Randy Cyphers

COMMENTARY
PRACTICAL AND EXPLANATORY ON THE
WHOLE BIBLE

COMMENTARY

PRACTICAL AND EXPLANATORY

ON THE

WHOLE BIBLE

REV. ROBERT JAMIESON, D.D.
PROFESSOR OF THEOLOGY, ABERDEEN, SCOTLAND

REV. A. R. FAUSSET, A.M.
ST. CUTHBERT'S, YORK, ENGLAND

REV. DAVID BROWN, D.D.
ST. PAUL'S, GLASGOW, SCOTLAND

ZONDERVAN
PUBLISHING HOUSE
OF THE ZONDERVAN CORPORATION
GRAND RAPIDS, MICHIGAN 49506

Completely reset from new type,
with minor revisions and improvements
in the references, etc.

Zondervan Publishing House
Grand Rapids, Michigan

First printing of revised edition 1961
Nineteenth printing 1982
ISBN 0-310-26570-3

Printed in the United States of America

A WORD ABOUT THIS NEW EDITION

If we had no other worthy estimation of this time-honored "J. F. & B." *Commentary*, that of C. H. Spurgeon should be sufficient to make us go out and buy this new edition at once—"It contains so great a variety of information that if a man had no other exposition he would find himself at no great loss if he possessed this and used it diligently. I have of it a very high opinion . . . and I consult it continually and with great interest."

There is much to commend this *must* of inexhaustible subjects for every Bible student. It is sound theologically—most spiritual in character—notable for its clarity—of a high standard scholastically. While there are many excellent commentaries to consult, there is no question that this—Jamieson, Fausset and Brown's *Commentary on the Whole Bible*—is the most outstanding one-volume Bible commentary ever published.

If your means are limited, there is no need to be concerned about scarcity of books. Invest in this one volume, and you will be amazed at the inexhaustible supply of material you will find on any Bible book, verse or theme, within the covers of this single book. Without hesitation we proclaim it to be the treasure store of Bible information *par excellence*.

For this new edition, the type has been completely reset in a larger, more readable typeface, and many minor improvements have been made for the convenience of the reader. These refinements include the substitution of readily recognizable Arabic numerals instead of Roman numerals for the chapter numbers, and the employment of the modern forms of abbreviations and references in current use. These improvements, and the larger, more readable type, all enhance the value of this new edition for today's readers and students.

Cromwell Close,   HERBERT LOCKYER, D.D., R.S.L., F.R.G.S.
Bromley, Kent, England

INTRODUCTION

TO THE PENTATEUCH AND HISTORICAL BOOKS

THE Pentateuch, the name by which the first five books of the Bible are designated, is derived from two Greek words, *pente*, "five," and *teuchos*, a "volume," thus signifying the fivefold volume. Originally these books formed one continuous work, as in the Hebrew manuscripts they are still connected in one unbroken roll. At what time they were divided into five portions, each having a separate title, is not known, but it is certain that the distinction dates at or before the time of the *Septuagint* translation. The names they bear in our English version are borrowed from the LXX, and they were applied by those Greek translators as descriptive of the principal subjects—the leading contents of the respective books. In the later Scriptures they are frequently comprehended under the general designation, *The Law, The Book of the Law*, since, to give a detailed account of the preparations for, and the delivery of, the divine code, with all the civil and sacred institutions that were peculiar to the ancient economy, is the object to which they are exclusively devoted. They have always been placed at the beginning of the Bible, not only on account of their priority in point of time, but as forming an appropriate and indispensable introduction to the rest of the sacred books. The numerous and oft-recurring references made in the later Scriptures to the events, the ritual, and the doctrines of the ancient Church would have not only lost much of their point and significance, but have been absolutely unintelligible without the information which these five books contain. They constitute the groundwork or basis on which the whole fabric of revelation rests, and a knowledge of the authority and importance that is thus attached to them will sufficiently account for the determined assaults that infidels have made on these books, as well as for the zeal and earnestness which the friends of the truth have displayed in their defense.

The Mosaic origin of the Pentateuch is established by the concurring voices both of Jewish and Christian tradition; and their unanimous testimony is supported by the internal character and statements of the work itself. That Moses did keep a written record of the important transactions relative to the Israelites is attested by his own express affirmation. For in relating the victory over the Amalekites, which he was commanded by divine authority to record, the language employed, "write this for a memorial in a book [*Hebrew*, the book]" (Exod. 17:14), shows that that narrative was to form part of a register already in progress, and various circumstances combine to prove that this register was a continuous history of the special goodness and care of divine providence in the choice, protection, and guidance of the Hebrew nation. First, there are the repeated assertions of Moses himself that the events which checkered the experience of that people were written down as they occurred (see Exod. 24:4–7; 34:27; Num. 33:2). Secondly, there are the testimonies borne in various parts of the later historical books to the Pentateuch as a work well known, and familiar to all the people (see Josh. 1:8; 8:34; 23:6; 24:26; I Kings 2:3, etc.). Thirdly, frequent references are made in the works of the prophets to the facts recorded in the books of Moses (cf. Isa. 1:9 with Gen. 19:1; 12:2 with Exod. 15:2; 51:2 with Gen. 12:2; 54:9 with Gen. 8:21; Hos. 9:10 cf. with Num. 25:3; 11:8 with Genesis 19:24; 12:4 with Genesis 32:24, 25; 12:12 with Genesis 28:5; 29:20; Joel 1:9 cf. with Num. 15:4–7; 28:7–14; Deut. 12:6, 7; 16:10, 11; Amos 2:9 cf. with Num. 21:21; 4:4 with Num. 28:3; 4:11 with Gen. 19:24; 9:13 with Lev. 26:5; Mic. 6:5 cf. with Num. 22:25; 6:6 with Lev. 9:2, 6:15 with Lev. 26:16, etc.). Fourthly, the testimony of Christ and the Apostles is repeatedly borne to the books of Moses (Matt. 19:7; Luke 16:29; 24:27; John 1:17; 7:19; Acts 3:22; 28:23; Rom. 10:5). Indeed the references are so numerous, and the testimonies so distinctly borne to the existence of the Mosaic books throughout the whole history of the Jewish nation, and the unity of character, design, and style pervading these books is so clearly perceptible, notwithstanding the rationalistic assertions of their forming a series of separate and unconnected fragments, that it may with all safety be said, there is immensely stronger and more varied evidence in proof of their being the authorship of Moses than of any of the Greek or Roman classics being the productions of the authors whose names they bear. But admitting that the Pentateuch was written by Moses, an important question arises, as to whether the books which compose it have reached us in an authentic form; whether they exist genuine and entire as they came from the hands of their author. In answer to this question, it might be sufficient to state that, in the public and periodical rehearsals of the law in the solemn religious assemblies of the people, implying the existence of numerous copies, provision was made for preserving the integrity of "The Book of the Law." But besides this, two remarkable facts, the one of which occurred before and the other after the captivity, afford conclusive evidence of the genuineness and authenticity of the Pentateuch. The first is the discovery in the reign of Josiah of the autograph copy which was deposited by Moses in the ark of the testimony, and the second is the schism of the Samaritans, who erected a temple on Mount Gerizim, and who, appealing to the

5

Mosaic law as the standard of their faith and worship equally with the Jews, watched with jealous care over every circumstance that could affect the purity of the Mosaic record. There is the strongest reason, then, for believing that the Pentateuch, as it exists now, is substantially the same as it came from the hands of Moses. The appearance of a later hand, it is true, is traceable in the narrative of the death of Moses at the close of Deuteronomy, and some few interpolations, such as inserting the altered names of places, may have been made by Ezra, who revised and corrected the version of the ancient Scriptures. But, substantially, the Pentateuch is the genuine work of Moses, and many, who once impugned its claims to that character, and looked upon it as the production of a later age, have found themselves compelled, after a full and unprejudiced investigation of the subject, to proclaim their conviction that its authenticity is to be fully relied on.

The genuineness and authenticity of the Pentateuch being admitted, the inspiration and canonical authority of the work follow as a necessary consequence. The admission of Moses to the privilege of frequent and direct communion with God (Exod. 25:22; 33:3; Num. 7:89; 9:8); his repeated and solemn declarations that he spoke and wrote by command of God; the submissive reverence that was paid to the authority of his precepts by all classes of the Jewish people, including the king himself (Deut. 17:18; 27:3); and the acknowledgment of the divine mission of Moses by the writers of the New Testament, all prove the inspired character and authority of his books. The Pentateuch possessed the strongest claims on the attention of the Jewish people, as forming the standard of their faith, the rule of their obedience, the record of their whole civil and religious polity. But it is interesting and important to all mankind, inasmuch as besides revealing the origin and early development of the divine plan of grace, it is the source of all authentic knowledge, giving the true philosophy, history, geography, and chronology of the ancient world. Finally, the Pentateuch "is indispensable to the whole revelation contained in the Bible; for Genesis being the legitimate preface to the law; the law being the natural introduction to the Old Testament; and the whole a prelude to the gospel revelation, it could not have been omitted. What the four Gospels are in the New, the five books of Moses are in the Old Testament."

GENESIS, the book of the origin or production of all things, consists of two parts: the first, comprehended in chs. 1-11, gives a general history; the second, contained in the subsequent chapters, gives a special history. The two parts are essentially connected; the one, which sets out with an account of the descent of the human race from a single pair, the introduction of sin into the world, and the announcement of the scheme of divine mercy for repairing the ruins of the fall, was necessary to pave the way for relating the other, viz., the call of Abraham, and the selection of his posterity for carrying out the gracious purpose of God. An evident unity of method, therefore, pervades this book, and the information contained in it was of the greatest importance to the Hebrew people, as without it they could not have understood the frequent references made in their law to the purposes and promises of God regarding themselves. The arguments that have been already adduced as establishing the Mosaic origin of the Pentateuch prove of course that Moses was the author of Genesis. The few passages on which the rationalists grounded their assertions that it was the composition of a later age have been successfully shown to warrant no such conclusion; the use of Egyptian words and the minute acquaintance with Egyptian life and manners, displayed in the history of Joseph, harmonize with the education of Moses, and whether he received his information by immediate revelation, from tradition, or from written documents, it comes to us as the authentic work of an author who wrote as he was inspired by the Holy Ghost (II Pet. 1:21).

EXODUS, a "going forth," derives its name from its being occupied principally with a relation of the departure of the Israelites from Egypt, and the incidents that immediately preceded as well as followed that memorable migration. Its authorship by Moses is distinctly asserted by himself (Exod. 24:4), as well as by our Lord (Mark 12:26; Luke 20:37). Besides, the thorough knowledge it exhibits of the institutions and usages of the ancient Egyptians and the minute geographical details of the journey to Sinai, establish in the clearest manner the authenticity of this book.

LEVITICUS. So called from its treating of the laws relating to the ritual, the services, and sacrifices of the Jewish religion, the superintendence of which was entrusted to the Levitical priesthood. It is chiefly, however, the duties of the priests, "the sons of Aaron," which this book describes; and its claim to be the work of Moses is established by the following passages:—II Chron. 30:16; Neh. 8:14; Jer. 7:22-23; Ezek. 20:11; Matt. 8:4; Luke 2:22; John 8:5; Rom. 10:4; 13:9; II Cor. 6:16; Gal. 3:12; I Pet. 1:16.

NUMBERS. This book is so called because it contains an account of the enumeration and arrangement of the Israelites. The early part of it, from chs. 1-10, appears to be a supplement to Leviticus, being occupied with relating the appointment of the Levites to the sacred offices. The journal of the march through the wilderness is then given as far as ch. 21:20; after which the early incidents of the invasion are narrated. One direct quotation only from this book (ch. 16:5) is made in the New Testament (II Tim. 2:19); but indirect references to it by the later sacred writers are very numerous.

DEUTERONOMY, the *second law*, a title which plainly shows what is the object of this book, viz., a recapitulation of the law. It was given in the form of public addresses to the people; and as Moses spoke in the prospect of his speedy removal, he enforced obedience to it by many forcible appeals to the Israelites, concerning their long and varied experience both of the mercies and the judgments of God. The minute notices of the heathen people with whom they had come in contact, but who afterward disappeared from the pages of history, as well as the accounts of the fertility and products of Canaan, and the counsels respecting the conquest of that country, fix the date of this book and the time of its composition by the hand of Moses. The close, however, must have been added by another; and, indeed, it is supposed by some to have formed the original preface to the Book of Joshua.

JOSHUA. The title of this book is derived from the pious and valiant leader whose achievements it relates and who is commonly supposed to have been its author. The objections to this idea are founded chiefly on the clause, "unto this day," which occurs several times (ch. 4:9; 6:25; 8:28). But this, at least in the case of Rahab, is no valid reason for rejecting the idea of his authorship; for assuming what is most probable, that this book was composed toward the close of Joshua's long career, or compiled from written documents left by him, Rahab might have been still alive. A more simple and satisfactory way of accounting for the frequent insertion of the clause, "unto this day," is the opinion that it was a comment introduced by Ezra, when revising the sacred canon; and this difficulty being removed, the direct proofs of the book having been produced by a witness of the transactions related in it, the strong and vivid descriptions of the passing scenes, and the use of the words "we" and "us," (ch. 5:1-6), viewed in connection with the fact, that, after his farewell address to the people, Joshua "wrote these words in the book of the law of God"—all afford strong presumptive proof that the entire book was the work of that eminent individual. Its inspiration and canonical authority are fully established by the repeated testimonies of other Scripture writers (cf. ch. 6:26 with I Kings 16:34; cf. ch. 10:13 with Hab. 3:11; ch. 3:14 with Acts 7:45; 6:17-23 with Heb. 11:30; ch. 2 with Jas. 2:25; Ps. 44:2; 68:12-14; 78:54-55). As a narrative of God's faithfulness in giving the Israelites possession of the promised land, this history is most valuable, and bears the same character as a sequel to the Pentateuch, that the Acts of the Apostles do to the Gospels.

JUDGES is the title given to the next book, from its containing the history of those non-regal rulers who governed the Hebrews from the time of Joshua to that of Eli, and whose functions in time of peace consisted chiefly in the administration of justice, although they occasionally led the people in their wars against their public enemies. The date and authorship of this book are not precisely known. It is certain, however, that it preceded the Second Book of Samuel (cf. ch. 9:35 with II Sam. 11:21), as well as the conquest of Jerusalem by David (cf. ch. 1:21 with II Sam. 5:6). Its author was in all probability Samuel, the last of the judges (see ch. 19:1; 21:25), and the date of the first part of it is fixed in the reign of Saul, while the five chapters at the close might not have been written till after David's establishment as king in Israel (see ch. 18:31). It is a fragmentary history, being a collection of important facts and signal deliverances at different times and in various parts of the land, during the intermediate period of 300 years between Joshua and the establishment of the monarchy. The inspired character of this book is confirmed by allusions to it in many passages of Scripture (cf. ch. 4:2; 6:14 with I Sam. 12:9-12; ch. 9:53 with II Sam. 11:21; ch. 7:25 with Ps. 83:11; cf. ch. 5:4-5 with Ps. 7:5; ch. 13:5; 16:17 with Matt. 2:13-23; Acts 13:20; Heb. 11:32).

RUTH is properly a supplement to the preceding book, to which, in fact, it was appended in the ancient Jewish canon. Although it relates an episode belonging to the time of the Judges, its precise date is unknown. It appears certain, however, that it could not have been written prior to the time of Samuel (see ch. 4:17-22), who is generally supposed to have been its author; and this opinion, in addition to other reasons on which it rests, is confirmed by ch. 4:7, where it is evident that the history was not compiled till long after the transactions recorded. The inspiration and canonical authority of the book is attested by the fact of Ruth's name being inserted by Matthew in the Saviour's genealogy.

THE FIRST AND SECOND BOOKS OF SAMUEL. The two were, by the ancient Jews, conjoined so as to make one book, and in that form could be called the Book of Samuel with more propriety than now, the second being wholly occupied with the relation of transactions that did not take place till after the death of that eminent judge. Accordingly, in the *Septuagint* and the *Vulgate*, it is called the First and Second Books of Kings. The early portion of the First Book, down to the end of the twenty-fourth chapter, was probably written by Samuel; while the rest of it and the whole of the Second, are commonly ascribed to Nathan and Gad, founding the opinion on I Chron. 29:29. Commentators, however, are divided about this, some supposing that the statements in ch. 2:26; 3:1, indicate the hand of the judge himself, or a contemporary; while some think, from ch. 6:18; 12:5; 27:6, that its composition must be referred to a later age. It is probable, however, that these supposed marks of an after period were interpolations of Ezra. This uncertainty, however, as to the authorship does not affect the inspired authority of the book, which is indisputable, being quoted in the New Testament (Acts 13:22; Heb. 1:5), as well as in many of the Psalms.

THE FIRST AND SECOND BOOKS OF KINGS, in the ancient copies of the *Hebrew* Bible, constitute one book. Various titles have been given them; in the *Septuagint* and the *Vulgate* they are called the Third and Fourth Books of Kings. The authorship of these books is unknown; but the prevailing opinion is that they were compiled by Ezra, or one of the later prophets, from the ancient documents that are so frequently referred to in the course of the history as of public and established authority. Their inspired character was acknowledged by the Jewish Church, which ranked them in the sacred canon; and, besides, it is attested by our Lord, who frequently quotes from them (cf. I Kings 17:9; II Kings 5:14 with Luke 4:24–27; I Kings 10:1 with Matt. 12:42).

THE FIRST AND SECOND BOOKS OF CHRONICLES were also considered as one by the ancient Jews, who called them "words of days," i.e., diaries or journals, being probably compiled from those registers that were kept by the king's historiographers of passing occurrences. In the *Septuagint* the title given them is *Paraleipomenon*, "of things omitted," i.e., the books are supplementary because many things unnoticed in the former books are here recorded; and not only the omissions are supplied, but some narratives extended while others are added. The authorship is commonly ascribed to Ezra, whose leading object seems to have been to show the division of families, possessions, etc., before the captivity, with a view to the exact restoration of the same order after the return from Babylon. Although many things are restated and others are exact repetitions of what is contained in Kings, there is so much new and important information that, as Jerome has well said, the Chronicles furnish the means of comprehending parts of the New Testament, which must have been unintelligible without them. They are frequently referred to by Christ and the Apostles as forming part of "the Word of God" (see the genealogies in Matt. 1; Luke 3; cf. II Chron. 19:7 with I Pet. 1:17; II Chron. 24:19–21 with Matt. 23:32–35).

EZRA was, along with Nehemiah, reckoned one book by the ancient Jews, who called them the First and Second Books of Ezra, and they are still designated by Roman Catholic writers the First and Second Books of Esdras. This book naturally divides itself into two parts or sections, the one contained in the first six chapters, and which relates the circumstances connected with the return of the first detachment of Babylonish exiles under Zerubbabel with the consequent rebuilding of the temple and the re-establishment of the divine service. The other part, embraced in the four concluding chapters, narrates the journey of a second caravan of returning captives under the conduct of Ezra himself, who was invested with powers to restore, in all its splendor, the entire system of the Jewish ritual. The general opinion of the Church in every succeeding age has been that Ezra was the author of this book. The chief objection is founded on ch. 5:4, where the words, "then said," etc., have occasioned a surmise that the first portion of the book was not written by Ezra, who did not go to Jerusalem for many years after. But a little attention will show the futility of this objection, as the words in question did not refer to the writer, but were used by Tatnai and his associates. The style and unity of object in the book clearly prove it to have been the production of but one author. The canonical authority of this book is well established; but another under the name of Ezra is rejected as apocryphal.

NEHEMIAH appears to have been the author of this book, from his usually writing in his own name, and indeed, except in those parts which are unmistakably later editions or borrowed from public documents, he usually employs the first person. The major portion of the book is occupied with a history of Nehemiah's twelve years' administration in Jerusalem, after which he returned to his duties in Shushan. At a later period he returned with new powers and commenced new and vigorous measures of reform, which are detailed in the later chapters of the book.

ESTHER derives its name from the Jewess, who, having become wife of the king of Persia, employed her royal influence to effect a memorable deliverance for the persecuted Church of God. Various opinions are embraced and supported as to the authorship of this book, some ascribing it to Ezra, to Nehemiah, or to Mordecai. The preponderance of authorities is in favor of the last. The historical character of the book is undoubted, since, besides many internal evidences, its authenticity is proved by the strong testimony of the feast of Purim, the celebration of which can be traced up to the events which are described in this book. Its claim, however, to canonical authority has been questioned on the ground that the name of God does not once occur in it. But the uniform tradition both of the Jewish and the Christian Churches supports this claim, which nothing in the book tends to shake; while it is a record of the superintending care of divine providence over his chosen people, with which it is of the utmost importance the Church should be furnished. The name of God is strangely enough omitted, but the presence of God is felt throughout the history; and the whole tone and tendency of the book is so decidedly subservient to the honor of God and the cause of true religion that it has been generally received by the Church in all ages into the sacred canon.

INTRODUCTION

TO THE POETICAL BOOKS

HEBREW poetry is unique in its kind; in essence, the most sublime; in form, marked by a simplicity and ease which flow from its sublimity. "*The Spirit of the* LORD *spake by me* [the Hebrew poet], *and his word was in my tongue*" (II Sam. 23:2). Even the music was put under the charge of spiritually gifted men; and one of the chief musicians, Heman, is called "the king's seer in the words of God" (I Chron. 25:1, 5). King David is stated to have *invented instruments of music* (Amos 6:5). There is not in Hebrew poetry the artistic rhythm of form which appears in the classical poetry of Greece and Rome, but it amply makes up for this by its fresh and graceful naturalness.

Early specimens of Hebrew poetry occur; e.g., Lamech's sceptical parody of Enoch's prophecy, or, as others think, lamentation for a homicide committed in those lawless times in self-defense (Gen. 4:23; cf. Jude 14; Exod. 32:18; Num. 21:14, 15, 17, 18, 27; 23:7, 8, 18; 24:3, 15). The poetical element appears much more in the Old than in the New Testament. The poetical *books* are exclusively those of the Old Testament; and in the Old Testament itself, the portions that are the most fundamental (e.g., the Pentateuch of Moses, the lawgiver, in its main body), are those which have in them least of the poetical element in form. Elijah, the father of the prophets, is quite free of poetical art. The succeeding prophets were not strictly poets, except in so far as the ecstatic state in inspiration lifted them to poetic modes of thought and expression. The prophet was more of an inspired teacher than a poet. It is when the sacred writer acts as the representative of the *personal experiences* of the children of God and of the Church, that poetry finds its proper sphere.

The use of poetry in Scripture was particularly to supply the want not provided for by the law, viz., of *devotional forms* to express in private, and in public joint worship, *the feelings* of pious Israelites. The schools of the prophets fostered and diffused a religious spirit among the people; and we find them using lyric instruments to accompany their prophesyings (I Sam. 10:5). However, it was David, who specially matured the lyric effusions of devotion into a perfection which they had not before attained.

Another purpose which Psalmody, through David's inspired productions, served, was to *draw forth from under the typical forms of legal services their hidden essence and spirit, adapting them to the various spiritual exigencies of individual and congregational life. Nature,* too, is in them shown to speak the glory and goodness of the invisible, yet ever present God. A handbook of devotion was furnished to the Israelite whereby he could enter into the true spirit of the services of the sanctuary, and so feel the need of that coming Messiah, of whom especially the Book of Psalms testifies throughout. We also, in our Christian dispensation, need its help in our devotions. Obliged as we are, notwithstanding our higher privileges in most respects, to walk by faith rather than by sight in a greater degree than they, we find the Psalms, with their realizing expression of the felt nearness of God, the best repertory whence to draw *divinely sanctioned language*, wherewith to express our prayers and thanksgivings to God, and our breathings after holy communion with our fellow saints.

As to the objection raised against the spirit of revenge which breathes in some psalms, the answer is: a wide distinction is to be drawn between personal vindictiveness and the desire for God's honor being vindicated. Personal revenge, not only in the other parts of Scripture, but also in the Psalms, in theory and in practice, is alike reprobated (Exod. 23:4–5; Lev. 19:18; Job 31:29–30; Ps. 7:4, 5, 8, 11, 12; Prov. 25:21–22), which corresponds to David's practice in the case of his unrelenting enemy (I Sam. 24:5–6; 26:8–10). On the other hand, the people of God have always desired that whatever mars the cause of God, as for instance the prosperity of the enemies of God and His Church, should be brought to an end (Ps. 10:12; 30:27; 40:16, 79:6, 10). It is well for us, too, in our dispensation of love, to be reminded by these psalms of the danger of lax views as to God's hatred of sin; and of the need there is that we should altogether enter into the mind of God on such points at the same time that we seek to convert all men to God (cf. I Sam. 16:1; Ps. 139:21; Isa. 66:24; Rev. 14:10).

Some psalms are composed of twenty-two parallel sentences or strophes of verses, beginning with words of which the initial letters correspond with the Hebrew letters (twenty-two) in their order (cf. Ps. 37 and 119). So also Lamentations. This arrangement was designed as a help to the memory and is found only in such compositions as do not handle a distinct and progressive subject, but a series of pious reflections, in the case of which the precise order was of less moment. The Psalmist in adopting it does not slavishly follow it; but, as in the 25th Psalm, he deviates from it, so as to make the form, when needful, bend to the sense. Of these poems there are twelve in all in the Hebrew Bible (Ps. 25, 34, 37, 111, 112, 119, 145; Prov. 31:10–31; Lam. 1, 2, 3, 4).

The great excellence of the Hebrew principle of versification, viz., parallelism, or "thought rhythm"

(*Ewald*), is that, while the poetry of every other language, whose versification depends on the regular recurrences of certain sounds, suffers considerably by translation, Hebrew poetry, whose rhythm depends on the parallel correspondence of similar *thoughts*, loses almost nothing in being translated —the Holy Spirit having thus presciently provided for its ultimate translation into every language, without loss to the sense. Thus our *English Version*, Job and Psalms, though but translations, are eminently poetical. On parallelism, see my Introduction to Job. Thus also a clue is given to the *meaning* in many passages, the sense of the word in one clause being more fully set forth by the corresponding word in the succeeding parallel clause. In the Masoretic punctuation of the Hebrew, the metrical arrangement is marked by the distinctive accents. It accords with the divine inspiration of Scripture poetry, that the *thought* is more prominent than the form, the kernel than the shell. The Hebrew poetic rhythm resembled our blank verse, without, however, metrical *feet*. There is a *verbal rhythm* above that of prose; but as the true Hebrew pronunciation is lost, the rhythm is but imperfectly recognized.

The peculiarity of the Hebrew poetical age is that it was *always historic* and *true, not mythical*, as the early poetical ages of all other nations. Again, its poetry is distinguished from prose by the use of *terms decidedly poetic*. David's lament over Jonathan furnishes a beautiful specimen of another feature found in Hebrew poetry, *the strophe:* three strophes being marked by the recurrence three times of the dirge sung by the chorus; the first dirge sung by the whole body of singers, representing Israel; the second, by a chorus of damsels; the third, by a chorus of youths (II Sam. 1:17–27).

The lyrical poetry, which is the predominant style in the Bible and is especially terse and sententious, seems to have come from an earlier kind resembling the more modern Book of Proverbs (cf. Gen. 4:23–24). The Oriental mind tends to embody thought in pithy gnomes, maxims, and proverbs. "The poetry of the Easterns is a string of pearls. Every word has life. Every proposition is condensed wisdom. Every thought is striking and epigrammatical" (Kitto, *Biblical Cyclopædia*). We are led to the same inference from the term *Maschal*, a "proverb" or "similitude," being used to designate *poetry in general*. "Hebrew poetry, in its origin, was a painting to the eye, a parable or teaching by likenesses discovered by the popular mind, expressed by the popular tongue, and adopted and polished by the national poet." Solomon, under inspiration, may have embodied in his Proverbs such of the pre-existing popular wise sayings as were sanctioned by the Spirit of God.

The Hebrew title for the Psalms, *Tehilim*, means "hymns," i.e., joyous praises (sometimes accompanied with dancing Exod. 15; Judg. 5), not exactly answering to the LXX title, *Psalms*, i.e., "lyrical odes," or songs accompanied by an instrument. The title, *Tehilim*, "hymns," was probably adopted on account of *the use made of the Psalms in divine service*, though only a part can be strictly called songs of praise, others being *dirges*, and very many *prayers* (whence in Ps. 72:20, David styles all his previous compositions, "the *prayers* of David"). Sixty-five bear the title, "lyrical odes" (*Mizmorim*), while only one is styled *Tehilah* or "Hymn." From the title being Psalms in the LXX and New Testament, and also in the *Peshito*, it is probable that Psalms (*Mizmorim*) or lyrical odes, was the old title before *Tehilim*.

Epic poetry, as having its proper sphere in a *mythical heroic age*, has no place among the Hebrews of the Old Testament Scripture age. For in their earliest ages, viz. the patriarchal, *not fable* as in Greece, Rome, Egypt, and all heathen nations, but *truth* and *historic reality* reigned; so much so, that the poetic element, which is the offspring of the imagination, is found less in those earlier, than in the later, ages. The Pentateuch is almost throughout historic prose. In the subsequent uninspired age, in Tobit we have some approach to the Epos.

Drama, also, in the full modern sense, is not found in Hebrew literature. This was due, not to any want of intellectual culture, as is fully shown by the high excellence of their lyric and didactic poetry, but to their earnest character, and to the solemnity of the subjects of their literature. The dramatic element appears in Job, more than in any other book in the Bible; there are the *dramatis personæ*, a plot, and the "denouement" prepared for by Elihu, the fourth friend's speech, and brought about by the interposition of Jehovah Himself. Still it is not a strict drama, but rather an inspired debate on a difficult problem of the divine government exemplified in Job's case, with historic narrative, prologue, and epilogue. The Song of Solomon, too, has much of the dramatic cast. See my Introductions to Job and Song of Solomon. The *style* of many psalms is very dramatic, transitions often occurring from one to another person, without introduction, and especially from speaking indirectly *of* God to addresses *to* God; thus in Psalm 32:1–2, David makes a general introduction, "Blessed is the man whose iniquity is forgiven," etc.; then in vss. 3–7, he passes to addressing God directly; then in vs. 8, without preface God is introduced, directly speaking, in answer to the previous prayer; then in vss. 10–11, again he resumes indirect speaking *of* God, and addresses himself in conclusion to the righteous. These quick changes of person do not startle us, but give us a stronger sense of his habitual converse with God than any assertions could do. Cf. also in Psalm 132:8–10, the prayer, "Arise, O Lord, into *thy rest;* thou, and the ark of thy strength. Let thy *priests be clothed with righteousness; and let thy saints shout for joy.* For thy servant *David's* sake turn not away the face of thine anointed," with God's direct answer, which follows in almost the words of the prayer, "The Lord hath sworn unto *David*," etc. "This is *my rest* for ever [vs. 14]. I will *clothe her priests with salvation:* and *her saints shall shout aloud for joy.*" Thus also in Psalm 2, various personages are introduced, dramatically acting and speaking—the confederate nations, Jehovah, the Messiah, and the Psalmist.

A frequent feature is *the alternate succession of parts,* adapting the several psalms to alternate recitation by two *semi-choruses* in the temple worship, followed by a *full chorus* between the parts or at the end. (So Ps. 107:15, 21, 31). De Burgh, in his valuable commentary on the Psalms, remarks, "Our cathedral service exemplifies the form of chanting the Psalms, except that the *semi-chorus* is alternately *a whole verse,* instead of alternating, as of old, *the half verse;* while *the full chorus* is the 'gloria' at the end of each Psalm."

In conclusion, besides its unique point of excellence, its divine inspiration, Hebrew poetry is characterized as being essentially national, yet eminently catholic, speaking to the heart and spiritual sensibilities of universal humanity. Simple and unconstrained, it is distinguished by a natural freshness which is the result of its genuine truthfulness. The Hebrew poet sought not self or his own fame, as did heathen poets, but he was inspired by the Spirit of God to meet a pressing want which his own and his nation's spiritual aspirations after God made to be at once a necessity and a delight. Cf. II Samuel 23:1-2, "The sweet Psalmist of Israel said, The Spirit of the LORD spake by me," etc.

Ewald rightly remarks that several odes of the highest poetic excellence are not included (e.g., the songs of Moses, Exod. 15 and 32; of Deborah, Judg. 5; of Hannah, I Sam. 2:1-10; of Hezekiah, Isa. 38:9-20; of Habakkuk, Hab. 3; and even David's dirge over Saul and Jonathan, II Sam. 1:17-18). The selection of the Psalms collected in one book was made not so much with reference to the beauty of the pieces, as to their adaptation for public worship. Still one overruling Spirit ordered the selection and arrangement of the contents of the book, as one pervading tone and subject appear throughout, Christ in His own inner life as the God-man, and in His past, present, and future relations to the Church and the world. Isaac Taylor well calls the Psalms, "The Liturgy of the spiritual life"; and Luther, "A Bible in miniature."

The *principle of the order* in which the Psalms are given to us, though not always discoverable, is in some cases clear, and shows the arrangement to be unmistakably the work of the Spirit, not merely that of the collector. Thus Psalm 22 plainly portrays the dying agonies of Messiah; Psalm 23, His peaceful rest in Paradise after His death on the cross; and Psalm 24, His glorious ascension into heaven.

INTRODUCTION

TO THE PROPHETICAL BOOKS

THIS constitutes the second division, the others being the Law and Hagiographa. It included Joshua, Judges, I and II Samuel, I and II Kings, called *the former prophets;* and Isaiah, Jeremiah, Ezekiel, etc., to Malachi, *the latter prophets.* Daniel is excluded, because, though highly endowed with prophetic gifts, he *had not filled the prophetic office:* his book is therefore classed with the Hagiographa. Ezra probably commenced, and others subsequently completed, the arrangement of the canon. The prophets were not mere predictors. Their *Hebrew* name, *nabi,* comes from a root "to boil up as a fountain" (Gesenius); hence the fervor of inspiration (II Pet. 1:21). Others interpret it as from an *Arabic* root (Exod. 4:16, "spokesman" of God, the Holy Ghost supplying him with words); communicated by *dreams* (Joel. 2:28; Job 33:14-17 — no instance of this occurs in Isaiah); or *visions,* the scene being made to pass before their mind (Isa. 1:1); or *trance, ecstasy* (Num. 24:4, 16; Ezek. 1:3; 3:14); not depriving them, however, of free conscious agency (Jer. 20:7, 9; I Cor. 14:32).

These PECULIAR FORMS of inspiration distinguish *prophets,* strictly so called, from Moses and others, though inspired (Num. 12:6-8). Hence their name *seers.* Hence, too, the poetical cast of their style, though less restricted, owing to their practical tendency, by the outward forms observed in strictly poetical books. Hence, too, the union of music with prophesying (I Sam. 10:5). This ecstatic state, though exalted, is not the highest: for Jesus Christ was never in it, nor Moses. It was rendered necessary by the frailty of the prophets, and the spiritual obtuseness of the people. It accordingly predominates in the Old Testament, but is subordinate in the New Testament, where the Holy Ghost by the fulness of His ordinary gifts renders the extraordinary less necessary. After the time of the Mosaic economy, the idea of a prophet was regularly connected with the prophetic *office*—not conferred by men, but by God. In this they differ from mystics whose pretended inspiration is for themselves: prophetism is *practical,* not dreamy and secluded; the prophet's inspiration is theirs only as God's messengers to the people. His ordinary servants and *regular* teachers of the people were the priests; the prophets distinguished from them by inspiration, were designed to *rouse* and *excite.* In Israel, however, as distinguished from Judah (as there was no true priesthood) the prophets were the *regular* and only ministers of God. Prophecy in Israel needed to be supported more powerfully: therefore the "schools" were more established; and more striking prophetic deeds (e.g., Elijah's and Elisha's) are recorded, than in Judah. The law was their basis (Isa. 8:16, 20), both its form and spirit (Deut. 4:2; 13:1–3); at times they looked forward to a day when its ever living spirit would break its then imperfect form for a freer and more perfect development (Jer. 3:16; 31:31); but they altered not a tittle in their own days. Eichorn well calls Moses' song (Deut. 32) the Magna Charta of prophecy. The fulfilment of their predictions was to be the *sign* of their being real prophets of God (Deut. 18:22); also, their speaking in the name of no other but the true God (Deut. 18:20). Prophecy was the only sanctioned indulgence of the craving after knowledge of future events, which is so prevalent in the East (Deut. 18:10–11). For a momentary inspiration the mere beginning of spiritual life sufficed, as in Balaam's case; but for a continuous mission, the prophet must be converted (Isa. 6:7). In Samuel's days (I Sam. 10:8; 19:20) begin the prophetic "schools." These were associations of men, more or less *endowed with the Spirit,* in which the feebler were helped by those of greater spiritual powers: so at Beth-el and Gilgal (II Kings 2:3; 4:38; 6:21). Only the leaders stood in immediate communion with God, while the rest were joined to Him through their mediation (I Kings 19:15; II Kings 8:13); the former acted through the latter as their instruments (I Kings 19:16; II Kings 9:1–2). The bestowal of prophetic gifts was not, however, limited to these schools (Amos 7:14–15).

As to SYMBOLIC ACTIONS, many of them are not *actual* but only parts of the prophetic *visions,* internal not external facts, being impossible or indecent (Jer. 13:1–10; 25:12–38; Hos. 1:2–11). Still the internal actions, when possible and proper, were often expressed externally (I Kings 22:11). Those purely internal express the subject more strikingly than a naked statement could.

Other CRITERIA of a true prophet, besides the two above, were, *the accordance of his addresses with the law;* his *not promising prosperity without repentance;* his *own assurance of his divine mission* (sometimes received reluctantly, Jer. 20:8, 9; Jer. 26:12), *producing that inward assurance of the truth in others,* which is to them a stronger proof from the Spirit of God, than even outward miracles and arguments: his pious life, fortitude in suffering, and freedom from fanaticism, confirm these criteria. Miracles, though proofs, are not to be trusted without the negative criteria (Deut. 13:2). Predictions fulfilled in the prophet's lifetime established his authority thenceforth (I Sam. 3:19; Jer. 22:11–12; Ezek. 12:12–13; 24).

As to their PROMULGATION, it was usually oral, before the assembled people, and afterwards revised in writing. The second part of Isaiah and Ezekiel 40–48 were probably not given orally, but in writing. Before Isaiah's and his contemporaries' time, prophecies were not *written,* as not being intended for universal use. But now a larger field was opened. To the worldly power of heathen nations which threatened to destroy the theocracy is henceforth opposed the kingdom of God, about to conquer all through Messiah, whose coming concerns all ages. The lesser prophets give the quintessence of the prophecies of their respective authors. An instance of the mode of collecting and publishing prophecies occurs (Jer. 36:4–14). Those of the later prophets rest on those of the earlier (Zech. 1:4; 7:7, 12). Ewald fancies that a great number of prophetic rolls have been lost. But the fact of the prophets often alluding to writings which we have, and never to those which it can be *proved* we have not, makes it likely that we have all those predictions which were committed to writing; the care bestowed on them as divine, and the exact knowledge of them long after (Jer. 26:18, 19), confirm this view.

The ARRANGEMENT is chronological; but as the twelve lesser prophets are regarded as one work, and the three last of them lived later than Jeremiah and Ezekiel, the former are put after the latter. The lesser prophets are arranged chronologically, except Hosea, who being the largest, is placed first, though some were earlier than he; also Jonah, who seems to have been the earliest of *the latter prophets.*

As to THE MESSIAH, no *single* prophet gives a complete view of Him: this is made up of the various aspects of Him in different prophecies combined; just as His life in the Gospels is one under a fourfold aspect. In the first part of Isaiah, addressed to the whole people, the prominent idea is His triumph, as King, the design being there to remove their fears of the surrounding nations; in the second, addressed to the elect remnant, He is exhibited as Prophet and Priest, Himself being the sacrifice.

INTRODUCTION

TO THE PROPHETS OF THE RESTORATION

THE prophetic *gift* existed long before the prophetic *office* was instituted. Thus Enoch had the former (Jude 14); so Abraham is called "a prophet" (Gen. 20:7) as are also the patriarchs (Ps. 105:15). The office was first instituted under the Mosaic economy; but even then the *gift* was not always connected with the office; e.g., Daniel was endowed largely with the gift, but was never called to the office, as living in a heathen court where he could not have exercised it. So David (Matt. 13:35; 27:35). Hence the writings of both are classed with the Hagiographa, not with the prophets. Moreover, though the office ceased with the close of the Old Testament dispensation, the gift continued, and was among the leading charisms of the New Testament Church. "Prophet" (in *Hebrew* from a root, "to gush out like a fountain") meant one acting as spokesman for another (Exod. 7:1); so, one speaking authoritatively for God as *interpreter* of His will. "Seer" was the more ancient term (I Samuel 9:9), implying that he spake by a divine communication *presented either to his senses or his mind:* as "prophet" indicated his *authority* as speaking for God.

Christ was the only fountain of prophecy (I Pet. 1:11; Rev. 19:10; also Acts 16:7, the oldest reading, "the Spirit *of Jesus*"), and declared God's will to men by His Holy Spirit acting on the minds of the prophets. Thus the history of the Church is the history of God's revelations of Himself in His Son to man. The three divisions of this history, the Patriarchal, the Mosaic, and the Christian dispensations, are characterized each by a distinct mode of God's manifestations—i.e., by a distinct form of the prophetic gift. The *theophanic* mode characterizes the Patriarchal dispensation: God revealing Himself in *visible appearances* or *theophanies.* The *theopneustic* mode, the Mosaic: God revealing Himself through *God-inspired men.* The *theologic* mode, the Christian: God revealing Himself, not merely at intervals as before, but permanently by *inspired writings* ("the oracles of God," I Pet. 4:11).

In the *first* or patriarchal age, men work no miracles, unlike all other primeval histories, which abound in miracles wrought by men: a proof of genuineness. All the miracles are wrought by God without man's intervention; and the divine communications are usually by direct utterance, whence the prophetic gift is rare, as God in this dispensation only exceptionally employs the prophetic agency of men in it: only in Genesis 20:7, is the term "prophet" found. In the *second* or Mosaic dispensation, God withdraws Himself more from direct communication with man and manifests Himself through human instruments. Instead of working miracles *directly*, Moses, Joshua, etc., are His agents. So in His communications He speaks not directly, but through Moses and his successors. The theocracy needed a new form of prophetic gift: *God-inspired (theopneustic) men* must speak and act for God, the Head of the theocracy, as His administrators; the prophetic *gift* is therefore now connected with the prophetic *office.* These prophets accordingly are *acting,* not *writing,* prophets. The latter did not arise till the later ages of this second dispensation. Moses *acted* as a legislator; Joshua, the Judges, and Samuel as executive prophets; David and Solomon as devotional prophets. Even in the case of the writing prophets of the latter half of the Mosaic dispensation, their *primary* duty was to speak and act. Their writing had reference more to the use of the New Testament dispensation than to their own (I Pet. 1:12). So that even in their case the characteristic of the Mosaic dispensation was *theopneustic,* rather than *theologic.* The *third,* or Christian dispensation, is *theologic,* i.e., a revelation of God by inspired *writings.* Cf. I Peter 4:11; II Peter 1:16–21, where he contrasts "the old time" when "holy men *spake* by the Holy Ghost" with our time when we have the "sure word of prophecy"; or, as it may be translated, "the word of prophecy confirmed [to us]." Thus God now reveals His will, not by direct *theophanies,* as in the first dispensation; not by *inspired men,* as in the second; but by the written *word* which *liveth* and *abideth* for ever (as opposed to the desultory manifestations of God, and the noncontinuance in life of the prophets, under the two former dispensations respectively, I Pet. 1:23; II Pet. 3:2, 16). The next form shall be the return of the theophanic manifestations on earth, in a more perfect and abiding form than in the first age (Rev. 21:3).

The history of the prophetic office under the Mosaic dispensation falls into three divisions. The first ends with the age of Samuel and has no regular succession of prophets, these not being needed while *God Himself* ruled the people without an hereditary executive. The second period extends from Samuel to Uzziah, 800 B.C., and is the age of prophets of action. Samuel combined in himself the three elements of the theocracy, being a judge, a priest, and a prophet. The creation of a human king rendered the formal office of prophet more necessary as a counterpoise to it. Hence the age of the kings is the age of the prophets. But at this stage they were prophets of action, rather than of writing. Towards the close of this second period, the devotional and Messianic prophecies of David and Solomon prepared the way for the third period (from 800 B.C. to 400 B.C.), which began

13

under Uzziah, and which was the age of written prophecy. In this third period the prophets turn from the present to the future, and so the Messianic element grows more distinct. Thus in these three shorter periods the grand characteristics of the three great dispensations reappear. The first is *theophanic;* the second, *theopneustic;* and the third, *theologic.* Just as the great organic laws of the world reappear in smaller departments, the law of the tree developing itself in miniature forms in the structure of the leaf, and the curve of the planet's orbit reappearing in the line traced by the projected cannon-ball [MOORE].

Samuel probably enacted rules giving a permanent form to the prophetic order; at least in his time the first mention occurs of "schools of the prophets." These were all near each other, and in Benjamin, viz, in Bethel, Gilgal, Ramah, and Jericho. Had the prophet been a mere foreteller of events, such schools would have been useless. But he was also God's representative to ensure the due execution of the Mosaic ritual in its purity; hence arose the need of schools wherein to study that divinely ordained institution. God mostly chose His prophets from those thus educated, though not exclusively, as the cases of Amos (Amos 7:14) and Elisha (I Kings 19:19) prove. The fact that the humblest might be called to the prophetic office acted as a check to the hereditary kingly power and a stimulus to seeking the qualifications needed for so exalted an office. The Messianic Psalms towards the close of this second period form the transition between the prophets of *action* and the prophets of *word,* the men who were busy only with the present, and the men who looked out from the present into the glorious future.

The third period, that from Uzziah to Malachi, includes three classes of prophets: (1) Those of the ten tribes; (2) Those of the Gentiles; (3) Those of Judah. In the first class were Hosea and Amos. Few of the *writing* prophets belonged to Israel. They naturally gathered about the seat of the theocracy in Judah. Hence those of the ten tribes were mostly prophets of action. Under the second class fall Jonah, Nahum, and Obadiah, who were witnesses for God's authority over the Gentile world, as others witnessed for the same in the theocracy. The third class, those of Judah, have a wider scope and a more hopeful, joyous tone. They fall into five divisions: (1) *Those dwelling in Judah at the highest point of its greatness* during its separate state; viz., the century between Uzziah and Hezekiah, 800–700 B.C., Isaiah, Joel, and Micah. (2) The declining period of Judah, from Manasseh to Zedekiah, e.g., Zephaniah and Habakkuk. (3) *The captivity:* Jeremiah. (4) *The exile,* when the future was all that the eye could rest on with hope; e.g., Ezekiel and Daniel, who are chiefly prophets of the future. (5) *The restoration:* to which period belong the three last writing prophets of the Old Testament, Haggai, Zechariah, and Malachi. John the Baptist long subsequently belonged to the same dispensation, but he wrote nothing (Matt. 11:9–11); like Elijah, he was a prophet of action and preaching, preparing the way for the prophets of *word,* as John did for the Incarnate Word.

To understand the spirit of each prophet's teaching, his historical position and the circumstances of the time must be considered. The captivity was designed to eradicate the Jews' tendency to idolatry and to restore the theocratic spirit which recognized God as the only ruler, and the Mosaic institutions as His established law, for a time until Messiah should come. Hence the prophets of the restoration are best illustrated by comparison with the histories of Ezra and Nehemiah, contemporaries of Malachi.

Of the three prophets of the restoration, two, Haggai and Zechariah, are at the beginning of the period, and the remaining one, Malachi, is at the close. The exile was not one complete deportation of the people, but a series of deportations extending over a century and a half. So the restoration was not accomplished at once, but in successive returns extending over a century. Hence arises the different tone of Haggai and Zechariah at its beginning, and of Malachi at its close. The first return took place in the first year of Cyrus, 536 B.C.; 42,360 persons returned under Sheshbazzar or Zerubbabel and Joshua (Ezra 2:64). They built an altar and laid the foundations of the temple. They were interrupted by the misrepresentations of the Samaritans, and the work was suspended for fourteen years. The death of Smerdis gave an opportunity of renewing the work, seventy years after the destruction of the first temple. This was the time when Haggai and Zechariah arose, the former to incite to the immediate rebuilding of the temple and restoration of the Mosaic ritual, the latter to aid in the work and to unfold the grand future of the theocracy as an incentive to present labor. The impossibility of observing the Mosaic ritual in the exile generated an anti-theocratic indifference to it in the young who were strangers to the Jerusalem worship, from which the nation had been debarred for upwards of half a century. Moreover, the gorgeous pomp of Babylon tended to make them undervalue the humble rites of Jehovah's worship at that time. Hence there was need of a Haggai and a Zechariah to correct these feelings by unfolding the true glory of the theocratic institutions.

The next great epoch was the return of Ezra, 458 B.C., eighty years after the first expedition under Zerubbabel. Thirteen years later, 445 B.C., Nehemiah came to aid Ezra in the good work. It was now that Malachi arose to second these works, three-fourths of a century after Haggai and Zechariah. As their work was that of *restorers,* his was that of a *reformer.* The estates of many had become mortgaged, and depression of circumstances had led many into a sceptical spirit as to the service of God. They not only neglected the temple of worship, but took heathen wives, to the wrong of their Jewish wives and the dishonor of God. Therefore, besides the reformation of *civil* abuses and the rebuilding of the wall, effected through Nehemiah's exertions, a *religious* reformer was needed such as was Ezra, who reformed the ecclesiastical abuses, established synagogues, where regular instruction in the law could be received, restored the Sabbath, and the Passover, and the dignity of the priesthood, and generated a reverence for the written law, which afterwards became a superstition. Malachi aided in this good work by giving it his prophetical authority. How thoroughly the work was effected is proved by the utter change in the national character. Once always prone to idolatry, ever since the captivity they have abhorred it. Once loving kingly rule, now contrary to the ordinary course of history, they became submissive to priestly rule. Once negligent of the written Word, now they regarded it with reverence sometimes bordering on superstition. Once fond of foreign alliances, henceforth they shrank with abhorrence from all foreigners. Once fond of agriculture, now they became a trading people. From being pliable before, they now became intensely bigoted and nationally intolerant. Thus the restoration from Babylon moulded the national character more than any event since the exodus from Egypt.

Now the distinction between Judah and the ten tribes of Israel disappears. So in the New Testament the *twelve* tribes are mentioned (Acts 26:7; Jas. 1:1). The theocratic feeling generated at the restoration drew all of the elect nation round the seat of the theocracy, the metropolis of the true religion, Jerusalem. Malachi tended to promote this feeling; thus his prophecy, though addressed to the people of Jerusalem, is called "the word of the Lord to *Israel*."

The long silence of prophets from Malachi to the times of Messiah was calculated to awaken in the Jewish mind the more earnest desire for Him who was to exceed infinitely in word and deed all the prophets, His forerunners. The three prophets of the restoration being the last of the Old Testament, are especially distinct in pointing to Him who, as the great subject of the New Testament, was to fulfil all the Old Testament.

LIST OF ABBREVIATIONS AND CONTRACTIONS USED IN THIS WORK

THE Capital Letters of the Roman alphabet, A. B. C. D., designate the various manuscripts used by critics for the correction of the printed text.

A.—Used to designate the Alexandrian manuscript, which is so called from the place of its origin, the city of Alexandria, in Egypt.

B.—The Vatican manuscript, which is kept in the Vatican Library, at Rome.

C.—The Ephraim manuscript, so called from Ephraim, a Mesopotamian saint of the age of Constantine.

D.—The Beza manuscript, presented to the University of Cambridge, in England, by Theodore Beza, A.D. 1581.

A. D.—*Anno Domini.* In the year of our LORD.

App.—Appendix.

B. C.—Before Christ.

Ch. and Chs.—Chapter and Chapters.

Cf.—Compare. [*French: Confer.*]

Ed.—Edition.

E. g. *exempli gratia*—For example.

ibid.—ibidem. In the same place.

i. e.—*id est.* That is.

lib.—*liber.* Book.

lit.—literal, or literally.

LXX.—the Seventy, or the Septuagint.

MS. and MSS.—Manuscript and manuscripts, respectively.

N. B.—Take notice.

N. T.—New Testament.

O. T.—Old Testament.

p. and pp.—Page and pages, respectively.

q. d.—*quasi dicat.* As if he should say.

Quinct. Curt.—Quinctius Curtius.

Sept.—The Septuagint Greek version of the Old Testament.

Talm.—Talmud.

Virg. Georg.—The Georgics of Virgil.

CONTENTS

OLD TESTAMENT

	page			page
GENESIS	17	ECCLESIASTES		474
EXODUS	53	THE SONG OF SOLOMON		488
LEVITICUS	84	ISAIAH		503
NUMBERS	108	JEREMIAH		595
DEUTERONOMY	140	LAMENTATIONS		661
JOSHUA	166	EZEKIEL		667
JUDGES	184	DANIEL		730
RUTH	202	HOSEA		765
I SAMUEL	205	JOEL		782
II SAMUEL	228	AMOS		789
I KINGS	247	OBADIAH		802
II KINGS	269	JONAH		805
I CHRONICLES	292	MICAH		811
II CHRONICLES	311	NAHUM		821
EZRA	337	HABAKKUK		827
NEHEMIAH	345	ZEPHANIAH		833
ESTHER	355	HAGGAI		839
JOB	361	ZECHARIAH		844
PSALMS	405	MALACHI		868
PROVERBS	458			

NEW TESTAMENT

	page		page
MATTHEW	879	I TIMOTHY	1349
MARK	951	II TIMOTHY	1372
LUKE	987	TITUS	1384
JOHN	1024	PHILEMON	1390
THE ACTS	1080	HEBREWS	1393
ROMANS	1138	JAMES	1446
I CORINTHIANS	1185	I PETER	1460
II CORINTHIANS	1229	II PETER	1484
GALATIANS	1256	I JOHN	1494
EPHESIANS	1278	II JOHN	1512
PHILIPPIANS	1300	III JOHN	1514
COLOSSIANS	1313	JUDE	1515
I THESSALONIANS	1329	REVELATION	1521
II THESSALONIANS	1340		

A PRACTICAL
AND EXPLANATORY COMMENTARY

THE FIRST BOOK OF MOSES CALLED

GENESIS

CHAPTER 1

Vss. 1, 2. THE CREATION OF HEAVEN AND EARTH. **1. In the beginning**—a period of remote and unknown antiquity, hid in the depths of eternal ages; and so the phrase is used in Proverbs 8:22, 23. **God**—the name of the Supreme Being, signifying in *Hebrew*, "Strong," "Mighty." It is expressive of omnipotent power; and by its use here in the *plural* form, is obscurely taught at the opening of the Bible, a doctrine clearly revealed in other parts of it, viz., that though God is one, there is a plurality of persons in the Godhead—Father, Son, and Spirit, who were engaged in the creative work (Prov. 8:27; John 1:3, 10; Eph. 3:9; Heb. 1:2; Job 26:13). **created**—not formed from any pre-existing materials, but made out of nothing. **the heaven and the earth**—the universe. This first verse is a general introduction to the inspired volume, declaring the great and important truth that all things had a beginning; that nothing throughout the wide extent of nature existed from eternity, originated by chance, or from the skill of any inferior agent; but that the whole universe was produced by the creative power of God (Acts 17:24; Rom. 11:36). After this preface, the narrative is confined to the earth. **2. the earth was without form and void**—or in "confusion and emptiness," as the words are rendered in Isaiah 34:11. This globe, at some undescribed period, having been convulsed and broken up, was a dark and watery waste for ages perhaps, till out of this chaotic state, the present fabric of the world was made to arise. **the Spirit of God moved**—lit., continued brooding over it, as a fowl does, when hatching eggs. The immediate agency of the Spirit, by working on the dead and discordant elements, combined, arranged, and ripened them into a state adapted for being the scene of a new creation. The account of this new creation properly begins at the end of this second verse; and the details of the process are described in the natural way an onlooker would have done, who beheld the changes that successively took place.

3-5. THE FIRST DAY. **3. God said**—This phrase, which occurs so repeatedly in the account means: willed, decreed, appointed; and the determining will of God was followed in every instance by an immediate result. Whether the sun was created at the same time with, or long before, the earth, the dense accumulation of fogs and vapors which enveloped the chaos had covered the globe with a settled gloom. But by the command of God, light was rendered visible; the thick murky clouds were dispersed, broken, or rarefied, and light diffused over the expanse of waters. The effect is described in the name "day," which in *Hebrew* signifies "warmth," "heat"; while the name "night" signifies a "rolling up," as night wraps all things in a shady mantle. **4. divided the light from darkness**—refers to the alternation or succession of the one to the other, pro-

duced by the daily revolution of the earth round its axis. **5. first day**—a natural day, as the mention of its two parts clearly determines; and Moses reckons, according to Oriental usage, from sunset to sunset, saying not day and night as we do, but evening and morning.

6-8. SECOND DAY. **6. firmament**—an expanse—a beating out as a plate of metal: a name given to the atmosphere from its appearing to an observer to be the *vault* of heaven, supporting the weight of the *watery clouds*. By the creation of an atmosphere, the lighter parts of the waters which overspread the earth's surface were drawn up and suspended in the visible heavens, while the larger and heavier mass remained below. The air was thus "in the midst of the waters," i.e., separated them; and this being the apparent use of it, is the only one mentioned, although the atmosphere serves other uses, as a medium of life and light.

9-13. THIRD DAY. **9. let the waters under the heaven be gathered together into one place**—The world was to be rendered a terraqueous globe, and this was effected by a volcanic convulsion on its surface, the upheaving of some parts, the sinking of others, and the formation of vast hollows, into which the waters impetuously rushed, as is graphically described (Ps. 104:6-9) [HITCHCOCK]. Thus a large part of the earth was left "dry land," and thus were formed oceans, seas, lakes, and rivers which, though each having its own bed, or channel, are all connected with the sea (Job 38:10; Eccles. 1:7). **11. let the earth bring forth**—The bare soil was clothed with verdure, and it is noticeable that the trees, plants, and grasses—the three great divisions of the vegetable kingdom here mentioned—were not called into existence in the same way as the light and the air; they were made to grow, and they grew as they do still out of the ground—not, however, by the slow process of vegetation, but through the divine power, without rain, dew, or any process of labor—sprouting up and flourishing in a single day.

14-19. FOURTH DAY. **14. let there be lights in the firmament**—The atmosphere being completely purified, the sun, moon, and stars were for the first time unveiled in all their glory in the cloudless sky; and they are described as "in the firmament" which to the eye they appear to be, though we know they are really at vast distances from it. **16. two great lights**—In consequence of the day being reckoned as commencing at sunset—the moon, which would be seen first in the horizon, would appear "a great light," compared with the little twinkling stars; while its pale benign radiance would be eclipsed by the dazzling splendor of the sun; when his resplendent orb rose in the morning and gradually attained its meridian blaze of glory, it would appear "the greater light" that ruled the day. Both these lights may be said to be "made" on the fourth day—not created, indeed, for it is a different word that is here used, but constituted, appointed to the important and necessary office of serving as luminaries to the world, and regulating by their motions and their influence the progress and divisions of time.

20-23. FIFTH DAY. The signs of animal life appeared in the waters and in the air. **20. moving creature**—all oviparous animals, both among the finny and the feathery tribes—remarkable for their rapid and prodigious increase. **fowl**—means every flying thing: The word rendered "whales," includes also sharks, crocodiles, etc.; so that from the countless shoals of small fish to the great sea monsters, from the tiny insect to the king of birds, the waters and the air were suddenly made to swarm with creatures formed to live and sport in their respective elements.

24-31. SIXTH DAY. A farther advance was made by the creation of terrestrial animals, all the various species of which are included in three classes: (1) cattle, the herbivorous kind capable of labor or domestication. **24. beasts of the earth**—(2) wild animals, whose ravenous natures were then kept in check, and (3) all the various forms of **creeping things**—from the huge reptiles to the insignificant caterpillars. **26.** The last stage in the progress of creation being now reached—**God said, Let us make man**—words which show the peculiar importance of the work to be done, the formation of a creature, who was to be God's representative, clothed with authority and rule as visible head and monarch of the world. **In our image, after our likeness**—This was a peculiar distinction, the value attached to which appears in the words being twice mentioned. And in what did this image of God consist? Not in the erect form or features of man, not in his intellect, for the devil and his angels are, in this respect, far superior; not in his immortality, for he has not, like God, a past as well as a future eternity of being; but in the moral dispositions of his soul, commonly called *original righteousness* (Eccles. 7:29). As the new creation is only a restoration of this image, the history of the one throws light on the other; and we are informed that it is renewed after the image of God in knowledge, righteousness, and true holiness (Col. 3:10; Eph. 4:24). **28. Be fruitful,** etc.—The human race in every country and age has been the offspring of the first pair. Amid all the varieties found among men, some black, some copper-colored, others white, the researches of modern science lead to a conclusion, fully accordant with the sacred history, that they are all of one species and of one family (Acts 17:26). What power in the word of God! "He spake and it was done. He commanded and all things stood fast." "Great and manifold are thy works, Lord God Almighty! in wisdom hast thou made them all." We admire that wisdom, not only in the regular progress of creation, but in its perfect adaptation to the end. God is represented as pausing at every stage to look at His work. No wonder He contemplated it with complacency. Every object was in its right place, every vegetable process going on in season, every animal in its structure and instincts suited to its mode of life and its use in the economy of the world. He saw everything that He had made answering the plan which His eternal wisdom had conceived; and, **31. Behold it was very good.**

CHAPTER 2

Vs. 1. THE NARRATIVE OF THE SIX DAYS' CREATION CONTINUED. The course of the narrative is improperly broken by the division of the chapter.

1. the heavens—the firmament or atmosphere. **host**—a multitude, a numerous array, usually connected in Scripture with heaven only, but here with the earth also, meaning all that they contain. **were finished**—brought to completion. No permanent change has ever since been made in the course of the world, no new species of animals been formed, no law of nature repealed or added to. They could have been finished in a moment as well as in six days, but the work of creation was gradual for the instruction of man, as well, perhaps, as of higher creatures (Job 38:7).

2-7. THE FIRST SABBATH. **2. and he rested on the seventh day**—not to repose from exhaustion with labor (see Isa. 40:28), but ceased from working, an example equivalent to a command that we also should cease from labor of every kind. **3. blessed and sanctified the seventh day**—a peculiar distinction put upon it above the other six days, and showing it was devoted to sacred purposes. The institution of the Sabbath is as old as creation, giving rise to that weekly division of time which prevailed in the earliest ages. It is a wise and beneficent law, affording that regular interval of rest which the physical nature of man and the animals employed in his service requires, and the neglect of which brings both to premature decay. Moreover, it secures an appointed season for religious worship, and if it was necessary in a state of primeval innocence, how much more so now, when mankind has a strong tendency to forget God and His claims? **4. These are the generations of the heavens and the earth**—the history or account of their production. Whence did Moses obtain this account so different from the puerile and absurd fictions of the heathen? Not from any human source, for man was not in existence to witness it; not from the light of nature or reason, for though they proclaim the eternal power and Godhead by the things which are made, they cannot tell *how* they were made. None but the Creator Himself could give this information, and therefore it is through faith we understand that the worlds were framed by the word of God (Heb. 11:3). **rain, mist**—See on ch. 1:12. **7.** Here the sacred writer supplies a few more particulars about the first pair. **formed**—had FORMED MAN OUT OF THE DUST OF THE GROUND. Science has proved that the substance of his flesh, sinews, and bones, consists of the very same elements as the soil which forms the crust of the earth and the limestone that lies embedded in its bowels. But from that mean material what an admirable structure has been reared in the human body (Ps. 139:14). **breath of life**—lit., of lives, not only animal but spiritual life. If the body is so admirable, how much more the soul with all its varied faculties. **breathed into his nostrils the breath of life**—not that the Creator literally performed this act, but respiration being the medium and sign of life, this phrase is used to show that man's life originated in a different way from his body—being implanted directly by God (Eccles. 12:7), and hence in the new creation of the soul Christ breathed on His disciples (John 20:22).

8-17. THE GARDEN OF EDEN. **8. Eden**—was probably a very extensive region in Mesopotamia, distinguished for its natural beauty and the richness and variety of its produce. Hence its name, signifying "pleasantness." God planted a garden eastward, an extensive park, a paradise, in which the man was put to be trained under the paternal care of his Maker to piety and usefulness. **tree of life**—so called from its symbolic character as a sign and seal of immortal life. Its prominent position "in the midst of the garden," where it must have been an object of daily observation and interest, was admirably fitted to keep man habitually in mind of God and futurity. **9. tree of the knowledge of good and evil**—so called because it was a *test* of obedience by which our first parents were to be tried, whether they would be good or bad, obey God or break His commands. **17. thou shalt surely die**—no reason assigned for the prohibition, but death was to be the punishment of disobedience. A positive command like this was not only the simplest and easiest, but the only trial to which their fidelity could be exposed. **15. put the man into the garden of Eden to dress it**—not only to give him a pleasant employment, but to place him on his probation, and as the title of this garden, the garden of the Lord (ch. 13:10; Ezek. 28:13), indicates, it was in fact a temple in which he worshipped God, and was daily employed in offering the sacrifices of thanksgiving and praise.

18-25. THE MAKING OF WOMAN, AND INSTITUTION OF MARRIAGE. **18. it is not good for man to be alone**—In the midst of plenty and delights, he was conscious of feelings he could not gratify. To make him sensible of his wants, **19. God brought unto Adam**—not all the animals in existence, but those chiefly in his immediate neighborhood to be subservient to his use. **whatsoever Adam called every living creature, that was the name thereof**—His powers of perception and intelligence were supernaturally enlarged to know the characters, habits, and uses of each species that was brought to him. **20. but for Adam there was not found an help meet for him**—The design of this singular scene was to show him that none of the living creatures he saw were on an equal footing with himself, and that while each class came with its mate of the same nature, form, and habits, he alone had no companion. Besides, in giving names to them he was led to exercise his powers of speech and to prepare for social intercourse with his partner, a creature yet to be formed. **21. deep sleep**—probably an ecstasy or trance like that of the prophets, when they had visions and revelations of the Lord, for the whole scene was probably visible to the mental eye of Adam, and hence his rapturous exclamation. **took one of his ribs**—"She was not made out of his head to surpass him, nor from his feet to be trampled on, but from his side to be equal to him, and near his heart to be dear to him." **23. Woman**—in *Hebrew*— "man-ess." **one flesh**—The human pair differed from all other pairs, that by the peculiar formation of Eve, they were one. And this passage is appealed to by our Lord as the divine institution of marriage (Matt. 19:4, 5; Eph. 5:28). Thus Adam appears as a creature formed after the image of God—showing his *knowledge* by giving names to the animals, his *righteousness* by his approval of the marriage relation, and his *holiness* by his principles and feelings, and finding gratification in the service and enjoyment of God.

CHAPTER 3

Vss. 1-5. THE TEMPTATION. **1. the serpent**—The fall of man was effected by the seductions of a serpent. That it was a real serpent is evident from the plain and artless style of the history and from the many allusions made to it in the New Testament. But the material serpent was the instrument or tool of a higher agent, Satan or the devil, to whom the sacred writers apply from this incident the reproachful name of "the serpent"—"the old dragon."

Though Moses makes no mention of this wicked spirit—giving only the history of the visible world— yet in the fuller discoveries of the Gospel, it is distinctly intimated that Satan was the author of the plot (John 8:44; II Cor. 11:3; I John 3:8; I Tim. 2:14; Rev. 20:2). **more subtile**—Serpents are proverbial for wisdom (Matt. 10:16). But these reptiles were at first, probably, far superior in beauty as well as in sagacity to what they are in their present state. **He said**—There being in the pure bosoms of the first pair no principle of evil to work upon, a solicitation to sin could come only from *without*, as in the analogous case of Jesus Christ (Matt. 4:3); and as the tempter could not assume the human form, there being only Adam and Eve in the world, the agency of an inferior creature had to be employed. The dragon-serpent [BOCHART] seemed the fittest for the vile purpose; and the devil was allowed by Him who permitted the trial, to bring articulate sounds from its mouth. **unto the woman**—the object of attack, from his knowledge of her frailty, of her having been but a short time in the world, her limited experience of the animal tribes, and, above all, her being alone, unfortified by the presence and counsels of her husband. Though sinless and holy, she was a free agent, liable to be tempted and seduced. **yea, hath God said**—Is it true that He has restricted you in using the fruits of this delightful place? This is not like one so good and kind. Surely there is some mistake. He insinuated a doubt as to her sense of the divine will and appeared as "an angel of light" (II Cor. 11:14), offering to lead her to the true interpretation. It was evidently from her regarding him as specially sent on that errand, that, instead of being startled by the reptile's speaking, she received him as a heavenly messenger. **2. the woman said, We may eat of the fruit of the trees of the garden**—In her answer, Eve extolled the large extent of liberty they enjoyed in ranging at will amongst all the trees—one only excepted, with respect to which, she declared there was no doubt, either of the prohibition or the penalty. But there is reason to think that she had already received an injurious impression; for in using the words—"lest ye die," instead of "ye shall surely die"—she spoke as if the tree had been forbidden because of some poisonous quality of its fruit. The tempter, perceiving this, became bolder in his assertions. **4. Ye shall not surely die**—He proceeded, not only to assure her of perfect impunity, but to promise great benefits from partaking of it. **5. your eyes shall be opened**—His words meant more than met the ear. In one sense her eyes were opened; for she acquired a direful experience of "good and evil"—of the happiness of a holy, and the misery of a sinful, condition. But he studiously concealed this result from Eve, who, fired with a generous desire for knowledge, thought only of rising to the rank and privileges of her angelic visitants.

6-9. THE FALL. **6. And when the woman saw that the tree was good for food**—Her imagination and feelings were completely won; and the fall of Eve was soon followed by that of Adam. The history of every temptation, and of every sin, is the same; the outward object of attraction, the inward commotion of mind, the increase and triumph of passionate desire; ending in the degradation, slavery, and ruin of the soul (Jas 1:15; I John 2:16). **8. they heard the voice of the Lord God walking in the garden**—The divine Being appeared in the same manner as formerly—uttering the well-known tones of kindness, walking in some visible form—not running hastily, as one impelled by the influence of angry feelings. How beautifully expressive are these words of the familiar and condescending manner in which He had hitherto held intercourse with the first pair. **in the cool of the day**—lit., the breeze of the day—the evening. **hid themselves amongst the trees**—Shame, remorse, fear—a sense of guilt—feelings to which they had hitherto been strangers disordered their minds and led them to shun Him whose approach they used to welcome. How foolish to think of eluding His notice (Ps. 139:1-12). 10-13. THE EXAMINATION. **10. afraid, because . . . naked**—apparently, a confession—the language of sorrow; but it was evasive—no signs of true humility and penitence—each tries to throw the blame on another. **12. The woman . . . gave me**—He blames God [CALVIN]. As the woman had been given him for his companion and help, he had eaten of the tree from love to her; and perceiving she was ruined, was determined not to survive her [M'KNIGHT]. **13. beguiled**—cajoled by flattering lies. This sin of the first pair was heinous and aggravated—it was not simply eating an apple, but a love of self, dishonor to God, ingratitude to a benefactor, disobedience to the best of Masters—a preference of the creature to the Creator.

14-24. THE SENTENCE. **14. And the Lord God said unto the serpent**—The Judge pronounces a doom: first, on the material serpent, which is cursed above all creatures. From being a model of grace and elegance in form, it has become the type of all that is odious, disgusting, and low [LECLERC, ROSENMULLER]; or the curse has converted its natural condition into a punishment; it is now branded with infamy and avoided with horror; next, on the spiritual serpent, the seducer. Already fallen, he was to be still more degraded and his power wholly destroyed by the offspring of those he had deceived. **15. thy seed**—not only evil spirits, but wicked men. **seed of the woman**—the Messiah, or His Church [CALVIN, HENGSTENBERG]. **I will put enmity between thee and the woman**—God can only be said to do so by leaving "the serpent and his seed to the influence of their own corruption; and by those measures which, pursued for the salvation of men, fill Satan and his angels with envy and rage." **thou shalt bruise his heel**—The serpent wounds the heel that crushes him; and so Satan would be permitted to afflict the humanity of Christ and bring suffering and persecution on His people. **it shall bruise thy head**—The serpent's poison is lodged in its head; and a bruise on that part is fatal. Thus, fatal shall be the stroke which Satan shall receive from Christ, though it is probable he did not at first understand the nature and extent of his doom. **16. unto the woman he said, I will greatly multiply thy sorrow**—She was doomed as a wife and mother to suffer pain of body and distress of mind. From being the helpmeet of man and the partner of his affections, her condition would henceforth be that of humble subjection. **17-19. unto Adam he said**—made to gain his livelihood by tilling the ground; but what before his fall he did with ease and pleasure, was not to be accomplished after it without painful and persevering exertion. **till thou return unto the ground**—Man became mortal; although he did not die the moment he ate the forbidden fruit, his body underwent a change, and that would lead to dissolution; the union subsisting between his soul and God having already been dissolved, he had become liable to all the miseries of this life and to the pains of hell for ever. What a mournful chapter this is in the history of man! It gives the only true account of the origin of all the physical and moral evils that are

in the world; upholds the moral character of God; shows that man, made upright, fell from not being able to resist a slight temptation; and becoming guilty and miserable, plunged all his posterity into the same abyss (Rom. 5:12). How astonishing the grace which at that moment gave promise of a Saviour and conferred on her who had the disgrace of introducing sin the future honor of introducing that Deliverer (I Tim. 2:15). **20. Adam called his wife's name Eve**—probably in reference to her being a mother of the promised Saviour, as well as of all mankind. **21. God made coats of skins**—taught them to make these for themselves. This implies the institution of animal sacrifice, which was undoubtedly of divine appointment, and instruction in the only acceptable mode of worship for sinful creatures, through faith in a Redeemer (Heb. 9:22). **22. And God said, Behold, the man is become as one of us**—not spoken in irony as is generally supposed, but in deep compassion. The words should be rendered, "Behold, what has become [by sin] of the man who was as one of us!" Formed, at first, in our image to know good and evil—how sad his condition now. **and now, lest he put forth his hand, and take of the tree of life**—This tree being a pledge of that immortal life with which obedience should be rewarded, man lost, on his fall, all claim to this tree; and therefore, that he might not eat of it or delude himself with the idea that eating of it would restore what he had forfeited, the Lord sent him forth from the garden. **24. placed . . . cherubim**—The passage should be rendered thus:—"And he dwelt between the cherubim at the East of the Garden of Eden and a fierce fire or Shekinah unfolding itself to preserve the way of the tree of life." This was the mode of worship now established to show God's anger at sin and teach the mediation of a promised Saviour as the way of life, as well as of access to God. They were the same figures as were afterwards in the tabernacle and temple; and now, as then, God said, "I will commune with thee from between the cherubim" (Exod. 25:22).

CHAPTER 4

Vss. 1-26. BIRTH OF CAIN AND ABEL. **1. Eve said, I have gotten a man from the Lord**—i.e., "by the help of the Lord"—an expression of pious gratitude—and she called him Cain, i.e., "a possession," as if valued above everything else; while the arrival of another son reminding her of the misery she had entailed on her offspring, led to the name Abel, i.e., either weakness, vanity (Ps. 39:5), or grief, lamentation. Cain and Abel were probably twins; and it is thought that, at this early period, children were born in pairs (ch. 5:4) [CALVIN]. **Abel was a keeper of sheep**—lit., "feeder of a flock," which, in Oriental countries, always includes goats as well as sheep. Abel, though the younger, is mentioned first, probably on account of the pre-eminence of his religious character. **3. in process of time**—*Hebrew*, "at the end of days," probably on the Sabbath. **brought . . . an offering unto the Lord**—Both manifested, by the very act of offering, their faith in the being of God and in His claims to their reverence and worship; and had the kind of offering been left to themselves, what more natural than that the one should bring "of the fruits of the ground," and that the other should bring "of the firstlings of his flock and the fat thereof." **4. the Lord had respect unto Abel, not unto Cain,** etc.—The words, "had respect to," signify in *Hebrew*—"to look at any thing with a keen earnest glance," which has been translated, "kindle into a fire," so that the divine approval of Abel's offering was shown in its being consumed by fire (see ch. 15:17; Judg. 13:20). **7. If thou doest well, shalt thou not be accepted?**—A better rendering is, "Shalt thou not have the excellency?" which is the true sense of the words referring to the high privileges and authority belonging to the first-born in patriarchal times. **sin lieth at the door**—sin, i.e., a sin offering—a common meaning of the word in Scripture (as in Hos.4:8; II Cor. 5:21; Heb. 9:28). The purport of the divine rebuke to Cain was this, "Why art thou angry, as if unjustly treated? If thou doest well (i.e., wert innocent and sinless) a thank offering would have been accepted as a token of thy dependence as a creature. But as thou doest not well (i.e., art a sinner), a sin offering is necessary, by bringing which thou wouldest have met with acceptance and retained the honors of thy birthright." This language implies that previous instructions had been given as to the mode of worship; Abel offered through faith (Heb. 11:4). **unto thee shall be his desire**—The high distinction conferred by priority of birth is described (ch. 27:29); and it was Cain's conviction, that this honor had been withdrawn from him, by the rejection of his sacrifice, and conferred on his younger brother—hence the secret flame of jealousy, which kindled into a settled hatred and fell revenge. **8. And Cain talked with Abel his brother**—Under the guise of brotherly familiarity, he concealed his premeditated purpose till a convenient time and place occurred for the murder (I John 3:12; 9:10). **10. the voice of thy brother's blood crieth unto me**—Cain, to lull suspicion, had probably been engaging in the solemnities of religion when he was challenged directly from the Shekinah itself. **9. I know not**—a falsehood. One sin leads to another. **11, 12. now art thou cursed from the earth**—a curse superadded to the general one denounced on the ground for Adam's sin. **a fugitive**—condemned to perpetual exile—a degraded outcast—the miserable victim of an accusing conscience. **13, 14. And Cain said . . . My punishment is greater than I can bear**—What an overwhelming sense of misery; but no sign of penitence, nor cry for pardon. **every one that findeth me shall slay me**—This shows that the population of the world was now considerably increased. **15. whosoever slayeth Cain**—By a special act of divine forbearance, the *life* of Cain was to be spared in the then small state of the human race. **set a mark**—not any visible mark or brand on his forehead, but some *sign* or *token* of assurance that his life would be preserved. This sign is thought by the best writers to have been a wild ferocity of aspect that rendered him an object of universal horror and avoidance. **16. presence of the Lord**—the appointed place of worship at Eden. Leaving it, he not only severed himself from his relatives but forsook the ordinances of religion, probably casting off all fear of God from his eyes so that the last end of this man is worse than the first (Matt. 12:45). **land of Nod**—of flight or exile—thought by many to have been Arabia Petræa—which was cursed to sterility on his account. **17-22. builded a city**—It has been in cities that the human race has ever made the greatest social progress; and several of Cain's descendants distinguished themselves by their inventive genius in the arts. **19. Lamech took unto him two wives**—This is the first transgression of the law of marriage on record, and the practice of polygamy, like all other breaches of God's institutions, has been a fruitful source of corruption and misery. **23, 24. Lamech said unto his wives**—This speech is in a poetical

form, probably the fragment of an old poem, transmitted to the time of Moses. It seems to indicate that Lamech had slain a man in self-defense, and its drift is to assure his wives, by the preservation of Cain, that an *unintentional* homicide, as he was, could be in no danger. **26. men began to call upon the name of the Lord**—rather, by the name of the Lord. God's people, a name probably applied to them in contempt by the world.

CHAPTER 5

Vss. 1-32. GENEALOGY OF THE PATRIARCHS. **1. book of the generations** (See ch. 11:4). **Adam**—used here either as the name of the first man, or of the human race generally. **5. all the days . . . Adam lived**—The most striking feature in this catalogue is the longevity of Adam and his immediate descendants. Ten are enumerated in direct succession whose lives far exceed the ordinary limits with which we are familiar—the shortest being 365, and the longest 930 years. It is useless to inquire whether and what secondary causes may have contributed to this protracted longevity—vigorous constitutions, the nature of their diet, the temperature and salubrity of the climate; or, finally—as this list comprises only the true worshippers of God—whether their great age might be owing to the better government of their passions and the quiet, even tenor of their lives. Since we cannot obtain satisfactory evidence on these points, it is wise to resolve the fact into the sovereign will of God. We can, however, trace some of the important uses to which, in the early economy of Providence, it was subservient. It was the chief means of reserving a knowledge of God, of the great truths of religion, as well as the influence of genuine piety. So that, as their knowledge was obtained by tradition, they would be in a condition to preserve it in the greatest purity. **24. And Enoch walked with God**—a common phrase in Eastern countries denoting constant and familiar intercourse. **was not; for God took him**—In Hebrews 11:5, we are informed that he was translated to heaven—a mighty miracle, designed to effect what ordinary means of instruction had failed to accomplish, gave a palpable proof to an age of almost universal unbelief that the doctrines which he had taught (Jude 14, 15) were true and that his devotedness to the cause of God and righteousness in the midst of opposition was highly pleasing to the mind of God. **21. Enoch . . . begat Methuselah**—This name signifies, "He dieth, and the sending forth," so that Enoch gave it as prophetical of the flood. It is computed that Methuselah died in the year of that catastrophe. **26. Lamech**—a different person from the one mentioned in preceding chapter. Like his namesake, however, he also spoke in numbers on occasion of the birth of Noah—i. e., "rest" or "comfort." "The allusion is, undoubtedly, to the penal consequences of the fall in earthly toils and sufferings, and to the hope of a Deliverer, excited by the promise made to Eve. That this expectation was founded on a divine communication we infer from the importance attached to it and the confidence of its expression" [PETER SMITH]. **32. Noah was five hundred years old: and . . . begat**—That he and the other patriarchs were advanced in life before children were born to them is a difficulty accounted for probably from the circumstance that Moses does not here record their first-born sons, but only the succession from Adam through Seth to Abraham.

CHAPTER 6

Vss. 1-22. WICKEDNESS OF THE WORLD. **2. the sons of God saw the daughters of men**—By the former is meant the family of Seth, who were professedly religious; by the latter, the descendants of apostate Cain. Mixed marriages between parties of opposite principles and practice were necessarily sources of extensive corruption. The women, irreligious themselves, would as wives and mothers exert an influence fatal to the existence of religion in their household, and consequently the people of that later age sank to the lowest depravity. **3. flesh** —utterly, hopelessly debased. **And the Lord said, My spirit shall not always strive**—Christ, as God, had by His Spirit inspiring Enoch, Noah, and perhaps other prophets (I Pet. 3:20); II Pet. 2:5; Jude 14), preached repentance to the antediluvians; but they were incorrigible. **yet his days shall be an hundred and twenty years**—It was probable that the corruption of the world, which had now reached its height, had been long and *gradually* increasing, and this idea receives support from the long respite granted. **4. giants**—The term in *Hebrew* implies not so much the idea of great stature as of reckless ferocity, impious and daring characters, who spread devastation and carnage far and wide. **5, 6. God saw it . . . repented . . . grieved**—God cannot change (Mal. 3:6; Jas. 1:17); but, by language *suited to our nature and experience*, He is described as about to alter His visible procedure towards mankind—from being merciful and long-suffering, He was about to show Himself a God of judgment; and, as that impious race had filled up the measure of their iniquities, He was about to introduce a terrible display of His justice (Eccles. 8:11). **8. But Noah found grace in the eyes of the Lord**—favor. What an awful state of things when only one man or one family of piety and virtue was now existing among the professed sons of God! **9. Noah . . . just . . . and perfect**—not absolutely; for since the fall of Adam no man has been free from sin except Jesus Christ. But as living by faith he was just (Gal. 3:2; Heb. 11:7) and perfect—i.e., sincere in his desire to do God's will. **11. the earth was filled with violence** —In the absence of any well-regulated government it is easy to imagine what evils would arise. Men did what was right in their own eyes, and, having no fear of God, destruction and misery were in their ways. **13. And God said unto Noah**—How startling must have been the announcement of the threatened destruction! There was no outward indication of it. The course of nature and experience seemed against the probability of its occurrence. The public opinion of mankind would ridicule it. The whole world would be ranged against him. Yet, persuaded the communication was from God, through faith (Heb. 11:7), he set about preparing the means for preserving himself and family from the impending calamity. **14. Make thee an ark**—ark, a hollow chest (Exod.2:3). **gopher wood**—probably cypress, remarkable for its durability and abounding on the Armenian mountains. **rooms**—cabins or small cells. **pitch it within and without**—mineral pitch, asphalt, naphtha, or some bituminous substance, which, when smeared over and become hardened, would make it perfectly watertight. **15. And this is the fashion**—According to the description, the ark was not a ship, but an immense house in form and structure like the houses in the East, designed not to sail, but only to float. Assuming the cubit to be 21.888 inches, the ark would be 547 feet long, 91 feet 2 inches wide, and 47 feet 2 inches high.

16. A window—probably a skylight, formed of some transparent substance unknown. **in a cubit shalt thou finish it above**—a direction to raise the roof in the middle, seemingly to form a gentle slope for letting the water run off. **17-22. And, behold, I, even I, do bring a flood**—The repetition of the announcement was to establish its certainty (ch. 41:32). Whatever opinion may be entertained as to the operation of natural laws and agencies in the deluge, it was brought on the world by God as a punishment for the enormous wickedness of its inhabitants. **18. But with thee will I establish my covenant**—a special promise of deliverance, called a covenant, to convince him of the confidence to be reposed in it. The substance and terms of this covenant are related between vss. 19 and 21. **22. Thus did Noah**—He began without delay to prepare the colossal fabric, and in every step of his progress faithfully followed the divine directions he had received.

CHAPTER 7

Vss. 1-24. ENTRANCE INTO THE ARK. **1. And the Lord said unto Noah, Come thou and all thy house into the ark**—The ark was finished; and Noah now, in the spirit of implicit faith, which had influenced his whole conduct, waited for directions from God. **2, 3. Of every clean beast . . . fowls**—Pairs of every species of animals, except the tenants of the deep, were to be taken for the preservation of their respective kinds. This was the general rule of admission, only with regard to those animals which are styled "clean," three pairs were to be taken, whether of beasts or birds; and the reason was that their rapid multiplication was a matter of the highest importance, when the earth should be renovated, for their utility either as articles of food or as employed in the service of man. But what was the use of the seventh? It was manifestly reserved for sacrifice; and so that both during Noah's residence in the ark, and after his return to dry land, provision was made for celebrating the rites of worship according to the religion of fallen man. He did not, like many, leave religion behind. He provided for it during his protracted voyage. **4. For yet seven days**—A week for a world to repent! What a solemn pause! Did they laugh and ridicule his folly still? He whose eyes saw and whose heart felt the full amount of human iniquity and perverseness has told us of their reckless disregard (Luke 17:27). **9. There went in two and two**—Doubtless they were led by a divine impulse. The number would not be so large as at first sight one is apt to imagine. It has been calculated that there are not more than three hundred distinct species of beasts and birds, the immense varieties in regard to form, size, and color being traceable to the influence of climate and other circumstances. **16. and the Lord shut him in**—lit., "covered him round about." The "shutting him in" intimated that he had become the special object of divine care and protection, and that to those without the season of grace was over (Matt. 25:10). **17. the waters increased, and bare up the ark**—It seems to have been raised so gradually as to be scarcely perceptible to its occupants. **20. Fifteen cubits upward . . . and the mountains were covered**—twenty-two and a half feet above the summits of the highest hills. The language is not consistent with the theory of a partial deluge. **21. all flesh died . . . fowl . . . cattle, and . . . creeping thing**—It has been a uniform principle in the divine procedure, when judgments were abroad on the earth, to include every thing connected with the sinful objects of His wrath (ch. 19:25; Exod. 9:6). Besides, now that the human race was reduced to one single family, it was necessary that the beasts should be proportionally diminished, otherwise by their numbers they would have acquired the ascendancy and overmastered the few that were to repeople the world. Thus goodness was mingled with severity; the Lord exercises judgment in wisdom and in wrath remembers mercy. **24. an hundred and fifty days**—a period of five months. Though long before that every living creature must have been drowned, such a lengthened continuance of the flood was designed to manifest God's stern displeasure at sin and sinners. Think of Noah during such a crisis. We learn (Ezek. 14:14) that he was a man who lived and breathed habitually in an atmosphere of devotion; and having in the exercise of this high-toned faith made God his refuge, he did not fear "though the waters roared and were troubled; though the mountains shook with the swelling thereof."

CHAPTER 8

Vss. 1-14. ASSUAGING OF THE WATERS. **1. God remembered Noah**—The divine purpose in this awful dispensation had been accomplished, and the world had undergone those changes necessary to fit it for becoming the residence of man under a new economy of Providence. **every living thing . . . in the ark**—a beautiful illustration of Matthew 10:29. **and God made a wind to pass over the earth**—Though the divine will could have dried up the liquid mass in an instant, the agency of a wind was employed (Ps. 104:4)—probably a hot wind, which, by rapid evaporation, would again absorb one portion of the waters into the atmosphere; and by which, the other would be gradually drained off by outlets beneath. **4. seventh month**—of the year—not of the flood—which lasted only five months. **rested**—evidently indicating a calm and gentle motion. **upon the mountains of Ararat**—or Armenia, as the word is rendered (II Kings 19:37; Isa. 37:38). The mountain which tradition points to as the one on which the ark rested is now called Ara Dagh, the "finger mountain." Its summit consists of two peaks, the higher of which is 17,750 feet and the other 13,420 above the level of the sea. **5. And the waters decreased continually**—The decrease of the waters was for wise reasons exceedingly slow and gradual—the period of their return being nearly twice as long as that of their rise. **6. at the end of forty days**—It is easy to imagine the ardent longing Noah and his family must have felt to enjoy again the sight of land as well as breathe the fresh air; and it was perfectly consistent with faith and patience to make inquiries whether the earth was yet ready. **7. And he sent forth a raven**—The smell of carrion would allure it to remain if the earth were in a habitable state. But it kept hovering about the spot, and, being a solitary bird, probably perched on the covering. **8-11. Also he sent forth a dove**—a bird flying low and naturally disposed to return to the place of her abode. **10. again he sent forth a dove**—Her flight, judging by the time she was abroad, was pursued to a great distance, and the newly plucked olive leaf, she no doubt by supernatural impulse brought in her bill, afforded a welcome proof that the declivities of the hills were clear. **12. he . . . sent forth the dove: which returned not . . . any more**—In these results, we perceive a wisdom and prudence far superior to the inspiration of instinct—we discern the agency of God guiding all the movements of this bird for the in-

struction of Noah, and reviving the hopes of his household. **other seven days**—a strong presumptive proof that Noah observed the Sabbath during his residence in the ark. **13, 14. Noah removed the covering of the ark**—probably only as much of it as would afford him a prospect of the earth around. Yet for about two months he never stirred from his appointed abode till he had received the express permission of God. We should watch the leading of Providence to direct us in every step of the journey of life.

15-22. DEPARTURE FROM THE ARK. **15, 16. And God spake . . . Go forth**—They went forth in the most orderly manner—the human occupants first—then each species "after their kinds," lit., according to their families, implying that there had been an increase in the ark. **20. Noah builded an altar**—lit., "a high place"—probably a mound of earth, on which a sacrifice was offered. There is something exceedingly beautiful and interesting to know that the first care of this devout patriarch was to return thanks for the signal instance of mercy and goodness which he and his family had experienced. **took of every clean beast, and . . . fowl**—For so unparalleled a deliverance, a special acknowledgment was due. **21. The Lord smelled a sweet savour**—The sacrifice offered by a righteous man like Noah in faith was acceptable as the most fragrant incense. **Lord said in his heart**—same as "I have sworn that the waters of Noah should no more go over the earth" (Isa. 54:9). **for**—i.e., "though the imagination is evil"; instead of inflicting another destructive flood, I shall spare them—to enjoy the blessings of grace, through a Saviour. **22. While the earth remaineth**—The consummation, as intimated in II Peter 3:7, does not frustrate a promise which held good only during the continuance of that system. There will be no flood between this and that day, when the earth therein shall be burnt up [CHALMERS].

CHAPTER 9

Vss. 1-7. COVENANT. **1. And God blessed Noah** —Here is republished the law of nature that was announced to Adam, consisting as it originally did of several parts. **Be fruitful**, etc.—The first part relates to the transmission of life, the original blessing being reannounced in the very same words in which it had been promised at first. **2. And the fear of you and the dread of you**—The second part re-establishes man's dominion over the inferior animals; it was now founded not as at first in love and kindness, but in terror; this dread of man prevails among all the stronger as well as the weaker members of the animal tribes and keeps away from his haunts all but those employed in his service. **3. Every moving thing that liveth shall be meat for you**—The third part concerns the means of sustaining life; man was for the first time, it would seem, allowed the use of animal food. but the grant was accompanied with one restriction. **4. But flesh . . . the blood . . . shall ye not eat**—The sole intention of this prohibition was to prevent these excesses of cannibal ferocity in eating flesh of living animals, to which men in the earlier ages of the world were liable. **5. surely your blood of your lives will I require**—The fourth part establishes a new power for *protecting* life—the institution of the civil magistrate (Rom. 13:4), armed with public and official authority to repress the commission of violence and crime. Such a power had not previously existed in patriarchal society. **6. Whoso sheddeth man's blood . . . for in the image of**

God made he man—It is true that image has been injured by the fall, but it is not lost. In this view, a high value is attached to the life of every man, even the poorest and humblest, and an awful criminality is involved in the destruction of it.

8-29. RAINBOW. **13. I do set my bow in the cloud**—set, i.e., constitute or appoint. This common and familiar phenomenon being made the pledge of peace, its appearance when showers began to fall would be welcomed with the liveliest feelings of joy. **20. And Noah ... planted a vineyard**—Noah had been probably bred to the culture of the soil, and resumed that employment on leaving the ark. **21. And he drank of the wine, and was drunken**—perhaps at the festivities of the vintage season. This solitary stain on the character of so eminently pious a man must, it is believed, have been the result of age or inadvertency. **24.** This incident could scarcely have happened till twenty years after the flood; for Canaan, whose conduct was more offensive than that even of his father, was not born till after that event. It is probable that there is a long interval included between these verses and that this prophecy, like that of Jacob on his sons, was not uttered till near the close of Noah's life when the prophetic spirit came upon him; this presumption is strengthened by the mention of his death immediately after. **25. Cursed be Canaan**—This doom has been fulfilled in the destruction of the Canaanites—in the degradation of Egypt and the slavery of the Africans, the descendants of Ham. **26. Blessed be the Lord God of Shem**—rather, "Blessed of Jehovah, my God, be Shem,"—an intimation that the descendants of Shem should be peculiarly honored in the service of the true God—His Church being for ages established among them (the Jews), and of them, concerning the flesh, Christ came. They got possession of Canaan, the people of that land being made their "servants" either by conquest, or, like the Gibeonites, by submission. **27. God shall enlarge Japheth**—pointing to a vast increase in posterity and possessions. Accordingly his descendants have been the most active and enterprising, spread over the best and largest portion of the world, all Europe and a considerable part of Asia. **he shall dwell in the tents of Shem**—a prophecy being fulfilled at the present day, as in India British Government is established and the Anglo-Saxons being in the ascendancy from Europe to India, from India over the American continent. What a wonderful prophecy in a few verses (Isa. 46:10; I Peter 1:25)!

CHAPTER 10

Vss. 1-32. GENEALOGIES. **1. sons of Noah**—The historian has not arranged this catalogue according to seniority of birth; for the account begins with the descendants of Japheth, and the line of Ham is given before that of Shem though he is expressly said to be the youngest or younger son of Noah; and Shem was the elder brother of Japheth (vs. 21), the true rendering of that passage. **generations**, etc.—the narrative of the settlement of nations existing in the time of Moses, perhaps only the principal ones; for though the list comprises the sons of Shem, Ham, and Japheth, *all their descendants* are not enumerated. Those descendants, with one or two exceptions, are described by names indicative of tribes and nations and ending in the Hebrew *im*, or the English "ite." **5. the isles of the Gentiles**—a phrase by which the Hebrews described all countries which were accessible by sea (Isa. 11:11; 20:6; Jer. 25:22).

Such in relation to them were the countries of Europe, the peninsula of Lesser Asia, and the region lying on the east of the Euxine. Accordingly, it was in these quarters the early descendants of Japheth had their settlements. **6. sons of Ham**—emigrated southward, and their settlements were: Cush in Arabia, Canaan in the country known by his name, and Mizraim in Egypt, Upper and Lower. It is generally thought that his father accompanied him and personally superintended the formation of the settlement, whence Egypt was called "the land of Ham." **8. Nimrod**—mentioned as eclipsing all his family in renown. He early distinguished himself by his daring and successful prowess in hunting wild beasts. By those useful services he earned a title to public gratitude; and, having established a permanent ascendancy over the people, he founded the first kingdom in the world. **10. the beginning of his kingdom**—This kingdom, of course, though then considered great, would be comparatively limited in extent, and the towns but small forts. **11. Out of that land went forth Asshur**—or, as the *Margin* has it, "He [Nimrod] at the head of his army went forth into Assyria," i.e., he pushed his conquests into that country. **and builded Nineveh**—opposite the town of Mosul, on the Tigris, and the other towns near it. This raid into Assyria was an invasion of the territories of Shem, and hence the name "Nimrod," signifying "rebel," is supposed to have been conferred on him from his daring revolt against the divine distribution. **21. Unto Shem**—The historian introduces him with marked distinction as "the father of Eber," the ancestor of the Hebrews. **23. Aram**—In the general division of the earth, the countries of Armenia, Mesopotamia, and Syria, fell to his descendants. **24. Arphaxad**—The settlement of his posterity was in the extensive valley of Shinar, on the Tigris, towards the southern extremity of Mesopotamia, including the country of Eden and the region on the east side of the river. **25. Peleg; for in his days was the earth divided**—After the flood (ch. 11:10-16) the descendants of Noah settled at pleasure and enjoyed the produce of the undivided soil. But according to divine instruction, made probably through Eber, who seems to have been distinguished for piety or a prophetic character, the earth was divided and his son's name, "Peleg," was given in memory of that event (see Deut. 32:8; Acts 17:26). **32. These are the families of the sons of Noah after their generations, in their nations, etc.**—This division was made in the most orderly manner; and the inspired historian evidently intimates that the sons of Noah were ranged according to their nations, and every nation ranked by its families, so that every nation had its assigned territory, and in every nation the tribes, and in every tribe the families, were located by themselves.

CHAPTER 11

Vss. 1-32. CONFUSION OF TONGUES. **1. the whole earth was of one language**—The descendants of Noah, united by the strong bond of a common language, had not separated, and notwithstanding the divine command to replenish the earth, were unwilling to separate. The more pious and well-disposed would of course obey the divine will; but a numerous body, seemingly the aggressive horde mentioned (ch. 10:10), determined to please themselves by occupying the fairest region they came to. **2. land of Shinar**—The fertile valley watered by the Euphrates and Tigris was chosen as the center of their union and the seat of their power. **3. brick**—There being no stone in that quarter, brick is, and was, the only material used for building, as appears in the mass of ruins which at the Birs Nimroud may have been the very town formed by those ancient rebels. Some of these are sun-dried—others burnt in the kiln and of different colors. **slime**—bitumen, a mineral pitch, which, when hardened, forms a strong cement, commonly used in Assyria to this day, and forming the mortar found on the burnt-brick remains of antiquity. **4. a tower whose top may reach unto heaven**—a common figurative expression for great height (Deut. 1:28; 9:1-6). **6. now nothing will be restrained from them**—an apparent admission that the design was practicable, and would have been executed but for the divine interposition. **lest we be scattered**—To build a city and a town was no crime; but to do this to defeat the counsels of heaven by attempting to prevent emigration was foolish, wicked, and justly offensive to God. **7. confound their language**—lit., "their lip"; it was a failure in utterance, occasioning a difference in dialect which was intelligible only to those of the same tribe. Thus easily by God their purpose was defeated, and they were compelled to the dispersion they had combined to prevent. It is only from the Scriptures we learn the true origin of the different nations and languages of the world. By one miracle of tongues men were dispersed and gradually fell from true religion. By another, national barriers were broken down—that all men might be brought back to the family of God. **28. Ur** (now Orfa)—i.e., light, or fire. Its name probably derived from its being devoted to the rites of fire worship. Terah and his family were equally infected with that idolatry as the rest of the inhabitants (Josh. 24:15). **31. Sarai his daughter-in-law**—the same as Iscah, grand-daughter of Terah, probably by a second wife, and by early usages considered marriageable to her uncle, Abraham. **and they came unto Haran**—two days' journey south-southeast from Ur, on the direct road to the ford of the Euphrates at Rakka, the nearest and most convenient route to Palestine.

CHAPTER 12

Vss. 1-20. CALL TO ABRAM. **1. Now the Lord had said unto Abram**—It pleased God, who has often been found of them who sought Him not, to reveal Himself to Abraham perhaps by a miracle; and the conversion of Abraham is one of the most remarkable in Bible history. **Get thee out of thy country**—His being brought to the knowledge and worship of the true God had probably been a considerable time before. This call included two promises: the first, showing the land of his future posterity; and the second, that in his posterity all the earth was to be blessed. Abraham obeyed, and it is frequently mentioned in the New Testament as a striking instance of his faith (Heb. 11:8). **5. into the land of Canaan ... they came**—with his wife and an orphan nephew. Abram reached his destination in safety, and thus the first promise was made good. **6. the place of Sichem**—or Shechem, a pastoral valley then unoccupied (cf. ch. 33:18). **plain of Moreh**—rather, the "terebinth tree" of Moreh, very common in Palestine, remarkable for its wide-spreading branches and its dark green foliage. It is probable that in Moreh there was a grove of these trees, whose inviting shade led Abram to choose it for an encampment. **7. Unto thy seed will I give this land**—God was dealing with Abram not in his private and personal capacity merely, but with a view to high and important interests in future ages. That land his posterity was for centuries to inhabit as a peculiar people; the seeds of divine knowledge were to be sown there for the benefit of all mankind; and considered in its geographical situation, it was chosen in divine wisdom as the fittest of all lands to serve as the cradle of a divine revelation designed for the whole world. **and there builded he an altar unto the Lord**—By this solemn act of devotion he made an open profession of his religion, established the worship of the true God, and declared his faith in the promise. **10. there was a famine ... and Abram went down into Egypt**—did not go back to the place of his nativity, as regretting his pilgrimage and despising the promised land (Heb. 11:15), but withdrew for a while into a neighboring country. **11-13.** Sarai's complexion, coming from a mountainous country, would be fresh and fair compared with the faces of Egyptian women which were sallow. The counsel of Abram to her was true in words, but it was a deception, intended to give an impression that she was no more than his sister. His conduct was culpable and inconsistent with his character as a servant of God: it showed a reliance on worldly policy more than a trust in the promise; and he not only sinned himself, but tempted Sarai to sin also. **14. when Abram was come into Egypt**—It appears from the monuments of that country that at the time of Abram's visit a monarchy had existed for several centuries. The seat of government was in the Delta, the most northern part of the country, the very quarter in which Abram must have arrived. They were a race of shepherd kings, in close alliance with the people of Canaan. **15. the woman was taken into Pharaoh's house**—Eastern kings have for ages claimed the privilege of taking to their harem an unmarried woman whom they like. The father or brother may deplore the removal as a calamity, but the royal right is never resisted nor questioned. **16. he entreated Abram well for her sake**—The presents are just what one pastoral chief would give to another. **18-20.** Here is a most humiliating rebuke, and Abram deserved it. Had not God interfered, he might have been tempted to stay in Egypt and forget the promise (Ps. 105:13, 15). Often still does God rebuke His people and remind them through enemies that this world is not their rest.

CHAPTER 13

Vss. 1-18. RETURN FROM EGYPT. **1. went up ... south**—Palestine being a highland country, the entrance from Egypt by its southern boundary is a continual ascent. **2. very rich**—compared with the pastoral tribes to which Abraham belonged. An Arab sheik is considered rich who has a hundred or two hundred tents, from sixty to a hundred camels, a thousand sheep and goats respectively. And Abraham being very rich, must have far exceeded that amount of pastoral property. "Gold and silver" being rare among these peoples, his probably arose from the sale of his produce in Egypt. **3. went on his journeys**—His progress would be by slow marches and frequent encampments as he had to regulate his movements by the prospect of water and pasturage. **unto the place ... between Beth-el and Hai**—"a conspicuous hill—its topmost summit resting on the rocky slopes below, and distinguished by its olive groves—offering a natural base for the altar and a fitting shade for the tent of the patriarch" [STANLEY]. **4. there Abram called on the name of** the Lord—He felt a strong desire to reanimate his faith and piety on the scene of his former worship: it might be to express humility and penitence for his misconduct in Egypt or thankfulness for deliverance from perils—to embrace the first opportunity on returning to Canaan of leading his family to renew allegiance to God and offer the typical sacrifices which pointed to the blessings of the promise. **7. And there was a strife**—Abraham's character appears here in a most amiable light. Having a strong sense of religion, he was afraid of doing anything that might tend to injure its character or bring discredit on its name, and he rightly judged that such unhappy effects would be produced if two persons whom nature and grace had so closely connected should come to a rupture. Waiving his right to dictate, he gave the freedom of choice to Lot. The conduct of Abraham was not only disinterested and peaceable, but generous and condescending in an extraordinary degree, exemplifying the Scripture precepts (Matt. 6:32; Rom. 12:10, 11; Phil. 2:4). **10. Lot lifted up his eyes**—Travellers say that from the top of this hill, a little "to the east of Bethel," they can see the Jordan, the broad meadows on either bank, and the waving line of verdure which marks the course of the stream. **11. Then Lot chose him all the plain**—a choice excellent from a worldly point of view, but most inexpedient for his best interests. He seems, though a good man, to have been too much under the influence of a selfish and covetous spirit: and how many, alas! imperil the good of their souls for the prospect of worldly advantage. **14, 15. Lift up now thine eyes ... all the land which thou seest**—So extensive a survey of the country, *in all directions*, can be obtained from no other point in the neighborhood; and those plains and hills, then lying desolate before the eyes of the solitary patriarch, were to be peopled with a mighty nation "like the dust of the earth in number," as they were in Solomon's time (I Kings 4:20). **18. plain of Mamre ... built ... an altar**—grove of Mamre—the renewal of the promise was acknowledged by Abram by a fresh tribute of devout gratitude.

CHAPTER 14

Vss. 1-24. WAR. **1. And it came to pass**—This chapter presents Abram in the unexpected character of a warrior. The occasion was this: The king of Sodom and the kings of the adjoining cities, after having been tributaries for twelve years to the king of Elam, combined to throw off his yoke. To chastise their rebellion, as he deemed it, Chedorlaomer, with the aid of three allies, invaded the territories of the refractory princes, defeated them in a pitched battle where the nature of the ground favored his army (vs. 10), and hastened in triumph on his homeward march, with a large amount of captives and booty, though merely a stranger. **12. they took Lot ... and his goods, and departed**—How would the conscience of that young man now upbraid him for his selfish folly and ingratitude in withdrawing from his kind and pious relative! Whenever we go out of the path of duty, we put ourselves away from God's protection, and cannot expect that the choice we make will be for our lasting good. **13. there came one that had escaped**—Abram might have excused himself from taking any active concern in his "brother," i.e., nephew, who little deserved that he should incur trouble or danger on *his* account. But Abram, far from rendering evil for evil, resolved to take immediate measures for the

rescue of Lot. **14. And when Abram heard that his brother was taken captive, he armed his trained servants**—domestic slaves, such as are common in Eastern countries still and are considered and treated as members of the family. If Abram could spare three hundred and eighteen slaves and leave a sufficient number to take care of the flocks, what a large establishment he must have had. **15, 16. he divided himself ... by night**—This war between the petty princes of ancient Canaan is exactly the same as the frays and skirmishes between Arab chiefs in the present day. When a defeated party resolves to pursue the enemy, they wait till they are fast asleep; then, as they have no idea of posting sentinels, they rush upon them from different directions, strike down the tent poles—if there is any fight at all, it is the fray of a tumultuous mob—a panic commonly ensues, and the whole contest is ended with little or no loss on either side. **18. Melchizedek**—This victory conferred a public benefit on that part of the country; and Abram, on his return, was treated with high respect and consideration, particularly by the king of Sodom and Melchizedek, who seems to have been one of the few native princes, if not the only one, who knew and worshipped, "the most high God," whom Abram served. This king who was a type of the Saviour (Heb. 7:1), came to bless God for the victory which had been won, and in the name of God to bless Abram, by whose arms it had been achieved—a pious acknowledgment which we should imitate on succeeding in any lawful enterprise. **20. he gave him tithes of all**—Here is an evidence of Abram's piety, as well as of his valor; for it was to a priest or official mediator between God and him that Abram gave a tenth of the spoil—a token of his gratitude and in honor of a divine ordinance (Prov. 3:9). **21. the king of Sodom said ... Give me the persons**—According to the war customs still existing among the Arab tribes, Abram might have retained the recovered goods—and his right was acknowledged by the king of Sodom. But with honest pride, and a generosity unknown in that part of the world, he replied with strong phraseology common to the East, "I have lifted up mine hand [i.e., I have sworn] unto the Lord that I will not take from a thread even to a sandal-thong—that I will not take any thing that is thine, lest thou shouldst say, I have made Abram rich."

CHAPTER 15

Vss. 1-21. DIVINE ENCOURAGEMENT. **1. After these things**—the conquest of the invading kings. **the word of the Lord**—a phrase used, when connected with a vision, to denote a prophetic message. **Fear not, Abram**—When the excitement of the enterprise was over, he had become a prey to despondency and terror at the probable revenge that might be meditated against him. To dispel his fear, he was favored with this gracious announcement. Having such a promise, how well did it become him (and all God's people who have the same promise) to dismiss fears, and cast all burdens on the Lord (Ps. 27:3). **2. Lord God, what wilt thou give?**—To his mind the declaration, "I am thy exceeding great reward," had but one meaning, or was viewed but in one particular light, as bearing on the fulfilment of the promise, and he was still experiencing the sickness of hope deferred. **Eliezer of Damascus ... one born in my house is mine heir**—According to the usage of nomadic tribes, his chief confidential servant would be heir to his possessions and honors. But this man could have become his son only by adoption; and how sadly would that have come short of the parental hopes he had been encouraged to entertain! His language betrayed a latent spirit of fretfulness or perhaps a temporary failure in the very virtue for which he is so renowned—and absolute submission to God's time, as well as way, of accomplishing His promise. **4. This shall not be thine heir**—To the first part of his address no reply was given; but having renewed it in a spirit of more becoming submission, "whereby shall I know that I shall inherit it," he was delighted by a most explicit promise of Canaan, which was immediately confirmed by a remarkable ceremony. **9-12. Take me an heifer,** etc.—On occasions of great importance, when two or more parties join in a compact, they either observe precisely the same rites as Abram did, or, where they do not, they invoke the lamp as their witness. According to these ideas, which have been from time immemorial engraven on the minds of Eastern people, the Lord Himself condescended to enter into covenant with Abram. The patriarch did not pass between the sacrifice and the reason was that in this transaction he was bound to nothing. He asked a sign, and God was pleased to give him a sign, by which, according to Eastern ideas, He bound Himself. In like manner God has entered into covenant with us; and in the glory of the only begotten Son, who passed through between God and us, all who believe have, like Abram, a sign or pledge in the gift of the Spirit, whereby they may know that they shall inherit the heavenly Canaan.

CHAPTER 16

Vss. 1-16. BESTOWMENT OF HAGAR. **1. Now Sarai ... had a handmaid**—a female slave—one of those obtained in Egypt. **3. Sarai ... gave her to ... Abram to be his wife**—Wife is here used to describe an inferior, though not degrading, relation, in countries where polygamy prevails. In the case of these female slaves, who are the personal property of his lady, being purchased before her marriage or given as a special present to her, no one can become the husband's secondary wife without her mistress' consent or permission. This usage seems to have prevailed in patriarchal times; and Hagar, Sarai's slave, of whom she had the entire right of disposing, was given by her mistress' spontaneous offer, to be the secondary wife of Abram, in the hope of obtaining the long-looked—for heir. It was a wrong step—indicating a want of simple reliance on God—and Sarai was the first to reap the bitter fruits of her device. **5. And Sarai said ... My wrong be upon thee**—Bursts of temper, or blows, as the original may bear, took place till at length Hagar, perceiving the hopelessness of maintaining the unequal strife, resolved to escape from what had become to her in reality, as well as in name, a house of bondage. **7. And the angel of the Lord found her by a fountain**—This well, pointed out by tradition, lay on the side of the caravan road, in the midst of Shur, a sandy desert on the west of Arabia Petræa, to the extent of 150 miles, between Palestine and Egypt. By taking that direction, she seems to have intended to return to her relatives in that country. Nothing but pride, passion, and sullen obstinacy, could have driven any solitary person to brave the dangers of such an inhospitable wild; and she would have died, had not the timely appearance and words of the angel recalled her to reflection and duty. **11. Ishmael**—Like other Hebrew names, this had a signification, and it

is made up of two words—"God hears." The reason is explained. **12. he will be a wild man**—lit., "a wild ass man," expressing how the wildness of Ishmael and his descendants resembles that of the wild ass. **his hand will be against every man**—descriptive of the rude, turbulent, and plundering character of the Arabs. **dwell in the presence of all his brethren**—dwell, i.e., pitch tents; and the meaning is that they maintain their independence in spite of all attempts to extirpate or subdue them. **13. called the name**—common in ancient times to name places from circumstances; and the name given to this well was a grateful recognition of God's gracious appearance in the hour of her distress.

CHAPTER 17

Vss. 1-27. RENEWAL OF THE COVENANT. **1. Abram ... ninety years old and nine**—thirteen years after the birth of Ishmael. During that interval he had enjoyed the comforts of communion with God but had been favored with no special revelation as formerly, probably on account of his hasty and blameable marriage with Hagar. **the Lord appeared**—some visible manifestation of the divine presence, probably the Shekinah or radiant glory of overpowering effulgence. **I am the Almighty God**—the name by which He made Himself known to the patriarchs (Exod. 6:3), designed to convey the sense of "all-sufficient" (Ps. 16:5, 6; 73:25). **walk ... and be ... perfect**—upright, sincere (Ps. 51:6) in heart, speech, and behavior. **3. Abram fell on his face**—the attitude of profoundest reverence assumed by Eastern people. It consists in the prostrate body resting on the hands and knees, with the face bent till the forehead touches the ground. It is an expression of conscious humility and profound reverence. **4. my covenant is with thee**—Renewed mention is made of it as the foundation of the communication that follows. It is the covenant of grace made with all who believe in the Saviour. **5. but thy name shall be Abraham**—In Eastern countries a change of name is an advertisement of some new circumstance in the history, rank, or religion of the individual who bears it. The change is made variously, by the old name being entirely dropped for the new, or by conjoining the new with the old; or sometimes only a few letters are inserted, so that the altered form may express the difference in the owner's state or prospects. It is surprising how soon a new name is known and its import spread through the country. In dealing with Abraham and Sarai, God was pleased to adapt His procedure to the ideas and customs of the country and age. Instead of Abram, "a high father," he was to be called Abraham, "father of a multitude of nations" (Rev. 2:17). **6-8. I will give unto thee ... the land**—It had been previously promised to Abraham and his posterity (ch. 15:18). Here it is promised as an "everlasting possession," and was, therefore, a type of heaven, "the better country" (Heb. 11:16). **10. Every man child among you shall be circumcised**—This was the sign in the Old Testament Church as baptism is in the New, and hence the covenant is called "covenant of circumcision" (Acts 7:8; Rom. 4:11). The terms of the covenant were these: on the one hand Abraham and his seed were to observe the right of circumcision; and on the other, God promised, in the event of such observance, to give them Canaan for a perpetual possession, to be a God to him and his posterity, and that in him and his seed all nations should be blessed. **15, 16. As for Sarai ... I will**

...**give thee a son also of her**—God's purposes are gradually made known. A son had been long ago promised to Abraham. Now, at length, for the first time he is informed that it was to be a child of Sarai. **17. Abraham fell upon his face, and laughed**—It was not the sneer of unbelief, but a smile of delight at the improbability of the event (Rom. 4:20). **18. O that Ishmael might live before thee**—natural solicitude of a parent. But God's thoughts are not as man's thoughts. **19, 20.** The blessings of the covenant are reserved for Isaac, but common blessings were abundantly promised to Ishmael; and though the visible Church did not descend from his family, yet personally he might, and it is to be hoped *did*, enjoy its benefits.

CHAPTER 18

Vss. 1-8. ENTERTAINMENT OF ANGELS. **1. the Lord appeared**—another manifestation of the divine presence, more familiar than any yet narrated; and more like that in the fulness of time, when the Word was made flesh. **plains of Mamre**—rather, terebinth or oak of Mamre—a tall-spreading tree or grove of trees. **sat in the tent door**—The tent itself being too close and sultry at noon, the shaded open front is usually resorted to for the air that may be stirring. **2. lift up his eyes ... and, lo, three men**—Travellers in that quarter start at sunrise and continue till midday when they look out for some resting-place. **he ran to meet them**—When the visitor is an ordinary person, the host merely rises; but if of superior rank, the custom is to advance a little towards the stranger, and after a very low bow, turn and lead him to the tent, putting an arm round his waist, or tapping him on the shoulder as they go, to assure him of welcome. **3. My Lord, if now I have found favor**—The hospitalities offered are just of the kind that are necessary and most grateful, the refreshment of water, for feet exposed to dust and heat by the sandals, being still the first observed among the pastoral people of Hebron. **5. for therefore are ye come**—No questions were asked. But Abraham knew their object by the course they took—approaching directly in *front* of the chief sheik's tent, which is always distinguishable from the rest and thus showing their wish to be his guests. **6. Abraham hastened ... unto Sarah ... make cakes upon the hearth**—Bread is baked daily, no more than is required for family use, and always by the women, commonly the wife. It is a short process. Flour mixed with water is made into dough, and being rolled out into cakes, it is placed on the earthen floor, previously heated by a fire. The fire being removed, the cakes are laid on the ground, and being covered over with hot embers, are soon baked, and eaten the moment they are taken off. **7. Abraham ran unto the herd, and fetched a calf**—Animal food is never provided, except for visitors of a superior rank when a kid or lamb is killed. A calf is still a higher stretch of hospitality, and it would probably be cooked as is usually done when haste is required—either by roasting it whole or by cutting it up into small pieces and broiling them on skewers over the fire. It is always eaten along with boiled corn swimming in butter or melted fat, into which every morsel of meat, laid upon a piece of bread, is dipped, before being conveyed by the fingers to the mouth. **8. milk** —A bowl of camel's milk ends the repast. **he stood by them under the tree**—The host himself, even though he has a number of servants, deems it a necessary act of politeness to *stand* while his guests

are at their food, and Abraham evidently did this before he was aware of the real character of his visitors. 9-15. REPROOF OF SARAH. An inquiry about his wife, so surprising in strangers, the subject of conversation, and the fulfilment of the fondly cherished promise within a specified time, showed Abraham that he had been entertaining more than ordinary travellers (Heb. 13:2). **10. Sarah heard it in the tent door, which was behind him**—The women's apartment is in the back of the tent, divided by a thin partition from the men's. **12. Therefore Sarah laughed within herself**—Long delay seems to have weakened faith. Sarah treated the announcement as incredible, and when taxed with the silent sneer, she added falsehood to distrust. It was an aggravated offense (Acts 5:4), and nothing but grace saved her (Rom. 9:18).

16-22. DISCLOSURE OF SODOM'S DOOM. **16. the men rose ... Abraham went with them**—It is customary for a host to escort his guests a little way. **17. the Lord said, Shall I hide**—The chief stranger, no other than the Lord, disclosed to Abraham the awful doom about to be inflicted on Sodom and the cities of the plain for their enormous wickedness. **21. I will go down ... and see**—language used after the manner of men. These cities were to be made examples to all future ages of God's severity; and therefore ample proof given that the judgment was neither rash nor excessive (Ezek. 18:23; Jer. 18:7). 23-33. ABRAHAM'S INTERCESSION. **23. Abraham drew near, and said**, etc.—The scene described is full of interest and instruction—showing in an unmistakable manner the efficacy of prayer and intercession. (See also Prov. 15:8; Jas. 5:16). Abraham reasoned justly as to the rectitude of the divine procedure (Rom. 3:5, 6), and many guilty cities and nations have been spared on account of God's people (Matt. 5:13; 24:22). **33. the Lord ... left communing ... and Abraham returned unto his place**— Why did Abraham cease to carry his intercessions farther? Either because he fondly thought that he was now sure of the cities being preserved (Luke 13:9), or because the Lord restrained his mind from farther intercession (Jer. 7:16; 11:14). But there were not ten "righteous persons." There was only one, and he might without injustice have perished in the general overthrow (Eccles. 9:2). But a difference is sometimes made, and on this occasion the grace of God was manifested in a signal manner for the sake of Abraham. What a blessing to be connected with a saint of God!

CHAPTER 19

Vss. 1-38. LOT'S ENTERTAINMENT. **1. there came two angels**—most probably two of those that had been with Abraham, commissioned to execute the divine judgment against Sodom. **Lot sat in the gate of Sodom**—In Eastern cities it is the market, the seat of justice, of social intercourse and amusement, especially a favorite lounge in the evenings, the arched roof affording a pleasant shade. **2. turn in, I pray you ... tarry all night**—offer of the same generous hospitalities as described in the preceding chapter, and which are still spontaneously practised in the small towns. **And they said, Nay; but we will abide in the street all night**—Where there are no inns and no acquaintance, it is not uncommon for travellers to sleep in the street wrapped up in their cloaks. **3. entered into his house**—On removing to the plain, Lot intended at first to live in his tent apart from the people. But he was gradually drawn in, dwelt in the city, and he and his family were connected with the citizens by marriage ties. **4. men of Sodom, compassed the house**—Appalling proofs are here given of their wickedness. It is evident that evil communications had corrupted good manners; otherwise Lot would never have acted as he did. **12, 13. Hast thou here any besides? ... we will destroy this place** —Apostolic authority has declared Lot was "a righteous man" (II Pet. 2:8), at bottom good, though he contented himself with lamenting the sins that he saw, instead of acting on his own convictions, and withdrawing himself and family from such a sink of corruption. But favor was shown him: and even his bad relatives had, for his sake, an offer of deliverance, which was ridiculed and spurned (II Pet. 3:4). **15-17.** The kindly interest the angels took in the preservation of Lot is beautifully displayed. But he "lingered." Was it from sorrow at the prospect of losing all his property, the acquisition of many years? Or was it that his benevolent heart was paralyzed by thoughts of the awful crisis? This is the charitable way of accounting for a delay that would have been fatal but for the friendly urgency of the angel. **18, 19. Lot said ... Oh! not so, my Lord ... I cannot escape to the mountain**—What a strange want of faith and fortitude, as if He who had interfered for his rescue would not have protected him in the mountain solitude. **21. See, I have accepted thee concerning this ... also**—His request was granted him, the prayer of faith availed, and to convince him, from his own experience, that it would have been best and safest at once to follow implicitly the divine directions. **22. Haste ... for I cannot do any thing till thou be come thither**—The ruin of Sodom was suspended till he was secure. What care God does take of His people (Rev. 7:3)! What a proof of the love which God bore to a good though weak man! **24. Then the Lord rained ... brimstone and fire from ... heaven**—God, in accomplishing His purposes, acts immediately or mediately through the agency of means; and there are strong grounds for believing that it was in the latter way He effected the overthrow of the cities of the plain—that it was, in fact, by a volcanic eruption. The raining down of fire and brimstone from heaven is perfectly accordant with this idea since those very substances, being raised into the air by the force of the volcano, would fall in a fiery shower on the surrounding region. This view seems countenanced by Job. Whether it was miraculously produced, or the natural operation employed by God, it is not of much consequence to determine: it was a divine judgment, foretold and designed for the punishment of those who were sinners exceedingly. **26.** Lot was accompanied by his wife and two daughters. But whether it was from irresistible curiosity or perturbation of feeling, or that she was about to return to save something, his wife lingered, and while thus disobeying the parting counsel, "to look not back, nor stay in all the plain," the torrent of liquid lava enveloped her so that she became the victim of her supine indolence or sinful rashness. **27. Abraham gat up early in the morning,** etc.—Abraham was at this time in Mamre, near Hebron, and a traveller last year verified the truth of this passage. "From the height which overlooks Hebron, where the patriarch stood, the observer at the present day has an extensive view spread out before him towards the Dead Sea. A cloud of smoke rising from the plain would be visible to a person at Hebron now, and could have been, therefore, to Abraham as he looked toward

Sodom on the morning of its destruction by God" [HACKETT]. It must have been an awful sight, and is frequently alluded to in Scripture (Deut. 29:23; Isa. 13:19; Jude 7). "The plain which is now covered by the Salt or Dead Sea shows in the great difference of level between the bottoms of the northern and southern ends of the lake—the latter being 13 feet and the former 1300—that the southern end was of recent formation, and submerged at the time of the fall of the cities" [LYNCH]. **29. when God destroyed the cities,** etc.—This is most welcome and instructive after so painful a narrative. It shows if God is a "consuming fire" to the wicked, He is the friend of the righteous. He "remembered" the intercessions of Abraham, and what confidence should not this give us that He will remember the intercessions of a greater than Abraham in our behalf.

CHAPTER 20

Vss. 1-18. ABRAHAM'S DENIAL OF HIS WIFE. **1. Abraham journeyed from thence ... and dwelled between Kadesh and Shur**—Leaving the encampment, he migrated to the southern border of Canaan. In the neighborhood of Gerar was a very rich and well-watered pasture land. **2. Abraham said of Sarah his wife, She is my sister**—Fear of the people among whom he was, tempted him to equivocate. His conduct was highly culpable. It was deceit, deliberate and premeditated—there was no sudden pressure upon him—it was the second offense of the kind—it was a distrust of God every way surprising, and it was calculated to produce injurious effects on the heathen around. Its mischievous tendency was not long in being developed. **Abimelech** (father-king) **... sent and took Sarah**—to be one of his wives, in the exercise of a privilege claimed by Eastern sovereigns, already explained (ch. 12:19). **3. But God came to Abimelech in a dream**—In early times a dream was often made the medium of communicating important truths; and this method was adopted for the preservation of Sarah. **9. Then Abimelech called Abraham, and said ... What hast thou done?**—In what a humiliating plight does the patriarch now appear—he, a servant of the true God, rebuked by a heathen prince. Who would not rather be in the place of Abimelech than of the honored but sadly offending patriarch! What a dignified attitude is that of the king—calmly and justly reproving the sin of the patriarch, but respecting his person and heaping coals of fire on his head by the liberal presents made to him. **11. Abraham said ... I thought, Surely the fear of God is not in this place**—From the horrible vices of Sodom he seems to have taken up the impression that all other cities of Canaan were equally corrupt. There might have been few or none who feared God, but what a sad thing when men of the world show a higher sense of honor and a greater abhorrence of crimes than a true worshipper! **12. yet indeed she is my sister.** (See on ch. 11:3). What a poor defense Abraham made. The statement absolved him from the charge of direct and absolute falsehood, but he had told a moral untruth because there was an intention to deceive (cf. ch. 12:11-13). "Honesty is always the best policy." Abraham's life would have been as well protected without the fraud as with it: and what shame to himself, what distrust to God, what dishonor to religion might have been prevented! "Let us speak truth every man to his neighbor."

CHAPTER 21

Vss. 1-13. BIRTH OF ISAAC. **1. the Lord visited Sarah**—The language of the historian seems designedly chosen to magnify the power of God as well as His faithfulness to His promise. It was God's grace that brought about that event, as well as the raising of spiritual children to Abraham, of which the birth of this son was typical [CALVIN]. **3, 4. Abraham called the name of his son ... Isaac ... and circumcised**—God was acknowledged in the name which, by divine command, was given for a memorial (cf. ch. 17:19), and also in the dedication of the child by administering the seal of the covenant (cf. ch. 17: 10-12). **8. the child grew, and was weaned**—children are suckled longer in the East than in the Occident—boys usually for two or three years. **Abraham made a great feast,** etc.—In Eastern countries this is always a season of domestic festivity, and the newly weaned child is formally brought, in presence of the assembled relatives and friends, to partake of some simple viands. Isaac, attired in the symbolic robe, the badge of birthright, was then admitted heir of the tribe [ROSENMULLER]. **9. Sarah saw the son of Hagar ... mocking**—Ishmael was aware of the great change in his prospects, and under the impulse of irritated or resentful feelings, in which he was probably joined by his mother, treated the young heir with derision and probably some violence (Gal. 4:29). **10. Wherefore she said unto Abraham, Cast out this bondwoman**—Nothing but the expulsion of both could now preserve harmony in the household. Abraham's perplexity was relieved by an announcement of the divine will, which in everything, however painful to flesh and blood, all who fear God and are walking in His ways will, like him, promptly obey. This story, as the apostle tells us, in "an allegory," and the "persecution" by the son of the *Egyptian* was the commencement of the four hundred years' affliction of Abraham's seed by the *Egyptians.* **12. in all that Sarah hath said**—it is called the Scripture (Gal. 4:30). **13. also of the son of the bondwoman will I make a nation**—Thus Providence overruled a family brawl to give rise to two great and extraordinary peoples.

14-21. EXPULSION OF ISHMAEL. **14. Abraham rose up early,** etc.—early, that the wanderers might reach an asylum before noon. Bread includes all sorts of victuals—bottle, a leathern vessel, formed of the entire skin of a lamb or kid sewed up, with the legs for handles, usually carried over the shoulder. Ishmael was a lad of seventeen years, and it is quite customary for Arab chiefs to send out their sons at such an age to do for themselves: often with nothing but a few days' provisions in a bag. **wandered in the wilderness of Beer-sheba**—in the southern border of Palestine, but out of the common direction, a wide extending desert, where they lost their way. **15. the water was spent,** etc.—Ishmael sank exhausted from fatigue and thirst—his mother laid his head under one of the bushes to smell the damp while she herself, unable to witness his distress, sat down at a little distance in hopeless sorrow. **19. God opened her eyes**—Had she forgotten the promise (ch. 16:11)? Whether she looked to God or not, He regarded her and directed her to a fountain close beside her, but probably hid amid brushwood, by the waters of which her almost expiring son was revived. **20, 21. God was with the lad,** etc.—Paran (i.e., Arabia), where his posterity has ever dwelt (cf. ch. 16:12; also Isa. 48:19; I Pet. 1:25). **his mother took him a wife**—On a father's death, the mother looks out for a wife for her son, however young;

and as Ishmael was now virtually deprived of his father, his mother set about forming a marriage connection for him, it would seem, among her relatives.

22-34. COVENANT. **22. Abimelech and Phichol** —Here a proof of the promise (ch. 12:2) being fulfilled, in a native prince wishing to form a solemn league with Abraham. The proposal was reasonable, and agreed to. **25-31. Abraham reproved Abimelech because of a well**—Wells were of great importance to a pastoral chief and on the successful operation of sinking a new one, the owner was solemnly informed in person. If, however, they were allowed to get out of repair, the restorer acquired a right to them. In unoccupied lands the possession of wells gave a right of property in the land, and dread of this had caused the offense for which Abraham reproved Abimelech. Some describe four, others five, wells in Beer-sheba. **33. Abraham planted a grove**—*Hebrew,* of tamarisks, in which sacrificial worship was offered, as in a roofless temple. **34. Abraham sojourned in the Philistines' land**—a picture of pastoral and an emblem of Christian life.

CHAPTER 22

Vss. 1-19. OFFERING ISAAC. **1. God did tempt Abraham**—not incite to sin (Jas. 1:13), but try, prove —give occasion for the development of his faith (I Pet. 1:7). **and he said, ... Here I am**—ready at a moment's warning for God's service. **2. Take now thy son,** etc.,—Every circumstance mentioned was calculated to give a deeper stab to the parental bosom. To lose his only son, and by an act of his own hand, too!—what a host of conflicting feelings must the order have raised! But he heard and obeyed without a murmur (Gal. 1:16; Luke 14:26). **3. Abraham rose ... early,** etc.—That there might be no appearance of delay or reluctance on his part, he made every preparation for the sacrifice before setting out—the materials, the knife, and the servants to convey them. From Beer-sheba to Moriah, a journey of two days, he had the painful secret pent up in his bosom. So distant a place must have been chosen for some important reason. It is generally thought that "the place of which God had told him" was one of the hills of Jerusalem, on which the Great Sacrifice was afterwards offered. **4. on the third day Abraham lifted up his eyes, etc.**—Leaving the servants at the foot, the father and son ascended the hill, the one bearing the knife, and the other the wood for consuming the sacrifice. But there was no victim; and to the question so naturally put by Isaac, Abraham contented himself by replying, "My son, God will provide himself a lamb for a burnt offering." It has been supposed that the design of this extraordinary transaction was to show him, by action instead of words, the way in which all the families of the earth should be blessed; and that in his answer to Isaac, he anticipated some substitution. It is more likely that his words were spoken evasively to his son in ignorance of the issue, yet in unbounded confidence that that son, though sacrificed, would, in some miraculous way, be restored (Heb. 11:19). **9. Abraham built an altar,** etc.—Had not the patriarch been sustained by the full consciousness of acting in obedience to God's will, the effort would have been too great for human endurance; and had not Isaac, then upwards of twenty years of age displayed equal faith in submitting, this great trial could not have gone through. **11, 12. the angel ... called,** etc.—

The sacrifice was virtually offered—the intention, the purpose to do it, was shown in all sincerity and fulness. The Omniscient witness likewise declared His acceptance in the highest terms of approval; and the apostle speaks of it as actually made (Heb. 11:17; Jas. 2:21). **13-19. Abraham lifted up his eyes ... and behold ... a ram,** etc.—No method was more admirably calculated to give the patriarch a distinct idea of the purpose of grace than this scenic representation: and hence our Lord's allusion to it (John 8:56).

CHAPTER 23

Vss. 1, 2. AGE AND DEATH OF SARAH. **1. Sarah was an hundred and seven and twenty years old,** etc. —Sarah is the only woman in Scripture whose age, death, and burial are mentioned, probably to do honor to the venerable mother of the Hebrew people. **2. Abraham came to mourn for Sarah,** etc.—He came from his own tent to take his station at the door of Sarah's. The "mourning" describes his conformity to the customary usage of sitting on the ground for a time; while the "weeping" indicates the natural outburst of his sorrow.

3-20. PURCHASE OF A BURYING-PLACE. **3. Abraham stood up,** etc.—Eastern people are always provided with family burying-places; but Abraham's life of faith—his pilgrim state—had prevented him acquiring even so small a possession (Acts 7:5). **spake unto the sons of Heth**—He bespoke their kind offices to aid him in obtaining possession of a cave that belonged to Ephron—a wealthy neighbor. **9. Machpelah**—the "double" case. **10. Ephron dwelt** —lit., was "sitting" among the children of Heth in the gate of the city where all business was transacted. But, though a chief man among them, he was probably unknown to Abraham. **11-15. Ephron answered, Nay, my lord, etc.**—Here is a great show of generosity, but it was only a show; for while Abraham wanted only the cave, he joins "the field and the cave"; and though he offered them both as free gifts, he, of course, expected some costly presents in return, without which, he would not have been satisfied. The patriarch, knowing this, wished to make a purchase and asked the terms. **15. The land is worth four hundred shekels,** etc.—as if Ephron had said, "Since you wish to know the value of the property, it is so and so; but that is a trifle, which you may pay or not as it suits you." They spoke in the common forms of Arab civility, and this indifference was mere affectation. **16. Abraham weighed ... the silver**—The money, amounting to £50 (about $1,000), was paid in presence of the assembled witnesses; and it was weighed. The practice of weighing money, which is often in lumps or rings, each stamped with their weight, is still common in many parts of the East; and every merchant at the gates or the bazar has his scales at his girdle. **19. Abraham buried Sarah**—Thus he got possession of Machpelah and deposited the remains of his lamented partner in a family vault which was the only spot of ground he owned.

CHAPTER 24

Vss. 1-9. A MARRIAGE COMMISSION. **1. And Abraham was old ... take a wife**—His anxiety to see his son married was natural to his position as a pastoral chief interested in preserving the honor of his tribe, and still more as a patriarch who had regard to the divine promise of a numerous posterity. **3. thou shalt not take a wife,** etc.—Among pastoral tribes the matrimonial arrangements are made by the parents, and a youth must marry, not among strangers, but in his own tribe—custom giving him a claim, which is seldom or never resisted, to the hand of his first cousin. But Abraham had a far higher motive—a fear lest, if his son married into a Canaanitish family, he might be gradually led away from the true God. **said unto his eldest servant**— Abraham being too old, and as the heir of the promise not being at liberty to make even a temporary visit to his native land, was obliged to intrust this delicate mission to Eliezer, whom, although putting entire confidence in him, he on this occasion bound by a solemn oath. A pastoral chief in the present day would follow the same course if he could not go himself.

10-67. THE JOURNEY. **10. the servant took ten camels,** etc.—So great an equipage was to give the embassy an appearance worthy of the rank and wealth of Abraham; to carry provisions; to bear the marriage presents, which as usual would be distributed over several beasts; besides one or two spare camels in case of emergency. **went to Mesopotamia,** etc.—A stranger in those regions, who wishes to obtain information, stations himself at one of the wells in the neighborhood of a town, and he is sure to learn all the news of the place from the women who frequent them every morning and evening. Eliezer followed this course, and letting his camels rest, he waited till the evening time of water-drawing. **12. And he said, O Lord God of my master**—The servant appears worthy of the master he served. He resolves to follow the leading of Providence; and while he shows good sense in the tokens he fixes upon of ascertaining the temper and character of the future bride, he never doubts but that in such a case God will direct him. **15-21. before he had done speaking ... behold,** Rebekah came out—As he anticipated, a young woman unveiled, as in pastoral regions, appeared with her pitcher on her shoulder. Her comely appearance, her affable manners, her obliging courtesy in going down the steps to fetch water not only to him but to pour in into the trough for his camels, afforded him the most agreeable surprise. She was the very person his imagination had pictured, and he proceeded to reward her civility. **22. the man took a golden earring,** etc.—The ring was not for the ear, but the nose; and the armlets, such as young women in Syria and Arabia still appear daily at wells decked in. They are worn from the elbow to the wrist, commonly made of silver, copper, brass, or horn. **23-27. And said, Whose daughter art thou?** --After telling her name and family, the kind-hearted damsel hastened home to give notice of a stranger's arrival. **28. and told them of her mother's house these things** —the female apartments. This family was in an advanced stage of pastoral life, dwelling in a settled place and a fixed habitation. **29-31. Rebekah had a brother ... Laban ran out**—From what we know of his character, there is reason to believe that the sight of the dazzling presents increased both his haste and his invitation. **32-49. the man came into the house,** etc.—What a beautiful picture of piety, fidelity, and disinterestedness in a servant! He declined all attention to his own comforts till he had told his name and his errand. **50. Then Laban and Bethuel answered**—The brothers conduct all the marriage negotiations, their father being probably dead, and without consulting their sister. Their language seems to indicate they were worshippers of the true God. **53. And the servant brought forth jewels of silver, and ... gold**—These are the usual articles, with money, that form a woman's dowry among the pastoral tribes. Rebekah was betrothed and accompanied the servant to Canaan. **64. she lighted off the camel**—If Isaac was walking, it would have been most unmannerly for her to have continued seated; an inferior, if riding, always alights in presence of a person of rank, no exception being made for women. **65. she took a veil, and covered herself**—The veil is an essential part of female dress. In country places it is often thrown aside, but on the appearance of a stranger, it is drawn over the face, as to conceal all but the eyes. In a bride it was a token of her reverence and subjection to her husband. **67. And Isaac brought her into his mother's ... tent**—thus establishing her at once in the rights and honors of a wife before he had seen her features. Disappointments often take place, but when Isaac saw his wife, "he loved her."

CHAPTER 25

Vss. 1-6. SONS OF ABRAHAM. **1. Abraham took a wife**—rather, "had taken"; for Keturah is called Abraham's concubine, or secondary wife (I Chronicles 1:32); and as, from her bearing six sons to him, it is improbable that he married after Sarah's death; and also as he sent them all out to seek their own independence, during his lifetime, it is clear that this marriage is related here out of its chronological order, merely to form a proper winding up of the patriarch's history. **5, 6. Abraham gave all that he had unto Isaac ... unto the sons of the concubines ... Abraham gave gifts**—While the chief part of the inheritance went to Isaac, (the other sons, Ishmael included, migrated to "the East country," i.e., Arabia) but received each a portion of the patrimony, perhaps in cattle and other things; and this settlement of Abraham's must have given satisfaction, since it is still the rule followed among the pastoral tribes.

7-11. DEATH OF ABRAHAM. **7. these are the days of ... Abraham**—His death is here related, though he lived till Jacob and Esau were fifteen years, just one hundred years after coming to Canaan; "the father of the faithful," "the friend of God," died; and even in his death, the promises were fulfilled (cf. ch. 15:15). We might have wished some memorials of his deathbed experience; but the Spirit of God has withheld them—nor was it necessary; for (see Matt. 7:16) from earth he passed into heaven (Luke 16:22). Though dead he yet liveth (Matt. 22:32). **9, 10. his sons ... buried him**—Death often puts an end to strife, reconciles those who have been alienated, and brings rival relations, as in this instance, to mingle tears over a father's grave.

12-18. DESCENDANTS OF ISHMAEL. Before passing to the line of the promised seed, the historian gives a brief notice of Ishmael, to show that the promises respecting that son of Abraham were fulfilled—first, in the greatness of his posterity (cf. ch. 17:20); and, secondly, in their independence. **18. he died**—rather, "it [their lot] fell in the presence of his brethren" (cf. ch. 16:12).

19-35. HISTORY OF ISAAC. **19. these are the generations**—account of the leading events in his life. **21. Isaac entreated the Lord for his wife**—Though tried in a similar way to his father, he did not follow the same crooked policy. Twenty years he continued unblessed with offspring, whose seed was to be "as the stars." But in answer to their mutual prayers (I Pet. 3:7), Rebekah was divinely informed that she was to be the mother of twins, who should be the progenitors of two independent nations; that the descendants of the younger should be the more powerful and subdue those of the other (Rom. 9:12; II Chron. 21:8). **27. the boys grew**—from the first, opposite to each other in character, manners, and habits. **28.** The parents were divided in their affection; and while the grounds, at least of the father's partiality, were weak, the distinction made between the children led, as such conduct always does, to unhappy consequences. **29. Jacob sod pottage**—made of lentils or small beans, which are common in Egypt and Syria. It is probable that it was made of Egyptian beans, which Jacob had procured as a dainty; for Esau was a stranger to it. It is very palatable; and to the weary hunter, faint with hunger, its odor must have been irresistibly tempting. **31. Jacob said, Sell me ... thy birthright**—i.e., the rights and privileges of the first-born, which were very important, the chief being that they were the family priests (Exod. 4:22) and had a double portion of the inheritance (Deut. 21:17). **32. Esau said ... I am at the point to die**—i.e., I am running daily risk of my life; and of what use will the birthright be to me: so he despised or cared little about it, in comparison with gratifying his appetite—he threw away his religious privileges for a trifle; and thence he is styled "a profane person" (Heb. 12:16; also Job 31:7, 16; 6:13; Phil. 3:19). "There was never any meat, except the forbidden fruit, so dear bought, as this broth of Jacob" [BISHOP HALL].

CHAPTER 26

Vss. 1-35. SOJOURN IN GERAR. **1. And there was a famine in the land ... And Isaac went unto ... Gerar**—The pressure of famine in Canaan forced Isaac with his family and flocks to migrate into the land of the Philistines, where he was exposed to personal danger, as his father had been on account of his wife's beauty; but through the seasonable interposition of Providence, he was preserved (Ps. 105:14, 15). **12. Then Isaac sowed in that land**—During his sojourn in that district he farmed a piece of land, which, by the blessing of God on his skill and industry, was very productive (Isa. 65:13; Ps. 37:19); and by his plentiful returns he increased so rapidly in wealth and influence that the Philistines, afraid or envious of his prosperity, obliged him to leave the place (Prov. 27:4; Eccles. 4:4). This may receive illustration from the fact that many Syrian shepherds at this day settle for a year or two in a place, rent some ground, in the produce of which they trade with the neighboring market, till the owners, through jealousy of their growing substance, refuse to renew their lease and compel them to remove elsewhere. **15. all the wells which his father's servants had digged ... the Philistines had stopped,** etc.—The same base stratagem for annoying those against whom they have taken an umbrage is practiced still by choking the wells with sand or stones, or defiling them with putrid carcases. **17. valley of Gerar**—torrent-bed or wady, a vast undulating plain, unoccupied and affording good pasture. **18-22. Isaac digged again the wells of water**—The naming of wells by Abraham, and the hereditary right of his family to the property, the change of the names by the Philistines to obliterate the traces of their origin, the restoration of the names by Isaac, and the contests between the respective shepherds to the exclusive possession of the water, are circumstances that occur among the natives in those regions as frequently in the present day as in the time of Isaac. **26-33. Then Abimelech went to him**—As there was a lapse of ninety years between the visit of Abraham and of Isaac, the Abimelech and Phichol spoken of must have been different persons' official titles. Here is another proof of the promise (ch. 12:2) being fulfilled, in an overture of peace being made to him by the king of Gerar. By whatever motive the proposal was dictated—whether fear of his growing power, or regret for the bad usage they had given him, the king and two of his courtiers paid a visit to the tent of Isaac (Prov. 16:7). His timid and passive temper had submitted to the annoyances of his rude neighbors; but now that they wish to renew the covenant, he evinces deep feeling at their conduct, and astonishment at their assurance, or artifice, in coming near him. Being, however, of a pacific disposition, he forgave their offense, accepted their proposals, and treated them to the banquet by which the ratification of a covenant was usually crowned. **34. Esau ... took to wife**—If the pious feelings of Abraham recoiled from the idea of Isaac forming a matrimonial connection with a Canaanitish woman, that devout patriarch himself would be equally opposed to such a union on the part of his children; and we may easily imagine how much his pious heart was wounded, and the family peace destroyed, when his favorite but wayward son brought no less than two idolatrous wives among them—an additional proof that Esau neither desired the blessing nor dreaded the curse of God. These wives never gained the affections of his parents, and this estrangement was overruled by God for keeping the chosen family aloof from the dangers of heathen influence.

CHAPTER 27

Vss. 1-27. INFIRMITY OF ISAAC. **1. when Isaac was old, and his eyes were dim**—He was in his 137th year; and apprehending death to be near, he prepared to make his last will—an act of the gravest importance, especially as it included the conveyance through a prophetic spirit of the patriarchal blessing. **4. make ... savory meat**—perhaps to revive and strengthen him for the duty; or rather, "as eating and drinking" were used on all religious occasions, he could not convey the right, till he had eaten of the meat provided for the purpose by him who was to receive the blessing [ADAM CLARKE] (cf. ch. 18:7). **that my soul may bless thee**—It is difficult to imagine him ignorant of the divine purpose (cf. ch. 25:23). But natural affection, prevailing through age and infirmity, prompted him to entail the honors and powers of the birthright on his elder son; and perhaps he was not aware of what Esau had done (ch. 25:34). **5-10. Rebekah spake unto Jacob**—She prized the blessing as invaluable; she knew that God intended it for the younger son; and in her anxiety to secure its being conferred on the right object—on one who cared for religion—she acted in the sincerity of faith; but in crooked policy—with unenlightened zeal; on the false principle that the end would sanctify the means. **11. Jacob said, Esau my brother is an hairy man**—It is remarkable that his scruples were founded, not on the evil of the act, but on the risk and consequences of deception. **13-17. and his mother said, Upon me be thy curse**—His conscience being soothed by his mother, preparations were hastily made for carrying out the device; consisting, first, of a kid's flesh, which, made into a ragout, spiced with salt, onions, garlic, and lemon

juice, might easily be passed off on a blind old man, with blunted senses, as game; second, of pieces of goat's skin bound on his hands and neck, its soft silken hair resembling that on the cheek of a young man; third, of the long white robe—the vestment of the first-born, which, transmitted from father to son and kept in a chest among fragrant herbs and perfumed flowers used much in the East to keep away moths, his mother provided for him. **18-27. he came unto his father**—The scheme planned by the mother was to be executed by the son in the father's bedchamber; and it is painful to think of the deliberate falsehoods, as well as daring profanity, he resorted to. The disguise, though wanting in one thing, which had nearly upset the whole plot, succeeded in misleading Isaac; and while giving his paternal embrace, the old man was roused into a state of high satisfaction and delight. **27. the smell of my son is as of a field**—The aromatic odors of the Syrian fields and meadows, often impart a strong fragrance to the person and clothes, as has been noticed by many travellers.

28-46. THE BLESSING. **God give thee of the dew of heaven**—To an Oriental mind, this phraseology implied the highest flow of prosperity. The copious fall of dew is indispensable to the fruitfulness of lands, which would be otherwise arid and sterile through the violent heat; and it abounds most in hilly regions, such as Canaan, hence called the fat land (Neh. 9:25, 35). **plenty of corn and wine**—Palestine was famous for vineyards, and it produced varieties of corn, viz., wheat, barley, oats, and rye. **Let people serve thee**—fulfilled in the discomfiture of the hostile tribes that opposed the Israelites in the wilderness; and in the pre-eminence and power they attained after their national establishment in the promised land. This blessing was not realized to Jacob, but to his descendants; and the temporal blessings promised were but a shadow of those spiritual ones, which formed the grand distinction of Jacob's posterity. **30-35. Esau came in from his hunting**—Scarcely had the former scene been concluded, when the fraud was discovered. The emotions of Isaac, as well as Esau, may easily be imagined—the astonishment, alarm, and sorrow of the one—the disappointment and indignation of the other. But a moment's reflection convinced the aged patriarch that the transfer of the blessing was "of the Lord," and now irrevocable. The importunities of Esau, however, overpowered him; and as the prophetic afflatus was upon the patriarch, he added what was probably as pleasing to a man of Esau's character as the other would have been. **39, 40. Behold thy dwelling shall be the fatness of the earth**—The first part is a promise of temporal prosperity, made in the same terms as Jacob's—the second refers to the roving life of hunting freebooters, which he and his descendants should lead. Though Esau was not personally subject to his brother, his posterity were tributary to the Israelites, till the reign of Joram when they revolted and established a kingdom of their own (II Kings 8:20; II Chron. 21:8-10). **41. Esau hated Jacob**—It is scarcely to be wondered at that Esau resented the conduct of Jacob and vowed revenge. **The days of mourning for my father are at hand**—a common Oriental phrase for the death of a parent. **42-45. these words of Esau were told Rebekah**—Poor woman! she now early begins to reap the bitter fruits of her fraudulent device; she is obliged to part with her son, for whom she planned it, never, probably, seeing him again; and she felt the retributive justice of heaven fall upon him heavily in his own future family. **45. Why should I be deprived of you both**—This refers to the law of Goelism, by which the nearest of kin would be obliged to avenge the death of Jacob upon his brother. **46. Rebekah said to Isaac**—Another pretext her cunning had to devise to obtain her husband's consent to Jacob's journey to Mesopotamia; and she succeeded by touching the aged patriarch in a tender point, afflicting to his pious heart—the proper marriage of their younger son.

CHAPTER 28

Vss. 1-19. Jacob's Departure. **1. Isaac called Jacob and blessed him**—He entered fully into Rebekah's feelings, and the burden of his parting counsel to his son was to avoid a marriage alliance with any but the Mesopotamian branch of the family. At the same time he gave him a solemn blessing—pronounced before unwittingly, now designedly, and with a cordial spirit. It is more explicitly and fully given, and Jacob was thus acknowledged "the heir of the promise." **6-9. when Esau saw that Isaac had blessed Jacob**, etc.— Desirous to humor his parents and, if possible, get the last will revoked, he became wise when too late (see Matt. 25:10), and hoped by gratifying his parents in one thing to atone for all his former delinquencies. But he only made bad worse, and though he did not marry a "wife of the daughters of Canaan," he married into a family which God had rejected. It showed a partial reformation, but no repentance, for he gave no proofs of abating his vindictive purposes against his brother, nor cherishing that pious spirit that would have gratified his father—he was like Micah (see Judg. 17:13). **10. Jacob went out,** etc.—His departure from his father's house was an ignominious flight; and for fear of being pursued or waylaid by his vindictive brother, he did not take the common road, but went by lonely and unfrequented paths, which increased the length and dangers of the journey. **11. he lighted upon a certain place**—By a forced march he had reached Bethel, about forty-eight miles from Beer-sheba, and had to spend the night in the open field. **he took of the stones,** etc.—"The nature of the soil is an existing comment on the record of the stony territory where Jacob lay" [Clarke's Travels]. **12. he dreamed . . . and behold a ladder**—Some writers are of opinion that it was not a literal ladder that is meant, as it is impossible to conceive any imagery stranger and more unnatural than that of a ladder, whose base was on earth, while its top reached heaven, without having any thing on which to rest its upper extremity. They suppose that the little heap of stones, on which his head reclined for a pillow, being the miniature model of the object that appeared to his imagination, the latter was a gigantic mountain pile, whose sides, indented in the rock, gave it the appearance of a scaling ladder. There can be no doubt that this use of the original term was common among the early Hebrews; as Josephus, describing the town of Ptolemais (Acre), says it was bounded by a mountain, which, from its projecting sides, was called "the ladder," and the stairs that led down to the city are, in the original, termed a ladder (Neh. 3) thought they were only a flight of steps cut in the side of the rock. But whether the image presented to the mental eye of Jacob were a common ladder, or such a mountain pile as has been described, the design of this vision was to afford comfort, encouragement, and confidence to the

lonely fugitive, both in his present circumstances and as to his future prospects. His thoughts during the day must have been painful—he would be his own self-accuser that he had brought exile and privation upon himself—and above all, that though he had obtained the forgiveness of his father, he had much reason to fear lest God might have forsaken him. Solitude affords time for reflection; and it was now that God began to bring Jacob under a course of religious instruction and training. To dispel his fears and allay the inward tumult of his mind, nothing was better fitted than the vision of the gigantic ladder, which reached from himself to heaven, and on which the angels were continually ascending and descending from God Himself on their benevolent errands (John 1:51). **13. The Lord stood above it, and said**—That Jacob might be at no loss to know the purport of the vision, he heard the divine voice; and the announcement of His name, together with a renewal of the covenant, and an assurance of personal protection, produced at once the most solemnizing and inspiriting effect on his mind. **16. Jacob awaked out of his sleep**—His language and his conduct were alike that of a man whose mind was pervaded by sentiments of solemn awe, of fervent piety, and lively gratitude (Jer. 31:36). **18, 19. Jacob set up a stone**, etc.—The mere setting up of the stone might have been as a future memorial to mark the spot; and this practice is still common in the East, in memory of a religious vow or engagement. But the pouring oil upon it was a consecration. Accordingly he gave it a new name, Beth-el, "the house of God" (Hos. 12:4); and it will not appear a thing forced or unnatural to call a stone a house, when one considers the common practice in warm countries of sitting in the open air by or on a stone, as are those of this place, "broad sheets of bare rock, some of them standing like the cromlechs of Druidical monuments" [Stanley].

20-22. Jacob's Vow. **20. Jacob vowed a vow**— His words are not to be considered as implying a doubt, far less as stating the condition or terms on which he would dedicate himself to God. Let "if" be changed into "since," and the language will appear a proper expression of Jacob's faith—an evidence of his having truly embraced the promise. How edifying often to meditate on Jacob at Beth-el.

CHAPTER 29

Vss. 1-35. The Well of Haran. **1. Then Jacob went,** etc.—*Hebrew*, "lifted up his feet." He resumed his way next morning with a light heart and elastic step after the vision of the ladder; for tokens of the divine favor tend to quicken the discharge of duty (Neh. 8:10). **and came into the land,** etc.— Mesopotamia and the whole region beyond the Euphrates are by the sacred writers designated "the East" (Judg. 6:3; I Kings 4:32; Job 1:3). Between the first and the second clause of this verse is included a journey of four hundred miles. **2. And he looked,** etc.—As he approached the place of his destination, he, according to custom, repaired to the well adjoining the town where he would obtain an easy introduction to his relatives. **3. thither were all the flocks gathered: and a stone,** etc.—In Arabia, owing to the shifting sands and in other places, owing to the strong evaporation, the mouth of a well is generally covered, especially when it is private property. Over many is laid a broad, thick, flat stone, with a round hole cut in the middle, forming the mouth of the cistern. This hole is covered with a heavy stone which it would require two or three men to roll away. Such was the description of the well at Haran. **4. Jacob said, My brethren**—Finding from the shepherds who were reposing there with flocks and who all belonged to Haran, that his relatives in Haran were well and that one of the family was shortly expected, he enquired why they were idling the best part of the day there instead of watering their flocks and sending them back to pasture. **8. They said, We cannot until all the flocks be gathered**—In order to prevent the consequences of too frequent exposure in places where water is scarce, the well is not only covered, but it is customary to have all the flocks collected round it before the covering is removed in presence of the owner or one of his representatives; and it was for this reason that those who were reposing at the well of Haran with the three flocks were waiting the arrival of Rachel. **9-11. While he yet spake, Rachel came**—Among the pastoral tribes the young unmarried daughters of the greatest sheiks tend the flocks, going out at sunrise and continuing to watch their fleecy charges till sunset. Watering them, which is done twice a day, is a work of time and labor, and Jacob rendered no small service in volunteering his aid to the young shepherdess. The interview was affecting, the reception welcome, and Jacob forgot all his toils in the society of his Mesopotamian relatives. Can we doubt that he returned thanks to God for His goodness by the way? **12. Jacob told Rachel,** etc.—According to the practice of the East, the term "brother" is extended to remote degrees of relationship, as uncle, cousin, or nephew. **14-20. he abode a month**—Among pastoral people a stranger is freely entertained for three days; on the fourth day he is expected to tell his name and errand; and if he prolongs his stay after that time, he must set his hand to work in some way, as may be agreed upon. A similar rule obtained in Laban's establishment, and the wages for which his nephew engaged to continue in his employment was the hand of Rachel. **17. Leah tender-eyed**—i.e., soft blue eyes—thought a blemish. **Rachel beautiful and well-favored**—i.e., comely and handsome in form. The latter was Jacob's choice. **18. I will serve thee seven years for Rachel thy daughter**—A proposal of marriage is made to the father without the daughter being consulted, and the match is effected by the suitor either bestowing costly presents on the family, or by giving cattle to the value the father sets upon his daughter, or else by giving personal services for a specified period. The last was the course necessity imposed on Jacob; and there for seven years he submitted to the drudgery of a hired shepherd, with the view of obtaining Rachel. The time went rapidly away; for even severe and difficult duties become light when love is the spring of action. **21. Jacob said, Give me my wife**—At the expiry of the stipulated term the marriage festivities were held. But an infamous fraud was practised on Jacob, and on his showing a righteous indignation, the usage of the country was pleaded in excuse. No plea of kindred should ever be allowed to come in opposition to the claim of justice. But this is often overlooked by the selfish mind of man, and fashion or custom rules instead of the will of God. This was what Laban did, as he said, "It must not be so done in our country, to give the younger before the first-born." But, then, if that were the prevailing custom of society at Haran, he should have apprized his nephew of it at an early period in an honorable manner. This, however, is too much the way with the people of the East still. The duty of marrying

an elder daughter before a younger, the tricks which parents take to get off an elder daughter that is plain or deformed and in which they are favored by the long bridal veil that entirely conceals her features all the wedding day, and the prolongation for a week of the marriage festivities among the greater sheiks, are accordant with the habits of the people in Arabia and Armenia in the present day. **28. gave him Rachel also**—It is evident that the marriage of both sisters took place nearly about the same time, and that such a connection was then allowed, though afterwards prohibited (Lev. 18:18). **29. gave to Rachel his daughter Bilhah to be her maid**—A father in good circumstances still gives his daughter from his household a female slave, over whom the young wife, independently of her husband, has the absolute control. **31. Leah ... hated**—i.e., not loved so much as she ought to have been. Her becoming a mother ensured her rising in the estimation both of her husband and of society. **32-35. son ... called his name Reuben**—Names were also significant; and those which Leah gave to her sons were expressive of her varying feelings of thankfulness or joy, or allusive to circumstances in the history of the family. There was piety and wisdom in attaching a signification to names, as it tended to keep the bearer in remembrance of his duty and the claims of God.

CHAPTER 30

Vss. 1-24. DOMESTIC JEALOUSIES. **1. Rachel envied her sister**—The maternal relation confers a high degree of honor in the East, and the want of that status is felt as a stigma and deplored as a grievous calamity. **Give me children or else I die**—either be reckoned as good as dead, or pine away from vexation. The intense anxiety of Hebrew women for children arose from the hope of giving birth to the promised seed. Rachel's conduct was sinful and contrasts unfavorably with that of Rebekah (cf. ch. 25:22) and of Hannah (I Sam. 1:11). **3-9. Bilhah, ... Zilpah**—Following the example of Sarah with regard to Hagar, an example which is not seldom imitated still, she adopted the children of her maid. Leah took the same course. A bitter and intense rivalry existed between them, all the more from their close relationship as sisters; and although they occupied separate apartments, with their families, as is the uniform custom where a plurality of wives obtains, and the husband and father spends a day with each in regular succession, that did not allay their mutual jealousies. The evil lies in the system, which being a violation of God's original ordinance, cannot yield happiness. **20. Leah said, God hath endued me with a good dowry**—The birth of a son is hailed with demonstrations of joy, and the possession of several sons confers upon the mother an honor and respectability proportioned to their number. The husband attaches a similar importance to the possession, and it forms a bond of union which renders it impossible for him ever to forsake or to be cold to a wife who has borne him sons. This explains the happy anticipations Leah founded on the possession of her six sons. **21. afterwards, she bare a daughter**—The inferior value set on a daughter is displayed in the bare announcement of the birth.

25-43. JACOB'S COVENANT WITH LABAN. **25. when Rachel had borne Joseph**—Shortly after the birth of this son, Jacob's term of servitude expired, and feeling anxious to establish an independence for his family, he probably, from knowing that Esau was out of the way, announced his intention of returning to Canaan (Heb. 13:14). In this resolution the faith of Jacob was remarkable, for as yet he had nothing to rely on but the promise of God (cf. ch. 28:15). **27. Laban said ... I have learned**—His selfish uncle was averse to a separation, not from warmth of affection either for Jacob or his daughters, but from the damage his own interests would sustain. He had found, from long observation, that the blessing of heaven rested on Jacob, and that his stock had wonderfully increased under Jacob's management. This was a remarkable testimony that good men are blessings to the places where they reside. Men of the world are often blessed with temporal benefits on account of their pious relatives, though they have not always, like Laban, the wisdom to discern, or the grace to acknowledge it. **28. appoint me thy wages, and I will give it**—The Eastern shepherds receive for their hire not money, but a certain amount of the increase or produce of the flock; but Laban would at the time have done anything to secure the continued services of his nephew, and make a show of liberality, which Jacob well knew was constrained. **31. Jacob said, Thou shalt not give me any thing**—A new agreement was made, the substance of which was, that he was to receive remuneration in the usual way, but on certain conditions which Jacob specified. **32. I will pass through all thy flock to-day**—Eastern sheep being generally white, the goats black, and spotted or speckled ones comparatively few and rare, Jacob proposed to remove all existing ones of that description from the flock, and to be content with what might appear at the next lambing time. The proposal *seemed* so much in favor of Laban, that he at once agreed to it. But Jacob has been accused of taking advantage of his uncle, and though it is difficult to exculpate him from practising some degree of dissimulation, he was only availing himself of the results of his great skill and experience in the breeding of cattle. But it is evident from the next chapter (vss. 5-13) that there was something miraculous and that the means he had employed had been suggested by a divine intimation. **37. Jacob took rods**, etc.—There are many varieties of the hazel, some of which are more erect than the common hazel, and it was probably one of these varieties Jacob employed. The styles are of a bright red color, when peeled; and along with them he took wands of other shrubs, which, when stripped of the bark, had white streaks. These, kept constantly before the eyes of the female at the time of gestation, his observation had taught him would have an influence, through the imagination, on the future offspring. **38. watering troughs**—usually a long stone block hollowed out, from which several sheep could drink at once, but sometimes so small as to admit of only one drinking at a time.

CHAPTER 31

Vss. 1-21. ENVY OF LABAN AND SONS. **1. he heard the words of Laban's sons**—It must have been from rumor that Jacob got knowledge of the invidious reflections cast upon him by his cousins; for they were separated at the distance of three days' journey. **2. And Jacob beheld the countenance of Laban**—lit., was not the same as yesterday, and the day before, a common Oriental form of speech. The insinuations against Jacob's fidelity by Laban's sons, and the sullen reserve, the churlish conduct, of Laban himself, had made Jacob's situation, in his

uncle's establishment, most trying and painful. It is always one of the vexations attendant on worldly prosperity, that it excites the envy of others (Eccles. 4:4); and that, however careful a man is to maintain a good conscience, he cannot always reckon on maintaining a good name, in a censorious world. This, Jacob experienced; and it is probable that, like a good man, he had asked direction and relief in prayer. **3. the Lord said, ... Return unto the land of thy fathers**—Notwithstanding the ill usage he had received, Jacob might not have deemed himself at liberty to quit his present sphere, under the impulse of passionate fretfulness and discontent. Having been conducted to Haran by God (ch. 28:15) and having got a promise that the same heavenly Guardian would bring him again into the land of Canaan, he might have thought he ought not to leave it, without being clearly persuaded as to the path of duty. So ought we to set the Lord before us, and to acknowledge Him in all our ways, our journeys, our settlements, and plans in life. **4. Jacob sent and called Rachel and Leah**—His wives and family were in their usual residence. Whether he wished them to be present at the festivities of sheep-shearing, as some think; or, because he could not leave his flock, he called them both to come to him, in order that, having resolved on immediate departure, he might communicate his intentions. Rachel and Leah only were called, for the other two wives, being secondary and still in a state of servitude, were not entitled to be taken into account. Jacob acted the part of a dutiful husband in telling them his plans; for husbands that love their wives should consult with them and trust in them (Prov. 31:11). **6. ye know that ... I have served your father**—Having stated his strong grounds of dissatisfaction with their father's conduct and the ill requital he had got for all his faithful services, he informed them of the blessing of God that had made him rich notwithstanding Laban's design to ruin him; and finally, of the command from God he had received to return to his own country, that they might not accuse him of caprice, or disaffection to their family; but be convinced, that in resolving to depart, he acted from a principle of religious obedience. **14. Rachel and Leah answered**—Having heard his views, they expressed their entire approval; and from grievances of their own, they were fully as desirous of a separation as himself. They display not only conjugal affection, but piety in following the course described—"whatsoever God hath said unto thee, do." "Those that are really their husbands' helpmeets will never be their hindrances in doing that to which God calls them" [HENRY]. **17. Then Jacob rose up**—Little time is spent by pastoral people in removing. The striking down the tents and poles and stowing them among their other baggage; the putting their wives and children in *houdas* like cradles, on the backs of camels, or in panniers on asses; and the ranging of the various parts of the flock under the respective shepherds; all this is a short process. A plain that is covered in the morning with a long array of tents and with browsing flocks, may, in a few hours, appear so desolate that not a vestige of the encampment remains, except the holes in which the tent-poles had been fixed. **20. Jacob stole away**—The result showed the prudence and necessity of departing secretly; otherwise, Laban might have detained him by violence or artifice. **18. he carried the cattle of his getting**—i.e., his own and nothing more. He did not indemnify himself for his many losses by carrying off any thing of Laban's, but was content with what Providence had given him. Some may think that due notice should have been given; but when a man feels himself in danger—the law of self-preservation prescribes the duty of immediate flight, if it can be done consistently with conscience.

22-55. LABAN PURSUES JACOB—THEIR COVENANT AT GILEAD. **22. it was told Laban on the third day** —No sooner did the news reach Laban than he set out in pursuit, and he being not encumbered, advanced rapidly; whereas Jacob, with a young family and numerous flocks, had to march slowly, so that he overtook the fugitives after seven days' journey as they lay encamped on the brow of mount Gilead, an extensive range of hills forming the eastern boundary of Canaan. Being accompanied by a number of his people, he might have used violence had he not been divinely warned in a dream to give no interruption to his nephew's journey. How striking and sudden a change! For several days he had been full of rage, and was now in eager anticipation that his vengeance would be fully wreaked, when lo! his hands are tied by invisible power (Ps. 76:10). He did not dare to touch Jacob, but there was a war of words. **25-30. Laban said . . . What hast thou done?**—Not a word is said of the charge, (vs. 1). His reproaches were of a different kind. His first charge was for depriving him of the satisfaction of giving Jacob and his family the usual salutations at parting. In the East it is customary, when any are setting out to a great distance, for their relatives and friends to accompany them a considerable way with music and valedictory songs. Considering the past conduct of Laban, his complaint on this ground was hypocritical cant. But his second charge was a grave one—the carrying off his gods—*Hebrew*, teraphim, small images of human figures, used not as idols or objects of worship, but as talismans, for superstitious purposes. **31, 32. Jacob said, . . . With whomsoever thou findeth thy gods let him not live**— Conscious of his own innocence and little suspecting the misdeed of his favorite wife, he boldly challenged a search and denounced the heaviest penalty on the culprit. A personal scrutiny was made by Laban, who examined every tent; and having entered Rachel's last, he would have infallibly discovered the stolen images had not Rachel made an appeal to him which prevented further search. **34. Rachel had taken the images, and put them in the camel's furniture, and sat upon them**—The common pack-saddle is often used as a seat or a cushion, against which a person squatted on the floor may lean. **36, 37. Jacob was wroth**—Recrimination on his part was natural in the circumstances, and, as usual, when passion is high, the charges took a wide range. He rapidly enumerated his grievances for twenty years and in a tone of unrestrained severity described the niggard character and vexatious exactions of his uncle, together with the hardships of various kinds he had patiently endured. **38. The rams of thy flock have I not eaten**—Eastern people seldom kill the females for food except they are barren. **39. That which was torn of beasts I brought not unto thee**— The shepherds are strictly responsible for losses in the flock, unless they can prove these were occasioned by wild beasts. **40. in the day the drought . . . and the frost by night**—The temperature changes often in twenty-four hours from the greatest extremes of heat and cold, most trying to the shepherd who has to keep watch by his flocks. Much allowance must be made for Jacob. Great and long-continued provocations ruffle the mildest and most disciplined tempers. It is difficult to "be angry and sin not." But these two relatives, after having given utterance to their pent-up feelings, came at length to

a mutual understanding, or rather, God influenced Laban to make reconciliation with his injured nephew (Prov. 16:7). **44. Come thou, let us make a covenant**—The way in which this covenant was ratified was by a heap of stones being laid in a circular pile, to serve as seats, and in the center of this circle a large one was set up perpendicularly for an altar. It is probable that a sacrifice was first offered, and then that the feast of reconciliation was partaken of by both parties seated on the stones around it. To this day heaps of stones, which have been used as memorials, are found abundantly in the region where this transaction took place. **52. This heap be witness**—Objects of nature were frequently thus spoken of. But over and above, there was a solemn appeal to God; and it is observable that there was a marked difference in the religious sentiments of the two. Laban spake of the God of Abraham and Nahor, their common ancestors; but Jacob, knowing that idolatry had crept in among that branch of the family, swore by the "fear of his father Isaac." They who have one God should have one heart: they who are agreed in religion should endeavor to agree in everything else.

CHAPTER 32

Vss. 1, 2. VISION OF ANGELS. **1. angels of God meet him**—It is not said whether this angelic manifestation was made in a vision by day, or a dream by night. There is an evident allusion, however, to the appearance upon the ladder (cf. ch. 28:12), and this occurring to Jacob on his return to Canaan, was an encouraging pledge of the continued presence and protection of God (Ps. 34:7; Heb. 1:14). **2. Mahanaim**—two hosts or camps. The place was situated between mount Gilead and the Jabbok, near the banks of that brook.

3-32. MISSION TO ESAU. **3. Jacob sent messengers before him to Esau**—i.e., had sent. It was a prudent precaution to ascertain the present temper of Esau, as the road, on approaching the eastern confines of Canaan, lay near the wild district where his brother was now established. **the land of Seir**— a highland country on the east and south of the Dead Sea, inhabited by the Horites, who were dispossessed by Esau or his posterity (Deut. 11:12). When and in what circumstances he had emigrated thither, whether the separation arose out of the undutiful conduct and idolatrous habits of his wives, which had made them unwelcome in the tent of his parents, or whether his roving disposition had sought a country from his love of adventure and the chase, he was living in a state of power and affluence, and this settlement on the outer borders of Canaan, though made of his own free-will, was overruled by Providence to pave the way for Jacob's return to the promised land. **4. Thus shall ye speak unto my lord Esau**—The purport of the message was that, after a residence of twenty years in Mesopotamia, he was now returning to his native land, that he did not need any thing, for he had abundance of pastoral wealth, but that he could not pass without notifying his arrival to his brother and paying the homage of his respectful obeisance. Acts of civility tend to disarm opposition and soften hatred (Eccles. 10:4). **Thy servant Jacob**—He had been made *lord* over his brethren (cf. ch. 27:29). But it is probable he thought this referred to a spiritual superiority; or if to temporal, that it was to be realized only to his posterity. At all events, leaving it to God to fulfil that purpose, he deemed it prudent to assume the most kind and respectful bearing. **6. The messengers returned to Jacob**—Their report left Jacob in painful uncertainty as to what was his brother's views and feelings. Esau's studied reserve gave him reason to dread the worst. Jacob was naturally timid; but his conscience told him that there was much ground for apprehension, and his distress was all the more aggravated that he had to provide for the safety of a large and helpless family. **9-12. Jacob said, O God of my father Abraham**—In this great emergency, he had recourse to prayer. This is the first recorded example of prayer in the Bible. It is short, earnest, and bearing directly on the occasion. The appeal is made to God, as standing in a covenant relation to his family, just as we ought to put our hopes of acceptance with God in Christ. It pleads the special promise made to him of a safe return; and after a most humble and affecting confession of unworthiness, it breathes an earnest desire for deliverance from the impending danger. It was the prayer of a kind husband, an affectionate father, a firm believer in the promises. **13-23. took . . . a present for Esau his brother**—Jacob combined active exertions with earnest prayer; and this teaches us that we must not depend upon the aid and interposition of God in such a way as to supersede the exercise of prudence and foresight. Superiors are always approached with presents, and the respect expressed is estimated by the quality and amount of the gift. The present of Jacob consisted of 550 head of cattle, of different kinds, such as would be most prized by Esau. It was a most magnificent present, skilfully arranged and proportioned. The milch camels alone were of immense value; for the she-camels form the principal part of Arab wealth; their milk is a chief article of diet; and in many other respects they are of the greatest use. **16. every drove by themselves**—There was great prudence in this arrangement; for the present would thus have a more imposing appearance; Esau's passion would have time to cool as he passed each successive company; and if the first was refused, the others would hasten back to convey a timely warning. **17. he commanded the foremost**—The messengers were strictly commanded to say the same words, that Esau might be more impressed and that the uniformity of the address might appear more clearly to have come from Jacob himself. **21. himself lodged**—not the whole night, but only a part of it. **22. ford Jabbok** —now the *Zerka*—a stream that rises among the mountains of Gilead, and running from east to west, enters the Jordan, about forty miles south of the Sea of Tiberias. At the ford it is ten yards wide. It is sometimes forded with difficulty; but in summer it is very shallow. **he rose up and took**—Unable to sleep, he waded the ford in the night-time by himself; and having ascertained its safety, he returned to the north bank and sent over his family and attendants, remaining behind, to seek anew, in silent prayer, the divine blessing on the means he had set in motion. **24, 25. There wrestled a man with him** —This mysterious person is called an angel (Hos. 12:5) and God (vss. 28, 30; Hos. 12:4); and the opinion that is most supported is that he was "the angel of the covenant," who, in a visible form, appeared to animate the mind and sympathize with the distress of his pious servant. It has been a subject of much discussion whether the incident described was an actual conflict or a visionary scene. Many think that as the narrative makes no mention in express terms either of sleep, or dream, or vision, it was a real transaction; while others, considering the bodily exhaustion of Jacob, his great mental anxiety,

the kind of aid he supplicated, as well as the analogy of former manifestations with which he was favored —such as the ladder—have concluded that it was a vision [Calvin, Hessenberg, Hengstenberg]. The moral design of it was to revive the sinking spirit of the patriarch and to arm him with confidence in God, while anticipating the dreaded scenes of the morrow. To us it is highly instructive; showing that, to encourage us valiantly to meet the trials to which we are subjected, God allows us to ascribe to the efficacy of our faith and prayers, the victories which His grace alone enables us to make. **26. I will not let thee go, except thou bless me**—It is evident that Jacob was aware of the character of Him with whom he wrestled; and, believing that His power, though by far superior to human, was yet limited by His promise to do him good, he determined not to lose the golden opportunity of securing a blessing. And nothing gives God greater pleasure than to see the hearts of His people firmly adhering to Him. **28. Thy name shall be called no more Jacob, but Israel**—The old name was not to be abandoned; but, referring as it did to a dishonorable part of the patriarch's history, it was to be associated with another descriptive of his now sanctified and eminently devout character. **29. Jacob asked, Tell me . . thy name**—The request was denied that he might not be too elated with his conquest nor suppose that he had obtained such advantage over the angel as to make him do what he pleased. **31. halted upon his thigh**—As Paul had a thorn in the flesh given to humble him, lest he should be too elevated by the abundant revelations granted him, so Jacob's lameness was to keep him mindful of this mysterious scene, and that it was in gracious condescension the victory was yielded to him. In the greatest of these spiritual victories which, through faith, any of God's people obtain, there is always something to humble them. **32. the sinew which shrank**—the nerve that fastens the thigh-bone in its socket. The practice of the Jews in abstaining from eating this in the flesh of animals, is not founded on the law of Moses, but is merely a traditional usage. The sinew is carefully extracted; and where there are no persons skilled enough for that operation, they do not make use of the hind legs at all.

CHAPTER 33

Vss. 1-11. Kindness of Jacob and Esau. **1. behold, Esau came, and with him four hundred men**— Jacob having crossed the ford and ranged his wives and children in order—the dearest last, that they might be the least exposed to danger—awaited the expected interview. His faith was strengthened and his fears gone (Ps. 27:3). Having had power to prevail with God, he was confident of the same power with man, according to the promise (cf. ch. 32:28). **3. he bowed himself . . . seven times**—The manner of doing this is by looking towards a superior and bowing with the upper part of the body brought parallel to the ground, then advancing a few steps and bowing again, and repeating his obeisance till, at the seventh time, the suppliant stands in the immediate presence of his superior. The members of his family did the same. This was a token of profound respect, and, though very marked, it would appear natural; for Esau being the elder brother, was, according to the custom of the East, entitled to respectful treatment from his younger brother. His attendants would be struck by it, and according to Eastern habits, would magnify it in the hearing of their master. **4. Esau ran to meet him—** What a sudden and surprising change! Whether the sight of the princely present and the profound homage of Jacob had produced this effect, or it proceeded from the impulsive character of Esau, the cherished enmity of twenty years in a moment disappeared; the weapons of war were laid aside, and the warmest tokens of mutual affection reciprocated between the brothers. But doubtless, the efficient cause was the secret, subduing influence of grace (Prov. 21:1), which converted Esau from an enemy into a friend. **5. Who are those with thee?**—It might have been enough to say, They are my children; but Jacob was a pious man, and he could not give even a common answer but in the language of piety (Ps. 127:3; 113:9; 107:41). **11. He urged him and he took it**—In the East the acceptance by a superior is a proof of friendship, and by an enemy, of reconciliation. It was on both accounts Jacob was so anxious that his brother should receive the cattle; and in Esau's acceptance he had the strongest proofs of a good feeling being established that Eastern notions admit of.

12-20. THE PARTING. **12. And he said, Let us take our journey**—Esau proposed to accompany Jacob and his family through the country, both as a mark of friendship and as an escort to guard them. But the proposal was prudently declined. Jacob did not need any worldly state or equipage. Notwithstanding the present cordiality, the brothers were so different in spirit, character, and habits—the one so much a man of the world, and the other a man of God, that there was great risk of something occurring to disturb the harmony. Jacob having alleged a very reasonable excuse for the tardiness of his movements, the brothers parted in peace. **14. until come unto my lord**—It seems to have been Jacob's intention, passing round the Dead Sea, to visit his brother in Seir, and thus, without crossing the Jordan, go to Beersheba to Isaac; but he changed his plan, and whether the intention was carried out then or at a future period has not been recorded. **17. Jacob journeyed to Succoth**—i.e., "booths," that being the first station at which Jacob halted on his arrival in Canaan. His posterity, when dwelling in houses of stone, built a city there and called it Succoth, to commemorate the fact that their ancestor, "a Syrian ready to perish," was glad to dwell in booths. **18. Shalem**—i.e., "peace"; and the meaning may be that Jacob came into Canaan, arriving safe and sound at the city Shechem—a tribute to Him who had promised such a return (cf. ch. 28:15). But most writers take Shalem as a proper name—a city of Shechem, and the site is marked by one of the little villages about two miles to the northeast. A little further in the valley below Shechem "he bought a parcel of a field, where he spread his tent," thus being the first of the patriarchs who became a proprietor of land in Canaan. **19. an hundred pieces of money**—pieces, lit., "lambs"; probably a coin with the figure of a lamb on it. **20. and he erected ... an altar**—A beautiful proof of his personal piety, a most suitable conclusion to his journey, and a lasting memorial of a distinguished favor in the name "God, the God of Israel." Wherever we pitch a tent, God shall have an altar.

CHAPTER 34

Vss. 1-31. THE DISHONOR OF DINAH. **1-4.** Though freed from foreign troubles, Jacob met with a great domestic calamity in the fall of his only daughter.

According to Josephus, she had been attending a festival; but it is highly probable that she had been often and freely mixing in the society of the place and that she, being a simple, inexperienced, and vain young woman, had been flattered by the attentions of the ruler's son. There must have been time and opportunities of acquaintance to produce the strong attachment that Shechem had for her. **5. Jacob held his peace**—Jacob, as a father and a good man, must have been deeply distressed. But he could do little. In the case of a family by different wives, it is not the father, but the full brothers, on whom the protection of the daughters devolves—they are the guardians of a sister's welfare and the avengers of her wrongs. It was for this reason that Simeon and Levi, the two brothers of Dinah by Leah, appear the chief actors in this episode; and though the two fathers would have probably brought about an amicable arrangement of the affair, the hasty arrival of these enraged brothers introduced a new element into the negotiations. **6. Hamor**—i.e., "ass"; and it is a striking proof of the very different ideas which, in the East, are associated with that animal, which there appears sprightly, well proportioned, and of great activity. This chief is called Emmor (Acts 7:16). **7. the men were grieved, and ... very wroth**—Good men in such a case could not but grieve; but it would have been well if their anger had been less, or that they had known the precept "let not the sun go down upon your wrath." No injury can justify revenge (Deut. 32:35; Rom. 12:9); but Jacob's sons planned a scheme of revenge in the most deceitful manner. **8. Hamor communed with them**—The prince and his son seem at first sight to have acted honestly, and our feelings are enlisted on their side. They betray no jealousy of the powerful shepherds; on the contrary, they show every desire to establish friendly intercourse. But their conduct was unjustifiable in neither expressing regret nor restoring Dinah to her family; and this great error was the true cause of the negotiations ending in so unhappy a manner. **11. Shechem said unto her father ... and brethren**—The consideration of the proposal for marriage belonged to Jacob, and he certainly showed great weakness in yielding so much to the fiery impetuosity of his sons. The sequel shows the unhappy consequences of that concession. **12. Ask me never so much dowry and gift**—The gift refers to the presents made at betrothal, both to the bride elect and her relations (cf. ch. 24:53); the dowry to a suitable settlement upon her. **13. The sons of Jacob answered**—The honor of their family consisted in having the sign of the covenant. Circumcision was the external rite by which persons were admitted members of the ancient Church. But that outward rite could not make the Shechemites true Israelites; and yet it does not appear that Jacob's sons required anything more. Nothing is said of their teaching the people to worship the true God, but only of their insisting on their being circumcised; and it is evident that they did not seek to convert Shechem, but only made a show of religion—a cloak to cover their diabolical design. Hypocrisy and deceit, in all cases vicious, are infinitely more so when accompanied with a show of religion; and here the sons of Jacob, under the pretense of conscientious scruples, conceal a scheme of treachery as cruel and diabolical as was, perhaps, ever perpetrated. **20. Hamor and Shechem ... came unto the gate of their city**—That was the place where every public communication was made; and in the ready obsequious submission of the people to this measure we see an evidence either of the extraordinary affection for the governing family, or of the abject despotism of the East, where the will of a chief is an absolute command. **30. Jacob said ... Ye have troubled me**—This atrocious outrage perpetrated on the defenseless citizens and their families made the cup of Jacob's affliction overflow. We may wonder that, in speaking of it to his sons, he did not represent it as a heinous sin, an atrocious violation of the laws of God and man, but dwelt solely on the present consequences. It was probably because that was the only view likely to rouse the cold-blooded apathy, the hardened consciences of those ruffian sons. Nothing but the restraining power of God saved him and his family from the united vengeance of the people (cf. ch. 35:5). All his sons had not been engaged in the massacre. Joseph was a boy, Benjamin not yet born, and the other eight not concerned in it. Simeon and Levi alone, with their retainers, had been the guilty actors in the bloody tragedy. But the Canaanites would not be discriminating in their vengeance; and if *all* the Shechemites were put to death for the offense of their chief's son, what wonder if the natives should extend their hatred to all the family of Jacob; and who probably equalled, in number, the inhabitants of that village.

CHAPTER 35

Vss. 1-15. REMOVAL TO BETHEL. **1. God said unto Jacob, Arise,** etc.—This command was given seasonably in point of time and tenderly in respect of language. The disgraceful and perilous events that had recently taken place in the patriarch's family must have produced in him a strong desire to remove without delay from the vicinity of Shechem. Borne down by an overwhelming sense of the criminality of his two sons—of the offense they had given to God and the dishonor they had brought on the true faith; distracted, too, with anxiety about the probable consequences which their outrage might bring upon himself and family, should the Canaanite people combine to extirpate such a band of robbers and murderers; he must have felt this call as affording a great relief to his afflicted feelings. At the same time it conveyed a tender rebuke. **go up to Bethel**—Bethel was about thirty miles south of Shechem and was an ascent from a low to a highland country. There, he would not only be released from the painful associations of the latter place but be established on a spot that would revive the most delightful and sublime recollections. The pleasure of revisiting it, however, was not altogether unalloyed. **make there an altar unto God, that appeared** —It too frequently happens that early impressions are effaced through lapse of time, that promises made in seasons of distress, are forgotten; or, if remembered on the return of health and prosperity, there is not the same alacrity and sense of obligation felt to fulfil them. Jacob was lying under that charge. He had fallen into spiritual indolence. It was now eight or ten years since his return to Canaan. He had effected a comfortable settlement and had acknowledged the divine mercies, by which that return and settlement had been signally distinguished (cf. ch. 33:19). But for some unrecorded reason, his early vow at Bethel, in a great crisis of his life, remained unperformed. The Lord appeared now to remind him of his neglected duty, in terms, however, so mild, as awakened less the memory of his fault, than of the kindness of his heavenly Guardian; and how much Jacob felt the touching nature of the appeal to that memorable scene at Bethel, appears in the immediate preparations he made to *arise* and *go up* thither (Ps. 66:13). **2. Then Jacob said unto his household ... Put away the strange gods that are among you**—*Hebrew*, "gods of the stranger," of foreign nations. Jacob had brought, in his service, a number of Mesopotamian retainers, who were addicted to superstitious practices; and there is some reason to fear that the same high testimony as to the religious superintendence of his household could not have been borne of him as was done of Abraham (ch. 18:19). He might have been too negligent hitherto in winking at these evils in his servants; or, perhaps, it was not till his arrival in Canaan, that he had learnt, for the first time, that one nearer and dearer to him was secretly infected with the same corruption (ch. 31:34). Be that as it may, he resolved on an immediate and thorough reformation of his household; and in commanding them to put away the strange gods, he added, "be clean, and change your garments"; as if some defilement, from contact with idolatry, should still remain about them. In the law of Moses, many ceremonial purifications were ordained and observed by persons who had contracted certain defilements, and without the observance of which, they were reckoned unclean and unfit to join in the social worship of God. These bodily purifications were purely figurative; and as sacrifices were offered before the law, so also were external purifications, as appears from the words of Jacob; hence it would seem that types and symbols were used from the fall of man, representing and teaching the two great doctrines of revealed truth—viz., the atonement of Christ and the sanctification of our nature. **4. they gave unto Jacob all the strange gods ... and earrings**—Strange gods—the seraphim (cf. ch. 31:30), as well, perhaps, as other idols acquired among the Shechemite spoil—earrings of various forms, sizes, and materials, which are universally worn in the East, and, then as now, connected with incantation and idolatry (cf. Hos. 2:13). The decided tone which Jacob now assumed the probable cause of the alacrity with which those favorite objects of superstition were surrendered. **Jacob hid them under the oak**—or terebinth—a towering tree, which, like all others of the kind, was a striking object in the scenery of Palestine; and beneath which, at Shechem, the patriarch had pitched his tent. He hid the images and amulets, delivered to him by his Mesopotamian dependents, at the root of this tree. The oak being deemed a consecrated tree, to bury them at its root was to deposit them in a place where no bold hand would venture to disturb the ground; and hence it was called from this circumstance—"the plain of Meonenim"—i.e., the oak of enchantments" (Judg. 9:37); and from the great stone which Joshua set up—"the oak of the pillar" (Judg. 9:6). **5. the terror of God was upon the cities**—There was every reason to apprehend that a storm of indignation would burst from all quarters upon Jacob's family, and that the Canaanite tribes would have formed one united plan of revenge. But a supernatural panic seized them; and thus, for the sake of the "heir of the promise," the protecting shield of Providence was specially held over his family. **6. So Jacob came to this place ... that is, Bethel** —It is probable that this place was unoccupied ground when Jacob first went to it; and that after that period [CALVIN], the Canaanites built a town, to which they gave the name of Luz, from the profusion of almond trees that grew around. The name of Bethel, which would, of course, be confined to Jacob and his family, did not supersede the original one, till long after. It is now identified with the modern

Beitin and lies on the western slope of the mountain on which Abraham built his altar (Gen. 12:8). **7. El-Beth-el**—i.e., "the God of Bethel." **8. Deborah, Rebekah's nurse, died**—This event seems to have taken place before the solemnities were commenced. Deborah, a "bee," supposing her to have been fifty years on coming to Canaan, had attained the great age of 180. When she was removed from Isaac's household to Jacob's, is unknown. But it probably was on his return from Mesopotamia; and she would have been of invaluable service to his young family. Old nurses, like her, were not only honored, but loved as mothers; and, accordingly, her death was the occasion of great lamentation. She was buried under *the* oak—hence called "the terebinth of tears" (cf. I Kings 13:14). God was pleased to make a new appearance to him after the solemn rites of devotion were over. By this manifestation of His presence, God testified His acceptance of Jacob's sacrifice and renewed the promise of the blessings guaranteed to Abraham and Isaac; and the patriarch observed the ceremony with which he had formerly consecrated the place, comprising a sacramental cup, along with the oil that he poured on the pillar, and reimposing the memorable name. The whole scene was in accordance with the character of the patriarchal dispensation, in which the great truths of religion were exhibited to the senses, and "the world's grey fathers" taught in a manner suited to the weakness of an infantine condition. **13. God went up from him**—The presence of God was indicated in some visible form and His acceptance of the sacrifice shown by the miraculous descent of fire from heaven, consuming it on the altar.

16-27. BIRTH OF BENJAMIN—DEATH OF RACHEL, etc. **16. they journeyed from Beth-el**—There can be no doubt that much enjoyment was experienced at Bethel, and that in the religious observances solemnized, as well as in the vivid recollections of the glorious vision seen there, the affections of the patriarch were powerfully animated and that he left the place a better and more devoted servant of God. When the solemnities were over, Jacob, with his family, pursued a route directly southward and they reached Ephrath, when they were plunged into mourning by the death of Rachel, who sank in childbirth, leaving a posthumous son. A very affecting death, considering how ardently the mind of Rachel had been set on offspring (cf. ch. 30:1). **18. She called his name Ben-oni**—The dying mother gave this name to her child, significant of her circumstances; but Jacob changed it into Benjamin. This is thought by some to have been originally Benjamin, "a son of days," i.e., of old age. But with its present ending it means "son of the right hand," i.e., particularly dear and precious. **19. Ephrath, which is Beth-lehem**—The one the old, the other the later name, signifying "house of bread." **20. and Jacob set a pillar on her grave . . . unto this day**—The spot still marked out as the grave of Rachel exactly agrees with the Scriptural record, being about a mile from Bethlehem. Anciently it was surmounted by a pyramid of stones, but the present tomb is a Mohammedan erection. **22-26. Sons of Jacob . . . born to him in Padan-aram**—It is a common practice of the sacred historian to say of a company or body of men that which, though true of the majority, may not be applicable to every individual. (See Matt. 19:28; John 20:24; Heb. 11:13). Here is an example, for Benjamin was born in Canaan.

28, 29. DEATH OF ISAAC. **29. Isaac gave up the**

ghost—The death of this venerable patriarch is here recorded by anticipation for it did not take place till fifteen years after Joseph's disappearance. Feeble and blind though he was, he lived to a very advanced age; and it is a pleasing evidence of the permanent reconciliation between Esau and Jacob that they met at Mamre to perform the funeral rites of their common father.

CHAPTER 36

Vss. 1-43. POSTERITY OF ESAU. **1. these are the generations**—history of the leading men and events (cf. ch. 2:4). **Esau who is Edom**—A name applied to him in reference to the peculiar color of his skin at birth, rendered more significant by his inordinate craving for the *red* pottage and also by the fierce sanguinary character of his descendants (cf. Ezek. 25:12; Obad. 10). **2, 3. Esau took his wives of the daughters of Canaan**—There were three, mentioned under different names; for it is evident that Bashemath is the same as Mahalath (ch. 28:9), since they both stand in the relation of daughter to Ishmael and sister to Nebajoth; and hence it may be inferred that Adah is the same as Judith, Aholibamah as Bathsemath (ch. 26:34). It was not unusual for women, in that early age, to have two names, as Sarai was also Iscah; and this is the more probable in the case of Esau's wives, who of course would have to take new names when they went from Canaan to settle in mount Seir. **6, 7. Esau . . . went into the country from the face of his brother Jacob**—lit., "a country," without any certain prospect of a settlement. The design of this historical sketch of Esau and his family is to show how the promise (ch. 27:39, 40) was fulfilled. In temporal prosperity he far exceeds his brother; and it is remarkable that, in the overruling providence of God, the vast increase of his worldly substance was the occasion of his leaving Canaan and thus making way for the return of Jacob. **8. Thus dwelt Esau in mount Seir**—This was divinely assigned as his possession (Josh. 24:4; Deut. 2:5). **15-19. dukes**—The Edomites, like the Israelites, were divided into tribes, which took their names from his sons. The head of each tribe was called by a term which in our version is rendered "duke"—not of the high rank and wealth of a British peer, but like the sheiks or emirs of the modern East, or the chieftains of highland clans. Fourteen are mentioned who flourished contemporaneously. **20-30. Sons of Seir, the Horite**—native dukes, who were incorporated with those of the Edomite race. **24. This was that Anah that found the mules**—The word "mules" is, in several ancient versions, rendered "water springs"; and this discovery of some remarkable fountain was sufficient, among a wandering or pastoral people, to entitle him to such a distinguishing notice. **31-39. kings of Edom**—The royal power was not built on the ruins of the dukedoms, but existed at the same time. **40-43.** Recapitulation of the dukes according to their residences.

CHAPTER 37

Vss. 1-4. PARENTAL PARTIALITY. **1. Jacob dwelt in the land wherein his father was a stranger**—i.e., sojourner: father used collectively. The patriarch was at this time at Mamre, in the valley of Hebron (cf. ch. 35:27); and his dwelling there was continued in the same manner and prompted by the same motives as that of Abraham and Isaac (Heb. 11:13). **2. generations**—leading occurrences, in the domestic history of Jacob, as shown in the narrative about to be commenced. **Joseph ...was feeding the flock**—lit., Joseph being seventeen years old was a shepherd over the flock—he a lad, with the sons of Bilhah and Zilpah. Oversight or superintendence is evidently implied. This post of chief shepherd in the party might be assigned him either from his being the son of a principal wife or from his own superior qualities of character; and if invested with this office, he acted not as a gossiping telltale, but as a "faithful steward" in reporting the scandalous conduct of his brethren. **3. son of his old age**—Benjamin being younger, was more the son of his old age and consequently on that ground might have been expected to be the favorite. Literally rendered, it is "son of old age to him"—*Hebrew* phrase, for "a wise son"—one who possessed observation and wisdom above his years—an old head on young shoulders. **made him a coat of many colors**— formed in those early days by sewing together patches of colored cloth, and considered a dress of distinction (Judg. 5:30; II Sam. 13:18). The passion for various colors still reigns among the Arabs and other people of the East, who are fond of dressing their children in this gaudy attire. But since the art of interweaving various patterns was introduced, "the coats of colors" are different now from what they seem to have been in patriarchal times, and bear a close resemblance to the varieties of tartan. **4. could not speak peaceably unto him**—did not say "peace be to thee," the usual expression of good wishes among friends and acquaintances. It is deemed a sacred duty to give all this form of salutation; and the withholding of it is an unmistakable sign of dislike or secret hostility. The habitual refusal of Joseph's brethren, therefore, to meet him with "the *salaam*," showed how ill-disposed they were towards him. It is very natural in parents to love the youngest, and feel partial to those who excel in talents or amiableness. But in a family constituted as Jacob's—many children by different mothers—he showed great and criminal indiscretion.

5-36. THE DREAMS OF JOSEPH. **5. Joseph dreamed a dream**—Dreams in ancient times were much attended to, and hence the dream of Joseph, though but a mere boy, engaged the serious consideration of his family. But this dream was evidently symbolical. The meaning was easily discerned, and, from its being repeated under different emblems, the fulfilment was considered certain (cf. ch. 41:32), whence it was that "his brethren envied him, but his father observed the saying." **12. his brethren went to feed their father's flock in Shechem**—The vale of Shechem was, from the earliest mention of Canaan, blest with extraordinary abundance of water. Therefore did the sons of Jacob go from Hebron to this place, though it must have cost them near twenty hours' travelling—i.e., at the shepherd rate, a little more than fifty miles. But the herbage there was so rich and nutritious that they thought it well worth the pains of so long a journey, to the neglect of the grazing district of Hebron [VAN DE VELDE]. **13-17. Israel said, ...Do not thy brethren feed the flock in Shechem?**—Anxious to learn how his sons were doing in their distant encampment, Jacob despatched Joseph; and the youth,

accepting the mission with alacrity, left the vale of Hebron, sought them at Shechem, heard of them from a man in "the field," (the wide and richly cultivated plain of Esdraelon), and found that they had left that neighborhood for Dothan, probably being compelled by the detestation in which, from the horrid massacre, their name was held. **Joseph went after his brethren, and found them in Dothan**—*Hebrew, Dothaim,* or "two wells," recently discovered in the modern "Dothan," situated a few hours' distance from Shechem. **18. when they saw him afar off**—on the level grass-field, where they were watching their cattle. They could perceive him approaching in the distance from the side of Shechem, or rather, Samaria. **19. Behold, this dreamer cometh**—lit., "master of dreams"— a bitterly ironical sneer. Dreams being considered suggestions from above, to make false pretensions to having received one was detested as a species of blasphemy, and in this light Joseph was regarded by his brethren as an artful pretender. They already began to form a plot for his assassination, from which he was rescued only by the address of Reuben, who suggested that he should rather be cast into one of the wells, which are, and probably were, completely dried up in summer. **23. they stripped Joseph out of his coat ...of many colors**—Imagine him advancing in all the unsuspecting openness of brotherly affection. How astonished and terrified must he have been at the cold reception, the ferocious aspect, the rough usage of his unnatural assailants! A vivid picture of his state of agony and despair was afterwards drawn by themselves (cf. ch. 42:21). **25. they sat down to eat bread**—What a view does this exhibit of those hardened profligates! Their common share in this conspiracy is not the only dismal feature in the story. The rapidity, the almost instantaneous manner in which the proposal was followed by their joint resolution, and the cool indifference, or rather the fiendish satisfaction, with which they sat down to regale themselves, is astonishing. It is impossible that mere envy at his dreams, his gaudy dress, or the doting partiality of their common father, could have goaded them on to such a pitch of frenzied resentment or confirmed them in such consummate wickedness. Their hatred to Joseph must have had a far deeper seat. It must have been produced by dislike to his piety and other excellencies, which made his character and conduct a constant censure upon theirs, and on account of which they found that they could never be at ease till they had rid themselves of his hated presence. This was the true solution of the mystery, just as it was in the case of Cain (I John 3:12). **they lifted up their eyes, ... and, behold, a company of Ishmaelites**—They are called Midianites (vs. 28), and Medanites, *Hebrew* (vs. 36), being a travelling caravan composed of a mixed association of Arabians. Those tribes of Northern Arabia had already addicted themselves to commerce, and long did they enjoy a monopoly, the carrying trade being entirely in their hands. Their approach could be easily be seen; for, as their road, after crossing the ford from the transjordanic district, led along the south side of the mountains of Gilboa, a party seated on the plain of Dothan could trace them and their string of camels in the distance as they proceeded through the broad and gently sloping valley that intervenes. Trading in the produce of Arabia and India, they were in the regular course of traffic on their way to Egypt: and the chief articles of commerce in which this clan dealt were "spicery" from India, i.e., a species of resinous gum, called *storax*, "balm of Gilead," the juice of the balsam tree, a native of Arabia-Felix, and "myrrh," an Arabic gum of a strong, fragrant smell. For these articles there must have been an enormous demand in Egypt as they were constantly used in the process of embalmment. **26-28. Judah said, ... what profit is it if we slay our brother?**—The sight of these travelling merchants gave a sudden turn to the views of the conspirators; for having no wish to commit a greater degree of crime than was necessary for the accomplishment of their end, they readily approved of Judah's suggestion to dispose of their obnoxious brother as a slave. The proposal, of course, was founded on their knowledge that the Arabian merchants trafficked in slaves; and there is the clearest evidence furnished by the monuments of Egypt that the traders who were in the habit of bringing slaves from the countries through which they passed, found a ready market in the cities of the Nile. **they ... lifted up Joseph out of the pit, and sold him**—Acting impulsively on Judah's advice, they had their poor victim ready by the time the merchants reached them; and money being no part of their object, they sold him for "twenty pieces of silver." The money was probably in rings or pieces (shekels), and silver is always mentioned in the records of that early age before gold, on account of its rarity. The whole sum, if in shekel weight, did not exceed $20.00. **they brought Joseph into Egypt**—There were two routes to Egypt—the one was overland by Hebron, where Jacob dwelt, and by taking which, the fate of his hapless son would likely have reached the paternal ears; the other was directly westward across the country from Dothan to the maritime coast, and in this, the safest and most expeditious way, the merchants carried Joseph to Egypt. Thus did an overruling Providence lead this murderous conclave of brothers, as well as the slave-merchants—both following their own free courses—to be parties in an act by which He was to work out, in a marvellous manner, the great purposes of His wisdom and goodness towards His ancient Church and people. **29, 30. Reuben returned unto the pit**—He seems to have designedly taken a circuitous route, with a view of secretly rescuing the poor lad from a lingering death by starvation. His intentions were excellent, and his feelings no doubt painfully lacerated when he discovered what had been done in his absence. But the thing was of God, who had designed that Joseph's deliverance should be accomplished by other means than his. **31-33. they took Joseph's coat**—The commission of one sin necessarily leads to another to conceal it; and the scheme of deception which the sons of Jacob planned and practised on their aged father was a necessary consequence of the atrocious crime they had perpetrated. What a wonder that their cruel sneer, "thy son's coat," and their forced efforts to comfort him, did not awaken suspicion! But extreme grief, like every other passion, is blind, and Jacob, great as his affliction was, did allow himself to indulge his sorrow more than became one who believed in the government of a supreme and all-wise Disposer. **34. Jacob rent his clothes, and put sackcloth upon his loins**—the common signs of Oriental mourning. A rent is made in the skirt more or less long according to the afflicted feelings of the mourner, and a coarse rough piece of black sackcloth or

camel's hair cloth is wound round the waist. **35. and he said, For I will go down into the grave unto my son**—not the earth, for Joseph was supposed to be torn in pieces, but the unknown place—the place of departed souls, where Jacob expected at death to meet his beloved son.

CHAPTER 38

Vss. 1-30. JUDAH AND FAMILY. **1. at that time**—a formula frequently used by the sacred writers, not to describe any precise period, but an interval near about it. **2. Judah saw there a daughter of a certain Canaanite**—Like Esau, this son of Jacob, casting off the restraints of religion, married into a Canaanite family; and it is not surprising that the family which sprang from such an unsuitable connection should be infamous for bold and unblushing wickedness. **8. Judah said unto Onan ... marry her, and raise up seed to thy brother**—The first instance of a custom, which was afterwards incorporated among the laws of Moses, that when a husband died leaving a widow, his brother next of age was to marry her, and the issue, if any, was to be served heir to the deceased (cf. Deut. 25:5). **12. Judah ... went up unto his sheep-shearers**—This season, which occurs in Palestine towards the end of March, was spent in more than usual hilarity, and the wealthier masters invited their friends, as well as treated their servants, to sumptuous entertainments. Accordingly, it is said, Judah was accompanied by his friend Hirah. **Timnath**—in the mountains of Judah. **18. signet**, etc.—Bracelets, including armlets, were worn by men as well as women among the Hebrews. But the *Hebrew* word here rendered "bracelets," is everywhere else translated "lace" or "ribbon"; so that as the signet alone was probably more than an equivalent for the kid, it is not easy to conjecture why the other things were given in addition, except by supposing the perforated seal was attached by a ribbon to the staff. **24. Bring her forth, and let her be burnt**—In patriarchal times fathers seem to have possessed the power of life and death over the members of their families. The crime of adultery was anciently punished in many places by burning (Lev. 21:9; Judg. 15:6; Jer. 29:22). This chapter contains details, which probably would never have obtained a place in the inspired record, had it not been to exhibit the full links of the chain that connects the genealogy of the Saviour with Abraham; and in the disreputable character of the ancestry who figure in this passage, we have a remarkable proof that "He made himself of no reputation."

CHAPTER 39

Vss. 1-23. JOSEPH IN POTIPHAR'S HOUSE. **1. Potiphar**—This name, Potiphar, signifies one "devoted to the sun," the local deity of On or Heliopolis, a circumstance which fixes the place of his residence in the Delta, the district of Egypt bordering on Canaan. **officer**—lit., "prince of Pharaoh"—i.e., in the service of government. **captain of the guard**—The import of the original term has been variously interpreted, some considering it means "chief cook," others, "chief inspector of plantations"; but that which seems best founded is "chief of the executioners," "head of the police," the same as the captain of the watch, the *zabut* of modern Egypt [WILKINSON]. **bought him ... of the Ishmaelites**—The age, appearance, and intelligence of the Hebrew slave would soon cause him to be picked up in the market. But the unseen, unfelt influence of the great Disposer drew the attention of Potiphar towards him, in order that in the house of one so closely connected with the court, he might receive that previous training which was necessary for the high office he was destined to fill, and in the school of adversity learn the lessons of practical wisdom that were to be of greatest utility and importance in his future career. Thus it is that when God has any important work to be done, He always prepares fitting agents to accomplish it. **2. he was in the house of his master**—Those slaves who had been war captives were generally sent to labor in the field and subjected to hard treatment under the "stick" of taskmasters. But those who were bought with money were employed in domestic purposes, were kindly treated, and enjoyed as much liberty as the same class does in modern Egypt. **3. his master saw that the Lord was with him**—Though changed in condition, Joseph was not changed in spirit; though stripped of the gaudy coat that had adorned his person, he had not lost the moral graces that distinguished his character; though separated from his father on earth, he still lived in communion with his Father in heaven; though in the house of an idolater, he continued a worshipper of the true God. **5. the Lord blessed the Egyptian's house for Joseph's sake,** etc.—It might be—it probably was—that a special, a miraculous blessing was poured out on a youth who so faithfully and zealously served God amid all the disadvantages of his place. But it may be useful to remark that such a blessing usually follows in the ordinary course of things; and the most worldly, unprincipled masters always admire and respect religion in a servant when they see that profession supported by conscientious principle and a consistent life. **made him overseer in his house**—We do not know in what capacity Joseph entered into the service of Potiphar; but the observant eye of his master soon discovered his superior qualities and made him his chief, his confidential servant (cf. Eph. 6:7; Col. 3:23). The advancement of domestic slaves is not uncommon, and it is considered a great disgrace not to raise one who has been a year or two in the family. But this extraordinary advancement of Joseph was the doing of the Lord, though on the part of Potiphar it was the consequence of observing the astonishing prosperity that attended him in all that he did. **7. his master's wife cast her eyes upon Joseph**—Egyptian women were not kept in the same secluded manner as females are in most Oriental countries now. They were treated in a manner more worthy of a civilized people—in fact, enjoyed much freedom both at home and abroad. Hence Potiphar's wife had constant opportunity of meeting Joseph. But the ancient women of Egypt were very loose in their morals. Intrigues and intemperance were vices very prevalent among the them, as the monuments too plainly attest [WILKINSON]. Potiphar's wife was probably not worse than many of the same rank, and her infamous advances made to Joseph arose from her superiority of station. **9. How then can I do this great wickedness, and sin against God?**—This remonstrance, when all inferior arguments had failed, embodied the true principle of moral purity—a principle always sufficient where it exists, and

alone sufficient. **14. Then she called unto the men of her house**—Disappointed and affronted, she vowed revenge and accused Joseph, first to the servants of the house, and on his return to her lord. **See, he hath brought in an Hebrew ... to mock us**—an affected and blind aspersion of her husband for keeping in his house an Hebrew, the very abomination of Egyptians. **20. Joseph's master took him and put him into the prison**—the roundhouse, from the form of its construction, usually attached to the dwelling of such an officer as Potiphar. It was partly a subterranean dungeon (ch. 41:14), though the brick-built walls rose considerably above the surface of the ground, and were surmounted by a vaulted roof somewhat in the form of an inverted bowl. Into such a dungeon Potiphar, in the first ebullition of rage, threw Joseph and ordered him to be subjected further to as great harshness of treatment (Ps. 105:18) as he dared; for the power of masters over their slaves was very properly restrained by law, and the murder of a slave was a capital crime. **a place where the king's prisoners were bound**—Though prisons seem to have been an inseparable appendage of the palaces, this was not a common jail—it was the receptacle of state criminals; and, therefore, it may be presumed that more than ordinary strictness and vigilance were exercised over the prisoners. In general, however, the Egyptian, like other Oriental prisons, were used solely for the purposes of detention. Accused persons were cast into them until the charges against them could be investigated; and though the jailer was responsible for the appearance of those placed under his custody, yet, provided they were produced when called, he was never interrogated as to the way in which he had kept them. **21-23. The Lord ... gave him favour in the sight of the keeper of the prison,** etc. It is highly probable, from the situation of this prison (ch. 40:3), that the keeper might have been previously acquainted with Joseph and have had access to know his innocence of the crime laid to his charge, as well as with all the high integrity of his character. That may partly account for his showing so much kindness and confidence to his prisoner. But there was a higher influence at work; for "the Lord was with Joseph, and that which he did, the Lord made it to prosper."

CHAPTER 40

Vss. 1-8. TWO STATE PRISONERS. **1. the butler** —not only the cup-bearer, but overseer of the royal vineyards, as well as the cellars; having, probably, some hundreds of people under him. **baker**—or cook, had the superintendence of every thing relating to the providing and preparing of meats for the royal table. Both officers, especially the former, were, in ancient Egypt, always persons of great rank and importance; and from the confidential nature of their employment, as well as their access to the royal presence, they were generally the highest nobles or princes of the blood. **3. Pharaoh put them in ward,** etc.—Whatever was their crime, they were committed, until their case could be investigated, to the custody of the captain of the guard, i.e., Potiphar, in an outer part of whose house the royal prison was situated. **4. The captain of the guard charged Joseph with them**—not the keeper, though he was most favorably disposed; but Potiphar himself, who, it would seem, was by this time satisfied of the perfect innocence of the young Hebrew; though, probably, to prevent the exposure of his family, he deemed it prudent to detain him in confinement (see Ps. 37:5). **They continued a season in ward**—lit., "days," how long, is uncertain; but as they were called to account on the king's birthday, it has been supposed that their offense had been committed on the preceding anniversary [CALVIN]. **5-8. they dreamed a dream**—Joseph, influenced by the spirit of true religion, could feel for others (Eccles. 4:1; Rom. 12:15; Phil. 2:4). Observing them one day extremely depressed, he inquired the cause of their melancholy; and being informed it was owing to a dream they had respectively dreamed during the previous night, after piously directing them to God (Dan. 2:30; Isa. 26:10), he volunteered to aid them, through the divine help, in discovering the import of their vision. The influence of Providence must be seen in the remarkable fact of both officers dreaming such dreams in one night. He moves the spirits of men.

9-15. THE BUTLER'S DREAM. **9. In my dream, behold, a vine was before me**—The visionary scene described seems to represent the king as taking exercise and attended by his butler, who gave him a cooling draught. On all occasions, the kings of ancient Egypt were required to practice temperance in the use of wine [WILKINSON]; but in this scene, it is a prepared beverage he is drinking, probably the sherbet of the present day. Everything was done in the king's presence—the cup was washed, the juice of the grapes pressed into it; and it was then handed to him—not grasped; but lightly resting on the tips of the fingers. **12-15. Joseph said, ... This is the interpretation**—Speaking as an inspired interpreter, he told the butler that within three days he would be restored to all the honors and privileges of his office; and while making that joyful announcement, he earnestly bespoke the officer's influence for his own liberation. Nothing has hitherto met us in the record indicative of Joseph's feelings; but this earnest appeal reveals a sadness and impatient longing for release, which not all his piety and faith in God could dispel.

16-23. THE BAKER'S DREAM. **16. I had three white baskets**—The circumstances mentioned exactly describe his duties, which, notwithstanding numerous assistants, he performed with his own hands. **white**—lit., "full of holes,"—i.e., wicker baskets. The meats were carried to table upon the head in three baskets, one piled upon the other; and in the uppermost, the bakemeats. And in crossing the open courts, from the kitchen to the dining rooms, the removal of the viands by a vulture, eagle, ibis, or other rapacious bird, was a frequent occurrence in the palaces of Egypt, as it is an everyday incident in the hot countries of the East still. The risk from these carnivorous birds was the greater in the cities of Egypt, where being held sacred, it was unlawful to destroy them; and they swarmed in such numbers as to be a great annoyance to the people. **18, 19. Joseph answered and said, This is the interpretation**—The purport was that in three days his execution should be ordered. The language of Joseph describes minutely one form of capital punishment that prevailed in Egypt; viz., that the criminal was decapitated and then his headless body gibbeted on a tree by the highway till it was gradually devoured by the ravenous birds. **20-22. it came to pass the third day, which was Pharaoh's birthday**—This was a holiday season, celebrated at court with great magnificence and honored by a free pardon to prisoners. Accordingly, the issue happened to the butler and baker, as Joseph had foretold. Doubtless, he felt it painful to communicate such dismal tidings to the baker; but he could not help announcing what God had revealed to him; and it was for the honor of the true God that he should speak plainly. **23. yet did not the chief butler remember Joseph**—This was human nature. How prone are men to forget and neglect in prosperity, those who have been their companions in adversity (Amos 6:6)! But although reflecting no credit on the butler, it was wisely ordered in the providence of God that he should forget him. The divine purposes required that Joseph should obtain his deliverance in another way, and by other means.

CHAPTER 41

Vss. 1-24. PHARAOH'S DREAM. **1. at the end of two full years**—It is not certain whether these years are reckoned from the beginning of Joseph's imprisonment, or from the events described in the preceding chapter—most likely the latter. What a long time for Joseph to experience the sickness of hope deferred! But the time of his enlargement came when he had sufficiently learned the lessons of God designed for him; and the plans of Providence were matured. **Pharaoh dreamed**—Pharaoh, from an Egyptian word *Phre*, signifying the "sun," was the official title of the kings of that country. The prince, who occupied the throne of Egypt, was Aphophis, one of the Memphite kings, whose capital was On or Heliopolis, and who is universally acknowledged to have been a patriot king. Between the arrival of Abraham and the appearance of Joseph in that country, somewhat more than two centuries had elapsed. Kings sleep and dream, as well as their subjects. And this Pharaoh had two dreams in one night so singular and so similar, so distinct and so apparently significant, so coherent and vividly impressed on his memory, that his spirit was troubled. **8. he called for all the magicians of Egypt**—It is not possible to define the exact distinction between "magicians and wise men"; but they formed different branches of a numerous body, who laid claim to supernatural skill in occult arts and sciences, in revealing mysteries, explaining portents, and, above all, interpreting dreams. Long practice had rendered them expert in devising a plausible way of getting out of every difficulty and framing an answer suitable to the occasion. But the dreams of Pharaoh baffled their united skill. Unlike their Assyrian brethren (Dan. 2:4), they did not pretend to know the meaning of the symbols contained in them, and the providence of God had determined that they should all be nonplussed in the exercise of their boasted powers, in order that the inspired wisdom of Joseph might appear the more remarkable. **9-13. then spake the chief butler unto Pharaoh, saying, I do remember my faults**—This public acknowledgment of the merits of the young Hebrew would, tardy though it was, have reflected credit on the butler had it not been obviously made to ingratiate himself with his royal master. It is right to confess our faults against God, and against our fellow men when that confession is made in the spirit of godly sorrow and penitence. But this man was not much impressed with a sense of the fault he had committed against Joseph; he never thought of God, to whose goodness he was indebted for the prophetic announcement of his release, and in acknowledging his former fault against the king, he was practising the courtly art of pleasing his master. **14. Then Pharaoh sent and called Joseph**—Now that God's set time had come (Ps. 105:19), no human power nor policy could detain Joseph in prison. During his protracted confinement, he might have often been distressed with perplexing doubts; but the mystery of Providence was about to be cleared up, and all his sorrows forgotten in the course of honor and public usefulness in which his services were to be employed. **shaved himself**—The Egyptians were the only Oriental nation that liked a smooth chin. All slaves and foreigners who were reduced to that condition, were obliged, on their arrival in that country, to conform to the cleanly habits of the natives, by shaving their beards and heads, the latter of which were covered with a close cap. Thus prepared, Joseph was conducted to the palace, where the king seemed to have been anxiously waiting his arrival. **15, 16. Pharaoh said, . . . I have dreamed a dream**—The king's brief statement of the service required brought out the genuine piety of Joseph; disclaiming all merit, he ascribed whatever gifts or sagacity he possessed to the divine source of all wisdom, and he declared his own inability to penetrate futurity; but, at the same time, he expressed his confident persuasion that God would reveal what was necessary to be known. **17. Pharaoh said, In my dream, behold, I stood upon the bank of the river**—The dreams were purely Egyptian, founded on the productions of that country and the experience of a native. The fertility of Egypt being wholly dependent on the Nile, the scene is laid on the banks of that river; and oxen being in the ancient hieroglyphics symbolical of the earth and of food, animals of that species were introduced in the first dream. **18. there came up out of the river seven kine**—Cows now, of the buffalo kind, are seen daily plunging into the Nile; when their huge form is gradually emerging, they seem as if rising "out of the river." **and they fed in a meadow**—Nile grass, the aquatic plants that grow on the marshy banks of that river, particularly the lotus kind, on which cattle were usually fattened. **19. behold, seven other kine . . . poor and ill-favoured**—The cow being the emblem of fruitfulness, the different years of plenty and of famine were aptly represented by the different condition of those kine—the plenty, by the cattle feeding on the richest fodder; and the dearth, by the lean and famishing kine, which the pangs of hunger drove to act contrary to their nature. **22. I saw in my dream, and, behold, seven ears**—that is, of Egyptian wheat, which, when "full and good," is remarkable in size—a single seed sprouting into seven, ten, or fourteen stalks—and each stalk bearing an ear. **23. blasted with the east wind**—destructive everywhere to grain, but particularly so in Egypt; where, sweeping over the sandy deserts of Arabia, it comes in the character of a hot, blighting wind, that quickly withers all vegetation (cf. Ezek. 19:12; Hos. 13:15). **24. the thin ears devoured the seven good ears**—*devoured* is a different word from that used in vs. 4 and conveys the idea of destroying, by absorbing to themselves all the nutritious virtue of the soil around them.

25-36. JOSEPH INTERPRETS PHARAOH'S DREAMS. **25. Joseph said, . . . The dream . . . is one**—They both pointed to the same event—a remarkable dispensation of seven years of unexampled abundance, to be followed by a similar period of unparalleled dearth. The repetition of the dream in two different forms was designed to show the absolute certainty and speedy arrival of this public crisis; the interpretation was accompanied by several suggestions of practical wisdom for meeting so great an emergency as was impending. **33. Now therefore let Pharaoh look out a man**—The explanation given, when the key to the dreams was supplied, appears to have been satisfactory to the king and his courtiers; and we may suppose that much and anxious conversation arose, in the course of which Joseph might have been asked whether he had anything further to say. No doubt the providence of God provided the opportunity of his suggesting what was necessary. **34. and let him appoint officers over the land**—overseers, equivalent to the beys of modern Egypt. **take up the fifth part of the land**—i.e., of the land produce, to be purchased and stored by the government, instead of being sold to foreign corn merchants.

37-57. JOSEPH MADE RULER OF EGYPT. **38. Pharaoh said unto his servants**—The kings of ancient Egypt were assisted in the management of state affairs by the advice of the most distinguished members of the priestly order; and, accordingly, before admitting Joseph to the new and extraordinary office that was to be created, those ministers were consulted as to the expediency and propriety of the appointment. **a man in whom the Spirit of God is**—An acknowledgment of the being and power of the true God, though faint and feeble, continued to linger amongst the higher classes long after idolatry had come to prevail. **40. Thou shalt be over my house**—This sudden change in the condition of a man who had just been taken out of prison could take place nowhere, except in Egypt. In ancient as well as modern times, slaves have often risen to be its rulers. But the special providence of God had determined to make Joseph governor of Egypt; and the way was paved for it by the deep and universal conviction produced in the minds both of the king and his councillors, that a divine spirit animated his mind and had given him such extraordinary knowledge. **according unto thy word shall all my people be ruled**—lit., "kiss." This refers to the edict granting official power to Joseph, to be issued in the form of a firman, as in all Oriental countries; and all who should receive that order would kiss it, according to the usual Eastern mode of acknowledging obedience and respect for the sovereign [WILKINSON]. **41. Pharaoh said, . . . See, I have set thee over all the land**—These words were preliminary to investiture with the insignia of office, which were these: the signet ring, used for signing public documents, and its impression was more valid than the sign-manual of the king; the *kheilaat* or dress of honor, a coat of finely wrought linen, or rather cotton, worn only by the highest personages; the gold necklace, a badge of rank, the plain or ornamental *form* of it indicating the degree of rank and dignity; the privilege of riding in a state carriage, the second chariot; and lastly— **43. they cried before him, Bow the knee**—*abrech*, an Egyptian term, not referring to prostration, but signifying, according to some, "father" (cf. ch. 45:8); according to others, "native prince"—i.e., proclaimed him naturalized, in order to remove all popular dislike to him as a foreigner. **44.** These ceremonies of investiture were closed in usual form by the king in council solemnly ratifying the appointment. **I am Pharaoh, and without thee,** etc.—a proverbial mode of expression for great power. **45. Zaphnath-paaneah**—variously interpreted, "revealer of secrets"; "saviour of the land"; and from the hieroglyphics, "a wise man fleeing from pollution"—i.e., adultery. **gave him to wife Asenath, the daughter of**—His naturalization was completed by this alliance with a family of high distinction. On being founded by an Arab colony, Poti-pherah, like Jethro, priest of Midian, might be a worshipper of the true God; and thus Joseph, a pious man, will be freed from the charge of marrying an idolatress for worldly ends. **On**—called Aven (Ezek. 30:17) and also Beth-shemesh (Jer. 43:13). In looking at this profusion of honors heaped suddenly upon Joseph, it cannot be doubted that he would humbly yet thankfully acknowledge the hand of a special Providence in conducting him through all his checkered course to almost royal power; and we, who know more than Joseph did, cannot only see that his advancement was subservient to the most important purposes relative to the Church of God, but learn the great lesson that a Providence directs the minutest events of human life. **46. Joseph was thirty years old, when he stood before Pharaoh**—seventeen when brought into Egypt, probably three in prison, and thirteen in the service of Potiphar. **went out ... all the land**—made an immediate survey to determine the site and size of the storehouses required for the different quarters of the country. **47. the earth brought forth by handfuls**—a singular expression, alluding not only to the luxuriance of the crop, but the practice of the reapers grasping the ears, which alone were cut. **48. he gathered up all the food of the seven years**—It gives a striking idea of the exuberant fertility of this land, that, from the superabundance of the seven plenteous years, corn enough was laid up for the subsistence, not only of its home population, but of the neighboring countries, during the seven years of dearth. **50-52. unto Joseph were born two sons**—These domestic events, which increased his temporal happiness, develop the piety of his character in the names conferred upon his children. **53-56. The seven years of plenteousness ... ended**—Over and above the proportion purchased for the government during the years of plenty, the people could still have husbanded much for future use. But improvident as men commonly are in the time of prosperity, they found themselves in want, and would have starved by thousands had not Joseph anticipated and provided for the protracted calamity. **57. The famine was sore in all lands**—i.e., the lands contiguous to Egypt—Canaan, Syria, and Arabia.

CHAPTER 42

Vss. 1-38. JOURNEY INTO EGYPT. **1.** Now when **Jacob saw that there was corn in Egypt**—learned from common rumor. It is evident from Jacob's language that his own and his sons' families had suffered greatly from the scarcity; and through the increasing severity of the scourge, those men, who had formerly shown both activity and spirit, were sinking into despondency. God would not interpose miraculously when natural means of preser-

vation were within reach. **5. the famine was in the land of Canaan**—The tropical rains, which annually falling swell the Nile, are those of Palestine also; and their failure would produce the same disastrous effects in Canaan as in Egypt. Numerous caravans of its people, therefore, poured over the sandy desert of Suez, with their beasts of burden, for the purchase of corn; and among others, "the sons of Israel" were compelled to undertake a journey from which painful associations made them strongly averse. **6. Joseph was the governor**—in the zenith of his power and influence. **he it was that sold**—i.e., directed the sales; for it is impossible that he could give attendance in every place. It is probable, however, that he may have personally superintended the storehouses near the border of Canaan, both because that was the most exposed part of the country and because he must have anticipated the arrival of some messengers from his father's house. **Joseph's brethren came, and bowed down themselves before him**—His prophetic dreams were in the course of being fulfilled, and the atrocious barbarity of his brethren had been the means of bringing about the very issue they had planned to prevent (Isa. 60:14; Rev. 3:9, last clause). **7, 8. Joseph saw his brethren, and he knew them, ... but they knew not him**—This is not strange. They were full-grown men —he was but a lad at parting. They were in their usual garb—he was in his official robes. They never dreamt of him as governor of Egypt, while he had been expecting them. They had but one face—he had ten persons to judge by. **made himself strange unto them, and spake roughly**—It would be an injustice to Joseph's character to suppose that this stern manner was prompted by any vindictive feelings—he never indulged any resentment against others who had injured him. But he spoke in the authoritative tone of the governor in order to elicit some much-longed-for information respecting the state of his father's family, as well as to bring his brethren, by their own humiliation and distress, to a sense of the evils they had done to him. **9-14. Ye are spies**—This is a suspicion entertained regarding strangers in all Eastern countries down to the present day. Joseph, however, who was well aware that his brethren were not spies, has been charged with cruel dissimulation, with a deliberate violation of what he knew to be the truth, in imputing to them such a character. But it must be remembered that he was sustaining the part of a ruler; and, in fact, acting on the very principle sanctioned by many of the sacred writers, and our Lord Himself, who spoke parables (fictitious stories) to promote a good end. **15. By the life of Pharaoh**—It is a very common practice in Western Asia to swear by the life of the king. Joseph spoke in the style of an Egyptian and perhaps did not think there was any evil in it. But we are taught to regard all such expressions in the light of an oath (Matt. 5:34; Jas. 5:12). **17-24. put them ... into ward three days**—Their confinement had been designed to bring them to salutary reflection. And this object was attained, for they looked upon the retributive justice of God as now pursuing them in that foreign land. The drift of their conversation is one of the most striking instances on record of the power of conscience. **24. took ... Simeon, and bound him** —He had probably been the chief instigator—the most violent actor in the outrage upon Joseph; and if so, his selection to be the imprisoned and fettered hostage for their return would, in the present course of their reflections, have a painful significance. **25-28. Joseph commanded to fill their sacks with corn, and to restore every man's money**—This private generosity was not an infringement of his duty—a defrauding of the revenue. He would have a discretionary power—he was daily enriching the king's exchequer—and he might have paid the sum from his own purse. **27. inn**—a mere station for baiting beasts of burden. **he espied his money** —The discovery threw them into greater perplexity than ever. If they had been congratulating themselves on escaping from the ruthless governor, they perceived that now he would have a handle against them; and it is observable that they looked upon this as a judgment of heaven. Thus one leading design of Joseph was gained in their consciences being roused to a sense of guilt. **35. as they emptied their sacks, that behold, every man's ...money was in his sack**—It appears that they had been silent about the money discovery at the resting-place, as their father might have blamed them for not instantly returning. However innocent they knew themselves to be, it was universally felt to be an unhappy circumstance, which might bring them into new and greater perils. **36. Me have ye bereaved**—This exclamation indicates a painfully excited state of feeling, and it shows how difficult it is for even a good man to yield implicit submission to the course of Providence. The language does not imply that his missing sons had got foul play from the hands of the rest, but he looks upon Simeon as lost, as well as Joseph, and he insinuates it was by some imprudent statements of theirs that he was exposed to the risk of losing Benjamin also. **37. Reuben spake, ... Slay my two sons, if I bring him not to thee**—This was a thoughtless and unwarrantable condition—one that he never seriously expected his father would accept. It was designed only to give assurance of the greatest care being taken of Benjamin. But unforeseen circumstances might arise to render it impossible for all of them to preserve that young lad (Jas. 4:13), and Jacob was much pained by the prospect. Little did he know that God was dealing with him severely, but in kindness (Heb. 12:7, 8), and that all those things he thought against Him were working together for his good.

CHAPTER 43

Vss. 1-14. Preparations for a Second Journey to Egypt. **2. their father said, ... Go again, buy us a little food**—It was no easy matter to bring Jacob to agree to the only conditions on which his sons could return to Egypt (ch. 42:15). The necessity of immediately procuring fresh supplies for the maintenance of themselves and their families overcame every other consideration and extorted his consent to Benjamin joining in a journey, which his sons entered on with mingled feelings of hope and anxiety—of hope, because having now complied with the governor's demand to bring down their youngest brother, they flattered themselves that the alleged ground of suspecting them would be removed; and of apprehension that some ill designs were meditated against them. **11. take of the best fruits ... a present**— It is an Oriental practice never to approach a man of power without a present, and Jacob might remember how he pacified his brother (Prov. 21:14) —balm, spices, and myrrh (ch. 37:25), honey, which some think was *dibs*, a syrup made from

ripe dates [BOCHART]; but others, the honey of Hebron, which is still valued as far superior to that of Egypt; nuts, pistachio nuts, of which Syria grows the best in the world; almonds, which were most abundant in Palestine. **12. take double money**—the first sum to be returned, and another sum for a new supply. The restored money in the sacks' mouth was a perplexing circumstance. But it might have been done inadvertently by one of the servants—so Jacob persuaded himself—and happy it was for his own peace and the encouragement of the travellers that he took this view. Besides the duty of restoring it, honesty in their case was clearly the best—the safest policy. **14. God Almighty give you mercy before the man**—Jacob is here committing them all to the care of God and, resigned to what appears a heavy trial, prays that it may be overruled for good.

15-30. Arrival in Egypt. **15. stood before Joseph**—We may easily imagine the delight with which, amid the crowd of other applicants, the eye of Joseph would fix on his brethren and Benjamin. But occupied with his public duties, he consigned them to the care of a confidential servant till he should have finished the business of the day. **16. ruler of his house**—In the houses of wealthy Egyptians one upper man-servant was intrusted with the management of the house (cf. ch. 39:5). **slay, and make ready**—Hebrew, "kill a killing"—implying preparations for a grand entertainment (cf. ch. 31:54; I Sam. 25:11; Prov. 9:2; Matt. 22:4). The animals have to be killed as well as prepared at home. The heat of the climate requires that the cook should take the joints directly from the hands of the flesher, and the Oriental taste is, from habit, fond of newly killed meat. A great profusion of viands, with an inexhaustible supply of vegetables, was provided for the repasts, to which strangers were invited, the pride of Egyptian people consisting rather in the quantity and variety than in the choice or delicacy of the dishes at their table. **dine ... at noon**—The hour of dinner was at midday. **18. the men were afraid**—Their feelings of awe on entering the stately mansion, unaccustomed as they were to houses at all, their anxiety at the reasons of their being taken there, their solicitude about the restored money, their honest simplicity in communicating their distress to the steward and his assurances of having received their money in "full weight," the offering of their fruit-present, which would, as usual, be done with some parade, and the Oriental salutations that passed between their host and them—are all described in a graphic and animated manner.

31-34. The Dinner. **31. Joseph said, Set on bread**—equivalent to having dinner served, bread being a term inclusive of all victuals. The table was a small stool, most probably the usual round form, "since persons might even then be seated according to their rank or seniority, and the modern Egyptian table is not without its post of honor and a fixed gradation of place" [WILKINSON]. Two or at most three persons were seated at one table. But the host being the highest in rank of the company had a table to himself; while it was so arranged that an Egyptian was not placed nor obliged to eat from the same dish as a Hebrew. **32. Egyptians might not eat bread with the Hebrews; for that is an abomination**—The prejudice probably arose from the detestation in which, from the oppressions of the shepherd-kings, the nation held all of that occupation. **34. took and**

sent messes ... Benjamin's mess was five times— In Egypt, as in other Oriental countries, there were, and are, two modes of paying attention to a guest whom the host wishes to honor—either by giving a choice piece from his own hand, or ordering it to be taken to the stranger. The degree of respect shown consists in the quantity, and while the ordinary rule of distinction is a double mess, it must have appeared a very distinguished mark of favor bestowed on Benjamin to have no less than five times any of his brethren. **they drank, and were merry with him**—*Hebrew*, "drank freely" (same as Solomon's Song, 5:1, John 2:10). In all these cases the idea of intemperance is excluded. The painful anxieties and cares of Joseph's brethren were dispelled, and they were at ease.

CHAPTER 44

Vss. 1-34. POLICY TO STAY HIS BRETHREN. **1. And Joseph commanded the steward**—The design of putting the cup into the sack of Benjamin was obviously to bring that young man into a situation of difficulty or danger, in order thereby to discover how far the brotherly feelings of the rest would be roused to sympathize with his distress and stimulate their exertions in procuring his deliverance. But for what purpose was the money restored? It was done, in the first instance, from kindly feelings to his father; but another and further design seems to have been the prevention of any injurious impressions as to the character of Benjamin. The discovery of the cup in *his* possession, if there had been nothing else to judge by, might have fastened a painful suspicion of guilt on the youngest brother; but the sight of the money in each man's sack would lead all to the same conclusion, that Benjamin was just as innocent as themselves, although the additional circumstance of the cup being found in his sack would bring him into greater trouble and danger. **2. put my cup, the silver cup, in the sack's mouth** —It was a large goblet, as the original denotes, highly valued by its owner, on account of its costly material or its elegant finish and which had probably graced his table at the sumptuous entertainment of the previous day. **3. As soon as the morning was light, the men were sent away**—They commenced their homeward journey at early dawn (see on ch. 18:2); and it may be readily supposed in high spirits, after so happy an issue from all their troubles and anxieties. **4. When they were gone out of the city ... Joseph said unto his steward**—They were brought to a sudden halt by the stunning intelligence that an article of rare value was missing from the governor's house. It was a silver cup; so strong suspicions were entertained against them that a special messenger was despatched to search them. **5. Is not this it in which my lord drinketh**—not only kept for the governor's personal use, but whereby he divines. Divination by cups, to ascertain the course of futurity, was one of the prevalent superstitions of ancient Egypt, as it is of Eastern countries still. It is not likely that Joseph, a pious believer in the true God, would have addicted himself to this superstitious practice. But he might have availed himself of that popular notion to carry out the successful execution of his stratagem for the last decisive trial of his brethren. **6, 7. he overtook them, and he spake ... these words**—The steward's

words must have come upon them like a thunderbolt, and one of their most predominant feelings must have been the humiliating and galling sense of being made so often objects of suspicion. Protesting their innocence, they invited a search. The challenge was accepted. Beginning with the eldest, every sack was examined, and the cup being found in Benjamin's, they all returned in an indescribable agony of mind into the house of the governor, throwing themselves at his feet, with the remarkable confession, "God hath found out the iniquity of thy servants." **16-34. Judah said, What shall we say?**—This address needs no comment— consisting at first of short, broken sentences, as if, under the overwhelming force of the speaker's emotions, his utterance were choked, it becomes more free and copious by the effort of speaking, as he proceeds. Every word finds its way to the heart; and it may well be imagined that Benjamin, who stood there speechless like a victim about to be laid on the altar, when he heard the magnanimous offer of Judah to submit to slavery for his ransom, would be bound by a lifelong gratitude to his generous brother, a tie that seems to have become hereditary in his tribe. Joseph's behavior must not be viewed from any single point, or in separate parts, but as a whole—a well-thought, deep-laid, closely, connected plan; and though some features of it do certainly exhibit an appearance of harshness, yet the pervading principle of his conduct was real, genuine, brotherly kindness. Read in this light, the narrative of the proceedings describes the continuous, though secret, pursuit of one end; and Joseph exhibits, in his management of the scheme, a very high order of intellect, a warm and susceptible heart, united to a judgment that exerted a complete control over his feelings—a happy invention in devising means towards the attainment of his ends and an inflexible adherence to the course, however painful, which prudence required.

CHAPTER 45

Vss. 1-28. JOSEPH MAKING HIMSELF KNOWN. **1. Then Joseph could not refrain himself**—The severity of the inflexible magistrate here gives way to the natural feelings of the man and the brother. However well he had disciplined his mind, he felt it impossible to resist the artless eloquence of Judah. He saw a satisfactory proof, in the return of *all* his brethren on such an occasion, that they were affectionately united to one another; he had heard enough to convince him that time, reflection, or grace had made a happy improvement on their characters; and he would probably have proceeded in a calm and leisurely manner to reveal himself as prudence might have dictated. But when he heard the heroic self-sacrifice of Judah and realized all the affection of that proposal—a proposal for which he was totally unprepared—he was completely unmanned; he felt himself forced to bring this painful trial to an end. **he cried, Cause every man to go out from me**—In ordering the departure of witnesses of this last scene, he acted as a warm-hearted and real friend to his brothers—his conduct was dictated by motives of the highest prudence—that of preventing their early iniquities from becoming known either to the members of his household, or among the people of Egypt. **2. he wept aloud**—No doubt, from the fulness of highly excited feelings; but to indulge in vehement and long-continued transports of sobbing is the usual way in which the Orientals express their grief. **3. I am Joseph**—The emotions that now rose in his breast as well as that of his brethren—and chased each other in rapid succession—were many and violent. He was agitated by sympathy and joy; they were astonished, confounded, terrified; and betrayed their terror, by shrinking as far as they could from his presence. So "troubled" were they, that he had to repeat his announcement of himself; and what kind, affectionate terms he did use. He spoke of their having sold him—not to wound their feelings, but to convince them of his identity; and then, to reassure their minds, he traced the agency of an overruling Providence, in his exile and present honor. Not that he wished them to roll the responsibility of their crime on God; no, his only object was to encourage their confidence and induce them to trust in the plans he had formed for the future comfort of their father and themselves. **6. and yet there are five years, in the which there shall neither be earing nor harvest**—"Ear" is an *old* English word, meaning "to plough" (cf. I Sam. 8:12; Isa. 30:24). This seems to confirm the view given (ch. 41:57) that the famine was caused by an extraordinary drought, which prevented the annual overflowing of the Nile; and of course made the land unfit to receive the seed of Egypt. **14, 15. And he fell upon . . . Benjamin's neck**—The sudden transition from a condemned criminal to a fondled brother, might have occasioned fainting or even death, had not his tumultuous feelings been relieved by a torrent of tears. But Joseph's attentions were not confined to Benjamin. He affectionately embraced every one of his brothers in succession; and by those actions, his forgiveness was demonstrated more fully than it could be by words. **17-20. Pharaoh said unto Joseph, Say unto thy brethren**—As Joseph might have been prevented by delicacy, the king himself invited the patriarch and all his family to migrate into Egypt; and he made most liberal arrangements for their removal and their subsequent settlement. It displays the character of this Pharaoh to advantage, that he was so kind to the relatives of Joseph; but indeed the greatest liberality he could show could never recompense the services of so great a benefactor of his kingdom. **21. Joseph gave them wagons**—which must have been novelties in Palestine; for wheeled carriages were almost unknown there. **22. changes or raiment**—It was and is customary with great men, to bestow on their friends dresses of distinction, and in places where they are of the same description and quality, the value of these presents consists in their number. The great number given to Benjamin bespoke the warmth of his brother's attachment to him; and Joseph felt, from the amiable temper they now all displayed, he might, with perfect safety, indulge this fond partiality for his mother's son. **23. to his father he sent**—a supply of everything that could contribute to his support and comfort—the large and liberal scale on which that supply was given being intended, like the five messes of Benjamin, as a token of his filial love. **24. so he sent his brethren away**—In dismissing them on their homeward journey, he gave them this particular admonition: "See that ye fall not out by the way"—a caution that would be greatly needed; for not only during the journey would they be occupied in recalling the parts they had respectively acted in the events that led to Jo-

seph's being sold into Egypt, but their wickedness would soon have to come to the knowledge of their venerable father.

CHAPTER 46

Vss. 1-4. SACRIFICE AT BEER-SHEBA. **1. Israel took his journey with all that he had**—that is, his household; for in compliance with Pharaoh's recommendation, he left his heavy furniture behind. In contemplating a step so important as that of leaving Canaan, which at his time of life he might never revisit, so pious a patriarch would ask the guidance and counsel of God. With all his anxiety to see Joseph, he would rather have died in Canaan without that highest of earthly gratifications than leave it without the consciousness of carrying the divine blessing along with him. **came to Beer-sheba**—That place, which was in his direct route to Egypt, had been a favorite encampment of Abraham (ch. 21:33) and Isaac (ch. 26:25), and was memorable for their experience of the divine goodness; and Jacob seems to have deferred his public devotions till he had reached a spot so consecrated by covenant to his own God and the God of his fathers. **2. God spake unto Israel**—Here is a virtual renewal of the covenant and an assurance of its blessings. Moreover, here is an answer on the chief subject of Jacob's prayer and a removal of any doubt as to the course he was meditating. At first the prospect of paying a personal visit to Joseph had been viewed with unmingled joy. But, on calmer consideration, many difficulties appeared to lie in the way. He may have remembered the prophecy to Abraham that his posterity was to be afflicted in Egypt and also that his father had been expressly told *not* to go; he may have feared the contamination of idolatry to his family and their forgetfulness of the land of promise. These doubts were removed by the answer of the oracle, and an assurance given him of great and increasing prosperity. **3. I will there make of thee a great nation**—How truly this promise was fulfilled, appears in the fact that the seventy souls who went down into Egypt increased, in the space of 215 years, to 180,000. **4. I will also surely bring thee up again**—As Jacob could not expect to live till the former promise was realized, he must have seen that the latter was to be accomplished only to his posterity. To himself it was literally verified in the removal of his remains to Canaan; but, in the large and liberal sense of the words, it was made good only on the establishment of Israel in the land of promise. **Joseph shall put his hand upon thine eyes**—shall perform the last office of filial piety; and this implied that he should henceforth enjoy, without interruption, the society of that favorite son.

5-27. IMMIGRATION TO EGYPT. **5. Jacob rose up from Beer-sheba**—to cross the border and settle in Egypt. However refreshed and invigorated in spirit by the religious services at Beer-sheba, he was now borne down by the infirmities of advanced age; and, therefore, his sons undertook all the trouble and toil of the arrangements, while the enfeebled old patriarch, with the wives and children, was conveyed by slow and leisurely stages in the Egyptian vehicles sent for their accommodation. **6. goods, which they had gotten in the land**—not furniture, but substance—precious things. **7. daughters**—As Dinah was his only daughter, this must mean daughters-in-law. **all his seed, brought**

he with him—Though disabled by age from active superintendence, yet, as the venerable sheik of the tribe, he was looked upon as their common head and consulted in every step. **8-27. all the souls of the house of Jacob, which came into Egypt, were threescore and ten**—Strictly speaking, there were only sixty-six went to Egypt; but to these add Joseph and his two sons, and Jacob the head of the clan, and the whole number amounts to seventy. In the speech of Stephen (Acts 7:14) the number is stated to be seventy-five; but as that estimate includes five sons of Ephraim and Manasseh (I Chron. 7:14-20), born in Egypt, the two accounts coincide. **28-34. ARRIVAL TO EGYPT. 28. he sent Judah before him unto Joseph**—This precautionary measure was obviously proper for apprising the king of the entrance of so large a company within his territories; moreover, it was necessary in order to receive instruction from Joseph as to the *locale* of their future settlement. **29, 30. Joseph made ready his chariot**—The difference between chariot and wagon was not only in the lighter and more elegant construction of the former, but in the one being drawn by horses and the other by oxen. Being a public man in Egypt, Joseph was required to appear everywhere in an equipage suitable to his dignity; and, therefore, it was not owing either to pride or ostentatious parade that he drove his carriage, while his father's family were accommodated only in rude and humble wagons. **presented himself unto him**—in an attitude of filial reverence (cf. Exod. 22:17). The interview was a most affecting one—the happiness of the delighted father was now at its height; and life having no higher charms, he could, in the very spirit of the aged Simeon, have departed in peace. **31-34. Joseph said,...I will go up, and show Pharaoh**—It was a tribute of respect due to the king to inform him of their arrival. And the instructions which he gave them were worthy of his character alike as an affectionate brother and a religious man.

CHAPTER 47

Vss. 1-31. PRESENTATION AT COURT. **1. Joseph ...told Pharaoh, My father, and my brethren**—Joseph furnishes a beautiful example of a man who could bear equally well the extremes of prosperity and adversity. High as he was, he did not forget that he had a superior. Dearly as he loved his father and anxiously as he desired to provide for the whole family, he would not go into the arrangements he had planned for their stay in Goshen until he had obtained the sanction of his royal master. **2. he took some of his brethren**—probably the five eldest brothers: seniority being the least invidious principle of selection. **4. For to sojourn...are we come**—The royal conversation took the course which Joseph had anticipated (ch. 46:33), and they answered according to previous instructions—manifesting, however, in their determination to return to Canaan, a faith and piety which affords a hopeful symptom of their having become all, or most of them, religious men. **7. Joseph brought in Jacob his father**—There is a pathetic and most affecting interest attending this interview with royalty; and when, with all the simplicity and dignified solemnity of a man of God, Jacob signalized his entrance by imploring the divine blessing on the royal head,

it may easily be imagined what a striking impression the scene would produce (cf. Heb. 7:7). **8. Pharaoh said unto Jacob, How old art thou?**—The question was put from the deep and impressive interest which the appearance of the old patriarch had created in the minds of Pharaoh and his court. In the low-lying land of Egypt and from the artificial habits of its society, the age of man was far shorter among the inhabitants of that country than it had yet become in the pure bracing climate and among the simple mountaineers of Canaan. The Hebrews, at least, still attained a protracted longevity. **9. The days of the years of my pilgrimage**, etc.—Though 130 years, he reckons by days (cf. Ps. 90:12), which he calls *few*, as they appeared in retrospect, and *evil*, because his life had been one almost unbroken series of trouble. The answer is remarkable, considering the comparative darkness of the patriarchal age (cf. II Tim. 1:10). **11. Joseph placed his father and his brethren...in the best of the land**—best *pasture* land in lower Egypt. Goshen, "the land of verdure," lay along the Pelusiac or eastern branch of the Nile. It included a part of the district of Heliopolis, or "On," the capital, and on the east stretched out a considerable length into the desert. The ground included within these boundaries was a rich and fertile extent of natural meadow, and admirably adapted for the purposes of the Hebrew shepherds (cf. ch. 49:24; Ps. 34:10; 78:72). **13-15. there was no bread in all the land**—This probably refers to the second year of the famine (ch. 45:6) when any little stores of individuals or families were exhausted and when the people had become universally dependent on the government. At first they obtained supplies for payment. Before long money failed. **16. And Joseph said, Give your cattle**—"This was the wisest course that could be adopted for the preservation both of the people and the cattle, which, being bought by Joseph, was supported at the royal expense, and very likely returned to the people at the end of the famine, to enable them to resume their agricultural labors." **21. as for the people, he removed them to the cities**—obviously for the convenience of the country people, who were doing nothing, to the cities where the corn stores were situated. **22. Only the land of the priests, bought he not**—These lands were inalienable, being endowments by which the temples were supported. The priests for themselves received an annual allowance of provision from the state, and it would evidently have been the height of cruelty to withhold that allowance when their lands were incapable of being tilled. **23-28. Joseph said, Behold**, etc.—The lands being sold to the government (vss. 19, 20), seed would be distributed for the first crop after the famine; and the people would occupy them as tenants-at-will on the payment of a produce rent, almost the same rule as obtains in Egypt in the present day. **29-31. the time drew nigh that Israel must die**—One only of his dying arrangements is recorded; but that one reveals his whole character. It was the disposal of his remains, which were to be carried to Canaan, not from a mere romantic attachment to his native soil, nor, like his modern descendants, from a superstitious feeling for the soil of the Holy Land but from faith in the promises. His address to Joseph—"if I have found grace in thy sight," i.e., as the vizier of Egypt, his exacting a solemn oath that his wishes would be fulfilled and the peculiar form of that oath, all pointed significantly to the promise and showed the intensity of his desire to enjoy its blessings (cf. Num. 10:29). **Israel bowed himself upon the bed's head**—Oriental beds are mere mats, having no head, and the translation should be "the top of his staff," as the apostle renders it (Heb. 11:21).

CHAPTER 48

Vss. 1-22. Joseph's Visit to His Sick Father. **1. one told Joseph, Behold, thy father is sick**— Joseph was hastily sent for, and on this occasion he took with him his two sons. **2. Israel strengthened himself, and sat upon the bed**—In the chamber where a good man lies, edifying and spiritual discourse may be expected. **3, 4. God Almighty appeared unto me at Luz**—The object of Jacob, in thus reverting to the memorable vision at Bethel —one of the great landmarks in his history—was to point out the splendid promises in reserve for his posterity—to engage Joseph's interest and preserve his continued connection with the people of God, rather than with the Egyptians. **Behold, I will make thee fruitful**—This is a repetition of the covenant (ch. 28:13-15, 35:12). Whether these words are to be viewed in a limited sense, as pointing to the many centuries during which the Jews were occupiers of the Holy Land, or whether the words bear a wider meaning and intimate that the scattered tribes of Israel are to be reinstated in the land of promise, as their "everlasting possession," are points that have not yet been satisfactorily determined. **5. thy two sons, Ephraim and Manasseh**—It was the intention of the aged patriarch to adopt Joseph's sons as his own, thus giving him a double portion. The reasons for this procedure are stated (I Chron. 5:1, 2). **are mine** —Though their connections might have attached them to Egypt and opened to them brilliant prospects in the land of their nativity, they willingly accepted the adoption (Heb. 11:25). **9. Bring them, I pray thee, unto me, and I will bless them** —The apostle (Heb. 11:21) selected the blessing of Joseph's son as the chief, because the most comprehensive, instance of the patriarch's faith which his whole history furnishes. **13. Joseph took them both**—The very act of pronouncing the blessing was remarkable, showing that Jacob's bosom was animated by the spirit of prophecy. **21. Israel said unto Joseph, Behold, I die**—The patriarch could speak of death with composure, but he wished to prepare Joseph and the rest of the family for the shock. **but God shall be with you** —Jacob, in all probability, was not authorized to speak of their bondage—he dwelt only on the certainty of their restoration to Canaan. **22. moreover, I have given to thee one portion above thy brethren**—This was near Shechem (ch. 33:18; John 4:5; also Josh. 16:1; 20:7). And it is probable that the Amorites, having seized upon it during one of his frequent absences, the patriarch, with the united forces of his tribe, recovered it from them by his sword and his bow.

CHAPTER 49

Vss. 1-33. Patriarchal Blessing. **1. Jacob called unto his sons**—It is not to the sayings of the dying saint, so much as of the inspired prophet, that attention is called in this chapter. Under the immediate influence of the Holy Spirit he pronounced his prophetic benediction and described the condition of their respective descendants in the last days, or future times.

3-4. Reuben forfeited by his crime the rights and honors of primogeniture. His posterity never made any figure; no judge, prophet, nor ruler, sprang from this tribe.

5-7. Simeon and Levi were associate in wickedness, and the same prediction would be equally applicable to both their tribes. Levi had cities allotted to them (Josh. 21) in every tribe. On account of their zeal against idolatry, they were honorably "divided in Jacob"; whereas the tribe of Simeon, which was guilty of the grossest idolatry and the vices inseparable from it, were ignominiously "scattered."

8-12. Judah—A high pre-eminence is destined to this tribe (Num. 10:14; Judg. 1:2). Besides the honor of giving name to the Promised Land, David, and a greater than David—the Messiah— sprang from it. Chief among the tribes, "it grew up from a lion's whelp," i.e., a little power, till it became "an old lion"—i.e., calm and quiet, yet still formidable. **until Shiloh come**—Shiloh—this obscure word is variously interpreted to mean "the sent" (John 17:3), "the seed" (Isa. 11:1), the "peaceable or prosperous one" (Eph. 2:14)—i.e., the Messiah (Isa. 11:10; Rom. 15:12); and when He should come, "the tribe of Judah should no longer boast either an independent king or a judge of their own" [Calvin]. The Jews have been for eighteen centuries without a ruler and without a judge since Shiloh came, and "to Him the gathering of the people has been."

13. Zebulun was to have its lot on the seacoast, close to Zidon, and to engage, like that state, in maritime pursuits and commerce.

14-15. Issachar—a strong ass couching down between two burdens—i.e., it was to be active, patient, given to agricultural labors. It was established in lower Galilee— a "good land," settling down in the midst of the Canaanites, where, for the sake of quiet, they "bowed their shoulder to bear, and became a servant unto tribute."

16-18. Dan—though the son of a secondary wife, was to be "as one of the tribes of Israel." Dan— "a judge." **a serpent, . . . an adder**—A serpent, an adder, implies subtlety and stratagem; such was pre-eminently the character of Samson, the most illustrious of its judges.

19. Gad—This tribe should be often attacked and wasted by hostile powers on their borders (Judg. 10:8; Jer. 49:1). But they were generally victorious in the close of their wars.

20. Asher—"Blessed." Its allotment was the seacoast between Tyre and Carmel, a district fertile in the production of the finest corn and oil in all Palestine.

21. Naphtali—The best rendering we know is this, "Naphtali is a deer roaming at liberty; he shooteth forth goodly branches," or majestic antlers [Taylor's *Scripture Illustrations*], and the meaning of the prophecy seems to be that the tribe of Naphtali would be located in a territory so fertile and peaceable, that, feeding on the richest pasture, he would spread out, like a deer, branching antlers.

22-26. Joseph—**a fruitful bough**, etc.—denotes the extraordinary increase of that tribe (cf. Num. 1:33-35; Josh. 17:17; Deut. 33:17). The patriarch describes him as attacked by envy, revenge, temptation, ingratitude; yet still, by the grace of God, he triumphed over all opposition, so that he became the sustainer of Israel; and then he proceeds to shower blessings of every kind upon the head of this favorite son. The history of the tribes of Ephraim and Manasseh shows how fully these blessings were realized.

27-33. BENJAMIN shall ravin like a wolf.—This tribe in its early history spent its energies in petty or inglorious warfare and especially in the violent and unjust contest (Judg. 19, 20), in which it engaged with the other tribes, when, notwithstanding two victories, it was almost exterminated. **28. all these are the twelve tribes of Israel**—or ancestors. Jacob's prophetic words obviously refer not so much to the sons as to the tribes of Israel. **29. he charged them**—The charge had already been given and solemnly undertaken (ch. 47:31). But in mentioning his wishes now and rehearsing all the circumstances connected with the purchase of Machpelah, he wished to declare, with his latest breath, before all his family, that he died in the same faith as Abraham. **33. when Jacob had made an end of commanding his sons** —It is probable that he was supernaturally strengthened for this last momentous office of the patriarch, and that when the divine afflatus ceased, his exhausted powers giving way, he yielded up the ghost, and was gathered unto his people.

CHAPTER 50

Vss. 1-26. MOURNING FOR JACOB. **1. Joseph fell upon his father's face,** etc.—On him, as the principal member of the family, devolved the duty of closing the eyes of his venerable parent (cf. ch. 46:4) and imprinting the farewell kiss. **2. Joseph commanded his servants the physicians to embalm his father,** etc.—In ancient Egypt the embalmers were a class by themselves. The process of embalmment consisted in infusing a great quantity of resinous substances into the cavities of the body, after the intestines had been removed, and then a regulated degree of heat was applied to dry up the humors, as well as decompose the tarry materials which had been previously introduced. Thirty days were allotted for the completion of this process; forty more were spent in anointing it with spices; the body, tanned from this operation, being then washed, was wrapped in numerous folds of linen cloth—the joinings of which were fastened with gum, and then it was deposited in a wooden chest made in the form of a human figure. **3. the Egyptians mourned,** etc.—It was made a period of public mourning, as on the death of a royal personage. **4. Joseph spake unto the house of Pharaoh,** etc.—Care was taken to let it be known that the family sepulchre was provided before leaving Canaan and that an oath bound his family to convey the remains thither. Besides, Joseph deemed it right to apply for a special leave of absence; and being unfit, as a mourner, to appear in the royal presence, he made the request through the medium of others. **7-9. Joseph went up to bury his father**—a journey of 300 miles. The funeral cavalcade, composed of the nobility and military, with their equipages, would exhibit an imposing appearance. **10. they came to the threshing-floor of Atad,** etc.—"Atad" may be taken as a common noun, signifying "the plain of the thorn bushes." It was on the border between Egypt and Canaan; and as the last opportunity of indulging grief was always the most violent, the Egyptians made a prolonged halt at this spot, while the family of Jacob probably proceeded by themselves to the place of sepulture. **15-21. When Joseph's brethren saw that their father was dead, they said, Joseph will peradventure hate us,** etc.—Joseph was deeply affected by this communication. He gave them the strongest assurances of his forgiveness and thereby gave both a beautiful trait of his own pious character, as well as appeared an eminent type of the Saviour. **22, 23. Joseph dwelt in Egypt**—He lived eighty years after his elevation to the chief power witnessing a great increase in the prosperity of the kingdom, and also of his own family and kindred—the infant Church of God. **24. Joseph said unto his brethren, I die**—The national feelings of the Egyptians would have been opposed to his burial in Canaan; but he gave the strongest proof of the strength of his faith and full assurance of the promises, by "the commandment concerning his bones." **26. they embalmed him**—His funeral would be conducted in the highest style of Egyptian magnificence and his mummied corpse carefully preserved till the Exodus.

THE SECOND BOOK OF MOSES CALLED

EXODUS

CHAPTER 1

Vss. 1-22. INCREASE OF THE ISRAELITES. **1. Now these are the names**—(See on ch. 46:8-26). **7. children of Israel were fruitful**—They were living in a land where, according to the testimony of an ancient author, mothers produced three and four sometimes at a birth; and a modern writer declares "the females in Egypt, as well among the human race as among animals, surpass all others in fruitfulness." To this natural circumstance must be added the fulfilment of the promise made to Abraham. **8. Now there arose up a new king** —About sixty years after the death of Joseph a revolution took place—by which the old dynasty was overthrown, and upper and lower Egypt united into one kingdom. Assuming that the king formerly reigned in Thebes, it is probable that he would know nothing about the Hebrews; and that, as foreigners and shepherds, the new government would, from the first, regard them with dislike and scorn. **9. he said ... Behold, the ... children of Israel are more and mightier than we**—They had risen to great prosperity—as during the lifetime of Joseph and his royal patron, they had, probably, enjoyed a free grant of the land. Their increase and prosperity were viewed with jealousy by the new government; and as Goshen lay between Egypt and Canaan, on the border of which latter country were a number of warlike tribes, it was perfectly conformable to the suggestions of worldly policy that they should enslave and maltreat them, through apprehension of their joining in any invasion by those foreign rovers. The new king, who neither knew the name nor cared for the services of Joseph, was either *Amosis*, or one of his immediate successors [OSBURN]. **11. Therefore they did set over them taskmasters**—Having first obliged them, it is thought, to pay a ruinous rent and involved them in difficulties, that new government, in pursuance of its oppressive policy, degraded them to the condition of serfs—employing them exactly as the laboring people are in the present day (driven in companies or bands), in rearing the public works, with taskmasters, who anciently had sticks—now whips—to punish the indolent, or spur on the too languid. All public or royal buildings, in ancient Egypt, were built by captives; and on some of them was placed an inscription that no free citizen had been engaged in this servile employment. **they built for Pharaoh treasure cities**—These two store places were in the land of Goshen; and being situated near a border liable to invasion, they were fortified cities (cf. II Chron. 11-12). Pithom (*Greek, Patumos*), lay on the eastern Pelusiac branch of the Nile, about twelve Roman miles from Heliopolis; and Raamses, called by the LXX Heroöpolis, lay between the same branch of the Nile and the Bitter Lakes. These two fortified cities were situated, therefore, in the same valley; and the fortifications, which Pharaoh commanded to be built around both, had probably the same common object, of obstructing the entrance into Egypt, which this valley furnished the enemy from Asia [HENGSTENBERG]. **13, 14. The Egyptians . . .made their lives bitter with hard bondage, in mortar and in brick**—Ruins of great brick buildings are found in all parts of Egypt. The use of crude brick, baked in the sun, was universal in upper and lower Egypt, both for public and private buildings; *all* but the temples themselves were of crude brick. It is worthy of remark that more bricks bearing the name of Thothmes III, who is supposed to have been the king of Egypt at the time of the Exodus, have been discovered than of any other period [WILKINSON]. Parties of these brickmakers are seen depicted on the ancient monuments bearing "taskmasters," some standing, others in a sitting posture beside the laborers, with their uplifted sticks in their hands. **15. the king of Egypt spake to the Hebrew midwives**—Two only were spoken to—either they were the heads of a large corporation [LABORDE], or, by tampering with these two, the king designed to terrify the rest into secret compliance with his wishes [CALVIN]. **16. if it be a son, then ye shall kill him**—Opinions are divided, however, what was the method of destruction which the king did recommend. Some think that the "stools" were low seats on which these obstetric practitioners sat by the bedside of the Hebrew women; and that, as they might easily discover the sex, so, whenever a boy appeared, they were to strangle it, unknown to its parents; while others are of opinion that the "stools" were stone troughs, by the river side—into which, when the infants were washed, they were to be, as it were, accidentally dropped. **17. But the midwives feared God**—Their faith inspired them with

such courage as to risk their lives, by disobeying the mandate of a cruel tyrant; but it was blended with weakness, which made them shrink from speaking the truth, the whole truth, and nothing but the truth. **20. God dealt well with the midwives**—This represents God as rewarding them for telling a lie. This difficulty is wholly removed by a more correct translation. To make or build up a house in *Hebrew* idiom, means to have a numerous progeny. The passage then should be rendered thus: God protected the midwives, and the people waxed very mighty; and because the midwives feared, the Hebrews grew and prospered.

CHAPTER 2

Vss. 1-10. BIRTH AND PRESERVATION OF MOSES. **1. there went a man of the house of Levi,** etc.— Amram was the husband and Jochebed the wife (cf. ch. 6:2); Num. 26:59). The marriage took place, and two children, Miriam and Aaron, were born some years before the infanticidal edict. **2. the woman . . . bare a son,** etc. Some extraordinary appearance of remarkable comeliness led his parents to augur his future greatness. Beauty was regarded by the ancients as a mark of the divine favor. **hid him three months**—The parents were a pious couple, and the measures they took were prompted not only by parental attachment, but by a strong faith in the blessing of God prospering their endeavors to save the infant. **3. she took for him an ark of bulrushes**—papyrus, a thick, strong, and tough reed. **slime**—the mud of the Nile, which, when hardened, is very tenacious. **pitch**—mineral tar. Boats of this description are seen daily floating on the surface of the river, with no other caulking than Nile mud (cf. Isa. 18:2), and they are perfectly watertight, unless the coating is forced off by stormy weather. **flags**—a general term for sea- or river-weed. The chest was not, as is often represented, committed to the bosom of the water but laid on the bank, where it would naturally appear to have been drifted by the current and arrested by the reedy thicket. The spot is traditionally said to be the Isle of Rodah, near Old Cairo. **4. his sister**—Miriam would probably be a girl of ten or twelve years of age at the time. **5. the daughter of Pharaoh came down to wash herself at the river**—The occasion is thought to have been a religious solemnity which the royal family opened by bathing in the sacred stream. Peculiar sacredness was attached to those portions of the Nile which flowed near the temples. The water was there fenced off as a protection from the crocodiles; and doubtless the princess had an enclosure reserved for her own use, the road to which seems to have been well known to Jochebed. **walked along**—in procession or in file. **she sent her maid**—her immediate attendant. The term is different from that rendered "maidens." **6-9. when she had opened it, she saw the child**—The narrative is picturesque. No tale of romance ever described a plot more skilfully laid or more full of interest in the development. The expedient of the ark—the slime and pitch—the choice of the time and place—the appeal to the sensibilities of the female breast—the stationing of the sister as a watch of the proceedings—her timely suggestion of a nurse—and the engagement of the mother herself—all bespeak a more than ordinary measure of ingenuity as well as intense solicitude on the part of the parents. But the origin of the scheme was most probably owing to a divine suggestion, as its success was due to an overruling Providence, who not only preserved the child's life, but provided for his being trained in the nurture and admonition of the Lord. Hence it is said to have been done by faith (Heb. 11:23), either in the general promise of deliverance, or some special revelation made to Amram and Jochebed—and in this view, the pious couple gave a beautiful example of a firm reliance on the word of God, united with an active use of the most suitable means. **10. she brought him unto Pharaoh's daughter**—Though it must have been nearly as severe a trial for Jochebed to part with him the second time as the first, she was doubtless reconciled to it by her belief in his high destination as the future deliverer of Israel. His age when removed to the palace is not stated; but he was old enough to be well instructed in the principles of the true religion; and those early impressions, deepened by the power of divine grace, were never forgotten or effaced. **he became her son**—by adoption, and his high rank afforded him advantages in education, which in the Providence of God were made subservient to far different purposes from what his royal patroness intended. **she called his name Moses**—His parents might, as usual, at the time of his circumcision, have given him a name, which is traditionally said to have been Joachim. But the name chosen by the princess, whether of Egyptian or Hebrew origin, is the only one by which he has ever been known to the church; and it is a permanent memorial of the painful incidents of his birth and infancy.

11-25. HIS SYMPATHY WITH THE HEBREWS. **11. in those days, when Moses was grown**—not in age and stature only, but in power as well as in renown for accomplishments and military prowess (Acts 7:22). There is a gap here in the sacred history which, however, is supplied by the inspired commentary of Paul, who has fully detailed the reasons as well as extent of the change that took place in his worldly condition; and whether, as some say, his royal mother had proposed to make him co-regent and successor to the crown, or some other circumstances, led to a declaration of his mind, he determined to renounce the palace and identify himself with the suffering people of God (Heb. 11:24-29). The descent of some great sovereigns, like Diocletian and Charles V, from a throne into private life, is nothing to the sacrifice which Moses made through the power of faith. **he went out unto his brethren**—to make a full and systematic inspection of their condition in the various parts of the country where they were dispersed (Acts 7:23), and he adopted this proceeding in pursuance of the patriotic purpose that the faith, which is of the operation of God, was even then forming in his heart. **he spied an Egyptian smiting an Hebrew**—one of the taskmasters scourging a Hebrew slave without any just cause (Acts 7:24), and in so cruel a manner, that he seems to have died under the barbarous treatment —for the conditions of the sacred story imply such a fatal issue. The sight was new and strange to him, and though pre-eminent for meekness (Num. 12:3), he was fired with indignation. **12. he slew the Egyptian, and hid him in the sand**—This act of Moses may seem and indeed by some has been condemned as rash and unjustifiable—in plain terms, a deed ·of assassination. But we must not judge of his action in such a country and age by

the standard of law and the notions of right which prevail in our Christian land; and, besides, not only is it not spoken of as a crime in Scripture or as distressing the perpetrator with remorse, but according to existing customs among nomadic tribes, he was bound to avenge the blood of a brother. The person he slew, however, being a government officer, he had rendered himself amenable to the laws of Egypt, and therefore he endeavored to screen himself from the consequences by concealment of the corpse. **13, 14. two men of the Hebrews strove together**—His benevolent mediation in this strife, though made in the kindest and mildest manner, was resented, and the taunt of the aggressor showing that Moses' conduct on the preceding day had become generally known, he determined to consult his safety by immediate flight (Heb. 11:27). These two incidents prove that neither were the Israelites yet ready to go out of Egypt, nor Moses prepared to be their leader (Jas. 1:20). It was by the staff and not the sword—by the meekness, and not the wrath of Moses that God was to accomplish that great work of deliverance. Both he and the people of Israel were for forty years more to be cast into the furnace of affliction, yet it was therein that He had chosen them (Isa. 48:10). **15. Moses fled from the face of Pharaoh**—His flight took place in the second year of Thothmes I. **dwelt in the land of Midian**—situated on the eastern shore of the gulf of the Red Sea and occupied by the posterity of Midian the son of Cush. The territory extended northward to the top of the gulf and westward far across the desert of Sinai. And from their position near the sea, they early combined trading with pastoral pursuits (Gen. 37:28). The headquarters of Jethro are supposed to have been where Dahab-Madian now stands; and from Moses coming direct to that place, he may have travelled with a caravan of merchants. But another place is fixed by tradition in Wady Shuweib, or Jethro's valley, on the east of the mountain of Moses. **sat down by a well**—See on Genesis 29:3. **16-22. the priest of Midian**—As the officers were usually conjoined, he was the ruler also of the people called Cushites or Ethiopians, and like many other chiefs of pastoral people in that early age, he still retained the faith and worship of the true God. **seven daughters**—were shepherdesses to whom Moses was favorably introduced by an act of courtesy and courage in protecting them from the rude shepherds of some neighboring tribe at a well. He afterwards formed a close and permanent alliance with this family by marrying one of the daughters, Zipporah, "a little bird," called a Cushite or Ethiopian (Num. 12:1), and whom he doubtless obtained in the manner of Jacob by service. He had by her two sons, whose names were, according to common practice, commemorative of incidents in the family history. **23. the king of Egypt died: and the children of Israel sighed by reason of the bondage**—The language seems to imply that the Israelites had experienced a partial relaxation, probably through the influence of Moses' royal patroness; but in the reign of her father's successor the persecution was renewed with increased severity.

CHAPTER 3

Vss. 1-22. DIVINE APPEARANCE AND COMMISSION TO MOSES. **1. Now Moses kept the flock**—This employment he had entered on in furtherance of his matrimonial views (see on ch. 2:21), but it is probable he was continuing his service now on other terms like Jacob during the latter years of his stay with Laban (Gen. 30:28). **he led the flock to the back side of the desert**—i.e., on the west of the desert [Genesius], assuming Jethro's headquarters to have been at Dahab. The route by which Moses led his flock must have been west through the wide valley called by the Arabs, Wady-es-Zugherah [Robinson], which led into the interior of the wilderness. **Mountain of God**—so named either according to *Hebrew* idiom from its great height, as "great mountains," *Hebrew,* "mountains of God" (Ps. 36:6); "goodly cedars," *Hebrew,* "cedars of God" (Ps. 80:10); or some think from its being the old abode of "the glory"; or finally from its being the theater of transactions most memorable in the history of the true religion to Horeb—rather, Horeb-ward. Horeb, i.e., dry, desert, was the general name for the mountainous district in which Sinai is situated, and of which it is a part. (See on ch. 19). It was used to designate the region comprehending that immense range of lofty, desolate, and barren hills, at the base of which, however, there are not only many patches of verdure to be seen, but almost all the valleys, or *wadys*, as they are called, show a thin coating of vegetation, which, towards the south, becomes more luxuriant. The Arab shepherds seldom take their flocks to a greater distance than one day's journey from their camp. Moses must have gone at least two days' journey, and although he seems to have been only following his pastoral course, that region, from its numerous springs in the clefts of the rocks being the chief resort of the tribes during the summer heats, the Providence of God led him thither for an important purpose. **2, 3. the angel of the Lord appeared unto him in a flame of fire**—It is common in Scripture to represent the elements and operations of nature, as winds, fires, earthquakes, pestilence, everything enlisted in executing the divine will, as the "angels" or messengers of God. But in such cases God Himself is considered as really, though invisibly, present. Here the preternatural fire may be primarily meant by the expression "angel of the Lord"; but it is clear that under this symbol, the Divine Being was present, whose name is given (vss. 4, 6), and elsewhere called the angel of the covenant, Jehovah-Jesus. **out of the midst of a bush**—the wild acacia or thorn, with which that desert abounds, and which is generally dry and brittle, so much so, that at certain seasons, a spark might kindle a district far and wide into a blaze. A fire, therefore, being in the midst of such a desert bush was a "great sight." It is generally supposed to have been emblematic of the Israelites' condition in Egypt—oppressed by a grinding servitude and a bloody persecution, and yet, in spite of the cruel policy that was bent on annihilating them, they continued as numerous and thriving as ever. The reason was "God was in the midst of them." The symbol may also represent the present state of the Jews, as well as of the Church generally in the world. **4. when the Lord saw that he turned aside to see**—The manifestations which God anciently made of Himself were always accompanied by clear, unmistakable signs that the communications were really from heaven. This certain evidence was given to Moses. He saw a fire, but no human agent to kindle it; he heard a voice, but no human lips from

which it came; he saw no living Being, but One was in the bush, in the heat of the flames, who knew him and addressed him by name. Who could this be but the Divine Being? **5. put off thy shoes**—The direction was in conformity with a usage which was well known to Moses, for the Egyptian priests observed it in their temples, and it is observed in all Eastern countries where the people take off their shoes or sandals, as we do our hats. But the Eastern idea is not precisely the same as the Western. With us, the removal of the hat is an expression of reverence for the place we enter, or rather of Him who is worshiped there. With them the removal of the shoes is a confession of personal defilement and conscious unworthiness to stand in the presence of unspotted holiness. **6-8. I am the God ... come down to deliver**—The reverential awe of Moses must have been relieved by the divine Speaker (see on Matt. 22:32), announcing Himself in His covenant character, and by the welcome intelligence communicated. Moreover, the time, as well as all the circumstances of this miraculous appearance, were such as to give him an illustrious display of God's faithfulness to His promises. The period of Israel's journey and affliction in Egypt had been predicted (Gen. 15:13), and it was during the last year of the term which had still to run that the Lord appeared in the burning bush. **10-22. Come now therefore, and I will send thee**—Considering the patriotic views that had formerly animated the breast of Moses, we might have anticipated that no mission could have been more welcome to his heart than to be employed in the national emancipation of Israel. But he evinced great reluctance to it and stated a variety of objections, all of which were successfully met and removed—and the happy issue of his labors was minutely described.

CHAPTER 4

Vss. 1-31. Miraculous Change of the Rod, etc. **1. But behold**—*Hebrew,* "If," "perhaps," "they will not believe me."—What evidence can I produce of my divine mission? There was still a want of full confidence, not in the character and divine power of his employer, but in His presence and power always accompanying him. He insinuated that his communication might be rejected and he himself treated as an impostor. **2. the Lord said, ... What is that in thine hand?**—The question was put not to elicit information which God required, but to draw the particular attention of Moses. **A rod**—probably the shepherd's crook—among the Arabs, a long staff, with a curved head, varying from three to six feet in length. **6. Put now thine hand into thy bosom**—the open part of his outer robe, worn about the girdle. **9. take of the water of the river**—Nile. Those miracles, two of which were wrought then, and the third to be performed on his arrival in Goshen, were at first designed to encourage him as satisfactory proofs of his divine mission, and to be repeated for the special confirmation of his embassy before the Israelites. **10-13. I am not eloquent**—It is supposed that Moses labored under a natural defect of utterance or had a difficulty in the free and fluent expression of his ideas in the Egyptian language, which he had long disused. This new objection was also overruled, but still Moses, who foresaw the manifold difficulties of the undertaking, was anxious to be freed from the responsibility. **14. the anger of the Lord was kindled against Moses**—The Divine Being is not subject to ebullitions of passion; but His displeasure was manifested by transferring the honor of the priesthood, which would otherwise have been bestowed on Moses, to Aaron, who was from this time destined to be the head of the house of Levi (I Chron. 23:13). Marvellous had been His condescension and patience in dealing with Moses; and now every remaining scruple was removed by the unexpected and welcome intelligence that his brother Aaron was to be his colleague. God knew from the beginning what Moses would do, but He reserves this motive to the last as the strongest to rouse his languid heart, and Moses now fully and cordially complied with the call. If we are surprised at his backwardness amidst all the signs and promises that were given him, we must admire his candor and honesty in recording it. **18. Moses ... returned to Jethro**—Being in his service, it was right to obtain his consent, but Moses evinced piety, humility, and prudence, in not divulging the special object of his journey. **19. all the men are dead which sought thy life**—The death of the Egyptian monarch took place in the four hundred and twenty-ninth year of the Hebrew sojourn in that land, and that event, according to the law of Egypt, took off his proscription of Moses, if it had been publicly issued. **20. Moses took his wife and sons, and set them upon an ass**—*Septuagint*, "asses." Those animals are not now used in the desert of Sinai except by the Arabs for short distances. **returned**—entered on his journey towards Egypt. **he took the rod of God**—so called from its being appropriated to His service, and because whatever miracles it might be employed in performing would be wrought not by its inherent properties, but by a divine power following on its use. (Cf. Acts 3:12). **24. inn**—*Hebrew*, a halting-place for the night. **the Lord met him, and sought to kill him**—i.e., he was either overwhelmed with mental distress or overtaken by a sudden and dangerous malady. The narrative is obscure, but the meaning seems to be, that, led during his illness to a strict self-examination, he was deeply pained and grieved at the thought of having, to please his wife, postponed or neglected the circumcision of one of his sons, probably the younger. To dishonor that sign and seal of the covenant was criminal in any Hebrew, peculiarly so in one destined to be the leader and deliverer of the Hebrews; and he seems to have felt his sickness as a merited chastisement for his sinful omission. Concerned for her husband's safety, Zipporah overcomes her maternal feelings of aversion to the painful rite, performs herself, by means of one of the sharp flints with which that part of the desert abounds, an operation which her husband, on whom the duty devolved, was unable to do, and having brought the bloody evidence, exclaimed in the painful excitement of her feelings that from love to him she had risked the life of her child [CALVIN, BULLINGER, ROSENMULLER]. **26. So he let him go**—Moses recovered; but the remembrance of this critical period in his life would stimulate the Hebrew legislator to enforce a faithful attention to the rite of circumcision when it was established as a divine ordinance in Israel, and made their peculiar distinction as a people. **27. Aaron met him in the mount of God, and kissed him**—After a separation of forty years, their meeting would be mutually happy. Similar are the salu-

tations of Arab friends when they meet in the desert still; conspicuous is the kiss on each side of the head. **29. Moses and Aaron went**—towards Egypt, Zipporah and her sons having been sent back. (Cf. ch. 18:2). **gathered ... all the elders**—Aaron was spokesman, and Moses performed the appointed miracles—through which "the people," i.e., the elders, believed (I Kings 17:24; Josh. 3:2) and received the joyful tidings of the errand on which Moses had come with devout thanksgiving. Formerly they had slighted the message and rejected the messenger. Formerly Moses had gone in his own strength; now he goes leaning on God, and strong only through faith in Him who had sent him. Israel also had been taught a useful lesson, and it was good for both that they had been afflicted.

CHAPTER 5

Vss. 1-23. FIRST INTERVIEW WITH PHARAOH. **1. Moses and Aaron went in**—As representatives of the Hebrews, they were entitled to ask an audience of the king, and their thorough Egyptian training taught them how and when to seek it. **and told Pharaoh**—When introduced, they delivered a message in the name of the God of Israel. This is the first time He is mentioned by that national appellation in Scripture. It seems to have been used by divine direction (ch. 4:2) and designed to put honor on the Hebrews in their depressed condition (Heb. 11:16). **2. Pharaoh said, Who is the Lord**—rather "Jehovah." Lord was a common name applied to objects of worship; but Jehovah was a name he had never heard of; he estimated the character and power of this God by the abject and miserable condition of the worshippers and concluded that He held as low a rank among the gods as His people did in the nation. To demonstrate the supremacy of the true God over all the gods of Egypt, was the design of the plagues. **I know not the Lord, neither will I let Israel go**—As his honor and interest were both involved he determined to crush this attempt, and in a tone of insolence, or perhaps profanity, rejected the request for the release of the Hebrew slaves. **3. The God of the Hebrews hath met with us**—Instead of being provoked into reproaches or threats, they mildly assured him that it was not a proposal originating among themselves, but a duty enjoined on them by their God. They had for a long series of years been debarred from the privilege of religious worship, and as there was reason to fear that a continued neglect of divine ordinances would draw down upon them the judgments of offended heaven, they begged permission to go three days' journey into the desert—a place of seclusion—where their sacrificial observances would neither suffer interruption nor give umbrage to the Egyptians. In saying this, they concealed their ultimate design of abandoning the kingdom, and by making this partial request at first, they probably wished to try the king's temper before they disclosed their intentions any farther. But they said only what God had put in their mouths (ch. 3:12, 18), and this "legalizes the specific act, while it gives no sanction to the general habit of dissimulation" [CHALMERS]. **4. Wherefore do ye, Moses and Aaron, let the people from their works?** etc.— Without taking any notice of what they had said, he treated them as ambitious demagogues, who were appealing to the superstitious feelings of the people, to stir up sedition and diffuse a spirit of discontent, which spreading through so vast a body of slaves, might endanger the peace of the country. **6. Pharaoh commanded**—It was a natural consequence of the high displeasure created by this interview that he should put additional burdens on the oppressed Israelites. **taskmasters** —Egyptian overseers, appointed to exact labor of the Israelites. **officers**—Hebrews placed over their brethren, under the taskmasters, precisely analogous to the Arab officers set over the Arab Fellahs, the poor laborers in modern Egypt. **7. Ye shall no more give the people straw to make brick**—The making of bricks appears to have been a government monopoly as the ancient bricks are nearly all stamped with the name of a king, and they were formed, as they are still in Lower Egypt, of clay mixed with chopped straw and dried or hardened in the sun. The Israelites were employed in this drudgery; and though they still dwelt in Goshen and held property in flocks and herds, they were compelled in rotation to serve in the brick-quarries, pressed in alternating groups, just as the *fellaheen*, or peasants, are marched by press-gangs in the same country still. **let them go and gather straw for themselves**—The enraged despot did not issue orders to do an impracticable thing. The Egyptian reapers in the corn harvest were accustomed merely to cut off the ears and leave the stalk standing. **8. tale**—an appointed number of bricks. The materials of their labor were to be no longer supplied, and yet, as the same amount of produce was exacted daily, it is impossible to imagine more aggravated cruelty—a perfect specimen of Oriental despotism. **12. So the people were scattered**—It was an immense grievance to the laborers individually, but there would be no hindrance from the husbandmen whose fields they entered, as almost all the lands of Egypt were in the possession of the crown (Gen. 47:20). **13-19. taskmasters hasted them ... officers ... beaten**—As the nearest fields were bared and the people had to go farther for stubble, it was impossible for them to meet the demand by the usual tale of bricks. "The beating of the officers is just what might have been expected from an Eastern tyrant, especially in the valley of the Nile, as it appears from the monuments, that ancient Egypt, like modern China, was principally governed by the stick" [TAYLOR]. "The mode of beating was by the offender being laid flat on the ground and generally held by the hands and feet while the chastisement was administered" [WILKINSON]. (Deut. 25:2). A picture representing the Hebrews on a brick-field, exactly as described in this chapter, was found in an Egyptian tomb at Thebes. **20, 21. they met Moses. ... The Lord look upon you, and judge**—Thus the deliverer of Israel found that this patriotic interference did, in the first instance, only aggravate the evil he wished to remove, and that instead of receiving the gratitude, he was loaded with the reproaches of his countrymen. But as the greatest darkness is immediately before the dawn, so the people of God are often plunged into the deepest affliction when on the eve of their deliverance; and so it was in this case.

CHAPTER 6

Vss. 1-13. RENEWAL OF THE PROMISE. **1. Lord said unto Moses**—The Lord, who is long-suffering and indulgent to the errors and infirmities of His people, made allowance for the mortification of Moses as the result of this first interview and cheered him with the assurance of a speedy and successful termination to his embassy. **2. And God spake unto Moses**—For his further encouragement, there was made to him an emphatic repetition of the promise (ch. 3:20). **3. I ... God Almighty**—All enemies must fall, all difficulties must vanish before My omnipotent power, and the patriarchs had abundant proofs of this. **but by my name**, etc.—rather, interrogatively, by My name Jehovah was I not known to them? Am not I, the Almighty God, who pledged My honor for the fulfilment of the covenant, also the self-existent God who lives to accomplish it? Rest assured, therefore, that I shall bring it to pass. This passage has occasioned much discussion; and it has been thought by many to intimate that as the name Jehovah was not known to the patriarchs, at least in the full bearing or practical experience of it, the honor of the disclosure was reserved for Moses, who was the first sent with a message in the name of Jehovah, and enabled to attest it by a series of public miracles. **9-11. Moses spake so unto the children of Israel**—The increased severities inflicted on the Israelites seem to have so entirely crushed their spirits, as well as irritated them, that they refused to listen to any more communications (ch. 14:12). Even the faith of Moses himself was faltering; and he would have abandoned the enterprise in despair had he not received a positive command from God to revisit the people without delay, and at the same time renew their demand on the king in a more decisive and peremptory tone. **12. how then shall ... who am of uncircumcised lips?**—A metaphorical expression among the Hebrews, who, taught to look on the circumcision of any part as denoting perfection, signified its deficiency or unsuitableness by uncircumcision. The words here express how painfully Moses felt his want of utterance or persuasive oratory. He seems to have fallen into the same deep despondency as his brethren, and to be shrinking with nervous timidity from a difficult, if not desperate, cause. If he had succeeded so ill with the people, whose dearest interests were all involved, what better hope could he entertain of his making more impression on the heart of a king elated with pride and strong in the possession of absolute power? How strikingly was the indulgent forbearance of God displayed towards His people amid all their backwardness to hail His announcement of approaching deliverance! No perverse complaints or careless indifference on their part retarded the development of His gracious purposes. On the contrary, here, as generally, the course of His providence is slow in the infliction of judgments, while it moves more quickly, as it were, when misery is to be relieved or benefits conferred.

14-30. THE GENEALOGY OF MOSES. **14. These be the heads of their fathers' houses**—chiefs or governors of their houses. The insertion of this genealogical table in this part of the narrative was intended to authenticate the descent of Moses and Aaron. Both of them were commissioned to act so important a part in the events transacted in the court of Egypt and afterwards elevated to so high offices in the government and Church of God, that it was of the utmost importance that their lineage should be accurately traced. Reuben and Simeon being the oldest of Jacob's sons, a passing notice is taken of them, and then the historian advances to the enumeration of the principal persons in the house of Levi. **20. Amram took him Jochebed his father's sister to wife**—The *Septuagint* and *Syriac* versions render it his cousin. **23. Elisheba** —i.e., Elizabethan. These minute particulars recorded of the family of Aaron, while he has passed over his own, indicate the real modesty of Moses. An ambitious man or an impostor would have acted in a different manner.

CHAPTER 7

Vss. 1-25. Second Interview with Pharaoh. **1. the Lord said unto Moses**—He is here encouraged to wait again on the king—not, however, as formerly, in the attitude of a humble suppliant, but now armed with credentials as God's ambassador, and to make his demand in a tone and manner which no earthly monarch or court ever witnessed. **I have made thee a god**—made, i.e., set, appointed; "a god," i.e., he was to act in this business as God's representative, to act and speak in His name and to perform things beyond the ordinary course of nature. The Orientals familiarly say of a man who is eminently great or wise, "he is a god" among men. **Aaron thy brother shall be thy prophet**—i.e., interpreter or spokesman. The one was to be the vicegerent of God, and the other must be considered the speaker throughout all the ensuing scenes, even though his name is not expressly mentioned. **3. I will harden Pharaoh's heart**—This would be the *result*. But the divine message would be the *occasion*, not the *cause* of the king's impenitent obduracy. **4, 5. I may lay mine hand upon Egypt,** etc.—The succession of terrible judgments with which the country was about to be scourged would fully demonstrate the supremacy of Israel's God. **7. Moses was fourscore years**—This advanced age was a pledge that they had not been readily betrayed into a rash or hazardous enterprise, and that under its attendant infirmities they could not have carried through the work on which they were entering had they not been supported by a divine hand. **9. When Pharaoh shall speak unto you,** etc.—The king would naturally demand some evidence of their having been sent from God; and as he would expect the ministers of his own gods to do the same works, the contest, in the nature of the case, would be one of miracles. Notice has already been taken of the rod of Moses (ch. 4:2), but rods were carried also by all nobles and official persons in the court of Pharaoh. It was an Egyptian custom, and the rods were symbols of authority or rank. Hence God commanded His servants to use a rod. **10. Aaron cast down his rod before Pharaoh,** etc.—It is to be presumed that Pharaoh had demanded a proof of their divine mission. **11. Then Pharaoh also called the wise men and the sorcerers,** etc.—His object in calling them was to ascertain whether this doing of Aaron's was really a work of divine power or merely a feat of magical art. The magicians of Egypt in modern times have been long celebrated adepts in charming serpents, and particularly by pressing the nape of the neck, they throw them into a kind of catalepsy, which renders them stiff and immovable—thus seeming to change them into a rod. They conceal the serpent about their persons, and by acts of legerdemain produce it from their dress, stiff and straight as a rod. Just the same trick was played off by their ancient predecessors, the most renowned of whom, Jannes

and Jambres (II Tim. 3:8), were called in on this occasion. They had time after the summons to make suitable preparations—and so it appears they succeeded by their "enchantments" in practising an illusion on the senses. **12. but Aaron's rod swallowed up their rods.** This was what they could not be prepared for, and the discomfiture appeared in the loss of their rods, which were probably real serpents. **14. Pharaoh's heart is hardened**—Whatever might have been his first impressions, they were soon dispelled; and when he found his magicians making similar attempts, he concluded that Aaron's affair was a magical deception, the secret of which was not known to his wise men. **15. Get thee unto Pharaoh**—Now began those appalling miracles of judgment by which the God of Israel, through His ambassadors, proved His sole and unchallengeable supremacy over all the gods of Egypt, and which were the natural phenomena of Egypt, at an unusual season, and in a miraculous degree of intensity. The court of Egypt, whether held at Rameses, or Memphis, or Tanis in the field of Zoan (Ps. 78:12), was the scene of those extraordinary transactions, and Moses must have resided during that terrible period in the immediate neighborhood. **in the morning; lo, he goeth out unto the water,** etc.—for the purpose of ablutions or devotions perhaps; for the Nile was an object of superstitious reverence, the patron deity of the country. It might be that Moses had been denied admission into the palace; but be that as it may, the river was to be the subject of the first plague, and therefore he was ordered to repair to its banks with the miracle-working rod, now to be raised, not in demonstration, but in judgment, if the refractory spirit of the king should still refuse consent to Israel's departure for their sacred rites. **17-21. Aaron lifted up the rod and smote the waters,** etc.— Whether the water was changed into real blood, or only the appearance of it (and Omnipotence could effect the one as easily as the other), this was a severe calamity. How great must have been the disappointment and disgust throughout the land when the river became of a blood-red color, of which they had a national abhorrence; their favorite beverage became a nauseous draught, and the fish, which formed so large an article of food, were destroyed. The immense scale on which the plague was inflicted is seen by its extending to "the streams," or branches of the Nile —to the "rivers," the canals, the "ponds" and "pools," that which is left after an overflow, the reservoirs, and the many domestic vessels in which the Nile water was kept to filter. And accordingly the sufferings of the people from thirst must have been severe. Nothing could more humble the pride of Egypt than this dishonor brought on their national god. **22. The magicians ... did so with their enchantments,** etc.—Little or no pure water could be procured, and therefore their imitation must have been on a small scale—the only drinkable water available being dug among the sands. It must have been on a sample or specimen of water dyed red with some coloring matter. But it was sufficient to serve as a pretext or command for the king to turn unmoved and go to his house.

CHAPTER 8

Vss. 1-15. Plague of Frogs. **1. the Lord spake unto Moses, Go unto Pharaoh**—The duration of the first plague for a whole week must have satisfied all that it was produced not by any accidental causes, but by the agency of omnipotent power. As a judgment of God, however, it produced no good effect, and Moses was commanded to wait on the king and threaten him, in the event of his continued obstinacy, with the infliction of a new and different plague. As Pharaoh's answer is not given, it may be inferred to have been unfavorable, for the rod was again raised. **2. I will smite all thy borders with frogs**—Those animals, though the natural spawn of the river, and therefore objects familiar to the people, were on this occasion miraculously multiplied to an amazing extent, and it is probable that the ova of the frogs, which had been previously deposited in the mire and marshes, were miraculously brought to perfection at once. **3. bedchamber ... bed**—mats strewed on the floor as well as more sumptuous divans of the rich. **ovens**—holes made in the ground and the sides of which are plastered with mortar. **kneading-troughs** —Those used in Egypt were bowls of wicker or rush work. What must have been the state of the people when they could find no means of escape from the cold, damp touch and unsightly presence of the frogs, as they alighted on every article and vessel of food! **5, 6. Stretch forth thine hand with thy rod over the streams**, etc.— The miracle consisted in the reptiles leaving their marshes at the very time he commanded them. **7. the magicians did so with their enchantments**— required no great art to make the offensive reptiles appear on any small spot of ground. What they undertook to do already existed in abundance all around. They would better have shown their power by removing the frogs. **8. Pharaoh called, ... Intreat the Lord, that he may take away the frogs from me**—The frog, which was now used as an instrument of affliction, whether from reverence or abhorrence, was an object of national superstition with the Egyptians, the god Ptha being represented with a frog's head. But the vast numbers, together with their stench, made them an intolerable nuisance so that the king was so far humbled as to promise that, if Moses would intercede for their removal, he would consent to the departure of Israel, and in compliance with this appeal, they were withdrawn at the very hour named by the monarch himself. But many, while suffering the consequences of their sins, make promises of amendment and obedience which they afterwards forget; and so Pharaoh, when he saw there was a respite, was again hardened.

16-19. PLAGUE OF LICE. **16. smite the dust of the land**, etc.—Aaron's rod, by the direction of Moses, who was commanded by God, was again raised, and the land was filled with gnats, mosquitoes—that is the proper meaning of the original term. In ordinary circumstances they embitter life in Eastern countries, and therefore the *terrible* nature of this infliction on Egypt may be imagined when no precautions could preserve from their painful sting. The very smallness and insignificance of these fierce insects made them a dreadful scourge. The magicians never attempted any imitation, and what neither the blood of the river nor the nuisance of the frogs had done, the visitation of this tiny enemy constrained them to acknowledge "this is the finger of God," properly "gods," for they spoke as heathens.

20-32. PLAGUE OF FLIES. **20. Rise up early ... Pharaoh; lo, he cometh forth to the water**, etc.— Pharaoh still appearing obdurate, Moses was or-

dered to meet him while walking on the banks of the Nile and repeat his request for the liberation of Israel, threatening in case of continued refusal to cover every house from the palace to the cottage with swarms of flies—while, as a proof of the power that accomplished this judgment, the land of Goshen should be exempted from the calamity. The appeal was equally vain as before, and the predicted evil overtook the country in the form of what was not "flies," such as we are accustomed to, but divers sorts of flies (Ps. 78:45), the gad-fly, the cockroach, the Egyptian beetle, for all these are mentioned by different writers. They are very destructive, some of them inflicting severe bites on animals, others destroying clothes, books, plants, every thing. The worship of flies, particularly of the beetle, was a prominent part of the religion of the ancient Egyptians. The employment of these winged deities to chastise them must have been painful and humiliating to the Egyptians while it must at the same time have strengthened the faith of the Israelites in the God of their fathers as the only object of worship. **25-32. Pharaoh called for Moses, ... and said, Go ye, sacrifice to your God in the land**, etc.—Between impatient anxiety to be freed from this scourge and a reluctance on the part of the Hebrew bondsmen, the king followed the course of expediency; he proposed to let them free to engage in their religious rites within any part of the kingdom. But true to his instructions, Moses would accede to no such arrangement; he stated a most valid reason to show the danger of it; and the king having yielded so far as to allow them a brief holiday *across the border,* annexed to this concession a request that Moses would entreat with Jehovah for the removal of the plague. He promised to do so, and it was removed the following day. But no sooner was the pressure over than the spirit of Pharaoh, like a bent bow, sprang back to its wonted obduracy, and, regardless of his promise, he refused to let the people depart.

CHAPTER 9

Vss. 1-7. MURRAIN OF BEASTS. **3. Behold, the hand of the Lord is upon thy cattle**—A fifth application was made to Pharaoh in behalf of the Israelites by Moses, who was instructed to tell him that, if he persisted in opposing their departure, a pestilence would be sent among all the flocks and herds of the Egyptians, while those of the Israelites would be spared. As he showed no intention of keeping his promise, he was still a mark for the arrows of the Almighty's quiver, and the threatened plague of which he was forewarned was executed. But it is observable that in this instance it was not inflicted through the instrumentality or waving of Aaron's rod, but directly by the hand of the Lord, and the fixing of the precise time tended still further to determine the true character of the calamity (Jer. 12:4). **6. all the cattle of Egypt died**—not absolutely every beast, for we find (vss. 19, 21) that there were still some left; but a great many died of each herd—the mortality was frequent and widespread. The adaptation of this judgment consisted in the Egyptians venerating the more useful animals, such as the ox, the cow, and the ram; in all parts of the country temples were reared and divine honors paid to these domesticated beasts, and thus while the pestilence caused a great loss in money, it also struck a heavy blow at their superstition. **7. Pharaoh sent ... there was not one of the cattle of the Israelites dead**—The despatch of confidential messengers indicates that he would not give credit to vague reports, and we may conclude that some impression had been made on his mind by that extraordinary exemption, but it was neither a good nor a permanent impression. His pride and obstinacy were in no degree subdued.

8-17. PLAGUE OF BOILS. 8. Take to you handfuls of ashes, etc.—The next plague assailed the persons of the Egyptians, and it appeared in the form of ulcerous eruptions upon the skin and flesh (Lev. 13:20; II Kings 20:7; Job 2:7). That this epidemic did not arise from natural causes was evident from its taking effect from the particular action of Moses done in the sight of Pharaoh. The attitude he assumed was similar to that of Eastern magicians, who, "when they pronounce an imprecation on an individual, a village, or a country, take the ashes of cows' dung (that is, from a common fire) and throw them in the air, saying to the objects of their displeasure, such a sickness or such a curse shall come upon you" [ROBERTS]. Moses took ashes from the furnace—*Hebrew,* brick-kiln. The magicians, being sufferers in their own persons, could do nothing, though they had been called; and as the brick-kiln was one of the principal instruments of oppression to the Israelites, it was now converted into a means of chastisement to the Egyptians, who were made to read their sin in their punishment.

18-35. PLAGUE OF HAIL. 18. I will cause it to rain a very grievous hail, etc.—The seventh plague which Pharaoh's hardened heart provoked was that of hail, a phenomenon which must have produced the greatest astonishment and consternation in Egypt as rain and hailstones, accompanied by thunder and lightning, were very rare occurrences. **such as hath not been in Egypt**—In the Delta, or lower Egypt, where the scene is laid, rain occasionally falls between January and March—hail is not unknown, and thunder sometimes heard. But a storm, not only exhibiting all these elements, but so terrific that hailstones of immense size fell, thunder pealed in awful volleys, and lightning swept the ground like fire, was an unexampled calamity. **20, 21. He that feared the word of the Lord ... regarded not,** etc.—Due premonition, it appears, had been publicly given of the impending tempest—the cattle seem to have been sent out to graze, which is from January to April, when alone pasturage can be obtained, and accordingly the cattle were in the fields. This storm occurring at that season, not only struck universal terror into the minds of the people, but occasioned the destruction of all—people and cattle—which, in neglect of the warning, had been left in the fields, as well as of all vegetation. It was the more appalling because hailstones in Egypt are small and of little force; lightning also is scarcely ever known to produce fatal effects; and to enhance the wonder, not a trace of any storm was found in Goshen. **31, 32. the flax and the barley was smitten,** etc.—The peculiarities that are mentioned in these cereal products arise from the climate and physical constitution of Egypt. In that country flax and barley are almost ripe when wheat and rye (spelt) are green. And hence the flax must have been "bolled"—i.e., risen in stalk or podded in February, thus fixing the particular month when the event took place. Barley ripens about a

month earlier that wheat. Flax and barley are generally ripe in March, wheat and rye (properly, spelt) in April. **27-35. Pharaoh sent, and called for Moses and Aaron, and said unto them, I have sinned**—This awful display of divine displeasure did seriously impress the mind of Pharaoh, and, under the weight of his convictions, he humbles himself to confess he has done wrong in opposing the divine will. At the same time he calls for Moses to intercede for cessation of the calamity. Moses accedes to his earnest wishes, and this most awful visitation ended. But his repentance proved a transient feeling, and his obduracy soon became as great as before.

CHAPTER 10

Vss. 1-20. PLAGUE OF LOCUSTS. **1. show these my signs,** etc.—Sinners even of the worst description are to be admonished even though there may be little hope of amendment, and hence those striking miracles that carried so clear and conclusive demonstration of the being and character of the true God were performed in lengthened series before Pharaoh to leave him without excuse when judgment should be finally executed. **2. And that thou mayest tell ... of thy son, and of thy son's son,** etc.—There was a further and higher reason for the infliction of those awful judgments, viz., that the knowledge of them there, and the permanent record of them still, might furnish a salutary and impressive lesson to the Church down to the latest ages. Worldly historians might have described them as extraordinary occurrences that marked this era of Moses in ancient Egypt. But we are taught to trace them to their cause: the judgments of divine wrath on a grossly idolatrous king and nations. **4. to-morrow will I bring the locusts**—Moses was commissioned to renew the request, so often made and denied, with an assurance that an unfavorable answer would be followed on the morrow by an invasion of locusts. This species of insect resembles a large, spotted, red and black, double-winged grasshopper, about three inches or less in length, with the two hind legs working like hinged springs of immense strength and elasticity. Perhaps no more terrible scourge was ever brought on a land than those voracious insects, which fly in such countless numbers as to darken the land which they infest; and on whatever place they alight, they convert it into a waste and barren desert, stripping the ground of its verdure, the trees of their leaves and bark, and producing in a few hours a degree of desolation which it requires the lapse of years to repair. **7-11. Pharaoh's servants said**—Many of his courtiers must have suffered serious losses from the late visitations, and the prospect of such a calamity as that which was threatened and the magnitude of which former experience enabled them to realize, led them to make a strong remonstrance with the king. Finding himself not seconded by his counsellors in his continued resistance, he recalled Moses and Aaron, and having expressed his consent to their departure, inquired who were to go. The prompt and decisive reply, "all," neither man nor beast shall remain, raised a storm of indignant fury in the breast of the proud king. He would permit the grown-up men to go away; but no other terms would be listened to. **11. they were driven out from Pharaoh's presence**—In the East, when a person of authority and rank feels annoyed by a petition which he is unwilling to grant, he makes a signal to his attendants, who rush forward and, seizing the obnoxious suppliant by the neck, drag him out of the chamber with violent haste. Of such a character was the impassioned scene in the court of Egypt when the king had wrought himself into such a fit of uncontrollable fury as to treat ignominiously the two venerable representatives of the Hebrew people. **13. the Lord brought an east wind**—The rod of Moses was again raised, and the locusts came. They are natives of the desert and are only brought by an east wind into Egypt, where they sometimes come in sun-obscuring clouds, destroying in a few days every green blade in the track they traverse. Man, with all his contrivances, can do nothing to protect himself from the overwhelming invasion. Egypt has often suffered from locusts. But the plague that followed the wave of the miraculous rod was altogether unexampled. Pharaoh, fearing irretrievable ruin to his country, sent in haste for Moses, and confessing his sin, implored the intercession of Moses, who entreated the Lord, and a "mighty strong west wind took away the locusts."

21-29. PLAGUE OF DARKNESS. **21. Stretch out thine hand toward heaven, that there may be darkness**—Whatever secondary means were employed in producing it, whether thick clammy fogs and vapors, according to some; a sandstorm, or the *chamsin*, according to others; it was such that it could be almost perceived by the organs of touch, and so protracted as to continue for three days, which the *chamsin* does [HENSTENBERG]. The appalling character of this calamity consisted in this, that the sun was an object of Egyptian idolatry; that the pure and serene sky of that country was never marred by the appearance of a cloud. And here, too, the Lord made a marked difference between Goshen and the rest of Egypt. **24-26. Pharaoh called unto Moses, and said, Go ye, serve the Lord**—Terrified by the preternatural darkness, the stubborn king relents, and proposes another compromise—the flocks and herds to be left as hostages for their return. But the crisis is approaching, and Moses insists on every iota of his demand. The cattle would be needed for sacrifice—how many or how few could not be known till their arrival at the scene of religious observance. But the emancipation of Israel from Egyptian bondage was to be complete. **28. Pharaoh said . . . , Get thee from me**—The calm firmness of Moses provoked the tyrant. Frantic with disappointment and rage, with offended and desperate malice, he ordered him from his presence and forbade him ever to return. **29. Moses said, Thou hast spoken well.**

CHAPTER 11

Vss. 1-10. DEATH OF THE FIRST-BORN THREATENED. **1. the Lord said**—rather HAD said unto Moses. It may be inferred, therefore, that he had been apprised that the crisis had now arrived, that the next plague would so effectually humble and alarm the mind of Pharaoh, that he would "thrust them out thence altogether"; and thus the word of Moses (ch. 10:29), must be regarded as a prediction. **2, 3. Speak now in the ears of the people**—These verses, describing the communication which had been made in private to Moses, are inserted here as a parenthesis, and will be con-

sidered (ch. 12:35). **4. Thus saith the Lord, About midnight**—Here is recorded the announcement of the last plague made in the most solemn manner to the king, on whose hardened heart all his painful experience had hitherto produced no softening, at least no permanently good effect. **will I go out into the midst of Egypt**—language used after the manner of men. **5. all the first-born in the land . . . shall die**—The time, the suddenness, the dreadful severity of this coming calamity, and the peculiar description of victims, among both men and beasts, on whom it was to fall, would all contribute to aggravate its character. **the maid-servant that is behind the mill**—The grinding of the meal for daily use in every household is commonly done by female slaves and is considered the lowest employment. Two portable millstones are used for the purpose, of which the uppermost is turned by a small wooden handle, and during the operation the maid sits behind the mill. **6. shall be a great cry throughout all the land**—In the case of a death, people in the East set up loud wailings, and imagination may conceive what "a great cry" would be raised when death would invade every family in the kingdom. **7. against any of the children of Israel shall not a dog move his tongue**—No town or village in Egypt or in the East generally is free from the nuisance of dogs, who prowl about the streets and make the most hideous noise at any passers-by at night. What an emphatic significance does the knowledge of this circumstance give to this fact in the sacred record, that on the awful night that was coming, when the air should be rent with the piercing shrieks of mourners, so great and universal would be the panic inspired by the hand of God, that not a dog would move his tongue against the children of Israel! **8. all these thy servants shall . . . bow down themselves unto me**—This would be the effect of the universal terror; the hearts of the proudest would be humbled and do reverential homage to God, in the person of His representative. **went out . . . in a great anger**—Holy and righteous indignation at the duplicity, repeated falsehood, and hardened impenitence of the king; and this strong emotion was stirred in the bosom of Moses, not at the ill reception given to himself, but at the dishonor done to God (Matt. 19:8; Eph. 4:26).

CHAPTER 12

Vss. 1-10. THE PASSOVER INSTITUTED. **1. the Lord spake unto Moses**—rather, *had* spoken unto Moses and Aaron; for it is evident that the communication here described must have been made to them on or before the tenth of the month. **2. this month shall be unto you the beginning of months**—the first not only in order but in estimation. It had formerly been the seventh according to the reckoning of the civil year, which began in September, and continued unchanged, but it was thenceforth to stand first in the national religious year which began in March, April. **3. Speak ye unto all the congregation of Israel**—The recent events had prepared the Israelitish people for a crisis in their affairs, and they seem to have yielded implicit obedience at this time to Moses. It is observable that, amid all the hurry and bustle of such a departure, their serious attention was to be given to a solemn act of religion. **a lamb for an house**—a kid might be taken (vs. 5). The service was to be a domestic one, for the deliverance was to be from an evil threatened to every house in Egypt. **4. if the household be too little for the lamb,** etc.—It appears from Josephus that ten persons were required to make up the proper paschal communion. **every man, according to his eating** —It is said that the quantity eaten of the paschal lamb, by each individual, was about the size of an olive. **5. lamb ... without blemish**—The smallest deformity or defect made a lamb unfit for sacrifice—a type of Christ (Heb. 7:26; I Pet. 1:19). **a male of the first year**—Christ in the prime of life. **6. keep it up until the fourteenth day,** etc.—Being selected from the rest of the flock, it was to be separated four days before sacrifice; and for the same length of time was Christ under examination and His spotless innocence declared before the world. **kill it in the evening**—i.e., the interval between the sun's beginning to decline, and sunset, corresponding to our three o'clock in the afternoon. **7. take of the blood, and strike it on the two side-posts,** etc.—as a sign of safety to those within. The posts must be considered of tents, in which the Israelites generally lived, though some might be in houses. Though the Israelites were sinners as well as the Egyptians, God was pleased to accept the substitution of a lamb—the blood of which, being seen *sprinkled* on the doorposts, procured them mercy. It was to be on the sideposts and upper doorposts, where it might be *looked* to, not on the threshold, where it might be trodden under foot. This was an emblem of the blood of sprinkling (Heb. 12:24, 29). **8. roast with fire**—for the sake of expedition; and this difference was always observed between the cooking of the paschal lamb and the other offerings (II Chron. 35:13). **unleavened bread**—also for the sake of despatch (Deut. 16:3), but as a kind of corruption (Luke 12:1) there seems to have been a typical meaning under it (I Cor. 5:8). **bitter herbs**—lit., bitters—to remind the Israelites of their affliction in Egypt, and morally of the trials to which God's people are subject on account of sin. **9. Eat not of it raw**—i.e., with any blood remaining—a caveat against conformity to idolatrous practices. It was to be roasted whole, not a bone to be broken, and this pointed to Christ (John 19:36). **10. let nothing of it remain until the morning**—which might be applied in a superstitious manner, or allowed to putrefy, which in a hot climate would speedily have ensued; and which was not becoming in what had been offered to God.

11-14. THE RITE OF THE PASSOVER. **11. thus shall ye eat it; with your loins girded, your shoes on your feet**—as prepared for a journey. The first was done by the skirts of the loose outer cloth being drawn up and fastened in the girdle, so as to leave the leg and knee free for motion. As to the other, the Orientals never wear shoes indoors, and the ancient Egyptians, as appears from the monuments, did not usually wear either shoes or sandals. These injunctions seem to have applied chiefly to the first celebration of the rite. **it is the Lord's passover**—called by this name from the blood-marked dwellings of the Israelites being *passed* over figuratively be the destroying angel. **12. smite ... gods of Egypt**—perhaps used here for princes and grandees. But, according to Jewish tradition, the idols of Egypt were all on that night broken in pieces (see Num. 33:4; Isa. 19:1). **14. for a memorial,** etc.—The close analogy traceable in all points between the Jewish and Christian passovers is seen also in the cir-

cumstance that both festivals were instituted before the events they were to commemorate had transpired.

15-51. UNLEAVENED BREAD. **15. Seven days shall ye eat unleavened bread,** etc.—This was to commemorate another circumstance in the departure of the Israelites, who were urged to leave so hurriedly that their dough was unleavened (vs. 39), and they had to eat unleavened cakes (Deut. 16:3). The greatest care was always taken by the Jews to free their houses from leaven—the owner searching every corner of his dwelling with a lighted candle. A figurative allusion to this is made (I Cor. 5:7). The exclusion of leaven for seven days would not be attended with inconvenience in the East, where the usual leaven is dough kept till it becomes sour, and it is kept from one day to another for the purpose of preserving leaven in readiness. Thus even were there none in all the country, it could be got within twenty-four hours [HARMER]. **that soul shall be cut off**—excommunicated from the community and privileges of the chosen people. **16. there shall be an holy convocation**—lit., *calling* of the people, which was done by sound of trumpets (Num. 10:2), a sacred assembly—for these days were to be regarded as Sabbaths—excepting only that meat might be cooked on them (ch. 16:23). **17. ye shall observe,** etc.—The seven days of this feast were to commence the day after the passover. It was a distinct festival following that feast; but although this feast was instituted like the passover *before* the departure, the observance of it did not take place till *after*. **19. stranger**—No foreigner could partake of the passover, unless circumcised; the "stranger" specified as admissible to the privilege must, therefore, be considered a Gentile *proselyte*. **21-25. Then Moses called for all the elders of Israel,** etc.—Here are given special directions for the observance. **hyssop**—a small red moss [HASSELQUIST]. The caper-plant [ROYLE]. It was used in the sprinkling, being well adapted for such purposes, as it grows in bushes—putting out plenty of suckers from a single root. And it is remarkable that it was ordained in the arrangements of an all-wise Providence that the Roman soldiers should undesignedly, on their part, make use of this symbolical plant to Christ when, as our Passover, He was sacrificed for us. **none ... shall go out at the door of his house until the morning**—This regulation was peculiar to the first celebration, and intended, as some think, to prevent any suspicion attaching to them of being agents in the impending destruction of the Egyptians; there is an allusion to it (Isa. 26:20). **26. when your children shall say, ... What mean ye by this service**—Independently of some observances which were not afterwards repeated, the usages practised at this yearly commemorative feast were so peculiar that the curiosity of the young would be stimulated, and thus parents had an excellent opportunity, which they were enjoined to embrace, for instructing each rising generation in the origin and leading facts of the national faith. **27, 28. the people bowed the head, and worshipped**—All the preceding directions were communicated through the elders, and the Israelites, being deeply solemnized by the influence of past and prospective events, gave prompt and faithful obedience. **29. at midnight the Lord smote all the first-born in the land of Egypt**—At the moment when the Israelites were observing the newly instituted feast in the singular manner described, the threatened calamity overtook the Egyptians. It is more easy to imagine than describe the confusion and terror of that people suddenly roused from sleep and enveloped in darkness—none could assist their neighbors when the groans of the dying and the wild shrieks of mourners were heard everywhere around. The hope of every family was destroyed at a stroke. This judgment, terrible though it was, evinced the equity of divine retribution. For eighty years the Egyptians had caused the male children of the Israelites to be cast into the river, and now all their own first-born fell under the stroke of the destroying angel. They were made, in the justice of God, to feel something of what they had made His people feel. Many a time have the hands of sinners made the snares in which they have themselves been entangled, and fallen into the pit which they have dug for the righteous. "Verily there is a God that judgeth in the earth." **30. there was not a house where there was not one dead**—Perhaps this statement is not to be taken absolutely. The Scriptures frequently use the words "all," "none," in a comparative sense—and so in this case. There would be many a house in which there would be no child, and many in which the first-born might be already dead. What is to be understood is, that almost every house in Egypt had a death in it. **31. called for Moses and Aaron**—a striking fulfilment of the words of Moses (ch. 11:8), and showing that they were spoken under divine suggestion. **32. also take your flocks,** etc.—All the terms the king had formerly insisted on were now departed from; his pride had been effectually humbled. Appalling judgments in such rapid succession showed plainly that the hand of God was against him. His own family bereavement had so crushed him to the earth that he not only showed impatience to rid his kingdom of such formidable neighbors, but even begged an interest in their prayers. **34. people took ... kneading-troughs**—Having lived so long in Egypt, they must have been in the habit of using the utensils common in that country. The Egyptian kneading-trough was a bowl of wicker or rush-work, and it admitted of being hastily wrapped up with the dough in it and slung over the shoulder in their *hykes* or loose upper garments. **35. children of Israel borrowed of the Egyptians jewels of silver**—When the Orientals go to their sacred festivals, they always put on their *best jewels.* The Israelites themselves thought they were only going three days' journey to hold a feast unto the Lord, and in these circumstances it would be easy for them to *borrow* what was necessary for a sacred festival. But "borrow" conveys a wrong meaning. The word rendered *borrow* signifies properly to *ask, demand, require.* The Israelites had been kept in great poverty, having received little or no wages. They now insisted on full remuneration for all their labor, and it was paid in light and valuable articles adapted for convenient carriage. **36. the Lord gave the people favour in the sight of the Egyptians**—Such a dread of them was inspired into the universal minds of the Egyptians, that whatever they asked was readily given. **spoiled the Egyptians**—The accumulated earnings of many years being paid them at this moment, the Israelites were suddenly enriched, according to the promise made to Abraham (Gen. 15:14), and they left the country like a victorious army laden with spoil (Ps. 105:37; Ezek. 39:10). **37. The children of Israel journeyed from Rameses**—now generally

identified with the ancient Heroöpolis, and fixed at the modern *Abu*-Keisheid. This position agrees with the statement that the scene of the miraculous judgments against Pharaoh was "in the field of Zoan." And it is probable that, in expectation of their departure, which the king on one pretext or another delayed, the Israelites had been assembled there as a general rendezvous. In journeying from Rameses to Palestine, there was a choice of two routes—the one along the shores of the Mediterranean to El-Arish, the other more circuitous round the head of the Red Sea and the desert of Sinai. The latter Moses was directed to take (ch. 13:17). **to Succoth**—i.e., booths, probably nothing more than a place of temporary encampment. The Hebrew word signifies a covering or shelter formed by the boughs of trees; and hence, in memory of this lodgment, the Israelites kept the feast of tabernacles yearly in this manner. **six hundred thousand ... men**—It appears from Numbers 1 that the enumeration is of men above twenty years of age. Assuming, what is now ascertained by statistical tables, that the number of males above that age is as nearly as possible the half of the total number of males, the whole male population of Israel, on this computation, would amount to 1,200,000; and adding an equal number for women and children, the aggregate number of Israelites who left Egypt would be 2,400,000. **38. a mixed multitude went with them**—lit., a great rabble (see also Num. 11:4); Deut. 29:11); slaves, persons in the lowest grades of society, partly natives and partly foreigners, bound close to them as companions in misery, and gladly availing themselves of the opportunity to escape in the crowd. (Cf. Zech. 8:23). **40. the sojourning of the children of Israel ... was four hundred and thirty years**—The *Septuagint* renders it thus: "The sojourning of the children and of their fathers, which they sojourned in the land of Canaan and in the land of Egypt." These additions are important, for the period of sojourn in Egypt did not exceed 215 years; but if we reckon from the time that Abraham entered Canaan and the promise was made in which the sojourn of his posterity in Egypt was announced, this makes up the time to 430 years. **41. even the selfsame day**—implying an exact and literal fulfilment of the predicted period. **49. One law shall be to him that is homeborn, and unto the stranger**—This regulation displays the liberal spirit of the Hebrew institutions. Any foreigner might obtain admission to the privileges of the nation on complying with their sacred ordinances. In the Mosaic equally as in the Christian dispensation, privilege and duty were inseparably conjoined.

CHAPTER 13

Vss. 1, 2. THE FIRST-BORN SANCTIFIED. **2. Sanctify unto me all the first-born**—To sanctify means to consecrate, to set apart from a common to a sacred use. The foundation of this duty rested on the fact that the Israelites, having had their first-born preserved by a distinguishing act of grace from the general destruction that overtook the families of the Egyptians, were bound in token of gratitude to consider them as the Lord's peculiar property (cf. Heb. 12:23).

3-10. MEMORIAL OF THE PASSOVER. **3. Moses said unto the people, Remember this day**—The day that gave them a national existence and introduced them into the privileges of independence and freedom, deserved to live in the memories of the Hebrews and their posterity; and, considering the signal interposition of God displayed in it, to be held not only in perpetual, but devout remembrance. **house of bondage**—lit., house of slaves —i.e., a servile and degrading condition. **for by strength of hand the Lord brought you out from this place**—The emancipation of Israel would never have been obtained except it had been wrung from the Egyptian tyrant by the appalling judgments of God, as had been at the outset of his mission announced to Moses (ch. 3:19). **There shall no leavened bread**, etc.—The words are elliptical, and the meaning of the clause may be paraphrased thus:—"For by strength of hand the Lord brought you out from this place, in such haste that there could or should be no leavened bread eaten." **4. month Abib**—lit., a green ear, and hence the month Abib is the month of green ears, corresponding to the middle of our March. It was the best season for undertaking a journey to the desert region of Sinai, especially with flocks and herds; for then the winter torrents had subsided, and the wadies were covered with an early and luxuriant verdure. **5-7. when the Lord shall bring thee**—The passover is here instituted as a permanent festival of the Israelites. It was, however, only a prospective observance; we read of only one celebration of the passover during the protracted sojourn in the wilderness; but on their settlement in the promised land, the season was hallowed as a sacred anniversary, in conformity with the directions here given. **8. thou shalt show thy son in that day, saying**—The establishment of this and the other sacred festivals presented the best opportunities of instructing the young in a knowledge of His gracious doings to their ancestors in Egypt. **9. it shall be for a sign unto thee upon thine hand**, etc.—There is no reason to believe that the Oriental tattooing—the custom of staining the hands with the powder of Hennah, as Eastern females now do—is here referred to. Nor is it probable that either this practice or the phylacteries of the Pharisees—parchment scrolls, which were worn on their wrists and foreheads— had so early an existence. The words are to be considered only as a figurative mode of expression. **that the Lord's law may be in thy mouth**, etc.—i.e., that it may be the subject of frequent conversation and familiar knowledge among the people.

11-16. FIRSTLINGS OF BEASTS. **12. every firstling**, etc.—the injunction respecting the consecration of the first-born, as here repeated, with some additional circumstances. The firstlings of clean beasts, such as lambs, kids, and calves, if males, were to be devoted to God and employed in sacrifice. Those unclean beasts, as the ass's colt, being unfit for sacrifice, were to be redeemed (Num. 18:15).

17-21. JOURNEY FROM EGYPT. **17. God led them not through the way of the land of the Philistines, although that was near**, etc.—The shortest and most direct route from Egypt to Palestine was the usual caravan road that leads by Belbeis, El-Arish, to Ascalon and Gaza. The Philistines, who then possessed the latter, would have been sure to dispute their passage, for between them and the Israelites there was a hereditary feud (I Chron. 7:21, 22); and so early a commencement of hostilities would have discouraged or dismayed the unwarlike band which Moses led. Their faith was to be exercised and

strengthened, and from the commencement of their travels we observe the same careful proportion of burdens and trials to their character and state, as the gracious Lord shows to His people still in that spiritual journey of which the former was typical. **18. God led the people about through the way of the wilderness of the Red Sea**, etc.—This wondrous expanse of water is a gulf of the Indian ocean. It was called in Hebrew "the weedy sea," from the forest of marine plants with which it abounds. But the name of the Red Sea is not so easily traced. Some think it was given from its contiguity to the countries of Edom (red); others derive it from its coral rocks; while a third class ascribe the origin of the name to an extremely red appearance of the water in some parts, caused by a numberless multitude of very small mollusca. This sea, at its northern extremity, separates into two smaller inlets—the eastern called anciently the Elanitic gulf, now the gulf of Akaba; and the western the Heroöpolite gulf, now the gulf of Suez, which, there can be no doubt, extended much more to the north anciently than it does now. It was toward the latter the Israelites marched. **went up harnessed**—i.e., girded, equipped for a long journey. (See Psalm 105:37). The margin renders it "five in a rank," meaning obviously five large divisions, under five presiding officers, according to the usages of all caravans; and a spectacle of such a mighty and motley multitude must have presented an imposing appearance, and its orderly progress could have been effected only by the superintending influence of God. **19. Moses took the bones of Joseph with him**—in fulfilment of the oath he exacted from his brethren (Gen. 50:25, 26). The remains of the other patriarchs—not noticed from their obscurity—were also carried out of Egypt (Acts 7:16); and there would be no difficulty as to the means of conveyance—a few camels bearing these precious relics would give a true picture of Oriental customs, such as is still to be seen in the immense pilgrimages to Mecca. **20. encamped in Etham**—This place is supposed by the most intelligent travellers to be the modern Ajrud, where is a watering-place, and which is the third stage of the pilgrim caravans to Mecca. "It is remarkable that either of the different routes eastward from Heliopolis, or southward from Heroöpolis, equally admit of Ajrud being Etham. It is twelve miles northwest from Suez, and is literally on the edge of the desert" [PICTORIAL BIBLE]. **21, 22. the Lord went before them**—by a visible token of His presence, the Shekinah, in a majestic cloud (Ps. 78:14; Neh. 9:12; I Cor. 10:1), called the angel of God (ch. 14:19; 23:20-23; Ps. 99:6, 7; Isa. 63:8, 9).

CHAPTER 14

Vss. 1-41. GOD INSTRUCTS THE ISRAELITES AS TO THEIR JOURNEY. **2. Speak unto the children of Israel, that they turn and encamp**—The Israelites had now completed their three days' journey, and at Etham the decisive step would have to be taken whether they would celebrate their intended feast and return, or march onwards by the head of the Red Sea into the desert, with a view to a final departure. They were already on the borders of the desert, and a short march would have placed them beyond the reach of pursuit, as the chariots of Egypt could have made little progress over dry and yielding sand. But at Etham, instead of pursuing their journey eastward with the sea on their right, they were suddenly commanded to diverge to the south, keeping the gulf on their left; a route which not only detained them lingering on the confines of Egypt, but, in adopting it, they actually turned their backs on the land of which they had set out to obtain the possession. A movement so unexpected, and of which the ultimate design was carefully concealed, could not but excite the astonishment of all, even of Moses himself, although, from his implicit faith in the wisdom and power of his heavenly Guide, he obeyed. The object was to entice Pharaoh to pursue, in order that the moral effect, which the judgments on Egypt had produced in releasing God's people from bondage, might be still further extended over the nations by the awful events transacted at the Red Sea. **Pi-hahiroth**—the mouth of the defile, or pass—a description well suited to that of Bedea, which extended from the Nile and opens on the shore of the Red Sea. **Migdol**—a fortress or citadel. **Baal-zephon**—some marked site on the opposite or eastern coast. **3. the wilderness hath shut them in**—Pharaoh, who would eagerly watch their movements, was now satisfied that they were meditating flight, and he naturally thought from the error into which they appeared to have fallen by entering that defile, he could intercept them. He believed them now entirely in his power, the mountain chain being on one side, the sea on the other, so that, if he pursued them in the rear, escape seemed impossible. **5. the heart of Pharaoh and of his servants was turned against the people,** etc. —Alas, how soon the obduracy of this reprobate king reappears! He had been convinced, but not converted—overawed, but not sanctified by the appalling judgments of heaven. He bitterly repented of what he now thought a hasty concession. Pride and revenge, the honor of his kingdom, and the interests of his subjects, all prompted him to recall his permission to reclaim those runaway slaves and force them to their wonted labor. Strange that he should yet allow such considerations to obliterate or outweigh all his painful experience of the danger of oppressing that people. But those whom the Lord has doomed to destruction are first infatuated by sin. **6. he made ready his chariot**—His preparations for an immediate and hot pursuit are here described: a difference is made between "the chosen chariots and the chariots of Egypt." The first evidently composed the king's guard, amounting to six hundred, and they are called "chosen," lit., "third men"; three men being allotted to each chariot, the charioteer and two warriors. As to "the chariots of Egypt," the common cars contained only two persons, one for driving and the other for fighting"; sometimes only one person was in the chariot, the driver lashed the reins round his body and fought; infantry being totally unsuitable for a rapid pursuit, and the Egyptians having had no cavalry, the word "riders" is in the grammatical connection applied to war chariots employed, and these were of light construction, open behind, and hung on small wheels. **10. when Pharaoh drew nigh, the children of Israel lifted up their eyes**—The great consternation of the Israelites is somewhat astonishing, considering their vast superiority in numbers, but their deep dismay and absolute despair at the sight of this armed host receives a satisfactory explanation from the fact that the civilized state of Egyptian society required the absence of all arms, except when they were on service. If the Israelites were entirely unarmed at their departure, they could not think of making any resistance [WILKINSON & HENGSTENBERG]. **13, 14. Moses said, . . . Fear ye not, stand still, and see the salvation of the Lord**—Never, perhaps, was the

fortitude of a man so severely tried as that of the Hebrew leader in this crisis, exposed as he was to various and inevitable dangers, the most formidable of which was the vengeance of a seditious and desperate multitude; but his meek, unruffled, magnanimous composure presents one of the sublimest examples of moral courage to be found in history. And whence did his courage arise? He saw the miraculous cloud still accompanying them, and his confidence arose solely from the hope of a divine interposition, although, perhaps, he might have looked for the expected deliverance in every quarter, rather than in the direction of the sea. **15-18. the Lord said unto Moses, Wherefore criest thou unto me?** etc.—When in answer to his prayers, he received the divine command to go forward, he no longer doubted by what kind of miracle the salvation of his mighty charge was to be effected. **19. the angel of God,** i.e., the pillar of cloud. The slow and silent movement of that majestic column through the air, and occupying a position behind them must have excited the astonishment of the Israelites (Isa. 58:8). It was an effectual barrier between them and their pursuers, not only protecting them, but concealing their movements. Thus, the same cloud produced light (a symbol of favor) to the people of God, and darkness (a symbol of wrath) to their enemies (cf. II Cor. 2:16). **21. Moses stretched out his hand,** etc.—The waving of the rod was of great importance on this occasion to give public attestation in the presence of the assembled Israelites, both to the character of Moses and the divine mission with which he was charged. **the Lord caused . . . a strong east wind all that night**—Suppose a mere ebb tide caused by the wind, raising the water to a great height on *one side,* still as there was not only "dry land," but, according to the tenor of the sacred narrative, a wall on the right hand and on the left, it would be impossible on the hypothesis of such a natural cause to rear the wall on the *other.* The idea of divine interposition, therefore, is imperative; and, assuming the passage to have been made at Mount Attakah, or at the mouth of Wady-Tawarik, an *east* wind would cut the sea in that line. The *Hebrew* word *kedem,* however, rendered in our translation, "east," means, in its primary signification, *previous;* so that this verse might, perhaps, be rendered, "the Lord caused the sea to go back by a strong *previous* wind all that night"; a rendering which would remove the difficulty of supposing the host of Israel marched over on the sand, in the teeth of a rushing column of wind, strong enough to heap up the waters as a wall on each side of a dry path, and give the intelligible narrative of divine interference. **22. the children of Israel went into the midst of the sea,** etc.—It is highly probable that Moses, along with Aaron, first planted his footsteps on the untrodden sand, encouraging the people to follow him without fear of the treacherous walls; and when we take into account the multitudes that followed him, the immense number who through infancy and old age were incapable of hastening their movements, together with all the appurtenances of the camp, the strong and steadfast character of the leaders' faith was strikingly manifested (Josh. 2:10; 4:23; Ps. 66:6; 74:13; 106:9; 136:13; Isa. 63:11-13; I Cor. 10:1; Heb. 11:29). **23. the Egyptians pursued, and went in after them to the midst of the sea** — From the darkness caused by the intercepting cloud, it is probable that they were not aware on what ground they were driving: they heard the sound of the fugitives before them, and they pushed on with the fury of the avengers of blood, without dreaming that they were on the bared bed of the sea. **24. Lord looked ... through ... the cloud, and troubled them—** We suppose the fact to have been that the side of the pillar of cloud towards the Egyptians was suddenly, and for a few moments, illuminated with a blaze of light, which, coming as it were in a refulgent flash upon the dense darkness which had preceded, so frightened the horses of the pursuers that they rushed confusedly together and became unmanageable. "Let us flee," was the cry that resounded through the broken and trembling ranks, but it was too late; all attempts at flight were vain [BUSH]. **27. Moses stretched forth his hand over the sea,** etc.—What circumstances could more clearly demonstrate the miraculous character of this transaction than that at the waving of Moses' rod, the dividing waters left the channel dry, and on his making the same motion on the opposite side, they returned, commingling with instantaneous fury? Is such the character of any ebb tide? **28. there remained not so much as one of them** — It is surprising that, with such a declaration, some intelligent writers can maintain there is no evidence of the destruction of Pharaoh himself (Ps. 106:11). **30. Israel saw the Egyptians dead upon the sea-shore,** etc.—The tide threw them up and left multitudes of corpses on the beach; a result that brought greater infamy on the Egyptians, but that tended, on the other hand, to enhance the triumph of the Israelites, and doubtless enriched them with arms, which they had not before. The locality of this famous passage has not yet been, and probably never will be, satisfactorily fixed. Some place it in the immediate neighborhood of Suez; where, they say, the part of the sea is most likely to be affected by "a strong east wind"; where the road from the defile of Migdol (now Muktala) leads directly to this point; and where the sea, not above two miles broad, could be crossed in a short time. The vast majority, however, who have examined the spot, reject this opinion, and fix the passage, as does local tradition, about ten or twelve miles further down the shore at Wady-Tawarik. "The time of the miracle was the whole night, at the season of the year, too, when the night would be about its average length. The sea at that point extends from six and a half to eight miles in breadth. There was thus ample time for the passage of the Israelites from any part of the valley, especially considering their excitement and animation by the gracious and wonderful interposition of Providence in their behalf" [WILSON].

CHAPTER 15

Vss. 1-27. SONG OF MOSES. **1. Then sang Moses and the children of Israel**—The scene of this thanksgiving song is supposed to have been at the landing-place on the eastern shore of the Red Sea, at Ayoun Musa, the fountains of Moses. They are situated somewhat farther northward along the shore than the opposite point from which the Israelites set out. But the line of the people would be extended during the passage, and one extremity of it would reach as far north as these fountains, which would supply them with water on landing. The time when it was sung is supposed to have been the morning after the passage. This song is, by some hundred years, the oldest poem in the world. There is a sublimity and beauty in the language that is unexampled. But its unrivalled superiority arises not solely from the splendor of the diction. Its poetical excellencies have often drawn forth the admiration of the best judges, while the character of the event commemorated, and its being prompted by divine inspiration, contribute to give it an interest and sublimity peculiar to itself. **I will sing unto the Lord, for he hath triumphed gloriously**—Considering the state of servitude in which they had been born and bred, and the rude features of character which their subsequent history often displays, it cannot be supposed that the children of Israel generally were qualified to commit to memory or to appreciate the beauties of this inimitable song. But they might perfectly understand its pervading strain of sentiment; and, with the view of suitably improving the occasion, it was thought necessary that all, old and young, should join their united voices in the rehearsal of its words. As every individual had cause, so every individual gave utterance to his feelings of gratitude. **20. Miriam the prophetess**—so called from her receiving divine revelations (Num. 12:1; Mic. 6:4), but in this instance principally from her being eminently skilled in music, and in this sense the word "prophecy" is sometimes used in Scripture (I Chron. 25:1; I Cor. 11:5). **took a timbrel**—or tabret—a musical instrument in the form of a hoop, edged round with rings or pieces of brass to make a jingling noise and covered over with tightened parchment like a drum. It was beat with the fingers, and corresponds to our tambourine. **all the women went out after her with timbrels and with dances**—We shall understand this by attending to the modern customs of the East, where the dance—a slow, grave, and solemn gesture, generally accompanied with singing and the sound of the timbrel, is still led by the principal female of the company, the rest imitating her movements and repeating the words of the song as they drop from her lips. **21. Miriam answered them**—"them" in the *Hebrew* is masculine, so that Moses probably led the men and Miriam the women—the two bands responding alternately, and singing the first verse as a chorus. **22. wilderness of Shur** — comprehending all the western part of Arabia Petræa. The desert of Etham was a part of it, extending round the northern portion of the Red Sea, and a considerable distance along its eastern shore; whereas the "wilderness of Shur" (now Sudhr) was the designation of all the desert region of Arabia Petræa that lay next to Palestine. **23. when they came to Marah, they could not drink of the waters**—Following the general route of all travellers southward, between the sea and the tableland of the Tih (valley of wandering), Marah is almost universally believed to be what is now called Howarah, in Wady-Amarah, about thirty miles from the place where the Israelites landed on the eastern shore of the Red Sea—a distance quite sufficient for their march of three days. There is no other perennial spring in the intermediate space. The water still retains its ancient character, and has a bad name among the Arabs, who seldom allow their camels to partake of it. **25. the Lord showed him a tree, which when he had cast into the waters, the waters were made sweet** —Some travellers have pronounced this to be the Elvah of the Arabs—a shrub in form and flower resembling our hawthorn; others, the berries of the Ghurkhud—a bush found growing around all brackish fountains. But neither of these shrubs are known by the natives to possess such natural virtues. It is far more likely that God miraculously endowed some tree with the property of purifying the bitter water—a tree employed as the medium, but the sweetening was not dependent upon the nature or quality of the tree, but the power of God (cf. John 9:6). And hence the "statute and ordinance" that followed, which would have been singularly inopportune if no miracle had been wrought. **and there he proved them**—God now brought the Israelites into circumstances which would put their faith and obedience to the test (cf. Gen. 22:1). **27. they came to Elim, where were twelve wells of water**—supposed to be what is now called Wady-Ghurandel, the most extensive watercourse in the western desert—an oasis, adorned with a great variety of trees, among which the palm is still conspicuous, and fertilized by a copious stream. It is estimated to be a mile in breadth, but stretching out far to the northeast. After the weary travel through the desert, this must have appeared a most delightful encampment from its shade and verdure, as well as from its abundant supply of sweet water for the thirsty multitude. The palm is called "the tree of the desert," as its presence is always a sign of water. The palms in this spot are greatly increased in number, but the wells are diminished.

CHAPTER 16

Vss. 1-36. MURMURS FOR WANT OF BREAD. **1. they took their journey from Elim**—where they had remained several days. **came unto the wilderness of Sin**—It appears from Number 32, that several stations are omitted in this historical notice of the journey. This passage represents the Israelites as advanced into the great plain, which, beginning near El-Murkah, extends with a greater or less breadth to almost the extremity of the peninsula. In its broadest part northward of Tur it is called El-Kaa, which is probably the desert of Sin [ROBINSON]. **2. the whole congregation ... murmured against Moses and Aaron**—Modern travellers through the desert of Sinai are accustomed to take as much as is sufficient for the sustenance of men and beasts during forty days. The Israelites having been rather more than a month on their journey, their store of corn or other provisions was altogether or nearly exhausted; and there being no prospect of procuring any means of subsistence in the desert, except some wild olives and wild honey (Deut. 32: 13), loud complaints were made against the leaders. **3. Would to God we had died by the hand of the Lord in the land of Egypt**—How unreasonable and absurd the charge against Moses and Aaron! how ungrateful and impious against God! After all their experience of the divine wisdom, goodness, and power, we pause and wonder over the sacred narrative of their hardness and unbelief. But the expression of feeling is contagious in so vast a multitude, and there is a feeling of solitude and despondency in the desert which numbers cannot dispel; and besides, we must remember that they were men engrossed with the *present*—that the Comforter was not then given—and that they were destitute of all visible means of sustenance and cut off from every visible comfort, with only the promises of an *unseen* God to look to as the ground of their hope. And though we may lament they should tempt God in the wilderness and freely admit their sin in so doing, we can be at no loss for a reason why those who had all their lives been accustomed to walk by *sight* should, in circumstances of unparalleled difficulty and perplexity, find it hard to walk by *faith*. Do not even *we* find it difficult to walk by faith through the wilderness of this world, though in the light of a clearer revelation, and under a nobler leader than

Moses? [FISK]. (See I Cor. 10:11, 12). **4. Then said the Lord unto Moses**—Though the outbreak was immediately against the human leaders, it was indirectly against God: yet mark His patience, and how graciously He promised to redress the grievance. **I will rain bread from heaven**—Israel, a type of the Church which is from above, and being under the conduct, government, and laws of heaven, received their food from heaven also (Ps. 78:24). **that I may prove them, whether they will walk in my law, or no**—The grand object of their being led into the wilderness was that they might receive a religious training directly under the eye of God; and the first lesson taught them was a constant dependence on God for their daily nourishment. **13. at even the quails came up, and covered the camp**—This bird is of the gallinaceous kind, resembling the red partridge, but not larger than the turtledove. They are found in certain seasons in the places through which the Israelites passed, being migratory birds, and they were probably brought to the camp by "a wind from the Lord" as on another occasion (Num. 11;31). **13-31. and in the morning ... a small round thing ... manna**—There is a gum of the same name distilled in this desert region from the tamarisk, which is much prized by the natives, and preserved carefully by those who gather it. It is collected early in the morning, melts under the heat of the sun, and is congealed by the cold of night. In taste it is as sweet as honey, and has been supposed by distinguished travellers, from its whitish color, time, and place of its appearance, to be the manna on which the Israelites were fed: so that, according to the views of some, it was a production indigenous to the desert; according to others, there was a miracle, which consisted, however, only in the preternatural arrangements regarding its supply. But more recent and accurate examination has proved this gum of the tarfa-tree to be wanting in all the principal characteristics of the Scripture manna. It exudes only in small quantities, and not every year; it does not admit of being baked (Num. 11:8) or boiled (vs. 23). Though it may be exhaled by the heat and afterwards fall with the dew, it is a medicine, not food—it is well known to the natives of the desert, while the Israelites were strangers to theirs; and in taste as well as in the appearance of double quantity on Friday, none on Sabbath, and in not breeding worms, it is essentially different from the manna furnished to the Israelites. **32-36. Fill an omer of it to be kept for your generations**—The mere fact of such a multitude being fed for forty years in the wilderness, where no food of any kind is to be obtained, will show the utter impossibility of their subsisting on a natural production of the kind and quantity as this tarfa-gum; and, as if for the purpose of removing all such groundless speculations, Aaron was commanded to put a sample of it in a pot—a golden pot (Heb. 9:4)—to be laid before the Testimony—to be kept for future generations, that they might see the bread on which the Lord fed their fathers in the wilderness. But we have the bread of which that was merely typical (I Cor. 10:3; John 6:32).

CHAPTER 17

Vss. 1-7. THE PEOPLE MURMUR FOR WATER. **1. the children of Israel journeyed from the wilderness of Sin**—In the succinct annals of this book, those places only are selected for particular notice by the inspired historian, which were scenes memorable for their happy or painful interest in the history of the Israelites. A more detailed itinerary is given in the later books of Moses, and we find that here two stations are omitted (Num. 33). **according to the commandment of the Lord,** etc.—not given in oracular response, nor a vision of the night, but indicated by the movement of the cloudy pillar. The same phraseology occurs elsewhere (Num. 9:18, 19). **pitched in Rephidim**—now believed, on good grounds, to be Wady Feiran, which is exactly a day's march from Mount Sinai, and at the entrance of the Horeb district. It is a long circuitous defile about forty feet in breadth, with perpendicular granite rocks on both sides. The wilderness of Sin through which they approached to this valley is very barren, has an extremely dry and thirsty aspect, little or no water, scarcely even a dwarfish shrub to be seen, and the only shelter to the panting pilgrims is under the shadow of the great overhanging cliffs. **2, 3. the people did chide with Moses, and said, Give us water that we may drink,** etc.—The want of water was a privation, the severity of which we cannot estimate, and it was a great trial to the Israelites, but their conduct on this new occasion was outrageous; it amounted even to "a tempting of the Lord." It was an opposition to His minister, a distrust of His care, an indifference to His kindness, an unbelief in His providence, a trying of His patience and fatherly forbearance. **4. Moses cried unto the Lord, saying, What shall I do unto this people?**—His language, instead of betraying any signs of resentment or vindictive imprecation on a people who had given him a cruel and unmerited treatment, was the expression of an anxious wish to know what was the best to be done in the circumstances (cf. Matt. 5:44; Rom. 12:21). **5. the Lord said unto Moses,** etc.—not to smite the rebels, but the rock; not to bring a stream of blood from the breast of the offenders, but a stream of water from the granite cliffs. The cloud rested on a particular rock, just as the star rested on the house where the infant Saviour was lodged. And from the rod-smitten rock there forthwith gushed a current of pure and refreshing water. It was perhaps the greatest miracle performed by Moses, and in many respects bore a resemblance to the greatest of Christ's: being done without ostentation and in the presence of a few chosen witnesses (I Cor. 10:4). **7. called the name of the place**—Massah (temptation); Meribah (**chiding,** strife): the same word which is rendered "provocation" (Heb. 3:8).

8-16. ATTACK OF AMALEK. 8. Then came Amalek—Some time probably elapsed before they were exposed to this new evil; and the presumption of there being such an interval affords the only ground on which we can satisfactorily account for the altered, the better, and former spirit that animated the people in this sudden contest. The miracles of the manna and the water from the rock had produced a deep impression and permanent conviction that God was indeed among them; and with feelings elevated by the conscious experience of the Divine Presence and aid, they remained calm, resolute, and courageous under the attack of their unexpected foe. **fought with Israel**—The language implies that no occasion had been furnished for this attack; but, as descendants of Esau, the Amalekites entertained a deep-seated grudge against them, especially as the rapid prosperity and marvellous experience of Israel showed that the blessing contained in the birthright was taking effect. It seems to have been a mean, dastardly, insidious surprise on the rear (Num. 24: 20; Deut. 25:17), and an impious defiance of God.

9. Moses said unto Joshua—or Jesus (Acts 7:45; Heb. 4:8). This is the earliest notice of a young warrior destined to act a prominent part in the history of Israel. He went with a number of picked men. There is not here a wide open plain on which the battle took place, as according to the rules of modern warfare. The Amalekites were a nomadic tribe, making an irregular attack on a multitude probably not better trained than themselves, and for such a conflict the low hills and open country around this wady would afford ample space [ROBINSON]. **10-12. Moses . . . went up . . . the hill . . . held up his hand**—with the wonder-working rod; he acted as the standard-bearer of Israel, and also their intercessor, praying for success and victory to crown their arms—the earnestness of his feelings being conspicuously evinced amid the feebleness of nature. **13. Joshua discomfited Amalek**—Victory at length decided in favor of Israel, and the glory of the victory, by an act of national piety, was ascribed to God (cf. I John 5:4). **14-16. Write this for a memorial**—If the bloody character of this statute seems to be at variance with the mild and merciful character of God, the reasons are to be sought in the deep and implacable vengeance they meditated against Israel (Ps. 83:4).

CHAPTER 18

Vss. 1-27. VISIT OF JETHRO. **1-5. Jethro . . . came . . . unto Moses,** etc.—It is thought by many eminent commentators that this episode is inserted out of its chronological order, for it is described as occurring when the Israelites were "encamped at the mount of God." And yet they did not reach it till the third month after their departure from Egypt (ch. 19:1, 2; cf. Deut. 1:6, 9-15). **6. thy wife, and her two sons**—See on ch. 4:20. **7. Moses went out to meet his father-in-law,** etc.—Their salutations would be marked by all the warm and social greetings of Oriental friends (see on ch. 4:27)—the one going out to "meet" the other, the "obeisance," the "kiss" on each side of the head, the silent entrance into the tent for consultation; and their conversation ran in the strain that might have been expected of two pious men, rehearsing and listening to a narrative of the wonderful works and providence of God. **12. Jethro . . . took a burnt offering**—This friendly interview was terminated by a solemn religious service—the *burnt offerings* were consumed on the altar, and the *sacrifices* were *peace* offerings, used in a feast of joy and gratitude at which Jethro, as priest of the true God, seems to have presided, and to which the chiefs of Israel were invited. This incident is in beautiful keeping with the character of the parties, and is well worthy of the imitation of Christian friends when they meet in the present day. **13-26. on the morrow . . . Moses sat to judge the people, etc.**—We are here presented with a specimen of his daily morning occupations; and among the multifarious duties his divine legation imposed, it must be considered only a small portion of his official employments. He appears in this attitude as a type of Christ in His legislative and judicial characters. **the people stood by Moses from the morning unto the evening,** etc.—Governors in the East seat themselves at the most public gate of their palace or the city, and there, amid a crowd of applicants, hear causes, receive petitions, redress grievances, and adjust the claims of contending parties. **17. Moses' father-in-law said unto him, The thing . . . is not good**—not good either for Moses himself, for the maintenance of justice, or for the satisfaction and interests of the people. Jethro gave a prudent counsel as to the division of labor, and universal experience in the Church and State has attested the soundness and advantages of the principle. **23. If thou shalt do this thing, etc.**—Jethro's counsel was given merely in the form of a suggestion; it was not to be adopted without the express sanction and approval of a better and higher Counsellor; and although we are not informed of it, there can be no doubt that Moses, before appointing subordinate magistrates, would ask the mind of God, as it is the duty and privilege of every Christian in like manner to supplicate the divine direction in all his ways.

CHAPTER 19

Vss. 1-25. ARRIVAL AT SINAI. **1. In the third month**—according to Jewish usage, the *first* day of that month—"same day"—It is added, to mark the time more explicitly, i.e., forty-five days after Egypt—one day spent on the mount (vs. 3), one returning the people's answer (vss. 7, 8), three days of preparation, making the whole time fifty days from the first passover to the promulgation of the law. Hence the feast of pentecost, i.e., the fiftieth day, was the inauguration of the Old Testament church, and the divine wisdom is apparent in the selection of the same reason for the institution of the New Testament church (John 1:17; Acts 2:1). **2. were come to the desert of Sinai**—The desert has its provinces, or divisions, distinguished by a variety of names; and the "desert of Sinai" is that wild and desolate region which occupies the very center of the peninsula, comprising the lofty range to which the mount of God belongs. It is a wilderness of shaggy rocks of porphyry and red granite, and of valleys for the most part bare of verdure. **and there Israel camped before the mount**—Sinai, so called from Seneh, or acacia bush. It is now called Jebel Musa. Their way into the interior of the gigantic cluster was by Wady Feiran, which would lead the bulk of the hosts with their flocks and herds into the high valleys of Jebel Musa, with their abundant springs, especially into the great thoroughfare of the desert—the longest, widest, and most continuous of all the valleys, the Wady-es-Sheikh, while many would be scattered among the adjacent valleys; so that thus secluded from the world in a wild and sublime amphitheatre of rocks, they "camped before the mount." "In this valley—a long flat valley—about a quarter of a mile in breadth, winding northwards, Israel would find ample room for their encampment. Of all the wadys in that region, it seems the most suitable for a prolonged sojourn. The 'goodly tents' of Israel could spread themselves without limit" [BONAR]. **3-6. Moses went up unto God**—the Shekinah—within the cloud (ch. 33:20; John 1:18). **Thus shalt thou say to the house of Jacob, etc.**—The object for which Moses went up was to receive and convey to the people the message contained in these verses, and the purport of which was a general announcement of the terms on which God was to take the Israelites into a close and peculiar relation to Himself. In thus negotiating between God and His people, the highest post of duty which any mortal man was ever called to occupy, Moses was still but a servant. The only Mediator is Jesus Christ. **ye shall be unto me a kingdom of priests**—As the priestly order was set apart from the common mass, so the Israelites, compared

with other people, were to sustain the same near relation to God; a community of spiritual sovereigns. **an holy nation**—set apart to preserve the knowledge and worship of God. **7, 8. Moses came and called for the elders of the people**—The message was conveyed to the mighty multitude through their elders, who, doubtless, instructed them in the conditions required. Their unanimous acceptance was conveyed through the same channel to Moses, and by him reported to the Lord. Ah! how much self-confidence did their language betray! How little did they know what spirit they were of! **9-15. The Lord said unto Moses, Lo, I come . . . in a thick cloud, etc.**—The deepest impressions are made on the mind through the medium of the senses; and so He who knew what was in man signalized His descent at the inauguration of the ancient church, by all the sensible tokens of august majesty that were fitted to produce the conviction that He is the great and terrible God. The whole multitude must have anticipated the event with feelings of intense solemnity and awe. The extraordinary preparations enjoined, the ablutions and rigid abstinence they were required to observe, the barriers erected all round the base of the mount, and the stern penalties annexed to the breach of any of the conditions, all tended to create an earnest and solemn expectation which increased as the appointed day drew near. **16. on the third day, in the morning, that there were thunders and lightning, etc.**—The descent of God was signalized by every object imagination can conceive connected with the ideas of grandeur and of awe. But all was in keeping with the character of the law about to be proclaimed. As the mountain burned with fire, God was exhibited as a consuming fire to the transgressors of His law. The thunder and lightning, more awful amid the deep stillness of the region and reverberating with terrific peals among the mountains, would rouse the universal attention; a thick cloud was an apt emblem of the dark and shadowy dispensation (cf. Matt. 17:5). **the voice of a trumpet**—This gave the scene the character of a miraculous transaction, in which other elements than those of nature were at work, and some other than material trumpet was blown by other means than human breath. **17. Moses brought forth the people out of the camp to meet with God**—Wady-er-Raheh, where they stood, has a spacious sandy plain, immediately in front of Es-Suksafeh, considered by ROBINSON to be the mount from which the law was given. "We measured it, and estimate the whole plain at two geographical miles long, and ranging in breadth from one-third to two-thirds of a mile, or as equivalent to a surface of one square mile. This space is nearly doubled by the recess on the west, and by the broad and level area of Wady-es-Sheikh on the east, which issues at right angles to the plain, and is equally in view of the front and summit of the mount. The examination convinced us that here was space enough to satisfy all the requisitions of the Scripture narrative, so far as it relates to the assembling of the congregation to receive the law. Here, too, one can see the fitness of the injunction to set bounds around the mount, that neither man nor beast might approach too near, for it rises like a perpendicular wall." But Jebel Musa, the old traditional Sinai, and the highest peak, has also a spacious valley, Wady-Seba'iyeh, capable of holding the people. It is not certain on which of these two they stood. **21. the Lord said unto Moses, Go down, charge the people**—No sooner had Moses proceeded a little up the mount, than he was suddenly ordered to return, in order to keep the people from breaking through to gaze—a course adopted to heighten the impressive solemnity of the secne. The strict injunctions renewed to all, whatever their condition, at a time and in circumstances when the whole multitude of Israel were standing at the base of the mount, was calculated in the highest degree to solemnize and awe every heart.

CHAPTER 20

Vss. 1-26. THE TEN COMMANDMENTS. **1. God spake all these words**—The Divine Being Himself was the speaker (Deut. 5:12, 32, 33), in tones so loud as to be heard—so distinct as to be intelligible by the whole multitude standing in the valleys below, amid the most appalling phenomena of agitated nature. Had He been simply addressing rational and intelligent creatures, He would have spoken with the still small voice of persuasion and love. But He was speaking to those who were at the same time fallen and sinful creatures, and a corresponding change was required in the manner of God's procedure, in order to give a suitable impression of the character and sanctions of the law revealed from heaven (Rom. 11:5-9). **2. I am the Lord thy God** —This is a preface to the ten commandments—the latter clause being specially applicable to the case of the Israelites, while the former brings it home to all mankind; showing that the reasonableness of the law is founded in their eternal relation as creatures to their Creator, and their mutual relations to each other. **3. Thou shalt have no other gods before me**—in My presence, beside, or except Me. **4, 5. Thou shalt not make ... any graven image ... thou shalt not bow down thyself to them**—i.e., "make in order to bow." Under the auspices of Moses himself, figures of cherubim, brazen serpents, oxen, and many other things in the earth beneath, were made and never condemned. The mere making was no sin—it was the making with the intent to give idolatrous worship. **8. Remember the sabbath day**— implying it was already known, and recognized as a season of sacred rest. The first four commandments comprise our duties to God—the other six our duties to our fellow men; and as interpreted by Christ, they reach to the government of the heart as well as the lip (Matt. 5:17). "If a man do them he shall live in them." But, ah! what an *if* for frail and fallen man. Whoever rests his hope upon the law stands debtor to it all; and in this view every one would be without hope were not "the LORD OUR RIGHTEOUSNESS" (John 1:17). **18-21. all the people saw the thunderings and the lightnings**—They were eye and ear witnesses of the awful emblems of the Deity's descent. But they perceived not the Deity Himself. **19. let not God speak with us, lest we die**, etc.—The phenomena of thunder and lightning had been one of the plagues so fatal to Egypt, and as they heard God speaking to them now, they were apprehensive of instant death also. Even Moses himself, the mediator of the old covenant, did "exceedingly quake and fear" (Heb. 12:21). But doubtless God spake what gave *him* relief—restored him to a frame of mind fit for the ministrations committed to him; and hence immediately after he was enabled to relieve and comfort them with the relief and comfort which he himself had received from God (II Cor. 1:4). **22, 23. the Lord said unto Moses**—It appears from Deuteronomy 4:14-16, that this injunction was a conclusion drawn from the scene on Sinai—that as no similitude of God was

displayed then, they should not attempt to make any visible figure or form of Him. **24. An altar of earth thou shalt make unto me**—a regulation applicable to special or temporary occasions. **25. thou shalt not build it of hewn stone**, etc.—i. e., carved with figures and ornaments that might lead to superstition. **26. by steps**—a precaution taken for the sake of decency, in consequence of the loose, wide, flowing garments of the priests.

CHAPTER 21

Vss. 1-6. LAWS FOR MENSERVANTS. **1. judgments**—rules for regulating the procedure of judges and magistrates in the decision of cases and the trial of criminals. The government of the Israelites being a theocracy, those public authorities were the servants of the Divine Sovereign, and subject to His direction. Most of these laws here noticed were primitive usages, founded on principles of natural equity, and incorporated, with modifications and improvements, in the Mosaic code. **2-6. If thou buy an Hebrew servant**—Every Israelite was freeborn; but slavery was permitted under certain restrictions. An Hebrew might be made a slave through poverty, debt, or crime; but at the end of six years he was entitled to freedom, and his wife, if she had voluntarily shared his state of bondage, also obtained release. Should he, however, have married a female slave, she and the children, after the husband's liberation, remained the master's property; and if, through attachment to his family, the Hebrew chose to forfeit his privilege and abide as he was, a formal process was gone through in a public court, and a brand of servitude stamped on his ear (Ps. 40:6) for life, or at least till the Jubilee (Deut. 15:17).

7-36. LAWS FOR MAIDSERVANTS. **7. if a man sell his daughter**—Hebrew girls might be redeemed for a reasonable sum. But in the event of her parents or friends being unable to pay the redemption money, her owner was not at liberty to sell her elsewhere. Should she have been betrothed to him or his son, and either change their minds, a maintenance must be provided for her suitable to her condition as his intended wife, or her freedom instantly granted. **23-25. eye for eye**—The law which authorized retaliation—a principle acted upon by all primitive people—was a civil one. It was given to regulate the procedure of the public magistrate in determining the amount of compensation in every case of injury, but did not encourage feelings of private revenge. The later Jews, however, mistook it for a moral precept, and were corrected by our Lord (Matt. 5:38-42). **28-36. If an ox gore a man or a woman, that they die**—For the purpose of sanctifying human blood, and representing all injuries affecting life in a serious light, an animal that occasioned death was to be killed or suffer punishment proportioned to the degree of damage it had caused. Punishments are still inflicted on this principle in Persia and other countries of the East; and among a rude people greater effect is thus produced in inspiring caution, and making them keep noxious animals under restraint, than a penalty imposed on the owners. **30. If there be laid on him a sum of money**, etc.—Blood fines are common among the Arabs as they were once general throughout the East. This is the only case where a money compensation, instead of capital punishment, was expressly allowed in the Mosaic law.

CHAPTER 22

Vss. 1-31. LAWS CONCERNING THEFT. **1. If a man shall steal an ox, or a sheep**—The law respects the theft of cattle which constituted the chief part of their property. The penalty for the theft of a sheep which was slain or sold, was fourfold; for an ox fivefold, because of its greater utility in labor; but, should the stolen animal have been recovered alive, a *double* compensation was all that was required, because it was presumable he (the thief) was not a practised adept in dishonesty. A robber breaking into a house at *midnight* might, in self-defense, be slain with impunity; but if he was slain after *sunrise*, it would be considered murder, for it was not thought likely an assault would then be made upon the lives of the occupants. In every case where a thief could not make restitution, he was sold as a slave for the usual term. **6. If fire break out, and catch in thorns**—This refers to the common practice in the East of setting fire to the dry grass before the fall of the autumnal rains, which prevents the ravages of vermin, and is considered a good preparation of the ground for the next crop. The very parched state of the herbage and the long droughts of summer, make the kindling of a fire an operation often dangerous, and always requiring caution from its liability to spread rapidly. **stacks** —or as it is rendered "shocks" (Judg. 15:5; Job 5: 26), means simply a bundle of loose sheaves. **26, 27. If thou at all take thy neighbour's raiment to pledge**, etc.—From the nature of the case, this is the description of a poor man. No Orientals undress, but, merely throwing off their turbans and some of their heavy outer garments, they sleep in the clothes which they wear during the day. The bed of the poor is usually nothing else than a mat; and, in winter, they cover themselves with a cloak—a practice which forms the ground or reason of the humane and merciful law respecting the pawned coat. **28. gods**—a word which is several times in this chapter rendered "judges" or magistrates. **the ruler of thy people**—and the chief magistrate who was also the high priest, at least in the time of Paul (Acts 23:1-5).

CHAPTER 23

Vss. 1-33. LAWS CONCERNING SLANDER, ETC. **1. put not thine hand**—join not hands. **2. decline**—depart, deviate from the straight path of rectitude. **3. countenance**—adorn, embellish—thou shalt not varnish the cause even of a poor man to give it a better coloring than it merits. **10, 11. six years thou shalt sow thy land**—intermitting the cultivation of the land every seventh year. But it appears that even then there was a spontaneous produce which the poor were permitted freely to gather for their use, and the beasts driven out fed on the remainder, the owners of fields not being allowed to reap or collect the fruits of the vineyard or oliveyard during the course of this sabbatical year. This was a regulation subservient to many excellent purposes; for, besides inculcating the general lesson of dependence on Providence, and of confidence in His faithfulness to His promise respecting the triple increase on the sixth year (Lev. 25:20, 21), it gave the Israelites a practical proof that they held their properties of the Lord as His tenants, and must conform to His rules on pain of forfeiting the lease of them. **12. Six days thou shalt do thy work, and on the seventh day thou shalt rest**—This law is repeated lest any might suppose there was a relaxation of its observance during the sabbatical year. **13. make no mention of the name of other gods**, etc.—i.e., in common conversation, for a familiar use of them would tend to lessen horror of idolatry. **14-18. Three times ... keep a feast ... in the year**—This was the institution of the great religious festivals—"The feast of unleavened bread" or the passover—"the feast of harvest" or pentecost—"the feast of ingathering" or the feast of tabernacles, which was a memorial of the dwelling in booths in the wilderness, and which was observed "in the end of the year," or the seventh month (ch. 12:2). All the males were enjoined to repair to the tabernacle and afterwards the temple, and the women frequently went. The institution of this national custom was of the greatest importance in many ways: by keeping up a national sense of religion and a public uniformity in worship, by creating a bond of unity, and also by promoting internal commerce among the people. Though the absence of all the males at these three festivals left the country defenseless, a special promise was given of divine protection, and no incursion of enemies was ever permitted to happen on those occasions. **19. Thou shalt not seethe a kid in his mother's milk** —A prohibition against imitating the superstitious rites of the idolaters in Egypt, who, at the end of their harvest, seethed a kid in its mother's milk and sprinkled the broth as a magical charm on their gardens and fields, to render them more productive the following season. **20-25. Behold, I send an Angel before thee, to keep thee in the way**—The communication of these laws, made to Moses and by him rehearsed to the people, was concluded by the addition of many animating promises, intermingled with several solemn warnings that lapses into sin and idolatry would not be tolerated or passed with impunity. **my name is in him**—This angel is frequently called Jehovah and Elohim, i.e., God. **28. I will send hornets before thee**, etc. (Josh. 24: 12).—Some instrument of divine judgment, but variously interpreted, as hornets in a literal sense [BOCHART]. As a pestilential disease [ROSENMULLER]. As a terror of the Lord—an extraordinary dejection [JUNIUS]. **29, 30. I will not drive ... out ... in one year; lest the land become desolate**—Many reasons recommend a gradual extirpation of the former inhabitants of Canaan. But only one is here specified—the danger lest, in the unoccupied grounds, wild beasts should inconveniently multiply; a clear proof that the promised land was more than sufficient to contain the actual population of the Israelites.

CHAPTER 24

Vss. 1-18. DELIVERY OF THE LAW AND COVENANT. **3. Moses came and told the people all the words of the Lord**—The rehearsal of the foregoing laws and the ten commandments, together with the promises of special blessings in the event of their obedience, having drawn forth from the people a unanimous declaration of their consent, it was forthwith recorded as the conditions of the *national* covenant. The next day preparations were made for having it solemnly ratified, by building an altar and twelve pillars; the altar representing God, and the pillars the tribes of Israel—the two parties in this solemn compact—while Moses acted as typical mediator. **5. young men**—priests (ch. 19:22), probably the oldest sons of particular families, who acted under the direction of Moses. **oxen**—Other animals, though not mentioned, were offered in sacrifice

(Heb. 9:18-20). **6. Moses took half of the blood ... sprinkled**—Preliminary to this was the public reading of the law and the renewed acceptance of the terms by the people; then the sprinkling of the blood was the sign of solemn ratification—half on each party in the transaction. **8. Moses took the blood, and sprinkled it on the people**—probably on the twelve pillars, as representing the people (also the book, Heb. 9:19), and the act was accompanied by a public proclamation of its import. It was setting their seal to the covenant (cf. I Cor. 11:25). It must have been a deeply impressive, as well as instructive scene, for it taught the Israelites that the covenant was made with them only through the sprinkling of blood—that the divine acceptance of themselves and services, was only by virtue of an atoning sacrifice, and that even the blessings of the *national* covenant were promised and secured to them only through grace. The ceremonial, however, had a further and higher significance, as is shown by the apostle (see as above). **9. Then went up Moses, and Aaron**—in obedience to a command given (vss. 1, 2; also ch. 19:24), previous to the religious engagement of the people, now described. **Nadab, and Abihu**—the two oldest sons of Aaron. **seventy of the elders**—a select number; what was the principle of selection is not said; but they were the chief representatives, the most conspicuous for official rank and station, as well as for their probity and weight of character in their respective tribes. **10. they saw the God of Israel**—That there was no visible form or representation of the divine nature, we have expressly intimated (Deut. 4:15). But a symbol or emblem of His glory was distinctly, and at a distance, displayed before those chosen witnesses. Many think, however, that in this private scene was discovered, amid the luminous blaze, the faint adumbrated form of the humanity of Christ (Ezek. 1:26; cf. Gal. 3:24). **sapphire**—one of the most valuable and lustrous of the precious gems—of a sky-blue or light azure color and frequently chosen to describe the throne of God (see Ezek. 1:26; 10:1). **11. upon the nobles of the children of Israel he laid not his hand**—The "nobles," i.e., the elders, after the sprinkling of the blood, were not inspired with terror in presence of the calm, benign, radiant symbol of the divine majesty; so different from the terrific exhibitions at the giving of the law. The report of so many competent witnesses would tend to confirm the people's faith in the divine mission of Moses. **eat and drink**—feasted on the peace offering—on the remnants of the late sacrifices and libations. This feast had a prophetic bearing, intimating God's dwelling with men. **12. I will give thee tables of stone**—The ten commandments, which had already been spoken, were to be given in a permanent form. Inscribed on stone, for greater durability, by the hand of God Himself, they were thus authenticated and honored above the judicial or ceremonial parts of the law. **13. Moses went up into the mount of God**—He was called to receive the divine transcript. Joshua was taken a little higher, and it would be a great comfort for the leader to have his company during the six days he was in patient waiting for the call on the seventh or sabbath-day. **14. he said unto the elders, Tarry ye here for us**—There is a circular valley or hollow a good way up on the brow of Jebel Musa, which was their halting-place, while he alone was privileged to ascend the highest peak. The people stood below, as in the "outer court," the elders in the "holy place," Moses, as a type of Christ, in "the holy of holies." **18. Moses went into the midst of**

the cloud—the visible token of God's presence. Divine grace animated and supported him to enter with holy boldness. **Moses was in the mount forty days and forty nights**—The six days spent in waiting are not included. During that protracted period he was miraculously supported (Deut. 9:9), on a peak scarcely thirty paces in compass.

CHAPTER 25

Vss. 1-40. CONCERNING AN OFFERING. **1. the Lord spake unto Moses,** etc.—The business that chiefly occupied Moses on the mount, whatever other disclosures were made to him there, was in receiving directions about the tabernacle, and they are here recorded as given to him. **2. bring me an offering: of every man that giveth it willingly,** etc.—Having declared allegiance to God as their sovereign, they were expected to contribute to His state, as other subjects to their kings; and the "offering" required of them was not to be imposed as a tax, but to come from their own loyal and liberal feelings. **3. this is the offering which ye shall take of them**—the articles of which the offerings should consist. **brass**—rather copper, brass being a composite metal. **4. goats' hair**—or leather of goats' skin. **5. badgers' skins**—The badger was an unclean animal, and is not a native of the East—rather some kind of fish, of the leather of which sandals are made in the East. **shittim wood**—or *Shittah* (Isa. 41:19), the acacia, a shrub which grows plentifully in the deserts of Arabia, yielding a light, strong, and beautiful wood, in long planks. **7. ephod**—a square cloak, hanging down from the shoulders, and worn by priests. **8. a sanctuary; that I may dwell among them**—In one sense the tabernacle was to be a palace, the royal residence of the King of Israel, in which He was to dwell among His people, receive their petitions, and issue His responses. But it was also to be a place of worship, in which God was to record His name and to enshrine the mystic symbols of His presence. **9. According to all that I show thee, after the pattern of the tabernacle**—The proposed erection could be, in the circumstances of the Israelites, not of a fixed and stable but of a temporary and movable description, capable of being carried about with them in their various sojournings. It was made after "the pattern" shown to Moses, by which is now generally understood, not that it was an unheard-of novelty, or an entirely original structure, for it is ascertained to have borne resemblance in form and arrangements to the style of an Egyptian temple, but that it was so altered, modified, and purified from all idolatrous associations, as to be appropriated to right objects, and suggestive of ideas connected with the true God and His worship. **10. an ark**—a coffer or chest, overlaid with gold, the dimensions of which, taking the cubit at eighteen inches, are computed to be three feet nine inches in length, two feet three inches in breadth. **11. a crown**—a rim or cornice. **12. rings**—staples for the poles, with which it was to be carried from place to place. **15. staves shall be in the rings of the ark**—i.e., always remain in the rings, whether the ark be at rest or in motion. **16. the testimony**—that is, the two tables of stone, containing the ten commandments, and called "the testimony," because by it God did testify His sovereign authority over Israel as His people, His selection of them as the guardians of His will and worship, and His displeasure in the event of their transgressing His laws; while on their part, by receiving and depositing this law in its appointed place, they testified their acknowledgment of God's right to rule over them, and their submission to the authority of His law. The superb and elaborate style of the ark that contained "the testimony" was emblematic of the great treasure it held; in other words, the incomparable value and excellence of the Word of God, while its being placed in this chest further showed the great care which God has ever taken for preserving it. **17. thou shalt make a mercy seat of pure gold**—to serve as a lid, covering it exactly. It was "the propitiatory cover," as the term may be rendered, denoting that Christ, our great propitiation, has fully answered all the demands of the law, covers our transgressions, and comes between us and the curse of a violated law. **18. two cherubim**—The real meaning of these figures, as well as the shape or form of them, is not known with certainty— probably similar to what was afterwards introduced into the temple, and described in Ezekiel 10. They stretched out their wings, and their faces were turned towards the mercy seat, probably in a bowing attitude. The prevailing opinion now is, that those splendid figures were symbolical not of angelic but of earthly and human beings—the members of the Church of God interested in the dispensation of grace, the redeemed in every age—and that these hieroglyphic forms symbolized the qualities of the true people of God— courage, patience, intelligence, and activity. **22. there I will meet with thee, and I will commune with thee from above the mercy seat**—The Shekinah, or symbol of the Divine Presence, rested on the mercy seat, and was indicated by a cloud, from the midst of which responses were audibly given when God was consulted on behalf of His people. Hence God is described as "dwelling" or "sitting" between the cherubim. **23. table of shittim wood**—of the same material and decorations as the ark, and like it, too, furnished with rings for the poles on which it was carried. The staves, however, were taken out of it when stationary, in order not to encumber the priests while engaged in their services at the table. It was half a cubit less than the ark in length and breadth, but of the same height. **24. crown**—the moulding or ornamental rim, which is thought to have been raised above the level of the table, to prevent anything from falling off. **29. dishes**—broad platters. **spoons**—cups or concave vessels, used for holding incense. **covers**—both for bread and incense. **bowls**—cups; for though no mention is made of wine, libations were undoubtedly made to God, according to JOSEPHUS and the rabbins, once a week, when the bread was changed. **to cover withal**—rather to pour out withal. **30. showbread** lit., *presence bread*, so called because it was constantly exhibited before the Lord, or because the bread of His presence, like the angel of His presence, pointed symbolically to Christ. It consisted of twelve unleavened loaves, said traditionally to have been laid in piles of six each. This bread was designed to be a symbol of the full and never-failing provision which is made in the Church for the spiritual sustenance and refreshment of God's people. **31. candlestick**—lit., a lamp-bearer. It was so constructed as to be capable of being taken to pieces for facility in removal. The shaft or stock rested on a pedestal. It had seven branches, shaped like reeds or canes—three on each side, with one in the center—and worked out into knobs, flowers, and bowls, placed alternately. The figure represented on the arch of Titus gives the best idea of this candlestick. **33. knops**—old spelling for knobs—bosses. **37. they shall light the lamps** . . .

that they may give light—The light was derived from pure olive oil, and probably kept continually burning (cf. ch. 30:7; Lev. 24:2). **38. tongs**—snuffers. **39. a talent of pure gold**—in weight equivalent to 125 lbs. troy. **40. look that thou make them after their pattern**—This caution, which is repeated with no small frequency in other parts of the narrative, is an evidence of the deep interest taken by the Divine King in the erection of His palace or sanctuary; and it is impossible to account for the circumstance of God's condescending to such minute details, except on the assumption that this tabernacle was to be of a typical character, and eminently subservient to the religious instruction and benefit of mankind, by shadowing forth in its leading features the grand truths of the Christian Church.

CHAPTER 26

Vss. 1-37. TEN CURTAINS. **1. cunning work**—i.e., of elegant texture, richly embroidered. The word "cunning," in old English, is synonymous with skilful. **2. length**—Each curtain was to be fifteen yards in length and a little exceeding two in breadth. **3. The five curtains shall be coupled together one to another**, etc.—so as to form two grand divisions, each eleven yards wide. **6. taches**—clasps; supposed in shape, as well as in use, to be the same as hooks and eyes. **7-13. curtains of goats' hair**—These coarse curtains were to be one more in number than the others, and to extend a yard lower on each side, the use of them being to protect and conceal the richer curtains. **14. a covering . . . of rams' skins dyed red**—i. e., of Turkey red leather. **15-30. thou shalt make boards . . . rear up the tabernacle according to the fashion . . . which was showed thee**—The tabernacle, from its name as well as from its general appearance and arrangements, was a tent; but from the description given in these verses, the boards that formed its walls, the five (cross) bars that strengthened them, and the middle bar that "reached from end to end," and gave it solidity and compactness, it was evidently a more substantial fabric than a light and fragile tent, probably on account of the weight of its various coverings as well as for the protection of its precious furniture. **36. an hanging for the door of the tent**—Curtains of rich and elaborate embroidery, made by the women, are suspended over the doors or entrances of the tents occupied by Eastern chiefs and princes. In a similar style of elegance was the hanging finished which was to cover the door of this tabernacle —the chosen habitation of the God and King of Israel. It appears from verses 12, 22, 23, that the ark and mercy seat were placed in the west end of the tabernacle, and consequently the door or entrance fronted the east, so that the Israelites in worshipping Jehovah, turned their faces towards the west, that they might be thus figuratively taught to turn from the worship of that luminary which was the great idol of the nations, and to adore the God who made it and them [HEWLETT].

CHAPTER 27

Vss. 1-21. ALTAR FOR BURNT OFFERING. **1. altar of shittim wood**—The dimensions of this altar which was placed at the entrance of the sanctuary were nearly three yards square, and a yard and a half in height. Under the wooden frame of this chest-like altar the inside was hollow, and each corner was to be terminated by "horns"—angular projections, perpendicular or oblique, in the form of horns. The animals to be sacrificed were bound to these (Ps. 118:27), and part of the blood was applied to them. **3. shovels**—fire shovels for scraping together any of the scattered ashes. **basons**—for receiving the blood of the sacrifice to be sprinkled on the people. **fleshhooks**—curved, three-pronged forks (I Sam. 2: 13, 14). **fire-pans**—A large sort of vessel, wherein the sacred fire which came down from heaven (Lev. 9:24) was kept burning, while they cleaned the altar and the grate from the coals and ashes, and while the altar was carried from one place to another in the wilderness [PATRICK, SPENCER, LE CLERC]. **4. a grate of network of brass**—sunk latticework to support the fire. **5. put it under the compass of the altar beneath**—i.e., the grating in which they were carried to a clean place (Lev. 4: 12). **4. four brazen rings**—by which the grating might be lifted and taken away as occasion required from the body of the altar. **6, 7. staves . . . rings**—Those rings were placed at the side through which the poles were inserted on occasions of removal. **9. the court of the tabernacle**—The enclosure in which the edifice stood was a rectangular court, extending rather more than fifty yards in length and half that space in breadth, and the enclosing parapet was about three yards or half the height of the tabernacle. That parapet consisted of a connected series of curtains, made of fine twined linen yarn, woven into a kind of network, so that the people could see through; but that large curtain which overhung the entrance was of a different texture, being embroidered and dyed with variegated colors, and it was furnished with cords for pulling it up or drawing it aside when the priests had occasion to enter. The curtains of this enclosure were supported on sixty brazen pillars which stood on pedestals of the same metal, but their capitals and fillets were of silver, and the hooks on which they were suspended were of silver also. **19. pins**—were designed to hold down the curtains at the bottom, lest the wind should waft them aside. **20, 21. pure oil olive beaten**—i.e., such as runs from the olives when bruised and without the application of fire. **for the light . . . Aaron and his sons**—were to take charge of lighting it in all time coming. **shall order it from evening to morning**—The tabernacle having no windows, the lamps required to be lighted during the day. JOSEPHUS says that in his time only three were lighted; but his were degenerate times, and there is no Scripture authority for this limitation. But although the priests were obliged from necessity to light them by day, they might have let them go out at night had it not been for this express ordinance.

CHAPTER 28

Vss. 1-43. APPOINTMENT TO THE PRIESTHOOD. **1. take thou unto thee Aaron thy brother, and his sons with him**—Moses had hitherto discharged the priestly functions (Ps. 99:6), and he evinced the piety as well as humility of his character, in readily complying with the command to invest his brother with the sacred office, though it involved the perpetual exclusion of his own family. The appointment was a special act of God's sovereignty, so that there could be no ground for popular umbrage by the selection of Aaron's family, with whom the office was inalienably established and continued in unbroken succession till the introduction of the Christian era.

2-5. holy garments—No inherent holiness belonged either to the material or the workmanship. But they are called "holy" simply because they were not worn on ordinary occasions, but assumed in the discharge of the sacred functions (Ezek. 44:19). **for glory and for beauty**—It was a grand and sumptuous attire. In material, elaborate embroidery, and color, it had an imposing splendor. The tabernacle being adapted to the infantine aid of the church, it was right and necessary that the priests' garments should be of such superb and dazzling appearance, that the people might be inspired with a due respect for the ministers as well as the rites of religion. But they had also a further meaning; for being all made of linen, they were symbolical of the truth, purity, and other qualities in Christ that rendered Him such a high priest as became us. **6-14. ephod**—It was a very gorgeous robe made of byssus, curiously embroidered, and dyed with variegated colors, and further enriched with golden tissue, the threads of gold being either originally interwoven or afterwards inserted by the embroiderer. It was short—reaching from the breast to a little below the loins—and though destitute of sleeves, retained its position by the support of straps thrown over each shoulder. These straps or braces, connecting the one with the back, the other with the front piece of which the tunic was composed, were united on the shoulder by two onyx stones, serving as buttons, and on which the names of the twelve tribes were engraved, and set in golden encasements. The symbolical design of this was, that the high priest, who bore the names along with him in all his ministrations before the Lord, might be kept in remembrance of his duty to plead their cause, and supplicate the accomplishment of the divine promises in their favor. The ephod was fastened by a girdle of the same costly materials, i.e., dyed, embroidered, and wrought with threads of gold. It was about a handbreadth wide and wound twice round the upper part of the waist; it fastened in front, the ends hanging down at great length (Rev. 1:13). **15-29. thou shalt make the breastplate of judgment with cunning work**— a very splendid and richly embroidered piece of brocade, a span square, and doubled, to enable it the better to bear the weight of the precious stones in it. There were twelve different stones, containing each the name of a tribe, and arranged in four rows, three in each. The Israelites had acquired a knowledge of the lapidary's art in Egypt, and the amount of their skill in cutting, polishing, and setting precious stones, may be judged of by the diamond forming one of the engraved ornaments on this breastplate. A ring was attached to each corner, through which the golden chains were passed to fasten this brilliant piece of jewelry at the top and bottom tightly on the breast of the ephod. **30. thou shalt put in the breastplate of judgment the Urim and Thummim**—The words signify "lights" and "perfections"; and nothing more is meant than the precious stones of the breastplate already described (cf. ch. 39:8-21; Lev. 8:8). They received the name because the bearing of them qualified the high priest to consult the divine oracle on all public or national emergencies, by going into the holy place—standing close before the veil and putting his hand upon the Urim and Thummim, he conveyed a petition from the people and asked counsel of God, who, as the Sovereign of Israel, gave response from the midst of His glory. Little, however, is known about them. But it may be remarked that Egyptian judges wore on the breast of their official robes a representation of Justice, and the high priest in Israel long officiated also as a judge; so that some think the Urim and Thummim had a reference to his judicial functions. **31. the robe of the ephod all of blue**—It was the middle garment, under the ephod and above the coat. It had a hole through which the head was thrust, and was formed carefully of one piece, such as was the robe of Christ (John 19: 23). The high priest's was of a sky-blue color. The binding at the neck was strongly woven, and it terminated below in a fringe, made of blue, purple, and scarlet tassels, in the form of a pomegranate, interspersed with small bells of gold, which tinkled as the wearer was in motion. **34. a golden bell and a pomegranate**—The bells were hung between the pomegranates, which are said to have amounted to seventy-two, and the use of them seems to have been to announce to the people when the high priest entered the most holy place, that they might accompany him with their prayers, and also to remind himself to be attired in his official dress, to minister without which was death. **36-38. mitre**—crown-like cap for the head, not covering the entire head, but adhering closely to it, composed of fine linen. The Scripture has not described its form, but from JOSEPHUS we may gather that it was conical in shape, as he distinguishes the mitres of the common priests by saying that they were *not* conical—that it was encircled with swathes of blue embroidered, and that it was covered by one piece of fine linen to hide the seams. **plate**—lit., a petal of a flower, which seems to have been the figure of this golden plate, which was tied with a ribbon of blue on the front of the mitre, so that every one facing him could read the inscription. **39. coat of fine linen**—a garment fastened at the neck, and reaching far down the person, with the sleeves terminating at the elbow. **girdle of needlework**—a piece of fine twined linen, richly embroidered, and variously dyed. It is said to have been very long, and being many times wound round the body, it was fastened in front and the ends hung down, which, being an impediment to a priest in active duty, were usually thrown across the shoulders. This was the outer garment of the common priests. **40. bonnets**—turbans. **42. linen breeches**—drawers, which encompassed the loins and reached halfway down the thighs. They are seen very frequently represented in Egyptian figures.

CHAPTER 29

Vss. 1-35. CONSECRATING THE PRIESTS AND THE ALTAR.—**1. hallow them, to minister unto me in the priest's office**—The act of inaugurating the priests was accompanied by ceremonial solemnities well calculated not only to lead the people to entertain exalted views of the office, but to impress those functionaries themselves with a profound sense of its magnitude and importance. In short, they were taught to know that the service was for them as well as for the people; and every time they engaged in a new performance of their duties, they were reminded of their personal interest in the worship, by being obliged to offer for themselves, before they were qualified to offer as the representatives of the people. **this is the thing that thou shalt do**—Steps are taken at the beginning of a society, which would not be repeated when the social machine was in full motion; and Moses, at the opening of the tabernacle, was employed to discharge functions which in later periods would have been regarded as sacrilege

and punished with instant death. But he acted under the special directions of God. **4-10. Aaron and his sons thou shalt bring unto the door of the tabernacle**—as occupying the intermediate space between the court where the people stood, and the dwelling-place of Israel's king, and therefore the fittest spot for the priests being duly prepared for entrance, and the people witnessing the ceremony of inauguration. **wash them with water. And ... take the garments**—The manner in which these parts of the ceremonial were performed is minutely described, and in discovering their symbolical import, which indeed, is sufficiently plain and obvious, we have inspired authority to guide us. It signified the necessity and importance of moral purity or holiness (Isa. 52:11; John 13:10; II Cor. 7:1; I Pet. 3:21). In like manner, the investiture with the holy garments signified their being clothed with righteousness (Rev. 19:8) and equipped as men active and well prepared for the service of God; the anointing the high priest with oil denoted that he was to be filled with the influences of the Spirit, for the edification and delight of the church (Lev. 10:7; Ps. 45:7; Isa. 61:1; I John 2:27), and as he was officially a type of Christ (Heb. 7:26; John 3:34; also Matt. 3:16; 11:29). **Thou shalt cause a bullock to be brought before the tabernacle**—This part of the ceremonial consisted of three sacrifices: (1) The sacrifice of a bullock, as a sin offering; and in rendering it, the priest was directed to put his hand upon the head of his sacrifice, expressing by that act a consciousness of personal guilt, and a wish that it might be accepted as a vicarious satisfaction. (2) The sacrifice of a ram as a burnt offering—(vss. 15-18)—The ram was to be wholly burnt, in token of the priest's dedication of himself to God and His service. The sin offering was first to be presented, and *then* the burnt offering; for until guilt be removed, no acceptable service can be performed. (3) There was to be a peace offering, called the ram of consecration (vss. 19-22). And there was a marked peculiarity in the manner in which this other ram was to be disposed of. The former was for the glory of God—this was for the comfort of the priest himself; and as a sign of a mutual covenant being ratified, the blood of the sacrifice was divided—part sprinkled on the altar round about, and part upon the persons and garments of the priests. Nay, the blood was, by a singular act, directed to be put upon the extremities of the body, thereby signifying that the benefits of the atonement would be applied to the whole nature of man. Moreover, the flesh of this sacrifice was to be divided, as it were, between God and the priest—part of it to be put into his hand to be waved up and down, in token of its being offered to God, and then it was to be burnt upon the altar; the other part was to be eaten by the priests at the door of the tabernacle—that feast being a symbol of communion or fellowship with God. These ceremonies, performed in the order described, showed the qualifications necessary for the priests. (See Heb. 7:26, 27; 10:14). **35. seven days shalt thou consecrate them**—The renewal of these ceremonies on the return of every day in the seven, with the intervention of a Sabbath, was a wise preparatory arrangement, in order to afford a sufficient interval for calm and devout reflection (Heb. 9:1; 10:1).

36, 37. CONSECRATION OF THE ALTAR. **36. thou shalt cleanse the altar**—The phrase, "when thou hast made an atonement for it," should be, *upon* it; and the purport of the direction is, that during all the time they were engaged as above from day to day in offering the appointed sacrifices, the greatest care was to be taken to keep the altar properly cleansed —to remove the ashes, and sprinkle it with the prescribed unction that, at the conclusion of the whole ceremonial, the altar itself should be consecrated as much as the ministers who were to officiate at it (Matt. 23:19). It was thenceforth associated with the services of religion.

38–46. INSTITUTION OF DAILY SERVICE. 38. two lambs of the first year day by day continually—The sacred preliminaries being completed, Moses was instructed in the end or design to which these preparations were subservient, viz., the worship of God; and hence the institution of the morning and evening sacrifice. The institution was so imperative, that in no circumstances was this daily oblation to be dispensed with; and the due observance of it would secure the oft-promised grace and blessing of their heavenly King.

CHAPTER 30

VSS. 1-38. THE ALTAR OF INCENSE. **1. thou shalt make an altar to burn incense upon**, etc.—Its material was to be like that of the ark of the testimony, but its dimensions very small. **2. foursquare**—the meaning of which is not that it was to be entirely of a cubical form, but that upon its upper and under surface, it showed four equal sides. It was twice as high as it was broad, being twenty-one inches broad and three feet six inches high. It had "horns"; its top or flat surface was surmounted by an ornamental ledge or rim, called a crown, and it was furnished at the sides with rings for carriage. Its only accompanying piece of furniture was a golden censer or pan, in which the incense was set fire to upon the altar. Hence it was called the altar of incense, or the "golden altar," from the profuse degree in which it was gilded or overlaid with the precious metal. This splendor was adapted to the early age of the church, but in later times, when the worship was to be more spiritual, the altar of incense is prophetically described as not of gold but of wood, and double the size of that in the tabernacle, because the church should be vastly extended (Mal. 1:11). **6. thou shalt put it before the veil that is by the ark of the testimony**—which separated the holy from the most holy place. The altar was in the middle between the table of showbread and the candlestick next the holy of holies, at equal distances from the north and south walls; in other words, it occupied a spot on the outside of the great partition veil, but directly in front of the mercy seat, which was within that sacred enclosure; so that although the priest who ministered at this altar could not behold the mercy seat, he was to look towards it, and present his incense in that direction. This was a special arrangement, and it was designed to teach the important lesson that, though we cannot with the eye of sense, see the throne of grace, we must "direct our prayer to it and look up" (cf. II Cor. 3:14; Heb. 10:20; Rev. 4:1). **7. Aaron shall burn thereon sweet incense**—lit., incense of spices— Strong aromatic substances were burnt upon this altar to counteract by their odoriferous fragrance the offensive fumes of the sacrifices; or the incense was employed in an offering of tributary homage which the Orientals used to make as a mark of honor to kings; and as God was Theocratic Ruler of Israel, *His* palace was not to be wanting in a usage of such significance. Both these ends were served by this altar—that of fumigating the apartments of

the sacred edifice, while the pure lambent flame, according to Oriental notions, was an honorary tribute to the majesty of Israel's King. But there was a far higher meaning in it still; for as the tabernacle was not only a palace for Israel's King, but a place of worship for Israel's God, this altar was immediately connected with a religious purpose. In the style of the sacred writers, incense was a symbol or emblem of prayer (Ps. 141:2; Rev. 5:8; 8:3). From the uniform combination of the two services, it is evident that the incense was an emblem of the prayers of sincere worshippers ascending to heaven in the cloud of perfume; and, accordingly, the priest who officiated at this altar typified the intercessory office of Christ (Luke 1:10; Heb. 7:25). **8. Aaron shall burn incense**—seemingly limiting the privilege of officiating at the altar of incense to the high priest alone, and there is no doubt that he and his successors exclusively attended this altar on the great religious festivals. But "Aaron" is frequently used for the whole priestly order, and in later times, any of the priests might have officiated at this altar in rotation (Luke 1:9). **every morning ... at even**— In every period of the national history this daily worship was scrupulously observed. **9. Ye shall offer no strange incense**—i.e., of a different composition from that of which the ingredients are described so minutely. **11-16. When thou takest the sum of the children of Israel,** etc.—Moses did so twice, and doubtless observed the law here prescribed. The tax was not levied from women, minors, old men (Num. 1:42, 45), and the Levites (Num. 1:47), they being not numbered. Assuming the shekel of the sanctuary to be about half an ounce troy, though nothing certain is known about it, the sum payable by each individual was fifty cents. This was not a voluntary contribution, but a ransom for the soul or lives of the people. It was required from all classes alike, and a refusal to pay implied a wilful exclusion from the privileges of the sanctuary, as well as exposure to divine judgments. It was probably the same impost that was exacted from our Lord (Matt. 17:24-27), and it was usually devoted to repairs and other purposes connected with the services of the sanctuary. **18-21. Thou shalt ... make a laver of brass**—Though not actually forming a component part of the furniture of the tabernacle, this vase was closely connected with it; and though from standing at the entrance it would be a familiar object, it possessed great interest and importance from the baptismal purposes to which it was applied. No data are given by which its form and size can be ascertained; but it was probably a miniature pattern of Solomon's—a circular basin. **his foot**—supposed not to be the pedestal on which it rested, but a trough or shallow receptacle below, into which the water, let out from a cock or spout, flowed; for the way in which all Eastern people wash their hands or feet is by pouring upon them the water which falls into a basin. This laver was provided for the priests alone. But in the Christian dispensation, all believers are priests, and hence the apostle exhorts them how to draw near to God (Josh. 13:10; Heb. 10:22). **22-33. Take thou also ... principal spices,** etc.—Oil is frequently mentioned in Scripture as an emblem of sanctification, and anointing with it a means of designating objects as well as persons to the service of God. Here it is prescribed by divine authority, and the various ingredients in their several proportions described which were to compose the oil used in consecrating the furniture of the tabernacle. **myrrh**—a fragrant and medicinal gum from a little known tree in Arabia. **sweet cinnamon**—produced from a species of laurel or sweet bay, found chiefly in Ceylon, growing to a height of twenty feet: this spice is extracted from the inner bark, but it is not certain whether that mentioned by Moses is the same as that with which we are familiar. **sweet calamus**—or sweet cane, a product of Arabia and India, of a tawny color in appearance; it is like the common cane and strongly odoriferous. **cassia** —from the same species of tree as the cinnamon— some think the outer bark of that tree. All these together would amount to 120 lbs. troy weight. **hin** —a word of Egyptian origin, equal to ten pints. Being mixed with the olive oil—no doubt of the purest kind—this composition probably remained always in a liquid state, and the strictest prohibition issued against using it for any other purpose than anointing the tabernacle and its furniture. **34-38. the Lord said unto Moses, Take unto thee sweet spices**—These were: stacte, the finest myrrh; onycha, supposed to be an odoriferous shell; galbanum, a gumresin from an umbelliferous plant. **frankincense**—a dry, resinous, aromatic gum, of a yellow color, which comes from a tree in Arabia, and is obtained by incision of the bark. This incense was placed within the sanctuary, to be at hand when the priest required to burn on the altar. The art of compounding unguents and perfumes was well known in Egypt, where sweet-scented spices were extensively used not only in common life, but in the ritual of the temples. Most of the ingredients here mentioned have been found on minute examination of mummies and other Egyptian relics; and the Israelites, therefore, would have the best opportunities of acquiring in that country the skill in pounding and mixing them which they were called to exercise in the service of the tabernacle. But the recipe for the incense as well as for the oil in the tabernacle, though it receives illustration from the customs of Egypt, was peculiar, and being prescribed by divine authority, was to be applied to no common or inferior purpose.

CHAPTER 31

Vss. 1-18. BEZALEEL AND AHOLIAB. **2. See, I have called**—Though the instructions about the tabernacle were privately communicated to Moses, it was plainly impossible that he could superintend the work in person, amid the multiplicity of his other duties. A head director or builder was selected by God Himself; and the nomination by such high authority removed all ground of jealousy or discontent on the part of any who might have thought their merits overlooked (cf. Matt. 18:1). **by name Bezaleel**—signifying "in the shadow or protection of God"; and, as called to discharge a duty of great magnitude—to execute a confidential trust in the ancient Church of God, he has his family and lineage recorded with marked distinction. He belonged to the tribe of Judah, which, doubtless for wise and weighty reasons, God all along delighted to honor; and he was the grandson of Hur, a pious patriot (ch. 17:12), who was associated, by a special commission, with Aaron in the government of the people during the absence of Moses. Moreover, it may be noticed that a Jewish tradition affirms Hur to be the husband of Miriam; and if this tradition may be relied on, it affords an additional reason for the appointment of Bezaleel emanating from the direct authority of God. **3-5. I have filled him with the spirit of God**—It is probable that he was nat-

urally endowed with a mechanical genius, and had acquired in Egypt great knowledge and skill in the useful, as well as liberal, arts so as to be a first-class artisan, competent to take charge of both the plain and ornamental work, which the building of the sacred edifice required. When God has any special work to be accomplished, He always raises up instruments capable of doing it; and it is likely that He had given to the son of Uri that strong natural aptitude and those opportunities of gaining mechanical skill, with an ultimate view to this responsible office. Notwithstanding that his grand duty was to conform with scrupulous fidelity to the pattern furnished, there was still plenty of room for inventive talent and tasteful exactness in the execution; and his natural and acquired gifts were enlarged and invigorated for the important work. **6. I have given with him Aholiab**—He belonged to the tribe of Dan, one of the least influential and honorable in Israel; and here, too, we can trace the evidence of wise and paternal design, in choosing the colleague or assistant of Bezaleel from an inferior tribe (cf. I Cor. 12:14-25; also Mark 6:7). **all that are wisehearted I have put wisdom**—At that period, when one spirit pervaded all Israel, it was not the man full of heavenly genius who presided over the work; but all who contributed their skill, experience, and labor, in rendering the smallest assistance, showed their piety and devotedness to the divine service. In like manner, it was at the commencement of the Christian Church (Acts 6:5; 18:2). **12-17. Verily my sabbaths ye shall keep**—The reason for the fresh inculcation of the fourth commandment at this particular period was, that the great ardor and eagerness, with which all classes betook themselves to the construction of the tabernacle, exposed them to the temptation of encroaching on the sanctity of the appointed day of rest. They might suppose that the erection of the tabernacle was a sacred work, and that it would be a high merit, an acceptable tribute, to prosecute the undertaking without the interruption of a day's repose; and therefore the caution here given, at the commencement of the undertaking, was a seasonable admonition. **18. tables of stone, written with the finger of God**— containing the ten commandments (ch. 24:12), called "tables of testimony," because God testified His will in them.

CHAPTER 32

Vss. 1-35. THE GOLDEN CALF. **1. when the people saw that Moses delayed**—They supposed that he had lost his way in the darkness or perished in the fire. **the people gathered themselves together unto Aaron**—rather "against" Aaron in a tumultuous manner, to compel him to do what they wished. The incidents related in this chapter disclose a state of popular sentiment and feeling among the Israelites that stands in singular contrast to the tone of profound and humble reverence they displayed at the giving of the law. Within a space of little more than thirty days, their impressions were dissipated. Although they were still encamped upon ground which they had every reason to regard as holy; although the cloud of glory that capped the summit of Sinai was still before their eyes, affording a visible demonstration of their being in close contact, or rather in the immediate presence, of God, they acted as if they had entirely forgotten the impressive scenes of which they had been so recently the witnesses. **said unto him, Up, make** us gods; which shall go before us—The *Hebrew* word rendered "gods" is simply the name of God in its plural form. The image made was single, and therefore it would be imputing to the Israelites a greater sin than they were guilty of, to charge them with renouncing the worship of the true God for idols. The fact is, that they required, like children, to have something to strike their senses, and as the Shekinah, "the glory of God," of which they had hitherto enjoyed the sight, was now veiled, they wished for some visible material object as the symbol of the divine presence, which should go before them as the pillar of fire had done. **2. Aaron said, ... Break off ... earrings**—It was not an Egyptian custom for young men to wear earrings, and the circumstance, therefore, seems to point out "the mixed rabble," who were chiefly *foreign* slaves, as the ringleaders in this insurrection. In giving direction to break their earrings, Aaron probably calculated on gaining time; or, perhaps, on their covetousness and love of finery proving stronger than their idolatrous propensity. If such were his expectations, they were doomed to signal disappointment. Better to have calmly and earnestly remonstrated with them, or to have preferred duty to expediency, leaving the issue in the hands of Providence. **3. all the people brake off the golden earrings**—The Egyptian rings, as seen on the monuments, were round massy plates of metal; and as they were rings of this sort the Israelites wore, their size and number must, in the general collection, have produced a large store of the precious metal. **4. fashioned it with a graving tool, after he had made it a molten calf**—The words are transposed, and the rendering should be, "he framed with a graving tool the image to be made, and having poured the liquid gold into the mould, he made it a molten calf." It is not said whether it was of life size, whether it was of solid gold or merely a wooden frame covered with plates of gold. This idol seems to have been the god Apis, the chief deity of the Egyptians, worshipped at Memphis under the form of a live ox, three years old. It was distinguished by a triangular white spot on its forehead and other peculiar marks. Images of it in the form of a whole ox, or of a calf's head on the end of a pole, were very common; and it makes a great figure on the monuments where it is represented in the van of all processions, as borne aloft on men's shoulders. **they said, These be thy gods, O Israel, which brought thee up out of the land of Egypt**—It is inconceivable that they, who but a few weeks before had witnessed such amazing demonstrations of the true God, could have suddenly sunk to such a pitch of infatuation and brutish stupidity, as to imagine that human art or hands could make a god that should go before them. But it must be borne in mind, that though by election and in name they were the people of God, they were as yet, in feelings and associations, in habits and tastes, little, if at all different, from Egyptians. They meant the calf to be an image, a visible sign or symbol of Jehovah, so that their sin consisted not in a breach of the FIRST, but of the SECOND commandment. **5, 6. Aaron made proclamation, and said, To-morrow is a feast to the Lord**—a remarkable circumstance, strongly confirmatory of the view that they had not renounced the worship of Jehovah, but in accordance with Egyptian notions, had formed an image with which they had been familiar, to be the visible symbol of the divine presence. But there seems to have been much of the revelry that marked the feasts of the heathen.

7-14. the Lord said unto Moses, Go, get thee down—Intelligence of the idolatrous scene enacted at the foot of the mount was communicated to Moses in language borrowed from human passions and feelings, and the judgment of a justly offended God was pronounced in terms of just indignation against the gross violation of the so recently promulgated laws. **make of thee a great nation**—Care must be taken not to suppose this language as betokening any change or vacillation in the divine purpose. The covenant made with the patriarchs had been ratified in the most solemn manner; it *could* not and never was intended that it *should* be broken. But the manner in which God spoke to Moses served two important purposes—it tended to develop the faith and intercessory patriotism of the Hebrew leader, and to excite the serious alarm of the people, that God would reject them and deprive them of the privileges they had fondly fancied were so secure. **15-18. Moses turned, and went down from the mount**—The plain, Er-Raheh, is not visible from the top of Jebel Musa, nor can the mount be descended on the side towards that valley; hence Moses and his companion, who on duty had patiently waited his return in the hollow of the mountain's brow, heard the shouting some time before they actually saw the camp. **19. Moses' anger waxed hot, and he cast the tables out of his hands**—The arrival of the leader, like the appearance of a specter, arrested the revellers in the midst of their carnival, and his act of righteous indignation when he dashed on the ground the tables of the law, in token that as they had so soon departed from their covenant relation, so God could withdraw the peculiar privileges that He had promised them—that act, together with the rigorous measures that followed, forms one of the most striking scenes recorded in sacred history. **20. he took the calf which they had made, and burnt it in the fire,** etc.—It has been supposed that the gold was dissolved by *natron* or some chemical substance. But there is no mention of solubility here, or in Deuteronomy 9:21; it was "burned in the fire," to cast it into ingots of suitable size for the operations which follow—"grounded to powder"; the powder of malleable metals can be ground so fine as to resemble dust from the wings of a moth or butterfly; and these dust particles will float in water for hours, and in a running stream for days. These operations of grinding were intended to show contempt for such worthless gods, and the Israelites would be made to remember the humiliating lesson by the state of the water they had drunk for a time [NAPIER]. Others think that as the idolatrous festivals were usually ended with great use of sweet wine, the nauseous draught of the gold dust would be a severe punishment (ch. II Kings 23:6, 15; II Chron. 15:16; 34:7). **22. Aaron said, Let not the anger of my lord wax hot**—Aaron cuts a poor figure, making a shuffling excuse and betraying more dread of the anger of Moses than of the Lord (cf. Deut. 9:20). **25. naked**—either unarmed and defenseless, or ashamed from a sense of guilt. Some think they were literally naked, as the Egyptians performed some of their rites in that indecent manner. **26-28. Moses stood in the gate of the camp, and said**—The camp is supposed to have been protected by a rampart after the attack of the Amalekites. **Who is on the Lord's side? let him come unto me**—The zeal and courage of Moses was astonishing, considering he opposed an intoxicated mob. The people were separated into two divisions, and those who were the boldest and most obstinate in vindicating their idolatry were put to death, while the rest, who withdrew in shame or sorrow, were spared. **29. Consecrate yourselves to-day to the Lord**—or, ye have consecrated yourselves to-day. The Levites, notwithstanding the dejection of Aaron, distinguished themselves by their zeal for the honor of God and their conduct in doing the office of executioners on this occasion; and this was one reason that they were appointed to a high and honorable office in the service of the sanctuary. **30-33. Moses said unto the people, Ye have sinned a great sin**—Moses labored to show the people the heinous nature of their sin, and to bring them to repentance. But not content with that, he hastened more earnestly to intercede for them. **32. blot me . . . out of thy book**—an allusion to the registering of the living, and erasing the names of those who die. What warmth of affection did he evince for his brethren! How fully was he animated with the true spirit of a patriot, when he professed his *willingness* to die for them. But Christ actually died for His people (Rom. 5:8). **35. the Lord plagued the people, because they made the calf**—No immediate judgments were inflicted, but this early lapse into idolatry was always mentioned as an aggravation of their subsequent apostasies.

CHAPTER 33

Vss. 1-23. THE LORD REFUSES TO GO WITH THE PEOPLE. **1. the Lord said**—rather "had" said unto Moses. The conference detailed in this chapter must be considered as having occurred prior to the pathetic intercession of Moses, recorded at the close of the preceding chapter; and the historian, having mentioned the fact of his earnest and painful anxiety, under the overhelming pressure of which he poured forth that intercessory prayer for his apostate countrymen, now enters on a detailed account of the circumstances. **3. I will not go up . . . lest I consume thee**—Here the Lord is represented as determined to do what He afterwards did not. (See on ch. 32:10). **4. when the people heard these evil tidings**— from Moses on his descent from the mount. **5. put off thy ornaments**—In seasons of mourning, it is customary with Eastern people to lay aside all gewgaws and divest themselves of their jewels, their gold, and every thing rich and splendid in their dress. This token of their sorrow the Lord required of His offending people. **that I may know what to do unto thee**—The language is accommodated to the feeble apprehensions of men. God judges the state of the heart by the tenor of the conduct. In the case of the Israelites, He cherished a design of mercy; and the moment He discerned the first symptoms of contrition, by their stripping off their ornaments, as penitents conscious of their error and sincerely sorrowful, this fact added its weight to the fervency of Moses' prayers, and gave them prevalence with God in behalf of the people. **7. Moses took the tabernacle, and pitched it without the camp**—Not the tabernacle, of which a pattern had been given him, for it was not yet erected, but his own tent—conspicuous as that of the leader—in a part of which he heard cases and communed with God about the people's interests; hence called "the tabernacle of the congregation," and the withdrawal of which, in abhorrence from a polluted camp, was regarded as the first step in the total abandonment with which God had threatened them. **8. all the people rose up, and stood every man at his tent door**—Its removal produced deep and universal consternation; and it is easy to conceive how anxiously all eyes would be directed towards it; how rapidly the happy intelligence would spread, when a phenomenon was witnessed from which an encouraging hope could be founded. **9-11. the cloudy pillar descended, and stood at the door of the tabernacle**—How would the downcast hearts of the people revive—how would the tide of joy swell in every bosom, when the symbolic cloud was seen slowly and majestically to descend and stand at the entrance of the tabernacle! **as Moses entered**—It was when he appeared as their mediator, when he repaired from day to day to intercede for them, that welcome token of assurance was given that his advocacy prevailed, that Israel's sin was forgiven, and that God would again be gracious. **18-23. I beseech thee, show me thy glory**—This is one of the most mysterious scenes described in the Bible: he had, for his comfort and encouragement, a splendid and full display of the divine majesty, not in its unveiled effulgence, but as far as the weakness of humanity would admit. The face, hand, back parts, are to be understood figuratively.

CHAPTER 34

Vss. 1-35. THE TABLES ARE RENEWED. **1. the like unto the first**—God having been reconciled to repentant Israel, through the earnest intercession, the successful mediation of Moses, means were to be taken for the restoration of the broken covenant. Intimation was given, however, in a most intelligible and expressive manner, that the favor was to be restored with some memento of the rupture; for at the former time God Himself had provided the materials, as well as written upon them. Now, Moses was to prepare the stone tables, and God was only to retrace the characters originally inscribed for the use and guidance of the people. **2. present thyself . . . to me in the top of the mount**—Not absolutely the highest peak; for as the cloud of the Shekinah usually abode on the summit, and yet (vs. 5) it "descended," the plain inference is that Moses was to station himself at a point not far distant, but still below the loftiest pinnacle. **3. no man shall come up with thee . . . neither . . . flocks nor herds**—All these enactments were made in order that the law might be a second time renewed with the solemnity and sanctity that marked its first delivery. The whole transaction was ordered so as to impress the people with an awful sense of the holiness of God; and that it was a matter of no trifling moment to have subjected Him, so to speak, to the necessity of re-delivering the law of the ten commandments. **4. Moses . . . took in his hand the two tables of stone**—As he had no attendant to divide the labor of carrying them, it is evident that they must have been light, and of no great dimensions—probably flat slabs of shale or slate, such as abound in the mountainous region of Horeb. An additional proof of their comparatively small size appears in the circumstance of their being deposited in the ark of the most holy place (ch. 25:10). **5. the Lord descended in the cloud**—After graciously hovering over the tabernacle, it seems to have resumed its usual position on the summit of the mount. It was the shadow of God manifest to the outward senses; and, at the same time, of God manifest in the flesh. The emblem of a cloud seems to have been chosen to signify that, although He was pleased to make known much about himself, there was more veiled from mortal view. It was to check presumption and engender awe and give a humble sense of human attainments in divine knowledge, as now man sees, but darkly. **6. the Lord passed by before him**—in this remarkable scene, God performed what He had promised to Moses the day before. **proclaimed, The Lord . . . merciful and gracious**—At an earlier period He had announced Himself to Moses, in the glory of His self-existent and eternal majesty, as "I am"; now He makes Himself known in the glory of His grace and goodness—attributes that were to be illustriously displayed in the future history and experience of the church. Being about to republish His law—the sin of the Israelites being forgiven and the deed of pardon about to be signed and sealed by renewing the terms of the former covenant—it was the most fitting time to proclaim the extent of the divine mercy which was to be displayed, not in the case of Israel only, but of all who offend. **8-26. Moses bowed . . . and worshipped**—In the East, people bow the head to royalty, and are silent when it passes by, while in the West, they take off their hats and shout. **9. he said, If now I have found grace in thy sight, O Lord, let my Lord, I pray thee, go among us**—On this proclamation, he, in the overflowing benevolence of his heart, founded an earnest petition for the Divine Presence being continued with the people; and God was pleased to give His favorable answer to his intercession by a renewal of His promise under the form of a covenant, repeating the leading points that formed the conditions of the former national compact. **27, 28. the Lord said unto Moses, Write thou these words**—i. e., the ceremonial and judicial injunctions comprehended above (vss. 11-26); while the rewriting of the ten commandments on the newly prepared slabs was done by God Himself (cf. Deut. 10:1-4). **he was there with the Lord forty days and forty nights**—as long as formerly, being sustained for the execution of his special duties by the miraculous power of God. A special cause is assigned for his protracted fast on this second occasion (Deut. 9:18). **29. Moses wist not that the skin of his face shone while he talked with him**—It was an intimation of the exalted presence into which he had been admitted and of the glory he had witnessed (II Cor. 3:18); and in that view, it was a badge of his high office as the ambassador of God. No testimonial needed to be produced. He bore his credentials on his very face; and whether this extraordinary effulgence was a permanent or merely temporary distinction, it cannot be doubted that this reflected glory was given him as an honor before all the people. **30. they were afraid to come nigh him**—Their fear arose from a sense of guilt— the beaming radiance of his countenance made him appear to their awe-struck consciences a flaming minister of heaven. **33. he put a veil upon his face**—That veil was with the greatest propriety removed when speaking with the Lord, for every one appears unveiled to the eye of Omniscience; but it was replaced on returning to the people—and this was emblematic of the dark and shadowy character of that dispensation (II Cor. 3:13, 14).

CHAPTER 35

Vss. 1-35. Contributions to the Tabernacle. **1. Moses gathered all the congregation of the children of Israel**, etc.—On the occasion referred to in the opening of this chapter, the Israelites were specially reminded of the design to erect a magnificent tabernacle for the regular worship of God, as well as of the leading articles that were required to furnish that sacred edifice. (See on chs. 25, 27, 30, 31). **20, 21. all the congregation of Israel departed**

from the presence of Moses—No exciting harangues were made, nor had the people Bibles at home in which they could compare the requirements of their leader and see if these things were so. But they had no doubt as to his bearing to them the will of God, and they were impressed with so strong a sense of its being their duty, that they made a spontaneous offer of the best and most valuable treasures they possessed. **they came, every one whose heart stirred him up**—One powerful element doubtless of this extraordinary open-hearted liberality was the remembrance of their recent transgression, which made them "zealous of good works" (cf. II Cor. 7: 11). But along with this motive, there were others of a higher and nobler kind—a principle of love to God and devotedness to His service, an anxious desire to secure the benefit of His presence, and gratitude for the tokens of His divine favor: it was under the combined influence of these considerations that the people were so willing and ready to pour their contributions into that exchequer of the sanctuary. **every one whom his spirit made willing** —Human nature is always the same, and it is implied that while an extraordinary spirit of pious liberality reigned in the bosoms of the people at large, there were exceptions—some who were too fond of the world, who loved their possessions more than their God, and who could not part with these; no, not for the service of the tabernacle. **22. they came, both men and women**, etc.—lit., "the men over and above the women"; a phraseology which implies that the women acted a prominent part, presented their offerings *first*, and then were followed by as many of their male companions as were similarly disposed. **brought bracelets**, etc.—There was in that early age no money in the form of coins or bullion. What money passed current with the merchant consisted of rings which were weighed, and principally of ornaments for personal decoration. Astonishment at the abundance of their ornaments is at an end when we learn that costly and elegant ornaments abounded in proportion as clothing was simple and scarce among the Egyptians, and some, entirely divested of clothing, yet wore rich necklaces [Hengstenberg]. Among people with Oriental sentiments and tastes, scarcely any stronger proof could have been given of the power of religion than their willingness not only to lay aside, but to devote those much-valued trinkets to the house of God; and thus all, like the Eastern sages, laid the best they had at the service of God. **30. See, the Lord hath called by name Bezaleel the son of Uri**, etc.—Moses had made this communication before. But now that the collection had been made, the materials were contributed, and the operations of building about to be commenced, it was with the greatest propriety he reminded the people that the individuals entrusted with the application of their gold and silver had been nominated to the work by authority to which all would bow. **35. Them hath he filled with wisdom of heart**—A statement which not only testifies that skill in art and science is a direct gift from God, but that weaving was especially the business of men in Egypt (see ch. 38:22; 39:22, 27). And in perfect harmony with the testimony of the monuments is the account given by Moses to the artists who were divinely taught the arts necessary for the embellishment of the tabernacle. Others, whose limited means did not admit of these expensive contributions, offered their gratuitous services in fabricating such articles of tapestry as were needed; arts which the Israelitish females learned as bondwomen, in the houses of Egyptian princes.

CHAPTER 36

Vss. 1-38. Offerings Delivered to the Workmen. **1. Then wrought Bezaleel and Aholiab, and Aholiab, and every wise-hearted man,** etc.—Here is an illustrious example of zeal and activity in the work of the Lord. No unnecessary delay was allowed to take place; and from the moment the first pole was stuck in the ground till the final completion of the sacred edifice, he and his associates labored with all the energies both of mind and body engaged in the work. And what was the mainspring of their arduous and untiring diligence? They could be actuated by none of the ordinary motives that give impulse to human industry, by no desire for the acquisition of gain; no ambition for honor; no view of gratifying a mere love of power in directing the labors of a large body of men. They felt the stimulus—the strong irresistible impulse of higher and holier motives—obedience to the authority, zeal for the glory, and love to the service of God. **3. they brought yet unto him free offerings every morning,** etc.—Moses, in common with other Oriental magistrates, had his morning levees for receiving the people (see on ch. 18:13); and it was while he was performing his magisterial duties that the people brought unto him freewill offerings every morning. Some who had nothing but their manual labor to give would spend a great part of the night in hastening to complete their self-imposed task before the early dawn; others might find their hearts constrained by silent meditations on their beds to open their coffers and give a part of their hoarded treasure to the pious object. All whose hearts were touched by piety, penitence, or gratitude, repaired with eager haste into the presence of Moses, not as heretofore, to have their controversies settled, but to lay on his tribunal their contributions to the sanctuary of God (II Cor. 9:7). **they** [the workmen] **received of Moses all the offering which the children of Israel had brought,** etc.—It appears that the building was begun after the first few contributions were made; it was progressively carried on, and no necessity occurred to suspend operations even for the shortest interval, from want of the requisite materials. **5. they spake unto Moses, saying, The people bring much more than enough,** etc. —By the calculations which the practised eyes of the workmen enabled them to make, they were unanimously of the opinion that the supply already far exceeded the demand and that no more contributions were required. Such a report reflects the highest honor on their character as men of the strictest honor and integrity, who, notwithstanding they had command of an untold amount of the most precious things and might, without any risk of human discovery, have appropriated much to their own use, were too high principled for such acts of peculation. Forthwith, a proclamation was issued to stop further contributions. **35. he made a veil of blue**—the second or inner veil, which separated the holy from the most holy place, embroidered with cherubim and of great size and thickness. **37. made an hanging for the . . . door**—Curtains of elaborately wrought needlework are often suspended over the entrance to tents of the great nomad sheiks, and throughout Persia, at the entrance of summer tents, mosques, and palaces. They are preferred as cooler and more elegant than wooden doors. This chapter contains an instructive narrative: it is the first instance of donations made for the worship of God, given from the wages of the people's sufferings and toils. They are accept-able to God (Phil. 4:18), and if the Israelites showed such liberality, how much more should those whose privilege it is to live under the Christian dispensation (I Cor. 6:20; 16:2).

CHAPTER 37

Vss. 1-29. Furniture of the Tabernacle. **1. Bezaleel made the ark**—The description here given of the things within the sacred edifice is almost word for word the same as that contained in chapter 25. It is not on that account to be regarded as a useless repetition of minute particulars; for by the enumeration of these details, it can be seen how exactly everything was fashioned according to the "pattern shown on the mount"; and the knowledge of this exact correspondence between the prescription and the execution was essential to the purposes of the fabric. **6-10. made the mercy seat of pure gold**—To construct a figure, whether the body of a beast or a man, with two extended wings, measuring from two to three feet from tip to tip, with the hammer, out of a solid piece of gold, was what few, if any, artisans of the present day could accomplish. **17-22. he made the candlestick of pure gold**—Practical readers will be apt to say, "Why do such works with the hammer, when they could have been cast so much easier—a process they were well acquainted with?" The only answer that can be given is, that it was done according to order. We have no doubt but there were reasons for so distinctive an order, something significant, which has not been revealed to us [Napier]. The whole of that sacred building was arranged with a view to inculcate through every part of its apparatus the great fundamental principles of revelation. Every object was symbolical of important truth—every piece of furniture was made the hieroglyphic of a doctrine or a duty—on the floor and along the sides of that movable edifice was exhibited, by emblematic signs addressed to the eye, the whole remedial scheme of the gospel. How far this spiritual instruction was received by every successive generation of the Israelites, it may not be easy to determine. But the tabernacle, like the law of which it was a part, was a schoolmaster to Christ. Just as the walls of schools are seen studded with pictorial figures, by which the children, in a manner level to their capacities and suited to arrest their volatile minds, are kept in constant and familiar remembrance of the lessons of piety and virtue, so the tabernacle was intended by its furniture and all its arrangements to serve as a "shadow of good things to come." In this view, the minute description given in this chapter respecting the ark and mercy seat, the table of showbread, the candlestick, the altar of incense, and the holy oil, were of the greatest utility and importance; and though there are a few things that are merely ornamental appendages, such as the knops and the flowers, yet, in introducing these into the tabernacle, God displayed the same wisdom and goodness as He has done by introducing real flowers into the kingdom of nature to engage and gratify the eye of man.

CHAPTER 38

Vss. 1-31. Furniture of the Tabernacle. **1. the altar of burnt offering**—The repetitions are continued, in which may be traced the exact conformity of the execution to the order. **8. laver of brass . . . of the looking glasses of the women**—The word *mirrors* should have been used, as those implements, usually round, inserted into a handle of wood, stone, or metal, were made of brass, silver, or bronze, highly polished [WILKINSON]. It was customary for the Egyptian women to carry mirrors with them to the temples; and whether by taking the looking glasses of the Hebrew women Moses designed to put it out of their power to follow a similar practice at the tabernacle, or whether the supply of brass from other sources in the camp was exhausted, it is interesting to learn how zealously and to a vast extent they surrendered those valued accompaniments of the female toilet. **of the women assembling . . . at the door**—not priestesses but women of pious character and influence, who frequented the courts of the sacred building (Luke 2: 37), and whose parting with their mirrors, like the cutting the hair of the Nazarites, was their renouncing the world for a season [HENGSTENBERG]. **9. the court**—It occupied a space of one hundred and fifty feet by seventy-five, and it was enclosed by curtains of fine linen about eight feet high, suspended on brazen or copper pillars. Those curtains were secured by rods fastened to the top, and kept extended by being fastened to pins stuck in the ground. **10. hooks**—The hooks of the pillars in the court were for hanging up the carcasses of the sacrificial beasts —those on the pillars at the entry of the tabernacle were for hanging the sacerdotal robes and other things used in the service. **11. sockets**—mortices or holes in which the end of the pillars stood. **17. chapiters**—or capitals of the pillars, were wooden posts which ran along their top, to which were attached the hooks for the hangings. **18. the height in the breadth**—or in the measure. The sense is that the hangings of the court gate, which was twenty cubits wide, were of the same height as the hangings all round the court [WALL]. **21. This is the sum of the tabernacle**—Having completed his description of the component parts of the tabernacle, the inspired historian digresses into a statement respecting the gold and silver employed in it, the computation being made according to an order of Moses—by the Levites, under the direction of Ithamar, Aaron's youngest son. **24. twenty and nine talents, and seven hundred and thirty shekels**—equivalent to approximately $450,000. **25. the silver of them that were numbered**—603,550 men at 50 cents each would contribute 301,775 dollars. It may seem difficult to imagine how the Israelites should be possessed of so much wealth in the desert; but it should be remembered that they were enriched first by the spoils of the Egyptians, and afterwards by those of the Amalekites. Besides, it is highly probable that during their sojourn they traded with the neighboring nations who bordered on the wilderness [HEWLETT].

CHAPTER 39

Vss. 1-43. GARMENTS OF THE PRIESTS. **1. cloths of service**—official robes. The ephod of the high priest, the robe of the ephod, the girdle of needlework, and the embroidered coat were all of fine linen; for on no material less delicate could such elaborate symbolical figures have been portrayed in embroidery, and all beautified with the same brilliant colors. (See on ch. 28). **3. cut the gold into wires to work it**—i.e., the metal was beaten with a hammer into thin plates—cut with scissors or some other instrument into long slips—then rounded into filaments or threads. "Cloth of golden tissue is not uncommon on the monuments, and specimens of it have been found rolled about mummies; but it

is not easy to determine whether the gold thread was originally interwoven or subsequently inserted by the embroiderer" [TAYLOR]. **30. a writing, like to the engravings of a signet**—The seal-ring worn both by ancient and modern Egyptians on the little finger of the right hand, contained, inscribed on a cornelian or other precious stone, along with the owner's name, a religious sentiment or sacred symbol, intimating that he was the servant of God, or expressive of trust in Him. And it was to this practice the inscription on the high priest alludes (cf. Exod. 28:11). **34. the covering of rams' skin dyed red**—(See ch. 25:7). It was probably red morocco leather and "badgers' skins," rather "the skins of the *tahash*, supposed to be the dugong, or dolphin of the Red Sea, the skin of which is still used by the Arabs under the same appellation" [Goss]. **43. Moses did look upon all the work, and, behold, they had done it as the Lord had commanded**—A formal inspection was made on the completion of the tabernacle, not only with a view to have the work transferred from the charge of the workmen, but to ascertain whether it corresponded with "the pattern." The result of a careful and minute survey showed that every plank, curtain, altar, and vase had been most accurately made of the form, and in the place designed by the Divine Architect—and Moses, in accepting it of their hands, thanked God for them, and begged Him to bless them.

CHAPTER 40

Vss. 1-38. THE TABERNACLE REARED AND A-NOINTED. **2. On the first day of the first month**—From a careful consideration of the incidents recorded to have happened after the exodus (ch. 12:2; 13:4; 19:1; 20:18; 34:28, etc.), it has been computed that the work of the tabernacle was commenced within six months after that emigration; and consequently, that other six months had been occupied in building it. So long a period spent in preparing the materials of a movable pavilion, it would be difficult to understand, were it not for what we are told of the vast dimensions of the tabernacle, as well as the immense variety of curious and elaborate workmanship which its different articles of furniture required. **the tabernacle**—the entire edifice. **the tent**—the covering that surmounted it (vs. 19). **15. anoint them, as thou didst anoint their fathers**—The sacred oil was used, but it does not appear that the ceremony was performed exactly in the same manner; for although the anointing oil was sprinkled over the garments both of Aaron and his sons (ch. 29:21; Lev. 8:30), it was not poured over the heads of the latter. This distinction was reserved for the high priest (ch. 29:7; Lev. 8:12; Ps. 133:2). **16. Thus did Moses: according to all that the Lord commanded him**—On his part, the same scrupulous fidelity was shown in conforming to the "pattern" in the disposition of the furniture, as had been displayed by the workmen in the erection of the edifice. **33. So Moses finished the work**—Though it is not expressly recorded in this passage, yet, from what took place on all similar occasions, there is reason to believe that on the inauguration day the people were summoned from their tents— were all drawn up as a vast assemblage, yet in calm and orderly arrangement, around the newly erected tabernacle. **34. a cloud**—lit., *"The"* cloud,—the mystic cloud which was the well-known symbol of the Divine Presence. After remaining at a great distance from them on the summit of the mount, it appeared to be in motion; and if many among them had a secret misgiving about the issue, how the fainting heart would revive, the interest of the moment intensely increase, and the tide of joy swell in every bosom, when that symbolic cloud was seen slowly and majestically descending towards the plain below and covering the tabernacle. The entire and universal concealment of the tabernacle within the folds of an impervious cloud was not without a deep and instructive meaning; it was a protection to the sacred edifice from the burning heats of the Arabian climate; it was a token of the Divine Presence; and it was also an emblem of the Mosaic dispensation, which, though it was a revelation from heaven, yet left many things hid in obscurity; for it was a dark cloud compared with the bright cloud, which betokened the clearer and fuller discoveries of the divine character and glory in the gospel (Matt. 17:5). **the glory of the Lord filled the tabernacle**—i. e., light and fire, a created splendor, which was the peculiar symbol of God (I John 1:5). Whether this light was inherent in the cloud or not, it emanated from it on this occasion, and making its entry, not with the speed of a lightning flash as if it were merely an electric spark, but in majestic splendor, it passed through the outer porch into the interior of the most holy place (I Kings 8:10; John 1:14). Its miraculous character is shown by the fact, that, though "it filled the tabernacle," not a curtain or any article of furniture was so much as singed. **35. Moses was not able to enter into the tent of the congregation**— How does this circumstance show the incapacity of man, in his present state, to look upon the unveiled perfections of the Godhead! Moses could not endure the unclouded effulgence, nor the sublimest of the prophets (Isa. 6:5). But what neither Moses nor the most eminent of God's messengers to the ancient church through the weakness of nature could endure, we can all now do by an exercise of faith; looking unto Jesus, who reflected with chastened radiance the brightness of the Father's glory; and who, having as the Forerunner for us, entered within the veil, has invited us to come boldly to the mercy seat. While Moses was compelled, through the influence of overwhelming awe, to stand aloof and could not enter the tabernacle, Christ entered into the holy place not made with hands; nay, He is Himself the true tabernacle, filled with the glory of God, ever with the grace and truth which the Shekinah typified. What great reason we have to thank God for Jesus Christ, who, while He Himself was the brightness of the Father's glory, yet exhibited that glory in so mild and attractive a manner, as to allure us to draw near with confidence and love into the Divine Presence! **36. when the cloud was taken**

up from over the tabernacle—In journeying through the sandy, trackless deserts of the East, the use of torches, exhibiting a cloud of smoke by day and of fire by night, has been resorted to from time immemorial. The armies of Darius and Alexander were conducted on their marches in this manner [FABER]. The Arab caravans in the present day observe the same custom; and materials for these torches are stored up among other necessary preparations for a journey. Live fuel, hoisted in chafing-dishes at the end of long poles, and being seen at a great distance, serves, by the smoke in the daytime and the light at night, as a better signal for march than the sound of a trumpet, which is not heard at the extremities of a large camp [LABORDE]. This usage, and the miracle related by Moses, mutually illustrate each other. The usage leads us to think that the miracle was necessary, and worthy of God to perform; and, on the other hand, the miracle of the cloudy pillar, affording double benefit of shade by day and light at night, implies not only that the usage was not unknown to the Hebrews, but supplied all the wants which they felt in common with other travellers through those dreary regions [FABER, HESS, GRANDPIERRE]. But its peculiar appearance, unvarying character, and regular movements, distinguished it from all the common atmospheric phenomena. It was an invaluable boon to the Israelites, and being recognized by all classes among that people as the symbol of the Divine Presence, it guided their journeys and regulated their encampments (cf. Ps. 29 and 105). **38. the cloud of the Lord was upon the tabernacle,** etc.— While it had hitherto appeared sometimes in one place, sometimes in another, it was now found on the tabernacle only; so that from the moment that sanctuary was erected, and the glory of the Lord had filled the sacred edifice, the Israelites had to look to the place which God had chosen to put His name there, in order that they might enjoy the benefit of a heavenly Guide (Num. 9:15-23). In like manner, the church had divine revelation for its guide from the first—long before the WORD of God existed in a written form; but ever since the setting up of that sacred canon, it rests on that as its tabernacle and there only is it to be found. It accompanies us wherever we are or go, just as the cloud led the way of the Israelites. It is always accessible and can be carried in our pockets when we walk abroad; it may be engraven on the inner tablets of our memories and our hearts; and so true, faithful, and complete a guide is it, that there is not a scene of duty or of trial through which we may be called to pass in the world, but it furnishes a clear, a safe, and unerring direction (Col. 3:16).

THE THIRD BOOK OF MOSES CALLED

LEVITICUS

CHAPTER I

Vss. 1-17. BURNT OFFERINGS OF THE HERD. **1. the Lord . . . spake . . . out of the tabernacle**—The laws that are contained in the previous record were delivered either to the people publicly from Sinai,

or to Moses privately, on the summit of that mountain; but on the completion of the tabernacle, the remainder of the law was announced to the Hebrew leader by an audible voice from the divine glory, which surmounted the mercy seat. **2. Speak unto the children of Israel, and say unto them**—If the subject of communication were of a temporal nature, the Levites were excluded; but if it were a spiritual matter, all the tribes were comprehended under this name (Deut. 27:12). **If any man of you bring an offering unto the Lord**—The directions given here relate solely to voluntary or freewill offerings—those rendered over and above such, as being of standing and universal obligation, could not be dispensed with or commuted for any other kind of offering (Exod. 29:38; ch. 23:37; Num. 28:3, 11-27, etc.). **bring your offering of the cattle,** etc.—i.e., those animals that were not only tame, innocent and gentle, but useful and adapted for food. This rule excluded horses, dogs, swine, camels, and asses, which were used in sacrifice by some heathen nations, beasts and birds of prey, as also hares and deers. **3. a burnt sacrifice**—so called from its being wholly consumed on the altar; no part of it was eaten either by the priests or the offerer. It was designed to propitiate the anger of God incurred by original sin, or by particular transgressions; and its entire combustion indicated the self-dedication of the offerer—his whole nature—his body and soul—as necessary to form a sacrifice acceptable to God (Rom. 12:1; Phil. 1:20). This was the most ancient as well as the most conspicuous mode of sacrifice. **a male without blemish**—No animal was allowed to be offered that had any deformity or defect. Among the Egyptians, a minute inspection was made by the priest; and the bullock having been declared perfect, a certificate to that effect being fastened to its horns with wax, was sealed with his ring, and no other might be substituted. A similar process of examining the condition of the beasts brought as offerings, seems to have been adopted by the priests in Israel (John 6:27). **at the door of the tabernacle**—where stood the altar of burnt offering (Exod. 40:6). Every other place was forbidden, under the highest penalty (ch. 17:4). **4. shall put his hand upon the head**—This was a significant act which implied not only that the offerer devoted the animal to God, but that he confessed his consciousness of sin and prayed that his guilt and its punishment might be transferred to the victim. **and it shall be**—that is, "that it may be an acceptable atonement." **5. he shall kill the bullock**—The animal should be killed by the offerer, not by the priest, for it was not his duty in case of voluntary sacrifices; in later times, however, the office was generally performed by Levites. **before the Lord**—on the spot where the hands had been laid upon the animal's head, on the north side of the altar. **sprinkle the blood**—This was to be done by the priests. The blood being considered the life, the effusion of it was the essential part of the sacrifice; and the sprinkling of it—the application of the atonement—made the person and services of the offerer acceptable to God. The skin having been stripped off, and the carcass cut up, the various pieces were disposed on the altar in the manner best calculated to facilitate their being consumed by the fire. **8. the fat**—that about the kidneys especially, which is called "suet." **9. but his inwards and his legs shall he wash in water,** etc.—This part of the ceremony was symbolical of the *inward* purity, and the holy *walk,* that became acceptable worshippers. **a sweet savour unto the Lord**—is an expression of the offerer's piety, but especially as a sacrificial type of Christ. **10-13. if his offering be of the flocks**—Those who could not afford the expense of a bullock might offer a ram or a he-goat, and the same ceremonies were to be observed in the act of offering. **14-17. if the burnt**

sacrifice ... be of fowls—The gentle nature and cleanly habits of the dove led to its selection, while all other fowls were rejected, either for the fierceness of their disposition or the grossness of their taste; and in this case, there being from the smallness of the animal no blood for waste, the priest was directed to prepare it *at* the altar and sprinkle the blood. This was the offering appointed for the poor. The fowls were always offered in pairs, and the reason why Moses ordered two turtledoves or two young pigeons, was not merely to suit the convenience of the offerer, but according as the latter was in season; for pigeons are sometimes quite hard and unfit for eating, at which time turtledoves are very good in Egypt and Palestine. The turtledoves are not restricted to any age because they are always good when they appear in those countries, being birds of passage; but the age of the pigeons is particularly marked that they might not be offered to God at times when they are rejected by men [HARMER]. It is obvious, from the varying scale of these voluntary sacrifices, that the disposition of the offerer was the thing looked to — not the costliness of his offering.

CHAPTER 2

Vss. 1-16. THE MEAT OFFERINGS. **1. when any will offer a meat offering**—or gift—distinguishing a bloodless from a bloody sacrifice. The word "meat," however, is improper, as its meaning as now used is different from that attached at the date of our English translation. It was then applied not to "flesh," but "food," generally, and here it is applied to the flour of wheat. The meat offerings were intended as a thankful acknowledgment for the bounty of Providence; and hence, although meat offerings accompanied some of the appointed sacrifices, those here described being voluntary oblations, were offered alone. **pour oil upon it**—Oil was used as butter is with us—symbolically it meant the influences of the Spirit, of which oil was the emblem, as incense was of prayer. **2. shall burn the memorial**—rather "for a memorial,' i.e., a part of it. **3. the remnant of the meat offering shall be Aaron's and his sons'**—The circumstance of a portion of it being appropriated to the use of the priests distinguishes this from a burnt offering. They alone were to partake of it within the sacred precincts, as among "the most holy things." **4. if thou bring an oblation of a meat offering baken in the oven**—generally a circular hole excavated in the floor, from one to five feet deep, the sides of which are covered with hardened plaster, on which cakes are baked of the form and thickness of pancakes. (See on Genesis 18:6.) The shape of Eastern ovens varies considerably according to the nomadic or settled habits of the people. **5. baken in a pan**—a thin plate, generally of copper or iron, placed on a slow fire, similar to what the country people in Scotland called a "girdle" for baking oatmeal cakes. **6. part it in pieces, and pour oil thereon**—Pouring oil on bread is a common practice among Eastern people, who are fond of broken bread dipped in oil, butter, and milk. Oil only was used in the meat offerings, and probably for a symbolic reason. It is evident that these meat offerings were previously prepared by the offerer, and when brought, the priest was to take it from his hands and burn a portion on the altar. **11. ye shall burn no leaven, nor any honey, in any offering of the Lord**—Nothing sweet or sour was to be offered. In the warm climates of the East leavened bread soon spoils, and hence it was regarded as the emblem of hypocrisy or corruption. Some, however, think that the prohibition was that leaven and honey were used in the idolatrous rites of the heathen. **12. the oblation of the first-fruits**—voluntary offerings made by individuals out of their increase, and leaven and honey might be used with these (ch. 23:17; Num. 15:20). Though presented at the altar, they were not consumed, but assigned by God for the use of the priests. **13. every ... meat offering shalt thou season with salt**—The same reasons which led to the prohibition of leaven, recommended the use of salt—if the one soon putrefies, the other possesses a strongly preservative property, and hence it became an emblem of incorruption and purity, as well as of a perpetual covenant—a perfect reconciliation and lasting friendship. No injunction in the whole law was more sacredly observed than this application of salt; for besides other uses of it that will be noticed elsewhere, it had a typical meaning referred to by our Lord concerning the effect of the Gospel on those who embrace it (Mark 9:49, 50); as when plentifully applied it preserves meat from spoiling, so will the Gospel keep men from being corrupted by sin. And as salt was indispensable to render sacrifices acceptable to God, so the Gospel, brought home to the hearts of men by the Holy Ghost, is indispensably requisite to their offering up of themselves as living sacrifices [BROWN]. **14. a meat offering of thy first-fruits**—From the mention of green ears, this seems to have been a voluntary offering before the harvest—the ears being prepared in the favorite way of Eastern people, by parching them at the fire, and then beating them out for use. It was designed to be an early tribute of pious thankfulness for the earth's increase, and it was offered according to the usual directions.

CHAPTER 3

Vss. 1-17. The Peace Offering of the Herd. **1. if his oblation be a sacrifice of peace offering,** etc.—"Peace" being used in Scripture to denote prosperity and happiness generally, a peace offering was a voluntary tribute of gratitude for health or other benefits. In this view it was eucharistic, being a token of thanksgiving for benefits already received, or it was sometimes votive, presented in prayer for benefits wished for in the future. **of the herd**—This kind of offering being of a festive character, either male or female, if without blemish, might be used, as both of them were equally good for food, and, if the circumstances of the offerer allowed it, it might be a calf. **2. he shall lay his hand upon the head of his offering**—Having performed this significant act, he killed it before the door of the tabernacle, and the priests sprinkled the blood round about upon the altar. **3. he shall offer of the sacrifice of the peace offering**—The peace offering differed from the oblations formerly mentioned in this respect: while the burnt offering was wholly consumed on the altar, and the freewill offering was partly consumed and partly assigned to the priests; in this offering the fat alone was burnt; only a small part was allotted to the priests while the rest was granted to the offerer and his friends, thus forming a sacred feast of which the Lord, His priests, and people conjointly partook, and which was symbolical of the spiritual feast, the sacred communion which, through Christ, the great peace offering, believers enjoy. (See further on chs. 19, 22.) **the fat that covereth the inwards**—

i.e., the web-work that presents itself first to the eye on opening the belly of a cow. **the fat ... upon the inwards**—adhering to the intestines, but easily removable from them; or, according to some, that which was next the ventricle. **4-11. the two kidneys ... of the flock ... the whole rump**—There is, in Eastern countries, a species of sheep the tails of which are not less than four feet and a half in length. These tails are of a substance between fat and marrow. A sheep of this kind weighs sixty or seventy English pounds weight, of which the tail usually weighs fifteen pounds and upwards. This species is by far the most numerous in Arabia, Syria, and Palestine, and, forming probably a large portion in the flocks of the Israelites, it seems to have been the kind that usually bled on the Jewish altars. The extraordinary size and deliciousness of their tails give additional importance to this law. To command by an express law the tail of a certain sheep to be offered in sacrifice to God, might well surprise us; but the wonder ceases, when we are told of those broad-tailed Eastern sheep, and of the extreme delicacy of that part which was so particularly specified in the statute [PAXTON]. **12. if his offering be a goat**—Whether this or any of the other two animals were chosen, the same general directions were to be followed in the ceremony of offering. **17. ye eat neither fat nor blood**—The details given above distinctly define the fat in animals which was not to be eaten, so that all the rest, whatever adhered to other parts, or was intermixed with them, might be used. The prohibition of blood rested on a different foundation, being intended to preserve their reverence for the Messiah, who was to shed His blood as an atoning sacrifice for the sins of the world [BROWN].

CHAPTER 4

Vss. 1, 2. Sin Offering of Ignorance. **2. If a soul shall sin through ignorance against any of the commandments of the Lord**—a soul—an individual. All sins may be considered, in a certain sense, as committed "through ignorance," error, or misapprehension of one's true interests. The sins, however, referred to in this law were unintentional violations of the ceremonial laws,— breaches made through haste, or inadvertency of some negative precepts, which, if done knowingly and wilfully, would have involved a capital punishment. **do against any of them**—To bring out the meaning, it is necessary to supply, "he shall bring a sin offering."

3-35. Sin Offering for the Priest. **3. If the priest that is anointed do sin**—i.e., the high priest, in whom, considering his character as typical mediator, and his exalted office, the people had the deepest interest; and whose transgression of any part of the divine law, therefore, whether done unconsciously or heedlessly, was a very serious offense, both as regarded himself individually, and the influence of his example. He is the person principally meant, though the common order of the priesthood was included. **according to the sin of the people**—i.e., bring guilt on the people. He was to take a young bullock (the age and sex being expressly mentioned), and having killed it according to the form prescribed for the burnt offerings, he was to take it into the holy place and sprinkle the atoning blood seven times before the veil, and tip with the crimson fluid the horns of the golden altar of incense, on his way to the court of the priests,— a solemn ceremonial appointed only for very grave and heinous offenses, and which betokened that his sin, though done in ignorance, had vitiated all his services; nor could any official duty he engaged in be beneficial either to himself or the people, unless it were atoned for by blood. **11. the skin of the bullock, and all his flesh**—In ordinary circumstances, these were perquisites of the priests. But in the expiation necessary for a sin of the high priest, after the fat of the sacrifice was offered on the altar, the carcass was carried without the camp, in order that the total combustion of it in the place of ashes might the more strikingly indicate the enormity of the transgression, and the horror with which he regarded it (cf. Heb. 13:12, 13). **13. if the whole congregation of Israel sin through ignorance**—In consequence of some culpable neglect or misapprehension of the law, the people might contract national guilt, and then national expiation was necessary. The same sacrifice was to be offered as in the former case, but with this difference in the ceremonial, that the elders or heads of the tribes, as representing the people and being the principal aggressors in misleading the congregation, laid their hands on the head of the victim. The priest then took the blood into the holy place, where, after dipping his finger in it seven times, he sprinkled the drops seven times before the veil.—This done, he returned to the court of the priests, and ascending the altar, put some portion upon its horns; then he poured it out at the foot of the altar. The fat was the only part of the animal which was offered on the altar; for the carcass, with its appurtenances and offals, was carried without the camp, into the place where the ashes were deposited, and there consumed with fire. **22-26. When a ruler hath sinned, and done somewhat through ignorance against any of the commandments**—Whatever was the form of government, the king, judge, or subordinate, was the party concerned in this law. The trespass of such a civil functionary being less serious in its character and consequences than that either of the high priest or the congregation, a sin offering of inferior value was required—"a kid of the goats"; and neither was the blood carried into the sanctuary, but applied only to the altar of burnt offering; nor was the carcass taken without the camp; it was eaten by the priests-in-waiting. **27-34. if any one of the common people sin through ignorance**—In this case the expiatory offering appointed was a female kid, or a ewe lamb without blemish; and the ceremonies were exactly the same as those observed in the case of the offending ruler. In these two latter instances, the blood of the sin offering was applied to the altar of burnt offering—the place where bloody sacrifices were appointed to be immolated. But the transgression of a high priest, or of the whole congregation, entailing a general taint on the ritual of the tabernacle, and vitiating its services, required a further expiation; and therefore, in these cases, the blood of the sin offering was applied to the altar of incense. **35. it shall be forgiven him**—None of these sacrifices possessed any intrinsic value sufficient to free the conscience of the sinner from the pollution of guilt, or to obtain his pardon from God; but they gave a formal deliverance from a secular penalty (Heb. 9:13, 14); and they were figurative representations of the full and perfect sin offering which was to be made by Christ.

CHAPTER 5

Vs. 1. Trespass Offerings for Concealing Knowledge. **1. if a soul ... hear the voice of swearing**—or, according to some, "the words of adjuration." A proclamation was issued calling any one who could give information, to come before the court and bear testimony to the guilt of a criminal; and the manner in which witnesses were interrogated in the Jewish courts of justice was not by swearing them directly, but adjuring them by reading the words of an oath: "the voice of swearing." The offense, then, for the expiation of which this law provides, was that of a person who neglected or avoided the opportunity of lodging the information which it was in his power to communicate. **2, 3. Touching Any Thing Unclean. 2. if a soul touch any unclean thing**—A person who, unknown to himself at the time, came in contact with any thing unclean, and either neglected the requisite ceremonies of purification or engaged in the services of religion while under the taint of ceremonial defilement, might be afterwards convinced that he had committed an offense. **4-19. For Swearing. 4. if a soul swear**—a rash oath, without duly considering the nature and consequences of the oath, perhaps inconsiderately binding himself to do anything wrong, or neglecting to perform a vow to do something good. In all such cases a person might have transgressed one of the divine commandments unwittingly, and have been afterwards brought to a sense of his delinquency. **5. it shall be, when he shall be guilty ... that he shall confess that he hath sinned in that thing**—make a voluntary acknowledgment of his sin from the impulse of his own conscience, and before it come to the knowledge of the world. A previous discovery might have subjected him to some degree of punishment from which his spontaneous confession released him, but still he was considered guilty of trespass, to expiate which he was obliged by the ceremonial law to go through certain observances. **6-14. he shall bring his trespass offering unto the Lord for his sins which he hath sinned**—A trespass offering differed from a sin offering in the following respects—that it was appointed for persons who had either done evil unwittingly, or were in doubt as to their own criminality; or felt themselves in such a special situation as required sacrifices of that kind [BROWN]. The trespass offering appointed in such cases was a female lamb or kid; if unable to make such an offering, he might bring a pair of turtledoves or two young pigeons—the one to be offered for a sin offering, the other for a burnt offering; or if even *that* was beyond his ability, the law would be satisfied with the tenth part of an ephah of fine flour without oil or frankincense. **15, 16. sin through ignorance, in the holy things of the Lord**, etc.—This is a case of sacrilege committed ignorantly, either in not paying the full due of tithes, first-fruits, and similar tribute in eating of meats, which belonged to the priests alone—or he was required, along with the restitution in money, the amount of which was to be determined by the priest, to offer a ram for a trespass offering, as soon as he came to the knowledge of his involuntary fraud. **17-19. if a soul sin ... though he wist it not, yet he is guilty**—This also refers to holy things, and it differs from the preceding in being one of the *doubtful* cases, i.e., where conscience suspects, though the understanding be in doubt whether criminality or sin has been committed. The Jewish rabbis give, as an example, the case of a person who, knowing that "the fat of the inwards" is not to be eaten, religiously abstained from the use of it; but should a dish happen to have been at table in which he had reason to suspect some portion of that meat was intermingled, and he had, inadvertently, partaken of that unlawful viand, he was bound to bring a ram as a trespass offering. These provisions were all designed to impress the conscience with the sense of responsibility to God and keep alive on the hearts of the people a salutary fear of doing any secret wrong.

CHAPTER 6

Vss. 1-7. Trespass Offering for Sins Done Wittingly. **2. If a soul sin, and commit a trespass against the Lord**—This law, the record of which should have been joined with the previous chapter, was given concerning things stolen, fraudulently gotten, or wrongfully kept. The offender was enjoined to make restitution of the articles to the rightful owner, along with a fifth part out of his own possessions. But it was not enough thus to repair the injury done to a neighbor and to society; he was required to bring a trespass offering, as a token of sorrow and penitence for having hurt the cause of religion and of God. That trespass offering was a ram without blemish, which was to be made on the altar of burnt offerings, and the flesh belonged to the priests. This penalty was equivalent to a mitigated fine; but being associated with a sacred duty, the form in which the fine was inflicted served the important purpose of rousing attention to the claims and reviving a sense of responsibility to God.

8-13. The Law of the Burnt Offering. **9. Command Aaron and his sons, saying, This . . . law of the burnt offering**—In this passage Moses received instructions to be delivered to the priests respecting their official duties, and first the burnt offering—*Hebrew*, "a sacrifice, which went up in smoke." The daily service consisted of two lambs, one offered in the morning at sunrise, the other in the evening, when the day began to decline. Both of them were consumed on the altar by means of a slow fire, before which the pieces of the sacrifice were so placed that they fed it all night. At all events, the observance of this daily sacrifice on the altar of burnt offering was a daily expression of national repentance and faith. The fire that consumed these sacrifices had been kindled from heaven at the consecration of the tabernacle, and to keep it from being extinguished and the sacrifices from being burned with common fire, strict injunctions are here given respecting not only the removal of the ashes, but the approaching near to the fireplace in garments that were not officially "holy."

14-18. The Law of the Meat Offering. **14. this is the law of the meat offering**—Though this was a provision for the priests and their families, it was to be regarded as "most holy"; and the way in which it was prepared was: on any meat offerings being presented, the priest carried them to the altar, and taking a handful from each of them as an oblation, he salted and burnt it on the altar; the residue became the property of the priests, and was the food of those whose duty it was to attend on the service. They themselves as well as the vessels from which they ate were typically holy, and they were not at liberty to partake of the meat offering while they labored under any ceremonial defilement.

19-23. The High Priest's Meat Offering. **20. This is the offering of Aaron, and of his sons**—the daily meat offering of the high priest; for though his sons are mentioned along with him, it was probably only those of his descendants who succeeded him in that high office that are meant. It was to be offered, one half of it in the morning and the other half in the evening—being daily laid by the ministering priest on the altar of burnt offering, where, being dedicated to God, it was wholly consumed. This was designed to keep him and the other attendant priests in constant remembrance, that though they were typically expiating the sins of the people, their own persons and services could meet with acceptance only through faith, which required to be daily nourished and strengthened from above.

21-30. The Law of the Sin Offering. **25. This is the law of the sin offering**—It was slain, and the fat and inwards, after being washed and salted, were burnt upon the altar. But the rest of the carcass belonged to the officiating priest. He and his family might feast upon it—only, however, within the precincts of the tabernacle; and none else were allowed to partake of it but the members of a priestly family—and not even they, if under any ceremonial defilement. The flesh on all occasions was boiled or sodden, with the exception of the paschal lamb, which was roasted; and if an earthen vessel had been used, it being porous and likely to imbibe some of the liquid particles, it was to be broken; if a metallic pan had been used it was to be scoured and washed with the greatest care, not because the vessels had been defiled, but the reverse —because the flesh of the sin offering having been boiled in them, those vessels were now too sacred for ordinary use. The design of all these minute ceremonies was to impress the minds, both of priests and people, with a sense of the evil nature of sin and the care they should take to prevent the least taint of its impurities clinging to them.

CHAPTER 7

Vss. 1-27. The Law of the Trespass Offering. **1. Likewise this is the law of the trespass offering**— This chapter is a continuation of the laws that were to regulate the duty of the priests respecting the trespass offerings. The same regulations obtained in this case as in the burnt offerings—part was to be consumed on the altar, while the other part was a perquisite of the priests—some fell exclusively to the officiating minister, and was the fee for his services; others were the common share of all the priestly order, who lived upon them as their provision, and whose meetings at a common table would tend to promote brotherly harmony and friendship. **8. the priest shall have to himself the skin of the burnt offering which he hath offered**— All the flesh and the fat of the burnt offerings being consumed, nothing remained to the priest but the skin. It has been thought that this was a patriarchal usage, incorporated with the Mosaic law, and that the right of the sacrificer to the skin of the victim was transmitted from the example of Adam (see on Gen. 3:21). **11-14. this is the law of the sacrifice of peace offerings**—Besides the usual accompaniments of other sacrifices, leavened bread was offered with the peace offerings, as a thanksgiving, such bread being common at feasts. **15-17. the flesh of the sacrifice of his peace offerings . . . shall be eaten the same day that it is offered**—The flesh of the sacrifices was eaten on the day of the offering or on the day following. But if any part of it remained till the third day, it was, instead of being made use of, to be burned with fire. In the East, butcher-meat is generally eaten the day it is killed, and it is rarely kept a second day, so that as a prohibition was issued against any of the flesh in the peace offerings being used on the third day, it has been thought, not without reason, that this injunction must have been given to prevent a superstitious notion arising that there was some virtue or holiness belonging to it. **18. if any of the flesh of the sacrifice . . . be eaten at all on the third day, it shall not be accepted, neither . . . imputed**—The sacrifice will not be acceptable to God nor profitable to him that offers it. **20. cut off from his people**—i.e., excluded from the privileges of an Israelite—lie under a sentence of excommunication. **21. abominable unclean thing**—Some copies of the Bible read, "any reptile." **22-27. Ye shall eat no manner of fat**—See on ch. 3:17.

28-38. THE PRIESTS' PORTION. **29. He that offereth the sacrifice of his peace offerings unto the Lord**—In order to show that the sacrifice was voluntary, the offerer was required to bring it with his own hands to the priest. The breast having been waved to and fro in a solemn manner as devoted to God, was given to the priests; it was assigned to the use of their order generally, but the right shoulder was the perquisite of the officiating priest. **35-38. This is the portion of the anointing of Aaron**—These verses contain a general summing up of the laws which regulate the privileges and duties of the priests. The word "anointing" is often used as synonymous with "office" or "dignity." So that the "portion of the anointing of Aaron" probably means the provision made for the maintenance of the high priest and the numerous body of functionaries which composed the sacerdotal order. **in the day when he presented them to minister unto the Lord**, etc.–i.e., from the day they approached the Lord in the duties of their ministry.

CHAPTER 8

Vss. 1-36. MOSES CONSECRATES AARON AND HIS SONS. **2. Take Aaron and his sons**—The consecration of Aaron and his sons had been ordered long before (Exod. 29), but it is now described with all the details of the ceremonial, as it was gone through after the tabernacle was completed and the regulations for the various sacrifices enacted. **3-5. gather thou all the congregation together**, etc.—It was manifestly expedient for the Israelitish people to be satisfied that Aaron's appointment to the high dignity of the priesthood was not a personal intrusion, nor a family arrangement between him and Moses; and nothing, therefore, could be a more prudent or necessary measure, for impressing a profound conviction of the divine origin and authority of the priestly institution, than to summon a general assembly of the people, and in their presence perform the solemn ceremonies of inauguration, which had been prescribed by divine authority. **6. Moses . . . washed them with water**—At consecration they were subjected to entire ablution, though on ordinary occasions they were required, before entering on their duties, only to wash their hands and feet. This symbolical ablution was designed to teach them the necessity of inward purity, and the imperative obligation on those who bore the vessels and conducted the services of the sanctuary to be holy. **7-9. he put upon him the coat, and girded him with the girdle**—The splendor of the official vestments, together with the gorgeous tiara of the high priest, was intended, doubtless, in the first instance, to produce in the minds of the

people a high respect for the ministers of religion; and in the next, from the predominant use of linen, to inculcate upon Aaron and his sons the duty of maintaining unspotted righteousness in their characters and lives. **10-12. took the anointing oil,** etc.—which was designed to intimate that persons who acted as leaders in the solemn services of worship should have the unction of the Holy One both in His gifts and graces. **14-17. brought the bullock for the sin offering,** etc.—a timely expression of their sense of unworthiness—a public and solemn confession of their personal sins and a transference of their guilt to the typical victim. **18-21. brought the ram,** etc.—as a token of their entire dedication to the service of God. **22-30. brought the other ram,** etc.—After the sin offering and burnt offering had been presented on their behalf, this was their peace offering, by which they declared the pleasure which they felt in entering upon the service of God and being brought into close communion with Him as the ministers of His sanctuary, together with their confident reliance on His grace to help them in all their sacred duties. **33. ye shall not go out of the door of the tabernacle of the congregation,** etc.—After all these preliminaries, they had still to undergo a week's probation in the court of the tabernacle before they obtained permission to enter into the interior of the sacred building. During the whole of that period the same sacrificial rites were observed as on the first day, and they were expressly admonished that the smallest breach of any of the appointed observances would lead to the certain forfeiture of their lives.

CHAPTER 9

Vss. 1-24. THE PRIESTS' ENTRY INTO OFFICE. **1, 2. Moses called . . . Take thee a young calf for a sin offering**—The directions in these sacred things were still given by Moses, the circumstances being extraordinary. But he was only the medium of communicating the divine will to the newly made priests. The first of their official acts was the sacrifice of another sin offering to atone for the defects of the inauguration services; and yet that sacrifice did not consist of a bullock—the sacrifice appointed for some particular transgression, but of a calf, perhaps not without a significant reference to Aaron's sin in the golden calf. Then followed a burnt offering, expressive of their voluntary and entire self-devotement to the divine service. The newly consecrated priests having done this on their own account, they were called to offer a sin offering and burnt offering for the people, ending the ceremonial by a peace offering, which was a sacred feast. This injunction "to make an atonement for himself and for the people" (*Septuagint,* "for thy family"), at the commencement of his sacred functions, furnishes a striking evidence of the divine origin of the Jewish system of worship. In all false or corrupt forms of religion, the studied policy has been to inspire the people with an idea of the sanctity of the priesthood as in point of purity and favor with the Divinity far above the level of other men. But among the Hebrews the priests were required to offer for the expiation of their own sins as well as the humblest of the people. This imperfection of Aaron's priesthood, however, does not extend to the gospel dispensation: for our great High Priest, who has entered for us into "the true tabernacle," "knew no sin" (Heb. 10:10, 11). **8. Aaron . . . went unto the altar, and slew the calf of the sin offering**—

Whether it had been enjoined the first time, or was unavoidable from the divisions of the priestly labor not being as yet completely arranged, Aaron, assisted by his sons, appears to have slain the victims with his own hands, as well as gone through all the prescribed ritual at the altar. **17-21. meat offering . . . wave offering**—It is observable that there is no notice taken of these in the offerings the priests made for themselves. They could not bear their own sins: and therefore, instead of eating any part of their own sin offering, as they were at liberty to do in the case of the people's offering, they had to carry the whole carcasses *"without* the camp and burn them with fire." **22. Aaron lifted up his hand . . . and blessed**—The pronouncing of a benediction on the people assembled in the court was a necessary part of the high priest's duty, and the formula in which it was to be given is described (Num. 6:23-27). **came down from offering**—The altar was elevated above the level of the floor, and the ascent was by a gentle slope (Exod. 20:26). **23. Moses and Aaron went into the tabernacle**—Moses, according to the divine instructions he had received, accompanied Aaron and his sons to initiate them into their sacred duties. Their previous occupations had detained them at the altar, and they now entered in company into the sacred edifice to bear the blood of the offerings within the sanctuary. **the glory of the Lord appeared unto all the people**—perhaps in a resplendent effulgence above the tabernacle as a fresh token of the divine acceptance of that newly established seat of His worship. **24. there came a fire out from . . . the Lord**—A flame emanating from that resplendent light that filled the holy place flashed upon the brazen altar and kindled the sacrifices. This miraculous fire—for the descent of which the people had probably been prepared, and which the priests were enjoined never to let go out (ch. 6:13)—was a sign, not only of the acceptance of the offerings and of the establishment of Aaron's authority, but of God's actual residence in that chosen dwelling-place. The moment the solemn though welcome spectacle was seen, a simultaneous shout of joy and gratitude burst from the assembled congregation, and in the attitude of profoundest reverence they worshipped "a present Deity."

CHAPTER 10

Vss. 1-20. Nadab and Abihu Burnt. **1. the sons of Aaron,** etc.—If this incident occurred at the solemn period of the consecrating and dedicating the altar, these young men assumed an office which had been committed to Moses; or if it were some time after, it was an encroachment on duties which devolved on their father alone as the high priest. But the offense was of a far more aggravated nature than such a mere informality would imply. It consisted not only in their venturing unauthorized to perform the incense service—the highest and most solemn of the priestly offices—not only in their engaging together in a work which was the duty only of one, but in their presuming to intrude into the holy of holies, to which access was denied to all but the high priest alone. In this respect, "they offered strange fire before the Lord"; they were guilty of a presumptuous and unwarranted intrusion into a sacred office which did not belong to them. But their offense was more aggravated still; for instead of taking the fire which was put into their censers from the brazen altar, they seem to have been content with common fire and thus perpetrated an

act which, considering the descent of the miraculous fire they had so recently witnessed and the solemn obligation under which they were laid to make use of that which was specially appropriated to the service of the altars, they betrayed a carelessness, an irreverence, a want of faith, most surprising and lamentable. A precedent of such evil tendency was dangerous, and it was imperatively necessary, therefore, as well for the priests themselves as for the sacred things, that a marked expression of the divine displeasure should be given for doing that which "God commanded them not." **2. there went out fire from the Lord, and devoured them**—rather, killed them; for it appears (vs. 5) that neither their bodies nor their robes were consumed. The expression, "from the Lord," indicates that this fire issued from the most holy place. In the destruction of these two young priests by the infliction of an awful judgment, the wisdom of God observed the same course, in repressing the first instance of contempt for sacred things, as he did at the commencement of the Christian dispensation (Acts 5: 1-11). **3. Moses said . . . This is it that the Lord spoke . . . I will be sanctified in them that come nigh me**—"They that come nigh me," points, in this passage, directly to the priests; and they had received repeated and solemn warnings as to the cautious and reverent manner of their approach into the divine prescence (Exod. 19:22; 29:44; ch. 8:35). **Aaron held his peace**—The loss of two sons in so sudden and awful a manner was a calamity overwhelming to parental feelings. But the pious priest indulged in no vehement ebullition of complaint and gave vent to no murmur of discontent, but submitted in silent resignation to what he saw was "the righteous judgment of God." **4, 5. Moses called Mishael and Elzaphan**—The removal of the two corpses for burial without the camp would spread the painful intelligence throughout all the congregation. The interment of the priestly vestments along with them, was a sign of their being polluted by the sin of their irreligious wearers; and the remembrance of so appalling a judgment could not fail to strike a salutary fear into the hearts both of priests and people. **6. Uncover not your heads**—They who were ordered to carry out the two bodies, being engaged in their sacred duties, were forbidden to remove their turbans, in conformity with the usual customs of mourning; and the prohibition, "neither rend your garments," was, in all probability, confined also to their official costume. For at other times the priests wore the ordinary dress of their countrymen and, in common with their families, might indulge their private feelings by the usual signs or expressions of grief. **8-11. Do not drink wine nor strong drink**—This prohibition, and the accompanying admonitions, following immediately the occurrence of so fatal a catastrophe, has given rise to an opinion entertained by many, that the two disobedient priests were under the influence of intoxication when they committed the offense which was expiated only by their lives. But such an idea, though the presumption is in its favor, is nothing more than conjecture. **12-15. Moses spake unto Aaron,** etc.—This was a timely and considerate rehearsal of the laws that regulated the conduct of the priests. Amid the distractions of their family bereavement, Aaron and his surviving sons might have forgotten or overlooked some of their duties. **16-20. Moses diligently sought the goat of the sin offering, and, behold, it was burnt**—In a sacrifice presented, as that had been, on behalf of the people, it was the duty of the priests, as typically representing them and bearing their sins, to have eaten the flesh after the blood had been sprinkled upon the altar. Instead of using it, however, for a sacred feast, they had burnt it without the camp; and Moses, who discovered this departure from the prescribed ritual, probably from a dread of some farther chastisements, challenged, not Aaron, whose heart was too much lacerated to bear a new cause of distress but his two surviving sons in the priesthood for the great irregularity. Their father, however, who heard the charge and by whose directions the error had been committed, hastened to give the explanation. The import of his apology is, that all the duty pertaining to the presentation of the offering had been duly and sacredly performed, except the festive part of the observance, which privately devolved upon the priest and his family; and that this had been omitted, either because his heart was too dejected to join in the celebration of a cheerful feast, or that he supposed, from the appalling judgments that had been inflicted, that all the services of that occasion were so vitiated that he did not complete them. Aaron was decidedly in the wrong. By the express command of God, the sin offering was to be eaten in the holy place; and no fanciful view of expediency or propriety ought to have led him to dispense at discretion with a positive statute. The law of God was clear and, where that is the case, it is sin to deviate a hair's breadth from the path of duty. But Moses sympathized with his deeply afflicted brother and, having pointed out the error, said no more.

CHAPTER 11

Vss. 1-47. Beasts That May and May Not Be Eaten. **1. the Lord spake unto Moses and to Aaron** —These laws, being addressed to both the civil and ecclesiastical rulers in Israel, may serve to indicate the twofold view that is to be taken of them. Undoubtedly the first and strongest reason for instituting a distinction among meats was to discourage the Israelites from spreading into other countries, and from general intercourse with the world—to prevent them acquiring familiarity with the inhabitants of the countries bordering on Canaan, so as to fall into their idolatries or be contaminated with their vices: in short, to keep them a distinct and peculiar people. To this purpose, no difference of creed, no system of polity, no diversity of language or manner, was so subservient as a distinction of meats founded on religion; and hence the Jews, who were taught by education to abhor many articles of food freely partaken of by other people, never, even during periods of great degeneracy, could amalgamate with the nations among which they were dispersed. But although this was the principal foundation of these laws, dietetic reasons also had weight; for there is no doubt that the flesh of many of the animals here ranked as unclean, is everywhere, but especially in warm climates, less wholesome and adapted for food than those which were allowed to be eaten. These laws, therefore, being subservient to sanitary as well as religious ends, were addressed both to Moses and Aaron. **3-7. Whatsoever parteth the hoof, and is cloven-footed, and cheweth the cud**— Ruminating animals by the peculiar structure of their stomachs digest their food more fully than others. It is found that in the act of chewing the cud, a large portion of the poisonous properties of noxious plants eaten by them, passes off by the

salivary glands. This power of secreting the poisonous effects of vegetables, is said to be particularly remarkable in cows and goats, whose mouths are often sore, and sometimes bleed, in consequence. Their flesh is therefore in a better state for food, as it contains more of the nutritious juices, is more easily digested in the human stomach, and is consequently more easily assimilated. Animals which do not chew the cud, convert their food less perfectly; their flesh is therefore unwholesome, from the gross animal juices with which they abound, and is apt to produce scorbutic and scrofulous disorders. But the animals that may be eaten are those which "part the hoof as well as chew the cud," and this is another means of freeing the flesh of the animal from noxious substances. "In the case of animals with parted hoofs, when feeding in unfavorable situations a prodigious amount of fœtid matter is discharged, and passes off between the toes; while animals with undivided hoofs, feeding on the same ground, become severely affected in the legs, from the poisonous plants among the pasture" [Whitlaw's *Code of Health*]. All experience attests this, and accordingly the use of ruminating animals (that is, those which both chew the cud and part the hoof) has always obtained in most countries though it was observed most carefully by the people who were favored with the promulgation of God's law. **4. the camel**—It does to a certain extent divide the hoof, for the foot consists of two large parts, but the division is not complete; the toes rest upon an elastic pad on which the animal goes; as a beast of burden its flesh is tough. An additional reason for its prohibition might be to keep the Israelites apart from the descendants of Ishmael. **5. the coney**—not the rabbit, for it is not found in Palestine or Arabia, but the hyrax, a little animal of the size and general shape of the rabbit, but differing from it in several essential features. It has no tail, singular, long hairs bristling like thorns among the fur on its back; its feet are bare, its nails flat and round, except those on each inner toe of the hind feet, which are sharp and project like an awl. It does not burrow in the ground but frequents the clefts of rocks. **6. the hare**—Two species of hare must have been pointed at: the Sinai hare—the hare of the desert, small and generally brown; the other, the hare of Palestine and Syria, about the size and appearance of that known in our own country. Neither the hare nor the coney are really ruminating. They only appear to be so from working the jaws on the grasses they live on. They are not cloven-footed; and besides, it is said that from the great quantity of down upon them, they are very much subject to vermin—that in order to expel these, they eat poisonous plants, and if used as food while in that state, they are most deleterious [Whitlaw]. **7. the swine**—It is a filthy, foul-feeding animal, and it lacks one of the natural provisions for purifying the system, "it cheweth not the cud"; in hot climates indulgence in swine's flesh is particularly liable to produce leprosy, scurvy, and various cutaneous eruptions. It was therefore strictly avoided by the Israelites. Its prohibition was further necessary to prevent their adopting many of the grossest idolatries practised by neighboring nations. **9. These shall ye eat ... whatsoever hath fins and scales**— "The fins and scales are the means by which the excrescences of fish are carried off, the same as in animals by perspiration. I have never known an instance of disease produced by eating such fish; but those that have no fins and scales cause, in hot climates, the most malignant disorders when eaten; in many cases they prove a mortal poison" [WHIT-LAW]. **12. Whatsoever hath no fins nor scales,** etc. —Under this classification frogs, eels, shellfish of all descriptions, were included as unclean; "many of the latter (shellfish) enjoy a reputation they do not deserve, and have, when plentifully partaken of, produced effects which have led to a suspicion of their containing something of a poisonous nature." **13-19. these are they which ye shall have in** particularly ranked in the class unclean; all those **abomination among the fowls**—All birds of prey are which feed on flesh and carrion. No less than twenty species of birds, all probably then known, are mentioned under this category, and the inference follows that all which are not mentioned were allowed; that is, fowls which subsist on vegetable substances. From our imperfect knowledge of the natural history of Palestine, Arabia, and the contiguous countries at that time, it is not easy to determine exactly what some of the prohibited birds were; although they must have been all well known among the people to whom these laws were given. **the ossifrage**—*Hebrew*, "bone-breaker," rendered in the Septuagint *griffon,* supposed to be the *Gypœtos barbatus,* the Lammer Geyer of the Swiss—a bird of the eagle or vulture species, inhabiting the highest mountain ranges in Western Asia as well as Europe. It pursues as its prey the chamois, ibex, or marmot, among rugged cliffs, till it drives them over a precipice—thus obtaining the name of "bone-breaker." **the ospray**—the black eagle, among the smallest, but swiftest and strongest of its kind. **the vulture**—The word so rendered in our version means more probably "the kite" or "glede" and describes a varying but majestic flight, exactly that of the kite, which now darts forward with the rapidity of an arrow, now rests motionless on its expanded wings in the air. It feeds on small birds, insects, and fish. **the kite**—the vulture. In Egypt and perhaps in the adjoining countries also, the kite and vulture are often seen together flying in company, or busily pursuing their foul but important office of devouring the carrion and relics of putrefying flesh, which might otherwise pollute the atmosphere. **after his kind**—i.e., the prohibition against eating it extended to the whole species. **the raven**—including the crow, the pie. **the owl**—It is generally supposed the ostrich is denoted by the original word. **the nighthawk**—a very small bird, with which, from its nocturnal habits, many superstitious ideas were associated. **the cuckoo**—Evidently some other bird is meant by the original term, from its being ranged among rapacious birds. DR. SHAW thinks it is the safsaf; but that, being a graminivorous and gregarious bird, is equally objectionable. Others think that the sea mew, or some of the small sea-fowl, is intended. **the hawk**—The *Hebrew* word includes every variety of the falcon family—as the goshawk, the jerhawk, the sparrow hawk, etc. Several species of hawks are found in Western Asia and Egypt, where they find inexhaustible prey in the immense numbers of pigeons and turtledoves that abound in those quarters. The hawk was held pre-eminently sacred among the Egyptians; and this, besides its rapacious disposition and gross habits, might have been a strong reason for its prohibition as an article of food to the Israelites. **the little owl**—or horned owl, as some render it. The common barn owl, which is well known in the East. It is the only bird of its kind here referred to, although the word is thrice mentioned in our version. **cormorant**—supposed to be the gull. **the**

great owl—according to some, the Ibis of the Egyptians. It was well known to the Israelites, and so rendered by the *Septuagint* (Deut. 14:16; Isa. 34:11): according to PARKHURST, the bittern, but not determined. **the swan**—found in great numbers in all the countries of the Levant. It frequents marshy places—the vicinity of rivers and lakes. It was held sacred by the Egyptians, and kept tame within the precincts of heathen temples. It was probably on this account chiefly that its use as food was prohibited. MICHAELIS considers it the goose. **the pelican**—remarkable for the bag or pouch under its lower jaw which serves not only as a net to catch, but also as a receptacle of food. It is solitary in its habits and, like other large aquatic birds, often flies to a great distance from its favorite haunts. **the gier eagle**—Being here associated with waterfowl, it has been questioned whether any species of eagle is referred to. Some think, as the original name *racham* denotes "*tenderness,*" "*affection,*" the halcyon or kingfisher is intended [CALMET]. Others think that it is the bird now called the *rachami,* a kind of Egyptian vulture, abundant in the streets of Cairo and popularly called Pharaoh's fowl. It is white in color, in size like a raven, and feeds on carrion; it is one of the foulest and filthiest birds in the world. **the stork**—a bird of benevolent temper and held in the highest estimation in all Eastern countries; it was declared unclean, probably, from its feeding on serpents and other venomous reptiles, as well as rearing its young on the same food. **the heron**—The word so translated only occurs in the prohibited list of food and has been variously rendered—the crane, the plover, the woodcock, the parrot. In this great diversity of opinion nothing certain can be affirmed regarding it. Judging from the group with which it is classified, it must be an aquatic bird that is meant. It may as well be the heron as any other bird, the more especially as herons abound in Egypt and in the Hauran of Palestine. **the lapwing**—or hoopoe—found in warm regions, a very pretty but filthy species of bird. It was considered unclean, probably from its feeding on insects, worms, and snails. **the bat**—the great or Ternat bat, known in the East, noted for its voracity and filthiness. **20. All fowls that creep,** etc.—By "fowls" here are to be understood all creatures with wings and "going upon all fours," not a restriction to animals which have exactly four feet, because many "creeping things" have more than that number. The prohibition is regarded generally as extending to insects, reptiles, and worms. **21. Yet these may ye eat of every flying creeping thing that goeth upon all four, which have legs above their feet**—Nothing short of a scientific description could convey more accurately the nature "of the locust after its kind." They were allowed as lawful food to the Israelites, and they are eaten by the Arabs, who fry them in olive oil.—When sprinkled with salt, dried, smoked, and fried, they are said to taste not unlike red herrings. **26. every beast ... not cloven-footed**—The prohibited animals under this description include not only the beasts which have a single hoof, as horses and asses, but those also which divided the foot into paws, as lions, tigers, etc. **29. the weasel**—rather, the mole. **the mouse**—From its diminutive size it is placed among the reptiles instead of the quadrupeds. **the tortoise**—a lizard, resembling very nearly in shape, and in the hard pointed scales of the tail, the shaketail. **30. the ferret**—the *Hebrew* word is thought by some to signify the newt or chameleon, by others the frog.

the chameleon—called by the Arabs the warral, a green lizard. **the snail**—a lizard which lives in the sand, and is called by the Arabs *chulca,* of an azure color. **the mole**—Another species of lizard is meant, probably the chameleon. **31-35. whosoever doth touch them, when . . . dead, shall be unclean until the even**—These regulations must have often caused annoyance by suddenly requiring the exclusion of people from society, as well as the ordinances of religion. Nevertheless they were extremely useful and salutary, especially as enforcing attention to cleanliness. This is a matter of essential importance in the East, where venomous reptiles often creep into houses and are found lurking in boxes, vessels, or holes in the wall; and the carcass of one of them, or a dead mouse, mole, lizard, or other unclean animal, might be inadvertently touched by the hand, or fall on clothes, skin-bottles, or any article of common domestic use. By connecting, therefore, the touch of such creatures with ceremonial defilement, which required immediately to be removed, an effectual means was taken to prevent the bad effects of venom and all unclean or noxious matter. **47. make a difference between the unclean and the clean**—i.e., between animals used and not used for food. It is probable that the laws contained in this chapter were not entirely new, but only gave the sanction of divine enactment to ancient usages. Some of the prohibited animals have, on physiological grounds, been everywhere rejected by the general sense or experience of mankind; while others may have been declared unclean from their unwholesomeness in warm countries of from some reasons, which are now imperfectly known, connected with contemporary idolatry.

CHAPTER 12

Vss. 1-8. WOMAN'S UNCLEANNESS BY CHILDBIRTH. **2. If a woman,** etc.—The mother of a boy was ceremonially unclean for a week, at the end of which the child was circumcised (Gen. 17:12; Rom. 4:11-13); the mother of a girl for two weeks—a stigma on the sex (I Tim. 2:14, 15) for sin, which was removed by Christ; everyone who came near her during that time contracted a similar defilement. After these periods, visitors might approach her though she was still excluded from the public ordinances of religion. **6-8. the days of her purifying**—Though the occasion was of a festive character, yet the sacrifices appointed were not a peace offering, but a burnt offering and sin offering, in order to impress the mind of the parent with recollections of the origin of sin, and that the child inherited a fallen and sinful nature. The offerings were to be presented the day after the period of her separation had ended—i.e., forty-first for a boy, eighty-first for a girl. **bring two turtles,** etc.—(See on ch. 5:7). This was the offering made by Mary, the mother of Jesus, and it affords an incontestable proof of the poor and humble condition of the family (Luke 2:22-24).

CHAPTER 13

Vss. 1-59. THE LAWS AND TOKENS IN DISCERNING LEPROSY. **2. When a man shall have in the skin,** etc.—The fact of the following rules for distinguishing the plague of leprosy being incorporated with the Hebrew code of laws, proves the existence of the odious disease among that people. But a short time, little more than a year (if so long a period had elapsed since the exodus) when symptoms of leprosy seem extensively to have appeared among them; and as they could not be very liable to such a cutaneous disorder amid their active journeyings and in the dry open air of Arabia, the seeds of the disorder must have been laid in Egypt, where it has always been endemic. There is every reason to believe that this was the case: that the leprosy was not a family complaint, hereditary among the Hebrews, but that they got it from intercourse with the Egyptians and from the unfavorable circumstances of their condition in the house of bondage. The great excitement and irritability of the skin in the hot and sandy regions of the East produce a far greater predisposition to leprosy of all kinds than in cooler temperatures; and cracks or blotches, inflammations or even contusions of the skin, very often lead to these in Arabia and Palestine, to some extent, but particularly in Egypt. Besides, the subjugated and distressed state of the Hebrews in the latter country, and the nature of their employment, must have rendered them very liable to this as well as to various other blemishes and misaffections of the skin; in the production of which there are no causes more active or powerful than a depressed state of body and mind, hard labor under a burning sun, the body constantly covered with the excoriating dust of brickfields, and an impoverished diet—to all of which the Israelites were exposed while under the Egyptian bondage. It appears that, in consequence of these hardships, there was, even after they had left Egypt, a general predisposition among the Hebrews to the contagious forms of leprosy—so that it often occurred as a consequence of various other affections of the skin. And hence all cutaneous blemishes or blains—especially such as had a tendency to terminate in leprosy—were watched with a jealous eye from the first [GOOD's *Study of Medicine*]. A swelling, a pimple, or bright spot on the skin, created a strong ground of suspicion of a man's being attacked by the dreaded disease. **then he shall be brought unto Aaron the priest,** etc.—Like the Egyptian priests, the Levites united the character of physician with that of the sacred office; and on the appearance of any suspicious eruptions on the skin, the person having these was brought before the priest—not, however, to receive medical treatment, though it is not improbable that some purifying remedies might be prescribed, but to be examined with a view to those sanitary precautions which it belonged to legislation to adopt. **3-6. the priest shall look on the plague in the skin of the flesh,** etc. —The leprosy, as covering the person with a white, scaly scurf, has always been accounted an offensive blemish rather than a serious malady in the East, unless when it assumed its less common and malignant forms. When a Hebrew priest, after a careful inspection, discovered under the cutaneous blemish the distinctive signs of contagious leprosy, the person was immediately pronounced unclean, and is supposed to have been sent out of the camp to a lazaretto provided for that purpose. If the symptoms appeared to be doubtful, he ordered the person to be kept in domestic confinement for seven days, when he was subjected to a second examination; and if during the previous week the eruption had subsided or appeared to be harmless, he was instantly discharged. But if the eruption continued unabated and still doubtful, he was put under surveillance another week; at the end of which the character of the disorder never failed to manifest itself, and he was either doomed to perpetual exclusion from society or allowed to go at large. A person who had thus been detained on suspicion, when at length set at liberty, was obliged to "wash his clothes," as having been tainted by ceremonial pollution; and the purification through which he was required to go was, in the spirit of the Mosaic dispensation, symbolical of that inward purity it was instituted to promote. **7, 8. But if the scab spread much abroad in the skin**—Those doubtful cases, when they assumed a malignant character, appeared in one of two forms, apparently according to the particular constitution of the skin or of the habit generally. The one was "somewhat dark"— i.e., the obscure or dusky leprosy, in which the natural color of the hair (which in Egypt and Palestine is black) is not changed, as is repeatedly said in the sacred code, nor is there any depression in the dusky spot, while the patches, instead of keeping stationary to their first size, are perpetually enlarging their boundary. The patient laboring under this form was pronounced unclean by the Hebrew priest or physician, and hereby sentenced to a separation from his family and friends—a decisive proof of its being contagious. **9-37. if the rising be white**—This BRIGHT WHITE leprosy is the most malignant and inveterate of all the varieties the disease exhibits, and it was marked by the following distinctive signs:—A glossy white and spreading scale, upon an elevated base, the elevation depressed in the middle, but without a change of color; the black hair on the patches participating in the whiteness, and the scaly patches themselves perpetually enlarging their boundary. Several of these characteristics, taken separately, belong to other blemishes of the skin as well; so that none of them was to be taken alone, and it was only when the whole of them concurred that the Jewish priest, in his capacity of physician, was to pronounce the disease a malignant leprosy. If it spread over the entire frame without producing any ulceration, it lost its contagious power by degrees; or, in other words, it ran through its course and exhausted itself. In that case, there being no longer any fear of further evil, either to the individual himself or to the community, the patient was declared clean by the priest, while the dry scales were yet upon him, and restored to society. If, on the contrary, the patches ulcerated and quick or fungous flesh sprang up in them, the purulent matter of which, if brought into contact with the skin of other persons, would be taken into the constitution by means of absorbent vessels, the priest was at once to pronounce it an inveterate leprosy. A temporary confinement was them declared to be totally unnecessary, and he was regarded as unclean for life [DR. GOOD]. Other skin affections, which had a tendency to terminate in leprosy, though they were not decided symptoms when alone, were: "a boil" (vss. 18-23); "a hot burning," i.e., a fiery inflammation or carbuncle (vss. 24-28); and "a dry scall" (vss. 29-37), when the leprosy was distinguished by being deeper than the skin and the hair became thin and yellow. **38, 39. If a man ... or a woman have in the skin of their flesh bright spots**—This modification of the leprosy is distinguished by a dull white color, and it is entirely a cutaneous disorder, never injuring the constitution. It is described as not penetrating below the skin of the flesh and as not rendering necessary an exclusion from society. It is evident, then, that this common form of leprosy is not contagious; otherwise Moses would have prescribed as strict a quarantine in this as in the other cases. And hereby we see the great superiority of the Mosaic

law (which so accurately distinguished the characteristics of the leprosy and preserved to society the services of those who were laboring under the uncontagious forms of the disease) over the customs and regulations of Eastern countries in the present day, where all lepers are indiscriminately proscribed and are avoided as unfit for free intercourse with their fellow men. **40, 41. bald ... forehead bald**—The falling off of the hair, when the baldness commences in the back part of the head, is another symptom which creates a suspicion of leprosy. But it was not of itself a decisive sign unless taken in connection with other tokens, such as a "sore of a reddish white color." The Hebrews as well as other Orientals were accustomed to distinguish between the forehead baldness, which might be natural, and that baldness which might be the consequence of disease. **45. the leper in whom the plague is, his clothes shall be rent,** etc.—The person who was declared affected with the leprosy forthwith exhibited all the tokens of suffering from a heavy calamity. Rending garments and uncovering the head were common signs of mourning. As to "the putting a covering upon the upper lip," that means either wearing a moustache, as the Hebrews used to shave the upper lip [CALMET], or simply keeping a hand over it. All these external marks of grief were intended to proclaim, in addition to his own exclamation "Unclean!" that the person was a leper, whose company every one must shun. **46. he shall dwell alone; without the camp**—in a lazaretto by himself, or associated with other lepers (II Kings 7:3, 8). **47-59. The garment ... that the ... leprosy is in**—It is well known that infectious diseases, such as scarlet fever, measles, the plague, are latently imbibed and carried by the clothes. But the language of this passage clearly indicates a disease to which clothes themselves were subject, and which was followed by effects on them analogous to those which malignant leprosy produces on the human body—for similar regulations were made for the rigid inspection of suspected garments by a priest as for the examination of a leprous person. It has long been conjectured and recently ascertained by the use of a lens, that the leprous condition of swine is produced by myriads of minute insects engendered in their skin; and regarding all leprosy as of the same nature, it is thought that this affords a sufficient reason for the injunction in the Mosaic law to destroy the clothes in which the disease, after careful observation, seemed to manifest itself. Clothes are sometimes seen contaminated by this disease in the West Indies and the southern parts of America [WHITLAW's *Code of Health*]; and it may be presumed that, as the Hebrews were living in the desert where they had not the convenience of frequent changes and washing, the clothes they wore and the skin mats on which they lay, would be apt to breed infectious vermin, which, being settled in the stuff, would imperceptibly gnaw it and leave stains similar to those described by Moses. It is well known that the wool of sheep dying of disease, if it had not been shorn from the animal while living, and also skins, if not thoroughly prepared by scouring, are liable to the effects described in this passage. The stains are described as of a greenish or reddish color, according, perhaps, to the color or nature of the ingredients used in preparing them; for acids convert blue vegetable colors into red and alkalies change then into green [BROWN]. It appears, then, that the leprosy, though sometimes inflicted as a miraculous judgment (Num. 12:10; II Kings 5:27) was a natural disease, which is known in Eastern countries still; while the rules prescribed by the Hebrew legislator for distinguishing the true character and varieties of the disease and which are far superior to the method of treatment now followed in those regions, show the divine wisdom by which he was guided. Doubtless the origin of the disease is owing to some latent causes in nature; and perhaps a more extended acquaintance with the archæology of Egypt and the natural history of the adjacent countries, may confirm the opinion that leprosy results from noxious insects or a putrid fermentation. But whatever the origin or cause of the disease, the laws enacted by divine authority regarding it, while they pointed in the first instance to sanitary ends, were at the same time intended, by stimulating to carefulness against ceremonial defilement, to foster a spirit of religious fear and inward purity.

CHAPTER 14

Vss. 1-57. The Rites and Sacrifices in Cleansing of the Leper. **2. law of the leper in the day of his cleansing**—Though quite convalescent, a leper was not allowed to return to society immediately and at his own will. The malignant character of his disease rendered the greatest precautions necessary to his re-admission among the people. One of the priests most skilled in the diagnostics of disease [Grotius], being deputed to attend such outcasts, the restored leper appeared before this official, and when after examination a certificate of health was given, the ceremonies here described were forthwith observed outside the camp. **4. two birds**—lit., sparrows. The *Septuagint*, however, renders the expression "little birds"; and it is evident that it is to be taken in this generic sense from their being specified as "clean"—a condition which would have been altogether superfluous to mention in reference to sparrows. In all the offerings prescribed in the law, Moses ordered only common and accessible birds; and hence we may presume that he points here to such birds as sparrows or pigeons, as in the desert it might have been very difficult to procure wild birds alive. **cedar wood, and scarlet, and hyssop**—The cedar here meant was certainly not the famous tree of Lebanon, and it is generally supposed to have been the juniper, as several varieties of that shrub are found growing abundantly in the clefts and crevices of the Sinaitic mountains. A stick of this shrub was bound to a bunch of hyssop by a scarlet ribbon, and the living bird was to be so attached to it, that when they dipped the branches in the water, the tail of the bird might also be moistened, but not the head nor the wings, that it might not be impeded in its flight when let loose. **5. the priest shall command that one of the birds be killed ... over running water**—As the blood of a single bird would not have been sufficient to immerse the body of another bird, it was mingled with spring water to increase the quantity necessary for the appointed sprinklings, which were to be repeated *seven times*, denoting a complete purification. (See II Kings 5:10; Ps. 51:2; Matt. 8:4; Luke 5:14.) The living bird being then set free, in token of the leper's release from quarantine, the priest pronounced him clean; and this official declaration was made with all solemnity, in order that the mind of the leper might be duly impressed with a sense of the divine goodness, and that others might be satisfied they might safely hold intercourse with him. Several other purifications had to be gone through

during a series of seven days, and the whole process had to be repeated on the seventh, ere he was allowed to re-enter the camp. The circumstance of a priest being employed seems to imply that instruction suitable to the newly recovered leper would be given, and that the symbolical ceremonies used in the process of cleansing leprosy would be explained. How far they were then understood we cannot tell. But we can trace some instructive analogies between the leprosy and the disease of sin, and between the rites observed in the process of cleansing leprosy and the provisions of the Gospel. The chief of these analogies is that as it was only when a leper exhibited a certain change of state that orders were given by the priest for a sacrifice, so a sinner must be in the exercise of faith and penitence ere the benefits of the gospel remedy can be enjoyed by him. The slain bird and the bird let loose are supposed to typify, the one the death, and the other the resurrection of Christ; while the sprinklings on him that had been leprous typified the requirements which led a believer to cleanse himself from all filthiness of the flesh and spirit, and to perfect his holiness in the fear of the Lord. **10-20. on the right day he shall take two he-lambs without blemish, and one ewe-lamb of the first year without blemish**—The purification of the leper was not completed till at the end of seven days, after the ceremonial of the birds and during which, though permitted to come into the camp, he had to tarry abroad out of his tent, from which he came daily to appear at the door of the tabernacle with the offerings required. He was presented before the Lord by the priest that made him clean. And hence it has always been reckoned among pious people the first duty of a patient newly restored from a long and dangerous sickness to repair to the church to offer his thanksgiving, where his body and soul, in order to be an acceptable offering, must be presented by our great Priest, whose blood alone makes any clean. The offering was to consist of two lambs, the one was to be a sin offering and the an ephah of fine flour (two pints $= \frac{1}{10}$) and one log (half pint) of oil (ch. 2:1). One of the lambs was for a trespass offering, which was necessary from the inherent sin of his nature or from his defilement of the camp by his leprosy previous to his expulsion; and it is remarkable that the blood of the trespass offering was applied exactly in the same particular manner to the extremities of the restored leper, as that of the ram in the consecration of the priests. The parts sprinkled with this blood were then anointed with oil—a ceremony which is supposed to have borne this spiritual import: that while the blood was a token of forgiveness, the oil was an emblem of healing—as the blood of Christ justifies, the influence of the Spirit sanctifies. Of the other two lambs the one was to be a sin offering and the other a burnt offering, which had also the character of a thank offering for God's mercy in his restoration. And this was considered to make atonement "for him"; i.e., it removed that ceremonial pollution which had excluded him from the enjoyment of religious ordinances, just as the atonement of Christ restores all who are cleansed through faith in His sacrifice to the privileges of the children of God. **21-32. if he be poor, and cannot get so much; then he shall take one lamb**—a kind and considerate provision for an extension of the privilege to lepers of the poorer class. The blood of their smaller offering was to be applied in the same process of purification and they were as publicly and completely cleansed as those who brought a costlier offering (Acts 10:34). **34-48. leprosy in a house**—This law was prospective, not to come into operation till the settlement of the Israelites in Canaan. The words, "I put the leprosy," has led many to think that this plague was a judicial infliction from heaven for the sins of the owner; while others do not regard it in this light, it being common in Scripture to represent God as doing that which He only permits in His providence to be done. Assuming it to have been a natural disease, a new difficulty arises as to whether we are to consider that the house had become infected by the contagion of leprous occupiers; or that the leprosy was in the house itself. It is evident that the latter was the true state of the case, from the furniture being removed out of it on the first suspicion of disease on the walls. Some have supposed that the name of leprosy was analogically applied to it by the Hebrews, as we speak of cancer in trees when they exhibit corrosive effects similar to what the disease so named produces on the human body; while others have pronounced it a mural efflorescence or species of mildew on the wall apt to be produced in very damp situations, and which was followed by effects so injurious to health as well as to the stability of a house, particularly in warm countries, as to demand the attention of a legislator. Moses enjoined the priests to follow the same course and during the same period of time for ascertaining the true character of this disease as in human leprosy. If found leprous, the infected parts were to be removed. If afterwards there appeared a risk of the contagion spreading, the house was to be destroyed altogether and the materials removed to a distance. The stones were probably rough, unhewn stones, built up without cement in the manner now frequently used in fences and plastered over, or else laid in mortar. The oldest examples of architecture are of this character. The very same thing has to be done still with houses infected with mural salt. The stones covered with the nitrous incrustation must be removed, and if the infected wall is suffered to remain, it must be plastered all over anew. **48-57. the priest shall pronounce the house clean, because the plague is healed**—The precautions here described show that there is great danger in warm countries from the house leprosy, which was likely to be increased by the smallness and rude architecture of the houses in the early ages of the Israelitish history. As a house could not contract any impurity in the sight of God, the "atonement" which the priest was to make for it must either have a reference to the sins of its occupants or to the ceremonial process appointed for its purification, the very same as that observed for a leprous person. This solemn declaration that it was "clean," as well as the offering made on the occasion, was admirably calculated to make known the fact, to remove apprehension from the public mind, as well as relieve the owner from the aching suspicion of dwelling in an infected house.

CHAPTER 15

Vss. 1-18. UNCLEANNESS OF MEN. **2. When any man hath a running issue**—This chapter describes other forms of uncleanness, the nature of which is sufficiently intelligible in the text without any explanatory comment. Being the effects of licentiousness, they properly come within the notice of the legislator, and the very stringent rules here

prescribed, both for the separation of the person diseased and for avoiding contamination from anything connected with him, were well calculated not only to prevent contagion, but to discourage the excesses of licentious indulgence. **9. what saddle . . . he rideth upon that hath the issue shall be unclean**—(See on Gen. 31:34). **12. the vessel of earth that he toucheth which hath the issue shall be broken**—It is thought that the pottery of the Israelites, like the earthenware jars in which the Egyptians kept their water, was unglazed and consequently porous, and that it was its porousness which, rendering it extremely liable to imbibe small particles of impure matter, was the reason why the vessel touched by an unclean person was ordered to be broken. **13, 14. then he shall number to himself seven days for his cleansing**—Like a leprous person he underwent a week's probation, to make sure he was completely healed. Then with the sacrifices prescribed, the priest made an atonement for him, i.e., offered the oblations necessary for the removal of his ceremonial defilement, as well as the typical pardon of his sins.

19-33. UNCLEANNESS OF WOMEN. **19. if a woman have an issue**—Though this, like the leprosy, might be a natural affection, it was anciently considered contagious and entailed a ceremonial defilement which typified a moral impurity. This ceremonial defilement had to be removed by an appointed method of ceremonial expiation, and the neglect of it subjected any one to the guilt of defiling the tabernacle, and to death as the penalty of profane temerity. **31-33. Thus shall ye separate the children of Israel from their uncleanness**—The divine wisdom was manifested in inspiring the Israelites with a profound reverence for holy things; and nothing was more suited to this purpose than to debar from the tabernacle all who were polluted by any kind of uncleanness, ceremonial as well as natural, mental as well as physical. The better to mark out that people as His family, His servants and priests, dwelling in the camp as in a holy place, consecrated by His presence and His tabernacle, He required of them complete purity, and did not allow them to come before Him when defiled, even by involuntary or secret impurities, as a want of respect due to His majesty. And when we bear in mind that God was training a people to live in His presence in some measure as priests devoted to His service, we shall not consider these rules for the maintenance of personal purity either too stringent or too minute (I Thess. 4:4).

CHAPTER 16

Vss. 1-34. HOW THE HIGH PRIEST MUST ENTER INTO THE HOLY PLACE. **1. after the death of the two sons of Aaron, when they offered before the Lord, and died**—It is thought by some that this chapter has been transposed out of its right place in the sacred record, which was immediately after the narrative of the deaths of Nadab and Abihu. That appalling catastrophe must have filled Aaron with painful apprehensions lest the guilt of these two sons might be entailed on his house, or that other members of his family might share the same fate by some irregularities or defects in the discharge of their sacred functions. And, therefore, this law was established, by the due observance of whose requirements the Aaronic order would be securely maintained and accepted in the priesthood. **2. Speak unto Aaron thy brother, that he come not at all**

times into the holy place within the veil, etc.—Common priests went every day into the part of the sanctuary *without* the veil to burn incense on the golden altar. But none except the high priest was allowed to enter *within* the veil, and that only once a year with the greatest care and solemnity. This arrangement was evidently designed to inspire a reverence for the most holy place, and the precaution was necessary at a time when the presence of God was indicated by sensible symbols, the impression of which might have been diminished or lost by daily and familiar observation. **I will appear in the cloud**—i.e., the smoke of the incense which the high priest burnt on his yearly entrance into the most holy place: and this was the cloud which at that time covered the mercy seat. **3, 4. Thus shall Aaron come into the holy place**—As the duties of the great day of atonement led to the nearest and most solemn approach to God, the directions as to the proper course to be followed were minute and special. **with a young bullock . . . and a ram**—These victims he brought alive, but they were not offered in sacrifice till he had gone through the ceremonies described between this and the eleventh verse. He was not to attire himself on that occasion in the splendid robes that were proper to his sacred office, but in a plain dress of linen, like the common Levites, for, as he was then to make atonement for his own sins, as well as for those of the people, he was to appear in the humble character of a suppliant. That plain dress was more in harmony with a season of humiliation (as well as lighter and more convenient for the duties which on that occasion he had singly to perform) than the gorgeous robes of the pontificate. It showed that when all appeared as sinners, the highest and lowest were then on a level, and that there is no distinction of persons with God. **5-10. shall take of the congregation . . . two kids of the goats . . . and one ram**—The sacrifices were to be offered by the high priest respectively for himself and the other priests, as well as for the people. The bullock (vs. 3) and the goats were for sin offerings and the rams for burnt offerings. The goats, though used in different ways, constituted only one offering. They were both presented before the Lord, and the disposal of them determined by lot, which Jewish writers have thus described: The priest, placing one of the goats on his right hand and the other on his left, took his station by the altar, and cast into an urn two pieces of gold exactly similar, inscribed, the one with the words "for the Lord," and the other for "Azazel" (the scapegoat). After having well shaken them together, he put both his hands into the box and took up a lot in each: that in his right hand he put on the head of the goat which stood on his right, and that in his left he dropped on the other. In this manner the fate of each was decided. **11-14. Aaron shall bring the bullock of the sin offering which is for himself,** etc.—The first part of the service was designed to solemnize his own mind, as well as the minds of the people, by offering the sacrifices for their sins. The sin offerings being slain had the sins of the offerer judicially transferred to them by the imputation of his hands on their head (ch. 4); and thus the young bullock, which was to make atonement for himself and the other priests (called "his house," Ps. 135: 19), was killed by the hands of the high priest. While the blood of the victim was being received into a vessel, taking a censer of live coals in his right hand and a platter of sweet incense in his left, he, amid the solemn attention and the anxious prayers of the assembled multitude, crossed the porch and the holy place, opened the outer veil which led into the holy of holies and then the inner veil. Standing before the ark, he deposited the censer of coals on the floor, emptied the plate of incense into his hand, poured it on the burning coals; and the apartment was filled with fragrant smoke, intended, according to Jewish writers, to prevent any presumptuous gazer prying too curiously into the form of the mercy seat, which was the Lord's throne. The high priest having done this, perfumed the sanctuary, returned to the door, took the blood of the slain bullock, and, carrying it into the holy of holies, sprinkled it with his finger once upon the mercy seat "eastward,"—i.e., on the side next to himself; and seven times "before the mercy seat,"—i.e., on the front of the ark. Leaving the coals and the incense burning, he went out a second time, to sacrifice at the altar of burnt offering the goat which had been assigned as a sin offering for the people; and carrying its blood into the holy of holies, made similar sprinklings as he had done before with the blood of the bullock. While the high priest was thus engaged in the most holy place, none of the ordinary priests were allowed to remain within the precincts of the tabernacle. The sanctuary or holy place and the altar of burnt offering were in like manner sprinkled seven times with the blood of the bullock and the goat. The object of this solemn ceremonial was to impress the minds of the Israelites with the conviction that the whole tabernacle was stained by the sins of a guilty people, that by their sins they had forfeited the privileges of the divine presence and worship, and that an atonement had to be made as the condition of God's remaining with them. The sins and shortcomings of the past year having polluted the sacred edifice, the expiation required to be annually renewed. The exclusion of the priests indicated their unworthiness and the impurities of their service. The mingled blood of the two victims being sprinkled on the horns of the altar indicated that the priests and the people equally needed an atonement for their sins. But the sanctuary being thus ceremonially purified, and the people of Israel reconciled by the blood of the consecrated victim, the Lord continued to dwell in the midst of them, and to honor them with His gracious presence. **20-22. he shall bring the live goat**—Having already been presented before the Lord (vs. 10), it was now brought forward to the high priest, who, placing his hands upon its head, and "having confessed over it all the iniquities of the people of Israel, and all their transgressions in all their sins," transferred them by this act to the goat as their substitute. It was then delivered into the hands of a person, who was appointed to lead him away into a distant, solitary, and desert place, where in early times he was let go, to escape for his life; but in the time of Christ, he was carried to a high rock twelve miles from Jerusalem, and there, being thrust over the precipice, he was killed. Commentators have differed widely in their opinions about the character and purpose of this part of the ceremonial; some considering the word "Azazel," with the LXX and our translators, to mean, "the scapegoat"; others, "a lofty, precipitous rock" [BOCHART]; others, "a thing separated to God" [EWALD, THOLUCK]; while others think it designates Satan [GESENIUS, HENGSTENBERG]. This last view is grounded on the idea of both goats forming one and the same sacrifice of atonement, and it is supported by Zechariah 3, which presents a striking commentary on this passage. Whether there was in this peculiar ceremony any reference to an Egyptian superstition about Typhon, the spirit of evil, inhabiting the wilderness, and the design was to ridicule it by sending a cursed animal into his gloomy dominions, it is impossible to say. The subject is involved in much obscurity. But in any view there seems to be a typical reference to Christ who bore away our sins. **23-28. Aaron shall come into the tabernacle of the congregation, and shall put off the linen garments**—On the dismissal of the scapegoat, the high priest prepared for the important parts of the service which still remained; and for the performance of these he laid aside his plain linen clothes, and, having bathed himself in water, he assumed his pontifical dress. Thus gorgeously attired, he went to present the burnt offerings which were prescribed for himself and the people, consisting of the two rams which had been brought with the sin offerings, but reserved till now. The fat was ordered to be burnt upon the altar; the rest of the carcasses to be cut down and given to some priestly attendants to burn without the camp, in conformity with the general law for the sin offerings (ch. 4:8-12; 8:14-17). The persons employed in burning them, as well as the conductor of the scapegoat, were obliged to wash their clothes and bathe their flesh in water before they were allowed to return into the camp. **29-34. this shall be a statute for ever unto you, that in the seventh month, on the tenth day of the month, ye shall afflict your souls**—This day of annual expiation for all the sins, irreverences, and impurities of all classes in Israel during the previous year, was to be observed as a solemn fast, in which "they were to afflict their souls"; it was reckoned a sabbath—kept as a season of "holy convocation," or, assembling for religious purposes. All persons who performed any labor were subject to the penalty of death. It took place on the tenth day of the seventh month, corresponding to our third of October; and this chapter, together with chapter 23:27-32, as containing special allusion to the observances of the day, was publicly read. The rehearsal of these passages appointing the solemn ceremonial was very appropriate, and the details of the successive parts of it (above all the spectacle of the public departure of the scapegoat under the care of its leader) must have produced salutary impressions both of sin and of duty that would not be soon effaced.

CHAPTER 17

Vss. 1-16. BLOOD OF BEASTS MUST BE OFFERED AT THE TABERNACLE DOOR. **3. What man ... killeth an ox**—The Israelites, like other people living in the desert, would not make much use of animal food; and when they did kill a lamb or a kid for food, it would almost always be, as in Abraham's entertainment of the angels, an occasion of a feast, to be eaten in company. This was what was done with the peace offerings, and accordingly it is here enacted, that the same course shall be followed in slaughtering the animals as in the case of those offerings, viz., that they should be killed publicly, and after being devoted to God, partaken of by the offerers. This law, it is obvious, could only be observable in the wilderness while the people were encamped within an accessible distance from the tabernacle. The reason for it is to be found in the strong addictedness of the Israelites to idolatry at the time of their departure from Egypt; and as it would have been easy for any by killing an animal to sacrifice privately to a favorite object of worship,

a strict prohibition was made against their slaughtering at home. (See on Deut. 12:13.) **5. To the end that the children of Israel may bring their sacrifices, which they offer in the open field**—"They" is supposed by some commentators to refer to the Egyptians, so that the verse will stand thus: "the children of Israel may bring their sacrifices which they (the Egyptians) offer in the open field." The law is thought to have been directed against those whose Egyptian habits led them to imitate this idolatrous practice. **7. they shall no more offer their sacrifices unto devils**—lit., "goats." The prohibition evidently alludes to the worship of the hirei-footed kind, such as Pan, Faunus, and Saturn, whose recognized symbol was a goat. This was a form of idolatry enthusiastically practised by the Egyptians, particularly in the nome or province of Mendes. Pan was supposed especially to preside over mountainous and desert regions, and it was while they were in the wilderness that the Israelites seem to have been powerfully influenced by a feeling to propitiate this idol. Moreover, the ceremonies observed in this idolatrous worship were extremely licentious and obscene, and the gross impurity of the rites gives great point and significance to the expression of Moses, "they have gone a-whoring." **8, 9. Whatsoever man ... offereth ... And bringeth it not unto the door of the tabernacle**—Before the promulgation of the law, men worshipped wherever they pleased or pitched their tents. But after that event the rites of religion could be acceptably performed only at the appointed place of worship. This restriction with respect to place was necessary as a preventive of idolatry; for it prohibited the Israelites, when at a distance, from repairing to the altars of the heathen, which were commonly in groves or fields. **10. I will even set my face against that soul that eateth blood, and will cut him off from among his people**—The face of God is often used in Scripture to denote His anger (Ps. 34:16; Rev. 6:16; Ezek. 38:18). The manner in which God's face would be set against such an offender was, that if the crime were public and known, he was condemned to death; it it were secret, vengeance would overtake him. (See on Gen. 9:4.) But the practice against which the law is here pointed was an idolatrous rite. The Zabians, or worshippers of the heavenly host, were accustomed, in sacrificing animals, to pour out the blood and eat a part of the flesh at *the place* where the blood was poured out (and sometimes the blood itself) believing that by means of it, friendship, brotherhood, and familiarity were contracted between the worshippers and the deities. They, moreover, supposed that the blood was very beneficial in obtaining for them a vision of the demon during their sleep, and a revelation of future events. The prohibition against eating blood, viewed in the light of this historic commentary and unconnected with the peculiar terms in which it is expressed, seems to have been levelled against idolatrous practices, as is still farther evident from Ezek. 33:25, 26, I Cor. 10:20, 21. **11. the life of the flesh is in the blood; and I have given it to you upon the altar, to make an atonement for your souls**—God, as the sovereign author and proprietor of nature, reserved the blood to Himself and allowed men only one use of it—in the way of sacrifices. **13, 14. whatsoever man ... hunteth**—It was customary with heathen sportsmen, when they killed any game or venison, to pour out the blood as a libation to the god of the chase. The Israelites, on the contrary, were enjoined, instead of leaving it exposed, to cover it with dust and, by this means, were effectually debarred from all the superstitious uses to which the heathen applied it. **15, 16. every soul that eateth that which died of itself** (Exod. 22:31; ch. 11:30; Acts 15:20), **be unclean until the even**—i.e., from the moment of his discovering his fault until the evening. This law, however, was binding only on an Israelite. (See Deut. 14:21.)

CHAPTER 18

Vss. 1-30. UNLAWFUL MARRIAGES. **2-4. I am the Lord your God**—This renewed mention of the divine sovereignty over the Israelites was intended to bear particularly on some laws that were widely different from the social customs that obtained both in Egypt and Canaan; for the enormities, which the laws enumerated in this chapter were intended to put down, were freely practised or publicly sanctioned in both of those countries; and, indeed, the extermination of the ancient Canaanites is described as owing to the abominations with which they had polluted the land. **5. Ye shall therefore keep my statutes and my judgments; which if a man do, he shall live in them**—A special blessing was promised to the Israelites on condition of their obedience to the divine law; and this promise was remarkably verified at particular eras of their history, when pure and undefiled religion prevailed among them, in the public prosperity and domestic happiness enjoyed by them as a people. Obedience to the divine law always, indeed, ensures temporal advantages; and this, doubtless, was the primary meaning of the words, "which if a man do, he shall live in them." But that they had a higher reference to spiritual life is evident from the application made of them by our Lord (Luke 10:28) and the apostle (Rom. 10:2). **6. None of you shall approach to any that is near of kin**—Very great laxity prevailed amongst the Egyptians in their sentiments and practice about the conjugal relation, as they not only openly sanctioned marriages between brothers and sisters, but even between parents and children. Such incestuous alliances Moses wisely prohibited, and his laws form the basis upon which the marriage regulations of this and other Christian nations are chiefly founded. This verse contains a general summary of all the particular prohibitions; and the forbidden intercourse is pointed out by the phrase, "to approach to." In the specified prohibitions that follow, all of which are included in this general summary, the prohibited familiarity is indicated by the phrases, to "uncover the nakedness," to "take," and to "lie with." The phrase in this sixth verse, therefore, has the same identical meaning with each of the other three, and the marriages in reference to which it is used are those of consanguinity or too close affinity, amounting to incestuous connections. **18. Neither shalt thou take a wife to her sister, to vex her.** The original is rendered in the margin, "neither shalt thou take one wife to another to vex her," and two different and opposite interpretations have been put upon this passage. The marginal construction involves an express prohibition of polygamy; and, indeed, there can be no doubt that the practice of having more wives than one is directly contrary to the divine will. It was prohibited by the original law of marriage, and no evidence of its lawfulness under the Levitical code can be discovered, although Moses—from "the hardness of their hearts"—tolerated it in the people of a rude and early age. The second interpretation forms the ground upon which the "vexed question"

has been raised in our times respecting the lawfulness of marriage with a deceased wife's sister. Whatever arguments may be used to prove the unlawfulness or inexpediency of such a matrimonial relation, the passage under consideration cannot, on a sound basis of criticism, be enlisted in the service; for the crimes with which it is here associated warrant the conclusion that it points not to marriage with a deceased wife's sister, but with a sister in the wife's lifetime, a practice common among the ancient Egyptians, Chaldeans, and others. **21. thou shalt not let any of thy seed pass through the fire to Molech, etc.**—Molech, or Moloch, which signifies "king," was the idol of the Ammonites. His statue was of brass, and rested on a pedestal or throne of the same metal. His head, resembling that of a calf, was adorned with a crow, and his arms were extended in the attitude of embracing those who approached him. His devotees dedicated their children to him; and when this was to be done, they heated the statue to a high pitch of intensity by a fire within, and then the infants were either shaken over the flames, or passed through the ignited arms, by way of lustration to ensure the favor of the pretended deity. The fire-worshippers asserted that all children who did not undergo this purifying process would die in infancy; and the influence of this Zabian superstition was still so extensively prevalent in the days of Moses, that the divine lawgiver judged it necessary to prohibit it by an express statute. **neither shalt thou profane the name of thy God**—by giving it to false or pretended divinities; or, perhaps, from this precept standing in close connection with the worship of Molech, the meaning rather is, Do not, by devoting your children to him, give foreigners occasion to blaspheme the name of your God as a cruel and sanguinary deity, who demands the sacrifice of human victims, and who encourages cruelty in his votaries. **24. Defile not yourselves in any of these things**—In the preceding verses seventeen express cases of incest are enumerated; comprehending eleven of affinity, and six of consanguinity, together with some criminal enormities of an aggravated and unnatural character. In such prohibitions it was necessary for the instruction of a people low in the scale of moral perception, that the enumeration should be very specific as well as minute; and then, on completing it, the divine lawgiver announces his own views of these crimes, without any exception or modification, in the remarkable terms employed in this verse. **in all these the nations are defiled which I cast out before you,** etc.—Ancient history gives many appalling proofs that the enormous vices described in this chapter were very prevalent, nay, were regularly practised from religious motives in the temples of Egypt and the groves of Canaan; and it was these gigantic social disorders that occasioned the expulsion, of which the Israelites were, in the hands of a righteous and retributive Providence, the appointed instruments (Gen. 15:16). The strongly figurative language of "the land itself vomiting out her inhabitants," shows the hopeless depth of their moral corruption. **25 therefore I do visit the iniquity thereof upon it; and the land itself vomiteth out its inhabitants**—The Canaanites, as enormous and incorrigible sinners, were to be exterminated; and this extermination was manifestly a judicial punishment inflicted by a ruler whose laws had been grossly and perseveringly outraged. But before a law can be disobeyed, it must have been previously in existence; and hence a law, prohibiting all the horrid crimes enumerated above—a law obligatory upon the Canaanites as well as other nations—was already known and in force before the Levitical law of incest was promulgated. Some general law, then, prohibiting these crimes must have been published to mankind at a very early period of the world's history; and that law must either have been the moral law, originally written on the human heart, or a law on the institution of marriage revealed to Adam and known to the Canaanites and others by tradition or otherwise. **29. the souls that commit them shall be cut off**—This strong denunciatory language is applied to all the crimes specified in the chapter without distinction: to incest as truly as to bestiality, and to the eleven cases of affinity as fully as to the six of consanguinity. Death is the punishment sternly denounced against all of them. No language could be more explicit or universal; none could more strongly indicate intense loathing and abhorrence. **30. Therefore shall ye keep mine ordinance, that ye commit not any one of these abominable customs**—In giving the Israelites these particular institutions, God was only redelivering the law imprinted on the natural heart of man; for there is every reason to believe that the incestuous alliances and unnatural crimes prohibited in this chapter were forbidden to all men by a law expressed or understood from the beginning of the world, or at least from the era of the flood, since God threatens to condemn and punish, in a manner so sternly severe, these atrocities in the practice of the Canaanites and their neighbors, who were not subject to the laws of the Hebrew nation.

CHAPTER 19

Vss. 1-37. A REPETITION OF SUNDRY LAWS. **2. Speak unto all the congregation of the children of Israel**—Many of the laws enumerated in this chapter had been previously announced. As they were, however, of a general application, not suited to particular classes, but to the nation at large, so Moses seems, according to divine instructions, to have rehearsed them, perhaps on different occasions and to successive divisions of the people, till "all the congregation of the children of Israel" were taught to know them. The will of God in the Old as well as the New Testament Church was not locked up in the repositories of an unknown tongue, but communicated plainly and openly to the people. **Ye shall be holy: for I . . . am holy**—Separated from the world, the people of God were required to be holy, for His character, His laws, and service were holy. (See I Pet. 1:15.) **3. Ye shall fear every man his mother and his father, and keep my sabbaths**—The duty of obedience to parents is placed in connection with the proper observance of the Sabbaths, both of them lying at the foundation of practical religion. **5-8. if ye offer a sacrifice of peace offerings unto the Lord, ye shall offer it at your own will**—Those which included thank offerings, or offerings made for vows, were always freewill offerings. Except the portions which, being waved and heaved, became the property of the priests (see ch. 3), the rest of the victim was eaten by the offerer and his friend, under the following regulations, however, that, if thank offerings, they were to be eaten on the day of their presentation; and if a freewill offering, although it might be eaten on the second day, yet if any remained of it till the third day, it was to be burnt, or deep criminality was incurred by the person who then ventured to partake of it. The reason of this strict prohibition

seems to have been to prevent any mysterious virtue being superstitiously attached to meat offered on the altar. **9, 10. when ye reap the harvest of your land, thou shalt not wholly reap the corners of thy field**—The right of the poor in Israel to glean after reapers, as well as to the unreaped corners of the field, was secured by a positive statute; and this, in addition to other enactments connected with the ceremonial law, formed a beneficial provision for their support. At the same time, proprietors were not obliged to admit them into the field until the grain had been carried off the field; and they seem also to have been left at liberty to choose the poor whom they deemed the most deserving or needful (Ruth 2:2, 8). This was the earliest law for the benefit of the poor that we read of in the code of any people; and it combined in admirable union the obligation of a public duty with the exercise of private and voluntary benevolence at a time when the hearts of the rich would be strongly inclined to liberality. **11-16. Ye shall not steal**—A variety of social duties are inculcated in this passage, chiefly in reference to common and little-thought-of vices to which mankind are exceedingly prone; such as committing petty frauds, or not scrupling to violate truth in transactions of business, ridiculing bodily infirmities, or circulating stories to the prejudice of others. In opposition to these bad habits, a spirit of humanity and brotherly kindness is strongly enforced. **17. thou shalt in any wise rebuke thy neighbour**—Instead of cherishing latent feelings of malice or meditating purposes of revenge against a person who has committed an insult or injury against them, God's people were taught to remonstrate with the offender and endeavor, by calm and kindly reason, to bring him to a sense of his fault. **not suffer sin upon him**—lit., that ye may not participate in his sin. **18. thou shalt love thy neighbour as thyself**—The word "neighbour" is used as synonymous with "fellow creature." The Israelites in a later age restricted its meaning as applicable only to their own countrymen. This narrow interpretation was refuted by our Lord in a beautiful parable (Luke 10:30). **19. Thou shalt not let thy cattle gender with a diverse kind**—This prohibition was probably intended to discourage a practice which seemed to infringe upon the economy which God has established in the animal kingdom. **thou shalt not sow thy field with mingled seed**—This also was directed against an idolatrous practice, viz., that of the ancient Zabians, or fire-worshippers, who sowed different seeds, accompanying the act with magical rites and invocations; and commentators have generally thought the design of this and the preceding law was to put an end to the unnatural lusts and foolish superstitions which were prevalent among the heathen. But the reason of the prohibition was probably deeper: for those who have studied the diseases of land and vegetables tell us, that the practice of mingling seeds is injurious both to flowers and to grains. "If the various genera of the natural order Gramineæ, which includes the grains and the grasses, should be sown in the same field, and flower at the same time, so that the pollen of the two flowers mix, a spurious seed will be the consequence, called by the farmers *chess*. It is always inferior and unlike either of the two grains that produced it, in size, flavor, and nutritious principles. Independently of contributing to disease the soil, they never fail to produce the same in animals and men that feed on them" [WHITLAW]. **neither shall a garment mingled of linen and woollen come upon thee**—Although this precept, like the other two with which it is associated, was in all probability designed to root out some superstition, it seems to have had a farther meaning. The law, it is to be observed, did not prohibit the Israelites wearing many different kinds of cloths together, but only the two specified; and the observations and researches of modern science have proved that "wool, when combined with linen, increases its power of passing off the electricity from the body. In hot climates, it brings on malignant fevers and exhausts the strength; and when passing off from the body, it meets with the heated air, inflames and excoriates like a blister" [WHITLAW]. (See Ezek. 44:17, 18.) **23-25. ye shall count the fruit thereof as uncircumcised; three years ... it shall not be eaten of**—"The wisdom of this law is very striking. Every gardener will teach us not to let fruit trees bear in their earliest years, but to pluck off the blossoms: and for this reason, that they will thus thrive the better, and bear more abundantly afterwards. The very expression, 'to regard them as uncircumcised,' suggests the propriety of pinching them off; I do not say *cutting* them off, because it is generally the hand, and not a knife, that is employed in this operation" [MICHAELIS]. **26. shall not eat any thing with the blood**—(See on ch. 17:10.) **neither ... use enchantment, nor observe times**—The former refers to divination by serpents—one of the earliest forms of enchantment, and the other means the observation, lit., of *clouds*, as a study of the appearance and motion of clouds was a common way of foretelling good or bad fortune. Such absurd but deep-rooted superstitions often put a stop to the prosecution of serious and important transactions, but they were forbidden especially as implying a want of faith in the being, or of reliance on the providence of God. **27. Ye shall not round the corners of your heads**, etc.—It seems probable that this fashion had been learned by the Israelites in Egypt, for the ancient Egyptians had their dark locks cropped short or shaved with great nicety, so that what remained on the crown appeared in the form of a circle surrounding the head, while the beard was dressed into a square form. This kind of coiffure had a highly idolatrous meaning; and it was adopted, with some slight variations, by almost all idolaters in ancient times. (Jer. 9:25, 26; 25:23, where "in the utmost corners" means having the corners of their hair cut.) Frequently a lock or tuft of hair was left on the hinder part of the head, the rest being cut round in the form of a ring, as the Turks, Chinese, and Hindoos do at the present day. **neither shalt thou mar**, etc.—The Egyptians used to cut or shave off their whiskers, as may be seen in the coffins of mummies, and the representations of divinities on the monuments. But the Hebrews, in order to separate them from the neighboring nations, or perhaps to put a stop to some existing superstition, were forbidden to imitate this practice. It may appear surprising that Moses should condescend to such minutiæ as that of regulating the fashion of the hair and the beard—matters which do not usually occupy the attention of a legislator—and which appear widely remote from the province either of government or of a religion. A strong presumption, therefore, arises that he had in mind by these regulations to combat some superstitious practices of the Egyptians. **28. Ye shall not make any cuttings in your flesh for the dead**—The practice of making deep gashes on the face and arms and legs, in time of bereavement, was universal among the heathen, and it was deemed a becoming mark of respect for the dead, as well as a sort of propitiatory

offering to the deities who presided over death and the grave. The Jews learned this custom in Egypt, and though weaned from it, relapsed in a later and degenerate age into this old superstition (Isa. 15:2; Jer. 16:6; 41:5). **nor print any marks upon you**—by *tattooing*—imprinting figures of flowers, leaves, stars, and other fanciful devices on various parts of their person—the impression was made sometimes by means of a hot iron, sometimes by ink or paint, as is done by the Arab females of the present day and the different castes of the Hindoos. It it probable that a strong propensity to adopt such marks in honor of some idol gave occasion to the prohibition in this verse; and they were wisely forbidden, for they were signs of apostasy; and, when once made, they were insuperable obstacles to a return. (See allusions to the practice, Isa. 44:5; Rev. 13:17; 14: 1.) **30. keep my sabbaths, and reverence my sanctuary**—This precept is frequently repeated along with the prohibition of idolatrous practices, and here it stands closely connected with the superstitions forbidden in the previous verses. **31. Regard not them that have familiar spirits**—The *Hebrew* word, rendered "familiar spirit," signifies the belly, and sometimes a leathern bottle, from its similarity to the belly. It was applied in the sense of this passage to ventriloquists, who pretended to have communication with the invisible world. The Hebrews were strictly forbidden to consult them as the vain but high pretensions of those impostors were derogatory to the honor of God and subversive of their covenant relations with Him as His people. **neither seek after wizards**—fortunetellers, who pretended, as the *Hebrew* word indicates, to prognosticate by palmistry (or an inspection of the lines of the hand) the future fate of those who applied to them. **33, 34. if a stranger sojourn with thee in your land, ye shall not vex him**—The Israelites were to hold out encouragement to strangers to settle among them, that they might be brought to the knowledge and worship of the true God; and with this in view, they were enjoined to treat them not as aliens, but as friends, on the ground that they themselves, who were strangers in Egypt, were at first kindly and hospitably received in that country. **37. I am the Lord**—This solemn admonition, by which these various precepts are repeatedly sanctioned, is equivalent to "I, your Creator—your Deliverer from bondage, and your Sovereign, who have wisdom to establish laws, have power also to punish the violation of them." It was well fitted to impress the minds of the Israelites with a sense of their duty and God's claims to obedience.

CHAPTER 20

Vss. 1-27. GIVING ONE'S SEED TO MOLECH. **2. Whosoever ... giveth any of his seed unto Molech** [see on ch. 18:21], **the people of the land shall stone him with stones**, etc.—Criminals who were condemned to be stoned were led, with their hands bound, without the gates to a small eminence, where was a large stone placed at the bottom. When they had approached within ten cubits of the spot, they were exhorted to confess, that, by faith and repentance, their souls might be saved. When led forward to within four cubits, they were stripped almost naked, and received some stupefying draught, during which the witnesses prepared, by laying aside their outer garments, to carry into execution the capital sentence which the law bound them to do. The criminal, being placed on the edge of the precipice, was then pushed backwards, so that he fell down the perpendicular height on the stone lying below: if not killed by the fall, the second witness dashed a large stone down upon his breast, and then the "people of the land," who were bystanders, rushed forward, and with stones completed the work of death (Matt. 21:44; Acts 7:58). **4. If the people of the land do any ways hide their eyes from the man,** etc.—i.e., connive at their countrymen practising the horrid rites of Molech. Awful was it that any Hebrew parents could so violate their national covenant, and no wonder that God denounced the severest penalties against them and their families. **7-19. Sanctify yourselves therefore, and be ye holy**—The minute specification of the incestuous and unnatural crimes here enumerated shows their sad prevalence amongst the idolatrous nations around, and the extreme proneness of the Israelites to follow the customs of their neighbors. It is to be understood, that, whenever mention is made that the offender was "to be put to death" without describing the mode, stoning is meant. The only instance of another form of capital punishment occurs in verse 14, that of being burnt with fire; and yet it is probable that even here death was first inflicted by stoning, and the body of the criminal afterwards consumed by fire (Josh. 7:15). **20. they shall die childless**—Either by the judgment of God they shall have no children, or their spurious offspring shall be denied by human authority the ordinary privileges of children in Israel. **24. I . . . have separated you from other people**—Their selection from the rest of the nations was for the all-important end of preserving the knowledge and worship of the true God amid the universal apostasy; and as the distinction of meats was one great means of completing that separation, the law about making a difference between clean and unclean beasts is here repeated with emphatic solemnity.

CHAPTER 21

Vss. 1-24. OF THE PRIESTS' MOURNING. **1. There shall none be defiled for the dead among his people**—The obvious design of the regulations contained in this chapter was to keep inviolate the purity and dignity of the sacred office. Contact with a corpse, or even contiguity to the place where it lay, entailing ceremonial defilement (Num. 19:14), all mourners were debarred from the tabernacle for a week; and as the exclusion of a priest during that period would have been attended with great inconvenience, the whole order were enjoined to abstain from all approaches to the dead, except at the funerals of relatives, to whom affection or necessity might call them to perform the last offices. Those exceptional cases, which are specified, were strictly confined to the members of their own family, within the nearest degrees of kindred. **4. But he shall not defile himself**—"for any other," as the sense may be fully expressed. "The priest, in discharging his sacred functions, might well be regarded as a chief man among his people, and by these defilements might be said to profane himself" [BISHOP PATRICK]. The word rendered "chief man" signifies also "a husband"; and the sense according to others is, "But he being a husband, shall not defile himself by the obsequies of a wife" (Ezek. 44:25). **5. They shall not make baldness upon their heads . . . nor . . . cuttings in their flesh**—The superstitious marks of sorrow, as well as the violent excesses in which the heathen indulged at the death of

their friends, were forbidden by a general law to the Hebrew people (ch. 19:28). But the priests were to be laid under a special injunction, not only that they might exhibit examples of piety in the moderation of their grief, but also by the restraint of their passions, be the better qualified to administer the consolations of religion to others, and show, by their faith in a blessed resurrection, the reasons for sorrowing not as those who have no hope. **7-9. They shall not take a wife that is a whore, or profane**—Private individuals might form several connections, which were forbidden as inexpedient or improper in priests. The respectability of their office, and the honor of religion, required unblemished sanctity in their families as well as themselves, and departures from it in their case were visited with severer punishment than in that of others. **10-15. he that is the high priest among his brethren . . . shall not uncover his head, nor rend his clothes**—The indulgence in the excepted cases of family bereavement, mentioned above, which was granted to the common priests, was denied to him; for his absence from the sanctuary for the removal of any contracted defilement could not have been dispensed with, neither could he have acted as intercessor for the people, unless ceremonially clean. Moreover, the high dignity of his office demanded a corresponding superiority in personal holiness, and stringent rules were prescribed for the purpose of upholding the suitable dignity of his station and family. The same rules are extended to the families of Christian ministers (I Tim. 3:2; Titus 1:6). **16-24. Whosoever he be . . . that hath any blemish, let him not approach to offer the bread of his God**—As visible things exert a strong influence on the minds of men, any physical infirmity or malformation of body in the ministers of religion, which disturbs the associations or excites ridicule, tends to detract from the weight and authority of the sacred office. Priests laboring under any personal defect were not allowed to officiate in the public service; they might be employed in some inferior duties about the sanctuary but could not perform any sacred office. In all these regulations for preserving the unsullied purity of the sacred character and office, there was a typical reference to the priesthood of Christ (Heb. 7:26).

CHAPTER 22

Vss. 1-9. THE PRIESTS IN THEIR UNCLEANNESS. **2. Speak unto Aaron and to his sons, that they separate themselves from the holy thing**—"To separate" means, in the language of the Mosaic ritual, "to abstain"; and therefore the import of this injunction is that the priests should abstain from eating that part of the sacrifices which, though belonging to their order, was to be partaken of only by such of them as were free from legal impurities. **that they profane not my holy name in those things which they hallow unto me,** etc.—i.e., let them not, by their want of due reverence, give occasion to profane my holy name. A careless or irreverent use of things consecrated to God tends to dishonor the name and bring disrespect on the worship of God. **3. Whosoever he be . . . that goeth unto the holy things**—The multitude of minute restrictions to which the priests, from accidental defilement, were subjected, by keeping them constantly on their guard lest they should be unfit for the sacred service, tended to preserve in full exercise the feeling of awe and submission to the authority of God.

The ideas of sin and duty were awakened in their breasts by every case to which either an interdict or an injunction was applied. But why enact an express statute for priests disqualified by the leprosy or polluting touch of a carcass, when a general law was already in force which excluded from society all persons in that condition? Because priests might be apt, from familiarity, to trifle with religion, and in committing irregularities or sins, to shelter themselves under the cloak of the sacred office. This law, therefore, was passed, specifying the chief forms of temporary defilement which excluded from the sanctuary, that priests might not deem themselves entitled to greater license than the rest of the people; and that so far from being in any degree exempted from the sanctions of the law, they were under greater obligations, by their priestly station, to observe it in its strict letter and its smallest enactments. **4-6. wash his flesh with water**—Any Israelite who had contracted a defilement of such a nature as debarred him from the enjoyment of his wonted privileges, and had been legally cleansed from the disqualifying impurity, was bound to indicate his state of recovery by the immersion of his whole person in water. Although all ceremonial impurity formed a ground of exclusion, there were degrees of impurity which entailed a longer or shorter period of excommunication, and for the removal of which different rites required to be observed according to the trivial or the malignant nature of the case. A person who came inadvertently into contact with an unclean animal was rendered unclean for a specified period; and then, at the expiry of that term, he washed, in token of his recovered purity. But a leper was unclean so long as he remained subject to that disease, and on his convalescence, he also washed, not to cleanse himself, for the water was ineffectual for that purpose, but to signify that he was clean. Not a single case is recorded of a leper being restored to communion by the use of water; it served only as an outward and visible sign that such a restoration was to be made. The Book of Leviticus abounds with examples which show that in all the ceremonial washings, as uncleanness meant loss of privileges, so baptism with water indicated a restoration to those privileges. There was no exemption; for as the unclean Israelite was exiled from the congregation, so the unclean priest was disqualified from executing his sacred functions in the sanctuary; and in the case of both, the same observance was required—a formal intimation of their being readmitted to forfeited privileges was intimated by the appointed rite of baptism. If any one neglected or refused to perform the washing, he disobeyed a positive precept, and he remained in his uncleanness; he forbore to avail himself of this privilege, and was therefore said to be "cut off" from the presence of the Lord. **8. dieth of itself**—The feelings of nature revolt against such food. It might have been left to the discretion of the Hebrews, who it may be supposed (like the people of all civilized nations) would have abstained from the use of it without any positive interdict. But an express precept was necessary to show them that whatever died naturally or from disease, was prohibited to them by the operation of that law which forbade them the use of any meat with its blood.

10-16. Who of the Priests' House May Eat of Them. 10. There shall no stranger eat the holy thing—The portion of the sacrifices assigned for the support of the officiating priests was restricted to the exclusive use of his own family. A temporary guest or a hired servant was not at liberty to eat of them; but an exception was made in favor of a bought or home-born slave, because such was a stated member of his household. On the same principle, his own daughter, who married a husband not a priest, could not eat of them. However, if a widow and childless, she was reinstated in the privileges of her father's house as before her marriage. But if she had become a mother, as her children had no right to the privileges of the priesthood, she was under a necessity of finding support for them elsewhere than under her father's roof. **13. there shall no stranger eat thereof**—The interdict recorded (vs. 10) is repeated to show its stringency. All the Hebrews, even the nearest neighbors of the priest, the members of his family excepted, were considered strangers in this respect, so that they had no right to eat of things offered at the altar. **14. if a man eat of the holy things unwittingly**—A common Israelite might unconsciously partake of what had been offered as tithes, firstfruits, etc., and on discovering his unintentional error, he was not only to restore as much as he had used, but be fined in a fifth part more for the priests to carry into the sanctuary. **15, 16. they shall not profane the holy things of the children of Israel**—There is some difficulty felt in determining to whom "they" refers. The subject of the preceding context being occupied about the priests, it is supposed by some that this relates to them also; and the meaning then is that the whole people would incur guilt through the fault of the priests, if they should defile the sacred offerings, which they would have done had they presented them while under any defilement [CALVIN]. According to others, "the children of Israel" is the nominative in the sentence; which thus signifies, the children of Israel shall not profane or defile their offerings, by touching them or reserving any part of them, lest they incur the guilt of eating what is divinely appointed to the priests alone [CALMET].

17-33. The Sacrifices Must Be without Blemish. 19. Ye shall offer at your own will—rather, to your being accepted. **a male without blemish**—This law (ch. 1:3) is founded on a sense of natural propriety, which required the greatest care to be taken in the selection of animals for sacrifice. The reason for this extreme caution is found in the fact that sacrifices are either an expression of praise to God for His goodness, or else they are the designed means of conciliating or retaining His favor. No victim that was not perfect in its kind could be deemed a fitting instrument for such purposes if we assume that the significance of sacrifices is derived entirely from their relation to Jehovah. Sacrifices may be likened to gifts made to a king by his subjects, and hence the reasonableness of God's strong remonstrance with the worldly-minded Jews (Mal. 1:8). If the tabernacle, and subsequently the temple, were considered the palace of the great King, then the sacrifices would answer to presents as offered to a monarch on various occasions by his subjects; and in this light they would be the appropriate expressions of their feelings towards their sovereign. When a subject wished to do honor to his sovereign, to acknowledge allegiance, to appease his anger, to supplicate forgiveness, or to intercede for another, he brought a present; and all the ideas involved in sacrifices correspond to these sentiments—those of gratitude, of worship, of prayer, of confession and atonement [BIB. SAC]. **23. that mayest thou offer**, etc.—The passage should be rendered thus: if thou offer it either for a freewill offering, or for a vow, it shall not be accepted. This sacrifice being required to be "without blemish," symbolically implied that the people of God were to dedicate themselves wholly with sincere purposes of heart, and its being required to be "perfect to be accepted," led them typically to Him without whom no sacrifice could be offered acceptable to God. **27, 28. it shall be seven days under the dam**—Animals were not considered perfect nor good for food till the eighth day. As sacrifices are called the bread or food of God (vs. 25), to offer them immediately after birth, when they were unfit to be eaten, would have indicated a contempt of religion; and besides, this prohibition, as well as that contained in the following verse, inculcated a lesson of humanity or tenderness to the dam, as well as secured the sacrifices from all appearance of unfeeling cruelty.

CHAPTER 23

Vss. 1-4. OF SUNDRY FEASTS. **2. Speak unto the children of Israel, . . . concerning the feasts of the Lord**— lit., "the times of assembling, or solemnities" (Isa. 33:20); and this is a preferable rendering, applicable to all sacred seasons mentioned in this chapter, even the day of atonement, which was observed as a fast. They were appointed by the direct authority of God and announced by a public proclamation, which is called "the joyful sound" (Ps. 89:15). Those "holy convocations" were evidences of divine wisdom, and eminently subservient to the maintenance and diffusion of religious knowledge and piety. **3. Six days shall work be done; but the seventh day is the sabbath of rest**—(See on Exod. 20:8, 9.) The Sabbath has the precedence given to it, and it was to be "a holy convocation," observed by families "in their dwellings"; where practicable, by the people repairing to the door of the tabernacle; at later periods, by meeting in the schools of the prophets, and in synagogues. **4. These are the feasts of the Lord, which ye shall proclaim in their seasons**—Their observance took place in the parts of the year corresponding to our March, May, and September. Divine wisdom was manifested in fixing them at those periods; in winter, when the days were short and the roads broken up, a long journey was impracticable; while in summer the harvest and vintage gave busy employment in the fields. Besides, another reason for the choice of those seasons probably was to counteract the influence of Egyptian associations and habits. And God appointed more sacred festivals for the Israelites in the month of September than the people of Egypt had in honor of their idols. These institutions, however, were for the most part prospective, the observance being not binding on the Israelites during their wanderings in the wilderness, while the regular celebration was not to commence till their settlement in Canaan.
5-8. THE PASSOVER. the Lord's passover—(See Exod. 12:2, 14, 18.) The institution of the passover was intended to be a perpetual memorial of the circumstances attending the redemption of the Israelites, while it had a typical reference to a greater redemption to be effected for God's spiritual people. On the first and last days of this feast, the people were forbidden to work; but while on the Sabbath they were not to do *any* work, on feast days they were permitted to dress meat—and hence the prohibition is restricted to "no servile work."

At the same time, those two days were devoted to "holy convocation"—special seasons of social devotion. In addition to the ordinary sacrifices of every day, there were to be "offerings by fire" on the altar (see on Num. 28:19), while unleavened bread was to be eaten in families all the seven days (see I Cor. 5:8).
9-14. THE SHEAF OF FIRST FRUITS. 10. ye shall bring a sheaf of the first-fruits of your harvest unto the priest—A sheaf, lit., an omer, of the first-fruits of the barley harvest. The barley being sooner ripe than the other grains, the reaping of it formed the commencement of the general harvest season. The offering described in this passage was made on the sixteenth of the first month, the day following the first Passover Sabbath, which was on the fifteenth (corresponding to the beginning of our April); but it was reaped after sunset on the previous evening by persons deputed to go with sickles and obtain samples from different fields. These, being laid together in a sheaf or loose bundle, were brought to the court of the temple, where the grain was winnowed, parched, and bruised in a mortar. Then, after some incense had been sprinkled on it, the priest waved it aloft before the Lord towards the four different points of the compass, took a part of it and threw it into the fire of the altar—all the rest being reserved to himself. It was a proper and beautiful act, expressive of dependence on the God of nature and providence—common among all people, but more especially becoming the Israelites, who owed their land itself as well as all it produced to the divine bounty. The offering of the wave-sheaf sanctified the whole harvest (Rom. 11:16). At the same time, this feast had a typical character, and pre-intimated the resurrection of Christ (I Cor. 15:20), who rose from the dead on the very day the first-fruits were offered.
15-22. FEAST OF PENTECOST. **15. ye shall count unto you from the morrow after the sabbath**—i.e., after the first day of the passover week, which was observed as a Sabbath. **16. number fifty days**—The forty-ninth day after the presentation of the first-fruits, or the fiftieth, including it, was the feast of Pentecost. (See also Exod. 23:16; Deut. 16:9.) **17. Ye shall bring out of your habitations two wave loaves of two tenth deals,** etc.—These loaves were made of "fine" or wheaten flour, the quantity contained in them being somewhat more than ten pounds in weight. As the wave-sheaf gave the signal for the commencement, the two loaves solemnized the termination of the harvest season. They were the first-fruits of that season, being offered unto the Lord by the priest in name of the whole nation. (See on Exod. 34:22.) The loaves used at the Passover were unleavened; those presented at Pentecost were leavened—a difference which is thus accounted for, that the one was a memorial of the bread hastily prepared at their departure, while the other was a tribute of gratitude to God for their daily food, which was leavened. **21. ye shall proclaim on the selfsame day, that it may be an holy convocation unto you: ye shall do no servile work therein**—Though it extended over a week, the first day only was held as a Sabbath, both for the national offering of first-fruits and a memorial of the giving of the law. **22. thou shalt not make clean riddance of the corners of thy fields when thou reapest,** etc.—(See on ch. 19:9.) The repetition of this law here probably arose from the priests reminding the people, at the presentation of the first-fruits, to unite piety to God with charity to the poor.
23-25. FEAST OF TRUMPETS. **In the seventh**

month, the first day of the month, shall ye have a sabbath—That was the first day of the ancient civil year. **a memorial of blowing of trumpets**—Jewish writers say that the trumpets were sounded thirty successive times, and the reason for the institution was for the double purpose of announcing the commencement of the new year, which was (vs. 25) to be religiously observed (see Num. 29:3), and of preparing the people for the approaching solemn feast. **27-32. there shall be a day of atonement ... and ye shall afflict your souls**—an unusual festival, at which the sins of the whole year were expiated. (See ch. 16:29-34.) It is here only stated that the severest penalty was incurred by the violation of this day. **33-44. the feast of tabernacles, for seven days unto the Lord**—This festival, which was instituted in grateful commemoration of the Israelites having securely dwelt in booths or tabernacles in the wilderness, was the third of the three great annual festivals, and, like the other two, it lasted a week. It began on the fifteenth day of the month, corresponding to the end of our September and beginning of October, which was observed as a Sabbath; and it could be celebrated only at the place of the sanctuary, offerings being made on the altar every day of its continuance. The Jews were commanded during the whole period of the festival to dwell in booths, which were erected on the flat roofs of houses, in the streets or fields; and the trees made use of are by some stated to be the citron, the palm, the myrtle, and the willow, while others maintain the people were allowed to take any trees they could obtain that were distinguished for verdure and fragrance. While the solid branches were reserved for the construction of the booths, the lighter branches were carried by men, who marched in triumphal procession, singing psalms and crying "Hosanna!" which signifies, "Save, we beseech thee!" (Ps. 118:15, 25, 26). It was a season of great rejoicing. But the ceremony of drawing water from the pool, which was done on the last day, seems to have been the introduction of a later period (John 7:37). That last day was the eighth, and, on account of the scene at Siloam, was called "the great day of the feast." The feast of ingathering, when the vintage was over, was celebrated also on that day, and, as the conclusion of one of the great festivals, it was kept as a sabbath.

CHAPTER 24

Vss. 1-23. OIL FOR THE LAMPS. **2. Command the children of Israel**—This is the repetition of a law previously given (Exod. 27:20, 21). **pure oil olive beaten**—or cold-drawn, which is always of great purity. **3, 4. Aaron shall order it from the evening unto the morning**—The daily presence of the priests was necessary to superintend the cleaning and trimming. **upon the pure candlestick**—so called because of pure gold. This was symbolical of the light which ministers are to diffuse through the Church. **5-9. take fine flour, and bake twelve cakes**—for the showbread, as previously appointed (Exod. 25:30). Those cakes were baked by the Levites, the flour being furnished by the people (I Chron. 9:32; 23:29), oil, wine, and salt being the other ingredients (ch. 2:13). **two tenth deals**—i.e., of an ephah—thirteen and a half pounds weight each; and on each row or pile of cakes some frankincense was strewed, which, being burnt, led to the showbread being called "an offering made by fire." Every Sabbath a fresh supply was furnished;

hot loaves were placed on the altar instead of the stale ones, which, having lain a week, were removed, and eaten only by the priests, except in cases of necessity (I Sam. 21:3-6; also Luke 6:3,4). **10. the son of an Israelitish woman**, etc.—This passage narrates the enactment of a new law, with a detail of the circumstances which gave rise to it. The "mixed multitude" that accompanied the Israelites in their exodus from Egypt creates a presumption that marriage connections of the kind described were not infrequent. And it was most natural, in the relative circumstances of the two people, that the father should be an Egyptian and the mother an Israelite. **11. the Israelitish woman's son blasphemed the name of the Lord**—A youth of this half-blood, having quarrelled with an Israelite, vented his rage in some horrid form of impiety. It was a common practice among the Egyptians to curse their idols when disappointed in obtaining the object of their petitions. The Egyptian mind of this youth thought the greatest insult to his opponent was to blaspheme the object of his religious reverence. He spoke disrespectfully of One who sustained the double character of the King as well as the God of the Hebrew people; and as the offense was a new one, he was put in ward till the mind of the Lord was ascertained as to his disposal. **14. Bring forth him that hath cursed without the camp**—All executions took place without the camp; and this arrangement probably originated in the idea that, as the Israelites were to be "a holy people," all flagrant offenders should be thrust out of their society. **let all that heard him lay their hands upon his head**, etc.—The imposition of hands formed a public and solemn testimony against the crime, and at the same time made the punishment legal. **16. as well the stranger, as he that is born in the land, when he blasphemeth the name of the Lord, shall be put to death**—Although strangers were not obliged to be circumcised, yet by joining the Israelitish camp, they became amenable to the law, especially that which related to blasphemy. **17-22. he that killeth any man shall surely be put to death**—These verses contain a repetition of some other laws, relating to offenses of a social nature, the penalties for which were to be inflicted, not by the hand of private parties, but through the medium of the judges before whom the cause was brought. **23. the children of Israel did as the Lord commanded**—The chapter closes with the execution of Shelomith's son—and stoning having afterwards become the established punishment in all cases of blasphemy, it illustrates the fate of Stephen, who suffered under a false imputation of that crime.

CHAPTER 25

Vss. 1-7. SABBATH OF THE SEVENTH YEAR. **2-4. When ye come into the land which I give unto you**—It has been questioned on what year, after the occupation of Canaan, the sabbatic year began to be observed. Some think it was the seventh year after their entrance. But others, considering that as the first six years were spent in the conquest and division of the land (Joshua 5:12), and that the sabbatical year was to be observed after six years of agriculture, maintain that the observance did not commence till the fourteenth year. **the land keep a sabbath unto the Lord**—This was a very peculiar arrangement. Not only all agricultural processes were to be intermitted every seventh year, but the cultivators had no right to the soil. It lay entirely fallow, and its spontaneous produce was the common property of the poor and the stranger, the cattle and game. This year of rest was to invigorate the productive powers of the land, as the weekly Sabbath was a refreshment to men and cattle. It commenced immediately after the feast of ingathering, and it was calculated to teach the people, in a remarkable manner, the reality of the presence and providential power of God.

8-23. THE JUBILEE. **thou shalt number seven sabbaths of years**—This most extraordinary of all civil institutions, which received the name of "Jubilee" from a *Hebrew* word signifying a musical instrument, a horn or trumpet, began on the tenth day of the seventh month, or the great day of atonement, when, by order of the public authorities, the sound of trumpets proclaimed the beginning of the universal redemption. All prisoners and captives obtained their liberties, slaves were declared free, and debtors were absolved. The land, as on the sabbatic year, was neither sowed nor reaped, but allowed to enjoy with its inhabitants a sabbath of repose; and its natural produce was the common property of all. Moreover, every inheritance throughout the land of Judea was restored to its original owner. **ye shall hallow the fiftieth year**—Much difference of opinion exists as to whether the jubilee was observed on the forty-ninth, or, in round numbers, it is called the fiftieth. The prevailing opinion, both in ancient and modern times, has been in favor of the latter. **12. ye shall eat the increase thereof out of the field,** etc.—All that the ground yielded spontaneously during that period might be eaten for their necessary subsistence, but no persons were at liberty to hoard or form a private stock in reserve. **13. ye shall return every man unto his possession,** etc.—Inheritances, from whatever cause, and how frequently soever they had been alienated, came back into the hands of the original proprietors. This law of entail, by which the right heir could never be excluded, was a provision of great wisdom for preserving families and tribes perfectly distinct, and their genealogies faithfully recorded, in order that all might have evidence to establish their right to the ancestral property. Hence the tribe and family of Christ were readily discovered at his birth. **17. Ye shall not oppress one another, but thou shalt fear thy God**—This, which is the same as vs. 14, related to the sale or purchase of possessions and the duty of paying an honest and equitable regard, on both sides, to the limited period during which the bargain could stand. The object of the legislator was, as far as possible, to maintain the original order of families, and an equality of condition among the people. **21, 22. I will command my blessing upon you in the sixth year, and it shall bring forth fruit for three years,** etc.—A provision was made, by the special interposition of God, to supply the deficiency of food which would otherwise have resulted from the suspension of all labor during the sabbatic year. The sixth year was to yield a miraculous supply for three continuous years. And the remark is applicable to the year of Jubilee as well as the sabbatic year. (See allusions to this extraordinary provision in II Kings 19:29; Isa. 37:30.) None but a legislator who was conscious of acting under divine authority would have staked his character on so singular an enactment as that of the sabbatic year; and none but a people who had witnessed the fulfilment of the divine promise would been induced to suspend their agricultural preparations on a recurrence of a periodical Jubilee.

23-28. The land shall not be sold for ever—or, "be quite cut off," as the margin better renders it. The land was God's, and, in prosecution of an important design, He gave it to the people of His choice, dividing it among their tribes and families—who, however, held it of Him merely as tenants at will and had no right or power of disposing of it to strangers. In necessitous circumstances, individuals might effect a temporary sale. But they possessed the right of redeeming it, at *any time,* on payment of an adequate compensation to the present holder; and by the enactments of the Jubilee they recovered it free—so that the land was rendered inalienable. (See an exception to this law, ch. 27: 20.) **29-31. if a man sell a dwelling house in a walled city, then he may redeem it within a whole year after it is sold**—All sales of houses were subject to the same condition. But there was a difference between the houses of villages (which, being connected with agriculture, were treated as parts of the land) and houses possessed by trading people or foreigners in walled towns, which could only be redeemed within the year after the sale; if not then redeemed, these did not revert to the former owner at the Jubilee. **32-34. Notwithstanding the cities of the Levites,** etc.—The Levites, having no possessions but their towns and their houses, the law conferred on them the same privileges that were granted to the lands of the other Israelites. A certain portion of the lands surrounding the Levitical cities was appropriated to them for the pasturage of their cattle and flocks (Num. 35:4, 5). This was a permanent endowment for the support of the ministry and could not be alienated for any time. The Levites, however, were at liberty to make exchanges among themselves; and a priest might sell his house, garden, and right of pasture to another priest, but not to an Israelite of another tribe (Jer. 41:7-9). **35-38. if thy brother be waxen poor, ... relieve him**—This was a most benevolent provision for the poor and unfortunate, designed to aid them or alleviate the evils of their condition. Whether a native Israelite or a mere sojourner, his richer neighbor was required to give him food, lodging, and a supply of money without usury. Usury was severely condemned (Ps. 15:5; Ezek. 18:8, 17), but the prohibition cannot be considered as applicable to the modern practice of men in business, borrowing and lending at legal rates of interest. **39-46. if thy brother ... be waxen poor, and be sold unto thee, thou shalt not compel him to serve as a bound-servant**—An Israelite might be compelled, through misfortune, not only to mortgage his inheritance, but himself. In the event of his being reduced to this distress, he was to be treated not as a slave, but a hired servant whose engagement was temporary, and who might, through the friendly aid of a relative, be redeemed at any time before the Jubilee. The ransom money was determined on a most equitable principle. Taking account of the number of years from the proposal to redeem and the Jubilee, of the current wages of labor for that time, and multiplying the remaining years by that sum, the amount was to be paid to the master for his redemption. But if no such friendly interposition was made for a Hebrew slave, he continued in servitude till the year of Jubilee, when, as a matter of course, he regained his liberty, as well as his inheritance. Viewed in the various aspects in which it is presented in this chapter, the Jubilee was an admirable institution, and subservient in an eminent degree to uphold the interests of religion, social order, and freedom among the Israelites.

CHAPTER 26

Vss. 1, 2. OF IDOLATRY. **1. Ye shall make you no idols**—Idolatry had been previously forbidden (Exod. 20:4, 5), but the law was repeated here with reference to some particular forms of it that were very prevalent among the neighboring nations. **a standing image**—i.e., upright pillar. **image of stone** —i.e., an obelisk, inscribed with hieroglyphical and superstitious characters; the former denoting the common and smaller pillars of the Syrians or Canaanites; the latter, pointing to the large and elaborate obelisks which the Egyptians worshipped as guardian divinities, or used as stones of adoration to stimulate religious worship. The Israelites were enjoined to beware of them. **2. Ye shall keep my sabbaths, and reverence my sanctuary**—Very frequently, in this Book of the Law, the Sabbath and the sanctuary are mentioned as antidotes to idolatry.

3-13. A BLESSING TO THE OBEDIENT. **3. If ye walk in my statutes**—In that covenant into which God graciously entered with the people of Israel, He promised to bestow upon them a variety of blessings, so long as they continued obedient to Him as their Almighty Ruler; and in their subsequent history that people found every promise amply fulfilled, in the enjoyment of plenty, peace, a populous country, and victory over all enemies. **4. I will give you rain in due season, and the land shall yield her increase**—Rain seldom fell in Judea except at two seasons—the former rain at the end of autumn, the seedtime; and the latter rain in spring, before the beginning of harvest (Jer. 5:24). **5. your threshing shall reach unto the vintage, and the vintage shall reach unto the sowing time**, etc.—The barley harvest in Judea was about the middle of April; the wheat harvest about six weeks after, or in the beginning of June. After the harvest came the vintage, and fruit gathering towards the latter end of July. Moses led the Hebrews to believe that, provided they were faithful to God, there would be no idle time between the harvest and vintage, so great would be the increase. (See Amos 9:13.) This promise would be very animating to a people who had come from a country where, for three months, they were pent up without being able to walk abroad because the fields were under water. **10. ye shall eat old store**—Their stock of old corn would be still unexhausted and large when the next harvest brought a new supply. **13. I have broken the bands of your yoke, and made you go upright**— a metaphorical expression to denote their emancipation from Egyptian slavery.

14-39. A CURSE TO THE DISOBEDIENT. **But if ye will not hearken unto me,** etc.—In proportion to the great and manifold privileges bestowed upon the Israelites would be the extent of their national criminality and the severity of their national punishments if they disobeyed. **16. I will even appoint over you terror**—the falling sickness [PATRICK]. **consumption, and the burning ague**—Some consider these as symptoms of the same disease—consumption followed by the shivering, burning, and sweating fits that are the usual concomitants of that malady. According to the Septuagint, ague is "the jaundice," which disorders the eyes and produces great depression of spirits. Others, however, consider the word as referring to a scorching wind; no certain explanation can be given. **18. if ye will not yet for all this hearken unto me, then I will punish you seven times more**—i.e., with far more severe and protracted calamities. **19. will make your**

heaven as iron, and your earth as brass—No figures could have been employed to convey a better idea of severe and long-continued famine. **22. I will also send wild beasts among you**—This was one of the four judgments threatened (Ezek. 14:21; see also II Kings 2:4). **your highways shall be desolate** —Trade and commerce will be destroyed—freedom and safety will be gone—neither stranger nor native will be found on the roads (Isa. 33:8). This is an exact picture of the present state of the Holy Land, which has long lain in a state of desolation, brought on by the sins of the ancient Jews. **26. ten women shall bake your bread in one oven,** etc.—The bread used in families is usually baked by women, and at home. But sometimes also, in times of scarcity, it is baked in public ovens for want of fuel; and the scarcity predicted here would be so great, that one oven would be sufficient to bake as much as ten women used in ordinary occasions to provide for family use; and even this scanty portion of bread would be distributed by weight (Ezek. 4:16). **29. ye shall eat the flesh of your sons**—The revolting picture was actually exhibited at the siege of Samaria, at the siege of Jerusalem by Nebuchadnezzar (Lam. 4:10), and at the destruction of that city by the Romans. (See on Deut. 28.) **30. I will destroy your high places**—Consecrated enclosures on the tops of mountains, or on little hillocks, raised for practising the rites of idolatry. **cut down your images**—According to some, those images were made in the form of chariots (II Kings 23:11); according to others, they were of a conical form, like small pyramids. Reared in honor of the sun, they were usually placed on a very high situation, to enable the worshippers to have a better view of the rising sun. They were forbidden to the Israelites, and when set up, ordered to be destroyed. **cast your carcasses upon the carcasses of your idols,** etc. —Like the statues of idols, which, when broken, lie neglected and contemned, the Jews during the sieges and subsequent captivity often wanted the rites of sepulture. **31. I will make your cities waste**—This destruction of its numerous and flourishing cities, which was brought upon Judea through the sins of Israel, took place by the forced removal of the people during, and long after, the captivity. But it is realized to a far greater extent now. **bring your sanctuaries unto desolation, and I will not smell the savour of your sweet odours**—the tabernacle and temple, as is evident from the tenor of the subsequent clause, in which God announces that He will not accept or regard their sacrifices. **33. I will scatter you among the heathen,** etc.—as was done when the elite of the nation were removed into Assyria and placed in various parts of the kingdom. **34. Then shall the land enjoy her sabbaths, as long as it lieth desolate,** etc.—A long arrear of sabbatic years had accumulated through the avarice and apostasy of the Israelites, who had deprived their land of its appointed season of rest. The number of those sabbatic years seems to have been seventy, as determined by the duration of the captivity. This early prediction is very remarkable, considering that the usual policy of the Assyrian conquerors was to send colonies to cultivate and inhabit their newly acquired provinces. **38. the land of your enemies shall eat you up,** etc.—On the removal of the ten tribes into captivity, they never returned, and all traces of them were lost. **40-45. If they shall confess their iniquity,** etc.—This passage holds out the gracious promise of divine forgiveness and favor on their repentance, and their happy restoration to their land, in memory of the covenant made with their fathers (Rom. 2). **46. These are the statutes and judgments and laws**—It has been thought by some that the last chapter was originally placed after the twenty-fifth [ADAM CLARKE], while others consider that the next chapter was added as an appendix, in consequence of many people being influenced by the promises and threats of the preceding one, to resolve that they would dedicate themselves and their possessions to the service of God [CALMET].

CHAPTER 27

Vss. 1-18. CONCERNING VOWS. **2-8. When a man shall make a singular vow**, etc.—Persons have, at all times and in all places, been accustomed to present votive offerings, either from gratitude for benefits received, or in the event of deliverance from apprehended evil. And Moses was empowered, by divine authority, to prescribe the conditions of this voluntary duty. **the persons shall be for the Lord,** etc.—better rendered thus:—"According to thy estimation, the persons shall be for the Lord." Persons might consecrate themselves or their children to the divine service, in some inferior or servile kind of work about the sanctuary (I Sam. 3:1). In the event of any change, the persons so devoted had the privilege in their power of redeeming themselves; and this chapter specifies the amount of the redemption money, which the priest had the discretionary power of reducing, as circumstances might seem to require. Those of mature age, between twenty and sixty, being capable of the greatest service, were rated highest; young people, from five till twenty, less, because not so serviceable; infants, though devotable by their parents before birth (I Samuel 1:11), could not be offered nor redeemed till a month after birth; old people were valued below the young, but above children; and the poor—in no case freed from payment, in order to prevent the rash formation of vows—were rated according to their means. **9-13. if it be a beast, whereof men bring an offering unto the Lord** —a clean beast. After it had been vowed, it could neither be employed in common purposes nor exchanged for an equivalent—it must be sacrificed—or if, through some discovered blemish, it was unsuitable for the altar, it might be sold, and the money applied for the sacred service. If an unclean beast—such as an ass or camel, for instance— had been vowed, it was to be appropriated to the use of the priest at the estimated value, or it might be redeemed by the person vowing on payment of that value, and the additional fine of a fifth more. **14-16. when a man shall sanctify his house to be holy unto the Lord,** etc.—In this case, the house

having been valued by the priest and sold, the proceeds of the sale were to be dedicated to the sanctuary. But if the owner wished, on second thought, to redeem it, he might have it by adding a fifth part to the price. **16-24. if a man shall sanctify unto the Lord some part of a field of his possession,** etc.—In the case of acquired property in land, if not redeemed, it returned to the donor at the Jubilee; whereas the part of a hereditary estate, which had been vowed, did not revert to the owner, but remained attached in perpetuity to the sanctuary. The reason for this remarkable difference was to lay every man under an obligation to redeem the property, or stimulate his nearest kinsman to do it, in order to prevent a patrimonial inheritance going out from any family in Israel. **26, 27. Only the firstlings of the beasts**—These, in the case of clean beasts, being consecrated to God by a universal and standing law (Exod. 13:12; 34:19), could not be devoted; and in that of unclean beasts were subject to the rule mentioned (vss. 11, 12). **28, 29. no devoted thing, that a man shall devote unto the Lord of all that he hath, . . . shall be sold or redeemed**—This relates to vows of the most solemn kind—the devotee accompanying his vow with a solemn imprecation on himself not to fail in accomplishing his declared purpose. **shall surely be put to death**—This announcement imported not that the person was to be sacrificed or doomed to a violent death; but only that he should remain till death unalterably in the devoted condition. The preceding regulations were evidently designed to prevent rashness in vowing (Eccles. 5: 4) and to encourage serious and considerate reflection in all matters between God and the soul (Luke 21:4). **30-33. all the tithe of the land, whether of the seed of the land**—This law gave the sanction of divine authority to an ancient usage (Gen. 14:20; 28:22). The whole produce of the land was subjected to the tithe tribute—it was a yearly rent which the Israelites, as tenants, paid to God, the owner of the land, and a thank offering they rendered to Him for the bounties of His providence. (See Prov. 3: 9; I Cor. 9:11; Gal. 6:6.) **32. whatsoever passeth under the rod,** etc.—This alludes to the mode of taking the tithe of cattle, which were made to pass singly through a narrow gateway, where a person with a rod, dipped in ochre, stood, and counting them, marked the back of every tenth beast, whether male or female, sound or unsound. **34. These are the commandments,** etc.—The laws contained in this book, for the most part ceremonial, had an important spiritual bearing, the study of which is highly instructive (Rom. 10:4; Heb. 4:2; 12:18). They imposed a burdensome yoke (Acts 15:10), but yet in the infantine age of the Church formed the necessary discipline of "a schoolmaster to Christ."

THE FOURTH BOOK OF MOSES CALLED

NUMBERS

CHAPTER 1

Vss. 1-54. MOSES NUMBERING THE MEN OF WAR. **1. on the first day of the second month,** etc.—Thirteen months had elapsed since the exodus.

About one month had been occupied in the journey; and the rest of the period had been passed in encampment among the recesses of Sinai, where the transactions took place, and the laws, religious and civil, were promulgated, which are contained in the two preceding books. As the tabernacle was erected on the first day of the first month, and the order here mentioned was given on the first day of the second, some think the laws in Leviticus were all given in one month. The Israelites having been formed into a separate nation, under the special government of God as their King, it was necessary, before resuming their march towards the promised land, to put them into good order. And accordingly Moses was commissioned, along with Aaron, to take a census of the people. This census was incidentally noticed (Exod. 38:26), in reference to the poll tax for the works of the tabernacle; but it is here described in detail, in order to show the relative increase and military strength of the different tribes. The enumeration was confined to those capable of bearing arms, and it was to be made with a careful distinction of the tribe, family, and household to which every individual belonged. By this rule of summation many important advantages were secured: an exact genealogical register was formed, the relative strength of each tribe was ascertained, and the reason found for arranging the order of precedence in march as well as disposing the different tribes in camp around the tabernacle. The promise of God to Abraham was seen to be fulfilled in the extraordinary increase of his posterity, and provision made for tracing the regular descent of the Messiah. **3. Aaron shall number them by their armies**—or companies. In their departure from Egypt they were divided into five grand companies (Exod. 13:18), but from the sojourn in the wilderness to the passage of the Jordan, they were formed into four great divisions. The latter is here referred to. **4-16. with you there shall be a man of every tribe**, etc.—The social condition of the Israelites in the wilderness bore a close resemblance to that of the nomad tribes of the East in the present day. The head of the tribe was a hereditary dignity, vested in the oldest son or some other to whom the right of primogeniture was transferred, and under whom were other inferior heads, also hereditary, among the different branches of the tribe. The Israelites being divided into twelve tribes, there were twelve chiefs appointed to assist in taking the census of the people. **5. these are the names of the men that shall stand with you,** etc.—Each is designated by adding the name of the ancestors of his tribe, the people of which were called "Beni-Reuben, Beni-Levi," sons of Reuben, sons of Levi, according to the custom of the Arabs still, as well as other nations which are divided into clans, as the Macs of Scotland, the Aps of Wales, and the O's and the Fitz's of Ireland [CHALMERS]. **16-18. These were the renowned**—lit., the called of the congregation, summoned by name; and they entered upon the survey the very day the order was given. **by their polls**—individually, one by one. **19. As the Lord commanded Moses,** etc.—The numbering of the people was not an act sinful in itself, as Moses did it by divine appointment; but David incurred guilt by doing it without the authority of God. (See on II Sam. 24:10.) **20-44. These are those that were numbered**—In this registration the tribe of Judah appears the most numerous; and accordingly, as the pre-eminence had been assigned to it by Jacob, it got the precedence in all the encampments of Israel. Of the two half tribes of Joseph, who is seen to be "a fruitful bough," that of Ephraim was the larger, as had been predicted. The relative increase of all, as in the two just mentioned, was owing to the special blessing of God, conformably to the

prophetic declaration of the dying patriarch. But the divine blessing is usually conveyed through the influence of secondary causes; and there is reason to believe that the relative populousness of the tribes would, under God, depend upon the productiveness of the respective localities assigned to them. **45, 46. all they that were numbered were six hundred thousand,** etc.—What an astonishing increase from seventy-five persons who went down to Egypt about 215 years before, and who were subjected to the greatest privations and hardships! And yet this enumeration was restricted to men from 20 years and upwards. Including women, children, and old men, together with the Levites, the whole population of Israel, on the ordinary principles of computation, amounted to about 2,400,000. **47-54. But the Levites ... were not numbered among them**—They were obliged to keep a register of their own. They were consecrated to the priestly office, which in all countries has been exempted customarily, and in Israel by the express authority of God, from military service. The custody of the things devoted to the divine service was assigned to them so exclusively, that "no stranger"—i.e., no person, not even an Israelite of any other tribe, was allowed, under penalty of death, to approach these. Hence they encamped round the tabernacle in order that there should be no manifestation of the divine displeasure among the people. Thus the numbering of the people was subservient to the separation of the Levites from those Israelites who were fit for military service, and to the practical introduction of the law respecting the first-born, for whom the tribe of Levi became a substitute.

CHAPTER 2

Vss. 1-34. THE ORDER OF THE TRIBES IN THEIR TENTS. **2. Every man ... shall pitch by his own standard, with the ensign of their father's house**—Standards were visible signs of a certain recognized form for directing the movements of large bodies of people. As the Israelites were commanded to encamp "each by his own standard, with the ensign of their father's house," the direction has been considered as implying that they possessed three varieties: (1) the great tribal standards, which served as rallying points for the twelve large clans of the people; (2) the standards of the subdivided portions; and, (3) those of families or houses. The latter must have been absolutely necessary, as one ensign only for a tribe would not have been visible at the extremities of so large a body. We possess no authentic information as to their forms, material, colors, and devices. But it is probable that they might bear some resemblance to those of Egypt, only stripped of any idolatrous symbols. These were of an umbrella or a fanlike form, made of ostrich feathers, shawls, etc., lifted on the points of long poles, which were borne, either like the sacred central one, on a car, or on men's shoulders, while others might be like the beacon lights which are set on poles by Eastern pilgrims at night. Jewish writers say that the standards of the Hebrew tribes were symbols borrowed from the prophetic blessing of Jacob—Judah's being a lion, Benjamin's a wolf, etc.; and that the ensigns or banners were distinguished by their colors—the colors of each tribe being the same as that of the precious stone representing that tribe in the breastplate of the high priest. **far off about the tabernacle of the congregation shall they pitch**—i.e., over against, at a reverential distance. The place of every tribe is successively and specifically described because each had a certain part assigned both in the order of march and the disposition of the encampment. **3. on the east side toward the rising of the sun shall they of the standard of the camp of Judah pitch,** etc.—Judah, placed at the head of a camp composed of three tribes rallying under its standard, was said to have combined the united colors in the high priest's breastplate, but called by the name of Judah. They were appointed to occupy the east side and to take the lead in the march, which, for the most part, was in an easterly direction. **Nahshon** [or Naasson (Matt. 1:4)] **shall be captain**—It appears that the twelve men who were called to superintend the census were also appointed to be the captains of their respective tribes—a dignity which they owed probably to the circumstances, formerly noticed, of their holding the hereditary office of head or "prince." **5. those that pitch next unto him**—i.e., on the one side. **7. Then the tribe of Zebulun**—on the other side. While Judah's tribe was the most numerous, those of Issachar and Zebulun were also very numerous; so that the association of those three tribes formed a strong and imposing van. **10-31. On the south side the standard of the camp of Reuben**—The description given of the position of Reuben and his attendant tribes on the south, of Ephraim and his associates on the west, of Dan and his confederates on the north, with that of Judah on the east, suggests the idea of a square or quadrangle, which, allowing one square cubit to each soldier while remaining close in the ranks, has been computed to extend over an area of somewhat more than twelve square miles. But into our calculations of the occupied space must be taken not only the fighting men, whose numbers are here given, but also the families, tents, and baggage. The tabernacle or sacred tent of their Divine King, with the camp of the Levites around it (see on ch. 3:38), formed the center, as does the chief's in the encampment of all nomad people. In marching, this order was adhered to, with some necessary variations. Judah led the way, followed, it is most probable, by Issachar and Zebulun. Reuben, Simeon, and Gad formed the second great division. They were followed by the central company, composed of the Levites, bearing the tabernacle. Then the third and posterior squadron consisted of Ephraim, Manasseh, and Benjamin, while the hindmost place was assigned to Dan, Asher, and Naphtali. Thus Judah's, which was the most numerous, formed the van: and Dan's, which was the next in force, brought up the rear; while Reuben's and Ephraim's, with the tribes associated with them respectively, being the smallest and weakest, were placed in the center. (See on ch. 10:14.)

CHAPTER 3

Vss. 1-51. THE LEVITES' SERVICE. **1. These ... are the generations of Aaron and Moses,** etc.—This chapter contains an account of their families; and although that of Moses is not detailed like his brother's, his children are included under the general designation of the Amramites (vs. 27), a term which comprehends all the descendants of their common father Amram. The reason why the family of Moses was so undistinguished in this record is that they were in the private ranks of the Levites, the dignity of the priesthood being conferred exclusively on the posterity of Aaron; and

hence, as the sacerdotal order is the subject of this chapter, Aaron, contrary to the usual style of the sacred history, is mentioned before Moses. **in the day that the Lord spake with Moses in mount Sinai** —This is added, because at the date of the following record the family of Aaron was unbroken. **2-4. these are the names of the sons of Aaron**—All the sons of Aaron, four in number, were consecrated to minister in the priest's office. The two oldest enjoyed but a brief term of office (Lev. 10:1, 2; ch. 26: 61); but Eleazar and Ithamar, the other two, were dutiful, and performed the sacred service during the lifetime of their father, as his assistants, and under his superintendence. **5-10. Bring the tribe of Levi near**—The *Heb.* word "bring near" is a sacrificial term, denoting the presentation of an offering to God; and the use of the word, therefore, in connection with the Levites, signifies that they were devoted as an offering to the sanctuary, no longer to be employed in any common offices. They were subordinate to the priests, who alone enjoyed the privilege of entering the holy place; but they were employed in discharging many of the humbler duties which belonged to the sanctuary, as well as in various offices of great utility and importance to the religion and morals of the people. **9. they are wholly given unto him out of the children of Israel,** etc.—The priests hold the place of God, and the Levites are the servants of God in the obedience they render to the priests. **11-13. I have taken the Levites,** etc.—The consecration of this tribe did not originate in the legislative wisdom of Moses, but in the special appointment of God, who chose them as substitutes for the first-born. By an appointment made in memory of the last solemn judgment on Egypt (from which the Israelitish households were miraculously exempt) all the first-born were consecrated to God (Exod. 13:12; 22:29), who thus, under peculiar circumstances, seemed to adopt the patriarchal usage of appointing the oldest to act as the priest of the family. But the privilege of redemption that was allowed the first-born opened the way for a change; and accordingly, on the full organization of the Mosaic economy, the administration of sacred things formerly committed to the first-born was transferred from them to the Levites, who received that honor partly as a tribute to Moses and Aaron, partly because this tribe had distinguished themselves by their zeal in the affair of the golden calf (Exod. 32:29), and also because, being the smallest of the tribes, they could ill find suitable employment and support in the work. (See on Deut. 33:9.) The designation of a special class for the sacred offices of religion was a wise arrangement; for, on their settlement in Canaan, the people would be so occupied that they might not be at leisure to wait on the service of the sanctuary, and sacred things might, from various causes, fall into neglect. But the appointment of an entire tribe to the divine service ensured the regular performance of the rites of religion. The subsequent portion of the chapter relates to the formal substitution of this tribe. **I am the Lord**— i.e., I decree it to be so; and being possessed of sovereign authority, I expect full obedience. **14-27. Number the children of Levi**—They were numbered as well as the other tribes; but the enumeration was made on a different principle—for while in the other tribes the number of males was calculated from twenty years and upward, in that of Levi they were counted from a month old and upward. The reason for the distinction is obvious. In the other tribes the survey was made for purposes of war, from which the Levites were totally exempt. But the Levites were appointed to a work on which they entered as soon as they were capable of instruction. They are mentioned under the names of Gershon, Kohath, and Merari, sons of Levi, and chiefs or ancestral heads of three subdivisions into which this tribe was distributed. Their duties were to assist in the conveyance of the tabernacle when the people were removing the various encampments, and to form its guard while stationary—the Gershonites being stationed on the west, the Kohathites on the south, and the families of Merari on the north. The Kohathites had the principal place about the tabernacle, and charge of the most precious and sacred things—a distinction with which they were honored, probably, because the Aaronic family belonged to this division of the Levitical tribe. The Gershonites, being the oldest, had the next honorable post assigned them, while the burden of the drudgery was thrown on the division of Merari. **32. chief**—rather, chiefs of the Levites. Three persons are mentioned as chiefs of these respective divisions. And Eleazar presided over them; whence he is called "the second priest" (II Kings 25:18); and in the case of the high priest's absence from illness or other necessary occasions, he performed the duties (I Kings 4:4). **38. those that encamp,** etc.—That being the entrance side, it was the post of honor, and consequently reserved to Moses and the priestly family. But the sons of Moses had no station here. **39. twenty and two thousand**—The result of this census, though made on conditions most advantageous to Levi, proved it to be by far the smallest in Israel. The separate numbers stated in verses 22, 28, 34, when added together, amount to 22,300. The omission of the 300 is variously accounted for—by some, because they might be first-born who were already devoted to God and could not be counted as substitutes; and by others, because in Scripture style, the sum is reckoned in round numbers. The most probable conjecture is, that as *Heb.* letters are employed for figures, one letter was, in the course of transcription, taken for another of like form but smaller value. **40-51. Number all the first-born of the males of the children of Israel,** etc.—The principle on which the enumeration of the Levites had been made was now to be applied to the other tribes. The number of their male children, from a month old and upward, was to be reckoned, in order that a comparison might be instituted with that of the Levites, for the formal adoption of the latter as substitutes for the first-born. The Levites, amounting to 22,000, were given in exchange for an equal number of the first-born from the other tribes, leaving an excess of 273; and as there were no substitutes for these, they were redeemed at the rate of five shekels for each (ch. 18:15, 16). Every Israelite would naturally wish that his son might be redeemed by a Levite without the payment of this tax, and yet some would have to incur the expense, for there were not Levites enough to make an equal exchange. Jewish writers say the matter was determined by lot, in this manner: Moses put into an urn 22,000 pieces of parchment, on each of which he wrote "a son of Levi," and 273 more, containing the words, "five shekels." These being shaken, he ordered each of the first-born to put in his hand and take out a slip. If it contained the first inscription, the boy was redeemed by a Levite; if the latter, the parent had to pay. The ransom money, which, reckoning the shekel at half a dollar, would amount to $2.50 each, was appropriated to the use of the

sanctuary. The excess of the general over the Levitical first-born is so small, that the only way of accounting for it is, by supposing those first-born only were counted as were males remaining in their parents' household, or that those first-born only were numbered which had been born since the departure from Egypt, when God claimed all the first-born as his special property. **41. the cattle of the Levites**—These, which they kept to graze on the glebes and meadows in the suburbs of their cities, to supply their families with dairy produce and animal food, were also taken as an equivalent for all the firstlings of the cattle which the Israelites at that time possessed. In consequence of this exchange the firstlings were not brought then, as afterwards, to the altar and the priests.

CHAPTER 4

Vss. 1-49. OF THE LEVITES' SERVICE. **2, 3. sons of Kohath, from thirty years old and upward** —This age was specifically fixed (see on ch. 8:24) as the full maturity of bodily energy to perform the laborious duties assigned them in the wilderness, as well as of mental activity to assist in the management of the sacred services. And it was the period of life at which John the Baptist and Christ entered on their respective ministries. **even unto fifty**—The term perscribed for active duty was a period of twenty years, at the end of which they were exempted from the physical labors of the office, though still expected to attend in the tabernacle (ch. 8:26). **all that enter into the host**—so called from their ranks, and their special duty as guards of the tabernacle. The *Heb.* word, however, signifies also a station of office; and hence the passage may be rendered, "All that enter into the sacerdotal office" (vs. 23). **4-15. This shall be the service of the sons of Kohath,** etc.—They are mentioned first, from their close connection with Aaron; and the special department of duty assigned them during the journeyings of Israel accorded with the charge they had received of the precious contents of the tabernacle. But these were to be previously covered by the common priests, who, as well as the high priest, were admitted on such necessary occasions into the holy place. This was an exception to the general rule, which prohibited the entrance of any but the high priest. But when the cloud removed from the tabernacle, the sanctuary might be entered by the common priests, as to them was reserved the exclusive privilege of packing the sacred utensils; and it was not till the holy things were thus ready for carriage, that the Kohathites were allowed to approach. **5. covering veil**—the inner veil, which separated the holy from the most holy place. (See on Exod. 36:3.) **6. covering of badgers' skins**—(See on Exod. 25:5.) The covering, however, referred to was not that of the tabernacle, but one made for the special purpose of protecting the ark. **put in the staves**—These golden staves were now taken out. (See on Exod. 25:15, compared with I Kings 8:8.) The *Hebrew* word rendered "put in," signifies also "dispose," and probably refers here to their insertion through the openings in the coverings made for receiving them, to preserve them from the touch of the carriers as well as from the influence of the weather. It is worthy of notice that the coverings did not consist of canvas or coarse tarpauling, but of a kind which united beauty with decency. **7. continual showbread**—Though the people were in the wilderness fed upon manna, the sacred loaves were constantly made of corn, which was probably raised in small quantities from the verdant patches of the desert. **10. a bar**—or bier, formed of two poles fastened by two crosspieces and borne by two men, after the fashion of a sedan chair. **12. instruments of ministry**—the official dress of the priests (Exod. 31:10). **13. shall take away the ashes from the altar,** etc.—The necessity of removing ashes from the altar plainly implies that sacrifices were offered in the wilderness (cf. Exod. 18:12; 24:4), though that rebellious race seems frequently to have neglected the duty (Amos 5:25). No mention is made of the sacred fire; but as, by divine command, it was to be kept constantly burning, it must have been transferred to some pan or brazier under the covering, and borne by the appointed carriers. **15. the sons of Kohath shall come to bear it, but they shall not touch any holy thing, lest they die**—The mode of transport was upon the shoulders of the Levites (see on ch. 7:9), although afterwards wheeled vehicles were employed (II Samuel 6:3; I Chron. 15:12). And it was allowed to touch the covering, but not the things covered, on the penalty of death, which was inflicted more than once (I Sam. 6:19; II Samuel 6:6, 7). This stern denunciation was designed to inspire a sentiment of deep and habitual reverence in the minds of those who were officially engaged about holy things. **16. to the office of Eleazar . . . pertaineth the oil for the light, and the sweet incense,** etc.—He was charged with the special duty of superintending the squadron who were employed in the carrying of the sacred furniture; besides, to his personal care were committed the materials requisite for the daily service, and which it was necessary he should have easily at his command (Exod. 29:38). **17-20. Cut ye not off the tribe of the families of the Kohathites from among the Levites,** etc.—a solemn admonition to Moses and Aaron to beware, lest, by any negligence on their part, disorder and improprieties should creep in, and to take the greatest care that all the parts of this important service be apportioned to the proper parties, lest the Kohathites should be disqualified for their high and honorable duties. The guilt of their death would be incurred by the superintending priest, if he failed to give proper directions or allowed any irreverent familiarity with sacred things. **24-28. This is the service of the families of the Gershonites,** etc.— They were appointed to carry "the curtains of the tabernacle"—i.e., the goats' hair covering of the tent—the ten curious curtains and embroidered hangings at the entrance, with their red morocco covering, etc. **28. their charge shall be under the hand of Ithamar the son of Aaron,** etc.—The Levites were generally subject to the official command of the priests in doing the ordinary work of the tabernacle. But during the journeyings Eleazar, who was next in succession to his father, took the special charge of the Kohathites, while his brother Ithamar had the superintendence of the Gershonites and Merarites. **29-33. As for the sons of Merari**—They carried the coarser and heavier appurtenances, which, however, were so important and necessary, that an inventory was kept of them—not only on account of their number and variety, but of their comparative commonness and smallness, which might have led to their being lost or missing through carelessness, inadvertency, or neglect. It was a useful lesson, showing that God disregards nothing pertaining to His service, and that even in the least and most trivial matters, He requires the duty of faithful obedience. **34-49. Moses and Aaron and**

the chief of the congregation numbered the sons of the Kohathites, etc.—This enumeration was made on a different principle from that which is recorded in the preceding chapter. That was confined to the males from a month old and upward, while this was extended to all capable of service in the three classes of the Levitical tribe. In considering their relative numbers, the wisdom of Divine Providence appears in arranging that, whereas in the Kohathites and Gershonites, whose burdens were few and easier, there were but about a third part of them which were fit for service; the Merarites, whose burdens were more and heavier, had above one-half of them fit for this work [POOLE]. The small population of this tribe, so inferior to that of the other tribes, is attempted to be explained (see on ch. 3: 39).

CHAPTER 5

Vss. 1-4. THE UNCLEAN TO BE REMOVED OUT OF THE CAMP. **2. Command the children of Israel, that they put out of the camp every leper**—The exclusion of leprous persons from the camp in the wilderness, as from cities and villages afterwards, was a sanitary measure taken according to prescribed rules (Lev. 13, 14). This exclusion of lepers from society has been acted upon ever since; and it affords almost the only instance in which any kind of attention is paid in the East to the prevention of contagion. The usage still more or less prevails in the East among people who do not think the least precaution against the plague or cholera necessary; but judging from personal observation, we think that in Asia the leprosy has now much abated in frequency and virulence. It usually appears in a comparatively mild form in Egypt, Palestine, and other countries where the disorder is, or was, endemic. Small societies of excluded lepers live miserably in paltry huts. Many of them are beggars, going out into the roads to solicit alms, which they receive in a wooden bowl; charitable people also sometimes bring different articles of food, which they leave on the ground at a short distance from the hut of the lepers, for whom it is intended. They are generally obliged to wear a distinctive badge that people may know them at first sight and be warned to avoid them. Other means were adopted among the ancient Jews by putting their hand on their mouth and crying, "Unclean, unclean." But their general treatment, as to exclusion from society, was the same as now described. The association of the lepers, however, in this passage, with those who were subject only to ceremonial uncleanness, shows that one important design in the temporary exile of such persons was to remove all impurities that reflected dishonor on the character and residence of Israel's King. And this vigilant care to maintain external cleanliness in the people was typically designed to teach them the practice of moral purity, or cleansing themselves from all filthiness of the flesh and spirit. The regulations made for ensuring cleanliness in the camp suggest the adoption of similar means for maintaining purity in the church. And although, in large communities of Christians, it may be often difficult or delicate to do this, the suspension or, in flagrant cases of sin, the total excommunication of the offender from the privileges and communion of the church is an imperative duty, as necessary to the moral purity of the Christian as the exclusion of the leper from the camp was to physical health and ceremonial purity in the Jewish church.

5-10. RESTITUTION ENJOINED. **6. When a man or a woman shall commit any sin that men commit, to do a trespass against the Lord**—This is a wrong or injury done by one man to the property of another, and as it is called "a trespass against the Lord," it is implied, in the case supposed, that the offense has been aggravated by prevaricating—by a false oath, or a fraudulent lie in denying it, which is a "trespass" committed against God, who is the sole judge of what is falsely sworn or spoken (Acts 5:3, 4). **and that person be guilty**—i.e., from the obvious tenor of the passage, conscience-smitten, or brought to a sense and conviction of his evil conduct. (See on Lev. 6:4.) In that case there must be: first, confession, a penitential acknowledgment of sin; secondly, restitution of the property, or the giving of an equivalent, with the additional fine of a fifth part, both as a compensation to the person defrauded, and as a penalty inflicted on the injurer, to deter others from the commission of similar trespasses. (See on Exod. 22:1.) The difference between the law recorded in that passage and this is that the one was enacted against flagrant and determined thieves, the other against those whose necessities might have urged them into fraud, and whose consciences were distressed by their sin. This law also supposes the injured party to be dead, in which case, the compensation due to his representatives was to be paid to the priest, who, as God's deputy, received the required satisfaction. **9, 10. every offering . . . shall be his**—Whatever was given in this way, or otherwise, as by freewill offerings, irrevocably belonged to the priest.

11-31. THE TRIAL OF JEALOUSY. **if any man's wife go aside**—This law was given both as a strong discouragement to conjugal infidelity on the part of a wife, and a sufficient protection of her from the consequences of a hasty and groundless suspicion on the part of the husband. His suspicions, however, were sufficient in the absence of witnesses (Lev. 20:10) to warrant the trial described; and the course of proceeding to be followed was for the jealous husband to bring his wife unto the priest with an offering of barley meal, because none were allowed to approach the sanctuary empty-handed (Exod. 23:15). On other occasions, there were mingled with the offering, oil which signified joy, and frankincense which denoted acceptance (Ps. 141:2). But on the occasion referred to, both these ingredients were to be excluded, partly because it was a solemn appeal to God in distressing circumstances, and partly because it was a sin offering on the part of the wife, who came before God in the character of a real or suspected offender. **17. the priest shall take holy water**—Water from the laver, which was to be mixed with dust—an emblem of vileness and misery (Gen. 3:14; Ps. 22:15). **in an earthen vessel**—This fragile ware was chosen because, after being used, it was broken in pieces (Lev. 6:28; 11:33). All the circumstances of this awful ceremony—her being placed with her face toward the ark—her uncovered head, a sign of her being deprived of the protection of her husband (I Cor. 11:7)—the bitter potion being put into her hands preparatory to an appeal to God—the solemn adjuration of the priest (vss. 19-22), all were calculated in no common degree to excite and appall the imagination of a person conscious of guilt. **21. The Lord make thee a curse, etc.**—a usual form of imprecation (Isa. 65:15; Jer. 29:22). **22. the woman shall say, Amen, Amen**—The Israelites were accustomed, instead of formally repeating the words of an oath merely to say, "Amen," a "so be

it" to the imprecations it contained. The reduplication of the word was designed as an evidence of the woman's innocence, and a willingness that God would do to her according to her desert. **23, 24. write these curses in a book**—The imprecations, along with her name, were inscribed in some kind of record—on parchment, or more probably on a wooden tablet. **blot them out with the bitter water** —If she were innocent, they could be easily erased, and were perfectly harmless; but if guilty, she would experience the fatal effects of the water she had drunk. **29. This is the law of jealousies**—Adultery discovered and proved was punished with death. But strongly suspected cases would occur, and this law made provision for the conviction of the guilty person. It was, however, not a trial conducted according to the forms of judicial process, but an ordeal through which a suspected adulteress was made to go—the ceremony being of that terrifying nature, that, on the known principles of human nature, guilt or innocence could not fail to appear. From the earliest times, the jealousy of Eastern people has established ordeals for the detection and punishment of suspected unchastity in wives. The practice was deep-rooted as well as universal. And it has been thought, that the Israelites being strongly biassed in favor of such usages, this law of jealousies "was incorporated among the other institutions of the Mosaic economy, in order to free it from the idolatrous rites which the heathens had blended with it." Viewed in this light, its sanction by divine authority in a corrected and improved form exhibits a proof at once of the wisdom and condescension of God.

CHAPTER 6

Vss. 1-22. THE LAW OF THE NAZARITE IN HIS SEPARATION. **2-6. When either man or woman . . . shall vow a vow of a Nazarite**—i.e., "a separated one," from a Hebrew word, to separate. It was used to designate a class of persons who, under the impulse of extraordinary piety and with a view to higher degrees of religious improvement, voluntarily renounced the occupations and pleasures of the world to dedicate themselves unreservedly to the divine service. The vow might be taken by either sex, provided they had the disposal of themselves (ch. 30:4), and for a limited period—usually a month or a lifetime (Judg. 13:5; 16:17). We do not know, perhaps, the whole extent of abstinence they practised. But they separated themselves from three things in particular— viz., from wine, and all the varieties of vinous produce; from the application of a razor to their head, allowing their hair to grow; and from pollution by a dead body. The reasons of the self-restrictions are obvious. The use of wine tended to inflame the passions, intoxicate the brain, and create a taste for luxurious indulgence. The cutting off the hair being a recognized sign of uncleanness (Lev. 14:8, 9), its unpolled luxuriance was a symbol of the purity he professed. Besides, its extraordinary length kept him in constant remembrance of his vow, as well as stimulated others to imitate his pious example. Moreover, contact with a dead body, disqualifying for the divine service, the Nazarite carefully avoided such a cause of unfitness, and, like the high priest, did not assist at the funeral rites of his nearest relatives, preferring his duty to God to the indulgence of his strongest natural affections. **8-11 if any man die suddenly by him, and he hath defiled the head of**

his consecration—Cases of sudden death might occur to make him contract pollution; and in such circumstances he was required, after shaving his head, to make the prescribed offerings necessary for the removal of ceremonial defilement (Lev. 15: 13; ch. 19:11). But by the terms of this law an accidental defilement vitiated the whole of his previous observances, and he was required to begin the period of his Nazaritism afresh. But even this full completion did not supersede the necessity of a sin offering at the close. Sin mingles with our best and holiest performances, and the blood of sprinkling is necessary to procure acceptance to us and our services. **13-20. when the days of his separation are fulfilled,** etc.—On the accomplishment of a limited vow of Nazaritism, Nazarites might cut their hair wherever they happened to be (Acts 18:18); but the hair was to be carefully kept and brought to the door of the sanctuary. Then after the presentation of sin offerings and burnt offerings, it was put under the vessel in which the peace offerings were boiled; and the priest, taking the shoulder (Lev. 7:32), when boiled, and a cake and wafer of the meat offering, put them on the hands of the Nazarites to wave before the Lord, as a token of thanksgiving, and thus released them from their vow.

23-27. The Form of Blessing the People. Speak unto Aaron and unto his sons, saying, On this wise ye shall bless the congregation of Israel, etc. —This passage records the solemn benediction which God appointed for dismissing the people at the close of the daily service. The repetition of the name "Lord" or "Jehovah" three times, expresses the great mystery of the Godhead—three persons, and yet one God. The expressions in the separate clauses correspond to the respective offices of the Father, to "bless and keep us"; of the Son, to be "gracious to us"; and of the Holy Ghost, to "give us peace." And because the benediction, though pronounced by the lips of a fellow man, derived its virtue, not from the priest but from God, the encouraging assurance was added, "I the Lord will bless them."

CHAPTER 7

Vss. 1-89. The Princes' Offerings. 1. the day that Moses had fully set up the tabernacle—Those who take the word "day" as literally pointing to the exact date of the completion of the tabernacle, are under a necessity of considering the sacred narrative as disjointed, and this portion of the history from the seventh to the eleventh chapters as out of its place—the chronology requiring that it should have immediately followed the fortieth chapter of Exodus, which relates that the tabernacle was reared on the first day of the first month of the second year. But that the term "day" is used in a loose and indeterminate sense, as synonymous with *time*, is evident from the fact that not one day but several days were occupied with the transactions about to de described. So that this chapter stands in its proper place in the order of the history; after the tabernacle and its instruments (the altar and its vessels) had been anointed (Lev. 8:10), the Levites separated to the sacred service—the numbering of the people, and the disposal of the tribes about the tabernacle, in a certain order, which was observed by the princes in the presentation of their offerings. This would fix the period of the imposing ceremonial described in this chapter about a month after the completion of the tabernacle. **2, 3. the princes**

of Israel . . . brought their offering before the Lord —The finishing of the sacred edifice would, it may well be imagined, be hailed as an auspicious occasion, diffusing great joy and thankfulness throughout the whole population of Israel. But the leading men, not content with participating in the general expression of satisfaction, distinguished themselves by a movement, which, while purely spontaneous, was at the same time so appropriate in the circumstances and so equal in character, as indicates it to have been the result of concerted and previous arrangement. It was an offer of the means of carriage, suitable to the migratory state of the nation in the wilderness, for transporting the tabernacle from place to place. In the pattern of that sacred tent exhibited on the mount, and to which its symbolic and typical character required a faithful adherence, no provision had been made for its removal in the frequent journeyings of the Israelites. That not being essential to the plan of the divine architect, it was left to be accomplished by voluntary liberality; and whether we look to the judicious character of the gifts, or to the public manner in which they were presented, we have unmistakable evidence of the pious and patriotic feelings from which they emanated and the extensive interest the occasion produced. The offerers were "the princes of Israel, heads of the house of their fathers," and the offering consisted of six covered wagons or little cars, and twelve oxen, two of the princes being partners in a wagon, and each furnishing an ox. **4, 5. The Lord spake unto Moses, saying, Take it of them, that they may be to do the service of the tabernacle of the congregation**—They exhibited a beautiful example to all who are great in dignity and in wealth, to be foremost in contributing to the support and in promoting the interests of religion. The strictness of the injunctions Moses had received to adhere with scrupulous fidelity to the divine model of the tabernacle probably led him to doubt whether he was at liberty to act in this matter without orders. God, however, relieved him by declaring His acceptance of the freewill offerings, as well as by giving instructions as to the mode of their distribution among the Levites. It is probable that in doing so, He merely sanctioned the object for which they were offered, and that the practical wisdom of the offerers had previously determined that they should be distributed "unto the Levites, to every man according to his service"; i.e., more or fewer were assigned to each of the Levitical divisions, as their department of duty seemed to require. This divine sanction it is of great importance to notice, as establishing the principle, that while in the great matters of divine worship and church government we are to adhere faithfully to the revealed rule of faith and duty, minor arrangements respecting them may be lawfully made, according to the means and convenience of God's people in different places. "There is a great deal left to human regulation—appendages of undoubted convenience, and which it were as absurd to resist on the ground that an express warrant cannot be produced for them, as to protest against the convening of the people to divine service, because there is no Scripture for the erection and ringing of a church bell" [Chalmers]. **6-9. Moses took the wagons and the oxen**—The *Heb.* word seems to be fairly rendered by the word "wagons." Wheel carriages of some kind are certainly intended; and as they were covered, the best idea we can form of them is, that they bore some resemblance to our covered wagons. That wheel carriages were anciently used in Egypt, and in what is now Asiatic Turkey, is attested, not only by history, but by existing sculptures and paintings. Some of these the Israelites might have brought with them at their departure; and others, the skilful artisans, who did the mechanical work of the tabernacle, could easily have constructed, according to models with which they had been familiar. Each wagon was drawn by two oxen, and a greater number does not seem to have been employed on any of the different occasions mentioned in Scripture. Oxen seem to have been generally used for draught in ancient times among other nations as well as the Hebrews; and they continue still to be employed in dragging the few carts which are in use in some parts of Western Asia [KITTO]. **gave them unto the Levites** —The principle of distribution was natural and judicious. The Merarites had twice the number of wagons and oxen appropriated to them that the Gershonites had, obviously because, while the latter had charge only of the coverings and hangings (the light but precious and richly-embroidered drapery) the former were appointed to transport all the heavy and bulky materials (the boards, bars, pillars, and sockets) in short, all the larger articles of furniture. Whoever thinks only of the enormous weight of metal, the gold, silver, brass, etc., that were on the bases, chapiters, and pillars, etc., will probably come to the conclusion that four wagons and eight oxen were not nearly sufficient for the conveyance of so vast a load. Besides, the Merarites were not very numerous, as they amounted only to 3200 men from thirty years and upward; and, therefore, there is reason to suppose that a much greater number of wagons would afterwards be found necessary, and be furnished, than were given on this occasion [CALMET]. Others, who consider the full number of wagons and oxen to be stated in the sacred record, suppose that the Merarites may have carried many of the smaller things in their hands—the sockets, for instance, which being each a talent weight, was one man's burden (II Kings 5:23). The Kohathites had neither wheeled vehicles nor beasts of burden assigned them, because, being charged with the transport of the furniture belonging to the holy place, the sacred worth and character of the vessels entrusted to them (see on ch. 4:15) demanded a more honorable mode of conveyance. These were carried by those Levites shoulder-high. Even in this minute arrangement every reflecting reader will perceive the evidence of divine wisdom and holiness; and a deviation from the prescribed rule of duty led, in one recorded instance, to a manifestation of holy displeasure, calculated to make a salutary and solemn impression (II Sam. 6:6-13). **10, 11. the princes offered for dedicating of the altar,** etc.—"Altar" is here used in the singular for the plural; for it is evident, from the kind of offerings, that the altars of burnt offering and incense are both referred to. This was not the first or proper dedication of those altars, which had been made by Moses and Aaron some time before. But it might be considered an additional *dedication*— those offerings being the first that were made for particular persons or tribes. **They shall offer . . . , each prince on his day,** etc.—Eastern princes were accustomed anciently, as they are in Persia still on a certain yearly festival, to sit upon their thrones in great state, when the princes and nobles, from all parts of their dominions, appear before them with tributary presents, which form a large proportion of their royal revenue. And in the offering of all gifts or presents to great personages, every article is presented singly and with ostentatious display. The tabernacle being the palace of their great King, as well as the sanctuary of their God, the princes of Israel may be viewed, on the occasion under notice, as presenting their tributary offerings, and in the same manner of successive detail, which accords with the immemorial usages of the East. A day was set apart for each, as much for the imposing solemnity and splendor of the ceremony, as for the prevention of disorder and hurry; and it is observable that, in the order of offering, regard was paid to priority not of birth, but of rank and dignity as they were ranked in the camp—beginning at the east, proceeding to the south, then to the west, and closing with the north, according to the course of the sun. **12-17. He that offered his offering the first day was Nahshon . . . of the tribe of Judah,** etc.—Judah having had the precedence assigned to it, the prince or head of that tribe was the first admitted to offer as its representative; and his offering, as well as that of the others, is thought, from its costliness, to have been furnished not from his own private means, but from the general contributions of each tribe. Some parts of the offering, as the animals for sacrifice, were for the ritual service of the day, the peace offerings being by much the most numerous, as the princes and some of the people joined with the priests afterwards in celebrating the occasion with festive rejoicing. Hence the feast of dedication became afterwards an anniversary festival. Other parts of the offering were intended for permanent use, as utensils necessary in the service of the sanctuary; such as an immense platter and bowl (Exod. 25:29). Being of silver, they were to be employed at the altar of burnt offering, or in the court, not in the holy place, all the furniture of which was of solid or plated gold; and there was a golden spoon, the contents of which show its destination to have been the altar of incense. The word rendered "spoon" means a hollow cup, in the shape of a hand, with which the priests on ordinary occasions might lift a quantity from the incense-box to throw on the altar-fire, or into the censers; but on the ceremonial on the day of the annual atonement no instrument was allowed but the high priest's own hands (Lev. 16:12). **18. On the second day Nethaneel . . . prince of Issachar, did offer**—This tribe being stationed on the right side of Judah, offered next through its representative; then Zebulun, which was on the left side; and so on in orderly succession, every tribe making the same kind of offering and in the same amount, to show that, as each was under equal obligation, each rendered an equal tribute. Although each offering made was the same in quantity as well as quality, a separate notice is given of each, as a separate day was appointed for the presentation, that equal honor might be conferred on each, and none appear to be overlooked or slighted. And as the sacred books were frequently read in public, posterity, in each successive age, would feel a livelier interest in the national worship, from the permanent recognition of the offerings made by the ancestors of the respective tribes. But while this was done in one respect, as subjects offering tribute to their king, it was in another respect, a purely religious act. The vessels offered were for a sacrificial use—the animals brought were clean and fit for sacrifice, both symbolically denoting, that while God was to dwell among them as their Sovereign, they were a holy people, who by this offering dedicated themselves to God. **48. On the seventh day**—Surprise has been expressed by some that this work of presentation was continued on the Sabbath. But assuming that the seventh day referred to was a Sabbath (which is uncertain), the work was of a directly religious character, and perfectly in accordance with the design of the sacred day. **84-88. This was the dedication of the altar**—The inspired historian here sums up the separate items detailed in the preceding narrative, and the aggregate amount is as follows: 12 silver chargers, each weighing 130 shekels = 1560; 12 silver bowls, each 70 shekels = 840: total weight. A silver charger at 130 shekels, reduced to troy weight, made 75 oz., 9 dwts., 168.31 gr.; and a silver bowl at 70 shekels amounts to 40 oz., 12 dwts., 2121.31 gr. The total weight of the 12 chargers is therefore 905 oz., 16 dwts., 33.11 gr., and that of the 12 bowls 487 oz., 14 dwts., 204.31 gr.; making the total weight of silver vessels 1393 oz., 10 dwts., 237.31 gr. with an approximate value of $1200. The 12 golden spoons, allowing each to be 5 oz., 16 dwts., 3.31 gr., would have a value of about $1000. All this would make a grand total of about $2200. Besides these the offerings comprised 12 bullocks, 12 rams, 12 lambs, 24 goats, 60 rams, 60 he-goats, 60 lambs—amounting in all to 240. So large a collection of cattle offered for sacrifice on one occasion proves both the large flocks of the Israelites and the abundance of pastures which were then, and still are, found in the valleys that lie between the Sinaitic Mountains. All travellers attest the luxuriant verdure of those extensive wadies; and that they were equally or still more rich in pasture anciently, is confirmed by the numerous flocks of the Amalekites, as well as of Nabal, which were fed in the wilderness of Paran (I Sam. 15:9). **89. And when Moses was gone into the tabernacle of the congregation to speak with him**—As a king gives private audience to his minister, so special license was granted to Moses, who, though not a priest, was admitted into the sanctuary to receive instructions from his heavenly King as occasion demanded. **then he heard the voice of one speaking to him**—Though standing on the outer side of the veil, he could distinctly hear it, and the mention of this circumstance is important as the fulfilment, at the dedication of the tabernacle, of a special promise made by the Lord Christ Himself, the Angel of the Covenant, commanding its erection (Exod. 25:22). It was the reward of Moses' zeal and obedience; and, in like manner, to all who love Him and keep His commandments He will manifest Himself (John 14:21).

CHAPTER 8

Vss. 1-4. How the Lamps Are to Be Lighted. **1. the Lord spake unto Moses**—The order of this chapter suggests the idea that the following instructions were given to Moses while he was within the tabernacle of the congregation, after the princes had completed their offering. But from the tenor of the instructions, it is more likely that they were given immediately after the Levites had been given to the priests (see on chaps. 3, 4), and that the record of these instructions had been postponed till the narrative of other transactions in the camp had been made [Patrick]. **2. Speak unto Aaron,** etc.—The candlestick, which was made of one solid, massive piece of pure gold, with six lamps supported on as many branches, a seventh in the center surmounting the shaft itself (Exod. 25:31; 37:17), and completed according to the pattern shown in the mount,

was now to be lighted, when the other things in the sanctuary began to be applied to religious service. It was Aaron's personal duty, as the servant of God, to light His house, which, being without windows, required the aid of lights (II Pet. 1:19.) And the course he was ordered to follow was first to light the middle lamp from the altar-fire, and then the other lamps from each other—a course symbolical of all the light of heavenly truth being derived from Christ, and diffused by His ministers throughout the world (Rev. 4:5). **the seven lamps shall give light over against the candlestick**—The candlestick stood close to the boards of the sanctuary, on the south side, in full view of the table of showbread on the north (Exod. 26:35), having one set of its lamps turned towards the east, and another towards the west; so that all parts of the tabernacle were thus lighted up.

5-22. The Consecration of the Levites. **Take the Levites ... and cleanse them**—This passage describes the consecration of the Levites. Although the tribe was to be devoted to the divine service, their hereditary descent alone was not a sufficient qualification for entering on the duties of the sacred office. They were to be set apart by a special ceremony, which, however, was much simpler than that appointed for the priests; neither washing nor anointing, nor investiture with official robes, was necessary. Their purification consisted, along with the offering of the requisite sacrifices (Lev. 1:4; 3:2; 4:4), in being sprinkled by water mixed with the ashes of a red heifer (ch. 19:9), and shaved all over, and their clothes washed—a combination of symbolical acts which was intended to remind them of the mortification of carnal and wordly desires, and the maintenance of that purity in heart and life which became the servants of God. **9. thou shalt gather the whole assembly of the children of Israel together,** etc.—As it was plainly impossible that the whole multitude of the Israelites could do this, a select portion of them must be meant. This party, who laid their hands upon the Levites, are supposed by some to have been the first-born, who by that act, transferred their peculiar privilege of acting as God's ministers to the Levitical tribe; and by others, to have been the princes, who thus blessed them. It appears, from this passage, that the imposition of hands was a ceremony used in consecrating persons to holy offices in the ancient, as, from the example of our Lord and His apostles, it has been perpetuated in the Christian Church. **11-13. Aaron shall offer the Levites**—*Heb.*, as a wave offering; and it has been thought probable that the high priest, in bringing the Levites one by one to the altar, directed them to make some simple movements of their persons, analogous to what was done at the presentation of the wave offerings before the Lord. Thus were they first devoted as an offering to God, and by Him surrendered to the priests to be employed in His service. The consecration ceremonial was repeated in the case of every Levite who was taken (as was done at a later period) to assist the priests in the tabernacle and temple. (See on II Chron. 29:34.) **14. the Levites shall be mine**—i.e., exempt from all military duty or secular work—free from all pecuniary imposition and wholly devoted to the custody and service of the sanctuary. **15. after that, shall the Levites go in to do the service of the tabernacle of the congregation**—into the court, to assist the priests; and at removal into the tabernacle—i.e., into the door of it—to receive the covered furniture. **19. to make an atonement for the**

children of Israel, etc.–to aid the priests in that expiatory work; or, as the words may be rendered,
"to make redemption for" the Levites being exchanged or substituted for the first-born for this important end, that there might be a sanctified body of
men appointed to guard the sanctuary, and the
people not allowed to approach or presumptuously
meddle with holy things, which would expose them
to the angry judgments of Heaven. **24. from
twenty-five years old**, etc.–cf. ch. 4:3). They
entered on their work in their 25th year, as pupils
and probationers, under the superintendence and
direction of their senior brethren; and at 30 they
were admited to the full discharge of their official
functions. **25. from the age of fifty they shall
cease waiting upon the service thereof**, etc.–i.e., on
the laborious and exhausting parts of their work.
26. But shall minister with their brethren–in the
performance of easier and higher duties, instructing
and directing the young, or superintending important trusts. "They also serve who only wait"
[MILTON].

CHAPTER 9

Vss. 1-5. THE PASSOVER ENJOINED. **2. Let the
children of Israel also keep the passover at his appointed season**, etc.–The date of this command to
keep the passover in the wilderness was given
shortly after the erection and consecration of the
tabernacle and preceded the numbering of the
people by a month. (Cf. vs. 1 with ch. 1:1, 2.)
But it is narrated after that transaction in order to
introduce the notice of a particular case, for which
a law was provided to meet the occasion. This was
the first observance of the passover since the exodus;
and without a positive injunction, the Israelites were
under no obligation to keep it till their settlement
in the land of Canaan (Exod. 12:25). The anniversary was kept on the exact day of the year on
which they, twelve months before, had departed
from Egypt; and it was marked by all the peculiar
rites–the he-lamb and the unleavened bread. The
materials would be easily procured–the lambs from
their numerous flocks and the meal for the unleavened bread, by the aid of Jethro, from the land
of Midian, which was adjoining their camp (Exod.
3:1). But their girded loins, their sandalled feet,
and their staff in their hand, being mere circumstances attending a hurried departure and not essential to the rite, were not repeated. It is supposed
to have been the only observance of the feast during
their 40 years' wandering; and Jewish writers say
that, as none could eat the passover except they
were circumcised (Exod. 12:43, 44, 48), and cir-
cumsion was not practised in the wilderness, there
could be no renewal of the paschal solemnity.
A SECOND PASSOVER ALLOWED. Vss. 6-14.
**there were certain men who were defiled by the
dead body of a man**–To discharge the last offices
to the remains of deceased relatives was imperative;
and yet attendance on a funeral entailed ceremonial
defilement, which led to exclusion from all society
and from the camp for seven days. Some persons
who were in this situation at the arrival of the first
paschal anniversary, being painfully perplexed
about the course of duty because they were temporarily disqualified at the proper season, and having
no opportunity of supplying their want were liable
to a total privation of all their privileges, laid their
case before Moses. Jewish writers assert that these
men were the persons who had carried out the dead

bodies of Nadab and Abihu. **8. Moses said unto
them, Stand still, and I will hear what the Lord will
command concerning you**–A solution of the difficulty was soon obtained, it being enacted, by divine
authority, that to those who might be disqualified
by the occurrence of a death in their family circle
or unable by distance to keep the passover on the
anniversary day, a special license was granted of
observing it by themselves on the same day and
hour of the following month, under a due attendance
to all the solemn formalities. (See on II Chron.
30:2.) But the observance was imperative on all
who did not labor under these impediments. **14.
if a stranger shall sojourn among you, and will keep
the passover**–Gentile converts, or proselytes, as
they were afterwards called, were admitted, if
circumcised, to the same privileges as native Israelites, and were liable to excommunication if they
neglected the passover. But circumcision was an
indispensable condition; and whoever did not submit to that rite, was prohibited, under the sternest
penalties, from eating the passover.
15-23. A CLOUD GUIDES THE ISRAELITES. **the
cloud covered the tabernacle**–The inspired historian
here enters on an entirely new subject, which might
properly have formed a separate chapter, beginning at this verse and ending at vs. 29 of the following chapter [CALMET]. The cloud was a visible
token of God's special presence and guardian care of
the Israelites (Exod. 14:20; Ps. 105:39). It was
easily distinguishable from all other clouds by its
peculiar form and its fixed position; for from the day
of the completion of the tabernacle it rested by day
as a dark, by night as a fiery, column on that part of
the sanctuary which contained the ark of the testimony (Lev. 16:2). **17. when the cloud was taken up**–
i.e., rose to a higher elevation, so as to be conspicuous at the remotest extremities of the camp.
That was a signal for removal; and, accordingly, it
is properly called (vs. 18) "the commandment of the
Lord." It was a visible token of the presence of
God; and from it, as a glorious throne, He gave the
order. So that its motion regulated the commencement and termination of all the journeys of the
Israelites. (See on Exod. 14:19.) **19. when the
cloud tarried long upon the tabernacle, ... then
Israel kept the charge of the Lord and journeyed
not**–A desert life has its attractions, and constant
movements create a passionate love of change.
Many incidents show that the Israelites had strongly
imbibed this nomad habit and were desirous of
hastening to Canaan. But still the phases of the
cloud indicated the command of God: and whatsoever irksomeness they might have felt in remaining long stationary in camp, "when the cloud tarried
upon the tabernacle many days, they kept the
charge of the Lord, and journeyed not." Happy
for them had they always exhibited this spirit of
obedience! and happy for all if, through the wilderness of this world, we implicitly follow the leadings
of God's Providence and the directions of God's
Word!

CHAPTER 10

Vss. 1-36. THE USE OF THE SILVER TRUMPETS.
2. Make thee two trumpets of silver–These
trumpets were of a long form, in opposition to that
of the Egyptian trumpets, with which the people
were convened to the worship of Osiris and which
were curved like rams' horns. Those which Moses
made, as described by Josephus and represented

the arch of Titus, were straight, a cubit or more in length, the tubes of the thickness of a flute. Both extremities bore a close resemblance to those in use among us. They were of solid silver—so as, from the purity of the metal, to give a shrill, distinct sound; and there were two of them, probably because there were only two sons of Aaron; but at a later period the number was greatly increased (Josh. 6:8; II Chron. 5:12). And although the camp comprehended 2,500,000 of people, two trumpets would be quite sufficient, for sound is conveyed easily through the pure atmosphere and reverberated strongly among the valleys of the Sinaitic hills. **3. when they shall blow with them**—There seem to have been signals made by a difference in the loudness and variety in the notes, suited for different occasions, and which the Israelites learned to distinguish. A simple uniform sound by both trumpets summoned a general assembly of the people; the blast of a single trumpet convoked the princes to consult on public affairs; notes of some other kind were made to sound an alarm, whether for journeying or for war. One alarm was the recognized signal for the eastern division of the camp (the tribes of Judah, Issachar, and Zebulun) to march; two alarms gave the signal for the southern to move; and, though it is not in our present *Hebrew* text, the Septuagint has, that on three alarms being sounded, those on the west; while on four blasts, those on the north decamped. Thus the greatest order and discipline were established in the Israelitish camp—no military march could be better regulated. **8. Thet sons of Aaron the priests shall blow with the trumpets,** etc.—Neither the Levites nor any in the common ranks of the people could be employed in this office of signal-giving. In order to attract greater attention and more faithful observance, it was reserved to the priests alone, as the Lord's ministers; and as anciently in Persia and other Eastern countries the alarm trumpets were sounded from the tent of the sovereign, so were they blown from the tabernacle, the visible residence of Israel's King. **9. If ye go to war**—In the land of Canaan, either when attacked by foreign invaders or when they went to take possession according to the divine promise, "ye [i.e., the priests] shall blow an alarm." This advice was accordingly acted upon (ch. 31:6; II Chron. 13:12); and in the circumstances it was an act of devout confidence in God. A solemn and religious act on the eve of a battle has often animated the hearts of those who felt they were engaged in a good and just cause; and so the blowing of the trumpet, being an ordinance of God, produced that effect on the minds of the Israelites. But more is meant by the words—viz., that God would, as it were, be aroused by the trumpet to bless with His presence and aid. **10. Also in the days of your gladness, and in your solemn days**—Festive and thanksgiving occasions were to be ushered in with the trumpets, as all feasts afterwards were (Ps. 81:3; II Chron. 29:27) to intimate the joyous and delighted feelings with which they engaged in the service of God. **11. It came to pass on the twentieth day of the second month in the second year,** etc.—The Israelites had lain encamped in Wady-Er-Rahah and the neighboring valleys of the Sinaitic range for the space of 11 months and 29 days. (Cf. Exod. 19:1.) Besides the religious purposes of the highest importance to which their long sojourn at Sinai was subservient, Israelites, after the hardships and oppression of Egyptian servitude, required an interval of rest and refreshment. They were neither physi-

cally nor morally in a condition to enter the lists with the warlike people they had to encounter before obtaining possession of Canaan. But the wondrous transactions at Sinai—the arm of Jehovah so visibly displayed in their favor—the covenant entered into, and the special blessings guaranteed, beginning a course of moral and religious education which moulded the character of this people—made them acquainted with their high destiny and inspired them with those noble principles of divine truth and righteousness which alone make a great nation. **12. wilderness of Paran**—It stretched from the base of the Sinaitic group, or from Et-Tyh, over that extensive plateau to the southwestern borders of Palestine. **13-27. the children of Israel took their journey ... by the hand of Moses**—It is probable that Moses, on the breaking up of the encampment, stationed himself on some eminence to see the ranks defile in order through the embouchure of the mountains. The marching order is described (ch. 2); but, as the vast horde is represented here in actual migration, let us notice the extraordinary care that was taken for ensuring the safe conveyance of the holy things. In the rear of Judah, which, with the tribes of Issachar and Zebulun, led the van, followed the Gershonites and Merarites with the heavy and coarser materials of the tabernacle. Next in order were set in motion the flank divisions of Reuben and Ephraim. Then came the Kohathites, who occupied the center of the moving mass, bearing the sacred utensils on their shoulder. They were so far behind the other portions of the Levitical body that these would have time at the new encampment to rear the framework of the tabernacle before the Kohathites arrived. Last of all, Dan, with the associated tribes, brought up the rear of the immense caravan. Each tribe was marshalled under its prince or chief and in all their movements rallied around its own standard. **29. Hobab, the son of Raguel the Midianite**—called also Reuel (the same as Jethro). Hobab, the son of this Midianite chief and brother-in-law to Moses, seems to have sojourned among the Israelites during the whole period of their encampment at Sinai and now on their removal proposed returning to his own abode. Moses urged him to remain, both for his own benefit from a religious point of view, and for the useful services his nomad habits could enable him to render. **31. Leave us not, I pray thee ... and thou mayest be to us instead of eyes**—The earnest importunity of Moses to secure the attendance of this man, when he enjoyed the benefit of the directing cloud, has surprised many. But it should be recollected that the guidance of the cloud, though it showed the general route to be taken through the trackless desert, would not be so special and minute as to point out the places where pasture, shade, and water were to be obtained and which were often hid in obscure spots by the shifting sands. Besides, several detachments were sent off from the main body; the services of Hobab, not as a single Arab, but as a prince of a powerful clan, would have been exceedingly useful. **32. if thou go with us ... what goodness the Lord will show unto us, the same will we do unto thee**—A strong inducement is here held out; but it seems not to have changed the young man's purpose, for he departed and settled in his own district. (See on Judg. 1:16; I Sam. 15:6.) **33. they departed ... three days' journey**—the first day's progress being very small, about 18 or 20 miles. **ark of the covenant went before them**—It was carried in the center, and hence some eminent commentators think the passage should be rendered, "the ark went in their presence," the cloud above upon it being conspicuous in their eyes. But it is probable that the cloudy pillar, which, while stationary, rested upon the ark, preceded them in the march—as, when in motion at one time (Exod. 14:19) it is expressly said to have shifted its place. **35, 36. when the ark set forward that Moses said, Rise up, Lord, and let thine enemies be scattered—** Moses, as the organ of the people, uttered an appropriate prayer both at the commencement and the end of each journey. Thus all the journeys were sanctified by devotion; and so should our prayer be, "If thy presence go not with us, carry us not hence."

CHAPTER 11

Vss. 1-35. MANNA LOATHED. **1. When the people complained it displeased the Lord . . .**— Unaccustomed to the fatigues of travel and wandering into the depths of a desert, less mountainous but far more gloomy and desolate than that of Sinai, without any near prospect of the rich country that had been promised, they fell into a state of vehement discontent, which was vented at these irksome and fruitless journeyings. The displeasure of God was manifested against the ungrateful complainers by fire sent in an extraordinary manner. It is worthy of notice, however, that the discontent seems to have been confined to the extremities of the camp, where, in all likelihood, "the mixed multitude" had their station. At the intercession of Moses, the appalling judgment ceased, and the name given to the place, "Taberah" (a burning), remained ever after a monument of national sin and punishment. (See on vss. 34, 35.) **4. the mixed multitude that was among them fell a lusting—**These consisted of Egyptians. To dream of banquets and plenty of animal food in the desert becomes a disease of the imagination; and to this excitement of the appetite no people are more liable than the natives of Egypt. But the Israelites participated in the same feelings and expressed dissatisfaction with the manna on which they had hitherto been supported, in comparison with the vegetable luxuries with which they had been regaled in Egypt. **5. We remember the fish, which we did eat in Egypt freely—** (See on Exod. 7:21). The people of Egypt are accustomed to an almost exclusive diet of fish, either fresh or sun-dried, during the hot season in April and May—the very season when the Israelites were travelling in this desert. Lower Egypt, where were the brick-kilns in which they were employed, afforded great facilities for obtaining fish in the Mediterranean, the lakes, and the canals of the Nile. **cucumbers—**The Egyptian species is smooth, of a cylindrical form, and about a foot in length. It is highly esteemed by the natives and when in season is liberally partaken of, being greatly mellowed by the influence of the sun. **melons—** The watermelons are meant, which grow on the deep, loamy soil after the subsidence of the Nile; and as they afford a juicy and cooling fruit, all classes make use of them for food, drink, and medicine. **leeks—**by some said to be a species of grass cresses, which is much relished as a kind of seasoning. **onions—**the same as ours; but instead of being nauseous and affecting the eyes, they are sweet to the taste, good for the stomach, and form to a large extent the aliment of the laboring classes. **garlic—**is now nearly if not altogether extinct in Egypt although it seems to have grown anciently in

great abundance. The herbs now mentioned form a diet very grateful in warm countries where vegetables and other fruits of the season are much used. We can scarcely wonder that both the Egyptian hangers-on and the general body of the Israelites, incited by their clamors, complained bitterly of the want of the refreshing viands in their toilsome wanderings. But after all their experience of the bounty and care of God, their vehement longing for the luxuries of Egypt was an impeachment of the divine arrangements; and if it was the sin that beset them in the desert, it became them more strenuously to repress a rebellious spirit, as dishonoring to God and unbecoming their relation to Him as a chosen people. **6-9. But now . . . there is nothing . . . beside this manna—**Daily familiarity had disgusted them with the sight and taste of the monotonous food; and, ungrateful for the heavenly gift, they longed for a change of fare. It may be noticed that the resemblance of the manna to coriander seed was not in the color, but in the size and figure; and from its comparison to bdellium, which is either a drop of white gum or a white pearl, we are enabled to form a better idea of it. Moreover, it is evident, from the process of baking into cakes, that it could not have been the natural manna of the Arabian desert, for that is too gummy or unctuous to admit of being ground into meal. In taste it is said (Exod. 16:31), to have been like "wafers made with honey," and here to have the taste of fresh oil. The discrepancy in these statements is only apparent; for in the latter the manna is described in its raw state; in the former, after it was ground and baked. The minute description given here of its nature and use was designed to show the great sinfulness of the people in being dissatisfied with such excellent food, furnished so plentifully and gratuitously. **10-15. Moses said unto the Lord, Wherefore hast thou afflicted thy servant,** etc.—It is impossible not to sympathize with his feelings although the tone and language of his remonstrances to God cannot be justified. He was in a most distressing situation—having a mighty multitude under his care, with no means of satisfying their clamorous demands. *Their* conduct shows how deeply they had been debased and demoralized by long oppression: while *his* reveals a state of mind agonized and almost overwhelmed by a sense of the undivided responsibilities of his office. **16, 17. the Lord said unto Moses, Gather unto me seventy men of the elders—**(Exod. 3:16; 5:6; 24:9; 18:21, 24; Lev. 4:15). An order of seventy was to be created, either by a selection from the existing staff of elders or by the appointment of new ones, empowered to assist him by their collective wisdom and experience in the onerous cares of government. The Jewish writers say that this was the origin of the Sanhedrim, or supreme appellate court of their nation. But there is every reason to believe that it was only a temporary expedient, adopted to meet a trying exigency. **17. I will come down—**i.e., not in a visible manner or by local descent, but by the tokens of the divine presence and operations. **and I will take of the spirit which is upon thee—**The spirit means the gifts and influences of the Spirit (ch. 27: 18; Joel 2:28; John 7:39; I Cor. 14:12), and by "taking the spirit of Moses, and putting it upon them," is not to be understood that the qualities of the great leader were to be in any degree impaired but that the elders would be endowed with a portion of the same gifts, especially of prophecy (vs. 25)— i.e., an extraordinary penetration in discovering hidden and settling difficult things. **18-20. say tho** unto the people, Sanctify yourselves against to-morrow, and ye shall eat flesh—i.e., "prepare yourselves," by repentance and submission, to receive to-morrow the flesh you clamor for. But it is evident that the tenor of the language implied a severe rebuke and that the blessing promised would prove a curse. 21-23. Moses said, The people, among whom I am, are six hundred thousand .... Shall the flocks and herds be slain for them, to suffice them?—The great leader, struck with a promise so astonishing as that of suddenly furnishing, in the midst of the desert, more than two millions of people with flesh for a whole month, betrayed an incredulous spirit, surprising in one who had witnessed so many stupendous miracles. But it is probable that it was only a feeling of the moment—at all events, the incredulous doubt was uttered only to himself—and not, as afterwards, publicly and to the scandal of the people. (See on ch. 20:10.) It was, therefore, sharply reproved, but not punished. 24. Moses . . . gathered the seventy men of the elders of the people, etc.—The tabernacle was chosen for the convocation, because, as it was there God manifested Himself, there His Spirit would be directly imparted—there the minds of the elders themselves would be inspired with reverential awe and their office invested with greater respect in the eyes of the people. 25. when the spirit rested upon them, they prophesied, and did not cease—As those elders were constituted civil governors, their "prophesying" must be understood as meaning the performance of their civil and sacred duties by the help of those extraordinary endowments they had received; and by their not "ceasing" we understand, either that they continued to exercise their gifts uninterruptedly the first day (see I Sam. 19:24), or that these were permanent gifts, which qualified them in an eminent degree for discharging the duty of public magistrates. 26-29. But there remained two of the men in the camp—They did not repair with the rest to the tabernacle, either from modesty in shrinking from the assumption of a public office, or being prevented by some ceremonial defilement. They, however, received the gifts of the Spirit as well as their brethren; and when Moses was urged to forbid their prophesying, his answer displayed a noble disinterestedness as well as zeal for the glory of God akin to that of our Lord (Mark 9:39). 31-35. There went forth a wind from the Lord, and brought quails from the sea, etc.—These migratory birds (see on Exodus 16:13) were on their journey from Egypt, when "the wind from the Lord," an east wind (Ps. 78:26) forcing them to change their course, wafted them over the Red Sea to the camp of Israel. let them fall a day's journey—If the journey of an individual is meant, this space might be thirty miles; if the inspired historian referred to the whole host, ten miles would be as far as they could march in one day in the sandy desert under a vertical sun. Assuming it to be twenty miles this immense cloud of quails (Exod. 16:13) covered a space of forty miles in diameter. Others reduce it to sixteen. But it is doubtful whether the measurement be from the center or the extremities of the camp. It is evident, however, that the language describes the countless number of these quails. as it were two cubits high—Some have supposed that they fell on the ground above each other to that height—a ⁿpposition which would leave a vast quantity use-... as food to the Israelites, who were forbidden to ... ʸy animal that died of itself or from which the ... ʸas not poured out. Others think that, be-... ⁱusted with a long flight, they could not fly

more than three feet above the earth, and so were easily felled or caught. A more recent explanation applies the phrase, "two cubits high," not to the accumulation of the mass, but to the size of the individual birds. Flocks of large red-legged cranes, three feet high, measuring seven feet from tip to tip, have been frequently seen on the western shores of the Gulf of Akaba, or eastern arm of the Red Sea [STANLEY, SHUBERT]. 32. people stood up—rose up in eager haste—some at one time, others at another—some, perhaps through avidity, both day and night. ten homers—ten asses' loads; or, "homers" may be used indefinitely (as in Exod. 8:14; Judg. 15:16); and "ten" for many: so that the phrase "ten homers" is equivalent to great heaps. The collectors were probably one or two from each family; and, being distrustful of God's goodness, they gathered not for immediate consumption only, but for future use. In eastern and southern seas, innumerable quails are often seen, which, when weary, fall down, covering every spot on the deck and rigging of vessels; and in Egypt they come in such myriads that the people knock them down with sticks. spread them all abroad for themselves—salted and dried them for future use, by the simple process to which they had been accustomed in Egypt. 33. while the flesh was yet between their teeth, ere it was chewed—lit., cut off—i.e., before the supply of quails, which lasted a month (vs. 20), was exhausted. The probability is, that their stomachs, having been long inured to manna (a light food), were not prepared for so sudden a change of regimen—a heavy, solid diet of animal food, of which they seem to have partaken to so intemperate a degree as to produce a general surfeit, and fatal consequences. On a former occasion their murmurings for flesh were raised (Exod. 16) because they were in want of food. Here they proceeded, not from necessity, but wanton, lustful desire; and their sin, in the righteous judgment of God, was made to carry its own punishment. 34. called the name of that place Kibrothhattaavah—lit., the graves of lust, or those that lusted; so that the name of the place proves that the mortality was confined to those who had indulged inordinately. 35. Hazeroth—The extreme southern station of this route was a watering-place in a spacious plain, now Ain Haderah.

CHAPTER 12

Vss. 1-9. MIRIAM'S AND AARON'S SEDITION. 1. an Ethiopian woman—*Heb.*, a Cushite woman—Arabia was usually called in Scripture the land of Cush, its inhabitants being descendants of that son of Ham (see on Exod. 2:15) and being accounted generally a vile and contemptible race (Amos 9:7). The occasion of this seditious outbreak on the part of Miriam and Aaron against Moses was the great change made in the government by the adoption of the seventy rulers. Their irritating disparagement of his wife (who, in all probability, was Zipporah, and not a second wife he had recently married) arose from jealousy of the relatives, through whose influence the innovation had been first made (Exod. 18), while they were overlooked or neglected. Miriam is mentioned before Aaron as being the chief instigator and leader of the sedition. 2. Hath the Lord indeed spoken only by Moses? hath he not also spoken by us?—The prophetical name and character was bestowed upon Aaron (Exod. 4:15, 16) and Miriam (Exod. 15:20); and, therefore, they considered the conduct of Moses, in exercising an exclusive authority in this matter, as an encroachment on their rights (Micah 6:4). **3. the man Moses was very meek**—(Exod. 14:13; 21:7; 32:12, 13; Deut. 9:18). This observation might have been made to account for Moses taking no notice of their angry reproaches and for God's interposing so speedily for the vindication of His servant's cause. The circumstance of Moses recording an eulogium on a distinguishing excellence of his own character is not without a parallel among the sacred writers, when forced to it by the insolence and contempt of opponents (II Cor. 11:5; 12:11, 12). But it is not improbable that, as this verse appears to be a parenthesis, it may have been inserted as a gloss by Ezra or some later prophet. Others, instead of "very meek," suggest "very afflicted," as the proper rendering. **4. the Lord spake suddenly unto Moses, and unto Aaron, and unto Miriam**—The divine interposition was made thus openly and immediately, in order to suppress the sedition and prevent its spreading among the people. **5. the Lord came down in the pillar of the cloud, and stood in the door of the tabernacle**—without gaining admission, as was the usual privilege of Aaron, though it was denied to all other men and women. This public exclusion was designed to be a token of the divine displeasure. **6. Hear now my words**—A difference of degree is here distinctly expressed in the gifts and authority even of divinely commissioned prophets. Moses, having been set over all God's house, (i.e., His church and people), was consequently invested with supremacy over Miriam and Aaron also and privileged beyond all others by direct and clear manifestations of the presence and will of God. **8. with him will I speak mouth to mouth**—immediately, not by an interpreter, nor by visionary symbols presented to his fancy. **apparently**—plainly and surely. **not in dark speeches**—parables or similitudes. **the similitude of the Lord shall he behold**—not the face or essence of God, who is invisible (Exod. 33:20; Col. 1:15; John 1:18); but some unmistakable evidence of His glorious presence (Exod. 33:2; 34:5). The latter clause should have been conjoined with the preceding one, thus: "not in dark speeches, and in a figure shall he behold the Lord." The slight change in the punctuation removes all appearance of contradiction to Deuteronomy 4:15.

10-16. HER LEPROSY. 10. the cloud departed from the tabernacle—i.e., from the door to resume its permanent position over the mercy seat. **Miriam became leprous**—This malady in its most malignant form (Ex. 4:6; II Kings 5:27) as its color, combined with its sudden appearance, proved, was inflicted as a divine judgment; and she was made the victim, either because of her extreme violence or because the leprosy on Aaron would have interrupted or dishonored the holy service. **11-13.** On the humble and penitential submission of Aaron, Moses interceded for both the offenders, especially for Miriam, who was restored; not, however, till she had been made, by ther exclusion, a public example. **14. her father had but spit in her face, should she not be ashamed seven days?**—The Jews, in common with all people in the East, seem to have had an intense abhorrence of spitting, and for a parent to express his displeasure by doing so on the person of one of his children, or even on the ground in his presence, separated that child as unclean from society for seven days. **15. the people journeyed not till Miriam was brought in again**—Either not to crush her by a sentence of overwhelming severity or not to expose her, being a prophetess, to popular

contempt. **16 pitched in the wilderness of Paran**—The station of encampments seems to have been Rithma (ch. 33:19).

CHAPTER 13

VSS. 1-35. THE NAMES OF THE MEN WHO WERE SENT TO SEARCH THE LAND. **1, 2. The Lord spake unto Moses, Send thou men, that they may search the land, of Canaan**—Cf. Deuteronomy 1:22, whence it appears, that while the proposal of delegating confidential men from each tribe to explore the land of Canaan emanated from the people who petitioned for it, the measure received the special sanction of God, who granted their request at once as a trial, and a punishment of their distrust. **3. those men were heads of the children of Israel**—Not the princes who are named (ch. 10), but chiefs, leading men though not of the first rank. **16. Oshea**—i.e., a desire of salvation. Jehoshua, by prefixing the name of God, means "divinely appointed," "head of salvation," "Saviour," the same as Jesus. **17. Get you up this way . . . , and go up into the mountain**—Mount Seir (Deut. 1:2), which lay directly from Sinai across the wilderness of Paran, in a northeasterly direction into the southern parts of the promised land. **20. Now the time was the time of the first grapes**—This was in August, when the first clusters are gathered. The second are gathered in September, and the third in October. The spies' absence for a period of forty days determines the grapes they brought from Eshcol to have been of the second period. **21-24. So they . . . searched the land**—They advanced from south to north, reconnoitering the whole land. **the wilderness of Zin**—a long level plain, or deep valley of sand, the monotony of which is relieved by a few tamarisk and rethem trees. Under the names of El Ghor and El Araba, it forms the continuation of the Jordan valley, extending from the Dead Sea to the Gulf of Akaba. **Rehob**—or, Beth-rehob, was a city and district situated, according to some, eastward of Sidon; and, according to others, it is the same as El Hule, an extensive and fertile champaign country, at the foot of Anti-libanus, a few leagues below Paneas. **as men come unto Hamath**—or, "the entering in of Hamath" (II Kings 14:25), now the valley of Balbeck, a mountain pass or opening in the northern frontier, which formed the extreme limit in that direction of the inheritance of Israel. From the mention of these places, the route of the scouts appears to have been along the course of the Jordan in their advance; and their return was by the western border through the territories of the Sidonians and Philistines. **22. unto Hebron**—situated in the heart of the mountains of Judah, in the southern extremity of Palestine. The town or "cities of Hebron," as it is expressed in the *Heb.*, consists of a number of sheikdoms distinct from each other, standing at the foot of one of those hills that form a bowl round and enclose it. "The children of Anak," mentioned in this verse, seem to have been also chiefs of townships; and this coincidence of polity, existing in ages so distant from each other, is remarkable [VERE MONRO]. Hebron (Kirjath-Arba, Gen. 23:2) was one of the oldest cities in the world. **Zoan**—(the Tanis of the Greeks). It was situated on one of the eastern branches of the Nile, near the lake Menzala, and was the early royal residence of the Pharaohs. It boasted a higher antiquity than any other city in Egypt. Its name, which signifies flat and level, is descriptive of its situation in the low grounds of the Delta. **23. they came unto the brook of Eshcol**—i.e., "the torrent of the cluster." Its location was a little to the southwest of Hebron. The valley and its sloping hills are still covered with vineyards, the character of whose fruit corresponds to its ancient celebrity. **and cut down from thence a branch with one cluster of grapes**—The grapes reared in this locality are still as magnificent as formerly—they are said by one to be equal in size to prunes, and compared by another to a man's thumb. One cluster sometimes weights 10 or 12 pounds. The mode of carrying the cluster cut down by the spies, though not necessary from its weight, was evidently adopted to preserve it entire as a specimen of the productions of the promised land; and the impression made by the sight of it would be all the greater because the Israelites were familiar only with the scanty vines and small grapes of Egypt. **26. they came . . . to Kadesh**—an important encampment of the Israelites. But its exact situation is not definitely known, nor is it determined whether it is the same or a different place from Kadesh-barnea. It is supposed to be identical with Ain-el-Weibeh, a famous spring on the eastern side of the desert [ROBINSON], or also with Petra [STANLEY]. **27, 28. they told him, and said, We came unto the land whither thou sentest us, and surely it floweth with milk and honey**—The report was given publicly in the audience of the people, and it was artfully arranged to begin their narrative with commendations of the natural fertility of the country in order that their subsequent slanders might the more readily receive credit. **29. The Amalekites dwell in the land of the south**—Their territory lay between the Dead and the Red Seas, skirting the borders of Canaan. **Hittites . . . dwell in the mountains**—Their settlements were in the southern and mountainous part of Palestine (Gen. 23:7). **the Canaanites dwell by the sea**—The remnant of the original inhabitants, who had been dispossessed by the Philistines, were divided into two nomadic hordes—one settled eastward near the Jordan; the other westward, by the Mediterranean. **32. a land that eateth up the inhabitants**—i.e., an unhealthy climate and country. Jewish writers say that in the course of their travels they saw a great many funerals, vast numbers of the Canaanites being cut off at that time, in the providence of God, by a plague or the hornet (Joshua 24:12). **men of a great stature**—This was evidently a false and exaggerated report, representing, from timidity or malicious artifice, what was true of a few as descriptive of the people generally. **33. there we saw the giants, the sons of Anak**—The name is derived from the son of Arba—a great man among the Arabians (Josh. 15:14), who probably obtained his appellation from wearing a splendid collar or chain round his neck, as the word imports. The epithet "giant" evidently refers here to stature. (See on Gen. 6:4.) And it is probable the Anakims were a distinguished family, or perhaps a select body of warriors, chosen for their extraordinary size. **we were in our own sight as grasshoppers**—a strong Orientalism, by which the treacherous spies gave an exaggerated report of the physical strength of the people of Canaan.

CHAPTER 14

Vss. 1-45. **1. THE PEOPLE MURMUR AT THE SPIES' REPORT. all the congregation lifted up their** voice and cried—Not literally all, for there were some exceptions. **2-4. Would God that we had died in Egypt**—Such insolence to their generous leaders, and such base ingratitude to God, show the deep degradation of the Israelites, and the absolute necessity of the decree that debarred that generation from entering the promised land. They were punished by their wishes being granted to die in that wilderness. A leader to reconduct them to Egypt is spoken of (Neh. 9:17) as actually nominated. The sinfulness and insane folly of their conduct are almost incredible. Their conduct, however, is paralleled by too many among us, who shrink from the smallest difficulties and rather remain slaves to sin than resolutely try to surmount the obstacles that lie in their way to the Canaan above. **5. Moses and Aaron fell on their faces**—as humble and earnest suppliants—either to the people, entreating them to desist from so perverse a design;—or rather, to God, as the usual and only refuge from the violence of that tumultuous and stiff-necked rabble—and a hopeful means of softening and impressing their hearts. **6. Joshua . . . and Caleb, which were of them that searched the land, rent their clothes**—The two honest spies testified their grief and horror, in the strongest manner, at the mutiny against Moses and the blasphemy against God; while at the same time they endeavored, by a truthful statement, to persuade the people of the ease with which they might obtain possession of so desirable a country, provided they did not, by their rebellion and ingratitude, provoke God to abandon them. **8. a land flowing with milk and honey**—a general expression, descriptive of a rich and fertile country. The two articles specified were among the principal products of the Holy Land. **9. their defence is departed**—*Heb.*, their shadow. The Sultan of Turkey and the Shah of Persia are called "the shadow of God," "the refuge of the world." So that the meaning of the phrase, "their defence is departed" from them, is, that the favor of God was now lost to those whose iniquities were full (Gen. 15:16), and transferred to the Israelites. **10. the glory of the Lord appeared**—It was seasonably manifested on this great emergency to rescue His ambassadors from their perilous situation. **11. the Lord said, . . . I will smite them with the pestilence**—not a final decree, but a threatening, suspended, as appeared from the issue, on the intercession of Moses and the repentance of Israel. **17. let the power of my Lord be great**—be magnified. **21. all the earth shall be filled with the glory of the Lord**—This promise, in its full acceptation, remains to be verified by the eventual and universal prevalence of Christianity in the world. But the terms were used restrictively in respect to the occasion, to the report which would spread over all the land of the "terrible things in righteousness" which God would do in the infliction of the doom described, to which that rebellious race was now consigned. **ten times**—very frequently. **24. my servant Caleb**—Joshua was also excepted, but he is not named because he was no longer in the ranks of the people, being a constant attendant on Moses. **because he had another spirit, and hath followed me fully**—Under the influence of God's Spirit, Caleb was a man of bold, generous, heroic courage, above worldly anxieties and fears. **25. (Now the Amalekites and the Canaanites dwelt in the valley)** —i.e., on the other side of the Idumean mountain, at whose base they were then encamped. Those nomad tribes had at that time occupied it with a determination to oppose the further progress of the

Hebrew people. Hence God gave the command that they seek a safe and timely retreat into the desert, to escape the pursuit of those resolute enemies, to whom, with their wives and children, they would fall a helpless prey because they had forfeited the presence and protection of God. The 25th verse forms an important part of the narrative and should be freed from the parenthetical form which our English translators have given it. **30. save Caleb . . . and Joshua**—These are specially mentioned, as honorable exceptions to the rest of the scouts, and also as the future leaders of the people. But it appears that some of the old generation did not join in the mutinous murmuring, including in that number the whole order of the priests (Josh. 14:1). **34. ye shall known my breach of promise**—i.e., in consequence of your violation of the covenant betwixt you and Me, by breaking the terms of it, it shall be null and void on My part, as I shall withhold the blessings I promised in that covenant to confer on you on condition of your obedience. **36-38. those men that did bring up the evil report upon the land, died by the plague before the Lord**—Ten of the spies were struck dead on the spot—either by the pestilence, or some other judgment. This great and appalling mortality clearly betokened the hand of the Lord. **40-45. they rose up early in the morning, and gat them into the top of the mountain**—Notwithstanding the tidings that Moses communicated and which diffused a general feeling of melancholy and grief throughout the camp, the impression was of very brief continuance. They rushed from one extreme of rashness and perversity to another, and the obstinacy of their rebellious spirit was evinced by their active preparations to ascend the hill, notwithstanding the divine warning they had received not to undertake that enterprise. **for we have sinned**—i.e., realizing our sin, we now repent of it, and are eager to do as Caleb and Joshua exhorted us—or, as some render it, *though* we have sinned, we trust God will yet give us the land of promise. The entreaties of their prudent and pious leader, who represented to them that their enemies, scaling the other side of the valley, would post themselves on the top of the hill before them, were disregarded. How strangely perverse the conduct of the Israelites, who, shortly before, were afraid that, though their Almighty King was with them, they could not get possession of the land; and yet now they act still more foolishly in supposing that, though God were not with them, they could expel the inhabitants by their unaided efforts. The consequences were such as might have been anticipated. The Amalekites and Canaanites, who had been lying in ambuscade expecting their movement, rushed down upon them from the heights and became the instruments of punishing their guilty rebellion. **even unto Hormah**—The name was afterwards given to that place in memory of the immense slaughter of the Israelites on this occasion.

CHAPTER 15

Vss. 1-41. THE LAW OF SUNDRY OFFERINGS. **1, 2. The Lord spake unto Moses, saying, Speak unto the children of Israel**—Some infer from vs. 23 that the date of this communication must be fixed towards the close of the wanderings in the wilderness; and, also, that all the sacrifices prescribed in the law were to be offered only after the settlement in Canaan. **3. make an offering by fire unto the**

Lord, a burnt offering—It is evident that a peace offering is referred to because this term is frequently used in such a sense (Exod. 18:12; Lev. 17:5). **4. tenth deal**—i.e., an omer, the tenth part of an ephah (Exod. 16:36). **fourth part of an hin of oil**—This element shows it to have been different from such meat offerings as were made by themselves, and not merely accompaniments of other sacrifices. **6-12. two tenth deals**—The quantity of flour was increased because the sacrifice was of superior value to the former. The accessory sacrifices were always increased in proportion to the greater worth and magnitude of its principal. **13-16. a stranger**—one who had become a proselyte. There were scarcely any of the national privileges of the Israelites, in which the Gentile stranger might not, on conforming to certain conditions, fully participate. **19. when ye eat of the bread of the land, ye shall offer up an heave offering**—The offering prescribed was to precede the act of eating. **unto the Lord**—i.e., the priests of the Lord (Ezek. 44:30). **20. heave offering of the threshing-floor**—meaning the corn on the threshing-floor—i.e., after harvest. **so shall ye heave it**—to the priests accompanying the ceremony with the same rites. **22. if ye have erred and not observed all these commandments,** etc.—respecting the performance of divine worship, and the rites and ceremonies that constitute the holy service. The law relates only to any omission and consequently is quite different from *that* laid down in Leviticus 4:13, which implies a transgression or positive neglect of some observances required. *This* law relates to private parties or individual tribes; *that* to the whole congregation of Israel. **24-26. if aught be committed by ignorance**—The Mosaic ritual was complicated, and the ceremonies to be gone through in the various instances of purification which are specified, would expose a worshipper, through ignorance, to the risk of omitting or neglecting some of them. This law includes the stranger in the number of those for whom the sacrifice was offered for the sin of general ignorance. **27-29. if any soul sin through ignorance**—not only in common with the general body of the people, but his personal sins were to be expiated in the same manner. **30. the soul that doeth aught presumptuously**—*Heb. with an high or uplifted hand*—i.e., knowingly, wilfully, obstinately. In this sense the phraseology occurs (Exod. 14:8; Lev. 26:21; Ps. 19:13). **the same reproacheth the Lord**—sets Him at open defiance and dishonors His majesty. **31. his iniquity shall be upon him**—The punishment of his sins shall fall on himself individually; no guilt shall be incurred by the nation, unless there be a criminal carelessness in overlooking the offense. **32-34. a man that gathered sticks upon the sabbath day**—This incident is evidently narrated as an instance of presumptuous sin. The mere gathering of sticks was not a sinful act and might be necessary for fuel to warm him or to make ready his food. But its being done on the Sabbath altered the entire character of the action. The law of the Sabbath being a plain and positive commandment, this transgression of it was a known and wilful sin, and it was marked by several aggravations. For the deed was done with unblushing boldness in broad daylight, in open defiance of the divine authority—in flagrant inconsistency with His religious connection with Israel, as the covenant people of God; and it was an application to improper purposes of time, which God had consecrated to Himself and the solemn duties of religion. The offender was brought before the rulers, who, on hearing the painful report, were at a loss to determine what ought to be done. That they should have felt any embarrassment in such a case may seem surprising, in the face of the sabbath law (Exod. 31:14). Their difficulty probably arose from this being the first public offense of the kind which had occurred; and the appeal might be made to remove all ground of complaint—to produce a more striking effect, so that the fate of this criminal might be a beacon to warn all Israelites in the future. **35, 36. The Lord said, The man shall surely be put to death**—The Lord was King, as well as God of Israel, and the offense being a violation of the law of the realm, the Sovereign Judge gave orders that this man should be put to death; and, moreover, He required the whole congregation unite in executing the fatal sentence. **38. bid them that they make fringes in the border of their garments**—These were narrow strips, in a wing-like form, wrapped over the shoulders and on various parts of the attire. "Fringe," however, is the English rendering of two distinct Hebrew words—the one meaning a narrow lappet or edging, called the "hem" or "border" (Matt. 23:5; Luke 8:44), which, in order to make it more attractive to the eye and consequently more serviceable to the purpose described, was covered with a riband of blue or rather purple color; the other term signifies strings with tassels at the end, fastened to the corners of the garment. Both of these are seen on the Egyptian and Assyrian frocks; and as the Jewish people were commanded by express and repeated ordinances to have them, the fashion was rendered subservient, in their case, to awaken high and religious associations—to keep them in habitual remembrance of the divine commandments. **41. I am the Lord your God**—The import of this solemn conclusion is, that though He was displeased with them for their frequent rebellions, for which they would be doomed to forty years' wanderings, He would not abandon them but continue His divine protection and care of them till they were brought into the land of promise.

CHAPTER 16

Vss. 1-30. THE REBELLION OF KORAH. **1, 2. Now Korah, the son of Izhar**—Izhar, brother of Amram (Exod. 6:18), was the second son of Kohath, and for some reason unrecorded he had been supplanted by a descendant of the fourth son of Kohath, who was appointed prince or chief of the Kohathites (Ch. 3:30). Discontent with the preferment over him of a younger relative was probably the originating cause of this seditious movement on the part of Korah. **Dathan, and Abiram, ... and On**—These were confederate leaders in the rebellion, but On seems to have afterwards withdrawn from the conspiracy. **took men**—The latter mentioned individuals, being all sons of Reuben, the eldest of Jacob's family, had been stimulated to this insurrection on the pretext that Moses had, by an arbitrary arrangement, taken away the right of primogeniture, which had vested the hereditary dignity of the priesthood in the first-born of every family, with a view of transferring the hereditary exercise of the sacred functions to a particular branch of his own house; and that this gross instance of partiality to his own relations, to the permanent detriment of others, was a sufficient ground for refusing allegiance to his government. In addition to this grievance, another cause of jealousy and dissatisfaction that rankled in the

breasts of the Reubenites was the advancement of Judah to the leadership among the tribes. These malcontents had been incited by the artful representations of Korah (Jude 11), with whom the position of their camp on the south side afforded them facilities of frequent intercourse. In addition to his feeling of personal wrongs, Korah participated in their desire (if he did not originate the attempt) to recover their lost rights of primogeniture. When the conspiracy was ripe, they openly and boldly declared its object, and at the head of 250 princes, charged Moses with an ambitious and unwarrantable usurpation of authority, especially in the appropriation of the priesthood, for they disputed the claim of Aaron also to pre-eminence. **3. they gathered themselves together against Moses and against Aaron**—The assemblage seems to have been composed of the whole band of conspirators; and they grounded their complaint on the fact that the whole people, being separated to the divine service (Exod. 19:6), were equally qualified to present offerings on the altar, and that God, being graciously present among them by the tabernacle and the cloud, evinced His readiness to receive sacrifices from the hand of any others as well as from theirs. **4. when Moses heard it he fell upon his face**—This attitude of prostration indicated not only his humble and earnest desire that God would interpose to free him from the false and odious imputation, but also his strong sense of the daring sin involved in this proceeding. Whatever feelings may be entertained respecting Aaron, who had formerly headed a sedition himself, it is impossible not to sympathize with Moses in this difficult emergency. But he was a devout man, and the prudential course he adopted was probably the dictate of that heavenly wisdom with which, in answer to his prayers, he was endowed. **5-11. he spake unto Korah and unto all his company**—They were first addressed, not only because they were a party headed by his own cousin and Moses might hope to have more influence in that quarter, but because they were stationed near the tabernacle; and especially because an expostulation was the more weighty coming from him who was a Levite himself, and who was excluded along with his family from the priesthood. But to bring the matter to an issue, he proposed a test which would afford a decisive evidence of the divine appointment. **Even to-morrow**—lit., "in the morning," the usual time of meeting in the East for the settlement of public affairs. **the Lord will show who are his, ... even him whom he hath chosen will he cause to come near unto him**—i.e., will bear attestation to his ministry by some visible or miraculous token of His approval. **6. Take your censers, Korah, and all his company**, etc.—i.e., since you aspire to the priesthood, then go, perform the highest function of the office—that of offering incense; and if you are accepted—well. How magnanimous the conduct of Moses, who was now as willing that God's people should be priests, as formerly that they should be prophets (Ch. 11:29). But he warned them that they were making a perilous experiment. **12-14. Moses sent to call Dathan and Abiram**—in a separate interview, the ground of their mutiny being different; for while Korah murmured against the exclusive appropriation of the priesthood to Aaron and his family, they were opposed to the supremacy of Moses in civil power. They refused to obey the summons; and their refusal was grounded on the plausible pretext that their stay in the desert was prolonged for some secret and selfish purposes of the leader, who was conducting them like blind men wherever it suited him. **15. Moses was very wroth**—Though the meekest of all men, he could not restrain his indignation at these unjust and groundless charges; and the higly excited state of his feeling was evinced by the utterance of a brief exclamation in the mixed form of a prayer and an impassioned assertion of his integrity. (Cf. I Sam. 12:3.) **and said unto the Lord, Respect not thou their offering**—He calls it *their* offering, because, though it was to be offered by Korah and his Levitical associates, it was the united appeal of all the mutineers for deciding the contested claims of Moses and Aaron. **16-18. Moses said unto Korah, Be thou and all thy company before the Lord**—i.e., at "the door of the tabernacle" (vs. 18), that the assembled people might witness the experiment and be properly impressed by the issue. **two hundred and fifty censers** —probably the small platters, common in Egyptian families, where incense was offered to household deities and which had been among the precious things borrowed at their departure. **20. 21 the Lord spake unto Moses and Aaron, saying, Separate yourselves from among this congregation**—Curiosity to witness the exciting spectacle attracted a vast concourse of the people, and it would seem that the popular mind had been incited to evil by the clamors of the mutineers against Moses and Aaron. There was something in their behavior very offensive to God; for after His glory had appeared—as at the installation of Aaron (Lev. 9:23), so now for his confirmation in the sacred office—He bade Moses and Aaron withdraw from the assembly "that He might consume them in a moment." **22. they fell upon their faces, and said, O God, the God of the spirits of all flesh**—The benevolent importunity of their prayer was the more remarkable that the intercession was made for their enemies. **24-26. Speak unto the congregation, . . . Get you up from about the tabernacle**—Moses was attended in the execution of this mission by the elders. The united and urgent entreaties of so many dignified personages produced the desired effect of convincing the people of their crime, and of withdrawing them from the company of men who were doomed to destruction, lest, being partakers of their sins, they should perish along with them. **27. the tabernacle of Korah, Dathan, and Abiram**—Korah being a Kohathite, his tent could not have been in the Reubenite camp, and it does not appear that he himself was on the spot where Dathan and Abiram stood with their families. Their attitude of defiance indicated their daring and impenitent character, equally regardless of God and man. **28-34. Moses said, Hereby ye shall know that the Lord hath sent me to do all these works**—The awful catastrophe of the earthquake which, as predicted by Moses, swallowed up those impious rebels in a living tomb, gave the divine attestation to the mission of Moses and struck the spectators with solemn awe. **35. there came out a fire from the Lord**—i.e., from the cloud—This seems to describe the destruction of Korah and those Levites who with him aspired to the functions of the priesthood. (See on ch. 26:11, 58; I Chron. 6:22, 37.) **37-39. Speak unto Eleazar** —He was selected lest the high priest might contract defilement from going among the dead carcasses. **the brazen censers . . . made broad plates to be a memorial**—The altar of burnt offerings, being made of wood and covered with brass, this additional covering of broad plates not only rendered it doubly secure against the fire, but served as a warning-beacon to deter all from future invasions of the

priesthood. **41. the children of Israel murmured against Moses and against Aaron, saying, Ye have killed the people of the Lord**—What a strange exhibition of popular prejudice and passion—to blame the leaders for saving the rebels! Yet Moses and Aaron interceded for the people—the high priest perilling his own life in doing good to that perverse race. **48. he stood between the living and the dead** —The plague seems to have begun in the extremities of the camp. Aaron, in this remarkable act, was a type of Christ.

CHAPTER 17

Vss. 1-13. AARON'S ROD FLOURISHES. **2. Speak unto the children of Israel**—The controversy with Moses and Aaron about the priesthood was of such a nature and magnitude as required a decisive and authoritative settlement. For the removal of all doubts and the silencing of all murmuring in the future regarding the holder of the office, a miracle was wrought of a remarkable character and permanent duration; and in the manner of performing it, all the people were made to have a direct and special interest. **take of every one . . . princes . . . twelve rods**—As the princes, being the oldest sons of the chief family, and heads of their tribes, might have advanced the best claims to the priesthood, if that sacred dignity was to be shared among all the tribes, they were therefore selected, and being twelve in number—that of Joseph being counted only one—Moses was ordered to see that the name of each was inscribed—a practice borrowed from the Egyptians—upon his rod or wand of office. The name of Aaron rather than of Levi was used, as the latter name would have opened a door of controversy among the Levites; and as there was to be one rod only for the head of each tribe, the express appointment of a rod for Aaron determined him to be the head of that tribe, as well as that branch or family of the tribe to which the priestly dignity should belong. These rods were to be laid in the tabernacle close to the ark (cf. vs. 10 and Heb. 9:4), where a divine token was promised that would for all time terminate the dispute. **6. the rod of Aaron was among their rods**—either one of the twelve, or, as many suppose, a thirteenth in the midst (Heb. 9:4). The rods were of dry sticks or wands, probably old, as transmitted from one head of the family to a succeeding. **8. Moses went into the tabernacle**—being privileged to do so on this occasion by the special command of God; and he there beheld the remarkable spectacle of Aaron's rod—which, according to Josephus, was a stick of an almond tree, bearing fruit in three different stages at once—buds, blossoms, and fruit. **10. Bring Aaron's rod again before the testimony, to be kept for a token against the rebels**—For if, after all admonitions and judgments, seconded by miracles, the people should still rebel, they would certainly pay the penalty by death. **12, 13. Behold we die, we perish**—an exclamation of fear, both from the remembrance of former judgments, and the apprehension of future relapses into murmuring. **cometh any thing near**—i.e., nearer than he ought to do; an error into which many may fall. Will the stern justice of God overtake every slight offense? We shall all be destroyed. Some, however, regard this exclamation as the symptom or a new discontent, rather than the indication of a reverential and submissive spirit. Let us fear and sin not.

CHAPTER 18

Vss. 1-7. THE CHARGE OF THE PRIESTS AND LEVITES. **1. the Lord said unto Aaron, Thou and thy sons and thy father's house with thee shall bear the iniquity of the sanctuary**—Security is here given to the people from the fears expressed (ch. 17:12), by the responsibility of attending to all sacred things being devolved upon the priesthood, together with the penalties incurred through neglect; and thus the solemn responsibilities annexed to their high dignity, of having to answer not only for their own sins, but also for the sins of the people, were calculated in a great measure to remove all feeling of envy at the elevation of Aaron's family, when the honor was weighed in the balance with its burdens and dangers. **2-7. thy brethren also of the tribe of Levi**—The departments of the sacred office, to be filled respectively by the priests and Levites, are here assigned to each. To the priests was committed the charge of the sanctuary and the altar, while the Levites were to take care of everything else about the tabernacle. The Levites were to attend the priests as servants—bestowed on them as "gifts" to aid in the service of the tabernacle—while the high and dignified office of the priesthood was a "service of gift." "A stranger," i.e., one, neither a priest nor a Levite, who should intrude into any departments of the sacred office, should incur the penalty of death.

8-20. THE PRIESTS' PORTION. **8-13. the Lord spake unto Aaron, I also have given thee the charge of my heave offerings**—A recapitulation is made in this passage of certain perquisites specially appropriated to the maintenance of the priests. They were parts of the votive and freewill offerings, including both meat and bread, wine and oil, and the first-fruits, which formed a large and valuable item. **14. Every thing devoted in Israel shall be thine**—provided it was adapted for food or consumable by use; for the gold and silver vessels that were dedicated as the spoils of victory were not given to the priests, but for the use and adornment of the sacred edifice. **19. it is a covenant of salt**—i.e., a perpetual ordinance. This figurative form of expression was evidently founded on the conservative property of salt, which keeps meat from corruption; and hence it became an emblem of inviolability and permanence. It is a common phrase among Oriental people, who consider the eating of salt a pledge of fidelity, binding them in a covenant of friendship. Hence the partaking of the altar meats, which were appropriated to the priests on condition of their services and of which salt formed a necessary accompaniment, was naturally called a covenant of salt (Lev. 2:13).

21-32. THE LEVITES' PORTION. **21, 22. I have given to the children of Levi all the tenth in Israel for an inheritance, for their service which they serve**—Neither the priests nor the Levites were to possess any allotments of land but to depend entirely upon Him who liberally provided for them out of His own portion; and this law was subservient to many important purposes—such as that, being exempted from the cares and labors of worldly business, they might be exclusively devoted to His service; that a bond of mutual love and attachment might be formed between the people and the Levites, who, as performing religious services for the people, derived their subsistence from them; and further, that being the more easily dispersed among the different tribes, they might be more useful in instructing and directing the people. **23. But the Levites shall do**

the service of the congregation: they shall bear their iniquity—They were to be responsible for the right discharge of those duties that were assigned to them, and consequently to bear the penalty that was due to negligence or carelessness in the guardianship of the holy things. **26. the Levites... offer... a tenth of the tithe**—Out of their own they were to pay tithes to the priests equally as the people gave to them. The best of their tithes was to be assigned to the priests, and afterwards they enjoyed the same liberty to make use of the remainder that other Israelites had of the produce of their threshing-floors and winepresses. **32. ye shall bear no sin by reason of it,** etc.—Neglect in having the best entailed sin in the use of such unhallowed food, and the holy things would be polluted by the reservation to themselves of what should be offered to God and the priests.

CHAPTER 19

Vss. 1-22. THE WATER OF SEPARATION. **2. This is the ordinance of the law**—an institution of a peculiar nature ordained by law for the purification of sin, and provided at the public expense because it was for the good of the whole community. **Speak unto the children of Israel, that they bring thee a red heifer without spot,** etc.—This is the only case in which the color of the victim is specified. It has been supposed the ordinance was designed in opposition to the superstitious notions of the Egyptians. That people never offered a vow but they sacrificed a red bull, the greatest care being taken by their priests in examining whether it possessed the requisite characteristics, and it was an annual offering to Typhon, their evil being. By the choice, both of the sex and the color, provision was made for eradicating from the minds of the Israelites a favorite Egyptian superstition regarding two objects of their animal worship. **3. ye shall give her unto Eleazar, that he may bring her forth without the camp**—He was the second or deputy high priest, and he was selected for this duty because the execution of it entailed temporary defilement, from which the acting high priest was to be preserved with the greatest care. It was led "forth without the camp," in accordance with the law regarding victims laden with the sins of the people, and thus typical of Christ (Heb. 13:12; also Lev. 24:14). The priest was to sprinkle the blood "seven times" before—lit., *towards or near* the tabernacle, a description which seems to imply either that he carried a portion of the blood in a basin to the door of the tabernacle (Lev. 4:17), or that in the act of sprinkling he turned his face towards the sacred edifice, being disqualified through the defiling influence of this operation from approaching close to it. By this attitude he indicated that he was presenting an expiatory sacrifice, for the acceptance of which he hoped, in the grace of God, by looking to the mercy seat. Every part of it was consumed by fire except the blood used in sprinkling, and the ingredients mixed with the ashes were the same as those employed in the sprinkling of lepers (Lev. 14:4-7). It was a water of separation—i.e., of "sanctification" for the people of Israel. **7. the priest shall be unclean until the even**—The ceremonies prescribed show the imperfection of the Levitical priesthood, while they typify the condition of Christ when expiating our sins (II Cor. 5:21). **11-22. He that toucheth the dead body of any man shall be unclean**—This law is noticed here to show the uses to which the water of separation was applied. The case of a death is one; and as in every family which sustained a bereavement the members of the household became defiled, so in an immense population, where instances of mortality and other cases of uncleanness would be daily occurring, the water of separation must have been in constant requisition. To afford the necessary supply of the cleansing mixture, the Jewish writers say that a red heifer was sacrificed every year, and that the ashes, mingled with the sprinkling ingredients, were distributed through all the cities and towns of Israel. **12. He shall purify himself . . . the third day**—The necessity of applying the water on the third day is inexplicable on any natural or moral ground; and, therefore, the regulation has been generally supposed to have had a typical reference to the resurrection, on that day, of Christ, by whom His people are sanctified; while the process of ceremonial purification being extended over seven days, was intended to show that sanctification is progressive and incomplete till the arrival of the eternal Sabbath. Every one knowingly and presumptuously neglecting to have himself sprinkled with this water was guilty of an offense which was punished by excommunication. **14. when a man dieth in a tent,** etc.—The instances adduced appear very minute and trivial; but important ends, both of a religious and of a sanitary nature, were promoted by carrying the idea of pollution from contact with dead bodies to so great an extent. While it would effectually prevent that Egyptianized race of Israelites imitating the superstitious custom of the Egyptians, who kept in their houses the mummied remains of their ancestors, it ensured a speedy interment to all, thus not only keeping burial-places at a distance, but removing from the habitations of the living the corpses of persons who died from infectious disorders, and from the open field the unburied remains of strangers and foreigners who fell in battle. **21. he that sprinkleth . . . ; and he that toucheth the water of separation shall be unclean until even**—The opposite effects ascribed to the water of separation—of cleansing one person and defiling another—are very singular, and not capable of very satisfactory explanation. One important lesson, however, was thus taught, that its purifying efficacy was not inherent in itself, but arose from the divine appointment, as in other ordinances of religion, which are effectual means of salvation, not from any virtue in them, or in him that administers them, but solely through the grace of God communicated thereby.

CHAPTER 20

Vss. 1-29. THE DEATH OF MIRIAM. **1. Then came the children of Israel . . . into the desert of Zin in the first month**—i.e., of the fortieth year (cf. vss. 22, 23, with ch. 33:38). In this history only the principal and most important incidents are recorded, those confined chiefly to the first or second and the last years of the journeyings in the wilderness, thence called Et-Tih. Between the last verse of the preceding and the first verse of this chapter there is a long and undescribed interval of thirty-seven years. **the people abode in Kadesh**—supposed to be what is now known as Ain El-Weibeh, three springs surrounded by palms. (See on ch. 13:26.) It was their second arrival after an interval of thirty-eight years (Deut. 11:16). The old generation had nearly all died, and the new one encamped in it with the view of entering the prom-

ised land, not, however, as formerly on the south, but by crossing the Edomite region on the east. **Miriam died there**—four months before Aaron. **2-13. there was no water for the congregation**—There was at Kadesh a fountain, En-Mishpat (Gen. 14:7), and at the first encampment of the Israelites there was no want of water. It was then either partially dried up by the heat of the season, or had been exhausted by the demands of so vast a multitude. **6. Moses and Aaron went from the presence of the assembly**—Here is a fresh ebullition of the untamed and discontented spirit of the people. The leaders fled to the precincts of the sanctuary, both as an asylum from the increasing fury of the highly excited rabble, and as their usual refuge in seasons of perplexity and danger, to implore the direction and aid of God. **8. Take the rod**—which had been deposited in the tabernacle (ch. 17:10), the wonder-working rod by which so many miracles had been performed, sometimes called "the rod of God" (Exod. 4:20), sometimes Moses' (vs. 11) or Aaron's rod (Exod. 7:12). **10.** [Moses] **said unto them, Hear now, ye rebels, must we fetch you water out of this rock?**—The conduct of the great leader on this occasion was hasty and passionate (Ps. 106:33). He had been directed to *speak* to the rock, but he *smote it twice* in his impetuosity, thus endangering the blossoms of the rod, and, instead of speaking to the *rock,* he spoke to the *people* in a fury. **11. the congregation drank, and their beasts**—Physically the water afforded the same kind of needful refreshment to both. But from a religious point of view, this, which was only a common element to the cattle, was a sacrament to the people (I Cor. 10:3, 4)—It possessed a relative sanctity imparted to it by its divine origin and use. **12. The Lord spake unto Moses and Aaron, Because ye believed me not,** etc.—The act of Moses in smiting twice betrayed a doubt, not of the power, but of the will of God to gratify such a rebellious people, and his exclamation seems to have emanated from a spirit of incredulity akin to Sarai's (Gen. 18:13). These circumstances indicate the influence of unbelief, and there might have been others unrecorded which led to so severe a chastisement. **13. This is the water of Meribah**—The word Kadesh is added to to distinguish it from another Meribah (Exod. 17:7). **14-16. Moses sent messengers . . . to the king of Edom**—The encampment at Kadesh was on the confines of the Edomite territory, through which the Israelites would have had an easy passage across the Arabah by Wady-el-Ghuweir, so that they could have continued their course around Moab, and approached Palestine from the east [ROBERTS]. The Edomites, being the descendants of Esau and tracing their line of descent from Abraham as their common stock, were recognized by the Israelites as brethren, and a very brotherly message was sent to them. **17. we will go by the king's highway**—probably Wady-el-Ghuweir [ROBERTS], through which ran one of the great lines of road, constructed for commercial caravans, as well as for the progress of armies. The engineering necessary for carrying them over marshes or mountains, and the care requisite for protecting them from the shifting sands, led to their being under the special care of the state. Hence the expression, "the king's highway," which is of great antiquity. **19. if I and my cattle drink of thy water, then I will pay for it**—From the scarcity of water in the warm climates of the East, the practice of levying a tax for the use of the wells is universal; and the jealousy of the natives, in guarding the collected treasures of rain, is often so great that water cannot be procured for money. **21. Edom refused to give Israel passage through his border,** etc.—A churlish refusal obliged them to take another route. (See on chapter 21:4; Deut. 2:4; Judg. 11:18; see also I Sam. 14:47; II Sam. 8:14, which describe the retribution that was taken.) **22. the children of Israel . . . came unto mount Hor**—now Gebel Haroun, the most striking and lofty elevation in the Seir range, called emphatically "the mount" (vs. 28). It is conspicuous by its double top. **24-28. Aaron shall be gathered unto his people**—In accordance with his recent doom, he, attired in the high priest's costume, was commanded to ascend that mountain and die. But although the time of his death was hastened by the divine displeasure as a punishment for his sins, the *manner* of his death was arranged in tenderness of love, and to do him honor at the close of his earthly service. His ascent of the mount was to afford him a last look of the camp and a distant prospect of the promised land. The simple narrative of the solemn and impressive scene implies, though it does not describe, the pious resignation, settled faith, and inward peace of the aged pontiff. **26. strip Aaron of his garments**—i.e., his pontifical robes, in token of his resignation. (See Isa. 22:20-25.) **put them on his son**—as the inauguration into his high office. Having been formerly anointed with the sacred oil, that ceremony was not repeated, or, as some think, it was done on his return to the camp. **28. Aaron died there in the top of the mount**—(See on Deut. 10:6). A tomb has been erected upon or close by the spot where he was buried. **29. When all the congregation saw that Aaron was dead**—Moses and Eleazar were the sole witnesses of his departure. According to the established law, the new high priest could not have been present at the funeral of his father without contracting ceremonial defilement (Lev. 21:11). But that law was dispensed with in the extraordinary circumstances. The people learned the event not only from the recital of the two witnesses, but from their visible signs of grief and change; and this event betokened the imperfection of the Levitical priesthood (Heb. 7:12). **they mourned for Aaron thirty days**—the usual period of public and solemn mourning. (See on Deut. 34:8.)

CHAPTER 21

Vss. 1-35. Israel Attacked by the Canaanites. **1. King Arad the Canaanite**—rather, the Canaanite king of Arad—an ancient town on the southernmost borders of Palestine, not far from Kadesh. A hill called Tell Arad marks the spot. **heard tell that Israel came by the way of the spies**—in the way or manner of spies, stealthily, or from spies sent by himself to ascertain the designs and motions of the Israelites. The Septuagint and others consider the *Heb.* word "spies" a proper name, and render it: "Came by the way of Atharim towards Arad" [KENNICOTT]. **he fought against Israel, and took some of them prisoners**—This discomfiture was permitted to teach them to expect the conquest of Canaan not from their own wisdom and valor, but solely from the favor and help of God (Deut. 9:4; Ps. 44:3, 4). **2, 3. Israel vowed a vow unto the Lord**—Made to feel their own weakness, they implored the aid of Heaven, and, in anticipation of it, *devoted* the cities of this king to future destruction. The nature and consequence

of such anathemas are described (Lev. 27; Deut. 13). This vow of extermination against Arad gave name to the place Hormah (slaughter and destruction) though it was not accomplished till after the passage of the Jordan. Others think Hormah the name of a town mentioned (Josh. 12:14). **4. they journeyed from mount Hor**—On being refused the passage requested, they returned through the Arabah, "the way of the Red Sea," to Elath, at the head of the eastern gulf of the Red Sea, and thence passed up through the mountains to the eastern desert, so as to make the circuit of the land of Edom (ch. 33:41, 42). **the soul of the people was much discouraged because of the way**—Disappointment on finding themselves so near the confines of the promised land without entering it; vexation at the refusal of a passage through Edom and the absence of any divine interposition in their favor; and above all, the necessity of a retrograde journey by a long and circuitous route through the worst parts of a sandy desert and the dread of being plunged into new and unknown difficulties—all this produced a deep depression of spirits. But it was followed, as usually, by a gross outburst of murmuring at the scarcity of water, and of expressions of disgust at the manna. **5. our soul loatheth this light bread**—i.e., bread without substance or nutritious quality. The refutation of this calumny appears in the fact, that on the strength of this food they performed for forty years so many and toilsome journeys. But they had been indulging a hope of the better and more varied fare enjoyed by a settled people; and disappointment, always the more bitter as the hope of enjoyment seems near, drove them to speak against God and against Moses (I Cor. 10:9). **6. The Lord sent fiery serpents among the people**—That part of the desert where the Israelites now were—near the head of the gulf of Akaba—is greatly infested with venomous reptiles, of various kinds, particularly lizards, which raise themselves in the air and swing themselves from branches; and scorpions, which, being in the habit of lying in long grass, are particularly dangerous to the barelegged, sandalled people of the East. The only known remedy consists in sucking the wound, or, in the case of cattle, in the application of ammonia. The exact species of serpents that caused so great mortality among the Israelites cannot be ascertained. They are said to have been "fiery," an epithet applied to them either from their bright, vivid color, or the violent inflammation their bite occasioned. **7-9. the people came to Moses, and said, We have sinned**—The severity of the scourge and the appalling extent of mortality brought them to a sense of sin, and through the intercessions of Moses, which they implored, they were miraculously healed. He was directed to make the figure of a serpent in brass, to be elevated on a pole or standard, that it might be seen at the extremities of the camp and that every bitten Israelite who looked to it might be healed. This peculiar method of cure was designed, in the first instance, to show that it was the efficacy of God's power and grace, not the effect of nature or art, and also that it might be a type of the power of faith in Christ to heal all who look to Him because of their sins (John 3:14, 15; see also on II Kings 18: 4). **10. the children of Israel set forward**—along the eastern frontier of the Edomites, encamping in various stations. **12. pitched in the valley**—lit., the woody brook-valley of Zared (Deut. 2:13; Isa. 15:7; Amos 6:14). This torrent rises among the mountains to the east of Moab, and flowing west, empties itself into the Dead Sea. Ije-Abarim is supposed to have been its ford [CALMET]. **13. pitched on the other side of Arnon**—now El-Mojib, a deep, broad, and rapid stream, dividing the dominions of the Moabites and Amorites. **14. book of the wars of the Lord**—A fragment or passage is here quoted from a poem or history of the wars of the Israelites, principally with a view to decide the position of Arnon. **15. Ar**—the capital of Moab. **16. from thence they went to Beer**—i.e., a well. The name was probably given to it afterwards, as it is not mentioned (ch. 33). **17, 18. Then Israel sang**—This beautiful little song was in accordance with the wants and feelings of travelling caravans in the East, where water is an occasion both of prayer and thanksgiving. From the princes using their official rods only, and not spades, it seems probable that this well was concealed by the brushwood or the sand, as is the case with many wells in Idumea still. The discovery of it was seasonable, and owing to the special interposition of God. **21-23, Israel sent messengers unto Sihon**—The rejection of their respectful and pacific message was resented—Sihon was discomfited in battle—and Israel obtained by right of conquest the whole of the Amorite dominions. **24. from Arnon unto the Jabbok**—now the Zurka. These rivers formed the southern and northern boundaries of his usurped territory. **for the border of . . . Ammon was strong**—a reason stated for Sihon not being able to push his invasion further. **25. Israel dwelt in all the cities**—after exterminating the inhabitants who had been previously doomed (Deut. 2:34). **26. Heshbon**—(Song of Sol. 7:4)—situated sixteen English miles north of the Arnon, and from its ruins it appears to have been a large city. **27-30. Wherefore they that speak in proverbs**—Here is given an extract from an Amorite song exultingly anticipating an extension of their conquests to Arnon. The quotation from the poem of the Amorite bard ends at verse 28. The two following verses appear to be the strains in which the Israelites expose the impotence of the usurpers. **29. people of Chemosh**—the name of the Moabite idol (I Kings 11:7-33; II Kings 23:13; Jer. 48:46). **he**—i.e., their god, hath surrendered his worshippers to the victorious arms of Sihon. **33. they turned and went up by the way of Bashan**—a name given to that district from the richness of the soil—now Batanea or El-Bottein—a hilly region east of the Jordan lying between the mountains of Hermon on the north and those of Gilead on the south. **Og**—a giant, an Amoritish prince, who, having opposed the progress of the Israelites, was defeated. **34. The Lord said unto Moses, Fear him not**—a necessary encouragement, for his gigantic stature (Deut. 3:11) was calculated to inspire terror. He and all his were put to the sword.

CHAPTER 22

Vss. 1-20. BALAK'S FIRST MESSAGE FOR BALAAM REFUSED. **1. Israel . . . pitched in the plains of Moab**—so called from having formerly belonged to that people, though wrested from them by Sihon. It was a dry, sunken, desert region on the east of the Jordan valley, opposite Jericho. **2. Balak**—i.e., empty. Terrified (Deut. 2:25; Exod. 15:15) at the approach of so vast a multitude and not daring to encounter them in the field, he resolved to secure their destruction by other means. **4. elders of Midian**—called kings (ch. 31:8) and

princes (Josh. 13:21). The Midianites, a distinct people on the southern frontier of Moab, united with them as confederates against Israel, their common enemy. **5. He sent messengers therefore unto Balaam**—i.e., "lord" or "devourer" of people, a famous soothsayer (Josh. 13:22). **son of Beor,** or, in the Chaldee form, *Bosor*—i.e., "destruction." **Pethor**—a city of Mesopotamia, situated on the Euphrates. **6. Come . . . , curse me this people**—Among the heathen an opinion prevailed that prayers for evil or curses would be heard by the unseen powers as well as prayers for good, when offered by a prophet or priest and accompanied by the use of certain rites. Many examples are found in the histories of the Greeks and Romans of whole armies being devoted to destruction, and they occur among the natives of India and other heathen countries still. In the Burmese war, magicians were employed to curse the British troops. **7. the elders of Moab and . . . of Midian departed with the rewards of divination**—like the fee of a fortune-teller, and being a royal present, it would be something handsome. **8-14. Lodge here this night, and I will bring you word again, as the Lord shall speak unto me,** etc.—God usually revealed His will in visions and dreams; and Balaam's birth and residence in Mesopotamia, where the remains of patriarchal religion still lingered, account for his knowledge of the true God. His real character has long been a subject of discussion. Some, judging from his language, have thought him a saint; others, looking to his conduct, have described him as an irreligious charlatan; and a third class consider him a novice in the faith, who had a fear of God, but who had not acquired power over his passions [HENGSTENBERG]. **13. the Lord refuseth to give me leave to go with you**—This answer has an *appearance* of being good, but it studiously concealed the reason of the divine prohibition, and it intimated his own willingness and desire to go—if permitted. Balak despatched a second mission, which held out flattering prospects, both to his avarice and his ambition (Gen. 31:30). **19. tarry ye also here this night, that I may know what the Lord will say unto me more**—The divine will, as formerly declared, not being according to his desires, he hoped by a second request to bend it, as he had already bent his own conscience, to his ruling passions of pride and covetousness. The permission granted to Balaam is in accordance with the ordinary procedure of Providence. God often gives up men to follow the impulse of their own lusts; but there is no approval in thus leaving them to act at the prompting of their own wicked hearts (Josh. 13:27).

21-41. THE JOURNEY. **21. Balaam . . . saddled his ass**—probably one of the white sprightly animals which persons of rank were accustomed to ride. The saddle, as usually in the East, would be nothing more than a pad or his outer cloak. **22. God's anger was kindled because he went**—The displeasure arose partly from his neglecting the condition on which leave was granted him—viz., to wait till the princes of Moab "came to call him," and because, through desire for "the wages of unrighteousness," he entertained the secret purpose of acting in opposition to the solemn charge of God. **24. the angel of the Lord stood in a path of the vineyards**—The roads which lead through fields and vineyards are so narrow that in most parts a man could not pass a beast without care and caution. A stone or mud fence flanks each side of these roads, to prevent the soil being washed off by the rains. **28. the Lord** opened the mouth of the ass—to utter, like a parrot, articulate sounds, without understanding them. That this was a visionary scene is a notion which seems inadmissible, because of the improbability of a vision being described as an actual occurrence in the middle of a plain history. Besides, the opening of the ass's mouth must have been an external act, and that, with the manifest tenor of Peter's language, strongly favors the literal view. The absence of any surprise at such a phenomenon on the part of Balaam may be accounted for by his mind being wholly engrossed with the prospect of gain, which produced "the madness of the prophet." "It was a miracle, wrought to humble his proud heart, which had to be first subjected in the school of an ass before he was brought to attend to the voice of God speaking by the angel" [CALVIN]. **34, 35. I have sinned . . . if it displease thee, I will get me back again**—Notwithstanding this confession, he evinced no spirit of penitence, as he speaks of desisting only from the outward act. The words "go with the men" was a mere withdrawal of farther restraint, but the terms in which leave was given are more absolute and peremptory than those in verse 20. **36, 37. when Balak heard that Balaam was come, he went out to meet him**—Politeness requires that the higher the rank of the expected guest, greater distance is to be gone to welcome his arrival. **38. the word that God putteth in my mouth, that shall I speak**—This appears a pious answer. It was an acknowledgment that he was restrained by a superior power. **39. Kirjath-huzoth**—a city of streets. **40. Balak offered oxen and sheep**—made preparations for a grand entertainment to Balaam and the princes of Midian. **41. high places of Baal**—eminences consecrated to the worship of Baal-peor (ch. 25:3) or Chemosh.

CHAPTER 23

Vss. 1-30. BALAK'S SACRIFICES. 1. Balaam said unto Balak, Build me here seven altars—Balak, being a heathen, would naturally suppose these altars were erected in honor of Baal, the patron deity of his country. It is evident, from verse 4 that they were prepared for the worship of the true God; although in choosing the high places of Baal as their site and rearing a number of altars (II Kings 18:22; Isa. 17:8; Jer. 11:13; Hos. 8:11; 10:1), instead of one only, as God had appointed, Balaam blended his own superstitions with the divine worship. The heathen, both in ancient and modern times, attached a mysterious virtue to the number *seven;* and Balaam, in ordering the preparation of so many altars, designed to mystify and delude the king. **3. Stand by thy burnt offering**—as one in expectation of an important favor. **peradventure the Lord will come to meet me: and whatsoever he showeth me**—i.e., makes known to me by word or sign. **he went to an high place**—apart by himself, where he might practise rites and ceremonies, with a view to obtain a response of the oracle. **4–6. God met Balaam**—not in compliance with his incantations, but to frustrate his wicked designs and compel him, contrary to his desires and interests, to pronounce the following benediction. **7. took up his parable**—i.e., spoke under the influence of inspiration, and in the highly poetical, figurative, and oracular style of a prophet. **brought me from Aram**—This word, joined with "the mountains of the East," denotes the upper portion of Mesopotamia, lying on the east of Moab. The East enjoyed an infamous no-

toriety for magicians and soothsayers (Isa. 2:6). **8. How shall I curse, whom God hath not cursed?**—A divine blessing has been pronounced over the posterity of Jacob; and therefore, whatever prodigies can be achieved by my charms, al magical skill, all human power, is utterly impotent to counteract the decree of God. **9. from the top**—lit., "a bare place" on the rocks, to which Balak had taken him, for it was deemed necessary to see the people who were to be devoted to destruction. But that commanding prospect could contribute nothing to the accomplishment of the king's object, for the destiny of Israel was to be a distinct, peculiar people, separated from the rest of the nations in government, religion, customs, and divine protection (Deut. 33:28). So that although I might be able to gratify your wishes against other people, I can do nothing against them (Exod. 19:5; Lev. 20:24). **10. Who can count the dust of Jacob?**—an Oriental hyperbole for a very populous nation, as Jacob's posterity was promised to be (Gen. 13:16; 28:14). **the number of the fourth part of Israel**—i.e., the camp consisted of four divisions; every one of these parts was formidable in numbers. **Let me die the death of the righteous**—*Heb.,* of Jeshurun; or, the Israelites. The meaning is: they are a people happy, above all others, not only in life, but at death, from their knowledge of the true God, and their hope through His grace. Balaam is a representative of a large class in the world, who express a wish for the blessedness which Christ has promised to His people but are averse to imitate the mind that was in Him. **13-15. Come, . . . with me unto another place, from whence thou mayest see them**—Surprised and disappointed at this unexpected eulogy on Israel, Balak hoped that, if seen from a different point of observation, the prophet would give utterance to different feelings; and so, having made the same solemn preparations, Balaam retired, as before, to wait the divine afflatus. **14. he brought him into the field of Zophim . . . top of Pisgah**—a flat surface on the summit of the mountain range, which was cultivated land. Others render it "the field of sentinels," an eminence where some of Balak's guards were posted to give signals [CALMET]. **18. Rise up**—As Balak was already standing (vs. 17), this expression is equivalent to "now attend to me." The counsels and promises of God respecting Israel are unchangeable; and no attempt to prevail on Him to reverse them will succeed, as they may with a man. **21. He hath not beheld iniquity in Jacob**—Many sins were observed and punished in this people. But no such universal and hopeless apostasy had as yet appeared, to induce God to abandon or destroy them. **the Lord his God is with him**—has a favor for them. **and the shout of a king is among them**—such joyful acclamations as of a people rejoicing in the presence of a victorious prince. **22. he hath as it were the strength of an unicorn**—Israel is not as they were at the Exodus, a horde of poor, feeble, spiritless people, but powerful and invincible as a *reem*—i.e., a rhinoceros (Job 39:9; Ps. 22:21; 92:10). **23. Surely there is no enchantment against Jacob**—No art can ever prevail against a people who are under the shield of Omnipotence, and for whom miracles have been and yet shall be performed, which will be a theme of admiration in succeeding ages. **26. All that the Lord speaketh, that I must do**—a remarkable confession that he was divinely constrained to give utterances different from what it was his purpose and inclination to do. **28. Balak brought Balaam unto the top of Peor**—or, Beth-peor (Deut. 3:29), the eminence on which a temple of Baal stood. **that looketh toward Jeshimon**—the desert tract in the south of Palestine, on both sides of the Dead Sea.

CHAPTER 24

Vss. 1-25. BALAAM FORETELLS ISRAEL'S HAPPINESS. **1. to seek for**—i.e., to use enchantments. His experience on the two former occasions had taught him that these superstitious accompaniments of his worship were useless, and therefore he now simply looked towards the camp of Israel, either with a secret design to curse them, or to await the divine afflatus. **2. he saw Israel abiding in his tents according to their tribes**—i.e., in the orderly distribution of the camp (ch. 2). **the spirit of God came upon him**—Before the regular ministry of the prophets was instituted, God made use of various persons as the instruments through whom He revealed His will, and Balaam was one of these (Deut. 23:5). **3. the man whose eyes are open**—i.e., a seer (I Sam. 9:9), a prophet, to whom the visioned future was disclosed—sometimes when falling into a sleep (Gen. 15:12-15), frequently into "a trance." **5-7. How goodly are thy tents, ... O Israel!**—a fine burst of admiration, expressed in highly poetical strains. All travellers describe the beauty which the circular area of Bedouin tents impart to the desert. How impressive, then, must have been the view, as seen from the heights of Abarim, of the immense camp of Israel extended over the subjacent plains. **6. As the valleys**—*Heb.,* brooks, the watercourses of the mountains. **lign aloes**—an aromatic shrub on the banks of his native Euphrates, the conical form of which suggested an apt resemblance to a tent. The redundant imagery of these verses depicts the humble origin, rapid progress, and prosperity of Israel. **7. his king shall be higher than Agag**—The Amalekites were then the most powerful of all the desert tribes, and Agag a title common to their kings. **10-14. Balak's anger was kindled against Balaam, and he smote his hands together**—The "smiting of the hands together" is, among Oriental people, an indication of the most violent rage (see Ezek. 21:17; 22:13) and ignominious dismissal. **15. he took up his parable**—or prophecy, uttered in a poetical style. **17. I shall see him**—rather, "I do see" or "I have seen him"—a prophetic sight, like that of Abraham (John 8:56). **him**—i.e., Israel. **there shall come a Star out of Jacob, and a Sceptre shall rise out of Israel**—This imagery, in the hieroglyphic language of the East, denotes some eminent ruler—primarily David; but secondarily and pre-eminently, the Messiah (see on Gen. 49:10). **corners**—border, often used for a whole country (Exod. 8:2; Ps. 74:17). **children of Sheth**—some prince of Moab; or, according to some, "the children of the East." **18. Edom shall be a possession**—This prophecy was accomplished by David (II Sam. 8:14). **Seir**—seen in the south, and poetically used for Edom. The double conquest of Moab and Edom is alluded to (Ps. 60:8; 108:9). **19. Out of Jacob shall come he that shall have dominion** David, and particularly Christ. **that remaineth of the city**—those who flee from the field to fortified places (Ps. 60:9). **20. Amalek ... his latter end shall be that he perish for ever**—Their territory was seen at the remote extremity of the desert. (See on Exod. 17:14; also I Sam. 15.) **21. Kenites ... nest in a rock**—Though securely established among the clefts in the high rocks of En-

gedi towards the west, they should be gradually reduced by a succession of enemies till the Assyrian invader carried them into captivity (Judg. 1:16; 4:11; 16:17; also II Kings 15:29; 17:6). **23. who shall live when God doeth this!**—Few shall escape the desolation that shall send a Nebuchadnezzar to scourge all those regions. **24. Chittim**—the countries lying on the Mediterranean, particularly Greece and Italy (Dan. 11:29, 30). The Assyrians were themselves to be overthrown—first, by the Greeks under Alexander the Great and his successors; secondly, by the Romans. **Eber**—the posterity of the Hebrews (Gen. 10:24). **he also shall perish**—i.e., the conqueror of Asher and Eber, namely, the Greek and Roman empires. **25. Balaam rose up, and went ... to his place**—Mesopotamia, to which, however, he did not return. (See on ch. 31:8.)

CHAPTER 25

Vss. 1-18. THE ISRAELITES' WHOREDOM AND IDOLATRY WITH MOAB. **1. Israel abode in Shittim**—a verdant meadow, so called from a grove of acacia trees which lined the eastern side of the Jordan. (See ch. 33:49.) **3. Israel joined himself unto Baal-peor**—Baal was a general name for "lord," and Peor for a "mount" in Moab. The real name of the idol was Chemosh, and his rites of worship were celebrated by the grossest obscenity. In participating in this festival, then, the Israelites committed the double offense of idolatry and licentiousness. **4. The Lord said unto Moses, Take all the heads of the people, and hang them up**—Israelite criminals, who were capitally punished, were first stoned or slain, and *then* gibbeted. The persons ordered here for execution were the principal delinquents in the Baal-peor outrage—the subordinate officers, rulers of tens or hundreds. **before the Lord**—for vindicating the honor of the true God. **against the sun**—i.e., as a mark of public ignominy; but they were to be removed towards sunset (Deut. 21:23). **5. judges of Israel**—the seventy elders, who were commanded not only to superintend the execution within their respective jurisdictions, but to inflict the punishment with their own hands. (See on I Sam. 15:33.) **6, 7. behold, one of the children of Israel ... brought ... a Midianitish woman**—This flagitious act most probably occurred about the time when the order was given and before its execution. **who were weeping before the door of the tabernacle**—Some of the rulers and well-disposed persons were deploring the dreadful wickedness of the people and supplicating the mercy of God to avert impending judgments. **8. the plague**—some sudden and widespread mortality. **9. those that died in the plague were twenty and four thousand**—Only 23,000 perished (I Cor. 10:8) from pestilence. Moses includes those who died by the execution of the judges. **10-13. Phinehas ... hath turned my wrath away**—This assurance was a signal mark of honor that the stain of blood, instead of defiling, confirmed him in office and that his posterity should continue as long as the national existence of Israel. **14. Zimri, ... a prince ... among the Simeonites**—The slaughter of a man of such high rank is mentioned as a proof of the undaunted zeal of Phinehas, for there might be numerous avengers of his blood. **17. Vex the Midianites, and smite them**—They seem to have been the most guilty parties. (Cf. ch. 22:4; 31:8.) **18. they vex you with their wiles**—Instead of open war, they plot insidious ways of accomplishing your ruin by idolatry and corruption. **their sister—** their countrywoman.

CHAPTER 26

Vss. 1-51. Israel Numbered. **1. after the plague**—That terrible visitation had swept away the remnant of the old generation, to whom God sware in His wrath that they should not enter Canaan (Ps. 95:11). **2. Take the sum of all the congregation**—The design of this new census, after a lapse of thirty-eight years, was primarily to establish the vast multiplication of the posterity of Abraham in spite of the severe judgments inflicted upon them; secondarily, it was to preserve the distinction of families and to make arrangements, preparatory to an entrance into the promised land, for the distribution of the country according to the relative population of the tribes. **7. These are the families of the Reubenites**—the principal households, which were subdivided into numerous smaller families. Reuben had suffered great diminution by Korah's conspiracy and other outbreaks. **10. the earth opened her mouth and swallowed them up together with Korah**—rather, the things of Korah. (See on ch. 16:32-35; cf. Ps. 106:17.) **11. Notwithstanding the children of Korah died not**—Either they were not parties to their father's crime, or they withdrew from it by timely repentance. His descendants became famous in the time of David, and are often mentioned in the Psalms, also in I Chronicles 6:22, 38. **12. The sons of Simeon**—It is supposed that this tribe had been pre-eminent in the guilt of Baal-peor and had consequently been greatly reduced in numbers.

Thus God's justice and holiness, as well as His truth and faithfulness, were strikingly displayed: His justice and holiness in the sweeping judgments that reduced the ranks of some tribes; and His truth and faithfulness in the extraordinary increase of others so that the posterity of Israel continued a numerous people. **53. the land shall be divided according to the number of names**—The portion of each tribe was to be greater or less, according to its populousness. **54. To many thou shalt give the more**—i.e., to the more numerous tribes a larger allotment shall be granted. **according to those that were numbered**—the number of persons twenty years old at the time of the census being made, without taking into account either the increase of those who might have attained that age, when the land should be actually distributed, or the diminution from that amount, occasioned during the war of invasion. **55. the land shall be divided by lot**—The appeal to the lot did not place the matter beyond the control of God; for it is at His disposal (Prov. 16:33), and He has fixed to all the bounds of their habitation. The manner in which the lot was taken has not been recorded. But it is evident that the lot was cast for determining the section of the country in which each tribe should be located—not the quantity of their possessions. In other words, when the lot had decided that a particular tribe was to be settled in the north or the south, the east or the west, the extent of territory was allocated according to the rule (vs. 54). **58. families of the Levites**—The census of this tribe was taken separately, and on a different principle from the rest. (See Exod. 6:16-19). **62. twenty and three thousand**—so that there was an increase of a thousand (ch. 3:39). **males from a month old**

and upward—(See on ch. 3:15.) **64. among these there was not a man . . . numbered . . . in the wilderness of Sinai**—The statement in this verse must not be considered absolute. For, besides Caleb and Joshua, there were alive at this time Eleazar and Ithamar, and in all probability a considerable number of Levites, who had no participation in the popular defections in the wilderness. The tribe of Levi, having neither sent a spy into Canaan, nor being included in the enumeration at Sinai, must be regarded as not coming within the range of the fatal sentence; and therefore it would exhibit a spectacle not to be witnesed in the other tribes of many in their ranks above sixty years of age.

Tribes	Chap. 1	Chap. 26	In-crease	De-crease
Reuben	46,500	43,730	—	2,770
Simeon	59,300	22,200	—	37,100
Gad	45,650	40,500	—	5,150
Judah	74,600	76,500	1,900	—
Issachar	54,400	64,300	9,900	—
Zebulun	57,400	60,500	3,100	—
Ephraim ..	40,500	32,500	—	8,000
Manasseh ..	32,200	52,700	20,500	—
Benjamin ..	35,400	45,600	10,200	—
Dan	62,700	64,400	1,700	—
Asher	41,500	53,400	11,900	—
Naphtali ..	53,400	45,400	—	8,000
	603,550	601,730	59,200	61,020

Total decrease 1,820

CHAPTER 27

Vss. 1-11. The Daughters of Zelophehad Ask for an Inheritance. **4. Give unto us a possession among the brethren of our father**—Those young women perceived that the males only in families had been registered in the census. Because there were none in their household, their family was omitted. So they made known their grievance to Moses, and the authorities conjoined with him in administering justice. The case was important; and as the peculiarity of daughters being the sole members of a family would be no infrequent or uncommon occurrence, the law of inheritance, under divine authority, was extended not only to meet all similar cases, but other cases also—such as when there were no children left by the proprietor, and no brothers to succeed him. A distribution of the promised land was about to be made; and it is interesting to know the legal provision made in these comparatively rare cases for preserving a patrimony from being alienated to another tribe. (See on ch. 36:6, 7.) **3. Our father died in the wilderness, and he was not . . . in the company of . . . Korah**—This declaration might be necessary because his death might have occurred about the time of that rebellion; and especially because, as the children of these conspirators were involved along with their fathers in the awful punishment, their plea appeared the more proper and forcible that their father did not die for any cause that doomed his family to lose their lives or their inheritance. **died in his own sin**—i.e., by the common law of mortality to which men, through sin, are subject.

12-17. Moses, Being Told of His Approaching Death, Asks for a Successor. **12. The Lord said unto Moses, Get thee up into this mount Abarim,** and see the land—Although the Israelites were now on the confines of the promised land, Moses was not privileged to cross the Jordan, but died on one of the Moabitic range of mountains, to which the general name of Abarim was given (ch. 33:47). The privation of this great honor was owing to the unhappy conduct he had manifested in the striking of the rock at Meribah; and while the pious leader submitted with meek acquiescence to the divine decree, he evinced the spirit of genuine patriotism in his fervent prayers for the appointment of a worthy and competent successor. **16. God of the spirits of all flesh, set a man over the congregation**—The request was most suitably made to God in this character, as the Author of all the intellectual gifts and moral graces with which men are endowed, and who can raise up qualified persons for the most arduous duties and the most difficult situations. 18-23. JOSHUA APPOINTED TO SUCCEED HIM. **18. Take Joshua . . . a man in whom is the spirit, and lay thine hand upon him**—A strong testimony is here borne to the personality of the divine Spirit— the imposition of hands was an ancient ceremony. (See on Gen. 48:14; Lev. 1:4; I Tim. 4:14.) **20. Thou shalt put some of thine honour upon him**— In the whole history of Israel there arose no prophet or ruler in all respects like unto Moses till the Messiah appeared, whose glory eclipsed all. But Joshua was honored and qualified in an eminent degree, through the special service of the high priest, who asked counsel for him after the judgment of Urim before the Lord.

CHAPTER 28

Vss. 1-31. OFFERINGS TO BE OBSERVED. **2. Command the children of Israel, and say unto them** —The repetition of several laws formerly enacted, which is made in this chapter, was seasonable and necessary, not only on account of their importance and the frequent neglect of them, but because a new generation had sprung up since their first institution and because the Israelites were about to be settled in the land where those ordinances were to be observed. **My offering, and my bread**—used generally for the appointed offerings, and the import of the prescription is to enforce regularity and care in their observance. **9, 10. This is the burnt offering of every sabbath**—There is no previous mention of a Sabbath burnt offering, which was additional to the daily sacrifices. **11-15. In the beginnings of your months ye shall offer up a burnt offering unto the Lord**—These were held as sacred festivals; and though not possessing the character of solemn feasts, they were distinguished by the blowing of trumpets over the sacrifices (ch. 10:10), by the suspension of all labor except the domestic occupations of women (Amos 8:5), by the celebration of public worship (II Kings 4:23), and by social or family feasts (I Sam. 20:5). These observations are not prescribed in the law though they obtained in the practice of a later time. The beginning of the month was known, not by astronomical calculations, but, according to Jewish writers, by the testimony of messengers appointed to watch the first visible appearance of the new moon; and then the fact was announced through the whole country by signal-fires kindled on the mountain tops. The new-moon festivals having been common among the heathen, it is probable that an important design of their institution in Israel was to give the minds of that people a better direction;

and assuming this to have been one of the objects contemplated, it will account for one of the kids being offered unto the Lord (vs. 15), not unto the moon, as the Egyptians and Syrians did. The Sabbath and the new moon are frequently mentioned together. **16-25. in the fourteenth day of the first month is the passover**—The law for that great annual festival is given (Lev. 23:5), but some details are here introduced, as certain specified offerings are prescribed to be made on each of the seven days of unleavened bread. **26, 27. in the day of the first fruits . . . offer the burnt offering**—A new sacrifice is here ordered for the celebration of this festival, in addition to the other offering, which was to accompany the first fruits (Lev. 23:18).

CHAPTER 29

Vss. 1-40. THE OFFERING AT THE FEAST OF TRUMPETS. **1. in the seventh month**—of the ecclesiastical year, but the first month of the civil year, corresponding to our September. It was, in fact, the New Year's Day, which had been celebrated among the Hebrews and other contemporary nations with great festivity and joy and ushered in by a flourish of trumpets. This ordinance was designed to give a religious character to the occasion by associating it with some solemn observances. (Cf. Exod. 12:2; Lev. 23:24.) **it is a day of blowing the trumpets unto you**—This made it a solemn preparation for the sacred feasts—a greater number of which were held during this month than at any other season of the year. Although the institution of this feast was described before, there is more particularity here as to what the burnt offering should consist of; and, in addition to it, a sin offering is prescribed. The special offerings, appointed for certain days, were not to interfere with the offerings usually requisite on these days, for in verse 6 it is said that the daily offerings, as well as those for the first day of the month, were to take place in their ordinary course. **7-11. ye shall have on the tenth day of this seventh month an holy convocation**— This was the great day of atonement. Its institution, together with the observance to which that day was devoted, was described (Lev. 16:29, 30). But additional offerings seem to be noticed, viz., the large animal sacrifice for a general expiation, which was a sweet savor unto the Lord, and the sin offering to atone for the sins that mingled with that day's services. The prescriptions in this passage appear supplementary to the former statement in Leviticus. **12-34. on the fifteenth day**—was to be held the feast of booths or tabernacles. (See on Lev. 23:34, 35.) The feast was to last seven days, the first and last of which were to be kept as Sabbaths, and a particular offering was prescribed for each day, the details of which are given with a minuteness suited to the infant state of the church. Two things are deserving of notice: First, that this feast was distinguished by a greater amount and variety of sacrifices than any other—partly because, occurring at the end of the year, it might be intended to supply any past deficiencies—partly because, being immediately after the ingathering of the fruits, it ought to be a liberal acknowledgment —and partly, perhaps, because God consulted the weakness of mankind, who naturally grow weary both of the charge and labor of such services when they are long continued, and made them every day less toilsome and expensive [PATRICK]. Secondly, it will be remarked that the sacrifices varied in a progressive ratio of decrease every day. **after the manner**—according to the ritual order appointed by divine authority—that for meat offerings (vss. 3-10), and drink offerings. (See on ch. 28:7, 14.) **35-40. On the eighth day ye shall have a solemn assembly**—The feast of tabernacles was brought to a close on the eighth day, which was the great day (Lev. 23: 39). Besides the common routine sacrifices, there were special offerings appointed for that day though these were fewer than on any of the preceding days; and there were also, as was natural on that occasion when vast multitudes were convened for a solemn religious purpose, many spontaneous gifts and services, so that there was full scope for the exercise of a devout spirit in the people, both for their obedience to the statutory offerings, and by the presentation of those which were made by free will or in consequence of vows. **39. These things ye shall do unto the Lord in your set feasts**—From the statements made in this and the preceding chapter, it appears that the yearly offerings made to the altar at the public expense, without taking into account a vast number of voluntary vow and trespass offerings, were calculated at the following amount: —goats, 15; kids, 21; rams, 72; bullocks, 132; lambs, 1,101; sum total of animals sacrificed at public cost, 1,241. This, of course, is exclusive of the prodigious addition of lambs slain at the passover, which in later times, according to Josephus, amounted in a single year to the immense number of 255,600.

CHAPTER 30

Vss. 1-16. VOWS ARE NOT TO BE BROKEN. **1. This is the thing which the Lord hath commanded** —The subject of this chapter relates to vowing, which seems to have been an ancient usage, allowed by the law to remain, and by which some people declared their intention of offering some gift on the altar or abstaining from particular articles of meat or drink, of observing a private fast, or doing something to the honor or in the service of God, over and above what was authoritatively required. In verse 39 of the preceding chapter, mention was made of "vows and freewill offerings," and it is probable, from the explanatory nature of the rules laid down in this chapter, that these were given for the removal of doubts and difficulties which conscientious persons had felt about their obligation to perform their vows in certain circumstances that had arisen. **2. If a man vow a vow unto the Lord** —A mere secret purpose of the mind was not enough to constitute a vow; it had to be actually expressed in words; and though a purely voluntary act, yet when once the vow was made, the performance of it, like that of every other promise, became an indispensable duty—all the more because, referring to a sacred thing, it could not be neglected without the guilt of prevarication and unfaithfulness to God. **he shall not break his word**—lit., profane his word—render it vain and contemptible (Ps. 55:20; 89:34). But as it would frequently happen that parties would vow to do things which were neither good in themselves nor in their power to perform, the law ordained that their natural superiors should have the right of judging as to the propriety of those vows, with discretionary power to sanction or interdict their fulfilment. Parents were to determine in the case of their children, and husbands in that of their wives—being, however, allowed only a day for deliberation after

the matter became known to them; and their judgment, if unfavorable, released the devotee from all obligation. **3. If a woman also vow a vow unto the Lord, and bind herself by a bond, being in her father's house in her youth**—Girls only are specified; but minors of the other sex, who resided under the parental roof, were included, according to Jewish writers, who also consider the name "father" as comprehending all guardians of youth. We are also told that the age at which young people were deemed capable of vowing was 13 for boys and 12 for girls. The judgment of a father or guardian on the vow of any under his charge might be given either by an expressed approval or by silence, which was to be construed as approval. But in the case of a husband who, after silence from day to day, should ultimately disapprove or hinder his wife's vow, the sin of non-performance was to be imputed to him and not to her. **9. every vow of a widow**— In the case of a married woman, who, in the event of a separation from her husband, or of his death, returned, as was not uncommon, to her father's house, a doubt might have been entertained whether she was not, as before, subject to paternal jurisdiction and obliged to act with the paternal consent. The law ordained that the vow was binding if it had been made in her husband's lifetime, and he, on being made aware of it, had not interposed his veto; as, for instance, she might have vowed, when not a widow, that she would assign a portion of her income to pious and charitable uses, of which she might repent when actually a widow; but by this statute she was required to fulfil the obligation, provided her circumstances enabled her to redeem the pledge. The rules laid down must have been exceedingly useful for the prevention or cancelling of rash vows, as well as for giving a proper sanction to such as were legitimate in their nature, and made in a devout, reflecting spirit.

CHAPTER 31

Vss. 1-54. THE MIDIANITES SPOILED AND BALAAM SLAIN. **1, 2. the Lord spake unto Moses, Avenge the children of Israel of the Midianites**—a semi-nomad people, descended from Abraham and Keturah, occupying a tract of country east and southeast of Moab, which lay on the eastern coast of the Dead Sea. They seem to have been the principal instigators of the infamous scheme of seduction, planned to entrap the Israelites into the double crime of idolatry and licentiousness, by which, it was hoped, the Lord would withdraw from that people the benefit of His protection and favor. Moreover, the Midianites had rendered themselves particularly obnoxious by entering into a hostile league with the Amorites (Josh. 13:21). The Moabites were at this time spared in consideration of Lot (Deut. 2:9) and because the measure of their iniquities was not yet full. God spoke of avenging "the children of Israel"; Moses spoke of avenging the Lord, as dishonor had been done to God and an injury inflicted on His people. The interests were identical. God and His people have the same cause, the same friends, and the same assailants. This, in fact, was a religious war, undertaken by the express command of God against idolaters, who had seduced the Israelites to practise their abominations. **3. Arm some of yourselves**—This order was issued but a short time before the death of Moses. The announcement to him of that approaching event seems to have accelerated, rather than retarded, his warlike preparations. **5. there were delivered**—i.e., drafted, chosen, an equal amount from each tribe, to prevent the outbreak of mutual jealousy or strife. Considering the numerical force of the enemy, this was a small quota to furnish. But the design was to exercise their faith and animate them to the approaching invasion of Canaan. **6. Moses sent ... Eleazar the priest, to the war**—Although it is not expressly mentioned, it is highly probable that Joshua was the general who conducted this war. The presence of the priest, who was always with the army (Deut. 20:2), was necessary to preside over the Levites, who accompanied the expedition, and to inflame the courage of the combatants by his sacred services and counsels. **holy instruments**—As neither the ark nor the Urim and Thummim were carried to the battlefield till a later period in the history of Israel, the "holy instruments" must mean the "trumpets" (ch. 10:9). And this view is agreeable to the text, by simply changing "and" into "even," as the *Hebrew* particle is frequently rendered. **7. they slew all the males**—This was in accordance with a divine order in all such cases (Deut. 20:13). But the destruction appears to have been only partial—limited to those who were in the neighborhood of the Hebrew camp and who had been accomplices in the villainous plot of Baal-peor, while a large portion of the Midianites were absent on their pastoral wanderings or had saved themselves by flight. (Cf. Judg. 6:1.) **8. the kings of Midian**—so called, because each was possessed of absolute power within his own city or district—called also dukes or princes of Sihon (Josh. 13:21), having been probably subject to that Amorite ruler, as it is not uncommon in the East to find a number of governors or pachas tributary to one great king. **Zur**—father of Cozbi (ch. 25:15). **Balaam also ... they slew with the sword**—This unprincipled man, on his dismissal from Balak, set out for his home in Mesopotamia (ch. 24:25). But, either diverging from his way to tamper with the Midianites, he remained among them without proceeding further, to incite them against Israel and to watch the effects of his wicked counsel; or, learning in his own country that the Israelites had fallen into the snare which he had laid and which he doubted not would lead to their ruin, he had, under the impulse of insatiable greed, returned to demand his reward from the Midianites. He was an object of merited vengeance. In the immense slaughter of the Midianitish people—in the capture of their women, children, and property and in the destruction of all their places of refuge—the severity of a righteous God fell heavily on that base and corrupt race. But, more than all others, Balaam deserved and got the just reward of his deeds. His conduct had been atrociously sinful, considering the knowledge he possessed, and the revelations he had received, of the will of God. For any one in his circumstances to attempt defeating the prophecies he had himself been the organ of uttering, and plotting to deprive the chosen people of the divine favor and protection, was an act of desperate wickedness, which no language can adequately characterize. **13. Moses, and Eleazar the priest, ... went forth to meet them without the camp**—partly as a token of respect and congratulation on their victory, partly to see how they had executed the Lord's commands, and partly to prevent the defilement of the camp by the entrance of warriors stained with blood. **14-18. Moses was wroth with the officers of the host**—The displeasure of the great leader, though it appears the ebullition of a fierce and sanguinary

temper, arose in reality from a pious and enlightened regard to the best interests of Israel. No order had been given for the slaughter of the women, and in ancient war they were commonly reserved for slaves. By their antecedent conduct, however, the Midianitish women had forfeited all claims to mild or merciful treatment; and the sacred character, the avowed object of the war (vss. 2, 3), made their slaughter necessary without any special order. But why "kill every male among the little ones"? It was designed to be a war of extermination, such as God Himself had ordered against the people of Canaan, whom the Midianites equalled in the enormity of their wickedness. **19-24. abide without the camp seven days; whosoever hath killed any person ... purify both yourselves and your captives**—Though the Israelites had taken the field in obedience to the command of God, they had become defiled by contact with the dead. A process of purification was to be undergone, as the law required (Lev. 15:13; ch. 19:9-12), and this purifying ceremony was extended to dress, houses, tents, to everything on which a dead body had lain, which had been touched by the blood-stained hands of the Israelitish warriors, or which had been the property of idolaters. This became a standing ordinance in all time coming (Lev. 6:28; 11:33; 15:12). **25-39. Take the sum of the prey that was taken**—i.e., of the captives and cattle, which, having been first lumped together according ot ancient usage (Exod. 15:9; Judg. 5:30), were divided into two equal parts: the one to the people at large, who had sustained a common injury from the Midianites and who were all liable to serve: and the other portion to the combatants, who, having encountered the labors and perils of war, justly received the largest share. From both parts, however, a certain deduction was taken for the sanctuary, as a thank offering to God for preservation and for victory. The soldiers had greatly the advantage in the distribution; for a five-hundredth part only of their half went to the priest, while a fiftieth part of the congregation's half was given to the Levites. **32. the booty, being the rest of the prey which the men of war had caught**—Some of the captives having been killed (vs. 17) and part of the cattle taken for the support of the army, the total amount of the booty remaining was in the following proportions: —Sheep, 675,000—half to soldiers, 337,500; deducted to God, 675; half to congregation, 337,500; deducted to the Levites, 6,750. Beeves, 72,000—half to soldiers, 36,000; deducted to God, 72; half to congregation, 36,000; deducted to the Levites, 720. Asses, 61,000—half to soldiers, 30,500; deducted to God, 61; half to congregation, 30,500; deducted to the Levites, 610. Persons, 32,000—half to soldiers, 16,000, deducted to God, 32; half to congregation, 16,000; deducted to the Levites, 320. **48—54. officers ... said ... there lacketh not one man of us**—A victory so signal, and the glory of which was untarnished by the loss of a single Israelitish soldier, was an astonishing miracle. So clearly betokening the direct interposition of Heaven, it might well awaken the liveliest feelings of grateful acknowledgment to God (Ps. 44:2, 3). The oblation they brought for the Lord "was partly an atonement" or reparation for their error (vss. 14-16), for it could not possess any expiatory virtue, and partly a tribute of gratitude for the stupendous service rendered them. It consisted of the "spoil," which, being the acquisition of individual valor, was not divided like the "prey," or livestock, each soldier retaining it in lieu of pay; it was offered by the "captains" alone, whose pious feelings were evinced by the dedication of the spoil which fell to their share. There were jewels to the amount of 16,750 shekels, or about $305,000.

CHAPTER 32

Vss. 1-42. The Reubenites and Gadites Ask for an Inheritance. **1. the land of Jazer, and the land of Gilead**—A complete conquest had been made of the country east of the Jordan, comprising "the land of Jazer," which formed the southern district between the Arnon and Jabbok and "the land of Gilead," the middle region between the Jabbok and Jarmouk, or Hieromax, including Bashan, which lay on the north of that river. The whole of this region is now called the Belka. It has always been famous for its rich and extensive pastures, and it is still the favorite resort of the Bedouin shepherds, who frequently contend for securing to their immense flocks the benefit of its luxuriant vegetation. In the camp of ancient Israel, Reuben and Gad were pre-eminently pastoral; and as these two tribes, being placed under the same standard, had frequent opportunities of conversing and arranging about their common concerns, they united in preferring a request that the transjordanic region, so well suited to the habits of a pastoral people, might be assigned to them. **6-19. Moses said unto the children of Gad and to the children of Reuben, Shall your brethren go to war, and shall ye sit here**—Their language was ambiguous; and Moses, suspicious that this proposal was an act of unbelief, a scheme of self-policy and indolence to escape the perils of warfare and live in ease and safety, addressed to them a reproachful and passionate remonstrance. Whether they had really meditated such a withdrawal from all share in the war of invasion, or the effect of their leader's expostulation was to drive them from their original purpose, they now, in answer to his impressive appeal, declared it to be their sincere intention to co-operate with their brethren; but, if so, they ought to have been more explicit at first. **16. they came near**—The narrative gives a picturesque description of this scene. The suppliants had shrunk back, dreading from the undisguised emotions of their leader that their request would be refused. But, perceiving, from the tenor of his discourse, that his objection was grounded only on the supposition that they would not cross the Jordan to assist their brethren, they became emboldened to approach him with assurances of their goodwill. **We will build sheepfolds here for our cattle, and cities for our little ones**—i.e., rebuild, repair. It would have been impossible within two months to found new cities, or even to reconstruct those which had been razed to the ground. Those cities of the Amorites were not absolutely demolished, and they probably consisted only of mud-built, or dry-stone walls. **17. and our little ones shall dwell in the fenced cities, because of the inhabitants of the land**—There was good policy in leaving a sufficient force to protect the conquered region lest the enemy should attempt reprisals; and as only 40,000 of the Reubenites and the Gadites, and a half of Manasseh, passed over the Jordan (Josh. 4:13), there were left for the security of the new possessions 70,580 men, besides women and children under 20 years (cf. ch. 26:17). **We ourselves will go ready armed**—i.e., all of us in a collective body, or as many as may be deemed necessary, while the rest of our number shall remain at home to provide for the sustenance and secure the protection of our families and flocks. (See on Josh. 4:12, 13.) **20-33. Moses said unto them, If ye will do this thing**—with sincerity and zeal. **go before the Lord to war**—The phrase was used in allusion to the order of march in which the tribes of Reuben and Gad immediately preceded the ark (Num. 10:18-21), or to the passage over the Jordan, in which the ark stood in mid-channel, while all the tribes marched by in succession (Josh. 3:4), of course including those of Reuben and Gad, so that, literally, they *passed over before the Lord* and before the rest of Israel (Josh. 4:13). Perhaps, however, the phrase is used merely in a general sense to denote their marching on an expedition, the purpose of which was blessed with the presence, and destined to promote the glory, of God. The displeasure which Moses had felt on the first mention of their proposal had disappeared on the strength of their solemn assurances. But a lurking suspicion of their motives seems still to have been lingering in his mind—he continued to speak to them in an admonitory strain; and he concluded by warning them that in case of their failing to redeem their pledge, the judgments of an offended God would assuredly fall upon them. This emphatic caution against such an eventuality throws a strong doubt on the honesty of their first intentions; and yet, whether through the opposing attitude or the strong invectives of Moses they had been brought to a better state of mind, their final reply showed that now all was right. **28-32. concerning them Moses commanded**—The arrangement itself, as well as the express terms on which he assented to it, was announced by the leader to the public authorities. The pastoral country the two tribes had desired was to be granted them on condition that they would lend their aid to their brethren in the approaching invasion of Canaan. If they refused or failed to perform their promise, those possessions should be forfeited, and they themselves compelled to go across the Jordan and fight for a settlement like the rest of their brethren. **33. half the tribe of Manasseh**—It is nowhere explained in the record how they were incorporated with the two tribes, or what broke this great tribe into two parts, of which one was left to follow the fortunes of its brethren in the settled life of the western hills, while the other was allowed to wander as a nomadic tribe over the pasture lands of Gilead and Bashan. They are not mentioned as accompanying Reuben and Gad in their application to Moses; neither were they included in his first directions (vs. 25); but as they also were a people addicted to pastoral pursuits and possessed as immense flocks as the other two, Moses invited the half of them to remain, in consequence, probably, of finding that this region was more than sufficient for the pastoral wants of the others, and he may have given them the preference, as some have conjectured, for their valorous conduct in the contests with the Amorites (cf. vs. 39, with Josh. 17:1). **34-36. the children of Gad built**—(see on vs. 16)—Dibon, identified with Dheban, now in ruins, an hour's distance from the Arnon (Mojeb). **Ataroth** (crowns)—There are several towns so called in Scripture, but this one in the tribe of Gad has not been identified. Aroer, now Arair, standing on a precipice on the north bank of the Arnon. **35. Atroth, Shophan, and Jaazer . . . :**—Jaazer, near a famed fountain, Ain Hazier, the waters of which flow into Wady Schaib, about 15 miles from Hesbon. Beth-nimrah, now Nimrin; Heshbon, now Hesban; Elealeh (the high), now Elaal; Kirjathaim (the double city); Nebo, now Neba, near the mountain of that name; Baal-meon, now Myoun, in ruins, where was a temple of Baal (Josh. 13:17; Jer. 48:23); Shibmah, or Shebam (vs. 2), near Heshbon, famous for vines (Isa. 16:9, 10; Jer. 48:32). **38. (their names being changed)**—either because it was the general custom of conquerors to do so; or, rather, because from the prohibition to *mention the names of other gods* (Exod. 23:13), as Nebo and Baal were, it was expedient on the first settlement of the Israelites to obliterate all remembrance of those idols. (See on Josh. 13:17-20.) **39. Gilead**—now Jelud. **41. Havoth-jair**—i.e., tent-villages. Jair, who captured them, was a descendant of Manasseh on his mother's side (I Chron. 1:21, 22). **42. Nobah**—also a distinguished person connected with the eastern branch of this tribe.

CHAPTER 33

Vss. 1-15. Two and Forty Journeys of the Israelites—from Egypt to Sinai. **1. These are the journeys of the children of Israel**—This chapter may be said to form the winding-up of the history of the travels of the Israelites through the wilderness; for the three following chapters relate to matters connected with the occupation and division of the promised land. As several apparent discrepancies will be discovered on comparing the records here given of the journeyings from Sinai with the detailed accounts of the events narrated in the Book of Exodus and the occasional notices of places that are found in that of Deuteronomy, it is probable that this itinerary comprises a list of only the *most important* stations in their journeys—those where they formed prolonged encampments, and whence they dispersed their flocks and herds to pasture on the adjacent plains till the surrounding herbage was exhausted. The catalogue extends from their departure out of Egypt to their arrival on the plains of Moab. **went forth ... with their armies**—i.e., a vast multitude marshalled in separate companies, but regular order. **2. Moses wrote their goings out according to their journeys by the commandment of the Lord**—The wisdom of this divine order is seen in the importance of the end to which it was subservient—viz., partly to establish the truth of the history, partly to preserve a memorial of God's marvellous interpositions on behalf of Israel, and partly to confirm their faith in the prospect of the difficult enterprise on which they were entering, the invasion of Canaan. **3. Rameses**—generally identified with Heroöpolis, now the modern Abu-Keisheid (see on Exod. 12:37), which was probably the capital of Goshen, and, by direction of Moses, the place of general rendezvous previous to their departure. **4. upon their gods**—used either according to Scripture phraseology to denote their rulers (the first-born of the king and his princes) or the idolatrous objects of Egyptian worship. **5. pitched in Succoth**—i.e., booths—a place of no note except as a temporary halting-place, at Birketel-Hadji, the Pilgrim's Pool [CALMET]. **6. Etham**—edge, or border of all that part of Arabia Petræa which lay contiguous to Egypt and was known by the general name of Shur. **7. Pi-hahiroth, Baal-zephon, and Migdol**—(See on Exod. 14:1-4). **8. Marah**—thought to be Ain Howarah, both from its position and the time (three days) it would take them with their children and flocks to march from the water of Ayun Musa to that spot. **9. Elim**—

supposed to be Wady Ghurundel. (See on Exod. 15:27.) **10. encamped by the Red Sea**—The road from Wady Ghurundel leads into the interior, in consequence of a high continuous ridge which excludes all view of the sea. At the mouth of Wady-et-Tayibeh, after about three days' march, it opens again on a plain along the margin of the Red Sea. The minute accuracy of the Scripture narrative, in corresponding so exactly with the geographical features of this region, is remarkably shown in describing the Israelites as proceeding by the only practicable route that could be taken. This plain, where they encamped, was the Desert of Sin (see on Exod. 16:1). **12-14. Dophkah ... Alush ... Rephidim**—These three stations, in the great valleys of El Sheikh and Feiran, would be equivalent to four days' journey for such a host. Rephidim (Exod. 17:6) was in Horeb, the burnt region—a generic name for a hot, mountainous country. **15. wilderness of Sinai**—the Wady Er-Raheh.

16-56. From Sinai to Kadesh and Plains of Moab. **16-37. Kibroth-Hattaavah** (the graves of lust, see on ch. 11:4-34)—The route, on breaking up the encampment at Sinai, led down Wady Sheikh; then crossing Jebel-et-Tih, which intersected the peninsula, they descended into Wady Zalaka, pitching successively at two brief, though memorable, stations (Deut. 9:22); then they encamped at Hazeroth (unwalled villages), supposed to be at Ain-Hadera (ch. 11:35). Kadesh or Kadesh-barnea, is supposed to be the great valley of the Ghor, and the city Kadesh to have been situated on the border of this valley [BURCKHARDT, ROBINSON]. But as there are no less than *eighteen stations* inserted between Hazeroth and Kadesh, and only eleven days were spent in performing that journey (Deut. 1:2), it is evident that the intermediate stations here recorded belong to another and totally different visit to Kadesh. The first was when they left Sinai in the second month (ch. 1:11; ch. 13:20), and were in Kadesh in August (Deut. 1:45), and "abode many days" in it. Then, murmuring at the report of the spies, they were commanded to return into the desert "by the way of the Red Sea." The arrival at Kadesh, mentioned in this catalogue, corresponds to the *second* sojourn at that place, being the *first* month, or April (ch. 20:1). Between the two visits there intervened a period of thirty-eight years, during which they wandered hither and thither through all the region of El-Tih (wanderings), often returning to the same spots as the pastoral necessities of their flocks required; and there is the strongest reason for believing that the stations named between Hazeroth (vs. 8) and Kadesh (vs. 36) belong to the long interval of wandering. No certainty has yet been attained in ascertaining the locale of many of these stations. There must have been more than are recorded; for it is probable that those only are noted where they remained some time, where the tabernacle was pitched, and where Moses and the elders encamped, the people being scattered for pasture in various directions. From Ezion-geber, for instance, which stood at the head of the gulf of Akaba, to Kadesh, could not be much less than the whole length of the great valley of the Ghor, a distance of not less than 100 miles, whatever might be the exact situation of Kadesh; and, of course, there must have been several intervening stations, though none are mentioned. The incidents and stages of the rest of the journey to the plains of Moab are sufficiently explicit from the preceding chapters. **Rithmah**—the place of the broom, a station possibly in some wady extending westward of the Ghor (ch. 10:40). **Rimmon-parez,** or Rimmon—a city of Judah and Simeon (Josh. 15:32); Libnah, so called from its white poplars (Joshua 10:29), or, as some think, a white hill between Kadesh and Gaza (Josh. 10:29); Rissah (Elarish); mount Shapher (Cassius); Moseroth, adjacent to mount Hor, in Wady Mousa. Ezion-geber, near Akaba, a seaport on the western shore of the Elanitic gulf; Wilderness of Zin, on the east side of the peninsula of Sinai; Punon, in the rocky ravines of mount Hor and famous for the mines and quarries in its vicinity as well as for its fruit trees, now Tafyle, on the border of Edom; Abarim, a ridge of rugged hills northwest of the Arnon—the part called Nebo was one of its highest peaks—opposite Jericho. (See on Deut. 10:6.) **50-53. ye shall drive out all the inhabitants of the land from before you**—not, however, by expulsion, but extermination (Deut. 7:1). **destroy all their pictures**—obelisks for idolatrous worship (see on Lev. 26:1). **and destroy all their molten images**—by metonymy for all their groves and altars, and materials of worship on the tops of hills. **54. ye shall divide the land by lot**—The particular locality of each tribe was to be determined in this manner while a line was to be used in measuring the proportion (Josh. 18:10; Ps. 16:5, 6). **55. But if ye will not drive out the inhabitants of the land from before you**—No associations were to be formed with the inhabitants; otherwise, "if ye let remain, they will be pricks in your eyes, and thorns in your sides"—i.e., they would prove troublesome and dangerous neighbors, enticing to idolatry, and consequently depriving you of the divine favor and blessing. The neglect of the counsel against union with the idolatrous inhabitants became fatal to them. This earnest admonition given to the Israelites in their peculiar circumstances conveys a salutary lesson to us to allow no lurking habits of sin to remain in us. That spiritual enemy must be eradicated from our nature; otherwise it will be ruinous to our present peace and future salvation.

CHAPTER 34

Vss. 1-29. THE BORDERS OF THE LAND OF CANAAN. **2. this is the ... land of Canaan**—The details given in this chapter mark the general boundary of the inheritance of Israel west of the Jordan. The Israelites never actually possessed all the territory comprised within these boundaries, even when it was most extended by the conquests of David and Solomon. **3-5. your south quarter**—The line which bounded it on the south is the most difficult to trace. According to the best biblical geographers, the leading points here defined are as follows: The southwest angle of the southern boundary should be where the wilderness of Zin touches the border of Edom, so that the southern boundary should extend eastward from the extremity of the Dead Sea, wind around the precipitous ridge of Akrabbim (scorpions), thought to be the high and difficult Pass of Safeh, which crosses the stream that flows from the south into the Jordan—i.e., the great valley of the Arabah, reaching from the Dead to the Red Sea. **river of Egypt** —the ancient brook Sihor, the Rhinocolura of the Greeks, a little to the south of El-Arish, where this wady gently descends towards the Mediterranean (Josh. 13:3). **6. the western border**—There is no uncertainty about this boundary, as it is universally allowed to be the Mediterranean, which is called

"the great sea" in comparison with the small inland seas or lakes known to the Hebrews. **7-9. north border**—The principal difficulty in understanding the description here arises from what our translators have called mount Hor. The Hebrew words, however, *Hor-ha-Hor,* properly signify "the mountain of the mountain"—"the high double mountain," which, from the situation, can mean nothing else than the mountain Amana (Song of Sol. 4:8), a member of the great Lebanon range (Josh. 13:5). **entrance of Hamath**—The northern plain between those mountain ranges, now the valley of Balbeck (see on ch. 13:21-24). **Zedad**—identified as the present Sudud (Ezek. 17:15). **Ziphron**—(sweet odor); **Hazar-enan**—(village of fountains); but the places are unknown. "An imaginary line from mount Cassius, on the coast along the northern base of Lebanon to the entering into the Bekaa (Valley of Lebanon) at the Kamosa Hermel," must be regarded as the frontier that is meant [VAN DE VELDE]. **10-12. east border**—This is very clearly defined. Shepham and Riblah, which were in the valley of Lebanon, are mentioned as the boundary line, which commenced a little higher than the sources of the Jordan. Ain is supposed to be the source of that river; and thence the eastern boundary extended along the Jordan, the sea of Chinnereth (Lake of Tiberias), the Jordan; and again terminated at the Dead Sea. The line being drawn on the east of the river and the seas included those waters within the territory of the western tribes. **13-15. The two tribes and the half tribe have received their inheritance on this side Jordan**—The conquered territories of Sihon and Og, lying between the Arnon and mount Hermon, were allotted to them—that of Reuben in the most southerly part, Gad north of it, and the half Manasseh in the northernmost portion. **16-29. names of the men ... who shall divide the land**—This appointment by the Lord before the Jordan tended not only to animate the Israelites' faith in the certainty of the conquest, but to prevent all subsequent dispute and discontent, which might have been dangerous in presence of the natives. The nominees were ten princes for the nine and a half tribes, one of them being selected from the western section of Manasseh, and all subordinate to the great military and ecclesiastical chiefs, Joshua and Eleazar. The names are mentioned in the exact order in which the tribes obtained possession of the land, and according to *brotherly* connection.

CHAPTER 35

Vss. 1-5. EIGHT AND FORTY CITIES GIVEN TO THE LEVITES. **2. give unto the Levites of the inheritance of their possession cities to dwell in** —As the Levites were to have no territorial domain allocated to them like the other tribes on the conquest of Canaan, they were to be distributed throughout the land in certain cities appropriated to their use; and these cities were to be surrounded by extensive suburbs. There is an apparent discrepancy between verses 4 and 5, with regard to the extent of these suburbs; but the statements in the two verses refer to totally different things—the one to the extent of the suburbs from the walls of the city, the other to the space of 2000 cubits from their extremity. In point of fact, there was an extent of ground, amounting to 3000 cubits, measured from the wall of the city. One thousand were most probably occupied with outhouses for the accommodation of shepherds and other servants, with gardens, vineyards, or oliveyards. And these which were portioned out to different families (I Chron. 6:60) might be sold by one Levite to another, but not to any individual of another tribe (Jer. 32:7). The other two thousand cubits remained a common for the pasturing of cattle (Lev. 25:34) and, considering their number, that space would be fully required.

6-8. CITIES OF REFUGE. there shall be six cities for refuge, which ye shall appoint for the manslayer—The establishment of those privileged sanctuaries among the cities of the Levites is probably traceable to the idea, that they would be the most suitable and impartial judges—that their presence and counsels might calm or restrain the stormy passions of the blood avenger—and that, from their being invested with the sacred character, they might be types of Christ, in whom sinners find a refuge from the destroyer (see Deut. 4:43; Josh. 20:8). **the cities which ye shall give shall be of the possession of the children of Israel**—The burden of furnishing those places for the residence and support of the Levitical order was to fall in equitable proportions upon the different tribes (see ch. 33:54; Josh. 20:7).

9-34. THE BLOOD AVENGER. that the slayer may flee thither, which killeth any person at unawares—The practice of Goelism, i.e., of the nearest relation of an individual who was killed being bound to demand satisfaction from the author of his death, existed from a very remote antiquity (Gen. 4:14; 27:45). It seems to have been an established usage in the age of Moses; and although in a rude and imperfect state of society, it is a natural and intelligible principle of criminal jurisprudence, it is liable to many great abuses; the chief of the evils inseparable from it is that the kinsman, who is bound in duty and honor to execute justice, will often be precipitate—little disposed, in the heat of passion or under the impulse of revenge, to examine into the circumstances of the case, to discriminate between the premeditated purpose of the assassin and the misfortune of the unintentional homicide. Moreover, it had a tendency, not only to foster a vindictive spirit, but in case of the Goel being unsuccessful in finding his victim, to transmit animosities and feuds against his descendants from one generation to another. This is exemplified among the Arabs in the present day. Should an Arab of one tribe happen to kill one of another tribe, there is "blood" between the tribes, and the stain can only be wiped out by the death of some individual of the tribe with which the offense originated. Sometimes the penalty is commuted by the payment of a stipulated number of sheep or camels. But such an equivalent, though offered, is as often refused, and blood has to be repaid only by blood. This practice of Goelism obtained among the Hebrews to such an extent that it was not perhaps expedient to abolish it; and Moses, while sanctioning its continuance, was directed, by divine authority, to make some special regulations, which tended both to prevent the unhappy consequences of sudden and personal vengeance, and, at the same time, to afford an accused person time and means of proving his innocence. This was the humane and equitable end contemplated in the institution of cities of refuge. There were to be six of these legalized asyla, three on the east of Jordan, both because the territory there was equal in length, though not in breadth, to Canaan, and because it might be more convenient for some to take refuge across the border. They were appoint-

ed for the benefit, not of the native Israelites only, but of all resident strangers. **16-21. If he smite him with an instrument of iron so that he die,** etc.—Various cases are here enumerated in which the Goel or avenger was at liberty to take the life of the murderer; and every one of them proves a premeditated purpose. **22-28. But if he thrust him suddenly without enmity, or have cast upon him any thing without laying of wait,** etc.—Under the excitement of a sudden provocation, or violent passion, an injury might be inflicted issuing in death; and for a person who had thus undesignedly committed slaughter, the Levitical cities offered the benefit of full protection. Once having reached the nearest, for one or other of them was within a day's journey of all parts of the land, he was secure. But he had to "abide in it." His confinement within its walls was a wise and salutary rule, designed to show the sanctity of human blood in God's sight, as well as to protect the manslayer himself, whose presence and intercourse in society might have provoked the passions of the deceased's relatives. But the period of his release from this confinement was not until the death of the high priest. That was a season of public affliction, when private sorrows were sunk or overlooked under a sense of the national calamity, and when the death of so eminent a servant of God naturally led all to serious consideration about their own mortality. The moment, however, that the refugee broke through the restraints of his confinement and ventured beyond the precincts of the asylum, he forfeited the privilege, and, if he was discovered by his pursuer, he might be slain with impunity. **29-34. these things shall be for a statute of judgment unto you throughout your generations**—The law of the blood avenger, as thus established by divine authority, was a vast improvement on the ancient practice of Goelism. By the appointment of cities of refuge, the manslayer was saved, in the meantime, from the blind and impetuous fury of vindictive relatives; but he might be tried by the local court, and, if proved guilty on sufficient evidence, condemned and punished as a murderer, without the possibility of deliverance by any pecuniary satisfaction. The enactment of Moses, which was an adaptation to the character and usages of the Hebrew people, secured the double advantage of promoting the ends both of humanity and of justice.

CHAPTER 36

Vss. 1-13. THE INCONVENIENCE OF THE INHERITANCE. **1. the chief fathers of the families of the children of Gilead**—Being the tribal governors in Manasseh, they consulted Moses on a case that affected the public honor and interests of their tribe. It related once more to the daughters of Zelophehad. Formerly they had applied, at their own instance, to be recognized, for want of male heirs in their family, as entitled to inherit their father's property; now the application was made on behalf of the tribe to which they belonged—that steps might be taken to prevent the alienation of their patrimony by their alliance with husbands of another tribe. The unrestricted marriages of daughters in such circumstances threatened seriously to affect the tenure of land in Israel, as their inheritance would go to their children, who, by the father's side, would belong to another tribe, and thus lead, through a complication of interests and the confusion of families, to an evil for which even the Jubilee could not afford a remedy. (See on Lev. 25:13.) **5-12. Moses commanded the children of Israel according to the word of the Lord**—The plea appeared just and reasonable; and, accordingly an enactment was made by which the daughters of Zelophehad, while left to the free choice of their husbands, were restricted to marry not only within their own tribe, but *within the family* of their father's tribe—i.e., one of their cousins. This restriction, however, was imposed only on those who were heiresses. The law was not applicable to daughters in different circumstances (I Chron. 23:22)—for they might marry into another tribe; but if they did so, they were liable to forfeit their patrimonial inheritance, which, on the death of their father or brothers, went to the nearest of the family kinsmen. Here was an instance of progressive legislation (see also Exod. ch. 18:27) in Israel, the enactments made being suggested by circumstances. But it is deserving of special notice that those additions to, or modifications of, the law were confined to civil affairs; while the slightest change was inadmissible in the laws relating to worship or the maintenance of religion. **13. These are the commandments and the judgments, which the Lord commanded by the hand of Moses unto the children of Israel in the plains of Moab**—The Israelitish encampment was on an extensive plateau north of the Arnon, which, though wrested from the Moabites by Sihon and Og, still retained the name of its original possessors. The particular site, as indicated by the words "Jordan near Jericho," is now called El-Koura—a large plain lying not far from Nebo, between the Arnon and a small tributary stream, the Wael [BURCKHARDT]. It was a desert plain on the eastern bank, and marked only by groves of the wild, thorny acacia tree.

THE FIFTH BOOK OF MOSES CALLED

DEUTERONOMY

CHAPTER 1

Vss. 1-46. MOSES' SPEECH AT THE END OF THE FORTIETH YEAR. **1. These be the words which Moses spake unto all Israel**—The mental condition of the people generally in that infantine age of the Church, and the greater number of them being of young or tender years, rendered it expedient to repeat the laws and counsels which God had given. Accordingly, to furnish a recapitulation of the leading branches of their faith and duty was among the last public services which Moses rendered to Israel. The scene of their delivery was on the plains of Moab where the encampment was pitched "on this side Jordan," or, as the Hebrew word may be rendered "on the bank of the Jordan." **in the wilderness, in the plain**—the Arabah, a desert plain, or steppe, extended the whole way from the Red Sea north to the Sea of Tiberias. While the high tablelands of Moab were "cultivated fields," the Jordan valley, at the foot of the mountains where Israel was encamped, was a part of the great desert plain, little more inviting than the desert of Arabia. The locale is indicated by the names of the most prominent places around it. Some of these places are unknown to us. The Hebrew word, *Suph*, red (for "sea," which our translators have inserted, is not in the original, and Moses was now farther from the Red Sea than ever), probably meant a place noted for its reeds (Num. 21:14). **Tophel**—identified as Tafyle or Tafeilah, lying between Bozrah and Kerak. Hazeroth is a different place from that at which the Israelites encamped after leaving "the desert of Sinai." **2. There are eleven days' journey from Horeb**—Distances are computed in the East still by the hours or days occupied by the journey. A day's journey on foot is about twenty miles—on camels, at the rate of three miles an hour, thirty miles—and by caravans, about twenty-five miles. But the Israelites, with children and flocks, would move at a slow rate. The length of the Ghor from Ezion-geber to Kadesh is 100 miles. The days here mentioned were not necessarily successive days [ROBINSON], for the journey can be made in a much shorter period. But this mention of the *time* was made to show that the great number of years spent in travelling from Horeb to the plain of Moab was not owing to the length of the way, but to a very different cause; viz., banishment for their apostasy and frequent rebellions. **mount Seir**—the mountainous country of Edom. **3-8. in the fortieth year . . . Moses spake unto the children of Israel**, etc.—This impressive discourse, in which Moses reviewed all that God had done for His people, was delivered about a month before his death, and after peace and tranquillity had been restored by the complete conquest of Sihon and Og. **Ashtaroth**—the royal residence of Og, so called from Astarte (the moon), the tutelary goddess of the Syrians. Og was slain at Edrei—now Edhra, the ruins of which are fourteen miles in circumference [BURCKHARDT]; its general breadth is about two leagues. **5. On this side Jordan, in the land of Moab, began Moses to declare this law**—declare, i.e., explain this law. He follows the same method here that he elsewhere observes; viz., that of first enumerating the marvellous doings of God in behalf of His people, and reminding them what an unworthy requital they had made for all His kindness—then he rehearses the law and its various precepts. **6. The Lord our God spake unto us in Horeb, saying, Ye have dwelt long enough in this mount**—Horeb was the general name of a mountainous district—lit., "the parched or burnt region," whereas Sinai was the name appropriated to a particular peak. About a year had been spent among the recesses of that wild solitude, in laying the foundation, under the immediate direction of God, of a new and peculiar community, as to its social, political, and, above all, religious character; and when this purpose had been accomplished, they were ordered to break up their encampment in Horeb. The command given them was to march straight to Canaan, and possess it. **8. I have set the land before you**—lit., before your faces—it is accessible—there is no impediment to your occupation. The order of the journey as indicated by the places mentioned would have led to a course of invasion, the opposite of what was eventually followed; viz., from the seacoast eastward—instead of from the Jordan westward (see on Num. 20:1). **7. the mount of the Amorites**—the hilly tract lying next to Kadesh-barnea in the south of Canaan. **to the land of the Canaanites, and unto Lebanon**—i.e., Phœnicia, the country of Sidon, and the coast of the Mediterranean—from the Philistines to Lebanon. The name Canaanite is often used synonymously with that of Phœnician. **9-18. I spake unto you at that time, saying, I am not able to bear you myself alone**—a little before their arrival in Horeb. Moses addresses that new generation as the representatives of their fathers, in whose sight and hearing all the transactions he recounts took place. A reference is here made to the suggestion of Jethro (Exod. 18:18). In noticing his practical adoption of a plan by which the administration of justice was committed to a select number of subordinate officers, Moses, by a beautiful allusion to the patriarchal blessing, ascribed the necessity of that memorable change in the government to the vast increase of the population. **ye are this day as the stars ... for multitude**—This was neither an Oriental hyperbole nor a mere empty boast. Abraham was told (Gen. 15:5, 6) to look to the stars, and though they *appear* innumerable, yet those seen by the naked eye amount, in reality, to no more than 3010 in both hemispheres. The Israelites already far exceeded that number, being at the last census above 600,000. It was a seasonable memento, calculated to animate their faith in the accomplishment of other parts of the divine promise. **19-21. we went through all that great and terrible wilderness**—of Paran, which included the desert and mountainous space lying between the wilderness of Shur westward, or towards Egypt and mount Seir, or the land of Edom eastwards; between the land of Canaan northwards, and the Red Sea southwards; and thus it appears to have comprehended really the wilderness of Sin and Sinai [FISK]. It is called by the Arabs El Tih, "the wandering." It is a dreary waste of rock and of calcareous soil covered with black sharp flints; all travellers, from a feeling of its complete isolation from the world, describe it as a great and terrible wilderness. **22-33. ye came ... and said, We will send men before us, and they shall search us out the land**—The proposal to despatch spies emanated from the people through unbelief; but Moses, believing them sincere, gave his cordial assent to this measure, and God on being consulted permitted them to follow the suggestion (see on Num. 13:1, 2). The issue proved disastrous to them, only through their own sin and folly. **28. the cities are great, and walled up to heaven**—an Oriental metaphor, meaning very high. The Arab marauders roam about on horseback, and hence the walls of St. Catherine's monastery on Sinai are so lofty that travellers are drawn up by a pulley in a basket. **Anakims**—(see on Num. 13:33). The honest and uncompromising language of Moses, in reminding the Israelites of their perverse conduct and outrageous rebellion at the report of the treacherous and faint-hearted scouts, affords a strong evidence of the truth of this history as well as of the divine authority of his mission. There was great reason for his dwelling on this dark passage in their history, as it was their unbelief that excluded them from the privilege of entering the promised land (Heb. 3:19); and that unbelief was a marvellous exhibition of human perversity, considering the miracles

which God had wrought in their favor, especially in the daily manifestations they had of His presence among them as their leader and protector. **34-36. the Lord heard the voice of your words, and was wroth**—In consequence of this aggravated offense (unbelief followed by open rebellion), the Israelites were doomed, in the righteous judgment of God, to a life of wandering in that dreary wilderness till the whole adult generation had disappeared by death. The only exceptions mentioned are Caleb and Joshua, who was to be Moses' successor. **37. Also the Lord was angry with me for your sakes**—This statement *seems* to indicate that it was on this occasion Moses was condemned to share the fate of the people. But we know that it was several years afterwards that Moses betrayed an unhappy spirit of distrust at the waters of strife (Ps. 106:32, 33). This verse must be considered therefore as a parenthesis. **39. your children ... who in that day had no knowledge between good and evil**—All ancient versions read "to-day" instead of "that day"; and the sense is—"your children who now know," or "who know not *as yet* good or evil." As the children had not been partakers of the sinful outbreak, they were spared to obtain the privilege which their unbelieving parents had forfeited. God's ways are not as man's ways. **40-45. turn you, and take your journey into the wilderness by the ... Red Sea**—This command they disregarded, and, determined to force an onward passage in spite of the earnest remonstrances of Moses, they attempted to cross the heights then occupied by the combined forces of the Amorites and Amalekites (cf. Num. 14:43), but were repulsed with great loss. People often experience distress even while in the way of duty. But how different their condition who suffer in situations where God is with them from the feelings of those who are conscious that they are in a position directly opposed to the divine will! The Israelites were grieved when they found themselves involved in difficulties and perils; but their sorrow arose not from a sense of the guilt so much as the sad effects of their perverse conduct; and "though they wept," they were not true penitents. So the Lord would not hearken to their voice, nor give ear unto them. **46. So ye abode at Kadesh many days**—That place had been the site of their encampment during the absence of the spies, which lasted forty days, and it is supposed from this verse that they prolonged their stay there after their defeat for a similar period.

CHAPTER 2

Vss. 1-37. THE STORY IS CONTINUED. **1. Then we turned, and took our journey into the wilderness by the way of the Red Sea.** After their unsuccessful attack upon the Canaanites, the Israelites broke up their encampment at Kadesh, and journeying southward over the west desert of Tih as well as through the great valley of the Ghor and Arabah, they extended their removals as far as the gulf of Akaba. **we compassed mount Seir many days**—In these few words Moses comprised the whole of that wandering nomadic life through which they passed during 38 years, shifting from place to place, and regulating their stations by the prospect of pasturage and water. Within the interval they went northward a second time to Kadesh, but being refused a passage through Edom and opposed by the Canaanites and Amalekites, they again had no alternative but to traverse once more the great Arabah southwards to the Red Sea, where turning to the left and crossing the long, lofty mountain chain to the eastward of Ezion-geber (Num. 21:4, 5), they issued into the great and elevated plains, which are still traversed by the Syrian pilgrims in their way to Mecca. They appear to have followed northward nearly the same route, which is now taken by the Syrian hadji, along the western skirts of this great desert, near the mountains of Edom [ROBINSON]. It was on entering these plains they received the command, "Ye have compassed this mountain (this hilly tract, now Jebel Shera) long enough, turn ye northward." **4. the children of Esau which dwell in Seir ... shall be afraid of you**—The same people who had haughtily repelled the approach of the Israelites from the western frontier were alarmed now that they had come round upon the weak side of their country. **5. Meddle not with them**—i.e., "which dwell in Seir" (vs. 4)—for there was another branch of Esau's posterity, viz., the Amalekites, who were to be fought against and destroyed (Gen. 36:12; Exod. 17: 14; Deut. 25:17). But the people of Edom were not to be injured, either in their persons or property. And although the approach of so vast a nomadic horde as the Israelites naturally created apprehension, they were to take no advantage of the prevailing terror to compel the Edomites to accept whatever terms they imposed. They were merely to pass "through" or along their border, and to buy meat and water of them for money (vs. 6). The people, kinder than their king, did sell them bread, meat, fruits, and water in their passage along their border (vs. 29), in the same manner as the Syrian caravan of Mecca is now supplied by the people of the same mountains, who meet the pilgrims as at a fair or market on the hadji route [ROBINSON]. Although the Israelites still enjoyed a daily supply of the manna, there was no prohibition against their eating other food when opportunity afforded. Only they were not to cherish an inordinate desire for it. Water is a scarce commodity and is often paid for by travellers in those parts. It was the more incumbent on the Israelites to do so,' as, by the blessing of God, they possessed plenty of means to purchase, and the long-continued experience of the extraordinary goodness of God to them, should inspire such confidence in Him as would suppress the smallest thought of resorting to fraud or violence in supplying their wants. **8-18. we passed ... through the way of the plain**—the Arabah or great valley, from Elath (trees), (the Ailah of the Greeks and Romans). The site of it is marked by extensive mounds of rubbish. Ezion-geber, now Akaba, both were within the territory of Edom; and after making a circuit of its southeastern boundary, the Israelites reached the border of Moab on the southeast of the Salt Sea. They had been forbidden by divine command to molest the Moabites in any way; and this special honor was conferred on that people not on their own account, for they were very wicked, but in virtue of their descent from Lot. (See on ch. 23:3.) Their territory comprised the fine country on the south, and partly on the north of the Arnon. They had won it by their arms from the original inhabitants, the Emims, a race, terrible, as their name imports, for physical power and stature (Gen. 14:5), in like manner as the Edomites had obtained their settlement by the overthrow of the original occupiers of Seir, the Horims (Gen. 14: 6), who were troglodytes, or dwellers in caves. Moses alluded to these circumstances to encourage his countrymen to believe that God would much more enable them to expel the wicked and accursed

Canaanites. At that time, however, the Moabites, having lost the greater part of their possessions through the usurpations of Sihon, were reduced to the small but fertile region between the Zered and the Arnon. **13. Now rise up, and get you over the brook Zered**—The southern border of Moab, *Zered* (woody), now Wady Ahsy, separates the modern district of Kerak from Jebal, and, indeed, forms a natural division of the country between the north and south. Ar, called in later times Rabbah, was the capital of Moab and situated 25 miles south of the Arnon on the banks of a small but shady stream, the Beni-Hamed. It is here mentioned as representative of the country dependent on it, a rich and well-cultivated country, as appears from the numerous ruins of cities, as well as from the traces of tillage still visible on the fields. **16. all the men of war were consumed and dead from among the people**—The outbreak at Kadesh on the false report of the spies had been the occasion of the fatal decree by which God doomed the whole grown-up population to die in the wilderness; but that outbreak only filled up the measure of their iniquities. For that generation, though not universally abandoned to heathenish and idolatrous practices, yet had all along displayed a fearful amount of ungodliness in the desert, which this history only hints at obscurely, but which is expressly asserted elsewhere (Ezek. 20:25, 26; Amos 5:25, 27; Acts 7:42, 43). **19-37. when thou comest nigh over against the children of Ammon, distress them not, nor meddle with them**—The Ammonites, being kindred to the Moabites, were, from regard to the memory of their common ancestor, to remain undisturbed by the Israelites. The territory of this people had been directly north from that of Moab. It extended as far as the Jabbok, having been taken by them from a number of small Canaanitish tribes, viz., the Zamzummins, a bullying, presumptuous band of giants, as their name indicates; and the Avims, the aborigines of the district extending from Hazerim or Hazeroth (El Hudhera) even unto Azzah (Gaza), but of which they had been dispossessed by the Caphtorim (Philistines), who came out of Caphtor (Lower Egypt) and settled in the western coast of Palestine. The limits of the Ammonites were now compressed; but they still possessed the mountainous region beyond the Jabbok (Josh. 11:2). What a strange insight does this parenthesis of four verses give into the early history of Palestine! How many successive wars of conquest had swept over its early state—what changes of dynasty among the Canaanitish tribes had taken place long prior to the transactions recorded in this history! **24. Rise ye up ... and pass over the river Arnon**—At its mouth, this stream is 82 feet wide and 4 deep. It flows in a channel banked by perpendicular cliffs of sandstone. At the date of the Israelitish migration to the east of the Jordan, the whole of the fine country lying between the Arnon and the Jabbok including the mountainous tract of Gilead, had been seized by the Amorites, who, being one of the nations doomed to destruction (see ch. 7:2; 20:16), were utterly exterminated. Their country fell by right of conquest into the hands of the Israelites. Moses, however, considering this doom as referring solely to the Amorite possessions west of Jordan, sent a pacific message to Sihon, requesting permission to go through his territories, which lay on the east of that river. It is always customary to send messengers before to prepare the way; but the rejection of Moses' request by Sihon and his opposition to the advance of the Israelites (Num. 21:

23; Judg. 11:26) drew down on himself and his Amorite subjects the predicted doom on the first pitched battlefield with the Canaanites. It secured to Israel not only the possession of a fine and pastoral country, but, what was of more importance to them, a free access to the Jordan on the east.

CHAPTER 3

Vss. 1-20. CONQUEST OF OG, KING OF BASHAN. **1. we turned, and went up the way to Bashan**— Bashan (fruitful or flat), now El-Bottein, lay situated to the north of Gilead and extended as far as Hermon. It was a rugged mountainous country, valuable however for its rich and luxuriant pastures. **Og the king of Bashan came out against us** —Without provocation, he rushed to attack the Israelites, either disliking the presence of such dangerous neighbors, or burning to avenge the overthrow of his friends and allies. **2. The Lord said unto me, Fear him not; for I will deliver him, and all his people, and his land, into thy hand**—His gigantic appearance and the formidable array of forces he will bring to the field, need not discourage you; for, belonging to a doomed race, he is destined to share the fate of Sihon. **3-8.** Argob was the capital of a district in Bashan of the same name, which, together with other 59 cities in the same province, were conspicuous for their lofty and fortified walls. It was a war of extermination. Houses and cities were razed to the ground; all classes of people were put to the sword; and nothing was saved but the cattle, of which an immense amount fell as spoil into the hands of the conquerors. Thus, the two Amorite kings and the entire population of their dominions were extirpated. The whole country east of the Jordan—first upland downs from the torrent of the Arnon on the south to that of the Jabbok on the north; next the high mountain tract of Gilead and Bashan from the deep ravine of Jabbok—became the possession of the Israelites. **9. Hermon**—now Jebel-Es-Sheick —the majestic hill on which the long and elevated range of Anti-Lebanon terminates. Its summit and the ridges on its sides are almost constantly covered with snow. It is not so much one high mountain as a whole cluster of mountain peaks, the highest in Palestine. According to the survey taken by the English Government Engineers in 1840, they were about 9376 feet above the sea. Being a mountain chain, it is no wonder that it should have received different names at different points from the different tribes which lay along the base—all of them designating extraordinary height: Hermon, the lofty peak, "Sirion," or in an abbreviated form "Sion" (ch. 4:48), the upraised "Shenir," the glittering breastplate of ice. **11. only Og king of Bashan remained of the remnant of giants**—lit., of Rephaim. He was not the last giant, but the only living remnant in the transjordanic country (Josh. 15:14), of a certain gigantic race, supposed to be the most ancient inhabitants of Palestine. **behold, his bedstead was a bedstead of iron**—Although beds in the East are with the common people nothing more than a simple mattress, bedsteads are not unknown. They are in use among the great, who prefer them of iron or other metals, not only for strength and durability, but for the prevention of the troublesome insects which in warm climates commonly infest wood. Taking the cubit at half a yard, the bedstead of Og would measure 13½ feet, so that as

beds are usually a little larger than the persons who occupy them, the stature of the Amorite king may be estimated at about 11 or 12 feet; or he might have caused his bed to be made much larger than was necessary, as Alexander the Great did for each of his foot soldiers, to impress the Indians with an idea of the extraordinary strength and stature of his men [LECLERC]. But how did Og's bedstead come to be in Rabbath, of the children of Ammon? In answer to this question, it has been said, that Og had, on the eve of engagement, conveyed it to Rabbath for safety. Or it may be that Moses, after capturing it, may have sold it to the Ammonites, who had kept it as an antiquarian curiosity till their capital was sacked in the time of David. This is a most unlikely supposition, and besides renders it necessary to consider the latter clause of this verse as an interpolation inserted long after the time of Moses. To avoid this, some eminent critics take the Hebrew word rendered "bedstead" to mean "coffin." They think that the king of Bashan having been wounded in battle, fled to Rabbath, where he died and was buried; hence the dimensions of his "coffin" are given [DATHE, ROS]. **12. this land, which we possessed at that time, from Aroer ... gave I unto the Reubenites and to the Gadites**—The whole territory occupied by Sihon was parcelled out among the pastoral tribes of Reuben and Gad. It extended from the north bank of the Arnon to the south half of mount Gilead—a small mountain ridge, now called Djelaad, about six or seven miles south of the Jabbok, and eight miles in length. The northern portion of Gilead and the rich pasture lands of Bashan—a large province, consisting, with the exception of a few bleak and rocky spots, of strong and fertile soil—was assigned to the half tribe of Manasseh. **14. Jair the son of Manasseh took all the country of Argob**—The original inhabitants of the province north of Bashan, comprising sixty cities (vs. 4), not having been extirpated along with Og, this people were afterwards brought into subjection by the energy of Jair. This chief, of the tribe of Manasseh, in accordance with the pastoral habits of his people, called these newly acquired towns by a name which signifies "Jair's Bedouin Villages of Tents." **unto this day**—This remark must evidently have been introduced by Ezra, or some of the pious men who arranged and collected the books of Moses. **15. I gave Gilead unto Machir**—It was only the half of Gilead (vss. 12, 13) which was given to the descendants of Machir, who was now dead. **16. from Gilead**—i.e., not the mountainous region, but the town Ramothgilead, **even unto the river Arnon half the valley** —The word "valley" signifies a wady, either filled with water or dry, as the Arnon is in summer, and thus the proper rendering of the passage will be—"even to the half middle of the river Arnon" (cf. Josh. 12:2). This prudent arrangement of the boundaries was evidently made to prevent all disputes between the adjacent tribes about the exclusive right to the water. **25. I pray thee, let me go over, and see the good land that is beyond Jordan, that goodly mountain, and Lebanon**—The natural and very earnest wish of Moses to be allowed to cross the Jordan was founded on the idea that the divine threatening might be conditional and revertible. "That goodly mountain" is supposed by Jewish writers to have pointed to the hill on which the temple was to be built (chapter 12:5; Exod. 15:2). But biblical scholars now, generally, render the words—"that goodly mountain, even Lebanon," and consider it to be mentioned as typifying the beauty of Palestine, of which hills and mountains were so prominent a feature. **26. speak no more unto me of this matter** —i.e., My decree is unalterable.

CHAPTER 4

Vss. 1-13. An Exhortation to Obedience. **1. hearken, O Israel, unto the statutes and unto the judgments which I teach you**—By statutes were meant all ordinances respecting religion and the rites of divine worship; and by judgments, all enactments relative to civil matters. The two embraced the whole law of God. **2. Ye shall not add unto the word which I command you**—by the introduction of any heathen superstition or forms of worship different from those which I have appointed (ch. 12:32; Num. 15:39; Matt. 15:9). **neither shall ye diminish aught from it**—by the neglect or omission of any of the observances, however trivial or irksome, which I have prescribed. The character and provisions of the ancient dispensation were adapted with divine wisdom to the instruction of that infant state of the church. But it was only a temporary economy; and although God here authorizes Moses to command that all its institutions should be honored with unfailing observance, this did not prevent Him from commissioning other prophets to alter or abrogate them when the end of that dispensation was attained. **3, 4. Your eyes have seen what the Lord did because of Baal-peor . . . the Lord thy God hath destroyed them from among you**—It appears that the pestilence and the sword of justice overtook only the guilty in that affair (Num. 25) while the rest of the people were spared. The allusion to that recent and appalling judgment was seasonably made as a powerful dissuasive against idolatry, and the fact mentioned was calculated to make a deep impression on people who knew and felt the truth of it. **5, 6. this is your wisdom and your understanding in the sight of the nations, which shall hear all these statutes**—Moses predicted that the faithful observance of the laws given them would raise their national character for intelligence and wisdom. In point of fact it did do so; for although the heathen world generally ridiculed the Hebrews for what they considered a foolish and absurd exclusiveness, some of the most eminent philosophers expressed the highest admiration of the fundamental principle in the Jewish religion—the unity of God; and their legislators borrowed some laws from the constitution of the Hebrews. **7-9. what nation is there so great**—Here he represents their privileges and their duty in such significant and comprehensive terms, as were peculiarly calculated to arrest their attention and engage their interest. The former, their national advantages, are described (vss. 7, 8), and they were twofold: 1. God's readiness to hear and aid them at all times; and 2. the excellence of that religion in which they were instructed, set forth in the "statutes and judgments so righteous" which the law of Moses contained. Their duty corresponding to these pre-eminent advantages as a people, was also twofold: 1. their own faithful obedience to that law; and 2. their obligation to imbue the minds of the young and rising generation with similar sentiments of reverence and respect for it. **10. the day thou stoodest before the Lord . . . in Horeb**— The delivery of the law from Sinai was an era never to be forgotten in the history of Israel. Some of those whom Moses was addressing had been present, though very young; while the rest were federally

represented by their parents, who in their name and for their interest entered into the national covenant. **12. ye heard the voice of the words, but saw no similitude**—Although articulate sounds were heard emanating from the mount, no form or representation of the Divine Being who spoke was seen to indicate His nature or properties according to the notions of the heathen.

14-40. A Particular Dissuasive against Idolatry. **15. Take . . . good heed . . . for ye saw no manner of similitude**—The extreme proneness of the Israelites to idolatry, from their position in the midst of surrounding nations already abandoned to its seductions, accounts for their attention being repeatedly drawn to the fact that God did not appear on Sinai in any visible form; and an earnest caution, founded on that remarkable circumstance, is given to beware, not only of making representations of false gods, but also any fancied representation of the true God. **16-19. Lest ye corrupt yourselves, and make you a graven image**—The things are here specified of which God prohibited any image or representation to be made for the purposes of worship; and, from the variety of details entered into, an idea may be formed of the extensive prevalence of idolatry in that age. In whatever way idolatry originated, whether from an intention to worship the true God through those things which seemed to afford the strongest evidences of His power, or whether a divine principle was supposed to reside in the things themselves, there was scarcely an element or object of nature but was deified. This was particularly the case with the Canaanites and Egyptians, against whose superstitious practices the caution, no doubt, was chiefly directed. The former worshipped Baal and Astarte, the latter Osiris and Isis, under the figure of a male and a female. It was in Egypt that animal worship most prevailed, for the natives of that country deified among beasts the ox, the heifer, the sheep, and the goat, the dog, the cat, and the ape; among birds, the ibis, the hawk, and the crane; among reptiles, the crocodile, the frog, and the beetle; among fishes, all the fish of the Nile; some of these, as Osiris and Isis, were worshipped over all Egypt, the others only in particular provinces. In addition they embraced the Zabian superstition, the adoration of the Egyptians, in common with that of many other people, extending to the whole starry host. The very circumstantial details here given of the Canaanitish and Egyptian idolatry were owing to the past and prospective familiarity of the Israelites with it in all these forms. **20. But the Lord hath taken you, and brought you forth out of the iron furnace**—i.e., furnace for smelting iron. A furnace of this kind is round, sometimes 30 feet deep, and requiring the highest intensity of heat. Such is the tremendous image chosen to represent the bondage and affliction of the Israelites [Rosen-muller]. **to be unto him a people of inheritance**— His peculiar possession from age to age; and therefore for you to abandon His worship for that of idols, especially the gross and debasing system of idolatry that prevails among the Egyptians, would be the greatest folly—the blackest ingratitude. **26. I call heaven and earth to witness against you**—This solemn form of adjuration has been common in special circumstances among all people. It is used here figuratively, or as in other parts of Scripture where inanimate objects are called up as witnesses (ch. 32:1; Isa. 1:2). **28. there ye shall serve gods, the work of men's hands**—The compulsory measures of their tyrannical conquerors would force them into idolatry, so that their choice would become their punishment. **30. in the latter days, if thou turn to the Lord thy God**—either towards the destined close of their captivities, when they evinced a returning spirit of repentance and faith, or in the age of Messiah, which is commonly called "the latter days," and when the scattered tribes of Israel shall be converted to the Gospel of Christ. The occurrence of this auspicious event will be the most illustrious proof of the truth of the promise made in verse 31. **41-43. Then Moses severed three cities on this side Jordan**—(See on Josh. 20:7, 8). **44-49. this is the law which Moses set before the children of Israel**—This is a preface to the rehearsal of the law, which, with the addition of various explanatory circumstances, the following chapters contain. **46. Beth-peor**—i.e., house or temple of Peor. It is probable that a temple of this Moabite idol stood in full view of the Hebrew camp, while Moses was urging the exclusive claims of God to their worship, and this allusion would be very significant if it were the temple where so many of the Israelites had grievously offended. **49. The springs of Pisgah**—more frequently Ashdoth-pisgah (ch. 3:17; Josh. 12:3; 13:20), the roots or foot of the mountains east of the Jordan.

CHAPTER 5

Vss. 1-29. A COMMEMORATION OF THE COVENANT IN HOREB. **1. Hear, O Israel, the statutes and judgments**—Whether this rehearsal of the law was made in a solemn assembly, or as some think at a general meeting of the elders as representatives of the people, is of little moment; it was addressed either directly or indirectly to the Hebrew people as principles of their peculiar constitution as a nation; and hence, as has been well observed, "the Jewish law has no obligation upon Christians, unless so much of it as given or commanded by Jesus Christ; for whatever in this law is conformable to the laws of nature, obliges us, not as given by Moses, but by virtue of an antecedent law common to all rational beings" [BISHOP WILSON]. **3. The Lord made not this covenant with our fathers, but with us**—The meaning is, "not with our fathers" only, "but with us" also, assuming it to be "a covenant" of grace. It may mean "not with our fathers" at all, if the reference is to the peculiar establishment of the covenant of Sinai; a law was not given to them as to us, nor was the covenant ratified in the same public manner and by the same solemn sanctions. Or, finally, the meaning may be "not with our fathers" who died in the wilderness, in consequence of their rebellion, and to whom God did not give the rewards promised only to the faithful; but "with us," who alone, strictly speaking, shall enjoy the benefits of this covenant by entering on the possession of the promised land. **4. The Lord talked with you face to face in the mount**—not in a visible and corporeal form, of which there was no trace (ch. 4:12, 15), but freely, familiarly, and in such a manner that no doubt could be entertained of His presence. **5. I stood between the Lord and you at that time**—as the messenger and interpreter of thy heavenly King, bringing near two objects formerly removed from each other at a vast distance, viz., God and the people (Gal. 10:19). In this character Moses was a type of Christ, who is the only mediator between God and men (I Tim. 11:5), the Mediator of a better covenant (Heb. 8:6; 9:15; 12:24). **to show you the word of the Lord**

—not the ten commandments—for they were proclaimed directly by the Divine Speaker Himself, but the statutes and judgments which are repeated in the subsequent portion of this book. **6-20. I am the Lord thy God**—The word "Lord" is expressive of authority or dominion; and God, who by natural claim as well as by covenant relation was entitled to exercise supremacy over His people Israel, had a sovereign right to establish laws for their government. The commandments which follow are, with a few slight verbal alterations, the same as formerly recorded (Exod. 20), and in some of them there is a distinct reference to that promulgation. **12. Keep the sabbath day to sanctify it, as the Lord thy God hath commanded thee**—i.e., keep it in mind as a sacred institution of former enactment and perpetual obligation. **14. that thy manservant and thy maidservant may rest as well as thou**—This is a different reason for the observance of the Sabbath from what is assigned in Exodus 20, where that day is stated to be an appointed memorial of the creation. But the addition of another motive for the observance does not imply any necessary contrariety to the other; and it has been thought probable that, the commemorative design of the institution being well known, the other reason was specially mentioned on this repetition of the law, to secure the privilege of sabbatic rest to servants, of which, in some Hebrew families, they had been deprived. In this view, the allusion to the period of Egyptian bondage (vs. 15), when they themselves were not permitted to observe the Sabbath either as a day of rest or of public devotion, was peculiarly seasonable and significant, well fitted to come home to their business and bosoms. **16. that it may go well with thee**—This clause is not in Exodus, but admitted into Ephesians 6:3. **21. Neither shalt thou desire thy neighbour's wife, ... house, his field**—An alteration is here made in the words (see Exod. 20), but it is so slight ("wife" being put in the first clause and house in the second) that it would not have been worth while noticing it, except that the interchange proves, contrary to the opinion of some eminent critics, that these two objects are included in one and the same commandment. **22. he added no more**—(Exod. 20:1). The pre-eminence of these ten commandments was shown in God's announcing them directly: other laws and institutions were communicated to the people through the instrumentality of Moses. **23-28. And ... ye came near unto me**—(See on Exod. 20:19). **29. Oh, that there were such an heart in them, that they would fear me**—God can bestow such a heart, and has promised to give it, wherever it is asked (Jer. 32:40). But the wish which is here expressed on the part of God for the piety and steadfast obedience of the Israelites did not relate to them as individuals, so much as a nation, whose religious character and progress would have a mighty influence on the world at large.

CHAPTER 6

Vss. 1-25. MOSES EXHORTS ISRAEL TO HEAR GOD AND TO KEEP HIS COMMANDMENTS. **1. Now these are the commandments, the statutes, and the judgments which the Lord your God commanded to teach you, that ye might do them ... whither ye go to possess it**—The grand design of all the institutions prescribed to Israel was to form a religious people, whose national character should be distinguished by that fear of the Lord their God which would ensure their divine observance of His worship and their steadfast obedience to His will. The basis of their religion was an acknowledgment of the unity of God with the understanding and the love of God in the heart (vss. 4, 5). Compared with the religious creed of all their contemporaries, how sound in principle, how elevated in character, how unlimited in the extent of its moral influence on the heart and habits of the people! Indeed, it is precisely the same basis on which rests the purer and more spiritual form of it which Christianity exhibits (Matt. 22:37; Mark 12:30; Luke 10:27). Moreover, to help in keeping a sense of religion in their minds, it was commanded that its great principles should be carried about with them wherever they went, as well as meet their eyes every time they entered their homes. A further provision was made for the earnest inculcation of them on the minds of the young by a system of parental training, which was designed to associate religion with all the most familiar and oft-recurring scenes of domestic life. It is probable that Moses used the phraseology in the seventh verse merely in a figurative way, to signify assiduous, earnest, and frequent instruction; and perhaps he meant the metaphorical language in the eighth verse to be taken in the same sense also. But as the Israelites interpreted it literally, many writers suppose that a reference was made to a superstitious custom borrowed from the Egyptians, who wore jewels and ornamental trinkets on the forehead and arm, inscribed with certain words and sentences, as amulets to protect them from danger. These, it has been conjectured, Moses intended to supersede by substituting sentences of the law; and so the Hebrews understood him, for they have always considered the wearing of the *Tephilim* or frontlets a permanent obligation. The form was as follows: Four pieces of parchment, inscribed, the first with Exodus 13:2-10; the second with Exodus 13:11-16; the third with Deuteronomy 6:1-8; and the fourth with Deuteronomy 11:18-21, were enclosed in a square case or box of tough skin, on the side of which was placed the Hebrew letter (*shin*), and bound round the forehead with a thong or ribbon. When designed for the arms, those four texts were written on one slip of parchment, which, as well as the ink, was carefully prepared for the purpose. With regard to the other usage supposed to be alluded to, the ancient Egyptians had the lintels and imposts of their doors and gates inscribed with sentences indicative of a favorable omen [WILKINSON]; and this is still the case, for in Egypt and other Mohammedan countries, the front doors of houses—in Cairo, for instance—are painted red, white, and green, bearing conspicuously inscribed upon them such sentences from the Koran, as "God is the Creator," "God is one, and Mohammed is his prophet." Moses designed to turn this ancient and favorite custom to a better account and ordered that, instead of the former superstitious inscriptions, there should be written the words of God, persuading and enjoining the people to hold the laws in perpetual remembrance. **20-25. when thy son asketh thee in time to come, saying**—The directions given for the instruction of their children form only an extension of the preceding counsels.

CHAPTER 7

Vss. 1-26. ALL COMMUNION WITH THE NATIONS FORBIDDEN. **1. the Hittites**—This people were de-

scended from Heth, the second son of Canaan (Gen. 10:15), and occupied the mountainous region about Hebron, in the south of Palestine. **the Girgashites** —supposed by some to be the same as the Gergesenes (Matt. 8:28), who lay to the east of Lake Gennesareth; but they are placed on the west of Jordan (Josh 24:11), and others take them for a branch of the large family of the Hivites, as they are omitted in nine out of ten places where the tribes of Canaan are enumerated; in the tenth they are mentioned, while the Hivites are not. **the Amorites**—descended from the fourth son of Canaan. They occupied, besides their conquest on the Moabite territory, extensive settlements west of the Dead Sea, in the mountains. **the Canaanites**—located in Phoenicia, particularly about Tyre and Sidon, and being sprung from the oldest branch of the family of Canaan, bore his name. **the Perizzites**—i.e., *villagers,* a tribe who were dispersed throughout the country and lived in unwalled towns. **the Hivites**—who dwelt about Ebal and Gerizim, extending towards Hermon. They are supposed to be the same as the Avims. **the Jebusites**—resided about Jerusalem and the adjacent country. **seven nations greater and mightier than thou**—Ten were formerly mentioned (Gen. 15:19-21). But in the lapse of near five hundred years, it cannot be susprising that some of them had been extinguished in the many intestine feuds that prevailed among those warlike tribes. It is more than probable that some, stationed on the east of Jordan, had fallen under the victorious arms of the Israelites. **2-6. thou shalt smite them, and utterly destroy them; thou shalt make no covenant with them**—This relentless doom of extermination which God denounced against those tribes of Canaan cannot be reconciled with the attributes of the divine character, except on the assumption that their gross idolatry and enormous wickedness left no reasonable hope of their repentance and amendment. If they were to be swept away like the antediluvians or the people of Sodom and Gomorrah, as incorrigible sinners who had filled up the measure of their iniquities, it mattered not to them in what way the judgment was inflicted; and God, as the Sovereign Disposer, had a right to employ any instruments that pleased Him for executing His judgments. Some think that they were to be exterminated as unprincipled usurpers of a country which God had assigned to the posterity of Eber and which had been occupied ages before by wandering shepherds of that race, till, on the migration of Jacob's family into Egypt through the pressure of famine, the Canaanites overspread the whole land, though they had no legitimate claim to it, and endeavored to retain possession of it by force. In this view their expulsion was just and proper. The strict prohibition against contracting any alliances with such infamous idolaters was a prudential rule, founded on the experience that "evil communications corrupt good manners," and its importance or necessity was attested by the unhappy examples of Solomon and others in the subsequent history of Israel. **5. thus shall ye deal with them; ye shall destroy their altars, ...**—The removal of the temples, altars, and everything that had been enlisted in the service, or might tend to perpetuate the remembrance, of Canaanite idolatry, was likewise highly expedient for preserving the Israelites from all risk of contamination. It was imitated by the Scottish Reformers, and although many ardent lovers of architecture and the fine arts have anathematized their proceedings as vandalism, yet there was profound wisdom in the favorite maxim of Knox—"pull down the nests, and the rooks will disappear." **6-10. For thou art an holy people unto the Lord thy God**—i.e., set apart to the service of God, or chosen to execute the important purposes of His providence. Their selection to this high destiny was neither on account of their numerical amount (for, till after the death of Joseph, they were but a handful of people); nor because of their extraordinary merits (for they had often pursued a most perverse and unworthy conduct); but it was in consequence of the covenant or promise made with their pious forefathers; and the motives that led to that special act were such as tended not only to vindicate God's wisdom, but to illustrate His glory in diffusing the best and most precious blessings to all mankind. **11-26. Thou shalt therefore keep the commandments, and the statutes, and the judgments, which I command thee this day**—In the covenant into which God entered with Israel, He promised to bestow upon them a variety of blessings so long as they continued obedient to Him as their heavenly King. He pledged His veracity that His infinite perfections would be exerted for this purpose, as well as for delivering them from every evil to which, as a people, they would be exposed. That people accordingly were truly happy as a nation, and found every promise which the faithful God made to them amply fulfilled, so long as they adhered to that obedience which was required of them. See a beautiful illustration of this in Psalm 144:12-15. **15. the evil diseases of Egypt**—(See Exod. 15:26). Besides those with which Pharaoh and his subjects were visited, Egypt has always been dreadfully scourged with diseases. The testimony of Moses is confirmed by the reports of many modern writers, who tell us that, notwithstanding its equal temperature and sereneness, that country has some indigenous maladies which are very malignant, such as ophthalmia, dysentery, smallpox, and the plague. **20. God will send the hornet among them**—(See on Josh. 24:11-13). **22. lest the beasts of the field increase upon thee**—(See on Exod. 23:28-30). The omnipotence of their Almighty Ruler could have given them possession of the promised land at once. But, the unburied corpses of the enemy and the portions of the country that might have been left desolate for a while, would have drawn an influx of dangerous beasts. This evil would be prevented by a progressive conquest and by the use of ordinary means, which God would bless.

CHAPTER 8

Vss. 1-20. AN EXHORTATION TO OBEDIENCE. **1. All the commandments which I command thee this day shall ye observe to do, that ye may live**—In all the wise arrangements of our Creator duty has been made inseparably connected with happiness; and the earnest enforcement of the divine law which Moses was making to the Israelites was in order to secure their being a happy (because a moral and religious) people: a course of prosperity is often called life (Gen. 17:18; Prov. 3:2). **live, and multiply**—This reference to the future increase of their population proves that they were too few to occupy the land fully at first. **2. thou shalt remember all the way which the Lord thy God led thee these forty years in the wilderness**—The recapitulation of all their checkered experience during that long period was designed to awaken lively impressions of the goodness of God. First, Moses showed

them the object of their protracted wanderings and varied hardships. These were trials of their obedience as well as chastisements for sin. Indeed, the discovery of their infidelity, inconstancy, and their rebellions and perverseness which this varied discipline brought to light, was of eminently practical use to the Israelites themselves, as it has been to the church in all subsequent ages. Next, he enlarged on the goodness of God to them, while reduced to the last extremities of despair, in the miraculous provision which, without anxiety or labor, was made for their daily support (see on Exod. 16:12). Possessing no nutritious properties inherent in it, this contributed to their sustenance, as indeed all food does (Matt. 4:4) solely through the ordinance and blessing of God. This remark is applicable to the means of spiritual as well as natural life. **4. Thy raiment waxed not old upon thee, neither did thy foot swell, these forty years**—What a striking miracle was this! No doubt the Israelites might have brought from Egypt more clothes than they wore at their outset; they might also have obtained supplies of various articles of food and raiment in barter with the neighboring tribes for the fleeces and skins of their sheep and goats; and in furnishing them with such opportunities the care of Providence appeared. But the strong and pointed terms which Moses here uses (see also ch. 29:5) indicate a special or miraculous interposition of their loving Guardian in preserving them amid the wear and tear of their nomadic life in the desert. Thirdly, Moses expatiated on the goodness of the promised land. **7. For the Lord thy God bringeth thee into a good land**—All accounts, ancient and modern, concur in bearing testimony to the natural beauty and fertility of Palestine, and its great capabilities if properly cultivated. **a land of brooks of water, of fountains and depths that spring out of valleys and hills**—These characteristic features are mentioned first, as they would be most striking; and all travellers describe how delightful and cheerful it is, after passing through the barren and thirsty desert, to be among running brooks and swelling hills and verdant valleys. It is observable that water is mentioned as the chief source of its ancient fertility. **8. A land of wheat, and barley**—These cereal fruits were specially promised to the Israelites in the event of their faithful allegiance to the covenant of God (Ps. 81:16; 147:14). The wheat and barley were so abundant as to yield sixty and often an hundredfold (Gen. 26:12; Matt. 13:8). **vines, and fig trees, and pomegranates**—The limestone rocks and abrupt valleys were entirely covered, as traces of them still show, with plantations of figs, vines, and olive trees. Though in a southern latitude, its mountainous formations tempered the excessive heat, and hence, figs, pomegranates, etc., were produced in Palestine equally with wheat and barley, the produce of northern regions. **honey**—The word honey is used often in a loose, indeterminate sense, very frequently to signify a syrup of dates or of grapes, which under the name of *dibs* is much used by all classes, wherever vineyards are found, as a condiment to their food. It resembles thin molasses, but is more pleasant to the taste [ROBINSON]. This is esteemed a great delicacy in the East, and it was produced abundantly in Palestine. **9. a land whose stones are iron**—The abundance of this metal in Palestine, especially among the mountains of Lebanon, those of Kesraoun, and elsewhere, is attested not only by Josephus, but by Volney, Buckingham, and other travellers. **brass**—not the alloy brass, but the ore of copper. Although the mines may now be exhausted or neglected, they yielded plenty of those metals anciently (I Chron. 22:3; 29:2-7; Isa. 60:17). **11-20. Beware that thou forget not the Lord**—After mentioning those instances of the divine goodness, Moses founded on them an argument for their future obedience. **15. Who led thee through that great and terrible wilderness, wherein were fiery serpents, and scorpions**—Large and venomous reptiles are found in great numbers there still, particularly in autumn. Travelers must use great caution in arranging their tents and beds at night; even during the day the legs not only of men, but of the animals they ride, are liable to be bitten. **who brought thee forth water out of the flinty rock**—(See on chap. 9:21).

CHAPTER 9

Vss. 1-25. MOSES DISSUADES THEM FROM THE OPINION OF THEIR OWN RIGHTEOUSNESS. **1. this day**—means *this time*. The Israelites had reached the confines of the promised land, but were obliged, to their great mortification, to return. But now they certainly were to enter it. No obstacle could prevent their possession; neither the fortified defenses of the towns, for the resistance of the gigantic inhabitants of whom they had received from the spies so formidable a description. **cities great and fenced up to heaven**—Oriental cities generally cover a much greater space than those in Europe; for the houses often stand apart with gardens and fields intervening. They are almost all surrounded with walls built of burnt or sun-dried bricks, about forty feet in height. All classes in the East, but especially the nomad tribes, in their ignorance of engineering and artillery, would have abandoned in despair the idea of an assault on a walled town, which today need to be demolished in a few hours. **4. Speak not thou in thine heart, ... saying, For my righteousness the Lord hath brought me in to possess this land**—Moses takes special care to guard his countrymen against the vanity of supposing that their own merits had procured them the distinguished privilege. The Canaanites were a hopelessly corrupt race, and deserved extermination; but history relates many remarkable instances in which God punished corrupt and guilty nations by the instrumentality of other people as bad as themselves. It was not for the sake of the Israelites, but for His own sake, for the promise made to their pious ancestors, and in furtherance of high and comprehensive purposes of good to the world, that God was about to give them a grant of Canaan. **7. Remember, and forget not, how thou provokedst the Lord**—To dislodge from their minds any presumptuous idea of their own righteousness, Moses rehearses their acts of disobedience and rebellion committed so frequently, and in circumstances of the most awful and impressive solemnity, that they had forfeited all claims to the favor of God. The candor and boldness with which he gave, and the patient submission with which the people bore, his recital of charges so discreditable to their national character, has often been appealed to as among the many evidences of the truth of this history. **8. Also in Horeb**—rather, even in Horeb, where it might have been expected they would have acted otherwise. **12-29. Arise, get thee down quickly from hence: for the people ... have corrupted themselves**—With a view to humble them effectually, Moses proceeds to particularize some of the most

atrocious instances of their infidelity. He begins with the impiety of the golden calf—an impiety which, while their miraculous emancipation from Egypt, the most stupendous displays of the Divine Majesty that were exhibited on the adjoining mount, and the recent ratification of the covenant by which they engaged to act as the people of God, were fresh in memory, indicated a degree of inconstancy or debasement almost incredible. **17. I took the two tables, ... and broke them before your eyes**—not in the heat of intemperate passion, but in righteous indignation, from zeal to vindicate the unsullied honor of God, and by the suggestion of His Spirit to intimate that the covenant had been broken, and the people excluded from the divine favor. **18. I fell down before the Lord**—The sudden and painful reaction which this scene of pagan revelry produced on the mind of the pious and patriotic leader can be more easily imagined than described. Great and public sins call for seasons of extraordinary humiliation, and in his deep affliction for the awful apostasy, he seems to have held a miraculous fast as long as before. **20. The Lord was very angry with Aaron to have destroyed him**—By allowing himself to be overborne by the tide of popular clamor, Aaron became a partaker in the guilt of idolatry and would have suffered the penalty of his sinful compliance, had not the earnest intercession of Moses on his behalf prevailed. **21. I cast the dust thereof into the brook that descended out of the mount**—i.e., the smitten rock (El Leja) which was probably contiguous to, or a part of, Sinai. It is too seldom borne in mind that though the Israelites were supplied with water from this rock when they were stationed at Rephidim (Wady Feiran), there is nothing in the Scripture narrative which should lead us to suppose that the rock was in the immediate neighborhood of that place (see on Exod. 17:5, 6). The water on this smitten rock was probably the brook that descended from the mount. The water may have flowed at the distance of many miles from the rock, as the winter torrents do now through the wadies of Arabia Petræa (Ps. 78:15, 16). And the rock may have been smitten at such a height, and at a spot bearing such a relation to the Sinaitic valleys, as to furnish in this way supplies of water to the Israelites during the journey from Horeb by the way of mount Seir and Kadesh-barnea (ch. 1:1, 2). On this supposition new light is, perhaps, cast on the figurative language of the apostle, when he speaks of "the rock following" the Israelites (I Cor. 10:4) [WILSON'S LAND OF THE BIBLE]. **25. Thus I fell down before the Lord forty days and forty nights, as I fell down at the first**—After the enumeration of various acts of rebellion, he had mentioned the outbreak at Kadesh-barnea, which, on a superficial reading of this verse, would seem to have led Moses to a third and protracted season of humiliation. But on a comparison of this passage with Numbers 14:5, the subject and language of this prayer show that only the second act of intercession (vs. 18) is now described in fuller detail.

CHAPTER 10

Vss. 1-22. GOD'S MERCY IN RESTORING THE TWO TABLES. **1. At that time the Lord said unto me, Hew thee two tables of stone like unto the first**—It was when God had been pacified through the intercessions of Moses with the people who had so greatly offended Him by the worship of the golden calf. The obedient leader executed the orders he had received as to the preparation both of the hewn stones, and the ark or chest in which those sacred archives were to be laid. **3. I made an ark of shittim wood**—It appears, however, from Exodus 37:1, that the ark was not framed till his return from the mount, or most probably, he gave instructions to Bezaleel, the artist employed on the work, before he ascended the mount,—that, on his descent, it might be finished, and ready to receive the precious deposit. **4, 5. he wrote on the tables, according to the first writing**—i.e., not Moses, who under the divine direction acted as amanuensis, but God Himself who made this inscription a second time with His own hand, to testify the importance He attached to the ten commandments. Different from other stone monuments of antiquity, which were made to stand upright and in the open air, those on which the divine law was engraven were portable, and designed to be kept as a treasure. Josephus says that each of the tables contained five precepts. But the tradition generally received, both among Jewish and Christian writers is, that one table contained four precepts, the other six. **I . . . put the tables in the ark which I had made; there they be, as the Lord commanded me**—Here is another minute, but important circumstance, the public mention of which at the time attests the veracity of the sacred historian. **6-9. the children of Israel took their journey from Beeroth of the children of Jaakan to Mosera**—So sudden a change from a spoken discourse to a historical narrative has greatly puzzled the most eminent biblical scholars, some of whom reject the parenthesis as a manifest interpolation. But it is found in the most ancient Hebrew MSS., and, believing that all contained in this book was given by inspiration and is entitled to profound respect, we must receive it as it stands, although acknowledging our inability to explain the insertion of these encampment details in this place. There is another difficulty in the narrative itself. The stations which the Israelites are said successively to have occupied are enumerated here in a different order from Numbers 33:31. That the names of the stations in both passages are the same there can be no doubt; but, in Numbers, they are probably mentioned in reference to the *first* visit of the Hebrews during the long wandering southwards, before their return to Kadesh the second time; while here they have a reference to the *second* passage of the Israelites, when they again marched south, in order to compass the land of Edom. It is easy to conceive that Mosera (Hor) and the wells of Jaakan might lie in such a direction that a nomadic horde might, in different years, at one time take the former *first* in their way, and at another time the latter [ROBINSON]. **10-22.** Moses here resumes his address, and having made a passing allusion to the principal events in their history, concludes by exhorting them to fear the Lord and serve Him faithfully. **16. Circumcise therefore the foreskin of your heart**—Here he teaches them the true and spiritual meaning of that rite, as was afterwards more strongly urged by Paul (Rom. 2:25, 29), and should be applied by us to our baptism, which is "not the putting away of the filth of the flesh, but the answer of a good conscience toward God."

CHAPTER 11

Vss. 1-32. AN EXHORTATION TO OBEDIENCE. **1. Therefore thou shalt love the Lord thy God, and**

keep his charge—The reason for the frequent repetition of the same or similar counsels is to be traced to the infantine character and state of the church, which required line upon line and precept upon precept. Besides, the Israelites were a headstrong and perverse people, impatient of control, prone to rebellion, and, from their long stay in Egypt, so violently addicted to idolatry, that they ran imminent risk of being seduced by the religion of the country to which they were going, which, in its characteristic features, bore a strong resemblance to that of the country they had left. **2-9. I speak not to your children which have not known . . . But your eyes have seen all the great acts of the Lord which he did**—Moses is here giving a brief summary of the marvels and miracles of awful judgment which God had wrought in effecting their release from the tyranny of Pharaoh, as well as those which had taken place in the wilderness. He knew that he might dwell upon these, for he was addressing many who had been witnesses of those appalling incidents. For it will be remembered that the divine threatening that they should die in the wilderness, and its execution, extended only to males from 20 years and upward, who were able to go forth to war. No males under 20 years of age, no females, and none of the tribe of Levi, were objects of the denunciation (see Num. 14:28-30; 16:49). There might, therefore, have been many thousands of the Israelites at that time of whom Moses could say, "Your eyes have seen all the great acts which He did"; and with regard to those the historic review of Moses was well calculated to stir up their minds to the duty and advantages of obedience. **10-12. For the land, whither thou goest in to possess it, is not as the land of Egypt, from whence ye came out**—The physical features of Palestine present a striking contrast to those of the land of bondage. A widely extending plain forms the cultivated portion of Egypt, and on the greater part of this low and level country rain never falls. This natural want is supplied by the annual overflow of the Nile, and by artificial means from the same source when the river has receded within its customary channel. Close by the bank the process of irrigation is very simple. The cultivator opens a small sluice on the edge of the square bed in which seed has been sown, making drill after drill; and when a sufficient quantity of water has poured in, he shuts it up with his foot. Where the bank is high, the water is drawn up by hydraulic engines, of which there are three kinds used, of different power, according to the subsidence of the stream. The water is distributed in small channels or earthen conduits, simple in construction, worked by the foot, and formed with a mattock by the gardener who directs their course, and which are banked up or opened, as occasion may require, by pressing in the soil with the foot. Thus was the land watered in which the Israelites had dwelt so long. Such vigilance and laborious industry would not be needed in the promised land. Instead of being visited with moisture only at one brief season and left during the rest of the year under a withering blight, every season it would enjoy the benign influences of a genial climate. The hills would attract the frequent clouds, and in the refreshing showers the blessing of God would especially rest upon the land. **A land which the Lord thy God careth for**—i.e., watering it, as it were, with His own hands, without human aid or mechanical means. **14. the first rain and the latter rain**—The early rain commenced in autumn, i.e., chiefly during the months of September and October, while the latter rain fell in the spring of the year, i.e., during the months of March and April. It is true that occasional showers fell all the winter; but, at the autumnal and vernal seasons, they were more frequent, copious, and important; for the early rain was necessary, after a hot and protracted summer, to prepare the soil for receiving the seed; and the latter rain, which shortly preceded the harvest, was of the greatest use in invigorating the languishing powers of vegetation (Jer. 5:24; Amos 4:7; Jas. 5:7). **15-17. I will send grass in thy fields for thy cattle**—Undoubtedly the special blessing of the former and the latter rain was one principal cause of the extraordinary fertility of Canaan in ancient times. That blessing was promised to the Israelites as a temporal reward for their fidelity to the national covenant. It was threatened to be withdrawn on their disobedience or apostasy; and most signally is the execution of that threatening seen in the present sterility of Palestine. Mr. Lowthian, an English farmer, who was struck during his journey from Joppa to Jerusalem by not seeing a blade of grass, where even in the poorest localities of Britain some wild vegetation is found, directed his attention particularly to the subject, and pursued the inquiry during a month's residence in Jerusalem, where he learned that a miserably small quantity of milk is daily sold to the inhabitants at a dear rate, and that chiefly asses' milk. "Most clearly," says he, "did I perceive that the barrenness of large portions of the country was owing to the cessation of the early and latter rain, and that the absence of grass and flowers made it no longer the land (vs. 9) flowing with milk and honey." **18-25. lay up these my words in your heart and in your soul, and bind them**—(See on ch. 6:8). **Every place whereon the soles of your feet shall tread shall be yours**—not as if the Jews should be lords of the world, but of very place within the promised land. It should be granted to them and possessed by them, on conditions of obedience:—**from the wilderness**—the Arabah on the south; **Lebanon**—the northern limit; **Euphrates**—their boundary on the east. Their grant of dominion extended so far, and the right was fulfilled to Solomon. **even unto the uttermost sea**—the Mediterranean. **26-32. Behold, I set before you this day a blessing and a curse**—(See on ch. 27:11).

CHAPTER 12

Vss. 1-15. MONUMENTS OF IDOLATRY TO BE DESTROYED. **1. These are the statutes and judgments which ye shall observe**—Having in the preceding chapter inculcated upon the Israelites the general obligation to fear and love God, Moses here enters into a detail of some special duties they were to practise on their obtaining possession of the promised land. **2. Ye shall utterly destroy all the places, wherein the nations which ye shall possess served their gods**—This divine command was founded on the tendencies of human nature; for to remove out of sight everything that had been associated with idolatry, that it might never be spoken of and no vestige of it remain, was the only effectual way to keep the Israelites from temptations to it. It is observable that Moses does not make any mention of temples, for such buildings were not in existence at that early period. The "places" chosen as the scene of heathen worship were situated either on the summit of a lofty mountain, or on some artificial mound, or in a grove, planted with particular trees,

such as oaks, poplars, and elms (Isa. 57:5-7; Hos. 4:13). The reason for the selection of such sites was both to secure retirement and to direct the attention upward to heaven; and the "place" was nothing else than a consecrated enclosure, or at most, a canopy or screen from the weather. **3. ye shall overthrow their altars**—piles of turf or small stones. **and break their pillars**—Before the art of sculpture was known, the statues of idols were only rude blocks of colored stones. **5. unto the place which the Lord thy God shall choose ... to put his name there ... thou shalt come**—They were forbidden to worship either in the impure superstitious manner of the heathen, or in any of the places frequented by them. A particular place for the general rendezvous of all the tribes would be chosen by God Himself; and the choice of one common place for the solemn rites of religion was an act of divine wisdom, for the security of the true religion. It was admirably calculated to prevent the corruption which would otherwise have crept in from their frequenting groves and high hills—to preserve uniformity of worship and keep alive their faith in Him to whom all their sacrifices pointed. The place was successively Mizpeh, Shiloh, and especially Jerusalem. But in all the references made to it by Moses, the name is never mentioned. This studied silence was maintained partly lest the Canaanites within whose territories it lay might have concentrated their forces to frustrate all hopes of obtaining it; partly lest the desire of possessing a place of such importance might have become a cause of strife or rivalry amongst the Hebrew tribes, as about the appointment to the priesthood (Num. 16). **7. there ye shall eat before the Lord**—of the things mentioned (vs. 6); but of course, none of the parts assigned to the priests before the Lord—in the place where the sanctuary should be established, and in those parts of the Holy City which the people were at liberty to frequent and inhabit. **12. ye shall rejoice before the Lord your God, ye, your sons, and your daughters ...**—Hence it appears that, although males only were commanded to appear before God at the annual solemn feasts (Exod. 23:17), the women were allowed to accompany them (I Sam. 1:3-23). **15. Notwithstanding thou mayest kill and eat flesh in all thy gates**—Every animal designed for food, whether ox, goat, or lamb, was during the abode in the wilderness ordered to be slain as a peace offering at the door of the tabernacle; its blood to be sprinkled, and its fat burnt upon the altar by the priest. The encampment, being then round about the altar, made this practice, appointed to prevent idolatry, easy and practicable. But on the settlement in the promised land, the obligation to slay at the tabernacle was dispensed with. The people were left at liberty to prepare their meat in their cities or homes. **according to the blessing of the Lord thy God which he hath given thee**—The style of living should be accommodated to one's condition and means—profuse and riotous indulgence can never secure the divine blessing. **the unclean and the clean may eat thereof**—The unclean here are those who were under some slight defilement, which, without excluding them from society, yet debarred them from eating any of the sacred meats (Lev. 7:20). They were at liberty freely to partake of common articles of food. **of the roebuck**—the gazelle. **and as of the hart**—The Syrian deer (*Cervus barbatus*) is a species between our red and fallow deer, distinguished by the want of a bis-antler, or second branch on the horns, reckoning from below, and for a spotted livery which is effaced only in the third or fourth year.

16-25. BLOOD PROHIBITED. **ye shall not eat the blood; ye shall pour it upon the earth as water**—The prohibition against eating or drinking blood as an unnatural custom accompanied the announcement of the divine grant of animal flesh for food (Gen. 9:4), and the prohibition was repeatedly renewed by Moses with reference to the great objects of the law (Lev. 17:2), the prevention of idolatry, and the consecration of the sacrificial blood to God. In regard, however, to the blood of animals slain for food, it might be shed without ceremony and poured on the ground as a common thing like water—only for the sake of decency, as well as for preventing all risk of idolatry, it was to be covered over with earth (Lev. 17:13), in opposition to the practice of heathen sportsmen, who left it exposed as an offering to the god of the chase. **22-28. Even as the roebuck and the hart is eaten, so shalt thou eat them**...—Game when procured in the wilderness had not been required to be brought to the door of the tabernacle. The people were now to be as free in the killing of domestic cattle as of wild animals. The permission to hunt and use venison for food was doubtless a great boon to the Israelites, not only in the wilderness, but on their settlement in Canaan, as the mountainous ranges of Lebanon, Carmel, and Gilead, on which deer abounded in vast numbers, would thus furnish them with a plentiful and luxuriant repast.

26-32. HOLY THINGS TO BE EATEN IN THE HOLY PLACE. **Only thy holy things which thou hast**—The tithes mentioned (vs. 17) are not to be considered ordinary tithes, which belonged to the Levites, and of which private Israelites had a right to eat; but they are other extraordinary tithes or gifts, which the people carried to the sanctuary to be presented as peace offerings, and on which, after being offered and the allotted portion given to the priest, they feasted with their families and friends (Lev. 27:30). **29-32. Take heed to thyself that thou be not snared by following them ... saying, How did these nations serve their gods?**—The Israelites, influenced by superstitious fear, too often endeavored to propitiate the deities of Canaan. Their Egyptian education had early impressed that bugbear notion of a set of local deities, who expected their dues of all who came to inhabit the country which they honored with their protection, and severely resented the neglect of payment in all newcomers [WARBURTON]. Taking into consideration the prevalence of this idea among them, we see that against an Egyptian influence was directed the full force of the wholesome caution with which this chapter closes.

CHAPTER 13

Vss. 1-5. ENTICERS TO IDOLATRY TO BE PUT TO DEATH. **1. If there arise among you a prophet**—The special counsels which follow arose out of the general precept contained in the last verse of the preceding chapter; and the purport of them is, that every attempt to seduce others from the course of duty which that divine standard of faith and worship prescribes must not only be strenuously resisted, but the seducer punished by the law of the land. This is exemplified in three cases of enticement to idolatry. **a prophet**—i.e., some notable person laying claim to the character and authority of the prophetic office (Num. 12:6; I Sam. 10:6), performing feats of dexterity or power in support of his pretensions, or even predicting events which occurred as he foretold; as, for instance, an eclipse which a knowledge of natural science might enable him to anticipate (or, as Caiaphas, John 18:14). Should the aim of such a one be to seduce the people from the worship of the true God, he is an impostor and must be put to death. No prodigy, however wonderful, no human authority, however great, should be allowed to shake their belief in the divine character and truth of a religion so solemnly taught and so awfully attested (cf. Gal. 1:8). The modern Jews appeal to this passage as justifying their rejection of Jesus Christ. But He possessed all the characteristics of a true prophet, and He was so far from alienating the people from God and His worship that the grand object of His ministry was to lead to a purer, more spiritual and perfect observance of the law.

6-18. WITHOUT REGARD TO NEARNESS OF RELATION. **6. If thy brother ... entice thee secretly**—This term being applied very loosely in all Eastern countries (Gen. 20:13), other expressions are added to intimate that no degree of kindred, however intimate, should be allowed to screen an enticer to idolatry, to conceal his crime, or protect his person. Piety and duty must overcome affection or compassion, and an accusation must be lodged before a magistrate. **9. thou shalt surely kill him**—not hastily, or in a private manner, but after trial and conviction; and his relative, as informer, was to cast the first stone (see on ch. 17:7; Acts 7:58). It is manifest that what was done in secret could not be legally proved by a single informer; and hence Jewish writers say that spies were set in some private part of the house, to hear the conversation and watch the conduct of a person suspected of idolatrous tendencies. **12-18. Certain men, the children of Belial**—lawless, designing demagogues (Judg. 19:22; I Sam. 1:16; 25:25), who abused their influence to withdraw the inhabitants of the city to idol worship. **14. Then shalt thou inquire**—i.e., the magistrate, to whom it officially belonged to make the necessary investigation. In the event of the report proving true, the most summary proceedings were to be commenced against the apostate inhabitants. The law in this chapter has been represented as stern and sanguinary, but it was in accordance with the national constitution of Israel. God being their King, idolatry was treason, and a city turned to idols put itself into a state, and incurred the punishment, of rebellion. **16. it shall be an heap for ever; it shall not be built again**—Its ruins shall be a permanent monument of the divine justice, and a beacon for the warning and terror of posterity. **17. there shall cleave naught of the cursed thing to thine hand**—No spoil shall be taken from a city thus solemnly devoted to destruction. Every living creature must be put to the sword—everything belonging to it reduced to ashes—that nothing but its infamy may remain.

CHAPTER 14

Vss. 1, 2. GOD'S PEOPLE MUST NOT DISFIGURE THEMSELVES IN MOURNING. **1. ye shall not cut yourselves ... for the dead**—It was a common practice of idolaters, both on ceremonial occasions of their worship (I Kings 18:28), and at funerals (cf. Jer. 16:6; 41:5), to make ghastly incisions on their faces and other parts of their persons with their finger nails or sharp instruments. The making a large bare space between the eyebrows was another heathen custom in honor of the dead (see on Lev. 19:27, 28; 21:5). Such indecorous and degrading usages, being extravagant and unnatural expressions of hopeless sorrow (I Thess. 4:13), were to be carefully avoided by the Israelites, as derogatory to the character, and inconsistent with the position, of those who were the people of God. **3-21. WHAT MAY BE EATEN, AND WHAT NOT. Thou shalt not eat any abominable thing**—i.e., anything forbidden as unclean (see on Lev. 11). Of BEASTS. **4-8. The hart**—(see on ch. 12:15). **fallow deer**—The Hebrew word (*Jachmur*) so rendered, does not represent the fallow deer, which is unknown in Western Asia, but an antelope (*Oryx leucoryx*), called by the Arabs, jazmar. It is of a white color, black at the extremities, and a bright red on the thighs. It was used at Solomon's table. **wild goat** —The word *akko* is different from that commonly used for a wild goat (I Sam. 24:2; Ps. 104:18; Prov. 5:19), and it is supposed to be a goat-deer, having the body of a stag, but the head, horns, and beard of a goat. An animal of this sort is found in the East, and called *Lerwee* [SHAW'S TRAVELS]. **pygarg** —a species of antelope (*Oryx addax*) with white buttocks, wreathed horns two feet in length, and standing about three feet seven inches high at the shoulders. It is common in the tracks which the Israelites had frequented [SHAW]. **wild ox**—supposed to be the *Nubian Oryx*, which differs from the *Oryx leucoryx* (formerly mentioned) by its black color; and it is, moreover, of larger stature and more slender frame, with longer and more curved horns. It is called *Bekkar-El-Wash* by the Arabs. **chamois**—rendered by the Sept. Cameleopard; but, by others who rightly judge it must have been an animal more familiar to the Hebrews, it is thought to be the Kebsch (*Ovis tragelaphus*), rather larger than a common sheep, covered not with wool, but with reddish hair—a Syrian sheep-goat. Of BIRDS. **11-20. Of all clean birds ye shall eat**—(see on Lev. 11:21). **13. glede**—thought to be the same as that rendered "*Kulture*" (Lev. 11:14). **the cuckow**— more probably the sea-gull. **the swan**—rather the goose (MICHAELIS). **gier eagle**—The Hebrew word *Rachemah* is manifestly identical with *Rachamah*, the name which the Arabs give to the common vulture of Western Asia and Egypt. (*Neophron percnopterus.*) **cormorant**—rather the *plungeon;* a seafowl. **the lapwing**—the upupa or hoop: a beautiful bird, but of the most unclean habits. **21. Ye shall not eat of any thing that dieth of itself**—(see on Leviticus 17:15; 22:8). **thou shalt give it unto the stranger that is in thy gates**—not a proselyte, for he, as well as an Israelite, was subject to this law; but a heathen traveller or sojourner. **Thou shalt not seethe a kid in his mother's milk**—This is the third place in which the prohibition is repeated. It was pointed against an annual pagan ceremony (see on Exod. 23:19; 34:26). **22-27. Thou shalt truly tithe all the increase of thy seed**—The dedication of a tenth part of the year's produce in everything was then a religious duty. It was to be brought as an offering to the sanctuary; and, where distance prevented its being taken in kind, it was by this statute convertible into money. **28-29. At the end of three years ... the Levite ... shall come, etc.**— The Levites having no inheritance like the other tribes, the Israelites were not to forget them, but honestly to tithe their increase. Besides the tenth of all the land produce, they had forty-eight cities, with the surrounding grounds, "the best of the land," and a certain proportion of the sacrifices as

their allotted perquisites. They had, therefore, if not an affluent, yet a comfortable and independent, fund for their support.

CHAPTER 15

Vss. 1-11. THE SEVENTH YEAR A YEAR OF RE-LEASE FOR THE POOR. **1. At the end of every seven years**—during the last of the seven, i.e., the sabbatical year (Exod. 21:2; 23:11; Lev. 25:4; Jer. 34:14). **2. Every creditor that lendeth ought unto his neighbour shall release it**—not by an absolute discharge of the debt, but by passing over that year without exacting payment. The relief was temporary and peculiar to that year during which there was a total suspension of agricultural labor. **he shall not exact it ... of his brother**—i.e., an Israelite, so called in opposition to a stranger or foreigner. **because it is called the Lord's release**—The reason for acquitting a debtor at that particular period proceeded from obedience to the command, and a regard for the honor, of God; an acknowledgment of holding their property of Him, and gratitude for His kindness. **3. Of a foreigner thou mayest exact it again**—Admission to all the religious privileges of the Israelites was freely granted to heathen proselytes, though this spiritual incorporation did not always imply an equal participation of civil rights and privileges (Lev. 25:44; Jer. 34:14; cf. I Chron. 22:2; II Chron. 2:17). **4. Save when there shall be no poor man among you**—Apparently a qualifying clause added to limit the application of the foregoing statement; so that "the brother" to be released pointed to a poor borrower, whereas it is implied that if he were rich, the restoration of the loan might be demanded even during that year. But the words may properly be rendered (as on marg.) to the *end, in order that there may be no poor among you*—i.e., that none be reduced to inconvenient straits and poverty by unseasonable exaction of debts at a time when there was no labor and no produce, and that all may enjoy comfort and prosperity, which will be the case through the special blessing of God on the land, provided they are obedient. **7-11. If there be among you a poor man ... thou shalt not harden thine heart**—Lest the foregoing law should prevent the Israelites lending to the poor, Moses here admonishes them against so mean and selfish a spirit and exhorts them to give in a liberal spirit of charity and kindness, which will secure the divine blessing (Rom. 12:8; II Cor. 9:7). **11. For the poor shall never cease out of the land**— Although every Israelite on the conquest of Canaan became the owner of property, yet in the providence of God who foresaw the event, it was permitted, partly as a punishment of disobedience and partly for the exercise of benevolent and charitable feelings, that "the poor should never cease out of the land."

12-19. HEBREW SERVANTS' FREEDOM. 12. if thy brother, an Hebrew man, or an Hebrew woman, be sold unto thee—The last extremity of an insolvent debtor, when his house or land was not sufficient to cancel his debt, was to be sold as a slave with his family (Lev. 25:39; II Kings 4:1; Neh. 5:1-13; Job 24:9; Matt. 18:25). The term of servitude could not last beyond six years. They obtained their freedom either after six years from the time of their sale or before the end of the seventh year. At the year of jubilee, such slaves were emancipated even if their six years of service were not completed. **13-15. thou shalt not let him go away empty**—A seasonable and wise provision for enabling a poor unfortunate to regain his original status in society, and the motive urged for his kindness and humanity to the Hebrew slave was the remembrance that the whole nation was once a degraded and persecuted band of helots in Egypt. Thus, kindness towards their slaves, unparalleled elsewhere in those days, was inculcated by the Mosaic law; and in all their conduct towards persons in that reduced condition, leniency and gentleness were enforced by an appeal which no Israelite could resist. **16, 17. if he say unto thee, I will not go away from thee**—If they declined to avail themselves of the privilege of release and chose to remain with their master, then by a peculiar form of ceremony they became a party to the transaction, voluntarily sold themselves to their employer, and continued in his service till death. **18. he hath been worth a double hired servant to thee**—i.e., he is entitled to double wages because his service was more advantageous to you, being both without wages and for a length of time, whereas hired servants were engaged yearly (Lev. 25:53), or at most for three years (Isa. 16:14). **19. All the firstling males of thy herd and of thy flock thou shalt sanctify unto the Lord thy God**—(See on Exod. 22:30). **thou shalt do not work with the firstling of thy bullock**—i.e., the second firstlings (see on ch. 12:17, 18; 14:23).

CHAPTER 16

Vss. 1-22. The Feast of the Passover. **1. Observe the month of Abib**—or first-fruits. It comprehended the latter part of our March and the beginning of April. Green ears of the barley, which were then full, were offered as first fruits, on the second day of the passover. **for in the month of Abib the Lord thy God brought thee out of Egypt by night**—This statement is apparently at variance with the prohibition (Exod. 12:22) as well as with the recorded fact that their departure took place in the *morning* (Exod. 13:3; Num. 33:3). But it is susceptible of easy reconciliation. Pharaoh's permission, the first step of emancipation, was extorted during the night, the preparations for departure commenced, the rendezvous at Rameses made, and the march entered on in the morning. **2. Thou shalt therefore sacrifice the passover**—not the paschal lamb, which was strictly and properly the passover. The whole solemnity is here meant, as is evident from the mention of the additional victims that required to be offered on the subsequent days of the feast (Num. 28:18, 19; II Chron. 35:8, 9), and from the allusion to the continued use of unleavened bread for seven days, whereas the passover itself was to be eaten at once. The words before us are equivalent to "thou shalt observe the feast of the passover." **3. seven days shalt thou eat unleavened bread**—a sour, unpleasant, unwholesome kind of bread, designed to be a memorial of their Egyptian misery and of the haste with which they departed, not allowing time for their morning dough to ferment. **5, 6. Thou mayest not sacrifice the passover within any of thy gates**—The passover was to be observed nowhere but in the court of the tabernacle or temple, as it was not a religious feast or sacramental occasion merely, but an actual sacrifice (Exod. 12:27; 23:18; 34:25). The blood had to be sprinkled on the altar and in the place where the true Passover was afterwards to be sacrificed for us at even, at the going down of the sun—lit., be-

tween the evenings. **at the season**—i.e., the month and day, though not perhaps the precise hour. The immense number of victims that had to be immolated on the eve of the passover—i.e., within a space of four hours—has appeared to some writers a great difficulty. But the large number of officiating priests, their dexterity and skill in the preparation of the sacrifices, the wide range of the court, the extraordinary dimensions of the altar of burnt offering and orderly method of conducting the solemn ceremonial, rendered it easy to do that in a few hours, which would otherwise have required as many days. **7. thou shalt roast and eat it**—(See on Exod. 12:8; cf. II Chron. 35:13). **thou shalt turn in the morning, and go unto thy tents**—The sense of this passage, on the first glance of the words, seems to point to the morning after the first day—the passover eve. Perhaps, however, the divinely appointed duration of this feast, the solemn character and important object, the journey of the people from the distant parts of the land to be present, and the recorded examples of their continuing all the time (II Chron. 30:21), (though these may be considered extraordinary, and therefore exceptional occasions), may warrant the conclusion that the leave given to the people to return home was to be on the morning after the completion of the seven days. **9-12. Seven weeks shalt thou number**—The feast of weeks, or a week of weeks: the feast of pentecost (see on Exod. 34:22; Lev. 23:10; Acts 2:1). As on the second day of the passover a sheaf of new barley, reaped on purpose, was offered, so on the second day of pentecost a sheaf of new wheat was presented as first fruits (Exod. 23:16; Num. 28:26), a freewill, spontaneous tribute of gratitude to God for His temporal bounties. This feast was instituted in memory of the giving of the law, that spiritual food by which man's soul is nourished (Deut. 8:3). **13-17. Thou shalt observe the feast of tabernacles seven days**—(See on Exod. 23:16; Lev. 23:34; Num. 29:12). Various conjectures have been formed to account for the appointment of this feast at the conclusion of the whole harvest. Some imagine that it was designed to remind the Israelites of the time when they had no cornfields to reap but were daily supplied with manna; others think that it suited the convenience of the people better than any other period of the year for dwelling in booths; others that it was the time of Moses' second descent from the mount; while a fourth class are of opinion that this feast was fixed to the time of the year when the Word was made flesh and *dwelt*—lit., *tabernacled*—among us (Josh. 1:14), Christ being actually born at that season. **15. in all the works of thine hands . . . repoice**—i.e., praising God with a warm and elevated heart. According to Jewish tradition, no marriages were allowed to be celebrated during these great festivals, that no personal or private rejoicings might be mingled with the demonstrations of public and national gladness. **16. Three times in a year shall all thy males appear before the Lord thy God**—No *command* was laid on women to undertake the journeys, partly from regard to the natural weakness of their sex, and partly to their domestic cares. **18-20. Judges and officers shalt thou make**—These last meant heralds or bailiffs, employed in executing the sentence of their superiors. **in all thy gates**—The gate was the place of public resort among the Israelites and other Eastern people, where business was transacted and cases decided. The Ottoman Porte derived its name from the administration of justice at its gates. **21. Thou shalt not plant thee a grove**—A grove has in

Scripture a variety of significations—a group of overshadowing trees, or a grove adorned with altars dedicated to a particular deity, or a wooden image in a grove (Judg. 6:25; II Kings 23:4-6). They might be placed near the earthen and temporary altars erected in the wilderness, but they could not exist either at the tabernacle or temples. They were places, which, with their usual accompaniments, presented strong allurements to idolatry; and therefore the Israelites were prohibited from planting them. **22. Neither shalt thou set up any image**—erroneously rendered so for "pillar"; pillars of various kinds, and materials of wood or stone were erected in the neighborhood of altars. Sometimes they were conical or oblong, at other times they served as pedestals for the statues of idols. A superstitious reverence was attached to them, and hence they were forbidden.

CHAPTER 17

Vs. 1. Things Sacrificed Must Be Sound. **1. Thou shalt not sacrifice ... any bullock or sheep wherein is blemish**—Under the name of bullock were comprehended bulls, cows, and calves; under that of sheep, rams, lambs, kids, he and she-goats. An ox, from mutilation, was inadmissible. The qualifications required in animals destined for sacrifice are described (Exod. 12:5; Lev. 1:3). 2-7. Idolaters Must Be Slain. **2-7. If there be found among you ... man or woman, that hath wrought wickedness**—The grand object contemplated in choosing Israel was to preserve the knowledge and worship of the one true God; and hence idolatry of any kind, whether of the heavenly bodies or in some grosser form, is called "a transgression of His covenant." No rank or sex could palliate this crime. Every reported case, even a flying rumor of the perpetration of so heinous an offense, was to be judicially examined; and if proved by the testimony of competent witnesses, the offender was to be taken without the gates and stoned to death, the witnesses casting the first stone at him. The object of this special arrangement was partly to deter the witnesses from making a rash accusation by the prominent part they had to act as executioners, and partly to give a public assurance that the crime had met its due punishment. 8-13. The Priests and Judges to Determine Controversies. **8-13. If there arise a matter too hard for thee in judgment**—In all civil or criminal cases, where there was any doubt or difficulty in giving a decision, the local magistrates were to submit them by reference to the tribunal of the Sanhedrim—the supreme council, which was composed partly of civil and partly of ecclesiastical persons. "The priests and Levites," should rather be "the priests—the Levites"; i.e., the Levitical priests, including the high priest, who were members of the legislative assembly; and who, as forming one body, are called "the judge." Their sittings were held in the neighborhood of the sanctuary because in great emergencies the high priest had to consult God by Urim (Num. 27:21). From their judgment there was no appeal; and if a person were so perverse and refractory as to refuse obedience to their sentences, his conduct, as inconsistent with the maintenance of order and good government, was then to be regarded and punished as a capital crime.

14-20. The Election and Duty of a King. **14. When thou ... shalt say, I will set a king over me**—In the following passage Moses *prophetically* announces a revolution which should occur at a later period in the national history of Israel. No sanction or recommendation was indicated; on the contrary, when the popular clamor had effected that constitutional change on the theocracy by the appointment of a king, the divine disapproval was expressed in the most unequivocal terms (I Sam. 8:7). Permission at length was granted, God reserving to Himself the nomination of the family and the person who should be elevated to the regal dignity (I Sam. 9:15; 10:24; 16:12; I Chron. 28:4). In short, Moses foreseeing that his ignorant and fickle countrymen, insensible to their advantages as a peculiar people, would soon wish to change their constitution and be like other nations, provides to a certain extent for such an emergency and lays down the principles on which a king in Israel must act. He was to possess certain indispensable requisites. He was to be an Israelite, of the same race and religion, to preserve the purity of the established worship, as well as be a type of Christ, a spiritual king, one of their brethren. **15. thou mayest not set a stranger over thee, which is not thy brother**—i.e., by their free and voluntary choice. But God, in the retributions of His providence, did allow foreign princes to usurp the dominion (Jer. 38:17; Matt. 22:17). **16. he shall not multiply horses to himself**—The use of these animals was not absolutely prohibited, nor is there any reason to conclude that they might not be employed as part of the state equipage. But the multiplication of horses would inevitably lead to many evils, to increased intercourse with foreign nations, especially with Egypt, to the importation of an animal to which the character of the country was not suited, to the establishment of an Oriental military despotism, to proud and pompous parade in peace, to a dependence upon Egypt in time of war, and a consequent withdrawal of trust and confidence in God. (II Sam. 8:4; I Kings 10:26; II Chron. 1:16; 9:28; Isa. 31:3.) **17. Neither shall he multiply wives to himself, that his heart turn not away**—There were the strongest reasons for recording an express prohibition on this point, founded on the practice of neighboring countries in which polygamy prevailed, and whose kings had numerous harems; besides, the monarch of Israel was to be absolutely independent of the people and had nothing but the divine law to restrain his passions. The mischievous effects resulting from the breach of this condition were exemplified in the history of Solomon and other princes, who, by trampling on the restrictive law, corrupted themselves as well as the nation. **neither shall he greatly multiply ... silver and gold**—i.e., the kings were forbidden to accumulate money for private purposes. **18-20. he shall write him a copy of this law in a book**—The original scroll of the ancient Scriptures was deposited in the sanctuary under the strict custody of the priests (see on ch. 31:26; II Kings 22:8). Each monarch, on his accession, was to be furnished with a true and faithful copy, which he was to keep constantly beside him, and daily peruse it, that his character and sentiments being cast into its sanctifying mould, he might discharge his royal functions in the spirit of faith and piety, of humility and a love or righteousness. **that he may prolong his days in his kingdom, he, and his children**—From this it appears that the crown in Israel was to be hereditary, unless forfeited by personal crime.

CHAPTER 18

Vss. 1-8. The Lord Is the Priests' and the Levites' Inheritance. **1. The priests the Levites ... shall eat the offerings**—As the tribe of Levi had no inheritance allotted them like the other tribes but were wholly consecrated to the priestly office, their maintenance was to arise from tithes, first fruits, and certain portions of the oblations presented on the altar, which God having by express appointment reserved to Himself made over, after being offered, to His ministers. **3 this shall be the priests' due from the people**—All who offered sacrifices of thanksgiving or peace offerings (Lev. 7: 31-33) were ordered to give the breast and shoulder as perquisites to the priests. Here "the two cheeks" or head and "the maw" or stomach, deemed anciently a great dainty, are specified. But whether this is a new injunction, or a repetition of the old with the supplement of more details, it is not easy to determine. **6-8. if a Levite ... come with all the desire of his mind**—It appears that the Levites served in rotation from the earliest times; but, from their great numbers, it was only at infrequent intervals they could be called into actual service. Should any Levite, however, under the influence of eminent piety, resolve to devote himself wholly and continually to the sacred duties of the sanctuary, he was allowed to realize his ardent wishes; and as he was admitted to a share of the work, so also to a share of the remuneration. Though he might have private property, that was to form no ground for withholding or even diminishing his claim to maintenance like the other ministering priests. The reason or principle of the enactment is obvious (I Cor. 9:13). At the same time, while every facility was afforded for the admission of such a zealous and self-denying officer, this admission was to be in an orderly manner: he was to minister "as all his brethren"—i.e., a Gershonite with Gershonites; a Merarite with Merarites; so that there might be no derangement of the established courses.

9-14. The Abominations of the Nations Are to Be Avoided. **9-14. thou shalt not learn to do after the abominations of those nations**—(See on Lev. 18:21; 19:26-31; 20:6). In spite of this express command, the people of Canaan, especially the Philistines, were a constant snare and stumbling block to the Israelites, on account of their divinations and superstitious practices.

15-19. Christ the Prophet Is to Be Heard. **15-19. The Lord thy God will raise up unto thee a prophet**—The insertion of this promise, in connection with the preceding prohibition, might warrant the application (which some make of it) to that order of true prophets whom God commissioned in unbroken succession to instruct, to direct, and warn His people; and in this view the purport of it is, "There is no need to consult with diviners and soothsayers, as I shall afford you the benefit of divinely appointed prophets, for judging of whose credentials a sure criterion is given" (vss. 20-22). But the prophet here promised was pre-eminently the Messiah, for He alone was "like unto Moses (see on ch. 34:10) in His mediatorial character; in the peculiar excellence of His ministry; in the number, variety, and magnitude of His miracles; in His close and familiar communion with God; and in His being the author of a new dispensation of religion." This prediction was fulfilled 1500 years afterwards and was expressly applied to Jesus Christ by Peter (Acts 3:22, 23), and by Stephen (Acts 7:37). **19. whosoever will not hearken unto my words which he shall speak in my name, I will require it of him**—The direful consequences of unbelief in Christ, and disregard of His mission, the Jewish people have been experiencing during 1800 years.

CHAPTER 19

Vss. 1-13. Of the Cities of Refuge. **2. Thou shalt separate three cities in the midst of thy land**—Goelism, or the duty of the nearest kinsmen to avenge the death of a slaughtered relative, being the customary law of that age (as it still is among the Arabs and other people of the East), Moses incorporated it in an improved form with his legislative code. For the protection of the unintentional homicide, he provided certain cities of refuge —three had been destined for this purpose on the east of Jordan (ch. 4:41; Num. 35:11); three were to be invested with the same privilege on the west of that river when Canaan should be conquered. **in the midst of the land**—in such a position that they would be conspicuous and accessible, and equidistant from the extremities of the land and from each other. **3. Thou shalt prepare thee a way**—The roads leading to them were to be kept in good condition and the brooks or rivers to be spanned by good bridges; the width of the roads was to be 32 cubits; and at all the crossroads signposts were to be erected with the words, *Mekeleth, Mekeleth,* "refuge, refuge," painted on them. **divide the coasts of thy land ... into three parts**—the whole extent of the country from the south to the north. The three cities on each side of Jordan were opposite to each other, "as two rows of vines in a vineyard" (see on Josh. 20:7, 8). **6. Lest the avenger of blood pursue the slayer, while his heart is hot**—This verse is a continuation of the third (for vss. 4, 5, which are explanatory, are in a parenthetical form), and the meaning is that if the kinsman of a person inadvertently killed should, under the impulse of sudden excitement and without inquiring into the circumstances, inflict summary vengeance on the homicide, however guiltless, the law tolerated such an act; it was to pass with impunity. But to prevent such precipitate measures, the cities of refuge were established for the reception of the homicide, that "innocent blood might not be shed in thy land" (vs. 10). In the case of premeditated murder (vss. 11, 12), they afforded no immunity; but, if it were only manslaughter, the moment the fugitive was within the gates, he found himself in a safe asylum (Num. 35:26-28; Josh. 20:6). **8, 9. And if the Lord thy God enlarge thy coast**—Three additional sanctuaries were to be established in the event of their territory extending over the country from Hermon and Gilead to the Euphrates. (See on Gen. 15:18; Exod. 23:31.) But it was obscurely hinted that this last provision would never be carried into effect, as the Israelites would not fulfil the conditions, viz., "that of keeping the commandments, to love the Lord, and walk ever in his ways." In point of fact, although that region was brought into subjection by David and Solomon, we do not find that cities of refuge were established; because those sovereigns only made the ancient inhabitants tributary, instead of sending a colony of Israelites to possess it. The privilege of sanctuary cities, however, was given only for Israelites; and besides, that conquered territory did not remain long under the power of the Hebrew kings.

14. The Landmark Is Not to Be Removed. **14. Thou shalt not remove thy neighbour's land-**

mark, which they of old have set in thine inheritance—The state of Palestine in regard to enclosures is very much the same now as it has always been. Though gardens and vineyards are surrounded by dry stone walls or hedges of prickly-pear, the boundaries of arable fields are marked by nothing but by a little trench, a small cairn, or a single erect stone, placed at certain intervals. It is manifest that a dishonest person could easily fill the gutter with earth, or remove these stones a few feet without much risk of detection and so enlarge his own field by a stealthy encroachment on his neighbor's. This law, then, was made to prevent such trespasses.

15. Two WITNESSES REQUIRED. **15. One witness shall not arise against a man for any iniquity**—The following rules to regulate the admission of testimony in public courts are founded on the principles of natural justice. A single witness shall not be admitted to the condemnation of an accused person.

16-21. PUNISHMENT OF A FALSE WITNESS. But if convicted of perjury, it will be sufficient for his own condemnation, and his punishment shall be exactly the same as would have overtaken the object of his malignant prosecution. (See on Exod. 21:24; Lev. 24:20.)

CHAPTER 20

Vss. 1-20. THE PRIESTS' EXHORTATION TO ENCOURAGE THE PEOPLE TO BATTLE. **1. When thou goest out to battle against thine enemies**—In the approaching invasion of Canaan, or in any just and defensive war, the Israelites had reason to expect the presence and favor of God. **2. when ye are come nigh unto the battle, the priest shall approach and speak unto the people**—Jewish writers say that there was a war priest appointed by a special ceremonial to attend the army. It was natural that the solemn objects and motives of religion should have been applied to animate patriotism, and so give additional impulse to valor; other people have done this. But in the case of Israel, the regular attendance of a priest on the battlefield was in accordance with their theocratic government, in which everything was done directly by God through His delegated ministers. It was the province of this priest to sound the trumpets (Num. 10:9; 31:6), and he had others under him who repeated at the head of each battalion the exhortations which he addressed to the warriors in general. The speech (vss. 3, 4) is marked by a brevity and expressiveness admirably suited to the occasion, viz., when the men were drawn up in line. **4. your God is he that goeth with you, to fight for you against your enemies, to save you**—According to Jewish writers, the ark was always taken into the field of combat. But there is no evidence of this in the sacred history; and it must have been a sufficient ground of encouragement to be assured that God was on their side. **5. the officers shall speak unto the people**—lit., *Shoterim,* who are called "scribes" or "overseers" (Exod. 5:6). They might be keepers of the muster-roll, or perhaps rather military heralds, whose duty it was to announce the orders of the generals (II Chron. 26:11). This proclamation (vss. 5, 8) must have been made previous to the priest's address, as great disorder and inconvenience must have been occasioned if the serried ranks were broken by the departure of those to whom the privilege was granted. Four grounds of exemption are expressly mentioned: (1) The dedication of a new house, which, as in all Oriental countries still, was an important event, and celebrated by festive and religious ceremonies (Neh. 12:27); exemption for a year. (2) The planting of a vineyard. The fruit of the first three years being declared unfit for use, and the first fruits producible on the fourth, the exemption in this case lasted at least four years. (3) The betrothal of a wife, which was always a considerable time before marriage. It was deemed a great hardship to leave a house unfinished, a new property half cultivated, and a recently contracted marriage; and the exemptions allowed in these cases were founded on the principle that a man's heart being deeply engrossed by something at a distance, he would not be very enthusiastic in the public service. (4) The ground of exemption was cowardice. From the composition of the Israelitish army, which was an irregular militia, all above twenty years being liable to serve, many totally unfit for war must have been called to the field; and it was therefore a prudential arrangement to rid the army of such unwarlike elements—persons who could render no efficient service, and the contagion of whose craven spirit might lead to panic and defeat. **9. they shall make captains of the armies to lead the people**—When the exempted parties have withdrawn, the combatants shall be ranged in order of battle. **10-20. When thou comest nigh unto a city to fight against it, then proclaim peace unto it**—An important principle is here introduced into the war law of Israel regarding the people they fought against and the cities they besieged. With "the cities of those people which God doth give thee" in Canaan, it was to be a war of utter extermination (vss. 17, 18). But when on a just occasion, they went against other nations, they were first to make a proclamation of peace, which if allowed by a surrender, the people would become dependent, and in the relation of tributaries the conquered nations would receive the highest blessings from alliance with the chosen people; they would be brought to the knowledge of Israel's God and of Israel's worship, as well as a participation of Israel's privileges. But if the besieged city refused to capitulate and be taken, a universal massacre was to be made of the males while the women and children were to be preserved and kindly treated (vss. 13, 14). By this means a provision was made for a friendly and useful connection being established between the captors and the captives; and Israel, even through her conquests, would prove a blessing to the nations. **19. thou shalt not destroy the trees thereof by forcing an axe against them**—In a protracted siege, wood would be required for various purposes, both for military works and for fuel. But fruit-bearing trees were to be carefully spared; and, indeed, in warm countries like India, where the people live much more on fruit than we do, the destruction of a fruit tree is considered a sort of sacrilege. **20. thou shalt build bulwarks against the city that maketh war with thee**—It is evident that some sort of military engines were intended; and accordingly we know, that in Egypt, where the Israelites learned their military tactics, the method of conducting a siege was by throwing up banks, and making advances with movable towers, or with the testudo [WILKINSON].

CHAPTER 21

Vss. 1-9. EXPIATION OF UNCERTAIN MURDER. **1. If one be found slain ... lying in the field, and** it be not known who hath slain him—The ceremonies here ordained to be observed on the discovery of a slaughtered corpse show the ideas of sanctity which the Mosaic law sought to associate with human blood, the horror which murder inspired, as well as the fears that were felt lest God should avenge it on the country at large, and the pollution which the land was supposed to contract from the effusion of innocent, unexpiated blood. According to Jewish writers, the Sanhedrim, taking charge of such a case, sent a deputation to examine the neighborhood. They reported to the nearest town to the spot where the body was found. An order was then issued by their supreme authority to the elders or magistrates of that town, to provide the heifer at the civic expense and go through the appointed ceremonial. The engagement of the public authorities in the work of expiation, the purchase of the victim heifer, the conducting it to a "rough valley" which might be at a considerable distance, and which, as the original implies, was a wady, a perennial stream, in the waters of which the polluting blood would be wiped away from the land, and a desert withal, incapable of cultivation; the washing of the hands, which was an ancient act symbolical of innocence—the whole of the ceremonial was calculated to make a deep impression on the Jewish, as well as on the Oriental, mind generally; to stimulate the activity of the magistrates in the discharge of their official duties; to lead to the discovery of the criminal, and the repression of crime.

10-23. THE TREATMENT OF A CAPTIVE TAKEN TO WIFE. **10-14. When thou goest to war .. and seest among the captives a beautiful woman ... that thou wouldest have her to be thy wife**—According to the war customs of all ancient nations, a female captive became the slave of the victor, who had the sole and unchallengeable control of right to her person. Moses improved this existing usage by special regulations on the subject. He enacted that, in the event that her master was captivated by her beauty and contemplated a marriage with her, a month should be allowed to elapse, during which her perturbed feelings might be calmed, her mind reconciled to her altered condition, and she might bewail the loss of her parents, now to her the same as dead. A month was the usual period of mourning with the Jews, and the circumstances mentioned here were the signs of grief—the shaving of the head, the allowing the nails to grow uncut, the putting off her gorgeous dress in which ladies, on the eve of being captured, arrayed themselves to be the more attractive to their captors. The delay was full of humanity and kindness to the female slave, as well as a prudential measure to try the strength of her master's affections. If his love should afterwards cool and he become indifferent to her person, he was not to lord it over her, neither to sell her in the slave-market, nor retain her in a subordinate condition in his house; but she was to be free to go where her inclinations led her. **15-17. If a man have two wives, one beloved, and another hated**—In the original and all other translations, the words are rendered "have had," referring to events that have already taken place; and that the "had" has, by some mistake, been omitted in our version, seems highly probable from the other verbs being in the past tense—"hers that was hated," not "hers that is hated"; evidently intimating that she (the first wife) was dead at the time referred to. Moses, therefore, does not here legislate upon the case of a man who has two wives at the same time, but on

that of a man who has married twice in succession, the second wife after the decease of the first; and there was an obvious necessity for legislation in these circumstances; for the first wife, who was hated, was dead, and the second wife, the favorite, was alive; and with the feelings of a stepmother, she would urge her husband to make her own son the heir. This case has no bearing upon polygamy, which there is no evidence that the Mosaic code legalized. **18-21. If a man have a stubborn and rebellious son**—A severe law was enacted in this case. But the consent of both parents was required as a prevention of any abuse of it; for it was reasonable to suppose that they would not both agree to a criminal information against their son except from absolute necessity, arising from his inveterate and hopeless wickedness; and, in that view, the law was wise and salutary, as such a person would be a pest and nuisance to society. The punishment was that to which blasphemers were doomed; for parents are considered God's representatives and invested with a portion of his authority over their children. **22, 23. if a man have committed a sin ... and thou hang him on a tree**—Hanging was not a Hebrew form of execution—gibbeting is meant—but the body was not to be left to rot or be a prey to ravenous birds: it was to be buried "that day," either because the stench in a hot climate would corrupt the air, or the spectacle of an exposed corpse bring ceremonial defilement on the land.

CHAPTER 22

Vss. 1-4. OF HUMANITY TOWARD BRETHREN. **1. Thou shalt not see thy brother's ox or his sheep go astray, and hide thyself from them ...**—"Brother" is a term of extensive application, comprehending persons of every description; not a relative, neighbor, or fellow countryman only, but any human being, known or unknown, a foreigner, and even an enemy (Exod. 23:4). The duty inculcated is an act of common justice and charity, which, while it was taught by the law of nature, was more clearly and forcibly enjoined in the law delivered by God to His people. Indifference or dissimulation in the circumstances supposed would not only be cruelty to the dumb animals, but a violation of the common rights of humanity; and therefore the dictates of natural feeling, and still more the authority of the divine law, enjoined that the lost or missing property of another should be taken care of by the finder, till a proper opportunity occurred of restoring it to the owner.

5-12. THE SEX TO BE DISTINGUISHED BY APPAREL. **5. The woman shall not wear that which pertaineth unto a man, neither shall a man put on a woman's garment**—Though disguises were assumed at certain times in heathen temples, it is probable that a reference was made to unbecoming levities practised in common life. They were properly forbidden; for the adoption of the habiliments of the one sex by the other is an outrage on decency, obliterates the distinctions of nature by fostering softness and effeminacy in the man, impudence and boldness in the woman as well as levity and hypocrisy in both; and, in short, it opens the door to an influx of so many evils that all who wear the dress of another sex are pronounced "an abomination unto the Lord." **6, 7. If a bird's nest chance to be before thee**—This is a beautiful instance of the humanizing spirit of the Mosaic law, in checking a tendency to wanton destructiveness and encouraging a spirit of kind and compassionate tenderness to the tiniest creatures. But there was wisdom as well as humanity in the precept; for, as birds are well known to serve important uses in the economy of nature, the extirpation of a species, whether of edible or ravenous birds, must in any country be productive of serious evils. But Palestine, in particular, was situated in a climate which produced poisonous snakes and scorpions; and the deserts and mountains would have been overrun with them as well as immense swarms of flies, locusts, mice, and vermin of various kinds if the birds which fed upon them were extirpated [MICHAELIS]. Accordingly, the counsel given in this passage was wise as well as humane, to leave the hen undisturbed for the propagation of the species, while the taking of the brood occasionally was permitted as a check to too rapid an increase. **8. thou shalt make a battlement for thy roof, that thou bring not blood upon thine house, if any man fall from thence**—The tops of houses in ancient Judea, as in the East still, were flat, being composed of branches or twigs laid across large beams, and covered with a cement of clay or strong plaster. They were surrounded by a parapet breast high. In summer the roof is a favorite resort for coolness, and accidents would frequently happen from persons incautiously approaching the edge and falling into the street or court; hence it was a wise and prudent precaution in the Jewish legislator to provide that a stone balustrade or timber railing round the roof should form an essential part of every new house. **9. Thou shalt not sow thy vineyard with divers seeds**—(See on Lev. 19:19). **10. Thou shalt not plough with an ox and an ass together**—Whether this association, like the mixture of seeds, had been dictated by superstitious motives and the prohibition was symbolical, designed to teach a moral lesson (II Cor. 6:14), may or may not have been the case. But the prohibition prevented a great inhumanity still occasionally practised by the poorer sort in Oriental countries. An ox and ass, being of different species and of very different characters, cannot associate comfortably, nor unite cheerfully in drawing a plough or a wagon. The ass being much smaller and his step shorter, there would be an unequal and irregular draft. Besides, the ass, from feeding on coarse and poisonous weeds, has a fetid breath, which its yoke-fellow seeks to avoid, not only as poisonous and offensive, but producing leanness, or, if long continued, death; and hence, it has been observed always to hold away its head from the ass and to pull only with one shoulder. **11. thou shalt not wear a garment of divers sorts**—The essence of the crime (Zeph. 1:8) consisted, not in wearing a woollen and a linen robe, but in the two stuffs being woven together, according to a favorite superstition of ancient idolaters (see on Lev. 19:19). **12. thou shalt make thee fringes upon the four quarters**—or, according to some eminent biblical interpreters, *tassels on the coverlet of the bed.* The precept is not the same as Num. 15:38. **13-30. If a man take a wife, etc.**—The regulations that follow might be imperatively needful in the *then* situation of the Israelites; and yet, it is not necessary that *we* should curiously and impertinently inquire into them. So far was it from being unworthy of God to leave such things upon record, that the enactments must heighten our admiration of His wisdom and goodness in the management of a people so perverse and so given to irregular passions. Nor is it a better argument that the Scriptures were not written by inspiration of God to

object that this passage, and others of a like nature, tend to corrupt the imagination and will be abused by evil-disposed readers, than it is to say that the sun was not created by God, because its light *may* be abused by wicked men as an assistant in committing crimes which they have meditated [HORNE].

CHAPTER 23

Vss. 1-25. WHO MAY AND WHO MAY NOT ENTER INTO THE CONGREGATION. **1. He that is wounded . . ., shall not enter into the congregation of the Lord**—"To enter into the congregation of the Lord" means either admission to public honors and offices in the Church and State of Israel, or, in the case of foreigners, incorporation with that nation by marriage. The rule was that strangers and foreigners, for fear of friendship or marriage connections with them leading the people into idolatry, were not admissible till their conversion to the Jewish faith. But this passage describes certain limitations of the general rule. The following parties were excluded from the full rights and privileges of citizenship: (1) Eunuchs—It was a very ancient practice for parents in the East by various arts to mutilate their children, with a view to training them for service in the houses of the great. (2) Bastards—such an indelible stigma in both these instances was designed as a discouragement to practices that were disgraceful, but too common from intercourse with foreigners. (3) Ammonites and Moabites—without provocation they had combined to engage a soothsayer to curse the Israelites; and had further endeavored, by ensnaring them into the guilt and licentious abominations of idolatry, to seduce them from their allegiance to God. **3. even to the their tenth generation shall they not enter**—Many eminent writers think that this law of exclusion was applicable only to males; at all events that a definite is used for an indefinite number (Neh. 13:1; Ruth 4:10; II Kings 10:2). Many of the Israelites being established on the east side of Jordan in the immediate neighborhood of those people, God raised this partition wall between them to prevent the consequences of evil communications. More favor was to be shown to Edomites and Egyptians—to the former from their near relationship to Israel; and to the latter, from their early hospitalities to the family of Jacob, as well as the many acts of kindness rendered them by private Egyptians at the Exodus (Exod. 12:36). The grandchildren of Edomite or Egyptian proselytes were declared admissible to the full rights of citizenship as native Israelites; and by this remarkable provision, God taught His people a practical lesson of generosity and gratitude for special deeds of kindness, to the forgetfulness of all the persecution and ill services sustained from those two nations. **9-14. When the host goeth forth against thine enemies, keep thee from every wicked thing**—from the excesses incident to camp life, as well as from habits of personal neglect and impurity. **15, 16. Thou shalt not deliver unto his master the servant which has escaped from his master unto thee**—evidently a servant of the Canaanites or some of the neighboring people, who was driven by tyrannical oppression, or induced, with a view of embracing the true religion, to take refuge in Israel. **19, 20. Thou shalt not lend upon usury to thy brother . . . Unto a stranger thou mayest lend upon usury**—The Israelites lived in a simple state of society, and hence they were encouraged to lend to each other in a friendly way without any hope of gain. But the case was different with foreigners, who, engaged in trade and commerce, borrowed to enlarge their capital, and might reasonably be expected to pay interest on their loans. **21, 22. When thou shalt vow a vow**—(See on Num. 30:2). **24, 25. When thou comest into thy neighbour's vineyard, then thou mayest eat grapes thy fill at thine own pleasure**—Vineyards, like cornfields mentioned in the next verse, were often unenclosed. In vine-growing countries grapes are amazingly cheap; and we need not wonder, therefore, that all within reach of a person's arm, was free; the quantity plucked was a loss never felt by the proprietor, and it was a kindly privilege afforded to the poor and wayfaring man.

CHAPTER 24

Vss. 1-22. OF DIVORCES. **1. When a man hath taken a wife, and married her, and it come to pass that she find no favour in his eyes**—It appears that the practice of divorces was at this early period very prevalent amongst the Israelites, who had in all probability become familiar with it in Egypt [LANE]. The usage, being too deep-rooted to be soon or easily abolished, was tolerated by Moses (Matt. 19:8). But it was accompanied under the law with two conditions, which were calculated greatly to prevent the evils incident to the permitted system; viz.: (1) The act of divorcement was to be certified on a written document, the preparation of which, with legal formality, would afford time for reflection and repentance; and (2) In the event of the divorced wife being married to another husband, she could not, on the termination of that second marriage, be restored to her first husband, however desirous he might be to receive her. **5. When a man hath taken a new wife, he shall not go out to war**—This law of exemption was founded on good policy and was favorable to matrimony, as it afforded a full opportunity for the affections of the newly married pair being more firmly rooted, and it diminished or removed occasions for the divorces just mentioned. **6. No man shall take the nether or the upper millstone to pledge**—The "upper" stone being concave, covers the "nether" like a lid; and it has a small aperture, through which the corn is poured, as well as a handle by which it is turned. The propriety of the law was founded on the custom of grinding corn every morning for daily consumption. If either of the stones, therefore, which composed the handmill was wanting, a person would be deprived of his necessary provision. **7. If a man be found stealing any of his brethren**—(See on Exod. 21:16). **8, 9. Take heed in the plague of leprosy**—(See on Lev. 13:14). **10-13. When thou dost lend thy brother anything, thou shalt not go into his house to fetch his pledge**—The course recommended was, in kind and considerate regard, to spare the borrower's feelings. In the case of a poor man who had pledged his cloak, it was to be restored before night, as the poor in Eastern countries have commonly no other covering for wrapping themselves in when they go to sleep than the garment they have worn during the day. **14, 15. Thou shalt not oppress a hired servant that is poor and needy**—Hired servants in the East are paid at the close of the day; and for a master to defraud the laborer of his hire, or to withhold it wrongfully for a night, might have subjected a poor man with his family to suffering and was therefore an injustice to be avoided (Lev. 19:13). **16-18 The**

fathers shall not be put to death for the children—The rule was addressed for the guidance of magistrates, and it established the equitable principle that none should be responsible for the crimes of others. **19-22. When thou cuttest down thine harvest in thy field**—The grain, pulled up by the roots or cut down with a sickle, was laid in loose sheaves; the fruit of the olive was obtained by striking the branches with long poles; and the grape clusters, severed by a hook, were gathered in the hands of the vintager. Here is a beneficent provision for the poor. Every forgotten sheaf in the harvest field was to lie; the olive tree was not to be beaten a second time; nor were grapes to be gathered, in order that, in collecting what remained, the hearts of the stranger, the fatherless, and the widow might be gladdened by the bounty of Providence.

CHAPTER 25

Vss. 1-19. STRIPES MUST NOT EXCEED FORTY. **2. if the wicked man be worthy to be beaten**—In judicial sentences, which awarded punishment short of capital, scourging, like the Egyptian bastinado, was the most common form in which they were executed. The Mosaic law, however, introduced two important restrictions; viz.: (1) The punishment should be inflicted in presence of the judge instead of being inflicted in private by some heartless official; and (2) The maximum amount of it should be limited to forty stripes, instead of being awarded according to the arbitrary will or passion of the magistrate. The Egyptian, like Turkish and Chinese rulers, often applied the stick till they caused death or lameness for life. Of what the scourge consisted at first we are not informed; but in later times, when the Jews were exceedingly scrupulous in adhering to the letter of the law and, for fear of miscalculation, were desirous of keeping within the prescribed limit, it was formed of three cords, terminating in leathern thongs, and thirteen strokes of this counted as thirty-nine stripes (II Cor. 11:24). **4. Thou shalt not muzzle the ox when he treadeth out the corn**—In Judea, as in modern Syria and Egypt, the larger grains are beaten out by the feet of oxen, which, yoked together, day after day trod round the wide open spaces which form the threshing-floors. The animals were allowed freely to pick up a mouthful, when they chose to do so: a wise as well as humane regulation, introduced by the law of Moses (cf. I Cor. 9:9; I Tim. 5:17, 18). **5-10. the wife of the dead shall not marry without unto a stranger; her husband's brother . . . shall take her to him to wife**—This usage existed before the age of Moses (Gen. 38:8). But the Mosaic law rendered the custom obligatory (Matt. 22:25) on younger brothers, or the nearest kinsman, to marry the widow (Ruth 4:4), by associating the natural desire of perpetuating a brother's name with the preservation of property in the Hebrew families and tribes. If the younger brother declined to comply with the law, the widow brought her claim before the authorities of the place at a public assembly (the gate of the city); and he having declared his refusal, she was ordered to loose the thong of his shoe—a sign of degradation—following up that act by spitting on the ground—the strongest expression of ignominy and contempt among Eastern people. The shoe was kept by the magistrate as an evidence of the transaction, and the parties separated. **13-16. Thou shalt not have . . . divers weights**—Weights were anciently made of stone and are frequently used still by Eastern shopkeepers and traders, who take them out of the bag and put them in the balance. The man who is not cheated by the trader and his bag of divers weights must be blessed with more acuteness than most of his fellows [ROBERTS]. (Cf. Prov. 16:11; 20:10.) **17-19. Remember what Amalek did**—This cold-blooded and dastardly atrocity is not narrated in the previous history (Exod. 17:14). It was an unprovoked outrage on the laws of nature and humanity, as well as a daring defiance of that God who had so signally shown His favor towards Israel.

CHAPTER 26

Vss. 1-15. THE CONFESSION OF HIM THAT OFFERS THE BASKET OF FIRST FRUITS. **2. Thou shalt take of the first of all the fruit of the earth**—The Israelites in Canaan, being God's tenants at will, were required to give Him tribute in the form of first fruits and tithes. No Israelite was at liberty to use any productions of his field until he had presented the required offerings. The tribute began to be exigible after the settlement in the promised land, and it was yearly repeated at one of the great feasts (Lev. 2:14; 23:10; 23:15; Num. 28: 26; ch. 16:9). Every master of a family carried it on his shoulders in a little basket of osier, peeled willow, or palm leaves, and brought it to the sanctuary. **5. thou shalt say . . . , A Syrian ready to perish was my father**—rather, a wandering Syrian. The ancestors of the Hebrews were nomad shepherds, either Syrians by birth as Abraham, or by long residence as Jacob. When they were established as a nation in the possession of the promised land, they were indebted to God's unmerited goodness for their distinguished privileges, and in token of gratitude they brought this basket of first fruits. **11. thou shalt rejoice**—feasting with friends and the Levites, who were invited on such occasions to share in the cheerful festivities that followed oblations (ch. 12:7; 16:10-15). **12-15. When thou hast made an end of tithing all the tithes of thine increase the third year**—Among the Hebrews there were two tithings. The first was appropriated to the Levites (Numbers 18:21). The second, being the tenth of what remained, was brought to Jerusalem in kind; or it was converted into money, and the owner, on arriving in the capital, purchased sheep, bread, and oil (ch. 14:22, 23). This was done for two consecutive years. But this second tithing was eaten at home, and the third year distributed among the poor of the place (ch. 14:28, 29). **13. thou shalt say before the Lord thy God, I have brought away the hallowed things out of mine house**—This was a solemn declaration that nothing which should be devoted to the divine service had been secretly reserved for personal use. **14. I have not eaten thereof in my mourning**—in a season of sorrow, which brought defilement on sacred things; under a pretense of poverty, and grudging to give any away to the poor. **neither . . . for any unclean use**—i.e., any common purpose, different from what God had appointed and which would have been a desecration of it. **nor given aught thereof for the dead**—on any funeral service, or, to an *idol,* which is a dead thing.

CHAPTER 27

Vss. 2-10. THE PEOPLE ARE TO WRITE THE LAW UPON STONES. **2. it shall be on the day when**

ye shall pass over Jordan—"Day" is often put for "time"; and it was not till some days after the passage that the following instructions were acted upon. **thou shalt set thee up great stones, and plaister them with plaister**—These stones were to be taken in their natural state, unhewn, and unpolished—the occasion on which they were used not admitting of long or elaborate preparation; and they were to be daubed over with paint or whitewash, to render them more conspicuous. Stones and even rocks are seen in Egypt and the peninsula of Sinai, containing inscriptions made 3000 years ago, in paint or plaister. By some similar method those stones may have been inscribed, and it is most probable that Moses learned the art from the Egyptians. **3. thou shalt write upon them all the words of this law**—It might be, as some think, the Decalogue; but a greater probability is that it was "the blessings and curses," which comprised in fact an epitome of the law (Josh. 8:34). **5-10. there shalt thou build an altar . . . of whole stones**—The stones were to be in their natural state, as if a chisel would communicate pollution to them. The stony pile was to be so large as to contain all the conditions of the covenant, so elevated as to be visible to the whole congregation of Israel; and the religious ceremonial performed on the occasion was to consist: first, of the elementary worship needed for sinful men; and secondly, of the peace offerings, or lively, social feasts, that were suited to the happy people whose God was the Lord. There were thus, the law which condemned, and the typical expiation—the two great principles of revealed religion.

11-13. THE TRIBES DIVIDED ON GERIZIM AND EBAL. **11-13. These shall stand upon mount Gerizim to bless the people . . . these shall stand upon mount Ebal to curse**—Those long, rocky ridges lay in the province of Samaria, and the peaks referred to were near Shechem (Nablous), rising in steep precipices to the height of about 800 feet and separated by a green, well-watered valley of about 500 yards wide. The people of Israel were here divided into two parts. On mount Gerizim (now Jebel-et-Tur) were stationed the descendants of Rachel and Leah, the two principal wives of Jacob, and to them was assigned the most pleasant and honorable office of pronouncing the benedictions; while on the twin hill of Ebal (now Imad-el-Deen) were placed the posterity of the two secondary wives, Zilpah and Bilhah, with those of Reuben, who had lost the primogeniture, and Zebulun, Leah's youngest son; to them was committed the necessary but painful duty of pronouncing the maledictions (see on Judg. 9:7). The ceremony might have taken place on the lower spurs of the mountains, where they approach more closely to each other; and the course observed was as follows: Amid the silent expectations of the solemn assembly, the priests standing round the ark in the valley below, said aloud, looking to Gerizim, "Blessed is the man that maketh not any graven image," when the people ranged on that hill responded in full simultaneous shouts of "Amen"; then turning round to Ebal, they cried, "Cursed is the man that maketh any graven image"; to which those that covered the ridge answered, "Amen." The same course at every pause was followed with all the blessings and curses (see on Josh. 8:33, 34). These curses attendant on disobedience to the divine will, which had been revealed as a law from heaven, be it observed, are given in the form of a *declaration,* not a *wish,* as the words should be rendered, "Cursed is he," and not, "Cursed be he."

CHAPTER 28

Vss. 1-68. The Blessings for Obedience. **1. if thou shalt hearken diligently unto the voice of the Lord thy God**—In this chapter the blessings and curses are enumerated at length, and in various minute details, so that on the first entrance of the Israelites into the land of promise, their whole destiny was laid before them, as it was to result from their obedience or the contrary. **2. all these blessings shall come on thee**—Their national obedience was to be rewarded by extraordinary and universal prosperity. **7. flee before thee seven ways**—i.e., in various directions, as always happens in a rout. **10. called by the name of the Lord**—They are really and actually His people (ch. 14:1; 26:18). **11. the Lord shall make thee plenteous in goods**—Beside the natural capabilities of Canaan, its extraordinary fruitfulness was traceable to the special blessing of Heaven. **12. The Lord shall open unto thee his good treasure**—The seasonable supply of the early and latter rain was one of the principal means by which their land was so uncommonly fruitful. **thou shalt lend unto many nations, and thou shalt not borrow**—i.e., thou shalt be in such affluent circumstances, as to be capable, out of thy superfluous wealth, to give aid to thy poorer neighbors. **13, 14. the head, and not the tail**—an Oriental form of expression, indicating the possession of independent power and great dignity and acknowledged excellence (Isa. 9:14; 19:15). **15-20. But ... if thou wilt not hearken unto the voice of the Lord**—Curses that were to follow them in the event of disobedience are now enumerated, and they are almost exact counterparts of the blessings which were described in the preceding context as the reward of a faithful adherence to the covenant. **21. pestilence**—some fatal epidemic. There is no reason, however, to think that the plague, which is the great modern scourge of the East, is referred to. **22. a consumption**—a wasting disorder; but the modern tuberculosis is almost unknown in Asia. **fever ... inflammation ... extreme burning**—Fever is rendered "burning ague" (Lev. 26:16), and the others mentioned along with it evidently point to those febrile affections which are of malignant character and great frequency in the East. **the sword**—rather "dryness,"—the effect on the human body of such violent disorders. **blasting, and with mildew**—two atmospheric influences fatal to grain. **23. heaven ... brass ... earth ... iron**—strong Oriental figures used to describe the effects of long-continued drought. This want of regular and seasonable rain is allowed by the most intelligent observers to be one great cause of the present sterility of Palestine. **24. the rain of thy land powder and dust**—an allusion probably to the dreadful effects of tornadoes in the East, which, raising the sands in immense twisted pillars, drive them along with the fury of a tempest. These shifting sands are most destructive to cultivated lands; and in consequence of their encroachments, many once fertile regions of the East are now barren deserts. **27. the botch of Egypt**—a troublesome eruption, marked by red pimples, to which, at the rising of the Nile, the Egyptians are subject. **emerods**—fistulæ or piles. **scab**—scurvy. **itch**—the disease commonly known by that name; but it is far more malignant in the East than is ever witnessed in our part of the world. **28. madness, and blindness, and astonishment of heart**—They would be bewildered and paralyzed with terror at the extent of their calamities. **29-33. thou shalt grope at noonday**—a

general description of the painful uncertainty in which they would live. During the middle ages the Jews were driven from society into hiding-places which they were afraid to leave, not knowing from what quarter they might be assailed and their children dragged into captivity, from which no friend could rescue, and no money ransom them. **35. the Lord shall smite thee in the knees, and in the legs**—This is an exact description of elephantiasis, a horrible disease, something like leprosy, which attacks particularly the lower extremities. **35. The Lord shall smite thee in the knees, and in** shows how widespread would be the national calamity; and at the same time how hopeless, when he who should have been their defender shared the captive fate of his subjects. **there shalt thou serve other gods, wood and stone**—The Hebrew exiles, with some honorable exceptions, were seduced or compelled into idolatry in the Assyrian and Babylonish captivities (Jer. 44:17-19). Thus, the sin to which they had too often betrayed a perverse fondness, a deep-rooted propensity, became their punishment and their misery. **37. thou shalt become an astonishment, a proverb, and a byword among all nations whither the Lord shall ...**—The annals of almost every nation, for eighteen hundred years, afford abundant proofs that this has been, as it still is, the case—the very name of Jew being a universally recognized term for extreme degradation and wretchedness. **49. The Lord shall bring a nation against thee from far**—the invasion of the Romans—"they came from far." The soldiers of the invading army were taken from France, Spain, and Britain—then considered "the end of the earth." Julius Severus, the commander, afterwards Vespasian and Hadrian, left Britain for the scene of contest. Moreover, the ensign on the standards of the Roman army was "an eagle"; and the dialects spoken by the soldiers of the different nations that composed that army were altogether unintelligible to the Jews. **50. A nation of fierce countenance**—a just description of the Romans, who were not only bold and unyielding, but ruthless and implacable. **51. he shall eat the fruit of thy cattle, etc.**—According to the Jewish historian, every district of the country through which they passed was strewn with the wrecks of their devastation. **52. he shall besiege thee ... until thy high and fenced walls come down**—All the fortified places to which the people betook themselves for safety were burnt or demolished, and the walls of Jerusalem itself razed to the ground. **53-57. thou shalt eat the fruit of thine own body**—(See on II Kings 6:29; Lam. 4:10). Such were the dreadful extremities to which the inhabitants during the siege were reduced that many women sustained a wretched existence by eating the flesh of their own children. Parental affection was extinguished, and the nearest relatives were jealously avoided, lest they should discover and demand a share of the revolting viands. **62. ye shall be left few in number**—There has been, ever since the destruction of Jerusalem, only an inconsiderable remnant of Jews existing in that land—aliens in the land of their fathers; and of all classes of the inhabitants they are the most degraded and miserable beings, dependent for their support on contributions from other lands. **63. ye shall be plucked from off the land**—Hadrian issued a proclamation, forbidding any Jews to reside in Judea, or even to approach its confines. **64. the Lord shall scatter thee among all people**—There is, perhaps, not a country in the world where Jews are not to be found. Who that looks on this condition of the

Hebrews is not filled with awe, when he considers the fulfilment of this prophecy? **68. The Lord shall bring thee into Egypt again with ships**—The accomplishment of this prediction took place under Titus, when, according to Josephus, multitudes of Jews were transported in ships to the land of the Nile, and sold as slaves. "Here, then, are instances of prophecies delivered above three thousand years ago; and yet, as we see, being fulfilled in the world at this very time; and what stronger proofs can we desire of the divine legation of Moses? How these instances may affect others I know not; but for myself, I must acknowledge, they not only convince but amaze and astonish me beyond expression; they are truly, as Moses foretold (vss. 45, 46) they would be, 'a sign and a wonder for ever' " [BISHOP NEWTON].

CHAPTER 29

Vss. 1-29. AN EXHORTATION TO OBEDIENCE. **1. These are the words of the covenant**—The discourse of Moses is continued, and the subject of that discourse was Israel's covenant with God, the privileges it conferred, and the obligations it imposed. **beside the covenant which he made with them in Horeb**—It was substantially the same; but it was renewed now, in different circumstances. They had violated its conditions. Moses rehearses these, that they might have a better knowledge of its conditions and be more disposed to comply with them. **2. Moses called unto all Israel, . . . Ye have seen all that the Lord did . . .**—This appeal to the experience of the people, though made generally, was applicable only to that portion of them who had been very young at the period of the Exodus, and who remembered the marvellous transactions that preceded and followed that era. Yet, alas! those wonderful events made no good impression upon them (vs. 4). They were strangers to that grace of wisdom which is liberally given to all who ask it; and their insensibility was all the more inexcusable that so many miracles had been performed which might have led to a certain conviction of the presence and the power of God with them. The preservation of their clothes and shoes, the supply of daily food and fresh water—these continued without interruption or diminution during so many years' sojourn in the desert. They were miracles which unmistakably proclaimed the immediate hand of God and were performed for the express purpose of training them to a practical knowledge of, and habitual confidence in, Him. Their experience of this extraordinary goodness and care, together with their remembrance of the brilliant successes by which, with little exertion or loss on their part, God enabled them to acquire the valuable territory on which they stood, is mentioned again to enforce a faithful adherence to the covenant, as the direct and sure means of obtaining its promised blessings. **10-29. Ye stand this day, all of you, before the Lord**—The whole congregation of Israel, of all ages and conditions, all—young as well as old; menials as well as masters; native Israelites as well as naturalized strangers—all were assembled before the tabernacle to renew the *Sinaitic* covenant. None of them were allowed to consider themselves as exempt from the terms of that national compact, lest any lapsing into idolatry might prove a root of bitterness, spreading its noxious seed and corrupt influence all around (cf. Heb. 12:15). It was of the greatest consequence thus to reach the heart and conscience of everyone, for some might delude themselves with

the vain idea that by taking the oath (vs. 12) by which they engaged themselves in covenant with God, they would surely secure its blessings. Then, even though they would not rigidly adhere to His worship and commands, but would follow the devices and inclinations of their own hearts, yet they would think that He would wink at such liberties and not punish them. It was of the greatest consequence to impress all with the strong and abiding conviction, that while the covenant of grace had special blessings belonging to it, it at the same time had curses in reserve for transgressors, the infliction of which would be as certain, as lasting and severe. This was the advantage contemplated in the law being rehearsed a second time. The picture of a once rich and flourishing region, blasted and doomed in consequence of the sins of its inhabitants, is very striking, and calculated to awaken awe in every reflecting mind. Such is, and long has been, the desolate state of Palestine; and, in looking at its ruined cities, its blasted coast, its naked mountains, its sterile and parched soil—all the sad and unmistakable evidences of a land lying under a curse—numbers of travellers from Europe, America, and the Indies ("strangers from a far country," vs. 22) in the present day see that the Lord has executed His threatening. Who can resist the conclusion that it has been inflicted "because the inhabitants had forsaken the covenant of the Lord God of their fathers, . . . and the anger of the Lord was kindled against this land, to bring upon it all the curses that are written in this book"? **29. The secret things belong unto the Lord**—This verse has no apparent connection with the thread of discourse. It is thought to have been said in answer to the looks of astonishment or the words of inquiry as to whether they would be ever so wicked as to deserve such punishments. The recorded history of God's providential dealings towards Israel presents a wonderful combination of "goodness and severity." There is much of it involved in mystery too profound for our limited capacities to fathom; but, from the comprehensive wisdom displayed in those parts which have been made known to us, we are prepared to enter into the full spirit of the apostle's exclamation, "How unsearchable are his judgments" (Rom. 11:33).

CHAPTER 30

Vss. 1-10. GREAT MERCIES PROMISED UNTO THE PENITENT. **1-3. when all these things are come upon thee, . . . and [thou] shalt return . . . then the Lord thy God will turn thy captivity**—The hopes of the Hebrew people are ardently directed to this promise, and they confidently expect that God, commiserating their forlorn and fallen condition, will yet rescue them from all the evils of their long dispersion. They do not consider the promise as fulfilled by their restoration from the captivity in Babylon, for Israel was not then scattered in the manner here described—"among all the nations," unto the utmost parts of heaven" (vs. 4). When God recalled them from that bondage, all the Israelites were not brought back. They were not multiplied above their fathers (vs. 5), nor were their hearts and those of their children circumcised to love the Lord (vs. 6). It is not, therefore, of the Babylonish captivity that Moses was speaking in this passage; it must be of the dispersed state to which they have been doomed for 1800 years. This prediction may have been partially accomplished on the return of the Israelites from Babylon;

for, according to the structure and design of Scripture prophecy, it may have pointed to several similar eras in their national history; and this view is sanctioned by the prayer of Nehemiah (Neh. 1: 8, 9). But undoubtedly it will receive its full and complete accomplishment in the conversion of the Jews to the Gospel of Christ. At the restoration from the Babylonish captivity, that people were changed in many respects for the better. They were completely weaned from idolatry; and this outward reformation was a prelude to the higher attainments they are destined to reach in the age of Messiah, "when the Lord God will circumcise their hearts and the hearts of their seed to love the Lord." The course pointed out seems clearly to be this: that the hearts of the Hebrew people shall be circumcised (Col. 2:2); in other words, by the combined influences of the Word and spirit of God, their hearts will be touched and purified from all their superstition and unbelief. They will be converted to the faith of Jesus Christ as their Messiah—a spiritual deliverer, and the effect of their conversion will be that they will return and obey the voice (the Gospel, the evangelical law) of the Lord. The words may be interpreted either wholly in a spiritual sense (John 11:51, 52), or, as many think, in a literal sense also (Rom. 11). They will be recalled from all places of the dispersion to their own land and enjoy the highest prosperity. The mercies and favors of a bountiful Providence will not then be abused as formerly (ch. 31:20; 32:15). They will be received in a better spirit and employed to nobler purposes. They will be happy, "for the Lord will again repoice over them for good, as He rejoiced over their fathers."

11-14. THE COMMANDMENT IS MANIFEST. **11-14. For this commandment . . . is not hidden . . . , neither is it far off**—That law of loving and obeying God, which was the subject of Moses' discourse, was well known to the Israelites. They could not plead ignorance of its existence and requirements. It was not concealed as an impenetrable mystery in heaven, for it had been revealed; nor was it carefully withheld from the people as a dangerous discovery; for the youngest and humblest of them were instructed in those truths, which were subjects of earnest study and research among the wisest and greatest of other nations. They were not under a necessity of undertaking long journeys or distant voyages, as many ancient sages did in quest of knowledge. They enjoyed the peculiar privilege of a familiar acquaintance with it. It was with them a subject of common conversation, engraven on their memories, and frequently explained and inculcated on their hearts. The apostle Paul (Rom. 10:6-8) has applied this passage to the Gospel, for the law of Christ is substantially the same as that of Moses, only exhibited more clearly in its spiritual nature and extensive application; and, accompanied with the advantages of Gospel grace, it is practicable and easy.

15-20. DEATH AND LIFE ARE SET BEFORE THE ISRAELITES. **15-20. See, I have set before thee this day, life and good, and death and evil**—the alternative of a good and happy, or a disobedient and miserable life. Love of God and compliance with His will are the only ways of securing the blessings and avoiding the evils described. The choice was left to them, and in urging upon them the inducements to a wise choice, Moses warmed as he proceeded into a tone of solemn and impressive earnestness similar to that of Paul to the elders of Ephesus (Acts 20:26, 27).

CHAPTER 31

Vss. 1-8. MOSES ENCOURAGES THE PEOPLE AND JOSHUA. **1. Moses went and spake**—It is probable that this rehearsal of the law extended over several successive days; and it might be the last and most important day on which the return of Moses to the place of assembly is specially noticed. In drawing his discourse towards a conclusion, he adverted to his advanced age; and although neither his physical nor intellectual powers had suffered any decay (ch. 34:7), yet he knew, by a special revelation, that the time had arrived when he was about to be withdrawn from the superintendence and government of Israel. **2-8. also the Lord hath said**—should be "*for* the Lord hath said" thou shalt not go over this Jordan. While taking a solemn leave of the people, he exhorted them not to be intimidated by the menacing opposition of enemies; to take encouragement from the continued presence of their covenanted God; and to rest assured that the same divine power, which had enabled them to discomfit their first assailants on the east of Jordan, would aid them not less effectually in the adventurous enterprise which they were about to undertake, and by which they would obtain possession of "the land which He had sworn unto their fathers to give them."

9-13. HE DELIVERS THE LAW TO THE PRIESTS, TO READ IT EVERY SEVENTH YEAR TO THE PEOPLE. **9-13. Moses wrote this law, and delivered it unto the priests**—The law thus committed to writing was either the whole book of Deuteronomy, or the important part of it contained between the twenty-seventh and thirtieth chapters. It was usual in cases of public or private contract for two copies of the engagement to be made—one to be deposited in the national archives or some secure place for reference, should occasion require. The other was to remain in the hands of the contracting parties (Jer. 32:12-14). The same course was followed on this renewal of the covenant between God and Israel. Two written copies of the law were prepared, the one of which was delivered to the public representatives of Israel; viz., the priests and the elders. **the priests, . . . who bare the ark of the covenant**—In all ordinary journeys, it was the common duty of the Levites to carry the ark and its furniture (Num. 4: 15); but, on solemn or extraordinary occasions, that office was discharged by the priests (Josh. 3:3-8; 6:6; I Chron. 15:11, 12). **all the elders of Israel**—They were assistants to the priests and overseers to take care of the preservation, rehearsal, and observance of the law. **10, 11. At the end of every seven years, . . . thou shalt read this law**—At the return of the sabbatic year and during the feast of tabernacles, the law was to be publicly read. This order of Moses was a future and prospective arrangement; for the observance of the sabbatic year did not commence till the conquest and peaceful occupation of Canaan. The ordinance served several important purposes. For, while the people had opportunities of being instructed in the law every Sabbath and daily in their own homes, this public periodical rehearsal at meetings in the courts of the sanctuary, where women and children of twelve years were present (as they usually were at the great festivals), was calculated to produce good and pious impressions of divine truth amid the sacred associations of the time and place. Besides, it formed a public guarantee for the preservation, integrity, and faithful transmission of the Sacred Book to successive ages. **14-15. the Lord said** unto Moses, ... call Joshua, and present yourselves in the tabernacle of the congregation—Joshua had been publicly designated to the office of commander by Moses; and God was pleased to confirm his appointment by the visible symbols of His presence and approval. As none but the priests were privileged to enter the sanctuary, it is probable that this significant manifestation of the cloudy pillar was made while the leaders stood at the door of the tabernacle. 16-22. the Lord said unto Moses, ... this people will rise up—In this remarkable interview, Moses was distinctly apprised of the infidelity of Israel, their corruptions of the true religion through intercourse with the idolatrous inhabitants of Canaan (Amos 5:26), and their chastisements in consequence of those national defections. 17. Then my anger shall be kindled, ... and I will hide my face from them—an announcement of the withdrawal of the divine favor and protection of which the Shekinah was the symbol and pledge. It never appeared in the second temple; and its non-appearance was a prelude of "all the evils that came upon them, because their God was not among them." 19. Now therefore write ye this song—National songs take deep hold of the memories and have a powerful influence in stirring the deepest feelings of a people. In accordance with this principle in human nature, a song was ordered to be composed by Moses, doubtless under divine inspiration, which was to be learnt by the Israelites themselves and to be taught to their children in every age, embodying the substance of the preceding addresses, and of a strain well suited to inspire the popular mind with a strong sense of God's favor to their nation. 26. Take this book of the law, and put it in the side of the ark—The second copy of the law (see on vs. 9) was deposited for greater security and reverence in a little chest *beside* the ark of the covenant, for there was nothing contained within it but the tables of stone (I Kings 8:9). Others think it was put *within* the ark, it being certain, from the testimony of Paul (Heb. 9:4), that there were once other things inside the ark, and that this was the copy found in the time of Josiah (II Kings 22:8).

CHAPTER 32

Vss. 1-43. Moses' Song, Which Sets Forth the Perfections of God. 1. Give ear, O ye heavens; ... hear, O earth—The magnificence of the exordium, the grandeur of the theme, the frequent and sudden transitions, the elevated strain of the sentiments and language, entitle this song to be ranked amongst the noblest specimens of poetry to be found in the Scriptures. 2, 3. My doctrine shall drop ...—The language may justly be taken as uttered in the form of a wish or prayer, and the comparison of wholesome instruction to the pure, gentle, and insinuating influence of rain or dew, is frequently made by the sacred writers (Isa. 5:6; 55:10, 11). 4. He is the Rock—a word expressive of power and stability. The application of it in this passage is to declare that God had been true to His covenant with their fathers and them. Nothing that He had promised had failed; so that if their national experience had been painfully checkered by severe and protracted trials, notwithstanding the brightest promises, that result was traceable to their own undutiful and perverse conduct; not to any vacillation or unfaithfulness on the part of God (Jas. 1:17), whose procedure was marked by justice

and judgment, whether they had been exalted to prosperity or plunged into the depths of affliction. 5. They have corrupted themselves—i.e., the Israelites by their frequent lapses and their inveterate attachment to idolatry. their spot is not the spot of his children—This is an allusion to the marks which idolaters inscribe on their foreheads or their arms with paint or other substances, in various colors and forms—straight, oval, or circular, according to the favorite idol of their worship. 6. is not he thy father that hath bought thee—or emancipated thee from Egyptian bondage. and made thee—advanced the nation to unprecedented and peculiar privileges. 8, 9. When the Most High divided to the nations their inheritance—In the division of the earth, which Noah is believed to have made by divine direction (Gen. 10:5; ch. 2:5-9; Acts 17:26, 27), Palestine was reserved by the wisdom and goodness of Heaven for the possession of His peculiar people and the display of the most stupendous wonders. The theater was small, but admirably suited for the convenient observation of the human race—at the junction of the two great continents of Asia and Africa, and almost within sight of Europe. From this spot as from a common center the report of God's wonderful works, the glad tidings of salvation through the obedience and sufferings of His own eternal Son, might be rapidly and easily wafted to every part of the globe. he set the bounds of the people according to the number of the children of Israel—Another rendering, which has received the sanction of eminent scholars, has been proposed as follows: "When the Most High divided to the nations their inheritance, when He separated the sons of Adam and set the bounds of every people, the children of Israel were few in numbers, when the Lord chose that people and made Jacob His inheritance" (cf. ch. 30:5; Gen. 34:30; Ps. 105:9-12). 10. found him in a desert land—took him into a covenant relation at Sinai, or rather "sustained," "provided for him" in a desert land. a waste howling wilderness—a common Oriental expression for a desert infested by wild beasts. 11. As an eagle ... fluttereth over her young—This beautiful and expressive metaphor is founded on the extraordinary care and attachment which the female eagle cherishes for her young. When her newly fledged progeny are sufficiently advanced to soar in their native element, she, in their first attempts at flying, supports them on the tip of her wing, encouraging, directing, and aiding their feeble efforts to longer and sublimer flights. So did God take the most tender and powerful care of His chosen people; He carried them out of Egypt and led them through all the horrors of the wilderness to the promised inheritance. 13, 14. He made him ride on the high places ...—All these expressions seem to have peculiar reference to their home in the transjordanic territory, that being the extent of Palestine that they had seen at the time when Moses is represented as uttering these words. "The high places" and "the fields" are specially applicable to the tablelands of Gilead as are the allusions to the herds and flocks, the honey of the wild bees which hive in the crevices of the rocks, the oil from the olive as it grew singly or in small clumps on the tops of hills where scarcely anything else would grow, the finest wheat (Ps. 81:16; 147:14), and the prolific vintage. 15. But Jeshurun waxed fat, and kicked—This is a poetical name for Israel. The metaphor here used is derived from a pampered animal, which, instead of being tame and gentle, becomes mischievous and vicious, in consequence of good living and kind treatment. So did the Israelites conduct themselves by their various acts of rebellion, murmuring, and idolatrous apostasy. **17. They sacrificed unto devils**—(See on Lev. 17:7). **21. those which are not a people**—i.e., not favored with such great and peculiar privileges as the Israelites (or, rather poor, despised heathens). The language points to the future calling of the Gentiles. **23. I will spend mine arrows upon them**—War, famine, pestilence (Ps. 77:17) are called in Scripture the arrows of the Almighty. **29. Oh, . . . that they would consider their latter end**—The terrible judgments, which, in the event of their continued and incorrigible disobedience, would impart so awful a character to the close of their national history. **32. vine of Sodom . . . grapes of gall**—This fruit, which the Arabs call "Lot's Sea Orange," is of a bright yellow color and grows in clusters of three or four. When mellow, it is tempting in appearance, but on being struck, explodes like a puffball, consisting of skin and fiber only. **44-47. Moses . . . spake all the words of this song in the ears . . .**—It has been beautifully styled "the Song of the Dying Swan" [Lowth]. It was designed to be a national anthem, which it should be the duty and care of magistrates to make well known by frequent repetition, to animate the people to right sentiments towards a steadfast adherence to His service. **48-51. Get thee up . . . and die . . . Because ye trespassed . . . at Meribah**—(See on Num. 20:12). **52. thou shalt see the land, but thou shalt not go thither** —(Num. 27:12). Notwithstanding so severe a disappointment, not a murmur of complaint escapes his lips. He is not only resigned but acquiescing; and in the near prospect of his death, he pours forth the feelings of his devout heart in sublime strains and eloquent blessings.

CHAPTER 33

Vss. 1-28. THE MAJESTY OF GOD. **1. Moses the man of God**—This was a common designation of a prophet (I Sam. 2:27; 9:6), and it is here applied to Moses, when, like Jacob, he was about to deliver ministerially before his death, a prophetic benediction to Israel. **2-4. The Lord came**—Under a beautiful metaphor, borrowed from the dawn and progressive splendor of the sun, the Majesty of God is sublimely described as a divine light which appeared in Sinai and scattered its beams on all the adjoining region in directing Israel's march to Canaan. In these descriptions of a *theophania*, God is represented as coming from the south, and the allusion is in general to the thunderings and lightnings of Sinai; but other mountains in the same direction are mentioned with it. The location of Seir was on the east of the Ghor; mount Paran was either the chain on the west of the Ghor, or rather the mountains on the southern border of the desert towards the peninsula [ROBINSON]. (Cf. Judg. 5:4, 5; Ps. 68:7, 8; Hab. 3:3.) **ten thousands of saints**—rendered by some, "with the ten thousand of Kadesh," or perhaps better still, "from Meribah" [EWALD]. **a fiery law**—so called both because of the thunder and lightning which accompanied its promulgation (Exod. 19:16-18; ch. 4:11), and the fierce, unrelenting curse denounced against the violation of its precepts (II Cor. 3:7-9). Notwithstanding those awe-inspiring symbols of Majesty that were displayed on Sinai, the law was really given in kindness and love (vs. 3), as a means of promoting both the temporal and eternal welfare of the people. And it was "the inheritance of the congregation of Jacob," not only from the hereditary obligation under which that people were laid to observe it, but from its being the grand distinction, the peculiar privilege of the nation. **6. Let Reuben live, and not die**—Although deprived of the honor and privileges of primogeniture, he was still to hold rank as one of the tribes of Israel. He was more numerous than several other tribes (Num. 1:21; 2:11). Yet gradually he sank into a mere nomadic tribe, which had enough to do merely "to live and not die." Many eminent biblical scholars, resting on the most ancient and approved manuscripts of the Septuagint, consider the latter clause as referring to Simeon; "and Simean, let his men be few," a reading of the text which is in harmony with other statements of Scripture respecting this tribe (Num. 25: 6-14; 1:23; 26:14; Josh. 19:1). **7. this is the blessing of Judah**—Its general purport points to the great power and independence of Judah, as well as its taking the lead in all military expeditions. **8-10. of Levi he said**—The burden of this blessing is the appointment of the Levites to the dignified and sacred office of the priesthood (Lev. 10:11; ch. 22:8; 17:8-11), a reward for their zeal in supporting the cause of God, and their unsparing severity in chastising even their nearest and dearest relatives who had participated in the idolatry of the molten calf (Exod. 32:25-28; cf. Mal. 2:4-6). **12. of Benjamin he said**—A distinguishing favor was conferred on this tribe in having its portion assigned near the temple of God. **between his shoulders**—i.e., on his sides or borders. Mount Zion, on which stood the city of Jerusalem, belonged to Judah; but Mount Moriah, the site of the sacred edifice, lay in the confines of Benjamin. **13-17. of Joseph he said**—The territory of this tribe, diversified by hill and dale, wood and water, would be rich in all the productions—olives, grapes, figs, etc., which are reared in a mountainous region, as well as in the grain and herbs that grow in the level fields. "The firstling of the bullock and the horns of the unicorn" (rhinceros), indicate glory and strength, and it is supposed that under these emblems were shadowed forth the triumphs of Joshua and the new kingdom of Jeroboam, both of whom were of Ephraim (cf. Gen. 58:20). **18, 19. Rejoice, Zebulun, in thy going out**—on commercial enterprises and voyages by sea. **and, Issachar in thy tents**—preferring to reside in their maritime towns. **shall suck of the abundance of the seas, and of treasures hid in the sand**—Both tribes should traffic with the Phœnicians in gold and silver, pearl and coral, especially in *murex*, the shellfish that yielded the famous Tyrian dye, and in glass, which was manufactured from the sand of the river Belus, in their immediate neighborhood. **20, 21. of Gad he said**—Its possessions were larger than they would have been had they lain west of Jordan; and this tribe had the honor of being settled by Moses himself in the first portion of land conquered. In the forest region, south of the Jabbok, "he dwelt as a lion" (cf. Gen. 30:11; 49:19). Notwithstanding, they faithfully kept their engagement to join the "heads of the people" in the invasion of Canaan. **22. Dan is a lion's whelp**—His proper settlement in the south of Canaan being too small, he by a sudden and successful irruption, established a colony in the northern extremity of the land. This might well be described as the leap of a young lion from the hills of Bashan. **23. of Naphtali he said**—The pleasant and fertile territory of this tribe lay to "the west," on the borders of lakes Merom and Chinnereth, and to "the south" of the northern Danites.

24, 25. of Asher he said—The condition of this tribe is described as combining all the elements of earthly felicity. **dip his foot in oil**—These words allude either to the process of extracting the oil by foot presses, or to his district as particularly fertile and adapted to the culture of the olive. **shoes of iron and brass**—These shoes suited his rocky coast from Carmel to Sidon. Country people as well as ancient warriors had their lower extremities protected by metallic greaves (I Sam. 17:6; Eph. 6:15) and iron-soled shoes. **26-29. There is none like unto the God of Jeshurun**—The chapter concludes with a congratulatory address to Israel on their peculiar happiness and privilege in having Jehovah for their God and protector. **who rideth upon the heaven in thy help**—an evident allusion to the pillar of cloud and fire, which was both the guide and shelter of Israel. **28. the fountain of Jacob**—The posterity of Israel shall dwell in a blessed and favored land.

CHAPTER 34

Vss. 1-12. Moses from Mount Nebo Views the Land. **1. Moses went up from the plains of Moab**—This chapter appears from internal evidence to have been written subsequently to the death of Moses, and it probably formed, at one time, an introduction to the Book of Joshua. **unto the mountain of Nebo, to the top of Pisgah**—lit., the head or summit of *the Pisgah*,—i.e., the height (cf. Num. 23:14; ch. 3:17-27; 4:49). The general name given to the whole mountain range east of Jordan, was Abarim (cf. ch. 32:49), and the peak to which Moses ascended was dedicated to the heathen Nebo, as Balaam's standing-place had been consecrated to Peor. Some modern travellers have fixed on Jebel-Attarus, a high mountain south of the Jabbok (Zurka), as the Nebo of this passage [BURCKHARDT, SEETZEN, etc.]. But it is situated too far north for a height which, being described as "over against Jericho," must be looked for above the last stage of the Jordan. **the Lord showed him all the land of Gilead**—That pastoral region was discernible at the northern extremity of the mountain-line on which he stood, till it ended, far beyond his sight in Dan. Westward, there were on the horizon, the distant hills of "all Naphtali." Coming nearer, was "the land of Ephraim and Manasseh." Immediately

opposite was "all the land of Judah," a title at first restricted to the portion of this tribe, beyond which were "the utmost sea" (the Mediterranean) and the Desert of the "South." These were the four great marks of the future inheritance of his people, on which the narrative fixes our attention. Immediately below him was "the circle" of the plain of Jericho, with its oasis of palm trees; and far away on his left, the last inhabited spot before the great desert "Zoar." The foreground of the picture alone was clearly discernible. There was no miraculous power of vision imparted to Moses. That he should see all that is described is what any man could do, if he attained sufficient elevation. The atmosphere of the climate is so subtle and free from vapor that the sight is carried to a distance of which the beholder, who judges from the more dense air of Europe, can form no idea [VERE MONRO]. But between him and that "good land," the deep valley of the Jordan intervened; "he was not to go over thither." **5. So Moses ... died**—After having governed the Israelites forty years. **6. he buried him**—or, "he was buried in a valley," i.e., a ravine or gorge of the Pisgah. Some think that he entered a cave and there died, being, according to an ancient tradition of Jews and Christians, buried by angels (Jude 9; Num. 21:20). **6. no man knoweth of his sepulchre unto this day**—This concealment seems to have been owing to a special and wise arrangement of Providence, to prevent its being ranked among "holy places," and made the resort of superstitious pilgrims or idolatrous veneration, in after ages. **8. wept for Moses ... thirty days**—Seven days was the usual period of mourning, but for persons in high rank or official eminence, it was extended to thirty (Gen. 50:3-10; 20:29). **9. Joshua ... was full of the spirit of wisdom**—He was appointed to a peculiar and extraordinary office. He was not the successor of Moses, for he was not a prophet or civil ruler, but the general or leader, called to head the people in the war of invasion and the subsequent allocation of the tribes. **10-12. there arose not a prophet since**—In whatever light we view this extraordinary man, the eulogy pronounced in these inspired words will appear just. No Hebrew prophet or ruler equalled him in character or official dignity, or in knowledge of God's will and opportunities of announcing it.

THE BOOK OF

JOSHUA

CHAPTER 1

Vss. 1-18. The Lord Appoints Joshua to Succeed Moses. **1. Now after the death of Moses**—Joshua, having been already appointed and designated leader of Israel (Num. 27:18-23), in all probability assumed the reins of government *immediately* "after the death of Moses." **the servant of the Lord**—This was the official title of Moses as invested with a special mission to make known the will of God; and it conferred great honor and authority. **the Lord spake unto Joshua**—probably during the period of public mourning, and

either by a direct revelation to the mind of Joshua, or by means of Urim and Thummim (Num. 27:21). This first communication gave a pledge that the divine instructions which, according to the provisions of the theocracy, had been imparted to Moses, would be continued to the new leader, though God might not perhaps speak to him "mouth to mouth" (Num. 12:8). **Joshua**—The original name, Oshea, (Num. 13:8), which had been, according to Eastern usage, changed like those of Abram and Sarai (Gen. 17:5-15) into Jehoshua or Joshua (i.e., "God's salvation") was significant of the services he was to render, and typified those of a greater Saviour (Heb.

4:8). **Moses' minister**—i.e., his official attendant, who, from being constantly employed in important services and early initiated into the principles of the government, would be well trained for undertaking the leadership of Israel. **2-9. now therefore arise, go over this Jordan**—Joshua's mission was that of a military leader. This passage records his call to begin the work, and the address contains a literal repetition of the promise made to Moses (Deut. 11: 24, 25; 31:6-8, 23). **3, 4. Every place that the sole of your foot shall tread upon, that have I given you**—meaning, of course, not universal dominion, but only the territory comprised within the boundaries here specified (see on Deut. 19:8, 9). **all the land of the Hittites**—These occupied the southern extremities and were the dominant tribe of Canaan. Their superior power and the extent of their dominions are attested by the mention of them under the name of Khita, on the Assyrian inscriptions, and still more frequently on the Egyptian inscriptions of the 18th and 19th Dynasties. What life and encouragement must have been imparted to Joshua by the assurance that his people, who had been overwhelmed with fear of that gigantic race, should possess "all the land of the Hittites"! **5-9. There shall not any man be able to stand before thee**—Canaan was theirs by a divine grant; and the renewed confirmation of that grant to Joshua when about to lead the people into it, intimated not only a certain but an easy conquest. It is remarkable, however, that his courage and hope of victory were made to depend (see on Deut. 17:19) on his firm and inflexible adherence to the law of God, not only that regarding the extirpation of the Canaanites, but the whole divine code. **10-18. Then Joshua commanded the officers of the people**—These were the Shoterim (see on Exod. 5:6; Deut. 20:5). **11. command the people, saying, Prepare you victuals**—not manna, which, though it still fell, would not keep; but corn, sheep, and articles of food procurable in the conquered countries. **for within three days ye shall pass over this Jordan**—i.e., the third day according to *Hebrew* idiom)—the time allotted for getting ready before the encampment in Abel-Shittim broke up and they removed to the desert bank of the river where no victuals were available. At the same time Joshua himself convened the two and a half tribes which had settled east of Jordan, to remind them of their promise (Num. 32:1-42) to assist their brethren in the conquest of western Canaan. Their readiness to redeem their pledge and the terms in which they answered the appeal of Joshua displayed to great advantage their patriotic and pious feelings at so interesting a crisis. **14. ye shall pass . . . armed**—i.e., officered or marshalled under five leaders in the old and approved caravan order (see on Exod. 13:18). **all the mighty men of valour**—The words are not to be interpreted strictly as meaning the whole, but only the flower or choice of the fighting men (see on ch. 4:12, 13).

CHAPTER 2

Vss. 1-7. Rahab Receives and Conceals the Two Spies. **1. Joshua . . . sent . . . two men to spy secretly**—Faith is manifested by an active, persevering use of means (Jas. 2:22); and accordingly Joshua, while confident in the accomplishment of the divine promise (ch. 1:3), adopted every precaution which a skilful general could think of to render his first attempt in the invasion of Canaan successful. Two spies were despatched to reconnoitre

the country, particularly in the neighborhood of Jericho; for in the prospect of investing that place, it was desirable to obtain full information as to its site, its approaches, the character, and resources of its inhabitants. This mission required the strictest privacy, and it seems to have been studiously concealed from the knowledge of the Israelites themselves, lest any unfavorable or exaggerated report, publicly circulated, might have dispirited the people, as that of the spies did in the days of Moses. **Jericho**—Some derive this name from a word signifying "*new moon,*" in reference to the crescent-like plain in which it stood, formed by an amphitheater of hills; others from a word signifying "*its scent,*" on account of the fragrance of the balsam and palm trees in which it was embosomed. Its site was long supposed to be represented by the small mudwalled hamlet Er-Riha; but recent researches have fixed on a spot about half an hour's journey westward, where large ruins exist about six or eight miles distant from the Jordan. It was for that age a strongly fortified town, the key of the eastern pass through the deep ravine, now called Wady-Kelt, into the interior of Palestine. **they . . . came into an harlot's house**—Many expositors, desirous of removing the stigma of this name from an ancestress of the Saviour (Matt. 1:5), have called her a hostess or tavern-keeper. But Scriptural usage (Lev. 21:7-14; Deut. 23:18; Judg. 11:1; I Kings 3:16), the authority of the Septuagint, followed by the apostles (Heb. 11:31; Jas. 2:25), and the immemorial style of Eastern khans, which are never kept by women, establish the propriety of the term employed in our version. Her house was probably recommended to the spies by the convenience of its situation, without any knowledge of the character of the inmates. But a divine influence directed them in the choice of that lodging-place. **2, 3. it was told the king**—by the sentinels who at such a time of threatened invasion would be posted on the eastern frontier and whose duty required them to make a strict report to headquarters of the arrival of all strangers. **4-6. the woman took the two men, and hid them**—lit., "him," i.e., each of them in separate places, of course previous to the appearance of the royal messengers and in anticipation of a speedy search after her guests. According to Eastern manners, which pay an almost superstitious respect to a woman's apartment, the royal messengers did not demand admittance to search but asked her to bring the foreigners out. **6. she had brought them up to the roof of the house, and hid them with the stalks of flax**—Flax, with other vegetable productions, is at a certain season spread out on the flat roofs of Eastern houses to be dried in the sun; and, after lying awhile, it is piled up in numerous little stacks, which, from the luxuriant growth of the flax, rise to a height of three or four feet. Behind some of these stacks Rahab concealed the spies. **5. the time of shutting the gates**—The gates of all Oriental cities are closed at sunset, after which there is no possibility either of admission or egress. **the men went out**—This was a palpable deception. But, as lying is a common vice among heathen people, Rahab was probably unconscious of its moral guilt, especially as she resorted to it as a means for screening her guests; and she might deem herself bound to do it by the laws of Eastern hospitality, which make it a point of honor to preserve the greatest enemy, if he has once eaten one's salt. Judged by the divine law, her answer was a sinful expedient; but her infirmity being united with faith, she was graciously pardoned and her service accepted (Jas. 2:25). **7.**

the men pursued after them the way to Jordan unto the fords—That river is crossed at several well-known fords. The first and second immediately below the sea of Galilee; the third and fourth immediately above and below the pilgrims' bathing-place, opposite Jericho. as soon as they which pursued after them were gone, they shut the gate—This precaution was to ensure the capture of the spies, should they have been lurking in the city. 8-21. THE COVENANT BETWEEN HER AND THEM. 8-13. she came up unto them upon the roof and said—Rahab's dialogue is full of interest, as showing the universal panic and consternation of the Canaanites on the one hand (ch. 24:11; Deut. 2:25), and her strong convictions on the other, founded on a knowledge of the divine promise, and the stupendous miracles that had opened the way of the Israelites to the confines of the promised land. She was convinced of the supremacy of Jehovah, and her earnest stipulations for the preservation of her relatives amid the perils of the approaching invasion, attest the sincerity and strength of her faith. 14. the men answered, Our life for yours, if ye utter not this our business—This was a solemn pledge—a virtual oath, though the name of God is not mentioned; and the words "if ye utter not this our business," were added, not as a condition of their fidelity, but as necessary for her safety, which might be endangered if the private agreement was divulged. 15. her house was upon the town wall—In many Oriental cities houses are built on the walls with overhanging windows; in others the town wall forms the back wall of the house, so that the window opens into the country. Rahab's was probably of this latter description, and the cord or rope sufficiently strong to bear the weight of a man. 16-21. she said—rather "she had said," for what follows must have been part of the previous conversation. Get you to the mountain—A range of white limestone hills extends on the north, called Quarantania (now Jebel-karantu), rising to a height of from 1200 to 1500 feet, and the sides of which are perforated with caves. Some one peak adjoining was familiarly known to the inhabitants as "the mountain." The prudence and propriety of the advice to flee in that direction rather than to the ford, were made apparent by the sequel. 21. she bound the scarlet line in the window—probably soon after the departure of the spies. It was not formed, as some suppose, into network, as a lattice, but simply to hang down the wall. Its red color made it conspicuous, and it was thus a sign and pledge of safety to Rahab's house, as the bloody mark on the lintels of the houses of the Israelites in Egypt to that people.

CHAPTER 3

Vss. 1-6. JOSHUA COMES TO JORDAN. 1. Joshua rose early in the morning—On the day following that on which the spies had returned with their encouraging report, the camp was broken up in "Shittim" (the acacia groves), and removed to the eastern bank of the Jordan. The duration of their stay is indicated (vs. 2), being, according to *Hebrew* reckoning, only one entire day, including the evening of arrival and the morning of the passage; and such a time would be absolutely necessary for so motley an assemblage of men, women, and children, with all their gear and cattle to make ready for going into an enemy's country. 2-4. the officers went through the host; And they commanded the people—The instructions given at this time and in

this place were different from those described (ch. 1:11). When ye see the ark..., and the priests of the Levites bearing it...—The usual position of the ark, when at rest, was in the center of the camp; and, during a march, in the middle of the procession. On this occasion it was to occupy the van, and be borne, not by the Kohathite Levites, but the priests, as on all solemn and extraordinary occasions (cf. Num. 4:15; ch. 6:6; I Kings 8:3-6). then ye shall...go after it. Yet there shall be a space between you and it—These instructions refer exclusively to the advance into the river. The distance which the people were to keep in the rear of the ark was nearly a mile. Had they crowded too near the ark, the view would have been intercepted, and this intervening space, therefore, was ordered, that the chest containing the sacred symbols might be distinctly visible to all parts of the camp, and be recognized as their guide in the untrodden way. 5. Joshua said unto the people—rather "had said," for as he speaks of "to-morrow," the address must have been made previous to the day of crossing, and the sanctification was in all probability the same as Moses had commanded before the giving of the law, consisting of an outward cleansing (Exod. 19:10-15) preparatory to that serious and devout state of mind with which so great a manifestation should be witnessed. 6. Joshua spake unto the priests—This order to the priests would be given privately, and involving as it did an important change in the established order of march, it must be considered as announced in the name and by the authority of God. Moreover, as soon as the priests stepped into the waters of Jordan, they were to stand still. The ark was to accomplish what had been done by the rod of Moses.

7, 8. THE LORD ENCOURAGES JOSHUA. 7, 8. the Lord said to Joshua, This day will I...magnify thee in the sight of all Israel—Joshua had already received distinguished honors (Exod. 24:13; Deut. 31:7). But a higher token of the divine favor was now to be publicly bestowed on him, and evidence given in the same unmistakable manner that his mission and authority were from God as was that of Moses (Exod. 14:31).

9-13. JOSHUA ENCOURAGES THE PEOPLE. 9-13. Come hither, and hear the words of the Lord—It seems that the Israelites had no intimation how they were to cross the river till shortly before the event. The premonitory address of Joshua, taken in connection with the miraculous result exactly as he had described it, would tend to increase and confirm their faith in the God of their fathers as not a dull, senseless, inanimate thing like the idols of the nations, but a Being of life, power, and activity to defend them and work for them.

14-17. THE WATERS OF JORDAN ARE DIVIDED. 14. And it came to pass, when the people removed from their tents...—To understand the scene described we must imagine the band of priests with the ark on their shoulders, standing on the depressed edge of the river, while the mass of the people were at a mile's distance. Suddenly the whole bed of the river was dried up; a spectacle the more extraordinary in that it took place in the time of harvest, corresponding to our April or May—when "the Jordan overfloweth all its banks." The original words may be more properly rendered "fills all its banks." Its channel, snow-fed from Lebanon, was at its greatest height—brimful; a translation which gives the only true description of the state of Jordan in harvest as observed by modern travellers. The river about Jericho is, in ordinary appearance, about 50 or 60 yards in breadth. But as seen in harvest, it is twice as broad; and in ancient times, when the hills on the right and left were much more drenched with rain and snow than since the forests have disappeared, the river must, from a greater accession of water, have been broader still than at harvest-time in the present day. **16. the waters which came down from above**—i.e., the Sea of Galilee "stood and rose up in a heap," a firm, compact barrier (Exod. 15:8; Ps. 18:13), "very far," high up the stream; "from the city Adam, that is beside Zaretan," near mount Sartabeh, in the northern part of the Ghor (I Kings 7:46); i.e., a distance of thirty miles from the Israelitish encampment; and "those that came down towards the sea of the desert"—the Dead Sea—failed and were cut off (Ps. 114:2, 3). The river was thus dried up as far as the eye could reach. This was a stupendous miracle; Jordan takes its name, "the Descender," from the force of its current, which, after passing the Sea of Galilee, becomes greatly increased as it plunges through twenty-seven "horrible rapids and cascades," besides a great many lesser through a fall of 1000 feet, averaging from four to five miles an hour [LYNCH]. When swollen "in time of harvest," it flows with a vastly accelerated current. **16. the people passed over right against Jericho**—The exact spot is unknown; but it cannot be that fixed by Greek tradition—the pilgrims' bathing-place—both because it is too much to the north, and the eastern banks are there sheer precipices 10 or 15 feet high. **17. the priests ... and all the Israelites passed over on dry ground**—the river about Jericho has a firm pebbly bottom, on which the host might pass, without inconvenience when the water was cleared off.

CHAPTER 4

Vss. 1-8. TWELVE STONES TAKEN FOR A MEMORIAL OUT OF JORDAN. **1, 2. the Lord spake unto Joshua, Take you twelve men**—each representing a tribe. They had been previously chosen for this service (ch. 3:12), and the repetition of the command is made here solely to introduce the account of its execution. Though Joshua had been divinely instructed to erect a commemorative pile, the representatives were not apprised of the work they were to do till the time of the passage. **4, 5. Joshua called the twelve men**—They had probably, from a feeling of reverence, kept back, and were standing on the eastern bank. They were now ordered to advance. Picking up each a stone, probably as large as he could carry, from around the spot "where the priests stood," they pass over before the ark and deposit the stones in the place of next encampment (vss. 19, 20), viz., Gilgal. **6, 7. That this may be a sign among you**—The erection of cairns, or huge piles of stones, as monuments of remarkable incidents has been common among all people, especially in the early and crude periods of their history. They are the established means of perpetuating the memory of important transactions, especially among the nomadic people of the East. Although there be no inscription engraved on them, the history and object of such simple monuments are traditionally preserved from age to age. Similar was the purpose contemplated by the conveyance of the twelve stones to Gilgal: it was that they might be a standing record to posterity of the miraculous passage of the Jordan. **8. the children of Israel did so as Joshua commanded**—i.e., it was done by their twelve representatives.

9. TWELVE STONES SET UP IN THE MIDST OF JORDAN. **9. Joshua set up twelve stones ... in the place where the feet of the priests ... stood**—In addition to the memorial just described, there was another memento of the miraculous event, a duplicate of the former, set up in the river itself, on the very spot where the ark had rested. This heap of stones might have been a large and compactly built one and visible in the ordinary state of the river. As nothing is said where these stones were obtained, some have imagined that they might have been gathered in the adjoining fields and deposited by the people as they passed the appointed spot. **they are there unto this day**—at least twenty years after the event, if we reckon by the date of this history (ch. 24:26), and much later, if the words in the latter clause were inserted by Samuel or Ezra.

10-13. THE PEOPLE PASS OVER. **10. the priests which bare the ark stood in the midst of Jordan**—This position was well calculated to animate the people, who probably crossed *below* the ark, as well as to facilitate Joshua's execution of the minutest instructions respecting the passage (Num. 27:21-23). The unfaltering confidence of the priests contrasts strikingly with the conduct of the people, who "hasted and passed over." Their faith, like that of many of God's people, was, through the weakness of nature, blended with fears. But perhaps their "haste" may be viewed in a more favorable light, as indicating the alacrity of their obedience, or it might have been enjoined in order that the the whole multitude might pass in one day. **11. the ark of the Lord passed over, and the priests, in the presence of the people**—The ark is mentioned as the efficient cause; it had been the first to move—it was the last to leave; and its movements arrested the deep attention of the people, who probably stood on the opposite bank, wrapt in admiration and awe of this closing scene. It was a great miracle, greater even than the passage of the Red Sea in this respect: that, admitting the fact, there is no possibility of rationalistic insinuations as to the influence of natural causes in producing it, as have been made in the former case. **12, 13. the children of Reuben ... passed over armed before the children of Israel**—There is no precedency to the other tribes indicated here; for there is no reason to suppose that the usual order of march was departed from; but these are honorably mentioned to show that, in pursuance of their promise (ch. 1:16-18), they had sent a complement of fighting men to accompany their brethren in the war of invasion. **to the plains of Jericho**—That part of the Arabah or Ghor, on the west, is about seven miles broad from the Jordan to the mountain entrance at Wady-Kelt. Though now desert, this valley was in ancient times richly covered with wood. An immense palm forest, seven miles long, surrounded Jericho.

14-24. GOD MAGNIFIES JOSHUA. **14-17. On that day the Lord magnified Joshua in the sight of all Israel**—It appeared clear from the chief part he acted, that he was the divinely appointed leader; for even the priests did not enter the river or quit their position, except at his command; and thenceforward his authority was as firmly established as that of his predecessor. **18. it came to pass, when the priests that bare the ark ... were come out of the midst of Jordan ... that the waters of Jordan returned unto their place**—Their crossing, which was the final act, completed the evidence of the miracle; for then, and not till then, the suspended laws of nature were restored, the waters returned to their place, and the river flowed with as full a current as before. **19. the people came out of Jordan on the tenth day of the first month**–i.e., the month Nisan, four days before the passover, and the very day when the paschal lamb required to be set apart, the providence of God having arranged that the entrance into the promised land should be at the feast. **and encamped in Gilgal**–The name is here given by anticipation (see on ch. 5:9). It was a tract of land, according to Josephus, fifty stadia (6½ miles) from Jordan, and ten stadia (1¼ miles) from Jericho, at the eastern outskirts of the palm forest, now supposed to be the spot occupied by the village Riha. **20-24. those twelve stones which they took out of Jordan, did Joshua pitch in Gilgal**–Probably to render them more conspicuous, they might be raised on a foundation of earth or turf. The pile was designed to serve a double purpose–that of impressing the heathen with a sense of the omnipotence of God, while at the same time it would teach an important lesson in religion to the young and rising Israelites in after ages.

CHAPTER 5

Vs. 1. THE CANAANITES AFRAID. **1. the kings of the Amorites, which were on the side of Jordan westward, and all the kings of the Canaanites which were by the sea**–Under the former designation were included the people who inhabited the mountainous region, and under the latter those who were on the seacoast of Palestine. **heard that the Lord had dried up the waters of Jordan . . . that their heart melted**–They had probably reckoned on the swollen river interposing for a time a sure barrier of defense. But seeing it had been completely dried up, they were completely paralyzed by so incontestable a proof that God was on the side of the invaders. In fact, the conquest had already begun in the total prostration of spirit among the native chiefs. "Their heart melted," but unhappily not into faith and penitent submission. 2-12. CIRCUMCISION IS RENEWED. **2. At that time**–on the encampment being made after the passage. **the Lord said unto Joshua, Make thee sharp knives**–Stone knives, collect and make them ready. Flints have been used in the early times of all people; and although the use of iron was known to the Hebrews in the days of Joshua, probably the want of a sufficient number of metallic implements dictated the employment of flints on this occasion (cf. Exod. 4:25). **circumcise again the children of Israel the second time**–lit., return and circumcise. The command did not require him to repeat the operation on those who had undergone it, but to resume the observance of the rite, which had been long discontinued. The language, however, evidently points to a general circumcising on some previous occasion, which, though unrecorded, must have been made before the celebration of the passover at Sinai (cf. Exod. 12:48; Num. 9:5), as a mixed multitude accompanied the camp. "The second time" of general circumcising was at the entrance into Canaan. **3. at the hill**–probably one of the argillaceous hills that form the highest terrace of the Jordan, on a rising ground at the palm forest. **4-7. this is the cause why Joshua did circumcise**–The omission to circumcise the children born in the wilderness might have been owing to the incessant movements of the people; but it is most generally thought that the true cause was a temporary suspension of the covenant with the unbelieving race who, being rejected of the Lord, were doomed to

perish in the wilderness, and whose children had to bear the iniquity of their fathers (Num. 14:33), though, as the latter were to be brought into the promised land, the covenant would be renewed with them. **8. when they had done circumcising all the people**–As the number of those born in the wilderness and uncircumcised must have been immense, a difficulty is apt to be felt how the rite could have been performed on such a multitude in so short a time. But it has been calculated that the proportion between those already circumcised (under twenty when the doom was pronounced) and those to be circumcised, was one to four, and consequently the whole ceremony could easily have been performed in a day. Circumcision being the sign and seal of the covenant, its performance was virtually an investment in the promised land, and its being delayed till their actual entrance into the country was a wise and gracious act on the part of God, who postponed this trying duty till the hearts of the people, animated by the recent astonishing miracle, were prepared to obey the divine will. **they abode in their places . . . till they were whole**–It is calculated that, of those who did not need to be circumcised, more than 50,000 were left to defend the camp if an attack had been then made upon it. **9. the Lord said unto Joshua, This day have I rolled away the reproach of Egypt**–The taunts industriously cast by that people upon Israel as *nationally* rejected by God by the cessation of circumcision and the renewal of that rite was a practical announcement of the restoration of the covenant [KEIL]. *Gilgal*–No trace either of the name or site is now to be found; but it was about two miles from Jericho [JOSEPHUS], and well suited for an encampment by the advantages of shade and water. It was the first place pronounced "holy" in the Holy Land (vs. 15). **10. kept the passover on the fourteenth day of the month at even**–The time fixed by the law (see Exod. 12:18; Lev. 23:5; Num. 28:16). Thus the national existence was commenced by a solemn act of religious dedication. **11, 12. they did eat of the old corn of the land**–found in storehouses of the inhabitants who had fled into Jericho. **parched corn**–new grain (see on Lev. 23:10), probably lying in the fields. This abundance of food led to the discontinuance of the manna; and the fact of its then ceasing, viewed in connection with its seasonable appearance in the barren wilderness, is a striking proof of its miraculous origin. 13-15. AN ANGEL APPEARS TO JOSHUA. **13. when Joshua was by Jericho**–in the immediate vicinity of that city, probably engaged in surveying the fortifications, and in meditating the best plan of a siege. **there stood a man over against him with his sword drawn**–It is evident from the strain of the context that this was not a mere vision, but an actual appearance; the suddenness of which surprised, but did not daunt, the intrepid leader. **14. the host of the Lord**–either the Israelitish people (Exod. 7:4; 12:41; Isa. 55:4), or the angels (Ps. 148:2), or both included, and the Captain of it was the angel of the covenant, whose visible manifestations were varied according to the occasion. His attitude of equipment betokened his approval of, and interest in, the war of invasion. **Joshua fell on his face . . . , and did worship**–The adoption by Joshua of this absolute form of prostration demonstrates the sentiments of profound reverence with which the language and majestic bearing of the stranger inspired him. The real character of this personage was disclosed by His accepting the homage of worship (cf. Acts 10:25, 26; Rev. 19:10), and still further in the command, "Loose thy shoe from off thy foot" (Exod. 3:5).

CHAPTER 6

Vss. 1-7. JERICHO SHUT UP. **1. Now Jericho was straitly shut up**—This verse is a parenthesis introduced to prepare the way for the directions given by the Captain of the Lord's host. **See, I have given into thine hand Jericho**—The language intimates that a purpose already formed was about to be carried into immediate execution; and that, although the king and inhabitants of Jericho were fierce and experienced warriors, who would make a stout and determined resistance, the Lord promised a certain and easy victory over them. **3-5. ye shall compass the city, all ye men of war.... Thus shalt thou do six days...**—Directions are here given as to the mode of procedure. *Heb.*, "horns of jubilee"; i.e., the bent or crooked trumpets with which the jubilee was proclaimed. It is probable that the horns of this animal were used at first; and that afterwards, when metallic trumpets were introduced, the primitive name, as well as form of them, was traditionally continued. The design of this whole proceeding was obviously to impress the Canaanites with a sense of the divine omnipotence, to teach the Israelites a memorable lesson of faith and confidence in God's promises, and to inspire sentiments of respect and reverence for the ark as the symbol of His presence. The length of time during which those circuits were made tended the more intensely to arrest the attention, and to deepen the impressions, both of the Israelites and the enemy. The number seven was among the Israelites the symbolic seal of the covenant between God and their nation [KEIL, HENGSTENBERG]. **6, 7. Joshua...called the priests**—The pious leader, whatever military preparations he had made, surrendered all his own views, at once and unreservedly, to the declared will of God.

8-19. THE CITY COMPASSED SIX DAYS. **8-11. the seven priests bearing the seven trumpets... passed on before the Lord**—before the ark, called "the ark of the covenant," for it contained the tables on which the covenant was inscribed. The procession was made in deep and solemn silence, conforming to the instructions given to the people by their leader at the outset, that they were to refrain from all acclamation and noise of any kind until he should give them a signal. It must have been a strange sight; no mound was raised, no sword drawn, no engine planted, no pioneers undermining —here were armed men, but no stroke given; they must walk and not fight. Doubtless the people of Jericho made themselves merry with the spectacle [BISHOP HALL]. **12-14. Joshua rose early in the morning, and the priests took up the ark of the Lord**—The second day's procession seems to have taken place in the morning. In all other respects, the arrangements of the first day continued to be the rule followed on the other six. **15. on the seventh day they rose early about the dawning of the day, and compassed the city...seven times**—on account of the seven circuits they had to make that day. It is evident, however, that the militia only of the Israelites had been called to the march—for it is inconceivable that two millions of people could have gone so frequently round the city in a day. **16. it came to pass at the seventh time,...Joshua said unto the people,**

Shout; for the Lord hath given you the city—This delay brought out their faith and obedience in so remarkable a manner, that it is celebrated by the apostle (Heb. 11:30). **17-19. the city shall be accursed**—(See on Lev. 27:28, 29). **The *cherem*, or** anathema, was a devotion to utter destruction (Deut. 7:2; 20:17; I Sam. 15:3). When such a ban was pronounced against a hostile city, the men and animals were killed—no booty was allowed to be taken. The idols and all the precious ornaments on them were to be burned (Deut. 7:25; cf. I Chron. 14:12). Everything was either to be destroyed or consecrated to the sanctuary. Joshua pronounced this ban on Jericho, a great and wealthy city, evidently by divine direction. The severity of the doom, accordant with the requirements of a law which was holy, just, and good, was justified, not only by the fact of its inhabitants being part of a race who had filled up their iniquities, but by their resisting the light of the recent astonishing miracle at the Jordan. Besides, as Jericho seems to have been defended by reinforcements from all the country (ch. 24:11), its destruction would paralyze all the rest of the devoted people, and thus tend to facilitate the conquest of the land; showing, as so astounding a military miracle did, that it was done, not by man, but by the power and through the anger, of God. **18. and ye, in any wise keep yourselves from the accursed thing**—Generally they were at liberty to take the spoil of other cities that were captured (Deut. 2:35; 3:7; ch. 8:27). But this, as the first fruits of Canaan, was made an exception; nothing was to be spared but Rahab and those in her house. A violation of these stringent orders would not only render the guilty persons obnoxious to the curse, but entail distress and adversity upon all Israel, by provoking the divine displeasure. These were the instructions given, or repeated (Deut. 13:17; 7:26), previous to the last act of the siege.

20, 21. THE WALLS FALL DOWN. **20. So the people shouted when the priests blew with the trumpets**—Towards the close of the seventh circuit, the signal was given by Joshua, and on the Israelites' raising their loud war cry, the walls fell down, doubtless burying multitudes of the inhabitants in the ruins, while the besiegers, rushing in, consigned everything animate and inanimate to indiscriminate destruction (Deut. 20:16, 17.) Jewish writers mention it as an immemorial tradition that the city fell on the Sabbath. It should be remembered that the Canaanites were incorrigible idolaters, addicted to the most horrible vices, and that the righteous judgment of God might sweep them away by the sword, as well as by famine or pestilence. There was mercy mingled with judgment in employing the sword as the instrument of punishing the guilty Canaanites, for while it was directed against one place, time was afforded for others to repent.

22-25. RAHAB IS SAVED. **22, 23. Joshua had said...Go into the harlot's house, and bring out thence the woman, and all that she hath**—It is evident that the town walls were not demolished universally, at least all at once, for Rahab's house was allowed to stand until her relatives were rescued according to promise. **they brought out all her kindred, and left them without the camp of Israel**—a temporary exclusion, in order that they might be cleansed from the defilement of their native idolatries and gradually trained for admission into the society of God's people. **24. burned the city...and all...therein**—except the silver, gold, and other metals, which, as they would not burn, were added to the treasury of the sanctuary.

25. she [Rahab] **dwelleth in Israel unto this day**—a proof that this book was written not long after the events related.

26, 27. THE REBUILDER OF JERICHO CURSED. **26.** Joshua **adjured them at that time**—i.e., imposed upon his countrymen a solemn oath, binding on themselves as well as their posterity, that they would never rebuild that city. Its destruction was designed by God to be a permanent memorial of His abhorrence of idolatry and its attendant vices. **Cursed be the man ... that riseth up and buildeth this city Jericho**—i.e., makes the daring attempt to build. **he shall lay the foundation thereof in his first-born, and in his youngest son shall he set up the gates of it**—shall become childless—the first beginning being marked by the death of his oldest son, and his only surviving child dying at the time of its completion. This curse was accomplished 550 years after its denunciation (See on I Kings 16: 34.)

CHAPTER 7

Vs. 1. ACHAN'S TRESPASS. **1.** the children of Israel **committed a trespass in the accursed thing**—There was one transgressor against the *cherem,* or ban, on Jericho, and his transgression brought the guilt and disgrace of sin upon the whole nation. **Achan**—called afterwards Achar (trouble) (I Chron. 2:7). **Zabdi**—or Zimri (I Chron. 2:6). **Zerah**—or Zarah, son of Judah and Tamar (Gen. 38:30.) His genealogy is given probably to show that from a parentage so infamous the descendants would not be carefully trained in the fear of God.

2-26. THE ISRAELITES SMITTEN AT AI. **2.** Joshua **sent men from Jericho to Ai**—After the sacking of Jericho, the next step was to penetrate into the hills above. Accordingly, spies went up the mountain pass to view the country. The precise site of Ai, or Hai, is indicated with sufficient clearness (Gen. 12:8; 13:3) and has been recently discovered in an isolated tell, called by the natives Tell-el-hajar, "the mount of stones," at two miles', or thirty-five minutes' distance, east-southeast from Bethel [VAN DE VELDE]. **Beth-aven**—("house of vanity")—a name afterwards given derisively (Hos. 4:15; 5:8; 10:5), on account of its idolatries, to Bethel, "house of God," but here referred to another place, about six miles east of Bethel and three north of Ai. **3.** Let not all the people go up, ... for they are but few—As the population of Ai amounted to 12,000 (ch. 8:25), it was a considerable town; though in the hasty and distant reconnoitre made by the spies, it probably appeared small in comparison to Jericho; and this may have been the reason for their proposing so small a detachment to capture it. **4, 5.** they fled before the men of Ai—An unexpected resistance, and the loss of thirty-six of their number diffused a panic, which ended in an ignominious rout. **chased them from before the gate even unto Shebarim**—i.e., unto the "breakings" or "fissures" at the opening of the passes. **and smote them in the going down**—i.e., the declivity or slope of the deep, rugged, adjoining wady. **wherefore the hearts of the people melted, and became as water**—It is evident that the troops engaged were a tumultuary, undisciplined band, no better skilled in military affairs than the Bedouin Arabs, who become disheartened and flee on the loss of ten or fifteen men. But the consternation of the Israelites arose from another cause—the evident displeasure of God, who withheld that aid on which they had confidently reckoned. **6-9.** Joshua rent his clothes,

and fell to the earth ... before the ark ..., he and the elders—It is evident, from those tokens of humiliation and sorrow, that a solemn fast was observed on this occasion. The language of Joshua's prayer is thought by many to savor of human infirmity and to be wanting in that reverence and submission he owed to God. But, although apparently breathing a spirit of bold remonstrance and complaint, it was in reality the effusion of a deeply humbled and afflicted mind, expressing his belief that God could not, after having so miraculously brought His people over Jordan into the promised land, intend to destroy them, to expose them to the insults of their triumphant enemies, and bring reproach upon His own name for inconstancy or unkindness to His people, or inability to resist their enemies. Unable to understand the cause of the present calamity, he owned the hand of God. **10-15.** the Lord said unto Joshua, Get thee up—The answer of the divine oracle was to this effect: the crisis is owing not to unfaithfulness in Me, but sin in the people. The conditions of the covenant have been violated by the reservation of spoil from the doomed city; wickedness, emphatically called folly, has been committed in Israel (Ps. 14:1), and dissimulation, with other aggravations of the crime, continues to be practised. The people are liable to destruction equally with the accursed nations of Canaan (Deut. 7:26). Means must, without delay, be taken to discover and punish the perpetrator of this trespass that Israel may be released from the ban, and things be restored to their former state of prosperity. **16-18.** So Joshua rose up early, and brought Israel by their tribes—i.e., before the tabernacle. The lot being appealed to (Prov. 16:33), he proceeded in the inquiry from heads of tribes to heads of families, and from heads of households in succession to one family, and to particular persons in that family, until the criminal was found to be Achan, who, on Joshua's admonition, confessed the fact of having secreted for his own use, in the floor of his tent, spoil both in garments and money. How dreadful must have been his feelings when he saw the slow but certain process of discovery! (Num. 32:23). **19.** Joshua said unto Achan, My son, give ... glory to God—a form of adjuration to tell the truth. **21.** a goodly Babylonish garment—lit., a mantle of Shinar. The plain of Shinar was in early times celebrated for its gorgeous robes, which were of brilliant and various colors, generally arranged in figured patterns, probably resembling those of modern Turkish carpets, and the colors were either interwoven in the loom or embroidered with the needle. **two hundred shekels of silver**—about $200.00 according to the old Mosaic shekel, or the half of that sum, reckoning by the common shekel. **a wedge of gold**—lit., an ingot or bar in the shape of a tongue worth about $500.00. **22, 23.** Joshua sent messengers, and they ran unto the tent—from impatient eagerness not only to test the truth of the story, but to clear Israel from the imputation of guilt. Having discovered the stolen articles, they laid them out before the Lord, "as a token of their belonging to Him" on account of the ban. **24-26.** Joshua, and all Israel with him, took Achan—He with his children and all his property, cattle as well as movables, were brought into one of the long broad ravines that open into the Ghor, and after being stoned to death (Num. 15:30-35), his corpse, with all belonging to him, was consumed to ashes by fire. "All Israel" was present, not only as spectators, but active agents, as many as possible, in inflicting the punishment—thus testifying their abhorrence of the sacrilege, and their intense solicitude to regain the divine favor. As the divine law expressly forbade the children to be put to death for their father's sins (Deut. 24:16), the conveyance of Achan's "sons and daughters" to the place of execution might be only as spectators, that they might take warning by the parental fate; or, if they shared his punishment (ch. 22:20), they had probably been accomplices in his crime, and, indeed, he could scarcely have dug a hole within his tent without his family being aware of it. **they raised over him a great heap of stones**—It is customary to raise cairns over the graves of criminals or infamous persons in the East still. **the name of that place was called, The valley of Achor** [trouble], **unto this day** —So painful an episode would give notoriety to the spot, and it is more than once noted by the sacred writers of a later age (Isa. 65:10; Hos. 2:15).

CHAPTER 8

Vss. 1-28. GOD ENCOURAGES JOSHUA. **1. The Lord said unto Joshua, Fear not**—By the execution of justice on Achan, the divine wrath was averted, the Israelites were reassured, defeat was succeeded by victory; and thus the case of Ai affords a striking example of God's disciplinary government, in which chastisements for sin are often made to pave the way for the bestowment of those temporal benefits, which, on account of sin, have been withdrawn, or withheld for a time. Joshua, who had been greatly dispirited, was encouraged by a special communication promising him (see ch. 1:6; Deut. 31:6-8) success in the next attempt, which, however, was to be conducted on different principles. **take all the people of war with thee, and arise, go up to Ai**— The number of fighting men amounted to 600,000, and the whole force was ordered on this occasion, partly because the spies, in their self-confidence, had said that a few were sufficient to attack the place (ch. 7:3), partly to dispel any misgivings which the memory of the late disaster might have created, and partly that the circumstance of the first spoil obtained in Canaan being shared among all, might operate both as a reward for obedience in refraining from the booty of Jericho, and as an incentive to future exertions (Deut. 6:10). The rest of the people, including the women and children, remained in the camp at Gilgal. Being in the plains of Jericho, it was an ascent to Ai, which was on a hill. **I have given into thy hand the king of Ai, and his people, and his city, and his land . . . lay thee an ambush for the city**—God assured him of its capture, but allowed him to follow his own tactics in obtaining the possession. **3. So Joshua . . . chose out thirty thousand mighty men of valour**— Joshua despatched 30,000 men under cover of night, to station themselves at the place appointed for the ambuscade. Out of this number a detachment of 5000 was sent forward to conceal themselves in the immediate precincts of the town, in order to seize the first opportuny of throwing themselves into it. **4. behind the city**—is rendered (vs. 9) "on the west of Ai." **9. between Beth-el and Ai**—Bethel, though lying quite near in the direction of west by north, cannot be seen from Tell-el-hajar; two rocky heights rise between both places, in the wady El-Murogede, just as the laying of an ambush to the west of Ai would require [VAN DE VELDE, ROBINSON]. **10. Joshua . . . numbered the people**— i.e., the detachment of liers-in-wait; he did this, to be furnished with clear evidence afterwards, that

the work had been done without any loss of men, whereby the people's confidence in God would be strengthened and encouragement given them to prosecute the war of invasion with vigor. **he and the elders of Israel**—the chief magistrates and rulers, whose presence and official authority were necessary to ensure that the cattle and spoil of the city might be equally divided between the combatants and the rest of the people (Num. 31:27)—a military rule in Israel, that would have been very liable to be infringed, if an excited soldiery, eager for booty, had been left to their own will. **11-14. there was a valley** [lit., "*the* valley"] **between them and Ai. Joshua went that night into the midst of the valley**— The deep and steep-sided glen to the north of Tell-el-hajar, into which one looks down from the tell, fully agrees with this account [VAN DE VELDE]. Joshua himself took up his position on the north side of "the ravine"—the deep chasm of the wady El-Murogede; "*that* night"—means, while it was dark, probably after midnight, or very early in the morning (John 20:1). The king of Ai, in the early dawn, rouses his slumbering subjects and makes a hasty sally with all his people who were capable of bearing arms, once more to surprise and annihilate them. **at a time appointed**—either an hour concocted between the king and people of Ai and those of Beth-el, who were confederates in this enterprise, or perhaps they had fixed on the same time of day, as they had fought successfully against Israel on the former occasion, deeming it a lucky hour (Judg. 20: 38). **but he wist not that there were liers in ambush against him behind the city**—It is evident that this king and his subjects were little experienced in war; otherwise they would have sent out scouts to reconnoitre the neighborhood; at all events, they would not have left their town wholly unprotected and open. Perhaps an ambuscade may have been a war stratagem hitherto unknown in that country, and among that people. **15-17. Joshua and all Israel made as if they were beaten before them**—the pretended flight in the direction of the wilderness— i.e., southeast, into the Ghor, the desert valley of the Jordan, decoyed all the inhabitants of Ai out of the city, while the people of Beth-el hastened to participate in the expected victory. It is supposed by some, from "the city," and not "cities," being spoken of, that the effective force of Beth-el had been concentrated in Ai, as the two places were closely contiguous, and Ai the larger of the two. (See on ch. 12:16.) It may be remarked, however, that the words, "or Beth-el," are not in the Sept., and are rejected by some eminent scholars, as an interpolation not found in the most ancient MSS. **18-25. Joshua stretched out the spear that he had in his hand toward the city**—The uplifted spear had probably a flag, or streamer on it, to render it the more conspicuous from the height where he stood. At the sight of this understood signal the ambush nearest the city, informed by their scouts, made a sudden rush and took possession of the city, telegraphing to their brethren by raising a smoke from the walls. Upon seeing this, the main body, who had been feigning a flight, turned round at the head of the pass upon their pursuers, while the 25,000 issuing from their ambuscade, fell back upon their rear. The Ai-ites surprised, looked back, and found their situation now desperate. **23. the king of Ai they took alive, and brought him to Joshua**— to be reserved for a more ignominious death, as a greater criminal in God's sight than his subjects. In the mingled attack from before and behind, all the men were massacred. **24. all the Israelites re-**

turned unto Ai, and smote it with the edge of the sword—the women, children, and old persons left behind, amounting, in all, to 12,000 people. Joshua drew not his hand back—Perhaps, from the long continuance of the posture, it might have been a means appointed by God, to animate the people, and kept up in the same devout spirit as Moses had shown, in lifting up his hands, until the work of slaughter had been completed—the ban executed. (See on Exod. 17:11, 12.) 28. Joshua burnt Ai, and made it an heap for ever—"For ever" often signifies "a long time" (Gen. 6:3). One of the remarkable things with regard to the tell we have identified with Ai is its name—the tell of the heap of stones—a name which to this day remains [VAN DE VELDE]. 29. THE KING HANGED. 29. The king of Ai he hanged on a tree—i.e., gibbeted. In ancient, and particularly Oriental wars, the chiefs, when taken prisoners, were usually executed. The Israelites were obliged, by the divine law, to put them to death. The execution of the king of Ai would tend to facilitate the conquest of the land, by striking terror into the other chiefs, and making it appear a judicial process, in which they were inflicting the vengeance of God upon His enemies. take his carcass down . . . and raise thereon a great heap of stones—It was taken down at sunset, according to the divine command (Deut. 21:23), and cast into a pit dug "at the entering of the gate," because that was the most public place. An immense cairn was raised over his grave—an ancient usage, still existing in the East, whereby is marked the sepulchre of persons whose memory is infamous. 30, 31. JOSHUA BUILDS AN ALTAR. 30, 31. Then Joshua built an altar unto the Lord God of Israel in mount Ebal—(See on Deut. 27:1, 2). This spot was little short of twenty miles from Ai. The march through a hostile country and the unmolested performance of the religious ceremonial observed at this mountain, would be greatly facilitated, through the blessing of God, by the disastrous fall of Ai. The solemn duty was to be attended to at the first convenient opportunity after the entrance into Canaan (Deut. 27:2); and with this in view Joshua seems to have conducted the people through the mountainous region that intervened though no details of the journey have been recorded. Ebal was on the north, opposite to Gerizim, which was on the south side of the town Sichem (Nablous). an altar of whole stones—according to the instructions given to Moses (Exod. 20:25; Deut. 27:5). over which no man hath lifted up any iron—i.e., iron tool. The reason for this was that every altar of the true God ought properly to have been built of earth (Exod. 20:24); and if it was constructed of stone, rough, unhewn stones were to be employed that it might retain both the appearance and nature of earth, since every bloody sacrifice was connected with sin and death, by which man, the creature of earth, is brought to earth again [KEIL]. they offered thereon burnt offerings unto the Lord, and sacrificed peace offerings—This had been done when the covenant was established (Exod. 24:5); and by the observance of these rites (Deut. 27:6), the covenant was solemnly renewed—the people were reconciled to God by the burnt offering, and this feast accompanying the peace or thank offering, a happy communion with God was enjoyed by all the families in Israel. 32. he wrote there upon the stones a copy of the law—(see on Deut. 27:2-8); i.e., the blessings and curses of the law. Some think that the stones which contained this inscription were the stones of the altar: but this verse

seems rather to indicate that a number of stone pillars were erected alongside of the altar, and on which, after they were plastered, this duplicate of the law was inscribed. 33. all Israel, and their elders, and officers, and their judges, stood on this side the ark and on that side—One half of Israel was arranged on Gerizim, and the other half on Ebal—along the sides and base of each. before the priests the Levites—in full view of them. 34. afterward he read all the words of the law—caused the priests or Levites to read it (Deut. 27:14). Persons are often said in Scripture to do that which they only command to be done. 35. There was not a word of all that Moses commanded, which Joshua read not—It appears that a much larger portion of the law was read on this occasion than the brief summary inscribed on the stones; and this must have been the essence of the law as contained in Deuteronomy (Deut. 4:44; 6:9; 27:8). It was not written on the stones, but on the plaster. The immediate design of this rehearsal was attained by the performance of the act itself. It only related to posterity, in so far as the record of the event would be handed down in the Book of Joshua, or the documents which form the groundwork of it [HENGSTENBERG]. Thus faithfully did Joshua execute the instructions given by Moses. How awfully solemn must have been the assemblage and the occasion! The eye and the ear of the people being both addressed, it was calculated to leave an indelible impression; and with spirits elevated by their brilliant victories in the land of promise, memory would often revert to the striking scene on mounts Ebal and Gerizim, and in the vale of Sychar.

CHAPTER 9

Vss. 1-29. THE KINGS COMBINE AGAINST ISRAEL. 1. all the kings which were on this side—i.e., the western side of Jordan—in the hills, and in the valleys, and in all the coasts of the great sea—This threefold distinction marks out very clearly a large portion of Canaan. The first designates the hill country, which belonged afterwards to the tribes of Judah and Ephraim: the second, all the low country from Carmel to Gaza; and the third, the shores of the Mediterranean, from the Isthumus of Tyre to the plain of Joppa. (As for the tribes mentioned, see on ch. 3:10.) heard (*thereof*)—that is, of the sacking of Jericho and Ai, as well as the rapid advance of the Israelites into the interior of the country. 2. they gathered themselves together, to fight with Joshua and with Israel, with one accord—Although divided by separate interests and often at war with each other, a sense of common danger prompted them to suspend their mutual animosities, that by their united forces they might prevent the land from falling into the hands of foreign masters. 3-15. THE GIBEONITES OBTAIN A LEAGUE BY CRAFT. 3-15. when the inhabitants of Gibeon heard—This town, as its name imports, was situated on a rocky eminence, about six miles northwest from Jerusalem, where the modern village of El-Jib now stands. It was the capital of the Hivites, and a large important city (ch. 10:2). It seems to have formed, in union with a few other towns in the neighborhood, a free independent state (vs. 17) and to have enjoyed a republican government (vs. 11). They did work wilily—They acted with dexterous policy, seeking the means of self-preservation, not by force, which they were convinced would be unavailing, but by artful diplomacy. took old

sacks upon their asses—Travellers in the East transport their luggage on beasts of burden; the poorer sort stow all their necessaries, food, clothes, utensils together, in a woollen or hair-cloth sack, laid across the shoulders of the beast they ride upon. **wine bottles, old, and rent, and bound up**—Goatskins, which are better adapted for carrying liquor of any kind fresh and good, than either earthenware, which is porous, or metallic vessels, which are soon heated by the sun. These skin bottles are liable to be rent when old and much used; and there are various ways of mending them—by inserting a new piece of leather, or by gathering together the edges of the rent and sewing them in the form of a purse, or by putting a round flat splinter of wood into the hole. **5. old shoes and clouted**—Those who have but one ass or mule for themselves and baggage frequently dismount and walk—a circumstance which may account for the worn shoes of the pretended travellers. **bread ... dry and mouldy**—This must have been that commonly used by travellers—a sort of biscuit made in the form of large rings, about an inch thick, and four or five inches in diameter. Not being so well baked as our biscuits, it becomes hard and mouldy from the moisture left in the dough. It is usually soaked in water previous to being used. **6-14. they went to Joshua unto the camp at Gilgal**—Arrived at the Israelitish headquarters, the strangers obtained an interview with Joshua and the elders, to whom they opened their business. **7. the men of Israel said unto the Hivites, Peradventure ye dwell among us**—The answer of the Israelites implied that they had no discretion, that their orders were imperative, and that if the strangers belonged to any of the native tribes, the idea of an alliance with them was unlawful since God had forbidden it (Exod. 23:32; 34:12; Deut. 7:2). **9. From a very far country thy servants are come, because of the name of the Lord thy God**—They pretended to be actuated by religious motives in seeking to be allied with His people. But their studied address is worthy of notice in appealing to instances of God's miraculous doings at a distance, while they pass by those done in Canaan, as if the report of these had not yet reached their ears. **14, 15. the men took of their victuals, and asked not counsel at the mouth of the Lord**—The mouldy appearance of their bread was, after examination, accepted as guaranteeing the truth of the story. In this precipitate conclusion the Israelites were guilty of excessive credulity and culpable negligence, in not asking by the high priest's Urim and Thummim the mind of God, before entering into the alliance. It is not clear, however, that had they applied for divine direction they would have been forbidden to spare and connect themselves with any of the Canaanite tribes who renounced idolatry and embraced and worshipped the true God. At least, no fault was found with them for making a covenant with the Gibeonites; while, on the other hand, the violation of it was severely punished (II Sam. 21:1; and ch. 11:19, 20). **16, 17. at the end of three days ... they heard that they were their neighbours, and dwelt among them**—This information was obtained in their further progress through the country; for as vs. 17 should be rendered, "when the children of Israel journeyed, they came to their cities." Gibeon was about eighteen or twenty miles from Gilgal; *Chephirah* (ch. 18:26; Ezra 2:25; Neh. 7:29); Beeroth (II Samuel 4:2), now *El Berich,* about twenty minutes' distance from El Jib (Gibeon); Kirjath-jearim, "the city of forests," now Kuryet-el-Enab [Robinson]. **18-27. the children of Israel smote**

them not—The moral character of the Gibeonites' stratagem was bad. The princes of the congregation did not vindicate either the expediency or the lawfulness of the connection they had formed; but they felt the solemn obligations of their oath; and, although the popular clamor was loud against them, caused either by disappointment at losing the spoils of Gibeon, or by displeasure at the apparent breach of the divine commandment, they determined to adhere to their pledge, "because they had sworn by the Lord God of Israel." The Israelitish princes acted conscientiously; they felt themselves bound by their solemn promise; but to prevent the disastrous consequences of their imprudent haste, they resolved to degrade the Gibeonites to a servile condition as a means of preventing their people from being ensnared into idolatry, and thus acted up, as they thought, to the true spirit and end of the law. **27. hewers of wood and drawers of water**—The menials who performed the lowest offices and drudgery in the sanctuary; whence they were called Nethinims (I Chron. 9:2; Ezra 2:43; 8: 20); i.e., given, appropriated. Their chastisement thus brought them into the possession of great religious privileges (Ps. 84:10).

CHAPTER 10

Vss. 1-5. Five Kings War against Gibeon. **1. Adoni-zedek**—"lord of righteousness,"—nearly synonymous with Melchizedek, "king of righteousness." These names were common titles of the Jebusite kings. **Jerusalem**—The original name, "Salem" (Gen. 14:18; Ps. 76:2), was superseded by that here given, which signifies "a peaceful possession," or "a vision of peace," in allusion, as some think, to the strikingly symbolic scene (Gen. 22:14) represented on the mount whereon that city was afterwards built. **inhabitants of Gibeon had made peace with Israel, and were among them**—i.e., the Israelites—had made an alliance with that people, and acknowledging their supremacy, were living on terms of friendly intercourse with them. **2. they feared greatly**—The dread inspired by the rapid conquests of the Israelites had been immensely increased by the fact of a state so populous and so strong as Gibeon having found it expedient to submit to the power and the terms of the invaders. **as one of the royal cities**—Although itself a republic (ch. 9:3), it was large and well fortified, like those places in which the chiefs of the country usually established their residence. **3. Wherefore Adonizedek ... sent, ... saying, Come up unto me, and help me**—A combined attack was meditated on Gibeon, with a view not only to punish its people for their desertion of the native cause, but by its overthrow to interpose a barrier to the farther inroads of the Israelites. This confederacy among the mountaineers of Southern Palestine was formed and headed by the king of Jerusalem, because his territory was most exposed to danger, Gibeon being only six miles distant, and because he evidently possessed some degree of pre-eminence over his royal neighbors. **5. the five kings of the Amorites**—The settlement of this powerful and warlike tribe lay within the confines of Moab; but having also acquired extensive possessions on the southwest of the Jordan, their name, as the ruling power, seems to have been given to the region generally (II Sam. 21:2), although Hebron was inhabited by Hittites or Hivites (ch. 11:19), and Jerusalem by Jebusites (ch. 15:63). **6-9.** Joshua Rescues It. **6-8. the men of Gib-**

eon sent unto Joshua— Their appeal was urgent and
their claim to protection irresistible, on the ground,
not only of kindness and sympathy, but of justice.
In attacking the Canaanites, Joshua had received
from God a general assurance of success (ch. 1:5).
But the intelligence of so formidable a combination
among the native princes seems to have depressed
his mind with the anxious and dispiriting idea that
it was a chastisement for the hasty and inconsiderate alliance entered into with the Gibeonites. It
was evidently to be a struggle of life and death, not
only to Gibeon, but to the Israelites. And in this
view the divine communication that was made to
him was seasonable and animating. He seems to
have asked the counsel of God and received an
answer, before setting out on the expedition. **9.**
Joshua therefore came upon them suddenly—This
is explained in the following clause, where he is
described as having accomplished, by a forced
march of picked men, in one night, a distance of
twenty-six miles, which, according to the slow pace
of Eastern armies and caravans, had formerly been
a three days' journey (ch. 9:17).

10, 11. GOD FIGHTS AGAINST THEM WITH HAIL-
STONES. **10, 11. the Lord discomfited them**—*Heb.*,
terrified, confounded the Amorite allies, probably
by a fearful storm of lightning and thunder. So the
word is usually employed (I Sam. 7:10; Ps. 18:13;
144:6). **and slew them with a great slaughter at**
Gibeon—This refers to the attack of the Israelites
upon the besiegers. It is evident that there had
been much hard fighting around the heights of
Gibeon, for the day was far spent before the enemy
took to flight. **chased them along the way that**
goeth up to Beth-horon—i.e., the House of Caves,
of which there are still traces existing. There were
two contiguous villages of that name, upper and
nether. Upper Beth-horon was nearest Gibeon—
about ten miles distant, and approached by a gradual ascent through a long and precipitous ravine.
This was the first stage of the flight. The fugitives
had crossed the high ridge of Upper Beth-horon, and
were in full flight down the descent to Beth-horon
the Nether. The road between the two places is
so rocky and rugged that there is a path made by
means of steps cut in the rock [ROBINSON]. Down
this pass Joshua continued his victorious rout.
Here it was that the Lord interposed, assisting His
people by means of a storm, which, having been
probably gathering all day, burst with such irresistible fury, that "they were more which died with
hailstones than they whom the children of Israel
slew with the sword." The Oriental hailstorm is
a terrific agent; the hailstones are masses of ice,
large as walnuts, and sometimes as two fists; their
prodigious size, and the violence with which they
fall, make them always very injurious to property,
and often fatal to life. The miraculous feature of
this tempest, which fell on the Amorite army, was
the entire preservation of the Israelites from its
destructive ravages.

12-15. THE SUN AND MOON STAND STILL AT THE
WORD OF JOSHUA. **12-15. Then spake Joshua to the**
Lord . . . and . . . he said in the sight of all Israel,
Sun, stand thou still . . . and thou, Moon—The inspired author here breaks off the thread of his history of this miraculous victory to introduce a quotation from an ancient poem, in which the mighty acts
of that day were commemorated. The passage,
which is parenthetical, contains a *poetical* description of the victory which was miraculously gained
by the help of God, and forms an extract from "the
book of Jasher," i.e., "the upright"—an anthology,

or collection of national songs, in honor of renowned and eminently pious heroes. The language
of a poem is not to be literally interpreted; and
therefore, when the sun and moon are personified,
addressed as intelligent beings, and represented as
standing still, the explanation is that the light of the
sun and moon was supernaturally prolonged by the
same laws of refraction and reflection that ordinarily cause the sun to appear above the horizon, when
it is in reality below it [KEIL, BUSH]. Gibeon (a hill)
was now at the back of the Israelites, and the height
would soon have intercepted the rays of the setting
sun. The valley of Ajalon (stags) was before them,
and so near that it was sometimes called "the valley
of Gibeon" (Isa. 28:21). It would seem, from vs.
14, that the command of Joshua was in reality a
prayer to God for the performance of this miracle;
and that, although the prayers of eminently good
men like Moses often prevailed with God, never
was there on any other occasion so astonishing a
display of divine power made in behalf of His
people, as in answer to the prayer of Joshua.
Verse 15 is the end of the quotation from Jasher;
and it is necessary to notice this, as the fact described in it is recorded in due course, and the same
words, by the sacred historian (vs. 43).

16-27. THE FIVE KINGS HANGED. **16-27. these**
five kings . . . hid themselves in a cave [*Heb.*, the
cave] **at Makkedah**—The pursuit was continued,
without interruption, to Makkedah at the foot of
the western mountains, where Joshua seems to have
halted with the main body of his troops while a detachment was sent forward to scour the country in
pursuit of the remaining stragglers, a few of whom
succeeded in reaching the neighboring cities. The
last act, probably the next day, was the disposal of
the prisoners, among whom the five kings were
consigned to the infamous doom of being slain
(Deut. 20:16, 17); and then their corpses were
suspended on five trees till the evening. **24. put**
your feet upon the necks of these kings—not as a
barbarous insult, but a symbolical action, expressive of a complete victory (Deut. 33:29; Ps. 110:5;
Mal. 4:3).

28-42. SEVEN MORE KINGS CONQUERED. **28-42.**
that day Joshua took Makkedah—In this and the
following verses is described the rapid succession of
victory and extermination which swept the whole of
southern Palestine into the hands of Israel. "All
these kings and their land did Joshua take *at one*
time, because the Lord God of Israel fought for
Israel. And Joshua returned, and all Israel with
him, unto the camp to Gilgal."

CHAPTER 11

VSS. 1-9. DIVERS KINGS OVERCOME AT THE WA-
TERS OF MEROM. **1-9. And it came to pass, when**
Jabin king of Hazor had heard those things—The
scene of the sacred narrative is here shifted to the
north of Canaan, where a still more extensive confederacy was formed among the ruling powers to
oppose the further progress of the Israelites. Jabin
("the Intelligent"), which seems to have been a
hereditary title (Judg. 4:2), took the lead, from
Hazor being the capital of the northern region (vs.
10). It was situated on the borders of lake Merom.
The other cities mentioned must have been in the
vicinity though their exact position is unknown. **2.**
the kings that were on the north of the mountains—
the Anti-libanus district. **the plains south of Chin-**
neroth—the northern part of the Arabah, or valley

of the Jordan. **the valley**—the low and level country, including the plain of Sharon. **borders of Dor on the west**—the highlands of Dor, reaching to the town of Dor on the Mediterranean coast, below mount Carmel. **3. the Canaanites on the east and on the west**—a particular branch of the Canaanitish population who occupied the western bank of the Jordan as far northward as the Sea of Galilee, and also the coasts of the Mediterranean Sea. **under Hermon**—now Jebel-es-sheikh. It was the northern boundary of Canaan on the east of the Jordan. **land of Mizpeh**—now Cœlo-Syria. **4, 5. they went out, ... as the sand upon the seashore in multitude**—The chiefs of these several tribes were summoned by Jabin, being all probably tributary to the kingdom of Hazor. Their combined forces, according to Josephus, amounted to 300,000 infantry, 10,000 cavalry, and 20,000 war chariots. **with horses and chariots very many**—The war chariots were probably like those of Egypt, made of wood, but nailed and tipped with iron. These appear for the first time in the Canaanite war, to aid this last determined struggle against the invaders; and "it was the use of these which seems to have fixed the place of rendezvous by the lake Merom (now Huleh), along whose level shores they could have full play for their force." A host so formidable in numbers, as well as in military equipments, was sure to alarm and dispirit the Israelites. Joshua, therefore, was favored with a renewal of the divine promise of victory (vs. 6), and thus encouraged, he, in the full confidence of faith, set out to face the enemy. **6. to-morrow, about this time, will I deliver them up all slain before Israel**—As it was impossible to have marched from Gilgal to Merom in one day, we must suppose Joshua already moving northward and within a day's distance of the Canaanite camp, when the Lord gave him this assurance of success. With characteristic energy he made a sudden advance, probably during the night, and fell upon them like a thunderbolt, when scattered along the rising grounds (Sept.), before they had time to rally on the plain. In the sudden panic "the Lord delivered them into the hand of Israel, who smote them, and chased them." The rout was complete; some went westward, over the mountains, above the gorge of the Leontes, to Sidon and Misrephothmaim (glass-smelting houses), in the neighborhood, and others eastward to the plain of Mizpeh. **8. they left none remaining**—of those whom they overtook. All those who fell into their hands alive were slain. **9. Joshua did unto them as the Lord** [vs. 6] **bade him**—Houghing the horses is done by cutting the sinews and arteries of their hinder legs, so that they not only become hopelessly lame, but bleed to death. The reasons for this special command were that the Lord designed to lead the Israelites to trust in Him, not in military resources (Ps. 20:7); to show that in the land of promise there was no use of horses; and, finally, to discourage their travelling as they were to be an agricultural, not a trading, people. **11. he burnt Hazor with fire**—calmly and deliberately, doubtless, according to divine direction. **13. as for the cities that stood still in their strength**—lit., "on their heaps." It was a Phœnician custom to build cities on heights, natural or artificial [HENGSTENBERG]. **16. So Joshua took all that land**—Here follows a general view of the conquest. The division of the country there into five parts; viz., the hills, the land of Goshen, i.e., a pastoral land near Gibeon (ch. 10:41); the valley, the plains and the mountains of Israel. **17. from the mount Halak** [*Heb.*, "the smooth mountain"]. **that**

goeth up to Seir—an irregular line of white naked hills, about eighty feet high, and seven or eight geographical miles in length that cross the whole Ghor, eight miles south of the Dead Sea, probably "the ascent of Akrabbim" [ROBINSON]. **unto Baalgad in the valley of Lebanon**—the city or temple of the god of destiny, in Baalbec. **23. Joshua took the whole land**—The battle of the lake of Merom was to the north what the battle of Beth-horon was to the south; more briefly told and less complete in its consequences; but still the decisive conflict by which the whole northern region of Canaan fell into the hands of Israel [STANLEY].

CHAPTER 12

Vss. 1-6. THE TWO KINGS WHOSE COUNTRIES MOSES TOOK AND DISPOSED OF. **1. Now these are the kings of the land which the children of Israel smote, and possessed their land on the other side Jordan**—This chapter contains a recapitulation of the conquests made in the promised land, with the additional mention of some places not formerly noted in the sacred history. The river Arnon on the south and mount Hermon on the north were the respective boundaries of the land acquired by the Israelites beyond Jordan (see on Num. 21:21; Deut. 2:36; 3:6-16).

7-24. THE ONE AND THIRTY KINGS ON THE WEST SIDE OF JORDAN, WHICH JOSHUA SMOTE. **7. Baalgad ... even unto ... Halak**—(see on ch. 11:17). A list of thirty-one chief towns is here given; and, as the whole land contained a superficial extent of only fifteen miles in length by fifty in breadth, it is evident that these capital cities belonged to petty and insignificant kingdoms. With a few exceptions, they were not the scenes of any important events recorded in the sacred history, and therefore do not require a particular notice.

CHAPTER 13

Vss. 1-33. BOUNDS OF THE LAND NOT YET CONQUERED. **1. Now Joshua was old and stricken in years**—He was probably above a hundred years old; for the conquest and survey of the land occupied about seven years, the partition one; and he died at the age of 110 years (ch. 24:29). The distribution, as well as the conquest of the land, was included in the mission of Joshua; and his advanced age supplied a special reason for entering on the immediate discharge of that duty; viz., of allocating Canaan among the tribes of Israel—not only the parts already won, but those also which were still to be conquered. **2-6. This is the land that yet remaineth**—i.e., to be acquired. This section forms a parenthesis, in which the historian briefly notices the districts yet unsubdued; viz., first, the whole country of the Philistines—a narrow tract stretching about sixty miles along the Mediterranean coast, and that of the Geshurites to the south of it (I Sam. 27:8). Both included that portion of the country "from Sihor, which is before Egypt," a small brook near El-Arish, which on the east was the southern boundary of Canaan, to Ekron, the most northerly of the five chief lordships or principalities of the Philistines. **also the Avites: From** [on] **the south**—The two clauses are thus connected in the Septuagint and many other versions. On being driven out (Deut. 2:23), they established themselves in the south of Philistia. The second division of the unconquered country comprised **all the land of the Canaanites, and Mearah** [the cave] **that is beside** the Sidonians—a mountainous region of Upper Galilee, remarkable for its caves and fastnesses, eastward unto Aphek (now Afka), in Lebanon, to the borders of the Amorites—a portion of the northeastern territory that had belonged to Og. The third district that remained unsubdued was: 5. all the land of the Giblites—Their capital was Gebal or Bylbos (*Gr.*), on the Mediterranean, forty miles north of Sidon. all Lebanon, toward the sunrising —i.e., Anti-libanus; the eastern ridge, which has its proper termination in Hermon. entering into Hamath—the valley of Baalbec. 6, 7. All the inhabitants of the hill country from Lebanon unto Misrephoth-main (see on ch. 11:8)—i.e., "all the Sidonians and Phœnicians." them will I drive out —The fulfilment of this promise was conditional. In the event of the Israelites proving unfaithful or disobedient, they would not subdue the districts now specified; and, in point of fact, the Israelites never possessed them though the inhabitants were subjected to the power of David and Solomon. only divide thou it by lot unto the Israelites for an inheritance—The parenthetic section being closed, the historian here resumes the main subject of this chapter—the order of God to Joshua to make an immediate allotment of the land. The method of distribution by lot was, in all respects, the best that could have been adopted, as it prevented all ground of discontent, as well as charges of arbitrary or partial conduct on the part of the leaders; and its announcement in the life of Moses (Num. 33:54), as the system according to which the allocations to each tribe should be made, was intended to lead the people to the acknowledgment of God as the proprietor of the land and as having the entire right to its disposal. Moreover, a solemn appeal to the lot showed it to be the dictate not of human, but divine, wisdom. It was used, however, only in determining the part of the country where a tribe was to be settled—the extent of the settlement was to be decided on a different principle (Num. 26: 54). The overruling control of God is conclusively proved because each tribe received the possession predicted by Jacob (Gen. 49) and by Moses (Deut. 33). 8. With whom—*Heb.*, him. The antecedent is evidently to Manasseh, not, however, the half tribe just mentioned, but the other half; for the historian, led, as it were, by the sound of the word, breaks off to describe the possessions beyond Jordan already assigned to Reuben, Gad, and the half of Manasseh (see on Num. 32; Deut. 3:8-17). It may be proper to remark that it was wise to put these boundaries on record. In case of any misunderstanding or dispute arising about the exact limits of each district or property, an appeal could always be made to this authoritative document, and a full knowledge as well as grateful sense obtained of what they had received from God (Ps. 16:5, 6).

CHAPTER 14

VSS. 1-5. THE NINE TRIBES AND A HALF TO HAVE THEIR INHERITANCE BY LOT. 1. these are the countries which the children of Israel inherited in the land of Canaan—This chapter forms the introduction to an account of the allocation of the land west of Jordan, or Canaan proper, to the nine tribes and a half. It was also made by lot in presence of a select number of superintendents, appointed according to divine directions given to Moses (see on Num. 34:16-29). In everything pertaining to civil government, and even the division of the land, Joshua was

the acknowledged chief. But in a matter to be determined by lot, a solemn appeal was made to God, and hence Eleazar, as high priest, is named before Joshua. 4. The children of Joseph were two tribes, Manasseh and Ephraim—As two and a half tribes were settled on the east Jordan, and the Levites had no inheritance assigned them in land, there would have been only eight and a half tribes to provide for. But Ephraim and Manasseh, the two sons of Joseph, had been constituted two tribes (Gen. 48:5), and although Levi was excluded, the original number of the tribes of Israel was still preserved. 5. the children of Israel . . . divided the land—i.e., they made the preliminary arrangements for the work. A considerable time was requisite for the survey and measurement.

6-15. CALEB BY PRIVILEGE REQUESTS AND OBTAINS HEBRON. 6-11. Then the children of Judah came to Joshua in Gilgal; and Caleb . . . said—This incident is recorded here because it occurred while the preparations were being made for casting the lots, which, it appears, were begun in Gilgal. The claim of Caleb to the mountains of Hebron as his personal and family possessions was founded on a solemn promise of Moses, forty-five years before (Num. 14:24; Deut. 1:36), to give him that land on account of his fidelity. Being one of the nominees appointed to preside over the division of the country, he might have been charged with using his powers as a commissioner to his own advantage, had he urged his request in private; and therefore he took some of his brethren along with him as witness of the justice and propriety of his conduct. 12. give me this mountain, whereof the Lord spake in that day—this highland region. for thou heardest in that day how the Anakims were there—The report of the spies, who tried to kindle the flame of sedition and discontent, related chiefly to the people and condition of this mountain district, and hence it was promised as the reward of Caleb's truth, piety, and faithfulness. 13, 14. Joshua blessed him, and gave unto Caleb Hebron for an inheritance—Joshua, who was fully cognizant of all the circumstances, not only admitted the claim, but in a public and earnest manner prayed for the divine blessing to succor the efforts of Caleb in driving out the idolatrous occupiers. 15. Kirjath-arba—i.e., the city of Arba, a warrior among the native race remarkable for strength and stature. the land had rest from war— Most of the kings having been slain and the natives dispirited, there was no general or systematic attempt to resist the progress and settlement of the Israelites.

CHAPTER 15

VSS. 1-12. BORDERS OF THE LOT OF JUDAH. 1. This then was the lot of the tribe of the children of Judah—In what manner the lot was drawn on this occasion the sacred historian does not say; but it is probable that the method adopted was similar to that described in ch. 18. Though the general survey of the country had not been completed, some rough draft or delineation of the first conquered part must have been made, and satisfactory evidence obtained that it was large enough to furnish three cantons, before all the tribes cast lots for them; and they fell to Judah, Ephraim, and the halftribe of Manasseh. The lot of Judah came first, in token of the pre-eminence of that tribe over all the others; and its destined superiority thus received the visible sanction of God. The territory, assigned to it as a possession, was large and extensive, being bounded on the south by the wilderness of Zin, and the southern extremity of the Salt Sea (Num. 34:3-5); on the east, by that sea, extending to the point where it receives the waters of the Jordan; on the north, by a line drawn nearly parallel to Jerusalem, across the country, from the northern extremity of the Salt Sea to the southern limits of the Philistine territory, and to the Mediterranean; and on the west this sea was its boundary, as far as Sihor (Wady El-Arish). **2. the bay**—*Heb.*, "tongue." It pushes its waters out in this form to a great distance [ROBINSON]. **3. Maaleh-akrabbim**—*Heb.*, "the ascent of scorpions"; a pass in the "bald mountain" (see on ch. 11:17), probably much infested by these venomous reptiles. **5. the end**—i.e., the mouth of the Jordan. **6. Beth-hogla**—now Ain Hadjla, a fine spring of clear and sweet water, at the northern extremity of the Dead Sea, about two miles from the Jordan [ROBINSON]. **Beth-arabah**—the house or place of solitude, in the desert of Judah (vs. 61). **stone of Bohan the son of Reuben**—the sepulchral monument of a Reubenite leader, who had been distinguished for his bravery, and had fallen in the Canaanite war. **7. Achor**—(see on ch. 7:26). **Adummim**—a rising ground in the wilderness of Jericho, on the south of the little brook that flowed near Jericho (ch. 16:1). **En-shemesh**—the fountain of the sun; "either the present well of the apostle, below Bethany, on the road to Jericho, or the fountain near to St. Saba" [ROBINSON]. **En-rogel**—the fuller's fountain, on the southeast of Jerusalem, below the spot where the valleys of Jehoshaphat and Hinnom unite.

13-15. CALEB'S PORTION AND CONQUEST. **13. unto Caleb he gave a part among the children of Judah**—(See on ch. 14:6-15). **14. drove thence the three sons of Anak**—rather three chiefs of the Anakim race. This exploit is recorded to the honor of Caleb, as the success of it was the reward of his trust in God. **15. Debir**—oracle. Its former name, Kirjath-sepher, signifies "city of the book," being probably a place where public registers were kept.

16-20. OTHNIEL, FOR HIS VALOR, HAS ACHSAH TO WIFE. **16-20. He that smiteth Kirjath-sepher**—This offer was made as an incentive to youthful bravery (see on I Sam. 17:25); and the prize was won by Othniel, Caleb's *younger* brother (Judg. 1:13; 3:9). This was the occasion of drawing out the latent energies of him who was destined to be the first judge in Israel. **18. as she came unto him**—i.e., when about to remove from her father's to her husband's house. She suddenly alighted from her travelling equipage—a mark of respect to her father, and a sign of making some request. She had urged Othniel to broach the matter, but he not wishing to do what appeared like evincing a grasping disposition, she resolved herself to speak out. Taking advantage of the parting scene when a parent's heart was likely to be tender, she begged (as her marriage portion consisted of a field which, having a southern exposure, was comparatively an arid and barren waste) he would add the adjoining one, which abounded in excellent springs. The request being reasonable, it was granted; and the story conveys this impoitant lesson in religion, that if earthly parents are ready to bestow on their children that which is good, much more will our heavenly Father give every necessary blessing to them who ask Him.

21-63. CITIES OF JUDAH. **21-63. the uttermost cities of the tribe of the children of Judah**—There is given a list of cities within the tribal territory of Judah, arranged in four divisions, corresponding to the districts of which it consisted—the cities in the southern part (21-32), those in the lowlands (33-47), those in the highlands (48-60), and those in the desert (61, 62). One gets the best idea of the relative situation of these cities by looking at the map.

CHAPTER 16

VSS. 1-4. THE GENERAL BORDERS OF THE SONS OF JOSEPH. **1. the lot of the children of Joseph fell**—*Heb.*, went forth, referring either to the lot as drawn out of the urn, or to the tract of land thereby assigned. The first four verses describe the territory allotted to the family of Joseph in the rich domains of central Palestine. It was drawn in one lot, that the brethren might be contiguously situated; but it was afterwards divided. The southern boundary only is described here; that on the north being irregular and less defined (ch. 17:10, 11), is not mentioned. **water of Jericho** (II Kings 2:19)—at the joint of its junction with the Jordan. **mount Beth-el**—the ridge south of Beth-el. Having described the position of Joseph's family generally the historian proceeds to define the territory; first, that of Ephraim.

5-9. THE BORDERS OF THE INHERITANCE OF EPHRAIM. **5-9. the border of their inheritance … was Ataroth-addar**—Ataroth-addar (now Atara), four miles south of Jetta [ROBINSON], is fixed on as a center, through which a line is drawn from Upper Beth-honon to Michmethah, showing the western limit of their actual possessions. The tract beyond that to the sea was still unconquered. **6, 7. Michmethah on the north side**—The northern boundary is traced from this point eastward to the Jordan. **8. from Tappuah westward unto the river Kanah**—It is retraced from east to west, to describe the prospective and intended boundary, which was to reach to the sea. Kanah (reedy) flows into the Mediterranean. **9. separate cities for the children of Ephraim were among the inheritance of Manasseh**—(ch. 17:9), because it was found that the tract allotted to Ephraim was too small in proportion to its population and power. **10. they drave not out the Canaanites … but the Canaanites dwell among the Ephraimites unto this day, and serve under tribute**—This is the first mention of the fatal policy of the Israelites, in neglecting the divine command (Deut. 20:16) to exterminate the idolaters.

CHAPTER 17

VSS. 1-6. LOT OF MANASSEH. **1. There was also a lot for the tribe of Manasseh**—Ephraim was mentioned, as the more numerous and powerful branch of the family of Joseph (Gen. 48:19, 20); but Manasseh still retained the right of primogeniture and had a separate inheritance assigned. **Machir**—his descendants. **the father of Gilead**—Though he had a son of that name (Num. 26:29; 27:1), yet, as is evident from the use of the *Heb.* article, reference is made, not to the person, but the province of Gilead. "Father" here means lord or possessor of Gilead. This view is confirmed by the fact that it was not Machir, but his descendants, who subdued Gilead and Bashan (Num. 32:41; Deut. 3:13-15). These Machirites had their portion on the east side of Jordan. The western portion of land, allotted to the tribe of Manasseh, was divided into ten portions because the male descendants who had sons consisted of five families, to which, consequently, five shares were given; and the sixth family, viz., the posterity of Hepher, being all women, the five daughters of Zelophehad were, on application to the valuators, endowed each with an inheritance in land (see on Num. 27:1).

7-11. THIS COAST. **7-11. the coast of Manasseh was from Asher to Michmethah**—The southern boundary is here traced from the east. Asher (now Yasir), the starting-point, was a town fifteen Roman miles east of Shechem, and anciently a place of importance. **9. the coast descended unto the river Kanah, southward of the river**—The line which separated the possessions of the two brothers from each other ran to the south of the stream. Thus the river was in the territory of Manasseh; but the cities which were upon the river, though all were within the limits of Manasseh's possessions, were assigned partly to Ephraim, and partly to Manasseh; those on the south side being given to the former; those upon the north to the latter [KEIL]. It appears (vs. 10) that Manasseh was still further interlaced with other neighboring tribes. **11. Beth-shean and her towns**—Gr., Scythopolis (now Beisan), in the valley of the Jordan, towards the east end of the plain of Jezreel. "Beth-shean" means "house of rest," so called from its being the halting-place for caravans travelling between Syria or Midian, and Egypt, and the great station for the commerce between these countries for many centuries. **Ibleam and her towns**—in the neighborhood of Megiddo (II Kings 9:27). **the inhabitants of Dor and her towns**—(now Tantoura), anciently a strong fortress; a wall of wild precipitous rock defended the shore fortifications against attack from the land side. **En-dor and her towns**—situated on a rocky eminence, four Roman miles south of Tabor. **Taanach and ... Megiddo**—These were near to each other, and they are generally mentioned in Scripture together. They were both royal and strongly fortified places (see on Judg. 1:27). **three countries**—districts or provinces. It is computed that Manasseh possessed in Asher and Issachar portions of ground to the extent of more than 200 square miles.

12, 13. CANAANITES NOT DRIVEN OUT. **12, 13. Manasseh could not drive out the inhabitants of those cities**—probably due to indolence, a love of ease. Perhaps a mistaken humanity, arising from a disregard or forgetfulness of the divine command, and a decreasing principle of faith and zeal in the service of God, were the causes of their failure.

14-18. THE CHILDREN OF JOSEPH ASK FOR ANOTHER LOT. **14-18. the children of Joseph spake unto Joshua**—The two tribes join in laying a complaint before the leader, as to the narrow boundaries of their allotment and its insufficiency to be the residence of tribes so vastly increased. But Joshua's answer was full of wisdom as well as patriotism. Knowing their character, he treated them accordingly, and sarcastically turned all their arguments against themselves. Thus he rebuked their unbelief and cowardice. **mount Ephraim**—called so here by anticipation. The Gilboa range between Beth-shean and the plain of Jezreel is meant, anciently covered with an extensive forest. **chariots of iron**—unusually strengthened with that metal, and perhaps armed with projecting scythes.

CHAPTER 18

Vs. 1. THE TABERNACLE SET UP AT SHILOH. **1. the whole congregation ... assembled together at** **Shiloh**—The main body of the Israelites had been diminished by the separation of the three tribes, Judah, Ephraim, and Manasseh into their respective allotments; and the country having been in a great measure subdued, the camp was removed to Shiloh —now Seilun. It was twenty or twenty-five miles north of Jerusalem, twelve north of Bethel, and ten south of Shechem, and embosomed in a rugged and romantic glen. This sequestered spot in the heart of the country might have been recommended by the dictates of convenience. There the allotment of the territory could be most conveniently made, north, south, east, and west, to the different tribes. But "the tabernacle of the congregation was also set up there," and its removal therefore must have been made or sanctioned by divine intimation (Deut. 12:11). It remained in Shiloh for more than 300 years (I Sam. 4:1-11).

2-9. THE REMAINDER OF THE LAND DESCRIBED. **2. there remained ... seven tribes which had not yet received their inheritance**—The selection of Shiloh for the seat of worship, together with the consequent removal of the camp thither, had necessarily interrupted the casting of lots, which was commenced by fixing localities for the tribes of Judah and Joseph. Various causes led to a long delay in resuming it. The satisfaction of the people with their change to so pleasant and fertile a district, their preference of a nomad life, a love of ease, and reluctance to renew the war, seem to have made them indifferent to the possession of a settled inheritance. But Joshua was too much alive to the duty laid on him by the Lord to let matters continue in that state; and accordingly, since a general conquest of the land had been made, he resolved to proceed immediately with the lot, believing that when each tribe should receive its inheritance, a new motive would arise to lead them to exert themselves in securing the full possession. **3. How long are ye slack to go to possess the land which the Lord God of your fathers hath given you**—This reproof conveys an impression that the seven tribes were dilatory to a criminal extent. **4-9. Give out from among you three men for each tribe**—Though the lot determined the part of the country where each tribe was to be located, it could not determine the extent of territory which might be required; and the dissatisfaction of the children of Joseph with the alleged smallness of their possession gave reason to fear that complaints might arise from other quarters, unless precautions were taken to make a proper distribution of the land. For this purpose a commission was given to twenty-one persons— three chosen from each of the seven tribes which had not yet received their inheritance, to make an accurate survey of the country. "The men went and passed through the land, and described it by cities into seven parts in a book" (vs. 9); dividing the land according to its value, and the worth of the cities which it contained, into seven equal portions. This was no light task to undertake. It required learning and intelligence which they or their instructors had, in all probability, brought with them out of Egypt. Accordingly, Josephus says that the survey was performed by men expert in geometry. And, in fact, the circumstantial account which is given of the boundaries of each tribe and its situation, well proves it to have been the work of no mean or incompetent hands.

10. DIVIDED BY LOT. **10. Joshua cast lots for them in Shiloh before the Lord**—before the tabernacle, where the divine presence was manifested, and which associated with the lot the idea of divine

sanction. **11. the lot of ... Benjamin came up**—It has been supposed that there were two urns or vessels, from which the lots were drawn: one containing the names of the tribes, the other containing those of the seven portions; and that the two were drawn out simultaneously. **the coast of their lot came forth between the children of Judah and the children of Joseph**—Thus the prophecy of Moses respecting the inheritance of Benjamin was remarkably accomplished. (See on Deut. 33:12.)

CHAPTER 19

Vss. 1-9. THE LOT OF SIMEON. **1. the second lot came forth to Simeon**—The next lot that was drawn at Shiloh, gave the tribe of Simeon his inheritance within the territory, which had been assigned to that of Judah. The knowledge of Canaan possessed by the Israelites, when the division of the land commenced, was but very general, being derived from the rapid sweep they had made over it during the course of conquest; and it was on the ground of that rough survey alone that the distribution proceeded, by which Judah received an inheritance. Time showed that this territory was too large (vs. 9), either for their numbers, however great, to occupy and their arms to defend, or too large in proportion to the allotments of the other tribes. Justice therefore required (what kind and brotherly feeling readily dictated) a modification of their possession; and a part of it was appropriated to Simeon. By thus establishing it within the original domain of another tribe, the prophecy of Jacob in regard to Simeon was fulfilled (Gen. 49:7); for from its boundaries being not traced, there is reason to conclude that its people were divided and dispersed among those of Judah; and though one group of its cities named (2-6), gives the idea of a compact district, as it is usually represented by mapmakers, the other group (7, 8) were situated, two in the south, and two elsewhere, with tracts of the country around them.

10-16. OF ZEBULUN. **10-14. the third lot came up for the children of Zebulun**—The boundaries of the possession assigned to them extended from the Lake of Chinnereth (Sea of Galilee) on the east, to the Mediterranean on the west. Although they do not seem at first to have touched on the western shore—a part of Manasseh running north into Asher (ch. 17:10)—they afterwards did, according to the prediction of Moses (Deut. 33:19). The extent from north to south cannot be very exactly traced; the sites of many of the places through which the boundary line is drawn being unknown. Some of the cities were of note.

17-23. OF ISSACHAR. **17-20. the fourth lot came out to Issachar**—Instead of describing the boundaries of this tribe, the inspired historian gives a list of its principal cities. These cities are all in the eastern part of the plain of Esdraelon.

24-31. OF ASHER. **24-31. the fifth lot came out for the tribe of the children of Asher**—The western boundary is traced from north to south through the cities mentioned; the site of them, however, is unknown. **to Carmel ... and Shihor-libnath**—i.e., the black or muddy river; probably the Nahr Belka, below Dor (Tantoura); for that town belonged to Asher (ch. 17:10). Thence the boundary line turned eastward to Beth-dagon, a town at the junction of Zebulun and Naphtali, and ran northwards as far as Cabul, with other towns, among which is mentioned (vs. 28) "great Zidon," so called on ac-

count of its being even then the flourishing metropolis of the Phœnicians. Though included in the inheritance of Asher, this town was never possessed by them (Judg. 1:31). **29. and then the coast turneth to Ramah**—now El-Hamra, which stood where the Leontes (Litany) ends its southern course and flows westward. **and to the strong city Tyre**—The original city appears to have stood on the mainland, and was well fortified. From Tyre the boundary ran to Hosah, an inland town; and then, passing the unconquered district of Achzib (Judg. 1:31), terminated at the seacoast.

32-39. OF NAPHTALI. **32-39. the sixth lot came out to the children of Naphtali**—Although the cities mentioned have not been discovered, it is evident, from Zaanannim, which is by Kedesh, i.e., on the northwest of Lake Merom (Judg. 4:11), that the boundary described (vs. 34) ran from the southwest towards the northeast, up to the sources of the Jordan. **Aznoth-tabor**—on the east of Tabor towards the Jordan, for the border ran thence to Hukkok, touching upon that of Zebulun; and as the territory of Zebulun did not extend as far as the Jordan, Aznoth-tabor and Hukkok must have been border towns on the line which separated Naphtali from Issachar. **to Judah upon Jordan toward the sunrising**—The sixty cities, Havoth-jair, which were on the eastern side of the Jordan, opposite Naphtali, were reckoned as belonging to Judah, because Jair, their possessor, was a descendant of Judah (I Chron. 2:4-22) [KEIL].

40-48. OF DAN. **40-46. the seventh lot came out for the tribe ... of Dan**—It lay on the west of Benjamin and consisted of portions surrendered by Judah and Ephraim. Its boundaries are not stated, as they were easily distinguishable from the relative position of Dan to the three adjoining tribes. **47. the children of Dan went up to fight against Leshem**—The Danites, finding their inheritance too small, decided to enlarge its boundaries by the sword; and, having conquered Leshem (Laish), they planted a colony there, calling the new settlement by the name of Dan (see on Judg. 18).

49-51. THE CHILDREN OF ISRAEL GIVE AN INHERITANCE TO JOSHUA. **50. According to the word of the Lord, they gave him the city which he asked**—It was most proper that the great leader should receive an inheritance suited to his dignity, and as a reward for his public services. But the gift was not left to the spontaneous feelings of a grateful people. It was conferred "according to the word of the Lord"—probably an unrecorded promise, similar to what had been made to Caleb (ch. 14:9). **Timnath-serah**—or Heres, on Mount Gaash (Judg. 2:9). Joshua founded it, and was afterwards buried there (ch. 24:30). **51. These are the inheritances**—This verse is the formal close of the section which narrates the history of the land distribution; and to stamp it with due importance, the names of the commissioners are repeated, as well as the spot where so memorable a transaction took place.

CHAPTER 20

Vss. 1-6. THE LORD COMMANDS THE CITIES OF REFUGE. **1. The Lord spake unto Joshua, ... Appoint out for you cities of refuge**—(See Num. 35:9-28; Deut. 19:1-13). The command here recorded was given on their going to occupy their allotted settlements. The sanctuaries were not temples or altars, as in other countries, but inhabited cities; and the design was not to screen criminals, but only to afford the homicide protection from the vengeance of the deceased's relatives until it should have been ascertained whether the death had resulted from accident and momentary passion, or from premeditated malice. The institution of the cities of refuge, together with the rules prescribed for the guidance of those who sought an asylum within their walls, was an important provision, tending to secure the ends of justice as well as of mercy. **4. he that doth flee unto one of those cities shall stand at the entering of the gate of the city**—It was the place of public resort, and on arriving there he related his tale of distress to the elders, who were bound to give him shelter and the means of support, until the local authorities (vs. 6), having carefully investigated the case, should have pronounced the decision. If found guilty, the manslayer was surrendered to the blood-avenger; if extenuating circumstances appeared, he was to remain in the city of refuge, where he would be safe from the vindictive feelings of his pursuers; but he forfeited the privilege of immunity the moment he ventured beyond the walls. **6. until the death of the high priest**—His death secured the complete deliverance of the manslayer from his sin, only because he had been anointed with the holy oil (Num. 35:25), the symbol of the Holy Ghost; and thus the death of the earthly high priest became a type of that of the heavenly one (Heb. 9:14, 15).

7-9. THE ISRAELITES APPOINT BY NAME THE CITIES OF REFUGE. **7-9. they appointed ... cities**—There were six: three on the west, and three on the east, of Jordan. In the first instance, they were a provision of the criminal law of the Hebrews, necessary in the circumstances of that people (see on Num. 35:9-15; Deut. 19). At the same time they were designed also typically to point out the sinner's way to Christ (Heb. 6:18).

CHAPTER 21

Vss. 1-8. EIGHT AND FORTY CITIES GIVEN BY LOT OUT OF THE OTHER TRIBES UNTO THE LEVITES. **1. Then came near the heads of the fathers of the Levites**—The most venerable and distinguished members of the three Levitical families, on behalf of their tribe, applied for the special provision that had been promised them to be now awarded (see on Num. 35:1-5). Their inheritance lay within the territory of every tribe. It was assigned in the same place and manner, and by the same commissioners as the other allotments. While the people, knowing the important duties they were to perform, are described (vs. 3) as readily conceding this "peculiar" to them, it had most probably been specified and reserved for their use while the distribution of the land was in progress. **4-8. the lot came out for the families of the Kohathites**—The Levites were divided into Kohathites, Gershonites, and Merarites. Among the former the family of Aaron were exclusively appointed to the priesthood, and all the rest were ranked in the common order of Levites. The first lot was drawn by the Kohathites; and the first of theirs again by the priests, to whom thirteen cities were granted, and ten to the rest of the Kohathites (vs. 5); thirteen to the Gershonites (vs. 6), and twelve to the Merarites (vs. 7).

9-42. THE CITIES OF THE PRIESTS. **9-40. they gave ... these cities which are here mentioned by name**—It was overruled by the unerring providence of the Divine Lawgiver that the cities of the priests lay within the territories of Judah and Benjamin. This was a provision, the admirable wisdom and

propriety of which were fully manifested on the schism that took place in the reign of Rehoboam. **41. All the cities of the Levites within the possession of the children of Israel were forty and eight cities with their suburbs**—This may appear too great a proportion compared with those of the other tribes. But it must be borne in mind that the list given here contains the names of every Levitical city (see on I Chron. 6:39-66); whereas only those cities of the other tribes are mentioned which lay on the frontier or along the boundary line. Besides, the Levites were not the exclusive inhabitants of those forty-eight cities; for there must have been also a considerable number of people kept there to cultivate the glebe lands and tend the cattle. Still further, the Levitical cities had nothing but "their suburbs—a limited circuit of ground—round about them"; whereas the other cities in Israel possessed a group of independent villages (see chaps. 17-19).

43-45. GOD GAVE THEM REST. **43-45. the Lord gave unto Israel all the land which he sware to give unto their fathers**—This is a general winding up of the history from chapter 13, which narrates the occupation of the land by the Israelites. All the promises made, whether to the people or to Joshua (ch. 1:5), had been, or were in the course of being fulfilled; and the recorded experience of the Israelites (vs. 45), is a ground of hope and confidence to the people of God in every age, that all other promises made to the Church will, in due time, be accomplished.

CHAPTER 22

Vss. 1-9. JOSHUA DISMISSES THE TWO TRIBES AND A HALF, WITH A BLESSING. **1. Then Joshua called the Reubenites, and the Gadites, and the half tribe of Manasseh**—The general war of invasion being ended and the enemy being in so dispirited and isolated a condition that each tribe, by its own resources or with the aid of its neighboring tribe, was able to repress any renewed hostilities, the auxiliary Israelites from the eastern side of the Jordan were now discharged from service. Joshua dismissed them with high commendations for their fidelity and earnest admonitions to cultivate perpetual piety in life. The redundancy of the language is remarkable. It shows how important, in the judgment of the venerable leader, a steadfast observance of the divine law was to personal happiness, as well as national prosperity. **3. Ye have not left your brethren these many days unto this day**—for the space of seven years. **4-7. get you unto your tents**—i.e., home; for their families had been left in fortified towns (Num. 32:17). **8. he spake unto them, saying, Return with much riches**—in cattle, clothes, and precious metals. **divide the spoil of your enemies with your brethren**—See on Numbers 31:25-39.

10. THEY BUILD THE ALTAR OF TESTIMONY ON THEIR JOURNEY. **10. when they came unto the borders of Jordan, that are in the land of Canaan, the children of Reuben ... built there an altar**—This altar was probably an immense pile of stones and earth. The generality of our translators supposes that it was reared on the banks of the Jordan, within the limits of Canaan proper. But a little closer examination seems to make the conclusion irresistible that its position was on the eastern side of the river, for these two reasons; first, because it is said (vs. 11) to have been built "over against," or in the sight of the land of Canaan—not within it;

and secondly, because the declared motive of the transjordanic Israelites in erecting it was to prevent their brethren in Canaan ever saying, "in time to come, What have ye to do with the Lord God of Israel? For the Lord hath made Jordan a border between us and you . . . ." Such a taunt would be obviously prevented or confuted by the two tribes and a half having on the eastern side of Jordan, within their own land, a facsimile of the altar at Shiloh, as a witness that they acknowledged the same God and practised the same rites of worship as the brethren in Canaan.

11-29. CONTENTION THEREUPON. **11-29. and the children of Israel heard say**—Fame speedily spread intelligence of what the transjordanic tribes had done. The act being suspected of some idolatrous design, the tribes rose in a mass, and repairing to the tabernacle at Shiloh, resolved to declare war against the two tribes and a half as apostates from God. On calmer and more mature consideration, however, they determined, in the first instance, to send a deputation consisting of the son of the high priest, and ten eminent persons from each tribe, to make inquiry into this rumored rebellion against God (Deut. 13:13-15). The quality of the deputies evinced the deep solicitude that was felt on the occasion to maintain the purity of the divine worship throughout Israel. In the presumptive belief that the two tribes and a half had really built an altar, the deputies expressed astonishment at their so soon falling into such a heinous crime as that of violating the unity of divine worship (Exod. 20:24; 17:8, 9; Deut. 12:5-13). They reminded their eastern brethren of the disastrous consequences that were entailed on the nation at large by the apostasy at Peor and by the sin of Achan, and finally exhorted them, if they felt the want of the tabernacle and altar and repented of their rash choice in preferring worldly advantages to religious privileges, to remove to the western side of the Jordan, where all the tribes would form a united and obedient community of worshippers. **21. Then the children of Reuben . . . answered**—repudiating, in the strongest terms, the alleged crime, and deponing that so far from entertaining the intention imputed to them, their only object was to perpetuate the memory of their alliance with Israel, and their adherence to the worship of Israel's God.

30-34. THE DEPUTIES SATISFIED. **33, 34. the thing pleased the children of Israel**—The explanation not only gave perfect satisfaction to the deputies, but elicited from them expressions of unbounded joy and thankfulness. "This day we perceive that the Lord is among us," i.e., by His gracious presence and preventing goodness, which has kept you from falling into the suspected sin and rescued the nation from the calamity of a fratricidal war or providential judgments. This episode reflects honor upon all parties and shows that piety and zeal for the honor and worship of God animated the people that entered Canaan to an extent far beyond what was exemplified in many other periods of the history of Israel.

CHAPTER 23

Vss. 1, 2. JOSHUA'S EXHORTATION BEFORE HIS DEATH. **1. a long time after the Lord had given rest unto Israel from all their enemies**—about fourteen years after the conquest of Canaan, and seven after the distribution of that country among the tribes. **2. Joshua called for all Israel**—The clause which follows seems to restrict this general expres-

sion as applicable only to the officers and representatives of the people. The place of assembly was most probably Shiloh. The occasion of convening it was the extreme age and approaching death of the venerable leader; and the purport of this solemn address was to animate the chosen people and their posterity to a faithful and unswerving continuance in the faith and worship of the God of Israel.

3. BY FORMER BENEFITS. **ye have seen all that the Lord your God hath done unto all these nations because of you**—The modesty and humility of Joshua are remarkably displayed at the commencement of this address. Dismissing all thoughts of his personal services, he ascribed the subjugation and occupation of Canaan entirely to the favoring presence and aid of God; and in doing so, he spoke not more piously than truly. This had been promised (Deut. 1:30; 3:22); and the reality of the divine aid was seen in the rapid overthrow of the Canaanites, which had already led to the division of the whole land among the tribes.

5-11. BY PROMISES. **5-11. the Lord your God, he shall expel them from before you, as the Lord your God has promised you**, etc.—The actual possessions which God had given were a pledge of the complete fulfilment of His promise in giving them the parts of the country still unconquered. But the accomplishment of the divine promise depended on their inviolable fidelity to God's law—on their keeping resolutely aloof from all familiar intercourse and intimate connections with the Canaanites, or in any way partaking of their idolatrous sins. In the event of their continuing in steadfast adherence to the cause of God, as happily distinguished the nation at that time, His blessing would secure them a course of brilliant and easy victories (Lev. 26:7; Deut. 28:7; 32:30). **11. Take good heed, therefore, that ye love the Lord your God**—The sum of his exhortation is comprised in the love of God, which is the end or fulfilment of the law (Deut. 6:5; 11:13; Matt. 22:37).

12. BY THREATENINGS IN CASE OF DISOBEDIENCE. **12. Else if ye do in any wise go back, and cleave unto the remnant of these nations**—By "going back" is meant transgression of the divine law; and as marriage connections with the idolatrous Canaanites would present many and strong temptations to transgress it, these were strictly prohibited (Exod. 34:12-16; Deut. 7:3). With his eye, as it were, upon those prohibitions, Joshua threatens them with the certain withdrawal of the divine aid in the further expulsion of the Canaanites (a threat founded on Exod. 23:33; Numb. 33:55; Deut. 7:16).

CHAPTER 24

Vs. 1. JOSHUA ASSEMBLING THE TRIBES. **1. Joshua gathered all the tribes of Israel to Shechem**—Another and final opportunity of dissuading the people against idolatry is here described as taken by the aged leader, whose solicitude on this account arose from his knowledge of the extreme readiness of the people to conform to the manners of the surrounding nations. This address was made to the representatives of the people convened at Shechem, and which had already been the scene of a solemn renewal of the covenant (ch. 8:30, 35). The transaction now to be entered upon being in principle and object the same, it was desirable to give it all the solemn impressiveness which might be derived from the memory of the former ceremonial, as well as from other sacred associations of the place (Gen. 12:6, 7; 33:18-20; 35:2-4). **they** presented themselves before God—It is generally assumed that the ark of the covenant had been transferred on this occasion to Shechem; as on extraordinary emergencies it was for a time removed (Judg. 20:1-18; I Sam. 4:3; II Sam. 15:24). But the statement, not necessarily implying this, may be viewed as expressing only the religious character of the ceremony [HENGSTENBERG].

2-13. RELATES GOD'S BENEFITS. **2. Joshua said unto all the people**—His address briefly recapitulated the principal proofs of the divine goodness to Israel from the call of Abraham to their happy establishment in the land of promise; it showed them that they were indebted for their national existence as well as their peculiar privileges, not to any merits of their own, but to the free grace of God. **Your fathers dwelt on the other side of the flood**—The Euphrates, viz., at Ur. **Terah, the father of Abraham, and the father of Nahor**—(see on Gen. 11:27). Though Terah had three sons, Nahor only is mentioned with Abraham, as the Israelites were descended from him on the mother's side through Rebekah and her nieces, Leah and Rachel. **served other gods**—conjoining, like Laban, the traditional knowledge of the true God with the domestic use of material images (Gen. 31:19, 34). **3. I took your father Abraham from the other side of the flood, and led him throughout all the land of Canaan**—It was an irresistible impulse of divine grace which led the patriarch to leave his country and relatives, to migrate to Canaan, and live a "stranger and pilgrim" in that land. **4. I gave unto Esau mount Seir**—(see on Gen. 36:8, 9.) In order that he might be no obstacle to Jacob and his posterity being the exclusive heirs of Canaan. **12. I sent the hornet before you**—a particular species of wasp which swarms in warm countries and sometimes assumes the scourging character of a plague; or, as many think, it is a figurative expression for uncontrollable terror (Exod. 23:27, 28). **14-28. Now therefore fear the Lord, and serve him in sincerity and in truth**—After having enumerated so many grounds for national gratitude, Joshua calls on them to declare, in a public and solemn manner, whether they will be faithful and obedient to the God of Israel. He avowed this to be his own unalterable resolution, and urged them, if they were sincere in making a similar avowal, "to put away the strange gods that were among them"—a requirement which seems to imply that some were suspected of a strong hankering for, or concealed practice of, the idolatry, whether in the form of Zabaism, the fire-worship of their Chaldean ancestors, or the grosser superstitions of the Canaanites. **26. Joshua wrote these words in the book of the law of God**—registered the engagements of that solemn covenant in the book of sacred history. **took a great stone**—ac-

cording to the usage of ancient times to erect stone pillars as monuments of public transactions. **set it up there under an oak**—or terebinth, in all likelihood, the same as that at the root of which Jacob buried the idols and charms found in his family. **that was by the sanctuary of the Lord**—either the spot where the ark had stood, or else the place around, so called from that religious meeting, as Jacob named Beth-el the house of God.

14-33. HIS AGE AND DEATH. **29, 30. Joshua ... died**—Lightfoot computes that he lived seventeen, others twenty-seven years, after the entrance into Canaan. He was buried, according to the Jewish practice, within the limits of his own inheritance. The eminent public services he had long rendered to Israel and the great amount of domestic comfort and national prosperity he had been instrumental in diffusing among the several tribes, were deeply felt—were universally acknowledged; and a testimonial in the form of a statue or obelisk would have been immediately raised to his honor, in all parts of the land, had such been the fashion of the times. The brief but noble epitaph by the historian is, Joshua, "the servant of the Lord." **31. Israel served the Lord all the days of Joshua**—The high and commanding character of this eminent leader had given so decided a tone to the sentiments and manners of his contemporaries and the memory of his fervent piety and many virtues continued so vividly impressed on the memories of the people, that the sacred historian has recorded it to his immortal honor. "Israel served the Lord all the days of Joshua, and all the days of the elders that overlived Joshua." **32. the bones of Joseph**—They had carried these venerable relics with them in all their migrations through the desert, and deferred the burial, according to the dying charge of Joseph himself, till they arrived in the promised land. The sarcophagus, in which his mummied body had been put, was brought thither by the Israelites, and probably buried when the tribe of Ephraim had obtained their settlement, or at the solemn convocation described in this chapter. **in a parcel of ground which Jacob bought ... for an hundred pieces of silver**—*Kestitah,* translated, "piece of silver," is supposed to mean a lamb, the weights being in the form of lambs or kids, which were, in all probability, the earliest standard of value among pastoral people. The tomb that now covers the spot is a Mohammedan *Welce,* but there is no reason to doubt that the precious deposit of Joseph's remains may be concealed there at the present time. **33. Eleazar the son of Aaron died, and they buried him ... in mount Ephraim**—The sepulchre is at the modern village Awertah, which, according to Jewish travellers, contains the graves also of Ithamar, the brother of Phinehas, the son of Eleazar [VAN DE VELDE].

THE BOOK OF

JUDGES

CHAPTER 1

Vss. 1-3. THE ACTS OF JUDAH AND SIMEON. **1. Now after the death of Joshua**—probably not a long period, for the Canaanites seem to have taken ad-

vantage of that event to attempt recovering their lost position, and the Israelites were obliged to renew the war. **the children of Israel asked the Lord**—The divine counsel on this, as on other occasions, was sought by Urim and Thummim, by applying to the high priest, who, according to Josephus, was Phinehas. **saying, Who shall go up for us against the Canaanites first**—The elders, who exercised the government in their respective tribes, judged rightly, that in entering upon an important expedition, they should have a leader nominated by divine appointment; and in consulting the oracle, they adopted a prudent course, whether the object of their inquiry related to the choice of an individual commander, or to the honor of precedency among the tribes. **2. the Lord said, Judah shall go up**—The predicted pre-eminence (Gen. 49:8) was thus conferred upon Judah by divine direction, and its appointment to take the lead in the ensuing hostilities was of great importance, as the measure of success by which its arms were crowned, would animate the other tribes to make similar attempts against the Canaanites within their respective territories. **I have delivered the land into his hand**—not the whole country, but the district assigned for his inheritance. **3. Judah said unto Simeon, Come up with me . . . , that we may fight against the Canaanites**—Being conterminous tribes (Josh. 19:1, 2), they had a common interest, and were naturally associated in this enterprise.

4-21. Adoni-bezek Justly Requited. **Bezek**—This place lay within the domain of Judah, about twelve miles south of Jerusalem. **5. found Adoni-bezek**—i.e., lord of Bezek—he was "found," i.e., surprised and routed in a pitched battle, whence he fled; but being taken prisoner, he was treated with a severity unusual among the Israelites, for they "cut off his thumbs and great toes." Barbarities of various kinds were commonly practised on prisoners of war in ancient times, and the object of this particular mutilation of the hands and feet was to disable them for military service ever after. The infliction of such a horrid cruelty on this Canaanite chief would have been a foul stain on the character of the Israelites if there were not reason for believing it was done by them as an act of retributive justice, and as such it was regarded by Adoni-bezek himself, whose conscience read his atrocious crimes in their punishment. **7. Threescore and ten kings**—So great a number will not appear strange, when it is considered that anciently every ruler of a city or large town was called a king. It is not improbable that in that southern region of Canaan, there might, in earlier times, have been even more till a turbulent chief like Adoni-bezek devoured them in his insatiable ambition. **8. Now the children of Judah had fought against Jerusalem, and had taken it**—The capture of this important city, which ranks among the early incidents in the war of invasion (Josh. 15:63), is here noticed to account for its being in the possession of the Judahites; and they brought Adoni-bezek thither, in order, probably, that his fate being rendered so public, might inspire terror far and wide. Similar inroads were made into the other unconquered parts of Judah's inheritance. The story of Caleb's acquisition of Hebron is here repeated (Josh. 15:16-19). **16. the children of the Kenite, Moses' father-in-law, went up out of the city of palm trees with the children of Judah**—called "the Kenite," as probably descended from the people of that name (Num. 24:21, 22). If he might not himself, his posterity did accept the invitation of Moses (Num. 10:32) to accompany the Israelites to Canaan. Their first encampment was in the "city of palm trees"—not Jericho, of course, which was utterly destroyed, but the surrounding district, perhaps En-gedi, in early times called Hazezon-tamar (Gen. 14:7), from the palm-grove

which sheltered it. Thence they removed for some unknown cause, and associating themselves with Judah, joined in an expedition against Arad, in the southern part of Canaan (Num. 21:1). On the conquest of that district, some of this pastoral people pitched their tents there, while others migrated to the north (ch. 4:17). **17-29. And Judah went with Simeon his brother**—The course of the narrative is here resumed from verse 9, and an account given of Judah returning the services of Simeon (vs. 3), by aiding in the prosecution of the war within the neighboring tribes. **slew the Canaanites that inhabited Zephath**—or Zephathah (II Chron. 14:10), a valley lying in the southern portion of Canaan. **Hormah**—destroyed in fulfilment of an early vow of the Israelites (see on Num. 21:1-3). The confederate tribes, pursuing their incursions in that quarter, came successively to Gaza, Askelon, and Ekron, which they took. But the Philistines seem soon to have regained possession of these cities. **19. the Lord was with Judah; . . . but they could not drive out the inhabitants of the valley**—The war was of the Lord, whose omnipotent aid would have ensured their success in every encounter, whether on the mountains or the plains, with foot soldiers or cavalry. It was distrust, the want of a simple and firm reliance on the promise of God, that made them afraid of the iron chariots (see on Josh. 11:4-9). **21. the children of Benjamin did not drive out the Jebusites that inhabited Jerusalem**—Judah had expelled the people from their part of Jerusalem (vs. 8). The border of the two tribes ran through the city—Israelites and natives must have been closely intermingled.

22-26. Some Canaanites Left. **22, 23. the house of Joseph**—the tribe of Ephraim, as distinguished from Manasseh (vs. 27). **24. the spies . . . said, . . . Show us, . . . the entrance into the city**—i.e., the avenues to the city, and the weakest part of the walls. **we will show thee mercy**—The Israelites might employ these means of getting possession of a place which was divinely appropriated to them: they might promise life and rewards to this man, though he and all the Canaanites were doomed to destruction (Josh. 2:12-14); but we may assume the promise was suspended on his embracing the true religion, or quitting the country, as he did. If they had seen him to be firmly opposed to either of these alternatives, they would not have constrained him by promises any more than by threats to betray his countrymen. But if they found him disposed to be serviceable, and to aid the invaders in executing the will of God, they might promise to spare him. **26. Luz**—(See on Gen. 12:8, 28:19). **27-36.** The same course of subjugation was carried on in the other tribes to a partial extent, and with varying success. Many of the natives, no doubt, during the progress of this exterminating war, saved themselves by flight and became, it is thought, the first colonists in Greece, Italy, and other countries. But a large portion made a stout resistance and retained possession of their old abodes in Canaan. In other cases, when the natives were vanquished, avarice led the Israelites to spare the idolaters, contrary to the express command of God; and their disobedience to His orders in this matter involved them in many troubles which this book describes.

CHAPTER 2

Vss. 1-10. An Angel Sent to Rebuke the People at Bochim. **1, 2, an angel . . . came from**

Gilgal to Bochim—We are inclined to think, from the authoritative tone of his language, that he was the Angel of the Covenant (Exod. 23:20; Josh. 5: 14); the same who appearerd in human form and announced himself captain of the Lord's host. His coming from Gilgal had a peculiar significance, for there the Israelites made a solemn dedication of themselves to God on their entrance into the promised land; and the memory of that religious engagement, which the angel's arrival from Gilgal awakened, gave emphatic force to his rebuke of their apostasy. Bochim, "the weepers," was a name bestowed evidently in allusion to this incident or the place, which was at or near Shiloh. **I said, I will never break my covenant with you . . . but ye have not obeyed my voice**—The burden of the angel's remonstrance was that God would inviolably keep His promise; but they, by their flagrant and repeated breaches of their covenant with Him, had forfeited all claim to the stipulated benefits. Having disobeyed the will of God by voluntarily courting the society of idolaters and placing themselves in the way of temptation, He left them to suffer the punishment of their misdeeds. **4, 5. when the Lord spake these words . . . the people lifted up their voice, and wept**—The angel's expostulation made a deep and painful impression. But the reformation was but temporary, and the gratifying promise of a revival which this scene of emotion held out, was, ere long, blasted by speedy and deeper relapses into the guilt of defection and idolatry. **6-10. And when Joshua had let the people go**—This passage is a repetition of Joshua 24:29-31. It was inserted here to give the reader the reasons which called forth so strong and severe a rebuke from the angel of the Lord. During the lifetime of the first occupiers, who retained a vivid recollection of all the miracles and judgments which they had witnessed in Egypt and the desert, the national character stood high for faith and piety. But, in course of time, a new race arose who were strangers to all the hallowed and solemnizing experience of their fathers, and too readily yielded to the corrupting influences of the idolatry that surrounded them.

11-19. WICKEDNESS OF THE NEW GENERATION AFTER JOSHUA. 11-19. the children of Israel did evil in the sight of the Lord—This chapter, together with the first eight verses of the next, contains a brief but comprehensive summary of the principles developed in the following history. An attentive consideration of them, therefore, is of the greatest importance to a right understanding of the strange and varying phases of Israelitish history, from the death of Joshua till the establishment of the monarchy. **served Baalim**—The plural is used to include all the gods of the country. **13. Ashtaroth**—Also a plural word, denoting all the female divinities, whose rites were celebrated by the most gross and revolting impurities. **14. the anger of the Lord was hot against Israel, and he delivered them into the hands of the spoilers that spoiled them**—Adversities in close and rapid succession befell them. But all these calamities were designed only as chastisements—a course of correctional discipline by which God brought His people to see and repent of their errors; for as they returned to faith and allegiance, He "raised up judges" (vs. 16), **which delivered them out of the hand of those that spoiled them**—The judges who governed Israel were strictly God's vicegerents in the government of the people, He being the supreme ruler. Those who were thus elevated retained the dignity as long as

they lived; but there was no regular, unbroken succession of judges. Individuals, prompted by the inward, irresistible impulse of God's Spirit when they witnessed the depressed state of their country, were roused to achieve its deliverance. It was usually accompanied by a special call, and the people seeing them endowed with extraordinary courage or strength, accepted them as delegates of Heaven, and submitted to their sway. Frequently they were appointed only for a particular district, and their authority extended no farther than over the people whose interests they were commissioned to protect. They were without pomp, equipage, or emoluments attached to the office. They had no power to make laws; for these were given by God; nor to explain them, for that was the province of the priests—but they were officially upholders of the law, defenders of religion, avengers of all crimes, particularly of idolatry and its attendant vices.

CHAPTER 3

Vss. 1-4. NATIONS LEFT TO PROVE ISRAEL. **1. these are the nations which the Lord left, to prove Israel**—This was the special design of these nations being left, and it evinces the direct influence of the theocracy under which the Israelites were placed. These nations were left for a double purpose: in the first instance, to be instrumental, by their inroads, in promoting the moral and spiritual discipline of the Israelites; and also to subserve the design of making them acquainted with war, in order that the young, more especially, who were total strangers to it, might learn the use of weapons and the art of wielding them.

5-7. BY COMMUNION WITH THESE THE ISRAELITES COMMIT IDOLATRY. **5-7. the children of Israel dwelt among the Canaanites**—The two peoples by degrees came to be on habits of intercourse. Reciprocal alliances were formed by marriage till the Israelites, relaxing the austerity of their principles, showed a growing conformity to the manners and worship of their idolatrous neighbors.

8-11. OTHNIEL DELIVERS ISRAEL. **8-11. sold them**—i.e., delivered them into the hand of Chushan-rishathaim, or Chushan, "the wicked." This name had been probably given him from his cruel and impious character. **served Chushan-rishathaim eight years**—by the payment of a stipulated tribute yearly, the raising of which must have caused a great amount of labor and privation. **9. when the children of Israel cried unto the Lord**—In their distress they had recourse to earnest prayer, accompanied by humble and penitent confession of their errors. **Othniel**—(See on Josh. 15:17; ch. 1: 13). His military experience qualified him for the work, while the gallant exploits he was known to have performed, gained him the full confidence of his countrymen in his ability as a leader. **10. The Spirit of the Lord came upon him, and he judged Israel, and went out to war**—Impelled by a supernatural influence, he undertook the difficult task of government at this national crisis—addressing himself to promote a general reformation of manners, the abolition of idolatry, and the revival of pure religion. After these preliminary measures, he collected a body of choice warriors to expel the foreign oppressors. **the Lord delivered Chushan-rishathaim king of Mesopotamia into his hand; and his hand prevailed against Chushan-rishathaim**—No details are given of this war, which, considering the resources of so potent a monarch, must have been a determined struggle. But the Israelitish arms were crowned through the blessing of God with victory, and Canaan regained its freedom and independence. **11. Othniel ... died**—How powerful the influence of one good man is, in church or state, is best found in his loss [BISHOP HALL].

12-30. EHUD SLAYS EGLON. 12-14. the children of Israel did evil again in the sight of the Lord—The Israelites, deprived of the moral and political influences of Othniel, were not long in following their native bias to idolatry. **the Lord strengthened Eglon king of Moab**—The reigning monarch's ambition was to recover that extensive portion of his ancient territory possessed by the Israelites. In conjunction with his neighbors, the Ammonites and the Amalekites, sworn enemies of Israel, he first subjected the eastern tribes; then crossing the Jordan, he made a sudden incursion on western Canaan, and in virtue of his conquests, erected fortifications in the territory adjoining Jericho [JOSEPHUS], to secure the frontier, and fixed his residence there. This oppressor was permitted, in the providence of God, to triumph for eighteen years. **15. Ehud son of Gera**—descended from Gera, one of Benjamin's sons (Gen. 46:21). **left-handed**—This peculiarity distinguished many in the Benjamite tribe (ch. 20:16). But the original word is rendered in some versions "both-handed," a view countenanced by I Chron. 12:2. **by him the children of Israel sent a present unto Eglon the king of Moab**—the yearly tribute, which, according to Eastern fashion, would be borne with ostentatious ceremony and offered (vs. 18) by several messengers. **16. Ehud made him a dagger ... and he did gird it ... upon his right thigh**—The sword was usually worn on the left side; so that Ehud's was the more likely to escape detection. **19. quarries**—rather graven images (Deut. 7:25; Jer. 8:19; 51:52); statues of Moabite idols, the sight of which kindled the patriotic zeal of Ehud to avenge this public insult to Israel on its author. **I have a secret errand unto thee, O king; who said, Keep silence**—"Privacy"—a signal for all to withdraw. **20. a summer parlour**—*Heb.*, chamber of cooling—one of those retired edifices which Oriental grandees usually have in their gardens, and in which they repose during the heat of the day. **21. Ehud put forth his left hand**—The whole circumstance of this daring act—the death of Eglon without a shriek, or noise—the locking of the doors—the carrying off the key—the calm, unhurried deportment of Ehud—show the strength of his confidence that he was doing God service. **27. he blew a trumpet in the mount of Ephraim**—summoned to arms the people of that mountainous region, which, adjoining the territory of Benjamin, had probably suffered most from the grievous oppression of the Moabites. **28. they went down after him, and took the fords**—(See on Josh. 2:7). With the view of preventing all escape to the Moabite coast, and by the slaughter of 10,000 men, Ehud rescued his country from a state of ignominious vassalage. **31. after him was Shamgar**—No notice is given of the tribe or family of this judge; and from the Philistines being the enemy that roused him into public service, the suffering seems to have been local—confined to some of the western tribes. **slew ... six hundred men with an oxgoad**—This instrument is eight feet long and about six inches in circumference. It is armed at the lesser end with a sharp prong for driving the cattle, and on the other with a small iron paddle for removing the clay which encumbers the plough in working. Such an instrument, wielded by a strong

arm, would do no mean execution. We may suppose, however, for the notice is very fragmentary, that Shamgar was only the leader of a band of peasants, who by means of such implements of labor as they could lay hold of at the moment, achieved the heroic exploit recorded.

CHAPTER 4

Vss. 1-17. DEBORAH AND BARAK DELIVER ISRAEL FROM JABIN AND SISERA. 1. The children of Israel again did evil in the sight of the Lord, when Ehud was dead—The removal of the zealous judge Ehud again left his infatuated countrymen without the restraint of religion. **2. Jabin, king of Canaan**—Jabin, a royal title (Josh. 11:1). The second Jabin built a new capital on the ruins of the old (Josh. 11:10, 11). The northern Canaanites had recovered from the effect of their disastrous overthrow in the time of Joshua, and now triumphed in their turn over Israel. This was the severest oppression to which Israel had been subjected. But it fell heaviest on the tribes in the north, and it was not till after a grinding servitude of twenty years that they were awakened to view it as the punishment of their sins and to seek deliverance from God. **4. Deborah, a prophetess**—A woman of extraordinary knowledge, wisdom, and piety, instructed in divine knowledge by the Spirit and accustomed to interpret His will; who acquired an extensive influence, and was held in universal respect, insomuch that she became the animating spirit of the government and discharged all the special duties of a judge, except that of military leader. **wife of Lapidoth**—rendered by some "a woman of splendors." **5. she dwelt under the palm tree**—or, collectively, palm grove. It is common still in the East to administer justice in the open air, or under the canopy of an umbrageous tree. **6. she sent and called Barak**—by virtue of her official authority as judge. **Kedesh-naphtali**—situated on an eminence, little north of the Sea of Galilee, and so called to distinguish it from another Kedesh in Issachar. **Hath not the Lord of Israel commanded**—a Hebrew form of making an emphatic communication. **Go and draw toward Mount Tabor**—an isolated mountain of Galilee, northeast corner of the plain of Esdraelon. It was a convenient place of rendezvous, and the enlistment is not to be considered as limited to 10,000, though a smaller force would have been inadequate. **8. Barak said unto her, If thou wilt go with me, then I will go**—His somewhat singular request to be accompanied by Deborah was not altogether the result of weakness. The Orientals always take what is dearest to the battlefield along with them; they think it makes them fight better. The policy of Barak, then, to have the presence of the prophetess is perfectly intelligible as it would no less stimulate the valor of the troops, than sanction, in the eyes of Israel, the uprising against an oppressor so powerful as Jabin. **9. the Lord shall sell Sisera into the hand of a woman**—This was a prediction which Barak could not understand at the time; but the strain of it conveyed a rebuke of his unmanly fears. **11. Now Heber the Kenite ... pitched his tent**—It is not uncommon, even in the present day, for pastoral tribes to feed their flocks on the extensive commons that lie in the heart of inhabited countries in the East (see on ch. 1:16). **plain of Zaanaim**—This is a mistranslation for "the oaks of the wanderers." The site of the encampment was under a grove of oaks, or terebinths, in the upland valley of Kedesh. **13. the river of Kishon**—The plain on its bank was chosen as the battlefield by Sisera himself, who was unconsciously drawn thither for the ruin of his army. **14. Barak went down from mount Tabor**—It is a striking proof of the full confidence Barak and his troops reposed in Deborah's assurance of victory, that they relinquished their advantageous position on the hill and rushed into the plain in face of the iron chariots they so much dreaded. **15. the Lord discomfited Sisera**—*Heb.*, threw his army into confusion; men, horses, and chariots being intermingled in wild confusion. The disorder was produced by a supernatural panic (see on ch. 5:20). **so that Sisera lighted down off his chariot, and fled away on his feet**—His chariot being probably distinguished by its superior size and elegance, would betray the rank of its rider, and he saw therefore that his only chance of escape was on foot. **16. But Barak pursued ... unto Harosheth**—Broken and routed, the main body of Sisera's army fled northward; others were forced into the Kishon and drowned (see on ch. 5:21). **17, 18. Sisera fled ... to the tent of Jael**—According to the usages of nomadic people, the duty of receiving the stranger in the sheik's absence devolves on his wife, and the moment the stranger is admitted into his tent, his claim to be defended or concealed from his pursuers is established. **19. she ... gave him drink, and covered him**—Sisera reckoned on this as a pledge of his safety, especially in the tent of a friendly sheik. This pledge was the strongest that could be sought or obtained, after he had partaken of refreshments, and been introduced in the inner or women's apartment. **20. he said unto her, ... when any man doth come and inquire of thee and say, Is there any man here? thou shalt say, No**—The privacy of the harem, even in a tent, cannot be intruded on without express permission. **21. Then Jael took a nail of the tent**—most probably one of the pins with which the tent ropes are fastened to the ground. Escape was almost impossible for Sisera. But the taking of his life by the hand of Jael was murder. It was a direct violation of all the notions of honor and friendship that are usually held sacred among pastoral people, and for which it is impossible to conceive a woman in Jael's circumstances to have had any motive, except that of gaining favor with the victors. Though predicted by Deborah, it was the result of divine foreknowledge only—not the divine appointment or sanction; and though it is praised in the song, the eulogy must be considered as pronounced not on the moral character of the woman and her deed, but on the public benefits which, in the overruling providence of God, would flow from it.

CHAPTER 5

Vss. 1-31. DEBORAH AND BARAK'S SONG OF THANKSGIVING. **1. Then sang Deborah and Barak ... on that day**—This noble triumphal ode was evidently the composition of Deborah herself. **2-3.** The meaning is obscurely seen in our version; it has been better rendered thus, "Praise ye Jehovah; for the free are freed in Israel—the people have willingly offered themselves" [ROBINSON]. **4, 5.** Allusion is here made, in general terms, to God's interposition on behalf of His people. **Seir ... the field of Edom**—represent the mountain range and plain extending along the south from the Dead Sea to the Elanitic Gulf. **thou wentest out**—indicates

the storm to have proceeded from the south or southeast. **6-8.** The song proceeds in these verses to describe the sad condition of the country, the oppression of the people, and the origin of all the national distress in the people's apostasy from God. Idolatry was the cause of foreign invasion and internal inability to resist it. **9.** expresses gratitude to the respective leaders of the tribes which participated in the contest; but, above all, to God, who inspired both the patriotic disposition and the strength. **Speak**—i.e., join in this song of praise. **white asses**—Those which are purely white are highly prized, and being costly, are possessed only by the wealthy and great. "Ye that sit in judgment," has been rendered, "ye that repose on tapestries." **11-14.** The wells which are at a little distance from towns in the East, are, in unsettled times, places of danger. But in peace they are scenes of pleasant and joyous resort. The poetess anticipates that this song may be sung, and the righteous acts of the Lord rehearsed at these now tranquil "places of drawing water." Deborah now rouses herself to describe, in terms suitable to the occasion, the preparation and the contest, and calls in a flight of poetic enthusiasm on Barak to parade his prisoners in triumphal procession. Then follows a eulogistic enumeration of the tribes which raised the commanded levy, or volunteered their services—the soldiers of Ephraim who dwelt near the mount of the Amalekites, the small quota of Benjamin; "the governors," valiant leaders "out of Machir," the western Manasseh; and out of Zebulun. **15.** Then comes a reproachful notice of the tribes which did not obey the summons to take the field against the common enemy of Israel. By the "divisions," i.e., the watercourses which descend from the eastern hills unto the Jordan and Dead Sea. **For the divisions of Reuben there were great thoughts of heart**—They felt the patriotic impulse and determined, at first, to join the ranks of their western brethren, but resiled from the purpose, preferring their peaceful shepherd songs to the trumpet sound of war. **17. Gilead abode beyond Jordan**—i.e., Both Gad and the eastern half to Manasseh chose to dwell at ease in their Havoth-jair, or villages of tents, while Dan and Asher, both maritime tribes, continued with their ships and in their "breaches" (havens). The mention of these craven tribes is concluded (vs. 18) with a fresh burst of commendation on Zebulun and Naphtali. **19-22.** describes the scene of battle and the issue. It would seem (vs. 19) that Jabin was reinforced by the troops of other Canaanite princes. The battlefield was near Taanach (now Ta'annuk), on a tell or mound in the level plain of Megiddo (now Leijun), on its southwestern extremity, by the left bank of the Kishon. **they took no gain of money**—They obtained no plunder. **the stars in their courses fought**—A fearful tempest burst upon them and threw them into disorder. **the river of Kishon swept them away**—The enemy was defeated near "the waters of Megiddo"—the sources and side streams of the Kishon: they that fled had to cross the deep and marshy bed of the torrent, but the Lord had sent a heavy rain—the waters suddenly rose—the warriors fell into the quicksands, and sinking deep into them, were drowned or washed into the sea [VAN DE VELDE]. **22. Then were the horse hoofs broken by the means of the prancings**—Anciently, as in many parts of the East still, horses were not shod. The breaking of the hoofs denotes the hot haste and heavy irregular tramp of the routed foe. **23. Curse ye Meroz**—a village on the confines of

Issachar and Naphtali, which lay in the course of the fugitives, but the inhabitants declined to aid in their destruction. **24-27.** is a most graphic picture of the treatment of Sisera in the tent of Jael. **butter** —curdled milk; a favorite beverage in the East. **28-30.** In these verses a sudden transition is made to the mother of the Canaanite general, and a striking picture is drawn of a mind agitated between hope and fear—impatient of delay, yet anticipating the news of victory and the rewards of rich booty. **the lattice**—a lattice window—common to the houses in warm countries for the circulation of air. **her wise ladies**—maids of honor. **to every man a damsel or two**—Young maidens formed always a valued part of Oriental conquerors' war-spoils. But Sisera's mother wished other booty for him; namely, the gold-threaded, richly embroidered, and scarlet-colored cloaks which were held in such high esteem. The ode concludes with a wish in keeping with the pious and patriotic character of the prophetess.

CHAPTER 6

Vss. 1-6. THE ISRAELITES, FOR THEIR SINS, OP-PRESSED BY MIDIAN. **1. the Lord delivered them into the hand of Midian**—Untaught by their former experiences, the Israelites again apostatized, and new sins were followed by fresh judgments. Midian had sustained a severe blow in the time of Moses (Num. 31:1-18); and the memory of that disaster, no doubt, inflamed their resentment against the Israelites. They were wandering herdsmen, called "children of the East," from their occupying the territory east of the Red Sea, contiguous to Moab. The destructive ravages they are described as at this time committing in the land of Israel are similar to those of the Bedouin Arabs, who harass the peaceful cultivators of the soil. Unless composition is made with them, they return annually at a certain season, when they carry off the grain, seize the cattle and other property; and even life itself is in jeopardy from the attacks of those prowling marauders. The vast horde of Midian-ites that overran Canaan made them the greatest scourge which had ever afflicted the Israelites. **made ... dens ... in the mountains and caves**—not, of course, excavating them, for they were there already, but making them fit for habitation.

7-10. A PROPHET REBUKES THEM. **the Lord sent a prophet unto the children of Israel**—The curse of the national calamity is authoritatively traced to their infidelity as the cause.

11-16. AN ANGEL SENDS GIDEON TO DELIVER THEM. **there came an angel of the Lord**—He appeared in the character and equipments of a travel-ler (vs. 21), who sat down in the shade to enjoy a little refreshment and repose. Entering into conversation on the engrossing topic of the times, the grievous oppression of the Midianites, he began urging Gideon to exert his well-known prowess on behalf of his country. Gideon, in replying, ad-dresses him at first in a style equivalent (in *Hebrew*) to "sir," but afterwards gives to him the name usually applied to God. **an oak**—*Hebrew*, "the oak"—as famous in after-times. **Ophrah**—a city in the tribe of Manasseh, about sixteen miles north of Jericho, in the district belonging to the family of Abiezer (Josh. 17:2). **his son Gideon threshed wheat by the wine press**—This incident tells em-phatically the tale of public distress. The small quantity of grain he was threshing, indicated by his

using a flail instead of the customary treading of cattle—the unusual place, near a wine press, under a tree, and on the bare ground, not a wooden floor, for the prevention of noise—all these circumstances reveal the extreme dread in which the people were living. **13. if the Lord be with us, why then is all this befallen us?**—Gideon's language betrays want of reflection, for the very chastisements God had brought on His people showed His presence with, and His interest in, them. **14. the Lord looked upon him, and said, Go in this thy might ... have not I sent thee?**—The command and the promise made Gideon aware of the real character of his visitor; and yet like Moses, from a sense of humility, or a shrinking at the magnitude of the undertaking, he excused himself from entering on the enterprise. And even though assured that, with the divine aid, he would overcome the Midianites as easily as if they were but one man, he still hesitates and wishes to be better assured that the mission was really from God. He resembles Moses also in the desire for a sign; and in both cases it was the rarity of revelations in such periods of general corruption that made them so desirous of having the fullest conviction of being addressed by a heavenly mes-senger. The request was reasonable, and it was graciously granted.

17-32. GIDEON'S PRESENT CONSUMED BY FIRE. **18. Depart not hence, I pray thee, until I ... bring forth my present**—*Hebrew*, my *mincha*, or meat offering; and his idea probably was to prove, by his visitor's partaking of the entertainment, whether or not he was more than man. **19. Gideon went in, and made ready a kid; ... the flesh he put in a basket, and he put the broth in a pot**—(See on Gen. 18). The flesh seems to have been roasted, which is done by cutting it into kobab, i.e., into small pieces, fixed on a skewer, and put before the fire. The broth was for immediate use; the other, brought in a hand-basket was intended to be a future supply to the traveller. The miraculous fire that consumed it and the vanishing of the stranger, not by walking, but as a spirit in the fire, filled Gideon with awe. A consciousness of demerit fills the heart of every fallen man at the thought of God, with fear of His wrath; and this feeling was in-creased by a belief prevalent in ancient times, that whoever saw an angel would forthwith die. The acceptance of Gideon's sacrifice betokened the ac-ceptance of his person; but it required an express assurance of the divine blessing, given in some un-known manner, to restore his comfort and peace of mind. **24-32. it came to pass the same night, that the Lord said unto him**—The transaction in which Gideon is here described as engaged was not en-tered on till the night after the vision. **Take thy father's ... second bullock**—The Midianites had probably reduced the family herd; or, as Gideon's father was addicted to idolatry, the best may have been fattened for the service of Baal; so that the second was the only remaining one fit for sacrifice to God. **throw down the altar of Baal that thy father hath**—standing upon his ground, though kept for the common use of the townsmen. **cut down the grove that is by it**—dedicated to Ashtaroth. With the aid of ten confidential servants he demolished the one altar and raised on the ap-pointed spot the altar of the Lord; but, for fear of opposition, the work had to be done under cover of night. A violent commotion was excited next day, and vengeance vowed against Gideon as the perpetrator. "Joash, his father, quieted the mob in a manner similar to that of the town clerk of

Ephesus. It was not for them to take the matter into their own hands. The one, however, made an appeal to the magistrate; the other to the idolatrous god himself" [CHALMERS].

33-39. THE SIGNS. **33. all the Midianites... pitched in Jezreel**—The confederated troops of Midian, Amalek, and their neighbors, crossing the Jordan to make a fresh inroad on Canaan, encamped in the plains of Esdraelon (anciently Jezreel). The southern part of the Ghor lies in a very low level, so that there is a steep and difficult descent into Canaan by the southern wadies. Keeping this in view, we see the reason why the Midianite army, from the east of Jordan, entered Canaan by the northern wadies of the Ghor, opposite Jezreel. **34. the Spirit of the Lord came upon Gideon**—Called in this sudden emergency into the public service of his country, he was supernaturally endowed with wisdom and energy commensurate with the magnitude of the danger and the difficulties of his position. His summons to war was enthusiastically obeyed by all the neighboring tribes. On the eve of a perilous enterprise, he sought to fortify his mind with a fresh assurance of a divine call to the responsible office. The miracle of the fleece was a very remarkable one—especially, considering the copious dews that fall in his country. The divine patience and condescension were wonderfully manifested in reversing the form of the miracle. Gideon himself seems to have been conscious of incurring the displeasure of God by his hesitancy and doubts; but He bears with the infirmities of His people.

CHAPTER 7

Vss. 1-8. GIDEON'S ARMY. **1. Jerubbaal**—This had now become Gideon's honorable surname, "the enemy of Baal." **well**—rather "spring of Harod," i.e., "fear, trembling"—probably the same as the fountain in Jezreel (I Sam. 29:1). It was situated not far from Gilboa, on the confines of Manasseh, and the name "Harod" was bestowed on it with evident reference to the panic which seized the majority of Gideon's troops. The host of the Midianites were on the northern side of the valley, seemingly deeper down in the descent towards the Jordan, near a little eminence. **2. the Lord said unto Gideon, The people... are too many**—Although the Israelitish army mustered only 32,000—or one-sixth of the Midianitish host—the number was too great, for it was the Lord's purpose to teach Israel a memorable lesson of dependence on Him. **3. Now therefore..., proclaim in the ears of the people, saying, Whosoever is fearful..., let him return**—This proclamation was in terms of an established law (Deut. 20:8). **4. too many**—Two reductions were ordered, the last by the application of a test which was made known to Gideon alone. **bring them down unto the water**—When the wandering people in Asia, on a journey or in haste, come to water, they do not stoop down with deliberation on their knees, but only bend forward as much as is necessary to bring their hand in contact with the stream, and throw it up with rapidity, and at the same time such address, that they do not drop a particle. The Israelites, it seems, were acquainted with the practice; and those who adopted it on this occasion were selected as fit for a work that required expedition. The rest were dismissed according to the divine direction. **7. the Lord said, By the three hundred men that lapped**

will I save you—It is scarcely possible to conceive a more severe trial than the command to attack the overwhelming forces of the enemy with such a handful of followers. But Gideon's faith in the divine assurance of victory was steadfast, and it is for this he is so highly commended (Heb. 11:32). **8. the host of Midian was beneath him in the valley**—Attention to the relative position of the parties is of the greatest importance to an understanding of what follows.

9-15. HE IS ENCOURAGED BY THE DREAM AND THE INTERPRETATION OF THE BARLEY CAKE. **9-10. Arise, get thee down unto the host... But if thou fear to go down, go thou with Phurah thy servant**—In ancient times it was reckoned no degradation for persons of the highest rank and character to act as spies on an enemy's camp; and so Gideon did on this occasion. But the secret errand was directed by God, who intended that he should hear something which might animate his own valor and that of his troops. **11. the outside of the armed men that were in the host**—"Armed," means embodied under the five officers established by the ordinary laws and usages of encampments. The camp seems to have been unprotected by any rampart, since Gideon had no difficulty in reaching and overhearing a conversation, so important to him. **12. the valley like grasshoppers for multitude; and the Midianites and the Amalekites... lay along in their camels without number**—a most graphic description of an Arab encampment. They lay wrapt in sleep, or resting from their day's plunder, while their innumerable camels were stretched round about them. **13. I dreamed a dream, and, lo, a cake of barley bread tumbled into the host of Midian**—This was a characteristic and very expressive dream for an Arab in the circumstances. The rolling down the hill, striking against the tents, and overturning them, naturally enough connected it in his mind with the position and meditated attack of the Israelitish leader. The circumstance of the cake, too, was very significant. Barley was usually the food of the poor, and of beasts; but most probably, from the widespread destruction of the crops by the invaders, multitudes must have been reduced to poor and scanty fare. **15. when Gideon heard the telling of the dream, and the interpretation... he worshipped**—The incident originated in the secret overruling providence of God, and Gideon, from his expression of pious gratitude, regarded it as such. On his mind, as well as that of his followers, it produced the intended effect—that of imparting new animation and impulse to their patriotism.

16-24. HIS STRATAGEM AGAINST MIDIAN. **16. he divided the three hundred men into three companies**—The object of dividing his forces was, that they might seem to be surrounding the enemy. The pitchers were empty to conceal the torches, and made of earthenware, so as to be easily broken; and the sudden blaze of the held-up lights—the loud echo of the trumpets, and the shouts of Israel, always terrifying (Num. 23:21), and now more terrible than ever by the use of such striking words, broke through the stillness of the midnight air. The sleepers started from their rest; not a blow was dealt by the Israelites; but the enemy ran tumultuously, uttering the wild, discordant cries peculiar to the Arab race. They fought indiscriminately, not knowing friend from foe. The panic being universal, they soon precipitately fled, directing their flight down to the Jordan, by the foot of the mountains of Ephraim, to places known as the "house of the acacia," and "the meadow of the dance." **23. the men of Israel gathered themselves together**—These were evidently the parties dismissed, who having lingered at a little distance from the scene of contest, now eagerly joined in the pursuit southwestward through the valley. **24. Gideon sent messengers throughout all mount Ephraim**—The Ephraimites lay on the south and could render seasonable aid. **Come . . . , take before them the waters unto Beth-barah** (See on ch. 3:28)—These were the northern fords of the Jordan, to the east-northeast of wady Maleh. **the men of Ephraim gathered themselves together . . . unto Beth-barah**—A new conflict ensued, in which two secondary chiefs were seized and slain on the spots where they were respectively taken. The spots were named after these chiefs, Oreb, "the Raven," and Zeeb, "the Wolf"—appropriate designations of Arab leaders.

CHAPTER 8

Vss. 1-9. THE EPHRAIMITES OFFENDED, BUT PACIFIED. **1. the men of Ephraim said, Why hast thou served us thus?**—Where this complaint was made, whether before or after the crossing of the Jordan, cannot be determined. By the overthrow of the national enemy, the Ephraimites were benefited as largely as any of the other neighboring tribes. But, piqued at not having been sharers in the glory of the victory, their leading men could not repress their wounded pride; and the occasion only served to bring out an old and deep-seated feeling of jealous rivalry that subsisted between the tribes (Isa. 9:21). The discontent was groundless, for Gideon acted according to divine directions. Besides, as their tribe was conterminous with that of Gideon, they might, had they been really fired with the flame of patriotic zeal, have volunteered their services in a movement against the common enemy. **2, 3. he said, What have I done now in comparison of you?**—His mild and truly modest answer breathes the spirit of a great as well as good man, who was calm, collected, and self-possessed in the midst of most exciting scenes. It succeeded in throwing oil on the troubled waters (Prov. 16:1), and no wonder, for in the height of generous self-denial, it ascribes to his querulous brethren a greater share of merit and glory than belonged to himself (I Cor. 13:4; Philemon 2:3). **4. Gideon came to Jordan, and passed over**—much exhausted, but eager to continue the pursuit till the victory was consummated. **5. he said unto the men of Succoth**—i.e., a place of tents or booths. The name seems to have been applied to the whole part of the Jordan valley on the west, as well as on the east side of the river, all belonging to the tribe of Gad (cf. Gen. 33:17; I Kings 7:46; with Josh. 13:27). Being diligent in the common cause of all Israel, he had a right to expect support and encouragement from his countrymen everywhere. **6. the princes of Succoth said, Are the hands of Zebah and Zalmunna now in thine hand**—an insolent as well as a time-serving reply. It was insolent because it implied a bitter taunt that Gideon was counting with confidence on a victory which they believed he would not gain; and it was time-serving, because living in the near neighborhood of the Midianite sheiks, they dreaded the future vengeance of those roving chiefs. This contumelious manner of acting was heartless and disgraceful in people who were of Israelitish blood. **7. I will tear your flesh with the thorns of the wilderness and with briers**—a cruel torture, to which

captives were often subjected in ancient times, by having thorns and briers placed on their naked bodies and pressed down by sledges, or heavy implements of husbandry being dragged over them. **8. he went up thence to Penuel, and spake unto them likewise**—a neighboring city, situated also in the territory of Gad, near the Jabbok, and honored with this name by Jacob (Gen. 32: 30, 31). **9. he spake . . . , When I come again in peace I will break down this tower**—Intent on the pursuit, and afraid of losing time, he postponed the merited vengeance till his return. His confident anticipation of a triumphant return evinces the strength of his faith; and his specific threat was probably provoked by some proud and presumptuous boast, that in their lofty watchtower the Penuelites would set him at defiance.

10-27. ZEBAH AND ZALMUNNA TAKEN. **10. Now Zebah und Zalmunna were in Karkor**—a town on the eastern confines of Gad. The wreck of the Midianite army halted there. **11. Gideon went up by the way of them that dwelt in tents on the east**—He tracked the fugitives across the mountain range of Gilead to the northeast of the Jabbok, and there came upon them unexpectedly while they were resting secure among their own nomadic tribes. Jogbehah is supposed to be Ramoth-gilead; and, therefore, the Midianites must have found refuge at or near Abela, "Abel-cheramim," the plain of the vineyards. **12. when Zebah and Zalmunna fled, he pursued after them**—A third conflict took place. His arrival at their last quarters, which was by an unwonted path, took the fugitives by surprise, and the conquest of the Midianite horde was there completed. **13. Gideon returned from battle before the sun was up**—He seems to have returned by a nearer route to Succoth, for what is rendered in our version "before the sun was up," means "the heights of Heres, the sun-hills." **14. he described**—wrote the names of the seventy princes or elders. It was from them he had received so inhospitable a treatment. **16. he took . . . the thorns of the wilderness and briers, and with them he taught the men of Succoth**—By refusing his soldiers refreshment, they had committed a public crime, as well as an act of inhumanity, and were subjected to a horrible punishment, which the great abundance and remarkable size of the thorn bushes, together with the thinness of clothing in the East, has probably suggested. **18. Then said he unto Zebah and Zalmunna, What manner of men were they whom ye slew at Tabor?**—This was one of the countless atrocities which the Midianite chiefs had perpetrated during their seven years' lawless occupancy. It is noticed now for the first time when their fate was about to be determined. **each one resembled the children of a king**—An Orientalism for great beauty, majesty of appearance, uncommon strength, and grandeur of form. **19. They were my brethren, even the sons of my mother**—That is, uterine brothers; but, in all countries where polygamy prevails, "the son of my mother" implies a closeness of relationship and a warmth of affection never awakened by the looser term, "brother." **20. he said unto Jether his first-born, Up, and slay them**—The nearest of kin was the blood avenger; but a magistrate might order any one to do the work of the executioner; and the person selected was always of a rank equal or proportioned to that of the party doomed to suffer (I Kings 2:29). Gideon intended, then, by the order to Jether, to put an honor on his son, by employing him to slay two enemies of his country; and on the youth declining, he performed the bloody deed himself. **22, 23. the men of Israel** said unto Gideon, **Rule thou over us ... Gideon said unto them, the Lord shall rule over you**—Their unbounded admiration and gratitude prompted them, in the enthusiasm of the moment, to raise their deliverer to a throne, and to establish a royal dynasty in his house. But Gideon knew too well, and revered too piously the principles of the theocracy, to entertain the proposal for a moment. Personal and family ambition was cheerfully sacrificed to a sense of duty, and every worldly motive was kept in check by a supreme regard to the divine honor. He would willingly act as judge, but the Lord alone was King of Israel. **24-26. Gideon said unto them, I would desire a request of you** —This was the contribution of an earring (sing.). As the ancient Arabians (Ishmaelites and Midianites being synonymous terms, Gen. 37:25, 28) were gorgeously adorned with barbaric pearl and gold, an immense amount of such valuable booty had fallen into the hands of the Israelitish soldiers. The contribution was liberally made, and the quantity of gold given to him equalled about $25,000.00 in today's measure. **ornaments**—crescent-like plates of gold suspended from the necks, or placed on the breasts of the camels. **collars**—rather earrings, or drops of gold or pearl. **purple**—a royal color. The ancient, as well as modern Arabs, adorned the necks, breasts, and legs, of their riding animals with sumptuous housing. **27. Gideon made an ephod thereof, and put it in his city, ... Ophrah**—That no idolatrous use was in view, nor any divisive course from Shiloh contemplated, is manifest from verse 33. Gideon proposed, with the gold he received, to make an ephod for his use *only* as a civil magistrate or ruler, as David did (I Chron. 15:27), and a magnificent pectoral or breastplate also. It would seem, from the history, that he was not blamable in making this ephod, as a civil robe or ornament merely, but that it *afterward* became an object to which religious ideas were attached; whereby it proved a snare, and consequently an evil, by *perversion,* to Gideon and his house [TAYLOR'S FRAGMENT]. 28. MIDIAN SUBDUED. **28. Thus was Midian subdued before the children of Israel**—This invasion of the Arab hordes into Canaan was as alarming and desolating as the irruption of the Huns into Europe. It was the severest scourge ever inflicted upon Israel; and both it and the deliverance under Gideon lived for centuries in the minds of the people (Ps. 83:11).

CHAPTER 9

VSS. 1-6. ABIMELECH IS MADE KING BY THE SHECHEMITES. **1. Abimelech the son of Jerubbaal went to Shechem**—The idolatry which had been stealthily creeping into Israel during the latter years of Gideon was now openly professed; Shechem was wholly inhabited by its adherents; at least, idolaters had the ascendency. Abimelech, one of Gideon's numerous sons, was connected with that place. Ambitious of sovereign power, and having plied successfully the arts of a demagogue with his maternal relatives and friends, he acquired both the influence and money by which he raised himself to a throne. **communed ... with all the family of the house of his mother's father**—Here is a striking instance of the evils of polygamy—one son has connections and interests totally alien to those of his brothers. **2. Whether is better for you, either that all the sons of Jerubbaal, ... or that one reign over you**—a false insinuation, artfully contrived to stir up jealousy and alarm. Gideon

had rejected, with abhorrence, the proposal to make himself or any of his family king, and there is no evidence that any of his other sons coveted the title. **4. the house of Baal-berith**—either the temple, or the place where this idol was worshipped; Baal-berith, "god of the covenant," by invocation of whom the league of cities was formed. **Abimelech hired vain and light persons, which followed him**—idle, worthless vagabonds, the scum of society, who had nothing to lose, but much to gain from the success of a revolutionary movement. **5. went unto ... Ophrah, and slew his brethren ... upon one stone**—This is the first mention of a barbarous atrocity which has, with appalling frequency, been perpetrated in the despotic countries of the East—that of one son of the deceased monarch usurping the throne and hastening to confirm himself in the possession by the massacre of all the natural or legitimate competitors. Abimelech slew his brethren *on one stone,* either by dashing them from one rock, or sacrificing them on one stone altar, in revenge for the demolition of Baal's altar by their father. This latter view is the more probable, from the Shechemites (vs. 24) aiding in it. **threescore and ten persons**—A round number is used, but it is evident that two are wanting to complete that number. **6. all the men of Shechem ..., and all the house of Millo**—i.e., a mound or rampart, so that the meaning is, all the men in the house or temple; namely, the priests of Baal. **made Abimelech king, by the plain of the pillar**—rather, by the oak near a raised mound—so that the ceremony of coronation might be conspicuous to a crowd.

7-21. JOTHAM BY A PARABLE REPROACHES THEM. **7. he ... stood in the top of mount Gerizim, and lifted up his voice**—The spot he chose was, like the housetops, the public place of Shechem; and the parable drawn from the rivalry of the various trees was appropriate to the diversified foliage of the valley below. Eastern people are exceedingly fond of parables and use them for conveying reproofs—which they could not give in any other way. The top of Gerizim is not so high in the rear of the town, as it is nearer to the plain. With a little exertion of voice, he could easily have been heard by the people of the city; for the hill so overhangs the valley, that a person from the side or summit would have no difficulty in speaking to listeners at the base. Modern history records a case, in which soldiers on the hill shouted to the people in the city and endeavored to instigate them to an insurrection. There is something about the elastic atmosphere of an Eastern clime which causes it to transmit sound with wonderful celerity and distinctness [HACKETT]. **13. wine, which cheereth God and man**—not certainly in the same manner. God might be said to be "cheered" by it, when the sacrifices were accepted, as He is said also to be honored by oil (vs. 9). **21. Jotham ... went to Beer**—the modern village El-Bireh, on the ridge which bounds the northern prospect of Jerusalem.

22-49. GAAL'S CONSPIRACY. **22. When Abimelech had reigned three years**—His reign did not, probably at first, extend beyond Shechem; but by stealthy and progressive encroachments he subjected some of the neighboring towns to his sway. None could "reign" in Israel, except by rebellious usurpation; and hence the reign of Abimelech is expressed in the original by a word signifying "despotism," not that which describes the mild and divinely authorized rule of the judge. **23. Then God sent an evil spirit between Abimelech and the men of Shechem**—In the course of providence.

jealousy, distrust, secret disaffection, and smothered rebellion appeared among his subjects disappointed and disgusted with his tyranny; and God permitted those disorders to punish the complicated crimes of the royal fratricide and idolatrous usurper. **26. Gaal . . . came with his brethren . . . , and the men of Shechem put their confidence in him**—An insurrection of the original Canaanites, headed by this man, at last broke out in Shechem. **28-45. would to God this people were under my hand**—He seems to have been a boastful, impudent, and cowardly person, totally unfit to be a leader in a revolutionary crisis. The consequence was that he allowed himself to be drawn into an ambush—was defeated—the city of Shechem destroyed and strewn with salt. The people took refuge in the stronghold, which was set on fire, and all in it perished. **50-57. ABIMELECH SLAIN. 50. Then went Abimelech to Thebez, and encamped against Thebez**—now Tubas—not far from Shechem. **51. all the men and women . . . gat them up to the top of the tower**—The Canaanite forts were generally mountain fastnesses or keeps, and they often had a strong tower which served as a last refuge. The Assyrian bas-reliefs afford counterparts of the scene here described so vivid and exact, that we might almost suppose them to be representations of the same historic events. The besieged city—the strong tower within—the men and *women* crowding its battlements—the fire applied to the doors, and even the huge fragments of stone dropping from the hands of one of the garrison on the heads of the assailants—are all well represented to the life—just as they are here described in the narrative of inspired truth [Goss].

CHAPTER 10

VSS. 1-5. TOLA JUDGES ISRAEL IN SHAMIR. **1. after Abimelech there arose to defend Israel, Tola**—i.e., to save. Deliverance was necessary as well from intestine usurpation as from foreign aggression. **the son of Puah**—He was uncle to Abimelech by the father's side, and consequently brother of Gideon; yet the former was of the tribe of Issachar, while the latter was of Manasseh. They were, most probably, uterine brothers. **dwelt in Shamir in mount Ephraim**—As a central place, he made it the seat of government. **3. Jair, a Gileadite**—This judge was a different person from the conqueror of that northeastern territory, and founder of Havoth-jair, or "Jair's villages." (Num. 32:41; Deut. 3:14; Josh. 13:3; I Chron. 2:22.) **4. he had thirty sons that rode on thirty ass colts**—This is a characteristic trait of Eastern manners in those early times; and the grant of a village to each of his thirty sons was a striking proof of his extensive possessions. His having thirty sons is no conclusive evidence that he had more than one wife, much less that he had more than one at a time. There are instances, in this country, of men having as many children by two successive wives. **6-9. ISRAEL OPPRESSED BY THE PHILISTINES AND AMMONITES. 6. the children of Israel did evil again in the sight of the Lord**—This apostasy seems to have exceeded every former one in the grossness and universality of the idolatry practised. **7. Philistines, and . . . the children of Ammon**—The predatory incursions of these two hostile neighbors were made naturally on the parts of the land respectively contiguous to them. But the Ammonites, animated with the spirit of conquest, carried their arms across the Jordan; so that the central

and southern provinces of Canaan were extensively desolated. **10-15. THEY CRY TO GOD. 10. The children of Israel cried unto the Lord, We have sinned against thee**—The first step of repentance is confession of sin, and the best proof of its sincerity is given by the transgressor, when he mourns not only over the painful consequences which have resulted from his offenses to himself, but over the heinous evil committed against God. **11. the Lord said . . . , Did I not deliver you from the Egyptians**—The circumstances recorded in this and the following verses were not probably made through the high priest, whose duty it was to interpret the will of God. **12. Maonites**—i.e., Midianites. **16-18. THEY REPENT; GOD PITIES THEM. they put away the strange gods . . . and served the Lord; and his soul was grieved for the misery of Israel**—On their abandonment of idolatry and return to purity of worship, God graciously abridged the term of national affliction and restored times of peace. **17, 18. the children of Ammon were gathered together**—From carrying on guerrilla warfare, the Ammonites proceeded to a continued campaign. Their settled aim was to wrest the whole of the trans-jordanic territory from its actual occupiers. In this great crisis, a general meeting of the Israelitish tribes was held at Mizpeh. This Mizpeh was in eastern Manasseh (Josh. 11:3).

CHAPTER 11

VSS. 1-3. JEPHTHAH. **1. Jephthah**—"opener." **son of an harlot**—a concubine, or foreigner; implying an inferior sort of marriage prevalent in Eastern countries. Whatever dishonor might attach to his birth, his own high and energetic character rendered him early a person of note. **Gilead begat Jephthah** —His father seems to have belonged to the tribe of Manasseh (I Chron. 7:14, 17). **2. Thou shalt not inherit in our father's house**—As there were children by the legitimate wife, the son of the secondary one was not entitled to any share of the patrimony, and the prior claim of the others was indisputable. Hence, as the brothers of Jephthah seem to have resorted to rude and violent treatment, they must have been influenced by some secret ill-will. **3. Jephthah . . . dwelt in the land of Tob**—on the north of Gilead, beyond the frontier of the Hebrew territories (II Sam. 10:6, 8). **there were gathered vain men to Jephthah**—idle, daring, or desperate. **and went out with him**—followed him as a military chief. They led a freebooting life, sustaining themselves by frequent incursions on the Ammonites and other neighboring people, in the style of Robin Hood. The same kind of life is led by many an Arab or Tartar still, who as the leader of a band, acquires fame by his striving or gallant adventures. It is not deemed dishonorable when the expeditions are directed against those out of his own tribe or nation. Jephthah's mode of life was similar to that of David when driven from the court of Saul. **4-11. THE GILEADITES COVENANT WITH JEPHTHAH. 4. in process of time**—on the return of the season. **the children of Ammon made war against Israel**—Having prepared the way by the introduction of Jephthah, the sacred historian here resumes the thread of his narrative from ch. 10:17. The Ammonites seem to have invaded the country, and active hostilities were inevitable. **5, 6. the elders of Gilead went to fetch Jephthah**—All eyes were directed towards him as the only person possessed of the qualities requisite for the preservation of the country in this time of imminent danger; and a deputation of the chief men was despatched from the Hebrew camp at Mizpeh to solicit his services. **7-9. Jephthah said, Did not ye hate me?**—He gave them at first a haughty and cold reception. It is probable that he saw some of his brothers among the deputies. Jephthah was now in circumstances to make his own terms. With his former experience, he would have shown little wisdom or prudence without binding them to a clear and specific engagement to invest him with unlimited authority, the more especially as he was about to imperil his life in their cause. Although ambition might, to a certain degree, have stimulated his ready compliance, it is impossible to overlook the piety of his language, which creates a favorable impression that his roving life, in a state of social manners so different from ours, was not incompatible with habits of personal religion. **10, 11. the elders of Israel said unto Jephthah, The Lord be witness between us**—Their offer being accompanied by the most solemn oath, Jephthah intimated his acceptance of the mission, and his willingness to accompany them. But to make "assurance doubly sure," he took care that the pledge given by the deputies in Tob should be ratified in a general assembly of the people at Mizpeh—and the language of the historian, "Jephthah uttered all his words before the Lord," seems to imply that his inauguration with the character and extraordinary office of judge was solemnized by prayer for the divine blessing, or some religious ceremonial.

12-28. His Embassy to the King of Ammon. **12-28. Jephthah sent messengers unto the king of the children of Ammon**—This first act in his judicial capacity reflects the highest credit on his character for prudence and moderation, justice and humanity. The bravest officers have always been averse to war; so Jephthah, whose courage was indisputable, resolved not only to make it clearly appear that hostilities were forced upon him, but to try measures for avoiding, if possible, an appeal to arms: and in pursuing such a course he was acting as became a leader in Israel (Deut. 20:10-18). **13. the king of Ammon answered . . . , Because Israel took away my land**—(See on Deut. 2:19-37). The subject of quarrel was a claim of right advanced by the Ammonite monarch to the lands which the Israelites were occupying. Jephthah's reply was clear, decisive, and unanswerable;—first, those lands were not in the possession of the Ammonites when his countrymen got them, and that they had been acquired by right of conquest from the Amorites; secondly, the Israelites had now, by a lapse of 300 years of undisputed possession, established a prescriptive right to the occupation; and thirdly, having received a grant of them from the Lord, his people were entitled to maintain their right on the same principle that guided the Ammonites in receiving, from their god Chemosh, the territory they now occupied. This diplomatic statement, so admirable for the clearness and force of its arguments, concluded with a solemn appeal to God to maintain, by the issue of events, the cause of right and justice. **28. Howbeit the king of Ammon hearkened not unto the words of Jephthah**—His remonstrances to the aggressor were disregarded, and war being inevitable, preparations were made for a determined resistance.

29-31. His Vow. **29. Then the Spirit of the Lord came upon Jephthah**—The calm wisdom, sagacious forethought, and indomitable energy which he was enabled to display, were a pledge to

himself and a convincing evidence to his countrymen, that he was qualified by higher resources than his own for the momentous duties of his office. **he passed over Gilead, and Manasseh**—the provinces most exposed and in danger, for the purpose of levying troops, and exciting by his presence a widespread interest in the national cause. Returning to the camp at Mizpeh, he then began his march against the enemy. There he made his celebrated vow, in accordance with an ancient custom for generals at the outbreak of a war, or on the eve of a battle, to promise the god of their worship a costly oblation, or dedication of some valuable booty, in the event of victory. Vows were in common practice also among the Israelites. They were encouraged by the divine approval as emanating from a spirit of piety and gratitude; and rules were laid down in the law for regulating the performance. But it is difficult to bring Jephthah's vow within the legitimate range (see on Lev. 27:28). **31. whatsoever cometh forth of the doors of my house to meet me**—This evidently points not to an animal, for that might have been a dog; which, being unclean, was unfit to be offered; but to a person, and it looks extremely as if he, from the first, contemplated a human sacrifice. Bred up as he had been, beyond the Jordan, where the Israelitish tribes, far from the tabernacle, were looser in their religious sentiments, and living latterly on the borders of a heathen country where such sacrifices were common, it is not improbable that he may have been so ignorant as to imagine that a similar immolation would be acceptable to God. His mind, engrossed with the prospect of a contest, on the issue of which the fate of his country depended, might, through the influence of superstition, consider the dedication of the object dearest to him the most likely to ensure success. **shall surely be the Lord's; and** [or] **I will offer it up for a burnt offering**—The adoption of the latter particle, which many interpreters suggest, introduces the important alternative, that if it were a person, the dedication would be made to the service of the sanctuary; if a proper animal or thing, it would be offered on the altar.

32, 33. He Overcomes the Ammonites. **32. Jephthah passed over unto the children of Ammon . . . , and the Lord delivered them into his hands**—He met and engaged them at Aroer, a town in the tribe of Gad, upon the Arnon. A decisive victory crowned the arms of Israel, and the pursuit was continued to Abel (plain of the vineyards), from south to north, over an extent of about sixty miles. **34. Jephthah came to Mizpeh unto his house, and, behold, his daughter came out to meet him with timbrels and with dances**—The return of the victors was hailed, as usual, by the joyous acclaim of a female band (I Sam. 18:6), the leader of whom was Jephthah's daughter. The vow was full in his mind, and it is evident that it had not been communicated to anyone, otherwise precautions would doubtless have been taken to place another object at his door. The shriek, and other accompaniments of irrepressible grief, seem to indicate that her life was to be forfeited as a sacrifice; the nature of the sacrifice (which was abhorrent to the character of God) and distance from the tabernacle does not suffice to overturn this view, which the language and whole strain of the narrative plainly support; and although the lapse of two months might be supposed to have afforded time for reflection, and a better sense of his duty, there is but too much reason to conclude that he was impelled to the fulfilment by the dictates of a pious but unenlightened conscience.

CHAPTER 12

Vss. 1-3. THE EPHRAIMITES QUARRELLING WITH JEPHTHAH. **1. the men of Ephraim gathered themselves together**—*Heb.*, "were summoned." **and went northward**—After crossing the Jordan, their route from Ephraim was, strictly speaking, in a northeasterly direction, toward Mizpeh. **the men of Ephraim . . . said unto Jephthah, Wherefore . . . didst [thou] not call us?**—This is a fresh development of the jealous, rash, and irritable temper of the Ephraimites. The ground of their offense now was their desire of enjoying the credit of patriotism although they had not shared in the glory of victory. **2. when I called you, ye delivered me not out of their hands**—The straightforward answer of Jephthah shows that their charge was false; their complaint of not being treated as confederates and allies entirely without foundation; and their boast of a ready contribution of their services came with an ill grace from people who had purposely delayed appearing till the crisis was past. **3. when I saw that ye delivered me not, I put my life in my hands**—A common form of speech in the East for undertaking a duty of imminent peril. This Jephthah had done, having encountered and routed the Ammonites with the aid of his Gileadite volunteers alone; and since the Lord had enabled him to conquer without requiring assistance from any other tribe, why should the Ephraimites take offense? They ought rather to have been delighted and thankful that the war had terminated without their incurring any labor and danger.

4-15. DISCERNED BY THE WORD SIBBOLETH, ARE SLAIN BY THE GILEADITES. **4. the men of Gilead smote Ephraim, because they said, Ye Gileadites are fugitives of Ephraim**—The remonstrances of Jephthah, though reasonable and temperate, were not only ineffectual, but followed by insulting sneers that the Gileadites were reckoned both by the western Manassites and Ephraimites as outcasts—the scum and refuse of their common stock. This was addressed to a peculiarly sensitive people. A feud immediately ensued. The Gileadites, determined to chastise this public affront, gave them battle; and having defeated the Ephraimites, they chased their foul-mouthed but cowardly assailants out of the territory. Then rushing to the fords of the Jordan, they intercepted and slew every fugitive. The method adopted for discovering an Ephraimite was by the pronunciation of a word naturally suggested by the place where they stood. "Shibboleth," means a stream; "Sibboleth," a burden. The Eastern tribe had, it seems, a dialectical provincialism in the sound of Shibboleth; and the Ephraimites could not bring their organs to pronounce it. **7. Jephthah died**—After a government of six years, this mighty man of valor died; and however difficult it may be for us to understand some passages in his history, he has been ranked by apostolic authority among the worthies of the ancient church. He was followed by a succession of minor judges, of whom the only memorials preserved relate to the number of their families and their state.

CHAPTER 13

Vs. 1. ISRAEL SERVES THE PHILISTINES FORTY YEARS. **1. the Lord delivered them into the hand of the Philistines forty years**—The Israelites were represented (ch. 10:6, 7) as having fallen universally into a state of gross and confirmed idolatry, and in chastisement of this great apostasy, the Lord raised up enemies that harassed them in various quarters, especially the Ammonites and Philistines. The invasions and defeat of the former were narrated in the two chapters immediately preceding this; and now the sacred historian proceeds to describe the inroads of the latter people. The period of Philistine ascendency comprised forty years, reckoning from the time of Elon till the death of Samson.

2-10. AN ANGEL APPEARS TO MANOAH'S WIFE. **2. Zorah**—a Danite town (Josh. 15:33) lying on the common boundary of Judah and Dan, so that it was near the Philistine border. **3. the angel of the Lord**—The messenger of the covenant, the divine personage who made so many remarkable appearances of a similar kind already described. **5. thou shalt conceive, and bear a son**—This predicted child was to be a Nazarite. The mother was, therefore, for the sake of her promised offspring, required to practice the rigid abstinence of the Nazarite law (see on Num. 6:3). **he shall begin to deliver Israel out of the hands of the Philistines**—a prophecy encouraging to a patriotic man; the terms of it, however, indicated that the period of deliverance was still to be distant. **6-8. then Manoah entreated the Lord**—On being informed by his wife of the welcome intimation, the husband made it the subject of earnest prayer to God. This is a remarkable instance, indicative of the connection which God has established between prayer and the fulfilment of His promises.

11-14. THE ANGEL APPEARS TO MANOAH. **11. Art thou the man that spakest unto the woman?**—Manoah's intense desire for the repetition of the angel's visit was prompted not by doubts or anxieties of any kind, but was the fruit of lively faith, and of his great anxiety to follow out the instructions given. Blessed was he who had not seen, yet had believed.

15-23. MANOAH'S SACRIFICE. **15. Manoah said unto the angel . . . , I pray thee, let us detain thee, until we shall have made ready a kid**—The stranger declined the intended hospitality and intimated that if the meat were to be an offering, it must be presented to the Lord. Manoah needed this instruction, for his purpose was to offer the prepared viands to him, not as the Lord, but as what he imagined him to be, not even an angel (vs. 16), but a prophet or merely human messenger. It was on this account, and not as rejecting divine honors, that he spoke in this manner to Manoah. The angel's language was exactly similar to that of our Lord (Matt. 19:17). **17. Manoah said unto the angel . . . , What is thy name?**—Manoah's request elicited the most unequivocal proofs of the divinity of his supernatural visitor—in his name "secret" (in the *Marg.* wonderful), and in the miraculous flame that betokened the acceptance of the sacrifice.

24, 25. SAMSON BORN. **24. the woman bare a son, and called his name Samson**—The birth of this child of promise, and the report of the important national services he was to render, must, from the first, have made him an object of peculiar interest and careful instruction. **25. the Spirit of the Lord began to move him at times**—not, probably, as it moved the prophets, who were charged with an inspired message, but kindling in his youthful bosom a spirit of high and devoted patriotism. **Eshtaol**—the free city. It, as well as Zorah, stood on the border between Judah and Dan.

CHAPTER 14

Vss. 1-5. SAMSON DESIRES A WIFE OF THE PHI-
LISTINES. **1, 2. Timnath**—now Tibna, about three
miles from Zorah, his birthplace. **saw a woman
. . . of the Philistines; and told his father and his
mother, and said, . . . get her for me to wife**—In
the East parents did, and do in many cases still,
negotiate the marriage alliances for their sons.
During their period of ascendency, the Philistine
invaders had settled in the towns; and the intercourse between them and the Israelites was often
of such a friendly and familiar character as to issue
in matrimonial relations. Moreover, the Philistines
were not in the number of the seven devoted
nations of Canaan—with whom the law forbade
them to marry. **3. Is there never a woman among
the daughters of thy brethren**—i.e., of thine own
tribe—a Danite woman. **Samson said . . . , Get her
for me, for she pleaseth me well**—lit., "she is right
in mine eyes"—not by her beautiful countenance or
handsome figure, but *right or fit for his purpose.*
And this throws light on the historian's remark in
reference to the resistance of his parents: they
"knew not that it was of the Lord, that he sought
an occasion against the Phillistines"—rather *from*
the Philistines—originating on their side. The
Lord, by a course of retributive proceedings, was
about to destroy the Philistine power, and the means
which He meant to employ was not the forces of a
numerous army, as in the case of the preceding
judges, but the miraculous prowess of the single-
handed champion of Israel. In these circumstances, the provocation to hostilities could only
spring out of a *private* quarrel, and this marriage
scheme was doubtless suggested by the secret influence of the Spirit as the best way of accomplishing the intended result.

6-9. HE KILLS A LION. **5-9. a young lion**—*Heb.,*
a lion in the pride of his youthful prime. The wild
mountain passes of Judah were the lairs of savage
beasts; and most or all the "lions" of Scripture occur in that wild country. His rending and killing
the shaggy monster, without any weapon in his
hand, were accomplished by that superhuman
courage and strength which the *occasional* influences of the Spirit enabled him to put forth, and by
the exertion of which, in such private incidental
circumstances, he was gradually trained to confide
in them for the more public work to which he was
destined. **7. he went down, and talked with the
woman**—The social intercourse between the youth
of different sexes is extremely rare and limited in
the East, and generally so after they are betrothed.
8. after a time he returned to take her—probably
after the lapse of a year—the usual interval between
the ceremonies of betrothal and marriage. It was
spent by the bride elect with her parents in preparation for the nuptials—and at the proper time the
bridegroom returned to take her home. **he turned
aside to see the carcass of the lion; and, behold,
there was a swarm of bees and honey in the carcass of the lion**—In such a climate, the myriads of
insects and the ravages of birds of prey, together
with the influences of the solar rays, would, in a
few months, put the carcass in a state inviting to
such cleanly animals as bees.

10, 11. HIS MARRIAGE FEAST. **10. his father
went down**—The father is mentioned as the head
and representative of Samson's relatives. **Samson
made there a feast**—The wedding festivity lasted a
week. The men and women were probably entertained in separate apartments—the bride, with her
female relatives, at her parents' house; Samson, in
some place obtained for the occasion, as he was a
stranger. A large number of paranymphs, or
"friends of the bridegroom," furnished, no doubt,
by the bride's family, attended his party, ostensibly
to honor the nuptials, but really as spies on his
proceedings.

12-18. HIS RIDDLE. **12-18. I will now put forth
a riddle**—Riddles are a favorite Oriental amusement
at festive entertainments of this nature, and rewards
are offered to those who give the solution. Samson's riddle related to honey in the lion's carcass.
The prize he offered was thirty *sindinim,* or shirts,
and thirty changes of garments, probably woolen.
Three days were passed in vain attempts to unravel
the enigma. The festive week was fast drawing to
a close when they secretly enlisted the services of
the newly married wife, who having got the secret,
revealed it to her friends. **18. If ye had not
ploughed with my heifer, ye had not found out my
riddle**—a metaphor borrowed from agricultural
pursuits, in which not only oxen but cows and
heifers were, and continue to be, employed in dragging the plough. Divested of metaphor, the meaning is taken by some in a criminal sense, but probably means no more than that they had resorted to
the aid of his wife—an unworthy expedient, which
might have been deemed by a man of less noble
spirit and generosity as releasing him from the
obligation to fulfil his bargain.

19, 20. HE SLAYS THIRTY PHILISTINES. **19, 20.
went down to Askelon, and slew thirty men**—This
town was about twenty-four miles west by southwest from Timnah; and his selection of this place,
which was dictated by the Divine Spirit, was probably owing to its bitter hostility to Israel. **took
their spoil**—The custom of stripping a slain enemy
was unknown in Hebrew warfare. **20. Samson's
wife was given to his companion, whom he had used
as his friend**—i.e., "the friend of the bridegroom,"
who was the medium of communicating during the
festivities between him and his bride. The acceptance of her hand, therefore, was an act of base
treachery, that could not fail to provoke the just
resentment of Samson.

CHAPTER 15

Vss. 1, 2. SAMSON IS DENIED HIS WIFE. **1. in
the time of wheat harvest**—i.e., about the end of our
April, or the beginning of our May. The shocks
of grain were then gathered into heaps, and lying
on the field or on the threshing-floors. It was the
dry season, dry far beyond our experience, and the
grain in a most combustible state. **Samson visited
his wife with a kid**—It is usual for a visitor in the
East to carry some present; in this case, it might be
not only as a token of civility, but of reconciliation.
he said—i.e., to himself. It was his secret purpose.
into the chamber—the female apartments or harem.
**2. her father said, I verily thought that thou hadst
utterly hated her**—This allegation was a mere sham—
a flimsy pretext to excuse his refusal of admittance.
The proposal he made of a marriage with her
younger sister was but an insult to Samson, and one
which it was unlawful for an Israelite to accept
(Lev. 18:18).

3-8. HE BURNS THE PHILISTINES' CORN. **3.
Samson said . . . , Now shall I be more blameless
than the Philistines**—This nefarious conduct provoked the hero's just indignation, and he resolved to
take signal vengeance. **4. went and caught three**

hundred foxes—rather jackals; an animal between a wolf and a fox, which, unlike our fox, a solitary creature, prowls in large packs or herds and abounds in the mountains of Palestine. The collection of so great a number would require both time and assistance. **took firebrands**—torches or matches, which would burn slowly, retaining the fire, and blaze fiercely when blown by the wind. He put two jackals together, tail by tail, and fastened tightly a fire-match between them. At nightfall he lighted the firebrand and sent each pair successively down from the hills, into the "Shefala," or plain of Philistia, lying on the borders of Dan and Judah, a rich and extensive corn district. The pain caused by the fire would make the animals toss about to a wide extent, kindling one great conflagration. But no one could render assistance to his neighbor: the devastation was so general, the panic would be so great. **6. Who hath done this**—The author of this outrage, and the cause that provoked such an extraordinary retaliation, soon became known; and the sufferers, enraged by the destruction of their crops, rushing with tumultuous fury to the house of Samson's wife, "burnt her and her father with fire." This was a remarkable retribution. To avoid this menace, she had betrayed her husband; and by that unprincipled conduct, eventually exposed herself to the horrid doom which, at the sacrifice of conjugal fidelity, she had sought to escape. **7. Samson said . . . , Though ye have done this, yet will I be avenged of you**—By that act the husbandmen had been the instruments in avenging his private and personal wrongs. But as a judge, divinely appointed to deliver Israel, his work of retribution was not yet accomplished. **8. smote them hip and thigh**—a proverbial expression for a merciless slaughter.

9-13. He Is Bound by the Men of Judah, and Delivered to the Philistines. **8. he went down and dwelt in the top of the rock Etam**—rather went down and dwelt in the cleft—i.e., the cave or cavern of the cliff Etam. **9. Then the Philistines went up**—to the high land of Judah. **and spread themselves in Lehi**—now El-Lekieh, abounding with limestone cliffs; the sides of which are perforated with caves. The object of the Philistines in this expedition was to apprehend Samson, in revenge for the great slaughter he had committed on their people. With a view of freeing his own countrymen from all danger from the infuriated Philistines, he allowed himself to be bound and surrendered a fettered prisoner into their power. Exulting with joy at the near prospect of riddance from so formidable an enemy, they went to meet him. But he exerted his superhuman strength, and finding a new (or moist) jawbone of an ass, he laid hold of it, and with no other weapon, slew a thousand men at a place which he called Ramath-lehi—i.e., the hill of the jawbone. **16. With the jawbone of an ass, heaps upon heaps, with the jaw of an ass have I slain a thousand men**—The inadequacy of the weapon plainly shows this to have been a miraculous feat, "a case of supernatural strength," just as the gift of prophecy is a case of supernatural knowledge [CHALMERS]. **19. a hollow place . . . in the jaw**—in Lehi—taking the word as a proper noun, marking the place. **there came water thereout; and when he had drunk, his spirit came again**—His strength, exhausted by the violent and long-continued exertion, was recruited by the refreshing draft from the spring; and it was called En-hakkore, the "supplication well," a name which records the piety of this heroic champion.

CHAPTER 16

Vss. 1-3. **1. Samson Carries Away the Gates of Gaza. Gaza**—now Guzzah, the capital of the largest of the five Philistine principal cities, about fifteen miles southwest of Ashkelon. The object of this visit to this city is not recorded, and unless he had gone in disguise, it was a perilous exposure of his life in one of the enemy's strongholds. It soon became known that he was there; and it was immediately resolved to secure him; but deeming themselves certain of their prey, the Gazites deferred the execution of their measure till the morning. **3. Samson . . . arose at midnight, and took the doors of the gate of the city**—A ruinous pile of masonry is still pointed out as the site of the gate. It was probably a part of the town wall, and as this ruin is "toward Hebron," there is no improbability in the tradition. **carried them up to the top of an hill, that is before Hebron**—That hill is El-Montar; but by Hebron in this passage is meant "the mountains of Hebron"; for otherwise Samson, had he run night and day from the time of his flight from Gaza, could only have come on the evening of the following day within sight of the city of Hebron. The city of Gaza was, in those days, probably not less than three-quarters of an hour distant from El-Montar. To have climbed to the top of this hill with the ponderous doors and their bolts on his shoulders, through a road of thick sand, was a feat which none but a Samson could have accomplished [VAN DE VELDE].

4-14. Delilah Corrupted by the Philistines. **4. he loved a woman in the valley of Sorek**—The location of this place is not known, nor can the character of Delilah be clearly ascertained. Her abode, her mercenary character, and her heartless blandishments afford too much reason to believe she was a profligate woman. **5. the lords of the Philistines**—The five rulers deemed no means beneath their dignity to overcome this national enemy. **Entice him, and see wherein his great strength lieth**—They probably imagined that he carried some amulet about his person, or was in the possession of some important secret by which he had acquired such herculean strength; and they bribed Delilah, doubtless by a large reward, to discover it for them. She undertook the service and made several attempts, plying all her arts of persuasion or blandishment in his soft and communicative moods, to extract his secret. **7. Samson said . . . , If they bind me with seven green withs**—Vine tendrils, pliant twigs, or twists made of crude vegetable stalks are used in many Eastern countries for ropes at the present day. **8. she bound him with them**—probably in a sportive manner, to try whether he was jesting or in earnest. **9. there were men lying in wait, abiding . . . in the chamber**—The *Heb.*, literally rendered, is, "in the inner or most secret part of the house." **10. And Delilah said**—To avoid exciting suspicion, she must have allowed some time to elapse before making this renewed attempt. **12. new ropes**—It is not said of what material they were formed; but from their being dried, it is probable they were of twigs, like the former. The *Hebrew* intimates that they were twisted, and of a thick, strong description. **13. If thou weavest the seven locks of my head**—braids or tresses, into which, like many in the East, he chose to plait his hair. Working at the loom was a female employment; and Delilah's appears to have been close at hand. It was of a very simple construction; the woof was driven into the warp, not by a reed, but by a wooden spatula. The extremity of the web was fastened to a pin or stake fixed in the wall or ground; and while Delilah sat squatting at her loom, Samson lay stretched on the floor, with his head reclining on her lap—a position very common in the East. **went away with the pin of the beam, and with the web**—i.e., the whole weaving apparatus. 15-20. HE IS OVERCOME. **15-20. she pressed him daily with her words**—Though disappointed and mortified, this vile woman resolved to persevere; and conscious how completely he was enslaved by his passion for her, she assailed him with a succession of blandishing arts, till she at length discovered the coveted secret. **17. if I be shaven, then my strength will go from me**—His herculean powers did not arise from his hair, but from his peculiar relation to God as a Nazarite. His unshorn locks were a sign of his Nazaritism, and a pledge on the part of God that his supernatural strength would be continued. **19. she called for a man, and she caused him to shave off the seven locks of his head**—It is uncertain, however, whether the ancient Hebrews cut off the hair to the same extent as Orientals now. The word employed is sometimes the same as that for shearing sheep, and therefore the instrument might be only scissors. **20. he wist not that the Lord was departed from him**—What a humiliating and painful spectacle! Deprived of the divine influences—degraded in his character—and yet, through the infatuation of a guilty passion, scarcely awake to the wretchedness of his fallen condition!

21, 22. THE PHILISTINES TOOK HIM AND PUT OUT HIS EYES. **21. the Philistines took him, and put out his eyes**—To this cruel privation prisoners of rank and consequence have commonly been subjected in the East. The punishment is inflicted in various ways, by scooping out the eyeballs, by piercing the eye, or destroying the sight by holding a red-hot iron before the eyes. His security was made doubly sure by his being bound with fetters of brass (copper), not of leather, like other captives. **he did grind in the prison-house**—This grinding with hand millstones being the employment of menials, he was set to it as the deepest degradation. **22. Howbeit the hair on his head began to grow again**—It is probable that he had now reflected on his folly; and becoming a sincere penitent, renewed his Nazarite vow. "His hair grew together with his repentance, and his strength with his hairs" [BISHOP HALL].

23-25. THEIR FEAST TO DAGON. **23. the lords of the Philistines gathered to offer a great sacrifice unto Dagon**—It was a common practice in heathen nations, on the return of their solemn religious festivals, to bring forth their war prisoners from their places of confinement or slavery; and, in heaping on them every species of indignity, they would offer their grateful tribute to the gods by whose aid they had triumphed over their enemies. Dagon was a sea-idol, usually represented as having the head and upper parts human, while the rest of the body resembled a fish. 26-31. HIS DEATH. **27. there were upon the roof about three thousand men and women, that beheld while Samson made sport**—This building seems to have been similar to the spacious and open amphitheaters well known among the Romans and still found in many countries of the East. They are built wholly of wood. The standing-place for the spectators is a wooden floor resting upon two pillars and rising on an inclined plane, so as to enable all to have a view of the area in the center.

In the middle there are two large beams, on which the whole weight of the structure lies, and these beams are supported by two pillars placed almost close to each other, so that when these are unsettled or displaced, the whole pile must tumble to the ground. **28. Samson called unto the Lord**—His penitent and prayerful spirit seems clearly to indicate that this meditated act was not that of a vindictive suicide, and that he regarded himself as putting forth his strength in his capacity of a public magistrate. He must be considered, in fact, as dying for his country's cause. His death was not designed or sought, except as it might be the inevitable consequence of his great effort. His prayer must have been a silent ejaculation, and, from its being revealed to the historian, approved and accepted of God. **31. Then his brethren and all the house of his father came down and took him, and brought him up, and buried him**—This awful catastrophe seems to have so completely paralyzed the Philistines, that they neither attempted to prevent the removal of Samson's corpse, nor to molest the Israelites for a long time after. Thus the Israelitish hero rendered by his strength and courage signal services to his country, and was always regarded as the greatest of its champions. But his slavish subjection to the domination of his passions was unworthy of so great a man and lessens our respect for his character. Yet he is ranked among the ancient worthies who maintained a firm faith in God (Heb. 11:32).

CHAPTER 17

Vss. 1-4. MICAH RESTORING THE STOLEN MONEY TO HIS MOTHER, SHE MAKES IMAGES. **1. a man of mount Ephraim**—i.e., the mountainous parts of Ephraim. This and the other narratives that follow form a miscellaneous collection, or appendix to the Book of Judges. It belongs to a period when the Hebrew nation was in a greatly disordered and corrupt state. This episode of Micah is connected with chapter 1:34. It relates to his foundation of a small sanctuary of his own—a miniature representation of the Shiloh tabernacle—which he stocked with images modelled probably in imitation of the ark and cherubim. Micah and his mother were sincere in their intention to honor God. But their faith was blended with a sad amount of ignorance and delusion. The divisive course they pursued, as well as the will-worship they practised, subjected the perpetrators to the penalty of death. **3. a graven image and a molten image**—The one carved from a block of wood or stone, to be plated over with silver; the other, a figure formed of the solid metal cast into a mould. It is observable, however, that only 200 shekels were given to the founder. Probably the expense of making two such figures of silver, with their appurtenances (pedestals, bases, etc.), might easily cost, in those days, 200 shekels, which would be a sum not adequate to the formation of large statues [TAYLOR'S FRAGMENT]. **5. the man Micah had a house of gods**—*Hebrew*, "a house of God"—a domestic chapel, a private religious establishment of his own. **an ephod**—(see on Exod. 28:4). **teraphim**—tutelary gods of the household (see on Gen. 31:19, 30). **consecrated one of his sons, who became his priest**—The assumption of the priestly office by any one out of the family of Aaron was a direct violation of the divine law (Num. 3:10; 16:17; Deut. 21:5; Heb. 5:4). **6. every man did that which was right in his own eyes**—From want of a settled government, there was no one to call him to account. No punishment followed any crime. **7. Bethlehem-judah**—so called in contradistinction to a town of the same name in Zebulun (Josh. 19:15). **of the family** [i.e., tribe] **of Judah**—Men of the tribe of Levi might connect themselves, as Aaron did (Exod. 6:23), by marriage with another tribe; and this young Levite belonged to the tribe of Judah, by his mother's side, which accounts for his being in Bethlehem, not one of the Levitical cities. **8. the man departed . . . to sojourn where he could find a place**—A competent provision being secured for every member of the Levitical order, his wandering about showed him to have been a person of a roving disposition or unsettled habits. In the course of his journeying he came to the house of Micah, who, on learning what he was, engaged his permanent services. **10. Micah said unto him, Dwell with me, be unto me a father**—a spiritual father, to conduct the religious services of my establishment. He was to receive, in addition to his board, a salary of ten shekels of silver. **a suit of apparel**—not only dress for ordinary use, but vestments suitable for the discharge of his priestly functions. **12. Micah consecrated the Levite**—*Hebrew*, "filled his hand." This act of consecration was not less unlawful for Micah to perform than for this Levite to receive (see on ch. 18:30). **13. Now know I that the Lord will do me good**—The removal of his son, followed by the installation of this Levite into the priestly office, seems to have satisfied his conscience, that by what he deemed the orderly ministrations of religion he would prosper. This expression of his hope evinces the united influence of ignorance and superstition.

CHAPTER 18

Vss. 1-26. THE DANITES SEEK OUT AN INHERITANCE. **1-6. In those days . . . the Danites sought them an inheritance to dwell in**—The Danites had a territory assigned them as well as the other tribes. But either through indolence, or a lack of energy, they did not acquire the full possession of their allotment, but suffered a considerable portion of it to be wrested out of their hands by the encroachments of their powerful neighbors, the Philistines. In consequence, being straitened for room, a considerable number resolved on trying to effect a new and additional settlement in a remote part of the land. A small deputation, being despatched to reconnoitre the country, arrived on their progress northward at the residence of Micah. Recognizing his priest as one of their former acquaintances, or perhaps by his provincial dialect, they eagerly enlisted his services in ascertaining the result of their present expedition. His answer, though apparently promising, was delusive, and really as ambiguous as those of the heathen oracles. This application brings out still more clearly and fully than the schism of Micah the woeful degeneracy of the times. The Danites expressed no emotions either of surprise or of indignation at a Levite daring to assume the priestly functions, and at the existence of a rival establishment to that of Shiloh. They were ready to seek, through means of the teraphim, the information that could only be lawfully applied for through the high priest's Urim. Being thus equally erroneous in their views and habits as Micah, they show the low state of religion, and how much superstition prevailed in all parts of the land. **7-10. the five men departed, and came to Laish**—or Leshem (Josh. 19:47). supposed to have been peopled by a colony of Zidonians. The place

was very secluded—the soil rich in the abundance and variety of its produce, and the inhabitants, following the peaceful pursuits of agriculture, lived in their fertile and sequestered valley, according to the Zidonian style of ease and security, happy among themselves, and maintaining little or no communication with the rest of the world. The discovery of this northern paradise seemed, to the delight of the Danite spies, an accomplishment of the priest's prediction. They hastened back to inform their brethren in the south both of the value of their prize, and how easily it could be made their prey. **11. there went from thence of the family of the Danites . . . six hundred men**—This was the collective number of the men who were equipped with arms to carry out this expeditionary enterprise, without including the families and furniture of the emigrants (vs. 21). Their journey led them through the territory of Judah, and their first halting-place was "behind," that is, on the west of Kirjath-jearim, on a spot called afterwards "the camp of Dan." Prosecuting the northern route, they skirted the base of the Ephraimite hills. On approaching the neighborhood of Micah's residence, the spies having given information that a private sanctuary was kept there, the priest of which had rendered them important service when on their exploring expedition, it was unanimously agreed that both he and the furniture of the establishment would be a valuable acquisition to their proposed settlement. A plan of spoliation was immediately formed. While the armed men stood sentinels at the gates, the five spies broke into the chapel, pillaged the images and vestments, and succeeded in bribing the priest also by a tempting offer to transfer his services to their new colony. Taking charge of the ephod, the teraphim, and the graven image, he "went in the midst of the people"—a central position assigned him in the march, perhaps for his personal security; but more probably in imitation of the place appointed for the priests and the ark, in the middle of the congregated tribes, on the marches through the wilderness. This theft presents a curious medley of low morality and strong religious feeling. The Danites exemplified a deep-seated principle of our nature—that men have religious affections, which must have an object on which these may be exercised, while they are often not very discriminating in the choice of the objects. In proportion to the slender influence religion wields over the heart, the greater is the importance attached to external rites; and in the exact observance of these, the conscience is fully satisfied, and seldom or never molested by reflections on the breach of minor morals. **22-26. the men that were in the houses near to Micah's house were gathered together**—The robbers of the chapel being soon detected, a hot pursuit was forthwith commenced by Micah, at the head of a considerable body of followers. The readiness with which they joined in the attempt to recover the stolen articles affords a presumption that the advantages of the chapel had been open to all in the neighborhood; and the importance which Micah, like Laban, attached to his teraphim, is seen by the urgency with which he pursued the thieves, and the risk of his life in attempting to procure their restoration. Finding his party, however, not a match for the Danites, he thought it prudent to desist, well knowing the rule which was then prevalent in the land, that

They should take who had the power,
And they should keep who could.

THEY WIN LAISH. 27-29. **27. they . . . came unto Laish . . . smote them** [the inhabitants] **. . . and burnt the city**—"We are revolted by this inroad and massacre of a quiet and secure people. Nevertheless, if the original grant of Canaan to the Israelites gave them the warrant of a divine commission and command for this enterprise, that sanctifies all and legalizes all" [CHALMERS]. This place seems to have been a dependency of Zidon, the distance of which, however, rendered it impossible to obtain aid thence in the sudden emergency. **28-29. they built a city, and . . . called the name of that city Dan**—It was in the northern extremity of the land, and hence the origin of the phrase, "from Dan to Beersheba." 30, 31. THEY SET UP IDOLATRY. **30. the children of Dan set up the graven image**—Their distance secluded them from the rest of the Israelites, aud doubtless this, which was their apology for not going to Shiloh, was the cause of perpetuating idolatry among them for many generations.

CHAPTER 19

Vss. 1-15. A LEVITE GOING TO BETHLEHEM TO FETCH HIS WIFE. **1. it came to pass in those days**—The painfully interesting episode that follows, together with the intestine commotion the report of it produced throughout the country, belongs to the same early period of anarchy and prevailing disorder. **a certain Levite . . . took a concubine**—The priests under the Mosaic law enjoyed the privilege of marrying as well as other classes of the people. It was no disreputable connection this Levite had formed; for a nuptial engagement with a concubine-wife (though, as wanting in some outward ceremonies, it was reckoned a secondary or inferior relationship) possessed the true essence of marriage; it was not only lawful, but sanctioned by the example of many good men. **2. his concubine . . . went away from him unto her father's house**—The cause of the separation assigned in our version rendered it unlawful for her husband to take her back (Deut. 24:4); and according to the uniform style of sentiment and practice in the East, she would have been put to death, had she gone to her father's family. Other versions concur with Josephus, in representing the reason for the flight from her husband's house to be, that she was disgusted with him, through frequent brawls. **3. And her husband arose, and went after her to speak friendly unto her**—*Hebrew*, speak to her heart, in a kindly and affectionate manner, so as to rekindle her affection. Accompanied by a servant, he arrived at the house of his father-in-law, who rejoiced to meet him, in the hope that a complete reconciliation would be brought about between his daughter and her husband. The Levite, yielding to the hospitable importunities of his father-in-law, prolonged his stay for days. **8. tarried** [with reluctance] **until afternoon**—lit., "the decline of the day." People in the East, who take little or nothing to eat in the morning, do not breakfast till from 10 to 12 A.M., and this meal the hospitable relative had purposely protracted to so late a period as to afford an argument for urging a further stay. **9. the day draweth toward evening**—*Hebrew*, "the pitching time of day." Travellers who set out at daybreak usually halt about the middle of the afternoon the first day, to enjoy rest and refreshment. It was, then, too late a time to commence a journey. But duty, perhaps, obliged the Levite to indulge no further delay. **10. the man . . . departed, and came over**

against Jebus—The note, "which is Jerusalem," must have been inserted by Ezra or some later hand. Jebus being still, though not entirely (ch. 1:8) in the possession of the old inhabitants, the Levite resisted the advice of his attendant to enter it and determined rather to press forward to pass the night in Gibeah, which he knew was occupied by Israelites. The distance from Bethlehem to Jerusalem is about six miles. The event showed that it would have been better to have followed the advice of his attendant—to have trusted themselves among aliens than among their own countrymen. **13. in Gibeah, or in Ramah**—The first of these places was five miles northeast, the other from four to five north of Jerusalem. **15. when he went in he sat him down in a street of the city**—The towns of Palestine at this remote period could not, it seems, furnish any establishment in the shape of an inn or public lodging-house. Hence we conclude that the custom, which is still frequently witnessed in the cities of the East, was then not uncommon, for travellers who were late in arriving and who had no introduction to a private family, to spread their bedding in the streets, or wrapping themselves up in their cloaks, pass the night in the open air. In the Arab towns and villages, however, the sheik, or some other person, usually comes out and urgently invites the strangers to his house. This was done also in ancient Palestine (Gen. 18:4; 19:2). That the same hospitality was not shown in Gibeah seems to have been owing to the bad character of the people.

16-21. AN OLD MAN ENTERTAINS HIM AT GIBEAH. **16. there came an old man from his work out of the field at even, which was also of mount Ephraim**—Perhaps his hospitality was quickened by learning the stranger's occupation, and that he was on his return to his duties at Shiloh. **19. there is no want of anything**—In answering the kindly inquiries of the old man, the Levite deemed it right to state that he was under no necessity of being burdensome on anyone, for he possessed all that was required to relieve his wants. Oriental travellers always carry a stock of provisions with them; and knowing that even the khans or lodging-houses they may find on their way afford nothing beyond rest and shelter, they are careful to lay in a supply of food both for themselves and their beasts. Instead of hay, which is seldom met with, they used chopped straw, which, with a mixture of barley, beans, or the like, forms the provender for cattle. The old man, however, in the warmth of a generous heart, refused to listen to any explanation, and bidding the Levite keep his stocks for any emergency that might occur in the remainder of his journey, invited them to accept of the hospitalities of his house for the night. **20. only lodge not in the street**—As this is no rare or singular circumstance in the East, the probability is that the old man's earnest dissuasive from such a procedure arose from his acquaintance with the infamous practices of the place.

22-28. THE GIBEAHITES ABUSE HIS CONCUBINE TO DEATH. **22. certain sons of Belial beset the house**—The narrative of the horrid outrage that was committed—of the proposal of the old man—the unfeeling, careless, and in many respects, inexplicable conduct of the Levite towards his wife, disclose a state of morality that would have appeared incredible, did it not rest on the testimony of the sacred historian. Both men ought to have protected the women in the house, even though at the expense of their lives, or thrown themselves on God's providence. It should be noted, however, that the guilt of such a foul outrage is not fastened on the general population of Gibeah. **29. divided her ... into twelve pieces**—The want of a regular government warranted an extraordinary step; and certainly no method could have been imagined more certain of rousing universal horror and indignation than this terrible summons of the Levite.

CHAPTER 20

Vss. 1-7. THE LEVITE, IN A GENERAL ASSEMBLY, DECLARES HIS WRONG. **1. all ... the congregation was gathered as one man**—In consequence of the immense sensation the horrid tragedy of Gibeah had produced, a national assembly was convened, at which "the chief of all the people" from all parts of the land, including the eastern tribes, appeared as delegates. **Mizpeh**—the place of convention (for there were other Mizpehs), was in a town situated on the confines of Judah and Benjamin (Josh. 15: 38; 18:26). Assemblies were frequently held there afterwards (I Samuel 7:11; 10:17); and it was but a short distance from Shiloh. The phrase, "unto the Lord," may be taken in its usual sense, as denoting consultation of the oracle. This circumstance, together with the convention being called "the assembly of the people of God," seems to indicate, that amid the excited passions of the nation, those present felt the profound gravity of the occasion and adopted the best means of maintaining a becoming deportment. **3. Now the children of Benjamin heard that the children of Israel were gone up to Mizpeh**—Some suppose that Benjamin had been passed over, the crime having been perpetrated within the territory of that tribe; and that, as the concubine's corpse had been divided into twelve pieces—two had been sent to Manasseh, one respectively to the western and eastern divisions. It is more probable that Benjamin had received a formal summons like the other tribes, but chose to treat it with indifference, or haughty disdain. **4-7. the Levite, the husband of the woman that was slain, answered and said**—The injured husband gave a brief and unvarnished recital of the tragic outrage, from which it appears that force was used, which he could not resist. His testimony was doubtless corroborated by those of his servant and the old Ephraimite. There was no need of strong or highly colored description to work upon the feelings of the audience. The facts spoke for themselves and produced one common sentiment of detestation and vengeance.

8. THEIR DECREE. **8. all the people arose as one man**—The extraordinary unanimity that prevailed shows, that notwithstanding great disorders had broken out in many parts, the people were sound at the core; and remembering their national covenant with God, they now felt the necessity of wiping out so foul a stain on their character as a people. It was resolved that the inhabitants of Gibeah should be subjected to condign punishment. But the resolutions were conditional. For as the common law of nature and nations requires that an inquiry should be made and satisfaction demanded, before committing an act of hostility or vengeance, messengers were despatched through the whole territory of Benjamin, demanding the immediate surrender or execution of the delinquents. The request was just and reasonable; and by refusing it the Benjamites virtually made themselves a party in the quarrel. It must not be supposed that the people of this tribe were insensible or indifferent to

the atrocious character of the crime that had been committed on their soil. But their patriotism or their pride was offended by the hostile demonstration of the other tribes. The passions were inflamed on both sides; but certainly the Benjamites incurred an awful responsibility by the attitude of resistance they assumed. **14-17. the children of Benjamin gathered themselves out of the cities unto Gibeah**—Allowing their valor to be ever so great, nothing but blind passion and unbending obstinacy could have impelled them to take the field against their brethren with such a disparity of numbers. **16. left-handed: every one could sling stones at an hair-breadth, and not miss**—The sling was one of the earliest weapons used in war. The Hebrew sling was probably similar to that of the Egyptian, consisting of a leather thong, broad in the middle, with a loop at one end, by which it was firmly held with the hand; the other end terminated in a lash, which was let slip when the stone was thrown. Those skilled in the use of it, as the Benjamites were, could hit the mark with unerring certainty. A good sling could carry its full force to the distance of 200 yards. 18-28. THE ISRAELITES LOSE FORTY THOUSAND. **18-28. the children of Israel arose, and went up to the house of God**—This consultation at Shiloh was right. But they ought to have done it at the commencement of their proceedings. Instead of this, all their plans were formed, and never doubting, it would seem, that the war was just and inevitable, the only subject of their inquiry related to the precedency of the tribes—a point which it is likely was discussed in the assembly. Had they asked counsel of God sooner, their expedition would have been conducted on a different principle—most probably by reducing the number of fighting men, as in the case of Gideon's army. As it was, the vast number of volunteers formed an excessive and unwieldy force, unfit for strenuous and united action against a small, compact, and well-directed army. A panic ensued, and the confederate tribes, in two successive engagements, sustained great losses. These repeated disasters (notwithstanding their attack on Benjamin had been divinely authorized) overwhelmed them with shame and sorrow. Led to reflection, they became sensible of their guilt in not repressing their national idolatries, as well as in too proudly relying on their superior numbers and the precipitate rashness of this expedition. Having humbled themselves by prayer and fasting, as well as observed the appointed method of expiating their sins, they were assured of acceptance as well as of victory. The presence and services of Phinehas on this occasion help us to ascertain the chronology thus far, that the date of the occurrence must be fixed shortly after the death of Joshua.

29-48. THEY DESTROY ALL THE BENJAMITES, EXCEPT SIX HUNDRED. **29-48. Israel set liers in wait round about Gibeah**—A plan was formed of taking that city by stratagem, similar to that employed in the capture of Ai. **33. Baal-tamar**—a palm grove, where Baal was worshipped. The main army of the confederate tribes was drawn up there. **out of the meadows of Gibeah**—*Heb.*, "the caves of Gibeah." **34. there came against Gibeah ten thousand chosen men**—This was a third division, different both from the ambuscade and the army, who were fighting at Baal-tamar. The general account stated in verse 35 is followed by a detailed narrative of the battle, which is continued to the end of the chapter. **45. they turned and fled towards the wilderness unto the rock of Rimmon**—Many of the fugitives found refuge in the caves of this rocky mountain, which is situated to the northeast of Beth-el. Such places are still sought as secure retreats in times of danger; and until the method of blowing up rocks by gunpowder became known, a few men could in such caves sustain a siege for months. **46. all which fell that day of Benjamin were twenty and five thousand men**—On comparing this with verse 35, it will be seen that the loss is stated here in round numbers and is confined only to that of the third day. We must conclude that 1000 had fallen during the two previous engagements, in order to make the aggregate amount given (vs. 15). **48. the men of Israel turned again upon the children of Benjamin, and smote them with the edge of the sword**—This frightful vengeance, extending from Gibeah to the whole territory of Benjamin, was executed under the impetuous impulse of highly excited passions. But doubtless the Israelites were only the agents of inflicting the righteous retributions of God; and the memory of this terrible crisis, which led almost to the extermination of a whole tribe, was conducive to the future good of the whole nation.

CHAPTER 21

Vss. 1-15. THE PEOPLE BEWAIL THE DESOLATION OF ISRAEL. **2. the people came to the house of God, ... and lifted up their voices, and wept**—The characteristic fickleness of the Israelites was not long in being displayed; for scarcely had they cooled from the fierceness of their sanguinary vengeance, than they began to relent and rushed to the opposite extreme of self-accusation and grief at the desolation which their impetuous zeal had produced. Their victory saddened and humbled them. Their feelings on the occasion were expressed by a public and solemn service of expiation at the house of God. And yet this extraordinary observance, though it enabled them to find vent for their painful emotions, did not afford them full relief, for they were fettered by the obligation of a religious vow, heightened by the addition of a solemn anathema on every violator of the oath. There is no previous record of this oath; but the purport of it was, that they would treat the perpetrators of this Gibeah atrocity in the same way as the Canaanites, who were doomed to destruction; and the entering into this solemn league was of a piece with the rest of their inconsiderate conduct in this whole affair. **6. There is one tribe cut off from Israel this day**—i.e., in danger of becoming extinct; for, as it appears from verse 7, they had massacred all the women and children of Benjamin, and 600 men alone survived of the whole tribe. The prospect of such a blank in the cata-

logue of the twelve tribes, such a gap in the national arrangements, was too painful to contemplate, and immediate measures must be taken to prevent this great catastrophe. **8. there came none to the camp from Jabesh-gilead to the assembly**—This city lay within the territory of eastern Manasseh, about fifteen miles east of the Jordan, and was, according to Josephus, the capital of Gilead. The ban which the assembled tribes had pronounced at Mizpeh seemed to impose on them the necessity of punishing its inhabitants for not joining the crusade against Benjamin; and thus, with a view of repairing the consequences of one rash proceeding, they hurriedly rushed to the perpetration of another, though a smaller tragedy. But it appears (vs. 11) that, besides acting in fulfilment of their oath, the Israelites had the additional object by this raid of supplying wives to the Benjamite remnant. This shows the intemperate fury of the Israelites in the indiscriminate slaughter of the women and children. 16-21. THE ELDERS CONSULT HOW TO FIND WIVES FOR THOSE THAT WERE LEFT. **16. the elders of the congregation said, How shall we do for wives for them that remain**—Though the young women of Jabesh-gilead had been carefully spared, the supply was found inadequate, and some other expedient must be resorted to. **17. There must be an inheritance for them that are escaped of Benjamin**—As they were the only rightful owners of the territory, provision must be made for transmitting it to their legitimate heirs, and a new act of violence was meditated (vs. 19); the opportunity for which was afforded by the approaching festival—a feast generally supposed to be the feast of tabernacles. This, like the other annual feasts, was held in Shiloh, and its celebration was attended with more social hilarity and holiday rejoicings than the other feasts. **19. on the east side of the highway that goeth up from Bethel to Shechem**—The exact site of the place was described evidently for the direction of the Benjamites. **21. daughters of Shiloh come out to dance in dances**—The dance was anciently a part of the religious observance. It was done on festive occasions, as it is still in the East, not in town, but in the open air, in some adjoining field, the women being by themselves. The young women being alone indulging their light and buoyant spirits, and apprehensive of no danger, facilitated the execution of the scheme of seizing them, which closely resembles the Sabine rape in Roman history. The elders undertook to reconcile the families to the forced abduction of their daughters. And thus the expression of their public sanction to this deed of violence afforded a new evidence of the evils and difficulties into which the unhappy precipitancy of the Israelites in this crisis had involved them.

THE BOOK OF

RUTH

CHAPTER 1

Vss. 1-5. ELIMELECH, DRIVEN BY FAMINE INTO MOAB, DIES THERE. **1. in the days when the judges ruled**—The beautiful and interesting story which

this book relates belongs to the early times of the judges. The precise date cannot be ascertained. **2. Elimelech**—signifies "My God is king." **Naomi**—"fair or pleasant"; and their two sons, Mahlon and Chilion, are supposed to be the same as Joash and Saraph (I Chron. 4:22). **Ephrathites** —The ancient name of Bethlehem was Ephrath (Gen. 35:19; 48:7), which was continued after the occupation of the land by the Hebrews, even down to the time of the prophet Micah (Micah 5:2). **Bethlehem-judah**—so called to distinguish it from a town of the same name in Zebulun. The family, compelled to emigrate to Moab through pressure of a famine, settled for several years in that country. After the death of their father, the two sons married Moabite women. This was a violation of the Mosaic law (Deut. 7:3; 23:3; Ezra 9:2; Neh. 13:23); and Jewish writers say that the early deaths of both the young men were divine judgments inflicted on them for those unlawful connections.

6-18. NAOMI, RETURNING HOME, RUTH ACCOMPANIES HER. **6, 7. Then she arose with her daughters-in-law, that she might return from the country of Moab**—The aged widow, longing to enjoy the privileges of Israel, resolved to return to her native land as soon as she was assured that the famine had ceased, and made the necessary arrangements with her daughters-in-law. **8. Naomi said unto her two daughters-in-law, Go, return each to her mother's house**—In Eastern countries women occupy apartments separate from those of men, and daughters are most frequently in those of their mother. **the Lord deal kindly with you, as ye have dealt with the dead**—i.e., with my sons, your husbands, while they lived. **9. The Lord grant that ye may find rest**—enjoy a life of tranquillity, undisturbed by the cares, incumbrances, and vexatious troubles to which a state of widowhood is peculiarly exposed. **Then she kissed them**—the Oriental manner when friends are parting. **11. are there yet any more sons in my womb, that they may be your husbands?**—This alludes to the ancient custom (Gen. 38:26) afterwards expressly sanctioned by the law of Moses (Deut. 25:5), which required a younger son to marry the widow of his deceased brother. **12, 13. Turn again, my daughters, go your way**—That Naomi should dissuade her daughters-in-law so strongly from accompanying her to the land of Israel may appear strange. But it was the wisest and most prudent course for her to adopt: first, because they might be influenced by hopes which could not be realized; second, because they might be led, under temporary excitement, to take a step they might afterwards regret; and, third, because the sincerity and strength of their conversion to the true religion, which she had taught them, would be thoroughly tested. **13. the hand of the Lord is gone out against me**—i.e., I am not only not in a condition to provide you with other husbands, but so reduced in circumstances that I cannot think of your being subjected to privations with me. The arguments of Naomi prevailed with Orpah, who returned to her people and her gods. But Ruth clave unto her; and even in the pages of Sterne, that great master of pathos, there is nothing which so calls forth the sensibilities of the reader as the simple effusion he has borrowed from Scripture—of Ruth to her mother-in-law [CHALMERS].

19-22. THEY COME TO BETHLEHEM. **19-22. all the city was moved about them**—The present condition of Naomi, a forlorn and desolate widow, presented so painful a contrast to the flourishing state of prosperity and domestic bliss in which she had been at her departure. **in the beginning of barley harvest**—corresponding to the end of our March.

CHAPTER 2

VSS. 1-3. RUTH GLEANS IN THE FIELD OF BOAZ. **2. Ruth . . . said unto Naomi, Let me now go to the field, and glean**—The right of gleaning was conferred by a positive law on the widow, the poor, and the stranger (see on Lev. 19:9, 10; Deut. 24:19, 21). But liberty to glean *behind the reapers* was not a right that could be claimed; it was a privilege granted or refused according to the good will or favor of the owner. **3. her hap was to light on a part of the field belonging unto Boaz**—Fields in Palestine being unenclosed, the phrase signifies that portion of the open ground which lay within the landmarks of Boaz.

4-23. HE TAKES KNOWLEDGE OF HER, AND SHOWS HER FAVOR. **4. Boaz came from Bethlehem, and said unto the reapers, The Lord be with you**—This pious salutation between the master and his laborers strongly indicates the state of religious feeling among the rural population of Israel at that time, as well as the artless, happy, and unsuspecting simplicity which characterized the manners of the people. The same patriarchal style of speaking is still preserved in the East. **5. his servant that was set over the reapers**—an overseer whose special duty was to superintend the operations in the field, to supply provision to the reapers, and pay them for their labor in the evening. **7. she said, . . . Let me glean and gather after the reapers among the sheaves**—Various modes of reaping are practised in the East. Where the crop is thin and short, it is plucked up by the roots. Sometimes it is cut with the sickle. Whether reaped in the one way or the other, the grain is cast into sheaves loosely thrown together, to be subjected to the process of threshing, which takes place, for the most part, immediately after the reaping. Field labors were begun early in the morning—before the day became oppressively hot. **she tarried a little in the house**—i.e., the field tent, erected for the occasional rest and refreshment of the laborers. **8, 9. said Boaz unto Ruth, . . . bide here fast by my maidens**—The reaping was performed by women while the assortment of sheaves was the duty of menservants. The same division of harvest labor obtains in Syria still. Boaz not only granted to Ruth the full privilege of gleaning after his reapers, but provided for her personal comfort. **go unto the vessels, and drink of that which the young men have drawn**—Gleaners were sometimes allowed, by kind and charitable masters, to partake of the refreshments provided for the reapers. The vessels alluded to were skin bottles, filled with water—and the bread was soaked in vinegar (vs. 14); a kind of poor, weak wine, sometimes mingled with a little olive oil—very cooling, as would be required in harvest-time. This grateful refection is still used in the harvest-field. **14. he reached her parched corn, and she did eat, and was sufficed, and left**—some of the new grain, roasted on the spot, and fit for use after being rubbed in the hands—a favorite viand in the East. He gave her so much, that after satisfying her own wants, she had some (vs. 18) in reserve for her mother-in-law. **16. let fall also some of the handfuls on purpose for her**—The gleaners in the East glean with much success; for a great quantity of corn is scattered in the reaping, as well as in their manner of carrying it. One may judge, then, of the large quantity which Ruth would gather in consequence of the liberal orders given to the servants. These extraordinary marks of favor were not only given from a kindly disposition, but from regard to her good character and devoted attachment to her venerable relative. **17. and beat out that she had gleaned**— When the quantity of grain was small, it was beat out by means of a stick. **an ephah**—supposed to contain about a bushel. **20. the man is . . . one of our next kinsmen**—*Heb.,* "one of our redeemers"— on whom it devolves to protect us, to purchase our lands, and marry you, the widow of his next kinsman. She said, "one of them," not that there were many in the same close relationship, but that he was a very near kinsman, one other individual only having the precedence. **21. all my harvest**—both barley and wheat harvests. The latter was at the end of May or the beginning of June. **22. Naomi said unto Ruth . . . , It is good . . . that thou go out with his maidens**—a prudent recommendation to Ruth to accept the generous invitation of Boaz, lest, if she were seen straying into other fields, she might not only run the risk of rude treatment, but displease him by seeming indifferent to his kind liberality. Moreover, the observant mind of the old matron had already discerned, in all Boaz' attentions to Ruth, the germs of a stronger affection, which she wished to increase.

CHAPTER 3

Vss. 1-13. By Naomi's Instructions, Ruth Lies at Boaz's Feet, Who Acknowledges the Duty of a Kinsman. **2. he winnoweth barley to-night in the threshing-floor**—The winnowing process is performed by throwing up the grain, after being trodden down, against the wind with a shovel. The threshing-floor, which was commonly on the harvest-field, was carefully leveled with a large cylindric roller and consolidated with chalk, that weeds might not spring up, and that it might not chop with drought. The farmer usually remained all night in harvest-time on the threshing-floor, not only for the protection of his valuable grain, but for the winnowing. That operation was performed in the evening to catch the breezes which blow after the close of a hot day, and which continue for the most part of the night. This duty at so important a season the master undertakes himself; and, accordingly, in the simplicity of ancient manners, Boaz, a person of considerable wealth and high rank, laid himself down to sleep on the barn floor, at the end of the heap of barley he had been winnowing. **4. go in, and uncover his feet, and lay thee down**—Singular as these directions may appear to us, there was no impropriety in them, according to the simplicity of rural manners in Bethlehem. In ordinary circumstances these would have seemed indecorous to the world; but in the case of Ruth, it was a method, doubtless conformable to prevailing usage, of reminding Boaz of the duty which devolved on him as the kinsman of her deceased husband. Boaz probably slept upon a mat or skin; Ruth lay crosswise at his feet—a position in which Eastern servants frequently sleep in the same chamber or tent with their master; and if they want a covering, custom allows them that benefit from part of the covering on their master's bed. Resting, as the Orientals do at night, in the same clothes they wear during the day, there was no indelicacy in a stranger, or even a woman, putting the extremity of this cover over her. **9. I am Ruth thine handmaid: spread therefore thy skirt over thine handmaid; for thou art a near kinsman**—She had already drawn part of the mantle over her; and she asked him now to do it, that the act might become his own. To spread a skirt over one

is, in the East, a symbolical action denoting protection. To this day in many parts of the East, to say of anyone that he put his skirt over a woman, is synonymous with saying that he married her; and at all the marriages of the modern Jews and Hindoos, one part of the ceremony is for the bridegroom to put a silken or cotton cloak around his bride. **15. Bring the veil that thou hast upon thee, and hold it**—Eastern veils are large sheets—those of ladies being of red silk; but the poorer or common class of women wear them of blue, or blue and white striped linen or cotton. They are wrapped round the head, so as to conceal the whole face except one eye. **17. six measures of barley**—*Heb.,* "six *seahs,*" a *seah* contained about two gallons and a half, six of which must have been rather a heavy load for a woman.

CHAPTER 4

Vss. 1-5. Boaz Calls into Judgment the Next Kinsman. **1. Then went Boaz up to the gate of the city**—a roofed building, unenclosed by walls; the place where, in ancient times, and in many Eastern towns still, all business transactions are made, and where, therefore, the kinsman was most likely to be found. No preliminaries were necessary in summoning one before the public assemblage; no writings and no delay were required. In a short conversation the matter was stated and arranged— probably in the morning as people went out, or at noon when they returned from the field. **2. he took ten men of the elders of the city**—as witnesses. In ordinary circumstances, two or three were sufficient to attest a bargain; but in cases of importance, such as matrimony, divorce, conveyancing of property, it was the Jewish practice to have ten (I Kings 21: 8). **3. Naomi . . . selleth a parcel of land**—i.e., entertains the idea of selling. In her circumstances she was at liberty to part with it (Lev. 25:25). Both Naomi and Ruth had an interest in the land during their lives; but Naomi alone was mentioned, not only because she directed all the negotiations, but because the introduction of Ruth's name would awaken a suspicion of the necessity of marrying her, before the first proposition was answered. **4. there is none to redeem it beside thee; and I am after thee** —(See on Deut. 25:5-10). The redemption of the land of course involved a marriage with Ruth, the widow of the former owner.

6-8. He Refuses the Redemption. **6. The kinsman said, I cannot redeem it . . . , lest I mar mine own inheritance**—This consequence would follow, either, first, from his having a son by Ruth, who, though heir to the property, would not bear his name; his name would be extinguished in that of her former husband; or, secondly, from its having to be subdivided among his other children, which he had probably by a previous marriage. This right, therefore, was renounced and assigned in favor of Boaz, in the way of whose marriage with Ruth the only existing obstacle was now removed. **7, 8. a man plucked off his shoe**—Where the kinsman refused to perform his duty to the family of his deceased relation, the widow was directed to pull off the shoe with some attendant circumstances of contemptuous disdain. But, as in this case, there was no refusal, the usual ignominy was spared; and the plucking off the shoe, the only ceremony observed, was a pledge of the transaction being completed.

9-12. He Marries Ruth. **9. Boaz said unto the**

elders, Ye are witnesses this day that I have bought all that was . . . Chilion's and Mahlon's, of the hand of Naomi—Although the widow of Chilion was still living, no regard was paid to her in the disposal of her husband's property. From her remaining in Moab, she was considered to have either been married again, or to have renounced all right to an inheritance with the family of Elimelech. **10. Ruth the Moabitess . . . have I purchased to be my wife—** This connection Boaz not only might form, since Ruth had embraced the true religion, but he was under a legal necessity of forming it. **11. all the people and the elders said, We are witnesses—**A multitude, doubtless from curiosity or interest, were present on the occasion. There was no signing of deeds; yet was the transfer made, and complete security given, by the public manner in which the whole matter was carried on and concluded. **the Lord make the woman that is come into thine house**

like Rachel and Leah—This was the usual bridal benediction. **12. let thy house be like the house of Pharez—**i.e., as honorable and numerous as his. He was the ancestor of the Bethlehem people, and his family one of the five from which the tribe of Judah sprang. 13-17. SHE BEARS OBED. **17. Obed—**means "servant." **18-22. these are the generations of Pharez—**i.e., his descendants. This appendix shows that the special object contemplated by the inspired author of this little book was to preserve the memory of an interesting domestic episode, and to trace the genealogy of David. There was an interval of 380 years between Salmon and David. It is evident that whole generations are omitted; the leading personages only are named, and grandfathers are said, in Scripture language, to beget their grandchildren, without specifying the intermediate links.

THE FIRST BOOK OF

SAMUEL

CHAPTER 1

Vss. 1-8. OF ELKANAH AND HIS TWO WIVES. **1. a certain man of Ramathaim-zophim—**The first word being in the dual number, signifies the double city—the old and new town of Ramah (vs. 19). There were five cities of this name, all on high ground. This city had the addition of Zophim attached to it, because it was founded by Zuph, "an Ephrathite," that is a native of Ephratha. Bethlehem, and the expression of Ramathaim-zophim must, therefore, be understood as Ramah in the land of Zuph in the hill country of Ephratha. Others, considering "mount Ephraim" as pointing to the locality in Joseph's territory, regard "Zophim" not as a proper but a common noun, signifying watchtowers, or watchmen, with reference either to the height of its situation, or its being the residence of prophets who were watchmen (Ezek. 3:17). Though a native of Ephratha or Bethlehem-judah, Elkanah was a Levite (I Chron. 6:33, 34). Though of this order, and a good man, he practised polygamy. This was contrary to the original law, but it seems to have been prevalent among the Hebrews in those days, when there was no king in Israel, and every man did what seemed right in his own eyes. **3. this man went up out of his city yearly to worship in Shiloh—**In that place was the "earth's one sanctuary," and thither he repaired at the three solemn feasts, accompanied by his family at one of them—probably the passover. Although a Levite, he could not personally offer a sacrifice—that was exclusively the office of the priests; and his piety in maintaining a regular attendance on the divine ordinances is the more worthy of notice because the character of the two priests who administered them was notoriously bad. But doubtless he believed, and acted on the belief, that the ordinances were "effectual means of salvation, not from any virtue in them, or in those who administered them, but from the grace of God being communicated through them." **4. when . . . Elkanah offered, he gave to Peninnah . . . portions—**The offerer received back

the greater part of the peace offerings, which he and his family or friends were accustomed to eat at a social feast before the Lord. (See on Lev. 3: 7; Deut. 12:12.) It was out of these consecrated viands Elkanah gave portions to all the members of his family; but "unto Hannah he gave a worthy portion"; i.e., a larger choice, according to the Eastern fashion of showing regard to beloved or distinguished guests. (See on ch. 9:23, 24; also Gen. 43:45.) **6. her adversary provoked her sore—** The conduct of Peninnah was most unbecoming. But domestic broils in the houses of polygamists are of frequent occurrence, and the most fruitful cause of them has always been jealousy of the husband's superior affection, as in this case of Hannah. 9-18. HANNAH'S PRAYER. **9-11. she prayed . . . and vowed a vow—**Here is a specimen of the intense desire that reigned in the bosoms of the Hebrew women for children. This was the burden of Hannah's prayer; and the strong preference she expressed for a male child originated in her purpose of dedicating him to the tabernacle service. The circumstance of his birth bound him to this; but his residence within the precincts of the sanctuary would have to commence at an earlier age than usual, in consequence of the Nazarite vow. **12-18. Eli marked her mouth—**The suspicion of the aged priest seems to indicate that the vice of intemperance was neither uncommon nor confined to one sex in those times of disorder. This mistaken impression was immediately removed, and, in the words, "God grant," or rather, "will grant," was followed by an invocation which, as Hannah regarded it in the light of a prophecy pointing to the accomplishment of her earnest desire, dispelled her sadness, and filled her with confident hope. The character and services of the expected child were sufficiently important to make his birth a fit subject for prophecy. 20. SAMUEL BORN. **20. called his name Samuel** —doubtless with her husband's consent. The names of children were given sometimes by the fathers, and sometimes by the mothers (see on Gen. 4:1, 26; 5:29; 19:37; 21:3); and among the early Hebrews, they were commonly compound names, one part including the name of God. **21. the man Elkanah ... went up to offer ... his vow**—The solemn expression of his concurrence in Hannah's vow was necessary to make it obligatory. (See on Num. 30.) **22. But Hannah went not up**—Men only were obliged to attend the solemn feasts (Exod. 23: 17). But Hannah, like other pious women, was in the habit of going, only she deemed it more prudent and becoming to defer her next journey till her son's age would enable her to fulfil her vow. **24. three bullocks**—*Sept.* renders it "a bullock of three years old"; which is probably the true rendering.

CHAPTER 2

Vss. 1-11. Hannah's Song in Thankfulness to God. **1. Hannah prayed, and said**—Praise and prayer are inseparably conjoined in Scripture (Col. 4:2; I Tim. 2:1). This beautiful song was her tribute of thanks for the divine goodness in answering her petition. **mine horn is exalted in the Lord**—Allusion is here made to a peculiarity in the dress of Eastern women about Lebanon, which seems to have obtained anciently among the Israelite women, that of wearing a tin or silver horn on the forehead, on which their veil is suspended. Wives, who have no children, wear it projecting in an oblique direction, while those who become mothers forthwith raise it a few inches higher, inclining towards the perpendicular, and by this slight but observable change in their headdress, make known, wherever they go, the maternal character which they now bear. **5. they that were hungry ceased**—i.e., to hunger. **the barren hath born seven**—i.e., many children. **6. he bringeth down to the grave, and bringeth up**—i.e., He reduces to the lowest state of degradation and misery, and restores to prosperity and happiness. **8. He raiseth up the poor out of the dust, and lifteth up the beggar from the dunghill**—The dunghill, a pile of horse, cow, or camel offal, heaped up to dry in the sun, and used as fuel, was, and is, one of the common haunts of the poorest mendicants; and the change that had been made in the social position of Hannah, appeared to her grateful heart as auspicious and as great as the elevation of a poor despised beggar to the highest and most dignified rank. **inherit the throne of glory**—i.e., possesses seats of honor. **10. the Lord shall judge the ends of the earth ... exalt the horn of his anointed**—This is the first place in Scripture where the word "anointed," or Messiah, occurs; and as there was no king in Israel at the time, it seems the best interpretation to refer it to Christ. There is, indeed, a remarkable resemblance between the song of Hannah and that of Mary (Luke 1:46). **11. the child did minister unto the Lord before Eli the priest**—He must have been engaged in some occupation suited to his tender age, as in playing upon the cymbals, or other instruments of music; in lighting the lamps, or similar easy and interesting services.

12-17. The Sin of Eli's Sons. **12. Now the sons of Eli were sons of Belial**—not only careless and irreligious, but men loose in their actions, and vicious and scandalous in their habits. Though professionally engaged in sacred duties, they were not only strangers to the power of religion in the heart, but they had thrown off its restraints, and even ran, as is sometimes done in similar cases by the sons of eminent ministers, to the opposite extreme of reckless and open profligacy. **13. the priest's custom with the people**—When persons wished to present a sacrifice of peace offering on the altar, the offering was brought in the first instance to the priest, and as the Lord's part was burnt, the parts appropriated respectively to the priests and offerers were to be sodden. But Eli's sons, unsatisfied with the breast and shoulder, which were the perquisites appointed to them by the divine law (Exod. 29:27; Lev. 7:31, 32), not only claimed part of the offerer's share, but rapaciously seized them previous to the sacred ceremony of heaving or waving (see on Lev. 7:34); and moreover they committed the additional injustice of taking up with their fork those portions which they preferred, while still raw. Pious people revolted at such rapacious and profane encroachments on the dues of the altar, as well as what should have gone to constitute the family and social feast of the offerer. The truth is, the priests having become haughty and unwilling in many instances to accept invitations to those feasts, presents of meat were sent to them; and this, though done in courtesy at first, being, in course of time, established into a right, gave rise to all the rapacious keenness of Eli's sons.

18-26. Samuel's Ministry. **18. But Samuel ministered before the Lord, being a child**—This notice of his early services in the outer courts of the tabernacle was made to pave the way for the remarkable prophecy regarding the high priest's family. **girded with a linen ephod**—A small shoulder-garment or apron, used in the sacred service by the inferior priests and Levites; sometimes also by judges or eminent persons, and hence allowed to Samuel, who, though not a Levite, was devoted to God from his birth. **19. his mother made him a little coat, and brought it to him from year to year**—Aware that he could not yet render any useful service to the tabernacle, she undertook the expense of supplying him with wearing apparel. All weaving stuffs, manufacture of cloth, and making of suits were anciently the employment of women. **20. Eli blessed Elkanah and his wife**—This blessing, like that which he had formerly pronounced, had a prophetic virtue; which, before long, appeared in the increase of Hannah's family (vs. 21), and the growing qualifications of Samuel for the service of the sanctuary. **22. the women that assembled at the door of the tabernacle**—This was an institution of holy women of a strictly ascetic order, who had relinquished worldly cares and devoted themselves to the Lord; an institution which continued down to the time of Christ (Luke 2:37). Eli was, on the whole, a good man, but lacking in the moral and religious training of his family. He erred on the side of parental indulgence; and though he reprimanded them (see on Deut. 21:18-21), yet, from fear or indolence, he shrank from laying on them the restraints, or subjecting them to the discipline, their gross delinquencies called for. In his judicial capacity, he winked at their flagrant acts of maladministration and suffered them to make reckless encroachments on the constitution, by which the most serious injuries were inflicted both on the rights of the people and the laws of God. **25. they hearkened not unto the voice of their father,** *because* [it should be *therefore*] **the Lord would slay them**—It was not God's preordination, but their own wilful and impenitent disobedience which was the cause of their destruction.

27-35. A Prophecy against Eli's House. **27. there came a man of God unto Eli, and said ...**

there shall not be an old man in thine house—So much importance has always, in the East, been attached to old age, that it would be felt to be a great calamity, and sensibly to lower the respectability of any family which could boast of few or no old men. The prediction of this prophet was fully confirmed by the afflictions, degradation, poverty, and many untimely deaths with which the house of Eli was visited after its announcement (see on ch. 4:11; 14:3; 22:18-23; I Kings 2:27). **31. I will cut off thine arm, and the arm of thy father's house**—By the withdrawal of the high priesthood from Eleazar, the elder of Aaron's two sons (after Nadab and Abihu were destroyed), that dignity had been conferred on the family of Ithamar, to which Eli belonged, and now that his descendants had forfeited the honor, it was to be taken from them and restored to the elder branch. **32. thou shalt see an enemy in my habitation**—A successful rival for the office of high priest shall rise out of another family (II Sam. 15:35; I Chron. 24:3; 29:22). But the marginal reading, "thou shalt see the affliction of the tabernacle," seems to be a preferable translation.

CHAPTER 3

Vss. 1-10. THE LORD APPEARS TO SAMUEL IN A VISION. **1. the child Samuel ministered unto the Lord before Eli**—His ministry consisted, of course, of such duties in or about the sanctuary as were suited to his age, which is supposed now to have been about twelve years. Whether the office had been specially assigned him, or it arose from the interest inspired by the story of his birth, Eli kept him as his immediate attendant; and he resided not *in* the sanctuary, but in one of the tents or apartments around it, assigned for the accommodation of the priests and Levites, *his* being near to that of the high priest. **the word of the Lord was precious in those days**—It was very rarely known to the Israelites; and in point of fact only two prophets are mentioned as having appeared during the whole administration of the judges (Judg. 4:4; 6:8). **there was no open vision**—no publicly recognized prophet whom the people could consult, and from whom they might learn the will of God. There must have been certain indubitable evidences by which a communication from heaven could be distinguished. Eli knew them, for he may have received them, though not so frequently as is implied in the idea of an "open vision." **3. ere the lamp of God went out in the temple of the Lord**—The "temple" seems to have become the established designation of the tabernacle, and the time indicated was towards the morning twilight, as the lamps were extinguished at sunrise (see on Lev. 6:12, 13). **5. he ran unto Eli, and said, Here am I, for thou calledst me**—It is evident that his sleeping chamber was close to that of the aged high priest and that he was accustomed to be called during the night. The three successive calls addressed to the boy convinced Eli of the divine character of the speaker, and he therefore exhorted the child to give a reverential attention to the message. The burden of it was an extraordinary premonition of the judgments that impended over Eli's house; and the aged priest, having drawn the painful secret from the child, exclaimed, "It is the Lord; let him do what seemeth him good." Such is the spirit of meek and unmurmuring submission in which we ought to receive the dispensations of God, however severe and afflictive. But, in order to form a right estimate of Eli's language

and conduct on this occasion, we must consider the overwhelming accumulation of judgments denounced against his person, his sons, his descendants —his altar, and nation. With such a threatening prospect before him, his piety and meekness were wonderful. In his personal character he seems to have been a good man, but his sons' conduct was flagrantly bad; and though his misfortunes claim our sympathy, it is impossible to approve or defend the weak and unfaithful course which, in the retributive justice of God, brought these adversities upon him.

CHAPTER 4

Vss. 1-11. ISRAEL OVERCOME BY THE PHILISTINES. **1. the word of Samuel came to all Israel**—The character of Samuel as a prophet was now fully established. The want of an "open vision" was supplied by him, for "none of his words were let fall to the ground" (ch. 3:19); and to his residence in Shiloh all the people of Israel repaired to consult him as an oracle, who, as the medium of receiving the divine command, or by his gift of a prophet, could inform them what was the mind of God. It is not improbable that the rising influence of the young prophet had alarmed the jealous fears of the Philistines. They had kept the Israelites in some degree of subjection ever since the death of Samson and were determined, by further crushing, to prevent the possibility of their being trained by the counsels, and under the leadership, of Samuel, to reassert their national independence. At all events, the Philistines were the aggressors (vs. 2). But, on the other hand, the Israelites were rash and inconsiderate in rushing to the field without obtaining the sanction of Samuel as to the war, or having consulted him as to the subsequent measures they took. **Israel went out against the Philistines to battle**—i.e., to resist this new incursion. **Eben-ezer ... Aphek**—Aphek, which means "strength," is a name applied to any fort or fastness. There were several Apheks in Palestine; but the mention of Eben-ezer determines this "Aphek" to be in the south, among the mountains of Judah, near the western entrance of the pass of Beth-horon, and consequently on the borders of the Philistine territory. The first encounter at Aphek being unsuccessful, the Israelites determined to renew the engagement in better circumstances. **3-9. Let us fetch the ark of the covenant of the Lord out of Shiloh unto us**—Strange that they were so blind to the real cause of the disaster and that they did not discern, in the great and general corruption of religion and morals (ch. 2 and 7:3; Ps. 78:58), the reason why the presence and aid of God were not extended to them. Their first measure for restoring the national spirit and energy ought to have been a complete reformation—a universal return to purity of worship and morals. But, instead of cherishing a spirit of deep humiliation and sincere repentance, instead of resolving on the abolition of existing abuses, and the re-establishing of the pure faith, they adopted what appeared an easier and speedier course—they put their trust in ceremonial observances, and doubted not but that the introduction of the ark into the battlefield would ensure their victory. In recommending this extraordinary step, the elders might recollect the confidence it imparted to their ancestors (Num. 10:35; 14:44), as well as what had been done at Jericho. But it is more probable that they were influenced by the heathenish ideas of their idolatrous neighbors, who carried their idol Dagon, or his sacred symbols, to their wars, believing that the power of their divinities was inseparably associated with, or residing in, their images. In short, the shout raised in the Hebrew camp, on the arrival of the ark, indicated very plainly the prevalence among the Israelites at this time of a belief in national deities—whose influence was local, and whose interest was especially exerted in behalf of the people who adored them. The joy of the Israelites was an emotion springing out of the same superstitious sentiments as the corresponding dismay of their enemies; and to afford them a convincing, though painful proof of their error, was the ulterior object of the discipline to which they were now subjected—a discipline by which God, while punishing them for their apostasy by allowing the capture of the ark, had another end in view—that of signally vindicating His supremacy over all the gods of the nations.

12-22. ELI HEARING THE TIDINGS. 13. Eli sat upon a seat by the wayside—The aged priest, as a public magistrate, used, in dispensing justice, to seat himself daily in a spacious recess at the entrance gate of the city. In his intense anxiety to learn the issue of the battle, he took up his usual place as the most convenient for meeting with passers-by. His seat was an official chair, similar to those of the ancient Egyptian judges, richly carved, superbly ornamented, high, and *without a back*. The calamities announced to Samuel as about to fall upon the family of Eli were now inflicted in the death of his two sons, and after his death, by that of his daughter-in-law, whose infant son received a name that perpetuated the fallen glory of the church and nation. The public disaster was completed by the capture of the ark. Poor Eli! He was a good man, in spite of his unhappy weaknesses. So strongly were his sensibilities enlisted on the side of religion, that the news of the capture of the ark proved to him a knell of death; and yet his overindulgence, or sad neglect of his family—the main cause of all the evils that led to its fall—has been recorded, as a beacon to warn all heads of Christian families against making shipwreck on the same rock.

CHAPTER 5

Vss. 1, 2. THE PHILISTINES BRING THE ARK INTO THE HOUSE OF DAGON. **1. Ashdod**—or Azotus, one of the five Philistine satrapies, and a place of great strength. It was an inland town, thirty-four miles north of Gaza, now called Esdud. **2. the house of Dagon**—Stately temples were erected in honor of this idol, which was the principal deity of the Philistines, but whose worship extended over all Syria, as well as Mesopotamia and Chaldea; its name being found among the Assyrian gods on the cuneiform inscriptions [RAWLINSON]. It was represented under a monstrous combination of a human head, breast, and arms, joined to the belly and tail of a fish. The captured ark was placed in the temple of Dagon, right before this image of the idol.

3-5. DAGON FALLS DOWN. 3. they of Ashdod arose early—They were filled with consternation when they found the object of their stupid veneration prostrate before the symbol of the divine presence. Though set up, it fell again, and lay in a state of complete mutilation; its head and arms, severed from the trunk, were lying in distant and separate places, as if violently cast off, and only the fishy part remained. The degradation of their idol, though concealed by the priests on the former occasion, was now more manifest and infamous. It lay in the attitude of a vanquished enemy and a suppliant, and this picture of humiliation significantly declared the superiority of the God of Israel. **5. Therefore neither the priests . . . nor any . . . tread on the threshold of Dagon**—A superstitious ceremony crept in, and in the providence of God was continued, by which the Philistines contributed to publish this proof of the helplessness of their god. **unto this day**—The usage continued in practice at the time when this history was written—probably in the later years of Samuel's life.

6-12. THE PHILISTINES ARE SMITTEN WITH EMERODS. 6. the hand of the Lord was heavy upon them of Ashdod—The presumption of the Ashdodites was punished by a severe judgment that overtook them in the form of a pestilence. **smote them with emerods**—bleeding piles, hemorrhoids (Ps. 78:66), in a very aggravated form. As the heathens generally regarded diseases affecting the secret parts of the body as punishments from the gods for trespasses committed against themselves, the Ashdodites would be the more ready to look upon the prevailing epidemic as demonstrating the anger of God, already shown against their idol. **7. the ark of God shall not abide with us**—It was removed successively to several of the large towns of the country, but the same pestilence broke out in every place and raged so fiercely and fatally that the authorities were forced to send the ark back into the land of Israel. **11. they sent**—i.e., the magistrates of Ekron. **12. the cry of the city went up to heaven**—The disease is attended with acute pain, and it is far from being a rare phenomenon in the Philistian plain [VAN DE VELDE].

CHAPTER 6

Vss. 1-9. THE PHILISTINES COUNSEL HOW TO SEND BACK THE ARK. **1. the ark . . . was in the country of the Philistines seven months**—Notwithstanding the calamities which its presence had brought on the country and the people, the Philistine lords were unwilling to relinquish such a prize, and tried every means to retain it with peace and safety, but in vain. **2. the Philistines called for the priests and the diviners**—The designed restoration of the ark was not, it seems, universally approved of, and many doubts were expressed whether the prevailing pestilence was really a judgment of Heaven. The priests and diviners united all parties by recommending a course which would enable them easily to discriminate the true character of the calamities, and at the same time to propitiate the incensed Deity for any acts of disrespect which might have been shown to His ark. **4. Five golden emerods**—Votive or thank offerings were commonly made by the heathen in prayer for, or gratitude after, deliverance from lingering or dangerous disorders, in the form of metallic (generally silver) models or images of the diseased parts of the body. This is common still in Roman Catholic countries, as well as in the temples of the Hindoos and other modern heathen. **five golden mice**—This animal is supposed by some to be the jerboa or jumping-mouse of Syria and Egypt [BOCHART]; by others, to be the short-tailed field mouse, which often swarms in prodigious numbers and commits great ravages in the cultivated fields of Palestine. **5. give glory unto** the God of Israel—By these propitiatory presents, the Philistines would acknowledge His power and make reparation for the injury done to His ark. **lighten his hand . . . from off your gods**—Elohim for god. **6. Wherefore then do ye harden your hearts, as the Egyptians and Pharaoh hardened their hearts** —The memory of the appalling judgments that had been inflicted on Egypt was not yet obliterated. Whether preserved in written records, or in floating tradition, they were still fresh in the minds of men, and being extensively spread, were doubtless the means of diffusing the knowledge and fear of the true God. **7. make a new cart**—Their object in making a new one for the purpose seems to have been not only for cleanliness and neatness, but from an impression that there would have been an impropriety in using one that had been applied to meaner or more common services. It appears to have been a covered wagon (see on II Sam. 6:3). **two milch kine**—Such untrained heifers, wanton and vagrant, would pursue no certain and regular path, like those accustomed to the yoke, and therefore were most unlikely of their own spontaneous motion to prosecute the direct road to the land of Israel. **bring their calves home from them**—The strong natural affection of the dams might be supposed to stimulate their return homewards, rather than direct their steps in a foreign country. **8. take the ark of the Lord, and lay it upon the cart**—This mode of carrying the sacred symbol was forbidden; but the ignorance of the Philistines made the indignity excusable (see on II Sam. 6:6). **put the jewels . . . in a coffer by the side thereof**—The way of securing treasure in the East is still in a chest, chained to the house wall or some solid part of the furniture. **9. Beth-shemesh**—i.e., "house of the sun," now Ain Shems [ROBINSON], a city of priests in Judah, in the southeast border of Dan, lying in a beautiful and extensive valley. Josephus says they were set a-going near a place where the road divided into two— the one leading back to Ekron, where were their calves, and the other to Beth-shemesh. Their frequent lowings attested their ardent longing for their young, and at the same time the supernatural influence that controlled their movements in a contrary direction. **12. the lords of the Philistines went after them**—to give their tribute of homage, to prevent imposture, and to obtain the most reliable evidence of the truth. The result of this journey tended to their own deeper humiliation, and the greater illustration of God's glory. **14. they clave** —i.e., the Beth-shemites, in an irrepressible outburst of joy. **offered the kine**—Though contrary to the requirements of the law (Lev. 1:3; 22:19), these animals might properly be offered, as consecrated by God Himself; and though not beside the tabernacle, there were many instances of sacrifices offered by prophets and holy men on extraordinary occasions in other places. **17-18. these are the golden emerods . . . and the mice**—There were five representative images of the emerods, corresponding to the five principal cities of the Philistines. But the number of the golden mice must have been greater, for they were sent from the walled towns as well as the country villages. **unto the great stone of Abel**—*Abel* or Aben means "stone," so that without resorting to *italics*, the reading should be, "the great stone." **19. he smote the men of Beth-shemesh, because they had looked into the ark**—In the ecstasy of delight at seeing the return of the ark, the Beth-shemesh reapers pried into it beneath the wagon cover; and instead of covering it up again, as a sacred utensil, they let it remain exposed

to common inspection, wishing it to be seen, in order that all might enjoy the triumph of seeing the votive offerings presented to it, and gratify curiosity with the sight of the sacred shrine. This was the offense of those Israelites (Levites, as well as common people), who had treated the ark with less reverence than the Philistines themselves. **he smote of the people fifty thousand and threescore and ten men**—Beth-shemesh being only a village, this translation *must* be erroneous, and should be, "he smote fifty out of a thousand," being only 1400 in all who indulged this curiosity. God, instead of decimating, according to an ancient usage, slew only a twentieth part; i.e., according to Josephus, 70 out of 1400 (see on Num. 4:18-22). **21. Kirjath-jearim** —"the city of woods," also called Kirjath-baal (Josh. 15:60; 18:14; I Chron. 13:6, 7). This was the nearest town to Beth-shemesh; and being a place of strength, it was a more fitting place for the residence of the ark. Beth-shemesh being in a low plain, and Kirjath-jearim on a hill, explains the message, "Come ye down, and fetch it up to you."

CHAPTER 7

Vss. 1-2. THE ARK AT KIRJATH-JEARIM. **1. the men of Kirjath-jearim**—"the city of woods," also Kirjath-baal (Josh. 15:60; 18:14; I Chron. 13:5, 6). It was the nearest town to Beth-shemesh and stood on a hill. This was the reason of the message (ch. 6:21), and why this was chosen for the convenience of people turning their faces to the ark (I Kings 8: 29-35; Ps. 28:2; Dan. 6:10). **brought it into the house of Abinadab**—Why it was not transported at once to Shiloh where the tabernacle and sacred vessels were remaining, is difficult to conjecture. **sanctified . . . his son**—He was not a Levite, and was therefore only set apart or appointed to be keeper of the place. **2. the ark abode in Kirjath-jearim . . . twenty years**—It appears, in the subsequent history, that a much longer period elapsed before its final removal from Kirjath-jearim (II Sam. 6; I Chron. 13). But that length of time had passed when the Israelites began to revive from their sad state of religious decline. The capture of the ark had produced a general indifference either as to its loss or its recovery. **all the house of Israel lamented after the Lord**—They were then brought, doubtless by the influence of Samuel's exhortations, to renounce idolatry, and to return to the national worship of the true God.

3-6. THE ISRAELITES, THROUGH SAMUEL'S INFLUENCE, SOLEMNLY REPENT AT MIZPEH. **3-6. Samuel spake unto all the house of Israel**—A great national reformation was effected through the influence of Samuel. Disgusted with their foreign servitude, and panting for the restoration of liberty and independence, they were open to salutary impressions; and convinced of their errors, they renounced idolatry. The re-establishment of the faith of their fathers was inaugurated at a great public meeting, held at Mizpeh in Judah, and hallowed by the observance of impressive religious solemnities. The drawing water, and pouring it out before the Lord, seems to have been a symbolical act by which, in the people's name, Samuel testified their sense of national corruption, their need of that moral purification of which water is the emblem, and their sincere desire to pour out their hearts in repentance before God. **Samuel judged . . . Israel in Mizpeh**—At the time of Eli's death he could not have much exceeded twenty years of age; and although his character and position must have given him great influence, it does not appear that hitherto he had done more than prophets were wont to do. Now he entered on the duties of a civil magistrate. **7-14. WHILE SAMUEL PRAYS, THE PHILISTINES ARE DISCOMFITED. 7-11. when the Philistines heard . . .**—The character and importance of the national convention at Mizpeh were fully appreciated by the Philistines. They discerned in it the rising spirit of religious patriotism among the Israelites that was prepared to throw off the yoke of their domination. Anxious to crush it at the first, they made a sudden incursion while the Israelites were in the midst of their solemn celebration. Unprepared for resistance, they besought Samuel to supplicate the divine interposition to save them from their enemies. The prophet's prayers and sacrifice were answered by such a tremendous storm of thunder and lightning that the assailants, panic-struck, were disordered and fled. The Israelites, recognizing the hand of God, rushed courageously on the foe they had so much dreaded and committed such immense havoc, that the Philistines did not for long recover from this disastrous blow. This brilliant victory secured peace and independence to Israel for twenty years, as well as the restitution of the usurped territory. **12. Samuel took a stone, and set it between Mizpeh and Shen**—on an open spot between the town and "the crag" (some well-known rock in the neighborhood). A huge stone pillar was erected as a monument of their victory (Lev. 26:1). The name—Eben-ezer—is thought to have been written on the face of it.

CHAPTER 8

Vss. 1-18. OCCASIONED BY THE ILL-GOVERNMENT OF SAMUEL'S SONS, THE ISRAELITES ASK A KING. 1. when Samuel was old—He was now about fifty-four years of age, having discharged the office of sole judge for twelve years. Unable, from growing infirmities, to prosecute his circuit journeys through the country, he at length confined his magisterial duties to Ramah and its neighborhood, delegating to his sons as his deputies (ch. 7:15) the administration of justice in the southern districts of Palestine, their provincial court being held at Beersheba. The young men, however, did not inherit the high qualities of their father. Having corrupted the fountains of justice for their own private aggrandizement, a deputation of the leading men in the country lodged a complaint against them in headquarters, accompanied with a formal demand for a change in the government. The limited and occasional authority of the judges, the disunion and jealousy of the tribes under the administration of those rulers, had been creating a desire for a united and permanent form of government; while the advanced age of Samuel, together with the risk of his death happening in the then unsettled state of the people, was the occasion of calling forth an expression of this desire now. **6. the thing displeased Samuel when they said, Give us a king to judge us**—Personal and family feelings might affect his views of this public movement. But his dissatisfaction arose principally from the proposed change being revolutionary in its character. Though it would not entirely subvert their theocratic government, the appointment of a visible monarch would necessarily tend to throw out of view their unseen King and Head. God intimated, through Samuel, that their request would, in anger, be granted, while at the same time he apprised them of some of the evils that would result from their choice. **11. This will be the manner of the king**—The following is a very just and graphic picture of the despotic governments which anciently and still are found in the East, and into conformity with which the Hebrew monarchy, notwithstanding the restrictions prescribed by the law, gradually slid. **He will take your sons, and appoint them for himself**—Oriental sovereigns claim a right to the services of any of their subjects at pleasure. **some shall run before his chariots**—The royal equipages were, generally throughout the East (as in Persia they still are), preceded and accompanied by a number of attendants who ran on foot. **12. he will appoint him captains**—In the East, a person must accept any office to which he may be nominated by the king, however irksome it may be to his taste or ruinous to his interests. **13. he will take your daughters to be confectionaries**—Cookery, baking, and the kindred works are, in Eastern countries, female employment, and thousands of young women are occupied with these offices in the palaces even of petty princes. **14-18. he will take your fields . . .**—The circumstances mentioned here might be illustrated by exact analogies in the conduct of many Oriental monarchs in the present day. **19-22. Nevertheless the people refused to obey the voice of Samuel**—They sneered at Samuel's description as a bugbear to frighten them. Determined, at all hazards, to gain their object, they insisted on being made like all the other nations, though it was their glory and happiness to be unlike other nations in having the Lord for their King and Lawgiver (Num. 23:9; Deut. 33:28). Their demand was conceded, for the government of a king had been provided for in the law; and they were dismissed to wait the appointment, which God had reserved to Himself (Deut. 17:14-20).

CHAPTER 9

Vss. 1-14. SAUL, DESPAIRING TO FIND HIS FATHER'S ASSES, COMES TO SAMUEL. 1. a mighty man of power—i.e., of great wealth and substance. The family was of high consideration in the tribe of Benjamin, and therefore Saul's words must be set down among the common forms of affected/humility, which Oriental people are wont to use. **2. Saul, a choice young man, and a goodly**—He had a fine appearance; for it is evident that he must have been only a little under seven feet tall. A gigantic stature and an athletic frame must have been a popular recommendation at that time in that country. **3. the asses of Kish Saul's father were lost. And Kish said to Saul . . . , arise, go seek the asses**—The probability is that the family of Kish, according to the immemorial usage of Oriental shepherds in the purely pastoral regions, had let the animals roam at large during the grazing season, at the close of which messengers were despatched in search of them. Such travelling searches are common; and, as each owner has his own stamp marked on his cattle, the mention of it to the shepherds he meets gradually leads to the discovery of the strayed animals. This ramble of Saul's had nothing extraordinary in it, except its *superior* directions and issue, which turned its uncertainty into certainty. **4, 5. he passed through mount Ephraim**—This being situated on the north of Benjamin, indicates the direction of Saul's journey. The district explored means the whole of the mountainous region, with its valleys and defiles, which belonged to Ephraim.

Turning apparently southwards—probably through the verdant hills between Shiloh and the vales of Jordan (Shalisha and Shalim)—he approached again the borders of Benjamin, scoured the land of Zuph, and was proposing to return, when his servant recollected that they were in the immediate neighborhood of the man of God, who would give them counsel. **6. there is in this city a man of God**—Ramah was the usual residence of Samuel, but several circumstances, especially the mention of Rachel's sepulchre, which lay in Saul's way homeward, lead to the conclusion that "this city" was not the Ramah where Samuel dwelt. **peradventure he can show us our way that we should go**—It seems strange that a dignified prophet should be consulted in such an affair. But it is probable that at the introduction of the prophetic office, the seers had discovered things lost or stolen, and thus their power for higher revelations was gradually established. **7. Saul said to his servant, But behold, if we go, what shall we bring the man?**—According to Eastern notions, it would be considered a want of respect for any person to go into the presence of a superior man of rank or of official station without a present of some kind in his hand, however trifling in value. **the bread is spent in our vessels**—Shepherds, going in quest of their cattle, put up in a bag as much flour for making bread as will last sometimes for thirty days. It appears that Saul thought of giving the man of God a cake from his travelling bag, and this would have been sufficient to render the indispensable act of civility—the customary tribute to official dignity. **8. the fourth part of a shekel of silver**—rather more than quarter. Contrary to our Western notions, money is in the East the most acceptable form in which a present can be made to a man of rank. **9. seer . . . Prophet**—The recognized distinction in latter times was, that a seer was one who was favored with visions of God—a view of things invisible to mortal sight; and a prophet foretold future events. **11. as they went up the hill**—The modern village, Er-Rameh, lies on an eminence; and on their way they met a band of young maidens going out to the well, which, like all similar places in Palestine, was beyond the precincts of the town. From these damsels they learned that the day was devoted to a festival occasion, in honor of which Samuel had arrived in the city; that a sacrifice had been offered, which was done by prophets in extraordinary circumstances at a distance from the tabernacle, and that a feast was to follow—implying that it had been a peace offering, and that, according to the venerable practice of the Israelites, the man of God was expected to ask a special blessing on the food in a manner becoming the high occasion. **14. Samuel came out against them for to go up to the high place**—Such were the simple manners of the times that this prophet, the chief man in Israel, was seen going to preside at a high festival undistinguished either by his dress or equipage from any ordinary citizen.

15-27. GOD REVEALS TO SAMUEL SAUL'S COMING, AND HIS APPOINTMENT TO THE KINGDOM. 15. Now the Lord had told Samuel in his ear a day before—The description of Saul, the time of his arrival, and the high office to which he was destined, had been secretly intimated to Samuel from heaven. The future king of Israel was to fight the battles of the Lord and protect His people. It would appear that they were at this time suffering great molestation from the Philistines, and that this was an additional reason of their urgent demands for the appointment of a king (see on ch. 10:5; 13:3). **18. Tell me, I**

pray thee, where the seer's house is—Satisfying the stranger's inquiry, Samuel invited him to the feast, as well as to sojourn till the morrow; and, in order to reconcile him to the delay, he assured him that the strayed asses had been recovered. **20. on whom is all the desire of Israel? Is it not on thee, and on thy father's house?**—This was a covert and indirect premonition of the royal dignity that awaited him; and, though Saul's answer shows that he fully understood it, he affected to doubt that the prophet was in earnest. **21. And Saul answered and said, Am not I a Benjamite, of the smallest of the tribes of Israel . . .**—By selecting a king from this least and nearly extinct tribe (Judg. 20), divine wisdom designed to remove all grounds of jealousy among the other tribes. **22. Samuel took Saul and his servant and brought them into the parlour**—The toilworn but noble-looking traveller found himself suddenly seated among the principal men of the place and treated as the most distinguished guest. **24. the cook took up the shoulder . . . , and set it before Saul. And Samuel said, Behold that which is left; set it before thee, and eat**—i.e., reserved (see on Gen. 18:6; 43:34). This was, most probably, the right shoulder; which, as the perquisite of the sacrifice, belonged to Samuel, and which he had set aside for his expected guest. In the sculptures of the Egyptian shambles, also, the first joint taken off was always the right shoulder for the priest. The meaning of those distinguished attentions must have been understood by the other guests. **25. Samuel communed with Saul upon the top of the house**—Saul was taken to lodge with the prophet for that night. Before retiring to rest, they communed on the flat roof of the house, the couch being laid there (Josh. 2:6), when, doubtless, Samuel revealed the secret and described the peculiar duties of a monarch in a nation so related to the Divine King as Israel. Next morning early, Samuel roused his guest, and conveying him on his way towards the skirts of the city, sought, before parting, a *private* interview—the object of which is narrated in the next chapter.

CHAPTER 10

Vss. 1-27. SAMUEL ANOINTS SAUL, AND CONFIRMS HIM BY THE PREDICTION OF THREE SIGNS. **1. Then Samuel took a vial of oil**—This was the ancient (Judg. 9:8) ceremony of investiture with the royal office among the Hebrews and other Eastern nations. But there were two unctions to the kingly office; the one in private, by a prophet (ch. 16:13), which was meant to be only a prophetic intimation of the person attaining that high dignity—the more public and formal inauguration (II Sam. 2:4; 5:3) was performed by the high priest, and perhaps with the holy oil, but that is not certain. The first of a dynasty was thus anointed, but not his heirs, unless the succession was disputed (I Kings 1:39; II Kings 11:12; 23:30; II Chron. 23:11). **kissed him**—This salutation, as explained by the words that accompanied it, was an act of respectful homage, a token of congratulation to the new king (Ps. 2:12). **2. When thou art departed from me to-day**—The design of these specific predictions of what should be met with on the way, and the number and minuteness of which would arrest attention, was to confirm Saul's reliance on the prophetic character of Samuel, and lead him to give full credence to what had been revealed to him as the word of God. **Ra sepulchre**—near Bethlehem (see on Gen. **Zelzah**—or Zelah, now *Bet-jalah*, in the ne hood of that town. **3. the plain**—or the oak of Tabor, not the celebrated mount, for that was far distant. **three men going up to God to Bethel**—apparently to offer sacrifices there at a time when the ark and the tabernacle were not in a settled abode, and God had not yet declared the permanent place which He should choose. The kids were for sacrifice, the loaves for the offering, and the wine for the libations. **5. the hill of God**—probably Geba (ch. 13:3), so called from a school of the prophets being established there. The company of prophets were, doubtless, the pupils at this seminary, which had probably been instituted by Samuel, and in which the chief branches of education taught were a knowledge of the law, and of psalmody with instrumental music, which is called "prophesying" (here and in I Chron. 25:1, 7). **6. the Spirit of the Lord will come upon thee**—lit., rush upon thee, suddenly endowing thee with a capacity and disposition to act in a manner far superior to thy previous character and habits; and instead of the simplicity, ignorance, and sheepishness of a peasant, thou wilt display an energy, wisdom, and magnanimity worthy of a prince. **8. thou shalt go down before me to Gilgal**—This, according to Josephus, was to be a standing rule for the observance of Saul while the prophet and he lived; that in every great crisis, such as a hostile incursion on the country, he should repair to Gilgal, where he was to remain seven days, to afford time for the tribes on both sides Jordan to assemble, and Samuel to reach it. **9. when he had turned his back to go from Samuel, God gave him another heart**—Influenced by the words of Samuel, as well as by the accomplishment of these signs, Saul's reluctance to undertake the onerous office was overcome. The fulfilment of the two first signs is passed over, but the third is specially described. The spectacle of a man, though more fit to look after his father's cattle than to take part in the sacred exercises of the young prophets—a man without any previous instruction, or any known taste, entering with ardor into the spirit, and skilfully accompanying the melodies of the sacred band, was so extraordinary a phenomenon, that it gave rise to the proverb, "Is Saul also among the prophets?" (see on ch. 19:24). The prophetic spirit had come upon him; and to Saul it was as personal and experimental an evidence of the truth of God's word that had been spoken to him, as converts to Christianity have in themselves from the sanctifying power of the Gospel. **12. But who is their father?**—The *Sept.* reads, "Who is his father?" referring to Saul the son of Kish. **17. Samuel called the people together . . . at Mizpeh**—a shaft-like hill near Hebron, 500 feet in height. The national assemblies of the Israelites were held there. A day having been appointed for the election of a king, Samuel, after having charged the people with a rejection of God's institution and a superseding of it by one of their own, proceeded to the nomination of the new monarch. As it was of the utmost importance that the appointment should be under the divine direction and control, the determination was made by the miraculous lot, tribes, families, and individuals being successively passed until Saul was found. His concealment of himself must have been the result either of innate modesty, or a sudden nervous excitement under the circumstances. When dragged into view, he was seen to possess all those corporeal advantages which a rude people desiderate in their sovereigns; and the exhibition of which gained for the prince the favorable opinion of Samuel also. In the midst of the national

enthusiasm, however, the prophet's deep piety and genuine patriotism took care to explain "the manner of the kingdom," i.e., the royal rights and privileges, together with the limitations to which they were to be subjected; and in order that the constitution might be ratified with all due solemnity, the charter of this constitutional monarchy was recorded and laid up "before the Lord," i.e., deposited in the custody of the priests, along with the most sacred archives of the nation. **26. Saul also went home to Gibeah**—near Geba. This was his place of residence (see on Judg. 20), about five miles north of Jerusalem. **there went . . . a band of men, whose hearts God had touched**—who feared God and regarded allegiance to their king as a conscientious duty. They are opposed to "the children of Belial." **27. the children of Belial said, How shall this man save us? And they despised him, and brought him no presents**—In Eastern countries, the honor of the sovereign and the splendor of the royal household are upheld, not by a fixed rate of taxation, but by presents brought at certain seasons by officials, and men of wealth, from all parts of the kingdom, according to the means of the individual, and of a customary registered value. Such was the tribute which Saul's opponents withheld, and for want of which he was unable to set up a kingly establishment for a while. But "biding his time," he bore the insult with a prudence and magnanimity which were of great use in the beginning of his government.

CHAPTER 11

Vss. 1-4. NAHASH OFFERS THEM OF JABESH-GILEAD A REPROACHFUL CONDITION. **1. Then Nahash the Ammonite came up**—Nahash (serpent); (see on Judg. 8:3). The Ammonites had long claimed the right of original possession in Gilead. Though repressed by Jephthah (Judg. 11:33), they now, after ninety years, renew their pretensions; and it was the report of their threatened invasion that hastened the appointment of a king (ch. 12:12). **Make a covenant with us, and we will serve thee**—They saw no prospect of aid from the western Israelites, who were not only remote, but scarcely able to repel the incursions of the Philistines from themselves. **2. thrust out all your right eyes**—lit., scoop or hollow out the ball. This barbarous mutilation is the usual punishment of usurpers in the East—inflicted on chiefs; sometimes, also, even in modern history, on the whole male population of a town. Nahash meant to keep the Jabeshites useful as tributaries, whence he did not wish to render them wholly blind, but only to deprive them of their right eye, which would disqualify them for war. Besides, his object was, through the people of Jabesh-gilead, to insult the Israelitish nation. **3, 4. send messengers unto all the coasts of Israel**—a curious proof of the general dissatisfaction that prevailed as to the appointment of Saul. Those Gileadites deemed him capable neither of advising nor succoring them; and even in his own town the appeal was made to the people—not to the prince.

5-11. THEY SEND TO SAUL, AND ARE DELIVERED. **7. he took a yoke of oxen, and hewed them in pieces**—(see on Judg. 19.) This particular form of war-summons was suited to the character and habits of an agricultural and pastoral people. Solemn in itself, the denunciation that accompanied it carried a terrible threat to those that neglected to obey it. Saul conjoins the name of Samuel with his own, to lend the greater influence to the measure, and to strike greater terror unto all contemners of the order. The small contingent furnished by Judah suggests that the disaffection to Saul was strongest in that tribe. **8. Bezek**–This place of general muster was not far from Shechem, on the road to Beth-shan, and nearly opposite the ford for crossing to Jabesh-gilead. The great number on the muster roll showed the effect of Saul's wisdom and promptitude. **11. on the morrow Saul put the people in three companies**–Crossing the Jordan in the evening, Saul marched his army all night, and came at daybreak on the camp of the Ammonites, who were surprised in three different parts, and totally routed. This happened before the seven days' truce expired.

12-15. SAUL CONFIRMED KING. **12, 13. the people said . . . , Who is he that said, Shall Saul reign over us?**–The enthusiastic admiration of the people, under the impulse of grateful and generous feelings, would have dealt summary vengeance on the minority who opposed Saul, had not he, either from principle or policy, shown himself as great in clemency as in valor. The calm and sagacious counsel of Samuel directed the popular feelings into a right channel, by appointing a general assembly of the militia, the really effective force of the nation, at Gilgal, where, amid great pomp and religious solemnities, the victorious leader was confirmed in his kingdom.

CHAPTER 12

Vss. 1-5. SAMUEL TESTIFIES HIS INTEGRITY. **1. Samuel said unto all Israel**–This public address was made after the solemn re-instalment of Saul, and before the convention at Gilgal separated. Samuel, having challenged a review of his public life, received a unanimous testimony to the unsullied honor of his personal character, as well as the justice and integrity of his public administration. **5. the Lord is witness against you, and his anointed is witness**–that, by their own acknowledgment, he had given them no cause to weary of the divine government by judges, and that, therefore, the blame of desiring a change of government rested with themselves. This was only insinuated, and they did not fully perceive his drift.

6-16. HE REPROVES THE PEOPLE FOR INGRATITUDE. **7. Now therefore stand still, that I may reason with you**–The burden of this faithful and uncompromising address was to show them, that though they had obtained the change of government they had so importunely desired, their conduct was highly displeasing to their heavenly King; nevertheless, if they remained faithful to Him and to the principles of the theocracy, they might be delivered from many of the evils to which the new state of things would expose them. And in confirmation of those statements, no less than in evidence of the divine displeasure, a remarkable phenomenon, on the invocation of the prophet, and of which he gave due premonition, took place. **11. Bedan**–The *Sept.* reads "Barak"; and for "Samuel," some versions read "Samson," which seems more natural than that the prophet should mention himself to the total omission of the greatest of the judges. (Cf. Heb. 11:32).

17-25. HE TERRIFIES THEM WITH THUNDER IN HARVEST-TIME. **17. Is it not wheat harvest to-day?** That season in Palestine occurs at the end of June or beginning of July, when it seldom or never rains, and the sky is serene and cloudless. There could

not, therefore, have been a stronger or more appropriate proof of a divine mission than the phenomenon of rain and thunder happening, without any prognostics of its approach, upon the prediction of a person professing himself to be a prophet of the Lord, and giving it as an attestation of his words being true. The people regarded it as a miraculous display of divine power, and, panic-struck, implored the prophet to pray for them. Promising to do so, he dispelled their fears. The conduct of Samuel, in this whole affair of the king's appointment, shows him to have been a great and good man who sank all private and personal considerations in disinterested zeal for his country's good and whose last words in public were to warn the people, and their king, of the danger of apostasy and disobedience to God.

CHAPTER 13

Vss. 1, 2. SAUL'S SELECTED BAND. **1. Saul reigned one year**–(*see Marg*). The transactions recorded in the eleventh and twelfth chapters were the principal incidents comprising the first year of Saul's reign; and the events about to be described in this happened in the second year. **2. Saul chose him three thousand men of Israel**–This band of picked men was a bodyguard, who were kept constantly on duty, while the rest of the people were dismissed till their services might be needed. It seems to have been his tactics to attack the Philistine garrisons in the country by different detachments, rather than by risking a general engagement; and his first operations were directed to rid his native territory of Benjamin of these enemies.

3, 4. HE CALLS THE HEBREWS TO GILGAL AGAINST THE PHILISTINES. **3. Jonathan** [God-given] **smote the garrison of the Philistines . . . in Geba**– Geba and Gibeah were towns in Benjamin, very close to each other (Josh. 18:24, 28). The word rendered "garrison" is different from that of verse 23; ch. 14:1, and signifies, lit., something erected; probably a pillar or flagstaff, indicative of Philistine ascendency. That the secret demolition of this standard, so obnoxious to a young and noblehearted patriot, was the feat of Jonathan referred to, is evident from the words, "the Philistines heard of it," which is not the way we should expect an attack on a fortress to be noticed. **Saul blew the trumpet throughout all the land**–This, a well-known sound, was the usual Hebrew war-summons; the first blast was answered by the beacon fire in the neighboring places. A second blast was blown– then answered by a fire in a more distant locality, whence the proclamation was speedily diffused over the whole country. As the Philistines resented what Jonathan had done as an overt attempt to throw off their yoke, a levy, en masse, of the people was immediately ordered, the rendezvous to be the old camping-ground at Gilgal.

5. THE PHILISTINES' GREAT HOST. **5. The Philistines gathered themselves together to fight with Israel, thirty thousand chariots, and six thousand horsemen**–Either this number must include chariots of every kind–or the word "chariots" must mean the men fighting in them (II Sam. 10:18; I Kings 20:21; I Chron. 19:18); or, as some eminent critics maintain, *Sheloshim*, thirty, has crept into the text, instead of *Shelosh*, three. The gathering of the chariots and horsemen must be understood to be on the Philistine plain, before they ascended the western passes and pitched in the heart of the Benjamite hills, in "Michmash," (now Mukmas), a "steep

precipitous valley" [ROBINSON], eastward from Beth-aven (Beth-el).

6, 8. THE ISRAELITES' DISTRESS. 6. When the men of Israel saw that they were in a strait—Though Saul's gallantry was unabated, his subjects displayed no degree of zeal and energy. Instead of venturing an encounter, they fled in all directions. Some, in their panic, left the country (vs. 7), but most took refuge in the hiding-places which the broken ridges of the neighborhood abundantly afford. The rocks are perforated in every direction with "caves," and "holes," and "pits"—crevices and fissures sunk deep in the rocky soil, subterranean granaries or dry wells in the adjoining fields. The name of Michmash (hidden treasure) seems to be derived from this natural peculiarity [STANLEY]. **8. he [Saul] tarried seven days**—He was still in the eastern borders of his kingdom, in the valley of Jordan. Some bolder spirits had ventured to join the camp at Gilgal; but even the courage of those stout-hearted men gave way in prospect of this terrible visitation; and as many of them were stealing away, he thought some immediate and decided step must be taken.

9-16. SAUL, WEARY OF WAITING FOR SAMUEL, SACRIFICES. 9. Saul said, Bring hither a burnt offering to me, and peace offerings—Saul, though patriotic enough in his own way, was more ambitious of gaining the glory of a triumph to himself than ascribing it to God. He did not understand his proper position as king of Israel; and although aware of the restrictions under which he held the sovereignty, he wished to rule as an autocrat, who possessed absolute power both in civil and sacred things. This occasion was his first trial. Samuel waited till the last day of the seven, in order to put the constitutional character of the king to the test; and, as Saul, in his impatient and passionate haste knowingly transgressed (vs. 12) by invading the priest's office and thus showing his unfitness for his high office (as he showed nothing of the faith of Gideon and other Hebrew generals), he incurred a threat of the rejection which his subsequent way-wardness confirmed. **15, 16. Samuel . . . gat him . . . unto Gibeah . . . and Saul, and Jonathan his son, and the people that were present with them, abode in Gibeah**—Saul removed his camp thither, either in the hope that, it being his native town, he would gain an increase of followers or that he might enjoy the counsels and influence of the prophet. **17. the spoilers came out of the camp of the Philistines in three companies**—ravaging through the three valleys which radiate from the uplands of Michmash to Ophrah on the north, through the pass of Beth-horon on the west, and down the ravines of Zeboim (the hyænas), towards the Ghor or Jordan valley on the east. **19. Now there was no smith found throughout . . . Israel**—The country was in the lowest state of depression and degradation. The Philistines, after the great victory over the sons of Eli, had become the virtual masters of the land. Their policy in disarming the natives has been often followed in the East. For repairing any serious damage to their agricultural implements, they had to apply to the neighboring forts. "Yet they had a file," as a kind of privilege, for the purpose of sharpening sundry smaller utensils of husbandry.

CHAPTER 14

Vss. 1-14. JONATHAN MIRACULOUSLY SMITES THE PHILISTINES' GARRISON. **1. the Philistines' garrison**

—*Marg.*, the standing camp "in the passage of Mich-mash" (ch. 13:16, 23), now Wady Es-Suweinit. "It begins in the neighborhood of Betin (Beth-el) and El-Bireh (Beetroth), and as it breaks through the ridge below these places, its sides form precipitous walls. On the right, about a quarter of an acre below, it again breaks off, and passes between high perpendicular precipices" [ROBINSON]. **2. Saul tarried in the uttermost part or Gibeah**—*Heb.*, Geba, entrenched, along with Samuel and Ahiah the high priest, on the top of one of the conical or spherical hills which abound in the Benjamite territory, and favorable for an encampment, called Migron (a precipice). **4. between the passages**—i.e., the deep and great ravine of Suweinit. **Jonathan sought to go over unto the Philistines' garrison**—a distance of about three miles running between two jagged points; *Heb.*, "teeth of the cliff." **there was a sharp rock on the one side, and a sharp rock on the other side . . . Bozez**—(shining) from the aspect of the chalky rock. **Seneh**—(the thorn) probably from a solitary acacia on its top. They are the only rocks of the kind in this vicinity; and the top of the crag towards Michmash was occupied as the post of the Philistines. The two camps were in sight of each other; and it was up the steep rocky sides of this isolated eminence that Jonathan and his armorbearer (vs. 6) made their adventurous approach. This enterprise is one of the most gallant that history or romance records. The action, viewed in itself, was rash and contrary to all established rules of military discipline, which do not permit soldiers to fight or to undertake any enterprise that may involve important consequences without the order of the generals. **6. it may be that the Lord will work for us**—This expression did not imply a doubt; it signified simply that the object he aimed at was not in his own power—but it depended upon God—and that he expected success neither from his own strength nor his own merit. **9, 10. if they say, Come up unto us; then we will go up: for the Lord hath delivered them into our hand**—When Jonathan appears here to prescribe a sign or token of God's will, we may infer that the same spirit which inspired this enterprise suggested the means of its execution, and put into his heart what to ask of God. (See on Gen. 24:12-14.) **11. Behold, the Hebrews come forth out of their holes**—As it could not occur to the sentries that two men had come with hostile designs, it was a natural conclusion that they were Israelite deserters. And hence no attempt was made to hinder their ascent, or stone them. **14. that first slaughter, which Jonathan and his armourbearer made, was about twenty men, within as it were an half acre of land, which a yoke of oxen might plough**—This was a very ancient mode of measurement, and it still subsists in the East. The men who saw them scrambling up the rock had been surprised and killed, and the spectacle of twenty corpses would suggest to others that they were attacked by a numerous force. The success of the adventure was aided by a panic that struck the enemy, produced both by the sudden surprise and the shock of an earthquake. The feat was begun and achieved by the faith of Jonathan, and the issue was of God. **16. the watchmen of Saul . . . looked**—The wild disorder in the enemies' camp was described and the noise of dismay heard on the heights of Gibeah. **17-19. Then said Saul unto the people that were with him, Number now, and see who is gone from us**—The idea occurred to him that it might be some daring adventurer belonging to his own little troop, and it would be easy to discover him. **Saul said unto Ahiah, Bring hither the ark of God**—There is no evidence that the ark had been brought from Kirjath-jearim. The *Sept.* version is preferable; which, by a slight variation of the text, reads, "the ephod;" i.e., the priestly cape, which the high priest put on when consulting the oracle. That this should be at hand is natural, from the presence of Ahiah himself, as well as the nearness of Nob, where the tabernacle was then situated. **Withdraw thine hand**—The priest, invested with the ephod, prayed with raised and extended hands. Saul, perceiving that the opportunity was inviting, and that God appeared to have sufficiently declared in favor of His people, requested the priest to cease, that they might immediately join in the contest. The season for consultation was past—the time for prompt action was come. **20-22. Saul and all the people**—All the warriors in the garrison at Gibeah, the Israelite deserters in the camp of the Philistines, and the fugitives among the mountains of Ephraim, now all rushed to the pursuit, which was hot and sanguinary. **23. So the Lord saved Israel that day; and the battle passed over unto Beth-aven**—i.e., Beth-el. It passed over the forest, now destroyed, on the central ridge of Palestine, then over to the other side from the eastern pass of Michmash (vs. 31), to the western pass of Aijalon, through which they escaped into their own plains. **24. Saul had adjured the people**—Afraid lest so precious an opportunity of effectually humbling the Philistine power might be lost, the impetuous king laid an anathema on any one who should taste food until the evening. This rash and foolish denunciation distressed the people, by preventing them taking such refreshments as they might get on the march, and materially hindered the successful attainment of his own patriotic object. **25. all they of the land came to a wood; and there was honey**—The honey is described as "upon the ground," "dropping" from the trees, and in honeycombs—indicating it to be bees' honey. "Bees in the East are not, as in England, kept in hives; they are all in a wild state. The forests literally flow with honey; large combs may be seen hanging on the trees as you pass along, full of honey" [ROBERTS]. **31-34. the people were very faint. And the people flew upon the spoil**—at evening, when the time fixed by Saul had expired. Faint and famishing, the pursuers fell voraciously upon the cattle they had taken, and threw them on the ground to cut off their flesh and eat them raw, so that the army, by Saul's rashness, were defiled by eating blood, or living animals; probably, as the Abyssinians do, who cut a part of the animal's rump, but close the hide upon it, and nothing mortal follows from that wound. They were painfully conscientious in keeping the king's order for fear of the curse, but had no scruple in transgressing God's command. To prevent this violation of the law, Saul ordered a large stone to be rolled, and those that slaughtered the oxen to cut their throats on that stone. By laying the animal's head on the high stone, the blood oozed out on the ground, and sufficient evidence was afforded that the ox or sheep was dead before it was attempted to eat it. **36-46. the people rescued Jonathan, that he died not**—When Saul became aware of Jonathan's transgression in regard to the honey, albeit it was done in ignorance and involved no guilt, he was, like Jephthah, about to put his son to death, in conformity with his vow. But the more enlightened conscience of the army prevented the tarnishing the glory of the day by the blood of the young hero, to whose faith and valor it was chiefly due. **47, 48. So Saul**

...fought against all his enemies on every side—This signal triumph over the Philistines was followed, not only by their expulsion from the land of Israel, but by successful incursions against various hostile neighbors, whom he harassed though he did not subdue them.

CHAPTER 15

Vss. 1-6. SAUL SENT TO DESTROY AMALEK. **1. Samuel also said unto Saul, The Lord sent me to anoint thee . . . : now therefore hearken unto . . . the Lord**—Several years had been passed in successful military operations against troublesome neighbors. During these Saul had been left to act in a great measure at his own discretion as an independent prince. Now a second test is proposed of his possessing the character of a theocratic monarch in Israel; and in announcing the duty required of him, Samuel brought before him his official station as the Lord's vicegerent, and the peculiar obligation under which he was laid to act in that capacity. He had formerly done wrong, for which a severe rebuke and threatening were administered to him (ch. 13:13, 14). Now an opportunity was afforded him of retrieving that error by an exact obedience to the divine command. **2, 3. Amalek**—the powerful tribe which inhabited the country immediately to the eastward of the northern Cushites. Their territory extended over the whole of the eastern portion of the desert of Sinai to Rephidim—the earliest opponent (Deut. 25:18; Exod. 17:8-16)—the hereditary and restless enemy of Israel (Num. 14:45; Judg. 3:13; 6:3), and who had not repented (ch. 14: 48) of their bitter and sleepless hatred during the 500 years that had elapsed since their doom was pronounced. Being a people of nomadic habits, they were as plundering and dangerous as the Bedouin Arabs, particularly to the southern tribes. The national interest required, and God, as KING OF ISRAEL, decreed that this public enemy should be removed. Their destruction was to be without reservation or exception. **I remember**—I am reminded of what Amalek did—perhaps by the still remaining trophy or memorial erected by Moses (Exod. 17:15, 16). **4. Saul gathered the people together**—The alacrity with which he entered on the necessary preparations for the expedition gave a fair, but delusive promise of faithfulness in its execution. **Telaim**—or Telem, among the uttermost cities of the tribe of Judah towards the coast of Edom (Josh. 15:21, 24). **5. Saul came to a city of Amalek**—probably their capital. **laid wait in the valley**—following the strategic policy of Joshua at Ai (Josh. 6). **6. Kenites**—(See on Judg. 1:16). In consequence, probably, of the unsettled state of Judah, they seem to have returned to their old desert tracts. Though now intermingled with the Amalekites, they were not implicated in the offenses of that wicked race; but for the sake of their ancestors, between whom and those of Israel there had been a league of amity, a timely warning was afforded them to remove from the scene of danger.

7-9. HE SPARES AGAG AND THE BEST OF THE SPOIL. **7-9. Saul smote the Amalekites**—His own view of the proper and expedient course to follow was his rule, not the command of God. **8. he took Agag . . . alive**—This was the common title of the Amalekite kings. He had no scruple about the apparent cruelty of it, for he made fierce and indiscriminate havoc of the people. But he spared Agag, probably to enjoy the glory of displaying so distinguished a captive, and, in like manner, the most valuable portions of the booty, as the cattle. By this wilful and partial obedience to a positive command, complying with it in some parts and violating it in others, as suited his own taste and humor, Saul showed his selfish, arbitrary temper, and his love of despotic power, and his utter unfitness to perform the duties of a delegated king in Israel. **10, 11. God Rejects Him for Disobedience. 10, 11. Then came the word of the Lord unto Samuel, saying, It repenteth me that I have set up Saul**—Repentance is attributed in Scripture to Him when bad men give Him cause to alter His course and method of procedure, and to treat them as if He did "repent" of kindness shown. To the heart of a man like Samuel, who was above all envious considerations, and really attached to the king, so painful an announcement moved all his pity and led him to pass a sleepless night of earnest intercession. **12. Saul came to Carmel**—in the south of Judah (Josh. 15:55; ch. 25:2). **12. he set him up a place**—i.e., a pillar (II Samuel 18:18); lit., a *hand*—indicating that whatever was the form of the monument, it was surmounted, according to the ancient fashion, by the figure of a hand, the symbol of power and energy. The erection of this vainglorious trophy was an additional act of disobedience. His pride had overborne his sense of duty in first raising this monument to his own honor, and then going to Gilgal to offer sacrifice to God. **13. Saul said unto him, Blessed be thou of the Lord; I have performed the commandment of the Lord**—Saul was either blinded by a partial and delusive self-love, or he was, in his declaration to Samuel, acting the part of a bold and artful hypocrite. He professed to have fulfilled the divine command, and that the blame of any defects in the execution lay with the people. Samuel saw the real state of the case, and in discharge of the commission he had received before setting out, proceeded to denounce his conduct as characterized by pride, rebellion, and obstinate disobedience. When Saul persisted in declaring that he had obeyed, alleging that the animals, whose bleating was heard, had been reserved for a liberal sacrifice of thanksgiving to God, his shuffling, prevaricating answer called forth a stern rebuke from the prophet. It well deserved it—for the destination of the spoil to the altar was a flimsy pretext—a gross deception, an attempt to conceal the selfishness of the original motive under the cloak of religious zeal and gratitude. **24. I feared the people, and obeyed their voice**—This was a different reason from the former he had assigned. It was the language of a man driven to extremities, and even had it been true, the principles expounded by Samuel showed that it could have been no extenuation of the offense. The prophet then pronounced the irreversible sentence of the rejection of Saul and his family. He was judicially cut off for his disobedience. **24. 25. I have sinned ... turn again with me, that I may worship the Lord**—The erring, but proud and obstinate monarch was now humbled. He was conscience-smitten for the moment, but his confession proceeded not from sincere repentance, but from a sense of danger and desire of averting the sentence denounced against him. For the sake of public appearance, he besought Samuel not to allow their serious differences to transpire, but to join with him in a public act of worship. Under the influence of his painfully agitated feelings, he designed to offer sacrifice, partly to express his gratitude for the recent victory,

and partly to implore mercy and a reversal of his doom. It was, from another angle, a politic scheme, that Samuel might be betrayed into a countenancing of his design in reserving the cattle for sacrificing. Samuel declined to accompany him. **27. he laid hold upon the skirt of his mantle**—the *moil,* upper tunic, official robe. In an agony of mental excitement, he took hold of the prophet's dress to detain him; the rending of the mantle was adroitly pointed to as a significant and mystical representation of his severance from the throne. **29. the Strength of Israel will not lie**—*Heb.,* "He that gives a victory to Israel," a further rebuke of his pride in rearing the Carmel trophy, and an intimation that no loss would be sustained in Israel by his rejection. **31. Samuel turned again after Saul**—not to worship along with him; but first, that the people might have no ground, on pretense of Saul's rejection, to withdraw their allegiance from him; and secondly, to compensate for Saul's error, by executing God's judgment upon Agag. **32. Agag came unto him delicately**—or cheerfully, since he had gained the favor and protection of the king. **33. Samuel hewed Agag**—This cruel tyrant met the retribution of a righteous Providence. Never has it been unusual for great or official personages in the East to perform executions with their own hands. Samuel did it "before the Lord" in Gilgal, appointing that same mode of punishment (hitherto unknown in Israel) to be used towards him, which he had formerly used towards others.

CHAPTER 16

Vss. 1-10. **Samuel Sent by God to Bethlehem. 1. the Lord said unto Samuel, How long wilt thou mourn for Saul**—Samuel's grief on account of Saul's rejection, accompanied, doubtless, by earnest prayers for his restitution, showed the amiable feelings of the man; but they were at variance with his public duty as a prophet. The declared purpose of God to transfer the kingdom of Israel into other hands than Saul's was not an angry menace, but a fixed and immutable decree; so that Samuel ought to have sooner submitted to the peremptory manifestation of the divine will. But to leave him no longer room to doubt of its being unalterable, he was sent on a private mission to anoint a successor to Saul (see on ch. 10:1). The immediate designation of a king was of the greatest importance for the interests of the nation in the event of Saul's death, which, to this time, was dreaded; it would establish David's title and comfort the minds of Samuel and other good men with a right settlement, whatever contingency might happen. **I have provided me a king**—The language is remarkable, and intimates a difference between this and the former king. Saul was the people's choice—the fruit of their wayward and sinful desires for their own honor and aggrandizement. The next was to be a king who would consult the divine glory, and selected from that tribe to which the pre-eminence had been early promised (Gen. 49:10). **2. How can I go?**—This is another instance of human infirmity in Samuel. Since God had sent him on this mission, He would protect him in the execution. **I am come to sacrifice**—It seems to have been customary with Samuel to do this in the different circuits to which he went, that he might encourage the worship of God. **3. call Jesse to the sacrifice**—i.e., the social feast that followed the peace offering. Samuel, being the offerer, had a right to invite any guest he pleased. **4. the elders of the town trembled at his coming**—Bethlehem was an obscure town, and not within the usual circuit of the judge. The elders were naturally apprehensive, therefore, that his arrival was occasioned by some extraordinary reason, and that it might entail evil upon their town, in consequence of the estrangement between Samuel and the king. **5. sanctify yourselves**—by the preparations described (Exod. 19:14, 15). The elders were to sanctify themselves. Samuel himself took the greatest care in the sanctification of Jesse's family. Some, however, think that the former were invited only to join in the sacrifice, while the family of Jesse were invited by themselves to the subsequent feast. **6-10. Samuel said, Surely the Lord's anointed is before him**—Here Samuel, in consequence of taking his impressions from the external appearance, falls into the same error as formerly (ch. 10:24).

11-14. He Anoints David. **11. There remaineth yet the youngest, and, behold, he keepeth the sheep**—Jesse having evidently no idea of David's wisdom and bravery, spoke of him as the most unfit. God, in His providence, so ordered it, that the appointment of David might the more clearly appear to be a divine purpose, and not the design either of Samuel or Jesse. David having not been sanctified with the rest of his family, it is probable that he returned to his pastoral duties the moment the special business on which he had been summoned was done. **12. he was ruddy,...**—Josephus says that David was ten, while most modern commentators are of the opinion that he must have been fifteen years of age. **13. Then Samuel took the horn of oil, and anointed him**—This transaction must have been strictly private. **14-18. The Spirit of the Lord departed from Saul, and an evil spirit from the Lord troubled him**—His own gloomy reflections, the consciousness that he had not acted up to the character of an Israelitish king, the loss of his throne, and the extinction of his royal house, made him jealous, irritable, vindictive, and subject to fits of morbid melancholy. **19. Saul sent messengers unto Jesse, and said, Send me David**—In the East the command of a king is imperative; and Jesse, however reluctant and alarmed, had no alternative but to comply. **20. Jesse took an ass laden with bread, and a bottle of wine, and a kid, and sent them...unto Saul**—as a token of homage and respect. **21. David came to Saul**—Providence thus prepared David for his destiny, by placing him in a way to become acquainted with the manners of the court, the business of government, and the general state of the kingdom. **became his armourbearer**—This choice, as being an expression of the king's partiality, shows how honorable the office was held to be. **23. David took an harp, and played with his hand: so Saul was refreshed, and was well**—The ancients believed that music had a mysterious influence in healing mental disorders.

CHAPTER 17

Vss. 1-3. The Israelites and Philistines Being Ready to Battle. **1. the Philistines gathered together their armies**—twenty-seven years after their overthrow at Michmash. Having now recovered their spirits and strength, they sought an opportunity of wiping out the infamy of that national disaster, as well as to regain their lost ascendency over Israel. **Shocoh**—now Shuweikeh, a town in the western plains of Judah (Josh. 15:35), nine Roman

miles from Eleutheropolis, toward Jerusalem [Robinson]. **Azekah**—a small place in the neighborhood. **Ephes-dammim**—or Pas-dammim (I Chron. 11:13), "the portion or effusion of blood," situated between the other two. **2. valley of Elah**—i.e., the Terebinth, now Wady Er-Sumt [Robinson]. Another valley somewhat to the north, now called Wady Beit Hanina, has been fixed on by the tradition of ages.

4-11. Goliath Challenges a Combat. **4-11. a champion**—*Heb.*, a "man between two"; i.e., a person who, on the part of his own people, undertook to determine the national quarrel by engaging in single combat with a chosen warrior in the hostile army. **5. helmet of brass**—The Philistine helmet had the appearance of a row of feathers set in a tiara, or metal band, to which were attached scales of the same material, for the defense of the neck and the sides of the face [Osborn]. **a coat of mail**—a kind of corslet, quilted with leather or plates of metal, reaching only to the chest, and supported by shoulder straps, leaving the shoulders and arms at full liberty. **6. greaves of brass**—boots, terminating at the ankle, made in one plate of metal, but round to the shape of the leg, and often lined with felt or sponge. They were useful in guarding the legs, not only against the spikes of the enemy, but in making way among thorns and briers. **a target of brass**—a circular frame, carried at the back, suspended by a long belt which crossed the breast from the shoulders to the loins. **7. staff of his spear**—rather under five feet long, and capable of being used as a javelin (ch. 19:10). It had an iron head. **one bearing a shield**—In consequence of their great size and weight, the Oriental warrior had a trusty and skilful friend, whose office it was to bear the large shield behind which he avoided the missile weapons of the enemy. He was covered, cap-a-pie, with defensive armor, while he had only two offensive weapons—a sword by his side and a spear in his hand. **8-11. I defy the armies of Israel...; give me a man, that we may fight together**—In cases of single combat, a warrior used to go out in front of his party, and advancing towards the opposite ranks, challenge someone to fight with him. If his formidable appearance, or great reputation for physical strength and heroism, deterred any from accepting the challenge, he used to parade himself within hearing of the enemy's lines, specify in a loud, boastful, bravado style, defying them, and pouring out torrents of abuse and insolence to provoke their resentment.

12-58. David Accepts the Challenge, and Slays Him. **17. Take now for thy brethren an ephah of this parched corn, and these ten loaves**—In those times campaigns seldom lasted above a few days at a time. The soldiers were volunteers or militia, who were supplied with provisions from time to time by their friends at home. **18. carry these ten cheeses to the captain**—to enlist his kind attention. Oriental cheeses are very small; and although they are frequently made of so soft a consistence as to resemble curds, those which David carried seem to have been fully formed, pressed, and sufficiently dried to admit of their being carried. **take their pledge**—Tokens of the soldiers' health and safety were sent home in the convenient form of a lock of their hair, or piece of their nail, or such like. **20. David left the sheep with a keeper**—This is the only instance in which the hired shepherd is distinguished from the master or one of his family. **trench**—some feeble attempt at a rampart. It appears (see *Marg.*) to have been formed by a line of carts or chariots, which, from the earliest times, was the practice of nomad people. **22. left his carriage in the hand of the keeper of the carriage**—to make his way to the standard of Judah. **25. make his father's house free in Israel**—His family should be exempted from the impositions and services to which the general body of the Israelites were subjected. **34-36. a lion, and a bear**—There were two different rencontres, for those animals prowl alone. The bear must have been a Syrian bear, which is believed to be a distinct species, or perhaps a variety, of the brown bear. The beard applies to the lion alone. Those feats seem to have been performed with no weapons more effective than the rude staves and stones of the field, or his shepherd's crook. **37. The Lord that delivered me**—It would have been natural for a youth, and especially an Oriental youth, to make a parade of his gallantry. But David's piety sank all consideration of his own prowess and ascribed the success of those achievements to the divine aid, which he felt assured would not be withheld from him in a cause which so intimately concerned the safety and honor of His people. **Saul said unto David, Go, and the Lord be with thee**—The pious language of the modest but valiant youth impressed the monarch's heart. He felt that it indicated the true military confidence for Israel, and, therefore, made up his mind, without any demur, to sanction a combat on which the fate of his kingdom depended, and with a champion supporting his interests apparently so unequal to the task. **38, 39. Saul armed David with his armour**—The ancient Hebrews were particularly attentive to the personal safety of their warriors, and hence Saul equipped the youthful champion with his own defensive accoutrements, which would be of the best style. It is probable that Saul's coat of mail, or corslet, was a loose shirt, otherwise it could not have fitted both a stripling and a man of the colossal stature of the king. **40. brook**—wady. **bag**—or scrip for containing his daily food. **sling**—The sling consisted of a double rope with a thong, probably of leather, to receive the stone. The slinger held a second stone in his left hand. David chose five stones, as a reserve, in case the first should fail. Shepherds in the East carry a sling and stones still, for the purpose of driving away, or killing, the enemies that prowl about the flock. **42-47. the Philistine said . . . said David to the Philistine**—When the two champions met, they generally made each of them a speech, and sometimes recited some verses, filled with allusions and epithets of the most opprobrious kind, hurling contempt and defiance at one another. This kind of abusive dialogue is common among the Arab combatants still. David's speech, however, presents a striking contrast to the usual strain of these invectives. It was full of pious trust, and to God he ascribed all the glory of the triumph he anticipated. **49. smote the Philistine in his forehead**—At the opening for the eyes—that was the only exposed part of his body. **51. cut off his head**—not as an evidence of the giant's death, for his slaughter had been effected in presence of the whole army, but as a trophy to be borne to Saul. The heads of slain enemies are always regarded in the East as the most welcome tokens of victory. **52 Shaaraim**—(See Josh. 15:36). **54. tent**—the sacred tabernacle. David dedicated the sword of Goliath as a votive offering to the Lord. **55-58. Saul . . . said unto Abner . . . whose son is this youth?**—A young man is more spoken of in many Eastern countries by his

father's name than his own. The growth of the beard, and other changes on a now full-grown youth, prevented the king from recognizing his former favorite minstrel.

CHAPTER 18

Vss. 1-4. JONATHAN LOVES DAVID. **1. the soul of Jonathan was knit with the soul of David**—They were nearly of an age. The prince had taken little interest in David as a minstrel; but his heroism and modest, manly bearing, his piety and high endowments, kindled the flame not of admiration only, but of affection, in the congenial mind of Jonathan. **2. Saul would let him go no more home**—He was established as a permanent resident at court. **3. Then Jonathan and David made a covenant**—Such covenants of brotherhood are frequent in the East. They are ratified by certain ceremonies, and in presence of witnesses, that the persons covenanting will be sworn brothers for life. **4. Jonathan stripped himself of the robe that was upon him, and gave it to David**—To receive any part of the dress which had been *worn* by a sovereign, or his eldest son and heir, is deemed, in the East, the *highest* honor which can be conferred on a subject (see on Esther 6:8). The girdle, being connected with the sword and the bow, may be considered as being part of the military dress, and great value is attached to it in the East. **5-9. SAUL ENVIES HIS PRAISE. 6. the women came out of all the cities of Israel**—in the homeward march from the pursuit of the Philistines. This is a characteristic trait of Oriental manners. On the return of friends long absent, and particularly on the return of a victorious army, bands of women and children issue from the towns and villages, to form a triumphal procession, to celebrate the victory, and, as they go along, to gratify the soldiers with dancing, instrumental music, and extempore songs, in honor of the generals who have earned the highest distinction by feats of gallantry. The Hebrew women, therefore, were merely paying the customary gratulations to David as the deliverer of their country, but they committed a great indiscretion by praising a subject at the expense of their sovereign. **9. Saul eyed David**—i.e., invidiously, with secret and malignant hatred. **10-12. SEEKS TO KILL HIM. 10. on the morrow the evil spirit from God came upon Saul**—This rankling thought brought on a sudden paroxysm of his mental malady. **he prophesied**—The term denotes one under the influence either of a good or a bad spirit. In the present it is used to express that Saul was in a frenzy. David, perceiving the symptoms, hastened, by the soothing strains of his harp, to allay the stormy agitation of the royal mind. But before its mollifying influence could be felt, Saul hurled a javelin at the head of the young musician. **there was a javelin in Saul's hand**—Had it been followed by a fatal result, the deed would have been considered the act of an irresponsible maniac. It was repeated more than once ineffectually, and Saul became impressed with a dread of David as under the special protection of Providence. **13-16. FEARS HIM FOR HIS GOOD SUCCESS. 13. Therefore Saul removed him from him**—sent him away from the court, where the principal persons, including his own son, were spellbound with admiration of the young and pious warrior. **and made him captain over a thousand**—gave him a military commission, which was intended to be an honorable exile. But this post of duty served only to draw out before the public the extraordinary and varied qualities of his character, and to give him a stronger hold of the people's affections.

17-21. HE OFFERS HIM HIS DAUGHTER FOR A SNARE. 17. Saul said to David, Behold my elder daughter Merab, her will I give thee to wife—Though bound to this already, he had found it convenient to forget his former promise. He now holds it out as a new offer, which would tempt David to give additional proofs of his valor. But the fickle and perfidious monarch broke his pledge at the time when the marriage was on the eve of being celebrated, and bestowed Merab on another man (see on II Sam. 21:8); an indignity as well as a wrong, which was calculated deeply to wound the feelings and provoke the resentment of David. Perhaps it was intended to do so, that advantage might be taken of his indiscretion. But David was preserved from this snare. **20. Michal, Saul's daughter, loved David**—This must have happened some time after. **they told Saul, and the thing pleased him**—Not from any favor to David, but he saw that it would be turned to the advancement of his malicious purposes, and the more so when, by the artful intrigues and flattery of his spies, the loyal sentiments of David were discovered. **25. The king desireth not any dowry**—In Eastern countries the husband *purchases* his wife either by gifts or services. As neither David nor his family were in circumstances to give a suitable dowry for a princess, the king intimated that he would be graciously pleased to accept some gallant deed in the public service. **a hundred foreskins of the Philistines**—Such mutilations on the bodies of their slain enemies were commonly practised in ancient war, and the number told indicated the glory of the victory. Saul's willingness to accept a public service had an air of liberality, while his choice of so difficult and hazardous a service seemed only putting a proper value on gaining the hand of a king's daughter. But he covered unprincipled malice against David under this proposal, which exhibited a zeal for God and the covenant of circumcision. **26. the days were not expired**—The period within which this exploit was to be achieved was not exhausted. **27. David ... slew of the Philistines two hundred men**—The number was doubled, partly to show his respect and attachment to the princess, and partly to oblige Saul to the fulfilment of his pledge. **29. Saul was yet the more afraid of David**—because Providence had visibly favored him, by not only defeating the conspiracy against his life, but through his royal alliance paving his way to the throne.

CHAPTER 19

Vss. 1-7. JONATHAN DISCLOSES HIS FATHER'S PURPOSE TO KILL DAVID. 1. Saul spake to Jonathan his son, and to all his servants, that they should kill David—The murderous design he had secretly cherished he now reveals to a few of his intimate friends. Jonathan was among the number. He prudently said nothing at the time, but secretly apprised David of his danger; and waiting till the morning, when his father's excited temper would be cooled, he stationed his friend in a place of concealment, where, overhearing the conversation, he might learn how matters really stood and take immediate flight, if necessary. **4-7. Jonathan spake good of David**—He told his father he was committing a great sin to plot against the life of a man who had rendered the most invaluable services to his

country and whose loyalty had been uniformly steady and devoted. The strong remonstrances of Jonathan produced an effect on the impulsive mind of his father. As he was still susceptible of good and honest impressions, he bound himself by an oath to relinquish his hostile purpose; and thus, through the intervention of the noble-minded prince, a temporary reconciliation was effected, in consequence of which David was again employed in the public service.

8-17. SAUL'S MALICIOUS RAGE BREAKS OUT AGAINST DAVID. 8-10. David went out, and fought with the Philistines, and slew them with a great slaughter—A brilliant victory was gained over the public enemy. But these fresh laurels of David reawakened in the moody breast of Saul the former spirit of envy and melancholy. On David's return to court, the temper of Saul became more fiendish than ever; the melodious strains of the harp had lost all their power to charm; and in a paroxysm of uncontrollable frenzy he aimed a javelin at the person of David—the missile having been thrown with such force that it pierced the chamber wall. David providentially escaped; but the king, having now thrown off the mask and being bent on aggressive measures, made his son-in-law's situation everywhere perilous. **11, 12. Saul sent messengers unto David's house, to watch him, and to slay him**—The fear of causing a commotion in the town, or favoring his escape in the darkness, seemed to have influenced the king in ordering them to patrol till the morning. This infatuation was overruled by Providence to favor David's escape; for his wife, secretly apprised by Jonathan, who was aware of the design, or by spying persons in court livery watching the gate, let him down through a window (see on Josh. 2:15). **13, 14. Michal took an image, and laid it in the bed**—"an image," lit., "the teraphim," and laid, not in the bed, but literally on the "divan"; and "the pillows," i.e., the cushion, which usually lay at the back of the divan and was stuffed with "goat's hair," she took from its bolster or heading at the upper part of the divan. This she placed lower down, and covered with a mantle, as if to foster a proper warmth in a patient; at the same time spreading the goat's hair skin so as to resemble human hair in a dishevelled state. The pretext was that David lay there sick. The first messengers of Saul, keeping at a respectable distance, were deceived; but the imposition was detected on a closer inspection. **15. Bring him to me in the bed**—a portable couch or mattress.

18-23. DAVID FLEES TO SAMUEL. 18-21. David fled, ... and came to Samuel to Ramah—Samuel was living in great retirement, superintending the school of the prophets, established in the little hamlet of Naioth, in the neighborhood of Ramah. It was a retreat congenial to the mind of David; but Saul, having found out his asylum, sent three successive bodies of men to apprehend him. The character of the place and the influence of the sacred exercises produced such an effect on them that they were incapable of discharging their commission, and were led, by a resistless impulse, to join in singing the praises of God. Saul, in a fit of rage and disappointment, determined to go himself. But, before reaching the spot, his mental susceptibilities were roused even more than his messengers, and he was found, before long, swelling the ranks of the young prophets. This singular change can be ascribed only to the power of Him who can turn the hearts of men even as the rivers of water. **24. SAUL PROPHESIES. 24. lay down naked—**

i.e., divested of his armor and outer robes—in a state of trance. Thus God, in making the wrath of man to praise Him, preserved the lives of all the prophets, frustrated all the purposes of Saul, and preserved the life of His servant.

CHAPTER 20

Vss. 1-10. DAVID CONSULTS WITH JONATHAN FOR HIS SAFETY. **1. David fled from Naioth in Ramah, and came and said before Jonathan**—He could not remain in Naioth, for he had strong reason to fear that when the religious fit, if we may so call it, was over, Saul would relapse into his usual fell and sanguinary temper. It may be thought that David acted imprudently in directing his flight to Gibeah. But he was evidently prompted to go thither by the most generous feelings—to inform his friend of what had recently occurred, and to obtain that friend's sanction to the course he was compelled to adopt. Jonathan could not be persuaded there was any real danger after the oath his father had taken; at all events, he felt assured his father would do nothing without telling him. Filial attachment naturally blinded the prince to defects in the parental character and made him reluctant to believe his father capable of such atrocity. David repeated his unshaken convictions of Saul's murderous purpose, but in terms delicately chosen (vs. 3), not to wound the filial feelings of his friend; while Jonathan, clinging, it would seem, to a hope that the extraordinary scene enacted at Naioth might have wrought a sanctified improvement on Saul's temper and feelings, undertook to inform David of the result of his observations at home. **5. David said to Jonathan, Behold tomorrow is the new moon, and I should not fail to sit with the king at meat**—The beginning of a new month or moon was always celebrated by special sacrifices, followed by feasting, at which the head of a family expected all its members to be present. David, both as the king's son-in-law and a distinguished courtier, dined on such occasions at the royal table, and from its being generally known that David had returned to Gibeah, his presence in the palace would be naturally expected. This occasion was chosen by the two friends for testing the king's state of feeling. As a suitable pretext for David's absence, it was arranged that he should visit his family at Bethlehem, and thus create an opportunity of ascertaining how his non-appearance would be viewed. The time and place were fixed for Jonathan reporting to David; but as circumstances might render another interview unsafe, it was deemed expedient to communicate by a concerted signal.

11-23. THEIR COVENANT RENEWED BY OATH. **11. Jonathan said to David, Come, let us go into the field**—The private dialogue, which is here detailed at full length, presents a most beautiful exhibition of these two amiable and noble-minded friends. Jonathan was led, in the circumstances, to be the chief speaker. The strength of his attachment, his pure disinterestedness, his warm piety, his invocation to God (consisting of a prayer and a solemn oath combined), the calm and full expression he gave of his conviction that his own family were, by the divine will, to be disinherited, and David elevated to the possession of the throne, the covenant entered into with David on behalf of his descendants, and the imprecation (vs. 16) denounced on any of them who should violate his part of the conditions, the reiteration of this covenant on both

sides (vs. 17) to make it indissoluble—all this indicates such a power of mutual affection, such magnetic attractiveness in the character of David, such susceptibility and elevation of feeling in the heart of Jonathan, that this interview for dramatic interest and moral beauty stands unrivalled in the records of human friendship. **19. when thou hast stayed three days**—either with your family at Bethlehem, or wherever you find it convenient. **come to the place where thou didst hide thyself when the business was in hand**—*Heb.*, "in the day or time of the business," when the same matter was under inquiry formerly (ch. 19:22). **remain by the stone Ezel**—*Heb.*, "the stone of the way"; a sort of milestone which directed travellers. He was to conceal himself in some cave or hiding-place near that spot. **23. as touching the matter which thou and I have spoken of**—The plan being concerted, the friends separated for a time, and the amiable character of Jonathan again peers out in his parting allusion to their covenant of friendship.

24-40. SAUL, MISSING DAVID, SEEKS TO KILL JONATHAN. **25. the king sat upon his seat, as at other times . . . by the wall**—The left-hand corner at the upper end of a room was and still is in the East, the most honorable place. The person seated there has his left arm confined by the wall, but his right hand is at full liberty. From Abner's position next the king, and David's seat being left empty, it would seem that a state etiquette was observed at the royal table, each of the courtiers and ministers having places assigned them according to their respective gradations of rank. **Jonathan arose**—either as a mark of respect on the entrance of the king, or in conformity with the usual Oriental custom for a son to stand in presence of his father. **26. he is not clean**—No notice was taken of David's absence, as he might be laboring under some ceremonial defilement. **27. on the morrow, which was the second day of the month**—The time of the moon's appearance being uncertain—whether at midday, in the evening, or at midnight, the festival was extended over two days. Custom, not the law, had introduced this. **Saul said unto Jonathan his son, Wherefore cometh not the son of Jesse**—The question was asked, as it were, casually, and with as great an air of indifference as he could assume. And Jonathan having replied that David had asked and obtained his permission to attend a family anniversary at Bethlehem, the pent-up passions of the king burst out in a most violent storm of rage and invective against his son. **30. Thou son of the perverse rebellious woman**—This is a striking Oriental form of abuse. Saul was not angry with his wife; it was the son alone, upon whom he meant, by this style of address, to discharge his resentment. The principle on which it is founded seems to be, that to a genuine filial instinct it is a more inexpiable offense to hear the name or character of a parent traduced, than any personal reproach. This was, undoubtedly, one cause of "the fierce anger" in which the high-minded prince left the table without tasting a morsel. **33. Saul cast a javelin at him**—This is a sad proof of the maniacal frenzy into which the unhappy monarch was transported. **35. Jonathan went out into the field at the time appointed**—or, "at the place appointed." **36. he said unto his lad, Run, find out now the arrows which I shoot**—The direction given aloud to the attendant was the signal preconcerted with David. It implied danger. **40. Jonathan gave his artillery unto his lad**—i.e., his missive weapons. The French word *artillerie*, signifies "archery." The term is still used in England, in the designation of the "artillery company of London," the association of archers, though they have long disused bows and arrows. Jonathan's boy being despatched out of the way, the friends enjoyed the satisfaction of a final meeting.

41, 42. JONATHAN AND DAVID LOVINGLY PART. **41, 42. David ... fell on his face and bowed three times**—a token of homage to the prince's rank; but on a close approach, every other consideration was sunk in the full flow of the purest brotherly affection. **42. Jonathan said to David, Go in peace**— The interview being a stolen one, and every moment precious, it was kindness in Jonathan to hasten his friend's departure.

CHAPTER 21

Vss. 1-7. DAVID, AT NOB, OBTAINS OF AHIMELECH HALLOWED BREAD. **1. Then came David to Nob to Ahimelech**—Nob, a city of the priests (ch. 22:19), was in the neighborhood of Jerusalem, on the Mount of Olives—a little north of the top, and on the northeast of the city. It is computed to have been about five miles distant from Gibeah. Ahimelech, the same as Ahiah, or perhaps his brother, both being sons of Ahitub (cf. ch. 14:3, with ch. 22: 4-11, 20). His object in fleeing to this place was partly for the supply of his necessities, and partly for comfort and counsel, in the prospect of leaving the kingdom. **Ahimelech was afraid at the meeting of David**—suspecting some extraordinary occurrence by his appearing so suddenly, and in such a style, for his attendants were left at a little distance. **2. The king hath commanded me a business, and hath said unto me, Let no man know**—This was a direct falsehood, extorted through fear. David probably supposed, like many other persons, that a lie is quite excusable which is told for the sole purpose of saving the speaker's life. But what is essentially sinful, can never, from circumstances, change its immoral character; and David had to repent of this vice of lying (Ps. 119:29). **4. there is hallowed bread**—There would be plenty of bread in his house; but there was no time to wait for it. "The hallowed bread" was the old shew-bread, which had been removed the previous day, and which was reserved for the use of the priests alone (Lev. 24:9). Before entertaining the idea that this bread could be lawfully given to David and his men, the high priest seems to have consulted the oracle (ch. 22:10) as to the course to be followed in this emergency. A dispensation to use the hallowed bread was specially granted by God Himself. **5. these three days**—as required by law (Exod. 19:15). David and his attendants seem to have been lurking in some of the adjoining caves, to elude pursuit, and to have been, consequently, reduced to great extremities of hunger. **the bread is in a manner common**—i.e., now that it is no longer standing on the Lord's table. It is eaten by the priests, and may also, in our circumstances, be eaten by us. **yea, though it were sanctified this day in the vessel**—i.e., though the hallowed bread had been but newly placed on the vessel, the ritual ordinance would have to yield to the great law of necessity and mercy (see on Matt. 12:3; Mark 2:25; Luke 6:3). **6. there was no bread there—in the tabernacle.** The removal of the old and the substitution of the new bread was done on the Sabbath (Lev. 24:8), the loaves being kept warm in an oven heated the previous day. **7. Doeg, an Edomite**—who had embraced the Hebrew religion. **detained before the Lord**—at the tabernacle, perhaps, in the perform-

ance of a vow, or from its being the Sabbath, which rendered it unlawful for him to prosecute his journey. **the chiefest of the herdsmen that belonged to Saul**—Eastern monarchs anciently had large possessions in flocks and herds; and the office of the chief shepherd was an important one.

9. HE TAKES GOLIATH'S SWORD. **9. sword of Goliath**—(See on ch. 18:54). **behind the ephod**—in the place allowed for keeping the sacred vestments, of which the ephod is mentioned as the chief. The giant's sword was deposited in that safe custody as a memorial of the divine goodness in delivering Israel. **There is none like that**—not only for its size and superior temper, but for its being a pledge of the divine favor to him, and a constant stimulus to his faith.

10-15. AT GATH HE FEIGNS HIMSELF MAD. **10. David ... fled ... to Achish the king of Gath**— which was one of the five principalities of the Philistines. In this place his person must have been known, and to venture into that country, he their greatest enemy, and with the sword of Goliath in his hand, would seem to have been a perilous experiment; but, doubtless, the protection he received implies that he had been directed by the divine oracle. Achish was generous (ch. 27:6). He might wish to weaken the resources of Saul, and it was common in ancient times for great men to be harbored by neighboring princes. **13. feigned himself mad**—It is supposed to have been an attack of epilepsy, real or perhaps only pretended. This disease is relieved by foaming at the mouth. **let his spittle fall down upon his beard**—No wonder that Achish supposed him insane, as such an indignity, whether done by another, or one's self, to the beard, is considered in the East an intolerable insult.

CHAPTER 22

Vss. 1-8. DAVID'S KINDRED AND OTHERS RESORT TO HIM AT ADULLAM. **1. David ... escaped to the cave Adullam**—supposed to be that now called Deir-Dubban, a number of pits or underground vaults, some nearly square, and all about fifteen or twenty feet deep, with perpendicular sides, in the soft limestone or chalky rocks. They are on the borders of the Philistine plain at the base of the Judea mountains, six miles southwest from Bethlehem, and well adapted for concealing a number of refugees. **his brethren and all his father's house ... went down**—to escape the effects of Saul's rage, which seems to have extended to all David's family. From Bethlehem to Deir-Dubban it is, indeed, a descent all the way. **2. every one that was in distress**—(See on Judg. 11:3). **3. David went thence to Mizpeh of Moab**—Mizpeh signifies a watchtower, and it is evident that it must be taken in this sense here, for (vs. 4) it is called "the hold" or fort. The king of Moab was an enemy of Saul (ch. 14:47), and the great-grandson of Ruth, of course, was related to the family of Jesse. David, therefore, had less anxiety in seeking an aylum within the dominions of this prince than those of Achish, because the Moabites had no grounds for entertaining vindictive feelings against him, and their enmity to Saul rendered them the more willing to receive so illustrious a refugee from his court. **5. the prophet Gad said unto David, Abide not in the hold**—This sound advice, no doubt, came from a higher source than Gad's own sagacity. It was right to appear publicly among the people of his own tribe, as one conscious of innocence and trusting in God; and it was expedient that, on the death of Saul, his friends might be encouraged to support his interest. **forest of Harath**—southwest of Jerusalem. **6. Saul abode ... under a tree in Ramah**—lit., "under a grove on a hill." Oriental princes frequently sit with their court under some shady canopy in the open air. A spear was the early scepter. **7. Hear now, ye Benjamites**—This was an appeal to stimulate the patriotism or jealousy of his own tribe, from which he insinuated it was the design of David to transfer the kingdom to another. This address seems to have been made on hearing of David's return with his four hundred men to Judah. A dark suspicion had risen in the jealous mind of the king that Jonathan was aware of this movement, which he dreaded as a conspiracy against the crown.

9-16. DOEG ACCUSES AHIMELECH. **9. Doeg ... set over the servants**—*Sept.*, the mules of Saul. **10. he inquired of the Lord for him**—Some suppose that this was a malicious fiction of Doeg to curry favor with the king, but Ahimelech seems to acknowledge the fact. The poor simple-minded high priest knew nothing of the existing family feud between Saul and David. The informer, if he knew it, said nothing of the cunning artifice by which David obtained the aid of Ahimelech. The *facts looked* against him, and the whole priesthood along with him were declared abettors of conspiracy.

17-19. SAUL COMMANDS TO KILL THE PRIESTS. **17. the footmen that stood about him**—his bodyguard, or his runners (ch. 8:11; II Sam. 15:1; I Kings 1:5; I Kings 14:28), who held an important place at court (II Chronicles 12:10). But they chose rather to disobey the king than to offend God by imbruing their hands in the blood of his ministering servants. A foreigner alone (Ps. 52:1-3) could be found willing to be the executioner of this bloody and sacrilegious sentence. Thus was the doom of the house of Eli fulfilled. **19. Nob, the city of the priests, smote he with the edge of the sword**—The barbarous atrocities perpetrated against this city seem to have been designed to terrify all the subjects of Saul from affording either aid or an asylum to David. But they proved ruinous to Saul's own interest, as they alienated the priesthood and disgusted all good men in the kingdom.

20-23. ABIATHAR ESCAPES AND FLEES AFTER DAVID. **20. one of the sons of Ahimelech ... escaped**—This was Abiathar, who repaired to David in the forest of Hareth, rescuing, with his own life, the high priest's vestments (ch. 23:6, 9). On hearing his sad tale, David declared that he had dreaded such a fatal result from the malice and intriguing ambition of Doeg; and, accusing himself as having been the occasion of all the disaster to Abiathar's family, David invited him to remain, because, firmly trusting himself in the accomplishment of the divine promise, David could guarantee protection to him.

CHAPTER 23

Vss. 1-6. DAVID RESCUES KEILAH. **1. Then they told David**—rather, "now they had told"; for this information had reached him previous to his hearing (vs. 6) of the Nob tragedy. **Keilah**—a city in the west of Judah (Josh. 15:44), not far from the forest of Hareth. **and they rob the threshing-floors**—These were commonly situated on the fields and were open to the wind (Judg. 6:11; Ruth 3:2). **2. David inquired of the Lord**—most probably through Gad (II Sam. 24; I Chron. 21:9), who was present in David's camp (ch. 22:5), probably by the recom-

mendation of Samuel. To repel unprovoked assaults on unoffending people who were engaged in their harvest operations, was a humane and benevolent service. But it was doubtful how far it was David's duty to go against a public enemy without the royal commission; and on that account he asked, and obtained, the divine counsel. A demur on the part of his men led David to renew the consultation for their satisfaction; after which, being fully assured of his duty, he encountered the aggressors and, by a signal victory, delivered the people of Keilah from further molestation. **6. an ephod**—in which was the Urim and Thummim (Exod. 28:30). It had, probably, been committed to his care, while Ahimelech and the other priests repaired to Gibeah, in obedience to the summons of Saul.

7-13. SAUL'S COMING, AND TREACHERY OF THE KEILITES. **7. it was told Saul that David was come to Keilah**—Saul imagined himself now certain of his victim, who would be hemmed within a fortified town. The wish was father to the thought. How wonderfully slow and unwilling to be convinced by all his experience, that the special protection of Providence shielded David from all his snares! **8. Saul called all the people together to war**—not the united tribes of Israel, but the inhabitants of the adjoining districts. This force was raised, probably, on the ostensible pretext of opposing the Philistines, while, in reality, it was secretly to arouse mischief against David. **9. he said to Abiathar the priest, Bring hither the ephod**—The consultation was made, and the prayer uttered, by means of the priest. The alternative conditions here described have often been referred to as illustrating the doctrine of God's foreknowledge and preordination of events.

14-18. DAVID ESCAPES TO ZIPH. **14, 15. David abode in the wilderness ... of Ziph**—A mountainous and sequestered region generally called a wilderness, and took its name from some large town in the district. Two miles southeast of Hebron, and in the midst of a level plain, is Tell-ziph, an isolated and conical hillock, about 100 feet high, probably the acropolis [VAN DE VELDE], or the ruins [ROBINSON] of the ancient city of Ziph, from which the surrounding wilderness was called. It seems, anciently, to have been covered by an extensive woods. The country has for centuries lost its woods and forests, owing to the devastations caused by man. **16. Jonathan went to David into the wood, and strengthened his hand in God**—by the recollection of their mutual covenant. What a victory over natural feelings and lower considerations must the faith of Jonathan have won, before he could seek such an interview and give utterance to such sentiments! To talk with calm and assured confidence of himself and family being superseded by the man who was his friend by the bonds of a holy and solemn covenant, could only have been done by one who, superior to all views of worldly policy, looked at the course of things in the spirit and through the principles of that theocracy which acknowledged God as the only and supreme Sovereign of Israel. Neither history nor fiction depicts the movements of a friendship purer, nobler, and more self-denying than Jonathan's!

19-29. SAUL PURSUES HIM. **19-23. Then came up the Ziphites to Saul, saying, Doth not David hide himself with us?**—From the tell of Ziph a panorama of the whole surrounding district is to be seen. No wonder, then, that the Ziphites saw David and his men passing to and fro in the mountains of the wilderness. Spying him at a distance when he ventured to show himself on the hill of Hachilah, "on the right hand of the wilderness," i.e., the south side of Ziph, they sent in haste to Saul, to tell him of the lurking place of his enemy [VAN DE VELDE]. **25. David ... came down into a rock, and abode in the wilderness of Maon**—Tell Main, the hillock on which was situated the ancient Maon (Josh. 15:55), and from which the adjoining wilderness took its name, is one mile north, ten east from Carmel. The mountain plateau seems here to end. It is true the summit ridge of the southern hills runs out a long way further towards the southwest; but towards the southeast the ground sinks more and more down to a tableland of a lower level, which is called "the plain to the right hand [i.e., to the south] of the wilderness" [VAN DE VELDE]. **29. David went up from thence, and dwelt in strongholds at En-gedi**—i.e., "the spring of the wild goats or gazelles"—a name given to it from the vast number of ibexes or Syrian chamois which inhabit these cliffs on the western shore of the Dead Sea (Josh. 15:62). It is now called Ain Jiddy. On all sides the country is full of caverns, which might then serve as lurking places for David and his men, as they do for outlaws at the present day [ROBINSON].

CHAPTER 24

Vss. 1-7. DAVID IN A CAVE AT EN-GEDI CUTS OFF SAUL'S SKIRT, BUT SPARES HIS LIFE. **2. Saul ... went ... to seek David ... upon the rocks of the wild goats**—Nothing but the blind infatuation of fiendish rage could have led the king to pursue his outlawed son-in-law among those craggy and perpendicular precipices, where were inaccessible hiding places. The large force he took with him seemed to give him every prospect of success. But the overruling providence of God frustrated all his vigilance. **3. he came to the sheepcotes**—most probably in the upper ridge of Wady Chareitun. There a large cave—I am quite disposed to say the cave—lies hardly five minutes to the east of the village ruin, on the south side of the wady. It is high upon the side of the calcareous rock, and it has undergone no change since David's time. The same narrow natural vaulting at the entrance; the same huge natural chamber in the rock, probably the place where Saul lay down to rest in the heat of the day; the same side vaults, too, where David and his men were concealed. There, accustomed to the obscurity of the cavern, they saw Saul enter, while, blinded by the glare of the light outside, he saw nothing of him whom he so bitterly persecuted. **4-7. the men of David said ... Behold the day of which the Lord said unto thee, Behold, I will deliver thine enemy into thine hand**—God had never made any promise of delivering Saul into David's hand; but, from the general and repeated promises of the kingdom to him, they concluded that the king's death was to be effected by taking advantage of some such opportunity as the present. David steadily opposed the urgent instigations of his followers to put an end to his and their troubles by the death of their persecutor (a revengeful heart would have followed their advice, but David rather wished to overcome evil with good, and heap coals of fire upon his head); he, however, cut off a fragment from the skirt of the royal robe. It is easy to imagine how this dialogue could be carried on and David's approach to the king's person could have been effected without arousing suspicion. The bustle and noise of Saul's military men and their beasts, the number of

cells or divisions in these immense caverns (and some of them far interior) being enveloped in darkness, while every movement could be seen at the cave's mouth—the probability that the garment David cut from might have been a loose or upper cloak lying on the ground, and that Saul might have been asleep—these facts and presumptions will be sufficient to account for the incidents detailed.

8-15. HE URGES THEREBY HIS INNOCENCY. **8. David also arose ... and went out of the cave, and cried after Saul**—The closeness of the precipitous cliffs, though divided by deep wadies, and the transparent purity of the air enable a person standing on one rock to hear distinctly the words uttered by a speaker standing on another (Judg. 9:7). The expostulation of David, followed by the visible tokens he furnished of his cherishing no evil design against either the person or the government of the king, even when he had the monarch in his power, smote the heart of Saul in a moment and disarmed him of his fell purpose of revenge. He owned the justice of what David said, acknowledged his own guilt, and begged kindness to his house. He seems to have been naturally susceptible of strong, and, as in this instance, of good and grateful impressions. The improvement of his temper, indeed, was but transient—his language that of a man overwhelmed by the force of impetuous emotions and constrained to admire the conduct, and esteem the character, of one whom he hated and dreaded. But God overruled it for ensuring the present escape of David. Consider his language and behavior. This language —"a dead dog," "a flea," terms by which, like Eastern people, he strongly expressed a sense of his lowliness and the entire committal of his cause to Him who alone is the judge of human actions, and to whom vengeance belongs, his steady repulse of the vindictive counsels of his followers; the relentings of heart which he felt even for the apparent indignity he had done to the person of the Lord's anointed; and the respectful homage he paid the jealous tyrant who had set a price on his head—evince the magnanimity of a great and good man, and strikingly illustrate the spirit and energy of his prayer "when he was in the cave" (Ps. 142).

CHAPTER 25

Vss. 1-9. SAMUEL DIES. **1. Samuel died**—After a long life of piety and public usefulness, he left behind him a reputation which ranks him among the greatest of Scripture worthies. **buried him in his house at Ramah**—i.e., his own mausoleum. The Hebrews took as great care to provide sepulchers anciently as people do in the East still, where every respectable family has its own house of the dead. Often this is in a little detached garden, containing a small stone building (where there is no rock), resembling a house, which is called the sepulcher of the family—it has neither door nor window. **David arose, and went down to the wilderness of Paran**—This removal had probably no connection with the prophet's death; but was probably occasioned by the necessity of seeking provision for his numerous followers. **the wilderness of Paran**—stretching from Sinai to the borders of Palestine in the southern territories of Judea. Like other wildernesses, it presented large tracts of natural pasture, to which the people sent their cattle at the grazing season, but where they were liable to constant and heavy depredations by prowling Arabs. David and his men earned their subsistence by making reprisals on the cattle of these freebooting Ishmaelites; and, frequently for their useful services, they obtained voluntary tokens of acknowledgment from the peaceful inhabitants. **2. in Carmel**—now **Kurmul.** The district takes its name from this town, now a mass of ruins; and about a mile from it is Tell Main, the hillock on which stood ancient Maon. **the man was very great**—His property consisted in cattle, and he was considered wealthy, according to the ideas of that age. **3. he was of the house of Caleb**—of course, of the same tribe with David himself; but many versions consider Caleb (dog) not as a proper, but a common noun, and render it, "he was snappish as a dog." **4-9. Nabal did shear his sheep, and David sent out ten young men . . .**—David and his men lurked in these deserts, associating with the herdsmen and shepherds of Nabal and others and doing them good offices, probably in return for information and supplies obtained through them. Hence when Nabal held his annual sheepshearing in Carmel, David felt himself entitled to share in the festival and sent a message, recounting his own services and asking for a present. "In all these particulars we were deeply struck with the truth and strength of the biblical description of manners and customs almost identically the same as they exist at the present day. On such a festive occasion, near a town or village, even in our own time, an Arab sheik of the neighboring desert would hardly fail to put in a word either in person or by message; and his message, both in form and substance, would be only a transcript of that of David" [ROBINSON].

10-13. THE CHURLISH ANSWER PROVOKES HIM. 10-12. Nabal answered David's servants . . . Who is David? . . .—Nabal's answer seems to indicate that the country was at the time in a loose and disorderly state. David's own good conduct, however, as well as the important services rendered by him and his men, were readily attested by Nabal's servants. The preparations of David to chastise his insolent language and ungrateful requital are exactly what would be done in the present day by Arab chiefs, who protect the cattle of the large and wealthy sheep-masters from the attacks of the marauding border tribes or wild beasts. Their protection creates a claim for some kind of tribute, in the shape of supplies of food and necessaries, which is usually given with great good-will and gratitude; but when withheld, is enforced as a right. Nabal's refusal, therefore, was a violation of the established usages of the place. **13. two hundred men abode by the stuff**—This addition to his followers was made after his return into Judah (see on ch. 22:2).

14-35. ABIGAIL PACIFIES HIM. 14-18. Then Abigail made haste—The prudence and address of Nabal's wife were the means of saving him and family from utter destruction. She acknowledged the demand of her formidable neighbors; but justly considering, that to atone for the insolence of her husband, a greater degree of liberality had become necessary, she collected a large amount of food, accompanying it with the most valued products of the country. **bottles**—goatskins, capable of holding a great quantity. **parched corn**—It was customary to eat parched corn when it was fully grown, but not ripe. **19. she said unto her servants, Go on before me; behold, I come after you**—People in the East always try to produce an effect by their presents, loading on several beasts what might be easily carried by one, and bringing them forward, article by article, in succession. Abigail not only sent her servants in this way, but resolved to go in person,

following her present, as is commonly done, to watch the impression which her munificence would produce. **23. she hasted, and lighted off the ass, and fell before David on her face**—Dismounting in presence of a superior is the highest token of respect that can be given; and it is still an essential act of homage to the great. Accompanying this act of courtesy with the lowest form of prostration, she not only by her attitude, but her language, made the fullest amends for the disrespect shown by her husband, as well as paid the fullest tribute of respect to the character and claims of David. **25. Nabal**—signifying *fool,* gave pertinence to his wife's remark. **26. let thine enemies . . . be as Nabal**—be as foolish and contemptible as he. **29. the soul of my lord shall be bound in the bundle of life with the Lord thy God**—An Orientalism, expressing the perfect security of David's life from all the assaults of his enemies, under the protecting shield of Providence, who had destined him for high things. **32-35. David said to Abigail, Blessed be the Lord**—Transported by passion and blinded by revenge, he was on the eve of perpetrating a great injury. Doubtless, the timely appearance and prudent address of Abigail were greatly instrumental in changing his purpose. At all events, it was the means of opening his eyes to the moral character of the course on which he had been impetuously rushing; and in accepting her present, he speaks with lively satisfaction as well as gratitude to Abigail, for having relieved him from bloodshed.

36-44. NABAL'S DEATH. 36. he held a feast in his house, like the feast of a king—The sheepshearing season was always a very joyous occasion. Masters usually entertained their shepherds; and even Nabal, though of a most niggardly disposition, prepared festivities on a scale of sumptuous liberality. The modern Arabs celebrate the season with similar hilarity. **37, 38. in the morning . . . his wife had told him these things, that his heart died within him**—He probably fainted from horror at the perilous situation in which he had unconsciously placed himself; and such a shock had been given him by the fright to his whole system, that he rapidly pined and died. **39-42. the Lord hath returned the wickedness of Nabal upon his own head**—If this was an expression of pleasure, and David's vindictive feelings were gratified by the intelligence of Nabal's death, it was an instance of human infirmity which we may lament; but perhaps he referred to the unmerited reproach (vss. 10, 11), and the contempt of God implied in it. **David sent and communed with Abigail, to take her to wife**—This unceremonious proceeding was quite in the style of Eastern monarchs, who no sooner take a fancy for a lady than they despatch a messenger to intimate their royal wishes that she should henceforth reside in the palace; and her duty is implicitly to obey. David's conduct shows that the manners of the Eastern nations were already imitated by the great men in Israel; and that the morality of the times which God permitted, gave its sanction to the practice of polygamy. His marriage with Abigail brought him a rich estate. **44. Michal**—By the unchallengeable will of her father, she who was David's wife was given to another. But she returned and sustained the character of his wife when he ascended the throne.

CHAPTER 26

Vss. 1-4. SAUL COMES TO THE HILL OF HACHILAH AGAINST DAVID. **1. the Ziphites came unto Saul to**

Gibeah—This people seem to have thought it impossible for David to escape, and therefore recommended themselves to Saul, by giving him secret information (see on ch. 23:19). The knowledge of their treachery makes it appear strange that David should return to his former haunt in their neighborhood; but, perhaps he did it to be near Abigail's possessions, and under the impression that Saul had become mollified. But the king had relapsed into his old enmity. Though Gibeah, as its name imports, stood on an elevated position, and the desert of Ziph, which was in the hilly region of Judea, may have been higher than Gibeah, it was still necessary to descend in leaving the latter place; thence Saul (vs. 2) " went down to the wilderness of Ziph." **4-5. David . . . sent out spies . . . and David arose and came to the place where Saul had pitched**—Having obtained certain information of the locality, he seems, accompanied by his nephew (vs. 6), to have hid himself, perhaps disguised, in a neighboring wood, or hill, on the skirts of the royal camp towards night, and waited to approach it under covert of the darkness.

5-25. DAVID STAYS ABISHAI FROM KILLING SAUL, BUT TAKES HIS SPEAR AND CRUSE. **5. Saul lay in the trench, and the people pitched round about him**—Among the nomad people of the East, the encampments are usually made in a circular form. The circumference is lined by the baggage and the men, while the chief's station is in the center, whether he occupy a tent or not. His spear, stuck in the ground, indicates his position. Similar was the disposition of Saul's camp—in this hasty expedition he seems to have carried no tent, but to have slept on the ground. The whole troop was sunk in sleep around him. **8-12. Then said Abishai to David, God hath delivered thine enemy into thine hand**—This midnight stratagem shows the activity and heroic enterprise of David's mind, and it was in unison with the style of warfare in ancient times. **let me smite him . . . even to the earth at once**—The ferocious vehemence of the speaker is sufficiently apparent from his language, but David's magnanimity soared far above the notions of his followers. Though Saul's cruelty and perfidy and general want of right principle had sunk him to a low pitch of degradation, yet that was no reason for David's imitating him in doing wrong. Besides, he was the sovereign; David was a subject. Though God had rejected him from the kingdom, it was in every way the best and most dutiful course, instead of precipitating his fall by imbruing their hands in his blood and thereby contracting the guilt of a great crime, to wait the awards of that retributive providence which sooner or later would take him off by some sudden and mortal blow. He who, with impetuous haste was going to exterminate Nabal, meekly spared Saul. But Nabal refused to give a tribute to which justice and gratitude, no less than custom, entitled David. Saul was under the judicial infatuation of heaven. Thus David withheld the hand of Abishai; but, at the same time, he directed him to carry off some things which would show where they had been, and what they had done. Thus he obtained the best of victories over him, by heaping coals of fire on his head. **11. the spear that is at his bolster, and the cruse of water**—The Oriental spear had, and still has, a spike at the lower extremity, intended for the purpose of sticking the spear into the ground when the warrior is at rest. This common custom of Arab sheiks was also the practice of the Hebrew chiefs. **at his bolster**—lit., "at his head"; perhaps, Saul as a sovereign had the

distinguished luxury of a bolster carried for him. A "cruse of water" is usually, in warm climates, kept near a person's couch, as a drink in the nighttime is found very refreshing. Saul's cruse would probably be of superior materials, or more richly ornamented than common ones, and therefore by its size or form be easily distinguished. **13-20. Then David . . . stood on the top of a hill afar off . . . and cried to the people**—(See on Judg. 9:7). The extraordinary purity and elasticity of the air in Palestine enable words to be distinctly heard that are addressed by a speaker from the top of one hill to people on that of another, from which it is separated by a deep intervening ravine. Hostile parties can thus speak to each other, while completely beyond the reach of each other's attack. It results from the peculiar features of the country in many of the mountain districts. **15. David said to Abner, Art not thou a valiant man: . . . wherefore then hast thou not kept thy lord the king?**—The circumstance of David having penetrated to the center of the encampment, through the circular rows of the sleeping soldiers, constituted the point of this sarcastic taunt. This new evidence of David's moderation and magnanimous forbearance, together with his earnest and kindly expostulation, softened the obduracy of Saul's heart. **19. If the Lord have stirred thee up against me**—By the evil spirit He had sent, or by any spiritual offenses by which we have mutually displeased Him. **let him accept an offering**—i.e., let us conjointly offer a sacrifice for appeasing His wrath against us. **if they be the children of men**—The prudence, meekness, and address of David in ascribing the king's enmity to the instigations of some malicious traducers, and not to the jealousy of Saul himself, is worthy of notice. **saying, Go, serve other gods**—This was the drift of their conduct. By driving him from the land and ordinances of the true worship, into foreign and heathen countries, they were exposing him to all the seductions of idolatry. **20. as when one doth hunt a partridge**—People in the East, in hunting the partridge and other game birds, pursue them, till observing them becoming languid and fatigued after they have been put up two or three times, they rush upon the birds stealthily and knock them down with bludgeons [SHAW'S TRAVELS]. It was exactly in this manner that Saul was pursuing David. He drove him from time to time from his hiding-place, hoping to render him weary of his life, or obtain an opportunity of accomplishing his destruction. **25. So David went on his way**—Notwithstanding this sudden relenting of Saul, David placed no confidence in his professions or promises, but wisely kept at a distance and awaited the course of Providence.

CHAPTER 27

VSS. 1-4. SAUL HEARING THAT DAVID WAS FLED TO GATH, SEEKS NO MORE FOR HIM. **1. David said in his heart, . . . there is nothing better for me than that I should speedily escape into the land of the Philistines**—This resolution of David's was, in every respect, wrong: (1) It was removing him from the place where the divine oracle intimated him to remain (ch. 22:5); (2) It was rushing into the idolatrous land, for driving him into which he had denounced an imprecation on his enemies (ch. 26: 19); (3) It was a withdrawal of his counsel and aid from God's people. It was a movement, however, overruled by Providence to detach him from his country and to let the disasters impending over

Saul and his followers be brought on by the Philistines. **2. Achish, the son of Maoch, king of Gath** —The popular description of this king's family creates a presumption that he was a different king from the reigning sovereign on David's first visit to Gath. Whether David had received a special invitation from him or a mere permission to enter his territories, cannot be determined. It is probable that the former was the case. From the universal notoriety given to the feud between Saul and David, which had now become irreconcilable, it might appear to Achish good policy to harbor him as a guest, and so the better pave the way for the hostile measures against Israel which the Philistines were at this time meditating. 5-12. DAVID BEGS ZIKLAG OF ACHISH. **5. let them give me a place in some town in the country**— It was a prudent arrangement on the part of David; for it would prevent him being an object of jealous suspicion, or of mischievous plots among the Philistines. It would place his followers more beyond the risk of contamination by the idolatries of the court and capital; and it would give him an opportunity of making reprisals on the freebooting tribes that infested the common border of Israel and the Philistines. **6. Ziklag**—Though originally assigned to Judah (Josh. 15:31), and subsequently to Simeon (Josh. 19:5), this town had never been possessed by the Israelites. It belonged to the Philistines, who gave it to David. **8. David ... went up, and invaded the Geshurites**—(See Josh. 13:2). **and the Girzites**—or the Gerizi [GESENIUS], (Josh. 12:12), some Arab horde which had once encamped there. **and the Amalekites**—Part of the district occupied by them lay on the south of the land of Israel (Judg. 5:14; 12:15). **10. Achish said, Whither have ye made a road to-day?**—i.e., *raid*, a hostile excursion for seizing cattle and other booty. **David said, Against the south of Judah, and against the south of the Jerahmeelites**—Jerahmeel was the great-grandson of Judah, and his posterity occupied the southern portion of that tribal domain. **the south of the Kenites**—the posterity of Jethro, who occupied the south of Judah (Judg. 1:16; Num. 24:21). The deceit practised upon his royal host and the indiscriminate slaughter committed, lest any one should escape to tell the tale, exhibit an unfavorable view of this part of David's history.

CHAPTER 28

Vss. 1-6. ACHISH'S CONFIDENCE IN DAVID. **1. The Philistines gathered their armies together for warfare, to fight with Israel**—The death of Samuel, the general dissatisfaction with Saul, and the absence of David, instigated the cupidity of those restless enemies of Israel. **Achish said to David, Know thou assuredly that thou shalt go out with me to battle**—This was evidently to try him. Achish, however, seems to have thought he had gained the confidence of David and had a claim on his services. **2. Surely thou shalt know what thy servant can do** —This answer, while it seemed to express an apparent cheerfulness in agreeing to the proposal, contained a studied ambiguity—a wary and politic generality. **Therefore will I make thee keeper of mine head**—or my life; i.e., captain of my bodyguard—an office of great trust and high honor. **3. Now Samuel was dead ...**—This event is here alluded to as affording an explanation of the secret and improper methods by which Saul sought information and direction in the present crisis of his

affairs. Overwhelmed in perplexity and fear, he yet found the common and legitimate channels of communication with Heaven shut against him. And so, under the impulse of that dark, distempered, superstitious spirit which had overmastered him, he resolved, in desperation, to seek the aid of one of those fortune-telling impostors whom, in accordance with the divine command (Lev. 19:31; 20:6, 27; Deut. 18:11), he had set himself formerly to exterminate from his kingdom. **4. the Philistines ... pitched in Shunem**—Having collected their forces for a last grand effort, they marched up from the seacoast and encamped in the "valley of Jezreel." The spot on which their encampment was fixed was Shunem (Josh. 19:18), now Sulem, a village which still exists on the slope of a range called "Little Hermon." On the opposite side, on the rise of Mount Gilboa, hard by "the spring of Jezreel," was Saul's army—the Israelites, according to their wont, keeping to the heights, while their enemies clung to the plain. 7-25. SAUL SEEKS A WITCH, WHO, BEING ENCOURAGED BY HIM, RAISES UP SAMUEL. **7. Then said Saul unto his servants, Seek me a woman that hath a familiar spirit**—From the energetic measures which he himself had taken for extirpating the dealers in magical arts (the profession having been declared a capital offense), his most attached courtiers might have had reason to doubt the possibility of gratifying their master's wish. Anxious inquiries, however, led to the discovery of a woman living very secluded in the neighborhood, who had the credit of possessing the forbidden powers. To her house he repaired by night in disguise, accompanied by two faithful servants. **En-dor**—"the fountain of the circle"—that figure being constantly affected by magicians—was situated directly on the other side of the Gilboa range, opposite Tabor; so that, in this midnight adventure, Saul had to pass over the shoulder of the ridge on which the Philistines were encamped. **8. bring me him up, whom I shall name unto thee**—This pythoness united to the arts of divination a claim to be a necromancer (Deut. 18:11); and it was her supposed power in calling back the dead of which Saul was desirous to avail himself. Though she at first refused to listen to his request, she accepted his pledge that no risk would be incurred by her compliance. It is probable that his extraordinary stature, the deference paid him by his attendants, the easy distance of his camp from Endor, and the proposal to call up the great prophet and first magistrate in Israel (a proposal which no private individual would venture to make), had awakened her suspicions as to the true character and rank of her visitor. The story has led to much discussion whether there was a real appearance of Samuel or not. On the one hand, the woman's profession, which was forbidden by the divine law, the refusal of God to answer Saul by any divinely constituted means, the well-known age, figure, and dress of Samuel, which she could easily represent herself, or by an accomplice—his apparition being evidently at some distance, being muffled, and not actually seen by Saul, whose attitude of prostrate homage, moreover, must have prevented him distinguishing the person though he had been near, and the voice seemingly issuing out of the ground, and coming along to Saul—and the vagueness of the information, imparted much which might have been reached by natural conjecture as to the probable result of the approaching conflict—the woman's representation—all of this has led many to think that this was a mere deception. On the other hand, many eminent writers (considering that the apparition came before her arts were put in practice; that she herself was surprised and alarmed; that the prediction of Saul's own death and the defeat of his forces was confidently made), are of opinion that Samuel really appeared. **24. the woman had a fat calf . . . and she hasted, and killed it . . .**—(See on Gen. 18:1-8). **25. Then they rose up, and went away that night**—Exhausted by long abstinence, overwhelmed with mental distress, and now driven to despair, the cold sweat broke on his anxious brow, and he sank helpless on the ground. But the kind attentions of the woman and his servants having revived him, he returned to the camp to await his doom.

CHAPTER 29

Vss. 1-5. David Marching with the Philistines to Fight with Israel. **1. Aphek**—(Josh. 12:8), in the tribe of Issachar, and in the plain of Esdraelon. A person who compares the Bible account of Saul's last battle with the Philistines, with the region around Gilboa, has the same sort of evidence that the account relates what is true, that a person would have that such a battle as Waterloo really took place. Gilboa, Jezreel, Shunem, En-dor, are all found, still bearing the same names. They lie within sight of each other. Aphek is the only one of the cluster not yet identified. Jezreel on the northern slope of Gilboa, and at the distance of twenty minutes to the east, is a large fountain, and a smaller one still nearer; just the position which a chieftain would select, both on account of its elevation and the supply of water needed for his troops [Hackett's Scripture Illustrated]. **2. David and his men passed on in the rereward with Achish**—as the commander of the lifeguards of Achish, who was general of this invading army of the Philistines. **3. these days, or these years**—He had now been with the Philistines a full year and four months (ch. 27:7), and also some years before. It has been thought that David kept up a private correspondence with his Philistine prince, either on account of his native generosity, or in the anticipation that an asylum in his territories would sooner or later be needed. **4. the princes of the Philistines were wroth with him**—It must be considered a happy circumstance in the overruling providence of God to rescue David out of the dangerous dilemma in which he was now placed. But David is not free from censure in his professions to Achish (vs. 8), to do what he probably had not the smallest purpose of doing—of fighting with Achish against his enemies. It is just an instance of the unhappy consequences into which a false step—a departure from the straight course of duty—will betray everyone who commits it. **9. notwithstanding the princes of the Philistines have said**—The Philistine government had constitutional checks—or at least the king was not an absolute sovereign; but his authority was limited—his proceedings liable to be controlled by "the powerful barons of that rude and early period—much as the kings of Europe in the Middle Ages were by the proud and lawless aristocracy which surrounded them" [Chalmers].

CHAPTER 30

Vss. 1-5. The Amalekites Spoil Ziklag. **1. Amalekites had invaded the south, and Ziklag**—

While the strength of the Philistine forces was poured out of their country into the plain of Esdraelon, the Amalekite marauders seized the opportunity of the defenseless state of Philistia to invade the southern territory. Of course, David's town suffered from the ravages of these nomad plunderers, in revenge for his recent raid upon their territory. **2. they slew not any, either great or small, but carried them away**—Their conduct seems to stand in favorable contrast to that of David (ch. 27:11). But their apparent clemency did not arise from humane considerations. It is traceable to the ancient war usages of the East, where the men of war, on the capture of a city, were unsparingly put to death, but there were no warriors in Ziklag at the time. The women and boys were reserved for slaves, and the old people were spared out of respect to age. **3. David and his men came to the city, and, behold, it was burned with fire**—The language implies that the smoke of the conflagration was still visible, and the sacking very recent.

6-15. But David, Encouraged by God, Pursues Them. **6. David was greatly distressed**—He had reason, not only on his own personal account (vs. 5), but on account of the vehement outcry and insurrectionary threats against him for having left the place so defenseless that the families of his men fell an unresisting prey to the enemy. Under the pressure of so unexpected and widespread a calamity, of which he was upbraided as the indirect occasion, the spirit of any other leader guided by ordinary motives would have sunk; "but David encouraged himself in the Lord his God." His faith supplied him with inward resources of comfort and energy, and through the seasonable inquiries he made by Urim, he inspired confidence by ordering an immediate pursuit of the plunderers. **9. came to the brook Besor**—now Wady Gaza, a winter torrent, a little to the south of Gaza. The bank of a stream naturally offered a convenient rest to the soldiers, who, through fatigue, were unable to continue the pursuit. **11-15. they found an Egyptian in the field, and brought him to David**—Old and homeborn slaves are usually treated with great kindness. But a purchased or captured slave must look to himself; for, if feeble or sick, his master will leave him to perish rather than encumber himself with any additional burden. This Egyptian seems to have recently fallen into the hands of an Amalekite, and his master having belonged to the marauding party that had made the attack on Ziklag, he could give useful information as to the course taken by them on their return. **14. the Cherethites**—i.e., the Philistines (Ezek. 25:16; Zeph. 2:5). **15. Swear unto me by God**—Whether there was still among these idolatrous tribes a lingering belief in one God, or this Egyptian wished to bind David by the God whom the Hebrews worshipped, the solemn sanction of an oath was mutually recognized.

16-31. And Recovers His Two Wives and All the Spoil. **16. they were spread abroad upon all the earth**—Believing that David and all his men of war were far away, engaged with the Philistine expedition, they deemed themselves perfectly secure and abandoned themselves to all manner of barbaric revelry. The promise made in answer to the devout inquiries of David (vs. 8) was fulfilled. The marauders were surprised and panic-stricken. A great slaughter ensued—the people as well as the booty taken from Ziklag was recovered, besides a great amount of spoil which they had collected in a wide, freebooting excursion. **21. David came to the two hundred men, which were so faint that they could not** follow—This unexpected accession of spoil was nearly proving an occasion of quarrel through the selfish cupidity of some of his followers, and serious consequences might have ensued had they not been prevented by the prudence of the leader, who enacted it as a standing ordinance—the equitable rule—that all the soldiers should share alike (see on Num. 31:11, 27). **26. when David came to Ziklag, he sent of the spoil to the elders of Judah** —This was intended as an acknowledgment to the leading men in those towns and villages of Judah which had ministered to his necessities in the course of his various wanderings. It was the dictate of an amiable and grateful heart; and the effect of this well-timed liberality was to bring a large accession of numbers to his camp (I Chron. 12:22). The enumeration of these places shows what a numerous and influential party of adherents to his cause he could count within his own tribe.

CHAPTER 31

Vss. 1-7. Saul Having Lost His Army at Gilboa, and His Sons Being Slain, He and His Armorbearer Kill Themselves. **1. Now the Philistines fought against Israel**—In a regular engagement, in which the two armies met (ch. 28:1-4), the Israelites were forced to give way, being annoyed by the arrows of the enemy, which, destroying them at a distance before they came to close combat, threw them into panic and disorder. Taking advantage of the heights of Mount Gilboa, they attempted to rally, but in vain. Saul and his sons fought like heroes; but the onset of the Philistines being at length mainly directed against the quarter where they were, Jonathan and two brothers, Abinadab or Ishui (ch. 14:49) and Melchishua, overpowered by numbers, were killed on the spot. **3. the battle went sore against Saul . . .** —He seems to have bravely maintained his ground for some time longer; but exhausted with fatigue and loss of blood, and dreading that if he fell alive into the enemy's hands, they would insolently maltreat him (Josh. 8:29; 10:24; Judg. 8:21), he requested his armorbearer to despatch him. However, that officer refused to do so. Saul then falling on the point of his sword killed himself; and the armorbearer, who, according to Jewish writers, was Doeg, following the example of his master, put an end to his life also. They died by one and the same sword—the very weapon with which they had massacred the Lord's servants at Nob. **6. So Saul died** [see on I Chron. 10:13, 14;

Hos. 13:11], **and his three sons**—The influence of a directing Providence is evidently to be traced in permitting the death of Saul's three eldest and most energetic sons, particularly that of Jonathan, for whom, had he survived his father, a strong party would undoubtedly have risen and thus obstructed the path of David to the throne. **and all his men, that same day together**—his servants or bodyguard (I Chron. 10:6). **7. the men of Israel that were on the other side of the valley**—probably the valley of Jezreel—the largest and southernmost of the valleys that run between Little Hermon and the ridges of the Gilboa range direct into the Jordan valley. It was very natural for the people in the towns and villages there to take fright and flee, for had they waited the arrival of the victors, they must, according to the war usages of the time, have been deprived either of their liberty or their lives.

8-10. The Philistines Triumph over Their Dead Bodies. **8. on the morrow, when the Philistines came to strip the slain, that they found Saul and his three sons fallen**—On discovering the corpses of the slaughtered princes on the battlefield, the enemy reserved them for special indignities. They consecrated the armor of the king and his sons to the temple of Ashtaroth, fastened their bodies on the temple of Shen, while they fixed the royal heads ignominiously in the temple of Dagon (I Chron. 10:10); thus dividing the glory among their several deities. **10. to the wall**—(II Sam. 21:12)—"the street" of Beth-shan. The street was called from the temple which stood in it. And they had to go along it to the wall of the city (see Josh. 17:11).

11-13. The Men of Jabesh-gilead Recover the Bodies and Bury Them at Jabesh. **11-13. the inhabitants of Jabesh-gilead heard of that which the Philistines had done**—Mindful of the important and timely services Saul had rendered them, they gratefully and heroically resolved not to suffer such indignities to be inflicted on the remains of the royal family. **12. valiant men arose, and went all night, and took the body of Saul and the bodies of his sons** —Considering that Beth-shan is an hour and a half's distance, and by a narrow upland passage, to the west of the Jordan—the whole being a journey from Jabesh-gilead of about ten miles, they must have made all haste to travel thither to carry off the headless bodies and return to their own side of the Jordan in the course of a single night. **burnt them**—This was not a Hebrew custom. It was probably resorted to on this occasion to prevent all risk of the Bethshanites coming to disinter the royal remains for further insult.

THE SECOND BOOK OF

SAMUEL

CHAPTER 1

Vss. 1-16. An Amalekite Brings Tidings of Saul's Death. **1. David had abode two days in Ziklag**—Though greatly reduced by the Amalekite incendiaries, that town was not so completely sacked and destroyed, but David and his 600 followers, with their families, could still find some accommodation. **2-12. a man came out of the camp from**

Saul—As the narrative of Saul's death, given in the last chapter, is inspired, it must be considered the true account, and the Amalekite's story a fiction of his own, invented to ingratiate himself with David, the presumptive successor to the throne. David's question, "How went the matter?" evinces the deep interest he took in the war—an interest that sprang from feelings of high and generous patriotism—not from views of ambition. The Amalekite, however, judging him to be actuated by a selfish principle, fabricated a story improbable and inconsistent, which he thought would procure him a reward. Having probably witnessed the suicidal act of Saul, he thought of turning it to his own account, and suffered the penalty of his grievously mistaken calculation (cf. vs. 9 with I Sam. 31:4, 5). **10. the crown**—a small metallic cap or wreath, which encircled the temples, serving the purpose of a helmet, with a very small horn projecting in front, as the emblem of power. **the bracelet that was on his arm**—the armlet worn above the elbow; an ancient mark of royal dignity. It is still worn by kings in some Eastern countries. **13-15. David said unto the young man . . . , Whence art thou?**—The man had at the outset stated who he was. But the question was now formally and judicially put. The punishment inflicted on the Amalekite may seem too severe, but the respect paid to kings in the West must not be regarded as the standard for that which the East may think due to royal station. David's reverence for Saul, as the Lord's anointed, was in his mind a principle on which he had faithfully acted on several occasions of great temptation. In present circumstances it was especially important that his principle should be publicly known; and to free himself from the imputation of being in any way accessory to the execrable crime of regicide was the part of a righteous judge, no less than of a good politician.

17-27. DAVID LAMENTS SAUL AND JONATHAN. 17. David lamented with this lamentation—It has always been customary for Eastern people, on the death of great kings and warriors, to celebrate their qualities and deeds in funeral songs. This inimitable pathetic elegy is supposed by many writers to have become a national war-song, and to have been taught to the young Israelites under the name of "The Bow," in conformity with the practice of Hebrew and many classical writers in giving titles to their songs from the principal theme (Ps. 22; 56; 60; 80; 100). Although the words "use of" are a supplement by our translators, they may be rightly introduced, for the natural sense of this parenthetical verse is, that David took immediate measures for instructing the people in the knowledge and practice of archery, their great inferiority to the enemy in this military arm having been the main cause of the late national disaster. **19. The beauty of Israel**—lit., the gazelle or antelope of Israel. In Eastern countries, that animal is the chosen type of beauty and symmetrical elegance of form. **how are the mighty fallen!**—This forms the chorus. **21. let there be no dew, neither let there be rain**—To be deprived of the genial atmospheric influences which, in those anciently cultivated hills, seem to have reared plenty of first fruits in the corn harvests, was specified as the greatest calamity the lacerated feelings of the poet could imagine. The curse seems still to lie upon them; for the mountains of Gilboa are naked and sterile. **the shield of the mighty is vilely cast away**—To cast away the shield was counted a national disgrace. Yet, on that fatal battle of Gilboa, many of the Jewish soldiers, who had displayed unflinching valor in former battles, forgetful of their own reputation and their country's honor, threw away their shields and fled from the field. This dishonorable and cowardly conduct is alluded to with exquisitely touching pathos. **24. Ye daughters of Israel, weep over Saul, who clothed you in scarlet, with other delights . . .**—The fondness for dress, which anciently distinguished Oriental women, is their characteristic still. It appears in their love of bright, gay, and divers colors, in profuse display of ornaments, and in various other forms. The inmost depths of the poet's feeling are stirred, and his amiable disposition appears in the strong desire to celebrate the good qualities of Saul, as well as Jonathan. But the praises of the latter form the burden of the poem, which begins and ends with that excellent prince.

CHAPTER 2

VSS. 1-7. DAVID, BY GOD'S DIRECTION, GOES UP TO HEBRON, AND IS MADE KING OVER JUDAH. **1. David inquired of the Lord**—By Urim (I Sam. 23:6, 9; 30:7, 8). He knew his destination, but he knew also that the providence of God would pave the way. Therefore he would take no step in such a crisis of his own and the nation's history, without asking and obtaining the divine direction. He was told to go into Judah, and fix his headquarters in Hebron, whither he accordingly repaired with his now considerable force. There his interests were very powerful; for he was not only within his own tribe, and near chiefs with whom he had been long in friendly relations (see on I Sam. 30:26-31), but Hebron was the capital and center of Judah, and one of the Levitical cities; the inhabitants of which were strongly attached to him, both from sympathy with his cause ever since the massacre at Nob, and from the prospect of realizing in his person their promised pre-eminence among the tribes. The princes of Judah, therefore, offered him the crown over their tribe, and it was accepted. More could not, with prudence, be done in the circumstances of the country (I Chron. 11:3). **5-7. David sent messengers unto the men of Jabesh-gilead**—There can be no doubt that this message of thanks for their bold and dangerous enterprise in rescuing the bodies of Saul and his sons was an expression of David's personal and genuine feeling of satisfaction. At the same time, it was a stroke of sound and timely policy. In this view the announcement of his royal power in Judah, accompanied by the pledge of his protection of the men of Jabesh-gilead, should they be exposed to danger for their adventure at Bethshan, would bear an important significance in all parts of the country and hold out an assurance that he would render them the same timely and energetic succor that Saul had done at the beginning of his reign.

8-17. ABNER MAKES ISH-BOSHETH KING OVER ISRAEL. 8-17. Abner, son of Ner, captain of Saul's host, took Ish-bosheth—Here was the establishment of a rival kingdom, which, however, would probably have had no existence but for Abner. **Ish-bosheth**—or Esh-baal (I Chron. 8:33; 9:39). The Hebrews usually changed names ending with Baal into Bosheth (shame) (cf. Judg. 9:53 with ch. 11:21). This prince was so called from his imbecility. **Abner**—was first cousin of Saul, commander of the forces, and held in high respect throughout the country. Loyalty to the house of his late master was mixed up with opposition to David and views of personal ambition in his originating this factious movement. He, too, was alive to the importance of securing the eastern tribes; so, taking Ish-bosheth across the Jordan, he proclaimed him king at Mahanaim, a town on the north bank of the Jabbok, hallowed in patriarchal times by the divine presence (Gen. 32:2). There he rallied the tribes around the standard of the unfortunate son of Saul. **9. over Gilead**—used in a loose sense for the land beyond Jordan. **Ashurites**—the tribe of Asher in the extreme north. **Jez-**

reel—the extensive valley bordering on the central tribes. **over all Israel . . . 10. But Judah**—David neither could nor would force matters. He was content to wait God's time and studiously avoided any collision with the rival king, till, at the lapse of two years, hostilities were threatened from that quarter. **12. Abner . . . and the servants of Ish-bosheth . . . went out from Mahanaim to Gibeon**—This town was near the confines of Judah, and as the force with which Abner encamped there seemed to have some aggressive design, David sent an army of observation, under the command of Joab, to watch his movements. **14. Abner said to Joab, Let the young men now arise, and play before us**—Some think that the proposal was only for an exhibition of a little tilting match for diversion. Others suppose that, both parties being reluctant to commence a civil war, Abner proposed to leave the contest to the decision of twelve picked men on either side. This fight by championship instead of terminating the matter, inflamed the fiercest passions of the two rival parties; a general engagement ensued, in which Abner and his forces were defeated and put to flight.

19-22. ASAHEL SLAIN. 19. Asahel pursued after Abner—To gain the general's armor was deemed the grandest trophy. Asahel, ambitious of securing Abner's, had outstripped all other pursuers, and was fast gaining on the retreating commander. Abner, conscious of possessing more physical power, and unwilling that there should be "blood" between himself and Joab, Asahel's brother, twice urged him to desist. The impetuous young soldier being deaf to the generous remonstrance, the veteran raised the pointed butt of his lance, as the modern Arabs do when pursued, and, with a sudden back-thrust, transfixed him on the spot, so that he fell, and lay weltering in his blood. But Joab and Abishai continued the pursuit by another route till sunset. On reaching a rising ground, and receiving a fresh reinforcement of some Benjamites, Abner rallied his scattered troops and earnestly appealed to Joab's better feelings to stop the further effusion of blood, which, if continued, would lead to more serious consequences—a destructive civil war. Joab, while upbraiding his opponent as the sole cause of the fray, felt the force of the appeal and led off his men; while Abner probably dreading a renewal of the attack when Joab should learn his brother's fate, and vow fierce revenge, endeavored, by a forced march, to cross the Jordan that night. On David's side the loss was only nineteen men, besides Asahel. But of Ish-bosheth's party there fell three hundred and sixty. This skirmish is exactly similar to the battles of the Homeric warriors, among whom, in the flight of one, the pursuit by another, and the dialogue held between them, there is vividly represented the style of ancient warfare.

CHAPTER 3

Vss. 1-5. SIX SONS BORN TO DAVID. 1. there was long war between the house of Saul and the house of David—The rival parties had varying success, but David's interest steadily increased; less, however, by the fortunes of war, than a growing adherence to him as the divinely designated king. **2. unto David were sons born in Hebron**—The six sons mentioned had all different mothers. **3. Chileab**—(his father's picture)—called also Daniel (I Chron. 3:1). **Maacah, the daughter of Talmai king of Geshur**—a region in Syria, north of Israel. This marriage seems to have been a political match,

made by David, with a view to strengthen himself against Ish-bosheth's party, by the aid of a powerful friend and ally in the north. Piety was made to yield to policy, and the bitter fruits of this alliance with a heathen prince he reaped in the life of the turbulent Absalom. **5. Eglah, David's wife**—This addition has led many to think that Eglah was another name for Michal, the *first* and *proper* wife, who, though she had no family after her insolent ridicule of David (ch. 6:23), might have had a child before.

6-12. ABNER REVOLTS TO DAVID. 6-11. Abner made himself strong for the house of Saul—In the East, the wives and concubines of a king are the property of his successor to this extent, that for a private person to aspire to marry one of them would be considered a virtual advance of pretensions to the crown (see on I Kings 2:17). It is not clear whether the accusation against Abner was well or ill founded. But he resented the charge as an indignity, and, impelled by revenge, determined to transfer all the weight of his influence to the opposite party. He evidently set a full value on his services, and seems to have lorded it over his weak nephew in a haughty, overbearing manner. **12. Abner sent messengers to David**—Though his language implied a secret conviction, that in supporting Ish-bosheth he had been laboring to frustrate the divine purpose of conferring the sovereignty of the kingdom on David, this acknowledgment was no justification either of the measure he was now adopting, or of the motives that prompted it. Nor does it seem possible to uphold the full integrity and honor of David's conduct in entertaining his secret overtures for undermining Ish-bosheth, except we take into account the divine promise of the kingdom, and his belief that the secession of Abner was a means designed by Providence for accomplishing it. The demand for the restoration of his wife Michal was perfectly fair; but David's insisting on it at that particular moment, as an indispensable condition of his entering into any treaty with Abner, seems to have proceeded not so much from a lingering attachment as from an expectation that his possession of her would incline some adherents of the house of Saul to be favorable to his cause. **17-21. Abner had communication with the elders of Israel**—He spoke the truth in impressing their minds with the well-known fact of David's divine designation to the kingdom. But he acted a base and hypocritical part in pretending that his present movement was prompted by religious motives, when it sprang entirely from malice and revenge against Ish-bosheth. The particular appeal of the Benjamites was a necessary policy; their tribe enjoyed the honor of giving birth to the royal dynasty of Saul; they would naturally be disinclined to lose that *prestige*. They were, besides, a determined people, whose contiguity to Judah might render them troublesome and dangerous. The enlistment of their interest, therefore, in the scheme, would smooth the way for the adhesion of the other tribes; and Abner enjoyed the most convenient opportunity of using his great influence in gaining over that tribe while escorting Michal to David with a suitable equipage. The mission enabled him to cover his treacherous designs against his master—to draw the attention of the elders and people to David as uniting in himself the double recommendation of being the nominee of Jehovah, no less than a connection of the royal house of Saul, and, without suspicion of any dishonorable motives, to advocate policy of terminating the civil discord, by bestowing the sovereignty on the husband of Michal. In the same character of public ambassador, he was received and feted by David; and while, ostensibly, the restoration of Michal was the sole object of his visit, he busily employed himself in making private overtures to David for bringing over to his cause those tribes which he had artfully seduced. Abner pursued a course unworthy of an honorable man and though his offer was accepted by David, the guilt and infamy of the transaction were exclusively his.

22-30. Joab Kills Abner. 24. Joab came to the king and said, What hast thou done?—Joab's knowledge of Abner's wily character might have led him to doubt the sincerity of that person's proposals and to disapprove the policy of relying on his fidelity. But undoubtedly there were other reasons of a private and personal nature which made Joab displeased and alarmed by the reception given to Abner. The military talents of that general, his popularity with the army, his influence throughout the nation, rendered him a formidable rival. In the event of his overtures being carried out, the important service of bringing over all the other tribes to the king of Judah would establish so strong a claim on the gratitude of David, that his accession would inevitably raise a serious obstacle to the ambition of Joab. To these considerations was added the remembrance of the blood-feud that existed between them since the death of his brother Asahel (ch. 2:23). Determined, therefore, to get Abner out of the way, Joab feigned some reason, probably in the king's name, for recalling him, and, going out to meet him, stabbed him unawares; not within Hebron, for it was a city of refuge, but at a noted well in the neighborhood. **31. David said to Joab, and to all the people that were with him, Rend your clothes; gird you with sackcloth**—David's sorrow was sincere and profound, and he took occasion to give it public expression by the funeral honors he appointed for Abner. **King David himself followed the bier**—a sort of wooden frame, partly resembling a coffin, and partly a hand-barrow. **33, 34. the king lamented over Abner**—This brief elegy is an effusion of indignation as much as of sorrow. As Abner had stabbed Asahel in open war, Joab had not the right of the Goel. Besides, he had adopted a lawless and execrable method of obtaining satisfaction (see on I Kings 2:5). The deed was an insult to the authority, as well as most damaging to the prospects of the king. But David's feelings and conduct on hearing of the death, together with the whole character and accompaniments of the funeral solemnity, tended not only to remove all suspicion of guilt from him, but even to turn the tide of popular opinion in his favor, and to pave the way for his reigning over all the tribes more honorably than by the treacherous negotiations of Abner.

CHAPTER 4

Vss. 1-2. Baanah and Rechab Slay Ish-bosheth, and Bring His Head to Hebron. **4. Jonathan, Saul's son, had a son that was lame of his feet**—This is mentioned as a reason why, according to Oriental notions, he was considered unfit for exercising the duties of sovereignty. **5. Rechab and Baanah went and came about the heat of the day to the house of Ish-bosheth . . .**—It is still a custom in the East to allow their soldiers a certain quantity of corn, together with some pay; and these two captains very naturally went to the palace the day before to fetch wheat, in order to distribute it to the sol-

diers, that it might be sent to the mill at the accustomed hour in the morning. **7. when they came into the house, he lay on his bed**—Rechab and Baanah came in the heat of the day, when they knew that Ish-bosheth, their master, would be resting on his divan; and as it was necessary, for the reason just given, to have the corn the day before it was needed, their coming at that time, though it might be a little earlier than usual, created no suspicion, and attracted no notice [Harmer]. **gat them away through the plain all night**—i.e., the valley of the Jordan, through which their way lay from Mahanaim to Hebron. **8. They brought the head of Ish-bosheth unto David . . . , and said, Behold the head of Ish-bosheth**—Such bloody trophies of rebels and conspirators have always been acceptable to princes in the East, and the carriers have been liberally rewarded. Ish-bosheth being a usurper, the two assassins thought they were doing a meritorious service to David by removing the only existing obstacle to the union of the two kingdoms.

10-12. David Causes Them to Be Put to Death. 12. slew them, and cut off their hands and their feet—as the instruments in perpetrating their crime. The exposure of the mutilated remains was intended as not only a punishment of their crime, but also the attestation of David's abhorrence.

CHAPTER 5

Vss. 1-5. The Tribes Anoint David King over Israel. **1. Then came all the tribes of Israel**—a combined deputation of the leading authorities in every tribe. David possessed the first and indispensable qualification for the throne; viz., that of being an Israelite (Deut. 17:15). Of his military talent he had furnished ample proof, and the people's desire for his assumption of the government of Israel was further increased by their knowledge of the will and purpose of God, as declared by Samuel (I Sam. 16: 11-13). **3. King David made a league with them in Hebron before the Lord**—(see on I Sam. 10:25). This formal declaration of the constitution was chiefly made at the commencement of a new dynasty, or at the restoration of the royal family after a usurpation (II Kings 11:17), though circumstances sometimes led to its being renewed on the accession of any new sovereign (I Kings 12:4). It seems to have been accompanied by religious solemnities.

6-12. He Takes Zion from the Jebusites. 6. the king and his men went to Jerusalem unto the Jebusites—The first expedition of David, as king of the whole country, was directed against this place, which had hitherto remained in the hands of the natives. It was strongly fortified and deemed so impregnable that the blind and lame were sent to man the battlements, in derisive mockery of the Hebrew king's attack, and to shout, "David cannot come in hither." To understand the full meaning and force of this insulting taunt, it is necessary to bear in mind the depth and steepness of the valley of Gihon, and the lofty walls of the ancient Canaanitish fortress. **7. stronghold of Zion**—Whether Zion be the southwestern hill commonly so called, or the peak now level on the north of the temple mount, it is the towering height which catches the eye from every quarter—"the hill fort," "the rocky hold" of Jerusalem. **8. Whosoever getteth up to the gutter**—This is thought by some to mean a subterranean passage; by others a spout through which water was poured upon the fire which the besiegers often applied to the woodwork at the gateways, and by the projections of which a skilful climber might make his ascent good; a third class render the words, "whosoever dasheth them against the precipice" (I Chron. 11:6). **9. David dwelt in the fort . . .**—Having taken it by storm, he changed its name to "the city of David," to signify the importance of the conquest, and to perpetuate the memory of the event. **David built round about from Millo and inward**—probably a row of stone bastions placed on the northern side of Mount Zion, and built by David to secure himself on that side from the Jebusites, who still lived in the lower part of the city. The house of Millo was perhaps the principal corner tower of that fortified wall. **11, 12. Hiram . . . sent carpenters and masons**—The influx of Tyrian architects and mechanics affords a clear evidence of the low state to which, through the disorders of long-continued war, the better class of artisans had declined in Israel.

13-16. ELEVEN SONS BORN TO HIM. **13. David took him more concubines and wives**—In this conduct David transgressed an express law, which forbade the king of Israel to multiply wives unto himself (Deut. 17:17).

17-25. HE SMITES THE PHILISTINES. **17. when the Philistines heard that they had anointed David king over Israel**—During the civil war between the house of Saul and David, those restless neighbors had remained quiet spectators of the contest. But now, jealous of David, they resolved to attack him before his government was fully established. **18. valley of Rephaim**—i.e., of giants, a broad and fertile plain, which descends gradually from the central mountains towards the northwest. It was the route by which they marched against Jerusalem. The "hold" to which David went down "was some fortified place where he might oppose the progress of the invaders," and where he signally defeated them. **21. there they left their images**—probably their lares or household deities, which they had brought into the field to fight for them. They were burnt as ordained by law (Deut. 7:5). **22. the Philistines came up yet again**—The next year they renewed their hostile attempt with a larger force, but God manifestly interposed in David's favor. **24. the sound of a going in the tops of the mulberry trees**—now generally thought not to be mulberry trees, but some other tree, most probably the poplar, which delights in moist situations, and the leaves of which are rustled by the slightest movement of the air (ROYLE].

CHAPTER 6

Vss. 1-5. DAVID FETCHES THE ARK FROM KIR-JATH-JEARIM ON A NEW CART. **1. Again David gathered together all the chosen men of Israel**—(See ch. 5:1). The object of this second assembly was to commence a national movement for establishing the ark in Jerusalem, after it had continued nearly fifty years in the house of Abinadab (see on I Chron. 13:1-5). **2. from Baale of Judah**—A very large force of picked men were selected for this important work lest the undertaking might be opposed or obstructed by the Philistines. Besides, a great concourse of people accompanied them out of veneration for the sacred article. The journey *to* Baale, which is related (I Chron. 13:6), is here presupposed, and the historian describes the course of the procession *from* that place to the capital. **3. they set the ark of God upon a new cart**—or covered wagon (see on I Sam. 6:7). This was a hasty and inconsiderate procedure, in violation of an express statute (see on Num. 4:14, 15; 7:9; 18:3).

6-11. UZZAH SMITTEN. **6. they came to Nachon's threshing-floor**—or Chidon's (I Chron. 13:9). The Chaldee version renders the words, "came to the place prepared for the reception of the ark," i.e., near the city of David (vs. 13). **the oxen shook it**—or stumbled (I Chron. 13:9). Fearing that the ark was in danger of being overturned, Uzzah, under the impulse of momentary feeling, laid hold of it to keep it steady. Whether it fell and crushed him, or some sudden disease attacked him, he fell dead upon the spot. This melancholy occurrence not only threw a cloud over the joyous scene, but entirely stopped the procession; for the ark was left where it then was, in the near neighborhood of the capital. It is of importance to observe the proportionate severity of the punishments attending the profanation of the ark. The Philistines suffered by diseases, from which they were relieved by their oblations, because the law had not been given to them; the Beth-shemites also suffered, but not fatally; their error proceeded from ignorance or inadvertency. But Uzzah, who was a Levite, and well instructed, suffered death for his breach of the law. The severity of Uzzah's fate may seem to us too great for the nature and degree of the offense. But it does not become us to sit in judgment on the dispensations of God; and, besides, it is apparent that the divine purpose was to inspire awe of His majesty, a submission to His law, and a profound veneration for the symbols and ordinances of His worship. **9. David was afraid of the Lord that day . . .**—His feelings on this alarming judgment were greatly excited on various accounts, dreading that the displeasure of God had been provoked by the removal of the ark, that the punishment would be extended to himself and people, and that they might fall into some error or neglect during the further conveyance of the ark. He resolved, therefore, to wait for more light and direction as to the path of duty. An earlier consultation by Urim would have led him right at the first, whereas in this perplexity and distress, he was reaping the fruits of inconsideration and neglect. **11. Obed-edom the Gittite**—a Levite (I Chron. 15:18, 21, 24; 16:5; 26:4). He is called a Gittite, either from his residence at Gath, or more probably from Gath-rimmon, one of the Levitical cities (Josh. 21: 24, 25).

12-19. DAVID AFTERWARDS BRINGS THE ARK TO ZION. **12. it was told King David, saying, The Lord hath blessed the house of Obed-edom and all that pertaineth unto him, because of the ark of God**—The lapse of three months not only restored the agitated mind of the monarch to a tranquil and settled tone, but led him to a discovery of his former error. Having learned that the ark was kept in its temporary resting-place not only without inconvenience or danger, but with great advantage, he resolved forthwith to remove it to the capital, with the observance of all due form and solemnity (I Chron. 15:1-13). It was transported now on the shoulders of the priests, who had been carefully prepared for the work, and the procession was distinguished by extraordinary solemnities and demonstrations of joy. **13. when they that bare the ark . . . had gone six paces**—Some think that four altars were hastily raised for the offering of sacrifices at the distance of every six paces (but see I Chron. 15:26). **14. David danced before the Lord**—The Hebrews, like other ancient people, had their sacred dances, which were performed on their solemn anniversaries and other great occasions of commemorating some special token of the divine goodness and favor. **with all his might**—intimating violent efforts of leaping, and divested of his royal mantle—in a state of undress—conduct apparently unsuitable to the gravity of age or the dignity of a king. But it was unquestionably done as an act of religious homage, his attitudes and dress being symbolic, as they have always been in Oriental countries, of penitence, joy, thankfulness, and devotion. **17. they brought in the ark of the Lord, and set it in his place in the midst of the tabernacle that David had pitched for it**—The old tabernacle remained at Gibeon (I Chron. 16:39; 21:29; II Chron. 1:3). Probably it was not removed because it was too large for the temporary place the king had appropriated, and because he contemplated the building of a temple. **18. he blessed the people**—in the double character of prophet and king (see on I Kings 8:55, 56). **19. cake of bread**—unleavened and slender. **a good piece of flesh**—roast beef.

20-23. MICHAL'S BARRENNESS. **Michal . . . came out to meet David . . .**—Proud of her royal extraction, she upbraided her husband for lowering the dignity of the crown and acting more like a buffoon than a king. But her taunting sarcasm was repelled in a manner that could not be agreeable to her feelings while it indicated the warm piety and gratitude of David.

CHAPTER 7

Vss. 1-3. NATHAN APPROVES THE PURPOSE OF DAVID TO BUILD GOD A HOUSE. **2. the king said unto Nathan the prophet, See now, I dwell in an house of cedar**—The palace which Hiram had sent men and materials to build in Jerusalem had been finished. It was magnificent for that age, though made wholly of wood: houses in warm countries not being required to possess the solidity and thickness of walls which are requisite for dwellings in regions exposed to rain and cold. Cedar was the rarest and most valuable timber. The elegance and splendor of his own royal mansion, contrasted with the mean and temporary tabernacle in which the ark of God was placed, distressed the pious mind of David. **3. Nathan said to the king, Go, do all that is in thine heart**—The piety of the design commended it to the prophet's mind, and he gave his hasty approval and encouragement to the royal plans. The prophets, when following the impulse of their own feelings, or forming conjectural opinions, fell into frequent mistakes. (See on I Sam. 16:6; II Kings 4:27.)

4-17. GOD APPOINTS HIS SUCCESSOR TO BUILD IT. **4-17. it came to pass that night, that the word of the Lord came unto Nathan**—The command was given to the prophet on the night immediately following; i.e., before David could either take any measures or incur any expenses. **11. Also the Lord telleth thee that he will make thee an house**—As a reward for his pious purpose, God would increase and maintain the family of David and secure the succession of the throne to his dynasty. **12. I will set up thy seed after thee . . .**—It is customary for the *oldest son born after the father's succession to the throne* to succeed him in his dignity as king. David had several sons by Bath-sheba born after his removal to Jerusalem (ch. 5:14-16; cf. I Chron. 3:5). But by a special ordinance and promise of God, his successor was to be a son born after this time; and the departure from the established usage of the East in fixing the succession, can be accounted for on no other known ground, except the fulfilment of the divine promise. **13. He shall build an house for my name, and I will establish the throne of his kingdom for ever**—This declaration referred, in its primary appli-

cation, to Solomon, and to the temporal kingdom of David's family. But in a larger and sublimer sense, it was meant of David's Son of another nature (Heb. 1:8).

18-29. DAVID'S PRAYER AND THANKSGIVING. **18. Then went King David in, and sat before the Lord**—Sitting was anciently an attitude for worship (Exod. 17:12; I Sam. 4:13; I Kings 19:4). As to the particular attitude David sat, most probably, *upon his heels*. It was the posture of the ancient Egyptians before the shrines; it is the posture of deepest respect before a superior in the East. Persons of highest dignity sit thus when they do sit in the presence of kings and it is the only sitting attitude assumed by the modern Mohammedans in their places and rites of devotion. **19. is this the manner of man, O Lord God?**—i.e., is it customary for men to show such condescension to persons so humble as I am? (See on I Chron. 17:17). **20. what can David say more unto thee?**—i.e., my obligations are greater than I can express.

CHAPTER 8

Vss. 1, 2. DAVID SUBDUES THE PHILISTINES, AND MAKES THE MOABITES TRIBUTARY. **1. David took Metheg-ammah out of the hand of the Philistines**—that is, Gath and her suburban towns (I Chron. 18:1). That town had been "a bridle" by which the Philistines kept the people of Judah in check. David used it now as a barrier to repress that restless enemy. **2. he smote Moab and measured them with a line**—This refers to a well-known practice of Eastern kings, to command their prisoners of war, particularly those who, notorious for the atrocity of their crimes or distinguished by the indomitable spirit of their resistance, had greatly incensed the victors, to lie down on the ground. Then a certain portion of them, which was determined by lot, but most commonly by a measuring line, were put to death. Our version makes him put two-thirds to death, and spare one-third. The *Septuagint* and *Vulgate* make one-half. This war usage was not, perhaps, usually practised by the people of God; but Jewish writers assert that the cause of this particular severity against this people was their having massacred David's parents and family, whom he had, during his exile, committed to the king of Moab.

3-14. HE SMITES HADADEZER AND THE SYRIANS. **3. Zobah**—(I Chron. 18:3). This kingdom was bounded on the east by the Euphrates, and it extended westward from that river, perhaps as far north as Aleppo. It was long the chief among the petty kingdoms of Syria, and its king bore the hereditary title of Hadadezer or Hadarezer (Hadad—helped). **as he went to recover his border at the river Euphrates**—in accordance with the promises God made to Israel that He would give them all the country as far as the Euphrates (Gen. 15:18; Num. 24:17). In the first compaign David signally defeated Hadadezer. Besides a great number of foot-prisoners, he took from him an immense amount of booty in chariots and horses. Reserving only a small number of the latter, he hamstrung the rest. The horses were thus mutilated because they were forbidden to the Hebrews, both in war and agriculture. So it was of no use to keep them. Besides, their neighbors placed much dependence on cavalry, but having, for want of a native breed, to procure them by purchase, the greatest damage that could be done to such enemies was to render their horses serviceable in war. (See also Gen. 46:6; Josh.

9.) A king of Damascene-Syria came to Hadad-ezer's succor; but David routed those auxiliary forces also, took possession of their country, put garrisons into their fortified towns, and made them tributary. **9. Toi king of Hamath**—Cœle-Syria; northwards, it extended to the city Hamath on the Orontes, which was the capital of the country. The Syrian prince, being delivered from the dread of a dangerous neighbor, sent his son with valuable presents to David to congratulate him on his victories, and solicit his alliance and protection. **10. Joram**—or Hadoram (I Chron. 18:10). **11. Which also King David did dedicate unto the Lord**—Eastern princes have always been accustomed to hoard up vast quantities of gold. This is the first instance of a practice uniformly followed by David of reserving, after defraying expenses and bestowing suitable rewards upon his soldiers, the remainder of the spoil taken in war, to accumulate for the grand project of his life—the erection of a national temple at Jerusalem. **13. David gat him a name when he returned from smiting of the Syrians**—Instead of Syrians, the *Sept.* version reads Edomites, which is the true reading, as is evident from verse 14. This conquest, made by the army of David, was due to the skilful generalship and gallantry of Abishai and Joab. (I Chron. 18:12; cf. Ps. 60, title.) The valley was the ravine of salt (the Ghor), adjoining the Salt Mountain, at the southwestern extremity of the Dead Sea, separating the ancient territories of Judah and Edom [Robinson].

15-18. His Reign. 15. David executed judgment and justice unto all his people—Though involved in foreign wars, he maintained an excellent system of government at home, the most eminent men of the age composing his cabinet of ministers. **16. Joab . . . was over the host**—by virtue of a special promise (ch. 5:8). **recorder**—historiographer or daily annalist, an office of great trust and importance in Eastern countries. **17. Zadok . . . and Ahimelech . . . were the priests**—On the massacre of the priests at Nob, Saul conferred the priesthood on Zadok, of the family of Eleazar (I Chron. 6:50), while David acknowledged Ahimelech, of Ithamar's family, who fled to him. The two high priests exercised their office under the respective princes to whom they were attached. But, on David's obtaining the kingdom over all Israel, they both retained their dignity; Ahimelech officiating at Jerusalem, and Zadok at Gibeon (I Chron. 16:39). **18. Cherethites**—i.e., Philistines (Zeph. 2:5). **Pelethites**—from Pelet (I Chron. 12:3). They were the valiant men who, having accompanied David during his exile among the Philistines, were made his bodyguard.

CHAPTER 9

Vss. 1-12. David Sends for Mephibosheth. **1. David said, Is there yet any that is left of the house of Saul**—On inquiry, Saul's land steward was found, who gave information that there still survived Mephibosheth, a son of Jonathan, who was five years old at his father's death, and whom David, then wandering in exile, had never seen. His lameness (ch. 4:4) had prevented him from taking any part in the public contests of the time. Besides, according to Oriental notions, the younger son of a crowned monarch has a preferable claim to the succession over the son of a mere heir-apparent; and hence his name was never heard of as the rival of his uncle Ish-bosheth. His insignificance had led to his being lost ight of, and it was only through Ziba that David

learned of his existence, and the retired life he passed with one of the great families in transjordanic Canaan who remained attached to the fallen dynasty. Mephibosheth was invited to court, and a place at the royal table on public days was assigned him, as is still the custom with Eastern monarchs. Saul's family estate, which had fallen to David in right of his wife (Num. 27:8), or been forfeited to the crown by Ish-bosheth's rebellion (ch. 12:8), was provided (vs. 11; also ch. 19:28), for enabling Mephibosheth to maintain an establishment suitable to his rank, and Ziba appointed steward to manage it, on the condition of receiving one-half of the produce in remuneration for his labor and expense, while the other moiety was to be paid as rent to the owner of the land (ch. 19:29). **10. Ziba had fifteen sons and twenty servants**—The mention of his sons and the slaves in his house was to show that Mephibosheth would be honored with an equipage "as one of the king's sons." **12. Mephibosheth had a young son, whose name was Micah**—Whether born before or after his residence in Jerusalem, cannot be ascertained. But through him the name and memory of the excellent Jonathan was preserved (see on I Chron. 8:34, 35; 9:40, 41).

CHAPTER 10

Vss. 1-5. David's Messengers, Sent to Comfort Hanun, Are Disgracefully Treated. **2. Then said David, I will show kindness unto Hanun, the son of Nahash, as his father showed kindness unto me**—It is probable that this was the Nahash against whom Saul waged war at Jabesh-gilead (I Sam. 11:11). David, on leaving Gath, where his life was exposed to danger, found an asylum with the king of Moab; and as Nahash, king of the Ammonites, was his nearest neighbor, it may be that during the feud between Saul and David, he, through enmity to the former, was kind and hospitable to David. **3. the princes of the children of Ammon said unto Hanun**—Their suspicion was not warranted either by any overt act or by any cherished design of David: it must have originated in their knowledge of the denunciations of God's law against them (Deut. 23:3-6), and of David's policy in steadfastly adhering to it. **4. Hanun took David's servants and shaved off the one-half of their beards**—From the long flowing dress of the Hebrews and other Orientals, the curtailment of their garments must have given them an aspect of gross indelicacy and ludicrousness. Besides, a knowledge of the extraordinary respect and value which has always been attached, and the gross insult that is implied in any indignity offered, to the beard in the East, will account for the shame which the deputies felt, and the determined spirit of revenge which burst out in all Israel on learning the outrage. Two instances are related in the modern history of Persia, of similar insults by kings of haughty and imperious temper, involving the nation in war; and we need not, therefore, be surprised that David vowed revenge for this wanton and public outrage. **5. Tarry at Jericho**—or in the neighborhood, after crossing the fords of the Jordan.

6-14. The Ammonites Overcome. **6. when the children of Ammon saw that they stank before David**—To chastise those insolent and inhospitable Ammonites, who had violated the common law of nations, David sent a large army under the command of Joab, while they, informed of the impending attack, made energetic preparations to repel it by engaging the services of an immense number of Syrian mercenaries. **Beth-rehob**—the capital of the low-lying region between Lebanon and Anti-Lebanon. **Zoba**—(see on ch: 8. 3). **of King Maachah**—His territories lay on the other side of Jordan, near Gilead (Deut. 3:14). **Ish-tob**—i.e., the men of Tob—the place of Jephthah's marauding adventures (see also I Chron. 19:6; Ps. 60, title). As the Israelite soldiers poured into the Ammonite territory, that people met them at the frontier town of Medeba (I Chron. 19:7-9), the native troops covering the city, while the Syrian mercenaries lay at some distance encamped in the fields. In making the attack, Joab divided his forces into two separate detachments—the one of which, under the command of his brother, Abishai, was to concentrate its attack upon the city, while he himself marched against the overwhelming host of mercenary auxiliaries. It was a just and necessary war that had been forced on Israel, and they could hope for the blessing of God upon their arms. With great judgment the battle opened against the mercenaries, who could not stand against the furious onset of Joab, and not feeling the cause their own, consulted their safety by flight. The Ammonites, who had placed their chief dependence upon a foreign aid, then retreated to entrench themselves within the walls of the town.—**14. So Joab returned and came to Jerusalem**—Probably the season was too far advanced for entering on a siege.

15-19. THE SYRIANS DEFEATED. **16. Hadadezer sent and brought out the Syrians that were beyond the river**—This prince had enjoyed a breathing-time after his defeat (ch. 8:3). But alarmed at the increasing power and greatness of David, as well as being an ally of the Ammonites, he levied a vast army not only in Syria, but in Mesopotamia, to invade the Hebrew kingdom. Shobach, his general, in pursuance of this design, had marched his troops as far as Kelam, a border town of eastern Manasseh, when David, crossing the Jordan by forced marches, suddenly surprised, defeated, and dispersed them. As a result of this great and decisive victory, all the petty kingdoms of Syria submitted and became his tributaries (see on I Chron. 19).

CHAPTER 11

Vss. 1. JOAB BESIEGES RABBAH. **1. at the time when kings go forth to battle**—The return of spring was the usual time of commencing military operations. This expedition took place the year following the war against the Syrians; and it was entered upon because the disaster of the former campaign having fallen chiefly upon the Syrian mercenaries, the Ammonites had not been punished for their insult to the ambassadors. **David sent Joab and his servants . . . they destroyed the children of Ammon**—The powerful army that Joab commanded ravaged the Ammonite country and committed great havoc both on the people and their property, until having reached the capital, they besieged Rabbah—"Rabbah" denotes a great city. This metropolis of the Ammonites was situated in the mountainous tract of Gilead, not far from the source of the Arnon. Extensive ruins are still found on its site.

2-12. DAVID COMMITS ADULTERY WITH BATH-SHEBA. **2. it came to pass in an eventide, that David arose from off his bed**—The Hebrews, like other Orientals, rose at daybreak, and always took a nap during the heat of the day. Afterwards they lounged in the cool of the evening on their flat-roofed terraces. It is probable that David had ascended to enjoy the open-air refreshment earlier than usual. **3. one said**—lit., he said to himself, "Is not this Bath-sheba?" etc. She seems to have been a celebrated beauty, whose renown had already reached the ears of David, as happens in the East, from reports carried by the women from harem to harem. **Bath-sheba, the daughter of Eliam**—or Ammiel (I Chron. 3:5), one of David's worthies (ch. 23: 34), and son of Ahithophel. **4. David sent messengers, and took her**—The despotic kings of the East, when they take a fancy for a woman, send an officer to the house were she lives, who announces it to be the royal pleasure she should remove to the palace. An apartment is there assigned to her; and if she is made queen, the monarch orders the announcement to be made that he has made choice of her to be queen. Many instances in modern Oriental history show the ease and despatch with which such secondary marriages are contracted, and a new beauty added to the royal seraglio. But David had to make a promise, or rather an express stipulation, to Bath-sheba, before she complied with the royal will (I Kings 1:13, 15, 17, 28); for in addition to her transcendent beauty, she appears to have been a woman of superior talents and address in obtaining the object of her ambition; in her securing that her son should succeed on the throne; in her promptitude to give notice of her pregnancy; in her activity in defeating Adonijah's natural expectation of succeeding to the crown; in her dignity as the king's mother—in all this we see very strong indications of the ascendency she gained and maintained over David, who, perhaps, had ample leisure and opportunity to discover the punishment of this unhappy connection in more ways than one [TAYLOR'S CALMET]. **5. the woman conceived, and sent and told David**—Some immediate measures of concealing their sin were necessary, as well for the king's honor as for her safety, for death was the punishment of an adulteress (Lev. 20:10). **8. David said to Uriah, Go down to thy house**—This sudden recall, the manner of the king, his frivolous questions (vs. 7), and his urgency for Uriah to sleep in his own house, probably awakened suspicions of the cause of this procedure. **there followed him a mess of meat from the king**—A portion of meat from the royal table, sent to one's own house or lodgings, is one of the greatest compliments which an Eastern prince can pay. **9. But Uriah slept at the door of the king's house**—It is customary for servants to sleep in the porch or long gallery; and the guards of the Hebrew king did the same. Whatever his secret suspicions might have been, Uriah's refusal to indulge in the enjoyment of domestic pleasure, and his determination to sleep "at the door of the king's house," arose (vs. 11) from a high and honorable sense of military duty and propriety. But, doubtless, the resolution of Uriah was overruled by that Providence which brings good out of evil, and which has recorded this sad episode for the warning of the church.

14-27. URIAH SLAIN. **14, 15. David wrote a letter to Joab, and sent it by the hand of Uriah . . . Set ye Uriah in the forefront of the hottest battle**—The various arts and stratagems by which the king tried to cajole Uriah, till at last he resorted to the horrid crime of murder—the cold-blooded cruelty of despatching the letter by the hands of the gallant but much-wronged soldier himself, the enlistment of Joab to be a partaker of his sin, the heartless affectation of mourning, and the indecent haste of his marriage with Bath-sheba—have left an indelible stain upon the character of David, and exhibit a painfully humiliating proof of the awful lengths to which the best of men may go when they forfeit the restraining grace of God.

CHAPTER 12

Vss. 1-6. NATHAN'S PARABLE. **1. the Lord sent Nathan unto David**—The use of parables is a favorite style of speaking among Oriental people, especially in the conveyance of unwelcome truth. This exquisitely pathetic parable was founded on a common custom of pastoral people who have pet lambs, which they bring up with their children, and which they address in terms of endearment. The atrocity of the real, however, far exceeded that of the fictitious offense. **5. the man that hath done this thing shall surely die**—This punishment was more severe than the case deserved, or than was warranted by the divine statute (Exod. 22:1. The sympathies of the king had been deeply enlisted, his indignation aroused, but his conscience was still asleep; and at the time when he was most fatally indulgent to his own sins, he was most ready to condemn the delinquencies and errors of others.

7-23. HE APPLIES IT TO DAVID, WHO CONFESSES HIS SIN, AND IS PARDONED. **7. Nathan said to David, Thou art the man**—These awful words pierced his heart, aroused his conscience, and brought him to his knees. The sincerity and depth of his penitent sorrow are evinced by the Psalms he composed [32; 51; 103]. He was pardoned, so far as related to the restoration of the divine favor. But as from his high character for piety, and his eminent rank in society, his deplorable fall was calculated to do great injury to the cause of religion, it was necessary that God should testify His abhorrence of sin by leaving even His own servant to reap the bitter temporal fruits. David was not himself doomed, according to his own view of what justice demanded (vs. 5); but he had to suffer a quadruple expiation in the successive deaths of four sons, besides a lengthened train of other evils. **8. I gave thee thy master's house, and thy master's wives**—The phraseology means nothing more than that God in His providence had given David, as king of Israel, everything that was Saul's. The history furnishes conclusive evidence that he never actually married any of the wives of Saul. But the harem of the preceding king belongs, according to Oriental notions, as a part of the regalia to his successor. **11. I will raise up evil against thee out of thine own house,** ... The prophet speaks of God threatening to do what He only permitted to be done. The fact is, that David's loss of character by the discovery of his crimes, tended, in the natural course of things, to diminish the respect of his family, to weaken the authority of his government, and to encourage the prevalence of many disorders throughout his kingdom. **15-23. the Lord struck the child** ... **and it was very sick**—The first visible chastisement inflicted on David appeared on the person of that child which was the evidence and monument of his guilt. His domestics were surprised at his conduct, and in explanation of its singularity, it is necessary to remark that the custom in the East is to leave the nearest relative of a deceased person to the full and undisturbed indulgence of his grief, till on the third or fourth day at farthest (John 11:17). Then the other relatives and friends visit him, invite him to eat, lead him to a bath, and bring him a change of dress, which is necessary from his having sat or lain on the ground. The surprise of David's servants, then,

who had seen his bitter anguish while the child was sick, arose apparently from this, that when he found it was dead, he who had so deeply lamented arose of himself from the earth, without waiting for their coming to him, immediately bathed and anointed himself, instead of appearing as a mourner, and after worshiping God with solemnity, returned to his wonted repast, without any interposition of others.

24, 25. SOLOMON IS BORN. **24. Bath-sheba** ... **bare a son, and he called his name Solomon**—i.e., peaceable. But Nathan gave him the name of Jedediah, by command of God, or perhaps only as an expression of God's love. This love and the noble gifts with which he was endowed, considering the criminality of the marriage from which he sprang, is a remarkable instance of divine goodness and grace.

26-31. RABBAH IS TAKEN. **26. Joab fought against Rabbah**—The time during which this siege lasted, since the intercourse with Bath-sheba, and the birth of at least one child, if not two, occurred during the progress of it, probably extended over two years. **27. the city of waters**—Rabbah, like Aroer, was divided into two parts—one the lower town, insulated by the winding course of the Jabbok, which flowed almost round it, and the upper and stronger town, called the royal city. "The first was taken by Joab, but the honor of capturing so strongly a fortified place as the other was an honor reserved for the king himself." **28. encamp against the city, and take it**—It has always been characteristic of Oriental despots to monopolize military honors; and as the ancient world knew nothing of the modern refinement of kings gaining victories by their generals, so Joab sent for David to command the final assault in person. A large force was levied for the purpose. David without much difficulty captured the royal city and obtained possession of its immense wealth. **lest I take the city, and it be called after my name**—The circumstance of a city receiving a new name after some great person, as Alexandria, Constantinople, Hyderabad, is of frequent occurrence in the ancient and modern history of the East. **30. he took the king's crown from off his head**—While the treasures of the city were given as plunder to his soldiers, David reserved to himself the crown, which was of rarest value. Its great weight makes it probable that it was like many ancient crowns, not worn, but suspended over the head, or fixed on a canopy on the top of the throne. **the precious stones**—*Hebrew,* "stone" was a round ball composed of pearls and other jewels, which was in the crown, and probably taken out of it to be inserted in David's own crown. **31. he brought forth the people** ... **and put them under saws** ... This excessive severity and employment of tortures, which the Hebrews on no other occasion are recorded to have practised, was an act of retributive justice on a people who were infamous for their cruelties (I Sam. 11:2; Amos 1:13).

CHAPTER 13

Vss. 1-5. AMNON LOVES TAMAR. **1. Tamar**—daughter of David by Maachah (ch. 3:3). **2. for she was a virgin**—Unmarried daughters were kept in close seclusion from the company of men; no strangers, nor even their relatives of the other sex, being permitted to see them without the presence of witnesses. Of course, Amnon must have seen Tamar, for he had conceived a violent passion for her, which, though forbidden by the law (Lev. 18:11), yet with the sanction of Abraham's example (Gen.

20:12), and the common practice in neighboring countries for princes to marry their half sisters, he seems not to have considered an improper connection. But he had no means of making it known to her, and the pain of that disappointment preying upon his mind produced a visible change in his appearance and health. **3. Jonadab, the son of Shimeah**—or Shammah (I Sam. 16:9). By the counsel and contrivance of this scheming cousin a plan was devised for obtaining an unrestricted interview with the object of his attachment. **4. my brother Absalom's sister**—In Eastern countries, where polygamy prevails, the girls are considered to be under the special care and protection of their uterine brother, who is the guardian of their interests and their honor, even more than their father himself (see on Gen. 34:6-25).

6-27. HE DEFILES HER. **6. Amnon lay down, and made himself sick**—The Orientals are great adepts in feigning sickness, whenever they have any object to accomplish. **let Tamar my sister come and make me a couple of cakes**—To the king Amnon spoke of Tamar as "his sister," a term artfully designed to hoodwink his father; and the request appeared so natural, the delicate appetite of a sick man requiring to be humored, that the king promised to send her. The cakes seem to have been a kind of fancy bread, in the preparation of which Oriental ladies take great delight. Tamar, flattered by the invitation, lost no time in rendering the required service in the house of her sick brother. **12-14. do not force me**—The remonstrances and arguments of Tamar were so affecting and so strong, that had not Amnon been violently goaded on by the lustful passion of which he had become the slave, they must have prevailed with him to desist from his infamous purpose. In bidding him, however, "speak to the king, for he will not withhold me from thee," it is probable that she urged this as her last resource, saying anything she thought would please him, in order to escape for the present out of his hands. **15. Then Amnon hated her exceedingly**—It is not unusual for persons instigated by violent and irregular passions to go from one extreme to another. In Amnon's case the sudden revulsion is easily accounted for; the atrocity of his conduct, with all the feelings of shame, remorse, and dread of exposure and punishment, now burst upon his mind, rendering the presence of Tamar intolerably painful to him. **17. bolt the door after her**—The street door of houses in the East is always kept barred—the bolts being of wood. In the great mansions, where a porter stands at the outside, this precaution is dispensed with; and the circumstance, therefore, of a prince giving an order so unusual shows the vehement perturbation of Amnon's mind. **18. garment of divers colours**—As embroidery in ancient times was the occupation or pastime of ladies of the highest rank, the possession of these parti-colored garments was a mark of distinction; they were worn exclusively by young women of royal condition. Since the art of manufacturing cloth stuffs has made so great progress, dresses of this variegated description are now more common in the East. **19. Tamar put ashes on her head, and rent her garment of divers colours . . . laid her hand on her head, and went on crying**—i.e., sobbing. Oriental manners would probably see nothing beyond a strong sense of the injury she had sustained, if Tamar actually rent her garments. But, as her veil is not mentioned, it is probable that Amnon had turned her out of doors without it, and she raised her hand with the design to conceal her face. By these signs, especially the rending of her

distinguishing robe, Absalom at once conjectured what had taken place. Recommending her to be silent about it and not publish her own and her family's dishonor, he gave no inkling of his angry feelings to Amnon. But all the while he was in secret "nursing his wrath to keep it warm," and only "biding his time" to avenge his sister's wrongs, and by the removal of the heir-apparent perhaps further also his ambitious designs. **20. So Tamar remained desolate in her brother Absalom's house**—He was her natural protector, and the children of polygamists lived by themselves, as if they constituted different families. **23. Absalom had sheepshearers in Baal-hazor, which is beside Ephraim**—A sheepshearing feast is a grand occasion in the East. Absalom proposed to give such an entertainment at his estate in Baal-hazor, about eight miles northeast of Jerusalem near a town called Ephraim (Josh. 11:10). He first invited the king and his court; but the king declining, on account of the heavy expense to which the reception of royalty would subject him, Absalom then limited the invitation to the king's sons, which David the more readily agreed to, in the hope that it might tend to the promotion of brotherly harmony and union.

28-36. AMNON IS SLAIN. **28. Absalom had commanded his servants, saying . . . when Amnon's heart is merry with wine . . . kill him, fear not**—On a preconcerted signal from their master, the servants, rushing upon Amnon, slew him at the table, while the rest of the brothers, horror-struck, and apprehending a general massacre, fled in affrighted haste to Jerusalem. **29. every man gat him upon his mule**—This had become the favorite equipage of the great. King David himself had a state mule (I Kings 1:33). The Syrian mules are, in activity, strength, and capabilities, still far superior to ours. **30. tidings came to David, saying, Absalom hath slain all the king's sons**—It was natural that in the consternation and tumult caused by so atrocious a deed, an exaggerated report should reach the court, which was at once plunged into the depths of grief and despair. But the information of Jonadab, who seems to have been aware of the plan, and the arrival of the other princes, made known the real extent of the catastrophe.

37-39. ABSALOM FLEES TO TALMAI. **37. Absalom fled, and went to Talmai**—The law as to premeditated murder (Num. 35:21) gave him no hope of remaining with impunity in his own country. The cities of refuge could afford him no sanctuary, and he was compelled to leave the kingdom, taking refuge at the court of Geshur, with his maternal grandfather, who would, doubtless, approve of his conduct.

CHAPTER 14

Vss. 1-21. JOAB INSTRUCTS A WOMAN OF TEKOAH. **2. Joab sent to Tekoah, and fetched thence a wise woman**—The king was strongly attached to Absalom; and having now got over his sorrow for the violent death of Amnon, he was desirous of again enjoying the society of his favorite son, who had now been three long years absent. But a dread of public opinion and a regard to the public interests made him hesitate about recalling or pardoning his guilty son; and Joab, whose discerning mind perceived this struggle between parental affection and royal duty, devised a plan for relieving the scruples, and, at the same time, gratifying the wishes, of his master. Having procured a countrywoman of superior intelligence and address, he directed her to seek an audience of the king, and by soliciting his royal interposition in the settlement of a domestic grievance, convinced him that the life of a murderer might in some cases be saved. Tekoah was about twelve miles south of Jerusalem, and six south of Bethlehem; and the design of bringing a woman from such a distance was to prevent either the petitioner being known, or the truth of her story easily investigated. Her speech was in the form of a parable—the circumstances—the language—the manner—well suited to the occasion, represented a case as like David's as it was policy to make it, so as not to be prematurely discovered. Having got the king pledged, she avowed it to be her design to satisfy the royal conscience, that in pardoning Absalom he was doing nothing more than he would have done in the case of a stranger, where there could be no imputation of partiality. The device succeeded; David traced its origin to Joab; and, secretly pleased at obtaining the judgment of that rough, but generally sound-thinking soldier, he commissioned him to repair to Geshur and bring home his exiled son. **7. they shall quench my coal which is left**—The life of man is compared in Scripture to a light. To quench the light of Israel (ch. 21:17) is to destroy the king's life; to ordain a lamp for any one (Ps. 132:17) is to grant him posterity; to quench a coal signifies here the extinction of this woman's only remaining hope that the name and family of her husband would be preserved. The figure is a beautiful one; a coal live, but lying under a heap of embers—all that she had to rekindle her fire—to light her lamp in Israel. **9. the woman said . . . O king, the iniquity be on me** —i.e., the iniquity of arresting the course of justice and pardoning a homicide, whom the Goel was bound to slay wherever he might find him, unless in a city of refuge. This was exceeding the royal prerogative, and acting in the character of an absolute monarch. The woman's language refers to a common precaution taken by the Hebrew judges and magistrates, solemnly to transfer from themselves the responsibility of the blood they doomed to be shed, either to the accusers or the criminals (ch. 1:16; 3:28); and sometimes the accusers took it upon themselves (Matt. 27:25). **13-17. Wherefore, then, hast thou thought such a thing against the people of God . . .**—Her argument may be made clear in the following paraphrase:—You have granted me the pardon of a son who had slain his brother, and yet you will not grant to your subjects the restoration of Absalom, whose criminality is not greater than my son's, since he killed his brother in similar circumstances of provocation. Absalom has reason to complain that he is treated by his own father more sternly and severely than the meanest subject in the realm; and the whole nation will have cause for saying that the king shows more attention to the petition of a humble woman than to the wishes and desires of a whole nation. The death of my son is a private loss to my family, while the preservation of Absalom is the common interest of all Israel, who now look to him as your successor on the throne.

22-33. JOAB BRINGS ABSALOM TO JERUSALEM. 22. To-day thy servant knoweth that I have found grace in thy sight—Joab betrayed not a little self-ishness amid his professions of joy at this act of grace to Absalom, and flattered himself that he now brought both father and son under lasting obligations. In considering this act of David, many extenuating circumstances may be urged in favor of it; the provocation given to Absalom; his being now

in a country where justice could not overtake him; the risk of his imbibing a love for heathen principles and worship; the safety and interests of the Hebrew kingdom; together with the strong predilection of the Hebrew people for Absalom, as represented by the stratagem of Joab—these considerations form a plausible apology for David's grant of pardon to his bloodstained son. But, in granting this pardon, he was acting in the character of an Oriental despot rather than a constitutional king of Israel. The feelings of the father triumphed over the duty of the king, who, as the supreme magistrate, was bound to execute impartial justice on every murderer, by the express law of God (Gen. 9:6; Num. 35:30, 31), which he had no power to dispense with (Deut. 18: 18; Josh. 1:8; I Sam. 10:25). **25. But in all Israel there was none to be so much praised as Absalom for his beauty**—This extraordinary popularity arose not only from his high spirit and courtly manners, but from his uncommonly handsome appearance. One distinguishing feature, seemingly an object of great admiration, was a profusion of beautiful hair. Its extraordinary luxuriance compelled him to cut it "at every year's end"; lit., "at times," "from time to time," when it was found to weigh 200 shekels— equal to 112 oz. troy; but as "the weight was after the king's shekel," which was less than the common shekel, the rate has been reduced as low as 3 lbs. 2 oz. [BOCHART], and even less by others. **28. So Absalom dwelt two full years in Jerusalem, and saw not the king's face**—Whatever error David committed in authorizing the recall of Absalom, he displayed great prudence and command over his feelings afterwards—for his son was not admitted into his father's presence but was confined to his own house and the society of his own family. This slight severity was designed to bring him to sincere repentance, on perceiving that his father had not fully pardoned him, as well as to convince the people of David's abhorrence of his crime. Not being allowed to appear at court, or to adopt any state, the courtiers kept aloof; even his cousin did not deem it prudent to go into his society. For two full years his liberty was more restricted, and his life more apart from his countrymen while living in Jerusalem, than in Geshur; and he might have continued in this disgrace longer, had he not, by a violent expedient, determined (vs. 30) to force his case on the attention of Joab, through whose kind and powerful influence a full reconciliation was effected between him and his father.

CHAPTER 15

Vss. 1-9. ABSALOM STEALS THE HEARTS OF ISRAEL. **1. Absalom prepared him chariots and horses, and fifty men to run before him**—This was assuming the state and equipage of a prince. The royal guards, called runners, avant-couriers, amounted to fifty (I Kings 1:5). The chariot, as the Hebrew indicates, was of a magnificent style; and the horses, a novelty among the Hebrew people, only introduced in that age as an appendage of royalty (Ps. 32:9; 66:12), formed a splendid retinue, which would make him "the observed of all observers." **2. Absalom rose up early, and stood beside the way of the gate**—Public business in the East is always transacted early in the morning—the kings sitting an hour or more to hear causes or receive petitions, in a court held anciently, and in many places still, in the open air at the city gateway; so that, as those whose circumstances led them to wait on King David required to be in attendance on his morning levees,

Absalom had to rise up early and stand beside the way of the gate. Through the growing infirmities of age, or the occupation of his government with foreign wars, many private causes had long lain undecided, and a deep feeling of discontent prevailed among the people. This dissatisfaction was artfully fomented by Absalom, who addressed himself to the various suitors; and after briefly hearing their tale, he gratified everyone with a favorable opinion of his case. Studiously concealing his ambitious designs, he expressed a wish to be invested with official power, only that he might accelerate the course of justice and advance the public interests. His professions had an air of extraordinary generosity and disinterestedness, which, together with his fawning arts in lavishing civilities on all, made him a popular favorite. Thus, by forcing a contrast between his own display of public spirit and the dilatory proceedings of the court, he created a growing disgust with his father's government, as weak, careless, or corrupt, and seduced the affections of the multitude, who neither penetrated the motive nor foresaw the tendency of his conduct. **7. after forty years**—It is generally admitted that an error has here crept into the text, and that instead of forty, we should read with the Syriac and Arabic versions, and Josephus, "four years"—i.e., after Absalom's return to Jerusalem, and his beginning to practice the base arts of gaining popularity. **my vow which I have vowed unto the Lord**—during his exile in Geshur. The purport of it was, that whenever God's providence should pave the way for his re-establishment in Jerusalem, he would offer a sacrifice of thanksgiving. Hebron was the spot selected for the performance of this vow, ostensibly as being his native place (ch. 3:3), and a famous high place, where sacrifices were frequently offered before the temple was built; but really as being in many respects the most suitable for the commencement of his rebellious enterprise. David, who always encouraged piety and desired to see religious engagements punctually performed, gave his consent and his blessing.

10-12. He Forms a Conspiracy. **10. Absalom sent spies throughout all the tribes of Israel**—These emissaries were to sound the inclination of the people, to further interests of Absalom, and exhort all the adherents of his party to be in readiness to join his standard as soon as they should hear that he had been proclaimed king. As the summons was to be made by the sound of trumpets, it is probable that care had been taken to have trumpeters stationed on the heights, and at convenient stations—a mode of announcement that would soon spread the news over all the country of his inauguration to the throne. **11. with Absalom went two hundred men ... that were called**—From their quality, reputation, and high standing, such as would create the impression that the king patronized the movement and, being aged and infirm, was willing to adopt his oldest and noblest son to divide with him the cares and honors of government. **12. Absalom sent for Ahithophel**—who he knew was ready to join the revolt, through disgust and revenge, as Jewish writers assert, at David's conduct towards Bath-sheba, who was his granddaughter. **Giloh**—near Hebron. **the conspiracy was strong**—The rapid accession of one place after another in all parts of the kingdom to the party of the insurgents, shows that deep and general dissatisfaction existed at this time against the person and government of David. The remnant of Saul's partisans, the unhappy affair of Bath-sheba, the overbearing insolence and crimes of Joab, negligence and obstruction in the administration of justice—these were some of the principal causes that contributed to the success of this widespread insurrection.

13-37. David Flees from Jerusalem. **14. David said .. ., Arise, and let us flee**—David, anxious for the preservation of the city which he had beautified, and hopeful of a greater support throughout the country, wisely resolved on leaving Jerusalem. **18. all the Gittites, six hunderd men**—These were a body of foreign guards, natives of Gath, whom David, when in the country of the Philistines, had enlisted in his service, and kept around his person. Addressing their commander, Ittai, he made a searching trial of their fidelity in bidding them (vs. 19) abide with the new king. **23. the brook Kidron**—a winter torrent that flows through the valley between the city and the eastern side of the Mount of Olives. **24. Zadok also and all the Levites .. ., bearing the ark**—Knowing the strong religious feelings of the aged king, they brought it to accompany him in his distress. But as he could not doubt that both the ark and their sacred office would exempt them from the attacks of the rebels, he sent them back with it—not only that they might not be exposed to the perils of uncertain wandering—for he seems to place more confidence in the symbol of the divine presence than in God Himself—but that, by remaining in Jerusalem, they might render him greater service by watching the enemy's movements. **30. David went up by the ascent of mount Olivet**—The same pathway over that mount has been followed ever since that memorable day. **had his head covered**—with a mourning wrapper. The humility and resignation of David marked strongly his sanctified spirit, induced by contrition for his transgressions. He had fallen, but it was the fall of the upright; and he rose again, submitting himself meekly in the meantime to the will of God [Chalmers]. **31. David said, Turn, O Lord, ... the counsel of Ahithophel**—this senator being the mainstay of the conspiracy. **32. when David was come to the top of the mount, where he worshipped**—looking towards Jerusalem, where were the ark and tabernacle. **Hushai the Archite**—A native of Archi, on the frontiers of Benjamin and Ephraim (Josh. 16:2). Comparing the prayer against Ahithophel with the counsel to Hushai, we see how strongly a spirit of fervent piety was combined in his character with the devices of an active and far-seeing policy.

CHAPTER 16

Vss. 1-4. Ziba, by False Suggestions, Claims His Master's Inheritance. **1. Ziba the servant of Mephibosheth met him**—This crafty man, anticipating the certain failure of Absalom's conspiracy, took steps to prepare for his future advancement on the restoration of the king. **a bottle of wine**—a large goatskin vessel. Its size made the supply of wine proportioned to the rest of his present. **2. The asses be for the king's household to ride on**—The royal fugitives were moving on foot, not from inability to procure conveyances, but as being suitable to their present state of humiliation and penitence. **3. To-day shall the house of Israel restore me the kingdom of my father**—Such a hope might not unnaturally arise at this period of civil distraction, that the family of David would destroy themselves by their mutual broils, and the people reinstate the old dynasty. There was an air of plausibility in Ziba's story. Many, on whom the king had conferred favors, were now deserting him. No wonder, therefore, that in the excitement of momentary feeling, believing, on the report of a slanderer, Mephibosheth to be among the number, he pronounced a rash and unrighteous judgment by which a great injury was inflicted on the character and interests of a devoted friend. 5-19. SHIMEI CURSES DAVID. **5. when King David came to Bahurim**—a city of Benjamin (ch. 3: 16; 19:16). It is, however, only the confines of the district that are here meant. **Shimei, a man of the family of Saul**—The misfortune of his family, and the occupation by David of what they considered their rightful possessions, afforded a natural, if not a justifiable cause for this ebullition of rude insults and violence. He upbraided David as an ambitious usurper, and charged him, as one whose misdeeds had recoiled upon his own head, to surrender a throne to which he was not entitled. His language was that of a man incensed by the wrongs that he conceived had been done to his house. David was guiltless of the crime of which Shimei accused him; but his conscience reminded him of other flagrant iniquities; and he, therefore, regarded the cursing of this man as a chastisement from heaven. His answer to Abishai's proposal evinced the spirit of deep and humble resignation—the spirit of a man who watched the course of Providence, and acknowledged Shimei as the instrument of God's chastening hand. One thing is remarkable, that he acted more independently of the sons of Zeruiah in this season of great distress than he could often muster courage to do in the days of his prosperity and power. **13. went along on the hill's side over against him**—as he descended the rough road on the eastern side of the Mount of Olives, "went along the side"—lit., the rib of the hill. **threw stones at him** —as a mark of contempt and insult. **cast dust**—As if to add insult to injury, clouds of dust were thrown by this disloyal subject in the path of his unfortunate sovereign. **14. refreshed themselves there**—i.e., in the city of Bahurim. **15-19. Hushai said unto Absalom, God save the king**—Hushai's devotion to David was so well known, that his presence in the camp of the conspirators excited great surprise. Professing, however, with great address, to consider it his duty to support the cause which the course of Providence and the national will had seemingly decreed should triumph, and urging his friendship for the father as a ground of confidence in his fidelity to the son, he persuaded Absalom of his sincerity, and was admitted among the councillors of the new king. 20-23. AHITHOPHEL'S COUNSEL. **20. Give counsel among you what we shall do**—This is the first cabinet council on record, although the deference paid to Ahithophel gave him the entire direction of the proceedings. **21 Ahithophel said unto Absalom** —This councillor saw that now the die was cast; half measures would be inexpedient. To cut off all possibility of reconciliation between the king and his rebellious son, he gave this atrocious advice regarding the treatment of the royal women who had been left in charge of the palace. Women, being held sacred, are generally left inviolate in the casualties of war. The history of the East affords only one parallel to this infamous outrage of Absalom.

CHAPTER 17

Vss. 1-14. AHITHOPHEL'S COUNSEL OVERTHROWN BY HUSHAI. **1. Moreover Ahithophel said unto Absalom**—The recommendation to take prompt and decisive measures before the royalist forces could be collected and arranged, evinced the deep political sagacity of this councillor. The adoption of his advice would have extinguished the cause of David; and it affords a dreadful proof of the extremities to which the heartless prince was, to secure his ambitious objects, prepared to go, that the parricidal counsel "pleased Absalom well, and all the elders of Israel." It was happily overruled, however, by the address of Hushai, who saw the imminent danger to which it would expose the king and the royal cause. He dwelt upon the warlike character and military experience of the old king—represented him and his adherents as mighty men, who would fight with desperation; and who, most probably, secure in some stronghold, would be beyond reach, while the smallest loss of Absalom's men at the outset might be fatal to the success of the conspiracy. But his dexterity was chiefly displayed in that part of his counsel which recommended a general levy throughout the country; and that Absalom should take command of it in person—thereby flattering at once the pride and ambition of the usurper. The bait was caught by the vainglorious and wicked prince. **12. we will light upon him as the dew falleth upon the ground**— No image could have symbolized the sudden onset of an enemy so graphically to an Oriental mind as the silent, irresistible, and rapid descent of this natural moisture on every field and blade of grass. **13. all Israel shall bring ropes to that city**—In besieging a town, hooks or cranes were often thrown upon the walls or turrets, by which, with ropes attached to them, the besiegers, uniting all their force, pulled down the fortifications in a mass of ruins. **14. The counsel of Hushai is better than the counsel of Ahithopel**—The reasons specified being extremely plausible, and expressed in the strong hyperbolical language suited to dazzle an Oriental imagination, the council declared in favor of Hushai's advice; and their resolution was the immediate cause of the discomfiture of the rebellion, although the council itself was only a link in the chain of causation held by the controlling hand of the Lord. 15-22. SECRET INTELLIGENCE SENT TO DAVID. **16. send quickly, and tell David**—Apparently doubting that his advice would be followed, Hushai ordered secret intelligence to be conveyed to David of all that transpired, with an urgent recommendation to cross the Jordan without a moment's delay, lest Ahithophel's address and influence might produce a change on the prince's mind, and an immediate pursuit be determined on. **17. by En-rogel**— the fuller's well in the neighborhood of Jerusalem, below the junction of the valley of Hinnom with that of Jehoshaphat. **18. and came to a man's house in Bahurim, which had a well in his court**—The court was that of the house, and the well an empty cistern. All the houses of the better class are furnished with such reservoirs. Nothing could more easily happen than that one of these wells, in consequence of a deficiency of water, should become dry and it would then answer as a place of retreat, such as David's friends found in the man's house at Bahurim. The spreading of a covering over the well's mouth for the drying of corn is a common practice. 23-29. AHITHOPHEL HANGS HIMSELF. **23. when Ahithophel saw that his counsel was not followed** —His vanity was wounded, his pride mortified on finding that his ascendency was gone; but that chagrin was aggravated by other feelings—a painful conviction that through the delay which had been resolved on, the cause of Absalom was lost. Hastening home, therefore, he arranged his private affairs, and knowing that the storm of retributive vengeance would fall chiefly upon him as the instigator and prop of the rebellion, he hanged himself. It may be remarked that the Israelites did not, at that time, refuse the rites of sepulture even to those who died by their own hands. He had an imitator in Judas, who resembled him in his treason, as well as in his infamous end. **24. Then David came to Mahanaim**—in the high eastern country of Gilead, the seat of Ish-bosheth's government. **Absalom passed over Jordan** —It is not said how long an interval elapsed, but there must have been sufficient time to make the intended levy throughout the kingdom. **25. Amasa**—By the genealogy it appears that this captain stood in the same relation to David as Joab, both being his nephews. Of course, Amasa was Absalom's cousin, and though himself an Israelite, his father was an Ishmaelite (I Chron. 2:17). Nahash is thought by some to be another name of Jesse, or according to others, the name of Jesse's wife. **27. when David was come to Mahanaim**— The necessities of the king and his followers were hospitably ministered to by three chiefs, whose generous loyalty is recorded with honor in the sacred narrative. **Shobi**—must have been a brother of Hanun. Disapproving, probably, of that young king's outrage upon the Israelite ambassadors, he had been made governor of Ammon by David on the conquest of that country. **Machir**—(See ch. 9: 4). Supposed by some to have been a brother of Bath-sheba, and Barzillai, a wealthy old grandee, whose great age and infirmities made his loyal devotion to the distressed monarch peculiarly affecting. The supplies they brought, which (besides beds for the weary) consisted of the staple produce of their rich lands and pastures, may be classified a follows: eatables—wheat, barley, flour, beans, lentils, sheep, and cheese; drinkables—"honey and butter" or cream. which, being mixed together, form a thin, diluted beverage, light, cool, and refreshing. Being considered a luxurious refreshment (Song of Sol. 4:11), the supply of it shows the high respect that was paid to David by his loyal and faithful subjects at Mahanaim. **29. in the wilderness**—spread out beyond the cultivated tablelands into the steppes of Hauran.

CHAPTER 18

Vss. 1-4. David Reviewing the Armies. **1. David numbered the people that were with him**— The hardy mountaineers of Gilead came in great numbers at the call of their chieftains, so that, although without money to pay any troops, David soon found himself at the head of a considerable army. A pitched battle was now inevitable. But so much depending on the life of the king, he was not allowed to take the field in person; and he therefore divided his forces into three detachments under Joab, Abishai, and Ittai, the commander of the foreign guards. 5-13. Gives Them Charge of Absalom. **5. Deal gently for my sake with the young man, even with Absalom**—This affecting charge, which the king gave to his generals, proceeded not only from his overwhelming affection for his children, but from his consciousness that this rebellion was the chastisement of his own crimes, Absalom being merely an instrument in the hand of retributive Providence;—and also from his piety, lest the unhappy prince should die with his sins unrepented of. **6. wood of Ephraim**—This wood, of course, was on the

east of Jordan. Its name was derived, according to some, from the slaughter of the Ephraimites by Jephthah—according to others, from the connection of blood with the transjordanic Manasseh. **7. the people of Israel were slain**—This designation, together with the immense slaughter mentioned later, shows the large extent to which the people were enlisted in this unhappy civil contest. **8. the wood devoured more people that the sword**—The thick forest of oaks and terebinths, by obstructing the flight, greatly aided the victors in the pursuit. **9. Absalom met the servants of David**—or was overtaken. "It is necessary to be continually on one's guard against the branches of trees; and when the hair is worn in large locks floating down the back, as was the case with a young man of the party to which I belonged, any thick boughs interposing in the path might easily dislodge a rider from his seat, and catch hold of his flowing hair" [Hartley]. Some, however, think that the sacred historian points not so much to the hair, as to the *head* of Absalom, which, being caught while running between two branches, was enclosed so firmly that he could not disengage himself from the hold, nor make use of his hands. **the mule that was under him went away**—The Orientals, not having saddles as we do, do not sit so firmly on the beasts they ride. Absalom quitting his hold of the bridle, apparently to release himself when caught in the oak, the mule escaped. **11. Joab said unto the man that told him, . . . I would have given thee ten shekels of silver and a girdle**— i.e., would have raised him from the ranks to the status of a commissioned officer. Besides a sum of money, a girdle, curiously and richly wrought, was among the ancient Hebrews a mark of honor, and sometimes bestowed as a reward of military merit. This soldier, however, who may be taken as a fair sample of David's faithful subjects, had so great a respect for the king's wishes, that no prospect of reward would have tempted him to lay violent hands on Absalom. But Joab's stern sense of public duty, which satisfied him that there could be neither safety to the king, nor peace to the kingdom, nor security to him and other loyal subjects, so long as that turbulent prince lived, overcame his sensibilities, and looking upon the charge given to the generals as more befitting a parent than a prince, he ventured to disobey it. 14-32. He Is Slain by Joab. **14. he took three darts . . . and thrust them through the heart of Absalom**—The deed, partially done by Joab, was completed by his bodyguard. Being a violation of the expressed wish, as well as of all the fond paternal feelings of David, it must have been deeply offensive to the king, nor was it ever forgotten (I Kings 2:5); and yet there is the strongest reason for believing that Joab, in doing it, was actuated by a sincere regard to the interests of David, both as a man and a monarch. **16. Joab blew the trumpet . . . and held back the people**—Knowing that by the death of the usurper there was no occasion for further bloodshed, he put an end to the pursuit and thereby evinced the temperate policy of his conduct. However harsh and unfeeling to the king Joab may appear, there can be no doubt that he acted the part of a wise statesman in regarding the peace and welfare of the kingdom more than his master's private inclinations, which were opposed to strict justice as well as his own interests. Absalom deserved to die by the divine law (Deut. 21:18, 21), as well as being an enemy to his king and country; and no time was more fitting than when he met that death in open battle.

17. they took Absalom, and cast him into a great pit . . . and laid a very great heap of stones upon him—The people of the East indicate their detestation of the memory of an infamous person by throwing stones at the place where he is buried. The heap is increased by the gradual accumulation of stones which passers-by add to it. **18. Absalom in his lifetime had . . . reared for himself a pillar**—lit., *hand.* In the valley of Jehoshaphat, on the east of Jerusalem, is a tomb or cenotaph, said to be this "pillar" or monument: it is twenty-four feet square, dome-topped, and reaches forty feet in height. This may occupy the spot, but cannot itself be the work of Absalom, as it evidently bears the style of a later architecture. **19. Then said Ahimaaz . . . Let me . . . run and bear the king tidings**—The reasons why Joab declined to accept Ahimaaz' offer to bear intelligence of the victory to David, and afterwards let him go along with another, are variously stated by commentators—but they are of no importance. Yet the alacrity of the messengers, as well as the eager excitement of the expectants, is graphically described. **23. by the way of the plain**—or *ciccar,* circle. This word is only used elsewhere in connection with the valley of the Jordan. It is possible that there may have been a place or region so called on the tablelands of Gilead, as the *Septuagint* seems to indicate. Or Mahanaim may have been so situated, with the regard to the battlefield, as to be more easily accessible by a descent to the plain of the Jordan, than over the hills themselves. Or the word may signify (as EWALD explains) a manner of quick running [STANLEY]. **24. David sat between the two gates**—i.e., in the tower-house on the wall that overhung the gate of Mahanaim. Near it was a watchtower, on which a sentinel was posted, as in times of war, to notify every occurrence. The delicacy of Ahimaaz' communication was made up by the unmistakable plainness of Cushi's. The death of Absalom was a heavy trial, and it is impossible not to sympathize with the outburst of feeling by which David showed that all thoughts of the victory he had won as a king were completely sunk in the painful loss he had sustained as a father. The extraordinary ardor and strength of his affection for this worthless son break out in the redundancy and vehemence of his mournful ejaculations.

CHAPTER 19

Vss . 1-8. JOAB CAUSES THE KING TO CEASE MOURNING. **3. the people gat them by stealth . . . to the city**—The rumor of the king's disconsolate condition spread a universal and unseasonable gloom. His troops, instead of being welcomed back (as a victorious army always was) with music and other demonstrations of public joy, slunk secretly and silently into the city, as if ashamed after the commission of some crime. **4. the king covered his face** —one of the usual signs of mourning (see on ch. 15: 30). **7. Thou hast shamed . . . the faces of all thy servants**—by withdrawing thyself to indulge in grief, as if their services were disagreeable and their devotion irksome to thee. Instead of hailing their return with joy and gratitude, thou hast refused them the small gratification of seeing thee. Joab's remonstrance was right and necessary, but it was made with harshness. He was one of those persons who spoil their important services by the insolence of their manners, and who always awaken a feeling of obligation in those to whom they render any serv-

ices. He spoke to David in a tone of hauteur that ill became a subject to show towards his king. **7. Now . . . arise, go forth, and speak comfortably unto thy servants**—The king felt the truth of Joab's reprimand; but the threat by which it was enforced, grounded as it was on the general's unbounded popularity with the army, showed him to be a dangerous person; and that circumstance, together with the violation of an express order to deal gently for his sake with Absalom, produced in David's mind a settled hatred, which was strongly manifested in his last directions to Solomon. **8. the king arose, and sat in the gate**—He appeared daily in the usual place for the hearing of causes. **all the people came before the king**—i.e., the loyal natives who had been faithful to his government, and fought in his cause. **Israel had fled**—i.e., the adherents of Absalom, who, on his defeat, had dispersed and saved themselves by flight.

9-43. THE ISRAELITES BRING THE KING BACK. **9. all the people were at strife throughout the tribes of Israel**—The kingdom was completely disorganized. The sentiments of three different parties are represented in verses 9 and 10: the royalists, the adherents of Absalom who had been very numerous, and those who were indifferent to the Davidic dynasty. In these circumstances the king was right in not hastening back, as a conqueror, to reascend his throne. A re-election was, in some measure, necessary. He remained for some time on the other side of Jordan, in expectation of being invited back. That invitation was given without, however, the concurrence of Judah. David, disappointed and vexed by his own tribe's apparent lukewarmness, despatched the two high priests to rouse the Judahites to take a prominent interest in his cause. It was the act of a skilful politician. Hebron having been the seat of the rebellion, it was graceful on his part to encourage their return to allegiance and duty; it was an appeal to their honor not to be the last of the tribes. But this separate message, and the preference given to them, occasioned an outburst of jealousy among the other tribes that was nearly followed by fatal consequences. **13. And say ye to Amasa,** etc.—This also was a dextrous stroke of policy. David was fully alive to the importance, for extinguishing the rebellion, of withdrawing from that cause the only leader who could keep it alive; and he, therefore, secretly intimated his intention to raise Amasa to the command of the army in the place of Joab, whose overbearing haughtiness had become intolerable. The king justly reckoned, that from natural temper as well as gratitude for the royal pardon, he would prove a more tractable servant; and David, doubtless, intended in all sincerity to fulfil this promise. But Joab managed to retain his high position (see on ch. 20). **14. he bowed the heart of all the men of Judah**—i.e., Amasa, who had been won over, used his great influence in re-attaching the whole tribe of Judah to the interest of David. **15. Judah came to Gilgal**—the most convenient place where preparations could be made for bringing the king and court over the Jordan. **16. Shimei . . . a thousand men of Benjamin with him**—This display of his followers was to show what force he could raise against or in support of the king. Expressing the deepest regret for his former outrageous conduct, he was pardoned on the spot; and although the son of Zeruiah urged the expediency of making this chief a public example, his officiousness was repulsed by David with magnanimity, and with the greater confidence that he felt himself now re-established in the kingdom (see on I Kings 2:8,9). **17. Ziba, the**

servant of the house of Saul—He had deceived his master; and when ordered to make ready the ass for the lame prince to go and meet the king, he slipped away by himself to pay court first; so that Mephibosheth, being lame, had to remain in Jerusalem till the king's arrival. **18. ferry boat**—probably rafts, which are still used on that part of the river. **20. I am come the first . . . of all the house of Joseph**—i.e., before all the rest of *Israel* (Ps. 77:15; 80:1; 81: 5; Zech. 10:6). **24-30. Mephibosheth . . . came down to meet the king.** The reception given to Mephibosheth was less creditable to David. The sincerity of that prince's grief for the misfortunes of the king cannot be doubted. "He had neither dressed his feet"—not taken the bath, "nor trimmed his beard." The Hebrews cut off the hair on the upper lip (see on Lev. 13:45), and cheeks, but carefully cherished it on the chin from ear to ear. Besides dyeing it black or red colors, which, however, is the exception, and not the rule in the East, there are various modes of trimming it: they train it into a massy bushy form, swelling and round; or they terminate it like a pyramid, in a sharp point. Whatever the mode, it is always trimmed with the greatest care; and they usually carry a small comb for the purpose. The neglect of this attention to his beard was an undoubted proof of the depth of Mephibosheth's grief. The king seems to have received him upbraidingly, and not to have been altogether sure either of his guilt or innocence. It is impossible to commend the cavalier treatment, any more than to approve the partial award, of David in this case. If he were too hurried and distracted by the pressure of circumstances to inquire fully into the matter, he should have postponed his decision; for if by "dividing the land" (vs. 29) he meant that the former arrangement should be continued by which Mephibosheth was acknowledged the proprietor, and Ziba the farmer, it was a hardship inflicted on the owner to fix him with a tenant who had so grossly slandered him. But if by "dividing the land," they were now to share alike, the injustice of the decision was greatly increased. In any view, the generous, disinterested spirit displayed by Mephibosheth was worthy a son of the noble-hearted Jonathan. **31-40. Barzillai the Gileadite**—The rank, great age, and chivalrous devotion of this Gileadite chief wins our respect. His declining to go to court, his recommendation of his son, his convoy across the Jordan, and his parting scene with the king, are interesting incidents. What mark of royal favor was bestowed on Chimham has not been recorded; but it is probable that David gave a great part of his personal patrimony in Bethlehem to Chimham and his heirs in perpetuity (Jer. 41:17). **35. the voice of singing men and singing women**—Bands of professional musicians form a prominent appendage to the courts of Oriental princes. **37. buried by the grave of my father and my mother**—This is an instance of the strong affection of people in the East towards the places of sepulture appropriated to their families. **40-43. the king went on to Gilgal, . . . and all the people of Judah conducted the king, and also half the people of Israel**—Whether from impatience to move on or from some other cause, David did not wait till all the tribes had arrived to conduct him on his return to the capital. The procession began as soon as Amasa had brought the Judahite escort, and the preference given to this tribe produced a bitter jealousy, which was nearly kindling a civil war fiercer than that which had just ended. A war of words ensued between the tribes—Israel resting their argument on their superior numbers; "they had ten

parts in the king," whereas Judah had no more than one. Judah grounded their right to take the lead, on the ground of their nearer relationship to the king. This was a claim dangerous to the house of David; and it shows the seeds were already sown for that tribal dissension which, before long, led to the dismemberment of the kingdom.

CHAPTER 20

Vss. 1-9. SHEBA MAKES A PARTY IN ISRAEL. 1. Sheba . . . a Benjamite—Though nothing is known of this man, he must have been a person of considerable power and influence, before he could have raised so sudden and extensive a sedition. He belonged to the tribe of Benjamin, where the adherents of Saul's dynasty were still numerous; and perceiving the strong disgust of the other tribes with the part assumed by Judah in the restoration, his ill-designing heart resolved to turn it to the overthrow of David's authority in Israel. **every man to his tents**—This proverbial expression may have had its foundation in the fact, that many of the Israelite peasantry adhered to the custom of the patriarchs who tilled land, and yet lived in tents, as Syrian peasants often do still. This was the usual watchword of national insurrection, and from the actual temper of the people, it was followed by effects beyond what he probably anticipated. **2. from Jordan even to Jerusalem**—The quarrel had broken out shortly after the crossing of the Jordan, between Judah and the other tribes, who withdrew; so that Judah was left nearly alone to conduct the king to the metropolis. **3. the king took the ten women his concubines**—Jewish writers say that the widowed queens of Hebrew monarchs were not allowed to marry again but were obliged to pass the rest of their lives in strict seclusion. David treated his concubines in the same manner after the outrage committed on them by Absalom. They were not divorced, for they were guiltless; but they were no longer publicly recognized as his wives; nor was their confinement to a sequestered life a very heavy doom, in a region where women have never been accustomed to go much abroad. **4. Then said the king to Amasa, Assemble me the men of Judah within three days**—Amasa is now installed in the command which David had promised him. The revolt of the ten tribes, probably, hastened the public declaration of this appointment, which he hoped would be popular with them, and Amasa was ordered within three days to levy a force from Judah sufficient to put down the insurrection. The appointment was a blunder, and the king soon perceived his error. The specified time passed, but Amasa could not muster the men. Dreading the loss of time, the king gave the commission to Abishai, and not to Joab—a new affront, which, no doubt, wounded the pride of the stern and haughty old general. But he hastened with his attached soldiers to go as second to his brother, determined to take the first opportunity of wreaking his vengeance on his successful rival. **8. Amasa went before them**—Having collected some forces, he by a rapid march overtook the expedition at Gibeon, and assumed the place of commander; in which capacity, he was saluted, among others, by Joab. **Joab's garment, that he had put on, was girded unto him**—in the fashion of travelers and soldiers. **a sword . . . and, as he went forth, it fell out**—i.e., out of the scabbard. According to Josephus, he let it drop on purpose as he was accosting Amasa, that stooping, as it were accidentally, to pick it up, he might salute the new general with the naked sword in his hand, without exciting any suspicion of his design. "He went forth" in a ceremonious manner to meet Amasa, now commander-in-chief, in order to seem to render to that officer, whom he considered as usurping his post, a conspicuous honor and homage. **9. took Amasa by the beard with the right hand to kiss him**—This act, common with two friends on meeting when one of them returns from a journey, indicates respect as well as kindliness, and the performance of it evinced the deep hypocrisy of Joab, who thereby put Amasa off his guard. No wonder, then, that while this act of friendly gratulation after long absence occupied Amasa's attention, he did not perceive the sword that was in Joab's *left* hand. The action of Joab was indeed a high compliment, but neither suspicious nor unusual and to this compliment, Amasa paying attention and no doubt returning it with suitable politeness, he could little expect the fatal event that Joab's perfidy produced.

10-13. AMASA IS SLAIN. 10. smote him . . . in the fifth rib—the seat of the liver and bowels, where wounds are mortal. **struck him not again**—i.e., despatched him at the first blow. **11. He that favoureth Joab, and he that is for David, let him go after Joab** —It is a striking proof of Joab's unrivalled influence over the army, that with this villainous murder perpetrated before their eyes they unanimously followed him as their leader in pursuit of Sheba. A soldier conjoined his name with David's, and such a magic spell was in the word "Joab," that all the people "went on"—Amasa's men as well as the rest. The conjunction of these two names is very significant. It shows that the one could not afford to do without the other—neither Joab to rebel against David, nor David to get rid of Joab, though hating him.

14, 15. JOAB PURSUES SHEBA UNTO ABEL. 14. he went through all the tribes of Israel unto Abel— beating up for recruits. But there the prompt marches of Joab overtook and hemmed him in by a close siege of the place. **15. Abel of Beth-maachah** —a verdant place—the addition of "Maachah" betokening that it belonged to the district Maachah, which lay far up the Jordan at the foot of Lebanon.

16-22. A WISE WOMAN SAVES THE CITY BY SHEBA'S HEAD. 16. Then cried a wise woman— The appeal of this woman, who, like Deborah, was probably a judge or governess of the place, was a strong one. **18. They were wont to speak in old time**—The translation of the margin gives a better meaning, which is to this effect: When the people saw thee lay siege to Abel, they said, Surely he will ask if we will have peace, for the law (Deut. 20:10) prescribes that he should offer peace to strangers, much more then to Israelitish cities; and if he do this, we shall soon bring things to an amicable agreement, for we are a peaceable people. The answer of Joab brings out the character of that ruthless veteran as a patriot at heart, who, on securing the author of this insurrection, was ready to put a stop to further bloodshed and release the peaceable inhabitants from all molestation.

23-26. DAVID'S GREAT OFFICERS. 23. Now Joab was over all the host of Israel—David, whatever his private wishes, found that he possessed not the power of removing Joab; so winking at the murder of Amasa, he re-established that officer in his former post of commander-in-chief. The enumeration of David's cabinet is here given to show that the government was re-established in its wonted course.

CHAPTER 21

VSS. 1-9. THE THREE YEARS' FAMINE FOR THE GIBEONITES CEASE BY HANGING SEVEN OF SAUL'S SONS. 1. the Lord answered, It is for Saul, and for his bloody house, because he slew the Gibeonites— The sacred history has not recorded either the time or the reason of this massacre. Some think that they were sufferers in the atrocity perpetrated by Saul at Nob (I Sam. 22:19), where many of them may have resided as attendants of the priests; while others suppose it more probable that the attempt was made afterwards, with a view to regain the popularity he had lost throughout the nation by that execrable outrage. **2. in his zeal to the children of Israel and Judah**—Under pretense of a rigorous and faithful execution of the divine law regarding the extermination of the Canaanites, he set himself to expel or destroy those whom Joshua had been deceived into sparing. His real object seems to have been, that the possessions of the Gibeonites, being forfeited to the crown, might be divided among his own people (cf. I Sam. 22:7). At all events, his proceeding against this people was in violation of a solemn oath, and involving *national* guilt. The famine was, in the wise and just retribution of Providence, made a *national* punishment, since the Hebrews either assisted in the massacre, or did not interpose to prevent it; since they neither endeavored to repair the wrong, nor expressed any horror of it; and since a general protracted chastisement might have been indispensable to inspire a proper respect and protection to the Gibeonite remnant that survived. **6. Let seven men of his sons be delivered unto us, and we will hang them up unto the Lord**— The practice of the Hebrews, as of most Oriental nations, was to slay first, and afterwards to suspend on a gibbet, the body not being left hanging after sunset. The king could not refuse this demand of the Gibeonites, who, in making it, were only exercising their right as blood-avengers; and, although through fear and a sense of weakness they had not hitherto claimed satisfaction, yet now that David had been apprised by the oracle of the cause of the long-prevailing calamity, he felt it his duty to give the Gibeonites full satisfaction—hence their specifying the number seven—which was reckoned full and complete. And if it should seem unjust to make the descendants suffer for a crime which, in all probability, originated with Saul himself, yet his sons and grandsons might be the instruments of his cruelty, the willing and zealous executors of this bloody *raid*. **the king said, I will give them**—David cannot be charged with doing this as an indirect way or ridding himself of rival competitors for the throne, for those delivered up were only collateral branches of Saul's family, and never set up any claim to the sovereignty. Moreover, David was only granting the request of the Gibeonites as God had bidden him do. **8. the five sons of Michal the daughter of Saul whom she brought up for Adriel** —Merab, Michal's sister, was the wife of Adriel; but Michal adopted and brought up the boys under her care. **9. they hanged them in the hill before the Lord**—Deeming themselves not bound by the criminal law of Israel (Deut. 21:22, 23), their intention was to let the bodies hang until God, propitiated by this offering, should send rain upon the land, for the want of it had occasioned the famine. It was a heathen practice to gibbet men with a view of appeasing the anger of the gods in seasons of famine, and the Gibeonites, who were a remnant of the Amorites (vs. 2), though brought to the knowledge of the true God, were not, it seems, free from this superstition. God, in His providence, suffered the Gibeonites to ask and inflict so barbarous a retaliation, in order that the oppressed Gibeonites might obtain justice and some reparation of their wrongs, especially that the scandal brought on the name of the true religion by the violation of a solemn national compact might be wiped away from Israel, and that a memorable lesson should be given to respect treaties and oaths.

10, 11. RIZPAH'S KINDNESS UNTO THE DEAD. **10. Rizpah . . . took sackcloth, and spread it for her upon the rock**—She erected a tent near the spot, in which she and her servants kept watch, as the relatives of executed persons were wont to do, day and night, to scare the birds and beasts of prey away from the remains exposed on the low-standing gibbets.

12-22. DAVID BURIES THE BONES OF SAUL AND JONATHAN IN THEIR FATHER'S SEPULCHER. **12. David went and took the bones of Saul and the bones of Jonathan his son,** etc.—Before long, the descent of copious showers, or perhaps an order of the king, gave Rizpah the satisfaction of releasing the corpses from their ignominious exposure; and, incited by her pious example, David ordered the remains of Saul and his sons to be transferred from their obscure grave in Jabesh-gilead to an honorable interment in the family vault at Zelah or Zelzah (I Sam. 10:2), now Beit-jala. **15-22. Moreover the Philistines had yet war again with Israel**—Although the Philistines had completely succumbed to the army of David, yet the appearance of any gigantic champions among them revived their courage and stirred them up to renewed inroads on the Hebrew territory. Four successive contests they provoked during the latter period of David's reign, in the first of which the king ran so imminent a risk of his life that he was no longer allowed to encounter the perils of the battlefield.

CHAPTER 22

Vss. 1-51. DAVID'S PSALM OF THANKSGIVING FOR GOD'S POWERFUL DELIVERANCE AND MANIFOLD BLESSINGS. The song contained in this chapter is the same as the eighteenth Psalm, where the full commentary will be given. It may be sufficient simply to remark that Jewish writers have noticed a great number of very minute variations in the language of the song as recorded here, from that embodied in the Book of Psalms—which may be accounted for by the fact that this, the first copy of the poem, was carefully revised and altered by David afterwards, when it was set to the music of the tabernacle. This inspired ode was manifestly the effusion of a mind glowing with the highest fervor of piety and gratitude, and it is full of the noblest imagery that is to be found within the range even of sacred poetry. It is David's grand tribute of thanksgiving for deliverance from his numerous and powerful enemies, and establishing him in the power and glory of the kingdom.

CHAPTER 23

Vss. 1-7. DAVID PROFESSES HIS FAITH IN GOD'S PROMISES. **1. Now these be the last words of David**—Various opinions are entertained as to the precise meaning of this statement, which, it is obvious, proceeded from the compiler or collector of the sacred canon. Some think that, as there is no division of chapters in the Hebrew Scriptures, this introduction was intended to show that what follows is no part of the king's poetical compositions; while still others consider it the last of his utterances as an inspired writer. **raised up on high**—from an obscure family and condition to a throne. **the anointed of the God of Jacob**—chosen to be king by the special appointment of that God, to whom, by virtue of an ancient covenant, the people or Israel owed all their peculiar destiny and distinguished privileges. **the sweet psalmist of Israel**—i.e., delightful, highly esteemed. **2. The Spirit of the Lord spake by me**—Nothing can more clearly show that all that is excellent in spirit, beautiful in language, or grand in prophetic imagery, which the Psalms of David contain, were owing, not to his superiority in natural talents or acquired knowledge, but to the suggestion and dictates of God's Spirit. **3. the Rock of Israel**—This metaphor, which is commonly applied by the sacred writers to the Almighty, was very expressive to the minds of the Hebrew people. Their national fortresses, in which they sought security in war, were built on high and inaccessible rocks. **spake to me**—either preceptively, giving the following counsels respecting the character of an upright ruler in Israel, or prophetically, concerning David and his royal dynasty, and the great Messiah, of whom many think this is a prophecy, rendering the words, "he that ruleth"—"there shall be a ruler over men." **4. as the tender grass springing out of the earth by clear shining after rain**—Little patches of grass are seen rapidly springing up in Palestine after rain; and even where the ground has been long parched and bare, within a few days or hours after the enriching showers begin to fall, the face of the earth is so renewed that it is covered over with a pure fresh mantle of green. **5. Although my house be not so with God, yet he hath made with me an everlasting covenant, ordered in all things and sure**—"the light of the morning," i.e., the beginning of David's kingdom, was unlike the clear brilliant dawn of an Eastern day but was overcast by many black and threatening clouds; neither he nor his family had been like the tender grass springing up from the ground and flourishing by the united influences of the sun and rain; but rather like the grass that withereth and is prematurely cut down. The meaning is: although David's house had not flourished in an uninterrupted course of worldly prosperity and greatness, according to his hopes; although great crimes and calamities had beclouded his family history; some of the most promising branches of the royal tree had been cut down in his lifetime and many of his successors should suffer in like manner for their personal sins; although many reverses and revolutions may overtake his race and his kingdom, yet it was to him a subject of the highest joy and thankfulness that God will inviolably maintain His covenant with his family, until the advent of his greatest Son, the Messiah, who was the special object of his desire, and the author of his salvation. **6. But the sons of Belial shall be all of them as thorns**—i.e., the wicked enemies and persecutors of this kingdom of righteousness. They resemble those prickly, thorny plants which are twisted together, whose spires point in every direction, and which are so sharp and strong that they cannot be touched or approached without danger; but hard instruments and violent means must be taken to destroy or uproot them. So God will remove or destroy all who are opposed to this kingdom. **8-39.** A CATALOGUE OF HIS MIGHTY MEN. **8.**

These be the names of the mighty men whom David had—This verse should be translated thus: He who sits in the seat of the Tachmonite (i.e., of Jashobeam the Hachmonite), who was chief among the captains, the same is Adino the Eznite; he lift up his spear against eight hundred, whom he slew at one time. The text is corrupt in this passage; the number eight hundred should be three hundred [DAVIDSON'S HERM.]. Under Joab he was chief or president of the council of war. The first or highest order was composed of him and his two colleagues, Eleazar and Shammah. Eleazar seems to have been left to fight the Philistines alone; and on his achieving the victory, they returned to the spoil. In like manner Shammah was left to stand alone in his glory, when the Lord, by him, wrought a great victory. It is not very easy to determine whether the exploits that are afterwards described were performed by the first or the second three. **15. the well of Bethlehem**—An ancient cistern, with four or five holes in the solid rock, at about ten minutes' distance to the north of the eastern corner of the hill of Bethlehem, is pointed out by the natives as Bir-Daoud; that is, David's well. Dr. ROBINSON doubts the identity of the well; but others think that there are no good grounds for doing so. Certainly, considering this to be the ancient well, Bethlehem must have once extended ten minutes further to the north, and must have lain in times of old, not as now, on the summit, but on the northern rise of the hill; for the well is *by* or (I Chron. 11:7) *at* the gate. I find in the description of travellers, that the common opinion is, that David's captains had come from the southeast, in order to obtain, at the risk of their lives, the so-much-longed-for water; while it is supposed that David himself was then in the great cave that is not far to the southeast of Bethlehem; which cave is generally held to have been that of Adullam. But (Josh. 15:35) Adullam lay "in the valley"; that is, in the undulating plain at the western base of the mountains of Judea and consequently to the southwest of Bethlehem. Be this as it may, David's *men* had in any case to break through the host of the Philistines, in order to reach the well; and the position of Bir-Daoud agrees well with this [VAN DE VELDE]. **19. the first three**—The mighty men or champions in David's military staff were divided into three classes—the highest, Jashobeam, Eleazar, and Shammah; the second class, Abishai, Benaiah, and Asahel; and the third class, the thirty, of which Asahel was the chief. There are thirty-one mentioned in the list, including Asahel; and these added to the two superior orders make thirty-seven. Two of them, we know, were already dead; viz., Asahel and Uriah; and if the dead, at the drawing up of the list, amounted to seven, then we might suppose a legion of honor, consisting of the definite number thirty, where the vacancies, when they occurred, were replaced by fresh appointments.

CHAPTER 24

Vss. 1-9. DAVID NUMBERS THE PEOPLE. **1. again the anger of the Lord was kindled against Israel, and he moved David against them to say, Go, number Israel and Judah**—"Again" carries us back to the former tokens of His wrath in the three years' famine. God, though He cannot tempt any man (Jas. 1:13), is frequently described in Scripture as doing what He merely permits to be done; and so, in this case, He permitted Satan to tempt David. Satan was the active mover, while God only withdrew His supporting grace, and the great tempter prevailed against the king. (See Exod. 7:13; I Sam. 26:19; ch. 16:10; Ps. 105:25; Isa. 7:17, etc.) The order was given to Joab, who, though not generally restrained by religious scruples, did not fail to present, in strong terms (see on I Chron. 21:3), the sin and danger of this measure. He used every argument to dissuade the king from his purpose. The sacred history has not mentioned the objections which he and other distinguished officers urged against it in the council of David. But it expressly states that they were all overruled by the inflexible resolution of the king. **5. they passed over Jordan**—This census was taken first in the eastern parts of the Hebrew kingdom; and it would seem that Joab was accompanied by a military force, either to aid in this troublesome work, or to overawe the people who might display reluctance or opposition. **the river of Gad**—"Wady" would be a better term. It extends over a course estimated at about sixty miles. which, though in summer almost constantly dry, exhibits very evident traces of being swept over by an impetuous torrent in winter (see on Deut. 2:36). **6. the land of Tahtim-hodshi**—i.e., the land lately acquired; viz., that of the Hagrites conquered by Saul (I Chron. 5-10). The progress was northward. Thence they crossed the country, and, proceeding along the western coast to the southern extremities of the country, they at length arrived in Jerusalem, having completed the enumeration of the whole kingdom in the space of nine months and twenty days. **9. Joab gave up the sum of the number of the people unto the king**—The amount here stated, compared with I Chron. 21:5, gives a difference of 300,000. The discrepancy is only apparent, and admits of an easy reconciliation; thus (see I Chron. 27), there were twelve divisions of generals, who commanded monthly, and whose duty was to keep guard on the royal person, each having a body of troops consisting of 24,000 men, which, together, formed an army of 288,000; and as a separate detachment of 12,000 was attendant on the twelve princes of the twelve tribes mentioned in the same chapter, so both are equal to 300,000. These were not reckoned in this book, because they were in the actual service of the king as a regular militia. But I Chronicles 21:5 joins them to the rest, saying, "all those of Israel were one million, one hundred thousand"; whereas the author of Samuel, who reckons only the eight hundred thousand, does not say, "all those of Israel," but barely "and Israel were," etc. It must also be observed that, exclusive of the troops before mentioned, there was an army of observation on the frontiers of the Philistines' country, composed of 30,000 men, as appears from chapter 6:1; which, it seems, were included in the number of 500,000 of the people of Judah by the author of Samuel. But the author of Chronicles, who mentions only 470,000, gives the number of that tribe exclusive of those thirty thousand men, because they were not all of the tribe of Judah, and therefore he does not say, "all those of Judah," as he had said, "all those of Israel," but only, "and those of Judah." Thus both accounts may be reconciled [DAVIDSON].

10-14. HE, HAVING THREE PLAGUES PROPOUNDED BY GAD, REPENTS, AND CHOOSES THREE DAYS' PESTILENCE. **10. David's heart smote him after that he had numbered the people. And David said unto the Lord, I have sinned**—The act of numbering the people was not in itself sinful; for Moses did it by the express authority of God. But David acted not only independently of such order of sanction,

n II Sam. 16:11; also on 12:8.) Solomon's
...tion was roused; he in a moment penetrated
...ful scheme, and from his associating the
...of Abiathar and Joab, he seems to have sus-
or known that those deep schemers had been
...ompters of Adonijah. **23-25. God do so to**
...**d more also**—the common form of introducing
...nn oath. **if Adonijah have not spoken this**
...**against his own life**—Whether there was a trea-
...e design to conceal under this request or not,
...t, according to Eastern notions, was criminal,
...d dangerous consequence to the state. There
...ground of censure upon Solomon for cruelty
...cipitation in this instance. He had pardoned
...ijah's former conspiracy; but this new attempt
...ebellion against the viceroy appointed by the
...King and called for condign punishment.
...ffice of executioner was among the Hebrews, as
...her ancient countries of the East, performed
...emoniously and privately—often without any
...ous warning—by the captain of the guard, or
...of his officers (Matt. 14:10). **26, 27. unto**
...**thar the priest said the king**—This functionary,
...e counsellor or accomplice of Adonijah, had
...rved to share his fate. But partly from regard
...s priestly dignity, and partly from his long asso-
...ons with the late king, Solomon pronounced on
...the mitigated sentence of banishment to his
...ntry estate at Anathoth, and thereby, as God's
...gerent, deprived him of his office and its emolu-
...ts. The sacred writer notices the remarkable
...lment. Abiathar's degradation from the high
...esthood (see on ch. 4:4), of the doom denounced
...inst the house of Eli (I Sam. 2:30).
...28-45. JOAB SLAIN. **28. Then tidings came to**
...b—The execution of these sentences respectively
...Adonijah and Abiathar prepared Joab for his
...e. Death, due to his great crimes (Num. 35:33),
...uld long ago have been inflicted, had not his pow-
...and popularity with the army been too formi-
...ble for the old king. He now fled to the altar,
...hich, though a recognized asylum, afforded no
...nctuary to the rebel and murderer (Exod. 21:14).
...nd, as he refused to leave it, he seems to have
...erished some faint hope that a religious scruple
...ould have been felt at the thought of violating the
...nctity of the place by bloodshed. Benaiah, not
...king to assume any responsibility, referred the
...atter to Solomon, who determined that the law
...hould take its course (Deut. 19:13). **33. Their**
...**lood shall . . . return upon the head of Joab**, etc.
...—A reference is here made to the curse publicly and
...olemnly pronounced by King David (II Sam. 3:28,
...9). **34. Benaiah . . . went up, and fell upon him**—
...According to the terms of the statute (Exod. 21:14),
...nd the practice in similar cases (II Kings 11:15),
...he criminal was to be dragged from the altar and
...slain elsewhere. But the truth is, that the sanctity
...of the altar was violated as much by the violence
...used in forcing the criminal from the place as in
...shedding his blood there; the express command of
...God authorized the former and therefore by impli-
...cation permitted the latter. **was buried in his own**
house—or family vault, at his property in the wilderness of Judah. His interment was included in the
king's order, as enjoined in the divine law (Deut. 21:
23).
34-46. SHIMEI PUT TO DEATH. **36. the king**
sent and called for Shimei—He was probably residing at Bahurim, his native place. But, as he was a
suspicious character, Solomon condemned him
henceforth to live in Jerusalem, on the penalty of
death, for going without the gates. He submitted

to this confinement for three years, when, violating
his oath, he was arrested and put to death by Solomon for perjury, aggravated by his former crime of
high treason against David. **46. the kingdom was**
established in the hand of Solomon—Now, by the
death of Shimei, *all* the leaders of the rival factions
had been cut off.

CHAPTER 3

Vs. 1. SOLOMON MARRIES PHARAOH'S DAUGHTER.
1. Solomon made affinity with Pharaoh—This was a
royal title, equivalent to sultan, and the personal
name of this monarch is said to have been Vaphres.
The formation, on equal terms, of this matrimonial
alliance with the royal family of Egypt, shows the
high consideration to which the Hebrew kingdom
had now arisen. Rosellini has given, from the
Egyptian monuments, what is supposed to be a
portrait of this princess. She was received in
the land of her adoption with great éclat; for the
Song of Solomon and the forty-fifth Psalm are
supposed to have been composed in honor of this
occasion, although they may both have a higher
typical reference to the introduction of the Gentiles into the church. **brought her into the city**
of David—i.e., Jerusalem. She was not admissible into the stronghold of Zion, the building
where the ark was (Deut. 23:7, 8). She seems to
have been lodged at first in his mother's apartments
(Song of Sol. 3:4; 8:2), as a suitable residence
was not yet provided for her in the new palace
(ch. 7:8; 9:24; II Chron. 8:11). **building . . . the**
wall of Jerusalem—Although David had begun
(Ps. 51:18), it was, according to Josephus, reserved
for Solomon to extend and complete the fortifications of the city. It has been questioned whether
this marriage was in conformity with the law (see
on Exod. 34:16; Deut. 7:3; Ezra 10:1-10; Neh. 13:
26). But it is nowhere censured in Scripture, as are
the connections Solomon formed with other foreigners (ch. 11:1-3); whence it may be inferred that
he had stipulated for her abandonment of idolatry,
and conforming to the Jewish religion (Ps. 45:10,
11).
2-5. HIGH PLACES BEING IN USE HE SACRIFICES
AT GIBEON. **3. Solomon loved the Lord**—This declaration, illustrated by what follows, affords undoubted evidence of the young king's piety; nor is
the word "only," which prefaces the statement, to be
understood as introducing a qualifying circumstance
that reflected any degree of censure upon him.
The intention of the sacred historian is to describe
the generally prevailing mode of worship before
the temple was built. The "high places" were
altars erected on natural or artificial eminences,
probably from the idea that men were brought
nearer to the Deity. They had been used by the
patriarchs, and had become so universal among the
heathen that they were almost identified with idolatry. They were prohibited in the law (Lev. 17:3, 4;
Deut. 12:13, 14; Jer. 7:31; Ezek. 6:3, 4; Hos. 10:8).
But, so long as the tabernacle was migratory and
the means for the national worship were merely
provisional, the worship on those high places was
tolerated. Hence, as accounting for their continuance, it is expressly stated (vs. 2) that God had not
yet chosen a permanent and exclusive place for his
worship. **4. the king went to Gibeon to sacrifice**
there—The old tabernacle and the brazen altar which
Moses had made in the wilderness were there (I
Chron. 16:39; 21:29; II Chron. 1:3-6). The royal

but from motives unworthy of the delegated king
of Israel; from pride and vainglory; from self-confidence and distrust of God; and, above all, from
ambitious designs of conquest, in furtherance of
which he was determined to force the people into
military service, and to ascertain whether he could
muster an army sufficient for the magnitude of the
enterprises he contemplated. It was a breach of the
constitution, an infringement of the liberties of the
people, and opposed to that divine policy which
required that Israel should continue a separate people. His eyes were not opened to the heinousness
of his sin till God had spoken unto him by His commissioned prophet. **13. Shall seven years of famine**
come unto thee—i.e., in addition to the three that
had been already, with the current year included
(see on I Chron. 21:11, 12). **14. David said, . . . Let**
us fall now into the hand of the Lord—His overwhelming sense of his sin led him to acquiesce in the
punishment denounced, notwithstanding its apparent
excess of severity. He proceeded on a good principle in choosing the pestilence. In pestilence he
was equally exposed, as it, was just and right he
should be, to danger as his people, whereas, in war
and famine, he possessed means of protection superior to them. Besides, he thereby showed his trust,
founded on long experience, in the divine goodness.
15-25. HIS INTERCESSION TO GOD; THE PLAGUE
CEASES. **15. from the morning**—rather *that* morning when Gad came, till the end of the three days.
there died of the people . . . seventy thousand men
—Thus was the pride of the vainglorious monarch,
confiding in the number of his population, deeply
humbled. **16. the Lord repented him of the evil**—
God is often described in Scripture as repenting
when He ceased to pursue a course He had begun.
17. David . . . said [or had said], I have sinned . . .
but these sheep, what have they done?—The guilt
of numbering the people lay exclusively with David.
But in the body politic as well as natural, when the

head suffers, all the members suffer along with it;
and, besides, although David's sin was the immediate
cause, the great increase of national offenses at this
time had (vs. 1) kindled the anger of the Lord. **18.**
Araunah—or Ornan (I Chron. 21:18), the Jebusite,
one of the ancient inhabitants, who, having become
a convert to the true religion, retained his house and
possessions. He resided on Mount Moriah, the
spot on which the temple was afterwards built (II
Chron. 3:1); but that mount was not then enclosed
in the town. **21. to build an altar unto the Lord,**
that the plague may be stayed—It is evident that the
plague was not stayed till after the altar was built,
and the sacrifice offered, so that what is related (vs.
16) was by anticipation. Previous to the offering of
this sacrifice, he had seen the destroying angel as
well as offered the intercessory prayer (vs. 17).
This was a sacrifice of expiation; and the reason
why he was allowed to offer it on Mount Moriah
was partly in gracious consideration to his fear of
repairing to Gibeon (I Chron. 21:29, 30), and partly
in anticipation of the removal of the tabernacle and
the erection of the temple there (II Chron. 3:1). **23.**
All these things did Araunah, as a king, give—Indicating, as the sense is, that this man had been anciently a heathen king or chief, but was now a proselyte who still retained great property and influence
in Jerusalem, and whose piety was evinced by the
liberality of his offers. The words, "as a king," are
taken by some to signify simply, "he gave with royal
munificence." **24. Nay; . . . I will . . . buy it of thee**
at a price—The sum mentioned here, about fifty
dollars, was paid for the floor, oxen and wood instruments only, whereas the large sum (I Chron. 21:
25) was paid afterwards for the whole hill, on which
David made preparations for building the temple.
25. David offered burnt offerings and peace offer-
ings—There seem to have been two sacrifices; the
first expiatory, the second a thanksgiving for the
cessation of the pestilence (see on I Chron. 21:26).

THE FIRST BOOK OF

THE KINGS

CHAPTER 1

Vss. 1-4. ABISHAG CHERISHES DAVID IN HIS EX-
TREME AGE. **1. Now King David was old**—He was
in the seventieth year of his age (II Samuel 5:4, 5).
But the wear and tear of a military life, bodily
fatigue, and mental care, had prematurely, if we
may say it, exhausted the energies of David's strong
constitution (I Sam. 16:12). In modern Palestine
and Egypt the people, owing to the heat of the
climate, sleep each in a *separate* bed. They only
depart from this practice for medical reasons (Eccles. 4:11). The expedient recommended by David's physicians is the regimen still prescribed in
similar cases in the East, particularly among the
Arab population, not simply to give heat, but "to
cherish," as they are aware that the inhalation of
young breath will give new life and vigor to the
worn-out frame. The fact of the health of the
young and healthier person being, as it were, stolen
to support that of the more aged and sickly is well
established among the medical faculty. And hence

the prescription for the aged king was made in a
hygienic point of view for the prolongation of his
valuable life, and not merely for the comfort to be
derived from the natural warmth imparted to his
withered frame [TENT and KHAN]. The polygamy
of the age and country may account for the introduction of this practice; and it is evident that Abishag was made a concubine or secondary wife to
David (see on ch. 2:22). **3. a Shunammite**—Shunem, in the tribe of Issachar (Josh. 19:18), lay on an
eminence in the plain of Esdraelon, five miles south
of Tabor. It is now called Sulam.
5-31. ADONIJAH USURPS THE KINGDOM. **5. Then**
Adonijah the son of Haggith exalted himself—Nothing is said as to the origin or rank of Haggith, so
that it is probable she was not distinguished by family descent. Adonijah, though David's fourth son
(II Sam. 3:4; I Chron. 3:2), was now the oldest
alive; and his personal attractions and manners (I
Sam. 9:2) not only recommended him to the leading
men about court, but made him the favorite of his
father, who, though seeing him assume an equipage

becoming only the heir-presumptive to the throne (II Sam. 15:1), said nothing; and his silence was considered by many, as well as by Adonijah, to be equivalent to an expression of consent. The sinking health of the king prompted him to take a decisive step in furtherance of his ambitious designs. **7. he conferred with Joab**—The anxiety of Adonijah to secure the influence of a leader so bold, enterprising, and popular with the army was natural, and the accession of the hoary commander is easily accounted for from his recent grudge at the king (see on II Sam. 19:13). **and with Abiathar the priest**—His influence was as great over the priests and Levites—a powerful body in the kingdom—as that of Joab over the troops. It might be that both of them thought the crown belonged to Adonijah by right of primogeniture, from his mature age and the general expectations of the people (ch. 2:15). **8. But Zadok the priest**—He had been high priest in the tabernacle at Gibeon under Saul (I Chron. 16:39). David, on his accession, had conjoined him and Abiathar equal in the exercise of their high functions (II Sam. 8:17; 15:24; 29:35). But it is extremely probable that some cause of jealousy or discord between them had arisen, and hence each lent his countenance and support to opposite parties. **Benaiah**—Distinguished for his bravery (I Sam. 23:20), he had been appointed captain of the king's bodyguard (II Sam. 8:18; 20:23; I Chron. 18:17), and was regarded by Joab as a rival. **Nathan the prophet**—He was held in high estimation by David, and stood on the most intimate relations with the royal family (II Sam. 12:25). **Shimei**—probably the person of this name who was afterwards enrolled among Solomon's great officers (ch. 4:18). **Rei**—supposed to be the same as Ira (II Sam. 20:26). **and the mighty men**—the select band of worthies. **9. En-rogel**—situated (Josh. 15:7-10) east of Jerusalem, in a level place, just below the junction of the valley of Hinnom with that of Jehoshaphat. It is a very deep well, measuring 125 feet in depth; the water is sweet, but not very cold, and it is at times quite full to overflowing. The Orientals are fond of enjoying festive repasts in the open air at places which command the advantage of shade, water, and verdure; and those *fêtes champêtres* are not cold collations, but magnificent entertainments, the animals being killed and dressed on the spot. Adonijah's feast at En-rogel was one of this Oriental description, and it was on a large scale (II Sam. 3:4, 5; 5:14-16; I Chron. 14:1-7). At the accession of a new king there were sacrifices offered (I Sam. 11:15). But on such an occasion it was no less customary to entertain the grandees of the kingdom and even the populace in a public manner (I Chron. 12:23-40). There is the strongest probability that Adonijah's feast was purely political, to court popularity and secure a party to support his claim to the crown. **11-27. Nathan spake unto Bath-sheba . . . let me . . . give thee counsel,** etc.—The revolt was defeated by this prophet, who, knowing the Lord's will (II Sam. 7:12; I Chron. 22:9), felt himself bound, in accordance with his character and office, to take the lead in seeing it executed. Hitherto the succession of the Hebrew monarchy had not been settled. The Lord had reserved to Himself the right of nomination (Deut. 17:15), which was acted upon in the appointments both of Saul and David; and in the case of the latter the rule was so far modified that his posterity were guaranteed the perpetual possession of the sovereignty (II Sam. 7:12). This divine purpose was known throughout the kingdom; but no intimation had been made as to whether the right of inheritance was to belong to the oldest son. Adonijah, in common with the people generally, expected that this natural arrangement should be followed in the Hebrew kingdom as in all others. Nathan, who was aware of the old king's solemn promise to Solomon, and, moreover, that this promise was sanctioned by the divine will, saw that no time was to be lost. Fearing the effects of too sudden excitement in the king's feeble state, he arranged that Bath-sheba should go first to inform him of what was being transacted without the walls, and that he himself should follow to confirm her statement. The narrative here not only exhibits the vivid picture of a scene within the interior of a palace, but gives the impression that a great deal of Oriental state ceremonial had been established in the Hebrew court. **20. the eyes of all Israel are upon thee, that thou shouldest tell them who shall sit on the throne**—When the kings died without declaring their will, then their oldest son succeeded. But frequently they designated long before their death which of their sons should inherit the throne. The kings of Persia, as well as of other Eastern countries, have exercised the same right in modern and even recent times. **21. I and my son . . . shall be counted offenders**—i.e., slain, according to the barbarous usage of the East towards all who are rivals to the throne. **28-31. Then King David answered and said, Call me Bath-sheba**—He renews to her the solemn pledge he had given, in terms of solemnity and impressiveness which show that the aged monarch had roused himself to the duty the emergency called for.

32-49. Solomon, by David's Appointment, Is Anointed King. **33. cause Solomon my son to ride upon mine own mule**—Directions were forthwith given for the immediate coronation of Solomon. A procession was to be formed by the "servants of their lord"—i.e., the king's bodyguard. Mules were then used by all the princes (II Sam. 13:29); but there was a state mule of which all subjects were forbidden, under pain of death, to make use, without special permission; so that its being granted to Solomon was a public declaration in his favor as the future king (see on Esther 6:8, 9). **bring him down to Gihon**—a pool or fountain on the west of Jerusalem (see on II Chron. 32:30), chosen as equally public for the counter proclamation. **34. anoint him**—done only in the case of a new dynasty or disputed succession (see on I Sam. 16:13; II Sam. 2:4). **35. Then ye shall come up after him, that he may come and sit upon my throne**—The public recognition of the successor to the throne, during the old king's lifetime, is accordant with the customs of the East. **39. an horn of oil out of the tabernacle**—It was the sacred oil (Exod. 30:22) with which the kings were anointed. **40. all the people came up after him**—i.e., from the valley to the citadel of Zion. **41. Adonijah, and all the guests that were with him, heard it as they had made an end of eating**—The loud shouts raised by the populace at the joyous proclamation at Gihon, and echoed by assembled thousands, from Zion to En-rogel, were easily heard at that distance by Adonijah and his confederates. The arrival of a trusty messenger, who gave a full detail of the coronation ceremony, spread dismay in their camp. The wicked and ambitious plot they had assembled to execute was dissipated, and every one of the conspirators consulted his safety by flight.

50-53. Adonijah, Fleeing to the Horns of the Altar, Is Dismissed by Solomon. **50. Adonijah . . . went and caught hold on the horns of the altar**—most probably the altar of burnt offering which had been erected on Mount Zion, where Abiathar,

one of his partisans, presided as high priest. The horns or projections at the four corners of the altar, to which the sacrifices were bound, and which were tipped with the blood of the victim, were symbols of grace and salvation to the sinner. Hence the altar was regarded as a sanctuary (Exod. 21:14), but not to murderers, rebels, or deliberate perpetrators. Adonijah, having acted in opposition to the will of the reigning king, was guilty of rebellion, and stood self-condemned. Solomon spared his life on the express condition of his good behavior—living in strict privacy, leading a quiet, peaceable life, and meddling with the affairs of neither the court nor the kingdom. **53. they brought him down**—from the ledge around the altar on which he was standing. **he bowed himself**—i.e., did homage to Solomon as king.

CHAPTER 2

Vss. 1-11. David Dies. **1. David . . . charged his son**—The charge recorded here was given to Solomon just before his death and is different from the farewell address delivered in public some time before (I Chron. 28:29). It is introduced with great solemnity. **2. I go the way of all the earth**—a beautiful and impressive periphrasis for death. **be thou strong, . . . and show thyself a man**—This counsel is similar to the apostolic direction (I Cor. 16:13) and refers to the fortitude or strength of mind that was required to discharge the onerous functions of king. **3. keep the charge of the Lord thy God**—i.e., the divine law in all its ceremonial as well as moral requirements. But particular reference was intended to its political institutions, as it was only by strictly maintaining the conduct that became the Hebrew monarch (Deut. 17:10-20), that he would secure the blessing of peace and prosperity to his reign (see on Deut. 4:6; 29:10-21). **4. there shall not fail thee . . . a man on the throne of Israel**—a reference to the promise made to David of the sovereignty being vested perpetually in his lineage (II Sam. 7:11-16), which was confirmed to Solomon afterwards (see on ch. 9:5), and repeated with reference to its spiritual meaning long after (Jer. 33:17). **5, 6. thou knowest also what Joab . . . did**—The insolent and imperious conduct of that general had not only been deeply offensive to the feelings (II Sam. 18:5-15; 19:5-7), but calculated to bring reproach on the character, to injure the prospects, and endanger the throne of David. Passing over the injuries committed directly against himself, David dwelt with strong feelings on the base assassination of Abner and Amasa. **shed the blood of war in peace,** etc.—The obvious meaning is, that in peace he acted towards them as if they had been in a state of warfare; but perhaps these graphic expressions might be designed to impress Solomon's mind more strongly with a sense of the malice, treachery, and cruelty by which those murders were characterized. **6. Do . . . according to thy wisdom**—Joab's immense popularity with the army required that any proceedings instituted against him should be taken with great prudence and deliberation. **8. thou hast with thee Shimei**—Though David promised him a pardon, which being enforced by the presence of a thousand followers, could not have been well refused, he warned his son against Shimei as a turbulent and dangerous character. It must not be supposed that in these dying instructions David was evincing a fierce, vindictive spirit. He is rather to be considered as acting in the character of a king and magistrate, in noticing crimes which he had not been in a condition to punish, and pointing out persons
would be under a necessity to rid
ous to the state. The grateful r
lai's kindness was, however, a per
does honor to the warmth of his hea
as to Mephibosheth, the son of J
than, would imply the previous dea
9. for thou art a wise man—Solomo
indications of wisdom before his m
ment with the heavenly gift (see o
his own sagacity would dictate the co
be followed in any new offense tha
commit. **10. So David slept wit**
about six months after the coronati
(cf. II Sam. 5:5, with I Chron. 29:2
val was spent in developing his ideas
the future glory of the kingdom and
the permanent worship of God (see o
et seq.). **was buried in the city of**
chres were not allowed within the prec
Jerusalem, however, formed an excep
even there, the privilege was reserved
royal family (Acts 2:29). Tradition
bones of David repose on Mount Zion,
aret of a small mosque points out the
tradition has fixed. His was a noble,
and a humbling history. He was a go
his life was deformed by various crime
gross character. But there were many
noble traits in his character; he was an ea
of the divine law; his reign was signalize
important services that contributed to th
God and the exaltation of His kingdom
name, as the sweet Psalmist of Israel, will
honor to the latest age of the Church.

12-24. Solomon Succeeds Him. **12.**
Solomon up on the throne of David his fa
ascension to the royal dignity was made u
happiest auspices. Having been born afte
ther became monarch of the *whole* kingd
claim, according to the notions of Oriental
was preferable to that of all, *even* his elder br
The Hebrew kingdom enjoyed internal pros
it was respected and renowned abroad, and So
well knew how to improve these advantages.
18. Adonijah . . . came to Bath-sheba—Her qu
to him betrays an apprehension which his r
conduct might well warrant; but his pious ackn
edgment of the divine will seemed apparently
indicate so entire an acquiescence in the settlem
of the succession, that, in her womanly simplic
she perceived not the deep cunning and evil desi
that was concealed under his request and readi
undertook to promote his wishes. **19, 20. Bath-**
sheba . . . went unto King Solomon—The filial rev-
erence and the particular act of respect, which Solomon rendered, were quite in accordance with the sentiments and customs of the East. The right hand is the place of honor; and as it expressly said to have been assigned to "the king's mother," it is necessary to remark that, when a husband dies his widow acquires a higher dignity and power, as a mother over her son, than she ever possessed before. Besides, the dignity of "king's mother" is a state office, to which certain revenues are attached. The holder has a separate palace or court, as well as possesses great influence in public affairs; and as the dignity is held for life, it sometimes happens, in consequence of deaths, that the person enjoying it may not be related to the reigning sovereign by natural maternity. Bath-sheba had evidently been invested with this honorable office. **22. why dost thou ask Abishag . . . ask for him the kingdom also**

—(See
indign
the a
names
pecte
the p
me, a
a sol
word
sonal
the a
and
is no
or p
Ado
was
divi
The
in c
unc
prev
one
Abi
as
des
to
cia
hin
co
vic
me
ful
pr
ag

Jo
o
fa
w
e
c

progress was of public importance. It was a season of national devotion. The king was accompanied by his principal nobility (II Chron. 1:2); and, as the occasion was most probably one of the great annual festivals which lasted seven days, the rank of the offerer and the succession of daily oblations may help in part to account for the immense magnitude of the sacrifices. **5. In Gibeon the Lord appeared to Solomon in a dream**—It was probably at the close of this season, when his mind had been elevated into a high state of religious fervor by the protracted services. Solomon felt an intense desire, and he had offered an earnest petition, for the gift of wisdom. In sleep his thoughts ran upon the subject of his prayer, and he dreamed that God appeared to him and gave him the option of every thing in the world—that he asked wisdom, and that God granted his request. His dream was but an imaginary repetition of his former desire, but God's grant of it was real.

6-15. HE CHOOSES WISDOM. **6. Solomon said** —i.e., had dreamed that he said. **7. I am but a little child**—not in age, for he had reached manhood (ch. 2:9) and must have been at least twenty years old; but he was raw and inexperienced in matters of government. **10. the speech pleased the Lord**—It was Solomon's waking prayers that God heard and requited, but the acceptance was signified in this vision. **15. behold, it was a dream**—The vivid impression, the indelible recollection he had of this dream, together with the new and increased energy communicated to his mind, and the flow of worldly prosperity that rushed upon him, gave him assurance that it came by divine inspiration and originated in the grace of God. The wisdom, however, that was asked and obtained was not so much of the heart as of the head—it was wisdom not for himself personally, but for his office, such as would qualify him for the administration of justice, the government of a kingdom, and for the attainment of general scientific knowledge.

16-28. HIS JUDGMENT BETWEEN TWO HARLOTS. **16. Then came there two women**—Eastern monarchs, who generally administer justice in person, at least in all cases of difficulty, often appeal to the principles of human nature when they are at a loss otherwise to find a clue to the truth or see clearly their way through a mass of conflicting testimony. The modern history of the East abounds with anecdotes of judicial cases, in which the decision given was the result of an experiment similar to this of Solomon upon the natural feelings of the contending parties.

CHAPTER 4

1-6. SOLOMON'S PRINCES. **1. So King Solomon was king over all Israel**—This chapter contains a general description of the state and glory of the Hebrew kingdom during the more flourishing or later years of his reign. **2. these were the princes**—or chief officers, as is evident from two of them marrying Solomon's daughters. **Azariah the son of Zadok the priest**—rather, the prince, as the *Hebrew* word frequently signifies (Gen. 41:45; Exod. 2:16; II Sam. 8:18); so that from the precedency given to his person in the list, he seems to have been prime minister, the highest in office next the king. **3. scribes**—i.e., secretaries of state. Under David, there had been only one. The employment of three functionaries in this department indicates either improved regulations by the division of labor, or a great increase of business, occasioned by the grow-

ing prosperity of the kingdom, or a more extensive correspondence with foreign countries. **recorder**—i.e., historiographer, or annalist—an office of great importance in Oriental courts, and the duties of which consisted in chronicling the occurrences of every day. **4. Benaiah ... was over the host**—formerly captain of the guard. He had succeeded Joab as commander of the forces. **Zadok and Abiathar were the priests**—Only the first discharged the sacred functions; the latter had been banished to his country seat and retained nothing more than the name of high priest. **5. over the officers**—i.e., the provincial governors enumerated in vss. 17-19. **principal officer, and the king's friend**—perhaps president of the privy council, and Solomon's confidential friend or favorite. This high functionary had probably been reared along with Solomon. That he should heap those honors on the sons of Nathan was most natural, considering the close intimacy of the father with the late king, and the deep obligations under which Solomon personally lay to the prophet. **6. Ahishar was over the household**—steward or chamberlain of the palace. **Adoniram**—or Adoram (II Sam. 20:24; ch. 12:18), or Hadoram (II Chron. 10: 18), **was over the tribute**—not the collection of money or goods, but the levy of compulsory laborers (cf. ch: 5:13, 14).

7-21. HIS TWELVE OFFICERS. **7. Solomon had twelve officers over all Israel.** The royal revenues were raised according to the ancient, and still, in many parts, existing usage of the East, not in money payments, but in the produce of the soil. There would be always a considerable difficulty in the collection and transmission of these tithes (I Sam. 8:15). Therefore, to facilitate the work, Solomon appointed twelve officers, who had each the charge of a tribe or particular district of country, from which, in monthly rotation, the supplies for the maintenance of the king's household were drawn, having first been deposited in "the store cities" which were erected for their reception (ch. 9:19; II Chron. 8:4, 6). **8. The son of Hur**—or, as the margin has it, *Benhur, Bendekar.* In the rural parts of Syria, and among the Arabs, it is still common to designate persons not by their own names, but as the sons of their fathers. **21. Solomon reigned over all kingdoms, from the river**—All the petty kingdoms between the Euphrates and the Mediterranean were tributary to him. Similar is the statement in vs. 24. **24. from Tiphsah**—i.e., Thapsacus, a large and flourishing town on the west bank of the Euphrates, the name of which was derived from a celebrated ford near it, the lowest on that river. **even to Azzah**—i.e., Gaza, on the southwestern extremity, not far from the Mediterranean. **22. Solomon's provision for one day**—not for the king's table only, but for all connected with the court, including, besides the royal establishment, those of his royal consorts, his principal officers, his bodyguards, his foreign visitors, etc. The quantity of fine floor used is estimated at 240 bushels: that of meal or common flour at 480. The number of cattle required for consumption, besides poultry and several kinds of game (which were abundant on the mountains) did not exceed in proportion what is needed in other courts of the East. **25. every man under his vine and ... fig tree**—This is a common and beautiful metaphor for peace and security (Mic. 4:4; Zech. 3:10), founded on the practice, still common in modern Syria. of training these fruit trees up the walls and stairs of houses, so as to make a shady arbor, beneath which the people sit and relax. **26. forty thousand stalls**—for the royal mews (see on II Chron. 9:25). **28.**

Barley ... and straw—Straw is not used for litter, but barley mixed with chopped straw is the usual fodder of horses. **dromedaries**—one-humped camels, distinguished for their great fleetness. 29-34. His Wisdom. **29. God gave Solomon wisdom and understanding exceeding much, and largeness of heart**—i.e., high powers of mind, great capacity for receiving, as well as aptitude for communicating, knowledge. **30. Solomon's wisdom excelled the wisdom of all the children of the east country**—i.e., the Arabians, Chaldeans, and Persians (Gen. 25:6). **all the wisdom of Egypt**—Egypt was renowed as the seat of learning and sciences, and the existing monuments, which so clearly describe the ancient state of society and the arts, show the high culture of the Egyptian people. **31. wiser than all men**—i.e., all his contemporaries, either at home or abroad. **than Ethan**—or Jeduthun, of the family of Merari (I Chron. 6:44). **Heman**—(I Chron. 15: 17-19)—the chief of the temple musicians and the king's seers (I Chron. 25:5); the other two are not known. **the sons of Mahol**—either another name for Zerah (I Chron. 2:6); or taking it as a common noun, signifying a dance, a chorus, "the sons of Mahol" signify persons eminently skilled in poetry and music. **32. he spake three thousand proverbs**—embodying his moral sentiments and sage observations on human life and character. **songs ... a thousand and five**—Psalm 72, 127, 132, and the Song of Songs are his. **33. he spake of trees, from the cedar ... to the hyssop**—all plants, from the greatest to the least. The Spirit of God has seen fit to preserve comparatively few memorials of the fruits of his gigantic mind. The greater part of those here ascribed to him have long since fallen a prey to the ravages of time, or perished in the Babylonish captivity, probably because they were not inspired.

CHAPTER 5

Vss. 1-6. Hiram Sends to Congratulate Solomon. **1. Hiram ... sent his servants unto Solomon**—the grandson of David's contemporary [Kitto]; or the same Hiram [Winer and others]. The friendly relations which the king of Tyre had cultivated with David are here seen renewed with his son and successor, by a message of condolence as well as of congratulation on his accession to the throne of Israel. The alliance between the two nations had been mutually beneficial by the encouragement of useful traffic. Israel, being agricultural, furnished corn and oil, while the Tyrians, who were a commercial people, gave in exchange their Phœnician manufactures, as well as the produce of foreign lands. A special treaty was now entered into in furtherance of that undertaking which was the great work of Solomon's splendid and peaceful reign. **6. command thou that they hew me cedar trees out of Lebanon**—Nowhere else could Solomon have procured materials for the woodwork of his contemplated building. The forests of Lebanon, adjoining the seas in Solomon's time, belonged to the Phœnicians, and the timber being a lucrative branch of their exports, immense numbers of workmen were constantly employed in the felling of trees as well as the transportation and preparation of the wood. Hiram stipulated to furnish Solomon with as large a quantity of cedars and cypresses as he might require and it was a great additional obligation that he engaged to render the important service of having it brought down, probably by the Dog river, to the seaside, and conveyed along the coast

in floats; i.e., the logs being bound together, to the harbor of Joppa (II Chron. 2:16), whence they could easily find the means of transport to Jerusalem. **my servants shall be with thy servants**—The operations were to be on so extensive a scale that the Tyrians alone would be insufficient. A division of labor was necessary, and while the former would do the work that required skilful artisans, Solomon engaged to supply the laborers. 7-12. Furnishes Timber to Build the Temple. **7. Blessed be the Lord**—This language is no decisive evidence that Hiram was a worshipper of the true God, as he might use it only on the polytheistic principle of acknowledging Jehovah as the God of the Hebrews (see on II Chron. 2:12). **8. Hiram sent to Solomon, saying, I have considered the things ... and I will do**—The contract was drawn out formally in a written document (II Chron. 2:11), which, according to Josephus, was preserved both in the Jewish and Tyrian records. **10. fir trees**—rather, the cypress. **11. food to his household**—This was an annual supply for the palace, different from that mentioned in II Chron. 2:10, which was for the workmen in the forests. 13-18. Solomon's Workmen and Laborers. **13. Solomon raised a levy out of all Israel**—The renewed notice of Solomon's divine gift of wisdom (vs. 12) is evidently introduced to prepare for this record of the strong but prudent measures he took towards the accomplishment of his work. So great a stretch of arbitrary power as is implied in this compulsory levy would have raised great discontent, if not opposition, had not his wise arrangement of letting the laborers remain at home two months out of three, added to the sacredness of the work, reconciled the people to this forced labor. The carrying of burdens and the irksome work of excavating the quarries was assigned to the remnant of the Canaanites (ch. 9:20; II Chron. 8:7-9) and war prisoners made by David—amounting to 153,600. The employment of persons of that condition in Eastern countries for carrying on any public work, would make this part of the arrangements the less thought of. **17. brought great stones**—The stone of Lebanon is "hard, calcareous, whitish and sonorous, like free-stone" [Shaw]. The same white and beautiful stone can be obtained in every part of Syria and Palestine. **hewed stones**—or neatly polished, as the *Hebrew* word signifies (Exod. 20:25). Both Jewish and Tyrian builders were employed in hewing these great stones. **18. and the stone-squarers**—The margin, which renders it "the Giblites" (Josh. 13:5), has long been considered a preferable translation. This marginal translation also must yield to another which has lately been proposed, by a slight change in the *Hebrew* text, and which would be rendered thus: "Solomon's builders, and Hiram's builders, did hew them and bevel them" [Thenius]. These great bevelled or grooved stones, measuring some twenty, others thirty feet in length, and from five to six feet in breadth, are still seen in the substructures about the ancient site of the temple; and, in the judgment of the most competent observers, were those originally employed "to lay the foundation of the house."

CHAPTER 6

Vss. 1-4. The Building of Solomon's Temple. **2. the house which King Solomon built for the Lord**—The dimensions are given in cubits, which are to be reckoned according to the early standard (II

Chron. 3:3), or holy cubit (Ezek. 40:5; 43:13), a handbreadth longer than the common or later one. It is probable that the internal elevation only is here stated. **3. the porch**—or portico, extended across the whole front (see on II Chron. 3:4). **windows of narrow lights**—i.e., windows with lattices, capable of being shut and opened at pleasure, partly to let out the vapor of the lamps, the smoke of the frankincense, and partly to give light [KEIL].

5-10. THE CHAMBERS THEREOF. **5. against the wall of the house he built chambers**—On three sides, there were chambers in three stories, each story wider than the one beneath it, as the walls were narrowed or made thinner as they ascended, by a rebate being made, on which the beams of the side floor rested, without penetrating the wall. These chambers were approached from the right-hand side, in the interior of the under story, by a winding staircase of stone, which led to the middle and upper stories. **7. there was neither hammer nor axe nor any tool of iron heard in the house while it was in building**—A subterranean quarry has been very recently discovered near Jerusalem, where the temple stones are supposed to have been hewn. There is unequivocal evidence in this quarry that the stones were dressed there; for there are blocks very similar in size, as well as of the same kind of stone, as those found in the ancient remains. Thence, probably, they would be moved on rollers down the Tyropean valley to the very side of the temple [TENT and KHAN]. **9, 10. built the house**—The temple is here distinguished from the wings or chambers attached to it—and its roofing was of cedar wood. **10. chambers . . . five cubits high**—The height of the whole three stories was therefore about fifteen cubits. **they rested on the house with timber of cedar**—i.e., because the beams of the side-stones rested on the ledges of the temple wall. The wing was attached to the house; it was connected with the temple, without, however, interfering injuriously with the sanctuary [KEIL].

11-14. GOD'S PROMISES UNTO IT. **11. the word of the Lord came to Solomon**—probably by a prophet. It was very seasonable, being designed: first, to encourage him to go on with the building, by confirming anew the promise made to his father David (II Sam. 7); and secondly, to warn him against the pride and presumption of supposing that after the erection of so magnificent a temple, he and his people would always be sure of the presence and favor of God. The condition on which that blessing could alone be expected was expressly stated. The dwelling of God among the children of Israel refers to those symbols of His presence in the temple, which were the visible tokens of His spiritual relation to that people.

15-22. THE CEILING AND ADORNING OF IT. **15. he built the walls of the house within**—The walls were wainscotted with cedar wood—the floor paved with cypress planks—the interior was divided (by a partition consisting of folding doors, which were opened and shut with golden chains) into two apartments—the back or inner room, i.e., the most holy place, was twenty cubits long and broad—the front, or outer room, i.e., the holy place, was forty cubits. The cedar wood was beautifully embellished with figures in relievo, representing clusters of foliage, open flowers, cherubims, and palm trees. The whole interior was overlaid with gold, so that neither wood nor stone was seen; nothing met the eye but pure gold, either plain or richly chased. **31-35. for the entering of the oracle**—The door of the most holy place was made of solid olive tree and adorned with figures. The door of the holy place was made of cypress wood, the sides being of olive wood. **36. the inner court**—was for the priests. Its wall, which had a coping of cedar, is said to have been so low that the people could see over it.

37, 38. THE TIME TAKEN TO BUILD IT. **37. In the fourth year was the foundation laid**—The building was begun in the second month of the fourth year and completed in the eighth month of the eleventh year of Solomon's reign, comprising a period of seven and a half years, which is reckoned here in round numbers. It was not a very large, but a very splendid building, requiring great care, and ingenuity, and division of labor. The immense number of workmen employed, together with the previous preparation of the materials, serves to account for the short time occupied in the process of building.

CHAPTER 7

Vs. 1. BUILDING OF SOLOMON'S HOUSE. **1. Solomon was building his own house thirteen years**—The time occupied in building his palace was nearly double that spent in the erection of the temple, because neither had there been the same previous preparations for it, nor was there the same urgency as in providing a place of worship, on which the national well-being so much depended.

2-7. OF THE HOUSE OF LEBANON. **2. He built also the house of the forest of Lebanon**—It is scarcely possible to determine whether this was a different edifice from the former, or whether his house, the house of the forest of Lebanon, and the one for Pharaoh's daughter, were not parts of one grand palace. As difficult is it to decide what was the origin of the name; some supposing it was so called because built on Lebanon; others, that it was in or near Jerusalem, but contained such a profuse supply of cedar columns as to have occasioned this peculiar designation. We have a similar peculiarity of name in the building called the East India house, though situated in London. The description is conformable to the arrangement of Eastern palaces. The building stood in the middle of a great oblong square, which was surrounded by an enclosing wall, against which the houses and offices of those attached to the court were built. The building itself was oblong, consisting of two square courts, flanking a large oblong hall which formed the center, and was 100 cubits long, by 50 broad. This was properly the house of the forest of Lebanon, being the part where were the cedar pillars of this hall. In front was the porch of judgment, which was appropriated to the transaction of public business. On the one side of this great hall was the king's house; and on the other the harem or royal apartments for Pharaoh's daughter (Esther 2:3,9). This arrangement of the palace accords with the Oriental style of building, according to which a great mansion always consists of three divisions, or separate houses—all connected by doors and passages—the men dwelling at one extremity, the women of the family at the other, while public rooms occupy the central part of the building. **10. the foundation was of costly stones, even great stones**—Enormous stones, corresponding exactly with the dimensions given, are found in Jerusalem at this day. Not only the walls from the foundation to the roof-beams were built of large hewn stones, but the spacious court around the palace was also paved with great square stones. **12. for the inner court of the house of the Lord**—

should be, *as in* the inner court of the house of the Lord; the meaning is, that in this palace, as in the temple, rows of hewed stones and the cedar beams formed the enclosing wall.

13-51. HIRAM'S WORKS. **Solomon sent and fetched Hiram out of Tyre**—The Tyrians and other inhabitants on the Phœnician coast were the most renowed artists and workers in metal in the ancient world. **14. He was a widow's son of the tribe of Naphtali**—In II Chronicles 2:14 his mother is said to have been of the daughters of Dan. The apparent discrepancy may be reconciled thus: Hiram's mother, though belonging to the tribe of Dan, had been married to a Naphtalite, so that when married afterwards to a Tyrian, she might be described as a widow of the tribe of Naphtali. Or, if she was a native of the city Dan (Laish), she might be said to be of the daughters of Dan, as born in that place; and of the tribe of Naphtali, as really belonging to it. **a worker in brass**—This refers particularly to the works described in this chapter. But in II Chronicles 2:13 his artistic skill is represented as extending to a great variety of departments. In fact, he was appointed, from his great natural talents and acquired skill, to superintend all the works of art in the temple. **15-22. two pillars of brass of eighteen cubits high**—They were made of the brass (bronze) which was taken from the king of Zobah (I Chron. 18:8). In II Chronicles 3:15 they are said to have been thirty-five cubits high. There, however, their joint lengths are given; whereas here the length of the pillars is given separately. Each pillar was seventeen and a half cubits long, which is stated, in round numbers, as eighteen. Their dimensions in American measure are as follows: The pillars without the capitals measured thirty-two and a half feet long, and seven feet diameter; and if hollow, as WHISTON, in his translation of Josephus, thinks (Jer. 52:21), the metal would be about three and a half inches thick; so that the whole casting of one pillar must have been from sixteen to twenty tons. The height of the capitals was eight and three-fourths feet; and, at the same thickness of metal, would not weigh less than seven or eight tons each. The nature of the workmanship in the finishing of these capitals is described (vss. 17-22). The pillars, when set up, would stand forty feet in height [NAPIER'S METAL]. **17. nets of checker work**—i.e., branchwork, resembling the branches of palm trees, and *wreaths of chain-work*; i.e., plaited in the form of a chain, composing a sort of crown or garland. Seven of these were wound in festoons on one capital, and over and underneath them were fringes, one hundred in a row. Two rows of pomegranates strung on chains (II Chron. 3:16) ran round the capital (vs. 42; cf. II Chron. 4:12, 13; Jer. 52:23), which, itself, was of a bowl-like or globular form (vs. 41). These rows were designed to form a binding to the ornamental work—to keep it from falling asunder; and they were so placed as to be above the chain-work, and below the place where the branch-work was. **19. lily work**—beautiful ornaments, resembling the stalks, leaves, and blossoms of lilies—of large dimensions, as suited to the height of their position. **21. Jachin and ... Boaz**—These names were symbolical, and indicated the strength and stability—not so much of the material temple, for they were destroyed along with it (Jer. 52:17), as of the spiritual kingdom of God, which was embodied in the temple. **23-26. he made a molten sea**—In the tabernacle was no such vessel; the laver served the double purpose of washing the hands and feet of the priests as well as the parts of the sacri-

fices. But in the temple there were separate vessels provided for these offices. (See on II Chron. 4:6.) The molten sea was an immense semicircular vase, measuring seventeen and a half feet in diameter, and being eight and three-fourths feet in depth. This, at three and a half inches in thickness, could not weigh less than from twenty-five to thirty tons in one solid casting—and held from 16,000 to 20,000 gallons of water. The brim was all carved with lilywork or flowers, and oxen were carved or cut on the outside all round, to the number of 300; and it stood on a pedestal of twelve oxen. These oxen must have been of considerable size, like the Assyrian bulls, so that their corresponding legs would give thickness or strength to support so great a weight for, when the vessel was filled with water, the whole weight would be about 100 tons [NAPIER]. (See on II Chron. 4:5.) **27-39. he made ten bases of brass**—These were trucks or four-wheeled carriages, for the support and conveyance of the lavers. The description of their structure shows that they were elegantly fitted up and skilfully adapted to their purpose. They stood, not on the axles, but on four rests attached to the axles, so that the figured sides were considerably raised above the wheels. They were all exactly alike in form and size. The lavers which were borne upon them were vessels capable each of holding 300 gallons of water, upwards of a ton weight. The whole, when full of water, would be no less than two tons [NAPIER]. **40-45. And Hiram made the lavers, and the shovels, and the basins**—These verses contain a general enumeration of Hiram's works, as well as those already mentioned as other minor things. The Tyrian artists are frequently mentioned by ancient authors as skilful artificers in fashioning and embossing metal cups and bowls; and we need not wonder, therefore, to find them employed by Solomon in making the golden and brazen utensils for his temple and palaces. **46. In the plain of Jordan did the king cast them**—Zarthan or Zaretan (Josh. 3:16), or Zartanah (ch. 4:12), or Zeredathah (II Chron. 4:17), was on the bank of the Jordan in the territories of western Manasseh. Succoth was situated on the eastern side of Jordan, at the ford of the river near the mouth of the Jabbok. One reason assigned by commentators for the castings being made there is, that at such a distance from Jerusalem that city would not be annoyed by the smoke and noxious vapors necessarily occasioned by the process. [Note in BAGSTER'S BIBLE.] But the true reason is to be found in the nature of the soil; *Marg.,* the thickness of the ground. That part of the Jordan valley abounds with marl. Clay and sand are the moulding material still used for bronze. Such large quantities of metal as one of these castings would contain could not be fused in one furnace, but would require a series of furnaces, especially for such a casting as the brazen sea—the whole series of furnaces being filled with metal, and fused at one time, and all tapped together, and the metal let run into the mould. Thus a national foundry was erected in the plain of Jordan [NAPIER]. **48. the altar of gold**—i.e., the altar of incense. **49. candlesticks of pure gold**—made, probably, according to the model of that in the tabernacle, which, along with the other articles of furniture, were deposited with due honor, as sacred relics, in the temple. But these seem not to have been used in the temple service; for Solomon made new lavers tables, and candlesticks, ten of each. (See further regarding the dimensions and furniture of the temple, in II Chron. 3:5.)

CHAPTER 8

Vss. 1-12. The Dedication of the Temple. 2. at the feast in the month Ethanim—The public and formal inauguration of this national place of worship did not take place till eleven months after the completion of the edifice. The delay, most probably, originated in Solomon's wish to choose the most fitting opportunity when there should be a general rendezvous of the people in Jerusalem (vs. 2); and that was not till the next year. That was a jubilee year, and he resolved on commencing the solemn ceremonial a few days before the feast of tabernacles, which was the most appropriate of all seasons. That annual festival had been instituted in commemoration of the Israelites dwelling in booths during their stay in the winderness, as well as of the tabernacle, which was then erected, in which God promised to meet and dwell with His people, sanctifying it with His glory. As the tabernacle was to be superseded by the temple, there was admirable propriety in choosing the feast of tabernacles as the period for dedicating the new place of worship, and praying that the same distinguished privileges might be continued to it in the manifestation of the divine presence and glory. At the time appointed for the inauguration, the king issued orders for all the heads and representatives of the nation to repair to Jerusalem and take part in the august procession. The lead was taken by the king and elders of the people, whose march must have been slow, as priests were stationed to offer an immense number of sacrifices at various points in the line of road through which the procession was to go. Then came the priests bearing the ark and the tabernacle—the old Mosaic tabernacle which was brought from Gibeon. Lastly, the Levites followed, carrying the vessels and ornaments belonging to the old, for lodgment in the new, house of the Lord. There was a slight deviation in this procedure from the order of march established in the wilderness (Num. 3:31; 4:15); but the spirit of the arrangement was duly observed. The ark was deposited in the oracle; i.e., the most holy place, under the wings of the cherubim—not the Mosaic cherubim, which were firmly attached to the ark (Exod. 37:7, 8), but those made by Solomon, which were far larger and more expanded. **8. they drew out the staves**—a little way, so as to project (see on Exod. 25:15; Num. 4:6); and they were left in that position. The object was, that these projecting staves might serve as a guide to the high priest, in conducting him to that place where, once a year, he went to officiate before the ark; otherwise he might miss his way in the dark, the ark being wholly overshadowed by the wings of the cherubim. **9. There was nothing in the ark save the two tables of stone**—Nothing else was ever in the ark, the articles mentioned (Heb. 9:4) being not *in*, but *by* it, being laid in the most holy place before the testimony (Exod. 16:33; Num. 17:10). **10, 11. the cloud filled the house of the Lord**—The cloud was the visible symbol of the divine presence, and its occupation of the sanctuary was a testimony of God's gracious acceptance of the temple as of the tabernacle (Exod. 40:34). The dazzling brightness, or rather, perhaps, the dense portentous darkness of the cloud, struck the minds of the priests, as it formerly had done Moses, which such astonishment and terror (Lev. 16:2-13; Deut. 4:24; Exod. 40:35) that they could not remain. Thus the temple became the place where the divine glory was revealed, and the king of Israel established his royal residence. **12-21. Solomon's Blessing. 12. Then spake**

Solomon—For the reassurance of the priests and people, the king reminded them that the cloud, instead of being a sign ominous of evil, was a token of approval. **The Lord said**—not in express terms, but by a continuous course of action (Exod. 13:21; 24:16; Num. 9:15). **13. I have surely built thee an house**—This is an apostrophe to God, as perceiving His approach by the cloud, and welcoming Him to enter as guest or inhabitant of the fixed and permanent dwelling-place, which, at His command, had been prepared for His reception. **14. the king turned his face about**—From the temple, where he had been watching the movement of the mystic cloud, and while the people were standing, partly as the attitude of devotion, partly out of respect to royalty, the king gave a fervent expression of praise to God for the fulfilment of His promise (II Sam. 7:6-16).

22-61. His Prayer. 22. Solomon stood before the altar—This position was in the court of the people, on a brazen scaffold erected for the occasion (II Chron. 6:13), fronting the altar of burnt offering, and surrounded by a mighty concourse of people. Assuming the attitude of a suppliant, kneeling (vs. 54, cf. II Chron. 6:24) and with uplifted hands, he performed the solemn act of consecration—an act remarkable, among other circumstances, for this, that it was done, not by the high priest or any member of the Aaronic family, but by the king in person, who might minister *about*, though not *in*, holy things. This sublime prayer, which breathes sentiments of the loftiest piety blended with the deepest humility, naturally bore a reference to the national blessing and curse contained in the law—and the burden of it—after an ascription of praise to the Lord for the bestowment of the former, was an earnest supplication for deliverance from the latter. He specifies seven cases in which the merciful interposition of God would be required; and he earnestly bespeaks it on the condition of people praying towards that holy place. The blessing addressed to the people at the close is substantially a brief recapitulation of the preceding prayer.

62-64. His Sacrifice of Peace Offering. 62. the king, and all Israel ... offered sacrifice before the Lord—This was a burnt offering with its accompaniments, and being the first laid on the altar of the temple, was, as in the analogous case of the tabernacle, consumed by miraculous fire from heaven (see on II Chron. 7:12). On remarkable occasions, the heathens sacrificed hecatombs (a hundred animals), and even chiliombs (a thousand animals), but the public sacrifices offered by Solomon on this occasion surpassed all the other oblations on record, without taking into account those presented by private individuals, which, doubtless, amounted to a large additional number. The large proportion of the sacrifices were peace offerings, which afforded the people an opportunity of festive enjoyment. **63. So the king and all the children of Israel dedicated the house of the Lord**—The dedication was not a ceremony ordained by the law, but it was done in accordance with the sentiments of reverence naturally associated with edifices appropriated to divine worship. **64. The same day did the king hallow the middle of the court**—i.e., the whole extent of the priests' court—the altar of burnt offerings, though large (II Chron. 4:1), being totally inadequate for the vast number of sacrifices that distinguished this occasion. It was only a temporary erection to meet the demands of an extraordinary season, in aid of the established altar, and removed at the conclusion of the sacred festival.

65. THE PEOPLE JOYFUL. 65. from the entering in of Hamath unto the river of Egypt—i.e., from one extremity of the kingdom to the other. The people flocked from all quarters. **seven days and seven days, even fourteen days**—The first seven were occupied with the dedication, and the other seven devoted to the feast of tabernacles (II Chron. 7:9). The particular form of expression indicates that the fourteen days were not continuous. Some interval occurred in consequence of the great day of atonement falling on the tenth of the seventh month (vs. 2), and the last day of the feast of tabernacles was on the twenty-third (II Chron. 7:10), when the people returned to their homes with feelings of the greatest joy and gratitude "for all the goodness that the LORD had done for David his servant, and for Israel his people."

CHAPTER 9

VSS. 1-9. GOD'S COVENANT IN A SECOND VISION WITH SOLOMON. **1. And it came to pass, when Solomon had finished the building of the house**—This first verse is connected with the eleventh, all that is contained between verses 2-10 being parenthetical. **2. That** [rather, *for*] **the Lord appeared**—This appearance was, like the former one at Gibeon, most probably made in a supernatural vision, and on the night immediately following the dedication of the temple (II Chron. 7:12). The strain of it corresponds to this view, for it consists of direct answers to his solemn inaugural prayer (vs. 3 is in answer to ch. 8:29; vss. 4, 5 is in answer to ch. 8:25, 26; vss. 6-9 to ch. 8:33-46, see also Deut. 29:22-24). **8. this house, which is high**—"high," either in point of situation, for it was built on a hill, and therefore conspicuous to every beholder; or "high" in respect to privilege, honor, and renown; or this "house of the Most High," notwithstanding all its beauty and magnificence, shall be destroyed, and remain in such a state of ruin and degradation as to be a striking monument of the just judgment of God. The record of this second vision, in which were rehearsed the conditions of God's covenant with Solomon and the consequences of breaking them, is inserted here as a proper introduction to the narrative about to be given of this king's commercial enterprises and ambitious desire for worldly glory; for this king, by encouraging an influx of foreign people and a taste for foreign luxuries, rapidly corrupted his own mind and that of his subjects, so that they turned from following God, they and their children (vs. 6).

10-23. THE MUTUAL PRESENTS OF SOLOMON AND HIRAM. **10. at the end of twenty years**—Seven and a half years were spent in building the temple, and twelve and a half or thirteen in the erection of his palace (ch. 7:1; II Chron. 8:1). This verse is only a recapitulation of the first, necessary to recover the thread of connection in the narrative. **11. Solomon gave Hiram twenty cities in the land of Galilee**—According to Josephus, they were situated on the northwest of it, adjacent to Tyre. Though lying within the boundaries of the promised land (Gen. 15:18; Josh. 1:4), they had never been conquered till then, and were inhabited by Canaanite heathens (Judg. 4:2-13, II Kings 15:29). They were probably given to Hiram, whose dominions were small, as a remuneration for his important services in furnishing workmen, materials, and an immense quantity of *wrought* gold (vs. 14) for the temple and other buildings [MICHAELIS]. The gold, however, as others think, may have been the amount of forfeits paid to Solomon by Hiram for not being able to answer the riddles and apothegms, with which, according to Josephus, in their private correspondence, the two sovereigns amused themselves. Hiram having refused these cities, probably on account of their inland situation making them unsuitable to his maritime and commercial people, Solomon satisfied his ally in some other way; and, taking these cities into his own hands, he first repaired their shattered walls, then filled them with a colony of Hebrews (II Chron. 8:2). **15-24. this is the reason of the levy**—A levy refers both to men and money, and the necessity for Solomon making it arose from the many gigantic works he undertook to erect. **Millo**—part of the fort of Jerusalem on Mount Zion (II Sam. 5:9; I Chron. 11:8), or a row of stone bastions around Mount Zion, Millo being the great corner tower of that fortified wall (ch. 11:27; II Chron. 32:5). **the wall of Jerusalem**—either repairing some breaches in it (ch. 11:27), or extending it so as to enclose Mount Zion. **Hazor**—fortified on account of its importance as a town in the northern boundary of the country. **Megiddo**—(now Leijun) —Lying in the great caravan road between Egypt and Damascus, it was the key to the north of Palestine by the western lowlands, and therefore fortified. **Gezer**—on the western confines of Ephraim, and, though a Levitical city, occupied by the Canaanites. Having fallen by right of conquest to the king of Egypt, who for some cause attacked it, it was given by him as a dowry to his daughter, and fortified by Solomon. **17. Beth-horon the nether**—situated on the way from Joppa to Jerusalem and Gibeon; it required, from so public a road, to be strongly garrisoned. **18. Baalath**—Baalbek. **Tadmor**—Palmyra, between Damascus and the Euphrates, was rebuilt and fortified as a security against invasion from northern Asia. In accomplishing these and various other works which were carried on throughout the kingdom, especially in the north, where Rezon of Damascus, his enemy, might prove dangerous, he employed vast numbers of the Canaanites as galley slaves (II Chron. 2:18), treating them as prisoners of war, who were compelled to do the drudgery and hard labor, while the Israelites were only engaged in honorable employment. **23. These were the chief of the officers**—(See on II Chron. 8: 10).

24-28. SOLOMON'S YEARLY SACRIFICES. **24, 25. three times in a year**—viz., at the passover, pentecost, and feast of tabernacles (II Chron. 8:13; 31:3). The circumstances mentioned in these two verses form a proper conclusion to the record of his buildings and show that his design in erecting those at Jerusalem was to remedy defects existing at the commencement of his reign (see on ch. 3:1-4). **26. Ezion-geber, which is beside Eloth**—These were neighboring ports at the head of the eastern or Elanitic branch of the Red Sea. Tyrian ship-carpenters and sailors were sent there for Solomon's vessels (see on II Chron. 8). **Ezion-geber**—i.e., the giant's backbone; so called from a reef of rocks at the entrance of the harbor. **Eloth**—Elim or Elath; i.e., "the trees"—a grove of terebinthes still exists at the head of the gulf. **28. Ophir**—a general name, like the East or West Indies with us, for all the southern regions lying on the African, Arabian, or Indian seas, in so far as at that time known [HEEREN]. **gold, four hundred and twenty talents**—(See on II Chron. 8:18). At 125 pounds Troy, or 1500 ounces to the talent, and £4 to the ounce, this would make £2,604,000, or about $12,350,000.

CHAPTER 10

Vss. 1-13. THE QUEEN OF SHEBA ADMIRES THE WISDOM OF SOLOMON. **1. the queen of Sheba**—Some think her country was the Sabean kingdom of Yemen, of which the capital was Saba, in Arabia Felix; others, that it was in African Ethiopia, i.e., Abyssinia, towards the south of the Red Sea. The opinions preponderate in favor of the former. This view harmonizes with the language of our Lord, as Yemen means "South"; and this country, extending to the shores of the Indian ocean, might in ancient times be considered "the uttermost parts of the earth." **heard of the fame of Solomon**—doubtless by the Ophir fleet. **concerning the name of the Lord**—meaning either his great knowledge of God, or the extraordinary things which God had done for him. **hard questions**—enigmas or riddles. The Orientals delight in this species of intellectual exercise and test wisdom by the power and readiness to solve them. **2. she came to Jerusalem with a very great train, with camels**—A long train of those beasts of burden forms the common way of travelling in Arabia; and the presents specified consist of the native produce of that country. Of course, a royal equipage would be larger and more imposing than an ordinary caravan. **6. It was a true report that I heard in mine own land of thy acts and of thy wisdom**—The proofs she obtained of Solomon's wisdom—not from his conversation only, but also from his works; the splendor of his palace; the economy of his kitchen and table; the order of his court; the gradations and gorgeous costume of his servants; above all, the arched viaduct that led from his palace to the temple (II Kings 16:18), and the remains of which have been recently discovered [ROBINSON]—overwhelmed her with astonishment. **9. Blessed be the Lord thy God**—(See on ch. 5:7.) It is quite possible, as Jewish writers say, that this queen was converted, through Solomon's influence, to the worship of the true God. But there is no record of her making any gift or offering in the temple. **10. she gave the king an hundred and twenty talents of gold**—$3,500,000. **11. almug trees**—Parenthetically, along with the valuable presents of the queen of Sheba, is mentioned a foreign wood, which was brought in the Ophir ships. It is thought by some to be the sandalwood; by others, to be the deodar—a species of fragrant fir, much used in India for sacred and important works. Solomon used it for stairs in his temple and palace (II Chron. 9:11), but chiefly for musical instruments. **13. King Solomon gave unto the queen of Sheba all her desire, whatsoever she asked, beside**—i.e., Solomon not only gave his illustrious guest all the insight and information she wanted; but, according to the Oriental fashion, he gave her ample remuneration for the presents she had brought.

14-29. HIS RICHES. **14. Now the weight of gold that came to Solomon in one year**—666 talents, equal to about $20,000,000. The sources whence this was derived are not mentioned; nor was it the full amount of his revenue; for this was "Beside that he had of the merchantmen, and of the traffic of the spice merchants, and of all the kings of Arabia, and of the governors of the country." The great encouragement he gave to commerce was the means of enriching his royal treasury. By the fortifications which he erected in various parts of his kingdom, (particularly at such places as Thapsacus, one of the passages of Euphrates, and at Tadmor, in the Syrian desert), he gave complete security to the caravan trade from the depredations of the Arab marauders; and it was reasonable that, in return for this protection, he should exact a certain toll or duty for the importation of foreign goods. A considerable revenue, too, would arise from the use of the store cities and khans he built; and it is not improbable that those cities were emporia, where the caravan merchants unloaded their bales of spices and other commodities and sold them to the king's factors, who, according to the modern practice in the East, retailed them in the Western markets at a profit. "The revenue derived from the tributary kings and from the governors of the country" must have consisted in the tribute which all inferior magistrates periodically bring to their sovereigns in the East, in the shape of presents of the produce of their respective provinces. **16, 17. two hundred targets, six hundred shekels**—These defensive arms were anciently made of wood and covered with leather; those were covered with fine gold. $6,000 worth of gold was used in the gilding of each target—**$1800 for each shield.** They were intended for the state armory of the palace (see on ch. 14:26). **18-26. a great throne of ivory**—It seems to have been made not of solid ivory, but veneered. It was in the form of an armchair, with a carved back. The ascent to it was by six steps, on each of which stood lions, in place of a railing—while a lion, probably of gilt metal, stood at each side, which, we may suppose from the analogy of other Oriental thrones, supported a canopy. A golden footstool is mentioned (II Chron. 9:18) as attached to this throne, whose magnificence is described as unrivalled. **22. a navy of Tarshish**—Tartessus in Spain. There gold, and especially silver, was obtained, anciently, in so great abundance that it was nothing accounted of in the days of Solomon. But Tarshish came to be a general term for the West (Jonah 1). **at sea**—on the Mediterranean. **once in three years**—i.e., every third year. Without the mariner's compass they had to coast along the shore. The ivory, apes, and peacocks might have been purchased, on the outward or homeward voyage, on the north coast of Africa, where the animals were to be found. They were particularized, probably as being the rarest articles on board. **26-29.**—(See on II Chron. 1:14-17.)

CHAPTER 11

Vss. 1-8. SOLOMON'S WIVES AND CONCUBINES IN HIS OLD AGE. **1. But King Solomon loved many strange women**—Solomon's extraordinary gift of wisdom was not sufficient to preserve him from falling into grievous and fatal errors. A fairer promise of true greatness, a more beautiful picture of juvenile piety, never was seen than that which he exhibited at the commencement of his reign. No sadder, more humiliating, or awful spectacle can be imagined than the besotted apostasy of his old age; and to him may be applied the words of Paul (Gal. 3:3), of John (Rev. 3:17), and of Isaiah (14:21). A love of the world, a ceaseless round of pleasure, had insensibly corrupted his heart, and produced, for a while at least, a state of mental darkness. The grace of God deserted him; and the son of the pious David—the religiously trained child of Bathsheba (Prov. 31:1-3), and pupil of Nathan, instead of showing the stability of sound principle and mature experience became at last an old and foolish king (Eccles. 4:13). His fall is traced to his "love of many strange women." Polygamy was tolerated among the ancient Hebrews; and, although in most countries of the East, the generality of men, from convenience and economy, confine themselves to one woman, yet a number of wives is reckoned as an indication of wealth and importance, just as a numerous stud of horses and a grand equipage are among us. The sovereign, of course, wishes to have a more numerous harem than any of his subjects; and the female establishments of many Oriental princes have, both in ancient and modern times, equalled or exceeded that of Solomon's. It is probable, therefore, that, in conformity with Oriental notions, he resorted to it as a piece of state magnificence. But in him it was unpardonable, as it was a direct and outrageous violation of the divine law (Deut. 17:17), and the very result which that statute was ordained to prevent was realized in him. His marriage with the daughter of Pharaoh is not censured either here or elsewhere (see on ch. 3:1). It was only his love for many strange women; for women, though in the East considered inferiors, exert often a silent but powerful seductive influence over their husbands in the harem, as elsewhere, and so it was exemplified in Solomon. **3. he had seven hundred wives, princesses**—They were, probably, according to an existing custom, the daughters of tributary chiefs, given as hostages for good conduct of their fathers. **concubines**—were legitimate, but lower or secondary wives. These the chief or first wife regards without the smallest jealousy or regret, as they look up to her with feelings of respectful submission. Solomon's wives became numerous, not all at once, but gradually. Even at an early period his taste for Oriental show seems to have led to the establishment of a considerable harem (Song of Sol. 6:8). **4. when Solomon was old**—He could not have been more than fifty. **his wives turned away his heart after other gods**—Some, considering the lapse of Solomon into idolatry as a thing incredible, regard him as merely humoring his wives in the practice of their superstition; and, in countenancing their respective rites by his presence, as giving only an outward homage—a sensible worship, in which neither his understanding nor his heart was engaged. The apology only makes matters worse, as it implies an adding of hypocrisy and contempt of God to an open breach of His law. There seems no possibility of explaining the language of the sacred historian, but as intimating that Solomon became an actual and open idolater, worshipping images of wood or stone in sight of the very temple which, in early life, he had erected to the true God. Hence that part of Olivet was called the high place of Tophet (Jer. 7:30-34), and the hill is still known as the Mount of Offense, of the Mount of Corruption (II Kings 23:13). **5-7. Ashtoreth** [Astarte], **Milcolm** [Molech], **and Chemosh**—He built altars for these three; but, although he is described (vs. 8) as doing the same for "all his strange wives," there is no evidence that they had idols distinct from these; and there is no trace whatever of Egyptian idolatry. **8. burnt incense and sacrificed unto their gods**—The first was considered a higher act of homage, and is often used as synonymous with worship (II Kings 22:17; 23:5).

9-13. GOD THREATENS HIM. **9. the Lord was angry with Solomon**—The divine appearance, first at Gibeon, and then at Jerusalem, after the dedication of the temple, with the warnings given him on both occasions, had left Solomon inexcusable; and it was proper and necessary that on one who had been so signally favored with the gifts of Heaven, but who had grossly abused them, a terrible judgment should fall. The divine sentence was announced to him probably by Ahijah; but there was mercy mingled with judgment, in the circumstance,

that it should not be inflicted on Solomon personally—and that a remnant of the kingdom should be spared—"for David's sake, and for Jerusalem's sake, which had been chosen" to put God's name there; not from a partial bias in favor of either, but that the divine promise might stand (II Sam. 7). **13. I will give one tribe to thy son**—There were left to Rehoboam the tribes of Judah, Benjamin, and Levi (II Chron. 11:12, 13); and multitudes of Israelites, who, after the schism of the kingdom, established their residence within the territory of Judah to enjoy the privileges of the true religion (ch. 12:17). These are all reckoned as one tribe.

14-40. SOLOMON'S ADVERSARIES. **14. the Lord stirred up an adversary**—i.e., permitted him, through the impulse of his own ambition, or revenge, to attack Israel. During the war of extermination, which Joab carried on in Edom (II Sam. 8:13), this Hadad, of the royal family, a mere boy when rescued from the sword of the ruthless conqueror, was carried into Egypt, hospitably entertained, and became allied with the house of the Egyptian king. In after years, the thought of his native land and his lost kingdom taking possession of his mind, he, on learning the death of David and Joab, renounced the ease, possessions, and glory of his Egyptian residence, to return to Edom and attempt the recovery of his ancestral throne. The movements of this prince seem to have given much annoyance to the Hebrew government; but as he was defeated by the numerous and strong garrisons planted throughout the Edomite territory, Hadad seems to have offered his services to Rezon, another of Solomon's adversaries (vss. 23-25). This man, who had been general of Hadadezer and, on the defeat of that great king, had succesfully withdrawn a large force, went into the wilderness, led a predatory life, like Jephthah, David, and others, on the borders of the Syrian and Arabian deserts. Then, having acquired great power, he at length became king in Damascus, threw off the yoke, and was "the adversary of Israel all the days of Solomon." He was succeeded by Hadad, whose successors took the official title of Benhadad from him, the illustrious founder of the powerful kingdom of Damascene-Syria. These hostile neighbors, who had been long kept in check by the traditional fame of David's victories, took courage; and breaking out towards the latter end of Solomon's reign, they must have not only disturbed his kingdom by their inroads, but greatly crippled his revenue by stopping his lucrative traffic with Tadmor and the Euphrates. **26-40. Jeroboam**—This was an internal enemy of a still more formidable character. He was a young man of talent and energy, who, having been appointed by Solomon superintendent of the engineering works projected around Jerusalem, had risen into public notice, and on being informed by a very significant act of the prophet Ahijah of the royal destiny which, by divine appointment, awaited him, his mind took a new turn. **29. clad**—rather wrapped up. The meaning is, "Ahijah, the Shilonite, the prophet, went and took a fit station *in the way*; and, in order that he might not be known, *he wrapped himself up*, so as closely to conceal himself, in a *new garment*, a *surtout*, which he afterwards tore in twelve pieces," Notwithstanding this privacy, the story, and the prediction connected with it, probably reached the king's ears; and Jeroboam became a marked man. His aspiring ambition, impatient for the death of Solomon, led him to form plots and conspiracies, in consequence of which he was compelled to flee to Egypt. Though chosen of God, he would not wait the course of God's providence, and therefore incurred the penalty of death by his criminal rebellion. The heavy exactions and compulsory labor (vs. 28) which Solomon latterly imposed upon his subjects, when his foreign resources began to fail, had prepared the greater part of the kingdom for a revolt under so popular a demagogue as Jeroboam. **40. Shishak—** He harbored and encouraged the rebellious refugee, and was of a different dynasty from the father-in-law of Solomon.

CHAPTER 12

Vss. 1-5. REFUSING THE OLD MEN'S COUNSEL. **1. Rehoboam went to Shechem**—He was the oldest, and perhaps the only son of Solomon, and had been, doubtless, designated by his father heir to the throne, as Solomon had been by David. The incident here related took place after the funeral obsequies of the late king and the period for public mourning had past. When all Israel came to make him king, it was not to exercise their old right of election (I Sam. 10:19-21), for, after God's promise of the perpetual sovereignty to David's posterity, their duty was submission to the authority of the rightful heir; but their object was, when making him king, to renew the conditions and stipulations to which their constitutional kings were subject (I Sam. 10:25). To the omission of such rehearsing which, under the peculiar circumstances in which Solomon was made king, they were disposed to ascribe the absolutism of his government. **Shechem**—This ancient, venerable, and central town was the place of convocation; and it is evident, if not from the appointment of that place, at least from the tenor of their language, and the concerted presence of Jeroboam, that the people were determined on revolt. **4. Thy father made our yoke grievous**—The splendor of Solomon's court and the magnitude of his undertakings being such, that neither the tribute of dependent states, nor the presents of foreign princes, nor the profits of his commercial enterprises, were adequate to carry them on, he had been obliged, for obtaining the necessary revenue, to begin a system of heavy taxation. The people looked only to the burdens, not to the benefits they derived from Solomon's peaceful and prosperous reign—and the evils from which they demanded deliverance were civil oppressions, not idolatry, to which they appear to have been indifferent or approving. **5. he said ..., Depart yet for three days**—It was prudent to take the people's demand into calm and deliberate consideration. Whether, had the advice of the sage and experienced counsellors been followed, any good result would have followed, it is impossible to say. It would at least have removed all pretext for the separation. But he preferred the counsel of his young companions (not in age, for they were all about forty-one, but inexperienced), who recommended prompt and decisive measures to quell the malcontents. **11. whips ... scorpions**—The latter, as contrasted with the former, are supposed to mean thongs thickly set with sharp iron points, used in the castigation of slaves. **15. the king hearkened not unto the people, for the cause was from the Lord—** That was the overruling cause. Rehoboam's weakness (Eccles. 2:18, 19) and inexperience in public affairs has given rise to the probable conjecture, that, like many other princes in the East, he had been kept secluded in the harem till the period of his accession (Eccles. 4:14), his father being either afraid of his aspiring to the sovereignty, like the two sons of David, or, which is more probable, afraid of

prematurely exposing his imbecility. The king's haughty and violent answer to a people already filled with a spirit of discontent and exasperation, indicated so great an incapacity to appreciate the gravity of the crisis, so utter a want of common sense, as to create a belief that he was struck with judicial blindness. It was received with mingled scorn and derision. The revolt was accomplished, and yet so quietly, that Rehoboam remained in Shechem, fancying himself the sovereign of a united kingdom, until his chief tax-gatherer, who had been most imprudently sent to treat with the people, had been stoned to death. This opened his eyes, and he fled for security to Jerusalem.

20-33. JEROBOAM MADE KING OVER THEM. **20. when all Israel heard that Jeroboam was come again** —This verse closes the parenthetical narrative begun at verse 2, and verses 21-24 resume the history from verse 1. Rehoboam determined to assert his authority by leading a large force into the disaffected provinces. But the revolt of the ten tribes was completed when the prophet Shemaiah ordered, in the Lord's name, an abandonment of any hostile measures against the revolutionists. The army, overawed by the divine prohibition, dispersed, and the king was obliged to submit. **25. Jeroboam built Shechem**—destroyed by Abimelech (Judg. 9:1-49). It was rebuilt, and perhaps fortified, by Jeroboam, as a royal residence. **built Penuel**—a ruined city with a tower (Judg. 8:9), east of Jordan, on the north bank of the Jabbok. It was an object of importance to restore this fortress (as it lay on the caravan road from Gilead to Damascus and Palmyra) and to secure his frontier on that quarter. **26. Jeroboam said in his heart, Now shall the kingdom return to the house of David** Having received the kingdom from God, he should have relied on the divine protection. But he did not. With a view to withdraw the people from the temple and destroy the sacred associations connected with Jerusalem, he made serious and unwarranted innovations on the religious observances of the country, on pretext of saving the people the trouble and expense of a distant journey. First, he erected two golden calves —the young bulls, Apis and Mnevis, as symbols (in the Egyptian fashion) of the true God, and the nearest, according to his fancy, to the figures of the cherubim. The one was placed at Dan, in the northern part of his kingdom; the other at Beth-el, the southern extremity, in sight of Jerusalem, and in which place he probably thought God was as likely to manifest Himself as at Jerusalem (Gen. 32; II Kings 2:2). The latter place was the most frequented—for the words (vs. 30) should be rendered, "the people even to Dan went to worship before the one" (Jer. 48:13; Amos 4:4, 5; 5:5; Hos. 5:8; 10: 8). The innovation was a sin because it was setting up the worship of God by symbols and images and departing from the place where He had chosen to put His name. Secondly, he changed the feast of tabernacles from the 15th of the seventh to the 15th of the eighth month. The ostensible reason might be, that the ingathering or harvest was later in the northern parts of the kingdom; but the real reason was to eradicate the old association with this, the most welcome and joyous festival of the year. **31. made priests of the lowest of the people**—lit., out of all the people, the Levites refusing to act. He himself assumed to himself the functions of the high priest, at least, at the great festival, probably from seeing the king of Egypt conjoin the royal and sacred offices, and deeming the office of the high priest too great to be vested in a subject.

CHAPTER 13

Vss. 1-22. Jeroboam's Hand Withers. **1. there came a man of God out of Judah**—Who this prophet was cannot be ascertained, He came by divine authoritiy. It could not be either Iddo or Ahijah, for both were alive after the events here related. **Jeroboam stood by the altar to burn incense**—It was at one of the annual festivals. The king, to give interest to the new ritual, was himself the officiating priest. The altar and its accompaniments would, of course, exhibit all the splendor of a new and gorgeously decorated temple. But the prophet foretold its utter destruction. **2. he cried against the altar**—which is put for the whole system of worship organized in Israel. **Behold, a child shall be born . . . Josiah by name**—This is one of the most remarkable prophecies recorded in the Scriptures; and, in its clearness, circumstantial minuteness, and exact prediction of an event that took place 360 years later, it stands in striking contrast to the obscure and ambiguous oracles of the heathen. Being publicly uttered, it must have been well known to the people; and every Jew who lived at the accomplishment of the event must have been convinced of the truth of a religion connected with such a prophecy as this. A present sign was given of the remote event predicted, in a visible fissure being miraculously made on the altar. Incensed at the man's license of speech, Jeroboam stretched out his hand and ordered his attendants to seize the bold intruder. That moment the king's arm became stiff and motionless, and the altar split asunder, so that the fire and ashes fell on the floor. Overawed by the effects of his impiety, Jeroboam besought the prophet's prayer. His request was acceded to, and the hand was restored to its healthy state. Jeroboam was artful, and invited the prophet to the royal table, not to do him honor or show his gratitude for the restoration of his hand, but to win, by his courtesy and liberal hospitality, a person whom he could not crush by his power. But the prophet informed him of a divine injunction expressly prohibiting him from all social intercourse with any in the place, as well as from returning the same way. The prohibition not to eat or drink in Beth-el was because all the people had become apostates from the true religion, and the reason he was not allowed to return the same way was lest he should be recognized by any whom he had seen in going. **11. Now there dwelt an old prophet in Beth-el**—If this were a true prophet, he was a bad man. **18. an angel spake unto me by the word of the Lord**—This circuitous mode of speaking, instead of simply saying, "the LORD spake to me," was adopted to hide an equivocation, to conceal a double meaning—an inferior sense given to the word angel—to offer a *seemingly superior* authority to persuade the prophet, while really the authority was secretly known to the speaker to be *inferior*. The "angel"—i.e., messenger, was his own sons, who were worshippers, perhaps priests, at Beth-el. As this man was governed by self-interest, and wished to curry favor with the king (whose purpose to adhere to his religious polity, he feared, might be shaken by the portents that had occurred), his hastening after the prophet of Judah, the deception he practised, and the urgent invitation by which, on the ground of a falsehood, he prevailed on the too facile man of God to accompany him back to his house in Beth-el, were to create an impression in the king's mind that he was an impostor, who acted in opposition to his own statement. **20-22. he cried unto the man of God that came from Judah**—rather, "it cried," i.e., the word of the Lord.

23-32. The Disobedient Prophet Slain by a Lion. **24. a lion met him by the way, and slew him**—There was a wood near Beth-el infested with lions (II Kings 2:24). This sad catastrophe was a severe but necessary judgment of God, to attest the truth of the message with which the prophet had been charged. All the circumstances of this tragic occurrence (the undevoured carcass, the untouched ass, the unmolested passers-by the lion, though standing there) were calculated to produce an irresistible impression that the hand of God was in it. **31. bury me in the sepulchre wherein the man of God is buried**—His motive in making this request was either that his remains might not be disturbed when the predicted events took place (see on II Kings 23:18), or he had some superstitious hope of being benefited at the resurrection by being in the same cave with a man of God.

CHAPTER 14

Vss. 1-20. Ahijah Denounces God's Judgments against Jeroboam. **1. At that time**—a phrase used often loosely and indefinitely in sacred history. This domestic incident in the family of Jeroboam probably occurred towards the end of his reign; his son Abijah was of age and considered by the people the heir to the throne. **2. Jeroboam said to his wife, Arise, I pray thee, and disguise thyself**—His natural and intense anxiety as a parent is here seen, blended with the deep and artful policy of an apostate king. The reason of this extreme caution was an unwillingness to acknowledge that he looked for information as to the future, not to his idols, but to the true God; and a fear that this step, if publicly known, might endanger the stability of his whole political system; and a strong impression that Ahijah, who was greatly offended with him, would, if consulted openly by his queen, either insult or refuse to receive her. For these reasons he selected his wife, as, in every view, the most proper for such a secret and confidential errand, but recommended her to assume the garb and manner of a peasant woman. Strange infatuation, to suppose that the God who could reveal futurity could not penetrate a flimsy disguise! **3. And take with thee ten loaves, and cracknels, and a cruse of honey, and go to him**—This was a present in unison with the peasant character she assumed. Cracknels are a kind of sweet seed-cake. The prophet was blind, but having received divine premonition of the pretended countrywoman's coming, he addressed her the moment she appeared as the queen, apprised her of the calamities which, in consequence of the ingratitude of Jeroboam, his apostasy, and outrageous misgovernment of Israel, impended over their house, as well as over the nation which too readily followed his idolatrous innovations. **8. thou hast not been as my servant David**—David, though he fell into grievous sins, repented and always maintained the pure worship of God as enjoined by the law. **10. I will bring evil upon the house of Jeroboam**—Strong expressions are here used to indicate the utter extirpation of his house; "him that is shut up and left in Israel," means those who were concealed with the greatest privacy, as the heirs of royalty often are where polygamy prevails; the other phrase, from the loose garments of the East having led to a different practice from what prevails in the West, cannot refer to men; it must signify either a very young boy, or rather, perhaps, a dog, so entire would be the destruction of Jeroboam's house that none, not even a dog, belonging to it should escape. This peculiar phrase occurs only in regard to the threatened extermination of a family (I Sam. 25:22-34). See the manner of extermination (ch. 16:4; 21:24). **12. the child shall die**—The death and general lamentation felt through the country at the loss of the prince were also predicted. The reason for the profound regret shown at his death arose, according to Jewish writers, from his being decidedly opposed to the erection of the golden calves, and using his influence with his father to allow his subjects the free privilege of going to worship in Jerusalem. **13. all Israel shall mourn for him, and bury him**—the only one of Jeroboam's family who should receive the rites of sepulture. **14. the Lord shall raise him up a king ... but what? even now**—viz., Baasha (ch. 15:27); he was already raised—he was in being, though not in power. **17. Tirzah**—a place of pre-eminent beauty (Song of Sol. 6:4), three hours' travelling east of Samaria, chosen when Israel became a separate kingdom, by the first monarch, and used during three short reigns as a residence of the royal house. The fertile plains and wooded hills in that part of the territory of Ephraim gave an opening to the formation of parks and pleasure grounds similar to those which were the "paradises" of Assyrian and Persian monarchs [STANLEY]. Its site is occupied by the large village of Taltise [ROBINSON]. As soon as the queen reached the gate of the palace, she received the intelligence that her son was dying, according to the prophet's prediction. **19. the rest of the acts of Jeroboam**—None of the threatenings denounced against this family produced any change in his policy or government.

21-24. REHOBOAM'S WICKED REIGN. **21. he reigned ... in Jerusalem**—Its particular designation as "the city which the LORD did choose out of all the tribes of Israel, to put his name there," "seems given here, both as a reflection on the apostasy of the ten tribes, and as a proof of the aggravated wickedness of introducing idolatry and its attendant vices there. **his mother's name was Naamah, an Ammonitess**—Her heathen extraction and her influence as queen mother are stated to account for Rehoboam's tendency to depart from the true religion. Led by the warning of the prophet (ch. 12:23), as well as by the large immigration of Israelites into his kingdom (ch. 12:17; II Chron. 11:16), he continued for the first three years of his reign a faithful patron of true religion (II Chron. 11:17). But afterwards he began and encouraged a general apostasy; idolatry became the prevailing form of worship, and the religious state of the kingdom in his reign is described by the high places, the idolatrous statues, the groves and impure rites that with unchecked license were observed in them. The description is suited to the character of the Canaanitish worship.

25-31. SHISHAK SPOILS JERUSALEM. **25, 26. Shishak king of Egypt came up**—He was the instrument in the hand of Providence for punishing the national defection. Even though this king had been Solomon's father-in-law, he was no relation of • Rehoboam's; but there is a strong probability that he belonged to another dynasty (see on II Chron. 12). He was the Sheshonk of the Egyptian monuments, who is depicted on a bas-relief at Karnak, as dragging captives, who, from their peculiar physiognomy, are universally admitted to be Jews. **29. Now the rest of the acts of Rehoboam ..., are they not written in the book of the chronicles?**—not the book so called and comprehended in the sacred

canon, but the national archives of Judah. **30. there was war between Rehoboam and Jeroboam**—The former was prohibited from entering on an aggressive war; but as the two kingdoms kept up a jealous rivalry, he might be forced into vigilant measures of defense, and frequent skirmishes would take place on the borders.

CHAPTER 15

Vss. 1-8. ABIJAM'S WICKED REIGN OVER JUDAH. **1. Abijam**—His name was at first Abijah (II Chron. 12:16); "Jah," the name of God, according to an ancient fashion, being conjoined with it. But afterwards, when he was found "walking in all the sins of his father," that honorable addition was withdrawn, and his name in sacred history changed into Abijam [LIGHTFOOT]. **2. Three years reigned he**—(cf. vs. 1 with vs. 9). Parts of years are often counted in Scripture as whole years. The reign began in Jeroboam's eighteenth year, continued till the nineteenth, and ended in the course of the twentieth. **his mother's name was Maachah**—or Michaiah (II Chron. 13:2), probably altered from the one to the other on her becoming queen, as was very common under a change of circumstances. She is called the daughter of Abishalom, or Absalom (II Chron. 11:21), of Uriel (II Chron. 13:2). Hence, it has been thought probable that Tamar, the daughter of Absalom (II Sam. 14:27; 18:18), had been married to Uriel, and that Maachah was their daughter. **3. his heart was not perfect with the Lord ... as the heart of David his father**—(Cf. ch. 11:4; 14:22). He was not positively bad at first, for it appears (vs. 15) that he had done something to restore the pillaged treasures of the temple. This phrase contains a comparative reference to David's heart. His doing that which was right in the eyes of the Lord (vs. 5) is frequently used in speaking of the kings of Judah, and means only that they did or did not do that which, in the general course and tendency of their government, was acceptable to God. It furnishes no evidence as to the lawfulness or piety of one specific act. **4. for David's sake did the Lord ... give him a lamp**—"A lamp" in one's house is an Oriental phrase for continuance of family name and prosperity. Abijam was not rejected only in consequence of the divine promise to David (see on ch. 11:13-36).

9-22. ASA'S GOOD REIGN. **his mother's name was Maachah**—She was properly his grandmother, and she is here called "the king's mother," from the post of dignity which at the beginning of his reign she possessed. Asa, as a constitutional monarch, acted like the pious David, laboring to abolish the traces and polluting practices of idolatry, and in pursuance of his impartial conduct, he did not spare delinquents even of the highest rank. **13. also Maachah his mother, even her he removed from being queen**—The sultana, or queen dowager, was not necessarily the king's natural mother (see ch. 2: 19), nor was Maachah. Her title, and the privileges connected with that honor and dignity which gave her precedency among the ladies of the royal family, and great influence in the kingdom, were taken away. She was degraded for her idolatry. **because she had made an idol in a grove**—A very obscene figure, and the grove was devoted to the grossest licentiousness. His plans of religious reformation, however, were not completely carried through, "the high places were not removed" (see on ch. 3:2). The suppression of this private worship on natural or artificial hills, though a forbidden service after the temple had been declared the exclusive place of worship, the most pious king's laws were not able to accomplish. **15. he brought in the things which his father had dedicated**—Probably the spoils which Abijam had taken from the vanquished army of Jeroboam (see on II Chron. 13:16). **and the things which himself had dedicated**—after his own victory over the Cushites (II Chron. 14:12). **16. there was war between Asa and Baasha king of Israel all their days**—Asa enjoyed a ten years' peace after Jeroboam's defeat by Abijam, and this interval was wisely and energetically spent in making internal reforms, as well as increasing the means of national defense (II Chron. 14:1-7). In the fifteenth year of his reign, however, the king of Israel commenced hostilities against him, and, invading his kingdom, erected a strong fortress at Ramah, which was near Gibeah, and only six Roman miles from Jerusalem. Afraid lest his subjects might quit his kingdom and return to the worship of their fathers, he wished to cut off all intercourse between the two nations. Ramah stood on an eminence overhanging a narrow ravine which separated Israel from Judah, and therefore he took up a hostile position in that place. **18-20. Then Asa took all the silver and the gold that were left in the . . . house of the Lord**—Asa's religious character is now seen to decline. He trusted not in the Lord (II Chron. 16:7). In this emergency Asa solicited the powerful aid of the king of Damascene-Syria; and to bribe him to break off his alliance with Baasha, he transmitted to him the treasure lying in the temple and palace. The Syrian mercenaries were gained. Instances are to be found, both in the ancient and modern history of the East, of the violation of treaties equally sudden and unscrupulous, through the presentation of some tempting bribe. Ben-hadad poured an army into the northern provinces of Israel, and having captured some cities in Galilee, on the borders of Syria, compelled Baasha to withdraw from Ramah back within his own territories. **18. Ben-hadad**—(See on ch. 11:24). **22. Then King Asa made a proclamation**—The fortifications which Baasha had erected at Ramah were demolished, and with the materials were built other defenses, where Asa thought they were needed—at Geba (now Jeba) and Mizpeh (now Neby Samuil)—about two hours' travelling north of Jerusalem. **23. in the time of his old age he was diseased in his feet**—(See on II Chron. 16:10-12), where an additional proof is given of his religious degeneracy.

25-34. NADAB'S WICKED REIGN. 25. Nadab the son of Jeroboam began to reign—No record is given of him, except his close adherence to the bad policy of his father. **27. Baasha smote him at Gibbethon**—This town, within the tribe of Dan, was given to the Levites (Josh. 19:44). It lay on the Philistine borders, and having been seized by that people, Nadab laid siege to recover it. **29. when he reigned, he smote all the house of Jeroboam**—It was according to a barbarous practice too common in the East, for a usurper to extirpate all rival candidates for the throne; but it was an accomplishment of Ahijah's prophecy concerning Jeroboam (ch. 14:10, 11).

CHAPTER 16

Vss. 1-8. JEHU'S PROPHECY AGAINST BAASHA. **1. Then the word of the Lord came to Jehu**—This is the only incident recorded in the life of this prophet. His father was also a prophet (II Chron. 16:7). **2.**

Forasmuch as I exalted thee—The doom he pronounced on Baasha was exactly the same as denounced against Jeroboam and his posterity. Though he had waded through slaughter to his throne, he owed his elevation to the appointment or permission of Him "by whom kings reign." **over my people Israel**—With all their errors and lapses into idolatry, they were not wholly abandoned by God. He still showed His interest in them by sending prophets and working miracles in their favor, and possessed a multitude of faithful worshippers in the kingdom of Israel. **7. also by the hand of the prophet Jehu**—This is not another prophecy, but merely an addition by the sacred historian, explanatory of the death of Baasha and the extinction of his family. The doom pronounced against Jeroboam (ch. 14:9), did not entitle him to take the execution of the sentence into his own hands; but from his following the same calf worship, he had evidently plotted the conspiracy and murder of that king in furtherance of his own ambitious designs; and hence, in his own assassination, he met the just reward of his deeds. The similitude to Jeroboam extends to their deaths as well as their lives—the reign of their sons, and the ruin of their families. **8. began Elah the son of Baasha to reign**—(cf. ch. 15:33). From this it will appear that Baasha died in the twenty-third year of his reign (see on ch. 15:2), and Elah, who was a prince of dissolute habits, reigned not fully two years.

9-22. ZIMRI'S CONSPIRACY. **9. Zimri . . . conspired against him**—During a carousal in the house of his chamberlain, Zimri slew him, and having seized the sovereignty, endeavored to consolidate his throne by the massacre of all the royal race. **15. did Zimri reign seven days**—The news of his conspiracy soon spread, and the army having proclaimed their general, Omri, king, that officer immediately raised the siege at Gibbethon and marched directly against the capital in which the usurper had established himself. Zimri soon saw that he was not in circumstances to hold out against all the forces of the kingdom; so, shutting himself up in the palace, he set it on fire, and, like Sardanapalus, chose to perish himself and reduce all to ruin, rather than that the palace and royal treasures should fall into the hands of his successful rival. The seven days' reign may refer either to the brief duration of his royal authority, or the period in which he enjoyed unmolested tranquillity in the palace. **19. For his sins which he sinned**—This violent end was a just retribution for his crimes. "His walking in the ways of Jeroboam" might have been manifested either by the previous course of his life, or by his decrees published on his ascension, when he made a strong effort to gain popularity by announcing his continued support of the calf worship. **21, 22. Then were the people divided into two parts**—The factions that ensued occasioned a four years' duration (cf. vs. 15 with vs. 23), of anarchy or civil war. Whatever might be the public opinion of Omri's merits a large body of the people disapproved of the mode of his election, and declared for Tibni. The army, • however, as usual in such circumstances (and they had the will of Providence favoring them), prevailed over all opposition, and Omri became undisputed possessor of the throne. **Tibni died**—The *Heb.* does not enable us to determine whether his death was violent or natural.

23-28. OMRI BUILDS SAMARIA. **23. In the thirty and first year of Asa . . . began Omri to reign**—The twelve years of his reign are computed from the beginning of his reign, which was in the twenty-seventh year of Asa's reign. He held a contested reign for four years with Tibni; and then, at the date stated in this verse, entered on a sole and peaceful reign of eight years. **he bought the hill Samaria of Shemer**—The palace of Tirzah being in ruins, Omri, in selecting the site of his royal residence, was naturally influenced by considerations both of pleasure and advantage. In the center of a wide amphitheatre of mountains, about six miles from Shechem, rises an oblong hill with steep, yet accessible sides, and a long flat top extending east and west, and rising 500 or 600 feet above the valley. What Omri in all probability built as a mere palatial residence, became the capital of the kingdom instead of Shechem. It was as though Versailles had taken the place of Paris, or Windsor of London. The choice of Omri was admirable, in selecting a position which combined in a union not elsewhere found in Palestine: strength, beauty, and fertility [STANLEY]. **two talents of silver**—$4,250.00. Shemer had probably made it a condition of the sale, that the name should be retained. But as city and palace were built there by Omri, it was in accordance with Eastern custom to call it after the founder. The Assyrians did so, and on a tablet dug out of the ruins of Nineveh, an inscription was found relating to Samaria, which is called Beth-khumri—the house of Omri [LAYARD]. (See on II Kings 17:5.) **25-27. But Omri wrought evil**—The character of Omri's reign and his death are described in the stereotyped form used towards all the successors of Jeroboam in respect both to policy as well as time. **29-33. Ahab the son of Omri did evil in the sight of the Lord above all that were before him**—The worship of God by symbols had hitherto been the offensive form of apostasy in Israel, but now gross idolatry is openly patronized by the court. This was done through the influence of Jezebel, Ahab's queen. She was "the daughter of Eth-baal, king of the Zidonians." He was priest of Ashtaroth or Astarte, who, having murdered Philetes, king of Tyre, ascended the throne of that kingdom, being the eighth king since Hiram. Jezebel was the wicked daughter of this regicide and idol priest—and, on her marriage with Ahab, never rested till she had got all the forms of her native Tyrian worship introduced into her adopted country. **32. reared up an altar for Baal**—i.e., the sun, worshipped under various images. Ahab set up one (II Kings 3:2), probably as the Tyrian Hercules, in the temple in Samaria. No human sacrifices were offered—the fire was kept constantly burning—the priests officiated barefoot. Dancing and kissing the image (ch. 19:18) were among the principal rites. **34. JOSHUA'S CURSE FULFILLED UPON HIEL THE BUILDER OF JERICHO. 34. In his days did Hiel the Beth-elite build Jericho**—(see on Josh. 6:26). The curse took effect on the family of this reckless man but whether his oldest son died at the time of laying the foundation, and the youngest at the completion of the work, or whether he lost all his sons in rapid succession, till, at the end of the undertaking, he found himself childless, the poetical form of the ban does not enable us to determine. Some modern commentators think there is no reference either to the natural or violent deaths of Hiel's sons; but that he began in presence of his oldest son, that some unexpected difficulties, losses, or obstacles, delayed the completion till his old age, when the gates were set up in the presence of his youngest son. But the curse *was* fulfilled more than 500 years after it was uttered; and from Jericho being

inhabited after Joshua's time (Judg. 3:13; II Sam. 10:5), it has been supposed that the act against which the curse was directed, was an attempt at the restoration of the walls—the very walls which had been miraculously cast down. It seems to have been within the territory of Israel; and the unresisted act of Hiel affords a painful evidence how far the people of Israel had lost all knowledge of, or respect for, the word of God.

CHAPTER 17

Vss. 1-7. ELIJAH, PROPHESYING AGAINST AHAB, IS SENT TO CHERITH. **1. Elijah the Tishbite**—This prophet is introduced as abruptly as Melchisedek—his birth, parents, and call to the prophetic office being alike unrecorded. He is supposed to be called the Tishbite from Tisbeh, a place east of Jordan. **who was of the inhabitants**—or residents of Gilead, implying that he was not an Israelite, but an Ishmaelite, as MICHAELIS conjectures, for there were many of that race on the confines of Gilead. The employment of a Gentile as an extraordinary minister might be to rebuke and shame the apostate people of Israel. **said unto Ahab**—The prophet appears to have been warning this apostate king how fatal both to himself and people would be the reckless course he was pursuing. The failure of Elijah's efforts to make an impression on the obstinate heart of Ahab is shown by the penal prediction uttered at parting. **before whom I stand**—i.e., whom I serve (Deut. 18:5). **there shall not be dew nor rain these years**—not absolutely; but the dew and the rain would not fall in the usual and necessary quantities. Such a suspension of moisture was sufficient to answer the corrective purposes of God, while an absolute drought would have converted the whole country into an uninhabitable waste. **but according to my word**—not uttered in spite, vengeance, or caprice, but as the minister of God. The impending calamity was in answer to his earnest prayer, and a chastisement intended for the spiritual revival of Israel. Drought was the threatened punishment of national idolatry (Deut. 11:16, 17; 28:23). **2, 3. the word of the Lord came unto him, saying, Get thee hence, and turn thee eastward**, etc.—At first the king may have spurned the prediction as the utterance of a vain enthusiast; but when he found the drought did last and increase in severity, he sought Elijah, who, as it was necessary that he should be far removed from either the violence or the importunities of the king, was divinely directed to repair to a place of retreat, perhaps a cave on "the brook Cherith, that is, before [east of] Jordan." Tradition points it out in a small winter torrent, a little below the ford at Beth-shan. **6. the ravens brought him bread**—The idea of such unclean and voracious birds being employed to feed the prophet has appeared to many so strange that they have labored to make out the *Orebim*, which in our version has been rendered ravens, to be as the word is used (in Ezekiel 27:27) merchants; or Arabians (II Chron. 21:16; Neh. 4:7); or, the citizens of Arabah, near Beth-shan (Josh. 15:6; 18:18). But the common rendering (ch. 18:19) is, in our opinion, preferable to these conjectures. And, if Elijah was miraculously fed by ravens, it is idle to inquire where they found the bread and the flesh, for God would direct them. After the lapse of a year, the brook dried up, and this was a new trial to Elijah's faith.

8-16. HE IS SENT TO A WIDOW OF ZAREPHATH. **8. the word of the Lord came to him**—Zarephath or

Sarepta, now Surafend, whither he was directed to go, was far away on the western coast of Palestine, about nine miles south of Sidon, and within the dominions of Jezebel's impious father, where the famine also prevailed. Meeting, at his entrance into the town, the very woman who was appointed by divine providence to support him, his faith was severely tested by learning from her that her supplies were exhausted and that she was preparing her last meal for herself and son. The Spirit of God having prompted him to ask, and her to grant, some necessary succor, she received a prophet's reward (Matt. 10:41, 42), and for the one meal afforded to him, God, by a miraculous increase of the little stock, afforded many to her.

17-24. He Raises Her Son to Life. **17. the son of the woman, the mistress of the house, fell sick**—A severe domestic calamity seems to have led her to think that, as God had shut up heaven upon a sinful land in consequence of the prophet, she was suffering on a similar account. Without answering her bitter upbraiding, the prophet takes the child, lays it on his bed, and after a very earnest prayer, had the happiness of seeing its restoration, and along with it, gladness to the widow's heart and home. The prophet was sent to this widow, not merely for his own security, but on account of her faith, to strengthen and promote which he was directed to go to her rather than to many widows in Israel, who would have eagerly received him on the same privileged terms of exception from the grinding famine. The relief of her bodily necessities became the preparatory means of supplying her spiritual wants, and bringing her and her son, through the teachings of the prophet, to a clear knowledge of God, and a firm faith in His word (Luke 4:25).

CHAPTER 18

Vss. 1-16. Elijah Meets Obadiah. **1. the third year**—In the New Testament, it is said there was no rain "for the space of three years and six months." The early rain fell in our March, the latter rain in our October. Though Ahab might have at first ridiculed Elijah's announcement, yet when neither of these rains fell in their season, he was incensed against the prophet as the cause of the national judgment, and compelled him, with God's direction, to consult his safety in flight. This was six months after the king was told there would be neither dew nor rain, and from this period the three years in this passage are computed. **Go, show thyself unto Ahab**—The king had remained obdurate and impenitent. Another opportunity was to be given him of repentance, and Elijah was sent in order to declare to him the cause of the national judgment, and to promise him, on condition of his removing it, the immediate blessing of rain. **2. Elijah went**—a marvellous proof of the natural intrepidity of this prophet, of his moral courage, and his unfaltering confidence in the protecting care of God, that he ventured to approach the presence of the raging lion. **there was a sore famine in Samaria**—Elijah found that the famine was pressing with intense severity in the capital. Corn must have been obtained for the people from Egypt or the adjoining countries, else life could not have been sustained for three years; but Ahab, with the chamberlain of his royal household, is represented as giving a personal search for pasture to his cattle. On the banks of the rivulets, grass, tender shoots of grass, might naturally be

expected; but the water being dried up, the verdure would disappear. In the pastoral districts of the East it would be reckoned a most suitable occupation still for a king or chief to go at the head of such an expedition. Ranging over a large tract of country, Ahab had gone through one district, Obadiah through another. **3. Obadiah feared the Lord greatly**—Although he did not follow the course taken by the Levites and the majority of pious Israelites at that time of emigration into Judah (II Chron. 11:13-16), he was a secret and sincere worshipper. He probably considered the violent character of the government, and his power of doing some good to the persecuted people of God as a sufficient excuse for his not going to worship in Jerusalem. **4. an hundred prophets**—not men endowed with the extraordinary gifts of the prophetic office, but who were devoted to the service of God, preaching, praying, praising, etc. (I Sam. 10:10-12). **fed them with bread and water**—These articles are often used to include sustenance of any kind. As this succor must have been given them at the hazard, not only of his place, but his life, it was a strong proof of his attachment to the true religion. **7-16. as Obadiah was in the way ... Elijah met him**—Deeming it imprudent to rush without previous intimation into Ahab's presence, the prophet solicited Obadiah to announce his return to Ahab. The commission, with a delicate allusion to the perils he had already encountered in securing others of God's servants, was, in very touching terms, declined, as unkind and peculiarly hazardous. But Elijah having dispelled all the apprehensions entertained about the Spirit's carrying him away, Obadiah undertook to convey the prophet's message to Ahab and solicit an interview. But Ahab, bent on revenge, or impatient for the appearance of rain, went himself to meet Elijah. **17, 18. Art thou he that troubleth Israel**—A violent altercation took place. Ahab thought to awe him into submission, but the prophet boldly and undisguisedly told the king that the national calamity was traceable chiefly to his own and his family's patronage and practice of idolatry. But, while rebuking the sins, Elijah paid all due respect to the high rank of the offender. He urged the king to convene, by virtue of his royal mandate, a public assembly, in whose presence it might be solemnly decided which was the troubler of Israel. The appeal could not well be resisted, and Ahab, from whatever motives, consented to the proposal. God directed and overruled the issue. **19. gather ... the prophets of Baal ... the prophets of the groves**—From the sequel it appears that the former only came. The latter, anticipating some evil, evaded the king's command. **which eat at Jezebel's table**—i.e., not at the royal table where she herself dined, but they were maintained from her kitchen establishment (see on I Sam. 20:24; ch. 4:22). They were the priests of Astarte, the Zidonian goddess. **20. mount Carmel**—is a bold, bluff promontory, which extends from the western coast of Palestine, at the bay of Acre, for many miles eastward, to the central hills of Samaria. It is a long range, presenting many summits, and intersected by a number of small ravines. The spot where the contest took place is situated at the eastern extremity, which is also the highest point of the whole ridge. It is called El-Mohhraka, "the Burning," or "the Burnt Place." No spot could have been better adapted for the thousands of Israel to have stood drawn up on those gentle slopes. The rock shoots up in an almost perpendicular wall of more than 200 feet in height, on the side of the vale of Esdraelon. This wall made it visible over the whole plain, and from all the surrounding heights, where gazing multitudes would be stationed. **21-40. Elijah said unto all the people, How long halt ye?**—They had long been attempting to conjoin the service of God with that of Baal. It was an impracticable union and the people were so struck with a sense of their own folly, or dread of the king's displeasure, that they "answered not a word." Elijah proposed to decide for them the controversy between God and Baal by an appeal, not to the authority of the law, for that would have no weight, but by a visible token from Heaven. As fire was the element over which Baal was supposed to preside, Elijah proposed that two bullocks should be slain and placed on separate altars of wood, the one for Baal, and the other for God. On whichever the fire should descend to consume it, the event should determine the true God, whom it was their duty to serve. The proposal, appearing every way reasonable, was received by the people with unanimous approval. The priests of Baal commenced the ceremony by calling on their god. In vain did they continue invoking their senseless deity from morning till noon, and from noon till evening, uttering the most piercing cries, using the most frantic gesticulations, and mingling their blood with the sacrifice. No reponse was heard. No fire descended. Elijah exposed their folly and imposture with the severest irony and, as the day was far advanced, commenced his operations. Inviting the people to approach and see the entire proceeding, he first repaired an old altar of God, which Jezebel had demolished. Then, having arranged the cut pieces of the bullock, he caused four barrels or jars of water to be dashed all over the altar and round in the trench. Once, twice, a third time this precaution was taken, and then, when he had offered an earnest prayer, the miraculous fire descended (Lev. 9:24; Judg. 6:21; 13:20; I Chron. 21:26; II Chron. 7:1), and consumed not only the sacrifice, but the very stones of the altar. The impression on the minds of the people was that of admiration mingled with awe; and with one voice they acknowledged the supremacy of Jehovah as the true God. Taking advantage of their excited feelings, Elijah called on them to seize the priestly impostors, and by their blood fill the channel of the river (Kishon), which, in consequence of their idolatries, the drought had dried up—a direction, which, severe and relentless as it seems, it was his duty as God's minister to give (Deut. 15:5; 18:20). The natural features of the mount exactly correspond with the details of this narrative. The conspicuous summit, 1635 feet above the sea, on which the altars were placed, presents an esplanade spacious enough for the king and the priests of Baal to stand on the one side, and Elijah on the other. It is a rocky soil, on which there is abundance of loose stones, to furnish the twelve stones of which the altar was built—a bed of thick earth, in which a trench could be dug; and yet the earth not so loose that the water poured into it would be absorbed; 250 feet beneath the altar plateau, there is a perennial fountain, which, being close to the altar of the Lord, might not have been accessible to the people; and whence, therefore, even in that season of severe drought, Elijah could procure those copious supplies of water which he poured over the altar. The distance between this spring and the site of the altar is so short, as to make it perfectly possible to go thrice thither and back again, whereas it would have been impossible *once* in an afternoon to fetch water from the sea [VAN DE VELDE]. The summit is 1000 feet above the Kishon,

which nowhere runs from the sea so close to the base of the mount as just beneath El-Mohhraka; so that the priests of Baal could, in a few minutes, be taken down to the brook (torrent), and slain there.

41-46. ELIJAH, BY PRAYER, OBTAINS RAIN. **42. Ahab went up to eat and to drink**—Ahab, kept in painful excitement by the agonizing scene, had eaten nothing all the day. He was recommended to refresh himself without a moment's delay; and, while the king was thus occupied, the prophet, far from taking rest, was absorbed in prayer for the fulfilment of the promise (vs. 1). **put his face between his knees**—a posture of earnest supplication still used. **43. Go up now, look toward the sea**—From the place of worship there is a *small eminence,* which, on the west and northwest side, intercepts the view of the sea [STANLEY, VAN DE VELDE]. It can be ascended in a few minutes, and presents a wide prospect of the Mediterranean. Six times the servant went up, but the sky was clear—the sea tranquil. On the seventh he described the sign of approaching rain. **44. Behold, there ariseth a little cloud out of the sea, like a man's hand**—The clearness of the sky renders the smallest speck distinctly visible; and this is in Palestine the uniform precursor of rain. It rises higher and higher, and becomes larger and larger with astonishing celerity, till the whole heaven is black, and the cloud bursts in a deluge of rain. **Prepare thy chariot, and get thee down, that the rain stop thee not**—either by the river Kishon being suddenly so swollen as to be impassable, or from the deep layer of dust in the arid plain being turned into thick mud, so as to impede the wheels. **45. Ahab rode, and went to Jezreel**—now Zerin, a distance of about ten miles. This race was performed in the midst of a tempest of rain. But all rejoiced at it, as diffusing a sudden refreshment over all the land of Jezreel. **46. Elijah . . . girded up his loins, and ran before Ahab**—It was anciently, and still is in some countries of the East, customary for kings and nobles to have runners before their chariots, who are tightly girt for the purpose. The prophet, like the Bedouins of his native Gilead, had been trained to run; and, as the Lord was with him, he continued with unabated agility and strength. It was, in the circumstances, a most proper service for Elijah to render. It tended to strengthen the favorable impression made on the heart of Ahab and furnished an answer to the cavils of Jezebel for it showed that he who was so zealous in the service of God, was, at the same time, devotedly loyal to his king. The result of this solemn and decisive contest was a heavy blow and great discouragement to the cause of idolatry. But subsequent events seem to prove that the impressions, though deep, were but partial and temporary.

CHAPTER 19

Vss. 1-3. ELIJAH FLEES TO BEER-SHEBA. **3. he arose and went for his life**—He entered Jezreel full of hope. But a message from the incensed and hard-hearted queen, vowing speedy vengeance for her slaughtered priests, dispelled all his bright visions of the future. It is probable, however, that in the present temper of the people, even she would not have dared to lay violent hands on the Lord's servant, and purposely threatened him because she could do no more. The threat produced the intended effect, for his faith suddenly failed him. He fled out of the kingdom into the southernmost part of the territories in Judah; nor did he deem himself safe even there, but, dismissing his servant, he resolved to seek refuge among the mountain recesses of Sinai, and there longed for death (Jas. 5:17). This sudden and extraordinary depression of mind arose from too great confidence inspired by the miracles wrought at Carmel, and by the disposition the people evinced there. Had he remained steadfast and immovable, the impression on the mind of Ahab and the people generally might have been followed by good results. But he had been exalted above measure (II Cor. 12:7-9), and being left to himself, the great prophet, instead of showing the indomitable spirit of a martyr, fled from his post of duty.

4-18. He Is Comforted by an Angel. 4. went a day's journey into the wilderness—on the way from Beer-sheba to Horeb—a wide expanse of sandhills, covered with the retem (not juniper, but broom shrubs), whose tall and spreading branches, with their white leaves, afford a very cheering and refreshing shade. His gracious God did not lose sight of His fugitive servant, but watched over him, and, miraculously ministering to his wants, enabled him, in a better but not wholly right frame of mind, by virtue of that supernatural supply, to complete his contemplated journey. In the solitude of Sinai, God appeared to instruct him. What doest thou here, Elijah? was a searching question addressed to one who had been called to so arduous and urgent a mission as his. By an awful exhibition of divine power, he was made aware of the divine speaker who addressed him; his attention was arrested, his petulance was silenced, his heart was touched, and he was bid without delay return to the land of Israel, and prosecute the Lord's work there. To convince him that an idolatrous nation will not be unpunished, He commissions him to anoint three persons who were destined in Providence to avenge God's controversy with the people of Israel. Anointing is used synonymously with appointment (Judg. 9:8), and is applied to all named, although Jehu alone had the consecrated oil poured over his head. They were all three destined to be eminent instruments in achieving the destruction of idolaters, though in different ways. But of the three commissions, Elijah personally executed only one; viz., the call of Elisha to be his assistant and successor, and by him the other two were accomplished (II Kings 8:7-13; 9:1-10). Having thus satisfied the fiery zeal of the erring but sincere and pious prophet, the Lord proceeded to correct the erroneous impression under which Elijah had been laboring, of his being the sole adherent of the true religion in the land; for God, who seeth in secret, and knew all that were His, knew that there were 7000 persons who had not done homage (lit., kissed the hand) to Baal. **16. Abel-meholah**—i.e., the meadow of dancing, in the valley of the Jordan.

19-21. Elisha Follows Elijah. 19. Elisha the son of Shaphat—Most probably he belonged to a family distinguished for piety, and for their opposition to the prevailing calf worship. **ploughing with twelve yoke of oxen**—indicating that he was a man of substance. **Elijah . . . cast his mantle upon him**—This was an investiture with the prophetic office. It is in this way that the Brahmins, the Persian Sooffees, and other priestly or sacred characters in the East are appointed—a mantle being, by some eminent priest, thrown across their shoulders. Elisha had probably been educated in the schools of the prophets. **20. what have I done to thee?**—i.e., Go, but keep in mind the solemn ceremony I have just performed on thee. It is not I, but God, who calls thee. Do not allow any earthly affection to detain you from obeying His call. **21. took a yoke of oxen**—Having hastily prepared (II Sam. 24:22) a farewell entertainment to his family and friends, he left his native place and attached himself to Elijah as his minister.

CHAPTER 20

Vss. 1-12. Ben-hadad Besieges Samaria. 1. Ben-hadad the king of Syria—This monarch was the son of that Ben-hadad who, in the reign of Baasha, made a raid on the northern towns of Galilee (ch. 15:20). The thirty-two kings that were confederate with him were probably tributary princes. The ancient kings of Syria and Phœnicia ruled only over a single city, and were independent of each other, except when one great city, as Damascus, acquired the ascendency, and even then they were allied only in time of war. The Syrian army encamped at the gates and besieged the town of Samaria. **2-3. Thus saith Ben-hadad, Thy silver and thy gold is mine**—To this message sent him during the siege, Ahab returned a tame and submissive answer, probably thinking it meant no more than an exaction of tribute. But the demand was repeated with greater insolence; and yet, from the abject character of Ahab, there is reason to believe he would have yielded to this arrogant claim also, had not the voice of his subjects been raised against it. Ben-hadad's object in these and other boastful menaces was to intimidate Ahab. But the weak sovereign began to show a little more spirit, as appears in his abandoning "my lord the king," for the single "tell him," and giving him a dry but sarcastic hint to glory no more till the victory is won. Kindling into a rage at the cool defiance, Ben-hadad gave orders for the immediate sack of the city. **12. as he was drinking, he and the kings in the pavilions**—booths made of branches of trees and brushwood; which were reared for kings in the camp, as they still are for Turkish pashas or agas in their expeditions [Keil]. **Set yourselves in array**—Invest the city.

13-20. The Syrians Are Slain. 13. behold, there came a prophet unto Ahab—Though the king and people of Israel had highly offended Him, God had not utterly cast them off. He still cherished designs of mercy towards them, and here, though unasked, gave them a signal proof of His interest in them, by a prophet's animating announcement that the Lord would that day deliver the mighty hosts of the enemy into his hand by means of a small, feeble, inadequate band. Conformably to the prophet's instructions, 232 young men went boldly out towards the camp of the enemy, while 7000 more, apparently volunteers, followed at some little distance, or posted themselves at the gate, to be ready to reinforce those in front if occasion required it. Ben-hadad and his vassals and princes were already, at that early hour—scarcely midday—deep in their cups; and though informed of this advancing company, yet confiding in his numbers, or it may be, excited with wine, he ordered with indifference the proud intruders to be taken alive, whether they came with peaceful or hostile intentions. It was more easily said than done; the young men smote right and left, making terrible havoc among their intended captors; and their attack, together with the sight of the 7000, who soon rushed forward to mingle in the fray, created a panic in the Syrian army, who immediately took up flight. Ben-hadad himself escaped the pursuit of the victors on a fleet horse, surrounded by a squadron of horse-guards.

This glorious victory, won so easily, and with such a paltry force opposed to overwhelming numbers, was granted that Ahab and his people might know (vs. 13) that God is the Lord. But we do not read of this acknowledgment being made, or of any sacrifices being offered in token of their national gratitude. **22. the prophet came to the king of Israel, and said**—The same prophet who had predicted the victory shortly reappeared, admonishing the king to take every precaution against a renewal of hostilities in the following campaign. **at the return of the year**—i.e., in spring, when, on the cessation of the rainy season, military campaigns (II Sam. 11:1), were anciently begun. It happened as the prophet had forewarned. Brooding over their late disastrous defeat, the attendants of Ben-hadad ascribed the misfortune to two causes—the one arose from the principles of heathenism which led them to consider the gods of Israel as "gods of the hills"; whereas their power to aid the Israelites would be gone if the battle was maintained on the plains. The other cause to which the Syrian courtiers traced their defeat at Samaria, was the presence of the tributary kings, who had probably been the first to take flight; and they recommended "captains to be put in their rooms." Approving of these recommendations, Ben-hadad renewed his invasion of Israel the next spring by the siege of Aphek in the valley of Jezreel (I Sam. 29:1, with 28:4), not far from Endor. **27. like two little flocks of kids**—Goats are never seen in large flocks, or scattered, like sheep; and hence the two small but compact divisions of the Israelite force are compared to goats, not sheep. Humanly speaking, that little handful of men would have been overpowered by numbers. But a prophet was sent to the small Israelite army to announce the victory, in order to convince the Syrians that the God of Israel was omnipotent everywhere, in the valley as well as on the hills. And, accordingly, after the two armies had pitched opposite each other for seven days, they came to an open battle. 100,000 Syrians lay dead on the field, while the fugitives took refuge in Aphek, and there, crowding on the city walls, they endeavored to make a stand against their pursuers; but the old walls giving way under the incumbent weight, fell and buried 27,000 in the ruins. Ben-hadad succeeded in extricating himself, and, with his attendants, sought concealment in the city, fleeing from chamber to chamber; or, as some think it, an inner chamber, i.e., a harem but seeing no ultimate means of escape, he was advised to throw himself on the tender mercies of the Israelitish monarch. **32. put ropes on their heads**—Captives were dragged by ropes round their necks in companies, as is depicted on the monuments of Egypt. Their voluntary attitude and language of submission flattered the pride of Ahab, who, little concerned about the dishonor done to the God of Israel by the Syrian king, and thinking of nothing but victory, paraded his clemency, called the vanquished king "his brother," invited him to sit in the royal chariot, and dismissed him with a covenant of peace. **34. streets for thee in Damascus**—implying that a quarter of that city was to be assigned to Jews, with the free exercise of their religion and laws, under a judge of their own. This misplaced kindness to a proud and impious idolater, so unbecoming a theocratic monarch, exposed Ahab to the same censure and fate as Saul (I Sam. 15:9, etc.). It was in opposition to God's purpose in giving him the victory.

35-42. A Prophet Reproves Him. **35. Smite me**—This prophet is supposed (vs. 8) to have been

Micaiah. The refusal of his neighbor to smite the prophet was manifestly wrong, as it was a withholding of necessary aid to a prophet in the discharge of a duty to which he had been called by God, and it was severely punished, as a beacon to warn others (see on ch. 13:2-24). The prophet found a willing assistant, and then, waiting for Ahab, leads the king unconsciously, in the parabolic manner of Nathan (II Samuel 12), to pronounce his own doom; and this consequent punishment was forthwith announced by a prophet (see on ch. 21). **39. a talent of silver**—about $ 2,000.00.

CHAPTER 21

Vss. 1-4. Naboth Refuses Ahab His Vineyard. **1. Naboth the Jezreelite had a vineyard, which was in Jezreel**—Ahab was desirous, from its contiguity to the palace, to possess it for a vegetable garden. He proposed to Naboth to give him a better in exchange, or to obtain it by purchase; but the owner declined to part with it. In persisting in his refusal, Naboth was not actuated by any feelings of disloyalty or disrespect to the king, but solely from a conscientious regard to the divine law, which, for important reasons, had prohibited the sale of a paternal inheritance; or if, through extreme poverty or debt, an assignation of it to another was unavoidable, the conveyance was made on the condition of its being redeemable at any time; at all events, of its reverting at the jubilee to the owner. In short, it could not be alienated from the family, and it was on this ground that Naboth (vs. 3) refused to comply with the king's demand. It was not, therefore, any rudeness or disrespect that made Ahab heavy and displeased, but his sulky and pettish demeanor betrays a spirit of selfishness that could not brook to be disappointed of a favorite object, and that would have pushed him into lawless tyranny had he possessed any natural force of character. **4. turned away his face**—either to conceal from his attendants the vexation of spirit he felt, or, by the affectation of great sorrow, rouse them to devise some means of gratifying his wishes.

5-16. Jezebel Causes Naboth to Be Stoned. **7. Dost thou now govern the kingdom of Israel?**—This is not so much a question as an exclamation—a sarcastic taunt; "A pretty king thou art! Canst thou not use thy power and take what thy heart is set upon?" **arise, and eat bread, and let thine heart be merry: I will give thee the vineyard**—After upbraiding Ahab for his pusillanimity and bidding him act as a king, Jezebel tells him to trouble himself no more about such a trifle; she would guarantee the possession of the vineyard. **8. So she wrote letters in Ahab's name, and sealed them with his seal**—The seal-ring contained the name of the king and gave validity to the documents to which it was affixed (Esther 8:8; Dan. 6:17). By allowing her the use of his signet-ring, Ahab passively consented to Jezebel's proceeding. Being written in the king's name, it had the character of a royal mandate. **sent the letters unto the elders and nobles that were in his city**—They were the civic authorities of Jezreel, and would, in all likelihood, be the creatures and fit tools of Jezebel. It is evident that, though Ahab had recently been in Jezreel, when he made the offer to Naboth, both he and Jezebel were now in Samaria (ch. 20:43). **9. Proclaim a fast**, etc.—Those obsequious and unprincipled magistrates did according to orders. Pretending that a heavy guilt lay on one, or some unknown party, who was charged with blaspheming God and the king and that Ahab was threatening vengeance on the whole city unless the culprit were discovered and punished, they assembled the people to observe a solemn fast. Fasts were commanded on extraordinary occasions affecting the public interests of the state (II Chron. 20:3; Ezra 8:21; Joel 1:14; 2:15; Jonah 3:5). The wicked authorities of Jezreel, by proclaiming the fast, wished to give an external appearance of justice to their proceedings and convey an impression among the people that Naboth's crime amounted to treason against the king's life. **set Naboth on high** —During a trial the panel, or accused person, was placed on a high seat, in the presence of all the court; but as the guilty person was supposed to be unknown, the setting of Naboth on high among the people must have been owing to his being among the distinguished men of the place. **13. there came in two men**—worthless fellows who had been bribed to swear a falsehood. The law required two witnesses in capital offenses (Deut. 17:6; 19:15; Num. 35:30; Matt. 26:60). Cursing God and cursing the king are mentioned in the law (Exod. 22:28) as offenses closely connected, the king of Israel being the earthly representative of God in His kingdom. **they carried him forth out of the city, and stoned him**—The law, which forbade cursing the rulers of the people, does not specify the penalty for this offense but either usage had sanctioned or the authorities of Jezreel had originated stoning as the proper punishment. It was always inflicted out of the city (Acts 7:58). **14-16. Jezebel said to Ahab, Arise, take possession**—Naboth's execution having been announced, and his family being involved in the same fatal sentence (II Kings 9:26), his property became forfeited to the crown, not by law, but traditionary usage (see on II Sam. 16:4). **Ahab rose to go down**—from Samaria to Jezreel.

17-29. ELIJAH DENOUNCES JUDGMENTS AGAINST AHAB AND JEZEBEL. 17-19. Hast thou killed, and also taken possession?—While Ahab was in the act of surveying his ill-gotten possession, Elijah, by divine commission, stood before him. The appearance of the prophet, at such a time, was ominous of evil, but his language was much more so (cf. Ezek. 45:8; 46:16-18). Instead of shrinking with horror from the atrocious crime, Ahab eagerly hastened to his newly acquired property. **In the place where dogs licked,** etc.—a righteous retribution of Providence. The prediction was accomplished, not in Jezreel, but in Samaria; and not on Ahab personally, in consequence of his repentance (vs. 29), but on his son (II Kings 9:25). The words "in the place where" might be rendered "in like manner as." **20. thou hast sold thyself to work evil**—i.e., allowed sin to acquire the unchecked and habitual mastery over thee (II Kings 17:17; Rom. 7:11). **21, 22. will make thine house,** etc.—see on ch. 15:29; 16: 3-12). Jezebel, though included among the members of Ahab's house, has her ignominious fate expressly foretold (see on II Kings 9:30). **27-29. Ahab . . . rent his clothes, and put sackcloth upon his flesh, and fasted, and lay in sackcloth, and went softly**—He was not obdurate, like Jezebel. This terrible announcement made a deep impression on the king's heart, and led, for a while, to sincere repentance. Going softly, i.e., barefoot, and with a pensive manner, within doors. He manifested all the external signs, conventional and natural, of the deepest sorrow. He was wretched, and so great is the mercy of God, that, in consequence of his humiliation, the threatened punishment was deferred.

CHAPTER 22

Vss. 1-36. AHAB SLAIN AT RAMOTH-GILEAD. 1. continued three years without war between Syria and Israel—The disastrous defeat of Ben-hadad had so destroyed his army and exhausted the resources of his country, that, however eager, he was unable to recommence active hostilities against Israel. But that his hereditary enmity remained unsubdued, was manifest by his breach of faith concerning the treaty by which he had engaged to restore all the cities which his father had seized (ch. 20:34). **2. Jehoshaphat the king of Judah came down to the king of Israel**—It was singular that a friendly league between the sovereigns of Israel and Judah should, for the first time, have been formed by princes of such opposite characters—the one pious, the other wicked. Neither this league nor the matrimonial alliance by which the union of the royal families was more closely cemented, met the Lord's approval (II Chron. 19:2). It led, however, to a visit by Jehoshaphat, whose reception in Samaria was distinguished by the most lavish hospitality (II Chron. 18:2). The opportunity of this visit was taken advantage of, to push an object on which Ahab's heart was much set. **3. Know ye that Ramoth in Gilead is ours**— a Levitical and free town on the north border of Gad (Deut. 4:43; Josh. 21:38), on the site of the present Salt Lake, in the province of Belka. It lay within the territories of the Israelitish monarch, and was unjustly alienated; but whether it was one of the cities usurped by the first Ben-hadad, which his son had promised to restore, or was retained for some other reasons, the sacred historian has not mentioned. In the expedition which Ahab meditated for the recovery of this town, the aid of Jehoshaphat was asked and promised (see on II Chron. 18:3). Previous to declaring hostilities, it was customary to consult the prophets (see on I Sam. 28); and Jehoshaphat having expressed a strong desire to know the Lord's will concerning this war, Ahab assembled four hundred of his prophets. These could not be either the prophets of Baal or of Ashteroth (ch. 18:19), but seem (vs. 12) to have been false prophets, who conformed to the symbolic calf worship of Jehovah. Being the creatures of Ahab, they unanimously predicted a prosperous issue to the war. But dissatisfied with them, Jehoshaphat inquired if there was any true prophet of the Lord. Ahab agreed, with great reluctance, to allow Micaiah to be summoned. He was the only true prophet then to be found residing in Samaria, and he had to be brought out of prison (vs. 26), into which, according to Josephus, he had been cast on account of his rebuke to Ahab for sparing the king of Syria. **10. a void place**—lit., a threshing-floor, formed at the gate of Samaria. **11. Zedekiah the son of Chenaanah made him horns of iron** —Small projections, of the size and form of our candle extinguishers (worn in many parts of the East as military ornaments), were worn by the Syrians of that time, and probably by the Israelite warriors also. Zedekiah, by assuming two horns, personated two heroes, and, pretending to be a prophet, wished in this manner to represent the kings of Israel and Judah in a military triumph. It was a symbolic action, to impart greater force to his language (see on Deut. 33:17); but it was little more than a flourish with a *spontoon* [CALMET'S FRAGMENT]. **14. what the Lord saith unto me, that will I speak**— On the way the messenger who conducted him to the royal presence informed him of the tenor of the prophecies already given and recommended him to agree with the rest, no doubt from the kindly motive of seeing him released from imprisonment. But Micaiah, inflexibly faithful to his divine mission as a prophet, announced his purpose to proclaim honestly whatever God should bid him. On being asked by the king, "Shall I go against Ramoth-gilead, or shall I forbear?" the prophet gave precisely the same answer as the previous oracles that had been consulted; but it must have been given in a sarcastic tone and in ironical mockery of their way of speaking. Being solemnly urged to give a serious and truthful answer, Micaiah then declared the visionary scene the Spirit had revealed to him;—"I saw all Israel scattered upon the hills as sheep that have not a shepherd." The purport of this was that the army of Israel would be defeated and dispersed; that Ahab would fall in the battle, and the people return without either being pursued or destroyed by the enemy. **18-23. Did I not tell thee that he would prophesy no good concerning me, but evil?**—Since Ahab was disposed to trace this unwelcome truth to personal enmity, Micaiah proceeded fearlessly to tell the incensed monarch in full detail what had been revealed to him. The Hebrew prophets, borrowing their symbolic pictures from earthly scenes, described God in heaven as a king in His kingdom. And as earthly princes do nothing of importance without asking the advice of their counsellors, God is represented as consulting about the fate of Ahab. This prophetic language must not be interpreted literally, and the command must be viewed as only a permission to the lying spirit (Rom. 11:34) [CALMET]. **24, 25. Zedekiah the son of Chenaanah went near, and smote Micaiah on the cheek**—The insolence of this man, the leader of the false prophets, seems to have been provoked by jealousy at Micaiah's assumed monopoly of the spirit of inspiration. This mode of smiting, usually with a shoe, is both severe and ignominious. The calm reply of the Lord's prophet consisted in announcing the fate of the false prophets who suffered as the advisers of the disastrous expedition. **26-28. Take Micaiah, ... Put this fellow in prison**—Ahab, under the impulse of vehement resentment, remands the prophet until his return. **bread of affliction, water of affliction**—i.e., the poorest prison fare. Micaiah submitted, but reiterated aloud, in the presence of all, that the issue of the war would be fatal to Ahab. **29-38. went up to Ramoth-gilead**—The king of Israel, bent on this expedition, marched, accompanied by his ally, with all his forces to the siege; but on approaching the scene of action, his courage failed, and, hoping to evade the force of Micaiah's prophecy by a secret stratagem, he assumed the uniform of a subaltern, while he advised Jehoshaphat to fight in his royal attire. The Syrian king, with a view either to put the speediest end to the war, or perhaps to wipe out the stain of his own humiliation (ch. 20:31), had given special instructions to his generals to single out Ahab, and to take or kill him, as the author of the war. The officers at first directed their assault on Jehoshaphat, but, becoming aware of their mistake, desisted. Ahab was wounded by a random arrow, which, being probably poisoned, and the state of the weather increasing the virulence of the poison, he died at sunset. The corpse was conveyed to Samaria; and, as the chariot which brought it was being washed, in a pool near the city, from the blood that had profusely oozed from the wound, the dogs, in conformity with Elijah's prophecy, came and licked it. Ahab was succeeded by his son Ahaziah.

THE SECOND BOOK OF

THE KINGS

CHAPTER 1

Vs. 1. MOAB REBELS. 1. Then Moab rebelled—Subdued by David (II Samuel 8:2), they had, in the partition of Israel and Judah, fallen to the share of the former kingdom. But they took advantage of the death of Ahab to shake off the yoke (see on ch. 3:6). The casualty that befell Ahaziah prevented his taking active measures for suppressing this revolt—which was accomplished as a providential judgment on the house of Ahab for all these crimes. **2-8. AHAZIAH'S JUDGMENT BY ELIJAH. 2-8. Ahaziah fell down through a lattice in his upper chamber**—This lattice was either a *part* of the wooden parapet, or fence, which surrounds the flat roofs of houses, and over which the king was carelessly leaning when it gave way; or it might be an opening like a skylight in the roof itself, done over with lattice-work, which, being slender or rotten, the king stepped on and slipped through. This latter supposition is most probably the true one, as Ahaziah did not fall either into the street or the court, but "in his upper chamber." **inquire of Baalzebub**—Anxious to learn whether he should recover from the effects of this severe fall, he sent to consult Baalzebub—i.e., the god of flies, who was considered the patron deity of medicine. A temple to that idol was erected at Ekron, which was resorted to far and wide, though it afterwards led to the destruction of the place (Zech. 9:5; Amos 1:8; Zeph. 2:4). "After visiting Ekron, 'the god of flies' is a name that gives me no surprise. The flies there swarmed, in fact so innumerably, that I could hardly get any food without these troublesome insects getting into it" [VAN DE VELDE]. **3. the angel of the Lord**—not *an* angel, but *the* angel, who carried on all communications between the invisible God and His chosen people [HENGSTENBERG]. This angel commissioned Elijah to meet the king's messengers, to stop them peremptorily on the idolatrous errand, and convey by them to the king information of his approaching death. This consultation of an idol, being a breach of the fundamental law of the kingdom (Exod. 20:3; Deut. 5:7), was a daring and deliberate rejection of the national reljgion. The Lord, in making this announcement of his death, designed that he should see in that event a judgment for his idolatry. **4. Thou shall not come down from that bed**—On being taken up, he had probably been laid on the divan—a raised frame, about three feet broad, extended along the sides of a room, covered with cushions and mattresses—serving, in short, as a sofa by day and a bed by night—and ascended by steps. **Elijah departed**—to his ordinary abode, which was then at Mount Carmel (ch. 2:25; I Kings 18:42). **5. the messengers turned back**—They did not know the stranger; but his authoritative tone, commanding attitude, and affecting message determined them at once to return. **8. an hairy man**—This was the description not of his person, as in the case of Esau, but of his dress, which consisted either of unwrought sheep or goatskins (Heb. 11:37), or of camel's haircloth—the coarser manufacture of this material—like our rough haircloth. The Dervishes and Bedouins are attired in this wild, uncouth manner, while their hair flows loose on the head, their shaggy cloak is thrown over their shoulders and tied in front on the breast, naked, except at the waist, round which is a skin girdle—a broad, rough leathern belt. Similar to this was the girdle of the prophets, as in keeping with their coarse garments and their stern, uncompromising office.

9-16. ELIJAH BRINGS FIRE FROM HEAVEN ON AHAZIAH'S MESSENGERS. **9. Then the king sent unto him a captain of fifty**—Any appearance of cruelty that there is in the fate of the two captains and their men will be removed, on a full consideration of the circumstances. God being the King of Israel, Ahaziah was bound to govern the kingdom according to the divine law; to apprehend the Lord's prophet, for discharging a commanded duty, was that of an impious and notorious rebel. The captains abetted the king in his rebellion; and they exceeded their military duty by contemptuous insults. **man of God**—In using this term, they either spoke derisively, believing him to be no true prophet; or, if they regarded him as a true prophet, the summons to him to surrender himself bound to the king was a still more flagrant insult; the language of the second captain being worse than that of the first. **10. let fire come down**—rather, "fire shall come down." Not to avenge a personal insult of Elijah, but an insult upon God in the person of His prophet; and the punishment was inflicted, not by the prophet, but by the direct hand of God. **15. he arose, and went down with him**—a marvellous instance of faith and obedience. Though he well knew how obnoxious his presence was to the king, yet, on receiving God's command, he goes unhesitatingly, and repeats, with his own lips, the unwelcome tidings conveyed by the messengers.

17, 18. AHAZIAH DIES, and IS SUCCEEDED BY JEHORAM. **17. Jehoram**—The brother of Ahaziah (see on ch. 3:1).

CHAPTER 2

Vss. 1-10. ELIJAH DIVIDES JORDAN. **1. when the Lord would take up Elijah**—A revelation of this event had been made to the prophet; but, unknown to him, it had also been revealed to his disciples, and to Elisha in particular, who kept constantly beside him. **Gilgal**—This Gilgal (Jiljil) was near Ebal and Gerizim—a school of the prophets was established there. At Beth-el there was also a school of the prophets, which Elijah had founded, notwithstanding that place was the headquarters of the calf worship; and at Jericho there was another. In travelling to these places, which he had done through the impulse of the Spirit (vss. 2, 4-6), Elijah wished to pay a farewell visit to these several institutions, which lay on his way to the place of ascension and, at the same time, from a feeling of humility and modesty, to be in solitude, where there would be no

eye-witnesses of his glorification. All his efforts, however, to prevail on his attendant to remain behind, were fruitless. Elisha knew that the time was at hand, and at every place the sons of the prophets spoke to him of the approaching removal of his master. Their last stage was at the Jordan. They were followed at a distance by fifty scholars of the prophets, from Jericho, who were desirous, in honor of the great occasion, to witness the miraculous translation of the prophet. The revelation of this striking event to so many was a necessary part of the dispensation; for it was designed to be under the law, like that of Enoch in the patriarchal age, a visible proof of another state, and a type of the resurrection of Christ. **3. take away thy master from they head**—an allusion to the custom of scholars sitting at the feet of their master—the latter being over their heads (Acts 22:3). **8. Elijah took his mantle, and wrapped it together, and smote the waters**—Like the rod of Moses, it had the divinely operating power of the Spirit. **9. Elijah said unto Elisha, Ask what I shall do for thee**—trusting either that it would be in his power to bequeath it, or that God, at his entreaty, would grant it. **let a double portion of thy spirit be upon me**—This request was not, as is commonly supposed, for the power of working miracles exceeding the magnitude and number of his master's, nor does it mean a higher endowment of the prophetic spirit; for Elisha was neither superior to, nor perhaps equally great with, his predecessor. But the phrase, "a double portion," was applied to the first-born, and therefore Elisha's request was, simply, to be heir to the prophetic office and gifts of his master. **10. Thou hast asked a hard thing**—an extraordinary blessing which *I* cannot, and God only, can give. Nevertheless he, doubtless by the secret directions of the Spirit, proposed to Elisha a sign, the observation of which would keep him in the attitude of an anxious waiter, as well as suppliant for the favor.

11-18. HE IS TAKEN UP TO HEAVEN IN A CHARIOT OF FIRE. **11. behold, there appeared a chariot of fire, and horses of fire**—some bright effulgence, which, in the eyes of the spectators, resembled those objects. **went up by a whirlwind**—a tempest or storm-wind accompanied with vivid flashes of fire, figuratively used for the divine judgments (Isa. 29:6). **12. Elisha saw it, and he cried, My father**—i.e., spiritual father, as the pupils of the prophets are called their sons. **the chariot of Israel, and the horseman thereof**—i.e., that as earthly kingdoms are dependent for their defense and glory upon warlike preparations, there a single prophet had done more for the preservation and prosperity of Israel than all her chariots and horsemen. **took hold of his own clothes and rent them**—in token of his grief for his loss. **13. He took up also the mantle of Elijah**—The transference of this prophetic cloak was, to himself, a pledge of his being appointed successor, and it was an outward token to others of the spirit of Elijah resting upon him. **14-18. smote the waters**—The waving of the mantle on the river, and the miraculous division of the waters consequent upon it, was an evidence that the Lord God of Elijah was with him, and as this miracle was witnessed by the scholars of the prophets from Jericho, they forthwith recognized the pre-eminence of Elisha, as now the prophet of Israel. **16-18. fifty strong men, let them go, we pray thee, and seek thy master**—Though the young prophets from Jericho had seen Elijah's miraculous passage of the Jordan, they had not witnessed the ascension. They imagined that he might have been cast by the whirlwind on some mountain or valley; or, if he had actually been admitted into heaven, they expected that his body would still be remaining somewhere on earth. In compliance with their importunity, he gave them permission, but told them what the result would be.

19-25. ELISHA HEALS THE WATERS. 20. Bring me a new cruse, and put salt therein—The noxious qualities of the water could not be corrected by the infusion of salt—for, supposing the salt was possessed of such a property, a whole spring could not be purified by a dishful for a day, much less in all future time. The pouring in of the salt was a symbolic act with which Elisha accompanied the word of the Lord, by which the spring was healed [KEIL]. **23, 24. there came forth little children**—i.e., the idolatrous, or infidel young men of the place, who affecting to disbelieve the report of his master's translation, sarcastically urged him to follow in the glorious career. **bald head**—an epithet of contempt in the East, applied to a person even with a bushy head of hair. The appalling judgment that befell them was God's interference to uphold his newly invested prophet.

CHAPTER 3

Vss. 1-3. JEHORAM'S EVIL REIGN OVER ISRAEL. 1. Jehoram the son of Ahab began to reign over Israel in Samaria the eighteenth year of Jehoshaphat —(cf. I Kings 22:51). To reconcile the statements in the two passages, we must suppose that Ahaziah, having reigned during the seventeenth and the greater part of the eighteenth year of Jehoshaphat, was succeeded by his brother Joram or Jehoram, in the end of that eighteenth year, or else that Ahaziah, having reigned two years in conjunction with his father, died at the end of that period when Jehoram ascended the throne. His policy was as hostile as that of his predecessors to the true religion; but he made some changes. Whatever was his motive for this alteration—whether dread of the many alarming judgments the patronage of idolatry had brought upon his father; or whether it was made as a small concession to the feelings of Jehoshaphat, his ally, he abolished idolatry in its gross form and restored the symbolic worship of God, which the kings of Israel, from the time of Jeroboam, had set up as a partition wall between their subjects and those of Judah.

4, 5. MESHA, KING OF MOAB, REBELS. 4-6. Mesha king of Moab, etc.—As his dominions embraced an extensive pasture country, he paid, as annual tribute, the wool of 100,000 lambs and 100,000 rams. It is still common in the East to pay custom and taxes in the fruits or natural produce of the land. **5. king of Moab rebelled**—This is a repetition of ch. 1:1, in order to introduce an account of the confederate expedition for crushing this revolt, which had been allowed to continue unchecked during the short reign of Ahaziah.

6-24. ELISHA PROMISES WATER AND VICTORY OVER MOAB. 6. King Jehoram . . . numbered Israel —made a levy from his own subjects, and at the same time sought an alliance with Jehoshaphat, which, as on the former occasion with Ahab, was readily promised (I Kings 22:4). **8, 9. Which way shall we go? And he answered, The way through the wilderness of Edom**—This was a long and circuitous route, by the southern bend of the Dead Sea. Jehoshaphat however preferred it, partly because the part of the Moabite territory at which they

would arrive, was the most defenseless; and partly because he would thereby enlist, in the expedition, the forces of the king of Edom. But, in penetrating the deep, rocky valley of Ahsy, which forms the boundary between Edom and Moab, the confederate army was reduced, both man and beast, to the greatest extremities for want of water. They were disappointed by finding the wady of this valley, the brook Zered (Deut. 2:13-18) [ROBINSON], dry. Jehoram was in despair. But the pious mind of Jehoshaphat inquired for a prophet of the Lord; and, on being informed that Elisha was at hand, "the three kings went down to him"; i.e., to his tent, which was either in the camp, or close by it. He had been directed thither by the Spirit of God for this special purpose. They went to him, not only as a mark of respect, but to supplicate for his assistance. **11. which poured water on the hands of Elijah**—i.e., was his servant—this being one of the common offices of a servant. The phrase is used here as synonymous with "a true and eminent prophet," who will reveal God's will to us. **13. What have I to do with thee**, etc.—Wishing to produce a deep spirit of humility and contrition, Elisha gave a stern repulse to the king of Israel, accompanied by a sarcastic sneer, in bidding him go and consult Baal and his soothsayers. But the distressed condition, especially the imploring language, of the royal suppliants, who acknowledged the hand of the Lord in this distress, drew from the prophet the solemn assurance, that solely out of respect to Jehoshaphat, the Lord's true servant, did he take any interest in Jehoram. **15. bring me a minstrel**—The effect of music in soothing the mind is much regarded in the East; and it appears that the ancient prophets, before entering their work, commonly resorted to it, as a preparative, by praise and prayer, to their receiving the prophetic afflatus. **the hand of the Lord**—a phrase significantly implying that the gift of prophecy was not a natural or inherent gift, but conferred by the power and grace of God. **16. Make this valley full of ditches**—capable of holding water. **17. Ye shall not see wind**—It is common in the East to speak of *seeing* wind, from the clouds of straw, dust, or sand, that are often whirled into the air, after a long drought. **20. when the meat offering was offered**— i.e., at the time of the morning sacrifice, accompanied, doubtless, with solemn prayers; and these led, it may be, by Elisha on this occasion, as on a similar one by Elijah (I Kings 18:36). **behold, there came water by the way of Edom**—Far from the Israelitish camp, in the eastern mountains of Edom, a great fall of rain—a kind of cloudburst took place, by which the wady was at once filled, but they saw neither the wind nor the rains. The divine interposition was shown by introducing the laws of nature to the determined end in the predetermined way [KEIL]. It brought not only aid to the Israelitish army in their distress, by a plentiful supply of water, but destruction on the Moabites, who, perceiving the water, under the refulgent rays of the morning sun, red like blood, concluded the confederate kings had quarrelled and deluged the field with their mutual slaughter; so that, rushing to their camp in full expectation of great spoil, they were met by the Israelites, who, prepared for battle, fought and pursued them. Their country was laid waste in the way, which has always been considered the greatest desolation in the East (vs. 24). **25. Kir-haresheth**— (now Kerak)—Castle of Moab—then, probably, the only fortress in the land. **27. took his eldest so͞** that should have reigned in his stead, and offered h' for a burnt offering, etc.—By this deed of horro͞ which the allied army drove the king of Moab, a divine judgment came upon Israel; that is, the besiegers feared the anger of God, which they had incurred by giving occasion to the human sacrifice forbidden in the law (Lev. 18:21; 20:3), and hastily raised the siege.

CHAPTER 4

Vss. 1-7. ELISHA AUGMENTS THE WIDOW'S OIL. **1. there cried a certain woman of the wives of the sons of the prophets**—They were allowed to marry as well as the priests and Levites. Her husband, not enjoying the lucrative profits of business, had nothing but a professional income, which, in that irreligious age, would be precarious and very scanty, so that he was not in a condition to provide for his family. **the creditor is come to take unto him my two sons to be bondmen**—By the enactment of the law, a creditor was entitled to claim the person and children of the insolvent debtor, and compel them to serve him as bondmen till the year of jubilee should set them free. **2. a pot**—or cruet of oil. This comprising her whole stock of domestic utensils, he directs her to borrow empty vessels not a few; then, secluding herself with her children, she was to pour oil from her cruse into the borrowed vessels, and, selling the oil, discharge the debt, and then maintain herself and family with the remainder. **6. the oil stayed**—i.e., ceased to multiply; the benevolent object for which the miracle had been wrought having been accomplished.

8-17. PROMISES A SON TO THE SHUNAMMITE. **8. Elisha passed to Shunem**—now Sulam, in the plain of Esdraelon, at the southwestern base of Little Hermon. The prophet, in his journey, was often entertained here by one of its pions and opulent inhabitants. **10. Let us make a little chamber**—not build, but prepare it. She meant a room in the *oleah*, the porch, or gateway (II Sam. 18:33; I Kings 17:19), attached to the front of the house, leading into the court and inner apartments. The front of the house, excepting the door, is a dead wall, and hence this room is called a chamber in the wall. It is usually appropriated to the use of strangers, or lodgers for a night, and, from its seclusion, convenient for study or retirement. **13. what is to be done for thee?**—Wishing to testify his gratitude for the hospitable attentions of this family, he announced to her the birth of a son "about this time next year." The interest and importance of such an intelligence can only be estimated by considering that Oriental women, and Jewish in particular, connect ideas of disgrace with barrenness, and cherish a more ardent desire for children than women in any other part of the world (Gen. 18:10-15).

18-37. RAISES HER DEAD SON. **19. My head, my head!**—The cries of the boy, the part affected, and the season of the year, make it probable that he had been overtaken by a stroke of the sun. Pain, stupor, and inflammatory fever are the symptoms of the disease, which is often fatal. **22. she called unto her husband**—Her heroic concealment of the death from her husband is not the least interesting feature of the story. **24. Drive, and go forward**—'s usual for women to ride on asses, accompanied a servant, who walks behind and drives the with his stick, goading the animal at the speed d by her mistress. The Shunammite had to urney of five or six hours to the top of **26. And she answered, It is well**—Her

answer was purposely brief and vague to Gehazi, for she reserved a full disclosure of her loss for the ear of the prophet himself. She had met Gehazi at the foot of the hill, and she stopped not in her ascent till she had disburdened her heavy-laden spirit at Elisha's feet. The violent paroxysm of grief into which she fell on approaching him, appeared to Gehazi an act of disrespect to his master; he was preparing to remove her when the prophet's observant eye perceived that she was overwhelmed with some unknown cause of distress. How great is a mother's love! how wondrous are the works of Providence! The Shunammite had not sought a son from the prophet—her child was, in every respect, the free gift of God. Was she then allowed to rejoice in the possession for a little, only to be pierced with sorrow by seeing the corpse of the cherished boy? Perish, doubt and unbelief! This event happened that "the works of God should be made manifest" in this prophet, "and for the glory of God." **29. take my staff ... and lay ... upon the face of the child**—The staff was probably an official rod of a certain form and size. Necromancers used to send their staff with orders to the messengers to let it come in contact with nothing by the way that might dissipate or destroy the virtue imparted to it. Some have thought that Elisha himself entertained similar ideas, and was under an impression that the actual application of his staff would serve as well as the touch of his hand. But this is an imputation dishonorable to the character of the prophet. He wished to teach the Shunammite, who obviously placed too great dependence upon him, a memorable lesson to look to God. By sending his servant forward to lay his staff on the child, he raised her expectations, but, at the same time, taught her that his own help was unavailing—"there was neither voice, nor hearing." The command, to salute no man by the way, showed the urgency of the mission, not simply as requiring the avoidance of the tedious and unnecessary greetings so common in the East (Luke 10:1), but the exercise of faith and prayer. The act of Gehazi was allowed to fail, in order to free the Shunammite, and the people of Israel at large, of the superstitious notion of supposing a miraculous virtue resided in any *person,* or in any *rod,* and to prove that it was only through earnest prayer and faith in the power of God and for His glory that this and every miracle was to be performed. **34. lay upon the child,** etc.—(see on I Kings 17:21; Acts 20:10). Although this contact with a dead body would communicate ceremonial uncleanness, yet, in performing the great moral duties of piety and benevolence, positive laws were sometimes dispensed with, particularly by the prophets. **35. the child sneezed seven times, and the child opened his eyes**—These were the first acts of restored respiration, and they are described as successive steps. Miracles were for the most part performed instantaneously; but sometimes, also, they were advanced progressively towards completion (I Kings 18:44, 45; Mark 8:24, 25).

38-41. PURIFIES DEADLY POTTAGE. **38. there was a dearth in the land**—(see on ch. 8:1). **the sons of the prophets were sitting before him**—When receiving instruction, the scholars sat under their masters. This refers to their being domiciled under the same roof (cf. ch. 6:1). **Set on the great pot**—As it is most likely that the Jewish would resemble the Egyptian "great pot," it is seen by the monumental paintings to have been a large goblet, with two long legs, which stood over the fire on the floor. The seethed pottage consisted of meat cut into small pieces, mixed with rice or meal and vegetables. **39. went out into the field to gather herbs**—Wild herbs are very extensively used by the people in the East, even by those who possess their own vegetable gardens. The fields are daily searched for mallow, asparagus, and other wild plants. **wild vine**—lit., "the vine of the field," supposed to be the *colocynth*, a cucumber, which, in its leaves, tendrils, and fruit, bears a strong resemblance to the wild vine. The "gourds," or fruit, are of the color and size of an orange bitter to the taste, causing colic, and exciting the nerves, eaten freely they would occasion such a derangement of the stomach and bowels as to be followed by death. The meal which Elisha poured into the pot was a symbolic sign that the noxious quality of the herbs was removed. **lap full**—The hyke, or large cloak, is thrown loosely over the left shoulder and fastened under the right arm, so as to form a lap or apron.

42-44. Satisfies a Hundred Men with Twenty Loaves. **43. They shall eat, and shall leave thereof**—This was not a miracle of Elisha, but only a prediction of one by the word of the Lord. Thus it differed widely from those of Christ (Matt. 15:37; Mark 8:8; Luke 9:17; John 6:12).

CHAPTER 5

Vss. 1-7. Naaman's Leprosy. **1. Naaman, captain of the host of the king of Syria, was a great man with his master**—highly esteemed for his military character and success. **and honourable**—rather, "very rich." **but he was a leper**—This leprosy, which, in Israel, would have excluded him from society, did not affect his free intercourse in the court of Syria. **2. a little maid**—who had been captured in one of the many predatory incursions which were then made by the Syrians on the northern border of Israel (see on I Sam. 30:8; ch. 13:21; 24:2). By this young Hebrew slave of his wife, Naaman's attention was directed to the prophet of Israel, as the person who would remove his leprosy.

Naaman, on communicating the matter to his royal master, was immediately furnished with a letter to the king of Israel, and set out for Samaria, carrying with him, as an indispensable preliminary in the East, very costly presents. **5. ten talents of silver**—$20,000 in silver, $60,000 in gold. **ten changes of raiment**—splendid dresses, for festive occasions—the honor being thought to consist not only in the beauty and fineness of the material, but on having a variety to put on one after another, in the same night. **7. when the king of Israel had read the letter, he rent his clothes**—According to an ancient practice among the Eastern people, the main object only was stated in the letter as was carried by the party concerned, while other circumstances were left to be explained at the interview. This explains Jehoram's burst of emotion—not horror at supposed blasphemy, but alarm and suspicion that this was merely made an occasion for a quarrel. Such a prince as he was would not readily think of Elisha, or, perhaps, have heard of his miraculous deeds.

8-15. Elisha Sends Him to Jordan, and He Is Healed. **8. when Elisha the man of God had heard that the king of Israel had rent his clothes, that he sent to the king, saying, . . . let him come to me**—This was the grand and ultimate object to which, in the providence of God, the journey of Naaman was subservient. When the Syrian general, with his imposing retinue, arrived at the prophet's house,

Elisha sent him a message to "go and wash in Jordan seven times." This apparently rude reception to a foreigner of so high dignity incensed Naaman to such a degree that he resolved to depart, scornfully boasting that the rivers of Damascus were better than all the waters of Israel. **11. strike his hand over the place**—i.e., wave it over the diseased parts of his body. It was anciently, and still continues to be, a very prevalent superstition in the East that the hand of a king, or person of great reputed sanctity, touching, or waved over a sore, will heal it. **12. Abana and Pharpar**—the Barrady and one of its five tributaries—uncertain which. The waters of Damascus are still highly extolled by their inhabitants for their purity and coldness. **14. Then went he down, and dipped himself seven times in Jordan**—Persuaded by his calmer and more reflecting attendants to try a method so simple and easy, he followed their instructions, and was cured. The cure was performed on the basis of God's covenant with Israel, by which the land, and all pertaining to it, was blessed. Seven was the symbol of the covenant [Keil].

15-19. Elisha Refuses Naaman's Gifts. **15. he returned to the man of God**—After the miraculous cure, Naaman returned to Elisha, to whom he acknowledged his full belief in the sole supremacy of the God of Israel and offered him a liberal reward. But to show that he was not actuated by the mercenary motives of the heathen priests and prophets, Elisha, though he accepted presents on other occasions (ch. 4:42), respectfully but firmly declined them on this, being desirous that the Syrians should see the piety of God's servants, and their superiority to all worldly and selfish motives in promoting the honor of God and the interests of true religion. **17. two mules' burden of earth**—with which to make an altar (Exod. 20:24) to the God of Israel. What his motive or his purpose was in this proposal—whether he thought that God could be acceptably worshipped only on his own *soil*; or whether he wished, when far away from the Jordan, to have the *earth* of Palestine to rub himself with, which the Orientals use as a substitute for water; or whether, by making such a request of Elisha, he thought the prophet's grant of it would impart some virtue; or whether, like the modern Jews and Mohammedans, he resolved to have a portion of this *holy earth* for his nightly pillow—it is not easy to say. It is not strange to find such notions in so newly a converted heathen. **18. goeth into the house of Rimmon**—a Syrian deity; probably the sun, or the planetary system, of which a pomegranate (*Heb., Rimmon*) was the symbol. **leaneth on my hand**—i.e., meaning the service which Naaman rendered as the attendant of his sovereign. Elisha's prophetic commission not extending to any but the conversion of Israel from idolatry, he makes no remark, either approving or disapproving, on the declared course of Naaman, but simply gives (vs. 19) the parting benediction.

20-27. Gehazi, by a Lie, Obtains a Present, but Is Smitten with Leprosy. **20. I will run after him, and take somewhat of him**—The respectful courtesy to Elisha, shown in the person of his servant, and the open-handed liberality of his gifts, attest the fulness of Naaman's gratitude; while the lie—the artful management is dismissing the bearers of the treasure, and the deceitful appearance before his master, as if he had not left the house—give a most unfavorable impression of Gehazi's character. **23. in two bags**—People in the East, when travelling, have their money, in certain sums, put up in bags. 2

leper as white as snow—(See on Lev. 13:3). This heavy infliction was not too severe for the crime of Gehazi. For it was not the covetousness alone that was punished; but, at the same time, it was the ill use made of the prophet's name to gain an object prompted by a mean covetousness, and the attempt to conceal it by lying [KEIL].

CHAPTER 6

Vss. 1-7. ELISHA CAUSES IRON TO SWIM. **1. the place where we dwell with thee**—Marg., "sit before thee." The one points to a common residence—the other to a common place of meeting. The tenor of the narrative shows the humble condition of Elisha's pupils. The place was either Beth-el or Jericho, probably the latter. The ministry and miracles of Elisha brought great accessions to his schools. **2. Let us go, we pray thee, unto Jordan**—whose wooded banks would furnish plenty of timber. **5. it was borrowed**—lit., begged. The scholar's distress arose from the consideration that it had been presented to him; and that, owing to his poverty, he could not procure another. **6. cut down a stick, and cast it in thither**—Although this means was used, it had no natural adaptation to make the iron swim. Besides, the Jordan is at Jericho so deep and rapid that there were 1000 chances to 1 against the stick falling into the hole of the axe-head. All attempts to account for the recovery of the lost implement on such a theory must be rejected. "The iron did swim"— only by the miraculous exertion of Elisha's power.

8-17. DISCLOSES THE KING OF SYRIA'S COUNSEL. **8. the king of Syria warred against Israel**—This seems to have been a sort of guerrilla warfare, carried on by predatory inroads on different parts of the country. Elisha apprised King Jehoram of the secret purpose of the enemy; so, by adopting precautionary measures, he was always enabled to anticipate and defeat their attacks. The frequency of his disappointments having led the Syrian king to suspect some of his servants of carrying on a treacherous correspondence with the enemy, he was informed about Elisha, whose apprehension he forthwith determined to effect. This resolution was, of course, grounded on the belief that however great the knowledge of Elisha might be, if seized and kept a prisoner, he could no longer give information to the king of Israel. **13. Dothan**—or Dothaim, a little north of Samaria (see on Gen. 37:17). **15. his servant said unto him, Alas, my master! how shall we do?**—When the Syrian detachment surrounded the place by night, for the apprehension of the prophet, his servant was paralyzed with fear. This was a new servant, who had only been with him since Gehazi's dismissal and consequently had little or no experience of his master's powers. His faith was easily shaken by so unexpected an alarm. **17. Elisha prayed, and said, O Lord, I pray thee, open his eyes that he may see**—The invisible guard of angels that encompass and defend us (Ps. 34:7). The opening of the eyes, which Elisha prayed for, were those of the Spirit, not of the body—the eye of faith sees the reality of the divine presence and protection where all is vacancy or darkness to the ordinary eye. The horses and chariots were symbols of the divine power (see on ch. 2:12); and their fiery nature denoted their supernatural origin; for fire, the most ethereal of earthly elements, is the most appropriate symbol of the Godhead [KEIL].

18-23. HIS ARMY SMITTEN WITH BLINDNESS. **18. Smite this people, I pray thee, with blindness**—

not a total and material blindness, for then they could not have followed him—but a mental hallucination (see on Gen. 19:11) so that they did not perceive or recognize him to be the object of their search. **19. This is not the way, neither is this the city**—This statement is so far true that, as he had now left the place of his residence, they would not have got him by that road. But the ambiguity of his language was purposely framed to deceive them; and yet the deception must be viewed in the light of a stratagem, which has always been deemed lawful in war. **he led them to Samaria**—When they arrived in the midst of the capital, their eyes, at Elisha's request, were opened, and they then became aware of their defenseless condition, for Jehoram had received private premonition of their arrival. The king, so far from being allowed to slay the enemies who were thus unconsciously put in his power, was recommended to entertain them with liberal hospitality and then dismiss them to their own country. This was humane advice; it was contrary to the usage of war to put war captives to death in cold blood, even when taken by the point of the sword, much more those whom the miraculous power and providence of God had unexpectedly placed at his disposal. In such circumstances, kind and hospitable treatment was every way more becoming in itself, and would be productive of the best effects. It would redound to the credit of the true religion, which inspired such an excellent spirit into its professors; and it would not only prevent the future opposition of the Syrians but make them stand in awe of a people who, they had seen, were so remarkably protected by a prophet of the Lord. The latter clause of verse 23 shows that these salutary effects were fully realized. A moral conquest had been gained over the Syrians.

24-33. BEN-HADAD BESIEGES SAMARIA. **Ben-hadad . . . besieged Samaria**—This was the predicted accomplishment of the result of Ahab's foolish and misplaced kindness (I Kings 20:42). **25. an ass's head was sold for fourscore pieces of silver**—Though the ass was deemed unclean food, necessity might warrant their violation of a positive law when mothers, in their extremity, were found violating the law of nature. The head was the worst part of the animal. Eighty pieces of silver, equal to $50.00. **the fourth part of a cab**—A cab was the smallest dry measure. The proportion here stated was nearly half a pint for $ 3.00. "Dove's dung" is thought by BOCHART to be a kind of pulse or pea, common in Judea, and still kept in the storehouses of Cairo and Damascus, and other places, for the use of it by pilgrim caravans; by LINNAEUS, and other botanists, it is said to be the root or white bulb of the plant *Ornithogalum umbellatum*, Star of Bethlehem. The sacred historian does not say that the articles here named were regularly sold at the rates described, but only that instances were known of such high prices being given. **26. as the king was passing**—to look at the defenses, or to give some necessary orders for manning the walls. **29. we boiled my son, and did eat him**—(See on Deut. 28:53). **30. had sackcloth within upon his flesh**—The horrid recital of this domestic tragedy led the king soon after to rend his garment, in consequence of which it was discovered that he wore a penitential shirt of haircloth. It is more than doubtful, however, if he was truly humbled on account of his own and the nation's sins; otherwise he would not have vowed vengeance on the prophet's life. The true explanation seems to be, that Elisha having counselled him not to surrender, with the promise, on condition of deep humiliation, of being delivered, and he having assumed the signs of contrition without receiving the expected relief, regarded Elisha who had proved false and faithless as the cause of all the protracted distress. **32. But Elisha sat in his house, and the elders sat with him**—The latter clause of vs. 33, which contains the king's impatient exclamation, enables us to account for the impetuous order he issued for the beheading of Elisha. Though Jehoram was a wicked king and most of his courtiers would resemble their master, many had been won over, through the prophet's influence, to the true religion. A meeting, probably a prayer-meeting, of those was held in the house where he lodged, for he had none of his own (I Kings 19:20, 21); and them he not only apprised of the king's design against himself, but disclosed to them the proof of a premeditated deliverance.

CHAPTER 7

Vss. 1-16. ELISHA PROPHESIES INCREDIBLE PLENTY IN SAMARIA. **1. Hear ye the word of the Lord**—This prediction, though uttered first to the assembled elders, was intimated to the king's messengers, who reported it to Jehoram (vs. 18). **Tomorrow, about this time, shall a measure of fine flour be sold for a shekel,** etc.—This may be estimated at a peck of fine flour for a dollar, and two pecks of barley at the same price. **in the gate of Samaria**—Vegetables, cattle, all sorts of country produce, are still sold every morning at the gates of towns in the East. **2. a lord on whose hand the king leaned**—When an Eastern king walks or stands abroad in the open air, he always supports himself on the arm of the *highest* courtier present. **if the Lord would make windows in heaven**—The scoffing infidelity of this remark, which was a sneer against not the prophet only, but the God he served, was justly and signally punished (see vs. 20). **3. there were four leprous men**—The account of the sudden raising of the siege and the unexpected supply given to the famishing inhabitants of Samaria, is introduced by a narrative of the visit and discovery, by these poor creatures, of the extraordinary flight of the Syrians. **leprous men at the entering in of the gate**—living, perhaps, in some lazar-house there (Lev. 13:4-6; Num. 5:3). **5. they rose up in the twilight**—i.e., the evening twilight (vs. 12). **the uttermost part of the camp of Syria**—i.e., the extremity nearest the city. **6, 7. the Lord had made the host of the Syrians to hear a noise of chariots**—This illusion of the sense of hearing, whereby the besiegers imagined the tramp of two armies from opposite quarters, was a great miracle which God wrought directly for the deliverance of His people. **8-11. these lepers ... did eat and drink**—After they had appeased their hunger and secreted as many valuables as they could carry, their consciences smote them for concealing the discovery and they hastened to publish it in the city. **10. horses tied, and asses tied, and the tents as they were**—The uniform arrangement of encampments in the East is to place the tents in the center, while the cattle are picketed all around, as an outer wall of defense; and hence the lepers describe the cattle as the first objects they saw. **12-15. the king ... said unto his servants, I will now show you what the Syrians have done**—Similar stratagems have been so often resorted to in the ancient and modern wars of the East that there is no wonder Jehoram's suspicions were awakened. But the scouts, whom he des-

patched, soon found unmistakable signs of the panic that had struck the enemy and led to a most precipitate flight. **17-20.** THE UNBELIEVING LORD TRODDEN TO DEATH. **17. the king appointed the lord on whose hand he leaned,** etc.—The news spread like lightning through the city, and was followed, as was natural, by a popular rush to the Syrian camp. To keep order at the gate, the king ordered his minister to keep guard; but the impetuosity of the famishing people could not be resisted. The lord was trodden to death, and Elisha's prophecy in all respects accomplished.

CHAPTER 8

Vss. 1-6. THE SHUNAMMITE'S LAND RESTORED. **1. Then spake Elisha unto the woman**—rather "had spoken." The repetition of Elisha's direction to the Shunammite is merely given as an introduction to the following narrative; and it probably took place before the events recorded in chaps. 5 and 6. **6. The Lord hath called for a famine**—All such calamities are chastisements inflicted by the hand of God; and this famine was to be of double duration to that one which happened in the time of Elijah (Jas. 5:17)—a just increase of severity, since the Israelites still continued obdurate and incorrigible under the ministry and miracles of Elisha (Lev. 26: 21, 24, 28). **2. she ... sojourned in the land of the Philistines seven years**—Their territory was recommended to her from its contiguity to her usual residence; and now that this state had been so greatly reduced, there was less risk than formerly from the seductions of idolatry; and many of the Jews and Israelites were residing there. Besides, an emigration thither was less offensive to the king of Israel than going to sojourn in Judah. **3. she went forth to cry unto the king for her house and for her land**—In consequence of her long-continued absence from the country, her possessions were occupied by her kindred, or had been confiscated by the crown. No statute in the law of Moses ordained that alienation. But the innovation seems to have been adopted in Israel. **4. the king talked with Gehazi**—Ceremonial pollution being conveyed by contact alone, there was nothing to prevent a conference being held with this leper at a distance; and although he was excluded from the *town* of Samaria, this reported conversation may have taken place at the gate or in one of the royal gardens. The providence of God so ordained that King Jehoram had been led to inquire, with great interest, into the miraculous deeds of Elisha, and that the prophet's servant was in the act of relating the marvellous incident of the restoration of the Shunammite's son when she made her appearance to prefer her request. The king was pleased to grant it; and a state officer was charged to afford her every facility in the recovery of her family possession out of the hands of the occupier. **7-15.** HAZAEL KILLS HIS MASTER, AND SUCCEEDS HIM. **7. Elisha came to Damascus**—He was directed thither by the Spirit of God, in pursuance of the mission formerly given to his master in Horeb (I Kings 19:15), to anoint Hazael king of Syria. On the arrival of the prophet being known, Ben-hadad, who was sick, sent to inquire the issue of his disease, and, according to the practice of the heathens in consulting their soothsayers, ordered a liberal present in remuneration for the service. **9. forty camels' burden**—The present, consisting of the rarest and most valuable produce of the land, would be liberal and magnificent. But it must not be supposed it was actually so large as to require forty camels to carry it. The Orientals are fond of display, and would, ostentatiously, lay upon forty beasts what might very easily have been borne by four. **Thy son Ben-hadad**—so called from the established usage of designating the prophet "father." This was the same Syrian monarch who had formerly persecuted him (see on ch. 6:13, 14). **10. Go, say . . ., Thou mayest certainly recover**—There was no contradiction in this message. This part was properly the answer to Ben-hadad's inquiry. The second part was intended for Hazael, who, like an artful and ambitious courtier, reported only as much of the prophet's statement as suited his own views (cf. vs. 14). **11. he settled his countenance steadfastly, until he was ashamed**—i.e., Hazael. The steadfast, penetrating look of the prophet seemed to have convinced Hazael that his secret designs were known. The deep emotions of Elisha were justified by the horrible atrocities which, too common in ancient warfare, that successful usurper committed in Israel (ch. 10:32; 13: 3, 4, 22). **15. took a thick cloth,** etc.—a coverlet. In the East, this article of bedding is generally a thick quilt of wool or cotton, so that, with its great weight, when steeped in water, it would be a fit instrument for accomplishing the murderous purpose, without leaving any marks of violence. It has been supposed by many that Hazael purposely murdered the king. But it is common for Eastern people to sleep with their faces covered with a mosquito net; and, in some cases of fever, they dampen the bedclothes. Hazael, aware of those chilling remedies being usually resorted to, might have, with an honest intention, spread a refreshing cover over him. The rapid occurrence of the king's death and immediate burial were favorable to his instant elevation to the throne.

16-23. JEHORAM'S WICKED REIGN. **16. Jehoram the son of Jehoshaphat . . . began to reign**—(See on ch. 3:1). His father resigned the throne to him two years before his death. **18. daughter of Ahab**—Athaliah, through whose influence Jehoram introduced the worship of Baal and many other evils into the kingdom of Judah (see II Chron. 21:2-20). This apostasy would have led to the total extinction of the royal family in that kingdom, had it not been for the divine promise to David (II Sam. 7). A national chastisement, however, was inflicted on Judah by the revolt of Edom, which, being hitherto governed by a tributary ruler (ch. 3:9; I Kings 22:47), erected the standard of independence (see on II Chron. 21:9).

24. AHAZIAH SUCCEEDS HIM. **24. Ahaziah his son reigned in his stead**—(See on II Chron. 22: 1-6).

CHAPTER 9

Vss. 1-23. JEHU IS ANOINTED. **1. Ramoth-gilead**—a city of great importance to the Hebrew people, east of Jordan, as a fortress of defense against the Syrians. Jehoram had regained it (ch. 8:29). But the Israelitish army was still encamped there, under the command of Jehu. **Elisha . . . called one of the children of the prophets**—This errand referred to the last commission given to Elijah in Horeb (I Kings 19:16). **box of oil**—(See I Sam. 10:1). **2. carry him to an inner chamber**—both to ensure the safety of the messenger and to prevent all obstruction in the execution of the business. **3. I have anointed thee king over Israel**—This was only

a part of the message; the full announcement of which is given (vss. 7-10). **flee, and tarry not**—for fear of being surprised and overtaken by the spies or servants of the court. **4. So the young man . . . went to Ramoth-gilead**—His ready undertaking of this delicate and hazardous mission was an eminent proof of his piety and obedience. The act of a-nointing being done through a commissioned prophet, was a divine intimation of his investiture with the sovereign power. But it was sometimes done long prior to the actual possession of the throne (I Sam. 16:13); and, in like manner, the commission had, in this instance, been given also a long time before to Elijah, who, for good reasons, left it in charge to Elisha; and he awaited God's time and command for executing it [POOLE]. **10. in the portion of Jezreel**—i.e., that had formerly been the vineyard of Naboth. **11. Is all well?** etc.—Jehu's attendants knew that the stranger belonged to the order of the prophets by his garb, gestures, and form of address; and soldiers such as they very readily concluded such persons to be crackbrained, not only from the sordid negligence of their personal appearance and their open contempt of the world, but from the religious pursuits in which their whole lives were spent, and the grotesque actions which they frequently performed (cf. Jer. 29:26). **13. they hasted, and took every man his garment**—the upper cloak which they spread on the ground, as a token of their homage to their distinguished commander (Matt. 21:7). **top of the stairs**—from the room where the prophet had privately anointed Jehu. That general returned to join his brother officers in the public apartment, who, immediately on learning his destined elevation, conducted him to the top of the stairs leading to the roof. This was the most conspicuous place of an Oriental structure that could be chosen, being at the very top of the gate-building, and fully in view of the people and military in the open ground in front of the building [KITTO]. The popularity of Jehu with the army thus favored the designs of Providence in procuring his immediate and enthusiastic proclamation as king, and the top of the stairs was taken as a most convenient substitute for a throne. **14, 15. Joram had kept Ramoth-gilead**—rather, was keeping, guarding, or besieging it, with the greater part of the military force of Israel. The king's wounds had compelled his retirement from the scene of action, and so the troops were left in command of Jehu. **16. So Jehu rode in a chariot, and went to Jezreel**—Full of ambitious designs, he immediately proceeded to cross the Jordan to execute his commission on the house of Ahab. **17. there stood a watchman on the tower of Jezreel**—The Hebrew palaces, besides being situated on hills had usually towers attached to them, not only for the pleasure of a fine prospect, but as posts of useful observation. The ancient watchtower of Jezreel must have commanded a view of the whole region eastward, nearly down to the Jordan. Beth-shan stands on a rising ground about six or seven miles below it, in a narrow part of the plain; and when Jehu and his retinue reached that point between Gilboa and Beth-shan, they could be fully descried by the watchman on the tower. A report was made to Joram in his palace below. A messenger on horseback was quickly despatched down into the plain to meet the ambiguous host and to question the object of their approach. "Is it peace?" We may safely assume that this messenger would meet Jehu at the distance of three miles or more. On the report made of his being detained and turned into the rear of the still advancing troops, a second messenger was in like manner despatched, who would naturally meet Jehu at the distance of a mile or a mile and a half down on the plain. He also being turned into the rear, the watchman now distinctly perceived "the driving to be like the driving of Jehu, the son of Nimshi; for he driveth furiously." The alarmed monarch, awakened to a sense of his impending danger, quickly summoned his forces to meet the crisis. Accompanied by Ahaziah, king of Judah, the two sovereigns ascended their chariots to make a feeble resistance to the impetuous onset of Jehu, who quickly from the plain ascended the steep northern sides of the site on which Jezreel stood, and the conflicting parties met in "the portion of Naboth the Jezreelite," where Joram was quickly despatched by an arrow from the strong arm of Jehu. We were impressed with the obvious accuracy of the sacred historian; the *localities* and *distances* being such as seem naturally to be required by the incidents related, affording just time for the transactions to have occurred in the order in which they are recorded [HOWE]. **25. cast him in the portion of the field of Naboth the Jezreelite,** etc.—according to the doom pronounced by divine authority on Ahab (I Kings 21:19), but which on his repentance was deferred to be executed on his son. **26. the blood of Naboth, and the blood of sons, saith the Lord**—Although their death is not expressly mentioned, it is plainly implied in the confiscation of his property (see on I Kings 21:16).

27-35. AHAZIAH IS SLAIN. 27. Ahaziah—was grandnephew to King Joram, and great-grandson to King Ahab. **Ibleam**—near Megiddo, in the tribe of Issachar (Josh. 17:11; Judg. 1:27); and Gur was an adjoining hill. **30. Jezebel painted her face**—lit., her eyes, according to a custom universal in the East among women, of staining the eyelids with a black powder made of pulverized antimony, or leadore mixed with oil, and applied with a small brush on the border, so that by this dark ligament on the edge, the largeness as well as the luster of the eye itself was thought to be increased. Her object was, by her royal attire, not to captivate, but to overawe Jehu. **35. found no more of her than the skull, and the palms of her hands,** etc.—The dog has a rooted aversion to prey on the human hands and feet.

36, 37. JEZEBEL EATEN BY DOGS. **36. he said, This is the word of the Lord**—(see on I Kings 21:23). Jehu's statement, however, was not a literal but a paraphrased quotation of Elijah's prophecy.

CHAPTER 10

Vss. 1-17. JEHU CAUSES SEVENTY OF AHAB'S CHILDREN TO BE BEHEADED. **1. Ahab had seventy sons in Samaria**—As it appears (vs. 13) that grandsons are included, it is probable that this number comprehended the whole posterity of Ahab. Their being all assembled in that capital might arise from their being left there on the king's departure for Ramoth-gilead, or from their taking refuge in some of the strongholds of that city on the news of Jehu's conspiracy. It may be inferred from the tenor of Jehu's letters that their first intention was to select the fittest of the royal family and set him up as king. Perhaps this challenge of Jehu was designed as a stroke of policy on his part to elicit their views, and to find out whether they were inclined to be pacific or hostile. The bold character of the man, and the rapid success of his conspiracy, terrified the civic authorities of Samaria and Jezreel into sub-

mission. **5. he that was over the house**—the governor or chamberlain of the palace. **the bringers-up of the children**—Anciently, and still also in many Eastern countries, the principal grandees were charged with the support and education of the royal princes. This involved a heavy expense which they were forced to bear, but for which they endeavored to find some compensation in the advantages of their connection with the court. **6. take ye the heads of the men, your master's sons**—The barbarous practice of a successful usurper slaughtering all who may have claims to the throne, has been frequently exemplified in the ancient and modern histories of the East. **8. Lay ye them in two heaps at the entering in of the gate,** etc.—The exhibition of the heads of enemies is always considered a glorious trophy. Sometimes a pile of heads is erected at the gate of the palace; and a head of peculiarly striking appearance selected to grace the summit of the pyramid. **9. said to all the people, Ye be righteous,** etc.—A great concourse was assembled to gaze on this novel and ghastly spectacle. The speech which Jehu addressed to the spectators was artfully framed to impress their minds with the idea that so wholesale a massacre was the result of the divine judgments denounced on the house of Ahab; and the effect of it was to prepare the public mind for hearing, without horror, of a similar revolting tragedy which was soon after perpetrated, viz., the extinction of all the influential friends and supporters of the dynasty of Ahab, including those of the royal house of Judah. **13. We are the brethren of Ahaziah**—i.e., not full, but step-brothers, sons of Jehoram by various concubines. Ignorant of the revolution that had taken place, they were travelling to Samaria on a visit to their royal relatives of Israel, when they were seized and put to death, because of the apprehension that they might probably stimulate and strengthen the party that still remained faithful in their allegiance to Ahab's dynasty. **children of the queen**—i.e., of the queen mother, or regent, Jezebel. **15-18. Jehonadab the son of Rechab**—(See on I Chron. 2:55). A person who, from his piety and simple primitive manner of life (Jer. 35), was highly esteemed, and possessed great influence in the country. Jehu saw in a moment the advantage that his cause would gain from the friendship and countenance of this venerable man in the eyes of the people, and accordingly paid him the distinguished attention of inviting him to a seat in his chariot. **give me thine hand**—not simply to aid him in getting up, but for a far more significant and important purpose—the giving, or rather joining hands, being the recognized mode of striking a league or covenant, as well as of testifying fealty to a new sovereign; accordingly, it is said, "he [Jehonadab] gave him [Jehu] his hand."

18-29. HE DESTROYS THE WORSHIPPERS OF BAAL. **19. call unto me all the prophets of Baal**—The votaries of Baal are here classified under the several titles of prophets, priests, and servants, or worshippers generally. They might be easily convened into one spacious temple, as their number had been greatly diminished both by the influential ministrations of Elijah and Elisha, and also from the late King Joram's neglect and discontinuance of the worship. Jehu's appointment of a solemn sacrifice in honor of Baal, and a summons to all his worshippers to join in its celebration, was a deep-laid plot, which he had resolved upon for their extinction, a measure in perfect harmony with the Mosaic law, and worthy of a constitutional king of Israel. It was done, however, not from religious, but purely political motives, because be believed that the existence and interests of the Baalites were inseparably bound up with the dynasty of Ahab and because he hoped that by their extermination he would secure the attachment of the far larger and more influential party who worshipped God in Israel. Jehonadab's concurrence must have been given in the belief of his being actuated solely by the highest principles of piety and zeal. **22. Bring forth vestments for all the worshippers of Baal**—The priests of Baal were clad, probably, in robes of white byssus while they were engaged in the functions of their office, and these were kept under the care of an officer in a particular wardrobe of Baal's temple. This treacherous massacre, and the means taken to accomplish it, are paralleled by the slaughter of the Janissaries and other terrible tragedies in the modern history of the East. **29. Howbeit from the sins of Jeroboam . . . Jehu departed not from after them**—Jehu had no intention of carrying his zeal for the Lord beyond a certain point, and as he considered it impolitic to encourage his subjects to travel to Jerusalem, he re-established the symbolic worship of the calves.

CHAPTER 11

Vss. 1-3. JEHOASH SAVED FROM ATHALIAH'S MASSACRE. **1. Athaliah**—(See on II Chron. 22:2). She had possessed great influence over her son, who, by her counsels, had ruled in the spirit of the house of Ahab. **destroyed all the seed royal**—all connected with the royal family who might have urged a claim to the throne, and who had escaped the murderous hands of Jehu (II Chron. 21:2-4; 22:1; ch. 10:13, 14). This massacre she was incited to perpetrate—partly from a determination not to let David's family outlive hers—partly as a measure of self-defense to secure herself against the violence of Jehu, who was bent on destroying the whole of Ahab's posterity to which she belonged (ch. 8:18-26); but chiefly from personal ambition to rule, and a desire to establish the worship of Baal. Such was the sad fruit of the unequal alliance between the son of the pious Jehoshaphat and a daughter of the idolatrous and wicked house of Ahab. **2. Jehosheba** —of Jehoshabeath (II Chron. 22:11). **daughter of King Joram**—not by Athaliah, but by a secondary wife. **stole him from among the king's sons which were slain**—either from among the corpses, he being considered dead, or out of the palace nursery. **hid him . . . in the bedchamber**—for the use of the priests, which was in some part of the temple (vs. 3), and of which Jehoiada and his wife had the sole charge. What is called, however, the bedchamber in the East is not the kind of apartment that we understand by the name, but a small closet, into which are flung during the day the mattresses and other bedding materials spread on the floors or divans of the sitting-rooms by day. Such a lumber-room was well suited to be a convenient place for the recovery of his wounds, and a hiding-place for the royal infant and his nurse.

4-12. HE IS MADE KING. **4. the seventh year**—viz., of the reign of Athaliah, and the rescue of Jehoash. **Jehoiada sent and fetched the rulers,** etc. —He could scarcely have obtained such a general convocation except at the time, or on pretext, of a public and solemn festival. Having revealed to them the secret of the young king's preservation and entered into a covenant with them for the overthrow of the tyrant, he then arranged with them the plan

and time of carrying their plot into execution (see on II Chron. 22:10-12; 23). The conduct of Jehoiada, who acted the leading and chief part in this conspiracy, admits of an easy and full justification; for, while Athaliah was a usurper, and belonged to a race destined by divine denunciation to destruction, even his own wife had a better and stronger claim to the throne; the sovereignty of Judah had been divinely appropriated to the family of David, and therefore the young prince on whom it was proposed to confer the crown, possessed an inherent right to it, of which a usurper could not deprive him. Moreover, Jehoiada was most probably the high priest, whose official duty it was to watch over the due execution of God's laws, and who in his present movement, was encouraged and aided by the countenance and support of the chief authorities, both civil and ecclesiastical, in the country. In addition to all these considerations, he seems to have been directed by an impulse of the Divine Spirit, through the counsels and exhortations of the prophets of the time.

13-16. ATHALIAH SLAIN. **13. Athaliah heard the noise of the guard and of the people**—The profound secrecy with which the conspiracy had been conducted rendered the unusual acclamations of the vast assembled crowd the more startling and roused the suspicions of the tyrant. **she came . . . into the temple of the Lord**—i.e., the courts, which she was permitted to enter by Jehoiada's directions (vs. 8) in order that she might be secured. **14. the king stood by a pillar**—or on a platform, erected for that purpose (II Chron. 6:13). **15. without the ranges** —i.e., fences, that the sacred place might not be stained with human blood.

17. JEHOIADA RESTORES GOD'S WORSHIP. **17. a covenant between the Lord and the king and the people**—The covenant with the Lord was a renewal of the national covenant with Israel (Exod. 19; 24; "to be unto him a people of inheritance," Deut. 4:6; 27:9). The covenant between the king and the people was the consequence of this, and by it the king bound himself to rule according to the divine law, while the people engaged to submit, to give him allegiance as the Lord's anointed. The immediate fruit of this renewal of the covenant was the destruction of the temple and the slaughter of the priests of Baal (see on ch. 10:27); the restoration of the pure worship of God in all its ancient integrity; and the establishment of the young king on the hereditary throne of Judah.

CHAPTER 12

Vss. 1-18. JEHOASH REIGNS WELL WHILE JEHOIADA LIVED. **2. Jehoash did that which was right in the sight of the Lord**—so far as related to his outward actions and the policy of his government. But it is evident from the sequel of his history that the rectitude of his administration was owing more to the salutary influence of his preserver and tutor, Jehoiada, than to the honest and sincere dictates of his own mind. **3. But the high places were not taken away**—The popular fondness for the private and disorderly rites performed in the groves and recesses of hills was so inveterate that even the most powerful monarchs had been unable to accomplish their suppression; no wonder that in the early reign of a young king, and after the gross irregularities that had been allowed during the maladministration of Athaliah, the difficulty of putting an end to the superstitions associated with "the high places" was greatly increased. **4. Jehoash said to the priests,** etc. There is here given an account of the measures which the young king took for repairing the temple by the levying of taxes: 1. "The money of every one that passeth the account," viz., half a shekel, as an offering to the Lord" (Exod. 30: 13). 2. "The money that every man is set at," i.e., the redemption-price of every one who had devoted himself or any thing belonging to him to the Lord, and the amount of which was estimated according to certain rules (Lev. 27:1-8). 3. Free-will or voluntary offerings made to the sanctuary. The first two were paid annually (see on II Chron. 24:5). **7-10. Why repair ye not the breaches of the house?**— This mode of collection not proving so productive as was expected (the dilatoriness of the priests was the chief cause of the failure), a new arrangement was proposed. A chest was placed by the high priest at the entrance into the temple, into which the money given by the people for the repairs of the temple was to be put by the Levites who kept the door. The object of this chest was to make a separation between the money to be raised for the building from the other moneys destined for the general use of the priests, in the hope that the people would be more liberal in their contributions when it was known that their offerings would be devoted to the special purpose of making the necessary repairs. The duty of attending to this work was no longer to devolve on the priests, but to be undertaken by the king. **11-13. they gave the money, being told, into the hands of them that did the work**—The king sent his secretary along with an agent of the high priest (II Chron. 24:11) to count the money in the chest from time to time, and deliver the amount to the overseers of the building, who paid the workmen and purchased all necessary materials. The custom of putting sums of certain amount in bags, which are labelled and sealed by a proper officer, is a common way of using the currency in Turkey and other Eastern countri·s. **13-16. Howbeit there were not made . . . bow ʒ,** etc.— When the repairs of the temple had been completed, the surplus was appropriated to the purchase of temple furniture. The integrity of the overseers of the work being undoubted, no account was exacted of the way in which they applied the money given to them, while other moneys levied at the temple were left to the disposal of the priests as the law directed (Lev. 5:16; Num. 5:8). **17, 18. Then Hazael . . . fought against Gath**—(See on II Chron. 24:23, 24). 19-21. He Is Slain. **20. his servants arose . . . and slew Joash in the house of Millo**—(See also II Chron. 24:25).

CHAPTER 13

Vss. 1-7. Jehoahaz's Wicked Reign over Israel. **1. Jehoahaz . . . reigned seventeen years**—Under his government, which pursued the policy of his predecessors regarding the support of the calf-worship, Israel's apostasy from the true God became greater and more confirmed than in the time of his father Jehu. The national chastisement, when it came, was consequently the more severe and the instruments employed by the Lord in scourging the revolted nation were Hazael and his son and general Ben-hadad, in resisting whose successive invasions the Israelitish army was sadly reduced and weakened. In the extremity of his distress, Jehoahaz besought the Lord, and was heard, not on his own

account (Ps. 66:18; Prov. 1:28; 15:8), but that of the ancient covenant with the patriarchs (vs. 23). **4. he saw the oppression of Israel**—i.e., commiserated the fallen condition of His chosen people. The divine honor and the interests of true religion required that deliverance should be granted them to check the triumph of the idolatrous enemy and put an end to their blasphemous taunts that God had forsaken Israel (Deut. 32:27; Ps. 12:4). **5. a saviour**—This refers neither to some patriotic defender nor some signal victory, but to the deliverance obtained for Israel by the two successors of Jehoahaz, viz., Joash, who regained all the cities which the Syrians had taken from his father (vs. 25); and Jeroboam, who restored the former boundaries of Israel (ch. 14:25). **6. there remained the grove**—Asherah—the idol set up by Ahab (I Kings 16:33), which ought to have been demolished (Deut. 7:5). **7. made them like the dust in threshing**—Threshing in the East is performed in the open air upon a level plot of ground, daubed over with a covering to prevent, as much as possible, the earth, sand, or gravel from rising; a great quantity of them all, notwithstanding this precaution, must unavoidably be taken up with the grain; at the same time the straw is shattered to pieces. Hence it is a most significant figure, frequently employed by Orientals to describe a state of national suffering, little short of extermination (Isa. 21:10; Mic. 4:12; Jer. 51:33). The figure originated in a barbarous war custom, which Hazael literally followed (Amos 1:3, 4; cf. II Sam. 8:31; Judg. 8:7).

8-25. Joash Succeeds Him. **8. his might**— This is particularly noticed in order to show that the grievous oppression from foreign enemies, by which the Israelites were ground down, was not owing to the cowardice or imbecility of their king, but solely to the righteous and terrible judgment of God for their foul apostasy. **12, 13. his might, wherewith he fought against Amaziah**—(See on ch. 14:8-14). The usual summary of his life and reign occurs rather early, and is again repeated in the account given of the reign of the king of Judah (ch. 14:15). **14-19. Elisha was fallen sick of his sickness whereof he died**—Every man's death is occasioned by some disease, and so was Elisha's. But in intimating it, there seems a contrast tacitly made between him and his prophetic predecessor, who did not die. **Joash the king of Israel came down unto him, and wept over his face**—He visited him where he was lying ill of this mortal sickness, and expressed deep sorrow, not from the personal respect he bore for the prophet, but for the incalculable loss his death would occasion to the kingdom. **my father, my father!** etc.—(See on ch. 2:12). These words seem to have been a complimentary phrase applied to one who was thought an eminent guardian and deliverer of his country. The particular application of them to Elisha, who, by his counsels and prayer, had obtained many glorious victories for Israel, shows that the king possessed some measure of faith and trust, which, though weak, was accepted, and called forth the prophet's dying benediction. **15. Take bow and arrows**— Hostilities were usually proclaimed by a herald, sometimes by a king or general making a public and formal discharge of an arrow into the enemy's country. Elisha directed Joash to do this, as a symbolical act, designed to intimate more fully and significantly the victories promised to the king of Israel over the Syrians. His laying his hands upon the king's hands was to represent the power imparted to the bow-shot as coming from the Lord through the medium of the prophet. His shooting the first arrow eastward—to that part of his kingdom which the Syrians had taken and which was east of Samaria—was a declaration of war against them for the invasion. His shooting the other arrows into the ground was in token of the number of victories he was taken to gain; but his stopping at the third betrayed the weakness of his faith; for, as the discharged arrow signified a victory over the Syrians, it is evident that the more arrows he shot the more victories he would gain. As he stopped so soon, his conquests would be incomplete. **20. Elisha died**—He had enjoyed a happier life than Elijah, as he possessed a milder character, and bore a less hard commission. His rough garment was honored even at the court. **coming in of the year**—i.e., the spring, the usual season of beginning campaigns in ancient times. Predatory bands from Moab generally made incursions at that time on the lands of Israel. The bearers of a corpse, alarmed by the appearance of one of these bands, hastily deposited, as they passed that way, their load in Elisha's sepulchre, which might be easily done by removing the stone at the mouth of the cave. According to the Jewish and Eastern custom, his body, as well as that of the man who was miraculously restored, was not laid in a coffin, but only swathed; so that the bodies could be brought into contact and the object of the miracle was to stimulate the king's and people of Israel's faith in the still unaccomplished predictions of Elisha respecting the war with the Syrians. Accordingly the historian forthwith records the historical fulfilment of the prediction (vss. 22-25), in the defeat of the enemy, in the recovery of the cities that had been taken, and their restoration to the kingdom of Israel.

CHAPTER 14

Vss. 1-6. AMAZIAH'S GOOD REIGN OVER JUDAH. **3-6. He did that which was right in the sight of the Lord, yet not like David his father**—The beginning of his reign was excellent, for he acted the part of a constitutional king, according to the law of God, yet not with perfect sincerity of heart (cf. II Chron. 25:2). As in the case of his father Joash, the early promise was belied by the devious course he personally followed in later life (see on II Chron. 20:14), as well as by the public irregularities he tolerated in the kingdom. **5. as soon as the kingdom was confirmed in his hand**—It was an act of justice no less than of filial piety to avenge the murder of his father. But it is evident that the two assassins must have possessed considerable weight and influence, as the king was obliged to retain them in his service, and durst not, for fear of their friends and supporters, institute proceedings against them until his power had been fully consolidated. **6. But the children of the murderers he slew not**—This moderation, inspired by the Mosaic law (Deut. 24:16), displays the good character of this prince; for the course thus pursued toward the families of the regicides was directly contrary to the prevailing customs of antiquity, according to which all connected with the criminals were doomed to unsparing destruction.
7. HE SMITES EDOM. **7. He slew of Edom in the valley of salt ten thousand**—In the reign of Joram the Edomites had revolted (see on ch. 8:20). But Amaziah, determined to reduce them to their former subjection, formed a hostile expedition against them, in which he routed their army and made himself master of their capital. **the valley of salt**—that part of the Ghor which comprises the salt and sandy plain to the south of the Dead Sea. **Selah**—lit.,

Selah—(rock) generally thought to be Petra. **Joktheel**—i.e., given or conquered by God. See the history of this conquest more fully detailed (II Chron. 25:6-16).
8-16. JOASH DEFEATS HIM. **8. Amaziah sent messengers to Jehoash, the son of Jehoahaz, son of Jehu, king of Israel**—This bold and haughty challenge, which was most probably stimulated by a desire of satisfaction for the outrages perpetrated by the discharged auxiliaries of Israel (II Chron. 25:13) on the towns that lay in their way home, as well as by revenge for the massacre of his ancestors by Jehu (ch. 9) sprang, there is little doubt, from pride and self-confidence, inspired by his victory over the Edomites. **9. Jehoash the king of Israel sent to Amaziah**—People in the East very often express their sentiments in a parabolic form, especially when they intend to convey unwelcome truths or a contemptuous sneer. This was the design of the admonitory fable related by Joash in his reply. The thistle, a low shrub, might be chosen to represent Amaziah, a petty prince; the cedar, the powerful sovereign of Israel, and the wild beast that trampled down the thistle the overwhelming army with which Israel could desolate Judah. But, perhaps, without making so minute an application, the parable may be explained generally, as describing in a striking manner the effects of pride and ambition, towering far beyond their natural sphere, and sure to fall with a sudden and ruinous crash. The moral of the fable is contained in vs. 10. **11. But Amaziah would not hear**—The sarcastic tenor of this reply incited the king of Judah the more; for, being in a state of judicial blindness and infatuation (II Chron. 25:20), he was immovably determined on war. But the superior energy of Joash surprised him ere he had completed his military preparations. Pouring a large army into the territory of Judah, he encountered Amaziah in a pitched battle, routed his army, and took him prisoner. Then having marched to Jerusalem, he not only demolished part of the city walls, but plundered the treasures of the palace and temple. Taking hostages to prevent any further molestation from Judah, he terminated the war. Without leaving a garrison in Jerusalem, he returned to his capital with all convenient speed, his presence and all his forces being required to repel the troublesome incursions of the Syrians.
17-20. HE IS SLAIN BY A CONSPIRACY. **19. they made a conspiracy against him in Jerusalem**—Amaziah's apostasy (II Chron. 25:27) was followed by a general maladministration, especially the disastrous issue of the war with Israel. The ruinous condition of Jerusalem, the plunder of the temple, and the loss of their children who were taken as hostages, lost him the respect and attachment not of the grandees only, but of his subjects generally, who were in rebellion. The king fled in terror to Lachish, a frontier town of the Philistines, where, however, he was traced and murdered. His friends had his corpse brought without any pomp or ceremony, in a chariot to Jerusalem, where he was interred among his royal ancestors.
21, 22. AZARIAH SUCCEEDS HIM. **21. all the people of Judah took Azariah**—or Uzziah (ch. 15:30; II Chron. 26:1). The popular opposition had been personally directed against Amaziah as the author of their calamities, but it was not extended to his family or heir. **22. He built Elath**—fortified that seaport. It had revolted with the rest of Edom, but was now recovered by Uzziah. His father, who did not complete the conquest of Edom, had left him that work to do.

23-29. JEROBOAM'S WICKED REIGN OVER ISRAEL.
23. Jeroboam, the son of Joash, the king of Israel—
This was Jeroboam II who, on regaining the lost
territory, raised the kingdom to great political power (vs. 25), but adhered to the favorite religious
policy of the Israelitish sovereigns (vs. 24). While
God granted him so great a measure of national
prosperity and eminence, the reason is expressly
stated (vss. 26, 27) to be that the purposes of the
divine covenant forbade as yet the overthrow of the
kingdom of the ten tribes (see on ch. 13:23).

CHAPTER 15

Vss. 1-4. AZARIAH'S REIGN OVER JUDAH. **1. In
the twenty and seventh year of Jeroboam**—It is
thought that the throne of Judah continued vacant
eleven or twelve years, between the death of Amaziah and the inauguration of his son Azariah. Being a child only four years old when his father was
murdered, a regency was appointed during Azariah's
minority. **began Azariah ... to reign**—The character of his reign is described by the brief formula
employed by the inspired historian, in recording the
religious policy of the later kings. But his reign
was a very active as well as eventful one, and is fully
related (II Chron. 26). Elated by the possession
of great power, and presumptuously arrogating to
himself, as did the heathen kings, the functions both
of the real and sacerdotal offices, he was punished
with leprosy, which, as the offense was capital (Num.
8:7), was equivalent to death, for this disease excluded him from all society. While Jotham, his
son, as his viceroy, administered the affairs of the
kingdom—being about fifteen years of age (cf. vs.
33)—he had to dwell in a place apart by himself
(see on ch. 7:3). After a long reign he died, and
was buried in the royal burying-field, though not in
the royal cemetery of "the city of David" (II Chron.
26:33).
8-16. ZECHARIAH'S REIGN OVER ISRAEL. **8. In
the thirty and eighth year of Azariah king of Judah
did Zechariah the son of Jeroboam reign over Israel**
—There was an interregnum from some unknown
cause between the reign of Jeroboam and the accession of his son, which lasted, according to some,
for ten or twelve years, according to others, for
twenty-two years, or more. This prince pursued
the religious policy of the calf-worship, and his
reign was short, being abruptly terminated by the
hand of violence. In his fate was fulfilled the
prophecy addressed to Jehu (ch. 10:30; also Hos. 1:
4), that his family would possess the throne of Israel for four generations; and accordingly Jehoahaz,
Joash, Jehoram, and Zechariah were his successors
—but there his dynasty terminated; and perhaps it
was the public knowledge of this prediction that
prompted the murderous design of Shallum. **13-17.
Shallum ... reigned a full month**—He was opposed
and slain by Menahem, who, according to Josephus,
was commander of the forces, which, on the report
of the king's murder, were besieging Tirzah, a town
twelve miles east of Samaria, and formerly a seat
of the kings of Israel. Raising the siege, he
marched directly against the usurper, slew him, and
reigned in his stead. **16. Menahem ... smote Tiphsah**—Thapsacus, on the Euphrates, the border city
of Solomon's kingdom (I Kings 4:24). The inhabitants refusing to open their gates to him, Menahem
took it by storm. Then having spoiled it, he committed the most barbarous excesses, without regard
either to age or sex.

17-21. MENAHEM'S REIGN. **17. reigned ten
years in Samaria**—His government was conducted
on the religious policy of his predecessors. **19. Pul
the king of Assyria**—This is the first Assyrian king
after Nimrod who is mentioned in biblical history.
His name has been recently identified with that of
Phalluka on the monuments of Nineveh, and that
of Menahem discovered also. **came against the
land**—Elsewhere it is said "Ephraim [Israel] went
to the Assyrian." The two statements may be reconciled thus: "Pul, of his own motion, induced,
perhaps, by the expedition of Menahem against
Thapsacus, advanced against the kingdom of Israel;
then Menahem sent him 1000 talents in order not
only to divert him from his plans of conquest, but
at the same time to purchase his friendship and aid
for the establishment of his own precarious sovereignty. So Menahem did not properly invite the
Assyrian into the land, but only changed the enemy
when marching against the country, by this tribute,
into a confederate for the security of his usurped
dominion. This the prophet Hosea, less concerned
about the historical fact than the disposition betrayed therein, might very well censure as a going of
Ephraim to the Assyrians (Hos. 5:13; 7:1; 8:9), and
a covenant-making with Asshur (ch. 12:1) [KEIL].
a thousand talents of silver—equal to $ 2,000.00.
This tribute, which Menahem raised by a tax on
the grandees of Israel, bribed Pul to return to his
own country (see on I Chron. 5:26).
22-24. PEKAHIAH'S REIGN. **23. Pekahiah ...
son of Menahem began to reign**—On comparing the
date given with Azariah's reign, it seems that several
months had intervened between the death of Menahem and the accession of Pekahiah, probably owing
to a contest about the throne. **25. with Argob and
Arieh**, etc.—Many commentators view these as the
captain's accomplices. But it is more probable that
they were influential friends of the king, who were
murdered along with him.
27-30. PEKAH'S REIGN. **29. in the days of
Pekah, king of Israel, came Tiglath-pileser**—This
monarch, who succeeded Pul on the throne of Assyria, is the only one of all the kings who does not
give his genealogy, and is therefore supposed to
have been an usurper. His annals have been discovered in the Nimroud mound—describing this expedition into Syria. The places taken are here
mentioned as they occurred and were conquered in
the progress of an invasion. **30. Hoshea the son of
Elah made a conspiracy ... and slew him**—He did
not, however, obtain possession of the kingdom till
about nine or ten years after the perpetration of this
crime [HALES].
30-38. JOTHAM'S REIGN OVER JUDAH. **30. in the
twentieth year of Jotham**—Jotham's reign lasted only
sixteen years, but the meaning is that the reign of
Hoshea began in the twentieth after the beginning
of Jotham's reign. The sacred historian, having not
yet introduced the name of Ahaz, reckoned the
date by Jotham, whom he had already mentioned
(see on II Chron. 27:8). **33. Five and twenty years
was he when he began to reign**—i.e., alone—for he
had ruled as his father's viceroy. **35. the higher
gate of the house of the Lord**—not the temple itself,
but one of its courts—probably that which led into
the palace (II Chron. 23:20). **37. the Lord began
to send against Judah, Rezin the king of Syria**, etc.
—This is the first intimation of the hostile feelings
of the kings of Israel and Syria, to Judah, which
led them to form an alliance and make joint preparations for war. However, war was not actually
waged till the reign of Ahaz.

CHAPTER 16

Vss. 1-16. AHAZ' WICKED REIGN OVER JUDAH.
**1-4. Ahaz ... did not that which was right in the
sight of the Lord**—The character of this king's reign,
the voluptuousness and religious degeneracy of all
classes of the people, are graphically portrayed in
the writings of Isaiah, who prophesied at that period.
The great increase of worldly wealth and luxury in
the reigns of Azariah and Jotham had introduced a
host of corruptions, which, during his reign, and
by the influence of Ahaz, bore fruit in the idolatrous
practices of every kind which prevailed in all parts
of the kingdom (see on II Chron. 28:24).   **3. walked
in the way of the kings of Israel**—This is descriptive
of the early part of his reign, when, like the kings
of Israel, he patronized the symbolic worship of God
by images but he gradually went farther into gross
idolatry (II Chron. 28:2).   **made his son to pass
through the fire**—(ch. 23:10).   The hands of the idol
Moloch being red-hot, the children were passed
through between them, which was considered a form
of lustration.   There is reason to believe that, in
certain circumstances, the children were burnt to
death (Ps. 106:37).   This was strongly prohibited
in the law (Lev. 18:21; 20:2-5; Deut. 18:10), although there is no evidence that it was practised in
Israel till the time of Ahaz.   **5. Then Rezin king of
Syria, and Pekah the son of Remaliah, king of Israel, came up to war against Jerusalem**—Notwithstanding their great efforts and military preparations, they failed to take it and, being disappointed,
raised the siege and returned home (cf. Isa. 7:1).
6. Rezin ... recovered Elath—which Azariah had
got into his possession (ch. 14:22).   **the Syrians
came to Elath, and dwelt there unto this day**—The
Septuagint version has "the Edomites," which the
most judicious commentators and travellers [ROBIN-
SON] prefer.   **7-9. So Ahaz sent messengers to
Tiglath-pileser**—In spite of the assurance given him
by Isaiah by two signs, the one immediate, the other
remote (Isa. 7:14; 8:4), that the confederate kings
would not prevail against him, Ahaz sought aid
from the Assyrian monarch, to purchase which he
sent the treasures of the palace and temple.   Tiglath-pileser marched against Damascus, slew Rezin
the king, and carried the people of Damascus into
captivity to Kir, which is thought to have been the
city Karine (now Kerend), in Media.   **10-16. Ahaz
went to Damascus to meet Tiglath-pileser**—This was
a visit of respect, and perhaps of gratitude.   During
his stay in that heathen city, Ahaz saw an altar with
which he was greatly captivated.   Forthwith a
sketch of it was transmitted to Jerusalem, with orders to Urijah the priest to get one constructed according to the Damascus model, and let this new
altar supersede the old one in the temple.   Urijah,
with culpable complaisance, acted according to his
instructions (vs. 16).   The sin in this affair consisted in meddling with, and improving according to
human taste and fancy, the altars of the temple, the
patterns of which had been furnished by divine authority (Exod. 25:40; 26:30; 27:1; I Chron. 28:19).
Urijah was one of the witnesses taken by Isaiah to
bear his prediction against Syria and Israel (Isa. 8:2).
17-19. HE SPOILS THE TEMPLE.   **17. cut off the
borders of the bases**, etc.—It is thought that he did
this to use the elaborate sculpture in adorning his
palace.   **18. the covert for the Sabbath**—the portico
through which the priests entered the temple on the
Sabbath.   **the king's entry without**—a private external entrance for the king into the temple.   The
change made by Ahaz consisted in removing both

of these into the temple from fear of the king of
Assyria, that, in case of a siege, he might secure the
entrance of the temple from him.

CHAPTER 17

Vss.1-6. HOSHEA'S WICKED REIGN.   **1. In the
twelfth year of Ahaz king of Judah, began Hoshea
... to reign**—The statement in ch. 15:30 may be
reconciled with the present passage in the following
manner: Hoshea conspired against Pekah in the
twentieth year of the latter, which was the eighteenth
of Jotham's reign.   It was two years before Hoshea
was acknowledged king of Israel, i.e., in the fourth
of Ahaz, and twentieth of Jotham.   In the twelfth
year of Ahaz his reign began to be tranquil and
prosperous [CALMET].   **2. he did evil ... but not as
the kings of Israel**—Unlike his predecessors from
the time of Jeroboam, he neither established the
rites of Baal, nor compelled the people to adhere to
the symbolic worship of the calves.   In these respects, Hoshea acted as became a constitutional king
of Israel.   Yet, through the influence of the nineteen princes who had swayed the scepter before him
(all of whom had been zealous patrons of idolatry,
and many of whom had been also infamous for personal crimes), the whole nation had become so completely demoralized that the righteous judgment of
an angry Providence impended over it.   **3. Against
him came up Shalmaneser**—or Shalman (Hos. 10:14),
the same as the Sargon of Isaiah.   Very recently the
name of this Assyrian king has been traced on the
Ninevite monuments, as concerned in an expedition
against a king of Samaria, whose name, though
mutilated, Colonel Rawlinson reads as Hoshea.   **4.
found conspiracy in Hoshea**—After having paid tribute for several years, Hoshea, determined on throwing off the Assyrian yoke, withheld the stipulated
tribute.   Shalmaneser, incensed at this rebellion,
proclaimed war against Israel.   This was in the sixth
year of Hoshea's reign.   **he had sent messengers to
So, king of Egypt**—the Sabaco of the classic historians, a famous Ethiopian who, for fifty years, occupied the Egyptian throne, and through whose aid
Hoshea hoped to resist the threatened attack of the
Assyrian conqueror.   But Shalmaneser, marching
against him, scoured the whole country of Israel, besieged the capital Samaria, and carried the principal
inhabitants into captivity in his own land, having
taken the king himself, and imprisoned him for life.
This ancient policy of transplanting a conquered
people into a foreign land, was founded on the idea
that, among a mixed multitude, differing in language
and religion, they would be kept in better subjection,
and have less opportunity of combining together to
recover their independence.   **6. carried Israel away**
—i.e., the remaining tribes (see on ch. 15:29).   **and
placed them**, etc.—This passage GESENIUS renders
thus, omitting the particle *by*, which is printed in
italics to show it is not in the original: "and placed
them in Halah, and on the Chabor, a river of Gozan,
and in the cities of the Medes."   Halah, the same
as Calah (Gen. 10:11, 12), in the region of the Lay-
cus or Zab river, about a day's journey from the
ruins of Nineveh.   Chabor is a river, and it is
remarkable that there is a river rising in the central
highlands of Assyria which retains this name
Khabour unchanged to the present day.   Gozan
(pasture) or Zozan, are the highlands of Assyria,
which afford pasturage.   The region in which
the Chabor and the Zab rise, and through which
they flow, is peculiarly of this character.   The
Nestorians repair to it with their numerous

flocks, spending the summer on the banks or in the highlands of the Chabor or the Zab. Considering the high authority we possess for regarding Gozan and Zozan as one name, there can be no doubt that this is the Gozan referred to in this passage. **cities of the Medes**—"villages," according to the Syriac and Vulgate versions, or "mountains," according to the Septuagint. The Medish inhabitants of Gozan, having revolted, had been destroyed by the kings of Assyria, and nothing was more natural than that they should wish to place in it an industrious people, like the captive Israelites, while it was well suited to their pastoral life [GRANT'S NESTORIANS].

7-41. SAMARIA TAKEN, AND ISRAEL FOR THEIR SINS CARRIED CAPTIVE. **7. For so it was, that the children of Israel had sinned**—There is here given a very full and impressive vindication of the divine procedure in punishing His highly privileged, but rebellious and apostate, people. No wonder that amid so gross a perversion of the worship of the true God, and the national propensity to do reverence to idols, the divine patience was exhausted; and that the God whom they had forsaken permitted them to go into captivity, that they might learn the difference between His service and that of their despotic conquerors. **24. the king of Assyria brought men from Babylon**, etc.—This was not Shalmaneser, but Esar-haddon (Ezek. 4:2). The places vacated by the captive Israelites he ordered to be occupied by several colonies of his own subjects from Babylon and other provinces. **from Cuthah**—the Chaldee form of Cush or Susiana, now Khusistan. **Ava**—supposed to be Ahivaz, situated on the river Karuns, which empties into the head of the Persian Gulf. **Hamath**—on the Orontes. **Sepharvaim**—Siphara, a city on the Euphrates above Babylon. **placed them in the cities of Samaria,** etc.—It must not be supposed that the Israelites were universally removed to a man. A remnant was left, chiefly however of the poor and lower classes, with whom these foreign colonists mingled; so that the prevailing character of society about Samaria was heathen, not Israelite. For the Assyrian colonists became masters of the land; and, forming partial intermarriages with the remnant Jews, the inhabitants became a mongrel race, no longer a people of Ephraim (Isa. 7:6). These people, imperfectly instructed in the creed of the Jews, acquired also a mongrel doctrine. Being too few to replenish the land, lions, by which the land had been infested (Judg. 14:5; I Sam. 17:34; I Kings 13:24; 20:36; Song of Sol. 4:8), multiplied and committed frequent ravages upon them. Recognizing in these attacks a judgment from the God of the land, whom they had not worshipped, they petitioned the Assyrian court to send them some Jewish priests who might instruct them in the right way of serving Him. The king, in compliance with their request, sent them one of the exiled priests of Israel, who established his headquarters at Beth-el and taught them how they should fear the Lord. It is not said that he took a copy of the Pentateuch with him, out of which he might teach them. *Oral teaching* was much better fitted for the superstitious people than instruction out of a written book. He could teach them more effectually by word of mouth. Believing that he would adopt the best and simplest method for them, it is unlikely that he took the written law with him, and so gave origin to the Samaritan copy of the Pentateuch [DAVIDSON'S CRITICISM]. Besides, it is evident from his being one of the exiled priests, and from his settlement at Beth-el, that he was not a Levite,

but one of the calf-worshipping priests. Consequently his instructions would be neither sound nor efficient. **29. Howbeit every nation made gods of their own**—These Assyrian colonists, however, though instructed in the worship, and acknowledging the being of the God of Israel, did not suppose Him to be the only God. Like other heathens, they combined His worship with that of their own gods; and as they formed a promiscuous society from different nations or provinces, a variety of idols was acknowledged among them. **30. Succoth-benoth**—i.e., the "tents or booths of the daughters," similar to those in which the Babylonian damsels celebrated impure rites (Amos 2:8). **Nergal**—The Jewish writers say this idol was in the form of a cock, and it is certain that a cock is often associated with a priest on the Assyrian monuments [LAYARD]. But modern critics, looking to the astrological character of Assyrian idolatry, generally consider Nergal as the planet Mars, the god of war. The name of this idol formed part of the appellation of two of the king of Babylon's princes (Jer. 39:3). **Ashima**—an idol under the form of an entirely bald he-goat. **31. Nibhaz**—under that of a dog—that Egyptian form of animal-worship having prevailed in ancient Syria, as is evident from the image of a large dog at the mouth of the Nahr-el-Kelb or Dog river. **Tartak**—According to the rabbis, it was in the form of an ass, but others understand it as a planet of ill-omen, probably Saturn. **Adrammelech**—supposed by some to be the same as Molech, and in Assyrian mythology to stand for the sun. It was worshipped in the form of a mule—others maintain in that of a peacock. **Anammelech**—worshipped in the form of a hare; others say in that of a goat. **34. Unto this day**—the time of the Babylonian exile, when this book was composed. Their religion was a strange medley or compound of the service of God and the service of idols. Such was the first settlement of the people, afterwards called Samaritans, who were sent from Assyria to colonize the land, when the kingdom of Israel, after having continued 356 years, was overthrown.

CHAPTER 18

Vss. 1-3. HEZEKIAH'S GOOD REIGN. **Hezekiah ... began to reign. Twenty and five years old**—According to this statement (cf. ch. 16:2), he must have been born when his father Ahaz was no more than eleven years old. Paternity at an age so early is not unprecedented in the warm climates of the south, where the human frame is matured sooner than in our northern regions. But the case admits of solution in a different way. It was customary for the later kings of Israel to assume their son and heir into partnership in the government during their lives; and as Hezekiah began to reign in the third year of Hoshea (vs. 1), and Hoshea in the twelfth year of Ahaz (ch. 17:1), it is evident that Hezekiah began to reign in the fourteenth year of Ahaz his father, and so reigned two or three years before his father's death. So that, at the beginning of his reign in conjunction with his father, he might be only twenty-two or three, and Ahaz a few years older than the common calculation makes him. Or th[e] case may be solved thus: As the ancient wri[ters] the computation of time, take notice of [the time] they mention, whether finished or newly [begun,] Ahaz might be near twenty-one years old [at the be]ginning of his reign, and near seventeen [years] at his death; while, on the other hand, when he began to reign, might be just entering into his twenty-fifth year, and so Ahaz would be near fourteen years old when his son Hezekiah was born —no uncommon age for a young man to become a father in southern latitudes [PATRICK].

4-37. HE DESTROYS IDOLATRY. **4. He removed the high places and brake the images**, etc.—The methods adopted by this good king for extirpating idolatry, and accomplishing a thorough reformation in religion, are fully detailed (II Chron. 20:3; 31:19). But they are indicated very briefly, and in a sort of passing allusion. **brake in pieces the brazen serpent**—The preservation of this remarkable relic of antiquity (Num. 21:5-10) might, like the pot of manna and Aaron's rod, have remained an interesting and instructive monument of the divine goodness and mercy to the Israelites in the wilderness; and it must have required the exercise of no small courage and resolution to destroy it. But in the progress of degeneracy it had become an object of idolatrous worship and as the interests of true religion rendered its demolition necessary, Hezekiah, by taking this bold step, consulted both the glory of God and the good of his country. **unto those days the children of Israel did burn incense to it**— It is not to be supposed that this superstitious reverence had been paid to it ever since the time of Moses, for such idolatry would not have been tolerated either by David or by Solomon in the early part of his reign, by Asa or Jehoshaphat had they been aware of such a folly. But the probability is, that the introduction of this superstition does not date earlier than the time when the family of Ahab, by their alliance with the throne of Judah, exercised a pernicious influence in paving the way for all kinds of idolatry. It is possible, however, as some think, that its origin may have arisen out of a misapprehension of Moses' language (Num. 21:8). Serpent-worship, how revolting soever it may appear, was an extensively diffused form of idolatry; and it would obtain an easier reception in Israel because many of the neighboring nations, such as the Egyptians and Phœnicians, adored idol gods in the form of serpents as the emblems of health and immortality. **5. He trusted in the Lord God of Israel**—without invoking the aid or purchasing the succor of foreign auxiliaries like Asa (I Kings 15:18, 19) and Ahaz (ch. 16:17; Isa. 7). **so that after him was none like him among all the kings of Judah**— Of course David and Solomon are excepted, they having had the sovereignty of the whole country. In the petty kingdom of Judah, Josiah alone had a similar testimony borne to him (ch. 23:25). But even he was surpassed by Hezekiah, who set about a national reformation at the beginning of his reign, which Josiah did not. The pious character and the excellent course of Hezekiah was prompted, among other secondary influences, by a sense of the calamities his father's wicked career had brought on the country, as well as by the counsels of Isaiah. **7. he rebelled against the king of Assyria**—i.e., the yearly tribute his father had stipulated to pay, he, with imprudent haste, withdrew. Pursuing the policy of a truly theocratic sovereign, he was, through the divine blessing which rested on his government, raised to a position of great public and national strength. Shalmaneser had withdrawn from Palestine, being engaged perhaps in a war with Tyre, or probably he was dead. Assuming, consequently, at full independent sovereignty which God had led on the house of David, he both shook off Assyrian yoke, and, by an energetic movement t the Philistines, recovered from that people

the territory which they had taken from his father Ahaz (II Chron. 28:18). **13. Sennacherib**—the son and successor of Shalmaneser. **all the fenced cities of Judah**—not absolutely all of them; for, besides the capital, some strong fortresses held out against the invader (vs. 17; ch. 19:8). The following account of Sennacherib's invasion of Judah and the remarkable destruction of his army, is repeated almost verbatim in II Chronicles 33; and Isaiah 36, 37. The expedition seems to have been directed against Egypt, the conquest of which was long a leading object of ambition with the Assyrian monarchs. But the invasion of Judah necessarily preceded, that country being the key to Egypt, the highway through which the conquerors from Upper Asia had to pass. Judah had also at this time formed a league of mutual defense with Egypt (vs. 24). Moreover, it was now laid completely open by the transplantation of Israel to Assyria. Overrunning Palestine, Sennacherib laid siege to the fortress of Lachish, which lay seven Roman miles from Eleutheropolis, and therefore southwest of Jerusalem on the way to Egypt [ROBINSON]. Among the interesting illustrations of sacred history furnished by the recent Assyrian excavations, is a series of bas-reliefs, representing the siege of a town, which the inscription on the sculpture shows to be Lachish, and the figure of a king, whose name is given, on the same inscription, as Sennacherib. The legend, sculptured over the head of the king, runs thus: "Sennacherib, the mighty king, king of the country of Assyria, sitting on the throne of judgment before the city of Lachish [Lakhisha], I give permission for its slaughter" [NINEVEH and BABYLON]. This minute confirmation of the truth of the Bible narrative is given not only by the name Lachish, which is contained in the inscription, but from the physiognomy of the captives brought before the king, which is unmistakably Jewish. **14. Hezekiah ... sent to Lachish, saying, ... that which thou puttest on me will I bear**—Disappointed in his expectations of aid from Egypt, and feeling himself unable to resist so mighty a conqueror who was menacing Jerusalem itself, Hezekiah made his submission. The payment of 300 talents of silver, and 30 talents of gold— $ 1,500,000.00—brought a temporary respite; but, in raising the imposed tribute, he was obliged not only to drain all the treasures of the palace and the temple, but even to strip the doors and pillars of the sacred edifice of the gold that adorned them.

SENNACHERIB BESIEGES JERUSALEM. **17. king of Assyria sent Tartan**—general (Isa. 20:1). **Rabsaris** —chief of the eunuchs. **Rab-shakeh**—chief cupbearer. These were the great officers employed in delivering Sennacherib's insulting message to Hezekiah. On the walls of the palace of Sennacherib, at Khorsabad, certain figures have been identified with the officers of that sovereign mentioned in Scripture. In particular, the figures, Rab-shakeh, Rabsaris, and Tartan, appear as full-length portraits of the persons holding those offices in the reign of Sennacherib. Probably they represent the very individuals sent on this embassy. **with a great host to Jerusalem**—Engaged in a campaign of three years in Egypt, Sennacherib was forced by the king of Ethiopia to retreat, and discharging his rage against Jerusalem, he sent an immense army to summon it to surrender. (See on II Chronicles 32: 30.) **the conduit of the upper pool, etc.**—the conduit which went from the reservoir of the Upper Gihon (Birket et Mamilla) to the lower pool, the Birket es Sultan. **the highway of the fuller's field**— the public road which passed by that district, which had been assigned them for carrying on their business without the city, on account of the unpleasant smell [KEIL]. **18. when they had called to the king**—Hezekiah did not make a personal appearance, but commissioned his three principal ministers to meet the Assyrian deputies at a conference outside the city walls. **Eliakim**—lately promoted to be master of the royal household (Isa. 22:20). **Shebna** —removed for his pride and presumption (Isa. 22:15) from that office, though still royal secretary. **Joah . . . the recorder**—i.e., the keeper of the chronicles, an important office in Eastern countries. **19. Rabshakeh said**—The insolent tone he assumed appears surprising. But this boasting, both as to matter and manner, his highly colored picture of his master's powers and resources, and the impossibility of Hezekiah making any effective resistance, heightened by all the arguments and figures which an Oriental imagination could suggest, has been paralleled in all, except the blasphemy, by other messages of defiance sent on similar occasions in the history of the East. **27. that they may eat,** etc.—This was designed to show the dreadful extremities to which, in the threatened siege, the people of Jerusalem would be reduced.

CHAPTER 19

Vss. 1-5. HEZEKIAH IN DEEP AFFLICTION. **1. when King Hezekiah heard it, he rent his clothes,** etc.—The rending of his clothes was a mode of expressing horror at the daring blasphemy—the assumption of sackcloth a sign of his mental distress—his entrance into the temple to pray, the refuge of a pious man in affliction—and the forwarding an account of the Assyrian's speech to Isaiah was to obtain the prophet's counsel and comfort. The expression in which the message was conveyed described, by a strong figure, the desperate condition of the kingdom, together with their own inability to help themselves; and it intimated also a hope, that the blasphemous defiance of Jehovah's power by the impious Assyrian might lead to some direct interposition for the vindication of His honor and supremacy to all heathen gods. **4. the living God**—is a most significant expression taken in connection with the senseless deities that Rabshakeh boasted were unable to resist his master's victorious arms.

6, 7. COMFORTED BY ISAIAH. **6. Isaiah said . . . Be not afraid**—The prophet's answer was most cheering, as it held out the prospect of a speedy deliverance from the invader. The blast, the rumor, the fall by the sword, contained a brief prediction that was soon fulfilled in all the three particulars—viz., the alarm that hastened his retreat, the destruction that overtook his army, and the violent death that suddenly ended his career.

8-13. SENNACHERIB SENDS A BLASPHEMOUS LETTER TO HEZEKIAH. **8. Rab-shakeh . . . found the king of Assyria warring against Libnah**—whether Lachish had fallen or not, is not said. But Sennacherib had transferred his battering-rams against the apparently neighboring fortress of Libnah (Josh. 10:29; cf. 31; 15:42), where the chief cup-bearer reported the execution of his mission. **9. when he heard say of Tirhakah . . ., Behold, he is come out to fight against thee,** etc. This was the "rumor" to which Isaiah referred. Tirhakah reigned in Upper Egypt, while So (or Sabaco) ruled in Lower Egypt. He was a powerful monarch, another Sesostris, and both he and Sabaco have left many monuments of their greatness. The name and figure of Tirhakah receiving war captives, are still seen in the Egyptian

temple of Medinet Abou. This was the expected succor which was sneered at (ch. 16:21) by Rabshakeh as "a bruised reed." Rage against Hezekiah for allying himself with Egypt, or the hope of being better able to meet this attack from the south, induced him, after hearing the rumor of Tirhakah's advance, to send a menacing letter to Hezekiah, in order that he might force the king of Judah to an immediate surrender of his capital. This letter, couched in the same vaunting and imperious style as the speech of Rab-shakeh, exceeded it in blasphemy, and contained a larger enumeration of conquered places, with the view of terrifying Hezekiah and showing him the utter hopelessness of all attempts at resistance.

14-34. HEZEKIAH'S PRAYER. **14. Hezekiah received the letter . . . and went up into the house of the Lord**—Hezekiah, after reading it, hastened into the temple, spread it in the childlike confidence of faith before the Lord, as containing taunts deeply affecting the divine honor, and implored deliverance from this proud defier of God and man. The devout spirit of this prayer, the recognition of the Divine Being in the plenitude of His majesty—so strikingly contrasted with the fancy of the Assyrians as to His merely local power—his acknowledgment of the conquests obtained over other lands, and of the destruction of their wooden idols, which, according to the Assyrian practice, were committed to the flames—because their tutelary deities were no gods; and the object for which he supplicated the divine interposition, that all the kingdoms of the earth might know that the Lord was the only God—this was an attitude worthy to be assumed by a pious theocratic king of the chosen people. **20. Then Isaiah . . . sent**—A revelation having been made to Isaiah, the prophet announced to the king that his prayer was heard. The prophetic message consisted of three different portions:—*First,* Sennacherib is apostrophized (vss. 21-28) in a highly poetical strain, admirably descriptive of the turgid vanity, haughty pretensions, and presumptuous impiety of the Assyrian despot. *Secondly,* Hezekiah is addressed (vss. 29-31), and a sign is given him of the promised deliverance—viz., that for two years the presence of the enemy would interrupt the peaceful pursuits of husbandry, but in the third year the people would be in circumstances to till their fields and vineyards and reap the fruits as formerly. *Thirdly,* the issue of Sennacherib's invasion is announced (vss. 32-34). **33. shall not come into this city**—nor approach near enough to shoot an arrow, not even from the most powerful engine which throws missiles to the greatest distance, nor shall he occupy any part of the ground before the city by a fence, a mantelet, or covering for men employed in a siege, nor cast (raise) a bank (mound) of earth, overtopping the city walls, whence he may see and command the interior of the city. None of these, which were the principal modes of attack followed in ancient military art, should Sennacherib be permitted to adopt. Though the army under Rabshakeh marched towards Jerusalem and encamped at a little distance with a view to blockade it, they delayed laying siege to it, probably waiting till the king, having taken Lachish and Libnah, should bring up his detachment, that with all the combined forces of Assyria they might invest the capital. So determined was this invader to conquer Judah and the neighboring countries (Isa. 10:7), that nothing but a divine interposition could have saved Jerusalem. It might be supposed that the powerful monarch who overran Palestine and carried away the tribes of Israel, would leave memorials of his deeds on sculptured slabs, or votive bulls. A long and minute account of this expedition is contained in the Annals of Sennacherib, a translation of which has recently been made into English, and, in his remarks upon it, Colonel Rawlinson says the Assyrian version confirms the most important features of the Scripture account. The Jewish and Assyrian narratives of the campaign are, indeed, on the whole, strikingly illustrative of each other [OUTLINES OF ASSYRIAN HISTORY].

35, 36. AN ANGEL DESTROYS THE ASSYRIANS. **35. in the morning ... they were all dead corpses**— It was the miraculous interposition of the Almighty that defended Jerusalem. As to the secondary agent employed in the destruction of the Assyrian army, it is most probable that it was effected by a hot south wind—such as to this day often envelops and destroys whole caravans. This conjecture is supported by verse 7, and Jeremiah 51:1. The destruction was during the night; the officers and soldiers, being in full security, were negligent; their discipline was relaxed; the camp-guards were not alert, or perhaps they themselves were the first taken off, and those who slept, *not wrapped up,* imbibed the poison plentifully. If this had been an evening of dissolute mirth (no uncommon thing in a camp), their joy (perhaps for a victory), or "the first night of their attacking the city," says Josephus, became, by its effects, one means of their destruction [CALMET'S FRAGMENT]. **36. So Sennacherib, king of Assyria ... went and returned** —the same way as he came (vs. 33). The route is described (Isa. 10). The early chariot track near Beyrouth is on the rocky edge of Lebanon, which is skirted by the ancient Lycus (Nahr-el Kelb). On the perpendicular face of the limestone rock, at different heights, are seen slabs with Assyrian inscriptions, which having been deciphered, are found to contain the name of Sennacherib. Thus, by the preservation of these tablets, the wrath of the Assyrian invaders is made to praise the Lord. **dwelt at Nineveh**—This statement implies a considerable period of time, and his Annals carry on his history at least five years after his disastrous campaign at Jerusalem. No record of his catastrophe can be found, as the Assyrian practice was to record victories alone. The sculptures give only the sunny side of the picture.

37. SENNACHERIB SLAIN. **37. as he was worshipping in the house of Nisroch**—Assarae, or Asshur, the head of the Assyrian Pantheon, represented not as a vulture-headed figure—that is now ascertained to be a priest—but as a winged figure in a circle, which was the guardian deity of Assyria. The king is represented on the monuments standing or kneeling beneath this figure, his hand raised in sign of prayer or adoration. **his sons smote him with the sword**—Sennacherib's temper, exasperated probably by his reverses, displayed itself in the most savage cruelty and intolerable tyranny over his subjects and slaves, till at length he was assassinated by his two sons, whom, it is said, he intended to sacrifice to pacify the gods and dispose them to grant him a return of prosperity. The parricides taking flight into Armenia, a third son, Esar-haddon, ascended the throne.

CHAPTER 20

VSS. 1-7. HEZEKIAH'S LIFE LENGTHENED. **1. In those days was Hezekiah sick**—As his reign lasted twenty-nine years (ch. 18:2), and his kingdom was invaded in the fourteenth (ch. 18:13), it is evident that this sudden and severe illness must have occurred in the very year of the Syrian invasion. Between the threatened attack and the actual appearance of the enemy, this incident in Hezekiah's history must have taken place. But according to the usage of the sacred historian, the story of Sennacherib is completed before entering on what was personal to the king of Judah (see also Isa. 38:39). **Set thine house in order**—Isaiah, being of the blood-royal, might have access to the king's private house. But since the prophet was commissioned to make this announcement, the message must be considered as referring to matters of higher importance than the settlement of the king's domestic and private affairs. It must have related chiefly to the state of his kingdom, he having not as yet any son (cf. vs. 6 with ch. 21:1). **for thou shalt die, and not live**—The disease was of a malignant character and would be mortal in its effects, unless the healing power of God should miraculously interpose. **2. he turned his face to the wall**—not like Ahab (I Kings 21:4), in fretful discontent, but in order to secure a better opportunity for prayer. **3. remember now how I have walked before thee,** etc.—The course of Hezekiah's thoughts was evidently directed to the promise made to David and his successors on the throne (I Kings 8:25). He had kept the conditions as faithfully as human infirmity admitted; and as he had been all along free from any of those great crimes by which, through the judgment of God, human life was often suddenly cut short, his great grief might arise partly from the love of life, partly from the obscurity of the Mosaic dispensation, where life and immortality had not been fully brought to light, and partly from his plans for the reformation of his kingdom being frustrated by his death. He pleaded the fulfilment of the promise. **4. afore Isaiah was gone out into the middle court**—of the royal castle. **5. Thus saith ... the God of David thy father**—An immediate answer was given to his prayer, containing an assurance that the Lord was mindful of His promise to David and would accomplish it in Hezekiah's experience, both by the prolongation of his life, and his deliverance from the Assyrians. **on the third day**—The perfect recovery from a dangerous sickness, within so short a time, shows the miraculous character of the cure (see his thanksgiving song, Isaiah 38:9). The disease cannot be ascertained; but the text gives no hint that the plague was raging then in Jerusalem; and although Arab physicians apply a cataplasm of figs to plague-boils, they also do so in other cases, as figs are considered useful in ripening and soothing inflammatory ulcers.

8-20. THE SUN GOES TEN DEGREES BACKWARD. **8. Hezekiah said unto Isaiah, What will be the sign that the Lord shall heal me**—His recovery in the course of nature was so unlooked for, that the king asked for some token to justify his reliance on the truth of the prophet's communication; and the sign he specified was granted to him. The shadow of the sun went back upon the dial of Ahaz the ten degrees it had gone down. Various conjectures have been formed as to this dial. The word in the original is "degrees," or "steps," and hence many commentators have supposed that it was a stair, so artfully contrived, that the shadows on the steps indicated the hours and course of the sun. But it is more probable that it was a proper instrument, and, from the Hebrews having no term to designate it, that it was one of the foreign novelties imported from Babylon by Ahaz. It seems to have been of such magnitude, and so placed in the court, that

Isaiah could point to it, and the king see it, from his chamber. The retrogression of the sun's shadow on the dial was miraculously accomplished by the omnipotent power of God; but the phenomenon was temporary, local, confined to the notice, and intended for the satisfaction, only of Hezekiah and his court. **12-19. Berodach-baladan**—(Isa. 39), the first king of Babylon mentioned in sacred history; formerly its rulers were viceroys of the Assyrian monarchs. This individual threw off the yoke, and asserting his independence, made with varying success, a long and obstinate resistance [RAWLINSON'S OUTLINES]. The message of congratulation to Hezekiah, was, in all likelihood, accompanied with proposals for a defensive alliance against their common Assyrian enemy. The king of Judah, flattered with this honor, showed the ambassadors all his treasures, his armory and warlike stores; and his motive for this was evidently that the Babylonian deputies might be the more induced to prize his friendship. **13. the silver, and the gold**—He paid so much tribute to Sennacherib as exhausted his treasury (cf. 18:16). But, after the destruction of Sennacherib, presents were brought him from various quarters, out of respect to a king who, by his faith and prayer, saved his country; and besides, it is by no means improbable that from the corpses in the Assyrian camp, all the gold and silver he had paid might be recovered. The vain display, however, was offensive to his divine liege lord, who sent Isaiah to reprove him. The answer he gave the prophet (vs. 14) shows how he was elated by the compliment of their visit; but it was wrong, as presenting a bait for the cupidity of these rapacious foreigners, who, at no distant period, would return and pillage his country, and transfer all the possessions he ostentatiously displayed to Babylon, as well as his posterity to be court attendants in that country—(see on II Chron. 32:31). **19. Good is the word of the Lord**—indicating a humble and pious resignation to the divine will. The concluding part of his reply was uttered after a pause and was probably an ejaculation to himself, expressing his thankfulness, that, though great afflictions should befall his descendants, the execution of the divine judgment was to be suspended during his own lifetime. **20. pool and a conduit**—(See on II Chron. 32:30).

CHAPTER 21

Vss. 1-18. MANASSEH'S WICKED REIGN, AND GREAT IDOLATRY. **1. Manasseh was twelve years old when he began to reign**—He must have been born three years after his father's recovery; and his minority, spent under the influence of guardians who were hostile to the religious principles and reforming policy of his father, may account in part for the anti-theocratic principles of his reign. The work of religious reformation which Hezekiah had zealously carried on was but partially accomplished. There was little appearance of its influence on the heart and manners of the people at large. On the contrary, the true fear of God had vanished from the mass of the people; corruption and vice increased, and were openly practised (Isa. 28:7, etc.) by the degenerate leaders, who, having got the young prince Manasseh into their power, directed his education, trained him up in their views, and seduced him into the open patronage of idolatry. Hence, when he became sovereign, he introduced the worship of idols, the restoration of high places, and the erection of altars or pillars to Baal, and the

placing, in the temple of God itself, a graven image of Asherah, the sacred or symbolic tree, which represented "all the host of heaven." This was not idolatry, but pure star worship, of Chaldaic and Assyrian origin [KEIL]. The sun, as among the Persians, had chariots and horses consecrated to it (ch. 23:11); and incense was offered to the stars on the housetops (ch. 23:12; II Chron. 33:5; Jer. 19:13; Zeph. 1:5), and in the temple area with the face turned toward the sunrise (Ezek. 8:16). **5. the two courts of the house of the Lord**—the court of the priests and the large court of the people. **6. made his son pass through the fire**—(See on ch. 16:3). **observed times**—from an observation of the clouds. **used enchantments**—jugglery and spells. **dealt with familiar spirits**—*Sept.*, ventriloquists, who pretended to ask counsel of a familiar spirit and gave the response received from him to others. **and wizards** —wise or knowing ones, who pretended to reveal secrets, to recover things lost and hidden treasure, and to interpret dreams. A great influx of these impostors had, at various times, poured from Chaldea into the land of Israel to pursue their gainful occupations, especially during the reigns of the latter kings; and Manasseh was not only their liberal patron, but zealous to appear himself an adept in the arts. He raised them to be an influential class at his court, as they were in that of Assyria and Babylon, where nothing was done till they had ascertained the lucky hour and were promised a happy issue. **7. And he set a graven image**—The placing of the Asherah within the precincts of the temple, which was dedicated to the worship of the true God, is dwelt upon as the most aggravated outrage of the royal idolater. **8. Neither will I make the feet of Israel move . . . out of the land which I gave their fathers**—alluding to the promise (II Sam. 7:10). **only if they will observe**, etc.—This condition was expressed from the first plantation of Israel in Canaan. But that people not only did not keep it, but through the pernicious influence of Manasseh, were seduced into greater excesses of idolatrous corruption than even the original Canaanites. **10-17. the Lord spake by his servants the prophets**—These were Hosea, Joel, Nahum, Habakkuk, and Isaiah. Their counsels, admonitions, and prophetic warnings, were put on record in the national chronicles (II Chron. 33:18) and now form part of the sacred canon. **12. whosoever heareth of it, both his ears shall tingle**—a strong metaphorical form of announcing an extraordinary and appalling event (see I Sam. 3:11; Jer. 19:3; also Hab. 1:5). **13. the line of Samaria, and the plummet of the house of Ahab** —Captives doomed to destruction were sometimes grouped together and marked off by means of a measuring-line and plummet (II Sam. 8:2; Isa. 34:11; Amos 7:7); so that the line of Samaria means the line drawn for the destruction of Samaria; the plummet of the house of Ahab, for exterminating his apostate family; and the import of the threatening declaration here is that Judah would be utterly destroyed, as Samaria and the dynasty of Ahab had been. **I will wipe Jerusalem**, etc.—The same doom is denounced more strongly in a figure unmistakably significant. **14. I will forsake the remnant of mine inheritance**—The people of Judah, who of all the chosen people alone remained. The consequence of the Lord's forsaking them would be their fall into the power of their enemies. **16. Moreover, Manasseh shed innocent blood**—Not content with the patronage and the practice of idolatrous abomination, he was a cruel persecutor of all who did not conform. The land was deluged with the blood of good men; among whom it is traditionally said Isaiah suffered a horrid death, by being sawn asunder (see on Heb. 11:37).

19-26. AMON'S WICKED REIGN. **18. Amon his son reigned in his stead**—This prince continued the idolatrous policy of his father; and, after an inglorious reign of two years, he was massacred by some of his own domestics. The people slew the regicide conspirators and placed his son Josiah on the throne.

CHAPTER 22

Vss. 1, 2. JOSIAH'S GOOD REIGN. **1. Josiah was eight years old when he began to reign**—Happier than his grandfather Manasseh, he seems to have fallen during his minority under the care of better guardians, who trained him in the principles and practice of piety; and so strongly had his young affections been enlisted on the side of true and undefiled religion, that he continued to adhere all his life, with undeviating perseverance, to the cause of God and righteousness.

3-7. HE PROVIDES FOR THE REPAIR OF THE TEMPLE. **3. in the eighteenth year of King Josiah**—Previous to this period, he had commenced the **work** of national reformation. The preliminary steps had been already taken; not only the builders were employed, but money had been brought by all the people and received by the Levites at the door, and various other preparations had been made. But the course of this narrative turns on one interesting incident which happened in the eigthteenth year of Josiah's reign, and hence that date is specified. In fact the whole land was thoroughly purified from every object and all traces of idolatry. The king now addressed himself to the repair and embellishment of the temple and gave directions to Hilkiah the high priest to take a general survey, in order to ascertain what was necessary to be done (see on II Chron. 34:8-15).

8-15. HILKIAH FINDS THE BOOK OF THE LAW. **8. Hilkiah said ... I have found the book of the law in the house of the Lord**, etc.—i.e., the law of Moses—the Pentateuch. It was the temple copy which, had been laid (Deut. 31:25, 26) beside the ark in the most holy place. During the ungodly reigns of Manasseh and Amon—or perhaps under Ahaz, when the temple itself had been profaned by idols, and the ark also (II Chron. 35:3) removed from its site—it was somehow lost, and was now found again during the repair of the temple [KEIL]. Delivered by Hilkiah the discoverer to Shaphan the scribe, it was by the latter shown and read to the king. It is thought, with great probability, that the passage read to the king, and by which the royal mind was so greatly excited, was a portion of Deuteronomy, the 28th, 29th, and 30th chapters, in which is recorded a renewal of the national covenant, and an enumeration of the terrible threats and curses denounced against all who violated the law, whether prince or people. The impressions of grief and terror which the reading produced on the mind of Josiah have seemed to many unaccountable. But, as it is certain from the extensive and familiar knowledge displayed by the prophets, that there were numbers of other copies in popular circulation, the king must have known its sacred contents in some degree. But he might have been a stranger to the passage read him, or the reading of it might, in the peculiar circumstances, have found a way to his heart in a manner that he never felt before. His

strong faith in the divine word, and his painful consciousness that the woeful and long-continued apostasies of the nation had exposed them to the infliction of the judgments denounced, must have come with overwhelming force on the heart of so pious a prince. **12-15. the king commanded ... Go, inquire of the Lord for me,** etc.—The agitated feelings of the king prompted him to ask immediate counsel how to avert those curses under which his kingdom lay; and forthwith a deputation of his principal officers was sent to one endowed with the prophetic spirit. **Ahikam**—a friend of Jeremiah (Jer. 26:24). **14. Achbor**—or Abdon (II Chron. 34:20), a man of influence at court (Jer. 26:22). The occasion was urgent, and therefore they were sent—not to Zephaniah (Zeph. 1:1), who was perhaps young—nor to Jeremiah, who was probably absent at his house in Anathoth, but to one who was at hand and known for her prophetic gifts—to Huldah, who was probably at this time a widow. Her husband Shallum was grandson of one Harhas, "keeper of the wardrobe." If this means the priestly wardrobe, he must have been a Levite. But it probably refers to the royal wardrobe. **she dwelt ... in the college**—rather in *the Misnah*, taking the original word as a proper name, not a school or college, but a particular suburb of Jerusalem. She was held in such veneration that Jewish writers say she and Jehoiada the priest were the only persons not of the house of David (II Chron. 24:16) who were ever buried in Jerusalem. **15. she said unto them, Thus saith the Lord God of Israel, Tell the man that sent you**—On being consulted, she delivered an oracular response in which judgment was blended with mercy; for it announced the impending calamities that at no distant period were to overtake the city and its inhabitants. But at the same time the king was consoled with an assurance that this season of punishment and sorrow should not be during his lifetime, on account of the faith, penitence, and pious zeal for the divine glory and worship which, in his public capacity and with his royal influence, he had displayed.

CHAPTER 23

Vss. 1-3. JOSIAH CAUSES THE LAW TO BE READ. **1. the king sent, and they gathered unto him all the elders**—This pious and patriotic king, not content with the promise of his own security, felt, after Huldah's response, an increased desire to avert the threatened calamities from his kingdom and people. Knowing the richness of the divine clemency and grace to the penitent, he convened the elders of the people, and placing himself at their head, accompanied by the collective body of the inhabitants, went in solemn procession to the temple, where he ordered the book of the law to be read to the assembled audience, and covenanted, with the unanimous concurrence of his subjects, to adhere steadfastly to all the commandments of the Lord. It was an occasion of solemn interest, closely connected with a great national crisis, and the beautiful example of piety in the highest quarter would exert a salutary influence over all classes of the people in animating their devotions and encouraging their return to the faith of their fathers. **2. he read in their ears**—i.e., caused to be read. **3. all the people stood to the covenant**—i.e., they agreed to the proposals made; they assented to what was required of them.

4-28. HE DESTROYS IDOLATRY. **4. the king**

commanded Hilkiah, etc.—i.e., the high priest and other priests, for there was not a variety of official gradations in the temple. **all the vessels,** etc.—the whole apparatus of idol worship. **burned them without Jerusalem**—The law required them to be consigned to the flames (Deut. 7:25). **in the fields of Kidron**—most probably that part of the valley of Kidron, where lies Jerusalem and the Mount of Olives. It is a level, spacious basin, abounding at present with plantations [ROBINSON]. The brook winds along the east and south of the city, the channel of which is throughout a large portion of the year almost or wholly dry, except after heavy rains, when it suddenly swells and overflows. There were emptied all the impurities of the temple (II Chron. 29:15, 16) and the city. His reforming predecessors had ordered the mutilated relics of idolatry to be thrown into that receptacle of filth (I Kings 15:13; II Chron. 15:16; 30:14); but Josiah, while he imitated their piety, far outstripped them in zeal; for he caused the ashes of the burnt wood and the fragments of the broken metal to be collected and conveyed to Beth-el, in order thenceforth to associate ideas of horror and aversion with that place, as odious for the worst pollutions. **5. put down the idolatrous priests**—*Hebrew, chemarim,* "scorched," i.e., Guebres, or fire-worshippers, distinguished by a girdle (Ezek. 23:14-17) or belt of wool and camel's hair, twisted round the body twice and tied with four knots, which had a symbolic meaning, and made it a supposed defense against evil. **them also that burned incense unto Baal, to the sun, and to the moon,** etc.—or Baal-shemesh—for Baal was sometimes considered the sun. This form of false worship was not by images, but pure star-worship, borrowed from the old Assyrians. **and**—rather, "even" to all the host of heaven. **6. brought out the grove**—i.e., Asherah, the mystic tree, placed by Manasseh in the temple, removed by him after his conversion, but replaced in the sanctuary by his wicked son Amon. Josiah had it taken to Kidron, burnt the wood, ground the metal about it to powder, and strewed the ashes "on the graves of the children of the people." The poor were buried in a common on part of the valley of Kidron. But reference is her made to the graves "of those that had sacrificed" (II Chron. 34:4). **7. brake down the houses of the sodomites**—not solid houses, but tents, called elsewhere Succoth-benoth, the booths of the young women who were devoted to the service of Asherah, for which they made embroidered hangings, and in which they gave themselves to unbridled revelry and lust. Or the hangings might be for Asherah itself, as it is a popular superstition in the East to hang pieces of cloth on trees. **8. he brought all the priests out of the cities of Judah, and defiled the high places,** etc.—Many of the Levitical order, finding in the reigns of Manasseh and Amon the temple worship abolished and the tithes and other offerings alienated, had been betrayed into the folly of officiating on high places, and presenting such sacrifices as were brought to them. These irregularities, even though the object of that worship was the true God, were prohibited in the law (Deut. 12: 11). Those who had been guilty of this sin, Josiah brought to Jerusalem. Regarding them as defiled, he debarred them from the service of the temple, but gave them an allowance out of the temple revenues, like the lame and disabled members of the priesthood (Lev. 21:21, 22). **from Geba to Beer-sheba**—the most northern and the most southern places in Judah—meaning all parts of the kingdom. **the high places ... which were in the enter-**

ing in of the gate of Joshua—The governor's house and gate were on the left of the city gate, and close by the entrance of that civic mansion-house were public altars, dedicated, it might be, to the true God, but contrary to His own ordinance of worship (Isa. 57:8). **10. Topheth**—so called from Toph—a drum. It is the prevailing opinion among Jewish writers that the cries of the terrified children made to pass through the fire in that place of idolatrous horror were drowned by the sound of that instrument. **11. took away the horses which the kings of Judah had given to the sun**—Among the people who anciently worshipped the sun, horses were usually dedicated to that divinity, from the supposed idea that the sun himself was drawn in a chariot by horses. In some cases these horses were sacrificed; but more commonly they were employed either in the sacred processions to carry the images of the sun, or for the worshippers to ride in every morning to welcome his rise. It seems that the idolatrous kings, Ahaz, Manasseh, and Amon, or their great officers, proceeded on these horses early on each day from the east gate of the temple to salute and worship the sun at his appearing above the horizon. **12. the altars that were on the top of the upper chamber of Ahaz**—Altars were reared on the flat roofs of houses, where the worshippers of "the host of heaven" burnt incense (Zeph. 1:5; Jer. 19:13). Ahaz had reared altars for this purpose on the *oleah,* or upper chamber of his palace, and Manasseh on some portion of the roof of the temple. Josiah demolished both of these structures. **13. the high places ... which Solomon ... had builded**—(See on I Kings 11:7). **the right hand of the mount of corruption**—The Mount of Olives is a hilly range on the east of Jerusalem. This range has three summits, of which the central one is the Mount of Corruption, so called from the idol temples built there, and of course the hill on the right hand denotes the southernmost peak. Josiah is said not to have destroyed, but only defiled, "the high places on the hill of corruption." It is most propable that Hezekiah had long before demolished the idolatrous temples erected there by Solomon but, as the superstitious people continued to regard the spot as consecrated ground, Josiah defiled it. **14. filled their places with the bones of men**—Every monument of idolatry in his dominion he in like manner destroyed, and the places where they stood he defiled by strewing them with dead men's bones. The presence of a dead carcass rendered both persons and places unclean in the eyes both of Jews and heathens. **15-20. Moreover, the altar that was at Beth-el,** etc.—Not satisfied with the removal of every vestige of idolatry from his own dominion, this zealous iconoclast made a tour of inspection through the cities of Samaria and all the territory formerly occupied by the ten tribes, destroying the altars and temples of the high places, consigning the Asherim to the flames, putting to death the priests of the high places, and showing his horror at idolatry by ransacking the sepulchers of idolatrous priests, and strewing the burnt ashes of their bones upon the altars before he demolished them. **16. according to the word of the Lord, which the man of God proclaimed,** etc.—In carrying on these proceedings, Josiah was prompted by his own intense hatred of idolatry. But it is remarkable that this act was predicted 326 years before his birth, and his name also was expressly mentioned, as well as the very place where it should be done (I Kings 13:2). This is one of the most remarkable prophecies contained in the Bible. **17. What title is that that I see?**—The king's attention, probably, had been arrested by a tombstone more conspicuous than the rest around it, bearing on an inscription the name of him that lay beneath; and this prompted his curiosity to make the inquiry. **the men of the city**—not the Assyrian colonists—for they could know nothing about the ancient transactions of the place—but some of the old people who had been allowed to remain, and perhaps the tomb itself might not then have been discoverable, through the effects of time and neglect, had not some "Old Mortality" garnished the sepulcher of the righteous. **21-23. the king commanded all the people, saying, Keep the passover unto the Lord your God,** etc.—It was observed with great solemnity and was attended not only by his own subjects, but by the remnant people from Israel (see on II Chron. 35:1-19). Many of the Israelites who were at Jerusalem might have *heard of,* if they did *not hear,* the law read by Josiah. It is probable that they might even have procured a copy of the law, stimulated as they were to the better observance of Jehovah's worship by the unusual and solemn transactions at Jerusalem. **26. Notwithstanding, the Lord turned not from the fierceness of his wrath,** etc. The national reformation which Josiah carried on was acquiesced in by the people from submission to the royal will; but they entertained a secret and strong hankering after the suppressed idolatries. Though outwardly purified, their hearts were not right towards God, as appears from many passages of the prophetic writings; their thorough reform was hopeless; and God, who saw no sign of genuine repentance, allowed His decree (ch. 21:12-15) for the subversion of the kingdom to take fatal effect. **29. In his days Pharaoh-nechoh**—(See II Chron. 35: 20-27).

CHAPTER 24

Vss. 1-7. JEHOIAKIM PROCURES HIS OWN RUIN. 1. Nebuchadnezzar—the son of Nabopolassar, the founder of the Chaldee monarchy. This invasion took place in the fourth year of Jehoiakim's, and the first of Nebuchadnezzar's reign (Jer. 25:1; cf. 46:2). The young king of Assyria being probably detained at home on account of his father's demise, despatched, along with the Chaldean troops on his border, an army composed of the tributary nations that were contiguous to Judea, to chastise Jehoiakim's revolt from his yoke. But this hostile band was only an instrument in executing the divine judgment (vs. 2) denounced by the prophets against Judah for the sins of the people; and hence, though marching by the orders of the Assyrian monarch, they are described as sent by the Lord (vs. 3). **4. the Lord would not pardon**—(see on ch. 23:26; Jer. 15:1). **6. Jehoiakim slept with his fathers**—This phraseology can mean nothing more than that he died; for he was not buried with his royal ancestors; and whether he fell in battle, or his body was subjected to posthumous insults, he was, according to the prediction (Jer. 22:19), not honored with the rites of sepulture (Jer. 36:30). **Jehoiachin his son reigned in his stead**—The very brief reign of this prince, which lasted only three months, during which he was a humble vassal of the Assyrians, is scarcely deserving to be taken into account, and therefore is in no way contradictory to the prophetic menace denounced against his father (Jer. 36:30). **7. the king of Egypt**—i.e., Pharaoh-nechoh. **8, 9. JEHOIACHIN SUCCEEDS HIM. 8. Jehoiachin** —i.e., "God appointed," contracted into *Jeconiah*

and *Coniah* (Jer. 22:24). **eighteen years old when he began to reign**—At the age of eight his father took him into partnership in the government (II Chron. 36:9). He began to reign alone at eighteen. **9. he did that which was evil in the sight of the Lord** —Untaught by experience, and deaf to the prophetic warnings, he pursued the evil courses which had brought so many disasters upon the royal family as well as the people of Judah. This bad character is figuratively but strongly depicted (Ezek. 19:5-7).

10-16. JERUSALEM TAKEN. 10. At that time—within three months after his accession to the throne. It was the spring of the year (II Chron. 36:10); so early did he indicate a feeling hostile to the interests of his Assyrian liege lord, by forming a league with Egypt. Nebuchadnezzar sent his generals to besiege Jerusalem, as Jeremiah had foretold (22:18; 24:30), and soon after he followed in person. Convinced of the hopelessness of making any effectual resistance, Jehoiachin, going to the camp of the besiegers, surrendered (vs. 12), in the expectation, probably, of being allowed to retain his throne as a vassal of the Assyrian empire. But Nebuchadnezzar's clemency towards the kings of Judah was now exhausted, so that Jehoiachin was sent as a captive to Babylon, according to Jeremiah's prediction (22: 24), accompanied by the queen mother (the same who had held that dignity under Jehoahaz) (ch. 23: 31), his generals, and officers. This happened in the eighth year of Nebuchadnezzar's reign, computing from the time when he was associated with his father in the government. Those that were left consisted chiefly of the poorer sort of people and the unskilled workmen. The palace and the temple were ransacked. The smaller golden vessels had been taken on the first capture of Jerusalem and placed by Nebuchadnezzar in the temple of his god as tokens of victory. They were used by Belshazzar at his impious feast, for the purpose of rewarding his army with these trophies, among which were probably the golden candlesticks, the ark, etc. (cf. II Chron. 36:7; Dan. 1:2). Now the gold plating was torn off all the larger temple furniture. **13. as the Lord had said**—(cf. ch. 20:17; Isa. 39:6; Jer. 15:13; 17:3). The elite of the nation for rank, usefulness, and moral worth, all who might be useful in Babylon or dangerous in Palestine, were carried off to Babylon, to the number of ten thousand (vs. 14). These are specified (vss. 15, 16), warriors, 7000; craftsmen and smiths, 1000; king's wives, officers, and princes, also priests and prophets (Jer. 29:1; Ezek. 1:1), 2000; equal to 10,000 captives in all.

17-20. ZEDEKIAH'S EVIL REIGN. 17. the king of Babylon made Mattaniah, his father's brother, king in his stead—Adhering to his former policy of maintaining a show of monarchy, Nebuchadnezzar appointed the third and youngest son of Josiah (I Chron. 3:15), full brother of Jehoahaz, and uncle of the captive Jehoiachin. But, according to the custom of conquerors, who changed the names of the great men they took captives in war, in token of their supremacy, he gave him the new name of Zedekiah—i.e., "The righteous of God." This being a purely Hebrew name, it seems that he allowed the puppet king to choose his own name, which was confirmed. His heart towards God was the same as that of Jehoiakim, impenitent and heedless of God's word. **20. through the anger of the Lord ... he cast them out from his presence**—i.e., in the course of God's righteous providence, his policy as king would prove ruinous to his country. **Zedekiah rebelled against the king of Babylon**—instigated by ambassadors from the neighboring states who came to congratulate him on his ascension to the throne (cf. Jer. 17:3, with 28:1), and at the same time get him to join them in a common league to throw off the Assyrian yoke. Though warned by Jeremiah against this step, the infatuated and perjured (Ezek. 17:13) Zedekiah persisted in his revolt.

CHAPTER 25

Vss. 1-3. JERUSALEM AGAIN BESIEGED. **1. Nebuchadnezzar . . . came . . . against Jerusalem, and pitched against it**—Incensed by the revolt of Zedekiah, the Assyrian despot determined to put an end to the perfidious and inconstant monarchy of Judea. This chapter narrates his third and last invasion, which he conducted in person at the head of an immense army, levied out of all the tributary nations under his sway. Having overrun the northern parts of the country and taken almost all the fenced cities (Jer. 34:7), he marched direct to Jerusalem to invest it. The date of the beginning as well as the end of the siege is here carefully marked (cf. Ezek. 24:1; Jer. 39:1; 52:4-6); from which it appears, that, with a brief interruption caused by Nebuchadnezzar's marching to oppose the Egyptians who were coming to its relief but who retreated without fighting, the siege lasted a year and a half. So long a resistance was owing, not to the superior skill and valor of the Jewish soldiers, but to the strength of the city fortifications, on which the king too confidently relied (cf. Jer. 21; 37; 38). **pitched against it, and . . . built forts**—rather, perhaps, drew lines of circumvallation, with a ditch to prevent any going out of the city. On this rampart were erected his military engines for throwing missiles into the city. **3. on the ninth day of the fourth month the famine prevailed**—In consequence of the close and protracted blockade, the inhabitants were reduced to dreadful extremities; and under the maddening influence of hunger, the most inhuman atrocities were perpetrated (Lam. 2:20, 22; 4:9, 10; Ezek. 5:10). This was a fulfilment of the prophetic denunciations threatened on the apostasy of the chosen people (Lev. 26:29; Deut. 28:53-57; Jer. 15:2; 27:13; Ezek. 4:16).

4-30. ZEDEKIAH TAKEN. **4. the city was broken up**—i.e., a breach was effected, as we are elsewhere informed, in a part of the wall belonging to the lower city (II Chron. 32:5; 33:14). **the men of war fled by night by the way of the gate between two walls, which is by the king's garden**—The king's garden was (Neh. 3:15) at the pool of Siloam, i.e., at the mouth of the Tyropæon. A trace of the outermost of these walls appears to be still extant in the rude pathway which crosses the mouth of the Tyropæon, on a mound hard by the old mulberry tree, which marks the traditional spot of Isaiah's martyrdom [ROBINSON]. It is probable that the besiegers had overlooked this pass. **the king went . . . toward the plain**—i.e., the Ghor, or valley of Jordan, estimated at five hours' distance from Jerusalem. The plain near Jericho is about eleven or twelve miles broad. **6. they took the king, and brought him . . . to Riblah**—Nebuchadnezzar, having gone from the siege to oppose the auxiliary forces of Pharaoh-hophra, left his generals to carry on the blockade, he himself not returning to the scene of action, but taking up his station at Riblah in the land of Hamath (ch. 23:33). **they gave judgment upon him**—They, i.e., the counsel (Jer. 39:3, 13; Dan. 6:7, 8, 12), regarding him as a seditious and rebellious vassal, condemned him for violating his oath

and neglecting the announcement of the divine will as made known to him by Jeremiah (cf. Jer. 32:5; 34:2; 38:17). His sons and the nobles who had joined in his flight were slain before his eyes (Jer. 39:6; 52:10). In conformity with Eastern ideas, which consider a blind man incapable of ruling, his eyes were put out, and being put in chains, he was carried to perpetual imprisonment in Babylon (Jer. 52:11), which, though he came to it, as Ezekiel had foretold, he did not see (Jer. 32:5; Ezek. 12:13; 17:16). **8-18. on the seventh day of the month . . . came Nebuzar-adan**—(cf. Jer. 52:12). In attempting to reconcile these two passages, it must be supposed either that, though he had set out on the 7th, he did not arrive in Jerusalem till the 10th, or that he did not put his orders in execution till that day. His office as captain of the guard (Gen. 37:36; 39:1) called him to execute the awards of justice on criminals; and hence, although not engaged in the siege of Jerusalem (Jer. 39:13), Nebuzar-adan was despatched to rase the city, to plunder the temple, to lay both in ruins, demolish the fortifications, and transport the inhabitants to Babylon. The most eminent of these were taken to the king at Riblah (vs. 27) and executed, as instigators and abettors of the rebellion, or otherwise obnoxious to the Assyrian government. In their number were Seraiah, the high priest, grandfather of Ezra (Ezra 7:1), his sagan or deputy, a priest of the second order (Jer. 21:2; 29:25, 29; 37:3). **the three keepers of the door**—not mere porters, but officers of high trust among the Levites (ch. 22:4; I Chron. 9:26). **19. five men of them that were in the king's presence**—i.e., who belonged to the royal retinue. It is probable that there were five at first, and that other two were found afterwards (Jer. 52:25). **22-26. Nebuchadnezzar . . . made Gedaliah . . . ruler**—The people permitted to remain were, besides the king's daughters, a few court attendants and others (Jer. 40:7) too insignificant to be removed, only the peasantry who could till the land and dress the vineyards. Gedaliah was Jeremiah's friend (Jer. 26:24), and having, by the prophet's counsel, probably fled from the city as abandoned of God, he surrendered himself to the conqueror (Jer. 38:2, 17), and being promoted to the government of Judea, fixed his provincial court at Mizpeh. He was well qualified to surmount the difficulties of ruling at such a crisis. Many of the fugitive Jews, as well as the soldiers of Zedekiah who had accompanied the king in his flight to the plains of Jericho, left their retreats (Jer. 40: 11, 12) and flocked around the governor; who having counselled them to submit, promised them on complying with this condition, security on oath that they would retain their possessions and enjoy the produce of their land (Jer. 40:9). **25. Ishmael . . . of the seed royal came, and ten men with him, and smote Gedaliah**—He had found refuge with Baalis, king of the Ammonites, and he returned with a bad design, being either instigated by envy of a governor not descended from the house of David, or bribed by Baalis to murder Gedaliah. The generous governor, though apprised of his intentions, refused to credit the report, much less to sanction the proposal made by an attached friend to cut off Ishmael. The consequence was, that he was murdered by this same Ishmael, when entertaining him in his own house (Jer. 41:1). **26. and all the people . . . came to Egypt**—In spite of Jeremiah's dissuasions (Jer. 43:7, 8) they settled in various cities of that country (Jer. 44:1). **27. seven and thirtieth year of the captivity of Jehoiachin**—corresponding with the year of Nebuchadnezzar's death, and his son Evil-merodach's ascension to the throne. **Evil-merodach ... did lift up the head of Jehoiachin ... and spake kindly**—gave him liberty upon parole. This kindly feeling is said to have originated in a familiar acquaintance formed in prison, in which Evil-merodach had lain till his father's death, on account of some malversation while acting as regent during Nebuchadnezzar's seven years' illness (Dan. 4:32, 33). But doubtless the improvement in Zedekiah's condition is to be traced to the overruling providence and grace of Him who still cherished purposes of love to the house of David (II Sam. 7:14, 15). **29. Jeohiachin did eat ... continually before him**—According to an ancient usage in Eastern courts, he had a seat at the royal table on great days, and had a stated provision granted him for the maintenance of his exiled court.

THE FIRST BOOK OF

THE CHRONICLES

CHAPTER 1

Vss. 1-23. ADAM'S LINE TO NOAH. **1. Adam, ...**—"Begat" must be understood. Only that one member of the family is mentioned, who came in the direct order of succession. **4-23. Noah, Shem, Ham, and Japheth**—The three sons of this patriarch are enumerated, partly because they were the founders of the new world, and partly because the fulfilment of Noah's prophecy (Gen. 9:25-27) could not otherwise appear to have been verified. **12. Casluhim (of whom came the Philistines), and Caphtorim**—a better rendering is, "and Casluhim, of whom came the Philistim and Caphtorim." They were brethren, the sons of Casluhim, and at first dwelt together, whence their names are used interchangeably. The Caphtorim are described as inhabiting Azzah, or Gaza, the seat of the Philistines. **14. the Jebusite, etc.**—From this verse to verse 17 the names are not those of individuals, but of people who all sprang from Canaan; and as several of them became extinct or were amalgamated with their brethren, their national appellations are given instead of the personal names of their ancestors. **17. Uz, and Hul, and Gether, and Meshech**—or Mash; these were the children of Aram, and *grandsons* of Shem (Gen. 10:23). **18. Arphaxad begat Shelah**—Cainan, the father's name, is omitted here. (See on Luke 3:36). **19. Peleg**—(See on Gen. 10:25). **22. Ebal** —or Obal (Gen. 10:28).

24-28. SHEM'S LINE TO ABRAHAM. **24. Shem, etc.**—This comprises a list of ten, inclusive of Abraham.

29-31. SONS OF ISHMAEL. **29. These are their generations**—the heads of his twelve tribes. The great northern desert of Arabia, including the entire neck, was colonized by these tribes; and if we can recover, in the modern geography of this part of the country, Arab tribes bearing the names of those patriarchs, i.e., names corresponding with those preserved in the original catalogue of Scripture, we obtain at once so many evidences, not of mere similarity, but of absolute identification [FORSTER]. Nebaioth—gave rise to the Nabathæans of the classic, and the *Beni Nabat* of Oriental writers. Kedar —the Arab tribe, El Khedeyre, on the coast of Hedgar. **Abdeel**—Abdilla, the name of a tribe in Yemen. **30. Dumah**—Dumah and Tema, the great Arab tribes of Beni Teman. Thus this writer [HISTORICAL GEOGRAPHY OF ARABIA] traces the names of all the heads of the twelve tribes of Ishmael as perpetuated in the clans or tribes of the Arabs in the present day.

32, 33. SONS OF KETURAH. **32. sons of Keturah** —These became founders of nomadic tribes in the north of Arabia and Syria, as Midian of the Midianites (Gen. 36:35; Judg. 6:2). **and Shuah**—from whom Bildad sprang (Job 2:11).

34-42. POSTERITY OF ABRAHAM BY ESAU. **36. sons of Eliphaz**—the tribe Adites, in the center country of the Saracens, so called from his mother, Adah (Gen. 36:10). **Teman**—gave rise to the land of Teman, near the head of the Red Sea. **Omar**—the tribe Beni-Amma, settled at the northern point of Djebel Shera (Mount Seir). **Zephi**—the tribe Dzaf. **Gatam**—Katam, inhabited by the tribe Al Saruat, or "people of Sarah." **Kenaz**—the tribe Aenezes, a tribe whose settlement lies in the neighborhood of Syria. **Amalek**—the Beni Malak of Zohran, and the Beni Maledj of the Shat el Arab. **37. Reuel**— a powerful branch of the great Aeneze tribe, the *Rowalla* Arabs. **Shammah**—the great tribe Beni Shammar. In the same way, the names of the other kings and dukes are traced in the modern tribes of Arabia. But it is unnecessary to mention any more of these obscure nomads, except to notice that Jobab (vs. 44), one of the kings of Edom, is considered to be Job, and that his seat was in the royal city of Dinahab (Gen. 36:32), identified with O'Daeb, a well-known town in the center of Al Dahna, a great northern desert in the direction of Chaldea and the Euphrates [FORSTER].

CHAPTER 2

Vss. 1, 2. SONS OF ISRAEL. Vss. 3-12. POSTERITY OF JUDAH. **3. The sons of Judah**—His descendants are enumerated first, because the right and privileges of the primogeniture had been transferred to him (Gen. 49:8), and because from his tribe the Messiah was to spring. **6. Zimri, and Ethan, and Heman, and Calcol, and Dara**—These five are here stated to be the sons of Zerah, i.e., of Ezra, whence they were called Ezrahites (I Kings 4:31). In that passage they are called "the sons of Mahol," which, however, is to be taken not as a proper name, but appellatively for "sons of music, dancing," etc. The traditional fame of their great sagacity and acquirements had descended to the time of Solomon and formed a standard of comparison for showing the superior wisdom of that monarch. Jewish writers say that they were looked up to as prophets by their countrymen during the abode in Egypt. **7. the sons of Carmi**—He was the son of Zimri, or Zabdi, as he is called (Josh. 7:1). **Achar** —or Achan (Josh. 7:1). This variety in the form of the name is with great propriety used here, since Achar means "troubler."

13-17. CHILDREN OF JESSE. **15. David the seventh**—As it appears (I Sam. 16:10; 17:12) that Jesse had eight sons, the presumption is from David being mentioned here as the seventh son of his father, that one of them had died at an early age, without leaving issue. **17. Jether the Ishmaelite**—(cf. II Sam. 17:25). In that passage he is called Ithra an Israelite; and there seems no reason why, in the early days of David, anyone should be specially distinguished as an Israelite. The presumption is in favor of the reading followed by the *Sept.,* which calls him "Jetra the Jezreelite." The circumstance of his settling in another tribe, or of a woman marrying out of her own tribe, was sufficiently rare and singular to call for the statement that Abigail was married to a man of Jezreel.

18-55. POSTERITY OF CALEB. **18. Caleb the son of Hezron**—The notices concerning this person appear confused in our version. In vs. 19 he is said to be the father of Hur, whereas in vs. 50 he is called "the son of Hur." The words in this latter passage have been transposed in the copying, and should be read thus, "Hur the son of Caleb." **begat children of Azubah his wife, and of Jerioth**—The former was his spouse, while Jerioth seems to have been a secondary wife, and the mother of the children whose names are here given. On the death of his principal wife, he married Ephrath, and by her had Hur. **21. Hezron . . . daughter of Machir the father of Gilead**—i.e., chief of that town, which with the lands adjacent was no doubt the property of Machir, who was so desirous of a male heir. He was grandson of Joseph. The wife of Machir was of the tribe of Manasseh (Num. 26:29). **22. Jair, who had three and twenty cities in the land of Gilead**—As the son of Segub and the grandson of Hezron, he was of the tribe of Judah; but from his maternal descent he is called (Num. 32:41; Deut. 3: 14) "the son of Manasseh." This designation implies that his inheritance lay in that tribe in right of his grandmother; in other words, his *maternal* and *adopting* great-grandfather was Machir the son of Manasseh. Jair, inheriting his property, was his lineal representative; and accordingly this is expressly stated to be the case; for the village group of "Havoth-Jair" was awarded to him in that tribe, in consequence of his valiant and patriotic exploits. This arrangement, however, took place previous to the law (Num. 36), by which it was enacted that heiresses were to marry in their own tribe. But this instance of Jair shows that in the case of a man obtaining an inheritance in another tribe it required him to become thoroughly incorporated with it as a representative of the family through which the inheritance was received. He had been adopted into Manasseh, and it would never have been imagined that he was other than "a son of Manasseh" naturally, had not this passage given information supplementary to that of the passage in Numbers. **23. he took**—rather "he had taken." This statement is accounting for his acquisition of so large a territory; he got it by right of conquest from the former possessors. **Kenath**—This place, along with its group of surrounding villages, was gained by Nobah, one of Jair's officers sent by him to capture it (Num. 32:1, 2). **All these belonged to the sons of Machir**—In their number Jair is included as having completely identified himself by his marriage and residence in Gilead with the tribe of Manasseh. **24. Caleb-ephratah**—so called from uniting the names of husband and wife (vs. 19), and supposed to be the same as was afterwards called Bethlehem-ephratah. **Ashur, the father of Tekoa**—(II Sam. 14:2-4). He is

called the father, either from his being the first founder, or perhaps the ruler, of the city. **34. Sheshan had no sons, but daughters**—either he had no sons alive at his death, or his family consisted wholly of daughters, of whom Ahlai (vs. 31) was one, she being specially mentioned on account of the domestic relations about to be noted. **35 Sheshan gave his daughter to Jarha his servant to wife**—The adoption and marriage of a foreign slave in the family where he is serving, is far from being a rare or extraordinary occurrence in Eastern countries. It is thought, however, by some to have been a connection not sanctioned by the law of Moses [MICHAELIS]. But this is not a well-founded objection, as the history of the Jews furnishes not a few examples of foreign proselytes in the same manner obtaining an inheritance in Israel; and doubtless Jarha had previously embraced the Jewish faith in place of the grovelling idolatries of his native Egypt. In such a case, therefore, there could be no legal difficulty. Being a foreign slave, he had no inheritance in a different tribe to injure by this connection; while his marriage with Sheshan's daughter led to his adoption into the tribe of Judah, as well as his becoming heir of the family property. **42. the sons of Caleb**—(cf. vss. 18, 25). The sons here noticed are the fruit of his union with a third wife. **55. the families of the scribes**—either civil or ecclesiastical officers of the Kenite origin, who are here classed with the tribe of Judah, not as being descended from it, but as dwelling within its territory, and in a measure incorporated with its people. **Jabez**—a place in Judah (ch. 4:9). **Kenites that came of Hemath**—who settled in Judah, and were thus distinguished from another division of the Kenite clan which dwelt in Manasseh (Judg. 4:11).

CHAPTER 3

VSS. 1-9. SONS OF DAVID. **1-3. Now these were the sons of David which were born unto him in Hebron**—It is of consequence for the proper understanding of events in the domestic history of David, to bear in mind the place and time of his sons' birth. The oldest son, born *after* his father's *accession* to the sovereign authority, is according to Eastern notions, the proper heir to the throne. And hence the natural aspirations of ambition in Ammon, who was long unaware of the alienation of the crown, and could not be easily reconciled to the claims of a younger brother being placed above his own (see on II Sam. 3:1-5). **3. Eglah his wife**—supposed to be another name of Michal, who, though she had no son after her mockery of David for dancing before the ark, might have had one previous to that time. She has the title of wife appended to her name because she was his proper wife; and the mention of her name last probably arose from the circumstance that, having been withdrawn from David and married to another husband but afterwards restored, she had in reality become the last of his wives. **5. four, of Bath-shua the daughter of Ammiel**—or Bath-sheba (II Sam. 11:3), and there her father is called Eliam. Of course Solomon was not her "only son," but he is called so (Prov. 4:3) from the distinguished affection of which he was the object; and though the oldest, he is named the last of Bath-sheba's children. **6. Elishama and Eliphelet**—Two sons of the same name are twice mentioned (vs. 8). They were the children of different mothers, and had probably some title or epithet appended by which the one was distinguished from the other. Or, it might be, that the former two were dead, and their names had been given to sons afterwards born to preserve their memories. **8. nine**—The number of David's sons born after his removal to Jerusalem, was eleven (II Sam. 5:14), but only nine are mentioned here: two of them being omitted, either in consequence of their early deaths or because they left no issue.

10-16. HIS LINE TO ZEDEKIAH. **10. Solomon's son was Rehoboam**, etc.—David's line is here drawn down to the captivity, through a succession of good and bad, but still influential and celebrated, monarchs. It has rarely happened that a crown has been transmitted from father to son, in lineal descent, for seventeen reigns. But this was the promised reward of David's piety. There is, indeed, observable some vacillation towards the close of this period—the crown passing from one brother to another, an even from uncle to nephew—a sure sign of disorderly times and a disjointed government. **15. Zedekiah**—called the son of Josiah (cf. Jer. 1:3; 37:1), but in II Chronicles 36:19 he is described as the brother of Jehoiachin, who was the son of Jehoiakim, and consequently the *grandson* of Josiah. Words expressive of affinity or relationship are used with great latitude in the Hebrew. **Shallum**—No king of this name is mentioned in the history of Josiah's sons (II Kings 23 and 14), but there is a notice of Shallum the son of Josiah (Jer. 22:11), who reigned in the stead of his father, and who is generally supposed to be Jehoahaz, a younger son, here called the fourth, of Josiah.

17-24. SUCCESSORS OF JECONIAH. **17. the sons of Jeconiah; Assir**—rather, "Jeconiah the prisoner, or captive." This record of his condition was added to show that Salathiel was born during the captivity in Babylon (cf. Matt. 1:12). Jeconiah was written childless (Jer. 22:30), a prediction which (as the words that follow explain) meant that this unfortunate monarch should have no son succeeding him on the throne. **18. Malchiram also**—As far as Jeconiah, everything is plain; but there is reason to suspect that the text in the subsequent verses has been dislocated and disarranged. The object of the sacred historian is to trace the royal line through Zerubbabel; yet, according to the present reading, the genealogical stem cannot be drawn from Jeconiah downwards. The following arrangement of the text is given as removing all difficulties [DAVIDSON'S HERM.] vs. 17. And the sons of Jeconiah the the captive, Salathiel (Shealtiel, Ezra 3:2; Neh. 12:1; Hag. 1:12, 14; 2:2) his son; vs. 18. And the sons of Salathiel; Zerubbabel and Shimei; and the sons of Zerubbabel; Meshullam, Hananiah, and Shelomith their sister. vs. 19. And Hashubah, and Ohel, and Berechiah, and Hasadiah, Jushab-hezed. vs. 20. And Malchiram, and Rephaiah, and Shenazar, Jecamiah, Hoshama, and Nedabiah. vs. 21. The sons of Hananiah; Pelatiah and Jesaiah; the sons of Rephaiah; his son Arnan, his son Obadiah, his son Shecaniah.

CHAPTER 4

VSS. 1-8. POSTERITY OF JUDAH BY CALEB THE SON OF HUR. **1. the sons of Judah**—i.e., the descendants —for with the exception of Pharez, none of those here mentioned were his immediate sons. Indeed, the others are mentioned solely to introduce the name of Shobal, whose genealogy the historian intended to trace (ch. 2:52).

9-20. OF JABEZ, AND HIS PRAYER. **9. Jabez**—

was, as many think, the son of Coz, or Kenaz, and is here eulogized for his sincere and fervent piety, as well, perhaps, as for some public and patriotic works which he performed. The Jewish writers affirm that he was an eminent doctor in the law, whose reputation drew so many scribes around him that a town was called by his name (ch. 2:55); and to the piety of his character this passage bears ample testimony. The memory of the critical circumstances which marked his birth was perpetuated in his name (cf. Gen. 35:15); and yet, in the development of his high talents or distinguished worth in later life, his mother must have found a satisfaction and delight that amply compensated for all her early trials. His prayer which is here recorded, and which, like Jacob's, is in the form of a vow (Gen. 28:20), seems to have been uttered when he was entering on an important or critical service, for the successful execution of which he placed confidence neither on his own nor his people's prowess, but looked anxiously for the aid and blessing of God. The enterprise was in all probability the expulsion of the Canaanites from the territory he occupied; and as this was a war of extermination, which God Himself had commanded, His blessing could be the more reasonably asked and expected in preserving them from all the evils to which the undertaking might expose him. In the words, "that it may not grieve me," and which might be more literally rendered, "that I may have no more sorrow," there is an allusion to the meaning of his name—Jabez— signifying grief; and the import of this petition is, Let me not experience the grief which my name implies, and which my sins may well produce. **10. God granted him that which he requested**—Whatever was the kind of undertaking which roused his anxieties, Jabez enjoyed a remarkable degree of prosperity, and God, in this instance, proved that He was not only the hearer, but the answerer of prayer. **13. the sons of Kenaz**—the grandfather of Caleb, who from that relationship is called a Kenezite (Num. 32:12). **14. Joah, the father of the valley of Carashim**—lit., the father of the inhabitants of the valley—the valley of craftsmen, as the word denotes. They dwelt together, according to a custom which, independently of any law, extensively prevails in Eastern countries for persons of the same trade to inhabit the same street or the same quarter, and to follow the same occupation from father to son, through many generations. Their occupation was probably that of carpenters, and the valley where they lived seems to have been in the neighborhood of Jerusalem (Neh. 11:35). **17, 18. she bare Miriam**—It is difficult, as the verses stand at present, to see who is meant. The following readjustment of the text clears away the obscurity: "These are the sons of Bithiah the daughter of Pharaoh, which Mered took, and she bare Miriam, and his wife Jehudijah bare Jezreel," etc. **Jehudijah**—the Jewess, to distinguish her from his other wife, who was an Egyptian. This passage records a very interesting fact—the marriage of an Egyptian princess to a descendant of Caleb. The marriage must have taken place in the wilderness. The barriers of a different national language and national religion kept the Hebrews separate from the Egyptians; but they did not wholly prevent intimacies, and even occasional intermarriages between private individuals of the two nations. Before such unions, however, could be sanctioned, the Egyptian party must have renounced idolatry, and this daughter of Pharaoh, as appears from her name, had become a convert to the worship of the God of Israel.

**21-23. POSTERITY OF SHELAH. 21. Laadah...
the father ... of the house of them that wrought fine
linen**—Here, again, is another incidental evidence
that in very early times certain trades were followed
by particular families among the Hebrews, apparently in hereditary succession. Their knowledge of the
art of linen manufacture had been, most probably,
acquired in Egypt, where the duty of bringing up
families to the occupations of their forefathers was
a compulsory obligation, whereas in Israel, as in
many parts of Asia to this day, it was optional,
though common. **22, 23. had the dominion in
Moab, and Jashubi-lehem**—"And these are ancient
things" seems a strange rendering of a proper name;
and, besides, it conveys a meaning that has no bearing on the record. The following improved
translation has been suggested: "Sojourned in Moab,
but returned to Bethlehem and Adaberim-athekim.
These and the inhabitants of Netaim and Gedera
were potters employed by the king in his own work."
Gedera or Gederoth, and Netaim, belonged to the
tribe of Judah, and lay on the southeast border of
the Philistines' territory (Josh. 15-36; II Chron. 28:
18).

24-43. OF SIMEON. 24. The sons of Simeon—
They are classed along with those of Judah, as their
possession was partly taken out of the extensive territory of the latter (Josh. 19:1). The difference in
several particulars of the genealogy given here from
that given in other passages is occasioned by some
of the persons mentioned having more than one
name. **27. his brethren had not many children**—
(see on Num. 1:22; 26:14). **31-43. These were their
cities unto the reign of David**—In consequence of
the sloth or cowardice of the Simeonites, some of the
cities within their allotted territory were only nominally theirs. They were never taken from the Philistines until David's time, when, the Simeonites
having forfeited all claim to them, he assigned them
to his own tribe of Judah (I Sam. 27:6). **38, 39.
increased greatly, and they went to the entrance of
Gedor**—Simeon having only a part of the land of
Judah, they were forced to seek accommodation
elsewhere; but their establishment in the new and
fertile pastures of Gederah was soon broken up; for,
being attacked by a band of nomad plunderers, they
were driven from place to place till some of them
effected by force a settlement on Mount Seir.

CHAPTER 5

**Vss. 1-10. THE LINE OF REUBEN. 1. Now the
sons of Reuben**—In proceeding to give this genealogy, the sacred historian states, in a parenthesis
(vss. 1, 2), the reason why it was not placed first, as
Reuben was the oldest son of Jacob. The birthright, which by a foul crime he had forfeited, implied not only dominion, but a double portion (Deut.
21:17); and both of these were transferred to Joseph,
whose two sons having been adopted as the children
of Jacob (Gen. 48:5), received each an allotted portion, as forming two distinct tribes in Israel. Joseph
then was entitled to the precedency; and yet, as his
posterity was not mentioned first, the sacred historian judged it necessary to explain that "the genealogy was not to be reckoned after the birthright,"
but with a reference to a superior honor and privilege that had been conferred on Judah—not the
man, but the tribe, whereby it was invested with the
pre-eminence over all the other tribes, and out of it
was to spring David with his royal lineage, and especially the great Messiah (Heb. 7:14). These were

the two reasons why, in the order of enumeration,
the genealogy of Judah is introduced before that of
Reuben. **9. Eastward he inhabited unto the entering in of the wilderness from the river Euphrates**—
The settlement was on the east of Jordan, and the
history of this tribe, which never took any part in
the public affairs or movements of the nation, is
comprised in "the multiplication of their cattle in
the land of Gilead," in their wars with the Bedouin
sons of Hagar, and in the simple labors of pastoral
life. They had the right of pasture over an extensive mountain range—the great wilderness of
Kedemoth (Deut. 2:26) and the Euphrates being a
security against their enemies.

**11-26. THE LINE OF GAD. 11-15. the children of
Gad dwelt over against them**—The genealogy of the
Gadites and the half-tribe of Manasseh (vs. 24) is
given along with that of the Reubenites, as these
three were associated in a separate colony. **16.
Sharon**—The term Sharon was applied as descriptive
of any place of extraordinary beauty and productiveness. There were three places in Palestine so
called. This Sharon lay east of the Jordan. **upon
their borders**—i.e., of Gilead and Bashan: Gilead
proper, or at least the largest part, belonged to the
Reubenites; and Bashan, the greatest portion of it,
belonged to the Manassites. The Gadites occupied
an intermediate settlement on the land which lay
upon their borders. **17. All these were reckoned ...
in the days of Jotham**—His long reign and freedom
from foreign wars as well as intestine troubles were
favorable for taking a census of the people. **and in
the days of Jeroboam**—the second of that name. **18
-22. Hagarites**—or Hagarenes, originally synonymous with Ishmaelites, but afterwards applied to a
particular tribe of the Arabs (cf. Ps. 83:6). **Jetur**—
His descendants were called Itureans, and the country Auranitis, from Hauran, its chief city. These,
who were skilled in archery, were invaded in the
time of Joshua by a confederate army of the tribes
of Reuben, Gad, and half Manasseh, who, probably
incensed by the frequent raids of those marauding
neighbors, took reprisals in men and cattle, dispossessed almost all of the original inhabitants, and
colonized the district themselves. Divine Providence favored, in a remarkable manner, the Hebrew army in this just war. **26. the God of Israel
stirred up the spirit of Pul**—the Phal-luka of the
Ninevite monuments (see on II Kings 15:19). **and
the spirit of Tilgath-pilneser**—the son of the former.
By then the transjordanic tribes, including the other
half of Manasseh, settled in Galilee, were removed
to Upper Media. This was the *first* captivity (II
Kings 15:29).

CHAPTER 6

Vss. 1-48. LINE OF THE PRIESTS. 5. Uzzi—It is
supposed that, in his days, the high priesthood was,
for unrecorded reasons, transferred from Eleazar's
family to Ithamar's, in which it continued for
several generations. **10. he it is that executed the
priest's office in the temple that Solomon built in
Jerusalem**—It is doubtful whether the person in favor
of whom this testimony is borne be Johanan or Azariah. If the former, he is the same as Jehoiada,
who rendered important public services (II Kings
11); if the latter, it refers to the worthy and independent part he acted in resisting the unwarrantable
encroachments of Uzziah (II Chron. 26:17). **in the
temple that Solomon built**—described in this particular manner to distinguish it from the second

temple, which was in existence at the time when this history was written. **14. Azariah begat Seraiah**—He filled the supreme pontifical office at the destruction of Jerusalem, and, along with his deputy and others, he was executed by Nebuchadnezzar's orders at Riblah (II Kings 25:18, 21). The line of high priests, under the first temple, which from Zadok amounted to twelve, terminated with him. **16-48. The sons of Levi; Gershom**, etc.—This repetition (see vs. 1) is made, as the historian here begins to trace the genealogy of the Levitical families who were not priests. The list is a long one, comprising the chiefs or heads of their several families until David's reign, who made a new and different classification of them by courses. **20. Zimmah his son**—his grandson (vs. 42). **24. Uriel**—or Zephaniah (vs. 36). **27. Elkanah**—the father of the prophet Samuel (I Sam. 1:1). **28. the sons of Samuel**—are here named Vashni and Abiah. The first-born is called Joel (I Sam. 8:2); and this name is given to him in verse 33 of this chapter. It is now generally thought by the best critics that, through an error of the copyists, an omission has been made of the oldest son's name, and that Vashni, which is not the name of a person, merely signifies "and the second." This critical emendation of the text makes all clear, as well as consistent with other passages relating to the family of Samuel. **32. before the dwelling place ...**—i.e., in the tent which David had erected for receiving the ark after it was removed from the house of Obed-edom. This was a considerable time before the temple was built. **they waited on their office according to their order**—which David, doubtless by the direction of the Holy Spirit, had instituted for the better regulation of divine worship. **33. Shemuel**—i.e., Samuel. This is the exact representation of the Hebrew name. **39. his brother Asaph**—They were brothers naturally, both being descended from Levi, as well as officially, both being of the Levitical order. **42. Ethan**—or Jeduthun (ch. 9:16; II Chron. 35:15). **48. Their brethren also, the Levites, were appointed unto all manner of service**—Those of them who were endowed with musical tastes and talents were employed in various other departments of the temple service.

49-81. OFFICE OF AARON AND HIS SONS. 49. But Aaron and his sons offered, etc.—The office and duties of the high priests having been already described, the names of those who successively filled that important office are recorded. **60. thirteen cities**—No more than eleven are named here; but two additional ones are mentioned (Josh. 21:16, 17), which makes up the thirteen. **61. unto the sons of Kohath which were left**—i.e., in addition to the priests belonging to the same family and tribe of Levi. **by lot, ten cities**—(Josh. 21:26). The sacred historian gives an explanation (vs. 66). Eight of these are mentioned, but only two of them are taken out of the half tribe of Manasseh (vs. 70). The names of the other two are given (Josh. 21:21), where full and detailed notices of these arrangements may be found. **62. to the sons of Gershom**—Supply "the children of Israel gave." **67. they gave unto them of the cities of refuge**—The names of the cities given here are considerably different from those applied to them (Josh. 21:14). In the lapse of centuries, and from the revolutions of society, changes might have been expected to take place in the form or dialectic pronunciation of the names of those cities; and this will sufficiently account for the variations that are found in the lists as enumerated here and in an earlier book. As to these cities themselves that were assigned to the Le-

vites, they were widely remote and separated—partly in fulfilment of Jacob's prophecy (Gen. 49:7), and partly that the various districts of the country might obtain a competent supply of teachers who might instruct the people in the knowledge, and animate them to the observance, of a law which had so important a bearing on the promotion both of their private happiness and their national prosperity.

CHAPTER 7

Vss. 1-5. SONS OF ISSACHAR. **1. Jashub**—or Job (Gen. 46:13). **2. whose number was in the days of David two and twenty thousand and six hundred**—Although a census was taken in the reign of David by order of that monarch, it is not certain that the sacred historian had it in mind, since we find here the tribe of Benjamin enumerated, which was not taken in David's time; and there are other points of dissimilarity. **3. five: all of them chief men**—Four only are mentioned; so that as they are stated to be five, in this number the father, Izrahiah, must be considered as included; otherwise one of the names must have dropped out of the text. They were each at the head of a numerous and influential division of their tribe. **5. fourscore and seven thousand**—exclusive of the 58,600 men which the Tola branch had produced (vs. 24), so that in the days of David the tribe would have contained a population of 45,600. This large increase was owing to the practice of polygamy, as well as the fruitfulness of the women. A plurality of wives, though tolerated among the Hebrews, was confined chiefly to the great and wealthy; but it seems to have been generally esteemed a privilege by the tribe of Issachar, "for they had many wives and sons."

6-12. OF BENJAMIN. **6. The sons of Benjamin**—Ten are named in Genesis 46:21, but only five later (ch. 8:1; Num. 26:38). Perhaps five of them were distinguished as chiefs of illustrious families, but two having fallen in the bloody wars waged against Benjamin (Judg. 20:46), there remained only three branches of this tribe, and these only are enumerated. **Jediael**—or Asbel (Gen. 46:21). **7. the sons of Bela**—Each of them was chief or leader of the family to which he belonged. In an earlier period seven great families of Benjamin are mentioned (Num. 26:38), five of them being headed by these five sons of Benjamin, and two descended from Bela. Here five families of Bela are specified, whence we are led to conclude that time or the ravages of war had greatly changed the condition of Benjamin, or that the five families of Bela were subordinate to the other great divisions that sprang directly from the five sons of the patriarch. **12. Shuppim also, and Huppim**—They are called Muppim and Huppim (Gen. 46:21) and Hupham and Shupham (Num. 26:39). They were the children of Ir, or Iri (vs. 7). **and Hushim, the** sons [son] **of Aher**—Aher signifies "another," and some eminent critics, taking Aher as a common noun, render the passage thus, "and Hushim, another son." Shuppim, Muppim, and Hushim are plural words, and therefore denote not individuals, but the heads of their respective families; and as they were not comprised in the above enumeration (vss. 7, 9) they are inserted here in the form of an appendix. Some render the passage, "Hushim, the son of another," i.e., tribe or family. The name occurs among the sons of Dan (Gen. 46:23), and it is a presumption in favor of this being the true rendering, that after having recorded the genealogy of Naphtali (vs. 13) the sacred historian adds, "the sons of Bilhah, the handmaid, who was the mother of Dan and Naphtali." We naturally expect, therefore, that these two will be noticed together, but Dan is not mentioned at all, if not in this passage.

13. OF NAPHTALI. 13. Shallum—or Shillem (Gen. 46:24). **sons of Bilhah**—As Dan and Naphtali were her sons, Hushim, as well as these enumerated in vs. 13, were her grandsons.

14-40. OF MANASSEH. 14. The sons of Manasseh—or descendants; for Ashriel was a grandson, and Zelophehad was a generation farther removed in descent (Num. 26:33). The text, as it stands, is so confused and complicated that it is exceedingly difficult to trace the genealogical thread, and a great variety of conjectures have been made with a view to clear away the obscurity. The passage should probably be rendered thus: "The sons of Manasseh were Ashriel, whom his Syrian concubine bare to him, and Machir, the father of Gilead (whom his wife bare to him). Machir took for a wife Maachah, sister to Huppim and Shuppim." **21. whom the men of Gath . . . slew,** etc.—This interesting little episode gives us a glimpse of the state of Hebrew society in Egypt; for the occurrence narrated seems to have taken place before the Israelites left that country. The patriarch Ephraim was then alive, though he must have arrived at a very advanced age; and the Hebrew people, at all events those of them who were his descendants, still retained their pastoral character. It was in perfect consistency with the ideas and habits of Oriental shepherds that they should have made a raid on the neighboring tribe of the Philistines for the purpose of plundering their flocks. For nothing is more common among them than hostile incursions on the inhabitants of towns, or on other nomad tribes with whom they have no league of amity. But a different view of the incident is brought out, if, instead of "because," we render the Hebrew particle "when" they came down to take their cattle, for the tenor of the context leads rather to the conclusion that "the men of Gath" were the aggressors, who, making a sudden foray on the Ephraimite flocks, killed the shepherds including several of the sons of Ephraim. The calamity spread a deep gloom around the tent of their aged father, and was the occasion of his receiving visits of condolence from his distant relatives, according to the custom of the East, which is remarkably exemplified in the history of Job (Job 2:11; cf. John 11:19).

CHAPTER 8

Vss. 1-32. SONS AND CHIEF MEN OF BENJAMIN. 1. Now Benjamin begat, etc.—This chapter contains some supplementary particulars in addition to what has been already said regarding the tribe of Benjamin (ch. 7:6). The names of many of the persons mentioned are different from those given by Moses—a diversity which may be accounted for in part on grounds formerly stated, viz., either that the persons had more than one name, or that the word "sons" is used in a loose sense for grandsons or descendants. But there are other circumstances to be taken into account in considering the details of this chapter; viz., first, that the genealogies of the Benjamites were disordered or destroyed by the almost total extermination of this tribe (Judg. 20.); secondly, that a great number of Benjamites, born in Assyria, are mentioned here, who returned from the long captivity in Babylon, and established themselves—some

in Jerusalem, others in different parts of Judea. There were more returned from Babylon of the families belonging to this tribe than to any other except Judah; and hence many strange names are here introduced; some of which will be found in the list of the restored exiles (cf. Ezra 2). **6. these are the sons of Ehud**—most probably the judge of Israel (Judg. 3:15). His descendants, who had at first been established in Geba in Benjamin, emigrated in a body under the direction of Gera (vs. 7) to Manahath, where their increased numbers would find more ample accommodation. Manahath was within the territory of Judah. **8. Shaharaim begat children in the country of Moab**—He had probably been driven to take refuge in that foreign land on the same calamitous occasion that forced Elimelech to emigrate thither (Ruth 1:1). But, destitute of natural affection, he forsook or divorced his two wives, and in the land of his sojourn married a third, by whom he had several sons. But there is another explanation given of the conduct of this Benjamite polygamist. His children by Hushim are mentioned (vs. 11), while his other wife is unnoticed. Hence it has been thought probable that it is Baara who is mentioned under the name of Hodesh, so called because her husband, after long desertion, returned and cohabited with her as before. **28. These dwelt in Jerusalem**—The ordinary and stated inhabitants of Jerusalem were Judahites, Benjamites, and Levites. But at the time referred to here, the chiefs or heads of the principal families who are enumerated (vss. 14-27) established themselves in the city after their return from the captivity.

33-40. STOCK OF SAUL AND JONATHAN. 33. Ner begat Kish—The father of Ner, though not mentioned here, is stated (ch. 9:35) to have been Jehiel. Moreover, the father of Kish is said (I Sam. 9:1) to have been Abiel, the son of Zeror, whence it would seem that Abiel and Ner were names of the same person. **Abinadab**—the same as Ishui (I Sam. 14:49). **Esh-baal**—that is, Ishbosheth. **34. Meribbaal**—that is, Mephibosheth. **36. Jehoada**—or Jara (ch. 9:42). **40. mighty men of valour, archers**—(see on Judg. 20-16). Great strength as well as skill was requisite in ancient archery, as the bow, which was of steel, was bent by treading with the feet, and pulling the string with both hands.

CHAPTER 9

Vss. 1-26. ORIGINAL REGISTERS OF ISRAEL AND JUDAH'S GENEALOGIES. 1. all Israel were reckoned by genealogies—From the beginning of the Hebrew nation, public records were kept, containing a registration of the name of every individual, as well as the tribe and family to which he belonged. "The book of the kings of Israel and Judah" does not refer to the two canonical books that are known in Scripture by that name, but to authenticated copies of those registers, placed under the official care of the sovereigns; and as a great number of the Israelites (vs. 3) took refuge in Judah during the invasion of Shalmaneser, they carried the public records along with them. The genealogies given in the preceding chapters were drawn from the public records in the archives both of Israel and Judah; and those given in this chapter relate to the period subsequent to the restoration; whence it appears (cf. ch. 3:17-24) that the genealogical registers were kept during the captivity in Babylon. These genealogical tables, then, are of the highest authority for truth and correctness, the earlier portion being extracted from the authenticated records of the nation; and as to those which belong to the time of the captivity, they were drawn up by a contemporary writer, who, besides enjoying the best sources of information, and being of the strictest integrity, was guided and preserved from all error by divine inspiration. **2. the first inhabitants that dwelt in their possessions**—This chapter relates wholly to the first returned exiles. Almost all the names recur in Nehemiah (chap. 11), although there are differences which will be explained there. The same division of the people into four classes was continued after, as before the captivity; viz., the priests, Levites, natives, who now were called by the common name of Israelites, and the Nethinims (Josh. 9:27; Ezra 2:43; 8:20). When the historian speaks of "the first inhabitants that dwelt in their possessions," he implies that there were others who afterwards returned and settled in possessions not occupied by the first. Accordingly, we read of a great number returning successively under Ezra, Nehemiah, and at a later period. And some of those who returned to the ancient inheritance of their fathers, had lived before the time of the captivity (Ezra 3:12; Hag. 2:4, 10). **18. the king's gate**—The king had a gate from his palace into the temple (II Kings 16:18), which doubtless was kept constantly closed except for the monarch's use; and although there was no king in Israel on the return from the captivity, yet the old ceremonial was kept up, probably in the hope that the scepter would, ere long, be restored to the house of David. It is an honor by which Eastern kings are distinguished, to have a gate exclusively devoted to their own special use, and which is kept constantly closed, except when he goes out or returns (Ezek. 44:2). There being no king then in Israel, this gate would be always shut.

CHAPTER 10

Vss. 1-7. Saul's Overthrow and Death. **1. Now the Philistines fought against Israel**—The details of this chapter have no relation to the preceding genealogies and seem to be inserted solely to introduce the narrative of David's elevation to the throne of the whole kingdom. The parallel between the books of Samuel and Chronicles commences with this chapter, which relates the issue of the fatal battle of Gilboa almost in the very same words as I Samuel 31. **3. the battle went sore against Saul; and the archers hit him, and he was wounded**—The *Heb.* words may be thus rendered: The archers found (attacked) him, and he feared the archers. He was not wounded, at least not dangerously, when he resolved on committing suicide. The deed was the effect of sudden terror and overwhelming depression of spirits [CALMET]. **4. his armour-bearer would not for he was sore afraid**— He was, of course, placed in the same perilous condition as Saul. But it is probable that the feelings that restrained him from complying with Saul's wish were a profound respect for royalty, mingled with apprehension of the shock which such a catastrophe would give to the national feelings and interests. **6. Saul died, and his three sons, and all his house**—his sons and courtiers who were there engaged in the battle. But it appears that Ish-bosheth and Mephibosheth were kept at Gibeah on account of their youth.

8-14. The Philistines Triumph over Him. **10. put his armour in the house of their gods**—It was common among the heathen to vow to a national or

favorite deity, that, in the event of a victory, the armor of the enemy's king, or of some eminent leader, should be dedicated to him as an offering of gratitude. Such trophies were usually suspended on the pillars of the temple. **fastened his head in the temple of Dagon**—while the trunk or headless corpse was affixed to the wall of Beth-shan (I Sam. 31:10). **13. Saul died for his transgression which he committed against the Lord**—in having spared the king of the Amalekites and taken the flocks of the people as spoils, as well as in having consulted a pythoness. Both of these acts were great sins—the first as a violation of God's express and positive command, and the second as contrary to a well-known statute of the kingdom (Lev. 19:31). **14. And inquired not of the Lord**—He had done so in form (I Sam. 28:6), but not in the spirit of a humble penitent, nor with the believing confidence of a sincere worshipper. His inquiry was, in fact, a mere mockery, and his total want of all right religious impressions was manifested by his rushing from God to a wretched impostor in the service of the devil.

CHAPTER 11

Vss. 1-3. David Made King. **1. Then all Israel gathered themselves to David unto Hebron**—This event happened on the death of Ish-bosheth (see on II Sam. 5:1-3). The convention of the estates of the kingdom, the public and solemn homage of the representatives of the people, and the repeated anointing of the new king in their presence and by their direction, seem to have been necessary to the general acknowledgment of the sovereign on the part of the nation (cf. I Sam. 11:15).

4-9. He Wins the Castle of Zion from the Jebusites by Joab's Valor. **4. David and all Israel went to . . . Jebus**—(See on II Sam. 5:6-13). **8. Joab repaired the rest of the city**—David built a new town to the north of the old one on Mount Zion; but Joab was charged with a commission to restore the part that had been occupied by the ancient Jebus, to repair the breaches made during the siege, to rebuild the houses which had been demolished or burned in the sacking of the town, and to preserve all that had escaped the violence of the soldiery. This work of reconstruction is not noticed elsewhere [CALMET].

10-47. A Catalogue of His Worthies. **10. These . . . are the chief of the mighty men**—(See on II Sam. 23:8-39). They are here described as those who held strongly with him (Marg.) to make him king, etc. In these words the sacred historian assigns a reason for introducing the list of their names, immediately after his account of the election of David as king, and the conquest of Jerusalem; viz., that they assisted in making David king. In the original form of the list, and the connection in which it occurs in Samuel, there is no reference to the choice of a king; and even in this passage it is only in the clause introduced into the superscription that such a reference occurs [KEIL]. **11-13. Jashobeam, an Hachmonite**—or son of Hachmoni. He is called also son of Zabdiel (ch. 27:2), so that, strictly speaking, he was the grandson of Hachmoni (cf. ch. 27:32). **lifted up his spear against three hundred, slain by him at one time**—The feat is said (II Sam. 23:8) to have been a slaughter of eight hundred in one day. Some endeavor to reconcile the statements in that passage and in this by supposing that he slew eight hundred on one occasion and three hundred on another; while others conjecture that he attacked a body of eight hundred, and, having slain three hundred of them, the rest fled [LIGHTFOOT]. **12. the three mighties**—Only two are mentioned; viz., Jashobeam and Eleazar—the third, Shammah (II Sam. 23:11), is not named in this passage. **13. He was with David at Pas-dammim**—It was at the time when he was a fugitive in the wilderness, and, parched with thirst under the burning heat of noonday, he wistfully thought of the cool fountain of his native village. This is a notice of the achievement, to which Eleazar owed his fame, but the details are found only in II Sam. 23:9-11, where it is further said that he was aided by the valor of Shammah, a fact corroborated in the passage before us (vs. 14), where it is recorded of the heroes, that "they set themselves in the midst of that parcel." As the singular number is used in speaking of Shammah (II Sam. 23:12), the true view seems to be that when Eleazar had given up from exhaustion, Shammah succeeded, and by his fresh and extraordinary prowess preserved the field. **barley**—or lentils (II Sam. 23:11). Ephes-dammim was situated between Shocoh and Azekah, in the west of the Judahite territory. These feats were performed when David acted as Saul's general against the Philistines. **15-19. David longed and said, Oh that one would give me drink . . . of the well of Beth-lehem**—(See II Sam. 23:15). This chivalrous act evinces the enthusiastic devotion of David's men, that they were ready to gratify his smallest wish at the risk of their lives. It is probable that, when uttering the wish, David had no recollection of the military posted at Bethlehem. It is generally taken for granted that those who fought a way to the well of Bethlehem were the three champions just mentioned. But this is far from being clear. On the contrary, it would seem that three different heroes are referred to, for Abishai (vs. 20) was one of them. The camp of the Philistines was in the valley of Rephaim (vs. 15), which lay on the west of Jerusalem, but an outpost was stationed at Bethlehem (vs. 16), and through this garrison they had to force a passage. **21. howbeit he attained not to the first three**—(See on II Sam. 23:19). **22. Benaiah . . . of Kabzeel**—a town in the south of Judah (Josh. 15:21; Neh. 11:25). It is said that "he had done many acts"—though three only are mentioned as specimens of his daring energy and fearless courage. **slew two lionlike men of Moab**—lit., lions of God, i.e., great lions or champions. This gallant feat was probably achieved in David's hostile invasion of Moab (II Sam. 8:2). **also he went down and slew a lion in a pit in a snowy day**—probably a cave into which Benaiah had taken refuge from the snowstorm, and in which he encountered a savage lion which had its lair there. In a spacious cave the achievement would be far greater than if the monster had been previously snared or cabined in a pit. **23. he went down**—the ordinary phraseology for expressing an engagement in battle. The encounter of Benaiah with this gigantic Egyptian reminds us, in some respects, of David's combat with Goliath. At least, the height of this giant, which was about eight feet, and his armor, resembled his of Gath. **with a staff**—i.e., having no other weapon in his hand than his walking stick. **25. David set him over his guard**—the Cherethites and Pelethites that composed the small bodyguard in immediate attendance on the king. **26. Also the valiant men of the armies**—This was the third degree of military rank, and Asahel was their chief; the names of few of those mentioned are historically known. **27. Shammoth**—Between this name and Hebez, that of Elikah has evidently fallen out, as we may see (II Sam. 23:25) [BERTHEAU].

30. Maharai—chief of the detachment of the guards who attended on the king in the tenth month—January—(ch. 27:13; II Sam. 23:28). **39. Naharai**—armorbearer to Joab (II Sam. 23:37). The non-occurrence of Joab's name in any of the three catalogues is most probably to be accounted for by the circumstance that his office as commander-in-chief raised him to a position superior to all these orders of military knighthood. **41. Uriah the Hittite**—The enrolment of this name in such a list, attesting, as it does, his distinguished merits as a brave and devoted officer, aggravates the criminality of David's outrage on his life and honor. The number of the names from verses 26 to 41 (exclusive of Asahel and Uriah, who were dead) is thirty, and from verses 41 to 47 is sixteen—making together forty-eight (see on ch. 27). Of those mentioned (vss. 26-41), the greater part belonged to the tribes of Judah and Benjamin; the sixteen names (vss. 41-47) are all associated with places unknown, or with cities and districts on the east of the Jordan. The northern tribes do not appear to have furnished any leaders [BERTHEAU].

CHAPTER 12

Vss. 1-22. The Companies That Came to David at Ziklag. **1-7. Now these are they that came to David to Ziklag**—There are three lists given in this chapter, arranged, apparently, according to the order of time when the parties joined the standard of David. **while he yet kept himself close because of Saul**—i.e., when the king's jealousy had driven him into exile from the court and the country. **Ziklag**—(See on I Sam. 27:6). It was during his retirement in that Philistine town that he was joined in rapid succession by the heroes who afterwards contributed so much to the glory of his reign. **2. of Saul's brethren of Benjamin**—i.e., of the tribe of Benjamin (cf. vs. 29), but some of them might be relatives of the king. This movement to which the parties were led, doubtless by the secret impulse of the Spirit, was of vast importance to the cause of David, as it must have been founded on their observation of the evident withdrawing of God's blessing from Saul, and His favoring presence with David, to whom it was universally known the Divine King of Israel had given the crown in reversion. The accession of the Benjamites who came first and their resolution to share his fortunes must have been particularly grateful to David. It was a public and emphatic testimony by those who had enjoyed the best means of information to the unblemished excellence of his character, as well as a decided protest against the grievous wrong inflicted by causelessly outlawing a man who had rendered such eminent services to his country. **4. Ismaiah the Gibeonite**—It appears that not only the Canaanites who were admitted into the congregation (Josh. 9), but people of the tribe of Benjamin, were among the inhabitants of Gibeon. The mention of "the Gederathite," probably from Gaderah (Josh. 15:36), in the lowlands of Judah; of the Korhites (vs. 6), from Korah (ch. 2:43); and of Gedor (vs. 7), a town in Judah, to the southwest of Bethlehem (cf. ch. 4: 4), shows that this first list contains men of Judah as well as Benjamin [BERTHEAU]. **8-13. of the Gadites there separated themselves unto David**—i.e., from the service of Saul and from the rest of the Gadites who remained steadfast adherents of his cause. **into the hold**—or fortress, i.e., of Ziklag, which was in the wilderness of Judah. **whose faces**

were like the faces of lions, etc.–A fierce, lion-like countenance (II Sam. 1:23), and great agility in pursuit (II Sam. 2:18), were qualities of the highest estimation in ancient warfare. **14. one of the least was over an hundred, and the greatest over a thousand**–David, while at Ziklag, had not so large an amount of forces as to give to each of these the command of so many men. Another meaning, therefore, must obviously be sought, and excluding *was,* which is a supplement by our translators, the import of the passage is, that one of the least could discomfit a hundred, and the greatest was worth a thousand ordinary men; a strong hyperbole to express their uncommon valor. **15. These are they that went over Jordan in the first month**–i.e., in spring, when the swollen river generally fills up the banks of its channel (see on Josh. 3:15; 4:19; 5:10). **they put to flight all them of the valleys**–This was probably done at the time of their separating themselves and their purpose being discovered, they had to cut their passage through the opposing adherents of Saul, both on the eastern and western banks. The impossibility of taking the fords at such a time, and the violent rapidity of the current, make this crossing of the Jordan–in whatever way these Gadites accomplished it–a remarkable feat. **16. the children of Benjamin and Judah**–It is probable that the Benjamites invited the Judahites to accompany them, in order to prevent David being suspicious of them. Their anticipations, as the result showed, were well founded. He did suspect them, but the doubts of David as to their object in repairing to him, were promptly dispelled by Amasai or Amasa, who, by the secret impulse of the Spirit, assured him of their strong attachment and their zealous service from a unanimous conviction that his cause was owned and blessed of God (I Sam. 18: 12-14). **19-22. there fell some of Manasseh**–The period of their accession is fixed as the time when David came with the Philistines against Saul to battle, "but they helped them not" (see on I Sam. 29:4). **20. As he went to Ziklag**–If those Manassites joined him on his return to Ziklag, after his dismissal from the Philistine army, then their arrival took place before the battle of Gilboa could have been fought (cf. I Sam. 29:11). Convinced of the desperate state of Saul's affairs, they abandoned him, and resolved to transfer their allegiance to David. But some learned men think that they came as fugitives from that disastrous field [CALMET and EWALD]. **captains of the thousands ... of Manasseh**–Those seven were commanders of the large military divisions of their tribe. **21, 22. they helped David against the band**–i.e., the Amalekites who had pillaged Ziklag in David's absence. This military expedition was made by all his men (I Sam. 30: 9), who, as David's early helpers, are specially distinguished from those who are mentioned in the latter portion of the chapter. **the host of God**–i.e., a great and powerful army. **23-40. THE ARMIES THAT CAME TO HIM AT HEBRON. 23. these are the numbers of the bands ... that came to David to Hebron**–after the death of Ish-bosheth (II Sam. 5:1). **to turn the kingdom of Saul to him according to the word of the Lord**–(ch. 10:14; 11:3, 10). The account commences with the southern tribes, Levi being associated with Judah and Simeon, as the great majority of the leading men in this tribe resided in Judah; and, after recounting the representatives of the northern tribes, it concludes with those on the east of Jordan. **27. Jehoiada, the leader of the Aaronites**–not the high priest, for that was Abiathar (I Sam. 23:9), but the

leader of the Aaronite warriors, supposed to be the father of Benaiah (ch. 11:22). **29. Benjamin ... 3000**–This small number shows the unpopularity of the movement in this tribe; and, indeed, it is expressly stated that the mass of the population had, even after Ish-bosheth's death, anxiously endeavored to secure the crown in the family of Saul. **32. children of Issachar, ... that had understanding of the times,** etc.–Jewish writers say that the people of this tribe were eminent for their acquirements in astronomical and physical science; and the object of the remark was probably to show that the intelligent and learned classes were united with the military, and had declared for David. **33. Zebulun ... could keep rank**–i.e., were more disciplined soldiers than the rest. **not of double heart**–Though their numbers were large, all were in a high degree well affected to David. **38. all the rest also of Israel were of one heart to make David king**–i.e., entertained a unanimous desire for his elevation. **39. 40. there they were with David three days, eating and drinking**–According to the statements made in the preceding verses, the number of armed warriors assembled in Hebron on this occasion amounted to 300,000. Supplies of provisions were abundantly furnished, not only by the people of the neighborhood, but from distant parts of the country, for all wished the festivities to be on a scale of liberality and magnificence suitable to the auspicious occasion.

CHAPTER 13

Vss. 1-8. DAVID FETCHES THE ARK FROM KIRJATH-JEARIM. **1-3. David consulted ... And let us bring again the ark of our God**–Gratitude for the high and splendid dignity to which he had been elevated would naturally, at this period, impart a fresh animation and impulse to the habitually fervent piety of David; but, at the same time, he was animated by other motives. He fully understood his position as ruler under the theocracy, and, entering on his duties, he was resolved to fulfil his mission as a constitutional king of Israel. Accordingly, his first act as a sovereign related to the interests of religion. The ark being then the grand instrument and ornament of it, he takes the opportunity of the official representatives of the nation being with him, to consult them about the propriety of establishing it in a more public and accessible locality. The assembly at which he spoke of this consisted of the Sheloshim, princes of thousands (II Sam. 6:1). During the reign of the late king, the ark had been left in culpable neglect. Consequently the people had, to a great extent, been careless about the ordinances of divine worship, or had contented themselves with offering sacrifices at Gibeon, without any thought of the ark, though it was the chief and most vital part of the tabernacle. The duty and advantages of this religious movement suggested by the king were apparent, and the proposal met with universal approval. **2. If it seem good unto you, and ... it be of the Lord**–i.e., I shall conclude that this favorite measure of mine is agreeable to the mind of God, if it receive your hearty concurrence. **let us send abroad to our brethren everywhere**–He wished to make it known throughout the country, in order that there might be a general assembly of the nation, and that preparations might be made on a scale and of a kind suitable to the inauguration of the august ceremonial. **and with them also to the priests and Levites ... in their cities and suburbs**–(See on

Num. 35). The original terms, "Let us send," imply immediate execution; and, doubtless, the publication of the royal edict would have been followed by the appointment of an early day for the contemplated solemnity, had it not been retarded by a sudden invasion of the Philistines, who were twice repulsed with great loss (II Sam. 5:17), by the capture of Jerusalem, and the transference of the seat of government to that city. Finding, however, soon after, peace restored and his throne established, he resumed his preparations for removing the ark to the metropolis. **5. from Shihor of Egypt**—(Josh. 15:4, 47; Num. 34:5; I Kings 8:65; II Kings 24:7; II Chron. 7:8); a small brook flowing into the Mediterranean, near the modern El-arish, which forms the southern boundary of Palestine. **unto the entering of Hemath**—the defile between the mountain ranges of Syria and the extreme limit of Palestine on the north. **6-14. David went up, and all Israel, to Baalah**—(See on II Sam. 6:1-11). **6. whose name is called on it**—rather, "who is worshipped there" (II Sam. 6:2).

CHAPTER 14

Vss. 1, 2. Hiram's Kindness to David; David's Felicity. **1. Now Hiram king of Tyre**—The alliance with this neighboring king, and the important advantages derived from it, were among the most fortunate circumstances in David's reign. The providence of God appeared concurrent with His promise in smoothing the early course of his reign. Having conquered the Jebusites and made Zion the royal residence, he had now, along with internal prosperity, established an advantageous treaty with a neighboring prince; and hence, in immediate connection with the mention of this friendly league, it is said, "David perceived that the Lord had confirmed him king over Israel." **2. his kingdom was lifted up on high, because of his people Israel**—This is an important truth, that sovereigns are invested with royal honor and authority, not for their own sakes so much as for that of their people. But while it is true of all kings, it was especially applicable to the monarchs of Israel, and even David was made to know that all his glory and greatness were given only to fit him, as the minister of God, to execute the divine purposes towards the chosen people.

3-7. His Wives. **3. David took more wives at Jerusalem**—(See on II Samuel 3:5). His concubines are mentioned (ch. 3:9), where also is given a list of his children (vss. 5-8), and those born in Jerusalem (II Sam. 5:14-16). In that, however, the names of Eliphalet and Nogah do not occur, and Beeliada appears to be the same as Eliada.

8-17. His Victories over the Philistines. **8. all the Philistines went up to seek David**—in the hope of accomplishing his ruin (for so the phrase is used, I Sam. 23:15; 24:2, 3) before his throne was consolidated. Their hostility arose, both from a belief that his patriotism would lead him, erelong, to wipe out the national dishonor at Gilboa, and by fear, that in any invasion of their country, his thorough knowledge of their weak points would give him superior advantages. They resolved, therefore, to surprise and crush him before he was fairly seated on his throne. **11. they came to Baal-perazim; and David smote them there**—In an engagement fought at Mount Perazim (Isa. 28:21), in the valley of Rephaim, a few miles west of Jerusalem, the Philistines were defeated and put to flight. **12. when they had left their gods**—(See on

II Sam. 5:21). **13. the Philistines yet again spread themselves**—They renewed the campaign the next season, taking the same route. David, according to divine directions, did not confront them. **14. Go not up after them**—The text in II Samuel 5:23, more correctly has, "Go, not up." **turn away from them**—i.e., by stealing round a baca-grove, come upon their rear. **15. for God is gone forth before thee**—"a sound of going in the tops of the mulberry trees," i.e., the rustling of the leaves by a strong breeze suddenly rising, was the sign by which David was divinely apprised of the precise moment for the attack. The impetuosity of his onset was like the gush of a pent-up torrent, which sweeps away all in its course; and in allusion to this incident the place got its name. **16. from Gibeon . . . to Gazer**—Geba or Gibea (II Sam. 5:25), now Yefa, in the province of Judah. The line from this to Gazer was intersected by the roads which led from Judah to the cities of the Philistines. To recover possession of it, therefore, as was effected by this decisive battle, was equivalent to setting free the whole mountain region of Judah as far as their most westerly slope [Bertheau].

CHAPTER 15

Vss. 1-24. David Brings the Ark from Obed-edom. **1. David made him houses in the city of David**—Through the liberality of his Tyrian ally (ch. 14:1), David was enabled to erect not only a palace for himself, but to furnish suitable accommodation for his numerous family. Where polygamy prevails, each wife has a separate house or suite of apartments for herself and children. **prepared a place for the ark of God, and pitched for it a tent**—i.e., made an entirely new one upon the model of the former. The old tabernacle, which Moses had constructed in the wilderness and which had hitherto served the purpose of a sacred covering, was to be left at Gibeon, either because of the unwillingness of the inhabitants to part with such a venerable relic, or because there was no use for it in Jerusalem, where a more solid and sumptuous edifice was contemplated. If it appear surprising that David "made him houses" before he prepared this new tabernacle, it should be remembered that he had received no divine intimation respecting such a work. **2. Then David said, None ought to carry the ark of God but the Levites**—After the lapse of three months (ch. 13:14) the purpose of transporting the ark to Jerusalem was resumed. Time and reflection had led to a discovery of the cause of the painful catastrophe that marred the first attempt. In preparing for the solemn procession that was now to usher the sacred symbol into its resting-place, David took special care that the carriage should be regulated in strict conformity to the law (Num. 4:5, 15; 7:9; 10:17). **3. David gathered all Israel together**—Some are of opinion that this was done on one of the three great festivals, but at whatever time the ceremonial took place, it was of great importance to summon a general convocation of the people, many of whom, from the long-continued disorders of the kingdom, might have had little or no opportunity of knowing anything of the ark, which had been allowed to remain so long in obscurity and neglect. **4. David assembled the children of Aaron, and the Levites**—The children of Aaron were the two priests (vs. 11), Zadok and Abiathar, heads of the two priestly houses of Eleazar and Ithamar, and colleagues in the high priesthood (II Sam. 20:25). The Levites were the chiefs of their father's house (vs. 12); four belonging to the Kohathite branch, on whose shoulders the ark was to be borne; viz., Uriel, Shemaiah—descended from Elizaphan or Elzaphan—(Exod. 6: 22), Hebron (Exod. 6:18; ch. 6:2), and Amminadab from Uzziel (Exod. 6:22). **12. sanctify yourselves** —This special sanctification, which was required on all grave and important occasions, consisted in observing the strictest abstinence, as well as cleanliness, both in person and dress (see on Gen. 35:2; Exod. 19:10, 15); and in the neglect of these rules no step could have been taken (II Chron. 30:3). **16-24. David spake to the chief of the Levites to appoint . . . singers with instruments**—These eminent Levites were instructed to train the musicians and singers who were under them, for the solemn procession. The performers were ranged in three choirs or bands, and the names of the principal leaders are given (vss. 17, 18, 21), with the instruments respectively used by each. "Ben" (vs. 18) is omitted (vs. 20). Either it was used merely as a common noun, to intimate that Zechariah was the son of Jaaziel or Aziel, or Ben is the same as Azaziah. **22. Chenaniah, chief of the Levites**—He was not of the six heads of the Levitical families, but a chief in consequence of his office, which required learning, without regard to birth or family. **instructed about the song**—He directed all these bands as to the proper time when each was to strike in or change their notes; or, as some render the passage, "He led the burdens, for he was skilled," i.e., in the custom which it was necessary to observe in the carriage of the holy things [BERTHEAU]. **23. Berechiah and Elkanah were doorkeepers**—who marched immediately in front, while Obed-edom and Jeiel went in the rear, of the ark. **25. So David and the elders . . . and captains . . . went**—The pious design of David in ordering all his principal ministers and officers to take part in this solemn work and imparting so much pomp and imposing ceremony to the procession, was evidently to inspire the popular mind with a profound veneration for the ark and to give the young especially salutary impressions of religion, which would be renewed by the remembrance that they had been witnesses of the august solemnity in which the king and the highest aristocracy of the land participated, vying with all other classes to do honor to the God of Israel. **26. it came to pass,** etc.—(See on II Sam. 6:13-23). **they offered seven bullocks and seven rams**—The Levites seem to have entered on this duty with fear and trembling; and finding that they might advance without any such indications of divine wrath as Uzza had experienced (ch. 13:10), they offered an ox and a fatted sheep immediately after starting (II Sam. 6:13), and seven bullocks and seven rams—a perfect sacrifice— at the close of the procession (ch. 16:1). It is probable that preparations had been made for the offering of similar sacrifices at regular intervals along the way. **27. a robe of fine linen**—*Hebrew, Butz*—is rather supposed in the later books to denote cotton. **an ephod**—a shoulder garment, a cincture or cape over his dress. It was worn by the priests, but was not so peculiar to them as to be forbidden others (I Sam. 2:18; 22:18). **29. Michal . . . saw . . . David dancing and playing**— His movements would be slow and solemn, suitable to the grave and solemn character of the music. Though his royal robes were laid aside, he was attired like the other officials, showing a becoming humility in the immediate presence of God. The feelings manifested by Michal were only an ebullition of spleen from a proud and passionate woman.

CHAPTER 16

Vss. 1-6. DAVID'S FESTIVAL SACRIFICE AND LIBERALITY TO THE PEOPLE. **2. he blessed the people in the name of the Lord**—The king commended their zeal, supplicated the divine blessing upon them, and ordered the remains of the thank offerings which had been profusely sacrificed during the procession, to be distributed in certain proportions to every individual, that the ceremonial might terminate with appropriate festivities (Deut. 12:7). **3. flagon of wine**—The two latter words are a supplement by our translators, and the former is, in other versions, rendered not a "flagon," but a "cake," a confection, as the *Septuagint* renders it, made of flour and honey. **4-6. he appointed certain of the Levites to minister before the ark of the Lord**—No sooner was the ark deposited in its tent than the Levites, who were to officiate in the choirs before it, entered upon their duties. A select number of the musicians were chosen for the service from the list (ch. 15:19-21) of those who had taken a prominent part in the recent procession. The same arrangement was to be observed in their duties, now that the ark again was stationary; Asaph, with his associates, composing the first or principal company, played with cymbals; Zechariah and his colleagues, with whom were conjoined Jeiel and Obed-edom, forming the second company, used harps and similar instruments. **5. Jeiel**—is the same as Aziel (ch. 15:20). **6. Benaiah also and Jahaziel**—The name of the former is mentioned among the priests (ch. 15:24), but not the latter. The office assigned to them was that of blowing trumpets at regular intervals before the ark and in the tabernacle.

7-43. HIS PSALM OF THANKSGIVING. **7. Then on that day David delivered first this psalm**—Among the other preparations for this solemn inauguration, the royal bard had composed a special hymn for the occasion. Doubtless it had been previously in the hands of Asaph and his assistants, but it was now publicly committed to them as they entered for the first time on the performance of their sacred duties. It occupies the greater part of this chapter (vss. 8-36), and seems to have been compiled from other psalms of David, previously known to the Israelites, as the whole of it will be found, with very slight variations, in Psalms 96; 105:1-15; 106:47, 48. In the form, however, in which it is given by the sacred historian, it seems to have been the first psalm given for use in the tabernacle service. Abounding, as it does, with the liveliest ascriptions of praise to God for the revelation of His glorious character and the display of His marvellous works and containing, as it does, so many pointed allusions to the origin, privileges, and peculiar destiny of the chosen people, it was admirably calculated to animate the devotions and call forth the gratitude of the assembled multitude. **36. all the people said, Amen**—(Cf. Ps. 72:19, 20; 106:48). In the former, the author of the doxology utters the amen himself, while in the latter the people are exhorted to say amen. This may arise from the fact that the latter psalm originally concluded with the injunction to say amen. But in this historical account of the festival, it was necessary to relate that the people obeyed this injunction on the occasion referred to, and therefore the words "let them praise," were altered into "and they praised" [BERTHEAU]. **37-42. So he left there, before the covenant of the Lord, Asaph and his brethren,** etc.—The sequel of the chapter describes the appointment of the sacred musicians and their respective duties. **38. Obed-edom with their** brethren—Hosah, mentioned at the close of the verse, and a great number besides (see on ch. 26). **to be porters**—doorkeepers. **39, 40. And Zadok ... before the tabernacle ... at Gibeon**—While the above-mentioned officers under the superintendence of Abiathar, were appointed to officiate in Jerusalem, whither the ark had been brought, Zadok and the priests subordinate to him were stationed at Gibeon to perform the sacred service before the ancient tabernacle which still remained there. **continually morning and evening**—as the law enjoined (Exod. 29:38; Num. 28:3, 6). **and do according to all that is written in the law**—(See Num. 28). Thus, in the time of David, the worship was performed at two places, where the sacred things that had been transmitted from the age of Moses were preserved. Before the Ark in Jerusalem, Asaph and his brethren officiated as singers, Obed-edom and Hosah served as doorkeepers, and Benaiah and Jehaziel blew the trumpets. While at the tabernacle and burnt offering in Gibeon, Heman and Jeduthun presided over the sacred music, the sons of Jeduthun were doorkeepers, and Zadok, with his suite of attendant priests, offered the sacrifices.

CHAPTER 17

Vss. 1-10. DAVID FORBIDDEN TO BUILD GOD A HOUSE. **1. as David sat in his house**—The details of this chapter were given in nearly similar terms (II Sam. 7). The date was towards the latter end of David's reign, for it is expressly said in the former book to have been at the cessation of all his wars. But as to narrate the preparations for the removal of the ark and the erection of the temple was the principal object of the historian, the exact chronology is not followed. **5. I ... have gone from tent to tent, and from one tabernacle to another**—The literal rendering is, "I was walking in a tent and in a dwelling." The evident intention (as we may see from vs. 6) was to lay stress upon the fact that God was a *Mithhallek* (a travelling God) and went from one place to another with His *tent* and His entire *dwelling* (the dwelling included not merely the tent, but the fore-courts with the altar of burnt offerings, etc.) [BERTHEAU]. **6 spake I a word to any of the judges**—In I Sam. 7:7 it is "any of the tribes" of Israel. Both are included. But the judges "who were commanded to feed the people," form the more suitable antithesis to David. **Why have ye not built me an house of cedars?**—i.e., a solid and magnificent temple. **7. Thus saith the Lord of hosts, I took thee from the sheepcote**—a round tower of rude construction, high walled, but open at the top, in which sheep are often enclosed at night to protect them from wild beasts. The meaning is, I elevated you to the throne from a humble condition solely by an act of divine grace, and not from any antecedent merits of your own (see on I Sam. 16:11), and I enabled you to acquire renown, equal or superior to any other monarch. Your reign will ever be afterwards regarded as the best and brightest era in the history of Israel, for it will secure to the nation a settled inheritance of prosperity and peace, without any of the oppressions or disorders that afflicted them in early times. **9, 10. at the beginning, and since the time I commanded judges**—i.e., including the whole period from Joshua to Saul. **I tell thee that the Lord will build thee an house**—This was the language of Nathan himself, who was specially directed to assure David, not only of personal blessing and prosperity, but of a continuous

line of royal descendants. **11. I will raise up thy seed**—(II Sam. 7:12). **13. I will not take my mercy away from him, as I took it from him that was before thee**—My procedure in dealing with him will be different from My disposal of Saul. Should his misconduct call for personal chastisement, I shall spare his family. If I see it necessary to withdraw My favor and help for a time, it will be a corrective discipline only to reform and restore, not to destroy. (On this passage some have founded an argument for Solomon's repentance and return to God.) **14. I will settle him in my house**—over My people Israel. **and in my kingdom**—God here asserts His right of supreme sovereignty in Israel. David and Solomon, with their successors, were only the vicegerents whom He nominated, or, in His providence, permitted. **his throne shall be established for evermore**—The posterity of David inherited the throne in a long succession—but not always. In such a connection as this, the phrase "for evermore" is employed in a restricted sense (see on Lam. 3:31). We naturally expect the prophet to revert to David before concluding, after having spoken (vs. 12) of the building of Solomon's temple. The promise that his house should be blessed was intended as a compensation for the disappointment of his wish to build the temple, and hence this assurance is appropriately repeated at the conclusion of the prophet's address [BERTHEAU]. **15. According to all ... this vision**—The revelation of the divine will was made to the prophet in a dream. **16. David the king ... sat before the Lord, and said**—(See on II Sam. 7:18-19).

CHAPTER 18

Vss. 1, 2. DAVID SUBDUES THE PHILISTINES AND MOABITES. **1. David ... took Gath and her towns**—The full extent of David's conquests in the Philistine territory is here distinctly stated, whereas in the parallel passage (II Sam. 8:1) it was only described in a general way. Gath was the "Methegammah," or "arm-bridle," as it is there called—either from its supremacy as the capital over the other Philistine towns, or because, in the capture of that important place and its dependencies, he obtained the complete control of his restless neighbors. **2. he smote Moab**—The terrible severities by which David's conquest of that people was marked, and the probable reason of their being subjected to such a dreadful retribution, are narrated (II Sam. 8:2). **the Moabites ... brought gifts**—i.e., became tributary to Israel.

3-17. DAVID SMITES HADADEZER AND THE SYRIANS. **3. Hadarezer**—or Hadadezer (II Sam. 8:3), which was probably the original form of the name, was derived from Hadad, a Syrian deity. It seems to have become the official and hereditary title of the rulers of that kingdom. **Zobah**—Its situation is determined by the words "unto" or "towards Hamath," a little to the northeast of Damascus, and is supposed by some to be the same place as in earlier times was called Hobah (Gen. 14:15). Previous to the rise of Damascus, Zobah was the capital of the kingdom which held supremacy among the petty states of Syria. **as he went to establish his dominion by the river Euphrates**—Some refer this to David, who was seeking to extend his possessions in one direction towards a point bordering on the Euphrates, in accordance with the promise (Gen. 15:18; Num. 24:17). But others are of opinion that, as David's name is mentioned (vs. 4), this reference is most applicable to Hadadezer. **4-8. David took from him a thousand chariots**—(See on II Sam. 8:3-14). In that passage David is said to have taken 700 horsemen, whereas here it is said that he took 7000. This great discrepancy in the text of the two narratives seems to have originated with a transcriber in confounding the two Hebrew letters which indicate the numbers, and in neglecting to mark or obscure the points over one of them. We have no means of ascertaining whether 700 or 7000 be the more correct. Probably the former should be adopted [DAVIDSON'S HERM.]. **but reserved of them an hundred chariots**—probably to grace a triumphal procession on his return to Jerusalem, and after using them in that way, destroy them like the rest. **8. from Tibhath and from Chun** —These places are called Betah and Berothai (II Sam. 8:8). Perhaps the one might be the Jewish, the other the Syrian, name of these towns. Neither their situation nor the connection between them is known. The Arabic version makes them to be Emesa (now Hems) and Baal-bek, both of which agree very well with the relative position of Zobah. **9-13. Tou**—or Toi—whose dominions border on those of Hadadezer. (See on II Sam. 8:9-12; I Kings 11:15.) **17. the Cherethites and the Pelethites**—who formed the royal bodyguard. The Cherethites were, most probably, those brave men who all along accompanied David while among the Philistines, and from that people derived their name (I Sam. 30:14; Ezek. 25:16; Zeph. 12:5) as well as their skill in archery—while the Pelethites were those who joined him at Ziklag, took their name from Pelet, the chief man in the company (ch. 12:3), and, being Benjamites, were expert in the use of the sling.

CHAPTER 19

Vss. 1-5. DAVID'S MESSENGERS, SENT TO COMFORT HANUN, ARE DISGRACEFULLY TREATED. **1. after this**—This phrase seems to indicate that the incident now to be related took place immediately, or soon after the wars described in the preceding chapter. But the chronological order is loosely observed, and the only just inference that can be drawn from the use of this phrase is, that some farther account is to be given of the wars against the Syrians. **Nahash the king of the children of Ammon died**—There had subsisted a very friendly relation between David and him, begun during the exile of the former, and cemented, doubtless, by their common hostility to Saul. **3. are not his servants come unto thee for to search?**—i.e., thy capital, Rabbah (II Sam. 10:3). **4. shaved them**— not completely, but only the half of their face. This disrespect to the beard, and indecent exposure of their persons by their clothes being cut off from the girdle downwards, was the grossest indignity to which Jews, in common with all Orientals, could be subjected. No wonder that the men were ashamed to appear in public—that the king recommended them to remain in seclusion on the border till the mark of their disgrace had disappeared— and then they might, with propriety, return to the court.

6-15. JOAB AND ABISHAI OVERCOME THE AMMONITES. **6. when the children of Ammon saw that they had made themselves odious to David**—One universal feeling of indignation was roused throughout Israel, and all classes supported the king in his determination to avenge this unprovoked insult on

the Hebrew nation. **Hanun . . . sent a thousand talents of silver**—a sum equal to about $2,000,000 to procure the services of foreign mercenaries. **chariots and horsemen out of Mesopotamia, . . . Syria-maachah, and . . . Zobah**—The Mesopotamian troops did not arrive during this campaign (vs. 16). Syria-maachah lay on the north of the possessions of the transjordanic Israelites, near Gilead. **Zobah** —(see on ch. 18:3). **7. they hired thirty and two thousand chariots**—*Heb.*, riders, or cavalry, accustomed to fight either on horseback or in chariots, and occasionally on foot. Accepting this as the true rendering, the number of hired auxiliaries mentioned in this passage agrees exactly with the statement in II Samuel 10:6. 20,000, 12,000 (from Tob), equal to 32,000, and 1000 with the king of Maachah. **8. David . . . sent Joab, and all the host of the mighty men**—All the forces of Israel, including the great military orders, were engaged in this war. **9. children of Ammon . . . put the battle in array before the gate of the city**—i.e., outside the walls of Medebah, a frontier town on the Arnon. **the kings that were come were by themselves in the field**—The Israelitish army being thus beset by the Ammonites in front, and by the Syrian auxiliaries behind, Joab resolved to attack the latter—the more numerous and formidable host—while he directed his brother Abishai, with a suitable detachment, to attack the Ammonites. Joab's address before the engagement displays the faith and piety that became a commander of the Hebrew people. The mercenaries being defeated, the courage of the Ammonites failed; so that, taking flight, they entrenched themselves within the fortified walls.

16-19. SHOPHACH SLAIN BY DAVID. **16. And when the Syrians saw that they were put to the worse**—(See on II Samuel 10:15-19). **18. David slew of the Syrians seven thousand men**—(Cf. II Samuel 10:18, which has seven hundred chariots). Either the text in one of the books is corrupt [KEIL, DAVIDSON], or the accounts must be combined, giving this result—7000 horsemen, 7000 chariots, and 40,000 footmen [KENNICOTT, HOUBIGANT, CALMET].

CHAPTER 20

Vss. 1-3. RABBAH BESIEGED BY JOAB, SPOILED BY DAVID, AND THE PEOPLE TORTURED. **1. at the time when kings go out to battle**—in spring, the usual season in ancient times for entering on a *campaign;* i.e., a year subsequent to the Syrian war. **Joab led forth the power of the army, and wasted the country . . . of Ammon**—The former campaign had been disastrous, owing chiefly to the hired auxiliaries of the Ammonites; and as it was necessary, as well as just, that they should be severely chastised for their wanton outrage on the Hebrew ambassadors, Joab ravaged their country and invested their capital, Rabbah. After a protracted siege, Joab took one part of it, the lower town or "city of waters," insulated by the winding course of the Jabbok. Knowing that the fort called "the royal city" would soon fall, he invited the king to come in person, and have the honor of storming it. The knowledge of this fact (mentioned in II Sam. 12:26) enables us to reconcile the two statements—"David tarried at Jerusalem" (vs. 1), and "David and all the people returned to Jerusalem" (vs. 3). **2. David took the crown of their king . . . , and found it to weigh a talent of gold**—equal to 125 lbs. Some think that *Malcom*, rendered in our version "their king," should be taken as a proper name, Milcom or

Molech, the Ammonite idol, which, of course, might bear a heavy weight. But, like many other state crowns of Eastern kings, the crown got at Rabbah was not worn on the head, but suspended by chains of gold above the throne. **precious stones**—*Heb.*, a stone, or cluster of precious stones, which was set on David's head. **3. cut them with saws, etc.**—The Hebrew word, "cut them," is, with the difference of the final letter, the same as that rendered "put them," in the parallel passage of Samuel; and many consider that putting them to saws, axes, etc., means nothing more than that David condemned the inhabitants of Rabbah to hard and penal servitude.

4-8. THREE OVERTHROWS OF THE PHILISTINES AND THREE GIANTS SLAIN. **4. war at Gezer**—or Gob (see II Sam. 21:18-22).

CHAPTER 21

Vss. 1-13. DAVID SINS IN NUMBERING THE PEOPLE. **1. Satan stood up against Israel**—God, by withdrawing His grace at this time from David (see on II Sam. 24:1), permitted the tempter to prevail over him. As the result of this successful temptation was the entail of a heavy calamity as a punishment from God upon the people, it might be said that "Satan stood up against Israel." **number Israel**—In the act of taking the census of a people, there is not only no evil, but much utility. But numbering Israel—that people who were to become as the stars for multitude, implying a distrust of the divine promise, was a sin; and though it had been done with impunity in the time of Moses, at that enumeration each of the people had contributed "half a shekel towards the building of the tabernacle," that there might be no plague among them when he numbered them (Exod. 30:12). Hence the numbering of that people was in itself regarded as an undertaking by which the anger of God could be easily aroused; but when the arrangements were made by Moses for the taking of the census, God was not angry because the people were numbered for the express purpose of the tax for the sanctuary, and the money which was thus collected ("the atonement money," Exod. 30:16) appeased Him. Everything depended, therefore, upon the design of the census [BERTHEAU]. The sin of David numbering the people consisted in its being either to gratify his pride to ascertain the number of warriors he could muster for some meditated plan of conquest; or, perhaps, more likely still, to institute a regular and permanent system of taxation, which he deemed necessary to provide an adequate establishment for the monarchy, but which was regarded as a tyrannical and oppressive exaction—an innovation on the liberty of the people—a departure from ancient usage unbecoming a king of Israel. **3. why will he be a cause of trespass to Israel?**—or bring an occasion of punishment on Israel. In *Heb.*, the word sin is often used synonymously with the punishment of sin. In the course of Providence, the people frequently suffer for the misconduct of their rulers. **5. Joab gave the sum of the number of the children of Israel**—It amounted to one million one hundred thousand men in Israel, capable of bearing arms, inclusive of the 300,000 military (ch. 27), which, being already enlisted in the royal service, were not reckoned (II Sam. 24:9), and to 470,000 men in Judah, omitting 30,000 which formed an army of observation stationed on the Philistine frontier (II Sam. 6:1). So large a population at this early period, considering the limited extent of the country and comparing it with the earlier census (Num. 26), is a striking proof of the fulfilment of the promise (Gen. 15:5). **6. Levi and Benjamin counted he not**—If this census was ordered with a view to the imposition of taxes, this alone would account for Levi, who were not warriors (vs. 5), not being numbered (see on Num. 1:47-55). The population of Benjamin had been taken (see on ch. 7:6-11), and the register preserved in the archives of that tribe. This, however, was taken on another occasion, and by other agency than that of Joab. The non-numbering of these two tribes might have originated in the special and gracious providence of God, partly because Levi was devoted to His service, and Benjamin had become the least of all the tribes (Judg. 21); and partly because God foresaw that they would remain faithful to the house of David in the division of the tribes, and therefore He would not have them diminished [POOLE]. From the course followed in this survey (see on II Samuel 24: 4-8), it would appear that Judah and Benjamin were the last tribes that were to be visited; and that, after the census in Judah had been finished, Joab, before entering on that of Benjamin, had to return to Jerusalem, where the king, now sensible of his great error, gave orders to stop all further proceedings in the business. Not only the remonstrance of Joab at the first, but his slow progress in the survey (II Sam. 24:8) showed the strong repugnance and even horror of the old general at this unconstitutional measure. **9. the Lord spake unto Gad, David's seer**—Although David was himself endowed with a prophetic gift, yet, in matters relating to himself or his kingdom, he was in the habit of consulting the Lord through the medium of the priests; and when he failed to do so, a prophet was sent on extraordinary occasions to admonish or chastise him. Gad, a private friend, was occasionally employed as the bearer of these prophetic messages. **11, 12. Choose thee,** etc.—To the *three* evils these correspond in beautiful agreement: *three* years, *three* months, *three* days [BERTHEAU]. (See on II Samuel 24:13.) **13. let me fall now into the hand of the Lord . . . let me not fall into the hand of man**—Experience had taught him that human passion and vengeance had no bounds, whereas our wise and gracious Father in heaven knows the kind, and regulates the extent, of chastisement which every one needs. **14, 15. So the Lord . . . sent an angel unto Jerusalem to destroy it**—The infliction only of the pestilence is here noticed, without any account of its duration or its ravages, while a minute description is given of the visible appearance and menacing attitude of the destroying angel. **stood by the threshing-floor of Ornan the Jebusite**—Ornan was probably his Hebrew or Jewish, Araunah his Jebusite or Canaanitish, name. Whether he was the old king of Jebus, as that title is given to him (II Sam. 24:23), or not, he had been converted to the worship of the true God, and was possessed both of property and influence. **16. David and the elders . . . clothed in sackcloth, fell upon their faces**—They appeared in the garb and assumed the attitude of humble penitents, confessing their sins, and deprecating the wrath of God.

18-30. HE BUILDS AN ALTAR. **18. the angel of the Lord commanded Gad to say**—The order about the erection of an altar, as well as the indication of its site, is described (II Sam. 24:18) as brought directly by Gad. Here we are informed of the quarter whence the prophet got his commission. It is only in the later stages of Israel's history that we find angels employed in communicating the divine will to the prophets. **20, 21. Ornan was threshing wheat**—If the census was entered upon in autumn, the beginning of the civil year, the nine and a half months it occupied would end at wheat-harvest. The common way of threshing corn is by spreading it out on a high level area, and driving backwards and forwards upon it two oxen harnessed to a clumsy sledge with three rollers and some sharp spikes. The driver sits on his knees on the box, while another person is employed in drawing back the straw and separating it from the grain underneath. By this operation the chaff is very much chopped, and the grain threshed out. **23. I give thee . . . the threshing instruments for wood**—i.e., to burn the sacrifice of the oxen. Very little real import—the *haste* and the *value* of the present offered —can be understood in this country. The offering was made for *instant* use. Ornan, hereby hoping to terminate the pestilence without a moment's delay, "gave all," oxen, the large threshing machine, and the wheat. **25. David gave . . . for the place six hundred shekels of gold**—At first he bought only the cattle and the threshing instruments, for which he paid fifty shekels of silver (II Sam. 24:24); afterwards he purchased the whole property, Mount Moriah, on which the future temple stood. High in the center of the mountain platform rises a remarkable rock, now covered by the dome of "the Sakrah." It is irregular in its form, and measures about sixty feet in one direction and fifty feet in the other. It is the natural surface of Mount Moriah and is thought by many to be the rock of the threshing-floor of Araunah, selected by David, and continued by Solomon and Zerubbabel as "the unhewn stone" on which to build the altar [BARTLETT'S "WALKS ABOUT JERUSALEM," STANLEY]. **26. David built there an altar**—He went in procession with his leading men from the royal palace, down Mount Zion, and through the intervening city. Although he had plenty of space on his own property, he was commanded, under peremptory *direction*, to go a considerable distance from his home, up Mount Moriah, to erect an altar on premises which he had to buy. It was on or close to the spot where Abraham had offered up Isaac. **answered him by fire from heaven**—(See Lev. 9:24; I Kings 18:21-23; II Kings 1:12; II Chron. 7:1). **28. when David saw that the Lord had answered him . . . , he sacrificed there**—or, he continued to sacrifice there. Perceiving his sacrifice was acceptable, he proceeded to make additional offerings there, and seek favor by prayer and expiatory rites; for the dread of the menacing angel destroying Jerusalem while he was absent in the center of worship at Gibeon, especially reverence for the Divine Being, led him to continue his adorations in that place which God (II Chron. 3:1) had hallowed by the tokens of His presence and gracious acceptance.

CHAPTER 22

Vss. 1-5. DAVID PREPARES FOR BUILDING THE TEMPLE. **1. David said, This is the home of the Lord God**—By the miraculous sign of fire from heaven, and perhaps other intimations, David understood it to be the will of God that the national place of worship should be fixed there, and he forthwith proceeded to make preparations for the erection of the temple on that spot. **2. David commanded to gather together the strangers**—partly the descendants of the old Canaanites (II Chron. 8:7-

10), from whom was exacted a tribute of bond-service, and partly war captives (II Chron. 2:7), reserved for the great work he contemplated. 6-19. HE INSTRUCTS SOLOMON. **6. Then he called for Solomon . . . and charged him**—The earnestness and solemnity of this address creates an impression that it was given a little before the old king's decease. He unfolded his great and long cherished plan, enjoined the building of God's house as a sacred duty on him as his son and successor, and described the resources that were at command for carrying on the work. The vast amount of personal property he had accumulated in the precious metals must have been spoil taken from the people he had conquered, and the cities he had sacked.

CHAPTER 23

Vs. 1. DAVID MAKES SOLOMON KING. **1. when David was old . . . he made Solomon . . . king**—This brief statement, which comprises the substance of I Kings 1:32-48, is made here solely to introduce an account of the preparations carried on by David during the latter years of his life for providing a national place of worship. 2-6. NUMBER AND DISTRIBUTION OF THE LEVITES. **2. he gathered together all the princes of Israel**—All important measures relating to the public interest were submitted for consideration to a general assembly of the representatives of the tribes (ch. 13: 1; 15:25; 22:17; 26). **3. the Levites were numbered . . . thirty and eight thousand**—Four times their number at the early census taken by Moses (see on Num. 4 and 26). It was, in all likelihood, this vast increase that suggested and rendered expedient that classification, made in the last year of David's reign, which the present and three subsequent chapters describe. **by their polls, man by man**—Women and children were not included. **4. twenty and four thousand were to set forward the work of the house of the Lord**—They were not to preside over all the services of the temple. The Levites were subject to the priests, and they were superior to the Nethinim and other servants, who were not of the race of Levi. But they had certain departments of duty assigned, some of which are here specified. **5. praised the Lord with the instruments which I made**—David seems to have been an inventor of many of the musical instruments used in the temple (Amos 6:5). **6. David divided them into courses among the sons of Levi**—These are enumerated according to their fathers' houses, but no more of these are mentioned here than the twenty-four thousand who were engaged in the work connected with the Lord's house. The fathers' houses of those Levites corresponded with the classes into which they [JOSEPHUS' ANTIQUITIES] as well as the priests were divided (see on ch. 24: 20-31; 26:20-28). 7-11. SONS OF GERSHON. **7-11. the Gershonites** —They had nine fathers' houses, six descended from Laadan, and three from Shimei. 12-20. OF KOHATH. **12. The sons of Kohath**— He was the founder of nine Levitical fathers' houses. **13. Aaron was separated**—as high priest (see on ch. 25:1-19). **14. concerning Moses**—His sons were ranked with the Levites generally, but not introduced into the distinctive portion of the descendants of Levi, who were appointed to the special functions of the priesthood.

21-23. OF MERARI. **21-23. The sons of Merari** —They comprised six fathers' houses. Summing them together, Gershon founded nine fathers' houses, Kohath nine, and Merari six: total, twenty-four.

24. OFFICE OF THE LEVITES. **24. These were the sons of Levi . . . that did the work . . . from the age of twenty years and upward**—The enumeration of the Levites was made by David (vs. 3) on the same rule as that followed by Moses (Num. 4:3), viz., from thirty years. But he saw afterwards that this rule might be beneficially relaxed, and that the enrolment of Levites for their proper duties might be made from twenty years of age. The ark and tabernacle being now stationary at Jerusalem, the labor of the Levites was greatly diminished, as they were no longer obliged to transport its heavy furniture from place to place. The number of 38,000 Levites, exclusive of priests, was doubtless more than sufficient for the ordinary service of the tabernacle. But this pious king thought that it would contribute to the glory of the Lord to employ as many officers in his divine service as possible. These first rules, however, which David instituted, were temporary, as very different arrangements were made after the ark had been deposited in the tabernacle of Zion.

CHAPTER 24

Vss. 1-19. DIVISION OF THE SONS OF AARON INTO FOUR AND TWENTY ORDERS. **1. Now these are the divisions of the sons of Aaron**—(See on ch. 23:6). **2. Nadab and Abihu died before their father**—i.e., not in his presence, but during his lifetime (see Marg. Ref). **therefore Eleazar and Ithamar executed the priest's office**—In consequence of the death of his two oldest sons without issue, the descendants of Aaron were comprised in the families of Eleazar and Ithamar. Both of these sons discharged the priestly functions as assistants to their father. Eleazar succeeded him, and in his line the high priesthood continued until it was transferred to the family of Ithamar, in the person of Eli. **3. Zadok . . . and Ahimelech of the sons of Ithamar**—This statement, taken in connection with verse 6, is not a little perplexing, since (II Sam. 15:24, 35; 20:25) Abiathar is mentioned as the person conjoined in David's time with Zadok, in the collegiate exercise of the high priesthood. Some think that the words have been transposed, reading Abiathar, the son of Ahimelech. But there is no ground for regarding the text as faulty. The high priests of the line of Ithamar were the following: Ahiah or Ahimelech, his son Abiathar, his son Ahimelech. We frequently find the grandfather and grandson called by the same name (see list of high priests of the line of Eleazar, ch. 5:30-41). Hence the author of the Chronicles was acquainted with Ahimelech, son of Abiathar, who, for some reason, discharged the duties of high priest in David's reign, and during the lifetime of his father (for Abiathar was living in the time of Solomon, I Kings 2:27) [KEIL]. **4. there were more chief men found**—The *Heb.* may be translated, "There were more men as to heads of the sons of Eleazar." It is true, in point of fact, that by the census the number of individuals belonging to the family of Eleazar was found greater than in that of Ithamar. And this, of necessity, led to there being more fathers' houses, and consequently more chiefs or presidents in the former. **5. Thus were they divided by lot**—This method of allocation

was adopted manifestly to remove all cause of jealousy as to precedence and the right of performing particular duties. **6. one principal household** —The marg. reading is preferable, "one house of the father." The lot was cast in a deliberate and solemn manner in presence of the king, the princes, the two high priests, and the chiefs of the priestly and Levitical families. The heads of families belonging to Eleazar and Ithamar were alternately brought forward to draw, and the name of each individual, as called, registered by an attendant secretary. To accommodate the casting of the lots to the inequality of the number, there being sixteen fathers' houses of Eleazar, and only eight of Ithamar, it was arranged that every house of Ithamar should be followed by two of Eleazar, or, what is the same thing, that every two houses of Eleazar should be followed by one of Ithamar. If, then, we suppose a commencement to have been made by Eleazar, the order would be as follows: one and two, Eleazar; three, Ithamar; four and five, Eleazar; six, Ithamar; seven and eight, Eleazar; nine, Ithamar; and so forth [BERTHEAU]. The lot determined also the order of the priests' service. That of the Levites was afterwards distributed by the same arrangement (vs. 31).

CHAPTER 25

Vss. 1-7. NUMBER AND OFFICE OF THE SINGERS. **1. David and the captains of the host**—i.e., the princes (ch. 23:2; 24:6). It is probable that the king was attended on the occasion of arranging the singers by the same parties that are mentioned as having assisted him in regulating the order of the priests and Levites. **2. according to the order of the king**—*Heb.*, "by the hands of the king," i.e., "according to the king's order," under the personal superintendence of Asaph and his colleagues. **which prophesied**—i.e., in this connection, played with instruments. This metaphorical application of the term "prophecy" most probably originated in the practice of the prophets, who endeavored to rouse their prophetic spirit by the animating influence of music (see on II Kings 3:15). It is said that Asaph did this "according to David's order," because by royal appointment he officiated in the tabernacle on Zion (ch. 16:37-41), while other leaders of the sacred music were stationed at Gibeon. **5. Heman the king's seer**—The title of seer or prophet of David is also given to Gad (ch. 21:9), and to Jeduthun (II Chron. 29:15), in the words (*marg. matters*) of God. **to lift up the horn**—i.e., to blow loudly in the worship of God; or perhaps it means nothing more than that he presided over the wind instruments, as Jeduthun over the harp. Heman had been appointed at first to serve at Gibeon (ch. 16:41). But his destination seems to have been changed at a subsequent period. **God gave to Heman fourteen sons and three daughters**— The daughters are mentioned, solely because from their musical taste and talents they formed part of the choir (Ps. 68:25). **6, 7. All these were under the hands of their father**—Asaph had four sons, Jeduthun six, and Heman fourteen, equal to twenty-four; making the musicians with their brethren the singers, an amount of 288. For, like the priests and Levites, they were divided into twenty-four courses of twelve men each, equal to 288, who served a week in rotation; and these, half of whom officiated every week with a proportionate number of assistants, were skilful and experienced musicians, capable of leading and instructing the general musical corps, which comprised no less than 4000 (ch. 23:5).

8-31. THEIR DIVISION BY LOT INTO FOUR AND TWENTY ORDERS. 8. they cast lots, ward against ward—"Ward" is an old English word for division or company. The lot was cast to determine the precedence of the classes or divisions over which the musical leaders presided; and, in order to secure an impartial arrangement of their order, the master and his assistants, the teacher and his scholars, in each class or company took part in this solemn casting of lots. In the first catalogue given in this chapter the courses are classed according to their employment as musicians. In the second, they are arranged in the order of their service.

CHAPTER 26

VSS. 1-12. DIVISIONS OF THE PORTERS. 1, 2. Concerning the divisions of the porters—There were 4000 (ch. 23:6), all taken from the families of the Kohathites and Merarites (vs. 14), divided into twenty-four courses—as the priests and musicians. **Meshelemiah the son of Kore, of the sons of Asaph** —Seven sons of Meshelemiah are mentioned (vs. 2), whereas eighteen are given (vs. 9), but in this latter number his relatives are included. **5. God blessed him**—i.e., Obed-edom. The occasion of the blessing was his faithful custody of the ark (II Sam. 6:11, 12). The nature of the blessing (Ps. 127:5) consisted in the great increase of progeny by which his house was distinguished; seventy-two descendants are reckoned. **6. mighty men of valour**—The circumstance of physical strength is prominently noticed in this chapter, as the office of the porters required them not only to act as sentinels of the sacred edifice and its precious furniture against attacks of plunderers or popular insurrection— to be, in fact, a military guard—but, after the temple was built, to open and shut the gates, which were extraordinarily large and ponderous. **10. Simri the chief ... though ... not the first-born**—probably because the family entitled to the right of primogeniture had died out, or because there were none of the existing families which could claim that right. **12. Among these were the divisions of the porters, even among the chief men** —These were charged with the duty of superintending the watches, being heads of the twenty-four courses of porters.

13-19. THE GATES ASSIGNED BY LOT. 13. they cast lots—Their departments of duty, such as the gates they should attend to, were allotted in the same manner as those of the other Levitical bodies, and the names of the chiefs or captains are given, with the respective gates assigned them. **15. the house of Asuppim**—or collections, probably a storehouse, where were kept the grain, wine, and other offerings for the sustenance of the priests. **16. the gate Shallecheth**—probably the rubbish gate, through which all the accumulated filth and sweepings of the temple and its courts were poured out. **by the causeway of the going up**—probably the ascending road which was cast up or raised from the deep valley between Mount Zion and Moriah, for the royal egress to the place of worship (II Chron. 9:4). **ward against ward**— Some refer these words to Shuppim and Hosah, whose duty it was to watch both the western gate and the gate Shallecheth, which was opposite, while others take it as a general statement applicable to all the guards, and intended to intimate that they were posted at regular distances

from each other, or that they all mounted and relieved guard at the same time in uniform order. **17-19. Eastward were six Levites**—because the gate there was the most frequented. There were four at the north gate; four at the south, at the storehouse which was adjoining the south, and which had two entrance gates, one leading in a southwesterly direction to the city, and the other direct west, two porters each. At the Parbar towards the west, there were six men posted—four at the causeway or ascent (vs. 16), and two at Parbar, amounting to twenty-four in all, who were kept daily on guard. **Parbar**—is, perhaps, the same as Parvar (suburbs, II Kings 23: 11), and if so, this gate might be so called as leading to the suburbs [CALMET].

20-28. LEVITES THAT HAD CHARGE OF THE TREASURES. 20. of the Levites, Ahijah—The heading of this section is altogether strange as it stands, for it looks as if the sacred historian were going to commence a new subject different from the preceding. Besides, "Ahijah, whose name occurs after" the Levites, is not mentioned in the previous lists. It is totally unknown and is introduced abruptly without further information; and lastly, Ahijah must have united in his own person those very offices of which the occupants are named in the verses that follow. The reading is incorrect. The *Septuagint* has this very suitable heading, "And their Levitical brethren over the treasures," etc. [BERTHEAU]. The names of those who had charge of the treasure-chambers at their respective wards are given, with a general description of the precious things committed to their trust. Those treasures were immense, consisting of the accumulated spoils of Israelitish victories, as well as of voluntary contributions made by David and the representatives of the people.

29-32. OFFICERS AND JUDGES. 29. officers and judges—The word rendered "officers" is the term which signifies scribes or secretaries, so that the Levitical class here described were magistrates, who, attended by their clerks, exercised judicial functions; there were 6000 of them (ch. 23:4), who probably acted like their brethren on the principle of rotation, and these were divided into three classes—one (vs. 29) for the outward business over Israel; one (vs. 30), consisting of 1700, for the west of Jordan "in all business of the Lord, and in the service of the king"; and the third (vss. 31, 32), consisting of 2700, "rulers for every matter pertaining to God, and affairs of the king."

CHAPTER 27

VSS. 1-15. TWELVE CAPTAINS FOR EVERY MONTH. 1. came in and went out month by month—Here is an account of the standing military force of Israel. A militia formed, it would seem, at the beginning of David's reign (see on vs. 7) was raised in the following order: Twelve legions, corresponding to the number of tribes, were enlisted in the king's service. Each legion comprised a body of 24,000 men, whose term of service was a month in rotation, and who were stationed either at Jerusalem or in any other place where they might be required. There was thus always a force sufficient for the ordinary purposes of state, as well as for resisting sudden attacks or popular tumults; and when extraordinary emergencies demanded a larger force, the whole standing army could easily be called to arms, amounting to 288,000, or to 300,000, including the 12,000 officers that naturally attended on the twelve princes (vss.

16-24). Such a military establishment would be burdensome neither to the country nor to the royal treasury; for attendance on this duty being a mark of honor and distinction, the expense of maintenance would be borne probably by the militiaman himself, or furnished out of the common fund of his tribe. Nor would the brief period of actual service produce any derangement of the usual course of affairs; for, on the expiry of the term, every soldier returned to the pursuits and duties of private life during the other eleven months of the year. Whether the same individuals were always enrolled, cannot be determined. The probability is, that provided the requisite number was furnished, no stricter scrutiny would be made. A change of men might, to a certain degree, be encouraged, as it was a part of David's policy to train all his subjects to skill in arms; and to have made the enlistment fall always on the same individuals would have defeated that purpose. To have confined each month's levy rigidly within the limits of one tribe might have fallen hard upon those tribes which were weak and small. The rotation system being established, each division knew its own month, as well as the name of the commander under whom it was to serve. These commanders are styled, "the chief fathers," i.e., the hereditary heads of tribes who, like chieftains of clans, possessed great power and influence. **captains of thousands and hundreds**—The legions of 24,000 were divided into regiments of 1000, and these again into companies of 100 men, under the direction of their respective subalterns, there being, of course, twenty-four captains of thousands, and 240 centurions. **and their officers**—the Shoterim, who in the army performed the duty of the commissariat, keeping the muster roll, etc. **2, 3. Jashobeam the son of Zabdiel**—(See on ch. 11:11; II Sam. 23:8). Hachmoni was his father, Zabdiel probably one of his ancestors; or there might be different names of the same individual. In the rotation of the military courses, the dignity of precedence, not of authority, was given to the hero. **4. second month was Dodai**—or Dodo. Here the text seems to require the supplement of "Eleazar the son of Dodo" (II Sam. 23:9). **7. Asahel**—This officer having been slain at the very beginning of David's reign, his name was probably given to this division in honor of his memory, and his son was invested with the command.

16-24. PRINCES OF THE TWELVE TRIBES. **16. over the tribes of Israel: the ruler**—This is a list of the hereditary chiefs or rulers of tribes at the time of David's numbering the people. Gad and Asher are not included; for what reason is unknown. The tribe of Levi had a prince (vs. 17), as well as the other tribes; and although it was ecclesiastically subject to the high priest, yet in all civil matters it had a chief or head, possessed of the same authority and power as in the other tribes, only his jurisdiction did not extend to the priests. **18. Elihu**—probably the same as Eliab (I Sam. 16:16). **23. But David took not the number of them from twenty years old and under**—The census which David ordered did not extend to all the Israelites; for to contemplate such an enumeration would have been to attempt an impossibility (Gen. 28:14), and besides would have been a daring offense to God. The limitation to a certain age was what had probably quieted David's conscience as to the *lawfulness* of the measure, while its *expediency* was strongly pressed upon his mind by the army arrangements he had in view. **24. neither was the number put in the account of the chronicles of King David**—either

because the undertaking was not completed, Levi and Benjamin not having been numbered (ch. 21: 6), or the full details in the hands of the enumerating officers were not reported to David, and, consequently, not registered in the public archives. **the chronicles**—were the daily records or annals of the king's reign. No notice was taken of this census in the historical register, as from the public calamity with which it was associated it would have stood as a painful record of the divine judgment against the king and the nation. **25. over the king's treasures** —Those treasures consisted of gold, silver, precious stones, cedar-wood, etc.; those which he had *in* Jerusalem as distinguished from others *without* the city. **the storehouses in the fields**—Grain covered over with layers of straw is frequently preserved in the fields under little earthen mounds, like our potato pits. **27. the vineyards**—These seem to have been in the vine-growing districts of Judah, and were committed to two men of that quarter. **winecellars**—The wine is deposited in jars sunk in the court of the house. **28. olive trees and the sycamore trees ... in the low plains**—i.e., the Shephela, the rich, low-lying ground between the Mediterranean and the mountains of Judah. **29. herds that fed in Sharon**—a fertile plain between Cæsarea and Joppa. **30. camels**—These were probably in the countries east of the Jordan, and hence an Ishmaelite and Nazarite were appointed to take charge of them. **31. rulers of the substance that was King David's**—How and when the king acquired these demesnes and this variety of property—whether it was partly by conquests, or partly by confiscation, or by his own active cultivation of waste lands—is not said. It was probably in all these ways. The management of the king's private possessions was divided into twelve parts, like his public affairs and the revenue derived from all these sources mentioned must have been very large.

CHAPTER 28

Vss. 1-8. DAVID EXHORTS THE PEOPLE TO FEAR GOD. **1. David assembled all the princes of Israel**— i.e., the representatives of the people, the leading men of the kingdom, who are enumerated in this verse according to their respective rank or degree of authority. **princes of the tribes**—(ch. 27:16-22). Those patriarchal chiefs are mentioned first as being the highest in rank—a sort of hereditary noblesse. **the captains of the companies**—the twelve generals mentioned (ch. 27:1-15). **the stewards**, etc.—(ch. 27:25-31). **the officers**—*Hebrew*, eunuchs, or attendants on the court (I Sam. 8:15; I Kings 22:9; II Kings 22:18); and besides Joab, the commander-in-chief of the army, the heroes who had no particular office (ch. 11; II Sam. 23). This assembly, a very mixed and general one, as appears from the parties invited, was more numerous and entirely different from that mentioned (ch. 23:2). **2. Hear me, my brethren**—This was the style of address becoming a constitutional king of Israel (Deut. 17:20; I Sam. 30:23; II Sam. 5:1). **I had it in mine heart**—I proposed or designed. **to build an house of rest**—a solid and permanent temple. **for the footstool of our God**—God seated between the cherubim, at the two extremities of the ark, might be said to be enthroned in His glory, and the coverlet of the ark to be His footstool. **and had made ready for the building**—The immense treasures which David had amassed and the elaborate preparations he had made, would have been amply sufficient for the erection of the temple of which he presented the model to Solomon. **3. thou hast been a man of war, and hast shed much blood**—The church or spiritual state of the world, of which the temple at Jerusalem was to be a type, would be presided over by One who was to be pre-eminently the Prince of Peace, and therefore would be represented not so fitly by David, whose mission had been a preparatory one of battle and conquest, as by his son, who should reign in unbroken peace. **4, 5. he hath chosen Solomon**—The spirit of David's statement is this:—It was not my ambition, my valor, or my merit that led to the enthronement of myself and family; it was the grace of God which chose the tribe, the family, the person—myself in the first instance, and now Solomon, to whom, as the Lord's anointed, you are all bound to submit. Like that of Christ, of whom he was a type, the appointment of Solomon to the kingdom above all his brethren was frequently pre-intimated (ch. 17:12; 22:9; II Sam. 7:12-14; 12:24, 25; II Kings 1:13). **7. I will establish his kingdom for ever, if he be constant to do my commandments**—The same condition is set before Solomon by God (I Kings 3:14; 9:4). **8. Now . . . in the sight of all Israel, . . . keep, and seek for all the commandments of the Lord,** etc.—This solemn and earnest exhortation to those present, and to all Israel through their representatives, to continue faithful in observing the divine law as essential to their national prosperity and permanence, is similar to that of Moses (Deut. 39:15-20). **9-20. HE ENCOURAGES SOLOMON TO BUILD THE TEMPLE. 9, 10. And thou, Solomon my son**—The royal speaker now turns to Solomon, and in a most impressive manner presses upon him the importance of sincere and practical piety. **know thou**—He did not mean head knowledge, for Solomon possessed that already, but that experimental acquaintance with God which is only to be obtained by loving and serving Him. **11. Then David gave to Solomon . . . the pattern**—He now put into the hands of his son and successor the plan or model of the temple, with the elevations, measurements, apartments, and chief articles of furniture, all of which were designed according to the pattern given him by divine revelation (vs. 19). **12. the pattern of all that he had by the spirit**—rather, with him in spirit; i.e., was floating in his mind. **15, 16. the candlesticks of silver**—Solomon made them all of gold—in this and a few minor particulars departing from the letter of his father's instructions, where he had the means of executing them in a more splendid style. There was only one candlestick and one table in the tabernacle, but ten in the temple. **18. the chariot of the cherubim**—The expanded wings of the cherubim formed what was figuratively styled the throne of God, and as they were emblematical of rapid motion, the throne or seat was spoken of as a chariot (Ps. 18:10; 99:1). It is quite clear that in all these directions David was not guided by his own taste, or by a desire for taking any existing model of architecture, but solely by a regard to the express revelation of the divine will. In a vision, or trance, the whole edifice, with its appurtenances, had been placed before his eyes so vividly and permanently, that he had been able to take a sketch of them in the models delivered to Solomon. **20. Be strong and of good courage**—The address begun in verse 9 is resumed and concluded in the same strain. **21. behold, the courses of the priests and Levites**—They were, most probably, represented in this assembly though they are not named. **also the**

princes and all the people—i.e., as well the skilful, expert, and zealous artisan, as the workman who needs to be directed in all his labors.

CHAPTER 29

Vss. 1-9. DAVID CAUSES THE PRINCES AND PEOPLE TO OFFER FOR THE HOUSE OF GOD. **1. Solomon . . . is yet young and tender**—Though Solomon was very young when he was raised to the sovereign power, his kingdom escaped the woe pronounced (Eccles. 10:16). Mere childhood in a prince is not always a misfortune to a nation, as there are instances of the government being wisely administered during a minority. Solomon himself is a most illustrious proof that a young prince may prove a great blessing; for when he was but a mere child, with respect to his age, no nation was happier. His father, however, made this address before Solomon was endowed with the divine gift of wisdom, and David's reference to his son's extreme youth, in connection with the great national undertaking he had been divinely appointed to execute, was to apologize to this assembly of the estates—or, rather, to assign the reason of his elaborate preparations for the work. **3, 4. Moreover . . . I have of mine own proper good,** etc.—In addition to the immense amount of gold and silver treasure which David had already bequeathed for various uses in the service of the temple, he now made an additional contribution destined to a specific purpose—that of overlaying the walls of the house. This voluntary gift was from the private fortune of the royal donor, and had been selected with the greatest care. The gold was "the gold of Ophir," then esteemed the purest and finest in the world (Job 22:24; 28:16; Isa. 13:12). The amount was 3000 talents of gold and 7000 talents of refined silver. **5. who then is willing to consecrate his service**—*Heb.,* fill his hand; i.e., make an offering (Exod. 32:29; Lev. 8:33; I Kings 13:33). The meaning is, that whoever would contribute voluntarily, as he had done, would be offering a freewill offering to the Lord. It was a sacrifice which every one of them could make, and in presenting which the offerer himself would be the priest. David, in asking freewill offerings for the temple, imitated the conduct of Moses in reference to the tabernacle (Exod. 25:1-8). **6-8. Then the chief of the fathers**—or heads of the fathers (ch. 24: 31; 27:1). **princes of the tribes**—(ch. 27:16-22). **the rulers of the king's work**—those who had charge of the royal demesnes and other possessions (ch. 27: 25-31). **offered willingly**—Influenced by the persuasive address and example of the king, they acted according to their several abilities, and their united contributions amounted to the gross sum—of gold worth about $125,000,000; and of silver, about $17,000,000, besides brass and iron. **7. drams**—rather, *darics,* a Persian coin, with which the Jews from the time of the captivity became familiar, and which was afterwards extensively circulated in the countries of Western Asia. It is estimated as equal in value to about $5.00 in American currency. **of brass eighteen thousand talents, and one hundred thousand talents of iron**—In Scripture, iron is always referred to as an article of comparatively low value, and of greater abundance and cheaper than bronze [NAPIER]. **8. and they with whom precious stones were found**—rather, "whatever was found along with it of precious stones they gave" [BERTHEAU]. These gifts were deposited in the hands of Jehiel, whose family was charged with the treasures of the house of the Lord (ch:26:21).

10-25. HIS THANKSGIVING. **10. Wherefore David blessed the Lord**—This beautiful thanksgiving prayer was the effusion overflowing with gratitude and delight at seeing the warm and widespread interest that was now taken in forwarding the favorite project of his life. Its piety is displayed in the fervor of devotional feeling—in the ascription of all worldly wealth and greatness to God as the giver, in tracing the general readiness in contributing to the influence of His grace, in praying for the continuance of this happy disposition among the people, and in solemnly and earnestly commending the young king and his kingdom to the care and blessing of God. **16. all this store that we have prepared**—It may be useful to exhibit a tabular view of the treasure laid up and contributions stated by the historian as already made towards the erection of the proposed temple. Omitting the brass and iron, and precious stones, which, though specified partly (vs. 7), are represented in other portions as "without weight" (ch. 22:3, 14), we shall give in this table only the amount of gold and silver. Taking the talent of gold as worth approximately $25,000 and the talent of silver as $1,700, we arrive at the following amounts of contributions:

Sum accumulated and in public treasury (22:14):
Gold	$2,500,000,000
Silver	1,700,000,000

Contributed by David personally (29:4):
Gold	82,000,000
Silver	12,000,000

Contributed by assembled rulers (29:7):
Gold	125,000,000
Silver	17,000,000

A grand total of approximately $4,436,000,000. Though it has been the common practice of Eastern monarchs to hoard vast sums for the accomplishment of any contemplated project, this amount so far exceeds not only every Oriental collection on record, but even the bounds of probability, that it is very generally allowed that either there is a corruption of the text in ch. 22:14, or that the reckoning of the historian was by the Babylonian, which was only a half, or the Syrian, which was only a fifth part, of the Hebrew talent. This would bring the Scripture account more into accordance with the statements of Josephus, as well as within the range of credibility. **20. all the congregation . . . worshipped the Lord, and the king**—Though the external attitude might be the same, the sentiments of which it was expressive were very different in the two cases —of divine worship in the one, of civil homage in the other. **21, 22. they sacrificed . . . And did eat and drink**—After the business of the assembly was over, the people, under the exciting influence of the occasion, still remained, and next day engaged in the performance of solemn rites, and afterwards feasted on the remainder of the sacrifices. **before the Lord**—either in the immediate vicinity of the ark, or, perhaps, rather in a religious and devout spirit, as partaking of a sacrificial meal. **made Solomon . . . king the second time**—in reference to the first time, which was done precipitately on Adonijah's conspiracy (I Kings 1:35). **they . . . anointed . . . Zadok**—The statement implies that his appointment met the popular approval. His elevation as sole high priest was on the disgrace of Abiathar, one of Adonijah's accomplices. **23. Solomon sat on the throne of the Lord**—As king of Israel, he was the Lord's vicegerent. **24. submitted themselves**—*Heb.*, put their hands under Solomon, according to the custom still practised in the East of putting a hand under the king's extended hand and kissing the back of it (II Kings 10:15).

26-30. HIS REIGN AND DEATH. **26. Thus David . . . reigned**—(See I Kings 2:11).

THE SECOND BOOK OF

THE CHRONICLES

CHAPTER 1

Vss. 1-6. SOLEMN OFFERING OF SOLOMON AT GIBEON. **2. Then Solomon spake unto all Israel**— The heads, or leading officers, who are afterwards specified, were summoned to attend their sovereign in a solemn religious procession. The date of this occurrence was the second year of Solomon's reign, and the high place at Gibeon was chosen for the performance of the sacred rites, because the tabernacle and all the ancient furniture connected with the national worship were deposited there. Zadok was the officiating high priest (I Chron. 16:39). It is true that the ark had been removed and placed in a new tent which David had made for it at Jerusalem. But the brazen altar, "before the tabernacle of the Lord," on which the burnt offerings were appointed by the law to be made, was at Gibeon; and although David had been led by extraordinary events and tokens of the divine presence to sacrifice on the threshing-floor of Araunah, Solomon considered it his duty to present his offerings on the legally appointed spot "before the tabernacle," and on the time-honored altar prepared by the skill of Bezaleel in the wilderness (Exod. 38:1). **6. offered a thousand burnt offerings**—This holocaust he offered, of course, by the hands of the priests. The magnitude of the oblation became the rank of the offerer on this occasion of national solemnity.

7-13. HIS CHOICE OF WISDOM IS BLESSED BY GOD. **7. In that night did God appear unto Solomon**—(See on I Kings 3:5).

14-17. HIS STRENGTH AND WEALTH. **14. Solomon gathered chariots and horsemen**—His passion for horses was greater than that of any Israelitish monarch before or after him. His stud comprised 1400 chariots and 12,000 horses. This was a prohibited indulgence, whether as an instrument of luxury or power. But it was not merely for his own use that he imported the horses of Egypt. The immense equestrian establishment he erected was not for show merely, but also for profit. The Egyptian breed of horses was highly valued; and being as fine as the Arabian, but larger and more powerful, they were well fitted for being yoked in chariots. These were light but compact and solid vehicles, without springs. From the price stated (vs. 17) as given for a chariot and a horse, it appears that the chariot cost four times the value of a horse. A horse brought 150 shekels, which amounts to about $100.00., while a chariot brought 600 shekels, equal to about $400. As an Egyptian chariot was usually drawn by two horses, a chariot and pair would cost about $600. As the Syrians, who were fond of the Egyptian breed of horses, could import them into their own country only through Judea, Solomon early perceived the commercial advantages to be derived from this trade, and established a monopoly.

His factors or agents purchased them in the markets or fairs of Egypt and brought them to the "chariot cities," the depots and stables he had erected on the frontiers of his kingdom, such as Beth-marcaboth, "the house of chariots," and Hazor-susah, "the village of horses" (Josh. 19:5; I Kings 10:28). **17. brought ... for all the kings of the Hittites**—A branch of this powerful tribe, when expelled from Palestine, had settled north of Lebanon, where they acquired large possessions contiguous to the Syrians.

CHAPTER 2

Vss. 1, 2. SOLOMON'S LABORERS FOR BUILDING THE TEMPLE. **1. Solomon determined to build**— The temple is the grand subject of this narrative, while the palace—here and in other parts of this book—is only incidentally noticed. The duty of building the temple was reserved for Solomon before his birth. As soon as he became king, he addressed himself to the work, and the historian, in proceeding to give an account of the edifice, begins with relating the preliminary arrangements. 3-10. HIS MESSAGE TO HURAM FOR SKILFUL ARTIFICERS. **3. Solomon sent to Huram**—The correspondence was probably conducted on both sides in writing (vs. 11; see also on I Kings 5:8). **As thou didst deal with David my father**—This would seem decisive of the question whether the Huram then reigning in Tyre was David's friend (see on I Kings 5:1-6). In opening the business, Solomon grounded his request for Tyrian aid on two reasons: 1. The temple he proposed to build must be a solid and permanent building because the worship was to be continued in perpetuity; and therefore the building materials must be of the most durable quality. 2. It must be a magnificent structure because it was to be dedicated to the God who was greater than all gods; and, therefore, as it might seem a presumptuous idea to erect an edifice for a Being "whom the heaven and the heaven of heavens do not contain," it was explained that Solomon's object was not to build a house for Him to dwell in, but a temple in which His worshippers might offer sacrifices to His honor. No language could be more humble and appropriate than this. The pious strain of sentiment was such as became a king of Israel. **7. Send me now therefore a man cunning to work**—Masons and carpenters were not asked for. Those whom David had obtained (I Chron. 14:1) were probably still remaining in Jerusalem, and had instructed others. But he required a master of works; a person capable, like Bezaleel (Exod. 35:31), of superintending and directing every department; for, as the division of labor was at that time little known or observed, an overseer had to be possessed of very versatile talents and experience. The things specified, in which he was to be skilled, relate not to the building, but the furniture of the temple. Iron,

which could not be obtained in the wilderness when the tabernacle was built, was now, through intercourse with the coast, plentiful and much used. The cloths intended for curtains were, from the crimson or scarlet-red and hyacinth colors named, evidently those stuffs, for the manufacture and dyeing of which the Tyrians were so famous. "The graving," probably, included embroidery of figures like cherubim in needlework, as well as wood carving of pomegranates and other ornaments. **8. Send me ... cedar trees,** etc.—The cedar and cypress were valued as being both rare and durable; the algum or almug trees (likewise a foreign wood), though not found on Lebanon, are mentioned as being procured through Huram (see on I Kings 10:11). **10. behold, I will give to thy servants ... beaten wheat**—Wheat, stripped of the husk, boiled, and saturated with butter, forms a frequent meal with the laboring people in the East (cf. I Kings 5:11). There is no discrepancy between that passage and this. The yearly supplies of wine and oil, mentioned in the former, were intended for Huram's court in return for the cedars sent him; while the articles of meat and drink specified here were for the workmen on Lebanon. 11-18. HURAM'S KIND ANSWER. **11. Because the Lord hath loved his people,** etc.—This pious language creates a presumption that Huram might have attained some knowledge of the true religion from his long familiar intercourse with David. But the presumption, however pleasing, may be delusive (see on I Kings 5:7-12). **13, 14. I have sent a cunning man**—(See on I Kings 7:13-51). **17, 18. Solomon numbered all the strangers,** etc.—(See on I Kings 5:13, 18).

CHAPTER 3

Vss. 1, 2. PLACE AND TIME OF BUILDING THE TEMPLE. **1. Mount Moriah, where the Lord appeared unto David**—These words seem to intimate that the region where the temple was built was *previously* known by the name of Moriah (Gen. 22: 2), and do not afford sufficient evidence for affirming, as has been done [STANLEY], that the name was *first* given to the mount, in *consequence* of the vision seen by David. Mount Moriah was one summit of a range of hills which went under the general name of Zion. The platform of the temple is now, and has long been, occupied by the haram, or sacred enclosure, within which stand the three mosques of Omar (the smallest), of El Aksa, which in early times was a Christian church, and of Kubbet el Sakhara, "The dome of the rock," so called from a huge block of limestone rock in the center of the floor, which, it is supposed, formed the elevated threshing-floor of Araunah, and on which the great brazen altar stood. The site of the temple, then, is so far established for an almost universal belief is entertained in the authenticity of the tradition regarding the rock El Sakhara; and it has also been conclusively proved that the area of the temple was identical on its western, eastern, and southern sides with the present enclosure of the haram [ROBINSON]. "That the temple was situated *somewhere* within the oblong enclosure on Mount Moriah, all topographers are agreed, although there is not the slightest vestige of the sacred fane now remaining; and the greatest diversity of sentiment prevails as to its exact position within that large area, whether in the center of the haram, or in its southwest corner [BARCLAY]. Moreover, the full extent of the temple area is a problem that remains to be solved, for the platform of Mount Moriah being too narrow for the extensive buildings and courts attached to the sacred edifice, Solomon resorted to artificial means of enlarging and levelling it, by erecting vaults, which, as Josephus states, rested on immense earthen mounds raised from the slope of the hill. It should be borne in mind at the outset that the grandeur of the temple did not consist in its colossal structure so much as in its internal splendor, and the vast courts and buildings attached to it. It was not intended for the reception of a worshipping assembly, for the people always stood in the outer courts of the sanctuary.

3-7. MEASURES AND ORNAMENTS OF THE HOUSE. **3. these are the things wherein Solomon was instructed for the building of the house of God**—by the written plan and specifications given him by his father. The measurements are reckoned by cubits, "after the first measure," i.e., the old Mosaic standard. But there is great difference of opinion about this, some making the cubit eighteen, others twenty-one inches. The temple, which embodied in more solid and durable materials the ground-form of the tabernacle (only being twice as large), was a rectangular building, seventy cubits long from east to west, and twenty cubits wide from north to south. **4. the porch**—The breadth of the house, whose length ran from east to west, is here given as the measure of the length of the piazza. The portico would thus be from thirty to thirty-five feet long, and from fifteen to seventeen and a half feet broad. **the height was an hundred and twenty cubits**—This, taking the cubit at eighteen inches, would be 180 feet; at twenty-one inches, 210 feet; so that the porch would rise in the form of a tower, or two pyramidal towers, whose united height was 120 cubits, and each of them about 90 or 105 feet high [STIEGLITZ]. This porch would thus be like the propylæum or gateway of the palace of Khorsabad [LAYARD], or at the temple of Edfou. **5. the greater house**—i.e., the holy places, the front or outer chamber (see on I Kings 6:17). **6. he garnished the house with precious stones for beauty**—better, he paved the house with precious and beautiful marble [KITTO]. It may be, after all, that these were stones with veins of different colors for decorating the walls. This was an ancient and thoroughly Oriental kind of embellishment. There was an under pavement of marble, which was covered with planks of fir. The whole interior was lined with boards, richly decorated with carved work, clusters of foliage and flowers, among which the pomegranate and lotus (or water-lily) were conspicuous; and overlaid, excepting the floor, with gold, either by gilding or in plates (I Kings 6).

8-13. DIMENSIONS, ETC., OF THE MOST HOLY HOUSE. **8. the most holy house**—It was a perfect **cube** (cf. I Kings 6:20). **overlaid it with . . . gold, amounting to six hundred talents**—equal to about $16,000,000. **10-13. two cherubim**—These figures in the tabernacle were of pure gold (Exod. 25) and overshadowed the mercy seat. The two placed in the temple were made of olive wood, overlaid with gold. They were of colossal size, like the Assyrian sculptures; for each, with expanded wings, covered a space of ten cubits in height and length—two wings touched each other, while the other two reached the opposite walls; their faces were inward, i.e., towards the most holy house, conformably to their use, which was to veil the ark.

14-17. VEIL AND PILLARS (see on I Kings 6:21). The united height is here given; and though the exact dimensions would be thirty-six cubits, each

column was only seventeen cubits and a half, a half cubit being taken up by the capital or the base. They were probably described as they were lying together in the mould before they were set up [POOLE]. They would be from eighteen to twenty-one feet in circumference, and stand forty feet in height. These pillars, or obelisks, as some call them, were highly ornamented, and formed an entrance in keeping with the splendid interior of the temple.

CHAPTER 4

Vs. 1. ALTAR OF BRASS. **1. he made an altar of brass**—Steps must have been necessary for ascending so elevated an altar, but the use of these could be no longer forbidden (Exod. 20:26) after the introduction of an official costume for the priests (Exod. 28:42). It measured thirty-five feet by thirty-five, and in height seventeen and a half feet. The thickness of the metal used for this altar is nowhere given; but supposing it to have been three inches, the whole weight of the metal would not be under two hundred tons [NAPIER].

2-5. MOLTEN SEA. **2. he made a molten sea**——(See on I Kings 7:23-26), as in that passage "knops" occur instead of "oxen." It is generally supposed that the rows of ornamental knops were in the form of ox heads. **3. Two rows of oxen were cast, when it was cast**—The meaning is, that the circular basin and the brazen oxen which supported it were all of one piece, being cast in one and the same mould. There is a difference in the accounts given of the capacity of this basin, for while in I Kings 7:26 it is said that two thousand baths of water could be contained in it, in this passage no less than three thousand are stated. It has been suggested that there is here a statement not merely of the quantity of water which the basin held, but that also which was necessary to work it, to keep it flowing as a fountain; that which was required to fill both it and its accompaniments. In support of this view, it may be remarked that different words are employed: the one in I Kings 7:26 rendered *contained;* the two here rendered, *received* and *held.* There was a difference between *receiving* and *holding.* When the basin played as a fountain, and all its parts were filled for that purpose, the latter, together with the sea itself, *received* 3000 baths; but the sea exclusively *held* only 2000 baths, when its contents were restricted to those of the circular basin. It received and held 3000 baths [CALMENT'S FRAGMENT].

6-18. THE TEN LAVERS, CANDLESTICKS, AND TABLES. **6. ten lavers**—(See on I Kings 7:27-39). The laver of the tabernacle had probably been destroyed. The ten new ones were placed between the porch and the altar, and while the molten sea was for the priests to cleanse their hands and feet, these were intended for washing the sacrifices. **7. ten candlesticks**—(See on I Kings 7:49). The increased number was not only in conformity with the characteristic splendor of the edifice, but also a standing emblem to the Hebrews, that the growing light of the word was necessary to counteract the growing darkness in the world [LIGHTFOOT]. **11. Huram made**—(See on I Kings 7:40-45).

CHAPTER 5

Vs. 1. THE DEDICATED TREASURES. **1. Solomon brought in all the things that David his father had** dedicated—the immense sums and the store of valuable articles which his father and other generals had reserved and appropriated for the temple (I Chron. 22:14; 26:26).

2-13. BRINGING UP OF THE ARK OF THE COVENANT. **2, 3. Then Solomon assembled . . . in the feast which was in the seventh month**—The feast of the dedication of the temple was on the eighth day of that month. This is related, word for word, the same as in I Kings 8:1-10. **9. there it is unto this day**—i.e., at the time when this history was composed; for after the Babylonish captivity there is no trace of either ark or staves. **11. all the priests that were present . . . did not then wait by course**—The rotation system of weekly service introduced by David was intended for the ordinary duties of the priesthood; on extraordinary occasions, or when more than wonted solemnity attached to them, the priests attended in a body. **12. the Levites which were the singers**—On great and solemn occasions, such as this, a full choir was required, and their station was taken with scrupulous regard to their official parts: the family of Heman occupied the central place, the family of Asaph stood on his right, and that of Jeduthun on his left; the place allotted to the vocal department was a space between the court of Israel and the altar in the east end of the priests' court. **with them an hundred and twenty priests sounding with trumpets**—The trumpet was always used by the priests, and in the divine service it was specially employed in calling the people together during the holy solemnities, and in drawing attention to new and successive parts of the ritual. The number of trumpets used in the divine service could not be less than two (Num. 10:2), and their greatest number never exceeded the precedent set at the dedication of the temple. The station where the priests were sounding with trumpets was apart from that of the other musicians; for while the Levite singers occupied an orchestra east of the altar, the priests stood at the marble table on the southwest of the altar. There both of them stood with their faces to the altar. The manner of blowing the trumpets was, first, by a long plain blast, then by one with breakings and quaverings, and then by a long plain blast again [BROWN'S JEWISH ANTIQUITIES]. **13. the house was filled with a cloud**—(See on I Kings 8:10, 11).

CHAPTER 6

Vss. 1-41. SOLOMON BLESSES THE PEOPLE AND PRAISES GOD. **1. The Lord hath said that he would dwell in the thick darkness**—This introduction to Solomon's address was evidently suggested by the remarkable incident recorded at the close of the last chapter: the phenomenon of a densely opaque and uniformly shaped cloud, descending in a slow and majestic manner and filling the whole area of the temple. He regarded it himself, and directed the people also to regard it, as an undoubted sign and welcome pledge of the divine presence and acceptance of the building reared to His honor and worship. He referred not to any particular declaration of God, but to the cloud having been all along in the national history of Israel the recognized symbol of the divine presence (Exod. 16:10; 24:16; 40:34; Num. 9:15; I Kings 8:10, 11). **13. Solomon had made a brazen scaffold**—a sort of platform. The *Hebrew* term rendered scaffold, being the same as that used to designate the basin, suggests the idea that this throne might bear some resemblance, in

form or structure, to those lavers in the temple, being a sort of round and elevated pulpit, placed in the middle of the court, and in front of the altar of burnt offering. **upon it he stood, and kneeled down upon his knees**—After ascending the brazen scaffold, he assumed those two attitudes in succession, and with different objects in view. He stood while he addressed and blessed the surrounding multitude (vss. 3-11). Afterwards he knelt down and stretched out his hands towards heaven, with his face probably turned towards the altar, while he gave utterance to the beautiful and impressive prayer which is recorded in the remainder of this chapter. It is deserving of notice that there was no seat in this pulpit—for the king either stood or knelt all the time he was in it. It is not improbable that it was surmounted by a canopy, or covered by a veil, to screen the royal speaker from the rays of the sun. **18-21. how much less this house which I have built! Have respect therefore to the prayer of thy servant**—No person who entertains just and exalted views of the spiritual nature of the Divine Being will suppose that he can raise a temple for the habitation of Deity, as a man builds a house for himself. Nearly as improper and inadmissible is the idea that a temple can contribute to enhance the glory of God, as a monument may be raised in honor of a great man. Solomon described the true and proper use of the temple, when he entreated that the Lord "would hearken unto the supplications of His servant and His people Israel, which they should make towards this place." In short, the grand purpose for which the temple was erected was precisely the same as that contemplated by churches—to afford the opportunity and means of public and social worship, according to the ritual of the Mosaic dispensation—to supplicate the divine mercy and favor—to render thanks for past instances of goodness, and offer petitions for future blessings (see on I Kings 8:22-61). This religious design of the temple—the ONE temple in the world—is in fact its standpoint of absorbing interest. **22. If a man sin against his neighbour, and an oath be laid upon him to make him swear, and the oath come before thine altar in this house**, etc.—In cases where the testimony of witnesses could not be obtained and there was no way of settling a difference or dispute between two people but by accepting the oath of the accused, the practice had gradually crept in and had acquired the force of consuetudinary law, for the party to be brought before the altar, where his oath was taken with all due solemnity, together with the imprecation of a curse to fall upon himself if his disavowal should be found untrue. There is an allusion to such a practice in this passage. **38. If they return to thee . . . in the land of their captivity . . . and pray toward their land, which thou gavest unto their fathers**—These words gave rise to the favorite usage of the ancient as well as modern Jews, of turning in prayer toward Jerusalem, in whatever quarter of the world they might be, and of directing their faces toward the temple when in Jerusalem itself or in any part of the holy land (I Kings 8:44). **41. arise, O Lord God, into thy resting place**—These words are not found in the record of this prayer in the First Book of Kings; but they occur in Psalm 132, which is generally believed to have been composed by David, or rather by Solomon, in reference to this occasion. "Arise" is a very suitable expression to be used when the ark was to be removed from the tabernacle in Zion to the temple on Mount Moriah. **into thy resting place**—The temple so called (Isa. 66:1), because it was a fixed and permanent mansion

(Ps. 132:14). **the ark of thy strength**—the abode by which Thy glorious presence is symbolized, and whence Thou dost issue Thine authoritative oracles, and manifest Thy power on behalf of Thy people when they desire and need it. It might well be designated the ark of God's strength, because it was through means of it the mighty miracles were wrought and the brilliant victories were won, that distinguish the early annals of the Hebrew nation. The sight of it inspired the greatest animation in the breasts of His people, while it diffused terror and dismay through the ranks of their enemies (cf. Ps. 78:61). **let thy priests . . . be clothed with salvation** —or with righteousness (Ps. 132:9), i.e., be equipped not only with the pure white linen garments Thou hast appointed for their robe of office, but also adorned with the moral beauties of true holiness, that their person and services may be accepted, both for themselves and all the people. Thus they would be "clothed with salvation," for that is the effect and consequence of a sanctified character. **42. turn not away the face of thine anointed**—i.e., of me, who by Thy promise and appointment have been installed as king and ruler of Israel. The words are equivalent in meaning to this: Do not reject my present petitions; do not send me from Thy throne of grace dejected in countenance and disappointed in heart. **remember the mercies of David thy servant**—i.e., the mercies promised to David, and in consideration of that promise, hear and answer my prayer (cf. Ps. 132:10).

CHAPTER 7

Vss. 1-3. GOD GIVES TESTIMONY TO SOLOMON'S PRAYER; THE PEOPLE WORSHIP. **1. the fire came down from heaven and consumed the burnt offering** —Every act of worship was accompanied by a sacrifice. The preternatural stream of fire kindled the mass of flesh, and was a token of the divine acceptance of Solomon's prayer (see on Lev. 9:24; I Kings 18:38). **the glory of the Lord filled the house** —The cloud, which was the symbol of God's presence and majesty, filled the interior of the temple (Exod. 40:35). **2. the priests could not enter**—Both from awe of the miraculous fire that was burning on the altar and from the dense cloud that enveloped the sanctuary, they were unable for some time to perform their usual functions (see on I Kings 8:10, 11). But afterwards, their courage and confidence being revived, they approached the altar and busied themselves in the offering of an immense number of sacrifices. **3. all the children of Israel . . . bowed themselves with their faces to the ground upon the pavement**—This form of prostration (that of lying on one's knees with the forehead touching the earth), is the manner in which the Hebrews, and Orientals in general, express the most profound sentiments of reverence and humility. The courts of the temple were densely crowded on the occasion, and the immense multitude threw themselves on the ground. What led the Israelites suddenly to assume that prostrate attitude on the occasion referred to, was the spectacle of the symbolical cloud slowly and majestically descending upon the temple, and then entering it.

4-11. SOLOMON'S SACRIFICES. **4. Then the king and all the people offered sacrifices**—Whether the individual worshippers slaughtered their own cattle, or a certain portion of the vast number of the Levitical order in attendance performed that work, as they

sometimes did, in either case the offerings were made through the priests, who presented the blood and the fat upon the altar (see on I Kings 8:62-64). **5. so the king and all the people dedicated the house of God**—The ceremonial of dedication consisted principally in the introduction of the ark into the temple, and in the sacrificial offerings that were made on a scale of magnitude suitable to the extraordinary occasion. All present, the king, the people, and the priests, took part according to their respective stations in the performance of the solemn service. The duty, of course, devolved chiefly on the priests, and hence in proceeding to describe their several departments of work, the historian says, generally, "the priests waited on their offices." While great numbers would be occupied with the preparation and offering of the victims, others sounded with their trumpets, and the different bands of the Levites praised the Lord with vocal and instrumental music, by the 136th Psalm, the oft-recurring chorus of which is, "for His mercy endureth for ever." **7. Solomon hallowed the middle of the court**—On this extraordinary occasion, when a larger number of animals were offered than one altar and the usual place of rings to which the animals were bound would admit, the whole space was taken in that was between the place of rings and the west end of the court to be used as a temporary place for additional altars. On that part of the spacious court holocausts were burning all round. **8. Solomon kept the feast seven days**—The time chosen for the dedication of the temple was immediately previous to the feast of tabernacles (see on I Kings 8:1-12). That season, which came after the harvest, corresponding to our September and October, lasted seven days, and during so prolonged a festival there was time afforded for the offering of the immense sacrifices enumerated. A large proportion of these were peace offerings, which afforded to the people the means of festive enjoyment. **all Israel . . . from the entering in of Hamath**—i.e., the defile at Lebanon. **unto the river of Egypt**—i.e., Rhinocorura, now El-Arish, the south boundary of Palestine. **10. on the three and twentieth day of the seventh month**—This was the last day of the feast of tabernacles.

12-22. GOD APPEARS TO HIM. **12. the Lord appeared to Solomon by night**—(See on I Kings 9:1-9). The dedication of the temple must have been an occasion of intense national interest to Solomon and his subjects. Nor was the interest merely temporary or local. The record of it is read and thought of with an interest that is undiminished by the lapse of time. The fact that this was the only temple of all nations in which the *true God* was worshipped imparts a moral grandeur to the scene and prepares the mind for the sublime prayer that was offered at the dedication. The pure theism of that prayer—its acknowledgment of the unity of God as well as of His moral perfections in providence and grace, came from the same divine source as the miraculous fire. They indicated sentiments and feelings of exalted and spiritual devotion, which sprang not from the unaided mind of man, but from the fountain of revelation. The reality of the divine presence was attested by the miracle, and that miracle stamped the seal of truth upon the theology of the temple worship.

CHAPTER 8

Vss. 1-6. SOLOMON'S BUILDINGS. **2. cities which Huram had restored . . . Solomon built them, etc.**—

These cities lay in the northwest of Galilee. Though included within the limits of the promised land, they had never been conquered. The right of occupying them Solomon granted to Huram, who, after consideration, refused them as unsuitable to the commercial habits of his subjects (see on I Kings 9:11). Solomon, having wrested them from the possession of the Canaanite inhabitants, repaired them and filled them with a colony of Hebrews. **3-6. Solomon went to Hamath-zobah**—Hamath was on the Orontes, in Cæle-Syria. Its king, Toi, had been the ally of David; but from the combination, Hamath and Zobah, it would appear that some revolution had taken place which led to the union of these two petty kingdoms of Syria into one. For what cause the resentment of Solomon was provoked against it, we are not informed, but he sent an armed force which reduced it. He made himself master also of Tadmor, the famous Palmyra in the same regiion. Various other cities along the frontiers of his extended dominions he repaired and fitted up, either to serve as store-places for the furtherance of his commercial enterprises, or to secure his kingdom from foreign invasion (see on ch. 1:14; I Kings 9:15-24).

7-11. The Canaanites Made Tributaries. 7. all the people that were left, etc.—The descendants of the Canaanites who remained in the country were treated as war prisoners, being obliged to "pay tribute or to serve as galley slaves" (ch. 2:18), while the Israelites were employed in no works but such as were of an honorable character. **10. two hundred and fifty that bare rule**—(Cf. I Kings 9:23). It is generally agreed that the text of one of these passages is corrupt. **11. Solomon brought up the daughter of Pharaoh out of the city of David unto the house he had built for her**—On his marriage with the Egyptian princess at the beginning of his reign, he assigned her a temporary abode in the city of David, i.e., Jerusalem, until a suitable palace for his wife had been erected. While that palace was in progress, he himself lodged in the palace of David, but he did not allow her to occupy it, because he felt that she being a heathen proselyte, and having brought from her own country an establishment of heathen maidservants, there would have been an impropriety in her being domiciled in a mansion which was or had been hallowed by the reception of the ark. It seems she was received on her arrival into his mother's abode (Song of Sol. 3:4; 8:2).

15-18. Solomon's Festival Sacrifices. 15. they departed not from the commandment of the king—i.e., David, in any of his ordinances, which by divine authority he established, either in regulating the courses of the priests and Levites, or in the destination of his accumulated treasures to the construction and adornment of the temple. **17. Then went Solomon to Ezion-geber, and to Eloth**—These two maritime ports were situated at the eastern gulf of the Red Sea, now called the Gulf of Akaba. Eloth is seen in the modern Akaba, Ezion-geber in El Gudyan [Robinson]. Solomon, determined to cultivate the arts of peace, was sagacious enough to perceive that his kingdom could become great and glorious only by encouraging a spirit of commercial enterprise among his subjects; and, accordingly, with that in mind he made a contract with Huram for ships and seamen to instruct his people in navigation. **18. Huram sent him . . . ships**—either sent him ship-*men*, able seamen, overland; or, taking the word "sent" in a looser sense, *supplied* him, i.e., *built* him ships—viz., in docks at Eloth (cf. I Kings 9:26, 27). This navy of Solomon was

manned by Tyrians, for Solomon had no seamen capable of performing distant expeditions. The Hebrew fishermen, whose boats plied on the Sea of Tiberias or coasted the shores of the Mediterranean, were not equal to the conducting of large vessels laden with valuable cargoes on long voyages and through the wide and unfrequented ocean. **four hundred and fifty talents of gold**—(Cf. I Kings 9:28). The text in one of these passages is corrupt.

CHAPTER 9

Vss. 1-12. The Queen of Sheba Visits Solomon; She Admires His Wisdom and Magnificence. **1. when the queen of Sheba heard of the fame of Solomon**—(See on I Kings 10:1-13). It is said that among the things in Jerusalem which drew forth the admiration of Solomon's royal visitor was "his ascent by which he went up into the house of the Lord." This was the arched viaduct that crossed the valley from Mount Zion to the opposite hill. In the commentary on the passage quoted above, allusion was made to the recent discovery of its remains. Here we give a full account of what, for boldness of conceptions for structure and magnificence, was one of the greatest wonders in Jerusalem. "During our first visit to the southwest corner of the area of the mosque, we observed several of the large stones jutting out from the western wall, which at first seemed to be the effect of a bursting of the wall from some mighty shock or earthquake. We paid little regard to this at the moment; but on mentioning the fact not long after to a circle of our friends, the remark was incidentally dropped that the stones had the appearance of having once belonged to a large arch. At this remark, a train of thought flashed across my mind, which I hardly dared to follow out until I had again repaired to the spot, in order to satisfy myself with my own eyes as to the truth or falsehood of the suggestion. I found it even so. The courses of these immense stones occupy their original position; their external surface is hewn to a regular curve; and, being fitted one upon another, they form the commencement or foot of an immense arch which once sprung out from this western wall in a direction towards Mount Zion, across the Tyropœon valley. This arch could only have belonged to the bridge, which, according to Josephus, led from this part of the temple to the Xystus (covered colonnade) on Zion; and it proves incontestably the antiquity of that portion from which it springs" [Robinson]. The distance from this point to the steep rock of Zion Robinson calculates to be about three hundred and fifty feet, the probable length of this ancient viaduct. Another writer adds, that "the arch of this bridge, if its curve be calculated with an approximation to the truth, would measure *sixty* feet, and must have been one of five sustaining the viaduct (allowing for the abutments on either side), and that the piers supporting the center arch of this bridge must have been of great altitude—not less, perhaps, than one hundred and thirty feet. The whole structure, when seen from the southern extremity of the Tyropœon, must have had an aspect of grandeur, especially as connected with the lofty and sumptuous edifices of the temple, and of Zion to the right and to the left [Isaac Taylor's Edition of Traill's Josephus].

13-28. His Riches. 13. Now the weight of gold that came to Solomon in one year—(See on I Kings 10:14-29). **six hundred and threescore and

six talents of gold—The sum named is equal to about $17,000,000; and if we take the proportion of silver (vs. 14), which is not taken into consideration, at 1 to 9, there would be about $2,000,000, making a yearly supply of nearly $19,000,000, being a vast amount for an infant effort in maritime commerce [NAPIER]. **21. the king's ships went to Tarshish**—rather, "the king's ships of Tarshish went" with the servants of Huram. **ships of Tarshish**—i.e., in burden and construction like the large vessels built for or used at Tarshish [CALMET'S FRAGMENTS]. **25. Solomon had four thousand stalls**—It has been conjectured [GESENIUS' HEBREW LEXICION] that the original term may signify not only stall or stable, but a number of horses occupying the same number of stalls. Supposing that ten were put together in one part, this would make 40,000. According to this theory of explanation, the historian in Kings refers to horses; while the historian in Chronicles speaks of the stalls in which they were kept. But more recent critics reject this mode of solving the difficulty, and, regarding the four thousand stalls as in keeping with the general magnificence of Solomon's establishments, are agreed in considering the text in Kings as corrupt, through the error of some copyist. **28. they brought unto Solomon horses out of Egypt**—(See on ch. 1:17). Solomon undoubtedly carried the Hebrew kingdom to its highest pitch of worldly glory. His completion of the grand work, the centralizing of the national worship at Jerusalem, whither the natives went up three times a year, has given his name a prominent place in the history of the ancient church. But his reign had a disastrous influence upon "the peculiar people," and the example of his deplorable idolatries, the connections he formed with foreign princes, the commercial speculations he entered into, and the luxuries introduced into the land, seem in a great measure to have altered and deteriorated the Jewish character.

CHAPTER 10

Vss. 1-15. REHOBOAM REFUSING THE OLD MEN'S GOOD COUNSEL. **1. Rehoboam went to Shechem**—(See on I Kings 12:1). This chapter is, with a few verbal alterations, the same as in I Kings. **3. And they sent**—rather, "for they had sent," etc. This is stated as the reason of Jeroboam's return from Egypt. **7. If thou be kind to this people, and please them, and speak good words to them**—In the Book of Kings, the words are, "If thou wilt be a servant unto this people, and wilt serve them." The meaning in both is the same, viz., If thou wilt make some reasonable concessions, redress their grievances, and restore their abridged liberties, thou wilt secure their strong and lasting attachment to thy person and government. **15. the king hearkened not unto the people, for the cause was of God**—Rehoboam, in following an evil counsel, and the Hebrew people, in making a revolutionary movement, each acted as free agents, obeying their own will and passions. But God, who permitted the revolt of the northern tribes, intended it as a punishment of the house of David for Solomon's apostasy. That event demonstrates the immediate superintendence of His providence over the revolutions of kingdoms; and thus it affords an instance, similar to many other striking instances that are found in Scripture, of divine predictions, uttered long before, being accomplished by the operation of human passions, and in the natural course of events.

CHAPTER 11

Vss. 1-17. REHOBOAM, RAISING AN ARMY TO SUBDUE ISRAEL, IS FORBIDDEN BY SHEMAIAH. **1-4. Rehoboam . . . gathered of the house of Judah and Benjamin . . . to fight against Israel**—(See on I Kings 12:21-24). **5. built cities for defence in Judah**—This is evidently used as the name of the southern kingdom. Rehoboam, having now a bitter enemy in Israel, deemed it prudent to lose no time in fortifying several cities that lay along the frontier of his kingdom. Jeroboam, on his side, took a similar precaution (I Kings 12:25). Of the fifteen cities named Aijalon, now Yalo, and Zorah, now Surah, between Jerusalem and Jabneh [ROBINSON], lay within the province of Benjamin. Gath, though a Philistine city, had been subject to Solomon. And Etham, which was on the border of Simeon, now incorporated with the kingdom of Israel, was fortified to repel danger from that quarter. These fortresses Rehoboam placed under able commanders and stocked them with provisions and military stores, sufficient, if necessary, to stand a siege. In the crippled state of his kingdom, he seems to have been afraid lest it might be made the prey of some powerful neighbors. **13-17. the priests and the Levites . . . resorted to him out of all their coasts**—This was an accession of moral power, for the maintenance of the true religion is the best support and safeguard of any nation; and as it was peculiarly the grand source of the strength and prosperity of the Hebrew monarchy, the great numbers of good and pious people who sought an asylum within the territories of Judah contributed greatly to consolidate the throne of Rehoboam. The cause of so extensive an emigration from the kingdom of Israel was the deep and daring policy of Jeroboam, who set himself to break the national unity by entirely abolishing, within his dominions, the religious institutions of Judaism. He dreaded an eventual reunion of the tribes if the people continued to repair thrice a year to worship in Jerusalem as they were obliged by law to do. Accordingly, on pretense that the distance of that city was too great for multitudes of his subjects, he fixed upon two more convenient places, where he established a new mode of worshipping God under gross and prohibited symbols. The priests and Levites, refusing to take part in the idolatrous ceremonies, were ejected from their living. Along with them a large body of the people who faithfully adhered to the instituted worship of God, offended and shocked by the impious innovations, departed from the kingdom. **15. he ordained him priests**—The persons he appointed to the priesthood were low and worthless creatures (I Kings 12:31; 13:33); any were consecrated who brought a bullock and seven rams (Ch. 13:9; Exod. 29:37). **for the high places**—Those favorite places of religious worship were encouraged throughout the country. **for the devils**—a term sometimes used for idols in general (Lev. 17:7). But here it is applied distinctively to the goat deities, which were probably worshipped chiefly in the northern parts of his kingdom, where the heathen Canaanites still abounded. **and for the calves**—figures of the ox gods Apis and Mnevis, with which Jeroboam's residence in Egypt had familiarized him. (See on I Kings 12:26-33.) **17. they strengthened the kingdom of Judah**—The innovating measures of Jeroboam were not introduced all at once. But as they were developed, the secession of the most excellent of his subjects began, and continuing to increase for three years, lowered the tone of religion in his kingdom, while it proportionally quickened its life and extended its influence in that of Judah.

18-23. HIS WIVES AND CHILDREN. **18. Rehoboam took Mahalath**—The names of her father and mother are given. Jerimoth, the father, must have been the son of one of David's concubines (I Chron. 3:9.) Abihail was, of course, his cousin, previous to their marriage. **20. after her he took Maachah ... daughter**—i.e., granddaughter (II Sam. 14:27) of Absalom, Tamar being, according to Josephus, her mother. (Cf. II Sam. 18:18.) **21. he took eighteen wives, and threescore concubines**—This royal harem, though far smaller than his father's, was equally in violation of the law, which forbade a king to "multiply wives unto himself." **22. made Abijah ... chief ... ruler among his brethren**—This preference seems to have been given to Abijah solely from the king's doting fondness for his mother and through her influence over him. It is plainly implied that Abijah was not the oldest of the family. In destining a younger son for the kingdom, without a divine warrant, as in Solomon's case, Rehoboam acted in violation of the law (Deut. 21:15). **23. he dealt wisely**—i.e., with deep and calculating policy (Exod. 1:10). **and dispersed of all his children ... unto every fenced city**—The circumstance of twenty-eight sons of the king being made governors of fortresses would, in our quarter of the world, produce jealousy and dissatisfaction. But Eastern monarchs ensure peace and tranquillity to their kingdom by bestowing government offices on their sons and grandsons. They obtain an independent provision, and being kept apart, are not likely to cabal in their father's lifetime. Rehoboam acted thus, and his sagacity will appear still greater if the wives he desired for them belonged to the cities where each son was located. These connections would bind them more closely to their respective places. In the modern countries of the East, particularly Persia and Turkey, younger princes were, till very lately, shut up in the harem during their father's lifetime; and, to prevent competition, they were blinded or killed when their brother ascended the throne. In the former country the old practice of dispersing them through the country as Rehoboam did, has been again revived.

CHAPTER 12

Vss. 1-12. REHOBOAM, FORSAKING GOD, IS PUNISHED BY SHISHAK. **1. when Rehoboam had established the kingdom, and had strengthened himself**—(See on ch. 11:17). During the first three years of his reign his royal influence was exerted in the encouragement of the true religion. Security and ease led to religious decline, which, in the fourth year, ended in open apostasy. The example of the court was speedily followed by his subjects, for "all Israel was with him," i.e., the people in his own kingdom. The very next year, the fifth of his reign, punishment was inflicted by the invasion of Shishak. **2. Shishak king of Egypt came up against Jerusalem**—He was the first king of the twenty-second or Bubastic Dynasty. What was the immediate cause of this invasion? Whether it was in resentment for some provocation from the king of Judah, or in pursuance of ambitious views of conquest, is not said. But the invading army was a vast horde, for Shishak brought along with his native Egyptians an immense number of foreign auxiliaries. **3. the Lubims**—the Libyans of northeastern Africa. **the**

Sukkiims—Some think these were the Kenite Arabs, dwellers in tents, but others maintain more justly that these were Arab troglodytes, who inhabited the caverns of a mountain range on the western coast of the Red Sea. **the Ethiopians**—from the regions south of Egypt. By the overwhelming force of numbers, they took the fortresses of Judah which had been recently put in a state of defense, and marched to lay siege to the capital. While Shishak and his army was before Jerusalem, the prophet Shemaiah addressed Rehoboam and the princes, tracing this calamity to the national apostasy and threatening them with utter destruction in consequence of having forsaken God (vs. 6). **6. the princes of Israel**—(cf. vs. 5, "the princes of Judah"). **7, 8. when the Lord saw that they humbled themselves**—Their repentance and contrition was followed by the best effects; for Shemaiah was commissioned to announce that the phial of divine judgment would not be fully poured out on them—that the entire overthrow of the kingdom of Judah would not take place at that time, nor through the agency of Shishak; and yet, although it should enjoy a respite from total subversion, it should become a tributary province of Egypt in order that the people might learn how much lighter and better is the service of God than that of idolatrous foreign despots. **9. So Shishak ... came up against Jerusalem**—After the parenthetical clause (vss. 5-8) describing the feelings and state of the beleaguered court, the historian resumes his narrative of the attack upon Jerusalem, and the consequent pillage both of the temple and the palace. **he took all**—i.e., everything valuable he found. The cost of the targets and shields has been estimated as about $1,200,000 [NAPIER'S METAL]. **the shields of gold**—(ch. 9:16) made by Solomon, were kept in the house of the forest of Lebanon (ch. 9:16). They seem to have been borne, like maces, by the guards of the palace, when they attended the king to the temple or on other public processions. Those splendid insignia having been plundered by the Egyptian conqueror, others were made of inferior metal and kept in the guardroom of the palace, to be ready for use; as, notwithstanding the tarnished glory of the court, the old state etiquette was kept up on public and solemn occasions. An account of this conquest of Judah, with the name of "king of Judah" in the cartouche of the principal captive, according to the interpreters, is carved and written in hieroglyphics on the walls of the great palace of Karnak, where it may be seen at the present day. This sculpture is about 2700 years old, and is of peculiar interest as a striking testimony from Egypt to the truth of Scripture history. **12. when he humbled himself, the wrath of the Lord turned from him**—The promise (vs. 7) was verified. Divine providence preserved the kingdom in existence, a reformation was made in the court, while true religion and piety were diffused throughout the land.

13-16. HIS REIGN AND DEATH. **13. Rehoboam strengthened himself ... and reigned**—The Egyptian invasion had been a mere predatory expedition, not extending beyond the limits of Judah, and probably, erelong, repelled by the invaded. Rehoboam's government acquired new life and vigor by the general revival of true religion, and his reign continued many years after the departure of Shishak. But "he prepared not his heart to seek the Lord," i.e., he did not adhere firmly to the good course of reformation he had begun, "and he did evil," for through the unhappy influence of his mother, a heathen foreigner, he had no doubt received in his youth a strong bias towards idolatry (see on I Kings 14:21-24).

CHAPTER 13

Vss. 1-20. Abijah, Succeeding, Makes War against Jeroboam, and Overcomes Him. **2. His mother's name also was Michaiah, the daughter of Uriel of Gibeah**—the same as Maachah (see on I Kings 15:2). She was "the daughter," i.e., granddaughter of Absalom (I Kings 15:2; cf. II Sam. 14), mother of Abijah, "mother," i.e., grandmother (I Kings 15:10, *marg.*) of Asa. **of Gibeah** probably implies that Uriel was connected with the house of Saul. **there was war between Abijah and Jeroboam**—The occasion of this war is not recorded (see I Kings 15:6, 7), but it may be inferred from the tenor of Abijah's address that it arose from his youthful ambition to recover the full hereditary dominion of his ancestors. No prophet now forbade a war with Israel (ch. 11:23) for Jeroboam had forfeited all claim to protection. **3. Abijah set the battle in array**—i.e., took the field and opened the campaign. **Abijah set the battle in array with ... four hundred thousand chosen men ... Jeroboam with eight hundred thousand**—These are, doubtless, large numbers, considering the smallness of the two kingdoms. It must be borne in mind, however, that Oriental armies are mere mobs—vast numbers accompanying the camp in hope of plunder, so that the gross numbers described as going upon an Asiatic expedition are often far from denoting the exact number of fighting men. But in accounting for the large number of soldiers enlisted in the respective armies of Abijah and Jeroboam, there is no need of resorting to this mode of explanation; for we know by the census of David the immense number of the population that was capable of bearing arms (I Chron. 21:5; cf. ch. 14:8; 17:14). **4-12. Abijah stood up upon Mount Zemaraim**—He had entered the enemy's territory and was encamped on an eminence near Beth-el (Josh. 18:22). Jeroboam's army lay at the foot of the hill, and as a pitched battle was expected, Abijah, according to the singular usage of ancient times, harangued the enemy. The speakers in such circumstances, while always extolling their own merits, poured out torrents of invective and virulent abuse upon the adversary. So did Abijah. He dwelt on the divine right of the house of David to the throne; and sinking all reference to the heaven-condemned offenses of Solomon and the divine appointment of Jeroboam, as well as the divine sanction of the separation, he upbraided Jeroboam as a usurper, and his subjects as rebels, who took advantage of the youth and inexperience of Rehoboam. Then contrasting the religious state of the two kingdoms, he drew a black picture of the impious innovations and gross idolatry introduced by Jeroboam, with his expulsion and impoverishment (ch. 11:14) of the Levites. He dwelt with reasonable pride on the pure and regular observance of the ancient institutions of Moses in his own dominion and concluded with this emphatic appeal: "O children of Israel, fight ye not against Jehovah, the God of your fathers, for ye shall not prosper." **13-17. But Jeroboam caused an ambushment to come about behind them**—The oration of Abijah, however animating an effect it might have produced on his own troops, was unheeded by the party to whom it was addressed; for while he was wasting time in useless words, Jeroboam had or-

dered a detachment of his men to move quietly round the base of the hill, so that when Abijah stopped speaking, he and his followers found themselves surprised in the rear, while the main body of the Israelitish forces remained in front. A panic might have ensued, had not the leaders "cried unto the Lord," and the priests "sounded with the trumpets"—the pledge of victory (Num. 10:9; 31:6). Reassured by the well-known signal, the men of Judah responded with a war shout, which, echoed by the whole army, was followed by an impetuous rush against the foe. The shock was resistless. The ranks of the Israelites were broken, for "God smote Jeroboam and all Israel." They took to flight, and the merciless slaughter that ensued can be accounted for only by tracing it to the rancorous passions enkindled by a civil war. **19. Abijah pursued after Jeroboam**—This sanguinary action widened the breach between the people of the two kingdoms. Abijah abandoned his original design of attempting the subjugation of the ten tribes, contenting himself with the recovery of a few border towns, which, though lying within Judah or Benjamin, had been alienated to the new or northern kingdom. Among these was Beth-el, which, with its sacred associations, he might be strongly desirous to wrest from profanation. **20. Neither did Jeroboam recover strength again in the days of Abijah**—The disastrous action at Zemaraim, which caused the loss of the flower and chivalry of his army, broke his spirits and crippled his power. **the Lord struck him, and he died**—i.e., Jeroboam. He lived, indeed, two years after the death of Abijah (I Kings 14:20; 15:9). But he had been threatened with great calamities upon himself and his house, and it is apparently to the execution of these threatenings, which issued in his death, that an anticipatory reference is here made.

CHAPTER 14

Vss. 1-5. Asa Destroys Idolatry. **1. In his days the land was quiet ten years**—This long interval of peace was the continued effect of the great battle of Zemaraim (cf. I Kings 15:11-14). **2. Asa did that which was good and right**—(cf. I Kings 15:14). Still his character and life were not free from faults (ch. 16:7, 10, 12). **3. brake down the images**—of Baal (see on ch. 34:4; Lev. 26:30). **cut down the groves**—rather, Asherim. **5. he took away ... the high places**—i.e., those devoted to idolatrous rites. **took away out of all the cities of Judah the high places and the images**—All public objects and relics of idolatry in Jerusalem and other cities through his kingdom were destroyed; but those high places where God was worshipped under the figure of an ox, as at Beth-el, were allowed to remain (I Kings 15:14); so far the reformation was incomplete.

6-8. Having Peace, He Strengthens His Kingdom with Forts and Armies. 6. he built fenced cities in Judah—(See on I Kings 15:22). **7. while the land is yet before us**—i.e., while we have free and undisputed progress everywhere; no foe is near; but, as this happy time of peace may not last always and the kingdom is but small and weak, let us prepare suitable defenses in case of need. He had also an army of 580,000 men. Judah furnished the heavily armed soldiers, and Benjamin the archers. This large number does not mean a body of professional soldiers but all capable of bearing arms and liable to be called into service.

9-15. He Overcomes Zerah, and Spoils the Ethiopians. **9. there came out against them Zerah the Ethiopian**—This could not have been from Ethiopia south of the cataracts of the Nile, for in the reign of Osorkon I., successor of Shishak, no foreign army would have been allowed a free passage through Egypt. Zerah must, therefore, have been chief of the Cushites, or Ethiopians of Arabia, as they were evidently a nomad horde who had a settlement of tents and cattle in the neighborhood of Gerar. **a thousand thousand, and three hundred chariots**—"Twenty camels employed to carry couriers upon them might have procured that number of men to meet in a short time. As Zerah was the aggressor, he had time to choose when he would summon these men and attack the enemy. Every one of these Cushite shepherds, carrying with them their own provisions of flour and water, as is their invariable custom, might have fought with Asa without eating a loaf of Zerah's bread or drinking a pint of his water" [Bruce's Travels]. **10. Asa went out against him, and they set the battle in array . . . at Mareshah**—one of the towns which Rehoboam fortified (ch. 11:8), near a great southern pass in the low country of Judah (Josh. 15:44). The engagement between the armies took place in a plain near the town, called "the valley of Zephathah," supposed to be the broad way coming down Beit Jibrin towards Tell Es-Safren [Robinson]. **11-13. Asa cried unto the Lord his God**—Strong in the confidence that the power of God was able to give the victory equally with few as with many, the pious king marched with a comparatively small force to encounter the formidable host of marauders at his southern frontier. Committing his cause to God, **he engaged** in the conflict—completely routed the enemy, and succeeded in obtaining, as the reward of his victory, a rich booty in treasure and cattle from the tents of this pastoral horde.

CHAPTER 15

Vss. 1-15. Judah Makes a Solemn Covenant with God. **1. Azariah the son of Oded**—This prophet, who is mentioned nowhere else, appears at this stage of the sacred story in the discharge of an interesting mission. He went to meet Asa, as he was returning from his victorious pursuit of the Ethiopians, and the congratulatory address here recorded was publicly made to the king in presence of his army. **2. The Lord is with you, while ye be with him**—You have had, in your recent signal success, a remarkable proof that God's blessing is upon you; your victory has been the reward of your faith and piety. If you steadfastly adhere to the cause of God, you may expect a continuance of His favor; but if you abandon it, you will soon reap the bitter fruits of apostasy. **3-6. Now for a long season Israel hath been without the true God,** etc.—Some think that Azariah was referring to the sad and disastrous condition to which superstition and idolatry had brought the neighboring kingdom of Israel. His words should rather be taken in a wider sense, for it seems manifest that the prophet had his eye upon many periods in the national history, when the people were in the state described—a state of spiritual destitution and ignorance—and exhibited its natural result as widespread anarchy, mutual dissension among the tribes, and general suffering (Judg. 9:23; 12:4; 20:21; II Chron. 13:17). These calamities God permitted to befall them as the punishment of their apostasy. Azariah's object in

these remarks was to establish the truth of his counsel (vs. 2), threatening, in case of neglecting it by describing the uniform course of the divine procedure towards Israel, as shown in all periods of their history. Then after this appeal to national experience, he concluded with an earnest exhortation to the king to prosecute the work of reformation so well begun. **7. Be ye strong**—Great resolution and indomitable energy would be required to persevere in the face of the opposition your reforming measures will encounter. **your work shall be rewarded**—What you do in the cause and for the glory of God will assuredly be followed by the happiest results both to yourself and your subjects. **8. when Asa heard . . . the prophecy of Oded the prophet**—The insertion of these words, "of Oded the prophet," is generally regarded as a corruption of the text. "The sole remedy is to erase them. They are, probably, the remains of a note, which crept in from the margin into the text" [Bertheau]. **he took courage**—Animated by the seasonable and pious address of Azariah, Asa became a more zealous reformer than ever, employing all his royal authority and influence to extirpate every vestige of idolatry from the land. **and out of the cities which he had taken from Mount Ephraim**—He may have acquired cities of Ephraim, the conquest of which is not recorded (ch. 17:2); but it has been commonly supposed that the reference is to cities which his father Abijah had taken in that quarter (ch. 13:19). **renewed the altar of the Lord . . . before the porch**—i.e., the altar of burnt offering. As this was done on or about the fifteenth year of the reign of this pious king, the renewal must have consisted in some splendid repairs or embellishments, which made it look like a new dedication, or in a reconstruction of a temporary altar, like that of Solomon (ch. 7:7), for extraordinary sacrifices to be offered on an approaching occasion. **9-15. he gathered all Judah and Benjamin**—Not satisfied with these minor measures of purification and improvement, Asa meditated a grand scheme which was to pledge his whole kingdom to complete the work of reformation, and with this in view he waited for a general assembly of the people. **and the strangers with them out of Ephraim and Manasseh**—The population of Asa's kingdom had been vastly increased by the continued influx of strangers, who, prompted by motives either of interest or of piety, sought in his dominions that security and freedom which they could not enjoy amid the complicated troubles which distracted Israel. **and out of Simeon**—Although a portion of that tribe, located within the territory of Judah, were already subjects of the southern kingdom, the general body of the Simeonites had joined in forming the northern kingdom of Israel. But many of them now returned of their own accord. **10. the third month**—when was held the feast of pentecost. On this occasion, it was celebrated at Jerusalem by an extraordinary sacrifice of 700 oxen and 7000 sheep, the spoil of the Ethiopians being offered. The assembled worshippers entered with great and holy enthusiasm into a national covenant "to seek the Lord God . . . with all their heart and with all their soul"; and, at the same time, to execute with rigor the laws which made idolatry punishable with death (Deut. 17:2-5; Heb. 10:28). The people testified unbounded satisfaction with this important religious movement, and its moral influence was seen in the promotion of piety, order, and tranquillity throughout the land. **18. the things which his father had dedicated**—probably part of the booty obtained by his signal victory over Jeroboam, but which, though dedicated, had hitherto been unrepresented. **and that he himself had dedicated**—of the booty taken from the Ethiopians. Both of these were now deposited in the temple as votive offerings to Him whose right hand and holy arm had given them the victory.

CHAPTER 16

Vss. 1-14. Asa, by a League with the Syrians, Diverts Baasha from Building Ramah. **1-6. In the six and thirtieth year of the reign of Asa, Baasha . . . came up**—Baasha had died several years before this date (I Kings 15:33), and the best biblical critics are agreed in considering this date to be calculated from the separation of the kingdoms, and coincident with the sixteenth year of Asa's reign. This mode of reckoning was, in all likelihood, generally followed in the book of the kings of Judah and Israel, the public annals of the time (vs. 11), the source from which the inspired historian drew his account. **Baasha . . . built Ramah**—i.e., fortified it. The blessing of God which manifestly rested at this time on the kingdom of Judah, the signal victory of Asa, the freedom and purity of religious worship, and the fame of the late national covenant, were regarded with great interest throughout Israel, and attracted a constantly increasing number of emigrants to Judah. Baasha, alarmed at this movement, determined to stem the tide; and as the high road to and from Jerusalem passed by Ramah, he made that frontier town, about six miles north of Asa's capital, a military station, where the vigilance of his sentinels would effectually prevent all passage across the boundary of the kingdom (see on I Kings 15:16-22; also Jer. 41:9). **4. Ben-hadad . . . sent the captains of his armies . . . and they smote . . . Abel-maim**—"The meadow of waters," supposed to have been situated on the marshy plain near the uppermost lake of the Jordan. The other two towns were also in the northern district of Palestine. These unexpected hostilities of his Syrian ally interrupted Baasha's fortifications at Ramah, and his death, happening soon after, prevented his resuming them. **7-10. Hanani the seer came to Asa . . . and said**—His object was to show the king his error in forming his recent league with Ben-hadad. The prophet represented the appropriation of the temple treasures to purchase the services of the Syrian mercenaries, as indicating a distrust in God most blameable with the king's experience. He added, that in consequence of this want of faith, Asa had lost the opportunity of gaining a victory over the united forces of Baasha and Benhadad, more splendid than that obtained over the Ethiopians. Such a victory, by destroying their armies, would have deprived them of all power to molest him in the future; whereas by his foolish and worldly policy, so unworthy of God's vicegerent, to misapply the temple treasures and corrupt the fidelity of an ally of the king of Israel, he had tempted the cupidity of the one, and increased the hostility of the other, and rendered himself liable to renewed troubles (I Kings 15:32). This rebuke was pungent and, from its truth and justness, ought to have penetrated and afflicted the heart of such a man as Asa. But his pride was offended at the freedom taken by the honest reprover of royalty, and in a burst of passionate resentment, he ordered Hanani to be thrown into prison. **10. Asa oppressed some of the people the same time**—The form or degree of this oppression is not recorded. The cause of his oppressing them was probably due to the same offense as that of Hanani—a strong expression of their dissatisfaction with his conduct in leaguing with Ben-hadad, or it may have been his maltreatment of the Lord's servant. **12. Asa . . . was diseased in his feet**—probably the gout. **his disease was exceeding great**—better, "moved upwards" in his body, which proves the violent and dangerous type of the malady. **yet in his disease he sought not to the Lord, but to the physicians**—most probably Egyptian physicians, who were anciently in high repute at foreign courts, and who pretended to expel diseases by charms, incantations, and mystic arts. Asa's fault consisted in his trusting to such physicians, while he neglected to supplicate the aid and blessing of God. The best and holiest men have been betrayed for a time into sins, but through repentance have risen again; and as Asa is pronounced a good man (ch. 15:17), it may be presumed that he also was restored to a better state of mind. **14. they buried him in his own sepulchre**—The tombs in the neighborhood of Jerusalem were excavated in the side of a rock. One cave contained several tombs or sepulchers. **laid him in the bed . . . filled with sweet odours and divers kinds of spices**—It is evident that a sumptuous public funeral was given him as a tribute of respect and gratitude for his pious character and patriotic government. But whether "the bed" means a state couch on which he lay exposed to public view, the odoriferous perfumes being designed to neutralize the offensive smell of the corpse, or whether it refers to an embalmment, in which aromatic spices were always used in great profusion, it is impossible to say. **they made a very great burning for him**—according to some, for consuming the spices. According to others, it was a magnificent pile for the cremation of the corpse—a usage which was at that time, and long after, prevalent among the Hebrews, and the omission of which in the case of royal personages was reckoned a great indignity (ch. 21:19; I Sam. 31:12; Jer. 34:5; Amos 6:10).

CHAPTER 17

Vss. 1-6. Jehoshaphat Reigns Well and Prospers. **1. Jehoshaphat . . . strengthened himself against Israel**—The temper and proceedings of the kings of Israel rendered it necessary for him to prepare vigorous measures of defense on the northern frontier of his kingdom. These consisted in filling all the fortresses with their full complement of troops and establishing military stations in various parts of the country, as well as in the cities of Mount Ephraim, which belonged to Jehoshaphat (ch. 15:8). **3-5. he walked in the first ways of his father David**—He imitated the piety of his great ancestor in the early part of his reign before he made those unhappy lapses which dishonored his character. **and sought not unto Baalim**—a term used for idols generally in contradistinction to the Lord God of his father. **and not after the doings of Israel**—He observed with scrupulous fidelity, and employed his royal influence to support the divine institutions as enacted by Moses, abhorring that spurious and unlawful calf-worship that now formed the established religion in Israel. Being thus far removed, alike from gross idolatry and Israelitish apostasy, and adhering zealously to the requirements of the divine law, the blessing of God rested on his government. Ruling in the fear of God, and for the good of his subjects,

"the Lord established the kingdom in his hand."
all Judah brought ... presents—This was customary
with the people generally at the beginning of a reign
(I Sam. 10:27), and with the nobles and high functionaries yearly afterwards. They were given in
the form of voluntary offerings, to avoid the odious
idea of a tax or tribute. **6. his heart was lifted up in
the ways of the Lord**—Full of faith and piety, he
possessed zeal and courage to undertake the reformation of manners, to suppress all the works and
objects of idolatry (see on ch. 20:33), and he held
out public encouragement to the pure worship of
God.
7-11. He Sends Levites to Teach in Judah.
**7-11. Also in the third year of his reign he sent to
his princes, ... to teach in the cities of Judah**—The
ordinary work of teaching devolved on the priests.
But extraordinary commissioners were appointed,
probably to ascertain whether the work had been
done or neglected. This deputation of five princes,
assisted by two priests and nine Levites, was to make
a circuit of the towns in Judah. It is the first practical measure we read of as being adopted by any
of the kings for the religious instruction of the
people. Time and unbroken opportunities were
afforded for carrying out fully this excellent plan of
home education, for the kingdom enjoyed internal
tranquillity as well as freedom for foreign wars.
It is conformable to the pious style of the sacred
historian to trace this profound peace to the "fear of
the Lord having fallen on all kingdoms of the lands
that were round about Judah." **the book of the
law**—i.e., either the whole Pentateuch or only the
book of Deuteronomy, which contains an abridg-
ment of it. **11. Also some of the Philistines brought
Jehoshaphat presents, and tribute silver**—either they
had been his tributaries, or they were desirous of
securing his valuable friendship, and now made a
voluntary offer of tribute. Perhaps they were the
Philistines who had submitted to the yoke of David
(II Sam. 8:1; Ps. 60:8). **the Arabians**—the nomad
tribes on the south of the Dead Sea, who, seeking
the protection of Jehoshaphat after his conquest of
Edom, paid their tribute in the way most suitable
to their pastoral habits—the present of so many
head of cattle.
12-19. His Greatness, Captains, and Armies.
14. these are the numbers—The warriors were arranged in the army according to their fathers'
houses. The army of Jehoshaphat, commanded by
five great generals and consisting of five unequal
divisions, comprised one million one hundred and
sixty thousand men, without including those who
garrisoned the fortresses. No monarch, since the
time of Solomon, equalled Jehoshaphat in the extent
of his revenue, in the strength of his fortifications,
and in the number of his troops.

CHAPTER 18

Vss. 1-34. Jehoshaphat and Ahab Go against
Ramoth-Gilead. **2. after certain years he went
down to Ahab to Samaria**—This is word for word,
the same as I Kings 22. (See commentary on that
chapter.)

CHAPTER 19

Vss. 1-4. Jehoshaphat Visits His Kingdom. **1.
Jehoshaphat ... returned to his house in peace**—
(See on ch. 18:16). Not long after he had resumed
the ordinary functions of royalty in Jerusalem, he

was one day disturbed by an unexpected and
ominous visit from a prophet of the Lord. This
was Jehu, of whose father we read in ch. 16:7. He
himself had been called to discharge the prophetic
office in Israel. But probably for his bold rebuke
to Baasha (I Kings 16:1), he had been driven by that
arbitrary monarch within the territory of Judah,
where we now find him with the privileged license of
his order, taking the same religious supervision of
Jehoshaphat's proceedings as he had formerly done
of Baasha's. At the interview here described, he
condemned, in the strongest terms, the king of Judah's imprudent and incongruous league with Ahab
—God's open enemy (I Kings 22:2)—as an unholy
alliance that would be conducive neither to the
honor and comfort of his house nor to the best interests of his kingdom. He apprised Jehoshaphat
that, on account of that grave offense, "wrath was
upon him from before the Lord," a judgment that
was inflicted soon after (see on ch. 20). The
prophet's rebuke, however, was administered in a
mingled strain of severity and mildness; for he interposed "a nevertheless" (vs. 3), which implied that
the threatened storm would be averted, in token of
the divine approval of his public efforts for the promotion of the true religion, as well as of the sincere
piety of his personal character and life. **4. he went
out again through the people**—This means his re-
appointing the commissioners of public instruction
(ch. 17:7-9), perhaps with new powers and a larger
staff of assistants to overtake every part of the land.
The complement of teachers required for that purpose would be easily obtained because the whole
tribe of Levites was now concentrated within the
kingdom of Judah.
5-7. His Instructions to the Judges. **5-7. he
set judges in the land**—There had been judicial
courts established at an early period. But Jehoshaphat was the first king who modified these institutions according to the circumstances of the now
fragmentary kingdom of Judah. He fixed local
courts in each of the fortified cities, these being the
provincial capitals of every district (see on Deut. 16:
18-20).
8-11. To the Priests and Levites. **8. set of
the Levites ... priests, and of the chief of the fathers
of Israel**—A certain number of these three classes
constituted a supreme court, which sat in Jerusalem
to review appellate cases from the inferior courts.
It consisted of two divisions: the first of which had
jurisdiction in ecclesiastical matters; the second, in
civil, fiscal, and criminal cases. According to
others, the two divisions of the supreme court ad-
judicated: the one according to the law contained in
the sacred books; the other according to the law
of custom and equity. As in Eastern countries at
the present day, the written and unwritten law are
objects of separate jurisdiction.

CHAPTER 20

Vss. 1-21. Jehoshaphat, Invaded by the Moabites, Proclaims a Fast. **1. the children of
Moab ... Ammon, and with them other beside the
Ammonites**—supposed to be rather the name of a
certain people called Mohammonim or Mehunim
(ch. 26:7), who dwelt in Mount Seir—either a branch
of the old Edomite race or a separate tribe who were
settled there. **2. from beyond the sea, on this side
Syria**—Instead of Syria, some versions read "Edom,"
and many able critics prefer this reading, both because the nomad tribes here mentioned were far

from Syria, and because express mention is made of Mount Seir, i.e., Edom. The meaning then is: this confederate horde was composed of the different tribes that inhabited the far distant regions bordering on the northern and eastern coasts of the Red Sea. Their progress was apparently by the southern point of the Dead Sea, as far as En-gedi, which, more anciently, was called Hazezon-tamar (Gen. 14:7). This is the uniform route taken by the Arabs in their marauding expeditions at the present day; and in coming round the southern end of the Dead Sea, they can penetrate along the low-lying Ghor far north, without letting their movements be known to the tribes and villages west of the mountain chain [ROBINSON]. Thus, anciently, the invading horde in Jehoshaphat's time had marched as far north as En-gedi, before intelligence of their advance was conveyed to the court. En-gedi is recognized in the modern Ainjidy and is situated at a point of the western shore, nearly equidistant from both extremities of the lake [ROBINSON]. **3, 4. Jehoshaphat ... proclaimed a fast throughout all Judah**— Alarmed by the intelligence and conscious of his total inability to repel this host of invaders, Jehoshaphat felt his only refuge was at the horns of the altar. He resolved to employ the aid of his God, and, in conformity with this resolution, he summoned all his subjects to observe a solemn fast at the sanctuary. It was customary with the Hebrew kings to proclaim fasts in perilous circumstances, either in a city, a district, or throughout the entire kingdom, according to the greatness of the emergency. On this occasion, it was a universal fast, which extended to infants (vs. 13; see also Joel 2:15, 16; Jonah 3:7). **5-13. Jehoshaphat stood ... in the house of the Lord, before the new court**—i.e., the great or outer court (ch. 4:9) called the new court, probably from having been at that time enlarged or beautified. **6. And said, O Lord God of our fathers**—This earnest and impressive prayer embraces every topic and argument which, as king and representative of the chosen people, he could urge. Then it concludes with an earnest appeal to the justice of God to protect those who, without provocation, were attacked and who were unable to defend themselves against overwhelming numbers. **14-18. Then upon Jahaziel ... came the Spirit of the Lord**—This prophet is not elsewhere mentioned, but his claim to the inspiration of a prophetic spirit was verified by the calm and distinct announcement he gave, both of the manner and the completeness of the deliverance he predicted. **16. they come up by the cliff of Ziz**—This seems to have been nothing else than the present pass which leads northwards, by an ascent from En-gedi to Jerusalem, issuing a little below Tekoa. The wilderness of Jeruel was probably the large flat district adjoining the desert of Tekoa, called el-Husasah, from a wady on its northern side [ROBINSON]. **18. Jehoshaphat bowed his head ... and all Judah, ...** —This attitude was expressive of reverence to God and His Word, of confidence in His promise, and thankfulness for so extraordinary a favor. **19. the Levites ... stood up to praise the Lord**—doubtless by the king's command. Their anthem was sung with such a joyful acclaim as showed that they universally regarded the victory as already obtained. **20, 21. as they went forth, Jehoshaphat stood ... Hear me, O Judah, and ye inhabitants of Jerusalem**—probably in the gate of Jerusalem, the place of general rendezvous; and as the people were on the eve of setting out, he exhorted them to repose implicit trust in the Lord and His prophet, not to be timid or desponding at sight

of the enemy, but to remain firm in the confident assurance of a miraculous deliverance, without their striking a single stroke. **he appointed singers ... that they should praise ... as they went out before the army**—Having arranged the line of procession, he gave the signal to move forwards. The Levites led the van with their musical instruments; and singing the 136th Psalm, the people went on, not as an army marching against an enemy, but returning in joyful triumph after a victory. **22-30. THE OVERTHROW OF HIS ENEMIES. 22. when they began to sing and to praise, the Lord set ambushments against the children of Ammon, Moab, and Mount Seir**—Some think that this was done by angels in human form, whose sudden appearance diffused an uncontrollable panic. Others entertain the more probable opinion that, in the camp of this vast horde, composed of different tribes, jealousies and animosities had sprung up, which led to widespread dissensions and fierce feuds, in which they drew the sword against each other. The consequence was, that as the mutual strife commenced when the Hebrew procession set out from Jerusalem, the work of destruction was completed before Jehoshaphat and his people arrived at the battlefield. Thus easy is it for God to make the wrath of man to praise Him, to confound the counsels of His enemies and employ their own passions in defeating the machinations they have devised for the overthrow of His Church and people. **24. when Judah came to the watchtower in the wilderness**—Most probably the conical hill, Jebel Fereidis, or Frank Mountain, from the summit of which they obtained the first view of the scene of slaughter. Jehoshaphat and his people found the field strewed with dead bodies, so that they had not to fight at all, but rather to take possession of an immense booty, the collection of which occupied three days. On the fourth they set out on their return to Jerusalem in the same order and joyful mood as they came. The place where they mustered previous to departure was, from their public thanksgiving service, called, "The Valley of Berachah" (benediction), now Wady Bereikut. **31-37. HIS REIGN. 31. Jehoshaphat reigned over Judah**—(See ch. 24:1). **32. he walked in the way of Asa his father, and departed not from it**— He was more steadfast and consistently religious (cf. ch. 15:18). **33. the high places were not taken away** —Those on which idolatry was practised were entirely destroyed (ch. 17:6); but those where the people, notwithstanding the erection of the temple, continued to worship the true God, prudence required to be slowly and gradually abolished, in deference to popular prejudice. **35-37. after this did Jehoshaphat ... join himself with Ahaziah ... to make ships**—A combined fleet was built at Eziongeber, the destination of which was to voyage to Tartessus, but it was wrecked. Jehoshaphat's motive for entering into this partnership was to secure a free passage through Israel, for the vessels were to be conveyed across the Isthmus of Suez, and to sail to the west of Europe from one of the ports of Palestine on the Mediterranean. Eliezar, a prophet, denounced this unholy alliance, and foretold, as divine judgment, the total wreck of the whole fleet. The consequence was, that although Jehoshaphat broke off—in obedience to the divine will—his league with Ahaziah, he formed a new scheme of a merchant fleet, and Ahaziah wished to be admitted a partner. The proposal of the Israelitish king was respectfully declined. The destination of this new fleet was to Ophir, because the

Israelitish seaports were not accessible to him for the Tartessus trade; but the ships, when just off the docks, were wrecked in the rocky creek of Eziongeber.

CHAPTER 21

Vss. 1-4. JEHORAM SUCCEEDS JEHOSHAPHAT. **1. Jehoshaphat slept with his fathers . . . Jehoram . . . reigned**—The late king left seven sons; two of them are in our version named Azariah; but in the Hebrew they appear considerably different, the one being spelt Azariah, and the other Azariahu. Though Jehoshaphat had made his family arrangements with prudent precaution, and while he divided the functions of royalty in his lifetime (cf. II Kings 8:16), as well as fixed the succession to the throne in his oldest son, he appointed each of the others to the government of a fenced city, thus providing them with an honorable independence. But this good intentions were frustrated; for no sooner did Jehoram find himself in the sole possession of sovereign power than, from jealousy, or on account of their connections, he murdered all his brothers, together with some leading influential persons who, he suspected, were attached to their interest, or would avenge their deaths. Similar tragedies have been sadly frequent in Eastern courts, where the heir of the crown looks upon his brothers as his most formidable enemies, and is therefore tempted to secure his power by their death.

5-7. HIS WICKED REIGN. **6. he walked . . . as did the house of Ahab, for he had the daughter of Ahab to wife**—The precepts and examples of his excellent father were soon obliterated by his matrimonial alliance with a daughter of the royal house of Israel. Through the influence of Athaliah he abolished the worship of the Lord, and encouraged an introduction of all the corruptions prevalent in the sister kingdom. The divine vengeance was denounced against him, and would have utterly destroyed him and his house, had it not been for a tender regard to the promise made to David (II Sam. 7; II Kings 8:19).

8-17. EDOM AND LIBNAH REVOLT. **8. the Edomites revolted**—That nation had been made dependent by David, and down to the time of Jehoshaphat was governed by a tributary ruler (I Kings 22:47; II Kings 3:9). But that king having been slain in an insurrection at home, his successor thought to ingratiate himself with his new subjects by raising the flag of independence [JOSEPHUS]. The attempt was defeated in the first instance by Jehoram, who possessed all the military establishments of his father; but being renewed unexpectedly, the Edomites succeeded in completely emancipating their country from the yoke of Judah (Gen. 27:40). Libnah, which lay on the southern frontier and towards Edom, followed the example of that country. **12-15. there came a writing to him from Elijah**—That prophet's translation having taken place in the reign of Jehoshaphat, we must conclude that the name of Elijah has, by the error of a transcriber, been put for that of Elisha. **13. hast made Judah and the inhabitants of Jerusalem . . . like to the whoredoms of the house of Ahab**—i.e., introduced the superstitions and vices of Phœnician idolatry (see on Deut. 13:6-14). On this account, as well as for his unnatural cruelties, divine vengeance was denounced against him, which was soon after executed exactly as the prophet had foretold. A series of overwhelming calamities befell this wicked king; for in addition to the revolts already mentioned, two

neighboring tribes (see ch. 17:11) made hostile incursions on the southern and western portions of his kingdom. His country was ravaged, his capital taken, his palace plundered, his wives carried off, and all his children slain except the youngest. He himself was seized with an incurable dysentery, which, after subjecting him to the most painful suffering for the unusual period of two years, carried him off, a monument of the divine judgment. To complete his degradation, his death was unlamented, his burial unhonored by his subjects. This custom, similar to what obtained in Egypt, seems to have crept in among the Hebrews, of giving funeral honors to their kings, or withholding them, according to the good or bad characters of their reign.

CHAPTER 22

Vss. 1-9. AHAZIAH SUCCEEDING JEHORAM, REIGNS WICKEDLY. **1. the inhabitants of Jerusalem made Ahaziah . . . king**—or Jehoahaz (ch. 21:17). All his older brothers having been slaughtered by the Arab marauders, the throne of Judah rightfully belonged to him as the only legitimate heir. **2. Forty and two years old was Ahaziah when he began to reign**—(Cf. II Kings 8:26). According to that passage, the commencement of his reign is dated in the twenty-second year of his age, and, according to this, in the forty-second year of the kingdom of his mother's family [LIGHTFOOT]. "If Ahaziah ascended the throne in the twenty-second year of his life, he must have been born in his father's nineteenth year. Hence, it may seem strange that he had older brothers; but in the East they marry early, and royal princes had, besides the wife of the first rank, usually concubines, as Jehoram had (ch. 21:17); he might, therefore, in the nineteenth year of his age, very well have several sons" [KEIL] (cf. ch. 21:20; II Kings 8:17). **Athaliah, the daughter of Omri**—more properly, granddaughter. The expression is used loosely, as the statement was made simply for the purpose of intimating that she belonged to that idolatrous race. **3, 4. his mother was his counsellor . . . they were his counsellors**—The facile king surrendered himself wholly to the influence of his mother and her relatives. Athaliah and her son introduced a universal corruption of morals and made idolatry the religion of the court and the nation. By them he was induced not only to conform to the religion of the northern kingdom, but to join a new expedition against Ramoth-gilead (see on II Kings 9:10). **5. went . . . to war against Hazael, king of Syria**—It may be mentioned as a very minute and therefore important confirmation of this part of the sacred history that the names of Jehu and Hazael, his contemporary, have both been found on Assyrian sculptures; and there is also a notice of Ithbaal, king of Sidon, who was the father of Jezebel. **6. Azariah . . . went down**—i.e., from Ramoth-gilead, to visit the king of Israel, who was lying ill of his wounds at Jezreel, and who had fled there on the alarm of Jehu's rebellion. **9. he sought Ahaziah, and they caught him (for he was hid in Samaria)** —(cf. II Kings 9:27-29). The two accounts are easily reconciled. "Ahaziah fled first to the garden-house and escaped to Samaria; but was here, where he had hid himself, taken by Jehu's men who pursued him, brought to Jehu, who was still near or in Jezreel, and at his command slain at the hill Gur, beside Ibleam, in his chariot; that is, mortally wounded with an arrow, so that he, again fleeing, expired at Megiddo" [KEIL]. Jehu left the corpse at the disposal of the king of Judah's attendants, who conveyed it to Jerusalem, and out of respect to his grandfather Jehoshaphat's memory, gave him an honorable interment in the tombs of the kings. **So the house of Ahaziah had no power to keep still the kingdom**—His children were too young to assume the reins of government, and all the other royal princes had been massacred by Jehu (vs. 8). 10-12. ATHALIAH, DESTROYING THE SEED ROYAL SAVE JOASH, USURPS THE KINGDOM. **10. Athaliah . . . arose and destroyed all the seed royal**—(See on II Kings 11:1-3.) Maddened by the massacre of the royal family of Ahab, she resolved that the royal house of David should have the same fate. Knowing the commission which Jehu had received to extirpate the whole of Ahab's posterity, she expected that he would extend his sword to her. Anticipating his movements, she resolved, as her only defense and security, to usurp the throne and destroy "the seed royal," both because they were hostile to the Phœnician worship of Baal, which she was determined to uphold, and because, if one of the young princes became king, his mother would supersede Athaliah in the dignity of queen mother. **12. he was with them hid in the house of God**—Certain persons connected with the priesthood had a right to occupy the buildings in the outer wall, and all within the outer wall was often called the temple. Jehoiada and his family resided in one of these apartments.

CHAPTER 23

Vss. 1-11. JEHOIADA MAKES JOASH KING. **1. in the seventh year Jehoiada . . . took the captains of hundreds, etc.**—(See on II Kings 11:4, 17). The five officers mentioned here had been probably of the royal guard, and were known to be strongly disaffected to the government of Athaliah. **2. chief of all the fathers of Israel**—This name is frequently used in Chronicles for Judah and Benjamin, now all that remained of Israel. Having cautiously entrusted the secret of the young prince's preservation to all the leading men in the kingdom, he enlisted their interest in the royal cause and got their pledge to support it by a secret oath of fidelity. **they came to Jerusalem**—The time chosen for the grand discovery was, probably, one of the annual festivals, when there was a general concourse of the nation at the capital. **4. This is the thing that ye shall do**—The arrangements made for defense are here described. The people were divided into three bodies; one attended as guards to the king, while the other two were posted at all the doors and gates, and the captains and military officers who entered the temple unarmed to lull suspicion, were furnished with weapons out of the sacred armory, where David had deposited his trophies of victory and which was reopened on this occasion. **8. Jehoiada . . . dismissed not the courses**—As it was necessary to have as large a disposable force as he could command on such a crisis, the high priest detained those who, in other circumstances, would have returned home on the expiry of their week of service. **11. Then they brought out the king's son, and put upon him the crown, and gave to him the testimony**—Some think that the original word rendered "testimony," as its derivation warrants, may signify here the regalia, especially the bracelet (II Sam. 1:10); and this view they support on the ground that "gave him" being supplemented, the text properly runs thus, "put upon him the crown and testimony." At the same time,

it seems equally pertinent to take "the testimony" in the usual acceptation of that term; and, accordingly, many are of opinion that a roll containing a copy of the law (Deut. 17:18) was placed in the king's hands, which he held as a scepter or truncheon. Others, referring to a custom of Oriental people, who when receiving a letter or document from a highly respected quarter, lift it up to their heads before opening it, consider that Joash, besides the crown, had the book of the law laid upon his head (see Job 31:35, 36). **God save the king**—lit., Long live the king.

12-15. ATHALIAH SLAIN. **12. Athaliah heard the noise of the people**—The unusual commotion, indicated by the blast of the trumpets and the vehement acclamations of the people, drew her attention, or excited her fears. She might have flattered herself that, having slain all the royal family, she was in perfect security; but it is just as likely that, finding on reflection, one had escaped her murderous hands, she might not deem it expedient to institute any inquiries; but the very idea would keep her constantly in a state of jealous suspicion and irritation. In that state of mind, the wicked usurper, hearing across the Tyropœon the outburst of popular joy, rushed across the bridge to the temple grounds, and, penetrating from a single glance the meaning of the whole scene, raised a shriek of "Treason!" **13. behold, the king stood at the pillar at the entering in**—The king's pillar was in the people's court, opposite that of the priests'. The young king, arrayed in the royal insignia, had been brought out of the inner, to stand forth in the outer court, to the public view. Some think that he stood on the brazen scaffold of Solomon, erected beside the pillar. **14, 15. Slay her not in the house of the Lord . . . and when she was come to the entering of the horse gate by the king's house, they slew her there**—The high priest ordered her immediately to be taken out of the temple grounds and put to death. "And they laid hands on her; and she went by the way by the which horses came into the king's house: and there was she slain" (II Kings 11:16). "Now, we are not to suppose that horses came into" the king's house "of residence, but into the king's (horses') house or hippodrome (the gate of the king's mules) [JOSEPHUS], he had built for them on the southeast of the temple, in the immediate vicinity of the horse gate in the valley of Kedron—a valley which was at that time a kind of desecrated place by the destruction of idols and their appurtenances" (II Kings 23:2, 6, 12), [BARCLAY'S CITY OF THE GREAT KING].

16. JEHOIADA RESTORES THE WORSHIP OF GOD, AND SETTLES THE KING. **16. Jehoiada made a covenant**—(See on II Kings 11:17).

CHAPTER 24

Vss. 1-14. JOASH REIGNS WELL ALL THE DAYS OF JEHOIADA. **1-3. Joash . . . began to reign**—(See on II Kings 12:1-3). **Jehoiada took for him two wives**—As Jehoiada was now too old to contract such new alliances, the generality of interpreters apply this statement to the young king. **4-14. Joash was minded to repair the house of the Lord**—(See on II Kings 12:4-16).

15, 16. JEHOIADA BEING DEAD. **15, 16. Jehoiada waxed old . . . and died**—His life, protracted to unusual longevity and spent in the service of his country, deserved some tribute of public gratitude, and this was rendered in the posthumous honors that were bestowed on him. Among the Hebrews, intramural interment was prohibited in every city but Jerusalem, and there the exception was made only to the royal family and persons of eminent merit, on whom the distinction was conferred of being buried in the city of David, among the kings, as in the case of Jehoiada.

17-22. Joash Falls into Idolatry. 17-22. Now came the princes of Judah, and made obeisance to the king—Hitherto, while Joash occupied the throne, his uncle had held the reins of sovereign power, and by his excellent counsels had directed the young king to such measures as were calculated to promote both the civil and religious interests of the country. The fervent piety, practical wisdom, and inflexible firmness of that sage counsellor exerted immense influence over all classes. But now that the helm of the state-ship was no longer steered by the sound head and firm hand of the venerable high priest, the real merits of Joash's administration appear; and for want of good and enlightened principle, as well as, perhaps, of natural energy of character, he allowed himself to be borne onward in a course which soon wrecked the vessel upon hidden rocks. **the king hearkened unto them,** etc.—They were secretly attached to idolatry, and their elevated rank affords sad proof how extensively and deeply the nation had become corrupted during the reigns of Jehoram, Ahaziah, and Athaliah. With strong professions of allegiance they humbly requested that they might not be subjected to the continued necessity of frequent and expensive journeys to Jerusalem, but allowed the privilege their fathers had enjoyed of worshipping God in high places at home. They framed their petition in this plausible and least offensive manner, well knowing that, if excused attendance at the temple, they might —without risk of discovery or disturbance—indulge their tastes in the observance of any private rites they pleased. The weak-minded king granted their petition; and the consequence was, that when they left the house of the Lord God of their fathers, they soon "served groves and idols." **18. wrath came upon Judah and Jerusalem**—The particular mention of Jerusalem as involved in the sin implies that the neglect of the temple and the consequent idolatry received not only the king's toleration, but his sanction; and it naturally occurs to ask how, at his mature age, such a total abandonment of a place with which all his early recollections were associated can be accounted for. It has been suggested that what he had witnessed of the conduct of many of the priests in the careless performance of the worship, and especially their unwillingness to collect the money, as well as apply a portion of their revenues for the repairs of the temple, had alienated and disgusted him [Leclerc]. **19. Yet he sent prophets** —Elisha, Micah, Jehu son of Hanani, Jahaziel son of Zechariah (ch. 20:14), Eliezar son of Dodavah (ch. 20:37), lived and taught at that time. But all their prophetic warnings and denunciations were unheeded. **20. the Spirit of God came upon Zechariah, the son of Jehoiada**—probably a younger son, for his name does not occur in the list of Aaron's successors (I Chron. 6). **stood above the people**— Being of the priestly order, he spoke from the inner court, which was considerably higher than that of the people. **and said unto them, Thus saith God, Why transgress ye the commandments of the Lord, that ye cannot prosper,** etc.—His near relationship to the king might have created a feeling of delicacy and reluctance to interfere; but at length he, too, was prompted by an irresistible impulse to protest

against the prevailing impiety. The bold freedom and energy of his remonstrance, as well as his denunciation of the national calamities that would certainly follow, were most unpalatable to the king; while they so roused the fierce passions of the multitude that a band of miscreants, at the secret instigation of Joash, stoned him to death. This deed of violence involved complicated criminality on the part of the king. It was a horrid outrage on a prophet of the Lord—base ingratitude to a family who had preserved his life—atrocious treatment of a true Hebrew patriot—an illegal and unrighteous exercise of his power and authority as a king. **22. when he died, he said, The Lord look upon it and require it**—These dying words, if they implied a vindictive imprecation, exhibit a striking contrast to the spirit of the first Christian martyr (Acts 7:60). But, instead of being the expression of a personal wish, they might be the utterance of a prophetic doom.

23-27. He Is Slain by His Servants. 23. at the end of the year the host of Syria came up—This invasion took place under the personal conduct of Hazael, whom Joash, to save the miseries of a siege, prevailed on to withdraw his forces by a large present of gold (II Kings 12:18). Most probably, also, he promised the payment of an annual tribute, on the neglect or refusal of which the Syrians returned the following year, and with a mere handful of men inflicted a total and humiliating defeat on the collected force of the Hebrews. **25. they left him in great diseases**—The close of his life was embittered by a painful malady, which long confined him to bed. **his own servants conspired against him**—These two conspirators (whose fathers were Jews, but their mothers aliens) were probably courtiers, who, having constant access to the bedchamber, could the more easily execute their design. **for the blood of the sons**—read "the son" of Jehoiada. Public opinion seems to have ascribed the disasters of his life and reign to that foul crime, and as the king had long lost the esteem and respect of his subjects, neither horror nor sorrow was expressed for his miserable end!

CHAPTER 25

Vss. 1-4. Amaziah Begins to Reign Well. 1. Amaziah was twenty and five years old, etc.—(See on II Kings 4:1-6).

5-10. Having Hired an Army of Israelites against the Edomites, at the Word of a Prophet He Loses a Hundred Talents and Dismisses Them. 5. Amaziah . . . made captains, etc.—As all who were capable of bearing arms were liable to serve, it was quite natural in making up the muster roll to class them according to their respective families and to appoint the officers of each corps from the same quarter; so that all the soldiers who formed a regiment were brothers, relatives, friends. Thus the Hebrew troops were closely linked together, and had strong inducements to keep steady in their ranks. **found them three hundred thousand choice men**—This was only a fourth part of Jehoshaphat's army (ch. 17:14-19), showing how sadly the kingdom of Judah had, in the space of eighty-two years, been reduced in population by foreign wars, no less than by internal corruptions. But the full amount of Amaziah's troops may not be here stated. **6. He hired also an hundred thousand mighty men of valour . . . for an hundred talents of silver**—This sum was paid into the treasury of Jehoahaz—not given as bounty to the mercenaries who were obliged to serve at the sovereign's call; their remuneration consisting only in the booty they might obtain. It was about $170,000 in our currency, or $17 per man, including officers—a very paltry pay, compared with the bounty given for a soldier in this country. But it must be remembered that in ancient times campaigns were short and the hazards of the service comparatively small. **7, 8. there came a man of God**—sent to dissuade Amaziah from the course he was following, on the ground that "the Lord is not with Israel." This statement was perfectly intelligible to the king. But the historian, writing long after, thought it might require explanation, and therefore added the comment, "with all the children of Ephraim." Idolatry had long been the prevailing religion in that kingdom, and Ephraim its headquarters. As to the other part of the prophet's advice (vs. 8), considerable obscurity hangs over it, as the text stands; and hence some able critics have suggested the insertion of "not" in the middle clause, so that the verse will be thus: "But if thou wilt go [alone], do, be strong for the battle; God shall *not* make thee fall before the enemy." **10. separated them ... the army ... out of Ephraim ... their anger was greatly kindled against Judah**—Amaziah, who knew his position as the Lord's viceroy, complied with the prophet's counsel, and, consenting to forfeit the purchase-money of the Israelitish soldiers, discharged them. Exasperated at this treatment, they resolved to indemnify themselves for the loss of their expected booty, and so on their return home they plundered all the towns in their way, committing great havoc both of life and property without any stoppage, as the king of Judah and his army had set out on their expedition (II Kings 14:7). **11. valley of salt**—This ravine lies to the south of the Dead Sea. The arms of Amaziah, in reward for his obedience to the divine will, were crowned with victory—ten thousand of the Edomites were slain on the field, and as many taken prisoners, who were put to death by precipitation "from the top of the rock." This rock might be situated in the neighborhood of the battlefield, but more probably it formed one of the high craggy cliffs of Selah (Petra), the capital of the Edomites, whither Amaziah marched directly from the Valley of Salt, and which he captured (II Kings 14:7). The savage cruelty dealt out to them was either in retaliation for similar barbarities inflicted on the Hebrews, or to strike terror into so rebellious a people for the future. The mode of execution, by dashing against stones (Ps. 137:9), was common among many ancient nations. **14-16. Amaziah ... brought the gods of the children of Seir**—The Edomites worshipped the sun under different forms and with various rites. But burning incense upon altars was a principal act of worship, and this was the very thing Amaziah is described as having with strange infatuation performed. Whether he had been captivated with the beauty of the images, or hoped by honoring the gods to disarm their spite at him for his conquest and harsh treatment of their votaries, his conduct in establishing these objects of religious homage in Jerusalem was foolish, ignorant, and highly offensive to God, who commissioned a prophet to rebuke him for his apostasy, and threaten him with the calamity that soon after befell him. **16. as he talked with him,** etc.—Those who were invested with the prophetic character were entitled to counsel kings. Amaziah, had he not been offended by unwelcome truths, would have admitted the claim of this prophet, who was probably the same that had given him counsel previous to the war with Edom. But victory had elated and blinded him.

17. HE PROVOKES JOASH TO HIS OVERTHROW. **17. Then Amaziah ... sent to Joash ... Come, let us see one another in the face**—(See on II Kings 14: 8-20).

CHAPTER 26

Vss. 1-8. UZZIAH SUCCEEDS AMAZIAH AND REIGNS WELL IN THE DAYS OF ZECHARIAH. **1. Then all the people of Judah took Uzziah**—(See on II Kings 14: 21, 22; 15:1-3). **2. He built Eloth**—or, "He it was who built Eloth." The account of the fortifications of this port on the Red Sea, which Uzziah restored to the kingdom of Judah (ch. 33:13), is placed before the chronological notices (vs. 3), either on account of the importance attached to the conquest of Eloth, or from the desire of the historian to introduce Uzziah as the king, who was known as the conqueror of Eloth. Besides, it indicates that the conquest occurred in the early part of his reign, that it was important as a port, and that Hebrew merchants maintained the old trade between it and the countries of the East [BERTHEAU]. **5. he sought God in the days of Zechariah**—a wise and pious counsellor, who was skilled in understanding the meaning and lessons of the ancient prophecies, and who wielded a salutary influence over Uzziah. **6, 7. he went forth and warred against the Philistines**—He overcame them in many engagements—dismantled their towns, and erected fortified cities in various parts of the country, to keep them in subjection. **Jabneh**—the same as Jabneel (Josh. 15:11). **Gur-baal**—thought by some to be Gerar, and by others Gebal. **8. the Ammonites gave gifts**—The countries east of the Jordan became tributary to him, and by the rapid succession and extent of his victories, his kingdom was extended to the Egyptian frontier.

9, 10. HIS BUILDINGS. **9. Uzziah built towers in Jerusalem,** etc.—whence resistance could be made, or missiles discharged against assailants. The sites of the principal of these towers were: at the corner gate (ch. 25:23), the northwest corner of the city; at the valley gate on the west, where the Joppa gate now is; at the "turning"—a curve in the city wall on the eastern side of Zion. The town, at this point, commanded the horse gate which defended Zion and the temple hill on the southeast [BERTHEAU]. **10. Also he built towers in the desert**—for the threefold purpose of defense, of observation, and of shelter to his cattle. He dug also a great many wells, for he loved and encouraged all branches of agriculture. Some of these "were in the desert," i.e., in the district to the southeast of Jerusalem, on the west of the Dead Sea, an extensive grazing district "in the low country" lying between the mountains of Judah and the Mediterranean; "and in the plains," east of the Jordan, within the territory of Reuben (Deut. 4:43; Josh. 20:8). **in Carmel**—This mountain, being within the boundary of Israel, did not belong to Uzziah; and as it is here placed in opposition to the vine-bearing mountains, it is probably used, not as a proper name, but to signify, as the word denotes, "fruitful fields" (*Margin*).

11-15. HIS HOST, AND ENGINES OF WAR. **11-15. an host of fighting men, who went out to war by bands**—He raised a strong body of militia, divided into companies or regiments of uniform size, which served in rotation. The enumeration was performed by two functionaries expert in the drawing up of military muster rolls, under the superintendence of Hananiah, one of the high officers of the crown. The army consisted of 307,500 picked men, under the command of two thousand gallant officers, chiefs or heads of fathers' houses, so that each fathers' house formed a distinct band. They were fully equipped with every kind of military accoutrements, from brazen helmets, a habergeon or coat of mail, to a sling for stones. **15. he made ... engines, invented by cunning men ... to shoot arrows and great stones**—This is the first notice that occurs in history of the use of machines for throwing projectiles. The invention is apparently ascribed to the reign of Uzziah, and PLINY expressly says they originated in Syria. **he was marvellously helped till he was strong**—He conducted himself as became the viceroy of the Divine King, and prospered.

16-21. HE INVADES THE PRIEST'S OFFICE, AND IS SMITTEN WITH LEPROSY. 16-21. he transgressed against the Lord, etc.—(See on II Kings 15:5.) This daring and wicked act is in both records traced to the intoxicating influence of overweening pride and vanity. But here the additional circumstances are stated, that his entrance was opposed, and strong remonstrances made (I Chron. 6:10) by the high priest, who was accompanied by eighty inferior priests. Rage and threats were the only answers he deigned to return, but God took care to vindicate the sacredness of the priestly office. At the moment the king lifted the censer, He struck him with leprosy. The earthquake mentioned (Amos 1:1) is said to have been felt at the moment [JOSEPHUS]. **21. dwelt in a several house**—in an infirmary [BERTHEAU]. **23. they buried him ... in the field of the burial which belonged to the kings**—He was interred not in, but near, the sepulcher of the kings, as the corpse of a leper would have polluted it.

CHAPTER 27

Vss. 1-4. JOTHAM, REIGNING WELL, PROSPERS. 1. Jotham was twenty and five years old—(See on II Kings 15:32-35). **His mother's name ... was Jerushah, the daughter of Zadok**—or descendant of the famous priest of that name. **2. he did that which was right**—The general rectitude of his government is described by representing it as conducted on the excellent principles which had guided the early part of his father's reign. **the people did yet corruptly**—(See II Kings 15:35); but the description here is more emphatic, that though Jotham did much to promote the good of his kingdom and aimed at a thorough reformation in religion, the widespread and inveterate wickedness of the people frustrated all his laudable efforts. **3. He built the high gate of the house of the Lord**—situated on the north—that portion of the temple hill which was high compared with the southern part—hence "the higher," or upper gate (II Kings 15:35). He built, i.e., repaired or embellished. **and on the wall of Ophel**—*Hebrew*, the Ophel, i.e., the mound, or eminence on the southeastern slope of the temple mount, a ridge lying between the valleys Kedron and Tyropœon, called "the lower city" [JOSEPHUS]. He "built much," having the same desire as his father to secure the defense of Jerusalem in every direction. **4. in the mountains of Judah, and in the forests he built castles and towers**—i.e., in the elevated and wooded spots where fortified cities could not be placed, he erected castles and towers.

5-9. HE SUBDUES THE AMMONITES. 5. He fought also with the king of the Ammonites—This invasion he not only repelled, but, pursuing the Ammonites

into their own territory, he imposed on them a yearly tribute, which, for two years, they paid. But when Rezin, king of Syria, and Pekah, king of Israel, combined to attack the kingdom of Judah, they took the opportunity of revolting, and Jotham was too distracted by other matters to attempt the reconquest (see on II Kings 15:37).

CHAPTER 28

Vss. 1-21. AHAZ, REIGNING WICKEDLY, IS AFFLICTED BY THE SYRIANS. 1-4. Ahaz was twenty years old—(See on II Kings 16:1-4). This prince, discarding the principles and example of his excellent father, early betrayed a strong bias to idolatry. He ruled with an arbitrary and absolute authority, and not as a theocratic sovereign: he not only forsook the temple of God, but embraced first the symbolic worship established in the sister kingdom, and afterwards the gross idolatry practised by the Canaanites. **5, 6. the Lord ... delivered him into the hand of the king of Syria ... he was also delivered into the hand of the king of Israel**—These verses, without alluding to the formation of a confederacy between the Syrian and Israelitish kings to invade the kingdom of Judah, or relating the commencement of the war in the close of Jotham's reign (II Kings 15:37), give the issue only of some battles that were fought in the early part of the campaign. **delivered him ... smote him ... he was also delivered**—i.e., his army, for Ahaz was not personally included in the number either of the slain or the captives. The slaughter of 120,000 in one day was a terrible calamity, which, it is expressly said (vs. 6), was inflicted as a judgment on Judah, "because they had forsaken the Lord God of their fathers." Among the slain were some persons of distinction: "Maaseiah the king's son" (the sons of Ahaz being too young to take part in a battle, this individual must have been a younger son of the late King Jotham); "Azrikam, the governor of the house," i.e., the palace; and "Elkanah that was next to the king," i.e., the vizier or prime minister (Gen. 41:40; Esther 10:3). These were all cut down on the field by Zichri, an Israelitish warrior, or, as some think, ordered to be put to death after the battle. A vast number of captives also fell into the power of the conquerors; and an equal division of war prisoners being made between the allies, they were sent off under a military escort to the respective capitals of Syria and Israel. **8. the children of Israel carried away captive of their brethren two hundred thousand**—These captives included a great number of women, boys, and girls, a circumstance which creates a presumption that the Hebrews, like other Orientals, were accompanied in the war by multitudes of non-combatants (see on Judg. 4:8). The report of these "brethren," being brought as captives to Samaria, excited general indignation among the better-disposed inhabitants; and Oded, a prophet, accompanied by the princes (vs. 12, compared with vs. 14), went out, as the escort was approaching, to prevent the disgraceful outrage of introducing such prisoners into the city. The officers of the squadron were, of course, not to blame; they were simply doing their military duty in conducting those prisoners of war to their destination. But Oded clearly showed that the Israelitish army had gained the victory—not by the superiority of their arms, but in consequence of the divine judgment against Judah. He forcibly exposed the enormity of the offense of keeping "their brethren" as slaves got in war. He protested earnestly against adding this great offense of unnatural and sinful cruelty (Lev. 25:43, 44; Mic. 2:8, 9) to the already overwhelming amount of their own national sins. Such was the effect of his spirited remonstrance and the opposing tide of popular feeling, that the armed men left the captives and the spoil before the princes and all the congregation." **15. the men which were expressed by name rose up**—These were either the "heads of the children of Ephraim" (mentioned vs. 12), or some other leading individuals chosen for the benevolent office. Under their kindly superintendence, the prisoners were not only released, but out of the spoils were comfortably relieved with food and clothing, and conveyed as far as Jericho on their way back to their own homes. This is a beautiful incident, and full of interest, as showing that even at this period of national decline, there were not a few who steadfastly adhered to the law of God. **16. At that time did King Ahaz send unto the kings of Assyria**—"kings," the plural for the singular, which is found in many ancient versions. "At that time," refers to the period of Ahaz' great distress, when, after a succession of defeats, he retreated within the walls of Jerusalem. Either in the same or a subsequent campaign, the Syrian and Israelitish allies marched there to besiege him (see on II Kings 16: 7-9). Though delivered from this danger, other enemies infested his dominions both on the south and the west. **17. again the Edomites had come and smitten Judah**—This invasion must have been after Rezin (at the beginning of the recent Syro-Israelitish war), had released that people from the yoke of Judah (ch. 15:11; cf. II Kings 16:6). **18. Gederoth**—on the Philistine frontier (Josh. 15:41). **Shocho**—or Socah (Josh. 15:35), now Shuweikeh, a town in the Valley of Judah (see on I Sam. 17:1). **Gimzo**—now Jimza, a little east of Ludd (Lydda) [ROBINSON]. All these disasters, by which the "Lord brought Judah low," were because of Ahaz, king of Israel (Judah), see ch. 21:2; 24:16; 28:27, who made Judah naked, and transgressed sore against the Lord. **20. Tilgath-pilneser ... distressed him, but strengthened him not**—i.e., Notwithstanding the temporary relief which Tilgath-pilneser afforded him by the conquest of Damascus and the slaughter of Rezin (II Kings 16:9), little advantage resulted from it, for Tilgath-pilneser spent the winter in voluptuous revelry at Damascus; and the connection formed with the Assyrian king was eventually a source of new and greater calamities and humiliation to the kingdom of Judah (vss. 2, 3). 22-27. HIS IDOLATRY IN HIS DISTRESS. **22. in the time of his distress did he trespass yet more against the Lord**—This infatuated king surrendered himself to the influence of idolatry and exerted his royal authority to extend it, with the intensity of a passion—with the ignorance and servile fear of a heathen (vs. 23) and a ruthless defiance of God (see on II Kings 16:10-20).

CHAPTER 29

Vss. 1, 2. HEZEKIAH'S GOOD REIGN. **1. Hezekiah began to reign**, etc.—(see on II Kings 18:1-3). His mother's name, which, in the passage referred to, appears in an abridged form, is here given in full. 3-11. HE RESTORES RELIGION. **3. in the first year of his reign, in the first month**—not the first month after his accession to the throne, but in Nisan, the first month of the sacred year, the season appointed for the celebration of the passover.

he opened the doors of the house of the Lord—which had been closed up by his father (ch. 28:24). **and repaired them**—or embellished them (cf. II Kings 18: 16). **4. the east street**—the court of the priests, which fronted the eastern gate of the temple. Assembling the priests and Levites there, he enjoined them to set about the immediate purification of the temple. It does not appear that the order referred to the removal of idols, for objects of idolatrous homage could scarcely have been put there, seeing the doors had been shut up; but in its forsaken and desolate state the temple and its courts had been polluted by every kind of impurity. **6. our fathers have trespassed**—Ahaz and the generation contemporary with him were specially meant, for they "turned away their faces from the habitation of the Lord," and whether or not they turned east to the rising sun, they abandoned the worship of God. They "shut up the doors of the porch," so that the sacred ritual was entirely discontinued. **8. Wherefore the wrath of the Lord was upon Judah and Jerusalem**—This pious king had the discernment to ascribe all the national calamities that had befallen the kingdom to the true cause, viz., apostasy from God. The country had been laid waste by successive wars of invasion, and its resources drained. Many families mourned members of their household still suffering the miseries of foreign captivity; all their former prosperity and glory had fled; and to what was this painful and humiliating state of affairs to be traced, but to the manifest judgment of God upon the kingdom for its sins? **10, 11. Now it is in mine heart to make a covenant with the Lord God**—Convinced of the sin and bitter fruits of idolatry, Hezekiah intended to reverse the policy of his father, and to restore, in all its ancient purity and glory, the worship of the true God. His commencement of this resolution at the beginning of his reign attests his sincere piety. It also proves the strength of his conviction that righteousness exalteth a nation; for, instead of waiting till his throne was consolidated, he devised measures of national reformation at the beginning of his reign and vigorously faced all the difficulties which, in such a course, he had to encounter, after the people's habits had so long been moulded to idolatry. His intentions were first disclosed to this meeting of the priests and Levites—for the agency of these officials was to be employed in carrying them into effect. 12-36. THE HOUSE OF GOD CLEANSED. **12. Then the Levites arose**—Fourteen chiefs undertook the duty of collecting and preparing their brethren for the important work of cleansing the Lord's house. Beginning with the outer courts—that of the priests and that of the people—the cleansing of these occupied eight days, after which they set themselves to purify the interior; but as the Levites were not allowed to enter within the walls of the temple, the priest brought all the sweepings out to the porch, where they were received by the Levites and thrown into the brook Kedron. This took eight days more. At the end of this period they repaired to the palace and announced that not only had the whole of the sacred edifice, within and without, undergone a thorough purification, but all the vessels which the late king had taken away and applied to a common use in his palace, had been restored, and "sanctified." **20. Then Hezekiah the king rose early, and gathered the rulers of the city**—His anxiety to enter upon the expiatory service with all possible despatch, now that the temple had been properly prepared for it, prevented his summoning all the representatives of Israel. The requisite number of victims having been provided, and the officers of the temple having sanctified themselves according to the directions of the law, the priests were appointed to offer sacrifices of atonement successively for "the kingdom," i.e., for the sins of the king and his predecessors; "for the sanctuary," i.e., for the sins of the priests themselves and for the desecration of the temple; "and for Judah," i.e., for the people who, by their voluntary consent, were involved in the guilt of the national apostasy. Animals of the kinds used in sacrifice were offered by sevens—that number indicating completeness. The Levites were ordered to praise God with musical instruments, which, although not originally used in the tabernacle, had been enlisted in the service of divine worship by David on the advice of the prophets Gad and Nathan, as well calculated to animate the devotions of the people. At the close of the special services of the occasion, viz., the offering of atonement sacrifices, the king and all civic rulers who were present joined in the worship. A grand anthem was sung (vs. 30) by the choir, consisting of some of the psalms of David and Asaph, and a great number of thank offerings, praise offerings, and freewill burnt offerings were presented at the invitation of the king. **31. Hezekiah . . . said, Now ye have consecrated yourselves unto the Lord, come near**— This address was made to the priests as being now, by the sacrifice of the expiation offerings, anew consecrated to the service of God and qualified to resume the functions of their sacred office (Exod. 28:41; 29:32). **the congregation brought in**—i.e., the body of civic rulers present. **34. the priests were too few, . . . wherefore their brethren the Levites did help them**—The skins of beasts intended as peace offerings might be taken off by the officers, because, in such cases, the carcass was not wholly laid upon the altar; but animals meant for burnt offerings which were wholly consumed by fire could be flayed by the priests alone, not even the Levites being allowed to touch them, except in cases of unavoidable necessity (ch. 35:11). The duty being assigned by the law to the priests (Lev. 1:6), was construed by consuetudinary practice as an exclusion of all others not connected with the Aaronic family. **for the Levites were more upright in heart to sanctify themselves than the priests**—i.e., displayed greater alacrity than the priests. This service was hastened by the irrepressible solicitude of the king. Whether it was that many of the priests, being absent in the country, had not arrived in time—whether from the long interruption of the public duties, some of them had relaxed in their wonted attentions to personal cleanliness, and had many preparations to make—or whether from some having participated in the idolatrous services introduced by Ahaz, they were backward in repairing to the temple—a reflection does seem to be cast upon their order as dilatory and not universally ready for duty (cf. ch. 30:15). Thus was the newly consecrated temple reopened to the no small joy of the pious king and all the people.

CHAPTER 30

Vss. 1-12. Hezekiah Proclaims a Passover. **1. Hezekiah sent to all . . . Judah . . . to come to . . . Jerusalem, to keep the passover**—This great religious festival had not been regularly observed by the Hebrews in their national capacity for a long time because of the division of the kingdom and the many disorders that had followed that unhappy event. Hezekiah longed extremely to see its observance revived; and the expression of his wishes having received a hearty response from the princes and chief men of his own kingdom, the preparatory steps were taken for a renewed celebration of the national solemnity. **letters also to Ephraim and Manasseh**—The names of these leading tribes are used for the whole kingdom of Israel. It was judged impossible, however, that the temple, the priests, and people could be all duly sanctified at the usual time appointed for the anniversary, viz., the fourteenth day of the first month (Nisan). Therefore it was resolved, instead of postponing the feast till another year, to observe it on the fourteenth day of the second month; a liberty which, being in certain circumstances (Num. 9:6-13) granted to individuals, might, it was believed, be allowed to all the people. Hezekiah's proclamation was, of course, authoritative in his own kingdom, but it could not have been made and circulated in all the towns and villages of the neighboring kingdom without the concurrence, or at least the permission, of the Israelitish sovereign. Hoshea, the reigning king, is described as, though evil in some respects, yet more favorably disposed to religious liberty than any of his predecessors since the separation of the kingdom. This is thought to be the meaning of the mitigating clause in his character (II Kings 17:2). **6. the posts**—i.e., runners, or royal messengers, who were taken from the king's bodyguard (ch. 23:1, 2). Each, well mounted, had a certain number of miles to traverse. Having performed his course, he was relieved by another, who had to scour an equal extent of ground; so that, as the government messengers were despatched in all directions, public edicts were speedily diffused throughout the country. The proclamation of Hezekiah was followed by a verbal address from himself, piously urging the duty, and setting forth the advantages, of a return to the pure faith and institutions which God had delivered to their ancestors through Moses. **the remnant of you that are escaped out of the hand of the kings of Assyria**—This implies that several expeditions against Israel had already been made by Assyrian invaders—by Pul (II Kings 15:19), but none of the people were then removed; at a later period by Tiglath-pileser, when it appears that numbers among the tribes east of Jordan (I Chron. 5:26), and afterwards in the northern parts of Israel (II Kings 15:20), were carried into foreign exile. The invasion of Shalmaneser cannot be alluded to, as it did not take place till the sixth year of Hezekiah's reign (II Kings 17:6; 18:9-12). **10 the posts passed from city to city**—It is not surprising that after so long a discontinuance of the sacred festival, this attempt to revive it should, in some quarters, have excited ridicule and opposition. Accordingly, among the tribes of Ephraim, Manasseh, and Zebulun, Hezekiah's messengers met with open insults and ill usage. Many, however, in these very districts, as well as throughout the kingdom of the ten tribes, generally complied with the invitation; while, in the kingdom of Judah, there was one unanimous feeling of high expectation and pious delight. The concourse that repaired to Jerusalem on the occasion was very great, and the occasion was ever after regarded as one of the greatest passovers that had ever been celebrated.

13-27. The Assembly Destroys the Altars of Idolatry. **14. they arose and took away the altars that were in Jerusalem**—As a necessary preparation for the right observance of the approaching solemnity, the removal of the altars, which Ahaz had erected in the city, was resolved upon (ch. 28:24); for, as the people of God, the Hebrews were bound to extirpate all traces of idolatry; and it was a happy sign and pledge of the influence of the Spirit pervading the minds of the people when they voluntarily undertook this important preliminary work. **15. the priests and Levites were ashamed**—Though the Levites are associated in this statement, the priests were principally referred to; those of them who had been dilatory or negligent in sanctifying themselves (ch. 29:34) were put to the blush and stimulated to their duty by the greater alacrity and zeal of the people. **16-18. the priests sprinkled the blood, which they received of the hand of the Levites**—This was a deviation from the established rules and practices in presenting the offerings of the temple. The reason was, that many present on the occasion having not sanctified themselves, the Levites slaughtered the paschal victims (see on ch. 35:5) for everyone that was unclean. At other times the heads of families killed the lambs themselves, the priests receiving the blood from their hands and presenting it on the altar. Multitudes of the Israelites, especially from certain tribes (vs. 18), were in this unsanctified state, and yet they ate the passover—an exceptional feature and one opposed to the law (Num. 9:6); but this exception was allowed in answer to Hezekiah's prayer (vss. 18-20). **20. the Lord . . . healed the people**—We imagine the whole affair to have been the following: In consequence of their transgressions they had cause to fear disease and even death (Lev. 15:31). Hezekiah prayed for the nation, which was on the point of being diseased, and might therefore be regarded as sick already [BERTHEAU]. **21. the children of Israel . . . kept the feast**—The time appointed by the law for the continuance of the feast was seven days; but in consequence of its having been allowed to fall so long into desuetude, they doubled the period of celebration and kept it fourteen days with unabated satisfaction and joy. Materials for the additional sacrificial meals were supplied by the munificence of the king and the princes. **24. and a great number of priests sanctified themselves**—so that there would be a sufficient number of hands for the additional services.

CHAPTER 31

Vss. 1-10. THE PEOPLE FORWARD IN DESTROYING IDOLATRY. **1. all Israel . . . present went out to the cities of Judah**—The solemnities of this paschal season left a deep and salutary impression on the minds of the assembled worshippers; attachment to the ancient institutions of their country was extensively revived; ardor in the service of God animated every bosom; and under the impulse of the devout feelings inspired by the occasion, they took measures at the close of the passover for extirpating idolatrous statues and altars out of every city, as at the beginning of the festival they had done in Jerusalem. **Judah and Benjamin**—denote the southern kingdom. **Ephraim also and Manasseh**—refer to the northern kingdom. This unsparing demolition of the monuments of idolatry would receive all encouragement from the king and public authorities of the former; and the force of the popular movement was sufficient to effect the same results among the tribes of Israel, whatever opposition the power of Hoshea or the invectives of some profane brethren might have made. Thus the reign of idolatry being completely overthrown and the pure worship of God re-established throughout the land,

the people returned every one to his own home, in the confident expectation that, through the divine blessing, they would enjoy a happy future of national peace and prosperity. **2. Hezekiah appointed the course of the priests**, etc.—The king now turned his attention to provide for the orderly performance of the temple-worship—arranging the priests and Levites in their courses, assigning to every one his proper place and functions—and issuing edicts for the regular payment of those dues from which the revenues of the sanctuary were derived. To set a proper example to his subjects, his own proportion was announced in the first instance, for to the king it belonged, out of his privy purse, to defray the expenses of the altar, both stated and occasional (Num. 28:3, 4, 9, 11, 19); and in making this contribution from his own means, Hezekiah followed the course which David and Solomon had taken before him (see on ch. 8:14; I Kings 9:25). Afterwards he reappointed the people's dues to the temple; and from its being necessary to issue a royal mandate in reference to this matter, it appears that the sacred tribute had been either totally neglected, or (as the idolatrous princes were known to appropriate it to their own purposes) the people had in many cases refused or evaded the duty. But with the improved state of public feeling, Hezekiah's commandment was readily obeyed, and contributions of first fruits and tithes were poured in with great liberality from all parts of Judah, as well as from Israel. The first fruits, even of some articles of produce that were unfit for sacrifice (Lev. 2:11), such as honey (*Marg.* dates), were appropriated to the priests (Num. 18:12, 13; Deut. 18:4). The tithes (Lev. 27:31) were intended for the support of the whole Levitical tribe (Num. 18:8, 20, 24). **6. and laid them by heaps**—The contributions began to be sent in shortly after the celebration of the passover, which had taken place in the middle of the second month. Some time would elapse before the king's order reached all parts of the kingdom. The wheat harvest occurred in the third month, so that the sheaves of that grain, being presented before any other, formed "the foundation," an under-layer in the corn stores of the temple. The first fruits of their land produce which were successively sent in all the summer till the close of the fruit and vintage season, i.e., the seventh month, continued to raise heap upon heap. **9. Hezekiah questioned with the priests and the Levites concerning the heaps**—The object of his inquiries was to ascertain whether the supplies afforded the prospect of a sufficient maintenance for the members of the sacred order. **10. Azariah . . . answered . . . we have had enough**—This is probably the person mentioned (ch. 26:17), and his reply was to the following purport: There has been an abundant harvest, and a corresponding plenty in the incoming of first fruits and tithes; the people have testified their gratitude to Him who has crowned the year with His goodness by their liberality towards His servants.

11-19. HEZEKIAH APPOINTS OFFICERS TO DISPOSE OF THE TITHES. **11. Hezekiah commanded to prepare chambers in the house of the Lord**—storehouses, granaries, or cellars; either the old ones, which had been allowed through neglect to fall into decay, were to be repaired, or additional ones built. Private individuals brought their own first fruits to the temple; but the tithes were levied by the Levites, who kept a faithful account of them in their several places of abode and transmitted the allotted proportion to the priests. Officers were appointed to distribute equal rations to all in the cities of the priests who, from age or other reasons, could not repair to the temple. With the exception of children under three years of age—an exception made probably from their being considered too young to receive solid food—lists were kept of the number and age of every male; of priests according to their fathers' house, and Levites from twenty years (see Num. 4:3; 28:24; I Chron. 23:24). But, besides, provision was also made for their wives, daughters, and servants. **18. for in their set office they sanctified themselves**—This is the reason assigned for providing for the wives and children out of the revenues of the sanctuary, that priests, withdrawing from those secular pursuits by which they might have maintained their households, devoted themselves entirely to the functions of the ministry. 20, 21. HIS SINCERITY OF HEART. **20. Hezekiah ... wrought that which was good and right**—He displayed the qualities of a constitutional king, in restoring and upholding the ancient institutions of the kingdom; while his zealous and persevering efforts to promote the cause of true religion and the best interests of his subjects entitled him to be ranked with the most illustrious of his predecessors (II Kings 18:15).

CHAPTER 32

Vss. 1-20. SENNACHERIB INVADES JUDAH. **1. After these things, and the establishment thereof**—i.e., the restoration of the temple-worship. The precise date is given, II Kings 18:13. Determined to recover the independence of his country, Hezekiah had decided to refuse to pay the tribute which his father had bound himself to pay to Assyria. **Sennacherib ... entered into Judah, and encamped against the fenced cities**—The whole land was ravaged; the strong fortresses of Ashdod (Isa. 20:1) and Lachish had fallen; the siege of Libnah had commenced, when the king of Judah, doubting his ability to resist, sent to acknowledge his fault, and offer terms of submission by paying the tribute. The commencement of this Assyrian war was disastrous to Hezekiah (II Kings 18:13). But the misfortunes of the early period of the war are here passed over, as the historian hastens to relate the remarkable deliverance which God wrought for His kingdom of Judah. **2-8. when Hezekiah saw that Sennacherib ... was purposed to fight against Jerusalem**—An account of the means taken to fortify Jerusalem against the threatened siege is given only in this passage. The polluting or filling up of wells, and the altering of the course of rivers, is an old practice that still obtains in the wars of the East. Hezekiah's plan was to cover the fountain-heads, so that they might not be discovered by the enemy, and to carry the water by subterranean channels or pipes into the city—a plan which, while it would secure a constant supply to the inhabitants, would distress the besiegers, as the country all around Jerusalem was very destitute of water. **4. So there was gathered much people ... who stopped all the fountains, and the brook that ran through the midst of the land**—"Where these various fountains were, we have now no positive means of ascertaining; though Enrogel, and the spring now called the Virgin's Fount, may well be numbered among them. *Josephus* mentions the existence of various fountains without the city, but does not mention any of them in this connection but Siloam. 'The brook,' however, is located with sufficient precision to enable us to trace it very definitely. We are told

that 'it ran through the midst of the land.' Now a stream running through either the Kedron or Hinnom Valley, could, in no proper sense, be said to run 'through the midst of the land,' but one flowing through the true Gihon valley, and separating Akra and Zion from Bezetha, Moriah, and Ophel, as a stream once, doubtless, did, could, with peculiar propriety, be said to run *through the midst of the land* on which the [Holy] City was built. And that this is the correct meaning of the phrase is not only apparent from the force of circumstances, but is positively so declared in the Septuagint, where, moreover, it is called a 'river,' which, at least, implies a much larger stream than the Kedron, and comports well with the marginal reading, where it is said to 'overflow through the midst of the land.' Previous to the interference of man, there was, no doubt, a very copious stream that gushed forth in the upper portion of that shallow, basin-like concavity north of Damascus Gate, which is unquestionably the upper extremity of the Gihon valley, and pursuing its meandering course through this valley, entered the Tyropœon at its great southern curve, down which it flowed into the valley of the Kedron" [BARCLAY'S CITY OF THE GREAT KING]. **5, 6. he strengthened himself**—He made a careful inspection of the city defenses for the purpose of repairing breaches in the wall here, renewing the masonry there, raising projecting machines to the towers, and especially fortifying the lower portion of Zion, i.e., Millo, "(in) the original city of David." "In" is a supplement of our translators, and the text reads better without it, for it was not the whole city that was repaired, but only the lower portion of Zion, or the original "city of David." **he ... gathered them together ... in the street**—i.e., the large open space at the gate of Eastern cities. Having equipped his soldiers with a full suit of military accoutrements, he addressed them in an animated strain, dwelling on the motives they had to inspire courage and confidence of success, especially on their consciousness of the favor and helping power of God. **9-20.** (See on II Kings 18:17-35; also 19: 8-34.) **18. they cried with a loud voice ... unto the people of Jerusalem ... on the wall**—It appears that the wall on the west side of the city reached as far to the side of the uppermost pool of Gihon at that time as it does now, if not farther; and the wall was so close to that pool that those sent to negotiate with the Assyrian general answered him in their own tongue (see on II Kings 18:27). 21-23. AN ANGEL DESTROYS THE ASSYRIANS. **21. an angel ... cut off all the mighty men**—(see on II Kings 19:35-37). 24-26. HEZEKIAH'S SICKNESS AND RECOVERY. **24. In those days Hezekiah was sick to the death**—(See on II Kings 20:1-11). 27-33. HIS RICHES AND WORKS. **he had exceeding much riches and honour**—(cf. II Kings 20:13; Isa. 39:2). A great portion of his personal wealth, like that of David and Uzziah, consisted in immense possessions of agricultural and pastoral produce. Besides, he had accumulated large treasures in gold, silver, and precious things, which he had taken as spoils from the Philistines, and which he had received as presents from neighboring states, among which he was held in great honor as a king under the special protection of Heaven. Much of his great wealth he expended in improving his capital, erecting forts, and promoting the internal benefit of his kingdom. **30. stopped the ... watercourse of Gihon, and brought it ... to the west side of the city,** etc.—(cf. II Kings 20:20). Particular notice is here taken of the aqueduct, as among the greatest of Hezekiah's works. "In exploring the subterranean channel conveying the water from Virgin's Fount to Siloam, I discovered a similar channel entering from the north, a few yards from its commencement; and on tracing it up near the Mugrabin gate, where it became so choked with rubbish that it could be traversed no farther, I there found it turn to the *west* in the direction of the south end of the cleft, or saddle, of Zion, and if this channel was not constructed for the purpose of conveying the waters of Hezekiah's aqueduct, I am unable to suggest any purpose to which it could have been applied. Perhaps the reason why it was not brought down on the Zion side, was that Zion was already well watered in its lower portion by the Great Pool, 'the lower pool of Gihon.' And accordingly *Williams* (HOLY CITY) renders this passage, 'He stopped the upper outflow of the waters of Gihon, and led them down westward to the city' " [BARCLAY'S CITY OF THE GREAT KING]. The construction of this aqueduct required not only masonic but engineering skill; for the passage was bored through a continuous mass of rock. Hezekiah's pool or reservoir made to receive the water within the northwest part of the city still remains. It is an oblong quadrangular tank, 240 feet in length, from 144 to 150 in breadth, but, from recent excavations, appears to have extended somewhat farther towards the north. **31. in the business of the ambassadors who sent . . . to inquire of the wonder that was done in the land,** etc.—They brought a present (vs. 23, see on II Kings 20:12, 13), and a letter of congratulation on his recovery, in which particular inquiries were made about the miracle of the sun's retrocession—a natural phenomenon that could not fail to excite great interest and curiosity at Babylon, where astronomy was so much studied. At the same time, there is reason to believe that they proposed a defensive league against the Assyrians. **God left him, to try him,** etc.—Hezekiah's offense was not so much in the display of his military stores and treasures, as in not giving to God the glory both of the miracle and of his recovery, and thus leading those heathen ambassadors to know Him.

CHAPTER 33

Vss. 1-10. MANASSEH'S WICKED REIGN. **1, 2. Manasseh . . . did that which was evil in the sight of the Lord**—(See on II Kings 21:1-16).
11-19. HE IS CARRIED UNTO BABYLON, WHERE HE HUMBLES HIMSELF BEFORE GOD, AND IS RESTORED TO HIS KINGDOM. **11. the captains of the host of the king of Assyria**—This king was Esarhaddon. After having devoted the first years of his reign to the consolidation of his government at home, he turned his attention to repair the loss of the tributary provinces west of the Euphrates, which, on the disaster and death of Sennacherib, had taken the opportunity of shaking off the Assyrian yoke. Having overrun Palestine and removed the remnant that were left in the kingdom of Israel, he despatched his generals, the chief of whom was Tartan (Isa. 20:1), with a portion of his army for the reduction of Judah also. In a successful attack upon Jerusalem, they took multitudes of captives, and got a great prize, including the king himself, among the prisoners. **took Manasseh among the thorns**—This may mean, as is commonly supposed, that he had hid himself among a thicket of briers and brambles. We know that the Hebrews sometimes took refuge from their enemies in thickets (I Sam. 13:6). But,

instead of the *Hebrew, Bacochim,* "among the thorns," some versions read *Bechayim,* "among the living," and so the passage would be "took him alive." **bound him with fetters, and carried him to Babylon**—The *Hebrew* word rendered "fetters" denotes properly two chains of brass. The humiliating state in which Manasseh appeared before the Assyrian monarch may be judged of by a picture on a tablet in the Khorsabad palace, representing prisoners led bound into the king's presence. "The captives represented appear to be inhabitants of Palestine. Behind the prisoners stand four persons with inscriptions on the lower part of their tunics; the first two are bearded, and seem to be accusers; the remaining two are nearly defaced; but behind the last appears the eunuch, whose office it seems to be to usher into the presence of the king those who are permitted to appear before him. He is followed by another person of the same race as those under punishment; his hands are manacled, and on his ankles are strong rings fastened together by a heavy bar" [NINEVEH AND ITS PALACES]. No name is given, and, therefore, no conclusion can be drawn that the figure represents Manasseh. But the people appear to be Hebrews, and this pictorial scene will enable us to imagine the manner in which the royal captive from Judah was received in the court of Babylon. Esar-haddon had established his residence there; for though from the many revolts that followed the death of his father, he succeeded at first only to the throne of Assyria, yet having some time previous to his conquest of Judah, recovered possession of Babylon, this enterprising king had united under his sway the two empires of Babylon and Chaldea and transferred the seat of his government to Babylon. **12, 13. when he was in affliction, he besought the Lord his God**—In the solitude of exile or imprisonment, Manasseh had leisure for reflection. The calamities forced upon him a review of his past life, under a conviction that the miseries of his dethronement and captive condition were owing to his awful and unprecedented apostasy (vs. 7) from the God of his fathers. He humbled himself, repented, and prayed for an opportunity of bringing forth the fruits of repentance. His prayer was heard; for his conqueror not only released him, but, after two years' exile, restored him, with honor and the full exercise of royal power, to a tributary and dependent kingdom. Some political motive, doubtless, prompted the Assyrian king to restore Manasseh, and that was most probably to have the kingdom of Judah as a barrier between Egypt and his Assyrian dominions. But God overruled this measure for higher purposes. Manasseh now showed himself, by the influence of sanctified affliction, a new and better man. He made a complete reversal of his former policy, by not only destroying all the idolatrous statues and altars he had formerly erected in Jerusalem, but displaying the most ardent zeal in restoring and encouraging the worship of God. **14. he built a wall without the city . . . on the west side of Gihon . . . even to the entering in at the fish gate**—"The well-ascertained position of the fish-gate, shows that the valley of Gihon could be no other than that leading northwest of Damascus gate, and gently descending southward, uniting with the Tyropœon at the northeast corner of Mount Zion, where the latter turns at right angles and runs towards Siloam. The wall thus built by Manasseh on the west side of the valley of Gihon, would extend from the vicinity of the northeast corner of the wall of Zion in a northerly direction, until it crossed over the valley to form a junction with the outer wall at the trench of Antonia, precisely in the quarter where the temple would be most easily assailed" [BARCLAY]. **17. the people did sacrifice still in the high places, yet unto the Lord their God only**—Here it appears that the worship on high places, though it originated in a great measure from the practice of heathenism, and too often led to it, did not necessarily imply idolatry.

20-25. HE DIES AND AMON SUCCEEDS HIM. **20, 21. Manasseh slept with his fathers ... Amon ... began to reign**—(See on II Kings 21:17-26).

CHAPTER 34

Vss. 1, 2. JOSIAH'S GOOD REIGN. **1. Josiah was eight years old**—(See on II Kings 22:1, 2). The testimony borne to the undeviating steadfastness of his adherence to the cause of true religion places his character and reign in honorable contrast with those of many of his royal predecessors.

3-7. HE DESTROYS IDOLATRY. **3. in the eighth year of his reign**—This was the sixteenth year of his age, and, as the kings of Judah were considered minors till they had completed their thirteenth year, it was three years after he had attained majority. He had very early manifested the piety and excellent dispositions of his character. In the twelfth year of his reign, but the twentieth of his age, he began to take a lively interest in the purgation of his kingdom from all the monuments of idolatry which, in his father's short reign, had been erected. At a later period, his increasing zeal for securing the purity of divine worship led him to superintend the work of demolition in various parts of his dominion. The course of the narrative in this passage is somewhat different from that followed in the Book of Kings. For the historian, having made allusion to the early manifestation of Josiah's zeal, goes on with a full detail of all the measures this good king adopted for the extirpation of idolatry; whereas the author of the Book of Kings sets out with the cleansing of the temple, immediately previous to the celebration of the passover, and embraces that occasion to give a general description of Josiah's policy for freeing the land from idolatrous pollution. The exact chronological order is not followed either in Kings or Chronicles. But it is clearly recorded in both that the abolition of idolatry began in the twelfth and was completed in the eighteenth year of Josiah's reign. Notwithstanding Josiah's undoubted sincerity and zeal and the people's apparent compliance with the king's orders, he could not extinguish a strongly rooted attachment to idolatries introduced in the early part of Manasseh's reign. This latent predilection appears unmistakably developed in the subsequent reigns, and the divine decree for the removal of Judah, as well as Israel, into captivity was irrevocably passed. **4. the graves of them that had sacrificed unto them.** He treated the graves themselves as guilty of the crimes of those who were lying in them [BERTHEAU]. **5. he burnt the bones of the priests upon their altars**—A greater brand of infamy could not have been put on idolatrous priests than the disinterment of their bones, and a greater defilement could not have been done to the altars of idolatry than the burning upon them the bones of those who had there officiated in their lifetime. **6. with their mattocks**—or "in their deserts"—so that the verse will stand thus: "And so did [viz., break the altars and burn the bones of priests] he in the cities of Manasseh, and Ephraim,

and Simeon, even unto Naphtali, in their deserted suburbs." The reader is apt to be surprised on finding that Josiah, whose hereditary possessions were confined to the kingdom of Judah, exercised as much authority among the tribes of Ephraim, Manasseh, Simeon, and others as far as Naphtali, as he did within his own dominion. Therefore, it is necessary to observe that, after the destruction of Samaria by Shalmaneser, the remnant that continued on the mountains of Israel maintained a close intercourse with Judah, and looked to the sovereigns of that kingdom as their natural protectors. Those kings acquired great influence over them, which Josiah exercised in removing every vestige of idolatry from the land. He could not have done this without the acquiescence of the people in the propriety of this proceeding, conscious that this was conformable to their ancient laws and institutions. The Assyrian kings, who were now masters of the country, might have been displeased at the liberties Josiah took beyond his own territories. But either they were not informed of his doings, or they did not trouble themselves about his religious proceedings, relating, as they would think, to the god of the land, especially as he did not attempt to seize upon any place or to disturb the allegiance of the people [CALMET].

8-18. HE REPAIRS THE TEMPLE. **in the eighteenth year of his reign ... he sent Shaphan**—(See on II Kings 22:3-9).

19-33. AND, CAUSING THE LAW TO BE READ, RENEWS THE COVENANT BETWEEN GOD AND THE PEOPLE. **19. when the king had heard the words of the law,** etc.—(See on II Kings 22:11-20; 23:1-3).

CHAPTER 35

Vss. 1-19. JOSIAH KEEPS A SOLEMN PASSOVER. **1. Moreover Josiah kept a passover**—(See on II Kings 23:21-23). The first nine verses give an account of the preparations made for the celebration of the solemn feast. The day appointed by the law was kept on this occasion (cf. ch. 30:2, 13). The priests were ranged in their courses and exhorted to be ready for their duties in the manner that legal purity required (cf. ch. 29:5). The Levites, the ministers or instructors of the people in all matters pertaining to the divine worship, were commanded (vs. 3) to "put the holy ark in the house which Solomon did build." Their duty was to transport the ark from place to place according to circumstances. Some think that it had been ignominiously put away from the sanctuary by order of some idolatrous king, probably Manasseh, who set a carved image in the house of God (ch. 33:7), or Amon; while others are of opinion that it had been temporarily removed by Josiah himself into some adjoining chamber, during the repairs on the temple. In replacing it, the Levites had evidently carried it upon their shoulders, deeming that still to be the duty which the law imposed on them. But Josiah reminded them of the change of circumstances. As the service of God was now performed in a fixed and permanent temple, they were not required to be bearers of the ark any longer; and, being released from the service, they should address themselves with the greater alacrity to the discharge of other functions. **4. prepare yourselves by the houses of your fathers, after your courses**—Each course or division was to be composed of those who belonged to the same fathers' house. **according to the writing of David and ... Solomon.** Their injunctions are recorded (ch. 8:14; I Chron. 23; 24; 25; 26). **5. stand in the holy place**—in the court of the priests, the place where the victims were killed. The people were admitted according to their families in groups or companies of several households at a time. When the first company entered the court (which consisted commonly of as many as it could well hold), the gates were shut and the offering was made. The Levites stood in rows from the slaughtering-places to the altar, and handed the blood and fat from one to another of the officiating priests (ch. 30:16-18). **6. So kill the passover**, etc. —The design of the minute directions given here was to facilitate the distribution of the paschal lambs. These were to be eaten by the respective families according to their numbers (Exod. 12:3). But multitudes of the people, especially those from Israel, having been reduced to poverty through the Assyrian devastations, were to be provided with the means of commemorating the passover. Therefore, the king enjoined the Levites that when the paschal lambs were brought to them to be killed (7-9) they should take care to have everything put in so orderly a train, that the lambs, after due presentation, might be easily delivered to the various families to be roasted and eaten by themselves apart. **7. Josiah gave to the people . . . lambs and kids**— These were in all probability destined for the poor; a lamb or a kid might be used at convenience (Exod. 12:5). **and . . . bullocks**—which were offered after the lambs on each of the successive days of the feast. **8. his princes**—They gave to the priests and Levites; as those of Hezekiah's princes (ch. 30:24). They were ecclesiastical princes; viz., Hilkiah the high priest (ch. 34:9), Zechariah, probably the second priest of the Eleazar (II Kings 16:18), and Jehiel of the Ithamar, line. And as the Levitical tribes were not yet sufficiently provided (vs. 9), some of their eminent brethren who had been distinguished in Hezekiah's time (ch. 31:12-15), gave a large additional contribution for the use of the Levites exclusively. **10. So the service was prepared**, etc. —All the necessary preparations having been completed, and the appointed time having arrived for the passover, the solemnity was celebrated. One remarkable feature in the account is the prominent part that was taken by the Levites in the preparation of the sacrifices; viz., the killing and stripping of the skins, which were properly the peculiar duties of the priests; but as those functionaries were not able to overtake the extraordinary amount of work and the Levites had been duly sanctified for the service, they were enlisted for the time in this priestly employment. At the passover in Hezekiah's time, the Levites officiated in the same departments of duty, the reason assigned for that deviation from the established rule being the unprepared state of many of the people (ch. 30:17). But on this occasion the whole people had been duly sanctified, and therefore the exceptional enlistment of the Levites' services must have been rendered unavoidably necessary from the multitudes engaged in celebrating the passover. **12. they removed the burnt offerings**—Some of the small cattle being designed for burnt offerings were put apart by themselves, that they might not be intermingled with the paschal lambs, which were carefully selected according to certain rules, and intended to be sacramentally eaten; and the manner in which those burnt offerings were presented seems to have been the following: "All the subdivisions of the different fathers' houses came one after another to the altar in solemn procession to bring to the

priests the portions which had been cut off, and the priests laid these pieces upon the fire of the altar of burnt offering." **13. they roasted the passover with fire according to the ordinance**—(See Exod. 12:7-9). This mode of preparation was prescribed by the law exclusively for the paschal lamb; the other offerings and thank offerings were cooked in pots, kettles, and pans (I Sam. 2:14). **divided them speedily among the people**—The haste was either owing to the multiplicity of the priests' business, or because the heat and flavor of the viands would have been otherwise diminished. Hence it appears that the meal consisted not of the paschal lambs alone, but of the meat of the thank offerings—for part of the flesh fell to the portion of the offerer, who, being in this instance, the king and the princes, were by them made over to the people, who were recommended to eat them the day they were offered, though not absolutely forbidden to do so on the next (Lev. 7:15-18). **14. afterwards they made ready for themselves, and for the priests**—The Levites rendered this aid to the priests solely because they were so engrossed the entire day that they had no leisure to provide any refreshments for themselves. **15. And the singers . . . , were in their place**—While the priests and people were so much engaged, the choir was not idle. They had to sing certain psalms, viz., 113 to 118 inclusive, once, twice, and even a third time, during the continuance of each company of offerers. As they could not leave their posts, for the singing was resumed as every fresh company entered, the Levites prepared for them also; for the various bands relieved each other in turn, and while the general choir was doing duty, a portion of the tuneful brethren, relieved for a time, partook of the viands that were brought them. **18. there was no passover like to that kept in Israel from the days of Samuel**—One feature by which this passover was distinguished was the liberality of Josiah. But what distinguished it above all preceding solemnities was, not the imposing grandeur of the ceremonies, nor the immensity of the assembled concourse of worshippers; for these, with the exception of a few from the kingdom of Israel, were confined to two tribes; but it was the ardent devotion of the king and people, the disregard of purely traditional customs, and the unusually strict adherence, even in the smallest minutiæ, to the forms of observance prescribed in the book of the law, the discovery of an original copy of which had produced so great a sensation. Instead of "from the days of Samuel," the author of the Book of Kings says, "from the days of the judges who judged Israel." The meaning is the same in both passages, for Samuel concluded the era of the judges. **all Judah and Israel were present** —The great majority of the people of the northern kingdom were in exile, but some of the remaining inhabitants performed the journey to Jerusalem on this occasion. 37,600 paschal lambs and kids were used, which, at ten to a company, would make 376,000 persons attending the feast. **19. In the eighteenth year of the reign of Josiah was this passover kept**—"It is said (II Kings 22:3) that Josiah sent Shaphan to Hilkiah in the eighth month of that year." If this statement rests upon an historical basis, all the events narrated here (from ch. 34:8 to ch. 35:19) must have happened in about the space of five months and a half. We should then have a proof that the eighteenth year of Josiah's reign was reckoned from the autumn (cf. ch. 29:3). "The eighth month" of the sacred year in the eighteenth year of his reign would be the second month of his eighteenth year, and the first month of the new year would be the seventh month [BERTHEAU].

20-27. HIS DEATH. 20. After all this, when Josiah had prepared the temple—He most probably calculated that the restoration of the divine worship, with the revival of vital religion in the land, would lead, according to God's promise and the uniform experience of the Hebrew people, to a period of settled peace and increased prosperity. His hopes were disappointed. The bright interval of tranquillity that followed his re-establishment of the true religion was brief. But it must be observed that this interruption did not proceed from any unfaithfulness in the divine promise, but from the state into which the kingdom of Judah had brought itself by the national apostasy, which was drawing down upon it the long threatened but long deferred judgments of God. **Necho king of Egypt came ap to fight against Carchemish by Euphrates**—Necho, son of Psammetichus, succeeded to the throne of Egypt in the twentieth year of Josiah. He was a bold and enterprising king, who entered with all his heart into the struggle which the two great powers of Egypt and Assyria had long carried on for the political ascendency. Each, jealous of the agressive movements of its rival, was desirous to maintain Palestine as a frontier barrier. After the overthrow of Israel, the kingdom of Judah became in that respect doubly important. Although the king and people had a strong bias for alliance with Egypt, yet from the time of Manasseh it had become a vassal of Assyria. Josiah, true to his political no less than his religious engagements, thought himself bound to support the interests of his Assyrian liege lord. Hence, when "Necho king of Egypt came up to fight Carchemish, Josiah went out against him." Carchemish, on the eastern side of the Euphrates, was the key of Assyria on the west, and in going thither the king of Egypt would transport his troops by sea along the coast of Palestine, northwards. Josiah, as a faithful vassal, resolved to oppose Necho's march across the northern parts of that country. They met in the "valley of Megiddo," i.e., the valley or plain of Esdraelon. The Egyptian king had come either by water or through the plains of Philistia, keeping constantly along the coast, round the northwest corner of Carmel, and so to the great plain of Megiddo. This was not only his direct way to the Euphrates, but the only route fit for his chariots, while thereby also he left Judah and Jerusalem quite to his right. In this valley, however, the Egyptian army had necessarily to strike across the country, and it was on that occasion that Josiah could most conveniently intercept his passage. To avoid the difficulty of passing the river Kishon, Necho kept to the south of it, and must, therefore, have come past Megiddo. Josiah, in following with his chariots and horsemen from Jerusalem, had to march northwards along the highway through Samaria by Kefr-Kud (the ancient Caper-Cotia) to Megiddo [VAN DE VELDE]. **21. But he sent ambassadors ... What have I to do with thee, thou king of Judah?**—Not wishing to spend time or strength in vain, Necho informed the king of Judah that he had no intention of molesting the Jews; that his expedition was directed solely against his old Assyrian enemy; and that he had undertaken it by an express commission from God. Commentators are not agreed whether it was really a divine commission given him through Jeremiah, or whether he merely used the name of God as an authority that Josiah would not refuse to obey. As he could not know the truth of Necho's declaration, Josiah did not sin in opposing him; or, if he sinned

at all, it was a sin of ignorance. The engagement took place. Josiah was mortally wounded. **24. took him out of that chariot, and put him in the second chariot**—the carriage he had for ordinary use, and which would be more comfortable for the royal sufferer than the war chariot. The death of this good king was the subject of universal and lasting regret. **25. Jeremiah lamented for Josiah,** etc.—The elegy of the prophet has not reached us; but it seems to have been long preserved among his countrymen and chanted on certain public occasions by the professional singers, who probably got the dirges they sang from a collection of funeral odes composed on the death of good and great men of the nation. The spot in the valley of Megiddo where the battle was fought was near the town of Hadadrimmon; hence the lamentation for the death of Josiah was called "the lamentation of Hadadrimmon in the valley of Megiddo," which was so great and so long continued, that the lamentation of Hadad passed afterwards into a proverbial phrase to express any great and extraordinary sorrow (Zech. 12:11).

CHAPTER 36

Vss. 1-4. JEHOAHAZ, SUCCEEDING, IS DEPOSED BY PHARAOH. 1. the people of the land took Jehoahaz—Immediately after Josiah's overthrow and death, the people raised to the throne Shallum (I Chron. 3:15), afterwards called Jehoahaz, in preference to his older brother Eliakim, from whom they expected little good. Jehoahaz is said (II Kings 23: 30) to have received at Jerusalem the royal anointing—a ceremony not usually deemed necessary in circumstances of regular and undisputed succession. But, in the case of Jehoahaz, it seems to have been resorted to in order to impart greater validity to the act of popular election; and, it may be, to render it less likely to be disturbed by Necho, who, like all Egyptians, would associate the idea of sanctity with the regal anointing. He was the youngest son of Josiah, but the popular favorite, probably on account of his martial spirit (Ezek. 19:3) and determined opposition to the aggressive views of Egypt. At his accession the land was free from idolatry; but this prince, instead of following the footsteps of his excellent father, adopted the criminal policy of his apostatizing predecessors. Through his influence, directly or indirectly used, idolatry rapidly increased (see on II Kings 23:32). **2. he reigned three months in Jerusalem**—His possession of sovereign power was of but very brief duration; for Necho determined to follow up the advantage he had gained in Judah; and, deeming it expedient to have a king of his own nomination on the throne of that country, he deposed the popularly elected monarch and placed his brother Eliakim or Jehoiakim on the throne, whom he anticipated to be a mere obsequious vassal. The course of events seems to have been this: on receiving intelligence after the battle of the accession of Jehoahaz to the throne, and perhaps also in consequence of the complaint which Eliakim brought before him in regard to this matter, Necho set out with a part of his forces to Jerusalem, while the remainder of his troops pursued their way at leisure towards Riblah, laid a tribute on the country, raised Eliakim (Jehoiakim) as his vassel to the throne, and on his departure brought Jehoahaz captive with him to Riblah. The old expositors mostly assumed that Necho, after the battle of Megiddo, marched directly against Carchemish, and then on his return came to Jerusalem. The improbability, indeed the impossibility, of his doing so appears from this: Carchemish was from four hundred to five hundred miles from Megiddo, so that within "three months" an army could not possibly make its way thither, conquer the fenced city of Carchemish, and then march back a still greater distance to Jerusalem, and take that city [KEIL]. **3. an hundred talents of silver**—about $170,000. **and a talent of gold**—about $25,000; total amount of tribute, about $195,000. **4. carried him** [Jehoahaz] **to Egypt**—There he died (Jer. 22:10-12).

5-8. JEHOIAKIM, REIGNING ILL, IS CARRIED INTO BABYLON. **5. Jehoiakim . . . did that which was evil in the sight of the Lord**—He followed the course of his idolatrous predecessors; and the people, to a great extent, disinclined to the reforming policy of his father, eagerly availed themselves of the vicious license which his lax administration restored. His character is portrayed with a masterly hand in the prophecy of Jeremiah (ch. 22:13-19). As the deputy of the king of Egypt, he departed further than his predecessor from the principles of Josiah's government; and, in trying to meet the insatiable cupidity of his master by grinding exactions from his subjects, he recklessly plunged into all evil. **6. Against him came up Nebuchadnezzar king of Babylon**—This refers to the first expedition of Nebuchadnezzar against Palestine, in the lifetime of his father Nabopolassar, who, being old and infirm, adopted his son as joint sovereign and despatched him, with the command of his army, against the Egyptian invaders of his empire. Nebuchadnezzar defeated them at Carchemish, drove them out of Asia, and reduced all the provinces west of the Euphrates to obedience—among the rest the kingdom of Jehoiakim, who became a vassal of the Assyrian empire (II Kings 24:1). Jehoiakim at the end of three years threw off the yoke, being probably instigated to revolt by the solicitations of the king of Egypt, who planned a new expedition against Carchemish. But he was completely vanquished by the Babylonian king, who stripped him of all his possessions between the Euphrates and the Nile (II Kings 24:7). Then marching against the Egyptian's ally in Judah, he took Jerusalem, carried away a portion of the sacred vessels of the temple, perhaps in lieu of the unpaid tribute, and deposited them in the temple of his god, Belus, at Babylon (Dan. 1:2; 5:2). Though Jehoiakim had been taken prisoner (and it was designed at first to transport him in chains to Babylon), he was allowed to remain in his tributary kingdom. But having given not long after some new offense, Jerusalem was besieged by a host of Assyrian dependents. In a sally against them Jehoiakim was killed (see on Kings 24:2-7; also Jer. 22:18, 19; 36:30). **9. Jehoiachin was eight years old**—called also Jeconiah or Coniah (Jer. 22:23)—"eight" should have been "eighteen," as appears from II Kings 24:8, and also from the full development of his ungodly principles and habits (see Ezek. 19:5-7). His reign being of so short duration cannot be considered at variance with the prophetic denunciation against his father (Jer. 36:30). But his appointment by the people gave umbrage to Nebuchadnezzar, who, "when the year was expired" (vs. 10)—i.e., in the spring when campaigns usually began—came in person against Jerusalem, captured the city, and sent Jehoiachin in chains to Babylon, removing at the same time all the nobles and most skilful artisans, and pillaging all the remaining treasures both of the temple and palace (see on II Kings 24:8-17).

11-21. ZEDEKIAH'S REIGN. **11. Zedekiah**—Nebuchadnezzar appointed him. His name, originally Mattaniah, was, according to the custom of Oriental conquerors, changed into Zedekiah. Though the son of Josiah (I Chron. 3:15; Jer. 1:2, 3; 37:1), he is called (vs. 10) the brother of Jehoiachin, i.e., according to the latitude of Hebrew style in words expressing affinity, his relative or kinsman (see on II Kings 24:18; 26:1-21). **13. who had made him swear**—Zedekiah received his crown on the express condition of taking a solemn oath of fealty to the king of Babylon (Ezek. 17:13); so that his revolt by joining in a league with Pharaoh-hophra, king of Egypt, involved the crime of perjury. His own pride and obdurate impiety, the incurable idolatry of the nation, and their reckless disregard of prophetic warnings, brought down on his already sadly reduced kingdom the long threatened judgments of God. Nebuchadnezzar, the executioner of the divine vengeance, commenced a third siege of Jerusalem, which, after holding out for a year and a half, was taken in the eleventh year of the reign of Zedekiah. It resulted in the burning of the temple, with, most probably, the ark, and in the overthrow of the kingdom of Judah (see on II Kings 25; Ezek. 12:13; 17:16). **21. until the land had enjoyed her sabbaths**—The return of every seventh year was to be held as a sabbatic year, a season of rest to all classes, even to the land itself, which was to be fallow. This divine institution, however, was neglected—how soon and how long, appears from the prophecy of Moses (Lev. 26:34), and of Jeremiah in this passage (see also *Marginal Reference*), which told that for divine retribution it was now to remain desolate seventy years. As the Assyrian conquerors usually colonized their conquered provinces, so remarkable a deviation in Palestine from their customary policy must be ascribed to the overruling providence of God.

22, 23. CYRUS' PROCLAMATION. **22. the Lord stirred up the spirit of Cyrus**—(See on Ezra 1:1-3).

THE BOOK OF

EZRA

CHAPTER 1

Vss. 1-6. PROCLAMATION OF CYRUS FOR BUILDING THE TEMPLE. **1. in the first year of Cyrus king of Persia**—The Persian empire, including Persia, Media, Babylonia, and Chaldea, with many smaller dependencies, was founded by Cyrus, 536 B.C. [HALES]. **that the word of the Lord by the mouth of Jeremiah might be fulfilled**—(See Jer. 25:12; 29: 10). This reference is a parenthetic statement of the historian, and did not form part of the proclamation. **2. The Lord God of heaven hath given me all the kingdoms of the earth**—Though this is in the Oriental style of hyperbole (see also Dan. 4:1), it was literally true that the Persian empire was the greatest ruling power in the world at that time. **he hath charged me to build him an house at Jerusalem**—The phraseology of this proclamation, independently of the express testimony of Josephus, affords indisputable evidence that Cyrus had seen (probably through means of Daniel, his venerable prime minister and favorite) those prophecies in which, 200 years before he was born, his name, his victorious career, and the important services he should render to the Jews were distinctly foretold (Isa. 44:28; 46:1-4). The existence of predictions so remarkable led him to acknowledge that all his kingdoms were gifts bestowed on him by "the Lord God of heaven," and prompted him to fulfil the duty which had been laid upon him long before his birth. This was the source and origin of the great favor he showed to the Jews. The proclamation, though issued "in the first year of Cyrus," did not take effect till the year following. **3. Who is there among you of all his people**—The purport of the edict was to grant full permission to those Jewish exiles, in every part of his kingdom, who chose, to return to their own country, as well as to recommend those of their countrymen who remained to aid the poor and feeble on their way, and contribute liberally towards the rebuilding of the temple. **5, 6. Then rose up the chief of the fathers**, etc.—The paternal and ecclesiastical chiefs of the later captivity, those of the tribes of Judah and Benjamin, with some also from other tribes (I Chron. 9:3), who retained their attachment to the pure worship of God, naturally took the lead in this movement. Their example was followed by all whose piety and patriotism were strong enough to brave the various discouragements attending the enterprise. They were liberally assisted by multitudes of their captive countrymen, who, born in Babylonia or comfortably established in it by family connections or the possession of property, chose to remain. It seems that their Assyrian friends and neighbors, too, either from a favorable disposition toward the Jewish faith, or from imitation of the court policy, displayed hearty good will and great liberality in aiding and promoting the views of the emigrants.

7-11. CYRUS RESTORES THE VESSELS. **7. Cyrus . . . brought forth the vessels of the house of the Lord**—Though it is said (II Kings 24:13) that these were *cut in pieces,* that would not be done to the large and magnificent vases; and, if they had been divided, the parts could be reunited. But it may be doubted whether the *Hebrew* word rendered *cut in pieces,* does not signify merely *cut off,* i.e., from further use in the temple. **8. Sheshbazzar, the prince of Judah**—i.e., Zerubbabel, son of Salathiel (cf. ch. 3:8; 5:16). He was born in Babylon and called by his family Zerubbabel, i.e., stranger or exile in Babylon. Sheshbazzar, signifying "fire-worshipper," was the name given him at court, as other names were given to Daniel and his friends. He was recognized among the exiles as hereditary prince of Judah. **11. All the vessels of gold and of silver were five thousand and four hundred**—The vessels here specified amount only to the number of 2499. Hence it is probable that the larger vases only are mentioned, while the inventory of the whole, including great and small, came to the gross sum stated in the text. **them of the captivity that were brought up from Babylon unto Jerusalem**—All the Jewish exiles did

not embrace the privilege which the Persian king granted them. The great proportion, born in Babylon, preferred continuing in their comfortable homes to undertaking a distant, expensive, and hazardous journey to a desolate land. Nor did the returning exiles all go at once. The first band went with Zerubbabel, others afterwards with Ezra, and a large number with Nehemiah at a still later period.

CHAPTER 2

VSS. 1-70. NUMBER OF THE PEOPLE THAT RETURNED. **1. children of the province**—i.e., Judea (ch. 5:8), so called as being now reduced from an illustrious, independent, and powerful kingdom to an obscure, servile, tributary province of the Persian empire. This name is applied by the sacred historian to intimate that the Jewish exiles, though now released from captivity and allowed to return into their own land, were still the subjects of Cyrus, inhabiting a province dependent upon Persia. **came again unto Jerusalem and Judah, every one unto his city**—either the city that had been occupied by his ancestors, or, as most parts of Judea were then either desolate or possessed by others, the city that was rebuilt and allotted to him now. **2. Which came with Zerubbabel**—He was the chief or leader of the first band of returning exiles. The names of other influential persons who were associated in the conducting of the caravans are also mentioned, being extracted probably from the Persian archives, in which the register was preserved: conspicuous in the number are Jeshua, the high priest, and Nehemiah. **3. The children**—This word, as used throughout this catalogue, means posterity or descendants. **5. children of Arah, seven hundred seventy and five**—The number is stated in Nehemiah 7 to have been only 652. It is probable that all mentioned as belonging to this family repaired to the general place of rendezvous, or had enrolled their names at first as intending to go; but in the interval of preparation, some died, others were prevented by sickness or insurmountable obstacles, so that ultimately no more than 652 came to Jerusalem. **23. The men of Anathoth**—It is pleasant to see so many of this Jewish town returning. It was a city of the Levites; but the people spurned Jeremiah's warning and called forth against themselves one of his severest predictions (Jer. 32:27-35). This prophecy was fulfilled in the Assyrian conquest. Anathoth was laid waste and continued a heap of ruins. But the people, having been brought during the captivity to a better state of mind, returned, and their city was rebuilt. **36-39. The priests**—Each of their families was ranged under its prince or head, like those of the other tribes. It will be remembered that the whole body was divided into twenty-four courses, one of which, in rotation, discharged the sacerdotal duties every week, and each division was called after the name of its first prince or chief. It appears from this passage that only four of the courses of the priests returned from the Babylonish captivity; but these four courses were afterwards, as the families increased, divided into twenty-four, which were distinguished by the names of the original courses appointed by David. Hence we find the course of Abijah or Abia (I Chron. 24:10) subsisting at the commencement of the Christian era (Luke 1: 5). **55. The children of Solomon's servants**—either the strangers that monarch enlisted in the building of the temple, or those who lived in his palace, which was deemed a high honor. **61, 62. the**

children of Barzillai—He preferred that name to that of his own family, deeming it a greater distinction to be connected with so noble a family, than to be of the house of Levi. But by this worldly ambition he forfeited the dignity and advantages of the priesthood. **63. Tirshatha**—a title borne by the Persian governors of Judea (see also Neh. 7:65-70; 8:9; 10: 1). It is derived from the Persian *torsh,* severe, and is equivalent to "your severity," "your awfulness." **64. The whole congregation together was forty-two thousand three hundred and threescore**—This gross amount is 12,000 more than the particular numbers given in the catalogue, when added together, come to. Reckoning up the smaller numbers, we shall find that they amount to 29,818 in this chapter, and to 31,089 in the parallel chapter of Nehemiah. Ezra also mentions 494 persons omitted by Nehemiah, and Nehemiah mentions 1765 not noticed by Ezra. If, therefore, Ezra's surplus be added to the sum in Nehemiah, and Nehemiah's surplus to the number in Ezra, they will both become 31,583. Subtracting this from 42,360, there will be a deficiency of 10,777. These are omitted because they did not belong to Judah and Benjamin, or to the priests, but to the other tribes. The servants and singers, male and female, are reckoned separately (vs. 65), so that putting all these items together, the number of all who went with Zerubbabel amounted to 50,000, with 8000 beasts of burden (ALTING, quoted DAVIDSON'S HERMENEUTICS). **68. some of the chief of the fathers, when they came to the house of the Lord, offered freely for the house of God,** etc.—The sight of a place hallowed by the most endearing and sacred associations, but now lying in desolation and ruins, made the well-springs of their piety and patriotism gush out afresh. Before taking any active measures for providing accommodation to themselves and their families, the chief among them raised a large sum by voluntary contributions towards the restoration of the temple. **69. drams of gold**—rather darics, a Persian coin (see on I Chron. 29:7). **priests' garments** (cf. Neh. 7:70). This—in the circumstances —was a very appropriate gift. In general, it may be remarked that presents of garments, or of any other usable commodities, however singular it may seem to us, is in harmony with the established notions and customs of the East.

CHAPTER 3

Vss. 1-13. THE ALTAR SET UP. **1. when the seventh month was come**—The departure of the returning exiles from Babylon took place in the spring. For some time after their arrival they were occupied in the necessary work of rearing habitations to themselves amid the ruins of Jerusalem and its neighborhood. This preliminary work being completed, they addressed themselves to rebuild the altar of burnt offering. As the seventh month of the sacred year was at hand—corresponding to the latter end of our September—when the feast of tabernacles (Lev. 23) fell to be observed, they resolved to celebrate that religious festival, just as if the temple had been fully restored. **2. Jeshua**—the grandson of Seraiah, the high priest, put to death by Nebuchadnezzar at Riblah (II Kings 25:18-21). His father, Josedech, had been carried captive to Babylon, and died there, some time before this. **Zerubbabel**— was, according to the order of nature, son of Pedaiah (I Chron. 3:17-19); but having been brought up by Salathiel, he was called his son. **builded the**

altar of the God of Israel, to offer burnt offerings thereon—This was of urgent and immediate necessity, in order, first, to make atonement for their sins; secondly, to obtain the divine blessing on their preparations for the temple, as well as animate their feelings of piety and patriotism for the prosecution of that national work. **3. they set the altar upon his bases**—They reared it upon its old foundation, so that it occupied as nearly as possible the site on which it had formerly stood. **they offered burnt offerings . . . morning and evening**—Deeming it their duty to perform the public rites of religion, they did not wait till the temple should be rebuilt and dedicated; but, at the outset, they resumed the daily service prescribed by the law (Exod. 29:38, 39; Lev. 6:9, 11), as well as observed the annual seasons of solemn observance.

4-7. OFFERINGS RENEWED. **4, 6. They kept also the feast of tabernacles . . . From the first day of the seventh month**—They revived at that time the daily oblation, and it was on the fifteenth day of that month the feast of tabernacles was held. **7. They gave . . . meat . . . drink, and oil, unto them of Zidon**—They opened negotiations with the Tyrians for workmen, as well as for timber, on the same terms and with the same views as Solomon had done (I Kings 5:11; II Chron. 2:15, 16).

8-13. THE FOUNDATION OF THE TEMPLE LAID. **8. appointed the Levites . . . to set forward the work** —i.e., to act as overseers of the workmen, and to direct and animate the laborers in the various departments. **9. Jeshua with his sons**—not the high priest, but a Levite (ch. 2:40). To these, as probably distinguished for their mechanical skill and taste, the duty of acting as overseer was particularly committed. **12. But many of the priests and Levites and chief of the fathers . . . wept with a loud voice**—Those painful emotions were excited by the sad contrast between the prosperous circumstances in which the foundations of the first temple had been laid and the desolate, reduced state of the country and city when the second was begun; between the inferior size and less costliness of the stones used in the foundations of the second (I Kings 7:9, 10), and the much smaller extent of the foundation itself, including all the appurtenances of the building (Hag. 2:3); between the comparative smallness of their present means and the immense resources of David and Solomon. Perhaps, however, the chief cause of grief was that the second temple would be destitute of those things which formed the great and distinguishing glory of the first; viz., the ark, the shekinah, the Urim and Thummim, etc. Not that this second temple was not a very grand and beautiful structure. But no matter how great its material splendor was, it was inferior in this respect to that of Solomon. Yet the glory of the second far outshone that of the first temple in another and more important point of view, viz., the receiving within its walls the incarnate Saviour (Hag. 2:9). **13. the people could not discern the shout of joy from the noise of the weeping**—Among Eastern people, expressions of sorrow are always very loud and vehement. It is indicated by wailing, the howl of which is sometimes not easily distinguishable from joyful acclamations.

CHAPTER 4

Vss. 1-6. THE BUILDING HINDERED. **1. the adversaries of Judah and Benjamin**—i.e., strangers settled in the land of Israel. **2. we seek your God, as ye do; and we do sacrifice unto him since the days of Esarhaddon . . . which brought us up hither**—A very interesting explanation of this passage has been recently obtained from the Assyrian sculptures. On a large cylinder, deposited in the British Museum, there is inscribed a long and perfect copy of the annals of Esarhaddon, in which the details are given of a large deportation of Israelites from Palestine, and a consequent settlement of Babylonian colonists in their place. It is a striking confirmation of the statement made in this passage. Those Assyrian settlers intermarried with the remnant of Israelite women, and their descendants, a mongrel race, went under the name of Samaritans. Though originally idolaters, they were instructed in the knowledge of God, so that they could say, "We seek your God"; but they served Him in a superstitious way of their own (see on II Kings 17:26-34, 41). **3. But Zerubbabel and Jeshua . . . said . . . Ye have nothing to do with us to build an house unto our God**—This refusal to co-operate with the Samaritans, from whatever motives it sprang, was overruled by Providence for ultimate good; for, had the two peoples worked together, familiar acquaintanceship and intermarriage would have ensued, and the result might have been a relapse of the Jews into idolatry. Most certainly, confusion and obscurity in the genealogical evidence that proved the descent of the Messiah would have followed; whereas, in their hostile and separate condition, were jealous observers of each other's proceedings, watching with mutual care over the preservation and integrity of the sacred books, guarding the purity and honor of the Mosaic worship, and thus contributing to the maintenance of religious knowledge and truth. **4. Then the people of the land weakened the hands of the people of Judah**, etc.—Exasperated by this repulse, the Samaritans endeavored by every means to molest the workmen as well as obstruct the progress of the building; and, though they could not alter the decree which Cyrus had issued regarding it, yet by bribes and clandestine arts indefatigably plied at court, they labored to frustrate the effects of the edict. Their success in those underhand dealings was great; for Cyrus, being frequently absent and much absorbed in his warlike expeditions, left the government in the hands of his son Cambyses, a wicked prince, and extremely hostile to the Jews and their religion. The same arts were assiduously practised during the reign of his successor, Smerdis, down to the time of Darius Hystaspes. In consequence of the difficulties and obstacles thus interposed, for a period of twenty years, the progress of the work was very slow. **6. in the reign of Ahasuerus, in the beginning of his reign, wrote they . . . an accusation**—Ahasuerus was a regal title, and the king referred to was successor of Darius, the famous Xerxes.

7-24. LETTER TO ARTAXERXES. **7. in the day of Artaxerxes wrote Bishlam**, etc.—The three officers named are supposed to have been deputy-governors appointed by the king of Persia over all the provinces subject to his empire west of the Euphrates. **the Syrian tongue**—or Aramæan language, called sometimes in our version, Chaldee. This was made use of by the Persians in their decrees and communications relative to the Jews (cf. II Kings 18:26; Isa. 36:11). The object of their letter was to press upon the royal notice the inexpediency and danger of rebuilding the walls of Jerusalem. They labored hard to prejudice the king's mind against that measure. **12. the Jews which came up from thee to us**—The name "Jews" was generally used after the return from the captivity, because the returning exiles belonged chiefly to the tribes of Judah and Benjamin. Although the edict of Cyrus permitted all who chose to return, a permission of which some of the Israelites availed themselves, the great body who went to settle in Judea were the men of Judah. **13. toll, tribute, and custom**—The first was a poll tax; the second was a property tax; the third the excise dues on articles of trade and merchandise. Their letter, and the edict that followed, commanding an immediate cessation of the work at the city walls, form the exclusive subject of narrative from vs. 7 to vs. 23. And now from this digression he returns at vs. 24 to resume the thread of his narrative concerning the building of the temple. **9. the Dinaites**—The people named were the colonists sent by the Babylonian monarch to occupy the territory of the ten tribes. "The great and noble Asnapper" was Esar-haddon. Immediately after the murder of Sennacherib, the Babylonians, Medes, Armenians, and other tributary people seized the opportunity of throwing off the Assyrian yoke. But Esar-haddon having, in the thirtieth year of his reign, recovered Babylon and subdued the other rebellious dependents, transported numbers of them into the waste cities of Samaria, most probably as a punishment of their revolt [HALES]. **14. we have maintenance from the king's palace**—lit., we are salted with the king's salt. "Eating a prince's salt" is an Oriental phrase, equivalent to "receiving maintenance from him." **24. Then ceased the work of the house of God**—It was this occurrence that first gave rise to the strong religious antipathy between the Jews and the Samaritans, which was afterwards greatly aggravated by the erection of a rival temple on Mount Gerizim.

CHAPTER 5

Vss. 1-17. ZERUBBABEL AND JESHUA SET FORWARD THE BUILDING OF THE TEMPLE IN THE REIGN OF DARIUS. **1. Then the prophets . . . prophesied . . . in the name of the God of Israel**—From the recorded writings of Haggai and Zechariah, it appears that the difficulties experienced and the many obstacles thrown in the way had first cooled the zeal of the Jews in the building of the temple, and then led to an abandonment of the work, under a pretended belief that the time for rebuilding it had not yet come (Hag. 1:2-11). For fifteen years the work was completely suspended. These two prophets upbraided them with severe reproaches for their sloth, negligence, and worldly selfishness (Hag. 1:4), threatened them with severe judgments if they continued backward, and promised that they would be blessed with great national prosperity if they resumed and prosecuted the work with alacrity and vigor. **Zechariah the son of Iddo**—i.e., grandson (Zech. 1:1). **2. Then rose up Zerubbabel . . . and Jeshua . . . and began to build the house of God**—The strong appeals and animating exhortations of these prophets gave a new impulse to the building of the temple. It was in the second year of the reign of Darius Hystaspes that the work, after a long interruption, was resumed. **3, 4. At the same time came to them Tatnai, governor on this side the river**—The Persian empire west of the Euphrates included at this time Syria, Arabia, Egypt, Phœnicia, and other provinces subject to Darius. The empire was divided into twenty provinces, called satrapies. Syria formed one satrapy, inclusive of Palestine, Phœnicia, and

Cyprus, and furnished an annual revenue of 350 talents. It was presided over by a satrap or viceroy, who at this time resided at Damascus. Though superior to the native governors of the Jews appointed by the Persian king, he never interfered with their internal government except when there was a threatened disturbance of order and tranquillity. Tatnai, the governor (whether this was a personal name or an official title is unknown), had probably been incited by the complaints and turbulent outrages of the Samaritans against the Jews; but he suspended his judgment, and he prudently resolved to repair to Jerusalem, that he might ascertain the real state of matters by personal inspection and inquiry, in company with another dignified officer and his provincial council. **5. But the eye of their God was upon the elders of the Jews,** etc.–The unusual presence, the imposing suite, the authoritative inquiries of the satrap appeared formidable, and might have produced a paralyzing influence or led to disastrous consequences, if he had been a partial and corrupt judge or actuated by unfriendly feelings towards the Jewish cause. The historian, therefore, with characteristic piety, throws in this parenthetical verse to intimate that God averted the threatening cloud and procured favor for the elders or leaders of the Jews, that they were not interrupted in their proceedings till communications with the court should be made and received. Not a word was uttered to dispirit the Jews or afford cause of triumph to their opponents. Matters were to go on till contrary orders arrived from Babylon. After surveying the work in progress, he inquired: first, by what authority this national temple was undertaken; and, secondly, the names of the principal promoters and directors of the undertaking. To these two heads of inquiry the Jews returned ready and distinct replies. Then having learned that it originated in a decree of Cyrus, who had not only released the Jewish exiles from captivity and permitted them to return to their own land for the express purpose of rebuilding the house of God, but, by an act of royal grace, had restored to them the sacred vessels which Nebuchadnezzar had carried off as trophies from the former temple, Tatnai transmitted all this information in an official report to his imperial master, accompanying it with a recommendatory suggestion that search should be made among the national archives at Babylon for the original decree of Cyrus, that the truth of the Jews' statement might be verified. The whole conduct of Tatnai, as well as the general tone of his despatch, is marked by a sound discretion and prudent moderation, free from any party bias, and evincing a desire only to do his duty. In all respects he appears in favorable contrast with his predecessor, Rehum (ch. 4:9). **8. the house of the great God, which is builded with great stones**—lit., "stones of rolling"–i.e., stones of such extraordinary size that they could not be carried–they had to be rolled or dragged along the ground. **13. Cyrus the king ... made a decree**–The Jews were perfectly warranted according to the principles of the Persian government to proceed with the building in virtue of Cyrus' edict. For everywhere a public decree is considered as remaining in force until it is revoked but the "laws of the Medes and Persians changed not." **16. Then came ... Sheshbazzar ... since that time even until now hath it been in building**–This was not a part of the Jews' answer–they could not have said this, knowing the building had long ceased. But Tatnai used these expressions in his report, either looking on the stoppage as a temporary interruption, or supposing that the Jews were always working a little, as they had means and opportunities.

CHAPTER 6

Vss. 1-12. DARIUS' DECREE FOR ADVANCING THE BUILDING. **1. Darius the king**–This was Darius **Hystaspes.** Great and interesting light has been thrown on the history of this monarch and the transaction of his reign, by the decipherment of the cuneatic inscriptions on the rocks at Behistun. **in the house of the rolls, where the treasures were laid up in Babylon**–An idea of the form of this Babylonian register house, as well as the manner of preserving public records within its repositories, can be obtained from the discoveries at Nineveh. Two small chambers were discovered in the palace of Koyunjik, which, from the fragments found in them, Mr. Layard considers "as a house of the rolls." After reminding his readers that the historical records and public documents of the Assyrians were kept on tablets and cylinders of baked clay, many specimens of which have been found, he goes on to say, "The chambers I am describing appear to have been a depository in the palace of Nineveh for such documents. To the height of a foot or more from the floor they were entirely filled with them; some entire, but the greater part broken into many fragments, probably by the falling in of the upper part of the building. They were of different sizes; the largest tablets were flat, and measured about 9 inches by 6½ inches; the smaller were slightly convex, and some were not more than an inch long, with but one or two lines of writing. The cuneiform characters on most of them were singularly sharp and well defined, but so minute in some instances as to be almost illegible without a magnifying glass. These documents appear to be of various kinds. The documents that have thus been discovered 'in the house of rolls' at Nineveh probably exceed all that have yet been afforded by the monuments of Egypt, and when the innumerable fragments are put together and transcribed, the publication of these records will be of the greatest importance to the history of the ancient world" [NINEVEH and BABYLON]. **2. Achmetha**–long supposed to be the capital of Greater Media–the Ecbatana of classical, the Hamadan of modern times, at the foot of the Elwund range of hills, where, for its coolness and salubrity, Cyrus and his successors on the Persian throne established their summer residence. There was another city, however, of this name, the Ecbatana of Atropatene, and the most ancient capital of northern Media, and recently identified by Colonel Rawlinson in the remarkable ruins of *Takht-i-Soleiman.* Yet as everything tends to show the attachment of Cyrus to his native city, the Atropatenian Ecbatana, rather than to the stronger capital of Greater Media, Colonel Rawlinson is inclined to think that he deposited there, in his fortress, the famous decree relating to the Jews, along with the other records and treasures of his empire [NINEVEH and PERSEPOLIS]. **8-10. of the king's goods, even of the tribute beyond the river ... expenses be given unto these men**–The decree granted them the privilege of drawing from his provincial treasury of Syria, to the amount of whatever they required for the furthering of the work and providing sacrifice for the service of the temple, that the priests might daily pray for the health of the king and the prosperity of the empire. **11. whosoever shall alter this word**–The warning was specially directed against the turbulent and fanatical Samaritans. The extremely favorable purport of this edict was no doubt owing in some measure to the influence of Cyrus, of whom Darius entertained a high admiration, and whose two daughters he had married. But it proceeded still more from the deep impressions made even on the idolatrous people of that country and that age, as to the being and providence of the God of Israel.

13-15. THE TEMPLE FINISHED. 13. Then Tatnai ... did speedily—A concurrence of favorable events is mentioned as accelerating the restoration of the temple and infusing a new spirit and energy into the workmen, who now labored with unabating assiduity till it was brought to a completion. Its foundation was laid in April, 536 B.C. (ch. 3:8-10), and it was completed on February 21, 515 B.C., being 21 years after it was begun [LIGHTFOOT].

16-18. FEASTS OF THE DEDICATION. 16. the the children of Israel ... kept the dedication ... with joy—The ceremonial was gone through with demonstrations of the liveliest joy. The aged who had wept at the laying of the foundation were most, if not all of them, now dead; and all rejoiced at the completion of this national undertaking. **17. twelve he-goats**—as at the dedication of the tabernacle (Num. 8:17). **18. they set the priests in their divisions, and the Levites in their courses ... as it is written in the book of Moses**—Although David arranged the priests and Levites in courses according to their families, it was Moses who assigned to the priests and Levites their rights and privileges, their stations and several duties.

19-22. AND OF THE PASSOVER. 21. all such as had separated themselves ... from the filthiness of the heathen—i.e., who had given satisfactory evidence of being true proselytes by not only renouncing the impure worship of idolatry, but by undergoing the rite of circumcision, a condition indispensable to a participation of the passover. **22. kept the feast ... with joy: for the Lord ... turned the heart of the king of Assyria unto them**—i.e., king of the Persian empire, which now included the possessions, and had surpassed the glory, of Assyria. The favorable disposition which Darius had evinced towards the Jews secured them peace and prosperity and the privileges of their own religion during the rest of his reign. The religious joy that so remarkably characterized the celebration of this feast, was testified by expressions of lively gratitude to God, whose overruling power and converting grace had produced so marvellous a change in the hearts of the mighty potentates, and disposed them, pagans though they were, to aid the cause and provide for the worship of the true God.

CHAPTER 7

Vss. 1-10. EZRA GOES UP TO JERUSALEM. 1. in the reign of Artaxerxes—the Ahasuerus of Esther. **Ezra the son of Seraiah**—i.e., grandson or great-grandson. Seraiah was the high priest put to death by Nebuchadnezzar at Riblah (II Kings 25:18). A period of 130 years had elapsed between that catastrophe and the journey of Ezra to Jerusalem. As a grandson of Seraiah, viz., Jeshua, who held the office of high priest, had accompanied Zerubbabel in the first caravan of returning exiles, Ezra must have been in all probability a grandson, descended, too, from a younger son, the older branch being in possession of the pontificate. **6. This Ezra ... was a ready scribe in the law of Moses**—The term "scribe" does not mean merely a penman, nor even an at-

torney well versed in forms of law and skilled in the method of preparing public or private deeds. He was a rabbi, or doctor, learned in the Mosaic law, and in all that related to the civil and ecclesiastical polity and customs of the Hebrew people. Scribes of this description possessed great authority and influence (cf. Matt. 23:25; Mark 12:28). **the king granted him all his request**—He left Babylon entrusted with an important commission to be executed in Jerusalem. The manner in which he obtained this office is minutely related in a subsequent passage. Here it is noticed, but with a pious acknowledgment of the divine grace and goodness which disposed the royal mind in favor of Ezra's patriotic objects. The Levites, etc., did not go at that time, but are mentioned here by anticipation. **8. he came to Jerusalem in the fifth month**—i.e., corresponding to the end of our July or beginning of our August. As he left Babylon on the Jewish New Year's Day (vs. 9), the journey must have occupied not less than four months—a long period—but it was necessary to move at a slow pace and by short, easy stages, as he had to conduct a large caravan of poor people, including women, children, and all their household gear (see on ch. 8). **10. Ezra had prepared his heart to seek the law of the Lord**, etc.—His reigning desire had been to study the divine law—its principles, institutions, privileges, and requirements; and now from love and zeal, he devoted himself, as the business of his life, to the work of instructing, reforming, and edifying others.

11-26. GRACIOUS COMMISSION OF ARTAXERXES. 11. this is the copy of the letter that the king Artaxerxes gave—The measure which this document authorized, and the remarkable interest in the Jews displayed in it, were most probably owing to the influence of Esther, who is thought to have been raised to the high position of queen a few months previous to the departure of Ezra [HALES]. According to others, who adopt a different chronology, it was more probably pressed upon the attention of the Persian court by Ezra, who, like Daniel, showed the prophecies to the king; or by some leading Jews on his accession, who, seeing the unsettled and disordered state of the colony after the deaths of Zerubbabel, Jeshua, Haggai, and Zechariah, recommended the appointment of a commission to reform abuses, suppress disorder, and enforce the observance of the law. **12. Artaxerxes, king of kings**—That title might have been assumed as, with literal truth, applicable to him, since many of the tributary princes of his empire still retained the name and authority of kings. But it was a probably a mere Orientalism, denoting a great and powerful prince, as the heaven of heavens signified the highest heaven, and vanity of vanities, the greatest vanity. This vainglorious title was assumed by the kings of Assyria, from whom it passed to the sovereigns of Persia. **unto Ezra the priest, a scribe of the law of the God of heaven**—The appointment of Ezra to this influential mission was of the highest importance to the Hebrew people, as a large proportion of them were become, in a great measure, strangers both to the language and the institutions of their forefathers. **14. sent of the king, and of his seven counsellors**—This was the fixed number of the privy council of the kings of Persia (Esther 1:10, 14). The document describes, with great clearness and precision, the nature of Ezra's commission and the extent of power and prerogatives with which he was invested. It gave him authority, in the first place, to organize the colony in Judea and institute a regular government, according to the laws of the Hebrew people,

but other Israelites are also included under these names, as they all were then occupying the territory formerly assigned to those two tribes. **It was the ninth month**—i.e., between the end of December and the beginning of January, which is the coldest and most rainy season of the year in Palestine. **all the people sat in the street**—i.e., the court. **10. Ezra the priest stood up, and said**—Having fully represented the enormity of their sin and urged them to dissolve their unlawful connections, he was gratified by receiving a prompt acknowledgment of the justice of his reproof and a promise of compliance with his recommendation. But as the weather was ungenial and the defaulters were too numerous to be passed in review at one time, it was resolved that a commission should be appointed to examine into the whole matter. These commissioners, assisted by the judges and elders of the respective cities, made a minute investigation into every case, and after three months' labor completely removed all traces of the abuse. Doubtless, an adequate provision was made for the repudiated wives and children, according to the means and circumstances of the husbands.

18-44. THOSE THAT HAD TAKEN STRANGE WIVES. **18. among the sons of the priests**—From the names of so many men of rank appearing in the following list, some idea may be formed of the great and complicated difficulties attending the reformatory work. **19. they gave their hands**—i.e., came under a solemn engagement, which was usually ratified by pledging the right hand (Prov. 6:1; Ezek. 17:18). The delinquents of the priestly order bound themselves to do like the common Israelites (vs. 25), and sought to expiate their sin by sacrificing a ram as a trespass offering.

THE BOOK OF
NEHEMIAH

CHAPTER 1

Vss. 1-3. NEHEMIAH, UNDERSTANDING BY HANANI THE AFFLICTED STATE OF JERUSALEM, MOURNS, FASTS, AND PRAYS. **1. Nehemiah the son of Hachaliah**—This eminently pious and patriotic Jew is to be carefully distinguished from two other persons of the same name—one of whom is mentioned as helping to rebuild the walls of Jerusalem (ch. 3:16), and the other is noticed in the list of those who accompanied Zerubbabel in the first detachment of returning exiles (Ezra 2:2; ch. 7:7). Though little is known of his genealogy, it is highly probable that he was a descendant of the tribe of Judah and the royal family of David. **in the month Chisleu**—answering to the close of November and the larger part of December. **Shushan the palace**—the capital of ancient Susiana, east of the Tigris, a province of Persia. From the time of Cyrus it was the favorite winter residence of the Persian kings. **2. Hanani, one of my brethren, came, he and certain men of Judah**—Hanani is called his brother (ch. 7:2). But as that term was used loosely by Jews as well as other Orientals, it is probable that no more is meant than that he was of the same family. According to Josephus, Nehemiah, while walking around the palace walls, overheard some persons conversing in the Hebrew language. Having ascertained that they had lately returned from Judea, he was informed by them, in answer to his eager inquiries, of the unfinished and desolate condition of Jerusalem, as well as the defenseless state of the returned exiles. The commissions previously given to Zerubbabel and Ezra extending only to the repair of the temple and private dwellings, the walls and gates of the city had been allowed to remain a mass of shattered ruins, as they had been laid by the Chaldean siege. 4-11. HIS PRAYER. **4. when I heard these words that I sat down ... and mourned, ... and fasted, and prayed**—The recital deeply affected the patriotic feelings of this good man, and no comfort could he find but in earnest and protracted prayer, that God would favor the purpose, which he seems to have secretly formed, of asking the royal permission to go to Jerusalem. **11. I was the king's cupbearer**—This officer, in the ancient Oriental courts, was always a person of rank and importance; and, from the confidential nature of his duties and his frequent access to the royal presence, he possessed great influence.

CHAPTER 2

Vss. 1-20. ARTAXERXES, UNDERSTANDING THE CAUSE OF NEHEMIAH'S SADNESS, SENDS HIM WITH LETTERS AND A COMMISSION TO BUILD AGAIN THE WALLS OF JERUSALEM. **1. it came to pass in the month Nisan**—This was nearly four months after he had learned the desolate and ruinous state of Jerusalem (ch. 1:1). The reasons for so long a delay cannot be ascertained. **I took up the wine, and gave it unto the king**—Xenophon has particularly remarked about the polished and graceful manner in which the cupbearers of the Median, and consequently the Persian, monarchs performed their duty of presenting the wine to their royal master. Having washed the cup in the king's presence and poured into his left hand a little of the wine, which they drank in his presence, they then handed the cup to him, not grasped, but lightly held with the tips of their thumb and fingers. This description has received some curious illustrations from the monuments of Assyria and Persia, on which the cupbearers are frequently represented in the act of handing wine to the king. **2. the king said unto me, Why is thy countenance sad?**—It was deemed highly unbecoming to appear in the royal presence with any weeds or signs of sorrow (Esther 4:2); and hence it was no wonder that the king was struck with the dejected air of his cupbearer, while that attendant, on his part, felt his agitation increased by his deep anxiety about the issue of the conversation so abruptly begun. But the piety and intense earnestness of the man immediately restored him to calm self-possession and enabled him to communicate, first, the cause of his sadness, and next, the patriotic wish of his heart to be the honored instrument of reviving the ancient glory of the city of his fathers. **6-9. the queen also sitting by him**—As the Persian monarchs did not admit their wives to be present at their state festivals, this must have been a private occasion. The queen referred to was probably Esther, whose presence would tend greatly to embolden Nehemiah in stating his request; and through her influence, powerfully exerted it may be supposed, also by her sympathy with the patriotic design, his petition was granted, to go as deputy-governor of Judea, accompanied by a military guard, and invested with full powers to obtain materials for the building in Jerusalem, as well as to get all requisite aid in promoting his enterprise. **6. I set him a time**—Considering the great despatch made in raising the walls, it is probable that this leave of absence was limited at first to a year or six months, after which he returned to his duties in Shushan. The circumstance of fixing a set time for his return, as well as entrusting so important a work as the refortification of Jerusalem to his care, proves the high favor and confidence Nehemiah enjoyed at the Persian court, and the great estimation in which his services were held. At a later period he received a new commission for the better settlement of the affairs of Judea and remained governor of that province for twelve years (ch. 5:14). **7. letters be given me to the governors beyond the river**—The Persian empire at this time was of vast extent, reaching from the Indus to the Mediterranean. The Euphrates was considered as naturally dividing it into two parts, eastern and western (see Ezra 5:3, 4). **8. according to the good hand of my God upon me**—The piety of Nehemiah appears in every circumstance. The conception of his patriotic design —the favorable disposition of the king, and the success of the undertaking are all ascribed to God. **9, 10. Sanballat the Horonite**—Horonaim being a town in Moab, this person, it is probable, was a Moabite. **Tobiah the servant, the Ammonite**—The term used indicates him to have been a freed slave, elevated to some official dignity. These were district magistrates under the government ȯf the satrap of Syria; and they seem to have been leaders of the Samaritan faction. **11, 12. So I came to Jerusalem, and was there three days**—Deeply affected with the desolations of Jerusalem, and uncertain what course to follow, he remained three days before informing any one of the object of his mission. At the end of the third day, accompanied with a few attendants, he made, under covert of night, a secret survey of the walls and gates. **13-15. I went out by night by the gate of the valley**—i.e., the Jaffa gate, near the tower of Hippicus. **even before the dragon well**— i.e., fountain on the opposite side of the valley. **and to the dung port**—the gate on the east of the city, through which there ran a common sewer to the brook Kedron and the valley of Hinnom. **14. Then** —i.e., after having passed through the gate of the Essenes. **I went on to the gate of the fountain**— i.e., Siloah, from which turning round the fount of Ophel. **to the king's pool; but there was no place for the beast that was under me to pass**—i.e., by the sides of this pool (Solomon's) there being water in the pool, and too much rubbish about it to permit the passage of the beast. **15. Then I went up . . . by the brook**—i.e., Kedron. **and entered by the gate of the valley, and so returned**—the gate leading to the valley of Jehoshaphat, east of the city. He went out by this gate, and having made the circuit of the city, went in by it again [BARCLAY'S CITY OF THE GREAT KING]. **16-18. the rulers knew not**—The

following day, having assembled the elders, Nehemiah produced his commission and exhorted them to assist in the work. The sight of his credentials, and the animating strain of his address and example, so revived their drooping spirits that they resolved immediately to commence the building, which they did, despite the bitter taunts and scoffing ridicule of some influential men.

CHAPTER 3

VSS. 1-32. THE NAMES AND ORDER OF THEM THAT BUILDED THE WALL OF JERUSALEM. **1. Then Eliashib the high priest**—the grandson of Jeshua, and the first high priest after the return from Babylon. **rose up, with his brethren the priests**—i.e., set an example by commencing the work—their labors being confined to the sacred localities. **they builded the sheep gate**—close to the temple. Its name arose either from the sheep-market, or from the pool of Bethesda, which was there (John 5:2). There the sheep were washed and then taken to the temple for sacrifice. **they sanctified it, and set up the doors** —Being the common entrance into the temple, and the first part of the building repaired, it is probable that some religious ceremonies were observed in gratitude for its completion. "It was the first-fruits, and therefore, in the sanctification of it, the whole lump and building was sanctified" [POOLE]. **the tower of Meah**—This word is improperly considered, in our version, as the name of a tower; it is the *Hebrew* word for "a hundred," so that the meaning is: they not only rebuilt the sheep gate, but also a hundred cubits of the wall, which extended as far as the tower of Hananeel. **2. next unto him builded the men of Jericho**, etc.—The wall was divided into portions, one of which was assigned respectively to each of the great families which had returned from the captivity. This distribution, by which the building was carried on in all parts simultaneously with great energy, was eminently favorable to despatch. "The villages where the restorers resided being mostly mentioned, it will be seen that this circumstance affords a general indication of the part of the wall upon which they labored, such places being on that side of the city nearest their place of abode; the only apparent exception being, perhaps, where they repaired more than their place. Having completed their first undertaking (if they worked any more), there being no more work to be done on the side next their residence, or having arrived after the repairs on that part of the city nearest them under operation were completed, they would go wherever their services would be required" [BARCLAY'S CITY OF THE GREAT KING]. **8. they fortified Jerusalem unto the broad wall**—or double wall, extending from the gate of Ephraim to the corner gate, 400 cubits in length, formerly broken down by Joash, king of Israel, but afterwards rebuilt by Uzziah, who made it so strong that the Chaldeans, finding it difficult to demolish, had left it standing. **12. Shallum . . . he and his daughters**—who were either heiresses or rich widows. They undertook to defray the expenses of a part of the wall next them. **13. the inhabitants of Zanoah** —There were two towns so called in the territory of Judah (Josh. 15:34, 56). **14. Beth-haccerem**—a city of Judah, supposed to be now occupied by Bethulia, on a hill of the same name, which is sometimes called also the mountain of the Franks, between Jerusalem and Tekoa. **16. the sepulchres of David, and to the pool that was made, and unto** the house of the mighty—i.e., along the precipitous cliffs of Zion [BARCLAY]. **19. at the turning of the wall**—i.e., the wall across the Tyropœon, being a continuation of the first wall, connecting Mount Zion with the temple wall [BARCLAY]. **25. the tower which lieth out from the king's high house**—i.e., watchtower by the royal palace [BARCLAY]. **26. the Nethinims**—Not only the priests and the Levites, but the common persons that belonged to the house of God, contributed to the work. The names of those who repaired the walls of Jerusalem are commemorated because it was a work of piety and patriotism to repair the holy city. It was an instance of religion and courage to defend the true worshippers of God, that they might serve Him in quietness and safety, and, in the midst of so many enemies, go on with this work, piously confiding in the power of God to support them [BISHOP PATRICK].

CHAPTER 4

Vss. 1-6. While the Enemies Scoff, Nehemiah Prays to God, and Continues the Work. **1. when Sanballat heard that we builded the wall, he was wroth**—The Samaritan faction showed their bitter animosity to the Jews on discovering the systematic design of refortifying Jerusalem. Their opposition was confined at first to scoffs and insults, in heaping which the governors made themselves conspicuous, and circulated all sorts of disparaging reflections that might increase the feelings of hatred and contempt for them in their own party. The weakness of the Jews in respect of wealth and numbers, the absurdity of their purpose apparently to reconstruct the walls and celebrate the feast of dedication in one day, the idea of raising the walls on their old foundations, as well as using the charred and mouldering debris of the ruins as the materials for the restored buildings, and the hope of such a parapet as they could raise being capable of serving as a fortress of defense—these all afforded fertile subjects of hostile ridicule. **3. if a fox go up**—The foxes were mentioned because they were known to infest in great numbers the ruined and desolate places in the mount and city of Zion (Lam. 5:18). **4, 5. Hear, O our God; for we are despised**—The imprecations invoked here may seem harsh, cruel, and vindictive; but it must be remembered that Nehemiah and his friends regarded those Samaritan leaders as enemies to the cause of God and His people, and therefore as deserving to be visited with heavy judgments. The prayer, therefore, is to be considered as emanating from hearts in which neither hatred, revenge, nor any inferior passion, but a pious and patriotic zeal for the glory of God and the success of His cause, held the ascendant sway. **6. all the wall was joined together unto the half thereof**—The whole circuit of the wall had been distributed in sections to various companies of the people, and was completed to the half of the intended height. 7-23. He Sets a Watch. **7. But ... when Sanballat ... heard that the walls ... were made up, and ... the breaches ... stopped**—The rapid progress of the fortifications, despite all their predictions to the contrary, goaded the Samaritans to frenzy. So they, dreading danger from the growing greatness of the Jews, formed a conspiracy to surprise them, demolish their works, and disperse or intimidate the builders. The plot being discovered, Nehemiah adopted the most energetic measures for ensuring the common safety, as well

as the uninterrupted building of the walls. Hitherto the governor, for the sake of despatch, had set all his attendants and guards on the work—now half of them were withdrawn to be constantly in arms. The workmen labored with a trowel in one hand and a sword in the other; and as, in so large a circuit, they were far removed from each other, Nehemiah (who was night and day on the spot, and, by his pious exhortations and example, animated the minds of his people) kept a trumpeter by his side, so that, on any intelligence of a surprise being brought to him, an alarm might be immediately sounded, and assistance rendered to the most distant detachment of their brethren. By these vigilant precautions, the counsels of the enemy were defeated, and the work was carried on apace. God, when He has important public work to do, never fails to raise up instruments for accomplishing it, and in the person of Nehemiah, who, to great natural acuteness and energy added fervent piety and heroic devotion, He provided a leader, whose high qualities fitted him for the demands of the crisis. Nehemiah's vigilance anticipated every difficulty, his prudent measures defeated every obstruction, and with astonishing rapidity this Jerusalem was made again "a city fortified."

CHAPTER 5

Vss. 1-5. The People Complain of Their Debt, Mortgage, and Bondage. **1. there was a great cry of the people ... against their brethren**—Such a crisis in the condition of the Jews in Jerusalem—fatigued with hard labor and harassed by the machinations of restless enemies, the majority of them poor, and the bright visions which hope had painted of pure happiness on their return to the land of their fathers being unrealized—must have been very trying to their faith and patience. But, in addition to these vexatious oppressions, many began to sink under a new and more grievous evil. The poor made loud complaints against the rich for taking advantage of their necessities, and grinding them by usurious exactions. Many of them had, in consequence of these oppressions, been driven to such extremities that they had to mortgage their lands and houses to enable them to pay the taxes to the Persian government, and ultimately even to sell their children for slaves to procure the means of subsistence. The condition of the poorer inhabitants was indeed deplorable; for, besides the deficient harvests caused by the great rains (Ezra 10:9; also Hag. 1:6-11), a dearth was now threatened by the enemy keeping such a multitude pent up in the city, and preventing the country people bringing in provisions. 6-19. The Usurers Rebuked. **6. I was very angry when I heard their cry and these words**—When such disorders came to the knowledge of the governor, his honest indignation was roused against the perpetrators of the evil. Having summoned a public assembly, he denounced their conduct in terms of just severity. He contrasted it with his own in redeeming with his money some of the Jewish exiles who, through debt or otherwise, had lost their personal liberty in Babylon. He urged the rich creditors not only to abandon their illegal and oppressive system of usury, but to restore the fields and vineyards of the poor, so that a remedy might be put to an evil the introduction of which had led to much actual disorder, and the continuance of which would inevitably prove ruinous to the newly restored colony, by violating the fundamental principles of the Hebrew constitution. The remonstrance was effectual. The conscience of the usurious oppressors could not resist the touching and powerful appeal. With mingled emotions of shame, contrition, and fear, they with one voice expressed their readiness to comply with the governor's recommendation. The proceedings were closed by the parties binding themselves by a solemn oath, administered by the priests, that they would redeem their pledge, as well as by the governor invoking, by the solemn and significant gesture of shaking a corner of his garment, a malediction on those who should violate it. The historian has taken care to record that the people did according to this promise. **14. Moreover from the time that I was appointed . . . I and my brethren have not eaten the bread of the governor**—We have a remarkable proof both of the opulence and the disinterestedness of Nehemiah. As he declined, on conscientious grounds, to accept the lawful emoluments attached to his government, and yet maintained a style of princely hospitality for twelve years out of his own resources, it is evident that his office of cupbearer at the court of Shushan must have been very lucrative. **15. the former governors . . . had taken . . . bread and wine, besides forty shekels of silver**—The income of Eastern governors is paid partly in produce, partly in money. "Bread" means all sorts of provision. The forty shekels of silver per day would amount to a yearly salary of about $9,000. **17. Moreover there were at my table an hundred and fifty of the Jews**—In the East it has been always customary to calculate the expense of a king's or grandee's establishment, not by the amount of money disbursed, but by the quantity of provisions consumed (see I Kings 4:22; 18:19; Eccles. 5:11).

CHAPTER 6

Vss. 1-19. SANBALLAT PRACTISES AGAINST NEHEMIAH BY INSIDIOUS ATTEMPTS. **2. Sanballat and Geshem sent unto me**—The Samaritan leaders, convinced that they could not overcome Nehemiah by open arms, resolved to gain advantage over him by deceit and stratagem. With this in view, under pretext of terminating their differences in an amicable manner, they invited him to a conference. The place of rendezvous was fixed "in *some one* of the villages in the plain of Ono." "In the villages" is, *Heb.,* "in Cephirim," or Cephirah, the name of a town in the territory of Benjamin (Josh. 9:17; 18:26). Nehemiah, however, apprehensive of some intended hischief, prudently declined the invitation. Though it was repeated four times, his uniform answer was that his presence could not be dispensed with from the important work in which he was engaged. This was one, though not the only, reason. The principal ground of his refusal was that his seizure or death at their hands would certainly put a stop to the further progress of the fortifications. **5-9. Then sent Sanballat his servant . . . the fifth time with an open letter in his hand**—In Western Asia, letters, after being rolled up like a map, are flattened to the breadth of an inch; and instead of being sealed, they are pasted at the ends. In Eastern Asia, the Persians make up their letters in the form of a roll about six inches long, and a bit of paper is fastened round it with gum, and sealed with an impression of ink, which resembles our printers' ink, but it is not so thick. Letters were,

and are still, sent to persons of distinction in a bag or purse, and even to equals they are enclosed—the tie being made with a colored ribbon. But to inferiors, or persons who are to be treated contemptuously, the letters were sent open—i.e., not enclosed in a bag. Nehemiah, accustomed to the punctillious ceremonial of the Persian court, would at once notice the want of the usual formality and know that it was from designed disrespect. The strain of the letter was equally insolent. It was to this effect: The fortifications with which he was so busy were intended to strengthen his position in the view of a meditated revolt: he had engaged prophets to incite the people to enter into his design and support his claim to be their native king; and, to stop the circulation of such reports, which would soon reach the court, he was earnestly besought to come to the wished-for conference. Nehemiah, strong in the consciousness of his own integrity, and penetrating the purpose of this shallow artifice, replied that there were no rumors of the kind described, that the idea of a revolt and the stimulating addresses of hired demagogues were stories of the writer's own invention, and that he declined now, as formerly, to leave his work. **10-14. Afterward I came unto the house of Shemaiah,** etc.—This man was the son of a priest, who was an intimate and confidential friend of Nehemiah. The young man claimed to be endowed with the gift of prophecy. Having been secretly bribed by Sanballat, he, in his pretended capacity of prophet, told Nehemiah that his enemies were that night to make an attempt upon his life. He advised him, at the same time, to consult his safety by concealing himself in the sanctuary, a crypt which, from its sanctity, was strong and secure. But the noble-minded governor determined at all hazards to remain at his post, and not bring discredit on the cause of God and religion by his unworthy cowardice in leaving the temple and city unprotected. This plot, together with a secret collusion between the enemy and the nobles of Judah who were favorably disposed towards the bad Samaritan in consequence of his Jewish connections (vs. 18), the undaunted courage and vigilance of Nehemiah were enabled, with the blessing of God, to defeat, and the erection of the walls thus built in troublous times (Dan. 9:25) was happily completed (vs. 15) in the brief space of fifty-two days. So rapid execution, even supposing some parts of the old wall standing, cannot be sufficiently accounted for, except by the consideration that the builders labored with the ardor of religious zeal, as men employed in the work of God.

CHAPTER 7

Vss. 1-4. NEHEMIAH COMMITS THE CHARGE OF JERUSALEM TO HANANI AND HANANIAH. **2. I gave my brother Hanani . . . charge over Jerusalem**—If, as is commonly supposed, Nehemiah was now contemplating a return to Shushan according to his promise, it was natural that he should wish to entrust the custody of Jerusalem and the management of its civic affairs to men on whose ability, experience, and fidelity, he could confide. Hanani, a near relative (ch. 1:2), was one, and with him was associated, as colleague, Hananiah, "the ruler of the palace"—i.e., the marshal or chamberlain of the viceregal court, which Nehemiah had maintained in Jerusalem. The high religious principle, as well as the patriotic spirit of those two men, recommended them as pre-eminently qualified for being invested with an official trust of such peculiar importance. **he ... feared God above many**—The piety of Hananiah is especially mentioned as the ground of his eminent fidelity in the discharge of all his duties and, consequently, the reason of the confidence which Nehemiah reposed in him; for he was fully persuaded that Hananiah's fear of God would preserve him from those temptations to treachery and unfaithfulness which he was likely to encounter on the governor's departure from Jerusalem. **3. Let not the gates of Jerusalem be opened until the sun be hot**, etc.—In the East it is customary to open the gates of a city at sunrise, and to bar them at sunset—a rule which is very rarely, and not except to persons of authority, infringed upon. Nehemiah recommended that the gates of Jerusalem should not be opened so early; a precaution necessary at a time when the enemy was practising all sorts of dangerous stratagems, to ensure that the inhabitants were all astir and enjoyed the benefit of clear broad daylight for observing the suspicious movements of any enemy. The propriety of regularly barring the gates at sunset was, in this instance, accompanied with the appointment of a number of the people to act as sentinels, each mounting guard in front of his own house. **4. Now the city was large and great**—The walls being evidently built on the old foundations, the city covered a large extent of surface, as all Oriental towns do, the houses standing apart with gardens and orchards intervening. This extent, in the then state of Jerusalem, was the more observable as the population was comparatively small, and the habitations of the most rude and simple construction—mere wooden sheds or coverings of loose, unmortared stones.

5-38. GENEALOGY OF THOSE WHO CAME AT THE FIRST OUT OF BABYLON. 5. my God put into mine heart to gather together the nobles, etc.—The arrangement about to be described, though dictated by mere common prudence, is, in accordance with the pious feelings of Nehemiah, ascribed not to his own prudence or reflection, but to the grace of God prompting and directing him. He resolved to prepare a register of the returned exiles, containing an exact record of the family and ancestral abode of every individual. While thus directing his attention, he discovered a register of the first detachment who had come under the care of Zerubbabel. It is transcribed in the following verses, and differs in some few particulars from that given in Ezra 2. But the discrepancy is sufficiently accounted for from the different circumstances in which the two registers were taken; that of Ezra having been made up at Babylon, while that of Nehemiah was drawn out in Judea, after the walls of Jerusalem had been rebuilt. The lapse of so many years might well be expected to make a difference appear in the catalogue, through death or other causes; in particular, one person being, according to Jewish custom, called by different names. Thus Hariph (vs. 24) is the same as Jorah (Ezra 2:18), Sia (vs. 47) the same as Siaha (Ezra 2:44), etc. Besides other purposes to which this genealogy of the nobles, rulers, and people was subservient, one leading object contemplated by it was to ascertain with accuracy the parties to whom the duty legally belonged of ministering at the altar and conducting the various services of the temple. For guiding to exact information in this important point of inquiry, the possession of the old register of Zerubbabel was invaluable.

39-73. OF THE PRIESTS. 39. The priests—It appears that only four of the courses of the priests

returned from the captivity; and that the course of Abia (Luke 1:5) is not in the list. But it must be noticed that these four courses were afterwards divided into twenty-four, which retained the names of the original courses which David appointed. **70. some of the chief of the fathers**, etc.—With verse 69 the register ends, and the thread of Nehemiah's history is resumed. He was the *tirshatha* or governor, and the liberality displayed by him and some of the leading men for the suitable equipment of the ministers of religion, forms the subject of the remaining portion of the chapter. Their donations consisted principally in garments. This would appear a singular description of gifts to be made by any one among us; but, in the East, a present of garments, or of any article of use, is conformable to the prevailing sentiments and customs of society. **drams of gold**—i.e., darics. A daric was a gold coin of ancient Persia. **71. pound of silver**—i.e., *mina* (sixty shekels, or about $45). **73. So ... all Israel, dwelt in their cities**—The utility of these genealogical registers was thus found in guiding to a knowledge of the cities and localities in each tribe to which every family anciently belonged.

CHAPTER 8

VSS. 1-8. RELIGIOUS MANNER OF READING AND HEARING THE LAW. **1. all the people gathered themselves together as one man**—The occasion was the celebration of the feast of the seventh month (ch. 7:73). The beginning of every month was ushered in as a sacred festival; but this, the commencement of the seventh month, was kept with distinguished honor as "the feast of trumpets," which extended over two days. It was the first day of the seventh ecclesiastical year, and the new year's day of the Jewish civil year, on which account it was held as "a great day." The place where the general concourse of people was held was "at the water gate," on the south rampart. Through that gate the Nethinims or Gibeonites brought water into the temple, and there was a spacious area in front of it. **they spake unto Ezra the scribe to bring the book of the law of Moses**—He had come to Jerusalem twelve or thirteen years previous to Nehemiah. He either remained there or had returned to Babylon in obedience to the royal order, and for the discharge of important duties. He had returned along with Nehemiah, but in a subordinate capacity. From the time of Nehemiah's appointment to the dignity of *tirshatha*, Ezra had retired into private life. Although cordially and zealously co-operating with the former patriot in his important measures of reform, the pious priest had devoted his time and attention principally toward producing a complete edition of the canonical Scriptures. The public reading of the Scriptures was required by the law to be made every seventh year; but during the long period of the captivity this excellent practice, with many others, had fallen into neglect, till revived·on this occasion. That there was a strong and general desire among the returned exiles in Jerusalem to hear the word of God read to them indicates a greatly improved tone of religious feeling. **4. Ezra .... stood upon a pulpit of wood**—Not made in the form known to us, but only a raised scaffold or platform, broad enough to allow fourteen persons to stand with ease upon it. Ezra's duty was very laborious, as he continued reading aloud from morning until midday, but his labor was lightened by the aid of the other priests present. Their presence was of importance, partly to show their cordial agreement with Ezra's declaration of divine truth; and partly to take their share with him in the important duty of publicly reading and expounding the Scripture. **5. when he opened it, all the people stood up**—This attitude they assumed either from respect to God's word, or, rather, because the reading was prefaced by a solemn prayer, which was concluded by a general expression of amen, amen. **7, 8. caused the people to understand the law ... gave the sense**—Commentators are divided in opinion as to the import of this statement. Some think that Ezra read the law in pure Hebrew, while the Levites, who assisted him, translated it sentence by sentence into Chaldee, the vernacular dialect which the exiles spoke in Babylon. Others maintain that the duty of these Levites consisted in explaining to the people, many of whom had become very ignorant, what Ezra had read.

9-15. THE PEOPLE COMFORTED. **9. This day is holy unto the Lord ... mourn not, nor weep**—A deep sense of their national sins, impressively brought to their remembrance by the reading of the law and its denunciations, affected the hearts of the people with penitential sorrow. But notwithstanding the painful remembrances of their national sins which the reading of the law awakened, the people were exhorted to cherish the feelings of joy and thankfulness associated with a sacred festival (see on Lev. 23:23-25). By sending portions of it to their poorer brethren (Deut. 16:11, 14; Esther 9:19), they would also enable them to participate in the public rejoicings.

16-18. THEY KEEP THE FEAST OF TABERNACLES. **16. the people went forth, and brought ... and made themselves booths,** etc.—(See on Lev. 23:34-44; Deut. 16:13-17). **17. since the days of Jeshua ... had not the children of Israel done so**—This national feast had not been neglected for so protracted a period. Besides that it is impossible that such a flagrant disregard of the law could have been tolerated by Samuel, David, and other pious rulers, its observance is sufficiently indicated (I Kings 8:2, 65; II Chron. 7:9) and expressly recorded (Ezra 3:4). But the meaning is, that the popular feelings had never been raised to such a height of enthusiastic joy since the time of their entrance into Canaan, as now on their return after a long and painful captivity. **18. Also day by day ... he read in the book of the law of God**—This was more than was enjoined (Deut. 31:10-12), and arose from the exuberant zeal of the time. **on the eighth day was a solemn assembly**—This was the last and great day of the feast (Num. 30:35). In later times, other ceremonies which increased the rejoicing were added (John 7:37).

CHAPTER 9

VSS. 1-3. A SOLEMN FAST AND REPENTANCE OF THE PEOPLE. **1. Now in the twenty and fourth day of this month**—i.e., on the second day after the close of the feast of tabernacles, which commenced on the fourteenth and terminated on the twenty-second (Lev. 23). The day immediately after that feast, the twenty-third, had been occupied in separating the delinquents from their unlawful wives, as well, perhaps, as in taking steps for keeping aloof in future from unnecessary intercourse with the heathen around them. For although this necessary measure of reformation had been begun formerly by Ezra (Ezra 10), and satisfactorily accomplished at that time (in so far as he had information of the

existing abuses, or possessed the power of correcting them) yet it appears that this reformatory work of Ezra had been only partial and imperfect. Many cases of delinquency had escaped, or new defaulters had appeared who had contracted those forbidden alliances; and there was an urgent necessity for Nehemiah again to take vigorous measures for the removal of a social evil which threatened the most disastrous consequences to the character and prosperity of the chosen people. A solemn fast was now observed for the expression of those penitential and sorrowful feelings which the reading of the law had produced, but which had been suppressed during the celebration of the feast; and the sincerity of their repentance was evinced by the decisive steps taken for the correction of existing abuses in the matter of marriage. **2. confessed their sins, and the iniquities of their fathers**—Not only did they read in their recent sufferings a punishment of the national apostasy and guilt, but they had made themselves partakers of their fathers' sins by following the same evil ways. **3. they ... read in the book of the law**—Their extraordinary zeal led them to continue this as before. **one fourth part of the day**—i.e., for three hours, twelve hours being the acknowledged length of the Jewish day (John 11:9). This solemn diet of worship, which probably commenced at the morning sacrifice, was continued for six hours, i.e., till the time of the evening sacrifice. The worship which they gave to the Lord their God, at this season of solemn national humiliation, consisted in acknowledging and adoring His great mercy in the forgiveness of their great and multiplied offenses, in delivering them from the merited judgments which they had already experienced or which they had reason to apprehend, in continuing amongst them the light and blessings of His word and worship, and in supplicating the extension of His grace and protection.

4-38. THE LEVITES CONFESS GOD'S MANIFOLD GOODNESS, AND THEIR OWN WICKEDNESS. **4. Then stood up upon the stairs**—the scaffolds or pulpits, whence the Levites usually addressed the people. There were probably several placed at convenient distances, to prevent confusion and the voice of one drowning those of the others. **cried with a loud voice unto the Lord**—Such an exertion, of course, was indispensably necessary, in order that the speakers might be heard by the vast multitude congregated in the open air. But these speakers were then engaged in expressing their deep sense of sin, as well as fervently imploring the forgiving mercy of God; and "crying with a loud voice" was a natural accompaniment of this extraordinary prayer meeting, as violent gestures and vehement tones are always the way in which the Jews, and other people in the East, have been accustomed to give utterance to deep and earnest feelings. **5. Then the Levites ... said, Stand up and bless the Lord your God**—If this prayer was uttered by all these Levites in common, it must have been prepared and adopted beforehand, perhaps, by Ezra; but it may only embody the substance of the confession and thanksgiving. **6. Thou, even thou, art Lord alone,** etc.—In this solemn and impressive prayer, in which they make public confession of their sins, and deprecate the judgments due to the transgressions of their fathers, they begin with a profound adoration of God, whose supreme majesty and omnipotence is acknowledged in the creation, preservation, and government of all. Then they proceed to enumerate His mercies and distinguished favors to them as a nation, from the period of the call of their great ancestor and the gracious promise intimated to him in the divinely bestowed name of Abraham, a promise which implied that he was to be the Father of the faithful, the ancestor of the Messiah, and the honored individual in whose seed all the families of the earth should be blessed. Tracing in full and minute detail the signal instances of divine interposition for their deliverance and their interest—in their deliverance from Egyptian bondage—their miraculous passage through the Red Sea—the promulgation of His law—the forbearance and long-suffering shown them amid their frequent rebellions—the signal triumphs given them over their enemies—their happy settlement in the promised land—and all the extraordinary blessings, both in the form of temporal prosperity and of religious privilege, with which His paternal goodness had favored them above all other people, they charge themselves with making a miserable requital. They confess their numerous and determined acts of disobedience. They read, in the loss of their national independence and their long captivity, the severe punishment of their sins. They acknowledge that, in all heavy and continued judgments upon their nation, God had done right, but they had done wickedly. And in throwing themselves on His mercy, they express their purpose of entering into a national covenant, by which they pledge themselves to dutiful obedience in future. **22. Moreover, thou gavest them kingdoms and nations**—i.e., put them in possession of a rich country, of an extensive territory, which had been once occupied by a variety of princes and people. **and didst divide them into corners**—i.e., into tribes. The propriety of the expression arose from the various districts touching at points or angles on each other. **the land of Sihon, and the land of the king of Heshbon**—Heshbon being the capital city, the passage should run thus: the land of Sihon or the land of the king of Heshbon. **32. Now therefore our God ... who keepest covenant and mercy**—God's fidelity to His covenant is prominently acknowledged, and well it might; for their whole national history bore testimony to it. But as this could afford them little ground of comfort or of hope while they were so painfully conscious of having violated it, they were driven to seek refuge in the riches of divine grace; and hence the peculiar style of invocation here adopted: "Now therefore, our God, the great, the mighty, and the terrible God, who *keepest covenant and mercy*." **36. Behold, we are servants this day**—Notwithstanding their happy restoration to their native land, they were still tributaries of a foreign prince whose officers ruled them. They were not, like their fathers, free tenants of the land which God gave them. **37. it yieldeth much increase unto the kings whom thou hast set over us because of our sins**—Our agricultural labors have been resumed in the land—we plough, and sow, and till, and Thou blessest the work of our hands with a plentifull return; but this increase is not for ourselves, as once it was, but for our foreign masters, to whom we have to pay large and oppressive tribute. **they have dominion over our bodies**—Their persons were liable to be pressed, at the mandate of their Assyrian conqueror, into the service of his empire, either in war or in public works. And our beasts are taken to do their pleasure. **38. we make a sure covenant, and write**—i.e., subscribe or sign it. This written document would exercise a wholesome influence in restraining their backslidings or in animating them to duty, by being a witness against them if in the future they were unfaithful to their engagements.

CHAPTER 10

Vss. 1-27. THE NAMES OF THOSE WHO SEALED THE COVENANT. **1. Nehemiah, the Tirshatha**—His name was placed first in the roll on account of his high official rank, as deputy of the Persian monarch. All classes were included in the subscription; but the people were represented by their elders (vs. 14), as it would have been impossible for every one in the country to have been admitted to the sealing. **28. THE REST OF THE PEOPLE BOUND THEMSELVES TO OBSERVE IT.** Those who were not present at the sealing ratified the covenant by giving their assent, either in words or by lifting up their hands, and bound themselves, by a solemn oath, to walk in God's law, imprecating a curse upon themselves in the event of their violating it. **29-39. POINTS OF THE COVENANT. 29. to observe and do all the commandments**, etc.—This national covenant, besides containing a solemn pledge of obedience to the divine law generally, specified their engagement to some particular duties, which the character and exigency of the times stamped with great urgency and importance, and which may be summed up under the following heads: that they abstain from contracting matrimonial alliances with the heathen; that they would rigidly observe the sabbath; that they would let the land enjoy rest and remit debts every seventh year; that they would contribute to the maintenance of the temple service, the necessary expenses of which had formerly been defrayed out of the treasury of the temple (I Chron. 26:20), and when it was drained, given out from the king's privy purse (II Chron. 31:3); and that they would make an orderly payment of the priests' dues. A minute and particular enumeration of the first fruits was made, that all might be made fully aware of their obligations, and that none might excuse themselves on pretext of ignorance from withholding taxes which the poverty of many, and the irreligion of others, had made them exceedingly prone to evade. **32. the third part of a shekel for the service of the house of our God**—The law required every individual above twenty years of age to pay half a shekel to the sanctuary. But in consequence of the general poverty of the people, occasioned by war and captivity, this tribute was reduced to a third part of a shekel. **34. we cast the lots ... for the wood offering**—The carrying of the wood had formerly been the work of the Nethinims. But few of them having returned, the duty was assigned as stated in the text. The practice afterwards rose into great importance, and Josephus speaks [WARS, 2. 17, sect. 6] of the Xylophoria, or certain stated and solemn times at which the people brought up wood to the temple. **38. the priest the son of Aaron shall be with the Levites, when the Levites take tithes**—This was a prudential arrangement. The presence of a dignified priest would ensure the peaceful delivery of the tithes; at least his superintendence and influence would tend to prevent the commission of any wrong in the transaction, by the people deceiving the Levites, or the Levites defrauding the priests. **the tithe of the tithes**—The Levites, having received a tenth of all land produce, were required to give a tenth of this to the priests. The Levites were charged with the additional obligation to carry the tithes when received, and deposit them in the temple stores, for the use of the priests. **39. we will not forsake the house of our God**—This solemn pledge was repeated at the close of the covenant as an expression of the intense zeal by which the people at this time were animated for the glory and the worship of God. Under the pungent feelings of sorrow and repentance for their national sins, of which apostasy from the service of the true God was the chief, and under the yet fresh and painful remembrance of their protracted captivity, they vowed, and (feeling the impulse of ardent devotion as well as of gratitude for their restoration) flattered themselves they would never forget their vow, to be the Lord's.

CHAPTER 11

Vss. 1, 2. The Rulers, Voluntary Men, and Every Tenth Man Chosen by Lot, Dwell at Jerusalem. **1. the rulers ... dwelt at Jerusalem**——That city being the metropolis of the country, it was right and proper that the seat of government should be there. But the exigency of the times required that special measures should be taken to insure the residence of an adequate population for the custody of the buildings and the defense of the city. From the annoyances of restless and malignant enemies, who tried every means to demolish the rising fortifications, there was some danger attending a settlement in Jerusalem. Hence the greater part of the returned exiles, in order to earn as well as secure the rewards of their duty, preferred to remain in the country or the provincial towns. To remedy this state of things, it was resolved to select every tenth man of the tribes of Judah and Benjamin by lot, to become a permanent inhabitant of the capital. The necessity of such an expedient commended it to the general approval. It was the more readily submitted to because the lot was resorted to on all the most critical conjunctures of the Jewish history, and regarded by the people as a divine decision (Prov. 18:18). This awakened strongly the national spirit; and patriotic volunteers came forward readily to meet the wishes of the authorities, a service which, implying great self-denial as well as courage, was reckoned in the circumstances of so much importance as entitled them to the public gratitude. No wonder that the conduct of these volunteers drew forth the tribute of public admiration; for they sacrificed their personal safety and comfort for the interests of the community because Jerusalem was at that time a place against which the enemies of the Jews were directing a thousand plots. Therefore, residence in it at such a juncture was attended with expense and various annoyances from which a country life was entirely free.

3-36. Their Names. **3. the chief of the province**—i.e., Judea. Nehemiah speaks of it, as it then was, a small appendix of the Persian empire. **in the cities of Judah dwelt every one in his possession in their cities**—The returned exiles, who had come from Babylon, repaired generally, and by a natural impulse, to the lands and cities throughout the country which had been anciently assigned them. **Israel**—This general name, which designated the descendants of Jacob before the unhappy division of the two kingdoms under Rehoboam, was restored after the captivity, the Israelites being then united with the Jews, and all traces of their former separation being obliterated. Although the majority of the returned exiles belonged to the tribes of Judah and Benjamin, they are here called Israel because a large number out of all the tribes were now intermingled, and these were principally the occupiers of the rural villages, while none but those of Judah and Benjamin resided in Jerusalem. **the Levites**—These took possession of the cities allotted to them, according as they had opportunity. **the Nethinims**—

A certain order of men, either Gibeonites or persons joined with them, who were devoted to the service of God. **4. at Jerusalem dwelt certain of the children of Judah**—The discrepancy that is apparent between this and the list formerly given in I Chron. 9:1-9, arose not only from the Jewish and Oriental practice of changing or modifying the names of persons from a change of circumstances, but from the alterations that must have been produced in the course of time. The catalogue in Chronicles contains those who came with the first detachment of returned exiles, while the list in this passage probably included also those who returned with Ezra and Nehemiah; or it was most probably made out afterwards, when several had died, or some, who had been inserted as going on the journey, remained, and others came in their stead. **9. overseer** i.e., captain or chief. **11. the ruler of the house of God**—assistant of the high priest (Num. 3: 32; 1 Chron. 9:11; II Chron. 19:11). **16. the oversight of the outward business of the house of God** —i.e., those things which were done outside, or in the country, such as the collecting of the provisions (I Chron. 26:29). **17. the principal to begin the thanksgiving in prayer**—i.e., the leader of the choir which chanted the public praise at the time of the morning and evening sacrifice. That service was always accompanied by some appropriate psalm, the sacred music being selected and guided by the person named. **22. the sons of Asaph, the singers were over the business of the house of God**—They were selected to take charge of providing those things which were required for the interior of the temple and its service, while to others was committed the care of the "outward business of the house of God" (vs. 16). This duty was very properly assigned to the sons of Asaph; for, though they were Levites, they did not repair in rotation to Jerusalem, as the other ministers of religion. Being permanent residents, and employed in duties which were comparatively light and easy, they were very competent to undertake this charge. **23. it was the king's commandment**—It was the will of the Persian monarch in issuing his edict that the temple service should be revived in all its religious fulness and solemnity. As this special provision for the singers is said to have been by the king's commandment, the order was probably given at the request or suggestion of Ezra or Nehemiah. **24. Pethahiah ... was at the king's hand in all matters concerning the people**—This person was entrusted with judicial power, either for the interest, or by the appointment, of the Persian monarch, and his duty consisted either in adjusting cases of civil dispute, or in regulating fiscal concerns. **25. some of the children of Judah dwelt at Kirjath-arba**—The whole region in which the villages here mentioned were situated had been completely devastated by the Chaldean invasion; and, therefore, it must be assumed, that these villages had been rebuilt before "the children dwelt in them." **36. And of the Levites were divisions in Judah, and in Benjamin**—Rather, there were divisions for the Levites; i.e., those who were not resident in Jerusalem were distributed in settlements throughout the provinces of Judah and Benjamin.

CHAPTER 12

Vss. 1-9. Priests and Levites Who Came Up with Zerubbabel. **1. these are the priests**—according to verse 7 "the chief of the priests," the heads of the twenty-four courses into which the priesthood was divided (I Chron. 24:1-20). Only four of the courses returned from the captivity (ch. 7:39-42; Ezra 2:36-39). But these were divided by Zerubbabel, or Jeshua, into the original number of twenty-four. Twenty-two only are enumerated here, and no more than twenty in verses 12-21. The discrepancy is due to the extremely probable circumstance that two of the twenty-four courses had become extinct in Babylon; for none belonging to them are reported as having returned (vss. 2-5). Hattush and Maadiah may be omitted in the account of those persons' families (vs. 12), for these had no sons. **Shealtiel**—or Salathiel. **Ezra**—This was most likely a different person from the pious and patriotic leader. If he were the same person, he would now have reached a very patriarchal age—and this longevity would doubtless be due to his eminent piety and temperance, which are greatly conducive to the prolongation of life, but, above all, to the special blessing of God, who had preserved and strengthened him for the accomplishment of the important work he was called upon to undertake in that critical period of the Church's history. **4. Abijah**—one of the ancestors of John the Baptist (Luke 1:5). **9. their brethren were over against them in the watches**—i.e., according to some, their stations—the places where they stood when officiating—"ward over against ward" (vs. 24); or, according to others, in alternate watches, in course of rotation.

10-47. SUCCESSION OF THE HIGH PRIESTS. **10. Jeshua begat Joiakim**, etc. This enumeration was of great importance, not only as establishing their individual purity of descent, but because the chronology of the Jews was henceforth to be reckoned, not as formerly by the reigns of their kings, but by the successions of their high priests. **11. Jaddua**—It is an opinion entertained by many commentators that this person was the high priest whose dignified appearance, solemn manner, and splendid costume overawed and interested so strongly the proud mind of Alexander the Great; and if he were not this person (as some object that this Jaddua was not in office till a considerable period after the death of Nehemiah), it might probably be his father, called by the same name. **12. in the days of Joiakim were priests, the chief of the fathers**—As there had been priests in the days of Jeshua, so in the time of Joiakim, the son and successor of Jeshua, the sons of those persons filled the priestly office in the place of their fathers, some of whom were still alive, though many were dead. **23. The sons of Levi ... were written in the book of the chronicles**—i.e., the public registers in which the genealogies were kept with great regularity and exactness. **27-43. at the dedication of the wall of Jerusalem**—This ceremony of consecrating the wall and gates of the city was an act of piety on the part of Nehemiah, not merely to thank God in a general way for having been enabled to bring the building to a happy completion, but especially because that city was the place which He had chosen. It also contained the temple which was hallowed by the manifestation of His presence, and anew set apart to His service. It was on these accounts that Jerusalem was called "the holy city," and by this public and solemn act of religious observance, after a long period of neglect and desecration, it was, as it were, restored to its rightful proprietor. The dedication consisted in a solemn ceremonial, in which the leading authorities, accompanied by the Levitical singers, summoned from all parts of the country, and by a vast concourse of people, marched in imposing procession round the city walls, and, pausing at intervals to engage in

united praises, prayer, and sacrifices, supplicated the continued presence, favor, and blessing on "the holy city." *"The assembly convened near Jaffa Gate, where the procession commences.* Then (vs. 31) I brought up the princes of Judah upon the wall (*near the Valley Gate*), and appointed two great companies of them that gave thanks, whereof one went on the right hand upon the wall towards the dung-gate (*through Bethzo*). And after them went Hoshaiah, and half of the princes of Judah. And (vs. 37) at the fountain-gate, which was over against them, they (*descending by the Tower of Siloam on the interior, and then reascending*) went up by the stairs of the city of David, at the going up of the wall, above the house of David, even unto the water-gate eastward (*by the staircase of the rampart, having descended to dedicate the fountain structures*). And the other company of them that gave thanks went over against them (*both parties having started from the junction of the first and second walls*), and I after them, and the half of the people upon the wall, from beyond the tower of the furnaces even unto the broad wall (*beyond the corner-gate*). And from above the gate of Ephraim, and above the old gate (*and the gate of Benjamin*), and above the fishgate, and the tower of Hananeel, and the tower of Meah, even unto the sheep-gate; and they stood still in the prison-gate (*or high gate, at the east end of the bridge*). So stood the two companies of them that gave thanks in the house of God, and I, and half of the rulers with me (*having thus performed the circuit of the investing walls*), and arrived in the courts of the temple" [BARCLAY'S CITY OF THE GREAT KING]. **43. the joy of Jerusalem was heard even afar off**—The events of the day, viewed in connection with the now repaired and beautified state of the city, raised the popular feeling to the highest pitch of enthusiasm, and the fame of their rejoicings was spread far and near. **44. portions of the law**—i.e., prescribed by the law. **for Judah rejoiced for the priests and ... Levites that waited**—The cause of this general satisfaction was either the full restoration of the temple service and the reorganized provision for the permanent support of the ministry, or it was the pious character and eminent gifts of the guardians of religion. **45. the singers and the porters kept ... the ward of the purification**—i.e., took care that no unclean person was allowed to enter within the precincts of the sacred building. This was the official duty of the porters (II Chron. 23:19), with whom, owing to the pressure of circumstances, it was deemed expedient that the singers should be associated as assistants. **47. all Israel ... sanctified holy things unto the Levites**, etc.—The people, selecting the tithes and first fruits, devoted them to the use of the Levites, to whom they belonged by appointment of the law. The Levites acted in the same way with the tithes due from them to the priests. Thus all classes of the people displayed a conscientious fidelity in paying the dues to the temple and the servants of God who were appointed to minister in it.

CHAPTER 13

Vss. 1-9. UPON THE READING OF THE LAW SEPARATION IS MADE FROM THE MIXED MULTITUDE. **1. On that day**—This was not immediately consequent on the dedication of the city wall and gates, but after Nehemiah's return from the Persian court to Jerusalem, his absence having extended over a considerable period. The transaction here described probably took place on one of the periodical occasions for the public readings of the law, when the people's attention was particularly directed to some violations of it which called for immediate correction. There is another instance afforded, in addition to those which have already fallen under our notice, of the great advantages resulting from the public and periodical reading of the divine law. It was an established provision for the religious instruction of the people, for diffusing a knowledge and a reverence for the sacred volume, as well as for removing those errors and corruptions which might, in the course of time, have crept in. **the Ammonite and the Moabite should not come into the congregation of God for ever**—i.e., not be incorporated into the Israelitish kingdom, nor united in marriage relations with that people (Deut. 23:3, 4). This appeal to the authority of the divine law led to a dissolution of all heathen alliances (ch. 9:2; Ezra 10:3). **4. before this**—The practice of these mixed marriages, in open neglect or violation of the law, had become so common, that even the pontifical house, which ought to have set a better example, was polluted by such an impure mixture. **Eliashib the priest . . . was allied unto Tobiah**—This person was the high priest (vs. 28; also ch. 3:1), who, by virtue of his dignified office, had the superintendence and control of the apartments attached to the temple. The laxity of his principles, as well as of his practice, is sufficiently apparent from his contracting a family connection with so notorious an enemy of Israel as Tobiah. But his obsequious attentions had carried him much farther; for to accommodate so important a person as Tobiah on his occasional visits to Jerusalem, Eliashib had provided him a splendid apartment in the temple. The introduction of so gross an impropriety can be accounted for in no other way than by supposing that in the absence of the priests and the cessation of the services, the temple was regarded as a common public building, which might, in the circumstances, be appropriated as a palatial residence. **6. But in all this was not I at Jerusalem**—Eliashib—concluding that, as Nehemiah had departed from Jerusalem, and, on the expiry of his allotted term of absence, had resigned his government, he had gone not to return—began to use great liberties, and, there being none left whose authority or frown he dreaded, allowed himself to do things most unworthy of his sacred office, and, which, though in unison with his own irreligious character, he would not have dared to attempt during the residence of the pious governor. Nehemiah resided twelve years as governor of Jerusalem, and having succeeded in repairing and refortifying the city, he at the end of that period returned to his duties in Shushan. How long he remained there is not expressly said, but "after certain days," which is a Scripture phraseology for a year or a number of years, he obtained leave to resume the government of Jerusalem; to his deep mortification and regret, he found matters in the neglected and disorderly state here described. Such gross irregularities as were practised, such extraordinary corruptions as had crept in, evidently imply the lapse of a considerable time. Besides, they exhibit the character of Eliashib, the high priest, in a most unfavorable light; for while he ought, by his office, to have preserved the inviolable sanctity of the temple and its furniture, his influence had been directly exercised for evil; especially he had given permission and countenance to a most indecent outrage—the appropriation of the best apartments in the sacred building to a heathen governor, one of the worst and most determined enemies of the people and the worship of

God. The very first reform Nehemiah on his second visit resolved upon, was the stopping of this gross profanation. The chamber which had been polluted by the residence of the idolatrous Ammonite was, after undergoing the process of ritual purification (Num. 15:9), restored to its proper use—a storehouse for the sacred vessels. **10-14. NEHEMIAH REFORMS THE OFFICERS IN THE HOUSE OF GOD. 10. And I perceived that the portions of the Levites had not been given them**—The people, disgusted with the malversations of Eliashib, or the lax and irregular performance of the sacred rites, withheld the tithes, so that the ministers of religion were compelled for their livelihood to withdraw to their patrimonial possessions in the country. The temple services had ceased; all religious duties had fallen into neglect. The money put into the sacred treasury had been squandered in the entertainment of an Ammonite heathen, an open and contemptuous enemy of God and His people. The return of the governor put an end to these disgraceful and profane proceedings. He administered a sharp rebuke to those priests to whom the management of the temple and its services was committed, for the total neglect of their duties, and the violation of the solemn promises which they had made to him at his departure. He upbraided them with the serious charge of having not only withheld from men their dues, but of having robbed God, by neglecting the care of His house and service. And thus having roused them to a sense of duty and incited them to testify their godly sorrow for their criminal negligence by renewed devotedness to their sacred work, Nehemiah restored the temple services. He recalled the dispersed Levites to the regular discharge of their duties; while the people at large, perceiving that their contributions would be no longer perverted to improper uses, willingly brought in their tithes as formerly. Men of integrity and good report were appointed to act as trustees of the sacred treasures, and thus order, regularity, and active service were re-established in the temple. **15-31. THE VIOLATION OF THE SABBATH. 15. In those days saw I in Judah some treading wine presses on the sabbath**—The cessation of the temple services had been necessarily followed by a public profanation of the Sabbath, and this had gone so far that labor was carried on in the fields, and fish brought to the markets on the sacred day. Nehemiah took the decisive step of ordering the city gates to be shut, and not to be opened, till the Sabbath was past; and in order to ensure the faithful execution of this order, he stationed some of his own servants as guards, to prevent the introduction of any commodities on that day. On the merchants and various dealers finding admission denied them, they set up booths outside the walls, in hopes of still driving a traffic with the peasantry; but the governor threatened, if they continued, to adopt violent measures for their removal. For this purpose a body of Levites was stationed as sentinels at the gate, with discretionary powers to protect the sanctification of the Sabbath. **24. could not speak in the Jews' language, but according to the language of each people** —a mongrel dialect imbibed from their mothers, together with foreign principles and habits. **25. cursed them**—i.e., pronounced on them an anathema which entailed excommunication. **smote . . . and plucked off their hair**—To cut off the hair of offenders seems to be a punishment rather disgraceful than severe; yet it is supposed that pain was added to disgrace, and that they tore off the hair with violence as if they were plucking a bird alive.

THE BOOK OF

ESTHER

CHAPTER 1

Vss. 1-22. AHASUERUS MAKES ROYAL FEASTS.
1. Ahasuerus—It is now generally agreed among
learned men that the Ahasuerus mentioned in this
episode is the Xerxes who figures in Grecian history.
3. made a feast unto all his princes and his servants
—Banquets on so grand a scale, and extending over
so great a period, have been frequently provided by
the luxurious monarchs of Eastern countries, both in
ancient and modern times. The early portion of
this festive season, however, seems to have been dedicated to amusement, particularly an exhibition of
the magnificence and treasures of the court, and it
was closed by a special feast of seven days' continuance, given within the gardens of the royal palace.
The ancient palace of Susa has been recently disin-
terred from an incumbent mass of earth and ruins;
and in that palace, which is, beyond all doubt, the
actual edifice referred to in this passage, there is a
great hall of marble pillars. "The position of the
great colonnade corresponds with the account here
given. It stands on an elevation in the center of the
mound, the remainder of which we may well imagine to have been occupied, after the Persian fashion,
with a garden and fountains. Thus the colonnade
would represent the 'court of the garden of the king's
palace' with its 'pillars of marble.' I am even inclined to believe the expression, 'Shushan the palace,' applies especially to this portion of the existing
ruins, in contradistinction to the citadel and the city
of Shushan" [LOFTUS' CHALDÆA AND SUSIANA]. **6.
Where were white, green, and blue hangings,** etc.—
The fashion, in the houses of the great, on festive
occasions, was to decorate the chambers from the
middle of the wall downward with damask or
velvet hangings of variegated colors suspended on
hooks, or taken down at pleasure. **the beds were of
gold and silver**—i.e., the couches on which, according to Oriental fashion, the guests reclined, and
which were either formed entirely of gold and silver
or inlaid with ornaments of those costly metals,
stood on an elevated floor of parti-colored marble.
7. they gave them drink in vessels of gold—There is
reason to believe from this account, as well as from
ch. 5:6, 7:2, 7, 8, where the drinking of wine occupies by far the most prominent place in the description, that this was a banquet rather than a feast. **9.
Also Vashti the queen made a feast for the women**—
The celebration was double; for, as according to the
Oriental fashion, the sexes do not intermingle in society, the court ladies were entertained in a separate
apartment by the queen. **10-12. On the seventh day,
when the heart of the king was merry with wine**—
As the feast-days advanced, the drinking was more
freely indulged in, so that the close was usually
marked by great excesses of revelry. **he commanded
. . . the seven chamberlains**—These were the eunuchs
who had charge of the royal harem. The refusal
of Vashti to obey an order which required her to
make an indecent exposure of herself before a company of drunken revellers, was becoming both the
modesty of her sex and her rank as queen; for, according to Persian customs, the queen, even more
than the wives of other men, was secluded from the
public gaze. Had not the king's blood been heated

with wine, or his reason overpowered by force of offended pride, he would have perceived that his own
honor, as well as hers, was consulted by her dignified conduct. **13. Then the king said to the wise
men**—These were probably the magi, without whose
advice as to the proper time of doing a thing the
Persian kings never did take any step whatever; and
the persons named in the following verse were the
"seven counsellors" (cf. Ezra 7:14) who formed the
state ministry. The combined wisdom of all, it
seems, was enlisted to consult with the king what
course should be taken after so unprecedented an
occurrence as Vashti's disobedience of the royal
summons. It is scarcely possible for us to imagine
the astonishment produced by such a refusal in a
country and a court where the will of the sovereign
was absolute. The assembled grandees were petri-
fied with horror at the daring affront. Alarm for
the consequences that might ensue to each of them
in his own household next seized on their minds;
and the sounds of bacchanalian revelry were hushed
into deep and anxious consultation what punishment
to inflict on the refractory queen. But a purpose
was to be served by the flattery of the king and the
enslavement of all women. The counsellors were
too intoxicated or obsequious to oppose the courtly
advice of Memucan. It was unanimously resolved,
with a wise regard to the public interests of the nation, that the punishment of Vashti could be nothing short of degradation from her royal dignity.
The doom was accordingly pronounced and made
known in all parts of the empire.

CHAPTER 2

Vss. 1-20. ESTHER CHOSEN TO BE QUEEN. **1.
After these things, when the wrath of King Ahasuerus was appeased**—On recovering from the violent
excitement of his revelry and rage, the king was
pierced with poignant regret for the unmerited treatment he had given to his beautiful and dignified
queen. But, according to the law, which made the
word of a Persian king irrevocable, she could not
be restored. His counsellors, for their own sake,
were solicitous to remove his disquietude, and hastened to recommend the adoption of all suitable
means for gratifying their royal master with another
consort of equal or superior attractions to those of
his divorced queen. In the despotic countries of the
East the custom obtains that when an order is sent
to a family for a young damsel to repair to the royal
palace, the parents, however unwilling, dare not refuse the honor for their daughter; and although they
know that when she is once in the royal harem, they
will never see her again, they are obliged to yield
a silent and passive compliance. On the occasion
referred to, a general search was commanded to be
made for the greatest beauties throughout the empire, in the hope that, from their ranks, the disconsolate monarch might select one for the honor
of succeeding to the royal honors of Vashti. The
damsels, on arrival at the palace, were placed under
the custody of "Hege, the king's chamberlain, keeper of the women," i.e., the chief eunuch, usually a
repulsive old man, on whom the court ladies are very

dependent, and whose favor they are always desirous to secure. **5. Now in Shushan the palace there was a certain Jew**—Mordecai held some office about the court. But his "sitting at the king's gate" (vs. 21) does not necessarily imply that he was in the humble condition of a porter; for, according to an institute of Cyrus, all state officers were required to wait in the outer courts till they were summoned into the presence-chamber. He might, therefore, have been a person of some official dignity. This man had an orphan cousin, born during the exile, under his care, who being distinguished by great personal beauty, was one of the young damsels taken into the royal harem on this occasion. She had the good fortune at once to gain the good-will of the chief eunuch. Her sweet and amiable appearance made her a favorite with all who looked upon her (vs. 15, last clause). Her Hebrew name (vs. 7) was Hadassah, i.e., myrtle, which, on her introduction into the royal harem, was changed to Esther, i.e., the star Venus, indicating beauty and good fortune [GENESIUS]. **11. Mordecai walked every day before the court of the women's house**—The harem is an inviolable sanctuary, and what is transacted within its walls is as much a secret to those without as if they were thousands of miles away. But hints were given him through the eunuchs. **12. Now when every maid's turn was come to go in to King Ahasuerus**—A whole year was spent in preparation for the intended honor. Considering that this took place in a palace, the long period prescribed, together with the profusion of costly and fragrant cosmetics employed, was probably required by state etiquette. **17. the king loved Esther above all the women**—The choice fell on Esther, who found favor in the eyes of Ahasuerus. He elevated her to the dignity of chief wife, or queen. The other competitors had apartments assigned them in the royal harem, and were retained in the rank of secondary wives, of whom Oriental princes have a great number. **he set the royal crown upon her head**—This consisted only of a purple ribbon, streaked with white, bound round the forehead. The nuptials were celebrated by a magnificent entertainment, and, in honor of the auspicious occasion, "he made a release to the provinces, and gave gifts, according to the state of the king." The dotation of Persian queens consisted in consigning to them the revenue of certain cities, in various parts of the kingdom, for defraying their personal and domestic expenditure. Some of these imposts the king remitted or lessened at this time.

21-23. MORDECAI, DISCOVERING A TREASON, IS RECORDED IN THE CHRONICLES. **21. In those days ...two of the king's chamberlains ... were wroth and sought to lay hand on the king, etc.**—This secret conspiracy against the king's life probably arose out of revenge for the divorce of Vashti, in whose interest, and at whose instigation, these eunuchs may have acted. Through the vigilance of Mordecai, whose fidelity, however, passed unnoticed, the design was frustrated, while the conspirators were condemned to be executed and as the matter was recorded in the court annals, it became the occasion afterwards of Mordecai's preferment to the place of power and influence for which, in furtherance of the national interests of the Jews, divine providence intended him.

CHAPTER 3

Vss. 1-15. HAMAN, ADVANCED BY THE KING, AND DESPISED BY MORDECAI, SEEKS REVENGE ON ALL THE JEWS. **1. After these things did Ahasuerus promote**

Haman ... and set his seat above all the princes—i.e., raised him to the rank of vizier, or prime confidential minister, whose pre-eminence in office and power appeared in the elevated state chair appropriated to that supreme functionary. Such a distinction in seats was counted of vast importance in the formal court of Persia. **2. all the king's servants, that were in the king's gate, bowed, and reverenced Haman**—Large mansions in the East are entered by a spacious vestibule, or gateway, along the sides of which visitors sit, and are received by the master of the house; for none, except the nearest relatives or special friends, are admitted farther. There the officers of the ancient king of Persia waited till they were called, and did obeisance to the all-powerful minister of the day. **But Mordecai bowed not, nor did him reverence**—The obsequious homage of prostration not entirely foreign to the manners of the East, had not been claimed by former viziers; but this minion required that all subordinate officers of the court should bow before him with their faces to the earth. But to Mordecai, it seemed that such an attitude of profound reverence was due only to God. Haman being an Amalekite, one of a doomed and accursed race, was, doubtless, another element in the refusal; and on learning that the recusant was a Jew, whose nonconformity was grounded on religious scruples, the magnitude of the affront appeared so much the greater, as the example of Mordecai would be imitated by all his compatriots. Had the homage been a simple token of civil respect, Mordecai would not have refused it; but the Persian kings demanded a sort of adoration, which, it is well known, even the Greeks reckoned it degradation to express. As Xerxes, in the height of his favoritism, had commanded the same honors to be given to the minister as to himself, this was the ground of Mordecai's refusal. **7. In the first month ... they cast Pur, that is, the lot**—In resorting to this method of ascertaining the most auspicious day for putting his atrocious scheme into execution, Haman acted as the kings and nobles of Persia have always done, never engaging in any enterprise without consulting the astrologers, and being satisfied as to the lucky hour. Vowing revenge but scorning to lay hands on a single victim, he meditated the extirpation of the whole Jewish race, who, he knew, were sworn enemies of his countrymen; and by artfully representing them as a people who were aliens in manners and habits, and enemies to the rest of his subjects, he procured the king's sanction of the intended massacre. One motive which he used in urging his point was addressed to the king's cupidity. Fearing lest his master might object that the extermination of a numerous body of his subjects would seriously depress the public revenue, Haman promised to make up the loss. **9. I will pay ten thousand talents of silver ... into the king's treasuries**—This sum, reckoning by the Babylonish talent, will be about $10,000,000 in our money; but estimated according to the Jewish talent, it will considerably exceed $15,000,000 an immense contribution to be made out of a private fortune. But classic history makes mention of several persons whose resources seem almost incredible. **10. the king took his ring from his hand, and gave it unto Haman**—There was a seal or signet in the ring. The bestowment of the ring, with the king's name and that of his kingdom engraven on it, was given with much ceremony, and it was equivalent to putting the sign manual to a royal edict. **12-15. Then were the king's scribes called ... and there was written**—The government secretaries were employed in making out the proclamation authorizing a universal massacre of the Jews on one day. It was translated into the dialects of all the people throughout the vast empire, and swift messengers were sent to carry it into all the provinces. On the day appointed, all Jews were to be put to death and their property confiscated; doubtless, the means by which Haman hoped to pay his stipulated tribute into the royal treasury. To us it appears unaccountable how any sane monarch could have given his consent to the extirpation of a numerous class of his subjects. But such acts of frenzied barbarity have, alas! been not rarely authorized by careless and voluptuous despots, who have allowed their ears to be engrossed and their policy directed by haughty and selfish minions, who had their own passions to gratify, their own ends to serve. **15. the king and Haman sat down to drink; but the city Shushan was perplexed**—The completeness of the word-painting in this verse is exquisite. The historian, by a simple stroke, has drawn a graphic picture of an Oriental despot, wallowing with his favorite in sensual enjoyments, while his tyrannical cruelties were rending the hearts and homes of thousands of his subjects.

CHAPTER 4

Vss. 1-14. MORDECAI AND THE JEWS MOURN. **1. When Mordecai perceived all that was done**—Relying on the irrevocable nature of a Persian monarch's decree (Dan. 6:15), Haman had made it known as soon as the royal sanction had been obtained; and Mordecai was, doubtless, among the first to hear of it. On his own account, as well as on that of his countrymen, this astounding decree must have been indescribably distressing. The acts described in this passage are, according to the Oriental fashion, expressive of the most poignant sorrow; and his approach to the gate of the palace, under the impulse of irrepressible emotions, was to make an earnest though vain appeal to the royal mercy. Access, however, to the king's presence was, to a person in his disfigured state, impossible: "for none might enter into the king's gate clothed with sackcloth." But he found means of conveying intelligence of the horrid plot to Queen Esther. **4. Then was the queen . . . grieved; and . . . sent raiment to . . . Mordecai**—Her object in doing so was either to qualify him for resuming his former office, or else, perhaps, of fitting him to come near enough to the palace to inform her of the cause of such sudden and extreme distress. **5. Then called Esther for Hatach, one of the king's chamberlains, whom he had appointed to attend upon her**—Communication with the women in the harem is very difficult to be obtained, and only through the medium of the keepers. The chief eunuch receives the message from the lips of the queen, conveys it to some inferior office of the seraglio. When the commission is executed, the subaltern communicates it to the superintendent, by whom it is delivered to the queen. This chief eunuch, usually an old man who has recommended himself by a long course of faithful service, is always appointed by the king; but it is his interest, as well as his duty, to ingratiate himself with the queen also. Accordingly, we find Hatach rendering himself very serviceable in carrying on those private communications with Mordecai who was thereby enabled to enlist Esther's powerful influence. **8. charge her that she should go in unto the king**—This language is exceedingly strong. As it can scarcely be supposed that Mordecai was still using authority

over Esther as his adopted daughter, he must be considered as imploring rather than commanding her, in the name of her brethren and in the name of her God, to make a direct appeal to the feelings of her royal husband. **11. whosoever, whether man or woman, shall come unto the king into the inner court, who is not called**—The Persian kings surrounded themselves with an almost impassable circle of forms. The law alluded to was first enacted by Deioces, king of Media, and afterwards, when the empires were united, adopted by the Persians, that all business should be transacted and petitions transmitted to the king through his ministers. Although the restriction was not intended, of course, to apply to the queen, yet from the strict and inflexible character of the Persian laws and the extreme desire to exalt the majesty of the sovereign, even his favorite wife had not the privilege of *entree*, except by special favor and indulgence. Esther was suffering from the severity of this law; and as, from not being admitted for a whole month to the king's presence, she had reason to fear that the royal affections had become alienated from her, she had little hope of serving her country's cause in this awful emergency. **13, 14. Then Mordecai commanded to answer Esther**—His answer was to this effect, that Esther need not indulge the vain hope she would, from her royal connection, escape the general doom of her race—that he (Mordecai) confidently believed God would interpose, and, if not through her, by some other deliverer, save His people; but that the duty evidently devolved on her, as there was great reason to believe that this was the design of Providence in her elevation to the dignity of queen, and therefore that she should go with a courageous heart, not doubting of success. **16. so will I go in unto the king, which is not according to the law**—The appeal of Mordecai was irresistible. Having appointed a solemn fast of three days, she expressed her firm resolution to make an appeal to the king, though she should perish in the attempt. **I . . . and my maidens**—It is probable that she had surrounded herself with Jewish maidens, or women who were proselytes to that religion.

CHAPTER 5

Vss. 1-14. ESTHER INVITES THE KING AND HAMAN TO A BANQUET. **1. Esther put on her royal apparel**—It was not only natural, but, on such occasions, highly proper and expedient, that the queen should decorate herself in a style becoming her exalted station. On ordinary occasions she might reasonably set off her charms to as much advantage as possible; but, on the present occasion, as she was desirous to secure the favor of one who sustained the twofold character of her husband and her sovereign, public as well as private considerations—a regard to her personal safety, no less than the preservation of her doomed countrymen—urged upon her the propriety of using every legitimate means of recommending herself to the favorable notice of Ahasuerus. **the king sat upon his royal throne in the royal house, over against the gate of the house**—The palace of this Persian king seems to have been built, like many more of the same quality and description, with an advanced cloister, over against the gate, made in the fashion of a large penthouse, supported only by one or two contiguous pillars in the front, or else in the center. In such open structures as these, in the midst of their guards and counsellors, are the *bashaws,* kadis, and other great officers, accustomed to distribute justice, and transact the public affairs of the provinces [SHAW'S TRAVELS]. In such a situation the Persian king was seated. The seat he occupied was not a *throne*, according to our ideas of one, but simply a chair, and so high that it required a footstool. It was made of gold, or, at least, inlaid with that metal, and covered with splendid tapestry, and no one save the king might sit down on it under pain of death. It is often found pictured on the Persepolitan monuments, and always of the same fashion. **2. the king held out to Esther the golden scepter that was in his hand**—This golden scepter receives an interesting illustration from the sculptured monuments of Persia and Assyria. In the bas-reliefs of Persepolis, copied by Sir Robert Ker Porter, we see King Darius enthroned in the midst of his court, and walking abroad in equal state; in either case he carries in his right hand a slender rod or wand, about equal in length to his own height, ornamented with a small knob at the summit. In the Assyrian alabasters, those found at Nimroud as well as those from Khorsabad, "the great king" is furnished with the same appendage of royalty, a slender rod, but destitute of any knob or ornament. On the Khorsabad reliefs the rod is painted red, *doubtless* to *represent gold;* proving that "the golden sceptre" was a simple wand of that precious metal, commonly held in the right hand, with one end resting on the ground, and that whether the king was sitting or walking. "The gold sceptre" has received little alteration or modification since ancient times [Goss]. It was extended to Esther as a token not only that her intrusion was pardoned, but that her visit was welcome, and a favorable reception given to the suit she had come to prefer. **touched the top of the sceptre**—This was the usual way of acknowledging the royal condescension, and at the same time expressing reverence and submission to the august majesty of the king. **3. it shall be even given thee to the half of the kingdom**—This mode of speaking originated in the Persian custom of appropriating for the maintenance of great men, or royal favorites, one city for his bread, another for his wine, a third for his clothes, etc., so that the phrase denoted great liberality. **4. let the king and Haman come this day unto the banquet that I have prepared for him**—There was great address in this procedure of Esther's; for, by showing such high respect to the king's favorite, she would the better insinuate herself into the royal affections; and gain a more suitable opportunity of making known her request. **8. let the king and Haman come to the banquet that I shall prepare**—The king ate alone, and his guests in an adjoining hall; but they were admitted to sit with him at wine. Haman being the only invited guest with the king and queen, it was natural that he should have been elated with the honor.

CHAPTER 6

Vss. 1-14. AHASUERUS REWARDS MORDECAI FOR FORMER SERVICE. 1. the king ... commanded to bring the book of records of the chronicles—In Eastern courts, there are scribes or officers whose duty it is to keep a journal of every occurrence worthy of notice. A book of this kind, abounding with anecdotes, is full of interest. It has been a custom with Eastern kings, in all ages, frequently to cause the annals of the kingdom to be read to them. It is resorted to, not merely as a pastime to while away the tedium of an hour, but as a source of instruction to the monarch, by reviewing the important incidents of his own life, as well as those of his ancestors. There was, therefore, nothing uncommon in this Persian monarch calling for the court journal. But, in his being unable to sleep at that particular juncture, in his ordering the book then to be read to him, and in his attention having been specially directed to the important and as yet unrewarded services of Mordecai, the immediate interposition of Providence is distinctly visible. **4. Now Haman was come into the outward court**—This was early in the morning. It is the invariable custom for kings in Eastern countries to transact business before the sun is hot, often in the open air, and so Haman was in all probability come officially to attend on his master. **6. What shall be done unto the man whom the king delighteth to honour?**—In bestowing tokens of their favor, the kings of Persia do not at once, and as it were by their own will, determine the kind of honor that shall be awarded; but they turn to the courtier standing next in rank to themselves, and ask him what shall be done to the individual who has rendered the service specified; and according to the answer received, the royal mandate is issued. **8. the royal apparel ... which the king useth to wear**—A coat which has been on the back of a king or prince is reckoned a most honorable gift, and is given with great ceremony. **the horse that the king rideth upon**—Persia was a country of horses, and the highbred charger that the king rode upon acquired, in the eyes of his venal subjects, a sort of sacredness from that circumstance. **and the crown royal which is set upon his head**—either the royal turban, or it may be a tiara, with which, on state processions, the horse's head was adorned. **9. delivered to the hand of one of the king's most noble princes ... array the man**—On grand and public occasions, the royal steed is led by the highest subject through the principal streets of the city, a ceremony which may occupy several hours. **11. Then Haman took**, etc.—This sudden reverse, however painful to Haman as an individual, is particularly characteristic of the Persian manners. **14. came the king's chamberlains, and hasted to bring Haman unto the banquet**—Besides the invitation given to an entertainment, a message is always sent to the guests, immediately at the day and hour appointed, to announce that all things are ready.

CHAPTER 7

Vss. 1-6. ESTHER PLEADS FOR HER OWN LIFE AND THE LIFE OF HER PEOPLE. 4. we are sold, I and my people, to be destroyed—i.e., by the cruel and perfidious scheme of that man, who offered an immense sum of money to purchase our extermination. Esther dwelt on his contemplated atrocity, in a variety of expressions, which both evinced the depth of her own emotions, and were intended to awaken similar feelings in the king's breast. **But if we had been sold for bondmen and bondwomen, I had held my tongue**—Though a great calamity to the Jews, the enslavement of that people might have enriched the national treasury; and, at all events, the policy, if found from experience to be bad, could be altered. But the destruction of such a body of people would be an irreparable evil, and all the talents Haman might pour into the treasury could not compensate for the loss of their services.

7-10. THE KING CAUSES HAMAN TO BE HANGED ON HIS OWN GALLOWS. 7. he saw that there was evil determined against him by the king—When the king of Persia orders an offender to be executed, and then rises and goes into the women's apartment, it is a sign that no mercy is to be hoped for. Even the sudden rising of the king in anger was the same as if he had pronounced sentence. **8. Haman was fallen upon the bed whereon Esther was**—We do not know the precise form of the couches on which the Persians reclined at table. But it is probable that they were not very different from those used by the Greeks and Romans. Haman, perhaps, at first stood up to beg pardon of Esther; but driven in his extremity to resort to an attitude of the most earnest supplication, he fell prostrate on the couch where the queen was recumbent. The king returning that instant was fired at what seemed an outrage on female modesty. **they covered Haman's face**—The import of this striking action is, that a criminal is unworthy any longer to look on the face of the king, and hence, when malefactors are consigned to their doom in Persia, the first thing is to cover the face with a veil or napkin. **9. Harbonah, one of the chamberlains, said before the king, Behold also, the gallows**—This eunuch had probably been the messenger sent with the invitation to Haman, and on that occasion had seen the gallows. The information he now volunteered, as well it may be from abhorrence of Haman's cold-blooded conspiracy as from sympathy with his amiable mistress, involved with her people in imminent peril. **10. So they hanged Haman on the gallows that he had prepared**—He has not been the only plotter of mischief whose feet have been taken in the net which they hid (Ps. 9:15). But never was condemnation more just, and retribution more merited, than the execution of that gigantic criminal.

CHAPTER 8

Vss. 1-6. MORDECAI ADVANCED. **1. On that day did . . . Ahasuerus give the house of Haman . . . unto Esther**—His property was confiscated, and everything belonging to him, as some compensation for the peril to which she had been exposed. **Mordecai came before the king**—i.e., was introduced at court and appointed one of the seven counsellors. Esther displayed great prudence and address in acknowledging Mordecai's relation to her at the moment most fitted to be of eminent service to him. **2. the king took off his ring . . . and gave it unto Mordecai**—By that act transferring to him all the power and authority which the ring symbolized, and promoting him to the high dignity which Haman had formerly filled. **Esther set Mordecai over the house of Haman**—as her steward or factor, to manage that large and opulent estate which had been assigned to her. **3. Esther spake yet again before the king, and fell down at his feet**—The king was then not reclining at table, but sitting on a divan, most probably in the Persian attitude, leaning back against the cushions, and one foot under him. **besought him with tears to put away the mischief of Haman**—i.e., to repeal the sanguinary edict which, at the secret instigation of Haman, had been recently passed (ch. 3:12). **4. Then the king held out the golden sceptre toward Esther**—in token that her request was accepted, and that she needed no longer to maintain the humble attitude of a suppliant. **5, 6. reverse the letters devised by Haman . . . to destroy the Jews**—The whole conduct of Esther in this matter is characterized by great tact, and the variety of expressions by which she describes her willing submission to her royal husband, the address with which she rolls the whole infamy of the meditated massacre on Haman, and the argument she draws from the king's sanction being surreptitiously obtained, that the decree

should be immediately reversed—all indicate the queen's wisdom and skill, and she succeeded in this point also.

7-14. AHASUERUS GRANTS TO THE JEWS TO DEFEND THEMSELVES. **8. Write . . . in the king's name, and seal it with the king's ring**—Hence it is evident that the royal ring had a seal in it, which, being affixed to any document, authenticated it with the stamp of royal authority. **which . . . may no man reverse**—This is added as the reason why he could not comply with the queen's request for a direct reversal of recall of Haman's letters; viz., that the laws of the Medes and Persians, once passed, were irrevocable. **10. sent . . . by posts . . . and riders on . . . camels, and young dromedaries**—The business being very urgent, the swiftest kind of camel would be employed, and so the word in the original denotes—the *wind-camel*. Young dromedaries also are used to carry expresses, being remarkable for the nimbleness and ease of their movements. Animals of this description could convey the new rescript of Ahasuerus over the length and breadth of the Persian empire in time to relieve the unhappy Jews from the ban under which they lay. **11-13. the king granted the Jews . . . to stand for their life . . . to slay . . . all . . . that would assault them**—The fixed and unalterable character claimed for Persian edicts often placed the king in a very awkward dilemma; for, however bitterly he might regret things done in a moment of haste and thoughtlessness, it was beyond even his power to prevent the consequences. This was the reason on account of which the king was laid under a necessity not to reverse, but to issue a contradictory edict; according to which it was enacted that if, pursuant to the first decree, the Jews were assaulted, they might, by virtue of the second, defend themselves and even slay their enemies. However strange and even ridiculous this mode of procedure may appear, it was the only one which, from the peculiarities of court etiquette in Persia, could be adopted. Instances occur in sacred (Dan. 6:14), no less than profane, history. Many passages of the Bible attest the truth of this, particularly the well-known incident of Daniel's being cast into the den of lions, in conformity with the rash decree of Darius, though, as it afterwards appeared, contrary to the personal desire of that monarch. That the law of Persia has undergone no change in this respect, and the power of the monarch not less immutable, appear from many anecdotes related in the books of modern travellers through that country.

15-17. MORDECAI'S HONORS, AND THE JEWS' JOY. **15. Mordecai went out . . . in royal apparel**—He was invested with the khelaat of official honor. A dress of blue and white was held in great estimation among the Persians; so that Mordecai, whom the king delighted to honor, was in fact arrayed in the royal dress and insignia. The variety and the kind of insignia worn by a favorite at once makes known to the people the particular dignity to which he has been raised.

CHAPTER 9

Vss. 1-19. THE JEWS SLAY THEIR ENEMIES WITH THE TEN SONS OF HAMAN. **1. in the twelfth month, . . . on the thirteenth day of the same**—This was the day which Haman's superstitious advisers had led him to select as the most fortunate for the execution of his exterminating scheme against the Jews. **2. The Jews gathered themselves . . . no man could withstand them**—The tables were now turned in their favor; and though their enemies made their long meditated attack, the Jews were not only at liberty to act on the defensive, but through the powerful influence enlisted on their side at court together with the blessing of God, they were everywhere victorious. **the fear of them fell upon all people**—This impression arose not alone from the consciousness of the all-powerful vizier being their countryman, but from the hand of God appearing so visibly interposed to effect their strange and unexpected deliverance. **5-16. Thus the Jews smote all their enemies** —The effect of the two antagonistic decrees was, in the meantime, to raise a fierce and bloody war between the Jews and their enemies throughout the Persian empire; but through the dread of Esther and Mordecai, the provincial governors universally favored their cause, so that their enemies fell in great numbers. **13. let it be granted to the Jews which are in Shushan to do to-morrow also according unto this day's decree**—Their enemies adroitly concealing themselves for the first day might have returned on the next, when they imagined that the privilege of the Jews was expired; so that that people would have been surprised and slain. The extension of the decree to another day at the queen's special desire has exposed her to the charge of being actuated by a cruel and vindictive disposition. But her conduct in making this request is capable of full vindication, on the ground (1) that Haman's sons having taken a prominent part in avenging their father's fall, and having been previously slain in the *melee*, the order for the exposure of their dead bodies on the gallows was only intended to brand them with public infamy for their malice and hatred to the Jews; and (2) the anti-Jewish party having, in all probability, been instigated through the arts or influence of Haman to acts of spiteful and wanton oppression, the existing state of feeling among the natives required some vigorous and decisive measure to prevent the outbreak of future aggressions. To order an extension, therefore, of the permissive edict to the Jews to defend themselves, was perhaps no more than affording an opportunity for their enemies to be publicly known. Though it led to so awful a slaughter of 75,000 of their enemies, there is reason to believe that these were chiefly Amalekites, in the fall of whom on this occasion, the prophecies (Exod. 17:14, 16; Deut. 25:19) against that doomed race were accomplished. **19. a day of ... feasting ... and of sending portions one to another**—The princes and people of the East not only invite their friends to feasts, but it is their custom to send a portion of the banquet to those who cannot well come to it, especially their relations, and those who are detained at home in a state of sorrow or distress.

20-32. THE TWO DAYS OF PURIM MADE FESTIVAL. **20. Mordecai wrote these things**—Commentators are not agreed what is particularly meant by "these things"; whether the letters following, or an account of these marvellous events to be preserved in the families of the Jewish people, and transmitted from one generation to another. **26. they called these days Purim, after the name of Pur**—Pur, in the Persian language, signifies lot; and the feast of Purim, or lots, has a reference to the time having been pitched upon by Haman through the decision of the lot. In consequence of the signal national deliverance which divine providence gave them from the infamous machinations of Haman, Mordecai ordered the Jews to commemorate that event by an anniversary festival, which was to last for two days, in accordance with the two days' war of defense they had to maintain. There was a slight difference in the time of this festival; for the Jews in the provinces, having defended themselves against their enemies on the thirteenth, devoted the fourteenth to festivity; whereas their brethren in Shushan, having extended that work over two days, did not observe their thanksgiving feast till the fifteenth. But this was remedied by authority, which fixed the fourteenth and fifteenth of Adar. It became a season of sunny memories to the universal body of the Jews; and, by the letters of Mordecai, dispersed through all parts of the Persian empire, it was established as an annual feast, the celebration of which is kept up still. On both days of the feast, the modern Jews read over the *Megillah* or Book of Esther in their synagogues. The copy read must not be printed, but written on vellum in the form of a roll; and the names of the ten sons of Haman are written on it a peculiar manner, being ranged, they say, like so many bodies on a gibbet. The reader must pronounce all these names in one breath. Whenever Haman's name is pronounced, they make a terrible noise in the synagogue. Some drum with their feet on the floor, and the boys have mallets with which they knock and make a noise. They prepare themselves for their carnival by a previous fast, which should continue three days, in imitation of Esther's; but they have mostly reduced it to one day [JENNING'S JEWISH ANTIQUITIES].

CHAPTER 10

VSS. 1-3. AHASUERUS' GREATNESS. MORDECAI'S ADVANCEMENT. **1. Ahasuerus laid a tribute**—This passage being an appendix to the history, and improperly separated from the preceding chapter, it might be that the occasion of levying this new impost arose out of the commotions raised by Haman's conspiracy. Neither the nature nor the amount of the tax has been recorded; only it was not a local tribute, but one exacted from all parts of his vast empire. **2. the declaration of the greatness of Mordecai**—The experience of this pious and excellent Jew verified the statement, "he that humbleth himself shall be exalted." From sitting contentedly at the king's gate, he was raised to the dignity of highest subject, the powerful ruler of the kingdom. Acting uniformly on the great principles of truth and righteousness, his greatness rested on a firm foundation. His faith was openly avowed, and his influence as a professor of the true religion was of the greatest usefulness for promoting the welfare of the Jewish people, as well as for advancing the glory of God. **3. Mordecai ... was next unto King Ahasuerus ... great among the Jews**, etc.—The elevation of this pious and patriotic Jew to the possession of the highest official power was of very great importance to the suffering church at that period; for it enabled him, who all along possessed the disposition, now to direct the royal influence and authority in promoting the interests and extending the privileges of his exiled countrymen. Viewed in this light, the providence of God is plainly traceable in all the steps that led to his unexpected advancement. This providential interposition is all the more remarkable, that, as in the analogous case of Joseph, it was displayed in making the ordinary and natural course of things lead to the most marvellous results. To use the pious words of an eminent prelate, "though in the whole of this episode there was no extraordinary manifestation of God's power, no particular cause or agent that was in its working advanced above the ordinary pitch of nature, yet the contrivance, and suiting these ordinary agents appointed by God, is in itself more admirable than if the same end had been effected by means that were truly miraculous." The sudden advancement of individuals from obscurity and neglect to the highest stations of power and influence is, in Eastern courts, no extraordinary nor infrequent occurrence. The caprice, the weak partiality of the reigning sovereign, or, it may be, his penetrating discernment in discovering latent energy and talent, has often "raised the beggar from the dunghill, and set him among princes." Some of the all-powerful viziers in modern Persia, and not a few of the beys in Egypt, have been elevated to their respective dignities in this manner. And, therefore, the advancement of "Mordecai, who was next unto Ahasuerus, and great among the Jews," was in perfect accordance with the rapid revolution of "the wheel of fortune" in that part of the world. But, considering all the circumstances of Mordecai's advancement, not only his gaining the favor of the king, but his being "accepted of the multitude of his brethren, it was beyond all controversy the doing of the Lord, and was truly marvellous in his people's eyes." **accepted of the multitude of his brethren**—Far from being envious of his grandeur, they blessed God for the elevation to official power of so good a man. **speaking peace to all his seed**—While his administration was conducted with a mild and impartial hand, he showed a peculiarly warm and friendly feeling to all his countrymen when asked his counsel or his aid.

THE BOOK OF

JOB

INTRODUCTION

JOB A REAL PERSON.—It has been supposed by some that the book of Job is an allegory, not a real narrative, on account of the artificial character of many of its statements. Thus the sacred numbers, *three* and *seven*, often occur. He had *seven* thousand sheep, *seven* sons, both before and after his trials; his *three* friends sit down with him *seven* days and *seven* nights; both before and after his trials he had *three* daughters. So also the number and form of the speeches of the several speakers seem to be artificial. The name of Job, too, is derived from an Arabic word signifying *repentance*.

But Ezekiel 14:14 (cf. vss. 16, 20) speaks of "Job" in conjunction with "Noah and Daniel," real persons. St. James (5:11) also refers to Job as an example of "patience," which he would not have been likely to do had Job been only a fictitious person. Also the names of persons and places are specified with a particularity not to be looked for in an allegory. As to the exact *doubling* of his possessions after his restoration, no doubt the *round* number is given for the exact number, as the latter approached near the former; this is often done in undoubtedly *historical* books. As to the studied number and form of the speeches, it seems likely that the arguments were *substantially* those which appear in the book, but that *the studied and poetic form* was given by Job himself, guided by the Holy Spirit. He lived one hundred and forty years after his trials, and nothing would be more natural than that he should, at his leisure, mould into a perfect form the arguments used in the momentous debate, for the instruction of the Church in all ages. Probably, too, the debate itself occupied several sittings; and the number of speeches assigned to each was arranged by preconcerted agreement, and each was allowed the interval of a day or more to prepare carefully his speech and replies; this will account for the speakers bringing forward their arguments in regular series, no one speaking out of his turn. As to the name Job—*repentance* (supposing the derivation correct)—it was common in old times to give a name from circumstances which occurred at an advanced period of life, and this is no argument against the reality of the person.

WHERE JOB LIVED.—Uz, according to GESENIUS, means a light, sandy soil, and was in the north of Arabia Deserta, between Palestine and the Euphrates, called by PTOLEMY (*Geography* 19) *Ausitai* or *Aisitai*. In Genesis 10:23; 22:21; 36:28; and I Chronicles 1:17, 42, it is the name of a man. In Jeremiah 25:20; Lamentations 4:21; and Job 1:1, it is a country. Uz, in Genesis 22:21, is said to be the son of Nahor, brother of Abraham—a different person from the one mentioned (Genesis 10:23), a grandson of Shem. The probability is that the country took its name from the latter of the two; for this one was the son of Aram, from whom the Arameans take their name, and these dwelt in Mesopotamia, between the rivers Euphrates and Tigris. Compare as to the dwelling of the sons of Shem in Genesis 10:30, "a mount *of the East*," answering to "men *of the East*" (Job 1:3). RAWLINSON, in his deciphering of the Assyrian inscriptions, states that "Uz is the prevailing name of the country at the mouth of the Euphrates." It is probable that Eliphaz the Temanite and the Sabeans dwelt in that quarter; and we know that the Chaldeans resided there, and not near Idumea, which some identify with Uz. The tornado from "the wilderness" (ch. 1:19) agrees with the view of it being Arabia Deserta. Job (ch. 1:3) is called "the greatest of the men of the East"; but Idumea was not east, but south of Palestine: therefore in Scripture language, the phrase cannot apply to that country, but probably refers to the north of Arabia Deserta, between Palestine, Idumea, and the Euphrates. So the Arabs still show in the Houran a place called Uz as the residence of Job.

THE AGE WHEN JOB LIVED.—EUSEBIUS fixes it two ages before Moses, i.e., about the time of Isaac: eighteen hundred years before Christ, and six hundred after the Deluge. Agreeing with this are the following considerations: 1. Job's length of life is patriarchal, two hundred years. 2. He alludes only to the earliest form of idolatry, viz., the worship of the sun, moon, and heavenly hosts (called *Saba*, whence arises the title Lord of *Sabaoth*, as opposed to Sabeanism) (ch. 31:26–28). 3. The number of oxen and rams sacrificed, *seven*, as in the case of Balaam. God would not have sanctioned this *after* the giving of the Mosaic law, though He might graciously accommodate Himself to existing customs *before* the law. 4. The language of Job is Hebrew, interspersed occasionally with Syriac and Arabic expressions, implying a time when all the Shemitic tribes spoke one common tongue and had not branched into different dialects, Hebrew, Syriac, and Arabic. 5. He speaks of the most ancient kind of writing, viz., sculpture. Riches also are reckoned by cattle. The Hebrew word, translated "a piece of money," ought rather be rendered "a lamb." 6. There is no allusion to the exodus from Egypt and to the miracles that accompanied it; nor to the destruction of Sodom and Gomorrah (PATRICK, however, thinks there is); though there is to the Flood (ch. 22:17); and these events, happening in Job's vicinity, would have been striking illustrations of the argument for God's interposition in destroying the wicked and vindicating the righteous, had Job and his friends known of them. Nor is there any *undoubted* reference to the Jewish law, ritual, and priesthood. 7. The religion of Job is that which prevailed among the patriarchs previous to the law; sacrifices performed by the head of the family; no officiating priesthood, temple, or consecrated altar.

THE WRITER.—All the foregoing facts accord with Job himself having been the author. The style of thought, imagery, and manners, are such as we should look for in the work of an Arabian emir. There is precisely that degree of knowledge of primitive tradition (see ch. 31:33, as to Adam) which was universally spread abroad in the days of Noah and Abraham, and which was subsequently embodied in the early chapters of Genesis. Job, in his speeches, shows that he was much more competent to compose the work than Elihu, to whom LIGHTFOOT attributes it. The style forbids its being attributed to Moses, to whom its composition is by some attributed, "whilst he was among the Midianites, about 1520 B.C." But the fact, that it, though not a Jewish book, appears among the Hebrew sacred writings, makes it likely that it came to the knowledge of Moses during the forty years which he passed in parts of Arabia, chiefly near Horeb; and that he, by divine guidance, introduced it as a sacred writing to the Israelites, to whom, in their affliction, the patience and restoration of Job were calculated to be a lesson of especial utility. That it is inspired appears from the fact that Paul (I Cor. 3:19) quotes it (Job 5:13) with the formula, "It is written." Cf. also James 4:10 and I Peter 5:6 with Job 22:29; Romans 11:34, 35 with Job 15:8. It is probably the oldest book in the world. It stands among the Hagiographa in the threefold division of Scripture into the Law, the Prophets, and the Hagiographa ("Psalms," Luke 24:44).

DESIGN OF THE BOOK.—It is a public debate in poetic form on an important question concerning the divine government; moreover the prologue and epilogue, which are in prose, shed the interest of a living history over the debate, which would otherwise be but a contest of abstract reasonings. To each speaker of the three friends *three* speeches are assigned. Job having no one to stand by him is allowed to reply to each speech of each of the three. Eliphaz, as the oldest, leads the way. Zophar, at his *third* turn, failed to speak, thus virtually owning himself overcome (ch. 27). Therefore Job continued his reply, which forms *three* speeches (chs. 26, 27, 28, 29–31). Elihu (chs. 32–37) is allowed *four* speeches. Jehovah makes *three* addresses (chs. 38–41). Thus, throughout there is a tripartite division. The whole is divided into *three* parts—the prologue, poem proper, and epilogue. The *poem*, into three—1. The dispute of Job and his three friends; 2. The address of Elihu; 3. The address of God. There are *three* series in the controversy, and in the same order. The epilogue (ch. 42) also is threefold; Job's justification, reconciliation with his friends, restoration. The speakers also in their successive speeches *regularly advance from less to greater vehemence*. With all this artificial composition, everything seems easy and natural.

The question to be solved, as exemplified in the case of Job, is, Why are the righteous afflicted consistently with God's justice? The doctrine of retribution after death, no doubt, is the great solution of the difficulty. And to it Job plainly refers in ch. 14:14, and ch. 19:25. The objection to this, that the explicitness of the language on the resurrection in Job is inconsistent with the obscurity on the subject in the early books of the Old Testament, is answered by the fact that Job enjoyed the divine vision (ch. 38:1; 42:5), and therefore, *by inspiration*, foretold these truths. Next, the revelations made outside of Israel being few needed to be the more explicit; thus Balaam's prophecy (Num. 24:17) was clear enough to lead the wise men *of the East* by the star (Matt. 2); and in the age before the written law, it was the more needful for God not to leave Himself without witness of the truth. Still Job evidently did not fully realize the significance designed by the Spirit in his own words (cf. I Pet. 1:11, 12). The doctrine, though existing, was not *plainly* revealed or at least understood. Hence he does not *mainly* refer to this solution. Yes, and *even now*, we need something *in addition* to this solution. David, who firmly believed in a future retribution (Ps. 16:10; 17:15), still felt the difficulty not *entirely* solved thereby (Ps. 83). The solution is not in Job's or in his three friends' speeches. It must, therefore, be in Elihu's. God will hold a final judgment, no doubt, to clear up all that seems dark in His present dealings; but He also *now* providentially and morally governs the world *and all the events of human life*. Even the comparatively righteous are not without sin which needs to be corrected. The justice and love of God administer the altogether deserved and merciful correction. Affliction to the godly is thus mercy and justice in disguise. The afflicted believer on repentance sees this. "*Via crucis, via salutis*." Though afflicted, the godly are happier *even now* than the ungodly, and when affliction has attained its end, it is removed by the Lord. In the Old Testament the consolations are more temporal and outward; in the New Testament, more spiritual; but in neither to the entire exclusion of the other. "Prosperity," says Bacon, "is the blessing of the Old Testament; adversity that of the New Testament, which is the mark of God's more especial favor. Yet even in the Old Testament, if you listen to David's harp, you shall hear as many hearse-like airs as carols; and the pencil of the Holy Ghost has labored more in describing the afflictions of Job than the felicities of Solomon. Prosperity is not without many fears and distastes; and adversity is not without comforts and hopes." This solution of Elihu is seconded by the addresses of God, in which it is shown God *must* be just (because He *is* God), as Elihu had shown *how* God can be just, and yet the righteous be afflicted. It is also acquiesced in by Job, who makes no reply. God reprimands the three friends, but not Elihu. Job's general course is approved; he is directed to intercede for his friends, and is restored to double his former prosperity.

POETRY.—In all countries poetry is the earliest form of composition as being best retained in the memory. In the East especially it was customary for sentiments to be preserved in a terse, proverbial, and poetic form (called *maschal*). Hebrew poetry is not constituted by the rhythm or meter, but in a form peculiar to itself:—1. In an alphabetical arrangement somewhat like our acrostic. For instance, Lamentations 1. 2. The same verse repeated at intervals; as in Psalms 42, 107. 3. Rhythm of gradation. *Psalms of degrees*, 120–134, in which the expression of the previous verse is resumed and carried forward in the next (Ps. 121). 4. The chief characteristic of Hebrew poetry is *parallelism*, or the correspondence of the same ideas in the parallel clauses. The earliest instance is Enoch's prophecy (Jude 14), and Lamech's parody of it (Gen. 4:23). Three kinds occur—(1) The synonymous parallelism, in which the second is a repetition of the first, with or without increase of force (Ps. 22:27; Isa. 15:1); sometimes with double parallelism (Isa. 1:15). (2) The antithetic, in which the idea of the second clause is the converse of that in the first (Prov. 10:1). (3) The synthetic, where there is a correspondence between different propositions, noun answering to noun, verb to verb, member to member, the sentiment, moreover, being not merely echoed, or put in contrast, but enforced by accessory ideas (Job 3:3–9). Also *alternate* (Isa. 51:19). "Desolation and destruction, famine and sword," i.e., desolation by famine, and destruction by the sword. *Introverted;* where the fourth answers to the first, and the third to the second (Matt. 7:6). Parallelism thus often affords a key to the interpretation. For fuller information, see Lowth ("Introduction to Isaiah," and "Lecture on Hebrew Poetry") and *Spirit of Hebrew Poetry* by Herder, translated by Marsh. The simpler and less artificial forms of parallelism prevail in Job—a mark of its early age.

CHAPTER 1

PART I—PROLOGUE OR HISTORICAL INTRODUCTION IN PROSE—CHAPTERS I, II

VSS. 1-5. THE HOLINESS OF JOB, HIS WEALTH, etc. **1. Uz**—north of Arabia Deserta, lying towards the Euphrates. It was in this neighborhood, and not in that of Idumea, that the Chaldeans and Sabeans who plundered him dwelt. The Arabs divide their country into the north, called Sham, or "the left"; and the south, called Yemen, or "the right"; for they faced east; and so the west was on their left, and the south on their right. Arabia Deserta was on the east, Arabia Petræa on the west, and Arabia Felix on the south. **Job**—The name comes from an *Arabic* word meaning "to return," viz., to God, "to repent," referring to his end [EICHORN]; or rather from a *Hebrew* word signifying one to whom enmity was shown, "greatly tried" [GESENIUS]. Significant names were often given among the Hebrews, from some event of later life (cf. Gen. 4:2, Abel—a "feeder" of sheep). So the emir of Uz was by general consent called Job, on account of his "trials." The only other person so called was a son of Issachar (Gen. 46:13). **perfect** —not absolute or faultless perfection (cf. 9:20); Eccles. 7:20), but *integrity, sincerity, and consistency* on the whole, in all relations of life (Gen. 6:9; 17:1; Prov. 10:9; Matt. 5:48). It was the fear of God that kept Job from evil (Prov. 8:13). **3. she-asses**—prized on account of their milk, and for riding (Judg. 5:10). Houses and lands are not mentioned among the emir's wealth, as nomadic tribes dwell in movable tents and live chiefly by pasture, the right to the soil not being appropriated by individuals. The "five hundred yoke of oxen" imply, however, that Job tilled the soil. He seems also to have had a dwelling in a town, in which respect he differed from the patriarchs. Camels are well called "ships of the desert," especially valuable for caravans, as being able to lay in a store of water that suffices them for days, and to sustain life on a very few thistles or thorns. **household**—(Gen. 26:14). The other rendering which the *Hebrew* admits, "husbandry," is not so probable. **men of the east**—denoting in Scripture those living east of Palestine; as the people of North Arabia Deserta (Judg. 6:3; Ezek. 25:4). **4. every one his day**—viz., the birth-

day (ch. 3:1). Implying the love and harmony of the members of the family, as contrasted with the ruin which soon broke up such a scene of happiness. The *sisters* are specified, as these feasts were not for revelry, which would be inconsistent with the presence of sisters. These latter were invited by the brothers, though they gave no invitations in return. **5. when the days of feasting were gone about**—i.e., at the end of all the birthdays collectively, when the banquets had gone round through all the families. **Job ... sanctified them**—by offering up as many expiatory burnt offerings as he had sons (Lev. 1:4). This was done "in the morning" (Gen. 22:3; Lev. 6:12). Jesus also began devotions early (Mark 1:35). The holocaust, or burnt offering, in patriarchal times, was offered (lit., "caused to ascend," referring to the smoke ascending to heaven) by each father of a family officiating as priest in behalf of his household. **cursed God**—The same *Hebrew* word means to "curse," and to "bless"; GESENIUS says, the original sense is to "kneel," and thus it came to mean bending the knee in order to invoke either a blessing or a curse. Cursing is a perversion of blessing, as all sin is of goodness. Sin is a degeneracy, not a generation. It is not, however, likely that Job should fear the possibility of his sons *cursing* God. The sense "bid farewell to," derived from the *blessing* customary at parting, seems sufficient (Gen. 47:10). Thus UMBREIT translates "may have dismissed God from their hearts"; viz., amid the intoxication of pleasure (Prov. 20:1). This act illustrates Job's "fear of God" (vs. 1).

6-12. SATAN, APPEARING BEFORE GOD, FALSELY ACCUSES JOB. **6. sons of God**—angels (ch. 38:7; I Kings 22:19). They present themselves to render account of their "ministry" in other parts of the universe (Heb. 1:14). **the Lord**—*Heb.*, JEHOVAH—the self-existing God, faithful to His promises. God says (Exod. 6:3) that He was not known to the patriarchs by this name. But, as the name occurs previously in Genesis 2:7-9, etc., what must be meant is, not until the time of delivering Israel by Moses was He known peculiarly and publicly in the *character* which the name means; viz., "making things to be," fulfilling the promises made to their forefathers. This name, therefore, here, is no objection against the antiquity of the Book of Job.

Satan—The tradition was widely spread that *he* had been the agent in Adam's temptation. Hence his name is given without comment. The feeling with which he looks on Job is similar to that with which he looked on Adam in Paradise: emboldened by his success in the case of one not yet fallen, he is confident that the piety of Job, one of a fallen race, will not stand the test. He had fallen himself (ch. 4:19; 15:15; Jude 6). In the Book of Job, Satan is first designated by *name:* "Satan," *Heb.,* "one who lies in wait"; an "adversary" in a court of justice (I Chron. 21:1; Ps. 109:6; Zech. 3:1); "accuser" (Rev. 12:10). He has the law of God on his side by man's sin, and against man. But Jesus Christ has fulfilled the law for us; justice is once more on man's side against Satan (Isa. 42:21); and so Jesus Christ can plead as our Advocate against the adversary. "Devil" is the *Greek* name—the "slanderer," or "accuser." He is subject to God, who uses his ministry for chastising man. In *Arabic,* Satan is often applied to a serpent (Gen. 3:1). He is called prince of this world (John 12:31); the god of this world (II Cor. 4:4); prince of the power of the air (Eph. 2:2). God here questions him, in order to vindicate His own ways before angels. **7. going to and fro**—rather, "hurrying rapidly to and fro." The original idea in *Arabic* is the heat of haste (Matt. 12:43; I Pet. 5:8). Satan seems to have had some peculiar connection with this earth. Perhaps he was formerly its ruler under God. Man succeeded to the vice royalty (Gen. 1: 26; Ps. 8:6). Man then lost it and Satan became prince of this world. The Son of man (Ps. 8:4)—the representative man, regains the forfeited inheritance (Rev. 11:15). Satan's replies are characteristically curt and short. When the angels appear before God, Satan is among them, even as there was a Judas among the apostles. **8. considered**—*Marg.* "set thine heart on"; i.e., considered attentively. No true servant of God escapes the eye of the adversary of God. **9. fear God for naught**—It is a mark of the children of Satan to sneer and not give credit to any for disinterested piety. Not so much God's gifts, as God Himself is "the reward" of His people (Gen. 15:1). **10. his substance is increased**—Lit., "spread out like a flood"; Job's herds covered the face of the country. **11. curse thee to thy face**—in antithesis to God's praise of him (vs. 8), "one that feareth God." Satan's words are too true of many. Take away their prosperity and you take away their religion (Mal. 3:14). **12. in thy power**—Satan has no power against man till God gives it. God would not touch Job with His own hand, though Satan asks this (vs. 11, "thine"), but He allows the enemy to do so.

13-22. JOB, IN AFFLICTION, BLESSES GOD, etc. **13. wine**—not specified in verse 4. The mirth inspired by the "wine" here contrasts the more sadly with the alarm which interrupted it. **14. the asses feeding beside them**—*Heb.,* "she-asses." A graphic picture of rural repose and peace; the more dreadful, therefore, by contrast is the sudden attack of the plundering Arabs. **15. Sabeans**—not those of Arabia Felix, but those of Arabia Deserta, descending from Sheba, grandson of Abraham and Keturah (Gen. 25:3). The Bedouin Arabs of the present day resemble, in marauding habits, these Sabeans (cf. Gen. 16:12). **I alone am escaped**—cunningly contrived by Satan. One in each case escapes (vss. 16, 17, 19), and brings the same kind of message. This was to overwhelm Job, and leave him no time to recover from the rapid succession of calamities—"misfortunes seldom come single." **16. fire of God** —Hebraism for "a mighty fire"; as "cedars of God"—

"lofty cedars." Not lightning, which would not consume *all* the sheep and servants. UMBREIT understands it of *the burning wind* of Arabia, called by the Turks "wind of poison." "The prince of the power of the air" is permitted to have control over such destructive agents. **17. Chaldeans**—not merely robbers as the Sabeans; but experienced in war, as is implied by "they *set in array* three bands" (Hab. 1:6-8). RAWLINSON distinguishes three periods: 1. When their seat of empire was in the south, towards the confluence of the Tigris and Euphrates. The Chaldean period, from 2300 B.C. to 1500 B.C. In this period was Chedorlaomer (Gen. 14), the Kudur of Hur or Ur of the Chaldees, in the Assyrian inscriptions, and the conqueror of Syria. 2. From 1500 to 625 B.C., the Assyrian period. 3. From 625 to 538 B.C. (when Cyrus the Persian took Babylon), the Babylonian period. "Chaldees" in *Hebrew*—*Chasaim.* They were akin, perhaps, to the Hebrews, as Abraham's sojourn in Ur, and the name "Chesed," a nephew of Abraham, imply. The *three* bands were probably in order to attack the three separate thousands of Job's camels (vs. 3). **19. wind from the wilderness**—south of Job's house. The tornado came the more violently along the desert, being uninterrupted (Isa. 21:1; Hos. 13:15). **the young men**—rather, "the young people"; including the daughters (so in Ruth 2:21). **20. Job arose**—not necessarily from sitting. Inward excitement is implied, and the beginning to do anything. He had heard the other messages calmly, but on hearing of the death of his children, *then* he arose; or, as EICHORN translates, he *started up* (II Sam. 13:31). The rending of the mantle was the conventional mark of deep grief (Gen. 37:34). Orientals wear a tunic or shirt, and loose pantaloons; and over these a flowing mantle (especially great persons and women). Shaving the head was also usual in grief (Jer. 41:5; Mic. 1:16). **21. Naked**—(I Tim. 6:7). "Mother's womb" is poetically the earth, the universal mother (Eccles. 5:15; 12:7; Ps. 139:15). Job herein realizes God's assertion (vs. 8) against Satan's (vs. 11). Instead of cursing, he blesses the name of JEHOVAH (*Hebrew*). The *name* of Jehovah, is Jehovah *Himself,* as manifested to us in His attributes (Isa. 9:6). **22. nor charged God foolishly** —rather, "allowed himself to commit no folly against God" [UMBREIT]. Chapter 2:10 proves that this is the meaning. Not as *marg.* "attributed no folly to God." Hasty words against God, though natural in the bitterness of grief, are *folly;* lit., an "insipid, unsavory" thing (ch. 6:6; Jer. 23:13, margin). Folly in Scripture is continually equivalent to wickedness. For when man sins, it is himself, not God, whom he injures (Prov. 8:36). We are to submit to trials, not because we see the reasons for them, nor yet as though they were matters of chance, but because *God wills* them, and has a right to send them, and has His own good reasons in sending them.

CHAPTER 2

Vss. 1-8. SATAN FURTHER TEMPTS JOB. **1. a day**—appointed for the angels giving an account of their ministry to God. The words "to present himself before the Lord" occur here, though not in 1:6, as Satan has now a special report to make as to Job. **3. integrity**—lit., "completeness"; so "perfect," another form of the same Hebrew word, ch. 11. **movedst . . . against**—So I Samuel 26:19; cf. I Chron. 21:1 with II Sam. 24:1. **4. Skin for skin**—a proverb.

Supply, "He will give." The "skin" is figurative for any outward good. Nothing outward is so dear that a man will not exchange it for some other outward good; "but" (not "yea") "life," the inward good, cannot be replaced; a man will sacrifice everything else for its sake. Satan sneers bitterly at man's egotism and says that Job bears the loss of property and children because these are mere *outward and exchangeable goods,* but he will give up all things, even his religion, in order to save his life, if you touch his bones and flesh. "Skin" and "life" are in antithesis [UMBREIT]. The martyrs prove Satan's sneer false. ROSENMULLER explains it not so well. A man willingly gives up *another's* skin (life) for *his own* skin (life). So Job might bear the loss of his children, etc., with equanimity, so long as he remained unhurt himself; but when touched in his own person, he would renounce God. Thus the first "skin" means the *other's* skin, i.e., body; the second "skin," *one's own,* as in Exodus 21:28. **6. but save**—rather, "only spare." Satan shows his ingenuity in inflicting pain, and also his knowledge of what man's body can bear without vital injury. **7. sore boils**—malignant boils; rather, as it is singular in the Hebrew, a "burning sore." Job was covered with one universal inflammation. The use of the potsherd agrees with this view. It was that form of leprosy called *black* (to distinguish it from the *white*), or *elephantiasis,* because the feet swell like those of the elephant. The *Arabic judham* (Deut. 28:35), where "sore botch" is rather the black burning boil (Isa. 1:6). **8. a potsherd**—not a piece of a broken earthen vessel, but an instrument made for scratching (the root of the *Hebrew* word is "scratch"); the sore was too disgusting to touch. "To sit in the ashes" marks the deepest mourning (Jonah 3:6); also humility, as if the mourner were nothing but dust and ashes; so Abraham (Gen. 18: 27).

9-13. JOB REPROVES HIS WIFE. **9. curse God**—rather "renounce" God. (*Note,* 1:5.) [UMBREIT]. However, it was usual among the heathens, when disappointed in their prayers accompanied with offerings to their gods, to reproach and *curse* them. **and die**—i.e., take thy farewell of God and so die For no good is to be got out of religion, either here or hereafter; or, at least, not in this life [GILL]. Nothing makes the ungodly so angry as to see the godly under trial not angry. **10. the foolish women** —Sin and folly are allied in Scripture (I Sam. 25:25; II Sam. 13:13; Ps. 14:1). **receive evil**—bear willingly (Lam. 3:39). **11. Eliphaz**—The view of RAWLINSON that "the names of Job's three friends represent the Chaldean times, about 700 B.C.," cannot be accepted. Eliphaz is an Idumean name, Esau's oldest son (Gen. 36:4); and Teman, son of Eliphaz (15), called "duke." EUSEBIUS places Teman in Arabia Petræa (but see *Note,* 6:19). Teman means "at the right hand"; and then the south, viz., part of Idumea; capital of Edom (Amos 1:12). Hebrew geographers faced the east, not the north as we do; hence with them "the right hand" was the south. Temanites were famed for wisdom (Jer. 49: 7). BARUCH mentions them as "authors of fables (viz., proverbs embodying the results of observation), and searchers out of understanding." **Bildad the Shuhite**—Shuah (a pit), son of Abraham and Keturah (Gen. 25:2). PTOLEMY mentions the region Syccea, in Arabia Deserta, east of Batanea. **Zophar the Naamathite**—not of the Naamans in Judah (Josh. 15:41), which was too distant; but some region in Arabia Deserta. FRETELIUS says there was a Naamath in Uz. **12. toward heaven**—They

threw ashes violently upwards, that they might fall on their heads and cover them—the deepest mourning (Josh. 7:6; Acts 22:23). **13. seven days . . . nights**—They did not remain in the same posture and without food, etc., all this time, but for most of this period daily and nightly. Sitting on the earth marked mourning (Lam. 2:10). Seven days was the usual length of it (Gen. 50:10; I Sam. 31:13). This silence may have been due to a rising suspicion of evil in Job; but chiefly because it is only ordinary griefs that find vent in language; extraordinary griefs are too great for utterance.

CHAPTER 3

THE POEM OR DEBATE ITSELF, 2-42:6; FIRST SERIES IN IT, 3-14; JOB FIRST 3

Vss. 1-19. JOB CURSES THE DAY OF HIS BIRTH AND WISHES FOR DEATH. **1. opened his mouth**—The Orientals speak seldom, and then sententiously; hence this formula expressing deliberation and gravity (Ps. 78:2). He formally began. **cursed his day**—the strict *Hebrew* word for "cursing": not the same as in ch. 1:5. Job cursed his birthday, but not his God. **2. spake**—*Hebrew,* "answered," i.e., not to any actual question that preceded, but to the question virtually involved in the case. His outburst is singularly wild and bold (Jer. 20:14). To desire to die so as to be free from sin is a mark of grace; to desire to die so as to escape troubles is a mark of corruption. He was ill-fitted to die who was so unwilling to live. But his trials were greater, and his light less, than ours. **3. the night** *in which* —rather "the night which said." The words in italics are not in the *Hebrew.* Night is personified and poetically made to speak. So in verse 7, and in Psalm 19:2. The birth of a male in the East is a matter of joy; often not so of a female. **4. let not God regard it**—rather, more poetically, "seek it out." "Let God stoop from His bright throne to raise it up from its dark hiding-place." The curse on the *day* in vs. 3, is amplified in vss. 4, 5; that on the *night,* in vss. 6-10. **5. Let . . . the shadow of death**— (deepest darkness, Isaiah 9:2). **stain**—This is a later sense of the verb [GESENIUS]; better the old and more poetic idea, "Let darkness (the ancient night of chaotic gloom) resume its rights over light (Gen. 1:2), and claim that day as its own." **a cloud** —collectively, a gathered mass of dark clouds. **the blackness of the day terrify it**—lit., the obscurations; whatever darkens the day [GESENIUS]. The verb in *Hebrew* expresses sudden terrifying. May it be suddenly affrighted at its own darkness. UMBREIT explains it as "magical incantations that darken the day," forming the climax to the previous clauses; vs. 8 speaks of "cursers of the day" similarly. But the former view is simpler. Others refer it to the poisonous simoom wind. **6. seize upon it**—as its prey, i.e., utterly dissolve it. **joined unto the days of the year**—rather, by poetic personification, "Let it not *rejoice* in the circle of days and nights and months, which form the circle of years." **7. solitary** —rather, unfruitful. "Would that it had not *given birth* to me." **8. them . . . that curse the day**—If "mourning" be the right rendering in the latter clause of this verse, these words refer to the hired mourners of the dead (Jer. 9:17). But the *Hebrew* for "mourning" elsewhere always denotes an animal, whether it be the crocodile or some huge serpent (Isa. 27:1), such as is meant by leviathan. Therefore, the expression, "cursers of day," refers to magicians, who were believed to be able by charms to make a day one of evil omen. (So Balaam, Num. 22:5.) This accords with UMBREIT's view (vs. 7); or to the Ethiopians and Atlantes, who "used to curse the sun at his rising for burning up them and their country" [HERODOTUS]. Necromancers claimed power to control or rouse wild beasts at will, as do the Indian serpent-charmers of our day (Ps. 58:5). Job does not say they had the power they claimed; but, supposing they had, may they curse the day. SCHUTTENS renders it by supplying words (?). Let those that are ready *for anything, call it* (the day) the raiser up of leviathan, i.e., of a host of evils. **9. dawning of the day**—lit., "eyelashes of morning." The Arab poets call the sun the eye of day. His early rays, therefore, breaking forth before sunrise, are the opening eyelids or eyelashes of morning. **12. Why did the knees prevent me?**—Old English for "anticipate my wants." The reference is to the solemn recognition of a newborn child by the father, who used to place it on his knees as his own, whom he was bound to rear (Gen. 30:3; 50:23; Isa. 66:12). **13. lain... quiet... slept**—a gradation. I should not only have *lain*, but been *quiet*, and not only *been quiet*, but *slept*. Death in Scripture is called sleep (Ps. 13:3); especially in the New Testament, where the resurrection-awakening is more clearly set forth (I Cor. 15:51; I Thess. 4:14; 5:10). **14. With kings... which built desolate places for themselves**—who built up for themselves what proved to be (not palaces, but) ruins! The wounded spirit of Job, once a great emir himself, sick of the vain struggles of mortal great men, after grandeur, contemplates the palaces of kings, now desolate heaps of ruins. His regarding the repose of death the most desirable end of the great ones of earth, wearied with heaping up perishable treasures, marks the irony that breaks out from the black clouds of melancholy [UMBREIT]. The "for themselves" marks their selfishness. MICHAELIS explains it weakly of mausoleums, such as are found still, of stupendous proportions, in the ruins of Petra of Idumea. **15. filled their houses with silver**—Some take this to refer to the treasures which the ancients used to bury with their dead. But see last verse. **16. untimely birth**—(Ps. 58:8); preferable to the life of the restless miser (Eccles. 6: 3-5). **17. the wicked**—the original meaning, "those ever restless," "full of desires" (Isa. 57:20, 21). **weary**—lit., "those whose strength is wearied out" (Rev. 14:13). **18. There are the prisoners rest**—from their chains. **19. servant**—The slave is there manumitted from slavery.

20-26. HE COMPLAINS OF LIFE BECAUSE OF HIS ANGUISH. **20. Wherefore giveth he light**—viz., God; often omitted reverentially (ch. 24:23; Eccles. 9:9). Light, i.e., life. The joyful light ill suits the mourners. The grave is most in unison with their feelings. **23. whose way is hid**—The picture of Job is drawn from a wanderer who has lost his way, and who is hedged in, so as to have no exit of escape (Hos. 2:6; Lam. 3:7, 9). **24. my sighing cometh before I eat**—i.e., prevents my eating [UMBREIT]; or, conscious that the effort to eat brought on the disease, Job must sigh before eating [ROSENMULLER]; or, sighing takes the place of good (Ps. 42:3) [GOOD]. But the first explanation accords best with the text. **my roarings are poured out like the waters**—an image from the rushing sound of water streaming. **25. the thing which I... feared is come upon me**—In the beginning of his trials, when he heard of the loss of one blessing, he feared the loss of another; and when he heard of the loss of that, he feared the loss of a third. **that which I was afraid of is come**

unto me—viz., the ill opinion of his friends, as though he were a hypocrite on account of his trials. **26. I was not in safety... yet trouble came**—referring, not to his former state, but to the *beginning* of his troubles. From that time I had no rest, there was no intermission of sorrows. "And" (not, "yet") a fresh trouble is coming, viz., my friends' suspicion of my being a hypocrite. This gives the starting-point to the whole ensuing controversy.

CHAPTER 4

Vss. 1-21. FIRST SPEECH OF ELIPHAZ. **Eliphaz** —the mildest of Job's three accusers. The greatness of Job's calamities, his complaints against God, and the opinion that calamities are proofs of guilt, led the three to doubt Job's integrity. **2. If we assay to commune**—Rather, two questions, "May we attempt a word with thee? Wilt thou be grieved at it?" Even pious friends often count that only a touch which we feel as a wound. **3. weak hands**—Isaiah 35:3; II Samuel 4:1. **5. thou art troubled**—rather, "unhinged," hast lost thy self-command (I Thess. 3: 3). **6. Is not this thy fear, thy confidence,** etc.— Does thy fear, thy confidence, come to nothing? Does it come only to this, that thou faintest now? Rather, by transposition, ""Is not thy fear (of God) thy hope? and the uprightness of thy ways thy confidence? If so, bethink thee, who ever perished being innnocent?" [UMBREIT]. But Luke 13:2, 3 shows that, though there *is* a retributive divine government even in this life, yet *we* cannot judge by the mere outward *appearance*. "One event is outwardly to the righteous and to the wicked" (Eccles. 9:2); but yet we must take it on trust, that God deals righteously even now (Ps. 37:25; Isa. 33: 16). Judge not by a part, but by the whole of a godly man's life, and by his end, even here (James 5:11). The one and the same outward event is altogether a different thing in its inward bearings on the godly and on the ungodly even here. Even prosperity, much more calamity, is a punishment to the wicked (Prov. 1:32). Trials are chastisements for their good (to the righteous) (Ps. 119:67, 71, 75). See Preface on the DESIGN of this book. **8. they that plough iniquity... reap the same**—(Prov. 22:8; Hos. 8:7; 10:13; Gal. 6:7, 8). **9. breath of his nostrils**—God's anger; a figure from the fiery winds of the East (ch. 1:16; Isa. 5:25; Ps. 18:8, 15). **10. lion**—i.e., wicked men, upon whom Eliphaz wished to show that calamities come in spite of their various resources, just as destruction comes on the lion in spite of his strength (Ps. 58:6; II Tim. 4:17). Five different *Hebrew* terms here occur for "lion." The raging of the lion (*the tearer*), and the roaring of the bellowing lion and the teeth of the *young lions*, not *whelps*, but grown up enough to hunt for prey. The *strong* lion, the whelps of the *lioness* (not the *stout lion,* as in *English Version*) [BARNES and UMBREIT]. The various phases of wickedness are expressed by this variety of terms: obliquely, Job, his wife, and children, may be hinted at by the lion, lioness, and whelps. The one verb, "are broken," does not suit both subjects; therefore, supply "the roaring of the bellowing lion *is* silenced." The strong lion dies of want at last, and the whelps, torn from the mother, are scattered, and the race becomes extinct. **12. a thing**—*Hebrew,* a "word." Eliphaz confirms his view by a divine declaration which was secretly and unexpectedly imparted to him. **a little**—lit., a whisper; implying the still silence around, and that more was conveyed than articulate words could utter (ch. 26:14; II Cor. 12:4). **13. In thoughts from the visions**—[So WINER]. While revolving night visions previously made to him (Dan. 2:29). Rather, "In my manifold (*Hebrew,* divided) thoughts, *before* the visions of the night commenced"; therefore not a delusive dream (Ps. 4:4) [UMBREIT]. **deep sleep**—(Gen. 2:21; 15:12). **16. It stood still**—At first the apparition glides before Eliphaz, then stands still, but with that shadowy indistinctness of form which creates such an impression of awe; a gentle murmur: not (*English Version*): *there was silence;* for in I Kings 19:12, the voice, as opposed to the previous storm, denotes a gentle, still murmur. **17. mortal man . . . a man**—Two *Hebrew* words for "man" are used; the first implying his feebleness; the second his strength. Whether feeble or strong, man is not righteous before God. **more just than God . . . more pure than his maker**—But this would be self-evident without an oracle. **18. folly**—Imperfection is to be attributed to the angels, in comparison with Him. The holiness of some of them had given way (II Pet. 2:4), and at best is but the holiness of a creature. Folly is the want of *moral* consideration [UMBREIT]. **19. houses of clay**—(II Cor. 5:1). Houses made of sun-dried clay bricks are common in the East; they are easily washed away (Matt. 7:27). Man's foundation is this dust (Gen. 3:19). **before the moth**—rather, "as before the moth," which devours a garment (ch. 13:28; Ps. 39:11; Isa. 50:9). Man, who cannot, in a physical point of view, stand before the very moth, surely cannot, in a moral, stand before God. **20. from morning to evening**—unceasingly; or, better, between the morning and evening of one short day (so Exod. 18:14; Isa. 38:12). "They are destroyed"; better, "they *would be* destroyed," if God withdrew His loving protection. Therefore man must not think to be *holy before God,* but to draw holiness and all things else *from God* (vs. 17). **21. their excellency**—(Ps. 39:11; 146:4; I Cor. 13:8). But UMBREIT, by an Oriental image from a bow, useless because unstrung. "*Their nerve* or *string* would be torn away." MICHAELIS, better in accordance with vs. 19, makes the allusion be to the *cords* of a tabernacle taken down (Isa. 33:20). **they die, even without wisdom**—rather, "They would perish, yet not according to wisdom," but according to arbitrary choice, if God were not infinitely wise and holy. The design of the spirit is to show that the continued existence of weak man proves the inconceivable wisdom and holiness of God, which alone save man from ruin [UMBREIT]. BENGEL shows from Scripture that God's holiness (*Hebrew, kadosh*) comprehends all His excellencies and attributes. DE WETTE loses the scope, in explaining it, of the shortness of man's life, contrasted with the angels "before they have attained to wisdom."

CHAPTER 5

Vss. 1-27. ELIPHAZ' CONCLUSION FROM THE VISION. **1. if there be any,** etc.—Rather, will He (God) reply to thee? Job, after the revelation just given, cannot be so presumptuous as to think God or any of the holy ones (Dan. 4:17; angels) round His throne, will vouchsafe a *reply* (a judicial expression) to his rebellious complaint. **2. wrath . . . envy** —fretful and passionate complaints, such as Eliphaz charged Job with (ch. 4:5; so Prov. 14:30). Not, the wrath *of God* killeth the foolish, and *His* envy, etc. **3. the foolish**—the wicked. I have seen the sinner spread his "root" wide in prosperity, yet cir-

cumstances "suddenly" occurred which gave occasion for his once prosperous dwelling being "cursed" as desolate (Ps. 37:35, 36; Jer. 17:8). **4. His children . . . crushed in the gate**—A judicial formula. The gate was the place of judgment and of other public proceedings (Ps. 127:5; Prov. 22:22; Gen. 23:10; Deut. 21:19). Such propylæa have been found in the Assyrian remains. Eliphaz obliquely alludes to the calamity which cut off Job's children. **5. even out of the thorns**—Even when part of the grain remains hanging on the thorn bushes (or, "is growing among thorns," Matthew 13:7), the hungry gleaner does not grudge the trouble of even taking it away, so clean swept away is the harvest of the wicked. **the robber**—as the Sabeans, who robbed Job. rather, translate "the thirsty," as the antithesis in the parallelism, "the hungry," proves. **6. Although**—rather, "for truly" [UMBREIT]. **affliction cometh not forth of the dust** —like a weed, of its own accord. Eliphaz hints that the cause of it lay with Job himself. **7. Yet**—rather, "Truly," or, *But* affliction does not come from chance, but is the appointment of God for sin; i.e., the original birth-sin of man. Eliphaz passes from the particular sin and consequent suffering of Job to the universal sin and suffering of mankind. Troubles spring from man's common sin by as necessary a law of natural consequences as sparks (*Hebrew,* sons of coal) fly upward. Troubles are many and fiery, as sparks (I Pet. 4:12; Isa. 43:2). UMBREIT for "sparks" has "birds of prey." **8.** Therefore (as affliction is ordered by God, on account of sin), "I would" have you to "seek unto God" (Isa. 8:19; Amos 5:8; Jer. 5:24). **11.** Connected with vs. 9. His "unsearchable" dealings are with a view to raise the humble and abase the proud (Luke 1:52). Therefore Job ought to turn humbly to Him. **12. enterprise**—lit., "realization." The *Hebrew* combines in the one word the two ideas, wisdom and happiness, "enduring existence" being the etymological and philosophical root of the combined notion [UMBREIT]. **13.** Paul (I Cor. 3: 19) quoted this clause with the formula establishing its inspiration, "it is written." He cites the exact *Hebrew* words, not as he usually does the LXX, *Greek* version (Ps. 9:15). Haman was hanged on the gallows he prepared for Mordecai (Esther 5:14; 7:10). The wise—i.e., the cunning. **is carried headlong**—Their scheme is precipitated before it is ripe. **14.** Judicial blindness often is sent upon keen men of the world (Deut. 28:29; Isa. 59:10; John 9: 39). **15.** "From the sword" which proceedeth "from their mouth" (Ps. 59:7; 57:4). **16. the poor hath hope**—of the interposition of God. **iniquity stoppeth her mouth**—(Ps. 107:42; Mic. 7:9, 10; Isa. 52:15). Especially at the last day, through shame (Jude 15; Matt. 22:12). The "mouth" was the offender (vs. 15), and the mouth shall then be stopped (Isa. 25:8) at the end. **17. happy**—not that the actual suffering is joyous; but the consideration of the *righteousness* of Him who sends it, and the *end* for which it is sent, make it a cause for thankfulness, not for complaints, such as Job had uttered (Heb. 12: 11). Eliphaz implies that the end in this case is to call back Job from the particular sin of which he takes for granted that Job is guilty. Paul seems to allude to this passage in Hebrews 12:5; so James 1: 12; Proverbs 3:12. Eliphaz does not give due prominence to this truth, but rather to *Job's sin.* It is Elihu alone (chs. 32-37) who fully dwells upon the truth, that affliction is mercy and justice in disguise, for the good of the sufferer. **18. he maketh sore, and bindeth up**—(Deut. 32:39; Hos. 6:1; I Sam. 2:

6). An image from binding up a wound. The healing art consisted much at that time in external applications. **19. in six ... yea, in seven**—(Prov. 6: 16; Amos 1:3). The *Hebrew* idiom fixes on a certain number (here "six"), in order to call attention as to a thing of importance; then increases the force by adding, with a "yea, nay seven," the next higher number; here "seven," the sacred and perfect number. In *all* possible troubles; not merely in the precise number "seven." **20. power**—(Jer. 5:12). *Hebrew*, hands. **of the sword**—(Ezek. 35:5, *Margin*). Hands are given to the sword personified as a living agent. **21.** (Ps. 31:20; Jer. 18:18.) **22. famine thou shalt laugh**—Not, in spite of destruction and famine, which is true (Hab. 3:17, 18), though not *the* truth meant by Eliphaz, but because those calamities shall not come upon thee. A different *Hebrew* word from that in vs. 20; there, famine *in general;* here, *the languid state* of those wanting proper nutriment [BARNES]. **23. in league with the stones of the field** —They shall not hurt the fertility of thy soil; nor the wild beasts thy fruits; spoken in Arabia Deserta, where stones abounded. *Arabia,* derived from *Arabah*—a desert plain. The first clause of this verse answers to the first clause of verse 22; and the last of this verse to the last of that verse. The full realization of this is yet future (Isa. 65:23, 25; Hos. 2:18). **24. know**—"Thou shalt rest in the assurance, that thine habitation is the abode of peace; and (if) thou numberest thine herd, thine expectations prove not fallacious" [UMBREIT]. "Sin" does not agree with the context. The *Hebrew* word—"to miss" a mark, said of archers (Judg. 20:16). The *Hebrew* for "habitation" primarily means "the fold for cattle"; and for "visit," often to "take an account of, to number." "Peace" is the common Eastern salutation; including inward and outward prosperity. **25. as the grass**—(Ps. 72:16). Properly, herb-bearing seed (Gen. 1:11, 12). **26. in a full age**—So "full of days" (42:17; Gen. 35:29). Not mere length of years, but ripeness for death, one's inward and outward full development not being prematurely cut short, is denoted (Isa. 65:22). "Thou shalt come," not lit., but expressing willingness to die. Eliphaz speaks from the Old Testament point of view, which made full years a reward of the righteous (Ps. 91:16; Exod. 20:12), and premature death the lot of the wicked (Ps. 55:23). The righteous are immortal till their work is done. To keep them longer would be to render them less fit to die. God takes them at their best (Isa. 57:1). The good are compared to wheat (Matt. 13:30). **cometh in**—lit., "ascends." The corn is lifted up off the earth and carried home; so the good man "is raised into the heap of sheaves" [UMBREIT]. **27. searched it ... for thy good**—lit., for thyself (Ps. 111:2; Prov. 2:4; 9:12).

CHAPTER 6

FIRST SERIES CONTINUED

Vss. 1-30. REPLY OF JOB TO ELIPHAZ. **2. thoroughly weighed**—Oh, that instead of censuring my complaints when thou oughtest rather to have sympathized with me, thou wouldst accurately compare my sorrow, and my misfortunes; these latter "outweigh in the balance" the former. **3. the sand**—(Prov. 27:3). **are swallowed up**—See *Margin.* So Psalm 77:4. But Job plainly is apologizing, not for not having had words *enough,* but for having spoken *too much* and *too boldly;* and the *Hebrew* is, "to speak rashly" [UMBREIT, GESENIUS, ROSENMULLER]. "Therefore were my words *so rash.*"

4. arrows ... within me—have pierced me. A poetic image representing the avenging Almighty armed with bow and arrows (Ps. 38:2, 3). Here the arrows are poisoned. Peculiarly appropriate, in reference to *the burning pains* which penetrated, like poison, into *the inmost parts*—("spirit"; as contrasted with mere *surface flesh wounds*) of Job's body. **set themselves in array**—a military image (Judg. 20: 33). All the terrors which the divine wrath can muster are set in array against me (Isa. 42:13). **5.** Neither wild animals, as the wild ass, nor tame, as the ox, are dissatisfied when well supplied with food. The braying of the one and the lowing of the other prove distress and want of palatable food. So, Job argues, if he complains, it is not without cause; viz., his pains, which are, as it were, disgusting food, which God feeds him with (end of verse 7). But he should have remembered a rational being should evince a better spirit than the brute. **6. unsavoury** —tasteless, insipid. Salt is a chief necessary of life to an Easterner, whose food is mostly vegetable. **the white**—lit., "spittle" (I Sam. 21:13), which the white of an egg resembles. **7.** To "touch" is contrasted with "meat." "My *taste* refused *even to touch* it, and yet am I *fed* with such *meat* of sickness." The second clause literally, is, "Such is like the sickness of my food." The natural taste abhors even to touch insipid food, and such forms my nourishment. For my sickness is like such nauseous food [UMBREIT]. (Ps. 42:3; 80:5; 102:9). No wonder, then, I complain. **8.** To desire death is no necessary proof of fitness for death. The ungodly sometimes desire it, so as to escape troubles, without thought of the hereafter. The godly desire it, in order to be with the Lord; but they patiently wait God's will. **9. destroy**—lit., grind or crush (Isa. 3:15). **let loose his hand**—God had put forth His hand only so far as to wound the *surface* of Job's flesh (ch. 1:12; 2:6); he wishes that hand to be *let loose,* so as to wound *deeply and vitally.* **cut me off**—metaphor from a weaver cutting off the web, when finished, from the thrum fastening it to the loom (Isa. 38:12). **10. I would harden myself** —rather, "I would *exult* in the pain," if I knew that that pain would hasten my death [GESENIUS]. UMBREIT translates the *Hebrew* of "Let Him not spare," as "unsparing"; and joins it with "pain." **concealed** —I have not disowned, in word or deed, the commands of the Holy One (Ps. 119:46; Acts 20:20). He says this in answer to Eliphaz' insinuation that he is a hypocrite. God is here called "the Holy One," to imply man's reciprocal obligation to be holy, as He is holy (Lev. 19:2). **11.** What strength have I, so as to warrant the hope of restoration to health? a hope which Eliphaz had suggested. "And what" but a miserable "end" of life is before me, "that I should" desire to "prolong life"? [UMBREIT]. UMBREIT and ROSENMULLER not so well translate the last words "to be patient." **12.** Disease had so attacked him that his strength would need to be hard as a stone, and his flesh like brass, not to sink under it. But he has only flesh, like other men. It must, therefore, give way; so that the hope of restoration suggested by Eliphaz is vain (see *Note,* 5:11). **13. Is not my help in me?**—The interrogation is better omitted. "There is no help in me!" For "wisdom," "deliverance" is a better rendering. "And deliverance is driven quite from me." **14. pity**—a proverb. Charity is the love which judges indulgently of our fellow men: it is put on a par with truth in Proverbs 3:3, for they together form the essence of moral perfection [UMBREIT]. It is the spirit of Christianity (I Pet. 4:8; I Cor. 13:7; Prov.

10:12; 17:17). If it ought to be used towards all men, much more towards friends. But he who does not use it forsaketh (renounceth) the fear of the Almighty (Jas. 2:13). **15.** Those whom I regarded as "my brethren," from whom I looked for faithfulness in my adversity, have disappointed me, as the streams failing from drought—wadies of Arabia, filled in the winter, but dry in the summer, which disappoint the caravans expecting to find water there. The fulness and noise of these temporary streams answer to the past large and loud professions of my friends; their dryness in summer, to the failure of the friendship when needed. The Arab proverb says of a treacherous friend, "I trust not in thy torrent" (Isa. 58:11, *Margin*). **streams of brooks**—rather, "the brook in the ravines which passes away." It has no perpetual spring of water to renew it (unlike "the fountain of living waters," Jer. 2:13; Isa. 33:16, at the end); and thus it passes away as rapidly as it arose. **16. blackish**—lit., Go as a mourner in black clothing (Ps. 34:14). A vivid and poetic image to picture the stream turbid and black with melted ice and snow, descending from the mountains into the valley. In the next clause, the snow dissolved is, in the poet's view, "hid" in the flood [UMBREIT]. **17. wax warm**—rather, at the time when. ("But they soon") [UMBREIT]. "they become narrower (flow in a narrower bed), they are silent (cease to flow noisily); in the heat (of the sun) they are consumed or vanish out of their place. First the stream flows more narrowly—then it becomes silent and still; at length every trace of water disappears by evaporation under the hot sun" [UMBREIT]. **18. turned aside**—rather, caravans (Hebrew travellers) turn aside from their way, by circuitous routes, to obtain water. They had seen the brook in spring full of water: and now in the summer heat, on their weary journey, they turn off their road by a devious route to reach the living waters, which they remembered with such pleasure. But, when "they go," it is "into a desert" [NOYES and UMBREIT]. Not as *English Version*, "They go to nothing," which would be a tame repetition of the drying up of the waters in verse 17; instead of waters, they find an "empty wilderness"; and, not having strength to regain their road, bitterly disappointed, they "perish." The terse brevity is most expressive. **19. the troops**—i.e., caravans. **Tema**—north of Arabia Deserta, near the Syrian desert; called from Tema son of Ishmael (Gen. 25:15; Isa. 21:14; Jer. 25:23), still so called by the Arabs. Verses 19, 20 give another picture of the mortification of disappointed hopes, viz., those of the caravans on the direct road, anxiously awaiting the return of their companions from the distant valley. The mention of the locality whence the caravans came gives living reality to the picture. "Sheba" refers here not to the marauders in North Arabia Deserta (ch. 1:15), but to the merchants (Ezek. 27:22) in the south, in Arabia Felix or Yemen, "afar off" (Jer. 6:20; Matt. 12:42; Gen. 10:28). Caravans are first mentioned in Genesis 37:25; men needed to travel thus in companies across the desert, for defense against the roving robbers and for mutual accommodation. "The companies waited for them," cannot refer to the caravans who had gone in quest of the waters; for verse 18 describes their utter destruction. **20.** lit., each had hoped; viz., that their companions would find water. The greater had been their hopes the more bitter now their disappointment; "they came thither," to the place, "and were ashamed"; lit., their countenances burn, an Oriental

phrase for the shame and consternation of deceived expectation; so "ashamed" as to disappointment (Rom. 5:5). **21.** As the dried-up brook is to the caravan, so are ye to me, viz., a nothing; ye might as well not be in existence [UMBREIT]. *The* Margin "like to them" or "it" (viz., the waters of the brook), is not so good a reading. **ye see, and are afraid**—Ye are struck aghast at the sight of my misery, and ye lose presence of mind. Job puts this mild construction on their failing to relieve him with affectionate consolation. **22.** And yet I did not ask you to "bring me" a gift; or to "pay for me out of your substance a reward" (to the Judge, to redeem me from my punishment); all I asked from you was affectionate treatment. **23. the mighty**—the oppressor, or creditor, in whose power the debtor was [UMBREIT]. **24, 25.** Irony—If you can "teach me" the right view, I am willing to be set right, and "hold my tongue"; and to be made to see my error. But then if your words be really the right words, how is it that they are so feeble? "Yet how feeble are the words of what you call the right view." So the *Hebrew* is used (in Mic. 2:10; 1:9). The *English Version*, "How powerful," etc., does not agree so well with the last clause of the verse. "And what will your arguings reprove?" lit., "the reproofs which proceed from you"; the emphasis is on *you; you* may find fault, who are not in *my* situation [UMBREIT]. **26. Do you imagine** [mean] **to reprove words and** [to reprove] **the speeches of one desperate, (which are) as wind**—mere nothings, not to be so narrowly taken to task? UMBREIT not so well takes the *Hebrew* for "as wind," as "sentiments"; making formal "sentiments" antithetical to mere "speeches," and supplying, not the word "reprove," but "would you regard," from the first clause. **27.** Ye overwhelm—lit., ye cause (supply, "your anger") [UMBREIT], a net, viz., of sophistry [NOYES and SCHUTTENS], to fall upon the desolate (one bereft of help, like the fatherless orphan); **and ye dig (a pit) for your friend,** i.e., try to ensnare him, to catch him in the use of unguarded language [NOYES]. (Ps. 57:6); metaphor from hunters catching wild beasts in a pit covered with brushwood to conceal it. UMBREIT from the *Syriac,* and answering to his interpretation of the first clause, has, "Would you be *indignant* against your friend?" The *Hebrew* in ch. 41:6, means to "feast upon." As the first clause asks, "Would you *catch him in a net?*" so this follows up the image, "And would you next *feast upon him,* and his miseries?" So LXX. **28. be content** —rather, be pleased to—look. Since you have so falsely judged my words, look upon me, i.e., upon my countenance: for (it is evident before your faces) if I lie; my countenance will betray me, if I be the hypocrite that you suppose. **29. Return**—rather, "retract" your charges: "Let it not be iniquity"; i.e., (retract) that injustice may not be done me. Yea retract, "my righteousness is in it"; i.e., my right is involved in this matter. **30.** Will you say that my guilt lies in the organ of speech, and will you call it to account? or, Is it that my taste (palate) or discernment is not capable to form a judgment of perverse things? Is it thus you will explain the fact of my having no consciousness of guilt? [UMBREIT].

CHAPTER 7

Vss. 1-21. JOB EXCUSES HIS DESIRE FOR DEATH. **1. appointed time**—better, "warfare," hard conflict with evil (so in Isa. 40:2; Dan. 10:1). Translate it "appointed time" (ch. 14:14). Job reverts to the sad picture of man, however great, which he had drawn (ch. 3:14), and details in this chapter the miseries which his friends will see, if, according to his request (ch. 6:28), they will look on him. Even the Christian soldier, "warring a good warfare," rejoices when it is completed (I Tim. 1:18; II Tim. 2: 3; 4:7, 8). **2. earnestly desireth**—*Hebrew*, "pants for the [evening] shadow." Easterners measure time by the length of their shadow. If the servant longs for the evening when his wages are paid, why may not Job long for the close of his hard service, when he shall enter on his "reward"? This proves that Job did not, as many maintain, regard the grave as a mere sleep. **3.** Months of comfortless misfortune. "I am made *to possess*," lit., "to be heir to." Irony. "To be heir to," is usually a matter of joy; but here it is the entail of an involuntary and dismal inheritance. "Months," for days, to express its long duration. **Appointed**—lit., "they have numbered to me"; marking well the unavoidable doom assigned to him. **4.** Lit., "When shall be the flight of the night?" [GESENIUS]. UMBREIT, not so well, "The night is long extended"; lit., measured out (so Margin). **5.** In elephantiasis maggots are bred in the sores (Acts 12:23; Isa. 14:11). **clods of dust**—rather, a crust of dried filth and accumulated corruption (ch. 2:7, 8). **my skin is broken and ... loathsome**—rather, comes together so as to heal up, and again breaks out with running matter [GESENIUS]. More simply the *Hebrew* is, "My skin rests (for a time) and (again) melts away" (Ps. 58:7). **6.** (Isa. 38:12.) Every day like the weaver's shuttle leaves a thread behind; and each shall wear, as he weaves. But Job's thought is that his days must swiftly be cut off as a web; **without hope,**—viz., of a recovery and renewal of life (ch. 14:19; I Chron. 29:15). **7.** Address to God. **Wind**—a picture of evanescence (Ps. 78:39). **shall no more see**—rather, "shall no more return to see good." This change from the different wish in ch. 3:17, etc., is most true to nature. He is now in a softer mood; a beam from former days of prosperity falling upon memory and the thought of the unseen world, where one is seen no more (vs. 8), drew from him an expression of regret at leaving this world of light (Eccles. 11:7); so Hezekiah (Isa. 38:11). Grace rises above nature (II Cor. 5:8). **8.** The eye of him who beholds me (present, not past), i.e., in the very act of beholding me, seeth me no more. **Thine eyes [are] upon me, and I [am] not.** He disappears, even while God is looking upon him. Job cannot survive the gaze of Jehovah (Ps. 104:32; Rev. 20:11). Not, "Thine eyes seek me and I am not to be found"; for God's eye penetrates even to the unseen world (Ps. 139:8). UMBREIT unnaturally takes "thine" to refer to one of the three friends. **9.** (II Sam. 12:23.) **the grave**—the Sheol, or place of departed spirits, not disproving Job's belief in the resurrection. It merely means, "He shall come up no more" in the present order of things. **10.** (Ps. 103:16.) The Oriental keenly loves his dwelling. In Arabian elegies the desertion of abodes by their occupants is often a theme of sorrow. Grace overcomes this also (Luke 18:29; Acts 4:34). **11.** Therefore, as such is my hard lot, I will at least have the melancholy satisfaction of venting my sorrow in words. The *Hebrew* opening words, "Therefore I, at all events," express self-elevation [UMBREIT]. **12-14.** Why dost thou deny me the comfort of care-assuaging sleep? Why scarest thou me with frightful dreams? **Am I a sea**—regarded in Old Testament poetry as a violent rebel against God, the Lord of nature, who therefore curbs his violence (Jer. 5:22). **or a whale**—or some

other sea monster (Isa. 27:1), that Thou needest thus to watch and curb me? The Egyptians watched the crocodile most carefully to prevent its doing mischief. **14.** The frightful dreams resulting from elephantiasis he attributes to God; the common belief assigned all night visions to God. **15.** UMBREIT translates, "So that I could wish to strangle myself—dead by my own hands." He softens this idea of Job's harboring the thought of suicide, by representing it as entertained only in agonizing dreams, and immediately repudiated with horror in next verse, "Yet that (self-strangling) I loathe." This is forcible and graphic. Perhaps the meaning is simply, "My soul chooses (even) strangling (or any violent death) rather than my life," lit., "my bones" (Ps. 35: 10); i.e., rather than the wasted and diseased skeleton, left to him. In this view, "I loathe it" (vs. 16) refers to his life. **16. Let me alone**—i.e., cease to afflict me for the few and vain days still left to me. **17.** (Ps. 8:4; 144:3.) Job means, "What is man that thou shouldst make him (of so much importance, and that thou shouldst expend such attention (heart-thought) upon him" as to make him the subject of so severe trials? Job ought rather to have reasoned from God's condescending so far to notice man as to try him, that there must be a wise and loving purpose in trial. David uses the same words, in their right application, to express wonder that God should do so much as He does for insignificant man. Christians who know God manifest in the man Christ Jesus may use them still more. **18.** With each new day (Ps. 73:14). It is rather God's mercies, not our trials, that are new every morning (Lam. 3:23). The idea is that of a shepherd taking count of his flock every morning, to see if all are there [COCCEIUS]. **19.** How long (like a jealous keeper) wilt thou never take thine eyes off (so the *Heb.* for "depart from") me? Nor let me alone for a brief respite (lit., "so long as I take to swallow my spittle"), an Arabic proverb, like our, "till I draw my breath." **20. I have sinned**—Yet what sin can I do against (to: ch. 35:6) thee (of such a nature that thou shouldst jealously watch and deprive me of all strength, as if thou didst fear me)? Yet thou art one who hast men ever in view, ever watchest them—O thou *Watcher* (vs. 12; Dan. 9:14) of men. Job had borne with patience his trials, as sent by God (ch. 1:21; ch. 2:10); only his reason cannot reconcile the ceaseless continuance of his mental and bodily pains with his ideas of the divine nature. **set me as a mark**—Wherefore dost thou make me thy point of attack? i.e., ever assail me with new pains? [UMBREIT]. (Lam. 3:12.) **21. for now**—very soon. **in the morning**—not the resurrection; for then Job will be found. It is a figure, from one seeking a sick man in the morning, and finding he has died in the night. So Job implies that, if God does not help him at once, it will be too late, for he will be gone. The reason why God does not give an immediate sense of pardon to awakened sinners is that they think they have a claim on God for it.

CHAPTER 8

FIRST SERIES—FIRST SPEECH OF BILDAD, MORE SEVERE AND COARSE THAN THAT OF ELIPHAZ

Vss. 1-22. THE ADDRESS OF BILDAD. **2. like a ... wind**—disregarding restraints, and daring against God. **3.** The repetition of "pervert" gives an emphasis galling to Job (ch. 34:12). "Wouldst thou have God (as thy words imply) pervert judgment," by letting thy sins go unpunished? He assumes

Job's guilt from his sufferings. **4. If**—Rather, "*Since* thy children have sinned against Him, and (*since*) He has cast them away for (*Hebrew, by the* hand of) their transgressions, (yet) if thou wouldst seek unto God, etc., if thou wert pure, etc., surely (even) now He would awake for thee." UMBREIT makes the apodosis to, "since thy children," etc., begin at "He has cast them away." Also, instead of "*for*," "He gave them up to (lit., *into* the hand of) their own guilt." Bildad expresses the justice of God, which Job had arraigned. Thy children have sinned; God leaves them to the consequence of their sin; most cutting to the heart of the bereaved father. **5. seek unto God betimes**—early. Make it the first and chief anxiety (Ps. 78:34; Hos. 5:15; Isa. 26:9; Prov. 8:17; 13:24). **6. He would awake for thee**—i.e., arise to thy help. God seemed to be asleep toward the sufferer (Ps. 35:23; 7:6; Isa. 51:9). **make . . . prosperous**—restore to prosperity thy (their) righteous habitation. Bildad assumes it to have been heretofore the habitation of guilt. **7. thy beginning**—the beginning of thy new happiness after restoration. **latter end**—(ch. 42:12; Prov. 23:18). **8, 9.** The sages of the olden time reached an age beyond those of Job's time (*Note,* 42:16), and therefore could give the testimony of a fuller experience. **of yesterday**—i.e., a recent race. We know nothing as compared with them because of the brevity of our lives; so even Jacob (Gen. 47:9). Knowledge consisted then in the results of observation, embodied in poetical proverbs, and handed down by tradition. Longevity gave the opportunity of wider observation. **a shadow**—(Ps. 144:4; I Chron. 29:15). **10. teach thee**—Chapter 6:24 had said, "Teach me." Bildad, therefore, says, "Since you want *teaching,* inquire of the fathers. They will teach thee." **utter words**—more than mere speaking; "put forth well-considered words." **out of their heart**—from observation and reflection; not merely, from their mouth: such, as Bildad insinuates, were Job's words. Verses 11, 12, 13 embody in poetic and sententious form (probably the fragment of an old poem) the observation of the elders. The double point of comparison between the ungodly and the paper-reed is: 1. the luxuriant prosperity at first; and, 2. the sudden destruction. **11. rush**—rather, paper-reed: the papyrus of Egypt, which was used to make garments, shoes, baskets, boats. and paper (a word derived from it) It and the flag or bulrush grow only in marshy places (such as are along the Nile). So the godless thrives only in external prosperity; there is in the hypocrite no inward stability; his prosperity is like the rapid growth of water plants. **12. not cut down**—Before it has ripened for the scythe, it withers more suddenly than any herb, having no self-sustaining power, once that the moisture is gone, which other herbs do not need in the same degree. So ruin seizes on the godless in the zenith of prosperity, more suddenly than on others who appear less firmly seated in their possessions [UMBREIT]. (Ps. 112:10.) **13. paths**—so "ways" (Prov. 1:19). **all that forget God**—the distinguishing trait of the godless (Ps. 9: 17; 50:22). **14. cut off**—so GESENIUS; or, to accord with the metaphor of the spider's "house," "The confidence (on which he builds) shall be laid in ruins" (Isa. 59:5, 6). **15. he shall hold it fast**—implying his eager grasp, when the storm of trial comes: as the spider "holds fast" by its web; but with this difference: the light spider is sustained by that on which it rests; the godless is not by the thin web on which he rests. The expression, "Hold fast," properly applies to the spider holding his web, but

is transferred to the man. Hypocrisy, like the spider's web, is fine-spun, flimsy, and woven out of its own inventions, as the spider's web out of its own bowels. An Arab proverb says, "Time destroys the well-built house, as well as the spider's web." **16. before the sun**—i.e., he (the godless) is green only before the sun rises; but he cannot bear its heat, and withers. So succulent plants like the gourd (Jonah 4:7, 8). But the widespreading in the garden does not quite accord with this. Better, "in sunshine"; the sun representing the smiling fortune of the hypocrite, during which he wondrously progresses [UMBREIT]. The image is that of weeds growing in rank luxuriance and spreading over even heaps of stones and walls, and then being speedily torn away. **17. seeth the place of stones**—*Hebrew,* "the house of stones"; i.e., the wall surrounding the garden. The parasite plant, in creeping towards and over the wall—the utmost bound of the garden—is said figuratively to "see" or regard it. **18. If He** (God) tear him away (properly, "to tear away rapidly and violently") from his place, "then it (the place personified) shall deny him" (Ps. 103:16). The very soil is ashamed of the weeds lying withered on its surface, as though it never had been connected with them. So, when the godless falls from prosperity, his nearest friends disown him. **19.** Bitter irony. The hypocrite boasts of joy. This then is his "joy" at the last. **and out of the earth** —others immediately, who take the place of the man thus punished; not *godly men* (Matt. 3:9). For the place of the weeds is among stones, where the gardener wishes no plants. But, *ungodly;* a fresh crop of weeds always springs up in the place of those torn up: there is no end of hypocrites on earth [UMBREIT]. **20.** Bildad regards Job as a righteous man, who has fallen into sin. **God will not cast away a perfect man**—(or godly man, such as Job was), if he will only repent. Those alone who persevere in sin God will not help (*Hebrew,* "take by the hand," Ps. 73:23; Isa. 41:13; 42:6) when fallen. **21. Till**—lit., "to the point that"; God's blessing on thee, when repentant, will go on increasing to the point that, or until, etc. **22.** The haters of Job are the wicked. They shall be clothed with shame (Jer. 3:25; Ps. 35:26; 109:29), at the failure of their hope that Job would utterly perish, and because they, instead of him, come to naught.

CHAPTER 9

FIRST SERIES

VSS. 1-35. REPLY OF JOB TO BILDAD. **2. I know that it is so**—that God does not "pervert justice" (8:3). But (even though I be sure of being in the right) how can a mere man assert his right—(be just) with God. The Gospel answers (Rom. 3:26). **3. If he** [God] **will contend with him**—lit., "*deign* to enter into judgment." **he cannot answer . . .**—He (man) would not dare, even if he had a thousand answers in readiness to one question of God's, to utter one of them, from awe of His Majesty. **4. wise in heart**—in understanding!—and mighty in power! God confounds the ablest arguer by His wisdom, and the mightiest by His power. **hardened himself** —or his neck (Prov. 29:1); i.e., defied God. To prosper, one must fall in with God's arrangements of providence and grace. **5. and they know not**—*Hebrew* for "suddenly, unexpectedly, before they are aware of it" (Ps. 35:8); "at unawares"; *Hebrew,* which "he knoweth not of" (Joel 2:14; Prov. 5:6). **6.** The earth is regarded, poetically, as resting on pillars, which tremble in an earthquake (Ps. 75:3; Isa. 24:20). The literal truth as to the earth is given (26:7). **7.** The sun, at His command, does not rise; viz., in an eclipse, or the darkness that accompanies earthquakes (vs. 6). **scaleth up**–i.e., totally covers as one would seal up a room, that its contents may not be seen. **8. spreadeth out**–(Isa. 40:22; Ps. 104:2). But throughout it is not so much God's creating, as His governing, power over nature that is set forth. A storm seems a struggle between Nature and her Lord! Better, therefore, "Who *boweth* the heavens alone," without help of any other. God descends from the bowed-down heaven to the earth (Ps. 18:9). The storm, wherein the clouds descend, suggests this image. In the descent of the vault of heaven, God has come down from His high throne and walks majestically over the mountain waves (*Hebrew*, "heights"), as a conqueror taming their violence. So "tread upon" (Deut. 33:29; Amos 4:13; Matt. 14:26). The Egyptian hieroglyphic for impossibility is a man walking on waves. **9. maketh**–rather, from the Arabic, "covereth up." This accords better with the context, which describes His boundless power as controller rather than as creator [UMBREIT]. **Arcturus**–the great bear, which always revolves about the pole, and never sets. The Chaldeans and Arabs, early named the stars and grouped them in constellations; often travelling and tending flocks by night, they would naturally do so, especially as the rise and setting of some stars mark the distinction of seasons. BRINKLEY, presuming the stars here mentioned to be those of Taurus and Scorpio, and that these were the cardinal constellations of spring and autumn in Job's time, calculates, by the precession of equinoxes, the time of Job to be 818 years after the deluge, and 184 before Abraham. **Orion**–*Hebrew,* "the fool"; in ch. 38:31 he appears fettered with "bands." The old legend represented this star as a hero, who presumptuously rebelled against God, and was therefore a fool, and was chained in the sky as a punishment; for its rising is at the stormy period of the year. He is Nimrod (the exceedingly impious rebel) among the Assyrians; Orion among the Greeks. Sabaism (worship of the heavenly hosts) and hero-worship were blended in his person. He first subverted the patriarchal order of society by substituting a chieftainship based on conquest (Gen. 10:9, 10). **Pleiades**–lit., "the heap of stars"; *Arabic,* "knot of stars." The various names of this constellation in the East express the close union of the stars in it (Amos 5:8). **chambers of the south**–the unseen regions of the southern hemisphere, with its own set of stars, as distinguished from those just mentioned of the northern. The true structure of the earth is here implied. **10.** Repeated from Eliphaz (ch. 5:9). **11. I see him not: he passeth on**–The image is that of a howling wind (Isa. 21:1). Like it when it bursts invisibly upon man, so God is felt in the awful *effects* of His wrath, but is not *seen* (John 3:8). Therefore, reasons Job, it is impossible to contend with Him. **12.** If "He taketh away," as in my case all that was dear to me, still a mortal cannot call Him to account. He only takes His own. He is an absolute King (Eccles. 8:4; Dan. 4:35). **13. If God**–rather,"God will not withdraw His anger," i.e., so long as a mortal obstinately resists [UMBREIT]. **the proud helpers**–The arrogant, who would help one contending with the Almighty, are of no avail against Him. **14. How much less shall I . . . ?**–who am weak–seeing that the mighty have to stoop before Him. Choose words (use a well-chosen speech, in order to reason) with Him.

15. (Ch. 10:15). Though I were conscious of no sin, yet I would not dare to say so, but leave it to His judgment and mercy to justify me (I Cor. 4:4). **16, 17. would I not believe that he had hearkened unto my voice**–who breaketh me (as a tree stript of its leaves) with a tempest. **19.** UMBREIT takes these as the words of God, translating, "What availeth the might of the strong?" "Here (saith he) behold! what availeth justice? Who will appoint me a time to plead?" (So Jer. 49:19). The last words certainly apply better to God than to Job. The sense is substantially the same if we make "me" apply to Job. The "lo!" expresses God's swift readiness for battle when challenged. **20. it**–(ch. 15:6; Luke 19:22); or "He." God. **21.** Lit., here (and in vs. 20), "I perfect! I should not know my soul! I would despise (disown) my life"; i.e., Though conscious of innocence, I should be compelled, in contending with the infinite God, to ignore my own soul and despise my past life as if it were guilty [ROSENMÜLLER]. **22. one thing**–"It is all one; whether perfect or wicked–He destroyeth." This was the point Job maintained against his friends, that the righteous and wicked alike are afflicted, and that great sufferings *here* do not prove great guilt (Luke 13:1-5; Eccles. 9:2). **23. If**–Rather, "While (His) scourge slays suddenly (the wicked, vs. 22), He laughs at (disregards; not derides) the pining away of the innocent." The only difference, says Job, between the innocent and guilty is, the latter are slain by a *sudden* stroke, the former pine away *gradually.* The translation, "trial," does not express the antithesis to "slay suddenly," as "pining away" does [UMBREIT]. **24.** Referring to righteous "judges," in antithesis to "the wicked" in the parallel first clause, whereas the wicked oppressor often has the earth given into his hand, the righteous judges are led to execution–culprits had their faces covered preparatory to execution (Esther 7:8). Thus the contrast of the wicked and righteous here answers to that in vs. 23. **if not, where and who?**–If God be *not* the cause of these anomalies, *where* is the cause to be found, and *who* is *he?* **25. a post**–a courier. In the wide Persian empire such couriers, on dromedaries or on foot, were employed to carry the royal commands to the distant provinces (Esther 3:13, 15; 8:14). "My days" are not like the slow caravan, but the fleet post. The "days" are themselves poetically said to "see no good," instead of Job in them (I Pet. 3:10). **26. swift ships**–rather, canoes of reeds or papyrus skiffs, used on the Nile, swift from their lightness (Isa. 18:2). **28.** The apodosis to 27–"If I say," etc. "I still am afraid of all my sorrows (returning), for I know that thou wilt (dost) not (by removing my sufferings) hold or declare me innocent. How then can "I leave off my heaviness"? **29.** The "if" is better omitted; I (am treated by God as) wicked; why then labor I in vain (to disprove His charge)? Job submits, not so much because he is *convinced* that God is *right,* as because God is *powerful* and he *weak* [BARNES]. **30. snow water**–thought to be more cleansing than common water, owing to the whiteness of snow (Ps. 51:7; Isa. 1:18). **never so clean**–Better, to answer to the parallelism of the first clause which expresses the cleansing material, "lye": the Arabs used alkali mixed with oil, as soap (Ps. 73:13; Jer. 2:22). **32.** (Eccles. 6:10; Isa. 45:9.) **33. daysman**–mediator or umpire; the imposition of whose hand expresses power to adjudicate between the persons. There might be one on a level with Job, the one party; but Job knew of none on a level with the Almighty, the other party (I Sam. 2:25). We Christians know of such a Mediator (not, however, in the sense of umpire on a level with both—the God-man, Christ Jesus (I Tim. 2:5). **34. rod**—not here the symbol of punishment, but of *power*. Job cannot meet God on fair terms so long as God deals with him on the footing of His almighty power. **35. it is not so with me**—As it now is, God not taking His rod away, I am not on such a footing of equality as to be able to vindicate myself.

CHAPTER 10

Vss. 1-22. Job's Reply to Bildad Continued. **1. leave my complaint upon myself**—rather, "I will *give loose* to my complaint" (ch. 7:11). **2. show me . . .**—Do not, by virtue of Thy mere sovereignty, treat me as guilty without showing me the reasons. **3.** Job is unwilling to think God can have pleasure in using His power to "oppress" the weak, and to treat man, the work of His own hands, as of no value (vs. 8; Ps. 138:8). **shine upon**—favor with prosperity (Ps. 50:2). **4-6.** Dost Thou see as feebly as man? i.e., with the same uncharitable eye, as, for instance, Job's friends? Is Thy time as short? Impossible! Yet one might think, from the rapid succession of Thy strokes, that Thou hadst no time to spare in overwhelming me. **7.** "Although Thou (the Omniscient) knowest," etc. (connected with vs. 6), "Thou searchest after my sin." **and . . . [that] none can deliver out of thine hand**—Therefore Thou hast no need to deal with me with the rapid violence which man would use (*Note,* vs. 6). **8. Made**—with pains; implying a work of difficulty and art; applying to God language applicable only to man. **together round about**—implying that the human body is a *complete unity,* the parts of which *on all sides* will bear the closest scrutiny. **9. clay**—Next verse proves that the reference here is, not so much to the *perishable* nature of the materials, as to their *wonderful fashioning* by the divine potter. **10.** In the organization of the body from its rude commencements, the original liquid gradually assumes a more solid consistency, like milk curdling into cheese (Ps. 139: 15, 16). Science reveals that the chyle circulated by the lacteal vessels is the supply to every organ. **11. fenced**—or "inlaid" (Ps. 139:15); curiously wrought" [Umbreit]. In the fœtus the skin appears first, then the flesh, then the harder parts. **12. visitation**—Thy watchful Providence, **spirit**—breath. **13. is with thee**—was Thy purpose. All God's dealings with Job in his creation, preservation, and present afflictions were part of His secret counsel (Ps. 139: 16; Acts 15:18; Eccles. 3:11). **14, 15.** Job is perplexed because God "marks" every sin of his with such ceaseless rigor. Whether "wicked" (godless and a hypocrite) or "righteous" (comparatively sincere), God condemns and punishes alike. **lift up my head**—in conscious innocence (Ps. 3:3). **see thou**—rather, "and seeing I see (I too well see) mine affliction," (which seems to prove me guilty) [Umbreit]. **16. increaseth**—rather, "(if) I *lift* up (my head) Thou wouldest hunt me, etc. [Umbreit]. **and again**—as if a lion should not kill his prey at once, but come back and torture it again. **17. witnesses**—His accumulated trials were like a succession of witnesses brought up in proof of his guilt, to wear out the accused. **changes and war**—rather, ("thou settest in array) against me host after host" (lit., "changes and a host," i.e,, a succession of hosts); viz., his afflictions, and then reproach upon reproach from his friends. **20.** But, since I was destined from my birth to these ills, at least give me a little

breathing time during the few days left me (ch. 9:34; 13:21; Ps. 39:13). **22.** The ideas of order and light, disorder and darkness, harmonize (Gen. 1:2). Three *Hebrew* words are used for darkness; in vs. 21 (1) the common word "darkness"; here (2) "a land of *gloom*" (from a *Hebrew* root, "to cover up"); (3) as "thick darkness" or blackness (from a root, expressing sunset). "Where the light thereof is like blackness." Its only sunshine is thick darkness. A bold figure of poetry. Job in a better frame has brighter thoughts of the unseen world. But his views at best wanted the definite clearness of the Christian's. Compare with his words here Revelation 21:23; 22: 5; II Timothy 1:10.

CHAPTER 11

FIRST SERIES

Vss. 1-20. First Speech of Zophar. **2.** Zophar assails Job for his empty words, and indirectly, the two friends, for their weak reply. Taciturnity is highly prized among Orientals (Prov. 10:8, 19). **3. lies**—rather, "vain boasting" (Isa. 16:6; Jer. 48:30). The "men" is emphatic; men of sense; in antithesis to "vain boasting." **mockest**—upbraidest God by complaints. **4. doctrine**—purposely used of Job's speeches, which sounded like lessons of doctrine (Deut. 32:2; Prov. 4:2). **thine**—addressed to God. Job had maintained his *sincerity* against his friends' suspicions, not *faultlessness.* **6. to that which is!** —Rather, "they are double to [man's] *wisdom*" [Michaelis]. So the *Hebrew* is rendered (Prov. 2:7). God's ways, which you arraign, if you were shown their secret wisdom, would be seen vastly to exceed that of men, including yours (I Cor. 1:25). **exacteth** —Rather, "God *consigns to oblivion* in thy favor much of thy guilt." **7.** Rather, "Penetrate to the perfections of the Almighty" (ch. 9:10; Ps. 139:6). **8. It**—the "wisdom" of God (vs. 6). The abruptness of the *Hebrew* is forcible: "The heights of heaven! What canst thou do" (as to attaining to them with thy gaze, Ps. 139:8)? **know**—viz., of His perfections. **10. cut off**—Rather, as in ch. 9:11, "pass over," as a storm; viz., rush upon in anger, **shut up** —in prison, with a view to trial. **gather together**— the parties for judgment: hold a judicial assembly; to pass sentence on the prisoners. **11.** (Ps. 94:11.) **consider**—so as to punish it. Rather, from the connection, vs. 6, "He seeth wickedness also, which man does not *perceive*"; lit., "But no (or save He) perceiveth it" [Umbreit]. God's "wisdom" (vs. 6), detects sin where Job's human eye cannot reach (vs. 8), so as to see any. **12. vain**—hollow. **would be**—"wants to consider himself wise"; opposed to God's "wisdom" (*Note,* vs. 11); refuses to see sin, where God sees it (Rom. 1:22). **wild ass's colt**—a proverb for untamed wildness (ch. 39:5, 8; Jer. 2:24; Gen. 16:12; *Hebrew,* "a wild-ass man"). Man wishes to appear wisely obedient to his Lord, whereas he is, from his birth, unsubdued in spirit. **13.** The apodosis to the "If" is at vs. 15. The preparation of the heart is to be obtained (Prov. 16:1) by stretching out the hands in prayer for it (Ps. 10:17; I Chron. 29:18). **14.** Rather, "if thou wilt put far away the iniquity in thine hand" (as Zaccheus did, Luke 19:8). The apodosis or conclusion is at vs. 15, "*then* shalt thou," etc. **15.** Zophar refers to Job's own words (ch. 10:15), "yet will I not lift up my head," even though righteous. Zophar declares, if Job will follow his advice, he may "lift up his face." **spot**—(Deut. 32:5). **steadfast**—lit., "run fast together," like metals which become firm and hard by fusion. The sinner on the contrary is wavering. **16.** Just as when the stream runs dry (ch. 6:17), the danger threatened by its wild waves is forgotten (Isa. 65:16) [UMBREIT]. **17. age**—days of life. **the noon-day**—viz., of thy former prosperity; which, in the poet's image, had gone on increasing, until it reached its height, as the sun rises higher and higher until it reaches the meridian (Prov. 4:18). **shine forth**—rather, "though now in darkness, thou shalt be as the morning"; or, "thy darkness (if any dark shade should arise on thee, it) shall be as the morning" (only the dullness of morning twilight, not nocturnal darkness) [UMBREIT]. **18.** The experience of thy life will teach thee there is hope for man in every trial. **dig**—viz., wells; the chief necessity in the East. Better, "though now *ashamed* (Rom. 5:5, opposed to the previous 'hope'), thou shalt then rest safely" [GESENIUS]. **19.** (Ps. 4:8; Prov. 3:24; Isa. 14:30); oriental images of prosperity. **19. make suit**—lit., stroke thy face, caress thee (Prov. 19:6). **20.** A warning to Job, if he would not turn to God. **The wicked**—i.e., obdurate sinners. **eyes ... fail**—i.e., in vain look for relief (Deut. 28:65). Zophar implies Job's only hope of relief is in a change of heart. **they shall not escape** —lit., "every refuge shall vanish from them. **giving up the ghost**—Their hope shall leave them as the breath does the body (Prov. 11:7).

CHAPTER 12

FIRST SERIES

Vss. 1-25. JOB'S REPLY TO ZOPHAR, chs. 12-14. **2. wisdom shall die with you**—Ironical, as if all the wisdom in the world was concentrated in them and would expire when they expired. Wisdom makes "a people": a foolish nation is "not a people" (Rom. 10:19). **3. not inferior**—not vanquished in argument and "wisdom" (ch. 13:2). **such things as these**—such commonplace maxims as you so pompously adduce. **4.** The unfounded accusations of Job's friends were a "mockery" of him. He alludes to Zophar's word, "mockest" (ch. 11:3). **his neighbour, who calleth ...**—rather, "I who *call* upon God *that he may answer* me favorably [UMBREIT]. **5.** Rather, "a torch" (lamp) is an object of contempt in the thoughts of him who rests securely (is at ease), though it was prepared for the falterings of the feet [UMBREIT]. (Prov. 25:19.) "Thoughts" and "feet" are in contrast; also rests "securely," and "falterings." The wanderer, arrived at his night-quarters, contemptuously throws aside the torch which had guided his uncertain steps through the darkness. As the torch is to the wanderer, so Job to his friends. Once they gladly used his aid in their need; now they in prosperity mock him in his need. **6. Job** shows that the matter of *fact* opposes Zophar's *theory* (ch. 11:14, 19, 20) that wickedness causes insecurity in men's "tabernacles." On the contrary, they who rob the "tabernacles" (dwellings) of others "prosper securely" in their own. **into whose hand ...** —rather, "who make a god of their own hand," i.e,, who regard their might as their only ruling principle [UMBREIT]. **7, 8.** Beasts, birds, fishes, and plants, reasons Job, teach that the violent live the most securely (vs. 6). The vulture lives more securely than the dove, the lion than the ox, the shark than the dolphin, the rose than the thorn which tears it. **speak to the earth**—rather, "the *shrubs* of the earth" [UMBREIT]. **9.** In all these

cases, says Job, the agency must be referred to Jehovah, though they may seem to man to imply imperfection (vs. 6; ch. 9:24). This is the only undisputed passage of the poetical part in which the name "Jehovah" occurs; in the historical parts it occurs frequently. **10.** The soul, i.e., the animal life. Man, reasons Job, is subjected to the same laws as the lower animals. **11.** As the mouth by tasting meats selects what pleases it, so the ear tries the words of others and retains what is convincing. Each chooses according to his taste. The connection with verse 12 is in reference to Bildad's appeal to the "ancients" (ch:8. 8). You are right in appealing to them, since "with them was wisdom," etc. But you select such proverbs of theirs as suit your views; so I may borrow from the same such as suit mine. **12. ancient**—aged (ch. 15:10). **13.** In contrast to, "with the ancient is wisdom" (vs. 12), Job quotes a saying of the ancients which suits his argument, "with Him (God) is (the true) wisdom" (Prov. 8:14); and by that "wisdom and strength" "He breaketh down," etc., as an absolute Sovereign, not allowing man to penetrate His mysteries; man's part is to bow to His unchangeable decrees (ch. 1: 21). The Mohammedan saying is, "if God will, and how God will." **14. shutteth up**—(Isa. 22:22). Job refers to Zophar's "shut up" (ch. 11:10). **15.** Probably alluding to the flood. **16.** (Ezek. 14:9). **18.** He looseth the authority of kings—the "bond" with which they bind their subjects (Isa. 45:1; Gen. 14:4; Dan. 2:21). **a girdle**—the *cord*, with which they are bound as captives, instead of the royal "girdle" they once wore (Isa. 22:21), and the bond they once bound others with. So "gird"—put on one the bonds of a prisoner instead of the ordinary girdle (John 21:18). **19. princes**—rather, "priests," as the *Hebrew* is rendered (Ps. 99:6). Even the sacred ministers of religion are not exempt from reverses and captivity. **the mighty**—rather, "the firm-rooted in power"; the *Arabic* root expresses ever-flowing *water* [UMBREIT]. **20. the trusty**—rather, "those secure in their eloquence"; e.g., the speakers in the gate (Isa. 3:3) [BEZA]. **understanding**—lit., "taste," i.e., insight or spiritual discernment, which experience gives the aged. The same *Hebrew* word is applied to Daniel's wisdom in interpretation (Dan. 2:14). **21.** Psalm 107:40 quotes, in its first clause, this verse and, in its second, the 24th verse of the chapter. **weakeneth the strength**—lit., "looseth the girdle"; Orientals wear flowing garments; when active strength is to be put forth, they gird up their garments with a girdle. Hence here—"He destroyeth their power" in the eyes of the people. **22.** (Dan. 2:22.) **23.** Isaiah 9:3; Psalm 107:38, 39, which Psalm quotes this chapter elsewhere. (See *Note*, vs. 21.) **straiteneth**—lit., "leadeth in," i.e., reduces. **24. heart**—intelligence. **wander in a wilderness**—figurative; not referring to any actual fact. This cannot be quoted to prove Job lived after Israel's wanderings in the desert. Psalm 107:4, 40 quotes this passage. **25.** Deuteronomy 28: 29; Psalm 107: 27 again quote Job, but in a different connection.

CHAPTER 13

Vss. 1-28. JOB'S REPLY TO ZOPHAR CONTINUED. **1. all this**—as to the dealings of Providence (ch. 12: 3). **3.** Job wishes to plead his cause before God (ch. 9:34, 35), as he is more and more convinced of the valueless character of his would-be "physicians" (ch. 16:2). **4. forgers of lies**—lit., "artful twisters of vain speeches" [UMBREIT]. **5.** (Prov. 17:28). The

Arabs say, "The wise are dumb; silence is wisdom." **7. deceitfully**—use fallacies to vindicate God in His dealings; as if the end justified the means. Their "deceitfulness" for God, against Job, was that they asserted he was a sinner, because he was a sufferer. **8. accept his person**—God's; i.e., be partial for Him, as when a judge favors one party in a trial, because of personal considerations. **contend for God**—viz., with fallacies and prepossessions against Job before judgment (Judg. 6:31). Partiality can never please the impartial God, nor the goodness of the cause excuse the unfairness of the arguments. **9.** Will the issue to you be good, when He searches out you and your arguments? Will you be regarded by Him as pure and disinterested? **mock**—(Gal. 6:7.) Rather, "Can you deceive Him as one man?" etc. **10.** If ye do, though secretly, act partially. (*Note*, vs. 8; Ps. 82:1, 2.) God can successfully vindicate His acts, and needs no fallacious argument of man. **11. make you afraid?**—viz., of employing sophisms in His name (Jer. 10:7, 10). **12. remembrances**—"proverbial maxims," so called because well remembered. **like unto ashes**—or, "parables of ashes"; the image of lightness and nothingness (Isa. 44:20). **bodies**—rather, "entrenchments"; those of clay, as opposed to those of stone, are easy to be destroyed; so the proverbs, behind which they entrench themselves, will not shelter them when God shall appear to reprove them for their injustice to Job. **13.** Job would wish to be spared their speeches, so as to speak out all his mind as to his wretchedness (vs. 14), happen what will. **14.** A proverb for, "Why should I anxiously desire to save my life?" [EICHORN]. The image in the first clause is that of a wild beast, which in order to preserve his prey, carries it in his teeth. That in the second refers to men who hold in the hand what they want to keep secure. **15. in him** —So the *margin* or *keri* reads. But the textual reading or *chetib* is "not," which agrees best with the context, and other passages wherein he says he has no hope (ch. 6:11; 7:21; 10:20; 19:10). "Though He slay me, and I dare no more hope, yet I will maintain," etc., i.e., "I desire to vindicate myself before Him," as not a hypocrite [UMBREIT and NOYES]. **16. He**—rather, "*This* also already speaks in my behalf (lit., "for my saving acquittal"), for an hypocrite would not wish to come before Him" (as I do) [UMBREIT]. (See last clause of vs. 15.) **17. my declaration**—viz., that I wish to be permitted to justify myself immediately before God. **with your ears**—i.e., attentively. **18. ordered**—implying a constant preparation for defense in his confidence of innocence. **19. if . . .**—Rather, *Then* would I hold my tongue and give up the ghost; i.e., if any one can contend with me and prove me false, I have no more to say. "I will be silent and die." Like our "I would stake my life on it" [UMBREIT]. **20.** Address to God. **not hide**—stand forth boldly to maintain my cause. **21.** (*Note*, 9:34; Ps. 39:10.) **22. call**—a challenge to the defendant to answer to the charges. **answer**—the defense begun. **speak**—as plaintiff. **answer**—to the plea of the plaintiff. Expressions from a trial. **23.** The catalogue of my sins ought to be great, to judge from the severity with which God ever anew crushes one already bowed down. Would that He would reckon them up! He then would see how much my calamities outnumber them. **sin?**—singular, "I am unconscious of a *single* particular sin, much less many" [UMBREIT]. **24. hidest . . . face**—a figure from the gloomy impression caused by the sudden clouding over of the sun. **enemy**—God treated Job as an enemy who must be robbed of power by ceaseless sufferings (ch. 7:17,

21). **25.** (Lev. 26:36; Ps. 1:4.) Job compares himself to a leaf already fallen, which the storm still chases hither and thither. **break**—lit., "shake with (Thy) terrors." Jesus Christ does not "break the bruised reed" (Isa. 42:3, 27:8). **26. writest**—a judicial phrase, to note down the determined punishment. The sentence of the condemned used to be *written down* (Isa. 10:1; Jer. 22:30; Ps. 149:9) [UMBREIT]. **bitter things**—bitter punishments. **makest me to posses**—or "inherit." In old age he receives possession of the inheritance of sin thoughtlessly acquired in youth. "To inherit *sins*" is to inherit the *punishments* inseparably connected with them in *Hebrew* ideas (Ps. 25:7). **27. stocks**—in which the prisoner's feet were made fast until the time of execution (Jer. 20:2). **lookest narrowly**—as an overseer would watch a prisoner. **print**—Either the stocks, or his disease, *marked* his *soles* (*Hebrew*, "roots") as the bastinado would. Better, thou drawest (or diggest) [GESENIUS] a line (or trench) [GESENIUS] round my soles, beyond which I must not move [UMBREIT]. **28.** Job speaks of himself in the third person, thus forming the transition to the *general* lot of man (ch. 14:1; Ps. 39:11; Hos. 5:12).

CHAPTER 14

Vss. 1-22. JOB PASSES FROM HIS OWN TO THE COMMON MISERY OF MANKIND. **1. woman**—feeble, and in the East looked down upon (Gen. 2:21). Man being born of one so frail must be frail himself (Matt. 11:11). **few days**—(Gen. 47:9; Ps. 90:10). Lit., "short of days." Man is the reverse of full of days and short of trouble. **2.** (Ps. 90:6; *Note*, ch. 8:9.) **3. open . . . eyes upon**—Not in graciousness; but, "Dost Thou sharply fix Thine eyes upon?" (*Note*, 7:20; also 1:7). Is one so frail as man worthy of such constant watching on the part of God? Zech. 12:4. **me**—so frail. **thee**—so almighty. **4.** A plea in mitigation. The doctrine of original sin was held from the first. "Man is unclean from his birth, how then can God expect perfect cleanness from such a one and deal so severely with me?" **5. determined**—(ch. 7:1; Isa. 10:23; Dan. 9:27; 11:36). **6. Turn**—viz., Thine eyes from watching him so jealously (vs. 3). **hireling**—(ch. 7:1). **accomplish**—rather, "enjoy." That he may at least enjoy the measure of rest of the hireling who though hard worked reconciles himself to his lot by the hope of his rest and reward [UMBREIT]. **7.** Man may the more claim a peaceful life, since, when separated from it by death, he never returns to it. This does not deny a future life, but a return to the *present condition* of life. Job plainly hopes for a future state (vs. 13; ch. 7:2). Still, it is but vague and trembling *hope*, not *assurance;* excepting the one bright glimpse in ch. 19:25. The Gospel revelation was needed to change fears, hopes, and glimpses into clear and definite certainties. **9. scent**—exhalation, which, rather than the humidity of water, causes the tree to germinate. In the antithesis to *man* the *tree* is personified, and volition is poetically ascribed to it. **like a plant**—"as if newly planted" [UMBREIT]; not as if trees and plants were a different species. **10. man . . . man**—Two distinct *Hebrew* words are here used; *Geber,* a *mighty* man: though mighty, he dies. *Adam,* a man of earth: because earthly, he gives up the ghost. **wasteth**—is reduced to nothing: he cannot revive in the present state, as the tree does. The cypress and pine, which when cut down do not revive, were the symbols of death among the Romans. **11. sea**—i.e., a lake, or pool formed from the outspreading of a river. Job lived near the Euphrates: and "sea" is applied to it (Jer. 51:36; Isa. 27:1). So of the Nile (Isa. 19:5). **fail**—utterly disappeared by drying up. The rugged channel of the once flowing water answers to the outstretched corpse ("lieth down," vs. 12) of the once living man. **12. heavens be no more**—This only implies that Job had no hope of living again in the *present* order of the world, not that he had no hope of life again in a new order of things. Psalm 102:26 proves that early under the Old Testament the dissolution of the present earth and heavens was expected (cf. Gen. 8:22). Enoch *before Job* had implied that the "saints shall live again" (Jude 14; Heb. 11:13-16). Even if, by this phrase, *Job* meant "never" (Ps. 89:29) in his gloomier state of feelings, yet the *Holy Ghost* has made him unconsciously (I Pet. 1: 11, 12) use language expressing the truth, that the resurrection is to be preceded by the dissolution of the heavens. In vss. 13-15 he plainly passes to brighter hopes of a world to come. **13.** Job wishes to be kept hidden in the grave until God's wrath against him shall have passed away. So while God's wrath is visiting the earth for the abounding apostasy which is to precede the second coming, God's people shall be hidden against the resurrection-glory (Isa. 26:19-21). **set time**—a decreed time (Acts 1:7). **14. shall he live?**—The answer implied is, *There is a hope that he shall, though not in the present order of life,* as is shown by the words following. Job had denied (vss. 10-12) that man shall live again in this present world. But hoping for a "set time," when God shall remember and raise him out of the hiding-place of the grave (vs. 13), he declares himself willing to "wait all the days of his appointed time" of continuance in the grave, however long and hard that may be. "Appointed time," lit., "warfare, hard service"; implying the *hardship* of being shut out from the realms of life, light, and God for the time he shall be in the grave (ch. 7:1). **change**—my release, as a soldier at his post released from duty by the relieving guard (*Note*, 10:17) [UMBREIT and GESENIUS], but elsewhere GESENIUS explains it, "renovation," as of plants in spring (vs. 7), but this does not accord so well with the metaphor in "appointed time" or "warfare." **15.** viz., at the resurrection (John 5:28; Ps. 17:15). **have a desire to**—lit., "become pale with anxious desire": the same word is translated "sore longedst after" (Gen. 31:30; Ps. 84:2), implying the utter unlikelihood that God would leave in oblivion the "creature of His own hands so fearfully and wonderfully made." It is objected that if Job knew of a future retribution, he would make it the *leading* topic in solving the problem of the permitted afflictions of the righteous. But, (1) "He did not intend to exceed the limits of what was *clearly revealed;* the doctrine was then in a vague form only; (2) The doctrine of God's moral government in *this* life, even *independently of the future,* needed vindication. **16.** Rather, "Yea, thou wilt number my steps, and wilt not (as now) jealously watch over my sin." Thenceforward, instead of severe watching for every sin of Job, God will guard him against every sin. "Number ... steps," i.e., minutely attend to them, that they may not wander" [UMBREIT] (I Sam. 2:9, Ps. 37: 23). **17. scaled up**—(ch. 9:7). Is shut up in eternal oblivion, i.e., God thenceforth will think no more of my former sins. *To cover* sins is to *completely forgive* them (Ps. 32:1; 85:2). Purses of money in the East are usually sealed. **sewest up**—rather, "coverest"; akin to an *Arabic* word, "to color over," to

forget wholly. **18. cometh to naught**—lit., "fadeth"; a poetical image from a leaf (Isa. 34:4). Here Job falls back into his gloomy bodings as to the grave. Instead of "and surely," translate "yet"; marking the transition from his brighter hopes. Even the solid mountain falls and crumbles away; man therefore cannot "hope" to escape decay or to live again in the present world (vs. 19). **out of his place**—so man (Ps. 103:16). **19.** The *Hebrew* order is more forcible: "Stones themselves are worn away by water." **things which grow out of**—rather, "*floods* wash away the dust of the earth." There is a gradation from "mountains" to "rocks" (vs. 18), then "stones," then last "dust of the earth"; thus the solid mountain at last disappears utterly. **20. prevailest**—dost overpower by superior strength. **passeth**—dieth. **changest countenance**—the change in the visage at death. Differently (Dan. 5:9). **21.** One striking trait is selected from the sad picture of the severance of the dead from all that passes in the world (Eccles. 9:5), viz., the utter separation of parents and children. **22.** "Flesh" and "soul" describe the whole man. Scripture rests the hope of a future life, not on the inherent immortality of the soul, but on the restoration of the *body* with the soul. In the unseen world, Job in a gloomy frame anticipates, man shall be limited to the thought of his own misery. "Pain is by personification, from *our* feelings while *alive,* attributed to the flesh and soul, as if the man could feel in his body when dead. It is the dead in general, not the wicked, who are meant here."

CHAPTER 15

SECOND SERIES

Vss. 1-35. SECOND SPEECH OF ELIPHAZ. **2. a wise man**—which Job claims to be. **vain knowledge** —*Hebrew,* "windy knowledge," lit., "of wind" (ch. 8:2). In Ecclesiastes 1:14, Hebrew "to catch wind," expresses to strive for what is vain. **east wind**—stronger than the previous "wind," for in that region the east wind is the most destructive of winds (Isa. 27:8). Thus here,—empty violence. **belly**—the inward parts, the breast (Prov. 18:8). **4. fear**—reverence for God (ch. 4:6; Ps. 2:11). **prayer**—meditation, in Psalm 104:34; so *devotion.* If thy views were right, reasons Eliphaz, that God disregards the afflictions of the righteous and makes the wicked to prosper, all devotion would be at an end. **5.** The sophistry of thine own speeches proves thy guilt. **6.** No *pious* man would utter such sentiments. **7**—I.e., Art thou wisdom personified? Wisdom existed before the hills; i.e., the eternal Son of God (Prov. 8:25; Ps. 90:2). Wast thou in existence before Adam? The farther back one existed, the nearer he was to the Eternal Wisdom. **8. secret,**—rather, "Wast thou a listener *in the secret council* of God?" The *Hebrew* means properly the *cushions* of a divan on which counsellors in the East usually sit. God's servants are admitted to God's secrets (Ps. 25:14; Gen. 18:17; John 15:15). **restrain** —Hebrew, didst thou take away, *or borrow,* thence (viz., from the divine secret council) thy wisdom? Eliphaz in this (vss. 8, 9) retorts Job's words upon himself (ch. 12:2, 3; 13:2). **9. in us**—or, "with us," Hebraism for "we are aware of." **10.** On our side, thinking with us are the aged. Job had admitted that wisdom is with them (ch. 12:12). Eliphaz seems to have been himself older than Job; perhaps the other two were also (ch. 32:6). Job, in ch. 30:1, does not refer to his three friends; it therefore forms no objection. The Arabs are proud of fulness of years. **11. consolations**—viz., the revelation which Eliphaz had stated as a consolatory reproof to Job, and which he repeats in vs. 14. **secret**—Hast thou some *secret* wisdom and source of consolation, which makes thee disregard those suggested by me? (vs. 8). Rather, from a different *Hebrew* root, Is the word of *kindness* or *gentleness* addressed by me treated by thee as valueless? [UMBREIT]. **12. wink** —i.e., why do thy eyes *evince pride*? (Prov. 6:13, Ps. 35:19). **13**—i.e., frettest against God and lettest fall rash words. **14.** Eliphaz repeats the revelation (ch. 4:17) in substance, but using Job's own words (ch. 14:1, *Note* on "born of a woman") to strike him with his own weapons. **15.** Repeated from ch. 4: 18; "servants" there are "saints"; here, viz., holy angels. **heavens**—lit., or else answering to "angels" (ch. 4:18; see *Note* there, and ch. 25:5). **16. filthy** —in *Arabic* "sour" (Ps. 14:3; 53:3), corrupted from his original purity. **drinketh**—(Prov. 19:28). **17.** In direct contradiction of Job's position (ch. 12:6, etc.), that the lot of the wicked was the most prosperous here, Eliphaz appeals (1) to his own experience, (2) to the wisdom of the ancients. **18.** Rather, "and which as handed down from their fathers, they have not concealed." **19.** Eliphaz speaks like a genuine Arab when he boasts that his ancestors had ever possessed the land unmixed with foreigners [UMBREIT]. His words are intended to oppose Job's (ch. 9:24); "the earth" in their case was *not* "given into the hand of the wicked." He refers to the division of the earth by divine appointment (Gen. 10:5; 25:32). Also he may insinuate that Job's sentiments had been corrupted from original purity by his vicinity to the Sabeans and Chaldeans [ROSENMULLER]. **20. travaileth**—rather, "trembleth of himself," though there is no real danger [UMBREIT]. **and the number of [his] years ...**—This gives the reason why the wicked man trembles continually; viz., because he knows not the moment when his life must end. **21.** An evil conscience conceives alarm at every sudden sound, though it be in a time of peace ("prosperity"), when there is no real danger (Lev. 26:36; Prov. 28:1; II Kings 7:6). **22. darkness**—viz., danger or calamity. Glancing at Job, who despaired of restoration: in contrast to good men when in darkness (Mic. 7:8, 9). **waited for of** —i.e., He is destined for the sword [GESENIUS]. Rather (in the night of danger), "he *looks anxiously towards* the sword," as if every sword was drawn against him [UMBREIT]. **23.** Wandereth *in anxious search* for bread. Famine in Old Testament depicts sore need (Isa. 5:13). Contrast the pious man's lot (ch. 5:20-22). **knoweth**—has the firm conviction. Contrast the same word applied to the pious (ch. 5: 24, 25). **ready at his hand**—an *Arabic* phrase to denote a thing's *complete readiness* and *full presence,* as if in the hand. **24. prevail**—break upon him suddenly and terribly, as a king, etc. (Prov. 6: 11). **25. stretcheth ... hand**—wielding the spear, as a bold rebel against God (ch .9:4; Isa. 27:4). **26. on his neck**—rather, "with outstretched neck," viz., that of the rebel [UMBREIT] (Ps. 75:5). **upon ... bucklers**—rather, "*with*—his (the rebel's, not God's) bucklers." The rebel and his fellows are depicted as joining shields together, to form a compact covering over their heads against the weapons hurled on them from a fortress [UMBREIT and GESENIUS]. **27.** The well-nourished body of the rebel is the sign of his prosperity. **collops**—masses of fat. He pampers and fattens himself with sensual indulgences; hence his rebellion against God (Deut. 32:15; I Sam. 2:29). **28.** The class of wicked here described is

that of robbers who plunder "cities," and seize on the houses of the banished citizens (Isa. 13:20). Eliphaz chooses this class because Job had chosen the same (ch. 12:6). **heaps**—of ruins. **29.** Rather, he shall not *increase* his riches; he has reached his highest point; his prosperity shall not continue. **perfection**—rather, "His *acquired* wealth—what he possesses—shall not *be extended,*" etc. **30. depart**— i.e., escape (vss. 22, 23). **branches**—viz., his offspring (ch. 1:18, 19; Ps. 37:35). **dry up**—The "flame" is the sultry wind in the East by which plants most full of sap are suddenly shrivelled. **his mouth**—i.e., God's wrath (Isa. 11:4). **31.** Rather, let him not trust in vanity or he will be deceived, etc. **vanity**—that which is unsubstantial. Sin is its own punishment (Prov. 1:31; Jer. 2:19). **32.** lit., "it (*the tree* to which he is compared, vs. 30, or else *his life*) shall not be filled up in its time"; i.e., "he shall be ended before his time." **shall not be green**—image from a withered tree; the childless extinction of the wicked. **33.** Images of incompleteness. The loss of the unripe grapes is poetically made the vine tree's own act, in order to express more pointedly that the sinner's ruin is the fruit of his own conduct (Isa. 3: 11; Jer. 6:19). **34.** Rather, The binding together of the hypocrites (wicked) shall be *fruitless* [UMBREIT]. Tabernacles of bribery, viz., dwellings of unjust judges, often reprobated in the Old Testament (Isa. 1:23). The "fire of God" that consumed Job's possessions (ch. 1:16) Eliphaz insinuates may have been on account of Job's bribery as an Arab sheik or emir. **35.** Bitter irony, illustrating the "unfruitfulness" (vs. 34) of the wicked. Their conceptions and birthgivings consist solely in mischief, etc. (Isa. 33:11). **prepareth**—hatcheth.

CHAPTER 16

SECOND SERIES

Vss. 1-22. JOB'S REPLY. **2.** (Ch. 13:4.) **3.** "Words of wind," *Hebrew.* He retorts upon Eliphaz his reproach (ch. 15:2). **emboldeneth**—lit., "What wearies you so that ye contradict"? i.e., What have I said to *provoke* you? etc. [SCHUTTENS]. Or, as better accords with the first clause, "Wherefore do ye weary yourselves contradicting?" [UMBREIT]. **4. heap up**—rather, marshal together (an army of) words. **shake ... head**—in mockery; it means *nodding,* rather than *shaking;* nodding is not with us, as in the East, a gesture of scorn (Isa. 37:22; Jer. 18: 16; Matt. 27:39). **5. strengthen ... with ... mouth** —bitter irony. In allusion to Eliphaz' boasted "consolations" (ch. 15:11). Opposed to strengthening with the *heart,* i.e., with real consolation. Translate, "I also (like you) could strengthen with the *mouth,*" i.e., with *heartless* talk: "And the moving of my lips (mere lip comfort) could console" (in the same fashion as you do) [UMBREIT]. "Hearty counsel" (Prov. 27:9) is the opposite. **6. eased**—lit., "What (portion of my sufferings) goes from me?" **7. But now**—rather, "ah!" **he**—God. **company**—rather, "band of *witnesses,*" viz., those who could attest his innocence (his children, servants, etc.). So the same *Hebrew* is translated next verse. UMBREIT makes his "band of witnesses" *himself,* for, alas! he had no other witness for him. But this is too recondite. **8. filled ... with wrinkles**—Rather (as also the same *Hebrew* word in ch. 22:16; *English Version,* "cut down"), "thou hast *fettered* me, thy witness" (*besides* cutting off my "band of witnesses," vs. 7), i.e., hast disabled me by pains from properly attesting my innocence. But another "witness" arises against him, viz., his "leanness" or wretched state of body, construed by his friends into a proof of his guilt. The radical meaning of the *Hebrew* is "to draw together," whence flow the double meaning "to bind" or "fetter," and in *Syriac,* "to wrinkle." **leanness**—meaning also "lie"; implying it was a *false* "witness." **9.** Image from a wild beast. So God is represented (ch. 10:16). **who hateth me**—rather, "and pursues me hard." Job would not ascribe "hatred" to God (Ps. 50:22). **mine enemy**—rather, "he sharpens, etc., *as an enemy*" (Ps. 7:12). Darts wrathful glances at me, like a foe (ch. 13:24). **10.** **gaped**—not in order to devour, but to mock him. To fill his cup of misery, the mockery of his friends (vs. 10) is added to the hostile treatment from God (vs. 9). **smitten ... cheek**—figurative for contemptuous abuse (Lam. 3:30; Matt. 5:39). **gathered themselves**—"conspired unanimously" [SCHUTTENS]. **11. the ungodly**—viz., his professed friends, who persecuted him with unkind speeches. **turned me over**—lit., cast me headlong into, etc. **12. I was at ease**—in past times (ch. 1). **by my neck**—as an animal does its prey (so ch. 10:16). **shaken**—violently; in contrast to his former "ease" (Ps. 102:10). Set me up (*again*). **mark**—(ch. 7:20; Lam. 3:12). God lets me always recover strength, so as to torment me ceaselessly. **13. his archers**—The image of previous verse is continued. God, in making me His "mark," is accompanied by the three friends, whose words wound like sharp arrows. **gall**—put for a vital part; so the liver (Lam. 2:11). **14.** The image is from storming a fortress by making breaches in the walls (II Kings 14:13). **a giant**—a mighty warrior. **15. sewed**—denoting the tight fit of the mourning garment; it was a sack with armholes closely sewed to the body. **horn**—image from horned cattle, which when excited tear the earth with their horns. The horn was the emblem of power (I Kings 22:11). Here, it is "in the *dust,*" which as applied to Job denotes *his humiliation* from former greatness. To throw one's self in the dust was a sign of mourning; this idea is here joined with that of excited despair, depicted by the fury of a horned beast. The Druses of Lebanon still wear horns as an ornament. **16. foul**—rather, "is red," i.e., flushed and heated [UMBREIT and NOYES]. **shadow of death**—i.e., darkening through many tears (Lam. 5:17). Job here refers to Zophar's implied charge (ch. 11:14). Nearly the same words occur as to Jesus Christ (Isa. 53:9). So vs. 10 above answers to the description of Jesus Christ (Ps. 12:13; Isa. 50:6, and vs. 4 to Ps. 22:7). He alone realized what Job aspired after, viz., outward *righteousness* of acts and inward *purity* of devotion. Jesus Christ as the representative man is typified in some degree in every servant of God in the Old Testament. **18. my blood**—i.e., my undeserved suffering. He compares himself to one murdered, whose blood the earth refuses to drink up until he is avenged (Gen. 4:10, 11; Ezek. 24:1, 8; Isa. 26:21). The Arabs say that the dew of heaven will not descend on a spot watered with innocent blood (cf. II Sam. 1:21). **no place**—no resting-place. "May my cry never stop!" May it go abroad! "Earth" in this verse in antithesis to "heaven" (vs. 19). May my innocence be as well known to *man* as it is even now to God! **19. Also now**—Even now, when I am so greatly misunderstood on earth, God in *heaven* is sensible of my innocence. **record**—*Hebrew,* "my witness." Amidst all his impatience, Job still trusts in God. **20.** *Hebrew,* more forcibly, "my mockers—my friends!" A heart-cutting paradox

[UMBREIT]. God alone remains to whom he can look for attestation of his innocence; plaintively with tearful eye, he supplicates for this. **21. one**—rather, He (God). "Oh, that He would plead for a man (viz., me) against God." Job quaintly says," God must support me against God; for He makes me to suffer, and He alone knows me to be innocent" [UMBREIT]. So God helped Jacob in wrestling against Himself (cf. 23:6; Gen. 32:25). *God* in Jesus Christ does plead with *God* for man (Rom. 8:26, 27). **as a man**—lit,. the Son of man. A prefiguring of the advocacy of Jesus Christ—a boon longed for by Job (ch. 9:33), though the spiritual pregnancy of his own words, designed for all ages, was but little understood by him (Ps. 80:17). **for his neighbour**—*Hebrew,* "friend." Job himself (ch. 42:8) pleaded as intercessor for his "friends," though "his scorners" (vs. 20); so Jesus Christ the Son of man (Luke 23:34); "for *friends*" (John 15:13-15). **22.** few—lit., "years *of number,*" i.e., few, opposed to *numberless* (Gen. 34:30).

CHAPTER 17

Vss. 1-16. JOB'S ANSWER CONTINUED. **1. breath ... corrupt**—result of elephantiasis. But UMBREIT, "my strength (spirit) is spent." **extinct**—Life is compared to an expiring light. "The light of my day is extinguished." **graves**—plural, to heighten the force. **2.** [UMBREIT], more emphatically, "had I only not to endure *mockery,* in the midst of their *contentions* I (mine eye) would remain quiet." "Eye continue," or *tarry all night* (*Hebrew*), is a figure taken from sleep at night, to express undisturbed *rest;* opposed to (ch. 16:20), when the eye of Job is represented as pouring out tears to God *without rest.* **3. Lay down**—viz., a pledge or security, i.e., be my surety; do Thou attest my innocence, since my friends only mock me (vs. 2). Both litigating parties had to lay down a sum as security before the trial. **put me in a surety**—Provide a surety for me (in the trial) with Thee. A presage of the "surety" (Heb. 7:22), or "one Mediator between God and man" (see *Note,* 16:21). **strike hands**—"who else (save God Himself) could strike hands with me?" i.e., be my securtiy (Ps. 119:122). The Hebrew strikes the hand of him for whom he goes security (Prov. 6:1). **4. their heart**—The *intellect* of his friends. **shalt ... exalt**—Rather imperative, exalt them not; allow them not to conquer [UMBREIT], (Isa. 6:9, 10). **5.** The *Hebrew* for "flattery" is "smoothness"; then it came to mean a *prey* divided by *lot,* because a smooth stone was used in casting the lots (Deut. 18:8), "a portion" (Gen. 14:24). Therefore translate, "He that delivers up his friend as a prey (which the conduct of my friends implies that they would do), even the eyes," etc. [NOYES] (Ch. 11:20). Job says this as to the sinner's *children,* retorting upon their reproach as to the cutting off of his (ch. 5:4; 15:30). This accords with the Old Testament dispensation of legal retribution (Exod. 20:5). **6. He**—God. The poet reverentially suppresses the name of God when speaking of calamities inflicted. **by-word**—(Deut. 28:37; Ps. 69:11). My awful punishment makes my name execrated everywhere, as if I must have been superlatively bad to have earned it. **aforetime ... tabret**—as David was honored (I Sam. 18:6). Rather from a different *Hebrew* root, "I am treated to my face as an object of disgust," lit., an object to be spit upon in the face (Num. 12:14). So *Raca* means (Matt. 5:22), [UMBREIT]. **7.** (Ps. 6:7; 31:9; Deut. 34:7.) **members**

—lit., "figures"; all the individual members being peculiar *forms* of the body; opposed to "shadow," which looks like a figure without solidity. **8. astonied**—at my unmerited sufferings. **against the hypocrite**—The upright shall feel their sense of justice wounded ("will be indignant") because of the prosperity of the wicked. By "hypocrite" or "ungodly," he perhaps glances at his false friends. **9.** The strength of religious principle is heightened by misfortune. The pious shall take fresh courage to persevere from the example of suffering Job. The image is from a warrior acquiring new courage in action (Isa. 40:30, 31; Phil. 1:14). **10.** "Return." If you have anything to advance really wise, though I doubt it, recommence your speech. For as yet I cannot find one wise man among you all. **11.** Only do not vainly speak of the restoration of health to me; for "my days are past." **broken off**—as the threads of the web cut off from the loom (Isa. 38:12). **thoughts** —lit., "possessions," i.e., all the feelings and fair hopes which my heart once nourished. These belong to the *heart,* as "purposes" to the *understanding;* the two together here describe the entire inner man. **12. They**—viz., *my friends* would change the night into day, i.e., would try to persuade me of the change of my misery into joy, which is impossible [UMBREIT] (ch. 11:17); (but) the light of prosperity (could it be enjoyed) would be short because of the darkness of adversity. Or better for "short," the *Hebrew* "near"; and the light of new prosperity should be near in the face of (before) the darkness of death;" i.e., they would persuade me that light is near, even though darkness approaches. **13.** Rather, "if I wait for this grave (Sheol, or the unseen world) as my house, and make my bed in the darkness (vs. 14), and say to corruption," rather, to the pit or grave, etc. (vs. 15.) Where then is my hope? [UMBREIT]. The apodosis is at vs. 15. **14. Thou art my father . . .**—expressing most intimate connection (Prov. 7:4). His diseased state made him closely akin to the grave and worm. **15.** Who shall see it fulfilled? viz., the "hope" (ch. 11:18) which they held out to him of restoration. **16. They** —viz., my hopes shall be buried with me. **bars**— (Isa. 38:10). Rather, the *wastes* or *solitudes* of the pit (sheol, the unseen world). **rest together**—the rest of me and my hope is in, etc. Both expire together. The word "rest" implies that man's ceaseless hopes only rob him of rest.

CHAPTER 18

SECOND SERIES

Vss. 1-21. REPLY OF BILDAD. **2. ye**—the other two friends of Job, whom Bildad charges with having spoken mere "words," i.e., empty speeches; opposed to "mark," i.e., come to *reason,* consider the question *intelligently;* and then let us speak. **3. beasts**— alluding to what Job said (ch. 12:7; so Isa. 1:3). **vile**—rather from a *Hebrew* root, "to stop up." "Stubborn," answering to the stupidity implied in the parallel first clause [UMBREIT]. Why should we give occasion by your empty speeches for our being mutually reputed, in the sight of Job and one another, as unintelligent? (ch. 17:4, 10). **4.** Rather, turning to Job, thou that tearest thyself in anger (ch. 5:2). **be forsaken**—become desolate. He alludes here to Job's words as to the "rock," crumbling away (ch. 14:18, 19); but in a different application. He says bitterly "for thee." Wert thou

not punished as thou art, and as thou art unwilling to bear, the eternal order of the universe would be disturbed and the earth become desolate through unavenged wickedness [UMBREIT]. Bildad takes it for granted Job is a great sinner (ch. 8:3-6; Isa. 24:5, 6). "Shall that which stands fast as a rock be removed for your special accommodation?" **5.** That (vs. 4) cannot be. The decree of God is unalterable, the light (prosperity) of the wicked shall at length be put out. **his fire**—alluding to Arabian hospitality, which prided itself on welcoming the stranger to the fire in the tent, and even lit fires to direct him to it. The ungodly shall be deprived of the means to show hospitality. His dwelling shall be dark and desolate! **6. candle**—the lamp which in the East is usually fastened to the ceiling. Oil abounds in those regions, and the lamp was kept burning all night, as now in Egypt, where the poorest would rather dispense with food than the night-lamp (Ps. 18:28). To put out the lamp was an image of utter desolation. **7.** "Steps of strength," *Hebrew,* for "His strong steps." A firm step marks health. To be straitened in steps is to be no longer able to move about at will (Prov. 4:12). **his own counsel**— Plans shall be the means of his fall (ch. 5:13). **8. he walketh upon**—rather, "he *lets himself go into* the net" [UMBREIT]. If the *English Version* be retained, then understand "snare" to be the pitfall, covered over with branches and earth, which when walked upon give way (Ps. 9:15, 35:8). **9. robber**— rather answering to "gin" in the parallel clause, "the *noose* shall hold him fast" [UMBREIT]. **11. Terrors** —often mentioned in this book (vs. 14; ch. 24:17; etc.). The terrors excited through an evil conscience are here personified. "Magor-missabib" (Jer. 20:3). **drive . . . to his feet**—rather, shall pursue (lit., "scatter," Hab. 3:14) him close at his heels (lit., "immediately after his feet," Hab. 3:5; I Sam. 25:42; *Hebrew*). The image is that of a pursuing conqueror who scatters the enemy [UMBREIT]. **12.** The *Hebrew* is brief and bold, "his strength is hungry." **destruction**—i.e., a great calamity (Prov. 1:27). **ready at his side**—close at hand to destroy him (Prov. 19:29). **13.** UMBREIT has "he" for "it," i.e., "in the rage of hunger he shall devour his own body"; or, "his own children" (Lam. 4:10). Rather, "destruction" from the last verse is nominative to "devour." **strength**—rather, "members" (lit., the "branches" of a tree). **the first-born of death**—a personification full of poetical horror. The first-born son held the chief place (Gen. 49:3); so here *the chiefest (most deadly) disease* that death has ever engendered (Isa. 14:30; "first-born of the poor"— the poorest). The Arabs call fever, "daughter of death." **14. confidence**—all that the father trusted in for domestic happiness, children, fortune, etc., referring to Job's losses. **rooted out**—suddenly torn away, it shall bring—i.e., he shall be brought; or, as UMBREIT better has, "*Thou* (God) shalt bring him *slowly.*" The *Hebrew* expresses, "to stride slowly and solemnly." The godless has a fearful death for long before his eyes, and is at last taken by it. Alluding to Job's case. The King of terrors, not like the heathen Pluto, the fabled ruler of the dead, but Death, with all its terrors to the ungodly, personified. **15. It**—"Terror" shall haunt, etc., and not as UMBREIT "another," which the last clause of the verse disproves. **none of his**—It is his no longer. **brimstone**—probably comparing the calamity of Job by the "fire of God" (ch. 1:16) to the destruction of guilty Sodom by fire and brimstone (Gen. 19:24). **16. Roots**—himself. **branch**—his children (ch. 8:12; 15:30; Mal. 4:1). **17. street**—Men shall not speak of him in meeting in the highways; rather, in the field or meadow; the shepherds shall no more mention his name—a picture from nomadic life [UMBREIT]. **18. light ... darkness**—existence—nonexistence. **19. nephew**—(so Isa. 14:22). But it is translated "grandson" (Gen. 21:23); translate "kinsman." **20. after ... before**—rather, "those in the West—those in the East"; i.e., all people; lit., those behind—those before"; for Orientals in geography turn with their faces to the east (not to the north as we), and back to the west; so that *before*—east; *behind*—north (so Zech. 14:8). **day**—of ruin (Obad. 12). **affrighted** —seized with terror (ch. 21:6; Isa. 13:8). **21.** (Ch. 8:22, *Marg.*)

CHAPTER 19

SECOND SERIES

Vss. 1-29. JOB'S REPLY TO BILDAD. **2. How long**, etc.—retorting Bildad's words (ch. 18:2). Admitting the punishment to be deserved, is it kind thus ever to be harping on this to the sufferer? And yet even this they have not yet proved. **3. These**—prefixed emphatically to numbers (Gen. 27:36). **ten**—i.e., often (Gen. 31:7). **make yourselves strange**—rather, *stun* me [GESENIUS]. (See *Marg.* for a different meaning.) **4. erred**—The *Hebrew* expresses *unconscious error*. Job was unconscious of wilful sin. **remaineth**—lit., passeth the night." An image from harboring an unpleasant guest for the night. I bear the consequences. **5. magnify**, etc.—Speak proudly (Obad. 12; Ezek. 35:13). **against me**—emphatically repeated (Ps. 38:16). **plead ... reproach** —*English Version* makes this part of the protasis, "if" being understood, and the apodosis beginning at vs. 6. Better with UMBREIT, If ye would become great heroes against me in truth, ye must *prove* (evince) against me my *guilt*, or *shame*, which you assert. In the *English Version* "reproach" will mean Job's *calamities*, which they "pleaded" against him as a "reproach," or proof of guilt. **6. compassed ... net**—alluding to Bildad's words (ch. 18:8). Know, that it is not that I as a wicked man have been caught in my "*own* net"; *it is God* who has compassed me in His—why, I know not. **7. wrong**—violence: brought on him by God. **no judgment**—God will not remove my calamities, and so vindicate my just cause; and my friends will not do *justice* to my past character. **8.** Image from a benighted traveller. **9. stripped ... crown**—image from a deposed king, deprived of his robes and crown; appropriate to Job, once an emir with all but royal dignity (Lam. 5:16; Ps. 89:39). **10. destroyed ... on every side**—"Shaken all round, so that I fall in the dust"; image from a tree uprooted by violent shaking from every side [UMBREIT]. The last clause accords with this (Jer. 1:10). **mine hope**—as to this life (in opposition to Zophar, ch. 11:18); not as to the world to come (vs. 25; ch. 14:15). **removed**—uprooted. **11. enemies**—(ch. 13:24; Lam. 2:5). **12. troops**—Calamities advance together like hostile troops (ch. 10:17). **raise up ... way**—An army must *cast up a way* of access before it, in marching against a city (Isa. 40:3). **13. brethren**—nearest kinsmen, as distinguished from "acquaintance." So "kinsfolk" and "familiar friends" (vs. 14) correspond in parallelism. The Arabic proverb is, "The brother, i.e., the true friend, is only known in time of need." **estranged**—lit., "turn away with disgust." Job again unconsciously uses language prefiguring the desertion of Jesus Christ (ch. 16:10; Luke 23:49; Ps. 38:11). **15. They that dwell**, etc.—rather, so-

journ: male servants, sojourning in his house. Mark the contrast. The stranger admitted to sojourn as a dependent treats the master as a stranger in his own house. **16. servant**—born in my house (as distinguished from those sojourning in it), and so altogether belonging to the family. Yet even he disobeys my call **mouth**—i.e., calling aloud; formerly a **nod** was enough. Now I no longer look for *obedience*, I try *entreaty*. **17. strange**—His breath by elephantiasis had become so strongly altered and offensive, that his wife turned away as estranged from him (vs. 13; ch. 17:1). **children ... of mine own body**—lit., "belly." But "loins" is what we should expect, not "belly" (womb), which applies to the woman. The "mine" forbids it being taken of his wife. Besides their children were dead. In ch. 3:10 the same words "my womb" mean, *my mother's womb:* therefore translate, "and I must entreat (as a suppliant) the children of my mother's womb"; i.e., my own brothers—a heightening of force, as compared with last clause of vs. 16 [UMBREIT]. Not only must I entreat suppliantly my *servant,* but my own *brothers* (Ps. 69:8). Here too, he unconsciously foreshadows Jesus Christ (John 7: 5). **18. young children**—So the *Hebrew* means (ch. 21:11). Reverence for age is a chief duty in the East. The word means "wicked" (ch. 16:11). So UMBREIT has it here, not so well. **I arose**—Rather, supply "if," as Job was no more in a state to stand up. "If I stood up (arose), they would speak against (abuse) me" [UMBREIT]. **19. inward**—confidential: lit., "men of my secret"—to whom I entrusted my most intimate confidence. **20.** Extreme meagerness. The bone seemed to stick in the skin, being seen through it, owing to the flesh drying up and falling away from the bone. The *Margin*, "as to my flesh," makes this sense clearer. The *English Version,* however, expresses the same: "*And* to my flesh," viz., which has fallen away from the bone, instead of firmly covering it. **skin of my teeth**—proverbial. I have *escaped* with bare life; I am whole *only with the skin of my teeth;* i.e., my gums alone are whole, the rest of the skin of my body is broken with sores (ch. 7:5; Ps. 102:5). Satan left Job his speech, in hope that he might therewith curse God. **21.** When God had made him such a piteous spectacle, his friends should spare him the additional persecution of their cruel speeches. **22. as God**—has persecuted me. Prefiguring Jesus Christ (Ps. 69:26). That God afflicts is no reason that man is to add to a sufferer's affliction (Zech. 1: 15). **satisfied with my flesh**—It is not enough that God afflicts my flesh literally (vs. 20), but you must "eat my flesh" metaphorically (Ps. 27:2); i.e., utter the worst calumnies, as the phrase often means in *Arabic.* **23.** Despairing of justice from his friends in his lifetime, he wishes his words could be preserved imperishably to posterity, attesting his hope of vindication at the resurrection. **printed**—not our modern printing, but engraven. **24. pen**—graver. **lead**—poured into the engraven characters, to make them better seen [UMBREIT]. Not on leaden plates; for it was "in the rock" that they were engraved. Perhaps it was the hammer that was of "lead," as sculptors find more delicate incisions are made by it, than by a harder hammer. FOSTER (*One Primev. Lang.*) has shown that the inscriptions on the rocks in Wady-Mokatta, along Israel's route through the desert, record the journeys of that people, as Cosmas Indicopleustes asserted, A.D. 535. **for ever**—as long as the rock lasts. **25. redeemer**—UMBREIT and others understand this and vs. 26, of God appearing as Job's avenger *before his death,* when his body would be wasted to a skeleton. But Job uniformly despairs of restoration and vindication of his cause in this life (ch. 17:15, 16). One hope alone was left, which the Spirit revealed—a vindication in a future life: it would be no full vindication if his soul alone were to be happy *without the body,* as some explain (vs. 26) *out of* the flesh." It was his body that had chiefly suffered: the resurrection of his body, therefore, alone could vindicate his cause: to see God with *his own eyes,* and in a renovated body (vs. 27), would disprove the imputation of guilt cast on him because of the sufferings of his present body. That this truth is not further dwelt on by Job, or noticed by his friends, only shows that it was *with him* a bright passing glimpse of *Old Testament* hope, rather than the steady light of *Gospel assurance; with us* this passage has a definite clearness, which it had not in *his* mind (see *Note,* 21:30). The idea in "redeemer" with Job is Vindicator (ch. 16:19; Num. 35:27), redressing his wrongs; also including at least with *us,* and probably with *him,* the idea of the predicted Bruiser of the serpent's head. Tradition would inform him of the prediction. Foster shows that the fall by the serpent is represented perfectly on the temple of Osiris at Philæ; and the resurrection on the tomb of the Egyptian Mycerinus, dating 4000 years back. Job's sacrifices imply sense of sin and need of atonement. Satan was the injurer of Job's body; Jesus Christ his Vindicator, the Living One who giveth life (John 5:21,26). **at the latter day**—Rather, "the Last," the peculiar title of Jesus Christ, though Job may not have known the pregnancy of his own inspired words, and may have understood merely *one that comes after* (I Cor. 15: 45; Rev. 1:17). Jesus Christ is *the last.* The day of Jesus Christ *the last day* (John 6:39). **stand**—rather, arise: as God is said to "raise up" the Messiah (Jer. 23:5; Deut. 18:15). **earth**—rather, dust: often associated with the body crumbling away in it (ch. 7:21; 17:16); therefore appropriately here. Above that very *dust* wherewith was mingled man's decaying body shall man's Vindicator arise. "Arise above the dust," strikingly expresses that fact that Jesus Christ *arose* first Himself *above the dust,* and then is to *raise* His people *above* it (I Cor. 15:20, 23). The Spirit intended in Job's words more than Job fully understood (I Pet. 1:12). Though He *seems,* in forsaking me, to be as one *dead,* He now truly "liveth" in heaven; hereafter He shall appear also above the *dust* of earth. The Goel or vindicator of blood was the nearest kinsman of the slain. So Jesus Christ took our flesh, to be our kinsman. Man lost life by Satan the "murderer" (John 8:44), here Job's persecutor (Heb. 2:14). Compare also as to *redemption of the inheritance* by the kinsman of the dead (Ruth 4:3-5; Eph. 1:14). **26.** Rather, though after my skin (is no more) this (body) is destroyed ("body" being omitted, because it was so wasted as not to deserve the name), yet *from* my flesh (*from my renewed body,* as the starting-point of vision, Song of Sol. 2:9; "looking out *from* the windows") "shall I see God." Next clause proves *bodily* vision is meant, for it specifies "mine eyes" [Rosenmuller, 2d ed.]. The *Hebrew* opposes "*in* my flesh." The "skin" was the first destroyed by elephantiasis, then the "body." **27. for myself**—for my advantage, as my friend. **not another**—Mine eyes shall behold Him, but *no longer* as one *estranged* from me, as now [Bengel]. **though**—better omitted: my reins (inward recesses of the heart) are consumed within me; i.e., pine with longing desire for that day (Ps. 84:2; 119:81). The Gentiles had but few revealed promises: how gracious that the

few should have been so explicit (cf. Num. 24:17; Matt. 2:2). **28.** Rather ye will then (when the Vindicator cometh) say, Why, etc. **root . . . in me**—The root of pious integrity, which was the *matter* at issue, whether it could be in one so afflicted, is found in me. Umbreit, with many MSS. and versions, reads "in him." "Or how found we in him *ground of contention."* **29.** "Wrath (the passionate violence with which the friends persecuted Job) bringeth," etc., lit., "is sin of the sword." **that ye may know**—Supply, "I say this." **judgment**—inseparably connected with the coming of the Vindicator. The "wrath" of God at His appearing for the temporal vindication of Job against the friends (ch. 42:7) is a pledge of the eternal wrath at the final coming to glorify the saints and judge their enemies (II Thess. 1:6-10; Isa. 25:8).

CHAPTER 20

SECOND SERIES

Vss. 1-29. Reply of Zophar. **2. Therefore**—Rather, the more excited I feel by Job's speech, the more *for that very reason* shall my reply be supplied by my calm consideration. Lit., "Notwithstanding; my calm thoughts (as in ch. 4:13) shall furnish my answer, because of the excitement (haste) within me" [Umbreit]. **3. check of my reproach**—i.e., the castigation intended as a reproach (lit., shame) to me. **spirit of . . . understanding**—my rational spirit; answering to "calm thoughts" (vs. 2). In spite of thy reproach urging me to "hastiness." I will answer in calm reason. **5. hypocrite**—lit., "the ungodly" (Ps. 37:36, 36). **6.** (Isa. 14:13; Obad. 3:4.) **7. dung** —in contrast to the haughtiness of the sinner (vs. 6); this strong term expresses disgust and the lowest degradation (Ps. 83:10; I Kings 14:10). **8.** (Ps. 73:20.) **9.** Rather "the eye followeth him, but can *discern* him no more." A *sharp-looking* is meant (ch. 28:7; ch. 7:10). **10. seek to please**—"Atone to the poor" (by restoring the property of which they had been robbed by the father) [De Wette]. Better than *English Version,* "The children" are reduced to the humiliating condition of "seeking the favor of those very poor," whom the father had oppressed. But Umbreit translates as *Margin.* **his hands**—rather, *their* (the children's) hands. **their goods**—the goods of the poor. Righteous retribution! (Exod. 20:5.) **11.** (Ps. 25:7), so *Vulgate.* Gesenius has "full of youth"; viz., *in the fulness of his youthful strength* he shall be laid in the dust. But "bones" plainly alludes to Job's disease, probably to Job's own words (ch. 19:20). Umbreit translates, "full of his *secret* sins," as in Psalm 90:8; his secret guilt in his time of seeming righteousness, like secret poison, at last lays him in the dust. The *English Version* is best. Zophar alludes to Job's own words (ch. 17:16). **with him**—His sin had so pervaded his nature that it accompanies him to the grave: for eternity the sinner cannot get rid of it (Rev. 22:11). **12. be**—"*taste sweet."* Sin's fascination is like poison sweet to the taste, but at last deadly to the vital organs (Prov. 20:17; ch. 9:17, 18). **hide . . . tongue**—seek to prolong the enjoyment by keeping the sweet morsel long in the mouth (so vs. 13). **14. turned**—*Hebrew* denotes a total change into a disagreeable contrary (Jer. 2:21; cf. Rev. 10:9, 10). **14. gall**—in which the poison of the asp was thought to lie. It rather is contained in a sack in the mouth. Scripture uses popular language, where no moral truth is thereby endangered. **15.** He is forced to disgorge his ill-gotten wealth. **16. shall suck**—It shall turn out that he has sucked the poison, etc.   **17. floods**—lit., "stream of floods," plentiful streams flowing with milk, etc. (ch. 29:6; Exod. 3:17).   Honey and butter are more fluid in the East than with us and are poured out from jars.   These "rivers" or waterbrooks are in the sultry East emblems of prosperity.   **18.** Image from food which is taken away from one before he can swallow it.   **restitution**—(So Prov. 6:31).   The parallelism favors the *Eng. Version* rather than the translation of Gesenius, "As a possession to be restored in which he rejoices not."   **he shall not rejoice**—His enjoyment of his ill-gotten gains shall then be at an end (vs. 5).   **19. oppressed**—whereas he ought to have espoused their cause (II Chron. 16:10).   **forsaken**—left helpless.   **house**—thus leaving the poor without shelter (Isa. 5:8; Mic. 2:2).   **20.** Umbreit translates, "His inward parts know no rest" from desires.   **his belly**—i.e., peace *inwardly.*   **not save**—lit., "not *escape* with that which," etc., alluding to Job's having been stripped of his all.   **21. look for**—rather, *because* his goods, i.e., prosperity *shall have* no *endurance.*   **22. shall be**—rather, "he is (feeleth) straitened."   The next clause explains in what respect.   **wicked**—Rather, "the whole hand of the *miserable* (whom he had oppressed) cometh upon him"; viz., the sense of his having oppressed the poor, now in turn comes with all its power (hand) on him.   This caused his "straitened" feeling even in prosperity.   **23.** Rather, "God shall cast (may God send) [Umbreit] upon him the fury of His wrath *to fill his belly!*"   **while . . . eating**—rather, "shall rain it upon him *for his food!*   Fiery rain, i.e., lightning (Ps. 11:6; alluding to Job's misfortune, ch. 1:16).   The force of the image is felt by picturing to one's self the opposite nature of a refreshing rain in the desert (Exod. 16:4; Ps. 68:9).   **24. steel**—rather, "brass."   While the wicked flees from one danger, he falls into a greater one from an opposite quarter [Umbreit].   **25. It is drawn**—Rather, "He (God) draweth (the sword, Josh. 5:13) and (no sooner has He done so, than) it cometh out of (i.e., passes right through) the (sinner's) body" (Deut. 32:41, 42; Ezek. 21:9, 10).   The *glittering* sword is a happy image for lightning.   **gall**—i.e., his life (ch. 16:13).   "Inflicts a deadly wound."   **terrors**—Zophar repeats Bildad's words (ch. 17:11; Ps. 88:16; 55:4).   **26.** "All darkness," i.e., every calamity that befalls the wicked shall be *hid* (in store for him) *in His* (God's) *secret places,* or treasures (Jude 13; Deut. 32:34).   **not blown**—not kindled by man's hands, but by God's (Isa. 30:33; LXX in Alexandrian MS. reads "unquenchable fire," Matt. 3:12).   Tact is shown by the friends in not expressly mentioning, but alluding under color of general cases, to Job's calamities; here (ch. 1:16) Umbreit explains it, *wickedness,* is a "self-igniting fire"; in it lie the principles of destruction.   **ill . . . tabernacle**—Every trace of the sinner must be obliterated (ch. 18:15).   **27.** All creation is at enmity with him, and proclaims his guilt, which he would fain conceal.   **28. increase**—prosperity.   Ill got—ill gone.   **flow away**—like waters that run dry in summer; using Job's own metaphor against himself (ch. 6:15-17; II Sam. 14:14; Mic. 1:4).   **his wrath**—God's   **29. appointed**—not as a matter of chance, but by the divine "decree" (*Margin*) and settled principle.

CHAPTER 21

SECOND SERIES

Vss. 1-34. Job's Answer.   **2. consolations**—If you will listen calmly to me, this will be regarded as

"consolations"; alluding to Eliphaz' boasted "consolations" ch. 15:11), which Job felt more as aggravations ("mockings," vs. 3) than consolations (ch. 16:2).   **3.** Lit., "*Begin* your mockings" (ch. 17:2).   **4.** Job's difficulty was not as to *man,* but as to *God,* why He so afflicted him, as if he were the guilty hypocrite which the friends alleged him to be.   Vulgate translates it, "my disputation."   **if it were**—rather, since this is the case.   **5. lay . . . hand upon . . . mouth**—(Prov. 30:32; Judg. 18:19).   So the heathen god of silence was pictured with his hand on his mouth.   There was enough in Job's case to awe them into silence (ch. 17:8).   **6. remember**—Think on it.   Can you wonder that I broke out into complaints, when the struggle was not with men, but with the Almighty?   Reconcile, if you can, the ceaseless woes of the innocent with the divine justice!   Is it not enough to make one tremble? [Umbreit].   **7.** The answer is Romans 2:4; I Timothy 1:16; Psalm 73:18; Ecclesiastes 8:11-13; Luke 2:35-end; Proverbs 16:4; Romans 9:22.   **old**—in opposition to the friends who asserted that sinners are "cut off" early (ch. 8:12, 14).   **8.** In opposition to ch. 18:19; 5:4.   **9.** Lit., "Peace from fear"; with poetic force.   Their house is *peace itself,* far removed from fear.   Opposed to the friends' assertion, as to the bad (ch. 15:21-24; 20:26-28), and conversely, the good (ch. 5:23, 24).   **10.** Rather, their cattle conceive.   The first clause of the verse describes an *easy conception,* the second, a happy *birth* [Umbreit].   **11.** "Send forth," viz., out of doors, to their happy sports under the skies, like a joyful flock sent to the pastures.   **little ones**—like lambkins.   **children**—somewhat older than the former.   **dance**—not formal dances; but skip, like lambs, in joyous and healthful play.   **12. take**—rather, *lift up the voice* (sing) to the note of [Umbreit].   **timbrel**—rather, tambourine.   **organ**—not the modern "organ," but the "pipe" (Gen. 4:21).   The first clause refers to stringed, the latter, to wind instruments; thus, with "the voice" all kinds of music are enumerated.   **13. wealth**—Old *English Version* for *prosperity.*   **in a moment**—not by a lingering disease.   Great blessings!   Lengthened life with prosperity, and a sudden painless death (Ps. 73:4).   **14. Therefore**—rather, *And yet* they are such as say, etc., i.e., say, not in so many words, but virtually, by their conduct (so the Gergesenes, Matt. 8:34).   How differently the godly (Isa. 2:3).   **ways**—The course of action, which God points out; as in Psalm 50:23; *Margin.*   **15.** (Cf. Jer. 2:20; *Margin;* Prov. 30:9; Exod. 5:2).   **what profit**—(ch. 35:3; Mal. 3:14; Ps. 73:13).   Sinners ask, not what is *right,* but what is for the *profit of self.*   They forget, "If religion cost self something, the want of it will cost self infinitely more."   **16. not in their hand**—but in the hand of God.   This is Job's difficulty, that God who has sinners' prosperity (good) in His hand should allow them to have it.   **is**—rather, "may the counsel of the wicked be far from me!" [Umbreit].   This naturally follows the sentiment of the first clause: Let me not hereby be thought to regard with aught but horror the ways of the wicked, however prosperous.   **17.** Job in this whole passage down to verse 21 quotes the assertion of the friends, as to the short continuance of the sinner's prosperity, not his own sentiments.   In verse 22 he proceeds to refute them.   "How oft is the candle" (lamp) etc., quoting Bildad's sentiment (ch. 18:5, 6), in order to question its truth (cf. Matt. 25:8).   **how oft**—"God distributeth," etc. (alluding to ch. 20:23, 29).   **sorrows**—Umbreit translates "snares," lit., "cords," which lightning in its twining motion resembles (Ps. 11:6).   **18.** Job alludes to a like sentiment of Bildad (ch. 18:18), using his own previous words (ch. 13:25). **19.** E-qually questionable is the friends' assertion that if the godless himself is not punished, the children are (ch. 18:19; 20:10); and that *God rewardeth him* here for his iniquity, and that *he shall know* it to his cost. So "know" (Hos. 9:7). **20.** Another questionable assertion of the friends, that the sinner sees his own and his children's destruction in his lifetime. **drink** –(Ps. 11:6; Isa. 51:17; Lam. 4:21.) **21.** The argument of the friends, in proof of vs. 20, What pleasure can he have from his house (children) when he is dead–("after him"; Eccles. 3:22). **when the number . . .**–(ch. 14:21). Or, rather, What hath he to do with his children, etc.? (so the *Hebrew* in Eccles. 3:1; 8:6). It is therefore necessary that "*his eyes should see* his and their destruction." **cut off**–rather, when the number of his *allotted* months is *fulfilled* (ch. 14:5). From an Arabic word, "arrow," which was used to draw lots with. Hence "arrow" –inevitable destiny [UMBREIT]. **22.** Reply of Job, "In all these assertions you try to teach God how He *ought* to deal with men, rather than prove that He does *in fact* so deal with them. Experience is against you. God gives prosperity and adversity as it pleases Him, not as man's wisdom would have it, on principles inscrutable to us" (Isa. 40:13; Rom. 11:34). **those . . . high**–the high ones, not only angels, but men (Isa. 2:12-17). **23.** Lit., in the bone of his perfection," i.e., the full strength of unimpaired prosperity [UMBREIT]. **24. breasts**–rather, skins, or vessels for fluids [LEE]. But [UMBREIT] "stations or resting-places of his herds near water"; in opposition to Zophar (ch. 20:17); the first clause refers to his abundant substance, the second to his vigorous health. **moistened**–comparing man's body to a well-watered field (Prov. 3:8; Isa. 58:11). **26.** (Eccles. 9:2.) **27.** Their wrongful thoughts against Job are stated by him in vs. 28. They do not honestly *name* Job, but *insinuate* his *guilt*. **28. ye say**–referring to Zophar (ch. 20:7). **the house**–referring to the fall of the *house* of Job's oldest son (ch. 1:19) and the destruction of his *family*. **prince** –The parallel "wicked" in the second clause requires this to be taken in a bad sense, *tyrant, oppressor* (Isa. 13:2), the same *Hebrew*, "nobles"–oppressors. **dwelling-places**–rather, pavilions, a tent containing many dwellings, such as a great emir, like Job, with many dependents, would have. **29.** Job, seeing that the friends will not admit him as an impartial judge, as they consider his calamities prove his guilt, begs them to ask the opinion of travellers (Lam. 1:12), who have the experience drawn from observation, and who are no way connected with him. Job opposes this to Bildad (ch. 8:8) and Zophar (ch. 20:4). **tokens**–rather, intimations (e.g., inscriptions, proverbs, signifying the results of their observation), testimony. Lit., "signs" or proofs in confirmation of the word spoken (Isa. 7:11). **30.** Their testimony (referring perhaps to those who had visited the region where Abraham who enjoyed a revelation then lived) is that "the wicked is (now) spared (reserved) against the day of destruction" (hereafter). The *Hebrew* does not so well agree with [UMBREIT] "in the day of destruction." Job does not deny sinners' *future* punishment, but their punishment *in this* life. They have their "good things" *now*. Hereafter, their lot, and that of the godly, shall be reversed (Luke 16:25). Job, by the Spirit, often utters truths which solve the difficulty under which he labored. His afflictions mostly clouded his faith, else he would have seen the solution furnished by his own words. This answers the objection, that if

he knew of the resurrection in ch. 19:25, and future retribution (ch. 21:30), why did he not draw his reasonings elsewhere from them, which he did not? God's righteous government, however, needs to be vindicated as to *this* life also, and therefore the Holy Ghost has caused the argument mainly to turn on it at the same time giving glimpses of a future fuller vindication of God's ways. **brought forth**–not "carried away safe" or "escape" (referring to *this life*), as UMBREIT has it. **wrath**–lit., "wraths," i.e., multiplied and fierce wrath. **31.** I.e., who dares to charge him openly with his bad ways? viz., in this present life. He shall, I grant (vs. 30), be "repaid" hereafter. **32. Yet**–rather, "and." **brought**–with solemn pomp (Ps. 45:15). **grave**–lit., "graves"; i.e., the place where the graves are. **remain in**–rather, *watch on* the tomb, or sepulchral mound. Even after death he seems still to live and watch (i.e., have his "remembrance" preserved) by means of the monument over the grave. In opposition to Bildad (ch. 18:17). **33.** As the classis saying has it, "The earth is light upon him." His repose shall be "sweet." **draw**–follow. He shall share the common lot of mortals; no worse off than they (Heb. 9:27). UMBREIT not so well (for it is not true of "*every* man"). "*Most* men follow in his bad steps, as countless such preceded him." **34. falsehood**–lit., "wickedness." **Your** boasted "consolations" (ch. 15:11) are contradicted by facts ("vain"); they therefore only betray your *evil intent* ("wickedness") against me.

CHAPTER 22

THIRD SERIES

Vss. 1-30. AS BEFORE, ELIPHAZ BEGINS. **1.** Eliphaz shows that man's goodness does not add to, or man's badness take from, the happiness of God; therefore it cannot be that God sends prosperity to some and calamities on others for His own advantage; the cause of the goods and ills sent must lie in the men themselves (Ps. 16:2; Luke 17:10; Acts 17: 25; I Chron. 29:14). So Job's calamities must arise from guilt. Eliphaz, instead of meeting the *facts*, tries to show that it *could not* be so. **2. as he that is wise**–rather, *yea* the *pious* man profiteth himself. So "understanding" or "wise"–*pious* (Dan. 12:3, 10; Ps. 14:2) [MICHAELIS]. **3. pleasure**–accession of happiness; God has pleasure in man's righteousness (Ps. 45:7), but He is not dependent on man's character for His happiness. **4.** Is the punishment inflicted on thee from fear of thee, in order to disarm thee? as Job had implied (*Notes*, 7:12, 20; 10:17). **will he enter . . . into judgment?**–Job had desired this (ch. 13:3, 21). He ought rather to have spoken as in Psalm 143:2. **5.** Heretofore Eliphaz had only insinuated, now he plainly asserts Job's guilt, merely on the ground of his sufferings. **6.** The crimes alleged, on a harsh inference, by Eliphaz against Job are such as he would think likely to be committed by a rich man. The Mosaic law (Exod. 22:26; Deut. 24:10) subsequently embodied the feeling that existed among the godly in Job's time against oppression of debtors as to their pledges. Here the case is not quite the same; Job is charged with taking a pledge where he had *no just claim to it;* and in the second clause, that pledge (the outer garment which served the poor as a covering by day and a bed by night) is represented as taken from one who had not "changes of raiment" (a common constituent of wealth in the East), but was poorly clad– "naked" (Matt. 25:36; Jas. 2:15); a sin the more heinous in a rich man like Job. **7.** Hospitality to the weary traveller is regarded in the East as a primary duty (Isa. 21:14). **8. mighty**—*Hebrew*, "man of *arm*" (Ps. 10:15; viz., Job). **honourable**—*Hebrew*, "accepted of countenance" (Isa. 3:3; II Kings 5:1); i.e., possessing authority. Eliphaz repeats his charge (ch. 15:28; so Zophar, ch. 20:19), that it was by violence Job wrung houses and lands from the poor, to whom now he refused relief (vss. 7, 9) [MICHAELIS]. **9. empty**—without their wants being relieved (Gen. 31:42). The Mosaic law especially protected the widow and fatherless (Exod. 22:22); the violation of it in their case by the great is a complaint of the prophets (Isa. 1:17). **arms**—supports, helps, on which one leans (Hos. 7:15). Thou hast robbed them of their only stay. Job replies in ch. 29:11-16. **10. snares**—alluding to Job's admission (ch. 19:6; cf. ch. 18:10; Prov. 22:5). **11. that**—so that thou. **abundance**—floods. Danger by floods is a less frequent image in this book than in the rest of the Old Testament (ch. 11:16; 27:20). **12.** Eliphaz says this to prove that God can from His height behold all things; gratuitously *inferring* that Job denied it, because he denied that the wicked are punished here. **height**—*Hebrew*, "head" i.e., elevation (ch. 11:8). **13.** Rather, *And yet* thou sayest, God does not *concern Himself with* ("know") human affairs (Ps. 73:11). **14.** "In the circuit of heaven" only, not taking any part in earthly affairs. Job is alleged as holding this Epicurean sentiment (Lam. 3:44; Isa. 29:15; 40:27; Jer. 23:24; Ezek. 8:12; Ps. 139:12). **15. marked**—Rather, Dost thou *keep to*? i.e., wish to follow (so *Hebrew*, II Sam. 22:22). If so, beware of sharing their end. **the old way**—the degenerate ways of the world before the flood (Gen. 6:5). **16. cut down**—rather, "fettered," as in ch. 16:8; i.e., arrested by death. **out of time**—prematurely, suddenly (ch. 15:32; Eccles. 7:17); lit., whose foundation was poured out (so as to become) a stream or flood. The solid earth passed from beneath their feet into a flood Gen. 7:11). **17.** Eliphaz designedly uses Job's own words (ch. 21:14,15). **do for them**—They think they can do everything for themselves. **18.** "Yet you say (ch. 21:16, see *Note*) that it is "*He* who filled their houses with good"— "their" "good is not in *their* hand," but comes from *God*. **but the counsel . . . is . . .**—rather, may the counsel be, etc. Eliphaz sarcastically quotes in continuation Job's words (ch. 21:16). Yet, after uttering this godless sentiment, thou dost hypocritically add, "May the counsel," etc. **19.** Triumph of the pious at the fall of the recent followers of the antediluvian sinners. While in the act of denying that God can do them any good or harm, they are cut off by Him. Eliphaz hereby justifies himself and the friends for their conduct to Job: not derision of the wretched, but joy at the vindication of God's ways (Ps. 107:42; Rev. 15:3; 16:7; 19:1, 2). **20.** The triumphant speech of the pious. If "substance" be retained, translate, rather as LXX, "Has not their substance been taken away, and . . . ? But the *Hebrew* is rather, "Truly our *adversary* is cut down" [GESENIUS]. The same opposition exists between the godly and ungodly seed as between the unfallen and restored Adam and Satan (*adversary*); this forms the groundwork of the book (chs. 1 and 2; Gen. 3: 15). **remnant**—all that "is left" of the sinner; repeated from 20:26, which makes UMBREIT'S rendering "glory" (*margin*), "excellency," less probable. **fire**—alluding to Job (ch. 1:16; 15:34; 18:15). First is mentioned destruction by *water* (vs. 16); here, by *fire* (II Pet. 3:5-7). **21.** Eliphaz takes it for granted, Job is not yet "acquainted" with God; lit., become a *companion* of God. Turn with familiar confidence to God. **and be**—*So* thou *shalt* be: the 2d *imperatively* expresses the consequence of obeying the 1st (Ps. 37:27). **peace**—prosperity and restoration to *Job*; true spiritually also to *us* (Rom. 5:1; Col. 1:20). **good**—(I Tim. 4:8). **22. lay up**—(Ps. 119:11). **23.** "Built up" anew, as a *restored* house. **thou shalt put away**—rather, If thou put away [MICHAELIS]. **24.** Rather, containing the protasis from the last clause of vs. 23, If thou exalt the glittering metal *as dust;* lit., "lay it on the dust"; to regard it of as little value as the dust on which it lies. The apodosis is at vs. 25, *Then* shall the Almighty be, etc. God will take the place of the wealth, in which thou didst formerly trust. **gold**—rather, "precious" or "glittering metal," parallel to "(gold) of Ophir," in the second clause [UMBREIT and MAURER]. **Ophir**—derived from a *Hebrew* word "dust," viz., gold dust. HEEREN thinks it a general name for the rich countries of the South, on the African, Indian, and especially the Arabian coast (where was the port Aphar. El Ophir, too, a city of Oman, was formerly the center of Arabian commerce). It is curious that the natives of Malacca still call their mines *Ophirs*. **stones of the brooks** —If thou dost let the gold of Ophir remain in its native valley among the stones of the brooks; i.e., regard it as of little worth as the stones, etc. The gold was washed down by mountain torrents and lodged among the stones and sand of the valley. **25.** Apodosis. **Yea**—rather, *Then* shall the Almighty be, etc. **defence**—rather, as the same *Hebrew* means in vs. 24 (see *Note*)—Thy *precious metals;* God will be to thee in the place of riches. **plenty of silver**—rather, "And shall be to thee in the place of *laboriously-obtained treasures* of silver" [GESENIUS]. Elegantly implying, it is less labor to find God than the hidden metals; at least to the humble seeker (ch. 28:12-28). But [MAURER] "the shining silver." **26. lift up . . . face**, etc.—repeated from Zophar (ch. 11:15). **27.** (Isa. 58:9, 14.) **pay thy vows** —which thou hast promised to God in the event of thy prayers being heard: God will give thee occasion to pay the former, by hearing the latter. **28. light**—success. **29.** Rather, When (thy ways; from vs. 28) are cast down (for a time), thou shalt (soon again have joyful cause to) say, There is lifting up (prosperity returns back to me) [MAURER]. **he**—God. **humble**—*Hebrew*, him that is of low eyes. Eliphaz implies that Job is not so now in his affliction; therefore it continues: with this he contrasts the blessed effect of being humble under it (Jas. 4:6, and I Pet. 5:5, probably quote this passage). Therefore it is better, I think, to take the first clause as referred to by "God resisteth the *proud.*" When (men) are cast down, thou shalt say (behold the effects of) *pride*. Eliphaz hereby justifies himself for attributing Job's calamities to his *pride*. "Giveth grace to the humble," answers to the second clause. **30. island**—i.e., dwelling. But the *Hebrew* expresses the *negative* (I Sam. 4:21); translate "Thus He (God) shall deliver him who was *not* guiltless," viz., one, who like Job himself on conversion shall be saved, but not because he was, as Job so constantly affirms of himself, guiltless, but because he *humbles* himself (vs. 29); an oblique attack on Job, even to the last. **and it**—Rather, "*he* (the *one* not heretofore guiltless) shall be delivered through the purity (acquired since conversion) of thy hands"; by thy intercession (as Gen. 18:26, etc.) [MAURER]. The irony is strikingly exhibited in Eliphaz unconsciously uttering words which exactly answer to what happened at last: he and the other two were "delivered" by God accepting the intercession of Job for them (ch. 42:7, 8).

CHAPTER 23

THIRD SERIES

Vss. 1-17. JOB'S ANSWER. **2. to-day**—implying, perhaps, that the debate was carried on through more days than one (see Introduction). **bitter**—(ch. 7:11; 10:1).—**my stroke**—the *hand* of God *on me* (*margin;* ch. 19:21; Ps. 32:4). **heavier than**—is so heavy that I cannot relieve myself adequately by groaning. **3.** The same wish as in ch. 13:3 (cf. Heb. 10:19-22). **Seat**—The idea in the *Hebrew* is *a well-prepared throne* (Ps. 9:7). **4. order**—state methodically (ch. 13:18; Isa. 43:26). **fill . . .**—I would have abundance of arguments to adduce. **5. he**—emphatic: it little matters what *man* may say of me, if only I know what *God* judges of me. **6.** An objection suggests itself, while he utters the wish (vs. 5). Do I hereby wish that He should plead against me with His omnipotence? Far from it! (ch. 9:19, 34; 13:21; 30:18). **strength**—so as to prevail with Him: as in Jacob's case (Hos. 12:3, 4). UMBREIT and MAURER better translate as in ch. 4:20 (I only wish that He) "would *attend* to me," i.e., give me a patient hearing as an ordinary judge, not using His omnipotence, but only His divine knowledge of my innocence. **7. There**—rather, Then: if God would "attend" to me (vs. 6). **righteous**—i.e., the result of my *dispute* would be, He would acknowledge me as *righteous.* **delivered**—from suspicion of guilt on the part of *my* Judge. **8.** But I wish in vain. For "behold," etc. **forward . . . backward**—rather, "to the east"—to the *west.*" The Hebrew geographers faced the east, i.e., sunrise: not the north, as we do. So "before" means east: "behind," west (so the Hindoos). *Para,* "before"—east: *Apara,* "behind" —west: *Daschina,* "the right hand"—south: *Bama,* "left"—north. A similar reference to sunrise appears in the name Asia, "sunrise," Europe, "sunset"; pure Babylonian names, as RAWLINSON shows. **9.** Rather, "To the north." **work**—God's glorious *works* are especially seen towards the north region of the sky by one in the northern hemisphere. The antithesis is between God *working* and yet *not* being *beheld:* as in ch. 9:11, between "He goeth by," and "I *see* Him *not.*" If the *Hebrew* bears it, the parallelism to the second clause is better suited by translating, as UMBREIT, "doth hide himself"; but then the antithesis to "behold" would be lost. **right hand** —"in the south." **hideth**—appropriately, of the unexplored south, then regarded as uninhabitable because of its heat (see ch. 34:29). **10. But**—correcting himself for the wish that his cause should be known before God. The omniscient One already *knoweth the way in me* (my *inward* principles: His *outward* way or course of acts is mentioned in vs. 11. So *in me,* ch. 4:21); though for some inscrutable cause He as yet hides Himself (vss. 8, 9). **when**—let Him only but try my cause, I shall, etc. **11. held**—fast by *His steps.* The law is in Old Testament poetry regarded as *a way,* God going before us as our guide, in whose footsteps we must tread (Ps. 17:5). **declined**—(Ps. 125:5). **12. esteemed**—rather, laid up, viz., as a treasure found (Matt. 13:44; Ps. 119:11); alluding to the words of Eliphaz (ch. 22:22). There was no need to tell me so; I have done so already (Jer. 15:16). **necessary** —"Appointed portion" (of food; as in Prov. 30:8). UMBREIT and MAURER translate, "More than my *law,*" my own will, in antithesis to "the words of His mouth" (John 6:38). Probably under the general term, "what is *appointed* to me" (the same *Hebrew* is in vs. 14), all that ministers to the ap-

petites of the body and carnal will is included. **13. in one mind**—notwithstanding my innocence, He is *unaltered* in His purpose of proving me guilty (ch. 9:12). **soul**—His *will* (Ps. 115:3). God's sovereignty. He has one great purpose; nothing is haphazard; everything has its proper place with a view to His purpose. **14. many such**—He has yet many more such ills in store for me, though hidden in His breast (ch. 10:13). **15.** God's decrees, impossible to be resisted, and leaving us in the dark as to what may come next, are calculated to fill the mind with holy awe [BARNES]. **16. soft**—faint; hath melted my courage. Here again Job's language is that of Jesus Christ (Ps. 22:14). **17.** Because I was not taken away by death from the evil to come (lit., "from before the face of the darkness," Isa. 57:1). Alluding to the words of Eliphaz (ch. 22:11), "darkness," i.e., calamity. "Cut off"; rather, in the *Arabic* sense, *brought to* the land of *silence;* my sad complaint hushed in death [UMBREIT]. "Darkness" in the second clause, not the same *Hebrew* word as in the first, "cloud," "obscurity." Instead of "covering the cloud (of evil) from my face," He "covers" me with it (ch. 22:11).

CHAPTER 24

Vss. 1-25. **1.** Why is it that, seeing that the times of punishment (Ezek. 30:3; "time" in the same sense) are not hidden from the Almighty, they who know Him (His true worshippers, ch. 18:21) do not see His days (of vengeance; Joel 1:15; II Pet. 3:10)? Or, with UMBREIT less simply, making the parallel clauses more nicely balanced, Why are not times of punishment hoarded up ("laid up"; ch. 21:19; *appointed*) by the Almighty? i.e., Why are they not so appointed as that man may now see them? as the second clause shows. Job does not doubt that they are appointed: nay, he asserts it (ch. 21:30); what he wishes is that God would let all now *see* that it is so. **2-24.** Instances of the wicked doing the worst deeds with seeming impunity. **Some**—the wicked. **landmarks**—boundaries between different pastures (Deut. 19:14; Prov. 22:28). **3. pledge**—alluding to ch. 22:6. Others really do, and with impunity, that which Eliphaz falsely charges the afflicted Job with. **4.** Lit., they push the poor out of their road in meeting them. Fig., they take advantage of them by force and injustice (alluding to the charge of Eliphaz (ch. 22:8; I Sam. 8:3). **poor**—in spirit and in circumstances (Matt. 5:3). **hide**—from the injustice of their oppressors, who have robbed them of their all and driven them into unfrequented places (ch. 20:19; 30:3-6; Prov. 28:28). **5. wild asses**—(ch. 11:12.) So Ishmael is called a wild ass-man; *Hebrew* (Gen. 16:12). These Bedouin robbers, with the unbridled wildness of the ass of the desert, go forth thither. Robbery is their lawless "work." The desert, which yields no food to other men, yields food for the robber and his children by the plunder of caravans. **rising betimes**—In the East travelling is begun very early, before the heat comes on. **6.** Like the wild asses (vs. 5), they (these Bedouin robbers) reap (metaphorically) their various grain (so the *Hebrew* for "corn" means). The wild ass does not let man pile his mixed provender up in a stable (Isa. 30:24); so these robbers find their food in the open air, at one time in the desert (vs. 5), at another in the fields. **the vintage of the wicked**—the vintage of robbery, not of honest industry. If we translate "belonging to the wicked," then it will imply that the wicked alone have vineyards, the "pious poor" (vs. 4) have none. "Gather" in *Hebrew,* is "gather late." As the first clause refers to the *early* harvest of corn, so the second to the vintage *late* in autumn. **7.** UMBREIT understands it of the Bedouin robbers, who are quite regardless of the comforts of life, "They pass the night naked, and uncovered," etc. But the allusion to ch. 22:6, makes the *English Version* preferable (see *Note* below, vs. 10). Frost is not uncommon at night in those regions (Gen. 31: 40). **8. They**—the plundered travellers. **embrace the rock**—take refuge under it (Lam. 4:5). **9. from the breast**—of the widowed mother. Kidnapping children for slaves. Here Job passes from wrongs in the desert to those done among the habitations of men. **pledge**—viz., the garment of the poor debtor, as next verse shows. **10.** (*Note,* ch. 22:6.) In vs. 7 a like sin is alluded to: but *there* he implies open **robbery of garments in the desert;** *here,* the more refined robbery in civilized life, under the name of a "pledge." Having stripped the poor, they make them besides labor in their harvest-fields and do not allow them to satisfy their hunger with any of the very corn which they carry to the heap. Worse treatment than that of the ox, according to Deut. 25:4. Translate: "they (the poor laborers) hungering carry the sheaves" [UMBREIT]. **11. Which**— "They," the poor, "press the oil within their wall"; viz., not only in the open fields (vs. 10), but also in the wall-enclosed vineyards and olive gardens of the oppressor (Isa. 5:5). Yet they are not allowed to quench their "thirst" with the grapes and olives. Here, *thirsty;* vs. 10, *hungry.* **12. Men**—rather, "mortals" (not the common *Hebrew* for "men"); so the Masoretic vowel points read as *English Version.* But the vowel points are modern. The true reading is, "The dying," answering to "the wounded" in the next clause, so *Syriac.* Not merely in the country (vs. 11), but also in the city there are oppressed sufferers, who cry for help in vain. "*From out* of the city;" i.e., they long to get forth and be free outside of it (Exod. 1:11; 2:23). **wounded**—by the oppressor (Ezek. 30:24). **layeth not folly**—takes no account of (by punishing) their *sin* ("folly" in Scripture; ch. 1:22). This is the gist of the whole previous list of sins (Acts 17:30). UMBREIT with *Syriac* reads by changing a vowel point, "Regards not their supplication." **13.** So far as to openly committed sins; now, those done in the dark. Translate: "There are those among them (the wicked) who rebel," etc. **light**—both literal and figurative (John 3:19, 20; Prov. 2:13). **paths thereof**—places where the light shines. **14. with the light**—at early dawn, while still dark, when the traveller in the East usually sets out, and the poor laborer to his work; the murderous robber lies in wait then (Ps. 10:8). **is as a thief**—*Thieves* in the East steal while men sleep at night; *robbers* murder at early dawn. The same man who steals at night, when light dawns not only robs, but murders to escape detection. **15.** (Prov. 7:9; Ps. 10:11.) **disguiseth**—puts a veil on. **16. dig through**—Houses in the East are generally built of sun-dried mud bricks (so Matt. 6:19). "Thieves break through," lit., "dig through" (Ezek. 12:7). **had marked**—Rather, as in ch. 9:7, "They shut themselves up (in their houses); lit., "they seal up." **for themselves**—for their own ends, viz., to escape detection. **know not**—shun. **17.** They shrink from the "morning" light, as much as other men do from *the blackest darkness* ("the shadow of *death*"). **if one know**—i.e., recognize them. Rather, "They know well (are familiar with) the terrors of," etc. [UMBREIT]. Or, as MAURER, "They know the terrors of (this) darkness," viz., of morning, the light,

which is as terrible to them as darkness ("the shadow of death") is to other men. **18-21.** In these verses Job quotes the opinions of his adversaries ironically; he quoted them so before. In vss. 22-24 he states his own observation as the opposite. You say, "The sinner is swift, i.e., swiftly passes away (as a thing floating) on the surface of the waters" (Eccles. 11:1; Hos. 10:7). **is cursed**—by those who witness their "swift" destruction. **beholdeth not**—"turneth not to"; figuratively, for He cannot enjoy his pleasant possessions (ch. 20:17; 15:33). **the way of the vineyards**—including his fields, fertile as vineyards; opposite to "the way of the desert. **19.** Arabian image; melted snow, as contrasted with the living fountain, quickly dries up in the sunburnt sand, not leaving a trace behind (ch. 6:16-18). The Hebrew is terse and elliptical to express the swift and utter destruction of the godless; (so) "the grave— they have sinned!" **20. The womb**—The very mother that bare him, and who is the last to "forget" the child that *sucked* her (Isa. 49:15), shall dismiss him from her memory (ch. 18:17; Prov. 10:7). The worm shall *suck,* i.e., "feed sweetly" on him as a delicate morsel (ch. 21:33). **wickedness**—i.e., the wicked; abstract for concrete (as ch. 5:16). **as a tree**—utterly (ch. 19:10); UMBREIT better, "as a staff." A broken staff is the emblem of irreparable ruin (Isa. 14:5; Hos. 4:12). **21.** The reason given by the friends why the sinner deserves such a fate. **barren**—without sons, who might have protected her. **widow**—without a husband to support her. **22-25.** Reply of Job to the opinion of the friends. Experience proves the contrary. Translate: "But He (God) prolongeth the life of (lit., draweth out at length; *Margin,* Ps. 36:10) the mighty with His (God's) power. He (the wicked) riseth up (from his sick bed) although he had given up hope of (lit., when he no longer believed in) life" (Deut. 28:66). **23.** Lit., "He (God omitted, as often; ch. 3:20; Eccles. 9:9; reverentially) giveth to him (the wicked, to be) in safety, or security." **yet**—Job means, How strange that God should so favor them, and yet have His eyes all the time open to their wicked ways (Prov. 15:3; Ps. 73:4)! **24.** Job repeats what he said (ch. 21:13), that sinners die in exalted positions, not the painful and lingering death we might expect, but a *quick and easy death.* Join "for a while" with "are gone," not as *English Version.* Translate: "A moment—and they are no more! They are brought low, as all (others) gather up their feet to die" (so the *Hebrew* of "are taken out of the way"). A natural death (Gen. 49:33). **ears of corn**—in a ripe and full age, not prematurely (ch. 5:26). **25.** (So ch. 9:24.)

CHAPTER 25

THIRD SERIES

Vss. 1-6. BILDAD'S REPLY. He tries to show Job's rashness (ch. 23:3), by arguments borrowed from Eliphaz (ch. 15:15), with which cf. ch. 11:17. **2.** Power and terror, i.e., terror-inspiring power. **peace in his high places**—implying that His power is such on high as to quell all opposition, not merely there, but on earth also. The Holy Ghost here shadowed forth Gospel truths (Col. 1:20; Eph. 1:10). **3. armies**—angels and stars (Isa. 40:26; Jer. 33:22; Gen. 15:5; countless, Dan. 7:10). **his light**—(Jas. 1:17). **4.** (ch. 4:17, 18; 14:4, 15:14.) **5.** "Look up even unto the moon" (ch. 15:15). "Stars" here answer to "saints" (angels) there; "the moon" here to "the heavens" there. Even the "stars," the most dazzling object to man's eye, and the angels, of which the stars are emblems (ch. 4:18; Rev. 9:1), are imperfect in His sight. Theirs is the light and purity but of creatures; His of the Creator. **6.** (ch. 4:19-21; 15:16). **worm . . . worm**—two distinct *Hebrew* words. The first, a worm bred in putridity; alluding to man's *corruption*. The second a crawling worm; implying that man is *weak and grovelling*.

CHAPTER 26

THIRD SERIES

Vss. 1-14. JOB'S REPLY. **2, 3. without power . . . no strength . . . no wisdom**—The negatives are used instead of the positives, *powerlessness*, etc., designedly (so Isa. 31:8; Deut. 32:21). Granting I am, as you say (ch. 18:17; 15:2), *powerlessness* itself, etc. *How hast thou helped* such a one? **savest**—supportest. **plentifully . . . the thing as it is**—rather, "abundantly—wisdom." Bildad had made great pretensions to abundant wisdom. How has he shown it? **4.** For whose instruction were thy words meant? If for me I know the subject (God's omnipotence) better than my instructor; vss. 5-14 is a sample of Job's knowledge of it. **whose spirit**—not that of God (ch. 32:8); nay, rather, the borrowed sentiment of Eliphaz (ch. 4:17-19; 15:14-16). **5-14.** As before in chs. 9 and 12, Job had shown himself not inferior to the friends' inability to describe God's greatness, so now he describes it as manifested in hell (the world of the dead), 5, 6; on earth, 7; in the sky, 8-11; the sea, 12; the heavens, 13. **Dead things are formed**—Rather, "The souls of the dead (Rephaim) tremble." Not only does God's power exist, as Bildad says (ch. 25:2), "in high places" (heaven), but reaches to the region of the dead. *Rephaim* here, and in Proverbs 21:16 and Isaiah 14:9, is from a *Hebrew* root, meaning "to be weak," hence "deceased"; in Genesis 14:5 it is applied to the Canaanite giants; perhaps in derision, to express their *weakness*, in spite of their gigantic size, as compared with Jehovah [UMBREIT]; or, as the imagination of the living magnifies apparitions, the term originally was applied to *ghosts*, and then to *giants* in general [MAGEE]. **from under**—UMBREIT joins this with the previous word tremble *from beneath* (so Isa. 14:9). But the Masoretic text joins it to "under the waters." Thus the place of the dead will be represented as "under the waters" (Ps. 18:4, 5); and the waters as under the earth (Ps. 24:2). MAGEE well translates thus: "The souls of the dead tremble; (the places) under the waters, and their inhabitants." Thus the Masoretic connection is retained; and at the same time the parallel clauses are evenly balanced. "The inhabitants of the places under the waters" are those in Gehenna, the lower of the two parts into which Sheol, according to the Jews, is divided; they answer to "destruction," i.e., the place of the wicked in vs. 6, as "Rephaim" (vs. 5) to "Hell" (Sheol) (vs. 6). Sheol comes from a *Hebrew* root—"ask," because it is insatiable (Prov. 27:20); or "ask as a loan to be returned," implying Sheol is but a *temporary* abode, previous to the resurrection; so for *English Version* "formed," LXX and *Chaldee* translate; *shall be born*, or *born again*, implying the dead are to be *given back* from Sheol and *born again into a new state* [MAGEE]. **6.**—(ch. 38:17; Ps. 139:8; Prov. 5:11). **destruction**—the abode of destruction, i.e., of lost souls. *Hebrew*, *Abaddon* (Rev. 9:11). **no covering**—from God's

eyes. **7.** Hint of the true theory of the earth. Its suspension in empty space is stated in the second clause. The north in particular is specified in the first, being believed to be the highest part of the earth (Isa. 14:13). The northern hemisphere or vault of *heaven* is included; often compared to a stretched-out canopy (Ps. 104:2). The chambers of the south are mentioned (ch. 9:9), i.e., the southern hemisphere, consistently with the earth's globular form. **8. in . . . clouds**—as if in airy vessels, which, though light, do not burst with the weight of water in them (Prov. 30:4). **9.** Rather, He *encompasseth* or *closeth*. God makes the clouds a veil to screen the glory not ony of His person, but even of the exterior of His throne from profane eyes. His agency is everywhere, yet He Himself is invisible (Ps. 18:11; 104:3). **10.** Rather, "He hath drawn a circular bound round the waters" (Prov. 8:27; Ps. 104:9). The horizon seems a circle. Indication is given of the globular form of the earth. **until the day . . .**—to the confines of light and darkness. When the light falls on our horizon, the other hemisphere is dark. UMBREIT and MAURER translate "He has *most perfectly* (lit., "to perfection") drawn the bound (taken from the first clause) between light and darkness" (cf. Gen. 1:4, 6, 9): where the bounding of the light from darkness is similarly brought into proximity with the bounding of the waters. **11. pillars**—poetically for the mountains which seem to bear up the sky (Ps. 104:32). **astonished**—viz., from terror. Personification. **his reproof**—(Ps. 104:7). The thunder, reverberating from cliff to cliff (Hab. 3:10; Nahum 1:5). **12. divideth**—(Psalm 74:13). Perhaps at creation (Gen. 1:9, 10). The parallel clause favors UMBREIT, "He stilleth." But the *Hebrew* means "He moves." Probably such a "moving" is meant as that at the assuaging of the flood by the wind which "God made to pass over" it (Gen. 8:1; Ps. 104:7). **the proud** —rather, its pride, viz., of the sea (ch. 9:13). **13.** UMBREIT less simply, "By His breath He maketh the heavens to revive": viz., His wind dissipates the clouds, which obscured the shining stars. And so the next clause in contrast, "His hand doth strangle," i.e., obscures the north constellation, the dragon. Pagan astronomy typified the flood trying to destroy the ark by the dragon constellation, about to devour the moon in its eclipsed crescent-shape like a boat (ch. 3:8, *Margin*). But better as *English Version* (Ps. 33:6). **crooked**—implying the oblique course, of the stars, or the ecliptic. "Fleeing" or "swift" [UMBREIT] (Isa. 27:1). This particular constellation is made to represent the splendor of all the stars. **14. parts**—Rather, "only the extreme boundaries of, etc., and how faint is the whisper that we hear of Him!" **thunder**—the entire fulness. In antithesis to "whisper" (I Cor. 13:9, 10, 12).

CHAPTER 27

Vss. 1-23. It was now Zophar's turn to speak. But as he and the other two were silent, virtually admitting defeat, after a pause Job proceeds. **1. parable**—applied in the East to a figurative sententious embodiment of wisdom in poetic form, a gnome (Ps. 49:4). **continued**—proceeded to put forth: implying elevation of discourse. **2.** (I Sam. 20:3.) **taken away . . . judgment**—words unconsciously foreshadowing Jesus Christ (Isa. 53:8; Acts 8:33). God will not give Job his right, by declaring his innocence. **vexed**—*Hebrew*, "made bitter" (Ruth 1:20). **3.** Implying Job's knowledge of the

fact that the living soul was breathed into man by
God (Gen. 2:7). "All the while." But MAURER,
"As yet all my breath is in me" (notwithstanding my
trials): the reason why I can speak so boldly. **4.**
(Ch. 6:28, 30). The "deceit" would be if he were
to admit guilt against the witness of his conscience.
5. justify you—approve of your views. **mine integrity**—which you deny, on account of my misfortunes. **6.** Rather, my "heart" (conscience) reproaches "not one of my days," i.e., I do not repent
of any of my days since I came into existence
[MAURER]. **7. Let . . . be**—Let mine enemy be accounted as wicked, i.e., He who opposes my asseveration of innocence must be regarded as actuated by criminal hostility. Not a curse on his
enemies. **8.** "What hope hath the hypocrite, notwithstanding all his gains, when?" etc. "Gained"
is antithetic to "taketh away." UMBREIT's translation is an unmeaning tautology. "When God cuts
off, when He *taketh away* his life." **taketh away**—
lit., "draws out" the soul from the body, which is,
as it were, its scabbard (ch. 4:21; Ps. 104:29; Dan.
7:15). Job says that he admits what Bildad said
(ch. 8:13) and Zophar (ch. 20:5). But he says the
very fact of his still calling upon God (vs. 10) amid
all his trials, which a hypocrite would not dare to
do, shows he is no "hypocrite." **9.** (Ps. 66:18.) **10.**
Alluding to ch. 22:26. **always call**—He may do so
in times of prosperity in order to be thought religious. But he will not, as I do, call on God in calamities verging on death. Therefore I cannot be a
"hypocrite" (ch. 19:25; 20:5; Ps. 62:8). **11-23.**
These words are contrary to Job's previous sentiments (*Notes,* ch. 21:22-33; 24:22-25). They therefore seem to be Job's statement, not so much of his
own sentiments, as of what Zophar would have said
had he spoken when his turn came (end of ch. 26).
So Job stated the friends' opinion (ch. 21:17-21;
24:18-21). The objection is, why, if so, does not
Job answer Zophar's opinion, as stated by himself?
The fact is, it is probable that Job tacitly, by giving,
in ch. 28, only a general answer, implies, that in
spite of the wicked *often* dying, as he said, in
prosperity, he does not mean to deny that the wicked
are *in the main* dealt with according to right, and
that God herein vindicates His moral government
even here. Job therefore states Zophar's argument
more strongly than Zophar would have done. But
by comparing vs. 13 with ch. 20:29 ("portion,"
"heritage"), it will be seen, it is Zophar's argument,
rather than his own, that Job states. Granting it to
be true, implies Job, you ought not to use it as an
argument to criminate *me.* For (ch. 28) the ways of
divine wisdom in afflicting the godly are inscrutable:
all that is sure to man is, the fear of the Lord is
wisdom (vs. 28). **by the hand**—rather, *concerning*
the hand of God, viz., what God does in governing
men. **with the Almighty**—the counsel or principle
which regulates God's dealings. **12.** "Ye yourselves see" that the wicked *often* are afflicted (though
often the reverse, ch. 21:33). But do you "vainly"
make this an argument to prove from my afflictions
that I am wicked? **13.** (*Note,* vs. 11.) **14.** His
family only increases to perish by sword or famine
(Jer. 18:21; ch. 5:20, the converse). **15.** Those that
escape war and famine (vs. 14) shall be buried by *the
deadly plague*—"death" (ch. 18:13; Jer. 15:2; Rev.
6:8). The plague of the Middle Ages was called
"the black death." *Buried by* it implies that they
would have none else but the death plague itself
(poetically personified) to perform their funeral
rites, i.e., would have no one. **his**—rather, their
widows. Transitions from *singular* to *plural* are

frequent. Polygamy is not implied. **16. dust . . .
clay**—images of multitudes (Zech. 9:3). Many
changes of raiment are a chief constituent of wealth
in the East. **17.** Introverted parallelism. (See my
introduction). Of the four clauses in the two verses,
1 answers to 4, 2 to 3 (so Matt. 7:6). **18.** (Ch. 8:14;
4:19.) The transition is natural from "raiment" (vs.
16) to the "house" of the "moth" in it, and of it,
when in its larva state. The *moth worm's house* is
broken whenever the "raiment" is shaken out, so
frail is it. **booth**—a bough-formed hut which the
guard of a vineyard raises for temporary shelter
(Isa. 1:8). **19. gathered**—buried honorably (Gen.
25:8; II Kings 22:20). But UMBREIT, agreeably to
vs. 18, which describes *the short continuance of the
sinner's prosperity,* "He layeth himself rich in his
bed, *and nothing is robbed from him,* he openeth his
eyes, and *nothing more is there.*" If *English Version* be retained, the first clause probably means,
rich though he be in *dying,* he shall not be honored
with a *funeral;* the second, When he opens his eyes
in the unseen world, it is only to see *his destruction:*
LXX reads for "not gathered," *He does not proceed,*
i.e., goes to his bed no more. So MAURER. **20.**
(Ch. 18:11; 22:11, 21.) Like a sudden violent flood
(Isa. 8:7, 8; Jer. 47:2): conversely (Ps. 32:6). **21.**
(Ch. 21:18; 15:2; Ps. 58:9.) **22. cast**—viz., thunderbolts (ch. 6:4; 7:20; 16:13; Ps. 7:12, 13). **23. clap
. . . hands**—for joy at his downfall (Lam. 2:15; Nah.
3:19). **hiss**—deride (Jer. 25:9). Job alludes to
Bildad's words (ch. 18:18).

CHAPTER 28

Vss. 1-28. JOB'S SPEECH CONTINUED. In ch. 27
Job had tacitly admitted that the statement of the
friends was often true, that God vindicated His
justice by punishing the wicked here; but still the
affliction of the godly remained unexplained. Man
has, by skill, brought the precious metals from their
concealment. But the Divine Wisdom, which
governs human affairs, he cannot similarly discover
(vs. 12, etc.). However, the image from the same
metals (ch. 23:10) implies Job has made some way
towards solving the riddle of his life; viz., that affliction is to him as the refining fire is to gold. **1. vein**
—a mine, from which it *goes forth, Hebrew,* is dug.
place for gold—a place where gold may be found,
which men refine. Not as English Version, "A
place—*where,*" (Mal. 3:3). Contrasted with gold
found in the bed and sand of rivers, which does not
need refining; as the gold *dug from a mine* does.
Golden ornaments have been found in Egypt, of the
times of Joseph. **2. brass**—i.e., copper; for brass is
a mixed metal of copper and zinc, of modern invention. Iron is less easily discovered, and
wrought, than copper; therefore copper was in common use long before iron. Copper-stone is called
"cadmium" by PLINY [NATURAL HISTORY 34:1; 36:
21]. Iron is fitly said to be taken out of the "earth"
(dust), for ore looks like mere earth. **3.** "Man
makes an end of darkness," by exploring the darkest
depths (with torches). **all perfection**—rather, carries out his search to the utmost perfection; most
thoroughly searches the stones of darkness and of
the shadow of death (thickest gloom); i.e., the stones,
whatever they be, embedded in the darkest bowels
of the earth [UMBREIT] (ch. 26:10). **4.** Three hardships in mining: 1. "A stream (flood) breaks out at
the side of the stranger"; viz., *the miner, a strange
newcomer* into places heretofore unexplored; his
surprise at the sudden stream breaking out *beside*

him is expressed (*English Version,* "from the inhabitant"); 2. "Forgotten (unsupported) by the foot they *hang,*" viz., by ropes, in descending. In the *Hebrew,* "Lo there" precedes this clause, graphically placing it as if before the eyes. "The waters" is inserted by *English Version.* "Are dried up," ought to be, "hang," "are suspended." *English Version* perhaps understood, waters of whose existence man was previously *unconscious,* and near which he *never trod;* and yet man's energy is such, that by pumps, etc., he soon causes them to "dry up and go away" [So HERDER]. 3. "Far away from men, they move with uncertain step"; they stagger; not "they are gone" [UMBREIT]. 5. Its fertile surface yields food; and yet "beneath it is turned up as it were with fire." So PLINY [NATURAL HISTORY, 33] observes on the ingratitude of man who repays the debt he owes the earth for food, by digging out its bowels. "Fire" was used in mining [UMBREIT]. *English Version* is simpler, which means precious stones which glow *like fire;* and so vs. 6 follows naturally (Ezek. 28:14). 6. Sapphires are found in alluvial soil near rocks and embedded in gneiss. The ancients distinguished two kinds: 1. The real, of transparent blue: 2. That improperly so called, opaque, with gold spots; i.e., lapis lazuli. To the latter, looking like gold dust, UMBREIT refers "dust of gold." *English Version* better, "The *stones* of the earth are, etc., and the *clods* of it (*Vulgate*) are gold"; the parallel clauses are thus neater. 7. **fowl** —rather, "ravenous bird," or "eagle," which is the most sharp-sighted of birds (Isa. 46:11). A vulture will spy a carcass at an amazing distance. The miner penetrates the earth by a way unseen by birds of keenest sight. 8. **lion's whelps**—lit., "the sons of pride," i.e., the fiercest beasts. **passed**—The *Hebrew* implies *the proud gait* of the lion. The miner ventures where not even the fierce lion dares to go in pursuit of his prey. 9. **rock**—flint. He puts forth his hand to cleave the *hardest rock.* **by the roots**— from their foundations, by undermining them. 10. *He cuts* channels to drain off the waters, which hinder his mining; and when the waters are gone, he is able to *see the precious things* in the earth. 11. **floods**—"He restrains *the streams* from *weeping*"; a poetical expression for the *trickling* subterranean *rills,* which impede him; answering to the first clause of vs. 10; so also the two latter clauses in each verse correspond. 12. Can man discover the Divine Wisdom by which the world is governed, as he can the treasures hidden in the earth? Certainly not. Divine Wisdom is conceived as a person (vss. 12-27) distinct from God (vs. 23; also in Prov. 8:23, 27). The Almighty Word, Jesus Christ, *we* know now, is that Wisdom. The order of the world was originated and is maintained by the breathing forth (Spirit) of Wisdom, unfathomable and unpurchasable by man. In verse 28, the only aspect of it, which relates to, and may be understood by, *man,* is stated. **understanding**—insight into the plan of the divine government. 13. Man can fix no price upon it, as it is nowhere to be found in man's abode (Isa. 38:11). Job implies both its valuable worth, and the impossibility of buying it at any price. 15. Not the usual word for "gold"; from *a Hebrew* root, "to shut up" with care; i.e., purest gold (I Kings 6:20, *Margin*). **weighed**—The precious metals were *weighed* out before coining was known (Gen. 23:16). 16. **gold of Ophir**—the most precious (*Note,* 22:24; Ps. 45:9). **onyx**—(Gen. 2:12.) More valued formerly than now. The term is Greek, meaning "thumb nail," from some resemblance in color. The *Arabic* denotes, of two colors, white preponderating. 17. **crystal**—Or else glass, if then known, very costly. From a root, "to be transparent." **jewels**—rather, vessels. 18. Red coral (Ezek. 27: 16). 18. **pearls**—lit., "what is frozen." Probably *crystal;* and vs. 17 will then be *glass.* **rubies**— UMBREIT translates "pearls" (see Lam. 4:1; Prov. 3: 15). The Urim and Thummim, the means of consulting God by the twelve stones on the high priest's breastplate, "the stones of the sanctuary" (Lam. 4:1), have their counterpart in this chapter; the precious stones symbolizing the "light" and "perfection" of the divine wisdom. 19. **Ethiopia**—*Cush* in the *Hebrew.* Either Ethiopia, or the south of Arabia, near the Tigris. 20. Verse 12 repeated with great force. 21. None can tell *whence* or *where, seeing* it, etc. **fowls**—The gift of divination was assigned by the heathen especially to birds. Their rapid flight heavenwards and keen sight originated the superstition. Job may allude to it. Not even the boasted divination of birds has an insight into it (Eccles. 10:20). But it may merely mean, as in vs. 7, It escapes the eye of the most keen-sighted bird. 22.—I.e., the abodes of *destruction* and of the *dead.* "Death" put for Sheol (ch. 30:23; 26:6, *Note;* Ps. 9: 13). **We have** [only] **heard**—the report of her. We have not *seen* her. In the land of the living (**vs.** 13) the workings of Wisdom are seen, though not herself. In the regions of the dead she is only *heard* of, her actings on nature not being seen (Eccles. 9:10). 23. God hath, and is Himself, wisdom. 24. "Seeth (all that is) under," etc. 25. God has adjusted the weight of the winds, so seemingly imponderable, lest, if too weighty, or too light, injury should be caused. He measureth out the waters, fixing their bounds, with wisdom as His counsellor (Prov. 8:27-31; Isa. 40:12). 26. The decree regulating at what time and place, and in what quantity, the rain should fall. **a way**—through the parted clouds (ch. 38:25; Zech. 10:1). 27. **declare**—manifest her, viz., in His works (Ps. 19:1, 2). So the approval bestowed by the Creator on His works (Gen. 1:10, 31); cf. the "rejoicing" of wisdom at the same (Prov. 8:30; which UMBREIT translates; "I was the skilful artificer by His side"). **prepared**—not *created,* for wisdom is from everlasting (Prov. 8); but "established" her as Governor of the world. **searched . . . out**—examined her works to see whether she was adequate to the task of governing the world [MAURER]. 28. Rather, *But* unto man, etc., *My* wisdom is that whereby all things are governed; *Thy* wisdom is *in fearing God and shunning evil,* and in feeling assured that My wisdom always acts aright, though thou dost not understand the principle which regulates it; e.g., in afflicting the godly (John 7:17). The friends, therefore, as not comprehending the Divine Wisdom, should not infer Job's guilt from his sufferings. Here alone in Job the name of God, *Adonai,* occurs; "Lord" or "master," often applied to Messiah in Old Testament. Appropriately here, in speaking of the Word or Wisdom, by whom the world was made (Prov. 8; John 1; Eccles. 24).

CHAPTER 29

Vss. 1-25. 1. Job pauses for a reply. None being made, he proceeds to illustrate the mysteriousness of God's dealings, as set forth (ch. 28) by his own case. 2. **preserved me**—from calamity. 3. **candle**—when His favor shone on me (*Note,* 18:6; Ps. 18:28). **darkness**—By His safeguard I passed secure through *dangers.* Perhaps alluding to the lights carried before caravans in nightly travels through deserts [Noyes]. **4. youth**—lit., "autumn"; the time of the ripe fruits of my prosperity. Applied to *youth,* as the Orientalists *began* their year with autumn, the most temperate season in the East. **secret**—when the intimate friendship of God rested on my tent (Prov. 3:32; Ps. 31:20; Gen. 18:17; John 15:15). The *Hebrew* often means a *divan for deliberation.* **6. butter**—rather, "cream," lit., "thick milk." Wherever I turned my steps, the richest milk and oil flowed in to me abundantly. Image from pastoral life. Literal *washing of the feet in milk* is not meant, as the second clause shows; *Margin,* "with me," i.e., "near" my path, wherever I walked (Deut. 32:13). Olives amidst *rocks* yield the best oil. Oil in the East is used for food, light, anointing, and medicine. **7-10.** The great influence Job had over young and old, and noblemen. **through . . . street**—rather, When I went out of my house, in the country (see ch. 1, prologue) to the gate (ascending), *up* to the city (which was on elevated ground), and when I prepared my (judicial) seat in *the market place.* The market place was the place of judgment, at the gate or propylæa of the city, such as is found in the remains of Nineveh and Persepolis (Isa. 59:14; Ps. 55:11; 127:5). **8. hid**—not lit.; rather, *stepped backwards,* reverentially. *The aged,* who were already seated, *arose and remained standing (Hebrew)* until Job seated himself. Oriental manners. **9.** (Ch. 4:2; *Note,* 21:5.) **Refrained**—stopped in the middle of their speech. **10.** *Margin,* "voice–hid," i.e., "hushed" (Ezek. 3:26). **Tongue cleaved . . .** i.e., awed by my presence, the emirs or sheiks were silent. **11. blessed**—extolled my virtues (Prov. 31:28). Omit "me" after "heard"; whoever *heard of* me (in general, not in the market place, 7-10) praised me. **gave witness** —to my honorable character. Image from a court of justice (Luke 4:22). "The eye"—i.e., "face to face"; antithesis to "ear"—i.e., report of me. **12-17.** The grounds on which Job was praised (vs. 11), his helping the afflicted (Ps. 72:12) who cried to him for help, as a judge, or as one possessed of means of charity. Translate; The fatherless who had none to help him. **13.** So far was I from sending "widows" away empty (ch. 22:9). **ready to perish** —(Prov. 31:6.) **14.** (Isa. 61:10; I Chron. 12:18.) **judgment**—justice. **diadem**—tiara. Rather, turban, head-dress. It and the full flowing outer mantle or "robe," are the prominent characteristics of an Oriental grandee's or high priest's dress (Zech. 3:5). So Job's righteousness especially characterized him. **15.** Lit., "the blind" (Deut. 27:18); "lame" (II Sam. 9:13); fig., also the spiritual support which the more enlightened gives to those less so (ch. 4:3; Heb. 12:13; Num. 10:31). **16.** So far was I from "breaking the arms of the *fatherless*," as Eliphaz asserts (ch. 22:9), I was a "father" to such. **the cause which I knew not**—rather—"of him whom I knew not," the stranger (Prov. 29:7 [Umbreit]; contrast Luke 18:1, etc.). Applicable to almsgiving (Ps. 41:1); but here primarily, judicial conscientiousness (ch. 31:13). **17.** Image from combating with wild beasts (ch. 4:11; Ps. 3:7). So compassionate was Job to the oppressed, so terrible to the oppressor! **jaws**—Job broke *his power,* so that he could do no more hurt, and tore from him the spoil, which he had torn from others. **18. I said**—in my heart (Ps. 30:6). **in**— rather, "*with* my nest"; as the second clause refers to long life. Instead of my family dying before me, as now, I shall live so long as to die with them: proverbial for long life. Job did realize his hope (ch. 42:16). However, *in* the bosom of my family, gives a good sense (Num. 24:21; Obad. 4). Use

"nest" for a *secure dwelling.* **sand**—(Gen. 22:17; Hab. 1:9). But LXX and Vulgate, and Jewish interpreters, favor the translation, "the phœnix bird." "Nest" in the parallel clause supports the reference to a bird. "Sand" for *multitude,* applies to men, rather than to *years.* The myth was, that the phœnix sprang from a nest of myrrh, made by his father before death, and that he then came from Arabia (Job's country) to Heliopolis (the city of the Sun) in Egypt, once in every 500 years, and there burnt his father [Herodotus, 2:73]. Modern research has shown that this was the Egyptian mode of representing hieroglyphically a particular chronological era or cycle. The death and revival every 500 years, and the reference to *the sun,* implies such a grand cycle commencing afresh from the same point in relation to the sun from which the previous one started. Job probably refers to this. **19.** Lit., "opened to the waters." Opposed to ch. 18:16. Vigorous health. **20.** My renown, like my bodily health, was continually fresh. **bow**—Metaphor from war, for, *my strength,* which gains me "renown," was ever renewed (Jer. 49:35). **21.** Job reverts with peculiar pleasure to his former dignity in assemblies (vss. 7-10). **22. not again**—did not contradict me. **dropped**—affected their minds, as the genial rain does the soil on which it gently drops (Amos 7:16; Deut. 32:2; Song of Sol. 4:11). **23.** Image of vs. 22 continued. They waited for my salutary counsel, as the dry soil does for the refreshing rain. **opened . . . mouth**—*panted for;* Oriental image (Ps. 119:131). The "early rain" is in autumn and onwards, while the seed is being sown. The "latter rain" is in March, and brings forward the harvest, which ripens in May or June. Between the early and latter rains, some rain falls, but not in such quantities as those rains. Between March and October no rain falls (Deut. 11:14; Jas. 5:7). **24.** When I relaxed from my wonted gravity (a virtue much esteemed in the East) and smiled, they could hardly credit it; and yet, notwithstanding my condescension, *they did not cast aside reverence* for *my gravity.* But the parallelism is better in Umbreit's translation, "I smiled kindly on those who trusted not," i.e., in times of danger I cheered those in despondency. And they could not cast down (by their despondency) my *serenity of countenance* (flowing from trust in God) (Prov. 16:15; Ps. 104: 15). The opposite phrase (Gen. 4:5, 6). "Gravity" cannot well be meant by "light of countenance." **25. I chose out their way**—i.e., I willingly went up to their assembly (from my country residence, vs. 7). **in the army**—as a king supreme in the midst of his army. **comforteth the mourners**—Here again Job unconsciously foreshadows Jesus Christ (Isa. 61:2, 3). Job's afflictions, as those of Jesus Christ, were fitting him for the office hereafter (Isa. 50:4; Heb. 2:18).

CHAPTER 30

Vss. 1-31. **1. younger**—not the three friends (ch. 15:10; 32:4, 6, 7). A general description: 1-8, the lowness of the persons who derided him; 9-15, the derision itself. Formerly old men rose to me (ch. 29:8). Now not only my *juniors,* who are bound to reverence me (Lev. 19:32), but even the mean and *base-born* actually *deride* me; opposed to, "smiled upon" (ch. 29:24). This goes farther than even the "mockery" of Job by *relations* and *friends* (ch. 12:4; 16:10, 20; 17:2, 6; 19:22). Orientals feel keenly any indignity shown by the young. Job speaks as ɔack in deference to the seniority of the friends *spoke.* **6. was afraid**–The root meaning in *ew is* "to crawl" (Deut. 32:24). **7. Days**–i.e., ged (ch. 15:10). **8.** Elihu claims inspiration, as inely commissioned messenger to Job (ch. 33:); and that claim is not contradicted in ch. 42. slate: "But the spirit (which God puts) in man, the inspiration . . ., is that which giveth . . ."; not mere "years" which give understanding . 2:6; John 20:22). **9. Great**–rather, old (vs. So *Hebrew,* in Gen. 25:23. "Greater, less" *the older, the younger.* **judgment**–what is **10.** Rather, I say. **opinion**–rather, knowl- **11.** Therefore Elihu was present from the **reasons**–lit., "understandings," i.e., the mean- ntended by words. **whilst**–I waited *until* you ld discover a suitable reply to Job. **13.** This been so ordered, "lest you should" pride your- s on having overcome him by your "wisdom" 9:23, the great aim of the Book of Job); and you may see, "God alone can thrust him down," confute him, "not man." So Elihu grounds his utation, not on the maxims of sages, as the nds did, but on his special commission from (vs. 8; ch. 33:4, 6). **14.** I am altogether un- udiced. For it is not I, whom he addressed. our speeches" have been influenced by irritation. Here Elihu turns from the friends to Job: and passes from the second person to the third; a sition frequent in a rebuke (ch. 18:3, 4). **they off**–Words were taken from them. **17. my** –for my part. **opinion**–knowledge. **18.** "I full of words," whereas the friends have not a d more to say. **the spirit**–(vs. 8; ch. 33:4; Jer. 9; Acts 18:5). **19. belly**–bosom: from which the rds of Orientalists in speaking seem to come re than with us; they speak gutturally. "Like w) wine (in fermentation) without a vent," to rk itself off. *New* wine is kept in new goatskin ttles. This fittingly applies to the *young* Elihu, contrasted with the *old* friends (Matt. 9:7). **20. freshed**–lit., "that there may be air to me" (I Sam. :23). **21.** "May I never accept. . . ." Elihu al- des to Job's words (ch. 13:8, 10), wherein he com- ains that the friends plead for God partially, "ac- pting His person." Elihu says he will not do so, t will act impartially between God and Job. And I will not give flattery . . . ." (Prov. 24:23). **. take me away**–as a punishment (Ps. 102:24).

CHAPTER 33

Vss. 1-33. ADDRESS TO JOB, AS (ch. 32) TO THE RIENDS. **2. mouth**–rather, "palate," whereby the aste *discerns.* Every man speaks with his mouth, ut few, as Elihu, *try* their words *with discrimina- ion* first, and only say what is really good (ch. 6:30; 2:11). **hath spoken**–rather, "proceeds to speak." . I will speak according to my inward conviction. **learly**–rather, "purely"; sincerely, not distorting he truth through passion, as the friends did. **4.** "The Spirit of God hath made me," as He did thee: latter clause of vs. 6 (Gen. 2:7). Therefore thou needest not fear me, as thou wouldest God (vs. 7; ch. 9:34). On the other hand, "the breath of the Almighty hath *inspired* me" (as ch. 32:8); not as *English Version,* "given me life"; therefore "I am according to thy wish (ch. 9:32, 33) in God's stead" to thee; a "daysman," umpire, or mediator, between God and thee. So Elihu was designed by the Holy Ghost to be a type of Jesus Christ (vss. 23-26). **5.** Images from a court of justice. **stand up**–alluding to Job's words (ch. 30:20). **6.** Note (vs. 4; ch. 31: 35; 13:3, 20, 21). **formed**–Though acting as God's representative, I am but a creature, like thyself. *Arabic,* "pressed together," as a mass of clay by the potter, in forming a vessel [UMBREIT]. *Hebrew* "cut off," as the portion taken from the clay to form it [MAURER]. **7. hand**–alluding to Job's words (ch. 13:21). **8. thy words**–(ch. 10:7; 16:17; 23:11, 12; 27:5, 6; 29:14). In ch. 9:30; 13:23, Job had acknowledged sin; but the general *spirit* of his words was to maintain himself to be "clean," and to charge God with injustice. He went too far on the opposite side in opposing the friends' false charge of hypocrisy. Even the godly, though willing to con- fess themselves sinners in *general,* often dislike sin in particular to be brought as a charge against them. Affliction is therefore needed to bring them to feel that sin *in them* deserves even worse than they suffer and that God does them no injustice. Then at last humbled under God they find, *affliction is for their real good,* and so at last it is taken away either here, or at least at death. To teach this is Elihu's mission. **9. clean**–spotless. **10. occasions**–for hostility: lit., "enmities" (ch. 13:24; 16:9; 19:11; 30:21). **11.** (Ch. 13:27.) **marketh**–narrowly watches (ch. 14:16; 7: 12; 31:4). **12. in this**–view of God and His govern- ment. It cannot be that God should jealously "watch" man, though "spotless," as an "enemy," or as one afraid of him as an equal. For "God is greater than man!" There must be sin in man, even though he be no hypocrite, which needs correction by suffering for the sufferer's good. **13.** (Isa. 45: 9.) **his matters**–ways. Our part is, not to "strive" with God, but to *submit.* To believe it is right be- cause He does it, not because *we see all the reasons* for His doing it. **14.** Translate, "Yet, man *regardeth* it not"; or rather, as UMBREIT, "Yea, twice (He repeats the warning)–if man gives no heed" to the first warning. Elihu implies that God's reason for sending affliction is because, when God has com- municated His will in various ways, man in pros- perity has not heeded it; God therefore must try what affliction will effect (John 15:2; Ps. 62:11; Isa. 28:10, 13). **15. slumberings**–light is opposed to "deep sleep." Elihu has in view Eliphaz (ch. 4:13), and also Job himself (ch. 7:14). "Dreams" in sleep, and "visions" of actual apparitions, were among the ways whereby God then spake to man (Gen. 20:3). **16. Lit.,** "sealeth (their ears) to Himself by warnings," i.e., with the sureness and secrecy of a seal He reveals His warnings [UMBREIT]. To seal up securely (ch. 37:7). On the "openeth," see ch. 36: 10. **17. purpose**–Margin, "work." So ch. 36:9. So "business" in a bad sense (I Sam. 20:19). Elihu alludes to Job's words (ch. 17:11). "Pride" is an open "pit" (vs. 18) which God hides or covers up, lest man should fall into it. Even the godly need to learn the lesson which trials teach, to "*humble* themselves under the mighty hand of God." **18. his soul**–his life. **the pit**–the grave; a symbol of hell. **perishing by the sword**–i.e., a violent death; in the Old Testament a symbol of the future punish- ment of the ungodly. **19.** When man does not heed warnings of the night, he is chastened, etc. The new thought suggested by Elihu is that affliction is *disciplinary* (ch. 36:10); *for the good* of the godly. **multitude**–so the *Margin, Hebrew* (KERI). Better with the text (CHETIB), "And with the perpetual (strong) *contest* of his bones"; the never-resting fever in his bones (Ps. 38:3) [UMBREIT]. 20. life–i.e., the appetite, which ordinarily sustains "life" (ch. 38:39; Ps. 107:18; Eccles. 12:5). The taking away of desire for food by sickness symbolizes the removal

a rich Arabian emir, proud of his descent. **dogs**– regarded with disgust in the East as unclean (I Sam. 17:43; Prov. 26:11). They are not allowed to enter a house, but run about wild in the open air, living on offal and chance morsels (Ps. 59:14, 15). Here again we are reminded of Jesus Christ (Ps. 22:16). "Their fathers, my coevals, were so mean and famished that I would not have associated them *with* (not to say, set them over) my dogs in guarding my flock." **2.** If their fathers could be of no profit to me, much less the sons, who are feebler than their sires; and in whose case the hope of attaining old age is utterly gone, so puny are they (ch. 5:26). [MAURER]. Even if they had "strength of hands," that could be now of no use to me, as all I want in my present affliction is sympathy. **3. solitary**–lit., *hard* as a rock; so translate, rather, "dried up," ema- ciated with hunger. Job describes the rudest race of Bedouins of the desert [UMBREIT]. **fleeing**–So LXX. Better, as *Syriac, Arabic,* and *Vulgate,* "*gnawers* of the wilderness." What they gnaw fol- lows in vs. 4. **in former time**–lit., the "*yesternight* of desolation and waste" (the most utter desolation; Ezek. 6:14); i.e., those deserts frightful as night to man, and even there from time immemorial. I think both ideas are in the words *darkness* [GESE- NIUS] and *antiquity* [UMBREIT]. (Isa. 30:33, *Mar- gin.*) **4. mallows**–rather, "salt-wort," which grows in deserts and is eaten as a salad by the poor [MAURER]. **by the bushes**–among the bushes. **juniper**–rather, a kind of broom, *Spartium junceum* [LINNÆUS], still called in Arabia, as in the *Hebrew* of Job, *retem,* of which the bitter roots are eaten by the poor. **5. they cried**–i.e., a cry is raised. Ex- pressing the contempt felt for this race by civilized and well-born Arabs. When these wild vagabonds make an incursion on villages, they are driven away, as thieves would be. **6.** They are forced "to dwell." **cliffs of the valleys**–rather, "in the gloomy (lit., gloom of) valleys," or wadies. To dwell in valleys is, in the East, a mark of wretchedness. The troglodytes, in parts of Arabia, lived in such dwel- lings as caves. **7. brayed**–like the wild ass (ch. 6:5 for food). The inarticulate tones of this uncivilized rabble are but little above those of the beast of the field. **gathered together**–rather, sprinkled here and there. Lit., "poured out," graphically picturing their disorderly mode of encampment, lying up and down behind the thorn-bushes. **nettles**–or bram- bles [UMBREIT]. **8. fools**–i.e., the impious and abandoned (I Sam. 25:25). **base**–nameless, low- born rabble. **viler than . . .**–rather, they were *driven* or *beaten out of the land.* The Horites in Mount Seir (Gen. 14:6, with which cf. Gen. 36:20, 21; Deut. 2:12, 22) were probably the aborigines, driven out by the tribe to which Job's ancestors be- longed; their name means troglodytæ, or "dwellers in caves." To these Job alludes here (vss. 1-8, and Gen. 24:4-8, which cf. together). **9.** (Ch. 17:6.) Strikingly similar to the derision Jesus Christ un- derwent (Lam. 3:14; Ps. 69:12). Here Job returns to the sentiment in vs. 1. It is to such I am become a song of "derision." **10. in my face**–rather, re- frain not to spit in deliberate contempt *before* my face. To spit at all in presence of another is thought in the East insulting, much more so when done to mark "abhorrence." Cf. the further insult to Jesus Christ (Isa. 50:6; Matt. 26:67). **11. He** –i.e., God; antithetical to *they; English Version* here follows the marginal reading (KERI). **my cord,**– image from a bow unstrung; opposed to ch. 29:20. The text (CHETIB), "*His* cord" or "reins" is better; "yea, each lets loose his reins" [UMBREIT]. **12. youth**–rather, a (low) *brood.* To rise on the right hand is to accuse, as that was the position of the accuser in court (Zech. 3:1; Ps. 109:6). **push . . . feet**–jostle me out of the way (ch. 24:4). **ways of** –i.e., their ways of (i.e., with a view to my) destruc- tion. Image, as in ch. 19:12, from a besieging army throwing up a way of approach for itself to a city. **13.** Image of an assailed fortress continued. They tear up the path by which succor might reach me. **set forward**–(Zech. 1:15). **they have no helper**– Arabic proverb for *contemptible* persons. Yet even such afflict Job. **14. waters**–(So II Sam. 5:20). But it is better to retain the image of vss. 12, 13. "They came (upon me) as through a wide *breach,*" viz., made by the besiegers in the wall of a fortress (Isa. 30:13) [MAURER]. **in the desolation**–"Amidst the crash" of falling masonry, or "with a shout like the crash" of, etc. **15. they**–terrors. **soul**–rather, my dignity [UMBREIT]. **welfare**–prosperity. **cloud** –(Ch. 7:9; Isa. 44:22). **16-23.** Job's outward ca- lamities affect his mind. **poured out**–in irrepress- ible complaints (Ps. 42:4; Josh. 7:5). **17.** In the *Hebrew,* night is poetically personified, as in ch. 3:3: "night pierceth my bones (so that they fall) *from* me" (not as *English Version, "in* me"; see vs. 30). **sinews**–so the *Arabic,* "veins," akin to the ***Hebrew;*** rather, gnawers, as in vs. 3 (*Note*), viz., my gnawing pains never cease. Effects of elephantiasis. **18. of my disease**–rather, "of God" (ch. 23:6). **garment changed**–from a robe of honor to one of mourning, literally (ch. 2:8; John 3:6) and metaphorically [UMBREIT]. Or rather, as SCHUTTENS, following up vs 17, My *outer* garment is changed into affliction; i.e., affliction has become my outer garment; it also bindeth me fast round (my throat) as the collar of the *inner* coat; i.e., it is both my inner and outer gar- ment. Observe the distinction between the inner and outer garments. The latter refers to his afflic- tions *from without* (vss. 1-13); the former his per- sonal afflictions (vss. 14-23). UMBREIT makes "God" subject to "bindeth," as in vs. 19. **19.** God is poetically said to do that which the mourner had done to himself (ch. 2:8). With lying in the ashes he had become, like them, in dirty color. **20. stand up**–the reverential attitude of a suppliant before a king (I Kings 8:14; Luke 18:11-13). **not**–supplied from the first clause. But the intervening affirm- ative "stand" makes this ellipsis unlikely. Rather, as in ch. 16:9 (not only dost thou refuse aid to me "standing" as a suppliant, but), *thou dost regard me with a frown:* eye me sternly. **22. liftest . . . to wind**–as a "leaf" or "stubble" (ch. 13:25). The moving pillars of sand, raised by the wind to the clouds, as described by travellers, would happily depict Job's agitated spirit, if it be to them that he alludes. **dissolvest . . . substance**–The *marginal He- brew* reading (KERI), "my wealth," or else "wis- dom," i.e., sense and spirit, or "my hope of *deliver- ance.*" But the text (CHETIB) is better: Thou dis- solvest me (with fear, Exod. 15:15) *in the crash* (of the whirlwind; as vs. 14, *Note*) [MAURER]. UM- BREIT translates as a verb, "Thou *terrifiest* me." **23.** This shows ch. 19:25 cannot be restricted to Job's hope of a *temporal* deliverance. **death**–as in ch. 28:22, the realm of the dead (Heb. 9:27; Gen. 3:19). **24.** Expressing Job's faith as to the state after death. Though one must go to the grave, yet He will no more afflict *in the ruin* of the body (so *Hebrew* for *grave*) there, if one has cried to Him when being destroyed. The "stretching of His hand" to punish after death answers antithetically to the raising "the cry" of prayer in the second clause. MAURER gives another translation which accords with the scope of vss. 24-31; if it be natural for one in affliction to ask aid, why should it be considered (by the friends) wrong in my case? "Nevertheless does not a man in ruin stretch out his hand" (imploring help, vs. 20; Lam. 1:17)? If one be in his calamity (destruction) is there not therefore a "cry" (for aid)? Thus in the parallelism "cry" answers to "stretch–hand"; "in his calamity," to "in ruin." The negative of the first clause is to be supplied in the second, as in vs. 25 (ch. 28:17). **25.** May I not be allowed to complain of my calamity, and beg relief, seeing that I myself sympathized with those "in trouble" (lit., "hard of day"; those who had a hard time of it). **26.** I may be allowed to crave help, seeing that, "when I looked for food (on account of my piety and charity), yet evil," etc. **light**—(ch. 22:28). **27. bowels**—regarded as the seat of deep feeling (Isa. 16:11). **boiled**—violently heated and agitated. **prevented**—Old English for unexpectedly came upon me, surprised me. **28. mourning**—rather, I move about *blackened,* though not by the sun; i.e., whereas many are blackened by the sun, I am, by the heat of God's wrath (so "boiled," vs. 27); the elephantiasis covering me with blackness of skin (vs. 30), as with the garb of mourning (Jer. 14:2). This striking enigmatic form of *Hebrew* expression occurs, Isaiah 29:9. **stood up**—as an innocent man crying for justice in an assembled court (vs. 20). **29. dragons . . . owls**—rather, "jackals," "ostriches," both of which utter dismal screams (Mic. 1:8); in which respect, as also in their living amidst solitudes (the emblem of desolation), Job is their brother and companion; i.e., resembles them. "Dragon," *Hebrew, tannim,* usually means the crocodile; so perhaps here, its open jaws lifted towards heaven, and its noise making it seem as if it mourned over its fate [BOCHART]. **30. upon me**—rather, as in vs. 17 (*Note*), my skin is black (and falls away) *from* me. **my bones**—(ch. 19:20; Ps. 102:5). **31. organ**—rather, *pipe* (ch. 21:12); "My joy is turned into the voice of weeping" (Lam. 5:15). These instruments are properly appropriated to joy (Isa. 30:29, 32), which makes their use now in sorrow the sadder by contrast.

CHAPTER 31

Vss. 1-40. **1.** Job proceeds to prove that he deserved a better lot. As in ch. 29, he showed his uprightness as an emir, or magistrate in *public* life, so in this chapter he vindicates his character in *private* life. **1-4.** He asserts his guarding against being allured to sin by his senses. **1. think**—rather, *cast* a (lustful) *look.* He not merely did not so, but put it out of the question by covenanting with his eyes against leading him into temptation (Prov. 6:25; Matt. 5:28). **2.** Had I let my senses tempt me to sin, "what portion (would there have been to me, i.e., must I have expected) from (lit. "of") God above, and what inheritance from (lit. "of") the Almighty," etc. [MAURER] (ch. 20:29; 27:13). **3.** Answer to the question in vs. 2. **strange**—extraordinary. **4.** Doth not he see . . . ? Knowing this, I could only have expected "destruction" (vs. 3), had I committed this sin (Prov. 5:21). **5.** Job's abstinence from evil deeds. **vanity**—i.e., falsehood (Ps. 12:2). **6.** Parenthetical. Translate: "Oh, that God would weigh me . . . *then* would He know . . ." **7.** Connected with vs. 6. **the way**—of God (ch. 23:11; Jer. 5:5). A godly life. **heart . . . after . . . eyes**—if my heart coveted, what my eyes beheld (Eccles. 11:9; Josh. 7:21). **hands**—(Ps. 24:4). **8.** Apodosis to vss. 5 and 7; the curses which he imprecates on himself, if he had done these things (Lev. 26:16; Amos 9:14; Ps. 128:2). **offspring**—rather, *what I plant,* my harvests. **9-12.** Job asserts his innocence of adultery. **deceived**—hath let itself be seduced (Prov. 7:8; Gen. 39:7-12). **laid wait**—until the husband went out. **10. grind**—turn the handmill. Be the most abject slave and concubine (Isa. 47:2; II Sam. 12-11). **11.** In the earliest times punished with death (Gen. 38:24). So in later times (Deut. 22:22). Heretofore he had spoken only of sins against conscience; now, one against the community, needing the cognizance of the judge. **12.** (Prov. 6:27-35; 8:6-23, 26, 27.) No crime more provokes God to send *destruction as a consuming fire;* none so desolates the soul. **13-23.** Job affirms his freedom from unfairness towards his servants, from harshness and oppression towards the needy. **despise the cause**—refused to do them justice. **14, 15.** Parenthetical; the reason why Job did not despise the cause of his servants. Translate: What then (had I done so) could I have done, when God arose (to call me to account); and when He visited (came to inquire), what could I have answered Him? **15.** Slaveholders try to defend themselves by maintaining the *original* inferiority of the slave. But Malachi 2:10; Acts 17:26; Ephesians 6:9, make the common origin of masters and servants the argument for brotherly love being shown by the former to the latter. **16. fail**—in the vain expectation of relief (ch. 11:20). **17.** Arabian rules of hospitality require the stranger to be helped first, and to the best. **18.** Parenthetical: asserting that he did the contrary to the things in vss. 16, 17. **he**—the orphan. **guided her**—viz., the widow, by advice and protection. On this and "a father," see ch. 29:16. **19. perish**—i.e., ready to perish (ch. 29:13). **20. loins**—The parts of the body benefited by Job are poetically described as thanking him; the loins before naked, when clad by me, wished me every blessing. **21.** "When (i.e., because) I saw" that I might calculate on the "help" of a powerful party in the court of justice—("gate"), if I should be summoned by the injured fatherless. **22.** Apodosis to vss. 13, 16, 17, 19, 20, 21. If I had done those crimes, I should have made a bad use of my influence (my arm, figuratively, vs. 21): therefore, if I have done them let my arm (literally) suffer. Job alludes to Eliphaz' charge (ch. 22:9). The first "arm" is rather the *shoulder.* The second "arm" is the *forearm.* **from the bone**—lit., "a reed"; hence the upper arm, above the elbow. **23. For**—i.e., the reason why Job guarded against such sins. *Fear of God,* though he could escape man's judgment (Gen. 39:9). UMBREIT more spiritedly translates, Yea, destruction and terror from God might have befallen me (had I done so): mere *fear* not being the motive. **highness**—majestic might. **endure**—I could have availed nothing against it. **24, 25.** Job asserts his freedom from trust in money (I Tim. 6:17). Here he turns to his duty towards God, as before he had spoken of his duty towards *himself* and his *neighbor.* Covetousness is covert idolatry, as it transfers the heart from the Creator to the creature (Col. 3:5). In vss. 26, 27 he passes to overt idolatry. **26.** If I looked unto the sun (as an object of worship) *because* he shined; or to the moon *because* she walked, etc. Sabaism (from *tsaba,* the heavenly hosts) was the earliest form of false worship. God is hence called in contradistinction, "Lord of Sabaoth." The sun, moon, and stars, the brightest objects in nature, and seen everywhere, were supposed to be visible representatives of the invisible God. They

had no temples, but were worshipped on high places and roofs of houses (Ezek. 8:16; Deut. 4:19; II Kings 23:5, 11). The *Hebrew* here for "sun" is *light.* Probably light was worshipped as the emanation from God, before its embodiments, the sun, etc. This worship prevailed in Chaldea; wherefore Job's exemption from the idolatry of his neighbors was the more exemplary. Our "Sun-day," "Mon-day," or Moon-day, bear traces of Sabaism. **27. enticed**—away from God to idolatry. **kissed . . . hand**—"adoration," literally means this. In worshipping they used to kiss the hand, and then throw the kiss, as it were, towards the object of worship (I Kings 19:18; Hos. 13:2). **28.** The Mosaic law embodied subsequently the feeling of the godly from the earliest times against idolatry, as deserving judicial penalties: being treason against the Supreme King (Deut. 13:9; 17:2-7; Ezek. 8:14-18). This passage therefore does not prove Job to have been subsequent to Moses. **29. lifted up himself**—in malicious triumph (Prov. 17:5; 24:17; Ps. 7:4). **30. mouth**—lit., "palate" (ch. 6:30, *Note*). **wishing**—lit., "so as to demand his (my enemy's) soul, i.e., life by a curse." This verse parenthetically confirms vs. 30. Job in the patriarchal age of the promise, anterior to the law, realizes the Gospel spirit, which was the end of the law (cf. Lev. 19:18; Deut. 23:6, with Matt. 5:43, 44). **31.** i.e., Job's household said, Oh, that we had Job's enemy to devour, we cannot rest satisfied till we have! But Job refrained from even wishing revenge (I Sam. 26:8; II Sam. 16:9, 10). So Jesus Christ (Luke 9:54, 55). But, better (see vs. 32), translated, "Who can show (lit., give) the man who was not satisfied with the flesh (meat) provided by Job?" He never let a poor man leave his gate without giving him enough to eat. **32. traveller**—lit., "way," i.e., wayfarers; so expressed to include all of every kind (II Sam. 12:4). **33. Adam**—translated by UMBREIT, "as men do" (Hos. 6, 7, where see *Margin*). But *English Version* is more natural. The very same word for "hiding" is used in Genesis 3:8, 10, of Adam *hiding* himself from God. Job elsewhere alludes to the flood. So he might easily know of the fall, through the two links which connect Adam and Abraham (about Job's time), viz., Methuselah and Shem. Adam is representative of fallen man's propensity to concealment (Prov. 28:13). It was *from God* that Job did not "hide his iniquity in his bosom," as on the contrary it was from God that "Adam" hid in his lurking-place. This disproves the translation, "as men"; for it is *from their fellow men* that "men" are chiefly anxious to hide their real character as guilty. MAGEE, to make the comparison with Adam more exact, for my "bosom" translates, "lurking-place." **34.** Rather, the apodosis to vs. 33, "Then let me be fear-stricken before a great multitude, let the contempt, etc., let me keep silence (the greatest disgrace to a patriot, heretofore so prominent in assemblies), and not go out," etc. A just retribution that he who hides his sin from God, should have it exposed before man (II Sam. 12:12). But Job had not been so exposed, but on the contrary was esteemed in the assemblies of the "tribes"—("families"); a proof, he implies, that God does not hold him guilty of hiding sin (ch. 24:16, contrast with ch. 29:21-25). **35.** Job returns to his wish (ch. 13:22; 19:23). Omit "is"; "Behold my *sign,*" i.e., my mark of subscription to the statements just given in my defense: the *mark* of signature was originally a *cross;* and hence the letter Tau or T. Translate, also "Oh, *that* the Almighty," etc. He marks "God" as the "One" meant in the first *clause.* Adversary, i.e., he who
contends with me, refers also to (
ness is designed to express "wł
judicially opposes me"—the Almi
had written a book—rather, "woul
charge." **36.** So far from hidin
"answer" or "charge" through fea
it on my shoulders" as a public ho
crown—not a mark of shame, bı
(Isa. 62:3). **37.** A good consci
princely dignity before man and f
approaching God. This can be
in Job's way (42:5, 6); but only
Christ (Heb. 10:22). **38.** Personifica
plaints of the unjustly ousted propr
ferred to the lands themselves (vs.
Hab. 2:11). If I have unjustly acq
24:2; Isa. 5:8). **furrows**—The specif
makes it likely, he implies in this, "I
laborer for *tillage";* as next verse, "If
for gathering in the fruits." Thu
clauses in vss. 38, 39, the 1st refers tc
ject as the 4th, the 2d is connected
introverted parallelism. Cf. James 5:4
alludes to this passage: cf. "Lord of
vs. 26 here. **39. lose . . . life**—not
"harassed to death;" until he gave m
gratis [MAURER]; as in Judges 16:16;
to languish" by taking away his me
[UMBREIT] (I Kings 21:19). **40.**
brambles, thorns. **cockle**—lit., "nox
The words . . . ended—i.e., in the cont
the friends. He spoke in the book aft
not to *them.* At vs. 37 would be the
clusion in strict art. But vss. 38-40 a
added by one whose mind in agitation
sense of innocence, even after it has
usual stopping point; this takes aw
pearance of rhetorical artifice. Hence
position by EICHORN of vss. 38-40 to foll
quite unwarranted.

CHAPTER 32

Vss. 1-22. SPEECH OF ELIHU (ch. 32-
Prose (poetry begins with "I am young"
cause . . .—and because they could not pro
that he was unrighteous. **2. Elihu**—mean
is Jehovah." In his name and characte
senger between God and Job, he foreshad
Christ (ch. 33:23-26). **Barachel**—meanir
blesses." Both names indicate the piety
family and their separation from idolaters.
—Buz was son of Nahor, brother of A
Hence was named a region in Arabia Dese
25:23). **Ram**—Aram, nephew of Buz. J
probably of an older generation than Elihu.
ever, the identity of names does not nec
prove the identity of persons. The partic
with which Elihu's descent is given, as con
with the others, led LIGHTFOOT to infer Elihu
author of the book. But the reason for partic
was, probably, that Elihu was *less known* th
three called "friends" of Job; and that it was
for the poet to mark especially him who was n
to solve the problem of the book. **rather than**
—i.e., was more eager *to vindicate himself than*
In ch. 4:17, Job denies *that man can be more*
than God. UMBREIT translates, "Before (in
presence of) God." **3.** Though silenced in
ment, they held their opinion still. **4. had sp**
—*Hebrew,* "in words" referring rather to *his*
"words" of reply, which he had long ago ready,

by affliction of lust, for things which foster the spiritual fever of pride. **soul**—desire. **21.** His flesh once prominent "can no more be seen." His bones once not seen now appear prominent. **stick out**—lit., "are bare." The *Margin, Hebrew* (KERI) reading. The text (CHETIB) reads it a noun (are become) "bareness." The KERI was no doubt an explanatory reading of transcribers. **22. destroyers**—angels of death commissioned by God to end man's life (II Sam. 24:16; Ps. 78:49). The *death pains* personified may, however, be meant; so "gnawers" (*Note*, ch. 30:17). **23.** Elihu refers to himself as the divinely-sent (ch. 32:8; 33:6) "messenger," the "interpreter" to explain to Job and vindicate God's righteousness; such a one Eliphaz had denied that Job could look for (ch. 5:1), and Job (ch. 9:33) had wished for such a "daysman" or umpire between him and God. The "messenger" of good is antithetical to the "destroyers" (vs. 23). **with him**—if there be vouchsafed *to the sufferer*. The office of the interpreter is stated "to show unto man *God's* uprightness" in His dealings; or, as UMBREIT, "man's upright course towards God" (Prov. 14:2). The former is better; Job maintained his own "uprightness" (ch. 16:17; 27:5, 6); Elihu on the contrary maintains God's, and that man's true uprightness lies in submission to God. "One among a thousand" is a man rarely to be found. So Jesus Christ (Song of Sol. 5:10). Elihu, the God-sent mediator of a *temporal* deliverance, is a type of the God-man Jesus Christ the Mediator of *eternal* deliverance: "the *messenger* of the covenant" (Mal. 3:1). This is the wonderful work of the Holy Ghost, that persons and events move in their own sphere in such a way as unconsciously to shadow forth Him, whose "testimony is the Spirit of prophecy"; as the same point may be center of a small and of a vastly larger concentric circle. **24.** Apodosis to vs. 23. **he**—God. **Deliver**—lit., "redeem"; in it and "ransom" there is reference to the *consideration*, on account of which God pardons and relieves the sufferers; here it is primarily the intercession of Elihu. But the language is too strong for its full meaning to be *exhausted* by this. The Holy Ghost has suggested language which receives its *full* realization only in the "eternal redemption found" by God in the price paid by Jesus Christ for it; i.e., His blood and meritorious intercession (Heb. 9:12). "Obtained," lit., "found"; implying the earnest zeal, wisdom, and faithfulness of the *finder*, and the newness and joyousness of the *finding*. Jesus Christ could not but have *found* it, but still His *seeking* it was needed [BENGEL], (Luke 15:8.) God the Father, is the Finder (Ps. 89:19). Jesus Christ the Redeemer, to whom He saith, *Redeem* (so *Hebrew*) him from going, etc. (II Cor. 5:19). **ransom**—used in a general sense by Elihu, but meant by the Holy Ghost in its strict sense as applied to Jesus Christ, of a *price* paid for deliverance (Exod. 21:30), an *atonement* (i.e., means of selling *at once*, i.e., reconciling *two* who are estranged), *a covering*, as of the ark with pitch, typical of what covers us sinners from wrath (Gen. 6:14; Ps. 32:1). The pit is primarily here the *grave* (Isa. 38:17), but the spiritual pit is mainly shadowed forth (Zech. 9:11). **25-28.** Effects of restoration to God's favor; lit., to Job a temporal revival; spiritually, an eternal *regeneration*. The striking words cannot be restricted to their temporal meaning, as used by Elihu (I Pet. 1:11, 12). **his flesh shall be fresher than a child's**—so Naaman, II Kings 5:14 spiritually, John 3:3-7. **26.** Job shall no longer pray to God, as he complains, in vain (ch. 23:3, 8, 9). True especially to the re-

deemed in Jesus Christ (John 16:23-27). **he** [Job] **shall see his face**—or, God shall make him to see His face [MAURER]. God shall no longer "hide His face" (ch. 13:24). True to the believer now (John 14:21, 22); eternally (Ps. 17:15; John 17:24). **his** [God's] **righteousness**—God will again make the restored Job no longer ("I perverted . . . right," vs. 27) doubt God's justice, but to justify Him in His dealings. The penitent justifies God (Ps. 51:4). So the believer is made to see God's righteousness in Jesus Christ (Isa. 45:24; 46:13). **27. he looketh**—God. Rather, with UMBREIT, "Now he (*the restored penitent*) *singeth joyfully* (answering to 'joy,' vs. 26; Ps. 51:12) before men, and saith," etc. (Prov. 25:20; Ps. 66:16; 116:14). **perverted**—made the straight crooked: as Job had misrepresented God's character. **profited**—lit., "was made even" to me; rather, "My punishment was not commensurate with my sin" (so Zophar, ch. 11:6); the reverse of what Job heretofore said (ch. 16:17; Ps. 103:10; Ezra 9:13). **28.** *Note*, vs. 24; rather, as *Hebrew* text (*English Version* reads as *Margin, Hebrew,* KERI, "his soul, his life"), "He hath delivered *my* soul . . . *my* life." Continuation of the penitent's testimony to the people. **light**—(vs. 30; ch. 3:16, 20; Ps. 56:13; Eccles. 11:7). **29.** Margin, "twice and thrice," alluding to vs. 14; once, by visions, vss. 15-17; secondly, by afflictions, vss. 19-22; now, by the "messenger," thirdly, vs. 23. **30.** Referring to vs. 28 (Ps. 50:13). **32. justify**—to do thee justice; and, if I can, consistently with it, to declare thee innocent. At vs. 33 Elihu pauses for a reply; then proceeds in ch. 34.

CHAPTER 34

Vss. 1-37. **1. answered**—proceeded. **2.** This chapter is addressed also to the "friends" as ch. 33, to Job alone. **3. palate** (*Note*, ch. 12:11; ch. 33:2). **4. judgment**—Let us select among the conflicting sentiments advanced, what will stand the test of examination. **5. judgment**—my right. Job's own words (ch. 13:18; 27:2). **6.** Were I to renounce my right (i.e., confess myself guilty), I should die. Job virtually had said so (ch. 27:4, 5; 6:28). MAURER, not so well, "Notwithstanding my right (innocence) I am treated as a liar," by God, by His afflicting me. **my wound**—lit., "mine arrow," viz., by which I am pierced. So "*my* stroke" (hand, *Margin*, ch. 23:2). My sickness (ch. 6:4; 16:13). **without transgression**—without fault of mine to deserve it (ch. 16:17). **7.** (Ch. 15:16.) Image from the camel. **scorning**—against God (ch. 15:4). **8.** Job virtually goes in company (makes common cause) with the wicked, by taking up their sentiments (ch. 9:22, 23, 30; 21: 7-15), or at least by saying, that those who act on such sentiments are unpunished (Mal. 3:14). To deny God's righteous government because we do not see the reasons of His acts, is virtually to take part with the ungodly. **9. with God**—in intimacy (Ps. 50: 18). **10.** The true answer to Job, which God follows up (ch. 38). Man is to *believe* God's ways are right, because they are His, not because we fully *see* they are so (Rom. 9:14; Deut. 32:4; Gen. 18:25). **11.** Partly here; fully, hereafter (Jer. 32:19; Rom. 2:6; I Pet. 1:17; Rev. 22:12). **12.** (Ch. 8:3.) In opposition to Job, vs. 5, will not—cannot. **13.** If the world were not God's property, as having been made by Him, but committed to His charge by some superior, it might be possible for Him to act unjustly, as He would not thereby be injuring Himself; but as it is, for God to act unjustly would undermine the whole order of the world, and so would injure God's own property (ch. 36:23). **disposed**— hath founded (Isa. 44:7), established the circle of the globe. **14, 15.** "If He were to set His heart on man," either to injure him, or to take strict account of his sins. The connection supports rather [UM-BREIT], "If He had regard to himself (only), and were to gather unto Himself (Ps. 104:29) man's spirit, etc. (which he sends forth, Ps. 104:30; Eccles. 12:7), all flesh must perish together," etc. (Gen. 3: 19). God's loving preservation of His creatures proves He cannot be selfish, and therefore cannot be unjust. **16.** In vs. 2, Elihu had spoken *to all* in general, now he calls Job's special attention. **17.** "Can even He who (in thy view) hateth right (justice) govern?" The government of the world would be impossible if injustice were sanctioned. God must be just, because He governs (II Sam. 23:3). **govern**—lit., "bind," viz., by authority (so "reign," *Margin*, I Sam. 9:17). UMBREIT translates for "govern," *repress wrath*, viz., against Job for his accusations. **most just**—rather, "Him who is at once mighty and just" (in His government of the world). **18.** Lit., (Is it fit) *to be said* to a king? It would be a gross outrage to reproach thus an earthly monarch, much more the King of kings (Exod. 22: 28). But MAURER with LXX and *Vulgate* reads, (It is not fit to accuse of injustice Him) *who says* to a king, Thou art wicked; to princes, Ye are ungodly; i.e., who punishes impartially the great, as the small. This accords with vs. 19. **19.** Acts 10:34; II Chron. 19:7; Prov. 22:2; ch. 31:15. **20. they**—"the rich" and "princes" who offend God. **the people**—viz., of the guilty princes: guilty also themselves. **at midnight**—image from a night attack of an enemy on a camp, which becomes an easy prey (Exod. 12: 29, 30). **without hand**—without *visible* agency, by the mere word of God (so ch. 20:26; Zech. 4:6; Dan. 2:34). **21.** God's omniscience and omnipotence enable Him to execute immediate justice. He needs not to be long on the "watch," as Job thought (ch. 7:12; II Chron. 16:9; Jer. 32:19). **22. shadow of death**—thick darkness (Amos 9:2, 3; Ps. 139:12). **23.** (I Cor. 10:13; Lam. 3:32; Isa. 27:8.) Better, as UMBREIT, "He does not (needs not to) *regard* (as in vs. 14; Isa. 41:20) man *long* (so *Hebrew*, Gen. 46: 29) in order that he may go (be brought by God) into judgment." Lit., *"lest* his (attention) upon men" (ch. 11:10, 11). So vs. 24, "without number" ought to be translated, "without (needing any) searching out," such as has to be made in human judgments. **24. break in pieces**—(Ps. 2:9; ch. 12: 18; Dan. 2:21). **25. Therefore**—because He knows all things (vs. 21). He knows their works, without a formal investigation (vs. 24). **in the night**—suddenly, unexpectedly (vs. 20). Fitly *in the night*, as it was in it that the godless hid themselves (vs. 22). UMBREIT, *less* simply, for "overturneth," translates, "walketh"; i.e., God is ever on the alert, discovering all wickedness. **26. striketh**—chasteneth. **as**—i.e., because they are wicked. **sight of others**—Sinners hid themselves in darkness; therefore they are punished before all, in open day. Image from the place of public execution (ch. 40:12; Exod. 14:30; II Sam. 12:12). **27, 28.** The grounds of their punishment in vs. 27; vs. 28 states in what respect they "considered not God's ways," viz., by *oppression*, whereby "they caused the cry," etc. **29.** (Prov. 16:7; Isa. 26:3.) **make trouble**—rather, condemn (Rom. 8:33, 34). MAURER, from the reference being only to *the godless*, in the next clause, and vs. 20 translates, "When God keeps quiet" (leaves men to *perish*) Ps. 83:1; [UMBREIT] from

the *Arabic* (*strikes to the earth*), "who shall condemn Him as unjust?" vs. 17. **hideth ... face**—(ch. 23:8, 9; Ps. 13:1). **it be done**— Whether it be against a guilty nation (II Kings 18:9-12) or an individual, that God acts so. **30.** "Ensnared" into sin (I Kings 12:28, 30). Or rather, "enthralled by further oppression," vss. 26-28. **31.** Job accordingly says so (ch. 40:3-5; Micah 7:9; Lev. 26:41). It was to lead him to this that Elihu was sent. Though no hypocrite, Job, like all, had sin; therefore through affliction he was to be brought to humble himself under God. All sorrow is a proof of the common heritage of sin, in which the godly shares; and therefore he ought to regard it as a merciful correction. UMBREIT and MAURER lose this by translating, as the *Hebrew* will bear, "Has any a right to say to God, I have borne chastisement and yet have not sinned?" (so vs. 6). **borne**—viz., the penalty of sin, as in Leviticus 5:1, 17. **offend**—lit., "to deal destructively or corruptly" (Neh. 1:7). **32.** ch. 10:2; Ps. 32:8; 19:12; 139:23, 24. **no more**—Prov. 28:13; Eph. 4:22. **33.** Rather, "should God recompense (sinners) according to thy mind? Then it is for thee to reject and to choose, and not me," UMBREIT; or as MAURER, *"For thou hast rejected* God's way of recompensing; state therefore thy way, *for thou must choose, not I,"* i.e., it is thy part, not mine, to show a better way than God's. **34, 35.** Rather, men ... will say to me, and the wise man (vs. 2, 10) who hearkens to me (will say), "Job hath spoken ...." **36.** Margin, not so well, "My father," Elihu addressing God. This title does not elsewhere occur in Job. **tried**—by calamities. **answers for wicked men**—(See *Note*, vs. 8.) Trials of the godly are not removed until they produce the effect designed. **37. clappeth ... hands**—in scorn (ch. 27:23; Ezek. 21:17). **multiplieth ... words**—(ch. 11:2; 35:16). To his original "sin" to correct which trials have been sent, "he adds *rebellion*," i.e., words arraigning God's justice.

CHAPTER 35

Vss. 1-16. **2. more than**—rather as in ch. 9:2; 25: 4: "I am righteous (lit., my righteousness is) before God." *English Version,* however, agrees with ch. 9:17; 16:12-17; 27:2-6. Ch. 4:17 is susceptible of either rendering. Elihu means Job said so, not in so many words, but *virtually*. **3.** Rather, explanatory of "this" in vs. 2, "That thou sayest (to thyself, as if a distinct person) What advantage is it (thy integrity) to thee? What profit have I (by integrity) more than (I should have) by my sin?" i.e., more than if I had sinned (ch. 34:9). Job had said that the wicked, who use *these very words,* do not suffer for it (ch. 21:13-15); whereby he virtually sanctioned their sentiments. The same change of persons from oblique to direct address occurs (ch. 19:28; 22:17). **4. companions**—those entertaining like sentiments with thee (ch. 34:8, 36). **5-8.** Elihu like Eliphaz (ch. 22:2, 3, 12) shows that God is too exalted in nature to be susceptible of benefit or hurt from the righteousness or sin of men respectively; it is themselves that they benefit by righteousness, or hurt by sin. **behold the clouds, which are higher than thou** —spoken with irony. Not only are they higher than thou, but thou canst not even reach them clearly with the eye. Yet these are not as high as God's seat. God is therefore too exalted to be dependent on man. Therefore He has no inducement to injustice in His dealings with man. When He afflicts, it must be from a different motive; viz., the good of the sufferer. **6. what doest**—how canst thou affect Him? **unto him**—that can hurt Him? (Jer. 7:19; Prov. 8: 36). **7.** (Ps. 16:2; Prov. 9:12; Luke 17:10.) **9.** (Eccles. 4:1.) Elihu states in Job's words (ch. 24: 12; 30:20) the difficulty; the "cries" of "the oppressed" not being heard might lead man to think that wrongs are not punished by Him. **10-13.** But the reason is that the innocent sufferers often do not humbly seek God for succor; so to their "pride" is to be laid the blame of their ruin; also because (13-16) they, as Job, instead of waiting God's time in pious trust, are prone to despair of His justice, when it is not immediately visible (ch. 33:19-26). If the sufferer would apply to God with a humbled, penitent spirit, He would hear. **Where . . .**—(Jer. 2:6, 8; Isa. 51:13). **songs**—of joy at deliverance (Ps. 42:8; 149:5; Acts 16:25). **in the night**—unexpectedly (ch. 34:20, 25). Rather, in calamity. **11.** Man's spirit, which distinguishes him from the brute, is the strongest proof of God's beneficence; by the use of it we may understand that God is the Almighty helper of all sufferers who humbly seek Him; and that they err who do not so seek Him. **fowls**—(ch. 28:21, *Note*). **12. There**—rather, *Then* (when none humbly casts himself on God, vs. 10). They cry proudly *against* God, rather than humbly *to* God. So, as the design of affliction is to humble the sufferer, there can be no answer until "pride" gives place to humble, penitent prayer (Ps. 10:4; Jer. 13: 17). **13.** Vanity, i.e., cries uttered in an unhumbled spirit, vs. 12, which applies in some degree to Job's cries; still more to those of the wicked (ch. 27:9; Prov. 15:29). **14.** Although thou sayest, thou shalt not see Him (as a *temporal* deliverer; for he did look for a Redeemer *after death*, ch. 19:25-27; which passage cannot consistently with Elihu's assertion here be interpreted of "seeing" a *temporal* "redeemer"), ch. 7:7; 9:11; 23:3, 8, 9; yet, judgment . . .; therefore trust . . . But the *Hebrew* favors MAURER, "*How much less* (will God . . . regard, vs. 13), since thou sayest, that He does not regard thee." So in ch. 4:19. Thus Elihu alludes to Job's words (ch. 19:7; 30:20). **judgment**—i.e., thy cause, thy right; as in Ps. 9:16; Prov. 31:5, 8. **trust**—rather, *wait thou* on Him, patiently, until He take up thy cause (Ps. 37:7). **15.** *As it is, because* Job waited *not* trustingly and patiently (vs. 14; Num. 20:12; Zeph. 3:2; Mic. 7:9), *God hath visited . . . ; yet still he has not taken* (severe) *cognizance of the great multitude* (English Version wrongly, "extremity") of sins; therefore Job should not complain of being punished with undue severity (ch. 7:20; 11: 6). MAURER translates: "Because His anger hath not visited (hath not immediately punished Job for his impious complaints), nor has He taken *strict* (great) cognizance of his *folly* (sinful speeches); therefore . . ." For "folly," UMBREIT translates with the Rabbins, "multitude" (English Version with LXX and *Vulgate* needlessly, "transgression." **16.** Apodosis to vs. 15. **in vain**—rashly.

CHAPTER 36

Vss. 1-33. **1, 2.** Elihu maintains that afflictions are to the godly disciplinary, in order to lead them to attain a higher moral worth, and that the reason for their continuance is not, as the friends asserted, on account of the sufferer's extraordinary guilt, but because the discipline has not yet attained its object, viz., to lead him to humble himself penitently before God (Isa. 9:13; Jer. 5:3). This is Elihu's *fourth* speech. He thus exceeds the ternary number of

the others. Hence his formula of politeness (vs. 2). Lit., Wait yet but a little for me." Bear with me a little farther. *I have yet* (much, ch. 32:18-20). There are Chaldeisms in this verse, agreeably to the view that the scene of the book is near the Euphrates and the Chaldees. **3. from afar**—not trite commonplaces, but drawn from God's mighty works. **ascribe righteousness**—whereas Job ascribed unrighteousness (ch. 34:10, 12). A man, in inquiring into God's ways, should at the outset *presume* they are all just, be *willing* to find them so, and *expect* that the result of investigation will prove them to be so; such a one will never be disappointed [BARNES]. **4.** I will not "speak wickedly for God," as the friends (ch. 13:4, 7, 8)—i.e., vindicate God by unsound arguments. **he that is perfect . . .**—Rather, as the parallelism requires, "a man of *integrity in sentiments* is with thee" (is he with whom thou hast to do). Elihu means himself, as opposed to the dishonest reasonings of the friends (ch. 21:34). **5.** Rather, *strength of understanding* (heart) the force of the repetition of "mighty"; as "mighty" as God is, none is too low to be "despised" by Him; for His "might" lies especially in "His strength of understanding," whereby He searches out the most minute things, so as to give to each his right. Elihu confirms his exhortation (ch. 35:14). **6. right . . . poor** —He espouses the cause of the afflicted. **7.** (I Pet. 3:12.) God does not forsake the godly, as Job implied, but "establishes," or *makes* them *sit* on the throne as kings (I Sam. 2:8; Ps. 113:7, 8). True of believers in the highest sense, already in part (I Pet. 2:9; Rev. 1:6); hereafter fully (Rev. 5:10; ch. 22:5). **and they are**—*that they may be.* **8-10.** If they be afflicted, it is no proof that they are hypocrites, as the friends maintain, or that God disregards them, and is indifferent whether men are good or bad, as Job asserts: God is thereby "disciplining them," and "showing them their sins," and if they bow in a right spirit under God's visiting hand, the greatest blessings ensue. **9.** **work**—transgression. **that . . . exceeded**—"In that they behaved themselves mightily (lit., "great"); i.e., presumptuously, or, at least, self-confidently. **10.** (Ch. 33:16-18, 23.) **11. serve**—i.e., worship; as in Isaiah 19:23. *God* is to be supplied (cf. Isa. 1:19, 20). **12.** (Ch. 33:18.) **without knowledge**—i.e., on account of their foolishness (ch. 4:20, 21). **13-15.** Same sentiment as vss. 11, 12, expanded. **13. hypocrites**—or, the ungodly [MAURER]; but "hypocrites" is perhaps a distinct class from the openly wicked (vs. 12). **heap up wrath**—of God against themselves (Rom. 2:5). UMBREIT translates, "nourish *their* wrath *against God*," instead of "crying" unto Him. This suits well the parallelism and the *Hebrew*. But *English Version* gives a good parallelism, "hypocrites" answering to "cry not" (ch. 27:8, 10); "heap up wrath" against themselves, to "He bindeth them" with fetters of affliction (vs. 8). **14.** Rather (Deut. 23:17), *Their life* is (ended) as that of (lit., "among") *the unclean,* prematurely and dishonorably. So the second clause answers to the first. A warning that Job make not common cause with the wicked (ch. 34:36). **15. poor**—*the afflicted* pious. **openeth . . . ears**—(vs. 10); so as to be *admonished* in their straits ("oppression") to seek God penitently, and so be "delivered" (ch. 33:16, 17, 23-27). **16.** Rather, "He *will* lead forth thee also out of *the jaws of* a strait" (Ps. 18:19; 118:5). The "broad place" expresses the *liberty,* and the well-supplied "table" the *abundance* of the prosperous (Ps. 23:5; Isa. 25:6). **17.** Rather, "But *if* thou art fulfilled (i.e., entirely filled) with the judgment of the wicked" (i.e., the *guilt* incurring judgment

[MAURER]; or rather, as UMBREIT, referring to ch. 34:5, 6, 7, 36, the *judgment pronounced on God by the guilty* in misfortunes), judgment (*God's judgment on the wicked*; Jer. 51:9, playing on the double meaning of "judgment") and justice shall closely follow each other [UMBREIT]. **18.** (Num. 16:45; Ps. 49:6, 7; Matt. 16:26.) Even the "ransom" by Jesus Christ (ch. 33:24) will be of no avail to wilful despisers (Heb. 10:26-29). **with his stroke**—(ch. 34: 26). UMBREIT translates, "Beware lest the wrath of God (thy severe calamity) *lead thee to scorn*" (ch. 34:7; 27:23). This accords better with the verb in the parallel clause, which ought to be translated, "Let not the great ransom (of money, which thou canst give) *seduce* thee (*Margin, Turn thee aside,* as if thou couldst deliver thyself from "wrath" by it). As the "scorn" in the first clause answers to the "judgment of the wicked" (vs. 17), so "ransom, seduce" to "will he esteem riches" (vs. 19). Thus, vs. 18 is the transition between vs. 17 and vs. 19. **19. forces of strength**—i.e., resources of wealth (Ps. 49:7; Prov. 11:4). **20. Desire**—rant for. Job had *wished for death* (ch. 3:3-9, etc.). **night**—(John 9:4). **when**—rather, "whereby." **cut off**—lit., "ascend," as the corn cut and lifted upon the wagon or stack (vs. 26); so "cut off," "disappear." **in their place**—lit., "under themselves"; so, without moving from their place, on the spot, suddenly (ch. 40:12) [MAURER]. UMBREIT's translation: "To *ascend* (which is really, as thou wilt find to thy cost, *to descend*) to the people *below*" (lit., "under themselves"), answers better to the parallelism and the *Hebrew*. Thou pantest for death as desirable, but it is a "night" or *region of darkness;* thy fancied *ascent* (amelioration) will prove a *descent* (deterioration) (ch. 10:22); therefore desire it not. **21. regard**—lit., "turn thyself to." **iniquity**—viz., presumptuous speaking against God (ch. 34:5, and above, vss. 17, 18, *Note*). **rather than**—to bear "affliction" with pious patience. Men think it an alleviation to complain against God, but this is adding sin to sorrow; it is sin, not sorrow, which can really hurt us (contrast Heb. 11:25). **22-25.** God is not to be impiously arraigned, but to be praised for His might, shown in His works. **exalteth**—rather, doeth lofty things, shows His exalted power [UMBREIT] (Ps. 21:13). **teacheth**—(Ps. 94:12, etc.). The connection is, returning to vs. 5, God's "might" is shown in His "wisdom"; He alone can *teach;* yet, because He, as a sovereign, explains not all His dealings, forsooth Job must presume to *teach Him* (Isa. 40:13, 14; Rom. 11:34; I Cor. 2:16). So the transition to vs. 23 is natural. UMBREIT with LXX translates, "Who is *Lord,*" wrongly, as this meaning belongs to later *Hebrew*. **23.** Job dared to *prescribe* to God what He should do (ch. 34:10, 13). **24.** Instead of arraigning, let it be thy fixed principle to *magnify* God in His works (Ps. 111:2-8; Rev. 15:3); these, which all may "see," may convince us that what we do not see is altogether wise and good (Rom. 1:20). **behold**—As "see," (vs. 25), shows; not, as MAURER, "sing," laud (*Note,* 33:27). **25.** "See," viz., with wondering admiration [MAURER]. **man may behold**— rather, (yet) *mortals* (a different *Hebrew* word from "man") behold it (only) from afar off," see but a small "part" (ch. 26:14). **26.** (Ch. 37:13.) God's greatness in heaven and earth: a reason why Job should bow under His afflicting hand. **26. know him not**—only in part (vs. 25; I Cor. 13:12). **his years**—(Ps. 90:2; 102:24, 27); applied to Jesus Christ (Heb. 1:12). **27, 28.** The marvellous formation of rain (so ch. 5:9, 10). **maketh small**—Rather, "He *draweth* (up) *to* Him, He *attracts*

(from the earth below) the drops of water; they (the drops of water) pour down rain, (*which is*) *His* vapor.*" "Vapor" is in apposition with "rain," marking the way in which rain is formed; viz., from the vapor drawn up by God into the air and then condensed into drops, which fall (Ps. 147:8). The suspension of such a mass of water, and its descent not in a deluge, but in *drops of vapory rain,* are the marvel. The selection of this particular illustration of God's greatness forms a fit prelude to the storm in which God appears (ch. 40:1). **28. abundantly** —lit., "upon many men." **29.** (ch. 37:5). God's marvels in thunder and lightnings. **29. spreadings** ...—the canopy of thick clouds, which covers the heavens in a storm (Ps. 105:39). **the noise** [crashing] **of his tabernacle**—viz., thunder; God being poetically said to have *His pavilion* amid dark clouds (Ps. 18:11; Isa. 40:22). **30. light**—lightning. **it**—His tabernacle. The light, in an instant spread over the vast mass of dark clouds, forms a striking picture. "Spread" is repeated from vs. 29 to form an antithesis. "He spreads not only *clouds,* but *light.*" **covereth the bottom** [*roots*] **of the sea**—viz., with the light. In the storm the depths of ocean are laid bare; so that "light" covers" them, at the same moment that it "spreads" across the dark sky. So in Psalm 18:14, 15, the discovering of "the channels of waters" follows the "lightnings." UMBREIT translates: "He spreadeth His light *upon Himself,* and *covereth Himself with* the roots of the sea" (Ps. 104:2). God's garment is woven of celestial light and of the watery depths, raised to the sky to form His cloudy canopy. The phrase, "cover Himself with the roots of the sea," is harsh; but the image is grand. **31.** These (rain and lightnings) are marvellous and *not* to be *understood* (vs. 29), yet necessary. "*For* by them He judgeth (chastiseth on the one hand), etc. (and on the other, by them) He giveth meat" (food), etc. (ch. 37:13; 38:23, 27; Acts 14:17). **32.** Rather, "He *covereth* (both) *His hands* with light (*lightning,* ch. 37:3, *Margin*), and giveth it a command *against his adversary*" (lit., the one "assailing" Him; Ps. 8:2; 139:20; 21:19). Thus, as in vs. 31, the twofold effects of His *waters* are set forth, so here, of His *light*; in the one hand, *destructive lightning* against the wicked; in the other, the *genial light* for good to His friends, etc. (vs. 33) [UMBREIT]. **33. noise**—rather, He revealeth it (lit., "announceth concerning it") to *His friend* (antithesis to *adversary,* vs. 32, so the *Hebrew* is translated, ch. 2:11); also to cattle and plants (lit., "that which shooteth up"; Gen. 40:10; 41:22). As the genial effect of "water" in the growth of food, is mentioned, vs. 31, so here that of "light" in cherishing *cattle* and *plants* [UMBREIT]. If *English Version,* "noise" be retained, translate, "His noise (thunder) announces concerning Him (His coming in the tempest), the cattle (to announce) concerning Him when He is in the act of *rising up*" (in the storm). Some animals give various intimations that they are sensible of the approach of a storm [*Virg. Georg.* I. 373, etc.].

CHAPTER 37

Vss. 1-24. **1. At this**—when I hear the thundering of the Divine Majesty. Perhaps the storm already had begun, out of which God was to address Job (ch. 38:1). **2. Hear attentively**—the thunder (noise), etc., and then you will feel that there is good reason to tremble. **sound**—*muttering* of the thunder. **3. directeth it**—however zigzag the lightning's course; or, rather, it applies to the pealing roll of the thunder. God's *all-embracing* power. **ends** —lit., "wings," "skirts," the habitable earth being often compared to an extended garment (ch. 38:13; Isa. 11:12). **4.** The thunderclap follows at an interval after the flash. **stay them**—He will not hold back the lightnings (vs. 3), when the thunder is heard [MAURER]. Rather, take "them" as the usual concomitants of thunder, viz., *rain and hail* [UMBREIT] (ch. 40:9). **5.** (Ch. 36:26; Ps. 65:6; 139:14). The sublimity of the description lies in this, that God is everywhere in the storm, directing it whither He will [BARNES]. See Psalm 29, where, as here, the "voice" of God is repeated with grand effect. The thunder in Arabia is sublimely terrible. **6. Be**—more forcible than "fall," as UMBREIT translates Genesis 1:3. **to the small rain . . .**—He saith, Be on the earth. The shower increasing from "small" to "great," is expressed by the *plural showers* (*Margin*), following the *singular shower*. Winter rain (Song of Sol. 2:11). **7.** In winter God stops man's out-of-doors activity. **sealeth**—closeth up (ch. 9:7). Man's "hands" are then tied up. **his work**—in antithesis to *man's own work* ("hand") which at other times engages men so as to make them liable to forget their dependence on God. UMBREIT more literally translates, That all men *whom He has made* (lit., "of His making") may be brought to acknowledgment. **8. remain**—rest in their lairs. It is beautifully ordered that during the cold, when they could not obtain food, many lie torpid, a state wherein they need no food. The desolation of the fields, at God's bidding, is poetically graphic. **9. south**—lit., "chambers"; connected with the south (ch. 9:9). The whirlwinds are poetically regarded as pent up by God in His southern chambers, whence He sends them forth (so ch. 38:22; Ps. 135:7). As to the southern whirlwinds (see Isa. 21:1; Zech. 9:14), they drive before them burning sands; chiefly from February to May. **the north**—lit., "scattering"; the north wind *scatters* the clouds. **10. the breath of God**—poetically, for the ice-producing north wind. **frost**—rather, ice. **straitened**—physically accurate; frost *compresses* or *contracts* the expanded liquid into a congealed mass (ch. 38:29, 30; Ps. 147:17, 18). **11-13.** How the thunderclouds are dispersed, or else employed by God, either for correction or mercy. **by watering**—by loading it with water. **wearieth**—*burdeneth* it, so that it falls in rain; thus "wearieth" answers to the parallel "scattereth" (cf. *Note,* vs. 9); a clear sky resulting alike from both. **bright cloud** —lit., "cloud of His light," i.e., of His lightning. UMBREIT for "watering," etc., translates; "*Brightness* drives away the clouds, His *light* scattereth the thick clouds"; the parallelism is thus good, but the *Hebrew* hardly sanctions it. **12.** **it**—the cloud of lightning. **counsels**—guidance (Ps. 148:8); lit., "steering"; the clouds obey God's guidance, as the ship does the helmsman. So the lightning (*Note,* 36:31, 32); neither is haphazard in its movements. **they**—*the clouds,* implied in the collective *singular* "it." **face of the world . . .**—in the face of the earth's circle. **13.** Lit., "He maketh it (the rain-cloud) find place," whether for correction, if (it be destined) for His land (i.e., for the part *inhabited by man,* with whom *God* deals, as opposed to the parts *uninhabited,* on which rain is at other times appointed to fall, ch. 38: 26, 27) or for mercy. "If it be destined for His land" is a parenthetical supposition [MAURER]. In *English Version,* this clause spoils the even balance of the antithesis between the "rod" (*Margin*) and "mercy" (Ps. 68:9; Gen. 7). **14.** (Ps. 111:2.) **15. when**—rather, "how." **disposed them**—lays His

charge on these "wonders" (vs. 14) to arise. **light**—lightning. **shine**—flash. How is it that *light* arises from the *dark* thundercloud? **16.** *Hebrew,* "*Hast thou understanding of* the balancings," etc., how the clouds are poised in the air, so that their watery gravity does not bring them to the earth? The condensed moisture, descending by gravity, meets a warmer temperature, which dissipates it into vapor (the tendency of which is to ascend) and so counteracts the descending force. **perfect in knowledge**—God; not here in the sense that Elihu uses it of himself (ch. 36:4). **17. Dost thou know—how, thy garments . . .**—i.e., how thy body grows warm, so as to affect thy garments with heat? **south wind**—lit., "region of the south." "When He *maketh still* (and sultry) the earth (i.e., the atmosphere) by (during) the south wind (Song of Sol. 4:16). **18. with him**—like as He does (ch. 40:15). **spread out**—given expanse to. **strong**—firm; whence the term "firmament" (Gen. 1:6; *Margin, expansion,* Isa. 44:24). **molten looking glass**—image of the bright smiling sky. Mirrors were then formed of molten polished metal, not glass. **19.** Men cannot explain God's wonders; we ought, therefore, to be dumb and not contend with God. If Job thinks we ought, "let him teach us, what we shall say." **order**—frame. **darkness**—of mind; ignorance. "The eyes are bewilderingly blinded, when turned in bold controversy with God towards the sunny heavens" (vs. 18) [UMBREIT]. **20.** What I a mortal say against God's dealings is not worthy of being told HIM. In opposition to Job's wish to "speak" before God (ch. 13:3, 18-22). **if . . . surely he shall be swallowed up**—The parallelism more favors UMBREIT, "Durst a man speak (before Him, complaining) *that he is* (without cause) *being destroyed?*" **21. cleanseth** i.e., *cleareth* the air of clouds. When the "bright light" of the sun, previously not seen through "clouds," suddenly shines out from behind them, owing to the wind clearing them away, the effect is dazzling to the eye; so if God's majesty, now hidden, were suddenly revealed in all its brightness, it would spread darkness over Job's eyes, anxious as he is for it (cf. *Note,* vs. 19) [UMBREIT]. It is because now man sees not the bright sunlight (God's dazzling majesty), owing to the intervening "clouds" (ch. 26:9), that they dare to wish to "speak" before God (vs. 20). Prelude to God's appearance (ch. 38:1). The words also hold true in a sense not intended by Elihu, but perhaps included by the Holy Ghost. Job and other sufferers cannot see the *light* of God's countenance through the *clouds* of trial: but the wind will soon clear them off, and God shall appear again: let them but wait patiently, for He still shines, though for a time they see Him not (see *Note,* 23:9). **22.** rather, golden splendor. MAURER translates "gold." *It* is found in northern regions. But *God* cannot be "found out," because of His "Majesty" (vs. 23). Thus ch. 28 corresponds; *English Version* is simpler. **the north**—Brightness is chiefly associated with it (*Note,* 23:9). Here, perhaps, because the north wind clears the air (Prov. 25:23). Thus this clause answers to the last of vs. 21; as the second of this verse to the first of vs. 21. Inverted parallelism. (See Isa. 14:13; Ps. 48:2). **with God**—splendor. **23. afflict**—oppressively, so as to "pervert *judgment*" as Job implied (*Note,* 8:3); but see end of *Note,* vs. 21, above. The reading, "He answereth not," i.e., gives no account of His dealings, is like a transcriber's correction, from ch. 33:13; *Margin.* **24. do**—rather, "*ought.*" **wise**—in their own conceits.

CHAPTER 38

Vss. 1-41. **1.** Jehovah appears unexpectedly in a whirlwind (already gathering ch. 37:1, 2), the symbol of "judgment" (Ps. 50:3, 4, etc.), to which Job had challenged Him. He asks him now to get himself ready for the contest. Can he explain the phenomena of God's *natural* government? How can he, then, hope to understand the principles of His *moral* government? God thus confirms Elihu's sentiment, that *submission to,* not *reasonings on,* God's ways is man's part. This and the *disciplinary* design of trial to the godly is the great lesson of this book. He does not solve the difficulty by reference to future retribution: for this was not the immediate question; *glimpses* of that truth were already given in chs. 14 and 19, the *full revelation* of it being reserved for Gospel times. Yet even *now* we need to learn the lesson taught by Elihu and God in Job. **2. this**—Job. **counsel**—impugning My divine wisdom in the providential arrangements of the universe. Such "words" (including those of the friends) rather obscure, than throw light on My ways. God is about to be Job's Vindicator, but must first bring him to a *right state of mind* for receiving relief. **3. a man**—*hero,* ready for battle (I Cor. 16:13), as he had wished (ch. 9:35; 13:22; 31: 37). The robe, usually worn flowing, was girt up by a girdle when men ran, labored, or fought (I Pet. 1:13). **4.** To understand the cause of things, man should have been present at their origin. The finite creature cannot fathom the infinite wisdom of the Creator (ch. 28:12; 15:7, 8). **hast [knowest] understanding**—(Prov. 4:1). **5. measures**—of its proportions. Image from an architect's plans of a building. **line**—of measurement (Isa. 28:17). The earth is formed on an all-wise *plan.* **6. foundations**—not *sockets,* as *Margin.* **fastened**—lit., "made to sink," as a foundation stone let down till it settles firmly in the clay (ch. 26:7). Gravitation makes and keeps the earth a sphere. **7.** So at the founding of Zerubbabel's temple (Ezra 3:10-13). So hereafter at the completion of the Church, the temple of the Holy Ghost (Zech. 4:7); as at its foundation (Luke 2:13, 14). **7. morning stars**—especially beautiful. The creation *morn* is appropriately associated with these, it being the *commencement* of this world's *day.* The stars are figuratively said to sing God's praises, as in Psalm 19:1; 148:3. They are symbols of the angels, bearing the same relation to our earth, as angels do to us. Therefore they answer to "sons of God," or angels, in the parallel. See *Note,* 25:5. **8. doors**—floodgates; these when opened caused the flood (Gen. 8:2); or else, *the shores.* **womb**—of chaos. The bowels of the earth. Image from childbirth (vss. 8, 9; Ezek. 32:2; Mic. 4:10). Ocean at its birth was wrapped in clouds as its swaddling bands. **10. brake up for**—i.e., appointed it. Shores are generally broken and abrupt cliffs. The *Greek* for *shore* means a *broken place.* I *broke off* or measured off for it *my limit,* i.e., the limit which I thought fit (ch. 26:10). **11. stayed**—*Hebrew,* "a limit shall be set to." **12-15.** Passing from creation to phenomena in the existing inanimate world. **12. Hast thou**—as God daily does. **commanded the morning**—to rise. **since thy days**—since thou hast come into being. **his place**—It varies in its place of rising from day to day, and yet it has its place each day according to fixed laws. **13. take hold of the ends . . .**—spread itself over the earth to its utmost bounds in a moment. **wicked**—who hate the light, and do their evil works in the dark (ch. 24:13). **shaken out of it**—The corners (*Hebrew,* "wings" or

"skirts") of it, as of a garment, are taken hold of by the dayspring, so as to shake off the wicked. **14.** Explaining the first clause of vs. 13, as vs. 15 does the second clause. As the plastic clay presents the various figures impressed on it by a seal, so the earth, which in the dark was void of all form, when illuminated by the dayspring, presents a variety of forms, hills, valleys, etc. **Turned** ("turns itself," *Hebrew*) alludes to the rolling cylinder seal, such as is found in Babylon, which leaves its impressions on the clay, as it is turned about; so the morning light rolling on over the earth. **they stand**—The forms of beauty, unfolded by the dawn, stand forth as a garment, in which the earth is clad. **15. their light**—by which they work; viz., darkness, which is *their day* (ch. 24:17), is extinguished by daylight. **high** —Rather, *The arm uplifted* for murder or other crime is broken; it falls down suddenly, powerless, through their fear of light. **16. springs**—fountains beneath the sea (Ps. 95:4, 5). **Search**—Rather, the inmost recesses; lit., "that which is only found by searching," the deep caverns of ocean. **17. seen**—The second clause heightens the thought in the first. Man during life does not even "see" the gates of the realm of the dead ("death," ch. 10:21); much less are they "opened" to him. But those are "naked before God" (ch. 26:6). So God doth (ch. 28:24). **19-38.** The marvels in heaven. **19.** "What is the way (to the place wherein) light dwelleth?" The origin of light and darkness. In Genesis 1, "light" is created distinct from, and previous to, light-emitting bodies, the luminaries of heaven. **20.** Dost thou know its place so well as to be able to *guide,* ("take" as in Isa. 36:17) it to (but UMBREIT, "*reach* it in") its own boundary, i.e., the limit between light and darkness (ch. 26:10)? **21.** Or without the interrogation, in an ironical sense [UMBREIT]. then—when I created light and darkness (ch. 15:7). **22. treasures**—storehouses, from which God draws forth snow and hail. Snow is vapor congealed in the air before it is collected in drops large enough to form hail. Its shape is that of a crystal in endless variety of beautiful figures. Hail is formed by rain falling through dry cold air. **23. against the time of trouble**—the time when I design to chastise men (Exod. 9:18; Josh. 10:11; Rev. 16:21; Isa. 28:17; Ps. 18:12, 13; Hag. 2:17). **24. is . . . parted**—parts, so as to diffuse itself over the whole earth, though seeming to come from one point. Light travels from the sun to the earth, ninety millions of miles, in eight minutes. **which scattereth**—rather, "And by what way the east wind (personified) spreads (scattereth) itself." The light and east wind are associated together, as both come from one quarter, and often arise together (Jonah 4:8). **25. waters**—Rain falls, not in a mass on one spot, but in countless separate canals in the air marked out for them. **way for the lightning**—(ch. 28:26.) **26.** Since rain falls also on places uninhabited by man, it cannot be that *man* guides its course. Such rain, though man cannot explain the reason for it, is not lost. *God* has some wise design in it. **27.** As though the desolate ground thirsted for God's showers. Personification. The beauty imparted to the uninhabited desert pleases God, for whom primarily all things exist, and He has ulterior designs in it. **28.** Can any visible origin of rain and dew be assigned by man? Dew is moisture, which was suspended in the air, but becomes condensed on reaching the—in the night—lower temperature of objects on the earth. **29.** Ch. 37:10. **30.** The unfrozen *waters are hid* under the frozen, as *with* a covering of *stone.* **frozen**—lit., "is taken"; the particles take hold of one another so as to cohere. **31. sweet influences**—the joy diffused by spring, the time when the Pleiades appear. The Eastern poets, Hafiz, Sadi, etc., describe them as "brilliant rosettes." GENESIUS translates: "bands" or "knot," which answers better the parallelism. But *English Version* agrees better with the *Hebrew*. The seven stars are closely "bound" together (*Note,* 9:9). "Canst thou bind or loose the tie?" "Canst thou loose the bonds by which the constellation Orion (represented in the East as an impious giant chained to the sky) is held fast?" (*Note,* 9:9). **32.** *Canst thou bring forth* from their places or *houses* (*Mazzaloth, Margin,* II Kings 23:5; to which *Mazzaroth* here is equivalent) into the sky the signs of the Zodiac at their respective seasons—the twelve lodgings in which the sun successively stays, or appears, in the sky? **Arcturus**—Ursa Major. **his sons**—the three stars in his tail. Canst thou make them appear in the sky? (ch. 9:9). The great and less Bear are called by the Arabs "Daughters of the Bier," the quadrangle being the bier, the three others the mourners. **33. ordinances**—which regulate the alternations of seasons, etc. (Gen. 8:22). **dominion**—*controlling influence* of the heavenly bodies, the sun, moon, etc., on the earth (on the tides, weather) (Gen. 1:16; Ps. 136:7-9). **34.** Jeremiah 14:22; above ch. 22:11, metaphorically. **35. Here we are**—at thy disposal (Isa. 6:8). **36. inward parts . . . heart**—But [UMBREIT] "dark clouds ("shining phenomena") [MAURER]—"meteor," referring to the consultation of these as signs of weather by the husbandman (Eccles. 11:4). But *Hebrew* supports *English Version.* The connection is, "Who hath given thee the intelligence to comprehend in any degree the phenomena just specified?" **heart**—not the usual *Hebrew* word, but one from a root "to view"; perception. **37.** Who appoints by his wisdom the due measure of the clouds? **stay**—rather, "empty"; lit., "lay down" or "incline" so as to pour out. **bottles of heaven**—rain-filled clouds. **38. groweth . . .**—rather, pour itself into a mass by the rain, like molten metal; then translate vs. 38, "Who is it that *empties,* etc., "when," etc.? *English Version,* however, is tenable: "*Is caked into a mass*" by heat, like molten metal, *before* the rain falls; "Who is it that *can empty* the rain vessels, and bring down rain *at such a time?*" (vs. 38). **39.** From this verse to ch. 39:30, the instincts of animals. Is it thou that givest it the instinct to hunt its prey? (Ps. 104:21.) **appetite**—lit., "life"; which depends on the *appetite* (ch. 33:20). **40. lie in wait**—for their prey (Ps. 10:9). **41.** Luke 12:24. Transition from the noble lioness to the croaking raven. Though man dislikes it, as of ill-omen, God cares for it, as for all His creatures.

CHAPTER 39

Vss. 1-30. **1.** Even wild beasts, cut off from all care of *man,* are cared for by *God* at their seasons of greatest need. Their instinct comes direct from God and guides them to help themselves in parturition; the very time when the herdsman is most anxious for his herds. **wild goats**—ibex (Ps. 104:18; I Sam. 24:2). **hinds**—fawns; most timid and defenseless animals, yet cared for by God. **2.** They bring forth with ease and do not need to reckon the months of pregnancy, as the shepherd does in the case of his flocks. **3.** "Bow themselves" in parturition; bend on their knees (I Sam. 4:19). **bring forth**—lit., "cause their young to cleave the womb

and break forth." **sorrows**—their young ones, the cause of their momentary pains. **4. are in good liking**—in good condition, grow up strong. **with corn**—rather, "in the field," without man's care. **return not**—being able to provide for themselves. **5. wild ass**—Two different *Hebrew* words are here used for the same animal, "the ass of the woods" and "the wild ass." (*Note,* 6:5; ch. 11:12, 24:5; Jer. 2:24.) **loosed the bands**—given its liberty to. Man can rob animals of freedom, but not, as God, give freedom, combined with subordination to fixed laws. **6. barren**—lit., "salt," i.e., unfruitful. (So *Margin,* Ps. 107:34.) **7. multitude**—rather, "din"; he sets it at defiance, being far away from it in the freedom of the wilderness. **driver**—who urges on the tame ass to work. The wild ass is the symbol of uncontrolled freedom in the East; even kings have, therefore, added its name to them. **8. The range**—lit., "searching," "that which it finds by searching is," etc. **9. unicorn**—Pliny (*Natural History* 8. 21), mentions such an animal; its figure is found depicted in the ruins of Persepolis. The *Hebrew reem* conveys the idea of *loftiness* and *power* (cf. *Ramah,* Indian *Ram,* Latin *Roma*). The rhinoceros was perhaps the original type of the unicorn. The Arab *rim* is a two-horned animal. Sometimes "unicorn" or *reem* is a mere poetical symbol or abstraction; but the buffalo is the animal referred to here, from the contrast to the tame ox, used in ploughing (vss. 10, 12). **abide**—lit., "pass the night." **crib**—(Isa. 1:3). **10. his band**—fastened to the horns, as its chief strength lies in the head and shoulders. **after thee**—obedient to thee; willing to follow, instead of being goaded on *before* thee. **11. thy labour**—rustic work. **12. believe**—trust **seed**—produce (I Sam. 8:15). **into thy barn**—rather, *gather* (the contents of) *thy threshing-floor* [MAURER]; the corn threshed on it. **13.** Rather, "the wing of the ostrich hen—lit., "the crying bird"; as the Arab name for it means "song"; referring to its night cries (ch. 30:29; Mic. 1:8) vibrating joyously. Is it not like the quill and feathers of *the pious bird*" (the stork)? [UMBREIT]. The *vibrating, quivering wing,* serving for sail and oar at once, is characteristic of the ostrich in full course. Its white and black feathers in the wing and tail are like the stork's. But, unlike that bird, the symbol of parental love in the East, it with seeming want of natural (pious) affection deserts its young. Both birds are poetically called by descriptive, instead of their usual appellative, names. **14.** Yet (unlike the stork) she "leaveth . . ." Hence called by the Arabs "the impious bird." However, the fact is, she lays her eggs with great care and hatches them, as other birds do; but in hot countries the eggs do not need so constant incubation; she therefore often leaves them and sometimes forgets the place on her return. Moreover, the outer eggs, intended for food, she feeds to her young; these eggs, lying separate in the sand, exposed to the sun, gave rise to the idea of her altogether leaving them. God describes her as she *seems to man;* implying, though she may seem foolishly to neglect her young, yet really she is guided by a sure instinct from God, as much as animals of instincts widely different. **16.** On a slight noise she often forsakes her eggs, and returns not, *as if* she were "hardened towards her young." **her labour**—in producing eggs, *is in vain,* (yet) *she has not disquietude* (about her young), unlike other birds, who, if one egg and another are taken away, will go on laying till their full number is made up. **17. wisdom**—such as God gives to other animals, and to man (ch. 35:11). The Arab proverb is, "foolish as an ostrich." Yet her very seeming want of wisdom is not without wise design of God, though man cannot see it; just as in the trials of the godly, which seem so unreasonable to Job, there lies hid a wise design. **18.** Notwithstanding her deficiencies, she has distinguishing excellences. **lifteth . . . herself**— for running; she cannot mount in the air. GESE-NIUS translates: "lashes herself" up to her course by flapping her wings. The old versions favor *English Version,* and the parallel "scorneth" answers to her *proudly* "lifting up herself." **19.** The allusion to "the horse" (vs. 18), suggests the description of him. Arab poets delight in praising the horse; yet it is not mentioned in the possessions of Job (chs. 1 and 42). It seems to have been at the time chiefly used for war, rather than "domestic purposes." **thunder**— poetically for, "he with arched neck inspires fear as thunder does." Translate, "majesty" [UMBREIT]. Rather "the trembling, quivering mane," answering to the "vibrating wing" of the ostrich (*Note,* vs. 13) [MAURER]. "Mane" in Greek also is from a root meaning "fear." *English Version* is more sublime. **20. make . . . afraid**—rather, "canst thou (as I do) make him *spring* as the *locust?*" So in Joel 2:4 the comparison is between *locusts* and *war-horses.* The heads of the two are so similar that the Italians call the locusts *cavaletta,* "little horse." **nostrils**— snorting furiously. **21. valley**—where the battle is joined. **goeth on**—goeth forth (Num. 1:3; 21:23). **23. quiver**—for the arrows, which they contain, and which are directed "against him." **glittering spear** —lit., "glittering of the spear," like "lightning of the spear" (Hab. 3:11). **shield**—rather, "lance." **24. swalloweth**—Fretting with impatience, he *draws the ground towards him* with his hoof, as if he would *swallow* it. The parallelism shows this to be the sense; not as MAURER, "scours over it." **neither believeth**—for joy. Rather, "he will not *stand still,* when the note of the trumpet" (soundeth). **25. saith**—poetically applied to his mettlesome neighing, whereby he shows his love of the battle. **smelleth** —snuffeth; discerneth (*Margin,* Isa. 11:3). **thunder** —thundering voice. **26.** The instinct by which some birds migrate to warmer climes before winter. Rapid flying peculiarly characterizes the whole hawk genus. **27. eagle**—It flies highest of all birds: thence called "the bird of heaven." **28. abideth**— securely (Ps. 91:1); it occupies the same abode mostly for life. **crag**—lit., "tooth" (*Margin,* I Sam. 14:5). **strong place**—citadel, fastness. **29. seeketh** —is on the lookout for. **behold**—The eagle descries its prey at an astonishing distance, by sight, rather than smell. **30.** Quoted partly by Jesus Christ (Matt. 24:28). The food of young eagles is the blood of victims brought by the parent, when they are still too feeble to devour flesh. **slain**—As the vulture chiefly feeds on carcasses, *it* is included probably in the eagle genus.

CHAPTER 40

Vss. 1-24. GOD'S SECOND ADDRESS. He had paused for a reply, but Job was silent. **1. the Lord**— *Hebrew,* JEHOVAH. **2. he that contendeth**—as Job had so often expressed a wish to do. Or, *rebuketh.* Does Job now still (after seeing and hearing of God's majesty and wisdom) wish to set, God right? **answer it**—viz., the questions I have asked. **3. Lord** —JEHOVAH. **4.** I am (too) vile (to reply). It is a very different thing to vindicate ourselves before God, from what it is before men. Job could do the

latter, not the former. **lay . . . hand upon . . . mouth**—I have no plea to offer (ch. 21:5; Judg. 18: 19). **5. Once . . . twice**—oftentimes, more than once (ch. 33:14, cf. with 29; Ps. 62:11): "I have spoken," viz., against God. **not answer**—not plead against Thee. **6. the Lord**—JEHOVAH. **7.** (*Note,* 38:3.) Since Job has not only spoken against God, but accused Him of injustice, God challenges him to try, could *he* govern the world, as *God* by His power doth, and punish the proud and wicked (vss. 7-14). **8.** Wilt thou not only contend with, but *set aside My judgment* or justice in the government of the world? **condemn**—declare Me unrighteous, in order *that thou mayest be* accounted *righteous* (innocent; undeservingly afflicted). **9. arm**—God's omnipotence (Isa. 53:1). **thunder**—God's voice (ch. 37:4). **10.** See, hast thou power and majesty like God's, to enable thee to judge and govern the world? **11. rage**—rather, pour out *the redundant floods of . . . .* **behold**—Try, canst thou, as God, by a mere *glance* abase the proud (Isa. 2:12, etc.)? **12. proud**—high (Dan. 4:37). **in their place**—on the spot; suddenly, before they can move from their place (*Note,* 34:26; 36:20). **13.** (Isa. 2:10.) *abase* and remove them out of the sight of men. **bind . . . faces**—i.e., shut up their persons [MAURER]. But it refers rather to the custom of binding a cloth over the faces of persons about to be executed (ch. 9:24; Esther 7:8). **in secret**—consign them to *darkness.* **14. confess**— rather, extol; "I also," who now *censure* thee. But since thou canst not do these works, thou must, instead of censuring, extol *My* government. **thine own . . . hand . . . save**—(Ps. 44:3). So as to eternal salvation by Jesus Christ (Isa. 59:16; 63:5). **15-24.** God shows that if Job cannot bring under control the lower animals (of which he selects the two most striking, behemoth on land, leviathan in the water), much less is he capable of governing the world. **15. behemoth**—The description in part agrees with the hippopotamus, in part with the elephant, but exactly in all details with neither. It is rather a poetical personification of the great *Pachydermata,* or *Herbivora* (so "he eateth grass"), the idea of the hippopotamus being predominant. In vs. 17, "the tail like a cedar," hardly applies to the latter (so also vss. 20, 23, "Jordan," a river which elephants alone could reach, but see *Note,* vs. 23). On the other hand, vss. 21, 22 are characteristic of the *amphibious* river horse. So leviathan (the twisting animal), ch. 41:1, is a generalized term for cetacea, pythons, saurians of the neighboring seas and rivers, including the crocodile, which is the most prominent, and is often associated with the river horse by old writers. "Behemoth" seems to be the Egyptian *Pehemout,* "water-ox," Hebraized, so-called as being like an ox, whence the Italian *bombarino.* **with thee**—as I made thyself. Yet how great the difference! The *manifold* wisdom and power of God! **he eateth grass**—marvellous in an animal living so much in the water; also strange, that such a monster should not be carnivorous. **16. navel**—rather, *muscles* of his belly; the weakest point of the elephant, therefore it is not meant. **17. like a cedar**—As the tempest *bends* the cedar, so it can move its smooth thick tail [UMBREIT]. But the cedar implies straightness and length, such as do not apply to the river horse's short tail, but perhaps to an extinct species of animal (see *Note,* vs. 15). **stones**—rather, *thighs.* **wrapped**— firmly *twisted together,* like a thick rope. **18. strong pieces**—rather, *tubes* of copper [UMBREIT]. **19.** Chief of the *works* of God; so "ways" (ch. 26:14; Prov. 8:22). **can make his sword to approach**— rather, has furnished him with his sword (*harpe*), viz., the *sickle-like* teeth with which he cuts down grain. *English Version,* however, is literally right. **20.** The mountain is not his *usual* haunt. BOCHART says it is *sometimes* found there(?). **beasts . . . play** –a graphic trait: though armed with such teeth, he lets the beasts play near him unhurt, for his food is grass. **21. lieth**–He leads an inactive life. **shady trees**–rather, lotus bushes; as vs. 22 requires. **22.** Translate: "lotus bushes." **23.** Rather, "(Though) a river be violent (overflow), he trembleth not"; (for though living on land, he can live in the water, too); he is secure, though a Jordan swell up to his mouth. "Jordan" is used for *any great river* (consonant with the "behemoth"), being a poetical generalization (*Note,* vs. 5). The author cannot have been a Hebrew as UMBREIT asserts, or he would not adduce the Jordan, where there were no river horses. He alludes to it as a name for *any* river, but not as one known to him, except by hearsay. **24.** Rather, "Will any take him by open force" (lit., "before his eyes"), "or pierce his nose with cords?" No; he can only be taken by guile, and in a pitfall (ch. 41:1, 2).

CHAPTER 41

Vss. 1-34. **1. leviathan**–lit., "the twisted animal," gathering itself in folds: a synonym to the Thannin (ch. 3:8, *Margin;* see Ps. 74:14; type of the Egyptian tyrant; Ps. 104:26; Isa. 27:1; the Babylon tyrant). A poetical generalization for all cetacean, serpentine, and saurian monsters (*Note,* 40:15, hence *all* the description applies to no *one* animal); especially the crocodile; which is naturally described after the *river horse,* as both are found in the Nile. **tongue . . . lettest down**–The crocodile has no tongue, or a very small one cleaving to the lower jaw. But as in fishing the tongue of the fish draws the baited hook to it, God asks, Canst thou in like manner take leviathan? **2. hook**–rather, a rope of rushes. **thorn**–rather, a ring or hook. So wild beasts were led about when caught (Isa. 37:29; Ezek. 29:4); fishes also were secured thus and thrown into the water to keep them alive. **3. soft words**–that thou mayest spare his life. No: he is untamable. **4.** Can he be tamed for domestic use (so ch. 39:10-12)? **5. a bird**–that is tamed. **6.** Rather, partners (viz., in fishing). **make a banquet**–The parallelism rather supports UMBREIT, "Do partners (in trade) *desire to purchase* him?" So the *Hebrew* (Deut. 2: 6). **merchants**–lit., "Canaanites," who were great merchants (Hos. 12:7, *Margin*). His hide is not penetrable, as that of fishes. **8.** If thou *lay . . . ,* thou wilt have reason ever to *remember . . . ,* and thou wilt never try it again. **9. the hope**–of taking *him.* **cast down**–with fear "at the (mere) sight of him." **10. fierce**–courageous. If a man *dare* attack one of My creatures (Gen. 49:9; Num. 24:9), who will dare (as Job has wished) oppose himself (Ps. 2:2) to Me, the Creator? This is the main drift of the description of leviathan. **11. prevented**–done Me a favor first: anticipated Me with service (Ps. 21:3). None can call Me to account ("stand before Me," vs. 10) as unjust, because I have withdrawn favors from him (as in Job's case): for none has laid Me under a prior obligation by conferring on Me something which was not already My own. What can man give to Him who possesses all, including man himself? Man cannot constrain the creature to be his "servant" (vs. 4), much less the Creator. **12. I will not conceal**–a resumption of the description broken off by the digression, which

formed an agreeable change. **his power**–lit., "the way," i.e., true proportion or expression *of his strength* (so *Hebrew,* Deut. 19:4). **comely proportion**–lit., "the comeliness of his structure" (his *apparatus:* so "suit of apparel" Judg. 17:10) [MAURER]. UMBREIT translates, "his armor." But that follows after. **13. discover**–rather, *uncover the surface* of his garment (*skin,* ch. 10:11): strip off the hard *outer coat* with which the inner skin is covered. **with**–rather, within his double jaws; lit., "bridle"; hence that into which the bridle is put, the double row of teeth; but "bridle" is used to imply that none dare put his hand in to insert a bridle where in other animals it is placed (vs. 4; ch. 39:10). **14. doors of . . . face**–his mouth. His teeth are sixty in number, larger in proportion than his body, some standing out, some serrated, fitting into each other like a comb [BOCHART]. **15.** Rather, his *furrows of shields* (as "tubes," "*channels,*" *Note,* 40:18), are, etc., i.e., the *rows of scales,* like *shields* covering him: he has seventeen such rows. **shut up**–firmly closed together. A musket ball cannot penetrate him, save in the eye, throat, and belly. **18.** Transate: "his sneezing, causeth a light to shine." Amphibious animals, emerging after having long held their breath under water, respire by violently expelling the breath like one sneezing: in the effort the *eyes* which are usually directed towards the sun, seem to flash fire; or it is the expelled *breath* that, in the sun, seems to emit light. **eyelids of morning**–The Egyptian hieroglyphics paint the *eyes of the crocodile* as the symbol for *morning,* because the eyes appear the first thing, before the whole body emerges from the deep [*Hor. Hierog.,* 1. 65. BOCHART]. **19. burning lamps**–"torches"; viz., in respiring (vs. 18), *seem* to go out. **20. seething**–boiling: lit., "blown under," under which a fire is blown. **21. kindleth coals**–poetical imagery (Ps. 18:8). **22. remaineth**–abideth permanently. His chief strength is in the neck. **sorrow**–anxiety or dismay personified. **is turned into joy**–rather, danceth, exulteth; wherever he goes, he spreads terror "before him." **23. flakes**–rather, dewlaps; that which *falls* down (*Margin*). They are "joined" *fast and firm,* together, not *hanging loose,* as in the ox. **are firm**–UMBREIT and MAURER, "are spread." **in themselves** –rather, upon him. **24. heart**–"In large beasts which are less acute in feeling, there is great firmness of the *heart,* and slower motion" [BOCHART]. The nether millstone, on which the upper turns, is especially hard. **25. he**–the crocodile: a type of the awe which the Creator inspires when He rises in wrath. **breakings**–viz., of the mind, i.e., terror. **purify themselves**–rather, they wander from the way, i.e., flee away bewildered [MAURER and UMBREIT]. **26. cannot hold**–on his hard skin. **habergeon**–coat of mail; *avail* must be taken by zeugma out of "hold," as the verb in the second clause: "hold" cannot apply to the "coat of mail." **27. iron . . . brass**–viz., weapons. **28. arrow**–lit., "son of the bow"; Oriental imagery (Lam. 3:13; *Margin*). **stubble**–Arrows produce no more effect than it would to throw stubble at him. **29. Darts**–rather, *clubs;* darts have been already mentioned. **30. stones**–rather, potsherds, i.e., the sharp and pointed scales on the belly, like broken pieces of pottery, **sharp-pointed things**–rather, *a threshing instrument,* but not on the *fruits* of the earth, but "on the *mire*"; irony. When he lies on the mire, he leaves the marks of his scales so imprinted on it, that one might fancy a threshing instrument with its sharp teeth had been drawn over it (Isa. 28:27). **31.** Whenever he moves. **sea**–the Nile (Isa. 19:5; Nah.

3:8). **pot of ointment**—the vessel in which it is mixed. Appropriate to the crocodile, which emits a musky smell. **32. path**—the foam on his track. **hoary**—as hair of the aged. **33. who**—being one who.... **34. beholdeth**—as their superior. **children of pride**—the proud and fierce beasts. So ch. 28:8; *Hebrew,* sons of pride. To humble the *pride* of man and to teach implicit submission, is the aim of Jehovah's speech and of the book; therefore with this as to leviathan, the type of God in His lordship over creation, He closes.

CHAPTER 42

Vss. 1-6. JOB'S PENITENT REPLY. **2.** In the first clause he owns God to be omnipotent over nature, as contrasted with his own feebleness, which God had proved (ch. 40:15; 41:34); in the second, that God is supremely just (which, in order to be governor of the world, He must needs be) in all His dealings, as contrasted with his own vileness (vs. 6), and incompetence to deal with the wicked as a just judge (ch. 40:8-14). **thought**—*purpose,* as in ch. 17:11; but it is usually applied to *evil devices* (ch. 21:27; Ps. 10:2): the ambiguous word is designedly chosen to express that, while to Job's finite view, God's plans seem bad, to the All-wise One they continue unhindered in their development, and will at last be seen to be as good as they are infinitely wise. No evil can emanate from the Parent of good (Jas. 1:13, 17); but it is His prerogative to overrule evil to good. **3.** I am the man! Job *in God's own words* (ch. 38: 2) expresses his deep and humble penitence. God's word concerning our guilt should be engraven on our hearts and form the groundwork of our confession. Most men in confessing sin palliate rather than confess. Job in omitting "by words" (ch. 38: 2), goes even further than God's accusation. Not merely my *words,* but my whole thoughts and ways were "without knowledge." **3. too wonderful**—I rashly denied that Thou hast any fixed plan in governing human affairs, merely because Thy plan was "too wonderful" for my comprehension. **4.** When I said, "Hear," etc., Job's *demand* (ch. 13:22) convicted him of being "without knowledge." God alone could speak thus to Job, not Job to God: therefore he quotes again God's words as the groundwork of retracting his own foolish words. **5. hearing of the ear**—(Ps. 18:44, *Margin*). *Hearing* and *seeing* are often in antithesis (ch. 29:11; Ps. 18:8). **seeth**—not God's *face* (Exod. 33:20), but His presence in the veil of a dark cloud (ch. 38:1). Job implies also that, besides this literal *seeing,* he now saw spiritually what he had indistinctly taken on hearsay before God's infinite wisdom. He "now" proves this; he had seen in a *literal* sense before, at the beginning of God's speech, but he had not seen *spiritually* till "now" at its close. **6. myself**—rather "I abhor," and retract *the rash speeches* I made against thee (vss. 3, 4) [UMBREIT].
7-17. EPILOGUE, in prose. **7. to Eliphaz**—because he was the foremost of the three friends; their speeches were but the echo of his. **right**—lit., "well-grounded," sure and true. Their spirit towards Job was unkindly, and to justify themselves in their unkindliness they used false arguments (ch. 13:7); (viz., that calamities always prove *peculiar* guilt); therefore, though it was "for God" they spake thus falsely, God "reproves" them, as Job said He would (ch. 13:10). **as . . . Job hath**—Job had spoken rightly in relation to *them* and their ar-

gument, denying their *theory,* and the *fact* which they alleged, that he was peculiarly guilty and a hypocrite; but wrongly in relation to *God,* when he fell into the opposite extreme of almost denying *all* guilt. This extreme *he* has now repented of, and therefore God speaks of him as now altogether "right." **8. seven**—(See Introduction). The number offered by the Gentile prophet (Num. 23:1). Job plainly lived before the legal priesthood, etc. The patriarchs acted as priests for their families; and sometimes as praying mediators (Gen. 20:17), thus foreshadowing the true Mediator (I Tim. 2:5), but sacrifice accompanies and is the groundwork on which the mediation rests. **him**—rather, "His *person* [face] only" (*Note,* 22:30). The "person" must be first accepted, before God can accept his offering and work (Gen. 4:4); *that* can be only through Jesus Christ. **folly**—impiety (ch. 1:22; 2:10). **9.** The forgiving spirit of Job foreshadows the love of Jesus Christ and of Christians to enemies (Matt. 5:44; Luke 23:34; Acts 7:60; 16:24, 28, 30, 31). **10. turned . . . captivity**—proverbial for *restored,* or *amply indemnified him for all he had lost* (Ezek. 16: 53; Ps. 14:7; Hos. 6:11). Thus the future vindication of man, body and soul, against Satan (ch. 1: 9-12), at the resurrection (ch. 19:25-27), has its earnest and adumbration in the temporal vindication of Job at last by Jehovah in person. **twice**—so to the afflicted literal and spiritual Jerusalem (Isa. 40:2, 60:7; 61:7; Zech. 9:12). As in Job's case, so in that of Jesus Christ, the glorious recompense follows the "intercession" for enemies (Isa. 53:12). **11.** It was Job's complaint in his misery that his "brethren," were "estranged" from him (ch. 19:13); these now return with the return of his prosperity (Prov. 14:20; 19:6, 7); the true friend loveth at all times (Prov. 17: 17; 18:24). "Swallow friends leave in the winter and return with the spring" [HENRY]. **eat bread**—in token of friendship (Ps. 41:9). **piece of money** —Presents are usual in visiting a man of rank in the East, especially after a calamity (II Chron. 32:23). *Hebrew, kesita.* MAGEE translates "*a lamb*" (the medium of exchange then before money was used), as it is in *Margin* of Genesis 33:19; Joshua 24:32. But it is from the *Arabic kasat,* "weighed out" [UMBREIT], not coined; so Genesis 42:35; 33:19; cf. with Genesis 23:15, makes it likely it was equal to four shekels; *Hebrew kashat,* "pure," viz., metal. The term, instead of the usual "shekel," etc., is a mark of antiquity. **earring**—whether for the nose or ear (Gen. 35:4; Isa. 3:21). Much of the gold in the East, in the absence of banks, is in the shape of ornaments. **12.** Probably by degrees, not all at once. **13.** The same number as before; perhaps by a second wife; in ch. 19:17 his wife is last mentioned. **14.** Names significant of his restored prosperity (Gen. 4:25; 5:29). Jemima, "daylight," after his "night" of calamity; but MAURER, "a dove." Kezia, "cassia," an aromatic herb (Ps. 45:8), instead of his offensive breath and ulcers. Keren-happuch, "horn of stibium," a paint with which females dyed their eyelids; in contrast to his "horn defiled in the dust" (ch. 16:15). The names also imply the beauty of his daughters. **15. inheritance among . . . brethren**—An unusual favor in the East to daughters, who, in the Jewish law, only inherited, if there were no sons (Num. 27:8), a proof of wealth and unanimity. **16.** LXX makes Job live 170 years after his calamity, and 240 in all. This would make him seventy at the time of his calamity, which added to 140 in *Hebrew* text makes up 210; a little more than the age (205) of Terah, father of Abraham, perhaps his contemporary. Man's length of life gradually shortened, till it reached threescore and ten in Moses' time (Ps. 90:10). **16. sons' sons**—a proof of divine favor (Gen. 50:23; Ps. 128:6; Prov. 17:6). **17. full of days**—*fully sated and contented* with all the happiness that life could give him; realizing what Eliphaz had painted as the lot of the godly (ch. 5:26; Ps. 91:16; Gen. 25:8; 35:29). LXX adds, "It is written, that he will rise again with those whom the Lord will raise up." Cf. Matthew 27:52, 53, from which it perhaps was derived spuriously.

THE BOOK OF

PSALMS

INTRODUCTION

THE Hebrew title of this book is *Tehilim*, "praises" or "hymns," for a leading feature in its contents is *praise*, though the word occurs in the title of only one Psalm (145). The Greek title (in the Septuagint, a translation made 200 years before Christ) is *psalmoi*, whence our word "Psalms." This corresponds to the Hebrew word *mizmoi* by which sixty-five Psalms are designated in their inscriptions, and which the Syriac, a language like the Hebrew, uses for the whole book. It means, as does also the Greek name, an ode, or song, whose singing is accompanied by an instrument, particularly the harp (cf. I Chron. 16:4–8; II Chron. 5:12, 13). To some Psalms, the Hebrew word (*shir*) "a song," is prefixed. Paul seems to allude to all these terms in Ephesians 5:19, "singing . . . in *psalms, hymns,* and spiritual *songs.*"

TITLES.—To more than a hundred Psalms are prefixed inscriptions, which give one or more (and in one case [Ps. 60] all) of these particulars: the direction to the musician, the name of the author or the instrument, the style of the music or of the poetry, the subject or occasion. The authority of these inscriptions has been disputed by some writers. They say that the earliest translators, as the Greek and Syriac, evince a disregard for their authority, by variations from a proper translation of some, altering others, and, in several instances, supplying titles to Psalms which, in Hebrew, had none. It is also alleged that the subject of a Psalm, as given in the title, is often inconsistent with its contents. But those translators have also varied from a right translation of many passages in the Bible, which all agree to be of good authority; and the alleged inconsistency may be shown, on more accurate investigation, not to exist. The admitted antiquity of these inscriptions, on the other hand, and even their obscurity, raise a presumption in their favor, while such prefaces to a composition accord with the usages of that age and part of the world (cf. Isa. 38:9).

"The Chief Musician" was the superintendent of the music (cf. I Chron. 15:21, *Margin*). "To" prefixed to this, means, "pertaining to" in his official character. This inscription is found in 53 Psalms and is attached to Habakkuk's prayer (Hab. 3). The same Hebrew preposition is prefixed to the name of the author and translated "of," as "a Psalm *of* David," "*of* Asaph," except that to "the sons of Korah," it is translated "for," which is evidently wrong, as the usual direction, "to the chief musician," is given, and no other authorship intimated. On the apparent exception to this last remark, see below, and Psalm 88 (title). The explanations of other particulars in the titles will be given as they occur.

AUTHORS.—This book is often called "The Psalms of David," he being the only author mentioned in the New Testament (Luke 20:42) and his name appearing in more titles than that of any other writer. Besides about one-half of the Psalms in which it thus appears, Psalms 2 and 95 are ascribed to him (Acts 4:25 and Heb. 4:7). He was probably the author of many others which appear without a name. He used great efforts to beautify the worship of the sanctuary. Among the 288 Levites he appointed for singing and performing instrumental music, we find mentioned the "sons of Korah" (I Chron. 9:19); including Heman (I Chron. 6:33–38); and also Asaph (39–44); and Ethan (15–19). God was doubtless pleased to endow these men with the inspiration of His Spirit, so that they used those poetic talents which their connection with the kindred art of music had led them to cultivate, in the production of compositions like those of their king and patron. To Asaph are ascribed twelve Psalms; to the sons of Korah, eleven, including the 88th, which is also ascribed to Heman, that being the only instance in which the name of the "son" (or descendant) is mentioned; and to Ethan, one. Solomon's name appears before the 72d and 127th; and that of Moses before the 90th. Special questions respecting authorship will be explained as they arise.

CONTENTS.—As the book contains 150 independent compositions, it is not susceptible of any logical analysis. The Jews having divided it into five books, corresponding to the Five Books of Moses (1st, 1–42; 2d, 43–72; 3d, 73–89; 4th, 90–106; 5th, 107–150), many attempts have been made to discover, in this division, some critical or practical value, but in vain. Sundry efforts have been made to classify the Psalms by subject. "Angus' Bible Hand-Book" is perhaps the most useful, and is appended.

Still the Psalms have a form and character peculiar to themselves; and with individual diversities of style and subject, they all assimilate to that form, and together constitute a consistent system of moral truth. They are all poetical, and of that peculiar parallelism (see Introduction to Poetical Books) which distinguished Hebrew poetry. They are all lyrical, or songs adapted to musical instruments, and all religious lyrics, or such as were designed to be used in the sanctuary worship.

The distinguishing feature of the Psalms is their devotional character. Whether their matter be didactic, historical, prophetical, or practical, it is made the ground or subject of prayer, or praise, or both. The doctrines of theology and percepts of pure morality are here inculcated. God's nature, attributes, perfections, and works of creation, providence, and grace, are unfolded. In the sublimest conceptions of the most exalted verse, His glorious supremacy over the principalities of heaven, earth, and hell, and His holy, wise, and powerful control of all material and immaterial agencies, are celebrated. The great covenant of grace resting on the fundamental promise of a Redeemer, both alike the provisions of God's exhaustless mercy, is set forth in respect of the doctrines of regeneration by the Spirit, forgiveness of sins, repentance toward God, and faith toward Jesus Christ, while its glorious results, involving the salvation of men "from the ends of the earth," are proclaimed in believing, prophetic prayer and thankful praise. The personal history of the authors, and especially David's in its spiritual aspects, is that of God's people generally. Christian biography is edifying only as it is truth illustrated in experience, such as God's Word and Spirit produce. It may be factitious in origin and of doubtful authenticity. But here the experience of the truly pious is detailed, under divine influence, and "in words which the Holy Ghost" taught. The whole inner life of the pious man is laid open, and Christians of all ages have here the temptations, conflicts, perplexities, doubts, fears, penitent moanings, and overwhelming griefs on the one hand, and the joy and hope of pardoning mercy, the victory over the seductions of false-hearted flatterers, and deliverance from the power of Satan on the other, with which to compare their own spiritual exercises. Here, too, are the fruits of that sovereign mercy, so often sought in earnest prayer, and when found, so often sung in rapturous joy, exhibited by patience in adversity, moderation in prosperity, zeal for God's glory, love for man, justice to the oppressed, holy contempt for the proud, magnanimity towards enemies, faithfulness towards friends, delight in the prosperity of Zion, and believing prayer for her enlargement and perpetuity.

The historical summaries of the Psalms are richly instructive. God's choice of the patriarchs, the sufferings of the Israelites in Egypt, their exodus, temptations of God, rebellions and calamities in the wilderness, settlement in Canaan, backslidings and reformations, furnish illustrations of God's providential government of His people, individually and collectively, tending to exalt His adorable grace and abase human pride. But the promises and prophecies connected with these summaries, and elsewhere presented in the Psalms, have a far wider reach, exhibiting the relations of the book to the great theme of promise and prophecy:

THE MESSIAH AND HIS KINGDOM.—David was God's chosen servant to rule His people, as the head at once of the State and the Church, the lineal ancestor, "according to the flesh," of His adorable Son, and His type, in His official relations, both in suffering and in triumph. Generally, David's trials by the ungodly depicted the trials of Christ, and his final success the success of Christ's kingdom. Typically, he uses language describing his feelings, which only finds its full meaning in the feelings of Christ. As such it is quoted and applied in the New Testament. And farther, in view of the great promise (II Sam. 7) to him and his seed, to which such frequent reference is made in the Psalms, David was inspired to know, that though his earthly kingdom should perish, his spiritual would ever endure, in the power, beneficence, and glory of Christ's. In repeating and amplifying that promise, he speaks not only as a type, but "being a prophet, and knowing that God had sworn with an oath to him, that of the fruit of his loins, according to the flesh, he would raise up Christ to sit on his throne," he "foretold the sufferings of Christ and the glory that should follow. His incarnation, humiliating sorrows, persecution, and cruel death are disclosed in the plaintive cries of a despairing sufferer; and His resurrection and ascension, His eternal priesthood, His royal dignity, His prophetical office, the purchase and bestowal of the gifts of the Spirit, the conversion of the nations, the establishment, increase, and perpetuity of the Church, the end of time, and the blessedness of the righteous who acknowledge, and the ruin of the wicked who reject this King in Zion, are predicted in the language of assured confidence and joy." While these great themes have supplied the people of God with a popular theology and a guide in religious experience and Christian morality, clothed in the language of devotion, they have provided an inspired liturgy in which the pious, of all creeds and sects, have, for nearly three thousand years, poured out their prayers and praises. The pious Jew, before the coming of Christ, mourned over the adversity, or celebrated the future glories, of Zion, in the words of her ancient king. Our Saviour, with His disciples, sang one of these hymns on the night on which He was betrayed; He took from one these words in which He uttered the dreadful sorrows of His soul, and died with those of another on His lips. Paul and Silas in the dungeon, primitive Christians in their covert places of worship, or the costly churches of a later day, and the scattered and feeble Christian flocks in the prevalence of darkness and error through the Middle Ages, fed their faith and warmed their love with these consoling songs. Now, throughout the Christian world, in untold forms of version, paraphrase, and imitation, by Papists and Protestants, Prelatists and Presbyterians, Independents, Baptists, Methodists— men of all lands and all creeds, in public and private worship, God is still adored in the sentiments expressed in these venerable Psalms. From the tone of sorrow and suffering which pervade their earlier portions we are gradually borne on amid alternate conflicts and triumphs, mournful complaints and awakening confidence; as we approach the close the tones of sorrow grow feebler, and those of praise wax louder and stronger—till, in the exulting strains of the last Psalm, the chorus of earth mingles with the hallelujahs of the multitude, which no man can number, in the sanctuary above.

Angus' or Bickersteth's arrangement may be profitably used as a guide for finding a Psalm on a special topic. It is a little modified, as follows:

1. Didactic. Good and bad men: Psalms 1, 5, 7, 9–12, 14, 15, 17, 24, 25, 32, 34, 36, 37, 50, 52, 53, 58, 73, 75, 84, 91, 92, 94, 112, 121, 125, 127, 128, 133; God's law: Psalms 19, 119; Human life vain: Psalms 39, 49, 90; Duty of rulers: Psalms 82, 101. –2. Praise. (1) For God's goodness generally to Israel: Psalms 46, 48, 65, 66, 68, 76, 81, 85, 98, 105, 124, 126, 129, 135, 136, 149; (2) To good men, Psalms 23, 34, 36, 91, 100, 103, 107, 117, 121, 145, 146; (3) Mercies to individuals: Psalms 9, 18, 22, 30, 40, 75, 103, 108, 116, 118, 138, 144; (4) For His attributes generally: Psalms 8, 19, 24, 29, 33, 47, 50, 65, 66, 76, 77, 93, 95–97, 99 104, 111,

113–115, 134, 139, 147, 148, 150. –3. Devotional—expressive of (1) Penitence: Psalms 6, 25, 32, 38, 51, 102, 130, 143; (2) Trust in trouble: Psalms 3, 16, 27, 31, 54, 56, 57, 61, 62, 71, 86; (3) Sorrow with hope: Psalms 13, 22, 69, 77, 88; (4) Of deep distress: Psalms 4, 5, 11, 28, 41, 55, 59, 64, 70, 109, 120, 140, 141, 143; (5) Feelings when deprived of religious privileges: Psalms 42, 43, 63, 84; (6) Desire for help: Psalms 7, 17, 26, 35, 44, 60, 74, 79, 80, 83, 89, 94, 102, 129, 137; (7) Intercession: Psalms 20, 67, 122, 132, 144. –4. Historical. Psalms 78, 105, 106. —5. Prophetical. Psalms 2, 16, 22, 40, 45, 68, 69, 72, 97, 110, 118.

Note.—The compiler of the following notes has omitted all references to authors, as needlessly encumbering the commentary. He has had before him the works of Calvin, Scott, Poole, Ainsworth, Cobbin, Geice, Vatablus, Tholuck, J. H. Michaelis, Rosenmuller, and Alexander. To the two last named he has been particularly indebted for the parallel passages. He has made a free use of the views advanced by these authors, and claims no credit for anything in the work except the conciseness united with fullness of exposition. Whoever attempts it will find it far easier to write a long commentary than a brief one.

PSALM 1

Vss. 1-6. The character and condition, and the present and future destiny, of the pious and the wicked are described and contrasted, teaching that true piety is the source of ultimate happiness, and sin of misery. As this is a summary of the teachings of the whole book, this Psalm, whether designedly so placed or not, forms a suitable preface. **1. Blessed**—lit., "oh, the happiness"—an exclamation of strong emotion, as if resulting from reflecting on the subject. The use of the plural may denote fulness and variety (II Chron. 9:7). **counsel . . . way . . . seat**—With their corresponding verbs, mark gradations of evil, as acting on the principles, cultivating the society, and permanently conforming to the conduct of the wicked, who are described by three terms, of which the last is indicative of the boldest impiety (cf. Ps. 26:4, 5; Jer. 15:17). **2. law**—all of God's word then written, especially the books of Moses (cf. Ps. 119:1, 55, 97, etc.). **3. like a tree**—(Jer. 17:7, 8). **planted**—settled, fast. **by**—or, over. **the rivers**—canals for irrigation. **shall prosper**—lit., "make prosper," brings to perfection. The basis of this condition and character is given (Ps. 32:1). **4. not so**—either as to conduct or happiness. **like the chaff**—which, by Eastern modes of winnowing against the wind, was utterly blown away.—**5. stand in the judgment**—be acquitted. They shall be driven from among the good (Matt. 25:45, 46). **6. knoweth the way**—attends to and provides for them (Ps. 101:6; Prov. 12:10; Hos. 13:5). **way of the wicked**—All their plans will end in disappointment and ruin (Ps. 37:13; 146:8; Prov. 4:19).

PSALM 2

Vss. 1-12. The number and authorship of this Psalm are stated (Acts 4:25; 13:33). Though the warlike events of David's reign may have suggested its imagery, the scenes depicted and the subjects presented can only find a fulfilment in the history and character of Jesus Christ, to which, as above cited and in Hebrews 1:5; 5:5, the New Testament writers most distinctly testify. In a most animated and highly poetical style, the writer, in "four stanzas of three verses each," sets forth the inveterate and furious, though futile, hostility of men to God and His anointed, God's determination to carry out His purpose, that purpose as stated more fully by His Son, the establishment of the Mediatorial kingdom, and the imminent danger of all who resist, as well as the blessing of all who welcome this mighty and triumphant king. **1. Why do the heathen . . .**—Beholding, in prophetic vision, the peoples and nations, as if in a tumultuous assembly, raging with a fury like the raging of the sea, designing to resist God's government, the writer breaks forth into an exclamation in which are mingled surprise at their folly, and indignation at their rebellion. **heathen**—nations generally, not as opposed to Jews. **people**—or, lit., "peoples," or races of men. **2.** The kings and rulers lead on their subjects. **set themselves**—take a stand. **take counsel**—lit., "sit together," denoting their deliberation. **anointed**—*Hebrew,* Messiah; *Greek,* Christ (John 1:41). Anointing, as an emblem of the gifts of the Holy Spirit, was conferred on prophets (Isa. 6:1); priests (Exod. 30:30); and kings (I Sam. 10:1; 16:13; I Kings 1:39). Hence this title well suited Him who holds all these offices, and was generally used by the Jews before His coming, to denote Him (Dan. 9:26). While the prophet has in view men's opposition generally, he here depicts it in its culminating aspect as seen in the events of Christ's great trial. Pilate and Herod, and the rulers of the Jews (Matt. 27:1; Luke 23:1-25), with the furious mob, are vividly portrayed. **3.** The rebellious purposes of men are more distinctly announced by this representation of their avowal in words, as well as actions. **bands . . . and . . . cords**—denote the restraints of government. **4.** By a figure whose boldness is only allowable to an inspired writer, God's conduct and language in view of this opposition are now related. **He that sitteth in the heavens**—enthroned in quiet dignities (cf. Ps. 29:10; Isa. 40:22). **shall laugh**—in supreme contempt; their vain rage excites His derision. He is still *the Lord,* lit., "Sovereign," though they rebel. **5. Then shall he speak**—His righteous indignation as well as contempt is roused. For God to speak is for Him to act, for what He resolves He will do (Gen. 1:3; Ps. 33:9). **vex them**—agitate or terrify them (Ps. 83:15). **6.** The purpose here declared, in its execution, involves their overthrow. **Yet**—lit., "and," in an adversative sense. **I have set**—anointed, or firmly placed, with allusion in the *Hebrew* to "casting an image in a mould." The sense is not materially varied in either case. **my king**—appointed by Me and for Me (Num. 27:18). **upon my holy hill of Zion**—Zion, selected by David as the abode of the ark and the seat of God's visible residence (I King 8:1); as also David, the head of the Church and nation, and type of Christ, was called holy, and the Church itself came to be thus named (Ps. 9:11; 51:18; 99:2; Isa. 8:18; 18:7, etc.). **7.** The king thus constituted declares the fundamental law of His kingdom, in the avowal of His Sonship, a relation involving His universal dominion. **this day have I begotten thee**—as II Samuel 7:14, "he shall be My son," is a solemn recognition of this relation. The interpretation of this passage to describe the inauguration of Christ as Mediatorial King, by no means impugns the Eternal Sonship of His divine nature. In Acts 13:33, Paul's quotation does not imply an application of this passage to the resurrection; for "raised up" in verse 32 is used as in Acts 2:30; 3:22, etc., to denote bringing Him into being as a man; and not that of resurrection, which it has only when, as in verse 34, allusion is made to His death (Rom. 1:4). That passage says He was declared as to His divine nature to be the Son of God, by the resurrection, and only teaches that that event manifested a truth already existing. A similar recognition of His Sonship is introduced in Hebrews 5:5, by these ends, and by others in Matthew 3:17; 17:5. **8.** The hopes of the rebels are thus overthrown, and not only so; the kingdom they opposed is destined to be coextensive with the earth. **heathen**—or, nations (vs. 1). **and the uttermost parts of the earth**—(Ps. 22:27); denotes universality. **9.** His enemies shall be subject to His terrible power (Job 4:9; II Thess. 2:8), as His people to His grace (Ps. 110:2, 3). **rod of iron**—denotes severity (Rev. 2:27). **a potter's vessel**—when shivered cannot be mended, which will describe utter destruction. **10-12. kings . . . judges**—For rulers generally (Ps. 148:11), who have been leaders in rebellion, should be examples of penitent submission, and with fear for His terrible judgments, mingled with trust in His mercy, acknowledge—**Kiss**—the authority of the Son. **perish from the way**—i.e., suddenly and hopelessly. **kindled but a little**—or, in a little time. **put their trust in him**—or take refuge in Him (Ps. 5:11). Men still cherish opposition to Christ in their hearts and evince it in their lives. Their ruin, without such trust, is inevitable (Heb. 10:29), while their happiness in His favor is equally sure.

PSALM 3

Vss. 1-8. For the historical occasion mentioned, cf. II Samuel, chaps. 15-17. David, in the midst of great distress, with filial confidence, implores God's aid, and anticipating relief, offers praise. **1. Lord . . . increased**—The extent of the rebellion (II Sam. 15:13) surprises and grieves him. **2. say of my soul**—i.e., of me (cf. Ps. 25:3). This use of "soul" is common; perhaps it arose from regarding the soul as man's chief part. **no help . . . in God** —rejected by Him. This is the bitterest reproach for a pious man, and denotes a spirit of malignant triumph. **Selah**—This word is of very obscure meaning. It probably denotes *rest* or *pause*, both as to the music and singing, intimating something emphatic in the sentiment (cf. Ps. 9:16). **3. But**— lit., "and" (Ps. 2:6). He repels the reproach by avowing his continued trust. **shield**—a favorite and often-used figure for protection. **my glory**—its source. **lifter up of mine head**—one who raises me from despondency. **4. cried . . . heard**—Such has been my experience. The latter verb denotes a gracious hearing or answering. **out of** [or, from] **his holy hill**—Zion (Ps. 2:6). His visible earthly residence. **5. the Lord sustained me**—lit., "will sustain me," the reason of his composure. **6. ten thousands of people**—or, myriads, any very great number (cf. II Sam. 16:18). **7. Arise, O Lord**—God is figuratively represented as asleep to denote His apparent indifference (Ps. 7:6). The use of "*cheekbone*" and "*teeth*" represents his enemies as fierce, like wild beasts ready to devour (Ps. 27:2), and smiting their ekbone (I Kings 22:24) denotes violence and in- **thou hast broken**—God took his part, utterly

depriving the enemy of power to injure. **8.** an ascription of praise to a delivering God, whose favor is an efficient benefit.

PSALM 4

Vss. 1-8. *On Neginoth,* i.e., stringed instruments, as the kind of musical accompaniment. On other parts of title, see Introduction. The historical occasion was probably the same as that of the foregoing. The writer, praying for further relief, admonishes his enemies of the vanity of attacking God's servant, exhorts them to repentance, and avows his confidence and peace in God's favor. **1. Hear**—as in Psalm 3:4. **God of my righteousness**—or, my righteousGod, as my holy hill (Ps. 2:6), who will act towards me on righteous principles. **thou hast enlarged**—expresses relief afforded in opposition to "distress," which is expressed by a word denoting straits or pressure. Past favor is a ground of hope for the future. **2. sons of men**—men of note or prominence (cf. II Chron. 21:9). **turn my glory**—or, royal dignity. **into shame**—or reproach. **vanity**—a foolish and hopeless enterprise (Ps. 2:1). **leasing**—a lie. **3. godly**—an object as well as subject of divine favor (cf. Ps. 105:14, 15). **4. Stand in awe**—(Eph. 4:26), from *Septuagint*—be angry. Both clauses are qualified by "not." **5.** Not only repent, but manifest penitence by sacrifices or righteousness or righteous sacrifices, etc. **6, 7.** Contrast true with vain confidence. **light of thy countenance**—figure for favor (Num. 6:26; Ps. 44:3; 81:16). **corn and wine**—lit., "new corn and wine." **increased**—an abundant harvest giving great joy (Isa. 9:3). **8. both lay me down, . . .**—or, will lie down at once, and sleep in sure confidence and quiet repose (Ps. 3:5).

PSALM 5

Vss. 1-12. *Upon Nehiloth*—flutes or wind instruments. The writer begs to be heard, on the ground of God's regard for His covenant people and true worshippers as contrasted with His holy hatred to the wicked. He prays for divine guidance, on account of his watchful, malignant, and deceitful enemies; and for their destruction as being also God's enemies. At the same time he expresses his confidence that God will extend aid to His people. **1. meditation**—moanings of that half-uttered form to which deep feeling gives rise—groanings, as in Romans 8:26, 27. **2. Hearken**—incline the ear (Ps. 10:17; cf. Ps. 61:2)—give close attention. **my cry**— i.e., for help (Ps. 61:2; Jer. 8:19). **my King**—thus by covenant relation interested in my cause. **3. direct**—lit., "set in order," as the shewbread was placed or set in order (Exod. 40:23). **4. For,** etc.—God only regards sincere worshippers. **evil**—or, the evil man. **dwell**—lodge, remain under protection. **5. foolish**—vainglorious and insolent. **iniquity**—especially such as denotes a negation, or defect, i.e., of moral principle. **6. leasing**—a lie, **the bloody . . . man**—lit., "man of blood"—murderer. **7. But**—as in Psalm 2:6, lit., "and." **house**—(I Chron. 9:23), the tabernacle. **temple**—lit., "palace," applied to God's residence, the Holy of Holies (I Sam. 3:3; II Sam. 22:7); the inner part of the tabernacle. **toward**—not in; the high priest alone was allowed to enter. **8. enemies**—lit., "watchers," (Ps. 27:11), hence special need of guidance. **in thy righteousness**—an attribute implying faithfulness in promises as well as threatenings. **make thy way straight**—i.e., make the way of providence plain. **9.** The wicked are not reliable because by nature they are full of wickedness, or lit., "wickednesses," of every kind (Rom. 8:7). **sepulchre**—a dwelling-place of corruption, emitting moral putridness. **flatter**—or, make smooth. **their tongue**—speaks deceitfully. **10. Destroy**—or, condemn them to destruction as guilty. **11. defendest**—(cf. *Margin*). **love thy name**—Thy manifested perfections (Ps. 9:10). **12. with favour**—or, acceptance, alluding to the favor shown to an acceptable offering and worshipper (Lev. 7:18, 19:7). **shield**—(cf. Ps. 3:3).

PSALM 6

Vss. 1-10. *On Neginoth* (cf. Psalm 4) *upon Sheminith*—the eighth—an instrument for the eighth key —or, more probably, the bass, as it is contrasted with Alamoth (the treble, Ps. 46) in I Chronicles 15:20, 21. In deep affliction the Psalmist appeals to God's mercy for relief from chastisement, which otherwise must destroy him, and thus disable him for God's service. Sure of a gracious answer, he triumphantly rebukes his foes.

1. He owns his ill desert in begging a relief from chastisement. **2. I am weak**—as a culled plant (Isa. 24:4). **my bones**—the very frame. **are vexed**—(Ps. 2:5)—shaken with fear. **3. how long?**—shall this be so (cf. Ps. 79:5). **but**—or, and. **thou**—The sentence is incomplete as expressive of strong emotion. **4. Return**—i.e., to my relief—or, "turn," as now having His face averted. **for thy mercies' sake**—to illustrate Thy mercy. **5.** (Cf. Ps. 115:17, 18; Isa. 38:18.) There is no incredulity as to a future state. The contrast is between this scene of life, and the grave or *Sheol,* the unseen world of the dead. **give ... thanks**—or, praise for mercies. **6.** By a strong figure the abundance as well as intensity of grief is depicted. **7. consumed**—or, has failed, denoting general debility (Ps. 13:3; 38:10). **waxeth old**—or, dim. **grief**—mingled with indignation. **8, 9.** Assured of God's hearing, he suddenly defies his enemies by an address indicating that he no longer fears them; **10.** and knows they will be disappointed and in their turn (cf. vs. 3) be terror-stricken or confounded.

PSALM 7

Vss. 1-17. *Shiggaion*—a plantive song or elegy. Though obscure in details, this title seems to intimate that the occasion of this Psalm was some event in David's persecution by Saul. He prays for relief because he is innocent, and God will be glorified in his vindication. He thus passes to the celebration of God's righteous government, in defending the upright and punishing the wicked, whose malignant devices will result in their own ruin; and, confident of God's aid, he closes with rejoicing.

1, 2. Though many enemies set upon him, one is singled out as prominent, and compared to a wild beast tearing his prey to pieces (cf. I Sam. 20:1; 23: 23; 26:19). **3. if I have done this**—i.e., the crime charged in the "words of Cush" (cf. I Sam. 24:9). **4. If I have injured my friend. yea, I have delivered ...** —This makes a good sense, but interrupts the course of thought, and hence it is proposed to render—"if I have spoiled my enemy"—in either case (cf. I Sam. 24:4-17; 31:8, 11. **5.** This is the consequence, if such has been his conduct. **mine**

honour—(cf. Ps. 3:3; 4:2)—my personal and official dignity. **6.** God is involved as if hitherto careless of him (Ps. 3:7; 9:18). **rage**—the most violent, like a flood rising over a river's banks. **the judgment ... commanded**—or, ordained; a just decision. **7. compass thee**—as those seeking justice. **return thou on high**—assume the judgment seat, to be honored as a just Ruler by them. **8.** Though not claiming innocence in general, he can confidently do so in this case, and in demanding from the Judge of all the earth a judgment, he virtually asks acquittal. **9. the hearts and reins**—the affections and motives of men, or the seat of them (cf. Ps. 16:7; 26:2); as we use heart and bosom or breast. **10. defence**—lit., "shield" (Ps. 5:12). **11. judgeth**—as in verse 8. **the wicked**—Though not expressed, they are implied, for they alone are left as objects of anger. **12, 13.** They are here distinctly pointed out, though by changing the person, a very common mode of speech, one is selected as a representative of wicked men generally. The military figures are of obvious meaning. **against the persecutors**—Some render "for burning," but the former is the best sense. Arrows for burning would be appropriate in besieging a town, not in warring against one man or a company in open fight. **14.** The first clause expresses the general idea that wicked men labor to do evil, the others carry out the figure fully. **15, 16.** I Samuel 18:17; 31:2 illustrate the statement whether alluded to or not. These verses are expository of verse 14, showing how the devices of the wicked end in disappointment, falsifying their expectations. **17. his righteousness**—(Ps. 5:8). Thus illustrated in the defense of His servant and punishment of the wicked.

PSALM 8

Vss. 1-19. *Upon* [or according to the] *Gittith,* probably means that the musical performance was directed to be according to a tune of that name; which, derived from *Gath,* a wine press, denotes a tune (used in connection with gathering the vintage) of a joyous character. All the Psalms to which this term is prefixed are of such a character. The Psalmist gives vent to his admiration of God's manifested perfections, by celebrating His condescending and beneficent providence to man as evinced by the position of the race, as originally created and assigned a dominion over the works of His hands.

1. thy name—perfections (Ps. 5:11; 7:17). **who hast set**—lit., "which set Thou Thy glory," etc., or "which glory of Thine set Thou," i.e., make it more conspicuous as if earth were too small a theater for its display. A similar exposition suits the usual rendering. **2.** So manifest are God's perfections, that by very weak instruments He conclusively sets forth His praise. Infants are not only wonderful illustrations of God's power and skill, in their physical constitution, instincts, and early developed intelligence, but also in their spontaneous admiration of God's works, by which they put to shame—**still**—or, silence men who rail and cavil against God. A special illustration of the passage is afforded in Matthew 21:16, when our Saviour *stilled* the cavillers by quoting these words; for the glories with which God invested His incarnate Son, even in His humiliation, constitute a most wonderful display of the perfections of His wisdom, love, and power. In view of the scope of verses 4-8 (see below), this quotation by our Saviour may be regarded as an exposition of the prophetical character of the words. **sucklings**—among the Hebrews were probably of an age to speak (cf. I Sam. 1:22-24; Mark 7:27). **ordained**—founded, or prepared, and perfected, which occurs in Matthew 21:16; taken from the *Septuagint,* has the same meaning. **strength**—In the quotation in the New Testament, *praise* occurs as the consequence or effect put for the cause (cf. Ps. 118:14). **avenger**—as in Psalm 44:16; one desirous of revenge, disposed to be quarrelsome, and so apt to cavil against God's government. **3, 4.** The allusion to the magnificence of the visible heavens is introduced for the purpose of illustrating God's condescension, who, though the mighty Creator of these glorious worlds of light, makes man the object of regard and recipient of favor. **man**—lit., "frail man," an allusion to his essential infirmity. **son of man**—only varies the form of speech. **visitest**—in favor (Ps. 65:10). This favor is now more fully illustrated. **5-8.** God has placed man next in dignity to angels, and but a little lower, and has crowned him with the empire of the world. **glory and honour**—are the attributes of royal dignity (Ps. 21:5; 45:3). The position assigned man is that described (Gen. 1:26-28) as belonging to Adam, in his original condition, the terms employed in detailing the subjects of man's dominion corresponding with those there used. In a modified sense, in his present fallen state, man is still invested with some remains of this original dominion. It is very evident, however, by the apostle's inspired expositions (Heb. 2:6-8: I Cor. 15:27, 28) that the language here employed finds its fulfilment only in the final exaltation of Christ's human nature. There is no limit to the "all things" mentioned, God only excepted, who "puts all things under." Man, in the person and glorious destiny of Jesus of Nazareth, the second Adam, the head and representative of the race, will not only be restored to his original position, but exalted far beyond it. "The last enemy, death," through fear of which, man, in his present estate, is "all his lifetime in bondage," "shall be destroyed." Then *all things* will have been put under his feet, "principalities and powers being made subject to him." This view, so far from being alien from the scope of the passage, is more consistent than any other; for man as a race cannot well be conceived to have a higher honor put upon him than to be thus exalted in the person and destiny of Jesus of Nazareth. And at the same time, by no other of His glorious manifestations has God more illustriously declared those attributes which distinguish His name than in the scheme of redemption, of which this economy forms such an important and essential feature. In the generic import of the language, as describing man's present relation to the works of God's hands, it may be regarded as typical, thus allowing not only the usual application, but also this higher sense which the inspired writers of the New Testament have assigned it. **9.** Appropriately, the writer closes this brief but pregnant and sublime song of praise with the terms of admiration with which it was opened.

PSALM 9

Vss. 1-20. *Upon Muth-labben,* or, *after the manner according to "death to the Son,"* by which some song was known, to whose air or melody the musician is directed to perform this Psalm. This mode of denoting a song by some prominent word or words is still common (cf. Ps. 22). The Psalmist praises God for deliverance from his enemies and celebrates the divine government, for providing security to God's people and punishment to the wicked. Thus encouraging himself, he prays for new occasions to recount God's mercies, and confident of His continued judgment on the wicked and vindication of the oppressed, he implores a prompt and efficient manifestation of the divine sovereignty.

1. Heartfelt gratitude will find utterance. **3-5. When . . . are turned back**—It is the result of God's power alone. He, as a righteous Judge (Ps. 7:11), vindicates His people. He rebukes by acts as well as words (Ps. 6:1; 18:15), and so effectually as to destroy the names of nations as well as persons. **6.** Lit., "As to the enemy finished are his ruins for ever. Thou [God] hast destroyed," etc. (I Sam. 15:3, 7; 27: 8, 9). The wicked are utterly undone. Their ruins shall never be repaired. **7, 8.** God's eternal possession of a throne of justice is contrasted with the ruin of the wicked. **9, 10.** The oppressed, and all who know Him (Ps. 5:3; 7:1), find Him a sure refuge. **11.** (Cf. Ps. 2:6; 3:4.) **12. for blood**—i.e., murders (Ps. 5:6), including all the oppressions of His people. **maketh inquisition**—(cf. Gen. 9:5). He will avenge their cause. **13. gates**—or, regions—**of death**—Gates being the entrance is put for the bounds. **14. gates . . . Zion**—The enclosure of the city (cf. Ps. 48:12; Isa. 23:12), or, church, as denoted by this phrase contrasted with that of death, carries out the idea of exaltation as well as deliverance. Signal favors should lead us to render signal and public thanks. **15, 16.** The undesigned results of the devices of the wicked prove them to be of God's overruling or ordering, especially when those results are destructive to the wicked themselves. **Higgaion**—means "meditation," and, combined with **Selah**, seems to denote a pause of unusual solemnity and emphasis (cf. Ps. 3:2). Though Selah occurs seventy-three times, this is the only case in which Higgaion is found. In the view which is given here of the retribution on the wicked as an instance of God's wise and holy ordering, we may well pause in adoring wonder and faith. **17. shall be turned**—or, shall turn, retreating under God's vengeance, and driven by Him to the extreme of destruction, even hell itself. Those who forget God are classed with the depraved and openly profane. **18.** (Cf. Ps. 13.) **the needy**—lit., "poor," as deprived of anything; hence miserable. **expectation of the poor**—or, meek, humble, made so by affliction. **19. Arise**—(cf. Ps. 4:7). **let not man**—(Ps. 8:4). **let . . . be judged**—and of course condemned. **20.** By their effectual subjection, make them to realize their frail nature Ps. 8:4), and deter them from all conceit and future rebellion.

PSALM 10

Vss. 1-18. The Psalmist mourns God's apparent indifference to his troubles, which are aggravated by the successful malice, blasphemy, pride, deceit, and profanity of the wicked. On the just and discriminating providence of God he relies for the destruction of their false security, and the defense of the needy. **1.** These are, of course, figurative terms (cf. Ps. 7:6; 13:1; etc.). **hidest**—Supply "thine eyes" or "face." **2.** Lit., "In pride of the wicked they (the poor or humble, vs. 17; Ps. 12:5) shall be taken in the devices they (the proud) have imagined. **3. his heart's** [or "soul's"] **desire**—i.e., his success in evil. **and blesseth . . .**—he (the wicked) blesseth the covetous, he despiseth the Lord. **4.** The face expresses the self-conceit, whose fruit is practical atheism (Ps. 14:1). **5, 6.** Such is his confidence in the permanence of his way or course of life, that he disregards God's providential government (*out of sight,* because he will not look, Isa. 26:11), sneers at his enemies, and boasts perpetual freedom from evil.   **7-10.** The malignity and deceit (Ps. 140:3) of such are followed by acts combining cunning, fraud, and violence (cf. Prov. 1:11, 18), aptly illustrated by the habits of the lion, and of hunters taking their prey. "Poor," in verses 8, 10, 14, represents a word peculiar to this Psalm, meaning the sad or sorrowful; in verse 9, as usual, it means the pious or meek sufferer.   **8. eyes . . . privily set**—He watches with half-closed eyes, appearing not to see.   **10. croucheth**—as a lion gathers himself into as small compass as possible to make the greater spring.   **fall by his strong ones**—The figure of the lion is dropped, and this phrase means the accomplices of the chief or leading wicked man.   **11.** As before, such conduct implies disbelief or disregard of God's government.   **12.** (Cf. Ps. 9:19; 3:7.)   **humble**—(Cf. vs. 17, and *Margin.*)   **lift up thine hand**—exert thy power.   **13, 14.** It is in vain to suppose God will overlook sin, however forbearing; for He carefully examines or beholds all wickedness, and will mark it by His providential (Thine hand) punishment.   **14. mischief and spit**—provocation and trouble of the sufferer (cf. Ps. 6:7; 7:14).   **committeth**—or, leaves (his burden) on Thee.   **15. arm**—power.   **till thou find none** —So far from not requiting (vss. 11, 13), God will utterly destroy the wicked and his deeds (Ps. 9:5, 6; 34:16; 37:36).   **16-18.** God reigns.   The wicked, if for a time successful, shall be cut off.   He hears and confirms the hearts of His suffering people (Ps. 112:7), executes justice for the feeble, and represses the pride and violence of conceited, though frail, men (cf. Ps. 9:16).

PSALM 11

Vss. 1-7.   On title, see *Introduction.*   Alluding to some event in his history, as in I Samuel 23:13, the Psalmist avows his confidence in God, when admonished to flee from his raging persecutors, whose destruction of the usual foundations of safety rendered all his efforts useless.   The grounds of his confidence are God's supreme dominion, His watchful care of His people, His hatred to the wicked and judgments on them, and His love for righteousness and the righteous.   **1. my soul**—me (Ps. 3:2).   **Flee**—lit., "flee ye"; i.e., he and his companion.   **as a bird to your mountain**—having as such no safety but in flight (cf. I Sam. 26:20; Lam. 3:52).   **2. privily**—lit., "in darkness," treacherously.   **3.** Lit., The foundations (i.e., of good order and law) will be destroyed, what has the righteous done (to sustain them)?   All his efforts have failed.   **4. temple . . . heaven**—The connection seems to denote God's heavenly residence; the term used is taken from the place of His visible earthly abode (Ps. 2:6; 3:4; 5:7).   Thence He inspects men with close scrutiny.   **5.** The trial of the righteous results in their approval, as it is contrasted with God's hatred to the wicked.   **6.** Their punishment is described by vivid figures denoting abundant, sudden, furious, and utter destruction (cf. Gen. 19:24; Job 18:15; Ps. 7:15; 9:15).   **cup**—is a frequent figure for God's favor or wrath (Ps. 16:5; 23:5; Matt. 20:22, 23).   **7. his countenance**—lit., "their faces"—a use of the plural applied to God, as in Genesis 1:26; 3:22; 11:7; Isaiah 6:8, etc., denoting the fulness of His perfections, or more probably originating in a reference to the trinity of persons.   "Faces" is used

as "eyes" (vs. 4), expressing here God's complacency towards the upright (cf. Ps. 34:15, 16).

PSALM 12

Vss. 1-8.   On title, see *Introduction* and Psalm 6.   The Psalmist laments the decrease of good men.   The pride and deceit of the wicked provokes God's wrath, whose promise to avenge the cause of pious sufferers will be verified even amidst prevailing iniquity.   **1. the faithful**—or lit., "faithfulness" (Ps. 31:23).   **2.** The want of it is illustrated by the prevalence of deceit and instability.   **3, 4.** Boasting (Dan. 7:25) is, like flattery, a species of lying.   **lips and . . . tongue** —for persons.   **5.** The writer intimates his confidence by depicting God's actions (cf. Ps. 9:19; 10:12) as coming to save the poor at whom the wicked sneer (Ps. 10:5).   **6. The words**—lit., "saying of" (vs. 5).   **seven times**—thoroughly (Dan. 3:19).   **7. them** —(*Margin.*)   **8.** The wicked roam undisturbed doing evil, when vileness and vile men are exalted.

PSALM 13

Vss. 1-6.   On title, see *Introduction.*   The Psalmist, mourning God's absence and the triumph of his enemies, prays for relief before he is totally destroyed, and is encouraged to hope his trust will not be in vain.   **1.** The forms of expression and figure here used are frequent (cf. Ps. 9:12, 18; 10:11, 12).   **How long . . . for ever**—Shall it be for ever?   **2.** The counsels or devices of his heart afford no relief.   **3. lighten mine eyes**—dim with weakness, denoting approaching death (cf. I Sam. 14:27-29; Ps. 6:7; 38:10).   **4. rejoice**—lit., "shout as in triumph."   **I am moved**— cast down from a firm position (Ps. 10:6).   **5, 6.** Trust is followed by rejoicing in the deliverance which God effects, and, instead of his enemy, he can lift the song of triumph.

PSALM 14

Vss. 1-7.   The practical atheism and total and universal depravity of the wicked, with their hatred to the good, are set forth.   Yet, as they dread God's judgments when He vindicates His people, the Psalmist prays for His delivering power.   **1.** Sinners are termed "fools," because they think and act contrary to right reason (Gen. 34:7; Josh. 7:15; Ps. 39:8; 74:18, 22).   **in his heart**—to himself (Gen. 6:12).   **2. looked**—in earnest inquiry.   **understand**—as opposed to fool.   **3. filthy**—lit., "spoiled," or, "soured," "corrupted" (Job. 15:16; Rom. 3:12).   **4-6.** Their conduct evinces indifference rather than ignorance of God; for when He appears in judgment, they are stricken with great fear.   **who eat up my people**—to express their beastly fury—(Prov. 30:14; Hab. 3:14).   To "call on the Lord" is to worship Him.   **7. captivity**—denotes any great evil.   **Zion**— God's abode, from which He revealed His purposes of mercy, as He now does by the Church (cf. 3:4; 20:2), and which He rules and in which He does all other things for the good of His people (Eph. 1:22).

PSALM 15

Vss. 1-5.   Those who are fit for communion with God may be known by a conformity to His law, which is illustrated in various important particulars.   **1. abide**—or, sojourn (cf. Ps. 5:4), where it means under God's protection here, as (Ps. 23:6, 27:4, 6) communion. **tabernacle**—seat of the ark (II Samuel 6:17), the symbol of God's presence. **holy hill**—(Cf. Ps. 2:6). **2. walketh**—(Cf. Ps. 1:1). **uprightly**—in a complete manner, as to all parts of conduct (Gen. 17:1), not as to degree. **worketh**—or, does. **righteousness**—what is right. **in his heart**—sincerely (Prov. 23:7). **3.** He neither slanders nor spreads slander. **4.** Love and hate are regulated by a regard to God. **sweareth . . . hurt**—or what so results (cf. Lev. 5:4). **5.** (Cf. Lev. 25:37; Deut. 23:19, 20.) **usury**—is derived from a verb meaning "to bite." All gains made by the wrongful loss of others are forbidden. **taketh reward . . .**—The innocent would not otherwise be condemned (cf. Exod. 23:8; Deut. 16:19). Bribery of all sorts is denounced. **doeth these . . .**—Such persons admitted to God's presence and favor shall never be moved (Ps. 10:6; 13:5).

PSALM 16

Vss. 1-11. *Michtam,* or, by the change of one letter, *Michtab*—a "writing," such as a poem or song (cf. Isa. 38:9). Such a change of the letter *m* for *b* was not unusual. The position of this word in connection with the author's name, being that usually occupied by some term, such as Psalm or song, denoting the style or matter of the composition, favors this view of its meaning, though we know not why this and Psalms 56-60 should be specially called "a writing." "A golden" (Psalm), or a "memorial" are explanations proposed by some—neither of which, however applicable here, appears adapted to the other Psalms where the term occurs. According to Peter (Acts 2:25) and Paul (Acts 13:35), this Psalm relates to Christ and expresses the feelings of His human nature, in view of His sufferings and victory over death and the grave, including His subsequent exaltation at the right hand of God. Such was the exposition of the best earlier Christian interpreters. Some moderns have held that the Psalm relates exclusively to David; but this view is expressly contradicted by the apostles; others hold that the language of the Psalm is applicable to David as a type of Christ, capable of the higher sense assigned it in the New Testament. But then the language of vs. 10 cannot be used of David in any sense, for "he saw corruption." Others again propose to refer the first part to David, and the last to Christ; but it is evident that no change in the subject of the Psalm is indicated. Indeed, the person who appeals to God for help is evidently the same who rejoices in having found it. In referring the whole Psalm to Christ, it is, however, by no means denied that much of its language is expressive of the feelings of His people, so far as in their humble measure they have the feelings of trust in God expressed by Him, their head and representative. Such use of His language, as recorded in His last prayer (John 17), and even that which He used in Gethsemane, under similar modifications, is equally proper. The propriety of this reference of the Psalm to Christ will appear in the scope and interpretation. In view of the sufferings before Him, the Saviour, with that instinctive dread of death manifested in Gethsemane, calls on God to "preserve" Him; He avows His delight in holiness and abhorrence of the wicked and their wickedness; and for "the joy that was set before Him, despising the shame," encourages Himself; contemplating the glories of the heritage appointed Him. Thus even death and the grave lose

their terrors in the assurance of the victory to be attained and "the glory that should follow."

1. Preserve me—keep or watch over my interests. **in thee . . . I . . . trust**—as one seeking shelter from pressing danger. **2. my soul**—must be supplied; expressed in similar cases (Ps. 42:5, 11). **my goodness . . . thee**—This obscure passage is variously expounded. Either one of two expositions falls in with the context. "My goodness" or merit is not on account of Thee—i.e., is not for Thy benefit. Then follows the contrast of vs. 3 (but is), in respect, or for the saints, etc.—i.e., it enures to them. Or, *my goodness*—or happiness is not *besides Thee*—i.e., without Thee I have no other source of happiness. Then, *"to the saints,"* etc., means that the same privilege of deriving happiness from God only is theirs. The first is the most consonant with the Messianic character of the Psalm, though the latter is not inconsistent with it. **3. saints**—or, persons consecrated to God, set apart from others to His service. **in the earth**—i.e., land of Palestine—the residence of God's chosen people—figuratively for the Church. **excellent**—or, nobles, distinguished for moral excellence. **4.** He expresses his abhorrence of those who seek other sources of happiness or objects of worship, and, by characterizing their rites by drink offerings of blood, clearly denotes idolaters. The word for "sorrows" is by some rendered idols; but, though a similar word to that for idols, it is not the same. In selecting such a term, there may be an allusion, by the author, to the sorrows produced by idolatrous practices. **5-7.** God is the chief good, and supplies all need (Deut. 10:9). **portion of mine inheritance and of my cup**—may contain an allusion to the daily supply of food, and also to the inheritance of Levi (Deut. 18:1, 2). **maintainest**—or, *drawest out* my lot—enlargest it. The next verse carries out this idea more fully. **7. given me counsel**—cared for me. **my reins**—the supposed seat of emotion and thought (Ps. 7:9, 26:2). **instruct me**—or, excite to acts of praise (Isa. 53:11, 12; Heb. 12:2). **8.** With God's presence and aid he is sure of safety (Ps. 10:6; 15:5; John 12:27, 28; Heb. 5:7, 8). **9. glory**—as heart (Ps. 7:5), for self. In Acts 2:26, after the Septuagint, *my tongue* as "the glory of the frame"—the instrument for praising God. **flesh**—If taken as opposed to soul (vs. 10), it may mean the body; otherwise, the whole person (cf. Ps. 63:1; 84: 2). **rest in hope**—(cf. *Margin*). **10. soul**—or, self. This use of soul for the person is frequent (Gen. 12:5; 46:26; Ps. 3:2; 7:2; 11:1), even when the body may be the part chiefly affected, as in Psalm 35:13; 105:18. Some cases are cited, as Leviticus 22:4; Numbers 6:6; 9:6, 10; 19:13; Haggai 2:13, etc., which seem to justify assigning the meaning of *body,* or dead body; but it will be found that the latter sense is given by some adjunct expressed or implied. In those cases *person* is the proper sense. **wilt not leave . . . hell**—abandon to the power of (Job 39:14; Ps. 49:10). Hell as (Gen. 42:38; Ps. 6:5; Jonah 2:2) the state or region of death, and so frequently—or the *grave itself* (Job 14:13, 17:13; Eccles. 9:10, etc.). So the *Greek Hades* (cf. Acts 2:27, 31). The context alone can settle whether the state mentioned is one of suffering and place of the damned (cf. Ps. 9:17; Prov. 5:5; 7:27). **wilt . . . suffer**—lit., "give" or "appoint." **Holy One**—(Ps. 4:3), one who is the object of God's favor, and so a recipient of divine grace which he exhibits—*pious.* **to see**—or, experience—undergo (Luke 2:26). **corruption**—Some render the word, *the pit,* which is possible, but for the obvious sense which the apostle's exposition (Acts 2:27; 13:36, 37) gives. The sense of the whole passage is clearly this: by the use of *flesh* and *soul,* the disembodied state produced by death is indicated; but, on the other hand, no more than the *state of death* is intended; for the last clause of vs. 10 is strictly parallel with the first, and *Holy One* corresponds to *soul,* and *corruption* to *hell.* As *Holy One,* or David (Acts 13:36, 37), which denotes the *person,* including soul and body, is used for *body,* of which only corruption can be predicated (cf. Acts 2:31); so, on the contrary, *soul,* which literally means the immaterial part, is used for the person. The language may be thus paraphrased, "In death I shall hope for resurrection; for I shall not be left under its dominion and within its bounds, or be subject to the corruption which ordinarily ensues." **11.** Raised from the dead, he shall die no more; death hath no more dominion over him. **Thou wilt show me**—guide me to attain. **the path of life**—or, "lives"—the plural denoting variety and abundance—immortal blessedness of every sort—as life often denotes. **in thy presence**—or, "before Thy faces." The frequent use of this plural form for faces may contain an allusion to the Trinity (Num. 6:25, 26; Ps. 17:15; 31:16). **at thy right hand**—to which Christ was exalted (Ps. 110:1; Acts 2:33; Col. 3:1; Heb. 1:3). In the glories of this state, He shall see of the travail (Isa. 53:10, 11; Phil. 2:9) of His soul, and be satisfied.

PSALM 17

Vss. 1-15. This Psalm is termed a prayer because the language of petition is predominant. With a just cause, sincerely presented, the writer prays for a just decision and help and protection. Pleading former mercies as a ground of hope, he urges his prayer in view of the malice, pride, rapacity, and selfishness of his foes, whose character is contrasted with his pious devotion and delight in God's favor. **2. sentence**—acquitting judgment. **from thy presence**—Thy tribunal. **things that are equal**—just and right, do Thou regard. **3. proved . . . visited . . . tried**—His character was most rigidly tested, at all times, and by all methods, affliction and others (Ps. 7:10). **purposed that . . .**—or, my mouth does not exceed my purpose—I am sincere. **4. works of men**—sinful practices. **by the word of thy lips**—as a guide (Ps. 119:9, 11, 95). **destroyer**—violent man. **5.** May be read as an assertion "my steps or goings have held on to Thy paths." **6. wilt hear me**—i.e., graciously (Ps. 3:4). **7. Show**—set apart as special and eminent (Exod. 8:18; Ps. 4:3). **thy right hand**—for Thy power. **8.** Similar figures, denoting the preciousness of God's people in His sight, in Deuteronomy 32:10, 11; Matthew 23:37. **9. compass me**—(cf. Ps. 118:10-12). **10. enclosed . . . fat**—are become proud in prosperity, and insolent to God (Deut. 32:15; Ps. 73:7). **11.** They pursue us as beasts tracking their prey. **12.** The figure made more special by that of a lion lurking. **13-15. disappoint**—lit., "come before," or, "encounter him." Supply "with" before "sword" (vs. 13), and "hand" (vs. 14). These denote God's power. **men . . . world**—all men of this present time. They appear, by fulness of bread and large families, to be prosperous; but (vs. 15) he implies this will be transient, contrasting his better portion in a joyful union with God hereafter.

PSALM 18

Vss. 1-50. "The servant of the LORD," which in the *Hebrew* precedes "David," is a significant part of the title (and not a mere epithet of David), denoting the inspired character of the song, as the production of one entrusted with the execution of God's will. He was not favored by God because he served Him, but served Him because selected and appointed by God in His sovereign mercy. After a general expression of praise and confidence in God for the future, David gives a sublimely poetical description of God's deliverance, which he characterizes as an illustration of God's justice to the innocent and His righteous government. His own prowess and success are celebrated as the results of divine aid, and, confident of its continuance, he closes in terms of triumphant praise. II Samuel 22 is a copy of this Psalm, with a few unimportant variations recorded there as a part of the history, and repeated here as part of a collection designed for permanent use.

1. I will love thee—with most tender affection. **2, 3.** The various terms used describe God as an object of the most implicit and reliable trust. **rock**—lit., "a cleft rock," for concealment. **strength**—a firm, immovable rock. **horn of my salvation**—The horn, as the means of attack or defense of some of the strongest animals, is a frequent emblem of power or strength efficiently exercised (cf. Deut. 33:17; Luke 1:69). **tower**—lit., "high place," beyond reach of danger. **to be praised**—for past favors, and worthy of confidence. **4. sorrows**—lit., "bands as of a net" (Ps. 116:3). **floods**—denotes multitude. **5. death**—and *hell* (cf. Ps. 16:10) are personified as man's great enemies (cf. Rev. 20:13, 14). **prevented**—encountered me, crossed my path, and endangered my safety. He does not mean he was in their power. **6.** He relates his methods to procure relief when distressed, and his success. **temple**—(Cf. Ps. 11:4). **7, 8.** God's coming described in figures drawn from His appearance on Sinai (cf. Deut. 32:22). **smoke out . . . his nostrils**—bitter in His wrath (cf. Ps. 74:1). **by it**—i.e., the fire (Exod. 19:18). **9. darkness**—or, a dense cloud (Exod. 19:16; Deut. 5:22). **10. cherub**—angelic agents (cf. Gen. 3:24), the figures of which were placed over the ark (I Sam. 4:4), representing God's dwelling; used here to enhance the majesty of the divine advent. *Angels* and *winds* may represent all rational and irrational agencies of God's providence (cf. Ps. 104:3, 4). **did fly**—Rapidity of motion adds to the grandeur of the scene. **12.** Out of this obscurity, which impresses the beholder with awe and dread, He reveals Himself by sudden light and the means of His terrible wrath (Josh. 10:11; Ps. 78:47). **13.** The storm breaks forth—thunder follows lightning, and hail with repeated lightning, as often seen, like balls or coals of fire, succeed (Exod. 9:23). **14.** The fiery brightness of lightning, in shape like burning arrows rapidly shot through the air, well represents the most terrible part of an awful storm. Before the terrors of such a scene the enemies are confounded and overthrown in dismay. **15.** The tempest of the air is attended by appropriate results on earth. The language, though not expressive of any special physical changes, represents the utter subversion of the order of nature. Before such a God none can stand. **16-19. from above**—As seated on a throne, directing these terrible scenes, God—**sent**—His hand (Ps. 144: 7), reached down to His humble worshipper, and delivered him. **many waters**—calamities (Job 30: 14; Ps. 124:4, 5). **prevented**—(vs. 5). **a large place**—denotes safety or relief, as contrasted with the straits of distress (Ps. 4:1). All his deliverance is ascribed to God, and this sublime poetical representation is given to inspire the pious with confidence and the wicked with dread. **20-24.** The statements of innocence, righteousness, etc., refer, doubtless, to his personal and official conduct and his purposes, during all the trials to which he was subjected in Saul's persecutions and Absalom's rebellions, as well as the various wars in which he had been engaged as the head and defender of God's Church and people. **upright before him**—In my relation to God I have been perfect as to all parts of His law. The perfection does not relate to degree. **mine iniquity**—perhaps the thought of his heart to kill Saul (I Sam. 24:6). That David does not allude to all his conduct, in all relations, is evident from Psalm 51:1, etc. **25-27.** God renders to men according to their deeds in a penal, not vindictive, sense (Lev. 26:23, 24). **merciful**—or, kind (Ps. 4:3). **froward**—contrary to. **the afflicted people**—i.e., the humbly pious. **high looks**—pide (Ps. 101:5; 131:1). **28.** *To give one light* is to make prosperous (Job. 18:5, 6; 21:17). **thou**—is emphatic, as if to say, I can fully confide in *Thee* for help. **29.** And this on past experience in his military life, set forth by these figures. **30-32.** God's perfection is the source of his own, which has resulted from his trust on the one hand, and God's promised help on the other. **tried**—"as metals are tried by fire and proved genuine" (Ps. 12:6). *Shield* (Ps. 3:3). *Girding* was essential to free motion on account of the looseness of Oriental dresses; hence it is an expressive figure for describing the gift of strength. **33-36.** God's help farther described—He gives swiftness to pursue or elude his enemies (Hab. 3:19); strength, protection, and a firm footing. **thy gentleness**— as applied to God—condescension—or, that which He gives, in the sense of *humility* (cf. Prov. 22:4). **enlarged my steps**—made ample room (cf. Prov. 4:12). **37-41.** In actual conflict, with God's aid, the defeat of his enemies is certain. A present and continued success is expressed. **that rose up against me**—lit., "insurgents" (Ps. 3:1; 44:5). **given me the necks**—lit., "backs of the necks"—make them retreat (Exod. 23:27; Josh. 7:8). **42.** This conquest was complete. **43-45.** Not only does He conquer civil foes, but foreigners, who are driven from their places of refuge. **submit . . .**—(cf. *Margin*)—i.e., show a forced subjection. **46. The Lord liveth**—contrasts Him with idols (I Cor. 8:4). **47, 48. avengeth me**—His cause is espoused by God as His own. **liftest me up**—to safety and honors. **49, 50.** Paul (Rom. 15:9) quotes from this doxology to show that under the Old Testament economy, others than the Jews were regarded as subjects of that spiritual government of which David was head, and in which character his deliverances and victories were typical of the more illustrious triumphs of David's greater Son. The language of vs. 50 justifies this view in its distinct allusion to the great promise (cf. II Sam. 7). In all David's successes he saw the pledges of a fulfilment of that promise, and he mourned in all his adversities, not only in view of his personal suffering, but because he saw in them evidences of danger to the great interests which were committed to his keeping. It is in these aspects of his character that we are led properly to appreciate the importance attached to his sorrows and sufferings, his joys and successes.

PSALM 19

Vss. 1-14. After exhibiting the harmonious revelation of God's perfections made by His works and His word, the Psalmist prays for conformity to the divine teaching.
1. the glory of God—is the sum of His perfections

(Ps. 24:7-10; Rom. 1:20). **firmament**—another word for "heavens" (Gen. 1:8). **handywork**—old English for "work of His hands." **2. uttereth**—pours forth—as a stream—a perpetual testimony. **3.** Though there is no articulate speech or words, yet without these their voice is heard (cf. *Margin*). **4. Their line—or** instruction—the influence exerted by their tacit display of God's perfections. Paul (Rom.10:18), quoting from the *Septuagint,* uses *sound,* which gives the same sense. **5, 6.** The sun, as the most glorious heavenly body, is specially used to illustrate the sentiment; and his vigorous, cheerful, daily, and extensive course, and his reviving heat (including light), well display the wondrous wisdom of his Maker. **7-9.** The law is described by six names, epithets, and effects. It is a rule, God's testimony for the truth, His special and general prescription of duty, fear (as its cause) and judicial decision. It is distinct and certain, reliable, right, pure, holy, and true. Hence it revives those depressed by doubts, makes wise the unskilled (II Tim. 3:15), rejoices the lover of truth, strengthens the desponding (Ps. 13:4; 34:6), provides permanent principles of conduct, and by God's grace brings a rich reward. **12-14.** The clearer our view of the law, the more manifest are our sins. Still for its full effect we need divine grace to show us our faults, acquit us, restrain us from the practice, and free us from the power, of sin. Thus only can our conduct be blameless, and our words and thoughts acceptable to God.

PSALM 20

Vss. 1-9. David probably composed this Psalm to express the prayers of the pious for his success as at once the head of the Church and nation. Like other compositions of which David in such relations is the subject, its sentiments have a permanent value —the prosperity of Christ's kingdom being involved, as well as typified, in that of Israel and its king.
1. hear thee—graciously (Ps. 4:1). **name of**—or manifested perfections, as power, wisdom, etc. **defend thee**—set thee on high from danger (Ps. 9:9; 18:3). **2. strengthen thee**—*sustain* in conflict; even physical benefits may be included, as courage for war, etc., as such may proceed from a sense of divine favor, secured in the use of spiritual privileges. **3. all thy offerings**—or gifts, vegetable offerings. **accept**—lit., "turn to ashes" (cf. I Kings 18:38). **Selah**—(Ps. 3:2). **4. thy counsel** —or plan. **5. salvation**—that wrought and experienced by him. **set up our banners**—(Num. 2:3, 10). In usual sense, or, as some render, *may we be made great.* **6.** He speaks as if suddenly assured of a hearing. **his anointed**—not only David personally, but as the specially appointed head of His Church. **his holy heaven**—or, lit., "the heavens of His holiness," where He resides (Ps. 2:6; 11:4). **saving . . . hand**—His power which brings salvation. **7. remember**—or cause to remember, mention thankfully (I Sam. 17:45; Ps. 33:16). **8. They**—i.e., who trust in horses, etc. **stand upright**—lit., "we have straightened ourselves up from our distress and fears." **9. let the king hear**—as God's representative, delivered to deliver. Perhaps a better sense is, "LORD, save the king; hear us when we call," or pray.

PSALM 21

Vss. 1-13. The pious are led by the Psalmist to celebrate God's favor to the king in the bounties already conferred and in prospective victories. The doxology added may relate to both Psalms; the preceding of petition, chiefly this of thanksgiving, ascribing honor to God for His display of grace and power to His Church in all ages, not only under David, but also under his last greatest successor, "the King of the Jews." **1. thy strength ... thy salvation**—as supplied by Thee. **2.** The sentiment affirmed in the first clause is reaffirmed by the negation of its opposite in the second. **3. preventest**—lit., "to meet here in good sense," or "friendship" (Ps. 59:10; cf. opposite, Ps. 17:13). **blessings of goodness**—which confer happiness. **crown of pure gold**—a figure for the highest royal prosperity. **4-6.** (Cf. II Sam. 7:13-16.) The glory and blessedness of the king as head of his line, including Christ, as well as in being God's specially selected servant, exceeded that of all others. **made him most blessed**—or set him "to be blessings," as Abraham (Gen. 12:2). **with thy countenance**—by sight of thee (Ps. 16:11), or by Thy favor expressed by the light of Thy countenance (Num. 6: 25), or both. **7.** The mediate cause is the king's faith, the efficient, God's mercy. **8.** The address is now made to the king. **hand**—denotes power, and —**right hand**—a more active and efficient degree of its exercise. **find out**—reach, lay hold of, indicating success in pursuit of his enemies. **9.** The king is only God's agent. **anger**—lit., "face," as appearing against them. **as a fiery oven**—as in it. **10. fruit**—children (Ps. 37:25; Hos. 9:16). **11.** This terrible overthrow, reaching to posterity, is due to their crimes (Exod. 20:5, 6). **12. turn their back**—lit., "place them [as to the] shoulder." **against the face of them**—The shooting against their faces would cause them to turn their backs in flight. **13.** The glory of all is ascribable to God alone.

PSALM 22

Vss. 1-31. The obscure words *Aijeleth Shahar* in this title have various explanations. Most interpreters agree in translating them by "hind of the morning." But great difference exists as to the meaning of these words. By some they are supposed (cf. Ps. 9) to be the name of the tune to which the words of the Psalm were set; by others, the name of a musical instrument. Perhaps the best view is to regard the phrase as enigmatically expressive of the subject—the sufferer being likened to a hind pursued by hunters in the early morning (lit., "the dawn of day")—or that, while *hind* suggests the idea of a meek, innocent sufferer, the addition of morning denotes relief obtained. The feelings of a pious sufferer in sorrow and deliverance are vividly portrayed. He earnestly pleads for divine aid on the ground of his relation to God, whose past goodness to His people encourages hope, and then on account of the imminent danger by which he is threatened. The language of complaint is turned to that of rejoicing in the assured prospect of relief from suffering and triumph over his enemies. The use of the words of the first clause of vs. 1 by our Saviour on the cross, and the quotation of vs. 18 by John (19: 24), and of vs. 22 by Paul (Heb. 2:12), as fulfilled in His history, clearly intimate the prophetical and Messianic purport of the Psalm. The intensity of the grief, and the completeness and glory of the deliverance and triumph, alike appear to be unsuitable representations of the fortunes of any less personage. In a general and modified sense (cf. on Ps. 16), the experience here detailed may be adapted to the case of all Christians suffering from spiritual foes, and delivered by divine aid, inasmuch as Christ in His human nature was their head and representative. **1.** A summary of the complaint. Desertion by God, when overwhelmed by distress, is the climax of the sufferer's misery. **words of my roaring**—shows that the complaint is expressed intelligently, though the term "roaring" is figurative, taken from the conduct of irrational creatures in pain. **2.** The long distress is evinced by—**am not silent**—lit., "not silence to me," either meaning, I continually cry; or, corresponding with "thou hearest not," or answerest not, it may mean, there is no rest or quiet to me. **3.** Still he not only refrains from charging God foolishly, but evinces his confidence in God by appealing to Him. **thou art holy**—or possessed of all the attributes which encourage trust, and the right object of the praises of the Church: hence the sufferer need not despair. **4, 5.** Past experience of God's people is a ground of trust. The mention of "our fathers" does not destroy the applicability of the words as the language of our Saviour's human nature. **6.** He who was despised and rejected of His own people, as a disgrace to the nation, might well use these words of deep abasement, which express not His real, but esteemed, value. **7, 8.** For the Jews used one of the gestures (Matt. 27:39) here mentioned, when taunting Him on the cross, and (vs. 43) reproached Him almost in the very language of this passage. **trusted on the Lord**—lit., "rolled"—i.e., his burden (Ps. 37:5; Prov. 16:3) on the Lord. This is the language of enemies sporting with his faith in the hour of his desertion. **shoot out** [or, open] **the lip**—(Cf. Ps. 35:21). **9, 10.** Though ironically spoken, the exhortation to trust was well founded on his previous experience of divine aid, the special illustration of which is drawn from the period of helpless infancy. **didst make me hope**—or lit., "made me secure." **11.** From this statement of reasons for the appeal, he renews it, pleading his double extremity, the nearness of trouble, and the absence of a helper. **12, 13.** His enemies, with the vigor of bulls and rapacity of lions, surround him, eagerly seeking his ruin. The force of both figures is greater without the use of any particle denoting comparison. **14, 15.** Utter exhaustion and hopeless weakness, in these circumstances of pressing danger, are set forth by the most expressive figures; the solidity of the body is destroyed, and it becomes like water; the bones are parted; the heart, the very seat of vitality, melts like wax; all the juices of the system are dried up; the tongue can no longer perform its office, but lies parched and stiffened (cf. Gen. 49:4; II Sam. 14:14; Ps. 58:8). In this, God is regarded as the ultimate source, and men as the instruments. **15. the dust of death**—of course, denotes the grave. We need not try to find the exact counterpart of each item of the description in the particulars of our Saviour's sufferings. Figurative language resembles pictures of historical scenes, presenting substantial truth, under illustrations, which, though not essential to the facts, are not inconsistent with them. Were any portion of Christ's terrible sufferings specially designed, it was doubtless that of the garden of Gethsemane. **16.** Evildoers are well described as dogs, which, in the East, herding together, wild and rapacious, are justly objects of great abhorrence. The last clause has been a subject of much discussion (involving questions as to the genuineness of the *Hebrew* word translated "pierce") which cannot be made intelligible to the English reader. Thought not quoted in the New Testament, the remarkable aptness of the description to the facts of the Saviour's history, together with difficulties attending any other mode of explaining the clause in the *Hebrew,* justify an adherence to the terms of our version and their obvious meaning. **17.** His emaciated frame, itself an item of his misery, is rendered more so as the object of delighted contemplation to his enemies. The verbs, *look* and *stare,* often occur as suggestive of feelings of satisfaction (cf. Ps. 27:13; 54:7; 118:7). **18.** This literally fulfilled prediction closes the sad picture of the exposed and deserted sufferer. **19, 20.** He now turns with unabated desire and trust to God, who, in His strength and faithfulness, is contrasted with the urgent dangers described. **my soul**—or self (cf. Ps. 3:2; 16:10). **my darling**—lit., "my only one," or, "solitary one," as desolate and afflicted (Ps. 25:16; 35:17). **21.** Deliverance pleaded in view of former help, when in the most imminent danger, from the most powerful enemy, represented by the unicorn or wild buffalo. **the lion's mouth**—(Cf. vs. 13.) The lion often used as a figure representing violent enemies; the connecting of the *mouth* intimates their rapacity. **22-24.** He declares his purpose to celebrate God's gracious dealings and publish His manifested perfections (name, Ps. 5:11), etc., and forthwith invites the pious (those who have a reverential fear of God) to unite in special praise for a deliverance, illustrating God's kind regard for the lowly, whom men neglect. *To hide the face* (or eyes) expresses a studied neglect of one's cause, and refusal of aid or sympathy (cf. Ps. 30:7; Isa. 1:15). **25, 26. My praise shall be of thee**—or, perhaps better, "from thee'—i.e., God gives grace to praise Him. With offering praise, he farther evinces his gratitude by promising the payment of his vows, in celebrating the usual festival, as provided in the law (Deut. 12:18; 16:11), of which the pious or humble, and they that seek the Lord (His true worshippers) shall partake abundantly, and join him in praise. In the enthusiasm produced by his lively feelings, he addresses such in words, assuring them of God's perpetual favor. *The dying of the heart* denotes death (I Sam. 25:37); so its living denotes life. **27-31.** His case illustrates God's righteous government. Beyond the existing time and people, others shall be brought to acknowledge and worship God; the *fat ones,* or the rich as well as the poor, the helpless who cannot keep themselves alive, shall together unite in celebrating God's delivering power, and transmit to unborn people the records of His grace. **it shall be accounted to the Lord for . . .** —or, it shall be told of the Lord to a generation. God's wonderful works shall be told from generation to generation. **that he hath done**—supply *it,* or *this*—i.e., what the Psalm has unfolded.

PSALM 23

Vss. 1-6. Under a metaphor borrowed from scenes of pastoral life, with which David was familiar, he describes God's providential care in providing refreshment, guidance, protection, and abundance, and so affording grounds of confidence in His perpetual favor. **1.** Christ's relation to His people is often represented by the figure of a shepherd (John 10:14; Heb. 13:20; I Pet. 2:25; 5:4), and therefore the opinion that He is *the Lord* here so described, and in Genesis 48:15; Psalm 80:1; Isaiah 40:11, is not without some good reason. **2. green pastures**—or, pastures of tender grass, are mentioned, not in respect to food, but as places of cool and refreshing rest. **the still waters**—are, lit., "waters of stillness," whose quiet flow invites to repose. They are contrasted with boisterous streams on the one hand, and stagnant, offensive pools on the other. **3.** To restore the soul is to revive or quicken it (Ps. 19:7), or relieve it (Lam. 1:11, 19). **paths of righteousness**—those of safety, as directed by God, and pleasing to Him. **for his name's sake**—or, regard for His perfections, pledged for His people's welfare. **4.** In the darkest and most trying hour God is near. **the valley of the shadow of death**—is a ravine overhung by high precipitous cliffs, filled with dense forests, and well calculated to inspire dread to the timid, and afford a covert to beasts of prey. While expressive of any great danger or cause of terror, it does not exclude the greatest of all, to which it is most popularly applied, and which its terms suggest. **thy rod and thy staff**—are symbols of a shepherd's office. By them he guides his sheep. **5, 6.** Another figure expresses God's provided care. **a table**—or, food, anointing **oil**—the symbol of gladness, and the overflowing **cup** (which represents abundance)—are prepared for the child of God, who may feast in spite of his enemies, confident that this favor will ever attend him. This beautiful Psalm most admirably sets before us, in its chief figure, that of a shepherd, the gentle, kind, and sure care extended to God's people, who, as a shepherd, both *rules and feeds them.* The closing verse shows that the blessings mentioned are spiritual.

PSALM 24

Vss. 1-10. God's supreme sovereignty requires a befitting holiness of life and heart in His worshippers; a sentiment sublimely illustrated by describing His entrance into the sanctuary, by the symbol of His worship—the ark, as requiring the most profound homage to the glory of His Majesty. **1. fulness**—everything. **world**—the habitable globe, with **they that dwell**—forming a parallel expression to the first clause. **2.** poetically represents the facts of Genesis 1:9. **3, 4.** The form of a question gives vivacity. *Hands, tongue,* and *heart* are organs of action, speech, and feeling, which compose character. **lifted up his soul**—is to set the affections (Ps. 25:1) on an object; here, **vanity**—or, any false thing, of which swearing falsely, or *to falsehood,* is a specification. **hill of the Lord**—(cf. Ps. 2:6, etc.). His Church—the true or invisible, as typified by the earthly sanctuary. **5. righteousness**—the rewards which God bestows on His people, or the grace to secure those rewards as well as the result. **6. Jacob** —By "Jacob," we may understand God's people (cf. Isa. 43:22; 44:2, etc.), corresponding to "the generation," as if he had said, "those who seek Thy face are Thy chosen people." **7-10.** The entrance of the ark, with the attending procession, into the holy sanctuary is pictured to us. The repetition of the terms gives emphasis. **Lord of hosts**—or fully, *Lord God of hosts* (Hos. 12:5; Amos 4:13), describes God by a title indicative of supremacy over all creatures, and especially the heavenly armies (Josh. 5:14; I Kings 22:19). Whether, as some think, the actual enlargement of the ancient gates of Jerusalem be the basis of the figure, the effect of the whole is to impress us with a conception of the matchless majesty of God.

PSALM 25

Vss. 1-22. The general tone of this Psalm is that of prayer for help from enemies. Distress, however, exciting a sense of sin, humble confession, supplication for pardon, preservation from sin, and divine guidance, are prominent topics. **1. lift up my soul**—(Ps. 24:4; 86:4), set my affections (cf. Col. 3:2). **2. not be ashamed**—by disappointment of hopes of relief. **3.** The prayer generalized as to all who *wait on God*—i.e., who expect His favor. On the other hand, the disappointment of the perfidious, who, unprovoked, have done evil, is invoked (cf. II Sam. 22:9). **4, 5.** On the ground of former favor, he invokes divine guidance, according to God's gracious ways of dealing and faithfulness. **6, 7.** Confessing past and present sins, he pleads for mercy, not on palliations of sin, but on God's well-known benevolence. **8, 9. upright**—acting according to His promise. **sinners**—the general term, limited by the **meek**—who are *penitent*. **in judgment**—rightly. **the way**—and **his way**—God's way of providence. **10. paths**—similar sense—His modes of dealing (cf. vs. 4). **mercy and truth**—(Job 14), God's grace in promising and faithfulness in performing. **11.** God's perfections of love, mercy, goodness, and truth are manifested (*his name*, cf. Ps. 9:10) in pardoning sin, and the greatness of sin renders pardon more needed. **12, 13.** What he asks for himself is the common lot of all the pious. The phrase—**inherit the earth**—(cf. Matt. 5:5), alluding to the promise of Canaan, expresses all the blessings included in that promise, temporal as well as spiritual. **14.** The reason of the blessing explained—the pious enjoy communion with God (cf. Prov. 3:21, 22), and, of course, learn His gracious terms of pardon. **15.** His trust in God is fixed. **net**—is frequently used as a figure for dangers by enemies (Ps. 9:15; 10:9). **16-19.** A series of earnest appeals for aid because God had seemed to desert him (cf. Ps. 13:1; 17:13, etc.), his sins oppressed him, his enemies had enlarged his troubles and multiplied, increasing in hate and violence (Ps. 9:8; 18:48). **20. keep my soul**—(Ps. 16:1). **put my trust**—flee for refuge (Ps. 2:12). **21.** In conscious innocence of the faults charged by his enemies, he confidently commits his cause to God. Some refer—**integrity . . .**—to God, meaning His covenant faithfulness. This sense, though good, is an unusual application of the terms. **22.** Extend these blessings to all Thy people in all their distresses.

PSALM 26

Vss. 1-12. After appealing to God's judgment on his avowed integrity and innocence of the charges laid by his enemies, the Psalmist professes delight in God's worship, and prays for exemption from the fate of the wicked, expressing assurance of God's favor. **1. Judge**—decide on my case—the appeal of innocence. **in mine integrity**—freedom from blemish (cf. Ps. 25:21). His confidence of perseverance results from trust in God's sustaining grace. **2.** He asks the most careful scrutiny of his affections and thoughts (Ps. 7:9), our motives. **3.** As often, the ground of prayer for present help is former favor. **4-8.** As exemplified by the fruits of divine grace, presented in his life, especially in his avoiding the wicked and his purposes of cleaving to God's worship. **wash mine hands**—expressive symbol of freedom from sinful acts (cf. Matt. 27:24). **the habitation of thy house**—where Thy house rests—as the tabernacle was not yet permanently fixed. **honour dwelleth**—conveys an allusion to the Holy of Holies. **9. Gather not . . .**—Bring me not to death. **bloody**

men—(cf. Ps. 5:6). **10.** Their whole conduct is that of violence and fraud. **11, 12. But . . .**—He contrasts his character and destiny with that of the wicked (cf. vss. 1, 2). **even place**—free from occasions of stumbling—safety in his course is denoted. Hence he will render to God his praise publicly.

PSALM 27

Vss. 1-14. With a general strain of confidence, hope, and joy, especially in God's worship, in the midst of dangers, the Psalmist introduces prayer for divine help and guidance. **1. light**—is a common figure for comfort. **strength**—or, stronghold—affording security against all violence. The interrogations give greater vividness to the negation implied. **2. eat . . . my flesh**—(Job 19:22; Ps. 14:4). The allusion to wild beasts illustrates their rapacity. **they stumbled**—"they" is emphatic; *not I*, but *they* were destroyed. **3.** In the greatest dangers. **in this**—i.e., then, in such extremity. **4, 5.** The secret of his confidence is his delight in communion with God (Ps. 16:11; 23:6), beholding the harmony of His perfections, and seeking His favor in His temple or palace; a term applicable to the tabernacle (cf. Ps. 5:7). There he is safe (Ps. 31:21; 61:5). The figure is changed in the last clause, but the sentiment is the same. **6. head be lifted up**—I shall be placed beyond the reach of my enemies. Hence he avows his purpose of rendering joyful thank offerings. **7.** Still pressing need extorts prayer for help. **cry with my voice**—denotes earnestness. Other things equal, Christians in earnest pray audibly, even in secret. **8.** The meaning is clear, though the construction in a literal translation is obscure. The *English Version* supplies the implied clause. To *seek God's face* is to seek His favor (Ps. 105:4). **9. Hide not . . .**—(Ps. 4:6; 22:24). Against rejection he pleads former mercy and love. **10.** In the extremity of earthly destitution (Ps. 31:11; 38:11), God provides (cf. Matt. 25:35). **11. thy way**—of providence. **a plain path**—(Ps. 26:12). **enemies**—lit., "watchers for my fall" (Ps. 5:8). **12. will**—lit., "soul," "desire" (Ps. 35:25). **enemies**—lit., "oppressors." Falsehood aids cruelty against him. **breathe out**—as being filled with it (Acts 9:1). **13.** The strong emotion is indicated by the incomplete sentence, for which the *English Version* supplies a proper clause; or, omitting that, and rendering, *yet I believed . . .*, the contrast of his faith and his danger is expressed. **to see**—is to experience (Ps. 22:17). **14. Wait . . .**—in confident expectation. The last clause is, lit., "and wait . . . ," as if expecting new measures of help.

PSALM 28

Vss. 1-9. An earnest cry for divine aid against his enemies, as being also those of God, is followed by the Psalmist's praise in assurance of a favorable answer, and a prayer for all God's people. **1. my rock**—(Ps. 18:2, 31). **be not silent to me**—lit., "from me," deaf or inattentive. **become like them . . .**—share their fate. **go down into the pit**—or, grave (Ps. 30:3). **2. lift up my hands**—a gesture of prayer (Ps. 63:4; 141:2). **oracle**—place of *speaking* (Exod. 25:22; Num. 7:89), where God answered His people (cf. Ps. 5:7). **3. Draw me not . . .**—implies punishment as well as death (cf. Ps. 26:9). Hypocrisy is the special *wickedness* mentioned. **4.** The imprecation is justified in vs. 5. The force of the passage is greatly enhanced by the accumulation of terms describing their sin. **endeavours**—points out their deliberate sinfulness. **5.** Disregard of God's judgments brings a righteous punishment. **destroy ... build ... up**—The positive strengthened by the negative form. **6. supplications**—or, cries for mercy. **7.** The repetition of heart denotes his sincerity. **8.** The distinction made between the people. **their strength**—and the **anointed**—may indicate Absalom's rebellion as the occasion. **9.** The special prayer for the people sustains this view. **feed them** —as a shepherd (Ps. 23:1, etc.).

PSALM 29

Vss. 1-11. Trust in God is encouraged by the celebration of His mighty power as illustrated in His dominion over the natural world, in some of its most terrible and wonderful exhibitions. **1. Give**—or, ascribe (Deut. 32:3). **mighty**—or, sons of the mighty (Ps. 89:6). Heavenly beings, as angels. **2. name**—as (Ps. 5:11; 8:1). **beauty of holiness**—the loveliness of a spiritual worship, of which the perceptible beauty of the sanctuary worship was but a type. **3. The voice of the Lord**—audible exhibition of His power in the tempest, of which thunder is a specimen, but not the uniform or sole example. **the waters**—the clouds or vapors (Ps. 18:11; Jer. 10:13). **4. powerful ... majesty**—lit., "in power, in majesty." **5, 6.** The tall and large cedars, especially of Lebanon, are shivered, utterly broken. The waving of the mountain forests before the wind is expressed by the figure of skipping or leaping. **7. divideth**—lit., "hews off." The lightning, like flakes and splinters hewed from stone or wood, flies through the air. **8. the wilderness**—especially Kadesh, south of Judea, is selected as another scene of this display of divine power, as a vast and desolate region impresses the mind, like mountains, with images of grandeur. **9.** Terror-stricken animals and denuded forests close the illustration. In view of this scene of awful sublimity, God's worshippers respond to the call of vs. 2, and speak or cry, "Glory!" By temple, or palace (God's residence, Ps. 5:7), may here be meant heaven, or the whole frame of nature, as the angels are called on for praise. **10, 11.** Over this terrible raging of the elements God is enthroned, directing and restraining by sovereign power; and hence the comfort of His people. "This awful God is ours, our Father and our Love."

PSALM 30

Vss. 1-12. Lit., "A Psalm-Song"—a composition to be sung with musical instruments, or without them—or, "*Song of the dedication* ... ," specifying the particular character of the Psalm. Some suppose that "*of David*" should be connected with the name of the composition, and not with "house"; and refer for the occasion to the selection of a site for the temple (I Chron. 21:26-30; 22:1). But "house" is never used absolutely for the temple, and "dedication" does not well apply to such an occasion. Though the phrase in the *Hebrew*, "dedication of the house of David," is an unusual form, yet it is equally unusual to disconnect the name of the author and the composition. As a "dedication of David's house" (as provided, Deut. 20:25), the scope of the Psalm well corresponds with the state of repose and meditation on his past trials suited to such an occasion (II Sam. 5:11; 7:2). For beginning

with a celebration of God's delivering favor, in which he invites others to join, he relates his prayer in distress, and God's gracious and prompt answer. **1. lifted me up**—as one is drawn from a well (Ps. 40:2). **2. healed me**—Affliction is often described as disease (Ps. 6:2; 41:4; 107:20), and so relief by healing. **3.** The terms describe extreme danger. **soul** —or, myself. **grave**—lit., "hell," as in Psalm 16:10. **hast kept me ... pit**—quickened or revived me from the state of dying (cf. Ps. 28:1). **4. remembrance**— the thing remembered or memorial. **holiness**—as the sum of God's perfections (cf. Ps. 22:3), used as *name* (Exod. 3:15; Ps. 135:13). **5.** Relatively, the longest experience of divine anger by the pious is momentary. These precious words have consoled millions. **6, 7.** What particular prosperity is meant we do not know; perhaps his accession to the throne. In his self-complacent elation he was checked by God's *hiding His face* (cf. Ps. 22:24; 27:9). **troubled** —confounded with fear (Ps. 2:5). **8-11.** As in Psalm 6:5; 88:10; Isaiah 38:18, the appeal for mercy is based on the destruction of his agency in praising God here, which death would produce. The terms expressing relief are poetical, and not to be pressed, though "dancing" is the translation of a word which means a *lute*, whose cheerful notes are contrasted with mourning, or (Amos 5:16) wailing. **sackcloth**— was used, even by kings, in distress (I Chron. 21:16; Isa. 37:1) but "gladness," used for a garment, shows the language to be figurative. **12.** Though—**my**—is supplied before—**glory**—it is better as in Psalm 16:10, to receive it as used for *tongue*, the organ of praise. The ultimate end of God's mercies to us is our praise to Him.

PSALM 31

Vss. 1-24. The prayer of a believer in time of deep distress. In the first part, cries for help are mingled with expressions of confidence. Then the detail of griefs engrosses his attention, till, in the assurance of strong but submissive faith, he rises to the language of unmingled joyful trust and exhorts others to like love and confidence towards God. **1.** Expresses the general tone of feeling of the Psalm. **2-4.** He seeks help in God's righteous government (Ps. 5:8), and begs for an attentive hearing, and speedy and effectual aid. With no other help and no claim of merit, he relies solely on God's regard to His own perfections for a safe guidance and release from the snares of his enemies. On the terms "rock," etc., cf. Ps. 17:2 18:2, 50; 20:6; 23:3; 25:21). **5, 6. commit my spirit**—my life, or myself. Our Saviour used the words on the Cross, not as prophetical, but, as many pious men have done, as expressive of His unshaken confidence in God. The Psalmist rests on God's faithfulness to His promises to His people, and hence avows himself one of them, detesting all who revere objects of idolatry (cf. Deut. 32:21; I Cor. 8:4). **7. hast known my soul ...** —had regard to me in trouble. **8. shut me up ... enemy**—abandon to (I Sam. 23:11). **large room**— place of safety (cf. Ps. 18:19). **9. 10. mine eye ...** denotes extreme weakness (cf. Ps. 6:7). **grief**—mingled sorrow and indignation (Ps. 6:7). **soul and ... belly**—the whole person. Though the effects ascribed to grief are not mere figures of speech—**spent ... consumed**—must be taken in the modified sense of *wasted* and *decayed*. **iniquity**—or, suffering by it (cf. on Ps. 40:12). **11. among**—or, lit., "from," or, "by" my enemies. The latter clauses describe the progress of his disgrace to the lowest degree, till **12.** he is forgotten as one dead, and contemned as a useless broken vessel. **13. For**—introduces further reasons for his prayer, the unjust, deliberate, and murderous purposes of his foes. **14-18.** In his profession of trust he includes the terms of the prayer expressing it. **times**—course of life. **deliver ... hand**—opposed to "shut me up . . ." of vs. 8. **Make ... shine**—(Cf. Num. 6:25; Ps. 4:6). Deprecating from himself, he imprecates on the wicked God's displeasure, and prays that their virulent persecution of him may be stopped. **19-21.** God displays openly His purposed goodness to His people. **the secret of thy presence**—or, *covering* of Thy countenance; the protection He thus affords; cf. Ps. 27:5 for a similar figure; "dwelling" used there for "presence" here. The idea of security further presented by the figure of a tent and a fortified city. **22. For I said** —lit., "And I said," in an adversative sense. I, thus favored, was despondent. **in my haste**—in my terror. **cut off ... eyes**—from all the protection of Thy presence. **23, 24. the Lord ... proud doer**—lit., "the Lord is keeping faith"—i.e., with His people, and is repaying, etc. Then let none despair, but take courage; their hopes shall not be in vain.

PSALM 32

Vss. 1-11. *Maschil*—lit., "giving instruction." The Psalmist describes the blessings of His forgiveness, succeeding the pains of conviction, and deduces from his own experience instruction and exhortation to others.
1, 2. (Cf. Rom. 4:6.) **forgiven**—lit., "taken away," opposed to *retain* (John 20:23). **covered**—so that God no longer regards the sin (Ps. 85:3). **imputeth**—charge to him, and treat him accordingly. **no guile** —or, *deceit,* no false estimate of himself, nor insincerity before God (cf. Rom. 8:1). **3, 4.** A vivid description of felt, but unacknowledged, sin. **When**—lit., "for," as in vs. 4. **thy hand**—of God, or, power in distressing him (Ps. 38:2). **moisture**—vital juices of the body, the parching heat of which expresses the anguish of the soul. On the other figures, cf. Psalm 6:2, 7; 31:9-11. If composed on the occasion of the fifty-first Psalm, this distress may have been protracted for several months. **5.** A prompt fulfilment of the purposed confession is followed by a prompt forgiveness. **6. For this**—i.e., my happy experience. **godly**—pious in the sense of Psalm 4:3. **a time**—(Isa. 55:6); when God's Spirit inclines us to seek pardon, He is ready to forgive. **floods ...**— denotes great danger (Ps. 18:17; 66:12). **7.** His experience illustrates the statement of vs. 6. **8.** Whether, as most likely, the language of David (cf. Ps. 51:13), or that of God, this is a promise of divine guidance. **I will ... mine eye**—or, My eye shall be on thee, watching and directing thy way. **9.** The latter clause, more literally, *"in that they come not near thee"*—i.e., *because* they will not come, etc., unless forced by bit and bridle. **10.** The sorrows of the impenitent contrasted with the peace and safety secured by God's mercy. **11.** The righteous and upright, or those conforming to the divine teaching for securing the divine blessing, may well rejoice with shouting.

PSALM 33

Vss. 1-22. A call to lively and joyous praise to God for His glorious attributes and works, as displayed in creation, and His general and special

providence, in view of which, the Psalmist, for all the pious, professes trust and joy and invokes God's mercy.
1-3. The sentiment falls in with Psalm 32:11 (cf. I Cor. 14:15). The instruments (Ps. 92:3; 144:9) do not exclude the voice. **a new song**—fresh, adapted to the occasion (Ps. 40:3; 96:1). **play skilfully**—(Cf. Ps. 15, 16, 21). **4-9.** Reasons for praise— first, God's truth, faithfulness, and mercy, generally; then, His creative power which all must honor. **In word and breath**—or, spirit, there may be an allusion to the Son (John 1:1) and Holy Spirit. **he spake**— lit., "said." **it was**—The addition of "done" weakens the sense (cf. Gen. 1:3-10). **10, 11.** In God's providence He thwarts men's purposes and executes His own. **heathen**—lit., "nations." **12-19.** The inference from the foregoing in vs. 12 is illustrated by God's special providence, underlying which is His minute knowledge of all men. **looketh**—intently (Isa. 14:16). **fashioneth**—or, forms, and hence knows and controls (Prov. 21:1). **alike**—without exception. **considereth**—or, understands; God knows men's motives. **16, 17.** Men's usual reliances in their greatest exigencies are, in themselves, useless. *On the war horse* (cf. Job 39:19-25). **a vain thing**—a lie, which deceives us. **18, 19.** Contrasted is God's guidance and power to save from the greatest earthly evil and its most painful precursor, and hence from all. **20-22. waiteth**—in earnest expectation. **holy name**—(Cf. Ps. 5:12; 22:22; 30:4). Our faith measures mercy (Matt. 9:29); and if of grace, it is no more of debt (Rom. 11:6).

PSALM 34

Vss. 1-22. On the title cf. I Samuel 21:13. Abimelech was the general name of the sovereign (Gen. 20:2). After celebrating God's gracious dealings with him, the Psalmist exhorts others to make trial of His providential care, instructing them how to secure it. He then contrasts God's care of His people and His punitive providence towards the wicked.
1-4. Even in distress, which excites supplication, there is always matter for praising and thanking God (cf. Eph. 5:20; Phil. 4:6). **make her boast**— glory (Ps. 105:3; cf. Gal. 6:14). **humble**—the pious, as in Psalm 9:12; 25:9. **magnify the Lord**—ascribe greatness to Him, an act of praise. **together**—alike (Ps. 33:15), or, equally, without exception. **delivered ... fears**—as well as actual evil (Ps. 64:1). **5-7.** God's favor to the pious generally, and to himself specially, is celebrated. **looked**—with desire for help. **lightened**—or, brightened, expressing joy, opposed to the downcast features of those who are ashamed or disappointed (Ps. 25:2, 3). **This poor man**—lit., "humble," himself as a specimen of such. **angel**—of the covenant (Isa. 63:9), of whom as a leader of God's host (Josh. 5:14; I Kings 22:19), the phrase—**encampeth ... —**is appropriate; or, "angel" used collectively for angels (Heb. 1:14). **8. taste and see**—try and experience. **9. that fear him**—who are pious—fear and love (Prov. 1:7; 9:10). **saints** —consecrated to His service (Isa. 40:31). **10. not want any good**—"good" is emphatic; they may be afflicted (cf. vs. 10); but this may be a *good* (II Cor. 4:17, 18; Heb. 12:10, 11). **11. children**—subjects of instruction (Prov. 1:8, 10). **12. What man**— Whoever desires the blessings of piety, let him attend. **13, 14.** Sins of thought included in those of speech (Luke 6:45), avoiding evil and doing good in our relations to men are based on a right relation

to God. **15. eyes of the Lord are upon**—(Ps. 32:8; 33:18). **16. face . . . against**—opposed to them (Lev. 17:10; 20:3). **cut off the remembrance**—utterly destroy (Ps. 109:13). **17, 18.** Humble penitents are objects of God's special tender regard (Ps. 51:19; Isa. 57:15). **20. bones**—framework of the body. **21, 22.** Contrast in the destiny of righteous and wicked; the former shall be delivered and never come into condemnation (John 5:24; Rom. 8:1); the latter are left under condemnation and desolate.

PSALM 35

Vss. 1-28. The Psalmist invokes God's aid, contrasting the hypocrisy, cunning, and malice of his enemies with his integrity and generosity. The imprecations of the first part including a brief notice of their conduct, the fuller exposition of their hypocrisy and malice in the second, and the earnest prayer for deliverance from their scornful triumph in the last, are each closed (vss. 9, 10, 18, 27, 28) with promises of praise for the desired relief, in which his friends will unite. The historical occasion is probably I Samuel 24.

1-3. God is invoked in the character of a warrior (Exod. 15:3; Deut. 32:41). **fight against**—lit., "devour my devourers." **stop the way against**—lit., "shut up" (the way), to meet or oppose, etc. **I . . . thy salvation**—who saves thee. **4.** (Cf. Psalm 9:17.) **devise my hurt**—purpose for evil to me. **5, 6.**—(Cf. Ps. 1:4)—a terrible fate; driven by wind on a slippery path in darkness, and hotly pursued by supernatural violence (II Sam. 24:16; Acts 12:23). **7, 8. net in a pit**—or, pit of their net—or, net-pit—as holy hill for hill of holiness—(Ps. 2:6)—a figure from hunting (Ps. 7:15). Their imprecations on impenitent rebels against God need no vindication; His justice and wrath are for such; His mercy for penitents. Cf. Psalms 7:16; 11:5, on the peculiar fate of the wicked here noticed. **9, 10. All my bones**—every part. **him that spoileth him**—(Cf. Ps. 10:2). **11. False witnesses**—lit., "Witnesses of injustice and cruelty" (cf. Ps. 11:5; 25:19). **12-14.** Though they rendered evil for good, he showed a tender sympathy in their affliction. **spoiling**—lit., "bereavement." The usual modes of showing grief are made, as figures, to express his sorrow. **prayer . . . bosom**—may denote either the posture—the head bowed—(cf. I Kings 18:42)—or, that the prayer was in secret. Some think there is a reference to the result—the prayer would benefit him if not them. **behaved**—lit., "went on" —denoting his habit. **heavily**—or, squalidly, his sorrowing occasioning neglect of his person. Altogether, his grief was that of one for a dearly loved relative. **15, 16.** On the contrary, they rejoiced in his affliction. *Halting,* or lameness, as in Psalm 38: 17 for any distress. **abjects**—either as cripples (cf. II Sam. 4:4), contemptible; or, degraded persons, such as had been beaten (cf. Job 30:1-8). **I knew it not**—either the persons, or, reasons of such conduct. **tear me, and ceased not**—lit., "were not silent"—showing that the *tearing* meant slandering. **mockers**—who were hired to make sport at feasts (Prov. 28:21). **17. darling**—(Cf. Ps. 22:20, 21.) **18.** (Cf. Ps. 22:22.) **19. enemies wrongfully**—by false and slanderous imputations. **wink with the eye**—an insulting gesture (Prov. 6:13). **without a cause** —manifests more malice than having a wrong cause. **20. deceitful matters**—or, words of deceit. **quiet in the land**—the pious lovers of peace. **21.** On the gesture cf. Psalm 22:7, and on the expressions of malicious triumph, cf. Psalms 10:13; 28:3. **23, 24.**

(Cf. Ps. 7:6; 26:1; II Thess. 1:6.) God's righteous government is the hope of the pious and terror of the wicked. **25. swallowed him up**—utterly destroyed him (Ps. 21:9; Lam. 2:16). **26. clothed**—covered wholly (Job 8:22). **27. favour . . . cause**—delight in it, as vindicated by Thee. **Let the Lord . . .** Let Him be greatly praised for His care of the just. **28.** In this praise of God's equitable government (Ps. 5:8) the writer promises ever to engage.

PSALM 36

Vss. 1-12. On *servant of the Lord,* cf. title of Psalm 18. The wickedness of man contrasted with the excellency of God's perfections and dispensations; and the benefit of the latter sought, and the evils of the former deprecated. **1.** The general sense of this difficult verse is, "that the wicked have no fear of God." The first clause may be rendered, "Saith transgression in my heart, in respect to the wicked, there is no fear," etc., i.e., such is my reflection on men's transgressions. **2-4.** This reflection detailed. **until his iniquity . . .**—lit., "for finding his iniquity for hating"; i.e., he persuades himself God will not so find it—"for hating" involving the idea of punishing. Hence his words of **iniquity** and **deceit, and** his bold rejection of all right principles of conduct. The climax is that he deliberately adopts and patronizes evil. The negative forms affirm more emphatically their contraries. **5, 6. mercy . . . and . . . faithfulness**—as mercy and truth (Ps. 25:10). **righteousness** [and] **judgments**—qualities of a good government (Ps. 5:8; 31:1). These all are set forth, by the figures used, as unbounded. **7. shadow of thy wings**—(Cf. Deut. 32:11; Ps. 91:1). **8. fatness**—richness. **thy house**—residence—for the privileges and blessings of communion with God (Ps. 23:6; 27:4). **river of thy pleasures**—plenteous supply—may allude to Eden. **9.** Light is an emblem of all blessings—given of God as a means to gain more. **10. that know thee**—right knowledge of God is the source of right affections and conduct. **11. foot of . . . hand . . . wicked**—all kinds of violent dealing. **12. There**—in the acting of violence, they are overthrown. A signal defeat.

PSALM 37

Vss. 1-40. A composed and uniform trust in God and a constant course of integrity are urged in view of the blessedness of the truly pious, contrasted in various aspects with the final ruin of the wicked. Thus the wisdom and justice of God's providence are vindicated, and its seeming inequalities, which excite the cavils of the wicked and the distrust of the pious, are explained. David's personal history abundantly illustrates the Psalm.

1, 2. The general sentiment of the whole Psalm is expressed. The righteous need not be vexed by the prosperity of the wicked; for it is transient, and their destiny undesirable. **3. Trust**—sure of safety. **shalt thou dwell**—or, dwell thou—repose quietly. **verily . . . fed**—or, feed on truth—God's promise (Ps. 36:5; cf. Hos. 12:1). **4. desires**—(Ps. 20:5; 21:2), what is lawful and right, really good (Ps. 84:11). **5. Commit thy way**—(Prov. 16:3). *Works*—what you have to do and cannot—set forth as a burden. **trust . . . in him**—lit., "on Him." *He will do* what you cannot (cf. Ps. 22:8; 31:6). He will not suffer your character to remain under suspicion. **7, 8. Rest in**—lit., "Be silent to the Lord." **and wait**—Be submissive—avoid petulance and murmurings, anger and rash doing. **9.** Two reasons: The prosperity of the wicked is short; and the pious, by humble trust, will secure all covenant blessing, denoted here by "inherit the earth" (cf. Ps. 25:13). **10, 11. shall not be** —lit., "is not"—is not to be found. **peace**—includes prosperity. **12. gnasheth . . . teeth**—in beastly rage. **13.** (Cf. Ps. 2:4.) **seeth**—knows certainly. **his day** —of punishment, long delayed, shall yet come (Heb. 10:37). **14, 15. sword, and . . . bow**—for any instruments of violence. **slay**—lit., "slaughter" (I Sam. 25:11). **poor and needy**—God's people (Ps. 10:17; 12:5). The punishment of the wicked as drawn on 'themselves—often mentioned (cf. Ps. 7:15, 16; 35:8). **16. riches**—lit., "noise and tumult," as incidental to much wealth (cf. Ps. 39:6). Thus the contrast with the "little" of one man is more vivid. **17.** Even the members of the body needed to hold weapons are destroyed. **18, 19.** God, who knows His people's changes, provides against evil and supplies all their need. **20.** While the wicked, however mighty, are destroyed, and that utterly, as smoke which vanishes and leaves no trace. **21, 22. payeth not**—not able; having grown poor (cf. Deut. 15:7). Ability of the one and inability of the other do not exclude moral dispositions. God's blessing or cursing makes the difference. **cut off**—opposed to "inherit the earth" (cf. Lev. 7:20, 21). **23, 24. steps**—way, or, course of life; as ordered by God, failures will not be permanent. **25, 26. his seed is blessed**—lit., "for a **blessing**" (Gen. 12:2; Ps. 21:6). This position is still true as the rule of God's economy (I Tim. 4:8; 6:6). **27-29.** The exhortation is sustained by the assurance of God's essential rectitude in that providential government which provides perpetual blessings for the good, and perpetual misery for the wicked. **30, 31.** The righteous described as to the elements of character, thought, word, and action. **steps**—or, goings—for conduct which is unwavering (Ps. 18:36). **32, 33.** The devices of the wicked against the good fail because God acquits them. **34.** On the contrary, the good are not only blessed, but made to see the ruin of their foes. **35, 36.** of which a picture is given, under the figure of a flourishing tree (cf. *Margin*), which soon withers. **he was not**—(Cf. vs. 10). **37.** By **the end** is meant reward (Prov. 23:18; 24:14), or expectation of success, as in vs. 38, which describes the *end of the wicked* in contrast, and that is *cut off* (cf. Ps. 73:17). **38. together**—at once— entirely (Ps. 4:8). **39, 40. strength**—(Ps. 27:1; 28:8). **trouble**—straits Ps. 9:9; 10:1). In trust and quietness is the salvation of the pious from all foes and all their devices.

PSALM 38

Vss. 1-22. *To bring to remembrance,* or, remind God of His mercy and himself of his sin. Appealing to God for relief from His heavy chastisement, the Psalmist avows his integrity before men, complains of the defection of friends and persecution of enemies, and in a submissive spirit, casting himself on God, with penitent confession he pleads God's covenant relation and his innocence of the charges of his enemies, and prays for divine comfort and help.

1-4. He deprecates deserved punishment, which is described (Ps. 6:1), under the figure of bodily disease. **arrows . . . and thy hand**—the sharp and heavy afflictions he suffered (Deut. 32:23). **iniq-**

uities—afflictions in punishment of sin (II Sam. 16:12; Ps. 31:10; 40:12). **gone over mine head** —as a flood. **5-8.** The loathsomeness, corruption, and wasting torture of severe physical disease set forth his mental anguish. It is possible some bodily disease was connected. The **loins** are the seat of strength. His exhaustion left him only the power to groan. **9.** That God can hear (Rom. 8:26). **10. My heart panteth**—as if barely surviving. **light . . . from me**—utter exhaustion (Ps. 6: 7; 13:3). **11, 12.** Friends desert, but foes increase in malignity. **seek after my life**—(I Sam. 20:1; 22:23). **13, 14.** He patiently submits, uttering no reproaches or replies (John 19:9) to their insulting speeches; **15-17.** for he is confident the **Lord**—lit., "Sovereign" (to whom he was a servant), would answer his prayer (Ps. 3:4; 4:1), and not permit their triumph in his partial halting, of which he was in danger. **18.** Consciousness of sin makes suffering pungent, and suffering, rightly received, leads to confession. **19, 20.** Still, while humbled before God, he is the victim of deadly enemies, full of malice and treachery. **enemies are lively**—lit., "of life," who would take my life, i.e., deadly. **21, 22.** (Cf. Ps. 22:19; 35:3.) All terms of frequent use. In this Psalm the language is generally susceptible of application to Christ as a sufferer, David, as such, typifying Him. This does not require us to apply the confessions of sin, but only the pains or penalties which He bore for us.

PSALM 39

Vss. 1-13. *To Jeduthun* (I Chron. 16:41, 42), one of the chief singers. His name mentioned, perhaps, as a special honor. Under depressing views of his frailty and the prosperity of the wicked, the Psalmist, tempted to murmur, checks the expression of his feelings, till, led to regard his case aright, he prays for a proper view of his condition and for the divine compassion.

1. I said—or, resolved. **will take heed**—watch. **ways**—conduct, of which the use of the tongue is a part (Jas. 1:26). **bridle**—lit., "muzzle" (cf. Deut. 25:4). **while . . . before me**—in beholding their prosperity (Ps. 37:10, 36). **2. even from good**—(Gen. 31:24), everything. **3.** His emotions, as a smothered flame, burst forth. **4-7.** Some take these words as those of fretting, but they are not essentially such. The tinge of discontent arises from the character of his suppressed emotions. But, addressing God, they are softened and subdued. **4. make me to know**— experimentally appreciate. **how frail I am**—lit., "when I shall cease." **5-6.** His prayer is answered in his obtaining an impressive view of the vanity of the life of all men, and their transient state. Their pomp is a mere image, and their wealth is gathered they know not for whom. **7.** The interrogation makes the implied negative stronger. Though this world offers nothing to our expectation, God is worthy of all confidence. **8-10.** Patiently submissive, he prays for the removal of his chastisement, and that he may not be a reproach. **11.** From his own case, he argues to that of all, that the destruction of man's enjoyments is ascribable to sin. **12, 13.** Consonant with the tenor of the Psalm, he prays for God's compassionate regard to him as a stranger here; and that, as such was the condition of his fathers, so, like them, he may be cheered instead of being bound under wrath and chastened in displeasure.

PSALM 40

Vss. 1-17. In this Psalm a celebration of God's deliverance is followed by a profession of devotion to His service. Then follows a prayer for relief from imminent dangers, involving the overthrow of enemies and the rejoicing of sympathizing friends. In Hebrews 10:5, etc., Paul quotes vss. 6-8 as the words of Christ, offering Himself as a better sacrifice. Some suppose Paul thus accommodated David's words to express Christ's sentiments. But the value of his quotation would be thus destroyed, as it would have no force in his argument, unless regarded by his readers as the original sense of the passage in the Old Testament. Others suppose the Psalm describes David's feelings in suffering and joy; but the language quoted by Paul, in the sense given by him, could not apply to David in any of his relations, for as a type the language is not adapted to describe any event or condition of David's career, and as an individual representing the pious generally, neither he nor they could properly use it (cf. on vs. 7 below). The Psalm must be taken then, as the sixteenth, to express the feelings of Christ's human nature. The difficulties pertinent to this view will be considered as they occur.

1-3. The figures for deep distress are illustrated in Jeremiah's history (Jer. 38:6-12). Patience and trust manifested in distress, deliverance in answer to prayer, and the blessed effect of it in eliciting praise from God's true worshippers, teach us that Christ's suffering is our example, and His deliverance our encouragement (Heb. 5:7, 8; 12:3; I Pet. 4:12-16). **inclined**—(the ear, Ps. 17:6), as if to catch the faintest sigh. **a new song**—(Ps. 33:3). **fear, and ... trust**—revere with love and faith. **4. Blessed**—(Ps. 1:1; 2:12). **respecteth**—lit., "turns towards," as an object of confidence. **turn aside**—from true God and His law to falsehood in worship and conduct. **5. be reckoned up in order**—(cf. Ps. 5:3; 33:14; Isa. 44:7), too many to be set forth regularly. This is but one instance of many. The use of the plural accords with the union of Christ and His people. In suffering and triumph, they are one with Him. **6-8.** In Paul's view this passage has more meaning than the mere expression of grateful devotion to God's service. He represents Christ as declaring that the sacrifices, whether vegetable or animal, general or special expiatory offerings, would not avail to meet the demands of God's law, and that He had come to render the required satisfaction, which he states was effected by "the offering of the body of Christ," for that is the "will of God" which Christ came to fulfil or do, in order to effect man's redemption. We thus see that the contrast to the unsatisfactory character assigned the Old Testament offerings in vs. 6 is found in the compliance with God's law (cf. vss. 7, 8). Of course, as Paul and other New Testament writers explain Christ's work, it consisted in more than being made under the law or obeying its precepts. It required an "obedience unto death," and that is the compliance here chiefly intended, and which makes the contrast with vs. 6 clear. **mine ears hast thou opened**—Whether allusion is made to the custom of boring a servant's ear, in token of voluntary and perpetual enslavement (Exod. 21:6), or that *the opening of the ear*, as in Isa. 48:8; 50:5 (though by a different word in *Hebrew*) denotes obedience by the common figure of hearing for obeying, it is evident that the clause is designed to express a devotion to God's will as avowed more fully in vs. 8, and already explained. Paul, however, uses the words, "a body hast thou prepared me," which are

found in the *Septuagint* in the place of the words, "*mine* ears hast thou opened." He does not lay any stress on this clause, and his argument is complete without it. It is, perhaps, to be regarded rather as an interpretation or free translation by the *Septuagint*, than either an addition or attempt at verbal translation. The *Septuagint* translators may have had reference to Christ's vicarious sufferings as taught in other Scriptures, as in Isaiah 53; at all events, the sense is substantially the same, as a body was essential to the required obedience (cf. Rom. 7:4; I Pet. 2:24). **7. Then**—in such case, without necessarily referring to order of time. **Lo, I come**—I am prepared to do, etc. **in the volume of the book**—*roll of the book*. Such rolls, resembling maps, are still used in the synagogues. **written of me**—or on me, prescribed to me (II Kings 22:13). The first is the sense adopted by Paul. In either case, the Pentateuch, or law of Moses, is meant, and while it contains much respecting Christ directly, as Genesis 3:15; 49:10; Deuteronomy 18:15, and, indirectly, in the Levitical ritual, there is nowhere any allusion to David. **9, 10.** Christ's prophetical office is taught. He "preached" the great truths of God's government of sinners. **I have preached**—lit., "announced good tidings." **11.** may be rendered as an assertion, that God *will not withhold* ... (Ps. 16:1). **12. evils**—inflicted by others. **iniquities**—or penal *afflictions,* and sometimes calamities in the wide sense. This meaning of the word is very common. (Ps. 31:11; 38:4; cf. Gen. 4:13, Cain's punishment; Gen. 19:15, that of Sodom; I Sam. 28:10, of the witch of Endor; also II Sam. 16:12; Job 19:29; Isa. 5:18; 53:11). This meaning of the word is also favored by the clause, "taken hold of me," which follows, which can be said appropriately of *sufferings,* but not of *sins* (cf. Job. 27:20; Ps. 69:24). Thus, the difficulties in referring this Psalm to Christ, arising from the usual reading of this verse, are removed. Of the terrible *afflictions,* or sufferings, alluded to and endured for us, cf. Luke 22:39-44, and the narrative of the scenes of Calvary. **my heart faileth me**—(Matt. 26:38), "My soul is exceeding sorrowful, even unto death." **cannot look up**—lit., "I cannot see," not denoting the depression of conscious guilt, as Luke 18:13, but exhaustion from suffering, as *dimness* of eyes (cf. Ps. 6:7; 13:3; 38:10). The whole context thus sustains the sense assigned to *iniquities*. **13.** (Cf. Ps. 22:19.) **14, 15.** The language is not necessarily imprecatory, but rather a confident expectation (Ps. 5:11), though the former sense is not inconsistent with Christ's prayer for the forgiveness of His murderers, inasmuch as their confusion and shame might be the very means to prepare them for humbly seeking forgiveness (cf. Acts. 2:37). **for a reward**—lit., "in consequence of." **Aha**—(Cf. Ps. 35:21, 25). **16.** (Cf. Psalm 35:27.) **love thy salvation**—delight in its bestowal on others as well as themselves. **17.** A summary of his condition and hopes. **thinketh upon**—or provides for me. "He was heard," "when he had offered up prayers and supplications with strong crying and tears, unto Him that was able to save him from death."

PSALM 41

Vss. 1-13. The Psalmist celebrates the blessedness of those who compassionate the poor, conduct strongly contrasted with the spite of his enemies and neglect of his friends in his calamity. He prays for God's mercy in view of his ill desert, and, in confi-

dence of relief, and that God will vindicate his cause, he closes with a doxology.
1-3. God rewards kindness to the poor (Prov. 19: 17). From vss. 2 and 11 it may be inferred that the Psalmist describes his own conduct, **poor**—in person, position, and possessions. **shall be blessed** —lit., "led aright," or "safely," prospered (Ps. 23:3). **upon the earth**—or land of promise (Ps. 25:13; 27: 3-9, etc.). The figures of vs. 3 are drawn from the acts of a kind nurse. **4. I said**—I asked the mercy I show. **heal my soul**—(Cf. Ps. 30:2). "Sin and suffering are united," is one of the great teachings of the Psalms. **5, 6.** A graphic picture of the conduct of a malignant enemy. **to see me**—as if to spy out my case. **he speaketh ... itself**—or, "he speaketh vanity as to his heart"—i.e., does not speak candidly, "he gathereth iniquity to him," collects elements for mischief, and then divulges the gains of his hypocrisy. **7, 8.** So of others, *all* act alike. **An evil disease**—lit., "a word of Belial," some slander. **cleaveth**—lit., "poured on him." **that he lieth**—*who has* now laid down, "he is utterly undone and our victory is sure." **9. mine ... friend**—lit., "man of my peace." **eat ... bread**—who depended on me or was well treated by me. **lifted up his heel**—in scornful violence. As David and his fortunes typified Christ and His (cf. *Introduction*), so these words expressed the treatment he received, and also that of his Son and Lord; hence, though not distinctly prophetical, our Saviour (John 13:18) applies them to Judas, "that the Scripture may be fulfilled." This last phrase has a wide use in the New Testament, and is not restricted to denote special prophecies. **10.** A lawful punishment of criminals is not revenge, nor inconsistent with their final good (cf. Ps. 40:14, 15). **11-13. favourest**—or tenderly lovest me (Gen. 34:19), evinced by relief from his enemies; and, farther, God recognizes his innocence by upholding him. **settest ... before thy face**—under thy watch and care, as God *before man's face* (Ps. 16:8) is an object of trust and love. **Blessed**—praised, usually applied to God. The word usually applied to men denotes *happiness* (Ps. 1:1; 32:1). With this doxology the first book closes.

PSALM 42

Vss. 1-11. *Maschil*—(Cf. Ps. 32, title). *For,* or *of* (cf. *Introduction*) the sons of Korah. The writer, perhaps one of this Levitical family of singers accompanying David in exile, mourns his absence from the sanctuary, a cause of grief aggravated by the taunts of enemies, and is comforted in hopes of relief. This course of thought is repeated with some variety of detail, but closing with the same refrain.
1, 2.—Cf. (Ps. 63:1.) **panteth**—desires in a state of exhaustion. **appear before God**—in acts of worship, the terms used in the command for the stated personal appearance of the Jews at the sanctuary. **3. Where is thy God?**—implying that He had forsaken him (cf. II Sam. 16:7; Ps. 3:2; 22:8). **4.** The verbs are properly rendered as futures, "I will remember," etc.,—i.e., the recollection of this season of distress will give greater zest to the privileges of God's worship, when obtained. **5.** Hence he chides his despondent soul, assuring himself of a time of joy. **help of his countenance**—or, face (cf. Num. 6:25; Ps. 4:6; 16:11). **6.** Dejection again described. **therefore**—i.e., finding no comfort in myself, I turn to Thee, even in this distant *"land of Jordan and the* (mountains) *Hermons,"* the country east of Jor-

dan. **hill Mizar**—as a name of a small hill contrasted with the mountains round about Jerusalem, perhaps denoted the contempt with which the place of exile was regarded. **7.** The roar of successive billows, responding to that of floods of rain, represented the heavy waves of sorrow which overwhelmed him. **8.** Still he relies on as constant a flow of divine mercy which will elicit his praise and encourage his prayer to God; **9, 10,** in view of which he dictates to himself a prayer based on his distress, aggravated as it was by the cruel taunts and infidel suggestions of his foes. **11.** This brings on a renewed self-chiding, and excites hopes of relief. **health** [or, help] **of my countenance**—(cf. vs. 5) who cheers me, driving away clouds of sorrow from my face. **my God**—It is He of whose existence and favor my foes would have me doubt.

PSALM 43

Vss. 1-5. Excepting the recurrence of the refrain, there is no good reason to suppose this a part of the preceding, though the scope is the same. It has always been placed separate.
1. Judge—or, vindicate (Ps. 10:18). **plead ... —** (Ps. 35:1). **ungodly**—neither in character or condition objects of God's favor (cf. Ps. 4:3). **2. God of my strength**—by covenant relation my stronghold (Ps. 18:1). **cast me off**—in scorn. **because**—or, in, i.e, in such circumstances of oppression. **3. light**— as in Psalm 27:1. **truth**—or, faithfulness (Ps. 25:5), manifest by fulfilling promises. *Light* and *truth* are personified as messengers who will bring him to the privileged place of worship. **tabernacles**—plural, in allusion to the various courts. **4. the altar** —as the chief place of worship. The mention of the harp suggests the prominence of praise in his offering.

PSALM 44

Vss. 1-26. In a time of great national distress, probably in David's reign, the Psalmist recounts God's gracious dealings in former times, and the confidence they had learned to repose in Him. After a vivid picture of their calamities, he humbly expostulates against God's apparent forgetfulness, reminding Him of their faithfulness and mourning their heavy sorrows.
1-3. This period is that of the settlement of Canaan (Josh. 24:12; Judg. 6:3). **have told**—or, related (cf. Exod. 10:2). **plantedst them**—i.e., our fathers, who are also, from the parallel construction of the last clause, to be regarded as the object of *"cast* them out," which means—lit., "send" them out, or, "extend them." *Heathen* and *people* denote the nations who were driven out to make room for the Israelites. **4. Thou art my King**—lit., "he who is my King," sustaining the same covenant relation as to the "fathers." **5.** The figure drawn from the habits of the ox. **6-8.** God is not only our sole help, but only worthy of praise. **thy name**—as in Psalm 5:11. **put ... to shame**—(cf. Ps. 6:10), disgraced. **9. But**—contrasting, *cast off* as abhorrent (Ps. 43:2). **goest not forth**—lit., "will not go" (II Sam. 5:23). In several consecutive verses the leading verb is *future,* and the following one *past* (in *Hebrew*), thus denoting the causes and effects. Thus (vss. 10, 11, 12), when defeated, spoiling follows; when delivered as sheep, dispersion follows, etc. **11.** The Babylonian captivity not necessarily meant. There were others (cf. I Kings 8:46). **13, 14.** (Cf. Deut. 28:37; Ps. 79:4). **15. shame of ... face**—

blushes in disgrace. **16.** Its cause, the taunts and presence of malignant enemies (Ps. 8:2). **17-19.** They had not apostatized totally—were still God's people. **declined**—turned aside from God's law. **sore broken**—crushed. **place of dragons**—desolate, barren, rocky wilderness (Ps. 63:10; Isa. 13:22), **shadow of death**—(Cf. Ps. 23:4). **20, 21.** A solemn appeal to God to witness their constancy. **stretched out . . . hands**—gesture of worship (Exod. 9:29; Ps. 88:9). **22.** Their protracted sufferings as God's people attests the constancy. Paul (Rom. 8:36) uses this to describe Christian steadfastness in persecution. **23-26.** This style of addressing God, as indifferent, is frequent (Ps. 3:7; 9:19; 13:1, etc.). However low their condition, God is appealed to, on the ground, and for the honor, of His mercy.

PSALM 45

Vss. 1-17. *Shoshannim*—lit., "Lilies," either descriptive of an instrument so shaped, or denoting some tune or air so called, after which the Psalm was to be sung (cf. Ps. 8, title). A *song of loves,* or, *of beloved ones* (plural and feminine)—a conjugal song. *Maschil* (cf. Ps. 32 and 42) denotes the didactic character of the Psalm; that it gives *instruction,* the song being of allegorical, and not literal, import. *The union and glories of Christ and his Church are described.* He is addressed as a king possessed of all essential graces, as a conqueror exalted on the throne of a righteous and eternal government, and as a bridegroom arrayed in nuptial splendor. The Church is portrayed in the purity and loveliness of a royally adorned and attended bride, invited to forsake her home and share the honors of her affianced lord. The picture of an Oriental wedding thus opened is filled up by representing the complimentary gifts of the wealthy with which the occasion is honored, the procession of the bride clothed in splendid raiment, attended by her virgin companions, and the entrance of the joyous throng into the palace of the king. A prediction of a numerous and distinguished progeny, instead of the complimentary wish for it usually expressed (cf. Gen. 24:60; Ruth 4:11, 12), and an assurance of a perpetual fame, closes the Psalm. All ancient Jewish and Christian interpreters regarded this Psalm as an allegory of the purport above named. In the Song of Songs the allegory is carried out more fully. Hosea (chs. 1-3) treats the relation of God and His people under the same figure, and its use to set forth the relation of Christ and His Church runs through both parts of the Bible (cf. Isa. 54:5; 62:4, 5; Matt. 22:3; 25:1; John 3:29; Eph. 5:25-32, etc.). Other methods of exposition have been suggested. Several Jewish monarchs, from Solomon to the wicked Ahab, and various foreign princes, have been named as the hero of the song. But to none of them can the terms here used be shown to apply, and it is hardly probable that any mere nuptial song, especially of a heathen king, would be permitted a place in the sacred songs of the Jews. The advocates for any other than the Messianic interpretation have generally silenced each other in succession, while the application of the most rigorous rules of a fair system of interpretation has but strengthened the evidences in its favor. The scope of the Psalm above given is easy and sustained by the explication of its details. The quotation of vss. 6, 7 by Paul (Heb. 1:8, 9), as applicable to Christ, *ought to be conclusive,* and their special exposition shows the propriety of such an application.

1. An animated preface indicative of strong emotion. *Lit.,* "*My heart overflows: a good matter I speak; the things which I have made,*" etc. **inditing** —lit., "boiling up," as a fountain overflows. **my tongue is the pen**—a mere instrument of God's use. **of a ready writer**—i.e., it is fluent. The theme is inspiring and language flows fast. **2.** To rich personal attractions is added grace of the lips, captivating powers of speech. This is given, and becomes a source of power and proves a blessing. Christ is a prophet (Luke 4:22). **3, 4.** The king is addressed as ready to go forth to battle. **sword**— (Cf. Rev. 1:16; 19:15.) **mighty**—(Cf. Isa. 9:6.) **glory and . . . majesty**—generally used as divine attributes (Ps. 96:6; 104:1; 111:3), or as specially conferred on mortals (Ps. 21:5), perhaps these typically. **ride prosperously**—or conduct a successful war. **because of**—for the interests of truth, etc. **meekness . . . righteousness**—without any connection—i.e., a righteousness or equity of government, distinguished by meekness or condescension (Ps. 18:35). **right hand**—or power, as its organ. **shall teach thee**— point the way to terrible things i.e., in conquest of enemies. **5.** The result. **people**—Whole nations are subdued. **6.** No lawful construction can be devised to change the sense here given and sustained by the ancient versions, and above all by Paul (Heb. 1:8). Of the perpetuity of this government, cf. II Samuel 7:13; Psalm 10:16; 72:5; 89:4; 110:4; Isaiah 9:7. **7.** As in vs. 6 the divine nature is made prominent, here the moral qualities of the human are alleged as the reason or ground of the mediatorial exultation. Some render "O God, thy God," instead of **God thy God**—but the latter is sustained by the same form (Ps. 50:7), and it was only of His human nature that the anointing could be predicated (cf. Isa. 61:3). **oil of gladness**—or token of gladness, as used in feasts and other times of solemn joy (cf. I Kings 1:39, 40). **fellows**—other kings. **8.** The king thus inaugurated is now presented as a bridegroom, who appears in garments richly perfumed, brought out from *ivory palaces,* His royal residence; by which, as indications of the happy bridal occasion, He has been gladdened. **9.** In completion of this picture of a marriage festival, female attendants or bridesmaids of the highest rank attend Him, while the queen, in rich apparel (vs. 13), stands ready for the nuptial procession. **10, 11.** She is invited to the union, for forming which she must leave her father's people. She representing, by the form of the allegory, the Church, this address is illustrated by all those scriptures, from Genesis 12:1 on, which speak of the people of God as a chosen, separate, and peculiar people. The relation of subjection to her spouse at once accords with the law of marriage, as given in Genesis 3:16; 18:12; Ephesians 5:22; I Peter 3:5, 6, and the relation of Church to Christ (Eph. 5:24). The love of the husband is intimately connected with the entire devotion to which the bride is exhorted. **12. daughter of Tyre**—(Ps. 9:14)—denotes the people. Tyre, celebrated for its great wealth, is selected to represent the richest nations, an idea confirmed by the next clause. These gifts are brought as means to conciliate the royal parties, representing the admitted subjection of the offerers. This well sets forth the exalted position of the Church and her head, whose moral qualities receive the homage of the world. The contribution of material wealth to sustain the institutions of the Church may be included (cf. "riches of the Gentiles," Ps. 72:10; Isa. 60:5-10). **13. the king's daughter**—a term of dignity. It may also intimate, with some allusion to the teaching of the allegory, that the bride of Christ, the Church, is the daughter of the great king, God. **within**—Not only is her outward raiment costly, but all her apparel is of the richest texture. **wrought gold**—gold embroidery, or cloth in which gold is woven. **14, 15.** The progress of the procession is described; according to the usual custom the bride and attendants are conducted to the palace. Some for the words—**in raiment of needlework**—propose another rendering, "on variegated (or embroidered) cloths" —i.e., in the manner of the East, richly wrought tapestry was spread on the ground, on which the bride walked. As the dress had been already mentioned, this seems to be a probable translation. **shall be brought**—in solemn form (cf. Job 10:19; 21:22). The entrance into the palace with great joy closes the scene. So shall the Church be finally brought to her Lord, and united amid the festivities of the holy beings in heaven. **16.** As earthly monarchs govern widely extended empires by viceroys, this glorious king is represented as supplying all the principalities of earth with princes of his own numerous progeny. **17.** The glories of this empire shall be as wide as the world and lasting as eternity. **therefore**—Because thus glorious, the praise shall be universal and perpetual. Some writers have taxed their ingenuity to find in the history and fortunes of Christ and His Church exact parallels for every part of this splendid allegory, not excepting its gorgeous Oriental imagery. Thus, by the dresses of the king and queen, are thought to be meant the eminent endowments and graces of Christ and His people. The attendant women, supposed (though inconsistently it might seem with the inspired character of the work) to be concubines, are thought to represent the Gentile churches, and the bride the Jewish, etc. But it is evident that we cannot pursue such a mode of interpretation. For, following the allegory, we must suspend to the distant future the results of a union whose consummation as a marriage is still distant (cf. Rev. 21:9). In fact, the imagery here and elsewhere sets before us the Church in two aspects. As a body, it is yet incomplete, the whole is yet ungathered. As a moral institution, it is yet imperfect. In the final catastrophe it will be complete and perfect. Thus, as a bride adorned, etc., it will be united with its Lord. Thus the union of Christ and the Church triumphant is set forth. On the other hand, in regard to its component parts, the relation of Christ as head, as husband, etc., already exists, and as these parts form an institution in this world, it is by His union with it, and the gifts and graces with which He endows it, that a spiritual seed arises and spreads in the world. Hence we must fix our minds only on the *one simple but grand truth, that Christ loves the Church, is head over all things for it, raises it in His exaltation to the highest moral dignity—a dignity of which every, even the meanest, sincere disciple will partake.* As to the *time,* then, in which this allegorical prophecy is to be fulfilled, it may be said that no periods of time are specially designated. The *characteristics* of the relation of Christ and His Church are indicated, and we may suppose that the whole process of His exaltation from the *declaration* of His Sonship, by His resurrection, to the grand catastrophe of the final judgment, with all the collateral blessings to the Church and the world, lay before the vision of the inspired prophet.

PSALM 46

Vss. 1-11. *Upon Alamoth*—most probably denotes the *treble,* or part sung by female voices, the word meaning "virgins"; and which was sung with some appropriately keyed instrument (cf. I Chron. 15:19-21; Ps. 6, title). The theme may be stated in Luther's well-known words, "A mighty fortress is our God." The great deliverance (II Kings 19:35; Isa. 37:36) may have occasioned its composition. **1. refuge**—lit., "a place of trust" (Ps. 2:12). **strength**—(Ps. 18:2). **present help**—lit., "a help He has been found exceedingly." **trouble**—as in Psalm 18:7. **2, 3.** The most violent civil commotions are illustrated by the greatest physical commotions. **swelling**—well represents the *pride* and haughtiness of insolent foes. **4.** God's favor is denoted by a **river** (cf. Ps. 36:8; Zech. 14:8; Rev. 22:1). **city of God, the holy place**—His earthly residence, Jerusalem and the temple (cf. Ps. 2:6, 3:4; 20:2; 48:2, etc.). God's favor, like a river whose waters are conducted in channels, is distributed to all parts of His Church. **most High**—denoting His supremacy (Ps. 17:2). **5. right early**—lit., "at the turn of morning, or change from night to day, a critical time (Ps. 30:5; cf. Isa. 37:36). **6.** (Cf. vs. 4.) **earth melted**—all powers dissolved by His mere word (Ps. 75:3; Hos. 2:22). **7. with us**—on our side; His presence is terror to our enemies, safety to us. **refuge**—high place (Ps. 9:9; cf. also Ps. 24:6, 10). **8. what desolations**—lit., "who hath put desolations," destroying our enemies. **9.** *The usual weapons of war* (Ps. 7:12), as well as those using them, are brought to an end. **10. Be still . . .** —lit., "Leave off to oppose Me and vex My people. I am over all for their safety". (cf. Isa. 2:11; Eph. 1:22).

PSALM 47

Vss. 1-9 Praise is given to God for victory, perhaps that recorded (II Chron. 20); and His dominions over all people, Jews and Gentiles, is asserted. **1. clap . . . hands . . . people**—lit., "peoples," or "nations" (cf. Deut. 32:43; Ps. 18:49; 98:9). **2, 3.** His universal sovereignty now exists, and will be made known. **under us**—i.e., His saints; Israel's temporal victories were types of the spiritual conquests of the true Church. **4. He shall . . . inheritance**—the heathen to be possessed by His Church (Ps. 2:8), as Canaan by the Jews. **excellency of Jacob**—lit., "pride," or, that in which he glories (not necessarily, though often, in a bad sense), the privileges of the chosen people—**whom he loved**—His love being the sole cause of granting them. **5-7.** God, victorious over His enemies, reascends to heaven, amid the triumphant praises of His people, who celebrate His sovereign dominion. This sovereignty is what the Psalm teaches; hence he adds—**sing . . . praises with understanding**—lit., "sing and play an instructive (Psalm)." The whole typifies Christ's ascension (cf. Ps. 68:18). **8, 9.** The instruction continued. **throne of . . . holiness**—or, holy throne (cf. on Ps. 2:6; 23:3). **princes**—who represent *peoples.* For—**even**—supply, "as," or, "to"—i.e., they all become united under covenant with Abraham's God. **shields**—as in Hosea 4:18, rulers.

PSALM 48

Vss. 1-14. This is a spirited Psalm and song (cf. Ps. 30), having probably been suggested by the same occasion as the foregoing. It sets forth the privileges and blessings of God's spiritual dominion as the terror of the wicked and joy of the righteous. **1. to be praised**—always: it is an epithet, as in

Psalm 18:3. **mountain of his holiness**—His Church (cf. Isa. 2:2, 3; 25:6, 7, 10); the sanctuary was erected first on Mount Zion, then (as the temple) on Moriah; hence the figure. **2, 3. situation**—lit., "elevation." **joy of . . .**—source of joy. **sides of the north**—poetically for eminent, lofty, distinguished, as the ancients believed the *north* to be the highest part of the earth (cf. Isa. 14:13). **palaces**—lit., "citadels." **refuge**—(Ps. 9:10; 18:3). He was so known in them because they enjoyed His presence. **4-6. For**—The reason is given. Though the kings (perhaps of Moab and Ammon, cf. Ps. 83:3-5) combined, a conviction of God's presence with His people, evinced by the unusual courage with which the prophets (cf. II Chron. 20:12-20) had inspired them, seized on their minds, and smitten with sudden and intense alarm, they fled astonished. **7. ships of Tarshish**—as engaged in a distant and lucrative trade, the most valuable. The phrase may illustrate God's control over all material agencies, whether their literal destruction be meant or not. **8.** This present experience assures of that perpetual care which God extends to His Church. **9. thought of**—lit., "compared," or considered, in respect of former dealings. **in the . . . temple**—in acts of solemn worship (cf. II Chron. 20:28). **10. According . . . praise**—i.e., As Thy perfections manifested (cf. Ps. 8:1; 20:1-7), demand praise, it shall be given, everywhere. **thy right hand . . .**—Thy righteous government is displayed by Thy power. **11. the daughters . . .**—*the small towns*, or the people, with the chief city, or rulers of the Church. **judgments**—decisions and acts of right government. **12-14.** The call to survey Zion, or the Church, as a fortified city, is designed to suggest "how well our God secures His fold." This security is perpetual, and its pledge is His guidance through this life.

PSALM 49

Vss. 1-20. This Psalm instructs and consoles. It teaches that earthly advantages are not reliable for permanent happiness, and that, however prosperous worldly men may be for a time, their ultimate destiny is ruin, while the pious are safe in God's care. **1-3.** All are called to hear what interests all. **world**—lit., "duration of life," the present time. **4. incline**—to hear attentively (Ps. 17:6; 31:2). **parable**—In *Hebrew* and *Greek* "parable" and "proverb" are translations of the same word. It denotes a *comparison*, or form of speech, which under one image includes many, and is expressive of a general truth capable of various illustrations. Hence it may be used for the *illustration* itself. For the former sense, "proverb" (i.e., one word for several) is the usual English term, and for the latter, in which comparison is prominent, "parable" (i.e., one thing laid by another). The distinction is not always observed, since here, and in Psalm 78:2; "proverb" would better express the style of the composition (cf. also Prov. 26:7, 9; Hab. 2:6; John 16:25, 29). Such forms of speech are often very figurative and also obscure (cf. Matt. 13:12-15). Hence the use of the parallel word—**dark saying**—or, riddle (cf. Ezek.17:2). **open**—is to explain. **upon the harp**—the accompaniment for a lyric. **5. iniquity**—or, calamity (Ps. 40:12). **of my heels**—lit., "my supplanters" (Gen. 27:36), or oppressors: "I am surrounded by the evils they inflict." **6.** They are vainglorious— **7-9.**—yet unable to save themselves or others. **it ceaseth for ever**—i.e., the ransom fails, the price is too precious, costly. **corruption**—lit., "pit," or,

"grave," thus showing that "soul" is used for life. **10. For he seeth**—i.e., corruption; then follows the illustration. **wise . . . fool**—(Ps. 14:1; Prov. 1:32; 10:1). **likewise**—alike altogether—(Ps 4:8)—die—all meet the same fate. **11.** Still infatuated and flattered with hopes of perpetuity, they call their lands, or "celebrate their names on account of (their) lands." **12.** Contrasted with this vanity is the frailty. However honored, man **abideth not**—lit., "lodgeth not," remains not till morning, but suddenly perishes as (wild) beasts, whose lives are taken without warning. **13.** Though their way is folly, others follow the same course of life. **14. Like sheep**—(cf. vs. 12) unwittingly, they—**are laid**—or, put., etc. **death shall feed on** [or, better, "shall rule"] **them**—as a shepherd (cf. "feed," Ps. 28:9, *Margin*). **have dominion over** [or, subdue] **them in the morning**—suddenly, or in their turn. **their beauty**—lit., "form" or shape. **shall consume**—lit., "is for the consumption" i.e., of the grave. **from their dwelling**—lit., "from their home (they go) to it," i.e., the grave. **15.** The pious, delivered from the—**power**—lit., "the hand," of death, are taken under God's care. **16-19.** applies this instruction. Be not anxious (Ps. 37:1, etc.), since death cuts off the prosperous wicked whom you dread. **Though . . . lived . . .**—lit., "For in his life he blessed his soul," or, himself (Luke 12:19, 16:25); yet (vs. 19); he has had his portion. **men will praise . . . thyself**—Flatterers enhance the rich fool's self-complacency; the form of address to him strengthens the emphasis of the sentiment. **20.** (Cf. vs. 12.) The *folly* is more distinctly expressed by *understandeth not*, substituted for *abideth not*.

PSALM 50

Vss. 1-23. In the grandeur and solemnity of a divine judgment, God is introduced as instructing men in the nature of true worship, exposing hypocrisy, warning the wicked, and encouraging the pious. **1-4.** The description of this majestic appearance of God resembles that of His giving the law (cf. Exod. 19:16; 20:18; Deut. 32:1). **4. from above**—lit., "above" (Gen. 1:7). **heavens . . . earth**—For all creatures are witnesses (Deut. 4:26; 30:19; Isa. 1:2). **5. my saints**—(Ps. 4:3)—**made**—[lit., "cut"] **a covenant . . .**—alluding to the dividing of a victim of sacrifice, by which covenants were ratified, the parties passing between the divided portions (cf. Gen. 15: 10, 18). **6.** The inhabitants of heaven, who well know God's character, attest His righteousness as a judge. **7. I will testify against**—i.e., for failure to worship aught. **thy God**—and so, by covenant as well as creation, entitled to a pure worship. **8-15.** However scrupulous in external worship, it was offered as if they conferred an obligation in giving God His own, and with a degrading view of Him as needing it. Reproving them for such foolish and blasphemous notions, He teaches them to *offer,* or lit., "sacrifice," thanksgiving, and pay, or perform, their vows—i.e., to bring, with the external symbolical service, the homage of the heart, and faith, penitence, and love. To this is added an invitation to seek, and a promise to afford, all needed help in trouble. **16-20. the wicked**—i.e., the formalists, as now exposed, and who lead vicious lives (cf. Rom. 2:21, 23). They are unworthy to use even the words of God's law. Their hypocrisy and vice are exposed by illustrations from sins against the seventh, eighth, and ninth commandments. **21, 22.** God, no longer (even in appearance) disregarding such, exposes their sins and threatens a terrible punishment. **forget God**—This denotes unmindfulness of His true character. **23. offereth praise**—(vs. 14), so that the external worship is a true index of the heart. **ordereth . . . aright**—acts in a straight, right manner, opposed to turning aside (Ps. 25:5). In such, pure worship and a pure life evince their true piety, and they will enjoy God's presence and favor.

PSALM 51

Vss. 1-19. On the occasion, cf. II Samuel 11:12. The Psalm illustrates true repentance, in which are comprised conviction, confession, sorrow, prayer for mercy, and purposes of amendment, and it is accompanied by a lively faith. **1-4.** A plea for mercy is a confession of guilt. **blot out**—as from a register. **transgressions**—lit., "rebellions" (Ps. 19:13; 32:1). **Wash me**—Purity as well as pardon is desired by true penitents. **For . . . before me**—Conviction precedes forgiveness; and, as a gift of God, is a plea for it (II Sam. 12:13; Ps. 32:5; I John 1:9). **Against thee**—chiefly, and as sins against others are violations of God's law, in one sense *only*. **that . . . judgest**—i.e., all palliation of his crime is excluded; it is the design in making this confession to recognize God's justice, however severe the sentence. **5, 6.** His guilt was aggravated by his essential, native sinfulness, which is as contrary to God's requisitions of inward purity as are outward sins to those for right conduct. **thou shalt make . . .**—may be taken to express God's gracious purpose in view of His strict requisition; a purpose of which David might have availed himself as a check to his native love for sin, and, in not doing so, aggravated his guilt. **truth . . . and . . . wisdom** —are terms often used for piety (cf. Job 28:28; Ps. 119:30). **7-12.** A series of prayers for forgiveness and purifying. **Purge . . . hyssop**—The use of this plant in the ritual (Exod. 12:22; Num. 19:6, 18) suggests the idea of atonement as prominent here; "purge" refers to vicarious satisfaction (Num. 19: 17-20). **Make . . . joy**—by forgiving me, which will change distress to joy. **Hide . . .**—Turn from beholding. **Create**—a work of almighty power. **in me**—lit., "to me," or, "for me"; bestow as a gift, a heart free from taint of sin (Ps. 24:4; 73:1). **renew** —implies that he had possessed it; the essential principle of a new nature had not been lost, but its influence interrupted (Luke 22:32); for vs. 11 shows that he had not lost God's presence and Spirit (I Sam. 16:13), though he had lost the "joy of his salvation" (vs. 12), for whose return he prays. **right spirit**—lit., constant, firm, not yielding to temptation. **free spirit**—"thy" ought not to be supplied, for the word "free" is, lit., "willing," and "spirit" is that of David. "Let a willing spirit uphold me," i.e., with a soul willingly conformed to God's law, he would be preserved in a right course of conduct. **13. Then** —Such will be the effect of this gracious work. **ways**—of providence and human duty (Ps. 18:21, 30; 32:8; Luke 22:32). **14. Deliver**—or, Free me (Ps. 39:8) from the *guilt* of murder (II Sam. 12:9, 10; Ps. 5:6). **righteousness**—as in Psalm 7:17; 31:1. **15. open . . . lips**—by removing my sense of guilt. **16.** Praise is better than sacrifice (Ps. 50:14), and implying faith, penitence, and love, glorifies God. In true penitents the joys of pardon mingle with sorrow for sin. **18. Do good . . .**—Visit not my sin on Thy Church. **build . . . walls**—is to show favor; cf. Psalm 89:40, for opposite form and idea. **19.**

God reconciled, material sacrifices will be acceptable (Ps. 4:5; cf. Isa. 1:11-17).

PSALM 52

Vss. 1-9. Cf. I Samuel 21:1-10; 22:1-10, for the history of the title. The first verse gives the theme; the boast of the wicked over the righteous is vain, for God constantly cares for His people. This is expanded by describing the malice and deceit, and then the ruin, of the wicked, and the happy state of the pious. **1. mighty man**—lit., hero. Doeg may be thus addressed, ironically, in respect of his might in slander. **2. tongue**—for self. **mischiefs**—evil to others (Ps. 5:9; 38:12). **working deceitfully**—(Ps. 10:7), as a keen, smoothly moving razor, cutting quietly, but deeply. **3, 4. all-devouring**—lit., swallowing, which utterly destroy (cf. Ps. 21:9; 35:25). **5. likewise**—or, so, also, as you have done to others God will do to you (Ps. 18:27). The following terms describe the most entire ruin. **6. shall . . . fear**—regard with religious awe. **laugh at him**—for his folly; **7.** for trusting in riches and being strong in—**wickedness** —lit., mischief (vs. 2), instead of trusting in God. **the man**—lit., the mighty man, or hero (vs. 1). **8.** The figure used is common (Ps. 1:3; Jer. 11:16). **green**—fresh. **house . . .**—in communion with God (cf. Ps. 27:4, 5). **for ever and ever**—qualifies mercy. **9. hast done**—i.e., what the context supplies, preserved me (cf. Ps. 22:31). **wait . . . name**—hope in Thy perfections, manifested for my good (Ps. 5:11; 20:1). **for it is good**—i.e., Thy name, and the whole method or result of its manifestation (Ps. 54:6; 69: 16).

PSALM 53

Vss. 1-6. *Upon Mahalath*—(cf. Ps. 88, title). Why this repetition of Psalm 14 is given we do not know. **1-4,** with few verbal changes, correspond with Psalm 14:1-4. **5.** Instead of assurances of God's presence with the pious, and a complaint of the wicked, Psalm 14:5, 6 portrays the ruin of the latter, whose "bones" even "are scattered" (cf. Ps. 141:7), and who are put to shame as contemptuously rejected of God.

PSALM 54

Vss. 1-7. Cf. title of Psalms 4 and 32; for the history, I Samuel 23:19, 29; 26:1-25. After an earnest cry for help, the Psalmist promises praise in the assurance of a hearing. **1. by thy name**—(Ps. 5:11), specially, power. **judge me**—as in Psalm 7:8; 26:1. **2.** (Cf. Ps. 4:1; 5: 1.) **3. strangers**—perhaps Ziphites. **oppressors**—lit., "terrible ones" (Isa. 13:11; 25:3). Such were Saul and his army. **not set . . . them**—acted as atheists, without God's fear (cf. Ps. 16:8). **4.** (Cf. Ps. 30:10.) **with them**—on their side, and for me (cf. Ps. 46:11). **5. He shall . . . evil**—or, Evil *shall return* on (Ps. 7:16) my enemies or watchers, i.e., to do me evil (Ps. 6:7). **in thy truth**—Thy verified promise. **6. I will freely . . .**—or, present a *free-will* offering (Lev. 7:16; Num. 15:3). **7. mine eye . . . desire**—(cf. Ps. 59:10; 112:8), expresses satisfaction in beholding the overthrow of his enemies as those of God, without implying any selfish or unholy feeling (cf. Ps. 52:6, 7).

PSALM 55

Vss. 1-23. In great terror on account of enemies, and grieved by the treachery of a friend, the Psalmist offers an earnest prayer for relief. He mingles confident assurances of divine favor to himself with invocations and predictions of God's avenging judgments on the wicked. The tone suits David's experience, both in the times of Saul and Absalom, though perhaps neither was exclusively before his mind. **1. hide not thyself . . .**—(cf. Ps. 13:1; 27:9), withhold not help. **2.** The terms of the last clause express full indulgence of grief. **3. oppression**—lit., "persecution." **they . . . iniquity**—lit., "they make evil doings slide upon me." **4, 5.** express great alarm. **come upon** [or lit., "into"] **me. 6. be at rest**—lit., "dwell," i.e., permanently. **7, 8.** Even a wilderness is a safer place than exposure to such evils, terrible as storm and tempest. **9. Destroy**—lit., "swallow" (Ps. 21:9). **divide their tongues**—or, confound their speech, and hence their counsels (Gen. 11:7). **the city**—perhaps Jerusalem, the scene of anarchy. **10, 11,** which is described in detail (cf. Ps. 7:14-16). **Wickedness**—lit., "Mischief," evils resulting from others (Ps. 5:9; 52:2, 7). **streets**—or lit., "wide places," markets, courts of justice, and any public place. **12-14.** This description of treachery does not deny, but aggravates, the injury from enemies. **guide**—lit., "friend" (Prov. 16:28: 17: 9). **acquaintance**—in *Hebrew*, a yet more intimate associate. **in company**—lit., "with a crowd," in a festal procession. **15. Let death . . .**—or, "Desolations are on them." **let them go**—(lit., "they will go"). **quick**—or, living in the midst of life, death will come (cf. Num. 16:33). **among them**—or, within them, in their hearts (Ps. 5:9; 49:11). **16-18.** God answers his constant and repeated prayers. **many with me**—i.e., by the context, fighting with me. **19.** God hears the wicked in wrath. **abideth** [or, sitteth] **of old**—enthroned as a sovereign. **Because . . . no changes**—Prosperity hardens them (Ps. 73:5). **20, 21.** The treachery is aggravated by hypocrisy. The changes of number, vss. 15, 23, and here, enliven the picture, and imply that the chief traitor and his accomplices are in view together. **22. thy burden**—lit., "gift," what is assigned you. **he shall sustain**—lit., "supply food," and so all need (Ps. 57: 25; Matt. 6:11). **to be moved**—from the secure position of His favor (cf. Ps. 10:6). **23. bloody . . . days**—(cf. Ps. 5:6; 51:14), deceit and murderous dispositions often united. The threat is directed specially (not as a general truth) against the wicked, then in the writer's view.

PSALM 56

Vss. 1-13. *Upon Jonath-elem-rechokim*—lit., "upon the dove of silence" of distant places; either denoting a melody (cf. on Ps. 9) of that name, to which this Psalm was to be performed; or it is an enigmatical form of denoting the subject, as given in the history referred to (I Sam. 21:11, etc.), David being regarded as an uncomplaining, meek dove, driven from his native home to wander in exile. Beset by domestic and foreign foes, David appeals confidently to God, recites his complaints, and closes with joyful and assured anticipations of God's continued help. **1, 2. would swallow**—lit., "pants as a raging beast" (Acts 9:1). **enemies**—watchers (Ps. 54:5). **most**

High—As it is not elsewhere used absolutely for God, some render the word here, arrogantly, or proudly, as qualifying "those who fight," etc. **3. in** [or lit., "unto"] **thee**—to whom he turns in trouble. **4. in God . . . his word**—By His grace or aid (Ps. 60: 12; 108:13), or, "I will boast in God as to His word"; in either case His word is the special matter and cause of praise. **flesh**—for mankind (Ps. 65:2; Isa. 31:3), intimating frailty. **5, 6.** A vivid picture of the conduct of malicious enemies. **7. Shall they escape . . . ?**—or better, "Their escape is by iniquity." **cast . . . people**—humble those who so proudly oppose Thy servant. **8.** God is mindful of his exile and remembers his tears. The custom of *bottling the tears* of mourners as a memorial, which has existed in some Eastern nations, may explain the figure. **9. God is for me**—or, on my side (Ps. 118: 6; 124:1, 2); hence he is sure of the repulse of his foes. **12. I will render praises**—will pay what I have vowed. **13.** The question implies an affirmative answer, drawn from past experience. **falling**—as from a precipice. **before God**—in His favor during life.

PSALM 57

Vss. 1-11. *Al-taschith*—"Destroy not." This is perhaps an enigmatical allusion to the critical circumstances connected with the history, for which cf. I Samuel 22:1; 26:1-3. In Moses' prayer (Deut. 9:26) it is a prominent petition deprecating God's anger against the people. This explanation suits the 58th and 59th also. Asaph uses it for the 75th, in the scope of which there is allusion to some emergency. *Michtam*—(Cf. Ps. 16). To an earnest cry for divine aid, the Psalmist adds, as often, the language of praise, in the assured hope of a favorable hearing. **1. my soul**—or self, or life, which is threatened. **shadow of thy wings**—(Ps. 17:8; 36:7). **calamities**—lit., "mischiefs" (Ps. 52:2; 55:10). **2. performeth**—or, completes what He has begun. **3. from . . . swallow me up**—that pants in rage after me (Ps. 56:2). **mercy and . . . truth**—(Ps. 25:10; 36:5), as messengers (Ps. 43:3) sent to deliver him. **4.** The mingled figures of wild beasts (Ps. 10:9; 17:12) and weapons of war (Ps. 11:2) heighten the picture of danger. **whose . . . tongue**—or slanders. **5.** This doxology illustrates his view of the connection of his deliverance with God's glory. **6.** (Cf. Ps. 7:15; 9:15, 16.) **7. I will . . . praise**—both with voice and instrument. **8. Hence**—he addresses his glory, or tongue (Ps. 16:9; 30:12), and his psaltery, or lute and harp. **I myself . . . early**—lit., "I will awaken dawn," poetically expressing his zeal and diligence. **9, 10.** As His mercy and truth, so shall His praise, fill the universe.

PSALM 58

Vss. 1-11. David's critical condition in some period of the Sauline persecution probably occasioned this Psalm, in which the Psalmist teaches that the innate and actual sinfulness of men deserves, and shall receive, God's righteous vengeance, while the pious may be consoled by the evidence of His wise and holy government of men. **1. O congregation**—lit., "Oh, dumb"—the word used is never translated "congregation." "Are ye dumb? ye should speak righteousness," may be the translation. In any case, the writer remonstrates with them, perhaps a council, who were assembled to try his cause, and bound to give a right decision. **2.** This they did not design; but **weigh ... violence**— or give decisions of violence. *Weigh* is a figure to express the acts of judges. **in the earth**—publicly. **3-5.** describe the wicked generally, who sin naturally, easily, malignantly, and stubbornly. **stoppeth her** [or, lit., "his"] **ear**—i.e., the wicked man (the singular used collectively), who thus becomes like the deaf adder which has no ear. **6.** He prays for their destruction, under the figure of ravenous beasts (Ps. 3:7; 7:2). **7. which run continually**—lit., "they shall go to themselves, utterly depart, as rapid mountain torrents. **he bendeth ... his arrows**—prepares it. The term for preparing a bow applied to arrows (Ps. 64:3). **let them ... pieces**—lit., "as if they cut themselves off"—i.e., become blunted and of no avail. **8, 9.** Other figures of this utter ruin; the last denoting rapidity. In a shorter time than pots feel the heat of thorns on fire—**he shall take them away as with a whirlwind**—lit., "blow him (them) away." **both living, ... wrath**—lit., "as the living" or fresh as the heated or burning—i.e., thorns—all easily blown away, so easily and quickly the wicked. The figure of the "snail" perhaps alludes to its loss of saliva when moving. Though obscure in its clauses, the general sense of the passage is clear. **10, 11. wash ... wicked**—denoting great slaughter. The joy of triumph over the destruction of the wicked is because they are God's enemies, and their overthrow shows that He reigneth (cf. Ps. 52:5-7; 54:7). In this assurance let heaven and earth rejoice (Ps. 96: 10; 97:1, etc.).

PSALM 59

Vss. 1-17. Cf. Psalm 57, and for history, I Sam. 19:11, etc. The scope is very similar to that of the 57th: prayer in view of malicious and violent foes, and joy in prospect of relief.
1. defend—(Cf. *Margin*). **rise up ... me**—(Cf. Ps. 17:7.) **2.** (Cf. Ps. 5:5; 6, 8.) **4, 5. prepare**, etc.— lit., "set themselves as in array." **awake**—(Cf. Ps. 3:7; 7:6), appeals to God in His covenant relation to His people (Ps. 9:18). **6, 7.** They are as ravening dogs seeking prey, and as such, "belch out"—i.e., slanders, their impudent barkings. **for who, say they**—For the full expression with the supplied words, cf. Psalm 84:5. **8.** (Cf. Ps. 2:4; 37:13.) **9.** By judicious expositors, and on good grounds, this is better rendered, "O my strength, on Thee will I wait" (vs. 17). **defence**—(Cf. Ps. 18:3). **10. prevent me** —(Ps. 21:3). **see my desire**—in their overthrow (Ps. 54:7). **enemies**—as in Psalm 5:8. **11. Slay them not**—at once (Judg. 2:21-23); but perpetuate their punishment (Gen. 4:12; Num. 32:13), by scattering or making them wander, and humble them. **12. let them even be ... taken in their pride**—while evincing it—i.e., to be punished for their lies, etc. **13.** Though delayed for wise reasons, the utter destruction of the wicked must come at last, and God's presence and power in and for His Church will be known abroad (I Sam. 17:46; Ps. 46:10, 11). **14, 15.** Meanwhile let the rapacious dogs prowl, they cannot hurt the pious; yea, they shall wander famished and sleepless. **grudge if ...**—lit., "they shall stay all night," i.e., obtain nothing. **16, 17.** Contrast the lot of God's servant, who employs his time in God's praise. **sing aloud ... in the morning** —when *they* retire famishing and disappointed, or it may denote delightful diligence in praise, as in Psalm 30:5.

PSALM 60

Vss. 1-12. *Shushan-eduth*—Lily of testimony. The lily is an emblem of beauty (cf. Ps. 45, title). As a description of the Psalm, those terms combined may denote a beautiful poem, witnessing—i.e., for God's faithfulness as evinced in the victories referred to in the history cited. *Aram-naharaim*—Syria of the two rivers, or Mesopotamia beyond *the river* (Euphrates) (II Sam. 10:16). *Aram-zobah*—Syria of Zobah (II Sam. 10:6), to whose king the king of the former was tributary. The war with Edom, by Joab and Abishai (II Chron. 18:12, 25), occurred about the same time. Probably, while doubts and fears alternately prevailed respecting the issue of these wars, the writer composed this Psalm, in which he depicts, in the language of God's people, their sorrows under former disasters, offers prayer in present straits, and rejoices in confident hope of triumph by God's aid.
1-3. allude to disasters. **cast ... off**—in scorn (Ps. 43:2; 44:9). **scattered**—broken our strength (cf. II Sam. 5:20). **Oh, turn thyself**—or, restore to us (prosperity). The figures of physical, denote great civil, commotions (Ps. 46:2, 3). **drink ... wine of astonishment**—lit., "of staggering"—i.e., made us weak (cf. Ps. 75:8; Isa. 51:17, 22). **4, 5.** Yet to God's banner they will rally, and pray that, led and sustained by His power (right hand, Ps. 17: 7; 20:6), they may be safe. **hear me**—or, hear us. **6-10. God hath spoken in** [or, "by"] **his holiness** —(Ps. 89:35; Amos 4:2), on the pledge of His attributes (Ps. 22:3; 30:4). Taking courage from God's promise to give them possession (Exod. 23:31; Deut. 11:24) (and perhaps renewed to him by special revelation), with triumphant joy he describes the conquest as already made. **Shechem, and ... Succoth** —as widely separated points, and—**Gilead ... and Manasseh**—as large districts, east and west of Jordan, represent the whole land. **divide ... and mete out**—means to have entire control over. **Ephraim** —denotes the military (Deut. 33:17); and—**Judah**— (the lawgiver, Gen. 49:10), the civil power. Foreign nations are then presented as subdued. **8. Moab** is a washpot—the most ordinary vessel. **over** [or, at] **Edom**—(as a slave) he casts his shoe. **Philistia, triumph ...** [or, rather, shout] **for me**—acknowledges subjection (cf. Ps. 108:9, "over Philistia will I triumph"). **9, 10.** He feels assured that, though once angry, God is now ready to favor His people. **who will lead me**—or, *who has led me*, as if the work were now begun. **Wilt not thou**—or, Is it not Thou? **11, 12.** Hence he closes with a prayer for success, and an assurance of a hearing.

PSALM 61

Vss. 1-8. *Neginah*—or, Neginoth (cf. Ps. 4, title). Separated from his usual spiritual privileges, perhaps by Absalom's rebellion, the Psalmist prays for divine aid, and, in view of past mercies, with great confidence of being heard.
1-3. From the end—i.e., places remote from the sanctuary (Deut. 28:64). **heart is overwhelmed**— lit., "covered over with darkness," or, distress. **to the rock** (Ps. 18:2; 40:2). **higher than I**—which otherwise I cannot ascend. **shelter ... and strong tower**—repeat the same sentiment. **4. I will abide** —So I desire to do (cf. Ps. 23:6). **trust in the covert ...**—*make* my refuge in the shadow (cf. Ps. 17:8; 36:7). **5. the heritage**—or, part in the spiritual blessings of Israel (Ps. 21:2-4). **vows**—implies

prayers. **6, 7. the king**–himself and his royal line ending in Christ. Mercy and truth personified, as in Psalm 40:11; 57:3. **abide before God**–lit., "sit as a king in God's presence," under His protection. **8.** Thus for new blessings will new vows of praise ever be paid.

PSALM 62

Vss. 1-12. *To Jeduthun*–(cf. Ps. 39, title). The general tone of this Psalm is expressive of confidence in God. Occasion is taken to remind the wicked of their sin, their ruin, and their meanness. **1. waiteth**–lit., "is silent," trusts submissively and confidently as a servant. **2.** The titles applied to God often occur (Ps. 9:9; 18:2). **be greatly moved** –(Ps. 10:6). No injury shall be permanent, though devised by enemies. **3.** Their destruction will come; as a tottering wall they already are feeble and failing. **bowing wall shall ye be**–better supply "are." Some propose to apply these phrases to describe the condition of "a man"–i.e., the pious suffer: thus, "Will ye slay him," etc.; but the other is a good sense. **4. his excellency**–or, elevation to which God had raised him (Ps. 4:2). This they try to do by lies and duplicity (Ps. 5:9). **5, 6.** (Cf. Ps. 1:2.) **not be moved**–not at all; his confidence has increased. **7. rock of my strength**–or strongest support (Ps. 7:10; 61:3). **8. pour out your heart**–give full expression to feeling (I Sam. 1:15; Job 30:16; Ps. 42:4). **ye people**–God's people. **9.** No kind of men are reliable, compared with God (Isa. 2:22; Jer. 17:5). **altogether**–alike, one as the other (Ps. 34:3). **10.** Not only are oppression and robbery, which are wicked means of wealth, no grounds of boasting; but even wealth, increasing lawfully, ought not to engross the heart. **11. once; twice**–(as in Job 33:14; 40:5), are used to give emphasis to the sentiment. God's power is tempered by His mercy, which it also sustains. **12. for thou renderest**–lit., "that Thou renderest," etc., connected with "I heard this," as the phrase–**"that power . . ."**–teaching that by His power He can show both mercy and justice.

PSALM 63

Vss. 1-11. The historical occasion referred to by the title was probably during Absalom's rebellion (cf. II Sam. 15:23, 28; 16:2). David expresses an earnest desire for God's favor, and a confident expectation of realizing it in his deliverance and the ruin of his enemies. **1. early . . . seek thee**–earnestly (Isa. 26:9). The figurative terms–dry and thirsty–lit., "weary," denoting moral destitution, suited his outward circumstances. **soul**–and–**flesh**–the whole man (Ps. 16:9, 10). **2.** The special object of desire was God's perfections as displayed in his worship (Ps. 27:4). **3.** Experiencing God's mercy, which exceeds all the blessings of life, his lips will be opened for his praise (Ps. 51:15). **4. Thus**–lit., "Truly," **will I bless**–praise Thee (Ps. 34:1). **lift up my hands**–in worship (cf. Ps. 28:2). **in thy name**–in praise of Thy perfections. **5-8.** Full spiritual blessings satisfy his desires, and acts of praise fill his thoughts and time. **night**–as well as day. Past favors assure him of future, and hence he presses earnestly near to God, whose power sustains him (Ps. 17:8; 60:5). **9, 10. those . . . to destroy it**–or lit., "to ruin," or, "for ruin"–i.e., such as seek to injure me (are) *for* ruin–appointed to it (cf. Ps. 35:8). **shall go . . . earth**–into the grave, or, to death; as their bodies are rep-

resented as a portion for–**foxes**–lit., "jackals." **11. the king**–i.e., David himself, and all who reverence God, "shall share a glorious part," while treacherous foes shall be for ever silenced (Ps. 62:4).

PSALM 64

Vss. 1-10. A prayer for deliverance from cunning and malicious enemies, with a confident view of their overthrow, which will honor God and give joy to the righteous. **1. preserve . . . fear**–as well as the danger producing it. **2. insurrection**–lit., "uproar," noisy assaults, as well as their secret counsels. **3, 4.** Similar figures for slander (Ps. 57:4; 59:7). **bend**–lit., "tread," or, prepared. The allusion is to the mode of bending a bow by treading on it; here, and in Psalm 58:7, transferred to arrows. **the perfect**–one innocent of the charges made (Ps. 18:23). **and fear not**–(Ps. 55:19), not regarding God. **5.** A sentiment here more fully presented, by depicting their deliberate malice. **6.** This is further evinced by their diligent efforts and deeply laid schemes. **7.** The contrast is heightened by representing God as using weapons like theirs. **8. their . . . tongue to fall . . .**–i.e., the consequences of their slanders, etc. (cf. Ps. 10:2; 31:16). **all that see . . . away**–Their partners in evil shall be terrified. **9, 10.** Men, generally, will acknowledge God's work, and the righteous, rejoicing in it, shall be encouraged to trust Him (Ps. 58:10).

PSALM 65

Vss. 1-13. This is a song of praise for God's spiritual blessings to His people and His kind providence over all the earth. **1. Praise waiteth for thee**–lit., "To Thee silence praise," or (cf. Ps. 62:1), To Thee silence is praise–i.e., Praise is waiting as a servant–it is due to Thee. So the last clause expresses the duty of paying vows. These two parts of acceptable worship, mentioned in Psalm 50:14, are rendered in Zion, where God chiefly displays His mercy and receives homage. **2.** All are encouraged to pray by God's readiness to hear. **3.** God's mercy alone delivers us from the burden of iniquities, by purging or expiating by an atonement the transgressions with which we are charged, and which are denoted by–**Iniquities**–or lit., "Words of iniquities." **4. dwell in thy courts; . . .** [and] **satisfied with the goodness . . . temple**–denote communion with God (Ps. 15:1; 23:6; cf. Ps. 5:7). This is a blessing for all God's people, as denoted by the change of number. **5. terrible things** –i.e., by the manifestation of justice and wrath to enemies, accompanying that of mercy to His people (Ps. 63:9-11; 64:7-9). **the confidence**–object of it. **of all . . . earth**–the whole world–i.e., deservedly such, whether men think so or not. **6-13.** God's great power and goodness are the grounds of this confidence. These are illustrated in His control of the mightiest agencies of nature and nations affecting men with awe and dread (Ps. 26:7; 98:1, etc.), and in His fertilizing showers, causing the earth to produce abundantly for man and beast. **outgoings of . . . rejoice**–*all* people from east to west. **visitest** –in mercy (cf. Ps. 8:4). **river of God**–His exhaustless resources. **thy paths**–ways of providence (Ps. 25:4, 10). **wilderness**–places, though not inhabited by men, fit for pasture (Lev. 16:21, 22; Job 24:5). **pastures**–(In vs. 12) is lit., "folds," or "enclosures for flocks"; and in vs. 13 it may be "lambs"–the same word used and so translated in Psalm 37:20; so that "the flocks are clothed with lambs" (a figure for abundant increase) would be the form of expression.

PSALM 66

Vss. 1-20. The writer invites all men to unite in praise, cites some striking occasions for it, promises special acts of thanksgiving, and celebrates God's great mercy. **1. Make . . . noise**—or, Shout. **2. his name**—as in Psalm 29:2. **make his praise glorious**—lit., "place honor, His praise," or, "as to His praise"—i.e., let His praise be such as will glorify Him, or, be honorable to Him. **3, 4.** A specimen of the praise. **How terrible**—(Cf. Ps. 65:8). **submit**—(Cf. *Margin*), show a forced subjection (Ps. 18:44), produced by terror. **5, 6.** The terrible works illustrated in Israel's history (Exod. 14:21). By this example let rebels be admonished. **7. behold the nations**—watch their conduct. **8, 9.** Here is, perhaps, cited a case of recent deliverance. **holdeth . . . in life**—lit., "putteth our soul in life"—i.e., out of danger (Ps. 30:3; 49:15). **to be moved** (Cf. Ps. 10:6; 55:22). **10-12.** Out of severe trials, God had brought them to safety (cf. Isa. 48:10; I Pet. 1:7). **affliction**—lit., "pressure," or, as in Psalm 55:3, oppression, which, laid on the —**loins**—the seat of strength (Deut. 33:11), enfeebles the frame. **men to ride over our heads** [made us to pass] **through fire . . .**—figures describing prostration and critical dangers (cf. Isa. 43:2; Ezek. 36:12). **wealthy**—lit., "overflowing," or, irrigated, and hence fertile. **13-15.** These full and varied offerings constitute the payment of vows (Lev. 22:18-23). **I will offer**—lit., "make to ascend"—alluding to the smoke of burnt offering, which explains the use of—**incense** —elsewhere always denoting the fumes of aromatics. **16-20.** With these he unites his public thanks, inviting those who fear God (Ps. 60:4; 61:5, His true worshippers) to hear. He vindicates his sincerity, inasmuch as God would not hear hypocrites, but had heard him. **he was extolled with my tongue**—lit., exaltation (was) under my tongue," as a place of deposit, whence it proceeded—i.e., honoring God was habitual. **If I regard iniquity**—lit., "see iniquity with pleasure."

PSALM 67

Vss. 1-7. A prayer that, by God's blessing on His people, His salvation and praise may be extended over the earth. **1. cause his face to shine**—show us favor (Num. 6:24, 25; Ps. 31:16). **2. thy way**—of gracious dealing (Isa. 55:8), as explained by—**saving health**—or lit., "salvation." **3-5.** *Thanks* will be rendered for the blessings of His wise and holy government (cf. Isa. 2:3, 4; 11:4). **6, 7.** The blessings of a fruitful harvest are mentioned as types of greater and spiritual blessings, under which all nations shall fear and love God.

PSALM 68

Vss. 1-35. This is a *Psalm-song* (cf. Psalm 30, title), perhaps suggested by David's victories, which secured his throne and gave rest to the nation. In general terms, the judgment of God on the wicked, and the equity and goodness of His government to the pious, are celebrated. The sentiment is illustrated by examples of God's dealings, cited from the Jewish history and related in highly poetical terms. Hence the writer intimates an expectation of equal and even greater triumphs and summons all nations to unite in praises of the God of Israel. The Psalm is evidently typical of the relation which God, in the person of His Son, sustains to the Church (cf. vs. 18). **1-3.** Cf. Numbers 10:35; Psalm 1:4; 22:14, on the figures here used. **before him**—as in vs. 2, *from* His presence, as dreaded; but in vs. 3, *in* His presence, as under His protection (Ps. 61:7). **the righteous**— all truly pious, whether of Israel or not. **4. extol him . . . heavens**—lit., "cast up for Him who rideth in the deserts," or "wilderness" (cf. vs. 7), alluding to the poetical representation of His leading His people in the wilderness as a conqueror, before whom a way is to be prepared, or "cast up" (cf. Isa. 40:3; 62: 10). **by his name JAH**—or, Jehovah, of which it is a contraction (Exod. 15:3; Isa. 12:2) (*Hebrew*). **name**—or, perfections (Ps. 9:10; 20:1), which—**5, 6.** are illustrated by the protection to the helpless, vindication of the innocent, and punishment of rebels, ascribed to Him. **setteth the solitary in families**— lit., "settleth the lonely" (as wanderers) "at home." Though a general truth, there is perhaps allusion to the wandering and settlement of the Israelites. **rebellious dwell in a dry land**—removed from all the comforts of home. **7, 8.** (Cf. Exod. 19:16-18.) **thou wentest**—in the pillar of fire. **thou didst march** —lit., "in Thy tread," Thy majestic movement. **even Sinai itself**—lit., "that Sinai," as in Judg. 5:5. **9, 10. a plentiful rain**—a rain of gifts, as manna and quails. **Thy congregation**—lit., "troop," as in II Sam. 23:11, 13—the military aspect of the people being prominent, according to the figures of the context. **therein**—i.e., in the land of promise. **the poor**—Thy humble people (vs. 9; cf. Ps. 10:17; 12:5). **11. gave the word**—i.e., of triumph. **company**—or, choir of females, celebrating victory (Exod. 15:20). **12. Kings of armies**—i.e., with their armies. **she that . . . at home**—Mostly women so remained, and the ease of victory appears in that such, without danger, quietly enjoyed the spoils. **13.** Some translate this, "When ye shall lie between the borders, ye shall . . . ," comparing the peaceful rest in the borders or limits of the promised land to the proverbial beauty of a gentle dove. Others understand by the word rendered "pots," the smoked sides of caves, in which the Israelites took refuge from enemies in the times of the judges; or, taking the whole figuratively, the rows of stones on which cooking vessels were hung; and thus that a contrast is drawn between their former low and afflicted state and their succeeding prosperity. In either case, a state of quiet and peace is described by a beautiful figure. **14.** Their enemies dispersed, the contrast of their prosperity with their former distress is represented by that of the snow with the dark and somber shades of Salmon. **15, 16.** Mountains are often symbols of nations (Ps. 46:2; 65:6). That of Bashan, northeast of Palestine, denotes a heathen nation, which is described as a "hill of God," or a great hill. Such are represented as envious of the hill (Zion) on which God resides; **17.** and, to the assertion of God's purpose to make it His dwelling, is added evidence of His protecting care. He is described as in the midst of His heavenly armies—**thousands of angels**— lit., "thousands of repetitions," or, thousands of thousands—i.e., of chariots. The word—**angels**—was perhaps introduced in our version, from Deuteronomy 33:2, and Galations 3:19. They are, of course, implied as conductors of the chariots. **as . . . Sinai, in the holy place**—i.e., He has appeared in Zion as once in Sinai. **18.** From the scene of conquest He ascends to His throne, leading—**captivity** [or, many captives (Judg. 5:12)] **captive. received gifts for men**—accepting their homage, even when forced, as that of rebels. **that the Lord God might dwell**—or lit., "to dwell, O LORD God" (cf. vs. 16)—i.e., to make this hill, His people or Church, His dwelling. This Psalm typifies the conquests of the Church under her divine leader, Christ. He, indeed, "who was with the Church in the wilderness" (Acts 7:38) is the *Lord*, described in this ideal ascension. Hence Paul (Eph. 4:8) applies this language to describe His real ascension, when, having conquered sin, death, and hell, the Lord of glory triumphantly entered heaven, attended by throngs of adoring angels, to sit on the throne and wield the scepter of an eternal dominion. The phrase—**received gifts for** [or lit., "among"] **men**—is by Paul, "gave gifts to men." Both describe the acts of a conqueror, who receives and distributes spoils. The Psalmist uses "receiving" as evincing the success, Paul "gave" as the act, of the conqueror, who, having subdued his enemies, proceeds to reward his friends. The special application of the passage by Paul was in proof of Christ's exaltation. What the Old Testament represents of His descending and ascending corresponds with His history. He who descended is the same who has ascended. As then ascension was an element of His triumph, so is it now; and He, who, in His humiliation, must be recognized as our vicarious sacrifice and the High Priest of our profession, must also be adored as Head of His Church and author of all her spiritual benefits. **19-21.** God daily and fully supplies us. The issues or escapes from death are under His control, who is the God that saves us, and destroys His and our enemies. **wound the head**—or, violently destroy (Num. 24:8; Ps. 110:6). **goeth on still in . . . trespasses**—perseveringly impenitent. **22.** Former examples of God's deliverance are generalized: as He has done, so He will do. **from Bashan**—the farthest region; and—**depths of the sea**—the severest afflictions. Out of all, God will bring them. The figures of vs. 23 denote the completeness of the conquest, not implying any savage cruelty (cf. II Kings 9:36; Isa. 63:1-6; Jer. 15:3). **24-27.** The triumphal procession, after the deliverance, is depicted. **They have seen**—impersonally, "There have been seen." **the goings of my God**—as leading the procession; the ark, the symbol of His presence, being in front. The various bands of music (vs. 25) follow, and all who are—**from** [or lit., "of"] **the fountain of Israel**—i.e., lineal descendants of Jacob, are invited to unite in the doxology. Then by one of the nearest tribes, one of the most eminent, and two of the most remote, are represented the whole nation of Israel, passing forward (Num. 7). **28, 29.** Thanks for the past, and confident prayer for the future victories of Zion are mingled in a song of praise. **thy temple at** [or lit., "over"] **Jerusalem**—His palace or residence (Ps. 5:7) symbolized His protecting presence among His people, and hence is the object of homage on the part of others. **30.** The strongest nations are represented by the strongest beasts (cf. *Margin*). **31 Princes**—or, lit., "fat ones," the most eminent from the most wealthy, and the most distant nation, represent the universal subjection. **stretch out** [or, make to run] **her hands**—denoting haste. **32-36.** To Him who is presented as riding in triumph through His ancient heavens and proclaiming His presence—to Him who, in nature,

and still more in the wonders of His spiritual government, out of His holy place (Ps. 43:3), is terrible, who rules His Church, and, by His Church, rules the world in righteousness—let all nations and kingdoms give honor and power and dominion evermore.

PSALM 69

Vss. 1-36. *Upon Shoshannim*—(cf. Ps. 45, title). Mingling the language of prayer and complaint, the sufferer, whose condition is here set forth, pleads for God's help as one suffering in His cause, implores the divine retribution on his malicious enemies, and, viewing his deliverance as sure, promises praise by himself, and others, to whom God will extend like blessings. This Psalm is referred to seven times in the New Testament as prophetical of Christ and the gospel times. Although the character in which the Psalmist appears to some in vs. 5 is that of a sinner, yet his *condition* as a *sufferer* innocent of alleged crimes sustains the *typical* character of the composition, and it may be therefore regarded throughout, as the 22d, as typically expressive of the feelings of our Saviour in the flesh.
1, 2—(Cf. Psalm 40:2.) **come in unto my soul**—lit., "come even to my soul," endanger my life by drowning (Jonah 2:5). **3**—(Cf. Psalm 6:6.) **mine eyes fail**—in watching (Ps. 119:82). **4. hate me . . .**—(Cf. John 15:25). On the number and power of his enemies (cf. Ps. 40:12). **then I restored . . . away**—i.e., he suffered wrongfully under the imputation of robbery. **5.** This may be regarded as an appeal, vindicating his innocence, as if he had said, "If sinful, thou knowest," etc. Though *David's condition* as a *sufferer* may *typify* Christ's, without requiring that a parallel be found *in character*. **6. for my sake**—lit., "in me," in my confusion and shame. **7-12.** This plea contemplates his relation to God as a sufferer in His cause. Reproach, domestic estrangement (Mark 3:21; John 7:5), exhaustion in God's service (John 2:17), revilings and taunts of base men were the sufferings. **wept (and chastened) my soul**—lit., "wept away my soul," a strongly figurative description of deep grief. **sit in the gate**—public place (Prov. 31:31). **13-15.** With increasing reliance on God, he prays for help, describing his distress in the figures of vss. 1, 2. **16-18.** These earnest terms are often used, and the address to God, as indifferent or averse, is found in Psalm 3:7; 22:24; 27:9, etc. **19, 20.** Calling God to witness his distress, he presents its aggravation produced by the want of sympathizing friends (cf. Isa. 63:5; Mark 14:50). **21.** Instead of such, his enemies increase his pain by giving him most distasteful food and drink. The Psalmist may have thus described by figure what Christ found in reality (cf. John 19:29, 30). **22, 23.** With unimportant verbal changes, this language is used by Paul to describe the rejection of the Jews who refused to receive the Saviour (Rom. 11:9, 10). The purport of the figures used is that blessings shall become curses, the "table" of joy (as one of food) a "snare," their "welfare," lit., "peaceful condition," or security, a "trap." Darkened eyes and failing strength complete the picture of the ruin falling on them under the invoked retribution. **continually to shake**—lit., "to swerve" or bend in weakness. **24, 25.** An utter desolation awaits them. They will not only be driven from their homes, but their homes—or lit., "palaces," indicative of wealth—shall be desolate (cf. Matt. 23:38). **26.** Though smitten of God (Isa. 53:4), men were not less guilty

in persecuting the sufferer (Acts 2:23). **talk to the grief**—in respect to, about it, implying derision and taunts. **wounded**—or, lit., "mortally wounded." **27, 28. iniquity**—or, punishment (Ps. 40:12). **come ... righteousness**—partake of its benefits. **book of the living**—or "life," with the next clause, a figurative mode of representing those saved, as having their names in a register (cf. Exod. 32:32; Isa. 4:3). **29. poor and sorrowful**—the afflicted pious, often denoted by such terms (cf. Ps. 10:17; 12:5). **set me ... high**—out of danger. **30, 31.** Spiritual are better than mere material offerings (Ps. 40:6; 50:8); hence a promise of the former, and rather contemptuous terms are used of the latter. **32, 33.** Others shall rejoice. "Humble" and poor, as in vs. 29. **your heart ...**—address to such (cf. Ps. 22:26). **prisoners**—peculiarly liable to be despised. **34-36.** The call on the universe for praise is well sustained by the prediction of the perpetual and extended blessings which shall come upon the covenant people of God. Though, as usual, the imagery is taken from terms used of Palestine, the whole tenor of the context indicates that the spiritual privileges and blessings of the Church are meant.

PSALM 70

Vss. 1-5. This corresponds to Psalm 40:13-17 with a very few variations, as "turn back" (vs. 3) for "desolate," and "make haste unto me" (vs. 5) for "thinketh upon me." It forms a suitable appendix to the preceding, and is called "a Psalm to bring to remembrance," as the 38th.

PSALM 71

Vss. 1-24. The Psalmist, probably in old age, appeals to God for help from his enemies, pleading his past favors, and stating his present need; and, in confidence of a hearing, he promises his grateful thanks and praise.
1-3. (Cf. Psalm 30:1-3.) **given commandment**—lit., "ordained," as in Psalm 44:4; 68:28. **rock ... fortress**—(Ps. 18:2). **4, 5. cruel man**—corrupt and ill-natured—lit., "sour." **trust**—place of trust. **6-9.** His history from early infancy illustrated God's care, and his wonderful deliverances were at once occasions of praise and ground of confidence for the future. **my praise ... of thee**—lit., "in" or "by Thee" (Ps. 22:25). **10, 11.** The craft and malicious taunts of his enemies now led him to call for aid (cf. on the terms used, II Sam. 17:12; Ps. 3:2; 7:2). **12.** (Cf. Ps. 22:19; 40:4.) **13.** (Cf. Ps. 35:4; 40:14.) **14-16.** The ruin of his enemies, as illustrating God's faithfulness, is his deliverance, and a reason for future confidence. **for I know ... thereof**—innumerable, as he had not time to count them. **in the strength ...**—or, relying on it. **thy righteousness**—or, faithful performance of promises to the pious (Ps. 7:17; 31:1). **17-21.** Past experience again encourages. **taught me ...**—by providential dealings. **is very high**—distinguished (Ps. 36:5; Isa. 55:9). **depths of the earth**—debased, low condition. **increase ...**—i.e., the great things done for me (vs. 19; cf. Ps. 40:5). **22-24.** To the occasion of praise he now adds the promise to render it. **will ... praise**—lit., "will thank." **even thy truth**—as to Thy truth or faithfulness.

PSALM 72

Vss. 1-19. *For,* or lit., "of Solomon." The closing verse rather relates to the 2d book of Psalms, of which this is the last, and was perhaps added by some collector, to intimate that the collection, to which, as chief author, David's name was appended, was closed. In this view, these may consistently be the productions of others included, as of Asaph, sons of Korah, and Solomon; and a few of David's may be placed in the latter series. The fact that here the usual mode of denoting authorship is used, is strongly conclusive that Solomon was the author, especially as no stronger objection appears than what has been now set aside. The Psalm, in highly wrought figurative style, describes the reign of a king as "righteous, universal, beneficent, and perpetual." By the older Jewish and most modern Christian interpreters, it has been referred to Christ, whose reign, present and prospective, alone corresponds with its statements. As the imagery of Psalm 2 was drawn from the martial character of David's reign, that of this is from the peaceful and prosperous state of Solomon's.
1. Give the king ...—a prayer which is equivalent to a prediction. **judgments**—the acts, and (figuratively) the principles of a right government (John 5:22; 9:39). **righteousness**—qualifications for conducting such a government. **king's son**—same person as a king—a very proper title for Christ, as such in both natures. **2,** etc. The effects of such a government by one thus endowed are detailed. **thy people ... and thy poor**—or, meek, the pious subjects of his government. **3.** As **mountains** and **hills** are not usually productive, they are here selected to show the abundance of peace, being represented as —**bringing**—or, lit., "bearing" it as a produce. **by righteousness**—i.e., by means of his eminently just and good methods of ruling. **4.** That peace, including prosperity, as an eminent characteristic of Christ's reign (Isa. 2:4; 9:6; 11:9), will be illustrated in the security provided for the helpless and needy, and the punishment inflicted on oppressors, whose power to injure or mar the peace of others will be destroyed (cf. Isa. 65:25; Zech. 9:10). **children of the needy**—for the needy (cf. sons of strangers, Ps. 18:45). **5. as long as ... endure**—lit., "with the sun," coeval with its existence, and *before,* or, *in presence of the moon,* while it lasts (cf. Gen. 11:28, "before Terah," lit., "in presence of," while he lived). **6.** A beautiful figure expresses the *grateful* nature of His influence; **7,** and, carrying out the figure, the results are described in an abundant production. **the righteous**—lit., "righteousness." **flourish**—lit., "sprout," or, "spring forth." **8.** The foreign nations mentioned (vss. 9, 10) could not be included in the limits, if designed to indicate the boundaries of Solomon's kingdom. The terms, though derived from those used (Exod. 23:31; Deut. 11:24) to denote the possessions of Israel, must have a wider sense. Thus, "ends of the earth" is never used of Palestine, but always of the world (cf. *Margin*). **9-11.** The extent of the conquests. **They that dwell in the wilderness**—the wild, untutored tribes of deserts. **bow ... dust**—in profound submission. The remotest and wealthiest nations shall acknowledge Him (cf. Ps. 45:12). **12-14.** They are not the conquests of arms, but the influences of humane and peaceful principles (cf. Isa. 9:7; 11:1-9; Zech. 9:9, 10). **15.** In his prolonged life he will continue to receive the honorable gifts of the rich, and the prayers of his people shall be made for him, and their praises given to him. **16.** The spiritual blessings, as often in Scripture, are set forth by material, the abundance of which is described by a figure, in which a "handful" (or lit., "a piece," or small portion) of corn in the most unpropitious lo-

cality, shall produce a crop, waving in the wind in its luxuriant growth, like the forests of Lebanon. **they of the city . . . earth**—This clause denotes the rapid and abundant increase of population—**of** [or, "from"] **the city**—Jerusalem, the center and seat of the typical kingdom. **flourish**—or, glitter as new grass—i.e., bloom.. This increase corresponds with the increased productiveness. So, as the gospel blessings are diffused, there shall arise increasing recipients of them, out of the Church in which Christ resides as head. **17. His name**—or, glorious perfections. **as long as the sun**—(Cf. vs. 5). **men shall be blessed**—(Gen. 12:3; 18:18). **18, 19.** These words close the Psalm in terms consistent with the style of the context, while **20** is evidently, from its prosaic style, an addition for the purpose above explained. **ended**—lit., "finished," or completed; the word never denotes fulfilment, except in a very late usage, as in Ezra 1:1; Daniel 12:7.

PSALM 73

Vss. 1-28. *Of Asaph*—(cf. *Introduction*). *God is good to His people.* For although the prosperity of the wicked, and the afflictions of the righteous, tempted the Psalmist to misgivings of God's government, yet the sudden and fearful ruin of the ungodly, seen in the light of God's revelation, reassures his heart; and, chiding himself for his folly, he is led to confide renewedly in God, and celebrate His goodness and love.

1. The abrupt announcement of the theme indicates that it is the conclusion of a perplexing mental conflict, which is then detailed (cf. Jer. 12:1-4). **Truly**—or, Surely it is so. **clean heart**—(Ps. 18:26) describes the true Israel. **2.** The figures express his wavering faith, by terms denoting tottering and weakness (cf. Ps. 22:5; 62:3). **3-9.** The prosperous wicked are insolently proud (Ps. 5:5). They die, as well as live, free from perplexities: pride adorns them, and violence is their clothing; indeed they are inflated with unexpected success. With all this—**They are corrupt**—or, lit., "they deride," they speak maliciously and arrogantly and invade even heaven with blasphemy (Rev. 13:6), and cover earth with slanders (Job 21:7-14). **10-12.** Hence God's people are confounded, turned hither (or back) and thither, perplexed with doubts of God's knowledge and care, and filled with sorrow. **prosper in the world**—lit., "secure for ever." **13, 14.** The Psalmist, partaking of these troubles, is especially disturbed in view of his own case, that with all his diligent efforts for a holy life, he is still sorely tried. **15.** Freed from idiomatic phrases, this verse expresses a supposition, as, "Had I thus spoken, I should," etc., intimating that he had kept his troubles to himself. **generation of thy children**—Thy people (I John 3:1). **offend**—lit., "deceive, mislead." **16, 17.** Still he—**thought**—lit., "studied," or, pondered this riddle; but in vain; it remained a toil (cf. *Margin*), till he—**went into the sanctuary**—to inquire (cf. Exod. 25:22; Ps. 5:7; 27:4). **18-20. their end**—future (Ps. 37:37, 38), which is dismal and terribly sudden (Prov. 1:27; 29:1), aggravated and hastened by terror. As one despises an unsubstantial dream, so God, waking up to judgment (Ps. 7:6; 44:23), despises their vain shadow of happiness (Ps. 39:6; Isa. 29:7). They are thrown into ruins as a building falling to pieces (Ps. 74:3). **21, 22.** He confesses how—**foolish**—lit., "stupid," and —**ignorant**—lit., "not discerning," had been his course of thought. **before thee**—lit., "with Thee," in conduct respecting Thee. **23.** Still he was *with God,*

as a dependent beneficiary, and so kept from falling (vs. 2). **24.** All doubts are silenced in confidence of divine guidance and future glory. **receive me to glory**—lit., "take for (me) glory" (cf. Ps. 68:18; Eph. 4:8). **25, 26.** God is his only satisfying good. **strength**—lit., "rock" (Ps. 18:2). **portion**—(Ps. 16:5; Lam. 3:24). **27, 28.** The lot of apostates, described by a figure of frequent use (Jer. 3:1, 3; Ezek. 23:35), is contrasted with his, who finds happiness in nearness to God (Jas. 4:8), and his delightful work the declaration of His praise.

PSALM 74

Vss. 1-23. If the historical allusions of vss. 6-8, etc., be referred, as is probable, to the period of the captivity, the author was probably a descendant and namesake of Asaph, David's contemporary and singer (cf. II Chron. 35:15; Ezra 2:41). He complains of God's desertion of His Church, and appeals for aid, encouraging himself by recounting some of God's mighty deeds, and urges his prayer on the ground of God's covenant relation to His people, and the wickedness of His and their common enemy. **1. cast . . . off**—with abhorrence (cf. Ps. 43:2; 44:9). There is no disavowal of guilt implied. The figure of fire to denote God's anger is often used; and here, and in Deuteronomy 29:20, by the word "smoke," suggests its continuance. **sheep . . . pasture**—(Cf. Ps. 80:1; 95:7). **2.** The terms to denote God's relation to His people increase in force: "congregation"—"purchased"—"redeemed"—"Zion," His dwelling. **3. Lift . . . feet**—(Gen. 29:1)—i.e., Come (to behold) the desolations (Ps. 73:19). **4. roar**—with bestial fury. **congregations**—lit., "worshipping assemblies." **ensigns**—lit., "signs"—substituted their idolatrous objects, or tokens of authority, for those articles of the temple which denoted God's presence. **5, 6.** Though some terms and clauses here are very obscure, the general sense is that the spoilers destroyed the beauties of the temple with the violence of woodmen. **was famous** —lit., "was known." **carved work**—(I Kings 6:29). **thereof**—i.e., of the temple, in the writer's mind, though not expressed till vs. 7, in which its utter destruction by fire is mentioned (II Kings 25:9; Isa. 64:11). **7. defiled**—or, profaned, as in Psalm 89:39. **8. together**—at once, all alike. **synagogues**—lit., "assemblies," for places of assembly, whether such as schools of the prophets (II Kings 4:23), or "synagogues" in the usual sense, there is much doubt. **9. signs**—of God's presence, as altar, ark, etc. (cf. vs. 4; II Chron. 36:18, 19; Dan. 5:2). **no more any prophet**—(Isa. 3:2; Jer. 40:1; 43:6). **how long**—this is to last. Jeremiah's prophecy (25:11), if published, may not have been generally known or understood. To the bulk of the people, during the captivity, the occasional and local prophetical services of Jeremiah, Ezekiel, and Daniel would not make an exception to the clause, "there is no more any prophet." **10.** (Cf. Ps. 31:1.) **how long . . . reproach**—us as deserted of God. **blaspheme thy name**—or, perfections, as power, goodness, etc. (Ps. 29:2). **11.** Why cease to help us? (Cf. Ps. 3:7; 7:6; 60:5). **12. For**—lit., "And," in an adversative sense. **13-15.** Examples of the "salvation wrought" are cited. **divide the sea**—i.e., Red Sea. **brakest . . . waters**—Pharaoh and his host (cf. Isa. 51:9, 10; Ezek. 29:3, 4). **heads of leviathan**—The word is a collective, and so used for many. **the people . . . wilderness**—i.e., wild beasts, as conies (Prov. 30:25, 26), are called a people. Others take the passages literally, that the sea monsters thrown out on dry land were food for the wandering Arabs. **cleave the fountain**—i.e., the rocks of Horeb and Kadesh—for fountains. **driedst up**—Jordan, and, perhaps, Arnon and Jabbok (Num. 21:14). **16, 17.** The fixed orders of nature and bounds of earth are of God. **18.** (Cf. vs. 10; Deut. 32:6.) The contrast is striking—that such a God should be thus insulted! **19. multitude**—lit., "beast," their flock or company of men (Ps. 68:10). **turtle-dove**—i.e., the meek and lonely Church. **congregation**—lit., "company," as above—thus the Church is represented as the spoiled and defeated remnant of an army, exposed to violence. **20.** And the prevalence of injustice in heathen lands is a reason for invoking God's regard to His promise (cf. Num. 14:21; Ps. 7:16; 18:48). **21. oppressed**—broken (Ps. 9:9). **return**—from seeking God. **ashamed**—(Ps. 35:4). **22, 23.** (Cf. Ps. 3:7; 7:6.) God hears the wicked to their own ruin (Gen. 4:10; 18:20).

PSALM 75

Vss. 1-10. *Al-taschith*—(Cf. Ps. 57, title). In impending danger, the Psalmist, anticipating relief in view of God's righteous government, takes courage and renders praise.
1. God's name or perfections are set forth by His wondrous works. **2, 3.** These verses express the purpose of God to administer a just government, and in a time of anarchy that He sustains the nation. Some apply the words to the Psalmist. **receive the congregation**—lit., "take a set time" (Ps. 102:13; Hos. 2:3), or an assembly at a set time—i.e., for judging. **Pillars of it**—(I Sam. 2:8). **4-8.** Here the writer speaks in view of God's declaration, warning the wicked. **Lift ... up the horn**—to exalt power, here, of the wicked himself—i.e., to be arrogant or self-elated. **speak ... neck**—insolently. **promotion**—lit., "a lifting up." God is the only right judge of merit. **in the hand ... a cup ... red**—God's wrath often thus represented (cf. Isa. 51:17; Jer. 25:15). **but the dregs**—lit., "surely the dregs, they shall drain it." **9, 10.** Contrasted is the lot of the pious who will praise God, and, acting under His direction, will destroy the power of the wicked, and exalt that of the righteous.

PSALM 76

Vss. 1-12. *On Neginoth*—(Cf. Ps. 4, title). This Psalm commemorates what the preceding anticipates: God's deliverance of His people by a signal interposition of power against their enemies. The occasion was probably the events narrated in II Kings 19:35; Isaiah 37. (Cf. Ps. 46.)
1, 2. These well-known terms denote God's people and Church and His intimate and glorious relations to them. **Salem**—(Gen. 14:18) is Jerusalem. **3. brake ... the arrows**—lit., "thunderbolts" (Ps. 78:48), from their rapid flight or ignition (cf. Ps. 18:14; Eph. 6:16). **the battle**—for arms (Hos. 2:18). **4. Thou**—God. **mountains of prey**—great victorious nations, as Assyria (Isa. 41:15; Ezek. 38:11, 12; Zech. 4:7). **5. slept their sleep**—died (Ps. 13:3). **none ... found ... hands**—are powerless. **6. chariot and horse**—for those fighting on them (cf. Ps. 68:17). **7. may ... sight**—contend with Thee (Deut. 9:4; Josh. 7:12). **8, 9.** God's judgment on the wicked is His people's deliverance (Ps. 9:12; 10:7). **10.** Man's wrath praises God by its futility before His

power. **restrain**—or, gird—i.e., Thyself, as with a sword, with which to destroy, or as an ornament to Thy praise. **11, 12.** Invite homage to such a God (II Chron. 32:23), who can stop the breath of kings and princes when He wills (Dan. 5:23).

PSALM 77

Vss. 1-20. *To Jeduthun*—(Cf. Ps. 39, title). In a time of great affliction, when ready to despair, the Psalmist derives relief from calling to mind God's former and wonderful works of delivering power and grace.
1, expresses the purport of the Psalm; **2,** his importunacy. **my sore ran ... night**—lit., "my hand was spread," or, stretched out (cf. Ps. 44:20). **ceased not**—lit., "grew not numb," or, feeble (Gen. 45:26; Ps. 38:8). **my soul ... comforted**—(cf. Gen. 37:35; Jer. 31:15). **3-9.** His sad state contrasted with former joys. **was troubled**—lit., "violently agitated," or disquieted (Ps. 39:6; 41:5). **my spirit was overwhelmed**—or, fainted (Ps. 107:5; Jonah 2:7). **holdest ... waking**—or, fast, that I cannot sleep. Thus he is led to express his anxious feelings in several earnest questions indicative of impatient sorrow. **10.** Omitting the supplied words, we may read, "This is my affliction—the years of," etc.—years being taken as parallel to affliction (cf. Ps. 90:15), as of God's ordering. **11, 12.** He finds relief in contrasting God's former deliverances. Shall we receive good at His hands, and not evil? Both are orderings of unerring mercy and unfailing love. **13. Thy way ... in the sanctuary**—God's ways of grace and providence (Ps. 22:3; 67:2), ordered on holy principles, as developed in His worship; or implied in His perfections, if "holiness" be used for "sanctuary," as some prefer translating (cf. Exod. 15:11). **14-20.** Illustrations of God's power in His special interventions for His people (Exod. 14), and, in the more common, but sublime, control of nature (Ps. 22:11-14; Hab. 3:14) which may have attended those miraculous events (Exod. 14:24). **Jacob and Joseph**—representing all. **water ... , footsteps**—may refer to His actual leading the people through the sea, though also expressing the mysteries of providence.

PSALM 78

Vss. 1-72. This Psalm appears to have been occasioned by the removal of the sanctuary from Shiloh in the tribe of Ephraim to Zion in the tribe of Judah, and the coincident transfer of pre-eminence in Israel from the former to the latter tribe, as clearly evinced by David's settlement as the head of the Church and nation. Though this was the execution of God's purpose, the writer here shows that it also proceeded from the divine judgment on Ephraim, under whose leadership the people had manifested the same sinful and rebellious character which had distinguished their ancestors in Egypt.
1. my people ... my law—the language of a religious teacher (vs. 2; Lam. 3:14; Rom. 2:16, 27; cf. Ps. 49:4). The history which follows was a "dark saying," or riddle, if left unexplained, and its right apprehension required wisdom and attention. **3-8.** This history had been handed down (Exod. 12:14; Deut. 6:20) for God's honor, and that the principles of His law might be known and observed by posterity. This important sentiment is reiterated in (vss. 7, 8) negative form. **testimony**—(Ps. 19:7.)

stubborn and rebellious–(Deut. 21:18.) set not their heart–on God's service (II Chron. 12:14). 9-11. The privileges of the first-born which belonged to Joseph (I Chron. 5:1, 2) were assigned to Ephraim by Jacob (Gen. 48:1). The supremacy of the tribe thus intimated was recognized by its position (in the marching of the nation to Canaan) next to the ark (Num. 2:18-24), by the selection of the first permanent locality for the ark within its borders at Shiloh, and by the extensive and fertile province given for its possession. Traces of this prominence remained after the schism under Rehoboam, in the use, by later writers, of *Ephraim* for *Israel* (cf. Hos. 5:3-14; 11:3-12). Though a strong, well-armed tribe, and, from an early period, emulous and haughty (cf. Josh. 17:14; Judg. 8:1-3; II Sam. 19:41), it appears, in this place, that it had rather led the rest in cowardice than courage; and had incurred God's displeasure, because, diffident of His promise, though often heretofore fulfilled, it had failed as a leader to carry out the terms of the covenant, by not driving out the heathen (Exod. 23:24; Deut. 31:16; II Kings 17:15). 12-14. A record of God's dealings and the sins of the people is now made. The writer gives the history from the exode to the retreat from Kadesh; then contrasts their sins with their reasons for confidence, shown by a detail of God's dealings in Egypt, and presents a summary of the subsequent history to David's time. Zoan–for Egypt, as its ancient capital (Num. 13:22; Isa. 19:11). 15, 16. There were two similar miracles (Exod. 17:6; Num. 20:11). great depths–and–rivers–denote abundance. 17-20. yet more–lit., "added to sin," instead of being led to repentance (Rom. 2:4). in their heart–(Matt. 15:19.) for their lust–lit., "soul," or, desire. provoking–and–tempted–illustrated by their absurd doubts, 19, 20, in the face of His admitted power. 21. fire–the effect of the "anger" (Num. 11:1). 22. (Cf. Heb. 8:8, 9.) 23-29. (Cf. Exod. 16; Num. 11.) angels' food–lit., "bread of the mighty" (cf. Ps. 105:40); so called, as it came from heaven. meat–lit., "victuals," as for a journey. their . . . desire–what they longed for. 30, 31. not estranged . . . lust–or, desire–i.e., were indulging it. slew . . . fattest–or, among the fattest; some of them–chosen–the young and strong (Isa. 40:31), and so none could resist. 33-39. Though there were partial reformations after chastisement, and God, in pity, withdrew His hand for a time, yet their general conduct was rebellious, and He was thus provoked to waste and destroy them, by long and fruitless wandering in the desert. lied . . . tongues–a feigned obedience (Ps. 18:44). heart . . . not right–or, firm (cf. vs. 8; Ps. 51:10). a wind . . . again–lit., "a breath," thin air (cf. Ps. 103:16; Jas. 4:14). 40, 41. There were ten temptations (Num. 14:22). limited–as in vss. 19, 20. Though some prefer "grieved" or "provoked." The retreat from Kadesh (Deut. 1:19-23) is meant, whether–turned–be for turning back, or to denote repetition of offense. 43. wrought–set or held forth. 45. The dog-fly or the mosquito. 46. caterpillar–the *Hebrew* name, from its voracity, and that of–locust–from its multitude. 47, 48. The additional effects of the storm here mentioned (cf. Exod. 9:23-34) are consistent with Moses' account. gave . . . cattle–lit., "shut up" (cf. Ps. 31:8). 49. evil angels–or, angels of evil–many were perhaps employed, and other evils inflicted. 50, 51. made a way–removed obstacles, gave it full scope. chief of their strength –lit., "first-fruits," or, "first-born" (Gen. 49:3; Deut. 21:17). Ham–one of whose sons gave name (*Mizraim, Hebrew*) to Egypt. 52-54. made his . . . forth

–or, brought them by periodical journeys (cf. Exod. 15:1). border of his sanctuary–or, holy border–i.e., region of which–this mountain–(Zion) was, as the seat of civil and religious government, the representative, used for the whole land, as afterwards for the Church (Isa. 25:6, 7). purchased–or, procured by His right hand or power (Ps. 60:5). 55. by line –or, the portion thus measured. divided them–i.e., the heathen, put for their possessions, so tents–i.e., of the heathen (cf. Deut. 6:11). 56, 57. a deceitful bow–which turns back, and so fails to project the arrow (I Sam. 1:22; Hos. 7:16). They relapsed. 58. Idolatry resulted from sparing the heathen (cf. vss. 9-11). 59, 60. heard–perceived (Gen. 11:7). abhorred–but not utterly. tent . . . placed–lit., "caused to dwell," set up (Josh. 18:1). 61. his strength–the ark, as symbolical of it (Ps. 96:6). 62. gave–or, shut up. his people–(vs. 48; I Sam. 4:10 -17). 63. fire–either figure of the slaughter (I Sam. 4:10), or a literal burning by the heathen.' given to marriage–lit., "praised"–i.e., as brides. 64. (Cf. I Sam. 4:17); and there were, doubtless, others. made no lamentation–either because stupefied by grief, or hindered by the enemy. 65. (Cf. Ps. 22:16; Isa. 42:13.) 66. And he smote . . . part–or, struck His enemies' back. The Philistines never regained their position after their defeats by David. 67, 68. tabernacle of Joseph–or, home, or, tribe, to which –tribe of Ephraim–is parallel (cf. Rev. 7:8). Its pre-eminence was, like Saul's, only permitted. Judah had been the choice (Gen. 49:10). 69. Exalted as–high palaces–or, mountains, and abiding as– the earth. 70-72. God's sovereignty was illustrated in this choice. The contrast is striking–humility and exaltation–and the correspondence is beautiful. following . . . ewes . . .–lit., "ewes giving suck" (cf. Isa. 40:11). On the pastoral terms, cf. Ps. 79:13.

PSALM 79

Vss. 1-13. This Psalm, like the 74th, probably despicts the desolations of the Chaldeans (Jer. 52:12-24). It comprises the usual complaint, prayer, and promised thanks for relief. 1. (Cf. Ps. 74:2-7.) 2, 3. (Cf. Jer. 15:3; 16:4.) 4. (Cf. Ps. 44:13; Jer. 42:18; Lam. 2:15.) 5. How long–(Ps. 13:1). be angry–(Ps. 74:1-10). jealousy burn–(Deut. 29:20). 6, 7. (Cf. Jer. 10:25.) Though we deserve much, do not the heathen deserve more for their violence to us (Jer. 51:3-5; Zech. 1:14)? The singular denotes the chief power, and the use of the plural indicates the combined confederates. called upon [or, by] thy name–proclaimed Thy attributes and professed allegiance (Isa. 12:4; Acts 2:21). 8. former iniquites–lit., "iniquities of former times." prevent [lit., "meet"] us–as in Psalm 21:3. 9. for . . . glory of thy name [and for] thy name's sake–both mean for illustrating Thy attributes, faithfulness, power, etc., purge . . . sins–lit., "provide atonement for us." Deliverance from sin and suffering, for their good and God's glory, often distinguish the prayers of Old Testament saints (cf. Eph. 1:7). 10. This ground of pleading often used (Exod. 32:12; Num. 14:13-16). blood . . . shed–(vs. 3). 11. prisoner–the whole captive people. power –lit., "arm" (Ps. 10:15). 12. into their bosom–The lap or folds of the dress is used by Eastern people for receiving articles. The figure denotes retaliation (cf. Isa. 65:6, 7). They reproached God as well as His people. 13. sheep . . . pasture (Cf. Ps. 74:1; 78:70).

PSALM 80

Vss. 1-19. *Shoshannim*—Lilies (Ps. 45, title). *Eduth*—Testimony, referring to the topic as a testimony of God to His people (cf. Ps. 19:7). This Psalm probably relates to the captivity of the ten tribes, as the former to that of Judah. Its complaint is aggravated by the contrast of former prosperity, and the prayer for relief occurs as a refrain through the Psalm.
1, 2. Joseph—for Ephraim (I Chron. 7:20-29; Ps. 78:67; Rev. 7:8), for Israel. **Shepherd**—(Cf. Gen. 49:24). **leadest** . . .—(Ps. 77:20). **dwellest . . . cherubim**—(Exod. 25:20); the place of God's visible glory, whence He communed with the people (Heb. 9: 5). **shine forth**—appear (Ps. 50:2; 94:1). **Before Ephraim** . . .—These tribes marched next the ark (Num. 2:18-24). The name of Benjamin may be introduced merely in allusion to that fact, and not because that tribe was identified with Israel in the schism (I Kings 12:16-21; cf. also Num. 10:24). **3. Turn us**—i.e., from captivity. **thy face to shine**—(Num. 6:25). **4. be angry**—(Cf. *Margin.*) **5. bread of tears**—still an Eastern figure for affliction. **6. strife**—object or cause of (Isa. 9:11). On last clause cf. Psalm 79:4; Ezekiel 36:4. **8-11. brought**—or plucked up, as by roots, to be replanted. **a vine**—(Ps. 78:47). The figure (Isa. 16:8) represents the flourishing state of Israel, as predicted (Gen. 28:14), and verified (I Kings 4:20-25). **12. hedges**—(Isa. 5: 5). **13. The boar**—may represent the ravaging Assyrian and the "wild beast" other heathen. **14, 15. visit this vine**—favorably (Ps. 8:4). **And the vineyard**—or, "And protect or guard what thy right hand," etc. **the branch**—lit., "over the Son of man," preceding this phrase, with "protect" or "watch." **for thyself**—a tacit allusion to the plea for help; for **16. it**—[the vine] or **they**—[the people] are suffering from Thy displeasure. **17. thy hand . . . upon**—i.e., strengthen (Ezra 7:6; 8:22). **man of . . . hand**—may allude to Benjamin (Gen. 35:18). The terms in the latter clause correspond with those of vs. 15, from "and the branch," etc., literally, and confirm the exposition given above. **18.** We need quickening grace (Ps. 71:20; 119:25) to persevere in Thy right worship (Gen. 4:26; Rom. 10:11). **19.** (Cf. vs. 3, O God; vs. 7, O God of hosts.)

PSALM 81

Vss. 1-16. *Gittith*—(Cf. Ps. 8, title). A festal Psalm, probably for the passover (cf. Matt. 26:30), in which, after an exhortation to praise God, He is introduced, reminding Israel of their obligations, chiding their neglect, and depicting the happy results of obedience.
1. our strength—(Ps. 38:7). **2.** unites the most joyful kinds of music, vocal and instrumental. **3. the new moon**—or the month. **the time appointed**—(Cf. Prov. 7:20). **5. a testimony**—The feasts, especially the passover, attested God's relation to His people. **Joseph**—for *Israel* (Ps. 80:1). **went out through**—or over, i.e., Israel in the exodus. **I heard**—change of person. The writer speaks for the nation. **language**—lit., "lip" (Ps. 14:1). An aggravation or element of their distress that their oppressors were foreigners (Deut. 28:49). **6.** God's language alludes to the burdensome slavery of the Israelites. **7. secret place**—the cloud from which He troubled the Egyptians (Exod. 14:24). **proved thee**—(Ps. 7:10; 17:3)—tested their faith by the miracle. **8.** (Cf. Ps. 50:7.) The reproof follows to vs. 12. **if thou wilt hearken**—He then propounds the terms

of His covenant: they should worship Him alone, who (vs. 10) had delivered them, and would still confer all needed blessings. **11, 12.** They failed, and He gave them up to their own desires and hardness of heart (Deut. 29:18; Prov. 1:30; Rom. 11:25). **13-16.** Obedience would have secured all promised blessings and the subjection of foes. In this passage, "should have," "would have," etc., are better, "should" and "would" expressing God's intention at the time, i.e., when they left Egypt.

PSALM 82

Vss. 1-8. Before the great Judge, the judges of the earth are rebuked, exhorted, and threatened.
1. congregation—(Cf. Exod. 12:3; 16:1). **of the mighty**—i.e., of God, of His appointment. **the gods**—or judges (Exod. 21:6; 22:9), God's representatives. **2. accept the persons**—lit., "lift up the faces," i.e., from dejection, or admit to favor and communion, regardless of merit (Lev. 19:15; Prov. 18:5). **3, 4.** So must good judges act (Ps. 10:14; 29:12). **poor and needy**—(Cf. Ps. 34:10; 41:1). **5.** By the wilful ignorance and negligence of judges, anarchy ensues (Ps. 11:3; 75:3). **out of course**—(Cf. *Margin*; Ps. 9:6; 62:2). **6, 7.** Though God admitted their official dignity (John 10:34), He reminds them of their mortality. **fall like** . . .—be cut off suddenly (Ps. 20:8; 91:7). **8.** As rightful sovereign of earth, God is invoked personally to correct the evils of His representatives.

PSALM 83

Vss. 1-18. *Of Asaph*—(Cf. Ps. 74, title). The historical occasion is probably that of II Chronicles 20:1, 2 (cf. Psalms 47, 48). After a general petition, the craft and rage of the combined enemies are described, God's former dealings recited, and a like summary and speedy destruction on them is invoked. **1.** God addressed as indifferent (cf. Ps. 35:22; 39: 12). **be not still**—lit., "not quiet," as opposed to action. **2. thine enemies**—as well as ours (Ps. 74:23; Isa. 37:23). **3. hidden ones**—whom God specially protects (Ps. 27:5; 91:1). **4. from being a nation**—utter destruction (Isa. 7:8; 23:1). **Israel**—here used for Judah, having been the common name. **5. they have consulted**—with heart, or cordially. **together**—all alike. **6-8. tabernacles**—for people (Ps. 78:67). **they**—all these united with the children of Lot, or Ammonites and Moabites (cf. II Chron. 20:1). **9-11.** Compare the similar fate of these (II Chron. 20:23) with that of the foes mentioned in Judges 7: 22, here referred to. They destroyed one another (Judg. 4:6-24; 7:25). Human remains form manure (cf. II Kings 9:37; Jer. 9:22). **12.** The language of the invaders. **houses**—lit., "residences," enclosures, as for flocks (Ps. 65:12). **of God**—as the proprietors of the land (II Chron. 20:11; Isa. 14:25). **13. like a wheel**—or, whirling of any light thing (Isa. 17:13), as stubble or chaff (Ps. 1:4). **14, 15.** Pursue them to an utter destruction. **16. that they may seek**—or as vs. 18, supply "men," since vss. 17, 18 amplify the sentiment of vs. 16, expressing more fully the measure of destruction, and the lesson of God's being and perfections (cf. II Chron. 20:29) taught to all men.

PSALM 84

Vss. 1-12. Cf. on titles of Psalms 8, 42. The writer describes the desirableness of God's worship and prays for a restoration to its privileges.

1. amiable—not lovely, but beloved. **tabernacles** —(Ps. 43:3). **2. longeth**—most intensely (Gen. 31: 30; Ps. 17:12). **fainteth**—exhausted with desire. **courts**—as tabernacles (vs. 1)—the whole building. **crieth out**—lit., "sings for joy"; but here, and Lamentations 2:19, expresses an act of sorrow as the corresponding noun (Ps. 17:1; 61:2). **heart and ... flesh**—as in Psalm 63:1. **3. thine altars**—i.e., of burnt offering and incense, used for the whole tabernacle. Its structure afforded facilities for sparrows and swallows to indulge their known predilections for such places. Some understand the statement as to the birds as a comparison: "as they find homes, so do I desire *thine altars*," etc. **4.** This view is favored by the language here, which, as in Psalms 15:1; 23:6, recognizes the blessing of membership in God's family by terms denoting a *dwelling in His house.* **5.** (Cf. Ps. 68:28.) **in whose heart ... ways** —i.e., who knows and loves the way to God's favor (Prov. 16:17; Isa. 40:3, 4). **6. valley of Baca**—or weeping. Through such, by reason of their dry and barren condition, the worshippers often had to pass to Jerusalem. As they might become wells, or fountains, or pools, supplied by refreshing rain, so the grace of God, by the exercises of His worship, refreshes and revives the hearts of His people, so that for sorrows they have "rivers of delight" (Ps. 36:8; 46:4). **7.** The figure of the pilgrim is carried out. As such daily refit their bodily strength till they reach Jerusalem, so the spiritual worshipper is daily supplied with spiritual strength by God's grace till he appears before God in heaven. **appeareth ... God**—the terms of the requisition for the attendance on the feasts (cf. Deut. 16:16). **9.** God is addressed as a shield (cf. vs. 11). **thine anointed**— David (1 Sam. 16:12). **10. I had ... doorkeeper**— lit., "I choose to sit on the threshold," the meanest place. **11, 12.** As a sun God enlightens (Ps. 27:1); as a shield He protects. **grace**—God's favor, its fruit—**glory**—the honor He bestows. **uprightly**— (Ps. 15:2; 18:23). **that trusteth**—constantly.

PSALM 85

Vss. 1-13. On the ground of former mercies, the Psalmist prays for renewed blessings, and, confidently expecting them, rejoices.

1. captivity—not necessarily the Babylonian, but any great evil (Ps. 14:7). **2, 3.** (Cf. Ps. 32:1-5.) To turn from the "fierceness," implies that He was reconcilable, though (**4-7**) having still occasion for the anger which is deprecated. **draw out**—or, prolong (Ps. 36:10). **8.** He is confident God will favor His penitent people (Ps. 51:17; 80:18). **saints**—as in Psalm 4:3, the "godly." **9.** They are here termed **"them that fear him";** and grace produces glory (Ps. 84:11). **10.** God's promises of "mercy" will be verified by His "truth" (cf. Ps. 25:10; 40:10); and the "work of righteousness" in His holy government shall be "peace" (Isa. 32:17). There is an implied contrast with a dispensation under which God's truth sustains His threatened wrath, and His righteousness inflicts misery on the wicked. **11.** Earth and heaven shall abound with the blessings of this government; **12-13,** and, under this, the deserted land shall be productive, and men be "set," or guided in God's holy ways. Doubtless, in this description of God's returning favor, the writer had in view that more glorious period, when Christ shall establish His government on God's reconciled justice and abounding mercy.

PSALM 86

Vss. 1-17. This is a prayer in which the writer, with deep emotion, mingles petitions and praises, now urgent for help, and now elated with hope, in view of former mercies. The occurrence of many terms and phrases peculiar to David's Psalms clearly intimates its authorship.

1, 2. poor and needy—a suffering child of God, as in Psalm 10:12, 17; 18:27. **I am holy**—or, godly, as in Psalm 4:3; 85:8. **4. lift up my soul**—with strong desire (Ps. 25:1). **5-7. unto all ... that call upon thee**—or, worship Thee (Ps. 50:15; 91:15) however undeserving (Exod. 34:6; Lev. 11:9-13). **8. neither ... works**—lit., "nothing like thy works," the "gods" have none at all. **9, 10.** The pious Jews believed that God's common relation to all would be ultimately acknowledged by all men (Ps. 45:12-16; 47: 9). **11. Teach**—Show, point out. **the way**—of Providence. **walk in thy truth**—according to its declarations. **unite my heart**—fix all my affections (Ps. 12: 2; Jas. 4:8). **to fear thy name**—(cf. vs. 12) to honor Thy perfections. **13, 14.** The reason: God had delivered him from death and the power of insolent, violent, and godless persecutors (Ps. 54:3; Ezek. 8: 12). **15.** Contrasts God with his enemies (cf. vs. 5). **16. son ... handmaid**—home-born servant (cf. Luke 15:17). **17. Show me**—lit., "Make with me a token," by Thy providential care. Thus in and by his prosperity his enemies would be confounded.

PSALM 87

Vss. 1-7. This triumphal song was probably occasioned by the same event as the 46th. The writer celebrates the glory of the Church, as the means of spiritual blessing to the nation.

1. His [i.e., God's] **foundation**—or, what He has founded, i.e., Zion (Isa. 14:32). **is in the holy mountains**—the location of Zion, in the wide sense, for the capital, or Jerusalem, being on several hills. **2. gates**—for the enclosures, or city to which they opened (Ps. 9:14; 122:2; cf. Ps. 132:13, 14). **3. spoken of** [or *in*] **thee**—i.e., the city of God (Ps. 46:4; 48: 2). **4.** This is what is spoken by God. **to them ... me**—lit., "for My knowers," they are true worshippers (Ps. 36:10; Isa. 19:21). These are mentioned as specimens. **this** [i.e., nation] ... **was born there**— Of each it is said, "This was born," or is a native of Zion, spiritually. **5.** The writer resumes—**This and that man**—lit., "man and man," or many (Gen. 14: 10; Exod. 8:10, 14), or all (Isa 44:5; Gal. 3:28). **the highest ... her**—God is her protector. **6.** The same idea is set forth under the figure of a register made by God (cf. Isa. 4:3). **7.** As in a great procession of those thus *written up,* or registered, seeking Zion (Isa. 2:3; Jer. 50:5), "the singers" and "players," or pipers, shall precede. **all my springs**—So each shall say, "All my sources of spiritual joy are in Thee" (Ps. 46:4; 84:6).

PSALM 88

Vss. 1-18. *Upon Mahalath*—either an instrument, as a lute, to be used as an accompaniment (*Leannoth,* for singing) or, as others think, an enigmatic title (cf. Ps. 5:22 and 45, titles), denoting the subject—i.e., "sickness or disease, for humbling," the idea of spiritual maladies being often represented by disease (cf. Ps. 6:5, 6; 22:14, 15, etc.). On the other terms, cf. Psalm 42:32. Heman and Ethan (Ps. 89, title) were David's singers (I Chron. 6:18, 33; 15:17), of the family of Kohath. If the persons alluded to (I Kings 4:31; I Chron. 2:6), they were probably adopted into the tribe of Judah. Though called a song, which usually implies joy (Ps. 83 :1), both the style and matter of the Psalm are very despondent; yet the appeals to God evince faith, and we may suppose that the word "song" might be extended to such compositions. **1, 2.** Cf. on the terms used, Psalms 22:2; 31:2. **3. grave**—lit., "hell" (Ps. 16:10), death in wide sense. **4. go . . . pit**—of destruction (Ps. 28:1). **as a man**—lit., "a stout man," whose strength is utterly gone. **5. Free . . . dead**—Cut off from God's care, as are the slain, who, falling under His wrath, are left, no longer sustained by His hand. **6.** Similar figures for distress in Psalms 63:9; 69:3. **7.** Cf. Psalm 38:2, on first, and Psalm 42:7, on last clause. **8.** Both cut off from sympathy and made hateful to friends (Ps. 31: 11). **9. Mine eye mourneth**—lit., "decays," or fails, denoting exhaustion (Ps. 6:7; 31:9). **I . . . called**—(Ps. 86:5, 7). **stretched out**—for help (Ps. 44:20). **10. shall the dead** [the remains of ghosts] **arise**—lit., "rise up," i.e., as dead persons. **11, 12** amplify the foregoing, the whole purport (as Ps. 6:5) being to contrast death and life as seasons for praising God. **13. prevent**—meet—i.e., he will diligently come before God for help (Ps. 18:41). **14.** On the terms (Ps. 27:9; 74:1; 77:7). **15. from . . . youth up**—all my life. With **16, 17** the extremes of anguish and despair are depicted. **18. into darkness**—Better omit "into"—mine acquaintances (are) darkness, the gloom of death, etc. (Job 17:13, 14).

PSALM 89

Vss. 1-52. *Of Ethan*—(see Ps. 88, title). This Psalm was composed during some season of great national distress, perhaps Absalom's rebellion. It contrasts the promised prosperity and perpetuity of David's throne (with reference to the great promise of II Sam. 7), with a time when God appeared to have forgotten His covenant. The picture thus drawn may typify the promises and the adversities of Christ's kingdom, and the terms of confiding appeal to God provided appropriate prayers for the divine aid and promised blessing. **1. mercies**—those promised (Isa. 55:3; Acts 13:34), and—**faithfulness**—i.e., in fulfilling them. **2. I have said**—expressed, as well as felt, my convictions (II Cor. 4:13). **3, 4.** The object of this faith expressed in God's words (II Sam. 7:11-16). **with** [or lit., "to"] **my chosen**—as the covenant is in the form of a promise. **6, 7.** This is worthy of our belief, for His faithfulness (is praised) by the congregation of saints or holy ones; i.e., angels (cf. Deut. 33:2; Dan. 8:13). **sons of the mighty**—(cf. Ps. 29:1). So is He to be admired on earth. **8-14.** To illustrate His power and faithfulness examples are cited from history. His control of the sea (the most mighty and unstable object in nature), and of Egypt (Ps. 87:4), the first great foe of Israel (subjected to utter helplessness from pride and insolence), are specimens. At the same time, the whole frame of nature founded and sustained by Him, Tabor and Hermon for east and west, and "north and south," together representing the whole world, declare the same truth as to His attributes. **rejoice in thy name**—praise Thy perfections by their very existence. **15.** His government of righteousness is served by "mercy" and "truth" as ministers (Ps. 85:10-13). **know the joyful sound**—understand and appreciate the spiritual blessings symbolized by the feasts to which the

people were called by the trumpet (Lev. 25:9, etc.). **walk . . . countenance**—live in His favor (Ps. 4:6; 44: 3). **16, 17. in** [or, "by"] **thy righteousness**—Thy faithful just rule. **glory** [or, "beauty"] **of their strength**—They shall be adorned as well as protected. **our horn**—exalt our power (Ps. 75:10; Luke 1:69). **18.** (Cf. *Margin*.) Thus is introduced the promise to "our shield," "our king," David. **19-37. Then** —when the covenant was established, of whose execution the exalted views of God now given furnish assurance. **thou . . . to thy holy one**—or godly saint, object of favor (Ps. 4:3). *Nathan* is meant (II Sam. 7:17; I Chron. 17:3-15). **laid help**—lit., "given help." David was chosen and then exalted. **20. I have found**—having sought and then selected him (I Sam. 16:1-6), **21,** will protect and sustain (Isa. 41:10), **22-25,** by restraining and conquering his enemies, and performing My gracious purpose of extending his dominion—**hand** [and] **right hand**—power (Ps. 17:7; 60:5). **sea, and . . . rivers**—limits of his empire (Ps. 72:8). **26, 27. first-born**—one who is chief, most beloved or distinguished (Exod. 4:22; Col. 1:15). In God's sight and purposes he was the first among all monarchs, and specially so in his typical relation to Christ. **28-37.** This relation is perpetual with David's descendants, as a whole typical in official position of his last greatest descendant. Hence though in personal relations any of them might be faithless and so punished, their typical relation shall continue. His oath confirms His promise, and the most enduring objects of earth and heaven illustrate its perpetual force (Ps. 72:5, 7, 17). **Once**—one thing (Ps. 27:4). **by my holiness**—as a holy God. **that I will not lie**—lit., "if I lie"—part of the form of swearing (I Sam. 24:6; II Sam. 3:35). **It shall . . . moon . . . heaven**—lit., "*As the moon,* and the witness in the sky is sure, i.e., the moon." **38-52** present a striking contrast to these glowing promises, in mournful evidences of a loss of God's favor. **38.** cast off—and *rejected* (cf. Ps. 15:4; 43:2; 44:9). **39.** An insult to the "crown," as of divine origin, was a profanation. **40-45.** The ruin is depicted under several figures—a vineyard whose broken "hedges," and "strongholds," whose ruins invite spoilers and invaders; a warrior, whose enemies are aided by God, and whose sword's "edge"—lit., rock or strength (Josh. 5:2) is useless; and a youth prematurely old. **days of his youth**—or, youthful vigor, i.e., of the royal line, or promised perpetual kingdom, under the figure of a man. **46. How long . . .**—(Cf. Ps. 13:1; 88:14; Jer. 4:4.) **47.** These expostulations are excited in view of the identity of the prosperity of this kingdom with the welfare of *all mankind* (Gen. 22:18; Ps. 72:17; Isa. 9:7; 11:1-10); for if such is the fate of this chosen royal line. **48. What man**—lit., "strong man—shall live?" and, indeed, have not all men been made in vain, as to glorifying God? **49-51.** The terms of expostulation are used in view of the actual appearance that God had forsaken His people and forgotten His promise, and the plea for aid is urged in view of the reproaches of His and His people's enemies (cf. Isa. 37: 17-35). **bear in my bosom**—as feeling the affliction of the people (Ps. 69:9). **footsteps**—ways (Ps. 56:6). **Blessed . . .**—denotes returning confidence (Ps. 34: 1-3). **Amen, and Amen**—closes the third book of Psalms.

PSALM 90

Vss. 1-17. Contrasting man's frailty with God's eternity, the writer mourns over it as the punishment of sin, and prays for a return of the divine favor.

A Prayer [mainly such] *of Moses the man of God*— (Deut. 33:1; Josh. 14:6); as such he wrote this (cf. titles of Psalm 18 and Psalm 36).

1. dwelling-place—home (cf. Ezek. 11:16), as a refuge (Deut. 33:27). **2. brought forth** [and] **formed** —both express the idea of production by birth. **3. to destruction**—lit., "even to dust" (Gen. 3:19), which is partly quoted in the last clause. **4.** Even were our days now 1000 years, as Adam's, our life would be but a moment in God's sight (II Pet. 3:8). **a watch** —or, third part of a night (cf. Exod. 14:24). **5, 6.** Life is like grass, which, though changing under the influence of the night's dew, and flourishing in the morning, is soon cut down and withereth (Ps. 103: 15; I Peter 1:24). **7, 8. For**—A reason, this is the infliction of God's wrath. **troubled**—lit., "confounded by terror" (Ps. 2:5). Death is by sin (Rom. 5:12). Though "secret," the light of God's countenance, as a candle, will bring sin to view (Prov. 20: 27; I Cor. 4:5). **9. are passed**—lit., "turn," as to depart (Jer. 6:4). **spend**—lit., "consume." **as a tale** —lit., a thought," or, "a sigh" (Ezek. 2:10). **10.** Moses' life was an exception (Deut. 34:7). **it is . . . cut off**—or, driven, as is said of the quails in using the same word (Num. 11:31). In view of this certain and speedy end, life is full of sorrow. **11.** The whole verse may be read as a question implying the negative, "No one knows what Thy anger can do, and what Thy wrath is, estimated by a true piety." **12.** This he prays we may know or understand, so as properly to number or appreciate the shortness of our days, that we may be wise. **13.** (Cf. Ps. 13: 2.) **let it repent**—a strong figure, as in Exodus 32: 12, imploring a change in His dealings. **14. early** —promptly. **15.** As have been our sorrows, so let our joys be great and long. **16. thy work**—or, providential acts. **thy glory**—(Ps. 8:5; 45:3), the honor accruing from Thy work of mercy to us. **17. let the beauty**—or sum of His gracious acts, in their harmony, be illustrated in us, and favor our enterprise.

PSALM 91

Vss. 1-16. David is the most probable author; and the pestilence, mentioned in II Sam. 24, the most probable of any special occasion to which the Psalm may refer. The changes of person allowable in poetry are here frequently made.

1. dwelleth in the secret place (Ps. 27:5; 31:20) denotes nearness to God. Such as do so abide or lodge secure from assaults, and can well use the terms of trust in vs. 2. **3. snares . . .** [and] **. . . noisome pestilence**—lit., "plagues of mischiefs" (Ps. 5:9; 52:7), are expressive figures for various evils. **4.** For the first figure cf. Deuteronomy 32:11; Mark 23:37. **buckler**—lit., "surrounding"—i.e., a kind of shield covering all over. **5. terror**—or, what causes it (Prov. 20:2). **by night**—then aggravated. **arrow** —i.e., of enemies. **7-8.** The security is more valuable, as being special, and, therefore, evidently of God; and while ten thousands of the wicked fall, the righteous are in such safety that they only see the calamity. **9-12.** This exemption from evil is the result of trust in God, who employs angels as ministering spirits (Heb. 1:14). **13.** Even the fiercest, strongest, and most insidious animals may be trampled on with impunity. **14-16.** God Himself speaks (cf. Ps. 46:10; 75:2, 3). All the terms to express safety and peace indicate the most undoubting confidence (cf. Ps. 18:2; 20:1; 22:5). **set his love**— that of the most ardent kind. **show him**—lit., "make him see" (Ps. 50:23; Luke 2:30).

PSALM 92

Vss. 1-15. *A Psalm-song*—(Cf. Ps. 30, title.) The theme: God should be praised for His righteous judgments on the wicked and His care and defense of His people. Such a topic, at all times proper, is specially so for the reflections of the Sabbath-day.

1. sing . . . name—celebrate Thy perfections. **2. in the morning, . . . every night**—diligently and constantly (Ps. 42:8). **loving-kindness**—lit., "mercy." **faithfulness**—in fulfilling promises (Ps. 89:14). **3.** In such a work all proper aid must be used. **with a . . . sound**—or, *on Higgaion* (cf. Ps. 9:16), perhaps an instrument of that name, from its sound resembling the muttered sound of meditation, as expressed also by the word. This is joined with the harp. **4. thy work**—i.e. of providence (Ps. 90:16, 17). **5. great . . . works**—correspond to *deep* or vast *thoughts* (Ps. 40:5; Rom. 11:23). **6. A brutish man knoweth not** i.e., God's works, so the Psalmist describes himself (Ps. 73:22) when amazed by the prosperity of the wicked, now understood and explained. **8.** This he does in part, by contrasting their ruin with God's exaltation and eternity. **most high**—as occupying the highest place in heaven (Ps. 7:7; 18:16). **9, 10.** A further contrast with the wicked, in the lot of the righteous, safety and triumph. **horn . . . exalt**—is to increase power (Ps. 75:5). **anointed . . . fresh** [or, new] **oil**—(Ps. 23:5) a figure for refreshment (cf. Luke 7:46). Such use of oil is still common in the East. **11. see . . .** [and] **. . . hear my desire**—or, lit., "look on" my enemies and hear of the wicked (cf. Ps. 27:11; 54:7)—i.e., I shall be gratified by their fall. **12-14.** The vigorous growth, longevity, utility, fragrance, and beauty of these noble trees, set forth the life, character, and destiny of the pious; **15,** and they thus declare God's glory as their strong and righteous ruler.

PSALM 93

Vss. 1-5. This and the six following Psalms were applied by the Jews to the times of the Messiah. The theme is God's supremacy in creation and providence.

1. God is described as a King entering on His reign, and, for robes of royalty, investing Himself with the glorious attributes of His nature. The result of His thus reigning is the durability of the world. **2-4.** His underived power exceeds the most sublime exhibitions of the most powerful objects in nature (Ps. 89:9). **5.** While His power inspires dread, His revealed will should secure our confidence (cf. Ps. 19:7; 25:10), and thus fear and love combined, producing all holy emotions, should distinguish the worship we offer in His house, both earthly and heavenly.

PSALM 94

Vss. 1-23. The writer, appealing to God in view of the oppression of enemies, rebukes them for their wickedness and folly, and encourages himself, in the confidence that God will punish evildoers, and favor His people.

1, 2. God's revenge is His judicial infliction of righteous punishment. **show thyself**—(Cf. *Margin*). **Lift up thyself**—or, "Arise," both figures representing God as heretofore indifferent (cf. Ps. 3:7; 22:16, 20). **3, 4.** In an earnest expostulation he expresses his desire that the insolent triumph of the wicked

may be ended. **5, 6. people** [and] **heritage**—are synonymous, the people being often called God's heritage. As justice to the weak is a sign of the best government, their oppression is a sign of the worst (Deut. 10:18; Isa. 10:2). **7.** Their cruelty is only exceeded by their wicked and absurd presumption (Ps. 10:11; 59:7). **8. ye brutish**—(Cf. Ps. 73:22; 92: 6). **9-11.** The evidence of God's providential government is found in His creative power and omniscience, which also assure us that He can punish the wicked in regard to all their vain purposes. **12, 13.** On the other hand He favors though He chastens, the pious, and will teach and preserve them till the prosperous wicked are overthrown. **14, 15.** This results from His abiding love (Deut. 32:15), which is further evinced by His restoring order in His government, whose right administration will be approved by the good. **16.** These questions imply that none other than God will help (Ps. 60:9), **17-19,** a fact fully confirmed by his past experience. **dwelt in silence**—as in the grave (Ps. 31:17). **my thoughts** —or, anxious cares. **20. throne**—power, rulers. **iniquity** [and] **mischief**—both denote evils done to others, as **21** explains. **22, 23.** Yet he is safe in God's care. **defence**—(Ps. 59:9). **rock of . . . refuge**—(Ps. 9:9; 18:2). **bring . . . iniquity**—(Cf. Ps. 5: 10; 7:16). **in their . . . wickedness**—while they are engaged in evil-doing.

PSALM 95

Vss. 1-11. David (Heb. 4:7) exhorts men to praise God for His greatness, and warns them, in God's words, against neglecting His service. **1.** The terms used to express the highest kind of joy. **rock**—a firm basis, giving certainty of salvation (Ps. 62:7). **2. come . . . presence**—lit., "approach," or, meet Him (Ps. 17:13). **3. above . . . gods**—esteemed such by men, though really nothing (Jer. 5:7; 10:10-15). **4, 5.** The terms used describe the world in its whole extent, subject to God. **6. come**—or, "enter," with solemn forms, as well as hearts. **7.** This relation illustrates our entire dependence (cf. Ps. 23:3; 74:1). The last clause is united by Paul (Heb. 3:7) to the following (cf. Ps. 81:8), **8-11,** warning against neglect; and this is sustained by citing the melancholy fate of their rebellious ancestors, whose provoking insolence is described by quoting the language of God's complaint (Num. 14:11) of their conduct at *Meribah* and *Massah,* names given (Exod. 17:7) to commemorate their strife and contention with Him (Ps. 78:18, 41). **err in their heart**—Their wanderings in the desert were but types of their innate ignorance and perverseness. **that they should not**—lit., "if they . . . ," part of the form of swearing (cf. Num. 14:30; Ps. 89:35).

PSALM 96

Vss. 1-13. The substance of this Psalm, and portions of the 97th, 98th, and 100th, are found in I Chronicles 16, which was used by David's directions in the dedication of the tabernacle on Mount Zion. The dispensation of the Messiah was typified by that event, involving, as it did, a more permanent seat of worship, and the introduction of additional and more spiritual services. Hence the language of these Psalms may be regarded as having a higher import than that pertinent to the occasion on which it was thus publicly used. **1-3.** All nations are invited to unite in this most

joyful praise. **new song**—lit., "fresh," or new mercies (Ps. 33:3; 40:3). **2. show forth**—lit., "declare joyful tidings." **salvation**—illustrates His glory in its wonders of love and mercy. **4, 5.** For He is not a local God, but of universal agency, while idols are nothing. **6. Honour and majesty**—are His attendants, declared in His mighty works, while power and grace are specially seen in His spiritual relations to His people. **7-9. Give**—or, ascribe (Ps. 29:1) due honor to Him, by acts of appointed and solemn worship in His house. **offering**—of thanks. **beauty of holiness**—(Ps. 29:2.) **fear . . . him**—(Ps. 2:11.) **10.** Let all know that the government of the world is ordered in justice, and they shall enjoy firm and lasting peace (cf. Ps. 72:3, 7; Isa. 9:6, 7). **11-13.** For which reason the universe is invoked to unite in joy, and even inanimate nature (Rom. 8:14-22) is poetically represented as capable of joining in the anthem of praise.

PSALM 97

Vss. 1-13. The writer celebrates the Lord's dominion over nations and nature, describes its effect on foes and friends, and exhorts and encourages the latter. **1-2.** This dominion is a cause of joy, because, even though our minds are oppressed with terror before the throne of the King of kings (Exod. 19:16; Deut. 5:22), we know it is based on righteous principles and judgments which are according to truth. **3-5.** The attending illustrations of God's awful justice on enemies (Ps. 83:14) are seen in the disclosures of His almighty power on the elements of nature (cf. Ps. 46:2; 77:17; Hab. 3:6, etc.). **6. heavens**—or, their inhabitants (Ps. 50:6), as opposed to "nations" in the latter clause (cf. Isa. 40:5; 66: 18). **7.** Idolaters are utterly put to shame, for if angels must worship Him, how much more those who worshipped them. **all ye gods**—lit., "all ye angels" (Ps. 8:5; 138:1; Heb. 1:6, 2:7). Paul quotes, not as a prophecy, but as language used in regard to the Lord Jehovah, who in the Old Testament *theophania* is the second person of the Godhead. **8, 9.** The exaltation of Zion's king is joy to the righteous and sorrow to the wicked. **daughters of Judah** —(Cf. Ps. 48:11). **above all gods**—(Ps. 95:3). **10-13.** Let gratitude for the blessings of providence and grace incite saints (Ps. 4:3) to holy living. Spiritual blessings are in store, represented by light (Ps. 27:1) and gladness. **sown**—to spring forth abundantly for such, who alone can and well may rejoice in the holy government of their sovereign Lord (cf. Ps. 30: 4; 32:11).

PSALM 98

Vss. 1-9. In view of the wonders of grace and righteousness displayed in God's salvation, the whole creation is invited to unite in praise. **1. gotten . . . victory**—lit., "made salvation," enabled Him to save His people. **right hand, and . . . arm**—denote power. **holy arm**—or, arm of holiness, the power of His united moral perfections (Ps. 22:3; 32:11). **2. salvation**—the result of His **righteousness** (Ps. 7:17; 31:1, and both are publicly displayed. **3.** The union of **mercy** and **truth** (Ps. 57:3; 85:10) secure the blessings of the promise (Gen. 12:3; 18: 18) to all the world (Isa. 52:10). **4-6 make a loud noise**—or, burst forth (Isa. 14:7; 44:23). **before . . . King**—hail Him as your sovereign; and while, with

every aid to demonstrate zeal and joy, intelligent
creatures are invited to praise, as in Psalm 96:11-13,
inanimate nature is also summoned to honor Him
who triumphs and rules in righteousness and equity.

PSALM 99

Vss. 1-9. God's government is especially exercised in and for His Church, which should praise
Him for His gracious dealings.
1. sitteth ... cherubim—(cf. I Sam. 4:4; Ps. 80:1).
tremble ... be moved—inspired with fear by His
judgments on the wicked. **2. great in Zion**—where
He dwells (Ps. 9:11). **3. thy ... name**—perfections
of justice, power, etc. **great and terrible**—producing dread (Deut. 10:17), and to be praised by those
over whom He is exalted (Ps. 97:9). **it is holy**—or,
He is holy (vss. 5, 9; Isa. 6:3). **4, 5.** To His wise
and righteous government all nations should render
honor. **king's ... judgment**—His power is combined with justice. **he is holy**—(cf. Ps. 22:3). **6-8.**
The experience of these servants of God is cited
for encouragement. **among ... priests, among ...
upon the Lord** [and] **He spake ... pillar**—may be referred to all three (cf. Exod. 18:19; Lev. 8:15; Deut.
5:5; I Sam. 9:13). **cloudy pillar**—the medium of divine intercourse (Exod. 33:9; Num. 12:5). Obedience was united with worship. God answered
them as intercessors for the people, who, though
forgiven, were yet chastened (Exod. 32:10, 34).

PSALM 100

Vss. 1-5. As closing this series (cf. on Ps. 94),
this Psalm is a general call on all the earth to render
exalted praise to God, the creator, preserver, and
benefactor of men.
1, 2. With thankful praise, unite service as the
subjects of a king (Ps. 2:11, 12). **3.** To the obligations of a creature and subject is added that of a
beneficiary (Ps. 95:7). **4.** Join joyfully in His public
worship. The terms are, of course, figurative (cf.
Ps. 84:2; 92:13; Isa. 66:23). **Enter**—or, Come with
solemnity (Ps. 95:6). **5.** The reason: God's eternal
mercy and truth (Ps. 25:8; 89:7).

PSALM 101

Vss. 1-8. In this Psalm the profession of the
principles of his domestic and political government
testifies, as well as actions in accordance with it, David's appreciation of God's mercy to him, and His
judgment on his enemies: and thus he sings or celebrates God's dealings.
2. He avows his sincere purpose, by God's aid, to
act uprightly (Gen. 17:1; Ps. 18:30). **3. set ... eyes**
—as an example to be approved and followed. **no
wicked thing**—lit., "word," plan or purpose of Belial (Ps. 41:8). **work of ... aside**—apostates. **not
cleave to me**—I will not be implicated in it (cf. Ps.
1:1-3). **4. A froward** [or, perverse] **heart**—(Ps. 18:
26). Such a temper I will not indulge, nor even
know evil or wickedness. **5, 6.** The slanderers and
haughty persons, so mischievous in society, I will
disown; but—**Mine eyes ... upon**—or, I will select
reliable and honest men for my servants. **7. not
dwell**—lit., "not sit," or tarry, or be established. **8.
will early**—or, diligently. **city of the Lord**—or, holy
place (Ps. 48:2), where wicked men shall not be tolerated.

PSALM 102

Vss. 1-28. *A prayer of the afflicted* ...—The general terms seem to denote the propriety of regarding the Psalm as suitably expressive of the anxieties
of any one of David's descendants, piously concerned for the welfare of the Church. It was probably David's composition, and, though specially
suggested by some peculiar trials, descriptive of future times. *overwhelmed*—(cf. Ps. 61:2). *complaint*—(Ps. 55:2). *pouring out the soul*—(Ps. 62:8).
The tone of complaint predominates, though in view
of God's promises and abiding faithfulness, it is
sometimes exchanged for that of confidence and
hope.
1-3. The terms used occur in Psalms 4:1; 17:1, 6;
18:6; 31:2, 10; 37:20. **4.** (Cf. Ps. 121:6.) **so that
I forget**—or, have forgotten, i.e., in my distress (Ps.
107:18), and hence strength fails. **5. voice ...
groaning**—effect put for cause, my agony emaciates
me. **6, 7.** The figures express extreme loneliness.
8. sworn against me—or lit., "by me," wishing others
as miserable as I am (Num. 5:21). **9. ashes**—a figure of grief, my bread; weeping or tears, my drink
(Ps. 80:5). **10. lifted ... cast me down**—or, cast me
away as stubble by a whirlwind (Isa. 64:6). **11.
shadow ... declineth**—soon to vanish in the darkness of night. **12.** Contrast with man's frailty (cf.
Ps. 90:1-7). **thy remembrance**—that by which
Thou art remembered, Thy promise. **13, 14.** Hence
it is here adduced. **for** [or, "when"] **... the set time
...**—the time promised, the indication of which is
the interest felt for Zion by the people of God. **15-
17.** God's favor to the Church will affect her persecutors with fear. **When the Lord shall build**—or
better, *Because* the Lord hath built, etc., as a reason
for the effect on others; for in thus acting and hearing the humble, He is most glorious. **18. people
... created**—(cf. Ps. 22:31), an organized body, as
a Church. **19-22.** A summary of what shall be
written. **For**—or, "That," as introducing the statement of God's condescension. **to loose ... appointed**—or, deliver them (Ps. 79:11). **To declare
...**—or, that God's name may be celebrated in the
assemblies of His Church, gathered from all nations
(Zech. 8:20-23), and devoted to His service. **23-28.**
The writer, speaking for the Church, finds encouragement in the midst of all his distresses. God's
eternal existence is a pledge of faithfulness to His
promises. **in the way**—of providence. **weakened**—
lit., "afflicted," and made fearful of a premature end,
a figure of the apprehensions of the Church, lest
God might not perform His promise, drawn from
those of a person in view of the dangers of early
death (cf. Ps. 89:47). Paul (Heb. 1:10) quotes vss.
26-28 as addressed to Christ in His divine nature.
The scope of the Psalm, as already seen, so far from
opposing, favors this view, especially by the sentiments of vss. 12-15 (cf. Isa. 60:1). The association
of the Messiah with a day of future glory to the
Church was very intimate in the minds of Old Testament writers; and with correct views of His nature
it is very consistent that He should be addressed as
the Lord and Head of His Church, who would
bring about that glorious future on which they ever
dwelt with fond delightful anticipations.

PSALM 103

Vss. 1-22. A Psalm of joyous praise, in which
the writer rises from a thankful acknowledgment of
personal blessings to a lively celebration of God's

gracious attributes, as not only intrinsically worthy of praise, but as specially suited to man's frailty. He concludes by invoking all creatures to unite in his song. **1. Bless . . .** —when God is the object, praise. **my soul**—myself (Ps. 3:3; 25:1), with allusion to the act, as one of intelligence. **all . . . within me**—(Deut. 6: 5). **his holy name**—(Ps. 5:11), His complete moral perfections. **2. forget not all**—not any, none of His benefits. **3. diseases**—as penal inflictions (Deut. 39:2; II Chron. 21:19). **4. redeemeth**—Cost is implied. **destruction**—lit., "pit of corruption" (Ps. 16: 10). **crowneth**—or, adorneth (Ps. 65:11). **tender mercies**—compassions (cf. Ps. 25:6; 40:11). **5.** By God's provision, the saint retains a youthful vigor like the eagles (Ps. 92:14; cf. Isa. 40:31). **6.** Lit., "righteousness and judgments," denoting various acts of God's government. **7. ways**—of providence, etc., as usual (Ps. 25:4; 67:2). **acts**—lit., "wonders" (Ps. 7:11; 78:17). **8-10.** God's benevolence implies no merit. He shows it to sinners, who also are chastened for a time (Exod. 34:6). **keep (anger)**—in Leviticus 19:18, bear a grudge (Jer. 3:5, 12). **11. great** —efficient. **12. removed . . . from us**—so as no longer to affect our relations to Him. **13. pitieth**—lit., "has compassion on." **14. he** [who formed, Ps. 94: 9] **knoweth our frame**—lit., "our form." **we are dust**—made of and tending to it (Gen. 2:7). **15, 16.** So short and frail is life that a breath may destroy it. **it is gone**—lit., "it is not." **know it no more**—no more recognize him (Ps. 90:6; Isa. 40:6-8). **17, 18.** For similar contrast cf. Psalms 90:2-6; 102:27, 28. **such . . . covenant**—limits the general terms preceding. **righteousness**—as usual (Ps. 7:17; 31:1). **19.** God's firm and universal dominion is a pledge that He will keep His promises (Ps. 11:4; 47:8). **20-22. do his commandments . . . word**—or, lit., "so as to hearken," etc., i.e., their acts of obedience are prompt, so that they are ever ready to hear, and know, and follow implicitly His declared will (cf. Deut. 26:17; Luke 1:19). **ye his hosts**—myriads, or armies, as corresponding to *angels* of *great power:* denoting multitudes also. **all his works**—creatures of every sort, everywhere.

PSALM 104

Vss. 1-35. The Psalmist celebrates God's glory in His works of creation and providence, teaching the dependence of all living creatures; and contrasting the happiness of those who praise Him with the awful end of the wicked. **1.** God's essential glory, and also that displayed by His mighty works, afford ground for praise. **2. light**—is a figurative representation of the glory of the invisible God (Matt. 17:2; I Tim. 6:16). Its use in this connection may refer to the first work of creation (Gen. 1:3). **stretchest out the heavens**— the visible heavens or sky which cover the earth as a curtain (Isa. 40:12). **3. in the waters**—or, it may be "with"; using this fluid for the beams, or frames, of His residence accords with the figure of clouds for His chariots, and wind as a means of conveyance. **walketh**—or, moveth (cf. Ps. 18:10, 11; Amos 9:6). **4.** This is quoted by Paul (Heb. 1:7) to denote the subordinate position of angels; i.e., they are only messengers as other and material agencies. **spirits** —lit., "winds." **flaming fire**—(Ps. 105:32) being here so called. **5.** The earth is firmly fixed by His power. **6-9.** These verses rather describe the wonders of the flood than the creation (Gen. 7:19, 20; II Pet. 3:5, 6). God's method of arresting the flood and making its waters subside is poetically called a

"rebuke" (Ps. 76:6; Isa. 50:2), and the process of their subsiding by undulations among the hills and valleys is vividly described. **10-13.** Once destructive, these waters are subjected to the service of God's creatures. In rain and dew from His chambers (cf. vs. 3), and fountains and streams, they give drink to thirsting animals and fertilize the soil. Trees thus nourished supply homes to singing birds, and the earth teems with the productions of God's wise agencies, **14, 15,** so that men and beasts are abundantly provided with food. **for the service**— lit., "for the culture," etc., by which he secures the results. **oil . . . shine**—lit., "makes his face to shine more than oil," i.e., so cheers and invigorates him, that outwardly he appears better than if anointed. **strengtheneth . . . heart**—gives vigor to man (cf. Judg. 19:5). **16-19.** God's care of even wild animals and uncultivated parts of the earth. **20-23.** He provides and adapts to man's wants the appointed times and seasons. **24-26.** From a view of the earth thus full of God's blessings, the writer passes to the sea, which, in its immensity, and as a scene and means of man's activity in commerce, and the home of countless multitudes of creatures, also displays divine power and beneficence. The mention of **leviathan**—(Job 40:20) heightens the estimate of the sea's greatness, and of His power who gives such a place for sport to one of His creatures. **27-30.** The entire dependence of this immense family on God is set forth. With Him, to kill or make alive is equally easy. To hide His face is to withdraw favor (Ps. 13:1). By His spirit, or breath, or mere word, He gives life. It is His constant providence which repairs the wastes of time and disease. **31-34.** While God could equally glorify His power in destruction, that He does it in preservation is of His rich goodness and mercy, so that we may well spend our lives in grateful praise, honoring to Him, and delightful to pious hearts (Ps. 147: 1). **35.** Those who refuse such a protector and withhold such a service mar the beauty of His works, and must perish from His presence. The Psalm closes with an invocation of praise, the translation of a Hebrew phrase, which is used as an English word, "Hallelujah," and may have served the purpose of a chorus, as often in our psalmody, or to give fuller expression to the writer's emotions. It is peculiar to Psalms composed after the captivity, as "Selah" is to those of an earlier date.

PSALM 105

Vss. 1-45. After an exhortation to praise God, addressed especially to the chosen people, the writer presents the special reason for praise, in a summary of their history from the calling of Abraham to their settlement in Canaan, and reminds them that their obedience was the end of all God's gracious dealings. **1. call . . . name**—(Ps. 79:6; Rom. 10:13). Call on Him, according to His historically manifested glory. After the example of Abraham, who, as often as God acquired for Himself a name in guiding him, *called* in solemn worship upon the name of the Lord (Gen. 12:8, 13:4). **among the people**— or, peoples (Ps. 18:49). **deeds**—or, wonders (Ps. 103:7). **3, 4.** Seeking God's favor is the only true mode of getting true happiness, and *His strength* is the only true source of protection (cf. Ps. 32:11; 40: 16). **Glory . . . name**—boast in His perfections. The world glories in its horses and chariots against the Church of God lying in the dust; but *our* hope is in the name, i.e., the power and love of God to His people, manifested in past deliverances. **5, 6. judgments . . . mouth**—His judicial decisions for the good and against the wicked. **chosen**—rather qualifies "children" than "Jacob," as a plural. **7.** Rather, "He, Jehovah, is our God." His title, JEHOVAH, implies that He, the unchangeable, self-existing Being, makes things to be, i.e., fulfils His promises, and therefore will not forsake His people. Though especially of His people, He is God over all. **8-11.** The covenant was often ratified. **commanded**—or, ordained (Ps. 68:28). **word**—answering to "covenant" in the parallel clause, viz., the word of promise, which, according to vs. 10, He set forth for an inviolable law. **to a thousand generations**—perpetually. A verbal allusion to Deuteronomy 7:9 (cf. Exod. 20:6). **9. Which covenant**—or, "Word" (vs. 8). **10, 11.** Alluding to God's promise to Jacob (Gen. 28:13). Out of the whole storehouse of the promises of God, only one is prominently brought forward, namely, that concerning the possession of Canaan. Everything revolves around this. The wonders and judgments have all for their ultimate design the fulfilment of this promise. **12-15. few . . . in number**—alluding to Jacob's words (Gen. 34: 30), "I being *few in number*." **yea, very few**—lit., "as a few," i.e., like fewness itself (cf. Isa. 1:9). **strangers**—sojourners in the land of their future inheritance, as in a strange country (Heb. 11:9). **13. from one nation to another**—and so from danger to danger; now in Egypt, now in the wilderness, and lastly in Canaan. Though a few strangers, wandering among various nations, God protected them. **14. reproved kings**—Pharaoh of Egypt and Abimelech of Gerar (Gen. 12:17; 20:3). **Touch not**—referring to Genesis 26:11, where Abimelech says of Isaac, "He that *toucheth* this man or his wife shall surely be put to death." **mine anointed**—as specially consecrated to Me (Ps. 2:2). The patriarch was the prophet, priest, and king of his family. **my prophets**—in a similar sense, cf. Genesis 20:7. The "anointed" are those vessels of God, consecrated to His service, "in whom (as Pharaoh said of Joseph, Gen. 41:38) the Spirit of God is" [HENGSTENBERG]. **16.** God ordered the famine. God **called for a famine**—as if it were a *servant*, ready to come at God's bidding. Cf. the centurion's words, as to disease being God's servant (Matt. 8:8, 9). **upon the land**—viz., Canaan (Gen. 41:54). **staff of bread**—what supports life ((Lev. 26:26; Ps. 104:15; Isa. 3:1). **17-21.** Joseph was sent of God (Gen. 45: 5). **hurt with fetters**—(Gen. 40:3). **was laid in iron**—lit., "his soul," or, he (Ps. 16:10) came into iron, or, he was bound to his grief (cf. Ps. 3:2; 11:1). Joseph is referred to as being an appropriate type of those "bound in affliction and iron" (Ps. 107:10). The "soul" is put for the whole person, because the soul of the captive suffers still more than the body. **his word came**—His prophecy (Gen. 41:11-20) to the officers came to pass, or was fulfilled (Judg. 13:12, 17; I Sam. 9:6, explain the form of speech). **the word** [or, saying, or decree] **of the Lord tried** [or, proved] **him**—by the afflictions it appointed him to endure before his elevation (cf. Gen. 41:40-43). **22. To bind**—Not literally *bind;* but *exercise over them absolute control,* as the parallel in the second clause shows; also Genesis 41:40, 44, in which not literal *fettering,* but *commanding obedience,* is spoken of. It refers to vs. 18. The soul that was once *bound* itself now *binds* others, even princes. The same moral *binding* is assigned to the saints (Ps. 149:8). **teach . . . senators wisdom**—the ground of his exaltation by Pharaoh was his *wisdom* (Gen. 41:39); viz.,

in state policy, and ordering well a kingdom. **23-25. Israel . . . and Jacob**—i.e., Jacob himself is meant, as vs. 24 speaks of "his people." Still, he came with his whole house (Gen. 46:6, 7). **sojourned**—(Gen. 47:4). **land of Ham**—or, Egypt (Ps. 78:51). **turned their heart**—God controls men's free acts (cf. I Sam. 10:9). "When Saul had turned his back to go from (God's prophet) Samuel, God *turned* (*Margin*) him to another heart" (see Exod. 1:8, etc.). Whatever evil the wicked man plots against God's people, God holds bound even his heart, so as not to lay a single plan except what God permits. Thus Isaiah (43:17) says it was *God* who *brought forth the army* of Pharaoh to pursue Israel to their own destruction (Exod. 4:21; 7:3). **26. Moses . . . chosen**—both what they were by divine choice (Psalm 78:70). **27. signs** —lit., "words of signs," or rather, as "words" in *Hebrew* means "things," "things of His signs," i.e., His marvellous tokens of power (Ps. 145:5, *Margin*). Cf. the same Hebraism (Ps. 65:3, *Margin*). **28-36.** The ninth plague is made prominent as peculiarly wonderful. **they rebelled not**—Moses and Aaron promptly obeyed God (Heb. 11:27); (cf. Exod. 7-11 and Ps. 78:44-51, with which this summary substantially agrees). Or, rather, the "darkness" here is figurative (Jer. 13:16), the literal plague of darkness (Exod. 10:22, 23) being only *alluded* to as the symbol of God's wrath which overhung Egypt as a dark cloud during all the plagues. Hence, it is placed first, out of the historical order. Thus, "They rebelled not (i.e., no longer) against His word," refers to *the Egyptians.* Whenever God sent a plague on them, *they were ready to let Israel go,* though refusing when the plague ceased. **His word** —His command to let Israel go [HENGSTENBERG]. Of the ten plagues, only eight are mentioned, the fifth, the murrain of beasts, and the sixth, the boils, being omitted. **29, 30.** He deprived them of their favorite "fish," and gave them instead, out of the water, loathsome "frogs," and (vs. 31) upon their land tormenting "flies" (the dog-fly, according to MAURER) and "lice" (gnats, HENGSTENBERG). **32. hail for rain**—instead of fertilizing showers, hail destructive to trees. This forms the transition to the vegetable kingdom. The locusts in vs. 34 similarly are destructive to plants. **gave them**—referring to Leviticus 26:4. "I *give* you rain in due season." His "gift" to Israel's foes is one of a very different kind from that bestowed on His people. **33. their coasts** —all their land (Ps. 78:54). **34. caterpillars**—lit., "the lickers up," devouring insects; probably the hairy-winged locust. **36. the chief**—lit., "the firstlings." The ascending climax passes from the food of man to man himself. The language here is quoted from Ps. 78:51. **37. with silver and gold**— *presented* them by the Egyptians, as an acknowledgment due for their labors in their bondage (cf. Exod. 12:35). **one feeble person**—or, stumbler, unfit for the line of march. Cf. "harnessed," i.e., accoutred and marshalled as an army on march (Exod. 13:18; Isa 5:27). **38**—(Cf. Exod. 12:33; Deut. 11:25.) **39. covering**—in sense of protection (cf. Exod. 13:21; Num. 10:34). In the burning sands of the desert the cloud protected the congregation from the heat of the sun; an emblem of God's protecting favor of His people, as interpreted by Isaiah (Isa. 4:5, 6; cf. Num. 9:16). **42-45.** The reasons for these dealings: (1) God's faithfulness to His covenant, "His holy promise" of Canaan, is the fountain whence flowed so many acts of marvellous kindness to His people (cf. vss. 8, 11). Exodus 2:24 is the fundamental passage [HENGSTENBERG]. (2) That they might be obedient. The observance of God's commands by

Abraham was the object of the covenant with him (Gen. 18:19), as it was also the object of the covenant with Israel, that they might observe God's statutes. **remembered . . . and Abraham**—or, "remembered His holy word (i.e., covenant confirmed) *with* Abraham." **inherited the labour**—i.e., the fruits of their labor; their corn and vineyards (Josh. 21:43-45).

PSALM 106

Vss. 1-48. This Psalm gives a detailed confession of the sins of Israel in all periods of their history, with special reference to the terms of the covenant as intimated (Ps. 105:45). It is introduced by praise to God for the wonders of His mercy, and concluded by a supplication for His favor to His afflicted people, and a doxology.

1. Praise . . . —(Ps. 104:24), begins and ends the Psalm, intimating the obligations of praise, however we sin and suffer. I Chron. 16:34-36 is the source from which the beginning and end of this Psalm is derived. **2.** His acts exceed our comprehension, as His praise our powers of expression (Rom. 11:33). Their unutterable greatness is not to keep us back, but to urge us the more to try to praise Him as best we can (Ps. 40:5; 71:15). **3.** The blessing is limited to those whose principles and acts are right. How "blessed" Israel would be now, if he had "observed God's statutes" (Ps. 105:45). **4, 5.** In view of the desert of sins to be confessed, the writer invokes God's covenant mercy to himself and the Church, in whose welfare he rejoices. The speaker, *me, I,* is not the Psalmist himself, but the people, the present generation (cf. vs. 6). **visit**—(Cf. Ps. 8:4.) **see the good**—participate in it (Ps. 37:13.) **thy chosen**—viz., Israel, God's elect (Isa. 43:20; 45:4). As God seems to have *forgotten* them, they pray that He would "remember" them with the favor which *belongs* to His own people, and which once they had enjoyed. **thine inheritance**—(Deut. 9:29; 32:9.) **6.** Cf. I Kings 8:47; Daniel 9:5, where the same three verbs occur in the same order and connection, the original of the two later passages being the first one, the prayer of Solomon in dedicating the temple. **sinned . . . fathers**—like them, and so partaking of their guilt. The terms denote a rising gradation of sinning (cf. Ps. 1:1). **with our fathers**—we and they together forming one mass of corruption. **7-12.** Special confession. Their rebellion at the sea (Exod. 14:11) was because they had not remembered nor understood God's miracles on their behalf. That God saved them in their unbelief was of His mere mercy, and for His own glory. **the sea . . . the Red Sea**—the very words in which Moses' song celebrated the scene of Israel's deliverance (Exod. 15:4). Israel began to rebel against God at the very moment and scene of its deliverance by God! **8. for his name's sake**—(Ezek. 20:14.) **9. rebuked**—(Ps. 104:7.) **as through the wilderness**—(Isa. 63:11-14.) **12. believed . . . his words**—This is said not to praise the Israelites, but God, who constrained even so unbelieving a people momentarily to "believe" while in immediate view of His wonders, a faith which they immediately afterwards lost (vs. 13; Exod. 14:31; 15:1). **13-15.** The faith induced by God's display of power in their behalf was short lived, and their new rebellion and temptation was visited by God with fresh punishment, inflicted by leaving them to the result of their own gratified appetites, and sending on them spiritual poverty (Num. 11:18). **They soon forgat**—lit., "They hasted, they forgat" (cf. Exod. 32:8). "They have turned aside *quickly* (or *hastily*) out of the

way." The haste of our desires is such that we can scarcely allow God one day. Unless He immediately answers our call, instantly then arise impatience, and at length despair. **his works**—(Deut. 11:3, 4; Dan. 9:14.) **his counsel**—They waited not for the development of God's counsel, or *plan for their deliverance,* at His own time, and in His own way. **14.** Lit., "lusted a lust" (quoted from Num. 11:4, *Margin*). Previously, there had been impatience as to *necessaries* of life; here it is *lusting* (Ps. 78:18). **15. but sent leanness**—rather, *"and* sent," i.e., *and thus, even in doing so,* the punishment was inflicted at the very time their request was granted. So Ps. 78:30, "While their meat was yet in their mouths, the wrath of God came upon them." **soul**—the animal soul, which craves for food (Num. 11:6; Ps. 107:18). This soul got its wish, and with it and in it its own punishment. The place was therefore called *Kibroth-hattaavah,* "the graves of lust," because there they buried the people who had lusted. Animal desires when gratified mostly give only a hungry craving for more (Jer. 2:13). **16-18.** All the congregation took part with Dathan, Korah, etc., and their accomplices (Num. 16:41). **Aaron the saint**—lit., "the holy one," as consecrated priest; not a moral attribute, but one designating his office as *holy* to the Lord. The rebellion was followed by a double punishment: (1) (vs. 17) of the *non-Levitical* rebels, the Reubenites, Dathan and Abiram, etc. (Deut. 11:6; Num. 26:10); these were swallowed up by the earth. **covered**—"closed upon them" (Num. 16:33). (2) Of the *Levitical* rebels, with Korah at their head (vs. 18; Num. 16:35; 26: 10); these had *sinned* by fire, and were punished by fire, as Aaron's (being high priest) sons had been (Lev. 10:2; Num. 16:1-35). **19-23.** From indirect setting God at naught, they pass to direct. **made**—though prohibited in Exod. 20:4, 5 to *make a likeness,* even of the true God. **calf**—called so in contempt. They would have made an ox or bull, but their idol turned out but a *calf;* an imitation of the divine symbols, the cherubim; or of the sacred bull of Egyptian idolatry. The idolatry was more sinful in view of their recent experience of God's power in Egypt and His wonders at Sinai (Exod. 32:1-6). Though intending to worship Jehovah under the symbol of the calf, yet as this was incompatible with His nature (Deut. 4:15-17), they in reality gave up Him, and so were given up by Him. Instead of the Lord of heaven, they had as their glory the image of an ox that does nothing but eat grass. **23. he said**—viz., to Moses (Deut. 9:13). With God, *saying* is as certain as *doing;* but His purpose, while full of wrath against sin, takes into account the mediation of Him of whom Moses was the type (Exod. 32:11-14; Deut. 9:18, 19). **Moses his chosen** —i.e., to be His servant (cf. Ps. 105:26). **in the breach**—as a warrior covers with his body the broken part of a wall or fortress besieged, a perilous place (Ezek. 13:5; 22:30). **to turn away** [or, prevent] **his wrath**—(Num. 25:11; Ps. 78:38.) **24-27.** The sin of refusing to invade Canaan, "the pleasant land" (Jer. 3:19; Ezek. 20:6; Dan. 8:9), "the land of beauty," was punished by the destruction of that generation (Num. 14:28), and the threat of dispersion (Deut. 4: 25; 28:32) afterwards made to their posterity, and fulfilled in the great calamities now bewailed, may have also been then added. **despised**—(Num. 14: 31.) **believed not his word**—by which He promised He would give them the land; but rather the word of the faithless spies (cf. Ps. 78:22). **lifted up his hand**—or, swore, the usual form of swearing (cf. Num. 14:30, *Margin*). **27. To overthrow**—lit., "To make them fall"; alluding to the words (Num. 14: 39). **among ... nations ... lands**—The "wilderness" was not more destructive to the *fathers* (vs. 26) than residence among the heathen ("nations") shall be to the children. Lev. 26:33, 38 is here, before the Psalmist's mind, the determination against the "seed" when rebellious, being not *expressed* in Num. 14:31-33, but *implied* in the determination against the fathers. **28-30. sacrifices of the dead**—i.e. of lifeless idols, contrasted with "the living God" (Jer. 10:3-10; cf. Ps. 115:4-7; I Cor. 12:2). On the words, "joined themselves to Baal-peor," see Numbers 25:2, 3, 5. Baal-peor, i.e. the possessor of Peor, the mountain on which *Chemosh*, the idol of Moab, was worshipped, and at the foot of which Israel at the time lay encamped (Num. 23:28). The name never occurs except in connection with that locality and that circumstance. **provoked**—excited grief and indignation (Ps. 6:7; 78:58). **stood**—as Aaron "stood between the living and the dead, and the plague was stayed" (Num. 16:48). **executed judgment**—lit., "judged," including sentence and act. **31. counted ... righteousness**—"a just and rewardable action." **for**—or, "unto," to the procuring of righteousness, as in Romans 4:2; 10:4. Here it was a particular act, not faith, nor its object Christ; and *what was procured* was not justifying righteousness, or what was to be rewarded with eternal life; for no one act of man's can be taken for complete obedience. But it was that which God approved and rewarded with a perpetual priesthood to him and his descendants (Num. 25:13; I Chron. 6:4, etc.). **32, 33.** (Cf. Num. 20:3-12; Deut. 1:37; 3:26). **went ill with** [lit., "was bad for"] **Moses**—His conduct, though under great provocation, was punished by exclusion from Canaan. **34-39.** They not only failed to expel the heathen, as God "commanded" (Exod. 23:32, 33), lit., "said (they should)," but conformed to their idolatries, and thus became spiritual adulterers (Ps. 73:27). **unto devils**—*Septuagint*, demons (cf. I Cor. 10:20), or evil spirits. **polluted with blood**—lit., "blood," or "murder" (Ps. 5:6; 26:9). **40-43.** Those nations first seduced and then oppressed them (cf. Judg. 1:34; 2:14; 3:30). Their apostasies ungratefully repaid God's many mercies till He finally abandoned them to punishment (Lev. 26:39). **44-46.** If, as is probable, this Psalm was written at the time of the captivity, the writer now intimates the tokens of God's returning favor. **repented**—(cf. Ps. 90:13). **made ... pitied**—(I Kings 8:50; Dan. 1:9). These tokens encourage the prayer and the promise of praise (Ps. 30:4), which is well closed by a doxology.

PSALM 107

Vss. 1-43. Although the general theme of this Psalm may have been suggested by God's special favor to the Israelites in their restoration from captivity, it must be regarded as an instructive celebration of God's praise for His merciful providence to all men in their various emergencies. Of these several are given—captivity and bondage, wanderings by land and sea, and famine; some as evidences of God's displeasure, and all the deliverances as evidence of His goodness and mercy to them who humbly seek Him.

1, 2. This call for thankful praise is the burden or chorus (cf. vs. 8, 15, etc.). **redeemed of the Lord**—(cf. Isa. 35:9, 10). **say**—i.e., that His mercy, etc. **hand of**—or, power of enemy. **3. gathered**—alluding to the dispersion of captives throughout the Babylonian empire. **from the south**—lit., "the sea," or, Red Sea (Ps. 114:3), which was on the south.

4-7. A graphic picture is given of the sufferings of those who from distant lands returned to Jerusalem; or, **city of habitation** may mean the land of Palestine. **fainted**—was overwhelmed (Ps. 61:3; 77:3). **8, 9.** To the chorus is added, as a reason for praise, an example of the extreme distress from which they had been delivered—extreme hunger, the severest privation of a journey in the desert. **10-16.** Their sufferings were for their rebellion against (Ps. 105: 28) the words, or purposes, or promises, of God for their benefit. When humbled they cry to God, who delivers them from bondage, described as a dark dungeon with doors and bars of metal, in which they are bound in iron—i.e., chains and fetters. **shadow of death**—darkness with danger (Ps. 23:4). **broken** —lit., "shivered" (Isa. 45:2). **17-22.** Whether the same or not, this exigency illustrates that dispensation of God according to which sin brings its own punishment. **are afflicted**—lit., "afflict themselves," i.e., bring on disease, denoted by loathing of food, and drawing **near unto** [lit., "even to"] **the gates** [or, domains, Ps. 9:16] **of death. sent his word** —i.e., put forth His power. **their destructions**— i.e., that which threatened them. To the chorus is added the mode of giving thanks, by a sacrifice and joyful singing (Ps. 50:14). **23-32.** Here are set forth the perils of seafaring, futility of man's, and efficiency of God's, help. **go ... sea**—alluding to the elevation of the land at the coast. **These see ... deep**—illustrated both by the storm He raises and the calm He makes with a word (Ps. 33:9). **waves thereof**—lit., "His waves" (God's, Ps. 42:7). **are ... end**—lit., "all their wisdom swallows up itself," destroys itself by vain and contradictory devices, such as despair induces. **He maketh ... calm**—or, to stand to stillness, or in quiet. Instead of acts of temple worship, those of the synagogue are here described, where the people with the **assembly**, or session of elders, convened for reading, singing, prayer, and teaching. **33-41.** God's providence is illustriously displayed in His influence on two great elements of human prosperity, the earth's productiveness and the powers of government. He punishes the wicked by destroying the sources of fertility, or, in mercy, gives fruitfulness to deserts, which become the homes of a busy and successful agricultural population. By a permitted misrule and tyranny, this scene of prosperity is changed to one of adversity. He rules rulers, setting up one and putting down another. **wander ... wilderness**—reduced to misery (Job 12:24). **42, 43.** In this providential government, good men will rejoice, and the cavils of the wicked will be stopped (Job 5:16; Isa. 52:15), and all who take right views will appreciate God's unfailing mercy and unbounded love.

PSALM 108

Vss. 1-13. This Psalm is composed of vss. 1-5 of Psalm 57:7-11; and vss. 6-12 of Psalm 60:5-12. The varieties are verbal and trivial, except that in vs. 9, "over Philistia will I triumph," differs from Psalm 60:8, the interpretation of which it confirms. Its altogether triumphant tone may intimate that it was prepared by David, omitting the plaintive portions of the other Psalms, as commemorative of God's favor in the victories of His people.

PSALM 109

Vss. 1-31. The writer complains of his virulent enemies, on whom he imprecates God's righteous punishment, and to a prayer for a divine interposition in his behalf appends the expression of his confidence and a promise of his praises. This Psalm is remarkable for the number and severity of its imprecations. Its evident typical character (cf. vs. 8) justifies the explanation of these already given, that as the language of David respecting his own enemies, or those of Christ, it has respect not to the penitent, but to the impenitent and implacable foes of good men, and of God and His cause, whose inevitable fate is thus indicated by inspired authority. **1. God of my praise**—its object, thus recognizing God as a certain helper. *Be not silent* (cf. Ps. 17:13; 28:1). **2. For the mouth ... opened** [or, They have opened a wicked mouth] **against me**—lit., "with me," i.e., Their intercourse is living, or, they slander me to my face (Matt. 26:59). **3.** (Cf. Ps. 35:7; 69:4.) **4, 5.** They return evil for good (cf. Ps. 27:12; Prov. 17:13). **I give myself unto prayer**—or lit., "I (am) prayer," or, as for me, prayer, i.e., it is my resource for comfort in distress. **6. over him**—one of his enemies prominent in malignity (Ps. 55:12). **let Satan stand**—as an accuser, whose place was the right hand of the accused (Zech. 3:1, 2). **7.** The condemnation is aggravated when prayer for relief is treated as a sin. **8.** The opposite blessing is long life (Ps. 91:16; Prov. 3:2). The last clause is quoted as to Judas by Peter (Acts 1:20). **office**—lit., "charge," *Septuagint,* and Peter, "oversight." **9, 10.** Let his family share the punishment, his children be as wandering beggars to prowl in their desolate homes, a greedy and relentless creditor grasp his substance, his labor, or the fruit of it, enure to strangers and not his heirs, and his unprotected, fatherless children fall in want, so that his posterity shall utterly fail. **13. posterity**—lit., "end," as in Psalm 37:38, or, what comes after; i.e., reward, or success, or its expectation, of which posterity was to a Jew a prominent part. **14, 15.** Added to the terrible overthrow following his own sin, let there be the imputation of his parents' guilt, that it may now come before God, for His meting out its full consequences, in cutting off the memory of them (i.e., the parents) from the earth (Ps. 34:16). **16.** Let God remember guilt, because he (the wicked) did not remember mercy. **poor and needy ... broken in heart**—i.e., pious sufferer (Ps. 34:18; 35:10; 40:17). **17-19.** Let his loved sin, cursing, come upon him in punishment (Ps. 35:8), thoroughly fill him as water and oil, permeating to every part of his system (cf. Num. 5:22-27), and become a garment and a girdle for a perpetual dress. **20. Let this ... reward**—or, wages, pay for labor, the fruit of the enemy's wickedness. **from the Lord**—as His judicial act. **21, 22. do ... for me**—i.e., kindness. **wounded**—lit., "pierced" (Ps. 69:16, 29). **23. like the shadow**—(Cf. Ps. 102:11). **tossed up and down**—or, driven (Exod. 10:19). **24, 25.** Taunts and reproaches aggravate his afflicted and feeble state (Ps. 22:6, 7). **26, 27.** Let my deliverance glorify Thee (cf. Ps. 59:13). **28-31.** In confidence that God's blessing would come on him, and confusion and shame on his enemies (Ps. 73:13), he ceases to regard their curses, and anticipates a season of joyful and public thanksgiving; for God is near to protect (Ps. 16:8, 34:6) the poor from all unrighteous judges who may condemn him.

PSALM 110

Vss. 1-7. The explicit application of this Psalm to our Saviour, by Him (Matt. 22:42-45) and by the

apostles (Acts 2:34; I Cor. 15:25; Heb. 1:13), and their frequent reference to its language and purport (Eph. 1:20-22; Phil. 2:9-11; Heb. 10:12, 13), leave no doubt of its purely prophetic character. Not only was there nothing in the position or character, personal or official, of David or any other descendant, to justify a reference to either, but utter severance from the royal office of all priestly functions (so clearly assigned the subject of this Psalm) positively forbids such a reference. The Psalm celebrates the exaltation of Christ to the throne of an eternal and increasing kingdom, and a perpetual priesthood (Zech. 6:13), involving the subjugation of His enemies and the multiplication of His subjects, and rendered infallibly certain by the word and oath of Almighty God. **1. The Lord said**—lit., "A saying of the Lord," (cf. Ps. 36:1), a formula, used in prophetic or other solemn or express declarations. **my Lord**—That the Jews understood this term to denote the Messiah their traditions show, and Christ's mode of arguing on such an assumption (Matt. 22:44) also proves. **Sit ... at my right hand**—not only a mark of honor (I Kings 2:19), but also implied participation of power (Ps. 45:9; Mark 16:19; Eph. 1:20). **Sit**—as a king (Ps. 29:10), though the position rather than posture is intimated (cf. Acts. 7:55, 56). **until I make ...**—The dominion of Christ over His enemies, as commissioned by God, and entrusted with all power (Matt. 28:18) for their subjugation, will assuredly be established (I Cor. 15:24-28). This is neither His government as God, nor that which, as the incarnate Saviour, He exercises over His people, of whom He will ever be Head. **thine enemies thy footstool**—an expression taken from the custom of Eastern conquerors (cf. Josh. 10:24; Judg. 1:7) to signify a complete subjection. **2. the rod of thy strength**—the rod of correction (Isa. 9:4; 10:15; Jer. 48:12), by which Thy strength will be known. This is His Word of truth (Isa. 2:3; 11:4), converting some and confounding others (cf. II Thess. 2:8). **out of Zion**—or, the Church, in which God dwells by His Spirit, as once by a visible symbol in the tabernacle on Zion (cf. Ps. 2:6). **rule thou ...**—over enemies now conquered. **in the midst**—once set upon, as by ferocious beasts (Ps. 22:16), now humbly, though reluctantly, confessed as Lord (Phil. 2:10, 11). **3. Thy people ... willing**—lit., "Thy people (are) free-will offerings"; for such is the proper rendering of the word "willing," which is a plural noun, and not an adjective (cf. Exod. 25:2; Ps. 54:6), also a similar form (Judg. 5:2-9). **in the day of thy power**—Thy people freely offer themselves (Rom. 12:1) in Thy service, enlisting under Thy banner. **in the beauties of holiness**—either as in Psalm 29:2, the loveliness of a spiritual worship, of which the temple service, in all its material splendors, was but a type; or more probably, the appearance of the worshippers, who, in this spiritual kingdom, are a nation of kings and priests (I Peter 2:9; Rev. 1:5), attending this Priest and King, clothed in those eminent graces which the beautiful vestments of the Aaronic priests (Lev. 16:4) typified. The last very obscure clause—**from the womb ... youth**—may, according to this view, be thus explained: The word "youth" denotes a period of life distinguished for strength and activity (cf. Eccles. 11:9)—the "dew" is a constant emblem of whatever is refreshing and strengthening (Prov. 19:12; Hos. 14:5). The Messiah, then, as leading His people, is represented as continually in the vigor of youth, refreshed and strengthened by the early dew of God's grace and

Spirit. Thus the phrase corresponds as a member of a parallelism with "the day of thy power" in the first clause. "In the beauties of holiness" belongs to this latter clause, corresponding to "Thy people" in the first, and the colon after "morning" is omitted. Others prefer: Thy youth, or youthful vigor, or body, shall be constantly refreshed by successive accessions of people as dew from the early morning; and this accords with the New Testament idea that the Church is Christ's body (cf. Micah 5:7). **4.** The perpetuity of the priesthood, here asserted on God's oath, corresponds with that of the kingly office just explained. **after the order**—(Heb. 7:15) after the similitude of Melchisedek, is fully expounded by Paul, to denote not only perpetuity, appointment of God, and a royal priesthood, but also the absence of priestly descent and succession, and superiority to the Aaronic order. **5. at thy right hand**—as Psalm 109:31, upholding and aiding, which is not inconsistent with vs. 1, where the figure denotes participation of power, for here He is presented in another aspect, as a warrior going against enemies, and sustained by God. **strike through**—smite or crush. **kings**—not common men, but their rulers, and so all under them (Ps. 2:2, 10). **6.** The person is again changed. The Messiah's conquests are described, though His work and God's are the same. As after a battle, whose field is strewn with corpses, the conqueror ascends the seat of empire, so shall He judge or rule among many nations, and subdue **the head** [or (as used collectively for many) the heads] **over many lands. wound**—lit., "smite," or "crush" (cf. vs. 5). **7.** As a conqueror, "faint, yet pursuing," He shall be refreshed by **the brook in the way,** and pursue to completion His divine and glorious triumphs.

PSALM 111

Vss. 1-10. The Psalmist celebrates God's gracious dealings with His people, of which a summary statement is given.

1. Praise ye the Lord—or, *Hallelujah* (Ps. 104:35). This seems to serve as a title to those of the later Psalms, which, like this, set forth God's gracious government and its blessed fruits. This praise claims the **whole heart** (Ps. 86:12), and is rendered publicly. **upright**—a title of the true Israel (Ps. 32: 11). **2.** His **works,** i.e., of providence and grace, are **sought**—or, carefully studied, by all desiring to know them. **3, 4. honourable and glorious**—lit., "honor and majesty," which illustrate His glorious perfections. **righteousness**—(Ps. 7:17; 31:1), which He has made memorable by wonders of love and mercy, in supplying the wants of His people according to covenant engagements. **6-8.** His power was shown especially in giving them the promised land, and His faithfulness and justice thus displayed are, like His precepts, reliable and of permanent obligation. **9.** The deliverance He provided accorded to His established covenant. Thus He manifested Himself in the sum of His perfections (Ps. 20:1, 7; 22:3) worthy of reverence. **10.** And hence love and fear of such a God is the chief element of true wisdom (cf. Prov. 1:7; 9:10).

PSALM 112

Vss. 1-10. This Psalm may be regarded as an exposition of Psalm 111:10, presenting the happiness of those who fear and obey God, and contrasting the fate of the ungodly.

1. True fear produces obedience and this happiness. **2, 3.** Temporal blessings follow the service of God, exceptions occurring only as they are seen by God to be inconsistent with those spiritual blessings which are better. **4. light**—figurative for relief (Ps. 27:1; 97:11). The **upright** are like God (Lev. 6:36; Ps. 111:4). **5-9.** Generosity, sound judgment in God, form a character which preserves from fear of evil and ensures success against enemies. While a man thus truly pious is liberal, he increases in substance. **not be moved**—(cf. Ps. 13:4; 15:5.) **heart is established**—or, firm in right principles. **see his desire**—(Ps. 50:23; 54:7.) **10.** Disappointed in their malevolent wishes by the prosperity of the pious, the wicked are punished by the working of their evil passions, and come to naught.

PSALM 113

Vss. 1-9. God's majesty contrasted with His condescension and gracious dealings towards the humble furnish matter and a call for praise. The Jews, it is said, used this and Psalms 114-118 on their great festivals, and called them the *Greater Hallel, or Hymn.*

1-3. Earnestness and zeal are denoted by the emphatic repetitions. **servants**—or, all the people of God. **name of the Lord**—perfections (Ps. 5:11; 111: 9). **From the rising . . .**—all the world. **4-6.** God's exaltation enhances His condescension; **7, 8,** which is illustrated as often in raising the worthy poor and needy to honor (cf. I Sam. 2:8; Ps. 44:25). **9.** On this special case, cf. I Sam. 2:21. Barrenness was regarded as a disgrace, and is a type of a deserted Church (Isa. 54:1). **the barren woman . . . house**—lit., "the barren of the house," so that the supplied words may be omitted.

PSALM 114

Vss. 1-8. The writer briefly and beautifully celebrates God's former care of His people, to whose benefit nature was miraculously made to contribute.

1-4. of strange language—(cf. Ps. 81:5). **skipped . . . rams**—(Ps. 29:6), describes the waving of mountain forests, poetically representing the *motion* of the mountains. The poetical description of the effect of God's presence on the sea and Jordan alludes to the history (Exod. 14:21; Josh. 3:14-17). **Judah** is put as a parallel to **Israel,** because of the destined, as well as real, prominence of that tribe. **5-8.** The questions place the implied answers in a more striking form. **at the presence of**—lit., "from before," as if affrighted by the wonderful display of God's power. Well may such a God be trusted, and great should be His praise.

PSALM 115

Vss. 1-18. The Psalmist prays that God would vindicate His glory, which is contrasted with the vanity of idols, while the folly of their worshippers is contrasted with the trust of God's people, who are encouraged to its exercise and to unite in the praise which it occasions.

1-3. The vindication of God's mercy and faithfulness (Ps. 25:10; 36:6) is the "glory" of His "name," which is desired to be illustrated in the deliverance of His people, as the implied mode of its manifestation. In view of the taunts of the heathen, faith in His dominion as enthroned in the heaven (Ps. 2:4; 11:4) is avowed. **Where is now . . .**

—"now" is "not a particle of time, but of entreaty," as in our forms of speech, "Come now," "See now," etc. **4-7.** (Cf. Isa. 40:18-20; 44:9-20.) **speak . . . throat**—lit., "mutter," not even utter articulate sounds. **8. every one that trusteth**—they who trust, whether makers or not. **9-13.** The repetitions imply earnestness. **14.** Opposed to the decrease pending and during the captivity. **15-17.** They were not only God's peculiar people, but as living inhabitants of earth, assigned the work of His praise as monuments of divine power, wisdom, and goodness. **18.** Hence let us fulfil the purpose of our creation, and evermore show forth His praise.

PSALM 116

Vss. 1-19. The writer celebrates the deliverance from extreme perils by which he was favored, and pledges grateful and pious public acknowledgments. **1, 2.** A truly grateful love will be evinced by acts of worship, which *calling on God* expresses (vs. 13: Ps. 55:16; 86:7; cf. Ps. 17:6; 31:2). **3, 4.** For similar figures for distress see Psalm 18:4, 5. **gat hold upon me**—Another sense ("found") of the same word follows, as we speak of disease *finding us,* and of our finding or catching disease. **5-8.** The relief which he asked is the result not of his merit, but of God's known pity and tenderness, which is acknowledged in assuring himself (his soul, Ps. 11:1; 16:10) of rest and peace. All calamities are represented by *death, tears,* and *falling of the feet* (Ps. 56:13). **9. walk before the Lord**—act, or live under His favor and guidance (Gen. 17:1; Ps. 61:7). **land of the living**—(Ps. 27:13). **10, 11.** Confidence in God opposed to distrust of men, as not reliable (Ps. 68:8, 9). He speaks from an experience of the result of his faith. **in my haste**—lit., "terror," or "agitation," produced by his affliction (cf. Ps. 31:22). **12-14.** These are modes of expressing acts of worship (cf. vs. 4; Ps. 50:14; Jonah 2:9). **the cup of salvation**—the drink offering which was part of the thank offering (Num. 15:3-5). **now**—(cf. Ps. 115:2). "Oh, that (I may do it)" in the presence, etc. **15, 16.** By the plea of being a home-born servant, he intimates his claim on God's covenant love to His people. **17-19.** An ampler declaration of his purpose, designating the place, the Lord's house, or earthly residence in Jerusalem.

PSALM 117

Vss. 1, 2. This may be regarded as a doxology, suitable to be appended to any Psalm of similar character, and prophetical of the prevalence of God's grace in the world, in which aspect Paul quotes it (Rom. 15:11; cf. Ps. 47:2; 66:8). **2. is great toward us**—lit., "prevailed over or protected us."

PSALM 118

Vss. 1-29. After invoking others to unite in praise, the writer celebrates God's protecting and delivering care towards him, and then represents himself and the people of God as entering the sanctuary and uniting in solemn praise, with prayer for a continued blessing. Whether composed by David on his accession to power, or by some later writer in memory of the restoration from Babylon, its tone is joyful and trusting, and, in describing the fortune and destiny of the Jewish Church and its visible head, it is typically prophetical of the Christian Church and her greater and invisible Head. **1-4.** The trine repetitions are emphatic (cf. vss. 10-12, 15, 16; Ps. 115:12, 13). **Let . . . say**—Oh! that Israel may say. **now**—as in Psalm 115:2; so in vss. 3, 4. After "now say" supply "give thanks." **that his mercy**—or *for* His mercy. **5. distress**—lit., "straits," to which **large place** corresponds, as in Psalm 4:1; 31:8. **6, 7.** Men are helpless to hurt him, if God be with him (Ps. 56:9), and, if enemies, they will be vanquished (Ps. 54:7). **8, 9.** Even the most powerful men are less to be trusted than God. **10-12.** Though as numerous and irritating as bees, by God's help his enemies would be destroyed. **as the fire of thorns**—suddenly. **in the name . . .**—by the power (Ps. 20:5; 124:8). **13-16.** The enemy is triumphantly addressed as if present. **rejoicing and salvation**—the latter as cause of the former. **right hand . . . is exalted**—His power greatly exerted. **17, 18.** He would live, because confident his life would be for God's glory. **19-21.** Whether an actual or figurative entrance into God's house be meant, the purpose of solemn praise is intimated, in which only the righteous would or could engage. **22, 23.** These words are applied by Christ (Matt. 21:42) to Himself, as the foundation of the Church (cf. Acts 4:11; Eph. 2:20; I Pet. 2:4, 7). It may here denote God's wondrous exaltation to power and influence of him whom the rulers of the nation despised. Whether (see above) David or Zerubbabel (cf. Hag. 2:2; Zech. 4:7-10) be primarily meant, there is here typically represented God's more wonderful doings in exalting Christ, crucified as an impostor, to be the Prince and Saviour and Head of His Church. **24. This is the day**—or period distinguished by God's favor of all others. **25. Save now**—*Hebrew, Hosannah* (cf. Ps. 115:2, etc., as to *now*) a form of prayer (Ps. 20:9), since, in our use, of praise. **26. he that cometh . . . Lord**—As above intimated, this may be applied to the visible head of the Jewish Church entering the sanctuary, as leading the procession; typically it belongs to Him of whom the phrase became an epithet (Mal. 3:1; Matt. 21:9). **27-29. showed us light**—or favor (Ps. 27:1; 97:11). With the sacrificial victim brought bound to the altar is united the more spiritual offering of praise (Ps. 50: 14, 23), expressed in the terms with which the Psalm opened.

PSALM 119

Vss. 1-176. This celebrated Psalm has several peculiarities. It is divided into twenty-two parts or stanzas, denoted by the twenty-two letters of the Hebrew alphabet. Each stanza contains eight verses, and the first letter of each verse is that which gives name to the stanza. Its contents are mainly praises of God's Word, exhortations to its perusal, and reverence for it, prayers for its proper influence, and complaints of the wicked for despising it. There are but two verses (122, 132) which do not contain some term or description of God's Word. These terms are of various derivations, but here used, for the most part, synonymously, though the use of a variety of terms seems designed, in order to express better the several aspects in which our relations to the revealed word of God are presented. The Psalm does not appear to have any relation to any special occasion or interest of the Jewish Church or nation, but was evidently "intended as a manual of pious thoughts, especially for instructing the young, and its peculiar artificial structure was probably adopted to aid the memory in retaining the language."

1. undefiled—lit., "complete," perfect, or sincere (cf. Ps. 37:37). **in** [or "of"] **the way**—course of life. **walk** [act] **in the law**—according to it (cf. Luke 1:6). **law**—from a word meaning "to teach," is a term of rather general purport, denoting the instruction of God's Word. **2. testimonies**—The word of God is so called, because in it He *testifies* for truth and against sin. **seek him**—i.e., a knowledge of Him, with desire for conformity to His will. **3. his ways** —the course He reveals as right. **4-6. precepts**—are those directions which relate to special conduct, from a word meaning "to inspect." **statutes**—or ordinances, positive laws of permanent nature. Both words originally denote rather positive than moral laws, such as derive force from the divine appointment, whether their nature or the reasons for them are apprehended by us or not. **commandments**—or institutions. The term is comprehensive, but rather denotes fundamental directions for conduct, both enjoining and forbidding. **have respect unto**—or regard carefully as to their whole purport. **7. judgments**—rules of conduct formed by God's judicial decisions; hence the wide sense of the word in the Psalms, so that it includes decisions of approval as well as condemnation. **8.** Recognizes the need of divine grace.

9. The whole verse may be read as a question; for, **by taking heed**—is better, "for" taking heed, i.e., so as to do it. The answer is implied, and inferable from vss. 5, 10, 18, etc., i.e., by God's grace. **10-16.** We must carefully treasure up the word of God, declare it to others, meditate on it, and heartily delight in it; and then by His grace we shall act according to it.

17-20. Life is desirable in order to serve God; that we may do so aright, we should seek to have our eyes opened to behold His truth, and earnestly desire fully to understand it. **21-24.** God will rebuke those who despise His word and deliver His servants from their reproach, giving them boldness in and by His truth, even before the greatest men.

25-27. Submitting ourselves in depression to God, He will revive us by His promises, and lead us to declare His mercy to others. **28-32. In order to** adhere to His word, we must seek deliverance from temptations to sin as well as from despondency. **enlarge** [or expand] **my heart**—with gracious affections.

33-38. To encourage us in prayer for divine aid in adhering to His truth, we are permitted to believe that by His help we shall succeed. **the way of thy statutes**—i.e., the way or manner of life prescribed by them. The help we hope to obtain by *prayer* is to be the basis on which our *resolutions* should rest. **Turn away mine eyes**—lit., "Make my eyes to pass, not noticing evil." **vanity**—lit., "falsehood;" all other objects of trust than God; idols, human power, etc. (Ps. 31:6; 40:4; 60:11; 62:9). **quicken . . . in thy way**—make me with *living* energy to pursue the way marked out by Thee. *Revive* me from the *death* of spiritual helplessness (vss. 17, 25, 40, 50; Ps. 116:3). **who is devoted to thy fear**—or better, "which (i.e., Thy word) is for Thy fear," for producing it. "Which is to those who fear Thee." God's word of promise belongs peculiarly to such (cf. Gen. 18:19; I Kings 2:4; 8:25) [HENGSTENBERG]. **39, 40.** Our hope of freedom from the *reproach of inconsistency* is in God's power, quickening us to live according to His Word, which He leads us to love. **for thy judgments are good**—The time must therefore be at hand when Thy justice will turn the "reproach" from Thy Church upon the world (Isa. 25:8; 66:5, Zeph. 2:8-10).

41-44. The sentiment more fully carried out. God's mercies and salvation, as revealed in His Word, provide hope of forgiveness for the past and security in a righteous course for the future. **42.** The possession of God's gift of "salvation" (vs. 41) will be the Psalmist's answer to the foe's "reproach," that his hope was a fallacious one. **45-48.** To freedom from reproach, when imbued with God's truth, there is added "great boldness in the faith," accompanied with increasing delight in the holy law itself, which becomes an element of happiness. **48. My hands . . . lift up unto . . . commandments**—i.e., I will *prayerfully* (Ps. 28:2) direct my heart to keep Thy commandments.

49-51. Resting on the promises consoles under affliction and the tauntings of the insolent. **49. upon which**—rather, "Remember Thy word unto Thy servant, *because,*" etc. So the *Hebrew* requires [HENGSTENBERG]. **50. for**—rather, "This is my comfort . . . *that,*" etc. [MAURER]. **hath quickened** —What the Word *has already done* is faith a pledge of what *it shall yet do.* **52-56,** The pious take comfort, when harassed and distressed by wickedness of men who forsake God's law, in remembering that the great principles of God's truth will still abide; and also God's "judgments of old" (vs. 52), i.e., His past interpositions in behalf of His people are a pledge that He will again interpose to deliver them; and they become the theme of constant and delightful meditation. The more we keep the more we love the law of God. **53. Horror** —rather, "vehement wrath" [HENGSTENBERG]. **54. songs**—As the exile sings songs of his home (Ps. 137: 3), so the child of God, "a stranger on earth," sings the songs of heaven, his true home (Ps. 39:12). In ancient times, laws were put in verse, to imprint them the more on the memory of the people. So God's laws are the believer's songs. **house of my pilgrimage**—present life (Gen. 17:8; 47:9; Heb. 11: 13). **56.** Rather, "This is peculiarly mine (*lit., to me*), *that* I keep Thy precepts" [HENGSTENBERG and MAURER].

57-60. Sincere desires for God's favor, penitence, and activity in a new obedience, truly evince the sincerity of those who profess to find God a portion (Num. 18:20; Ps. 16:5; Lam. 3:24). **58. favour**— Hebrew, "face" (Ps. 45:12). **59.** So the prodigal son, when reduced to straits of misery (Luke 15:17, 18). **61, 62.** This the more, if opposition of enemies, or love of ease is overcome in thus honoring God's law. **have robbed me**—better, surrounded me, either as forcible constraints like fetters, or as the cords of their nets. HENGSTENBERG translates, "snares." **62. At midnight**—HENGSTENBERG supposes a reference to the time when the Lord went forth to slay the Egyptian first-born (Exod. 11:4; 12: 29; cf. Job 34:20). But it rather refers to the Psalmist's own praises and prayers in the night-time. Cf. Paul and Silas (Acts 16:25; cf. Ps. 63:6). **63.** The communion of the saints. Delight in their company is an evidence of belonging to them (Ps. 16:3; Amos 3:3; Mal. 3:16). **64.** While opposed by the wicked, and opposing them, the pious delight in those who fear God, but, after all, rely for favor and guidance not on merit, but mercy.

65-67. The reliance on promises (vs. 49) is strengthened by experience of past dealings according with promises, and a prayer for guidance, encouraged by sanctified affliction. **66. Teach me good judgment and knowledge**—viz., in Thy word (so as to fathom its deep spirituality); for the corresponding expression (vss. 12, 64, 68), is, "Teach me Thy statutes." **67.** Referred by HENGSTENBERG to the chastening effect produced on the Jews' minds by the captivity (Jer. 31:18, 19). The truth is a general one (Job 5:6; John 15:2; Heb. 12:11). **68.** Cf. as to the Lord Jesus (Acts 10:38). **69, 70.** The crafty malice of the wicked, in slandering him, so far from turning him away, but binds him closer to God's Word, which they are too stupid in sin to appreciate. HENGSTENBERG refers the "lie" (vs. 69) to such slanders against the Jews during the captivity, as that in Ezra 4, of sedition. **fat as grease**—spiritually insensible (Ps. 17:10; 73:7; Isa. 6:10). **71, 72.** So also affliction of any kind acts as a wholesome discipline in leading the pious more highly to value the truth and promises of God.

73. As God made, so He can best control, us. So as to Israel, he owed to God his whole internal and external existence (Deut. 32:6). **74.** So when He has led us to rely on His truth, He will "make us to the praise of His grace" by others. "Those who fear Thee will be glad at my prosperity, as they consider my cause their cause" (Ps. 34:2; 142:7). **75-78. in faithfulness**—i.e., without in the least violating Thy faithfulness; because my sins deserved and needed fatherly chastisement. Enduring chastisement with a filial temper (Heb. 12:6-11), God's promises of mercy (Rom. 8:28) will be fulfilled, and He will give comfort in sorrow (Lam. 3:22; II Cor. 1:3, 4). **77. Let thy tender mercies come unto me**—As I am not able to come unto them. Those who fear Thee will be glad at my prosperity, as they consider my cause their cause" (Ps. 34:2; 142:7). **75-78. in faithfulness**—i.e., without in the least violating Thy faithfulness; because my sins deserved and needed fatherly chastisement. Enduring chastisement with a filial temper (Heb. 12:6-11), God's promises of mercy (Rom. 8:28) will be fulfilled, and He will give comfort in sorrow (Lam. 3:22; II Cor. 1:3, 4). **77. Let thy tender mercies come unto me**—As I am not able to come unto them. The wicked will be confounded. **78. but I will meditate in thy precepts**—and so shall not be "ashamed," i.e., put to shame (vs. 80). **79, 80.** Those who may have thought his afflictions an evidence of God's rejection will then be led to return to Him; as the friends of Job did on his restoration, having been previously led through his afflictions to doubt the reality of his religion. **Let my . . . be sound**—i.e., perfect, sincere. **ashamed**—disappointed in my hope of salvation.

81-83. In sorrow the pious heart yearns for the comforts of God's promises (Ps. 73:26; 84:2). **82. Mine eyes fail for thy word**—i.e., with yearning desire for Thy word. When the eyes fail, yet faith must not. **83. bottle in the smoke**—as a skin bottle dried and shriveled up in smoke, so is he withered by sorrow. Wine bottles of skin used to be hung up in smoke to dry them, before the wine was put in them [MAURER]. **84-87.** The shortness of my life requires that the relief afforded to me from mine enemies should be speedy. **85. pits**—plots for my destruction. **which**—rather, "who," i.e., "the proud"; "pits" is not the antecedent. **87. consumed me upon earth**—HENGSTENBERG translates, "in the land"; understanding "me" of the *nation* Israel, of which but a small remnant have been left. But *English Version* is simpler; either, "They have consumed me so as to leave almost nothing of me on earth"; or, "They have almost destroyed and prostrated me on the earth" [MAURER]. **87. I forsook not**—Whatever else I am forsaken of, I forsake not Thy precepts, and so am not mistaken of Thee (Ps. 39:5, 13; II Cor. 4:8, 9), and the injuries and insults of the wicked increase the need for it. But, however they act regardless of God's law, the pious, adhering to its teaching, receive quickening grace, and are sustained steadfast.

89-91. In all changes God's Word remains firm (I Pet. 1:25). Like the heavens, it continually attests God's unfailing power and unchanging care (Ps. 89:2). **is settled in**—i.e., stands as firmly as the heaven in which it dwells, and whence it emanated. **90.** (Ps. 33:9.) **91. They**—the heaven (vs. 89) and the earth (vs. 90). HENGSTENBERG translates, "They stand *for* thy judgment," i.e., ready, as obedient

servants, to execute them. The usage of this Psalm favors this view. But see Jeremiah 33:25. **92-94.** Hence the pious are encouraged and inclined to seek a knowledge of it, and persevere amidst the efforts of those planning and *waiting* to destroy them. **92. my delights**—plural, not merely *delight,* but equal to all other delights. **93.** The bounds of created perfection may be defined, but those of God's law in its nature, application, and influence, are infinite. There is no human thing so perfect but that something is wanting to it; its limits are narrow, whereas God's law is of infinite breadth, reaching to all cases, perfectly meeting what each requires, and to all times (Ps. 19:3, 6, 7-11; Eccles. 3:11). It cannot be cramped within any definitions of man's dogmatical systems. Man never outgrows the Word. It does not shock the ignorant man with declared anticipations of discoveries which he had not yet made; while in it the man of science finds his newest discoveries by tacit anticipations provided for. **97.** This characteristic love for God's law (cf. Ps. 1:2) ensures increase. **98-100,** of knowledge, both of the matter of all useful, moral truth, and an experience of its application. **98. wiser than mine enemies**—with all their carnal cunning (Deut. 4:6, 8). **they are ever with me**—The *Hebrew* is, rather *singular,* "it is ever with me"; the commandments forming ONE *complete whole,* Thy law. **100. more than the ancients**—Antiquity is no help against stupidity, where it does not accord with God's word [LUTHER] (Job 32:7-9). The Bible is the key of all knowledge, the history of the world, past, present, and to come (Ps. 111:10). he who does the will of God shall know of the doctrine (John 7:17). **understanding**—is practical skill (Ps. 2:10; 32:8). **101-104.** Avoidance of sinful courses is both the effect and means of increasing in divine knowledge (cf. Ps. 19:10).

105. Not only does the Word of God inform us of His will, but, as a light on a path in darkness, it shows us how to follow the right and avoid the wrong way. The lamp of the Word is not the sun. He would blind our eyes in our present fallen state; but we may bless God for the light shining as in a dark place, to guide us until the Sun of Righteousness shall come, and we shall be made capable of seeing Him (II Peter 1:19; Rev. 22:4). The lamp is fed with the oil of the Spirit. The allusion is to the lamps and torches carried at night before an Eastern caravan. **106-108.** Such was the national covenant at Sinai and in the fields of Moab. **108. free-will offerings**—the spontaneous expressions of his gratitude, as contrasted with the *appointed* "offerings" of the temple (Hos. 14:2; Heb. 13:15). He determines to pursue this way, relying on God's quickening power (vs. 50) in affliction, and a gracious acceptance of his "spiritual sacrifices of prayer and praise" (Ps. 50:5; 14, 23). **109, 110.** In the midst of deadly perils (the phrase is drawn from the fact that what we carry in our hands may easily slip from them, Judg. 12:3; I Sam. 28:21; Job 13:14; cf. I Sam. 19:5), and exposed to crafty enemies, his safety and guidance is in the truth and promises of God. **111, 112.** These he joyfully takes as his perpetual heritage, to perform the duties and receive the comforts they teach, evermore.

113. vain thoughts—better, unstable persons, lit., "divided men," those of a *divided,* doubting mind (Jas. 1:8); "a double-minded man" [HENGSTENBERG], skeptics, or, skeptical notions as opposed to the certainty of God's word. **114. hiding-place**—(Cf. Ps. 27:5). **shield**—(Ps. 3:3; 7-10). **hope in thy word**—confidently rest on its teachings and promises. **115-117.** Hence he fears not wicked men, nor dreads disappointment, sustained by God in making His law the rule of life. **Depart from me**—Ye can do nothing with me; *for,* etc. (Ps. 6:8). **118-120.** But the disobedient and rebellious will be visited by God's wrath, which impresses the pious with wholesome fear and awe. **their deceit is falsehood**—i.e., all their cunning deceit, wherewith they seek to entrap the godly, *is in vain.* **120.** The "judgments" are those on the wicked (vss. 119). Joyful hope goes hand in hand with fear (Hab. 3:16-18).

121-126. On the grounds of his integrity, desire for God's word, and covenant relation to Him, the servant of God may plead for His protecting care against the wicked, gracious guidance to the knowledge of truth, and His effective vindication of the righteous and their cause, which is also His own. **Be surety**—Stand for me against my oppressors (Gen. 43:9; Isa. 38:14). **127, 128. Therefore** [i.e., In view of these benefits, or, Because of the glory of Thy law, so much praised in the previous parts of the Psalm] **I love . . .,** [and] **Therefore** (repeated)—All its precepts, on all subjects, are estimable for their purity, and lead one imbued with their spirit to hate all evil (Ps. 19:10). The Word of God admits of no eclecticism; its least title is perfect (Ps. 12:6; Matt. 5:17-19).

129. wonderful—lit., "wonders," i.e., of moral excellence. **130. The entrance**—lit., "opening"; God's words, as an open door, let in light, or knowledge. Rather, as HENGSTENBERG explains it, *"The opening up,"* or, *"explanation of thy word."* To the natural man the doors of God's Word are shut. Luke 24: 27, 31; Acts 17:3; Eph. 1:18, confirm this view," "opening (i.e., explaining) and alleging," etc. **unto the simple**—those needing or desiring it (cf. Ps. 19: 7). **131-135.** An ardent desire (cf. Ps. 56:1, 2) for spiritual enlightening, establishment in a right course, deliverance from the wicked, and evidence of God's favor is expressed. **I opened my mouth, and panted**—as a traveller in a hot desert pants for the cooling breeze (Ps. 63:1; 84:2). **Look . . . upon me**—opposed to hiding or averting the face (cf. Ps. 25:15; 86:6; 102:17). **as thou usest to do**—or, "as it is *right* in regard to those who love Thy name." Such have a *right* to the manifestations of God's grace, resting on the nature of God as faithful to His promise to such, not on their own merits. **Order my steps**—*Make firm,* so that there be no halting (Ps. 40:2). **any iniquity**—vs. 34 (favors HENGSTENBERG, "any iniquitous man," any "oppressor." But the parallel first clause in this (vs. 33) favors *English Version* (Ps. 19:13). His hope of deliverance from *external* oppression of man (vs. 34) is founded on his deliverance from the *internal* "dominion of iniquity," in answer to his prayer (vs. 33). **136.** Zealous himself to keep God's law, he is deeply afflicted when others violate it (cf. vs. 53). Lit., "Mine eyes come down (dissolved) like waterbrooks" (Lam. 3:48; Jer. 9:1). **because . . .**—(Cf. Ezek. 9:4; Jer. 13:17).

137-139. God's justice and faithfulness in His government aggravate the neglect of the wicked, and more excite the lively zeal of His people. **139.** (Ps. 69:9.) **140. very pure**—lit., "refined," shown pure by trial. **141.** The pious, however despised of men, are distinguished in God's sight by a regard for His law. **142-144.** The principles of God's government are permanent and reliable, and in the deepest distress His people find them a theme of delightful meditation and a source of reviving power (vss. 17, 116). **law is the truth**—It therefore cannot deceive as to its promises. **everlasting**—(Ps. 111:3), though to outward appearance seeming dead.

145-149. An intelligent devotion is led by divine promises and is directed to an increase of gracious affections, arising from a contemplation of revealed truth. **prevented**—lit., "came before," anticipated not only the *dawn,* but even the usual periods of *the night;* when the nightwatches, which might be expected to find me asleep, come, they find me awake (Ps. 63:6; 77:4; Lam. 2:19). Such is the earnestness of the desire and love for God's truth. **quicken me** —revive my heart according to those principles of justice, founded on Thine own nature, and revealed in Thy law, which specially set forth Thy mercy to the humble as well as justice to the wicked (cf. vs. 30). **150-152.** Though the wicked are *near* to injure, because *far* from God's law, He is *near* to help, and faithful to His word, which abides for ever.

153-155. Though the remembering of God's law is not meritorious, yet it evinces a filial temper and provides the pious with promises to plead, while the wicked in neglecting His law, reject God and despise His promises (cf. Ps. 9:13; 43:1; 69:18). **154. Plead . . .**—HENGSTENBERG translates, "Fight my fight." (See Ps. 35:1; 43:1; Micah 7:9.) **156.** (Cf. vs. 149.) **157.** (Cf. vss. 86, 87, 95.) **158.** (Cf. vs. 136.) **transgressors**—or, lit., "traitors," who are faithless to a righteous sovereign and side with His enemies (cf. Ps. 25:3, 8). **159.** (Cf. vss. 121-126; 153-155.) **quicken . . .**—(vs. 88.) This prayer occurs here for the ninth time, showing a deep sense of frailty. **160.** God has been ever faithful, and the principles of His government will ever continue worthy of confidence. **from the beginning**—i.e., "every word *from Genesis* (called so by the Jews from its first words, 'In the beginning') to the end of the Scriptures is true." HENGSTENBERG translates more literally, "The *sum* of thy words is truth." The sense is substantially the same. The whole body of revelation is truth. "Thy Word is nothing but truth" [LUTHER].

161-165. (Cf. vss. 46, 86.) **161. awe**—reverential, not slavish fear, which could not coexist with love (vs. 163; I John 4:8). Instead of fearing his persecutors, he fears God's Word alone (Luke 12:4, 5). The Jews inscribe in the first page of the great Bible (Gen. 28), "How dreadful is this place! This is none other but the house of God, and this is the gate of heaven!" **162.** (Cf. Matt. 13:44, 45.) Though persecuted by the mighty, the pious are not turned from revering God's authority to seek their favor, but rejoice in the possession of this "pearl of great price," as great victors in spoils. Hating falsehood and loving truth, often, every day, praising God for it, they find peace and freedom from temptation. **163. lying**—i.e., as in vs. 29, unfaithfulness to the covenant of God with His people; apostasy. **nothing shall offend them**—or, *cause them* to offend (cf. *Margin*). **166-168.** As they keep God's law from motives of love for it, and are free from slavish fear, the are ready to subject their lives to His inspection. **168. all my ways are before thee**—I wish to order my ways as before Thee, rather than in reference to man (Gen. 19:1; Ps. 73:23). All men's ways are under God's eye (Prov. 5:21); the godly alone realize the fact, and live accordingly.

169, 170. The prayer for *understanding* of the truth precedes that for *deliverance.* The fulfilment of the first is the basis of the fulfilment of the second (Ps. 90:11-17). On the terms "cry" and "supplication" (cf. Ps. 6:9; 17:1). **171, 172. shall utter**—or, *pour* out praise (cf. Ps. 19:2); shall cause Thy praises to stream forth as from a bubbling, overflowing fountain. **My tongue shall speak of thy word**—lit., "answer Thy Word," i.e., with praise, *respond to Thy word.* Every expression in which we praise

God and His Word is a response, or acknowledgment, corresponding to the perfections of Him whom we praise. **173, 174.** (Cf. vss. 77, 81, 92.) **I have chosen**—in preference to all other objects of delight. **175.** Save me that I may praise Thee. **thy judgments**—as in vss. 149, 156. **176.** Though a wanderer from God, the truly pious ever desires to be drawn back to Him; and, though for a time negligent of duty, he never forgets the commandments by which it is taught. **lost**—therefore utterly helpless as to recovering itself (Jer. 50:6; Luke 15:4). Not only the sinner before conversion, but the believer after conversion, is unable to recover himself; but the latter, after temporary wandering, knows to whom to look for restoration. These last two verses seem to sum up the petitions, confessions, and professions of the Psalm. The writer desires God's favor, that he may praise Him for His truth, confesses that he has erred, but, in the midst of all his wanderings and adversities, professes an abiding attachment to the revealed Word of God, the theme of such repeated eulogies, and the recognized source of such great and unnumbered blessings. Thus the Psalm, though more than usually didactic, is made the medium of both parts of devotion—prayer and praise.

PSALM 120

Vss. 1-7. This is the first of fifteen Psalms (120-134) entitled "A Song of Degrees" (121st—lit., A song *for* the degrees), or *ascents*. It seems most probable they were designed for the use of the people when *going up* (cf. I Kings 12:27, 28) to Jerusalem on the festival occasions (Deut. 16:16), three times a year. David appears as the author of four, Solomon of one (127), and the other ten are anonymous, probably composed after the captivity. In this Psalm the writer acknowledges God's mercy, prays for relief from a malicious foe, whose punishment he anticipates, and then repeats his complaint.

2, 3. Slander and deceit charged on his foes implies his innocence. **tongue**—as in Psalm 52:2, 4. **4. Sharp arrows of the mighty**—destructive inflictions. **coals of juniper**—which retain heat long. This verse may be read as a description of the wicked, but better as their punishment, in reply to the question of vs. 3. **5.** A residence in these remote lands pictures his miserable condition. **6, 7.** While those who surrounded him were maliciously hostile, he was disposed to peace. This Psalm may well begin such a series as this, as a contrast to the promised joys of God's worship.

PSALM 121

Vss. 1-8. God's guardian care of His people celebrated.

1. I will lift up mine eyes—expresses desire (cf. Ps. 25:1), mingled with expectation. The last clause, read as a question, is answered, **2,** by avowing God to be the helper, of whose ability His creative power is a pledge (Ps. 115:15), to which, **3, 4,** His sleepless vigilance is added. **to be moved**—(Cf. Ps. 38:16; 66:9). **5. upon thy right hand**—a protector's place (Ps. 109:31; 110:5). **6-8.** God keeps His people at all times and in all perils. **nor the moon by night**—poetically represents the dangers of the night, over which the moon presides (Gen. 1:16). **thy going out . . .**—all thy ways (Deut. 28:19; Ps. 104: 23). **evermore**—includes a future state.

PSALM 122

Vss. 1-9. This Psalm might well express the sacred joy of the pilgrims on entering the holy city, where praise, as the religious as well as civil metropolis, is celebrated, and for whose prosperity, as representing the Church, prayer is offered.

1, 2. Our feet shall stand—lit., "are standing." **gates**—(Cf. Ps. 9:14; 87:2). **3-5. compact together**—all parts united, as in David's time. **testimony**—If "unto" is supplied, this may denote the ark (Exod. 25:10-21); otherwise the *act of going* is denoted, called a **testimony** in allusion to the requisition (Deut. 16:16), with which it was a compliance. **there are set thrones**—or, *do sit, thrones* used for the occupants, David's sons (II Sam. 8:18). **6, 7. Let peace**, including prosperity, everywhere prevail. **8, 9.** In the welfare of the city, as its civil, and especially the religious relations, was involved that of Israel. **now**—as in Psalm 115:2. Let me say—**house of . . . God**—in wider sense, the Church, whose welfare would be promoted by the good of Jerusalem.

PSALM 123

Vss. 1-4. An earnest and expecting prayer for divine aid in distress.

1. (Cf. Ps. 121:1.) **thou that dwellest**—lit., "sittest as enthroned" (cf. Ps. 2:4; 113:4, 5). **2.** Deference, submission, and trust, are all expressed by the figure. In the East, servants in attending on their masters are almost wholly directed by *signs,* which require the closest observance of the hands of the latter. The servants of God should look (1) to His directing hand, to appoint them their work; (2) to His supplying hand (Ps. 104:28), to give them their portion in due season; (3) to His protecting hand, to right them when wronged; (4) to His correcting hand (Isa. 9:13; I Pet. 5:6; cf. Gen. 16:6); (5) to His rewarding hand. **3. contempt**—was that of the heathen, and, perhaps, Samaritans (Neh. 1:3; 2:19). **4. of those that are at ease**—self-complacently, disregarding God's law, and despising His people.

PSALM 124

Vss. 1-8. The writer, for the Church, praises God for past, and expresses trust for future, deliverance from foes.

1, 2. on our side—for us (Ps. 56:9). **now**—or, "oh! let Israel . . ." **rose . . . against . . .**—(Ps. 3:1; 56:11). **3. Then**—i.e., the time of our danger. **quick**—lit., "living" (Num. 16:32, 33), description of ferocity. **4. 5.** (Cf. Ps. 18:4, 16.) The epithet **proud** added to **waters** denotes insolent enemies. **6, 7.** The figure is changed to that of a rapacious wild beast (Ps. 3:7), and then of a fowler (Ps. 91:3), and complete escape is denoted by breaking the net. **8.** (Cf. Ps. 121:2.) **name**—in the usual sense (Ps. 5:11; 20:1). He thus places over against the great danger the omnipotent God, and drowns, as it were in an anthem, the wickedness of the whole world and of hell, just as a great fire consumes a little drop of water [LUTHER].

PSALM 125

Vss. 1-5. God honors the confidence of His people, by protection and deliverance, and leaves hypocrites to the doom of the wicked.

1, 2. Mount Zion—as an emblem of permanence,

and locality of Jerusalem as one of security, represent the firm and protected condition of God's people (cf. Ps. 46:5), supported not only by Providence, but by covenant promise. Even the mountains shall depart, and the hills be removed, but God's kindness shall not depart, nor His covenant of peace be removed (Isa. 54:10). **They that trust**—(vs. 1) are "His people," (vs. 2). **3.** Though God may leave them for a time under the rod, or power (Ps. 2:9), and oppression of the wicked for a time, as a chastisement, He will not suffer them to be tempted so as to fall into sin (I Cor. 10:13). The wicked shall only prove a correcting rod to them, not a destroying sword; even this rod shall not *remain* ("rest") on them, lest they be tempted to despair and apostasy (Ps. 73:13, 14). God may even try His people to the uttermost: when nothing is before our eyes but pure despair, then He delivers us and gives life in death, and makes us blessed in the curse (II Cor. 1:8, 9) [LUTHER]. **the lot**—the possession, lit., "Canaan," spiritually, the heavenly inheritance of holiness and bliss which is appointed to the righteous. Sin's dominion shall not *permanently* come between the believer and his inheritance. **4.** (Cf. Ps. 7:10; 84:11.) **5.** Those who turn aside (under temptation) permanently show that they are hypocrites, and their lot or portion shall be with the wicked (Ps. 28:3). **crooked ways**—(Cf. Deut. 9:16; Mal. 2:8, 9). **their**—is emphatic; the "crooked ways" proceed from *their own* hearts. The true Israel is here distinguished from the false. Scripture everywhere opposes the Jewish delusion that mere outward descent would save (Rom. 2:28, 29; 9:6, 7; Gal. 6:16). The byways of sin from the way of life.

PSALM 126

Vss. 1-6. To praise for God's favor to His people is added a prayer for its continued manifestation.

1-3. The joy of those returned from Babylon was ecstatic, and elicited the admiration even of the heathen, as illustrating God's great power and goodness. **turned again the captivity**—i.e., restored from it (Job 39:12; Ps. 14:7; Prov. 12:14). HENGSTENBERG translates: "When the Lord turned Himself to the turning of Zion" (see *Margin*), God returns to His people when they return to Him (Deut. 30:2, 3). **4.** All did not return at once; hence the prayer for repeated favors. **as the streams in the south**—or, the torrents in the desert south of Judea, dependent on rain (Josh. 15:9), reappearing after dry seasons (cf. Job 6:15; Psalm 68:9). The point of comparison is joy at the reappearing of what has been so painfully missed. **5, 6.** As in husbandry the sower may cast his seed in a dry and parched soil with desponding fears, so those shall reap abundant fruit who toil in tears with the prayer of faith. (Cf. the history, Ezra 6:16, 22). **He that goeth forth**—lit., better, "He goes—he comes, he comes," etc. The repetition implies there is no end of weeping here, as there shall be no end of joy hereafter (Isa. 35:10). **precious seed**—rather, seed to be drawn from the seed-box for sowing; lit., "seed-draught." Cf. on this Psalm, Jer. 31:9, etc.

PSALM 127

Vss. 1-5. The theme of this Psalm, *that human enterprises only succeed by the divine blessing,* was probably associated with the building of the temple by Solomon, its author. It may have been adopted in this view, as suited to this series especially, as appropriately expressing the sentiments of God's worshippers in relation to the erection of the second temple.

1, 2 suggest the view of the theme given. **so he giveth his beloved sleep**—i.e., His providential care gives sleep which no efforts of ours can otherwise procure, and this is a reason for trust as to other things (cf. Matt. 6:26-32). **3-5.** Posterity is often represented as a blessing from God (Gen. 30:2, 18; I Samuel 1:19, 20). Children are represented as the defenders (arrows) of their parents in war, and in litigation. **adversaries in the gate**—or place of public business (cf. Job. 5:4; Ps. 69:12).

PSALM 128

Vss. 1-6. The temporal blessings of true piety. The 8th chapter of Zechariah is a virtual commentary on this Psalm. Cf. vs. 3 with Zechariah 8:5; and vs. 2 with Leviticus 26:16; Deuteronomy 28:33; Zechariah 8:10; and vs. 6 with Zechariah 8:4.

1. (Cf. Ps. 1:1.) **2. For thou shalt eat**—i.e., It is a blessing to live on the fruits of one's own industry. **3. by the sides**—or, within (Ps. 48:2). **olive plants**—are peculiarly luxuriant (Ps. 52:8). **5.** In temporal blessings the pious do not forget the richer blessings of God's grace, which they shall ever enjoy. **6.** Long life crowns all other temporal favors. As Psalm 125:5, this Psalm closes with a prayer for peace, with prosperity for God's people.

PSALM 129

Vss. 1-8. The people of God, often delivered from enemies, are confident of His favor, by their overthrow in the future.

1, 2. may Israel now say—or, oh! let Israel say (Ps. 124:1). Israel's youth was the sojourn in Egypt (Jer. 2:2; Hos. 2:15). **prevailed**—lit., "been able," i.e., to accomplish their purpose against me (Ps. 13:4). **3, 4.** The *ploughing* is a figure of scourging, which most severe physical infliction aptly represents all kinds. **the cords**—i.e., which fasten the plough to the ox; and *cutting* denotes God's arresting the persecution. **5, 6.** The ill-rooted roof grass, which withers before it grows up and procures for those gathering it no harvest blessing (Ruth 2:4), sets forth the utter uselessness and the rejection of the wicked.

PSALM 130

Vss. 1-8. The penitent sinner's hope is in God's mercy only.

1, 2. depths—for great distress (Ps. 40:2; 69:3). **3. shouldest mark**—or, take strict account (Job 10:14; 14:16), implying a confession of the existence of sin. **who shall stand**—(Ps. 1:6). *Standing* is opposed to the guilty sinking down in fear and self-condemnation (Mal. 3:2; Rev. 6:15, 16). The question implies a negative, which is thus more strongly stated. **4.** Pardon produces filial fear and love. Judgment without the hope of pardon creates fear and dislike. The sense of forgiveness, so far from producing licentiousness, produces holiness (Jer. 33:9; Ezek. 16:62, 63; I Pet. 2:16). "There is forgiveness with thee, not that thou mayest be presumed upon, but feared." **5, 6. wait for the Lord**—in expectation (Ps. 27:14). **watch for . . .**—in earnestness and anxiety. **7, 8. Let Israel . . .**—i.e., All are invited to seek and share divine forgiveness. **from all his iniquities**—or, punishments of them (Ps. 40, 12, etc.).

PSALM 131

Vss. 1-3. This Psalm, while expressive of David's pious feelings on assuming the royal office, teaches the humble, submissive temper of a true child of God. **1. eyes lofty**—a sign of pride (Ps. 18:27). **exercise myself**—lit., "walk in," of "meddle with." **2. Surely . . .**—The form is that of an oath or strongest assertion. Submission is denoted by the figure of a weaned child. As the child weaned by his mother from the breast, so I still the motions of pride in me (Matt. 18:3, 4; Isa. 11:8; 28:9). Hebrew children were often not weaned till three years old. **soul** —may be taken for desire, which gives a more definite sense, though one included in the idea conveyed by the usual meaning, *myself*.

PSALM 132

Vss. 1-18. The writer, perhaps Solomon (cf. vss. 8, 9), after relating David's pious zeal for God's service, pleads for the fulfilment of the promise (II Sam. 7:16), which, providing for a perpetuation of David's kingdom, involved that of God's right worship and the establishment of the greater and spiritual kingdom of David's greater Son. Of Him and His kingdom both the temple and its worship, and the kings and kingdom of Judah, were types. The congruity of such a topic with the tenor of this series of Psalms is obvious. **1-5.** This vow is not elsewhere recorded. It expresses, in strong language, David's intense desire to see the establishment of God's worship as well as of His kingdom. **remember David**—lit., "remember for David," i.e., all his troubles and anxieties on the matter. **habitation**—lit., "dwellings," generally used to denote the sanctuary. **6.** These may be the "words of David" and his pious friends, who, at Ephratah, or Bethlehem (Gen. 48:7), where he once lived, may have heard of the ark, which he found for the first time **in the fields of the wood**—or, *Jair*, or *Kirjath-jearim* (City of woods) (I Sam. 7:1; II Sam. 6:3, 4), whence it was brought to Zion. **7.** The purpose of engaging in God's worship is avowed. **8, 9.** The solemn entry of the ark, symbolical of God's presence and power, with the attending priests, into the sanctuary, is proclaimed in the words used by Solomon (II Chron. 6:41). **10-12. For thy servant David's sake** [i.e., On account of the promise made to him] **turn . . . anointed**—Repulse not him who, as David's descendant, pleads the promise to perpetuate his royal line. After reciting the promise, substantially from II Sam. 7:12-16 (cf. Acts 2:30, etc.), an additional plea, **13,** is made on the ground of God's choice of Zion (here used for Jerusalem) as His dwelling, inasmuch as the prosperity of the kingdom was connected with that of the Church (Ps. 122:8, 9). **14-18.** That choice is expressed in God's words, *I will sit* or *dwell*, or sit enthroned The joy of the people springs from the blessings of His grace, conferred through the medium of the priesthood. **make the horn . . . to bud** —enlarge his power. **a lamp**—the figure of prosperity (Ps. 18:10, 28; 89:17). With the confounding of his enemies is united his prosperity and the unceasing splendor of his crown.

PSALM 133

Vss. 1-3. The blessings of fraternal unity. **1, 2.** As the fragrant oil is refreshing, so this affords delight. The holy anointing oil for the high priest was olive oil mixed with four of the best spices (Exod. 30:22, 25, 30). Its rich profusion typified the abundance of the Spirit's graces. As the copious dew, such as fell on Hermon, falls in fertilizing power on the mountains of Zion, so this unity is fruitful in good works. **3. there**—i.e., in Zion, the Church; the material Zion, blessed with enriching dews, suggests this allusion the source of the influence enjoyed by the spiritual Zion. **commanded the blessing**—(Cf. Ps. 68:28).

PSALM 134

Vss. 1-3. **1, 2.** The pilgrim bands arriving at the sanctuary call on the priests, who **stand in the house of the Lord** at the time of the evening sacrifice, to unite in praising God in their name and that of the people, using appropriate gestures, to which the priests reply, pronouncing the Mosaic blessing which they alone could pronounce. A fit epilogue to the whole pilgrim-book, Psalms 120-134. **1. by night** —the *evening* service (Ps. 141:2), as opposed to *morning* (Ps. 92:2). **2. Lift up your hands**—(Cf. Ps. 28:2). **3.** After the manner directed (Num. 6:23). **out of Zion**—the Church, as His residence, and thus seat of blessings. Thus close the songs of degrees.

PSALM 135

Vss. 1-21. A Psalm of praise, in which God's relations to His Church, His power in the natural world, and in delivering His people, are contrasted with the vanity of idols and idol worship. **1-3.** In the general call for praise, the priests, **that stand in the house of the Lord,** are specially mentioned. **4-7.** God's choice of Israel is the first reason assigned for rendering praise; the next, His manifested greatness in creation and providence. **heaven, and . . . seas, and all . . . ends of the earth**—denote universality. **8, 9.** The last plague is cited to illustrate His "tokens and wonders." **10-12.** The conquest of Canaan was by God's power, not that of the people. **heritage**—or, possession. **13. name . . . memorial**—Each denote that by which God is made known. **14. will judge**—do justice (Ps. 72:2). **repent himself**—change His dealings (Ps. 90:13). **15-18.** (Cf. Ps. 115:4-8.) **are like unto them**—or, shall be like, etc. Idolaters become spiritually stupid and perish with their idols (Isa. 1:31). **19-21**—(Cf. Ps. 115:9-11.) There we have "trust" for "bless" here. **out of Zion**—(Cf. Ps. 110:2; 134:3.) From the Church, as a center, His praise is diffused throughout the earth.

PSALM 136

Vss. 1-26. The theme is the same as that of Psalm 135. God should be praised for His works of creation and providence, His deliverance and care of His people, and judgments on their enemies, and His goodness to all. The chorus to every verse is in terms of that of Psalm 106:1; 118:1-4, and was perhaps used as the *Amen* by the people, in worship (cf. I Chron. 16:36; Ps. 105:45).

1-3. The divine titles denote supremacy. **4. alone** —excluding all help. **5, 6. by** [or, "in"] **wisdom**— (Ps. 104:24). **made**—lit., "maker of." **above** [or, higher than] **the waters**—(Ps. 24:2). **12.** Cf. similar expressions (Exod. 3:20; Deut. 4:34, etc.). **15. overthrew**—lit., "shook off," as in Exodus 14:27, as a contemptuous rejection of a reptile. **23. remembered us**—or, for us (Ps. 132:1). **our low estate**— i.e., captivity. **24. And hath redeemed** [or, lit., "snatched"] **us**—alluding to the sudden deliverance effected by the overthrow of Babylon. **25.** To the special favors to His people is added the record of God's goodness to all His creatures (cf. Matt. 6:30). **26. God of heaven**—occurs but once (Jonah 1:9) before the captivity. It is used by the later writers as specially distinguishing God from idols.

PSALM 137

Vss. 1-9. This Psalm records the mourning of the captive Israelites, and a prayer and prediction respecting the destruction of their enemies. **1. rivers of Babylon**—the name of the city used for the whole country. **remembered Zion**—or, Jerusalem, as in Psalm 132:13. **2. upon the willows** —which may have grown there then, if not now; as the palm, which was once common, is now rare in Palestine. **3, 4.** Whether the request was in curiosity or derision, the answer intimates that a compliance was incongruous with their mournful feelings (Prov. 25:20). **5, 6.** For joyful songs would imply forgetfulness of their desolated homes and fallen Church. The solemn imprecations on the **hand** and **tongue,** if thus forgetful, relate to the cunning or skill in playing, and the power of singing. **7-9. Remember . . . the children of Edom**—(Cf. Ps. 132:1), i.e., to punish. **the day of Jerusalem**—its downfall (Lam. 4:21, 22; Obad. 11-13). **daughter of Babylon**—the people (Ps. 9:13). Their destruction had been abundantly foretold (Isa. 13:14; Jer. 51:23). For the terribleness of that destruction, God's righteous judgment, and not the passions of the chafed Israelites, was responsible.

PSALM 138

Vss. 1-8. David thanks God for His benefits, and anticipating a wider extension of God's glory by His means, assures himself of His continued presence and faithfulness. **1.** (Cf. Ps. 9:1.) **before the gods**—whether *angels* (Ps. 8:5); or *princes* (Exod. 21:6, Ps. 82:6; or *idols* (Ps. 97:7); denotes a readiness to worship the true God alone, and a contempt of all other objects of worship. **2.** (Cf. Ps. 5:7.) **thy word above all thy name**—i.e.,God's promise (II Sam. 7), sustained by His mercy and truth, exceeded all other manifestations of Himself as subject of praise. **3-5.** That promise, as an answer to his prayers in distress, revived and strengthened his faith; and, as the basis of other revelations of the Messiah, it will be the occasion of praise by all who hear and receive it (Ps. 68:29, 31; Isa. 4:3). **for great [is] the glory**— or, when the glory shall be great, in God's fulfilling His purposes of redemption. **6, 7.** On this general principle of God's government (Isa. 2:11; 57:15; 66: 2), he relies for God's favor in saving him, and overthrowing his enemies. **knoweth afar off**—their ways and deserts (Ps. 1:6). **8.** God will fulfil His promise.

PSALM 139

Vss. 1-24. After presenting the sublime doctrines of God's omnipresence and omniscience, the Psalmist appeals to Him, avowing his innocence, his abhorrence of the wicked, and his ready submission to the closest scrutiny. Admonition to the wicked and comfort to the pious are alike implied inferences from these doctrines.

PSALM 140

Vss. 1-13. The style of this Psalm resembles those of David in the former part of the book, presenting the usual complaint, prayer, and confident hope of relief. **1. evil man**—Which of David's enemies is meant is not important. **2-5.** This character of the wicked, and the devices planned against the pious, correspond to Psalm 10:7; 31:13; 58:4, etc. **sharpened . . . like a serpent**—not like a serpent does, but they are thus like a serpent in cunning and venom. **snare** [and] **net**—for threatening dangers (cf. Ps. 38:12; 57: 6). **6.** (Cf. Ps. 5:1-12; 16:2). **7. day of battle**—lit., "of armor," i.e., when using it. **8.** (Cf. Ps. 37:12; 66:7.) **lest they exalt themselves**—or, they will be exalted if permitted to prosper. **9.** Contrasts his head covered by God (vs. 7) with theirs, or (as head may be used for persons) with them, covered with the results of their wicked deeds (Ps. 7:16). **10.** (Cf. Ps. 11:6; 120:4.) **cast into the fire; into deep pits**—figures for utter destruction. **11. an evil speaker**—or, slanderer will not be tolerated (Ps. 101: 7). The last clause may be translated: "an evil (man) He (God) shall hunt," etc. **12.** (Cf. Ps. 9:4.) **13.** After all changes, the righteous shall have cause for praise. Such **shall dwell**—sit securely, under God's protection (Ps. 21:6; 41:12).

PSALM 141

Vss. 1-10. This Psalm evinces its authorship as the preceding, by its structure and the character of its contents. It is a prayer for deliverance from sins to which affliction tempted him, and from the enemies who caused it.

PSALM 142

Vss. 1-7. *Maschil*—(cf. Ps. 32, title). *When he was in the cave,* either of Adullam (I Sam. 22:1), or En-gedi (I Sam. 24:3). This does not mean that the Psalm was composed *in the cave,* but that the precarious mode of life, of which his refuge in caves was a striking illustration, occasioned the complaint, which constitutes the first part of the Psalm and furnishes the reason for the prayer with which it concludes, and which, as the prominent characteristic, gives its name. **1. with my voice**—audibly, because earnestly. **2.** (Cf. Ps. 62:8.) **complaint**—or, a sad musing. **3. thou knewest . . . path**—The appeal is indicative of conscious innocence; knowest it to be right, and that my affliction is owing to the snares of enemies, and is not deserved (cf. Ps. 42:4; 61:2). **4.** Utter desolation is meant. **right hand**—the place of a protector (Ps. 110:5). **cared for**—lit., "sought after," to do good. **5.** (Cf. Ps. 31:14; 62:7.) **6.** (Cf. Ps. 17:1.) **7.** (Cf. Ps. 25:17.) **that I may praise**—lit., "for praising," or that Thy name may be praised, i.e., by the righteous, who shall surround me with sympathizing joy (Ps. 35:27).

PSALM 143

Vss. 1-12. In structure and style, like the preceding (Psalms 104-142), this Psalm is clearly evinced to be David's. It is a prayer for pardon, and for relief from enemies; afflictions, as usual, producing confession and penitence. **1. in thy faithfulnes . . . and . . . righteousness**—or, God's regard to the claims which He has permitted His people to make in His covenant. **2. enter . . . judgment**—deal not in strict justice. **shall no . . . justified**—or, is no man justified, or innocent (Job 14: 3; Rom. 3:20). **3, 4.** The exciting reason for his prayer—his afflictions—led to confession as just made: he now makes the complaint. **as those that have been long dead**—deprived of life's comforts (cf. Ps. 40:15; 88:3-6). **5, 6.** The distress is aggravated by the contrast of former comfort (Ps. 22: 3-5), for whose return he longs. **a thirsty land**— which needs rain, as did his spirit God's gracious visits (Ps. 28:1; 89:17). **7. spirit faileth**—is exhausted. **8.** (Cf. Ps. 25:1-4; 59;16). **the way . . . walk**—i.e., the way of safety and righteousness (Ps. 142:3-6). **9.** (Cf. Ps. 31:15-20.) **10.** (Cf. Ps. 5:8; 27:11.) **land of uprightness**—lit., "an even land" (Ps. 26:12). **11.** (Cf. Ps. 23:3; 119:156). **12.** God's mercy to His people is often wrath to His and their enemies (cf. Ps. 31:17). **thy servant**—as chosen to be such, entitled to divine regard.

PSALM 144

Vss. 1-15. David's praise of God as his all-sufficient help is enhanced by a recognition of the intrinsic worthlessness of man. Confidently imploring God's interposition against his enemies, he breaks forth into praise and joyful anticipations of the prosperity of his kingdom, when freed from vain and wicked men.

PSALM 145

Vss. 1-21. A Psalm of praise to God for His mighty, righteous, and gracious government of all men, and of His humble and suffering people in particular. **1, 2.** (Cf. Ps. 30:1.) **bless thy name**—celebrate Thy perfections (Ps. 5:11). God is addressed as king, alluding to His government of men. **3.** (Cf. Ps. 18:3; 48:1.) **greatness**—as displayed in His works. **4. shall declare**—lit., "they shall declare," i.e., all generations. **5. I will speak**—or, muse (Ps. 77:12; 119:15). **thy wondrous works**—or, words of thy wonders, i.e., which described them (Ps. 105: 27, *Margin*. **6. terrible acts**—which produce dread or fear. **7. memory**—(Ps. 6:5), remembrance, or what causes to be remembered. **righteousness**—as in Psalm 143:1, goodness according to covenant engagement. **8, 9.** (Cf. 103:8; 111:4.) **over all . . .**— rests on all His works. **10. bless**—as in vs. 1, to praise with reverence, more than merely to praise. **11, 12.** The declaration of God's glory is for the extension of His knowledge and perfections in the world. **13.** (Cf. Dan. 4:3, 34.) **14.** (Cf. Ps. 37:17; 54:4.) **15, 16. eyes of . . . thee**—or, look with expecting faith (Ps. 104:27, 28). **17. holy . . . works** —lit., "merciful" or "kind, goodness" (Ps. 144:2) is the corresponding noun. **righteous**—in a similar relation of meaning to "righteousness" (vs. 7). **18,**

19. (Cf. Ps. 34:7, 10.) **20.** Those who fear Him (vs. 19) are those who are here said to love Him. **21.** (Cf. Ps. 23:21.) **all flesh**—(Ps. 65:2). The Psalm ends, as it began, with ascriptions of praise, in which the pious will ever delight to join.

PSALM 146

Vss. 1-10. An exhortation to praise God, who, by the gracious and faithful exercise of His power in goodness to the needy, is alone worthy of implicit trust.

PSALM 147

Vss. 1-20. This and the remaining Psalms have been represented as specially designed to celebrate the rebuilding of Jerusalem (cf. Neh. 6:16; 12:27). They all open and close with the stirring call for praise. This one specially declares God's providential care towards all creatures, and particularly His people. **1.** (Cf. Ps. 92:1; 135:3.) **2.** (Cf. Ps. 107:3; Isa. 11:12.) **3.** Though applicable to the captive Israelites, this is a general and precious truth. **wounds**— (Cf. *Margin*). **4, 5.** God's power in nature (Isa. 40: 26-28, and often) is presented as a pledge of His power to help His people. **telleth . . . stars**—what no man can do (Gen. 15:5). **6.** That power is put forth for the good of the meek and suffering pious, and confusion of the wicked (Ps. 146:8, 9). **7-9.** His providence supplies bountifully the wild animals in their mountain homes. **Sing . . . Lord**—lit., "Answer the Lord," i.e., in grateful praise to His goodness, thus declared in His acts. **10, 11.** The advantages afforded, as in war by the strength of the horse or the agility of man, do not incline God to favor any; but those who fear and, of course, trust Him, will obtain His approbation and aid. **12-14. strengthened . . . gates**—or, means of defense against invaders, **maketh . . . borders**—or, territories (Gen. 23:17; Isa. 54:12). **filleth thee . . .**—(Cf. *Margin*). **15-18.** God's Word, as a swift messenger, executes His purpose, for with Him to command is to perform (Gen. 1:3; Ps. 33:9), and He brings about the wonders of providence as easily as men cast crumbs. **morsels**—used as to food (Gen. 18:5), perhaps here denotes hail. **19, 20.** This mighty ruler and benefactor of heaven and earth is such especially to His chosen people, to whom alone (Deut. 4:32-34) He has made known His will, while others have been left in darkness. Therefore unite in the great hallelujah.

PSALM 148

Vss. 1-14. The scope of this Psalm is the same as that of the preceding. **1. heavens** [and] **heights**—are synonymous. **2. hosts**—(cf. Ps. 103:21). **4. heavens of heavens**—the very highest. **waters**—clouds, resting above the visible heavens (cf. Gen. 1:7). **5. praise the name**— as representing His perfections. **he commanded**— *He* is emphatic, ascribing creation to God alone. **6.** The perpetuity of the frame of nature is, of course, subject to Him who formed it. **a decree . . . pass**— His ordinances respecting them shall not change (Jer. 36:31), or perish (Job 34:20; Ps. 37:36). **7-10.** The call on the earth, as opposed to heaven, includes *seas* or *depths,* whose inhabitants the dragon, as one of the largest (cf. on leviathan, Ps. 104:26), is selected to represent. The most destructive and ungovernable agents of inanimate nature are introduced **fulfilling his word**—or, law, may be understood of each. Next the most distinguished productions of the vegetable world. **fruitful trees**—or, trees of fruit, as opposed to forest trees. Wild and domestic, large and small animals are comprehended. **11, 12.** Next all rational beings, from the highest in rank to little children. **princes**—or, military leaders. **13. Let them**—all mentioned. **excellent**—or, exalted (Isa. 12:4). **his glory**—majesty (Ps. 45:3). **above the earth and heaven**—*Their united* splendors fail to match His. **14. exalteth the horn** —established power (Ps. 75:5, 6). **praise of** [or lit., "for"] **his saints**—i.e., occasions for them to praise Him. They are further described as His people, and near Him, sustaining by covenanted care a peculiarly intimate relation.

PSALM 149

Vss. 1-9. This Psalm sustains a close connection with the foregoing. The chosen people are exhorted to praise God, in view of past favors, and also future victories over enemies, of which they are impliedly assured. **1.** (Cf. Ps. 96:1.) **2.** God had signalized His relation as a sovereign, in restoring them to their land. **3. in the dance**—(Ps. 30:11). The dance is connected with other terms, expressive of the great joy of the occasion. The word may be rendered *lute*, to which the other instruments are joined. **sing praises**—or, sing and play. **4. taketh pleasure** —lit., "accepts," alluding to acceptance of propitiatory offerings (cf. Ps. 7:18). **beautify . . .**—adorn the humble with faith, hope, joy, and peace. **5. in**

glory—the honorable condition to which they are raised. **upon their beds**—once a place of mourning (Ps. 6:6). **6. high (praise)**—or, deeds. They shall go forth as religious warriors, as once religious laborers (Neh. 4:17). **7.** The destruction of the incorrigibly wicked attends the propagation of God's truth, so that the military successes of the Jews, after the captivity, typified the triumphs of the Gospel. **9. the judgment written**—either in God's decrees, or perhaps as in Deuteronomy 32:41-43. **this honour** —i.e., to be thus employed, will be an honorable service, to be assigned **his saints**—or, godly ones (Ps. 16:3).

PSALM 150

Vss. 1-6. This is a suitable doxology for the whole book, reciting the "place, theme, mode, and extent of God's high praise." **1. in his sanctuary**—on earth. **firmament . . .**—which illustrates His power. **2. mighty acts**—(Ps. 145:4). **excellent greatness**—or, abundance of greatness. **3, 4. trumpet**—used to call religious assemblies; the **organs**—or pipe, a wind instrument, and the others were used in worship. **5. cymbals**—suited to loud praise (Neh. 12:27). **6.** LIVING VOICES SHALL TAKE UP THE FAILING SOUNDS OF DEAD INSTRUMENTS, AND AS THEY CEASE ON EARTH, THOSE OF INTELLIGENT RANSOMED SPIRITS AND HOLY ANGELS, AS WITH THE SOUND OF MIGHTY THUNDERS, WILL PROLONG ETERNALLY THE PRAISE, SAYING: "ALLELUIA! SALVATION, AND GLORY, AND HONOR, AND POWER, UNTO THE LORD OUR GOD"; ALLELUIA! FOR THE LORD GOD OMNIPOTENT REIGNETH." AMEN!

THE BOOK OF

PROVERBS

INTRODUCTION

I. THE NATURE AND USE OF PROVERBS.—A proverb is a pithy sentence, concisely expressing some well-established truth susceptible of various illustrations and applications. The word is of Latin derivation, literally meaning *for a word, speech, or discourse;* i.e., one expression for many. The *Hebrew* word for proverb (*mashal*) means a "comparison." Many suppose it was used, because the form or matter of the proverb, or both, involved the idea of *comparison.* Most of the proverbs are in couplets or triplets, or some modifications of them, the members of which correspond in structure and length, as if arranged to be compared one with another. They illustrate the varieties of parallelism, a distinguishing feature of *Hebrew* poetry. Cf. *Introduction* to Poetical Books. Many also clearly involve the idea of comparison in the sentiments expressed (cf. ch. 12:1-10; 25:10-15; 26:1-9). Sometimes, however, the designed omission of one member of the comparison, exercising the reader's sagacity or study for its supply, presents the proverb as a "riddle" or "dark saying" (cf. ch. 30:15-33; 1:6; Ps. 49:4). The sententious form of expression, which thus became a marked feature of the proverbial style, was also adopted for continuous discourse, even when not always preserving traces of comparison, either in form or matter (cf. chs. 1-9). In Ezekiel 17:1, 24:3, we find the same word properly translated "parable," to designate an illustrative discourse. Then the *Greek* translators have used a word, *parabola* (parable), which the gospel writers (except John) employ for our Lord's discourses of the same character, and which also seems to involve the idea of comparison, though that may not be its primary meaning. It might seem, therefore, that the proverbial and parabolic styles of writing were originally and essentially the same. The proverb is a "concentrated parable, and the parable an extension of the proverb by a full illustration." The proverb is thus the moral or theme of a parable, which sometimes precedes it, as in Matt. 19:30 (cf. ch. 20:1); or succeeds it, as in Matt. 22:1-16; Luke 15:1-10. The style being poetical, and adapted to the expression of a high order of poetical sentiment, such as prophecy, we find the same term used to designate such compositions (cf. Num. 23:7; Micah 2:4; Hab. 2:6).

Though the *Hebrews* used the same term for proverb and parable, the *Greek* employs two, though the sacred writers have not always appeared to recognize a distinction. The term for proverb is, *paroimia,* which the *Greek* translators employ for the title of this book, evidently with special reference to the later definition of a proverb, as a trite, sententious form of speech, which appears to be the best meaning of the term. John uses the same term to designate our Saviour's instructions, in view of their characteristic obscurity (cf. ch. 16:25–29, *Greek*), and even for his illustrative discourses (ch. 10:6), whose sense was not at once obvious to all his hearers. This form of instruction was well adapted to aid the learner. The parallel structure of sentences, the repetition, contrast, or comparison of thought, were all calculated to facilitate the efforts of memory; and precepts of practical wisdom which, extended into logical discourses, might have failed to make abiding impressions by reason of their length or complicated character, were thus compressed into pithy, and, for the most part, very plain statements. Such a mode of instruction has distinguished the written or traditional literature of all nations, and was, and still is, peculiarly current in the East.

In this book, however, we are supplied with a proverbial wisdom commended by the seal of divine inspiration. God has condescended to become our teacher on the practical affairs belonging to all the relations of life. He has adapted His instruction to the plain and unlettered, and presented, in this striking and impressive method, the great principles of duty to Him and to our fellow men. To the prime motive of all right conduct, the fear of God, are added all lawful and subordinate incentives, such as honor, interest, love, fear, and natural affection. Besides the terror excited by an apprehension of God's justly provoked judgments, we are warned against evil-doing by the exhibition of the inevitable temporal results of impiety, injustice, profligacy, idleness, laziness, indolence, drunkenness, and debauchery. To the rewards of true piety which follow in eternity, are promised the peace, security, love, and approbation of the good, and the comforts of a clear conscience, which render this life truly happy.

II. INSPIRATION AND AUTHORSHIP.—With no important exception, Jewish and Christian writers have received this book as the inspired production of Solomon. It is the first book of the Bible prefaced by the name of the author. The New Testament abounds with citations from the Proverbs. Its intrinsic excellence commends it to us as the production of a higher authority than the apocryphal writings, such as Wisdom or Ecclesiasticus. Solomon lived 500 years before the "seven wise men" of Greece, and 700 before the age of Socrates, Plato, and Aristotle. It is thus very evident, whatever theory of his sources of knowledge be adopted, that he did not draw upon any heathen repositories with which we are acquainted. It is far more probable, that by the various migrations, captivities, and dispersions of the Jews, heathen philosophers drew from this inspired fountain many of those streams which continue to refresh mankind amid the otherwise barren and parched deserts of profane literature.

As, however, the Psalms are ascribed to David, because he was the leading author, so the ascription of this book to Solomon is entirely consistent with the titles of chs. 30 and 31, which assign those chapters to Agur and Lemuel respectively. Of these persons we know nothing. This is not the place for discussing the various speculations respecting them. By a slight change of reading some propose to translate ch. 30:1: "The words of Agur, the son of her who was obeyed (i.e., the queen of) Massa"; and ch. 31:1: "The words of Lemuel, king of Massa"; but to this the earliest versions are contradictory, and nothing other than the strongest exegetical necessity ought to be allowed to justify a departure from a well-established reading and version when nothing useful to our knowledge is gained. It is better to confess ignorance than indulge in useless conjectures.

It is probable that out of the "three thousand proverbs" (I Kings 4:32) which Solomon spoke, he selected and edited chs. 1–24 during his life. Chs. 25–29 were also of his production, and copied out in the days of Hezekiah, by his "men," perhaps the prophets Isaiah, Hosea, and Micah. Such a work was evidently in the spirit of this pious monarch, who set his heart so fully on a reformation of God's worship. Learned men have endeavored to establish the theory that Solomon himself was only a collector; or that the other parts of the book, as these chapters, were also selections by later hands; but the reasons adduced to maintain these views have never appeared so satisfactory as to change the usual opinions on the subject, which have the sanction of the most ancient and reliable authorities.

III. DIVISIONS OF THE BOOK.—Such a work is, of course, not susceptible of any logical analysis. There are, however, some well-defined marks of division, so that very generally the book is divided into five or six parts.

1. The first contains nine chapters, in which are discussed and enforced by illustration, admonition, and encouragement the principles and blessings of wisdom, and the pernicious schemes and practices of sinful persons. These chapters are introductory. With few specimens of the proper proverb, they are distinguished by its conciseness and terseness. The sentences follow very strictly the form of parallelism, and generally of the synonymous species, only forty of the synthetic and four (ch. 3:32–35) of the antithetic appearing. The style is ornate, the figures bolder and fuller, and the illustrations more striking and extended.

2. The antithetic and synthetic parallelism to the exclusion of the synonymous distinguish chs. 10–22:16, and the verses are entirely unconnected, each containing a complete sense in itself.

3. Chs. 22:16–24 present a series of admonitions as if addressed to a pupil, and generally each topic occupies two or more verses.

4. Chs. 25–29 are entitled to be regarded as a distinct portion, for the reason given above as to its origin. The style is very much mixed; of the peculiarities, cf. parts 2 and 3.

5. Ch. 30 is peculiar not only for its authorship, but as a specimen of the kind of proverb which has been described as "dark sayings" or "riddles."

6. To a few pregnant but concise admonitions, suitable for a king, is added a most inimitable portraiture of female character. In both parts 5 and 6 the distinctive peculiarity of the original proverbial style gives place to the modifications already mentioned as marking a later composition, though both retain the concise and nervous method of stating truth, equally valuable for its deep impression and permanent retention by the memory.

CHAPTER 1

Vss. 1-33. After the title the writer defines the design and nature of the instructions of the book. He paternally invites attention to those instructions and warns his readers against the enticements of the wicked. In a beautiful personification, wisdom is then introduced in a most solemn and impressive manner, publicly inviting men to receive its teachings, warning those who reject, and encouraging those who accept, the proffered instructions. **1-4.** (Cf. *Introduction*, I.) **To know . . . instruction**—lit., "for knowing," i.e., such is the design of these writings. **wisdom**—or the use of the best means for the best ends, is generally employed in this book for true piety. **instruction**—discipline, by which men are trained. **to perceive** [lit., "for perceiving," the design (as above)] . . . **understanding** —i.e., words which enable one to discern good and evil. **To receive . . . of wisdom**—For receiving that discipline which *discretion* imparts. The *Hebrew* for wisdom differs from that of vs. 2, and denotes rather discreet counsel. Cf. the opposite traits of the fool (ch. 16:22). **justice . . . equity**—all the attributes of one upright in all his relations to God and man. **simple**—one easily led to good or evil; so the parallel. **young man**—one inexperienced. **subtilty** —or prudence (ch. 3:21; 5:21). **discretion**—lit., "device," both qualities, either good or bad, according to their use. Here good, as they imply wariness by which to escape evil and find good. **5, 6.** Such writings the wise, who pursue right ends by right means, will value. **learning**—not the act, but matter of it. **wise counsels**—or the art and principles of governing. **To understand**—so as to . . . such will be the result. **interpretation**—(Cf. *Margin*). **words of the wise**—(Cf. vs. 2). **dark sayings**—(Cf. Ps. 49: 4; John 16:25; and *Introduction*, I). **7. The fear of the Lord**—the principle of true piety (cf. ch. 2:5; 14: 26, 27; Job 28:28; Ps. 34:11; 111:10; Acts 9:31). **beginning**—first part, foundation. **fools**—the stupid and indifferent to God's character and government; hence the wicked. **8. My son**—This paternal form denotes a tender regard for the reader. Filial sentiments rank next to piety towards God, and ensure most distinguished rewards (cf. ch 6:20; Eph. 6:2, 3). On the figures of vs. 9, cf. Genesis 41:42; Song of Solomon 1:10; 4:9. **10-19.** A solemn warning against temptation. **10. entice**—lit., "open the way." **consent . . . not**—Sin is in consenting or yielding to temptation, not in being tempted. **11-14.** Murder and robbery are given as specific illustrations. **lay wait . . . lurk privily**—express an effort and hope for successful concealment. **swallow . . . grave**—utterly destroy the victim and traces of the crime (Num. 16:33; Ps. 55:15). Abundant rewards of villainy are promised as the fruits of this easy and safe course. **15, 16.** The society of the wicked (way or path) is dangerous. Avoid the beginnings of sin (ch. 4:14; Ps. 1:1; 119:101). **17-19.** Men warned ought to escape danger as birds instinctively avoid visibly spread nets. But stupid sinners rush to their own ruin (Ps. 9:16), and, greedy of gain, succeed in the very schemes which destroy them (I Tim. 6:10), not only failing to catch others, but procuring their own destruction. **20-33.** Some interpreters regard this address as the language of the Son of God under the name of Wisdom (cf. Luke 11:49). Others think that wisdom, as the divine attribute specially employed in acts of counsel and admonition, is here personified, and represents God. In either case the address is a most solemn and divine admonition, whose matter and spirit are eminently evangelical

and impressive (cf. *Note* on ch. 8). **20. Wisdom**—lit., "Wisdoms," the plural used either because of the unusual sense, or as indicative of the great excellency of wisdom (cf. ch. 9:1). **streets**—or most public places, not secretly. **21.** The publicity further indicated by terms designating places of most common resort. **22. simple ones**—(Cf. vs. 4.) **simplicity**—implying ignorance. **scorners**—(Ps. 1:1) —who despise, as well as reject, truth. **fools**— Though a different word is used from that of vs. 7, yet it is of the same meaning. **23. reproof**—implying conviction deserving it (cf. John 16:8, *Margin*). **pour out**—abundantly impart. **my spirit**—whether of wisdom personified, or of Christ, a divine agent. **24. stretched . . . hand**—Earnestness, especially in beseeching, is denoted by the figure (cf. Job 11:13; Ps. 68:31; 88:9). **25. set at naught**—rejected as of no value. **would none of**—lit., "were not willing or inclined to it." **26, 27.** In their extreme distress He will not only refuse help, but aggravate it by derision. **fear**—the object of it. **desolation**—lit., "a tumultuous noise," denoting their utter confusion. **destruction**—or calamity (vs. 26) compared to a whirlwind, as to fatal rapidity. **distress**—(Ps. 4:1; 44:11). **anguish**—a state of inextricable oppression, the deepest despair. **28.** Now no prayers or most diligent seeking will avail (ch. 8:17). **29, 30.** The sinner's infatuated rejection brings his ruin. **31. fruit . . . way**—result of conduct (Isa. 3:10; Ezek. 11: 21; Rom. 6:21; Gal. 6:7, 8). **be filled**—even to repletion (Ps. 123:4). **32, turning away**—i.e., from the call of vs. 23. **simple**—as in vs. 22. **prosperity** —quiet, implying indifference. **33. dwell safely**— lit., "in confidence" (Deut. 12:10). **be quiet**—or at ease, in real prosperity. **from fear**—without fear.

CHAPTER 2

Vss. 1-22. Men are invited to seek wisdom because it teaches those principles by which they may obtain God's guidance and avoid the society and influence of the wicked, whose pernicious courses are described. **1-5.** Diligence in hearing and praying for instruction must be used to secure the great principle of godliness, the fear of God. **1. hide . . . with thee**— lay up in store (cf. ch. 7:1). **2.** Listen attentively and reflect seriously (ch. 1:24; Ps. 130:2). **understanding**—right perception of truth. **3. Yea, if**— lit., "When if," i.e., in such a case. **knowledge**—or, discrimination. **understanding**—as in vs. 2. **4.** There must be earnest prayer and effort. **5. understand**—or, perceive intelligently. **find**—obtain. **6. For**—God is ready (Jas. 1:5; 4:8). **out of his mouth** —by revelation from Him. **7. sound wisdom**—lit., "substance," opposed to what is fictitious. According to the context, this may be assistance, as here corresponding with **buckler,** or safety, or wisdom, which procures it (cf. ch: 3:21; 8:14; 18:1; Job 6:13; 12:13). **layeth up**—provides, ever ready. **8. keepeth . . . way**—God defends the right way, and those in it. **saints**—objects of favor (cf. Ps. 4:3, etc.). He guides and guards them. **9. Then**—emphatic, in such a case. **righteousness . . . path**—all parts of duty to God and man. **10, 11.** Idea of vs. 9, amplified; on terms cf vs. 2 and vs. 4. **12-15. To deliver** —as from great danger (ch. 6:5). **way . . . man**— (Ps. 1:1). **froward things**—perversity (ch. 6:14; 23: 23), what is opposed to truth. **paths of uprightness** —or, plainness. **walk**—habitually act; **14,** and that with pleasure, in ignorance of good and pursuit of evil. **frowardness**—Not only their own perversity, but that of others is their delight. They love most the worst things. **15. crooked**—tortuous, unprincipled. **froward**—lit., (they) are going back, not only aside from right, but opposite to it. **16-19.** Deliverance from another danger. **the strange woman**—This term is often used for harlot, or loose woman (Judg. 11:1, 2), married (ch. 7:5, 19) or not (I Kings 11:1), so called, because such were, perhaps at first, foreigners, though "strange" may also denote whatever is opposed to right or proper, as *strange fire* (Num. 3:4); *strange incense* (Exod. 30:9). **flattereth**—lit., "smooths." **her words**—(Ps. 5:9). **17. guide . . . youth**—lawful husband (Jer. 3:4). **covenant . . . God**—of marriage made in God's name. **18. inclineth**—sinks down (cf. Num. 13:31). **the dead**—or shades of the departed (Ps. 88:10). **19.** i.e., such as remain impenitent (cf. Eccles. 7:26). **paths of life**—(Ps. 16:11), opposed to paths unto the dead. **20. That . . . way of good**—i.e., Such is the object of these warnings. **21, 22.** (Cf. Ps. 37:3, 9, 22, 27.) **transgressors**—or impious rebels (cf. Jer. 9:2). **rooted out**—utterly destroyed, as trees plucked up by the roots.

CHAPTER 3

Vss. 1-35. The study of truth commended. God must be feared, honored, and trusted, and filial submission, under chastisement, exhibited. The excellence of wisdom urged and illustrated by its place in the divine counsels. Piety enforced by a contrast of the destiny of the righteous and the wicked.

1. law [and] **commandments**—all divine instructions (cf. Ps. 119). **let thine heart keep**—or sincerely observe (ch. 4:13; 5:2). **2. length . . . life**—often promised as blessings (Ps. 21:4; 91:16). **peace**—includes prosperity (Ps. 125:5). **add**—abound to thee. **3. mercy and truth**—God's faithfulness to His promises is often expressed by these terms (Ps. 25:10; 57:3). As attributes of men, they express integrity in a wide sense (ch. 16:6; 20:28). **bind . . . write . . . heart**—outwardly adorn and inwardly govern motives. **4. favour**—grace, amiability (ch. 22:11; Ps. 45:2); united with this, **a good understanding**—(cf. *Margin*), a discrimination, which secures success. **in the sight . . . man**—such as God and man approve. **5. Trust . . . heart**—This is the center and marrow of true wisdom (ch. 22:19; 28:25). The positive duty has its corresponding negation in the admonition against self-confidence. **6. ways**—(Ps. 1:1.) **acknowledge**—by seeking His wise aid (ch. 16:3; Ps. 37:5; Jer. 9:23, 24). **direct**—lit., "make plain" (cf. Heb. 12:13). **7.** (Cf. ch. 27:2; Rom. 12:16.) **fear . . . evil**—reverentially regarding His law. **8. It**—This conduct. **health**—(Cf. *Margin*). **to thy navel** —for all the organs of nourishment. **marrow**—(Cf. *Margin*). **bones**—frame of body. True piety promotes bodily health. **9, 10.** (Cf. ch. 11:25; Exod. 23:19; Deut. 18:4; Isa. 32:8; II Cor. 9:13.) **presses** —or wine fats (Joel 2:24; 3:13). **11, 12.** The true intent of afflictions considered; they do not contradict the assertion of the blessed state of the pious (Job 5:17; Heb. 12:5, 6). **he delighteth**—or receiveth as denoting reconciliation regarding the offense which produced chastisement. **13. findeth**—lit., "reaches," or "obtains by seeking." **getteth**—lit., "draws out," as metals by digging. **14, 15.** The figure of vs. 13 carried out. **it**—i.e., wisdom. **merchandise**—acquisition by trading. **fine gold**—dug gold, solid as a nugget. **rubies**—gems, or pearls. **16, 17.** Wisdom personified as bringing the best blessings (cf. Matt. 6:33; I Tim. 4:8). **Her ways**—such

as she directs us to take. **18. Wisdom allegorized as a tree of life**—(Gen. 2:9; 3:22,) whose fruit preserves life, gives all that makes living a blessing. **19, 20.** The place of wisdom in the economy of creation and providence commends it to men, who, in proportion to their finite powers, may possess this invaluable attribute, and are thus encouraged by the divine example of its use to seek its possession. **21. sound wisdom**—(cf. ch. 2:7). **let . . . eyes**—i.e., these words of instruction. **22-24,** assign reasons in their value for happiness and ornament, guidance and support in dangers, both when waking and sleeping. **25. Be not**—or, You shall not be. **sudden fear**—what causes it (ch. 1:27), any unlooked-for evil (Ps. 46:3; 91:12; I Pet. 3:14). **desolation**—(ch. 1:27). **26.** The reason; such as are objects of God's favor. **be thy confidence**—lit., "in thy confidence," in the source of thy strength (cf. Nah. 3:9, for the same construction, *Hebrew*). **27, 28.** Promptly fulfil all obligations both of justice and charity (cf. Jas. 2:15, 16). **29, 30.** Do not abuse confidence and avoid litigation. **31. oppressor**—or man of mischief. The destiny of successful evildoers warns against desiring their lot (Ps. 37:1, 2, 35, 36). **32-35.** Reasons for the warning. **froward**—(ch. 2:15). **secret . . . righteous**—in their communion (Amos 3:7). **33. curse . . . wicked** —It abides with them, and will be manifested. **34.** The retribution of sinners, as in Ps. 18:26. **35. inherit**—as a portion. **shame**—or disgrace, as opposed to honor. **promotion**—(cf. *Margin*); as honor for well-doing makes men conspicuous, so fools are signalized by disgrace.

CHAPTER 4

Vss. 1-27. To an earnest call for attention to his teachings, the writer adds a commendation of wisdom, preceded and enforced by the counsels of his father and teacher. To this he adds a caution (against the devices of the wicked), and a series of exhortations to docility, integrity, and uprightness.

1, 2. (Cf. ch. 1:8.) **to know**—in order to know. **doctrine**—the matter of learning (ch. 1:5), such as he had received (Lam. 3:1). **3. father's son**—emphatic, a son specially regarded, and so called **tender**, as an object of special care (cf. I Chron. 22:7; 29:1); an idea further expressed by **only beloved**—(or, as an only son), (Gen. 22:2), though he had brothers (I Chron. 3:5). **4. He taught**—or directed me. **retain** —as well as receive. **keep . . . and live**—observe, that you may live (ch. 7:2). **5. Get**—as a possession not to be given up. **neither decline**—i.e., from obeying my word. **6.** Not only accept but love wisdom, who will keep thee from evil, and evil from thee. **7.** (Cf. Job 28:28.) **getting**—or possession; a desire for wisdom is wise. **8.** As you highly esteem her, she will raise you to honor. **embrace her**—with fond affection. **9. ornament**—such as the chaplet or wreath of conquerors. **deliver**—(Cf. Gen. 14:20.) The allusion to a shield, contained in the *Hebrew*, suggests protection as well as honor (cf. vs. 6). **10.** (Cf. ch. 2:1; 3:2.) **11, 12. way of wisdom**—which it prescribes. **led thee**—lit., "caused thee to tread," as a path (Ps. 107:7). **not be straitened**—have ample room (Ps. 18:36). **13**—(Cf. ch. 3:18.) The figure of laying hold with the hand suggests earnest effort. **14.** (Cf. Ps. 1:1.) Avoid all temptations to the beginning of evil. **16, 17.** The reason is found in the character of sinners, whose zeal to do evil is forcibly depicted (ch. 6:4; Ps. 36:5). They live by flagrant vices (ch. 1:13). Some prefer to render, "Their bread is wickedness, their drink violence" (cf. Job 15:16; 34:7). **18, 19.** As shining light increases from twilight to noonday splendor, so the course of the just increases in purity, but that of the wicked is as thickest darkness, in which one knows not on what he stumbles. **20-22.** (Cf. vss. 10, 13; ch. 3:8, etc.). **22. health ... flesh**—by preserving from vices destructive of health. **23. with all diligence**—or, above, or more than all, *custody* (cf. *Margin*), all that is kept (cf. Ezek. 38:7), because the heart is the depository of all wisdom and the source of whatever affects life and character (Matt. 12:35; 15:19). **24. a froward mouth**—i.e., a mouth, or words of ill nature. The *Hebrew* word differs from that used (ch. 2:15; 3:32). **perverse**—or, quarreling. **lips**—or, words. **25. Let ... before thee**—i.e., pursue a sincere and direct purpose, avoiding temptations. **26. Ponder**—Consider well; a wise course results from wise forethought. **27.** (Cf. vs. 25.) Avoid all by-paths of evil (Deut. 2:27; 17:11). A life of integrity requires attention to heart, speech, eyes, and conduct.

CHAPTER 5

Vss. 1-23. A warning against the seductive arts of wicked women, enforced by considering the advantages of chastity, and the miserable end of the wicked.
1. This connection of **wisdom** and **understanding** is frequent (ch. 2:2; 3:7); the first denotes the use of wise means for wise ends; the other, the exercise of a proper discrimination in their discovery. **2. regard**—or, observe. **keep**—preserve constantly. **3.** (Cf. ch. 2:16.) Her enticing promises are deceitful. **4. her end**—lit., "her future," in sense of reward, what follows (cf. Ps. 37:37; 73:17). Its nature is evinced by the use of figures, opposite those of vs. 3. The physical and moral suffering of the deluded profligate are notoriously terrible. **5. feet ... , steps**—i.e, course of life ends in death. **6. her ways ... know**—Some prefer, "that she may not ponder the path of life," etc.; but perhaps a better sense is, "her ways are varied, so as to prevent your knowledge of her true character, and so of true happiness." **8, 9.** Avoid the slightest temptation. **thine honour**—in whatever consisting, strength (ch. 3:13) or wealth. **thy years**—by cutting them off in dissipation. **unto the cruel**—for such the sensual are apt to become. **10. wealth**—lit., "strength," or the result of thy. **labours**—the fruit of thy painful exertions (Ps. 127:2). There may be a reference to slavery, a commuted punishment for death due the adulterer (Deut. 22: 22). **11. at the last**—the end, or reward (cf. vs. 4). **mourn**—roar in pain. **flesh and ... body**—the whole person under incurable disease. **12-14.** The ruined sinner vainly laments his neglect of warning and his sad fate in being brought to public disgrace. **evil**—for affliction, as in Genesis 19:20; 49:15. **15-20.** By figures, in which **well, cistern, and fountain**, represent the wife, and **rivers of waters** the children, men are exhorted to constancy and satisfaction in lawful conjugal enjoyments. In vs. 16, **fountains** (in the plural) rather denote the produce or waters of a spring, lit., "what is from a spring," and corresponds with "rivers of waters." **only thine own**—harlots' children have no known father. **wife ... youth**—married in youth. **loving ... roe**—other figures for a wife from the well-known beauty of these animals. **breasts**—(Cf. Song of Sol. 1:13; Ezek. 23: 3, 8). **ravished**—lit., "intoxicated," i.e., fully satisfied. **21.** The reason, God's eye is on you, **22, 23,** and He will cause sin to bring its punishment. **with-**

out instruction—lit., "in want of instruction," having refused it (cf. Job 13:18; Heb. 11:24). **go astray**—lit., "be drunken." The word "ravished" (vs. 19) here denotes fulness of punishment.

CHAPTER 6

Vss. 1-35. After admonitions against suretyship and sloth (cf. vss. 6-8), the character and fate of the wicked generally are set forth, and the writer (vss. 20-35) resumes the warnings against incontinence, pointing out its certain and terrible results. This train of thought seems to intimate the kindred of these vices.
1, 2. if—The condition extends through both verses. **be surety**—art pledged. **stricken ... hand**—bargained (cf. Job 17:3). **with a stranger**—i.e., for a friend (cf. ch. 11:15; 17:18). **3. come ... friend**—in his power. **humble ... sure thy friend**—urge as a supplant; i.e., induce the friend to provide otherwise for his debt, or secure the surety. **4, 5.** The danger requires promptness. **6-8.** The improvident sluggards usually want sureties. Hence, such are advised to industry by the ant's example. **9, 10.** Their conduct graphically described; **11,** and the fruits of their self-indulgence and indolence presented. **as ... travelleth**—lit., "one who walks backwards and forwards," i.e., a highwayman. **armed man**—i.e., one prepared to destroy. **12. A naughty person**—lit., "A man of Belial," or of worthlessness, i.e., for good, and so depraved, or wicked (cf. I Sam. 25:25; 30:22, etc.). Idleness and vice are allied. Though indolent in acts, he actively and habitually (**walketh**) is ill-natured in speech (ch. 4:24). **13, 14.** If, for fear of detection, he does not speak, he uses signs to carry on his intrigues. These signs are still so used in the East. **deviseth**—lit., "constructs, as an artisan." **mischief**—evil to others. **Frowardness**—as in ch. 2:14. **discord**—especially litigation. Cunning is the talent of the weak and lazy. **15.** *Suddenness* aggravates evil (cf. vs. 11; ch. 29:1). **calamity**—lit., "a crushing weight." **broken**—shivered as a potter's vessel; utterly destroyed (Ps. 2:9). **16-19. six ... seven**—a mode of speaking to arrest attention (ch. 30:15, 18; Job 5:19). **proud look**—lit., "eyes of loftiness" (Ps. 131:1). Eyes, tongue, etc., for persons. **speaketh**—lit., "breathes out," habitually speaks (Ps. 27:12; Acts 9:1). **20-23.** Cf. ch. 1:8; 3:3, etc.). **it**—(cf. vs. 23); denotes the instruction of parents (vs. 20), to which all the qualities of a safe guide and guard and ready teacher are ascribed. It prevents the ingress of evil by supplying good thoughts, even in dreams (ch. 3:21-23; Ps. 19:9; II Pet. 1:19). **reproofs**—(ch. 1:23) the convictions of error produced by instruction. **24.** A specimen of its benefit. By appreciating truth, men are not affected by lying flattery. **25.** One of the cautions of this instruction, avoid alluring beauty. **take** [or, ensnare] **... eyelids**—By painting the lashes, women enhanced beauty. **26.** The supplied words give a better sense than the old version: "The price of a whore is a piece of bread." **adulteress**—(cf. *Margin*), which the parallel and context (29-35) sustain. Of similar results of this sin, cf. ch. 5:9-12. **will hunt**—alluding to the snares spread by harlots (cf. ch. 7:6-8). **precious life**—more valuable than all else. **27-29.** The guilt and danger most obvious. **30, 31.** Such a thief is pitied, though heavily punished. **sevenfold**—(cf. Exod. 22:1-4), for many, ample (cf. Gen. 4:24; Matt. 18:21), even if all his wealth is taken. **32. lacketh understanding**—or, heart; destitute of moral principle and prudence.

33. dishonour—or, shame, as well as hurt of body (ch. 3:35). **reproach . . . away**—No restitution will suffice; **34, 35,** nor any terms of reconciliation be admitted. **regard** [or, accept] **any ransom.**

CHAPTER 7

Vss. 1-27. The subject continued, by a delineation of the arts of strange women, as a caution to the unwary. **1-4.** Similar calls (ch. 3:1-3; 4:10, etc.). **apple . . . eye**—pupil of eye, a custody (ch. 4:23) of special value. **Bind . . . fingers**—as inscriptions on rings. **5.** The design of the teaching (cf. ch.: 2:16; 6:24). **6. For**—or, "Since," introducing an example to illustrate the warning, which, whether a narrative or a parable, is equally pertinent. **window** [or, opening of the] . . . **casement**—or lattice. **looked**—lit., "watched earnestly" (Judg. 5:28). **7. simple**—as in ch. 1:4. **void of . . .**—(Cf. ch. 6:32.) **8. her corner** —where she was usually found. **went . . . house**—implying, perhaps, confidence in himself by his manner, as denoted in the word **"went"**—lit., "tread pompously." **9.** The time, **twilight**, ending in darkness. **black . . . night**—lit., "pupil," or, "eye," i.e., middle of night. **10. attire**—that of harlots was sometimes peculiar. **subtile**—or, wary, cunning. **11, 12. loud**—or, noisy, bustling. **stubborn**—not submissive. **without . . . streets, . . . corner**—(Cf. I Tim. 5:13; Titus 2:5.) **13-15.** The preparations for a feast do not necessarily imply peculiar religious professions. The offerer retained part of the victim for a feast (Lev. 3:9, etc.). This feast she professes was prepared for him whom she boldly addresses as one sought specially to partake of it. **16, 17. my bed**—or, couch, adorned in the costliest manner. **bed**—in vs. 17, a place for sleeping. **18-20.** There is no fear of discovery. **the day appointed**—perhaps, lit., "a full moon," i.e., a fortnight's time (cf. vs. 19). **21. caused . . . yield**—or, inclines. **flattering**—(Cf. ch. 5:3). **forced him**—by persuasion overcoming his scruples. **22. straightway**—quickly, either as ignorant of danger, or incapable of resistance. **23. Till** —He is now caught (ch. 6:26). **24.** The inferential admonition is followed, **26, 27,** by a more general allegation of the evils of this vice. Even the mightiest fail to resist her deathly allurements.

CHAPTER 8

Vss. 1-36. Contrasted with sensual allurements are the advantages of divine wisdom, which publicly invites men, offers the best principles of life, and the most valuable benefits resulting from receiving her counsels. Her relation to the divine plans and acts is introduced, as in ch. 3:19, 20, though more fully, to commend her desirableness for men, and the whole is closed by an assurance that those finding her find God's favor, and those neglecting ruin themselves. Many regard the passage as a description of the Son of God by the title, Wisdom, which the older Jews used (and by which He is called in Luke 11:49), as John 1:1, etc., describes Him by that of *Logos*, the Word. But the passage may be taken as a personification of wisdom: for, (1) Though described as with God, wisdom is not asserted to be God. (2) The use of personal attributes is equally consistent with a *personification*, as with the description of a real person. (3) The personal pronouns used accord with the gender (fem.) of wisdom constantly, and are never changed to that of the person

meant, as sometimes occurs in a corresponding use of *spirit*, which is neuter in Greek, but to which masculine pronouns are often applied (John 16:14), when the acts of the Holy Spirit are described. (4) Such a personification is agreeable to the style of this book (cf. chs. 1:20; 3:16, 17; 4:8; 6:20-22; 9:1-4), whereas no prophetical or other allusions to the Saviour or the new dispensation are found among the quotations of this book in the New Testament, and unless this be such, none exist. (5) Nothing is lost as to the importance of this passage, which still remains a most ornate and also solemn and impressive teaching of inspiration on the value of wisdom. **1-4.** The publicity and universality of the call contrast with the secrecy and intrigues of the wicked (ch. 7:8, etc.). **5. wisdom**—lit., "subtilty" in a good sense, or, prudence. **fools**—as ch. 1:22. **6. excellent things**—or, plain, manifest. **opening . . . things** —upright words. **7. For . . . truth**—lit., "My palate shall meditate," or (as Orientals did) "mutter," my thoughts expressed only to myself are truth. **wickedness**—specially falsehood, as opposed to truth. **8. in righteousness**—or, righteous (Ps. 9:8: 11:7). **froward**—lit., "twisted," or contradictory, i.e., to truth. **9. plain . . . understandeth**—easily seen by those who apply their minds. **that find**—implying search. **10. not silver**—preferable to it, so last clause implies comparison. **11.** (Cf. ch. 3:14, 15.) **12. prudence** —as in vs. 5. The connection of "wisdom" and "prudence" is that of the dictates of sound wisdom and its application. **find . . . inventions**—or, devices, discreet ways (ch. 1:4). **13.** For such is the effect of the fear of God, by which hatred to evil preserves from it. **froward mouth**—or, speech (ch. 2:12; 6: 14). **14.** It also gives the elements of good character in counsel. **sound wisdom**—(Ch. 2:7). **I . . . strength**—or, "As for me, understanding is strength to me," the source of power (Eccles. 9:16); good judgment gives more efficiency to actions; **15, 16,** of which a wisely conducted government is an example. **17. early**—or, diligently, which may include the usual sense of early in life. **18. durable riches . . . righteousness**—Such are the "riches," enduring sources of happiness in moral possessions (cf. ch. 3: 16). **19.** (Cf. vs. 11, 3:16). **20, 21.** The courses in which wisdom leads conduct to a true present prosperity (ch. 23:5). **22-31.** Strictly, God's attributes are part of Himself. Yet, to the poetical structure of the whole passage, this commendation of wisdom is entirely consonant. In order of time all His attributes are coincident and eternal as Himself. But to set forth the importance of wisdom as devising the products of benevolence and power, it is here assigned a precedence. As it has such in divine, so should it be desired in human, affairs (cf. ch. 3:19). **22. possessed**—or, created; in either sense, the idea of precedence. **in the beginning**—or simply, "beginning," in apposition with "me." **before . . . of** old—preceding the most ancient deeds. **23. I was set up**—ordained, or inaugurated (Ps. 2:6). The other terms carry out the idea of the earliest antiquity, and **24-29** illustrate it by the details of creation. **brought forth**—(Cf. Ps. 90:2). **abounding**—or, laden with water. **settled**—i.e., sunk in foundations. **fields**— or, out-places, deserts, as opposite to (habitable) **world. highest part**—or, sum, all particles together, **when he set . . . depth**—marked out the circle, according to the popular idea of the earth, as circular, surrounded by depths on which the visible concave heavens rested. **established . . . deep**—i.e., so as to sustain the waters above and repress those below the firmament (Gen. 1:7-11; Job 26:8). **comman**

ment—better, the shore, i.e., of the sea. **foundations** —figuratively denotes the solid structure (Job 38:4; Ps. 24:2). **30, 31. one brought up**—an object of special and pleasing regard. The bestowal of wisdom on men is represented by its finding a delightful residence and pleasing God. **32-36.** Such an attribute men are urged to seek. **watching . . . waiting**—lit., "so as to watch"; wait, denoting a most sedulous attention. **sinneth . . . me**—or better, missing me, as opposed to finding. **35.** (Cf. Luke 13:23, 24.) **love death**—act as if they did (cf. ch. 17:9).

CHAPTER 9

Vss. 1-18. The commendation of wisdom is continued, under the figure of a liberal host, and its provisions under that of a feast (cf. Luke 14:16-24). The character of those who are invited is followed by a contrasted description of the rejectors of good counsel; and with the invitations of wisdom are contrasted the allurement of the wicked woman. **1. house**—(cf. ch. 8:34). **her**—or, "its" (the house). **seven pillars**—the number seven for many, or a sufficiency (ch. 6:31). **2. mingled**—to enhance the flavor (ch. 23:30; Isa. 5:22). **furnished**—lit., "set out," "arranged." **3. maidens**—servants to invite (cf. Ps. 68:11; Isa. 40:9). **highest places**—ridges of heights, conspicuous places. **4-6.** (Cf. ch. 1:4; 6:32.) Wisdom not only supplies right but forbids wrong principles. **7, 8. shame**—(Cf. ch. 3:35.) **a blot**—or, stain on character. Bot terms denote the evil done by others to one whose faithfulness secures a wise man's love. **9.** The more a wise man learns, the more he loves wisdom. **10.** (Cf. ch. 1:7.) **of the holy**—lit., "holies," persons or things, or both. This knowledge gives right perception. **11.** (Cf. ch. 3:16-18; 4:10.) **12.** You are mainly concerned in your own conduct. **13. foolish woman**—or lit., "woman of folly," specially manifested by such as are described. **clamorous**—or, noisy (ch. 7:11). **knoweth nothing**—lit., "knoweth not what," i.e., is right and proper. **14. on a seat**—lit., "throne," takes a prominent place, impudently and haughtily. **15, 16.** to allure those who are right-minded, and who are addressed as in vs. 4, as **simple**—i.e., easily led (ch. 1:4) and unsettled, though willing to do right. **17.** The language of a proverb, meaning that forbidden delights are sweet and pleasant, as fruits of risk and danger. **18.** (Cf. ch. 2:18, 19; 7:27.)

CHAPTER 10

Vss. 1-32. Here begins the second part of the book, chs. 10-22:16, which, with the third, ch. 22:16-ch. 25, contains series of proverbs whose sense is complete in one or two verses, and which, having no logical connection, admit of no analysis. The parallelisms of chs. 10-15 are mostly antithetic; and those of chs. 16-22:16, synthetic. The evidences of art in the structure are very clear, and indicate, probably, a purpose of facilitating the labor of memorizing. **1. wise** [and] **foolish**—as they follow or reject the precepts of wisdom. **maketh . . . father**—or, gladdens a father. **heaviness**—or, grief. **2. Treasures . . . nothing**—i.e., Ill-gotten gains give no true happiness (cf. ch. 4:17; Matt. 6:19). **righteousness**—especially *beneficence* (Ps. 112:9). **death**—the greatest of all evils. **3.** (Cf. Ps. 37:16-20.) The last clause is better: "He will repel the greedy desires

of the wicked." **4. slack**—lit., "deceitful." failing of its purpose (cf. Hos. 7:16). **maketh rich**—(cf. vs. 22). **5. son**—as ch. 1:8, 10, and often. **sleepeth**—in indolence, and not for rest. **causeth shame**—lit., "is base" (cf. ch. 14:35; 17:2). **6. Blessings**—lit., "Praises." The last clause is better: "The mouth of the wicked covereth, or concealeth, violence, or mischievous devices," to be executed in due time (Ps. 5:9; 10:7; Rom. 3:14), and hence has no praises (cf. vs. 11). **7. blessed**—lit., "for a blessing," or praise. **shall rot**—lit., "be worm-eaten," useless and disgusting. **8. wise . . .**—(cf. ch. 9:8, 9, 16), opposed to **prating fool**—or, fool of lips of wicked language. **fall**—headlong, suddenly. **9. perverteth his ways**—acts deceitfully. **known**—discovered and punished. **10.** Two vices contrasted; hypocrisy, or insinuating evil against one (ch. 6:13; Ps. 35:19), and rashness of speech. In each case, the results are on the evildoers. **11. a well**—or, source of good to himself and others (John 7:37, 38). On last clause cf. vs. 6. **12. strifes**—or, litigations. **covereth**—by forgiveness and forbearance. **13. In the lips . . . found**—hence, not beaten, as the wicked-speaking fool. **void of understanding**—(ch. 6:32; 7:7). **14. lay up knowledge**—i.e., as treasures for good use. **mouth . . . destruction**—or, as to the mouth, etc., destruction is near; they expose themselves to evil by prating. **15.** Both by trusting in "uncertain riches" (I Tim. 6:17), or by the evils of poverty (ch. 30:9), men, not fearing God, fall into dangers. **16.** The industry of the righteous is alone truly successful, while the earnings of the wicked tempt and lead to sin. **17. keepeth**—observes (ch. 3:18; 4:22). **refuseth**—or, turns from reproof, which might direct him aright. **18.** Both vices must one day be known and punished, and hence their folly. **19.** Much speech involves risk of sin; hence the wisdom of restraining the tongue (Ps. 39:1; Jas. 1:26). **20.** Right speech is the fruit of a good heart, but the wicked show theirs to be useless. **21.** Fools not only fail to benefit others, as do the righteous, but procure their own ruin (cf. vss. 11, 17; Hos. 4:6). **22. it maketh . . .** "it" is emphatic. Riches from God are without the sorrow of ill-gotten wealth (cf. Eccles. 2:21-23; I Tim. 6:9, 10, 17). **23.** Sin is the pleasure of the wicked; wisdom that of the good. **24. it**—the very thing. The wicked get dreaded evil; the righteous, desired good. **25.** (Cf. Ps. 1:4; 37:9, 10, 36.) **righteous . . . foundation**—well laid and firm (Matt. 7:24, 25). **26.** i.e., causes vexation. **27.** (Cf. ch. 9:11; Ps. 55:23.) **28. gladness**—in confidence of realizing it. **expectation . . . perish**—in disappointment. **29. The way . . .** i.e., God's providence sustains the righteous and overthrows the wicked (Hos. 14:9). **30.** (Cf. ch. 12:3; Ps. 37:9-11; 102:28.) **earth**—or, land of promise. **31. bringeth forth**—lit., "germinates" as a plant. **froward**—(Cf. ch. 2:12, 14). **cut off** —as an unproductive plant. **32. know**—regard and provide for (Ps. 1:6). **frowardness**—all kinds of deceit and ill-nature. The word is plural.

CHAPTER 11

Vss. 1-31. **1.** (Cf. *Margin*.) The Hebrews used stones for weights. **just**—complete in measure. **2.** Self-conceit is unteachable; the humble grow wise (cf. ch. 16:18; 18:12). **3. guide**—to lead, as a shepherd (ch. 6:37; Ps. 78:52). **perverseness**—ill-nature. **destroy**—with violence. **4.** (Cf. ch. 10:2.) **wrath**—i.e., of God. **5. direct**—or, make plain; wicked ways are not plain (ch. 13:17). **6. deliver them**—i.e., from evil, which the wicked suffer by their own doings (ch. 5:22; Ps. 9:16). **7. expectation . . . perish**—for death cuts short all his plans (Luke 16:25). **hope of unjust**—better, "hope of wealth," or power (cf. Isa. 40:29, *Hebrew*). This gives an advance on the sentiment of the first clause. Even hopes of gain die with him. **8.** Perhaps the *trouble* prepared by the wicked, and which he inherits (cf. vs. 6). **9.** (Cf. Ps. 35:16; Dan. 11:32.) The just is saved by superior discernment. **10, 11.** The last may be a reason for the first. Together, they set forth the relative moral worth of good and bad men. **By the blessing**—implying active benevolence. **12. despiseth**—or, reviles, a course contrasted with the prudent silence of the wise. **holdeth his peace**—as if neither hearing nor telling. **13. tale-bearer**—(cf. *Margin*), one trading as a peddler in scandal, whose propensity to talk leads him to betray confidence. **14. counsel**—the art of governing (ch. 1:5). **counsellors**—lit., "one giving counsel"; the participle used as a collective. **15.** (Cf. ch. 6:1.) **suretiship**—(Cf. *Margin*), the actors put for the action, which may be lawfully hated. **16. retaineth**—or lit., "lay hold of as a support." Honor is to a feeble woman thus as valuable as riches to men. **17. merciful**—kind to others; opposed to cruel. Such benefit themselves by doing good to others (cf. ch. 24:5), while the cruel injure themselves as well as others. **flesh**—i.e., his body, by penuriousness (Col. 2:23). **18. a deceitful work**—or, wages, which fail to satisfy, or flee away (ch. 10:2; 23:5). **sure reward**—or, gain, as from trading (Hos. 10:12; Gal. 6:8, 9). **19.** Inference from vs. 18 (cf. vss. 5, 6; ch. 10:16). **20.** (Cf. vs. 5.) **froward**—as in ch. 2:15, opposed to the simplicity and purity of the **upright. in their way**—or, conduct. **21.** The combined power of the wicked cannot free them from just punishment, while the unaided children of the righteous find deliverance by reason of their pious relationship (Ps. 37:25, 26). **22.** Jewels were often suspended from the nose (Gen. 24:47; Isa. 3:21). Thus adorned, a hog disgusts less than a fair and indiscreet woman. **23.** (Cf. ch. 10:28.) The wrath is that of God. **24-31.** The scope of the whole is a comment on vs. 23. Thus liberality (vs. 24), by God's blessing, secures increase, while penuriousness, instead of expected gain, procures poverty. **25. liberal soul**—(Cf. *Margin*). **made fat**—prospers (ch. 28:25; Deut. 32:15; Luke 6:38). **watereth . . . watered**—a common figure for blessing. **26.** Another example of the truth of vs. 23; the miser loses reputation, though he saves corn. **selleth it**—i.e., at a fair price. **27. good** [and] **mischief**—i.e., of others. **procureth . . . seeketh**—implying success. **28.** (Cf. ch. 10:15; Ps. 49:6; I Tim. 6:17.) **righteous . . . branch**—(Ps. 1:3; Jer. 17:8.) **29. troubleth**—as ch. 15:27 explains, by greediness for gain (cf. vs. 17). **inherit . . . wind**—Even successful, his gains are of no real value. So the fool, thus acting, either comes to poverty, or heaps up for others. **30. a tree of life**—Blessings to others proceed from the works of the righteous (ch. 3:18). **winneth souls**—(Cf. *Margin*), to do them good as opposed to ch. 6:25; Ezek. 13:18 (cf. Luke 5:10). **31. Behold**—Thus calling attention to the illustrations (cf. vs. 23), the sentiment of which is confirmed even in time, not excluding future rewards and punishments.

CHAPTER 12

Vss. 1-28. **1. loveth knowledge**—as the fruit of instruction or training (ch. 1:2). **hateth reproof**—(Ch. 10:17.) **brutish**—stupid, regardless of his own welfare (Ps. 49:10; 73:22). **3.** Wickedness cannot

give permanent prosperity. **root . . . not be moved** —firm as a flourishing tree—(Ps. 1:3; 15:5; Jer. 17:8). **4. A virtuous woman**—in the wide sense of well disposed to all moral duties (ch. 31:10). **maketh ashamed**—i.e., by misconduct. **rottenness**—an incurable evil. **5. thoughts**—or, purposes. **are right** —lit., "are judgment," i.e., true decisions. **counsels** —(Cf. ch. 11:14.) **deceit**—contrary to truth and honesty. **6. The words**—or, expressed designs of the wicked are for evil purposes. **the mouth**—or, words of the righteous delivering instead of ensnaring men. **7.** Such conduct brings a proper return, by the destruction of the wicked and well-being of the righteous and his family. **8. despised**—as opposed to **commended** (ch. 11:12). **perverse heart**— or, wicked principles, as opposed to one of wisdom. **9. despised**—held in little repute, obscure (I Sam. 18: 23; Isa. 3:5). **hath a servant**—implying some means of honest living. **honoureth himself**—is self-conceited. **10. regardeth**—lit., "knoweth" (Ps. 1:6). **mercies . . . cruel**—as acts of compassion ungraciously rendered to the needy. The righteous more regards a beast than the wicked a man. **11.** The idler's fate is the result of indolence and want of principle (ch. 6:32; 7:7). **12. the wicked . . . evil**— They love the crafty arts of deception. **the root . . .** (**fruit**)—their own resources supply them; or, it may be rendered: "He (God) giveth, or sets (Ezek. 17:22) the root of the righteous," and hence it is firm: or, the verb is impersonal; "As to the root, (etc.), it is firm" (ch. 17:19). **13, 14.** The sentiment expanded. While the wicked, such as liars, flatterers, etc., fall by their own words, the righteous are unhurt. Their good conduct makes friends, and God rewards them. **15. The way . . . eyes**—The fool is self-conceited (cf. vs. 1; ch. 1:32; 10:17; Jas. 3:17). **16. prudent . . . shame**—He is slow to denounce his insulters (Jas. 1:19). **18. speaketh**—lit., "speaketh hastily," or indiscreetly (Ps. 106:33), as an angry man retorts harsh and provoking invectives. **tongue . . . health**—by soothing and gentle language. **19.** Words of truth are consistent, and stand all tests, while lies are soon discovered and exposed. **20. that imagine**—or, plan (ch. 3:29). They design a deceitful course, to which, with all its evils and dangers to others and themselves, the happiness of peacemakers is opposed (cf. Matt. 5:9; Rom. 12:18). **21. no evil**—(as in Ps. 91:10), under God's wise limitations (Rom. 8:28). **mischief**—as penal evil. **22. deal truly**—or, faithfully, i.e., according to promises (cf. John 3:21). **23. concealeth**—by his modesty (ch. 10:14; 11:13). **heart . . . proclaimeth**—as his lips speak his thoughts (cf. Eccles. 10:3). **24. slothful**—(Cf. *Margin*), so called because he fails to meet his promises. **under tribute**—not denoting legal taxes, but the obligation of dependence. **25. a good word**—one of comfort. **26. more excellent**—(cf. *Margin*); or, more successful, while the wicked fail; or, we may read it: "The righteous guides his friend, but," etc., i.e., The ability of the righteous to aid others is contrasted with the ruin to which the way of the wicked leads themselves. **27.** (Cf. vs. 24.) **took in hunting**—or, his venison. He does not improve his advantages. **the substance . . . precious**— or, the wealth of a man of honor is being diligent, or diligence. **precious**—lit., "honor" (Eccles. 10:1). **28.** (Cf. ch. 8:8, 20, etc.) A sentiment often stated; here first affirmatively, then negatively.

CHAPTER 13

Vss. 1-25. **1.** (Cf. ch. 6:1-5; 10:1, 17.) **2. shall eat**—i.e., obtain (ch. 12:14). **transgressors**—as in ch. 2:22. **violence**—or, mischief to themselves. **3. He ... mouth ... life**—because evil speeches may provoke violence from others. On last clause cf. ch. 10:14. **4.** (Cf. ch. 12:11, 27.) **5. loathsome ... shame**—better, causeth shame and reproach (cf. ch. 19:26), by slander, etc., which the righteous hates. **6.** A sentiment of frequent recurrence, that piety benefits and sin injures. **7.** In opposite ways men act hypocritically for gain of honor or wealth. **8.** Riches save some from punishment, while others suffer because they will not heed the rebuke of sloth, which makes and keeps them poor. **9. light ... lamp**—prosperity; the first, the greater, and it **rejoiceth**—burns brightly, or continues, while the other, at best small, soon fails. **10.** The obstinacy which attends self-conceit, produces contention, which the well-advised, thus evincing modesty, avoid. **11. by vanity**—or, nothingness, i.e., which is vain or useless to the public (as card playing or similar vices). **gathereth ... labour**—(cf. *Margin*), little by little, laboriously. **12. desire cometh**—is realized. **a tree of life**—or, cause of happiness. **13. the word**—i.e., of advice, or, instruction (cf. ch. 10:27; 11:31). **14.** (Cf. ch. 10:11.) **fountain**—or, source of life. **to depart**—(cf. ch. 1:2-4), or, for departing, etc., and so gives life. **15.** Right perception and action secure good will, while evil ways are difficult as a stony road. The wicked left of God find punishment of sin in sinning. **hard**—or, harsh (cf. Hebrew: Deut. 21:4; Jer. 5:15). **16. dealeth**—acts with foresight. **a fool ... folly**—for want of caution. **17. A wicked** [or, unfaithful] **messenger falleth into mischief**—or, by mischief, or evil, and so his errand fails. Contrasted is the character of the faithful, whose faithfulness benefits others. **18.** (Cf. ch. 10:17; 12:1.) **19.** Self-denial, which fools will not endure, is essential to success. **20.** The benefits of good and evil of bad society are contrasted. **21.** (Cf. ch. 11:31.) **good ... repaid**—or, He (God) will repay good. **22. wealth ... just**—While good men's estates remain in their families, God so orders that the gains of sinners enure to the just (cf. ch. 28:8; Ps. 37:18, 22, 26, etc.). **23.** The laboring poor prosper more than those who injudiciously or wickedly strive, by fraud and violence, to supersede the necessity of lawful labor. **24. spareth**—or, withholds. **rod**—of correction. **hateth**—or, acts as if he hated him (cf. ch. 3: 12; 8:36). **chasteneth ... betimes**—or, diligently seeks for him all useful discipline. **25.** The comparative temporal prosperity of the righteous and wicked, rather than contentment and discontent, is noted.

CHAPTER 14

Vss. 1-35. **1. Every wise ...**—lit., "The wisdoms" (cf. ch. 9:1) "of women," plural, a distributive form of speech. **buildeth ... house**—increases wealth, which the foolish, by mismanagement, lessen. **2. uprightness**—is the fruit of fearing God, as falsehood and ill-nature (ch. 2:15; 3:32) of despising Him and His law. **3. rod of pride**—i.e., the punishment of pride, which they evince by their words. The words of the wise procure good to them. **4. crib is clean**—empty; so "cleanness of teeth" denotes want of food (cf. Amos 4:6). Men get the proper fruit of their doings (Gal. 6:7). **5. A faithful witness ...**—one tested to be such. **utter** [or, breathe out] **lies**—i.e., habitually lies (ch. 6:19; cf. Acts 9:1). Or the sense is, that habitual truthfulness, or lying, will be evinced in witness-bearing. **6.** An humble, teachable spirit succeeds in seeking (ch. 8:9; John

7:17; Jas. 1:5, 6). **7.** Avoid the society of those who cannot teach you. **8.** Appearances deceive the thoughtless, but the prudent discriminate. **9. Fools ... sin**—or, Sin deludes fools. **righteous ... favour** —i.e., of God, instead of the punishment of sin. **10.** Each one best knows his own sorrows or joys. **11.** (Cf. ch. 12:7.) The contrast of the whole is enhanced by that of **house** and **tabernacle**, a permanent and a temporary dwelling. **12. end thereof**—or, reward, what results (cf. ch. 5:4). **ways of death**— leading to it. **13.** The preceding sentiment illustrated by the disappointments of a wicked or untimely joy. **14. filled ... ways**—receive retribution (ch. 1:31). **a good man ... himself**—lit., "is away from such," will not associate with him. **15. The simple ... word**—He is credulous, not from love, but heedlessness (ch. 13:16). **16.** (Cf. ch. 3:7; 28:14.) **rageth**—acts proudly and conceitedly. **17. He ... angry**—lit., "short of anger" (cf. vs. 29, opposite idea). **man ... hated**—i.e., the deliberate evildoer is more hated than the rash. **18. inherit**— as a portion (cf. 3:35). **are crowned**—lit., "are surrounded with it," abound in it. **19.** Describes the humbling of the wicked by the punishment their sins incur. **20.** This sad but true picture of human nature is not given approvingly, but only as a fact. **21.** For such contempt of the poor is contrasted as sinful with the virtuous compassion of the good. **22.** As usual, the interrogative negative strengthens the affirmative. **mercy and truth**—i.e., God's (Ps. 57:3; 61:7). **23. labour**—painful diligence. **talk ... penury**—idle and vain promises and plans. **24.** (Cf. ch. 3:16.) **foolishness ... folly**—Folly remains, or produces folly; it has no benefit. **25.** *Life* often depends on truth-telling. **a deceitful ... lies**—He that breathes out lies is deceit, not to be trusted (vs. 5). **26.** The blessings of piety descend to children (ch. 13:22; 20:7; Exod. 20:6). **27.** (Cf. ch. 13:14.) **fear of the Lord**—or, *law of the wise*, is wisdom (Ps. 111:10). **28.** The teaching of a true political economy. **29. slow ... understanding**—(Cf. vs. 17). **hasty**—(Cf. vs. 17). **exalteth folly**—makes it conspicuous, as if delighting to honor it. **30. A sound heart**—both literally and figuratively, a source of health; in the latter sense, opposed to the known effect of evil passions on health. **31. reproacheth his Maker**—who is the God of such, as well as of the rich (ch. 22:2; Job 31:15; and specially I Sam. 2:8; Ps. 113:7). **32. driven**—thrust out violently (cf. Ps. 35:5, 6). **hath hope**—trusteth (ch. 10:2; 11:4; Ps. 2: 12), implying assurance of help. **33. resteth**— preserved in quietness for use, while fools blazon their folly (ch. 12:23; 13:16). **34. Righteousness**— just principles and actions. **exalteth**—raises to honor. **is a reproach**—brings on them the ill-will of others (cf. ch. 13:6). **35. wise**—discreet or prudent. **causeth shame**—(ch. 10:5; 12:4) acts basely.

CHAPTER 15

Vss. 1-33. **1. soft**—tender or gentle. **turneth ... wrath**—from any one. **stir up**—as a smouldering fire is excited. **2. useth ... aright**—commends knowledge by its proper use. **poureth out**—utters abundantly (ch. 12:23), and so disgusts others. **3. beholding**—watching (cf. ch. 5:21; Ps. 66:7). **4. A wholesome tongue**—(cf. *Margin*), pacifying and soothing language. **tree of life**—(ch. 3:18; 11:30). **perverseness therein**—cross, ill-natured language. **breach ... spirit**—(cf. Isa. 65:14, *Hebrew*), grieves, instead of appeasing. **5.** (Cf. ch. 4:1; 10:17; 13:1-18.) **is prudent**—acts discreetly. **6. treasure**—implying utility. **trouble**—vexation and affliction. **7.** (Cf. ch. 10:20, 21.) **heart...not so**—not right, or vain. **8, 9. The sacrifice** [and] **prayer**—are acts of worship. **way...followeth...righteousness**—denote conduct. God's regard for the worship and deeds of the righteous and wicked respectively, so stated in Psalm 50:17; Isaiah 1:11. **10.** (Cf. ch. 10:17.) **the way**—that in which God would have him to go (ch. 2:13; Ps. 119:1). **11. Hell**—(Ps. 16:10.) **destruction**—or, Abaddon, the place of the destroyer. All the unseen world is open to God, much more men's hearts. **12.** (Cf. ch. 9:8.) **go unto the wise** —to be instructed. **13. maketh...countenance**—or, benefits the countenance. **spirit is broken**—and so the countenance is sad. **14.** (Cf. ch. 10:21, 22.) The wise grow wiser, the fools more foolish (ch. 9:9). **15.** The state of the heart governs the outward condition. **evil**—sad, contrasted with the cheerfulness of a feast. **16. trouble**—agitation, implying the anxieties and perplexities attending wealth held by worldlings (ch. 16:18; I Tim. 6:6). **17. dinner** [or, allowance (II Kings 25:30)] **of herbs**—and that the plainest. **and hatred**—cf. ch. 10:12, 18). **18.** (Cf. ch. 14:29; 16:32.) **19.** The difficulties of the slothful result from want of energy; the righteous find a **plain** [and open] **way**—lit., "a highway," by diligence (I Sam. 10:7; Ps. 1:3). **20.** (Cf. ch. 10:1.) **21. walketh uprightly**—and so finds his joy (ch. 3:6; 10:23). **22. Without counsel**—or, deliberation, implying a wise deference to the opinions of the wise and good, contrasted with rashness. **23.** Good advice blesses the giver and receiver. **24.** (Cf. Col. 3:2.) Holy purposes prevent sinning, and so its evils. **25.** The most desolate who have God's aid have more permanent good than the self-reliant sinner (ch. 2:22; 12:7). **border**—or, boundary for possessions (Ps. 78:54). **26. are pleasant words**—i.e., pleasing to God (ch. 8:8, 9). **27.** (Cf. ch. 11:17.) Avarice brings trouble to him and his. **hateth gifts**—or, bribes (Exod. 23:8; Ps. 15:5), and is not avaricious. **28.** (Cf. vs. 14; ch. 10:11.) Caution is the fruit of wisdom; rashness of folly. **29. far...wicked**—in His love and favor (Ps. 22:11; 119:155). **30. light of the eyes**—(ch. 13:9). What gives light rejoiceth the heart, by relieving from anxiety as to our course; so **good report**—or, doctrine (Isa. 28:9; 53:1), **maketh ...fat**—or, gives prosperity (ch. 3:13-17; 9:11). The last clause is illustrated by the first. **31, 32.** (Cf. ch. 10:17.) **reproof of life**—which leads to life. **abideth...wise**—is numbered among them. **refuseth**—or, neglects, passes by (ch. 1:25; 4:15). **despiseth...soul**—so acts as if esteeming its interests of no value. **33. The fear...wisdom**—Wisdom instructs in true piety. **before...humility**—(cf. Luke 24:26; I Pet. 1:11); opposite (cf. ch. 16:18).

CHAPTER 16

Vss. 1-33. **1. preparations**—schemes. **in man**—or lit., "to man," belonging, or pertaining to him. **the answer...Lord**—The efficient ordering is from God: "Man proposes; God disposes." **2. clean**—or, faultless. **weigheth**—or, tries, judges, implying that they are faulty (ch. 21:2; 24:12). **3.** (Cf. *Margin.*) Rely on God for success to your lawful purposes. **4. for himself**—"for its answer, or purpose," i.e., according to God's plan; the wicked are for the day of evil (Ps. 49:5; Jer. 17:18); sinning and suffering answer to each other, are indissolubly united. **5.** (Cf. ch. 3:32.) **6. By mercy and truth**—i.e., God's (Ps. 85:10); He effects the atonement, or covering of sin; and the principles of true piety in-

cline men to depart from evil; or, "mercy" and "truth" may be man's, indicative of the gracious tempers which work instrumentally in procuring pardon. **purged**—expiated (as in Lev. 16:33; Isa. 27:9, *Hebrew*). **7.** Persecutions, of course, excepted. **8.** (Cf. ch. 15:6, 16, 17.) **9.** (Cf. vs. 3.) **directeth**—establisheth. **10.** The last clause depends on the first, expressing the importance of equity in decisions, so authoritative. **11. are the Lord's... his work**—i.e., what He has ordered, and hence should be observed by men. **12.** Rulers are rightly expected, by their position, to hate evil; for their power is sustained by righteousness. **13.** A specification of the general sentiment of vs. 12. **14.** This wrath, so terrible and certain, like **messengers of death** (I Kings 2:25), can be appeased by the **wise**. **15. light of...countenance**—favor (Ps. 4:6). **life**—preserves it, or gives blessings which make it valuable. **the latter rain**—fell just before harvest and matured the crop; hence specially valuable (Deut. 11:14). **16.** (Cf. ch. 3:16; 4:5.) **17. The highway** —A common, plain road represents the habitual course of the righteous in departing from evil. **keepeth**—observes. **18, 19.** (Cf. ch. 15:33.) Haughtiness and pride imply self-confidence which produces carelessness, and hence the fall—lit., "sliding." **divide the spoil**—i.e., conquer. Avoid the society of the proud (Jas. 4:6). **20. handleth a matter**—wisely considers *the word*, i.e., of God (cf. ch. 13:13). **trusteth**—(Cf. Ps. 2:12; 118:8, 9.) **21. wise in heart** —who rightly consider duty. **sweetness of the lips** —eloquent discourse, persuades and instructs others. **22. Understanding**—or, discretion, is a constant source of blessing (ch. 13:14), benefiting others; but fools' best efforts are folly. **23.** The heart is the source of wisdom flowing from the mouth. **24.** (Cf. ch. 15:26.) Gentle, kind words, by soothing the mind, give the body health. **25.** (Cf. ch. 14:2.) **26.** Diligence is a duty due to one's self, for his wants require labor. **27. ungodly man**—(Cf. ch. 6:12.) **diggeth up evil**—labors for it. **in his lips... fire**—His words are calumniating (ch. 3:6). **28.** (Cf. ch. 6:14; 10-31.) **whisperer**—prater, tale-bearer (ch. 18:8; 26:20). **29. violent man**—or, man of mischief (ch. 3:31). **enticeth**—(ch. 1:10.) **30. He shutteth his eyes**—denoting deep thought (Ps. 64:6). **moving** [or, biting] **his lips**—a determined purpose (ch. 6:13). **31.** (Cf. ch. 20:29.) **if**—or, *which* may be supplied properly, or without it the sense is as in ch. 3:16; 4:10, that piety is blessed with long life. **32.** (Cf. ch. 14:29.) **taketh a city**—i.e., by fighting. **33.** Seemingly the most fortuitous events are ordered by God.

CHAPTER 17

Vss. 1-28. **1. sacrifices**—or, feasts made with part of them (cf. 7:14; Lev. 2:3; 7:31). **with**—lit., "of." **strife**—its product, or attendant. **2.** (Cf. ch. 14:35.) **causeth shame**—(ch. 10:5). **shall...inheritance**—i.e., share a brother's part (cf. Num. 27:4, 7). **3.** God only knows, as He tries (Ps. 12:6; 66:10) the heart. **4.** Wicked doers and speakers alike delight in calumny. **5.** (Cf. ch. 14:31.) **glad at calamities** —rejoicing in others' evil. Such are rightly punished by God, who knows their hearts. **6.** Prolonged posterity is a blessing, its cutting off a curse (ch. 13:22; Ps. 109:13-15), hence children may glory in virtuous ancestry. **7. Excellent speech**—(Cf. *Margin.*) Such language as ill suits a fool, as lying (ought to suit) a prince (ch. 16:12, 13). **8.** One so corrupt as to take a bribe evinces his high estimate of it by subjection to its influence (ch. 18:16; 19:6). **9. seekth love**—(Cf. *Margin*). The contrast is between the peacemaker and talebearer. **10.** Reproof more affects the wise than severe scourging, fools. **11.** Such meet just retribution (I Kings 2:25). **a cruel messenger**—one to inflict it. **12.** They are less rational in anger than wild beasts. **13.** (Cf. Ps. 7: 4; 35:12.) **evil**—injury to another (ch. 13:21). **14. letteth . . . water**—as a breach in a dam. **before . . . meddled with**—before strife has become sharp, or, by an explanation better suiting the figure, *rolls on*, or increases. **15. abomination . . . Lord**—as reversing His method of acting (ch. 3:32; 12:2). **16.** Though wealth cannot buy wisdom for those who do not love it, yet wisdom procures wealth (ch. 3:16; 14:24). **17.** To the second of these parallel clauses, there is an accession of meaning, i.e., that a brother's love is specially seen in adversity. **18.** (Cf. ch. 6:1-5; 11:15.) **in the presence . . .**—i.e., he either fails to consult his friend, or to follow his advice. **19. strife**—contention is, and leads to, sin. **he that exalteth his gate**—gratifies a vain love of costly building. **seeketh**—or, findeth, as if he sought (cf. "loveth death," ch. 8:36). **20.** The second clause advances on the first. The ill-natured fail of good, and the cavilling and fault-finding incur evil. **21.** (Cf. ch. 23:24.) Different words are rendered by **fool**, both denoting stupidity and impiety. **22.** (Cf. ch. 14:30; 15:13.) The effect of the mind on the body is well known. **drieth**—as if the marrow were exhausted. **medicine**—or, body, which better corresponds with bone. **23. a gift . . . bosom**—Money and other valuables were borne in a fold of the garment, called the bosom. **to pervert**—i.e., by bribery. **24. Wisdom . . . him**—ever an object of regard, while a fool's affections are unsettled. **25. a grief**—or cross, vexation (cf. vs. 21; ch. 10:1). **26. Also**—i.e., Equally to be avoided are other sins: punishing good subjects, or resisting good rulers. **27, 28.** Prudence of speech is commended as is an excellent or calm spirit, not excited to vain conversation.

CHAPTER 18

Vss. 1-24. **1. Through desire . . . seeketh**—i.e., seeks selfish gratification. **intermeddleth . . . wisdom** —or, rushes on (ch. 17:14) against all wisdom, or what is valuable (ch. 2:7). **2. that his heart . . . itself** —i.e., takes pleasure in revealing his folly (ch. 12:23; 15:2). **3.** So surely are sin and punishment connected (ch. 16:4). **wicked,** for "wickedness," answers to **ignominy,** or the state of such; and **contempt,** the feeling of others to them; and to **reproach,** a manifestation of contempt. **4.** Wise speech is like an exhaustless stream of benefit. **5. accept the person**—(Cf. Psalm 82:2). "It is not good" is to be supplied before to **overthrow. 6, 7.** The quarrelsome bring trouble on themselves. Their rash language ensnares them (ch. 6:2). **8.** (Cf. ch. 16: 28). **as wounds**—not sustained by the *Hebrew;* better, as "sweet morsels," which men gladly swallow. **innermost . . . belly**—the mind, or heart (cf. ch. 20:27 -30; Ps. 22:14). **9.** One by failing to get, the other by wasting wealth, grows poorer. **waster**—lit., "master of washing," a prodigal. **10. name of the Lord** —manifested perfections (Ps. 8:1; 20:2), as faithfulness, power, mercy, etc., on which men rely. **is safe**—lit., "set on high, out of danger" (Ps. 18:2; 91: 4). **11.** contrasts with vs. 10 (cf. ch. 10:15). Such is a vain trust (cf. Ps. 73:6). **12.** (Cf. ch. 15:33; 16: 18.) **13.** Hasty speech evinces self-conceit, and ensures shame (ch. 26:12). **14. infirmity**—bodily sick-

ness, or outward evil. The **spirit,** which sustains, being **wounded,** no support is left, except, as implied, in God. **15.** (Cf. ch: 1:5,15, 31.) **16.** (Cf. ch. 17:8, 23.) Disapproval of the fact stated is implied. **17.** One-sided statements are not reliable. **searcheth**—thoroughly (ch. 17:9, 19). **18. The lot** —whose disposal is of God (ch. 16:13), may, properly used, be a right mode of settling disputes. **19.** No feuds so difficult of adjustment as those of relatives; hence great care should be used to avoid them. **20.** (Cf. ch. 12:14; 13:2.) Men's words are the **fruit,** or, **increase of his lips,** and when good, benefit them. **satisfied with**—(Cf. ch. 1:31; 14:14.) **21. Death and life**—or, the greatest evil and good. **that love it**—i.e., the tongue, or its use for good or evil. **eat . . . fruit**—(Cf. vs. 19; Jas. 1:19.) **22.** The old versions supply "good" before the "wife," as the last clause and ch. 19:14 imply (cf. ch. 31:10). **23. the rich . . . roughly**—He is tolerated because rich, implying that the estimate of men by wealth is wrong. **24. A man . . . friendly**—better, "A man . . . (is) to, or may triumph (Ps. 108:9), or, shout for joy (Ps. 5:11), i.e., may congratulate himself." Indeed, there is a Friend who is better than a brother; such is the "Friend of sinners," who may have been before the writer's mind.

CHAPTER 19

Vss. 1-29. **1.** (Cf. ch. 28:6.) "Rich" for **fool** here. Integrity is better than riches (ch. 15:16, 17; 16:8). **2.** The last illustrates the first clause. Rashness, the result of ignorance, brings trouble. **3. perverteth . . . way**—turns him back from right (ch. 13: 6; Jas. 1:13); and he blames God for his failures. **4.** (Cf. ch. 14:20.) Such facts are often adduced with implied disapprobation. **5.** Cf. vs. 9, where **perish** explains **not escape** here (cf. Ps. 88:9, 10). **8.** (Cf. *Margin;* ch. 15:32.) **loveth . . . soul**—or, himself, which he evinces by regarding his best interests. **keepeth**—or, regards. **10.** (Cf. ch. 17:7.) The fool is incapable of properly using pleasure as knowledge, yet for him to have it is less incongruous than the undue elevation of servants. Let each abide in his calling (I Cor. 7:20). **11.** (Cf. ch. 14:29; 16:32.) This inculcation of a forgiving spirit shows that true religion is always the same (Matt. 5:22-24). **12.** (Cf. ch. 16:14, 15; 20:2.) A motive to submission to lawful authority. **13. calamity**—lit., "calamities," varied and many. **continual dropping**—a perpetual annoyance, wearing out patience. **14.** A contrast of men's gifts and God's, who, though author of both blessings, confers the latter by His more special providence. **and**—or, "but," implying that the evils of vs. 13 are only avoided by His care. **15. a deep sleep**—a state of utter indifference. **idle soul**—or, person (cf. ch. 10:4; 12:24). **16.** (Cf. ch. 10:17; 13: 13.) **despiseth . . . ways**—opposed to keeping or observing, neglects (ch. 16:17) (as unworthy of regard) his moral conduct. **17.** (Cf. ch. 14:21; Ps. 37:26). **hath pity**—shown by acts (cf. *Margin*). **18.** (Cf. ch. 13:24; 23:13.) **let not . . . spare**—lit., "do not lift up thy soul" (Ps. 24:4; 25:1), i.e., do not desire to his death; a caution to passionate parents against angry chastisement. **19.** Repeated efforts of kindness are lost on ill-natured persons. **20.** (Cf. ch. 13:18-20.) **latter end**—(Ch. 5:11.) In youth prepare for age. **21.** (Cf. ch. 16:1, 9; Ps. 33:10, 11.) The failure of man's devices is implied. **22. desire**—i.e., to do good, indicates a kind disposition (ch. 11:23); and the poor thus affected are better than liars, who say and do not. **23. The fear . . . life**—(Cf. ch. 3:2).

abide—or, remain contented (I Tim. 4:8). **not visited with evil**—(ch. 10:3; Ps. 37:25), as a judgment, in which sense *visit* is often used (Ps. 89:32; Jer. 6:15). **24. bosom**—lit., a wide dish in which the hand was plunged in eating (Matt. 26:23). Cf. ch. 26:15, the sentiment expressed with equal irony and less exaggeration. **25.** Such is the benefit of reproof; even the simple profit, much more the wise. **26.** Unfilial conduct often condemned (ch. 17:21-25; 20: 20; Deut. 21:18, 21). **27.** Avoid whatever leads from truth. **28. ungodly witness**—(cf. *Margin*), one false by bad principles (cf. ch. 6:12). **scorneth judgment**—sets at naught the dictates of justice. **devoureth**—lit., swalloweth, as something delightful. **29.** Their punishment is sure, fixed, and ready (cf. ch. 3:34; 10:13).

CHAPTER 20

Vss. 1-30. **1. mocker**—scorner. Such men are made by wine. **strong drink**—made by spicing wine (cf. Isa. 5:11, 22); and it may include wine. **raging** —or, boisterous as a drunkard. **deceived**—lit., "erring," or reeling. **2.** (Cf. ch. 19:12.) Men who resist authority injure themselves (Rom. 13:2). **3. to cease from strife**—or, better, "to dwell from or without strife," denoting the habit of life. **fool ... meddling**—(Ch. 17:14). **4. shall ... beg**—lit., "ask" (in this sense, Ps. 109:10). **5. Counsel ... water**— i.e., deeply hidden (ch. 18:4; Ps. 13:2). The wise can discern well. **6.** Boasters are unreliable. **goodness**—or, kind disposition. **7.** The conduct of good men proclaims their sound principles. God's covenant and their good example secure blessing to their children (ch. 4:26; Ps. 112:1, 2). **8.** As in ch. 14:35; 16:10, 15, this is the character of a good king, not of all kings. **9.** The interrogation in the affirmative strengthens the implied negation (cf. Job. 15:14; Eccles. 7:20). **10.** Various measures, implying that some are wrong (cf. ch. 11:1; 16:11). **11.** The conduct of children even is the best test of principle (cf. Matt. 7:16). **12.** Hence, of course, God will know all you do (Ps. 94:9). **13.** Activity and diligence contrasted with sloth (ch. 6:9; 10:11). **lest ... poverty**—lit., "be deprived of inheritance." **14. when ... his way**—implying that he goes about boasting of his bargains. **15.** The contrast denotes the greater value of knowledge (cf. ch. 3:14-16). **16. Take his garment** implies severe exaction, justified by the surety's rashness. **a strange woman**—by some readings "strangers," but the former here, and in ch. 27: 13, is allowable, and strengthens the sense. The debauchee is less reliable than the merely careless. **Bread ... sweet**—either as unlawfully (ch. 9:17) or easily obtained. **mouth ... gravel**—well expresses the pain and grief given at last. **18.** (Cf. ch. 15:22.) Be careful and considerate in important plans. **19.** Those who love to tell news will hardly keep secrets. **flattereth ... lips**—(cf. *Margin*; ch. 1:10). **meddle ... him**— lit., "join," or "associate with." **20. his lamp**—(Cf. ch. 13:9; 24:20). **21. gotten hastily**— contrary to God's providence (ch. 28:20), implying its unjust or easy attainment; hence the man is punished, or spends freely what he got easily (cf. vs. 17). **22.** (Cf. Ps. 27:14; Rom. 12:17-19.) **23.** (Cf. vs. 10; ch. 11:1.) **24. Man's goings**—lit., "Stately steppings of a strong man." **a man**—any common man. **understand** [or, perceive] **his ... way. 25. devoureth ... holy**—or, better, who rashly speaks promises, or devotes what is holy, consecrating any thing. This suits better the last clause, which expresses a similar view of the results of rashly vowing.

26. (Cf. vs. 8.) **bringeth ... over them**—The wheel was used for threshing grain. The figure denotes severity (cf. Amos 1:3). **27. The spirit ... Lord**— Men's minds are God's gifts, and thus able to search one another (cf. vs. 5; ch. 18:8, 17; I Cor. 2:11). **28.** (Cf. ch. 3:3; 16:6, 12.) **29.** Each age has its peculiar excellence (ch. 16:31). **30. blueness**—lit., "joining," the process of uniting the edges of a wound throws off purulent matter. **stripes ... belly**—So punishment provides healing of soul (ch. 18:8), by deterring from evil courses.

CHAPTER 21

Vss. 1-31. **1. rivers**—irrigating channels (Ps. 1:3), whose course was easily turned (cf. Deut. 11:10). God disposes even kings as He pleases (ch. 16:9; Ps. 33:15). **2.** (Cf. ch. 14:2; 16:2-25.) **3.** (Cf. Ps. 50:7-15; Isa. 1:11, 17.) **4. high look**—(Cf. *Margin*; Ps. 131:1). **proud heart**—or, heart of breadth, one that is swollen (cf. Ps. 101:5). **ploughing**—better "lamp," a frequent figure for prosperity (ch. 20:20); hence joy or delight. **5.** The contrast is between steady industry and rashness (cf. ch. 19:2). **6. The getting**—or, what is obtained (cf. Job 7:2; Jer. 22:13, *Hebrew*). **vanity ... to and fro**—as fleeting as chaff or stubble in the wind (cf. ch. 20:17-21; Ps. 62:10). Such gettings are unsatisfactory. **them ... death**— act as if they did (ch. 8:36; 17:19). **7. robbery**— or, destruction, especially oppression, of which they are authors. **shall destroy**—lit., "cut with a saw" (I Kings 7:9), i.e., utterly ruin them. Their sins shall be visited on them in kind. **to do judgment**— what is just and right. **8. of man**—any one; his way is opposed to truth, and also estranged from it. The pure proves himself such by his right conduct. **9. corner**—a turret or arbor on the roof. **brawling**— or contentious. **wide house**—lit., "house of fellowship," large enough for several families. **10.** So strongly hath the desire to do evil (Psalm 10:3; Eccles. 8:11), that he will not even spare his friend if in his way. **11.** (Cf. ch. 19:25.) That which the simple learn by the terrors of punishment, the wise learn by teaching. **12.** (Cf. Psalm 37:35-38; 73:17, 20.) **house**—family or interests. **overthroweth**— either supply "God" (cf. ch. 10:24), or the word is used impersonally. **13.** The principles of retribution, often taught (cf. Ps. 18:26; Matt. 7:1-12). **14.** The effect of bribery (ch. 17:23) is enhanced by secrecy, as the bribed person does not wish his motives made known. **15.** But the just love right and need no bribes. The wicked at last meet destruction, though for a time happy in concealing corruption. **16. the way of understanding**—(Cf. ch. 12:26; 14: 22). **remain**—i.e., rest as at a journey's end; death will be his unchanging home. **17.** Costly luxuries impoverish. **18.** (Cf. ch. 11:8.) By suffering what they had devised for the righteous, or brought on them, the wicked became their ransom, in the usual sense of substitutes (cf. Josh. 7:26; Esther 7:9). **19.** (Cf. vs. 9.) **wilderness**—pasture, though uninhabitable ground (Ps. 65:12). **20.** The wise, by diligence and care, lay up and increase wealth, while fools "spend" lit., "swallow it up," greedily. **21.** He who tries to act justly and kindly (Ps. 34:14) will prosper and obtain justice and honor. **22.** "Wisdom is better than strength" (Eccles. 7:19; 9:15). **strength ... thereof**—that in which they confide. **23.** (Cf. ch. 13:2, 3; Jas. 3:6-10.) **24.** The reproachful name is deserved by those who treat others with anger and contempt. **25. desire**—i.e. of ease and idleness brings him to starvation. **26.** The sin of covetousness marks the sluggard, as the virtue of benevolence the righteous. **27.** God regards the heart, and hypocrisy is more odious than open inconsistency. **wicked mind—or design** (ch. 1:4). **28.** (Cf. ch. 19:5.) **that heareth**—or heeds instruction, and so grows wise. **speaketh constantly**—or sincerely (cf. Hab. 1:5), and hence is believed (ch. 12:19; Jas. 1:19). **29. hardeneth his face**—is obstinate. **directeth ... way** —considers it, and acts advisedly. **30, 31.** Men's best devices and reliances are vain compared with God's, or without His aid (ch. 19:21; Ps. 20:7; 33: 17).

CHAPTER 22

Vss. 1-29. **1. A good name**—(Job 30:8, *Hebrew*); "good" is supplied here from Ecclesiastes 7:1. **loving favour**—kind regard, i.e., of the wise and good. **2.** Before God all are on the same footing (ch. 14: 31; 17:5). **3. are punished**—i.e., for their temerity; for the **evil** is not necessarily punitive, as the **prudent** might otherwise be its objects. **4. humility and the fear of the Lord**—are in apposition; one produces the other. On the results, cf. ch. 3:16; 8:18. **5. he that ... them**—Those who properly watch over their own souls are thus preserved from the dangers which attend the way of perverse men (ch. 16:17). **6. Train** —initiate, or early instruct. **the way**—lit., "his way," that selected for him in which he should go; for early training secures habitual walking in it. **7.** The influence of wealth sets aside moral distinctions is implied, and, of course, disapproved (cf. ch. 19:6; 21:14, etc.). **8.** (Cf. ch. 11:18; Ps. 109:16-20; Gal. 6:7, 8.) **the rod ... fail**—His power to do evil will be destroyed. **9. a bountiful eye**—i.e., a beneficent disposition. **for he giveth ... poor**—His acts prove it. **10. Cast out**—or drive away. Scorners foster strife by taunts and revilings. **11.** (Cf. *Margin*.) **pureness of heart**—and gentle, kind words win favor, even from kings. **12. preserve**—or guard. **knowledge**—its principles and possessors. **overthroweth** —utterly confounds and destroys the wicked. **13.** Frivolous excuses satisfy the indolent man's conscience. **14. The mouth**—or flattering speeches (ch. 5:3; 7:5) ensnare man, *as pits,* beasts. God makes their own sin their punishment. **15. is bound**—or firmly fixed. Chastisement deters from crime and so leads to reformation of principle. **16.** These two vices pertain to the same selfish feeling. Both are deservedly odious to God and incur punishment. **17.** Here begins another division of the book, marked by those encouragements to the pursuit of wisdom, which are found in the earlier chapters. It will be observed that from vs. 22 to ch. 24:12, the proverbs are generally expressed in two verses instead of one (cf. *Introduction*). **18.** These lessons must be laid up in the mind, and **fitted**, or better, fixed in the lips so as to be ever ready. **19. That ... Lord**—This is the design of the instruction. **20. excellent things** —or probably of former times. **counsels and knowledge**—both advice and instruction. **21.** Specially he desires to secure accuracy, so that his pupil may teach others. **22, 23.** Here follow ten precepts of two verses each. Though men fail to defend the poor, God will (ch. 17:5; Ps. 12:5). **in the gate**— place of public gathering (Job 5:4; Ps. 69:12). **24, 25.** (Cf. ch. 2:12-15; 4:14.) **a snare ... soul**—The unsuspecting are often misled by bad company. **26, 27.** (Cf. ch. 6:1; 17:18.) **should he take ...**—(i.e., the creditor. **28.** (Cf. ch. 23:10.) Do not entrench on others (Deut. 19:14; 27:17). **29.** Success rewards diligence (ch. 10:4; 21:5).

CHAPTER 23

Vss. 1-35. **1-3.** Avoid the dangers of gluttony. **put a knife**—an Eastern figure for putting restraint on the appetite. **are deceitful meat**—though well tasted, injurious. **4, 5.** (Cf. I Tim. 6:9, 10.) **thine own wisdom**—which regards riches intrinsically as a blessing. **Wilt ... eyes**—As the eyes fly after or seek riches, they are not, i.e., either become transitory or unsatisfying; fully expressed by their flying away. **6-8.** Beware of deceitful men, whose courtesies even you will repent of having accepted. **evil eye**—or purpose (ch. 22:9; Deut. 15:9; Matt. 6:23). **The morsel ... words**—i.e., disgusted with his true character, all pleasant intercourse will be destroyed. **9.** (Cf. ch. 9:8.) "Cast not your pearls ..." (Matt. 7:6). **10, 11.** (Cf. ch. 22:22, 23.) **redeemer**—or avenger (Lev. 25:25, 26; Num. 35:12), hence advocate (Job. 19:25). **plead ... thee**—(Cf. Job 31:21; Ps. 35:1; 68:5). **12.** Here begins another series of precepts. **13, 14.** While there is little danger that the use of the "divine ordinance of the rod" will produce bodily harm, there is great hope of spiritual good. **15, 16.** The pleasure afforded the teacher by the pupil's progress is a motive to diligence. **my reins**—(Cf. Ps. 7:9.) **17, 18.** (Cf. *Margin*.) The prosperity of the wicked is short. **an end**—or hereafter, another time, when apparent inequalities shall be adjusted (cf. Ps. 37:28-38). **19-21. guide ... way**—or direct thy thoughts to a right course of conduct (cf. ch. 4:4; 9:6). **riotous ... flesh**—prodigal, or eating more than necessary. Instead of "their flesh" (cf. *Margin*), better, "flesh to them," i.e., used for pleasure. **drowsiness**—the dreamy sleep of the slothful. **22. Hearken**—i.e., obey (ch. 1:8; Eph. 6:1). **despise ... old**—Adults revere the parents whom, as children, they once obeyed. **23. Buy**—lit., "get" (ch. 4:5). **truth**—generally and specially as opposed to errors of all kinds. **24, 25.** (Cf. ch. 10:1; 17:21, 25.) **26-35.** A solemn warning against whoredom and drunkenness (Hos. 4:11). **26. give ... heart**— This is the address of that divine wisdom so often presented (ch. 8:1; 9:3, etc.). **heart**—confidence. **observe**—keep. **my ways**—such as I teach you (ch. 3:17; 9:6). **27, 28. deep ditch**—a narrow pit, out of which it is hard to climb. **lieth in wait**—to ensnare men into the pit, as hunters entrap game (cf. ch. 22:14). **increaseth ... transgressors**—(ch. 5:8-10). The vice alluded to is peculiarly hardening to the heart. **29, 30.** This picture is often sadly realized now. **mixed wine**—(Cf. ch. 9:2; Isa. 5:11.) **31. when ... red**—the color denoting greater strength (cf. Gen. 49:11; Deut. 32:14). **giveth ... cup**—lit., "gives its eye," i.e., sparkles. **moveth ... aright**— Perhaps its foaming is meant. **32.** The acute miseries resulting from drunkenness contrasted with the temptations. **33, 34.** The moral effects: it inflames passion (Gen. 19:31, 35), lays open the heart, produces insensibility to the greatest dangers, and debars from reformation, under the severest sufferings. **35. awake**—i.e., from drunkenness (Gen. 9: 24). This is the language rather of acts than of the tongue.

CHAPTER 24

Vss. 1-34. **1, 2.** (Cf. ch. 23:3, 17; Ps. 37:1.) **studieth**—meditateth. **talk ... mischief**—Their expressed purposes are to do evil. **3, 4.** (Cf. ch. 14:1; Isa. 54:14.) **house**—including the family. **by knowledge ... riches**—(ch. 8:18; 21:20.) **5, 6.** The general statement (Eccles. 9:16, 18) is specially illustrated (cf. ch. 21:22; Ps. 144:1). **7.** (Cf. ch. 14:16.)

in the gate—(Cf. ch. 22:22.) **8.** So called even if he fails **to do evil. 9.** Same thought varied. **10.** Lit., "If thou fail in the day of straits (**adversity**), strait (or small) is thy strength," which is then truly tested. **11, 12.** Neglect of known duty is sin (Jas. 4:17). **ready** [lit., "bowing down"] **to be slain**—i.e., unjustly. God's retributive justice cannot be avoided by professed ignorance. **13, 14.** As delicious food whets the appetite, so should the rewards of wisdom excite us to seek it. **reward**—lit., "after part," the proper result (cf. ch. 23:18; Ps. 37:37, 38). **15, 16.** The plots of the wicked against the good, though partially, shall not be fully successful (Ps. 37:24); while the wicked, falling under penal evil, find no help. **seven times**—often, or many (ch. 6:16, 31; 9: 1). **17, 18.** Yet let none rejoice over the fate of evildoers, lest God punish their wrong spirit by relieving the sufferer (cf. ch. 17:5; Job 31:29). **19, 20.** (Ps. 37:1, 38; 18:28.) **candle**—or, prosperity; it shall come to an end (ch. 13:9; 20:20). **21, 22.** A warning against impiety and resistance to lawful rule (Rom. 13:1-7; I Pet. 2:17). **meddle ... change** —(Cf. *Margin*), lit., "mingle yourself," avoid the society of restless persons. **their calamity ...**—either what God and the king inflict, or what *changers* and their company suffer; better the first. **23. These ... wise**—lit., "are of the wise," as authors (cf. "Psalms of David," *Hebrew*). "These" refers to the verses following, to ch. 25. **to have respect**—lit., "to discern faces," show partiality, **24, 25,** of which an example is justifying the wicked, to which is opposed, rebuking him, which has a blessing. **26. kiss his lips**—love and obey, do homage (Ps. 2:12; Song of Sol. 8:1). **right answer**—lit., "plain (ch. 8: 9) words," opposed to deceptive, or obscure. **27. Prepare ... in the field**—Secure, by diligence, a proper support, and then build; provide necessaries, then comforts, to which a house rather pertained, in a mild climate, permitting the use of tents. **28.** Do not speak even truth needlessly against any, and never falsehood. **29.** Especially avoid retaliation (Matt. 5:43-45; Rom. 12:17). **30, 31.** A striking picture of the effects of sloth. **32-34.** From the folly of the sluggard learn wisdom (ch. 6:10, 11).

CHAPTER 25

Vss. 1-28. **1.** The character of these proverbs sustains the title (cf. *Introduction*). **also**—refers to the former part of the book. **copied out**—lit., "transferred," i.e., from some other book to this; not given from memory. **2.** God's unsearchableness impresses us with awe (cf. Isa. 45:15; Rom. 11:33). But kings, being finite, should confer with wise counsellors; **3.** Ye wisely keeping state secrets, which to common men are as inaccessible heights and depths. **4, 5.** As separating impurities from ore leaves pure silver, so taking from a king wicked counsellors leaves a wise and beneficent government. **before**—or, "in presence of," as courtiers stood about a king. **6, 7.** Do not intrude into the presence of the king, for the elevation of the humble is honorable, but the humbling of the proud disgraceful (Luke 14:8-10). **8.** (Cf. ch. 3:30.) **lest ... shame**—lest you do what you ought not, when shamed by defeat, or "lest thou art shut out from doing any thing." **9, 10.** (Cf. Matt. 5:25; *Margin*.) **secret**—i.e., of your opponent, for his disadvantage, and so you be disgraced, not having discussed your difficulties with him. **11. a word fitly**—lit., "quickly," as wheels roll, just in time. The comparison **as apples ... silver** gives a like sense. **apples ...**—either real apples of golden

color, in a silver network basket, or imitations on silver embroidery. **12.** Those who desire to know and do rightly, most highly esteem good counsel (ch. 9:9; 15:31). The listening ear is better than one hung with gold. **13.** Snow from mountains was used to cool drinks; so refreshing is a faithful messenger (ch. 13:17). **14. clouds**—lit., "vapors" (Jer. 10:13), clouds only in appearance. **a false gift**— promised, but not given. **15.** Gentleness and kindness overcome the most powerful and obstinate. **long forbearing**—or, slowness to anger (ch. 14:29; 15: 18). **16, 17.** A comparison, as a surfeit of honey produces physical disgust, so your company, however agreeable in moderation, may, if excessive, lead your friend to hate you. **18. A false witness** is as destructive to reputation, as such weapons to the body (ch. 24:28). **beareth ... witness**—lit., "answereth questions," as before a judge, against his **neighbor. 19.** *Treachery* annoys as well as deceives. **20.** Not only is the incongruity of songs (i.e., joyful) and sadness meant, but an accession of sadness, by want of sympathy, is implied. **21, 22.** (Cf. Matt. 5:44; Rom. 12:20.) As metals are melted by heaping coals upon them, so is the heart softened by kindness. **23.** Better, "As the north wind bringeth forth (Ps. 90:2) or produces rain, so does a concealed or slandering tongue produce anger." **24.** (Cf. ch. 21:9, 19). **25.** (Cf. vs. 13.) **good news**— i.e., of some loved interest or absent friend, the more grateful as coming from afar. **26.** From troubled fountains and corrupt springs no healthy water is to be had, so when the righteous are oppressed by the wicked, their power for good is lessened or destroyed. **27.** Satiety surfeits (vs. 16); so men who are self-glorious find shame. **is not glory**—"not" is supplied from the first clause, or "is grievous," in which sense a similar word is used (ch. 27:2). **28.** Such are exposed to the incursions of evil thoughts and successful temptations.

CHAPTER 26

Vss. 1-28. **1.** The incongruities of nature illustrate also those of the moral world. The fool's unworthiness is also implied (ch. 17:7; 19:10). **2.** Though not obvious to us, **the bird**—lit., "sparrow"—and **swallow**—have an object in their motions, so penal evil falls on none without a reason. **3.** The rod is as much needed by fools and as well suited to them, as whips and bridles are for beasts. **4, 5. Answer not**—i.e., approvingly by like folly. **Answer**—by reproof. **6.** A fool fails by folly as surely as if he were maimed. **drinketh damage**—i.e., gets it abundantly (Job 15:16; 34:7). **7. legs ... equal**—or, "take away the legs," or the legs ... are weak. In any case the idea is that they are the occasion of an awkwardness, such as the fool shows in using a parable or proverb (cf. *Introduction;* ch. 17:7). **8.** A stone, bound in a sling, is useless; so honor, conferred on a fool, is thrown away. **9.** As vexatious and unmanageble as a thorn in a drunkard's hand is a parable to a fool. He will be as apt to misuse is as to use it rightly. **10.** Various versions of this are proposed (cf. *Margin*). Better perhaps—"Much He injures (or lit., "wounds") all who reward," etc., i.e., society is injured by encouraging evil men. **transgressors**—may be rendered vagrants. The word *God* is improperly supplied. **11. returneth ... folly** —Though disgusting to others, the fool delights in his folly. **12.** The self-conceited are taught with more difficulty than the stupid. **13.** (Cf. ch. 22:13.) **14.** (Cf. ch. 6:10; 24:33.) He moves but does not leave his place. **15.** (Cf. ch. 19:24.) **16.** The thoughtless being ignorant of their ignorance are conceited. **17. meddleth**—as in ch. 20:19; 24:21; as either holding a dog by the ears or letting him go involves danger, so success in another man's strife or failure involves a useless risk of reputation, does no good, and may do us harm. **18, 19.** Such are reckless of results. **20, 21.** The talebearers foster (ch. 16:28), and the contentious excite, strife. **22.** (Cf. ch. 18:8.) **23.** *Warm professions* can no more give value to insincerity than silver coating to rude earthenware. **24. dissembleth**—though an unusual sense of the word (cf. *Margin*), is allowable, and better suits the context, which sets forth hypocrisy. **25.** Sentiment of vs. 24 carried out. **seven . . . heart** —i.e., very many (cf. ch. 24:16). **26, 27.** Deceit will at last be exposed, and the wicked by their own arts often bring on retribution (cf. ch. 12:13; Ps. 17:16; 9:17, etc.). **28.** Men hate those they injure. **lying tongue**—*lips* for the persons (cf. ch. 4:24; Ps. 12:3).

CHAPTER 27

Vss. 1-27. **1.** Do not confide implicitly in your plans (ch. 16:9; 19:21; Jas. 4:13-15). **2.** Avoid self-praise. **3.** The literal sense of **heavy,** applied to material subjects, illustrates its figurative, *grievous,* applied to moral. **a fool's wrath**—is unreasonable and excessive. **4. envy**—or, jealousy (cf. *Margin;* ch. 6: 34), is more unappeasable than the simpler bad passions. **5, 6. love**—not manifested in acts is useless; and even, if its exhibition by rebukes wounds us, such love is preferable to the frequent (cf. *Margin*), and hence deceitful, kisses of an enemy. **7.** The luxury of wealth confers less happiness than the healthy appetite of labor. **8.** Such are not only out of place, but out of duty and in danger. **9. rejoice the heart**—the organ of perceiving what pleases the senses. **sweetness . . . counsel**—or, wise counsel is also pleasing. **10.** Adhere to tried friends. The ties of blood may be less reliable than those of genuine friendship. **11.** The wisdom of children both reflects credit on parents and contributes to their aid in difficulties. **12, 13.** (Cf. ch. 20:16; 22:3). **14.** Excessive zeal in praising raises suspicions of selfishness. **15.** (Cf. ch. 19:13.) **very . . . day**—lit., "a day of showers." **16. hideth**—or, restrains (i.e., tries to do it); is as fruitless an effort, as that of holding the wind. **the ointment . . . right hand**—the organ of power (Ps. 17:7; 18:35). His right hand endeavors to repress perfume, but vainly. Some prefer: "His right hand comes on oil, i.e, cannot take hold." Such a woman cannot be tamed. **17. a man sharpeneth . . . friend**—i.e., conversation promotes intelligence, which the face exhibits. **18.** Diligence secures a reward, even for the humble servant. **19.** We may see our characters in the developed tempers of others. **20.** Men's cupidity is as insatiable as the grave. **21.** Praise tests character. **a man to his praise**—according to his praise, as he bears it. Thus vain men seek it, weak men are inflated by it, wise men disregard it, etc. **22.** The obstinate wickedness of such is incurable by the heaviest inflictions. **23, 24. flocks**—constituted the staple of wealth. It is only by care and diligence that the most solid possessions can be perpetuated (ch. 23:5). **25-27.** The fact that providential arrangements furnish the means of competence to those who properly use them is another motive to diligence (cf. Ps. 65:9-13). **The hay appeareth**—lit., "Grass appeareth" (Job 40:15; Ps. 104:14). **household**—lit., "house," the family (Acts 16:15; I Cor. 1:16).

CHAPTER 28

Vss. 1-28. A bad conscience makes men timid; the righteous are alone truly bold (ch. 14:26; Ps. 27:1). **2.** Anarchy producing contending rulers shortens the reign of each. **but by a man . . . prolonged**—or, "by a man of understanding—i.e., a good ruler—he who knows or regards the right, i.e., a good citizen, shall prolong (his days)." Good rulers are a blessing to the people. Bad government as a punishment for evil is contrasted with good as blessing to the good. **3. A poor man . . .**—Such, in power, exact more severely, and so leave subjects bare. **4. They that forsake . . . wicked**—Wrongdoers encourage one another. **5.** (Cf. John 7:17.) Ignorance of moral truth is due to unwillingness to know it. **6.** (Cf. ch. 10:6.) Riches cannot compensate for sin, nor the want of them affect integrity. **7.** (Cf. ch. 17:25.) **riotous men**—or, gluttons (ch. 23:20, 21). **8. usury . . . unjust gain**—(cf. *Margin*). The two terms, meaning nearly the same, may denote excessive interest. God's providence directs the proper use of wealth. **9.** (Cf. ch. 15:8; 21:27.) **hearing**— i.e., obeying. God requires sincere worshippers (Ps. 66:18; John 4:24). **10.** (Cf. ch. 26:27.) **11.** A poor but wise man can discover (and expose) the rich and self-conceited. **12. great glory**—or, cause for it to a people, for the righteous rejoice in good, and righteousness exalts a nation (ch. 14:34). **a man . . . hidden**—i.e., the good retire, or all kinds try to escape a wicked rule. **13.** (Cf. Ps. 32:3-5.) Concealment of sin delivers none from God's wrath, but He shows mercy to the humble penitent (Ps. 51:4). **14. feareth**—i.e., God, and so repents. **hardeneth his heart**—makes himself insensible to sin, and so will not repent (ch. 14:16; 29:1). **15.** The rapacity and cruelty of such beasts well represent some wicked men (cf. Ps. 7:2; 17:12). **16. The prince . . . understanding**—i.e., He does not perceive that oppression jeopards his success. Covetousness often produces oppression, hence the contrast. **17. doeth violence . . . blood . . .**—or, that is oppressed by the blood of *life* (Gen. 9:6), which he has taken. **to the pit**—the grave or destruction (ch. 1:12; Job 33:18-24; Ps. 143:7). **stay him**—sustain or deliver him. **18.** (Cf. ch. 10:9; 17:20.) Double dealing is eventually fatal. **19.** (Cf. ch. 10:4; 20:4.) **vain persons**—idle, useless drones, implying that they are also wicked (ch. 12:11; Ps. 26:14). **20. maketh haste . . . rich**—implying deceit or fraud (ch. 20:21), and so opposed to **faithful** or reliable. **21. respect of persons**—(ch. 24:23). Such are led to evil by the slightest motive. **22.** (Cf. vs. 20.) **evil eye**—in the general sense of ch. 23:6, here more specific for covetousness (cf. ch. 22:9; Matt. 20:15). **poverty . . . him**—by God's providence. **23.** (Cf. ch. 9:8, 9; 27:5.) Those benefited by reproof will love their monitors. **24.** (Cf. Matt. 15:4-6.) Such, though heirs, are virtually thieves, to be ranked with highwaymen. **25. of a proud heart**—lit., "puffed up of soul"—i.e., self-confident, and hence overbearing and litigious. **made fat**—or, prosperous (ch. 11:25; 16:20). **26.** (Cf. ch. 3:6-8.) **walketh wisely**—i.e., trusting in God (ch. 22:17-19). **27.** (Cf. ch. 11:24-26.) **hideth his eyes** —as the face (Ps. 27:9; 69:17), denotes inattention. **28.** The elevation of the wicked to power drives men to seek refuge from tyranny (cf. vs. 12; ch. 11:10; Ps. 12:8).

CHAPTER 29

Vss. 1-27. **1. hardeneth . . . neck**—obstinately refuses counsel (II Kings 17:14; Neh. 9:16). **destroyed**

–lit., "shivered" or "utterly broken to pieces." **without remedy**–lit., "without healing" or repairing. **2.** (Cf. ch. 11:10; 28:28.) **in authority**–(Cf. *Margin*), increased in power. **3.** (Cf. ch. 4:6, 7; 10:1, etc.) **4. by judgment**–i.e., righteous decisions, opposed to those procured by gifts (cf. ch. 28:21), by which good government is perverted. **land**–for nation. **5.** (Cf. ch. 26:28.) **spreadeth . . . feet**–By misleading him as to his real character, the flatterer brings him to evil, prepared by himself or others. **6. In** [or, By] **the transgression**–he is brought into difficulty (ch. 12:13), but the righteous go on prospering, and so sing or rejoice. **7. considereth**–lit., "knows," as Ps. 1:6. **the cause**–i.e., in courts of justice (cf. vs. 14). The voluntary neglect of it by the wicked (ch. 28:27) occasions oppression. **8. Scornful men** –those who contemptuously disregard God's law. **bring**–(Cf. *Margin*), kindle strife. **turn away** [i.e., abate] **wrath. 9. contendeth**–i.e., in law. **whether . . . laugh**–The fool, whether angry or good-humored, is unsettled; or referring the words to the wise man, the sense is, that all his efforts, severe or gentle, are unavailing to pacify the fool. **10. bloodthirsty**–(Cf. *Margin*), murderers (Ps. 5:6; 26:9). **hate . . .** (ch. 1:11; Gen. 3:4.) **seek . . . soul**–i.e.,) to preserve it. **11.** (Cf. ch. 12:16; 16:32.) **mind**–or spirit, for anger or any ill passion which the righteous restrain. **12.** His servants imitate him. **13.** (Cf. ch. 22:2.) **deceitful man**–lit., "man of vexations," an exactor. **the Lord . . . their eyes**–sustains their lives (I Sam. 14:27; Ps. 13:3); i.e., both depend on Him, and He will do justice. **14.** (Cf. ch. 20: 28; 25:5.) Such is the character of the King of kings (Ps. 72:4, 12). **15.** (Cf. ch. 13:24; 23:13.) **16.** (Cf. vss. 2, 12; Ps. 12:1-8.) **shall see . . . fall**–and triumph in it (Ps. 37:34-38; 58:10, 11). **17.** (Cf. vss. 3, 15; ch. 19:18.) **give thee rest**–peace and quiet (cf. vs. 9). **18. no vision**–instruction in God's truth, which was by prophets, through visions (I Sam. 3:1). **people perish**–(Cf. *Margin*), are deprived of moral restraints. **keepeth the law**–has, and observes, instruction (ch. 14:11, 34; Ps. 19:11). **19. A servant**–who lacks good principle. **corrected**–or discovered. **will not answer**–i.e., will not obey. **20.** (Cf. ch. 21:5.) **hasty in . . . words**–implying self-conceit (ch. 26:12). **21. become his son**–assume the place and privileges of one. **22.** (Cf. ch. 15:18.) Such are delighted by discord and violence. **23.** (Cf. ch. 16:18; 18:12.) **honour . . . spirit**–or, such shall lay hold on honor (ch. 11:16). **24 hateth . . . soul**–(Cf. ch. 8:36). **heareth cursing**–(Lev. 5:1), risks the punishment, rather than reveal truth. **25. The fear . . . snare**–involves men in difficulty (cf. vs. 6). **shall be safe**–(Cf. *Margin;* ch. 18:10.) **26.** (Cf. *Margin;* Ps. 27:8.) God alone will and can do exact justice. **27.** (Cf. ch. 3:32.) On last clause, cf. vs. 16; Psalm 37:12.

CHAPTER 30

Vss. 1-33. **1.** This is the title of this chapter (cf. *Introduction*). **the prophecy**–lit., "the burden" (cf. Isa. 13:1; Zech. 9:1), used for any divine instruction; not necessarily a prediction, which was only a kind of prophecy (I Chron. 15:27, *a song*). Prophets were inspired men, who spoke for God to man, or for man to God (Gen. 20:7; Exod. 7:14, 15, 16). Such, also, were the New Testament prophets. In a general sense, Gad, Nathan, and others were such, who were divine teachers, though we do not learn that they were ever predicted. **the man spake**–lit., "the

saying of the man"; an expression used to denote any solemn and important announcement (cf. II Sam. 23:1; Ps. 36:1; 110:1; Isa. 1:24, etc.). Ithiel and Ucal were perhaps pupils. **2-4. brutish**–stupid, a strong term to denote his lowly self-estimation; or he may speak of such as his natural condition, as contrasted with God's all-seeing comprehensive knowledge and almighty power. The questions of the last clause emphatically deny the attributes mentioned to be those of any creature, thus impressively strengthening the implied reference of the former to God (cf. Deut. 30:12-14; Isa. 40:12; Eph. 4:8). **5.** (Cf. Ps. 12:6; 119:140.) **6. Add . . . words** –implying that his sole reliance was on God's all-sufficient teaching. **reprove** [convict] **thee**–and so the falsehood will appear. **7-9.** A prayer for exemption from wickedness, and the extremes of poverty and riches, the *two things* mentioned. Contentment is implied as desired. **vanity**–all sorts of sinful acts (Job 11:11; Isa. 5:18). **be full . . . deny**–i.e., puffed up by the pride of prosperity. **take the name . . . vain**–This is not (*Hebrew*) the form (cf. Exod. 20:7), but "take" rather denotes laying violent hold on any thing; i.e. lest I assail God's name or attributes, as justice, mercy, etc., which the poor are tempted to do. **10. Accuse not**–Slander not (Ps. 10: 7). **curse . . . guilty**–lest, however lowly, he be exasperated to turn on thee, and your guilt be made to appear. **11-14.** Four kinds of hateful persons–(1) graceless children, (2) hypocrites, (3) the proud, (4) cruel oppressors (cf. on vs. 14, Ps. 14:4; 52:2)–are now illustrated; (1) vss. 15, 16, the insatiability of prodigal children and their fate; (2) vs. 17, hypocrisy, or the concealment of real character; (3 and 4) vs. 18-20, various examples of pride and oppression. **15, 16. horse-leech**–supposed by some to be the vampire (a fabulous creature), as being literally insatiable; but the other subjects mentioned must be taken as this, comparatively insatiable. The use of a fabulous creature agreeably to popular notions is not inconsistent with inspiration. **There are three . . . yea, four**–(Cf. ch. 6:16). **17. The eye**–for the person, with reference to the use of the organ to express mockery and contempt, and also as that by which punishment is received. **the ravens . . . eagles . . . eat**–either as dying unnaturally, or being left unburied, or both. **18-20.** Hypocrisy is illustrated by four examples of the concealment of all methods or traces of action, and a pertinent example of double dealing in actual vice is added, i.e., the **adulterous woman. she eateth . . . mouth**–i.e,, she hides the evidences of her shame and professes innocence. **21-23.** Pride and cruelty, the undue exaltation of those unfit to hold power, produce those vices which disquiet society (cf. ch. 19:10; 28:3). **heir . . . mistress**–i.e., takes her place as a wife (Gen. 16:4). **24-31.** These verses provide two classes of apt illustrations of various aspects of the moral world, which the reader is left to apply. By the first, diligence and providence are commended; the success of these insignificant animals being due to their instinctive sagacity and activity, rather than strength. **conies**–mountain mice, or rabbits. **spider**–tolerated, even in palaces, to destroy flies. **taketh . . . hands**–or, uses with activity the limbs provided for taking prey. The other class provides similes for whatever is majestic or comely, uniting efficiency with gracefulness. **32.** As none can hope, successfully, to resist such a king, suppress even the thought of an attempt. **lay . . . hand upon thy mouth**–"lay" is well supplied (Judg. 18:19; Job 29:9; 40:4). **33.** i.e., strife–or other ills, as surely arise from devising evil as natural effects from natural causes.

CHAPTER 31

Vss. 1-31. **1.** On the title of this, the 6th part of the book, cf. *Introduction.* **prophecy**—as in ch. 30: 1. **2. What, my son?**—i.e., What shall I say? Repetitions denote earnestness. **son . . . womb**—as our phrase, "my own son," a term of special affection. **son. . . vows**—as one dedicated to God; so the word *Lemuel* may mean. **3-9.** Succinct but solemn warnings against vices to which kings are peculiarly tempted, as carnal pleasures and oppressive and unrighteous government are used to sustain sensual indulgence. **3. strength**—mental and bodily resources for health and comfort. **thy ways**—or course of life. **to that . . . kings**—lit., "to the destroying of kings," avoid destructive pleasures (cf. ch. 5:9; 7:22, 27; Hos. 4:11). **4, 5.** Stimulants enfeeble reason, pervert the heart, and do not suit rulers, who need clear and steady minds, and well-governed affections (cf. ch. 20:1; 22:29). **pervert . . . afflicted**—They give unrighteous decisions against the poor. **6, 7.** The proper use of such drinks is to restore tone to feeble bodies and depressed minds (cf. Ps. 104:15). **8, 9. Open . . . cause**—Plead for those who cannot plead for themselves, as the orphan, stranger, etc. (cf. Ps. 72:12; Isa. 1:17). **appointed to destruction** —who are otherwise ruined by their oppressors (cf. ch. 29:14, 16). **10-31.** This exquisite picture of a truly lovely wife is conceived and drawn in accordance with the customs of Eastern nations, but its moral teachings suit all climes. In *Hebrew* the verses begin with the letters of the *Hebrew* alphabet in order (cf. *Introduction* to Poetical Books). **10. Who . . . woman?**—The question implies that such are rare, though not entirely wanting (cf. ch. 18:22; 19:14). **virtuous**—lit., "of strength," i.e., moral courage (cf. ch. 12:4; Ruth 3:11). **her price . . .**—(cf. ch. 3:15). **11. heart . . . trust in her**—He relies on her prudence and skill. **no need of spoil**—does not lack profit or gain, especially, that obtained by the risk of war. **12. do . . . good**—contribute good to him. **13, 14.** Ancient women of rank thus wrought with their hands; and such, indeed, were the customs of Western women a few centuries since. In the East also, the fabrics were articles of merchandise. **15.** She diligently attends to expending as well as gathering wealth; **16.,** and hence has means to purchase property. **17, 18.** To energy she adds a watchfulness in bargains, and a protracted and painful industry. The last clause may figuratively denote that her prosperity (cf. ch. 24:20) is not short lived. **19.** No work, however mean, if honest, is disdained. **20.** Industry enables her to be charitable. **21. scarlet**—or, purple, by reason of the dyes used, the best fabrics; as a matter of taste also; the color suits cold. **22. coverings of tapestry** —or, coverlets, i.e., for beds. **silk** [or, linen (cf. Exod. 26:1; 27:9)] **and purple**—i.e., the most costly goods. **23. in the gates**—(cf. ch. 22:22). His domestic comfort promotes his advancement in public dignity. **24. fine linen**—or, linen shirts, or the material for them. **girdles**—were often costly and highly valued (II Sam. 18:11). **delivereth**—or, giveth as a present or to sell. **25. Strength and honour** —*Strong* and *beautiful* is her clothing; or, figuratively, for moral character, vigorous and honorable. **shall rejoice . . . come**—in confidence of certain maintenance. **26.** Her conversation is wise and gentle. **27.** (Cf. I Tim. 5:14; Titus 2:5.) She adds to her example a wise management of those under her control. **28.** She is honored by those who best know her. **29.** The words are those of her husband, praising her. **virtuously**—(Cf. vs. 10.) **30. Favour** —or, Grace of personal manner. **beauty**—of face, or form (cf. ch. 11:22). True piety alone commands permanent respect and affection (I Pet. 3:3). **31.** The result of her labor is her best eulogy.

Nothing can add to the simple beauty of this admirable portrait. On the measure of its realization in the daughters of our own day rest untold results, in the domestic, and, therefore, the civil and religious, welfare of the people.

ECCLESIASTES; OR THE PREACHER

INTRODUCTION

THE Hebrew *title* is *Koheleth*, which the speaker in it applies to himself (ch. 1:12), "I, *Koheleth*, was king over Israel." It means an *Assembler* or *Convener of a meeting* and a *Preacher* to such a meeting. The feminine form of the *Hebrew* noun, and its construction once (ch. 7:27) with a feminine verb, show that it not only signifies *Solomon*, the Preacher to assemblies (in which case it is construed with the verb or noun masculine), but also *Divine Wisdom* (feminine in *Hebrew*) speaking by the mouth of the inspired king. In six cases out of seven it is construed with the masculine. Solomon was endowed with inspired wisdom (I Kings 3:5-14; 6:11, 12; 9:1, etc.; 11:9-11), specially fitting him for the task. The Orientals delight in such meetings for grave discourse. Thus the Arabs formerly had an assembly yearly, at Ocadh, for hearing and reciting poems. Cf. "Masters of assemblies" (Note, ch. 12:11, also 12:9). "The Preacher taught the people knowledge," probably *viva voce;* I Kings 4:34; 10:2, 8, 24; II Chron. 9:1, 7, 23, plainly refer to a somewhat public divan met for literary discussion. So "spake," thrice repeated (I Kings 4:32, 33), refers not to *written* compositions, but to addresses *spoken* in assemblies convened for the purpose. The Holy Ghost, no doubt, signifies also by the term that Solomon's doctrine is intended for the "great congregation," the Church of all places and ages (Ps. 22:25; 49:2-4).

Solomon was plainly *the author* (ch. 1:12, 16; 2:15; 12:9). That the Rabbins attribute it to Isaiah or Hezekiah is explicable by supposing that one or the other inserted it *in the canon.* The difference of its style, as compared with Proverbs and Song of Solomon, is due to the difference of subjects, and the different period of his life in which each was written; the Song, in the fervor of his first love to God; Proverbs, about the same time, or somewhat later; but Ecclesiastes in late old age, as the seal and testimony of repentance of his apostasy in the intervening period: Psalm 89:30, 33 proves his penitence. The substitution of the title *Koheleth* for Solomon (that is, *peace*), may imply that, having *troubled* Israel, meantime he forfeited his name of *peace* (I Kings 11:14, 23); but now, having repented, he wishes to be henceforth a *Preacher* of righteousness. The alleged foreign expressions in the *Hebrew* may have been easily imported, through the great intercourse there was with other nations during his long reign. Moreover, supposed Chaldaisms may be fragments preserved from the common tongue of which *Hebrew, Syriac, Chaldee,* and *Arabic* were offshoots.

THE SCOPE of Ecclesiastes is *to show the vanity of all mere human pursuits, when made the chief end, as contrasted with the real blessedness of true wisdom,* i.e., religion. The immortality of the soul is dwelt on incidentally, as subsidiary to the main scope. Moses' law took this truth for granted but drew its sanctions of rewards and punishments in accordance with the theocracy, which was under a special providence of God as the *temporal* King of Israel, from the *present life,* rather than the future. But after Israel chose an earthly king, God withdrew, in part, His extraordinary providence, so that under Solomon, temporal rewards did not invariably follow virtue, and punishments vice (cf. ch. 2:16; 3:19; 4:1; 5:8; 7:15; 8:14; 9:2, 11). Hence the need arises to show that these anomalies will be rectified hereafter, and this is the grand "conclusion," therefore, of the "whole" book, that, seeing there is a coming judgment, and seeing that present goods do not satisfy the soul, "man's whole duty is to fear God and keep his commandments" (ch. 12:13, 14), and meanwhile, to use, in joyful and serene sobriety, and not abuse, the present life (ch. 3:12, 13).

It is objected that sensual epicurism seems to be inculcated (ch. 3:12, 13, 22, etc.); but it is a contented, thankful enjoyment of God's present gifts that is taught, as opposed to a murmuring, anxious, avaricious spirit, as is proved by ch. 5:18, cf. with 11–15, not making them the *chief end* of life; not the joy of levity and folly; a misunderstanding which he guards against in ch. 7:2–6; 11:9; 12:1. Again, ch. 7:16; 9:2–10, might seem to teach fatalism and skepticism. But these are words put in the mouth of an objector; or rather, they were the language of Solomon himself during his apostasy, finding an echo in the heart of every sensualist, who *wishes* to be an unbeliever, and, who, therefore, sees difficulties enough in the world around wherewith to prop up his wilful unbelief. The answer is given (ch. 7:17, 18; 9:11, etc.; 11:1, 6; 12:13). Even if these passages be taken as words of Solomon, they are to be understood as forbidding a self-made "righteousness," which tries to constrain God to grant salvation to imaginary good works and external strictness with which it wearies itself; also, that speculation which tries to fathom all God's inscrutable counsels (ch. 8:17), and that carefulness about the future forbidden in Matt. 6:25.

THE CHIEF GOOD is that the possession of that which makes us happy, is to be sought as the *end,* for its own sake; whereas, all other things are but *means* towards it. Philosophers, who made it the great subject of inquiry, restricted it to the present life, treating the eternal as unreal, and only useful to awe the multitude with. But Solomon shows the vanity of all human things (so-called philosophy included) to satisfy the soul, and that heavenly wisdom alone is the chief good. He had taught so when young (Prov. 1:20; 8, 1, etc.); so also; in Song of Solomon, he had spiritualized the subject in an allegory; and now, after having long personally tried the manifold ways in which the wordly seek to reach happiness, he gives the fruit of his experience in old age.

It is divided into two parts—chs. 1–6:10 showing the vanity of earthly things; ch. 6:10 to ch. 12, the excellence of heavenly wisdom. Deviations from strict logical methods occur in these divisions, but in the main they are observed. The deviations make it the less stiff and artificial, and the more suited to all capacities. It is in poetry; the hemistichal division is mostly observed, but occasionally not so. The choice of epithets, imagery, inverted order of words, ellipses, parallelism, or, in its absence, similarity of diction, mark versification.

CHAPTER 1

Vss. 1-18. INTRODUCTION. **1. the Preacher**—and *Convener of assemblies* for the purpose. See my Preface. *Koheleth* in *Hebrew,* a symbolical name for *Solomon,* and of *Heavenly Wisdom* speaking through and identified with him. Verse 12 shows that "king of Jerusalem" is in apposition, not with "David," but "Preacher." **of Jerusalem**—rather, *in* Jerusalem, for it was merely his metropolis, not his whole kingdom. **2.** The theme proposed of the first part of his discourse. **Vanity of vanities**—Hebraism for the most utter vanity. So "holy of holies" (Exod. 26); "servant of servants" (Gen. 9:25). The repetition increases the force. **all**—Hebrew, "*the* all"; all without exception, viz., earthly things. **vanity**—not in themselves, for God maketh nothing in vain (I Tim. 4:4, 5), but vain when put in the place of God and made the *end,* instead of the *means* (Ps. 39:5, 6; 62:9; Matt. 6:33); vain, also, because of the "vanity" to which they are "subjected" by the fall (Rom. 8:20). **3. What profit ... labour**—i.e., "What profit" as to the chief good (Matt. 16:26). Labor is profitable *in its proper place* (Gen. 2:15; 3:19; Prov. 14:23). **under the**

sun—i.e., *in this life,* as opposed to the future world. The phrase often recurs, but only in Ecclesiastes. **4. earth ... for ever**—(Ps. 104:5). While the *earth* remains the same, the generations of *men* are ever changing; what lasting profit, then, can there be from the toils of one whose sojourn on earth, as an individual, is so brief? The "for ever" is comparative, not absolute (Ps. 102:26). **5.** (Ps. 19:5, 6.) "Panting" as the *Hebrew* for "hasteth"; metaphor, from a runner (Ps. 19:5, "a strong man") in a "race." It applies rather to the *rising* sun, which seems *laboriously* to mount up to the meridian, than to the setting sun; the accents too favor MAURER, "And (that too, returning) to his place, where panting he riseth." **6. according to his circuits**—i.e., it returns afresh to its former circuits, however many be its previous veerings about. The north and south winds are the two prevailing winds in Palestine and Egypt. **7.** By subterraneous cavities, and by evaporation forming rain-clouds, the fountains and rivers are supplied from the sea, into which they then flow back. The connection is: *Individual* men are continually changing, while the *succession of the race* continues; just as the sun, wind, and rivers are ever shifting about, while the cycle in which they move is invariable; they return to the point whence they set out. Hence is man, as in these objects of nature which are his analogue, with all the seeming changes "there is no new thing" (vs. 9). 8. MAURER translates, "All *words* are wearied out," i.e., are inadequate, as also, "man cannot express" all the things in the world which undergo this ceaseless, changeless cycle of vicissitudes: "The eye is not satisfied with seeing them," etc. But it is plainly a return to the idea (vs. 3) as to *man's* "labor," which is only wearisome and profitless; "no new" good can accrue from it (vs. 9); for as the sun, etc., so man's laborious works move in a changeless cycle. The **eye** and **ear** are two of the taskmasters for which man toils. But these are never "satisfied" (ch. 6:7; Prov. 27:20). Nor can they be so hereafter, for there will be nothing "new." Not so the chief good, Jesus Christ (John 4:13, 14; Rev. 21:5). 9. Rather, "no new thing *at all*"; as in Numbers 11:6. This is not meant in a general sense; but there is no new source of happiness (the subject in question) which can be devised; the same round of petty pleasures, cares, business, study, wars, etc., being repeated over and over again [HOLDEN]. 10. old time—[*Hebrew,* "ages"]. which was—The *Hebrew plural* cannot be joined to the verb *singular.* Therefore translate: "It hath been in the ages before; certainly it hath been before us" [HOLDEN]. Or, as MAURER: "That which has been (done) before us (in our presence, I Chron. 16:33), has been (done) already in the old times." 11. The reason why some things are thought "new," which are not really so, is the imperfect record that exists of preceding ages among their successors. those that . . . come after—i.e., those that live *still later* than the "things, rather the *persons* or generations, vs. 4, with which this verse is connected, the six intermediate verses being merely illustrations of vs. 4 [WEISS], that are to come" (ch. 2:16; 9:5). 12. Resumption of vs. 1, the intermediate verses being the introductory statement of his thesis. Therefore, "the Preacher" (*Koheleth*) is repeated. was king—instead of "am," because he is about to give the results of his *past* experience during his long reign. in Jerusalem—specified, as opposed to David, who reigned both in Hebron and Jerusalem; whereas Solomon reigned only in Jerusalem. "King of Israel in Jerusalem," implies that he reigned over *Israel and Judah combined;* whereas David, at Hebron, reigned only over *Judah,* and not, until he was settled in Jerusalem, over both Israel and Judah. 13. this sore travail—viz., that of "searching" out all things done under heaven." Not human wisdom in general, which comes afterwards (ch. 2:12, etc.), but laborious inquiries into, and speculations about, the works of men; e.g., political science. As man is doomed to get his bread, so his knowledge, by the sweat of his brow (Gen. 3:19) [GILL]. exercised—i.e., disciplined; lit., "that they may thereby *chastise* or *humble* themselves." 14. The reason is here given why investigation into man's "works" is only "sore travail" (vs. 13); viz., because all man's ways are vain (vs. 18) and cannot be mended (vs. 15). vexation of ["a preying upon" the] spirit—MAURER translates; "the pursuit of wind," as in ch. 5:16; Hosea 12:1, "Ephraim feedeth on wind." But old versions support the *English Version.* 15. Investigation (vs. 13) into human ways is vain labor, for they are hopelessly "crooked" and "cannot be made straight" by it (ch. 7:13). God, the chief good, alone can do this (Isa. 40:4; 45:2). wanting—(Dan. 5:27). numbered—so as to make a complete number; so equivalent to "supplied" [MAURER]. Or, rather, man's state is *utterly wanting;* and that which

is wholly defective cannot be numbered or calculated. The investigator thinks he can draw up, in accurate *numbers,* statistics of man's wants; but these, including the defects in the investigator's labor, are not partial, but total. **16. communed with . . . heart**—(Gen. 24:45.) **come to great estate**—Rather, "I *have magnified* and gotten" (lit., "added," increased), etc. **all . . . before me in Jerusalem**—viz., the priests, judges, and two kings that preceded Solomon. His wisdom exceeded that of all before Jesus Christ, the antitypical *Koheleth,* or "*Gatherer* of men,*" (Luke 13:34), and "Wisdom" incarnate (Matt. 11:19; 12:42). **had . . . experience**—lit., "had *seen*" (Jer. 2:31). Contrast with this glorying in worldly wisdom Jeremiah 9:23, 24. **17. wisdom . . . madness**—i.e., their effects, the works of human wisdom and folly respectively. "Madness," lit., "vaunting extravagance"; ch. 2:12; 7:25, etc., support *English Version* rather than DATHE, "splendid matters." "Folly is read by *English Version* with some MSS., instead of the present *Hebrew* text, "prudence." If *Hebrew* be retained, understand "prudence," *falsely so called* (I Tim. 6:20), "craft" (Dan. 8:25). **18. wisdom . . . knowledge**—not in general, for wisdom, etc., are most excellent in their place; but *speculative knowledge of man's ways* (vss. 13, 17), which, the farther it goes, gives one the more pain to find how "crooked" and "wanting" they are (vs. 15; ch. 12:12).

CHAPTER 2

Vss. 1-26. He next tries pleasure and luxury, retaining however, his worldly "wisdom" (ch. 3:9), but all proves "vanity" in respect to the chief good. **1. I said . . . heart**—(Luke 12:19). **thee**—my heart, I will test whether thou canst find that solid good in pleasure which was not in "worldly wisdom." But this also proves to be "vanity" (Isa. 50:11). **2. laughter**—including *prosperity,* and *joy* in general (Job 8:21). **mad**—i.e., *when made the chief good;* it is harmless in its proper place. **What doeth it?** —Of what avail is it in giving solid good? (ch. 7:6; Prov. 14:13). **3-11.** Illustration more at large of vss 1, 2. **3. sought**—I resolved, after search into many plans. **give myself unto**—lit., "to draw my flesh (body) to" wine (including all banquetings). Image from a captive drawn after a chariot in triumph (Rom. 6:16, 19; I Cor. 12:2); or, one "allured" (II Pet. 2:18, 19). **yet acquainting . . . wisdom**—lit., and my heart (still) *was behaving,* or *guiding itself,* with wisdom [GESENIUS]. MAURER translates: "*was weary of* (worldly) wisdom." But the end of vs. 9 confirms *English Version.* **folly**—viz., pleasures of the flesh, termed "mad," vs. 2. **all the days . . .**—(See *Margin* and ch. 6:12; Job. 15:20). **4.** (I Kings 7:1-8; 9:1, 19; 10:18, etc.) **vineyards**—(Song of Sol. 8:11.) **5. gardens**—*Hebrew,* "paradises," a foreign word; *Sanscrit,* "a place enclosed with a wall"; *Armenian* and *Arabic,* "a pleasure-ground with flowers and shrubs near the king's house, or castle." An earthly paradise can never make up for the want of the heavenly (Rev. 2:7). **6. pools**—artificial, for irrigating the soil (Gen. 2:10; Neh. 2:14; Isa. 1:30). Three such reservoirs are still found, called Solomon's cisterns, a mile and a half from Jerusalem. **wood that bringeth forth**—rather, "the grove that *flourisheth with* trees" [LOWTH]. **7. born in my house**—These were esteemed more trustworthy servants than those bought (Gen. 14:14; 15:2, 3; 17:12, 13, 27; Jer. 2:14), called *songs of* one's *handmaid* (Exod. 23:12; cf. Gen. 12:

16; Job 1:3). **8.** (I Kings 10:27; II Chron. 1:15; 9: 20). **peculiar treasure of kings and . . . provinces**—contributed by them, as tributary to him (I Kings 4: 21, 24) a poor substitute for the wisdom whose "gain is better than fine gold" (Prov. 3:14, 15). **singers**—so David (II Sam. 19:35). **musical instruments . . . of all sorts**—introduced at banquets (Isa. 5:12; Amos 6:5, 6); rather, "a princess and princesses," from an *Arabic* root. One regular wife, or queen (Esther 1: 9); Pharaoh's daughter (I Kings 3:1); other secondary wives, "princesses," distinct from the "concubines" (I Kings 11:3; Ps. 45:10; Song of Sol. 6:8) [WEISS, GENENIUS]. Had these been omitted, the enumeration would be incomplete. **9. great**—opulent (Gen. 24:35; Job. 1:3; see I Kings 10:23). **remained**—(vs. 3). **10. my labour**—in procuring pleasures. **this**—evanescent "joy" was my only "portion out of all my labor" (ch. 3:22; 5:18; 9:19; I Kings 10:5). **11.** But all these I felt were only "vanity," and of no "profit" as to the chief good. "Wisdom" (worldly *common sense*, sagacity), which still "remained with me" (vs. 9), showed me that these could not give solid happiness. **12.** He had tried (wordly) wisdom (ch. 1: 12-18) and folly (foolish pleasure) (vs. 1-11); he now compares them (vs. 12), and finds that while (worldly) **wisdom excelleth folly** (vss. 13, 14), yet the one event, death, befalls both (vs. 14-16), and that thus the wealth acquired by the wise man's "labor" may descend to a "fool" that hath not labored (vss. 18, 19, 21); therefore all his labor is vanity (vss. 22, 23). **what can the man do . . . already done**—(ch. 1:9.) Parenthetical. A future investigator can strike nothing out "new," so as to draw a different conclusion from what I draw by comparing "wisdom and madness." HOLDEN, with less ellipsis, translates, "What, O man, shall come after the king?" etc. Better, GROTIUS, "What man can come after (compete with) the king in the things which are done?" None ever can have the same means of testing what all earthly things can do towards satisfying the soul; namely, worldly wisdom, science, riches, power, longevity, all combined. **13, 14.** (Prov. 17:24.) The worldly "wise" man has *good sense* in managing his affairs, *skill* and *taste* in building and planting, and keeps within *safe* and *respectable* bounds in pleasure, while the "fool" is wanting in these respects ("darkness," equivalent to *fatal error, blind infatuation*), yet one event, death, happens to both (Job 21:26). **15. was I**—so anxious to become, etc. (II Chron. 1:10). **Then**—Since such is the case. **this**—viz., pursuit of (worldly) wisdom; it can never fill the place of the true wisdom (Job. 28:28; Jer. 8:9). **16. remembrance**—a great aim of the worldly (Gen. 11:4). The righteous alone attain it (Ps. 112:6; Prov. 10:7). **for ever**—no *perpetual* memorial. **that which now is**—MAURER, "In the days to come all things shall be *now long ago* forgotten." **17.** Disappointed in one experiment after another, he is weary of life. The backslider ought to have rather reasoned as the prodigal (Hos. 2:6, 7; Luke 15:17, 18). **grievous unto me**—(Job. 10:1.) **18, 19.** One hope alone was left to the disappointed worldling, the perpetuation of his name and riches, laboriously gathered, through his successor. For selfishness is mostly at the root of worldly parents' alleged providence for their children. But now the remembrance of how he himself, the piously reared child of David, had disregarded his father's dying charge (I Chron. 28:9), suggested the sad misgivings as to what Rehoboam, his son by an idolatrous Ammonitess, Naamah, should prove to be; a foreboding too fully realized (I Kings 12; 14:21-31). **20.** *I gave up as desperate*

all hope of solid fruit from *my labor*. **21.** Suppose "there is a man. . . ." **equity**—rather "with success," as the *Hebrew* is rendered (ch. 11:6), "prosper," though *Margin* gives "right" [HOLDEN and MAURER]. **evil**—not in itself, for this is the ordinary course of things, but "evil," as regards the chief good, that one should have toiled so fruitlessly. **22.** Same sentiment as in vs. 21, interrogatively. **23.** The only fruit he has is, not only sorrows *in* his days, but *all* his days are sorrows, and his travail (not only *has* griefs connected with it, but *is* itself), grief. **24.** *English Version* gives a seemingly Epicurean sense, contrary to the general scope. The *Hebrew*, lit. is, "It is *not good* for man that he should eat," etc., "and should make his soul see good" (or "*show* his soul, i.e., himself, happy"), etc. [WEISS]. According to HOLDEN and WEISS, ch. 3:12, 22 differ from this verse in the text and meaning; here he means, "It is not good that a man should feast himself, and falsely make as though his soul were happy"; he thus refers to a false *pretending* of happiness *acquired by and for one's self*; in ch. 3:12, 22 and 5: 18, 19, to *real seeing*, or *finding* pleasure *when God gives it*. There it is said to be *good* for a man to enjoy with satisfaction and thankfulness the blessings which God gives; here it is said *not* to be *good* to take an unreal pleasure to one's self by feasting, etc. **This also I saw**—I perceived by experience that good (real pleasure) is not to be taken at will, but comes only from the hand of God [WEISS] (Ps. 4:6; Isa. 57:19-21). Or as HOLDEN, "It is the appointment from the hand of God, that the sensualist has no solid satisfaction" (good). **25. hasten**—after indulgences (Prov. 7:23; 19:2), *eagerly pursue* such enjoyments. None can compete with me in this. If I, then, with all my opportunities of enjoyment, failed utterly to obtain solid pleasure of my own making, apart from God, who else can? God mercifully spares His children the sad experiment which Solomon made, by denying them the goods which they often desire. He gives them the fruits of Solomon's experience, without their paying the dear price at which Solomon bought it. **26.** True, literally, in the Jewish theocracy; and in some measure in all ages (Job 27:16,17; Prov. 13:22, 28:8). Though the retribution be not so visible and immediate now as then, it is no less real. Happiness even here is more truly the portion of the godly (Ps. 84:11; Matt. 5:5; Mark 10:29, 30; Rom. 8:28; I Tim. 4:8). **that he** [the sinner] **may give**—i.e., unconsciously and in spite of himself. The godly Solomon had satisfaction in his riches and wisdom, when God gave them (II Chron. 1). The backsliding Solomon had no happiness when he sought it in them apart from God; and the riches which he heaped up became the prey of Shishak (II Chron. 12).

CHAPTER 3

Vss. 1-22. Earthly pursuits are no doubt lawful in their proper time and order (vss. 1-8), but unprofitable when out of time and place; as for instance, when pursued as the solid and chief good (vss. 9, 10); whereas God makes everything beautiful in its season, which man obscurely comprehends (vs. 11). God allows man to enjoy moderately and virtuously His earthly gifts (vss. 12, 13). What consoles us amidst the instability of earthly blessings is, God's counsels are immutable (vs. 14). **1.** Man has his appointed cycle of seasons and vicissitudes, as the sun, wind, and water (ch. 1:5-7).

purpose—as there is a fixed "season" in God's "purposes" (e.g., He has fixed the "time" when man is "to be born," and "to die," vs. 2), so there is a lawful "time" for man to carry out his "purposes" and inclinations. God does not condemn, but approves of, the *use* of earthly blessings (vs. 12); it is the *abuse* that He condemns, the making them the chief end (I Cor. 7:31). The earth, without human desires, love, taste, joy, sorrow, would be a dreary waste, without water; but, on the other hand, the misplacing and excess of them, as of a flood, need control. Reason and revelation are given to control them. **2. time to die**—(Ps. 31:15; Heb. 9:27). **plant** —A man can no more reverse the times and order of "planting," and of "digging up," and transplanting, than he can alter the times fixed for his "birth" and "death." To try to "plant" *out of season* is vanity, however good *in season;* so to make earthly things *the chief end* is vanity, however good they be in order and season. GILL takes it, not so well, figuratively (Jer. 18:7, 9; Amos 9:15; Matt. 15:13). **3. time to kill**—viz., judicially, criminals; or, in wars of self-defense; not in malice. Out of this time and order, killing is murder. **to heal**—God has His times for "healing" (lit., Isa. 38:5, 21; fig., Deut. 32: 39; Hos. 6:1; spiritually, Ps. 147:3; Isa. 57:19). To *heal* spiritually, before the sinner feels his *wound,* would be out of time, and so injurious. **time to break down**—cities, as Jerusalem, by Nebuchadnezzar. **build up**—as Jerusalem, in the time of Zerubbabel; spiritually (Amos 9:11), "the set time" (Ps. 102:13-16). **4. mourn**—viz., for the dead (Gen. 23:2). **dance**—as David before the ark (II Sam. 6:12-14; Ps. 30:11); spiritually (Matt. 9:15; Luke 6: 21; 15:25). The Pharisees, by requiring sadness *out of time,* erred seriously. **5. cast away stones**—as out of a garden or vineyard (Isa. 5:2). **gather**—for building; fig., the Gentiles, once castaway stones, were in due time made parts of the spiritual building (Eph. 2:19, 20), and children of Abraham (Matt. 3: 9); so the restored Jews hereafter (Ps. 102:13, 14; Zech. 9:16). **refrain. . . . embracing**—(Joel 2:16: I Cor. 7:5, 6.) **6. time to get**—e.g., to gain honestly a livelihood (Eph. 4:23). **lose**—When God wills losses to us, then is our time to be content. **keep**—not to give to the idle beggar (II Thess. 3:10). **cast away**—in charity (Prov. 11:24); or to part with the dearest object, rather than the soul (Mark 9:43). To be careful is right in its place, but not when it comes between us and Jesus Christ (Luke 10:40-42). **7. rend**—garments, in mourning (Joel 2:13); fig., nations, as Israel from Judah, already foretold, in Solomon's time (I Kings 11:30, 31), to be "sewed" together hereafter (Ezek. 37:15, 22). **silence**—(Amos 5:13), in a national calamity, or that of a friend (Job. 2:13); also not to murmur under God's visitation (Lev. 10:3; Ps. 39:1, 2, 9). **8. hate**—e.g., sin, lusts (Luke 14:26); i.e., to love *God* so much more as to seem in comparison to *hate* "father or mother," when coming between us and God. **time of war . . . peace**—(Luke 14:31). **9.** But these earthly pursuits, while lawful in their season, are "unprofitable" when made by man, what God never intended them to be, the chief good. Solomon had tried to create an artificial forced joy, at times when he ought rather to have been serious; the result, therefore, of his labor to be happy, out of God's order, was disappointment. "A time to plant" (vs. 2) refers to his *planting* (ch. 2:5); "laugh" (vs. 4), to ch. 2:1, 2. "his mirth," "laughter"; "build up," "gather stones" (vss. 3, 5), to his "building" (ch. 2:4); "embrace," "love," to his "princess" (*Note,* ch. 2:8); "get" (perhaps also "gather," vss. 5, 6), to his "gath-

ering" (ch. 2:8). All these were of no "profit," because not in God's time and order of bestowing happiness. **10.** (Ch. 1:13.) **11. his time**—i.e. *in its* proper *season* (Ps. 1:3), opposed to worldlings putting earthly pursuits *out of their proper time and place* (*Note,* vs. 9). **set the world in their heart**—given them capacities to understand *the world* of nature as reflecting God's wisdom in its beautiful order and times (Rom. 1:19,20). "Everything" answers to "world," in the parallelism. **so that**—i.e., but in such a manner that man only sees a portion, not the whole "from beginning to end" (ch. 8:17; Job 26: 14; Rom. 11:33; Rev. 15:4). PARKHURST, for "world," translates: "Yet He hath put *obscurity in the midst of them,*" lit., "a secret," so man's mental *dimness of sight* as to the full mystery of God's works. So HOLDEN and WEISS. This incapacity for "finding out" (comprehending) God's work is chiefly the fruit of the fall. The worldling ever since, not knowing God's time and order, labors in vain, because out of time and place. **12. in them**—in God's works (vs. 11), as far as relates to man's duty. Man cannot fully comprehend them, but he ought joyfully to receive ("rejoice in") God's gifts, and "do good" with them to himself and to others. This is never out of season (Gal. 6:9, 10). Not sensual joy and self-indulgence (Phil. 4:4; Jas. 4:16, 17). **13.** Lit., "And also as to every man who eats," etc., "this is the gift of God" (vs. 22; ch. 5:18). When received as God's gifts, and to God's glory, the good things of life are enjoyed in their due time and order (Acts 2:46; I Cor. 10:31; I Tim. 4:3, 4). **14.** (I Sam. 3:12; II Sam. 23:5; Ps. 80:34; Matt. 24:35; Jas. 1:17.) **for ever**—as opposed to man's perishing labors (ch. 2:15-18). **any thing taken from it**—opposed to man's "crooked and wanting" works (ch. 1:15; 7:13). The event of man's labors depends wholly on God's immutable purpose. Man's part, therefore, is to do and enjoy every earthly thing *in its proper season* (vss. 12, 13), not setting aside God's order, but observing deep reverence towards God; for the mysteriousness and unchangeableness of God's purposes are designed to lead "man to fear before Him." Man knows not the event of each act; otherwise he would think himself independent of God. **15.** Resumption of ch. 1:9. Whatever changes there be, the succession of events is ordered by God's "everlasting" laws (vs. 14), and returns in a fixed cycle. **requireth that . . . past**—After many changes, God's law *requires* the return of the same cycle of events, as in *the past,* lit., "that which is driven on." LXX and *Syriac* translate: "God requireth (i.e., avengeth) the *persecuted* man"; a transition to vss. 16, 17. The parallel clauses of the verse support *English Version.* **16.** Here a difficulty is suggested. If God "requires" events to move in their perpetual cycle, why are the wicked allowed to deal unrighteously in the place where injustice ought least of all to be; viz., "the place of judgment" (Jer. 12:1)? **17.** Solution of it. There is a coming judgment in which God will vindicate His righteous ways. The sinner's "time" of his unrighteous "work" is short. God also has His "time" and "work" of judgment; and, meanwhile, is overruling, for good at last, what seems now dark. Man cannot now "find out" the plan of God's ways (vs. 11; Ps. 97:2). If judgment instantly followed every sin, there would be no scope for free-will, faith, and perseverance of saints in spite of difficulties. The previous darkness will make the light at last the more glorious. **there**—(Job 3:17-19) in eternity, in the presence of the Divine Judge, opposed to the "there," in the human place of judgment (vs. 16): so "from *thence*" (Gen. 49:24). **18.**

estate—The estate of fallen man is so ordered (these wrongs are permitted), that God might "manifest," i.e., thereby *prove* them, and that they might themselves see their mortal frailty, like that of the beasts. **sons of men**—rather, *sons of Adam*, a phrase used for *fallen men*. The toleration of injustice until the judgment is designed to "manifest" men's characters in their fallen state, to see whether the oppressed will bear themselves aright amidst their wrongs, knowing that the time is short, and there is a coming judgment. The oppressed share in death, but the comparison to "beasts" applies especially to *the ungodly oppressors* (Ps. 49:12, 20). They too need to be "manifested" (proved), whether, considering that they must soon die as the "beasts," and fearing the judgment to come, they will repent (Dan. 4:27). **19.** Lit., "For the sons of men (Adam) *are a mere chance*, as also the beast is a mere chance." These words can only be the sentiments of the skeptical oppressors. God's delay in judgment gives scope for the "manifestation" of their infidelity (ch. 8:11; Ps. 55:19; II Pet. 3:3, 4). They are "brute *beasts*," morally (vs. 18; Jude 10); and they end by maintaining that man, physically, has no pre-eminence over the beast, both alike being "fortuities." Probably this was the language of Solomon himself in his apostasy. He answers it in vs. 21. If vss. 19, 20 be *his* words, they express only that *as regards liability to death*, excluding the future judgment, as the skeptic oppressors do, man is on a level with the beast. Life is "vanity," if regarded independently of religion. But vs. 21 points out the vast difference between them in respect to the future destiny; also (vs. 17) beasts have no "judgment" to come. **breath** —vitality. **21. Who knoweth**—Not *doubt* of the destination of man's spirit (ch. 12:7); but "*how few*, by reason of the outward mortality to which man is as liable as the beast and which is the ground of the skeptic's argument, comprehend the wide difference between man and the beast" (Isa. 53:1). The *Hebrew* expresses the difference strongly, "The spirit of man that ascends, it belongeth to on high; but the spirit of the beast that descends, it belongeth to below, even to the earth." Their destinations and proper element differ utterly [WEISS]. **22.** (Cf. vs. 12; ch. 5:18.) Inculcating a thankful enjoyment of God's gifts, and a cheerful discharge of man's duties, founded on fear of God; not as the sensualist (ch. 11:9); not as the anxious money-seeker (ch. 2:23; 5:10-17). **his portion**—in the present life. If it were made his *main* portion, it would be "vanity" (ch. 2:1; Luke 16:25). **for who . . .**—Our ignorance as to the future, which is God's "time" (vs. 11), should lead us to use the present time in the best sense and leave the future to His infinite wisdom (Matt. 6:20, 25, 31-34).

CHAPTER 4

Vss. 1-16. 1. returned—viz., to the thought set forth (ch. 3:16; Job 35:9). **power**—MAURER, not so well, "violence." **no comforter**—twice said to express *continued* suffering without any to give comfort (Isa. 53:7). **2.** A profane sentiment if severed from its connection; but just in its bearing on Solomon's scope. If religion were not taken into account (ch. 3:17, 19), to die as soon as possible would be desirable, so as not to suffer or witness "oppressions"; and still more so, not to be born at all (ch. 7:1). Job (3:12; 21:7), David (Ps. 73:3, etc.), Jeremiah (12:1), Habakkuk (1:13), all passed through the same perplexity, until they went into the sanctuary, and looked beyond the present to the "judgment" (Ps. 73:17; Hab. 2:20; 3:17, 18). Then they saw the need of delay, before completely punishing the wicked, to give space for repentance, or else for accumulation of wrath (Rom. 2:15); and before completely rewarding the godly, to give room for faith and perseverance in tribulation (Ps. 92:7-12). Earnests, however, are often even now given, by partial judgments of the future, to assure us, in spite of difficulties, that God governs the earth. **3. not seen**—nor *experienced*. **4. right**—rather (as in ch. 2:21, *Note*), prosperous. Prosperity, which men so much covet, is the very source of provoking oppression (vs. 1) and "envy," so far is it from constituting the chief good. **5.** Still the **fool**, the *wicked* oppressor who "folds his hands together" *in idleness* (Prov. 6:10; 24:33), living on the means he wrongfully wrests from others, is not to be envied even in this life; for such a one "eateth his own flesh," i.e., is a *self-tormentor*, never satisfied, his spirit preying on itself (Isa. 9:20; 49:26). **6.** *Hebrew;* "One *open hand (palm) full of* quietness, than both *closed hands full of* travail." "Quietness" (mental tranquillity flowing from honest labor), opposed to "eating one's own flesh" (vs. 5), also opposed to anxious labor to gain (vs. 8; Prov. 15:16, 17; 16:8). **7.** A vanity described in vs. 8. **8. not a second**—no partner. **child**—"son or brother," put for any heir (Deut. 25:5-10). **eye**—(ch. 1:8.) The miser would not be able to give an account of his infatuation. **9. Two**—opposed to "one" (vs. 8). Ties of union, marriage, friendship, religious communion, are better than the selfish solitariness of the miser (Gen. 2:18). **reward**—Advantage accrues from their efforts being conjoined. TALMAN says, "A man without a companion is like a left hand without the right." **10. if they fall**—if *the one or other* fall, as may happen to *both*, viz., into any distress of body, mind, or soul. **11.** (I Kings 1:1.) The image is taken from man and wife, but applies universally to the *warm* sympathy derived from social ties. So Christian ties (Luke 24:32; Acts 28:15). **12. one**—enemy. **threefold cord**—proverbial for a *combination of many*—husband, wife, and children (Prov. 11:14); so Christians (Luke 10:1; Col. 2:2,19). Untwist the cord, and the separate threads are easily "broken." **13.** The "threefold cord" of social ties suggests the subject of *civil government*. In this case too, he concludes that kingly power confers no lasting happiness. The "wise" child, though a supposed case of Solomon, answers, in the event foreseen by the Holy Ghost, to Jeroboam, then a poor but valiant youth, once a "servant" of Solomon, and (I Kings 11:26-40) appointed by God through the prophet Ahijah to be heir of the kingdom of the ten tribes about to be rent from Rehoboam. The "old and foolish king" answers to Solomon himself, who had lost his wisdom, when, in defiance of two warnings of God (I Kings 3:14; 9:2-9), he forsook God. **will no more be admonished**—knows not yet how to take warning (see *Margin*). God had by Ahijah already intimated the judgment coming on Solomon (I Kings 11:11-13). **14. out of prison**—Solomon uses this phrase of a supposed case; e.g., Joseph raised from a dungeon to be lord of Egypt. His words are at the same time so framed by the Holy Ghost that they answer virtually to Jeroboam, who fled to escape a "prison" and death from Solomon, to Shishak of Egypt (I Kings 11:40). This unconscious presaging of his own doom, and that of Rehoboam, constitutes the irony. David's elevation from poverty and exile, under Saul (which may have been before Solomon's mind), had so far their counterpart in that of Jeroboam. **whereas . . . becometh poor**—rather, "though he (the youth) was born poor in his kingdom" (in the land where afterwards he was to reign). **15.** "I considered all the living," the present generation, in relation to ("with") the *"second youth"* (the *legitimate* successor of the "old king," as opposed to the "poor youth," the one *first* spoken of, about to be raised from poverty to a throne), i.e., Rehoboam. **in his stead**—the old king's. **16.** Notwithstanding their now worshipping the rising sun, the heir-apparent, I reflected that "there were no bounds, no stability (II Sam. 15:6; 20:1), no check on the love of innovation, of all that have been before them," i.e., the past generation; so "also they that come after," i.e., the next generation, "shall not rejoice in him," viz., Rehoboam. The parallel, "shall not rejoice," fixes the sense of "no bounds," *no permanent adherence,* though now men *rejoice* in *him.*

CHAPTER 5

Vss. 1-20. **1.** From vanity connected with kings, he passes to vanities (vs. 7) which may be fallen into convinced of the vanity of the creature, wish to worship the Creator. **Keep thy foot**—In going to worship, go with considerate, circumspect, reverent feeling. The allusion is to the taking off the shoes, or sandals, in entering a temple (Exod. 3:5; Josh. 5:15, which passages perhaps gave rise to the custom). WEISS needlessly reads, "Keep thy *feast days"* (Exod. 23:14, 17; the three great feasts). **hear**—rather, "To be ready (to draw nigh with the desire) to hear (obey) is a better sacrifice than the offering of fools" [HOLDEN]. *(Vulgate: Syriac.)* (Ps. 51:16, 17; Prov. 21:3; Jer. 6:20; 7:21-23; 14:12; Amos 5:21-24). The warning is against mere ceremonial self-righteousness, as in ch. 7:12. *Obedience* is the spirit of the law's requirements (Deut.10:12). Solomon sorrowfully looks back on his own neglect of this (cf. I Kings 8:63 with 11:4, 6). *Positive* precepts of God must be kept, but will not stand instead of obedience to His *moral* precepts. The last provided no sacrifice for *wilful* sin (Num. 15:30, 31; Heb. 10:26-29). **2. rash**—opposed to the *considerate reverence* ("keep thy foot," vs. 1). This verse illustrates vs. 1, as to *prayer* in the house of God ("before God," Isa. 1:12); so vss. 4-6 as to *vows.* The remedy to such vanities is stated (vs. 6). "Fear thou God." **God is in heaven**—Therefore He ought to be approached with carefully weighed words, by thee, a frail creature of earth. **3.** As much "business," engrossing the mind, gives birth to incoherent "dreams," so many words, uttered inconsiderately in prayer, give birth to and betray "a fool's speech" (ch. 10:14), [HOLDEN and WEISS]. But vs. 7 implies that the "dream" is not a comparison, but the *vain thoughts of the fool* (sinner, Ps. 73:20), arising from multiplicity of (worldly) "business." His "dream" is that God hears him for his much speaking (Matt. 6:7), independently of the frame of mind [*English Version* and MAURER]. "Fool's voice" answers to "dream" in the parallel; it comes by the many "words" flowing from the fool's "dream." **4.** Hasty words in *prayer* (vss. 2, 3) suggest the subject of hasty *vows.* A vow should not be hastily made (Judg. 11:35; I Sam. 14:24). When made, it must be kept (Ps. 76:11), even as God keeps His word to us (Exod. 12:41, 51; Josh. 21:45). **5.** (Deut. 23:21, 23.) **6. thy flesh**—Vow not with "thy mouth" a vow (e.g., fasting), which the lusts of the flesh (body, *Margin,* ch. 2:3) may tempt thee to break (Prov. 20:25). **angel**—the "messenger" of God (Job 33:23); minister (Rev. 1:20); i.e., the priest (Mal. 2:7) "be-

fore" whom a breach of a vow was to be confessed (Lev. 5:4, 5). We, Christians, in our vows (e.g., at baptism, the Lord's Supper, etc.) vow in the presence of Jesus Christ, "the angel of the covenant" (Mal. 3:1), and of ministering angels as witnesses (I Cor. 11:10; I Tim. 5:21). Extenuate not any breach of them as a slight error. **7.** (*Note,* vs. 3.) God's service, which ought to be our chief good, becomes by "dreams" (foolish fancies as of God's requirements of us in worship), and random "words," positive "vanity." The remedy is, whatever fools may do, "Fear *thou* God" (ch. 12:13). **8.** As in ch. 3:16, so here the difficulty suggests itself. If God is so exact in even punishing hasty words (vss. 1-6), why does He allow gross injustice? In the remote "provinces," the "poor" often had to put themselves for protection from the inroads of Philistines, etc., under chieftains, who oppressed them even in Solomon's reign (I Kings 12:4). **the matter**—lit., "the pleasure," or purpose (Isa. 53:10). Marvel not at this *dispensation of God's will,* as if He had abandoned the world. Nay, there is coming a capital judgment at last, and an earnest of it in partial punishments of in serving the King of kings, even by those who, sinners meanwhile. **higher than the highest**—(Dan. 7:18.) **regardeth**—(II Chron. 16:9.) **there be higher**—*plural,* i.e., the three persons of the Godhead, or else, "regardeth (not only the 'highest' kings, than whom He 'is higher,' but even the petty tyrants of the provinces, viz., the high ones who are above them" (the poor) [WEISS]. **9.** "The profit (produce) of the earth is (ordained) for (the common good of) all: even the king himself is served by (the fruits of) the field" (II Chron. 26:10). Therefore the common Lord of all, high and low, will punish at last those who rob the "poor" of their share in it (Prov. 22:22, 23; Amos 8:4-7). **10.** Not only will God punish at last, but meanwhile the oppressive gainers of "silver" find no solid "satisfaction" in it. **shall not be satisfied**—so the oppressor "eateth his own flesh" (ch. 4:1, 5, *Note).* **with increase**—is not satisfied with the gain that he makes. **11. they . . . that eat them**—the rich man's dependents (Ps. 23:5). **12.** Another argument against anxiety to gain riches. "Sleep . . . sweet" answers to "quietness" (ch. 4:6); "not suffer . . . sleep," to "vexation of spirit." Fears for his wealth, and an overloaded stomach without "laboring" (cf. ch. 4:5), will not suffer the rich oppressor to sleep. **13, 14.** Proofs of God's judgments even in this world (Prov. 11:31). The rich oppressor's wealth provokes enemies, robbers, etc. Then, after having kept it for an expected son, he loses it beforehand by misfortune ("by evil travail"), and the son is born to be heir of poverty. Ch. 2:19, 23 gives another aspect of the same subject. **16.** Even supposing that he loses not his wealth before death, *then* at last he must go stripped of it all (Ps. 49:17). **laboured for . . . wind**—(Hos. 12:1; I Cor. 9:26). **17. eateth**—appropriately put for "liveth" in general, as connected with vss. 11, 12, 18. **darkness**—oppposed to "light (joy) of countenance" (ch. 8:1; Prov. 16:15). **wrath**—fretfulness, lit., "His sorrow is much, and his infirmity (of body) and wrath." **18.** Returns to the sentiment (ch. 3:12, 13, 22); translate: "Behold the good which I have seen, and which is becoming" (in a man). **which God giveth**—viz., both the good of his labor and his life. **his portion**—legitimately. It is God's gift that makes it so when regarded as such. Such a one will use, not abuse, earthly things (I Cor. 7:31). Opposed to the anxious life of the covetous (vss. 10, 17). **19.** As vs. 18 refers to the "laboring" man (vs. 12), so vs. 19 to the "rich" man, who gets wealth not by "oppression" (vs. 8), but by "God's gift." He is distinguished also from the "rich" man (ch. 6:2) in having received by God's gift not only "wealth," but also "power to eat thereof," which that one has not. "To take his portion" limits him to the lawful use of wealth, not keeping back from God *His* portion while enjoying *his own*. **20.** He will not remember much, looking back with disappointment, as the ungodly do (ch. 2:11), on the days of his life. **answereth...in the joy**—God *answers* his prayers in giving him "power" to *enjoy* his blessings. GESENIUS and *Vulgate* translate, "For God (so) *occupies* him with joy," etc., that he thinks not much of the shortness and sorrows of life. HOLDEN, "Though God gives not much (as to real enjoyment), yet he remembers (with thankfulness) the days; for (he knows) God *exercises* him by the joy," etc. (tries him by prosperity), so *Margin*, but *English Version* is simplest.

CHAPTER 6

Vss. 1-12. **1. common**—or else more literally, —"great upon man," falls heavily upon man. **2. for his soul**—i.e., his enjoyment. **God giveth him not power to eat**—This distinguishes him from the "rich" man in ch. 5:19. "God hath given" distinguishes him also from the man who got his wealth by "oppression" (ch. 5:8, 10). **stranger**—those not akin, nay, even hostile to him (Jer. 51:51; Lam. 5:2; Hos. 7:9). He seems to have it in his "power" to do as he will with his wealth, but an unseen power gives him up to his own avarice: God wills that he should toil for "a stranger" (ch. 2:26), who has found favor in God's sight. **3.** Even if a man (of this character) have very many (equivalent to "a hundred," II Kings 10:1) children, and not have a "stranger" as his heir (vs. 2), and live long ("days of years") express the *brevity* of life *at its best*, Gen. 47:9), yet enjoy no real "good" in life, and lie unhonored, without "burial," at death (II Kings 9:26, 35), the embryo is better than he. In the East to be without burial is the greatest degradation. "Better the fruit that drops from the tree before it is ripe than that left to hang on till rotten" [HENRY]. **4. he**—rather "it," "the untimely birth." So "its" not "*his* name." **with vanity**—to no purpose; a type of the driftless existence of him who makes riches the chief good. **darkness**—of the abortive; a type of the unhonored death and dark future beyond the grave of the avaricious. **5. this**—*yet* "it has more rest than" the toiling, gloomy miser. **6.** If the miser's length of "life" be thought to raise him above the abortive, Solomon answers that long life, without enjoying real good, is but lengthened misery, and riches cannot exempt him from going whither "all go." He is fit neither for life, nor death, nor eternity. **7. man**—rather, "the man," viz., the miser (vss. 3-6). For not *all* men labor for the mouth, i.e., for selfish gratification. **appetite**—*Hebrew*, "the soul." The insatiability of the desire prevents that which is the only end proposed in toils, viz., self-gratification; "the man" thus gets no "good" out of his wealth (vs. 3). **8. For**—However [MAURER]. The "for" means (in contrast to the insatiability of the miser), *For what* else is the advantage which *the wise man hath above the fool*?" *What* (advantage, i.e., superiority, above him who knows not how to walk uprightly) *hath the poor who knoweth to walk before the living?* i.e., to use and enjoy life aright (ch. 5:18, 19), a cheerful, thankful, godly "walk" (Ps. 116:9). **9.** Answer to the question in vs. 8. This is the advantage: "Better is the sight of the eyes (the wise man's

godly enjoyment of present *seen* blessings) than the (fool's) wandering, lit., *walking* (Ps. 73:9), of the desire," i.e., vague, insatiable desires for what he has not (vs. 7; Heb. 13:5). **this**—restless wandering of desire, and not enjoying contentedly the present (I Tim. 6:6, 8). **10.** Part II begins here. Since man's toils are vain, what is the chief good? (vs. 12). The answer is contained in the rest of the book. "That which hath been (man's various circumstances) is named already (not only has existed, ch. 1:9; 3:15, but has received its just *name*, 'vanity,' long ago), and it is known that it (vanity) is man" (*Hebrew*, "Adam," equivalent to man "of *red* dust," as his Creator appropriately named him from his frailty). **neither may he contend...**—(Rom. 9:20.) **11.** "Seeing" that man cannot escape from the "vanity," which by God's "mighty" will is inherent in earthly things, and cannot *call in question* God's wisdom in these dispensations (equivalent to "contend," etc.), "what is man the better" of these vain things as regards the chief good? None whatever. **12. For who knoweth ...**—The ungodly know not what is really "good" during life, nor "what shall be after them," i.e., what will be the event of their undertakings (ch. 3: 22; 8:7). The godly might be tempted to "contend with God" (vs. 10) as to His dispensations; but they cannot fully know the wise purposes served by them now and hereafter. Their sufferings from the oppressors are more really good for them than cloudless prosperity; sinners are being allowed to fill up their measure of guilt. Retribution in part vindicates God's ways even now. The judgment shall make all clear. In ch. 7, he states what is good, in answer to this verse.

CHAPTER 7

Vss. 1-29. **1.** (See *Note*, ch. 6:12.) **name**—character; a godly mind and life; not mere *reputation* with man, but what a man *is* in the eyes of God, with whom the *name* and *reality* are one thing (Isa. 9:6). This alone is "good," while all else is "vanity" when made the chief end. **ointment**—used lavishly at costly banquets and peculiarly refreshing in the sultry East. The *Hebrew* for "name" and for "ointment," have a happy paronomasia, *Sheem, Shemen*. "Ointment" is fragrant only in the place where the person is whose head and garment are scented, and only for a time. The "name" given by God to His child (Rev. 3:12) is for ever and in all lands. So in the case of the woman who received an everlasting name from Jesus Christ, in reward for her precious ointment (Isa. 56:5; Mark 14:3-9). Jesus Christ Himself hath such a name, as the Messiah, equivalent to Anointed (Song of Sol. 1:3). **and the day of** [his] **death...**—not a general censure upon God for creating man; but, connected with the previous clause, death is to him, who hath a godly name, "better" than the day of his birth; "far better," as Philippians 1:23 has it. **2.** Proving that it is not a *sensual* enjoyment of earthly goods which is meant in ch. 3:13; 5:18. A thankful use of these is right, but frequent feasting Solomon had found dangerous to piety in his own case. So Job's fear (ch. 1:4, 5). The house of feasting often shuts out thoughts of God and eternity. The sight of the dead in the "house of mourning" causes "the living" to think of their own "end." **3. Sorrow**—such as arises from serious thoughts of eternity. **laughter**—reckless mirth (ch. 2:2). **by the sadness...better**—(Ps. 126: 5, 6; II Cor. 4:17; Heb. 12:10, 11). MAURER translates: "In sadness of countenance there is (may be) a good (*cheerful*) heart." So *Hebrew,* for "good," equivalent to "cheerful" (ch. 11:19); but the parallel clause supports *English Version.* **5.** (Ps. 141:4, 5). Godly reproof offends the flesh, but benefits the spirit. Fools' songs in the house of mirth please the flesh, but injure the soul. **6. crackling**—answers to the loud merriment of fools. It is the very fire consuming them which produces the seeming merry noise (Joel 2:5). Their light soon goes out in the black darkness. There is a paronomasia in the *Hebrew, Sirim* (thorns), *Sir* (pot). The wicked are often compared to "thorns" (II Sam. 23:6; Nah. 1:10). Dried cow-dung was the common fuel in Palestine; its slowness in burning makes the quickness of a fire of thorns the more graphic, as an image of the sudden end of fools (Ps. 118:12). **7. oppression**—recurring to the idea (ch. 3:16; 5:8). Its connection with vss. 4-6 is, the sight of "oppression" perpetrated by "fools" might tempt the "wise" to call in question God's dispensations, and imitate the folly (equivalent to "madness") described (vss. 5:6). WEISS, for "oppression," translates, "distraction," produced by merriment. But ch. 5:8 favors *English Version.* **a gift**—i.e., the sight of *bribery* in "places of judgment" (ch. 3:16) might cause the wise to lose their wisdom (equivalent to "heart"), (Job 12:6; 21:6, 7; 24:1, etc.). This suits the parallelism better than "a heart of gifts"; a benevolent heart, as WEISS. **8.** connected with vs. 7. Let the "wise" wait for "the end," and the "oppressions" which now (in "the beginning") perplex their faith, will be found by God's working to be overruled to their good. "Tribulation worketh *patience*" (Rom. 5:3), which is infinitely better than "the proud spirit" that prosperity might have generated in them, as it has in fools (Ps. 73:2, 3, 12-14, 17-26; Jas. 5:11). **9. angry**—impatient at adversity befalling thee, as Job was (ch. 5:2; Prov. 12:16). **10.** Do not call in question God's ways in making thy former days better than thy present, as Job did (ch. 29:2-5). The very putting of the question argues that heavenly "wisdom" (*Margin*) is not as much as it ought made the chief good with thee. **11.** Rather, "Wisdom, *as compared* with an inheritance, is good," i.e., is as good as an inheritance; "yea, better (lit., "and a profit") to them that see the sun" (i.e., *the living,* ch. 11:7; Job 3:16; Ps. 49:19). **12.** Lit., (To be) in (i.e., under) the *shadow* (Isa. 30:2) of wisdom (is the same as to be) in (under) the *shadow* of money; wisdom no less *shields* one from the ills of life than money does. **is, that**—rather, "the excellency of the knowledge *of* wisdom giveth life," i.e., life in the highest sense, here and herafter (Prov. 3:18; John 17:3; II Pet. 1:3). Wisdom (religion) cannot be lost as money can. It *shields* one in adversity, as well as prosperity; money, only in prosperity. The question in vs. 10 implies a want of it. **13.** *Consider* as to *God's work,* that it is impossible to alter His dispensations; *for who can,* etc. **straight . . . crooked**—Man cannot amend what God wills to be "wanting" and "adverse" (ch. 1:15; Job 12:14). **14. consider**—resumed from vs. 13. "Consider," i.e., regard it as "the work of God"; for "God has made (*Hebrew,* for 'set') this (adversity) also as well as the other" (prosperity). "Adversity" is one of the things which "God has made crooked," and which man cannot "make straight." He ought therefore to be "patient" (vs. 8). **after him**—equivalent to "that man may not find anything (to blame) after God" i.e., *after* "considering God's work," vs. 13). *Vulgate* and *Syriac, "against* Him" (cf. vs. 10; Rom. 3:4). **15.** An objection entertained

by Solomon "in the days of his vanity" (apostasy) (ch. 8:14; Job 21:7). **just . . . perisheth**—(I Kings 21:13.) *Temporal* not eternal death (John 10:28). But see *Note,* vs. 16; *"just"* is probably a *self-justiciary.* **wicked . . . prolongeth**—See the antidote to the abuse of this statement in ch. 8:12. **16.** HOLDEN makes vs. 16 the scoffing inference of the objector, and vs. 17 the answer of Solomon, now repentant. So (I Cor. 15:32) the skeptic's objection; (vs. 33) the answer. However, "Be not righteous over much," may be taken as Solomon's words, forbidding a *self-made* righteousness of outward performances, which would wrest salvation from God, instead of receiving it as the gift of His *grace.* It is a fanatical, pharisaical righteousness, separated from God; for the "fear of God" is in antithesis to it (vs. 18; ch. 5:3, 7; Matt. 6:1-7; 9:14; 23:23, 24; Rom. 10:3; I Tim. 4:3). **over wise**—(Job 11:12; Rom. 12:3, 16), presumptuously self-sufficient, as if acquainted with the whole of divine truth. **destroy thyself**—expose thyself to needless persecution, austerities and the wrath of God; hence to an untimely death. "Destroy thyself" answers to "perisheth" (vs. 15); "righteous over much," to "a just man." Therefore in vs. 15 it is *self-justiciary,* not a truly righteous man, that is meant. **17. over much wicked**—so worded, to answer to "righteous *over much.*" For if not taken thus, it would seem to imply that we *may* be wicked *a little.* "Wicked" refers to "wicked man" (vs. 15); "die before thy time," to "prolongeth his life," antithetically. There may be a wicked man spared to "live long," owing to his avoiding gross excesses (vs. 15). Solomon says, therefore, Be not so foolish (answering antithetically to "over wise," vs. 16), as to run to such excess of riot, that God will be provoked to cut off prematurely thy day of grace (Rom. 2:5). The precept is addressed to a *sinner.* Beware of aggravating thy sin, so as to make thy case desperate. It refers to the days of Solomon's "vanity" (apostasy, vs. 15), when only such a precept would be applicable. By LITOTES it includes, "Be not wicked *at all.*" **18. this . . . this**—the two opposite excesses (vs. 16, 17), fanatical, self-wise righteousness, and presumptuous, foolhardy wickedness. **he that feareth God shall come forth of them all**—shall escape all such extremes (Prov. 3:7). **19.** *Hebrew,* "The wisdom," i.e., the true wisdom, religion (II Tim. 3:15). **than ten mighty**—i.e., able and valiant generals (vs. 12; ch. 9:13-18; Prov. 21:22; 24:5). These "watchmen wake in vain, except the Lord keep the city" (Ps. 127:1). **20.** Referring to vs. 16. Be not self-righteous, seek not to make thyself "*just*" before God by a superabundance of self-imposed performances; "for true 'wisdom,' or 'righteousness,' shows that there is not a *just* man," etc. **21.** As therefore thou being far from perfectly "just" thyself, hast much to be forgiven by God, do not take too strict account, as the *self-righteous* do (vs. 16; Luke 18:9, 11), and thereby shorten their lives (vss. 15, 16), of words spoken against thee by others, e.g., thy servant: Thou art their "fellow servant" before God (Matt. 18:32-35). **22.** (I Kings 2:44.) **23. All this**—resuming the "all" in vs. 15; vss. 15-22 is therefore the fruit of his dearly bought experience in the days of his "vanity." **I will be wise**—I tried to "be wise," independently of God. But true wisdom was then "far from him," in spite of his *human* wisdom, which he retained by God's gift. So "over wise" (vs. 16). **24. That . . . far off . . . deep**—True wisdom is so when sought independently of "fear of God" (vs. 18; Deut. 30:12, 13; Job 11:7, 8; 28:12-20, 28; Ps. 64:6; Rom. 10:6, 7). **25.** Lit., "I turned myself and mine heart to." A phrase peculiar to Ecclesiastes, and appropriate to the penitent *turning* back to *commune with his heart* on his past life. **wickedness of folly**—He is now a step further on the path of penitence than in ch. 1: 17; 2:12, where "folly" is put without "wickedness" prefixed. **reason**—rather, *the right estimation* of things. HOLDEN translates also "foolishness (i.e., sinful folly, answering to 'wickedness' in the parallel) of madness" (i.e., of man's mad pursuits). **26.** "I find" that, of all my sinful follies, none has been so ruinous a snare in seducing me from God as idolatrous women (I Kings 11:3; 4; Prov. 5:3, 4; 22: 14). As "God's favor is better than life," she who seduces from God is "more bitter than death." **whoso pleaseth God**—as Joseph (Gen. 39:2, 3, 9). It is God's *grace* alone that keeps any from falling. **27. this**—viz., what follows in vs. 28. **counting one by one**—by comparing one thing with another [HOLDEN and MAURER]. **account**—a right estimate. But vs. 28 more favors GESENIUS. "Considering *women one by one.*" **28.** Rather, referring to his *past* experience, "Which my soul *sought* further, but I *found* not." **one man**—i.e., worthy of the name, "man," "upright"; not more than one in a thousand of my courtiers (Job 33:23; Ps. 12:1). Jesus Christ alone of men fully realizes the perfect ideal of "man." "Chiefest among ten thousand" (Song of Sol. 5:10). No *perfect* "woman" has ever existed, not even the Virgin Mary. Solomon, in the word "thousand," alludes to his three hundred wives and seven hundred concubines. Among these it was not likely that he should find the fidelity which *one* true wife pays to *one* husband. Connected with vs. 26, not an unqualified condemnation of the sex, as Proverbs 12:4; 31:10, etc., prove. **29.** The "only" way of accounting for the scarcity of even comparatively upright men and women is that, whereas God made man upright, they (men) have, etc. The only account to be "found" of the origin of evil, the great mystery of theology, is that given in Holy Writ (Gen. 2, 3). Among man's "inventions" was the one especially referred to in vs. 26, the bitter fruits of which Solomon experienced, the breaking of God's primeval marriage law, joining one man to *one* woman (Matt. 19:4, 5, 6). "Man" is *singular, viz.,* Adam; "they," *plural,* Adam, Eve, and their posterity.

CHAPTER 8

Vss. 1-17. **1.** Praise of true wisdom continued (ch. 7:11, etc.). "Who" is to be accounted "equal to the wise man?" "Who (like him) knoweth the interpretation" of God's providences (e.g., ch. 7:8, 13, 14), and God's word (e.g., ch. 7:29, *Note;* Prov. 1:6)? **face to shine**—(ch. 7:14; Acts 6:15.) *A sunny countenance,* the reflection of a tranquil conscience and serene mind. Communion with God gives it (Exod. 34:29, 30). **boldness**—austerity. **changed**—into a benign expression by true wisdom (religion) (Jas. 3:17). MAURER translates, "The *shining* (brightness) of his face is *doubled,*" arguing that the *Hebrew* noun for "boldness" is never used in a bad sense (Prov. 4:18). Or as *Margin,* "strength" (ch. 7:19; Isa. 40:31; II Cor. 3:18). But the adjective is used in a bad sense (Deut. 28:50). **2. the king's**—Jehovah, peculiarly the king of Israel in the theocracy; vss. 3, 4, prove it is not the earthly king who is meant. **the oath of God**—the covenant which God made with Abraham and renewed with David; Solomon remembered Ps. 89:35, "I have *sworn,*" etc. (vs. 36), and the penalties if David's children should forsake it (vss. 30-32); inflicted on

Solomon himself; yet God not "utterly" forsaking him (vss. 33, 34). **3. hasty**—rather, "Be not *terror-struck* so as to go out of His sight." Slavishly "terror-struck" is characteristic of the sinner's feeling toward God; he vainly tries to flee out of His sight (Ps. 139:7); opposed to the "shining face" of filial confidence (vs. 1; John 8:33-36; Rom. 8:2; I John 4:18). **stand not**—persist not. **for he doeth** —God inflicts what punishment He pleases on persisting sinners (Job 23:13; Ps. 115:3). True of none save God. **4.** God's very "word" is "power." So the gospel word (Rom. 1:16; Heb. 4:12). **who may say . . .**—(Job 9:12; 33:13; Isa. 45:9; Dan. 4:35.) Scripture does not ascribe such arbitrary power to earthly kings. **5. feel**—experience. **time**—the neglect of the right "times" causes much of the sinful folly of the spiritually unwise (3:1-11). **judgment** —the right manner [HOLDEN]. But as God's future "judgment" is connected with the "time for every purpose" in ch. 3:17, so it is here. The punishment of persisting sinners (vs. 3) suggests it. The wise man realizes the fact, that as there is a fit "time" for every purpose, so for the "judgment." This thought cheers him in adversity (ch. 7:14; 8:1). **6. therefore the misery . . .**—because the foolish sinner does not think of the right "times" and the "judgment." **7. he**—the sinner, by neglecting times (e.g., "the accepted *time,* and the day of salvation, II Cor. 6:2), is taken by surprise by the judgment (ch. 3:22; 6:12; 9:12). The godly wise observe the due times of things (ch. 3:1), and so, looking for the judgment, are not taken by surprise, though not knowing the precise "when" (I Thess. 5:2-4); they "know the time" to all saving purposes (Rom. 13:11). **8. spirit** —"breath of life" (ch. 3:19), as the words following require. Not "wind," as WEISS thinks (Prov. 30:4). This verse naturally follows the subject of "times" and "judgment" (vss. 6, 7). **discharge**—alluding to the liability to military service of all above twenty years old (Num. 1:3), yet many were exempted (Deut. 20:5-8). But in *that* war (death) there is no exemption. **those . . . given to**—lit., the *master* of it. Wickedness can get money for the sinner, but cannot deliver him from the death, temporal and eternal, which is its penalty (Isa. 28:15, 18). **9. his own hurt** —The tyrannical ruler "hurts" not merely his subjects, but *himself;* so Rehoboam (I Kings 12); but the "time" of "hurt" chiefly refers to eternal ruin, incurred by "wickedness," at "the *day* of death" (vs. 8), and the "*time*" of "judgment" (vs. 6; Prov. 8:36). **10. the wicked**—viz., rulers (vs. 9). **buried**—with funeral pomp by man, though little meriting it (Jer. 22:19); but this only formed the more awful contrast to their death, temporal and eternal, inflicted by God (Luke 16:22, 23). **come and gone from the place of the holy**—went to and came from *the place of judicature,* where they sat as *God's representatives* (Ps. 82:1-6), with pomp [HOLDEN]. WEISS translates, "Buried and *gone* (utterly), even from the holy place they departed." As Joab, by Solomon's command, was sent to the grave from the "holy place" *in the temple,* which was not a sanctuary to murderers (Exod. 21:14; I Kings 2:28, 31). The use of the very word "bury" there makes this view likely; still "who had come and gone" may be retained. Joab *came* to the altar, but had to *go* from it; so the "wicked rulers" (vs. 9) (including *high priests*) came to, and went from, *the temple,* on occasions of solemn worship, but did not thereby escape their doom. **forgotten**—(Prov. 10:7.) **11.** The reason why the wicked persevere in sin: God's delay in judgment (Matt. 24:48-51; II Pet. 3:8, 9). "They see not the smoke of the pit, therefore they dread not the fire" [SOUTH], (Ps. 55:19). Joab's escape from the punishment of his murder of Abner, so far from "leading him to repentance," as it ought (Rom. 2:4), led him to the additional murder of Amasa. **12.** He says this, lest the sinner should abuse the statement (ch. 7:15), "A wicked man *prolongeth* his life." **before him**—lit., "at His presence"; reverently serve Him, realizing His continual presence. **13. neither shall he prolong**—not a contradiction to vs. 12. The "prolonging" of his days there is only *seeming*, not *real*. Taking into account his eternal existence, his present days, however seemingly long, are really short. God's delay (vs. 11) exists only in man's short-sighted view. It gives scope to the sinner to repent, or else to fill up his full measure of guilt; and so, in either case, tends to the final vindication of God's ways. It gives exercise to the faith, patience, and perseverance of saints. **shadow**—(ch. 6:12; Job 8:9). **14.** An objection is here started (entertained by Solomon in his apostasy), as in ch. 3:16; 7:15, to the truth of retributive justice, from the fact of the just and the wicked not now receiving always according to their respective deserts; a cavil, which would seem the more weighty to men living under the Mosaic covenant of temporal sanctions. The objector adds, as Solomon had said, that the worldling's pursuits are "vanity" (vs. 10), "I *say* (not 'said') *this* also is vanity. Then I commend mirth," etc. [HOLDEN]. Vss. 14, 15 may, however, be explained as teaching a cheerful, thankful use of God's gifts "under the sun," i.e., not making them the *chief* good, as sensualists do, which ch. 2:2; 7:2, forbid; but in "the fear of God," as ch. 3:12; 5:18; 7:18; 9:7, opposed to the abstinence of the self-righteous ascetic (ch. 7:16), and of the miser (ch. 5:17). **15. no better thing . . .**—viz., for the "just" man, whose *chief* good is religion, not for the worldly. **abide**—Hebrew, "adhere"; not *for ever*, but it is the only sure good to be enjoyed from *earthly labors* (equivalent to "of his labor the days of his life"). Still, the language resembles the skeptical precept (I Cor. 15: 32), introduced only to be refuted; and "abide" is too strong language, perhaps, for a religious man to apply to "eating" and "mirth." **16.** Reply to vss. 14, 15. When I applied myself to observe man's toils after happiness (some of them so incessant as not to allow sufficient time for "sleep"), then (vs. 17, the apodosis) I saw that man cannot find out (the reason of) God's inscrutable dealings with the "just" and with the "wicked" here (vs. 14; ch. 3:11; Job 5: 9; Rom. 11:33); his duty is to acquiesce in them as good, because they are *God's*, though he *sees* not all the reasons for them (Ps. 73:16). It is enough to know "the righteous are in God's hand" (ch. 9:1). "Over wise" (ch. 7:16); i.e., Speculations above what is written are vain.

CHAPTER 9

Vss. 1-18. **1. declare**—rather, explore; the result of my exploring is this, that "the righteous, etc., are in the hand of God. No man knoweth either the love or hatred (of God to them) by all that is before them," i.e., by what is *outwardly* seen in His present dealings (ch. 8:14, 17). However, from the sense of the same words, in vs. 6, "love and hatred" seem to be the feelings *of the wicked towards the righteous*, whereby they caused to the latter comfort and sorrow. Translate: "Even the love and hatred" (exhibited towards the righteous, are in God's hand) (Ps. 76:10; Prov. 16:7). "No man knoweth all that is before them." **2. All things . . . alike**—not univer-

sally; but as to *death*. Vss. 2-10 are made by HOLDEN the objection of a skeptical sensualist. However, they may be explained as Solomon's language. He repeats the sentiment already implied in ch. 2:14; 3:20; 8:14. **one event**—not eternally; but *death* is common to all. **good**—morally. **clean**—ceremonially. **sacrificeth**—alike to Josiah who sacrificed to God, and to Ahab who made sacrifice to Him cease. **sweareth**—rashly and falsely. **3.** Translate, "There is an evil above all (evils) that are done," etc., viz., that not only "there is one event to all," but "also the heart of the sons of men" makes this fact a reason for "madly" persisting in "evil while they live, and after that," etc., sin is "madness." **the dead**—(Prov. 2:18; 9:18.) **4. For**—rather, "Nevertheless." *English Version* rightly reads as the *Margin, Hebrew,* "that is joined," instead of the text, "who is to be chosen?" **hope**—not of mere temporal good (Job 14:7); but of yet repenting and being saved. **dog**—metaphor for the vilest persons (I Sam. 24:14). **lion**—the noblest of animals (Prov. 30:30). **better**—as to hope of salvation; the noblest who die unconverted have no hope; the vilest, so long as they have life, have hope. **5. know that they shall die**—and may thereby be led "so to number their days, that they may apply their hearts to wisdom" (ch. 7:1-4; Ps. 90:12). **dead know not anything**—i.e., so far as their *bodily* senses and *worldly* affairs are concerned (Job 14:21; Isa. 63:16); also, they know no door of repentance open to them, such as is to all on earth. **neither . . . reward**—no advantage from their worldly labors (ch. 2:18-22; 4:9). **memory**—not of the righteous (Ps. 112:6; Mal. 3:16), but *the wicked*, who with all the pains to perpetuate their names (Ps. 49:11) are soon "forgotten" (ch. 8:10). **6. love, and . . . hatred . . .**—(referring to vs. 1, where see the *Note*). Not that these cease in a future world absolutely (Ezek. 32: 27; Rev. 22:11); but as the end of this verse shows, relatively to persons and things in this world. Man's love and hatred can no longer be exercised for good or evil in the same way as here; but the fruits of them remain. What he is at death he remains for ever. "Envy," too, marks the wicked as referred to, since it was therewith that they assailed the righteous (vs. 1, *Note*). **portion**—Their "portion" was "in this life" (Ps. 17:14), that they now "cannot have any more." **7.** Addressed to the "righteous wise," spoken of in vs. 1. Being "in the hand of God," who now accepteth "thy works" in His service, as He has previously accepted thy person (Gen. 4:4), thou mayest "eat . . . with a cheerful (not sensually 'merry') heart" (ch. 3:13; 5: 18; Acts 2:46). **8. white**—in token of joy (Isa. 61:3). Solomon was clad in *white* (JOSEPHUS, *Antiquities,* 8:7, 3); hence his attire is compared to the "*lilies*" (Matt. 6:29), typical of the spotless righteousness of Jesus Christ, which the redeemed shall wear (Rev. 3:18; 7:14). **ointment**—(Ps. 23:5), opposed to a gloomy exterior (II Sam. 14:2; Ps. 45:7; Matt. 6: 17); typical, also (ch. 7:1; Song of Sol. 1:3). **9. wife . . . lovest**—godly and true love, opposed to the "snares" of the "thousand" concubines (ch. 7:26, 28), "among" whom Solomon could not find the true love which joins one man to *one* woman (Prov. 5:15, 18, 19; 18:22; 19:14). **10.** "Whatsoever," viz., in the service of God. This and last verse plainly are the language of Solomon, not of a skeptic, as Holden would explain it. **hand . . .**—(*Margin,* Lev. 12:8; *Margin,* I Sam. 10:7.) **thy might**—diligence (Deut. 6:5; *Margin,* Jer. 48:10). **no work . . . in the grave**—(John 9:4; Rev. 14:13.) "The soul's playday is Satan's work-day; the idler the man the busier the tempter" [SOUTH]. **11.** This verse qualifies the sentiment, vss. 7-9. Earthly "enjoyments," however lawful in their place (ch. 3:1), are to give way when any work to be done for God requires it. Reverting to the sentiment (ch. 8:17), we ought, therefore, not only to work God's work "with might" (vs. 10), but also with the feeling that the event is wholly "in God's hand" (vs. 1). **race ... not to the swift**—(II Sam. 18:23); spiritually (Zeph. 3:19; Rom. 9:16). **nor ... battle to ... strong**—(I Sam. 17:47; II Chron. 14:9, 11, 15; Ps. 33:16.) **bread**—livelihood. **favour** —of the great. **chance**—seemingly, really Providence. But as man cannot "find it out" (ch. 3:11), he needs "with all might" to use opportunities. Duties are ours; events, God's. **12. his time**—viz., of death (ch. 7:15; Isa. 13:22). Hence the danger of delay in doing the work of God, as one knows not when his opportunity will end (vs. 10). **evil net**— fatal to them. The unexpected suddenness of the capture is the point of comparison. So the second coming of Jesus Christ, "as a snare" (Luke 21:35). **evil time**—as an "evil net," fatal to them. **13.** Rather, "I have seen wisdom of this kind also," i.e., exhibited in the way which is described in what follows [MAURER]. **14, 15.** (II Sam. 20:16-22.) **bulwarks** —military works of besiegers. **15. poor**—as to the temporal advantages of true wisdom, though it often saves others. It receives little reward from the world, which admires none save the rich and great. **no man remembered**—(Gen. 40:23.) **16.** Resuming the sentiment (ch. 7:19; Prov. 21:22; 24: 5). **poor man's wisdom is despised**—not the poor man mentioned in vs. 15; for *his* wisdom could not have saved the city, had "his words not been heard"; but poor men in general. So Paul (Acts 27:11). **17.** Though generally the poor wise man is not heard (vs. 16), yet "the words of wise men, when heard in quiet (when calmly given heed to, as in vs. 15), are more serviceable than," etc. **ruleth**—as the "great king" (vs. 14). Solomon reverts to "the rulers to their own hurt" (ch. 8:9). **18. one sinner,** etc.—(Josh. 7:1, 11, 12.) Though wisdom excels folly (vs. 16; ch. 7:19), yet a "little folly (equivalent to *sin*) can destroy much good," both in himself (ch. 10:1; Jas. 2:10) and in others. "Wisdom" must, from the antithesis to "sinner," mean religion. Thus typically, the "little city" may be applied to *the Church* (Luke 12:32; Heb. 12:22); the great king to *Satan* (John 12:31); the despised poor wise man, Jesus Christ (Isa. 53:2, 3; Mark 6:3; II Cor. 8:9; Eph. 1:7, 8; Col. 2:3).

CHAPTER 10

Vss. 1-20. **1.** Following up ch. 9:18. **him that is in reputation**—e.g., David (II Sam. 12:14); Solomon (I Kings 11); Jehoshaphat (II Chron. 18; 19:2); Josiah (II Chron. 35:22). The more delicate the perfume, the more easily spoiled is the ointment. Common oil is not so liable to injury. So the higher a man's religious character is, the more hurt is caused by a sinful folly in him. Bad savor is endurable in oil, but not in what professes to be, and is compounded by the perfumer ("apothecary") for, fragrance. "Flies" answer to "a little folly" (sin), appropriately, being *small* (I Cor. 5:6); also, "Beelzebub" means *prince of flies.* "Ointment" answers to "reputation" (ch. 7:1; Gen. 34:30). The verbs are *singular,* the noun *plural,* implying that *each* of the flies causes the stinking savor. **2.** (Ch. 2:14.) **right**—The right hand is more expert than

the left. The godly wise is more on his guard than the foolish sinner, though at times he slip. Better a diamond with a flaw, than a pebble without one. **3. by the way**—in his ordinary *course; in his simplest acts* (Prov. 6:12-14). That he "saith," *virtually,* "that he" himself, etc. [LXX]. But *Vulgate,* "He thinks that *every one* (*else* whom he meets) is a fool." **4. spirit**—anger. **yielding pacifieth**—(Prov. 15:1.) This explains "leave not thy place"; do not in a *resisting* spirit withdraw from thy post of duty (ch. 8:3). **5. as**—rather, "*by reason of* an error" [MAURER and HOLDEN]. **6. rich**—not in mere wealth, but in *wisdom,* as the antithesis to "folly" (for "foolish men") shows. So *Hebrew,* rich, equivalent to "liberal," in a good sense (Isa. 32:5). Mordecai and Haman (Esther 3:1, 2; 6:6-11). **7. servants upon horses**—the worthless exalted to *dignity* (Jer. 17:25); and vice versa (II Sam. 15:30). **8.** The fatal results to kings of such an unwise policy; the wrong done to others recoils on themselves (ch. 8:9); they fall into the pit which they dug for others (Esther 7: 10; Ps. 7:15; Prov. 26:27). Breaking through the wise fences of their throne, they suffer unexpectedly themselves; as when one is stung by a serpent lurking in the stones of his neighbor's garden wall (Ps. 80:12), which he maliciously pulls down (Amos 5: 19). **9. removeth stones**—viz., of an ancient building [WEISS]. His neighbor's landmarks [HOLDEN]. *Cuts out* from the quarry [MAURER]. **endangered**— by the splinters, or by the head of the hatchet, flying back on himself. Pithy aphorisms are common in the East. The sense is: Violations of true wisdom recoil on the perpetrators. **10. iron ... blunt**—in "cleaving wood" (vs. 9), answering to the "fool set in dignity" (vs. 6), who wants sharpness. More force has then to be used in both cases; but force without judgment "endangers" one's self. Translate, "If one hath blunted his iron" [MAURER]. The preference of rash to judicious counsellors, which entailed the pushing of matters by *force,* proved to be the "hurt" of Rehoboam (I Kings 12). **wisdom is profitable to direct**—to a prosperous issue. Instead of forcing matters by main "strength" to one's own hurt (ch. 9:16, 18). **11.** A "serpent will bite" if "enchantment" is not used; "and a babbling calumniator is no better." Therefore, as one may escape a serpent by charms (Ps. 58:4, 5), so one may escape the sting of a calumniator by discretion (vs. 12), [HOLDEN]. Thus, "without enchantment" answers to "not whet the edge" (vs. 10), both expressing, figuratively, *want of judgment.* MAURER translates, "There is no gain to the enchanter" (*Margin,* "*master of the tongue*") from his enchantments, because the serpent bites before he can use them; hence the need of continual caution. Vss. 8-10, caution in acting; vs. 11 and following verses, caution in speaking. **12. gracious**—Thereby he takes precaution against sudden injury (vs. 11). **swallow up himself**—(Prov. 10:8, 14, 21, 32; 12:13; 15:2; 22:11). **13.** Illustrating the *folly* and *injuriousness* of the fool's words; last clause of vs. 12. **14. full of words**—(ch. 5:2.) **a man cannot tell what shall be**—(ch. 3:22; 6:12; 8:7; 11:2; Prov. 27:1.) If man, universally (including the wise man), cannot foresee the future, much less can the fool; his "many words" are therefore futile. **15. labour ... wearieth** —(Isa. 55:2; Hab. 2:13.) **knoweth not how to go to the city**—proverb for *ignorance of the most ordinary matters* (vs. 3); spiritually, *the heavenly city* (Ps. 107:7; Matt. 7:13, 14). MAURER connects vs. 15 with the following verses. The labor (vexation) caused by the foolish (injurious princes, vss. 4-7) harasses him who "knows not how to go to the city," to ingratiate himself with them there. *English Version* is simpler. **16. a child**—given to pleasures; behaves with childish levity. Not *in years;* for a nation may be happy under a young prince, as Josiah. **eat in the morning**—the usual time for dispensing *justice* in the East (Jer. 21:12); here, given to feasting (Isa. 5:11; Acts 2:15). **17. son of nobles** —not merely in blood, but in virtue, the true nobility (Song of Sol. 7:1; Isa. 32:5, 8). **in due season**—(ch. 3:1), not until duty has first been attended to. **for strength**—to refresh the body, not for *revelry* (included in "drunkenness"). **18. building**—lit., "the joining of the rafters," viz., the kingdom (vs. 16; Isa. 3:6; Amos 9:11). **hands**—(ch. 4:5; Prov. 6:10.) **droppeth**—By neglecting to repair the roof in time, the rain gets through. **19.** Referring to vs. 18. Instead of repairing the breaches in the commonwealth (equivalent to "building"), the princes "make a feast for laughter (vs. 16), and wine maketh their *life* glad (Ps. 104:15), and (but) money supplieth (answereth their wishes by supplying) all things," i.e., they take bribes to support *their extravagance;* and hence arise the wrongs that are perpetrated (vss. 5, 6; ch. 3:16; Isa. 1:23; 5:23). MAURER takes "all things" of *the wrongs* to which princes are instigated by "money"; e.g., the heavy taxes, which were the occasion of Rehoboam losing ten tribes (I Kings 12: 4, etc.). **20. thought**—lit., "consciousness." **rich**— the great. The language, as applied to earthly princes knowing the "thought," is figurative. But it literally holds good of the King of kings (Ps. 139), whose consciousness of every evil thought we should ever realize. **bed-chamber**—the most secret place (II Kings 6:12). **bird of the air . . .**—proverbial (cf. Hab. 2:11; Luke 19:40); in a way as marvellous and rapid, as if birds or some winged messenger carried to the king information of the curse so uttered. In the East superhuman sagacity was attributed to birds (see my *Note,* Job 28:21; hence the proverb).

CHAPTER 11

Vss. 1-10. 1. Vs. 2 shows that *charity* is here inculcated. **bread**—bread-corn. As in the Lord's prayer, *all things needful for the body and soul.* Solomon reverts to the sentiment (ch. 9:10). **waters** —image from the custom of sowing seed by casting it from boats into the overflowing waters of the Nile, or in any marshy ground. When the waters receded, the grain in the alluvial soil sprang up (Isa. 32:20). "Waters" express *multitudes,* so vs. 2; Revelation 17:15; also the seemingly *hopeless* character of the recipients of the charity; but it shall prove at last to have been not thrown away (Isa. 49:4). **2. portion**—of thy bread. **seven**—the perfect number. **eight**—even *to more than seven:* i.e., to *many* (so "waters," vs. 1), nay, even to *very many* in need (Job 5:19; Micah 5:5). **evil**—The day may be near, when you will need the help of those whom you have bound to you by kindnesses (Luke 16:9). The very argument which covetous men use against liberality (viz., that bad times may come), the wise man uses for it. **3. clouds**—answering to "evil" (vs. 2), meaning, When the times of evil are fully ripe, evil *must* come; and speculations about it beforehand, so as to prevent one sowing seed of liberality, are vain (vs. 4). **tree**—Once the storm uproots it, it lies either northward or southward, according as it fell. So man's character is unchangeable, whether for hell or heaven, once that death overtakes him (Rev. 22:11,

14, 15). *Now* is his time for liberality, before the evil days come (ch. 12:1). **4.** Therefore sow thy charity in faith, without hesitancy or speculation as to results, because they may not seem promising (ch. 9:10). So in vs. 1, man is told to "cast his bread-corn" on the seemingly unpromising "waters" (Ps. 126:5, 6). The farmer would get on badly, who, instead of sowing and reaping, spent his time in watching the wind and clouds. **5. spirit**—How the *soul* animates the body! Thus the transition to the formation of the *body* "in the womb" is more natural, than if with MAURER we translate it "wind" (ch. 1:6; John 3:8). **bones . . . grow**—(Job 10:8, 9; Ps. 139:15, 16.) **knowest not the works of God**— (ch. 3:11; 8:17; 9:12.) **6. morning . . . evening**— early and late; when young and when old; in sunshine and under clouds. **seed**—of godly works (Hos. 10:12; II Cor. 9:10; Gal. 6:7). **prosper**—(Isa. 55: 10, 11.) **both . . . alike**—Both the unpromising and the promising sowing may bear good fruit in *others:* certainly they shall to the faithful *sower.* **7. light** —of life (ch. 7:11; Ps. 49:19). Life is enjoyable, especially to the godly. **8.** But while man thankfully enjoys life, "let him remember" it will not last for ever. The "many days of darkness," i.e., the unseen world (Job 10:21, 22; Ps. 88:12), also days of "evil" in this world (vs. 2), are coming; therefore sow the good seed while life and good days last, which are not too long for accomplishing life's duties. **All that cometh**—i.e., All that followeth in the *evil* and *dark days* is vain, as far as *work for God* is concerned (ch. 9:10). **9. Rejoice**—not *advice,* but *warning.* So I Kings 22:15, is irony; if thou dost rejoice (*carnally,* ch. 2:2; 7:2, not *moderately,* as in ch. 5:18), etc., then "know that . . . God will bring thee into judgment" (ch. 3:17; 12:14). **youth . . . youth**—distinct *Hebrew* words, *adolescence* or boyhood (before vs. 13), and full-grown *youth.* It marks the gradual progress in self-indulgence, to which the young especially are prone; they see the roses, but do not discover the thorns, until pierced by them. Religion will cost self-denial, but the want of it infinitely more (Luke 14: 28). **10. sorrow**—i.e., *the lusts* that end in "sorrow," opposed to "rejoice," and "heart cheer thee" (vs. 9), *Margin,* "anger," i.e., all "ways of thine heart"; "remove," etc., is thus opposed to "walk in," etc. (vs. 9). **flesh**—the bodily organ by which the sensual *thoughts* of the "heart" are embodied in *acts.* **childhood**—rather, "boyhood"; the same *Hebrew* word as the first, "youth" in vs. 9. A motive for self-restraint; the time is coming when the vigor of youth on which thou reliest, will seem vain, except in so far as it has been given to God (ch. 12:1). **youth**— lit., *the dawn* of thy days.

CHAPTER 12

Vss. 1-14. 1. As ch. 11:9, 10 showed what youths are to shun, so this verse shows what they are to follow. **Creator**—"Remember" that thou art not thine own, but God's property; for He has created thee (Ps. 100:3). Therefore serve Him with thy "all" (Mark 12:30), and with thy *best* days, not with the dregs of them (Prov. 8:17; 22:6; Jer. 3:4; Lam. 3:27). The *Hebrew* is "Creators," plural, implying the plurality of persons, as in Genesis 1:26; so *Hebrew,* "Makers" (Isa. 54:5). **while . . . not**—i.e., *before that* (Prov. 8:26) the evil days come; viz., calamity and old age, when one can no longer serve God, as in youth (ch. 11:2, 8). **no pleasure**—of a sensual kind (II Sam. 19:35; Ps. 90:10). Pleasure in God continues to the godly old (Isa. 46:4). **2.** Illustrating "the evil days" (Jer. 13:16). "Light," "sun," etc., express *prosperity;* "darkness," *pain and calamity* (Isa. 13:10; 30:26). **clouds . . . after . . . rain**—After rain sunshine (comfort) might be looked for, but only a brief glimpse of it is given, and the gloomy clouds (pains) return. **3. keepers of the house**—viz., *the hands and arms* which *protected* the body, as guards do a palace (Gen. 49:24; Job 4:19; II Cor. 5:1), are now palsied. **strong men . . . bow** —(Judg. 16:25, 30.) Like supporting pillars, *the feet and knees* (Song of Sol. 5:15); the *strongest* members (Ps. 147:10). **grinders**—the molar teeth. **cease** —are idle. **those that look out of the windows**—the eyes; the powers of vision, looking out from beneath the eyelids, which open and shut like the casement of a window. **4. doors**—*the lips,* which are closely *shut* together as *doors,* by old men in eating, for, if they did not do so, the food would drop out (Job 41:14; Ps. 141:3; Micah 7:5). **in the streets**—i.e., toward the street, "the *outer* doors" [MAURER and WEISS]. **sound of . . . grinding**—The teeth being almost gone, and the lips "shut" in eating, the sound of mastication is scarcely heard. **the bird**—the cock. In the East all mostly rise with the dawn. But the old are glad to rise from their sleepless couch, or painful slumbers still earlier, viz., when the cock crows, before dawn (Job. 7:4) [HOLDEN]. The least noise awakens them [WEISS]. **daughters of music**—the organs that produce and that enjoy music; the *voice* and *ear.* **5. that which is high**—The old are afraid of ascending a *hill.* **fears . . . in the way**—Even on the level *highway* they are full of fears of falling, etc. **almond . . . flourish**—In the East the hair is mostly dark. *The white head* of the old among the dark-haired is like *an almond tree,* with its white blossoms, among the dark trees around [HOLDEN]. The almond tree *flowers* on a leafless stock in *winter* (answering to *old age,* in which all the powers are dormant), while the other trees are flowerless. GESENIUS takes the *Hebrew* for *flourishes* from a different root, *casts off;* when the old man *loses* his gray hairs, as the almond tree *casts* its white flowers. **grasshoppers**—the dry, shrivelled, old man, his backbone sticking out, his knees projecting forwards, his arms backwards, his head down, and the apophyses enlarged, is like that insect. Hence arose the fable, that Tithonus in very old age was changed into a grasshopper [PARKHURST]. "The locust *raises itself* to fly"; the old man about to leave the body is like a locust when it is assuming its winged form, and is about to fly [MAURER]. **a burden**—viz., to himself. **desire shall fail**—satisfaction shall be abolished. For "desire," *Vulgate* has "the caper tree," provocative of lust; not so well. **long home**—(Job 16:22; 17:13.) **mourners**—(Jer. 9:17-20), hired for the occasion (Matt. 9:23). **6.** A double image to represent *death,* as in vss. 1-5, *old age:* (1) A *lamp* of frail material, but *gilded* over, often in the East hung from roofs by a *cord* of silk and *silver* interwoven; as the lamp is dashed down and broken, when the cord breaks, so man at death; the golden bowl of the lamp answers to *the skull,* which, from the vital preciousness of its contents, may be called "golden"; "the silver cord" is *the spinal marrow,* which is white

and precious as silver, and is attached to the brain. (2) *A fountain,* from which water is drawn by a *pitcher* let down by a rope wound round *a wheel;* as, when the pitcher and wheel are broken, water can no more be drawn, so life ceases when the vital energies are gone. The "fountain" *may* mean the right ventricle of the heart; the "cistern," the left; the pitcher, the veins; the wheel the aorta, or great artery [SMITH]. The circulation of the blood, whether known or not to Solomon, *seems* to be implied in the language put by the Holy Ghost into his mouth. This gloomy picture of old age applies to those who have not "remembered their Creator in youth." They have none of the consolations of God, which they might have obtained in youth; it is now too late to seek them. A good old age is a blessing to the godly (Gen. 15:15; Job 5:26; Prov. 16:31; 20:29). **7. dust**—the dust-formed body. **spirit**—surviving the body; implying its immortality (ch. 3:11). **8-12.** A summary of the first part. **13, 14.** A summary of the second. **Vanity . . .**—Resumption of the sentiment with which the book began (ch. 1:2; I John 2:17). **9. gave good heed**—lit., "he weighed." The "teaching the people" seems to have been *oral;* the "proverbs," *in writing.* There must then have been auditories *assembled to hear* the inspired *wisdom of the Preacher.* See the explanation of *Koheleth* in the *Introduction* and ch. 1 (I Kings 4:34). **that which is written . . .**—rather, (he sought) "*to write down* uprightly (or 'aright') words of truth" [HOLDEN and WEISS]. "Acceptable" means an agreeable style; "uprightly . . . truth," correct sentiment. 11. **goads**—piercing deeply into the mind (Acts 2:37; 9:5; Heb. 4:12); evidently *inspired words,* as the end of the verse proves. **fastened**—rather, on account of the *Hebrew* genders, (The words) "are fastened (in the memory) like nails" [HOLDEN]. **masters of assemblies**—rather, "the masters of collections (i.e., collectors of inspired sayings, Prov. 25:1), are given ('have published them as proceeding' [HOLDEN]) from one Shepherd," viz., the Spirit of Jesus Christ [WEISS], (Ezek. 37:24). However, the mention of "goads" favors the *English Version,* "masters of assemblies," viz., *under-shepherds,* inspired by *the Chief Shepherd* (I Pet. 5:2-4). SCHMIDT translates, "The masters of assemblies are fastened (made sure) as nails," so Isa. 22:23. **12.** (*Note,* ch. 1:18.) **many books**—of mere *human* composition, opposed to "by these"; these *inspired* writings are the only sure source of "admonition." **(over much) study**—in mere human books, wearies the body, without solidly profiting the soul. **13**—The grand inference of the whole book. **Fear God**—The antidote to following creature-idols, and "vanities," whether self-righteousness (ch. 7:16, 18), or wicked oppression and other evils (ch. 8:12, 13), or mad mirth (ch. 2:2; 7:2-5), or self-mortifying avarice (ch. 8:13, 17), or youth spent without God (ch. 11:9; 12:1). **this is the whole duty of man**—lit., "this is the whole man," the full ideal of man, as originally contemplated, realized wholly by Jesus Christ alone; and, through Him, by saints now in part, hereafter perfectly (I John 3:22-24; Rev. 22:14). **14.** The future judgment is the test of what is "vanity," what solid, as regards the chief good, the grand subject of the book.

THE SONG OF

SOLOMON

INTRODUCTION

THE Song of Solomon, called in the Vulgate and LXX, "The Song of Songs," from the opening words. This *title* denotes its *superior excellence*, according to the *Hebrew* idiom; so *holy of holies*, equivalent to most holy (Exod. 29:37); *the heaven of heavens*, equivalent to the highest heavens (Deut. 10:14). It is one of the five volumes (*megilloth*) placed immediately after the Pentateuch in MSS. of the Jewish Scriptures. It is also fourth of the Hagiographa (*Cetubim, writings*) or the third division of the Old Testament, the other two being the Law and the Prophets. The Jewish enumeration of the *Cetubim* is Psalms, Proverbs, Job, Canticles, Ruth, Lamentations, Ecclesiastes, Esther, Daniel, Ezra (including Nehemiah), and Chronicles. Its *canonicity* is certain; it is found in all Hebrew MSS. of Scripture; also in the Greek LXX; in the catalogues of Melito, bishop of Sardis, A.D. 170 (EUSEBIUS, H. E., iv. 26), and of others of the ancient Church.

Origen and Jerome tell us that the Jews forbade it to be read by any until he was thirty years old. It certainly needs a degree of spiritual maturity to enter aright into the holy mystery of love which it allegorically sets forth. To such as have attained this maturity, of whatever age they be, the Song of Songs is one of the most edifying of the sacred writings. Rosenmuller justly says, The sudden transitions of the bride from the court to the grove are inexplicable, on the supposition that it describes merely human love. Had it been the latter, it would have been positively objectionable, and never would have been inserted in the holy canon. The allusion to "Pharaoh's chariots" (ch. 1:9) has been made a ground for conjecturing that the love of Solomon and Pharaoh's daughter is the subject of the Song. But this passage alludes to a remarkable event in the history of the Old Testament Church, the deliverance from the hosts and chariots of Pharaoh at the Red Sea. (See, however, note there). The other allusions are quite opposed to the notion; the bride is represented at times as a shepherdess (ch. 1:7), "an abomination to the Egyptians" (Gen. 46:34); so also chapters 1:6; 3:4; 4:8; 5:7 are at variance with it. The Christian fathers, Origen and Theodoret, compared the teachings of Solomon to a ladder with three steps; Ecclesiastes, natural (the nature of sensible things, vain); Proverbs, moral; Canticles, mystical (figuring the union of Christ and the Church). The Jews compared Proverbs to the outer court of Solomon's temple, Ecclesiastes to the holy place, and Canticles to the holy of holies. Understood allegorically, the Song is cleared of all difficulty. "Shulamith" (ch. 6:13), the bride, is thus an appropriate name, *Daughter of Peace* being the feminine of Solomon, equivalent to the *Prince of Peace*. She by turns is a vinedresser, shepherdess, midnight inquirer, and prince's consort and daughter, and He a suppliant drenched with night-dews, and a king in His palace, in harmony with the various relations of the Church and Christ. As Ecclesiastes sets forth the vanity of love of the creature, Canticles sets forth the fullness of the love which joins believers and the Saviour. The entire economy of salvation, says Harris, aims at restoring to the world the lost spirit of love. God is love, and Christ is the embodiment of the love of God. As the other books of Scripture present severally their own aspects of divine truth, so Canticles furnishes the believer with language of holy love, wherewith his heart can commune with his Lord; and it portrays the intensity of Christ's love to him; the affection of love was created in man to be a transcript of the divine love, and the Song clothes the latter in words; were it not for this, we should be at a loss for language, having the divine warrant, wherewith to express, without presumption, the fervor of the love between Christ and us. The image of a bride, a bridegroom, and a marriage, to represent this spiritual union, has the sanction of Scripture throughout; nay, the spiritual union was *the original fact in the mind of God*, of which marriage is the transcript (Isa. 54:5; 62:5; Jer. 3:1, etc.; Ezek. 16 and 23; Matt. 9:15; 22:2; 25:1, etc.: John 3:29; II Cor. 11:2; Eph. 5:23–32, where Paul does not go from the marriage relation to the union of Christ and the Church as if the former were the first; but comes down from the latter as the first and best recognized fact on which the relation of marriage is based; Rev. 19:7; 21:2; 22:17). Above all, the Song seems to correspond to, and form a trilogy with, the 45th and 72d Psalms, which contain the same imagery; just as Psalm 37 answers to Proverbs, and Psalms 39 and 73 to Job. Love to Christ is the strongest, as it is the purest, of human passions, and therefore needs the strongest language to express it: to the pure in heart the phraseology, drawn from the rich imagery of Oriental poetry, will not only appear not indelicate or exaggerated, but even below the reality. A single emblem is a *type;* the actual rites, incidents, and persons of the Old Testament were appointed types of truths afterwards to be revealed. But the *allegory* is a continued metaphor, in which the circumstances are palpably often purely imagery, while the thing signified is altogether real. The clew to the meaning of the Song is not to be looked for in the allegory itself, but in other parts of Scripture. "It lies in the casket of revelation an exquisite gem, engraved with emblematical characters, with nothing literal thereon to break the consistency of their beauty" [BURROWES]. This accounts for the name of God not occurring in it. Whereas in the *parable* the writer narrates, in the *allegory* he never does so. The Song throughout consists of immediate addresses either of Christ to the soul, or of the soul to Christ. "The experimental knowledge of Christ's loveliness and the believer's love is the best commentary on the whole of this allegorical Song" [LEIGHTON]. Like the curiously wrought Oriental lamps, which do not reveal the beauty of their transparent emblems until lighted up within, so the types and allegories of Scripture, "the lantern to our path," need the inner light of the Holy Spirit of Jesus to reveal their significance. The details of the allegory are not to be too minutely pressed. In the Song, with an Oriental profusion of imagery, numbers of lovely, sensible objects are aggregated not strictly congruous, but portraying jointly by their very diversity the thousand various and seemingly opposite beauties which meet together in Christ.

The unity of subject throughout, and the recurrence of the same expressions (ch. 2:6, 7; 3:5; 8:3, 4; 2:16; 6:3; 7:10; 3:6; 6:10; 8:5), prove the unity of the poem, in opposition to those who make it consist of a number of separate erotic songs. The sudden transitions (e.g., from the midnight knocking at a humble cottage to a glorious description of the King) accord with the alternations in the believer's experience. However various the divisions assigned be, most commentators have observed four breaks (whatever more they have imagined), followed by four abrupt beginnings (ch. 2:7; 3:5; 5:1; 8:4). Thus there result five parts, all alike ending in full repose and refreshment. We read (I Kings 4:32) that Solomon's songs were "a thousand and *five.*" The odd number *five* added over the complete *thousand* makes it not unlikely that the "five" refers to the Song of songs, consisting of five parts.

It answers to the idyllic poetry of other nations. The Jews explain it of the union of Jehovah and ancient Israel; the allusions to the *temple* and the *wilderness* accord with this; some Christians of Christ and the Church; others of Christ and the individual believer. All these are true; for the Church is one in all ages, the ancient typifying the modern Church, and its history answering to that of each individual soul in it. Jesus "sees all, as if that all were one, loves one, as if that one were all." "The time suited the manner of this revelation; because types and allegories belonged to the old dispensation, which reached its ripeness under Solomon, when the temple was built" [MOODY STUART]. "The daughter of Zion at that time was openly married to Jehovah"; for it is thenceforth that the prophets, in reproving Israel's subsequent sin, speak of it as a breach of her marriage covenant. The songs heretofore sung by her were the preparatory hymns of her childhood; "the last and crowning 'Song of Songs' was prepared for the now mature maiden against the day of her marriage to the King of kings" [ORIGEN]. Solomon was peculiarly fitted to clothe this holy mystery with the lovely natural imagery with which the Song abounds; for "he spake of trees, from the cedar in Lebanon, even unto the hyssop that springeth out of the wall" (I Kings 4:33). A higher qualification was his knowledge of the eternal Wisdom or Word of God (Prov. 8), the heavenly bridegroom. David, his father, had prepared the way, in Psalms 45 and 72; the son perfected the allegory. It seems to have been written in early life, long before his declension; for after it a song of holy gladness would hardly be appropriate. It was the song of his first love, in the kindness of his youthful espousals to Jehovah. Like other inspired books, its sense is not to be restricted to that local and temporary one in which the writer may have understood it; it extends to all ages, and shadows forth everlasting truth (I Pet. 1:11, 12; II Pet. 1:20, 21).

> Oh that I knew how all thy lights combine, and the configurations of their glorie,
> Seeing not only how each verse doth shine, but all the constellations of the storie.—HERBERT

Three notes of time occur [MOODY STUART]: (1) The Jewish Church speaks of the Gentile Church (ch. 8:8) towards the end; (2) Christ speaks to the apostles (ch. 5:1) in the middle; (3) The Church speaks of the coming of Christ (ch. 1:2) at the beginning. Thus we have, in direct order, Christ about to come, and the cry for the advent; Christ finishing His work on earth, and the last supper; Christ ascended, and the call of the Gentiles. In another aspect we have: (1) In the individual soul the longing for the manifestation of Christ to it, and the various alternations in its experience (ch. 1:2, 4; 2:8; 3:1, 4, 6, 7) of His manifestation; (2) The abundant enjoyment of His sensible consolations, which is soon withdrawn through the bride's carelessness (ch. 5:1–3, etc.), and her longings after Him, and reconciliation (ch. 5:8–16; 6:3, etc.; 7:1, etc.); (3) Effects of Christ's manifestation on the believer; viz., assurance, labors of love, anxiety for the salvation of the impenitent, eagerness for the Lord's second coming (ch. 7:10, 12; 8:8–10, 14).

CHAPTER 1

Vss. 1-17. CANTICLE I.—THE BRIDE SEARCHING FOR AND FINDING THE KING. Ch. 1:2-2:7. **1. The song of songs**—The most excellent of all songs, *Hebrew* idiom (Exod. 29:37; Deut. 10:14). A foretaste on earth of the "new song" to be sung in glory (Rev. 5:9; 14:3; 15:2-4). **Solomon's**—"King of Israel," or "Jerusalem," is not added, as in the opening of Proverbs and Ecclesiastes, not because Solomon had not yet ascended the throne [MOODY STUART], but because his personality is hid under that of Christ, the true Solomon (equivalent to *Prince of Peace*). The earthly Solomon is not introduced, which would break the consistency of the allegory. Though the bride bears the chief part, the Song throughout is not hers, but that of her "Solomon." He animates her. He and she, the Head and the members, form but one Christ [ADELAIDE NEWTON]. Aaron prefigured Him as priest; Moses, as prophet; David, as a suffering king; Solomon, as the triumphant prince of peace. The camp in the wilderness represents the Church in the world; the peaceful reign of Solomon, after all enemies had been subdued, represents the Church in heaven, of which joy

the Song gives a foretaste. **2. him**—abruptly. She names him not, as is natural to one whose heart is full of some much desired friend: so Mary Magdalene at the sepulchre (John 20:15), as if everyone must know whom she means, the *one* chief object of her desire (Ps. 73:25; Matt. 13:44-46; Phil. 3:7, 8). **kiss**—the token of *peace* from the Prince of Peace (Luke 15:20); "our Peace" (Ps. 85:10; Col. 1:21; Eph. 2:14). **of his mouth**—marking the tenderest affection. For a king to permit his hands, or even garment, to be kissed, was counted a great honor; but that he should himself kiss another *with his mouth* is the greatest honor. God had in times past spoken by *the mouth* of His prophets, who had declared the Church's betrothal; the bride now longs for contact with *the mouth of the Bridegroom Himself* (Job 23:12; Luke 4:22; Heb. 1:1, 2). True of the Church before the first advent, longing for "the hope of Israel," "the desire of all nations"; also the awakened soul longing for the kiss of *reconciliation;* and further, the kiss that is the token of the *marriage contract* (Hos. 2:19, 20), and of *friendship* (I Sam. 20:41; John 14:21; 15:15). **thy love**—*Hebrew,* "loves," viz., tokens of love, loving blandishments. **wine**—which makes glad "the heavy heart" of one ready to perish, so that he "remembers his misery no more" (Prov. 31:6, 7). So, in a "better" sense, Christ's love (Hab. 3:17, 18). He gives the same praise to the bride's love, with the emphatic addition, "How much" (ch. 4:10). Wine was created by His first miracle (John 2), and was the pledge given of His love at the last supper. The spiritual wine is His blood and His spirit, the "new" and better wine of the kingdom (Matt. 26:29), which we can never drink to "excess," as the other (Eph. 5:18; cf. Ps. 23:5; Isa. 55:1). 3. Rather, "As regards the savor of thy ointments, it is good" [MAURER]. In ch. 4:10, 11, the Bridegroom reciprocates the praise of the bride in the same terms. **thy name**—Christ's *character and office* as the "Anointed" (Isa. 9:6; 61:1), as "the savor of ointments" are the graces that surround His *person* (Ps. 45:7, 8). Ecclesiastes 7:1, in its fullest sense, applies to Him. The holy anointing oil of the high priest, which it was death for anyone else to make (so Acts 4:12), implies the exclusive preciousness of Messiah's name (Exod. 30:23-28, 31-38). So Mary brake the box of precious ointment over Him, appropriately (Mark 14:5), the broken box typifying His body, which, when broken, diffused all grace: compounded of various spices, etc. (Col. 1:19; 2:9); of sweet odor (Eph. 5:2). **poured**—(Isa. 53:12; Rom. 5:5.) **therefore**—because of the manifestation of God's character in Christ (I John 4:9, 19). So the penitent woman (Luke 7:37, 38, 47). **virgins**—the pure in heart (II Cor. 11:2; Rev. 14:4). The same *Hebrew* is translated, "thy hidden ones" (Ps. 83:3). The "ointment" of the Spirit "poured forth" produces the "love of Christ" (Rom. 5:5). **4.** (1) The cry of ancient Israel for Messiah, e.g., Simeon, Anna, etc. (2) The cry of an awakened soul for the drawing of the Spirit, after it has got a glimpse of Christ's loveliness and its own helplessness. **Draw me**—The Father draws (John 6:44). The Son draws (Jer. 31:3; Hos. 11:4; John 12:32). "Draw" here, and "Tell" (vs. 7), reverently qualify the word "kiss" (vs. 2). **me, we**—No believer desires to go to heaven alone. We are converted as *individuals;* we follow Christ as joined in a *communion* of saints (John 1:41, 45). Individuality and community meet in the bride. **run**—Her earnestness kindles as she prays (Isa. 40:31; Ps. 119:32, 60). **after thee**—not before (John 10:4). **king . . . brought me into**—(Ps. 45:14, 15; John 10:16). He is the anointed *Priest* (vs. 3); *King* (vs. 4). **chambers**—Her prayer is answered even beyond her desires. Not only is she permitted to *run* after Him, but is brought into the inmost pavilion, where Eastern kings admitted none but the most intimate friends (Esther 4:11; 5:2; Ps. 27:5). The erection of the temple of Solomon was the first bringing of the bride into permanent, instead of migratory, chambers of the King. Christ's body on earth was the next (John 2:21), whereby believers are brought within the veil (Eph. 2:6; Heb. 10:19, 20). Entrance into the closet for prayer is the first step. The earnest of the future bringing into heaven (John 14:3). *His* chambers are the bride's also (Isa. 26:20). There are various *chambers, plural* (John 14:2). **be glad and rejoice**—*inward* and *outward* rejoicing. **in thee**—(Isa. 61:10; Phil. 4:1, 4). Not in *our* spiritual frames (Ps. 30:6, 7). **remember**—rather, "commemorate with praises" (Isa. 63:7). The mere *remembrance* of spiritual joys is better than the *present enjoyment* of carnal ones (Ps. 4:6, 7). **upright**—rather, "uprightly," "sincerely" (Ps. 58:1; Rom. 12:9); so Nathanael (John 1:47); Peter (John 21:17); or "deservedly" [MAURER]. **5. black**—viz., "as the tents of Kedar," equivalent to *blackness* (Ps. 120:5). She draws the

image from the black goatskins with which the Scenite Arabs ("Kedar" was in Arabia Petræa) cover their tents (contrasted with the splendid state tent in which *the King* was awaiting His bride according to Eastern custom); typifying the darkness of man's natural state. To feel this, and yet also feel one's self in Jesus Christ "comely as the curtains of Solomon," marks the believer (Rom. 7:18, etc.; 8:1); I Tim. 1:15, "I *am* chief"; so she says not merely, "I was," but "I am"; *still* black in herself, but comely through *His* comeliness put upon her (Ezek. 16:14). **curtains**—first, the hangings and veil in the temple of Solomon (Ezek. 16:10); then, also, the "fine linen which is the righteousness of saints" (Rev. 19:8), the white wedding garment provided by Jesus Christ (Isa. 61:10; Matt. 22:11; I Cor. 1:30; Col. 1:28; 2:10; Rev. 7:14). *Historically*, the dark tents of Kedar represent the Gentile Church (Isa. 60:3-7, etc.). As the vineyard at the close is transferred from the Jews, who had not kept their own, to the Gentiles, so the Gentiles are introduced at the commencement of the Song; for they were among the earliest inquirers after Jesus Christ (Matt. 2): the wise men from the East (Arabia, or Kedar). **daughters of Jerusalem**—professors, not the bride, or "the virgins," yet not enemies; invited to gospel blessings (ch. 3:10, 11); so near to Jesus Christ as not to be unlikely to find Him (ch. 5:8); desirous to seek Him with her (ch. 6:1; cf. ch. 6:13; 7:1, 5, 8). In ch. 7:8, 9, the bride's Beloved becomes *their* Beloved; not, however, of *all* of them (ch. 8:4; cf. Luke 23:27, 28). **6.** She feels as if her blackness was so great as to be gazed at by all. **mother's children**—(Matt. 10:36.) She is to forget "her own people and her father's house," i.e., the worldly connections of her unregenerate state (Ps. 45:10); they had maltreated her (Luke 15:15, 16). Children of the same mother, but not the same father [MAURER], (John 8:41-44). They made her a common keeper of vineyards, whereby the sun looked upon, i.e., burnt her; thus she did "not keep her own" vineyard, i.e., fair beauty. So the world, and the soul (Matt. 16:26; Luke 9:25). The believer has to watch against the same danger (I Cor. 9:27). So he will be able, instead of the self-reproach here, to say as in ch. 8:12. **7. my soul loveth**—more intense than "the virgins" and "the upright love thee" (vss. 3, 4; Matt. 22:37). To carry out the design of the allegory, the royal encampment is here represented as moving from place to place, in search of green pastures, under the *Shepherd King* (Ps. 23). The bride, having first enjoyed communion with him in the pavilion, is willing to follow Him into labors and dangers; arising from all absorbing love (Luke 14:26); this distinguishes her from the formalist (John 10:27; Rev. 14:4). **feedest**—tendest thy flock (Isa. 40:11; Heb. 13:20; I Peter 2:25; 5:4; Rev. 7:17.) No *single* type expresses all the office of Jesus Christ; hence arises the variety of *diverse* images used to portray the manifold aspects of Him: these would be quite incongruous, if the Song referred to the earthly Solomon. Her intercourse with Him is peculiar. She hears His voice, and addresses none but Himself. Yet it is through a veil; she sees Him not (Job 23:8, 9). If we would be fed, we must follow the Shepherd through the *whole* breadth of His Word, and not stay on *one* spot alone. **makest . . . to rest**—distinct from "feedest"; periods of rest are vouchsafed after labor (Isa. 4:6; 49:10; Ezek. 34:13-15). Communion in private must go along with public following of Him. **turneth aside**—rather one *veiled,* i.e., as a *harlot,* not His true bride (Gen. 38:15), [GESENIUS]; or as a *mourner* (II Sam. 15:30), [WEISS]; or as one *un-*

known [MAURER]. All imply estrangement from the Bridegroom. She feels estranged even among Christ's true servants, answering to "thy companions" (Luke 22:28), so long as she has not Himself present. The opposite spirit to I Corinthians 3:4. **8. If**—she ought to have *known* (John 14:8, 9). The confession of her ignorance and *blackness* (vs. 5) leads Him to call her "fairest" (Matt. 12:20). Her jealousy of letting even "His companions" take the place of Himself (vs. 7) led her too far. He directs her to follow them, as they follow Him (I Cor. 11:1; Heb. 6:10, 12); to use ordinances and the ministry; where *they* are, *He* is (Jer. 6:16; Matt. 18:19, 20; Heb. 10:25). Indulging in isolation is not the way to find Him. It was thus, literally, that Zipporah found her bridegroom (Exod. 2:16). The bride unhesitatingly asks the watchmen afterwards (ch. 3:3). **kids**—(John 21:15). Christ is to be found in active ministrations, as well as in prayer (Prov. 11:25). **shepherds' tents**—ministers in the sanctuary (Ps. 84: 1). **9. horses in Pharaoh's chariots**—celebrated for *beauty, swiftness,* and *ardor,* at the Red Sea (Exod. 14:15). These qualities, which *seem* to belong to the ungodly, *really* belong to the saints [MOODY STUART]. The allusion may be to the horses brought at a high price by Solomon out of Egypt (II Chron. 1:16, 17). So the bride is redeemed out of spiritual Egypt by the true Solomon, at an infinite price (Isa. 51:1; I Pet. 1:18, 19). But the deliverance from *Pharaoh at the Red Sea* accords with the allusion to the tabernacle (ch. 1:5; 3:6, 7); it rightly is put at the beginning of the Church's call. The *ardor* and *beauty* of the bride are the point of comparison; (vs. 4) "run"; (vs. 5) "comely." Also, like Pharaoh's horses, she forms a great company (Rev. 19:7, 14). As Jesus Christ is both Shepherd and Conqueror, so believers are not only His *sheep*, but also, as a Church *militant* now, His *chariots and horses* (ch. 6:4). **10. rows of jewels**—(Ezek. 16:11, 12, 13). OLERIUS says, Persian ladies wear two or three rows of pearls round the head, beginning on the forehead and descending down to the cheeks and under the chin, so that their faces seem to be set in pearls (Ezek. 16:11). The comparison to the horses (vs. 9) implies the vital energy of the bride; this verse, her superadded graces (Prov. 1:9; 4:9; I Tim. 2:9; II Pet. 1:5). **11. We**—the Trinity implied by the Holy Ghost, whether it was so by the writer of the Song or not (Gen. 1:26; Prov. 8:30; 30:4). "The Jews acknowledged God as king, and Messiah as king, in interpreting the Song, but did not know that these two are one" [LEIGHTON]. **make**—not merely *give* (Eph. 2:10). **borders of gold, with studs** [i.e., spots] **of silver**—Jesus Christ delights to give more "to him that hath" (Matt. 25:29). He crowns *His own work* in us (Isa. 26:12). The "borders" here are equivalent to "rows" (vs. 10); but here, the King seems to give the finish to her attire, by adding a *crown* (*borders,* or circles) of gold studded with silver spots, as in Esther 2:17. Both the *royal* and *nuptial* crown, or chaplet. The *Hebrew* for "spouse" (ch. 4:8) is *a crowned one* (Ezek. 16:12; Rev. 2:10). The crown is given at once upon conversion, in title, but in sensible possession afterwards (II Tim. 4:8). **12. While** —It is the presence of the Sun of Righteousness that draws out the believer's odors of grace. It was the sight of Him at table that caused the two women to bring forth their ointments for Him (Luke 7:37, 38; John 12:3; II Cor. 2:15). Historically fulfilled (Matt. 2:11); spiritually (Rev. 3:20); and in church worship (Matt. 18:20); and at the Lord's Supper especially, for here *public* communion with Him at table amidst His friends is spoken of, as vs. 4 refers

to *private* communion (I Cor. 10:16, 21); typically (Exod. 24:9-11); the future perfect fulfilment (Luke 22:30; Rev. 19:9). The allegory supposes the King to have stopped in His movements and to be seated with His friends on the divan. What grace that a table should be prepared for us, while still militant (Ps. 23:5)! **my spikenard**—not boasting, but *owning* the Lord's grace to and in her. The spikenard is a lowly herb, the emblem of humility. She rejoices that *He* is well pleased with her graces, His own work (Phil. 4:18). **13. bundle of myrrh**—abundant *preciousness (Greek),* (I Pet. 2:7). Even a *little* myrrh was costly; much more a *bundle* (Col. 2:9). BURROWES takes it of *a scent-box filled with liquid myrrh;* the liquid obtained by incision gave the tree its chief value. **he**—rather, "it"; it is the myrrh that lies in the bosom, as the cluster of camphire is in the vineyards (vs. 14). **all night**—an undivided heart (Eph. 3:17; contrast Jer. 4:14; Ezek. 16:15, 30). Yet on account of the everlasting covenant, God restores the adulteress (Ezek. 16:60, 62; Hos. 2:2, etc.). The night is the whole present dispensation till the everlasting day dawns (Rom. 13:12). Also, lit., "night" (Ps. 119:147, 148), the night of *affliction* (Ps. 42:8). **14. cluster**—Jesus Christ is one, yet *manifold* in His graces. **camphire**—or, "cypress." The hennah is meant, whose odorous flowers grow in clusters, of a color white and yellow softly blended; its bark is dark, the foliage light green. Women deck their persons with them. The loveliness of Jesus Christ. **vineyards**—appropriate in respect to Him who is "the vine." The spikenard was for the banquet (vs. 12); the myrrh was in her bosom continually (vs. 13); the camphire is in the midst of natural beauties, which, though lovely, are eclipsed by the one cluster, Jesus Christ, preëminent above them all. **En-gedi**—in South Palestine, near the Dead Sea (Josh. 15:62; Ezek. 47:10), famed for aromatic shrubs. **15. fair**—He discerns beauty in her, who had said, "I am black" (vs. 5), because of the everlasting covenant (Ps. 45:11; Isa. 62:5; Eph. 1:4, 5). **doves' eyes**—large and beautiful in the doves of Syria. The prominent features of her beauty (Matt. 10:16), gentleness, innocence, and constant love, emblem of the Holy Ghost, who changes us to *His own* likeness (Gen. 8:10, 11; Matt. 3:16). The opposite kind of eyes (Ps. 101:5; Matt. 20:15; II Pet. 2:14). **16.** *Reply of the Bride.* She presumes to call Him beloved, because He called her so first. Thou callest me "fair"; if I am so, it is not in myself; it is all from Thee (Ps. 90:17); but *Thou* art fair in Thyself (Ps. 45:2). **pleasant**—(Prov. 3:17) towards Thy friends (II Sam. 1:26). **bed . . . green**—the couch of green grass on which the King and His bride sit to "rest at noon." Thus her prayer in vs. 7 is here granted; a green oasis in the desert, always found near waters in the East (Ps. 23:2; Isa. 41:17-19). The scene is a kiosk, or summerhouse. *Historically,* the literal resting of the Babe of Bethlehem and His parents on the *green* grass provided for cattle (Luke 2). In this verse there is an incidental allusion, in vs. 15, to the offering (Luke 2:24). So the "cedar and fir" ceiling refers to the temple (I Kings 5:6-10; 6:15-18); type of the heavenly temple (Rev. 21:22). **17. our house** —see *Note,* vs. 16; but *primarily,* the kiosk (Isa. 11: 10), "His rest." Cedar is pleasing to the eye and smell, hard, and never eaten by worms. **fix**—rather, cypress, which is hard, durable, and fragrant, of a reddish hue [GENSIUS, WEISS, and MAURER]. Contrasted with the shifting "tents" (vs. 5), *His* house is "*our* house" (Ps. 92:13; Eph. 2:19; Heb. 3:6). Perfect oneness of Him and the bride (John 14:20; 17:21). There is the shelter of a princely roof from the sun (Ps. 121:6), without the confinement of walls, and amidst rural beauties. The carved ceiling represents the wondrous excellencies of His divine nature.

CHAPTER 2

Vss. 1-17. **1. rose**—if applied to Jesus Christ, it, with the white lily (lowly, II Cor. 8:9), answers to "white and ruddy" (ch. 5:10). But it is rather the *meadow-saffron:* the *Hebrew* means radically a plant with a *pungent bulb*, inapplicable to the *rose*. So *Syriac*. It is of a white and violet color [MAURER, GESENIUS, and WEISS]. The bride thus speaks of herself as lowly though lovely, in contrast with the lordly "apple" or citron tree, the bridegroom (vs. 3); so the "lily" is applied to her (vs. 2). **Sharon**—(Isa. 35:1, 2.) In North Palestine, between Mount Tabor and Lake Tiberias (I Chron. 5:16). LXX and *Vulgate* translate it, "a plain"; though they err in this, the *Hebrew* Bible not elsewhere favoring it, yet the parallelism to *valleys* shows that, in the proper name Sharon, there is here a tacit reference to its meaning of lowliness. Beauty, delicacy, and lowliness, are to be in her, as they were in Him (Matt. 11:29). **2.** *Jesus Christ to the Bride* (Matt. 10:16; John 15:19; I John 5:19). Thorns, equivalent to the wicked (II Sam. 23:6; Ps. 57:4). **daughters**—of men, not of God; not "the virgins." "If thou art the lily of Jesus Christ, take heed lest by impatience, rash judgments, and pride, thou thyself become a thorn" [LUTHER]. **3.** *Her reply.* **apple**—generic including the golden citron, pomegranate, and orange apple (Prov. 25:11). He combines the *shadow* and fragrance of the citron with the *sweetness* of the orange and pomegranate fruit. The foliage is perpetual; throughout the year a succession of blossoms, fruit, and perfume (Jas. 1:17). **among the sons**—parallel to "among the daughters" (vs. 2). He alone is ever fruitful among the fruitless wild trees (Ps. 89:6; Heb. 1:9). **I sat . . . with . . . delight**—lit., "I eagerly desired and sat" (Ps. 94:19; Mark 6:31; Eph. 2:6; I Pet. 1:8). **shadow**—(Ps. 121:5; Isa. 4:6; 25:4; 32:2). Jesus Christ interposes the shadow of His cross between the blazing rays of justice and us sinners. **fruit**—Faith plucks it (Prov. 3:18). Man lost the tree of life (Gen. 3). Jesus Christ regained it for him; he eats it partly now (Ps. 119:103; John 6:55, 57; I Pet. 2:3); fully hereafter (Rev. 2:7; 22:2, 14); not earned by the sweat of his brow, or by his righteousness (Rom. 10). Contrast the worldling's fruit (Deut. 32:32; Luke 15:16). **4.** Historically fulfilled in the joy of Simeon and Anna in the temple, over the infant Saviour (Luke 2), and that of Mary, too (cf. Luke 1:53); typified (Exod. 24:9-11). Spiritually, the bride or beloved is led (vs. 4) first *into the King's chambers,* thence is *drawn* after Him in answer to her prayer; is next received on a grassy couch under a cedar kiosk; and at last in a "banqueting hall," such as, Josephus says, Solomon had in his palace, "wherein all the vessels were of gold" (*Antiquities,* 8:5, 2). The transition is from holy retirement to *public* ordinances, church-worship, and the Lord's Supper (Ps. 36:8). The bride, as the queen of Sheba, is given "all her desire" (I Kings 10:13; Ps. 63:5; Eph. 3:8, 16-21; Phil. 4:19); type of the heavenly feast hereafter (Isa. 25:6, 9). **his banner . . . love**—After having rescued us from the enemy, our victorious captain (Heb. 2:10) seats us at the banquet under a banner inscribed with *His name,* "love" (I John 4:8). His love conquered us to Himself; this banner rallies round us the forces of Om-

nipotence, as our protection; it marks to what country we belong, heaven, the abode of love, and in what we most glory, the cross of Jesus Christ, through which we triumph (Rom. 8:37; I Cor. 15:57; Rev. 3:21). Cf. with *"over* me," *"underneath* are the everlasting arms" (Deut. 33:27). **5. flagons**—MAURER prefers translating, "dried raisin cakes"; from the *Hebrew* root "fire," viz., dried by heat. But the "house of *wine*" (*Margin,* vs. 4) favors "flagons"; the "new wine" of the kingdom, the Spirit of Jesus Christ. **apples**—from the tree (vs. 3), so sweet to her, the promises of God. **sick of love**—the highest degree of sensible enjoyment that can be attained here. It may be at an early or late stage of experience. Paul (II Cor. 12:7). In the last sickness of J. Welch, he was overheard saying, "Lord, hold thine hand, it is enough; thy servant is a clay vessel, and can hold no more" [FLEMING, *Fulf. Script.*]. In most cases this intensity of joy is reserved for the heavenly banquet. Historically, Israel had it, when the Lord's glory filled the tabernacle, and afterwards the temple, so that the priests could not stand to minister: so in the Christian Church, on Pentecost. The bride addresses *Christ* mainly, though in her rapture she uses the *plural,* "Stay *(ve)* me," speaking generally. So far from asking the withdrawal of the manifestations which had overpowered her, she asks for more: so *""fainteth for"* (Ps. 84:2); also Peter, on the mount of transfiguration (Luke 9:33), "Let us make . . . , *not knowing what he said.*" **6.** The "stay" she prayed for (vs. 5) is granted (Deut. 33:12, 27; Ps. 37:24; Isa. 41:16). None can pluck from that *embrace* (John 10:28-30). His hand keeps us from falling (Matt. 14:30, 31); to it we may commit ourselves (Ps. 31:5). **left hand**—is the inferior hand, by which the Lord less signally manifests His love, than by the right; the secret hand of ordinary providence, as distinguished from that of manifested grace (the "right"). They really go together, though sometimes they seem divided; here both are felt at once. THEODORET takes the left hand, equivalent to *judgment and wrath;* the right, equivalent to *honor and love.* The hand of justice no longer is lifted to smite, but is under the head of the believer to support (Isa. 42:21); the hand of Jesus Christ pierced by justice for our sin supports us. The charge not to disturb the beloved occurs thrice; but the sentiment here, "His left hand . . .," nowhere else fully; which accords with the intensity of joy (vs. 5) found nowhere else; in ch. 8:3, it is only conditional, *"should* embrace," not "doth." **7. by the roes**—not an oath but a solemn charge, to act as cautiously as the hunter would with the wild roes, which are proverbially timorous; he must advance with breathless circumspection, if he is to take them; so he who would not lose Jesus Christ and His Spirit, which is easily grieved and withdrawn, must be tender of conscience and watchful (Ezek. 16:43; Eph. 4:30; 5:15; I Thess. 5:19). In *Margin,* title of Psalm 22, Jesus Christ is called the *"Hind* of the morning," hunted to death by the dogs (cf. vss. 8, 9, where He is represented as bounding on the hills, Ps. 18:33). Here He is *resting,* but with a repose easily broken (Zeph. 3:17). It is thought a gross rudeness in the East to awaken one sleeping, especially a person of rank. **my love**—in *Hebrew, Feminine* for *Masculine,* the abstract for concrete, Jesus Christ being the embodiment of *love* itself (ch. 3:5; 8:7), where, as here, the context requires it to be applied to Him, not her. She too is "love" (ch. 7:6), for His love calls forth her love. Presumption in the convert is as grieving to the Spirit as despair. The *lovingness* and *pleasantness* of the hind and roe (Prov. 5:19) is included in this image of Jesus Christ.

CANTICLE II.—Ch. 2:8-3:5.—JOHN THE BAPTIST'S MINISTRY. **8. voice**—an exclamation of joyful surprise, evidently after a long silence. The restlessness of sin and fickleness in her had disturbed His rest with her, which she had professed not to wish disturbed "till He should please." He left her, but in sovereign grace unexpectedly heralds His return. She awakes, and at once recognizes His voice (I Sam. 3:9, 10; John 10:4); her sleep is not so sinfully deep as in ch. 5:2. **leaping**—bounding, as the roe does, over the roughest obstacles (II Sam. 2:18; I Chron. 12:8); as the father of the prodigal "had compassion and *ran*" (Luke 15:20). **upon the hills**—as the sunbeams glancing from hill to hill. So *Margin,* title of Jesus Christ (Ps. 22), "Hind of the *morning*" (type of His resurrection). Historically, the coming of the kingdom of heaven (the gospel dispensation), announced by John Baptist, is meant; *it* primarily is the garden or vineyard; the bride is called so in a secondary sense. "The voice" of Jesus Christ is indirect, through "the friend of the bridegroom" (John 3:29), John the Baptist. Personally, He is silent during John's ministration, who awoke the long slumbering Church with the cry, "Every *hill* shall be made low," in the spirit of Elias, on the "rent mountains" (I Kings 19:11; cf. Isa. 52:7). Jesus Christ is implied as coming with intense desire (Luke 22:15; Heb. 10:7). disregarding the mountain hindrances raised by man's sin. **9. he standeth**—after having bounded over the intervening space like a roe. He often stands near when our unbelief hides Him from us (Gen. 28:16; Rev. 3:14-20). His usual way; long promised and expected; sudden at last; so, in visiting the second temple (Mal. 3:1); so at Pentecost (Acts 2:1, 2); so in visiting an individual soul, Zaccheus (Luke 19:5, 6; John 3:8); and so, at the second coming (Matt. 24:48, 50; II Pet. 3:4, 10). So it shall be at His second coming (I Thess. 5:2, 3). **wall**—over the cope of which He is first seen; next, He looks *through* (not *forth;* for He is outside) at the windows, *glancing* suddenly and stealthily (not as *English Version,* "showing Himself") through the lattice. The prophecies, types, etc., are lattice glimpses of Him to the Old Testament Church, in spite of the *wall* of separation which sin had raised (John 8:56); clearer glimpses were given by John Baptist, but not unclouded (John 1: 26). The legal wall of partition was not to be removed until His death (Eph. 2:14, 15; Heb. 10:20). Even now, He is only seen by *faith,* through the windows of His Word and the lattice of ordinances and sacraments (Luke 24:35; John 14:21); not full vision (I Cor. 13:12); an incentive to our looking for His second coming (Isa. 33:17; Titus 2:13). **10, 11.** Loving reassurance given by Jesus Christ to the bride, lest she should think that He had ceased to love her, on account of her unfaithfulness, which had occasioned His temporary withdrawal. He allures her to brighter than worldly joys (Micah 2:10). Not only does the saint wish to depart to be with Him, but He still more desires to have the saint with Him above (John 17:24). Historically, the vineyard or garden of the King, here first introduced, is "the kingdom of heaven preached" by John the Baptist, before whom "the law and the prophets were" (Luke 16:16). **11. the winter**—the law of the covenant of works (Matt. 4:16). **rain is over**—(Heb. 12:18-24; I John 2:8). Then first the Gentile Church is called "beloved, which was not beloved" (Rom. 9:25). So "the winter" of estrangement and sin is "past" to the believer (Isa. 44:22; Jer. 50:20; II Cor. 5:17; Eph.

2:1). The rising "Sun of righteousness" dispels the "rain" (II Sam. 23:4; Ps. 126:5, Mal. 4:2). The winter in Palestine is past by April, but all the showers were not over till May. The time described here is that which comes directly after these last showers of winter. In the highest sense, the coming resurrection and deliverance of the earth from the *past* curse is here implied (Rom. 8:19; Rev. 21:4; 22:3). No more "clouds" shall then "return after the rain" (Eccles. 12:2; Rev. 4:3; cf. Gen. 9:13-17); "the rainbow round the throne" is the "token" of this. **12. flowers**—tokens of anger past, and of grace come. "The summoned bride is welcome," say some fathers, "to weave from them garlands of beauty, wherewith she may adorn herself to meet the King." Historically, the flowers, etc., only give promise; the fruit is not ripe yet; suitable to the preaching of John the Baptist, "The kingdom of heaven is *at hand";* not yet fully come. **the time of . . . singing**—the rejoicing at the advent of Jesus Christ. GREGORY NYSSENUS refers the *voice* of the turtledove to John the Baptist. It with the olive branch announced to Noah that "the rain was over and gone" (Gen. 8:11). So John the Baptist, spiritually. Its *plaintive* "voice" answers to his preaching of *repentance* (Jer. 8:6, 7). *Vulgate* and LXX translate, "The time of *pruning,"* viz., spring (John 15:2). The mention of the "turtle's" cooing better accords with our text. The turtledove is migratory (Jer. 8: 7), and "comes" early in May; emblem of love, and so of the Holy Ghost. Love, too, shall be the keynote of the "new *song*" hereafter (Isa 35:10; Rev. 1:5; 14:3; 19:6). In the individual believer now, joy and love are here set forth in their *earlier* manifestations (Mark 4:28). **13. putteth forth**—rather, ripens, lit., "makes red" [MAURER]. The unripe figs, which grow in winter, begin to ripen in early spring, and in June are fully matured [WEISS]. **vines with the tender grape**—rather, "the vines in *flower,"* lit., "a flower," in apposition with "vines" [MAURER]. The vine flowers were so sweet that they were often put, when dried, into new wine to give it flavor. Applicable to the first manifestations of Jesus Christ, "the true Vine," both to the Church and to individuals; as to Nathanael under *the fig tree* (John 1:48). **Arise . . .**—His call, described by the bride, ends as it began (vs. 10); it is a consistent whole; "love" from first to last (Isa. 52:1, 2; II Cor. 6:17, 18). "Come," in the close of Revelation 22:17, as at His earlier manifestation (Matt. 11:28). **14. dove**—here expressing endearment (Ps. 74:19). Doves are noted for *constant attachment;* emblems, also, in their soft, plaintive note, of *softened penitents* (Isa. 59:11; Ezek. 7:16); other points of likeness are their *beauty;* "their wings covered with silver and gold" (Ps. 68: 13), typifying the change in the converted; the *dovelike spirit,* breathed into the saint by the Holy Ghost, whose emblem is the dove; *the messages of peace* from God to sinful men, as Noah's dove, with the olive branch (Gen. 8), intimated that the flood of wrath was past; *timidity,* fleeing with fear from sin and self to the cleft Rock of Ages (*Margin,* Isa. 26:4; Hos. 11:11); *gregarious,* flocking together to the kingdom of Jesus Christ (Isa. 60:8); *harmless simplicity* (Matt. 10:16). **clefts**—the refuge of doves from storm and heat (Jer. 48:28; see Jer. 49:16). GESENIUS translates the *Hebrew* from a different root, "the refuges." But see, for "clefts," Exodus 33:18-23. It is only when we are *in* Christ Jesus that our "voice is *sweet*" (in prayer, ch. 4:3, 11; Matt. 10:20; Gal. 4:6, because it is *His* voice *in* us; also in speaking *of* Him, Mal. 3:16); and our countenance comely" (Exod. 34:29; Ps. 27:5; 71:3; Isa. 33:16;

II Cor. 3:18). **stairs**–(Ezek. 38:29). *Margin,* a steep rock, broken into stairs or terraces. It is in "secret places" and rugged scenes that Jesus Christ woos the soul from the world to Himself (Mic. 2:10; 7:14). So Jacob amid the stones of Bethel (Gen. 28:11-19); Moses at Horeb (Exod. 3); so Elijah (I Kings 19:9-13); Jesus Christ with the three disciples on a "high mountain apart," at the transfiguration (Matt. 17:1); John in Patmos (Rev. 1). "Of the eight beatitudes, five have an afflicted condition for their subject. As long as the waters are on the earth, we dwell in the ark; but when the land is dry, the dove itself will be tempted to wander" [JEREMY TAYLOR]. Jesus Christ does not invite her to leave the rock, but *in* it (Himself), yet in holy freedom to lay aside the timorous spirit, look up boldly as accepted in Him, pray, praise, and confess Him (in contrast to her shrinking from being *looked at,* ch. 1:6), (Eph. 6:19; Heb. 13:15; I John 4:18); still, though trembling, the voice and countenance of the soul in Jesus Christ are pleasant to Him. The Church found no cleft in the Sinaitic legal rock, though good in itself, wherein to hide; but in Jesus Christ stricken by God for us, as the rock smitten by Moses (Num. 20:11), there is a hiding-place (Isa. 32:2). *She* praised His "voice" (vss. 8, 10); it is thus that her voice also, though tremulous, is "sweet" to Him here. **15.** Transition to the vineyard, often formed in "stairs" (vs. 14), or terraces, in which, amidst the vine leaves, foxes hid. **foxes**–generic term, including jackals. They eat only grapes, not the vine flowers; but they need to be driven out *in time* before the grape is ripe. She had failed in watchfulness before (ch. 1:6); now when converted, she is the more jealous of *subtle* sins (Ps. 139:23). In spiritual winter certain evils are frozen up, as well as good; in the spring of revivals these start up unperceived, crafty, false teachers, spiritual pride, uncharitableness, etc. (Ps. 19:12; Matt. 13:26; Luke 8:14; II Tim. 2:17; Heb. 12:15). "Little" sins are parents of the greatest (Eccles. 10:1; I Cor. 5:6). Historically, John the Baptist spared not the *foxlike* Herod (Luke 13:32), who gave vinelike promise of fruit af first (Mark 6:20), at the cost of his life; nor the viper-Sadducees, etc.; nor the varied subtle forms of sin (Luke 3:7-14). **16. mine . . . his**–rather, "is *for me . . . for Him*" (Hos. 3:3), where, as here, there is the assurance of indissoluble union, in spite of temporary absence. Next verse, entreating Him to return, shows that He has gone, perhaps through her want of guarding against the "little sins" (vs. 15). The order of the clauses is reversed in ch. 6:3, when she is riper in faith; there she rests more on *her being His;* here, on *His being hers;* and no doubt her sense of love to Him is a pledge that she is His (John 14:21, 23; I Cor. 8:3); this is her consolation in His withdrawal now. **I am his**–by creation (Ps. 100:3), by redemption (John 17:10; Rom. 14:8; I Cor. 6:19). **feedeth** –as a "roe," or gazelle (vs. 17); instinct is sure to lead him back to his feeding-ground, where the lilies abound. So Jesus Christ, though now withdrawn, the bride feels sure will return to His favorite resting-place (ch. 7:10; Ps. 132:14). So hereafter (Rev. 21:3). Psalm 45, title, terms His lovely bride's "lilies" [HENGSTENBERG] pure and white, though among thorns (vs. 2). **17. Night** is the image of the present world (Rom. 13:12). "Behold men as if dwelling in subterranean cavern" [PLATO *Republic,* vii. 1]. **Until**–i.e., "Before that," etc. **break**–rather, "breathe"; referring to the refreshing breeze of dawn in the East; or to the air of *life,* which distinguishes morning from the deathlike stillness of night. MAURER takes this verse of the *approach of night,*

when the breeze arises after the heat of day (cf. *Margin,* Gen. 3:8, with Gen. 18:1), and the "shadows" are lost in night (Ps. 102:11); thus our life will be the *day;* death, the *night* (John 9:4). The *English Version* better accords with (ch. 3:1). "By *night*" (Rom. 13:12). **turn**–to me. **Bether**–Mountains of Bithron, separated from the rest of Israel by the Jordan (II Sam. 2:29), not far from Bethabara, where John baptized and Jesus was first manifested. Rather, as *Margin,* "of divisions," and LXX, *mountains intersected* with deep gaps, hard to pass over, separating the bride and Jesus Christ. In ch. 8:14 the mountains are *of spices,* on which the roe feeds, not *of separation;* for at His first coming He had to overpass the gulf made by sin between Him and us (Zech. 4:6, 7); in His second, He will only have to come down from the fragrant hill above to take home His prepared bride. Historically, in the ministry of John the Baptist, Christ's call to the bride was not, as later (ch. 4:8), "Come *with* me," but "Come *away,*" viz., to meet Me (vss. 2, 10, 13). Sitting in darkness (Matt. 4:16), she "waited" and "looked" eagerly for Him, the "great light" (Luke 1:79; 2:25, 38); at His rising, the shadows of the law (Col. 2:16, 17; Heb. 10:1) were to "flee away." So we wait for the second coming, when means of grace, so precious now, shall be superseded by the Sun of righteousness (I Cor. 13:10, 12; Rev. 21:22, 23). The Word is our light until then (II Pet. 1:19).

CHAPTER 3

Vss. 1-11. **1. By night**–lit., "By nights." Continuation of the longing for the dawn of the Messiah (ch. 2:17; Ps. 130:6; Mal. 4:2). The spiritual desertion here (ch. 2:17; 3:5) is not due to indifference, as in ch. 5:2-8. "As nights and dews are better for flowers than a continual sun, so Christ's absence (at times) giveth sap to humility, and putteth an edge on hunger, and furnisheth a fair field to faith to put forth itself" [RUTHERFORD]. Contrast ch. 1:13; Psalm 30:6, 7. **on . . . bed**–the secret of her failure (Isa. 64:7; Jer. 29:13; Amos 6:1, 4; Hos. 7:14). **loveth**–no want of sincerity, but of diligence, which she now makes up for by leaving her bed to seek Him (Ps. 22:2; 63:8; Isa. 26:9; John 20:17). Four times (vss. 1-4) she calls Jesus Christ, "Him whom my soul loveth," designating Him as *absent;* language of desire: "He loved me," would be language of *present* fruition (Rev. 1:5). In questioning the watchmen (vs. 3), she does not even name Him, so full is her heart of Him. Having found Him at dawn (for throughout *He* is the *morning*), she charges the daughters not to abridge by intrusion the period of His stay. Cf. as to the thoughtful seeking for Jesus Christ in the time of John the Baptist, in vain at first, but presently after successful (Luke 3:15-22; John 1:19-34). **found him not**–Oh, for such honest dealings with ourselves (Prov. 25:14; Jude 12)! **2. Wholly awake for God** (Luke 14:18-20; Eph. 5:14). "An honest resolution is often to (the doing of) duty, like a needle that draws the thread after it" [DURHAM]. Not a mere wish, that counts not the cost–to leave her easy bed, and wander in the dark night seeking Him (Prov. 13:4; Matt. 21:30; Luke 14:27-33). **the city**–Jerusalem, literally (Matt. 3:5; John 1:19), and spiritually the *Church* here (Heb. 12:22), in glory (Rev. 21:2). **broad ways**–open spaces at the gates of Eastern cities, where the public assembled for business. So, the assemblies of worshippers (ch. 8:2, 3; Prov. 1:20-23; Heb. 10:25). She had in her first awakening shrunk from them, seeking Jesus Christ alone; but she was desired to seek the footsteps of the flock (ch. 1:8), so now in her second trial she goes forth to them of herself. "The more the soul grows in grace, and the less it leans on ordinances, the more it prizes and profits by them" [MOODY STUART] (Ps. 73:16, 17). **found him not**—Nothing short of Jesus Christ can satisfy her (Job 23:8-10; Ps. 63:1, 2). **3. watchmen**—ministers (Isa. 62:6; Jer. 6:17; Ezek. 3:17; Heb. 13:17), fit persons to consult (Isa. 21:11; Mal. 2:7). **found me**—the general ministry of the Word "finds" individually souls in quest of Jesus Christ (Gen. 24:27, end of verse; Acts 16:14); whereas formalists remain unaffected. **4.** Jesus Christ is generally "found" near the watchmen and means of grace; but they are not Himself; the star that points to Bethlehem is not the Sun that has risen there; she hastens past the guideposts to the goal [MOODY STUART]. Not even angels could satisfy Mary, instead of Jesus Christ (John 20:11-16). **found him**—(Isa. 45:19; Hos. 6:1-3; Matt. 13:44-46). **held him . . .**—willing to be held; not willing, if not held (Gen. 32:26; Matt. 28:9; Luke 24:28, 29; Rev. 3:11). "As a little weeping child will hold its mother fast, not because it is stronger than she, but because her bowels constrain her not to leave it; so Jesus Christ yearning over the believer *cannot go*, because He *will* not" [DURHAM]. In ch. 1:4 it is He who leads the bride into His chambers; here it is she who leads Him into her mother's. There are times when the grace of Jesus Christ seems to draw us to Him; and others, when we with strong cries draw Him to us and ours. In the East one large apartment often serves for the whole family; so the bride here speaks of her mother's apartment and her own together. The mention of the "mother" excludes impropriety, and imparts the idea of heavenly love, pure as a sister's, while ardent as a bride's; hence the frequent title, "my sister-spouse." Our mother after the Spirit, is *the Church*, the new Jerusalem (John 3:5-8; Gal. 4:19, 26); for her we ought to pray continually (Eph. 3:14-19), also for the *national* Jerusalem (Isa. 62:6, 7; Rom. 10:1), also for the *human family*, which is our mother and kindred after the flesh; these our mother's children have evilly treated us (ch. 1:6); but, like our Father, we are to return good for evil (Matt. 5:44, 45), and so bring Jesus Christ home to them (I Pet. 2:12). **5.** So ch. 2:7; but *there* it was for the non-interruption of her own fellowship with Jesus Christ that she was anxious; *here* it is for the not grieving of the Holy Ghost, on the part of the daughters of Jerusalem. Jealously avoid levity, heedlessness, and offenses which would mar the gracious work begun in others (Matt. 18:7; Acts 2:42, 43; Eph. 4:30).

CANTICLE *III.*—Ch. 3:6-5:1.—THE BRIDEGROOM WITH THE BRIDE. Historically, the ministry of Jesus Christ on earth. **6.** New scene (vss. 6-11). The friends of the Bridegroom see a cortege approach. His palanquin and guard. **cometh out**—rather, "up from"; the wilderness was lower than Jerusalem [MAURER]. **pillars of smoke**—from the perfumes burned around Him and His bride. Image from Israel and the tabernacle (answering to "bed," vs. 7) marching through the desert with the pillar of smoke by day and fire by night (Exod. 14:20), and the pillars of smoke ascending from the altars of incense and of atonement; so Jesus Christ's righteousness, atonement, and ever-living intercession. Balaam, the last representative of patriarchism, was required to curse the Jewish Church, just as *it* afterwards would not succumb to Christianity without a struggle (Num. 22:41), but he had to bless in language

like that here (Num. 24:5, 6). Angels too joyfully ask the same question, when Jesus Christ with the tabernacle of His body (answering to *His bed,* vs. 7; John 1:14, "dwelt," *Greek* "tabernacled," John 2:21) ascends into heaven (Ps. 24:8-10); also when they see His glorious bride with Him (Ps. 68:18; Rev. 7:13-17). Encouragement to her; amid the darkest trials (vs. 1), she is still on the road to glory (vs. 11) in a palanquin "paved with love" (vs. 10); she is now in soul spiritually "coming," exhaling the sweet graces, faith, love, joy, peace, prayer, and praise; (the fire is lighted *within,* the "smoke" is seen *without,* Acts 4:13); it is in the *desert* of trial (vss. 1-3) she gets them; she is the "merchant" buying from Jesus Christ without money or price (Isa. 55:1; Rev. 3:18); just as myrrh and frankincense are got, not in Egypt, but in the Arabian sands and the mountains of Palestine. Hereafter she shall "come" (vss. 6, 11) in a glorified body, too (Phil. 3:21). Historically, Jesus Christ returning from the wilderness, full of the Holy Ghost (Luke 4:1, 14). The same, "Who is this," etc. (Isa. 63:1, 5). **7.** In vs. 6 the *wilderness* character of the Church is portrayed; in vss. 7, 8, its *militant* aspect. In vs. 9, 10, Jesus Christ is seen dwelling in believers, who are His "chariot" and "body." In vs. 11, the consummation in glory. **bed**—palanquin. His body, lit., guarded by a definite number of angels, *threescore,* or sixty (Matt. 26:53), from the wilderness (Matthew 4:1, 11), and continually (Luke 2:13; 22:43; Acts 1:10, 11); just as 600,000 of Israel guarded the Lord's tabernacle (Num. 2:17-32), one for every 10,000. In contrast to the "bed of sloth" (vs. 1). **valiant**—(Josh. 5:13, 14.) Angels guarding His *tomb* used like words (Mark 16:6). **of Israel**—true subjects, not mercenaries. **8. hold**—not actually grasping them, but having them girt on the thigh ready for use, like their Lord (Ps. 45:3). So believers too are guarded by angels (Ps. 91:11; Heb. 1:14), and they themselves need "every man" (Neh. 4:18) to be armed (Ps. 144:1, 2; II Cor. 10:4; Eph. 6:12, 17; I Tim. 6:12), and "expert" (II Cor. 2:11). **because of fear in the night**—Arab marauders often turn a wedding into mourning by a night attack. So the bridal procession of saints in the night of this wilderness is the chief object of Satan's assault. **9. chariot**—more elaborately made than the "bed" or travelling litter (vs. 7), from a *Hebrew* root, "to elaborate" [EWALD]. So the temple of "cedar of Lebanon," as compared with the temporary tabernacle of shittim wood (II Sam. 7:2, 6, 7; I Kings 5:14; 6:15-18), Jesus Christ's body is the antitype, "made" by the Father for Him (I Cor. 1:30; Heb. 10:5), the wood answering to His human nature, the gold, His divine; the two being but one Christ. **10. pillars**—supporting the canopy at the four corners; curtains at the side protect the person within from the sun. Pillars with silver sockets supported the veil that enclosed the holy of holies; emblem of Jesus Christ's *strength* (I Kings 7:21), *Margin,* "silver," emblem of His *purity* (Ps. 12:6); so the saints hereafter (Rev. 3:12). **bottom**—rather, *the back for resting or reclining on* (*Vulgate* and LXX) [MAURER]. So the floor and mercy seat, the *resting*-place of God (Ps. 132:14) in the temple, was gold (I Kings 6:30). **covering**—rather, *seat* as in Leviticus 15:9. Hereafter the saints shall share His *seat* (Rev. 3:21). **purple**—the veil of the holiest, partly purple, and the *purple* robe put on Jesus Christ, accord with *English Version,* "*covering.*" "Purple" (including scarlet and crimson) is the emblem of *royalty,* and of *His blood;* typified by the passover lamb's blood, and the wine when the twelve *sat* or *reclined* at the Lord's table.　**paved**—tesselated, like mosaic pavement, with the various acts and promises of love of Father, Son, and Holy Ghost (Zeph. 3: 17; I John 4:8, 16), in contrast with the tables of stone in the "midst" of the ark, covered with writings of stern command (cf. John 19:13); *this* is all grace and love to believers, who answer to "the daughters of Jerusalem" (John 1:17).　The exterior silver and gold, cedar, purple, and guards, may deter, but when the bride enters *within*, she rests on a pavement of love.　**11. Go forth**—(Matt. 25:6). **daughters of Zion**—spirits of saints, and angels (Isa. 61:10; Zech. 9:9).　**crown**—nuptial (Ezek. 16:8-12), (the Hebrews wore costly crowns or chaplets at weddings) (Ps. 2:6; Rev. 19:12).　The crown of thorns was once His nuptial chaplet, His blood the wedding wine-cup (John 19:5).　"His mother," that so crowned Him, is the *human race*, for He is "the Son of *man*," not merely the son of Mary.　The same mother reconciled to Him (Matt. 12:50), as the Church, travails in birth for souls, which she presents to Him as a crown (Phil. 4:1; Rev. 4:10). Not being ashamed to call the children brethren (Heb. 2:11-14), He calls *their* mother *His* mother (Ps. 22:9; Rom. 8:29; Rev. 12:1, 2).　**behold**—(II Thess. 1:10.)　**day of his espousals**—chiefly final marriage, when the number of the elect is complete (Rev. 6:11).　**gladness**—(Ps. 45:15; Isa. 62:5; Rev. 19:7).　MOODY STUART observes as to this Canticle (ch. 3:6-5:1), the center of the Book, these characteristics: (1) The bridegroom takes the chief part, whereas elsewhere the bride is the chief speaker. (2) Elsewhere He is either "King" or "Solomon"; here He is twice called "King Solomon."　The bride is six times here called the "spouse"; never so before or after; also "sister" four times, and, except in the first verse of the next Canticle, nowhere else. (3) He and she are never separate; no absence, no complaint, which abound elsewhere, are in this Canticle.

CHAPTER 4

Vss. 1-16.　1. Contrast with the bride's state by nature (Isa. 1:6) *her state by grace* (vss. 1-7), "perfect through His comeliness put upon her" (Ezek. 16: 14; John 15:3).　The praise of Jesus Christ, unlike that of the world, hurts not, but edifies; as His, not ours, is the glory (John 5:44; Rev. 4:10, 11).　Seven features of beauty are specified (vss. 1-5) ("lips" and "speech" are but one feature, vs. 3), the number for *perfection*.　To each of these is attached a comparison from nature: the resemblances consist not so much in outward likeness, as in the combined sensations of delight produced by contemplating these natural objects.　**doves**—the large melting eye of the Syrian dove appears especially beautiful amid the foliage of its native groves: so the bride's "eyes within her locks" (Luke 7:44).　MAURER for "locks," has "veil"; but locks suit the connection better: so the *Hebrew* is translated (Isa. 47:2).　The dove was the only bird counted "clean" for sacrifice.　Once the heart was "the cage of every unclean and hateful bird."　Grace makes the change.　**eyes**—(Matt. 6: 22; Eph. 1:18; contrast Matt. 5:28; Eph. 4:18; I John 2:16.)　Chaste and guileless (Matt. 10:16, *Margin*; John 1:47).　John the Baptist, historically, was the "turtledove" (ch. 2:12), with eye directed to the coming Bridegroom: his Nazarite unshorn hair answers to "locks" (John 1:29, 36).　**hair . . . goats** —The hair of goats in the East is fine like silk.　As long hair is her glory, and marks her subjection to

man (I Cor. 11:6-15), so the Nazarite's hair marked his subjection and separation unto God.　(Cf. 16:17, with II Cor. 6:17; Titus 2:14; I Pet. 2:9.)　Jesus Christ cares for the minutest concerns of His saints (Matt. 10:30).　**appear from**—lit., *"that lie down from"*; lying along the hillside, they seem to *hang from* it: a picture of the bride's hanging tresses. **Gilead**—beyond Jordan: there stood "the heap of witness" (Gen. 31:48).　**2. even shorn**—is translated (I Kings 6:25), "of one size"; so the point of comparison to *teeth* is their *symmetry* of form; as in "came up from the washing," the *spotless whiteness;* and in "twins," the *exact correspondence of the upper and lower teeth:* and in "none barren," *none wanting,* none without its fellow.　Faith is the tooth with which we eat the living bread (John 6:35, 54).　Contrast the teeth of sinners (Ps. 57:4; Prov. 30:14); also their end (Ps. 3:7; Matt. 25:30).　Faith leads the flock to the washing (Zech. 13:1; I Cor. 6:11; Titus 3:5).　**none . . . barren**—(II Pet. 1:8.) He who is begotten of God begets instrumentally other sons of God.　**3. thread**—like a delicate fillet. Not thick and white as the leper's lips (type of sin), which were therefore to be "covered," as "unclean" (Lev. 13:45).　**scarlet**—The blood of Jesus Christ (Isa. 6:5-9) cleanses the leprosy, and unseals the lips (Isa. 57:19; Hos. 14:2; Heb. 13:15).　Rahab's scarlet thread was a type of it (Josh. 2:18).　**speech**—not a separate feature from the *lips* (Zeph. 3:9; Col. 4:6). Contrast "uncircumcised lips" (Exod. 6:12).　MAURER and BURROWES translate, "thy mouth."　**temples**—rather, *the upper part of the cheek* next the temples: the seat of shamefacedness; so, "within thy locks," no display (I Cor. 11:5, 6, 15).　Mark of true penitence (Ezra 9:6; Ezek. 16:63).　Contrast Jer. 3:3; Ezek. 3:7.　**pomegranate**—When cut, it displays in rows seeds pellucid, like crystal, tinged with red.　Her modesty is not on the surface, but within, which Jesus Christ can see into.　**4. neck**— stately: in beautiful contrast to the blushing temples (vs. 3); not "stiff" (Isa. 48:4; Acts 7:51), as that of unbroken nature; nor "stretched forth" wantonly (Isa. 3:16); nor burdened with the legal yoke (Lam. 1:14; Acts 15:10); but erect in gospel freedom (Isa. 52:2).　**tower of David**—probably on Zion.　He was a man of war, preparatory to the reign of Solomon, the king of peace.　So warfare in the case of Jesus Christ and His saints precedes the coming rest. Each soul won from Satan by Him is a trophy gracing the bride (Luke 11:22); (each hangs on Him, Isa. 22:23, 24); also each victory of her faith.　As shields adorn a temple's walls (Ezek. 27:11), so necklaces hang on the bride's neck (Judg. 5:30; I Kings 10:16).　**5. breasts**—The bust is left open in Eastern dress.　The breastplate of the high priest was made of "two" pieces, folded one on the other, in which were the Urim and Thummim (*lights* and *perfection*).　"Faith and love" are the double breastplate (I Thess. 5:8), answering to "hearing the word" and "keeping it," in a similar connection with breasts (Luke 12:27, 28).　**roes**—He reciprocates her praise (ch. 2:9).　Emblem of *love* and *satisfaction* (Prov. 5:19).　**feed**—(Ps. 23:2.)　**among the lilies**—shrinking from thorns of strife, worldliness, and ungodliness (II Sam. 23:6; Matt. 13:7).　Roes feed *among*, not *on* the lilies: where these grow, there is moisture producing green pasturage.　The lilies represent her white dress (Ps. 45:14; Rev. 19:8). **6.** Historically, *the hill of frankincense* is Calvary, where, "through the eternal Spirit He offered Himself"; the mountain of myrrh is His embalmment (John 19:39) till the resurrection "day-break."　The 3d Canticle occupies the one cloudless day of His presence on earth, beginning from the night (ch. 2: 17) and ending with the night of His departure (ch. 4:6). His promise is almost exactly in the words of her prayer (ch. 2:17), (the same Holy Ghost breathing in Jesus Christ and His praying people), with the difference that she then looked for His visible coming. He now tells her that when He shall have gone from sight, He still is to be met with spiritually in prayer (Ps. 68:16; Matt. 28:20), until the everlasting day break, when we shall see face to face (I Cor. 13:10, 12). **7.** Assurance that He is going from her in love, not in displeasure (John 16:6, 7). **all fair**—still stronger than ch. 1:15; vs. 1. **no spot**—our privilege (Eph. 5:27; Col. 2:10); our duty (II Cor. 6:17; Jude 23; Jas. 1:27). **8.** Invitation to her to leave the border mountains (the highest worldly elevation) between the hostile lands north of Palestine and the Promised Land (Ps. 45:10; Phil. 3:13). **Amana**—south of Anti-Libanus; the river Abana, or Amana, was near Damascus (II Kings 5:12). **Shenir**—The whole mountain was called *Hermon;* the part held by the Sidonians was called *Sirion;* the part held by the Amorites, *Shenir* (Deut. 3:9). Infested by the devouring lion and the stealthy and swift leopard (Ps. 76:4; Eph. 6:11; I Pet. 5:8). Contrasted with the mountain of myrrh, etc. (vs. 6; Isa. 2:2); the good land (Isa. 35:9). **with me**—twice repeated emphatically. The presence of Jesus Christ makes up for the absence of all besides (Luke 18:29, 30; II Cor. 6:10). Moses was permitted to see Canaan from Pisgah; Peter, James, and John had a foretaste of glory on the mount of transfiguration. **9. sister . . . spouse**—This title is here first used, as He is soon about to institute the Supper, the pledge of the nuptial union. By the term "sister," carnal ideas are excluded; the ardor of a spouse's love is combined with the purity of a sister's (Isa. 54:5; cf. Mark 3:35). **one**—Even *one* look is enough to secure His love (Zech. 12: 10; Luke 23:40-43). Not merely the Church collectively, but each *one* member of it (Matt. 18:10, 14; Luke 15:7, 24, 32). **chain**—necklace (Isa. 62:3; Mal. 3:17), answering to the "shields" hanging in the tower of David (vs. 4). Cf. the "ornament" (I Pet. 3:4); "chains" (Prov. 1:9; 3:22). **10. love**—*Hebrew*, "loves"; manifold tokens of thy love. **much better**—answering to her "better" (ch. 1:2), but with *increased* force. An Amœbean pastoral character pervades the Song, like the classic Amœbean idylls and eclogues. **wine**—The love of His saints is a more reviving cordial to Him than wine; e.g., at the feast in Simon's house (Luke 7:36, 47; John 4:32; cf. Zech. 10:7). **smell of . . . ointments than all spices**—answering to her praise (ch. 1:3) with increased force. Fragrant, as being fruits of *His* Spirit in us (Gal. 5:22). **11. drop**—always ready to fall, being full of honey, though not always (Prov. 10:19) actually *dropping* (ch. 5:13; Deut. 32: 2; Matt. 12:34). **honeycomb**—(Prov. 5:3; 16:24). **under thy tongue**—not always *on*, but *under*, the tongue, ready to fall (Ps. 55:21). Contrast her former state (Ps. 140:3; Rom. 3:13). "Honey and milk" were the glory of the good land. The change is illustrated in the penitent thief. Contrast Matthew 27:44 with Luke 23:39, etc. It was literally with "one" eye, a sidelong glance of love "better than wine," that he refreshed Jesus Christ (vss. 9, 10). "To-day shalt thou be *with Me* (cf. vs. 8) in Paradise" (vs. 12), is the only joyous sentence of His seven utterances on the cross. **smell of . . . garments**—which are often perfumed in the East (Ps. 45:8). The perfume comes from Him on us (Ps. 133:2). We draw nigh to God in the perfumed garment of our elder brother (Gen. 27:27; see Jude 23).

Lebanon—abounding in odoriferous trees (Hos. 14: 5-7). **12.** The *Hebrew* has no "is." Here she is distinct from the garden (ch. 5:1), yet identified with it (vs. 16) as being one with Him in His sufferings. Historically the Paradise, into which the soul of Jesus Christ entered at death; and the tomb of Joseph, in which His body was laid amid "myrrh," etc. (vs. 6), situated in *a nicely kept* garden (cf. "gardener," John 20:15); "sealed" with a stone (Matt. 27:66); in which it resembles "wells" in the East (Gen. 29:3, 8). It was in a garden of light Adam fell; in a garden of darkness, Gethsemane, and chiefly that of the tomb, the second Adam retrieved us. Spiritually the garden is the gospel kingdom of heaven. Here all is ripe; previously (ch. 2:13) it was "the *tender* grape." The garden is His, though He calls the plants hers (vs. 13) by His gift (Isa. 61:3, end). **spring . . . fountain**—Jesus Christ (John 4:10) sealed, while He was in the sealed tomb: it poured forth its full tide on Pentecost (John 7:37-39). Still He is a sealed fountain until the Holy Ghost opens it to one (I Cor. 12:3). The Church also is "a garden enclosed" (Ps. 4:3; Isa. 5: 1, etc.). Contrast Psalm 80: 9-12. So "a spring" (Isa. 27:3; 58:11); "sealed" (Eph. 4:30; II Tim. 2: 19). As wives in the East are secluded from public gaze, so believers (Ps. 83:3; Col. 3:3). Contrast the open streams which "pass away" (Job. 6:15-18; II Pet. 2:17). **13. orchard**—*Hebrew*, "a paradise," i.e., a pleasure-ground and orchard. Not only flowers, but fruit trees (John 15:8; Phil. 1:11). **camphire**—not camphor (ch. 1:14), *hennah*, or cypress blooms. **14. calamus**—"sweet cane" (Exod. 30:23; Jer. 6:20). **myrrh and aloes**—Ointments are associated with His death, as well as with feasts (John 12:7). The bride's ministry of "myrrh and aloes" is recorded (John 19:39). **15. of**—This pleasure-ground is not dependent on mere reservoirs; it has a fountain *sufficient to water* many "gardens" (*plural*). **living** —(Jer. 17:8; John 4:13, 14; 7:38, 39.) **from Lebanon** —Though the fountain is lowly, the source is lofty; fed by the perpetual snows of Lebanon, refreshingly cool (Jer. 18:14), fertilizing the gardens of Damascus. It springs upon earth; its source is heaven. It is now not "sealed," but open "streams" (Rev. 22: 17). **16. Awake**—lit., "arise." All besides is ready; one thing alone is wanted—the breath of God. This follows rightly after His death (ch. 6:12; Acts 2). It is His call to the Spirit to come (John 14:16); in John 3:8, compared to "the wind"; quickening (John 6:63; Ezek. 27:9). Saints offer the same prayer (Ps. 85:6; Hab. 3:2). The north wind *"awakes,"* or *arises* strongly, viz., the Holy Ghost as a reprover (John 16:8-11); the south wind *"comes"* gently, viz., the Holy Ghost as the comforter (John 14:16). The west wind brings rain from the sea (I Kings 18:44, 45; Luke 12:54). The east wind is tempestuous (Job 27:21; Isa. 27:8) and withering (Gen. 41:23). These, therefore, are not wanted; but first the north wind clearing the air (Job 37:22; Prov. 25:23), and then the warm south wind (vs. 17); so the Holy Ghost first clearing away mists of gloom, error, unbelief, sin, which intercept the light of Jesus Christ, then infusing spiritual warmth (II Cor. 4:6), causing the graces to exhale their odor. **Let my beloved . . .** —*the bride's reply*. The fruit was now at length ripe; the last passover, which He had so desired, is come (Luke 22:7, 15, 16, 18), the only occasion in which He took charge of the preparations. **his**—answering to Jesus Christ's "My." She owns that the garden is His, and the fruits in her, which she does not in false humility deny (Ps. 66:16; Acts 21: 19; I Cor. 15:10) are His (John 15:8; Phil. 1:11).

CHAPTER 5

Vss. 1-16. **1.** Answer to her prayer (Isa. 65:24; Rev. 3:20). **am come**—already (ch. 4:16); "come" (Gen. 28:16). **sister . . . spouse**—As Adam's was created of his flesh, out of his opened side, there being none on earth on a level with him, so the bride out of the pierced Saviour (Eph. 5:30-32). **have gathered . . . myrrh**—His course was already complete; the myrrh, etc. (Matt. 2:11; 26:7-12; John 19: 39), emblems of the indwelling of the anointing Holy Ghost, were already gathered. **spice**—lit., "balsam." **have eaten**—answering to her "eat" (ch. 4:16). **honeycomb**—distinguished here from liquid "honey" dropping from trees. The last supper, here set forth, is one of *espousal,* a pledge of the future *marriage* (ch. 8:14; Rev. 19:9). Feasts often took place in gardens. In the absence of sugar, then unknown, honey was more widely used than with us. His eating honey with milk indicates His true, yet spotless, human nature from infancy (Isa. 7:15); and after His resurrection (Luke 24:42). **my wine**—(John 18:11)—a cup of wrath to Him, of mercy to us, whereby God's Word and promises become to us "milk" (Ps. 19:10; I Pet. 2:2). "My" answers to "His" (ch. 4:16). The "myrrh (emblem, by its bitterness, of *repentance*), honey, milk (*incipient faith*), wine" (*strong faith*), in reference to believers, imply that He accepts all their graces, however various in degree. **eat**—He desires to make us partakers in His joy (Isa. 55:1, 2; John 6:53-57; I John 1:3). **drink abundantly**—so as to be *filled* (Eph. 5:18; as Hag. 1:6). **friends**—(John 15:15). CANTICLE IV.—Ch. 5:2-8:4—FROM THE AGONY OF GETHSEMANE TO THE CONVERSION OF SAMARIA. **2.** Sudden change of scene from evening to midnight, from a betrothal feast to cold repulse. He has gone from the feast alone; night is come; He knocks at the door of His espoused; she hears, but in sloth does not shake off half-conscious drowsiness; viz., the disciples' torpor (Matt. 26:40-43), "the spirit willing, the flesh weak" (cf. Rom. 7; Gal. 5). Not *total* sleep. The lamp was burning beside the *slumbering* wise virgin, but wanted trimming (Matt. 25:5-7). It is *His* voice that rouses her (Jonah 1:6; Eph. 5:14; Rev. 3:20). Instead of bitter reproaches, He addresses her by the most endearing titles, "my sister, my love," etc. Cf. His thought of *Peter* after the denial (Mark 16:7). **dew**—which falls heavily in summer nights in the East (see Luke 9:58). **drops of the night**—(Ps. 22:2; Luke 22:44.) His death is not *expressed,* as unsuitable to the allegory, a song of love and joy; vs. 4 refers to the scene in the judgment hall of Caiaphas, when Jesus Christ employed the cock-crowing and look of love to awaken Peter's sleeping conscience, so that his "bowels were moved" (Luke 22:61, 62); vss. 5, 6, the disciples with "myrrh," etc. (Luke 24:1, 5), seeking Jesus Christ in the tomb, but finding Him not, for He has "withdrawn Himself" (John 7:34; 13:33); vs. 7, the trials by watchmen extend through the whole night of His withdrawal from Gethsemane to the resurrection; they took off the "veil" of Peter's disguise; also, literally the linen cloth from the young man (Mark 14:51); vs. 8, the sympathy of friends (Luke 23:27). **undefiled**—not polluted by spiritual adultery (Rev. 14:4; Jas. 4:4). **3.** Trivial excuses (Luke 14:18). **coat**—rather, the inmost vest, next the skin, taken off before going to bed. **washed . . . feet**—before going to rest, for they had been soiled, from the Eastern custom of wearing sandals, not shoes. Sloth (Luke 11:7) and despondency (Deut. 7:17-19). **4.** A key in the East is usually a piece of wood with

pegs in it corresponding to small holes in a wooden bolt within, and is put through a hole in the door, and thus draws the bolt. So Jesus Christ "puts forth His hand (viz., His Spirit, Ezek. 3:14), by (*Hebrew,* 'from,' so in ch. 2:9) the hole"; in "chastening" (Ps. 38:2; Rev. 3:14-22, singularly similar to this passage), and other unexpected ways letting Himself in (Luke 22:61, 62). **bowels . . . moved for him**—It is His which are first troubled for us, and which cause ours to be troubled for Him (Jer. 31:20; Hos. 11:8). **5. dropped with myrrh**—The best proof a bride could give her lover of welcome was to anoint herself (the back of the hands especially, as being the coolest part of the body) *profusely* with the *best* perfumes (Exod. 30:23; Esther 2:12; Prov. 7:17); "sweet-smelling" is in the *Hebrew* rather, "spontaneously exuding" from the tree, and therefore the *best.* She designed also to anoint Him, whose "head was filled with the drops of night" (Luke 24:1). The myrrh typifies *bitter* repentance, the fruit of the Spirit's unction (II Cor. 1:21, 22). **handles of the lock**—sins which closed the heart against Him. **6. withdrawn**—He *knocked* when she was sleeping; for to have left her *then* would have ended in the death sleep; He *withdraws* now that she is roused, as she needs correction (Jer. 2:17, 19), and can appreciate and safely bear it now, which she could not then. "The strong He'll strongly try" (I Cor. 10:13). **when he spake**—rather, *because of His speaking;* at the remembrance of His tender words (Job 29:2, 3, Ps. 27:13; 142:7), or *till He should speak.* **no answer**—(Job. 23:3-9; 30: 20; 34:29; Lam. 3:44.) Weak faith receives immediate comfort (Luke 8:44, 47, 48); strong faith is tried with delay (Matt. 15:22, 23). **7. watchmen**—historically, the Jewish priests, etc. (see *Note,* vs. 2); spiritually, ministers (Isa. 62:6; Heb. 13:17), faithful in "smiting" (Ps. 141:5), but (as she leaves them, vs. 8) too harsh; or, perhaps, unfaithful; disliking her zeal wherewith she sought Jesus Christ, first, with spiritual prayer, "opening" her heart to Him, and then in charitable works "about the city"; miscalling it fanaticism (Isa. 66:5), and taking away her veil (the greatest indignity to an Eastern lady), as though she were positively immodest. She had before sought Him by night in the streets, under strong affection (ch. 3:2-4), and so without rebuff from "the watchmen," found Him immediately; but now after sinful neglect, she encounters pain and delay. God forgives believers, but it is a serious thing to draw on His forgiveness; so the *growing reserve* of God towards Israel observable in Judges, as His people repeat their demands on His grace. **8. She** turns from the unsympathizing watchmen to humbler persons, not yet themselves knowing Him, but in the way towards it. Historically, His secret friends in the night of His withdrawal (Luke 23:27, 28). Inquirers *may* find ("*if* ye find") Jesus Christ before she who has grieved His Spirit finds Him again. **tell**—in prayer (Jas. 5:16). **sick of love**—from an opposite cause (ch. 2:5) than through excess of delight at His *presence;* now excess of pain at His *absence.* **9.** Her own beauty (Ezek. 16:14), and lovesickness for Him, elicit now their inquiry (Matt. 5:16); heretofore "other lords besides Him had dominion over them"; thus they had seen "no beauty in Him" (Isa. 26:13; 53:2). **10.** (I Peter 3:15.) **white and ruddy**—health and beauty. So David (equivalent to *beloved*), His forefather after the flesh, and type (I Sam. 17:42). "The Lamb" is at once His nuptial and sacrificial name (I Pet. 1:19; Rev. 19:7), characterized by white and red; *white,* His spotless manhood (Rev. 1:14). The *Hebrew* for *white* is properly "illuminated by the sun," white as the light" (cf. Matt. 17:2); *red,* in His blood-dyed garment as slain (Isa. 63:1-3; Rev. 5:6; 19:13). Angels are white, not red; the blood of martyrs does not enter heaven; His alone is seen there. **chiefest** —lit., "a standard-bearer"; i.e., as conspicuous above all others, as a standard-bearer is among hosts (Ps. 45:7; 89:6; Isa. 11:10; 55:4; Heb. 2:10; cf. II Sam. 18:3; Job 33:23; Phil. 2:9-11; Rev. 1:5). The chief of sinners needs the "chiefest" of Saviours. **11. head . . . gold**—*the Godhead* of Jesus Christ, as distinguished from His *heel,* i.e., His manhood, which was "bruised" by Satan; both together being one Christ (I Cor. 11:3). Also His sovereignty, as Nebuchadnezzar, the supreme king was "the head of gold" (Dan. 2:32-38; Col. 1:18), the highest creature, compared with Him, is brass, iron, and clay. "Preciousness" (*Greek,* I Pet. 2:7). **bushy**—*curled,* token of Headship. In contrast with her *flowing* locks (ch. 4:1), the token of her subjection to Him (Ps. 8:4-8; I Cor. 11:3, 6-15). The *Hebrew* is (pendulous as) the *branches of a palm,* which, when in leaf, resemble waving plumes of feathers. **black**—implying youth; no "gray hairs" (Ps. 102:27; 110:3, 4; Hos. 7:9). Jesus Christ was crucified in the prime of vigor and manliness. In heaven, on the other hand, His hair is "white," He being the Ancient of days (Dan. 7:9). These contrasts often concur in Him (vs. 10), "white and ruddy"; here the "raven" (vs. 12), the "dove," as both with Noah in the ark (Gen. 8); emblems of judgment and mercy. **12. as the eyes of doves**—rather, "as doves" (Ps. 68:13); bathing in "the rivers"; so combining in their "silver" feathers the *whiteness* of milk with the *sparkling brightness* of the water trickling over them (Matt. 3:16). The "milk" may allude to the white around the pupil of the eye. The "waters" refer to the eye as the fountain of *tears of sympathy* (Ezek. 16:5, 6; Luke 19:41). Vivacity, purity, and love, are the three features typified. **fitly set**—as a gem in a ring; as the precious stones in the high priest's breastplate. Rather, translate as *Vulgate* (the doves), *sitting at the fulness* of the stream; by the full stream; or, as MAURER (the eyes) "*set in fulness,* not sunk in their sockets (Rev. 5:6), ("seven," expressing *full* perfection), (Zech. 3:9; 4:10). **13. cheeks**—the seat of beauty, according to the *Hebrew* meaning [GESENIUS]. Yet men smote and spat on them (Isa. 50:6). **bed**—full, like the raised surface of the garden bed; fragrant with ointments, as beds with aromatic plants (lit., "balsam"). **sweet flowers** —rather, "*terraces* of aromatic herbs"—"*high-raised* parterres of sweet plants," in parallelism to "bed," which comes from a *Hebrew* root, meaning "elevation." **lips**—(Ps. 45:2; John 7:46.) **lilies**—red lilies. Soft and gentle (I Pet. 2:22, 23). How different lips were man's (Ps. 22:7)! **dropping . . . myrrh**—viz., His lips, just as the sweet dewdrops which hang in the calyx of the lily. **14. rings set with . . . beryl**— *Hebrew, Tarshish,* so called from the city. The ancient chrysolite, gold in color (LXX), our topaz, one of the stones on the high priest's breastplate, also in the foundation of New Jerusalem (Rev. 21; also Dan. 10:6). "Are as," is plainly to be supplied, as in vs. 13 a similiar ellipsis; not as MOODY STUART: "*have* gold rings." The hands bent in are compared to beautiful rings, in which beryl is set, as the nails are in the fingers. BURROWES explains the rings as *cylinders* used as signets, such as are found in Nineveh, and which resemble fingers. A ring is the token of sonship (Luke 15:22). A slave was not allowed to wear a *gold* ring. He imparts His sonship and freedom to us (Gal. 4:7); also of authority

(Gen. 41:42; cf. John 6:27). He seals us in the name of God with His signet (Rev. 7:2-4), cf. below, ch. 8:6, where she desires to be herself *a signet ring* on His arms; so "graven on the palms," etc., i.e., on the signet ring in His hand (Isa. 49:16; contrast Hag. 2:23, with Jer. 22:24). **belly**—BURROWES and MOODY STUART translate, "body." NEWTON, as it is elsewhere, "bowels"; viz., His compassion (Ps. 22: 14; Isa. 63:15; Jer. 31:20; Hos. 11:8). **bright**— lit., "elaborately wrought so as to shine," so His "prepared" body (Heb. 10:5); the "ivory palace" of the king (Ps. 45:8); spotless, pure, so the bride's "neck is as to tower of *ivory*" (ch. 7:4). **sapphires** —spangling in the girdle around Him (Dan. 10:5). "To the pure all things are pure." As in statuary to the artist the partly undraped figure is suggestive only of beauty, free from indelicacy, so to the saint the personal excellencies of Jesus Christ, typified under the ideal of the noblest human form. As, however, the bride and bridegroom are in public, the usual robes on the person, richly ornamented, are presupposed (Isa. 11:5). Sapphires indicate His *heavenly* nature (so John 3:13, "*is* in heaven"), even in His humiliation, *overlaying* or cast "over" His ivory human body (Exod. 24:10). Sky-blue in color, the *height* and *depth* of the love of Jesus Christ (Eph. 3:18). **15. pillars**—strength and steadfastness. Contrast man's "legs" (Eccles. 12:3). Allusion to the temple (I Kings 5:8, 9; 7:21), the "cedars" of "Lebanon" (Ps. 147:10). Jesus Christ's "legs" were not broken on the cross, though the thieves' were; on them rests the weight of our salvation (Ps. 75:3). **sockets of fine gold**—His sandals, answering to the bases of the pillars; "set up from everlasting" (Prov. 8:22, 23). From the head (vs. 11) to the feet, "of fine gold." He was tried in the fire and found without alloy. **countenance**—rather, *His aspect,* including both *mien* and *stature* (cf. *Margin,* II Sam. 23:21 with I Chron. 11:23). From the several *parts,* she proceeds to the general effect of the *whole* person of Jesus Christ. **Lebanon**—so called from its *white* limestone rocks. **excellent**— lit., "choice," i.e., fair and tall as the cedars on Lebanon (Ezek. 31:3, etc.). Majesty is the prominent thought (Ps. 21:5). Also the cedars' *duration* (Heb. 1:11); *greenness* (Luke 23:31), and refuge afforded by it (Ezek. 17:22, 23). **16.** Lit., "His *palate* is *sweetness,* yea, all over *loveliness,*" i.e, He is the *essence* of these qualities. **mouth**—so ch. 1:2, not the same as "lips" (vs. 13), His breath (Isa. 11:4; John 20:22). "All over," all the beauties scattered among creatures are transcendently concentrated in Him (Col. 1:19; 2:9). **my beloved**—for I love Him. **my friend**—for He loves me (Prov. 18:24). Holy boasting (Ps. 34:2; I Cor. 1:31).

CHAPTER 6

Vss. 1-13. **1.** Historically, at Jesus Christ's crucifixion and burial, Joseph of Arimathea, and Nicodemus, and others, joined with His professed disciples. By speaking of Jesus Christ, the bride does good not only to her own soul, but to others (*Note,* ch. 1:4; Mal. 3:16; Matt. 5:14-16). Cf. the hypocritical use of similar words (Matt. 2:8). **2. gone down**—Jerusalem was on a hill (answering to its *moral* elevation), and the gardens were at a little distance in the valleys below. **beds of spices**—(balsam) which He Himself calls the "mountain of myrrh," etc. (ch. 4:6), and again (ch. 8:14), the resting-place of His body amidst spices, and of His soul in paradise, and now in heaven, where He stands as High Priest for ever. Nowhere else in the Song is there mention of mountains of spices. **feed in . . . gardens**—i.e., in the churches, though He may have withdrawn for a time from the individual believer: she implies an invitation to the daughters of Jerusalem to enter His spiritual Church, and become lilies, made white by His blood. He is gathering some lilies now to plant on earth, others to transplant into heaven (ch. 5:1; Gen. 5:24; Mark 4: 28, 29; Acts 7:60). **3.** In speaking of Jesus Christ to others, she regains her own assurance. Lit., "I am *for* my beloved . . . *for me.*" Reverse order from ch. 2:16. She *now,* after the season of darkness, grounds her convictions on His love towards her, more than on hers towards Him (Deut. 33:3). *There,* it was the young believer concluding that she was His, from the sensible assurance that He was hers. **4. Tirzah**—meaning *pleasant* (Heb. 13:21); "well-pleasing" (Matt. 5:14); the royal city of one of the old Canaanite kings (Josh. 12:24); and after the revolt of Israel, the royal city of its kings, before Omri founded Samaria (I Kings 16:8, 15). No ground for assigning a later date than the time of Solomon to the Song, as Tirzah was even in his time the capital of the north (Israel), as Jerusalem was of the south (Judah). **Jerusalem**—residence of the kings of *Judah,* as Tirzah, of *Israel* (Ps. 48:1, etc.; 122:1-3; 125:1, 2). Loveliness, security, unity, and loyalty; also the union of Israel and Judah in the Church (Isa. 11:13; Jer. 3:18; Ezek. 37:16, 17, 22; cf. Heb. 12:22; Rev. 21:2, 12). **terrible**—awe-inspiring. Not only armed as a city on the defensive, but as an army on the offensive. **banners.** -(*Note,* ch. 5: 10; Ps. 60:4); Jehovah-nissi (II Cor. 10:4). **5.** (Ch. 4:9; Gen. 32:28; Exod. 32:9-14; Hos. 12:4.) This is the way "the army" (vs. 4) "overcomes" not only enemies, but Jesus Christ Himself, with eyes fixed on Him (Ps. 25:15; Matt. 11:12). Historically. vss. 3. 4, 5 represent the restoration of Jesus Christ to His Church at the resurrection; His sending her forth as an army, with new powers (Mark 16:15-18, 20); His rehearsing the *same* instructions (cf. vs. 6, *Note*) as when with them (Luke 24:44). **5. overcome**—lit., "have taken me by storm." **6.** Not vain repetition of ch. 4:1, 2. The use of the same words shows His love unchanged after her temporary unfaithfulness (Mal. 3:6). **8. threescore**—indefinite number, as in ch. 3:7. Not queens, etc., *of Solomon,* but witnesses of the espousals, rulers of the earth contrasted with the saints. who, though many, are but "one" bride (Isa. 52:15; Luke 22:25, 26; John 17:21; I Cor. 10:17). The one bride is contrasted with the many wives whom Eastern kings had in violation of the marriage law (I Kings 11:1-3). **9.** Hollow professors, like half wives, have no part in the one bride. **only one of her mother**—viz., "Jerusalem above" (Gal. 4:26). The "little sister" (ch. 8:8) is not inconsistent with her being "the only one"; for that sister is one with herself (John 10:16). **choice**—(Eph. 1:4; II Thess. 2:13.) As she exalted Him above all others (ch. 5:10), so He now her. **daughters . . . blessed her**—(Isa 8:18; 61:9; Ezek. 16:14; II Thess. 1:10.) So at her appearance after Pentecost (Acts. 4:13; 6:15; 24:25; 26:28). **10.** The words expressing the admiration of the daughters. Historically (Acts 5:24-39.) **as the morning**—As yet she is not come to the fulness of her light (Prov. 4:18). **moon**—shining in the night, by light borrowed from the sun; so the bride, in the darkness of this world, reflects the light of the Sun of righteousness (II Cor. 3:18). **sun**—Her light of justification is perfect, for it is His (II Cor. 5:21; I John 4:17). The moon has less light, and has only one half illumi-

nated; so the bride's sanctification is as yet imperfect. Her future glory (Matt. 13:43). **army**—(vs. 4). The climax requires this to be applied to the starry and angelic hosts, from which God is called Lord of Sabaoth. Her final glory (Gen. 15:5; Dan. 12:3; Rev. 12:1). The Church Patriarchal, "the morning"; Levitical, "the moon"; Evangelical, "the sun"; Triumphant, "the bannered army" (Rev. 19:14). **11.** The bride's words; for she everywhere is the narrator, and often soliloquizes, which He never does. The first garden (ch. 2:11-13) was that of spring, full of flowers and grapes not yet. ripe; the second, autumn, with spices (which are always connected with the person of Jesus Christ), and nothing unripe (ch. 4:13, etc.). The third here, of "nuts," from the previous autumn; the end of winter, and verge of spring; the Church in the upper room Acts 1:13, etc.), when one dispensation was just closed, the other not yet begun; the hard shell of the old needing to be broken, and its inner sweet kernel extracted [ORIGEN] (Luke 24:27, 32); waiting for the Holy Ghost to usher in spiritual spring. The *walnut* is meant, with a bitter outer husk, a hard shell, and sweet kernel. So the Word is distasteful to the careless; when awakened, the sinner finds the letter hard, until the Holy Ghost reveals the sweet inner spirit. **fruits of the valley**—MAURER translates, "the *blooming products* of the *river,"* i.e., the plants growing on the margin of the river flowing through the garden. She goes to watch the *first* sproutings of the various plants. **12.** Sudden outpourings of the Spirit on Pentecost (Acts 2), while the Church was using the means (answering to "the garden," vs. 11; John 3:8). **Ammi-nadib**—supposed to me one proverbial for swift driving. Similarly (ch. 1:9). Rather, *my willing people* (Ps. 110:3). A willing chariot bore a "willing people"; or Nadib is *the Prince,* Jesus Christ (Ps. 68:17). She is borne in a moment into His presence (Eph. 2:6). **13.** Entreaty of the daughters of Jerusalem to her, in her chariot-like flight from them (cf. II Kings 2:12; II Sam. 19:14). **Shulamite**—new name applied to her now for the first time. *Feminine* of Solomon, Prince of Peace; His bride, daughter of peace, accepting and proclaiming it (Isa. 52:7; John 14:27; Rom. 5:1; Eph. 2:17). Historically, this name answers to the time when, not without a divine design in it, the young Church met in *Solomon's* porch (Acts 3:11, 5:12). The entreaty, "Return, O Shulamite," answers to the people's desire to keep Peter and John, after the lame man was healed, when they were about to enter the temple. Their reply attributing the glory not to themselves, but to Jesus Christ, answers to the bride's reply here, "What will ye see" in me? "As it were," etc. She accepts the name Shulamite, as truly describing her. But adds, that though "one" (vs. 9), she is nevertheless "two." Her glories are her Lord's, beaming through her (Eph. 5:31, 32). The two armies are the family of Jesus Christ in heaven, and that on earth, joined and one with Him; the one militant, the other triumphant. Or Jesus Christ and His ministering angels are one army, the Church the other, both being one (John 17:21, 22). Allusion is made to Mahanaim (meaning *two hosts*), the scene of Jacob's victorious conflict by prayer (Gen. 32:2, 9, 22-30). Though she is peace, yet she has warfare here, between flesh and spirit within and foes without; her strength, as Jacob's at Mahanaim, is Jesus Christ and His host enlisted on her side by prayer; whence she obtains those graces which raise the admiration of the daughters of Jerusalem.

CHAPTER 7

Vss. 1-13. **thy feet**—rather, thy goings" (Ps. 17: 5). Evident allusion to Isaiah 52:7: "*How beautiful* . . . are the *feet* of him . . . that publisheth *peace*" (Shulamite, ch. 6:13). shoes—Sandals are richly jewelled in the East (Luke 15:22; Eph. 6:15). She is evidently "on the mountains," whither she was wafted (ch. 6:12), *above* the daughters of Jerusalem, who therefore portray her *feet* first. daughter—of God the Father, with whom Jesus Christ is one (Matt. 5:9), "children of (the) God" (of *peace*), equivalent to Shulamite (Ps. 45:10-15; II Cor. 6:18), as well as bride of Jesus Christ. **prince's**—therefore princely herself, freely giving the word of life to others, not sparing her "feet," as in ch. 5:3; Exod. 12:11. To act on the offensive is defensive to ourselves. **joints**—rather, "the rounding"; the full graceful curve of the hips in the female figure; like the *rounding* of a *necklace* (as the *Hebrew* for "jewels" means). Cf. with the *English Version*, Eph. 4:13-16; Col. 2:19. Or, applying it to the girdle binding together the robes round the hips (Eph. 6:14). **cunning workman**—(Ps. 139:14-16; Eph. 2:10, 22: 5:29, 30, 32). **2. navel**—rather, "girdle-clasp," called from the part of the person underneath. The "shoes" (vs. 1) prove that *dress* is throughout presupposed on all parts where it is usually worn. She is "a bride adorned for her husband"; the "uncomely parts," being most adorned (I Cor. 12:23). The girdle-clasp was adorned with red rubies resembling the "round goblet" (crater or *mixer*) of spice-mixed wine (not "liquor," ch. 8:2; Isa. 5:22). The wine of the "New Testament in His blood" (Luke 22:20). The spiritual exhilaration by it was mistaken for that caused by new wine (Acts 2:13-17; Eph. 5:18). **belly**—i.e., *the vesture* on it. As in Psalm 45:13, 14, gold and needlework compose the bride's attire, so golden-colored "wheat" and white "lilies" here. The ripe grain, in token of harvest joy, used to be decorated with lilies; so the accumulated spiritual food (John 6:35; 12:24), free from chaff, not fenced with thorns, but made attractive by lilies (believers, ch. 2:2; Acts 2:46, 47; 5:13, 14, in common partaking of it). Associated with the exhilarating wine-cup (Zech. 9:17), as here. **3.** The daughters of Jerusalem describe her in the same terms as Jesus Christ in ch. 4:5. The testimonies of heaven and earth coincide. **twins**—faith and love. **4. tower of ivory**—In ch. 4:4, Jesus Christ saith, "a tower of David builded for an armory." Strength and conquest are the main thought in His description; here, beauty and polished whiteness; contrast ch. 1. **fishpools**—seen by BURCKHARDT, clear (Rev. 22:1), deep, quiet, and full (I Cor. 2:10, 15). **Heshbon**—east of Jordan, residence of the Amorite king, Sihon (Num. 21:25, etc.), afterwards held by Gad. **Bath-rabbim**—"daughter of a multitude"; a crowded thoroughfare. Her eyes (ch. 4:1) are called by Jesus Christ, "doves' eyes," waiting on Him. But here, looked on by the daughters or Jerusalem, they are compared to a placid lake. She is calm even amidst the crowd (Prov. 8:2; John 16:33). **nose**—or, face. **tower of Lebanon**—a border fortress, watching the hostile Damascus. Towards Jesus Christ her face was full of holy shame (ch. 4:1, 3, *Notes*); towards spiritual foes, like a watchtower (Hab. 2:1; Mark 13:37; Acts 4:13), elevated, so that she looks not up from earth to heaven, but down from heaven to earth. If we retain "nose," discernment of spiritual fragrance is meant. **5. upon thee**—the head-dress "upon" her. **Carmel**—signifying a well-cultivated field (Isa. 35:2). In ch. 5:15 He is compared to

majestic Lebanon; she here, to *fruitful* Carmel. Her head-dress, or crown (II Tim. 4:8; I Pet. 5:4). Also the souls won by her (I Thess. 2:19, 20), a token of her fruitfulness. **purple**—royalty (Rev. 1:6). As applied to hair, it expresses the glossy splendor of black hair (lit., "pendulous hair") so much admired in the East (ch. 4:1). While the King compares her hair to the flowering hair of goats (the token of her *subjection*), the daughters of Jerusalem compare it to *royal* purple. **galleries**—(so ch. 1:17. *Margin;* Rev. 21:3.) But MAURER translates here, "flowing ringlets"; with these, as with "thongs" (so LEE, from the *Arabic* translates it) "the King is held" bound (ch. 6:5; Prov. 6:25). Her purple crowns of martyrdom especially captivated the King, appearing from His galleries (Acts 7:55, 56). As Samson's strength was in his locks (Judg. 16:17). Here first the daughters see the King themselves. **6.** Nearer advance of the daughters to the Church (Acts 2:47; 5: 13, end). Love to her is the first token of love to Him (I John 5:1, end). **delights**—fascinating charms to them and to the King (vs. 5; Isa. 62:4, Hephzibah). Hereafter, too (Zeph. 3:17; Mal. 3:12; Rev. 21:9). **7. palm tree**—(Ps. 92:12.) The sure sign of *water near* (Exod. 15:27; John 7:38). **clusters**—not of dates, as MOODY STUART thinks. The parallelism (vs. 8), "clusters of the vine," shows it is here clusters of grapes. Vines were often trained (termed "wedded") on other trees. **8.** The daughters are no longer content to admire, but resolve to lay hold of her fruits, high though these be. The palm stem is bare for a great height, and has its crown of fruit-laden boughs at the summit. It is the symbol of triumphant joy (John 12:13); so hereafter (Rev. 7:9). **breasts**—(Isa. 66:11.) **the vine**—Jesus Christ (Hos. 14:7, end; John 15:1). **nose**—i.e., breath; the Holy Ghost breathed into her *nostrils* by Him, whose "mouth is most sweet" (ch. 5:16). **apples**—citrons, off the tree to which He is likened (ch. 2:3). **9. roof of thy mouth**—thy voice (Prov. 15:23). **best wine**—the *new* wine of the gospel kingdom (Mark 14:25), poured out at Pentecost (Acts 2:4, 13, 17). **for my beloved**—(Ch. 4:10). Here first the daughters call Him theirs, and become one with the bride. The steps successively are (ch. 1:5) where they misjudge her (ch. 3:11; ch. 5:8, where the possibility of their finding Him, before she regained Him, is expressed; ch. 5:9 (ch. 6:1; 7:6, 9), (John 4:42). **causing . . . asleep to speak**—(Isa. 35:6; Mark 5:19, 20; Acts 2:47; Eph. 5:14.) Jesus Christ's first miracle turned water into "good wine kept until now" (John 2); just as the Gospel revives those asleep and dying under the law (Prov. 31:6; Rom. 7:9, 10, 24, 25; 8:1). **10.** Words of the daughters of Jerusalem and the bride, now united into one (Acts 4:32). They are mentioned again distinctly (ch. 8:4), as fresh converts were being added from among inquirers, and these needed to be charged not to grieve the Spirit. **his desire is toward me**—strong assurance. He so desires us, as to give us sense of His desire toward us (Ps. 139:17, 18; Luke 22:15; Gal. 2:20; I John 4: 16). **11. field**—the country. "The tender grape (MAURER translates, flowers) and vines" occurred before (ch. 2:13). But here she prepares for Him all kinds of fruit old and new; also, she anticipates in going forth to seek them, communion with Him in "loves." "Early" implies immediate earnestness. "The villages" imply distance from Jerusalem. At Stephen's death the disciples were scattered from it through Judea and Samaria, preaching the word (Acts 8). Jesus Christ was with them, confirming the word with miracles. They gathered the *old* fruits, of which Jesus Christ had sown the seed (John

4), as well as *new* fruits. **lodge**—forsaking *home* for Jesus Christ's sake (Matt. 19:29). **12.** (Mark 1:35; John 9:4; Gal. 6:10.) Assurance fosters diligence, not indolence. **13. mandrakes**—*Hebrew, audaim,* from a root meaning "to love"; love-apples, supposed to exhilarate the spirits and excite love. Only here and Genesis 30:14-16. *Atropa mandragora* of Linnaeus; its leaves like lettuce, but dark green, flowers purple, root forked, fruit of the size of an apple, ruddy and sweet-smelling, gathered in wheat harvest, **i.e., in May** (*Mariti*, ii. 195). **gates**—the entrance to the kiosk or summerhouse. Love "lays up" the best of everything for the person beloved (I Cor. 10:31; Phil. 3:8; I Pet. 4:11), thereby really, though unconsciously, laying up for itself (I Tim. 6:18, 19).

CHAPTER 8

Vss. 1-14. **1.** He had been a brother already. Why, then, this prayer here? It refers to the time after His resurrection, when the previous *outward* intimacy with Him was no longer allowed, but it was implied it should be renewed at the second coming (John 20:17). For this the Church here prays; meanwhile she enjoys *inward* spiritual communion with Him. The last who ever "kissed" Jesus Christ on earth was the traitor Judas. The bride's return with the King to her mother's house answers to Acts 8:25, after the mission to Samaria. The rest spoken of (vs. 4) answers to Acts 9:31. **that sucked... mother**—a brother born of the same mother; the closest tie. **2.** Her desire to bring Him into her home circle (John 1:41). **who would instruct me**—rather, "thou wouldest instruct me," viz., how I might best please thee (Isa. 11:2, 3; 50:4; Luke 12:12; John 14:26; 16:13). **spiced wine**—seasoned with aromatic perfumes. Jesus Christ ought to have our choicest gifts. Spices are never introduced in the song in His absence; therefore the time of His return from "the mountain of spices" (vs. 14) is contemplated. The cup of betrothal was given by Him at the last supper; the cup or marriage shall be presented by her at His return (Matt. 26:29). Till then the believer often cannot feel towards, or speak of, Him as he would wish. **3, 4.** The "left and right hand," etc., occurred only once actually (ch. 2:6), and here optatively. Only at His first manifestation did the Church palpably embrace Him; at His second coming there shall be again sensible communion with Him. The rest in vs. 4, which is a *spiritual* realization of the wish in vs. 3 (I Pet. 1:8), and the charge not to disturb it, close the 1st, 2d, and 4th canticles; not the 3d, as the bridegroom there takes charge Himself; nor the 5th, as, if *repose* formed its close, we might mistake the present state for our rest. The broken, longing close, like that of the whole Bible (Rev. 22:20), reminds us we are to be waiting for a Saviour to come. On "daughters of Jerusalem," see *Note*, ch. 7:10.

CANTICLE V.—Ch. 8:5-14.—FROM THE CALL OF THE GENTILES TO THE CLOSE OF REVELATION. **5. Who is this**—Words of the daughters of Jerusalem, i.e., the churches of Judea; referring to Paul, on his return from Arabia ("the wilderness"), whither he had gone after conversion (Gal. 1:15-24). **I raised thee... she... bare thee**—(Acts 26:14-16.) The first words of Jesus Christ to the bride since her going to the garden of nuts (ch. 6:9, 10); so His appearance to Paul is the only one since His ascension, vs. 13 is not an address of Him as *visible:* her reply implies He is not visible (I Cor. 15:8). Spiritually, she was

found in the moral wilderness (Ezek. 16:5, Hos. 13:5); but now she is "coming up from" it (Jer. 2:2; Hos. 2:14), especially in the last stage of her journey, her conscious weakness casting itself the more wholly on Jesus Christ (II Cor. 12:9). "Raised" (Eph. 2:1-7). Found ruined under the forbidden tree (Gen. 3); restored under the shadow of Jesus Christ crucified, "the green tree" (Luke 23:31), fruit-"bearing" by the cross (Isa. 53:11; John 12:24). Born again by the Holy Ghost" "there" (Ezek. 16:3-6). In this verse, *her dependence,* in the similar verse, ch. 3:6, etc., *His omnipotence to support her,* are brought out (Deut. 33:26). **6.** Implying approaching absence of the Bridegroom. **seal**—having her name and likeness engraven on it. His Holy Priesthood also in heaven (Exod. 28:6-12, 15-30); Heb. 4:14); "his heart" there answering to "thine heart" here, and "two shoulders" to "arm." (Cf. Jer. 22:24, with Hag. 2:23.) But the Holy Ghost (Eph. 1:13, 14). As in vs. 5, she was "leaning" on Him, i.e., her arm on His *arm,* her head on His *bosom;* so she prays now that before they part, her impression may be engraven both on His *heart* and His *arm,* answering to His *love* and His *power* (Ps. 77:15; see Gen. 38:18; Isa. 62:3). **love is strong as death**—(Acts 21:13; Rom. 8:35-39; Rev. 12:11.) This their love unto death flows from His (John 10:15; 15:13). **jealousy... the grave**—*Zealous love,* jealous of all that would come between the soul and Jesus Christ (I Kings 19:10; Ps. 106:30, 31; Luke 9:60; 14:26; I Cor. 16:22). **cruel**—rather, "unyielding" hard, as the grave will not let go those whom it once holds (John 10:28). **a most vehement flame**—lit., "the fire-flame of Jehovah" (Ps. 80:16; Isa. 6:6). Nowhere else is *God's* name found in the Song. The zeal that burnt in Jesus Christ (Ps. 69:9; Luke 12:49, 50) kindled in His followers (Acts 2:3; Rom. 15:30; Phil. 2:17). **7. waters**—in contrast with the "coals of fire" (vs. 6; I Kings 18:33-38). Persecutions (Acts 8:1) cannot quench love (Heb. 10:34; Rev. 12:15, 16). Our many provocations have not quenched His love (Rom. 8:33-39). **if... give all the substance... contemned**—Nothing short of Jesus Christ Himself, not even heaven without Him, can satisfy the saint (Phil. 3:8). Satan offers the world, as to Jesus Christ (Matt. 4:8), so to the saint, in vain (I John 2:15-17; 5:4). Nothing but our love in turn can satisfy Him (I Cor. 13:1-3). **8.** The Gentile Church (Ezek. 16:48). "We," i.e., the Hebrew Church, which heretofore admitted Gentiles to communion, only by becoming *Judaic proselytes.* Now first *idolatrous* Gentiles are admitted *directly* (Acts 11:17-26). Generally, the saint's anxiety for other souls (Mark 5:19; John 4:28, 29). **no breasts**—neither faith nor love as yet (*Note,* ch. 4:5), which "come by hearing" of Him who first loved us. Not yet fit to be His bride, and mother of a spiritual offspring. **what shall we do**—the chief question in the early Church at the first council (Acts 15). How shall "the elder brother" treat the "younger," already received by the Father (Luke 15:25-32)? Generally (II Sam. 15:15; John 9:4; Acts 9:6; Gal. 6:10). **In the day... spoken for**—i.e., when she shall be *sought in marriage* (Judg. 14:7), viz., by Jesus Christ, the heavenly bridegroom. **9. wall... door**—the very terms employed as to the Gentile question (Acts 14:27; Eph. 2:14). If she be a wall in Zion, founded on Jesus Christ (I Cor. 3:11), we will not "withstand God" (Acts 11:17; 15:8-11). But if so, we must not "build" (Acts 15:14-17) on her "wood, hay, stubble" (I Cor. 3:12), i.e., Jewish rites, etc., but "a palace of silver," i.e., all the highest privileges of church communion (Gal. 2:11-18;

Eph. 2:11-22). Image from the splendid turrets "built" on the "walls" of Jerusalem, and flanking the "door," or gateway. The Gentile Church is the "door," the type of catholic accessibleness (I Cor. 16:9); but it must be not a mere thoroughfare but furnished with a wooden framework, so as not merely to admit, but also to safely enclose: cedar is fragrant, beautiful, and enduring. **10.** The Gentile Church's joy at its free admission to gospel privileges (Acts 15:30, 31). She is one wall in the spiritual temple of the Holy Ghost, the Hebrew Church is the other; Jesus Christ, the common foundation, joins them (Eph. 2:11-22). **breasts . . . towers**—alluding to the silver palace, which the bridal virgins proposed to build on her (vs. 9). "Breasts" of consolation (Isa. 66:11); faith and love (I Thess. 5:8); opposed to her previous state, "no breasts" (vs. 8; II Thess. 1:3). Thus Ezekiel 16:46, 61 was fulfilled, both Samaria and the Gentiles being joined to the Jewish gospel Church. **favour**—rather, *peace.* The Gentile Church too is become the Shulamite (ch. 6: 13), or *peace*-enjoying bride of Solomon, i.e., Jesus Christ, the Prince of Peace (Rom. 5:1; Eph. 2:14). Reject not those whom God accepts (Num. 11:28; Luke 9:49; Acts 15:8, 9). Rather, superadd to such every aid and privilege (vs. 9). **11.** The joint Church speaks of Jesus Christ's vineyard. Transference of it from the Jews, who rendered not the fruits, as is implied by the silence respecting any, to the Gentiles (Matt. 21:33-43). **Baal-hamon**—equivalent to *the owner of a multitude;* so Israel in Solomon's day (I Kings 4:20); so Isa. 5:1, *"a very fruitful hill"* abounding in *privileges,* as in *numbers.* **thousand pieces**— viz., silverlings, or shekels. The vineyard had 1000 vines probably; a vine at a silverling (Isa. 7:23), referring to this passage. **12.** "mine" by grant of the true Solomon. Not merely "let out to keepers," as in the Jewish dispensation of *works,* but "mine" by *grace.* This is "before me," i.e., *in my power* [MAURER]. But though no longer under constraint of "keeping" the law as a mere letter and covenant of works, *love* to Jesus Christ will constrain her the more freely to render all to Solomon (Rom. 8:2-4; I Cor. 6:20; Gal. 5:13; I Pet. 2:16), after having paid what justice and His will require should be paid to others (I Cor. 7:29-31; 9:14). "Before me" may

also mean "I will never lose sight of it" (contrast ch. 1:6) [MOODY STUART]. She will not keep it for herself, though so freely given to her, but for His use and glory (Luke 19:13; Rom. 6:15; 14:7-9); I Cor. 12:7). Or the "two hundred" may mean a *double tithe* (two-tenths of the whole paid back by Jesus Christ) as the reward of grace for our surrender of *all* (the thousand) to Him (Gal. 6:7; Heb. 6:10); then she and "those that keep" are the same [ADELAIDE NEWTON]. But Jesus Christ pays back not merely *two tithes,* but *His all* for our all (I Cor. 3:21-23). **13.** Jesus Christ's address to her; now no longer visibly present. Once she "had not kept" her vineyard (ch. 1:6); now she "dwells" in it, not as its owner, but its superintendent under Jesus Christ, with vine-dressers ("companions"), e.g., Paul, etc. (Acts 15:25, 26), under her (vss. 11, 12); these ought to obey her when she obeys Jesus Christ. Her voice in prayer and praise is to be heard continually by Jesus Christ, if her voice before men is to be effective (ch. 2:14; end; Acts 6:4; 13:2, 3). **14.** (See *Note,* ch. 2:17.) As she began with longing for His first coming (ch. 1:2), so she ends with praying for His second coming (Ps. 130:6; Phil. 3:20, 21; Rev. 22:20). MOODY STUART makes the roe upon spices to be the musk-deer. As there are four gardens, so four mountains, which form not mere images, as Gilead, Carmel, etc., but part of the structure of the Song: (1) Bether, or *division* (ch. 2:17), God's justice *dividing* us from God. (2) Those "of leopards" (ch. 4:8), sin, the world, and Satan. (3) That "of myrrh and aloes" (ch. 4:6, 14), the sepulchre of Calvary. (4) Those "of spices," here answering to "the hill of frankincense" (ch. 4:6), where His *soul* was for the three days of His death, and heaven, where He is a High Priest now, offering incense for us on the fragrant mountain of His own finished work (Heb. 4:14, 7:25; Rev. 8:3, 4); thus He surmounts the other three mountains, God's justice, our sin, death. The mountain of spices is as much greater than our sins, as heaven is higher than earth (Ps. 103:11). The abrupt, unsatisfied close with the yearning prayer for His *visible* coming shows that the marriage is future, and that to wait eagerly for it is our true attitude (I Cor. 1:7; I Thess. 1:10; Titus 2:13; II Pet. 3:12).

THE BOOK OF THE PROPHET

ISAIAH

INTRODUCTION

ISAIAH, son of Amoz (not Amos); contemporary of Jonah, Amos, Hosea, in Israel, but younger than they; and of Micah, in Judah. His call to a higher degree of the prophetic office (ch. 6) is assigned to the last year of Uzziah, i.e., 754 B.C. The chapters 1–5 belong to the closing years of that reign; not, as some think, to Jotham's reign: in the reign of the latter he seems to have exercised his office only orally, and not to have left any *record* of his prophecies because they were not intended for all ages. Chs. 1–5 and 6 are all that was designed for the Church universal of the prophecies of the first twenty years of his office. New historical epochs, such as occurred in the reigns of Ahaz and Hezekiah, when the affairs of Israel became interwoven with those of the Asiatic empires, are marked by prophetic writings. The prophets had now to interpret the judgments of the Lord, so as to make the people conscious of His punitive justice, as also of His mercy. Chs. 7–10:4 belong to the reign of Ahaz. Chs. 36–39 are historical, reaching to the fifteenth year of Hezekiah; probably chs. 10–12 and all from ch. 13 to 26, inclusive, belong to the same reign; the historical section being appended to facilitate the right understanding of these prophecies; thus we have Isaiah's office extending from about 760 to 713 B.C., forty-seven years. Tradition (*Talmud*) represents him as having been sawn asunder by Manasseh with a wooden saw, for having said that he had seen Jehovah (Exod. 33:20; II Kings 21:16; Heb. 11:37). II Chronicles 32:32 seems to imply that Isaiah survived Hezekiah; but "first and last" is not added, as in II Chronicles 26:22, which makes it possible that his history of Hezekiah was only carried up to a certain point. The second part, chs. 40–66, containing complaints of gross idolatry, needs not to be restricted to Manasseh's reign, but is applicable to previous reigns. At the accession of Manasseh Isaiah would be eighty-four; and if he prophesied for eight years afterwards, he must have endured martyrdom at ninety-two; so Hosea prophesied for sixty years. And Eastern tradition reports that he lived to one hundred and twenty. The conclusive argument against the tradition is that, according to the inscription, all Isaiah's prophecies are included in the time from Uzziah to Hezekiah; and the internal evidence accords with this.

His WIFE is called the *prophetess*, i.e., endowed, as Miriam, with a prophetic gift.

His CHILDREN were considered by him as not belonging merely to himself; in their names, Shear-jashub, "the remnant shall return," and Maher-shalal-hash-baz, "speeding to the spoil, he hasteth to the prey," the two chief points of his prophecies are intimated to the people, the *judgments* of the Lord on the people and the world, and yet His *mercy* to the elect.

His GARMENT of sackcloth (ch. 20:2), too, was a silent preaching by fact; he appears as the embodiment of that repentance which he taught.

His HISTORICAL WORKS.—History, as written by the prophets, is retroverted prophecy. As the past and future alike proceed from the essence of God, an inspired insight into the past implies an insight into the future, and vice versa. Hence most of the Old Testament histories are written by prophets and are classed with their writings; the Chronicles being not so classed, cannot have been written by them, but are taken from historical monographs of theirs; e.g., Isaiah's life of Uzziah, II Chronicles 26:22; also of Hezekiah, II Chron. 32:32; of these latter all that was important for all ages has been preserved to us, while the rest, which was local and temporary, has been lost.

The INSCRIPTION (ch. 1:1) applies to the whole book and implies that Isaiah is the author of the second part (chs. 40–66), as well as of the first. Nor do the words, "concerning Judah and Jerusalem," oppose the idea that the inscription applies to the whole; for whatever he says against other nations, he says on account of their relation to Judah. So the inscription of Amos, "concerning *Israel*," though several prophecies follow against foreign nations. EWALD maintains that chs. 40–66, though spurious, were subjoined to the previous portion, in order to preserve the former. But it is untrue that the first portion is unconnected with those chapters. The former ends with the Babylonian exile (ch. 39:6), the latter begins with the coming redemption from it. The portion, chs. 40–46, has no heading of its own, a proof that it is closely connected with what precedes, and falls under the general heading in ch. 1:1. JOSEPHUS (*Antiquities*, 11. 1, sec. 1, 2) says that Cyrus was induced by the prophecies of Isaiah (ch. 44:28; 45:1, 13) to aid the Jews in returning and rebuilding the temple. Ezra 1 confirms this; Cyrus in his edict there plainly refers to the prophecies in the second portion, which assign the kingdoms to him from Jehovah, and the duty of rebuilding the temple. Probably he took from them his historical name Cyrus (*Coresh*). Moreover, *subsequent prophets imitate this second portion*, which EWALD assigns to later times; e.g., cf. Jeremiah 50:51 with Isaiah's predictions against Babylon. "The Holy One of Israel," occurring but three times elsewhere in the Old Testament, is a favorite expression in the second, as in the first portion of Isaiah: it expresses God's covenant faithfulness in fulfilling the promises therein: Jeremiah borrows the expression from him. Also Ecclesiasticus 48:22–25 ("comforted"), quotes ch. 40:1 as Isaiah's. Luke 4:17 quotes ch. 61:1, 2 as Isaiah's, and as read as such by Jesus Christ in the synagogue.

The DEFINITENESS of the prophecies is striking: As in the second portion of Isaiah, so in Micah 4:8–10, the *Babylonian* exile, and the deliverance from it, are foretold 150 years before any hostilities had arisen between Babylon and Judah. On the other hand, all the prophets who foretell the *Assyrian* invasion coincide in stating, that Judah should be delivered from *it*, not by Egyptian aid, but directly by the Lord. Again Jeremiah, in the height of the Chaldean prosperity, foretold its conquest by the Medes, who should enter Babylon through the dry bed of the Euphrates on a night of general revelry. No human calculation could have discovered these facts. EICHORN terms these prophecies "veiled historical descriptions," recognizing in spite of himself that they are more than general poetical fancies. Isaiah 53 was certainly written ages before the Messiah, yet it *minutely* portrays His sufferings: these cannot be Jewish inventions, for the Jews looked for a *reigning*, not a suffering, Messiah.

Rationalists are so far right that THE PROPHECIES ARE ON A GENERAL BASIS whereby they are distinguished from soothsaying. They rest on the essential idea of God. The prophets, penetrated by this inner knowledge of His character, became conscious of the eternal laws by which the world is governed: that sin is man's ruin, and must be followed by judgment, but that God's covenant mercy to His elect is unchangeable. Without prophetism, the elect remnant would have decreased, and even God's judgments would have missed their end, by not being recognized as such: they would have been unmeaning, isolated facts. Babylon was in Isaiah's days under Assyria; it had tried a revolt unsuccessfully: but the elements of its subsequent success and greatness were then existing. The Holy Ghost enlightened his natural powers to discern this its rise; and his spiritual faculties, to foresee its fall, the sure consequence, in God's eternal law, of the pride which pagan success generates—and also Judah's restoration, as the covenant people, with whom God, according to His essential character, would not be wroth for ever. True conversion is the prophet's grand remedy against all evils: in this alone consists his politics. Rebuke, threatening, and promise, regularly succeed one another. The idea at the basis of all is in ch. 26:7–9; Lev. 10:3; Amos 3:2.

The USE OF THE PRESENT AND PRETERITE in prophecy is no proof that the author is later than Isaiah. For *seers* view the future as present, and indicate what is *ideally* past, not really past; seeing things in the light of God, who "calls the things that are not as though they were." Moreover, as in looking from a height on a landscape, hills seem close together which are really wide apart, so, in events foretold, the *order, succession,* and *grouping* are presented, but the intervals of *time* are overlooked. The *time,* however, is sometimes marked (Jer. 25:12; Dan. 9:26). Thus the deliverance from Babylon, and that effected by Messiah, are in rapid transition grouped together by THE LAW OF PROPHETIC SUGGESTION; yet no prophet so confounds the two as to make Messiah the leader of Israel from Babylon. *To the prophet* there was probably no double sense; but to his spiritual eye the two events, though distinct, lay so near, and were *so analogous,* that he could not separate them in description without unfaithfulness to the picture presented before him. The more remote and antitypical event, however, viz., Messiah's coming, is that to which he always hastens, and which he describes with far more minuteness than he does the nearer type; e.g., Cyrus (cf. ch. 45:1 with 53). In some cases he takes his stand in the midst of events between (e.g.) the humiliation of Jesus Christ, which he views as *past,* and His glorification, as *yet to come,* using the future tense as to the latter (cf. ch. 53:4–9 with 10–12). Marks of the time of events are given sparingly in the prophets: yet, as to Messiah, definitely enough to create the general expectation of Him at the time that He was in fact born.

The CHALDÆISMS alleged against the genuineness of the second portion of Isaiah, are found more in the first and undoubted portion. They occur in all the Old Testament, especially in the poetical parts, which prefer unusual expressions, and are due to the fact that the patriarchs were surrounded by Chaldee-speaking people; and in Isaiah's time a few Chaldee words had crept in from abroad.

His SYMBOLS are few and simple, and his poetical images correct; in the prophets, during and after the exile, the reverse holds good; Haggai and Malachi are not exceptions; for, though void of bold images, their style, unlike Isaiah's, rises little above prose: a clear proof that our Isaiah was long before the exile. Of VISIONS, strictly so called, he has but one, that in ch. 6; even it is more simple than those in later prophets. But he often gives SIGNS, i.e., a present fact as pledge of the more distant future; God condescending to the feebleness of man (ch. 7:14; 37:30; 38:7).

The VARIETIES IN HIS STYLE do not prove spuriousness, but that he varied his style with his subject. The second portion is not so much addressed to his contemporaries, as to the future people of the Lord, the elect remnant, purified by the previous judgments. Hence its tenderness of style, and frequent repetitions (ch. 40:1): for comforting exhortation uses many words; so also the many epithets added to the name of God, intended as stays whereon faith may rest for comfort, so as not to despair. In both portions alike there are peculiarities characteristic of Isaiah; e.g., "to be called" equivalent to *to be:* the repetition of the same words, instead of synonyms, in the parallel members of verses; the interspersing of his prophecies with hymns: "the remnant of olive trees," etc., for the remnant of people who have escaped God's judgments. Also cf. ch. 65:25 with 11:6.

The CHRONOLOGICAL ARRANGEMENT favors the opinion that Isaiah himself collected his prophecies into the volume; not Hezekiah's men, as the *Talmud* guesses from Proverbs 25:1. All the portions, the dates of which can be ascertained, stand in the right place, except a few instances, where prophecies of similar contents are placed together: with the termination of the Assyrian invasion (chs. 36–39) terminated the public life of Isaiah. The second part is his prophetic legacy to the small band of the faithful, analogous to the last speeches of Moses and of Jesus Christ to His chosen disciples.

The EXPECTATION OF MESSIAH is so strong in Isaiah, that Jerome *ad Paulinum* calls his book not a prophecy, but the *gospel:* "He is not so much a prophet as an evangelist." Messiah was already shadowed forth in Genesis 49:10, as the Shiloh or *tranquillizer;* also in Psalms 2, 45, 72, 110. Isaiah brings it out more definitely; and, whereas they dwelt on His kingly office, Isaiah develops most His priestly and prophetic office; Psalm 110 also had set forth His priesthood, but His *kingly* rather than, as Isaiah, His *suffering,* priesthood. The latter is especially dwelt on in the second part, addressed to *the faithful elect;* whereas the first part, addressed to *the whole people,* dwells on Messiah's *glory,* the antidote to the fears which then filled the people, and the assurance that the kingdom of God, then represented by Judah, would not be overwhelmed by the surrounding nations.

His STYLE (HENGSTENBERG, *Christol.* 1) is simple and sublime; in imagery, intermediate between the poverty of Jeremiah and the exuberance of Ezekiel. He shows his command of it in varying it to suit his subject.

The FORM is mostly that of *Hebrew poetical parallelism,* with, however, a freedom unshackled by undue restrictions.

JUDAH, the less apostate people, rather than Israel, was the subject of his prophecies: his residence was mostly at Jerusalem. On his praises, see Ecclesiasticus 48:22–25. Christ and the apostles quote no prophet so frequently.

CHAPTER 1

Vss. 1-31. **1.** THE GENERAL TITLE OR PROGRAM applying to the entire book: this discountenances the Talmud tradition, that he was sawn asunder by Manasseh. **Isaiah**—equivalent to *"The Lord shall save";* significant of the subject of his prophecies. On "vision," see I Sam. 9:9; Num. 12:6; and my *Introduction.* **Judah and Jerusalem**—Other nations also are the subjects of his prophecies; but only in their relation to the Jews (chs. 13-23); so also the ten tribes of Israel are introduced only in the same relation (chs. 7-9). Jerusalem is particularly specified, being the site of the temple, and the center of the theocracy, and the future throne of Messiah (Ps.

48:2, 3, 9; Jer. 3:17). Jesus Christ is the "Lion of the tribe of Judah" (Rev. 5:5). **Uzziah**—called also Azariah (II Kings 14:21; II Chron. 26). The Old Testament prophecies spiritually interpret the histories, as the New Testament Epistles interpret the Gospels and Acts. Study them together, to see their spiritual relations. Isaiah prophesied for only a few years before Uzziah's death; but his prophecies of that period (chs. 1-6) apply to Jotham's reign also, in which he probably *wrote* none; for ch. 7 enters immediately on Ahaz' reign, after Uzziah in ch. 6; the prophecies under Hezekiah follow next. **2.** The very words of Moses (Deut. 32); this implies that the *law was the charter and basis of all prophecy* (ch. 8:20). **Lord**—*Jehovah;* in *Hebrew,* "the self-

existing and promise-fulfilling, unchangeable One."
The Jews never pronounced this holy name. but
substituted Adonai. The *English Version,* LORD in
capitals, marks the *Hebrew* Jehovah, though *Lord*
is rather equivalent to Adonai than Jehovah.
children—(Exod. 4:22.) **rebelled**—as sons (Deut. 21:
18) and as subjects, God being king in the theocracy
(ch. 63:10). "Brought up," lit., "elevated," viz., to
peculiar privileges (Jer. 2:6-8; Rom. 9:4, 5). **3.** (Jer.
8:7.) **crib**—the stall where it is fed (Prov. 14:4).
Spiritually the word and ordinances. **Israel**—The
whole nation, Judah as well as Israel, in the restricted sense. God regards His covenant people in
their designed unity. **not know**—viz.. his Owner, as
the parallelism requires; i.e., *not recognize* Him as
such (Exod. 19:5, equivalent to "my people," John
1:10, 11). **consider**—*attend* to his Master (ch. 41:8),
notwithstanding the spiritual *food* which He provides (answering to "crib" in the parallel clause).
4. people—the peculiar designation of God's elect
nation (Hos. 1:10), that *they* should be "laden with
iniquity" is therefore the more monstrous. Sin is
a *load* (Ps. 38:4; Matt. 11:28). **seed**—another appellation of God's elect (Gen. 12:7; Jer. 2:21),
designed to be a "holy seed" (ch. 6:13), but, awful
to say, "evildoers;" **children**—by adoption (Hos.
11:1), yet "evildoers"; not only so, but "corrupters"
of others (Gen. 6:12); the climax. So "nation—
people—seed—children." **provoked**—lit., "despised,"
viz., so as to provoke (Prov. 1:30, 31). **Holy One
of Israel**—the peculiar heinousness of their sin, that
it was against *their* God (Amos 3:2). **gone . . .
backward**—lit., "estranged" (Ps. 58:3). **5. Why**—
rather, as *Vulgate,* "On what part." Image from a
body covered all over with marks of blows (Ps. 38:
3). There is no part in which you have not been
smitten. **head . . . sick . . .**—not referring, as it is
commonly quoted, to their *sins,* but to the universality of their *punishment.* However, sin, the moral
disease of the *head* or intellect, and the *heart,* is
doubtless made its own punishment (Prov. 1:31;
Jer. 2:19; Hos. 8:11). "Sick," lit., is in a state of
sickness [GESENIUS]; "has *passed into* sickness"
[MAURER]. **6.** From the lowest to the highest of the
people; "the ancient and honorable, the *head;* the
prophet that teacheth lies, the tail." See Isaiah 9:
13-16. He first states their wretched condition, obvious to all (vss. 6-9); and then, not previously, their
irreligious state, the cause of it. **wounds**—judicially
inflicted (Hos. 5:13). **mollified with ointment**—The
art of medicine in the East consists chiefly in external
applications (Luke 10:34; Jas. 5:14). **7.** Judah had
not in Uzziah's reign recovered from the ravages of
the Syrians in Joash's reign (II Chron. 24:24), and
of Israel in Amaziah's reign (II Chron. 25:13, 23,
etc.). Compare Isaiah's contemporary (Amos 4:6-
11), where, as here (vss. 9, 10), Israel is compared to
"Sodom and Gomorrah," because of the judgments
on it by "fire." **in your presence**—before your eyes:
without your being able to prevent them. **desolate
. . .**—lit., "there is desolation, such as one might look
for from foreign" invaders. **8. daughter of Zion**—
the city (Ps. 9:14), Jerusalem and its inhabitants (II
Kings 19:21): "daughter," *feminine, singular* being
used as a neuter collective noun, equivalent to *sons*
(see below, *Margin,* ch. 12:6) [MAURER]. Metropolis
or "mother-city" is the corresponding term. The
idea of youthful beauty is included in "daughter."
left—as a *remnant* escaping the general destruction.
cottage—a hut, made to give temporary *shelter* to the
caretaker of the vineyard. **lodge**—not permanent.
besieged—rather, as "left," and vs. 9 require,
preserved, viz., from the desolation all round [MAU-

RER]. **9.** Jehovah of Sabaoth, i.e., God of the
angelic and starry hosts (Ps. 59:5; 147:4; 148:2).
The latter were objects of idolatry, called hence
Sabaism (II Kings 17:16). God is above even them
(I Chron. 16:26). "The groves" were symbols of
these starry hosts; it was their worship of Sabaoth
instead of the Lord of Sabaoth, which had caused
the present desolation (II Chron. 24:18). It needed
no less a power than His, to preserve even a "remnant." Condescending grace for the elect's sake,
since He has no need of us, seeing that He has countless hosts to serve Him. **10. Sodom**—spiritually
(Gen. 19; Jer. 23:14; Ezek. 16:46; Rev. 11:8). **11.**
God does not here absolutely disparage sacrifice,
which is as old and universal as sin (Gen. 3:21; 4:4),
and sin is almost as old as the world; but sacrifice,
unaccompanied with obedience of heart and life
(I Sam. 15:22; Ps. 50:9-13; 51:16-19; Hos. 6:6).
Positive precepts are only means; *moral* obedience
is the end. A foreshadowing of the gospel, when
the One real sacrifice was to supersede all the
shadowy ones, and "bring in everlasting righteousness" (Ps. 40:6, 7; Dan. 9:24-27; Heb. 10:1-14).
full—to satiety; weary of **burnt offerings**—burnt
whole, except the blood, which was sprinkled about
the altar. **fat**—not to be eaten by man, but burnt on
the altar (Lev. 3:4, 5, 11, 17). **12. appear before
me**—in the temple where the Shekinah, resting on the
ark, was the symbol of God's presence (Exod. 23:15;
Ps. 42:2). **who hath required this**—as if you were
doing God a service by such hypocritical offerings
(Job 35:7). God did require it (Exod. 23:17), but
not in this spirit (Micah 6:6, 7). **courts**—areas, in
which the worshippers were. None but priests
entered the temple itself. **13. oblations**—unbloody:
"meat (old English sense, not *flesh*) offerings," i.e.,
of flour, fruits, oil, etc. (Lev. 2:1-13). *Hebrew,
mincha.* **incense**—put upon the sacrifices, and
burnt on the altar of incense. Type of prayer (Ps.
141:2; Rev. 8:3). **new moons**—observed as festivals
(Num. 10:10; 28:11, 14) with sacrifices and blowing
of silver trumpets. **sabbaths**—both the seventh day
and the beginning and closing days of the great
feasts (Lev. 23:24-39). **away with**—bear, MAURER
translates, "I cannot *bear iniquity and* the solemn
meeting," i.e., the meeting associated with iniquity—
lit., the *closing* days of the feasts; so the great days
(Lev. 23:36; John 7:37). **14. appointed**—the sabbath, passover, pentecost, day of atonement, and
feast of tabernacles [HENGSTENBERG]; they alone
were fixed to certain times of the year. **weary**—
(ch. 43:24.) **15.** (Ps. 66:18; Prov. 28:9; Lam. 3:43,
44.) **spread . . . hands**—in prayer (I Kings 8:22).
Hebrew, "bloods," for *all* heinous sins, persecution
of God's servants especially (Matt. 23:35). It was
the vocation of the prophets to dispel the delusion,
so contrary to the law itself (Deut. 10:16), that outward ritualism would satisfy God. **16.** God saith
to the sinner, "Wash *you,*" etc., that he, finding his
inability to "make" himself "clean," may cry to *God,*
Wash me, cleanse me (Ps. 51:2, 7, 10). **before mine
eyes**—not mere outward reformation before *man's*
eyes, who cannot, as God, see into the heart (Jer.
32:19). **17. seek judgment**—*justice,* as magistrates,
instead of *seeking* bribes (Jer. 22:3, 16). **judge**—
vindicate (Ps. 68:5; Jas. 1:27). **18.** God deigns to
argue the case with us, that all may see the just, nay,
loving principle of His dealings with men (ch. 43:26).
scarlet—the color of Jesus Christ's robe when bearing our "sins" (Matt. 27:28). So Rahab's thread
(Josh. 2:18; cf. Lev. 14:4). The rabbins say that
when the lot used to be taken, a *scarlet* fillet was
bound on the scapegoat's head, and after the high

priest had confessed his and the people's sins over it, the fillet became *white:* the miracle ceased, according to them, forty years before the destruction of Jerusalem, i.e., exactly when Jesus Christ was crucified; a remarkable admission of adversaries. *Hebrew* for "scarlet" radically means *double-dyed;* so the *deep-fixed permanency* of sin in the heart, which no mere tears can wash away. **snow**—(Ps. 51:7.) Repentance is presupposed, before sin can be made white as snow (vss. 19, 20); *it* too is God's gift (Jer. 31:18, end; Lam. 5:21; Acts 5:31). **red**—refers to "blood" (vs. 15). **as wool**—restored to its original undyed whiteness. This verse shows that the old fathers did not look only for transitory promises (Article VII, BOOK OF COMMON PRAYER). For sins of ignorance, and such like, alone had trespass offerings appointed for them; greater guilt therefore needed a greater sacrifice, for, "without shedding of blood there was no remission"; but none such was appointed, and yet forgiveness was promised and expected; therefore spiritual Jews must have looked for the One Mediator of both Old Testament and New Testament, though dimly understood. **19, 20.** *Temporal* blessings in "the land of their possession" were prominent in the Old Testament promises, as suited to the childhood of the Church (Exod. 3:17). New Testament *spiritual* promises derive their imagery from the former (Matt. 5:5). **Lord hath spoken it**—Isaiah's prophecies rest on the law (Lev. 26:33). God alters not His word (Num. 23:19) **21. faithful**—as a wife (ch. 54:5; 62:5; Hos. 2: 19, 20). **harlot**—(Ezek. 16:28-35.) **righteousness lodged**—(II Pet. 3:13.) **murderers**—murderous *oppressors,* as the antithesis requires (*Note,* vs. 15; I John 3:15). **22.** Thy princes and people are degenerate in *solid worth,* equivalent to "silver" (Jer. 6; 28, 30; Ezek. 22:18, 19), and in their use of *the living Word,* equivalent to "wine" (Song of Sol. 7:9). **mixed**—lit., "circumcised." So the *Arabic,* "to murder" wine, equivalent to dilute it. **23. companions of thieves**—by connivance (Prov. 29:24). **gifts**—(Ezek. 22:12.) A nation's corruption begins with its rulers. **24. Lord ... Lord**—*Adonai,* JEHO-VAH. **mighty One of Israel**—mighty to take vengeance, as before, to save. **Ah**—indignation. **ease me**—My long tried patience will *find relief* in at last punishing the guilty (Ezek. 5:13). God's language condescends to human conceptions. **25. turn**— **hand**—not in wrath, but in *grace* (Zech. 13:7), "upon *thee,*" as vss. 26, 27 show; contrasted with the *enemies,* of whom He will *avenge* Himself (vs. 24). **purely**—lit., "as alkali purifies." **dross ... tin**—not *thy sins,* but the sinful *persons* (Jer. 6:29); "enemies" (vs. 24); degenerate princes (*Note,* vs. 22), intermingled with the elect "remnant" of grace. **tin**— *Hebrew, bedil,* here the alloy of lead, tin, etc., separated by smelting from the silver. The pious Bishop Bedell took his motto from this. **26.** As the degeneracy had shown itself most in the *magistrates* (vss. 17-23), so, at the "restoration," these shall be such as the theocracy "at the first" had contemplated, viz., after the Babylonish restoration in part and typically, but fully and antitypically under Messiah (ch. 32:1; 52:8; Jer. 33:7; Matt. 19:28). **faithful**—no longer "an harlot." **27. redeemed**—temporarily, civilly, and morally; type of the spiritual *redemption* by the *price* of Jesus Christ's blood (I Pet. 1:18, 19), the foundation of "judgment" and "righteousness," and so of pardon. The *judgment* and *righteousness* are God's first (ch. 42:21; Rom. 3: 26); so they become man's when "converted" (Rom. 8:3, 4); typified in the display of God's "justice," then exhibited in delivering His covenant people,

whereby justice or "righteousness" was produced in them. **converts**—so MAURER. But *Margin,* "they that return of her," viz., the remnant that return from captivity. However, as Isaiah had not yet expressly foretold the Babylonian captivity, the *English Version* is better. **28. destruction**—lit., "breaking into shivers" (Rev. 2:27). The prophets hasten forward to the final extinction of the ungodly (Ps. 37:20; Rev. 19:20; 20:15); of which antecedent judgments are types. **29. ashamed**—(Rom. 6:21.) **oaks**—Others translate the "terebinth" or "turpentine tree." Groves were dedicated to idols. Our Druids took their name from the *Greek* for "oaks." A sacred tree is often found in Assyrian sculpture; symbol of the starry hosts, Saba. **gardens**—planted enclosures for idolatry; the counterpart of the garden of Eden. **30. oak**—Ye shall be like the "oaks," the object of your "desire" (vs. 29). People become like the gods they worship; they never rise above their level (Ps. 135:18). So men's sins become their own scourges (Jer. 2:9). The leaf of the idol oak fades by a law of necessary consequence, having no living sap or "water" from God. So "garden" answers to "gardens" (vs. 29). **31. strong** —powerful rulers (Amos 2:9), **maker of it**—rather, his work. He shall be at once the fuel, "tow," and the cause of the fire, by kindling the first "spark." **both**—the wicked ruler, and "his work," which "is as a spark."

CHAPTER 2

Vss. 1-22. **1.** The inscription. **The word**—the revelation. **2.** Same as Micah 4. As Micah prophesied in Jotham's reign, and Isaiah in Uzziah's, Micah rests on Isaiah, whom he confirms: not vice versa. HENGSTENBERG on slight grounds makes Micah 4 the original. **last days**—i.e., Messiah's: especially the days yet to come, to which all prophecy hastens, when "the house of the God *of Jacob,*" viz., at Jerusalem, shall be the center to which the converted nations shall flock together (Matt. 13:32; Luke 2:31, 32; Acts 1:6, 7); where "the kingdom" of Israel is regarded as certain and the *time* alone uncertain (Ps. 68:15, 16; 72:8, 11). **mountain of the Lord's house ... in the top ...**—the temple on Mount Moriah: type of the Gospel, beginning at Jerusalem, and, like an object set on the highest hill, made so conspicuous that all nations are attracted to it. **flow**—as a broad stream (ch. 66:12). **3.** If the curse foretold against Israel has been literally fulfilled, so shall the promised blessing be literal. We Gentiles must not, while giving them the curse, deny them their peculiar blessing by spiritualizing it. The Holy Ghost shall be poured out for *a general* conversion then (Jer. 50:5; Zech. 8:21, 23; Joel 2:28). **from Jerusalem**—(Luke 24:47) an earnest of the future relations of Jerusalem to Christendom (Rom. 11:12, 15). **4. judge**—as a sovereign umpire, settling all controversies (cf. ch. 11:4). LOWTH translates work, conviction. **plowshares**— in the East resembling a short sword (ch. 9:6, 7; Zech. 9:10). **5.** The connection is: As Israel's high destiny is to be a blessing to all nations (Gen. 12:3), let Israel's children walk worthy of it (Eph. 5:8). **6. Therefore**—rather, "For": reasons why there is the more need of the exhortation in vs. 5. **thou**— transition to Jehovah: such rapid transitions are natural, when the mind is full of a subject. **replenished**—rather, filled, viz., with the superstitions of the East, Syria, and Chaldea. **soothsayers**—forbidden (Deut. 18:10-14). **Philistines**—southwest of

Palestine: antithesis to "the east." **please them-selves**—rather, join hands with, i.e., enter into alliances, matrimonial and national: forbidden (Exod. 23:32; Neh. 13:23, etc.). **7. gold**—forbidden to be heaped together (Deut. 17:17). Solomon disobeyed (I Kings 10:21, 27). **horses . . . chariots**—forbidden (Deut. 17:16). But Solomon disobeyed (I Kings 20:26). Horses could be used effectively for war in the plains of Egypt; not so in the hilly Judea. God designed there should be as wide as possible a distinction between Israel and the Egyptians. He would have His people wholly dependent on Him, rather than on the ordinary means of warfare (Ps. 20:7). Also horses were connected with idolatry (II Kings 23:11); hence His objection: so the transition to "idols" (vs. 8) is natural. **8.** (Hos. 8:4.) Not so much public idolatry, which was not sanctioned in Uzziah's and Jotham's reign, but (see II Kings 15:4, 35) as *private*. **9. mean**—in rank: not morally base: opposed to **"the great man." The** former is in *Hebrew, Adam,* the latter, *ish*. **boweth** —viz., to idols. *All* ranks were idolaters. **forgive . . . not**—a threat expressed by an imperative. Isaiah so identifies himself with God's will, that he prays for that which he knows God purposes. So Revelation 18:6. **10.** Poetical form of expressing that, such were their sins, they would be obliged by God's judgments to seek a hiding-place from His wrath (Rev. 6:15, 16). **dust**—equivalent to "caves of the earth," or dust (vs. 19). **for fear . . .**—lit., "from the face of the terror of the Lord." **11. lofty looks**— lit., "eyes of pride" (Ps. 18:27). **humbled**—by calamities. God will so vindicate His honor "in that day" of judgments, that none else "shall be exalted" (Zech. 14:9). **12.** Man has had many days: "the day of the Lord" shall come at last, beginning with judgment, a never-ending day in which God shall be "all in all" (I Cor. 15:28; II Pet. 3:10). **every**—not merely *person,* as *English Version* explains it, but every *thing* on which the nation prided itself. **13. cedars . . . oaks**—image for haughty nobles and princes (Amos 2:9; Zech. 11:1, 2; cf. Rev. 19:18-21). **Bashan**—east of Jordan, north of the river Jabbok, famous for fine oaks, pasture, and cattle. Perhaps in "oaks" there is reference to their idolatry (ch. 1: 29). **14. high . . . hills**—referring to the "high places" on which sacrifices were unlawfully offered, even in Uzziah's (equivalent to Azariah) reign (II Kings 15:4). Also, *places* of strength, fastnesses in which they trusted, rather than in God; so **15. tower . . . wall**—*Towers* were often made on the walls of cities. **fenced**—strongly fortified. **16. Tarshish**— *Tartessus* in southwest Spain, at the mouth of the Guadalquivir, near Gibraltar. It includes the adjoining region: a Phœnician colony; hence its connection with Palestine and the Bible (II Chron. 9:21). The name was also used in a wide sense for *the farthest west,* as our West Indies (ch. 66:19; Ps. 48:7; 72:10). "Ships of Tarshish" became a phrase for *richly laden* and *far-voyaging* vessels. The judgment shall be on all that minister to man's luxury (cf. Rev. 18:17-19). **pictures**—ordered to be destroyed (Num. 33:52). Still to be seen on the walls of Nineveh's palaces. It is remarkable that whereas all other ancient civilized nations, Egypt, Assyria, Greece, Rome, have left monuments in the fine arts, Judea, while rising immeasurably above them in the possession of "the living oracles," has left none of the former. The fine arts, as in modern Rome, were so often associated with polytheism, that God required His people in this, as in other respects, to be separate from the nations (Deut. 4:15-18). But *Vulgate* translation is perhaps better, "All

that is beautiful to the sight"; not only paintings, but all luxurious ornaments. One comprehensive word for all that goes before (cf. Rev. 18:12, 14, 16). **17.** Repeated from vs. 11, for emphatic confirmation. **18. idols**—lit., "vain things," "nothings" (I Cor. 8:4). Fulfilled to the letter. *Before* the Babylonian captivity the Jews were most prone to idolatry; in no instance, *ever since.* For the future fulfilment, see Zechariah 13:2; Revelation 13:15; 19:20. **19.** The fulfilment answers exactly to the threat (vs. 10). they—the idol-worshippers. **caves**—abounding in Judea, a hilly country; hiding-places in times of alarm (I Sam. 13:6). **shake . . . earth**—and the heavens also (Heb. 12:26). Figure for severe and universal judgments. **20. moles**—Others translate "mice." The sense is, *under ground,* in darkness. **bats**—unclean birds (Lev. 11:19), living amidst tenantless ruins (Rev. 11:13). **22.** The high ones (vss. 11, 13) on whom the people trust, shall be "brought low" (ch. 3:2); therefore "cease from" depending on them, instead of on the Lord (Ps. 146:3-5).

CHAPTER 3

Vss. 1-26. **1. For**—continuation of ch. 2:22. **Lord of hosts**—therefore able to do as He says. **doth** —present for future, so certain is the accomplishment. **stay . . . staff**—the same *Hebrew* word, the one masculine, the other feminine, an *Arabic* idiom for *all kinds of support.* What a change from the previous luxuries (ch. 2:7)! Fulfilled in the siege by Nebuchadnezzar and afterwards by Titus (Jer. 37: 21; 38:9). **2.** Fulfilled (II Kings 24:14). **prudent**— the *Hebrew* often means a "soothsayer" (Deut. 18: 10-14); thus it will mean, the diviners, on whom they rely, shall in that day fail. It is found in a good sense (Prov. 16:10), from which passage the Jews interpret it *a king;* "without" whom Israel long has been (Hos. 3:4). **ancient**—old and experienced (I Kings 12:6-8). **3. captain of fifty**—not only captains of thousands, and centurions of a hundred, but even semi-centurions of fifty, shall fail. **honourable** —lit., "of dignified aspect." **cunning**—skilful. The mechanic's business will come to a standstill in the siege and subsequent desolation of the state; artisans are no mean "stay" among a nation's safeguards. **eloquent orator**—rather, as *Vulgate,* "skilled in whispering," i.e., incantation (Ps. 58:5). See ch. 8:19 below; and *Note* on "prudent" (vs. 2) above. **4. children**—in ability for governing; antithesis to the "ancient" (see vs. 12; Eccles. 10:16). **babes**—in warlike might; antithesis to "the mighty" and "man of war." **5.** The anarchy resulting under such imbecile rulers (vs. 4); unjust exactions mutually; the forms of respect violated (Lev. 19:32). **base**—low-born. Compare the marks of "the last days" (II Tim. 3:2). **6.** Such will be the want of men of wealth and ability, that they will "take hold of" (ch. 4:1) the first man whom they meet, having any property, to make him "ruler." **brother**—one having no better hereditary claim to be ruler than the "man" supplicating him. **Thou hast clothing**— which none of us has. Changes of raiment are wealth in the East (II Kings 5:5). **ruin**—Let our ruined affairs be committed to thee to retrieve. **7. swear**—lit., "lift up," viz., his hand; the gesture used in solemn attestation. Or, his voice, i.e., answer; so *Vulgate.* **healer**—of the body politic, incurably diseased (ch. 1:6). **neither . . . clothing**—so as to relieve the people and maintain a ruler's dignity. A nation's state must be bad indeed, when none among men, naturally ambitious, is willing to accept office.

8. Reason given by the prophet, why all shrink from the government. **eyes of his glory**—to provoke His "glorious" Majesty before His "eyes" (cf. ch. 49: 5; Hab. 1:13). The *Syriac* and LOWTH, by a slight change of the *Hebrew*, translate, "the *cloud* of His glory," the Shekinah. **9. show**—The *Hebrew* means, "that which may be *known* by their countenances" [GESENIUS and WEISS]. But MAURER translates, "Their respect for person"; so *Syriac* and *Chaldee*. But the parallel word "declare" favors the other view. KIMCHI, from the *Arabic*, translates "their hardness" (Job 19:3, *Margin*), or impudence of countenance (Jer. 3:3). They have lost not only the substance of virtue, but its color. **witness**—lit., "corresponds" to them; their look answers to their inner character (Hos. 5:5). **declare**—(Jude 13). "Foaming *out* their own shame"; so far from making it a secret, "glorying" in it (Phil. 3:19). **unto themselves**—Cf. "in themselves" (Prov. 1:31; 8:36; Jer. 2:19; Rom. 1:27). **10.** The faithlessness of many is no proof that *all* are faithless. Though nothing but croaking of frogs is heard on the surface of the pool, we are not to infer there are no fish beneath [BENGEL]. (See ch. 1:19, 20.) **fruit of doings**—(Prov. 1:31) in a good sense (Gal. 6:8; Rev. 22:14). Not salvation by works, but by fruit-bearing faith (ch. 45:24; Jer. 23:6). GESENIUS and WEISS translate, *Declare as to* the righteous that, etc. MAURER, "Say that *the righteous is blessed.*" **11. ill**—antithesis to "well" (vs. 10); emphatic ellipsis of the words italicized. "Ill!" **hands**—his conduct; "hands" being the instrument of acts (Eccles. 8:12, 13). **12.** (See vs. 4.) **oppressors**—lit., "exactors," i.e., exacting princes (ch. 60:17). They who *ought* to be *protectors* are *exactors;* as unqualified for rule as "children," as effeminate as "women." Perhaps it is also implied that they were under the influence of their harem, the women of their court. **lead**—*Hebrew,* "call thee blessed"; viz., the false *prophets,* who flatter the people with promises of safety in sin; as the political "rulers" are meant in the first clause. **way of thy paths**—(Jer. 6:16.) The right way set forth in the law. "Destroy"—*Hebrew,* "Swallow up," i.e., cause so utterly to disappear that not a vestige of it is left. **13. standeth up**—no longer *sitting* in silence. **plead**—indignant against a wicked people (ch. 66:16; Ezek. 20:35). **14. ancients**—Hence they are spoken of as "taken away" (vss. 1, 2). **vineyard**—the Jewish theocracy (ch. 5:1-7; Ps. 80:9-13). **eaten up**—"burnt"; viz., by "oppressive exactions" (vs. 12). Type of the crowning guilt of the husbandmen in the days of Jesus Christ (Matt. 21:34-41). **spoil . . . houses**—(Matt. 23:14.) **15.** What right have ye to beat, etc. (Ps. 94:5; Mic. 3:2, 3). **grind**—by exactions, so as to leave them nothing. **faces**—persons; with the additional idea of it being *openly* and *palpably* done. "Presence," equivalent to (*Hebrew*) "face." **16.** Luxury had become great in Uzziah's prosperous reign (II Chron. 26:5). **stretched forth**—proudly elevated (Ps. 75:5). **wanton**—rather, "making the eyes to glance about," viz., wantonly (Prov. 6:13) [MAURER]. But LOWTH, "falsely setting off the eyes with paint." Women's eyelids in the East are often colored with stibium, or powder of lead (*Note,* Job 42:14; Jer. 4:30, *Margin*). **mincing**—tripping with short steps. **tinkling**—with their ankle-rings on both feet, joined by small chains, which sound as they walk, and compel them to take short steps; sometimes little bells were attached (vss. 18, 20). **17. smite with a scab**—lit., "make bald," viz., by disease. **discover**—cause them to suffer the greatest indignity that can befall female captives, viz. to be stripped naked, and

have their persons exposed (ch. 47:3; cf. with ch. 20:4). **18. bravery**—the finery. **tinkling**—(See vs. 16.) **cauls**—network for the head. Or else, from an *Arabic* root, "little suns," answering to the "tires" or neck-ornaments, "like the moon" (Judg. 8:21). The *chumarah* or crescent is also worn in front of the head-dress in West Asia. **19. chains**—rather, pendants, hanging about the neck, and dropping on the breast. **mufflers**—veils covering the face, with apertures for the eyes, close above and loosely flowing below. The word radically means "tremulous," referring to the changing effect of the spangles on the veil. **20. bonnets**—turbans. **ornaments of the legs**—the short stepping-chains from one foot to another, to give a measured gait; attached to the "tinkling ornaments" (vs. 16). **headbands**—lit., "girdles." **tablets**—rather, houses of the breath, i.e., smelling-boxes [*Vulgate*]. **earrings**—rather, amulets suspended from the neck or ears, with magic formulæ inscribed; the root means to "whisper" or "conjure." **21. nose jewels**—The cartilage between the nostrils was bored to receive them; they usually hung from the left nostril. **22.** Here begin *entire* articles of apparel. Those before were single ornaments. **changeable**—from a root, "to put off"; not worn commonly; put on and off on special occasions. So, dress-clothes (Zech. 3:4). **mantles**—fuller tunics with sleeves, worn over the common one, reaching down to the feet. **wimples**—i.e., mufflers, or hoods. In Ruth 3:15, veils; perhaps here, a broad cloak, or shawl, thrown over the head and body. **crisping pins**—rather, money bags (II Kings 5:23). **23. glasses**—mirrors of polished metal (Exod. 38:8). But LXX, a transparent, gauzelike, garment. **hoods**—miters, or diadems (ch. 62:3; Zech. 3:5). **veils**—large enough to cover the head and person. Distinct from the smaller veils ("mufflers") above (Gen. 24:65). Token of woman's subjection (I Cor. 11:10). **24. stink**—arising from ulcers (Zech. 14:12). **girdle**—to gird up the loose Eastern garments, when the person walked. **rent**—LXX, better, a "rope," an emblem of poverty; the poor have nothing else to gird up their clothes with. **well-set hair**—(I Pet. 3:3, 4.) **baldness**—(vs. 17.) **stomacher**—a broad plaited girdle. **sackcloth**—(II Sam. 3:31.) **burning**—a sunburnt countenance, owing to their hoods and veils being stripped off, while they had to work as captives under a scorching sun (Song of Sol. 1:6). **25. Thy men**—of Jerusalem. **26. gates**—The place of concourse personified is represented mourning for the loss of those multitudes which once frequented it. **desolate . . . sit upon . . . ground**—the very figure under which Judea was represented on medals after the destruction by Titus: a *female sitting* under a palm tree in a posture of grief; the motto, *Judæa capta* (Job 2:13; Lam. 2:10, where, as here primarily, the destruction by Nebuchadnezzar is alluded to).

CHAPTER 4

Vss. 1-6. **1. that day**—the calamitous period described in previous chapter. **seven**—indefinite number among the Jews. So many men would be slain, that there would be very many more women than men; e.g., seven women, contrary to their natural bashfulness, would sue to (equivalent to "take hold of," ch. 3:6) one man to marry them. **eat . . . own bread**—foregoing the privileges, which the law (Exod. 21:10) gives to wives, when a man has more than one. **reproach**—of being unwedded and childless; especially felt among the Jews, who were looking for "the seed of the woman," Jesus

Christ, described in vs. 2; ch. 54:1, 4; Luke 1:25. **2.** In contrast to those on whom vengeance falls, there is a manifestation of Jesus Christ to the "escaped of Israel" in His characteristic attributes, *beauty* and *glory,* typified in Aaron's garments (Exod. 28:2). Their *sanctification* is promised as the fruit of their being "written" in the book of life by sovereign love (vs. 3); the means of it are the "spirit of judgment" and that of "burning" (vs. 4). Their "defense" by the special presence of Jesus Christ is promised (vss. 5, 6). **branch**—the sprout of JEHOVAH. Messiah (Jer. 23:5; 33:15; Zech. 3:8; 6:12; Luke 1:78, *Margin*). The parallel clause does not, as MAURER objects, oppose this; for "fruit of the earth" answers to "branch"; He shall not be a dry, but a *fruit-bearing branch* (ch. 27:6; Ezek. 34:23-27). He is "of the *earth*" in His birth and death, while He is also "of the *Lord*" (*Jehovah*) (John 12:24). His name, "the Branch," chiefly regards His descent from David, *when the family was low and reduced* (Luke 2:4, 7, 24); a sprout with more than David's glory, springing as from a decayed tree (ch. 11:1; 53: 2; Rev. 22:16). **excellent**—Heb. 1:4; 8:6). **comely**—(Song of Sol. 5:15, 16; Ezek. 16:14). **escaped of Israel**—the elect remnant (Rom. 11:5); (1) in the return from Babylon; (2) in the escape from Jerusalem's destruction under Titus; (3) in the still future assault on Jerusalem, and deliverance of "the third part"; events mutually analogous, like concentric circles (Zech. 12:2-10; 13:8, 9, etc.; 14:2; Ezek. 39: 23-29; Joel 3). **3. left in Zion**—equivalent to the "escaped of Israel" (vs. 2). **shall be called**—shall *be* (ch. 9:6). **holy**—(ch. 52:1; 60:21; Rev. 21:27.) **written**—in the book of life, antitypically (Phil. 4:3; Rev. 3:5; 17:8). Primarily, in the *register* kept of *Israel's* families and tribes. **living**—not "blotted out from the registry, as *dead;* but written there as among the "escaped of Israel" (Dan. 12:1; Ezek. 13: 9). To the *elect of Israel,* rather than the saved in general, the *special* reference is here (Joel 3:17). **4. When**—i.e., After. **washed**—(Zech. 13:1). **filth**—moral (ch. 1:21-25). **daughters of Zion**—same as in ch. 3:16. **purged**—purified by judgments; destroying the ungodly, correcting and refining the godly. **blood**—(ch. 1:15.) **spirit**—Whatever God does in the universe, He does by His *Spirit,* "without the hand" of man (Job 34:20; Ps. 104:30). Here He is represented using His power as *Judge.* **burning**—(Matt. 3:11, 12). The same Holy Ghost, who sanctifies believers by the fire of affliction (Mal. 3:2, 3), dooms unbelievers to the fire of perdition (I Cor. 3:13-15). **5. create**—The "new creation" needs as much God's creative omnipotence, as the material creation (II Cor. 4:6; Eph. 2:10). So it shall be in the case of the Holy Jerusalem to come (ch. 65:17, 18). **upon**—The pillar of cloud stood over the tabernacle, as symbol of God's favor and presence (Exod. 13:21, 22; Ps. 91:1). Both on *individual families* ("every dwelling") and on the *general* sacred "assemblies" (Lev. 23:2). The "cloud" became a "fire" by night in order to be seen by the Lord's people. **upon all the glory**—"upon the glorious whole"; viz., the Lord's people and sanctuary [MAURER]. May it not mean, "Upon whatever the glory (the *Shekinah* spoken of in the previous clause) shall rest, there shall be a defense." The symbol of His presence shall ensure also safety. So it was to Israel against the Egyptians at the Red Sea (Exod. 14:19, 20). So it shall be to literal Jerusalem hereafter (Zech. 2:5). Also to the Church, the spiritual "Zion" (ch. 32:18; 33:15-17; Heb. 12:22). **tabernacle**—Christ's body (John 1:14). "The Word 'tabernacled' (*Greek* for 'dwelt') among us" (John

2:21; Heb. 8:2). It is a "shadow from the heat" and "refuge from the storm" of divine wrath against man's sins (ch. 25:4). Heat and storms are violent in the East; so that a portable tent is a needful part of a traveller's outfit. Such shall be God's wrath hereafter, from which the "escaped of Israel" shall be sheltered by Jesus Christ (ch. 26:20, 21; 32:2). **covert**—answering to "defense" (vs. 5). The *Hebrew* for *defense* in vs. 5, is "covering"; the lid of the ark or mercy seat was named from the same *Hebrew* word, *caphar;* the *propitiatory;* for it, being sprinkled with blood by the high priest once a year, on the day of atonement, *covered* the people typically from wrath. Jesus Christ is the true Mercy Seat, on whom the Shekinah rested, the *propitiatory,* or atonement, beneath whom the law is kept, as it was literally within the ark, and man is *covered* from the storm. The redeemed Israel shall also be, by union with Him, a tabernacle for God's glory, which, unlike that in the wilderness, shall not be taken down (ch. 38:20).

CHAPTER 5

Vss. 1-30. PARABLE OF JEHOVAH'S VINEYARD. A new prophecy; entire in itself. Probably delivered about the same time as chs. 2 and 3, in Uzziah's reign. Cf. vss. 15, 16 with ch. 2:17; and vs. 1 with ch. 3:14. However, the close of the chapter alludes *generally* to the still distant invasion of Assyrians in a later reign (cf. vs. 26 with ch. 7:18; and vs. 25 with ch. 9:12). When the time drew nigh, according to the ordinary prophetic usage, he handles the details *more particularly* (chs. 7, 8); viz., the calamities caused by the Syro-Israelitish invasion, and subsequently by the Assyrians whom Ahaz had invited to his help. **1. to**—rather, "concerning" [GESENIUS], i.e., in the person of My beloved, as His representative [VITRINGA]. Isaiah gives a hint of the distinction and yet unity of the Divine Persons (cf. *He* with *I,* vss. 2, 3). **of my beloved**—inspired by Him; or else, a tender song [CASTALIO]. By a slight change of reading "a song of His love" [HOUBIGANT]. "The Beloved" is Jehovah, the Second Person, the "Angel" of God the Father, not in His character as incarnate *Messiah,* but as *God of the Jews* (Exod. 23:20, 21; 32:34; 33:14). **vineyard**—ch. 3:14; Ps. 80:8, etc.). The Jewish covenant people, separated from the nations for His glory, as the object of His peculiar care (Matt. 20:1; 21:33). Jesus Christ in the "vineyard" of the New Testament Church is the same as the Old Testament Angel of the Jewish covenant. **fruitful hill**—lit., "a horn" ("peak," as the Swiss *shreckhorn*) *of the son of oil;* poetically, for *very fruitful.* Suggestive of isolation, security, and a sunny aspect. Isaiah alludes plainly to the Song of Solomon (Song of Sol. 6:3; 8:11, 12), in the words *"His* vineyard" and *"my* Beloved" (cf. ch. 26:20; 61:10, with Song of Solomon 1:4; 4:10). The transition from "branch" (ch. 4:2) to "vineyard" here is not unnatural. **2. fenced**—rather, "digged and trenched" the ground to prepare it for planting the vines [MAURER]. **choicest vine**—*Hebrew, sorek;* called still in Morocco, *serki;* the grapes had scarcely perceptible seeds; the Persian *kishmish* or *bedana,* i.e., without seed (Gen. 49:11). **tower**—to watch the vineyard against the depredations of man or beast, and for the use of the owner (Matt. 21:33). **winepress**—including the winefat; both hewn, for coolness, out of the rocky undersoil of the vineyard. **wild grapes**—The *Hebrew* expresses offensive putrefaction, answering to the corrupt state of the Jews.

Fetid fruit of the wild vine [MAURER], instead of "choicest" grapes. Of the poisonous monk's hood [GESENIUS]. The Arabs call the fruit of the nightshade "wolf-grapes" (Deut. 32:32, 33; II Kings 4:39-41). Jerome tries to specify the details of the parable; the "fence," *angels;* the "stones gathered out," *idols;* the "tower," the *temple* "in the midst" of Judea; the "winepress," the *altar.* **3. And now** ... —appeal of God to themselves, as in ch. 1:18; Mic. 6:3. So Jesus Christ, in Matthew 21:40, 41, alluding in the very form of expression to this, makes them pass sentence on themselves. God condemns sinners "out of their own mouth" (Deut. 32:6; Job 15:6; Luke 19: 22; Rom. 3:4). 4. God has done all that could be done for the salvation of sinners, consistently with His justice and goodness. The God of nature is, as it were, amazed at the unnatural fruit of so well-cared a vineyard. **5. go to**—i.e., attend to me. **hedge ... wall**—It had both; a proof of the care of the owner. But now it shall be trodden down by wild beasts (enemies) (Ps. 80:12, 13). **6. I will ... command**—The parable is partly dropped and Jehovah, as in vs. 7, is implied to be the Owner: for He alone, not an ordinary husbandman (Matt. 21:43; Luke 17:22), could give such a "command." **no rain**—antitypically, *the heaven-sent teachings of the prophets* (Amos 8:11). Not accomplished in the Babylonish captivity; for Jeremiah, Ezekiel, Daniel, Haggai, and Zechariah prophesied during or after it. But in gospel times. **7.** Isaiah here applies the parable. It is no mere *human* owner, nor *a literal* vineyard that is meant. **vineyard of the Lord**—His *only* one (Exod. 19:5; Amos 3:2). **pleasant**—"the plant of his delight"; just as the husbandman was at pains to select the *sorek,* or "choicest vine" (vs. 2); so God's election of the Jews. **judgment**—justice. The play upon words is striking in the *Hebrew,* "He looked for *mishpat,* but behold *mispat* (bloodshed); for *tsedaqua,* but behold *tseaqua* (the cry that attends anarchy, covetousness, and dissipation, vs. 8, 11, 12; compare the cry of the rabble by which justice was overborne in the case of Jesus Christ, Matt. 27:23, 24). **8-23.** SIX DISTINCT WOES AGAINST CRIMES. **8.** (Lev. 25:13; Mic. 2:2.) The jubilee restoration of possessions was intended as a guard against avarice. **till there be no place**—left for any one else. **that they may be**—rather, and ye be. **the earth**—the land. **9. In mine ears ... the Lord**—viz., has revealed it, as in ch. 22:14. **desolate**—lit., "a desolation," viz., on account of the national sins. **great and fair**—houses. **10. acres**—lit., "yokes"; as much as one yoke of oxen could plow in a day. **one**—only. **bath**—of wine; seven and a half gallons. **homer ... ephah**—Eight bushels of seed would yield only three pecks of produce (Ezek. 45:11). The ephah and bath, one-tenth of an homer. **11.** Second **Woe**—against intemperance. **early**—when it was regarded especially shameful to drink (Acts 2:15; I Thess. 5:7). Banquets for revelry began earlier than usual (Eccles. 10:16, 17). **strong drink**—*Hebrew, sichar,* implying intoxication. **continue**—drinking all day till evening. **12.** Music was common at ancient feasts (ch. 24:8, 9; Amos 6:5, 6). **viol**—an instrument with twelve strings (JOSEPHUS, *Antiquities* 8. 10). **tabret**—*Hebrew, toph,* from the use of which in drowning the cries of children sacrificed to Moloch, *Tophet* received its name. *Arabic, duf.* A kettle drum, or tambourine. **pipe**—flute or flageolet: from a *Hebrew* root "to bore through"; or else, "to dance" (cf. Job 21; 11-15). **regard not ... Lord**—a frequent effect of feasting (Job 1:5; Ps. 28:5). **work ... operation**—in punishing the guilty

(vs. 19; ch. 10:12). **13. are gone**—The prophet sees the *future* as if it were before his eyes. **no knowledge**—because of their foolish recklessness (vs. 12; ch. 1:3; Hos. 4:6; Luke 19:44). **famished**—awful contrast to their luxurious feasts (vss. 11, 12). **multitude**—plebeians in contradistinction to the "honorable men," or nobles. **thirst**—(Ps. 107:4, 5.) Contrast to their drinking (vs. 11). In their deportation and exile, they shall hunger and thirst. **14. hell**—the grave; *Hebrew, sheol; Greek, hades;* the unseen world of spirits. Not here, the place of torment. Poetically, it is represented as enlarging itself immensely, in order to receive the countless hosts of Jews, which should perish (Num. 16:30). **their**—i.e., of the Jewish people. **he that rejoiceth**—the drunken reveller in Jerusalem. **15.** (Cf. ch. 2:9, 11, 17.) *All* ranks, "mean" and "mighty" alike; so "honorable" and "multitude" (vs. 13). **16.** God shall be "exalted" in man's view, because of His manifestation of His "justice" in punishing the guilty. **sanctified**—*regarded as holy* by reason of His "righteous" dealings. **17. after their manner**—lit., according to their own word, i.e., *at will.* Otherwise, *as in their own pasture* [GESENIUS]: so the *Hebrew* in Micah 2:12. The lands of the Scenite tent-dwellers (Jer. 35:7). Arab shepherds in the neighborhood shall roam at large, the whole of Judea being so desolate as to become a vast pasturage. **waste ... fat ones**—the *deserted* lands of *the rich* (Ps. 22:29, "fat"), then gone into captivity; "strangers," i.e., nomad tribes shall make their flocks to feed on [MAURER]. Figuratively, "the lambs" are the pious, "the fat ones" the impious. So tender disciples of Jesus Christ (I John 21:15) are called "lambs"; being meek, harmless, poor, and persecuted. Cf. Ezekiel 39:18, where the fatlings are the rich and great (I Cor. 1:26, 27). The "strangers" are in this view the "other sheep not of" the Jewish "fold (John 10:16), the *Gentiles* whom Jesus Christ shall "bring" to be partakers of the rich privileges (Rom. 11:17) which the Jews ("fat ones," Ezek. 34:16) fell from. Thus "after their (own) manner" will express that the Christian Church should worship God in freedom, released from legal bondage (John 4:23; Gal. 5:1). **18.** Third **Woe**—against obstinate perseverance in sin, as if they wished to provoke divine judgments. **iniquity**—guilt, incurring punishment [MAURER]. **cords ... cart rope**—Rabbins say, "An evil inclination is at first like a fine *hair-string,* but the finishing like a *cart-rope.*" The antithesis is between the slender *cords* of sophistry, like the spider's web (ch. 59:5; Job 8:14), with which one sin *draws* on another, until he at last bind themselves with great guilt as with a *cart-rope.* They strain every nerve in sin. **vanity**—wickedness. **sin**—substantive, not a verb: they draw on themselves "sin" and its penalty recklessly. **19. work**—vengeance (vs. 12). Language of defiance to God. So Lamech's boast of impunity (Gen. 4:23, 24; cf. Jer. 17:15; II Pet. 3:3, 4). **counsel**—God's threatened purpose to punish. **20.** Fourth **Woe**—against those who confound the distinctions of right and wrong (cf. Rom. 1:28), "reprobate," *Greek,* "undiscriminating: the moral perception darkened." **bitter ... sweet**—sin is *bitter* (Jer. 2:19; 4:18; Acts 8:23; Heb. 12:15); though it seem sweet for a time (Prov. 9:17, 18). Religion is *sweet* (Ps. 119:103). **21.** Fifth **Woe**—against those who were so "wise in their own eyes" as to think they knew better than the prophet, and therefore rejected his warnings (ch. 29:14, 15). **22, 23.** Sixth **Woe**—against corrupt judges, who, "mighty" in drinking "wine" (a boast still not uncommon), if not in defending their country, obtain the means of self-indulgence by taking bribes ("reward"). The two verses are closely joined [MAURER]. **mingle strong drink**—not with *water*, but *spices* to make it intoxicating (Prov. 9:2, 5; Song of Sol. 8:2). **take away the righteousness**—set aside the just claims of those having a righteous cause. **24. Lit.**, "tongue of fire eateth" (Acts 2:3). **flame consumeth the chaff**—rather, withered grass falleth before the flame (Matt. 3:12). **root . . . blossom**—*entire* decay, both the hidden *source* and outward *manifestations* of prosperity, perishing (Job 18:16; Mal. 4:1). **cast away . . . law**—in its spirit, while retaining the letter. **25. anger . . . kindled**—(II Kings 22:13, 17.) **hills . . . tremble**—This probably fixes the date of this chapter, as it refers to the *earthquake in the days of Uzziah* (Amos 1:1; Zech. 14:5). The earth trembled as if conscious of the presence of God (Jer. 4:24; Hab. 3:6). **torn**—rather, were as dung (Ps. 83:10). **For all this . . .**—This burden of the prophet's strains, with dirge-like monotony, is repeated at ch. 9:12, 17, 21; 10:4. With all the past calamities, still heavier judgments are impending; which he specifies in the rest of the chapter (Lev. 26:14, etc.). **26. lift . . . ensign**—to call together the hostile nations to execute His *judgments* on Judea (ch. 10:5-7; 45:1). But for *mercy* to it, in ch. 11:12; 18:3. **hiss**—(cf. 7:18.) Bees were drawn out of their hives by the sound of a flute, or *hissing*, or *whistling* (Zech. 10:8). God will collect the nations round Judea like bees (Deut. 1:44; Ps. 118:12). **end of the earth**—the widely distant subject races of which the Assyrian army was made up (ch. 22:6). The ulterior fulfilment took place in the siege under Roman Titus. Cf. "end of the earth" (Deut. 28:49, etc.). So the pronoun is *singular* in the *Hebrew*, for "them," "their," "whose" (him, his, etc.), vss. 26, 27, 28, 29; referring to some *particular* nation and person [HORSLEY]. **27. weary**—with long marches (Deut. 25:18). **none . . . slumber**—requiring no rest. **girdle**—with which the ancient loose robes used to be girded for action. Ever ready for march or battle. **nor the latchet . . . broken**—The soles were attached to the feet, not by upper leather as with us, but by straps. So securely clad that not even a strap of their sandals gives way, so as to impede their march. **28. bent**—ready for battle. **hoofs . . . flint**—The ancients did not shoe their horses: hence the value of hard hoofs for long marches. **wheels**—of their chariots. The Assyrian army abounded in cavalry and chariots (ch. 22:6, 7; 36:8). **29. roaring**—their battle cry. **30. sorrow, and the light is darkened**—Otherwise, *puɐ ssǝɹ̣sɪp light* (i.e., hope and fear) alternately succeed (as usually occurs in an unsettled state of things), *and darkness arises in*, etc. [MAURER]. **heavens**—lit., "clouds," i.e., its sky is rather "clouds" than sky. Otherwise from a different *Hebrew* root, "in its destruction" or ruins. HORSLEY takes "sea . . . look unto the land" as a new image taken from mariners in a coasting vessel (such as all ancient vessels were), *looking for the* nearest *land,* which the *darkness* of the storm conceals, so that *darkness and distress* alone may be said to be visible.

CHAPTER 6

Vss. 1-13. VISION OF JEHOVAH IN HIS TEMPLE. Isaiah is outside, near the altar in front of the temple. The doors are supposed to open, and the veil hiding the Holy of Holies to be withdrawn, unfolding to his view a vision of God represented as an Eastern monarch, attended by seraphim as His min-

isters of state (I King 22:19), and with a robe and flowing train (a badge of dignity in the East), which filled the temple. This assertion that he had seen God was, according to tradition (not sanctioned by ch. 1:1; see *Introduction*), the pretext for sawing him asunder in Manasseh's reign (Heb. 11:37). Visions often occur in the other prophets: in Isaiah there is only this one, and it is marked by characteristic clearness and simplicity. **In . . . year . . . Uzziah died**—Either *literal* death, or *civil* when he ceased as a leper to exercise his functions as king [CHALDEE], (II Chron. 26:19-21). 754 B.C. [CALMET]; 578 [COMMON CHRONOLOGY.] This is not the first beginning of Isaiah's prophecies, but his inauguration to a higher degree of the prophetic office: vs. 9, etc., implies the tone of one who had already experience of the people's obstinacy. **Lord**—here *Adonai; Jehovah* in vs. 5; *Jesus Christ* is meant as speaking in vs. 10, according to John 12:41. Isaiah could only have "seen" *the Son,* not the divine essence (John 1:18). The words in vs. 10 are attributed by Paul (Acts 28:25, 26) to the *Holy Ghost.* Thus the Trinity in unity is implied; as also by the thrice "Holy" (vs. 3). Isaiah mentions the robes, temple, and seraphim, but not the form of God Himself. Whatever it was, it was different from the usual Shekinah: that was on the mercy seat, this on a throne; that a cloud and fire, of this no form is specified: over that were the cherubim, over this the seraphim; that had no clothing, this had a flowing robe and train. **2. stood**—not necessarily the posture of *standing;* rather, *were in attendance on Him* [MAURER], hovering on expanded wings. **the**—not in the *Hebrew.* **seraphim**—nowhere else applied to God's attendant angels; but to *the fiery flying* (not winged, but *rapidly moving*) serpents, which bit the Israelites (Num. 21: 6), called so from the poisonous *inflammation* caused by their bites. *Seraph* is to burn; implying the *burning* zeal, dazzling *brightness* (II Kings 2:11; 6: 17; Ezek. 1:13; Matt. 28:3) and serpent-like *rapidity* of the seraphim in God's service. Perhaps Satan's form as a *serpent* (*nachash*) in his appearance to man has some connection with his original form as a seraph of light. The head of the serpent was the symbol of *wisdom* in Egypt (cf. Num. 21:8; II Kings 18:4). The seraphim, with six wings and one face, can hardly be identified with the cherubim, which had four wings (in the temple only *two*) and four faces (Ezek. 1:5-12). (But cf. Rev. 4:8.) The "face" and "feet" imply a human form; something of a serpentine form (perhaps a basilisk's head, as in the temples of Thebes) may have been mixed with it: so the cherub was compounded of various animal forms. However, seraph may come from a root meaning "princely," applied in Daniel 10:13 to Michael [MAURER]; just as cherub comes from a root (changing *m* into *b*), meaning "noble." **twain** —Two wings alone of the six were kept ready for instant flight in God's service; two veiled their faces as unworthy to look on the holy God, or pry into His secret counsels which they fulfilled (Exod. 3:6; Job 4:18; 15:15); two covered their feet, or rather the whole of the *lower parts* of their persons—a practice usual in the presence of Eastern monarchs, in token of reverence (cf. Ezek. 1:11, *their bodies*). Man's service *a fortiori* consists in reverent waiting on, still more than in active service for, God. **3.** (Rev. 4:8.) The Trinity is implied (see *Note* on "Lord." vs. 1). God's *holiness* is the keynote of Isaiah's whole prophecies. **whole earth**—the *Hebrew* more emphatically, *the fulness of the whole earth* is His *glory* (Ps. 24:1; 72:19). **4. posts of . . . door**—rather, foundations of the thresholds. **house**

—temple. **smoke**—the Shekinah cloud (I Kings 8: 10; Ezekiel 10:4.) **undone**—(Exod. 33:20.) The same effect was produced on others by the presence of God (Judg. 6:22; 13:22; Job 42:5, 6; Luke 5:8; Rev. 1:17). **lips**—appropriate to the context which describes the praises of the *lips,* sung in alternate responses (Exod. 15:20, 21; vs. 3) by the seraphim: also appropriate to the office of *speaking* as the prophet of God, about to be committed to Isaiah (vs. 9). **seen**—not strictly Jehovah Himself (John 1:18; I Tim. 6:16), but the symbol of His presence. **Lord**—*Hebrew,* JEHOVAH. **6. unto me**—The seraph had been in the temple, Isaiah *outside of it.* **live coal**—lit., "a hot stone," used, as in some countries in our days, to roast meat with, e.g., the meat of the sacrifices. Fire was a symbol of purification, as it takes the dross out of metals (Mal. 3:2, 3). **the altar**—of burnt offering, in the court of the priests before the temple. The fire on it was at first kindled by God (Lev. 9:24), and was kept continually burning. **7. mouth . . . lips**—(Cf. *Note,* vs. 5). The *mouth* was touched because it was the part to be used by *the prophet* when inaugurated. So "*tongues* of fire" rested on the disciples (Acts. 2:3, 4) when they were being set apart to *speak* in various languages of Jesus. **iniquity**—conscious unworthiness of acting as God's messenger. **purged**—lit., "covered," i.e., expiated, not by any physical effect of fire to cleanse from sin, but in relation to the *altar sacrifices,* of which Messiah, who here commissions Isaiah, was in His death to be the antitype: it is implied hereby that it is only by sacrifice sin can be pardoned. **8. I . . . us**—The change of number indicates the Trinity (cf. Gen. 1:26; 11:7). Though not a sure *argument* for the doctrine, for the *plural may* indicate merely majesty, it *accords* with that truth proved elsewhere. **Whom . . . who**—implying that *few* would be willing to bear the self-denial which the delivering of such an unwelcome message to the Jews would require on the part of the messenger (cf. I Chron. 29:5). **Here am I**—prompt zeal, now that he has been specially qualified for it (vs. 7; ch. I Sam. 3:10, 11; Acts 9:6). **9. Hear . . . indeed**—*Hebrew,* "In hearing hear," i.e., *Though ye hear* the prophet's warnings *again and again,* ye are doomed, because of your perverse will (John 7:17), *not to understand.* Light enough is given in revelation to guide those sincerely seeking to *know,* in order that they may *do,* God's will; darkness enough is left to confound the wilfully blind (ch. 43:8). So in Jesus' use of parables (Matt. 13:14). **see . . . indeed**—rather, "though ye *see again and again,*" yet, etc. **10. Make . . . fat**—(Ps. 119:17.) "Render them the more hardened by thy warnings" [MAURER]. This effect is the fruit, not of *the truth* in itself, but of the corrupt state of *their hearts,* to which God here judicially gives them over (ch. 63: 17). GESENIUS takes the imperatives as futures. "Proclaim truths, the *result* of which proclamation *will be* their becoming the more hardened" (Rom. 1:28; Eph. 4:18); but this does not so well as the former set forth God as *designedly* giving up sinners to *judicial* hardening (Rom. 11:8; II Thess. 2:11). In the first member of the sentence, the order is, *the heart, ears, eyes;* in the latter, the reverse order, *the eyes, ears, heart.* It is from the *heart* that corruption flows into the *ears and eyes* (Mark 7:21, 22); but through *the eyes and ears healing* reaches the *heart* (Rom. 10:17), [BENGEL]. (Jer. 5:21; Ezek. 12: 2; Zech. 7:11; Acts 7:57; II Tim. 4:4.) In Matthew 13:15, the words are quoted in the *indicative,* "is waxed gross" (so the LXX), not the *imperative,*

"make fat"; God's word as to the future is as certain as if it were already fulfilled. To *see with one's eyes* will not convince a will that is opposed to the truth (cf. John 11:45, 46; 12:10, 11). "One must *love* divine things in order to *understand* them" [PASCAL]. **be healed**—of their spiritual malady, sin (ch. 1:6; Ps. 103:3; Jer. 17:14). **11. how long**—will this wretched condition of the nation being hardened to its destruction continue? **until**—(ch. 5:9)—fulfilled primarily at the Babylonish captivity, and more fully at the dispersion under the Roman Titus. **12.** (II Kings 25:21.) **forsaking**—abandonment of dwellings by their inhabitants (Jer. 4:29). **13. and it shall return, and . . . be eaten**—Rather, *but it shall be again* given over *to be consumed:* if even a tenth survive the first destruction, it shall be destroyed by a second (ch. 5:25; Ezek. 5:1-5, 12), [MAURER and HORSLEY]. In *English Version,* "return" refers to the poor remnant left in the land at the Babylonish captivity (II Kings 24:14; 25:12), which afterwards fled to Egypt in fear (II Kings 25:26), and subsequently *returned* thence along with others who had fled to Moab and Edom (Jer. 40:11, 12), and suffered under further divine judgments. **teil**—rather, *terebinth or turpentine tree* (ch. 1:29). **substance . . . when . . . cast . . . leaves**—rather, "As a *terebinth* or *oak in which, when they are cast down* (not 'cast their leaves,' Job 14:7), *the trunk* or *stock* remains, *so the holy seed* (Ezra 9:2) *shall be the stock of that* land." The seeds of vitality still exist in both the land and the scattered people of Judea, waiting for the returning spring of God's favor (Rom. 11:5, 23-29). According to Isaiah, not all Israel, but the *elect remnant alone,* is destined to salvation. God shows unchangeable severity towards sin, but covenant faithfulness in preserving a remnant, and to it Isaiah bequeaths the prophetic legacy of the second part of his book (ch. 40-66).

CHAPTER 7

Chapters 7, 8, and 9:1-7. PREDICTION OF THE ILL SUCCESS OF THE SYRO-ISRAELITISH INVASION OF JUDAH—AHAZ' ALLIANCE WITH ASSYRIA, AND ITS FATAL RESULTS TO JUDEA—YET THE CERTAINTY OF FINAL PRESERVATION AND OF THE COMING OF MESSIAH. In the Assyrian inscriptions the name of Rezin, king of Damascus, is found among the tributaries of Tiglath-pileser, of whose reign the annals of seventeen years have been deciphered. For the historical facts in this chapter, cf. II Kings 15:37-16:9. Rezin of Syria and Pekah of Israel, as confederates, advanced against Jerusalem. In the first campaign (II Chron. 28) they "smote Ahaz with a great slaughter." Their object was probably to unite the three kingdoms against Assyria. Egypt seems to have favored the plan, so as to interpose these confederate kingdoms between her own frontier and Assyria (cf. vs. 18, "Egypt"; and II Kings 17:4, Hoshea's league with Egypt). Rezin and Pekah may have perceived Ahaz' inclination towards Assyria rather than towards their own confederacy; this and the old feud between Israel and Judah (I Kings 12:16) occasioned their invasion of Judah. Ahaz, at the *second* inroad of his enemies (cf. II Chronicles 28 and II Kings 15:37, with ch. 16:5), smarting under his former defeat, applied to Tiglath-pileser, in spite of Isaiah's warning in this chapter, that he should rather rely on God; that king accordingly attacked Damascus, and slew Rezin (II Kings 9); and probably it was at the same time that he carried away part of Israel captive (II Kings 15:

29), unless there were *two* assaults on Pekah—that in II Kings 15:29, the earlier, and that in which Tiglath helped Ahaz subsequently [G. V. SMITH]. Ahaz was saved at the sacrifice of Judah's independence and the payment of a large tribute, which continued till the overthrow of Sennacherib under Hezekiah (ch. 37; II Kings 16:8, 17, 18; II Chron. 28:20). Ahaz' reign began about 741 B.C., and Pekah was slain in 738 [WINER]. **1. Ahaz**—In the first years of his reign the design of the two kings against Judah was carried out, which was formed in Jotham's reign (II Kings 15:37). **Syria**—*Hebrew, Aram* (Gen. 10: 22, 23), originally the whole region between the Euphrates and Mediterranean, including *Assyria*, of which *Syria* is an abbreviation; here the region round Damascus, and along Mount Libanus. **Jerusalem—** An actual siege of it took place, but was foiled (II Kings 16:5). **2. is confederate with**—rather, *is encamped upon* the territory of Ephraim [MAURER], or better, as Rezin was encamped against *Jerusalem*, *"is supported by"* [LOWTH] Ephraim, whose land lay between Syria and Judah. The mention of "David" alludes, in sad contrast with the present, to the time when David made Syria subject to him (II Sam. 8:6). **Ephraim**—the ten tribes. **as . . . trees of . . . wood—** a simultaneous agitation. **3. Go forth**—out of the city, to the place where Ahaz was superintending the works for defense and the cutting off of the water supply from the enemy, and securing it to the city. So ch. 22:9; II Chron. 32:4. **Shearjashub**—i.e., A remnant shall return (ch. 6:13). His very name (cf. vs. 14; ch. 8:3) was a standing memorial to Ahaz and the Jews that the nation should not, notwithstanding the general calamity (vss. 17-25; ch. 8:6-8), be utterly destroyed (ch. 10:21, 22). **conduit**—an aqueduct from the pool or reservoir for the supply of the city. At the foot of Zion was Fount Siloah (ch. 8:6; Neh. 3:15, John 9:7), called also Gihon, on the west of Jerusalem (II Chron. 32:30). Two pools were supplied from it, *the Upper,* or *Old* (ch. 22:11), or *King's* (Neh. 2:14), and *the Lower* (ch. 22:9), which received the superfluous waters of the upper. The upper pool is still to be seen, about seven hundred yards from the Jaffa gate. The highway leading to the fullers' field, which was in a position near water for the purposes of washing, previous to drying and bleaching, the cloth, was probably alongside the aqueduct. **4. Take heed,** etc.—i.e., *See that* thou be quiet (not seeking Assyrian aid in a fit of panic). **tails**—mere *ends* of firebrands, almost consumed themselves (about soon to fall before the Assyrians, vs. 8), therefore harmless. **smoking**—as about to go out; not *blazing*. **son of Remaliah**—Pekah, a usurper (II Kings 15:25). The Easterners express contempt by designating one, not by his own name, but by his father's, especially when the father is but little known (I Sam. 20:27, 31). **6. vex**—rather, "throw into consternation" [GESENIUS]. **make a breach—** rather, "cleave it asunder." Their scheme was to divide a large portion of the territory between themselves, and set up a vassal king of their own over the rest. **son of Tabeal**—unknown; a Syrian-sounding name, perhaps favored by a party in Jerusalem (ch. 3:6, 9, 12). **7.** (Ch. 8:10; Prov. 21:30.) **8. head—** i.e., in both Syria and Israel the *capital* shall remain as it is; they shall not conquer Judah, but each shall possess only his own dominions. **threescore and five . . . not a people**—As these words break the symmetry of the parallelism in this verse, either they ought to be placed after "Remaliah's son," in vs. 9, or else they refer to some older prophecy of Isaiah, or of Amos (as the Jewish writers represent), parenthetically; to which, in vs. 8, the words, "If ye will

not believe . . . not be established," correspond in parallelism. *One* deportation of Israel happened within one or two years from this time, under Tiglath-pileser (II Kings 15:29). *Another* in the reign of Hoshea, under Shalmaneser (II Kings 17:1-6), was about twenty years after. But the final one which utterly "broke" up Israel so as to be "not a people," accompanied by a colonization of Samaria with foreigners, was under Esar-haddon, who carried away Manasseh, king of Judah, also, in the twenty-second year of his reign, sixty-five years from the utterance of this prophecy (cf. Ezra 4:2, 3, 10, with II Kings 17:24; II Chron. 33:11) [USHER]. The event, though so far off, was enough to assure the people of Judah that as God, the Head of the theocracy, would *ultimately* interpose to destroy the enemies of His people, so they might rely on Him *now*. **9. believe, . . . be established**—There is a paronomasia, or play on the words, in the *Hebrew:* "if ye will not *confide,* ye shall not *abide*." Ahaz brought distress on himself by distrust in the Lord, and trust in Assyria. **11. Ask thee**—since thou dost not credit the prophet's words. **sign**—a miraculous token to assure thee that God will fulfil His promise of saving Jerusalem (ch. 37:30; 38:7, 8). "Signs," facts then present or near at hand as pledges for the more distant future, are frequent in Isaiah. **ask . . . in . . . depth**—lit., "Make deep, . . . ask it," i.e., Go to the depth of the earth or of *Hades* [*Vulgate* and LOWTH], or, Mount high for it (lit., "Make high"). So in Matthew 16:1. Signs in *heaven* are contrasted with the signs on earth and below it (raising the dead) which Jesus Christ had wrought (cf. Rom. 10:6, 7). He offers Ahaz the widest limits within which to make his choice. **12. neither . . . tempt**—hypocritical pretext of keeping the law (Deut. 6:16); "tempt," i.e., put God to the proof, as in Matthew 4:7, by seeking His miraculous interposition without warrant. But here there *was* the warrant of the prophet of God; to have asked a sign, when thus offered, would not have been a *tempting* of God. Ahaz' true reason for declining was his resolve not to do God's will, but to negotiate with Assyria, and persevere in his idolatry (II Kings 16:7, 8, 3, 4, 10). Men often excuse their distrust in God, and trust in their own devices, by *professed* reverence for God. Ahaz may have fancied that though Jehovah was the God of Judea and could work a sign there, that was no proof that the local god of Syria might not be more powerful. Such was the common heathen notion (ch. 10:10, 11:36:18-20). **13. Is it a small thing?**—Is it not enough for you (Num. 16:9)? The allusion to "David" is in order to contrast *his* trust in God with his degenerate descendant Ahaz' distrust. **weary**—try the patience of. **men**—prophets. Isaiah as yet had given no outward proof that he was from God; but now God has offered a sign, which Ahaz publicly rejects. The sin is therefore *now* not merely against "men," but openly against "God." Isaiah's manner therefore changes from mildness to bold reproof. **14. himself**—since thou wilt not ask a sign, nay, rejectest the offer of one. **you**—for the sake of the house of believing "David" (God remembering His everlasting covenant with David), not for unbelieving Ahaz' sake. **Behold**—arresting attention to the extraordinary prophecy. **virgin**—from a root, "to lie hid," virgins being closely kept from men's gaze in their parents' custody in the East. The *Hebrew,* and LXX here, and *Greek* (Matt. 1: 23), have the article, *the* virgin, some definite one known to the speaker and his hearers; primarily, the woman, then a virgin, about immediately to become the second wife, and bear a child, whose attainment of the age of discrimination (about three years) should be preceded by the deliverance of Judah from its two invaders; its fullest significancy is realized in *"the* woman" (Gen. 3:15), whose seed should bruise the serpent's head and deliver captive man (Jer. 31: 22; Mic. 5:3). Language is selected such as, while *partially* applicable to the immediate event, receives its *fullest*, most appropriate, and exhaustive accomplishment in Messianic events. The New Testament application of such prophecies is not a strained "accommodation"; rather the temporary fulfilment of an adaptation of the far-reaching prophecy to the present passing event, which foreshadows typically the great central end of prophecy, Jesus Christ (Rev. 19:10). Evidently the wording is such as to apply more fully to Jesus Christ than to the prophet's son; "virgin" applies, in its simplest sense, to the Virgin Mary, rather than to the prophetess who ceased to be a *virgin* when she "conceived"; "Immanuel," *God with us* (John 1:14; Rev. 21:3), cannot in a strict sense apply to Isaiah's son, but only to Him who is presently called expressly (ch. 9:6), "the Child, the Son, Wonderful (cf. ch. 8:18), the mighty *God."* Local and temporary features (as in vss. 15, 16) are added in every type; otherwise it would be no type, but the thing itself. There are resemblances to the great Antitype sufficient to be recognized by those who seek them; dissimilarities enough to confound those who do not desire to discover them. **call**–i.e., *she* shall, or as *Margin, thou, O Virgin, shalt call;* mothers often named their children (Gen. 4:1, 25; 19:37; 29:32). In Matthew 1:23 the expression is strikingly changed into, *"They* shall call"; when the prophecy received its *full* accomplishment, no longer is the name Immanuel restricted to the *prophetess'* view of His character, as in its partial fulfilment in her son; *all* shall then call (i.e., not literally), or *regard* Him as *peculiarly and most fitly characterized by the descriptive name,* "Immanuel" (I Tim. 3:16; Col. 2:9). **name**–not mere appellation, which neither Isaiah's son nor Jesus Christ bore literally; but what describes His manifested attributes; His *character* (so ch. 9:6). The name in its proper destination was not arbitrary, but characteristic of the individual; sin destroyed the faculty of perceiving the internal being; hence the severance now between the name and the character; in the case of Jesus Christ and many in Scripture, the Holy Ghost has supplied this want [OLSHAUSEN]. **15. Butter**– rather, curdled milk, the acid of which is grateful in the heat of the East (Job 20:17). **honey**–abundant in Palestine (Judg. 14:8; I Sam. 14:25; Matt. 3: 4). Physicians directed that the first food given to a child should be honey, the next milk [BARNAB. Ep.]. HORSLEY takes this as implying the real humanity of the Immanuel Jesus Christ, about to be fed as other infants (Luke 2:52). Verse 22 shows that besides the fitness of milk and honey for children, a state of *distress* of the inhabitants is *also* implied, when, by reason of the invaders, milk and honey, things produced *spontaneously,* shall be the only abundant articles of food [MAURER]. **that he may know**–rather, until He shall know. **evil . . . choose . . . good**–At about three years of age moral consciousness begins (cf. ch. 8:4; Deut. 1:39; Jonah 4:11). **16. For**–The deliverance implied in the name "Immanuel," and the cessation of distress as to food (vss. 14, 15), shall last only till the child grows to know good and evil; for. . . . **the land that . . . abhorrest . . . forsaken of . . . kings**–rather, desolate shall be the land, before whose two kings thou art alarmed [HENGSTENBERG and GENESIUS]. **the**

land–viz., Syria and Samaria regarded as one (II Kings 16:9; 15:30), just *two* years after this prophecy, as it foretells. HORSLEY takes it, "The land (Judah and Samaria) of (the former of) which thou art the plague (lit., "thorn") shall be forsaken," etc.; a prediction thus, that Judah and Israel (appropriately regarded as *one* "land") should cease to be kingdoms (Luke 2:1; Gen. 49:10) before Immanuel came.

17-25. FATAL CONSEQUENCES OF AHAZ' ASSYRIAN POLICY. Though temporary deliverance (ch. 7:16; 8:4) was to be given then, and final deliverance through Messiah, sore punishment shall follow the former. After subduing Syria and Israel, the Assyrians shall encounter Egypt (II Kings 23:29), and Judah shall be the battlefield of both (vs. 18), and be made tributary to that very Assyria (II Chron. 28: 20; II Kings 16:7, 8) now about to be called in as an ally (ch. 39:1-6). Egypt, too, should prove a fatal ally (ch. 36:6; 31:1, etc.). **18. hiss**–whistle, to bring bees to settle (*Note*, ch. 5:26). **fly**–found in numbers about the arms of the Nile and the canals from it (ch. 19:5-7; 23:3), here called "rivers." Hence arose the plague of flies (Exod. 8:21). Figurative, for *numerous* and *troublesome* foes from the remotest parts of Egypt, e.g., Pharaoh-necho. **bee**– (Deut. 1:44; Ps. 118:12.) As numerous in Assyria as the fly in marshy Egypt. Sennacherib, Esarhaddon, and Nebuchadnezzar fulfilled this prediction. **19. rest**–image of flies and bees kept up. The enemy shall overspread the land *everywhere*, even in "desolate valleys." **thorns**–wild, contrasted with "bushes," which were *valued* and objects of care (see *Margin*). **20. razor**–The Assyrians are to be God's *instrument* of devastating Judea, just as a razor sweeps away all hair before it (ch. 10:5; Ezek. 29:19, 20). **hired**–alluding to Ahaz' hiring (II Kings 16:7, 8) Tiglath-pileser against Syria and Israel; namely, **by them beyond the river**–viz., the Euphrates; the eastern boundary of Jewish geographical knowledge (Ps. 72:8); the river which Abram crossed; the Nile also may be included (vs. 18) [G. V. SMITH]. GESENIUS translates, "With a razor *hired in the parts beyond the river."* **head . . . feet**–the *whole* body, including the most honored parts. To cut the "beard" is the greatest indignity to an Easterner (ch. 50:6; II Sam. 10: 4, 5; Ezek. 5:1). **21-25. THE COMING DESOLATE STATE OF THE LAND OWING TO THE ASSYRIANS AND EGYPTIANS. nourish**–i.e., own. **young cow** –a heifer giving milk. *Agriculture* shall cease, and the land become one great *pasturage.* **22. abundance**–by reason of the wide range of land lying desolate over which the cows and sheep (including goats) may range. **butter**–thick milk, or *cream.* **honey**–(*Note,* vs. 15). Food of *spontaneous* growth will be the resource of the *few* inhabitants left. Honey shall be abundant as the bees will find the wild flowers abounding everywhere. **23. where there were . . .**–where up to that time there was so valuable a vineyard as to have in it 1000 vines, worth a silverling (*shekel,* about 50 cents; *a large price)* each, there shall be only briers (Song of Sol. 8:11). Vineyards are estimated by the number of the vines, and the goodness of the kind of vine. Judea admits of a high state of cultivation, and requires it, in order to be productive; its present barrenness is due to neglect. **24.** It shall become a vast hunting ground, abounding in wild beasts (cf. Jer. 49:19). **25. shall be**–rather, were once. **digged**–in order to plant and rear vines (ch. 5:6). **there shall not come**–i.e., none shall come who fear thorns, seeing that thorns shall abound on all sides [MAURER]. Otherwise, "Thou shalt not come *for fear of thorns*" [GESENIUS]. Only cattle shall be able to penetrate the briery ground. **lesser cattle**—sheep and goats.

CHAPTER 8

Chapters 8 and 9:1-7. The first seven verses of ch. 9 belong to this section. Ch. 8 continues the subject of ch. 7, but at a later preiod (cf. ch. 8:4 with ch. 7:16; implying that the interval till the accomplishment is shorter now than then. The tone of ch. 8:17, 21, 22, expresses calamity more immediate and afflictive than ch. 7:4, 15, 22. **1. great**—suitable, for letters large enough to be read by all. **roll**—rather, *tablet* of wood, metal, or stone (ch. 30: 8; Hab. 2:2); sometimes coated with wax, upon which characters were traced with a pointed instrument, or iron stylus; skins and papyrus were also used (ch. 19:7). **man's pen**—i.e., in ordinary characters which the humblest can read (so Hab. 2:2). *Hebrew, enosh* means a "common man," is contrasted with the *upper ranks* (Rev. 21:17; Rom. 3:5). Not in hieroglyphics. The object was that, after the event, all might see that it had been predicted by Isaiah. **concerning**—the title and subject of the prophecy. **Maher-shalal-hash-baz**—"They (i.e., the Assyrians) hasten to the spoil (viz., to spoil Syria and Samaria), they speed to the prey" [GESENIUS]. Otherwise, "The spoil (i.e., spoiler) hastens, the rapine speeds forward" [MAURER]. **2. I took**—rather, "The Lord said to me, that I should take," etc. [MAURER]. **Uriah**—an accomplice of Ahaz in idolatry, and therefore a witness not likely to assist the prophet of God in getting up a *prophecy after the event* (II Kings 16:10). The witnesses were in order that when the event should come, they might testify that the tablet containing the prophecy had been inscribed with it at the time that it professed. **Zechariah**—(II Chron. 29:13.) **3. prophetess**—perhaps the same as the "virgin" (ch. 7:14); in the interim married as Isaiah's second wife: this is in the primary and temporary sense. Immanuel is even in this sense distinct from Maher-shalal-hash-baz. Thus nineteen months at least intervene from the prophecy (ch. 7:14), nine before the birth of Immanuel, and ten from that time to the birth of Maher-shalal-hash-baz: adding eleven or twelve months *before* the latter could cry, "Father" (ch. 8:4), we have about three years in all, agreeing with ch. 7:15, 16. **4. before . . .**—within a year. **6. waters of Shiloah . . . softly**—Their source is on the southeast of Zion and east of Jerusalem. It means "sent," the water being *sent* through an aqueduct (John 9:7). Figurative for the mild, though now weak, sway of the house of David; in the highest sense Shiloah expresses the benignant sway of Jehovah in the theocracy, administered through David. Contrast to the violent Euphrates, "the river" that typifies Assyria (vs. 7; Rev. 17:15). "This people" refers both to *Israel,* which preferred an alliance with Rezin of Syria to one with the kings of Judah, and to *Judah,* a party in which seems to have favored the pretentions of the son of Tabeal against David's line (ch. 7:6; also to *Judah's desire to seek an Assyrian alliance* is included in the censure (cf. ch. 7:17). Verse 14 shows that both nations are meant; both alike rejected the divine Shiloah. Not "*My* people," as elsewhere, when God expresses favor, but "this people" (ch. 6:9). **7. therefore**—for the reason given in vs. 6, the Assyrian flood, which is first to overflood Syria and Samaria, shall rise high enough to reach rebel Judah also (vs. 8). **the**

river—Euphrates swollen in spring by the melting of the snow of the Armenian mountains (cf. vs. 6; ch. 7:20). **all his glory**—Eastern kings travel with a gorgeous retinue. **channels**—natural and artificial in the level region, Mesopotamia. **8. pass through**—The flood shall not stop at Syria and Samaria, but shall *penetrate into* Judea. **the neck**—When the waters reach to the neck, a man is near drowning; still the *head* is not said to be overflowed. Jerusalem, elevated on hills, is the head. The danger shall be so imminent as to reach near it at Sennacherib's invasion in Hezekiah's reign; but it shall be spared (ch. 30:28). **wings**—the extreme bands of the Assyrian amies, fulfilled (ch. 36:1; 37:25). **thy land, O Immanuel**—Though temporarily applied to Isaiah's son, in the *full* sense this is applicable only to Messiah, that Judea is *His,* was, and still is, a pledge that, however sorely overwhelmed, it shall be saved at last; the "head" is safe even now, waiting for the times of restoration (Acts 1:6); at the same time these words imply that, notwithstanding the temporary deliverance from Syria and Israel, implied in "Immanuel," the greatest calamities are to follow to Judah. **9. Associate yourselves**—rather, "Raise tumults," or, Rage, i.e., Do your worst [MAURER], referring perhaps to the attack of Rezin and Pekah on Jerusalem. **and . . . be broken in pieces**—rather, "yet ye shall be thrown into consternation." *Imperative* in the *Hebrew,* according to the idiom whereby the second of two imperatives implies the *future,* viz., the consequence of the action contained in the first (so ch. 6:9). The name "Immanuel" in vs. 8 (cf. vs. 10) suggests the thought of the ultimate safety of *Immanuel's land,* both from its present two invaders, and even from the Assyrians, notwithstanding the grievous flood wherewith the previous verses foretell they shall deluge it. The succession of the house of David cannot be set aside in Judah, for Immanuel Messiah is to be born in it as heir of David, of whom Isaiah's son is but a type (ch. 9:4, 6). **give ear . . . far countries**—witness the discomfiture of Judah's enemies. The prophecy probably looks on *also* to the final conspiracy of Antichrist and his supporters against the Heir of David's throne in the latter days and their utter overthrow [HORSLEY]. **gird yourselves . . . gird yourselves**—The repetition expresses vehemently the *certainty* of their being *thrown into consternation* (not as *English Version,* "broken in pieces"). **10. the word**—of command, for the assault of Jerusalem. **God is with us**—"Immanuel implies this (Num. 14:9; Ps. 46: 7). **11. with a strong hand**—or else, "when He grasped me with His hand" [HORSLEY]. MAURER, as *English Version,* "with the impetus of His hand," i.e., the felt impulse of His inspiration in my mind (Jer. 15:17; Ezek. 1:3; 3:14, 22; 37:1). **way of . . . people**—their distrust of Jehovah, and the panic which led them and Ahab to seek Assyrian aid. **12-16.** The words of Jehovah. **12. confederacy**—rather, a conspiracy; an appropriate term for the *unnatural* combination of *Israel* with *Syrian* foreigners against Judea and the theocracy, to which the former was bound by ties of blood and hereditary religion [MAURER]. **to all . . . say**—rather, of all which this people calleth a conspiracy [G. V. SMITH]. **their fear**—viz., object of fear: the hostile conspiracy. **be afraid**—rather [MAURER], "nor make others to be afraid." **13. Sanctify**—Honor His *holy* name by regarding Him as your only hope of safety (ch. 29:23; Num. 20:12). **him . . . fear**—"fear" lest you provoke His wrath by your fear of man and distrust of Him. **14. sanctuary**—inviolable asylum, like the altar of the temple (I Kings 1:50; 2:28; Ezek. 11:16; cf.

Prov. 18:10); viz., to those who fear and trust in Him. **but . . . offence**—i.e., a rock over which they should fall to their hurt; viz., those who would not believe. **both . . . houses**—Israel and Judah. Here again the prophecy expands beyond the temporary application in Ahaz' time. The very stone, Immanuel, which would have been a *sanctuary* on belief, becomes a fatal *stumbling block* through unbelief. Jesus Christ refers to this in Matthew 21:44. (Cf. Deut. 32:4, 15, 18, 30, 31, 37; Dan. 2:34; Rom. 9:33; I Pet. 2:8.) **gin**—trap, in which birds are unexpectedly caught (Luke 21:35; I Thess. 5:2). So at the destruction of Jerusalem under Titus. **15. stumble . . . taken**—images from the means used in taking wild animals. **16. Bind up . . . seal**—What Isaiah had before briefly noted by inscribing *Maher-shalal-hash-baz* in a *tablet,* fixed up in some public place, he afterwards wrote out more in detail in a *parchment roll* (ch. 30:8); this he is now to *seal up,* not merely in order that nothing may be added to, or taken from it, as being complete, but to imply that it relates to distant events, and is therefore to be a *sealed* and *not understood* testimony (ch. 6:9, 10), except in part among God's disciples," i.e., those who "sanctify the Lord" by obedient trust (Ps. 25: 14). Subsequent revelations would afterwards clear up what now was dark. So the Apocalypse explains what in Daniel was left unexplained (cf. Dan. 8:26; 12:9). "The words are closed up and *sealed* till the time of the end"; but Revelation 22:10, "*Seal not* the sayings of the prophecy . . . for the time is at hand" (cf. Rev. 5:1, 5, 9), **testimony**—attested by Uriah and Zechariah (vs. 2). **law**—the revelation just given, having the force of a law. **disciples**—not as MAURER, Uriah and Zechariah (cf. John 7:17; 15:15). **17. I**—Whatever the rest of the nation may do, I will look to Jehovah alone. **that hideth . . . face**—*though* He seems now to *withdraw His countenance* from *Judah* (the then representive of "the house of Jacob"). Let us *wait* and trust in, though we cannot see, Him (ch. 50:10; 54:8; Hab. 2:3; Luke 2:25, 38). **18. I and the children**—Isaiah means "salvation of Jehovah"; His children's names, also (ch. 7:3; 7:14; 8:3), were "signs" suggestive of the coming and final deliverance. **wonders**—i.e., symbols of the future (ch. 20:3; Zech. 3:8). "Behold I . . . me" is quoted in Hebrews 2:13 to prove *the manhood of the Messiah.* This is the *main* and *ultimate* fulfilment of the prophecy; its *temporary* meaning is applied to Ahaz' time. Isaiah typically, in vss. 17, 18, personates Messiah, who is at once "Father" and "Son," *Isaiah* and *Immanuel,* "Child" and "Mighty God," and is therefore called here a "wonder," as in ch. 9:6, "Wonderful." Hence in Hebrews 2:13, believers are called His "children"; but in vss. 11, 12, His 'brethren." On "the LORD hath given me," see John 6:37, 39; 10:29; 17:12. **which dwelleth in . . . Zion**—and will therefore protect *Jerusalem.* **19. Seek unto**—Consult in your national difficulties. **them . . . familiar spirits**—necromancers, spirit-charmers. So Saul, when he had forsaken God (I Sam. 28:7, etc.), consulted the witch of Endor in his difficulties. These follow in the wake of idolatry, which prevailed under Ahaz (II Kings 16:3, 4, 10). He copied the soothsaying as he did the idolatrous "altar" of Damascus (cf. Lev. 20:6, which forbids it, ch. 19:3). **wizards**—men claiming supernatural *knowledge;* from the old English, "*to wit,*" i.e., know. **peep**—rather "chirp faintly," as young birds do; this sound was generally ascribed to departed spirits; by ventriloquism the soothsayers caused a low sound to proceed as from a grave, or dead person. Hence the LXX renders

the *Hebrew* for necromancers here "ventriloquists" (cf. ch. 29:4). **mutter**—moan. **should not . . .**—The answer which Isaiah recommends to be given to those advising to have recourse to necromancers. **for the living . . .**—"should one, *for the safety* of the living, seek unto (consult) the dead?" [GESENIUS]. LOWTH renders it, "*In place of* (consulting) the living, should one consult the dead?" **20. To the law . . .** the revelation of God by His prophet (vs. 16), to which he directs them to refer those who would advise necromancy. **if they speak not . . . it is because** *English Version* understands "they" as the necromancers. But the *Hebrew* rendered "because" is not this but "who"; and "if not," ought rather to be "shall they not"; or, *truly they shall* speak according to this word, *who* have no *morning light* (so the *Hebrew,* i.e., prosperity after the night of sorrows) *dawning* on them [MAURER and G. V. SMITH]. They who are in the dark night of trial, without a dawn of hope, shall surely say so, Do not seek, as we did, to necromancy, but to the law," etc. *The law* perhaps includes here the *law of Moses,* which was the "Magna Charta" on which prophetism commented [KITTO]. **21, 22.** More detailed description of the despair, which they shall fall into, who sought necromancy instead of God; vs. 20 implies that *too late* they shall see how much better it would have been for them to have sought "to the law," etc. (Deut. 32:31). But now they are given over to despair. Therefore, while seeing the truth of God, they only "curse their King and God"; foreshadowing the future, like conduct of those belonging to the "kingdom of the beast," when they shall be visited with divine plagues (Rev. 16:11; cf. Jer. 18:12). **through it**—viz., the land. **hardly bestead**—oppressed with anxiety. **hungry**—a more grievous famine than the temporary one in Ahaz' time, owing to Assyria; *then* there was *some* food, but *none now* (ch. 7:15, 22; Lev. 26:3-5, 14-16, 20). **their king . . . God**—Jehovah, King of the Jews (Ps. 5:2; 68:24). **look upward . . . unto the earth**—Whether they look up to heaven, or down towards *the land of Judea,* nothing but despair shall present itself. **dimness of anguish**—darkness of distress (Prov. 1:27). **driven to darkness**—rather, *thick darkness* (Jer. 23:12). Driven onward, as by a sweeping storm. The Jewish rejection of "their King and God," Messiah, was followed by all these awful calamities.

CHAPTER 9

VSS. 1-7. CONTINUATION OF THE PROPHECY IN CHAPTER 8. **1. Nevertheless . . .**—rather, "*For* darkness shall not (continually) be on it (i.e., the land) on which there is (now) distress" [HENGSTENBERG and MAURER]. The "for" refers, not to the words immediately preceding, but to the consolations in ch. 8:9, 10, 17, 18. Do not despair, *for,* etc. **when at the first . . .**—rather, "as the former time has brought contempt on the land of Zebulun and Naphtali (viz., the deportation of their inhabitants under Tiglath-pileser, II Kings 15:29, a little before the giving of this prophecy); so shall the after-coming time bring honor to the way of the sea (the district around the lake of Galilee, the land beyond [but HENGSTENBERG, "by the side of"] Jordan (*Perea,* east of Jordan, belonging to Reuben, Gad, and half-Manasseh), the circle [but HENGSTENBERG, "Galilee"] (i.e., region) of the "Gentiles" [MAURER, HENGSTENBERG, etc.]. *Galil* in *Hebrew* is a "circle", "circuit," and from it came the name Galilee. North of Naphtali, inhabited by a mixed race of Jews and Gentiles of the bordering Phœnician race (Judg. 1:30; I Kings 9:11). Besides the recent deportation by Tiglath-pileser, it had been sorely smitten by Benhadad of Syria, 200 years before (I Kings 15:20). It was after the Assyrian deportation colonized with heathens, by Esar-haddon (II Kings 17:24). Hence arose the contempt for it on the part of the southern Jews of purer blood (John 1:46; 7:52). The same region which was so darkened once, shall be among the first to receive Messiah's light (Matt. 4:13, 15, 16). It was in despised Galilee that He first and most publicly exercised His ministry; from it were most of His apostles. Foretold in Deuteronomy 33:18, 19; Acts 2:7; Psalm 68:27, 28, Jerusalem, the theocratic capital, might readily have known Messiah; to compensate less favored Galilee, He ministered mostly there; Galilee's very debasement made it feel its need of a Saviour, a feeling not known to the self-righteous Jews (Matt. 9:13). It was appropriate, too, that He who was both "the Light to lighten the Gentiles, and the Glory of His people Israel," should minister chiefly on the border land of *Israel,* near the *Gentiles.* **2. the people**—the whole nation, Judah and Israel. **shadow of death**—the darkest misery of captivity. **3. multiplied . . . nation**—primarily, the rapid *increase* of Israelites after the return from Babylon; more fully and exhaustively the rapid spread of Christianity at first. **not increased the joy** —By a slight change in the *Hebrew, its* (joy) is substituted by some for *not,* because "not increased the joy" seems opposite to what immediately follows, "the joy," etc. HENGSTENBERG, retains *not* thus: "Whose joy thou hadst not increased," (i.e., hadst *diminished*). Others, "Hast thou not increased the joy?" The very difficulty of the reading, *not,* makes it less likely to be an interpolation. HORSLEY best explains it: The prophet sees in vision a shifting scene, comprehending at one glance the history of the Christian Church to remotest times—a land dark and thinly peopled—lit up by a sudden light—filled with new inhabitants—then struggling with difficulties, and again delivered by the utter and final overthrow of their enemies. The influx of Gentile converts (represented here by "Galilee of the Gentiles") soon was to be followed by the growth of corruption, and the final rise of Antichrist, who is to be destroyed, while God's people is delivered, as in the case of Gideon's victory over Midian, not by man's prowess, but by the special interposition of God. **before thee** —a phrase taken from sacrificial feasts; the tithe of harvest was eaten *before God* (Deut. 12:7; 14:26). **as men rejoice . . . divide . . . spoil**—referring to the judgments on the enemies of the Lord and His people, which usually accompany revelations of His grace. **4.** The occasion of the "joy," the deliverance not only of Ahaz and Judah from the Assyrian tribute (II Kings 16:8), and of Israel's ten tribes from the oppressor (II Kings 15:19), but of the Jewish Christian Church from its last great enemy. **hast** —the past time for the future, in prophetic vision; it expresses the *certainly* of the event. **yoke of his burden**—the yoke with which he was burdened. **staff of . . . shoulder**—the staff which strikes his shoulder [MAURER]; or the wood, like a yoke, on the neck of slaves, the badge of servitude [ROSENMULLER]. **day of Midian**—(Judg. 7:8-22). As Gideon with a handful of men conquered the hosts of Midian, so Messiah the "child" (vs. 6) shall prove to be the "Prince of peace," and the small Israel under Him shall overcome the mighty hosts of Antichrist (cf. Mic. 5:2-5), containing the same contrast, and alluding also to "the Assyrian," the then enemy of the Church, as here in Isaiah, the type of the last great

enemy. For further analogies between Gideon's victory and the Gospel, cf. II Corinthians 4:7, with Judges 7:22. As the "dividing of the spoil" (vs. 3) was followed by that which was "not joy," the making of the idolatrous ephod (Judg. 8:24-27), so the gospel victory was soon followed by apostasy at the first, and shall be so again after the millennial overthrow of Antichrist (Rev. 20:3, 7-9), previous to Satans' last doom (Rev. 20:10). **5. every battle . . .**—rather, "every greave of (the warrior who is) armed with greaves in the din of battle, and the martial garment (or cloak, called by the Latins *sagum*) rolled in blood, shall be for burning, (and) fuel for fire" [MAURER]. All warlike accoutrements shall be destroyed, as no longer required in the new era of peace (ch. 2:4, 11:6, 7; Ps. 46:9; Ezek. 39:9; Mic. 5: 5, 10; Zech. 9:9, 10). Cf. Malachi 4:1, as to the previous *burning* up of the wicked. **6. For**—the ground of these great expectations, **unto us**—for the benefit of the Jews first, and then the Gentiles (cf. "unto *you*" (Luke 2:11). **son . . . given**—(Ps. 2: 7.) God's gratuitous gift, on which man had no claim (John 3:16; Rom. 6:23). **government . . . upon . . . shoulder**—The ensign of office used to be worn *on the shoulder,* in token of *sustaining* the government (ch. 22:22). Here *the government on* Messiah's *shoulder* is in marked antithesis to the "yoke and staff" of the oppressor on Israel's "shoulder" (vs. 4). He shall receive the kingdom of the earth from the Father, to vindicate it from the misrule of those to whom it was entrusted to hold it for and under the Most High, but who sought to hold it in defiance of His right; the Father asserts His right by the Son, the "Heir of all things," who will hold it for Him (Dan. 7:13, 14). **name . . . called**—His *essential characteristics shall be.* **Wonderful**—*(Note,* ch. 8:18; *Judg.* 13:18; *Margin,* I Tim. 3:16.) **Counsellor**—(Ps. 16:7; Rom. 11:33, 34; I Cor. 1:24; Col. 2:3.) **mighty God**—(ch. 10:21; Ps. 24:8; Titus 2:13.) HORSLEY translates: "God the mighty man." "Unto us . . . God" is equivalent to "Immanuel" (ch. 7:14). **everlasting Father**—This marks Him as "Wonderful," that He is "a child," yet the "everlasting *Father*" (John 10:30; 14:9). Earthly kings leave their people after a short reign; He will reign over and bless them *for ever* [HENGSTENBERG]. **Prince of Peace**—*(Note,* vs. 5; Gen. 49:10; *Shiloh,* "The Tranquillizer.") Finally (Hos. 2:18). Even already He is "our peace" (Luke 2:14; Eph. 2: 14). **7. Of . . . increase . . . no end**—His princely rule shall perpetually increase and be unlimited (Dan. 2:44). **throne of David**—(I Kings 8:25; Ps. 2:6; 132:11; Jer. 3:17, 18; Ezek. 34:23-26; 37: 16, 22; Luke 1:32, 33; Acts 2:30). **judgment . . . justice**—It is not a kingdom of mere might, and triumph of force over enemies, but of righteousness (ch. 42:21 Ps. 45:6, 7), attainable only in and by Messiah. **zeal . . .**—including not only Christ's hidden spiritual victory over Satan at the first coming, but the open one accompanied with "judgments" on Antichrist and every enemy at the second coming (ch. 59:17; Ps. 9:6-8).

Vss. 8-21, and chap. 10:1-4. PROPHECY AS TO THE TEN TRIBES. Delivered a little later than the previous one. The chapters 9 and 10 ought to have been so divided. The present division into *chapters* was made by Cardinal Hugo, in A.D. 1250; and into *verses,* by Robert Stephens, the famous printer of Paris, in 1551. After the Assyrian invasion of Syria, that of Ephraim shall follow (II Kings 16:9); verses 8-11, 17-20, foretell the intestine discords in Israel after Hoshea had slain Pekah (A.D. 739), i.e., just after the Assyrian invasions, when for seven years it was stripped of magistrates and torn into factions. There are four strophes, each setting forth Ephraim's *crime* and consequent *punishment,* and ending with the formula, "For all this His anger is not turned away," etc. (vss. 12, 17, 21, and ch. 10:4). **8.** *Heading of the prophecy;* (vss. 8-12), the *first* strophe. **unto Jacob**–*against* the ten tribes [LOWTH]. **lighted upon**–fallen from heaven by divine revelation (Dan. 4:31). **9. know**–to their cost: experimentally (Hos. 9:7). **Samaria**–the capital of Ephraim (cf. as to phrase, ch. 1:1). **10. bricks**–in the East generally sun-dried, and therefore soon dissolved by rain. Granting, say the Ephraimites to the prophet's threat, that our affairs are in a ruinous state, we will restore them to more than their former magnificence. Self-confident unwillingness to see the judgments of God (ch. 26:11). **hewn stones**–(I Kings 5:17.) **sycamores**–growing abundantly on the low lands of Judea, and though useful for building on account of their antiseptic property (which induced the Egyptians to use them for the cases of their mummies), not very valuable. The *cedar,* on the other hand, was odorous, free from knots, durable, and precious (I Kings 10:27). "We will replace cottages with palaces." **11. adversaries of Rezin**–the Assyrians, who shall first attack Damascus, shall next advance "against *him*" (Ephraim). This is the punishment of Ephraim's pride in making light (vs. 10) of the judgment already inflicted by God through Tiglath-pileser (II Kings 15:29). A *second* Assyrian invasion (*Note* on the beginning of ch. 7) shall follow. The reading "princes" for "adversaries" in uncalled for. **join**–rather, "arm"; cover with armor [MAURER]. **his**–Rezin's. **12. Syrians**–Though now allies of Ephraim, after Rezin's death they shall join the Assyrians against Ephraim. "Together," in vs. 11, refers to this. Conquering nations often enlist in their armies the subject races (ch. 22:6; cf. II Kings 16:9; Jer 35:11), [ABEN-ERZA, GESENIUS]. HORSLEY less probably takes "Syrians before," as *the Syrians to the east,* i.e., not Rezin's subjects, but the *Assyrians:* "Aram" being the common name of Syrians and Assyrians. **Philistines**–of Palestine. **behind**–from the *west:* in marking the points of the compass, Orientalists face the east, which is *before* them: the west is *behind.* The *right hand* is the south: *the left,* the north. **devour**–as a ravenous beast (ch. 1:20; Jer. 10:25; 30:16; Num. 14:9). **For all this . . .**–The burden of each strophe. **13-17.** Second strophe. **turneth not**–the design of God's chastisements; not fulfilled in their case; a new cause for punishment (Jer. 2:20; 5:3). **14. head and tail**–proverbial for *the highest and lowest* (Deut. 28: 13, 44). **branch and rush**–another image for the same thought (ch. 19:15). The branch is *elevated* on the top of the tree: the rush is coarse and *low.* **15. ancient**–the older. **honourable**–the man of rank. **prophet . . . lies, . . . tail**–There were many such in Samaria (I Kings 22:6, 22, 23; cf. as to "tail," Rev. 9:19). **16. leaders . . .**–See *Margin,* and *Note,* ch. 3:12. **17. no joy**–the parallelism, "neither . . . mercy," shows that this means, He shall have *no such delight* in their youthful warriors, however much they be the nation's delight and reliance, as to *save* them from the enemy's sword (ch. 31:8; cf. Jer. 18:21). **fatherless,** etc.–not even the usual objects of His pity (Ps. 10:14, 18; 68:5; Jer. 49:11; Hos. 14:3) shall be spared. **hypocrite**–rather, a libertine, polluted [HORSLEY]. **folly**–wickedness (Ps. 14:1). **still**–Notwithstanding all these judgments, more remain. **18-21.** Third strophe. **burn**–not only *spreading* rapid-**eth**–maketh consumption, ly, but also *consuming* like fire; sin is its own punish-

ment. **briers . . . thorns**–emblem of the wicked; especially those of low rank (ch. 27:4; II Sam. 23:6). **forest**–from the humble *shrubbery* the flame spreads to the vast *forest;* it reaches *the high,* as well as *the low.* **mount up like . . . smoke**–rather. "They (*the thickets of the forest*) shall *lift themselves proudly aloft* [the *Hebrew* is from a *Syriac* root, a cock, expressing stateliness of motion, from his strutting gait, HORSLEY], in (in passing into) volumes of ascending smoke" [MAURER]. **19. darkened**–viz., with smoke (vs. 18). LXX and *Chaldee* render it, "is burnt up," so MAURER, from an *Arabic* root meaning "suffocating heat." **no man . . . spare . . . brother**–intestine discord snapping asunder the dearest ties of nature. **20. hungry**–not literally. Image from unappeasable hunger, to picture internal factions, reckless of the most tender ties (vs. 19), and insatiably spreading misery and death on every side (Jer. 19:9). **eat**–not literally, but *destroy* (Ps. 27:2; Job 19:22). **flesh of . . . arm**–those nearest akin: their former support (helper) (ch. 32:2) [MAURER]. **21. Manasseh, Ephraim**–the two sons of Joseph. So closely united as to form between them but one tribe; but now about to be rent into factions, thirsting for each other's blood. Disunited in all things else, but united "together against their brother Judah" (II Kings 15: 10, 30).

CHAPTER 10

Vss. 1-4. Fourth strophe. **1. them that decree** –viz., unrighteous judges. **write grievousness . . .** not the scribes, but the magistrates *who caused unjust decisions* (lit., "injustice" or "grievousness") *to be recorded* by them (ch. 65:6) [MAURER], (ch. 1:10, 23). **2. To turn aside . . .**–The effect of their conduct is to pervert the cause of the needy [HORSLEY]. In *English Version* "from judgment" means "from *obtaining justice.*" **take away the right**–"make plunder of the right" (rightful claim) [HORSLEY]. **3. what will ye do**–what way of escape will there be for you? **visitation**–of God's wrath (ch. 26:14; Job 35:15; Hos. 9:7). **from far**–from Assyria. **leave . . . glory**–rather, "deposit (for safekeeping) your *wealth*" [LOWTH]. So Psalm 49:17. **4. Without me** –not having Me to "flee to" (vs. 3). **bow down**– Bereft of strength they shall fall; or else, they shall lie down fettered. **under . . . under**–rather, "among" (lit., in the place of) [HORSLEY]. The "under" may be, however, explained, "trodden *under the* (feet of the) *prisoners* going into captivity," and "overwhelmed *under the* heaps of *slain* on the battlefield" [MAURER].

Chapters 10:5-34, and 11:12. DESTRUCTION OF THE ASSYRIANS; COMING OF MESSIAH; HYMN OF PRAISE. Verses 9, 11 show that Samaria was destroyed before this prophecy. It was written when Assyria proposed (a design which it soon after tried to carry out under Sennacherib) to destroy Judah and Jerusalem, as it had destroyed Samaria. This is the first part of Isaiah's prophecies under Hezekiah. Probably between 722 and 715 B.C. (see vs. 27). **5. O Assyrian . . .**–rather, "What, ho [but MAURER, *Woe to the*], Assyrian! He is the rod and staff of Mine anger (*My instrument in punishing;* Jer. 51:20; Ps. 17:13). In their hands is Mine indignation" [HORSLEY, after JEROME]. I have put into the Assyrians' hands the execution of Mine indignation against My people. **6. send him**–"Kings' hearts are in the hand of the Lord" (Prov. 21:1). **hypocritical** –polluted [HORSLEY]. **nation**–Judah, against whom Sennacherib was forming designs. **of my wrath**– objects of My wrath. **give . . . charge**–(Jer. 34:22.)

and to tread . . .—HORSLEY translates: "And then to make *him* (the Assyrian) a trampling under foot like the mire of the streets" (so vs. 12; ch.33:1; Zech. 10:5). But see ch. 37:26. **7. meaneth not so**—He is only thinking of his own schemes, while God is over-ruling them to *His* purposes. **think**—intend. Sin-ners' plans are no less culpable, though they by them unconsciously fulfil God's designs (Ps. 76:10; Mic. 4:12). So Joseph's brethren (Gen. 50:20; Prov. 16: 4). The *sinner's motive*, not the *result* (which de-pends on God), will be the test in judgment. **heart to destroy . . . not a few**—Sennacherib's ambition was not confined to Judea. His plan was also to con-quer Egypt and Ethiopia (ch. 20; Zech. 1:15). **8-11.** Vauntings of the Assyrians. Illustrated by the self-laudatory inscriptions of Assyria deciphered by HINCKS. **princes . . . kings**—Eastern satraps and gov-ernors of provinces often had the title and diadem of kings. Hence the title, "King of kings," implying the greatness of Him who was *over* them (Ezek. 26: 7; Ezra 7:12). **9. Is not . . . as**—Was there any one of these cities able to withstand me? Not one. So Rabshakeh vaunts (ch. 36:19). **Calno**—Calneh, built by Nimrod (Gen. 10:10), once his capital, on the Tigris. **Carchemish**—Circesium, on the Euphrates. Taken afterwards by Necho, king of Egypt; and re-taken by Nebuchadnezzar: by the Euphrates (Jer. 46: 2). **Hamath**—in Syria, north of Canaan (Gen. 10: 18). Taken by Assyria about 753 B.C. From it colonists were planted by Assyria in Samaria. **Ar-pad**—near Hamath. **Samaria**—now overthrown. **Da-mascus**—(ch. 17). **10, 11. found**—unable to resist me: *hath overcome* (so Ps. 21:8). **and whose**—rath-er, "and their." This clause, down to "Samaria," is parenthetical. **excel**—were more powerful. He regards Jerusalem as idolatrous, an opinion which it often had given too much ground for: Jehovah was in his view the mere *local* god of Judea, as Baal of the countries where it was adored, nay, inferior in power to some national gods (ch. 36:19, 20, 37:12). See in opposition, ch. 37:20; 46:1. **As my hand . . . shall I not,** *as* **I have**—a double protasis. Agitation makes one accumulate sentences. **12. whole work** —His entire plan is regard to the *punishment* of the Jews (vss. 5-7). **Zion**—the royal residence, the court, princes and nobles; as distinguished from "Je-rusalem," the *people* in general. **fruit**—the result of, i.e., the plants emanating from. **stout**—*Hebrew*, "greatness of," i.e., pride of. **glory**—haughtiness. **13. I am prudent**—He ascribes his success to his own prudence, not to God's providence. **removed the bounds**—set aside old, and substituted new bound-aries of kingdoms at will. · A criminal act, as Je-hovah Himself had appointed the boundaries of the nations (Deut. 32:8). **treasures**—"hoarded treas-ures" [HORSLEY]. **put down . . . inhabitants like . . .** —rather, "as a valiant man, I have brought down *(from their seats)* those *seated"* (viz., on thrones; as in Ps. 2:4; 29:10; 55:19. The *Hebrew* for "He that abideth," is *He that sitteth on a throne*); otherwise, "I have *brought down* (as *captives into Assyria,* which lay *lower* than Judea; therefore 'brought down,' cf. ch. 36:1, 10), *the inhabitants"* [MAURER]. **14. nest**—implying the ease with which he carried off all before him. **left**—by the parent bird. **none . . . moved . . . wing**—image from an angry bird resisting the robbery of its "nest." **peeped**—chirped even low (ch. 8:19). No resistance was offered me, or deed, or even *word.* **15. Shall the instrument boast** against Him who uses it? Through *free* in a sense, and carrying out his own plans, the Assyrian was unconsciously carrying out *God's* purposes. **shaketh it**—moves it back and forward, **staff . . . lift . . . it-**

self . . . no wood—rather, "as if the staff (*man*, the instrument of God's judgments on his fellow man) should set aside (Him who is) not wood" (*not a* mere instrument, as *man).* On "no wood" cf. Deut. 32:21, "that which is *not God";* ch. 31:8 shows that God is meant here by "not wood" [MAURER]. **16. fat ones**—(ch. 5:17.) The robust and choice soldiers of Assyria (Ps. 78:31, where "fattest" answers in the parallelism to "chosen," or "young men," *Mar-gin).* **leanness**—carrying out the image on "fat ones." *Destruction* (Ps. 106:15). Fulfilled (ch. 37:36). **his glory**—Assyria's *nobles.* So in ch. 5:13 *Margin;* ch. 8:7. **kindle**—a new image from *fire* consuming quickly dry materials (Zech. 12:6). **17, 18. light of Israel**—carrying out the image in the end of vs. 16. *Jehovah,* who is a *light* to *Israel,* shall be the "fire" (Deut. 4:24; Heb. 12:29) that shall ignite the "thorns," (the Assyrians, like dry fuel, a ready prey to flame). **18. glory of his forest**—The *common* soldiers, the *princes, officers,* etc., all alike *together,* shall be con-sumed *(Note,* ch. 9:18). **in one day**—(ch. 37:36.) **fruitful field**—lit., "Carmel," a rich mountain in the tribe of Asher. Figurative for Sennacherib's mighty army. Perhaps alluding to his own boasting words about to be uttered (ch. 37:24), "I will enter the forest of his Carmel." **soul and body**—prover-bial for utterly; the *entire* man is made up of *soul and body.* **as when a standard-bearer fainteth**— rather, "they shall be as when a *sick man* (from a *Syriac* root) wastes away." Cf. "leanness," i.e., wasting destruction (vs. 16) [MAURER]. Or, "there shall be an entire *dissipation,* like a perfect *melt-ing"* (viz., of the Assyrian army) [HORSLEY]. **19. rest**—those who shall survive the destruction of the host. **his forest**—same image as in vs. 18, for the once dense army. **child . . . write**—so few that a child might count them. **20-22.** The effect on the "remnant" (contrasted with the Assyrian remnant, vs. 19); viz., those who shall be left after the in-vasion of Sennacherib, will be a return from depend-ence on external idolatrous nations, as Assyria and Egypt (II Kings 18:21; 16:7-9), to the God of the theocracy; fulfilled in part in the pious Hezekiah's days; but from the *future* aspect under which Paul, in Rom. 9:27, 28 (cf. "short work" with "whole work," vs. 12, here), regards the whole prophecy, the "remnant," "who stay upon the Lord," probably will receive their fullest realization in the portion of Jews left after that Antichrist shall have been over-thrown, who shall "return" unto the Lord (ch. 6:13; 7:3; Zech. 12:9, 10; 14:2, 3; Zeph. 3:12). **21. mighty God**—(ch. 9:6) the God who shall have evinced such *might* in destroying Israel's enemies. As the As-syrians in Sennacherib's reign did not carry off *Judah* captive, the returning "remnant" cannot *mainly* refer to this time. **22. yet**—rather in the sense in which Paul quotes it (Rom. 9:27), "Though Israel be now numerous as the sand, a remnant *only* of them shall return"—the great majority shall perish. The reason is added, Because "the consumption (ful-ly completed destruction) *is* decreed (lit., *decided on, brought to an issue),* it overfloweth (ch. 30:28; 8:8) with *justice";* i.e., the infliction of just punish-ment (ch. 5:16) [MAURER]. **23. even determined**— "A consumption, *and whatever is determined,"* or *decreed* [MAURER]. **midst**—Zion, the central point of the earth as to Jehovah's presence. **land**—Israel. But LXX, "in the whole *habitable world."* So *English Version* (Rom. 9:28), "upon the *earth."* **24. Therefore**—Return to the main proposition, Assyr-ia's ultimate punishment, though employed as God's "rod" to chastise Judea for a time. **O my people**— God's tenderness towards His elect nation. **after**

the manner of Egypt—as Egypt and Pharaoh oppressed thee. Implying, too, as Israel was nevertheless *delivered* from them, so now it would be from the Assyrian Sennacherib. The antithesis in vs. 26 requires this interpretation [MAURER]. **25. For**—Be not afraid (vs. 24), *for* . . . —**indignation** . . . **cease**—The punishments of God against Israel shall be consummated and ended (ch. 26:20; Dan. 11:36). "Till the indignation be accomplished," etc. **mine anger**—shall turn to their (the Assyrians') destruction. **26. slaughter of**—"stroke upon." **Midian**—(ch. 9:4; Judg. 7:25). **as his rod was upon the sea**—rather, understanding "stroke" from the previous clause, "according to the stroke of His rod upon the Red Sea" (Exod. 14:16, 26). His "rod" on the Assyrian (vss. 24, 26) stands in bold contrast to the Assyrian used as a "rod" to strike others (vs. 5). **after the manner of Egypt**—as He lifted it up against Egypt at the Red Sea. **27. his burden**—the Assyrians' oppression (ch. 9:3). Judah was still tributary to Assyria; Hezekiah had not yet revolted, as he did in the beginning of Sennacherib's reign. **because of**—(Hos. 10:15.) **the anointing**—viz., Messiah (Dan. 9:24). Just as in ch. 9:4-6, the "breaking of the yoke of" the enemies' "burden and staff" is attributed to *Messiah,* "For unto us a child is born," etc., so it is here. MAURER not so well translates, "Because of the fatness"; an image of the Assyrians' fierce and wanton pride drawn from a well-fed bull tossing off the yoke (Deut. 32:15). So vs. 16 above, and ch. 5:17, *"fat* ones." **28-32.** Onward gradual march of Sennacherib's army towards Jerusalem, and the panic of the inhabitants vividly pictured before the eyes. **come to**—*come upon* as a sudden invader (Gen. 34:27). **Aiath**—same as Ai (Josh. 7:2; Neh. 7:32). In the north of Benjamin; so the other towns also; all on the line of march to Jerusalem. **Michmash**—nine miles northeast of Jerusalem. **laid up . . . carriages**—He has left his heavier *baggage* (so "carriages" for the *things carried,* Acts 21:15) at Michmash, so as to be more lightly equipped for the siege of Jerusalem. So I Sam. 17:22; 25:13; 30:24 [JEROME and MAURER]. **29. passage**—the jaws of the wady or defile at Michmash (I Sam. 13:23; 14: 4, 5). **lodging**—their quarters for the night, after having passed the defile which might have been easily guarded against them. **Ramah**—near Geba; seven miles from Jerusalem. **Gibeah of Saul**—his birthplace and residence, in Benjamin (I Sam. 11:4), distinct from Gibeah *of Judah* (Josh. 15:57). **30. daughter of Gallim**—*Gallim and her sons (Note,* ch. 1:8; II Kings 19:21). "Cry aloud in consternation." **Laish**—not the town in Dan (Judg. 18:7), but one of the same name near Jerusalem (I Maccabees 9:9). **Anathoth**—three miles from Jerusalem in Benjamin; the birthplace of Jeremiah. "Poor" is applied to it in pity, on account of the impending calamity. Others translate, Answer her, O Anathoth. **31. Madmenah**—not the city in Simeon (Josh. 15:31), but a village near Jerusalem. **removed**—fled from fear. **gather themselves to flee**—"put their goods in a place of safety" [MAURER]. **32. that day**—lit., "As yet *this* (one only) day (is allowed to the soldiers) for remaining (halting for rest) at Nob"; northeast of Jerusalem on Olivet; a town of the priests (Neh. 11: 32). **daughter**—rightly substituted for the Chetib reading, *house.* His "shaking his hand" in menace implies that he is now at Nob. *within sight of* Jerusalem. **33. bough**—lit., the "beauty" of the tree; "the beautiful branch." **high ones of stature**—"the upright *stem,*" as distinguished from the previous "boughs" [HORSLEY]. **34.** This verse and vs. 33 describe the sudden arrest and overthrow of Sen-

nacherib in the height of his success; vss. 18, 19; Ezek. 31:3, etc., 14, etc., contain the same image; "Lebanon" and its forest are the Assyrian army; the "iron" axe that fells the forest refers to the stroke which destroyed the one hundred and eighty-five thousand Assyrians (II Kings 19:35). The "Mighty One" is Jehovah (vs. 21; ch. 9:6).

CHAPTER 11

Vss. 1-16. From the local and temporary national deliverance the prophet passes by the law of suggestion in an easy transition to the end of all prophecy—the everlasting deliverance under Messiah's reign, not merely His first coming, but chiefly His second coming. The *language* and illustrations are still drawn from the temporary national subject, with which he began, but the glories described pertain to Messiah's reign. Hezekiah cannot, as some think, be the subject; for he was already come, whereas the "stem of Jesse" was yet future ("shall come") (cf. Mic. 4:11, etc.; 5:1, 2; Jer. 23:5, 6; 33:15, 16; Rom. 15:12). **1. rod**—When the proud "boughs" of "Lebanon" (ch. 10:33, 34, the Assyrians) are lopped, and the vast *"forests* cut down" amidst all this rage, a seemingly humble *rod* shall come out of Jesse (Messiah), who shall retrieve the injuries done by the Assyrian *"rod"* to Israel (ch. 10:5, 6, 18, 19). **stem**—lit., "the stump" of a tree cut close by the roots: happily expressing the *depressed* state of the royal house of David, owing to the hostile storm (ch. 10:18, 19), when Messiah should arise from it, to raise it to more than its pristine glory. Luke 2:7 proves this (ch. 53:2; *Note,* ch. 8:6; cf. Job 14:7, 8). **Branch**—Scion. He is nevertheless also the "root" (vs. 10; Rev. 5:5; 22:16. "Root and offspring" combines both, Zech. 3:8; 6:12). **2. Spirit of the Lord**—JEHOVAH. The Spirit by which the prophets spake: for Messiah was to be a *Prophet* (ch. 61:1; Deut. 18:15, 18). *Seven* gifts of the Holy Spirit are specified, to imply that the *perfection* of them was to be in Him. Cf. "the *seven* Spirits" (Rev. 1:4), i.e., the Holy Ghost in His *perfect fulness: seven* being the sacred number. The prophets had only a portion out of the *"fulness"* in the Son of God (John 1: 16; 3:34; Col. 1:19). **rest**—permanently; not merely *come* upon Him (Num. 11:25, 26). **wisdom**—(I Cor. 1:30; Eph. 1:17; Col. 2:3.) **understanding**—coupled with "wisdom," being its fruit. Discernment and discrimination (Matt. 22:18; John 2:25). **counsel . . . might**—the faculty of *forming* counsels, and that of *executing* them (ch. 28:29). Counsellor (ch. 9:6). **knowledge**—of the deep things of God (Matt. 11:27). The knowledge of Him gives us true knowledge (Eph. 1:17). **fear of the Lord**—reverential, obedient fear. The first step towards true "knowledge" (Job 28:28; Ps. 111:10). **3. make him of quick understanding**—lit., *quick-scented* in the fear of Jehovah"; endowed with a singular sagacity in discerning the genuine principle of religious fear of God, when it lies dormant in the yet unawakened sinner (Matt. 12:20; Acts 10; 16:14) [HORSLEY]. But MAURER, "He shall *delight* in the fear of God." The *Hebrew* means "to delight in the odors" of anything (Exod. 30:38; Amos 5:21); "smell," i.e., "delight in." **after . . . sight**—according to mere external appearances (John 7:24; 8:15; Jas. 2:1; I Sam. 16:7). Herein Messiah is represented a just Judge and Ruler (Deut. 1:16, 17). **reprove**—"decide," as the parallelism shows. **after . . . ears**—by mere plausible hearsays, but by the true merits of each case (John 6:64; Rev. 2:23). **4. judge**

—see that impartial justice is done them. **reprove** —"decide." But LOWTH, "work conviction in." "Judge" may mean here "rule," as in Psalm 67:4. Cf. "meek . . . earth" with Matthew 5:5, and Revelation 11:15. **earth**—its *ungodly* inhabitants, answering to "the wicked" in the parallel, and in antithesis to the "poor" and "meek," viz., in spirit, the humble pious (Matt. 5:3). It is at the same time implied that "the earth" will be extraordinarily wicked when He shall come to judge and reign. His reign shall therefore be ushered in with judgments on the apostates (Ps. 2:9-12; Luke 18:8; Rev. 2:27). **rod of . . . mouth**—condemning sentences which proceed from His mouth against the wicked (Rev. 1:16; 2:16; 19:15, 21). **breath of . . . lips**—his judicial decisions (ch. 30:28; Job 15:30; Rev. 19:20; 20:9-12). He as the Word of God (Rev. 19:13-15) comes to strike that blow which shall decide His claim to the kingdom, previously usurped by Satan, and "the beast" to whom Satan delegates his power. It will be a day of judgment to the Gentile dispensation, as the first coming was to the Jews. Cf. a type of the "rod" (Num. 17:2-10). **5. righteousness . . . girdle** —(Rev. 1:13; 19:11.) The antitypical High Priest (Exod. 28:4). The *girdle* secures firmly the rest of the garments (I Peter 1:13). So "truth" gives firm consistency to the whole character (Eph. 5:14). In ch. 59:17, "righteousness" is His *breastplate.* **6. wolf . . . lamb**—Each animal is coupled with that one which is its natural prey. A fit state of things under the "Prince of Peace" (ch. 65:25; Ezek. 34:25; Hos. 2:18). These may be figures for *men* of corresponding animal-like characters (Ezek. 22:27; 38:13; Jer. 5:6; 13:23; Matt. 7:15; Luke 10:3). Still a *literal* change in the relations of animals to man and each other, restoring the state in Eden, is a more likely interpretation. Cf. Genesis 2:19, 20, with Psalm 8:6-8, which describes the restoration to man, in the person of "the Son of man," of the lost dominion over the animal kingdom of which he had been designed to be the merciful vicegerent under God, for the good of his animal subjects (Rom. 8:19-22). **7. feed**—viz., "together"; taken from the second clause. **straw**—no longer *flesh and blood.* **8. play**—lit., "delight" himself in sport. **cockatrice** —a fabulous serpent supposed to be hatched from the egg of a cock. The *Hebrew* means a kind of adder, more venomous than the asp; BOCHART supposes the basilisk to be meant, which was thought to poison even with its breath. **9. my holy mountain**—Zion, i.e., Jerusalem. The seat of government and of Messiah's throne is put for the whole earth (Jer. 3:17). **sea**—As the waters find their way into every cavern of *its depths,* so Christianity shall pervade every recess of the earth (Hab. 2:14). As vss. 1-5 describe the *personal* qualities of *Messiah,* and vss. 6-9 the regenerating effects of His coming on *creation,* so vss. 10-16 the results of it in the restoration of His people, *the Jews,* and the conversion through them of *the Gentiles.* **10. root**— rather, "shoot from the root" (cf. *Note,* vs. 1; ch. 53:2; Rev. 5:5; 22:16). **stand**—permanently and prominently, as a banner lifted up to be the rallying point of an army or people (ch. 5:26; John 12:32). **the people**—*peoples,* answering to "the Gentiles" in the parallel member. **to it . . . seek**—diligently (Job 8:5). They shall give in their allegiance to the Divine King (ch. 2:2; 60:5; Zech. 2:11). HORSLEY translates, "Of *Him* shall the Gentiles *inquire; viz.,* in a religious sense, *resort as to an oracle for consultation* in difficulties (Zech. 14:16). Cf. Romans 15:12, which quotes this passage, "In *Him* shall the Gentiles trust." **rest**—resting-place (ch. 60:13; Ps.

132:8, 14; Ezek. 43:7). The sanctuary in the temple of Jerusalem was "the resting-place of the ark and of Jehovah." So the glorious Church which is to be is described under the image of an oracle to which all nations shall resort, and which shall be filled with the visible glory of God. **11. set . . . hand** —take in hand the work. **the second time**—Therefore the coming restoration of the Jews is to be distinct from that after the Babylonish captivity, and yet to resemble it. The first restoration was *literal,* therefore so shall the second be; the latter, however, it is implied here, shall be much more universal than the former (ch. 43:5-7; 49:12, 17, 18; Ezek. 37:21; Hos. 3:5; Amos 9:14, 15; Mic. 4:6, 7; Zeph. 3:19, 20; Zech. 10:10; Jer. 23:8). **Pathros**—one of the three divisions of Egypt, Upper Egypt. **Cush**—either Ethiopia, south of Egypt, now Abyssinia, or the southern parts of Arabia, along the Red Sea. **Elam** —Persia, especially the southern part of it now called Susiana. **Shinar**—Babylonian Mesopotamia, the plain between the Euphrates and the Tigris: in it Babel was begun (Gen. 10:1). In the Assyrian inscriptions RAWLINSON distinguishes three periods: 1. The Chaldean; from 2300 B.C. to 1500, in which falls Chedorlaomer (Gen. 14), called in the cuneiform characters Kudur of Hur, or Ur of the Chaldees, and described as the conqueror of Syria. The seat of the first Chaldean empire was in the south, towards the confluence of the Tigris and Euphrates. 2. The Assyrian, down to 625 B.C. 3. The Babylonian, from 625 to 538 B.C., when Babylon was taken by the Persian Cyrus. **islands of [. . . sea**— the far western regions beyond the sea [JEROME]. As to the "remnant" destined by God to survive the judgments on the nation, cf. Jeremiah 46:28. **12.** In the first restoration Judah alone was restored, with perhaps some few of Israel (the ten tribes): in the future restoration *both* are expressly specified (Ezek. 37:16-19; Jer. 3:18). To Israel are ascribed the "outcasts" (masculine); to Judah the "dispersed" (feminine), as the former have been longer and more utterly castaways (though not finally) than the latter (John 7:52). The masculine and feminine conjoined express the *universality* of the restoration. **13. envy . . . of Ephraim . . . Judah**—which began as early as the time (Judg. 8:1; 12:1, etc.) Joshua had sprung from, and resided among the Ephraimites (Num. 13:9; Josh. 19:50); the sanctuary was with them for a time (Josh. 18:1). The *jealousy* increased subsequently (II Sam. 2:8, etc.; 19:41; 20:2; 3:10); and even before David's time (I Sam. 11:8; 15:4), they had appropriated to themselves the national name Israel. It ended in disruption (I Kings 11:26, etc.; 12; cf. II Kings 14:9; Ps. 78:56-71). **adversaries of Judah**—rather, "the adversaries *from* Judah"; those of Judah *hostile to the Ephraimites* [MAURER]. The parallelism "the envy of Ephraim," viz., against Judah, requires this, as also what follows; viz., "Judah shall not vex Ephraim" (Ezek. 37:15, 17, 19). **14.** With united forces they shall subdue their foes (Amos 9:12). **fly**—as a bird of prey (Hab. 1:8). **upon the shoulders**—This expresses an attack made unexpectedly on one *from behind.* The image is the more apt, as the *Hebrew* for "shoulders" in Numbers 34:11 is used also of a maritime coast. They shall make a sudden victorious descent *upon their borders* southwest of Judea. **them of the east**—*Hebrew,* children of the East, the Arabs, who, always hostile, are not to be reduced under regular government, but are only to be despoiled (Jer. 49:28, 29). **lay . . . hand upon**—take possession of (Dan. 11:42). **Edom**—south of Judah, from the Dead Sea to the Red Sea. **Moab**

—east of Jordan and the Dead Sea. **Ammon**—east of Judea, north of Moab, between the Arnon and Jabbok. **15.** There shall be a second exodus, destined to eclipse even the former one from Egypt in its wonders. So the prophecies elsewhere (Ps. 68:22; Exod. 14:22; Zech. 10:11). The same deliverance furnishes the imagery by which the return from Babylon is described (ch. 48:20, 21). **destroy** —lit., "devote," or "doom," i.e., dry up; for what God dooms, perishes (Ps. 106:9; Nah. 1:4). **tongue of the Egyptian Sea**—the Bubastic branch of the Nile [VITRINGA]; but as the *Nile* was not the obstruction to the exodus, it is rather the west tongue or Heroöpolite fork of the *Red Sea*. **with . . . mighty wind**— such as the "strong east wind" (Exod. 14:21), by which God made a way for Israel through the Red Sea. The *Hebrew* for "mighty" means *terrible.* MAURER translates, "With the terror of His *anger*"; i.e., *His terrible anger.* **in the seven streams**—rather, "shall smite it (*divide it by smiting*) into seven (*many*) streams, so as to be easily crossed" [LOWTH]. So Cyrus divided the river Gyndes, which retarded his march against Babylon, into 360 streams, so that even a woman could cross it (HERODOTUS, 1. 189). "The river" is the Euphrates, the obstruction to Israel's return "from Assyria" (vs. 16), a type of all future impediments to the restoration of the Jews. **dry shod**—*Hebrew,* "in shoes." Even in sandals they should be able to pass over the once mighty river without being wet (Rev. 16:12). **16. highway** —clear of obstructions (ch. 19:23; 35:8). **like as . . . Israel . . . Egypt**—(ch. 51:10, 11; 63:12, 13.)

CHAPTER 12

Vss. 1-6. THANKSGIVING HYMN OF THE RESTORED AND CONVERTED JEWS. Just as Miriam, after the deliverance of the Red Sea (ch. 11:16), celebrated it with an ode of praise (Exod. 15). **2. Lord** JEHOVAH —*Jah, Jehovah.* The repetition of the name denotes emphasis, and the unchangeableness of God's character. **strength . . . song . . . salvation**—derived from Exodus 15:2; Psalm 118:14. The idea of *salvation* was peculiarly associated with the feast of *tabernacles* (see vs. 3). Hence the cry "Hosanna," "*Save, we beseech thee,*" that accompanied Jesus' triumphal entry into Jerusalem on that day (the fifteenth of the seventh month) (Matt. 21:9; cf. with Ps. 118:25, 26); the earnest of the perfected "salvation" which He shall bring to His people at His glorious second appearance at Jerusalem (Heb. 9:28). "He shall appear the second time without sin unto *salvation.*" Cf. Revelation 21:3, "The *tabernacle* of God is with men." Cf. Luke 9:33, "three tabernacles: one for *thee* . . ." (the transfiguration being a pledge of the future kingdom), (Ps. 118:15; Zech. 14:16). As the Jew was reminded by the feast of tabernacles of his wanderings in tents in the wilderness, so the Jew-Gentile Church to come shall call to mind, with thanksgiving, the various past ways whereby God has at last brought them to the heavenly "city of habitation" (Ps. 107:7). **3. draw water . . . salvation** —an expressive image in a hot country. On the last day of the feast of tabernacles the Jews used to bring water in a golden pitcher from the fountain of Siloam, and pour it, mingled with wine, on the sacrifice on the altar, with great rejoicing. This is the allusion in Jesus' words on "the last day of the feast" (John 7:2, 37-39). The pouring out of water indicated *repentance* (I Sam. 7:6; cf., as to the *Jews'* repentance hereafter, Zech. 12:10). There shall be a *latter* outpouring of the Spirit like the *former* one

on pentecost (Joel 2:23). **wells**—not mere *streams,* which may run dry, but ever-flowing *fountains* (John 4:14; 7:38), "Out of his belly (i.e., in and from himself)—*living* water" (ch. 42:18; Ps. 84:6; Zech. 13:1; Rev. 7:17). **4. make mention**—*Hebrew,* "cause it to be remembered." **5. Sing . . .**—alluding to Exod. 15:21. **6. inhabitant of Zion**—*Hebrew,* "inhabitress"; so "daughter of Zion," i.e., Zion and its people. **in the midst of thee**—of Jerusalem literally (Jer. 3:17; Ezek. 48:35; Zeph. 3:15, 17; Zech. 2:10).

CHAPTER 13

Vss. 1-22. CHAPTERS 13-23 CONTAIN PROPHECIES AS TO FOREIGN NATIONS.—CHAPTERS 13, 14, AND 27, AS TO BABYLON AND ASSYRIA. The predictions as to foreign nations are for the sake of the covenant people, to preserve them from despair, or reliance on human confederacies, and to strengthen their faith in God: also in order to extirpate narrow-minded nationality: God is Jehovah to Israel, not for Israel's sake alone, but that He may be thereby Elohim to the nations. These prophecies are in their right chronological place, in the beginning of Hezekiah's reign; then the nations of Western Asia, on the Tigris and Euphrates, first assumed a most menacing aspect. **1. burden**—*weighty* or *mournful* prophecy [GROTIUS]. Otherwise, simply, *the prophetical declaration,* from a *Hebrew* root *to put forth with the voice* anything, as in Numbers 23:7 [MAURER]. **of Babylon**—*concerning* Babylon. **2. Lift . . . banner**—(ch. 5:26; 11:10.) **the high mountain**— rather, "a bare (lit., bald, i.e., without trees) mountain"; from it the banner could be seen afar off, so as to rally together the peoples against Babylon. **unto them**—unto the Medes (vs. 17), the assailants of Babylon. It is remarkable that Isaiah does not *foretell* here the Jews' captivity in Babylon, but *presupposes* that event, and throws himself *beyond,* predicting *another* event still more future, the overthrow of the city of Israel's oppressors. It was now 174 years before the event. **shake . . . hand**—*beckon* with the hand—wave the hand to direct the nations to march against Babylon. **nobles**—Babylonian. Rather, in a bad sense, *tyrants;* as in ch. 14:5, "rulers" in parallelism to "the wicked"; and Job 21: 28 [MAURER]. **3. sanctified ones**—the Median and Persian soldiers *solemnly set apart* by Me for the destruction of Babylon, not *inwardly* "sanctified," but *designated* to fulfil God's *holy* purpose (Jer. 51: 27, 28; Joel 3:9, 11; where the *Hebrew* for *prepare* war is "sanctify" war). **for mine anger**—to execute it. **rejoice in my highness**—"Those who are *made to triumph for* My honor" [HORSLEY]. The heathen Medes could not be said to "rejoice in God's highness" MAURER translates, "My haughtily exulting ones" (Zeph. 3:11); a special characteristic of the Persians (HERODOTUS, 1. 88). They *rejoiced in their own highness,* but it was *His* that they were unconsciously glorifying. **4. the mountains**—viz., which separate Media and Assyria, and on one of which the banner to rally the hosts is supposed to be reared. **tumultuous noise**—The Babylonians are vividly depicted as hearing some unwonted sound like the din of a host; they try to distinguish the sounds, but can only perceive a *tumultuous noise.* **nations**—Medes, Persians, and Armenians composed Cyrus' army. **5. They**—viz., "Jehovah," and the armies which are "the weapons of His indignation." **far country**— Media and Persia, stretching to the far north and east. **end of heaven**—the far east (Ps. 19:6). **destroy**—rather, "to seize" [HORSLEY]. **6. day of the**

Lord—day of His vengeance on Babylon (ch. 2:12). Type of the future "day of wrath" (Rev. 6:17). **destruction**—lit., "a devastating tempest." **from the Almighty**—not from mere man; therefore irresistible. "Almighty," *Hebrew, Shaddai.* **7. faint . . . melt**—So Jeremiah 50:43; cf. Joshua 7:5. Babylon was taken by surprise on the night of Belshazzar's impious feast (Dan. 5:30). Hence the sudden *fainting and melting of hearts.* **8. pangs**—The *Hebrew* means also a "messenger." HORSLEY, therefore, with LXX translates, "The *heralds* (who bring word of the unexpected invasion) *are terrified."* MAURER agrees with *English Version*, lit., "they shall take hold of pangs and sorrows." **woman . . . travaileth** —(I Thess. 5:3.) **amazed**—the stupid, bewildered gaze of consternation. **faces . . . flames**—"their visages have the livid hue of flame" [HORSLEY]; with anguish and indignation. **9. cruel**—not strictly, but *unsparingly just;* opposed to *mercy.* Also answering to the cruelty (in the strict sense) of Babylon towards others (ch. 14:17) now about to be visited on itself. **the land**—"the earth" [HORSLEY]. The language from vs. 9 to vs. 13 can only primarily and *partially* apply to Babylon; fully and *exhaustively,* the judgments to come, hereafter, on the whole earth. Cf. vs. 10 with Matt. 24:29; Rev. 8:12. The sins of Babylon, *arrogancy* (vs. 11; ch. 4:11; 47:7, 8), *cruelty, false worship* (Jer. 50:38), *persecution of the people of God* (ch. 47:6), are peculiarly characteristic of the Antichristian world of the latter days (Dan. 11:32-37; Rev. 17:3, 6; 18:6, 7, 9-14, 24). **10. stars . . .** —fig. for *anarchy, distress,* and *revolutions* of kingdoms (ch. 34:4; Joel 2:10; Ezek. 32:7, 8; Amos 8:9; Rev. 6:12-14). There may be a *literal* fulfilment *finally,* shadowed forth under this imagery (Rev. 21:1). **constellations**—*Hebrew,* "a fool," or "impious one"; applied to the constellation *Orion,* which was represented as an impious giant (Nimrod deified, the founder of Babylon) chained to the sky. See *Note,* Job. 38:31. **11. world**—*the impious* of the world (cf. ch. 11:4). **arrogancy**—Babylon's besetting sin (Dan. 4:22, 30). **the terrible**—rather, tyrants [HORSLEY]. **12. man . . . precious**—I will so cut off Babylon's defenders, that *a single man* shall be as rare and precious as the finest gold. **13.** Image for mighty revolutions (ch. 24:19; 34:4; Hab. 3:6, 10; Hag. 2:6, 7; Rev. 20:11). **14. it**—Babylon. **roe**—gazelle; the most timid and easily startled. **no man taketh up**—sheep defenseless, *without a shepherd* (Zech. 13:7). **every man . . . to his own people** —The "mingled peoples" of foreign lands shall flee out of her (Jer. 50:16, 28, 37; 51:9). **15. found**—in the city. **joined**—"intercepted" [MAURER]. "Every one that has *withdrawn himself,"* viz., to hide in the houses [GESENIUS]. **16.** (Ps. 137:8, 9.) **17. Medes** —(Ch. 21:2; Jer. 51:11, 28.) At that time they were subject to Assyria; subsequently Arbaces, satrap of Media, revolted against the effeminate Sardanapalus, king of Assyria, destroyed Nineveh, and became king of Media, in the ninth century B.C. **not regard silver**—In vain will one try to buy his life from them for a ransom. The heathen Xenophon (*Cyrop.* 5, 1, 10) represents Cyrus as attributing this characteristic to the Medes, *disregard of riches.* A curious confirmation of this prophecy. **18. bows**— in the use of which the Persians were particularly skilled. **19. glory of kingdoms**—(Ch. 14:4; 47:5; Jer. 51:41.) **beauty of . . . excellency**—*Hebrew,* "the glory of the pride" of the Chaldees; it was their glory and boast. **as . . . Gomorrah**—as utterly (Jer. 49: 18; 50:40; Amos 4:11). Taken by Cyrus by clearing out the canal made for emptying the superfluous waters of the Euphrates, and directing the river into

this new channel, so that he was able to enter the city by the old bed in the night. **20.** literally fulfilled. **neither . . . Arabian pitch tent**—Not only shall it not be a permanent residence, but not even a *temporary* resting-place. The Arabs, through dread of evil spirits, and believing the ghost of Nimrod to haunt it, will not pass the night there (cf. vs. 21). **neither . . . shepherds**—The region was once most fertile; but owing to the Euphrates being now no longer kept within its former channels, it has become a stagnant marsh, unfit for flocks; and on the wastes of its ruins (bricks and cement) no grass grows. **21. wild beasts**—*Hebrew, tsiyim,* animals dwelling in arid wastes. Wild cats, remarkable for their howl [BOCHART]. **doleful creatures**—"howling beasts," lit., "howlings" [MAURER]. **owls**—rather, ostriches; a timorous creature, delighting in solitary deserts and making a hideous noise [BOCHART]. **satyrs**—sylvan demi-gods—half man, half goat—believed by the Arabs to haunt these ruins; probably animals of the goat-ape species [VITRINGA]. *Devil-worshippers,* who *dance* amid the ruins on a certain night [J. WOLFF]. **22. wild beasts of the islands**— rather, jackals; called by the Arabs "sons of howling"; an animal midway between a fox and a wolf [BOCHART and MAURER]. **cry**—rather, "answer," "respond" to each other, as wolves do at night, producing a most dismal effect. **dragons**—serpents of various species, which hiss and utter dolorous sounds. Fable gave them wings, because they stand with much of the body elevated and then dart swiftly. MAURER understands here another species of jackal. **her time . . . near**—though 174 years distant, yet "near" to Isaiah, who is supposed to be speaking to the Jews as if now captives *in* Babylon (ch. 14:1, 2).

CHAPTER 14

Vss. 1-3. THE CERTAINTY OF DELIVERANCE FROM BABYLON. 4-23. THE JEWS' TRIUMPHAL SONG THEREAT. "It moves in lengthened elegiac measure like a song of lamentation for the dead, and is full of lofty scorn" [HERDER] 24-27. CONFIRMATION OF THIS BY THE HEREFORETOLD DESTRUCTION OF THE ASSYRIANS UNDER SENNACHERIB; a pledge to assure the captives in Babylon that He who, with such ease, overthrew the Assyrian, could likewise effect His purpose as to Babylon. The Babylonian king, the subject of this prediction, is Belshazzar, as representative of the kingdom (Dan. 5). **1. choose**— "set His choice upon." A deliberate predilection [HORSLEY]. Their restoration is grounded on their *election* (see Ps. 102:13-22). **strangers**—proselytes (Esther 8:17; Acts 2:10; 17:4, 17). Tacitus, a heathen (*Hist.* 5. 5), attests the fact of numbers of the Gentiles having become Jews in his time. An earnest of the future effect on the heathen world of the Jews' spiritual restoration (ch. 60:4, 5, 10; Mic. 5:7; Zech. 14:16; Rom. 11:12). **2. the people**—of Babylon, primarily. Of the whole Gentile world ultimately (ch. 49:22; 66:20; 60:9). **their place**— Judea (Ezra 1). **possess**—receive in possession. **captives**—not by physical, but by moral might; the force of love, and regard to Israel's God (ch. 60:14). **3. rest**—(Ch. 28:12; Ezek. 28:25, 26.)

4-8. A CHORUS OF JEWS EXPRESS THEIR JOYFUL SURPRISE AT BABYLON'S DOWNFALL:—The whole earth rejoices; the cedars of Lebanon taunt him. **4. proverb**—The Orientals, having few books, embodied their thoughts in weighty, figurative, briefly expressed gnomes. Here a taunting song of triumph

(Mic. 2:4; Hab. 2:6). **the king**—the ideal representative of Babylon; perhaps Belshazzar (Dan. 5). The mystical Babylon is ultimately meant. **golden city**—rather, "the exactress of gold" [MAURER]. But the old translators read differently in the *Hebrew*, "oppression," which the parallelism favors (cf. ch. 3:5). **5. staff**—not the scepter (Ps. 2:9), but the staff with which one strikes others, as he is speaking of more tyrants than one (ch. 9:4; 10:24; 14:29) [MAURER]. **rulers**—tyrants, as the parallelism "the wicked" proves (cf. *Note*, ch. 13:2). **6. people**—the peoples subjected to Babylon. **is persecuted**—the *Hebrew* is rather *active*, "which persecuted them, without any to hinder him" [VULGATE, JEROME, and HORSLEY]. **7. they**—the once subject nations of the whole earth. HOUBIGANT places the stop after "fir trees" (vs. 8), "The very fir trees break forth," etc. But the parallelism is better in *English Version*. **8. the fir trees**—now left undisturbed. Probably a kind of evergreen. **rejoice at thee**—(Ps. 96: 12). *At thy fall* (Ps. 35:19, 24). **no feller**—as formerly, when thou wast in power (ch. 10:34; 37: 24).

9-11. THE SCENE CHANGES FROM EARTH TO HELL. Hades (the *Amenthes* of Egypt), the unseen abode of the departed; some of its tenants, once mighty monarchs, are represented by a bold personification as rising from their seats in astonishment at the descent among them of the humbled king of Babylon. This proves, in opposition to WARBURTON, *Div. Leg.,* that the belief existed among the Jews that there was a Sheol or Hades, in which the "Rephaim" or manes of the departed abode. **9. moved**—put into agitation. **for thee**—i.e., "at thee"; towards thee; explained by "to meet thee at thy coming" [MAURER]. **chief ones**—lit., "goats"; so rams, leaders of the flock; princes (Zech. 10:3). The idea of *wickedness* on a *gigantic* scale is included (Ezek. 34:17; Matt. 25:32, 33). MAGEE derives Rephaim (*English Version*, "the dead") from a *Hebrew* root, "to resolve into first elements"; so *the deceased* (ch. 26:14) *ghosts* (Prov. 21:16). These being magnified by the imagination of the living into gigantic stature, gave their name to *giants* in general (Gen. 6:4; 14:5; Ezek. 32:18, 21). "Rephaim," translated in LXX, "giants" (cf. *Note*, Job 26:5, 6). Thence, as the giant Rephaim of Canaan were notorious even in that guilty land, *enormous wickedness* became connected with the term. So the Rephaim came to be *the wicked spirits* in Gehenna, the lower of the two portions into which Sheol is divided. **10.** They taunt him and derive from his calamity consolation under their own (Ezek. 31:16). **weak**—as a shade bereft of blood and life. **Rephaim, "the dead,"** may come from a *Hebrew* root, meaning similarly "feeble," "powerless." The speech of the departed closes with the next verse. **11.** "Pomp" and music, the accompaniment of Babylon's former feastings (ch. 5:12; 24:8), give place to the corruption and the stillness of the grave (Ezek. 32:27). **worm**—that is bred in putridity. **worms**—properly those from which the crimson dye is obtained. Appropriate here; instead of the *crimson* coverlet, *over* thee shall be "worms." Instead of the gorgeous couch, *"under"* thee" shall be the maggot.

12-15. THE JEWS ADDRESS HIM AGAIN AS A FALLEN ONCE-BRIGHT STAR. The language is so framed as to apply to the Babylonian king primarily, and at the same time to shadow forth through him, the great final enemy, the man of sin, Antichrist, of Daniel, St. Paul, and St. John; he alone shall fulfil exhaustively all the lineaments here given. **12. Lucifer**—"day star." A title truly belonging to Christ

(Rev. 22:16), "the bright and morning star," and therefore hereafter to be assumed by Antichrist. GESENIUS, however, renders the *Hebrew* here as in Ezek. 21:12; Zech. 11:2, "howl." **weaken**—"prostrate"; as in Exodus 17:13, "discomfit." **13. above ... God**—In Daniel 8:10, "stars" express *earthly potentates.* "The stars" are often also used to express *heavenly principalities* (Job 38:7). **mount of the congregation**—the place of solemn *meeting* between God and His people in the temple at Jerusalem. In Daniel 11:37, and II Thessalonians 2:4, this is attributed to Antichrist. **sides of the north**—viz., the sides of Mount Moriah on which the temple was built; *north* of Mount Zion (Ps. 48:2). However, the parallelism supports the notion that the Babylonian king expresses himself according to his own, and not Jewish opinions (so in ch. 10:10) thus "mount of the congregation" will mean the *northern* mountain (perhaps in Armenia) fabled by the Babylonians to be *the common meeting-place of their gods.* "Both sides" imply *the angle* in which the sides meet; and so the expression comes to mean *"the extreme parts* of the north." So the Hindoos place the Meru, the dwelling-place of their gods, in the north, in the Himalayan mountains. So the Greeks, in the *northern* Olympus. The Persian followers of Zoroaster put the Ai-bordsch in the Caucasus north of them. The allusion to the stars harmonizes with this; viz., that those near the *North* Pole, the region of the aurora borealis (cf. *Note,* Job 23:9; 37:22 [MAURER, LXX, SYRIAC]. **14. clouds** —rather, "the cloud," singular. Perhaps there is a reference to the cloud, the symbol of the divine presence (ch. 4:5; Exod. 13:21). So this tallies with II Thess. 2:4, *"above* all that is called God"; as here *"above* ... the cloud"; and as the Shekinah-*cloud* was connected with the *temple,* there follows, "he *as God* sitteth in the *temple* of God," answering to "I will be *like the Most High"* here. Moreover, Revelation 17:4, 5, represents Antichrist as seated in BABYLON, to which city, literal and spiritual, Isaiah refers here. **15. to hell**—to Sheol (vs. 6), thou who hast said, "I will ascend into *heaven"* (Matt. 11:23). **sides of the pit**—antithetical to the "sides of the north" (vs. 13). Thus the reference is to the *sides* of the sepulcher round which the dead were arranged in niches. But MAURER here, as in vs. 13, translates, "the *extreme,"* or innermost *parts* of the sepulchre: as in Ezek. 32:23 (cf. I Sam. 24:3).

16-20. THE PASSERS-BY CONTEMPLATE WITH ASTONISHMENT THE BODY OF THE KING OF BABYLON CAST OUT, INSTEAD OF LYING IN A SPLENDID MAUSOLEUM, AND CAN HARDLY BELIEVE THEIR SENSES THAT IT IS HE. **16. narrowly look**—to be certain they are not mistaken. **consider**—"meditate upon" [HORSLEY]. **17. opened not ... prisoners**—But MAURER, as *Margin,* "Did not let his captives loose *homewards."* **18. All**—i.e., This is the *usual* practice. **in glory**—in a grand mausoleum. **house**—i.e., "sepulchre," as in Ecclesiastes 12:5; "grave" (vs. 19). To be excluded from the family sepulcher was a mark of infamy (ch. 34:3; Jer. 22:19; I Kings 13:22; II Chron. 21:20; 24:25; 28:27). **19. cast out of**—not that he had lain in the grave and was then *cast out of* it, but "cast out *without* a grave," *such as might have been expected by thee* ("thy"). **branch** —a useless *sucker* starting up from the root of a tree, and cut away by the husbandman. **raiment of those ... slain**—covered with gore, and regarded with abhorrence as unclean by the Jews. Rather, *"clothed* i.e., covered) *with* the slain"; as in Job 7:5. "My flesh is clothed with worms and clods of dust" [MAURER]. **thrust through**—i.e., "the slain v have been thrust through," etc. **stones of ... pit**—whose bodies are buried in sepulchers excavated amidst stones, whereas the king of Babylon is an *unburied* "carcass trodden under foot." **20. not ... joined with them**—whereas the princes slain with thee shall be buried, thou shalt not. **thou ... destroyed ... land**—Belshazzar (or *Naboned*) oppressed his land with wars and tyranny, so that he was much hated (Xenophon, *Cyrop*. 4. 6, 3; 7. 5, 32). **seed ... never be renowned**—rather, "shall not be named for ever"; the Babylonian dynasty shall end with Belshazzar; his family shall not be perpetuated [HORSLEY].

21-23. GOD'S DETERMINATION TO DESTROY BABYLON. **21. Prepare ...**—charge to the Medes and Persians, as if they were God's *conscious* instruments. **his children**—Belshazzar's (Exod. 20:5). **rise**—to occupy the places of their fathers. **fill ... with cities**—MAURER translates, "enemies," as the *Hebrew* means in I Samuel 28:16; Psalm 139:20; viz., lest they inundate the world with their armies. VITRINGA translates, "disturbers." In *English Version* the meaning is, "lest they fill the land with *such* cities" of pride as Babylon was. **22. against them**—the family of the king of Babylon. **name**—all the *male* representatives, so that the name shall become extinct (ch. 56:5; Ruth 4:5). **remnant**—all that is left of them. The dynasty shall cease (Dan. 5:28-31). Cf. as to Babylon in general, Jeremiah 51:62. **23. bittern**—rather, the hedgehog [MAURER and GESENIUS]. Strabo (16:1) states that enormous hedgehogs were found in the islands of the Euphrates. **pools**—owing to Cyrus turning the waters of the Euphrates over the country. **besom**—sweep-net [MAURER], (I Kings 14:10; II Kings 21:13.)

24-27. A FRAGMENT AS TO THE DESTRUCTION OF THE ASSYRIANS UNDER SENNACHERIB. This would comfort the Jews when captives in Babylon, being a pledge that God, who had *by that time* fulfilled the promise concerning Sennacherib (though now still future), would also fulfil His promise as to destroying Babylon, Judah's enemy. In this vs. 24 *the Lord's thought* (purpose) stands in antithesis to *the Assyrians' thoughts* (ch. 10:7). (See ch. 46:10, 11; I Sam. 15:29; Mal. 3:6.) **25. That**—My purpose, namely, "that." **break ... yoke**—(Ch. 10:27). **my mountains**—Sennacherib's army was destroyed on the mountains near Jerusalem (ch. 10:33, 34). God regarded Judah as peculiarly His. **26. This is ... purpose ... whole earth**—A hint that the prophecy embraces the present world of all ages in its scope, of which the purpose concerning Babylon and Assyria, the then representatives of the world power, is but a part. **hand ... stretched out upon**—viz., in punishment (ch. 5:25). **27.** (Dan. 4:35.)

28-32. PROPHECY AGAINST PHILISTIA. To comfort the Jews, lest they should fear that people; not in order to call the Philistines to repentance, since the prophecy was probably never circulated among them. They had been subdued by Uzziah or Azariah (II Chron. 26:6); but in the reign of Ahaz (II Chron. 28:18), they took several towns in south Judea. Now Isaiah denounces their final subjugation by Hezekiah. **28. In ... year ... Ahaz died**—726 B.C. Probably it was in this year that the Philistines threw off the yoke put on them by Uzziah. **29. Palestina**—lit., "the land of sojourners." **rod ... broken**—The *yoke* imposed by Uzziah (II Chron. 26:6) was thrown off under Ahaz (II Chron. 28:18). **serpent's root**—the stock of Jesse (ch. 11:1). Uzziah was doubtless regarded by the Philistines as a biting "serpent." But though the effects of his bite have been got rid of, a more deadly *viper*, or "cockatrice"

(lit., "viper's offspring," as Philistia would regard him), viz., Hezekiah awaits you (II Kings 18:8). **30. first-born of ... poor**—Hebraism, for the *most abject poor; the first-born* being the foremost of the family. Cf. "first-born of death" (Job 18:13), for the most *fatal death*. The Jews, heretofore exposed to Philistine invasions and alarms, shall be in safety. Cf. Psalm 72:4, "Children of the needy," expressing those "needy in *condition*." **feed**—image from a flock feeding in safety. **root**—radical destruction. **He shall slay**—Jehovah shall. The change of person, He after I, is a common Hebraism. **31. gate**—i.e., ye who throng the gate; the chief place of concourse in a city. **from ... north**—Judea, north and east of Palestine. **smoke**—from the signal-fire, whereby a hostile army was called together (the *Jews'* signal-fire is meant here, the "pillar of cloud and fire," (Exod. 13:21; Neh. 9:19); or else from the region devastated by fire [MAURER]. GESENIUS less probably refers it to the *cloud of dust* raised by the invading army. **none ... alone ... in ... appointed times**—Rather, "There shall not be *a straggler* among his (the enemy's) *levies.*" The Jewish host shall advance on Palestine in close array; none shall fall back or lag from weariness (ch. 5:26, 27), [LOWTH]. MAURER thinks the *Hebrew* will not bear the rendering "levies" or "armies." He translates, "There is not one (of the Philistine watch-guards) who will remain *alone* (exposed to the enemy) *at his post,*" through fright. On "alone," cf. Psalm 102:7; Hosea 8:9. **32. messengers of the nation**—When messengers come from Philistia to inquire as to the state of Judea, the reply shall be, that the Lord ... (Ps. 87:1, 5; 102:16). **poor**—(Zeph. 3:12).

CHAPTER 15

VSS. 1-9. CHAPS. 15 and 16 FORM ONE PROPHECY ON MOAB. LOWTH thinks it was delivered in the first years of Hezekiah's reign and fulfilled in the fourth when Shalmaneser, on his way to invade Israel, may have seized on the strongholds of Moab. Moab probably had made common cause with Israel and Syria in a league against Assyria. Hence it incurred the vengeance of Assyria. Jeremiah has introduced much of this prophecy into his 48th chapter. **1. Because**—rather, "Surely"; lit., (I affirm) that [MAURER]. **night**—the time best suited for a hostile incursion (ch. 21:4; Jer. 39:4). **Ar**—meaning in *Hebrew,* "the city"; the metropolis of Moab, on the south of the river Arnon. **Kir**—lit., a citadel; not far from Ar, towards the south. **2. He**—Moab personified. **Bajith**—rather, "to the *temple*" [MAURER]; answering to the "sanctuary" (ch. 16:12), in a similar context. **to Dibon**—Rather, as Dibon was in *a plain* north of the Arnon, "Dibon (is gone up) to the high places," the usual places of sacrifice in the East. Same town as Dimon (vs. 9). **to weep**—at the sudden calamity. **over Nebo**—rather "in Nebo"; not "on account of" Nebo (cf. vs. 3) [MAURER]. The town Nebo was adjacent to the mountain, not far from the northern shore of the Dead Sea. There it was that Chemosh, the idol of Moab, was worshipped (cf. Deut. 34:1). **Medeba**—south of Heshbon, on a hill east of Jordan. **baldness ... beard cut off**—The Orientals regarded the beard with peculiar veneration. To cut one's beard off is the greatest mark of sorrow and mortification (cf. Jer. 48:37). **3. tops of ... houses**—flat; places of resort for prayer, etc., in the East (Acts 10:9). **weeping abundantly**—"melting away in tears." HORSLEY prefers "descending to weep." Thus there is a "parallelism by alternate construction" [LOWTH], or *chiasmus;* "howl" refers to "tops of houses." "Descending to weep" to "streets" or squares, whither they descend from the housetops. **4. Heshbon**—an Amorite city, twenty miles east of Jordan; taken by Moab after the carrying away of Israel (cf. Jer. 48). **Elealeh**—near Heshbon, in Reuben. **Jahaz**—east of Jordan, in Reuben. Near it Moses defeated Sihon. **therefore**—because of the sudden overthrow of their cities. Even the armed men, instead of fighting in defense of their land, shall join in the general cry. **life . . .** rather, "his soul is grieved" (I Sam. 1:8) [MAURER]. **5. My**—The prophet himself is moved with pity for Moab. Ministers, in denouncing the wrath of God against sinners, should do it with tender sorrow, not with exultation. **fugitives**—fleeing from Moab, wander as far as to Zoar, on the extreme boundary south of the Dead Sea. HORSLEY translates, "her nobility," (Hos. 4:18). **heifer . . .**—i.e., raising their voices "like a heifer" (cf. Jer. 48:34, 36). The expression "three years old," implies one at its full vigor (Gen. 15:9), as yet not brought under the yoke; as Moab heretofore unsubdued, but now about to be broken. So Jeremiah 31:18; Hosea 4:13. MAURER translates, "Eglath (in *English Version,* "a heifer") *Shel-ishijah*" (i.e., *the third,* to distinguish it from two others of the same name). **by the mounting up**—up the ascent. **Luhith**—a mountain in Moab. **Horonaim**—a town of Moab not far from Zoar (Jer. 48:5). It means "the two poles," being near caves. **cry of destruction**—a cry appropriate to the destruction which visits their country. **6. For**—the cause of their flight southwards (II Kings 3:19, 25). "For" the northern regions and even the city Nimrim (the very name of which means "limpid waters," in Gilead near Jordan) are without water or herbage. **7. Therefore**—because of the devastation of the land. **abundance**—lit., "that which is over and above" the necessaries of life. **brook of . . . willows**—The fugitives flee from Nimrim, where the waters have failed, to places better watered. *Margin* has "valley of Arabians"; i.e., to the valley on the boundary between them and Arabia Petrea; now Wady-el Arabah. Arabia means a "desert." **8. Eglaim**—(Ezek. 47:10), *En-eglaim.* Not the Agalum of Eusebius, eight miles from Areopolis towards the south; the context requires a town on the very borders of Moab or beyond them. **Beer-elim**—lit., "the well of the Princes"—(so Num. 21:16-18). Beyond the east borders of Moab. **9. Dimon**—same as Dibon (vs. 2). Its waters are the Arnon. **full of blood**—The slain of Moab shall be so many. **bring more**—fresh calamities, viz., the "lions" afterwards mentioned (II Kings 17:25; Jer. 5:6; 15:3). VITRINGA understands Nebuchadnezzar as meant by "the lion"; but it is *plural,* "lions." The "more," or in *Hebrew,* "additions," he explains of the addition made to the waters of Dimon by the streams of *blood* of the slain.

CHAPTER 16

Vss. 1-14. CONTINUATION OF THE PROPHECY AS TO MOAB. **1. lamb**—advice of the prophet to the Moabites who had fled southwards to Idumea, to send to the king of Judah the tribute of lambs, which they had formerly paid to *Israel,* but which they had given up (II Kings 3:4, 5). David probably imposed this tribute before the severance of Judah and Is-

rael (II Sam. 8:2). Therefore Moab is recommended to gain the favor and protection of *Judah,* by paying it to the Jewish king. Type of the need of submitting to Messiah (Ps. 2:10-12; Rom. 12:1). **from Sela to**—rather, "from Petra *through* (lit., 'towards') the wilderness" [MAURER]. Sela means "a rock," *Petra* in *Greek;* the capital of Idumea and Arabia Petra; the dwellings are mostly hewn out of the rock. The country around was a vast common ("wilderness") or open pasturage, to which the Moabites had fled on the invasion from the west (ch. 15:7). **ruler of the land**—viz., of *Idumea,* i.e., the king of Judah; Amaziah had become master of Idumea and Sela (II Kings 14:7). **2. cast out of . . . nest**—rather, "as a *brood* cast out" (in apposition with "a wandering bird," or rather, *wandering birds),* viz., a brood just fledged and expelled from the nest in which they were hatched [HORSLEY]. Cf. ch. 10:14; Deuteronomy 32:11. **daughters of Moab**—i.e., the inhabitants of Moab. So II Kings 19:21; Psalm 48:11; Jeremiah 46:11; Lamentations 4:22 [MAURER]. **at the fords**—trying to cross the boundary river of Moab, in order to escape out of the land. EWALD and MAURER make "fords" a poetical expression for "*the dwellers* on Arnon," answering to the parallel clause of the same sense, "daughters of Moab." **3-5.** GESENIUS, MAURER, etc., regard these verses as an address of the fugitive Moabites to the Jews for protection; they translate vs. 4, "Let mine outcasts *of Moab* dwell with thee, Judah"; the protection will be refused by the *Jews,* for the pride of Moab (vs. 6). VITRINGA makes it an additional advice *to Moab,* besides paying tribute. Give shelter to the Jewish outcasts who take refuge in thy land (vss. 3, 4); so "mercy" will be shown thee in turn by whatever king sits on the "throne" of "David" (vs. 5). Isaiah foresees that Moab will be too *proud* to pay the tribute, or conciliate Judah by sheltering its outcasts (vs. 6); therefore judgment shall be executed. However, as Moab just before is represented as itself an *outcast* in Idumea, it seems incongruous that it should be called on to *shelter* Jewish outcasts. So that it seems rather to foretell the ruined state of Moab *when its people should beg the Jews for shelter,* but be refused for their pride. **make . . . shadow as . . . night . . . in . . . noonday**—emblem of a thick shelter from the glaring noonday heat (ch. 4:6; 25:4; 32:2). **bewray . . . wandereth**—Betray not the fugitive to his pursuer. **4.** Rather, "Let the outcasts of Moab dwell with thee" (Judah) [HORSLEY]. **4. for the extortioner . . .**—The Assyrian *oppressor* probably. **is at an end**—By the time that Moab begs Judah for shelter, Judah shall be in a condition to afford it, *for* the Assyrian oppressor shall have been "consumed out of the land." **5.** If Judah shelters the suppliant Moab, allowing him to remain in Idumea, a blessing will redound to Judah itself and its "throne." **truth . . . judgment . . . righteousness**—language so divinely framed as to apply to "the latter days" under King Messiah, when "the Lord shall bring again the captivity of Moab" (Ps. 72:2; 96:13; 98:9; Jer. 48:47; Rom. 11:12). **hasting**—"prompt in executing." **6. We**—Jews. We reject Moab's supplication for his pride. **lies**—false boasts. **not be so**—rather, "not right"; shall prove vain (ch. 25:10; Jer. 48:29, 30; Zeph. 2:8). "It shall not be so; his lies shall not so effect it." **7. Therefore**—all hope of being allowed shelter by the Jews being cut off. **foundations**—i.e., "ruins"; because, when houses are pulled down, the "foundations" alone are left (ch. 58:12). Jeremiah, in the parallel place (Jer. 48:31), renders it "men," who are the moral foundations or stay of a city. **Kir-**

hareseth—lit., "a citadel of brick." **surely they are stricken**—rather, joined with "mourn"; "Ye shall mourn *utterly* stricken" [MAURER and HORSLEY]. **8. fields**—vine-fields (Deut. 32:32). **vine of Sibmah**—near Heshbon: viz., languishes. **lords of . . . heathen**—The heathen princes, the Assyrians, etc., who invaded Moab, destroyed his vines. So Jeremiah in the parallel place (Jer. 48:32, 33). MAURER thinks the following words require rather the rendering, "Its (the vine of Sibmah) shoots (the wines got from them) overpowered (by its generous flavor and potency) the lords of the nations" (Gen. 49:11, 12, 22). **come . . ., Jazer**—They (the vine-shoots) reached even to Jazer, fifteen miles from Heshbon. **wandered**—They overran in wild luxuriance the wilderness of Arabia, encompassing Moab. **the sea**—the Dead Sea; or else some lake near Jazer now dry; in Jeremiah 48:32 called the sea of Jazer; but see *Note* there (Ps. 80:8-11). **9. I**—will bewail for its desolation, though I belong to another nation (*Note,* ch. 15:5). **with . . . weeping of Jazer**—as Jazer weeps. **shouting for . . . fallen**—rather, "*Upon* thy summer fruits and upon thy *luxuriant vines* the shouting (*the battle shout,* instead of the *joyous shout* of the grape-gatherers, usual at the vintage) is fallen" (vs. 10; Jer. 25:30; 51:14). In the parallel passage (Jer. 48:32) the words substantially express the same sense. "The *spoiler* is fallen upon thy summer fruits." **10. gladness**—such as is felt in gathering a rich harvest. There shall be *no harvest* or vintage owing to the desolation; therefore no "gladness." **11. bowels**—in Scripture the seat of yearning compassion. It means the inward seat of emotion, the heart, etc. (ch. 63:15; cf. ch. 15:5; Jer. 48:36.) **sound . . . harp**—as its strings vibrate when beaten with the plectrum or hand. **12. when it is seen that**—rather, "When Moab shall have *appeared* (before his gods; cf. Exod. 23:15), *when* he is weary (i.e., when he shall have fatigued himself with observing burdensome rites; I Kings 18:26, etc.), on the high place (cf. ch. 15:2), *and* shall come to his sanctuary (of the idol Chemosh on Mount Nebo) to pray, he shall not prevail"; he shall effect nothing by his prayers [MAURER]. **13. since that time**—rather, "respecting that time" [HORSLEY]. BARNES translates it, "*formerly*" in contrast to "but *now*" (vs. 14): heretofore former prophecies (Exod. 15:15; Num. 21:29) have been given as to Moab, of which Isaiah has given the substance: *but now* a definite and steady *time* also is fixed. **14. three years . . . hireling**—Just as a hireling has his fixed term of engagement, which neither he nor his master will allow to be added to or to be taken from, so the limit within which Moab is to fall is unalterably fixed (ch. 21:16). Fulfilled about the time when the Assyrians led Israel into captivity. The ruins of Elealeh, Heshbon, Medeba, Dibon, etc., still exist to confirm the inspiration of Scripture. The accurate *particularity of specification* of the places 3000 years ago, confirmed by modern research, is a strong testimony to the truth of prophecy.

CHAPTER 17

Vss. 1-11. PROPHECY CONCERNING DAMASCUS AND ITS ALLY SAMARIA, i.e., Syria and Israel, which had leagued together (chs. 7 and 8). Already, Tiglath-pileser had carried away the people of Damascus to Kir, in the fourth year of Ahaz (II Kings 16:9); but now in Hezekiah's reign a *farther* overthrow is foretold (Jer. 49:23; Zech. 9:1). Also, Shalmaneser

carried away Israel from Samaria to Assyria (II Kings 17:6; 18:10, 11) in the *sixth* year of Hezekiah of Judah (the ninth year of Hoshea of Israel). This prophecy was, doubtless, given previously in the *first* years of Hezekiah when the foreign nations came into nearer collision with Judah, owing to the threatening aspect of Assyria. **Damascus**—put before *Israel* (Ephraim, vs. 3), which is chiefly referred to in what follows, because it was the prevailing power in the league; with it Ephraim either stood or fell (ch. 7). **2. cities of Aroer**—i.e., the cities round Aroer, and under its jurisdiction [GESENIUS]. So "cities with their villages" (Josh. 15:44); "Heshbon and all her cities" (Josh. 13:17). Aroer was near Rabbah-ammon, at the river of Gad, an arm of the Jabbok (II Sam. 24:5), founded by the Gadites (Num. 32:34). **for flocks**—(Ch. 5:17). **3. fortress . . . cease**—The strongholds shall be pulled down (*Samaria* especially: Hos. 10:14; Mic. 1:6; Hab. 1:10). **remnant of Syria**—all that was left after the overthrow by Tiglath-pileser (II Kings 16:9). **as the glory of . . . Israel**—They shall meet with the same fate as Israel, their ally. **4. glory of Jacob**—the kingdom of Ephraim and all that they rely on (Hos. 12:2; Mic. 1:5). **fatness . . . lean**—(*Note,* ch. 10:16.) **5. harvestman . . .**—The inhabitants and wealth of Israel shall be swept away, and but few left behind just as the husbandman gathers the corn and the fruit, and leaves only a few gleaning ears and grapes (II Kings 18:9-11). **with his arm**—He collects the standing grain with one arm, so that he can cut it with the sickle in the other hand. **Rephaim**—a fertile plain at the southwest of Jerusalem toward Bethlehem and the country of the Philistines (II Sam. 5:18-22). **6. in it**—i.e., in the land of Israel. **two or three . . . in the top**—A few poor inhabitants shall be left in Israel, like the two or three olive berries left on the topmost boughs, which it is not worth while taking the trouble to try to reach. **7. look to his Maker**—instead of trusting in their *fortresses*—(vs. 3; Mic. 7:7). **8. groves**—A symbolical tree is often found in Assyrian inscriptions, representing *the hosts of heaven* (Saba), answering to Asteroth or Astarte, the queen of heaven, as Baal or Bel is the king. Hence the expression, "image of the grove," is explained (II Kings 21:7). **images**—lit., "images to the sun," i.e., to Baal, who answers to the sun, as Astarte to the hosts of heaven (II Kings 23:5; Job 31:26). **9. forsaken bough**—rather "the leavings of woods," what the axeman leaves when he cuts down the grove (cf. vs. 6). **which they left because of**—rather, "which (the enemies) shall leave for the children of Israel"; lit., "shall leave (in departing) *from before the face* of the children of Israel [MAURER]. But a few cities out of many shall be left to Israel, by the purpose of God, executed by the Assyrian. **10. forgotten . . . God of . . . salvation . . . rock**—(Deut. 32:15, 18). **plants**—rather, nursery grounds, pleasure-grounds [MAURER]. **set in**—rather, "set them," the pleasure-grounds. **strange slips**—cuttings of plants from far, and therefore valuable. **11. In the day . . . thy plant**—rather, "In the day of *thy planting*" [HORSLEY]. **shalt . . . make . . . grow**—MAURER translates, "Thou didst *fence* it," viz., the pleasure-ground. The parallel clause, "Make . . . flourish," favors *English Version.* As soon as thou plantest, it grows. **in the morning**—i.e., immediately after; so in Psalm 94:14, the *Hebrew,* "in the morning," is translated "early." **but . . . shall be a heap**—rather, "but (promising as was the prospect) the harvest *is gone*" [HORSLEY]. **in . . . day of grief**—rather, "in the day of (expected) *possession*" [MAURER]. "In the day of *inundation*"

[HORSLEY]. **of desperate sorrow**—rather, "And the sorrow shall be desperate or irremediable." In *English Version* "heap" and "sorrow" may be taken together by hendiadys. "The heap of the harvest shall be desperate sorrow" [ROSENMULLER].

Chap. 17:12-18:7. SUDDEN DESTRUCTION OF A GREAT ARMY IN JUDEA (viz., that of the Assyrian Sennacherib), AND ANNOUNCEMENT OF THE EVENT TO THE Ethiopian AMBASSADORS. The connection of this fragment with what precedes is: notwithstanding the calamities coming on Israel, the people of God shall not be utterly destroyed (ch. 6:12, 13); the Assyrian spoilers shall perish (ch. 17:13, 14). **12. Woe . . . multitude**—rather, "*Ho* (Hark)! *a noise* of," etc. The prophet in vision perceives the vast and mixed Assyrian hosts (*Hebrew*, "many *peoples*," see *Note*, ch. 5:26): on the hills of Judah (so "mountains," vs. 13): but at the "rebuke" of God, they shall "flee as chaff." **to the rushing . . . that make**—rather, "the roaring . . . roareth" (cf. ch. 8:7; Jer. 6:23). **13. shall . . . shall**—rather, "God rebuketh (Ps. 9:5) them, and they *flee—are chased*"; the event is set before the eyes as actually present, not future. **chaff of . . . mountains**—Threshing-floors in the East are in the open air on *elevated* places, so as to catch the wind which separates the chaff from the wheat (Ps. 88:13; Hos. 13:3). **rolling thing**—anything that rolls: *stubble*. **14. eventide . . . before morning**—fulfilled to the letter in the destruction "before morning" of the vast host that "at eventingtide" was such a *terror* ("trouble") to Judah; on the phrase see Psalm 90:6; 30:5. **he is not**—viz., the enemy. **us**—the Jews. A general declaration of the doom that awaits the foes of God's people (ch. 54:17).

CHAPTER 18

Isaiah announces the overthrow of Sennacherib's hosts and desires the Ethiopian ambassadors, now in Jerusalem, to bring word of it to their own nation; and he calls on the whole world to witness the event (vs. 3). As ch. 17:12-14 announced the presence of the foe, so ch. 18 foretells his overthrow. The heading in *English Version*, "God will destroy the Ethiopians," is a mistake arising from the wrong rendering "Woe," whereas the *Hebrew* does not express a threat, but is an *appeal* calling attention (ch. 55:1; Zech. 2:6): "Ho." He is not speaking *against* but *to* the Ethiopians, calling on them to hear his prophetical announcement as to the destruction of their enemies. **1. shadowing with wings**—rather, "land *of the winged bark*"; i.e., "barks with wing-like sails, answering to vessels of bulrushes" in vs. 2; the word "rivers," in the parallelism, also favors it; so LXX and *Chaldee* [EWALD]. "Land of the clanging sound of *wings*," i.e., armies, as in ch. 8:8; the rendering "bark," or "ship," is rather dubious [MAURER]. The armies referred to are those of Tirhakah, advancing to meet the Assyrians (ch. 37:9). In *English Version*, "shadowing" means *protecting*—stretching out its *wings* to defend a feeble people, viz., the Hebrews [VITRINGA]. The *Hebrew* for "wings" is the same as for the idol *Cneph*, which was represented in temple sculptures with wings (Ps. 91:4). **beyond**—Meroe, the island between the "rivers" Nile and Astaboras is meant, famed for its commerce, and perhaps the seat of the Ethiopian government, hence addressed here as representing the whole empire: remains of temples are still found, and the name of "Tirhakah" in the inscriptions. This island region was probably the chief part of Queen Candace's kingdom (Acts 8:27). For "beyond" others translate less literally "which borderest

on." **Ethiopia**—lit., Cush. HORSLEY is probably right that the *ultimate* and *fullest* reference of the prophecy is to the restoration of the Jews in the Holy Land through the instrumentality of some *distant* people skilled in navigation (vs. 2; ch. 60:9, 10; Ps. 45:15; 68:31; Zeph. 3:10). Phœnician voyagers coasting along would speak of all Western *remote* lands as "beyond" the Nile's mouths. "Cush," too, has a wide sense, being applied not only to Ethiopia, but Arabia Deserta and Felix, and along the Persian Gulf, as far as the Tigris (Gen. 2:13). **2. ambassadors**—messengers sent to Jerusalem at the time that negotiations passed between Tirhakah and Hezekiah against the expected attack of Sennacherib (ch. 37:9). **by . . . sea**—on the *Nile* (ch. 19:5): as what follows proves. **vessels of bulrushes**—light canoes, formed of papyrus, daubed over with pitch: so the "ark" in which Moses was exposed (Exod. 2: 3). **Go**—Isaiah tells them to take back the tidings of what God is about to do (vs. 4) against the common enemy of both Judah and Ethiopia. **scattered and peeled**—rather, "strong and energetic" [MAURER]. The *Hebrew* for "strong" is lit., drawn out (*Margin,* Ps. 36:10; Eccles. 2:3). "Energetic," lit., sharp (Hab. 1:8; *Margin,* the verb means to "sharpen" a sword, Ezek. 21:15, 16); also "polished." As HERODOTUS (3:20, 114) characterizes the Ethiopians as "the tallest and fairest of men," G. V. SMITH translates, "tall and comely"; lit., extended (ch. 45: 14, "men of stature") *and polished* (the Ethiopians had *smooth, glossy skins*). In *English Version* the reference is to the Jews, *scattered* outcasts, and loaded with indignity (lit., "having their hair torn off" HORSLEY). **terrible**—the *Ethiopians* famed for warlike prowess [ROSENMULLER]. The *Jews* who, because of God's plague, made others to fear the like (Deut. 28:37). Rather, "awfully remarkable" [HORSLEY]. God puts the "terror" of His people into the surrounding nations as at the first (Exod. 23:27; Josh. 2:9); so it shall be again in the latter days (Zech. 12: 2, 3). **from . . . beginning hitherto**—so *English Version* rightly. But GESENIUS, "to the terrible nation (of upper Egypt) and further beyond" (to the Ethiopians, properly so called). **meted out**—*Hebrew*, "of line." The measuring line was used in *destroying* buildings (ch. 34:11; II Kings 21:13; Lam. 2:8). Hence, actively, it means here "a people *meting out*," —an all-destroying people"; which suits the context better than "meted," passively [MAURER]. HORSLEY, understanding it of *the Jews*, translates it, "Expecting, expecting (in a continual attitude of expectation of Messiah) and trampled under foot"; a graphic picture of them. Most translate, *of strength, strength* (from a root, *to brace* the sinews), i.e., *a most powerful* people. **trodden down**—true of the Jews. But MAURER translates it actively, a people "treading under foot" all its enemies, i.e., *victorious* (ch. 14:25), viz., the Ethiopians. **spoiled**—"cut up." The Nile is formed by the junction of many streams in Abyssinia, the Atbara, the Astapus or Blue river (between which two rivers Meroe, the "Ethiopia" here meant, lies), and the Astaboras or White river; these streams *wash down* the soil along their banks in the "land" of Upper Egypt and deposit it on that of Lower Egypt. G. V. SMITH translates it, "Divide." HORSLEY takes it figuratively *of the conquering armies* which have often "spoiled" *Judea,* **3. see ye . . . hear ye**—rather, ye shall see—shall hear. Call to the whole earth to *be witnesses* of what *Jehovah* ("He") is about to do. He will "lift up an ensign," calling the Assyrian motley hosts together (ch. 5:26) on "the mountains" round Jerusalem, to their own destruction. This (ch. 18) declares the coming overthrow of those armies whose presence is announced in ch. 17:12, 13. The same motive, which led Hezekiah to seek aid from Egypt, led him to accept gladly the Ethiopian Tirhakah's aid (ch. 36: 6; 37:9). Ethiopia, Egypt, and Judea were probably leagued together against the common enemy, 713 B.C. See notes on ch. 22 where a difference of tone (as referring to a different period) as to Ethiopia is observable. HORSLEY takes the "ensign" to be the cross, and the "trumpet" the *Gospel trumpet,* which shall be sounded more loudly in the last days. **4. take . . . rest . . . consider**—I will *calmly look on* and not interpose, while all seems to promise success to the enemy; when fig., the sun's heat" and "the night dews" ripen their "harvest"; but "before" it reaches its maturity I will destroy it (vs. 5; Eccles. 8:11, 12). **like a clear heat**—rather, "at the time of the clear (serene) heat" [MAURER]. **upon herbs**—answering to "harvest" in the parallel clause. MAURER translates, "in the sunlight" (Job 31:26; 37:21; Hab. 3:4). **like . . . dew**—rather, "at the time of the dew-cloud." God's "silence" is mistaken by the ungodly for consent; His delay in taking vengeance for forgetfulness (Ps. 50:21); so it shall be before the vengeance which in the last day shall usher in the restoration of the Jews (ch. 34:1-8; 57:11, end of the verse; II Pet. 3:3-10). **5. For**—rather, "But. **perfect**—perfected. When the enemy's plans are on the verge of completion. **sour grape . . . flower**—rather, "when the flower shall become the ripening grape" [MAURER]. **sprigs**—the *shoots* with the grapes on them. God will not only disconcert their present plans, but prevent them forming any future ones. HORSLEY takes the "harvest" and vintage here as referring to purifying judgments which cause the excision of the ungodly from the earth, and the placing of the faithful in a state of peace *on the earth:* not the last judgment (John 15:2; Rev. 14:15-20). **6. birds . . . beasts** —transition from the image "sprigs," "branches," to the thing meant: the Assyrian soldiers and leaders shall be the prey of birds and beasts, the whole year through, "winter" and "summer," so numerous shall be their carcasses. HORSLEY translates the Hebrew which is *singular:* "upon *it,*" not "upon them"; the "it" refers to God's "dwelling-place" (vs. 4) in the Holy Land, which Antichrist ("the bird of prey" with the "beasts," his rebel hosts) is to possess himself of, and where he is to perish. **7. present . . . people scattered and peeled**—For the right rendering, see *Note* on vs. 2. The repetition of epithets enhances the honor paid to Jehovah by *so mighty a nation.* The Ethiopians, wonder-struck at such an interposition of Jehovah in behalf of His people, shall send gifts to Jerusalem in His honor (ch. 16:1; Ps. 68:31; 72:10). Thus translate: "a present—*from* a people." Or translate, as *English Version;* "the present" will mean "the people" of Ethiopia converted to God (Rom. 15:16). HORSLEY takes the people converted to Jehovah, as the Jews in the latter days. **place of the name**—where Jehovah peculiarly manifests His glory. Acts 2:10 and 8:27 show how worshippers came up to Jerusalem from Egypt" and "Ethiopia." Frumentius, an Egyptian, in the 4th century, converted Abyssinia to Christianity; and a Christian church, under an *abuna* or bishop, still flourishes there. The full accomplishment is probably still future.

CHAPTER 19

Vss. 1-25. Chaps. 19 and 20 are connected, but with an interval between. Egypt had been held by an Ethiopian dynasty, Sabacho, Sevechus, or Sabacho II, and Tirhakah, for forty or fifty years. Sevechus (called *So,* the ally of Hoshea, II Kings 17:4), retired from Lower Egypt on account of the resistance of the priests; and perhaps also, as the Assyrians threatened Lower Egypt. On his withdrawal, Sethos, one of the priestly caste, became supreme, having Tanis ("Zoan") or else Memphis as his capital, 718 B.C.; while the Ethiopians retained Upper Egypt, with Thebes as its capital, under Tirhakah. A third native dynasty was at Sais, in the west of Lower Egypt; to this at a later period belonged Psammetichus, the first who admitted Greeks into Egypt and its armies; he was one of the dodecarchy, a number of petty kings between whom Egypt was divided, and by aid of foreign auxiliaries overcame the rest, 670 B.C. To the divisions at this last time, GESENIUS refers vs. 2; and Psammetichus, vs. 4, "a cruel lord." The dissensions of the ruling castes are certainly referred to. But the time referred to is much earlier than that of Psammetichus. In vs. 1, the invasion of Egypt is represented as caused by "the LORD"; and in vs. 17, "Judah" is spoken of as "a terror to Egypt," which it could hardly have been *by itself.* Probably, therefore, the Assyrian invasion of Egypt under Sargon, when Judah was the ally of Assyria, and Hezekiah had not yet refused tribute as he did in the beginning of Sennacherib's reign, is meant. That Assyria was in Isaiah's mind appears from the way in which it is joined with Israel and Egypt in the worship of Jehovah (vss. 24, 25). Thus the dissensions referred to (vs. 2) allude to the time of the withdrawal of the Ethiopians from Lower Egypt, probably not without a struggle, espebetween 722-715 B.C., answering to 718 B.C., when Sethos usurped the throne and entered on the contest with the military caste, by the aid of the town populations: when the Saitic dynasty was another cause of division. Sargon's reign was between 722-715 B.C. answering to 718 B.C., when Sethos usurped his throne [G. V. SMITH]. **1. burden**—(*Note,* ch. 13:1.) **upon . . . cloud**—(Ps. 104: 3; 18:10.) **come upon Egypt**—to inflict vengeance. "Egypt," in *Hebrew, Misraim, plural* form, to express the two regions of Egypt. BUNSEN observes, The title of their kings runs thus: "Lord of Upper and Lower Egypt." **idols**—the bull, crocodile, etc. The idols poetically are said to be "moved" with fear at the presence of one mightier than even they were *supposed* to be (Exod. 12:12; Jer. 43:12). **2. set**—stir up. GENESIUS translates, "arm." **Egyptians against the Egyptians**—Lower against Upper: and Saitic against both. (See ch. 3:10.) NEWTON refers it to the civil wars between Apries and Amasis at the time of Nebuchadnezzar's invasion; also between Tachos, Nectanebus, and the Mendesians, just before Ochus subdued Egypt. **kingdom against kingdom**—The LXX has "nome against nome"; Egypt was divided into forty-two *nomes* or districts. **3. spirit**—*wisdom,* for which Egypt was famed (ch. 31: 2; I Kings 4:30; Acts 7:22); answering to "counsel" in the parallel clause. **fail**—lit., "be poured out," i.e., be made void (Jer. 19:7). They shall "seek" help from sources that can afford none, "charmers," etc. (ch. 8:19). **charmers**—lit., "those making a faint sound"; the soothsayers imitated the faint sound which was attributed to the spirits of the dead (*Note,* ch. 8:19). **4. cruel lord**—Sargon, in *Hebrew* it is *lords;* but *plural* is often used to express *greatness,* where one alone is meant (Gen. 39:2). The parallel word "king" (singular) proves it. NEWTON makes the *general* reference to be to Nebuchadnezzar, and a *particular* reference to Cambyses, son of

Cyrus (who killed the Egyptian god, Apis), and Ochus, Persian conquerors of Egypt, noted for their "fierce cruelty." GESENIUS refers it to Psammetichus, who had brought into Egypt Greek and other foreign mercenaries to subdue the other eleven princes of the dodecarchy. **5. the sea**—the Nile. Physical calamities, it is observed in history, often accompany political convulsions (Ezek. 30:12). The Nile shall "fail" to rise to its wonted height, the result of which will be barrenness and famine. Its "waters" at the time of the overflow resemble "a sea" (PLINY, *N.H.*, 85. 11); and it is still called *El-Bahr*, "the sea," by the Egyptians (ch. 18:2; Jer. 51:36). A public record is kept at Cairo of the daily rise of the water at the proper time of overflow, viz., August: if it rises to a less height than twelve cubits, it will not overflow the land, and famine must be the result. So, also, when it rises higher than sixteen; for the waters are not drained off in time sufficient to sow the seed. **6. they shall turn the rivers**—rather, "the streams shall become putrid"; i.e., the artificial streams made for irrigation shall become stagnant and offensive when the waters fail [MAURER]. HORSLEY, with LXX, translates, "And waters from the sea shall be drunk"; by the failure of the river-water they shall be reduced to sea-water. **brooks of defence**—rather, "canals of *Egypt*"; canals, lit., "Niles," *Nile canals,* the *plural* of the Egyptian term for the great river. The same *Hebrew* word, *Matzor,* whence comes *Mitzraim,* expresses *Egypt,* and a place of "defense." HORSLEY, as *English Version* translates it, "embanked canals," **reeds . . . flags**—the papyrus. "Reed and rush"; *utter* withering. **7. paper reeds**—rather, pastures, lit., "places naked" of wood, and famed for rich herbage, on the banks of the Nile [GESENIUS]. Cf. Gen. 13:10; Deut. 11:10. HORSLEY translates, "nakedness upon the river," descriptive of the appearance of a river when its bottom is bare and its banks stripped of verdure by long drought: so *Vulgate.* **the brooks**—the river. **mouth**—rather, "the source [VULGATE]. "Even close to the river's *side* vegetation shall be so withered as to be scattered in the shape of powder by the wind" (*English Version,* "driven away") [HORSLEY]. **8. fishers**—The Nile was famed for fish (Num. 11:5); many would be thrown out of employment by the failure of fishes. **angle**—a hook. Used in the "brooks" or canals, as the "net" was in "the waters" of the river itself. **9. fine flax**—GESENIUS, for "fine," translates, "combed"; fine linen was worn by the rich only (Luke 16:19). Egypt was famous for it (Exod. 9:31; I Kings 10:28; Prov. 7:16; Ezek. 27:7). The processes of its manufacture are represented on the Egyptian tombs. Israel learned the art in Egypt (Exod. 26:36). The cloth now found on the mummies was *linen,* as is shown by the microscope. WILKINSON mentions linen from Egypt which has 540 (or 270 double) threads in one inch in the warp; whereas some modern cambric has but 160 [BARNES]. **networks**—rather, *white cloth* (Esther 1:6; 8:16). **10. in the purposes**—rather, the foundations, i.e., "the nobles shall be broken" or brought low: so ch. 3:1; Psalm 11:3; cf. vs. 13, "*Their weaving-frames*" [HORSLEY]. "Dykes" call a prince "a *pillar* of the people" [MAURER]. "*Their weaving-frames*" [HORSLEY]. "Dykes" [BARNES]. **all that make sluices,** etc.—"makers of *dams,*" made to confine the waters which overflow from the Nile in artificial fishponds [HORSLEY]. "Makers of gain," i.e., the common people who have to earn their livelihood, as opposed to the "nobles" previously [MAURER]. **11.**

Zoan—The Greeks called it Tanis, a city of Lower Egypt, east of the Tanitic arms of the Nile, now *San*; it was one the Egyptian towns nearest to Palestine (Num. 13:22); the scene of Moses' miracles (Ps. 78: 12, 43). It, or else Memphis, was the capital under Sethos. **I am . . . son of the wise . . . kings**—Ye have no advice to suggest to Pharaoh in the crisis, notwithstanding that ye boast of descent from wise and royal ancestors. The priests were the usual "counsellors" of the Egyptian king. He was generally chosen from the priestly caste, or, if from the warrior caste, he was admitted into the sacred order, and was called a priest. The priests are, therefore, meant by the expression, "son of the wise, and of ancient kings"; this was their favorite boast (Herodotus, 2. 141; cf. Amos 7:14; Acts 23:6; Phil. 3:5). "Pharaoh" was the common name of all the kings: Sethos, probably, is here meant. **12. let them know** —i.e., How is it that, with all their boast of knowing the future (Diodorus, 1. 81), they do not know what Jehovah of hosts.... **13. Noph**—called also *Moph; Greek, Memphis* (Hos. 9:6); on the western bank of the Nile, capital of Lower Egypt, second only to Thebes in all Egypt: residence of the kings, until the Ptolemies removed to Alexandria; the word means the "port of the good" (Plutarch). The *military* caste probably ruled in it: "*they also* are deceived," in fancying their country secure from Assyrian invasion. **stay of . . . tribes**—rather, "cornerstone of her castes" [MAURER], i.e., the princes, the two ruling castes, the priests and the warriors: image from a building which rests mainly on its cornerstones (vs. 10, *Note:* ch. 28:16; Ps. 118:22; Num. 24: 17; *Margin:* Judg. 20:2; I Sam. 14:28, *Margin:* Zech. 10:4). **14. err in every work thereof**—referring to the anarchy arising from their internal feuds. HORSLEY translates, "with respect to all *His* (God's) work"; they misinterpreted God's dealings at every step. "Mingled" contains the same image as "drunken"; as one *mixes* spices with wine to make it intoxicating (ch. 5:22; Prov. 9:2,5), so Jehovah has poured among them a spirit of *giddiness,* so that they are as helpless as a "drunken man." **15. work for Egypt**—nothing which Egypt can do to extricate itself from the difficulty. **head or tail**—high or low (vss. 11-15, and 8-10). **branch or rush**—the lofty palm branch or the humble reed (ch. 9:14, 15; 10: 33, 34). **16. like . . . women**—timid and helpless (Jer. 51:30; Nah. 3:13). **shaking of . . . hand**—His judgments by means of the invaders (ch. 10:5, 32; 11:15). **17. Judah . . . terror unto Egypt**—not by itself: but at this time Hezekiah was the active subordinate ally of Assyria in its invasion of Egypt under Sargon. Similarly to the alliance of Judah with Assyria here is II Kings 23:29, where Josiah takes the field against Pharaoh-necho of Egypt, probably as ally of Assyria against Egypt [G. V. SMITH]. VITRINGA explains it that Egypt in its calamities would remember that prophets of Judah had foretold them, and so Judah would be "a terror unto Egypt." **thereof**—of Judah. **it**—Egypt. **18-22.** Suffering shall lead to repentance. Struck with "terror" and "afraid" (vs. 17) because of Jehovah's judgments, Egypt shall be converted to Him: nay, even Assyria shall join in serving Him; so that Israel, Assyria, and Egypt, once mutual foes, shall be bound together by the tie of a common faith as one people. So a similar issue from other prophecies (ch. 18:7; 23:18). **five cities**—i.e., *several* cities, as in ch. 17:6; 30:17; Gen. 43:34; Lev. 26:8. Rather, *five* definite *cities* of Lower Egypt (vss. 11, 13; ch. 30:4), which had close intercourse with the neighboring Jewish cities [MAURER]; some say, Heliopolis, Leontopolis (else Diospolis), Migdol, Daphne (Tahpanes), and Memphis. **language of Canaan**—i.e., of the Hebrews in Canaan, the language of revelation. Fig. for, They shall embrace the Jewish *religion:* so "a pure *language"* and *conversion to God* are connected in Zephaniah 3:9; as also the first confounding and multiplication of languages was the punishment of the making of gods at Babel, other than the One God. Pentecost (Acts 2:4) was the counterpart of Babel: the separation of nations is not to hinder the unity of faith; the full realization of this is yet future (Zech. 14:9; John 17:21). The next clause, "swear to the LORD of Hosts," agrees with this view; i.e., bind themselves to Him by solemn covenant (ch. 45:23; 65:16; Deut. 6:13). **city of destruction**—Onias; "city of the *sun,"* i.e., On, or Heliopolis; he persuaded Ptolemy Philometer (149 B.C.) to let him build a temple in the prefecture (nome) of Heliopolis, on the ground that it would induce Jews to reside there, and that the very site was foretold by Isaiah 600 years before. The reading of the *Hebrew* text is, however, better supported, "city of *destruction";* referring to Leontopolis, the site of Onias' temple: which casts a reproach on that city because *it* was about to contain a temple rivalling the only sanctioned temple, that at Jerusalem. MAURER, with some MSS., reads "city of *defense"* or *"deliverance";* viz., Memphis, or some such city, to which God was about to send "a saviour" (vs. 20), to "deliver them." **19. altar**—not for *sacrifice,* but as the "pillar" for *memorial* and worship (Josh. 22:22-26). Isaiah does not contemplate a *temple* in Egypt: for the only legal temple wat at Jerusalem; but, like the patriarchs, they shall have altars in various places. **pillar**—such as Jacob reared (Gen. 28:18; 35:14); it was a common practice in Egypt to raise obelisks commemorating divine and great events. **at the border**—of Egypt and Judah, to proclaim to both countries the common faith. This passage shows how the Holy Spirit raised Isaiah above a narrow-minded nationality to a charity anticipatory of gospel catholicity. **20. it**—the altar and pillar. **a sign**—(of the fulfilment of prophecy) to their contemporaries. **a witness**—to their descendants. **unto the Lord**—no longer, to their *idols,* but to *Jehovah.* **for they shall cry**—or, "a sign . . . *that they cried, . . .* and *He sent* to them a saviour"; probably, *Alexander the Great* (so "a great one"), whom the Egyptians welcomed as a deliverer (*Greek,* Soter, a title of the Ptolemies) out of the hands of the Persians, who under Cambyses had been their "oppressors." At Alexandria, called from him, the Old Testament was translated into Greek for the Greek-speaking Jews, who in large numbers dwelt in Egypt under the Ptolemies, his successors. Messiah is the antitype ultimately intended (cf. Acts 2:10, "Egypt"). **21. oblation**—unbloody. **22. return**—for heathen sin and idolatry are an *apostasy* from primitive truth. **heal**—as described (vss. 18-20). **23. highway**—free communication, resting on the highest basis, the common faith of both (vs. 18; ch. 11:16). Assyria and Egypt were joined under Alexander as parts of his empire: Jews and proselytes from both met at the feasts of Jerusalem. A type of gospel times to come. **serve with**—serve *Jehovah* with the Assyrians. So "serve" is used absolutely (Job 36:11). **24. third**—The three shall be joined as one nation. **blessing**—the source of blessings to other nations, and the object of their benedictions. **in the midst of the land**—rather, earth (Mic. 5:7). Judah is designed to be the grand center of the whole earth (Jer. 3:17). **25. Whom**—rather, "Which," viz., "the land," or "earth," i.e., the people of it [MAURER].

my people—the peculiar designation of Israel, the elect people, here applied to Egypt to express its entire admission to religious privileges (Rom. 9:24-26; I Pet. 2:9, 10). **work of my hands**—spiritually (Hos. 2:23; Eph. 2:10).

CHAPTER 20

Vss.1-6. CONTINUATION OF THE SUBJECT OF CHAPTER 19, BUT AT A LATER DATE. CAPTIVITY OF EGYPT AND ETHIOPIA. In the reign of Sargon (722-715 B.C.), the successor of Shalmaneser, an Assyrian invasion of Egypt took place. Its success is here foretold, and hence a party among the Jews is warned of the folly of their "expectation" of aid from Egypt or Ethiopia. At a later period (ch. 18), when Tirhakah of Ethiopia was their ally, the Ethiopians are treated as *friends,* to whom God announces the overthrow of the common Assyrian foe, Sennacherib. Egypt and Ethiopia in this chapter (vss. 3, 4) are represented as *allied together,* the result no doubt of fear of the common foe; previously they had been at strife, and the Ethiopian king had, just before Sethos' usurpation, withdrawn from occupation of part of Lower Egypt. Hence, "Egypt" is mentioned *alone* in ch. 19, which refers to a somewhat earlier stage of the same event: a delicate mark of truth. Sargon seems to have been the king who finished the capture of Samaria which Shalmaneser began; the alliance of Hoshea with So or Sabacho II of Ethiopia, and his refusal to pay the usual tribute, provoked Shalmaneser to the invasion. On clay cylindrical seals found in Sennacherib's palace at Koyunjik, the name of Sabacho is deciphered; the two seals are thought, from the inscriptions, to have been attached to the treaty of peace between Egypt and Assyria, which resulted from the invasion of Egypt by Sargon, described in this chapter; II Kings 18:10 curiously confirms the view derived from Assyrian inscriptions, that though Shalmaneser began, Sargon finished the conquest of Samaria; *"they* took it" (cf. II Kings 17:4-6). In Sargon's palace at Khorsabad, inscriptions state that 27,280 Israelites were led captive by the founder of the palace. While Shalmaneser was engaged in the siege of Samaria, Sargon probably usurped the supreme power and destroyed him; the siege began in 723 B.C., and ended in 721 B.C., the first year of Sargon's reign. Hence arises the paucity of inscriptions of the two predecessors of Sargon. Tiglath-pileser and Shalmaneser; the usurper destroyed them, just as Tiglath-pileser destroyed those of Pul (Sardanapalus), the last of the old line of Ninus; the names of his father and grandfather, which have been deciphered in the palace of his son Sennacherib, do not appear in the list of Assyrian kings, which confirms the view that he was a satrap who usurped the throne. He was so able a general that Hezekiah made no attempt to shake off the tribute until the reign of Sennacherib; hence Judah was not invaded now as the lands of the Philistines and Egypt were. After conquering Israel he sent his general, Tartan, to attack the Philistine cities, "Ashdod," etc., preliminary to his invasion of Egypt and Ethiopia; for the line of march to Egypt lay along the southwest coast of Palestine. The inscriptions confirm the prophecy; they tell us he received tribute from a Pharaoh of "Egypt"; besides destroying in part the Ethiopian "No-ammon," or Thebes (Nah. 3:8); also that he warred with the kings of "Ashdod," Gaza, etc., in harmony with Isaiah here; a memorial tablet of him is found in Cyprus also, showing that he extended his arms to that island. His reign was six or seven years in duration—722-715 B.C. [G. V. SMITH]. **1. Tartan**—probably the same general as was sent by Sennacherib against Hezekiah (II Kings 18:17). GESENIUS takes "Tartan" as a title. **Ashdod**—called by the Greeks Azotus (Acts 8:40); on the Mediterranean, one of the "five" cities of the Philistines. The taking of it was a necessary preliminary to the invasion of Egypt, to which it was the key in that quarter, the Philistines being allies of Egypt. So strongly did the Assyrians fortify it that it stood a twenty-nine years' siege, when it was retaken by the Egyptian Psammetichus. **sent**—Sargon himself remained behind engaged with the Phœnician cities, or else led the main force more directly into Egypt out of Judah [G. V. SMITH]. **2. by**—lit., "by the hand of" (cf. Ezek. 3:14). **sackcloth**—the loose outer garment of coarse dark hair-cloth worn by mourners (II Sam. 3:31) and by prophets, fastened at the waist by a girdle (Matt. 3:4; II Kings 1:8; Zech. 13:4). **naked**—rather, uncovered; he merely put off the outer sackcloth, retaining still the tunic or inner vest(I Sam. 19:24; Amos 2:16; John 21:7); an emblem to show that Egypt should be stripped of its possessions; the very dress of Isaiah was a silent exhortation to repentance. **3. three years**—Isaiah's symbolical action did not continue all this time, but *at intervals,* to keep it before the people's mind during that period [ROSENMULLER]. Rather, join "three years" with "sign," *a three years' sign,* i.e., a sign that a three years' calamity would come on Egypt and Ethiopia [BARNES], (ch. 8:18). This is the only instance of a strictly symbolical act performed by Isaiah. With later prophets, as Jeremiah and Ezekiel, such acts were common. In some cases they were performed, not literally, but only in prophetic vision. **wonder**—rather, "omen"; conveying a threat as to the future [G. V. SMITH]. **upon**—in reference to, against. **4. buttocks uncovered**—BELZONI says that captives are found represented thus on Egyptian monuments (ch. 47:2, 3; Nah. 3:5, 8, 9), whereas here, Egypt and Ethiopia are mentioned as in alliance. **5. they**—the Philistine allies of Egypt who trusted in it for help against Assyria. A warning to the party among the Jews, who, though Judah was then the subordinate ally of Assyria, were looking to Egypt as a preferable ally (ch. 30:7). Ethiopia was their "expectation"; for Palestine had not yet obtained, *but hoped* for alliance with it. Egypt was their "glory," i.e., boast (ch. 13:19); for the alliance with it was completed. **6. isle**—i.e., coast on the Mediterranean—Philistia, perhaps Phœnicia (cf. ch. 23:2; 11:11; 13:22, Ps. 72:10). **we**—emphatical; if Egypt, in which we trusted, was overcome, how shall *we,* a small weak state, escape?

CHAPTER 21

Vss. 1-10. REPETITION OF THE ASSURANCE GIVEN IN CHAPTERS 13 AND 14 TO THE JEWS ABOUT TO BE CAPTIVES IN BABYLON, THAT THEIR ENEMY SHOULD BE DESTROYED AND THEY BE DELIVERED. He does not narrate the event, but graphically supposes himself a watchman in Babylon, beholding the events as they pass. **1. desert**—the champaign between Babylon and Persia; it was once a *desert,* and it was to become so again. **of the sea**—The plain was covered with the water of the Euphrates like a "sea" (Jer. 51:13, 36; so ch. 11:15, the Nile), until Semiramis raised great dams against it. Cyrus removed these dykes, and so converted the whole country

again into a vast desert-marsh. **whirlwinds in the south**—(Job 37:9; Zech. 9:14.) The south wind comes upon Babylon from the deserts of Arabia, and its violence is the greater from its course being unbroken along the plain (Job 1:19). **desert**—the plain between Babylon and Persia. **terrible land**—Media; to guard against which was the object of Nitocris' great works (HERODOTUS, 1. 185). Cf. as to "terrible" applied to a wilderness, as being full of unknown dangers, Deuteronomy 1:29. **2. dealeth treacherously**—referring to the *military* stratagem employed by Cyrus in taking Babylon. It may be translated, "is repaid with treachery"; then the subject of the verb is *Babylon.* She is repaid in her own coin; ch. 33:1; Habakkuk 2:8, favor this. **Go up**—Isaiah abruptly recites the order which he hears God giving to the Persians, the instruments of His vengeance (ch. 13:3, 17). **Elam**—a province of Persia, the original place of their settlement (Gen. 10: 22), east of the Euphrates. The name "Persia" was not in use until the captivity; it means a "horseman"; Cyrus first trained the Persians in horsemanship. It is a mark of authenticity that the name is not found before Daniel and Ezekiel [BOCHART]. **thereof**—the "sighing" *caused* by Babylon (ch. 14:7, 8). **3.** Isaiah imagines himself among the exiles in Babylon and cannot help feeling moved by the calamities which come on it. So for Moab (ch. 15:5; 16:11). **pain**—(Cf. ch. 13:8; Ezek. 30:4, 19; Nah. 2:10.) **at the hearing**—The *Hebrew* may mean, "I was so bowed down that *I could not hear;* I was so dismayed that *I could not see"* (Gen. 16:2; Ps. 69:23) [MAURER]. **4. panted**—"is bewildered" [BARNES]. **night of my pleasure**—The prophet supposes himself one of the banqueters at Belshazzar's feast, on the night that Babylon was about to be taken by surprise; hence his expression, *"my pleasure"* (ch. 14:11; Jer. 51:39; Dan. 5). **5. Prepare the table**—viz., the feast in Babylon; during which Cyrus opened the dykes made by Semiramis to confine the Euphrates to one channel and suffered them to overflow the country, so that he could enter Babylon by the channel of the river. Isaiah first represents the king ordering the feast to be got ready. The suddenness of the irruption of the foe is graphically expressed by the rapid turn in the language to an alarm addressed to the Babylonian princes, "Arise," etc. (cf. ch. 22:13). MAURER translates, "*They prepare* the table," etc. But see ch. 8:9. **watch in ... watchtower**—rather, set the watch. This done, they thought they might feast in entire security. Babylon had many watchtowers on its walls. **anoint ... shield**—This was done to prevent the leather of the shield becoming hard and liable to crack. "Make ready for *defense";* the mention of the "shield" alone implies that it is the Babylonian revellers who are called on to prepare for instant *self-defense.* HORSLEY translates, "Gripe the oiled shield." **6.** God's direction to Isaiah to set a watchman to "declare" what he sees. But as in vs. 10, Isaiah himself is represented as the one who "declared." HORSLEY makes *him* the "watchman," and translates, "Come, let him who standeth on the watchtower report what he seeth." **7. chariot ...**—rather, a body of riders, (namely), some riding in pairs on horses (lit., "pairs of horsemen," i.e., two abreast), others on asses, others on camels (cf. vs. 9; ch. 22:6). "Chariot" is not appropriate to be joined, as *English Version* translates, with "asses"; the *Hebrew* means plainly in vs. 7, as in vs. 9, "a body of men riding." The Persians used asses and camels for war [MAURER]. HORSLEY translates, "One drawn in a car, with a pair of riders, drawn by an ass, drawn by a camel"; Cyrus is the man; the car drawn by a camel and ass yoked together and driven by two postilions, one on each, is the joint army of Medes and Persians under their respective leaders. He thinks the more ancient military cars were driven by men riding on the beasts that drew them; vs. 9 favors this. **8. A lion**—rather, "(The watchman) cried, I am *as* a lion"; so *as* is understood (ch. 62:5; Ps. 11:1). The point of comparison to "a lion" is in Revelation 10:3, the *loudness* of the cry. But here it is rather his *vigilance*. The lion's eyelids are short, so that, even when asleep, he seems to be on the watch, awake; hence he was painted on doors of temples as the symbol of watchfulness, guarding the place (*Hor. Apollo*) [HORSLEY]. **9. chariot of men**—chariots with men in them; or rather, the same body of riders, horsemen two abreast, as in vs. 7 [MAURER]. But HORSLEY, "The man drawn in a car with a pair of riders." The first half of this verse describes what the watchman *sees;* the second half, what the watchman *says,* in consequence of what he sees. In the interval between vss. 7 and 9, the overthrow of Babylon by the horsemen, or man in the car, is accomplished. The overthrow needed to be announced to the prophet by the watchman, owing to the great extent of the city. HERODOTUS (1. 131) says that one part of the city was captured some time before the other received the tidings of it. **answered**—not to something *said* previously, but in reference to the subject in the mind of the writer, to be collected from the preceding discourse: *proclaimeth* (Job 3:2; *Margin*, Dan. 2:26; Acts 5:8). **fallen ... fallen**—The repetition expresses emphasis and certainty (Ps. 92:9; 93:3; cf. Jer. 51:8; Rev. 18: 2). **images**—Bel, Merodach, etc. (Jer. 50:2; 51:44, 52). The Persians had no images, temples, or altars, and charged the makers of such with madness (HERODOTUS 1.131); therefore they dashed the Babylonian "images broken unto the ground." **10. my threshing**—i.e., my people (the Jews) trodden down by Babylon. **corn of my floor**—*Hebrew*, "my son of the floor," i.e., my people, treated as corn laid on the floor for threshing; implying, too, that by affliction, a remnant (grain) would be separated from the ungodly (chaff) [MAURER]. HORSLEY translates, "O thou object of my unremitting *prophetic pains.*" See ch. 28:27, 28. Some, from Jeremiah 51:33, make Babylon the object of the threshing; but Isaiah is plainly addressing his countrymen, as the next words show, not the Babylonians.

11, 12. A PROPHECY TO THE IDUMEANS WHO TAUNTED THE AFFLICTED JEWS IN THE BABYLONISH CAPTIVITY. One out of Seir asks, What of the night? Is there a hope of the dawn of deliverance? Isaiah replies, The morning is beginning to dawn (*to us*); but night is also coming (to you). Cf. Psalm 137:7. The Hebrew captives would be delivered, and taunting Edom punished. If the Idumean wish to ask again, he may do so; if he wishes an answer of peace for his country, then let him "return (repent), come" [BARNES]. **11. Dumah**—a tribe and region of Ishmael in Arabia (Gen. 25: 14; I Chron. 1:30); now called *Dumah the Stony*, situated on the confines of Arabia and the Syrian desert; a part put for the *whole* of Edom. VITRINGA thinks "Dumah," *Hebrew*, "silence," is here used for Idumea, to imply that it was soon to be reduced to *silence* or destruction. **Seir**—the principal mountain in Idumea, south of the Dead Sea, in Arabia Petraea. "He calleth" ought to be rather, "*There is a call* from Seir." **to me**—Isaiah. So the heathen Balak and Ahaziah received oracles from a Hebrew prophet. **Watchman**—the prophet (ch. 62:6; Jer.

6:17), so called, because, like a watchman on the lookout from a tower, he announces future events which he sees in prophetic vision (Hab. 2:1, 2). **what of the night**—What tidings have you to give as to the state of the night? Rather, "What *remains* of the night?" How much of it is past? [MAURER]. "Night" means calamity (Job 35:10; Mic. 3:6), which, then, in the wars between Egypt and Assyria, pressed sore on Edom; or on Judah (if, as BARNES thinks, the question is asked in mockery of the suffering Jews in Babylon). The *repetition* of the question marks, in the former view, the anxiety of the Idumeans. **12. Reply of the prophet, The *morning* (prosperity) *cometh,* and (soon after follows) *the night* (adversity). Though you, Idumeans, may have a gleam of prosperity, it will soon be followed by adversity again. Otherwise, as BARNES, "Prosperity cometh (to the Jews) to be quickly followed by adversity (to you, Idumeans, who exult in the fall of Jerusalem, have seized on the southern part of their land in their absence during the captivity, and now deride them by your question") (ch. 34:5-7). This view is favored by Obadiah 10-21. **if ye will inquire, inquire**—If ye choose to consult me again, do so (similar phrases occur in Genesis 43: 14; II Kings 7:4; Esther 4:16). **return, come**—"Be converted to God (and then), come" [GESENIUS]; you will then receive a more favorable answer.

13-17. PROPHECY THAT ARABIA WOULD BE OVERRUN BY A FOREIGN FOE WITHIN A YEAR. Probably in the wars between Assyria and Egypt; Idumea and Arabia lay somewhat on the intermediate line of march. **13. upon**—i.e., respecting. **forest**—not a grove of trees, but a region of thick underwood, rugged and inaccessible; for Arabia has no forest of trees. **travelling companies**—caravans: ye shall be driven through fear of the foe to unfrequented routes (ch. 33:8; Judg. 5:6; Jer. 49:8 is parallel to this passage). **Dedanim**—In North Arabia (Gen. 25:3; Jer. 25:23; Ezek. 25:13; 27:20; a different "Dedan" occurs Gen. 10:7). **14. Tema**—a kindred tribe: an oasis in that region (Jer. 25:23). The Temeans give water to the faint and thirsting Dedanites; the greatest act of hospitality in the burning lands of the East, where water is so scarce. **prevented**—i.e., anticipated the wants of the fugitive Dedanites by supplying bread (Gen. 14:18). **their bread**—rather, "*his* (the fugitive's) bread"; the bread *due to him*, necessary for his support; so "*thy grave*" (ch. 14:19), [MAURER]. **15. they**—the fugitive Dedanites and other Arabs. **16. years of ... hireling**—(*Note*, ch. 16:14.) **Kedar**—a wandering tribe (Ps. 120:5). North of Arabia Petrea, and south of Arabia Deserta; put for Arabia in general. **17. residue ... diminished**—The remnant of Arab warriors, famous in the bow, left after the invasion, shall be small.

CHAPTER 22

Vss. 1-14. PROPHECY AS TO AN ATTACK ON JERUSALEM: that by Sennacherib, in the 14th year of Hezekiah; vss. 8-11, the preparations for defense and securing of water exactly answer to those in II Chronicles 32:4, 5, 30. "Shebna," too (vs. 15), was scribe at this time (ch. 36:3) [MAURER]. The language of vss. 12, 13, and 14, as to the infidelity and consequent utter ruin of the Jews, seems rather to foreshadow the destruction by Nebuchadnezzar in Zedekiah's reign, and cannot be restricted to Hezekiah's time [LOWTH]. **1. of ... valley of vision**—rather, respecting the valley of visions; viz., Jerusalem, the seat of divine revelations and visions, "the nursery of prophets" [JEROME], (ch. 2:3; 29:1; Ezek. 23:4, *Margin:* Luke 13:33). It lay in a "valley" surrounded by hills higher than Zion and Moriah (Ps. 125:2; Jer. 21:13). **thee**—the people of Jerusalem personified. **housetops**—Panic-struck, they went up on the flat balustraded roofs to look forth and see whether the enemy was near, and partly to defend themselves from the roofs (Judg. 9:51, etc.). **2. art**—rather, wert; for it could not *now* be said to be "a joyous city" (ch. 32:13). The cause of their *joy* (vs. 13) may have been because Sennacherib had accepted Hezekiah's offer to renew the payment of tribute, and they were glad to have peace on any terms, however humiliating (II Kings 18:14-16), or on account of the alliance with Egypt. If the reference be to Zedekiah's time, the joy and feasting are not inapplicable, for this recklessness was a general characteristic of the unbelieving Jews (ch. 56:12). **not slain with the sword**—but with the famine and pestilence about to be caused by the coming siege (Lam. 4:9). MAURER refers this to the *plague* by which he thinks Sennacherib's army was destroyed, and Hezekiah was made sick (ch. 37:36; 38:1). But there is no authority for supposing that the Jews in the city suffered such extremities of plague at *this* time, when God destroyed their foes. BARNES refers it to those *slain in flight*, not in open honorable "battle"; vs. 3 favors this. **3. rulers**—rather, generals (Josh. 10:24; Judg. 11:6, 11). **bound**—rather, *"are taken."* **by the archers**—lit., "by the bow"; so ch. 21:17. Bowmen were the light troops, whose province it was to skirmish in front and (II Kings 6:22) pursue fugitives (II Kings 25:5); this verse applies better to the attack of Nebuchadnezzar than that of Sennacherib. **all ... in thee**—all found in the city (ch. 13:15), not merely the "rulers" or generals. **fled from far**—those who had *fled from distant parts* to Jerusalem as a place of safety; rather, *fled afar.* **4. Look ... from me**—Deep grief seeks to be alone; while others feast joyously, Isaiah mourns in prospect of the disaster coming on Jerusalem (Mic. 1:8, 9). **daughter ...**—(*Note,* ch. 1:8; Lam. 2:11). **5. trouble ... by the Lord**—i.e., sent by or from the Lord (*Note,* ch. 19:15; Luke 21:22-24). **valley of vision**—(*Note,* vs. 1). Some think a valley near Ophel is meant as about to be the scene of devastation (cf. ch. 32:13, 14, *Note*). **breaking ... walls**—i.e., "a day of breaking the walls" of the city. **crying to the mountains**—the mournful cry of the townsmen *reaches* to (MAURER translates, *towards)* the mountains, and is echoed back by them. Josephus describes in the very same language the scene at the assault of Jerusalem under Titus. To this the prophecy, probably, refers ultimately. If, as some think, the "cry" is that of those *escaping* to the mountains, cf. Matthew 13:14; 24:16, with this. **6. Elam**—the country stretching east from the Lower Tigris, answering to what was afterwards called Persia (*Note,* ch. 21:2). Later, Elam was a province of Persia (Ezra 4:9). In Sennacherib's time, Elam was subject to Assyria (II Kings 18:11), and so furnished a contingent to its invading armies. Famed for the bow (ch. 13:18; Jer. 49:35), in which the Ethiopians alone excelled them. **with chariots of men and horsemen**—i.e., they used the bow both *in* chariots and on horseback. "Chariots of men," i.e., chariots in which men are borne, war chariots (cf. *Note,* ch. 21:7, 9). **Kir**—another people subject to Assyria (II Kings 16:9); the region about the river Kur, between the Caspian and Black Seas. **uncovered**—took off for the battle the leather covering of the shield, intended to protect the embossed figures on it from dust or injury

during the march. "The quiver" and "the shield" express two classes—light and heavy armed troops. **7. valleys**—east, north, and south of Jerusalem: Hinnom on the south side was the richest valley. **in array at the gate**—Rabshakeh stood at the upper pool close to the city (ch. 36:11-13). **8. he discovered the covering**—rather, "the veil of Judah shall be taken off" [HORSLEY]: fig. for, exposing to shame as a captive (ch. 47:3; Nah. 3:5). Sennacherib dismantled all "the defensed cities of Judah" (ch. 36:1). **thou didst look**—rather, "thou shalt look." **house of ... forest**—The *house* of armory built of cedar from the *forest* of Lebanon by Solomon, on a slope of Zion called Ophel (I Kings 7:2; 10:17; Neh. 3:19). Isaiah says (vss. 8-13) his countrymen will look to their own strength *to defend* themselves, while others of them will drown their sorrows as to their country in *feasting,* but none will look to Jehovah. **9. Ye have seen**—rather, "Ye shall see." **city of David**—the upper city, on Zion, the south side of Jerusalem (II Sam. 5:7, 9; I Kings 8:1); surrounded by a wall of its own; but even in it there shall be "breaches." Hezekiah's preparations for defense accord with this (II Chron. 32:5). **ye gathered**—rather, "ye shall gather." **lower pool**—(*Note,* vs. 11.) Ye shall bring together into the city by subterranean passages cut in the rock of Zion, the fountain from which the lower pool (only mentioned here) is supplied. *Note,* ch. 7:3; II Kings 20: 20; II Chronicles 32:3-5, represent Hezekiah as having *stopped* the fountains to prevent the Assyrians getting water. But this is consistent with the passage here. The superflous waters of the lower pool usually flowed into Hinnom valley, and so through that of Jehoshaphat to the brook Kedron. Hezekiah built a wall round it, *stopped* the outflowing of its waters to debar the foe from the use of them, and turned them into the city. **10. numbered**— rather, "ye shall number," viz., in order to see which of them may be pulled down with the least loss to the city, and with most advantage for the repair of the walls and rearing of towers (II Chron. 32:5). **have ye broken down**—rather, "ye shall break down." **11. Ye made ... a ditch**—rather, "Ye shall make a reservoir" for receiving the *water.* Hezekiah surrounded Siloah, from which the old (or king's, or upper) pool took its rise, with a wall joined to the wall of Zion on both sides; between these two walls he made a new pool, into which he directed the waters of the former, thus cutting off the foe from his supply of water also. The opening from which the upper pool received its water was nearer Zion than the other from which the lower pool took its rise, so that the water which flowed from the former could easily be shut in by a wall, whereas that which flowed from the latter could only be brought in by subterranean conduits (cf. *Note,* vs. 9; ch. 7:3; II Kings 20:20; II Chron. 32:3-5, 30; Eccles. 48:17). Both were southwest of Jerusalem. **have not looked ... neither had respect**—answering by contrast to *"Thou didst look* to the armor, *ye have seen* (had respect, or regard to) the breaches" (vss. 8, 9). **maker thereof**—God, by whose command and aid these defenses were made, and who gave this fountain "long ago." G. V. SMITH translates, "Him who *doeth* it," i.e., has brought this danger on you— "Him who hath prepared it from afar," i.e., planned it even from a distant time. **12. did the Lord God call**—Usually the *priests* gave the summons to national mourning (Joel 1:14); now JEHOVAH Himself shall give it; the "call" shall consist in the presence of a terrible foe. Translate, "shall call." **baldness** —emblem of grief (Job 1:20; Mic. 1:16). **13. Not-**

withstanding Jehovah's "call to mourning" (vs. 12), many shall make the desperate state of affairs a reason for reckless revelry (ch. 5:11, 12, 14; Jer. 18: 12; I Cor. 15:32). **15-25.** Prophecy that Shebna Should Be Deposed from Being Prefect of the Palace, and Eliakim Promoted to the Office. In ch. 36:3, 22; 37:2, we find Shebna "a scribe," and no longer prefect of the palace ("over the household"), and Eliakim in that office, as is here foretold. Shebna is singled out as the subject of prophecy (the only instance of an *individual* being so in Isaiah), as being one of the irreligious faction that set at naught the prophet's warnings (ch. 28:33); perhaps it was he who advised the temporary ignominious submission of Hezekiah to Sennacherib. **15. Go, get thee unto** —rather, "Go in to" (i.e., into the house to). **treasurer**—"him who dwells in the tabernacle" [Jerome]; viz., in a room of the temple set apart for the treasurer. Rather, "the king's friend," or "*principal officer of the court*" (I Kings 4:5; 18:3; I Chron. 27:33, "the king's counsellor") [Maurer]. "This" is prefixed contemptuously (Exod. 32:1). **unto Shebna**—The *Hebrew* for "unto" indicates an accosting of Shebna *with an unwelcome message.* **16. What . . . whom**—The prophet accosts Shebna at the very place where he was building a grand sepulcher for himself and his family (cf. ch. 14:18; Gen. 23; 49:29; 50:13). "*What* (business) hast thou here, and *whom* hast thou (of thy family, who is likely to be buried) here, that thou *buildest*," etc., seeing that thou art soon to be deposed from office and carried into captivity? [Maurer]. **on high**—Sepulchers were made in the *highest* rocks (II Chron. 32:33, *Margin*). **habitation for himself**—cf. "his own house" (ch. 14:18). **17. carry . . . away with . . . captivity**—rather, "will cast thee away with a mighty throw" [Maurer]. "Mighty," lit., "of a man" (so Job 38:3). **surely cover**—viz., with shame, where thou art rearing a monument to perpetuate thy fame [Vitringa]. "Rolling will roll thee," i.e., will *continually* roll thee on, as a ball to be tossed away [Maurer]. Cf. vs. 18. **18. violently turn and toss** —lit., "whirling He will whirl thee," i.e., He will, *without intermission,* whirl thee [Maurer]. "He will whirl thee round and round, and (then) cast thee away," as a stone in a sling is first whirled round repeatedly, before the string is let go [Lowth]. **large country**—perhaps Assyria. **chariots . . . shall be the shame of thy lord's house**—rather, "thy splendid chariots shall be there, O thou disgrace of thy lord's house" [Noyes]; "chariots of thy glory" mean "thy magnificent chariots." It is not meant that he would have these in a distant land, as he had in Jerusalem, but that he would be borne thither in ignominy instead of in his magnificent chariots. The Jews say that he was tied to the tails of horses by the enemy, to whom he had designed to betray Jerusalem, as they thought he was mocking them; and so he died. **19. state**—office. **he**—God. A similar change of persons occurs in ch. 34:16. **20. son of Hilkiah**—supposed by Kimchi to be the same as Azariah, son of Hilkiah, who perhaps had two names, and who was "over the household" in Hezekiah's time (I Chron. 6:13). **21. thy robe**—of office. **girdle**—in which the purse was carried, and to it was attached the sword; often adorned with gold and jewels. **father**—i.e., a counsellor and friend. **22. key**—emblem of his office over the house; to "open" or "shut"; access rested with him. **upon . . . shoulder**—So keys are carried sometimes in the East, hanging from the kerchief on the shoulder. But the phrase is rather figurative for *sustain-*

ing the government on one's shoulders. Eliakim, as his name implies, is here plainly a type of the Godman Christ, the son of "David," of whom Isaiah (ch. 9:6) uses the same language as the former clause of this verse. In Revelation 3:7, the same language as the latter clause is found (cf. Job 12:14). **23. nail . . . sure place**—Large nails or pegs stood in ancient houses on which were suspended the ornaments of the family. The sense is: all that is valuable to the nation shall rest securely on him. In Ezra 9:8 "nail" is used of the large spike driven into the ground to fasten the cords of the tent to. **throne**— resting-place to his family, as applied to Eliakim; but "throne," in the strict sense, as applied to Messiah, the antitype (Luke 1:32, 33). **24.** Same image as in vs. 23. It was customary to "hang" the valuables of a house on nails (I Kings 10:16, 17, 21; Song of Solomon 4:4). **offspring and the issue**— rather, "the offshoots of the family, high and low" [Vitringa]. Eliakim would reflect honor even on the latter. **vessels of cups**—of small capacity: answering to the *low* and humble *offshoots.* **vessels of flagons**—larger vessels: answering to the *high offshoots.* **25. nail . . . fastened**—Shebna, who was *supposed* to be firmly fixed in his post. **burden . . . upon it**—All that were dependent on Shebna, all his emoluments and rank will fail, as when a peg is suddenly "cut down," the ornaments on it fall with it. Sin reaches in its effects even to the family of the guilty (Exod. 20:5).

CHAPTER 23

Vss. 1-18. Prophecy respecting Tyre. Menander, the historian, notices a siege of Tyre by Shalmaneser, about the time of the siege of Samaria. Sidon, Acco, and Old Tyre, on the mainland, were soon reduced; but New Tyre, on an island half a mile from the shore, held out for five years. Sargon probably finished the siege. Sennacherib does not, however, mention it among the cities which the Assyrian kings conquered (chs. 36, 37). The expression, "Chaldeans" (vs. 13), may imply reference to its siege under Nebuchadnezzar, which lasted thirteen years. Alexander the Great destroyed New Tyre after a seven months' siege. **1. Tyre**—*Hebrew, Tsur,* i.e., Rock. **ships of Tarshish**—ships of Tyre returning from their voyage to Tarshish, or Tartessus in Spain, with which the Phœnicians had much commerce (Ezek. 27:12-25). "Ships of Tarshish" is a phrase also used of large and distant-voyaging merchant vessels (ch. 2:16; I Kings 10:22; Ps. 48:7). **no house**—viz., left; such was the case as to Old Tyre, after Nebuchadnezzar's siege. **no entering**—There is *no* house to *enter* (ch. 24:10) [G. V. Smith]. Or, Tyre is so laid waste, that there is no possibility of *entering the harbor* [Barnes]; which is appropriate to the previous "ships." **Chittim**—Cyprus, of which the cities, including *Citium* in the south (whence came "Chittim"), were mostly Phœnician (Ezek. 27:6). The ships from Tarshish on their way to Tyre learn the tidings ("it is revealed to them") of the downfall of Tyre. At a later period Chittim denoted the islands and coasts of the Mediterranean (Dan. 11:30). **2. Be still**—"struck dumb with awe." Addressed to those already in the country, eye-witnesses of its ruin (Lam. 2:10); or, in contrast to the *busy din* of commerce once heard in Tyre; now all is hushed and *still.* **isle**— strictly applicable to New Tyre: in the sense *coast,* to the mainland city, Old Tyre (cf. vs. 6; ch. 20:6). **Zidon**—of which Tyre was a colony, planted when

Zidon was conquered by the Philistines of Ascalon. Zidon means a "fishing station"; this was its beginning. **replenished**—with wealth and an industrious population (Ezek. 27:3, 8, 23). Here "Zidon," as the oldest city of Phœnicia, includes all the Phœnician towns on the strip of "coast." Thus, Ethbaal, king of Tyre (Josephus, *Antiquities*, 8. 3, 2), is called king of the Sidonians (I Kings 16:31); and on coins Tyre is called the metropolis of the Sidonians. **3. great waters**—the wide waters of the sea. **seed**—"grain," or crop, as in I Samuel 8:15; Job 39:12. **Sihor**—lit., dark-colored; applied to the Nile, as the Egyptian *Jeor*, and the *Greek Melas*, to express the *dark*, turbid colors given to its waters by the fertilizing soil which it deposits at its yearly overflow (Jer. 2:18). **harvest of the river**—the growth of the Delta; the produce due to the overflow of the Nile: Egypt was the great granary of corn in the ancient world (Gen. 41; 42; 43). **her revenue**—Tyrian vessels carried Egyptian produce obtained in exchange for wine, oil, glass, etc., into various lands, and so made large profits. **mart**—(Ezek. 27:3.) No city was more favorably situated for commerce. **4. Zidon**—called on, as being the parent country of Tyre (vs. 12), and here equivalent to Phœnicia in general, to feel the shame (as it was esteemed in the East) of being now as childless as if she never had any. "I (no more now) travail, nor bring forth," etc. "Strength of the sea," i.e., stronghold, viz., New Tyre, on a rock (as "Tyre" means) surrounded by the sea (Ezek. 26:4; 15:17; so Venice was called "Bride of the sea"; Zech. 9:3). **5. As . . .**—rather, *"When* the report (shall reach) the people of Egypt, they shall be sorely pained at the report concerning Tyre" (viz., its overthrow). So JEROME, "When the Egyptians shall hear that so powerful a neighboring nation has been destroyed, they must know their own end is near" [LOWTH, etc.]. **6. Pass . . . over** —Escape from Tyre to your colonies as Tarshish (cf. vs. 12). The Tyrians fled to Carthage and elsewhere, both at the siege under Nebuchadnezzar and that under Alexander. **7. Is this** silent ruin all that is left of *your* once *joyous city* (vs. 12)? **antiquity**—The Tyrian priests boasted in Herodotus' time that their city had already existed 2300 years: an exaggeration, but still implying that it was *ancient* even then. **her own feet**—walking on foot as captives to an enemy's land. **8. Who**—answered in vs. 9, "The Lord of hosts." **crowning**—crown-giving; i.e., the city from which dependent kingdoms had arisen, as Tartessus in Spain, Citium in Cyprus, and Carthage in Africa (Ezek. 27:33). **traffickers**—lit., Canaanites, who were famed for commerce (cf. Hos. 12:7, *Margin*). **9.** Whoever be the instruments in overthrowing haughty sinners, God, who has all hosts at His command, is the First Cause (ch. 10:5-7). **stain** —rather, "to profane"; as in Exodus 31:14, the *Sabbath*, and other objects of religious reverence; so here, "the pride of all glory" may refer to the Tyrian temple of Hercules, the oldest in the world, according to Arrian (ch. 2:16); the prophet of the true God would naturally single out for notice the idol of Tyre [G. V. SMITH]. It may, however, be a *general* proposition; the destruction of Tyre will exhibit to all how God mars the luster of whatever is haughty (ch. 2:11). **10. a river**—*Hebrew*, "the river," viz., Nile. **daughter of Tarshish**—Tyre and its inhabitants (ch. 1:8), about henceforth, owing to the ruin of Tyre, to become inhabitants of its colony, Tartessus: they would *pour forth* from Tyre, as waters flow on when the barriers are removed [LOWTH]. Rather, Tarshish, or Tartessus and its inhabitants, as the phrase usually means: they had been kept in hard

bondage, working in silver and lead mines near Tarshish, by the parent city (Ezek. 26:17): but now "the bond of restraint" (for so "strength," *Margin*, girdle, i.e., bond, Ps. 2:3, ought to be translated) is removed, since Tyre is no more. **11. He**—Jehovah. **kingdoms**—the Phœnician cities and colonies. **the merchant city**—rather, *Canaan*, meaning the north of it, viz., Phœnicia. On their coins, they call their country *Canaan*. **12. he**—God. **rejoice**—riotously (vs. 7). **oppressed**—"deflowered"; laying aside the figure "taken by storm"; the Arabs compare a city never taken to an undefiled virgin (cf. Nah. 3:5, etc.). **daughter of Zidon**—Tyre: or else, sons of Zidon, i.e., the whole land and people of Phœnicia (*Note*, vs. 2) [MAURER]. **Chittim**—Citium in Cyprus (vs. 1). **there also . . . no rest**—Thy colonies, having been harshly treated by thee, will now repay thee in kind (*Note*, vs. 10). But VITRINGA refers it to the calamities which befell the Tyrians in their settlements subsequently, viz., Sicily, Corcyra, Carthage, and Spain, all flowing from the original curse of Noah against the posterity of Canaan (Gen. 9:25-27). **13. Behold**—Calling attention to the fact, so humiliating to Tyre, that a people of yesterday, like the Chaldees, should destroy the most ancient of cities, Tyre. **was not**—had no existence as a recognized nation; the Chaldees were previously but a rude, predatory people (Job 1:17). **Assyrian founded it**—The Chaldees ("them that dwell in the wilderness") lived a nomadic life in the mountains of Armenia originally (Arphaxad, in Gen. 10:22, refers to such a region of Assyria near Armenia), north and east of Assyria proper. Some may have settled in Mesopotamia and Babylonia very early and given origin to the astrologers called *Chaldees* in later times. But most of the people had been transferred only a little before the time of this prophecy from their original seats in the north to Mesopotamia, and soon afterwards to South Babylonia. "Founded it," means "assigned *it* (the land) to them who had (heretofore) dwelt in the wilderness" as a permanent settlement (so in Ps. 104:8) [MAURER]. It was the Assyrian policy to infuse into their own population of the plain the fresh blood of hardy mountaineers, for the sake of recruiting their armies. Ultimately the Chaldees, by their powerful priest-caste, gained the supremacy and established the later or Chaldean empire. HORSLEY refers it to Tyre, founded by an Assyrian race. **towers thereof**—viz., of Babylon, whose towers, HERODOTUS says, were "set up" by the Assyrians [BARNES]. Rather, "The *Chaldees* set up *their siege-towers"* against Tyre, made for the attack of high walls, from which the besiegers hurled missiles, as depicted in the Assyrian sculptures [G. V. SMITH]. **raised up**—rather, "They *lay bare,"* viz., the foundations of *her* (Tyre's) *palaces,* i.e., utterly overthrew them (Ps. 137:7). **14. strength**—stronghold (cf. Ezek. 26:15-18). **15. forgotten**—Having lost its former renown, Tyre shall be in obscurity. **seventy years**—(so Jer. 25:11, 12; 29:10). **days of one king** —i.e., a dynasty. The Babylonian monarchy lasted properly but seventy years. From the first year of Nebuchadnezzar to the taking of Babylon, by Cyrus, was seventy years; then the subjected nations would be restored to liberty. Tyre was taken in the middle of that period, but is classed in common with the rest, some conquered sooner and others later, all, however, alike to be delivered at the end of the period. So "king" is used for dynasty (Dan. 7:17; 8:20): Nebuchadnezzar, his son Evil-merodach, and his grandson, Belshazzar, formed the whole dynasty (Jer. 25:11, 12; 27:7; 29:10). **shall Tyre sing as . . .**

harlot—It shall be to Tyre as the song of the harlot, viz., a harlot that has been forgotten, but who attracts notice again by her song. Large marts of commerce are often compared to harlots seeking many lovers, i.e., they court merchants of all nations, and admit any one for the sake of gain (Nah. 3:4; Rev. 18:3). Covetousness is closely akin to idolatry and licentiousness, as the connection (Eph. 5:5; Col. 3:5) proves (cf. ch. 2:6-8, 16). **16.** Same figure to express that Tyre would again prosper and attract commercial intercourse of nations to her, and be the same joyous, self-indulging city as before. **17. visit**—not in wrath, but mercy. **hire**—image from a harlot: her *gains* by commerce. After the Babylonian dynasty was ended, Tyre was rebuilt; also, again, after the destruction under Alexander. **18. merchandise . . . holiness**—Her traffic and gains shall at last (long after the restoration mentioned in vs. 17) be consecrated to Jehovah. Jesus Christ visited the neighborhood of Tyre (Matt. 15:21); Paul found disciples there (Acts 21:3-6); it early became a Christian bishopric, but the full evangelization of that whole race, as of the Ethiopians (ch. 18), of the Egyptians and Assyrians (ch. 19), is yet to come (ch. 60:5). **not treasured**—but freely expended in His service. **them that dwell before the Lord**—the ministers of religion. But HORSLEY translates, "them that *sit* before Jehovah" as *disciples*. **durable clothing**—Changes of raiment constituted much of the wealth of former days.

CHAPTER 24

THE LAST TIMES OF THE WORLD IN GENERAL, AND OF JUDAH AND THE CHURCH IN PARTICULAR. The four chaps. 24-27 form one continuous poetical prophecy: descriptive of the dispersion and successive calamities of the Jews (ch. 24:1-12); the preaching of the Gospel by the first Hebrew converts throughout the world (vss. 13-16); the judgments on the adversaries of the Church and its final triumph (vss. 16-23); thanksgiving for the overthrow of the apostate faction (ch. 25), and establishment of the righteous in lasting peace (ch. 26); judgment on leviathan and entire purgation of the Church (ch. 27). Having treated of the *several nations in particular*—Babylon, Philistia, Moab, Syria, Israel, Egypt, Edom, and Tyre (the miniature representative of all, as all kingdoms flocked into it)—he passes to the last times of *the world at large* and of Judah the representative and future head of the churches.

Vss. 1-23. **1. the earth**—rather, *the land* of Judah (so in vss. 3, 5, 6; Joel 1:2). The desolation under Nebuchadnezzar prefigured that under Titus. **2. as with the people, so with the priest**—All alike shall share the same calamity: no favored class shall escape (cf. Ezek. 7:12, 13; Hos. 4:9; Rev. 6:15). **4. world**—the kingdom of Israel; as in ch. 13:11, Babylon. **haughty**—lit., "the height" of the people: abstract for concrete, i.e., the high people; even the nobles share the general distress. **5. earth**—rather, the land. **defiled under . . . inhabitans**—viz., with innocent blood (Gen. 4:11; Num. 35:33; Ps. 106:38). **laws . . . ordinance . . . everlasting covenant**—The *moral* laws, *positive* statutes, and *national* covenant designed to be for ever between God and them. **6. earth**—the land. **burned**—viz., with the consuming wrath of heaven: either internally, as in Job 30:30 [ROSENMILLER]; or externally, the prophet has before his eyes the people being consumed with the withering dryness of their doomed land (so Joel 1: 10, 12), [MAURER]. **7. mourneth**—because there are

none to drink it [BARNES]. Rather, is become vapid [HORSLEY]. **languisheth**—because there are none to cultivate it now. **8.** (Rev. 18:22.) **9. with a song**—the usual accompaniment of feasts. **strong drink**—(*Note*, ch. 5:11.) "Date wine" [HORSLEY]. **bitter**—in consequence of the national calamities. **10. city of confusion**—rather, desolation. What *Jerusalem* would be; by anticipation it is called so. HORSLEY translates, "The city is broken down; it is a ruin." **shut up**—through fear; or rather, choked up by ruins. **11. crying for wine**—to drown their sorrows in drink (ch. 16:9); Joel 1:5, written about the same time, resembles this. **12. with destruction**—rather "crash" [GESENIUS]. "With a great tumult the gate is battered down" [HORSLEY]. **13. the land**—Judea. Put the comma after "land," not after "people." "There shall be among the people (a remnant left), as the shaking (the after-picking) of an olive tree"; as in gathering olives, a few remain on the highest boughs (ch. 17:5, 6). **14. They**—those who are left: the remnant. **sing for the majesty of the Lord**—sing a thanksgiving for the goodness of the LORD, who has so mercifully preserved them. **from the sea**—from the distant lands beyond the sea, whither they have escaped. **15. in the fires**—VITRINGA translates, "in the *caves*." Could it mean *the fires of affliction* (I Peter 1:7)? They were exiles at the time. The fires only loose the carnal bonds off the soul, without injuring a hair, as in the case of Shadrach, Meshach, and Abed-nego. LOWTH reads, in the *islands* (Ezek. 26:18). Rather translate for "fires," "in the regions of morning light," i.e., the east, in antithesis to the "isles of the sea," i.e., the west [MAURER]. Wheresoever ye be scattered, east or west, still glorify the Lord (Mal. 1:11). **16.** Songs to God come in together to Palestine from distant lands, as a grand chorus. **glory to the righteous**—the burden of the songs (ch. 26:2, 7). Amidst exile, the loss of their temple, and all that is dear to man, their confidence in God is unshaken. These songs recall the joy of other times and draw from Jerusalem in her present calamities, the cry, "My leanness." HORSLEY translates, "glory to *the Just One*"; then My leanness expresses his sense of man's corruption, which led the Jews, the treacherous dealers" (Jer. 5:11), to crucify the Just One; and his deficiency of righteousness which made him need to be clothed with the righteousness of the Just One (Ps. 106:15). **treacherous dealers**—the foreign nations that oppress Jerusalem, and overcome it by stratagem (so in ch. 21:2) [BARNES]. **17.** This verse explains the wretchedness spoken of in vs. 16. Jeremiah (48:43, 44) uses the same words. They are proverbial; vs. 18 expressing that the inhabitants were nowhere safe; if they escaped one danger, they fell into another, and worse, on the opposite side (Amos 5:19). "Fear" is the term applied to the cords with feathers of all colors which, when fluttered in the air, scare beasts into the pitfall, or birds into the snare. HORSLEY makes the connection. Indignant at the treatment which the Just One received, the prophet threatens the guilty land with instant vengeance. **18. noise of . . . fear**—the shout designed to rouse the game and drive it into the pitfall. **windows . . . open**—taken from the account of the deluge (Gen. 7:11); *the flood-gates*. So the final judgments of fire on the apostate world are compared to the deluge (II Pet. 3:5-7). **19. earth**—the land: image from an earthquake. **20. removed like a cottage**—(*Note*, ch. 1:8.) Here, *a hanging couch*, suspended from the trees by cords, such as Niebuhr describes the Arab keepers of lands as having, to enable them to keep watch, and at the same time to be secure from wild beasts. Translate, "Shall wave to and fro like a hammock" swung about by the wind. **heavy upon it**—like an overwhelming burden. **not rise again**—not meaning, that it *never* would rise (vs. 23), but *in those convulsions* it would not rise, it would surely fall. **21. host of . . . high ones**—the heavenly host, i.e., either *the visible host of heaven* (the present economy of nature, affected by the sun, moon, and stars, the objects of idolatry, being abolished, ch. 65:17; 60: 19, simultaneously with the corrupt polity of men); or rather, the *invisible* rulers of the darkness of this world, as the antithesis to "kings of the earth" shows. Angels, moreover, preside, as it were, over kingdoms of the world (Dan. 10:13, 20, 21). **22. in the pit**—rather, for the pit [HORSLEY]. "In the *dungeon*" [MAURER]. Image from captives thrust together into a dungeon. **prison**—i.e., as in a prison. This sheds light on the disputed passage, I Peter 3:19, where also the *prison* is figurative: The "shutting up" of the Jews in Jerusalem under Nebuchadnezzar, and again under Titus, was to be followed by a *visitation* of mercy "after many days"—seventy years in the case of the former—the time is not yet elapsed in the case of the latter. HORSLEY takes "visited" in a bad sense, viz., in wrath, as in ch. 26:14; cf. ch. 29:6; the punishment being the heavier in the fact of the delay. Probably a double visitation is intended, deliverance to the elect, wrath to hardened unbelievers; as vs. 23 plainly contemplates judgments on proud sinners, symbolized by the "sun" and "moon." **23.** (Jer. 3:17.) Still future: of which Jesus' triumphal entry into Jerusalem amidst hosannas was a pledge. **his ancients**—the elders of His people; or in general, His ancient people, the Jews. After the overthrow of the world-kingdoms, Jehovah's shall be set up with a splendor exceeding the light of the sun and moon under the previous order of things (ch. 60:19, 20).

CHAPTER 25

Vss. 1-12. CONTINUATION OF CHAPTER 24. THANKSGIVING FOR THE OVERTHROW OF THE APOSTATE FACTION, AND THE SETTING UP OF JEHOVAH'S THRONE ON ZION. The restoration from Babylon and re-establishment of the theocracy was a type and pledge of this. **1. wonderful**—(Ch. 9:6). **counsels of old**—(Ch. 42:9; 46:10). Purposes planned long ago; here, as to the deliverance of His people. **truth**—*Hebrew, Amen;* covenant-keeping, faithful to promises; the peculiar characteristic of Jesus (Rev. 3:14). **2. a city . . . heap**—Babylon, type of the seat of Antichrist, to be destroyed in the last days (cf. Jer. 51:37, with Rev. 18, followed, as here, by the song of the saints' thanksgiving in Rev. 19). "Heaps" is a graphic picture of Babylon and Nineveh as they now are. **palace**—Babylon regarded, on account of its splendor, as a vast palace. But MAURER translates, "a citadel." **of strangers**—foreigners, whose capital pre-eminently Babylon was, the metropolis of the pagan world. "Aliens from the commonwealth of Israel, *strangers* from the covenants of promise" (ch. 29:5; Eph. 2:12; see in contrast, Joel 3:17). **never be built**—(Ch. 13:19, 20, etc.). **3. strong people**—This cannot apply to the Jews; but other nations on which Babylon had exercised its cruelty (ch. 14:12) shall worship Jehovah, awed by the judgment inflicted on Babylon (ch. 23:18). **city**—not Babylon, which shall then be destroyed, but collectively for the *cities* of the surrounding nations. **4. the poor . . . needy**—the Jews, exiles from their country (ch. 26:6; 41:17). **heat**—calamity (ch. 4:6; 32:2). **blast**—i.e., wrath. **storm**—*a tempest* of *rain,* a winter flood, rushing against and overthrowing the wall of a house. **5.** Translate, "As the heat in a dry land [is brought down by the shadow of a cloud, so] thou shalt bring down the tumult [the shout of triumph over their enemies] of strangers (foreigners); and as the heat by the shadow of the cloud [is brought low], so the branch [the offspring] of the terrible ones shall be brought low." PARKHURST translates the *Hebrew* for "branch," *the exulting song.* JEROME translates the last clause, "And as when the heat burns under a cloud, thou shalt make the branch of the terrible ones to wither"; the branch withering even under the friendly shade of a cloud typifies the wicked brought to ruin, not for want of natural means of prosperity, but by the immediate act of God. **6. in this mountain**—Zion: Messiah's kingdom was to begin, and is to have its central seat hereafter, at Jerusalem, as the common country of "all nations" (ch. 2:2, etc.). **all people** —(Ch. 56:7; Dan. 7:14; Luke 2:10). **feast**—image of felicity (Ps. 22:26, 27; Matt. 8:11; Luke 14, 15; Rev. 19:9; cf. Ps. 36:8; 87). **fat things**—delicacies; the rich mercies of God in Christ (ch. 55:2; Jer. 31:14; Job 36:16). **wines on the lees**—wine which has been long kept on the lees; i.e., the oldest and most generous wine (Jer. 48:11). **marrow**—the choicest dainties (Ps. 63:5). **well refined**—cleared of all dregs. **7. face of . . . covering**—image from mourning, in which it was usual to *cover* the face with a veil (II Sam. 15:30). "Face of covering," i.e., the covering itself; as in Job 41:13, "the face of his garment," the garment itself. The covering or veil is the mist of ignorance as to a future state, and the way to eternal life, which enveloped the nations (Eph. 4:18) and the unbelieving Jew (II Cor. 3:15). The *Jew,* however, is *first* to be converted before the conversion of *"all nations";* for it is "in *this* mountain," viz., Zion, that the latter are to have the veil taken off (Ps. 102:13, 15, 16, 21, 22; Rom. 11: 12). **8.** Quoted in I Corinthians 15:54, in support of the resurrection. **swallow up . . . in victory**—completely and permanently "abolish" (II Tim. 1:10; Rev. 20:14; 21:4; cf. Gen. 2:17; 3:22). **rebuke**—(Cf. Mark. 8:38; Heb. 11:26). **9.** "After death has been swallowed up for ever, the people of God, who had been delivered from the hand of death, shall say to the Lord, Lo, this is our *God,* whom unbelievers regarded as only a *man"* [JEROME]. "The words are so moulded as to point us specially to the person of the Son of God, who 'saves' us; as He vouchsafed to Israel temporal saving, so to His elect He appears for the purpose of conferring eternal salvation" [VITRINGA]. *The Jews,* however, have a special share in the words, This is *our* God (*Note,* vs. 6). "In day . . . glad . . . rejoice," cf. Psalm 118:24, which refers to the second coming of Jesus (cf. Ps. 118:26, with Luke 13:35). "Waited" is characteristic of God's people in all ages (Gen. 49:18; Titus 2:13). **10. rest** —as its *permanent protector;* on "hand" in this sense; cf. Ezra 7:6, 28. **Moab**—while Israel is being protected, the foe is destroyed; Moab is the representative of all the foes of God's people. **under him**—Rather, in his own place or country (Exod. 10:23; 16:29). **for the dunghill**—Rather, in the water of the dung-heap, in which straw was trodden to make it manure (Ps. 83:10). HORSLEY translates either, "in the waters of Madmenah," viz., for the making of bricks; or as LXX, "as the *threshing-floor* is trampled by the *corn-drag*" (see *Margin,* Mic. 4:11-13). **11. he**—*Jehovah* shall spread His hands to strike the foe on this side and on that, with as little effort as a swimmer spreads forth his arms to cleave a passage through the water [CALVIN]. (Zech. 5:3.) LOWTH takes "he" as Moab, who, in danger of sinking, shall strain every nerve to save himself; *but Jehovah* (and "he") shall cause him to sink ("bring down the pride" of Moab, ch. 16:6). **with the spoils of . . . hands**—lit., "the craftily acquired spoils" of his (Moab's) hands [BARNES]. Moab's pride, as well as the sudden gripe of his hands (viz., whereby he tries to save himself from drowning) [LOWTH]. "Together with *the joints* of his hands," i.e., though Moab struggle against Jehovah hand and foot [MAURER]. **12. fortress**—the strongholds of *Moab,* the representative of the foes of God's people [BARNES]. Babylon [MAURER]. The society of infidels represented as a city (Rev. 11:8).

CHAPTER 26

Vss. 1-21. CONNECTED WITH CHAPTERS 24, 25. SONG OF PRAISE OF ISRAEL AFTER BEING RESTORED TO THEIR OWN LAND. As the overthrow of the apostate faction is described in ch. 25, so the peace of the faithful is here described under the image of a well-fortified city. **1. strong city**—Jerusalem, strong in Jehovah's protection: type of the new Jerusalem (Ps. 48:1-3), contrasted with the overthrow of the ungodly foe (vss. 4-7, 12-14; Rev. 22:2, 10-12, etc.). **salvation . . . walls**—(Ch. 60:18; Jer. 3:23; Zech. 2:5). MAURER translates, "Jehovah makes His help serve as walls" (ch. 33:20, 21, etc.). **bulwarks**—the trench with the antemural earthworks exterior to the wall. **2.** Address of the returning people to the gates of Jerusalem (type of the heavenly city, Heb. 12:22); (Ps. 24:7, 9; 118:19). Antitypically (Rev. 22:14; 21: 25, 27). **righteous nation**—that had not apostatized during the captivity. HORSLEY translates, "The nation of the Just One," viz., the Jews. **3. mind**—stayed—(Ps. 112:7, 8). Jesus can create "perfect peace" within thy mind, though storms of trial rage without (ch. 57:19; Mark 4:39); as a city kept securely by a strong garrison within, though besieged without (so Phil. 4:7). "Keep," lit., guard as with a garrison. HORSLEY translates, (God's) workmanship (the *Hebrew* does not probably mean "mind," but "a thing *formed,*" Eph. 2:10), so constantly "supported"; or else "formed and supported (by Thee) Thou shalt preserve (it, viz., the righteous nation) in perpetual peace." **4. Lord JEHOVAH**—*Hebrew, Jah, Jehovah.* The union of the two names expresses in the highest degree God's unchanging love and power (cf. Ps. 68:4). This passage, and ch. 12:2; Exodus 6:3; Psalm 83:18, are the four in which the *English Version* retains the JEHOVAH of the original. MAURER translates, "For JAH (the eternal unchangeable One, Exodus 3: 14) is JEHOVAH, the rock of ages" (cf. ch. 45:17; Deut. 32:15; I Sam. 2:2). **5. lofty city**—Babylon; representative of the stronghold of the foes of God's people in all ages (ch. 25:2, 12; 13:14). **6. poor**—(ch. 25:4), the once afflicted Jewish captives. "Foot shall tread," is figurative for *exulting* in the fall of God's enemies (Rev. 18:20). **7. uprightness**—rather, "is direct," i.e., is directed by God to a *prosperous issue,* however many be their afflictions in the meantime (as in the case of the Jewish exiles); the context requires this sense (Ps. 34:19; Prov. 3:6; 11:5), [MAURER]: thus "way" means *God's dealings with the righteous* (Ps. 37:23). **most upright**—(Deut. 32: 4.) **dost weigh**—(I Sam. 2:3; Prov. 5:21.) Rather, thou dost make plain and level [MAURER], removing all obstacles (ch. 40:3, 4). **8. way of thy judgments**

—We have waited for Thy proceeding to *punish* the enemy (vss. 9, 10) [MAURER]. HORSLEY translates vss. 7, 8, "The path of *the Just One* is perfectly even; an even road Thou wilt level for the Just One, *even the path of Thy laws,* O Jehovah. We have expected Thee." **name . . . remembrance**—the manifested *character* of God by which He would be *remembered* (ch. 64:5; Exod. 3:15). **9. With . . . soul . . . I**—lit., "I . . . my soul," in apposition; the faithful Jews here speak *individually.* The overthrow of the foe and the restoration of the Jews are to follow upon *prayer* on the part of the latter and of all God's people (ch. 62:1-4, 6, 7; Ps. 102:13-17). **in the night**—(Ps. 63:6; Song of Sol. 3:1.) **world . . . learn . . . righteousness**—the remnant left after judgments (Ps. 58:10, 11; Zech. 14:16). **10. uprightness** —rather, as in vs. 7, "prosperity," answering to "favor" in the parallelism, and in antithesis to "judgments in the earth" (vs. 9); where prosperity attends the wicked as well as the just, "he will not learn righteousness," therefore *judgments* must be sent that he may "learn" it [MAURER]. **11. lifted up**—to punish the foes of God's people. They who *will* not see *shall* be made to "see" to their cost (ch. 5:12). **their envy at the** (i.e., Thy) **people**—LOWTH translates. "They shall see with confusion *Thy zeal for Thy* people." **fire of . . . enemies**—i.e., the fire to which Thine enemies are doomed (ch. 9:18). **12. peace**—God's favor, including all blessings, temporal and spiritual, opposed to their previous trials (Ps. 138:8). **13. other lords**—temporal; heathen kings (II Chron. 12:8; 28:5, 6), Nebuchadnezzar, etc. Spiritual also, idols and lusts (Rom. 6:16-18). **by thee only**—It is due to Thee alone, that we again worship Thee as our Lord [MAURER]. "(We are) Thine only, we will celebrate Thy name" [HORSLEY]. The sanctifying effect of affliction (Ps. 71:16; 119:67, 71). **14. They** —The "other lords" or tyrants (vs. 13). **shall not live**—viz., again. **deceased**—*Hebrew,* Rephaim; powerless, in the land of shades (ch. 14:9, 10). **therefore**—i.e., inasmuch as. Cf. "therefore" (Gen. 18:5; 19:8). **15. hast**—prophetical preterite (ch. 9:3). **hast removed . . . far . . . ends of . . . earth** —rather, "Thou hast extended far all the borders of the land" [VITRINGA]. **16. visited**—sought—**poured out** (Ps. 62:8), as a vessel emptying out all its contents. **prayer**—lit., a whispered prayer, *Margin,* a secret sighing to God for help (cf. Jer. 13:17; Deut. 8:16). **17.** An image of anguish accompanied with expectation, to be followed by joy that will cause the anguish utterly to be forgotten. Zion, looking for deliverance, seemingly in vain, but really about to be gloriously saved (Mic. 4:9, 10-13; 5:1-3; John 16:21, 22). **18. brought forth wind**—MICHAELIS explains this of the disease *empneumatosis.* Rather, "wind" is a figure for that which proves an *abortive effort.* The "we" is in antithesis to "Thy," "my" (vs. 19), what *we* vainly attempt, *God* will accomplish. **not wrought . . . deliverance in . . . earth** —lit., the land (Judea) is *not made security,* i.e., is not become a place of security from our enemies. **neither . . . world fallen**—The "world" at large, is in antithesis to "the earth," i.e., Judea. The world at enmity with the city of God has not been subdued. But MAURER explains "fallen," according to *Arabic* idiom, of the *birth* of a child, which is said to *fall* when being born; "inhabitants of the world (*Israel,* ch. 24:4; not the world in general) are not yet born"; i.e., the country as yet lies desolate, and is not yet populated. **19.** In antithesis to vs. 14, "They (Israel's foes) shall not live"; "Thy (Jehovah's) dead men (the Jews) shall live," i.e., primarily, *be restored, spiritually* (ch. 54:1-3), *civilly and nationally* (vs. 15); whereas Thy foes shall not; ultimately, and in the fullest scope of the prophecy, *restored to life literally* (Ezek. 37:1-14; Dan. 12:2). **together with my dead body**—rather, *my dead body*, or *bodies* (the Jewish nation personified, which had been spiritually and civilly dead; or the nation, as a parent, speaking of the *bodies* of her children individually, *Note*, vs. 9, "I," "My"): Jehovah's "dead" and "my dead" are one and the same [HORSLEY]. However, as Jesus is the antitype to Israel (Matt. 2:15), *English Version* gives a true sense, and one ultimately contemplated in the prophecy: *Christ's* dead body being raised again is the source of Jehovah's people (*all*, and especially believers, the spiritual Israelites) also being raised (I Cor. 15:20-22). **Awake**—(Eph. 5: 14), spiritually. **in dust**—prostate and dead, spiritually and nationally; also literally (ch. 25:12; 47:1). **dew**—which falls copiously in the East and supplies somewhat the lack of rain (Hos. 14:5). **cast out . . . dead**—i.e., shall bring them forth to life again. **20. enter . . . chambers**—When God is about to take vengeance on the ungodly, the saints shall be shut in by Him in a place of safety, as Noah and his family were in the days of the flood (Gen. 7:16), and as Israel was commanded not to go out of doors on the night of the slaying of the Egyptian first-born (Exod. 12:22, 23; Ps. 31:20; 83:3). The saints are calmly and confidently to await the issue (Exod. 14: 13, 14). **21.** (Mic. 1:3; Jude 14.) **disclose . . . blood**—(Gen. 4:10, 11; Job 16:18; Ezek. 24:7, 8). All the innocent blood shed, and all other wrongs done, so long seemingly with impunity, shall then be avenged (Rev. 16:6).

CHAPTER 27

Vss. 1-13. CONTINUATION OF CHAPTERS 24, 25, 26. At the time when Israel shall be delivered, and the ungodly nations punished, God shall punish also the great enemy of the Church. **1. sore**—rather, hard, well-tempered. **leviathan**—lit., in *Arabic*, "the twisted animal," applicable to every great tenant of the waters, sea-serpents, crocodiles, etc. In Ezekiel 29:3; 32:2; Daniel 7:1, etc.; Revelation 12:3, etc., potentates hostile to Israel are similarly described; antitypically and ultimately Satan is intended (Rev. 20:10). **piercing**—rigid [LOWTH]. Flying [MAURER and LXX]. Long, extended, viz., as the crocodile which cannot readily bend back its body [HOUBIGANT]. **crooked**—winding. **dragon**—*Hebrew, tenin*; the crocodile. **sea**—the Euphrates, or the expansion of it near Babylon. **2.** In that day when leviathan shall be destroyed, the vineyard (Ps. 80:8), the Church of God, purged of its blemishes, shall be *lovely* in God's eyes; to bring out this sense the better, LOWTH, by changing a *Hebrew* letter, reads "pleasant", "lovely," for "red wine." **sing**—a *responsive* song [LOWTH]. **unto her**—rather, concerning her (*Note*, ch. 5:1); viz., the Jewish state [MAURER]. **3. lest any hurt it**—attack it [MAURER]. "Lest aught be wanting in her" [HORSLEY]. **4. Fury is not in me**—i.e., I entertain no longer angry towards my vine. **who would set . . . in battle**—i.e., would that I had the briers, etc. (the wicked foe; ch. 9:18; 10:17; II Sam. 23:6), before me! "I would go through," or rather, "*against* them." **5. Or**—Else; the only alternative, if Israel's enemies wish to escape being "burnt together." **strength**—rather, the refuge which I afford [MAURER]. "Take hold," refers to the horns of the altar which fugitives often *laid hold* of as an asylum (I Kings 1:50; 2:28). Jesus is God's "strength", or "refuge" which sinners must repair

to and take hold of, if they are to have "peace" with God (ch. 45:24; Rom. 5:1; Eph. 2:14; cf. Job 22:21). **6. He**—Jehovah. Here the song of the Lord as to His vineyard (vss. 2-5) ends; and the prophet confirms the sentiment in the song, under the same image of a *vine* (cf. Ps. 92:13-15; Hos. 14:5, 6). **Israel . . . fill . . . world**—(Rom. 11:12.) **7. him . . . those**—Israel—Israel's enemies. Has God punished His people as severely as He has those enemies whom He employed to chastise Israel? No! Far from it. Israel, after trials, He will restore; Israel's enemies He will utterly destroy at last. **the slaughter of them that are slain by him**—rather, "Is *Israel* slain according to the slaughter of *the enemy slain?*" the slaughter wherewith the enemy is slain [MAURER]. **8. In measure**—not beyond measure; in moderation (Job 23:6; Ps. 6:1; Jer. 10:24; 30:11; 46: 28). **when it shooteth**—image from the vine; rather, passing from the image to the thing itself, "*when sending her away* (viz., Israel to exile; ch. 50:1, God only *putting* the adulteress *away* when He might justly have put her to death), Thou didst *punish* her" [GESENIUS]. **stayeth**—rather, as *Margin*, "*when He removeth it by* His rough wind in the day," etc. **east wind**—especially violent in the East (Job 27:21; Jer. 18:17). **9. By this**—exile of Israel (the "sending away," vs. 8). **purged**—expiated [HORSLEY]. **all the fruit**—This is the whole *benefit* designed to be brought about by the chastisement; namely, the removal of his (Israel's) sin (viz., object of idolatry; Deut. 9:21; Hos. 10:8). **when he**—Jehovah; at the destruction of Jerusalem by Nebuchadnezzar, His instrument. The Jews ever since have abhorred idolatry (cf. ch. 17:8). **not stand up**—shall rise no more [HORSLEY]. **10. city**—Jerusalem; the beating asunder of whose altars and images was mentioned in vs. 9 (cf. ch. 24:10-12). **calf feed**—(ch. 17:2); it shall be a vast wild pasture. **branches**—resuming the image of the vine (vs. 6). **11. boughs . . . broken off**—so the Jews are called (Rom. 11:17, 19, 20). **set . . . on fire**—burn them as fuel; "women" are specified, as probably it was their office to collect fuel and kindle the fire for cooking. **no understanding**—as to the ways of God (Deut. 32:28, 29; Jer. 5:21; Hos. 4:6). **12.** Restoration of the Jews from their dispersion, described under the image of fruits shaken from trees and collected. **beat off**—as fruit beaten off a tree with a stick (Deut. 24:20), and then gathered. **river**—Euphrates. **stream of Egypt**—on the confines of Palestine and Egypt (Num. 34:5; Josh. 15:4, 47), now *Wady el-Arish*, Jehovah's vineyard, Israel, extended according to His purpose from the Nile to the Euphrates (I Kings 4:21, 24; Ps. 72:8). **one by one** —gathered most carefully, not merely as a nation, but as *individuals*. **13. great trumpet**—image from the trumpets blown on the first day of the seventh month to summon the people to a holy convocation (Lev. 23:24). Antitypically, the gospel trumpet (Rev. 11:15; 14:6) which the Jews shall hearken to in the last days (Zech. 12:10; 13:1). As the passover in the first month answers to Christ's crucifixion, so the day of atonement and the idea of "salvation" connected with the feast of tabernacles in the same seventh month, answer to the *crowning* of "redemption" at His second coming; therefore *redemption* is put last in I Corinthians 1:30. **Assyria** —whither the ten tribes had been carried; Babylonia is mainly meant, to which Assyria at that time belonged; the two tribes were restored, and *some* of the ten accompanied them. However, "Assyria" is designedly used to point *ultimately* to the future restoration of the ten *fully*, never yet accomplished

(Jer. 3:18). **Egypt**—whither many had fled at the Babylonish captivity (Jer. 41:17, 18). Cf. as to the future restoration, ch. 11:11, 12, 16; 51:9-16 ("Rahab" being Egypt).

CHAPTER 28

Vss. 1-29. Chaps. 28-33 form almost one continuous prophecy concerning the destruction of Ephraim, the impiety and folly of Judah, the danger of their league with Egypt, the straits they would be reduced to by Assyria, from which Jehovah would deliver them on their turning to Him; ch. 28 refers to the time just before the sixth year of Hezekiah's reign, the rest not very long before his fourteenth year. **1. crown of pride**—*Hebrew* for *"proud crown* of the drunkards," etc. [Horsley], viz., Samaria, the capital of Ephraim, or Israel. "Drunkards," lit. (vss. 7, 8; ch. 5:11, 22; Amos 4:1; 6:1-6) and metaphorically, *like drunkards,* rushing on to their own destruction. **beauty . . . flower**—"whose glorious beauty or ornament is a fading flower." Carrying on the image of "drunkards"; it was the custom at feasts to wreathe the brow with *flowers;* so Samaria, "which is (not as English Version, 'which are') upon the head of the fertile valley," i.e., situated on a hill surrounded with the rich valleys as a garland (I Kings 16:24); but the garland is "fading," as garlands often do, because Ephraim is now close to ruin (cf. ch. 16:8); fulfilled 721 B.C. (II Kings 17:6, 24). **2. strong one**—the Assyrian (ch. 10:5). **cast down**—viz., Ephraim (vs. 1) and Samaria, its crown. **with . . . hand**—with violence (ch. 8:11). **3. crown . . . the drunkards**—rather, "the crown *of* the drunkards." **4.** Rather, "the fading flower, their glorious beauty (vs. 1), which is on the head of the fat (fertile) valley, shall be as the early fig" [G. V. Smith]. Figs usually ripened in August; but earlier ones (*Hebrew bikkurah,* Spanish *bokkore*) in June, and were regarded as a delicacy (Jer. 24:2; Hos. 9:10; Mic. 7:1). **while it is yet**—i.e., *immediately,* without delay; describing the *eagerness* of the Assyrian Shalmaneser, not merely to conquer, but to *destroy utterly* Samaria; whereas other conquered cities were often spared. **5-13.** The prophet now turns to Judah; a gracious promise to the remnant ("residue"); a warning lest through like sins Judah should share the fate of Samaria. **crown**—in antithesis to the *"fading* crown" of Ephraim (vss. 1, 3). **the residue**—primarily, *Judah,* in the prosperous reign of Hezekiah (II Kings 18:7), antitypically, *the elect of God;* as He here is called *their* "crown and diadem," so are they called *His* (ch. 62:3); a beautiful reciprocity. **6.** Jehovah will inspire their magistrates with justice, and their soldiers with strength of spirit. **turn . . . battle to . . . gate**—the defenders of their country who not only repel the foe from themselves, but drive him to the gates of his own cities (II Sam. 11:23; II Kings 18:8). **7.** Though Judah is to survive the fall of Ephraim, yet "they also" (the men of Judah) have perpetrated like sins to those of Samaria (ch. 5:3, 11), which must be chastised by God. **erred . . . are out of the way**—"stagger" . . . "reel." Repeated, to express the *frequency* of the vice. **priest . . prophet**—If the ministers of religion sin so grievously, how much more the other rulers (ch. 56-10, 12)! **vision**—even in that most sacred function of the prophet to declare God's will revealed to them. **judgment**—The priests had the administration of the law committed to them (Deut. 17:9; 19:17). It was against the law for the priests to take wine before entering

the tabernacle (Lev. 10:9; Ezek. 44:21). **9, 10.** Here the drunkards are introduced as scoffingly commenting on Isaiah's warnings: "Whom *will* he (does *Isaiah* presume to) teach knowledge? And whom will He make to understand *instruction?* Is it those (i.e., does he take us to be) just weaned, etc.? For (he is constantly repeating, as if to little children) precept upon precept," etc. **line**—a rule or law. [Maurer]. The repetition of sounds in *Hebrew. tzav latzav, tzav latzav, gav laqav, gav laquav,* expresses the scorn of the imitators of Isaiah's speaking; he spoke *stammering* (vs. 11). God's mode of teaching offends by its simplicity the pride of sinners (II Kings 5:11, 12; I Cor. 1:23). *Stammerers* as they were by drunkenness, and children in knowledge of God, they needed to be spoken to in the language of children, and "with stammering lips" (cf. Matt. 13:13). A just and merciful retribution. **11. For**—rather, "Truly." This is *Isaiah's reply to* the scoffers: Your drunken questions shall be answered by the severe lessons from God conveyed through the Assyrians and Babylonians; the dialect of these, though Semitic, like the Hebrew, was so far different as to sound to the Jews like the speech of *stammerers* (cf. ch. 33:19; 36:11). To them who will not understand God will speak still more unintelligibly. **12.** Rather, "He (Jehovah) who hath said to them." **this . . . the rest**—Reference may be primarily to "rest" from national warlike preparations, the Jews being at the time "weary" through various preceding calamities, as the Syro-Israelite invasion (ch. 7:8; cf. ch. 30:15; 22:8; 39:2; 36:1; II Kings, 18:8). But spiritually, the "rest" meant is that to be found in obeying those very "precepts" of God (vs. 10) which they jeered at (cf. Jer. 6:16; Matt. 11:29). **13. But**—rather, "Therefore," viz., because "they would not hear" (vs. 12). **that they might go**—the *designed result* to those who, from a defect of *the will,* so far from profiting by God's mode of instructing, "precept upon precept," etc., made it into a stumbling block (Hos. 6:5; 8:12; Matt. 13:14). **go, and fall**—image appropriately from "drunkards" (vs. 7, which they were) who in trying to "go" *forward* "fall *backward." ***14. scornful**—(*Note,* vss. 9, 10.) **15. said**—virtually, in your conduct, if not in words. **covenant**—There may be a tacit reference to their confidence in their "covenant" with the Assyrians in the early part of Hezekiah's prosperous reign, before he ceased to pay tribute to them, as if it ensured Judah from evil, whatever might befall the neighboring Ephraim (vs. 1). The *full* meaning is shown by the language ("covenant with death—hell," or *sheol*) to apply to all lulled in false security spiritually (Ps. 12:4; Eccles. 8:8; Jer. 8:11); the godly alone are in covenant with death (Job 5:23; Hos. 2:18; I Cor. 3:22). **overflowing scourge**—two metaphors: the hostile Assyrian armies like an overwhelming flood. **pass through**—viz., through Judea on their way to Egypt, to punish it as the protector of Samaria (II Kings 17:4). **lies**—*They* did not use these *words,* but Isaiah designates their sentiments by their true name (Amos 2:4). **16.** Lit., *Behold Me* as Him who *has laid;* viz., in My divine counsel (Rev. 13:8); none save I could lay it (ch. 63:5). **stone**—*Jesus Christ; Hezekiah* [Maurer], or *the temple* [Ewald], do not realize the full significance of the language; but only in type point to Him, in whom the prophecy receives its exhaustive accomplishment; whether *Isaiah* understood its fulness or not (I Peter 1:11, 12), the Holy Ghost plainly contemplated its fulfilment in Christ alone; so in ch. 32:1; cf. Genesis 49:24; Psalm 118:22; Matthew 21:42; Romans 10:11; Ephesians 2:20

tried—both by the devil (Luke 4:1-13) and by men (Luke 20:1-38), and even by God (Matt. 27:46); a stone of tested solidity to bear the vast superstructure of man's redemption. The *tested righteousness* of Christ gives its peculiar merit to His vicarious sacrifice. The connection with the context is; though a "scourge" shall visit Judea (vs. 15), yet God's gracious purpose as to the elect remnant, and His kingdom of which "Zion" shall be the center, shall not fail, because its rests on Messiah (Matt. 7: 24, 25; II Tim. 2:19). precious—lit. "of preciousness," so in the *Greek,* (I Pet. 2:7). *He is preciousness.* corner-stone—(I Kings 5:17; 7:9; Job 38:6); the stone laid at the corner where two walls meet and connecting them; often costly. make haste—flee in hasty alarm; but LXX has "be ashamed"; so Romans 9:33, and I Peter 2:6, "be confounded," substantially the same idea; he who rests on Him shall not have the shame of disappointment, nor flee in sudden panic (see ch. 30:15; 32:17). 17. line—the measuring-line of the plummet. HORSLEY translates, "I will appoint judgment for the rule, and justice for the plummet." As the cornerstone stands most perpendicular and exactly proportioned, so Jehovah, while holding out grace to believers in the Foundation-stone, will judge the scoffers (vs. 15) according to the exact *justice* of the law (cf. Jas. 2: 13). hail—divine judgment (ch. 30:30; 32:19). 18. disannulled—obliterated, as letters traced on a waxen tablet are obliterated by passing the stylus over it. trodden down—passing from the metaphor to "scourge" to the thing meant, the *army* which *treads down* its enemies. 19. From the time . . .—rather, "As often as it comes over (i.e., passes through), it shall overtake you" [HORSLEY]; like a flood returning *from time to time,* frequent hostile invasions shall assail Judah, after the deportation of the ten tribes. vexation . . . understand . . . report—rather, "It shall be a terror even to hear the mere report of it" [MAURER], (I Sam. 3:11). But G. V. SMITH, "Hard treatment (HORSLEY, dispersion) only shall make you to understand instruction"; they scorned at the simple way in which the prophet offered it (vs. 9); therefore, they must be taught by the severe teachings of adversity. 20. Proverbial, for they shall find all their sources of confidence fail them; all shall be hopeless perplexity in their affairs. 21. Perazim—In the valley of Rephaim (II Sam. 5:18, 20; I Chron. 14:11), there Jehovah, by David, *broke forth* as waters do, and made a *breach* among the *Philistines,* David's enemies, as *Perazim* means, expressing a sudden and complete overthrow. Gibeon—(I Chron. 14:16; II Sam. 5:25; *Margin);* not Joshua's victory (Josh. 10:10). strange—as being against His own people; judgment is not what God delights in; it is, though necessary, yet strange to Him (Lam. 3:33). work—punishing the guilty (ch. 10:12). 22. mockers—a sin which they had committed (vss. 9, 10). bands—their Assyrian bondage (ch. 10:27); Judah was then tributary to Assyria; or, "lest your punishment be made still more severe" (ch. 24:22). consumption—destruction (ch. 10:22, 23; Dan. 9:27). 23. Calling attention to the following illustration from husbandry (Ps. 49:1, 2). As the husbandman does his different kinds of work, each in its *right time* and *due proportion,* so God adapts His measures to the varying exigencies of the several cases: now mercy, now judgments; now punishing sooner, now later (an answer to the scoff that His judgments, being put off so long, would never come at all, ch. 5:19); His object being not to *destroy* His people any more than the farmer's object in threshing is to destroy his crop; this vindicates

God's "strange work" (vs. 21) in punishing His people. Cf. the same image, Jeremiah 24:6; Hosea 2:23; Matthew 3:12. 24. all day—emphatic; he is not *always* ploughing: he also "sows," and that, too, in accordance with sure rules (vs. 25). doth he open—supply "always." Is he *always harrowing?* 25. face—the "surface" of the ground: "made plain," or level, by harrowing. fitches—rather, dill, or fennel; *Nigella romana,* with black seed, easily beaten out, used as a condiment and medicine in the East. So the LXX, "cummin" was used in the same way. cast in . . . principal wheat—rather, *plant the wheat in rows* (for wheat was thought to yield the largest crop, by being planted sparingly; PLINY, H.N. 18. 21); [MAURER]; "sow the wheat regularly" [HORSLEY]. But GENESIUS, like *English Version,* "fat," or "principal," i.e., excellent wheat. appointed barley—rather, "barley in its appointed place [MAURER]. in their place—rather, "in its (the field's) border [MAURER]. 26. to discretion—in the due rules of husbandry; God first taught it to man (Gen. 3:23). 27. The husbandman uses the same discretion in threshing. The dill ("fitches") and cummin, leguminous and tender grains, are beaten out, not as wheat, etc., with the heavy corn drag ("threshing instrument"), but with "a staff"; heavy instruments would crush and injure the seed. cart wheel—two iron wheels armed with iron teeth, like a saw, joined together by a wooden axle. The "corndrag" was made of three or four wooden cylinders, armed with iron teeth or flint stones fixed underneath, and joined like a sledge. Both instruments cut the straw for fodder as well as separated the corn. staff—used also where they had but a small quantity of *corn;* the flail (Ruth 2:17). 28. Bread-corn—corn of which bread is made. bruised—*threshed* with the corn-drag (as contrasted with dill and cummin, "beaten with the staff"), or, "trodden out" by the hoofs of cattle driven over it on the threshing-floor [G. V. SMITH], (Deut. 25:4; Mic. 4:13). because—rather, "but" [HORSLEY]; though the corn is threshed with the heavy instrument, *yet* he will not always be thus threshing it. break it—"drive over it (continually) the wheel" [MAURER]. cart—threshing-drag. horsemen—rather, "horses"; used to tread out corn. 29. This also—The skill wherewith the husbandman duly adjusts his modes of threshing is given by God, as well as the skill (vs. 26) wherewith he tills and sows (vss. 24, 25). Therefore He must also be able to adapt His modes of treatment to the several moral needs of His creatures. His object in sending *tribulation* (derived from the Latin *tribulum,* a "thresh ing instrument," Luke 22:31; Romans 5:3) is to sever the moral chaff from the wheat, not to crush utterly; "His judgments are usually in the line of our offenses; by the nature of the judgments we may usually ascertain the nature of the sin" [BARNES].

CHAPTER 29

Vss. 1-24. COMING INVASION OF JERUSALEM: ITS FAILURE: UNBELIEF OF THE JEWS. This chapter opens the series of prophecies as to the invasion of Judea under Sennacherib, and its deliverance. 1. Ariel—Jerusalem; Ariel means "Lion of God," i.e., city rendered by God invincible: the lion is emblem of a mighty hero (II Sam. 23:20). Otherwise "Hearth of God," i.e., place where the altar fire continually burns to God (ch. 31:9; Ezek. 43:15, 16). add . . . year to year—ironically; suffer one year after another to glide on in the round of formal, heartless "sacrifices." Rather, "add yet another year" to the one just closed [MAURER]. Let a year elapse and a little more (ch. 32:10; *Margin*). **let . . . kill sacrifices**—rather, "let the beasts (of another year) go round" [MAURER]; i.e., after the completion of a year "I will distress Ariel." **2. Yet**—rather, "Then." **heaviness . . . sorrow**—rather, preserving the *Hebrew* paronomasia, "groaning" and "moaning." **as Ariel** —either, "the city shall be as *a lion* of *God*," i.e., it shall emerge from its dangers unvanquished; or "it shall be as the *altar of burnt offering*," consuming with fire the besiegers (vs. 6; ch. 30:30; 31:9; Lev. 10:2); or best, as the next verse continues the *threat*, and the promise of *deliverance* does not come till vs. 4, "it shall be like a hearth of burning," i.e., a scene of devastation by fire [G. V. SMITH]. The prophecy, probably, contemplates *ultimately*, besides the affliction and deliverance in Sennacherib's time, the destruction of Jerusalem by Rome, the dispersion of the Jews, their restoration, the destruction of the enemies that besiege the city (Zech. 14:2), and the final glory of Israel (vss. 17-24). **3. I**—*Jehovah*, acting through the Assyrian, etc., His instruments (ch. 10:5). **mount**—an artificial *mound* formed to outtop high walls (ch. 37:33); else *a station*, viz., of warriors, for the siege. **round about**—not *fully* realized under Sennacherib, but in the Roman siege (Luke 19:43; 21:20). **forts**—siege-towers (Deut. 20: 20). **4.** Jerusalem shall be as a captive, humbled to the dust. Her voice shall come from the earth as that of the spirit-charmers or necromancers (ch. 8: 19), faint and shrill, as the voice of the dead was supposed to be. Ventriloquism was doubtless the trick caused to make the voice appear to come from the earth (ch. 19:3). An appropriate retribution that Jerusalem, which consulted necromancers, should be made like them! **5. Moreover**—rather, "Yet"; yet in this extremity help shall come, and the enemy be scattered. **strangers**—foreign enemies, invaders (ch. 25:2). **it shall be**—viz., the destruction of the enemy. **at an instant**—in a moment (ch. 30: 23). **6. Thou**—the Assyrian army. **thunder . . .**— not literally, in the case of the Assyrians (ch. 37: 36); but figuratively for an awful judgment (ch. 30: 30; 28:17). The ulterior fulfilment, in the case of the Jews' foes in the last days, may be more literal (see as to "earthquake," Zech. 14:4). **7. munition** —fortress. **8.** Their disappointment in the very height of their confident expectation of taking Jerusalem shall be as great as that of the hungry man who in a dream fancies he eats, but awakes to hunger still (Ps. 73:20); their dream shall be dissipated on the fatal morning (ch. 37:36). **soul**—simply *his appetite*; he is still thirsty. **9. Stay**—rather, "Be astounded"; expressing the stupid and amazed incredulity with which the Jews received Isaiah's announcement. **wonder**—The second imperative, as often (ch. 8:9), is a threat; the first is a simple declaration of a fact, "Be astounded, since you choose to be so, at the prophecy, soon *you will be amazed* at the sight of the actual event" [MAURER]. **cry . . . out . . . cry**—rather, "Be ye blinded (since you choose to be so, though the light shines all round you), and soon ye shall be blinded" in good earnest to your sorrow [MAURER], (ch. 6:9, 10). **not with wine**— but with spiritual paralysis (ch. 51:17, 21). **ye . . . they**—The change from speaking *to*, to speaking *of* them, intimates that the prophet turns away from them to a greater distance, because of their stupid unbelief. **10.** Jehovah gives them up judicially to their own hardness of heart (cf. Zech. 14:13). Quoted by Paul, with variations from the LXX, Romans 11:8. See ch. 6:10; Psalm 69:23. **eyes; the prophets . . .**—rather, "hath closed your eyes, the

prophets; and your heads (*Margin*, see also ch. 3:2), the seers, He hath covered." The Orientals cover the head to sleep; thus "covered" is parallel to "closed your eyes" (Judg. 4:19). Covering the face was also preparatory to execution (Esther 7:8). This cannot apply to the time when Isaiah himself prophesied, but to subsequent times. **11. of all**—rather, "*the whole* vision." "Vision" is the same here as "revelation," or "law"; in ch. 28:15, the same *Hebrew* word is translated, "covenant" [MAURER]. **sealed**—(ch. 8:16), God seals up the truth so that even the learned, because they lack believing docility, cannot discern it (Matt. 13:10-17; 11:25). Prophecy remained comparatively a *sealed* volume (Dan. 12:4, 9), until Jesus, who "alone is worthy," "opened the seals" (Rev. 5:1-5, 9; 6:1). **12.** The unlearned succeed no better than the learned, not from want of human learning, as they fancy, but from not having the teaching of God (ch. 54:13; Jer. 31:34; John 6:45; I Cor. 2:7-10; 1 John 2:20). **13. precept of men**—instead of the precepts of God, given by His prophets; also worship external, and by rule, not heartfelt as God requires (John 4:24). Cf. Christ's quotation of this verse from the LXX. **14.** (Hab. 1:5; Acts 13:41.) The "*marvellous* work" is one of *unparalleled* vengeance on the hypocrites: cf. "*strange* work," ch. 28:21. The judgment, too, will visit the wise in that respect in which they most pride themselves; their *wisdom* shall be hid, i.e., shall no longer appear, so as to help the nation in its distress (cf. I Cor. 1:19). **15. seek deep to hide**— rather, "That seek to hide deeply," etc. (cf. ch. 30:1, 2). The reference is to the *secret* plan which many of the Jewish nobles had of seeking Egyptian aid against Assyria, contrary to the advice of Isaiah. At the same time the hypocrite in general is described, who, under a plausible exterior, tries to hide his real character, not only from men, but even from God. **16.** Rather, "Ah! your perverseness! just as if the potter should be esteemed as the clay!" [MAURER]. Or, "Ye invert (turn upside down) the order of things, putting yourselves instead of God," and vice versa, just as if the potter should be esteemed as the clay [HORSLEY], (ch. 45:9; 64:8). **17. turned**—as contrasted with *your* "turnings of things upside down" (vs. 16), there shall be other and better *turnings* or revolutions; the outpouring of the Spirit in the latter days (ch. 32:15); first on the Jews; which shall be followed by their national restoration (*Note*, vs. 2; Zech. 12:10); then on the Gentiles (Joel 2:28). **fruitful field**—lit., a Carmel (*Note*, ch. 10: 18). The moral change in the Jewish nation shall be as great as if the wooded Lebanon were to become a fruitful field, and vice versa. Cf. Matthew 11:12, *Greek*: "the kingdom of heaven *forces itself*," as it were, on man's acceptance; instead of men having to seek Messiah, as they had John, in a *desert*, He presents Himself before them with loving invitations; thus men's hearts, once a moral desert, are reclaimed so as to bear fruits of righteousness: vice versa, the ungodly who seemed prosperous, both in the moral and literal sense, shall be exhibited in their real barrenness. **18. deaf . . . blind**—(Cf. Matt. 11:5.) The spiritually blind, etc., are chiefly meant; "the book," as Revelation is called pre-eminently, shall be no longer "sealed," as is described (vs. 11), but the most unintelligent shall hear and see (ch. 35: 5). **19. meek**—rather, *the afflicted* godly: the idea is, *virtuous suffering* (ch. 61:1; Ps. 25:9; 37:11), [BARNES]. **poor among men**—i.e., the poorest of men, viz., the pious poor. **rejoice**—when they see their oppressors punished (vss. 20, 21), and Jehovah exhibited as their protector and rewarder (vss. 22-24; ch. 41:17; Jas. 2:5). **20. terrible**—viz., the persecutors among the Jewish nobles. **scorner**—(Ch. 28:14, 22.) **watch for**—not only commit iniquity, but watch for opportunities of committing it, and make it their whole study (see Mic. 2:1; Matt. 26:59; 27:1). **21.** Rather, "Who make a man guilty in his *cause*" [GESENIUS], i.e., unjustly condemn him. "A man" is in the *Hebrew a poor man*, upon whom such unjust condemnations might be practiced with more impunity than on the rich; cf. vs. 19, "the meek... the poor." **him that reproveth**—rather, pleadeth; one who has a suit at issue. **gate**—the place of concourse in a city, where courts of justice were held (Ruth 4:11; Prov. 31:23; Amos 5:10, 12). **just**—one who has a just cause; or, Jesus Christ, "the Just One" [HORSLEY]. **for a thing of naught**—rather, "through falsehood," "by a decision that is null in justice" [BARNES]. Cf. as to Christ, Proverbs 28:21; Matthew 26:15; Acts 3:13, 14; 8:33. **22.** Join "saith... concerning the house of Jacob." **redeemed**—out of Ur, a land of idolaters (Josh. 24:3). **not now**—After the moral revolution described (vs. 17), the children of Jacob shall no longer give cause to their forefathers to blush for them. **wax pale**—with shame and disappointment at the wicked degeneracy of his posterity, and fear as to their punishment. **23. But**—rather, "For." **he**—Jacob. **work of mine hands** —spiritually, as well as physically (ch. 19:25; 60:21; Eph. 2:10). By Jehovah's agency Israel shall be cleansed of its corruptions, and shall consist wholly of pious men (ch. 54:13, 14; 2:1; 60:21). **midst of him**—i.e., his land. Or else "His children" are the *Gentiles adopted among the Israelites. his lineal descendants* (Rom. 9:26; Eph. 3:6) [HORSLEY]. **24. They...that erred**—(Ch. 28:7.) **learn doctrine**—rather, shall receive discipline or instruction. "Murmuring" was the characteristic of Israel's rebellion against God (Exod. 16:8; Ps. 106:25). This shall be so no more. Chastisements, and, in HORSLEY's view, the piety of the Gentiles provoking the Jews to holy jealousy (Rom. 11:11, 14), shall then produce the desired effect.

CHAPTER 30

Vss. 1-32. CHAPTERS 30-32 REFER PROBABLY TO THE SUMMER OF 714 B.C., AS CHAPTER 29 TO THE PASSOVER OF THAT YEAR. Jewish ambassadors were now on their way to Egypt to seek aid against Assyria (ch. 30:2-6, 15; 31:1). Isaiah denounces this reliance on Egypt rather than on Jehovah. God had prohibited such alliances with heathen nations, and it was a leading part of Jewish polity that they should be a separate people (Exod. 23:32; Deut. 7:2). **1. take counsel**—rather, as vss. 4, 6 imply, "execute counsels." **cover... covering**—i.e., wrap themselves in reliances disloyal towards Jehovah. "Cover" thus answers to "seek to hide deeply their counsel from the Lord" (ch. 29:15). But the *Hebrew* is lit., "who pour out libations"; as it was by these that *leagues* were made (Exod. 24:8; Zech. 9:11), translate, "who make a league." **not of**—not suggested by My Spirit" (Num. 27:21; Josh. 9:14). **that they may add**—The *consequence* is here spoken of as their *intention*, so reckless were they of sinning: one sin entails the commission of another (Deut. 29:19). **2. walk**—are now setting out, viz., their ambassadors (vs. 4). **Egypt**—See *Note*, in the beginning of chs. 19 and 20. **Pharaoh**—the generic name of the kings of Egypt, as *Cæsar* was at Rome. The

word in Egyptian means "king" (JOSEPHUS, *Antiquities*, 8.6, 2). *Phra*, "the sun," was the hieroglyphic symbol and title of the king. **shadow**—image from shelter against heat: *protection* (Ps. 121:5, 6). **3. shame**—disappointment. Egypt, weakened by its internal dissensions, can give no solid help. **4. his**—Judah's (cf. ch. 9:21). **at Zoan**—are already arrived there on their errand to Pharaoh (see ch. 19:11). **came to Hanes**—are come there. West of the Nile, in central Egypt: Egyptian *Hnes;* the *Greek Heracleopolis:* perhaps the Anysis of HERODOTUS (2.137); according to GROTIUS, *Tahpanhes* contracted (Jer. 43:7-9); the seat of a reigning prince at the time, as was Zoan, hence the Jewish ambassadors go to both. **5.** (Jer. 2:36) **6. burden**—the prophecy as to, etc. [MAURER]; so LXX, the fresh inscription here marks emphatically the prediction that follows. Or, rather, Isaiah sees in vision, the ambassador's beasts *burdened* with rich presents *travelling southwards* (viz., to Egypt, Dan. 11:5, 6), and exclaims, Oh, the *burden of treasure* on the beasts! etc. (Hos. 8:9; 12:1). **land of trouble**—the desert between Palestine and Egypt, destitute of water and abounding in dangerous animals (Deut. 8:15; Jer. 2:6). **flying serpent** —(ch. 14:29), a species which springs like a dart from trees, on its prey. **will carry**—rather, present, "carry," viz., as presents to Egypt (I Kings 15:19) **young asses**—rather, full-grown asses [MAURER]. **7.** "Egypt is vanity, and to no purpose will they help" [G. V. SMITH]. **strength**—*Hebrew, Rabah*, a designation for Egypt (ch. 51:9; Ps. 87:4), implying her *haughty fierceness;* translate, "Therefore I call her Arrogance that sitteth still." She who boasted of the help she would give, when it came to the test, sat still (ch. 36:6). *English Version* agrees with vs. 15 and ch. 7:4. **8. table**—a tablet (Hab. 2:2), which should be set in public, containing the prophecy in a briefer form, to be read by all. **a book**—viz., a parchment roll, containing the prophecy in full, for the use of distant posterity. Its truth will be seen hereafter when the event has come to pass. See ch. 8:1, 16, *Notes*. **for ever and ever**—rather read, "For a *testimony* for ever" [CHALDEE, JEROME, LOWTH]: "testimony is often joined to the notion of *perpetuity* (Deut. 31:19, 21, 26). **9. lying**—unfaithful to Jehovah, whose covenant they had taken on them as His adopted *children* (ch. 59:13; Prov. 30:9). **10.** (Mic 2:6, 11; 3:5). **See not**—as you now do, foretelling misfortune. **Prophesy not... right things**—Not that they avowedly requested this, but their conduct *virtually* expressed it. No man, *professedly*, wished to be deceived; but many seek a kind of teaching which is deceit; and which, if they would examine, they might know to be such (I Kings 22:13). The Jews desired success to be foretold as the issue of their league with Egypt, though ill had been announced by God's prophet as the result; this constituted the "deceits." **11.** Depart from the true "way" (so in Acts 19:9, 23) of religion. **cause... to cease**—Let us hear no more of His name. God's *holiness* is what troubles sinners most. **12. Holy One**—Isaiah so little yields to their wicked prejudices that he repeats the very name and truth which they disliked. **this word**—Isaiah's exhortation to reliance on Jehovah. **oppression**—whereby they levied the treasures to be sent to conciliate Egypt (vs. 6). **perverseness**—in relying on Egypt, rather than on Jehovah. **13.** Image from a curve swelling out in a wall (Ps. 62:3); when the former gives way, it causes the downfall of the whole wall; so their policy as to Egypt. **14. he**—the enemy; or rather, God (Ps. 2:9; Jer. 19:11). **it**—the Jewish state. **potter's vessel**

—earthen and fragile. **sherd**—a fragment of the vessel large enough to take up a live coal, etc. **pit**—cistern or pool. The swell of the wall is at first imperceptible and gradual, but at last it comes to the crisis; so the decay of the Jewish state. **15. returning and rest**—turning back from your embassy to Egypt, and ceasing from warlike preparations. **quietness**—answering to "wait for Him" (God) (vs. 18). **16. flee**—not as fugitives, but we will *speed* our course; viz., against the Assyrians, by the help of cavalry supplied by Egypt (ch. 31:1). This was expressly against the Mosaic law (Deut. 17:16; cf. *Note*, ch. 2:7; Hos. 14:3). **shall ... flee**—lit., before your enemies; their sin and its punishment correspond. **17. One thousand**—A thousand *at once*, or, *As one man* [MAURER]. **rebuke**—the battle cry. **shall ye**—at the rebuke of five shall ye, viz., *all* (in contrast to the "one thousand") flee so utterly that even two shall not be left together, but each one shall be as solitary "as *a signal staff* [G. V. SMITH]. or a *banner on a hill*" (ch. 5:26; 11:12). The signal staff was erected to rally a nation in war. The remnant of Jews left would be beacons to warn all men of the justice of God, and the truth of His threatenings. GESENIUS (from Lev. 26:8; Deut. 32:30) arbitrarily inserts "ten thousand." "At the rebuke of five shall ten thousand of you flee." **18. therefore**—on account of your wicked perverseness (vs. 1, 2, 9, 15, 16), Jehovah will *delay* to be gracious [HORSLEY]. Rather, *wait or delay* in punishing, to give you time for repentance (vss. 13, 14, 17) [MAURER]. Or, "Yet therefore" (viz., because of the distress spoken of in the previous verses; that distress will lead the Jews to repentance, and so Jehovah will pity them) [GESENIUS]. **be exalted**—Men will have more elevated views of God's mercy; or else, "He will rise up to pity you" [G. V. SMITH]. Or [taking the previous clause as MAURER, "*Therefore* Jehovah will delay" in punishing you, "*in order that He may be gracious to you*," if ye repent], He will be *far removed* from you [so in Ps. 10:5, *far above out of sight*]; i.e., He will not immediately descend to punish, "in order that He may have mercy, etc. **judgment**—justice; faithfulness to His covenant. **wait**—cf. vs. 15, wait, viz., for His times of having mercy. **19.** (Ch. 65:9.) The restoration from Babylon only typifies the *full* accomplishment of the prophecy (vss. 18-33). **weep no more**—(ch. 25:8.) **thy cry**—(ch. 26:8, 9; Jer. 29:12-14). **20.** Rather, "The Lord will give"; the "though" is not in the original. **bread of adversity**—He will not deny you food enough to save you in your adversity (I Kings 22:27; Ps. 127:2). **be removed**—rather, "hide themselves"; they shall no more be forced to hide themselves from persecution, but shall be openly received with reverence [MAURER]. Contrast with this Psalm 74:9; Amos 8: 11. **21. word**—conscience, guided by the Holy Spirit (John 16:13). **22. covering of ... images**—rather, "images" (formed of wood or potter's clay, and) "covered with silver." Hezekiah, and afterwards Josiah, defiled them (II Kings 23:8, 10, 14, 16; II Chron. 31:1; cf. ch. 2:20; Deut. 7:25). **23. rain of**—rather, "*for thy* seed." Physical prosperity accompanies national piety; especially under the Old Testament. The *early* rain fell soon after the seed was sown in October or November; the *latter* rain in the spring, before the ripening of the corn. Both were needed for a good harvest. **increase**—the produce. **fat**—bread made of the best wheat flour (cf. Gen. 49:20; Deut. 32:14). **24 ear**—i.e. till. Asses were employed in tillage, as well as oxen (Deut. 22: 10). **clean**—rather, *salted* provender [GESENIUS]. The Arab proverb is, Sweet provender is as bread

to camels—salted provender as confectionery. The very cattle shall share the coming felicity. Or else, *well-fermented maslin,* i.e., provender formed of a mixture of various substances: grain, beans, vetches, hay, and salt. **winnowed**—not as it is usually given to cattle before it is separated from the chaff; the grain shall be so abundant that it shall be given winnowed. **shovel**—by which the grain was thrown up in the wind to separate it from the chaff. **fan**—an instrument for winnowing. **25.** Even the otherwise barren hills shall then be well watered (ch. 44: 3). **the day ...**—when the disobedient among *the Jews* shall have been slain, as foretold in vs. 16: "towers," i.e., mighty men (ch. 2:15). Or else, the *towers of the Assyrian Sennacherib,* or of *Babylon,* types of all enemies of God's people. **26.** Image from the heavenly bodies to express the increase of spiritual light and felicity. "Sevenfold" implies the *perfection* of that felicity, seven being the sacred number. It shall also be literally fulfilled hereafter in the heavenly city (ch. 60:19, 20; Rev. 21:23, 24; 22:5). **breach**—the wound, or calamity, sent by God on account of their sins (ch. 1:5). **27. name of ... Lord**—i.e., Jehovah Himself (Ps. 44:5; 54:1); represented as a storm approaching and ready to burst over the Assyrians (vss. 30, 31). **burden ... is heavy**—lit., "grievousness is the flame," i.e., the flame which darts from Him is grievous. Or else (as the Hebrew means an "uplifting") *the uprising cloud is grievous* [G. V. SMITH]; the gathering cloud gradually rising till it bursts. **28.** (Ch. 11:4; II Thess. 2:8.) **reach ... neck**—the most extreme danger; yet as the *head,* or capital of Judah, was to be spared (ch. 8: 8), so the head, or sovereign of Assyria, Sennacherib, should escape. **sieve of vanity**—Rather, the winnowing fan of destruction [LOWTH] (ch. 41:16). **bridle in ... jaws**—as prisoners are represented in the Assyrian inscriptions (ch. 37:29). **causing ... to err**—(ch. 63:17.) "People," *Hebrew,* "peoples," viz., the various races composing the Assyrian armies (ch. 5:26). **29. the night ... solemnity**—As in the passover night ye celebrate your deliverance from Egypt, so shall ye celebrate your rescue from Assyrian bondage. Translate, "*the* solemnity" (Exod. 12:42). **goeth with a pipe**—or flute. They used to go up to Jerusalem ("the mountain of the Lord," Zion) at the three feasts with music and gladness (Deut. 16:16; Ezra 2:65; Ps. 122:1-4). **30.** Jehovah's "glorious voice," raised against the enemy (vs. 27), is again mentioned here, in contrast with the music (vs. 29) with which His people shall come to worship Him. **lighting down of ... arm**—(V. 32; Ps. 38:2.) The descent of His arm in striking. **scattering**—viz., a blast that scatters, or an "inundation" [MAURER]. **31.** The Assyrian rod which beat shall itself be beaten, and that by the mere *voice* of the Lord, i.e., an unseen divine agency (ch. 10:5, 24). **32. grounded**—rather, decreed, appointed [MAURER]. **staff**—the avenging rod. **him**—the Assyrian; type of all God's enemies in every age. *Margin* and MAURER construe, "Every passing through (infliction, ch. 28:15) of the appointed rod, which, (etc.), shall be with tabrets," i.e., accompanied with joy on the part of the rescued peoples. **battles of shaking**—i.e., shock of battles (ch. 19:16; cf. "sift ... sieve," vs. 28). **with it**—viz., Assyria. **33. Tophet**—lit., "A place of abomination"; the valley of the sons of Hinnom, southeast of Jerusalem, where Israel offered human sacrifices to Moloch by fire; hence a place of burning (II Kings 23:10; Jer. 7:31). Latterly Ge-hinnom or Gehenna, i.e., valley of Hinnom, was the receptacle of the refuse of the city, to consume which fires were constantly burning. Hence it came to express hell, the place of torment. In the former sense it was a fit place to symbolize the funeral pyre of the Assyrian army (not that it actually perished there); the Hebrews did not burn, but buried their dead, but the heathen Assyrians are to be burnt as a mark of ignominy. In the latter sense Tophet is the receptacle "prepared for the devil (antitype to the king, ch. 14:12-15) and his angels," and unbelieving men (Matt. 5:22; 25:41; Mark 9:43, 44).

CHAPTER 31

Vss. 1-9. THE CHIEF STRENGTH OF THE EGYPTIAN ARMIES LAY IN THEIR CAVALRY. In their level and fertile plains horses could easily be used and fed (Exod. 14:9; I Kings 10:28). In hilly Palestine horses were not so easily had or available. The Jews were therefore the more eager to get Egyptian chariots as allies against the Assyrian cavalry. In Assyrian sculptures chariots are represented drawn by three horses, and with three men in them (see ch. 36:9; Ps. 20:7; Dan. 9:13). **2. he also is wise**—as well as the Egyptian priests, so famed for wisdom (Acts 7:22), but who are "fools" before Him (ch. 19:11). He not only devises, but executes what He devises without "calling back His words" (Num. 23: 19). **house**—the whole race. **help**—the Egyptian succor sought by the Jews. **3. not spirit**—not of divine power (Ps. 56:4; 146:3, 5; Zech. 4:6). **he that helpeth**—Egypt. **holpen**—Judah. **4.** (Ch. 42:13; Hos. 11:10.) **roaring on**—"growling over" his prey. **abase himself**—be disheartened or frightened. **5.** As in the image of "the lion," the point of comparison is the fearless might of Jehovah; so in that of the birds, it is His solicitous affection (Deut. 32:11; Ps. 91:4; Matt. 23:37). **flying**—Rather, "which defend" their young with their wings; "to fly" is a secondary meaning of the Hebrew word [MAURER]. "Hovering over" to protect their young [G. V. SMITH]. **passing over**—as the destroying angel *passing over, so as to spare* the blood-marked houses of the Israelites on the first passover (Exod. 12:13, 23, 27). He passed, or *leaped forward* [LOWTH], to *destroy* the enemy and to spare His people. **6.** The power and love of Jehovah, just mentioned, are the strongest incentives for returning to Him (Ezek. 16:62, 63; Hos. 6:1). **ye . . . Israel**—The change of person marks that when they return to the Lord, He will address them in more direct terms of communion in the second person; so long as they were *revolters,* God speaks *of* them, as more at a distance, in the third person, rather than *to* them. **7.** In the day of trial the idols will be found to render no help and will therefore be cast away. Cf. as to the future restoration and conversion of Israel simultaneously with the interposition of Jehovah in its defense, Zechariah 12:9-14; 13:1, 2. **for a sin**—i.e., whereby especially you contracted guilt (I Kings 12: 30). **8. Assyrian**—Sennacherib, representative of some powerful head of the ungodly in the latter ages [HORSLEY]. **sword, not of . . . mighty . . . mean man**—but by the unseen sword of God. **flee**—Sennacherib alone *fled* homewards after his army had been destroyed (ch. 37:37). **young men**—the flower of his army. **discomfited**—rather, "shall be subject to slavery"; lit., shall be liable to tribute, i.e., personal service (Deut. 20:11; Josh. 9:21) [MAURER]. Or, not so well, "shall melt away" [ROSENMULLER]. **9.** Rather, *"shall pass beyond* his strongholds"; he shall not stop to take refuge in it through fear (Judg. 20:47; Jer. 48:28) [GESENIUS]. **ensign**—the

banner of Jehovah protecting the Jews [MAURER]. **fire . . . furnace**—"light" and "fire," viz., of Jehovah's *altar* at Jerusalem (ch. 29:1). Perhaps "furnace," as distinguished from "fire," may mean that His *dwelling-place* (His hearth) was at Jerusalem (cf. ch. 4:5); or else the *fiery furnace* awaiting all the enemies who should attack Jerusalem.

CHAPTER 32

Vss. 1-20. MESSIAH'S KINGDOM; DESOLATIONS, TO BE SUCCEEDED BY LASTING PEACE, THE SPIRIT HAVING BEEN POURED OUT. The times of purity and happiness which shall follow the defeat of the enemies of Jehovah's people (vss. 1-8). The period of wrath before that happy state (vss. 9-14). The assurance of the final prosperity of the Church is repeated (vss. 15-20). **1. king**—not Hezekiah, who was already on the throne, whereas a *future* time is contemplated. If he be meant at all, it can only be as a type of Messiah the King, to whom alone the language is fully applicable (Hos. 3:5; Zech. 9:9; see ch. 11:3-5, *Notes*). The kingdom shall be transferred from the world kings, who have exercised their power *against* God, instead of *for* God, to the rightful King of kings (Ezek. 21:27; Dan. 7:13, 14). **princes**—subordinate; referring to all in authority under Christ in the coming kingdom on earth, e.g., the apostles, etc. (Luke 22:30; I Cor. 6:2; II Tim. 2:12; Rev. 2:26, 27; 3:21). **2. a man**—rather, *the man* Christ [LOWTH]; it is as "the Son of man" He is to reign, as as Son of man He suffered (Matt. 26:64; John 5:27; 19:5). Not as MAURER explains, *"every* one of the princes shall be," etc. **rivers**—as refreshing as water and cool shade are to the heated traveller (ch. 35:6, 7; 41:18). **3. them that see**—the seers or prophets. **them that hear**—the people under instruction (ch. 35:5, 6). **4. rash**—rather, the hasty; contrast "shall not make haste" (ch. 28:16); the reckless who will not take time to weigh religious truth aright. Or else, the well-instructed [HORSLEY]. **stammers**—those who speak confusedly on divine things (cf. Exod. 4:10-12; Jer. 1:6; Matt. 10:19, 20). Or, rather, those drunken *scorners* who in stammering style imitated Isaiah's warnings to mock them [MAURER] (ch. 28:7-11, 13, 14, 22; 29:20); in this view, translate, "speak *uprightly"* (agreeably to the divine law); not as *English Version,* referring to the distinctness of articulation, "plainly." **5. vile**—rather, "fool" [LOWTH]; i.e., ungodly (Ps. 14:1; 74:18). **liberal**—rather, "nobleminded." **churl**—rather, "fraudulent" [GESENIUS]. **bountiful**—religiously. The atheistic churl, who envies the believer his hope "full of immortality," shall no longer be held as a patriot struggling for the emancipation of mankind from superstition [HORSLEY]. **6. vile . . . villainy**—rather, "the (irreligious) fool—(his) folly." **will speak**—rather, present; for (so far is the "fool" from deserving the epithet "noble-minded") the fool "speaketh" folly and "worketh," etc. **hypocrisy**—rather, "profligacy" [HORSLEY]. **error**—impiety, perverse arguments. **hungry**—spiritually (Matt. 5:6). **7. churl**—"the fraudulent"; this verse refers to the last clause of vs. 5; as vs. 6 referred to its first clause. **speaketh right**—pleadeth a just cause (ch. 29:21); spiritually, "the poor man's cause" is the divine doctrine, his rule of faith and practice. **8. liberal**—rather, "noble-minded." **stand**—shall be approved under the government of the righteous King. **9-20.** Address to the women of Jerusalem who troubled themselves little about the political signs of the times, but lived a life of self-indulgence (ch. 3:16-23); the failure of food through the devastations of the enemy is here foretold, being what was most likely to affect them as mothers of families, heretofore accustomed to every luxury. VITRINGA understands "women—daughters" as the cities and villages of Judea (Ezek. 16). See Amos 6:1. **10. Many days and years**—rather, "In little more than a year" [MAURER]; lit., days upon a year (so ch. 29). **vintage shall fail** —through the arrival of the Assyrian invader. As the wheat harvest is omitted, Isaiah must look for the invasion in the summer or autumn of 714 B.C., when the wheat would have been secured already, and the later fruit "gathering," and vintage would be still in danger. **11. strip you**—of your gay clothing. (*Note*, ch. 2). **12. lament for . . . teats**—rather, shall smite on their breasts in lamentation "for thy pleasant fields" (Nah. 2:7) [MAURER]. "Teats" in *English Version* is used for fertile lands, which, like *breasts*, nourish life. The transition from "ye" to "they" (vss. 11, 12) is frequent. **13.** (Ch. 5:6; 7:23.) **houses of joy**—pleasure-houses outside of Jerusalem, not Jerusalem itself, but other cities destroyed by Sennacherib in his march (ch. 7:20-25). However, the prophecy, in its full accomplishment, refers to the *utter* desolation of Judea and its *capital* by Rome, and subsequently, previous to the second coming of the King (Ps. 118:26; Luke 13:35; 19:38); "the joyous city" is in this view, Jerusalem (ch. 22:2). **14. palaces**—most applicable to Jerusalem (*Note*, vs. 13). **multitude . . . left**—the noisy din of the city, i.e., the city with its noisy multitude shall lie forsaken [MAURER]. **forts**—rather, Ophel (i.e. the mound), the term applied specially to the declivity on the east of Zion, surrounded with its own wall (II Chron. 27:3; 33:14; II Kings 5:24), and furnished with "towers" (or watch-towers), perhaps referred to here (Neh. 3:26, 27). **for ever**—limited by thee, "until," etc., next verse, *for a long time*. **15.** This can only partially apply to the spiritual revival in Hezekiah's time; its full accomplishment belongs to the Christian dispensation, first at Pentecost (Joel 2:28; Acts 2:17), perfectly in coming times (Ps. 104: 30; Ezek. 36:26; 39:29; Zech. 12:10), when the Spirit shall be poured on Israel, and through it on the Gentiles (Mic. 5:7). **wilderness . . . fruitful field . . . forest**—when Judea, so long waste, shall be populous and fruitful, and the land of the enemies of God shall be desolate. Or, "the field, now fruitful, shall be but as a barren forest in comparison with what it shall be then" (ch. 29:17). The barren shall become fruitful by regeneration; those already regenerate shall bring forth fruits in such abundance that their former life shall seem but as a wilderness where no fruits were. **16. judgment**—justice. **wilderness**—then reclaimed. **fruitful field**—then become more fruitful (vs. 15); thus "wilderness" and "fruitful field" include the *whole* land of Judea. **17. work**—the effect (Prov. 14:34; Jas. 3:18). **peace**—internal and external. **18. sure . . . quiet**—free from fear of invasion. **19.** Lit., "But it shall hail with coming down of the forest, and in lowness shall the city (Nineveh) be brought low; i.e., humbled." The "hail" is Jehovah's wrathful visitation (ch. 30:30; 28: 2, 17). The "forest" is the Assyrian host, dense as the trees of a forest (ch. 10:18, 19, 33, 34; Zech. 11: 2). **20.** While the enemy shall be brought "low," the Jews shall cultivate their land in undisturbed prosperity. **all waters**—well-watered places (ch. 30: 25). The *Hebrew* translation, "beside," ought rather to be translated, "upon" (Eccles. 11:1), where the meaning is, "Cast thy seed upon the waters when the river overflows its banks; the seed will sink into

the mud and will spring up when the waters subside, and you will find it after many days in a rich harvest." Before sowing, they send oxen, etc., into the water to tread the ground for sowing. CASTALIO thinks there is an allusion to the Mosaic precept, not to plough with an ox and ass together, mystically implying that the Jew was to have no intercourse with Gentiles; the Gospel abolishes this distinction (Col. 3:11); thus the sense here is, Blessed are ye that sow the gospel seed without distinction of race in the teachers or the taught. But there is no need of supposing that the ox and ass here are *yoked together;* they are probably "sent forth" separately, as in ch. 30:24.

CHAPTER 33

Vss. 1-24. THE LAST OF ISAIAH'S PROPHECIES AS TO SENNACHERIB'S OVERTHROW (vs. 19). Vss. 1, 8, 9, describe the Assyrian spoiler; strong as he is, he shall fall before Jehovah who is stronger (vss. 2-6, 10-12). The time is the autumn of 713 B.C. **1. and thou**—i.e., though thou wast not spoiled—though thou wast not dealt treacherously with (*Note*, ch. 24:16), thy spoiling and treachery are therefore without excuse, being unprovoked. **cease**—When God has let thee do thy worst, in execution of His plans, thine own turn shall come (cf. ch. 10:12; 14: 2; Hab. 2:8; Rev. 13:10). **2. us; we . . . their . . . our**—He speaks interceding for His people, separating himself in thought for a moment from them, and immediately returns to his natural identification with them in the word "our." **every morning**—each day as it dawns, especially during our danger, as the parallel "time of trouble" shows. **3. the tumult** —the approach of Jehovah is likened to an advancing thunderstorm (ch. 29:6; 30:27), which is His voice (Rev. 1:15), causing the people to "flee." **nation**—the Assyrian levies. **4.** The invaders' "spoil" shall be left behind by them in their flight, and the Jews shall gather it. **caterpillar**—rather, the wingless locust; as it gathers; the *Hebrew* word for "gathers" is properly used of the gathering of the fruits of harvest (ch. 32:10). **running to and fro**—viz., in gathering harvest fruits. **he**—rather, "they." **them**—rather, "it," i.e., the prey. **6. wisdom**—sacred; i.e., piety. **thy**—Hezekiah's; or rather, Judea's. "His" refers to the same; such changes from the pronoun possessive of the second person to that of the third are common in Hebrew poetry. **treasure**—Not so much material wealth as piety shall constitute the riches of the nation (Prov. 10:22; 15:16). **7-9.** From the vision of future glory Isaiah returns to the disastrous present; the grief of "the valiant ones" (parallel to, and identical with, "the ambassadors of peace"), men of rank, sent with presents to sue for peace, but standing "without" the enemy's camp, their suit being rejected (II Kings 18:14, 18, 37). The highways deserted through fear, the cities insulted, the lands devastated. **cry**—(ch. 15:4). **8. broken . . . covenant**—When Sennacherib invaded Judea, Hezekiah paid him a large sum to leave the land; Sennacherib received the money and yet sent his army against Jerusalem (II Kings 18:14, 17). **despised**—make slight of as unable to resist him (ch. 10:9; 36:19); easily captures them. **9.** (Ch. 24: 4.) **Lebanon**—personified; the allusion may be to the Assyrian cutting down its choice trees (ch. 14:8; 37:24). **Sharon**—south of Carmel, along the Mediterranean, proverbial for fertility (ch. 35:2). **Bashan**—afterwards called Batanea (ch. 2:13). **fruits**—rather, understand "leaves"; they lie as desolate as in winter. **10.** The sight of His people's misery arouses Jehovah; He has let the enemy go far enough. **I**—emphatic; God Himself will do what man could not. **11. Ye**—the enemy. **conceive chaff** —ch. 26:18; 59:4.) **your breath**—rather, *your own spirit* of anger and ambition [MAURER], (ch. 30:28). **12.** (Ch. 9:19; Amos 2:1.) Perhaps alluding to their being about to be burnt on the funeral pyre (ch. 30: 33). **thorns**—the wicked (II Sam. 23:6, 7). **13. far off**—distant nations. **near**—the Jews and adjoining peoples (ch. 49:1). **14. sinners in Zion**—false professors of religion among the elect people (Matt. 22: 12). **hypocrites**—rather, the profane; the abandoned [HORSLEY]. **who**, etc.—If Jehovah's wrath could thus consume a host in one night, who could abide it, if continued for ever (Mark 9:46-48)? Fire is a common image for the divine judgments (ch. 29:6; 30:30). **among us**—If such awful judgments have fallen on those who knew not the true God, how infinitely worse shall sin fall on *us* who, amid religious privileges and profession, sin against God (Luke 12:47, 48; Jas 4:17)? **15.** In contrast to the trembling "sinners in Zion" (vs. 14), the righteous shall be secure amid all judgments; they are described according to the Old Testament standpoint of righteousness (Ps. 15:2; 24:4). **stoppeth ... ears** **... eyes**—"Rejoiceth not in iniquity" (I Cor. 13:6; contrast ch. 29:20; Ps. 10:3; Rom. 1:32). The senses are avenues for the entrance of sin (Ps. 119: 37). **16. on high**—heights inaccessible to the foe (ch. 26:1). **bread ... waters**—image from the expected siege by Sennacherib; however besieged by trials without, the godly shall have literal and spiritual food, as God sees good for them (ch. 41:17; Ps. 37: 25; 34:10; 132:15). **17. Thine**—the saints'. **king in ... beauty**—not as now, Hezekiah in sackcloth, oppressed by the enemy, but King Messiah (ch. 32: 1) "in His beauty" (Song of Sol. 5:10, 16; Rev. 4:3). **land ... very far off**—rather, the land in its remotest extent (no longer pent up as Hezekiah was with the siege); see *Margin*. For Jerusalem is made the scene of the king's glory (vs. 20, etc.), and it could not be said to be "very far off," unless the far-off land be *heaven*, the Jerusalem above, which is to follow the *earthly* reign of Messiah at literal Jerusalem (ch. 65:17-19; Jer. 3:17; Rev. 21:1, 2, 10). **18. meditate**—on the "terror" caused by the enemy, but now past. **where**, etc.—the language of the Jews exulting over their escape from danger. **scribe**—who enrolled the army [MAURER]; or, who prescribed the tribute to be paid [ROSENMULLER]; or, who kept an account of the spoil. "The principal scribe of the host" (II Kings 25:19; Jer. 52:25). The Assyrian records are free from the exaggerations of Egyptian records. Two scribes are seen in every Assyrian bas-relief, writing down the various objects brought to them, the heads of the slain, prisoners, cattle, sheep, etc. **receiver**—*Margin*, weigher. LAYARD mentions, among the Assyrian inscriptions, "a pair a scales for weighing the spoils." **counted ... towers**—he whose duty it was to reconnoitre and report the strength of the city to be besieged. **19. fierce people**—The Assyrians shall not be allowed to enter Jerusalem (II Kings 19:32). Or, thou shalt not any longer see fierce enemies threatening thee as previously; such as the Assyrians, Romans, and the last Antichristian host that is yet to assail Jerusalem (Deut. 28:49, 50; Jer. 5:15; Zech. 14:2). **stammering**—barbarous; so "deeper," etc., i.e., unintelligible. The Assyrian tongue differed only in dialect from the Hebrew, but in the Assyrian levies were many of non-Semitic race and language, as the Medes, Elamites, etc. (*Note*, ch. 28:11). **20. solem-**

nities—solemn assemblies at the great feasts (*Notes*, ch. 30:29; Ps. 42:4; 48:12). **not ... taken down ... removed**—image from captives "removed" from their land (ch. 36:17). There shall be no more "taking away" to an enemy's land. Or else, from nomads living in shifting tents. The saints, who sojourned once in tabernacles as pilgrims, shall have a "building of God—eternal in the heavens" (II Cor. 5:1; Heb. 11:9, 10; cf. ch. 54:2). **stakes**—driven into the ground; to these the "cords" were fastened. Christ's Church shall never fall (Matt. 16:18). So individual believers (Rev. 3:12). **21. there**—viz., in Jerusalem. **will be ... rivers**—Jehovah will be as a broad river surrounding our city (cf. ch. 19:6; Nah. 3:8), and this, too, a river of such a kind as no ship of war can pass (cf. ch. 26:1). Jerusalem had not the advantage of a river; Jehovah will be as one to it, affording all the advantages, without any of the disadvantages of one. **galley with oars**—war-vessels of a long shape, and propelled by oars; merchant vessels were broader and carried sail. **gallant**— same *Hebrew* word as for "glorious," previously; "mighty" will suit both places; a ship of war is meant. No "mighty vessel" will dare to pass where the "mighty Lord" stands as our defense. **22. Lord**—thrice repeated, as often: the Trinity (Num. 6:24-26). **judge ... lawgiver ... king**—perfect ideal of the theocracy, to be realized under Messiah alone; the judicial, legislative, and administrative functions as king to be exercised by Him in person (ch. 11:4; 32:1; Jas. 4:12). **23. tacklings**—Continuing the allegory in vs. 21, he compares the enemies' host to a war-galley which is deprived of the tacklings or cords by which the mast is sustained and the sail is spread; and which therefore is sure to be wrecked on "the broad river" (vs. 21), and become the prey of Israel. **they**—the tacklings, "hold not firm the base of the mast." **then**—when the Assyrian host shall have been discomfited. Hezekiah had given Sennacherib three hundred talents of silver, and thirty of gold (II Kings 18:14-16), and had stripped the temple of its gold to give it to him; this treasure was probably part of the prey found in the foe's camp. After the invasion, Hezekiah had so much wealth that he made an improper display of it (II Kings 20:13-15); this wealth, probably, was in part got from the Assyrian. **the lame**—Even the most feeble shall spoil the Assyrian camp (cf. ch. 35:6; II Sam. 5:6). **24. sick**—SMITH thinks the allusion is to the beginning of the pestilence by which the Assyrians were destroyed, and which, while sparing the righteous, affected some within the city ("sinners in Zion"); it may have been the sickness that visited Hezekiah (ch. 38). In the Jerusalem to come there shall be no "sickness," because there will be no "iniquity," it being forgiven (Ps. 103:3). The latter clause of the verse contains the cause of the former (Mark 2:5-9).

CHAPTER 34

Vss. 1-17. JUDGMENT ON IDUMEA. Chapters 34 and 35 form one prophecy, the former part of which denounces God's judgment against His people's enemies, of whom Edom is the representative; the second part, of the flourishing state of the Church consequent on those judgments. This forms the termination of the prophecies of the first part of Isaiah (chs. 36-39 being historical) and is a kind of summary of what went before, setting forth the one main truth, *Israel shall be delivered from all its foes, and happier times shall succeed under Messiah.* **1.**

All creation is summoned to hear God's judgments (Ezek. 6:3; Deut. 32:1; Ps. 50:4; Mic. 6:1, 2), for they set forth His glory, which is the end of creation (Rev. 15:3; 4:11). **that come forth of it**—answering to "all that is therein"; or *Hebrew,* "all whatever fills it," *Margin.* **2. utterly destroyed**—rather, doomed them to an utter curse [HORSLEY]. **delivered**—rather, appointed. **3. cast out**—unburied (ch. 14:19). **melted**—washed away as with a descending torrent. **4.** (Ps. 102:26; Joel 2:31; 3:15; Matt. 24:29.) **dissolved**—(II Pet. 3:10-12.) Violent convulsions of nature are in Scripture made the *images* of great changes in the human world (ch. 24: 19-21), and shall *literally* accompany them at the winding up of the present dispensation. **scroll**—Books were in those days sheets of parchment rolled together (Rev. 6:14). **fall down**—The stars shall fall when the heavens in which they are fixed pass away. **fig tree**—(Rev. 6:13). **5. sword**—(Jer. 46:10.) Or else, *knife* for sacrifice for God does not here appear as a warrior about with His sword, but as one about to sacrifice victims doomed to slaughter [VITRINGA], (Ezek. 39:17.) **bathed**—rather "intoxicated," viz., with anger (so Deut. 32:42). "In heaven" implies the place where God's *purpose* of wrath is formed in antithesis to its "coming down" in the next clause. **Idumea**—originally extending from the Dead Sea to the Red Sea; afterwards they obtained possession of the country east of Moab, of which Bozrah was capital. Petra or Selah, called Joktheel (II Kings 14:7), was capital of South Edom (*Note,* ch. 16:1). David subjugated Edom (II Sam. 8:13, 14). Under Jehoram they regained independence (II Chron. 21: 8). Under Amaziah they were again subdued, and Selah taken (II Kings 14:7). When Judah was captive in Babylon, Edom, in every way, insulted over her fallen mistress, killed many of those Jews whom the Chaldeans had left, and hence was held guilty of fratricide by God (Esau, their ancestor, having been brother to Jacob): this was the cause of the denunciations of the prophets against Edom (ch. 63:1, etc.; Jer. 49:7; Ezek. 25:12-14; 35:3-15; Joel 3:19; Amos 1:11, 12; Obadiah 8, 10, 12-18; Mal. 1:3, 4). Nebuchadnezzar humbled Idumea accordingly (Jer. 25: 15-21). **of my curse**—i.e., doomed to it. **to judgment**—i.e., to execute it. **6. filled**—glutted. The image of a sacrifice is continued. **blood . . . fat**—the parts especially devoted to God in a sacrifice (II Sam. 1:22). **famos . . . goats**—*sacrificial* animals: the Idumeans, of all classes, doomed to slaughter, are meant (Zeph. 1:7). **Bozrah**—called *Bostra* by the Romans, etc., assigned in Jeremiah 48:24 to Moab, so that it seems to have been at one time in the dominion of Edom, and at another in that of Moab (ch. 63:1; Jer. 49:13, 20, 22); it was strictly not in Edom, but the capital of Auranitis (the *Houran*). Edom seems to have extended its dominion so as to include it (cf. Lam. 4:21). **7. unicorns**—*Hebrew, reem:* conveying the idea of loftiness, power, and pre-eminence (see *Note,* Job 39:9), in the Bible. At one time the image in the term answers to a reality in nature; at another it symbolizes an abstraction. The rhinoceros was the original type. The Arab *rim* is two-horned: it was the oryx (the *leucoryx,* antelope, bold and pugnacious); but when accident or artifice deprived it of one horn, the notion of the unicorn arose. Here is meant the portion of the Edomites which was strong and warlike. **come down**—rather, "fall down," slain [LOWTH]. **with them**—with the "lambs and goats," the less powerful Edomites (vs. 6). **bullocks . . . bulls**—the young and old Edomites: *all* classes. **dust**—ground. **8. recompenses for the controversy of Zion**—i.e., the

year when God will retaliate on those who have contended with Zion. Her controversy is *His.* Edom had thought to extend its borders by laying hold of its neighbor's lands and has instigated Babylon to cruelty towards fallen Judah (Ps. 137:7; Ezek. 36:5); therefore Edom shall suffer the same herself (Lam. 4:21, 22). The final winding up of the controversy between God and all enemies of Him and His people is also foreshadowed (ch. 61: 2; 63:4; 66:14-16; Mal. 4:1, 3; II Thess. 1:7, 8, 9; Rev. 11:18; 18:20; 19:2). Images from the overthrow of Sodom and Gomorrah (Gen. 19:24-28; so Deut. 29:23; Jer. 49:17, 18). **10. It**—The burning pitch, etc. (vs. 9). **smoke . . . for ever**—(Rev. 14:11; 18:18; 19:3). **generation to generation**—(Mal. 1:4). **none . . . pass through**—Edom's original offense was: they would not let Israel *pass through* their land in peace to Canaan: God "*recompenses*" them in kind, no traveller shall *pass through* Edom. VOLNEY, the infidel, was forced to confirm the truth of this prophecy: "From the reports of the Arabs, southeast of the Dead Sea, *within thee days' journey* are upwards of thirty ruined towns, *absolutely deserted.*" **11. cormorant**—The *Hebrew* is rendered, in Psalm 102:6, "pelican," which is a seafowl, and cannot be meant here: some waterfowl (*katta,* according to BURCKHARDT) that tenants desert places is intended. **bittern**—rather, the hedgehog, or porcupine [GESENIUS] (ch. 14:23). **owl**—from its being enumerated among water birds in Leviticus 11:17; Deuteronomy 14:16. MAURER thinks rather the heron or crane is meant; from a *Hebrew* root, "to blow," as it utters a sound like the blowing of a horn (Rev. 18:2). **confusion**—devastation. **line . . . stones**—metaphor from an architect with line and *plummet-stone* (*Note,* ch. 18:2; 28:17); God will render to it the *exact measure of justice* without mercy (Jas. 2:13; II Kings 21:13; Lam. 2:8; Amos 7:7, 8). **emptiness** —desolation. Edom is now a waste of "stones." **12.** Rather, "As to her nobles, there shall be none there who shall declare a kingdom," i.e., a king [MAURER]; or else, "There shall be no one there whom they shall call to the kingdom" [ROSENMULLER] (ch. 3:6, etc.). Idumea was at first governed by dukes (Gen. 36:15); out of them the king was chosen when the constitution became a monarchy. **13. dragons**—(*Note,* ch. 13:21, 22.) **court for owls** —rather, "a dwelling for ostriches." **14. wild beasts of the desert . . . island**—rather, "wild cats" . . . "jackals" (ch. 13:21). **screech owl**—rather, "the night-specter"; in Jewish superstition a female, elegantly dressed, that carried off children by night. The text does not assert the *existence* of such objects of superstition, but describes the place as one which superstition would people with such beings. **15. great owl**—rather, the arrow-snake, so called from its darting on its prey [GESENIUS]. **lay**—viz., eggs. **gather under her shadow**—rather, "cherishes" her young under, etc. (Jer. 17:11). **16. book of the Lord**—the volume in which the various prophecies and other parts of Scripture began henceforward to be collected together (ch. 30:8; Dan. 9:2). **Seek**— (so ch. 8:16, 20; John 5:39; 7:52). **no one . . . fail**— of these prophecies (Matt. 5:18). **none shall want . . . mate**—image from *pairing* of animals mentioned, vs. 15 ("mate"); no prediction shall want a fulfilment as its companion. Or rather, "none of these wild animals (just spoken of) shall be wanting: none shall be without its mate" to pair and breed with, in desolate Idumea. **my . . . his**—Such changes of person are frequent in *Hebrew* poetry. **them**—the wild beasts. **17. cast . . . lot**—As conquerors apportion lands by lot, so Jehovah has appointed and marked out ("divided") Edom for the wild beasts (Num. 26: 55, 56; Josh. 18:4-6).

CHAPTER 35

Vss. 1-10. CONTINUATION OF THE PROPHECY IN CHAPTER 34. See *introduction* there. **1. solitary place**—lit., "a dry place," without springs of water. A *moral* wilderness is meant. **for them**—viz., on account of the punishment inflicted according to the preceding prophecy on the enemy; probably the blessings set forth in this chapter are included in the causes for joy (ch. 55:12). **rose**—rather, the meadow saffron, an autumnal flower with bulbous roots; so *Syriac* translation. **2. glory of Lebanon** —its ornament, viz., its cedars (ch. 10:34). **excellency of Carmel**—viz., its beauty. **Sharon**—famed for its fertility. **see ... glory of the Lord ... excellency**—(Ch. 40:5, 9.) While the wilderness which had neither "glory" nor "excellency" shall have both "given to it," the Lord shall have all the "glory" and "excellency" ascribed to *Him*, not to the transformed wilderness (Matt. 5:16). **3. Strengthen ... hands .... confirm .... knees**—The Hebrew for "strengthen" refers to the strength residing in the *hand* for grasping and holding a thing manfully; "confirm," to the firmness with which one keeps his ground, so as not to be dislodged by any other [MAURER]. Encourage the Jews, now desponding, by the assurance of the blessings promised. **4. fearful**—*Margin,* "hasty," i.e., with a heart fluttered with agitation. **with**—the *Hebrew* is more forcible than the *English Version:* "God will come, vengeance! even God, a recompense!" The sense is the same. **5, 6.** Language fig., descriptive of the joy felt at the deliverance from Assyria and Babylon; lit., true of the antitypical times of Messiah and His miracles (see *Margin references*). **6. leap**—lit., fulfilled (Acts 3:8; 14:10). **sing**—joyful thanksgiving. **in ... wilderness ... waters**—(ch. 41:18.) **7. parched ground** —rather, "the mirage (*Hebrew, Sharab,* the sun's heat) shall become a (real) lake." The sun's rays refracted on the glowing sands at midday give the appearance of a lake of water and often deceive the thirsty traveller (cf. Jer. 2:13; ch. 41:18). **dragons** —rather jackals. **each**—viz., jackal. **grass**—rather, "*a dwelling or receptacle* (answering to the previous habitation) for reeds." etc. (which only grow where there is water, Job 8:11). Where once there was no water, water shall abound. **8. highway**—such a causeway (*raised way,* from a *Hebrew* root, *to cast up*) as was used for the march of armies; valleys being filled up, hills and other obstructions removed (ch. 62:10; cf. ch. 40:3, 4). **way of holiness**—Hebraism for "the holy way." HORSLEY translates, "the way of the Holy One;" but the words that follow, and vs. 10, show it is the way leading the redeemed back to Jerusalem, both the literal and the heavenly (ch. 52:1; Joel 3:17; Rev. 21:27); still Christ at His coming again shall be the Leader on the way, for which reason it is called, "The way *of the Lord*" (ch. 40:3; Mal. 3:1). **it shall be for those: the wayfaring men**—rather, "He (the Holy One) shall be with them, walking in the way" [HORSLEY]. **though fools**—rather, "And (even) fools," i.e., the simple shall not go astray, viz., because "He shall be with them" (Matt. 11:25; I Cor. 1:26-28). **9. No lion**—such as might be feared on the way through the wilderness which abounded in wild beasts, back to Judea. Every danger shall be warded off the returning people (ch. 11:6-9; Ezek. 34:25; Hos. 2:18). Cf. spiritually, Proverbs 3:17.

10. Language: lit., applying to the return from Babylon; fig. and more fully to the completed redemption of both literal and spiritual Israel. **joy upon ... heads**—(Ps. 126:2.) Joy manifested in their countenances. Some fancy an allusion to the custom of pouring oil "upon the head," or wearing chaplets in times of public festivity (Eccles. 9:8).

CHAPTER 36

Vss. 1-22. SENNACHERIB'S INVASION; RABSHAKEH'S BLASPHEMOUS SOLICITATIONS; HEZEKIAH IS TOLD OF THEM. This and chaps. 37, 38, 39, form the historical appendix closing the first division of Isaiah's prophecies, and were added to make the parts of these referring to Assyria more intelligible. So ch. 52, in Jeremiah; cf. II Kings 25. The section occurs almost word for word in II Kings 18:13, 17-20; II Kings 18:14-16, however, is additional matter. Hezekiah's "writing" also is in Isaiah, not in Kings (ch. 38:9-20). We know from II Chronicles 32:32 that Isaiah wrote the acts of Hezekiah. It is, therefore, probable, that his record here (ch. 36-39) was incorporated into the Book of Kings by its compiler. Sennacherib lived, according to Assyrian inscriptions, more than twenty years after his invasion; but as Isaiah survived Hezekiah (II Chron. 32:32), who lived upwards of fifteen years after the invasion (ch. 38:5), the record of Sennacherib's death (ch. 37:38) is no objection to this section having come from Isaiah; II Chronicles 32 is probably an abstract drawn from Isaiah's account, as the chronicler himself implies (vs. 32). Pul was probably the last of the old dynasty, and Sargon, a powerful satrap, who contrived to possess himself of supreme power and found a new dynasty (see *Note*, ch. 20:1). No attempt was made by Judah to throw off the Assyrian yoke during his vigorous reign. The accession of his son Sennacherib was thought by Hezekiah the opportune time to refuse the long-paid tribute; Egypt and Ethiopia, to secure an ally against Assyria on their Asiatic frontier, promised help; Isaiah, while opposed to submission to Assyria, advised reliance on Jehovah, and not on Egypt, but his advice was disregarded, and so Sennacherib invaded Judea, 712 B.C. He was the builder of the largest of the excavated palaces, that of Koyunjik. HINCKS has deciphered his name in the inscriptions. In the third year of his reign, these state that he overran Syria, took Sidon and other Phœnician cities, and then passed to southwest Palestine, where he defeated the Egyptians and Ethiopians (cf. II Kings 18:21; 19:9). His subsequent retreat, after his host was destroyed by God, is of course suppressed in the inscriptions. But other particulars inscribed agree strikingly with the Bible; the capture of the "defensed cities of Judah," the devastation of the country and deportation of its inhabitants; the increased tribute imposed on Hezekiah—thirty talents of gold—this *exact number being given in both;* the silver is set down in the inscriptions at 800 talents, in the Bible 300; the latter may have been the actual amount carried off, the larger sum may include the silver from the temple doors, pillars, etc. (II Kings 18:16). **1. fourteenth** —the third of Sennacherib's reign. His ultimate object was Egypt, Hezekiah's ally. Hence he, with the great body of his army (II Chron. 32:9), advanced towards the Egyptian frontier, in southwest Palestine, and did not approach Jerusalem. **2. Rabshakeh** —In II Kings 18:17, Tartan and Rabsaris are joined with him. Rabshakeh was probably the chief leader; Rab is a title of authority. "chief—cup-bearer." **Lachish**—a frontier town southwest of Jerusalem, in Judah; represented as a great fortified city in a hilly and fruitful country in the Koyunjik bas-reliefs, now in the British Museum; also, its name is found on a slab over a figure of Sennacherib on his throne. **upper pool**—the side on which the Assyrians would approach Jerusalem coming from the southwest (*Note,* ch. 7:3). **3. Eliakim**—successor to Shebna, who had been "over the household," i.e., chief minister of the king; in ch. 22:15-20, this was foretold. **scribe**—secretary, **recorder**—lit., one who reminds; a remembrancer to keep the king informed on important facts, and to act as historiographer. In II Kings 18:18, the additional fact is given that the Assyrian envoys "called to the king," in consequence of which Eliakim, etc., "came out to them." **4. great king**—the usual title of the Persian and Assyrian kings, as they had many subordinate princes or kings under them over provinces (ch. 10:8). **5. counsel**—Egypt was famed for its wisdom. **6.** It was a similar alliance with So (i.e., Sabacho, or else Sevechus), the Ethiopian king of Egypt, which provoked the Assyrian to invade and destroy Israel, the northern kingdom, under Hoshea. **7.** The Assyrian mistakes Hezekiah's religious reforms whereby he took away the high places (II Kings 18:4) as directed *against Jehovah.* Some of the high places may have been dedicated to Jehovah, but worshipped under the form of an *image* in violation of the second commandment; the "brazen serpent," also (broken in pieces by Hezekiah, and called *Nehushtan,* "a piece of brass," because it was worshipped by Israel) was originally set up by *God's* command. Hence the Assyrian's allegation has a specious color: you cannot look for help from Jehovah, for your king has "taken away His altars." **to Jerusalem**—(Deut. 12:5, 11; John. 4:20.) **8. give pledges**—a taunting challenge. Only give the *guarantee* that you can supply as many as 2000 riders, and I will give thee 2000 horses. But seeing that you have not even this small number (*Note,* ch. 2:7), how can you stand against the hosts of Assyrian cavalry? The Jews tried to supply their weakness in this "arm" from Egypt (ch. 31:1). **9. captain**—a governor under a satrap; even *he* commands more horsemen than this. **10.** A boastful inference from the past successes of Assyria, designed to influence the Jews to surrender; their *own* principles bound them to yield to Jehovah's will. He may have heard from partisans in Judah what Isaiah had foretold (ch. 10:5, 6). **11. Syrian**—rather, *Aramean*: the language spoken north and east of Palestine, and understood by the Assyrians as belonging to the same family of languages as their own: nearly akin to *Hebrew* also, though not intelligible to the multitude (cf. II Kings 5:5-7). *Aram* means a "high land," and includes parts of Assyria as well as Syria. **Jews' language**—The men of Judah since the disruption of Israel, claimed the *Hebrew* as their own peculiarly, as if they were now the only true representatives of the whole Hebrew twelve tribes. **ears of ... people on ... wall**—The interview is within hearing distance of the city. The people crowd on the wall, curious to hear the Assyrian message. The Jewish rulers fear that it will terrify the people and therefore beg Rabshakeh to speak Aramean. **12.** Is it to *thy master* and *thee* that I am sent? Nay, it is to *the men on the wall* (to let them know (so far am I from wishing them *not* to hear, as *you* would wish), that unless they surrender, they shall be reduced to the direst extremities of famine in the siege (II Chron. 32:11, explains the word here), viz., to eat their own excrements: or, connecting,

"that they may eat," etc., with "sit upon the wall"; who, as they hold the wall, are knowingly exposing themselves to the direst extremities [MAURER]. Isaiah, as a faithful historian, records the filthy and blasphemous language of the Assyrians to mark aright the true character of the attack on Jerusalem. **13.** Rabshakeh speaks louder and plainer than ever to the men on the wall. **15.** The foes of God's people cannot succeed against them, unless they can shake their trust in Him (cf. vs. 10). **16. agreement ... by ... present**—rather, "make *peace* with me"; lit., "blessing" so called from the mutual *congratulations* attending the ratification of peace. So CHALDEE. Or else, "*Do homage* to me" [HORSLEY]. **come out**—surrender to me; then you may remain in quiet possession of your lands till my return from Egypt, when I will lead you away to a land fruitful as your own. Rabshakeh tries to soften, in the eyes of the Jews, the well-known Assyrian policy of weakening the vanquished by deporting them to other lands (Gen. 47:21; II Kings 17:6). **19. Hamath ... Arphad**—(*Note,* ch. 10:9.) **Sepharvaim**—lit., "the two scribes"; now Sipphara, on the east of Euphrates, above Babylon. It was a just retribution (Prov. 1:31; Jer. 2:19). Israel worshipped the gods of Sepharvaim, and so colonists of Sepharvaim were planted in the land of Israel (thenceforth called Samaria) by the Assyrian conqueror (II Kings 17:24; cf. Kings 18:34). **Samaria**—Shalmaneser began the siege against Hoshea, because of his conspiring with So of Egypt (II Kings 17:4). Sargon finished it; and, in his palace at Khorsabad, he has mentioned the number of Israelites carried captive—27, 280 [G. V. SMITH]. **20.** (Cf. ch. 10:11; II Chron. 32:19.) Here he contradicts his own assertion (vs. 10), that he had "come up against the land *with the Lord.*" Liars need good memories. He classes Jehovah with the idols of the other lands; nay, thinks Him inferior in proportion as Judah, under His tutelage, was less than the lands under the tutelage of the idols. **21. not a word**—so as not to enter into a war of words with the blasphemer (Exod. 14:14; Jude 9). **22. clothes rent**—in grief and horror at the blasphemy (Matt. 26:65).

CHAPTER 37

Vss. 1-38. CONTINUATION OF THE NARRATIVE IN CHAPTER 36. **1. sackcloth**—(*Note,* ch. 20:2.) **house of the Lord**—the sure resort of God's people in distress (Ps. 73:16, 17; 77:13). **2. unto Isaiah**—implying the importance of the prophet's position at the time; the chief officers of the court are deputed to wait on him (cf. II Kings 22:12-14). **3. rebuke**—i.e., the Lord's rebuke for His people's sins (Ps. 149:7; Hos. 5:9). **blasphemy**—blasphemous railing of Rabshakeh. **the children ...**—a proverbial expression for, We are in the most extreme danger and have no power to avert it (cf. Hos. 13:13). **4. hear**—take cognizance of (II Sam. 16:12). **reprove**—will punish him for the words, etc. (Ps. 50:21). **remnant**—the two tribes of the kingdom of Judah, Israel being already captive. Isaiah is entreated to act as intercessor with God. **6. servants**—lit., "youths," mere lads, implying disparagement, not an embassy of venerable elders. The *Hebrew* is different from that for "servants" in vs. 5. **blasphemed me**—(ch. 36:20.) **7. blast**—rather, "I will put a *spirit* (ch. 28:6; I Kings 22:23) into him," i.e., so influence his judgment that when he hears the report (vs. 9, concerning Tirhakah), he shall return [GESENIUS]; the "report" also of the destruction of his army at Jerusalem, reaching Sennacherib, while he was in the southwest of Palestine on the borders of Egypt, led him to retreat. **by the sword**—(vs. 38.) **8. returned** —to the camp of his master. **Libnah**—meaning *"whiteness,"* the *Blanche-garde* of the Crusaders [STANLEY]. EUSEBIUS and JEROME place it more south, in the district of Eleutheropolis, ten miles northwest of Lachish, which Sennacherib had captured (*Note*, ch. 36:2). Libnah was in Judea and given to the priests (I Chron. 6:54, 57). **9. Tirhakah** —(see *Notes*, ch. 17:12; 18:6). Egypt was in part governed by three successive Ethiopian monarchs, for forty or fifty years: Sabacho, Sevechus, and Tirhakah. Sevechus retired from Lower Egypt owing to the resistance of the priests, whereupon Sethos, a prince-priest, obtained supreme power with Tanis (Zoan in Scripture), or Memphis, as his capital. The Ethiopians retained Upper Egypt under Tirhakah, with Thebes as the capital. Tirhakah's fame as a conqueror rivalled that of Sesostris; he, and one at least of the Pharaohs of Lower Egypt, were Hezekiah's allies against Assyria. The tidings of his approach made Sennacherib the more anxious to get possession of Jerusalem before his arrival. **sent** —II Kings 19:9 more fully expresses Sennacherib's eagerness by adding "again." **10.** He tries to influence *Hezekiah himself,* as Rabshakeh had addressed the people. **God . . . deceive**—(Cf. Num. 23:19). **11. all lands**—(ch. 14:17). He does not dare to enumerate *Egypt* in the list. **12. Gozan**— in Mesopotamia, on the Chabour (II Kings 17:6; 18: 11). Gozan is the name of the *district,* Chabour of the *river.* **Haran**—more to the west. Abraham removed to it from Ur (Gen. 11:31); the *Carræ* of the Romans. **Rezeph**—farther west, in Syria. **Eden** —There is an ancient village, *Adna,* north of Bagdad. Some think Eden to be the name of a *region* (of Mesopotamia or its vicinity) *in* which was Paradise; Paradise was not Eden itself (Gen. 2:8). "A garden in Eden." **Telassar**—now Tel-afer, west of Mosul [LAYARD]. *Tel* means a "hill" in *Arabic* and *Assyrian* names. **13. Hena . . . Ivah**—in Babylonia. From *Ava* colonists had been brought to Samaria (II Kings 17:24). **14. spread**—unrolled the scroll of writing. God *"knows* our necessities before we ask Him," but He delights in our unfolding them to Him with filial confidence (II Chron. 20:3, 11-13). **16. dwellest**—the Shekinah, or fiery symbol of God's presence, *dwelling* in the temple with His people, is from *shachan,* "to dwell" (Exod. 25:22; Ps. 80:1; 99: 1). **cherubim**—derived by transposition from either a *Hebrew* root, *rachab,* to "ride"; or rather, *barach,* to "bless." They were formed out of the same mass of pure gold as the mercy seat itself (Exod. 25:19, *Margin*). The phrase, "dwellest between the cherubim," arose from their position at each end of the mercy seat, while the Shekinah, and the awful name, JEHOVAH, in written letters, were in the intervening space. They are so inseparably associated with the manifestation of God's glory, that whether the Lord is at rest or in motion, they always are mentioned with Him (Num. 7:89; Ps. 18:10). (1) They are first mentioned (Gen. 3:24) "on the edge of" (as "on the east" may be translated) Eden; the *Hebrew* for "placed" is properly to "place in a tabernacle," which implies that this was a local tabernacle in which the symbols of God's presence were manifested suitably to the altered circumstances in which man, after the fall, came before God. It was here that Cain and Abel, and the patriarchs down to the flood, presented their offerings: and it is called "the presence of the Lord" (Gen. 4:16). When those symbols were removed at the close of that early

patriarchal dispensation, small models of them were made for domestic use, called, in *Chaldee,* "seraphim" or "teraphim." (2) The cherubim, in the Mosaic tabernacle and Solomon's temple, were the same in form as those at the outskirts of Eden: compound figures, combining the distinguishing properties of several creatures: the ox, chief among the tame and useful animals; the lion among the wild ones; the eagle among birds; and man, the head of all (the original headship of man over the animal kingdom, about to be restored in Jesus Christ, Ps. 8:4-8, is also implied in this combination). They are, throughout Scripture, represented as distinct from God; they could not be likenesses of Him which He forbade in any shape. (3) They are introduced in the third or gospel dispensation (Rev. 4:6) as *living creatures* (not so well translated "beasts" in English Version), not angels, but beings closely connected with the redeemed Church. So also in Ezekiel 1 and 10. Thus, throughout the three dispensations, they seem to be symbols of those who in every age should officially study and proclaim the manifold wisdom of God. **thou alone**—lit., *"Thou art He who alone* art God of all the kingdoms"; whereas Sennacherib had classed Jehovah with the heathen gods, he asserts the nothingness of the latter and the sole lordship of the former. **17. ear . . . eyes**—singular, plural. When we wish to hear a thing we lend one ear; when we wish to see a thing we open *both* eyes. **18. have laid waste**—conceding the truth of the Assyrian's allegation (ch. 36:18-20), but adding the reason, "For they were no gods." **19. cast . . . gods into . . . fire**—The policy of the Assyrians in order to alienate the conquered peoples from their own countries was, both to deport them elsewhere, and to destroy the tutelary idols of their nation, the strongest tie which bound them to their native land. The Roman policy was just the reverse. **20.** The strongest argument to plead before God in prayer, *the honor of God* (Exod. 32:12-14; Ps. 83:18; Dan. 9:18, 19). **21.** Whereas thou hast prayed to me—i.e., hast not relied on thy own strength but on Me (cf. II Kings 19:20.) "That which thou hast prayed to Me against Sennacherib, I have heard" (Ps. 65:2). **22.** Transition to poetry: in parallelism. **virgin . . . daughter**—honorable terms. "Virgin" implies that the city is, as yet, inviolate. "Daughter" is an abstract collective *feminine* personification of the *population,* the child of the place denoted (*Note,* ch. 23:10; 1-8). *Zion and her inhabitants.* **shaken . . . head**—in scorn (Ps. 22:7; 109:25; Matt. 27:39). With us to shake the head is a sign of denial or displeasure; but gestures have different meanings in different countries (ch. 58:9; Ezek. 25:6; Zeph. 2:15). **23. Whom**—not an idol. **24. said**—virtually. Hast thou within thyself? **height**—imagery from the Assyrian felling of trees in Lebanon (ch. 14:8; 33:9); fig. for, "I have carried my victorious army through the regions most difficult of access, to the most remote lands." **sides** —rather, "recesses" [G. V. SMITH]. **fir trees**—not cypresses, as some translate; pine foliage and cedars are still found on the northwest side of Lebanon [STANLEY]. **height of . . . border**—In II Kings 19:23, "the lodgings of his borders." Perhaps on the ascent to the top there was a place of repose or caravansary, which bounded the usual attempts of persons to ascend [BARNES]. Here, simply, "its extreme height." **forest of . . . Carmel**—rather, "its thickest forest." "Carmel" expresses thick luxuriance (*Note,* ch. 10:18; 29:17). **25. digged, and drunk water**—In II Kings 19:24, it is *"strange* waters." I have marched into foreign lands where I had to dig wells for the supply of my armies; even the natural destitution of water there did not impede my march. **rivers of . . . besieged places**— rather, "the streams (artificial canals from the Nile) of *Egypt*." "With the sole of my foot," expresses that as soon as his vast armies *marched* into a region, the streams were *drunk up* by them; or rather, that the rivers proved no *obstruction* to the onward *march* of his armies. So ch. 19:4-6, referring to *Egypt*, "the river—*brooks of defense*—shall be dried up." HORSLEY translates the *Hebrew* for "besieged places," rocks. **26.** Reply of God to Sennacherib. **long ago**—join, rather, with "I have done it." Thou dost boast that it is all by *thy* counsel and might: but it is *I who, long ago, have ordered* it so (ch. 22: 11); thou wert but the instrument in My hands (ch. 10:5, 15). This was the reason why "the inhabitants were of small power before thee" (vs. 27), viz., that I ordered it so; yet thou art in My hands, and I know thy ways (vs. 28), and I will check thee (vs. 29). Connect also, "*I from ancient times have arranged* ('formed') it." However, *English Version* is supported by ch. 33:13; 45:6, 21; 48:5. **27. Therefore**—not because of thy power, but because I made them unable to withstand thee. **grass**—which easily withers (ch. 40:6; Ps. 37:2). **on . . . housetops**— which having little earth to nourish it fades soonest (Ps. 129:6-8). **corn blasted before it be grown up**— SMITH translates, "The cornfield (frail and tender), before the corn is grown." **28. abode**—rather, "sitting down" (Ps. 139:2). The expressions here describe a man's whole course of life (Deut. 6:7; 28:6; I Kings 3:7; Ps. 121:8). There is also a special reference to Sennacherib's first being *at home*, then *going forth against* Judah and Egypt, and *raging* against Jehovah (vs. 4). **29. tumult**—insolence. **hook in . . . nose**—Like a wild beast led by a ring through the nose, he shall be forced back to his own country (cf. Job 41:1, 2; Ezek. 19:4; 29:4; 38:4). In a bas-relief of Khorsabad, captives are led before the king by a cord attached to a hook, or ring, passing through the under lip or the upper lip, and nose. **30.** Addressed to Hezekiah. **sign**—a token which, when fulfilled, would assure him of the truth of the whole prophecy as to the enemy's overthrow. The two years, in which they were sustained by the spontaneous growth of the earth, were the two in which Judea had been already ravaged by Sennacherib (ch. 32:10). Thus translate: "Ye *did eat* (the first year) such as *groweth* of itself, and in the second year that . . . , but *in this third year* sow ye," etc., for in this year the land shall be delivered from the foe. The fact that Sennacherib moved his camp away *immediately after* shows that the first two years refer to the past, not to the future [ROSENMULLER]. Others, referring the first two years to the future, get over the difficulty of Sennacherib's *speedy* departure, by supposing that year to have been the sabbatical year, and the second year the jubilee; no indication of this appears in the context. **31. remnant**—Judah *remained* after the ten tribes were carried away; also those of Judah who should survive Sennacherib's invasion are meant. **33. with shields** —He did come near it, but was not allowed to conduct a proper siege. **bank**—a mound to defend the assailants in attacking the walls. **34.** (See vss. 29, 37; ch. 29:5-8.) **35. I will defend**—Notwithstanding *Hezekiah's* measures of defense (II Chron. 32:3-5), *Jehovah* was its true defender. **mine own sake** —since Jehovah's name was blasphemed by Sennacherib (vs. 23). **David's sake**—on account of His promise to David (Ps. 132:17, 18), and to Messiah, the heir of David's throne (ch. 9:7; 11:1). **36.** Some

attribute the destruction to the agency of the plague (*Note*, ch. 33:24), which may have caused Hezekiah's sickness, narrated immediately after; but ch. 33: 1, 4, proves that the Jews spoiled the corpses, which they would not have dared to do, had there been on them infection of a plague. The secondary agency seems, from ch. 29:6; 30:30, to have been a storm of hail, thunder, and lightning (cf. Exod. 9:22-25). The simoon belongs rather to Africa and Arabia than Palestine, and ordinarily could not produce such a destructive effect. Some few of the army, as II Chronicles 32:21 seems to imply, survived and accompanied Sennacherib home. HERODOTUS (2. 141) gives an account confirming Scripture in so far as the sudden discomfiture of the Assyrian army is concerned. The Egyptian priests told him that Sennacherib was forced to retreat from Pelusium owing to a multitude of field mice, sent by one of their gods, having gnawed the Assyrians' *bow-strings* and *shield-straps*. Cf. the language (vs. 33), "He shall not shoot an *arrow* there, nor come before it with *shields*," which the Egyptians corrupted into their version of the story. Sennacherib was as the time with a part of his army, not at Jerusalem, but on the Egyptian frontier, southwest of Palestine. The sudden destruction of the host near Jerusalem, a considerable part of his whole army, as well as the advance of the Ethiopian Tirhakah, induced him to retreat, which the Egyptians accounted for in a way honoring to their own gods. The mouse was the Egyptian emblem of destruction. The *Greek* Apollo was called *Sminthian*, from a Cretan word for "a mouse," as a tutelary god of agriculture, he was represented with one foot upon a mouse, since field mice hurt corn. The Assyrian inscriptions, of course, suppress their own defeat, but nowhere boast of having taken Jerusalem; and the only reason to be given for Sennacherib not having, amidst his many subsequent expeditions recorded in the monuments, returned to Judah, is the terrible calamity he had sustained there, which convinced him that Hezekiah was under the divine protection. RAWLINSON says, In Sennacherib's account of his wars with Hezekiah, inscribed with cuneiform characters in the hall of the palace of Koyunjik, built by him (140 feet long by 120 broad), wherein even the Jewish physiognomy of the captives is portrayed, there occurs a remarkable passage; after his mentioning his taking two hundred thousand captive Jews, he adds, "Then I prayed unto God"; the only instance of an inscription wherein the name of GOD occurs without a heathen adjunct. The 46th Psalm probably commemorates Judah's deliverance. It occurred in one "night," according to II Kings 19:35, with which Isaiah's words, "when they arose *early in the morning*," etc., are in undesigned coincidence. **they . . . they**—"the Jews" . . . "the Assyrians." **37. dwelt at Nineveh**—for about twenty years after his disaster, according to the inscriptions. The word, "dwelt," is consistent with any indefinite length of time. "Nineveh," so called from Ninus, i.e., Nimrod, its founder; his name means "exceedingly impious rebel"; he subverted the existing patriarchal order of society, by setting up a system of chieftainship, founded on conquest; the hunting field was his training school for war; he was of the race of Ham, and transgressed the limits marked by God (Gen. 10:8-11, 25), encroaching on Shem's portion; he abandoned Babel for a time, after the miraculous confusion of tongues and went and founded Nineveh; he was, after death, worshipped as Orion, the constellation (*Note*, Job 9:9; 38:31). **38. Nisroch**—*Nisr*, in *Semitic*, means "*eagle*"; the termination *och*, means "great." The eagle-headed human figure in Assyrian sculptures is no doubt Nisroch, the same as Asshur, the chief Assyrian god; the corresponding goddess was Asheera, or Astarte; this means a "grove," or sacred tree, often found as the symbol of the heavenly hosts (*Saba*) in the sculptures, as Asshur the *Eponymus* hero of Assyria (Gen. 10:11) answered to the sun or Baal, Belus, the title of office, "Lord." This explains "image of the grove" (II Kings 21:7). The eagle was worshipped by the ancient Persians and Arabs. **Esar-haddon**—In Ezra 4: 2 he is mentioned as having brought colonists into Samaria. He is also thought to have been the king who carried Manasseh captive to Babylon (II Chron. 33:11). He built the palace on the mound Nebbiyunus, and that called the southwest palace of Nimroud. The latter was destroyed by fire, but his name and wars are recorded on the great bulls taken from the building. He obtained his building materials from the northwest palaces of the ancient dynasty, ending in Pul.

CHAPTER 38

Vss. 1-22. Hezekiah's Sickness; Perhaps Connected with the Plague or Blast Whereby the Assyrian Army Had Been Destroyed. **1. Set . . . house in order**—Make arrangement as to the succession to the throne; for he had then no son; and as to thy other concerns. **thou shalt die**—speaking according to the ordinary course of the disease. His being spared fifteen years was not a change in God's mind, but an illustration of God's dealings being unchangeably regulated by the state of man in relation to Him. **2.** The couches in the East run along the walls of houses. He turned away from the spectators to hide his emotion and collect his thoughts for prayer. **3.** He mentions his past religious consistency, not as a boast or a ground for justification; but according to the Old Testament dispensation, wherein temporal rewards (as long life, etc., Exod. 20:12) followed legal obedience, he makes his religious conduct a plea for asking the prolongation of his life. **walked**—Life is a journey; the pious "walk with God" (Gen. 5:24; I Kings 9:4). **perfect**—sincere; not absolutely perfect, but *aiming* towards it (Matt. 5:45); single-minded in walking as in the presence of God (Gen. 17:1). The *letter* of the Old Testament legal righteousness was, however, a standard very much below the *spirit* of the law as unfolded by Christ (Matt. 5:20-48; II Cor. 3:6, 14, 17.) **wept sore**—Josephus says, the reason why he wept so sorely was that being childless, he was leaving the *kingdom* without a successor. How often our wishes, when gratified, prove curses! Hezekiah lived to have a son; that son was the idolater Manasseh, the chief cause of God's wrath against Judah, and of the overthrow of the kingdom (II Kings 23: 26, 27). **4.** In II Kings 20:4, the quickness of God's answer to the prayer is marked, "afore Isaiah had gone out into the middle court, the word of the Lord came to him"; i.e., before he had left Hezekiah, or at least when he had just left him, and Hezekiah was in the act of praying after having heard God's message by Isaiah (cf. ch. 65:24; Ps. 32:5; Dan. 9: 21). **5. God of David thy father**—God remembers the covenant with the father to the children (Exod. 20:5; Ps. 89:28, 29). **tears**—(Ps. 56:8). **days . . . years**—Man's *years*, however many, are but as so many *days* (Gen. 5:27). **6.** In II Kings 20:8, after this verse comes the statement which is put at the end, in order not to interrupt God's message (vss. 21,

22) by Isaiah (vss. 5-8). **will deliver**—The city was *already* delivered, but here assurance is given, that Hezekiah shall have *no more* to fear from the Assyrians. **7. sign**—a token that God would fulfil His promise that Hezekiah should "go up into the house of the Lord *the third day*" (II Kings 20:5, 8); the words in italics are not in Isaiah. **8. bring again**—cause to return (Josh. 10:12-14). In II Kings 20:9, 11, the choice is stated to have been given to Hezekiah, whether the shadow should go forward, or go back, ten degrees. Hezekiah replied, "It is a light thing (a less decisive miracle) for the shadow to go down (its usual direction) ten degrees: nay, but let it return backward ten degrees"; so Isaiah cried to Jehovah that it should be so, and it was so (cf. Josh. 10:12, 14). **sundial of Ahaz**—Herodotus (2.109) states that the sundial and the division of the day into twelve hours, were invented by the Babylonians; from them Ahaz borrowed the invention. He was one, from his connection with Tiglath-pileser, likely to have done so (II Kings 16:7, 10). "Shadow of the degrees" means the shadow made on the degrees. Josephus thinks these degrees were *steps ascending* to the palace of Ahaz; the time of day was indicated by the number of steps reached by the shadow. But probably a sundial, strictly so called, is meant; it was of such a size, and so placed, that Hezekiah, when convalescent, could witness the miracle from his chamber. Cf. vss. 21, 22 with II Kings 20:9, where translate, shall *this* shadow go forward, etc.; the dial was no doubt *in sight,* probably "in the middle court" (II Kings 20:4), the point where Isaiah turned back to announce God's gracious answers to Hezekiah. Hence this particular sign was given. The retrogression of the shadow may have been effected by refraction; a cloud denser than the air interposing between the gnomon and dial would cause the phenomenon, which does not take from the miracle, for God gave him the choice whether the shadow should go forward or back, and regulated the time and place. Bosanquet makes the 14th year of Hezekiah to be 689 b.c., the known year of a solar eclipse, to which he ascribes the recession of the shadow. At all events, there is no need for supposing any revolution of the relative positions of the sun and earth, but merely an effect produced on the shadow (II Kings 20:9-11); that effect was only *local,* and designed for the satisfaction of Hezekiah, for the Babylonian astronomers and king "sent to inquire of the wonder that was done *in the land*" (II Chron. 32:31), implying that it had not extended to their country. No mention of any instrument for marking time occurs before this dial of Ahaz, 700 b.c. The first mention of the "hour" is made by Daniel at Babylon (Dan. 3:6). **9-20.** The prayer and thanksgiving song of Hezekiah is only given here, not in the parallel passages of II Kings and II Chron.; vs. 9 is the heading or inscription. **10. cutting off**—Rosenmuller translates, "the meridian"; when the sun stands in the zenith: so "the perfect day" (Prov. 4:18). Rather, "in the *tranquility* of my days," i.e., that period of life when I might now look forward to a tranquil reign [Maurer]. The *Hebrew* is so translated (ch. 62:6, 7). **go to**—rather, "go *into*," as in ch. 46:2 [Maurer]. **residue of my years**—those which I had calculated on. God sends sickness to teach man not to calculate on the morrow, but to live more wholly to God, as if each day were the last. **11. Lord . . . Lord**—The repetition, as in vs. 19, expresses the excited feeling of the king's mind. **See the Lord** [Jehovah]—fig. for "to enjoy His good gifts." So, in a similar connection (Ps. 27:13). "I had fainted, unless I had

believed *to see the goodness of the Lord* in the land of the living"; (Ps. 34:12), "What man is he that desireth life that he may *see good?*" **world**—rather, translate: "among the inhabitants of the land of *stillness,*" i.e., Hades [MAURER], in parallel antithesis to "the land of the living" in the first clause. The *Hebrew* comes from a root, to "rest" or "cease" (Job 14:6). **12. age**—rather, as the parallel "shepherd's tent" requires *habitation,* so the *Arabic* [GESENIUS]. **departed**—is broken up, or shifted, as a tent to a different locality. The same image occurs (II Cor. 5:1; II Pet. 1:12, 13). He plainly expects to exist, and not *cease* to be in another state; as the shepherd still lives, after he has struck his tent and removed elsewhere. **I have cut off**—He attributes to *himself* that which is *God's* will with respect to him; because he *declares* that will. So Jeremiah is said to "root out" kingdoms, because he *declares* God's purpose of doing so (Jer. 1:10). The weaver cuts off his web from the loom when completed. Job 7:6 has a like image. The Greeks represented the Fates as spinning and cutting off the threads of each man's life. **he**—God. **with pining sickness**—rather, "from the thrum," or thread, which tied the loom to the weaver's beam. **from day . . . to night**—i.e., in the space of a single day between morning and night (Job 4:20). **13. I reckoned . . . that**—rather, *I composed* (my mind, during the night, expecting relief in the "morning," so Job 7:4): *for (that* is not, as in the *English Version,* to be supplied) as a lion He *was breaking* all my bones [VITRINGA] (Job 10:16; Lam. 3:10, 11). The *Hebrew,* in Psalm 131: 2, is rendered, "I quieted." Or else, "I made myself like a lion (viz., in roaring, through pain), He was so breaking my bones!" Poets often compare great groaning to a lion's roaring, so, next verse, he compares his groans to the sounds of other animals (Ps. 22:1) [MAURER]. **14.** Rather, "Like a swallow, or a crane" (from a root; "to disturb the water," a bird frequenting the water) [MAURER], (Jer. 8:7). **chatter**—twitter: broken sounds expressive of pain. **dove**—called by the Arabs the daughter of mourning, from its plaintive note (ch. 59:11). **looking upward**—to God for relief. **undertake for**—lit., "be surety for" me; assure me that I shall be restored (Ps. 119: 122). **15-20.** The second part of the song passes from prayer to thanksgiving at the prayer being heard. **What shall I say**—the language of one at a loss for words to express his sense of the unexpected deliverance. **both spoken . . . and . . . done it**—(Num. 23:19). Both promised and performed (I Thess. 5:24; Heb. 10:23). **himself**—No one else could have done it (Ps. 98:1). **go softly . . . in the bitterness**—rather, "*on account of* the bitterness"; I will behave myself humbly in remembrance of my past sorrow and sickness from which I have been delivered by God's mercy (see I Kings 21:27, 29). In Psalm 42:2, the same *Hebrew* verb expresses the slow and solemn gait of one going up to the house of God; it is found nowhere else, hence ROSENMULLER explains it, "I will reverently attend the sacred festivals in the temple"; but this ellipsis would be harsh; rather metaphorically the word is transferred to a *calm, solemn,* and *submissive* walk of life. **16. by these**—viz., *by God's benefits,* which are implied in the context (vs. 15, "He hath Himself done it" "unto me"). *All* "men live by these" benefits (Ps. 104:27-30), "and in all these is the life of my spirit," i.e., I also live by them (Deut. 8:3). **and** (wilt) **make me to live**—The *Hebrew is imperative,* "make me to live." In this view he adds a *prayer* to the confident hope founded on his comparative convalescence, which he expressed, "Thou *wilt* recover me" [MAU-

RER]. **17. for peace**—instead of the prosperity which I had previously. **great bitterness**—lit., "bitterness to me, bitterness"; expressing intense emotion. **in love**—lit., "attachment," such as *joins* one to another tenderly; "Thou hast been lovingly attached to me from the pit"; pregnant phrase for, Thy love has gone down to the pit, and drawn me out from it. The "pit" is here simply *death,* in Hezekiah's sense; realized in its fulness only in reference to the *soul's* redemption from hell by Jesus Christ (ch. 61:1), who went down to the pit for that purpose Himself (Ps. 88:4-6; Zech. 9:11, 12; Heb. 13:20). "Sin" and sickness are connected (Ps. 103:3; cf. ch. 53:4, with Matt. 8:17; 9:5, 6), especially under the Old Testament dispensation of temporal sanctions; but even now, sickness, though not invariably arising from sin *in individuals,* is connected with it in the general moral view. **cast . . . behind back**—consigned my sins to oblivion. The same phrase occurs (I Kings 14:9; Neh. 9:26; Ps. 50:17). Contrast Psalm 90:8, "Thou hast set our iniquities *before* thee, our secret sins *in the light of thy countenance.*" **18. death**—i.e., the dead; Hades and its inhabitants (Job 28:22; see *Note,* vs. 11), Plainly Hezekiah believed in a world of disembodied spirits; his language does not imply what skepticism has drawn from it, but simply that he regarded the disembodied state as one incapable of declaring the praises of God *before men,* for it is, *as regards this world,* an unseen land of stillness; "the living" alone can praise God *on earth,* in reference to which only he is speaking; ch. 57:1, 2 shows that at this time the true view of the blessedness of the righteous dead was held, though not with the full clearness of the Gospel, which "has brought life and immortality to light" (II Tim. 1:10). **hope for thy truth**—(Ps. 104:27). Their probation is at an end. They can no longer exercise faith and hope in regard to Thy faithfulness to Thy promises, which are limited to the present state. For "hope" ceases (even in the case of the godly) when sight begins (Rom. 8:24, 25); the ungodly have "no hope" (I Thess. 4:13). Hope in God's truth is one of the grounds of praise to God (Ps. 71:14; 119:49). Others translate, "cannot celebrate.". **19. living . . . living**—emphatic repetition, as in vss. 11, 17; his heart is so full of the main object of his prayer that, for want of adequate words, he repeats the same word. **father to the children**—one generation of the *living* to another. He probably, also, hints at his own desire to live until he should have a child, the successor to his throne, to whom he might make known and so perpetuate the memory of God's truth. **truth**—*faithfulness* to His promises; especially in Hezekiah's case, His promise of hearing prayer. **20. was ready**—not in the *Hebrew;* "Jehovah was for my salvation," i.e., saved me (cf. ch. 12:2). **we—I** and my people. **in the house of the Lord**—This song was designed, as many of the other Psalms, as a *form* to be used in public worship at stated times, perhaps on every anniversary of his recovery; hence "all the days of *our* life." **lump of figs**—a round cake of figs pressed into a mass (I Sam. 25:18). God works by means; the meanest of which He can make effectual. **boil**—inflamed ulcer, produced by the plague. **22. house of the Lord**—Hence he makes the praises to be sung there prominent in his song (vs. 20; Ps. 116:12-14, 17-19).

CHAPTER 39

Vss. 1-8. HEZEKIAH'S ERROR IN THE DISPLAY OF HIS RICHES TO THE BABYLONIAN AMBASSADOR. **1.**

Merodach-baladan—For 150 years before the overthrow of Nineveh by Cyaxares the Mede, a succession of rulers, mostly viceroys of Assyria, ruled Babylon, from the time of Nabonassar, 747 B.C. That date is called "the Era of Nabonassar." Pul or Phallukha was then expelled, and a new dynasty set up at Nineveh, under Tiglath-pileser. Semiramis, Pul's wife, then retired to Babylon, with Nabonassar, her son, whose advent to the throne of Babylon, after the overthrow of the old line at Nineveh, marked a new era. Sometimes the viceroys of Babylon made themselves, for a time, independent of Assyria; thus Merodach-baladan at this time did so, encouraged by the Assyrian disaster in the Jewish campaign. He had done so before, and was defeated in the first year of Sennacherib's reign, as is recorded in cuneiform characters in that monarch's palace of Koyunjik. Nabopolassar was the first who established, *permanently,* his independence; his son, Nebuchadnezzar, raised Babylon to the position which Nineveh once occupied; but from the want of stone near the Lower Euphrates, the buildings of Babylon, formed of sun-dried brick, have not stood the wear of ages as Nineveh has. **Merodach**—an idol, the same as the god of war and planet Mars (Jer. 50:2). Often kings took their names from their gods, as if peculiarly under their tutelage. So Belshazzar from Bel. **Baladan**—means "Bel is his lord." The chronicle of Eusebius contains a fragment of Berosus, stating that Acises, an Assyrian viceroy, usurped the supreme command at Babylon. Merodach- (or Berodach) baladan murdered him and succeeded to the throne. Sennacherib conquered Merodach-baladan and left Esar-haddon, his son, as governor of Babylon. Merodach-baladan would naturally court the alliance of Hezekiah, who, like himself, had thrown off the yoke of the Assyrian king, and who would be equally glad of the Babylonian alliance against Assyria; hence arose the excessive attention which he paid to the usurper. **sick**—An additional reason is given (II Chron. 32:31). "The princes of Babylon sent to inquire of the wonder that was done in the land"; viz., the recession of the shadow on Ahaz' sundial; to the Chaldean astronomers, such a fact would be especially interesting, the dial having been invented at Babylon. **2. glad**—It was not the mere act, but the spirit of it, which provoked God (II Chron. 32:25), "Hezekiah rendered not again according to the benefit done unto him, for *his heart was lifted up*"; also cf. vs. 31. God "tries" His people at different times by different ways, bringing out "all that is in their heart," to show them its varied corruptions. Cf. David in a similar case (I Chron. 21:1-8). **precious things**—rather, "the house of his (aromatic) spices"; from a *Hebrew* root, to "break to pieces," as is done to aromatics. **silver ... gold**—partly obtained from the Assyrian camp (ch. 33:4); partly from presents (II Chron. 32:23, 27-29). **precious ointment**—used for anointing kings and priests. **armour**—or else vessels in general; the parallel passage (II Chron. 32:27), "treasuries ... *for shields*," favors *English Version.* His arsenal. **3. What ... whence**—implying that any proposition coming from the idolatrous enemies of God, with whom Israel was forbidden to form alliance, should have been received with anything but *gladness.* Reliance on Babylon, rather than on God, was a similar sin to the previous reliance on Egypt (chs. 30 and 31). **far country**—implying that he had done nothing more than was proper in showing attention to strangers "from a far country. **4. All**—a frank confession of his

whole fault; the king submits his conduct to the scrutiny of a subject, because that subject was accredited by God. Contrast Asa (II Chron. 16:7-10). **5. Lord of hosts**—who has all thy goods at His disposal. **6. days come**—120 years afterwards. This is the first intimation that the Jews would be carried to *Babylon*—the first designation of their *place* of punishment. The general prophecy of Moses (Lev. 26:33; Deut. 28:64); the more particular one of Ahijah in Jeroboam's time (I Kings 14:15), "beyond the river"; and of Amos 5:27, "captivity beyond Damascus"; are now concentrated in this specific one as to "Babylon" (Mic. 4:10). It was an exact retribution in kind, that as Babylon had been the instrument of Hezekiah and Judah's sin, so also it should be the instrument of their punishment. **7. sons ... from thee**—The sons which Hezekiah (as Josephus tells us) wished to have (*Note,* ch. 28:3, on "wept sore") will be among the foremost in suffering. **eunuchs**—fulfilled (Dan. 1:2, 3, 7). **8. peace ... in my days**—The punishment was not, as in David's case (II Sam. 24:13-15), sent in his time. True repentance acquiesces in all God's ways and finds cause of thanksgiving in any mitigation.

CHAPTER 40

Vss. 1-31. SECOND PART OF THE PROPHECIES OF ISAIAH. The former were local and temporary in their reference. These belong to the distant future, and are world-wide in their interest; the deliverance from Babylon under Cyrus, which he here foretells by prophetic suggestion, carries him on to the greater deliverance under Messiah, the Saviour of Jews and Gentiles in the present eclectic Church, and the restorer of Israel and Head of the world-wide kingdom, literal and spiritual, ultimately. As Assyria was the hostile world power in the former part, which refers to Isaiah's own time, so Babylon is so in the latter part, which refers to a period long subsequent. The connecting link, however, is furnished (ch. 39:6) at the close of the former part. The latter part was written in the old age of Isaiah, as appears from the greater mellowness of style and tone which pervades it; it is less fiery and more tender and gentle than the former part. **1. Comfort ye**—twice repeated to give double assurance. Having announced the coming captivity of the Jews in Babylon. God now desires His servants, the prophets (ch. 52:7), to comfort them. The scene is laid in Babylon; the time, near the close of the captivity; the ground of comfort is the speedy ending of the captivity, the Lord Himself being their leader. **my people ... your God**—correlatives (Jer. 31:33; Hos. 1:9, 10). It is God's covenant relation with His people, and His "word" of promise (vs. 8) to their forefathers, which is the ground of His interposition in their behalf, after having for a time chastised them (ch. 54:8). **2. comfortably**—lit., "to the heart"; not merely to the intellect. **Jerusalem**—though then in ruins, regarded by God as about to be rebuilt; her *people* are chiefly meant, but the *city* is personified. **cry**—publicly and emphatically as a herald cries aloud (vs. 3). **warfare**—the *appointed time* of her misery (Job 7:1, *Margin:* 14:14; Dan. 10: 1). The ulterior and Messianic reference probably is *the definite time* when the legal economy of burdensome rites is at an end (Gal. 4:3, 4). **pardoned**—The *Hebrew* expresses that her iniquity is so *expiated* that God now *delights* in restoring her.

double for all her sins—This can only, in a very restricted sense, hold good of Judah's restoration after the first captivity. For how can it be said her "warfare was accomplished," when as yet the galling yoke of Antiochus and also of Rome was before them? The "double for her sins" must refer to the twofold captivity, the Assyrian and the Roman; at the coming close of this latter dispersion, and then only, can her "iniquity" be said to be "pardoned," or *fully* expiated [HOUBIGANT]. It does not mean double as much as she *deserved,* but *ample* punishment in her twofold captivity. Messiah is the antitypical Israel (cf. Matt. 2:15, with Hos. 11:1). He indeed has "received" of sufferings *amply* more than enough to expiate "for our sins" (Rom. 5:15, 17). Otherwise (cry unto her) "that she *shall* receive (*blessings*) of the Lord's hand double to the *punishment of all her sins*" (so "sin" is used, Zech. 14:19, *Margin*) [LOWTH]. *English Version* is simpler. **3. crieth in the wilderness**—So the LXX and Matt. 3:3 connect the words. The *Hebrew* accents, however, connect them thus: "In the wilderness prepare ye," etc., and the parallelism also requires this, "Prepare ye *in the wilderness,*" answering to "make straight *in the desert.*" Matthew was entitled, as under inspiration, to vary the connection, so as to bring out another sense, included in the Holy Spirit's intention; in Matthew 3:1, "John the Baptist, *preaching in the wilderness,*" answers thus to "The voice of one *crying in the wilderness.*" MAURER takes the participle as put for the finite verb (so in vs. 6), "A voice *crieth.*" The clause, "in the wilderness," alludes to Israel's passage through it from Egypt to Canaan (Ps. 68:7), Jehovah being their leader; so it shall be at the coming restoration of Israel, of which the restoration from Babylon was but a type (not the full realization; for their way from it was *not* through the "wilderness"). Where John preached (viz., in the wilderness; the type of this earth, a moral wilderness), *there* were the hearers who are ordered to prepare the way of the Lord, and *there* was to be the coming of the Lord [BENGEL]. John, though he was immediately followed by the suffering Messiah, is rather the herald of the coming *reigning* Messiah, as Malachi 4:5, 6 ("before *the great* and *dreadful day of the Lord*"), proves. Matthew 17:11 (cf. Acts 3:21) implies that John is not exclusively meant; and that though in one sense Elias has come, in another he is *yet to come.* John was the figurative Elias, coming "in the *spirit and power* of Elias" (Luke 1:17); John 1:21, where John the Baptist denies that he was the *actual* Elias, accords with this view. Malachi 4:5, 6 cannot have received its exhaustive fulfilment in John; the Jews always understood it of the literal Elijah. As there is another consummating advent of Messiah Himself, so perhaps there is to be of his forerunner Elias, who also was present at the transfiguration. **the Lord**—*Hebrew, Jehovah;* as this is applied to Jesus, He must be Jehovah (Matt. 3:3). **4.** Eastern monarchs send heralds before them in a journey to clear away obstacles, make causeways over valleys, and level hills. So John's duty was to bring back the people to obedience to the law and to remove all self-confidence, pride in national privileges, hypocrisy, and irreligion, so that they should be ready for His coming (Mal. 4:6; Luke 1:17). **crooked**—declivities. **5. see it**—The LXX for "it," has "the salvation of God." So Luke 3:6 (cf. Luke 2:30, i.e., Messiah); but the Evangelist probably took these words from ch. 52:10. **for**—rather, "All flesh shall see *that* the mouth of Jehovah hath spoken it" [BENGEL]. **6. The voice**—the same divine herald as

in vs. 3. **he**—one of those ministers or prophets (*Note,* vs. 1) whose duty it was, by direction of "the voice," to "comfort the Lord's afflicted people with the promises of brighter days." **All flesh is grass**—The connection is, "All *human* things, however goodly, are transitory: *God's* promises alone are steadfast" (vs. 8, 15, 17, 23, 24); this contrast was already suggested in vs. 5, "*All flesh . . . the mouth of the Lord.*" I Peter 1:24, 25 applies this passage distinctly to the gospel word of Messiah (cf. John 12:24; Jas. 1:10). **7. spirit of the Lord**—rather, "wind of Jehovah" (Ps. 103:16). The withering east wind of those countries sent by Jehovah (Jonah 4:8). **the people**—rather, this people [LOWTH], which may refer to the Babylonians [ROSENMULLER]; but better, *mankind in general,* as in ch. 42:5, so vs. 6, "*all* flesh"; *this whole race,* i.e., man. **9.** Rather, "Oh, thou that bringest good things *to Zion*; thou that bringest good tidings *to Jerusalem.*" "Thou" is thus the collective personification of the *messengers* who announce God's gracious purpose to Zion (*Note,* vs. 1); ch. 52:7 confirms this [VULGATE and GESENIUS]. If *English Version* be retained, the sense will be the glad message was first to be proclaimed to Jerusalem, and then from it as the center to all "Judea, Samaria, and the uttermost parts of the earth" (Luke 24:47, 49; Acts 1:8) [VITRINGA and HENGSTENBERG]. **mountain**—It was customary for those who were about to promulgate any great thing, to ascend a hill from which they could be seen and heard by all (Judg. 9:7; Matt. 5:1). **be not afraid**—to announce to the exiles that their coming return home is attended with danger in the midst of the Babylonians. The gospel minister must "open his mouth *boldly*" (Prov. 29:25; Eph. 6:19). **Behold**—especially at His second coming (Zech. 12:10; 14:5). **10. with strong hand**—rather, as a strong one [MAURER]. Or, against the strong one, viz., Satan (Matt. 12:29; Rev. 20:2, 3, 10) [VITRINGA]. **arm**—power (Ps. 89:13; 98:1). **for him**—i.e., He needs not to seek help for Himself from any external source, but by His own inherent power He gains rule for Himself (so vs. 14). **work**—rather, recompense which He gives for work (ch. 62:11; Rev. 22:12). **11. feed**—including all a shepherd's care—"tend" (Ezek. 34:23; Ps. 23:1; Heb. 13:20; I Pet. 2:25). **carry**—applicable to *Messiah's restoration of Israel,* as sheep scattered in all lands, and unable to move of themselves *to their own land* (Ps. 80:1; Jer. 23:3). As Israel was "carried from the womb" (i.e., in its earliest days) (ch. 63:9, 11, 12; Ps. 77:20), so it shall be in "old age" (its latter days) (ch. 46:3, 4). **gently lead**—as a thoughtful shepherd does the ewes "giving suck" (Margin) (Gen. 33:13, 14). **12.** Lest the Jews should suppose that He who was just before described as a "shepherd" is a mere man, He is now described as GOD. **Who**—Who else but GOD could do so? Therefore, though the redemption and restoration of His people, foretold here, was a work beyond man's power, they should not doubt its fulfilment since all things are possible to Him who can accurately *regulate the proportion of the waters* as if He had measured them with His hand (cf. vs. 15). But MAURER translates: "Who can measure . . ." i.e., How immeasurable are the works of God? The former is a better explanation (Job 28:25; Prov: 30: 4). **span**—the space from the end of the thumb to the end of the middle finger extended; God measures the vast heavens as one would measure a small object with his span. **dust of the earth**—All the *earth* is to Him but as a few grains of *dust contained in a small measure* (lit., the *third* part of a larger measure). **hills in a balance**—adjusted in their right proportions and places, as exactly as if He had *weighed* them out. **13.** Quoted in Romans 11: 34; I Corinthians 2:16. The *Hebrew* here for "directed" is the same as in vs. 12 for "meted out"; thus the sense is, "Jehovah measures out heaven with His span"; but who can measure Him? i.e., Who can *search out* His Spirit (*mind*) wherewith He searches out and accurately adjusts all things? MAURER rightly takes the *Hebrew* in the same sense as in vs. 12 (so Prov. 16:2; 21:2), "weigh," "ponder." "Direct," as in *English Version*, answers, however, better to "taught" in the parallel clause. **14. path of jugdment**—His wisdom, whereby He so beautifully adjusts the places and proportions of all created things. **15.** of—rather (hanging) *from* a bucket [MAURER]. **he taketh up ...as a very little thing**—rather, "are as a mere grain of dust which is taken up," viz., by the wind; lit., "one taketh up," impersonally (Exod. 16:14) [MAURER]. **isles**—rather, *lands* in general, answering to "the nations" in the parallel clause; perhaps *lands*, like Mesopotamia, enclosed by rivers [JEROME] (so ch. 42:15). However, *English Version*, "isles" answers well to "mountains" (vs. 12), both alike being lifted up by the power of God; in fact, "isles" are mountains upheaved from the bed of the sea by volcanic agency; only that he seems here to have passed from unintelligent creatures (vs. 12) to intelligent, as *nations* and *lands*, i.e., their inhabitants. **16.** All Lebanon's forest would not supply fuel enough to burn sacrifices worthy of the glory of God (ch. 66:1; I Kings 8:27; Ps. 50:8-13). **beasts** —which abounded in Lebanon. **17.** (Ps. 62:9; Dan. 4:35). **less than nothing**—MAURER translates, as in ch. 41:24, "of nothing" (*partitively*; or expressive of the *nature* of a thing), a mere nothing. **vanity**— emptiness. **18.** Which of the heathen idols, then, is to be compared to this Almighty God? This passage, if not written (as BARNES thinks) so late as the idolatrous times of Manasseh, has at least a prospective warning reference to them and subsequent reigns; the result of the chastisement of Jewish idolatry in the Babylonish captivity was that thenceforth after the restoration the Jews never fell into it. Perhaps these prophecies here may have tended to that result (see II Kings 23:26, 27). **19. graven**— rather, *an image* in general; for it is incongruous to say "melteth" (i.e., casts out of metal) a *graven* image (i.e., one of carved wood); so Jeremiah 10:14, "molten image." **spreadeth it over**—(*Note*, ch. 30: 22). **chains**—an ornament lavishly worn by rich Orientals (ch. 3:18, 19), and so transferred to their idols. Egyptian relics show that idols were suspended in houses by chains. **20. impoverished**—lit., "sunk" in circumstances. **no oblation**—*he* who cannot afford to overlay his idol with gold and silver (vs. 19). **tree ... not rot**—the cedar, cypress, oak, or ash (ch. 44:14). **graven**—of wood; not a *molten* one of metal. **not be moved**—that shall be durable. **21. ye**—who worship idols. The question emphatically implies, they *had* known. **from the beginning** —(Ch. 41:4, 26; 48:16.) God is the beginning (Rev. 1:8). The tradition handed down *from the very first*, of the creation of all things by God at the beginning, ought to convince you of His omnipotence and of the folly of idolatry. **22. It is he**—rather, connected with last verse, Have ye not known?— have ye not understood *Him* that sitteth ...? (vs. 26) [MAURER]. **circle**—applicable to the globular form of the earth, above which, and the vault of sky around it, He sits. For "upon" translate "above." **as grasshoppers**—or locusts in His sight (Num. 13: 33), as He looks down from on high (Ps. 33:13, 14;

113:4-6). **curtain**—referring to the awning which the Orientals draw over the open court in the center of their houses as a shelter in rain or hot weather. **23.** (Ps. 107:4; Dan. 2:21.) **judges**—i.e., rulers; for these exercised judicial authority (Ps. 2:10). The *Hebrew, shophtee*, answers to the Carthaginian chief magistrates, *suffetes*. **24. they**—the "princes and judges" (vs. 23) who oppose God's purposes and God's people. Often compared to tall trees (Ps. 37:35; Dan. 4:10). **not ... sown**—the seed, i.e., *race* shall become extinct (Nah. 1:14). **stock**—not even shall any shoots spring up from the stump when the tree has been cut down: no descendants whatever (Job 14:7; *Note*, ch. 11:1). **and ... also**—so LXX. But MAURER translates, "They *are* hardly (lit., not yet, as in II Kings 20:4) planted [etc.] *when* He (God) blows upon them." **blow**—The image is from the hot east wind (simoon) that "withers" vegetation. **whirlwind ... stubble**—(Ps. 83:13), refers to the rotatory action of the whirlwind on the stubble. **25.** (Cf. vs. 18.) **26. bringeth out ... host**—image from a general reviewing his army: He is Lord of Sabaoth, the heavenly hosts (Job 38:32). **calleth ... by names**—numerous as the stars are. God knows each in all its distinguishing *characteristics* —a sense which "name" often bears in Scripture; so in Genesis 2:19, 20, Adam, as *God's vicegerent*, called the beasts *by name* i.e., characterized them by their several *qualities*, which, indeed, He has imparted. **by the greatness ... faileth**—rather, "by reason of abundance of (their inner essential) force *and firmness of strength*, not one of them *is driven astray*"; referring to the sufficiency of the physical forces with which He has endowed the heavenly bodies, to prevent all disorder in their motions [HORSLEY]. In *English Version* the sense is, "He has endowed them with their peculiar *attributes* ('names') by the greatness of His might," *and the power of His strength* (the better rendering, instead of, "for that He is strong"). **27.** Since these things are so, thou hast no reason to think that thine interest ("way," i.e., condition, Ps. 37:5; Jer. 12:1) is disregarded by God. **judgment is passed over from** —rather, My cause is neglected by my God; He *passes by my case* in my bondage and distress without noticing it. **my God**—who especially might be expected to care for me. **28. known**—by thine own observation and reading of Scripture. **heard**—from tradition of the fathers. **everlasting ...**—These attributes of Jehovah ought to inspire His afflicted people with confidence. **no searching of his understanding**—therefore thy cause cannot, as thou sayest, escape His notice; though much in His ways is *unsearchable*, He cannot err (Job 11:7-9). He is never "faint" or "weary" with having the countless wants of His people ever before Him to attend to. **29.** Not only does He "not faint" (vs. 28) but He gives power to them who *do faint*. **no might ... increaseth strength**—a seeming paradox. They "have no might" *in themselves;* but *in Him* they have strength, and He "*increases*" that strength (II Cor. 12:9). **30. young men**—lit., "those selected"; men picked out on account of their youthful vigor for an enterprise. **31. mount up**—(II Sam. 1:23). Rather, "They shall put forth fresh feathers as eagles" are said to renovate themselves; the parallel clause, "renew their strength," confirms this. The eagle was thought to moult and renew his feathers, and with them his strength, in old age (so LXX, *Vulgate*, Ps. 103:5). However, *English Version* is favored by the descending climax, *mount up—run—walk;* in every attitude the praying, waiting child of God is "strong in the Lord" (Ps. 84:7; Mic. 4:5; Heb. 12:1).

CHAPTER 41

Vss. 1-29. ADDITIONAL REASONS WHY THE JEWS SHOULD PLACE CONFIDENCE IN GOD'S PROMISES OF DELIVERING THEM; HE WILL RAISE UP A PRINCE AS THEIR DELIVERER, WHEREAS THE IDOLS COULD NOT DELIVER THE HEATHEN NATIONS FROM THAT PRINCE. **1.** (Zech. 2:13.) God is about to argue the case; therefore let the nations listen in reverential silence. Cf. Genesis 28:16, 17, as to the spirit in which we ought to behave before God. **before me**—rather (turning), "towards me" [MAURER]. **islands**—including *all regions beyond sea* (Jer. 25:22), maritime regions, not merely isles in the strict sense. **renew ... strength**—Let them gather their strength for the argument; let them *adduce their strongest arguments* (cf. ch. 1:18; Job 9:32). "Judgment" means here, to decide the point at issue between us. **2. Who**—else but God? The fact that God "raiseth up" Cyrus and qualifies him for becoming the conqueror of the nations and deliverer of God's people, is a strong argument why they should trust in Him. The future is here prophetically represented as present or past. **the righteous man**—Cyrus; as ch. 44:28; 45:1-4, 13; 46:11, "from the *East*," prove. Called "righteous," not so much on account of his own equity (HERODOTUS, 3.89), as because he fulfilled *God's* righteous will in restoring the Jews from their unjust captivity. *Raised him up in righteousness.* The LXX takes the *Hebrew* as a noun "righteousness." MAURER translates, "Who raised up him whom salvation (national and temporal, the gift of God's 'righteousness') to the good, ch. 32:17; cf. ch. 45:8; 51:5) meets at his foot" (i.e., wherever he goes). Cyrus is said to come *from the East,* because Persia is east of Babylon; but in vs. 25, *from the north,* in reference to Media. At the same time the full sense of *righteousness,* or *righteous,* and of the whole passage, is realized only in Messiah, Cyrus' antitype (Cyrus *knew not* God, ch. 45:4). He goes forth as the Universal Conqueror of the "nations," in right-eousness making war (Ps. 2:8, 9; Rev. 19:11-15; 6:2; 2:26, 27). "The idols He shall utterly abol-ish" (cf. vs. 7:23, with ch. 2:18). Righteousness was always raised up from the East. Paradise was east of Eden. The cherubim were at the east of the garden. Abraham was called from the East. Ju-dea, the birthplace of Messiah, was in the East. **called ... to ... foot**—called him to attend His (God's) steps, i.e., follow His guidance. In Ezra 1:2, Cyrus acknowledges Jehovah as the Giver of his victories. He subdued the nations from the Euxine to the Red Sea, and even Egypt (says XENO-PHON). **dust**—(Ch. 17:13; 29:5; Ps. 18:42). Persia, Cyrus' country, was famed for the use of the "bow" (ch. 22:6). "Before him" means "gave them *into his power*" (Josh. 10:12). MAURER translates, "Gave his (the enemy's) sword to be dust, and his (the enemy's) bow to be as stubble" (Job 41:26, 29). **3.** Cyrus had not visited the regions of the Euphrates and westward until he visited them for conquest. So the gospel conquests penetrated regions where the name of God was unknown before. **4. Who**—else but God? **calling ... generations from ... begin-ning**—The origin and position of all nations are from God (Deut. 32:8; Acts 17:26); what is true of Cyrus and his conquests is true of all the movements of history *from the first;* all are from God. **with the last**—i.e., the last (ch. 44:6; 48:12). **5. feared**—that they would be subdued. **drew near, and came**—to-gether, for mutual defense. **6. Be of good courage** —Be not alarmed because of Cyrus, but make new

images to secure the favor of the gods against him. **7.** One workman encourages the other to be quick in finishing the idol, so as to avert the impending dan-ger. **nails**—to keep it steady in its place. Wisdom 13:15, 16, gives a similar picture of the folly of idolatry. **8.** Contrast between the idolatrous nations whom God will destroy by Cyrus, and Israel whom God will deliver by the same man for their fore-fathers' sake. **servant**—so termed as being chosen by God to worship Him themselves, and to lead other peoples to do the same (ch. 45:4). **Jacob ....** **chosen**—(Ps. 135:4.) **my friend**—lit., "loving me." **9.** Abraham, the father of the Jews, taken from the remote Ur of the Chaldees. Others take it of Israel, called out of Egypt (Deut. 4:37; Hos. 11:1). **from the chief men**—lit., "the elbows"; so *the joints;* hence *the root* which joins the tree to the earth; fig., those of ancient and *noble* stock. But the parallel clause "ends of the earth" favors GESENIUS, who trans-lates, "the *extremities* of the earth"; so JEROME. **10. be not dismayed**—lit., anxiously *to look at one anoth-er* in dismay. **right hand of my righteousness**—i.e., My right hand prepared in accordance with My righteousness (faithfulness to My promises) to up-hold thee. **11. ashamed**—put to the shame of de-feat (cf. ch. 54:17; Rom. 9:33). **12. seek ... and ... not find**—said of one so utterly put out of the way that not a trace of him can be found (Ps. 37:36). **thing of naught**—shall utterly perish. **13.** (Deut. 33: 26, 29.) **14. worm**—in a state of contempt and af-fliction, whom all loathe and tread on, the very ex-pression which Messiah, on the cross, applies to *Himself* (Ps. 22:6), so completely are the Lord and His people identified and assimilated. "God's people are as 'worms' in humble thoughts of them-selves, and in their enemies' haughty thoughts of them; worms, but not vipers, or of the serpent's seed" [HENRY] **men**—The parallelism requires the word "men" here to have associated with it the idea of *fewness* or *feebleness.* LOWTH translates, "Ye *mortals* of Israel." The LXX, "altogether dimin-utive." MAURER supports *English Version,* which the *Hebrew* text best accord with. **the Lord**—in general. **and thy redeemer**—in particular; a still stronger reason why He should "help" them. **15.** God will make Israel to destroy their enemies as the Eastern corn-drag (ch. 28:27, 28) bruises out the grain with its teeth, and gives the chaff to the winds to scatter. **teeth**—serrated, so as to cut up the straw for fodder and separate the grain from the chaff. **mountains ... hills**—kingdoms more or less power-ful that were hostile to Israel (ch. 2:14). **16. fan**—winnowed (cf. Matt. 3:12). **whirlwind ... scatter them**—(Job 27:21; 30:22). **17. poor and needy**—primarily, the exiles in Babylon. **water**—fig., re-freshment, prosperity after their affliction. The lan-guage is so constructed as only very partially to apply to the local and temporary event of the resto-ration from Babylon; but fully to be realized in the waters of life and of the Spirit, under the Gospel (ch. 30:25; 44:3; John 7:37-39; 4:14). God wrought no miracles that we read of, in any wilderness, during the return from Babylon. **faileth**—rather, *"is rigid"* or parched [HORSLEY]. **18.** Alluding to the waters with which Israel was miraculously sup-plied in the desert after having come out of Egypt. **high places**—bare of trees, barren, and unwatered (Jer. 4:11; 14:6). "High places ... valleys" spirit-ually express that in *all* circumstances, whether *ele-vated* or *depressed,* God's people will have refresh-ment for their souls, however little to be expected it might seem. **19.** (Ch. 32:15; 55:13). **shittah**—rather, the acacia, or Egyptian thorn, from which the gum Arabic is obtained [LOWTH]. **oil tree**—the olive. **fir tree**—rather, the cypress: grateful by its shade. **pine**—GESENIUS translates, "the holm.' **box tree**—not the shrub used for bordering flower-beds, but [GESENIUS] a kind of cedar, remarkable for the smallness of its cones, and the upward direction of its branches. **20. consider**—lit., "lay it (to heart)"; turn (their attention) to it. "They" refers to *all lands* (vs. 1; Ps. 64:9; 40:3). The effect on the Gentiles of God's open interposition hereafter in behalf of Israel shall be, they shall seek Israel's God (ch. 2:3; Zech. 8:21-23). **21.** A new challenge to the idolaters (see vss. 1, 7) to say, can their idols *predict future events* as Jehovah can (vss. 22-25, etc.)? **your strong reasons**—the reasons for idol-worship which you think especially strong. **22. what shall happen**—"Let them *bring near and declare future contingencies*" [HORSLEY]. **former things . . . the latter end of them**—show what former predictions the idols have given, that we may compare the event ("latter end") with them; or give new prophecies ("declare things to come") (ch. 42:9), [MAURER]. BARNES explains it more recondítely, "Let them foretell the *entire series* of events, showing, in their *order*, the things which shall *first* occur, as well as those which shall *finally* happen"; the false prophets tried to predict isolated events, having no mutual dependency; not a long *series* of events mutually and orderly connected, and stretching far into futurity. They did not even *try* to do this. None but God can do it (ch. 46:10; 44:7, 8). "Or . . . things to come" will, in this view, mean, Let them, if they cannot predict the *series*, even predict plainly *any detached* events. **23. do good . . . evil**—give any proof at all of your power, either to reward your friends or punish your enemies (Ps. 115:2-8). **that we may be dismayed, and behold it together**—MAU-RER translates, "That we (Jehovah and the idols) may look one another in the face (i.e., encounter one another, II Kings 14:8, 11), and see" our respective powers by a trial. HORSLEY translates, "Then the moment we behold, we shall be dismayed." "We" thus, and in *English Version*, refers to Jehovah and His worshippers. **24. of nothing**—(*Note*, ch. 40:17.) The *Hebrew* text is here corrupt; and *English Version* treats it. **abomination**—abstract for concrete: not merely *abominable*, but the *essence* of whatever is so (Deut. 18:12). **chooseth you**—as an object of worship. **25. raised up**—in purpose: not fulfilled till 150 years afterwards. **north**—In vs. 2, "from the East"; both are true: see the note there. **call . . . my name**—acknowledge Me as God, and attribute his success to Me; this he did in the proclamation (Ezra 1:2). This does not necessarily imply that Cyrus renounced idolatry, but hearing of Isaiah's prophecy given 150 years before, so fully realized in his own acts, he recognized God as the true God, but retained his idol (so Naaman, II Kings 5; cf. II Kings 17:33, 41; Dan. 3:28; 4:1-3, 34-37). **princes**—the Babylonian satraps or governors of provinces. **mortar**—"mire"; He shall tread them under foot as dirt (ch. 10:6). **26. Who**—of the idolatrous soothsayers? When this prophecy shall be fulfilled, all shall see that God foretold as to Cyrus, which none of the soothsayers have. **beforetime**—before the event occurred. **He is righteous**—rather, It is true; it was a true prophecy, as the event shows. "He is righteous," in *English Version*, must be interpreted, The fulfilment of the idol's words proves that *he is faithful*. **showeth . . .**—rather, "there was none (of the soothsayers) that showed . . . declared —no one has heard your words" foretelling the event. **27.** Rather, "I first will give to Zion and to Jeru-

salem the messenger of good tidings, Behold, behold them!" The clause, "Behold . . . them" (*the wished-for event is now present*) is inserted in the middle of the sentence as a detached exclamation, by an elegant transposition, the language being framed abruptly, as one would speak in putting vividly as it were, before the eyes of others, some joyous event which he had just learned [LUDOVICUS DE DIEU] (cf. ch. 40:9). None of the idols had foretold these events. Jehovah was the "first" to do so (see vs. 4). **28. no counsellor**—no one of the idolatrous soothsayers who could *inform* (Num. 24:14) *those who consulted* them what would take place. Cf. "*counsel* of His messenger" (ch. 44:26). **when I asked**—i.e., challenged them, in this chapter. **29. confusion**—"emptiness" [BARNES].

CHAPTER 42

Vss. 1-25. MESSIAH THE ANTITYPE OF CYRUS.— God's description of His character (vss. 1-4). God addresses Him directly (vss. 5-7). Address to the people to attend to the subject (vss. 8, 9). Call to all, and especially the exile Jews to rejoice in the coming deliverance (vss. 10-25). **1. my servant**— The law of prophetic suggestion leads Isaiah from Cyrus to the far greater Deliverer, behind whom the former is lost sight of. The express quotation in Matthew 12:18-20, and the description can apply to *Messiah* alone (Ps. 40:6; with which cf. Exod. 21:6; John 6:38; Phil. 2:7). Israel, also, in its highest ideal, is called the "servant" of God (ch. 49:3). But this ideal is realized only in the antitypical Israel, its representative-man and Head, Messiah (cf. Matt. 2:15, with Hos. 11:1). "Servant" was the position assumed by the Son of God throughout His humiliation. **elect**—chosen by God before the foundation of the world for an atonement (I Pet. 1:20; Rev. 13: 8). Redemption was no afterthought to remedy an unforeseen evil (Rom. 16:25, 26; Eph. 3:9, 11; II Tim. 1:9, 10; Titus 1:2, 3). In Matthew 12:18 it is rendered "My beloved"; *the only beloved Son*, beloved in a sense distinct from all others. *Election* and the *love* of God are inseparably joined. **my soul**—a human phrase applied to God, because of the intended union of humanity with the Divinity: "I Myself." **delighteth**—is well pleased with, and accepts, *as a propitiation*. God could have "delighted" in no created being *as a mediator* (cf. vs. 21; ch. 63:5; Matt. 3:17). **spirit upon him**—(Ch. 11:2; 61:1; Luke 4:18; John 3:34.) **judgment**—the gospel dispensation, founded on *justice*, the canon of the divine rule and principle of judgment called "the law" (ch. 2:3; cf. vs. 4; 51:4; 49:6). The Gospel has a discriminating *judicial* effect: *saving* to penitents: *condemnatory* to Satan, the enemy (John 12:31; 16: 11), and the wilfully impenitent (John 9:39). Matthew 12:18 has, "He shall *show*," for "He shall bring forth," or "*cause to go forth*." Christ both *produced* and *announced* His "judgment." The *Hebrew* dwells most on His *producing* it; Matthew on His *announcement* of it: the two are joined in Him. **2.** Matthew marks the kind of "cry" as that of *altercation* by quoting it, "He shall not *strive*" (ch. 53:7). **street**—LXX translates "outside." An image from an altercation in a house, loud enough to be heard *in the street* outside: appropriate of Him who "withdrew Himself" from the public fame created by His miracles to privacy (Matt. 12:15; vs. 34, there, shows another and sterner aspect of His character, which is also implied in the term "judgment"). **3. bruised**— "It pleased the Lord to *bruise* Him" (ch. 53:5, 10:

Gen. 3:15); so He can feel for *the bruised*. As vs. 2 described His unturbulent spirit towards His violent enemies (Matt. 12:14-16), and His utter freedom from love of notoriety, so vs. 3, His tenderness in cherishing the first spark of grace in the penitent (ch. 40:11). **reed**—fragile: easily "shaken with the wind" (Matt. 11:7). Those who are at best feeble, and who besides are oppressed by calamity or by the sense of sin. **break**—entirely crush or condemn. Cf. "bind up the broken-hearted" (ch. 50:4; 61:1; Matt. 11:28). **flax**—put for the lamp-*wick*, formed of flax. The believer is the *lamp* (so the *Greek*, Matt. 5:15; John 5:35): his conscience enlightened by the Holy Ghost is the *wick*. "Smoking" means dimly burning, smouldering, the flame not quite extinct. This expresses the positive side of the penitent's religion; as "bruised reed," the negative. Broken-hearted in himself, but not without some spark of flame: lit., from above. Christ will supply such a one with grace as with oil. Also, the light of nature smouldering in the Gentiles amidst the hurtful fumes of error. He not only did not quench, but cleared away the mists and superadded the light of revelation. See JEROME, ad Alg. Qu. 2. **truth** —Matthew 12:20 quotes it, "send forth judgment unto *victory*." Matthew, under the Spirit, gives the virtual sense, but varies the word, in order to bring out a fresh aspect of the same thing. Truth has in itself the elements of victory over all opposing forces. *Truth* is the *victory* of Him who is "the truth" (John 14:6). The *gospel judicial sifting* ("judgment") of believers and unbelievers, begun already in part (John 3:18, 19; 9:39), will be *consummated victoriously in truth* only at His second coming; vss. 13, 14, here, and Matthew 12:32, 36, 41, 42, show that there is reference to the *judicial* aspect of the Gospel, especially finally: besides the mild triumph of Jesus coming in mercy to the penitent *now* (vs. 2), there shall be *finally* the judgment on His enemies, when the "truth" shall be perfectly developed. Cf. ch. 61:1-3, where the two comings are similarly joined (Ps. 2:4-6, 8; Rev. 15:2, 4; 19:11-16). On "judgment," see *Note*, vs. 1. **4. fail**— faint; *man* in religion may become as the almost expiring flax-wick (vs. 3), but not so He in His purposes of grace. **discouraged**—lit., "broken," i.e., checked in zeal by discouragements (cf. ch. 49:4, 5). ROSENMULLER not so well translates, "He shall not be too slow on the one hand, nor *run too hastily* on the other." **judgment**—His true religion, the canon of His judgments and righteous reign. **isles . . . wait . . .**—The distant lands beyond sea shall put their *trust* in His gospel way of salvation. Matthew 12: 21 virtually gives the sense, with the inspired addition of another aspect of the same thing, "In his *name* shall the Gentiles *trust*" (as "wait for" here means, ch. 30:18). "His law" is not something distinct from Himself, but is indeed *Himself*, the manifestation of God's character ("name") in Christ, who is the *embodiment of the law* (ch. 42:21; Jer. 23:6; Rom. 10:4). "Isles" here, and in vs. 12, may refer to the fact that the populations of which the Church was primarily formed were Gentiles of the countries bordering on the Mediterranean. **5.** Previously God had spoken *of* Messiah; now (vss. 5-7) He speaks *to* Him. To show to all that He is able to sustain the Messiah in His appointed work, and that all might accept Messiah as commissioned by such a mighty God, He commences by announcing Himself as the Almighty Creator and Preserver of all things. **spread . . . earth**—(Ps. 136:6). **6. in righteousness**—rather, "for a righteous purpose" [LOWTH]. (See vs. 21). God "set forth" His Son

"to be a propitiation (so as) to declare His (God's) *righteousness*, that God might be just, and (yet) the justifier of him which believeth in Jesus" (Rom. 3: 25, 26; cf. *Note*, ch. 41:2; 45:13; 50:8, 9). **hold . . . hand**—cf. as to Israel, the type of Messiah, Hosea 11:3. **covenant**—the medium of the covenant, originally made between God and Abraham (ch. 49:8). "The mediator of a better covenant" (Heb. 8:6) than the law (see ch. 49:8; Jer. 31:33; 50:5). So the abstract "peace," for *peace-maker* (Mic. 5:5; Eph. 2:14). **the people**—Israel; as ch. 49:8, compared with vs. 6, proves (Luke 2:32). **7. blind**— spiritually (vss. 16, 18, 19; ch. 35:5; John 9:39). **prison**—(ch. 61:1, 2.) **darkness**—opposed to "light" (vs. 6; Eph. 5:8; I Pet. 2:9). **8.** God turns from addressing Messiah to the people. **Lord**—JEHOVAH: God's distinguishing and incommunicable name, indicating essential *being* and immutable faithfulness (cf. Exod. 6:3; Ps. 83:18; 96:5; Hos. 12:5). **my**— that is due to Me, and to Me alone. **9. former things** —Former predictions of God, which were now fulfilled, are here adduced as proof that they ought to trust in Him alone as God; viz., the predictions as to Israel's restoration from Babylon. **new**—viz., predictions as to Messiah, who is to bring all nations to the worship of Jehovah (vss. 1, 4, 6). **spring forth** —The same image from plants *just beginning to germinate* occurs in ch. 43:19; 58:8. Before there is *the slightest indication* to enable a sagacious observer to infer the coming event, God *foretells* it. **10. new song**—such as has never before been sung, called for by a new manifestation of God's grace, to express which no hymn for former mercies would be appropriate. The new song shall be sung when the Lord shall reign in Jerusalem, and all "nations shall flow unto it" (ch. 2:2; 26:1; Rev. 5:9; 14:3). **ye that go down to the sea**—whose conversion will be the means of diffusing the Gospel to distant lands. **all . . . therein**—all the living creatures *that fill* the sea (Ps. 96:11) [MAURER]. Or, *all sailors and voyagers* [GENESIUS]. But these were already mentioned in the previous clause: there he called on all who go *upon* the sea; in this clause all animals *in* the sea; so in vs. 11, he calls on the inanimate wilderness to lift up its voice. External nature shall be so renovated as to be in unison with the moral renovation. **11. cities**—in a region not wholly waste, but mainly so, with an oasis here and there. **Kedar**—in Arabia Deserta (ch. 21:16; Gen. 25:13). The Kedarenians led a nomadic, wandering life. So Kedar is here put in general for that class of men. **rock**—*Sela*, i.e. Petra, the metropolis of Idumea and the Nabathœan Ishmaelites. Or it may refer in general to those in Arabia Petræa, who had their dwellings cut out of the rock. **the mountains**—viz., of Paran, south of Sinai, in Arabic Petræa [VITRINGA]. **12. glory . . . islands**—(ch. 24:15). **13-16.** Jehovah will no longer restrain His wrath: He will go forth as a mighty warrior (Exod. 15:3) to destroy His people's and His enemies, and to deliver Israel (cf. Ps. 45:3). **stir up jealousy**—rouse His indignation. **roar**—image from the battle cry of a warrior. **14. long time**— viz., during the desolation of Israel (ch. 32:14). **holden my peace**—(Cf. Ps. 50:21; Hab. 1:2.) **cry like a travailing woman . . .**—Like a woman in parturition, who, after having restrained her breathing for a time, at last, overcome with labor-pain, lets out her voice with a panting sigh; so Jehovah will give full vent to His long pent-up wrath. Translate, instead of "destroy . . . devour"; *I will at once breathe hard and pant*, viz., giving loose to My wrath. **15.** I will destroy all My foes. **mountains**—in Palestine usually planted with vines and olives in terraces, up to their tops. **islands**—rather, "dry lands." God will destroy His foes, the heathen, and their idols, and *"dry up"* the fountains of their oracles, their doctrines and institutions, the symbol of which is *water,* and their schools which promoted idolatry [VITRINGA]. **16. blind**—God's people, Israel, in captivity, needing a guide. In the ulterior sense the New Testament Church, which was about to be led and enlightened by the Son of God as its leader and shepherd in the wilderness of the Roman empire, until it should reach a city of habitation. "A way ... they knew not," refers to the various means employed by Providence for the establishment of the Church in the world, such as would never have occurred to the mind of mere man. "Blind," they are called, as not having heretofore seen God's ways in ordering His Church. **make darkness light ...**—implies that the glorious issue would only be known by the event itself [VITRINGA]. The same holds good of the *individual* believer (ch. 30:21; Ps. 107:7; cf. Hos. 2:6, 14; Eph. 5:8; Heb. 13:5). **17. turned back ... ashamed**—disappointed in their trust; the same phrase occurs in Psalm 35:4. **18. deaf**—viz., to the voice of God. **blind**—to your duty and interest; wilfully so (vs. 20). In this they differ from "the blind" (vs. 16). The Jews are referred to. He had said, God would destroy the heathen idolatry; here he remembers that even Israel, His "servant" (vs. 19), from whom better things might have been expected, is tainted with this sin. **19. my servant**—viz., Israel. Who of the heathen is so blind? Considering Israel's high privileges, the heathen's blindness was as nothing compared with that of Israelite idolaters. **my messenger ... sent**—Israel was designed by God to be the herald of His truth to other nations. **perfect**—furnished with institutions, civil and religious, suited to their *perfect* well-being. Cf. the title, "Jeshurun," the *perfect* one, applied to Israel (cf. ch. 44:2), as the type of Messiah [VITRINGA]. Or translate, the *friend* of God, which Israel was by virtue of descent from Abraham, who was so called (ch. 41:8), [GESENIUS]. The language, "my servant" (cf. vs. 1), "messenger" (Mal. 3:1), "perfect" (Rom. 10:4; Heb. 2:10; I Peter 2:22), can, in the full antitypical sense, only apply to Christ. So vs. 21 plainly refers to Him. "Blind" and "deaf" in His case refer to His endurance of suffering and reproach, as though He neither saw nor heard (Ps. 38:13, 14). Thus there is a transition by contrast from the moral *blindness* of Israel (vs. 18) to the patient blindness and deafness of Messiah [HORSLEY]. **20. observest**—Thou dost not *keep* them. The "many things" are the many proofs which all along from the first God had given Israel of His goodness and His power (Deut. 4:32-38; 29:2-4; Psalms 78; 105). **he**—transition from the second to the third person. "Opening ... ears," i.e., though he (Israel) hath his ears open (*Note,* ch. 6:10). This language, too (*Note,* vs. 19), applies to Messiah as Jehovah's *servant* (ch. 50: 5; Ps. 40:6). **21. his righteousness**—not His people's, but His own; vs. 24 shows that they had no righteousness (ch. 45:24; 59:16). God is *well pleased* with His Son ("in whom My soul *delighteth,"* vs. 1), "who fulfils all *righteousness"* (Matt. 3:15) for them, and with them for His sake (cf. vs. 6; Ps. 71:16, 19; Matt. 5:17; Rom. 10:3; Phil. 3:9). Perhaps in God's "righteousness" here is included His *faithfulness to His promises* given to Israel's forefathers [ROSENMULLER]; because of this He is well pleased with Israel, even though displeased with their sin, which He here reproves; but that promise could only be based on the *righteousness of Messiah,* the promised seed, which is *God's* righteousness. **22. holes**

—caught by their foes in the *caverns* where they had sought refuge [BARNES]. Or bound in subterranean dungeons [MAURER]. **prison houses**—either literal prisons, or their own houses, whence they dare not go forth for fear of the enemy. The connection is: Notwithstanding God's favor to His people for His righteousness' sake (vs. 21), they have fallen into misery (the Babylonish and Romish captivities and their present dispersion), owing to their disregard of the divine law: spiritual imprisonment is included (vs. 7). **none saith, Restore**—There is no deliverer (ch. 63:5). **23.** A call that they should be warned by the past judgments of God to obey Him for the time to come. **24. Who**—Their calamity was not the work of chance, but *God's* immediate act for their sins. **Jacob ... Israel ... we**—change from the third to the first person; Isaiah first speaking to them as a prophet, distinct from them; then identifying himself with them, and acknowledging His share in the nation's sins (cf. Josh. 5:1). **25. him**—Israel (vs. 24). **strength of battle**—violence of war. **it**—the *battle* or war (cf. ch. 10:16). **knew not**—knew not the lesson of repentance which the judgment was intended to teach (ch. 5:13; 9:13; Jer. 5:3).

CHAPTER 43

Vss. 1-28. A Succession of Arguments Wherein Israel May Be Assured that, notwithstanding Their Perversity towards God (ch. 42:25), He Will Deliver. and Restore Them. **1. But now**—notwithstanding God's past just judgments for Israel's sins. **created**—not only in the general sense, but specially *created* as a peculiar people unto Himself (vss. 7, 15, 21; ch. 44:2, 21, 24). So believers, "created in Christ Jesus" (Eph. 2:10), "a peculiar people" (I Pet. 2:9). **redeemed**—a second argument why they should trust Him besides *creation.* The *Hebrew* means *to ransom by a price paid in lieu of the captives* (cf. vs. 3). Babylon was to be the ransom in this case, i.e., was to be destroyed, in order that they might be delivered; so Christ became a curse, doomed to death, that we might be redeemed. **called ... by ... name**—not merely "called" in general, as in ch. 42:6; 48:12; 51:2, but *designated as His own* peculiar people (cf. ch. 45:3, 4; Exod. 32:1; 33:12; John 10:3). **2. rivers ... not overflow thee** —so in passing Jordan, though at its *"overflow,"* when its "swellings" were especially dangerous (Josh. 3:15; Jer. 12:5). **waters ... fire**—a proverbial phrase for the extremest perils (Ps. 66:12; also Ps. 138:7). Literally fulfilled at the Red Sea (Exod. 14), and in the case of the three youths cast into the fiery furnace for conscience' sake (Dan. 3:25, 27). **3. Egypt for thy ransom**—Either Egypt or Israel must perish; God chose that Egypt, though so much more mighty, should be destroyed, in order that His people might be delivered; thus Egypt stood, *instead* of Israel, as a kind of "ransom." The *Hebrew, kopher,* means properly "that with which anything is overlaid," as the pitch with which the ark was overlaid; hence that which *covers over* sins, an atonement. Nebuchadnezzar had subdued Egypt, Ethiopia (*Hebrew, Cush*), and Saba (descended from Cush, Genesis 10:7, probably Meroe of Ethiopia, a great island formed by the Astaboras and the Nile, conquered by Cambyses, successor of Cyrus). Cyrus received these from God with the rest of the Babylonian dominions, in consideration of his being about to deliver Israel. However, the reference may be to the three years' war in which Sargon overcame these countries, and so had his attention diverted from Israel (see *Notes,* ch. 20) [VITRINGA]. But the reference is probably more general, viz., to *all* the instances in which Jehovah sacrificed mighty heathen nations, when the safety of Israel required it. **4. Since**—All along from the beginning; for there was never a time when Israel was not Jehovah's people. The apodosis should be at, "I will give." "Since ever thou wast precious in My sight, honorable, and that I loved thee, I will give," etc. [MAURER]. GESENIUS, as *English Version,* takes "Since" to mean, "Inasmuch as." If the apodosis be as in *English Version,* "Since thou wast precious" will refer to the time when God called His people out of Egypt, manifesting then first the love which He had from everlasting towards them (Jer. 31:3; Hos. 11:1); "honorable" and "loved," refer to *outward* marks of honor and love from God. **men ... people**—*other* nations for thee (so. vs. 3). **thy life**—thy person. **5.** (Deut. 30:3). **seed**—descendants scattered in all lands. VITRINGA understands it of the *spiritual* "seed" of the Church produced by mystical regeneration: for the expression is, "bring," not "bring back." This sense is perhaps included, but not to the exclusion of the literal Israel's restoration (Jer. 30:10, 11; Amos 9:9; Zech. 2:6-13). **6. Give up**—viz., My people. **sons ... daughters**—The feminine joined to the masculine expresses the complete *totality* of anything (Zech. 9:17). **7. called by my name**—belong to Israel, whose people, as sons of God, bear the name of their Father (ch. 44:5; 48:1). **for my glory**—(vs. 21; ch. 29:23). **8.** Solemn challenge given by God to the nations to argue with Him the question of His superiority to their idols, and His power to deliver Israel (ch. 41:1). **blind people**—the Gentiles, who also, like Israel (ch. 42:19), are blind (spiritually), though having eyes; i.e., natural faculties, whereby they might know God (Rom. 1:20, 21) [LOWTH]. Or else, the Jews [VITRINGA]. **9. who ... can declare this**—who among the idolatrous soothsayers hath predicted *this;* i.e., as to Cyrus being the deliverer of Israel? **former** —predictions, as in ch. 42:9 [MAURER]. Or, things that shall first come to pass (*Note,* ch 41:21, 22) [BARNES]. **let them bring forth their witnesses**—as I do mine (vs. 10). **justified**—declared veracious in their pretended prophecies. **or**—rather, "and"; let men hear their prediction and say, from the event, It is verified (*Note,* ch. 41:26). **10. Ye**—the Jews, to whom I have given predictions, verified by the event; and in delivering whom I have so often manifested My power (see vss. 3, 4; ch. 44:8). **and my servant** —i.e., the whole Jewish people (ch. 41:8). **believe** —trust in. **formed**—before I *existed* none of the false gods were *formed.* "Formed" applies to the idols, not to God. Revelation 1:11 uses the same language to prove the Godhead of *Jesus,* as Isaiah here to prove the Godhead of *Jehovah.* **11. Lord**—Jehovah. **saviour**—temporally, from Babylon: eternally, from sin and hell (Hos. 13:4; Acts 4:12). The same titles as are applied to God are applied to Jesus. **12. declared**—predicted the future (ch. 41:22, 23). **saved**—the nation, in past times of danger. **showed**—viz., that I was God. **when ... no strange god ...**—to whom the predictions uttered by Me could be assigned. "Strange" means *foreign,* introduced from abroad. **13. before**—lit., *from the time of* the first existence of day **let**—Old English for "hinder" (ch. 14:27). Rather, translate, "undo it" [HORSLEY]. **14. sent**—viz., the Medes and Persians (ch. 10:5, 6; 13:3). **brought down**—"made to go down" to the sea (ch. 42:10), in order to escape the impending destruction of Babylon. **nobles**—rather, "fugitives," viz., the foreigners who sojourned in

populous Babylon (ch. 13:14), distinct from the Chaldeans [MAURER]. **whose cry is in the ships**—exulting in their ships with the joyous sailors—cry, boastingly; their joy heretofore in their ships contrasts sadly with their present panic in fleeing to them (ch. 22:2; Zeph. 2:15). Babylon was on the Euphrates, which was joined to the Tigris by a canal, and flowed into the Persian Gulf. Thus it was famed for ships and commerce until the Persian monarchs, to prevent revolt or invasion, obstructed navigation by dams across the Tigris and Euphrates. **15. creator of Israel**—(vs. 1.) **your**—proved to be specially *yours* by delivering you. **16, 17.** Allusion to the deliverance of Israel and overthrow of Pharaoh in the Red Sea, the standing illustration of God's unchanging character towards His people (Exod. 14). **the power**—the might of the enemies' host, every mighty warrior. **they shall lie down together**—as Pharaoh's army sank "together" in a watery grave. **18.** So wonderful shall be God's future interpositions in your behalf, that all past ones shall be forgotten in comparison. Plainly the future restoration of Israel is the event ultimately meant. Thus the "former things" are such events as the destruction of Sennacherib and the return from Babylon. "Things of old" are events still more ancient, the deliverance from Egypt and at the Red Sea, and entry into Canaan [VITRINGA]. **19. new**—unprecedented in its wonderful character (ch. 42:9). **spring forth**—as a germinating herb: a beautiful image of the *silent* but *certain gradual growth* of events in God's providence (Mark 4:26-28). **way in ... wilderness**—just as Israel in the wilderness, between the Red Sea and Canaan, was guided, and supplied with water by Jehovah; but the "new" deliverance shall be attended with manifestations of God's power and love, eclipsing the old (cf. ch. 41:17-19). "I will open a way, not merely in the Red Sea, but in the wilderness of the whole world; and not merely one river shall gush out of the rock, but many, which shall refresh, not the bodies as formerly, but the souls of the thirsty, so that the prophecy shall be fulfilled: "With joy shall ye draw water out of the wells of salvation" [JEROME]. "A way" often stands for *the true religion* (Acts 9:2; 18:26). "Rivers" express the influences of the Holy Spirit (John 7:37-39). Israel's *literal* restoration hereafter is included, as appears by comparing ch. 11:15, 16. **20. beast**—image of idolaters, defiled with blood and pollutions, dwelling like dragons, etc., in the wastes of Gentile ignorance: even they shall be converted. Or else, lit., such copious floods of water shall be given by God in the desert, that the very beasts shall (in poetic language) praise the Lord (Ps. 148:10) [JEROME]. **dragons**—"serpents", or else jackals (*Note,* ch. 13: 22). **owls**—rather, ostriches. **21. This people**—viz., The same as "My people, My chosen" (see vss. 1, 7, Ps. 102:18). **my praise**—on account of the many and great benefits conferred on them, especially their restoration. **22. But**—Israel, *however,* is not to think that these divine favors are due to their own piety towards God. So the believer (Titus 3:5). **but**—rather, "for." **weary of me**—(Amos 8:5, 6; Mal. 1:13), though "*I* have not wearied thee" (vs. 23), yet "thou hast been weary of Me." **23. small cattle**—rather, the "lamb" or "kid," required by the law to be daily offered to God (Exod. 29:38; Num. 28:3). **sacrifices**—offered any way; whereas the *Hebrew* for holocaust, or "burnt offering," denotes that which *ascends* as an offering consumed by fire. **I have not caused thee to serve**—i.e., to render the the service of a *slave* (Matt. 11:30; Rom. 8:15; I

John 4:18; 5:3). **offering**—bloodless (Lev. 2:1, 2). **wearied**—antithetical to vs. 22, "*Thou* hast been weary of Me." Though God in the law required such offerings, yet not so as to "weary" the worshipper, or to exact them in cases where, as in the Babylonian captivity, they were physically unable to render them; God did not require them, save in subordination to the higher moral duties (Ps. 50:8-14; 51:16, 17; Mic. 6:3, 6-8). **24. bought**—for "sweet cane" (aromatic *calamus*) was not indigenous to Palestine, but had to be bought from foreign countries (Jer. 6:20). It was used among the Hebrews to make the sacred ointment (Exod. 30:23). It is often offered as a mark of hospitality. **filled**—satiated (Jer. 31:14). God deigns to use human language to adapt Himself to human modes of thought. **made me to serve**—though "I have not caused *thee* to serve" (vs. 23). Our sin made the Son of God to become "a *servant*." He *served* to save us from servile bondage (Phil. 2:7; Heb. 2:14, 15). **wearied me**—Though I have "not wearied thee" (vs. 23; see ch. 1:14). **25.** (Ch. 44:22.) **I, even I**—the God against whom your sin is committed, and who alone can and will pardon. **for mine own sake**—(ch. 48:9, 11). How abominable a thing sin is, since it is against such a God of grace! "Blotted out" is an image from an account-book, in which, when a debt is paid, the charge is *cancelled* or *blotted out*. **not remember ... sins**—(Jer. 31:34). When God forgives, He forgets; i.e., treats the sinner as if He had forgotten his sins. **26. Put me in remembrance**—Remind Me of every plea which thou hast to urge before Me in thy defense. Image from a trial (ch. 1:18; 41:1). Our strongest plea is to remind God of His own promises. So Jacob did at Mahanaim and Peniel (Gen. 32:9, 12). God, then, instead of "pleading against us with His great power," "will put His strength" in us (Job 23:6); we thus become "the Lord's *remembrancers*" (ch. 62:6, *Margin*). "*Declare* God's righteousness" vindicated in Jesus Christ "that thou mayest be justified" (Rom. 3:26; cf. ch. 20, and Ps. 143:2). **27. first father**—collectively for "most ancient *ancestors*," as the parallelism ("teachers") proves [MAURER]. Or, *thy chief religious ministers* or *priests* [GESENIUS]. *Adam*, the common father of all nations, can hardly be meant here, as it would have been irrelevant to mention *his* sin in an address to *the Jews specially*. *Abraham* is equally out of place here, as he is everywhere cited as an example of faithfulness, not of *sin*. However, taking the passage in its ultimate application to the Church at large, Adam may be meant. **teachers**—lit., "interpreters" between God and man, the priests (Job 33:23; Mal. 2:7). **28. profaned the princes**—(Ps. 89:39; Lam. 2:2, 6, 7). I have esteemed, or treated, them as persons not sacred. I have left them to suffer the same treatment as the common people, stripped of their holy office and in captivity. **princes of the sanctuary**—"governors of" it (I Chron. 24:5); directing its holy services; priests. **curse**—Hebrew, *cherim*, a solemn anathema, or excommunication. **reproaches**—(Ps. 123:3, 4).

CHAPTER 44

VSS. 1-28. CONTINUATION OF THE PREVIOUS CHAPTER (VSS. 1-5). **1. Yet**—Though thou hast sinned, *yet* hear God's gracious promise as to thy deliverance. **chosen**—(ch. 41:8). **2.** (Ch. 43:1, 7.) **formed ... from ... womb**—(So vs. 24; ch. 49:1, 5). The sense is similar to that in ch. 1:2, "I have nourished

and brought up children." **Jesurun**—A diminutive term of endearment applied to Israel. The full title of affection was *Israelun;* contracted it became Jeshurun, with an allusion to the *Hebrew* root, *jashar,* "upright," "perfect" (see *Note* on "He that is perfect," ch. 42:19) [GESENIUS], (Deut. 32:15). **3.** (Ch. 41:18). **him ... thirsty**—rather, "the land" (ch. 35: 6, 7), fig. for *man* thirsting after righteousness (Matt. 5:6). **floods**—the *abundant* influences of the Holy Spirit, stronger than "water." **spirit**—including all spiritual and temporal gifts, as the parallel, "blessing," proves (ch. 11:2; 32:15). **seed**—(ch. 59:21). **4. they**—thy "seed" and "offspring" (vs. 3). **as among**—needlessly inserted in *English Version*. Rather, "The seed shall spring up as willows among the grass beside canals of water" [HORSLEY]. Or, "They shall spring up among the grass (i.e., luxuriantly; for what grows in the midst of grass grows luxuriantly) as willows by the water-courses," which makes the parallel clauses better balanced [MAURER]. **5.** The third clause answers in parallelism to the first, the fourth to the second. **I am the Lord's**—(Jer. 50:5; I Cor. 6:19, 20; II Cor. 8:5). **call himself by the name of Jacob**—The Gentiles (as the result of the outpouring of the Holy Spirit on Israel, the Lord's "seed," first) shall join themselves to the children of Jacob, in order to worship their God (cf. ch. 43:7; Ps. 49:11). Or, "calls," i.e., invokes and celebrates *the name of Jacob*, attaches himself to his nation and religion [MAURER], (Ps. 24:6). **subscribe ... hand unto ... Lord**—in solemn and public covenant, pledging himself to God's service (cf. Neh. 9:38), before "witnesses" (Heb. 12:1), after the manner of a civil contract (Jer. 32:10, 12, 44). So the Christian in the sacraments [BARNES]. Lit., "shall fill his hand with letters (Exod. 32:15; Ezek. 2:10) in honor of Jehovah"; or "shall write upon his hand, I am Jehovah's" (cf. ch. 49:16; Rev. 13:16); alluding to the puncture with ink on the hand, whereby a soldier marked himself as bound to his commander; and whereby the Christians used to mark themselves with the name of Christ [LOWTH]. The former view is simpler. **surname himself ... Israel**—MAURER and GESENIUS interpret this as the *Hebrew* sanctions, answering to their rendering of the parallel second clause, "*calls blandly* (speaks in honorable terms of) the name of Israel." Retaining *English Version*, we must, from the *Hebrew* understand it thus, "Surname himself by the *honorable* name of Israel" (ch. 45:4). **6.** Here follows an argument for Jehovah, as the only God, and against the idols, as vanity (see *Notes*, ch. 41:4; 43:1, 10-12). **7.** Who but God can predict future events and declare also the *order* and time of each (*Note*, ch. 41:22, 23; 45:21)? **call**—"openly proclaim" (ch. 40:6) things to come [MAURER]. Or, "call forth" the event; command that it happen (ch. 46:11; 48:15), [BARNES]. **set ... in order**—There is no chance or confusion; all events occur in the *order* best fitted to subserve God's plans. **for me**—It is FOR GOD that all things exist and take place (Rev. 4:11). But MAURER translates, "Let him *set it forth* (Job 37:19) *to me.*" **since ... ancient people**—I have given the Jews predictions of the future ever since I appointed them as My people in ancient times; therefore they were qualified to be His witnesses (vs. 8). As to their being God's "ancient (everlasting) people," see Deuteronomy 32:7-9; Jeremiah 31:3; the type of the redeemed Church (Eph. 1:4). **8. be afraid**—lit., "be astounded," or "distracted with fear." **from that time**—viz., from the time that "I appointed the ancient people" (vs. 7). From the time of Abraham's call, his family were the depositories of the predictions of the Redeemer, whereas the promise of Cyrus was not heard of till Isaiah's time; therefore, the event to the prediction and accomplishment of which God appeals in proof of His sole Godhead, is the redemption of man by a descendant of Abraham, in whose person "the ancient people" was first formally "appointed." The deliverance of the Jews, by Cyrus, is mentioned afterwards only as an earnest of that greater mercy [HORSLEY]. **no God**—Hebrew, *tsur,* "rock" (Deut. 32:4); i.e., a stronghold to take refuge in, and a solid foundation to build on. **9.** (Ch. 40:18, 20; 41:29). **delectable things**—the idols in which they take such pride and delight. **not profit**—(Hab. 2:18). **they are their own witnesses**—contrasted with, *"Ye are My* witnesses" (vs. 8). "They," i.e., both the makers and the idols, are witnesses against themselves, for the idols palpably see and know nothing (Ps. 115:4-8). **that they may be ashamed**—the consequence deducible from the whole previous argument, not merely from the words immediately preceding, as in ch. 28:13; 36:12. I say all this to show that they are doomed to *perish with shame,* which is their only fitting end. **10. Who . . . ?**—Sarcastic question: "How debased the man must be who *forms* a god!" It is a contradiction in terms. A *made god,* worshipped by its maker (I Cor. 8:4)! **11. his fellows**—the associates of him who makes an idol; or of the idol (see Deut. 7:26; Ps. 115:8; Hos. 4:17). **they are of men**—They are mortal men themselves; what better, then, can the idol be than its maker? **gathered together . . . stand up**—as in a court of justice, to try the issue between God and them (*Note,* ch. 41:1, 21). **yet**—wrongly inserted in *English Version.* The issue of the trial shall be, "they shall fear," etc. **12. tongs**—rather, "prepareth (to be supplied) *an axe,"* viz., with which to cut down the tree designed as the material of the idol. The "smith" (*Hebrew,* "workman in iron") here answers to the "carpenter" (*Hebrew,* "workman in wood"). "He worketh it (*the axe,* not the idol, which was wood, not metal) in the coals," etc. The axe was *wrought,* not cast. The smith makes the axe for the carpenter. **hungry . . . . drinketh no water**—so eager is he to expedite his work while the iron is hot. If the god were worth anything, it would not let him grow "faint" with hunger and thirst. WILLIAMS, the missionary, states that the South Sea islanders when they make an idol abstain from food and drink. **13.** After the smith's work in preparing the instruments comes the carpenter's work in forming the idol. **rule**—rather, "line" [BARNES]. **with a line**—rather, a "pencil," [HORSLEY]. Lit., "red ochre," which he uses to mark on the wood the outline of the figure [LOWTH]. Or best, the stylus or graver, with which the incision of the outline is made [GESENIUS]. **planes**—rather, chisels or carving tools, for a plane would not answer for carving. **compass**—from a *Hebrew* root, "to make a circle"; by it, symmetry of form is secured. **according to . . . beauty of a man**—irony. The highest idea the heathen could form of a god was one of a form like their own. Jerome says, "The more handsome the statue the more august the god was thought." The incarnation of the Son of God condescends to this anthropomorphic feeling so natural to man, but in such a way as to raise man's thoughts up to the infinite God who "is a spirit." **that it may remain in . . . house**—the only thing it was good for; it could not hear nor save (cf. Wisdom 13:15). **14.** Description of the material out of which the idol is formed. **cypress**—rather, from *Hebrew* root, "to be hard," the holm-oak," an evergreen abundant in Palestine [GESENIUS]. **strengtheneth**—lit., "and he getteth strength

to himself in the trees of the forest;" i.e., he layeth in a *great store* of timber [LOWTH]. Or, *"chooseth,"* as "madest strong for thyself," i.e., hast chosen (Ps. 80:15, 17) [GESENIUS]. But *English Version* gives a good sense: "strengtheneth"; i.e., rears to maturity; a meaning suitable also to the context of Psalm 80:15, 17, where Israel is compared to a *vine* planted by Jehovah [MAURER]. **rain doth nourish it**—Though the man planted the tree, yet he could not make it grow. In preparing to make an idol, he has to depend on the true God for rain from heaven (Jer. 14:22). **15.** The same tree that furnishes the material for the god is in part used as fuel for a fire to cook his meals and warm himself! **thereto**—rather, "he falleth down before *them,"* i.e., such images [MAURER]. **16. part . . . part**—not distinct parts, but *the same part* of the wood (cf. vs. 17). **eateth**—i.e., cooks so as to eat (vs. 19). **I have seen**—I feel its power. **18. he . . .**—God hath given them over to judicial blindness; not His direct physical, but His providential agency in administering His moral government, is meant (ch. 6:9, 10). "Shut," lit., "daubed," plastered up; it is an Eastern custom in some cases to seal up the eyes of offenders. **19. considereth**—lit., "layeth it to heart," (ch. 42:25; Jer. 12:11). **abomination**—the scriptural term for an idol, not merely abominable, but the *essence* of what is so, in the eyes of a jealous God (I Kings 11:5, 7). **20. feedeth on ashes**—fig., for the idolater delights in what is vain (Prov. 15:14; Hos. 12:1). "Feedeth on wind." There is an allusion, perhaps, also, to the god being made of a tree, the half of which was *reduced to ashes by fire* (vss. 15, 16, 17); the idol, it is implied, was no better, and could, and ought, to have been reduced to ashes like the other half. **deceived heart**—The heart and will first go astray, then the intellect and life (Rom. 1:28; Eph. 4:18). **lie in . . . right hand**—Is not my handiwork (the idol) a self-deceit? **21. Remember**—"Be not like the idolaters who consider not in their heart" (vs. 19). **these**—things just said as to the folly of idol worship. **my servant**—not like the idolaters, slaves to the stock of a tree (vs. 19). See vss. 1:2. **thou . . . not . . . forgotten of me**—Therefore *thou* oughtest to "remember" Me. **22. blotted out**—the debt of *thy* sin from the account book in which it was entered (Exod. 32:32, 33; Rev. 20:12). **as a thick cloud**—scattered away by the wind (Ps. 103:12). **as a cloud**—a descending gradation. Not only the "thick cloud" of the heavier "transgressions," but the "cloud" ("vapor" [LOWTH], not so dense, but *covering* the sky as a mist) of the countless "sins." These latter, though not thought much of by man, need, as much as the former, to be cleared away by the Sun of righteousness; else they will be a *mist* separating us from heaven (Ps. 19:12, 13; I John 1:7-9). **return . . . for**—The antecedent redemption is the ground of, and motive to, repentance. We do not repent *in order that He may* redeem us, but *because He hath* redeemed us (Zech. 12:10; Luke 24:47; Acts 3:18, 19). He who believes in his being forgiven cannot but love (Luke 7:43, 47). **23.** Call to inanimate nature to praise God; for it also shall share in the coming deliverance from "the bondage of corruption" (Rom. 8:20, 21). **done it**—effected redemption for both the literal and spiritual Israel. **lower parts . . .**—antithetical to "heavens"; "mountains," "forest," and "tree," are the intermediate objects in a descending gradation (see Ps. 96:11, 12). **24-28.** Confirmation of His promises to the Church and Israel, by various instances of His omnipotence; among these the restoration of the Jews by Cyrus. **alone**—lit., "Who was with Me?" viz., when I did it; answering to "by Myself," in the parallel clause (cf. similar phrases, Hos. 8:4; John 5:30) [MAURER]. **25. tokens** —prognostics; the pretended miracles which they gave as *proofs* of their supernatural powers. **liars**— (Jer. 50:36). Conjurors; or, astrologers; men leading a retired contemplative life in order to study divination by the signs of the stars [VITRINGA]. **backward** —with shame at their predictions not being verified. "To turn away the face" is to *frustrate defeat* (ch. 36: 9; I Kings 2:15). The "wise men" are the diviners who, when Babylon was attacked by Cyrus, predicted his overthrow. **26. servant**—in a collective sense, for *the prophets* in general, who foretold the return from Babylon; answering to "His messengers" (*plural*, in the parallel clause) [MAURER]. Antitypically, and ultimately, *Messiah*, who is the consummating embodiment of all the prophets and messengers of God (Mal. 3:1; Matt. 21:34, 36, 37; John 10:36); hence the *singular*, "His servant." **counsel** —predictions; prophets' *counsels* concern the future (cf. "counsellor," ch. 41:28). **Jerusalem**—regarded prophetically, as lying in ruins. **27.** Referring to the Euphrates, which was turned into a different channel, close to Babylon, by Cyrus, who thereby took the city. "The deep" is applied to Euphrates as "sea" (Jer. 51:32, 36). "Rivers" refers to the artificial canals from the Euphrates made to irrigate the country; when it was turned off into a different bed (viz., a lake, forty miles square, which was originally formed to receive the superfluous water in an inundation), the canals became dry. **28. my shepherd**—type of Messiah (ch. 40:11; Ps. 23:1; 77:20; Ezek. 34:23). **all my pleasure**—so Messiah (ch. 42: 1; 53:10). This is the first time Cyrus is *named* expressly; and that, 150 years before the time when in 550 B.C. he began his reign. The name comes from the Persian *khorschid*, "the sun"; kings often taking their names from the gods; the sun was worshipped as a god in Persia. **saying**—rather, "and that saith"; construed with *God*, not with *Cyrus*. God's word is instantaneously efficient in accomplishing His will. **to . . . to**—or, "*of* Jerusalem . . . *of* the temple," as previously, the same *Hebrew* word is translated, "*of* Cyrus" [BARNES]. *English Version* is more graphic. Cyrus, according to JOSEPHUS, heard of this prophecy of Isaiah delivered so long before; hence he was induced to do that which was so contrary to Oriental policy, to aid in restoring the captive Jews and rebuilding their temple and city.

CHAPTER 45

Vss. 1-25. THE SUBJECT OF THE DELIVERANCE BY CYRUS IS FOLLOWED UP (vss. 1-7). These seven verses should have been appended to previous chapter, and the new chapter should begin with vs. 8, "Drop down . . ." [HORSLEY]. Reference to the deliverance by Messiah often breaks out from amidst the local and temporary details of the deliverance from Babylon, as the great ultimate end of the prophecy. **1. his anointed**—Cyrus is so called as being *set apart as king*, by God's providence, to fulfil His special purpose. Though kings were not *anointed* in Persia, the expression is applied to him in reference to the *Jewish* custom of setting apart kings to the regal office by anointing. **right hand . . . holden**—image from sustaining a feeble person by holding his right hand (ch. 42:6). **subdue nations**—viz., the Cilicians, Syrians, Babylonians, Lydians, Bactrians, etc.; his empire extended from Egypt and the Mediterranean to the Indian Ocean, and from Ethiopia to the Euxine Sea. **loose . . .**

loins—i.e., the girdle off the loins; and so *enfeeble* them. The loose outer robe of the Orientals, when girt fast round the loins, was the emblem of strength and preparedness for action; ungirt, was indicative of *feebleness* (Job 38:3; 12:21); "*weakeneth the strength* of the mighty" (*Margin*), "*looseth the girdle* of the strong." *The joints of* Belshazzar's *loins*, we read in Daniel 5:6, *were loosed* during the siege by Cyrus, at the sight of the mysterious handwriting on the palace walls. His being taken by surprise, *unaccoutred*, is here foretold. **to open . . . gates**—In the revelry in Babylon on the night of its capture, the inner gates, leading from the streets to the river, were left open; for there were walls along each side of the Euphrates with gates, which, had they been kept shut, would have hemmed the invading hosts in the bed of the river, where the Babylonians could have easily destroyed them. Also, the gates of the palace were left open, so that there was access to every part of the city; and such was its extent, that they who lived in the extremities were taken prisoners before the alarm reached the center of the palace. [HERODOTUS, 1. sec. 191]. **2. crooked . . . straight**—(ch. 40: 4), rather, "maketh mountains plain" [LOWTH], i.e., clear out of thy way all opposing persons and things. The KERI reads as in vs. 13, "make straight" (*Margin*). **gates of brass**—(Ps. 107:16.) HERODOTUS (1. sec. 179) says, Babylon had 100 massive gates, twenty-five on each of the four sides of the city, all, as well as their posts, of brass. **bars of iron**—with which the gates were fastened. **3. treasures of darkness**—i.e., hidden in subterranean places; a common Oriental practive. Sorcerers pretended to be able to show where such treasures were to be found; in opposition to their pretensions, God says, He will really give hidden treasures to Cyrus (Jer. 50:37; 51: 13). PLINY (*H. N.*, 33:3) says that Cyrus obtained from the conquest of Asia 34,000 pounds weight of gold, besides golden vases, and 500,000 talents of silver, and the goblet of Semiramis, weighing fifteen talents. **that thou mayest know**—viz., not merely that He was "the God of Israel," but that He was Jehovah, the true God. Ezra 1:1, 2 shows that the correspondence of the event with the prediction had the desired effect on Cyrus. **which call . . . thy name**—so long before designate thee by name (ch. 43:1). **4.** (*Note*, ch. 41:8; 43:14.) **surnamed**—i.e., designated to carry out My design of restoring Judah (see *Note,* ch. 44:5; 44:28; 45:1). MAURER here, as in ch. 44:5, translates, "I have *addressed thee by an honorable name.*" **hast not known me**—*previous* to My calling thee to this office; *after* God's call, Cyrus *did* know Him in some degree (Ezra 1:1-3). **5.** (Ch. 42:8; 43:3, 11; 44:8; 46:9.) **girded thee**—whereas "I will loose (the girdle off) the loins of kings" (vs. 1), *strengthening* thee, but *enfeebling* them before thee. **though . . . not known me**—(vs. 4.) God *knows* His elect before they are made to know Him (Gal. 4:9; John 15:16). **6.** From the rising to the setting of the sun, i.e., from *east* to *west*, the whole *habitable* world. It is not said, "from *north* to *south*," for that would not imply the *habitable* world, as, "from *east* to *west*" does (Ezra 1:1, etc.). The conquest of Jerusalem by Babylon, the capital of the world, and the overthrow of Babylon and restoration of the Jews by Cyrus, who expressly acknowledged himself to be but the instrument in God's hands, were admirably suited to secure, throughout the world, the acknowledgment of Jehovah as the only true God. **7. form . . . create**—*yatzar*, to give "form" to previously existing matter. *Bara*, to "create" from nothing the chaotic dark material.

light ... darkness–lit. (Gen. 1:1-3), emblematical also, *prosperity* to Cyrus, *calamity* to Babylon and the nations to be vanquished [GROTIUS]. Isaiah refers also to the Oriental belief in two coexistent, eternal principles, ever struggling with each other, light or good, and darkness or evil, *Oromasden* and *Ahrimanen*. God, here, in opposition, asserts His sovereignty over both [VITRINGA]. **create evil**–not *moral* evil (Jas. 1:13), but in contrast to "peace" in the parallel clause, *war, disaster* (cf. Ps. 65:7; Amos 3:6). **8. Drop**–viz., the fertilizing rain (Ps. 65:12). **skies**–clouds; lower than the "heavens." **righteousness**–i.e., the dews of the Holy Spirit, whereby "righteousness" shall "spring up." (See latter end of the verse.) **earth**–fig. for the *hearts of men* on it, *opened* for receiving the truth by the Holy Ghost (Acts 16:14). **them**–the earth and the heavens. HORSLEY prefers: "Let the earth open, and *let salvation and justice grow forth;* let *it bring them forth* together; I the Lord have created *him*" (vs. 13). MAURER translates, "Let all kinds of salvation (prosperity) be fruitful" (Ps. 72:3, 6, 7). The revival of religion after the return from Babylon suggests to the prophet the diffusion of *Messiah's Gospel*, especially in days still future; hence the elevation of the language to a pitch above what is applicable to the state of religion after the return. **9.** Anticipating the objections which the Jews might raise as to why God permitted their captivity, and when He did restore them, why He did so by a foreign prince, Cyrus, not a Jew (ch. 40:27, etc.), but mainly and ultimately, the objections about to be raised by the Jews against *God's sovereign act in adopting the whole Gentile world as His spiritual Israel* (vs. 8, referring to this *catholic* diffusion of the Gospel), as if it were an infringement of their nation's privileges; so Paul expressly quotes it (Rom. 9:4-8, 11-21). **Let ... strive**–Not in the *Hebrew*; rather, in apposition with "him," "A potsherd *among* the potsherds of the earth!" A creature fragile and worthless as the fragment of an earthen vessel, among others equally so, and yet presuming to strive with his Maker! *English Version* implies, it is appropriate for man to strive with man, in opposition to II Tim. 2:24 [GESENIUS]. **thy ... He**–shall thy work *say of thee*, He ... ? **10.** If it be wrong for a child, born in less favorable circumstances, to upbraid his parents with having given him birth, *a fortiori*, it is, to upbraid God for His dealings with us. Rather translate, "*a father ... a woman.*" The Jews considered themselves exclusively God's children and were angry that God should adopt the Gentiles besides. Woe to him who says to one already a father, Why dost thou beget other children? [HORSLEY]. **11. Ask ... command**–Instead of striving with Me in regard to My purposes, your wisdom is in prayer to *ask,* and even *command* Me, in so far as it is for My glory, and for your real good (Mark 11:24; John 16:23, 13, latter part of the verse; I John 3:22). **sons**–(ch. 54:13; Gal. 3:26). **work of my hands**–spiritually (Eph. 2:10); also literal Israel (ch. 60:21). MAURER translates, instead of "command," *Leave it to Me,* in My dealings concerning My sons and concerning the work of My hands, to do what I will with My own. LOWTH reads it interrogatively, Do ye presume to question Me and dictate to Me (see vss. 9, 10)? The same sense is given, if the words be taken in irony. But *English Version* is best. **12.** The same argument for prayer, drawn from God's omnipotence and consequent power, to grant any request, occurs in ch. 40:26-31. **I, even my hands**–so *Hebrew* (Ps. 41:2), "Thou ... thy hand" (both nominatives, in apposition). **13. him**–Cyrus, type of

Messiah, who redeems the captives of Satan "without money and without price" (ch. 55:1), "freely" (gratuitously) (ch. 52:3; 61:1; Zech. 9:11; Rom. 3: 24). **in righteousness**–to fulfil My righteous purpose (*Note,* ch. 41:2; 42:6; Jer. 23:6). **14.** The language but cursorily alludes to Egypt, Ethiopia, and Seba, being given to Cyrus as a ransom in lieu of Israel whom he restored (ch. 43:3), but mainly and fully describes *the gathering in of the Gentiles to Israel* (Acts 2:10, 11; 8:27-38), especially at Israel's future restoration (ch. 2:2; 14:1, 2; 19:18-22; 60:3-14; 49: 23; Ps. 68:31; 72:10, 11). **labour**–wealth acquired by labor (Jer. 3:24). **Sabeans ... of stature**–the men of Meroe, in Upper Egypt. HERODOTUS (3.30) calls the Ethiopians "the tallest of men" (*Note,* ch. 18:2; I Chron. 11:23). **thee**–Jerusalem ("my city," vs. 13). **in chains**–(Ps. 149:8). "The saints shall judge the world" (I Cor. 6:2) and "rule the nations with a rod of iron" (Zech. 4:12-19; Rev. 2:26, 27). The "chains," in the case of the obedient, shall be the *easy yoke* of Messiah; as "the sword of the Spirit" also is saving to the believer, condemnatory to the unbeliever (John 12:48; Heb. 4:12; Rev. 19:15). **God is in thee**–(Jer. 3:19). **15. God that hidest thyself**–HORSLEY, after JEROME, explains this as the confession of Egypt, etc., that *God is concealed in human form in the person of Jesus.* Rather, connected with vss. 9, 10, the prophet, contemplating the wonderful issue of the seemingly dark counsels of God, implies a censure on those who presume to question God's dealings (ch. 55:8, 9; Deut. 29:29). Faith still discerns, even under the veil, the covenant-keeping *God of Israel, the Saviour* (ch. 8:17). **16. ashamed**–*disappointed* in their expectation of help from their idols (*Note,* ch. 42:17; Ps. 97:7). **17. in the Lord**–(vss. 24, 25), contrasted with the idols which cannot give even temporary help (vs. 16); *in Jehovah* there is *everlasting* salvation (ch. 26: 4) **not ... ashamed**–opposed to the doom of the idolaters, who, in the hour of need, shall be "ashamed" (*Note,* vs. 16). **18.** (*Note,* vs. 12.) **not in vain** [but] **to be inhabited**–Therefore, Judah, lying waste during the Babylonish captivity, shall be peopled again by the exiles. The Jews, from this passage, infer that, after the resurrection, the earth shall be inhabited, for there can be no reason why the earth should *then* exist in vain any more than now (II Pet. 3:13). **19. not ... secret**–not like the heathen oracles which gave their responses from dark caverns, with studied obscurity (ch. 48:16). Christ plainly quotes these words, thereby identifying Himself with Jehovah (John 18:20). **I said not ... Seek ... in vain**–When I commanded you to seek Me (Jehovah did so, vs. 11, "Ask Me," etc.), it was not in order that ye might be sent empty away (Deut. 32:47). Especially in Israel's time of trial, God's interposition, in behalf of Zion hereafter, is expressly stated as about to be the answer to prayer (ch. 62:6, 7-10; Ps. 102:13-17, 19-21). So in the case of all believers, the spiritual Israel. **righteousness**–that which is veracious: not in the equivocal terms of heathen responses, fitly symbolized by the *"dark* places" from which they were uttered. **right**–true (*Note,* ch. 41:26). **20. escaped of the nations**–those of the nations who shall have escaped the slaughter inflicted by Cyrus. Now, at last, ye shall see the folly of "praying to a god that cannot save" (vs. 16). Ultimately, those that shall be "left of all the nations which shall come against Jerusalem" are meant (Zech. 14:16). They shall then all be converted to the Lord (ch. 66:23, 24; Jer. 3:17; Zech. 8:20-23). **21.** Challenge the worshippers of idols (ch. 41:1). **take counsel together**–as to the best arguments wherewith to defend the cause of idolatry. **who... from that time**—(Ch. 41:22, 23; *Note*, ch. 44:8). Which of the idols has done what God hath, viz., foretold, primarily as to Cyrus; ultimately as to the final restoration of Israel hereafter? The idolatry of Israel before Cyrus' time will have its counterpart in the Antichrist and the apostasy, which shall precede Christ's manifestation. **just... and... Saviour**—*righteous* in keeping His promises, and therefore a *Saviour* to His people. Not only is it not inconsistent with, but it is the result of, His *righteousness*, or *justice*, that He should *save* His redeemed (ch. 42:6, 21; Ps. 85:10, 11; Rom. 3:26). **22. Look... and be ye saved**—The second imperative expresses the result which will follow obedience to the first (Gen. 42:18); *ye shall be saved* (John 3:14, 15). Numbers 21:9: "If a serpent had bitten any man, when he *beheld* the serpent of brass he lived." What so simple as a look? Not *do* something, but *look* to the Saviour (Acts 16:30, 31). Believers look by faith, the eye of the soul. The look is that of one *turning* (see *Margin*) to God, as at once "Just and the Saviour" (vs. 21), i.e., the look of *conversion* (Ps. 22:27). **23. sworn by myself**—equivalent to, "As I live," as Romans 14:11 quotes it. So Numbers 14:21. God could swear by no greater, therefore He swears by Himself (Heb. 6:13, 16). **word... in righteousness**—rather, "the truth (*Note*, vs. 19) is gone forth from My mouth, the word (of promise), and it shall not return (i.e., which shall not be revoked)" [LOWTH]. But the accents favor *English Version.* **tongue... swear**—viz., an oath of allegiance to God as their true King (*Note*, ch. 19:18; 65:16). Yet to be fulfilled (Zech. 14:9). **24.** Rather, *"Only in Jehovah shall men say of me* (this clause is parenthetical), *is there righteousness"* (which includes *salvation*, vs. 21, "a *just* God and a *Saviour*," ch. 46:13), etc. [MAURER]. **strength**—viz., to save. **shall men come**—Those who have set themselves up against God shall come to Him in penitence for the past (ch. 19:22). **ashamed**—(vs. 16; ch. 54:17; 41:11.) **25. all... Israel**—the spiritual Israel (Rom. 2:29) and the literal Israel, i.e., the final remnant which shall *all be saved* (vs. 17; Rom. 11:26). **justified**—treated *as if* they were just, through Christ's righteousness and death (Jer. 23:5). **glory**—lit., "sing" in His praise (Jer. 9:24; I Cor. 1:31).

CHAPTER 46

Vss. 1-13. BABYLON'S IDOLS COULD NOT SAVE THEMSELVES, MUCH LESS HER. BUT GOD CAN AND WILL SAVE ISRAEL: CYRUS IS HIS INSTRUMENT. **1. Bel**—the same as the Phœnician Baal, i.e., lord, the chief god of Babylon; to it was dedicated the celebrated tower of Babylon, in the center of one of the two parts into which the city was divided, the palace being in the center of the other. Identical with the *sun*, worshipped on turrets, housetops, and other high places, so as to be nearer the heavenly hosts (*Saba*) (Jer. 19:13; 32:29; Zeph. 1:5). GESENIUS identifies Bel with the planet Jupiter, which, with the planet Venus (under the name Astarte or Astaroth), was worshipped in the East as the god of fortune, the most propitious star to be born under (*Note*, ch. 65:11). According to the Apocryphal book, *Bel and the Dragon*, Bel was cast down by Cyrus. **boweth... stoopeth**—falleth prostrate (ch. 10:4; I Sam. 5:3, 4; Ps. 20:8). **Nebo**—the planet Mercury or Hermes, in astrology. The scribe of heaven, answering to the Egyptian Anubis. The extensive

worship of it is shown by the many proper names compounded of it: Neb-uchadnezzar, Neb-uzaradan, Nab-onassar, etc. **were upon**—i.e., were *a burden* (supplied from the following clause) upon. It was customary to transport the gods of the vanquished to the land of the conquerors, who thought thereby the more effectually to keep down the subject people (I Sam. 5:1, etc.; Jer. 48:7; 49:3; Dan. 11:8). **carriages**—in the Old English sense of *the things carried, the images borne by you:* the lading (Acts 21:15), "carriages," not the vehicles, but the baggage. Or, the images *which used to be carried by you* formerly in your solemn processions [MAURER] **were heavy loaden**—rather, *are put as a load on* the beasts of burden [MAURER]. HORSLEY translates, "They who should have been your *carriers* (as Jehovah is to *His* people, vss. 3, 4) are become *burdens*" (see *Note*, vs. 4). **2. deliver**—from the enemies' hands. **burden**—their images laid on the beasts (vs. 1). **themselves**—the *gods*, here also distinguished from their images. **3.** in contrast to what precedes: Babylon's idols, so far from *bearing* its people safely are themselves *borne off, a burden* to the laden beast; but Jehovah *bears* His people in safety even from the womb to old age (ch. 63:9; Deut. 32:11; Ps. 71:6, 18). God compares Himself to a nurse tenderly carrying a child; contrast Moses' language (Num. 11:12). **4. old age**—As "your"—"you"—"you," are not in the *Hebrew*, the sentiment is more general than *English Version*, though of course it *includes* the Jews from the infancy to the more advanced age of their history (ch. 47:6). **I am he**—i.e. the same (Ps. 102:27; John 8:24; Heb. 13:8). **I will bear... carry**—Not only do I not need to be *borne* and *carried* Myself, as the idols (vs. 1). **5.** (Ch. 40:18, 25.) **6.** (Ch. 40:19, 20; 41:7.) They lavish gold out of their purses and spare no expense for their idol. Their profuseness shames the niggardliness of professors who worship God with what cost them nothing. Sin is always a costly service **7. cry... can... not... save**—(ch. 45:20, with which contrast vs. 19). **8. show yourselves men**—Renounce the *childishness* of idolatry as shown in what precedes (I Cor. 14:20; 16:13; Eph. 4:14). In order to be *manly* we must be *godly;* for man was made "in the image of God," and only rises to his true dignity when joined to God; *virtue* is derived from the *Latin vir*, "a man." **bring... to mind**—rather, lay it to heart. **transgressors**—addressed to the idolaters among the Jews. **9. former**—viz., proofs of the sole Godship of Jehovah, from predictions fulfilled, and interpositions of God in behalf of Israel (ch. 45:5). **10.** (Ch. 45:21; 41:22, 23; 44:26.) **yet**—not in the *Hebrew*. Translate, "What had not been done" [HORSLEY]. **do all my pleasure**—(Ch. 53:10; Rom. 9:19.) **11. ravenous bird**—Cyrus so called on account of the rapidity of his marches from the distant regions of Persia to pounce on his prey (see *Notes*, ch. 41:2, 25; Jer. 49:22; Ezek. 17:3). The standard of Cyrus, too, was a golden *eagle* on a spear (see the heathen historian, XENOPHON, 7, where almost the same word is used, *aetos*, as here, *ayit*). **executeth my counsel**—(ch. 44:28; 45:13). Babylon represents, mystically, the apostate faction: the destruction of its idols symbolizes the future general extirpation of all idolatry and unbelief. **purposed... also do it**—(ch. 43:13). **12. stout-hearted**—stubborn in resisting God (Ps. 76:5; Acts 7:51). **far from righteousness**—(ch. 59:9; Hab. 2:4). **13. near**—antithetical to "far" (vs. 12; ch. 51:5; 56:1; 61:10, 11; Rom. 10:6-8). **righteousness**—answering to "salvation" in the parallel clause; therefore it means here, "my righteous deliverance";

righteous, because proving the *truth* of God's promises, and so contrived as to not compromise, but vindicate, His righteousness (ch. 42:21; Rom. 3: 26). **Zion . . . my glory**—rather, "I will give salvation in Zion; to Israel (I will give) my glory" [HORSLEY]. (Ch. 63:11; Ps. 14:7; Luke 2:32).

CHAPTER 47

Vss. 1-15. THE DESTRUCTION OF BABYLON IS REPRESENTED UNDER THE IMAGE OF A ROYAL VIRGIN BROUGHT DOWN IN A MOMENT FROM HER MAGNIFICENT THRONE TO THE EXTREME OF DEGRADATION. **1. in the dust**--(*Note*, ch. 3:26; Job 2:13; Lam. 2:10). **virgin**—i.e., heretofore *uncaptured* [HERODOTUS, 1. 191]. **daughter of Babylon**—Babylon and its inhabitants (*Notes*, ch. 1:8; 37:22). **no throne**—The seat of empire was transferred to Shushan. Alexander intended to have made Babylon his seat of empire, but Providence defeated his design. He soon died; and Seleucia, being built near, robbed it of its inhabitants, and even of its name, which was applied to Seleucia. **delicate**—alluding to the effeminate debauchery and prostitution of all classes at banquets and religious rites [CURTIUS, 5.1; HERODOTUS, 1.199; BARUCH, 6.43]. **2. millstones**—like the *querns* or hand-mills, found in this country, before the invention of water-mills and windmills: a convex stone, made by the hand to turn in a concave stone, fitted to receive it, the corn being ground between them: the office of a female slave in the East; most degrading (Job 31:10; Matt. 24:41). **uncover thy locks**—rather, "take off thy veil" [HORSLEY]: perhaps the removal of the *plaited hair* worn round the women's temples is included; it, too, is a *covering* (I Cor. 11: 15); to remove it and the veil is the badge of the lowest female degradation; in the East the head is the seat of female modesty; the *face* of a woman is seldom, the whole *head* almost never, seen bare (*Note*, ch. 22:8). **make bare the leg**—rather "lift up (lit., "uncover"; as in lifting up the train the leg is uncovered) thy *flowing train.*" In Mesopotamia, women of low rank, as occasion requires, wade across the rivers with stript legs, or else entirely put off their garments and swim across. "Exchange thy rich, loose, queenly robe, for the most abject condition, that of one going to and fro through rivers as a slave, to draw water," etc. **uncover . . . thigh**—gather up the robe, so as to wade across. **3. not meet . . . as a man**—rather, "I will not meet a man," i.e., suffer man to intercede with me—give man an audience [HORSLEY]. Or, "I will not *make peace with* any man," before all are destroyed. Lit., "strike a league with"; a phrase arising from the custom of *striking* hands together in making a compact [MAURER], (*Note*, Prov. 17:18; 22:26; 11:15, *Margin*). Or else from *striking* the victims sacrificed in making treaties. **4. As for**—rather supply, "*Thus saith* our Redeemer" [MAURER]. LOWTH supposes this verse to be the exclamation of a chorus breaking in with praises, "Our Redeemer! Jehovah of hosts," etc. (Jer. 50:34). **5. Sit**—the posture of mourning (Ezra 9:4; Job 2:13; Lam. 2:10). **darkness**—mourning and misery (Lam. 3:2; Mic. 7:8). **lady of kingdoms**—mistress of the world (ch. 13:19). **6.** reason for God's vengeance on Babylon: in executing God's will against His people, she had done so with wanton cruelty (ch. 10:5, etc.; Jer. 50:17; 51: 33; Zech. 1:15). **polluted my inheritance**—(ch. 43: 28). **the ancient**—Even old age was disregarded by the Chaldeans, who treated all alike with cruelty (Lam. 4:16; 5:12) [ROSENMULLER]. Or, "the an-

cient" means Israel, worn out with calamities in the latter period of its history (ch. 46: 4), as its earlier stage of history is called its "youth" (ch. 54:6; Ezek. 16:60). **7. so that**—Through thy vain expectation of being a queen for ever, thou didst advance to such a pitch of insolence as not to believe "these things" (viz., as to thy overthrow, vss. 1-5) possible. **end of it**—viz., of thy insolence, implied in her words, "I shall be a lady for ever." **8. given to pleasures**—(*Note*, vs. 1.) In no city were there so many incentives to licentiousness. **I am . . . none . . . beside me**—(vs. 10.) Language of arrogance in man's mouth; fitting for God alone (ch. 45:6). See ch. 5:8, latter part. **widow . . . loss of children**—A state, represented as a female, when it has fallen is called a *widow*, because its *king* is no more; and *childless*, because it has no inhabitants; they having been carried off as captives (ch. 23:4; 54:1, 4, 5; Rev. 18:7, 8). **9. in a moment**—It should not decay slowly, but be suddenly and unexpectedly destroyed; in a single night it was taken by Cyrus. The prophecy was again literally fulfilled when Babylon revolted against Darius; and, in order to hold out to the last, each man chose one *woman* of his family, and strangled the rest, to save provisions. Darius impaled 3000 of the revolters. **in . . . perfection**—i.e., "in full measure." **for . . . for**—rather, "notwithstanding the . . . notwithstanding"; "in spite of" [LOWTH]. So "for" (Num. 14:11). Babylon was famous for "expiations or sacrifices, and other incantations, whereby they tried to avert evil and obtain good" [DIODORUS SICULUS]. **10. wickedness**—as in ch. 13:11, the *cruelty* with which Babylon treated its subject states. **None seeth me**—(Ps. 10:11; 94:7). "There is none to exact punishment from me." Sinners are not safe, though seeming secret. **Thy wisdom**—astrological and political (ch. 19:11, etc., as to Egypt). **perverted**—turns thee aside from the right and safe path. **11. from whence it riseth**—*Hebrew*, "the dawn thereof," i.e., its first rising. Evil shall come on thee without the least previous intimation [ROSENMULLER]. But *dawn* is not applied to "evil," but to *prosperity* shining out after misery (ch. 21:12). Translate, "Thou shalt not see any dawn" (of alleviation) [MAURER]. **put . . . off** rather, as *Margin*, "remove by *expiation*"; it shall be never ending. **not know**—unawares: which thou dost not apprehend. Proving the fallacy of thy divinations and astrology (Job 9:5; Ps. 35:8). **12. Stand**—forth: a scornful challenge to Babylon's magicians to show whether they can defend their city. **laboured**—The devil's service is a laborious yet fruitless one (ch. 55:2). **13. wearied**—(cf. 57:10; Ezek. 24:12). **astrologers**—lit., those who form *combinations* of the heavens; who watch conjunctions and oppositions of the stars. "Casters of the configurations of the sky" [HORSLEY]. GESENIUS explains it: the dividers of the heavens. In casting a nativity they observed four signs:—the *horoscope*, or sign which arose at the time one was born; the *mid-heaven; the sign opposite the horoscope* towards the west; and the *hypogee.* **monthly prognosticators**—those who at each new moon profess to tell thereby what is about to happen. Join, not as *English Version*, "save . . . from those things," etc.; but, "They that at new moons make known from (by means of) *them* the things that shall come upon thee" [MAURER]. **14.** (Ch. 29:6; 30:30.) **not . . . a coal**—Like stubble, they shall burn to a dead ash, without leaving a live coal or cinder (cf. ch. 30:14), so utterly shall they be destroyed. **15. Thus . . .**—Such shall be the fate of those astrologers who cost thee such an amount of trouble and money. **thy merchants, from thy youth**–i.e., with whom thou hast trafficked from thy earliest history, the foreigners sojourning in Babylon for the sake of commerce (ch. 13:14; Jer. 51:6, 9; Nah. 3:16, 17) [BARNES]. Rather, the *astrologers,* with whom Babylon had so many deal-' ings (vss. 12-14) [HORSLEY]. **to his quarter**–lit., "straight before him" (Ezek. 1:9, 12). The foreigners, whether soothsayers or merchants, shall flee home out of Babylon (Jer. 50:16).

CHAPTER 48

Vss. 1-22. THE THINGS THAT BEFALL BABYLON JEHOVAH PREDICTED LONG BEFORE, LEST ISRAEL SHOULD ATTRIBUTE THEM, IN ITS "OBSTINATE" PERVERSITY, TO STRANGE GODS (vss. 1-5). **1. the waters of Judah**–spring from the *fountain* of Judah (Num. 24:7; Deut. 33:28; Ps. 68:26; *Margin*). *Judah* has the "fountain" attributed to it, because it survived the ten tribes, and from it Messiah was to spring. **swear by . . . Lord**–(ch. 19:18; 45:23; 65: 16). **mention**–in prayers and praises. **not in truth**–(Jer. 5:2; John 4:24). **2. For**–Ye deserve these reproofs; "for" ye call yourselves citizens of "the holy city" (ch. 52:1), but not in truth (vs. 1; Neh. 11:1; Dan. 9:24); so the inscription on their coins of the time of the Maccabees. "Jerusalem the Holy." **3. former**–things which have happened in time past to Israel (ch. 42:9; 44:7, 8; 45:21; 46: 10). **suddenly**–They came to pass so unexpectedly that the prophecy could not have resulted from mere human sagacity. **4. obstinate**–*Hebrew*, "hard" (Deut. 9:27; Ezek. 3:7, *Margin*). **iron sinew**–inflexible (Acts 7:51). **brow brass**–shameless as a harlot (see Jer. 6:28; 3:3; Ezek. 3:7, *Margin*). **5.** (See *Notes*, vss., 1, 3.) **6. Thou . . .**–So "ye are my witnesses" (ch. 43:10). Thou canst testify the prediction was uttered long before the fulfilment: "see all this," viz., that the event answers to the prophecy. **declare**–make the fact known as a proof that Jehovah alone is God (ch. 44:8). **new things**–viz., the deliverance from Babylon by Cyrus, *new* in contradistinction from former predictions that had been fulfilled (ch. 42:9; 43:19). Antitypically, the prophecy has in view the "new things" of the gospel treasury (Song of Sol. 7:13; Matt. 13:52; II Cor. 5:17; Rev. 21:5). From this point forward, the prophecies as to Messiah's first and second advents and the restoration of Israel, have a *new* circumstantial distinctness, such as did not characterize the previous ones, even of Isaiah. Babylon. in this view, answers to the mystical Babylon of Revelation. **hidden**–which could not have been guessed by political sagacity (Dan. 2:22, 29; I Cor. 2:9, 10). **7.** Not like natural results from existing causes, the events when they took place were like acts of *creative* power, such as had never before been "from the beginning." **even before the day when**–rather [MAURER], "And before the day (of their occurrence) thou hast not heard of them"; i.e., by any human acuteness; they are only heard of by the present inspired announcement. **8. heardest not**–repeated, as also "knewest not," from last verse. **from that time** Mine anger *towards* thee. *first* thine ear did not open itself," viz., to *obey* them [ROSENMULLER]. "To open the ear" denotes obedient attention (ch. 50:5); or, "was not opened" to *receive* them; i.e., they were not *declared by Me to thee* previously, since, if thou hadst been informed of them, such is thy perversity, thou couldst not have been kept in check [MAURER]. In the former

view, the sense of the words following is, "For I knew that, if I had not foretold the destruction of Babylon so plainly that there could be no perverting of it, thou wouldst have perversely ascribed it to idols, or something else than to Me" (vs. 5). Thus they would have relapsed into idolatry, to cure them of which the Babylonian captivity was sent: so they had done (Exod. 32:4). After the return, and ever since, they have utterly forsaken idols. **wast called** –as thine appropriate appellation (ch. 9:6). **from the womb**–from the beginning of Israel's national existence (ch. 44:2). **9. refrain**–lit., "muzzle"; His wrath, after the return, was to be *restrained a while,* and then, because of their sins, let loose again (Ps. 78:38). **for thee**–i.e., *that*–omit *that*: "From the **10.** (*Note,* ch. 1:25.) **with silver**–rather, "*for* silver." I sought by affliction to purify thee, but thou wast not *as silver* obtained by melting, but as dross [GESENIUS]. Thy repentance is not complete: thou art not yet as refined silver. ROSENMULLER explains, "not as silver," not with *the intense heat* needed to melt silver (it being harder to melt than gold), i.e., not with the most extreme severity. The former view is better (ch. 1:25; 42:25; Ezek. 22:18-20, 22). **chosen**–or else [LOWTH], tried . . . proved: according to GESENIUS, lit., "to rub with the touchstone," or to cut in pieces so as to examine (Zech. 13:9; Mal. 3:3; I Peter 1:7). **11. how should my name**–MAURER, instead of "My name" from vs. 9, supplies "My glory" from the next clause; and translates, "How (shamefully) My glory has been profaned!" In *English Version* the sense is, "I will refrain (vs. 9, i.e., not utterly destroy thee), for why should I permit My name to be polluted, which it would be, if the Lord utterly destroyed His elect people" (Ezek. 20:9)? **not give my glory unto another**–If God forsook His people for ever, the heathen would attribute *their triumph over Israel to their idols;* so God's glory would be given *to another.* **12-15.** The Almighty, who has founded heaven and earth, can, and will, restore His people. **the first . . . last**–(ch. 41:4; 44:6). **13, spanned**– measured out (ch. 40:12). **when I call . . . stand up together**–(ch. 40:26; Jer. 33:25). But it is not their creation so much which is meant, as that, like *ministers* of God, the heavens and the earth are prepared at His command to *execute His decrees* (Ps. 119:91) [ROSENMULLER]. **14. among them**– among the gods and astrologers of the Chaldees (ch. 41:22; 43:9; 44:7). **Lord . . . loved him; he will . . .**–i.e., "He whom the Lord hath loved will do," etc. [LOWTH]; viz., Cyrus (ch. 44:28; 45:1, 13; 46:11). However, Jehovah's language of love is too strong to apply to Cyrus, except as type of *Messiah,* to whom alone it fully applies (Rev. 5:2-5). **his pleasure**–not Cyrus' own, but Jehovah's. **15. brought**–led him on his way. **he**–change from the first to the third person [BARNES]. *Jehovah* shall make his (Cyrus') way prosperous. **16. not . . . in secret**–(ch. 45:19). Jehovah foretold Cyrus' advent, not with the studied ambiguity of heathen oracles, but plainly. **from the time . . .**–From the moment that the purpose began to be accomplished in the raising up of Cyrus I was present. **sent me**– The prophet here speaks, claiming attention to his announcement as to Cyrus, on the ground of his mission from God and His Spirit. But he speaks not in his own person so much as in that of Messiah, to whom alone in the fullest sense the words apply (ch. 61:1; John 10:36). Plainly, ch. 49:1, which is the continuation of ch. 48 from vs. 16, where the change of speaker from God (vss. 1, 12-15) begins, is the language of Messiah. Luke 4:1, 14, 18, shows that the Spirit combined with the Father in sending the Son: therefore "His Spirit" is *nominative* to "sent," not *accusative*, following it. 17. **teacheth . . . to profit**—by affliction, such as the Babylonish captivity, and the present long-continued dispersion of Israel (Heb. 12:10). 18. **peace**—(Ps. 119:165). Cf. the desire expressed by the same Messiah (Matt. 23:37; Luke 19:42). **river**—(ch. 33: 21; 41:18), a river flowing from God's throne is the symbol of *free, abundant, and ever flowing blessings from Him* (Ezek. 47:1; Zech. 14:8; Rev. 22:1). **righteousness**—*religious prosperity*; the parent of "peace" or *national prosperity;* therefroe "peace" corresponds to "righteousness" in the parallelism (ch. 32:17). 19. **sand**—retaining the metaphor of "the sea" (vs. 18). **like the gravel thereof**—rather, as the *Hebrew*, "like that (the offspring) of its (the sea's) bowels"; referring to the countless living creatures, fishes, etc., of the sea, rather than the gravel [MAURER]. JEROME, *Chaldee*, and *Syriac* support *English Version*. **his name . . . cut off**—transition from the second person, "thy," to the third "his." Israel's name was cut off *as a nation* during the Babylonish captivity; also it is so now, to which the prophecy especially looks (Rom. 11: 20). 20. **Go . . . forth . . . end of the earth**—Primarily, a prophecy of their joyful deliverance from Babylon, and a direction that they should leave it when God opened the way. But the publication of it "to the ends of the earth" shows it has a more world-wide scope antitypically; Revelation 18:4 shows that the mystical Babylon is ultimately meant. **redeemed . . . Jacob**—(ch. 43:1; 44:22, 23). 21. Ezra, in describing the return, makes no mention of God cleaving the rock for them in the desert [KIMCHI]. The circumstances, therefore, of the deliverance from Egypt (Exod. 17:6; Num. 20:11; Ps. 78:15; 105:41) and of that from Babylon, are blended together; the language, while more immediately referring to the latter deliverance, yet, as being blended with circumstances of the former not strictly applicable to the latter, cannot *wholly* refer to either, but to the mystic deliverance of man under Messiah, and literally to the final restoration of Israel. 22. Repeated (ch. 57:21). All the blessings just mentioned (vs. 21) belong only to the godly, not to the wicked. Israel shall first cast away its wicked unbelief before it shall inherit *national prosperity* (Zech. 12:10-14; 13:1, 9; 14:3, 14, 20, 21). The sentiment holds good also as to *all* wicked men (Job 15:20-25, 31-34).

CHAPTER 49

Vss. 1-26. SIMILAR TO CHAPTER 42:1-7 (vss. 1-9). Messiah, as the ideal Israel (vs. 3), states the object of His mission, His want of success for a time, yet His certainty of ultimate success. 1. **O isles**—Messiah is here regarded as having been rejected by the Jews (vss. 4, 5), and as now turning to the Gentiles, to whom the Father hath given Him "for a light and salvation." "Isles" mean all regions *beyond sea*. **from the womb**—(ch. 44:2; Luke 1:31; John 10:36). **from . . . bowels . . . mention of my name**—His name "Jesus" (i.e., God-Saviour) was designated by God before His birth (Matt. 1:21). 2. **my mouth . . . sword**—(ch. 11:4; Rev. 19: 15). The double office of the Word of God, saving and damnatory, is implied (ch. 50:4; John 12:48; Heb. 4:12). **shaft**—(Ps. 45:5). "Polished," i.e., free from all rust, implies His unsullied purity. **in . . . quiver . . . hid me**—Like a sword in its scabbard,

or a shaft in the quiver, Messiah, before His appearing, was *hid* with God, ready to be drawn forth at the moment God saw fit [HENGSTENBERG]; also always *protected* by God, as the arrow by the quiver (ch. 51:16). 3. **Israel**—applied to Messiah, according to the true import of the name, *the Prince* who had power with *God* in wrestling in behalf of man, and who prevails (Gen. 32:28; Hos. 12:3, 4). He is also the ideal Israel, the representative man of the nation (cf. Matt. 2:15 with Hos. 11:1). **in whom . . . glorified**—John 14:13; 17:1-5). 4. **I**—Messiah. **in vain**—comparatively in the case of *the greater number* of His own countrymen. "He came unto His own, and His own received Him not" (ch. 53:1-3; Luke 19:14; John 1:11; 7:5). Only 120 disciples met after His personal ministry was ended (Acts 1:15). **yet . . . my judgment . . . with the Lord**—Ultimately, God will do justice to My cause, and *reward* (*Margin* for *work*, cf. ch. 40:10; 62:11) My labors and sufferings. He was never "discouraged" (ch. 42:4; 50:7, 10). He calmly, in spite of seeming ill success for the time, left the result with God, confident of final triumph (ch. 53: 10-12; I Peter 2:23). So the ministers of Christ (I Cor. 4:1-5; I Pet. 4:19). 5. The reason why He was confident that His work would be accepted and rewarded, viz., because He is "glorious in the eyes of Jehovah," etc. **to bring Jacob again to him**—(Matt. 15:24; Acts 3:26). **Though Israel be not gathered**—metaphor from a scattered flock which the shepherd gathers together again; or a hen and her chickens (Matt. 23:37). Instead of the text "not," the *Keri* has the similar *Hebrew* word, "to Him," which the parallelism favors: "And that Israel may be gathered *to Him*." **yet**—rather, parenthetically. "*For* I am glorious, etc., and My God is My strength." Then (vs. 6) resuming the words from the beginning of vs. 5, "He saith" (I repeat), etc. HORSLEY explains, "Notwithstanding the incredulity of the Jews, Messiah shall be glorified in the conversion of the Gentiles," reading as *English Version*: but if the *Keri* be read, "Israel shall at one time or other be gathered, notwithstanding their incredulity during Messiah's sojourn on earth." 6. **It is a light thing**—"It is too little that Thou shouldest," [HENGSTENBERG], i.e., It is not enough honor to Thee to raise up *Jacob* and *Israel*, but I design for Thee more, viz., that Thou shouldest be the means of enlightening the *Gentiles* (ch. 42:6, 7; 60: 3). **the preserved** —viz., those remaining after the judgments of God on the nation—the elect remnant of Israel reserved for mercy. LOWTH, with a slight but needless change of the *Hebrew*, translates for "tribes" and "preserved," the "scions"—the "branches." 7. **whom man despiseth**—*Hebrew*, "the despised of soul," i.e., by every soul, by all men (ch. 52:14, 15; 53:3; 50:6-9; Ps. 22:6). LOWTH translates, "whose *person* is despised." **abhorreth**—lit., who is an abomination to the nation (Luke 23:18-23). The Jews contemptuously call Him always *Tolvi*, "the crucified." I prefer, on account of *Goi*, the *Hebrew* term for *nation* being usually applied to the *Gentiles*, and that for *people* to the Jews (Hos. 1:9; so the *Greek* terms respectively also *Laos* and *Ethne*, Rom. 9:25), to take "nation" here collectively for the *Gentile* world, which also spurned Him (Ps. 2:1-3; Acts 4:25-27). **servant of rulers**—(Matt. 17:27.) He who would not exert His power against the rulers (Matt. 26:52, 53). **shall see**—viz., the fulfilment of God's promises (vss. 3, 6), *when* He shall be *a light to the Gentiles*. **arise**—to reverence Thee (Ps. 72:10, 11; Phil. 2:10). **princes also** —rather, for the parallelism, supply the ellipsis, thus,

"Princes *shall see* and shall worship." **faithful**—viz., to His promises. **choose thee**—as God's *elect* (ch. 42:1). **8.** Messiah is represented as having asked for the grace of God in behalf of sinners; this verse contains God the Father's favorable answer. **an acceptable time**—"In a time of grace" [HENGSTENBERG]. A limited time (ch. 61:2; II Cor. 6:2). The time judged by God to be the best fitted for effecting the purposes of His grace by Messiah. **heard thee**—(Ps. 2:8; Heb. 5:7). **day of salvation**—when "the fulness of time" (Gal. 4:4) shall have come. The day of salvation is "to-day" (Heb. 4:7). **helped**—given Thee the help needed to enable Thee, as man, to accomplish man's salvation. **preserve**—from the assaults and efforts of Satan, to divert Thee from Thy voluntary death to save man. **covenant of the people**—(*Note*, ch. 42:6). "The people," *in the singular*, is always applied exclusively to Israel. **establish the earth**—rather, "to restore the land," viz., Canaan to Israel. Spiritually, the restoration of *the Church* (the spiritual Israel) to the heavenly land forfeited by man's sin is also included. **cause to inherit . . . desolate heritages**—image from the desolate state of Judea during the Babylonish captivity. Spiritually, the Gentile world, a moral waste, shall become a garden of the Lord. Lit., Judea lying desolate for ages shall be possessed again by Israel (cf. ch. 61:7, "in their land"). *Jesus,* the antitype of, and bearing the same name as *Joshua* (Heb. 4:8), shall, like him, divide the land among its true heirs (ch. 54:3; 61:4). **9.** (Ch. 42:7; Zech. 9:12). **prisoners**—the Jews bound in legal bondage. **them . . . in darkness**—the Gentiles having no light as to the one true God [VITRINGA]. **Show yourselves**—not only see but be seen (Matt. 5:16; Mark 5:19). Come forth from the darkness of your prison into the light of the Sun of righteousness. **in the ways . . .**—In a desert there are no "ways," nor "high places," with "pastures"; thus the sense is: "They shall have their pastures, not in deserts, but in cultivated and inhabited places. Laying aside the figure, the churches of Christ at the first shall be gathered, not in obscure and unknown regions, but in the most populous parts of the Roman empire, Antioch, Alexandria, Rome, etc. [VITRINGA]. Another sense probably is the right one. Israel, on its way back to the Holy Land, shall not have to turn aside to devious paths in search of necessaries, but shall find them in *all places* wherever their route lies; so ROSENMULLER. God will supply them *as if* He should make the grass grow in the trodden *ways* and on the barren *high places* wherever their route lies; so ROSENMULLER. wants, both of literal Israel on their way to Palestine, and of the spiritual on their way to heaven, as their Shepherd (ch. 65:13; Matt. 5:6), also in heaven (Rev. 7:16, 17). **11. my**—All things are God's. **mountains a way**—I will remove all obstructions out of the way (ch. 40:4). **exalted**—i.e., cast up (ch. 57:14; 62:10); for instance, over valleys. VITRINGA explains "mountains" as *great kingdoms,* Egypt, Syria, etc., subjected to Rome, to facilitate the spreading of the Gospel; "highways," the *Christian doctrine* wherein those who join the Church walk, and which, at the time of Constantine, was to be raised into prominence before all, and publicly protected (ch. 35:8, 9). **12. Sinim**—The Arabians and other Asiatics called China *Sin,* or *Tchin;* the Chinese had no special name for themselves, but either adopted that of the reigning dynasty or some high-sounding titles. This view of "Sinim" suits the context which requires a people to be meant "from far," and distinct from those

"from the north and from the west" [GESENIUS]. **13.** So Revelation 12:12. God will have mercy on *the* afflicted, because of His compassion; on *His* afflicted, because of His covenant. **14. Zion**—the literal Israel's complaint, as if God had forsaken her in the Babylonian captivity; also in their dispersion previous to their future restoration; thereby God's mercy shall be called forth (ch. 63:15-19; Ps. 77:9, 10; 102:17). **15.** (Ch. 44:21; Ps. 103:13; Matt. 7:11). **16.** Alluding to the Jews' custom (perhaps drawn from Exod. 13:9) of puncturing on their hands a representation of their city and temple, in token of zeal for them [LOWTH], (Song of Sol 8:6). **17. Thy children**—Israel (vss. 20, 21; ch. 43: 6). JEROME reads, for "Thy children," "Thy builders"; they that destroyed thee shall hasten to build thee. **haste**—to rebuild thy desolate capital. **shall go forth**—Thy destroyers shall leave Judea to Israel in undisturbed possession. **18.** As Zion is often compared to a bride (ch. 54:5), so the accession of converts is like bridal ornaments ("jewels," ch. 62:3; Mal. 3:17). Her *literal* children are, however, more immediately meant, as the context refers to their restoration; and only secondarily to her *spiritual* children by conversion to Christ. Israel shall be the means of the final complete conversion of the nations (Micah 5:7; Rom. 11:12, 15). **as a bride**—viz., binds on her ornaments. **19. land of thy destruction**—thy land once the scene of destruction. **too narrow**—(Ch. 54:1, 2; Zech. 10:10.) **20. children . . . after . . . other**—rather, "the children of thy widowhood," i.e., the children of whom thou hast been bereft during their dispersion in other lands (*Note*, ch. 47:8) [MAURER]. **again**—rather, "yet." **give place**—rather, "stand close to me," viz., in order that we may be the more able to *dwell* in in the *narrow* place [HORSLEY]. Cf. as to Israel's *spiritual* children, and the extension of the gospel sphere, Romans 15:19, 24; II Corinthians 10:14-16. But vs. 22 (cf. ch. 66:20) shows that her literal children are primarily meant. GESENIUS translates. "Make room." **21. Who . . . ?**—Zion's joyful wonder at the unexpected restoration of *the ten tribes.* Secondarily, the accession of spiritual Israelites to the mother church of Jerusalem from the Gentiles is meant. This created surprise at first (Acts 10:45; 14:27; 15:3, 4). **lost . . . am desolate, a captive, and removing to and fro**—rather, "bereaved of . . . have been barren, an exile and outcast" [HORSLEY]. She had been "put away" by Jehovah, her husband (ch. 50:1); hence her wonder at the *children begotten to her.* **22. lift . . . hand**—i.e., beckon to (*Note,* ch. 13:2). **standard**—(Ch. 11:12). **bring . . . sons in . . . arms**—The Gentiles shall aid in restoring Israel to its own land (ch. 60: 4; 66:20). Children able to support themselves are carried on the shoulders in the East; but infants, in the arms, or astride on one haunch (ch. 60:12). "Thy sons" must be distinct from "the Gentiles," who *carry* them; and therefore cannot primarily refer to converts among the Gentiles. **23. lick . . . dust**—i.e., kiss thy feet in token of humble submission. **for they . . . not . . . ashamed . . . wait for me**—The restoration of Israel shall be in answer to their prayerful waiting on the Lord (ch. 30:18, 19; Ps. 102:16, 17; Zech. 12:10; 14:3). **24. the prey**—Israel, long a prey to mighty Gentile nations, whose oppression of her shall reach its highest point under Antichrist (Dan. 11:36, 37, 41, 45). **lawful captive**—the Jews justly consigned for their sins (ch. 50:1) as captives to the foe. Secondarily, Satan and Death are "the mighty" conquerors of man, upon whom his sin give them their "lawful" claim.

Christ answers that claim for the sinners, and so the captive is set free (Job 19:25; 14:14; Matt. 12:29; Hos. 6:2, where vs. 4 shows the *primary* reference is to *Israel's restoration,* to which *the resurrection* corresponds; Isa. 26:19; Eph. 4:8; Heb. 2:14, 15). Others not so well translate, "the captives taken from among the *just* Israelites." **25.** (Ch. 53:12; Ps. 68:18; Col. 2:15). **contend with him, ...** — (Ch. 54:17). **26. feed ... own flesh**–a phrase for *internal strifes* (ch. 9:20). **own blood**–a just retribution for their having shed the blood of God's servants (Rev. 16:6). **sweet wine**–i.e., must, or new wine, the pure juice which flows from the heap of grapes before they are pressed; the ancients could preserve it for a long time, so as to retain its flavor. It was so mild that it required a large quantity to intoxicate; thus the idea here is that *very much* blood would be shed (Rev. 14:10, 20). **all flesh shall ...**–the effect on the world of God's judgments (ch. 66:15, 16, 18, 19; Rev. 15:3, 4).

CHAPTER 50

Vss. 1-11. The Judgments on Israel Were Provoked by Their Crimes, yet They Are Not Finally Cast Off by God. **1. Where ... mother's divorcement**–Zion is "the mother"; the Jews are the children; and God the Husband and Father (ch. 54:5; 62:5; Jer. 3:14). Gesenius thinks that God means by the question to *deny* that He had given "a bill of divorcement" to her, as was often done on slight pretexts by a husband (Deut. 24:1), or that He had "sold" His and her "children," as a poor parent sometimes did (Exod. 21:7; II Kings 4:1; Neh. 5:5) under pressure of his "creditors"; that it was they who sold themselves through their own sins. Maurer explains, "*Show* the bill of your mother's divorcement, whom ...; produce the creditors to whom ye have been sold; so it will be seen that it was not from any caprice of Mine, but through your own fault, your mother has been put away, and you sold" (ch. 52:3). Horsley best explains (as the antithesis between "I" and "yourselves" shows, though Lowth translates, "Ye *are sold*") *I* have never given your mother a regular bill of divorcement; I have merely "put her away" for a time, and can, therefore, by right as her husband still take her back on her submission; I have not made you, the children, over to any "creditor" to satisfy a debt; I therefore still have the right of a father over you, and can take you back on repentance, though as rebellious children *you* have sold yourselves to sin and its penalty (I Kings 21:25). **bill ... whom**–rather, "the bill *with which* I have put her away" [Maurer]. **2. no man**–willing to believe in and obey Me (ch. 52:1, 3). The same Divine Person had "come" by His prophets in the Old Testament (appealing to them, but in vain, Jer. 7:25, 26), who was about to come under the New Testament. **hand shortened**–the Oriental emblem of weakness, as the long *streched-out hand* is of power (ch. 59:1). Notwithstanding your sins, I can still "redeem" you from your bondage and dispersion. **dry up ... sea**–(Exod. 14:21.) The second exodus shall exceed, while it resembles in wonders, the first (ch. 11:11, 15; 51:15). **make ... rivers ... wilderness**–turn the prosperity of Israel's foes into adversity. **fish stinketh**–the very judgment inflicted on their Egyptian enemies at the first exodus (Exod. 7:18, 21). **3. heavens ... blackness**–another of the judgments on Egypt to be repeated hereafter on the last enemy of God's people (Exod. 10:21). **sack-**

cloth–(Rev. 6:12). **4.** Messiah, as "the servant of Jehovah" (ch. 42:1), declares that the office has been assigned to Him of encouraging the "weary" exiles of Israel by "words in season" suited to their case; and that, whatever suffering it is to cost Himself, He does not shrink from it (vss. 5, 6), for that He knows His cause will triumph at last (vss. 7, 8). **learned**–not in mere human learning, but in divinely taught modes of instruction and eloquence (ch. 49:2; Exod. 4:11; Matt. 7:28, 29; 13:54). **speak a word in season**–(Prov. 15:23; 25:11.) Lit., "to succor by words," viz., in their season of need, the "weary" dispersed ones of Israel (Deut. 28:65-67). Also, the spiritual "weary" (ch. 42:3; Matt. 11:28). **wakeneth [me] morning ...**–Cf. "daily rising up early" (Jer. 7:25; Mark 1:35). The image is drawn from a master *wakening* his pupils early for instruction. **wakeneth ... ear**–prepares me for receiving His divine instructions. **as the learned**–as one taught by Him. He "learned obedience," experimentally, "by the things which He suffered"; thus gaining that practical learning which *adapted* Him for "speaking a word in season" to suffering men (Heb. 5:8). **5. opened ... ear**–(see *Note,* ch. 42:20; 48:8); i.e., hath made me *obediently attentive* (but Maurer, "hath *informed me of my duty*"), as a *servant* to his master (cf. Ps. 40:6-8, with Phil. 2:7; ch. 42:1; 49:3, 6; 52:13; 53:11; Matt. 20:28; Luke 22:27). **not rebellious**–but, on the contrary, most willing to do the Father's will in proclaiming and procuring salvation for man, at the cost of His own sufferings (Heb. 10:5-10). **6. smiters**–with scourges and with the open hand (ch. 52:14; Mark 14:65). Literally fulfilled (Matt. 27:26; 26:27; Luke 18:33). To "pluck the hair" is the highest insult that can be offered an Oriental (II Samuel 10:4; Lam. 3:30). "I gave" implies the voluntary nature of His sufferings; His example corresponds to His precept (Matt. 5:39). **spitting**–To spit in another's presence is an insult in the East, much more on one; most of all in the face (Job 30:10; Matt. 27:30; Luke 18:32). **7.** Sample of His not being "discouraged" (ch. 42:4; 49:5). **set ... face like ... flint**–set Myself resolutely, not to be daunted from My work of love by shame or suffering (Ezek. 3:8, 9). **8.** (Ch. 49:4.) The believer, by virtue of his oneness with Christ, uses the same language (Ps. 138:8; Rom. 8:32-34). But "justify" in *His* case, is God's judicial acceptance and vindication of Him on the ground of *His own* righteousness (Luke 23:44-47; Rom. 1:4; I Tim. 3:16, with which cf. I Pet. 3:18); in *their* case, on the ground of His righteousness and meritorious death *imputed* to them (Rom. 5:19). **stand together**–in judgment, to try the issue. **adversary**–lit., "master of my cause," i.e., who has real ground of accusation against me, so that he can demand judgment to be given in his favor (cf. Zech. 3:1, etc.; Rev. 12:10). **9.** (Cf. ch. 52:13, *Margin*; ch. 53:10; Ps. 118:6; Jer. 23:5). **as a garment**–(Ch. 51:6, 8; Ps. 102:26.) A leading constituent of wealth in the East is change of raiment, which is always liable to the inroads of the moth; hence the frequency of the image in Scripture. **10.** Messiah exhorts the godly after His example (ch. 49:4, 5; 42:4) when in circumstances of trial ("darkness," ch. 47:5), to trust in the arm of Jehovah alone. **Who is ...**–i.e., Whosoever (Judg. 7:3). **obeyeth ... servant**–viz., Messiah. The godly "honor the Son, even as they honor the Father" (John 5:23). **darkness**–(Mic. 7:8, 9.) God never had a son who was not sometimes in the dark. For even Christ, His only Son, cried out, "My God, My God, why hast Thou forsaken Me?" **light**–rather, splendor; bright sunshine; for the servant of God is never wholly without "light" [VITRINGA]. A godly man's way may be dark, but his end shall be peace and light. A wicked man's way may be bright, but his end shall be utter darkness (Ps. 112:4; 97:11; 37:24). **let him trust . . .**—as Messiah did (vss. 8, 9). **11.** In contrast to the godly (vs. 10), the wicked, in times of darkness, instead of trusting in God, trust in themselves (*kindle a light* for themselves to walk by) (Eccles. 11:9). The image is continued from vs. 10, "darkness"; human devices for salvation (ch. 19:21; 16:9, 25) are like the spark that goes out in an instant in darkness (cf. Job 18:6; 21:17, with Ps. 18:28). **sparks**—not a steady light, but blazing sparks extinguished in a moment. **walk**—not a command, but implying that *as surely as they would do so,* they should lie down in sorrow (Jer. 3:25). In exact proportion to mystic Babylon's previous "glorifying" of herself shall be her sorrow (Matt. 25:30; 8:12; Rev. 18:7).

CHAPTER 51

Vss. 1-23. ENCOURAGEMENT TO THE FAITHFUL REMNANT OF ISRAEL TO TRUST IN GOD FOR DELIVERANCE, BOTH FROM THEIR LONG BABYLONIAN EXILE, AND FROM THEIR PRESENT DISPERSION. **1. me**—the God of your fathers. **ye . . . follow after righteousness**—the godly portion of the nation; vs. 7 shows this (Prov. 15:9; I Tim. 6:11). "Ye follow righteousness," seek it therefore from Me, who "bring it near," and that a righteousness "not about to be abolished" (vss. 6, 7); look to Abraham, your father (vs. 2), as a sample of how righteousness before Me is to be obtained; I, the same God who blessed him, will bless you at last (vs. 3); therefore trust in Me, and fear not man's opposition (vss. 7, 8, 12, 13). The mistake of the Jews, heretofore, has been, not in that they "followed after righteousness," but in that they followed it "by the works of the law," instead of "by faith," as Abraham did (Rom. 9:31, 32; 10:3, 4; 4:2-5). **hole of . . . pit**—The idea is not, as it is often quoted, the inculcation of humility, by reminding men of the fallen state from which they have been taken, but that as Abraham, the *quarry,* as it were (cf. ch. 48:1), whence their nation was hewn, had been called out of a strange land to the inheritance of Canaan, and blessed by God, the same God is able to deliver and restore them also (cf. Matt. 3:9). **2. alone**—translate, "I called him when he was but one" (Ezek. 33:24). The argument is: the same God who had so blessed "one" individual, as to become a mighty nation (Gen. 12:1; 22:7), can also increase and bless the small remnant of Israel, both that left in the Babylonish captivity, and that left in the present and latter days (Zech. 14:2; "the residue" (ch. 13:8, 9). **3. For**—See for the argument, last *Note.* **the garden of the Lord**—restoration of the primeval paradise (Gen. 2:8; Ezek. 28:13; Rev. 2:7). **melody**—*Hebrew,* "psalm." God's praises shall again be heard. **4. my people**—the Jews. This reading is better than that of GESENIUS: "O peoples . . . nations," viz., the Gentiles. The Jews are called on to hear and rejoice in the extension of the true religion to the nations; for, at the first preaching of the Gospel, as in the final age to come, it was *from Jerusalem* that the gospel law was, and is, to go forth (ch. 2:3). **law . . . judgment**—the gospel dispensation and institutions (ch. 42:1, "judgment"). **make . . . to rest**—establish firmly; found. **light . . .**—(Ch. 42:6). **5. righteousness . . . near**—i.e., faithful fulfilment of the promised deliverance, answering to "salvation" in

the parallel clause (ch. 46:13; 56:1; Rom. 10:8, 9). Ye follow after "righteousness"; seek it therefore, from Me, and you will not have far to go for it (vs. 1). **arms**—put for Himself; *I by My might.* **judge**—(Ch. 2:3, 4; Ps. 98:9.) **isles . . .**—(Ch. 60:9.) **arm**—(Rom. 1:16), "the power of God unto (the Gentiles as well as the Jews) salvation." **6.** (Ch. 40:6, 8; Ps. 102:26; Heb. 1:11, 12.) **vanish away**—lit., "shall be torn asunder," as a *garment* [MAURER]; which accords with the context. **in like manner**—But GESENIUS, "Like a gnat"; like the smallest and vilest insect. JEROME translates, as *English Version,* and infers that "in like manner" as man, the heavens (i.e., the sky) and earth are not to be annihilated, but changed for the better (ch. 65:17). **righteousness**—My faithfully fulfilled promise (*Note,* vs. 5). **7. know righteousness**—(*Note,* vs. 1). **8.** (*Note,* ch. 50:9; Job 4:18-20.) Not that the *moth eats men up,* but they shall be destroyed by as insignificant instrumentality as the moth that eats a garment. **9.** Impassioned prayer of the exiled Jews. **ancient days**—(Ps. 44:1). **Rahab**—poetical name for Egypt (*Note,* ch. 30:7). **dragon**—*Hebrew, tannin.* The crocodile, an emblem of Egypt, as represented on coins struck after the conquest of Egypt by Augustus; or rather here, its king, Pharaoh (*Note,* ch. 27:1; Ps. 74:13, 14; Ezek. 32:2, *Margin;* 29:3). **10. it**—the arm. Art not Thou the same Almighty power that . . . ? **dried the sea**—the Red Sea (ch. 43:16; Exod. 14:21). **11.** (Ch. 35:10.) **Therefore**—assurance of faith; or else the answer of Jehovah corresponding to their prayer. As surely as God redeemed Israel out of Egypt, He shall redeem them from Babylon, both the literal in the age following, and mystical in the last ages (Rev. 18:20, 21). There shall be a second exodus (ch. 11:11-16; 27:12, 13). **singing**—image from the custom of singing on a journey when a caravan is passing along the extended plains in the East. **everlasting joy**—(Jude 24.) **sorrow . . . flee away**—(Rev. 21:4.) **12. comforteth**—(vs. 3; ch. 40:1.) **thou**—Zion. **son of man**—frail and dying as his *parent Adam.* **be made as grass**—wither as grass (ch. 40:6, 7). **13.** (Ch. 40:12, 26, 28), the same argument of comfort drawn from the omnipotence of the Creator. **as if . . . ready . . .**—lit., "when he directs," viz., his arrow, to destroy (Ps. 21:12; 7:13; 11:2) [MAURER]. **14. captive exile**—lit., one *bowed down* as a captive (ch. 10:4) [MAURER]. The scene is primarily Babylon, and the time near the close of the captivity. Secondarily, and antitypically, the mystical Babylon, the last enemy of Israel and the Church, in which they have long suffered, but from which they are to be gloriously delivered. **pit**—such as were many of the ancient dungeons (cf. Jer. 38:6, 11, 13; Gen. 37:20). **nor . . . bread . . . fail**—(Ch. 33:16; Jer. 37:21.) **15. divided . . . sea**—the Red Sea. The same *Hebrew* word as "make to rest" (vs. 4). Rather, "that terrify the sea," i.e., restrain it by My rebuke, "when its waves roar" [GESENIUS]. The *Hebrew* favors MAURER, "that terrify the sea so that the waves roar." The sense favors GESENIUS (Jer. 5:22; 31:35), or *English Version* (vss. 9, 10), which favors the special reference to the exodus from Egypt). **16.** Addressed to Israel, embodied in "the servant of Jehovah" (ch. 42:1), Messiah, its ideal and representative Head, through whom the elect remnant is to be restored. **put my words in thy mouth**—true of Israel, the depository of true religion, but fully realized only in Israel's Head and antitype, Messiah (ch. 49:2; 50:4, 5; 59:21; Deut. 18:18; John 3:34). **covered . . . in . . . shadow of . . . hand**—protected thee (*Note,* ch. 49:2). **plant**—rather, "fix" as a tabernacle; so it ought to be rendered (Dan. 11:45). The "new creation," now going on in the spiritual world by the Gospel (Eph. 2:10), and hereafter to be extended to the visible world, is meant (ch. 65:17; 66:22; cf. ch. 13:13; II Pet. 3:10-13). **Zion**—Its restoration is a leading part in the new creation to come (ch. 65:17, 19). **17.** (Ch. 52:1.) **drunk**—Jehovah's wrath is compared to an intoxicating draught because it confounds the sufferer under it, and makes him fall (Job 21:20; Ps. 60:3; 75:8; Jer. 25:15, 16; 49:12; Zech. 12:2; Rev. 14:10); ("poured out without mixture"; rather, the pure wine juice mixed with intoxicating drugs). **of trembling**—which produced trembling or intoxication. **wrung . . . out**—drained the last drop out; the dregs were the sediments from various substances, as honey, dates, and drugs, put into the wine to increase the strength and sweetness. **18.** Following up the image in vs. 17, intoxicated and confused by the cup of God's anger, she has none to guide her in her helpless state; she has not yet awakened out of the sleep caused by that draught. This cannot apply to the Babylonish captivity; for in it they had Ezekiel and Daniel, Ezra and Nehemiah, as "guides," and soon awoke out of that sleep; but it applies to the Jews now, and will be still more applicable in their coming oppression by Antichrist. **19. two**—classes of evils, for he enumerates *four*, viz., *desolation* and *destruction* to the land and state; *famine* and *the sword* to the people. **who shall be sorry for thee**—so as to give thee effectual relief: as the parallel clause, "By whom shall I comfort thee?" shows (Lam. 2:11-13). **20. head of all . . . streets**—(Lam. 2:19; 4:1). **wild bull**—rather, *oryx* [JEROME], or gazelle [GESENIUS], or wild goat [BOCHART]; commonly in the East taken in a net, of a wide sweep, into which the beasts were hunted together. The streets of cities in the East often have gates, which are closed at night; a person wishing to escape would be stopped by them and caught, as a wild animal in a net. **21. drunken . . . not with wine**—(ch. 29:9; cf. vss. 17, 20, here; Lam. 3:15). **22. pleadeth . . . cause**—(Ps. 35:1; Jer. 50:34; Mic. 7:9). **no more drink it**—(ch. 54:7-9).This cannot apply to Israel after the return from Babylon, but only to them after their final restoration. **23.** (Ch. 49:26; Jer. 25:15-29; Zech. 12:2.) **Bow down that . . . go over** —Conquerors often literally trod on the necks of conquered kings, as Sapor of Persia did to the Roman emperor Valerian (Josh. 10:24; Ps. 18:40; 66: 11, 12).

CHAPTER 52

Vss. 1-15. VERSES 1-13 CONNECTED WITH CHAPTER 51. Zion long in bondage (ch. 51:17-20) is called to put on beautiful garments appropriate to its future prosperity. **1. strength**—as thy adornment; answering to "beautiful garments" in the parallel clause. Arouse thyself from dejection and assume confidence. **the holy city**—(Neh. 11:1; Rev. 21:2.) **no more . . . unclean**—(ch. 35:8; 60:21; Joel 3:17; Rev. 21:27). A prophecy never yet fulfilled. **uncircumcised**—spiritually (Ezek. 44:9; Acts 7:51). **2. from the dust**—the seat of mourners (Job 2:12, 13). **arise, and sit**—viz., in a more dignified place: on a divan or a throne [LOWTH], after having shaken off the dust gathered up by the flowing dress when seated on the ground; or simply, "Arise, and sit erect" [MAURER]. **bands of . . . neck**—the yoke of thy captivity. **3.** As you became your foes' servants, without their paying any price for you (Jer. 15:13), so they shall release you without demanding

any price or reward (ch. 45:13), (where Cyrus is represented as doing so: a type of their final restoration gratuitously in like manner). So the spiritual Israel, "sold under sin," gratuitously (Rom. 7:14), shall be redeemed also gratuitously (ch. 55:1). **4. My people**—Jacob and his sons. **went down**—Judea was an elevated country compared with Egypt. **sojourn**—They went there to stay only till the famine in Canaan should have ceased. **Assyrian**—Sennacherib. Remember how I delivered you from Egypt and the Assyrian; what, then, is to prevent Me from delivering you out of Babylon (and the mystical Babylon and the Antichrist in the last days)? **without cause**—answering to "for naught" in vs. 5; it was an act of *gratuitous* oppression in the present case, as in that case. **5. what have I here**—i.e., what am I called on to do? The fact "that My people is taken away (into captivity; ch. 49:24, 25) for naught" (by *gratuitous* oppression, vs. 4; also vs. 3, where see *Note*) demands My interposition. **they that rule**—or "tyrannize", viz., Babylon, literal and mystical. **make . . . to howl**—or, raise a cry of exultation over them [MAURER]. **blasphemed**—viz., in Babylon: God's reason for delivering His people, not their goodness, but for the sake of His holy name (Ezek. 20:9, 14). **6. shall know in that day**—when Christ shall reveal Himself to Israel sensibly; the only means whereby their obstinate unbelief shall be overcome (Ps. 102:16; Zech. 12:10; 14:5). **7. beautiful . . . feet**—i.e., The *advent* of such a herald seen on the distant "mountains" (*Notes*, ch. 40:9; 41:27; 25:6, 7; Song of Sol. 2:17) *running in haste* with the long-expected good tidings, is most grateful to the desolated city (Nah. 1:15). **good tidings**—only partially applying to the return from Babylon. Fully, and antitypically, the Gospel (Luke 2:10, 11), "beginning at Jerusalem" (Luke 24:17), "the city of the great King" (Matt. 5:35), where Messiah shall, at the final restoration of Israel, "reign" as peculiarly Zion's God ("*Thy* God reigneth"; cf. Ps. 2:6). **8. watchmen**—set on towers separated by intervals to give the earliest notice of the approach of any messenger with tidings (cf. ch. 21:6-8). The *Hebrew* is more forcible than *English Version*, "The voice of thy watchmen" (exclamatory as in Song of Sol. 2:8). "They lift up their voice! together they sing." **eye to eye**—i.e., close at hand, and so clearly [GESENIUS]; Numbers 14:14, "face to face"; Numbers 12:8, "mouth to mouth." Cf. I Corinthians 13:12; Revelation 22:4, of which Simeon's sight of the Saviour was a prefiguration (Luke 2:30). The watchmen, spiritually, are ministers and others who pray for the peace of Jerusalem (ch. 62:6, 7), **bring again**—i.e., restore. Or else, "return to" [MAURER]. **9.** (Ch. 14:7, 8; 42:11.) **redeemed**—spiritually and nationally (ch. 48:20). **10. made bare . . . arm**—metaphor from warriors who bare their arm for battle (Ezek. 4:7). **all . . . earth . . . see . . . salvation of . . . God**—The deliverance wrought by God for Israel will cause all nations to acknowledge the Lord (ch. 66:18-20). The partial fulfilment (Luke 3:6) is a forerunner of the future complete fulfilment. **11.** (Ch. 48:20; Zech. 2:6, 7.) Long residence in Babylon made many loath to leave it: so as to mystical Babylon (Rev. 18:4). **ye . . . that bear . . . vessels of the Lord**—the priests and Levites, whose office it was to carry the vessels of the temple (Jer. 27:18). Nebuchadnezzar had carried them to Babylon (II Chron. 36:18). Cyrus restored them (Ezra 1:7-11). **be . . . clean**—by separating yourselves wholly from Babylonian idolaters, mystical and literal. **12. not . . . with haste**—as when ye left Egypt (Exod. 12:33, 39; Deut. 16:3; cf. *Note*, ch. 28:16). Ye shall have time to cleanse yourselves and make deliberate preparation for departure. **Lord**—Jehovah, as your Leader in front (ch. 40:3; Exod. 23:20; Mic. 2:13). **rereward**—lit., "gather up," i.e., to bring up the rear of your host. The transition is frequent from the glory of Messiah in His advent to reign, to His humiliation in His advent to suffer. Indeed, so are both advents accounted one, that He is not said, in His second coming, to be about to *return*, but to *come*. **13.** Here ch. 53 ought to begin, and ch. 52 end with vs. 12. This section, from here to end of ch. 53 settles the controversy with the Jews, if Messiah be the person meant; and with infidels, if written by Isaiah, or at any time before Christ. The correspondence with the life and death of Jesus Christ is so minute, that it could not have resulted from conjecture or accident. An impostor could not have shaped *the course of events* so as to have made his character and life appear to be a fulfilment of it. The writing is, moreover, *declaredly prophetic*. The quotations of it in the New Testament show: (1) that it was, before the time of Jesus, a recognized part of the Old Testament; (2) that it refers to Messiah (Matt. 8:17; Mark 15:28; Luke 22: 37; John 12:38; Acts 8:28-35; Rom. 10:16; I Peter 2:21-25). The indirect allusions to it still more clearly prove the Messianic interpretation; so universal was that interpretation, that it is simply *referred to* in connection with the atoning virtue of His death, without being formally quoted (Mark 9:12; Rom. 4:25; I Cor. 15:3; II Cor. 5:21; I Pet. 1:19; 2: 21-25; I John 3:5). The genuineness of the passage is certain; for the Jews *would* not have forged it, since it is opposed to *their* notion of Messiah, as a triumphant temporal prince. The Christians *could* not have forged it; for the Jews, the enemies of Christianity, are "our librarians" [PALEY]. The Jews try to evade its force by the figment of two Messiahs, one a suffering Messiah (Ben Joseph), the other a triumphant Messiah (Ben David). HILLEL maintained that Messiah has already come in the person of Hezekiah. BUXTORF states that many of the modern Rabbins believe that He has been come a good while, but will not manifest Himself because of the sins of the Jews. But the ancient Jews, as the Chaldee paraphrast, Jonathan, refer it to Messiah; so the *Medrasch Tauchuma* (a commentary on the Pentateuch); also Rabbi Moses Haddarschan (see HENG-STENBERG, *Christol.*). Some explain it of *the Jewish people*, either in the Babylonish exile, or in their present sufferings and dispersion. Others, the *pious portion* of the nation taken collectively, whose sufferings made a vicarious satisfaction for the ungodly. Others, Isaiah, or Jeremiah [GESENIUS], *prophets collectively*. But an *individual* is plainly described: he suffers *voluntarily, innocently,* patiently, and as the efficient cause of the righteousness of His people, which holds good of none other but Messiah (ch. 53:4-6, 9, 11; contrast Jeremiah 20:7; 15: 10-21; Psalm 137:8, 9). Ch. 53:9 can hold good of none other. The objection that the sufferings (ch. 53:1-10) referred to are represented as *past*, the glorification alone as future (ch. 52:13-15; 53:11, 12) arises from not seeing that the prophet takes his stand *in the midst* of the scenes which he describes as future. The greater nearness of the first advent, and the interval between it and the second, are implied by the use of the *past tense* as to the first, the *future* as to the second. **Behold**—awakening attention to the striking picture of Messiah that follows (cf. John 19:5, 14). **my servant**—Messiah (ch. 42:1). **deal prudently**—rather, "prosper" [GESE-NIUS] as the parallel clause favors (ch. 53:10). Or,

uniting both meanings, "shall reign well" [HENG-STENBERG]. This verse sets forth in the beginning the ultimate issue of His sufferings, the description of which follows: the conclusion (ch. 53:12) corresponds; the section (ch. 52:13; 53:12) begins as it ends with His final glory. **extolled**—elevated (Mark 16:19; Eph. 1:20-22; I Pet. 3:22). **14, 15.** Summary of Messiah's history, which is set forth more in detail in ch. 53. "Just as many were astonished (accompanied with *aversion,* Jer. 18:16; 19:8), etc.; his visage, etc.; so shall He sprinkle," etc.; Israel in this answers to its antitype Messiah, now "an *astonishment* and byword" (Deut. 28:37), hereafter about to be a blessing and means of salvation to many nations (ch. 2:2, 3; Mic. 5:7). **thee; his**—Such changes of persons are common in *Hebrew* poetry. **marred** —Hebrew, "disfigurement"; abstract for concrete; not only disfigured, but *disfigurement itself.* **more than man**—CASTELIO translates, "so that it was no longer that of a man" (cf. Ps. 22:6). The more perfect we may suppose the "body prepared" (Heb. 10:5) for Him by God, the sadder by contrast was the "marring" of His visage and form. **15. sprinkle many**—GESENIUS, for the antithesis to "be astonished," translates, "shall cause . . . to exult." But the word universally in the Old Testament means either *to sprinkle with blood,* as the high priest makes an expiation (Lev. 4:6; 16:18, 19); or *with water,* to purify (Ezek. 36:25; cf. as to the Spirit, Acts 2:33), both appropriate to Messiah (John 13:8; Heb. 9:13, 14; 10:22; 12:24; I Pet. 1:2). The antithesis is sufficient without any forced rendering. *Many* were astonished; so *many* (not merely men, but) *nations* shall be sprinkled. They were amazed at such an *abject person claiming to be Messiah*; yet it is He who shall *justify and purify.* Men were *dumb with the amazement of scorn* at one marred more than the lowest of men, yet the *highest*: even *kings* (ch. 49:7, 23) shall be *dumb with awe and veneration* ("shut . . . mouths"; Job 29:9, 10; Mic. 7: 16). **that . . . not . . . told them**—the reason why kings shall so venerate them; the wonders of redemption, which had not been before told them, shall then be announced to them, wonders such as they had never heard or seen parallelled (ch. 55:1; Rom. 15: 21; 16:25, 26).

CHAPTER 53

Vss. 1-12. MAN'S UNBELIEF: MESSIAH'S VICARIOUS SUFFERINGS, AND FINAL TRIUMPH FOR MAN. The speaker, according to HORSLEY, personates the repenting Jews in the latter ages of the world coming over to the faith of the Redeemer; the whole is their penitent confession. This view suits the context (ch. 52:7-9), which is not to be fully realized until Israel is restored. However, primarily, it is the abrupt exclamation of the prophet: "Who hath believed our report," that of Isaiah and the other prophets, as to Messiah? The infidel's objection from the unbelief of the Jews is anticipated and hereby answered: that unbelief and the cause of it (Messiah's humiliation, whereas *they* looked for One coming to reign) were foreseen and foretold. **1. report**—lit., "the thing heard," referring to which sense Paul says, "So, then, faith cometh by *hearing*" (Rom. 10:16, 17). **arm**—power (ch. 40:10; exercised in miracles and in saving men (Rom. 1:16; I Cor. 1:18). The prophet, as if present during Messiah's ministry on earth, is deeply moved to see *how few believed* on Him (ch. 49:4; Mark 6:6; 9:19; Acts 1:15). *Two* reasons are given why all *ought* to have believed: (1) The "report" of the "ancient prophets." (2) "The arm of Jehovah" exhibited in Messiah while on earth. In HORSLEY'S view, this will be the penitent confession of the Jews, "How few of our nation, in Messiah's days, believed in Him!" 2. tender plant—Messiah grew silently and insensibly, as a sucker from an ancient stock, seemingly dead (viz., the house of David, then in a decayed state) (*Note,* ch. 11:1). shall grow . . . hath—rather, "grew up . . . had." before him—before Jehovah. Though unknown to the world (John 1:11), Messiah was observed *by God,* who ordered the most minute circumstances attending His growth. root—i.e., sprout from a root. form—beautiful form: sorrow had marred His once beautiful form. and when we shall see—rather, joined with the previous words, "Nor comeliness (attractiveness) *that we should look* (with delight) on Him." there is—rather, "was." The studied reticence of the New Testament as to His form, stature, color, etc., was designed to prevent our dwelling on the bodily, rather than on His moral beauty, holiness, love, etc., also a providential protest against the making and veneration of images of Him. The letter of P. LENTULUS to the emperor Tiberius, describing His person, is spurious; so also the story of His sending His portrait to Abgar, king of Edessa; and the alleged impression of His countenance on the handkerchief of Veronica. The former part of this verse refers to His birth and childhood; the latter to His first public appearance [VITRINGA]. 3. rejected—"*forsaken* of men" [GESENIUS]. "Most abject of men." Lit., "He who *ceases* from men," i.e., is no longer regarded as a man [HENGSTENBERG]. (*Note,* ch. 52:14; 49:7.) man of sorrows—i.e., whose distinguishing characteristic was sorrows. acquainted with—familiar by constant contact with. grief—lit., "disease"; fig. for all kinds of *calamity* (Jer. 6:14); *leprosy* especially represented this, being a direct judgment from God. It is remarkable Jesus is not mentioned as having ever suffered under sickness. and we hid . . . faces—rather, *as one* who *causes* men *to hide* their faces from Him (in aversion) [MAURER]. Or, "He was as an hiding of the face before it," i.e., as a thing before which a man covers his face in disgust [HENGSTENBERG]. Or, "as one before whom is the covering of the face"; before whom one covers the face in disgust [GESENIUS]. we—the prophet identifying himself with the Jews. See HORSLEY'S view (*Note,* vs. 1). esteemed . . . not—*negative* contempt; the previous words express *positive.* 4. Surely . . . our griefs—lit., *"But yet* He hath *taken* (or *borne*) our *sicknesses,"* i.e., they who despised Him because of His human infirmities ought rather to have esteemed Him on account of them; for thereby "Himself took OUR *infirmities"* (bodily diseases). So Matthew 8:17 quotes it. In the *Hebrew* for "borne," or *took,* there is probably the double notion, He *took on Himself* vicariously (so vss. 5, 6, 8, 12), and so He *took away;* His perfect humanity whereby He was bodily afflicted *for us,* and *in all our afflictions* (ch. 63:9; Heb. 4:15) was the ground on which He cured the sick; so that Matthew's quotation is not a mere *accommodation.* See *Note* 42 of Archbishop MAGEE, *Atonement.* The *Hebrew* there may mean to *overwhelm with darkness;* Messiah's time of darkness was temporary (Matt. 27:45), answering to the *bruising of His heel;* Satan's is to be eternal, answering to the *bruising of his head* (cf. ch. 50:10). carried . . . sorrows—The notion of *substitution* strictly. "Carried," viz., as a burden. "Sorrows," i.e., pains of the *mind;* as "griefs" refer to pains of the *body* (Ps. 32:10; 38:17). Matthew 8:17 might seem to oppose this: "And bare our *sicknesses."* But he

uses "sicknesses" figuratively for *sins,* the cause of them. Christ took on Himself all man's "infirmities," so as to remove them; the bodily by direct miracle, grounded on His participation in human infirmities; those of the soul by His vicarious suffering, which did away with the *source* of both. Sin and sickness are ethically connected as cause and effect (ch. 33:24; Ps. 103:3; Matt. 9:2; John 5:14; Jas. 5:15). we did esteem him stricken—judicially [LOWTH], viz., for *His* sins; whereas it was for *ours.* "We thought Him to be a leper" [JEROME, VULGATE], leprosy being the direct divine judgment for guilt (Lev. 13; Num. 12:10, 15; II Chron. 26:18-21). smitten—by divine judgments. afflicted—for His sins; this was the point in which they so erred (Luke 23:34; Acts 3:17; I Cor. 2:8). He was, it is true, "afflicted," but not for *His* sins. 5. wounded—a bodily wound; not mere mental sorrow; lit., "pierced"; minutely appropriate to Messiah, whose hands, feet, and side were pierced (Ps. 22:16). *Margin,* wrongly, from a *Hebrew* root, translates, "tormented." for . . . for—(Rom. 4:25; II Cor. 5:21; Heb. 9:28; I Pet. 2:24; 3:18)—*the cause for which* He suffered not His own, but *our* sins. bruised—crushing inward and outward suffering (*Note,* vs. 10). chastisement—lit., the correction inflicted by a *parent on children* for their good (Heb. 12:5-8, 10, 11). Not *punishment* strictly; for this can have place only where there is guilt, which He had not; but He took *on Himself the chastisement whereby the peace* (reconciliation with our Father; Rom. 5:1; Eph. 2:14, 15, 17) *of the children of God was to be effected* (Heb. 2:14). upon him—as a burden; parallel to "hath borne" and "carried." stripes—minutely prophetical of His being *scourged* (Matt. 27: 26; I Pet. 2:24). healed—spiritually (Ps. 41:4; Jer. 8:22). 6. Penitent confession of believers and of Israel in the last days (Zech. 12:10). sheep . . . astray—(Ps. 119:176; I Pet. 2:25). The antithesis is, "In ourselves we were scattered; in Christ we are collected together; by nature we wander, driven headlong to destruction; in Christ we find the way to the gate of life" [CALVIN]. True, also, literally of Israel before its coming restoration (Ezek. 34:5, 6; Zech. 10:2, 6; cf. with Ezek. 34:23, 24; Jer. 23:4, 5; also Matt. 9:36). laid—"*hath made to light* on Him" [LOWTH]. Rather, "hath made to rush upon Him" [MAURER]. the iniquity—i.e., its *penalty;* or rather, as in II Corinthians 5:21; He was not merely a *sin offering* (which would destroy the antithesis to "righteousness"), but, "sin for us"; sin itself vicariously; the representative of *the aggregate sin* of all mankind; not *sins* in the *plural,* for the "sin" of the world is *one* (Rom. 5:16, 17); thus we are made not merely *righteous,* but *righteousness,* even "the righteousness *of God."* The innocent was punished *as if* guilty, that the guilty might be rewarded *as if* innocent. This verse could be said of no mere *martyr.* 7. oppressed—LOWTH translates, "It was *exacted,* and He was made answerable." The verb means, "to have payment of a debt sternly exacted" (Deut. 15:2, 3), and so *to be oppressed* in general; the *exaction* of the full penalty for our sins in His sufferings is probably alluded to. and . . . afflicted—or, *and yet He suffered,* or bore Himself patiently, etc. [HENGSTENBERG and MAURER]. LOWTH'S translation, "He was made answerable," is hardly admitted by the *Hebrew.* opened not . . . mouth—Jeremiah 11:19; and David in Psalms 38:13, 14; 39: 9, prefiguring Messiah (Matt. 26:63; 27:12, 14; I Pet. 2:23). 8. Rather, "He was taken away (i.e., cut off) by oppression and by a judicial sentence"; a hendiadys for, "by an oppressive judicial sentence"

[LOWTH and HENGSTENBERG]. GESENIUS not so well, "He was delivered from oppression and punishment" only by death. *English Version* also translates, "from . . . from," not "by . . . by." But "prison" is not true of Jesus, who was not *incarcerated;* restraint and *bonds* (John 18:24) more accord with the *Hebrew.* Acts 8:33; translate as LXX: "In His humiliation His judgment (legal trial) was taken away"; the virtual sense of the *Hebrew* as rendered by LOWTH and sanctioned by the inspired writer of Acts; He was treated as one so mean that a fair trial was denied Him (Matt. 26:59; Mark 14:55-59). HORSLEY translates, "After condemnation and judgment He was *accepted.*" **who . . . declare . . . generation**—who can set forth (the wickedness of) His generation? i.e., of His contemporaries [ALFORD on Acts 8:33], which suits best the parallelism, "the wickedness of His generation" corresponding to "oppressive judgment." But LUTHER, "His length of life," i.e., there shall be *no end of His future days* (vs. 10; Rom. 6:9). CALVIN includes *the days of His Church,* which is inseparable from Himself. HENGSTENBERG, "His posterity." He, indeed, shall be cut off, but His *race* shall be so numerous that none can fully declare it. CHRYSOSTOM, etc., "His eternal sonship and miraculous incarnation." **cut off**—implying a *violent death* (Dan. 9:26). **my people**—Isaiah, including himself among them by the word "my" [HENGSTENBERG]. Rather, JEHOVAH speaks in the person of His prophet, "*My* people," by the election of grace (Heb. 2:13). **was he stricken**—*Hebrew,* "the stroke (was laid) upon Him." GESENIUS says the *Hebrew* means "them"; the collective body, whether of the prophets or people, to which the Jews refer the whole prophecy. But JEROME, the SYRIAC, and ETHIOPIAC versions translate it "Him"; so it is *singular* in some passages; Psalm 11:7, *His*; Job 27:23, *Him*; Isaiah 44:15, *thereto.* The LXX, the *Hebrew, lamo,* "upon Him," read the similar words, *lamuth,* "unto death," which would at once set aside the Jewish interpretation, "upon *them.*" ORIGEN, who laboriously compared the *Hebrew* with the LXX, so read it, and urged it against the Jews of his day, who would have denied it to be the true reading if the word had not then really so stood in the *Hebrew* text [LOWTH]. If his sole authority be thought insufficient, perhaps *lamo* may imply that Messiah was the *representative of the collective body of all men;* hence the equivocal *plural-singular* form. **9.** Rather, "His grave was appointed," or "they appointed Him His grave" [HENGSTENBERG]; i.e., they *intended* (by crucifying Him with two thieves, Matt. 27:38) that He should have His grave "with the wicked." Cf. John 19:31, the denial of honorable burial being accounted a great ignominy (*Note,* ch. 14:19; Jer. 26:23). **and with . . . rich**—rather, "*but He was* with a rich man," etc. GESENIUS, for the parallelism to "the wicked," translates "ungodly" (the effect of *riches* being to make one ungodly); but the *Hebrew* everywhere means "rich," never by itself ungodly; the parallelism, too, is one of contrast; viz., between their *design* and the *fact,* as it was ordered by God (Matt. 27: 57; Mark 15:43-46; John 19:39, 40); two rich men honored Him at His death, Joseph of Arimathea, and Nicodemus. **in his death**—*Hebrew,* "deaths." LOWTH translates, "His tomb"; *bamoth,* from a different root, meaning "high places," and so mounds for sepulture (Ezek. 43:7). But all the versions oppose this, and the *Hebrew* hardly admits it. Rather translate, "*after* His death" [HENGSTENBERG]; as we say, "*at* His death." The *plural,* "deaths," intensifies the force; as Adam by sin "dying died" (Gen. 2:17, *Margin*); i.e., incurred death, physical and spiritual. So Messiah, His substitute, endured death in both senses; spiritual, during His temporary abandonment by the Father; physical, when He gave up the ghost. **because**—rather, as the sense demands (so in Job 16: 17), "*although* He had done no . . . " [HENGSTENBERG], (I Pet. 2:20-22; I John 8:5). **violence**—i.e., wrong. **10.** Transition from His humiliation to His exaltation. **pleased the Lord**—the secret of His sufferings. They were voluntarily borne by Messiah, in order that thereby He might "*do Jehovah's will*" (John 6:38; Heb. 10:7, 9), as to man's redemption; so at the end of the verse, "the *pleasure of the* LORD shall prosper in His hand." **bruise**—(see vs. 5); Genesis 3:15, was hereby fulfilled, though the *Hebrew* word for "bruise," there, is not the one used here. The word "Himself," in Matthew, implies a personal *bearing on Himself* of our maladies, spiritual and physical, which *included as a consequence* His ministration to our bodily ailments: these latter are the reverse side of sin; His bearing on Him our spiritual malady involved with it His bearing sympathetically, and healing, the outward: which is its fruits and its type. HENGSTENBERG rightly objects to MAGEE'S translation, "taken away," instead of "borne," that the parallelism to "carried" would be destroyed. Besides, the *Hebrew* word elsewhere, when connected with *sin,* means to bear it and its punishment (Ezek. 18:20). Matthew, elsewhere, also sets forth His vicarious atonement (Matt. 20: 28). **when thou . . .**—rather, as *Margin,* "when His soul (i.e., He) shall have made an offering . . . ." In *English Version* the change of person is harsh: from Jehovah, addressed in the second person (vs. 10), to Jehovah speaking in the first person in vs. 11. *Margin* rightly makes the prophet in the name of Jehovah Himself to speak in this verse. **offering for sin** —(Rom. 3:25; I John 2:2; 4:10.) **his seed**—His spiritual posterity shall be numerous (Ps. 22:30); nay, more, though He must die, He shall *see* them. A numerous posterity was accounted a high blessing among the Hebrews; still more so, for one to live to *see* them (Gen. 48:11; Ps. 128:6). **prolong . . . days** —also esteemed a special blessing among the Jews (Ps. 91:16). Messiah shall, after death, rise again to an endless life (Hos. 6:2; Rom. 6:9). **prosper**— (ch. 52:13, *Margin*). **11.** Jehovah is still speaking. **see of the travail**—He shall see such blessed fruits resulting from His sufferings as amply to repay Him for them (ch. 49:4, 5; 50:5, 9). The "satisfaction," in seeing the full fruit of His travail of soul in the conversion of Israel and the world, is to be realized in the last days (ch. 2:2-4). **his knowledge**—rather, *the knowledge* (experimentally) *of Him* (John 17:3; Phil. 3:10). **my . . . servant**—Messiah (ch. 42:1; 52: 13). **righteous**—the ground on which He justifies others, His own righteousness (I John 2:1). **justify** —treat *as if* righteous; forensically; on the ground of *His* meritorious suffering, not *their* righteousness. **bear . . . iniquities**—(vss. 4, 5), as the sinner's substitute. **12. divide**—as a conqueror dividing the spoil after a victory (Ps. 2:8; Luke 11:22). **him**—for Him. **with . . . great**—HENGSTENBERG translates, "I will give Him the mighty for a portion"; so LXX. But the parallel clause, "with the strong," favors *English Version.* His triumphs shall be not merely among the few and weak, but among the many and mighty. **spoil . . . strong**—(Col. 2:15; cf. Prov. 16: 19). "With the great; with the mighty," may mean, as a great and mighty hero. **poured out . . . soul**— i.e., His life, which was considered as residing in the blood (Lev. 17:11; Rom. 3:25). **numbered with . . .**—not that He *was* a transgressor, but He was *treated as* such, when crucified with thieves (Mark 15:28; Luke 22:37). **made intercession . . .**—This office He began on the cross (Luke 23:34), and now continues in heaven (ch. 59:16; Heb. 9:24; I John 2:1). Understand *because* before "He was numbered . . . He bare . . . made intercession." His meritorious death and intercession are the cause of His ultimate triumph. MAURER, for the parallelism, translates, "He was put on the same footing with the transgressors." But *English Version* agrees better with the *Hebrew*, and with the sense and fact as to Christ. MAURER'S translation would make a tautology after "He was numbered with the transgressors"; parallelism does not need so servile a repetition. "He *made intercession* for . . . ," answers to the parallel. "He *was numbered with* . . . ," as *effect* answers to *cause*, His intercession for sinners being the effect flowing from His having been numbered with them.

CHAPTER 54

Vss. 1-17. THE FRUIT OF MESSIAH'S SUFFERINGS, AND OF ISRAEL'S FINAL PENITENCE AT HER PAST UNBELIEF (ch. 53:6): HER JOYFUL RESTORATION AND ENLARGEMENT BY JEHOVAH, WHOSE WRATH WAS MOMENTARY, BUT HIS KINDNESS EVERLASTING. Israel converted is compared to a wife (vs. 5; ch. 62:5) put away for unfaithfulness, but now forgiven and taken home again. The converted Gentiles are represented as a new progeny of the long-forsaken but now restored wife. The pre-eminence of the Hebrew Church as the mother Church of Christendom is the leading idea; the conversion of the Gentiles is mentioned only as part of her felicity [HORSLEY]. **1.** **Sing**—for joy (Zeph. 3:14). **barren**—the Jewish Church once forsaken by God, and therefore during that time destitute of spiritual children (vs. 6). **didst not bear**—during the Babylonian exile primarily. Secondarily, and chiefly, during Israel's present dispersion. **the children**—the Gentiles adopted by special grace into the original Church (vs. 3; ch. 49:20, 21). **than . . . married wife**—than were her spiritual children, when Israel was still a married wife (under the law, before the Babylonian exile), before God put her away [MAURER]. So Paul contrasts the universal Church of the New Testament with the Church of the Old Testament legal dispensation, quoting this very passage (Gal. 4:27). But the full accomplishment of it is yet future. **2.** (Ch. 49:19, 20; Jer. 31:31-36, 38, 39.) Thy children shall be so many that thy borders must be extended to contain them. **curtains**—the cloth forming the covering of the tent. **spare not**—give abundantly the means for the enlargement of the Church (II Corinthians 9:5-7). **cords . . . stakes**—The more the tent is enlarged by lengthening the cords by which the cloth covering is fastened to the ground, the more the stakes supporting the tent need to be strengthened; the Church is not merely to seek new converts, but to strengthen those she has in the faith. The image is appropriate, as the tabernacle was the symbol of the old Israelitish Church (*Note,* ch. 33: 20). **3.** **break forth**—rather, burst forth with increase; thy offspring shall grow, answering to "thy seed" in the parallel clause. **thy seed**—Israel and her children, as distinguished from "the Gentiles." **desolate cities**—of Israel (ch. 44:26). **4.** (Ch. 41:10, 14.) **shame of thy youth**—Israel's *unfaithfulness* as wife of Jehovah, almost from her *earliest* history. **reproach of widowhood**—Israel's punishment in her consequent dismissal from God and barrenness of

spiritual children in Babylon and her present dispersion (vs. 1; ch. 49:21; Jer. 3:24, 25; 31:19; Hos. 2:2-5). **5.** (Ch. 62:5; Jer. 3:14). That God was Israel's "Maker," both as individuals and as the theocratic kingdom, is the pledge of assurance that He will be her Redeemer (ch. 43:1-3). *Hebrew,* "*makers . . . husbands*"; plural for *singular,* to denote excellency. **of Israel . . . whole earth**—Not until He manifests Himself as God *of Israel* shall He appear as God *of the whole earth* (Ps. 102:13, 15, 16; Zech. 14:5, 9). **6.** **called**—i.e., recalled: the prophetic past for the future. **forsaken**—that *had been* forsaken. **when thou**—or, "when *she* was rejected"; one who had been a wife of youth (Ezek. 16:8, 22, 60; Jer. 2:2) at the time when (*thou,* or) she was rejected for infidelity [MAURER]. "A wife of youth *but afterwards* rejected" [LOWTH]. **7.** **small moment**—as compared with Israel's coming *long* prosperity (ch. 26:20; 60:10). So the spiritual Israel (Ps. 30:5; II Cor. 4:17). **gather thee**—to Myself from thy dispersions. **8. In a little wrath**—rather, "In the overflowing of wrath"; as Proverbs 27:4, *Margin,* [GESENIUS]. The wrath, though but "for a moment," was overflowing while it lasted. **hid . . . face**—(ch. 8:17; Ps. 30:7). **everlasting**—in contrast to "for a moment." **9.** I am about to do the same in this instance as in Noah's flood. As I swore then that it should not return (Gen. 8:21; 9:11), and I kept that promise, so I swear now to My people, and will perform My promise, that there shall be no return of the deluge of My wrath upon them. LOWTH, on insufficient authority, reads (the same will I do now as), "in the days of Noah." **10.** (Ch. 51:6; Ps. 89: 33, 34; Rom. 11:29). **covenant of my peace**—(II Sam. 23:5). The covenant whereby I have made thee at peace with Me. **11. not comforted**—by anyone; none gave her help or comfort. **lay . . . with fair colours**—rather, "lay . . . in cement of *vermilion*" [LOWTH]. The *Hebrew* for "fair colors" means *stibium,* the paint with which Eastern women painted their eyelids and eyelashes (II Kings 9:30). The very cement shall be of the most beautiful color (Rev. 21:18-21). **12. windows**—rather, "battlements"; lit., "suns"; applied to battlements from their *radiated* appearance. **agates**—rather, rubies. **carbuncles**—lit., "sparkling gems"; the carbuncle when held to the sun becomes like a burning coal. **all thy borders**—rather, "thy whole circuit," consisting of *precious stones.* The glory of the Church on earth, when the Hebrew Church, according to the original design, shall be the metropolis of Christendom. **13.** Quoted by the Saviour (John 6:45), to prove that in order to come to Him, men must be "drawn" by the Father. So Jeremiah 31:34; Micah 4:2; I Corinthians 2:10; Hebrews 8:10; 10:16; I John 2:20. **great . . . peace**—generally (Ps. 119:165). Specially referring to the *peaceful prosperity* which shall prevail under Messiah in the latter days (ch. 2:4, 9:6). **14. righteousness**—the characteristic of the reign of Messiah (ch. 11:4, 5; Ps. 72:2, 4; Rev. 19:11). **far from oppression . . .**—far from *suffering oppression;* "for thou shalt have nothing to fear." **15. gather together . . .**—i.e., If it should happen that enemies "gather together" against thee (Ps. 2:2), they will *not* have been sent *by Me* (cf. Hos. 8:4) as instruments of My wrath (nay, it *will* be with My disapproval); for "whosoever shall gather together," etc. (Ps. 59:3). **fall for thy sake**—rather, "shall come over to thy side" [LOWTH]. Lit., *"fall to thee"* (Jer. 21:9; 39:9). To be *fully* fulfilled to Jerusalem hereafter (Zech. 14:16). **16.** The workman that forms "weapons against thee" (vs. 17) is wholly in My power, therefore thou needest not fear, having

Me on thy side. **for his work**—rather, "by his labor [HORSLEY]. "According to the exigencies of his work" [MAURER]. **waster to destroy**—(ch. 10: 5-7; 37:26, 27; 45:1-6). Desolating conquerors who use the "instruments" framed by "the smith." The repetition of the "I" implies, however, something in the latter half of the verse contrasted with the former understand it, therefore, thus: "I have in My power both him who frames arms and him who destroys *them* (arms)" [ROSENMULLER]. **17. tongue ... condemn**—image from a court of justice. Those who desire to "condemn" thee *thou* shalt "condemn" (Exod. 11:7; Josh. 10:21; Ps. 64:8; Rom. 8:1, 33). **righteousness ... of me**—(ch. 45:24; 46:13). Rather *(this is) their justification from Me.* Their enemies would "condemn" them, but I justify and vindicate them, and so they condemn their enemies.

CHAPTER 55

Vss. 1-13. THE CALL OF THE GENTILE WORLD TO FAITH THE RESULT OF GOD'S GRACE TO THE JEWS FIRST. **1. every one**—After the *special* privileges of Israel (ch. 54) there follow, as the consequence, the *universal* invitation to the Gentiles (Luke 24:47; Rom. 11:12, 15). **Ho**—calls the most earnest attention. **thirsteth**—has a keen sense of need (Matt. 5:6). **waters ... wine and milk**—a gradation. Not merely *water,* which is needed to maintain life at all, but *wine and milk* to strengthen, cheer, and nourish; the spiritual blessings of the Gospel are meant (ch. 25:6; Song of Sol. 5:1; John 7:37). "Waters," *plural,* to denote abundance (ch. 43:20; 44:3). **no money**—Yet, in vs. 2, it is said, "ye spend money." A seeming paradox. Ye are really spiritual bankrupts: but thinking yourselves to have money, viz., a devotion of your own making, ye lavish it on that "which is not bread," i.e., on idols, whether literal or spiritual. **buy ... without money**—another paradox. We are *bought,* but not with a *price* paid by ourselves (I Cor. 6:20; I Pet. 1:18, 19). In a different sense we are to "buy" salvation, viz., by parting with everything which comes between us and Christ who has bought it for us and by making it our own (Matt. 13:44, 46; Luke 12:33; Rev. 3:18). **2. not bread**—(Hab. 2:13). "Bread of deceit" (Prov. 20:17). Contrast this with the "bread of life" (John. 6:32, 35; also Luke 14:16-20). **satisfieth not**—(Eccles. 1:8; 4:8). **hearken ... and eat**—When two *imperatives* are joined, the second expresses the *consequence* of obeying the command in the first (Gen. 42:18). *By hearkening ye shall eat.* So in vs. 1, "buy and eat." By buying, and so making it your own, ye shall eat, i.e., *experimentally enjoy* it (John 6:53). Cf. the invitation (Prov. 9:5, 6; Matt. 22:4). **fatness**—(Ps. 36:8; 63:5). **3. me ... live**—by coming to *me* ye shall *live:* for "*I* am the *life*" (John 14:6). **everlasting covenant**—(Jer. 32:40; II Sam. 23:5). **with you ... David**—God's covenant is with the antitypical David, Messiah (Ezek. 34:23), and so with us by our identification with Him. **sure**—answering to "everlasting," irrevocable, unfailing, to be relied on (Ps. 89:2-4, 28, 29, 34-36; Jer. 33:20, 21; II Sam. 7:15, 16; II Cor. 1:18-20). **mercies of David**—the mercies of grace (ch. 63:7; John 1:16) which I covenanted to give to David, and especially to Messiah, his antitype. Quoted in Acts 13:34. **4. him**—the mystical David (Ezek. 37:24, 25; Jer. 30:9; Hos. 3:5). Given by God (ch. 49:6). **witness**—He bore witness even unto death for God, to His law, claims, and plan of redeeming love (John 18:

37; Rev. 1:5). Revelation is a "testimony"; because it is propounded to be received on the authority of the Giver, and not merely because it can be proved by arguments. **commander**—"preceptor" [HORSLEY]; "lawgiver" [BARNES]. **to the people**—rather, peoples. **5. thou**—Jehovah addresses Messiah. **call ... run**—God must *call,* before man can, or will, *run* (Song of Sol. 1:4; John 6:44). Not merely *come,* but *run* eagerly. **thou knowest not** —now as thy people (so in Matt. 7:23). **nation ... nations**—gradation; from Israel, one *nation,* the Gospel spread to many *nations,* and will do so more fully on Israel's conversion. **knew not thee**—(ch. 52:15; Eph. 2:11, 12). **because of ... thy God ... glorified thee**—(ch. 60:5, 9; Zech. 8:23); where similar language is directed to *Israel,* because of the identification of Israel with Messiah, who is the ideal Israel (Matt. 2:15; cf. with Hos. 11:1; see Acts 3:13). **6.** The condition and limit in the obtaining of the spiritual benefits (vss. 1-3): (1) Seek the Lord. (2) Seek Him while He is to be found (ch. 65:1; Ps. 32:6; Matt. 25:1-13; John 7-34; 8-21; II Cor. 6:2; Heb. 2:3; 3:13, 15). **call**—casting yourselves wholly on His mercy (Rom. 10:13). Stronger than "seek"; so "near" is more positive than "while He may be found" (Rom. 10:8, 9). **near**—propitious (Ps. 34:18; 145:18). **7. unrighteous**—*Hebrew,* "man of iniquity"; true of all men. The "wicked" sins more openly in "his way"; the "unrighteous" refers to the more subtle workings of sin in the "thoughts." All are guilty in the latter respect, thought many fancy themselves safe, because not openly "wicked in ways" (Ps. 94:11). The parallelism is that of gradation. The progress of the penitent is to be from negative reformation, "forsaking his way," and a farther step, "his thoughts," to positive repentance, "returning to the Lord" (the only true repentance, Zech. 12:10), and making God *his* God, along with the other children of God (the crowning-point; *appropriation* of God *to ourselves:* "to *our* God"). "Return" implies that man originally walked with God, but has apostatized. Isaiah saith, "*our* God," the God of the believing Israelites; those themselves redeemed desire others to come to *their* God (Ps. 34:8; Rev. 22:17). **abundantly pardon**—(lit., "multiply to pardon," still more than "have mercy"; God's graciousness is felt more and more the longer one knows Him (Ps. 130: 7). **8. For**—referring to vs. 7. You need not doubt His willingness "abundantly to pardon" (cf. vs. 12); *for,* though "the wicked" man's "*ways,*" and "the unrighteous man's *thoughts,*" are so aggravated as to seem unpardonable, God's "thoughts" and "ways" in pardoning are not regulated by the proportion of the former, as man's would be towards his fellow man who offended him; cf. the "for" (Ps. 25:11; Rom. 5:19). **9.** (Ps. 57:10; 89:2; 103:11.) "For" is repeated from vs. 8. But MAURER, after the negation, translates, "but." **10.** The hearts of men, once barren of spirituality, shall be made, by the outpouring of the Spirit under Messiah, to bear fruits of righteousness (ch. 5:6; Deut. 32:2; II Sam. 23:4; Ps. 72:6). **snow**—which covers plants from frost in winter; and, when melted in spring, waters the earth. **returneth not**—void; as in vs. 11; it returns not in the same shape, or without "accomplishing" the desired end. **bud**—germinate. **11.** (Matt. 24:35.) Rain may to us seem lost when it falls on a desert, but it fulfils some purpose of God. So the gospel word falling on the hard heart; it sometimes works a change at last; and even if not so, it leaves men without excuse. The full accomplishment of this verse, and vss. 12, 13, is, however, to be at the Jews' final restoration and conversion of the world (ch. 11:9-12; 60:1-5, 21). **12. go out**—from the various countries in which ye (the Jews) are scattered, to your own land (Ezek. 11:17). **led**—by Messiah, your "Leader" (vs. 4; ch. 52:12; Mic. 2:12, 13). **mountains ... trees ...** —images justly used to express the seeming sympathy of nature with. the joy of God's people. For, when sin is removed, the natural world shall be delivered from "vanity," and be renewed, so as to be in unison with the regenerated moral world (ch. 44:23; Ps. 98:8; Rom. 8:19-22). **13. thorn**—emblem of the wicked (II Sam. 23:6; Mic. 7:4). **fir tree**—the godly (ch. 60:13; Ps. 92:12). Cf. as to the change wrought Romans 6:19. **brier**—emblem of uncultivation (ch. 5:6). **myrtle**—*Hebrew, Hedes,* from which comes *Hedassah,* the original name of Esther. Type of the Christian Church; for it is a lowly, though beautiful, fragrant, and evergreen shrub (Ps. 92:13, 14). **for a name ... everlasting sign**—a perpetual memorial to the glory of Jehovah (Jer. 13:11; 33:9).

CHAPTER 56

Vss. 1-12. The Preparation Needed on the Part of Those Who Wish to Be Admitted to the Kingdom of God. **1. judgment**—equity. John the Baptist preached similarly a return to righteousness, as needed to prepare men for Messiah's first coming (Luke 3:3, 8-14). So it shall be before the second coming (Mal. 4:4-6). **near to come**—(Matt. 3:2; 4: 17), also as to the second coming (ch. 62:10, 11; Luke 21:28, 31; Rom. 13:11, 12; Heb. 10:25). **righteousness**—answering to "salvation" in the parallel clause; therefore it means *righteousness which bringeth salvation* (ch. 46:13; Rom. 3:25, 26). **2.** (Luke 12:43). **the man**—*Hebrew, enosh,* "a man in humble life," in contradistinction to *Hebrew, ish,* "one of high rank." Even the humblest, as "the stranger" and "the eunuch" (vss. 4, 6), are admissible to these privileges. **this ... it**—what follows: "keeping the Sabbath," etc. (ch. 58:13, 14; Ezek. 20:12). A proof that the Sabbath, in the *spirit* of its obligation, was to be binding under the Gospel (ch. 66:23). That gospel times are referred to is plain, from the blessing not being pronounced on the man who observed the *sacrificial* ritual of the Jewish law. **layeth hold**—image from one grasping firmly some precious object which he is afraid of having forcibly snatched from him. The "Sabbath" here includes all the ordinances of divine worship under the new gospel law. **keepeth ... hand ... from ... evil**—The observance of the second table of the law; as the "Sabbath" referred to the first table. Together, they form the whole duty of man, the worship of God and a holy life. **3.** God welcomes all believers, without distinction of persons, under the new economy (Acts 10:34, 35). **joined ... to ... Lord**—(Num. 18:4, 7). "Proselytes." **separated**—Proselytes from the Gentiles were not admitted to the same privileges as native Israelites. This barrier between Jews and Gentiles was to be broken down (Eph. 2:14-16). **eunuch**—(Acts 8:27, etc.). Eunuchs were chamberlains over harems, or court ministers in general. **dry tree**—barren (cf. Luke 23:31); not admissible into the congregation of Israel (Deut. 23:1-3). Under the Gospel the eunuch and stranger should be released from religious and civil disabilities. **4. please me**—sacrifice their own pleasure to mine. **take hold**—so "layeth hold" (*Note,* vs. 2). **5. in mine house**—the temple, the emblem of the Church (I Tim. 3:15).

They shall no longer be confined as proselytes were, to the outer court, but shall be admitted "into the holiest" (Heb. 10:19, 20). **a place**—lit., "a hand." **than of sons**—Though the eunuch is barren of *children* (vs. 3), I will give him a more lasting name than that of being father of sons and daughters (regarded as a high honor among the Hebrews) (John 1:12; 10:3; I John 3:1; Rev. 2:17; 3:12). **6. join ... Lord**—(Jer. 50:6). Conditions of admission to the privileges of adoption. **7. Even them**—(Eph. 2:11-13.) **to my holy mountain**—Jerusalem, the seat of the Lord's throne in His coming kingdom (ch. 2:2; Jer. 3:17). **joyful**—(Rom. 5:11). **burnt offerings ... sacrifices**—spiritual, of which the literal were types (Rom. 12:1; Heb. 13:15; I Pet. 2:5). **accepted**—(Eph. 1:6.) **altar**—(Heb. 13:10), spiritually, the Cross of Christ, which sanctifies our sacrifices of prayer and praise. **house ... for all people**—or rather, "peoples." No longer restricted to *one* favored people (Mal. 1:11; John 4:21, 23; I Tim. 2:8). To be fully realized at the second coming (ch. 2:2-4). No longer literal, but spiritual sacrifice, viz., "prayer" shall be offered (Ps. 141:2; 52:17; Mal. 1:11; Matt. 21:13). **8.** Jehovah will not only restore the scattered outcasts of Israel (ch. 11:12; Ps. 147:2) to their own land, but "will gather others ('strangers') to him (Israel), besides those gathered" (*Margin,* to his gathered; i.e., in addition to the Israelites collected from their dispersion), (John 10:16; Eph. 1:10; 2:19). **9. beasts**—Gentile idolatrous nations hostile to the Jews, summoned by God to chastise them (Jer. 12:7-9; 50:17; Ezek. 34:5): the Chaldeans and subsequently the Romans. The mention of the "outcasts of Israel" (vs. 8) brings in view the outcasting, caused by the sins of their rulers (vss. 10-12). **to devour**—viz., Israel. **10. His watchmen**—Israel's spiritual leaders (ch. 62:16; Ezek. 3:17). **dumb dogs**—image from bad shepherds' watchdogs, which fail to give notice, by barking, of the approach of wild beasts. **blind**—(Matt. 23:16). **sleeping, lying down**—rather, "dreamers, sluggards" [Lowth]. Not merely *sleeping* inactive, but under *visionary delusions.* **loving to slumber**—not merely slumbering involuntarily, but loving it. **11. greedy**—lit., "strong" (i.e., insatiable) *in appetite* (Ezek. 34:2, 3; Mic. 3:11). **cannot understand**—unable to comprehend the wants of the people, spiritually: so vs. 10, "*cannot bark.*" **look to ... own way**—i.e., their own selfish interests; not to the spiritual welfare of the people (Jer. 6:13; Ezek. 22:27). **from his quarter**—rather, "from the highest to the lowest" [Lowth]. "From his quarter"; i.e., from one end to the other of them, *one and all* (Gen. 19:4). **12. fetch wine**—language of the national teachers challenging one another to drink. Barnes translates, "I will take another cup" (ch. 5:11). **to-morrow ... .**—Their self-indulgence was *habitual* and *intentional:* not merely they drink, but they mean to continue so.

CHAPTER 57

Vss. 1-21. The Peaceful Death of the Righteous Few: the Ungodliness of the Many: a Believing Remnant Shall Survive the General Judgments of the Nation, and Be Restored By Him Who Creates Peace. In the midst of the excesses of the unfaithful watchmen (ch. 56:10, 11, 12), most of the few that are godly perish: partly by vexation at the prevailing ungodliness; partly by violent death in persecution: prophetical of the persecuting times of Manasseh, before God's judgments in causing the captivity in Babylon; and again those in the last age of the Church, before the final judgments on the apostasy (II Kings 21:16; Matt. 23:29-35, 37; Rev. 11:17). The *Hebrew* for "perisheth," and "is taken away," expresses a *violent death* (Mic. 7:2). **1. no man layeth it to heart** —as a public calamity. **merciful men**—rather, *godly men;* the subjects of mercy. **none considering**—viz., what was the design of Providence in removing the godly. **from the evil**—*Hebrew,* from the face of the evil, i.e., both from the moral evil on every side (ch. 56:10-12), and from the evils about to come in punishment of the national sins, foreign invasions, etc. (ch. 56:9; 57:13). So Ahijah's death is represented as a blessing conferred on him by God for his piety (I Kings 14:10-13; see also II Kings 22:20). **2.** Or, "he *entereth* into peace"; in contrast to the *persecutions* which he suffered in this world (Job 3:13, 17). *Margin* not so well translates, "he shall go in peace" (Ps. 37:37; Luke 2:29). **rest**—the calm rest of their bodies in their graves (called "beds," II Chron. 16:14; cf. Isa. 14:18; because they "sleep" in them, with the certainty of awakening at the resurrection, I Thess. 4: 14) is the emblem of the eternal "rest" (Heb. 4:9; Rev. 14:13). **each one walking in . . . uprightness** —This clause defines the character of those who at death "rest in their beds," viz., all who walk uprightly. **3. But . . . ye**—In contrast to "the righteous" and their end, he announces to the unbelieving Jews their doom. **sons of the sorceress**— i.e., ye that are addicted to sorcery: this was connected with the worship of false gods (II Kings 21: 6). No insult is greater to an Oriental than any slur cast on his *mother* (I Sam. 20:30; Job 30:8). **seed of the adulterer**—*Spiritual* adultery is meant: idolatry and apostasy (Matt. 16:4). **4. sport yourselves**—make a mock (ch. 66:5). Are ye aware of the glory of Him whom you mock, by mocking His servants ("the righteous," vs. 1)? (II Chron. 36: 16.) **make . . . wide mouth**—(Ps. 22:7, 13; 35:21; Lam. 2:16). **children of transgression . . .**—not merely *children of transgressors,* and a *seed of false parents,* but of *transgression* and *falsehood* itself, utterly unfaithful to God. **5. Enflaming yourselves** —burning with lust *towards idols* [GESENIUS]; or else (cf. *Margin*), *in the terebinth groves,* which the *Hebrew* and the parallelism favor (*Note,* ch. 1:29) [MAURER]. **under . . . tree**—(II Kings 17:10.) The tree, as in the Assyrian sculptures, was probably made an idolatrous symbol of *the heavenly hosts.* **slaying . . . children**—as a sacrifice to Molech, etc. (II Kings 17:31; II Chron. 28:3; 33:6). **in . . . valleys**—the valley of the son of Hinnom. Fire was put within a hollow brazen statue, and the child was put in his heated arms; kettle drums (*Hebrew, toph*) were beaten to drown the child's cries; whence the valley was called Tophet (II Chron. 33:6; Jer. 7:3). **under . . . clifts**—the gloom of caverns suiting their dark superstitions. **6.** The smooth stones, shaped as idols, are the gods chosen by thee as thy portion (Ps. 16:5). **meat offering**—not a bloody sacrifice, but one of meal and flour mingled with oil. "Meat" in Old English meant *food,* not *flesh,* as it means now (Lev. 14:10). **Should I receive comfort**— rather, "Shall I bear these things with patience?" [HORSLEY]. **7. Upon . . . high mountain . . . bed**— image from adultery, *open and shameless* (Ezek. 23:7); the "bed" answers to the idolatrous *altar,* the scene of their spiritual unfaithfulness to their divine husband (Ezek. 16:16, 25; 23:41). **8.** "Remembrance," i.e., memorials of thy idolatry: the objects which thou holdest in remembrance. *They hung*

up household tutelary gods "behind the doors"; the very place where God has directed them to write His laws "on the posts and gates" (Deut. 6:9; 11:20); a curse, too, was pronounced on putting up an image "in a secret place" (Deut. 27:15). **discovered thyself**—image from an adulteress. **enlarged . . . bed**—so as to receive the more paramours. **made . . . covenant**—with idols: in open violation of thy "covenant" with *God* (Exod. 19:5; 23:32). Or, "hast made assignations with them for thyself" [HORSLEY]. **thy bed . . . their bed**—The Jews' sin was twofold; they resorted to places of idolatry (*"their* bed"), and they received idols into the temple of God (*"thy* bed"). **where**—rather, "ever since that" [HORSLEY]. The *Hebrew* for *"where"* means *"room"* (*Margin*), a place; therefore, translate, "thou hast provided a place for it" (for "their bed"), viz., by admitting idolatrous altars in thy land [BARNES]; or "thou choosest a (convenient) place for thyself" in their bed [MAURER] (ch. 56:5). **9. the king**— *the idol* which they came to worship, perfumed with oil, like harlots (Jer. 4:30; Ezek. 23:16, 40). So "king" means idol (Amos 5:26; Zeph. 1:5); (*malcham* meaning "king") [ROSENMULLER]. Rather, *the king of Assyria* or *Egypt,* and other foreign princes, on whom Israel relied, instead of on God; the "ointment" will thus refer to the presents (Hos. 12:1), and perhaps the compliances with foreigners' idolatries, whereby Israel sought to gain their favor [LOWTH] (ch. 30:6; Ezek. 16: 33; 23:16; Hos. 7:11). **send . . . messengers far off**—not merely to neighboring nations, but to those "far off," in search of new idols, or else alliances. **even unto hell**—the lowest possible degradation. **10. greatness of . . . way**—the *length* of thy journey in seeking strange gods, or else foreign aid (Jer. 2:23, 24). Notwithstanding thy deriving no good from these long journeys (so, "send . . . *far off,*" vs. 9), thou dost not still give up hope (Jer. 2:25; 18:12). **hast found . . . life of . . . hand**—for "thou still findest life (i.e., vigor) enough in thy hand" to make new idols [MAURER], or to seek new alliance ("hand" being then taken for *strength* in general). **grieved**—rather, "therefore thou art not *weak*" [MAURER]; inasmuch as having "life in thy hand," thou art still strong in hope. **11.** Israel wished not to seem *altogether* to have denied God. Therefore they "lied" to Him. God asks, Why dost thou do so? "Whom dost thou fear? Certainly not *Me; for* thou hast not remembered Me." Translate, *"seeing that* thou hast not remembered Me." **laid it to . . . heart** —rather, "nor hast Me at heart"; hast no regard for Me; and that, because I have been long silent and have not punished thee. Lit., "Have I not held My peace, and that for long? and so thou fearest Me not" (Ps. 50:21; Eccles. 8:11). It would be better openly to renounce God, than to "flatter Him" with lies of false professions (Ps. 78:36) [LUDOVICUS DE DIEU]. However, ch. 51:12, 13 favors *English Version* of the whole verse; God's "silent" longsuffering, which was intended to lead them to repentance, caused them "not to fear Him" (Rom. 2:4, 5). **12. declare**—I will expose publicly thy (hypocritical) righteousness. I will show openly how vain thy works, in having recourse to idols, or foreign alliances, shall prove (vs. 3). **13. When thou criest**—In the time of thy trouble. **companies** —viz., of idols, collected by thee from every quarter; or else, of foreigners, summoned to thy aid. **wind . . . carry . . . away**—(Job 21:18; Matt. 7:27). **vanity**—rather, a breath [LOWTH]. **possess . . . land . . . inherit**—i.e., the literal land of Judea and Mount Zion; the believing remnant of Israel shall return and inherit the land. Secondarily, the heavenly inheritance, and the spiritual Zion (ch. 49:8; Ps. 37:9, 11; 69:35, 36; Matt. 5:5; Heb. 12:22). "He that putteth his trust in Me," of whatever extraction, shall succeed to the spiritual patrimony of the apostate Jew [HORSLEY]. **14. shall say**—The nominative is, "He that trusteth in Me" (vs. 13). The believing remnant shall have every obstacle to their return cleared out of the way, at the coming restoration of Israel, the antitype to the return from Babylon (ch. 35:8; 40:3, 4; 62:10, 11). **Cast . . . up**—a high road before the returning Jews. **stumbling block**—Jesus had been so to the Jews, but will not be so *then* any longer (I Cor. 1:23); their *prejudices* shall then be taken out of the way. **15.** The pride and self-righteousness of the Jews were the stumbling block in the way of their acknowledging Christ. The *contrition* of Israel in the last days shall be attended with God's interposition in their behalf. So their self-humiliation, in ch. 66: 2, 5, 10, etc., precedes their final prosperity (Zech. 12:6, 10-14); there will, probably, be a previous period of unbelief even after their return (Zech. 12:8, 9). **16. For**—referring to the promise in vss. 14, 15, of restoring Israel when "contrite" (Gen. 6:3; 8:21; Ps. 78:38, 39; 85:5; 103:9, 13, 14; Mic. 7:18). God "will not contend for ever" *with His people*, for their human spirit would thereby be utterly crushed, whereas God's object is to chasten, not to destroy *them* (Lam. 3:33, 34; Mic. 7:8, 9). *With the ungodly* He is "angry *every day*" (Ps. 7:11; Rev. 14:11). **spirit . . . before me**—i.e., the human spirit which *went forth from Me* (Num. 16:22), answering to "which I have made" in the parallel clause. **17. covetousness**—akin to idolatry; and, like it, having drawn off Israel's heart from God (ch. 2:7; 56:11; 58:3; Jer. 6:13; Col. 3:5). **hid me** —(ch. 8:17; 45:15). **went on frowardly**—the result of God's hiding His face (Ps. 81:12; Rom. 1:24, 26). **18.** Rather, "I have seen his ways (in sin), *yet* will I heal him," i.e., restore Israel spiritually and temporally (Jer. 33:6; 3:22; Hos. 14:4, 5 [HORSLEY]. However, the phrase, "his mourners," favors *English Version;* "his ways" will thus be his ways *of repentance;* and God's pardon on "seeing" them answers to the like promise (ch. 61:2, 3; Jer. 31:18, 20). **19. fruit of . . . lips**—i.e., thanksgivings which flow from the lips. I make men to return thanks to Me (Hos. 14:2; Heb. 13:15). **Peace, peace**—"*perfect* peace" (see *Margin*, ch. 26:3; John 14:27). Primarily, the cessation of the troubles now afflicting the *Jews,* as formerly, under the Babylonian exile. More generally, the peace which the Gospel proclaims both to Israel "that is near," and to the Gentiles who are "far off" (Acts 2:39; Eph. 2:17). **20. when it cannot rest**—rather, "*for* it can have no rest" (Job 15:20, etc.; Prov. 4:16, 17). *English Version* represents the sea as *occasionally* agitated; but the *Hebrew* expresses that it can *never* be at rest. **21.** (Ch. 48:22; II Kings 9:22). **my God**—The prophet, having God as *his* God, speaks in the person of Israel, prophetically regarded as having now *appropriated* God and His "peace" (ch. 11:1-3), warning the impenitent that, while they continue so, they can have no peace.

CHAPTER 58

Vss. 1-14. REPROOF OF THE JEWS FOR THEIR DEPENDENCE ON MERE OUTWARD FORMS OF WORSHIP. **1. aloud**—*Hebrew,* with the throat, i.e., with full voice, not merely from the lips (I Sam. 1:13). Speak loud enough to arrest attention. **my people**

—the Jews in Isaiah's time, and again in the time of our Lord, more zealous for externals than for inward holiness. ROSENMULLER thinks the reference to be to the Jews in the captivity practising their rites to gain God's favor and a release; and that hence, *sacrifices* are not mentioned, but only *fasting* and *Sabbath* observance, which they could keep though far away from the temple in Jerusalem. The same also applies to their present dispersion, in which they cannot offer *sacrifices,* but can only show their zeal in *fastings,* etc. Cf. as to our Lord's time, Matthew 6:16; 23; Luke 18:12. **2.** Put the stop at "ways"; and connect "as a nation that . . ." with what follows; "As a nation that did righteousness," thus answers to, "they ask of Me *just judgments*" (i.e., as a matter of justice *due to them,* salvation to themselves, and destruction to their enemies); and "forsook not the ordinance of their God," answers to "they desire the drawing near of God" (that *God would draw near* to exercise those "just judgments" in behalf of them, and against their enemies) [MAURER]. So JEROME, "In the confidence, as it were, of a good conscience, they demand a just judgment, in the language of the saints: Judge me, O Lord, for I have walked in mine integrity." So in Malachi 2:17, they affect to be scandalized at the impunity of the wicked, and impugn God's *justice* [HORSLEY]. Thus, "seek Me daily, and desire (*English Version* not so well, 'delight') to know My ways," refers to their requiring to know why God delayed so long in helping them. *English Version* gives a good, though different sense; viz., dispelling the delusion that God would be satisfied with outward observances, while the *spirit* of the law was violated and the heart unchanged (vss. 3-14; Ezek. 33:31, 32; cf. John 18:28), scrupulosity side by side with murder. The prophets were the commentators on the law, as their *Magna Charta,* in its inward spirit and not the mere letter. **3. Wherefore**—the words of the Jews: "Why is it that, when we fast, Thou dost not notice it" (by delivering us)? They think to lay God under *obligation* to their fasting (Ps. 73:13; Mal. 3:14). **afflicted . . . soul**—(Lev. 16:29). **Behold**—God's reply. **pleasure**—in antithesis to their boast of having "*afflicted* their soul"; it was only in outward show they really *enjoyed* themselves. GESENIUS not so well translates, "business." **exact . . . labours**—rather, "*oppressive* labors" [MAURER]. HORSLEY, with *Vulgate,* translates, "Exact the whole upon your *debtors*"; those who owe you labor (Neh. 5: 1-5, 8-10, etc.). **4. ye shall not fast**—rather, "ye do not fast at this time, so as to make your voice to be heard on high," i.e., in heaven; your aim in fasting is strife, not to gain the ear of God [MAURER] (I Kings 21:9, 12, 13). In *English Version* the sense is, If you wish acceptance with God, ye must not fast as ye now do, to make your voice heard high *in strife.* **5. for a man to afflict his soul**—The pain felt by abstinence is not the *end* to be sought, as if it were meritorious; it is of value only in so far as it leads us to amend our ways (vss. 6, 7). **bow . . . head . . . sackcloth**—to affect the outward tokens, so as to "*appear* to men to fast" (Matt. 6: 17, 18; I Kings 21:27; Esther 4:3). **6. loose . . . bands of wickedness**—i.e., to dissolve every tie wherewith one hath unjustly bound his fellow men (Lev. 25:49, etc.). Servitude, a fraudulent contract, etc. **undo . . . heavy burdens**—*Hebrew,* loose the bands of the yoke. **oppressed**—lit., "the broken." The expression, "to let go free," implies that those "broken" with the yoke of *slavery* are meant (Neh. 5:10-12; Jer. 34:9-11, 14, 16).

JEROME interprets it, broken with poverty; bankrupt. **7. deal**—distribute (Job 31:16-21). **cast out** —rather, reduced [HORSLEY]. **naked . . . cover him** —(Matt. 25:36). **flesh**—kindred (Gen. 29:14). Also brethren in common descent from Adam, and brethren in Christ (Jas. 2:15). "Hide . . . thyself," means to be strange towards them, and not to relieve them in their poverty (Matt. 15:5). **8. light**— emblem of prosperity (vs. 10; Job 11:17). **health** —lit., a long bandage, applied by surgeons to heal a wound (cf. ch. 1:6). Hence *restoration* from all past calamities. **go before thee**—Thy conformity to the divine covenant acts as a leader, conducting thee to peace and prosperity. **glory . . . reward**— like the pillar of cloud and fire, the symbol of God's "glory," which went *behind* Israel, separating them from their Egyptian pursuers (ch. 52:12; Exod. 14: 19, 20). **9. Then . . . call . . . answer**—when sin is renounced (ch. 65:24). When the Lord's call is *not* hearkened to, He will not hear our "call" (Ps. 66:18; Prov. 1:24, 28; 15:29; 28:9). **putting forth of . . . finger**—the finger of scorn pointed at simpleminded godly men. The middle finger was so used by the Romans. **speaking vanity**—every *injurious* speech [LOWTH]. **10. draw out thy soul**—"impart of thine own subsistence," or "sustenance" [HORSLEY]. "Soul" is figurative for "that wherewith thou sustainest thy soul," or "life." **light . . . in obscurity**—Calamities shall be suddenly succeeded by prosperity (Ps. 112:4). **11. satisfy . . . in drought**— (ch. 41:17, 18). Lit., "drought," i.e., parched places [MAURER]. **make fat**—rather, strengthen [NOYES]. *"Give thee the free use of* thy bones" [JEROME], *or, of thy strength* [HORSLEY]. **watered garden**—an Oriental picture of happiness. **fail not** —Hebrew, "deceive not"; as streams that disappoint the caravan which had expected to find water, as formerly, but find it dried up (Job 6:15-17). **12. they . . . of thee**—thy people, the Israelites. **old waste places**—the old ruins of Jerusalem (ch. 61:4; Ezek. 36:33-36). **foundations of many generations** —i.e., the buildings which had lain in ruins, even to their *foundations, for many ages;* called in the parallel passage (ch. 61:4), "the *former* desolations"; and in the preceding clause here, "the *old* waste places." The literal and spiritual restoration of Israel is meant, which shall produce like blessed results on the Gentile world (Amos 9:11, 12; Acts 15:16, 17). **be called**—appropriately: the name truly designating what thou shalt do. **breach**—the calamity wherewith God visited Israel for their sin (ch. 30:26; I Chron. 15:13). **paths to dwell in**— not that the *paths* were *to be dwelt in,* but *the paths leading to their dwellings* were to be restored; "paths, so as to dwell in *the land*" [MAURER]. **13.** (Ch. 56:2; Neh. 13:15-22.) The Sabbath, even under the new dispensation, was to be obligatory (ch. 66:23). **foot**—the instrument of motion (cf. Prov. 4:27); men are not to *travel* for mere pleasure on the Sabbath (Acts 1:12). The Jews were forbidden to travel on it farther than the tabernacle or temple. If thou keep thy foot from going on thy own ways and "doing thy pleasure . . ." (Exod. 20:10, 11). **my holy day**—God claims it as *His* day; to take it for our pleasure is to rob Him of His own. This is the very way in which the Sabbath is mostly broken; it is made a day of carnal pleasure instead of spiritual "delight." **holy of the Lord**—not the predicate, but the subject; "if thou call the holy (day) of Jehovah honorable"; if thou treat it as a day to be honored. **him**—or else, *it,* the Sabbath. **not doing . . . own way**—answering to, "turn away thy foot from the Sabbath."

nor finding . . . pleasure—answering to, "doing thy pleasure." "To keep the Sabbath in an idle manner is the sabbath of oxen and asses; to pass it in a jovial manner is the sabbath of the golden calf, when the people sat down to eat and drink, and rose again to play; to keep it in surfeiting and wantonness is the sabbath of Satan, the devil's holiday" [BISHOP ANDREWES]. **nor speaking . . . words**— answering to, *"call* Sabbath a delight . . . honorable." Man's *"own* words" would "call' it a "weariness"; it is the spiritual nature given from above which "calls it a delight" (Amos 8:5; Mal. 1:13). **14. delight . . . in . . . Lord**—God rewards in kind, as He punishes in kind. As we "delight" in keeping God's "Sabbath," so God will give us "delight" in Himself (Gen. 15:1; Job 22:21-26; Ps. 37:4). **ride upon . . . high places**—I will make thee *supreme lord* of the land; the phrase is taken from a conqueror riding in his chariot, and occupying the hills and fastnesses of a country [VITRINGA], (Deut. 32:13; Mic. 1:3; Hab. 3:19). Judea was a land of *hills;* the idea thus is, "I will restore thee to thine own land" [CALVIN]. The parallel words, "heritage of *Jacob,*" confirm this (Gen. 27:28, 29; 28:13-15). **mouth of . . . Lord . . . spoken it**—a formula to assure men of the fulfilment of any solemn promise which God has made (ch. 40:5).

CHAPTER 59

Vss. 1-21. THE PEOPLE'S SIN THE CAUSE OF JUDGMENTS: THEY AT LAST OWN IT THEMSELVES: THE REDEEMER'S FUTURE INTERPOSITION IN THEIR EXTREMITY. The reason why Jehovah does not deliver His people, notwithstanding their religious services (ch. 58:3), is not want of power on His part, but because of their sins (vss. 1-8); vss. 9-15 contain their confession; vss. 16-21, the consequent promise of the Messiah. **1. hand . . . shortened**—(*Note,* ch. 50:2). **ear heavy**—(ch. 6:10). **2. hid**—*Hebrew,* caused Him to hide (Lam. 3:44). **3.** (Ch. 1:15; Rom. 3:13-15.) **hands . . . fingers**—Not merely the "hands" perpetrate deeds of *grosser* enormity ("blood"), but the "fingers" commit more *minute* acts of "iniquity." **lips . . . tongue**—The *lips* "speak" *openly* "lies," the *tongue* "mutters" malicious *insinuations* ("perverseness"; perverse misrepresentations of others) (Jer. 6:28; 9:4). **4.** Rather, "No one calleth an adversary into court with justice," i.e., None bringeth a just suit: "No one pleadeth *with* truth." **they trust . . . iniquity**—(So Job 15:36; Ps. 7:14). **5. cockatrice**—probably the basilisk serpent, *cerastes.* Instead of crushing evil in the egg, they foster it. **spider's web**—This refers not to the spider's web being made to *entrap,* but to its *thinness,* as contrasted with substantial "garments," as vs. 6 shows. Their works are vain and transitory (Job 8:14; Prov. 11:18). **eateth . . . their eggs**—he who *partakes in their plans,* or *has anything to do with them,* finds them pestiferous. **that which is crushed** —The *egg, when it is broken,* breaketh out as a viper; their plans, however specious in their undeveloped form like the egg, when developed, are found pernicious. Though the viper is viviparous (from which "vi-per" is derived), yet during gestation, the young are included in eggs, which break at the birth [BOCHART]; however, metaphors often combine things without representing everything to the life. **6. not . . . garments**—like the "fig leaves" wherewith Adam and Eve vainly tried to cover their shame, as contrasted with "the coats of skins" which the Lord God made to clothe them with (ch. 64:6; Rom. 13:

14; Gal. 3:27; Phil. 3:9). The artificial self-deceiving sophisms of human philosophy (I Tim. 6:5; II Tim. 2:16, 23). **7. feet**—*All* their members are *active* in evil; in vs. 3, the "hands, fingers, lips, and tongue," are specified. **run . . . haste**—(Rom. 3:15). Contrast David's "running and hasting" in the ways of God (Ps. 119:32, 60). **thoughts**—not merely their acts, but their whole *thoughts*. **8. peace**—whether in relation to God, to their own conscience, or to their fellow men (ch. 57:20, 21). **judgment**—justice. **crooked**—the opposite of "straightforward" (Prov. 2:15; 28:18). **9. judgment far**—retribution in kind because *they* had shown "no *judgment* in their goings" (vs. 8). *"The vindication of our just rights"* by God is withheld by Him from us." **us**—In vs. 8 and previous verses, it was "they," the third person; here, "us . . . we," the first person. The nation here speaks: God thus making *them* out of their own mouth condemn themselves; just as *He* by His prophet had condemned them before. Isaiah includes himself with his people and speaks in their name. **justice**—God's *justice* bringing salvation (ch. 46:13). **light**—the dawn of returning prosperity. **obscurity**—adversity (Jer. 8:15). **10. grope**—fulfilling Moses' threat (Deut. 28:29). **stumble at noon . . . as . . . night**—There is no relaxation of our evils; at the time when we might look for the noon of relief, there is still the night of our calamity. **in desolate places**—rather, to suit the parallel words "at noonday," in fertile (lit., fat; Gen. 27:28) fields [GESENIUS] (where all is promising) *we are like the dead* (who have no hope left them); or, where *others* are prosperous, *we* wander about as dead men; true of all unbelievers (ch. 26:10; Luke 15:17). **11. roar**—moan plaintively, like a hungry bear which growls for food. **doves**—(ch. 38:14; Ezek. 7:16). **salvation**—retribution in kind: because not salvation, but "destruction" was "in their paths" (vs. 7). **12.** (Dan. 9:5, etc.). **thee . . . us**—antithesis. **with us**—i.e., we are *conscious* of them (*Margin,* Job 12:3; 15:9). **know**—acknowledge they are *our* iniquities. **13.** The *particulars* of the sins *generally* confessed in the preceding verse (ch. 48:8; Jer. 2:19, 20). The act, the word, and the thought of apostasy, are all here marked: *transgression* and *departing,* etc.; *lying* (cf. vs. 4), and *speaking,* etc.; *conceiving* and uttering *from the heart.* **14.** Justice and righteousness are put away from our legal courts. **in the street**—in the forum, the place of judicature, usually at the gate of the city (Zech. 8:16). **cannot enter**—is shut out from the forum, or courts of justice. **15. faileth**—is not to be found. **he that departeth . . . prey**—He that will not fall in with the prevailing iniquity exposes himself as a prey to the wicked (Ps. 10:8, 9). **Lord saw it**—The iniquity of Israel, so desperate as to require nothing short of Jehovah's interposition to mend it, typifies the same necessity for a Divine Mediator existing in the deep corruption of man; Israel, the model nation, was chosen to illustrate his awful fact. **16. no man**—viz., to atone by his righteousness for the unrighteousness of the people. "Man" is emphatic, as in I Kings 2:2; no representative man able to retrieve the cause of fallen men (ch. 41:28; 63:5, 6; Jer. 5:1; Ezek. 22:30). **no intercessor**—no one to interpose, "to help . . . uphold" (ch. 63:5). **his arm**—(ch. 40:10; 51:5). Not *man's* arm, but *His* alone (Ps. 98:1; 44:3). **his righteousness**—the "arm" of Messiah. He won the victory for us, not by mere *might* as God, but by His invincible *righteousness,* as man having "the Spirit without measure" (ch. 11:5; 42:6, 21; 51:8; 53:11; I John 2:1). **17.** Messiah is represented as a warrior armed at all points, going forth to vindicate His people.

Owing to the unity of Christ and His people, their armor is like His, except that they have no "garments of *vengeance"* (which is God's prerogative, Rom. 12:19), or "cloak of *zeal"* (in the sense of *judicial fury* punishing the wicked; this zeal belongs properly to God, II Kings 10:16; Rom. 10:2; Phil. 3:6; "zeal," in the sense of *anxiety for the Lord's honor,* they have, Num. 25:11, 13; Ps. 69:9; II Cor. 7:11; 9:2); and for "salvation," which is of God alone (Ps. 3:8), they have as their *helmet* "the hope of salvation" (I Thess. 5:8). The "helmet of salvation" is attributed to them (Eph. 6:14, 17) in a secondary sense; viz., derived from Him, and as yet only in *hope,* not fruition (Rom. 8:24). The *second coming* here, as often, is included in this representation of Messiah. His "zeal" (John 2:15-17) at His first coming was but a type of His zeal and vengeance against the foes of God at His second coming (II Thess. 1:8-10; Rev. 19:11-21). **18. deeds**—*Hebrew,* "recompenses"; "according as their *deeds demand"* [MAURER]. This verse predicts the judgments at the Lord's second coming, which shall precede the final redemption of His people (ch. 66:18, 15, 16). **islands**—(*Note,* ch. 41:1). Distant countries. **19.** (Ch. 45:6; Mal. 1:11). The result of God's judgments (ch. 26:9; 66:18-20). **like a flood** —(Jer. 46:7, 8; Rev. 12:15). **lift up a standard**—rather, from a different *Hebrew* root, shall put him to flight, drive him away [MAURER]. LOWTH, giving a different sense to the *Hebrew* for "enemy" from that in vs. 18, and a forced meaning to the *Hebrew* for "Spirit of the Lord," translates, "When He shall come as a river *straitened* in its course, which a *mighty wind* drives along." **20. to Zion**—Romans 11:26 quotes it, *"out of* Zion." Thus Paul, by inspiration, supplements the sense from Psalm 14:7: He was, and is come to *Zion,* first with redemption, being sprung as man *out of* Zion. LXX translates *"for the sake of* Zion." Paul applies this verse to the coming restoration of Israel spiritually. **them that turn from**—(Romans 11:26). "shall turn away ungodliness from Jacob"; so LXX, Paul herein gives the full sense under inspiration. *They* turn from transgression, because He first turns them from it, and it from them (Ps. 130:4; Lam. 5:21). **21. covenant with them . . . thee**—The covenant is with *Christ,* and with *them* only as united to Him (Heb. 2:13). Jehovah addresses Messiah the representative and ideal Israel. The literal and spiritual Israel are His seed, to whom the promise is to be fulfilled (Ps. 22:30). **spirit . . . not depart . . . for ever**—(Jer. 31:31-37; Matt. 28:20).

CHAPTER 60

Vss. 1-22. ISRAEL'S GLORY AFTER HER AFFLICTION. An ode of congratulation to Zion on her restoration at the Lord's second advent to her true position as the mother church from which the Gospel is to be diffused to the whole Gentile world; the first promulgation of the Gospel among the Gentiles, *beginning at Jerusalem,* is an earnest of this. The language is too glorious to apply to anything that as yet has happened **1. Arise**—from the dust in which thou hast been sitting as a mourning female captive (ch. 3:26; 52:1, 2). **shine**—impart to others the spiritual light now given thee (vs. 3). *Margin* and GESENIUS translate, "Be enlightened"; be resplendent with posterity; imperative for the future indicative, "Thou shalt be enlightened" (ch. 58:8, 10; Eph. 5:8, 14). **glory of the Lord**—not merely the Shekinah, or cloud of glory, such as rested above the ark in the old dispensation, but the glory of the Lord in person (Jer. 3:16, 17). **is risen**—as the sun (Mal. 4:2; Luke 1:78, *Margin*). **2. darkness . . . earth**—the *rest* of the earth: in contrast with *"light . . .* upon *thee"* (vs. 1). The earth will be afterwards enlightened through Israel (ch. 9:2). **be seen**—*conspicuously:* so the *Hebrew*. 3. (Ch. 2:3; 11:10; 43:6; 49:22; 66:12.) **kings**—(ch. 49:7, 23; 52:15). **thy rising**—rather, "thy sun-rising," i.e., to the brightness that riseth upon thee. **4. Lift up . . . eyes**—Jerusalem is addressed as a female with *eyes cast down* from grief. **all they . . . they**—The Gentile peoples come together to bring back the dispersed Hebrews, restore their city, and worship Jehovah with offerings. **nursed at thy side**—rather carried. . . . It is the custom in the East to carry the children astride on the hip, with the arms around the body (ch. 66:12). **5. see**—(vs. 4), viz., the bringing back of thy sons. **flow together**—rather, "overflow *with joy*" [LOWTH]; or, from a different *Hebrew* root, *"be bright with joy"* [GESENIUS] (Job 3:4). **fear**—rather, *beat with the agitation* of solemn joy at the marvellous sight [HORSLEY] (Jer. 33:9). **be enlarged**—*swell* with delight. Grief, on the contrary, *contracts* the heart. **abundance of . . . sea**—the *wealth* of the lands beyond *the sea*, as in Solomon's time, the type of the coming reign of the Prince of peace. **converted**—rather, *be turned*, instead of being turned to purposes of sin and idolatry. **forces**—rather, riches. **6. camels**—laden with merchandise; the camel is "the ship of the desert" (cf. ch. 30:6). **cover thee**—so many of them shall there be. **dromedaries**—They have one hunch on the back, whereas the *camel* has two: distinguished for swiftness (Jer. 2:23). **Midian**—east of the Elanitic branch of the Red Sea, and stretching northward along Mount Seir. Associated with the Ishmaelites in traffic (Gen. 37:25, 28). **Ephah**—part of Midian, east of the Dead Sea. It abounded in camels (Judg. 6:5). **Sheba**—in Arabia Felix, famed for frankincense and gold (Ps. 72:15; Jer. 6:20), which they traded in (ch. 45:14; Job 6:19; Ezek. 27: 22). **7. Kedar**—(ch. 21:16; Song of Sol. 1:5), in the south of Arabia Deserta, or north of Arabia Petræa; they traded in flocks (Ezek. 27:21). **Nebaioth**—son of Ishmael, as was Kedar. Father of the Nabatheans in Arabia Petræa. **minister**—by coming up as an acceptable sacrifice. **come up with acceptance**—i.e., acceptably. The rams *offering themselves* voluntarily (Ps. 68:30; Rom. 12:1; I Pet. 2:5), without waiting for any other priest, answer to believers strong in faith and lamblike meekness; and in the white fleecelike robe of sanctity [VITRINGA]. **house of my glory**—the temple (Ezek. 41; Hag. 2:7, 9; Mal. 3:1). **8.** The prophet, seeing in vision new hosts approaching quickly like a cloud of doves, asks who they are. 9. (*Note*, ch. 42:4.) **Tarshish first**—The ships of *Tartessus* (*Note*, ch. 2:16; 23:1, i.e., vessels that trade to the most distant regions) will be among the *foremost* to bring back the scattered Israelites (ch. 66:20). **their silver**—The nations among whom the Jews have been scattered shall help them with their money in returning (vss. 5-7, 11, 16), as was the case at the return from Babylon (Ezra 1:4; cf. Ps. 68:30, 31). **unto the name . . . to the Holy One**—rather, *because of* the name—*because of* the Holy One (cf. ch. 55:5) [LOWTH]. **10. kings . . . minister unto thee**—(vs. 7 above, *Note;* ch. 49:23). **in my wrath I smote thee**—(ch. 54:7, 8; 57:17). **11.** (Rev. 21:25.) The gates are ever open to receive new offerings and converts (ch. 26:2; Acts 14:27; Rev. 3:8). In time of *peace* the gates of a city are open: so, under the Prince of peace, there shall be no need of barring gates against invaders. **forces**—riches. **be**

brought—as willing captives to the truth; or, *if not willingly*, be brought by *judgments to submit to Israel* (vss. 12, 14). GESENIUS explains it, "may come *escorted by a retinue*." **12. For**—the reason which will lead Gentile kings and people to submit themselves; fear of the God in Israel (Zech. 14:17). **13. glory**—i.e., the *trees* which adorned Lebanon; emblem of men eminent in natural gifts, devoting all that is in them to the God of Israel (Hos. 14:5, 6). **fir . . . pine . . . box**—rather, "the cypress . . . ilex . . . cedar." **place of my sanctuary**—Jerusalem (Jer. 3:17). **place of my feet**—no longer the *ark* (Jer. 3:16), "the footstool" of Jehovah (Ps. 99:5; 132:7; I Chron. 28:2); but "the place of His throne, the place of the soles of His feet, where He will dwell in the midst of the children of Israel for ever," in the new temple (Ezek. 43:7). **14. The sons**—Their *fathers* who "afflicted" Israel having been cut off by divine judgments (ch. 14:1, 2; 49:23). **The Zion of the Holy One**—The royal court of the Holy One. [MAURER] translates, "Zion, *the sanctuary (holy place)* of Israel" (ch. 57:15; Ps. 46:4). **15. forsaken** —(Ps. 78:60, 61). **no man went through thee**—Thy land was so desolate that no traveller, or caravan, passed through thee; true only of Israel, not true of the Church (Lam. 1:4). **excellency**—glory, i.e., for ever honored. **16. suck**—Thou shalt draw to thyself and enjoy all that is valuable of the possessions of the Gentiles, etc. (ch. 49:23; 61:6; 66:11, 12). **know**—by the favors bestowed on thee, and through thee on the Gentiles. **17.** Poetically, with figurative allusion to the furniture of the temple; all things in that happy age to come shall be changed for the better. **exactors**—viz., of tribute. **righteousness**—All rulers in restored Jerusalem shall not only be peaceable and righteous, but shall be, as it were, "peace" and "righteousness" itself in their administration. **18.** (Ch. 2:4.) Not only shall thy walls keep thee *safe* from foes, but "Salvation" shall serve as thy walls, converting thy foes into friends, and so ensuring thee perfect safety (ch. 26:1, 2). **gates**—once the scene of "destruction" when victorious foes burst through them (Neh. 1:3); henceforth to be not only the scene of praises, but "Praise" itself; the "gates," as the place of public concourse, were the scene of thanksgivings (II Chron. 31:2; Ps. 9:14; 24:7; 100:4). "Judah," the favored tribe, means "praise." **19.** The sun and moon, the brightest objects by day and night, shall be eclipsed by the surpassing glory of God manifesting Himself to thee (ch. 30:26; Zech. 2:5; Rev. 21:23; 22:5). **20.** There shall be no national and spiritual obscuration again as formerly (Joel 2:10; Amos 8:9). **mourning . . . ended**—(ch. 25:8; Rev. 21:4). **21. all righteous**—(ch. 4:3; 52:1; Rev. 21:27). **inherit . . . land**—(ch. 49:8; 54:3; 65:9; Ps. 37:11, 22; Matt. 5:5). **branch of my planting**—(ch. 61:3; Ps. 92:13; Matt. 15:13). **work of my hands**—the converted Israelites (ch. 29:23; 45:11). **that I may be glorified**—the final end of all God's gracious dealings (ch. 49:3; 61:3). **22. little one**—Even one, and that the smallest in number and rank, shall be multiplied a thousandfold in both respects (Mic. 5:2; Matt. 13:31, 32). **his time**—not *our* time; *we* might wish to hasten it, but it will come in due time, as in the case of Jesus' first coming (Gal. 4:4); so in that of the restoration of Israel and the conversion of the world (ch. 66:8; Hab. 2:3; Acts 1:7; Heb. 10:37).

CHAPTER 61

Vss. 1-11. MESSIAH'S OFFICES: RESTORATION OF ISRAEL. Messiah announces His twofold commission to bring gospel mercy at His first coming, and judgments on unbelievers and comfort to Zion at His second coming (vss. 1-9); the language can be applied to Isaiah, comforting by his prophecies the exiles in Babylon, only in a subordinate sense. **1. is upon me; because . . . hath anointed me**–quoted by Jesus as His credentials in preaching (Luke 4:18-21). The Spirit *is* upon Me in preaching, because Jehovah *hath* anointed Me from the womb (Luke 1: 35), and at baptism, with the Spirit "without measure," and permanently "abiding" on Me (ch. 11:2; John 1:32; 3:34; Ps. 45:7; with which cf. I Kings 1: 39, 40; 19:16; Exod. 29:7). "Anointed" as *Messiah*, Prophet, Priest, and King. **good tidings**–as the word "gospel" means. **the meek**–rather, "the poor," as Luke 4:18 has it; i.e., those afflicted with calamity, poor in circumstances and in spirit (Matt. 11:5). **proclaim liberty**–(John 8:31-36). Language drawn from the deliverance of the Babylonian captives, to describe the deliverance from sin and death (Heb. 2:15;) also from the "liberty proclaimed" to all bond-servants in the year of jubilee (vs. 2; Lev. 25:10; Jer. 34:8, 9). **opening of the prison**–The *Hebrew* rather is, "the *most complete* opening," viz., of the *eyes* to them that are bound, i.e., deliverance from *prison*, for captives are as it were *blind* in the darkness of prison (ch. 14:17; 35:5; 42:7) [EWALD]. So Luke 4:18 and LXX interpret it. Luke 4:18, under inspiration, adds to this, for the fuller explanation of the *single* clause in the *Hebrew*, "to set at liberty them that are bruised"; thus expressing the *double* "opening" implied; viz., that of the eyes (John 9:39), and that of the prison (Rom. 6:18; 7:24, 25; Heb. 2:15). His miracles were *acted parables.* **2. acceptable year**–the year of jubilee on which "liberty was proclaimed to the captives" (vs. 1; II Cor. 6:2). **day of vengeance**–The "acceptable time of grace" is a "year"; the time of "vengeance" but "a day" (so ch. 34:8; 63:4; Mal. 4:1). Jesus (Luke 4:20, 21) "closed the book" before this clause; for the interval from His first to His second coming is "the acceptable year"; the day of vengeance" will not be till He comes again (II Thess. 1:7-9). **our God**–The saints call Him *"our* God"; for He cometh to "avenge" them (Rev. 6:10; 19:2). **all that mourn**–The "all" seems to include the *spiritual* Israelite mourners, as well as the *literal,* who are in vs. 3 called "them that mourn *in Zion,"* and to whom ch. 57:18 refers. **3. to appoint . . . to give**–The double verb, with the one and the same accusative, imparts glowing vehemence to the style. **beauty for ashes**–There is a play on the sound and meaning of the *Hebrew* words, *peer, epher,* lit., "ornamental headdress" or *tiara* (Ezek. 24:17), worn in times of joy, instead of a headdress of "ashes," cast on the head in mourning (II Sam. 13:19). **oil of joy**–Perfumed ointment was poured on the guests at joyous feasts (Ps. 23:5; 45:7, 8; Amos 6:6). On occasions of grief its use was laid aside (II Sam. 14:2). **garment of praise**–bright-colored garments, indicative of thankfulness, instead of those that indicate despondency, as sackcloth (John 16:20). **trees of righteousness**–*Hebrew,* terebinth trees; symbolical of men *strong* in righteousness, instead of being, as heretofore, bowed down as a reed with sin and calamity (ch. 1:29, 30; 42:3; I Kings 14:15; Ps. 1:3; 92: 12-14; Jer. 17:8). **planting of . . . Lord**–(*Note,* ch. 60:21). **that he might be glorified**–(John 15:8). **4. old wastes**–Jerusalem and the cities of Judah which long lay in ruins (*Note,* ch. 58:12). **5. stand** –shall wait on you as servants (ch. 14:1, 2; 60:10). **6. But ye**–as contrasted with the "strangers." *Ye* shall have no need to attend to your flocks and

lands: *strangers* will do that for you; *your* exclusive business will be the service of Jehovah as His "priests" (Exod. 19:6, which remains yet to be realized; cf. as to the spiritual Israel, ch. 66:21; I Pet. 2:5, 9; Rev. 1:6; 5:10). **Ministers**–(Ezek. 44: 11). **eat . . . riches of . . . Gentiles**–(ch. 60:5-11). **in their glory . . . boast yourselves**–rather, "in their splendor ye shall *be substituted* in their stead"; ye shall substitute yourselves [MAURER]. **7. double**– Instead of your past share, ye shall have not merely as much, but "double" as much reward (ch. 40:2; Zech. 9:12; cf. the third clause in this verse). **confusion**–rather, humiliation, or contumely. **rejoice** –They shall *celebrate with jubilation* their portion [MAURER]. Transition from the second to the third person. **in their land**–marking the reference to literal Israel, not to the Church at large. **everlasting joy**–(ch. 35:10). **8. judgment**–justice, which requires that I should restore My people, and give them double in compensation for their sufferings. **robbery for burnt offering**–rather, from a different *Hebrew* root, *the spoil of iniquity* [HORSLEY]. So in Job 5:6. Hating, as I do, the *rapine,* combined *with iniquity,* perpetrated on My people *by* their enemies, I will vindicate Israel. **direct . . . work in truth**–rather, "I will give them the *reward of their work"* (cf. *Margin,* ch. 40:10; 49:4; 62:11) in faithfulness. **9. known**–honorably; shall be *illustrious* (Ps. 67:2). **people**–rather, "peoples." **seed . . . blessed**–(ch. 65:23). **10. Zion** (vs. 3) gives thanks for God's returning favor (cf. Luke 1:46, 47; Hab. 3:18). **salvation . . . righteousness**–inseparably connected together. The "robe" is a loose mantle thrown over the other parts of the dress (Ps. 132:9, 16; 149:4; Rev. 21:2; 19:8). **decketh himself with ornaments**–rather "maketh himself a *priestly headdress,"* i.e., a magnificent headdress, such as was worn by the high priest, viz., a miter and a plate, or crown of gold worn in front of it [AQUILA, etc.]; appropriate to the "kingdom of priests," dedicated to the offering of spiritual sacrifices to God continually (Exod. 19:6; Rev. 5:10; 20:6). **jewels**–rather, ornaments in general [BARNES]. **11.** (Ch. 45:8, 55: 10, 11; Ps. 72:3; 85:11.) **bud**–the tender shoots. **praise**–(ch. 60:18; 62:7).

CHAPTER 62

Vss. 1-12. INTERCESSORY PRAYERS FOR ZION'S RESTORATION, ACCOMPANYING GOD'S PROMISES OF IT, AS THE APPOINTED MEANS OF ACCOMPLISHING IT. **1. I**–the prophet, as representative of all the praying people of God who love and intercede for Zion (cf. vss. 6, 7; Ps. 102:13-17), or else Messiah (cf. vs. 6). So Messiah is represented as unfainting in His efforts for His people (ch. 42:4; 50:7). **righteousness thereof**–not its own inherently, but imputed to it, for its restoration to God's favor: hence *"salvation"* answers to it in the parallelism. "Judah" is to be *"saved"* through "the Lord our (Judah's and the Church's) *righteousness"* (Jer. 23:6). **as brightness**– properly the bright shining of the rising sun (ch. 60: 19; 4:5; II Sam. 23:4; Prov. 4:18). **lamp**–blazing torch. **2.** (Ch. 11:10; 42:1-6; 49:7, 22, 23; 60:3, 5, 16.) **new name**–expression of thy new and improved condition (vs. 4), the more valuable and lasting as being conferred by Jehovah Himself (vs. 12; ch. 65:15; Rev. 2:17; 3:12). **3.** (Zech. 9:16) **in . . . hand of . . . Lord**–As a crown is worn on the *head,* not "in the hand," *hand* must here be figurative for "under the Lord's *protection*" (cf. Deut. 33:3). "All His saints are in thy hand." His people are *in His hand* at the same time that they are "a crown of glory" to Him (Rev. 6:2; 19:12); reciprocally, *He* is "a crown of glory and a diadem of beauty" to them (ch. 28:5; cf. Mal. 3:17). **4. be termed**–*be* "forsaken," so as that that term could be applicable to thee. **Hephzi-bah**–(II Kings 21:1), the name of Hezekiah's wife, a type of Jerusalem, as Hezekiah was of Messiah (ch. 32:1): "my delight is in her." **Beulah**–"Thou art married." See the same contrast of Zion's past and future state under the same figure (ch. 54:4-6; Rev. 21:2, 4). **land ... married**–to Jehovah as its *Lord and Husband:* implying not only ownership, but *protection* on the part of the Owner [HORSLEY]. **5. thy sons**–rather, changing the points, which are of no authority *in Hebrew,* "thy builder" or "restorer," i.e., God; for in the parallel clause, and in vs. 4, God is implied as being "married" to her; whereas her "sons" could hardly be said to marry their mother; and in ch. 49:18, they are said to be her *bridal ornaments,* not her husband. The *plural* form, builders, is used of God in reverence as "husbands" (*Note,* ch. 54:5). **over the bride**–in the possession of the bride (ch. 65:19; Jer. 32:41; Zeph. 3:17). **6. I**–Isaiah speaking in the person of the Messiah. **watchmen upon ... walls**–image from the watches set upon a city's wall to look out for the approach of a messenger with good tidings (ch. 52:7, 8); the good tidings of the return of the Jewish exiles from Babylon, prefiguring the return from the present dispersion (cf. ch. 21:6-11; 56:10; Ezek. 3:17; 33:7). The watches in the East are announced by a loud cry to mark the vigilance of the watchmen. **ye that ... mention ... Lord**–*Hebrew,* "ye that are the Lord's remembrancers"; God's servants who by their prayers "put God in remembrance" of His promises (ch. 43:26); we are required to *remind* God, as if God could, which He cannot, *forget* His promises (Ps. 119:49; Jer. 14:21). **7. no rest**–*Hebrew,* "silence"; keep not silence *yourselves,* nor let *Him* rest in silence. Cf. as to Messiah Himself, "I will not hold ... peace ... not rest" (vs. 1); Messiah's watchmen (vss. 6, 7) imitate *Him* (vs. 1) in intercessory "prayer without ceasing" for Jerusalem (Ps. 122:6; 51:18); also for the spiritual Jerusalem, the Church (Luke 18:1, 7; Rom. 1:9). **a praise**–(*Note,* ch. 61:11; Zeph. 3:20). **8. sworn by ... right hand**–His mighty instrument of accomplishing His will (cf. ch. 45:23; Heb. 6:13). **sons of ... stranger**–*Foreigners* shall no more rob thee of the fruit of thy labors (cf. ch. 65:21, 22). **9. eat ... and praise**–not consume it on their own lusts, and without thanksgiving. **drink it in ... courts**–They who have *gathered* the vintage shall drink it at the feasts held in the courts surrounding the temple (Deut. 12:17, 18; 14:23, etc.). **10.** What Isaiah in the person of Messiah had engaged in (vs. 1) unrestingly to seek, and what the watchmen were unrestingly to pray for (vs. 7), and what Jehovah solemnly promised (vss. 8, 9), is now to be fulfilled; the Gentile nations are commanded to "go through the gates" (either of their own cities [ROSENMULLER] or of Jerusalem [MAURER]), in order to remove all obstacles out of "the way of *the* people" (Israel) (*Note,* 57:14; 40:3; 52:10-12). **standard**–for the dispersed Jews to rally round, with a view to their return (ch. 49:22; 11:12). **11. salvation**–embodied in the Saviour (see Zech. 9:9), **his work**–rather, *recompense* (ch. 40:10). **12. Sought out**–*Sought after and highly prized* by Jehovah; answering to "not forsaken" in the parallel clause; no longer abandoned, but loved; image from a wife (vs. 4; Jer. 30:14).

CHAPTER 63

VSS. 1-19. MESSIAH COMING AS THE AVENGER, IN ANSWER TO HIS PEOPLE'S PRAYERS. Messiah, approaching Jerusalem after having avenged His people on His and their enemies, is represented under imagery taken from the destruction of "Edom," the type of the last and most bitter foes of God and His people (see ch. 34:5, etc.). **1. Who**–the question of the prophet in prophetic vision. **dyed**–scarlet with blood (vss. 2, 3; Rev. 19:13). **Bozrah**–(*Note,* ch. 34:6). **travelling**–rather, stately; lit., "throwing back the head" [GESENIUS]. **speak in righteousness**–answer of Messiah. I, who have in faithfulness given a promise of deliverance, am now about to fulfil it. Rather, speak *of* righteousness (ch. 45:19; 46:13); *salvation* being meant as the result of His "righteousness" [MAURER]. **save**–The same Messiah that destroys the unbeliever *saves* the believer. **2.** The prophet asks why His garments are "dyed" and "red." **winefat**–rather, the wine-press, wherein the grapes were trodden with the feet; the juice would stain the garment of him who trod them (Rev. 14:19, 20; 19:15). The image was appropriate, as the country round Bozrah abounded in grapes. This final blow inflicted by Messiah and His armies (Rev. 19:13-15) shall decide His claim to the kingdoms usurped by Satan, and by the "beast," to whom Satan delegates his power. It will be a day of judgment to the hostile Gentiles, as His first coming was a day of judgment to the unbelieving Jews. **3.** Reply of Messiah. For the image, see Lamentations 1: 15. He "treads the winepress" here not as a *sufferer,* but as an *inflicter* of vengeance. **will tread ... shall be ... will stain**– rather preterites," I trod ... trampled ... was sprinkled ... I stained." **blood**–lit., "spirted juice" of the grape, pressed out by treading [GESENIUS]. **4. is**–rather, "was." This assigns the reason why He has thus destroyed the foe (Zeph. 3:8). **my redeemed**–My people *to be redeemed.* **day ... year**–here, as in ch. 34:8; 61:2, the time of "vengeance" is described as a "day"; that of grace and of "recompense" to the "redeemed," as a "year." **5.** The same words as in ch. 59:16, except that *there* it is His "righteousness," here it is His "fury," which is said to have upheld Him. **6.** Rather, preterites, "I *trod* down ... *made* them drunk." The same image occurs ch. 51:17, 21-23; Psalm 75: 8; Jeremiah 25:26, 27. **will bring down ... strength to ... earth**–rather, "I *spilled* their life-*blood* (the same *Hebrew* words as in vs. 3) on the earth" [LOWTH and LXX]. **7.** Israel's penitential confession and prayer for restoration (Ps. 102: 17, 20), extending from this verse to the end of ch. 64. **loving-kindnesses ... praises ... mercies ... loving-kindnesses**–The *plurals* and the repetitions imply that language is inadequate to express the full extent of God's goodness. **us**–the dispersed Jews at the time just preceding their final restoration. **house of Israel**–of all ages; God was good not merely to the Jews now dispersed, but to Israel in every age of its history. **8. he**–Jehovah "said," i.e., thought, in choosing them as His covenant people; so "said" (Ps. 95:10). Not that God was ignorant that the Jews would not keep faith with Him; but God is here said, according to *human* modes of thought to *say within Himself* what He might *naturally* have expected, as the result of His goodness to the Jews; thus the enormity of their *unnatural* perversity is the more vividly set forth. **lie**–prove false to Me (cf. Ps. 44:17). **so**–in virtue of His having *chosen* them, He became their *Saviour.* So the "therefore" (Jer. 31:33). His eternal *choice* is the ground of His actually *saving* men (Eph. 1:3, 4). **9. he was afflicted**—*English Version* reads the *Hebrew* as the *Keri* (*Margin*) does, "There was affliction *to Him*." But the *Chetib* (text) reads, "There was *no* affliction" (the change in *Hebrew* being only of one letter); i.e., "In all their affliction there was no (utterly overwhelming) affliction" [GESENIUS]; or, for "*Hardly* had an affliction befallen them, *when* the angel of His presence saved them" [MAURER]; or, as best suits the parallelism, "In all their straits there was no straitness in His goodness to them" [HOUBIGANT], (Judg. 10:16; Mic. 2:7; II Cor. 6:12). **angel of his presence**—lit., "of His face," i.e., who stands before Him continually; Messiah (Exod. 14:19; 23: 20, 21; Prov. 8:30); language applicable to no *creature* (Exod. 32:34; 33:2, 14; Num. 20:16; Mal. 3:1). **bare them**—(ch. 46:3, 4; 40:11; Exod. 19:4; Deut. 32:11, 12). **10. vexed**—grieved (Ps. 78:40; 95:10; Acts 7:51; Eph. 4:30; Heb. 3:10, 17). **he fought**—rather, "He it was that fought," viz., the angel of His presence [HORSLEY], (Lam. 2:5). **11. remembered**—Notwithstanding *their* perversitiy, He forgot not *His* covenant of old; therefore He did not wholly forsake them (Lev. 26:40-42, 44, 45; Ps. 106: 45, 46); the Jews make this their plea with God, that He should not now forsake them. **saying**—God is represented, in human language, mentally speaking of Himself and His former acts of love to Israel, as His ground for pitying them notwithstanding their rebellion. **sea**—Red Sea. **shepherd**—Moses; or if the *Hebrew* be read *plural*, "shepherds," Moses, Aaron, and the other leaders (so Ps. 77:20). **put ... Spirit ... within him**—*Hebrew*, "in the inward parts of him," i.e., Moses; or it refers to the flock, "in the midst of his people" (Num. 11:17, 25; Neh. 9:20; Hag. 2:5). **12.** The *right hand* of Moses was but the instrument; the *arm* of God was the real mover (Exod. 15:6; 14:21). **dividing the water**—(Neh. 9: 11; Ps. 78:13). **13. deep**—lit., "the tossing and roaring sea." **wilderness**—rather, the open plain [HORSLEY], wherein there is no obstacle to cause a horse in its course the danger of stumbling. **14. As a beast ... rest**—image from a herd led "down" from the hills to a fertile and well-watered "valley" (Ps. 23:2); so God's Spirit "caused Israel to rest" in the promised land after their weary wanderings. **to make ... name**—(So. vs. 12; II Sam. 7:23). **15.** Here begins a fervent appeal to God to pity Israel now on the ground of His former benefits. **habitation of ... holiness**—(ch. 57:15; Deut. 26:15; II Chron. 30:27; Ps. 33:14; 80:14). **zeal ... strength**—evinced formerly for Thy people. **sounding of ... bowels**—*Thine emotions of compassion* (ch. 16:11; Jer. 31:20; 48:36; Hos. 11:8). **16. thou ... father**—of Israel, by right not merely of creation, but also of electing adoption (ch. 64:8; Deut. 32:6; I Chron. 29: 10). **though Abraham ... Israel**—It had been the besetting temptation of the Jews to rest on the mere privilege of their descent from faithful Abraham and Jacob (Matt. 3:9; John 8:39; 4:12); now at last they renounce this, to trust in God alone as their Father, notwithstanding all appearances to the contrary. Even though Abraham, our earthly father, on whom we have prided ourselves, disown us, *Thou* wilt not (ch. 49:15; Ps. 27:10). Isaac is not mentioned, because not *all* his posterity was admitted to the covenant, whereas all Jacob's was; Abraham is specified because he was the first father of the Jewish race. **everlasting**—an argument why He should help them, viz., because of His *everlasting immutability*. **17. made us to err**—i.e., "suffer" us to err and to be hardened in our heart. They do not mean to deny their own blameworthiness, but confess that through their

own fault God gave them over to a reprobate mind (ch. 6:9, 10; Ps. 119:10; Rom. 1:28). **Return**—(Num. 10:36; Ps. 90:13.) **18. people of ... holiness**—Israel dedicated as holy unto God (ch. 62:12; Deut. 7:6). **possessed**—viz., the Holy Land, or Thy "sanctuary," taken from the following clause, which is parallel to this (cf. ch. 64:10, 11; Ps. 74:6-8). **thy**—an argument why God should help them; their cause is *His* cause. **19. thine ... never**—rather, "We are Thine *from of old;* Thou barest not rule over them" [BARNES]. LOWTH translates, "We for long have been as those over whom Thou hast not ruled, who are not called by Thy name"; "for long" thus stands in contrast to "but a little while" (vs. 18). But the analogy of vs. 18 makes it likely that the first clause in this verse refers to the Jews, and the second to their foes, as *English Version* and BARNES translate it. The Jews' foes are aliens who have unjustly intruded into the Lord's heritage.

CHAPTER 64

Vss. 1-12. TRANSITION FROM COMPLAINT TO PRAYER. **1. rend ... heavens**—bursting forth to execute vengeance, suddenly descending on Thy people's foe (Ps. 18:9; 144:5; Hab. 3:5, 6). **flow down**—(Judg. 5:5; Mic. 1:4). **2.** Oh, that Thy wrath would consume Thy foes *as the fire.* Rather, "as the fire burneth *the dry brushwood*" [GESENIUS]. **3. When**—Supply from vs. 2, "As when." **terrible things**—(Ps. 65:5). **we looked not for**—far exceeding the expectation of any of our nation; unparalleled before (Exod. 34:10; Ps. 68:8). **camest down**—on Mount Sinai. **mountains flowed**—Repeated from vs. 1; they pray God to do the *very same things* for Israel now as in former ages. GESENIUS, instead of "flowed" here, and "flow" in vs. 1, translates from a different Hebrew root, "quake ... quaked"; but "fire" *melts* and *causes to flow*, rather than to *quake* (vs. 2). **4. perceived by the ear**—Paul (I Cor. 2:9) has for this, "nor have entered into the heart of man"; the virtual sense, sanctioned by his inspired authority; men might hear with the outward ear, but they could only by the Spirit "perceive" with the "heart" the spiritual significancy of God's acts, both those in relation to Israel, primarily referred to here, and those relating to the Gospel secondarily, which Paul refers to. **O God ... what he ... prepared**—rather, "nor hath eye seen *a god* beside thee *who doeth such things.*" They refer to God's *past* marvellous acts in behalf of Israel as a plea for His now interposing for His people; but the Spirit, as Paul by inspiration shows, contemplated *further* God's revelation in the Gospel, which abounds in marvellous paradoxes never before heard of by carnal ear, not to be understood by mere human sagacity, and when foretold by the prophets not fully perceived or credited; and even after the manifestation of Christ not to be understood save through the inward teaching of the Holy Ghost. These are partly past and present, and partly future; therefore Paul substitutes "prepared" for "doeth," though his context shows he includes all three. For "waiteth" he has "love Him"; godly *waiting* on Him must flow from love, and not mere fear. **5. meetest**—i.e., Thou makest peace, or enterest into covenant with him (*Note*, ch. 47:3). **rejoiceth and worketh**—i.e., who *with joyful willingness* worketh [GESENIUS] (Acts 10:35; John 7:17). **those**—Thou meetest "those," in apposition to "him" who represents a class whose characteristics "those that," etc., more fully describes. **remember thee in thy ways**—(ch. 26:8). **sinned**—lit., "tripped," carrying on the figure in "ways." **in those is continuance**—a plea to deprecate the *continuance* of God's *wrath;* it is not in Thy wrath that there is continuance (ch. 54:7, 8; Ps. 30:5; 103:9), but *in* Thy ways ("those"), viz., of covenant-mercy to Thy people (Mic. 7:18-20; Mal. 3:6); on the strength of the everlasting continuance of His covenant they infer by faith, "we shall be saved." God "remembered" for them His covenant (Ps. 106:45), though *they* often "remembered not" Him (Ps. 78:42). CASTELLIO translates, "we have sinned for long in them ('thy ways'), and could we then be saved?' But they hardly would use such a plea when their very object was to be saved. **6. unclean thing**—legally unclean, as a leper. True of Israel, everywhere now cut off by unbelief and by God's judgments from the congregation of the saints. **righteousness**—plural, "uncleanness" extended to *every particular act* of theirs, even to their prayers and praises. True of the best doings of the unregenerate (Phil. 3:6-8; Titus 1:15; Heb. 11:6). **filthy rags** —lit., a "menstruous rag" (Lev. 15:33; 20:18; Lam. 1:17). **fade...leaf**—(Ps. 90:5, 6). **7. stirreth**—*rouseth* himself from spiritual drowsiness. **take hold**—(ch. 27:5). **8. father**—(ch. 63:16). **clay... potter**—(ch. 29:16; 45:9). Unable to mould themselves aright, they beg the sovereign will of God to mould them unto salvation, even as He *made* them at the first, and is their "Father." **9.** (Ps. 74:1, 2). **we are...thy people**—(Jer. 14:9, 21). **10. holy cities**—No city but Jerusalem is called "the holy city" (ch. 48:2; 52:1); the *plural,* therefore, refers to *the upper and the lower parts* of the same city Jerusalem [VITRINGA]; or all Judea was holy to God, so its *cities* were deemed "holy" [MAURER]. But the parallelism favors VITRINGA. *Zion* and *Jerusalem* (the one city) answering to "holy cities." **11. house**—the temple. **beautiful**—includes the idea of *glorious* (Mark 13:1; Acts 3:2). **burned**—(Ps. 74:7; Lam. 2:7; II Chron. 36:19). Its destruction under Nebuchadnezzar prefigured that under Titus. **pleasant things**—*Hebrew,* "objects of desire"; our homes, our city, and all its dear associations. **12. for these things**—Wilt Thou, *notwithstanding* these calamities of Thy people, still refuse Thy aid (ch. 42:14)?

CHAPTER 65

Vss. 1-25. GOD'S REPLY IN JUSTIFICATION OF HIS DEALINGS WITH ISRAEL. In ch. 64:9, their plea was, "we are all Thy people." In answer, God declares that *others* (Gentiles) would be taken into covenant with Him, while His ancient people would be rejected. The Jews were slow to believe this; hence Paul says (Rom. 10:20) that Isaiah was "very bold" in advancing so unpopular a sentiment; he implies what Paul states (Rom. 2:28; 9:6, 7; 11:1-31), that "they are not *all* (in opposition to the Jews' plea, ch. 64:9) Israel which are of Israel." God's reason for so severely dealing with Israel is not changeableness in Him, but sin in them (vss. 2-7). Yet the whole nation shall not be destroyed, but only the wicked; a remnant shall be saved (vss. 8-10, 11-16). There shall be, finally, universal blessedness to Israel, such as they had prayed for (vss. 17-25). **1. I am sought**—*Hebrew,* "I have granted access unto Me to them," etc. (so Ezek. 14:3, "Should I be *inquired of*"; Eph. 2:18). **found**—Romans 10:20 renders this, "I was made manifest." As an in-

stance of the sentiment in the clause, "I am sought ..." see John 12:21; of the sentiment in this clause, Acts 9:5. Cf. as to the Gentile converts, Ephesians 2:12, 13. **Behold me**—(ch. 45:22). **nation ...not called by my name**—i.e., the Gentiles. God retorts in their own words (ch. 63:19) that their plea as being exclusively "called by His name" will not avail, for God's gospel invitation is not so exclusive (Rom. 9:25; 1:16). **2. spread out...hands**—inviting them earnestly (Prov. 1:24). **all...day**—continually, late and early (Jer. 7:13). **rebellious people**—Israel, whose rebellion was the occasion of God's turning to the Gentiles (Rom. 11:11, 12, 15). **way...not good**—i.e., the very reverse of good, very bad (Ezek. 36:31). **3. continually**—answering to "all the day" (vs. 2). God was continually inviting them, and they *continually* offending Him (Deut. 32:21). **to my face**—They made no attempt to hide their sin (ch. 3:9). Cf. *"before Me"* (Exod. 20:3). **in gardens**—(*Note,* ch. 1:29; 66:17; Lev. 17: 5). **altars of brick**—*Hebrew,* "bricks." .God had commanded His altars to be of *unhewn stone* (Exod. 20:25). This was in order to separate them, even in *external respects,* from idolaters; also, as all chiselling was forbidden, they could not inscribe superstitious symbols on them as the heathen did. Bricks were more easily so inscribed than stone; hence their use for the cuneiform inscriptions at Babylon, and also for idolatrous altars. Some, not so well, have supposed that the "bricks" here mean the flat brick-paved *roofs* of houses on which they sacrificed to the sun, etc. (II Kings 23:12; Jer. 19: 13). **4. remain among...graves**—viz., for purposes of necromancy, as if to hold converse with the dead (ch. 8:19, 20; cf. Mark 5:3); or, for the sake of purifications, usually performed at night among sepulchers, to appease the manes [MAURER]. **monuments**—*Hebrew,* "pass the night in *hidden recesses,"* either the idol's *inmost shrines* ("consecrated precincts") [HORSLEY], where they used to sleep, in order to have divine communications in dreams [JEROME]; or better, on account of the parallel "graves," *sepulchral caves* [MAURER]. **eat swine's flesh**—To eat it at all was contrary to God's law (Lev. 11:7), but it much increased their guilt that they ate it in idolatrous sacrifices (cf. ch. 66: 17). VARRO (*Re Rust.,* 2.4) says that swine were first used in sacrifices; the Latins sacrificed a pig to Ceres; it was also offered on occasion of treaties and marriages. **broth**—so called from the "pieces" (*Margin*) or fragments of bread over which the broth was poured [GESENIUS]; such broth, made of swine's flesh, offered in sacrifice, was thought to be especially acceptable to the idol and was used in magic rites. Or, "fragments (pieces) of abominable foods," etc. This fourth clause explains more fully the third, as the second does the first [MAURER]. **is in**—rather, lit., "is their vessels," i.e., constitute their vessels' contents. The Jews, in our Lord's days, and ever since the return from Babylon, have been free from idolatry; still the imagery from idolatrous abominations, as being the sin most loathsome in God's eyes and that most prevalent in Isaiah's time, is employed to describe the foul sin of Israel in all ages, culminating in their killing Messiah, and still rejecting Him. **5.** (Matt. 9:11; Luke 5:30; 18:11; Jude 19). Applicable to the hypocritical self-justifiers of our Lord's time. **smoke**—alluding to the smoke of their self-righteous sacrifices; the fire of God's *wrath* was kindled at the sight, and exhibited itself in the *smoke* that breathed forth from His nostrils; in *Hebrew* the nose is the seat of anger; and the nostrils distended in wrath, as it were, breathe forth smoke [ROSENMULLER] (Ps. 18:8). **6. written before me**—"it is decreed by Me," viz., what follows (Job 13:26), [MAURER]; or, their guilt is recorded before Me (cf. Dan. 7:10; Rev. 20:12; Mal. 3:16). **into . . . bosom**—(Ps. 79:12; Jer. 32:18; Luke 6:38). The Orientals used the loose fold of the garment falling on "the bosom" or lap, as a receptacle for carrying things. The sense thus is: I will repay their sin so *abundantly* that the hand will not be able to receive it; it will need the spacious *fold on the bosom* to contain it [ROSENMULLER]. Rather it is, "I will repay it to *the very person from whom it has emanated.*" Cf. "God did render the evil of the men of Shechem upon their heads" (Judg. 9: 57; Ps. 7:16) [GESENIUS]. **7.** Their sin had been accumulating from age to age until God at last repaid it in full. **mountains**—(ch. 57:7; Ezek. 18:6; 20:27, 28; Hos. 4:13). **their**—"Your" had preceded. From speaking *to,* He speaks *of* them; this implies growing alienation from them and greater distance. **work**—the full *recompense* of their work (so ch. 49: 4). **8. new wine**—*as if some grapes having good wine-producing juice in them,* be found in a cluster which the vinedresser was about to throw away as bad, and one saith, etc. **blessing**—i.e., good wine-producing juice (cf. Judg. 9:13; Joel 2:14). **so**—God will spare the godly "remnant," while the ungodly mass of the nation shall be destroyed (ch. 1: 9; 6:13; 10:21; 11:11, 12-16). **my servants**—the godly remnant. But HORSLEY, "for the sake of my *servant, Messiah.*" **9. seed**—"the holy seed" (ch. 6:13), a posterity from Jacob, designed to repossess the Holy Land, forfeited by the sin of the former Jews. **my mountains**—Jerusalem and the rest of Judea, peculiarly God's (cf. ch. 2:2; 11:9; 14:32). **it**—the Holy Land. **elect**—(vss. 15, 22.) **10. Sharon**—(*Notes,* ch. 33:9; 35:2). **Achor**—meaning "trouble"; a valley near Jericho, so called from the trouble caused to Israel by Achan's sin (Josh. 7:24). "The valley of Achor," proverbial for whatever caused calamity, shall become proverbial joy and prosperity (Hos. 2:15). **11. holy mountain**—Moriah, on which the temple was. **troop**—rather "Gad," the Babylonian god of fortune, the planet Jupiter, answering to Baal or Bel; the Arabs called it "the Greater Good Fortune"; and the planet Venus answering to Meni, "the Lesser Good Fortune" [GESENIUS, KIMCHI, etc.]. Tables were laid out for their idols with all kinds of viands, and a cup containing a mixture of wine and honey, in Egypt especially, on the last day of the year [JEROME]. **drink offering**—rather, mixed drink. **number**—rather, Meni; as goddess of fortune she was thought to *number* the fates of men. VITRINGA understands Gad to be the sun; Meni the moon, or Ashtaroth or Astarte (I Kings 11:33). **12. number**—"doom" you. Alluding to the "number," as Meni (vs. 11) means. Retribution in kind, the punishment answering to the sin (cf. II Chron. 36: 14-17). **I called, ye . . . not answer**—"I called," though "none had called" upon Me (ch. 64:7); yet even then none "answered" (Prov. 1:24). Contrast with this God and His people's mutual fellowship in prayer (vs. 24). **eat**—enjoy all blessings from me (Song of Sol. 5:1). **hungry**—(Amos 4:6; 8:11). This may refer to the siege of Jerusalem under Titus, when 1,100,000 are said to have perished by famine; thus vs. 15 will refer to God's people without distinction of Jew and Gentile receiving "another name," viz., that of *Christians* [HOUBI-GANT]. A farther fulfilment may still remain, just before the creation of the "new heavens and earth,"

as the context, vs. 17, implies. **14. howl**—(ch. 15:2; Matt. 8:12). **15. curse**—The name of "Jew" has been for long a formula of execration (cf. Jer. 29: 22); if one wishes to curse another, he can utter nothing worse than this, "God make thee what the Jew is!" Contrast the formula (Gen. 48:20) [MAURER]. **my chosen**—the elect Church, gathered from Jews and Gentiles, called by "another name," *Christians* (Acts 11:26). However (*Note,* vs. 13), as "My chosen," or "elect," in vs. 3, refers to the "seed of Jacob," *the believing Jews,* hereafter about to possess their land (vss. 19, 22), are *ultimately* meant by "My chosen," as contrasted with the unbelieving Jews ("ye"). These elect Jews shall be called by "another," or a *new name,* i.e., shall no longer be "forsaken" of God for unbelief, but shall be His "delight" and "married" to Him (ch. 62:2, 4). **thee**—unbelieving Israel. *Isaiah.* here speaks of God, whereas in the preceding sentences *God Himself* spake. This change of persons marks without design how completely the prophet realized God with him and in him, so that he passes, without formally announcing it, from God's words to his own, and vice versa, both alike being from God. **16. That he**—rather, "he who," etc. **blesseth . . .**—(Ps. 72:17; Jer. 4:2). **God of truth**—very God, as opposed to *false* gods; *Hebrew, Amen:* the very name of Messiah (II Cor. 1:20; Rev. 3:14), faithful to His promises (John 1:17; 6:32). Real, substantial, spiritual, eternal, as opposed to the shadowy types of the law. **sweareth . . .**—God alone shall be appealed to as God (ch. 19:18; Deut. 6:13; Ps. 63:11). **troubles**—i.e., sins, provocations [LOWTH]. Rather, *calamities* caused by your sins; so far from these visiting you again, the very *remembrance* of them is "hid from Mine eyes" by the magnitude of the blessings I will confer on you (vs. 17, etc.) [MAURER]. **17.** As Caleb inherited the same land which his feet trod on (Deut. 1:36; Josh. 14:9), so Messiah and His saints shall inherit the renovated earth which once they trod while defiled by the enemy (ch. 34:4; 51:16; 66:22; Ezek. 21:27; Ps. 2:8; 37:11; II Pet. 3:13; Heb. 12:26-28; Rev. 21: 1). **not be remembered**—See *Note* on "troubles," vs. 16; the words here answer to "the former . . . forgotten," etc. The former sorrows of the earth, under the fall, shall be so far from recurring, that their very remembrance shall be obliterated by the many mercies I will bestow on the new earth (Rev. 21:4-27). **18. rejoice for ever . . . Jerusalem**—(ch. 51:11). "Everlasting joy . . . Zion." Spiritually (I Thess. 5:16). **19.** (Ch. 62:5.) **weeping . . . no more**—(ch. 25:7, 8; 35:10; Rev. 7:17; 21:4), primarily, foretold of *Jerusalem;* secondarily, of *all* the redeemed. **20.** The longevity of men in the first age of the world shall be enjoyed again. **thence**—from that time forward. **infant of days**—i.e., an infant who shall only complete a few days; short-lived. **filled . . . days**—None shall die without attaining a full old age. **child . . . die . . . hundred years**—i.e., "he that dieth an hundred years old shall die a mere child" [LOWTH]. **sinner . . . hundred . . . be accursed**—"The sinner that dieth at an hundred years shall be deemed accursed," i.e., his death at so early an age, which in those days the hundredth year will be regarded, just as if it were mere childhood, shall be deemed the effect of God's special visitation in wrath [ROSENMULLER]. This passage proves that the better age to come on earth, though much superior to the present will not be a perfect state; sin and death shall have place in it (cf. Rev. 20:7, 8), but much less frequently than now. **21.** (*Note,* ch. 62:8; Amos 9:14.) **22.** They shall not experience the curse pronounced (Lev. 26:16; Deut. 28:30). **tree**—among the most *long-lived* of objects in nature. They shall live as long as the trees they "plant" (cf. ch. 61:3, end of verse; Ps. 92:12). **enjoy**—Hebrew, "consume," "wear out"; they shall live to enjoy the last of it (ch. 62:9). **23. bring forth for trouble**—lit., "for terror," i.e., "They shall not bring forth children for a *sudden death*" (Lev. 26:16; Jer. 15:8). **seed . . . blessed**—(ch. 61:9). **offspring with them**—(Hos. 9:12). "Their offspring shall be with themselves" [MAURER]; not "brought forth" only to be cut off by "sudden death" (see the parallel clause). **24.** Contrast ch. 64:7, "none . . . calleth," etc.; and *Note*, vs. 12, "I called, ye did not answer." MAURER translates, "They shall hardly (lit., "not yet") call, when (lit., "and") I will answer; they shall be still speaking, when I will hear" (Ps. 32:5; Dan 9:20, 21). **25.** (*Notes*, ch. 11:6-9). **and dust**—rather, "but dust," etc. The curse shall *remain* on the serpent [HORSLEY], (Gen. 3:14; Mic. 7: 17). *To lick the dust* is figurative of the utter and perpetual *degradation* of Satan and his emissaries (ch. 49:23; Ps. 72:9). Satan fell *self-tempted;* therefore no atonement was contrived for him, as there was for man, who fell by *his* temptation (Jude 6; John 8:44). From his peculiar connection with the earth and man, it has been conjectured that the exciting cause of his rebellion was God's declaration that human nature was to be raised into union with the Godhead; this was "the truth" concerning the person of the Son of God which "he abode not in"; it galled his pride that a lower race was to be raised to that which he had aspired to (I Tim. 3:6). How exultingly he might say, when man fell through him, "*God* would raise manhood into union with Himself; *I* have brought it down below the beasts by sin!" At that very moment and spot he was told that the seed of the abhorred race, man, should bruise his head (I John 3:8). He was raised up for this, to show forth God's glory (Exod. 9:16; Rom. 9:17). In his unfallen state he may have been God's vicegerent over the earth and the animal kingdom before man: this will account for his assuming the form of a serpent (Gen. 3). Man succeeded to that office (Gen. 2:19, 20), but forfeited it by sin, whence Satan became "prince of this world"; Jesus Christ supplants the usurper, and as "Son of man" regains the lost inheritance (Ps. 8: 4-8). The steps in Satan's overthrow are these: he is cast out, first, from heaven (Rev. 12:7-9) on earth; next, he is bound a thousand years (Rev. 20:2, 3); finally, he is cast into the lake of fire for ever (Rev. 20:10).

CHAPTER 66

Vss. 1-24. THE HUMBLE COMFORTED, THE UNGODLY CONDEMNED, AT THE LORD'S APPEARING: JERUSALEM MADE A JOY ON EARTH. This closing chapter is *the summary* of Isaiah's prophecies as to the last days, hence the similarity of its sentiments with what went before. **1. heaven . . . throne . . . where is . . . house . . . ye build**—The same sentiment is expressed, as a precautionary proviso for the majesty of God in deigning to own any earthly temple as His, as if He could be circumscribed by space (I Kings 8:27) in inaugurating the temple of stone; next, as to the temple of the Holy Ghost (Acts 7:48, 49); lastly here, as to "the tabernacle of God with men" (ch. 2:2, 3; Ezek. 43:4, 7; Rev. 21:3). **where**—rather, "what is this house that ye are building, etc.—what place is this for My rest?" [VITRINGA]. **2. have been**—viz., made by Me. Or,

absolutely, *were* things *made;* and therefore belong to Me, the Creator [JEROME]. **look**—have regard. **poor**—humble (ch. 57:15). **trembleth at . . . word**—(II Kings 22:11, 19; Ezra 9:4). The spiritual temple of the heart, though not superseding the outward place of worship, is God's favorite dwelling (John 14:23). In the final state in heaven there shall be "no temple," but "the Lord God" Himself (Rev. 21: 22). **3.** God loathes even the sacrifices of the wicked (ch. 1:11; Prov. 15:8; 28:9). **is as if**—LOWTH not so well omits these words: "He that killeth an ox (presently after) murders a man (as in Ezek. 23:39). But the omission in the *Hebrew* of "is as if"—increases the force of the *comparison*. *Human* victims were often offered by the heathen. **dog's neck**—an abomination according to the Jewish law (Deut. 23:18); perhaps made so, because dogs were venerated in Egypt. He does not honor this abomination by using the word "sacrifice," but uses the degrading term, "cut off a dog's neck" (Exod. 13:13; 34:20). Dogs as unclean are associated with swine (Matt. 7:6; II Pet. 2:22). **oblation**—unbloody: in antithesis to "swine's *blood*" (ch. 65:4). **burneth**—*Hebrew*, "he who offereth as a memorial oblation" (Lev. 2:2). **they have chosen**—opposed to the two first clauses of vs. 4: "as *they* have chosen their own ways, etc., so *I* will choose their delusions." **4. delusions**—(II Thess. 2:11), answering to "their own ways" (vs. 3; so Prov. 1:31). However, the *Hebrew* means rather "vexations," "calamities," which also the parallelism to "fears" requires; "choose *their* calamities" means, "choose the calamities which they thought to escape by their own ways." **their fears**—the things they feared, to avert which their idolatrous "abominations" (vs. 3) were practised. **I called . . . none . . . answer**—(*Notes*, ch. 65:12, 24; Jer. 7:13). **did . . . chose**—not only *did* the evil deed, but did it deliberately as a matter of *choice* (Rom. 1:32). "*They* chose that in which *I* delighted not"; therefore, "*I* will choose" that in which *they* delight not, the "calamities" and "fears" which they were most anxious to avert. **before mine eyes**—(*Note*, ch. 65:3). **5. tremble at . . . word**—the same persons as in vs. 2, the believing few among the Jews. **cast you out for my name's sake**—excommunicate, as if too polluted to worship with them (ch. 65:5). So in Christ's first sojourn on earth (Matt. 10:22; John 9:22, 34; 16:2; 15:21). So it shall be again in the last times, when the believing shall be few (Luke 18:8). **Let the Lord be glorified**—the mocking challenge of the persecutors, as if their violence towards you was from zeal for God. "Let the Lord show Himself glorious," viz., *by manifesting Himself in your behalf;* as the parallelism to, "He shall *appear to your joy*," requires (as in ch. 5:19; cf. ch. 28:15; 57:4). So again Christ on the cross (Matt. 27:42, 43). **appear to your joy**—giving you "joy" instead of your "rebuke" (ch. 25:8, 9). **6.** God, from Jerusalem and His "temple," shall take vengeance on the enemy (Ezek. 43: 1-8; Zech. 12:2, 3; 14:3, 19-21). The abrupt language of this verse marks the suddenness with which God destroys the hostile *Gentile* host outside: as vs. 5 refers to the confounding of the unbelieving *Jews*. **voice of noise**—i.e., the *Lord's* loud-sounding voice (Ps. 68:33; 29:3-9; I Thess. 4:16). **7. she**—Zion. **Before . . . travailed . . . brought forth**—The accession of numbers, and of prosperity to her, shall be *sudden beyond all expectation* and *unattended with painful effort* (ch. 54:1, 4, 5). Contrast with this case of the future Jewish Church the *travail-pains* of the *Christian* Church in bringing forth "a man-child" (Rev. 12:2, 5). A man-child's birth is in the East a matter of special joy, while that of a female is not so; therefore, it here means the *manly sons* of the restored Jewish Church, the *singular* being used collectively for the *plural:* or the many sons being regarded as *one* under Messiah, who shall then be manifested as their *one representative Head*. **8. earth**—rather, to suit the parallelism, "is a *country* (put for the *people* in it) *brought forth* in one day?" [LOWTH]. In *English Version* it means, The earth brings forth its productions gradually, not in one day (Mark 4:28). **at once**—In this case, contrary to the usual growth of the nations by degrees, Israel starts into maturity at once. **for**—rather, "is a nation born at once, *that* Zion has, so soon as she travailed, brought forth?" [MAURER]. **9. cause to bring forth, and shut**—rather, "Shall I who *beget*, restrain the birth?" [LOWTH], (ch. 37:3; Hos. 13:13); i.e., Shall I who have begun, not finish My work of restoring Israel? (I Sam. 3:12; Rom. 11:1; Phil. 1:6). **shut**—(cf. Rev. 3:7, 8). **10. love ... mourn for her**—(Ps. 102:14, 17, 20; 122:6). **11. suck**—(ch. 60:5, 16; 61:6; 49:23). **abundance**—*Hebrew*, "the *raylike flow* of her opulence," i.e., with the milk spouting out from her full breasts (answering to the parallel, "breast of her consolations") in raylike streams [GESENIUS]. **12. extend**—I will *turn* peace (prosperity) upon her, like a river turned in its course [GESENIUS]. Or, "I will *spread* peace *over* her as an *overflowing* river" [BARNES], (ch. 48:18). **flowing stream**—as the Nile by its overflow fertilizes the whole of Egypt. **borne upon ... sides**—(*Note*, ch. 60:4). **her ... her**—If "ye" refers to the Jews, translate, "ye shall be borne upon *their sides ... their knees*," viz., those of the *Gentiles*, as in ch. 49:22; and as "suck" (ch. 60:16) refers to the *Jews* sucking the *Gentile* wealth. However, *English Version* gives a good sense: The Jews, and all who love Jehovah (vs. 10), "shall suck, and be borne" by *her* as a mother. **13. mother**—(ch. 49:15). **comforteth**—(ch. 40:1, 2). **14. bones**—which once were "dried up" by the "fire" of God's wrath (Lam. 1:13), shall live again (Prov. 3:8; 15:30; Ezek. 37:1, etc.). **flourish ... herb**—Rom. 11:15-24). **known toward**—manifested in behalf of. **15.** (Ch. 9:5; Ps. 50:3; Hab. 3:5; II Thess. 1:8; II Pet. 3:7.) **chariots ... whirlwind**—Jer. 4:13). **render**—as the *Hebrew* elsewhere (Job 9:13; Ps. 78:38) means to allay or stay wrath. MAURER translates it so here: *He stays His anger with* nothing but *fury*, etc.; nothing short of pouring out all His fiery fury will satisfy His wrath. **fury**—"burning heat" [LOWTH], to which the parallel, "flames of fire," answers. **16.** Rather, "With fire will Jehovah judge, and with His sword (He will judge) all flesh." The parallelism and collocation of the *Hebrew* words favor this (ch. 65:12). **all flesh**—i.e., *all* who are the objects of His wrath. The *godly* shall be hidden by the Lord in a place of safety away from the scene of judgment (ch. 26:20, 21; Ps. 31:20; I Thess. 4:16, 17). **17. in ... gardens**—*Hebrew* and LXX rather require, "*for* (entering into) gardens," viz., to sacrifice there [MAURER]. **behind one tree** —rather, "following one," i.e., some idol or other, which, from contempt, he does not name [MAURER]. VITRINGA, etc., think the *Hebrew* for "one," *Ahhadh*, to be the name of the god; called *Adad* (meaning *One*) in Syria (cf. Acts 17:23). The idol's power was represented by inclined rays, as of the sun shining on the earth. GESENIUS translates, "following one," viz., *Hierophant* (priest), who led the rest in performing the sacred rites. **in ... midst**—viz., of the garden (cf. *Notes*, ch. 65:3, 4). **mouse**—legally unclean (Lev. 11:29) because it was an idol

to the heathen (see *Note*, ch. 37:36; I Sam. 6:4). Translate, "the fieldmouse," or "dormouse" [BOCHART]. The Pharisees with their self-righteous purifications, and all mere formalists, are included in the same condemnation, described in language taken from the idolatries prevalent in Isaiah's times. **18. know**—not in the *Hebrew*. Rather, understand the words by aposiopesis; it is usual in threats to leave the persons threatened to supply the hiatus from their own fears, owing to conscious guilt: "For I ... their works and thoughts ..." viz., will punish [MAURER]. **it shall come**—the time *is come* that I will, etc. [MAURER]. **gather ... nations**—against Jerusalem, where the *ungodly* Jews shall perish; and then the Lord at last shall fight for Jerusalem against those nations: and the survivors (vs. 19) shall "see God's glory" (Zech. 12:8, 9; 14:1-3, 9). **tongues**—which have been *many* owing to sin, being confounded at Babel, but which shall again be *one* in Christ (Dan. 7:14; Zeph. 3:9; Rev. 7:9, 10). **19. sign**—a *banner* on a high place, to indicate the place of meeting for the dispersed Jewish exiles, preparatory to their return to their land (ch. 5:26; 11:12; 62:10). **those that escape of them**—the Gentile survivors spared by God (*Note*, vs. 18; Zech. 14:16). Ch. 2:2, 3; Micah 5:7; and Zechariah 14:16-19 represent it, not that the Jews go as missionaries to the Gentiles, but that the Gentiles come up to Jerusalem to learn the Lord's ways there. **Tarshish**—Tartessus in Spain, in the west. **Pul**—east and north of Africa: probably the same as *Philæ*, an island in the Nile, called by the Egyptians *Pilak*, i.e., the border country, being between Egypt and Ethiopia [BOCHART]. **Lud**—the Libyans of Africa (Gen. 10:13), Ludim being son of Mizraim (Egypt): an Ethiopian people famous as bowmen (Jer. 46:9): employed as mercenaries by Tyre and Egypt (Ezek. 27:10; 30:5). **Tubal**—Tibarenians, in Asia Minor, south of the Caucasus, between the Black Sea and Araxes. Or, the Iberians [JOSEPHUS]. Italy [JEROME]. **Javan**—the Greeks; called Ionians, including all the descendants of Javan, both in Greece and in Asia Minor (Gen. 10:2-4). **my glory ... Gentiles**—(Mal. 1:11). **20. they**—the Gentiles (vs. 19). **bring ... your brethren** —the Jews, back to the Holy Land (ch. 49:22). It cannot mean the mere entrance of the Jews into the Christian Church; for such an entrance would be by *faith*, not upon "horses, litters, and mules" [HOUBIGANT]. "Offering" is metaphorical, as in Romans 15:16. **horses**—not much used by the Jews. The Gentiles are here represented as using *their* modes of conveyance to "bring" the Jews to Jerusalem. **chariots**—as these are not found in Oriental caravans, translate, "vehicles," viz., borne, not drawn on wheels. **litters**—covered sedans for the rich. **upon swift beasts**—dromedaries: from *Hebrew* root, "to dance," from their bounding motion, often accelerated by music [BOCHART]. Panniers were thrown across the dromedaries' back for poorer women [HORSLEY]. **21. of them**—the Gentiles. **priests ... Levites**—for spiritual worship: enjoying the direct access to God which was formerly enjoyed by the ministers of the temple alone (I Pet. 2:9; Rev. 1:6). **22.** (Ch. 65:17; II Pet. 3:13; Rev. 21:1.) **23.** Lit., "As often as the new moon (shall be) in its own new moon," i.e., every month (Zech. 14:16). **sabbath**—which is therefore perpetually obligatory on earth. **all flesh**—(Ps. 65:2; 72:11). **before me**—at Jerusalem (Jer. 3:16, 17). **24. go forth, and look**—as the Israelites looked at the carcasses of the Egyptians destroyed at the Red Sea (Exod. 14:30; cf. ch. 26:14-19; Ps. 58:10; 49:14;

Mal. 4:1-3). **carcasses ... —**(vs. 16), those slain by the Lord in the last great battle near Jerusalem (Zech. 12:2-9; 14:2-4); type of the final destruction of *all* sinners. **worm ... not die—**(Mark 9:44, 46, 48). Image of hell, from bodies left unburied in the valley of Hinnom (whence comes *Gehenna,* or hell), south of Jerusalem, where a *perpetual fire* was kept to consume the refuse thrown there (ch. 30:33). It shall not be inconsistent with true love for the godly to look with satisfaction on God's vengeance on the wicked (Rev. 14:10).

May God bless this Commentary, and especially its solemn close, to His glory, and to the edification of the writer and the readers of it, for Jesus' sake!

THE BOOK OF THE PROPHET

JEREMIAH

INTRODUCTION

JEREMIAH, son of Hilkiah, one of the ordinary priests, dwelling in Anathoth of Benjamin (ch. 1:1), not the Hilkiah the high priest who discovered the book of the law (II Kings 22:8); had he been the same, the designation would have been *"the* priest," or *"the* high priest." Besides, his residence at Anathoth shows that he belonged to the line of Abiathar, who was deposed from the high priesthood by Solomon (I Kings 2:26–35), after which the office remained in Zadok's line. Mention occurs of Jeremiah in II Chronicles 35:25; 36:12, 21. In 629 B.C. the thirteenth year of King Josiah, while still very young (ch. 1:5), he received his prophetical call in Anathoth (ch. 1:2); and along with Hilkiah the high priest, the prophetess Huldah, and the prophet Zephaniah, he helped forward Josiah's reformation of religion (II Kings 23:1–25). Among the first charges to him was one that he should go and proclaim God's message in Jerusalem (ch. 2:2). He also took an official tour to announce to the cities of Judah the contents of the book of the law, found in the temple (ch. 11:6) five years after his call to prophesy. On his return to Anathoth, his countrymen, offended at his reproofs, conspired against his life. To escape their persecutions (ch. 11:21), as well as those of his own family (ch. 12:6), he left Anathoth and resided at Jerusalem. During the eighteen years of his ministry in Josiah's reign he was unmolested; also during the three months of Jehoahaz or Shallum's reign (ch. 22:10–12). On Jehoiakim's accession it became evident that Josiah's reformation effected nothing more than a forcible repression of idolatry and the establishment of the worship of God outwardly. The priests, prophets, and people then brought Jeremiah before the authorities, urging that he should be put to death for his denunciations of evil against the city (ch. 26:8–11). The princes, however, especially Ahikam, interposed in his behalf (ch. 26:16, 24), but he was put under restraint, or at least deemed it prudent not to appear in public. In the fourth year of Jehoiakim (606 B.C.), he was commanded to write the predictions given orally through him, and to read them to the people. Being "shut up," he could not himself go into the house of the Lord (ch. 36:5); he therefore deputed Baruch, his amanuensis, to read them in public on the fast day. The princes thereupon advised Baruch and Jeremiah to hide themselves from the king's displeasure. Meanwhile they read the roll to the king, who was so enraged that he cut it with a knife and threw it into the fire; at the same time giving orders for the apprehension of the prophet and Baruch. They escaped Jehoiakim's violence, which had already killed the prophet Urijah (ch. 26:20–23). Baruch rewrote the words, with additional prophecies, on another roll (ch. 36:27–32). In the three months' reign of Jehoiachin or Jeconiah, he prophesied the carrying away of the king and the queen mother (ch. 13:18; 22:24–30; cf. II Kings 24:12). In this reign he was imprisoned for a short time by Pashur (ch. 20), the chief governor of the Lord's house; but at Zedekiah's accession he was free (ch. 37:4), for the king sent to him to "inquire of the Lord" when Nebuchadnezzar came up against Jerusalem (ch. 21:1–3, etc.; 37:3). The Chaldeans drew off on hearing of the approach of Pharaoh's army (ch. 37:5); but Jeremiah warned the king that the Egyptians would forsake him, and the Chaldeans return and burn up the city (ch. 37:7, 8). The princes, irritated at this, made the departure of Jeremiah from the city during the respite a pretext for imprisoning him, on the allegation of his deserting to the Chaldeans (ch. 38:1–5). He would have been left to perish in the dungeon of Malchiah, but for the intercession of Ebed-melech, the Ethiopian (ch. 38:6–13). Zedekiah, though he consulted Jeremiah in secret yet was induced by his princes to leave Jeremiah in prison (ch. 38:14–28) until Jerusalem was taken. Nebuchadnezzar directed his captain, Nebuzaradan, to give him his freedom, so that he might either go to Babylon or stay with the remnant of his people as he chose. As a true patriot, notwithstanding the forty and a half years during which his country had repaid his services with neglect and persecution, he stayed with Gedaliah, the ruler appointed by Nebuchadnezzar over Judea (ch. 40:6). After the murder of Gedaliah by Ishmael, Johanan, the recognized ruler of the people, in fear of the Chaldeans avenging the murder of Gedaliah, fled with the people to Egypt, and forced Jeremiah and Baruch to accompany him, in spite of the prophet's warning that the people should perish if they went to Egypt, but be preserved by remaining in their land (ch. 41, 42, and 43). At Tahpanhes, a boundary city on the Tanitic or Pelustan branch of the Nile, he prophesied the overthrow of Egypt (ch. 43:8–13). Tradition says he died in Egypt. According to the Pseudo-Epiphanius, he was stoned at Taphnæ or Tahpanhes. The Jews so venerated him that they believed he would rise from the dead and be the forerunner of Messiah (Matt. 16:14).

HAVERNICK observes that the combination of features in Jeremiah's character proves his divine mission; mild, timid, and susceptible of melancholy, yet intrepid in the discharge of his prophetic functions, not sparing the prince any more than the meanest of his subjects—the Spirit of prophecy controlling his natural temper and qualifying him for his hazardous undertaking, without doing violence to his individuality. Zephaniah, Habakkuk, Daniel, and Ezekiel were his contemporaries. The last forms a good contrast to Jeremiah, the Spirit in his case acting on a temperament as strongly marked by firmness as Jeremiah's was by shrinking and delicate sensitiveness. Ezekiel views the nation's sins as opposed to righteousness—Jeremiah, as productive of misery; the former takes the objective, the latter the subjective, view of the evils of the times. Jeremiah's style corresponds to his character: he is peculiarly marked by pathos, and sympathy with the wretched; his Lamentations illustrate this; the whole series of elegies has but one object—to express sorrow for his fallen country; yet the lights and images in which he presents this are so many, that the reader, so far from feeling it monotonous, is charmed with the variety of the plaintive strains throughout. The language is marked by Aramæisms, which probably was the ground of JEROME's charge that the style is "rustic." LOWTH denies the charge and considers him in portions not inferior to Isaiah. His heaping of phrase on phrase, the repetition of stereotyped forms—and these often *three times*—are due to his affected feelings and to his desire to intensify the expression of them; he is at times more concise, energetic, and sublime, especially against foreign nations, and in the rhythmical parts.

The principle of the arrangement of his prophecies is hard to ascertain. The order of kings was—Josiah (under whom he prophesied eighteen years), Jehoahaz (three months), Jehoiakim (eleven years), Jeconiah (three months), Zedekiah (eleven years). But his prophecies under Josiah (chs. 1–20) are immediately followed by a portion under Zedekiah (ch. 21). Again, ch. 24:8–10, as to Zedekiah, comes in the midst of the section as to Jehoahaz, Jehoiakim, and Jeconiah (chs. 22, 23, 25, etc.). So chs. 35, 36 as to Jehoiakim, follow chs. 27, 28, 29, 33, 34, as to Zedekiah; and ch. 45, dated the fourth year of Jehoiakim, comes after predictions as to the Jews who fled to Egypt after the overthrow of Jerusalem. EWALD thinks the present arrangement substantially Jeremiah's own; the various portions are prefaced by the same formula, "The word which came to Jeremiah from the Lord" (ch. 7:1; 11:1; 18:1; 21:1; 25:1; 30:1; 32:1; 34:1, 8; 35:1; 40:1; 44:1; cf. ch.14:1; 46:1; 47:1; 49:34). Notes of time mark other divisions more or less historical (ch. 26:1, 27:1; 36:1; 37:1). Two other portions are distinct of themselves (ch. 29:1; 45:1). Ch. 2 has the shorter introduction which marks the beginning of a strophe; ch. 3 seems imperfect, having as the introduction merely "saying" (*Hebrew*, ch. 3:1). Thus in the poetical parts, there are twenty-three sections divided into strophes of from seven to nine verses, marked some way thus, "The Lord said also unto me." They form five books: I. The Introduction, ch. 1. II. Reproofs of the Jews, chs. 2–24, made up of seven sections: (1) ch. 2; (2) 3–6; (3) 7–10; (4) 11–13; (5) 14–17; (6) 17–19, 20; (7) 21–24. III. Review of all nations in two sections: chs. 25 and 26–49, with a historical appendix of three sections, (1) ch. 26; (2) 27; (3) 28, 29. IV. Two sections picturing the hopes of *brighter times*, (1) chs. 30, 31; (2) 32, 33; and an historical appendix in three sections: (1) ch. 34:1–7; (2) 34:8–22; (3) 35. V. The conclusion, in two sections: (1) ch. 36:2; (2) 45. Subsequently, in Egypt, he added ch. 46:13–26 to the previous prophecy as to Egypt; also the three sections, chs. 37–39; 40–43; and 44. Ch. 52 was probably (see ch. 51:64) an appendix from a later hand, taken from II Kings 24:18, etc.; 25:30. The prophecies against the several foreign nations stand in a different order in the *Hebrew* from that of LXX; also the prophecies against them in the *Hebrew* (chs. 46–51) are in the LXX placed after ch. 25:14, forming chs. 26–31; the remainder of ch. 25 of the *Hebrew* is ch. 32 of LXX. Some passages in the *Hebrew* (ch. 27:19–22; 33:14–26; 39:4–14; 48:45–47) are not found in LXX; the Greek translators must have had a different recension before them; probably an earlier one. The *Hebrew* is probably the latest and fullest edition from Jeremiah's own hand. See *Note*, ch. 25:13.

The canonicity of his prophecies is established by quotations of them in the New Testament (see Matt. 2:17; 16:14; Heb. 8:8–12; on Matt. 27:9, see *Introduction to Zechariah*); also by the testimony of Ecclesiasticus 49:7, which quotes Jeremiah 1:10; of Philo, who quotes his word as an "oracle"; and of the list of canonical books in Melito, Origen, Jerome, and the Talmud.

CHAPTER 1

Vss. 1-19. THE GENERAL TITLE OR INTRODUCTION (vss. 1-3); probably prefixed by Jeremiah, when he collected his prophecies and gave them to his countrymen to take with them to Babylon [MICHAELIS]. **1. Anathoth**—a town in Benjamin, twenty stadia, i.e., two or three miles north of Jerusalem; now Anata (cf. Isa. 10:30, and the context, 28-32). One of the four cities allotted to the Kohathites in Benjamin (Josh. 21:18). Cf. I Kings 2:26, 27; a stigma was cast thenceforth on the whole sacerdotal family resident there; this may be alluded to in the words here, "the priests . . . in Anathoth." God chooses "the weak, base, and despised things" "to confound the mighty." **2, 3. Jehoiakim . . . Josiah . . . Zedekiah**—Jehoahaz and Jehoiachin are omitted for they reigned only three months each. The first and last of the kings under whom each prophet prophesied are often thus specified in the general title. See on these kings, and Jeremiah's life, my Introduction. **thirteenth . . . of his reign**—(ch. 25:3). **fifth month**

—(II Kings 25:8). **4-10.** *Jeremiah's call to the prophetical office.* **unto me**—other MSS. read "to him"; but *English Version* probably represents the true *Hebrew* text; this inscription was doubtless made by Jeremiah himself. **5. knew**—approved of thee as My chosen instrument (Exod. 33:12, 17; cf. Isa. 49:1, 5; Rom. 8:29). **sanctified**—rather, separated. The primary meaning is, "to set apart" from a common to a special use; hence arose the secondary sense, "to sanctify," ceremonially and morally. It is not here meant that Jehovah cleansed Jeremiah from original sin or regenerated him by His Spirit; but separated him to his peculiar *prophetical office,* including in its range, not merely the Hebrews, but also the nations hostile to them (ch. 25:12-38; 27:46-51), [HENDERSON]. Not the effect, but the predestination in Jehovah's secret counsel, is meant by the sanctification here (cf. Luke 1:15, 41; Acts 15:18; Gal. 1:15; Eph. 1:11). **6.** From the long duration of his office (vss. 2, 3; ch. 40:1, etc.; 43:8, etc.), it is supposed that he was at the time of his call under twenty-five years of age.

child—the same word is translated, "young man" (II Sam. 18:5). The reluctance often shown by inspired ministers of God (Exod. 4:10; 6:12, 30; Jonah 1:3) to accept the call, shows that they did not assume the office under the impulse of self-deceiving fanaticism, as false prophets often did. **7. to all that**—to all "to whom" [ROSENMULLER]. Rather, "to all *against* whom"; in a hostile sense (cf. vss. 8, 17, 18, 19) [MAURER]. Such was the perversity of the rulers and people of Judea at that time, that whoever would desire to be a faithful prophet needed to arm himself with an intrepid mind; Jeremiah was naturally timid and sensitive; yet the Spirit moulded him to the necessary degree of courage without taking away his peculiar individuality. **8.** (Ezek. 2:6; 3:9.) **I am with thee**—(Exod. 3:12; Josh. 1:5). **9. touched my mouth**—a symbolical act in supernatural vision, implying that God would give him *utterance,* notwithstanding *his* inability to speak (vs. 6). So Isaiah's lips were touched with a living coal (Isa. 6:7; cf. Ezek. 2:8, 9, 10; Dan. 10: 16). **10. set thee over**—lit., "appointed thee to the oversight." He was to have his eye upon the nations, and to *predict* their destruction, or restoration, according as their conduct was bad or good. Prophets are said to *do* that which they *foretell* shall be done; for their word is God's word; and His word is His instrument whereby He doeth all things (Gen. 1:3; Ps. 33:6, 9). Word and deed are one thing with Him. What His prophet *saith* is as certain as if it were *done.* The prophet's own consciousness was absorbed into that of God; so closely united to God did he feel himself, that Jehovah's words and deeds are described as his. In ch. 31:28, God is said to do what Jeremiah here is represented as doing (cf. ch. 18:7; I Kings 19:17; Ezek. 43:3). **root out**—(Matt. 15:13). **pull down**—change of metaphor from architecture (II Cor. 10:4). There is a play on the similar sounds, *linthosh, linthotz,* in the *Hebrew* for "root out . . . pull down." **build . . . plant**—restore upon their repenting. His predictions were to be chiefly, and in the first instance, denunciatory; therefore the destruction of the nations is put first, and with a greater variety of terms than their restoration. **11. rod**—shoot, or branch. **almond tree**—lit., "the wakeful tree," because it awakes from the sleep of winter earlier than the other trees, flowering in January, and bearing fruit in March; symbol of God's *early* execution of His purpose; vs. 12, "*hasten* My word" (cf. Amos 8:3). **12. hasten**—rather, "I will *be wakeful* as to My word," etc.; alluding to vs. 11, *the wakeful tree* [MAURER]. **13.** Another vision, signifying what is the "word" about to be "performed," and by what instrumentality. **seething**—lit., "blown under"; so *boiling* by reason of the flame under it kept brisk by blowing. An Oriental symbol of a raging war. **toward**—rather, "*from* the north." Lit., from the face of the region situated towards the north (cf. vss. 14, 15) [MAURER]. The pot in the north rested on one side, its mouth being about to pour forth its contents southwards, viz., on Judea. Babylon, though east of Judea, was regarded by the Hebrews as north, because they appropriated the term "east" to Arabia Deserta, stretching from Palestine to the Euphrates; or rather [BOCHART], the reference here is not to the site, but to the *route* of the Babylonians; not being able to cross the desert, they must enter the Holy Land by the northern frontier, through Riblah in Hamath (ch. 39:5; 52:9). **14. break forth**—"shall disclose itself." **Out of the north**—(ch. 4:6; 6:1, 22; 10:22; 25:9; Ezek. 26:7). The Chaldeans did not cast off the yoke of Assyria

till several years after, under Nabopolassar, 625 B.C.; but long previously they had so increased as to threaten Assyria, which was now grown weak, and other neighboring peoples. **15. families**—the tribes or clans composing the various kingdoms of Babylon; the specification of these aggravates the picture of calamity (ch. 25:9). **throne at . . . gates** —the usual place of administering *justice.* The conquering princes will set up their tribunal there (ch. 39:3, 5; 52:9). Or the reference is to the military pavilion (ch. 43:10) [MAURER]. **16. utter** —pronounce. *The judicial sentences, pronounced* against the Jews by the invading princes, would be virtually the "judgments of God" (Isa. 10:5). **works** —idols. **17. gird . . . loins**—resolutely prepare for thy appointed task. Metaphor from the flowing robes worn in the East, which have to be *girt up* with a girdle, so as not to incommode one, when undertaking any active work (Job 38:3; Luke 12:35; I Pet. 1:13). **dismayed . . . confound**—the same *Hebrew* word; lit., "to break." Be not *dismayed* at their faces (before them), lest I make thee *dismayed* before their faces (before them), i.e., "lest I should permit thee to be overcome by them" (cf. ch. 49:37). **18. defenced city . . .**—i.e., I will give thee strength which no power of thine enemies shall overcome (ch. 6:27; 15:20; Isa. 50:7; 54:17; Luke 21:15; Acts 6:10). **walls**—*plural,* to express the *abundant* strength to be given him. DE ROSSI'S MSS. read *singular,* "wall." **people of the land**—the general masses, as distinguished from the princes and priests.

CHAPTER 2

Vss. 1-37. EXPOSTULATION WITH THE JEWS, REMINDING THEM OF THEIR FORMER DEVOTEDNESS, AND GOD'S CONSEQUENT FAVOR, AND A DENUNCIATION OF GOD'S COMING JUDGMENTS FOR THEIR IDOLATRY. Probably in the thirteenth year of the reign of Josiah (ch. 1:2; cf. ch. 3:6, "*also . . . in . . . days* of Josiah"). The warning not to rely as they did on Egypt (vs. 18), was in accordance with Josiah's policy, who took part with Assyria and Babylon against Egypt (II Kings 23:29). Jeremiah, doubtless, supported the reformation begun by Josiah, in the previous year (the twelfth of his reign), and fully carried out in the eighteenth. **2. cry**—proclaim. **Jerusalem**—the headquarters and center of their idolatry; therefore addressed first. **thee**—rather, "I remember *in regard to thee*" [HENDERSON]; *for thee* [MAURER]. **kindness of thy youth**—not so much Israel's kindness towards God, as *the kindness which Israel experienced from God* in their early history (cf. Ezek. 16:8, 22, 60; 23:3, 8, 19; Hos. 2: 15). For Israel from the first showed perversity rather than *kindness* towards God (cf. Exod. 14:11, 12; 15:24; 32:1-7, etc.). The greater were God's favors to them from the first, the fouler was their ingratitude in forsaking Him (vss. 3, 5, etc.). **espousals**—the intervals between Israel's betrothal to God at the exodus from Egypt, and the formal execution of the marriage contract at Sinai. EWALD takes the "kindness" and "love" to be Israel's towards God at first (Exod. 19:8; 24:3; 35:20-29; 36:5; Josh. 24:16-17). But cf. Deuteronomy 32: 16, 17; and Ezekiel 16:5, 6, 15, 22 ("days of thy youth") implies that the *love* here meant was on God's side, not Israel's. **thou wentest after me in . . . wilderness**—the next act of God's love, His leading them in the desert without needing any strange god, such as they since worshipped, to help Him (Deut. 2:7; 32:12). Verse 6 shows it is *God's* "leading" of them, not *their* following after God in the wilderness, which is implied. **3. holiness unto the Lord**–i.e., was *consecrated to* the service of *Jehovah* (Exod. 19:5, 6). They thus answered to the motto on their high priest's breastplate, "Holiness to the Lord" (Deut. 7:6; 14:2, 21). **first-fruits of his increase**–i.e., of *Jehovah's* produce. As the *first-fruits* of the whole *produce* of the land were devoted to God (Exod. 23:19; Num. 18:12, 13), so Israel was devoted to Him as the first-fruit and representative nation among all nations. So the spiritual Israel (Jas. 1:18; Rev. 14:4). **devour**–carrying on the image of *first-fruits* which were *eaten* before the Lord by the priests as the Lord's representatives; all who *ate* (injured) Jehovah's first-fruits (Israel), contracted guilt: e.g., Amalek, the Amorites, etc., were extirpated for their guilt towards Israel. **shall come**–rather, "came." **4. Jacob ... Israel**–the whole nation. **families**–(*Note*, ch. 1:15). Hear God's word not only collectively, but individually (Zech. 12:12-14). **5. iniquity**–*wrong* done to them (Isa. 5:4; Mic. 6:3; cf. Deut. 32:4). **walked after vanity**–contrasted with "*walkest after me* in the wilderness" (vs. 2): then *I* was their guide in the barren desert; now they take *idols* as their guides. **vanity ... vain**–An idol is not only *vain* (impotent and empty), but *vanity* itself. Its worshippers acquire its character, becoming *vain* as it is (Deut. 7:26; Ps. 115:8). A people's character never rises above that of its gods, which are its "better nature" [BACON] (II Kings 17:15; Jonah 2:8). **6. Neither said they, Where ...**–The very words which *God* uses (Isa. 63:9, 11, 13), when, as it were, reminding Himself of His former acts of love to Israel as a ground for interposing in their behalf again. When *they* would not say, Where is Jehovah, etc., *God Himself* at last said it for them (cf. *Note*, vs. 2, above). **deserts ... pits**–The desert between Mount Sinai and Palestine abounds in chasms and pits, in which beasts of burden often sink down to the knees. "Shadow of death" refers to the *darkness* of the caverns amidst the rocky precipices (Deut. 8:15; 32:10). **7. plentiful**–lit., a land of Carmel, or well-cultivated land: a garden land, in contrast to the "land of deserts" (vs. 6). **defiled**–by idolatries (Judg. 2:10-17; Ps. 78:58, 59; 106:38). **you ... ye**–change to the second person from the third, "they" (vs. 6), in order to bring home the guilt to the living generation. **8.** The three leading classes, whose very office under the theocracy was to lead the people to God, disowned Him in the same language as the nation at large, "Where is the Lord?" (See vs. 6). The **priests**–whose office it was to expound the law (Mal. 2:6, 7). **handle**–are occupied with the law as the subject of their profession. **pastors**–civil, not religious: princes (ch. 3:15), whose duty it was to tend their people. **prophets**–who should have reclaimed the people from their apostasy, encouraged them in it by pretended oracles from Baal, the Phœnician false god. **by Baal**–in his name and by his authority (cf. ch. 11:21). **walked after things ... not profit**–answering to, "walked after *vanity*," i.e., idols (vs. 5; cf. vs. 11; Hab. 2:18). **9. yet plead**–viz., by inflicting still further judgments on you. **children's children**–Three MSS. and JEROME omit "children's"; they seem to have thought it unsuitable to read "children's children," when "children" had not preceded. But it is designedly so written, to intimate that the final judgment on the nation would be suspended *for* many generations [HORSLEY]. (Cf. Ezek. 20:35, 36; Mic. 6:2). **10. pass over the isles**–rather,

"cross over to the isles." **Chittim ... Kedar**–i.e., the heathen nations, *west* and *east.* Go where you will, you cannot find an instance of any heathen nation forsaking their own for other gods. Israel alone does this. Yet the heathen gods are false gods; whereas Israel, in forsaking Me for other gods, forsake their "glory" for unprofitable idols. **Chittim**–Cyprus, colonized by Phœnicians, who built in it the city of Citium, the modern *Chitti.* Then the term came to be applied to all maritime coasts of the Mediterranean, especially Greece (Num. 24:24; Isa. 23:1; Dan. 11:30). **Kedar**–descended from Ishmael; the Bedouins and Arabs, east of Palestine. **11. glory**–Jehovah, the glory of Israel (Ps. 106:20; Rom. 1:23). The Shekinah, or cloud resting on the sanctuary, was the symbol of "the glory of the Lord" (I Kings 8:11; cf. Rom. 9:4). The golden calf was intended as an image of the true God (cf. Exod. 32:4, 5), yet it is called an "idol" (Acts 7:41). It (like Roman Catholic images) was a violation of the *second* commandment, as the heathen multiplying of gods is a violation of the *first.* **not profit**–(vs. 8.) **12.** Impassioned personification (Isa. 1:2). **horribly afraid**–rather, "be horrified." **be ... very desolate**–rather, "be exceedingly aghast" at the monstrous spectacle. Lit., "to be dried up," or "devastated," (places devastated have such an unsightly look) [MAURER]. **13. two evils**–not merely *one* evil, like the idolaters who know no better; besides *simple* idolatry, My people *add* the sin of forsaking the true God whom they have known; the heathen, though having the sin of idolatry, are free from the further sin of changing the true God for idols (vs. 11). **forsaken me**–The *Hebrew* collocation brings out the only living God into more prominent contrast with idol nonentities. "*Me* they have forsaken, the Fountain," etc. (ch. 17:13; Ps. 36:9; John 4:14). **broken cisterns**–tanks for rain water, common in the East, where wells are scarce. The tanks not only cannot give forth an ever-flowing fresh supply as fountains can, but cannot even retain the water poured into them; the stonework within being broken, the earth drinks up the collected water. So, in general, all earthly, compared with heavenly, means of satisfying man's highest wants (Isa. 55:1, 2; cf. Luke 12:33). **14. is he a home-born slave**–No. "Israel is Jehovah's *son*, even His first-born" (Exod. 4:22). Verses 16, 18, and 36, and the absence of any *express* contrast of the two parts of the nation are against EICHORN'S view, that the prophet proposes to Judah, as yet spared, the case of Israel (the ten tribes) which had been carried away by Assyria as a warning of what they might expect if they should still put their trust in Egypt. "Were Israel's ten tribes of meaner birth than Judah? Certainly not. If, then, the former fell before Assyria, what can Judah hope from Egypt against Assyria?" "Israel" is rather here the whole of the remnant still left in their own land, i.e., Judah. "How comes it to pass that the nation which once was under God's special protection (vs. 3) is now left at the mercy of the foe as a worthless slave?" The prophet sees this event *as if* present, though it was still *future* to Judah (vs. 19). **15. lions**–the Babylonian princes (ch. 4:7; cf. Amos 3:4). The disaster from the Babylonians in the fourth year of Jehoiakim's reign, and again three years later when, relying on Egypt, he revolted from Nebuchadnezzar, is here referred to (ch. 46:2; II Kings 24:1, 2). **16. Noph ... Tahapanes**–*Memphis,* capital of Lower Egypt, on the west bank of the Nile, near the pyramids of Gizeh, opposite the site of modern Cairo. *Daphne,* on the Tanitic branch of the Nile, near Pelusium, on the frontier of Egypt towards Palestine. Isaiah 30:4 contracts it, *Hanes.* These two cities, one the capital, the other that with which the Jews came most in contact, stand for the whole of Egypt. *Tahapanes* takes its name from a goddess, Tphnet [CHAMPOLLION]. *Memphis* is from *Man-nofri,* "the abode of good men"; written in *Hebrew, Moph* (Hos. 9:6), or *Noph.* The reference is to the coming invasion of Judah by Pharaoh-necho of Egypt, on his return from the Euphrates, when he deposed Jehoahaz and levied a heavy tribute on the land (II Kings 23:33-35). Josiah's death in battle with the same Pharaoh is probably included (II Kings 23:29, 30). **have broken**—rather, *shall feed down* the crown, etc., i.e., affect with the greatest ignominy, such as *baldness* was regarded in the East (ch. 48:37; II Kings 2:23). Instead of "also," translate, "even" the Egyptians, in whom thou dost trust, shall miserably disappoint thy expectation [MAURER]. Jehoiakim was twice leagued with them (II Kings 23:34, 35): when he received the crown from them, and when he revolted from Nebuchadnezzar (II Kings 24:1, 2, 7). The Chaldeans, having become masters of Asia, threatened Egypt. Judea, situated between the contending powers, was thus exposed to the inroads of the one or other of the hostile armies; and unfortunately, except in Josiah's reign, took side with Egypt, contrary to God's warnings. **17.** Lit., "Has not thy forsaking the Lord . . . procured this (calamity) to thee?" So LXX: the Masoretic accents make "this" the *subject* of the verb, leaving the *object* to be understood. "Has not this procured (*it,* i.e., the impending calamity) unto thee, that hast forsaken?" etc. (ch. 4:18). **led** —(Deut. 32:10.) **the way**—The article expresses *the right* way, the way *of the Lord:* viz., the moral training which they enjoyed in the Mosaic covenant. **18. now**—used in a *reasoning* sense, not of *time.* **the way of Egypt**—What hast thou to do *with the way,* i.e., with going down *to Egypt; or what . . . with* going to *Assyria?* **drink . . . waters** —i.e., to seek *reinvigorating* aid from them; so vss. 13 and 36; cf. "waters," meaning *numerous forces* (Isa. 8:7). **Sihor**—i.e., the *black* river, in *Greek Melas* (black), the Nile: so called from the black deposit or soil it leaves after the inundation (Isa. 23:3). The LXX identifies it with Gihon, one of the rivers of Paradise. **the river**—*Euphrates,* called by pre-eminence, *the* river; figurative for the Assyrian power. In 625 B.C., the seventeenth year of Josiah, and the fourth of Jeremiah's office, the kingdom of Assyria fell before Babylon, therefore *Assyria* is here put for *Babylon* its successor: so in II Kings 23:29; Lamentations 5:6. There was doubtless a league between Judea and Assyria (i.e., Babylon), which caused Josiah to march against Pharaoh-necho of Egypt when that king went against Babylon: the evil consequences of this league are foretold in this verse and vs. 36. **19. correct . . . reprove**—rather, in the severer sense, "chastise . . . punish" [MAURER]. **backslidings**— "apostasies"; *plural,* to express the number and variety of their defections. The very confederacies they entered into were the occasion of their overthrow (Prov. 1:31; Isa. 3:9; Hos. 5:5). **know . . . see**—imperative for *futures: Thou shalt know and see* to thy cost. **my fear**—rather, "the fear *of Me.*" **20. I**—the *Hebrew* should be pointed as the second person *feminine,* a form common in Jeremiah: "*Thou* hast broken," etc. So LXX, and the sense requires it. **thy yoke . . . bands**—the yoke and bands which I laid *on thee,* My laws (ch. 5:5).

transgress—so the *Keri* and many MSS. read. But LXX and most authorities read, "I will not serve," i.e., obey. The sense of *English Version* is, "I broke thy yoke (in Egypt), etc., and (at that time) thou saidst, I will not trangress; whereas thou hast (since then) wandered" (from Me) (Exod. 19:8). **hill . . . green tree**—the scene of idolatries (Deut. 12: 2; Isa. 57:5, 7). **wanderest**—rather, "thou hast *bowed down* thyself" (for the act of adultery: figurative of shameless idolatry Exod. 34:15, 16; cf. Job 31:10). **21.** The same image as in Deuteronomy 32:32; Psalm 80:8, 9; Isaiah 5:1, etc. **unto me**—with respect to Me. **22. nitre**—not what is now so called, viz., saltpeter; but the *natron* of Egypt, a mineral alkali, an incrustation at the bottom of the lakes, after the summer heat has evaporated the water: used for washing (cf. Job 9:30; Prov. 25:20). **soap**—potash, the carbonate of which is obtained impure from burning different plants, especially the *kali* of Egypt and Arabia. Mixed with oil it was used for washing. **marked**—deeply ingrained, indelibly marked; the *Hebrew, catham,* being equivalent to *cathab.* Others translate, "is treasured up," from the *Arabic.* MAURER from a *Syriac* root, "is polluted." **23.** (Prov. 30:12). **Baalim**—plural, to express manifold excellency: cf. *Elohim.* **see**—consider. **the valley**—viz., of Hinnom, or Tophet, south and east of Jerusalem: rendered infamous by the human sacrifices to Moloch in it (cf. ch. 19:2, 6, 13, 14; 32:35; Isa. 30: 33, *Note*). **thou art**—omit. The substantive that follows in this verse (and also that in vs. 24) is in apposition with the preceding "thou." **dromedary** —rather, a young she-camel. **traversing**—lit., "enfolding"; making its ways *complicated* by wandering hither and thither, lusting after the male. Cf. as to the Jews' spiritual lust, Hosea 2:6, 7. **24.** (Ch. 14:6; Job 39:5). "A wild ass," agreeing with "thou" (vs. 23). **at her pleasure**—rather, "in her ardor," viz., in pursuit of a male, sniffing the wind to ascertain where one is to be found [MAURER]. **occasion**—either from a *Hebrew* root, "to meet"; "her meeting (with the male for sexual intercourse), who can avert it?" Or better from an *Arabic* root: "her *heat* (sexual impulse), who can allay it?" [MAURER]. **all they**—whichever of the males desire her company [HORSLEY]. **will not weary themselves**—have no need to weary themselves in searching for her. **her month**—in the *season of the year when her sexual impulse is strongest,* she puts herself in the way of the males, so that they have no difficulty in *finding* her. **25. Withhold . . .**—i.e., abstain from incontinence; fig. for idolatry [HOUBIGANT]. **unshod . . .**—do not run so violently in pursuing lovers, as to *wear out thy shoes:* do not "thirst" so incontinently after sexual intercourse. HITZIG thinks the reference is to penances performed *barefoot* to idols, and the *thirst* occasioned by loud and continued invocations to them. **no hope**—(ch. 18:12; Isa. 57:10). "It is hopeless," i.e., I am *desperately* resolved to go on in my own course. **strangers**—i.e., laying aside the metaphor, "strange gods" (ch. 3:13; Deut. 32:16). **26. is ashamed**—is *put to shame.* **thief**—(John 10:1). **Israel**—i.e., Judah (vs. 28). **27. Thou art my father** —(Contrast ch. 3:4; Isa. 64:8). **in . . . trouble they will say**—viz., to God (Ps. 78:34; Isa. 26:16). Trouble often brings men to their senses (Luke 15: 16-18). **23. But**—God sends them to the gods for whom they forsook Him, to see if *they* can help them (Deut. 32:37, 38; Judg. 10:14). **according to the number of thy cities**—Besides national deities, each city had its tutelary god (ch. 11:13). **29.**

plead with me—i.e., contend with Me for afflicting you (vss. 23, 35). **30.** (Ch. 5:3; 6:29; Isa. 1:5; 9:13.) **your children**—i.e., your people, you. **your ... sword ... devoured ... prophets**—(II Chron. 36:16; Neh. 9:26; Matt. 23:29, 31). **31.** The *Hebrew* collocation is, "O, the generation, ye," i.e., "O ye who now live." The generation needed only to be named, to call its degeneracy to view, so palpable was it. **wilderness**—in which all the necessaries of life are wanting. On the contrary, Jehovah was a never-failing source of supply for all Israel's wants in the wilderness, and afterwards in Canaan. **darkness**—lit., "darkness of Jehovah," the strongest *Hebrew* term for "darkness; the densest darkness"; cf. "land of the shadow of death" (vs. 6). **We are lords**—i.e., We are our own masters. We will worship what gods we like (Ps. 12:4; 82:6). But it is better to translate from a different *Hebrew* root: "We ramble at large," without restraint pursuing our idolatrous lusts. **32.** Oriental women greatly pride themselves on their ornaments (cf. Isa. 61:10). **attire**—girdles for the breast. **forgotten me**—(ch. 12:25; Hos. 8:14). **33. Why trimmest**—MAURER translates, *"How skilfully* thou dost prepare thy way...."* But see II Kings 9:30. "Trimmest" best suits the image of one *decking* herself as a harlot. **way**—course of life. **therefore**—accordingly. Or else, *"nay,* thou hast even ...." **also ... wicked ones**—*even* the wicked harlots, i.e., (laying aside the metaphor) even the Gentiles who are wicked, thou teachest to be still more so [GROTIUS]. **34. Also**—not only art thou polluted with idolatry. but *also* with the guilt of shedding innocent blood [MAURER]. ROSENMULLER not so well translates, "even in thy skirts ..."; i.e., there is no part of thee (*not even thy skirts*) that is not stained with innocent blood (ch. 19:4; II Kings 21:16; Ps. 106:38). See as to innocent blood shed, not as here in honor of idols, but of *prophets* for having reproved them (vs. 30; ch. 26:20-23). **souls**—i.e., persons. **search** —I did not need to "search deep" to find proof of thy guilt; for it was "upon all these" thy skirts. Not in deep caverns didst thou perpetrate these atrocities, but openly in the vale of Hinnom and within the precincts of the temple. **35.** (Vss. 23, 29.) **36. gaddest**—runnest to and fro, now seeking help from Assyria (II Chron. 28:16-21), now from Egypt (ch. 37; 7, 8; Isa. 30:3). **37. him**—Egypt. **hands upon ... head**—expressive of mourning (II Sam. 13:19). **in them**—in those stays in which thou trustest.

CHAPTER 3

Vss. 1-25. GOD'S MERCY NOTWITHSTANDING JUDAH'S VILENESS. Contrary to all precedent in the case of adultery, Jehovah offers a return to Judah, the spiritual adulteress (vss. 1-5). A new portion of the book, ending with ch. 6. Judah worse than Israel; yet both shall be restored in the last days (vss. 6-25). **1. They say**—rather, as *Hebrew,* "saying," in agreement with "the LORD"; vs. 37 of last chapter [MAURER]. Or, it is equivalent to, "Suppose this case." Some copyist may have omitted, "The word of the LORD came to me," *saying.* **shall he return unto her**—will he take her back? It was unlawful to do so (Deut. 24:1-4). **shall not**—Should not the land be polluted if this were done? **yet return**—(vs. 22; ch. 4:1; Zech. 1:3; cf. Ezek. 16:51, 58, 60.) "Nevertheless ..." (Isa. 50:1, *Note*). **2. high places**—the scene of idolatries which were spiritual adulteries. **In ... ways ... sat for them**—watching for lovers like a prostitute (Gen. 38:14, 21;

Prov. 7:12; 23:28; Ezek. 16:24, 25), and like an Arab who lies in wait for travellers. The Arabs of the desert, east and south of Palestine, are still notorious as robbers. **3. no latter rain**—essential to the crops in Palestine; withheld in judgment (Lev. 26:19; cf. Joel 2:23). **whore's forehead**—(ch. 8:12; Ezek. 3:8). **4. from this time**—not referring, as MICHAELIS thinks, to the reformation begun the year before, i.e., the twelfth of Josiah; it means—now at once, now at last. **me**—contrasted with the "stock" whom they had heretofore called on as "father" (ch. 2:27; Luke 15:18). **thou art**—rather, "thou wast." **guide of ... youth**—i.e., husband (ch. 2:2; Prov. 2:17; Hos. 2:7, 15). *Husband* and *father* are the two most endearing of ties. **5. he**— "thou," the second person, had preceded. The change to the third person implies a putting away of God to a *greater distance* from them; instead of repenting and forsaking their idols, they merely deprecate the continuance of their *punishment.* Verse 12 and Psalm 103:9, answer their question in the event of their penitence. **spoken and**—rather (God's reply to them), "Thou hast spoken (thus), *and yet* (all the while) thou hast done evil ...."* **as thou couldest**—with all thy might; with incorrigible persistency [CALVIN]. **6.** From here to ch. 6:30, is a new discourse, delivered in Josiah's reign. It consists of two parts, the former extending to ch. 4:3, in which he warns Judah from the example of Israel's doom, and yet promises Israel final restoration; the latter a threat of Babylonian invasion; as Nabopolassar founded the Babylonian empire, 625 B.C., the seventeenth of Josiah, this prophecy is perhaps not earlier than that date (ch. 4:5, etc.; 5:14, etc.; 6:1, etc.; 22); and probably not later than the second thorough reformation in the eighteenth year of the same reign. **backsliding**—lit., apostasy; not merely *apostate,* but *apostasy itself,* the essence of it (vss. 14, 22). **7. I said**—(II Kings 17:13). **sister** —(Ezek. 16:46; 23:2, 4). **8.** I saw that, though (whereas) it was for this very reason (namely), because backsliding (apostate) Israel had committed adultery I had put her away (II Kings 17:6, 18), and given her a bill of divorce, yet Judah, etc. (Ezek. 23: 11, etc.). **bill of divorce**—lit., "a writing of *cuttings* off." The *plural* implies the completeness of the severance. The use of this metaphor here, as in the former discourse (vs. 1), implies a close connection between the discourses. The epithets are characteristic; Israel "apostate" (as the *Hebrew* for "backsliding" is better rendered); Judah, not as yet utterly *apostate,* but *treacherous* or *faithless.* **also** —herself also, like Israel. **9. it**—Some take this verse of *Judah,* to whom the end of vs. 8 refers. But vs. 10 puts *Judah* in contrast to *Israel* in this verse. "Yet for all this," referring to the sad example of *Israel;* if vs. 9 referred to *Judah,* "she" would have been written in vs. 10, not "Judah." Translate, "It (the putting away of Israel) had come to pass through ... whoredom; and (i.e., for) she (Israel) had defiled the land" etc. [MAURER]. *English Version,* however, *may* be explained to refer to *Israel.* **lightness**—"infamy." [EWALD.] MAURER not so well takes it from the *Hebrew* root, "voice," "fame." **10. yet**—notwithstanding the lesson given in Israel's case of the fatal results of apostasy. **not ... whole heart**—The reformation in the eighteenth year of Josiah was not thorough on the part of the people, for at his death they relapsed into idolatry (II Chron. 34:33; Hos. 7:14). **11. justified herself** —has been made to appear almost just (i.e., comparatively innocent) by the surpassing guilt of Judah, who adds hypocrisy and treachery to her sin; and who had the example of Israel to warn her, but in vain (cf. Ezek. 16:51; 23:11). **more than**—in comparison with. **12. Go**—not actually; but turn and proclaim towards the north (Media and Assyria, where the ten tribes were located by Tiglath-pileser and Shalmaneser, II Kings 15:29; 17:6; 18:9, 11). **Return ... backsliding**—*Hebrew, Shubah, Meshubah,* a play on sounds. In order to excite Judah to godly jealousy (Rom. 11:14), Jehovah addresses the exiled ten tribes of Israel with a loving invitation. **cause ... anger to fall**—lit., I will not let fall My countenance (cf. Gen. 4:5, 6; Job 29:3), i.e., I will not *continue* to frown on you. **keep**—"anger" is to be supplied (*Note,* vs. 5). **13. Only acknowledge**—(Deut. 30:1, 3; Prov. 28:13.) **scattered thy ways ...**—(ch. 2:25). Not merely the calves at Bethel, but the idols in every direction, were the objects of their worship (Ezek. 16:15, 24, 25). **14. I am married**—lit., I am Lord, i.e., husband to you (so ch. 31:32; cf. Hos. 2:19, 20; Isa. 54: 5). GESENIUS, following the LXX version of ch. 31:32, and Paul's quotation of it in (Heb. 8:9), translates, "I have *rejected* you"; so the corresponding *Arabic,* and the idea of *lordship,* may pass into that of *looking down upon,* and so *rejecting.* But LXX in *this* passage translates, "I will be Lord over you." And the "for" has much more force in *English Version* than in that of GESENIUS. The *Hebrew* hardly admits the rendering *though* HENGSTENBERG]. **take you one of a city**—Though but *one or two* Israelites were in a (foreign) city, they shall not be forgotten; *all* shall be restored (Amos 9:9). So, in the spiritual Israel, God gathers one convert here, another there, into His Church; not the least one is lost (Matt. 18:14; Rom. 11:5; cf. ch. 24:40, 41). **family**—a clan or tribe. **15. pastors**—not religious, but civil rulers, as Zerubbabel, Nehemiah (ch. 23:4; 2:8). **16. they shall say no more**—The Jews shall no longer glory in the possession of the ark; it shall not be missed, so great shall be the blessings of the new dispensation. The throne of the Lord, *present Himself,* shall eclipse and put out of mind the ark of the covenant and the mercy seat between the cherubim, God's former throne. The ark, containing the two tables of the law, disappeared at the Babylonian captivity, and was not restored to the second temple, implying that the symbolical "glory" was to be superseded by a "greater glory" (Hag. 2:9). **neither ... visit it**—rather, "neither shall *it be missed*" (so in ch. 23: 4). **done**—rather, "neither shall it (the ark) *be made*" (i.e., be restored) any more" [MAURER]. **17. Jerusalem**—*the whole city,* not merely the temple. As it has been the center of the *Hebrew* theocracy, so it shall be the point of attraction to the whole earth (Isa. 2:2-4; Zech. 2:10, 11; 14:16-21). **throne of ... Lord**—The Shekinah, the symbol of God's peculiar nearness to Israel (Deut. 4:7) shall be surpassed by the antitype, God's own throne in Jerusalem (Ps. 2:6, 8; Ezek. 34:23, 24; Zech. 2:5). **imagination**—rather, as *Margin,* "the obstinacy" or stubbornness. **18. Judah ... Israel ... together**—Two distinct apostasies, that of Israel and that of Judah, were foretold (vss. 8, 10). The two have never been united since the Babylonish captivity; therefore their joint restoration must be still future (Isa. 11:12, 13; Ezek. 37:16-22; Hos. 1:11). **north**—(*V.,* 12). **land ... given ... inheritance**—(Amos 9:15). **19.** The good land covenanted to Abraham is to be restored to his seed. But the question arises, How shall this be done? **put ... among ... children**—the *Greek* for *adoption* means, lit., "putting among the sons." **the children**—i.e., My

children. "How shall I receive thee back into My family, after thou hast so long forsaken Me for idols?" The answer is, they would acknowledge Him as "Father," and no longer turn away from Him. God assumes the language of one wondering how so desperate apostates could be restored to His family and its privileges (cf. Ezek. 37:3; CALVIN makes it, How *the race of Abraham can be propagated again,* being as it were dead); yet as His purpose has decreed it so, He shows how it shall be effected, viz., they shall receive from Him the spirit of adoption to cry, "*My* Father" (John 1:12; Gal. 4:6). The elect are "children" already in God's purpose; this is the ground of the subsequent realization of this relationship (Eph. 1:5; Heb. 2: 13). **pleasant land**—(ch. 11:5; Ezek. 20:6; Dan. 11: 16, *Margin.* **heritage of ... hosts**—a heritage the most goodly of all nations [MAURER]; or a "heritage possessed by powerful hosts" (Deut. 4:38; Amos 2: 9). The rendering "splendors," instead of "hosts," is opposed by the fact that the *Hebrew* for "splendor" is not found in the *plural.* **20. Surely**—rather, But. **husband**—lit., "friend." **21.** In harmony with the preceding promises of God, the penitential confessions of Israel are heard. **high places**—The scene of their idolatries is the scene of their confessions. Cf. vs. 23, in which they cast aside their trust in these idolatrous high places. The publicity of their penitence is also implied (cf. ch. 7:29; 48:38). **22.** Jehovah's renewed invitation (vss. 12, 14) and their immediate response. **heal**—forgive (II Chron. 30:18, 20; Hos. 14:4). **unto thee**—rather, "in obedience to thee"; lit., for thee [ROSENMULLER]. **23. multitude of mountains**—i.e., the multitude of *gods* worshiped on them (cf. Ps. 121:1, 2, Margin). **24. shame**—i.e., the *idols,* whose worship only covers us with *shame* (ch. 11:13; Hos. 9:10). So far from bringing us "salvation," they have cost us our cattle and even our children, whom we have sacrificed to them. **25.** (Ezra 9:7).

CHAPTER 4

VSS. 1-31. CONTINUATION OF ADDRESS TO THE TEN TRIBES OF ISRAEL (VSS. 1, 2). THE PROPHET TURNS AGAIN TO JUDAH, TO WHOM HE HAD ORIGINALLY BEEN SENT (VSS. 3-31). **1. return ... return**—play on words. "If thou wouldest *return to thy land* (thou must first), *return (by conversion* and repentance) *to Me.*" **not remove**—no longer be an unsettled *wanderer* in a strange land. So Cain (Gen. 4:12, 14). **2. And thou**—rather, "And *if* (carried on from vs. 1) thou shalt swear, 'Jehovah liveth,' in truth ... ," i.e., if thou shalt *worship* Him (for we *swear* by the God whom we worship; cf. Deut. 6:13; 10:20; Isa. 19:18; Amos 8:14) in sincerity, etc. **and the nations**—Rather, this is apodosis to the "if"; *then* shall the nations bless themselves in (by) Him" (Isa. 65:16). The conversion of the nations will be the consequence of Israel's conversion (Ps. 102: 13, 15; Rom. 11:12, 15). **3.** Transition to Judah. Supply mentally. All which (the foregoing declaration as to Israel) applies to Judah. **and Jerusalem**—i.e., *and especially* the men of Jerusalem, as being the most prominent in Judea. **Break ... fallow ground**—i.e., Repent of your idolatry, and so be prepared to serve the Lord in truth (Hos. 10:12, Matt. 13:7). The unhumbled heart is like ground which may be improved, being let out to us for that purpose, but which is as yet fallow, overgrown with weeds, its natural product. **4.** Remove your natural corruption of heart (Deut. 10:16; 30:6; Rom. 2:29; Col. 2:11). **5. cry, gather together**—rather, "cry fully" i.e., loudly. The Jews are warned to take measures against the impending Chaldean invasion (cf. ch. 8:14). **6. Zion**—The standard *toward* Zion intimated that the people of the surrounding country were to fly *to* it, as being the strongest of their fortresses. **7. lion**—Nebuchadnezzar and the Chaldeans (ch. 2:15; 5:6; Dan. 7:14). **his thicket**—lair; Babylon. **destroyer of the Gentiles**—rather, "the nations" (ch. 25:9). **8.** Nothing is left to the Jews but to bewail their desperate condition. **anger . . . not turned back**—(Isa. 9:12, 17, 21). **9. heart**—The *wisdom* of the most leading men will be utterly at a loss to devise means of relief. **10. thou hast . . . deceived**—God, having even the false prophets in His hands, is here said to do that which for inscrutable purposes He *permits* them to do (Exod. 9:12; II Thess. 2:11; cf. ch. 8:15; which passage shows that the dupes of error were *self-prepared* for it, and that God's predestination did not destroy their moral freedom as voluntary agents). The false prophets foretold "peace," and the Jews believed them; God overruled this to His purposes (ch. 5:12; 14:13; Ezek. 14:9). **soul**—rather, "reacheth to the *life*." **11. dry wind**—the *simoom*, terrific and destructive, blowing from the southeast across the sandy deserts east of Palestine. Image of the invading Babylonian army (Hos. 13: 15). Babylon in its turn shall be visited by a similar "destroying wind" (ch. 51:1). **of . . . high places**—i.e., that sweeps over the high places. **daughter**—i.e., the *children* of my people. **not to fan**—a very different wind from those ordinary winds employed for fanning the grain in the open air. **12. full . . . from those places**—rather, "a wind *fuller* (i.e., more impetuous) *than* those *winds*" (which fan the corn) (vs. 11) [ROSENMULLER]. **unto me**—for *Me,* as My instrument for executing My purpose. **sentence**—judgments against them (ch. 1:16). **13. clouds**—continuing the metaphor in vss. 11:12. Clouds of sand and dust accompany the simoom, and after rapid gyrations ascend like a pillar. **eagles**—(Deut. 28:49; Hab. 1:8). **Woe unto us**—The people are graphically presented before us, without it being formally so stated, bursting out in these exclamations. **14.** Only one means of deliverance is left to the Jews—a thorough repentance. GESENIUS translates, "How long *wilt thou harbor* vain thoughts?" **vain thoughts**—viz., projects for deliverance, such as enlisting the Egyptians on their side. **15. For . . . from Dan**—The connection is: There is danger in delay; *for* the voice of a messenger announces the approach of the Chaldean enemy from Dan, the northern frontier of Palestine (ch. 8:16; cf. vs. 6; ch. 1:14). **Mount Ephraim**—which borders closely on Judah; so that the foe is coming nearer and nearer. Dan and Bethel in *Ephraim* were the two places where Jeroboam set up the idolatrous calves (I Kings 12:29); just retribution. **16.** The neighboring foreign "nations" are summoned to witness Jehovah's judgments on His rebel people (ch. 6:18, 19). **watchers**—i.e., besiegers (cf. II Sam. 11:16); observed or watched, i.e., besieged. **their voice**—the war shout. **17. keepers of a field**—metaphor from those who watch a field, to frighten away the wild beasts. **18.** (Ch. 2:17, 19; Ps. 107:17.) **this is thy wickedness**—i.e., the fruit of thy wickedness. **19.** The prophet suddenly assumes the language of the Jewish state personified, lamenting its affliction (ch. 10:19, 20; 9:1, 10; Isa. 15:5; cf. Luke 19:41). **at my very heart**—*Hebrew,* "at the walls of my heart"; the muscles round the heart. There is a

climax, the "bowels," the *pericardium,* the "heart" itself. **maketh . . . noise**—moaneth [HENDERSON]. **alarm**—the battle shout. **20. Destruction . . . cried**—Breach upon breach is announced (Ps. 42:7; Ezek. 7:26). The war "trumpet" . . . the battle shout . . . the "destructions" . . . the havoc throughout the whole land" . . . the spoiling of the shepherds' "tents" (ch. 10:20; or, "tents" means *cities,* which should be overthrown as easily as *tents* [CALVIN]), form a gradation. **21.** Judah in perplexity asks, How long is this state of things to continue? **22.** Jehovah's reply; they cannot be otherwise than miserable, since they persevere in sin. The repetition of clauses gives greater force to the sentiment. **wise . . . evil . . . to do good . . . no knowledge**—reversing the rule (Rom. 16:19) "wise unto . . . good, simple concerning evil." **23.** Graphic picture of the utter desolation about to visit Palestine. "I beheld, and lo!" four times solemnly repeated, heightens the awful effect of the scene (cf. Isa. 24: 19; 34:11). **without form and void**—reduced to the primeval chaos (Gen. 1:2). **24. mountains**—(Isa. 5:25). **moved lightly**—shook vehemently. **25. no man . . . birds**—No vestige of the human, or of the feathered creation, is to be seen (Ezek. 38:20; Zeph. 1:3). **26. fruitful place**—*Hebrew, Carmel.* **a wilderness**—*Hebrew,* "*the* wilderness," in contrast to "*the* fruitful place"; the great desert, where *Carmel* was, there is now *the desert* of Arabia [MAURER]. **cities**—in contrast to *the fruitful place* or field. **27. full end**—utter destruction: I will leave some hope of restoration (ch. 5:10, 18; 30:11; 46, 28; cf. Lev. 26:44). **28. For this**—on account of the desolations just described (Isa. 5:30; Hos. 4:3). **not repent**—(Num. 23:19). **29. whole city**—Jerusalem: to it the inhabitants of the country had fled for refuge; but when it, too, is likely to fall, they flee out of it to hide in the "thickets." HENDERSON translates, "*every* city." **noise**—The mere noise of the hostile horsemen shall put you to flight. **30. when thou art spoiled**—rather, "thou, O *destroyed* one" [MAURER]. **rentest . . . face with painting**—Oriental women paint their eyes with stibium, or antimony, to make them look full and sparkling, the black margin causing the white of the eyes to appear the brighter by contrast (II Kings 9:30). He uses the term "distendest" in derision of their effort to make their eyes look large [MAURER]; or else, "rentest," i.e., dost lacerate by puncturing the eyelid in order to make the antimony adhere [ROSENMULLER]. So the Jews use every artifice to secure the aid of Egypt against Babylon. **face**—rather, thy *eyes* (Ezek. 23:40). **31. anguish**—viz., occasioned by the attack of the enemy. **daughter of Zion**—There is peculiar beauty in suppressing the name of the person in trouble, until that trouble had been fully described [HENDERSON]. **bewaileth herself**—rather, "draweth her breath short" [HORSLEY]. "panteth." **spreadeth . . . hands**—(Lam. 1: 17).

CHAPTER 5

Vss. 1-31. THE CAUSE OF THE JUDGMENTS TO BE INFLICTED IS THE UNIVERSAL CORRUPTION OF THE PEOPLE. **1. a man**—As the pious Josiah, Baruch, and Zephaniah lived in Jerusalem at that time, Jeremiah must here mean the mass of the people, the king, his counsellors, the false prophets, and the priests, as distinguished from the faithful few, whom God had openly separated from the reprobate people; among the latter not even *one* just person was to be found (Isa. 9:16) [CALVIN]; the godly, moreover, were forbidden to intercede for them (ch. 7:16; cf. Gen. 18:23, etc.; Ps. 12:1; Ezek. 22:30). **see ... know**–look ... ascertain. **judgment**–justice, righteousness. **pardon it**–rather, *her.* **2.** (Titus 1:16.) **swear falsely**–not a judicial oath; but their profession of the worship of Jehovah is insincere (vs. 7; ch. 4:2). The reformation under Josiah was merely superficial in the case of the majority. **3. eyes upon the truth**– (Deut. 32:4; II Chron. 16:9). "Truth" is in contrast with "swear falsely" (vs. 2). The false-professing Jews could expect nothing but judgments from the God of truth. **stricken ... not grieved**–(ch. 2: 30; Isa. 1:5; 9:13). **refused ... correction**–(ch. 7: 28; Zeph. 3:2). **4. poor**–rather, *"the* poor." He supposes for the moment that this utter depravity is confined to the uninstructed poor, and that he would find a different state of things in the higher ranks: but there he finds unbridled profligacy. **5. they have known**–rather, "they must know." The prophet *supposes it as probable,* considering their position. **but these**–I found the very reverse to be the case. **burst ... bonds**–set God's law at defiance (Ps. 2:3). **6. lion ... wolf ... leopard**–the strongest, the most ravenous, and the swiftest, respectively, of beasts: illustrating the formidable character of the Babylonians. **of the evenings**– Others not so well translate, *of the deserts.* The *plural* means that it goes forth *every evening* to seek its prey (Ps. 104:20; Hab. 1:8; Zeph. 3:3). **leopard ... watch ... cities**–(Hos. 13:7). It shall lie in wait about their cities. **7.** It would not be consistent with God's holiness to let such wickedness pass unpunished. **sworn by**–(vs. 2; ch. 4:2); i.e., worshipped. **no gods**–(Deut. 32:21). **fed ... to the full**–so the *Keri (Hebrew Margin)* reads, God's bountifulness is contrasted with their apostasy (Deut. 32:15). Prosperity, the gift of God, designed to lead men to Him, often produces the opposite effect. The *Hebrew Chetib* (text) reads: "I bound them (to Me) by oath," viz., in the *marriage covenant,* sealed at Sinai between God and Israel; in contrast to which stands their "adultery"; the antithesis favors this. **adultery ... harlots' houses**–spiritually: idolatry in temples of idols; but literal prostitution is also included, being frequently part of idol worship: e.g., in the worship of the Babylonian *Mylitta.* **8. in the morning**–(Isa. 5:11). "Rising early in the morning" is a phrase for unceasing eagerness in any pursuit; such was the Jews' avidity after idol worship. MAURER translates from a different *Hebrew* root, "continually wander to and fro," inflamed with lust (ch. 2:23). But *English Version* is simpler (cf. ch. 13:27; Ezek. 22:11). **9.** (Vs. 29; ch. 9:9; 44:22.) **10.** Abrupt apostrophe to the Babylonians, to take Jerusalem, but *not to destroy the nation utterly (Note,* ch. 4: 27. **battlements**–rather, *tendrils* [MAURER]: the state being compared to a *vine* (ch. 12:-10), the stem of which was to be spared, while the tendrils (the chief men) were to be removed. **11.** (Ch. 3:20.) **12. belied**–denied. **It is not he**–rather, "(Jehovah) is not HE," i.e., the true and only God (ch. 14:22; Deut. 32:39; Isa. 43:10, 13). By their idolatry they virtually denied Him. Or, referring to what follows, and to vs. 9, "(Jehovah) is not," viz., about to be the punisher of our sins (ch. 14:13; Isa. 28: 15). **13.** Continuation of the unbelieving language of the Jews. **the prophets**–who prophesy punishment coming on us. **the word**–the Holy Spirit, who speaks through true prophets, is not in them [MAURER]. Or else, "There is no word (di-

vine communication) in them" (Hos. 1:2) [ROSENMULLER]. **thus ...**–Their ill-omened prophecies shall fall on themselves. **14. ye ... thy ... this people**–He turns away from addressing the people to the prophet; implying that He puts them to a distance from Him, and only communicates with them through His prophet (vs. 19). **fire ... wood**– Thy denunciations of judgments shall be fulfilled and shall consume them as fire does wood. In ch. 23:29 it is the *penetrating energy* of fire which is the point of comparison. **15.** (Ch. 1:15; 6:22.) Alluding to Deuteronomy 28:49, etc. **Israel**–i.e., Judah. **mighty**–from an *Arabic* root, "enduring." The fourfold repetition of "nation" heightens the force. **ancient**–The Chaldeans came originally from the Carduchian and Armenian mountains north of Mesopotamia, whence they immigrated into Babylonia; like all mountaineers, they were brave and hardy *(Note,* Isa. 23:13). **language ... knowest not**–Isaiah 36:11 shows that *Aramaic* was not understood by the *multitude,* but only by the educated classes [MAURER]. HENDERSON refers it to the *original language* of the Babylonians, which, he thinks, they brought with them from their native hills, akin to the Persic, not to the Aramaic, or any other Semitic tongue, the parent of the modern *Kurd.* **16. open sepulchre**–(Cf. Ps. 5:9). Their quiver is all-devouring, as the grave opened to receive the dead: as many as are the arrows, so many are the deaths. **17.** (Lev. 26:16.) **18.** (vs. 10; ch. 4:27.) **Nevertheless**–*Not even* in those days of judgments, will God utterly exterminate His people. **19.** Retribution in kind. As ye have forsaken Me (ch. 2:13), so shall ye be forsaken by Me. As ye have served strange (foreign) gods in your land, so shall ye serve strangers (foreigners) in a land not yours. Cf. the similar retribution in Deuteronomy 28:47, 48. **21. eyes ... ears, and**–Translate, "and yet" (cf. Deut. 29:4; Isa. 6:9). Having powers of perception, they did not use them: still they were responsible for the exercise of them. **22. sand**– Though made up of particles easily shifting about, I render it sufficient to curb the violence of the sea. Such is your monstrous perversity, that the raging, senseless sea sooner obeys Me, than ye do who profess to be intelligent [CALVIN], (Job 26:10; 38:10; 11; Prov. 8:29; Rev. 15:4). **23.** (Ch. 6:28.) **24. rain ... former ... latter**–The "former" falls from the middle of October to the beginning of December. The "latter," or spring rain in Palestine, falls before harvest in March and April, and is essential for ripening the crops (Deut. 11:14; Joel 2:23). **weeks of ... harvest**–the seven weeks between passover and pentecost, beginning on the 16th of Nisan (Deut. 16:9). By God's special providence no rain fell in Palestine during the harvest weeks, so that harvest work went on without interruption (see Gen. 8:22). **25.** National guilt had caused the suspension of these national mercies mentioned in vs. 24 (cf. ch. 3:3). **26.** (Prov. 1:11, 17, 18; Hab. 1:15.) **as he that setteth snares**–rather, "as fowlers crouch" [MAURER]. **trap**–lit., destruction: the instrument of destruction. **catch men**–not as Peter, to save (Luke 5:10), but to destroy men. **27. full of deceit** –full of treasures got by deceit. **rich**–(Ps. 73:12, 18-20). **28. shine**–the effect of fatness on the skin (Deut. 32:15). They live a life of self-indulgence. **overpass ... the wicked**–exceed even the Gentiles in wickedness (ch. 2:33; Ezek. 5:6, 7). **judge not ... fatherless**–(Isa. 1:23). **yet ... prosper**–(ch. 12:1). **29.** (Vs. 9; Mal. 3:5.) **30.** (Ch. 23:14; Hos. 6:10.) **31. bear rule by their means**–lit., according to their hands, i.e., under their guidance (I Chron. 25:3).

As a sample of the priests lending themselves to the deceits of the false prophets, to gain influence over the people, see ch. 29:24-32. **love to have it so—** (Mic. 2:11). **end thereof—**the fatal issue of this sinful course when divine judgments shall come.

CHAPTER 6

Vss. 1-30. ZION'S FOES PREPARE WAR AGAINST HER: HER SINS ARE THE CAUSE. **1. Benjamin—**Jerusalem was situated in the tribe of Benjamin, which was here separated from that of Judah by the valley of Hinnom. Though it was inhabited partly by Benjamites, partly by men of Judah, he addresses the former as being his own countrymen. **blow ...trumpet...Tekoa—***Tikehu, Tekoa* form a play on sounds. The birthplace of Amos. **Beth-haccerem—**meaning in *Hebrew,* "vineyard-house." It and Tekoa were a few miles south of Jerusalem. As the enemy came from the north, the inhabitants of the surrounding country would naturally flee southwards. The fire-signal on the hills gave warning of danger approaching. **2. likened—**rather, "I lay waste." Lit., "O comely and delicate one, I lay waste the daughter of Zion," i.e., thee. So Zechariah 3:9, "before *Joshua,*" i.e., before *thee* [MAURER]. **3. shepherds—**hostile leaders with their armies (ch. 1:15; 4:17; 49:20; 50:45). **feed—**They shall consume each one all that is near him; lit., "his *hand,*" i.e., the *place* which he occupies (Num. 2:17 *Note,* Isa. 56:5). **4, 5.** The invading soldiers encourage one another to the attack on Jerusalem. **Prepare—**lit., "Sanctify" war, i.e., Proclaim it formally with solemn rites; the invasion was solemnly ordered by God (cf. Isa. 13:3). **at noon—**the hottest part of the day when attacks were rarely made (ch. 15:8; 20:16). Even at this time they wished to attack, such is their eagerness. **Woe unto us—**The words of the invaders, mourning the approach of night which would suspend their hostile operations; still, even in spite of the darkness, at *night* they renew the attack (vs. 5). **6. cast** —*Hebrew,* "pour out"; referring to the emptying of the baskets of earth to make the *mound,* formed of "trees" and earthwork, to overtop the city walls. The "trees" were also used to make warlike engines. **this—**pointing the invaders to Jerusalem. **visited—** i.e., punished. **wholly oppression—**or join "wholly" with "visited," i.e., she is altogether (in her whole extent) to be punished [MAURER]. **7. fountain—**rather, a *well* dug, from which water springs; distinct from a natural spring or fountain. **casteth out—**causeth to flow; lit., causeth to dig, the cause being put for the effect (II Kings 21:16, 24; Isa. 57: 20). **me—**Jehovah. **8.** Tender appeal in the midst of threats. **depart—***Hebrew,* "be torn away"; Jehovah's affection making Him unwilling to depart; His attachment to Jerusalem was such that an effort was needed to tear Himself from it (Ezek. 23:18; Hos 9:12; 11:8). **9.** The Jews are the grapes, their enemies the unsparing gleaners. **turn back... hand—**again and again bring freshly gathered handfuls to the baskets; referring to the repeated carrying away of captives to Babylon (ch. 52:28-30; II Kings 24:14; 25:11). **10. ear is uncircumcised—** closed against the precepts of God by the foreskin of carnality (Lev. 26:41; Ezek. 44:7; Acts 7:51). **word...reproach—**(ch. 20:8). **11. fury of...Lord** —His denunciations against Judah communicated to the prophet. **weary with holding in—**(ch. 20:9). **I will pour—**or else imperative: the command of God (see vs. 12), "Pour it out" [MAURER]. **aged...**

full of days—The former means *one becoming old;* the latter a *decrepit old man* [MAURER] (Job 5:26; Isa. 65:20). **12.** The very punishments threatened by Moses in the event of disobedience to God (Deut. 28:30). **turned—**transferred. **13.** (Ch. 8: 10; Isa. 56:11; Mic. 3:11.) **14. hurt—**the spiritual *wound.* **slightly—**as if it were but a *slight* wound; or, *in a slight manner,* pronouncing all sound where there is no soundness. **saying—**viz., the prophets and priests (vs. 13). Whereas they ought to warn the people of impending judgments and the need of repentance, they say there is nothing to fear. **peace** —including soundness. All is *sound* in the nation's moral state, so all will be *peace* as to its political state (ch. 4:10; 8:11; 14:13; 23:17; Ezek. 13:5, 10; 22:28). **15.** ROSENMULLER translates, "They *ought to have been* ashamed, because ... but," etc.; the *Hebrew* verb often expressing, not the action, but the *duty* to perform it, Gen. 20:9; Mal. 2:7). MAURER translates, "They shall be put to shame, for they commit abomination; nay (the prophet correcting himself), there is no shame in them" (ch. 3:3; 8:12; Ezek. 3:7; Zeph. 3:5). **them that fall—**They shall fall with the rest of their people who are doomed to fall, i.e., I will now cease from words; I will execute vengeance [CALVIN]. **16.** Image from travellers who have lost their road, stopping and inquiring which is the right way on which they once had been, but from which they have wandered. **old paths—**Idolatry and apostasy are the modern way; the worship of God the *old* way. Evil is not coeval with good, but a *modern degeneracy* from good. The forsaking of God is not, in a true sense, a "way cast up" at all (ch. 18:15; Ps. 139:24; Mal. 4:4). **rest—**(Isa. 28:12; Matt. 11:29). **17. watchmen—**prophets, whose duty it was to announce impending calamities, so as to lead the people to repentance (Isa. 21:11; 58:1; Ezek. 3:17; Hab. 2:1). **18. congregation—**parallel to "nations"; it therefore means *the gathered peoples* who are invited to be witnesses as to how great is the perversity of the Israelites (vss. 16, 17), and that they deserve the severe punishment about to be inflicted on them (vs. 19). **what is among them—**what *deeds* are committed by the *Israelites* (vss. 16, 17) [MAURER]. Or, "what *punishments* are about to be inflicted on them" [CALVIN]. **19.** (Isa. 1:2.) **fruit of...thoughts—** (Prov. 1:31). **nor to my law, but rejected it—**lit., "and (as to) My law they have rejected it." The same construction occurs in Genesis 22:24. **20.** Lit., "To what purpose is this to Me, that incense cometh to Me?" **incense...cane—**(Isa. 43:24; 60: 6). No external services are accepted by God without obedience of the heart and life (ch. 7:21; Ps. 50:7-9; Isa. 1:11; Mic. 6:6, etc.). **sweet... sweet—**antithesis. Your *sweet* cane is not *sweet* to Me. The calamus. **21. stumbling-blocks—**instruments of the Jews' ruin (cf. Matt. 21:44; Isa. 8:14; I Pet. 2:8). God Himself ("I") *lays* them before the reprobate (Ps. 69:22; Rom. 1:28; 11:9). **fathers...sons...neighbour...friend—**indiscriminate ruin. **22. north...sides of the earth—**The ancients were little acquainted with the *north;* therefore it is called *the remotest regions* (as the *Hebrew* for "sides" ought to be translated, see *Note,* Isa. 14:13) *of the earth.* The Chaldees are meant (ch. 1:15; 5:15). It is striking that the very same calamities which the Chaldeans had inflicted on Zion are threatened as the retribution to be dealt in turn to themselves by Jehovah (ch. 50:41-43). **23. like the sea—**(Isa. 5:30). **as men for war—**not that they were *like* warriors, for they *were* warriors; but "arrayed *most perfectly as warriors*" [MAURER]. **24.**

fame thereof—the report of them. **25.** He address-es "the daughter of Zion" (vs. 23); caution to the citizens of Jerusalem not to expose themselves to the enemy by going outside of the city walls. **sword of the enemy**—lit., "there is a sword to the enemy"; the enemy hath a sword. **26. wallow . . . in ashes**—(ch. 25:34; Mic. 1:10). As they usually in mourning only "cast ashes on the head," *wallow-ing in them* means something more, viz., so entirely to cover one's self with ashes as to be like one who had rolled in them (Ezek. 27:30). **as for an only son**—(Amos 8:10; Zech. 12:10.) **lamentation**—lit., lamentation expressed by beating the breast. **27. tower . . . fortress**—(ch. 1:18), rather, "an assayer (and) explorer." By a metaphor from metallurgy in vss. 27-30, Jehovah, in conclusion, confirms the prophet in his office, and the latter sums up the description of the reprobate people on whom he had to work. The *Hebrew* for "assayer" (*English Version*, "tower") is from a root "to try" metals. "Ex-plorer" (*English Version*, "fortress") is from an *Arabic* root, "keen-sighted"; or a *Hebrew* root, "cutting," i.e., separating the metal from the dross [EWALD]. GESENIUS translates as *English Version*, "fortress," which does not accord with the previous "assayer." **28. grievous revolters**—lit., "contu-macious of the contumacious," i.e., most contuma-cious, the *Hebrew* mode of expressing a superlative. So "the strong among the mighty," i.e., the strongest (Ezek. 32:21). See ch. 5:23; Hosea 4:16. **walk-ing with slanders**—(ch. 9:4). "Going about for the purpose of slandering" [MAURER]. **brass . . .**—i.e., copper. It and "iron" being the baser and harder metals express the debased and obdurate character of the Jews (Isa. 48:4; 60:17). **29. bellows . . . burned**—So intense a heat is made that the very bellows are almost set on fire. ROSENMULLER trans-lates not so well from a *Hebrew* root, "pant" or "snort," referring to the sound of the bellows blown hard. **lead**—employed to separate the baser metal from the silver, as quicksilver is now used. In other words, the utmost pains have been used to purify Israel in the furnace of affliction, but in vain (ch. 5:3; I Pet. 1:7). **consumed of the fire**—In the *Chetib* or *Hebrew* text, the "consumed" is supplied out of the previous "burned." Translat-ing as ROSENMULLER, "pant," this will be inadmis-sible; and the *Keri* (*Hebrew margin*) division of the *Hebrew* words will have to be read, to get "is con-sumed of the fire." This is an argument for the translation, "are burned." **founder**—the refiner. **wicked . . . not plucked away**—answering to the dross which has no good metal to be separated, the mass being all dross. **30. Reprobate**—silver so full of alloy as to be utterly worthless (Isa. 1:22). The Jews were fit only for rejection.

CHAPTER 7

Vss. 1-34. CHAPTERS 7-9. DELIVERED IN THE BEGINNING OF JEHOIAKIM'S REIGN, ON THE OCCASION OF SOME PUBLIC FESTIVAL. The prophet stood at the gate of the temple in order that the multitudes from the country might hear him. His life was threatened, it appears from ch. 26:1-9, for this prophecy, denouncing the fate of Shiloh as about to befall the temple at Jerusalem. The prophecy given in detail here is summarily referred to there. After Josiah's death the nation relapsed into idol-atry through Jehoiakim's bad influence; the wor-ship of Jehovah was, however, combined with it (vss. 4, 10). **2. the gate**—i.e., the gate of the court

of Israel within that of the women. Those whom Jeremiah addresses came through the gate leading into the court of the women, and the gate leading into the outer court, or court of the Gentiles ("these gates"). **3. cause you to dwell**—permit you still to dwell (ch. 18:11; 26:13). **4.** The Jews falsely thought that because their temple had been chosen by Jehovah as His peculiar dwelling, it could never be destroyed. Men think that ceremonial observ-ances will supersede the need of holiness (Isa. 48:2; Mic. 3:11). The triple repetition of "the temple of Jehovah" expresses the intense confidence of the Jews (see ch. 22:29; Isa. 6:3). **these**—the temple buildings which the prophet points to with his finger (vs. 2). **5. For**—"But" [MAURER]. **judgment**—justice (ch. 22:3). **6. this place**—this city and land (vs. 7) **to your hurt**—so vs. 19; "to the confusion or their own faces" (ch. 13:10; Prov. 8:36). **7.** The apodosis to the "if . . . if" (vss. 5, 6). **to dwell**—to continue to dwell. **for ever and ever**—joined with "to dwell," not with the words "gave to your fathers" (cf ch. 3: 18; Deut. 4:40). **8. that cannot profit**—MAURER translates, "so that you profit nothing" (see vs. 4; ch. 5:31). **9, 10.** "Will ye steal . . . *and then* come and stand before Me?" **whom ye know not**—Ye have no grounds of "knowing" that *they* are gods; but I have manifested My Godhead by My law, by benefits conferred, and by miracles. This aggra-vates their crime [CALVIN] (Judg. 5:8). **10. And come**—And yet come (Ezek. 23:39). **We are deliv-ered**—viz., from all impending calamities. In spite of the prophet's threats, we have nothing to fear; we have offered our sacrifices, and therefore Jehovah will "deliver" us. **to do all these abominations**—viz., those enumerated (vs. 9). These words are not to be connected with "we are delivered," but thus: "Is it *with this design* that ye come and stand before Me in this house," in order that having offered your worthless sacrifices, ye may be taken into My favor and so do all these abominations (vs. 9) with im-punity? [MAURER]. **11. den of robbers**—Do you re-gard My temple as being what robbers make their den, viz., an asylum wherein ye may obtain impunity for your abominations (vs. 10)? **seen it**—viz., that ye treat My house as if it were a den of thieves. Jehovah implies more than is expressed, "I have seen *and will punish* it" (Isa. 56:7; Matt. 21:13). **12. my place . . . in Shiloh**—God caused His taber-nacle to be set up in Shiloh in Joshua's days (Josh. 18:1; Judg. 18:31). In Eli's time God gave the ark, which had been at Shiloh, into the hands of the Philistines (ch. 26:6; I Sam. 4:10, 11; Ps. 78:56-61). Shiloh was situated between Bethel and Shechem in Ephraim. **at the first**—implying that *Shiloh* ex-ceeded the Jewish temple in antiquity. But God's favor is not tied down to localities (Acts 7:44). **my people Israel**—Israel was *God's* people, yet He spared it not when rebellious: neither will He spare Judah, now that it rebels, though heretofore it has been His people. **13. rising . . . early**—implying un-wearied earnestness in soliciting them (vs. 25; ch. 11: 17; II Chron. 36:15). **14. I gave**—and I therefore can revoke the gift for it is still Mine (Lev. 25:23), now that ye fail in the only object for which it was given, the promotion of My glory. **Shiloh**—as I ceased to dwell there, transferring My temple to Je-rusalem; so I will cease to dwell at Jerusalem. **15. your brethren**—children of Abraham, as much as you. **whole seed of Ephraim**—They were superior to you in numbers and power: they were *ten* tribes: ye but *two*. "Ephraim," as the leading tribe, stands for the whole ten tribes (II Kings 17:23; Ps. 78:67, 68). **16.** When people are given up to judicial hardness of heart, intercessory prayer for them is unavailing (ch. 11:14; 14:11; 15:1; Exod. 32:10; I John 5:16). **17.** Jehovah leaves it to Jeremiah himself to decide, is there not good reason that prayers should not be heard in behalf of such rebels? **18. children . . . fathers . . . women**—Not merely isolated individuals practised idolatry; young and old, men and women, and whole families, contributed their joint efforts to promote it. Oh, that there were the same zeal for the worship of God as there is for error (ch. 44:17, 19: 19:13)! **cakes . . . queen of heaven**—Cakes were made of honey, fine flour, etc., in a round flat shape to resemble the disc of *the moon,* to which they were offered. Others read as *Margin,* "the frame of heaven," i.e., the planets generally; so LXX here; but elsewhere LXX translates, "queen of heaven." The Phœnicians called the moon *Ashtoreth* or *Astarte:* the wife of Baal or Moloch, the *king* of heaven. The male and female pair of deities symbolized the generative powers of nature; hence arose the introduction of prostitution in the worship. The Babylonians worshipped Ashtoreth as Mylitta, i.e., generative. Our Monday, or *Moonday,* indicates the former prevalence of moon-worship (*Note,* Isa. 65:11). **that they may provoke me** —implying *design:* in worshipping strange gods they seemed as if *purposely* to provoke Jehovah. **19.** Is it *I* that they provoke to anger? Is it not *themselves?* (Deut. 32:16, 21; Job 35:6, 8; Prov. 8:36). **20. beast . . . trees . . . ground**—Why doth God vent His fury on these? On account of man, for whom these were created, that the sad spectacle may strike terror into him (Rom. 8:20-22). **21. Put . . . burnt offerings unto . . . sacrifices . . . eat flesh**—*Add* the former (which the law required to be *wholly* burnt) to the latter (which were burnt only *in part*), and "eat flesh" even off the holocausts or burnt offerings. As far as I am concerned, saith Jehovah, you may do with one and the other alike. I will have neither (Isa. 1:11; Hos. 8:13; Amos 5:21, 22). **22.** Not contradicting the divine obligation of the legal sacrifices. But, "I did not require sacrifices, unless combined with moral obedience" (Ps. 50:8; 51:16, 17). The superior claim of the *moral* above the *positive* precepts of the law was marked by the ten commandments having been delivered first, and by the two tables of stone being deposited alone in the ark (Deut. 5:6). The negative in *Hebrew* often supplies the want of the comparative: not excluding the thing denied, but only implying the prior claim of the thing set in opposition to it (Hos. 6:6). "I will have mercy, and *not* sacrifice (I Sam. 15:22). Love to God is the supreme *end,* external observances only *means* towards that end. "The mere sacrifice was not *so much* what I commanded, as the sincere submission to My will gives to the sacrifice all its virtue" [MAGEE, *Atonement, Note* 57]. **23.** (Exod. 15:26; 19:5.) **24. hearkened not**—They did not give even a partial hearing to Me (Ps. 81:11, 12). **imagination**—rather, as *Margin,* "the stubbornness." **backward . . .**—(ch. 2:27; 32:33; Hos. 4: 16). **25. rising . . . early**—(vs. 13). **26. hardened . . . neck**—(Deut. 31:27; Isa. 48:4; Acts 7:51). **worse than their fathers**—(ch. 16:12). In vs. 22 He had said, "*your* fathers"; here He says, "*their* fathers"; the change to the third person marks growing alienation from them. He no longer addresses *themselves,* as it would be a waste of words in the case of such hardened rebels. **27. Therefore**—rather, *"Though* thou speak . . . yet they will not hearken" [MAURER], (Ezek. 2:7), a trial to the prophet's faith; though he knew his warnings would be unheeded, still he was to give them in obedience to

God. **28. unto them**—i.e., in reference to them. **a nation**—The word usually applied to the Gentile *nations* is here applied to the Jews, as being cast off and classed by God among the Gentiles. **nor receiveth correction**—(ch. 5:3). **truth . . . perished**— (ch. 9:3). **29.** Jeremiah addresses Jerusalem under the figure of a woman, who, in grief for her lost children, deprives her head of its chief ornament and goes up to the hills to weep (Judg. 11:37, 38; Isa. 15:2). **hair**—flowing locks, like those of a Nazarite. **high places**—The scene of her idolatries is to be the scene of her mourning (ch. 3:21). **generation of his wrath**—the generation with which He is wroth. So Isa. 10:6; "the people of My wrath." **30. set their abominations in the house**—(ch. 32:34; II Kings 21:4, 7; 23:4; Ezek. 8:5-14). **31. high places of Tophet**—the *altars* [HORSLEY] of Tophet; erected to Moloch, on the heights along the south of the valley facing Zion. **burn . . . sons**—(Ps. 106:38). **commanded . . . not**—put for, "I forbade expressly" (Deut. 17:3; 12:31). See ch. 2:23; Isaiah 30:33; *Notes.* **32. valley of slaughter**—so named because of the great slaughter of the Jews about to take place at Jerusalem: a just retribution of their sin in slaying their children to Moloch in Tophet. **no place**—no room, viz., to bury in, so many shall be those slain by the Chaldeans (ch. 19:11; Ezek. 6:5). **33. fray**— *scare* or *frighten* (Deut. 28:26). Typical of the last great battle between the Lord's host and the apostasy (Rev. 19:17, 18, 21). **34.** Referring to the joyous songs and music with which the bride and bridegroom were escorted in the procession to the home of the latter from that of the former; a custom still prevalent in the East (ch. 16:9; Isa. 24: 7, 8; Rev. 18:23).

CHAPTER 8

Vss. 1-22. THE JEW'S COMING PUNISHMENT; THEIR UNIVERSAL AND INCURABLE IMPENITENCE. **1.** The victorious Babylonians were about to violate the sanctuaries of the dead in search of plunder; for ornaments, treasures, and insignia of royalty were usually buried with kings. Or rather, their purpose was to do the *greatest dishonor* to the dead (Isa. 14: 19). **2. spread . . . before the sun . . .**—retribution in kind. The very objects which received their idolatries shall unconcernedly witness their dishonor. **lover . . . served . . . after . . . walked . . . sought . . . worshipped**—Words are accumulated, as if enough could not be said fully to express the mad fervor of their idolatry to the heavenly host (II Kings 23:5). **nor . . . buried**—(ch. 22:19). **dung**—(ch. 9:22; Ps. 83:10). **3.** The survivors shall be still worse off than the dead (Job 3:21, 22; Rev. 9:6). **which remain in all the places**—"in all places of them that remain, whither I . . . , i.e, in all places whither I have driven them that remain [MAURER]. **4.** "Is it not a natural instinct, that if one falls, he *rises again;* if one turns away (i.e., wanders from the way), he will *return* to the point from which he wandered? Why then does not Jerusalem do so?" He plays on the double sense of *return;* literal and metaphorical (ch. 3:12; 4:1). **5. slidden . . . backsliding**—rather, as the *Hebrew* is the same as in vs. 4, to which this verse refers, "turned away" with a perpetual *turning away.*" **perpetual**—in contrast to the "arise" (rise again," vs. 4). **refuse to return**—in contrast to, "shall he . . . not return" (vs. 4; ch. 5:3). **6. spake not aright**—i.e., not so as *penitently to confess* that they acted wrong. Cf. what follows. **every one . . . his course**—The *Keri* reads "course," but the *Chetib,* "courses." "They persevere in the *courses* whatever they have once entered on." Their wicked *ways* were *diversified*. **horse rusheth**—lit., "pours himself forth," as water that has burst its embankment. The *mad rapidity* of the war horse is the point of comparison (Job 39:19-25). **7.** The instinct of the migratory birds leads them with unfailing regularity to return every spring from their winter abodes in summer climes (Song of Sol. 2:12); but God's people will not return to Him even when the winter of His wrath is past, and He invites them back to the spring of His favor. **in the heaven**—emphatical. The birds whose very element is the *air*, in which they are never at rest, yet show a steady sagacity, which God's people do not. **times**—viz., of migrating, and of returning. **my people**—This honorable title aggravates the unnatural perversity of the Jews towards *their* God. **know not . . .** —(ch. 5:4, 5; Isa. 1:3). **8. law . . . with us**—(Rom. 2:17). Possessing the law, on which they prided themselves, the Jews might have become the wisest of nations; but by their neglecting its precepts, the law became given "in vain," as far as they were concerned. **scribes**—copyists. "In vain" copies were multiplied. MAURER translates, "The false pen of the scribes hath converted it [the law] into a lie." See *Margin*, which agrees with *Vulgate*. **9. dismayed**—confounded. **what wisdom**—lit., "the wisdom of what?" i.e., "wisdom in what respect?" the Word of the Lord being the only true source of wisdom (Ps. 119:98-100; Prov. 1:7; 9:10). **10-12.** Repeated from ch. 6:12-15. See a similar repetition, vs. 15; ch. 14:19. **inherit**—*succeed to the possession* of them. **11.** (Ezek. 13:10.) **13. surely consume**—lit., "gathering I will gather," or "consuming I will consume." **no grapes . . . nor figs**—(Joel 1:7; Matt. 21:19). **things that I have given . . . shall pass away**—rather, "I will appoint to them those who shall overwhelm (pass over) them," i.e., I will send the enemy upon them [MAURER]. *English Version* accords well with the context; Though their grapes and figs ripen, they shall not be allowed to enjoy them. **14. assemble**—for defense. **let us be silent**—not assault the enemy, but merely defend ourselves in quiet, until the storm blow over. **put us to silence**—brought us to that state that we can no longer resist the foe; implying silent despair. **water of gall**—lit., "water of the poisonous plant," perhaps the poppy (ch. 9:15; 23:15). **15.** Repeated (ch. 14:19). **We looked for**—owing to the expectations held out by the false prophets. **health**—healing; i.e., restoration from adversity. **16. his horses**—the Chaldean's. **was heard**—the prophetical past for the future. **from Dan**—bordering on Phœnicia. This was to be Nebuchadnezzar's route in invading Israel; the *cavalry* in advance of the infantry would scour the country. **strong ones**—a poetical phrase for *steeds*, peculiar to Jeremiah (ch. 47:3; cf. ch. 4: 13, 29; 6:23). **17. I**—Jehovah. **cockatrices**—basilisks (Isa. 11:8), i.e., enemies whose destructive power no means, by persuasion or otherwise, can counteract. Serpent-charmers in the East entice serpents by music, and by a particular pressure on the neck render them incapable of darting (Ps. 58:4, 5). **18.** (Isa. 22:4.) The lamentation of the prophet for the impending calamity of his country. **against sorrow**—or, *with respect to* sorrow. MAURER translates, "Oh, my exhilaration as to sorrow!" i.e., "Oh, that exhilaration (comfort, from an *Arabic* root, to *shine* as the rising sun) would shine upon me as to my sorrow!" **in me**—within me. **19.** The prophet in vision hears the cry of the exiled Jews, wondering that God should have delivered them up

to the enemy, seeing that He is Zion's king, dwelling in her (Mic. 3:11). In the latter half of the verse God replies that their own idolatry, not want of faithfulness on His part, is the cause. **because of them that dwell in a far country**—rather, "from a land of distances," i.e., a distant land (Isa. 39:3). *English Version* understands the cry to be of the Jews *in their own land*, because of the enemy *coming from their far-off country*. **strange vanities**—foreign gods. **20.** Proverbial. Meaning: One season of hope after another has passed, but the looked-for deliverance never came, and now all hope is gone. **21. black**—sad in visage with grief (Joel 2:6). **22. balm**—*balsam;* to be applied to the wounds of my people. Brought into Judea first from Arabia Felix, by the queen of Sheba, in Solomon's time (JOSEPHUS, *Antiquities* 8.2). The *opobalsamum* of Pliny; or else [BOCHART] the resin drawn from the terebinth. It abounded in Gilead, east of Jordan, where, in consequence, many "physicians" established themselves (ch. 46:11; 51:8; Gen. 37:25; 43:11). **health . . . recovered**—The *Hebrew* is lit., "lengthening out . . . gone up"; hence, *the long bandage applied* to bind up a wound. So the *Arabic* also [GESENIUS].

CHAPTER 9

Vss. 1-26. JEREMIAH'S LAMENTATION FOR THE JEWS' SINS AND CONSEQUENT PUNISHMENT. **1.** This verse is more fitly joined to the last chapter, as vs. 23 in the *Hebrew* (cf. Isa. 22:4; Lam. 1:1; 3:48). **2. lodging place**—a caravanserai for caravans, or companies travelling in the desert, remote from towns. It was a square building enclosing an open court. Though a lonely and often filthy dwelling, Jeremiah would prefer even it to the comforts of Jerusalem, so as to be removed from the pollutions of the capital (Ps. 55:7, 8). **3. bend . . . tongues . . . for lies**—i.e., with lies as their arrows; they direct lies on their tongue as their bow (Ps. 64:3, 4). **not valiant for . . . truth**—(ch. 7:28). MAURER translates, "They do not *prevail by* truth" or *faith* (Ps. 12:4). Their *tongue*, not *faith*, is their weapon. **upon . . . earth**—rather, "in the land." **know not me**—(Hos. 4:1). **4. supplant**—lit., "trip up by the heel" (Hos. 12:3). **walk with slanders**—(ch. 6:28). **5. weary themselves**—*are at laborious pains* to act perversely [MAURER]. Sin is a hard bondage (Hab. 2:13). **6. Thine**—God addresses Jeremiah, who dwelt in the midst of deceitful men. **refuse to know me**—Their ignorance of God is wilful (vs. 3; ch, 5:4, 5). **7. melt . . . try them**—by sending calamities on them. **for how shall I do**—"What *else* can I do for the sake of the daughter of My people?" [MAURER], (Isa. 1:25; Mal. 3:3). **8. tongue . . . arrow shot out**—rather, "a *murdering* arrow" [MAURER] (vs. 3). **speaketh peaceably . . . in heart . . . layeth . . . wait**—layeth his ambush [HENDERSON], (Ps. 55:21). **9.** (Ch. 5:9, 29.) **10.** Jeremiah breaks in upon Jehovah's threats of wrath with lamentation for his desolated country. **mountains**—once cultivated and fruitful: the hillsides were cultivated in terraces between the rocks. **habitations of . . . wilderness**—rather, "the pleasant herbage (lit., "the choice parts" of any thing) of the pasture plain." The *Hebrew* for wilderness expresses not a barren desert, but an untilled plain, fit for pasture. **burned up**—because no one waters them, the inhabitants being all gone. **none can pass through them**—much less *inhabit* them. **fowl**—(ch. 4:25). **11. And**—omit "And." Jehovah here resumes His speech from vs. 9. **heaps**—(*Note,* Isa. 25:2). **dragons**—jackals. **12.** Rather, "Who is a wise man? (i.e., *Whosoever* has inspired wisdom, II Peter 3:15); let him understand this (weigh well the evils impending, and the causes of their being sent); and he to whom the mouth of the Lord hath spoken (i.e., *whosoever is prophetically inspired*), let him declare it to his fellow countrymen," if haply they may be roused to repentance, the only hope of safety. **13.** Answer to the "for what the land perisheth" (vs. 12). **14.** (Ch. 7:24.) **Baalim**—plural of Baal, to express his supposed manifold powers. **fathers taught them**—(Gal. 1:14; I Pet. 1:18). We are not to follow the errors of the fathers, but the authority of Scripture and of God [JEROME]. **15. feed**—(ch. 8:14; 23:15; Ps. 80:5). **16. nor their fathers have known**—alluding to vs. 14, "Their fathers taught them" idolatry; therefore the children shall be scattered to a land which neither their fathers nor they have known. **send a sword after them**—Not even in flight shall they be safe. **17. mourning women**—hired to heighten lamentation by plaintive cries baring the breast, beating the arms, and suffering the hair to flow dishevelled (II Chron. 35:25; Eccles. 12: 5; Matt. 9:23). **cunning**—skilled in wailing. **18.** (Ch. 14:17.) **19.** The cry of "the mourning women." **spoiled**—laid waste. **dwellings ... cast us out**—fulfilling Leviticus 18:28; 20:22. CALVIN translates, "*The enemy* have cast down our habitations." **20. Yet**—rather, "Only" [HENDERSON]. This particle calls attention to what follows. **teach ... daughters wailing**—The deaths will be so many that there will be a lack of mourning women to bewail them. The mothers, therefore, must teach their daughters the science to supply the want. **21. death ... windows**—The death-inflicting soldiery, finding the doors closed, burst in by the windows. **to cut off ... children from ... streets**—Death cannot be said to enter the *windows* to cut off the children *in* the streets, but to cut them off, so as no more to play in the streets without (Zech. 8:5). **22. saith the Lord**—continuing the thread of discourse from vs. 20. **dung**—(ch. 8:2). **handful ... none ... gather them**—implying that the handful has been so trodden as to be not worth even the poor *gleaner's* effort to gather it. Or the Eastern custom may be referred to: the reaper cuts the grain and is followed by another who *gathers it.* This grain shall not be worth gathering. How galling to the pride of the Jews to hear that so shall their carcasses be trodden contemptuously under foot! **23. wisdom**—political sagacity; as if *it* could rescue from the impending calamities. **might**—military prowess. **24.** Nothing but an experimental knowledge of God will save the nation. **understandeth**—*theoretically;* in the intellect. **knoweth**—*practically:* so as to walk in My ways (ch. 22:16; Job 22: 21: I Cor. 1:31). **loving-kindness**—God's mercy is put in the first and highest place, because without it we should flee from God in fear and despair. **judgment ... righteousness**—*loving-kindness* towards the godly; *judgment* towards the ungodly; *righteousness* the most perfect fairness in all cases [GROTIUS]. *Faithfulness to His promises* to preserve the godly, as well as stern execution of judgment on the ungodly, is included in "righteousness." **in the earth**—contrary to the dogma of some philosophers, that God does not interfere in terrestrial concerns (Ps. 58:11). **in these ... I delight**—as well in doing them as in seeing them done by others (Mic. 6:8; 7:18). **25. with the uncircumcised**—rather, "all that are circumcised *in uncircumcision*" [HENDERSON]. The *Hebrew* is an *abstract* term, not a *concrete,* as *English Version*

translates, and as the pious "circumcised" is. The nations specified, Egypt, Judah, etc., were *outwardly* "circumcised," but *in heart* were "uncircumcised." The heathen nations were defiled, in spite of their literal circumcision, by idolatry. The Jews, with all their glorying in their spiritual privileges, were no better (ch. 4:4; Deut. 10:16; 30:6; Rom. 2:28, 29; Col. 2:11). However, Ezekiel 31:18; 32:19, *may* imply that the Egyptians were uncircumcised; and it is uncertain as to the other nations specified whether they were at that early time circumcised. HERODOTUS says the Egyptians were so; but others think this applies only to the priests and others having a sacred character, not to the mass of the nation; so *English Version* may be right (Rom. 2: 28, 29). **26. Egypt**—put first to degrade Judah, who, though in privileges above the Gentiles, by unfaithfulness sank below them. · Egypt, too, was the power in which the Jews were so prone to trust, and by whose instigation they, as well as the other peoples specified, revolted from Babylon. **in the utmost corners**—rather, "having the hair shaven (or *clipped*) in angles," i.e., having the beard on the cheek narrowed or *cut:* a Canaanitish custom, forbidden to the Israelites (Lev. 19:27; 21:5). The Arabs are hereby referred to (cf. ch. 25:23; 49:32), as the words in apposition show, "that dwell in the wilderness." **uncircumcised ... uncircumcised in the heart**—The addition of "in the heart" in *Israel's* case marks *its* greater guilt in proportion to its greater privileges, as compared with the rest.

CHAPTER 10

Vss. 1-25. CONTRAST BETWEEN THE IDOLS AND JEHOVAH. THE PROPHET'S LAMENTATION AND PRAYER. **1. Israel**—the Jews, the surviving representatives of the nation. **2.** EICHORN thinks the reference here to be to some celestial portent which had appeared at that time, causing the Jews' dismay. Probably the reference is general, viz., to the Chaldeans, famed as astrologers, through contact with whom the Jews were likely to fall into the same superstition. **way**—the precepts or ordinances (Lev. 18:3; Acts 9:2). **signs of heaven**—The Gentiles did not acknowledge a Great First Cause: many thought events depended on the power of the stars, which some, as PLATO, thought to be endued with spirit and reason. All heavenly phenomena, eclipses, comets, etc. are included. *one* **cutteth a tree ...**—rather, "It (that which they busy themselves about: a sample of their 'customs') is a tree cut out of the forest" [MAURER]. **4. fasten ... move not**—i.e., that it may stand upright without risk of falling, which the god (!) would do, if left to itself (Isa. 41:7). **5. upright**—or, "They are of turned work, resembling a palm tree" [MAURER]. The point of comparison between the idol and the palm is in the pillar-like uprightness of the latter, it having no branches except at the top. **speak not**—(Ps. 115:5). **cannot go**—i.e., walk (Ps. 115:7; Isa. 46:1, 7), **neither ... do good**—(Isa. 41:23). **6. none**—lit., no particle of nothing: nothing whatever; the strongest possible denial (Exod. 15:11; Ps. 86:8, 10). **7.** (Rev. 15:4). **to thee doth it appertain**—to Thee it properly belongs, viz., that Thou shouldest be "feared" (taken out of the previous "fear Thee") (cf. Ezek. 21:27). He alone is the *becoming* object of worship. To worship any other is unseemly and an infringement of His inalienable prerogative. **none**—nothing whatever (*Note,* vs. 6; Ps. 89:6). **8. altogether**—rather, all alike [MAURER].

Even the so-called "wise" men (vs. 7) of the Gentiles are on a level with the *brutes* and "foolish," viz., because they connive at the popular idolatry (cf. Rom. 1:21-28). Therefore, in Daniel and Revelation, the world power is represented under a bestial form. Man divests himself of his true humanity, and sinks to the level of the *brute*, when he severs his connection with God (Ps. 115:8; Jonah 2:8). **stock is a doctrine of vanities**—The stock (put for the worship of *all idols whatever*, made out of a stock) speaks for itself that the whole theory of idolatry is vanity (Isa. 44:9-11). CASTALIO translates, "the very wood itself confuting the vanity" (of the idol). **9.** Everything connected with idols is the result of human effort. **Silver spread**—(*Notes,* Isa. 30:22; 40:19). **Tarshish**—Tartessus, in Spain, famed for precious metals. **Uphaz**—(Dan. 10:5). As the *Septuagint* in the *Syrian Hexapla* in the *Margin,* Theodotus, the *Syrian* and *Chaldee versions* have "*Ophir,*" GESENIUS thinks "Uphaz" a colloquial corruption (one letter only being changed) for "Ophir." Ophir, in Genesis 10:29, is mentioned among Arabian countries. Perhaps Malacca is the country meant, the natives of which still call their gold mines Ophirs. HEEREN thinks Ophir the general name for the rich countries of the south, on the Arabian, African, and Indian coasts; just as our term, East Indies. **cunning**—skilful. **10. true God**—lit., "God Jehovah is truth"; not merely *true,* i.e., veracious, but *truth* in the reality of His essence, as opposed to the "vanity" or emptiness which all idols are (vss. 3, 8, 15; II Chron. 15: 3; Ps. 31:5; I John 5:20). **living God**—(John 5:26; I Tim. 6:17). He hath life *in Himself,* which no creature has. All else "live in Him" (Acts 17:28). In contrast to *dead* idols. **everlasting**—(Ps. 10:16). In contrast to the *temporary* existence of all other objects of worship. **11.** This verse is in *Chaldee,* Jeremiah supplying his countrymen with a formula of reply to Chaldee idolaters in the tongue most intelligible to the latter. There may be also derision intended in imitating their barbarous dialect. ROSENMULLER objects to this view, that not merely the words put in the mouths of the Israelites, but *Jeremiah's* own introductory words, "Thus shall ye say to them," are in *Chaldee,* and thinks it to be a *marginal* gloss. But it is found in all the oldest versions. It was an old *Greek* saying. "Whoever thinks himself a god besides the one God, let him make another world" (Ps. 96:5). **shall perish**—(Isa. 2:18; Zech. 13:2). **these heavens**—the speaker pointing to them with his fingers. **12.** Continuation of vs. 10, after the interruption of the thread of the discourse in vs. 11 (Ps. 136:5, 6). **13.** Lit., "At the voice of His giving forth," i.e., when He thunders. (Job 38:34; Ps. 29:3-5). **waters**—(Gen. 1:7)—above the firmament; heavy rains accompany thunder. **vapours . . . ascend**—(Ps. 135:7). **treasures**—His stores. **14. in his knowledge**—"is rendered brutish *by* his skill," viz., in idol-making (vss. 8, 9). Thus the parallel, "confounded *by* the graven image," corresponds (so ch. 51:17). Others not so well translate, "*without* knowledge," viz., of God (see Isa. 42:17; 45:16; Hos. 4:6). **15. errors** —deceptions; from a *Hebrew* root, "to stutter"; then meaning "to mock." **their visitation they**—When God shall punish the idol-worshippers (viz., by Cyrus), the idols themselves shall be destroyed [ROSENMULLER] (vs. 11). **16. portion**—from a *Hebrew* root, "to divide." God is *the all-sufficient Good* of His people (Num. 18:20; Ps. 16:5; 73:26; Lam. 3:24). **not like them**—not like the idols, a vain object of trust (Deut. 32:31). **former of all**

things—the Fashioner (as a potter, Isa. 64:8) of the universe. **rod of his inheritance**—The portion marked off as His inheritance by the measuring *rod* (Ezek. 48:21). As He is their portion, so are they His portion (Deut. 32:9). A reciprocal tie (cf. ch. 51:19; Ps. 74:2, *Margin*). Others make "rod" refer to the tribal rod or scepter. **17. wares** —thine effects or movable goods (Ezek. 12:3). Prepare for migrating as captives to Babylon. The address is to Jerusalem, as representative of the whole people. **inhabitant of the fortress**—rather, *inhabitress* of the fortress. Though thou now seemest to *inhabit* an impregnable *fortress,* thou shalt have to remove. "The land" is the champaign region opposed to the "fortified" cities. The "fortress" being taken, the whole "land" will share the disaster. HENDERSON translates, "Gather up thy *packages* from the ground." ROSENMULLER, for "fortress," translates, "siege," i.e., the besieged city. The various articles, in this view, are supposed to be lying about in confusion on the ground during the siege. **18. sling out**—expressing the violence and suddenness of the removal to Babylon. A similar image occurs in ch. 16:13; I Samuel 25:29; Isaiah 22:17, 18. **at this once**—at this time, now. **find it so**—find it by experience, i.e., feel it (Ezek. 6: 10). MICHAELIS translates, "I will bind them together (as in a sling) that they may reach the goal" (Babylon). *English Version* is best: "that they may find it so as I have said" (Num. 23:19; Ezek. 6:10). **19.** Judea bewails its calamity. **wound**—the stroke I suffer under. **I must bear**—not humble submission to God's will (Mic. 7:9), but sullen impenitence. Or, rather, it is prophetical of their ultimate acknowledgment of their guilt as the cause of their calamity (Lam. 3:39). **20. tabernacle is spoiled**— metaphor from the tents of nomadic life; as these are taken down in a few moments, so as not to leave a vestige of them, so Judea (ch. 4:20). **cords**— with which the coverings of the tent are extended. **curtains**—tent-curtains. **21. pastors**—the rulers, civil and religious. This verse gives the cause of the impending calamity. **22. bruit**—rumor of invasion. The antithesis is between the *voice of God* in His prophets to whom they turned a deaf ear, and the *cry of the enemy,* a new teacher, whom they must hear [CALVIN]. **north country**—Babylon (ch. 1:15). **23.** Despairing of influencing the people, he turns to God. **way of man not in himself**—(Prov. 16:1; 20:24; Jas. 4:13, 14). I know, O Jehovah, that the march of the Babylonian conqueror against me (Jeremiah identifying himself with his people) is not at his own discretion, but is overruled by Thee (Isa. 10:5-7; cf. vs. 19). **that walketh**—when he walketh, i.e., sets out in any undertaking. **direct . . . steps**—to give a prosperous issue to (Ps. 73: 23). **24, 25.** Since I (my nation) must be corrected (justice requiring it because of the deep guilt of the nation), I do not deprecate all chastisement, but pray only for moderation in it (ch. 30:11; Ps. 6:1; 38:1); and that the full tide of Thy fury may be poured out on the heathen invaders for their cruelty towards *Thy* people. Psalm 79:6, 7, a psalm to be referred to the time of the captivity, its composer probably repeated this from Jeremiah. The imperative, "Pour out," is used instead of the future, expressing vividly the *certainty* of the prediction, and that the word of God itself effects its own declarations. Accordingly, the Jews were restored after *correction;* the Babylonians were utterly extinguished. **know thee . . . call . . . on thy name**— *Knowledge* of God is the beginning of piety; *calling* on Him the fruit. **heathen . . . Jacob**—He reminds

God of the distinction He has made between His people whom *Jacob* represents, and the heathen aliens. *Correct* us as Thy adopted sons, the seed of Jacob; destroy them as outcasts (Zech. 1:14, 15, 21).

CHAPTER 11

Vss. 1-23. Epitome of the Covenant Found in the Temple in Josiah's Reign. Judah's Revolt from It, and God's Consequent Wrath. **2. this covenant**—alluding to the book of the law (Deut. 27: 28) found in the temple by Hilkiah the high priest, five years after Jeremiah's call to the prophetic office (II Kings 22:8 to 23:25). **Hear ye**—Others besides Jeremiah were to promulgate God's will to the people; it was the duty of the priests to read the law to them (Mal. 2:7). **3.** (Deut. 27:26; Gal. 3: 10.) **4. in the day**—i.e., when. The Sinaitic covenant was made some time after the exodus, but the two events are so connected as to be viewed as one. **iron furnace**—(Deut. 4:20; I Kings 8:51). "Furnace" expresses the searching ordeal; "iron,' the long duration of it. The furnace was *of earth,* not *of iron* (Ps. 12:6); a furnace, in heat and duration enough to melt even iron. God's deliverance of them from such an ordeal aggravates their present guilt. **do them**—viz., the words of the covenant (vs. 3). **so . . .**—(Lev. 26:3, 12). **5. oath**—(Ps. 105: 9, 10.) **as it is this day**—These are the concluding words of God to the Israelites when formerly brought out of Egypt, "Obey . . . , that I may *at this time* make good the promise I made to your fathers, to give . . ." [Maurer]. *English Version* makes the words apply to *Jeremiah's time,* "As ye know at this time, that God's promise has been fulfilled," viz., in Israel's acquisition of Canaan. **So be it**—*Hebrew, Amen.* Taken from Deuteronomy 27:15-26. Jeremiah hereby solemnly concurs in the justice of the curses pronounced there (see vs. 3). **6.** Jeremiah was to take a prophetic tour throughout Judah, to proclaim everywhere the denunciations in the book of the law found in the temple. **Hear . . . do**—(Rom. 2:13; Jas. 1:22.) **7. rising early**—(ch. 7:13). **8. imagination**—rather, stubbornness. **will bring**—The words, "even unto this day" (vs. 7), confirm *English Version* rather than the rendering of Rosenmuller: "I *brought* upon them." **words**—threats (vs. 3; Deut. 27:15-26). **9. conspiracy**—a *deliberate combination* against God and against Josiah's reformation. Their idolatry is not the result of a hasty impulse (Ps. 83:5; Ezek. 22:25). **11. cry unto me**—contrasted with "cry unto the gods," (vs. 12). **not hearken**—(Ps. 18:41; Prov. 1:28; Isa. 1.15; Mic. 3:4). **12. cry unto the gods . . . not save**—(Deut. 32:37, 38). Cf. this verse and beginning of vs. 13, ch. 2: 28. **in the time of their trouble**—i.e., calamity (ch. 2:27). **13. shameful thing**—*Hebrew,* "shame," viz., the idol, not merely shameful, but the *essence* of all that is shameful (ch. 3:24; Hos. 9:10), which will bring shame and confusion on yourselves [Calvin]. **14.** There is a climax of guilt which admits of no further intercessory prayer (Exod. 32:10, in the *Chaldee version,* "leave off praying"; ch. 7:16; I. Sam. 16:1; 15:35; I John 5:16). Our mind should be at one with God in all that He is doing, even in the rejection of the reprobate. **for their trouble**—on account of their trouble. Other MSS. read, "*in the time* of their trouble" a gloss from vs. 12. **15. my beloved**—My elect people, Judea; this aggravates their ingratitude (ch. 12:7). **lewdness with many**—(Ezek. 16:25). Rather, "that great (or,

manifold) enormity"; lit., the enormity, the manifold; viz., their idolatry, which made their worship of God in the temple a mockery (cf. ch. 7:10; Ezek. 23:39) [Henderson]. **holy flesh**—(Hag. 2:12-14; Titus 1:15), viz., the sacrifices, which, through the guilt of the Jews, were no longer *holy,* i.e., acceptable to God. The sacrifices on which they relied will, therefore, no longer protect them. Judah is represented as a priest's wife, who, by adultery, has forfeited her share in the flesh of the sacrifices, and yet boasts of her prerogative at the very same time [Horsley]. **when thou doest evil**—lit., "when thy evil" (is at hand). Piscator translates, "When thy *calamity* is at hand (according to God's threats). **thou gloriest**" (against God, instead of humbling thyself). *English Version* is best (cf. Prov. 2:14). **16. called thy name**—made thee. **olive**—(Ps. 52:8; Rom. 11:17). The "olive" is chosen to represent the adoption of Judah by the *free grace* of God, as its *oil* is the image of *richness* (cf. Ps. 23:5; 104:15). **with . . . noise of . . . tumult**—or, "*at the noise . . . ,*" viz., at the tumult of the invading army (Isa. 13:4) [Maurer]. Or, rather, "with the sound of a mighty voice," viz., that of God, i.e., the thunder; thus there is no confusion of metaphors. The tree stricken with lightning has "*fire kindled* upon it, and the branches are *broken,*" at one and the same time [Houbigant]. **17. that planted thee**—(ch. 2:21; Isa. 5:2). **against themselves**—The sinner's sin is to his own hurt (*Note, ch.* 7:19). **18, 19.** Jeremiah here digresses to notice the attempt on his life plotted by his townsmen of Anathoth. He had no suspicion of it, until Jehovah revealed it to him (ch. 12:6). **the Lord . . . thou**—The change of person from the third to the second accords with the excited feelings of the prophet. **then**—when I was in peril of my life. **their doings**—those of the men of Anathoth. His thus alluding to them, before he has mentioned their name, is due to his excitement. **19. lamb**—lit., a pet lamb, such as the Jews often had in their houses, for their children to play with; and the Arabs still have (II Sam. 12:3). His own *familiar* friends had plotted against the prophet. The language is exactly the same as that applied to Messiah (Isa. 53:7). Each prophet and patriarch exemplified in his own person some one feature or more in the manifold attributes and sufferings of the Messiah to come; just as the saints have done since His coming (Gal. 2:20; Phil. 3:10; Col. 1:24). This adapted both the more experimentally to testify of Christ. **devices**—(ch. 18:18). **tree with . . . fruit**—lit., in its fruit or food, i.e., when it is in fruit. Proverbial, to express the destruction of cause and effect together. The man is the tree; his teaching, the fruit. Let us destroy the prophet and his prophecies; viz., those threatening destruction to the nation, which offended them. Cf. Matthew 7: 17, which also refers to *prophets* and their *doctrines.* **20. triest . . . heart**—(Rev. 2:23). **revealed**—committed *my cause.* Jeremiah's wish for vengeance was not personal but ministerial, and accorded with God's purpose revealed to him against the enemies alike of God and of His servant (Ps. 37:34; 54:7; 112:8; 118:7). **21. Prophesy not**—(Isa. 30:10; Amos 2:12; Mic. 2:6). If Jeremiah had not uttered his denunciatory predictions, they would not have plotted against him. None were more bitter than his own fellow townsmen. Cf. the conduct of the Nazarites towards Jesus of Nazareth (Luke 4:24-29). **22.** The retribution of their intended murder shall be in kind; just as in Messiah's case (Ps. 69:8-28). **23.** (Ch. 23:12.) **the year of . . . visitation**—LXX translates, "*in* the year of their . . ." i.e., at the time when I shall visit them in wrath. JEROME supports *English Version.* "Year" often means *a determined time.*

CHAPTER 12

Vss. 1-17. CONTINUATION OF THE SUBJECT AT THE CLOSE OF CHAPTER 11. He ventures to expostulate with Jehovah as to the prosperity of the wicked, who had plotted against his life (vss. 1-4); in reply he is told that he will have worse to endure, and that from his own relatives (vss. 5, 6). The heaviest judgments, however, would be inflicted on the faithless people (vss. 7-13); and then on the nations co-operating with the Chaldeans against Judah, with, however, a promise of mercy on repentance (vss. 14-17). **1.** (Ps. 51:4.) **let me talk . . .**—only let me reason the case with Thee: inquire of Thee the causes why such wicked men as these plotters against my life prosper (cf. Job 12:6; 21:7; Psalm 37:1, 35; 73:3; Mal. 3:15). It is right, when hard thoughts of God's providence suggest themselves, to fortify our minds by *justifying God beforehand* (as did Jeremiah), even before we hear the *reasons* of His dealings. **2. grow**—lit., go on, progress. Thou givest them sure dwellings and increasing prosperity. **near in . . . mouth . . . far from . . . reins**—(Isa. 29:13; Matt. 15:8). Hypocrites. **3. knowest me**—(Ps. 139:1). **tried . . . heart**—(ch. 11:20). **toward thee**—rather, with Thee, i.e., entirely devoted to Thee; contrasted with the hypocrites (vs. 2), "near in . . . mouth, and far from . . . reins." This being so, how is it that I fare so ill, they so well? **pull . . . out**—containing the metaphor, from a "rooted tree" (vs. 2). **prepare**—lit., separate, or set apart as devoted. **day of slaughter** —(Jas. 5:5). **4. land mourn**—personification (ch. 14: 2; 23:10). **for the wickedness**—(Ps. 107:34). **beasts**—(Hos. 4:3). **He shall not see our last end**— *Jehovah* knows not what is about to happen to us (ch. 5:12) ROSENMULLER]. So LXX. (Ps. 10:11; Ezek. 8:12; 9:9). Rather, *"The prophet* (Jeremiah, to whom the whole context refers) shall not see our last end." We need not trouble ourselves about his boding predictions. We shall not be destroyed as he says (ch. 5:12, 13). **5.** Jehovah's reply to Jeremiah's complaint. **horses**—i.e., horsemen: the argument a fortiori. A proverbial phrase. The injuries done thee by the men of Anathoth ("the footmen") are small compared with those which the men of Jerusalem ("the horsemen") are about to inflict on thee. If the former weary thee out, how wilt thou contend with the king, the court, and the priests at Jerusalem? *wherein* **thou trustedst,** *they wearied thee*—English Version thus fills up the sentence with the italicized words, to answer to the parallel clause in the first sentence of the verse. The parallelism is, however, sufficiently retained with a less ellipsis: "If (it is only) in a land of peace thou art confident" [MAURER]. **swelling of Jordan**—In harvest time and earlier (April and May) it overflows its banks (Josh. 3:15), and fills the valley called the Ghor. Or, "the *pride* of Jordan," viz., its wooded banks abounding in lions and other wild beasts (ch. 49:19; 50:44; Zech. 11:3; cf. II Kings 6:2). MAUNDRELL says that between the Sea of Tiberias and Lake Merom the banks are so wooded that the traveller cannot see the river at all without first passing through the woods. If in the champaign country (alone) thou art secure, how wilt thou do when thou fallest into the wooded haunts of wild beasts? **6. even thy**

brethren—as in Christ's case (Ps. 69:8; John 1:11; 7: 5; cf. ch. 9:4; 11:19, 21; Matt. 10:36). Godly faithfulness is sure to provoke the ungodly, even of one's own family. **called a multitude after thee** —(Isa. 31:4). JEROME translates, "cry after thee with a loud (lit., full) voice." **believe . . . not . . . though . . . speak fair**—(Prov. 26:25). **7. I have forsaken**—Jehovah will forsake His temple and the people peculiarly His. The mention of God's close tie to them, as heretofore *His,* aggravates their ingratitude, and shows that their past spiritual privileges will not prevent God from punishing them. **beloved of my soul**—image from a *wife* (ch. 11:15; Isa. 54:5). **8. is unto me**—is become unto Me: behaves towards Me as a lion which roars against a man, so that he withdraws from the place where he hears it: so I withdrew from My people, once beloved, but now an object of abhorrence because of their rebellious cries against Me. **9. speckled bird**—Many translate, "a ravenous beast, the hyena"; the corresponding *Arabic* word means *hyena;* so LXX. But the *Hebrew* always elsewhere means "a bird of prey." The *Hebrew* for "speckled" is from a root "to color"; answering to the Jewish *blending together* with paganism the altogether *diverse* Mosaic ritual. The neighboring nations, *birds* of *prey* like herself (for she had sinfully assimilated herself to them), were ready to pounce upon her. **assemble . . . beasts of . . . field** —The Chaldeans are told to gather the surrounding heathen peoples as allies against Judah (Isa. 56:9; Ezek. 34:5). **10. pastors**—the Babylonian leaders (cf. vs. 12; ch. 6:3). **my vineyard**—(Isa. 5:1, 5). **trodden my portion**—(Isa. 63:18). **11. mourneth unto me**—i.e., before Me. EICHORN translates, "by reason of Me," because I have given it to desolation (vs. 7). **because no man layeth it to heart**—because none by repentance and prayer seek to deprecate God's wrath. Or, "yet none lays it to heart"; as in ch. 5:3 [CALVIN]. **12. high places**— Before, He had threatened the plains; now, the hills. **wilderness**—not an uninhabited desert, but high lands of pasturage, lying between Judea and Chaldea (ch. 4:11). **13.** Description in detail of the devastation of the land (Mic. 6:15). **they shall be ashamed of your**—The change of persons, in passing from indirect to direct address, is frequent in the prophets. Equivalent to, "Ye shall be put to the shame of disappointment at the smallness of your produce." **14-17.** Prophecy as to the surrounding nations, the Syrians, Ammonites, etc., who helped forward Judah's calamity: they shall share her fall; and, on their conversion, they shall share with her in the future restoration. This is a brief anticipation of the predictions in chs. 47, 48, 49. **14. touch**—(Zech. 2:8). **pluck them out . . . pluck out . . . Judah**—(Cf. end of vs. 16). During the thirteen years that the Babylonians besieged Tyre, Nebuchadnezzar, after subduing Cœlo-Syria, brought Ammon, Moab, etc., and finally Egypt, into subjection (JOSEPHUS, *Antiquities,* 10.9, sec. 7). On the restoration of these nations, they were to exchange places with the Jews. The latter were now in the midst of them, but on their restoration *they* were to be "in the midst of the Jews," i.e., as proselytes to the true God (cf. Mic. 5:7; Zech. 14: 16). "Pluck *them,*" viz., the Gentile nations: in a bad sense. "Pluck Judah": in a good sense; used to express the force which was needed to snatch Judah from the tyranny of those nations by whom they had been made captives, or to whom they had fled; otherwise they never would have let Judah go. Previously he had been forbidden to pray for the mass of the Jewish people. But here he speaks consolation to the elect remnant among them. Whatever the Jews might be, God keeps *His* covenant. **15.** A promise, applying to Judah, as well as to the nations specified (Amos 9:14). As to Moab, cf. ch. 48:47; as to Ammon, ch. 49:6. **16. swear by my name**—(ch. 4:2; Isa. 19:18; 65:16); i.e., confess solemnly the true God. **built**—be made spiritually and temporally prosperous: fixed in sure habitations (cf. ch. 24:6; 42:10; 45:4; Ps. 87:4, 5; Eph. 2:20, 21; I Pet. 2:5). **17.** (Isa. 60:12.)

CHAPTER 13

Vss. 1-27. SYMBOLICAL PROPHECY (vss. 1-7). Many of these figurative acts being either not possible, or not probable, or decorous, seem to have existed only in the mind of the prophet as part of his inward vision. [So CALVIN.] The world he moved in was not the sensible, but the spiritual, world. Inward acts were, however, when it was possible and proper, materialized by outward performance but not always, and necessarily so. The internal act made a naked statement more impressive and presented the subject when extending over long portions of space and time more concentrated. The interruption of Jeremiah's official duty by a journey of more than 200 miles twice is not likely to have *literally* taken place. **1. put it upon thy loins . . .**—expressing the close intimacy wherewith Jehovah had joined Israel and Judah to Him (vs. 11). **linen**—implying it was the inner garment next the skin, not the outer one. **put it not in water**—signifying the moral filth of His people, like the literal filth of a garment worn constantly next the skin, without being washed (vs. 10). GROTIUS understands a garment not bleached, but left in its native roughness, just as Judah had no beauty, but was adopted by the sole grace of God (Ezek. 16:4-6). "Neither wast thou washed in *water*," etc. **4. Euphrates**—In order to support the view that Jeremiah's act was outward, HENDERSON considers that the *Hebrew* Phrath here is *Ephratha,* the original name of Bethlehem, six miles south of Jerusalem, a journey easy to be made by Jeremiah. The non-addition of the word "river," which usually precedes *Phrath,* when meaning Euphrates, favors this view. But I prefer *English Version.* The Euphrates is specified as being near Babylon, the Jews' future place of exile. **hole**—typical of the prisons in which the Jews were to be confined. **the rock**—some well-known rock. A sterile region, such as was that to which the Jews were led away (cf. Isa. 7:19) [GROTIUS]. **6. after many days**—Time enough was given for the girdle to become unfit for use. So, in course of time, the Jews became corrupted by the heathen idolatries around, so as to cease to be witnesses of Jehovah; they must, therefore, be cast away as a "marred" or spoiled girdle. **9.** (Lev. 26:19.) **10. imagination**—rather, obstinacy. **11.** (Ch. 33:9; Exod. 19:5.) **glory**—an ornament to glory in. **12. A new image. Do we not . . . know . . . wine**—The "bottles" are those used in the East, made of skins; our word "hogshead," originally "oxhide," alludes to the same custom. As they were used to hold water, milk, and other liquids, what the prophet said (viz., that they should be all filled with wine) was not, as the Jews' taunting reply implied, a truism even *literally.* The figurative sense which is what Jeremiah chiefly meant, they affected not to understand. As wine intoxicates, so God's wrath and judgments shall reduce them

to that state of helpless distraction that they shall rush on to their own ruin (ch. 25:15; 49:12; Isa. 51: 17, 21, 22; 63:6). **13. upon David's throne**—lit., who sit *for David on his throne;* implying the succession of the Davidic family (ch. 22:4). **all**—indiscriminately of every rank. **14. dash**—(Ps. 2:9). As a potter's vessel (Rev. 2:27). **15. be not proud** —Pride was the cause of their contumacy, as humility is the first step to obedience (vs. 17; Ps. 10:4). **16. Give glory . . .**—Show by repentance and obedience to God, that you revere His majesty. So Joshua exhorted Achan to "give glory to God" by confessing his crime, thereby showing he revered the All-knowing God. **stumble**—image from travellers stumbling into a fatal abyss when overtaken by nightfall (Isa. 5:30; 59:9, 10; Amos 8:9). **dark mountains**—lit., mountains of twilight or gloom, which cast such a gloomy shadow that the traveller stumbles against an opposing rock before he sees it (John 11:10; 12:35). **shadow of death**—the densest gloom; death-shade (Ps. 44:19). *Light* and *darkness* are images of prosperity and adversity. **17. hear it**—my exhortation. **in secret**—as one mourning and humbling himself for their sin, not self-righteously condemning them (Phil. 3:18). **pride**—(*Note,* vs. 15; Job 33:17.) **flock**—(vs. 20), just as kings and leaders are called pastors. **18. king**—Jehoiachin or Jeconiah. **queen**—the queen mother who, as the king was not more than eighteen years old, held the chief power. Nehushta, daughter of Elnathan, carried away captive with Jehoiachin by Nebuchadnezzar (II Kings 24:8-15). **Humble yourselves**—i.e., Ye shall be humbled, or brought low (ch. 22:26; 28:2). **your principalities**—rather, "your *head ornament.*" **19. cities of the south**—viz., south of Judea; farthest off from the enemy, who advanced from the north. **shut up**—i.e., deserted (Isa. 24:10); so that none shall be left to open the gates to travellers and merchants again [HENDERSON]. Rather, *shut up so* closely by Nebuchadnezzar's forces, sent on before (II Kings 24: 10, 11), that none shall be allowed by the enemy to get out (cf. vs. 20). **wholly**—lit., "fully"; completely. **20. from . . . north**—Nebuchadnezzar and his hostile army (ch. 1:14; 6:22). **flock . . . given thee** —Jeremiah, amazed at the depopulation caused by Nebuchadnezzar's forces, addresses Jerusalem (a *noun of multitude,* which accounts for the blending of *plural* and *singular, Your* eyes . . . *thee* . . . *thy* flock), and asks where is the population (vs. 17, "flock") which God had given her? **21. captains,** *and* **as chief**—lit., "princes as to headship; or over thy head," viz., the Chaldeans. Rather, translate, "What wilt thou say when God will set them (the enemies, vs. 20) above thee, seeing that thou thyself hast accustomed them (to be) with thee as (thy) *lovers in the highest place* (lit., at thy head)? Thou canst not say God does thee wrong, seeing it was thou that gave occasion to His dealing so with thee, by so eagerly courting their intimacy." Cf. ch. 2: 18, 36; II Kings 23:29, as to the league of Judah with Babylon, which led Josiah to march against Pharaoh-necho, when the latter was about to attack Babylon [MAURER]. **sorrows**—pains, throes. **22. if thou say**—connecting this verse with "What wilt thou *say*" (vs. 21)? **skirts discovered**—i.e., are thrown up so as to expose the person (vs. 26; Isa. 3:17; Nah. 3:5). **heels made bare**—The sandal was fastened by a thong above the heel to the instep. The *Hebrew,* is, "are violently handled," or "torn off"; i.e., thou art exposed to ignominy. Image from an adulteress. **23. Ethiopian**—the Cushite of Abyssinia. Habit is second nature; as therefore it is morally impossible that the Jews can alter their inveterate habits of sin, nothing remains but the infliction of the extremest punishment, their expatriation (vs. 24). **24.** (Ps. 1:4.) **by the wind**—*before* the wind. **of the wilderness**—where the wind has full sweep, not being broken by any obstacle. **25. portion of thy measures**—the portion which I have measured out to thee (Job 20:29; Ps. 11:6). **falsehood**—(vs. 27), false gods and alliances with foreign idolaters. **26. discover ... upon thy face**—rather, "throw up thy skirts over thy face," or head; done by way of ignominy to captive women and to prostitutes (Nah. 3:5). The Jews' punishment should answer to their crime. As their sin had been perpetrated in the most public places, so God would expose them to the contempt of other nations most openly (Lam. 1:8). **27. neighings**—(ch. 5:8), image from the lust of horses; the lust after idols degrades to the level of the brute. **hills**—where, as being nearer heaven, sacrifices were thought most acceptable to the gods. **wilt thou not ... ? when**—lit., "*thou wilt not be* made clean *after how long a time yet.*" (So vs. 23.) Jeremiah *denies* the moral possibility of one so long hardened in sin becoming *soon* cleansed. But see ch. 32:17; Luke 18:27.

CHAPTER 14

Vss. 1-22. Prophecies on the Occasion of a Drought Sent in Judgment on Judea. **1.** Lit., "That which was the word of Jehovah to Jeremiah concerning. . . ." **drought**—lit., the "withholdings," viz., of rain (Deut. 11:17; II Chron. 7:13). This word should be used especially of the withholding of rain because *rain* is in those regions of all things the one chiefly needed (ch. 17:8, *Margin*). **2. gates** —*The place of public concourse* in each city looks sad, as being no longer frequented (Isa. 3:26; 24:4). **black**—i.e., they mourn (blackness being indicative of sorrow), (ch. 8:21). **unto the ground**—bowing towards it. **cry**—of distress (I Sam. 5:12; Isa. 24. 11). **3. little ones**—rather, "their inferiors," i.e., domestics. **pits**—cisterns for collecting rain water, often met with in the *East* where there are no springs. **covered ... heads**—(II Sam. 15:30). A sign of humiliation and mourning. **5.** The brute creation is reduced to the utmost extremity for the want of food. The "hind," famed for her affection to her young, abandons them. **6. wild asses**—They repair to "the high places" most exposed to the winds, which they "snuff in" to relieve their thirst. **dragons**—jackals [Henderson]. **eyes**—which are usually most keen in detecting grass or water from the "heights," so much so that the traveller guesses from their presence that there must be herbage and water near; but now "their eyes fail." Rather the reference is to the great boas and python serpents which raise a large portion of their body up in a vertical column ten or twelve feet high, to survey the neighborhood above the surrounding bushes, while with open jaws they drink in the air. These giant serpents originated the widely spread notions which typified the deluge and all destructive agents under the form of a dragon or monster serpent; hence, the dragon temples always near water, in Asia, Africa, and Britain; e.g., at Abury, in Wiltshire; a symbol of the ark is often associated with the dragon as the preserver from the waters [Kitto's *Biblical Cyclopædia*]. **7. do thou it**—what we beg of Thee; interpose to remove the drought. Jeremiah pleads in the name of his nation (Ps. 109:21). So "work for us," absolutely used (I Sam. 14:6). **for thy name's sake**—"for *our* backslidings are so many" that we cannot urge Thee for the sake of *our* doings, but for the glory of *Thy* name; lest, if Thou give us not aid, it should be said it was owing to Thy want of power (Josh. 7:9; Ps. 79:9; 106:8; Isa. 48: 9; Ezek. 20:44). The same appeal to God's mercy, "for *His* name's sake," as our only hope, since *our* sin precludes trust in ourselves, occurs in Psalm 25: 11. **8.** (Ch. 17:13.) **hope of Israel**—The reference is, not to the faith of *Israel* which had almost ceased, but to the promise and everlasting covenant of *God*. None but the true Israel make God their "hope." **turneth aside to tarry**—The *traveller* cares little for the land he tarries but a night in; but Thou hast promised to *dwell* always in the midst of Thy people (II Chron. 33:7, 8). Maurer translates, "spreadeth," viz., his tent. **9. astonied**—like a "mighty man," at other times able to help (Isa. 59: 1). but now *stunned* by a sudden calamity so as to disappoint the hopes drawn from him. **art in the midst of us**—(Exod. 29:45, 46; Lev. 26:11, 12). **called by thy name**—(Dan. 9:18, 19) as Thine own peculiar people (Deut. 9:29). **10.** Jehovah's reply to the prayer (vss. 7-9; ch. 2:23-25). **Thus**—*So greatly*. **loved**—(ch. 5:31.) **not refrained ... feet** —They did not obey God's command; "withhold thy foot" (ch. 2:25), viz., from following after idols. **remember ... iniquity**—(Hos. 8:13; 9:9). Their sin is so great, God must punish them. **11.** (Ch. 7: 16; Exod. 32:10.) **12.** **not hear**—because their prayers are hypocritical: their hearts are still idolatrous. God never refuses to hear *real* prayer (ch. 7: 21, 22; Prov. 1:28; Isa. 1:15; 58:3). **sword ... famine ... pestilence**—the three sorest judgments at once; any one of which would be enough for their ruin (II Sam. 24:12, 13). **13.** Jeremiah urges that much of the guilt of the people is due to the false prophets' influence. **assured peace**—solid and lasting peace. Lit., "peace of truth" (Isa. 39:8). **14.** (Ch. 23:21.) **15.** (Ch. 5:12, 13.) **say, Sword and famine ... consumed**—retribution in kind both to the false prophets and to their hearers (vs. 16). **16. none to bury**—(Ps. 79:3). **pour their wickedness**— i.e., the punishment incurred by their wickedness (ch. 2:19). **17.** (Ch. 9:1; Lam. 1:16.) Jeremiah is desired to weep ceaselessly for the calamities coming on his nation (called a "virgin," as being heretofore never under foreign yoke), (Isa. 23:4). **18. go about**—i.e., shall have to migrate into a land of exile. Horsley translates, "go *trafficking* about the land (see *Margin;* ch. 5:31; II Cor. 4:2; II Pet. 2:3), and take no knowledge" (i.e., pay no regard to the miseries before their eyes) (Isa. 1:3; 58:3). If the sense of the *Hebrew* verb be retained, I would with *English Version* understand the words as referring to the exile to Babylon; thus, "the prophet and the priest shall have to go to a strange land to *practise their religious traffic* (Isa. 56:11; Ezek. 34: 2, 3; Mic. 3:11). **19.** The people plead with God, Jeremiah being forbidden to do so. **no healing**— ch. 15:18). **peace ... no good**—(ch. 8:15). **20.** (Dan. 9:8.) **21. us**—"the throne of Thy glory" may be the object of "abhor not" ("reject not"); or "Zion" (vs. 19). **throne of thy glory**—Jerusalem, or, *the temple*, called God's "footstool" and "habitation" (I Chron. 28:2; Ps. 132:5). **thy covenant**— (Ps. 106:45; Dan. 9:19). **22. vanities**—idols (Deut. 32:21). **rain**—(Zech. 10:1, 2.) **heavens**—viz., of themselves without God (Matt. 5:45; Acts 14:17); they are not the First Cause, and ought not to be deified, as they were by the heathen. The disjunctive "or" favors CALVIN's explanation: "Not even the heavens themselves can give rain, much less can the idol vanities." **art not thou he**—viz., who canst give rain?

CHAPTER 15

VSS. 1-21. GOD'S REPLY TO JEREMIAH'S INTER-CESSORY PRAYER. **1. Moses ... Samuel**—eminent in intercessions (Exod. 32:11, 12; 1 Sam. 7:9; Ps. 99:6). **be toward**—could not be favorably inclined toward them. **out of my sight**—God speaks as if the people were present before Him, along with Jeremiah. **2. death**—deadly plague (ch. 18:21; 43:11; Ezek. 5:2, 12; Zech. 11:9). **3. appoint**—(Lev. 26:16). **kinds**—of punishments. **4. cause ... to be removed**—(Deut. 28:25; Ezek. 23:46). Rather, "I will give them up to vexation," I will cause them to wander so as nowhere to have repose [CALVIN], (II Chron. 29:8, "trouble," *Margin,* "commotion"). **because of Manasseh**—He was now dead, but the effects of his sins still remained. How much evil one bad man can cause! The evil fruits remain even after he himself has received repentance and forgiveness. The people had followed his wicked example ever since; and it is implied that it was only through the long-suffering of God that the penal consequences had been suspended up to the present time (cf. I Kings 14:16; II Kings 21:11, 23:26; 24:3, 4). **5. go aside ... how thou doest**—Who will turn aside (in passing by) to *salute* thee (to wish thee "peace")? **6. weary with repenting**—(Hos. 13:14; 11:8). I have so often *repented* of the evil that I threatened (ch. 26:19; Exod. 32:14; I Chron. 21:15), and have spared them, without My forbearance moving them to repentance, that I will not again change My purpose (God speaking in condescension to human modes of thought), but will take vengeance on them now. **7. fan**—tribulation—from *tribulum,* a thresh-ing instrument, which separates the chaff from the wheat (Matt. 3:12). **gates of the land**—i.e., the ex-treme bounds of the land through which the en-trance to and exit from it lie. MAURER translates, "I will fan," i.e., cast them forth "*to* the gates of the land" (Nah. 3:13). "In the gates"; *English Version* draws the image from a man cleaning corn with a fan; he stands at the gate of the threshing-floor in the open air, to remove the wheat from the chaff by means of the wind; so God threatens to remove Israel out of the bounds of the land [HOUBIGANT]. **8. Their widows**—My people's (vs. 7). **have brought**—prophetical past: I will bring. **mother of the young men**—"mother" is collective; after the "widows," He naturally mentions bereavement of their sons ("young men"), brought on the "mothers" by "the spoiler"; it was owing to the number of men slain that the "widows" were so many [CAL-VIN]. Others take "mother," as in II Samuel 20: 19, of Jerusalem, the metropolis; "I have brought on them, against the 'mother,' a young spoiler," viz., Nebuchadnezzar, sent by his father, Nabopolassar, to repulse the Egyptian invaders (II Kings 23:29; 24:1), and occupy Judea. But vs. 7 shows the future, not the past, is referred to; and "widows" being literal, "mother" is probably so, too. **at noonday**—the hottest part of the day, when military operations were usually suspended; thus it means *unexpectedly,* answering to the parallel, "suddenly"; *openly,* as others explain it, will not suit the parallel-ism (cf. Ps. 91:6). **it**—*English Version* seems to understand by "it" the mother city, and by "him"

the "spoiler"; thus "it" will be parellel to "city." Rather, "I will cause to fall upon *them* (the 'moth-ers' about to be bereft of their sons) suddenly *anguish* and terrors." **the city**—rather, from a root "heat," *anguish,* or consternation. So LXX. **9. borne seven**—(I Sam. 2:5). Seven being the perfect number indicates full fruitfulness. **languisheth**—because not even one is left of all her sons (vs. 8). **sun is gone down while ... yet day**—Fortune deserts her at the very height of her prosperity (Amos 8:9). **she ... ashamed**—The mothers (*she* being collective) are put to the shame of disappointed hopes through the loss of all their children. **10.** (Ch. 20:14; Job 3:1, etc.). Jeremiah seems to have been of a pecul-iarly sensitive temperament; yet the Holy Spirit enabled him to deliver his message at the certain cost of having his sensitiveness wounded by the enmities of those whom his words offended. **man of strife**—exposed to strifes on the part of "the whole earth" (Ps. 80:6). **I have neither lent ...**—prover-bial for, "I have given no cause for strife against me." **11.** Verily—lit., Shall it not be? i.e., Surely it shall be. **thy remnant**—the *final issue* of thy life; thy life, which now seems to thee so sad, shall eventuate in prosperity [CALVIN]. They who think that they shall be the surviving remnant, whereas thou shalt perish, shall themselves fall, whereas *thou shalt remain* and be favored by the conquerors [JUNIUS], (ch. 40:4, 5; 39:11, 12). The *Keri* reads, "I will *set* thee *free* (or as [MAURER], 'I will establish thee') for good" (ch. 14:11; Ezra 8:22; Ps. 119:122). **to entreat thee well**—lit., "to meet thee"; so "to be placable, nay, of their own accord to *anticipate in meeting* thee with kindness" [CALVIN]. I prefer this translation as according with the event (ch. 39: 11, 12; 40:4, 5). GESENIUS, from ch. 7:16; 27:18: Job 21:15, translates (not only will I relieve thee from the enemy's vexations, but) "I will make thine enemy (that now vexeth thee) *apply to thee with prayers*" (ch. 38:14; 42:2-6). **12. steel**—rather, *brass* or *copper,* which mixed with "iron" (by the Chalybes near the Euxine Pontus, far north of Palestine), formed the hardest metal, like our *steel.* Can *the Jews,* hardy like common iron though they be, break the still hardier *Chaldees* of the north (ch. 1:14), who resemble the Chalybian iron hardened with copper? Certainly not [CALVIN]. HENDERSON translates. "Can *one* break iron, (even) the northern iron, and brass," on the ground that *English Version* makes ordinary *iron* not so hard as brass. But it is not brass, but a particular mixture of iron and *brass,* which is represented as harder than *common iron,* which was probably then of inferior texture, owing to ignorance of modern modes of preparation. **13. Thy substance ... sins**—Judea's, not Jeremiah's. **without price**—God casts His people away as a thing *worth naught* (Ps. 44:12). So, on the con-trary, Jehovah, when about to restore His people, says, He will give Egypt, etc., for their "*ransom*" (Isa. 43:3). **even in all thy borders**—joined with "Thy substance ... treasures, as also with "all thy sins," their sin and punishment being commensurate (ch. 17:3). **14. thee**—MAURER supplies "them," viz., "thy treasures." EICHORN, needlessly, from *Syriac* and LXX, reads, "I will *make thee to serve* thine enemies"; a reading doubtless interpolated from ch. 17:4. **fire**—(Deut. 32:22). **15. thou knowest**—viz., my case; what wrongs my adversaries have done me (ch. 12:3). **revenge me**—(*Note,* ch. 11:20). The prophet in this had regard to, not his own personal feelings of revenge, but the cause of God; he speaks by inspiration God's will against the un-godly. Contrast in this the law with the gospel

(Luke 23:34; Acts 7:60). **take me not away in thy long-suffering**—By Thy long-suffering towards them, suffer them not meanwhile to take away my life. **for thy sake I have suffered rebuke**—the very words of the antitype, Jesus Christ (Ps. 69:7, 22-28), which last cf. with Jeremiah's prayer in the beginning of this verse. **16. eat**—(Ezek. 2:8; 3:1, 3; Rev. 10:9, 10). As soon as Thy words were found by me, I eagerly laid hold of and appropriated them. The *Keri* reads, "Thy *word.*" **thy word . . . joy**—(Job 23:12; Ps. 119:72, 111; cf. Matt. 13:44). **called by thy name**—I am Thine, Thy minister. So the antitype, Jesus Christ (Exod. 23:21). **17. My "rejoicing"** (vs. 16) was not that of the profane mockers (Ps. 1:1; 26:4, 5) at feasts. So far from having fellowship with these, he was expelled from society, and made to sit "alone," because of his faithful prophecies. **because of thy hand**—i.e., Thine inspiration (Isa. 8:11; Ezek. 1:3; 3:14). **filled me with indignation**—So ch. 6:11, "full of the fury of the Lord"; so full was he of the subject (God's "indignation" against the ungodly) with which God had inspired him, as not to be able to contain himself from expressing it. The same comparison by contrast between the effect of *inspiration*, and that of *wine*, both taking a man out of himself, occurs (Acts 2:13, 15, 18). **18.** (Ch. 30:15.) "Pain," viz., the perpetual persecution to which he was exposed, and his being left by God without consolation and "alone." Contrast his feeling here with that in vs. 16, when he enjoyed the full presence of God, and was inspired by His words. Therefore he utters words of his natural "infirmity" (so David, Ps. 77: 10) here; as before he spoke under the higher spiritual nature given him. **as a liar, and as**—rather, "as a *deceiving* (river) . . . waters that are not sure" (lasting); opposed to "living (perennial) waters" (Job 6:15). Streams that the thirsty traveller had calculated on being full in winter, but which disappoint him in his sorest need, having run dry in the heat of summer. Jehovah had promised Jeremiah protection from his enemies (ch. 1:18, 19); his infirmity suggests that God had failed to do so. **19.** God's reply to Jeremiah. **return . . . bring . . . again** —Jeremiah, by his impatient language, had left his proper posture towards God; God saith, "If thou wilt return (to thy former *patient* discharge of thy prophetic function) I will bring thee back" to thy former position: in the *Hebrew* there is a play of words, "*return . . . turn again*" (ch. 8:4; 4:1). **stand before me**—minister acceptably to Me (Deut. 10:8; I Kings 17:1; 18:15). **take . . . precious from . . . vile**—image from metals: "If thou wilt separate what is precious *in thee* (the divine graces imparted) from what is vile (thy natural corruptions, impatience, and hasty words), thou shalt be as My mouth": my mouthpiece (Exod. 4:16). **return not thou unto them**—Let not them lead you into their profane ways (as Jeremiah had spoken irreverently, vs. 18), but lead thou them to the ways of godliness (vss. 16, 17). Ezekiel 22:26 accords with the other interpretation, which, however, does not so well suit the context, "If thou wilt separate from the promiscuous mass the better ones, and lead them to conversion by faithful warnings . . . ." **20, 21.** The promise of ch. 1:18, 19, in almost the same words, but with the addition, adapted to the present attacks of Jeremiah's formidable enemies, "I will deliver thee out of . . . wicked . . . redeem . . . terrible"; the repetition is in order to assure Jeremiah that God is *the same now* as when He first made the promise, in opposition to the prophet's irreverent accusation of unfaithfulness (vs. 18).

CHAPTER 16

Vss. 1-21. CONTINUATION OF THE PREVIOUS PROPHECY. **2. in this place**—in Judea. The direction to remain single was (whether literally obeyed, or only in prophetic vision) to symbolize the coming calamities of the Jews (Ezek. 24:15-27) as so severe that the single state would be then (contrary to the ordinary course of things) preferable to the married (cf. I Cor. 7:8; 26:29; Matt. 24:19; Luke 23:29). **4. grievous deaths**—rather, deadly diseases (ch. 15: 2). **not . . . lamented**—so many shall be the slain (ch. 22:18). **dung**—(Ps. 83:10). **5.** (Ezek. 24:17, 22, 23.) **house of mourning**—(Mark 5:38). *Margin*, mourning-feast; such feasts were usual at funerals. The *Hebrew* means, in Amos 6:7, the *cry of joy* at a banquet; here, and Lamentations 2:19, the *cry of sorrow*. **6. cut themselves**—indicating extravagant grief (ch. 41:5; 47:5), prohibited by the law (Lev. 19:28). **bald**—(ch. 7:29; Isa. 22:12). **7. tear themselves**—rather, "break bread," viz., that eaten at the funeral-feast (Deut. 26:14; Job 42:11; Ezek. 24:17; Hos. 9:4). "Bread" is to be supplied, as in Lamentations 4:4; cf. "take" (food) (Gen. 42:33). **give . . . cup of consolation . . . for . . . father**—It was the Oriental custom for friends to send viands and wine (the "cup of consolation") to console relatives in mourning-feasts, e.g., to children upon the death of a "father" or "mother." **8. house of feasting**—joyous: as distinguished from mourning-feasts. Have no more to do with this people whether in mourning or joyous feasts. **9.** (Ch. 7:34; 25:10; Ezek 26:13). **10.** (Deut. 29:24; I Kings 9:8, 9). **11.** (Ch. 5:19; 13:22; 22:8, 9). **12. ye**—emphatic: so far from avoiding your fathers' bad example, ye have done worse (ch. 7:26; I Kings 14:9). **imagination**—rather, stubborn perversity. **that they may not hearken**—rather, connected with "ye": "ye have walked . . . so as not to hearken to Me." **13. serve other gods**—That which was their sin in their own land was their punishment in exile. Retribution in kind. They *voluntarily* forsook God for idols at home; they were *not allowed* to serve God, if they wished it, in captivity (Dan. 3 and 6). **day and night**—irony. You may there serve idols, which ye are so mad after, even to satiety, and without intermission. **14. Therefore**—So severe shall be the Jews' bondage that their deliverance from it shall be a greater benefit than that out of Egypt. The consolation is incidental here; the prominent thought is the *severity* of their punishment, so great that their rescue from it will be greater than that from Egypt [CALVIN]; so the context, vs. . 13, 17, 18, proves (ch. 23:7, 8; Isa. 43:18). **15. the north**—Chaldea. But while the return from Babylon is primarily meant, the return hereafter is the full and final accomplishment contemplated, as "from *all* the lands" proves. "*Israel*" was not, save in a very limited sense, "gathered from all the lands" at the return from Babylon (cf. ch. 24:6; 30:3; 32:15, *Notes*). **16. send for**—translate, "I will send many"; "I will give the commission to many" (II Chron. 17: 7). **fishers . . . hunters**—successive invaders of Judea (Amos 4:2; Hab. 1:14, 15). So "net" (Ezek. 12:13). As to "hunters," see Genesis 10:9; Micah 7:2. The Chaldees were famous in hunting, as the Egyptians, the other enemy of Judea, were in fishing. "Fishers" expresses the *ease* of their victory over the Jews as that of the angler over fishes; "hunters," the keenness of their pursuit of them into every cave and nook. It is remarkable, the same image is used in a good sense of the Jews' restoration, implying that just as their enemies were employed by God to take them in hand for destruction, so the same shall be employed for their restoration (Ezek. 47:9, 10). So spiritually, those once enemies by nature (*fishermen* many of them literally) were employed by God to be heralds of salvation, "catching men" for life (Matt. 4:19; Luke 5: 10; Acts 2:41; 4:4); cf. here vs. 19, "the Gentiles shall come unto thee" (II Cor. 12:16). **17.** (Ch. 32: 19; Prov. 5:21; 15:3.) **their iniquity**—the cause of God's judgments on them. **18. first . . . double**—HORSLEY translates, "I will recompense . . . *once and again*"; lit., the first time repeated: alluding to the two captivities—the Babylonian and the Roman. MAURER, "I will recompense their *former* iniquities (those *long ago* committed by their fathers) and their (own) *repeated* sins" (vss. 11, 12). *English Version* gives a good sense, "*First* (before "I bring them again into their land"), I will doubly (i.e., *fully and amply*, ch. 17:18; Isa. 40:2) recompense." **carcasses**—not sweet-smelling *sacrifices* acceptable to God, but "carcasses" offered to idols, an offensive odor to God: human victims (ch. 19:5; Ezek. 16:20), and unclean animals (Isa. 65:4; 66:17). MAURER explains it, "the carcasses" *of the idols:* their images void of sense and life. Cf. vss. 19, 20. Leviticus 26:30 favors this. **19, 20.** The result of God's judgments on the Jews will be that both the Jews when restored, and the Gentiles who have witnessed those judgments, shall renounce idolatry for the worship of Jehovah. Fulfilled partly at the return from Babylon, after which the Jews entirely renounced idols, and many proselytes were gathered in from the Gentiles, but not to be realized in its fulness till the final restoration of Israel (Isa. 2). **20.** indignant protest of Jeremiah against idols. **and they are no gods**—(ch. 2:11; Isa. 37:19; Gal. 4: 8). "They" refers to the idols. A *man* (a creature himself) making *God* is a contradiction in terms. *Vulgate* takes "they" thus: "Shall man make gods, though *men* themselves are not gods?" **21. Therefore**—In order that all may be turned from idols to Jehovah, He will now give awful proof of His divine power in the judgments He will inflict. **this once**—If the punishments I have heretofore inflicted *have* not been severe enough to teach them. **my name . . . Lord**—*Jehovah* (Ps. 83:18): God's incommunicable name, to apply which to idols would be blasphemy. Keeping His threats and promises (Exod. 6:3).

CHAPTER 17

Vss. 1-27. THE JEWS' INVETERATE LOVE OF IDOLATRY. The LXX omits the first four verses, but other *Greek* versions have them. **1.** The first of the four clauses relates to the third, the second to the fourth, by alternate parallelism. The sense is: They are as keen after idols as if their propensity was "graven with an iron pen (Job 19:24) on their hearts," or as if it were sanctioned by a law "inscribed with a diamond point" on their altars. The names of their gods used to be written on "the horns of the altars" (Acts 17:23). As the clause "on their hearts" refers to their *inward* propensity, so "on . . . altars," the *outward* exhibition of it. Others refer "on the horns of . . . altars" to their staining them with the blood of victims, in imitation of the Levitical precept (Exod. 29:12; Lev. 4:7, 18), but "written . . . graven," would thus be inappropriate. **table of . . . heart**—which God intended to be inscribed very differently, viz., with His truths (Prov. 3:3; II Cor. 3:3). **your**—Though "their"

preceded, He directly addresses them to charge the guilt home to them in particular. **2. children remember**—Instead of forsaking the idolatries of their fathers, they keep them up (ch. 7:18). This is given as proof that their sin is "graven upon . . . altars" (vs. 1), i.e., is not merely temporary. They corrupt their posterity after them. CASTALIO less probably translates, "They remember their altars as (fondly as) they do their children." **groves**—rather, images of Astarte, the goddess of the heavenly hosts, represented as a sacred tree, such as is seen in the Assyrian sculptures (II Kings 21:7; II Chron. 24:18). "Image of the grove." The *Hebrew* for "grove" is Asherah, i.e., Assarak, Astarte, or Ashtaroth. **by the green trees**—i.e., near them: the sacred trees (idol symbols) of Astarte being placed in the midst of natural trees: "green trees" is thus distinguished from "groves," *artificial* trees. HENDERSON, to avoid taking the same *Hebrew* particle in the same sentence differently, "by . . . upon" translates "images of Astarte *on* the green trees." But it is not probable that images, in the form of a sacred tree, should be hung *on* trees, rather than *near* them. **3. mountain**—Jerusalem, and especially Zion and the temple. **in the field**—As Jerusalem was surrounded by *mountains* (Ps. 125:2), the sense probably is, Ye rely on your mountainous position (ch. 3:23), but I will make "My mountain" to become as if it were *in a plain* (field), so as to give thy substance an easy prey to the enemy [CALVIN]. "Field" may, however, mean *all Judea;* it and "My mountain" will thus express *the country and its capital.* (GESENIUS translates, "together with," instead of "in"; as the Hebrew is translated in ch. 11: 19; Hosea 5:6; but this is not absolutely needed), "the substance" of both of which God "will give to the spoil." **thy high places**—corresponding in parallelism to "My mountain" (cf. Isa. 11:9), as "all thy borders," to "the field" (which confirms the view that "field" means *all Judea*). **for sin**—connected with high places" in *English Version*, viz., frequented for sin, i.e., for idolatrous sacrifices. But ch. 15: 13 makes the rendering probable, "I will give thy substance . . . to . . . spoil . . . *on account of thy sin throughout all thy borders.*" **4. even thyself**—rather, "owing to thyself," i.e., by thy own fault (ch. 15:13). **discontinue from**—be dispossessed of. Not only thy substance, but thyself shall be carried off to a strange land (ch. 15:14). **5.** Referring to the Jews' proneness to rely on Egypt, in its fear of Assyria and Babylon (Isa. 31:1, 3). **trusteth**—This word is emphatic. We may expect help from men, so far as God enables them to help us, but we must rest our trust in God alone (Ps. 62:5). **6. heath**—In Psalm 102:17; Isaiah 32:11; Habakkuk 3:9, the *Hebrew* is translated, "bare," "naked," "destitute"; but as the parallel in vs. 8 is "tree," some plant must be meant of which this is the characteristic epithet (see ch. 48:6, *Margin*), "a naked tree." ROBINSON translates, "the juniper tree," found in the Arabah or Great Valley, here called "the desert," south of the Dead Sea. The "heath" was one of the plants, according to PLINY (13.21; 16.26), excluded from religious uses, because it has neither fruit nor seed, and is neither sown nor planted. **not see . . . good**—(Job 20:17.) **salt land**—(Deut. 29:23), barren ground. **7.** (Ps. 34: 8; Prov. 16:20; Isa. 30:18.) Jeremiah first removed the weeds (false trusts), so that there might be room for the good grain [CALVIN]. **8.** (Ps. 1:3.) **shall not see**—i.e., feel. Answering to vs. 6; whereas the unbelievers "shall not see (even) when *good* cometh," the believer "shall not see (so as to be overwhelmed by it even) when heat (fiery trial) cometh." Trials shall come upon him as on all, nay, upon him especially (Heb. 12:6); but he shall not sink under them, because the Lord is his secret strength, just as the "roots spread out by a river" (or, "water course") draw hidden support from it (II Cor. 4:8-11). **careful**—anxious, as one desponding (Luke 12:29; I Pet. 5:7). **drought**—lit., withholding, viz., of rain (ch. 14:1); he here probably alludes to the drought which had prevailed, but makes it the type of all kinds of distress. **9. deceitful**—from a root, "supplanting," "tripping up insidiously by the heel," from which Jacob (Hos. 12:3) took his name. In speaking of the Jews' *deceit of heart,* he appropriately uses a term alluding to their forefather, whose deceit, but not whose faith, they followed. *His* "supplanting" was in order to obtain Jehovah's blessing. They plant Jehovah for "trust in man" (vs. 5), and then think to *deceive God,* as if it could escape His notice, that it is in *man,* not in Him, they trust. **desperately wicked**—"incurable" [HORSLEY], (Mic. 1:9). Trust in one's own heart is as foolish as in our fellow man (Prov. 28:26). **10.** Lest any should infer from vs. 9, "who can know it?" that even *the Lord* does not know, and therefore cannot punish, the hidden treachery of the heart, He says, "I the Lord search the heart," etc. (I Chron. 28:9; Ps. 7:9; Prov. 17:3; Rev. 2:23). **even to give**—*and that* in order that I may give (ch. 32:19). **11. partridge**—(I Sam. 26:20). *Hebrew* "korea," from a root, "to call," alluding to its cry; a name still applied to a bustard by the Arabs. Its nest is liable, being on the ground, to be trodden under foot, or robbed by carnivorous animals, notwithstanding all the beautiful manœuvres of the parent birds to save the brood. The translation, "sitteth on eggs *which it has not laid,*" alludes to the ancient notion that she stole the eggs of other birds and hatched them as her own; and that the young birds when grown left her for the true mother. It is not needful to make Scripture allude to an exploded notion, as if it were true. MAURER thinks the reference is to Jehoiakim's grasping cupidity (ch. 22:13-17). Probably the sense is more general; as previously He condemned trust in man (vs. 5), He now condemns another object of the deceitful hearts' trust, *unjustly gotten riches* (Ps. 39:6; 49:16, 17; 55:23). fool—(Prov. 23:5; Luke 12:20; "their folly" (Ps. 49:13). He himself, and all, shall at last perceive he was not the wise man he thought he was. **12. throne**—the temple of Jerusalem, the throne of Jehovah. Having condemned false objects of trust, *"high places* for sin" (vs. 3), and an "arm of flesh," he next sets forth Jehovah, and *His* temple, which was ever open to the Jews, as the true object of confidence, and sanctuary to flee to. HENDERSON makes Jehovah, in vs. 13, the subject, and this verse predicate, "A throne of glory, high from the beginning, the place of our sanctuary, the hope of Israel is Jehovah." "Throne" is thus used for Him who sits on it; cf. *thrones* (Col. 1:16). He is called a "sanctuary" to His people (Isa. 8:14; Ezek. 11:16). So *Syriac* and *Arabic.* **13. me**—"Jehovah." Though "Thee" precedes. This sudden transition is usual in the prophetic style, owing to the prophet's continual realization of Jehovah's presence. **all that forsake thee**—(Ps. 73:27; Isa. 1:28.) **written in the earth**—in the dust, i.e., shall be consigned to oblivion. So Jesus' significant writing "on the ground" (probably the accusers' names) (John 8:6). Names written in the dust are obliterated by a very slight wind. Their hopes and celebrity are wholly *in the earth,* not in the heavenly book of life (Rev.

13:8; 20:12, 15). The Jews, though boasting that they were the people of God, had no portion in heaven, no status before God and His angels. Contrast "written in heaven," i.e., in the muster-roll of its blessed citizens (Luke 10:20). Also, contrast "written in a book," and "in the rock *for ever"* (Job 19:23, 24). **living waters**—(ch. 2:13). **14-18.** Prayer of the prophet for deliverance from the enemies whom he excited by his faithful denunciations. **Heal . . . save**—not only *make me whole* (as to the evils of soul as well as body which I am exposed to by contact with ungodly foes, ch, 15:18), but *keep me so.* **my praise**—He whom I have to praise for past favors, and therefore to whom alone I look for the time to come. **15. Where is the word?**—(Isa. 5:19; Amos 5:18). Where is the fulfilment of the threats which thou didst utter as from God? A characteristic of the last stage of apostasy (II Peter 3:4). **16.** I have not refused Thy call of me to be a prophet (Jonah 1:3), however painful to me it was to utter what would be sure to irritate the hearers (ch. 1:4, etc.); therefore Thou shouldest not forsake me (ch. 15:15, etc.). **to follow thee**—lit., "after thee"; as an under-pastor following Thee, the Chief Shepherd (Eccles. 12:11; I Peter 5:4). **neither . . . desired**—I have not *wished* for the day of calamity, though I foretell it as about to come on my countrymen; therefore they have no reason for persecuting me. **thou knowest**—I appeal to Thee for the truth of what I assert. **that which came out of my lips**—my words (Deut. 23:23). *right* **before thee**—rather, "was before Thee"; was *known to Thee*—(Prov. 5:21). **17. a terror**—viz., by deserting me: all I fear is Thine abandoning me; if Thou art with me, I have no fear of evil from enemies. **18. destroy . . . destruction**—"break them with a double breach," *Hebrew* (ch. 14:17). On "double," see *Note,* ch. 16:18. **19-27.** Delivered in the reign of Jehoiakim, who undid the good effected by Josiah's reformation, especially as to the observance of the Sabbath [EICHORN]. **gate of . . . children of . . . people**—The gate next the king's palace, called *the gate of David,* and *the gate of the people,* from its being the principal thoroughfare: now the Jaffa gate. It is probably the same as "the gate of the fountain" at the foot of Zion, near which were the king's garden and pool (ch. 39:4; II Kings 25:4; Neh. 2:14; 3:15; 12:37). **20. kings**—He begins with the kings, as they ought to have repressed such a glaring profanation. **21. Take heed to yourselves**—lit., to your souls. MAURER explains, "as ye love your lives"; a phrase used here to give the greater weight to the command. **sabbath**—The non-observance of it was a chief cause of the captivity, the number of years of the latter, seventy, being exactly made to agree with the number of Sabbaths which elapsed during the 490 years of their possession of Canaan from Saul to their removal (Lev. 26:34, 35; II Chron. 36:21). On the restoration, therefore, stress was especially laid on Sabbath observance (Neh. 13:19). **Jerusalem**—It would have been scandalous anywhere; but in the capital, *Jerusalem,* it was an open insult to God. Sabbath-hallowing is intended as a symbol of holiness in general (Ezek. 20:12); therefore much stress is laid on it; the Jews' gross impiety is manifested in their setting God's will at naught, in the case of such an easy and positive command. **23.** (Ch. 7:24, 26.) **24.** A part put for the whole, "If ye keep the Sabbath and *My* other *laws."* **25. kings . . . in chariots**—The kingdom at this time had been brought so low that this promise here was a special favor. **remain**—*Hebrew,* be inhabited (vs. 6; Isa. 13:20). **26. plain . . .**

mountains ... south—(Josh. 15:1-4). The southern border had extended to the river of Egypt, but was now much curtailed by Egyptian invasions (II Chron. 35:20; 36:3, 4). The *Hebrew* for "south" means *dry;* the arid desert *south* of Judea is meant. The enumeration of all the parts of Judea, city, country, plain, hill, and desert, implies that no longer shall there be aught wanting of the integrity of the Jewish land (Zech. 7:7). **sacrifices**—As in vs. 22, one constituent of Judea's prosperity is mentioned, viz., its *kings* on David's throne, the pledge of God being its guardian; so in this verse another constituent, viz., its *priests*, a pledge of God being propitious to it (Ps. 107:22). **27. burden ... in ... gates ... fire in the gates**—retribution answering to the sin. The scene of their sin shall be the scene of their punishment (ch. 52:13; II Kings 25:9).

CHAPTER 18

Vss. 1-23. GOD, AS THE SOLE SOVEREIGN, HAS AN ABSOLUTE RIGHT TO DEAL WITH NATIONS ACCORDING TO THEIR CONDUCT TOWARDS HIM; ILLUSTRATED IN A TANGIBLE FORM BY THE POTTER'S MOULDING OF VESSELS FROM CLAY. **2. go down**—viz., from the high ground on which the temple stood, near which Jeremiah exercised his prophetic office, to the low ground, where some well-known (this is the force of "the") potter had his workshop. **3. wheels**—lit., "on *both stones.*" The potter's horizontal lathe consisted of two round plates, the lower one larger, the upper smaller; of stone originally, but afterwards of wood. On the upper the potter moulded the clay into what shapes he pleased. They are found represented in Egyptian remains. In Exodus 1:16 alone is the *Hebrew* word found elsewhere, but in a different sense. **4. marred**—spoiled. "*Of clay*" is the true reading, which was corrupted into "*as clay*" (*Margin*), through the similarity of the two *Hebrew* letters, and from vs. 6, "*as the clay.*" **6.** Refuting the Jews' reliance on their external privileges as God's elect people, as if God could never cast them off. But if the potter, a mere creature, has power to throw away a marred vessel and raise up other clay from the ground, a fortiori God, the Creator, can cast away the people who prove unfaithful to His election and can raise others in their stead (cf. Isa. 45:9; 64:8; Rom. 9:20, 21). It is curious that the *potter's field* should have been the purchase made with the price of Judas' treachery (Matt. 27:9, 10: a potter's vessel dashed to pieces, cf. Ps. 2:8, 9; Rev. 2:27), because of its failing to answer the maker's design, being the very image to depict God's sovereign power to give reprobates to destruction, not by caprice, but in the exercise of His righteous judgment. Matthew quotes Zechariah's words (Zech. 11:12, 13) *as Jeremiah's* because the latter (chs. 18, 19) was the source from which the former derived his summary in ch. 11:12, 13 [HENGSTENBERG]. **7. At what instant**—in a moment, when the nation least expects it. Hereby he reminds the Jews how marvellously God had delivered them from their original degradation, i.e., In one and the same day ye were the most wretched, and then the most favored of all people [CALVIN]. **8. their evil**—in antithesis to, "the evil that *I* thought to do." **repent**—God herein adapts Himself to human conceptions. The change is not in God, but in the circumstances which regulate God's dealings: just as we say the land recedes from us when we sail forth, whereas it is we who recede from the land (Ezek. 18:21; 33:11). God's unchangeable

principle is to do the best that can be done under all circumstances; if then He did not take into account the moral change in His people (their prayers, etc.), He would not be acting according to His own unchanging principle (vss. 9, 10). This is applied practically to the Jews' case (vs. 11; see ch. 26:3; Jonah 3:10). **11. frame evil**—alluding to the preceding image of "the potter," i.e., I, Jehovah, am now as it were the potter *framing* evil against you; but in the event of your repenting, it is in My power to *frame anew* My course of dealing towards you. **return ...**—(II Kings 17:13). **12. no hope**—Thy threats and exhortations are all thrown away (ch. 2:25). Our case is desperate; we are hopelessly abandoned to our sins and their penalty. In this and the following clauses, "We will walk after our own devices," Jeremiah makes them express the *real* state of the case, rather than the hypocritical subterfuges which *they* would have been inclined to put forth. So Isaiah 30:10, 11. **13.** (Ch. 2:10, 11.) Even among the heathen it was a thing unheard of, that a nation should lay aside its gods for foreign gods, though their gods are false gods. But Israel forsook the true God for foreign false gods. **virgin of Israel**—(II Kings 19:21). It enhances their guilt, that Israel was *the virgin* whom God had specially betrothed to Him. **horrible thing**—(ch. 5:30). **14.** Is there any man (living near it) who would leave the snow of Lebanon (i.e., the cool melted snow-water of Lebanon, as he presently explains), which cometh from the rock of the field (a poetical name for Lebanon, which towers aloft above the surrounding *field*, or comparatively plain country)? None. Yet Israel forsakes Jehovah, the living fountain close at hand, for foreign broken cisterns. Ch. 17:13; 2:13, accord with *English Version* here. MAURER translates, "Shall the snow of Lebanon *cease* from the rock *to water* (lit., forsake) My fields" (the whole land around being peculiarly Jehovah's)? *Lebanon* means the "white mountain"; so called from the perpetual snow which covers that part called Hermon, stretching northeast of Palestine. **that come from another place**—that come from far, viz., from the distant lofty rocks of Lebanon. HENDERSON translates, "the *compressed* waters," viz., contracted within a narrow channel while descending through the gorges of the rocks; "flowing" may in this view be rather "flowing down" (Song of Sol. 4:15). But the parallelism in *English Version* is better, "which cometh from the rock," "that cometh from another place." **be forsaken**—answering to the parallel, "Will a man leave ...." MAURER translates, "dry up," or "fail" (Isa. 19:5); the sense thus being, Will nature ever turn aside from its fixed course? The "cold waters" (cf. Prov. 25:25) refer to the perennial streams, fed from the partial melting of the snow in the hot weather. **15. Because**—rather, "And yet"; in defiance of the natural order of things. **forgotten me** —(ch. 2:32). This implies a previous knowledge of God, whereas He was unknown to the Gentiles; the Jews' forgetting of God, therefore, arose from determined perversity. **they have caused ... to stumble** —viz., the false prophets and idolatrous priests have. **ancient paths**—(ch. 6:16): the paths which their pious ancestors trod. Not antiquity indiscriminately, but the example of the fathers who trod the right way, is here commended. **them**—the Jews. **not cast up**—not duly prepared: referring to the raised center of the road. CALVIN translates, "not trodden." They had no precedent of former saints to induce them to devise for themselves a new worship. **16. hissing**—(I Kings 9:8). In sign of contempt.

That which was to be only the *event* is ascribed to the *purpose* of the people, although altogether different from what they would have been likely to hope for. Their *purpose* is represented as being the destruction of their country, because it was the *inevitable result* of their course of acting. **wag ... head**—in mockery (II Kings 19:21; Matt. 27:39). As "wag ... head" answers to "hissing," so "astonished" answers to "desolate," for which, therefore, MUNSTER and others rather translate, "an object of wonder" (ch. 19:8). **17. as with an east wind**—lit., "I will scatter them, *as an east wind*" (scatters all before it): a most violent wind (Job 27:21; Ps. 48:7; Isa. 27:8). Thirty-two MSS. read (without *as*), "*with* an east wind." **I will show them the back ... not ... face**—just retribution: as "they turned their back unto Me ... not their face" (ch. 2:27). **18.** (Ch. 11:19.) Let us bring a capital charge against him, as a false prophet; "for (whereas he foretells that this land shall be left without priests to teach the law, Malachi 2:7; without scribes to explain its difficulties; and without prophets to reveal God's will), the law shall not perish from the prophet ..."; since God has made these a lasting institution in His church, and the law declares they shall never perish (Lev. 6:18; 10:11; cf. ch. 5:12) [GROTIUS]. **the wise**—scribes and elders joined to the priests. Perhaps they mean to say, we must have right on our side, in spite of Jeremiah's words against us and our prophets (ch. 28:15, 16; 29:25, 32; 5:31); "for the law shall not perish ...." I prefer GROTIUS' explanation. **with ... tongue**—by a false accusation (Ps. 57:4; 64:3; 12:4; 50:19). "For the tongue" (*Margin*), i.e., for his speaking against us. "In the tongue," i.e., let us kill him, that he may speak no more against us [CASTALIO]. **19. Give heed**—contrasted with, "let us not give heed" (vs. 18). As *they* give no heed to me, do Thou, O Lord, give heed to me, and let my words at least have their weight with Thee. **20.** In the particulars here specified, Jeremiah was a type of Jesus Christ (Ps. 109:4, 5; John 15:25). **my soul** —my life; me (Ps. 35:7). **I stood before thee ... to turn away thy wrath**—so Moses (Ps. 106:23; cf. Ezek. 22:30). So Jesus Christ, the antitype of previous partial intercessors (Isa. 59:16). **21. pour out their blood by the force of the sword**—lit., "by the hands of the sword." So Ezekiel 35:5. MAURER with JEROME translates, "*deliver them* over to the power of the sword." But cf. Psalm 63:10, *Margin;* Isaiah 53:12. In this prayer he does not indulge in personal revenge, as if it were his own cause that was at stake; but he speaks under the dictation of the Spirit, ceasing to intercede, and speaking prophetically, knowing they were doomed to destruction as reprobates; for those not so, he doubtless ceased not to intercede. *We* are not to draw an example from this, which is a special case. **put to death**—or, as in ch. 15:2, "perish by the *death-plague*" [MAURER]. **men ... young men**—HORSLEY distinguishes the former as *married men* past middle age; the latter, the flower of *unmarried youth*. **22. cry**—by reason of the enemy bursting in: let their houses be no shelter to them in their calamities [CALVIN]. **digged ... pit**—(V. 20; Ps. 57:6; 119:85). **23. forgive not**—(Ps. 109:9, 10, 14). **blot out**—image from an account book (Rev. 20:12). **before thee**—Hypocrites suppose God is not near, so long as they escape punishment; but when He punishes, they are said to stand before Him, because they can no longer flatter themselves they can escape His eye (cf. Ps. 90:8). **deal thus**—exert Thy power against them [MAURER]. **time of thine anger**—

Though He seems to tarry, His time shall come at last (Eccles. 8:11, 12; II Peter 3:9, 10).

CHAPTER 19

Vss. 1-15. THE DESOLATION OF THE JEWS FOR THEIR SINS FORETOLD IN THE VALLEY OF HINNOM; THE SYMBOL OF BREAKING A BOTTLE. Referred by MAURER, etc., to the beginning of Zedekiah's reign. **1. bottle**—*Hebrew, bakuk,* so called from the gurgling sound which it makes when being emptied. **ancients**—elders. As witnesses of the symbolic action (vs. 10; Isa. 8:1, 2), that the Jews might not afterwards plead ignorance of the prophecy. The seventy-two elders, composing the Sanhedrim, or Great Council, were taken partly from "the priests," partly from the other tribes, i.e., "the people," the former presiding over spiritual matters, the latter over civil; the seventy-two represented the whole people. **2. valley of the son of Hinnom**—or Tophet, south of Jerusalem, where human victims were offered, and children made to pass through the fire, in honor of Molech. **east gate**—*Margin,* "sun gate," sunrise being in the *east.* MAURER translates, the "potter's gate." Through it lay the road to the valley of Hinnom (Josh. 15:8). The potters there formed vessels for the use of the temple, which was close by (cf. vss. 10, 14; ch. 18:2; Zech. 11:13). The same as "*the water gate* toward the east" (Neh. 3:26; 12:37); so called from the brook Kedron. CALVIN translates, as *English Version* and *Margin.* "It was monstrous perversity to tread the law under foot in so conspicuous a place, over which the sun daily rising reminded them of the light of God's law." **3.** The scene of their guilt is chosen as the scene of the denunciation against them. **kings**—the king and queen (ch. 13:18); or including the king's counsellors and governors under him. **tingle**—as if struck by a thunder peal (I Sam. 3:11; II Kings 21:12). **4.** (Isaiah 65:11.) **estranged this place**—devoted it to the worship of strange gods: alienating a portion of the sacred city from God, the rightful Lord of the temple, city, and whole land. **nor their fathers**—viz., the *godly* among them; their *ungodly* fathers God makes no account of. **blood of innocents**—slain in honor of Molech (ch. 7:31; Ps. 106: 37). **5. commanded not**—nay, more, I commanded the opposite (Lev. 18:21; see ch. 7:31, 32). **6. no more ... Tophet**—from *Hebrew, toph,* "drum"; for in sacrificing children to Molech drums were beaten to drown their cries. Thus the name indicated the *joy* of the people at the fancied propitiation of the god by this sacrifice; in antithesis to its joyless name subsequently. **valley of slaughter**—It should be the scene of slaughter, no longer of children, but of men; not of "innocents" (vs. 4), but of those who richly deserved their fate. The city could not be assailed without first occupying the valley of Hinnom, in which was the only fountain: hence arose the violent battle there. **7. make void the counsel**—defeat their plans for repelling the enemy (II Chron. 32:1-4; Isa. 19:3; 22:9, 11). Or their schemes of getting help by having recourse to idols [CALVIN]. **in this place**—The valley of Hinnom was to be the place of the Chaldean encampment; the very place where they looked for help from idols was to be the scene of their own slaughter. **8.** (*Note,* ch. 18:16.) **9.** (Deut. 28:53; Lam. 4:10.) **10. break ... bottle**—a symbolical action, explained in vs. 11. **the men**—the elders of the people and of the priests (vs. 1; cf. ch. 51:63, 64). **11. as one breaketh a potter's ves-**

sel—expressing God's absolute sovereignty (ch. 18:6; Ps. 2:9; Isa. 30:14, *Margin;* Lam. 4:2; Rom. 9:20, 21). **cannot be made whole again**—A broken potter's vessel cannot be restored, but a new one may be made of the same material. So God raised a new Jewish seed, not identical with the destroyed rebels, but by substituting another generation in their stead [GROTIUS]. **no place to bury**—(ch. 7:32). **12. make this city as Tophet**—i.e., as defiled with dead bodies as Tophet. **13. shall be defiled**—with dead bodies (vs. 12; II Kings 23:10). **because of all the houses**—Rather, (explanatory of the previous "the houses . . . and . . . houses"), "*even* all the houses," etc. [CALVIN]. **roofs**—being flat, they were used as high places for sacrifices to the sun and planets (ch. 32:29; II Kings 23:11, 12; Zeph. 1:5). The Nabateans, south and east of the Dead Sea, a nation most friendly to the Jews, according to Strabo, had the same usage. **14. court of the Lord's house**—near Tophet; the largest court, under the open air, where was the greatest crowd (II Chron. 20:5). **15. her towns**—the suburban villages and towns near Jerusalem, such as Bethany.

CHAPTER 20

Vss. 1-18. JEREMIAH'S INCARCERATION BY PASHUR, THE PRINCIPAL OFFICER OF THE TEMPLE, FOR PROPHESYING WITHIN ITS PRECINCTS; HIS RENEWED PREDICTIONS AGAINST THE CITY, etc., ON HIS LIBERATION. **1. son**—descendant. **of Immer**—one of the original "governors of the sanctuary and of the house of God," twenty-four in all, i.e., sixteen of the sons of Eleazar and eight of the sons of Ithamar (I Chron. 24:14). This Pashur is distinct from Pashur, *son of Melchiah* (ch. 21:1). The "captains" (Luke 22:4) seem to have been over the twenty-four guards of the temple, and had only the right of *apprehending* any who were guilty of delinquency within it; but the Sanhedrim had the *judicial power* over such delinquents [GROTIUS] (ch. 26:8, 10, 16). **2.** The fact that Pashur was of the same order and of the same family as Jeremiah aggravates the indignity of the blow (I Kings 22:24; Matt. 26:67). **stocks**—an instrument of torture with five holes, in which the neck, two hands, and two feet were thrust, the body being kept in a crooked posture (ch. 29:26). From a *Hebrew* root, to "turn," or "rack." This marks Pashur's cruelty. **high**—i.e., *the upper* gate (II Kings 15:35). **gate of Benjamin**—a gate in the temple wall, corresponding to the gate of Benjamin, properly so called, in the city wall, in the direction of the territory of Benjamin (ch. 7:2; 37:13; 38:7). The temple gate of Benjamin, being on a lofty position, was called "the high gate," to distinguish it from the city wall gate of Benjamin. **3. Pashur**—compounded of two roots, meaning "largeness" (and so "security") "*on every side*"; in antithesis to *Magor-missabib*, "terror *round about*" (vs. 10; ch. 6:25; 46:5; 49:29; Ps. 31:13). **4. terror . . . to all thy friends**—who have believed thy false promises (vs. 6). The sense must be in order to accord with "fear round about" (vs. 3). I will bring terror on thee and on all thy friends, that terror arising from thyself, viz., thy false prophecies. Thou and thy prophecies will be seen, to the dismay both of thee and thy dupes, to have caused their ruin and thine. MAURER'S translation is therefore not needed, "I will give up thee and all thy friends *to* terror." **5. strength**—i.e., resources. **labours**—fruits of labor, gain, wealth. **6. prophesied lies**—viz., that God cannot possibly leave this land with-out prophets, priests, and teachers ("the wise") (ch. 18:18; cf. ch. 5:31). **7.** Jeremiah's complaint, not unlike that of Job, breathing somewhat of human infirmity in consequence of his imprisonment. Thou didst promise never to give me up to the will of mine enemies, and yet Thou hast done so. But Jeremiah misunderstood God's promise, which was not that he should have nothing to suffer, but that God would deliver him out of sufferings (ch. 1:19). **deceived**—Others translate as *Margin*, "Thou hast *enticed*" or "*persuaded* me," viz., to undertake the prophetic office, "and I was persuaded," i.e., suffered myself to be persuaded to undertake what I find too hard for me. So the *Hebrew* word is used in a good sense (Gen. 9:27, *Margin; Prov.* 25:15; Hos. 2:14). **stronger than I**—Thou whose strength I could not resist hast laid this burden on me, and hast prevailed (hast made me prophesy, in spite of my reluctance) (ch. 1:5-7); yet, when I exercise my office, I am treated with derision (Lam. 3:14). **8.** Rather, "*Whenever* I speak, I cry out." *Concerning* violence and spoil, I (am compelled to) cry out," i.e., complain [MAURER]. *English Version* in the last clause is more graphic, "I cried violence and spoil" (ch. 6:7)! I could not speak in a calm tone; their desperate wickedness compelled me to "cry out." **because**—rather, "therefore," the apodosis of the previous sentence; *because* in discharging my prophetic functions, I not merely *spake*, but *cried; and cried, violence . . . ; therefore* the word of the Lord was made a reproach to me (vs. 7). **9.** *his word was*—or lit., "there was in my heart, as it were, a burning fire," i.e., the divine afflatus or impulse to speak was as . . . (Job 32:18, 19; Ps. 39:3). **weary with forbearing, and I could not**—"I labored to contain myself, but I could not" (Acts 18:5; cf. ch. 23:9; I Cor. 9:16, 17). **10. For**—not referring to the words immediately preceding, but to "I will not make mention of Him." The "defaming" or *detraction* of the enemy on every side (see Ps. 31:13) tempted him to think of prophesying no more. **Report . . . we will report**—The words of his adversaries one to the other; give any information against him (true or false) which will give color for accusing him; and "we will report it," viz., to the Sanhedrim, in order to crush him. **familiars**—lit., "men of my peace"; those who pretended to be on peaceable terms with me (Ps. 41:9). Jeremiah is a type of Messiah, referred to in that Psalm. (See ch. 38:22; Job 19:19; Ps. 55:13, 14; Luke 11:53, 54.) **watched for my halting**—(Ps. 35:15, *Margin*, "halting"; Ps. 38:17; 71:10, *Margin*). GESENIUS not so well translates, according to *Arabic* idiom, "those guarding my side" (i.e., my most intimate friends *always at my side*), in apposition to "familiars," and the subject of "say" (instead of "saying." The *Hebrew* means properly "side," then "halting," as the halt bend on one side. **enticed**—to commit some sin. **11. not prevail**—as they hoped to do (vs. 10; ch. 15:20). **prosper**—in their plot. **12. triest the righteous**—in latent contrast to the hasty judgments of men (ch. 11:20; 17:10). **opened**—i.e., committed (cf. II Kings 19:14; Ps. 35:1). **13. delivered . . . soul**—This deliverance took place when Zedekiah succeeded Jeconiah. **14-18.** The contrast between the spirit of this passage and the preceding *thanksgiving* is to be explained thus: to show how great was the deliverance (vs. 13), he subjoins a picture of what his wounded spirit *had been* previous to his deliverance; I *had said* in the time of my imprisonment, "Cursed be the day"; my feeling was that of Job (Job 3:3, 10, 11, whose words Jeremiah therefore copies). Though Jeremiah's zeal had been stirred up, not so much for self as for God's honor trampled on by the rejection of the prophet's words, yet it was intemperate when he made his birth a subject for *cursing,* which was really a ground for thanksgiving. **15. A man child**—The birth of a son is in the *East* a special subject of joy; whereas that of a daughter is often not so. **16. the cities**—Sodom and Gomorrah. **cry . . . morning . . . noontide**—i.e., Let him be kept in alarm the *whole day* (not merely at *night* when terrors ordinarily prevail, but in *daytime* when it is something extraordinary) with terrifying war shouts, as those in a besieged city (ch. 18:22). **17. he**—"that man" (vss. 15, 16). **from the womb**—i.e., at that time while I was still in the womb.

CHAPTER 21

Vss. 1-14. ZEDEKIAH CONSULTS JEREMIAH WHAT IS TO BE THE EVENT OF THE WAR: GOD'S ANSWER. Written probably when, after having repulsed the Egyptians who brought succors to the Jews (ch. 37: 5-8; II Kings 24:7), the Chaldees were a second time advancing against Jerusalem, but were not yet closely besieging it (vss. 4, 13) [ROSENMULLER]. This chapter probably ought to be placed between chs. 37 and 38; since what the "princes," in ch. 38:2, represent Jeremiah as having said, is exactly what we find in vs. 9 of this ch. 21. Moreover, the same persons as here (vs. 1) are mentioned in ch. 37:3; 38:1, viz., Pashur and Zephaniah. What is here more fully related is there simply referred to in the historical narrative. Cf. ch. 52:24; II Kings 25:18 [MAURER]. **Zedekiah**—a prince having some reverence for sacred things, for which reason he sends an honorable embassy to Jeremiah; but not having moral courage to obey his better impulses. **Pashur** —son of Melchiah, of the fifth order of priests, distinct from Pashur, son of Immer (ch. 20:1), of the sixteenth order (I Chron. 24:9, 14). **Zephaniah**—of the twenty-fourth order. They are designated, not by their father, but by their family (I Chron. 24:18). **2. Nebuchadrezzar**—the more usual way of spelling the name in Jeremiah than Nebuchadnezzar. From *Persiac* roots, meaning either "Nebo, the chief of the gods," or, "Nebo, the god of fire." He was son of Nabopolassar, who committed the command of the army against Egypt, at Carchemish, and against Judea, to the crown prince. **according to all his wondrous works**— Zedekiah hopes for God's special interposition, such as was vouchsafed to Hezekiah against Sennacherib (II Kings 19:35, 36). **he**—Nebuchadnezzar. **go up from us**—*rise up* from the siege which he sat down to lay (ch. 37:5, 11, *Margin*; Num. 16: 24; 27; I Kings 15:19, *Margin*). **4. God of Israel**—Those "wondrous works" (vs. 2) do not belong to you; *God* is faithful; it is *you* who forfeit the privileges of the covenant by unfaithfulness. "God will always remain *the God of Israel*, though He destroy thee and thy people" [CALVIN]. **turn back the weapons**—I will turn them to a very different use from what you intend them. With them you now fight against the Chaldees "without the walls" (the Jewish defenders being as yet able to sally forth more freely, and defend the fountains outside the walls in the valley under Mount Zion; see vs. 13; ch. 19:6, 7); but soon ye shall be driven back within the city [MAURER], and "in the midst" of it, I will cause all your arms to be gathered in one place ("I will assemble *them,*" viz., your arms) by the Chaldean conquerors [GROTIUS], who shall slay you with those

very arms [MENOCHIUS]. **5.** The Jews shall have not merely the Chaldees, but Jehovah Himself in wrath at their provocations, fighting against them. Every word enhances the formidable character of God's opposition, "I myself . . . outstretched hand . . . strong arm (no longer as in Exod. 6:6, and in the case of Sennacherib, in your behalf, but) in anger . . . fury . . . great wrath." **7. the people, and such** —rather, explanatory, "the people, viz., such as are left." **seek their life**—content with nothing short of their death; not content with plundering and enslaving them. **smite with . . . sword**—This was the fate of Zedekiah's sons and many of the Jewish nobles. Zedekiah himself, though not put to a violent death, died of grief. Cf. as to the accurate fulfilment, ch. 34:4; Ezek. 12:13; II Kings 25:6, 7. **8.** "Life," if ye surrender; "death," if ye persist in opposing the Chaldees (cf. Deut. 30:19). The individuality of Jeremiah's mission from God is shown in that he urges to unconditional surrender; whereas all former prophets had urged the people to oppose their invaders (Isa. 7:16; 37:33, 35). **9.** (Ch. 38:2, 17, 18.) **falleth to**—deserts to. **life . . . a prey**— proverbial, to make one's escape with life, like a valuable spoil or prey that one carries off; the narrowness of the escape, and the joy felt at it, are included in the idea (ch. 39:18). **10. set . . . face against**—determined to punish (Lev. 17:10). **12. house of David**—the royal family and all in office about the king. He calls them so, because it was the greater disgrace that they had so degenerated from the piety of their forefather, *David;* and to repress their glorying in their descent from him, as if they were therefore inviolable; but God will not spare them as apostates. **in the morning**—alluding to *the time* of dispensing justice (Job 24:17; Ps. 101:8); but the sense is mainly proverbial, for "with promptness" (Ps. 90:14; 143:8). MAURER translates, "every morning." **lest my fury . . . like fire**—Already it was kindled, and the decree of God gone forth against the city (vss. 4, 5), but the king and his house may yet be preserved by repentance and reformation. God urges to righteousness, not as if they can thereby escape punishment wholly, but as the condition of a *mitigation* of it. **13. inhabitant of the valley, and rock of the plain**—Jerusalem personified; situated for the most part on hills, with valleys at the bottom of them, as the valley of Hinnom, etc.; and beyond the valleys and mountains again, a position most fortified by nature, whence the inhabitants fancied themselves beyond the reach of enemies; but since God is "against" them, their position will avail nothing for them. The "valley" between Mount Zion and Moriah is called Tyropœon. ROBINSON takes, "rock of the plain" as Mount Zion, *on which* is a *level tract* of some extent. It is appropriately here referred to, being the site of the royal residence of the "house of David," addressed (vs. 12). **14. fruit of your doings** —(Prov. 1:31; Isa. 3:10, 11). **forest thereof**—viz., of your city, taken from vs. 13. "Forest" refers to the dense mass of houses built of cedar, etc. brought from Lebanon (ch. 22:7; 52:13; II Kings 25:9).

CHAPTER 22

Vss. 1-30. EXHORTATION TO REPENTANCE; JUDGMENT ON SHALLUM, JEHOIAKIM, AND CONIAH. Belonging to an earlier period than ch. 21, viz., the reigns of Shallum or Jehoahaz, Jehoiakim, and Jeconiah (vss. 10, 13, 20). Jeremiah often groups his prophecies, not by chronological order, but by *similarity of subjects;* thus vs. 3 in this chapter corresponds to ch. 21:12. GROTIUS thinks that Jeremiah here *repeats* to Zedekiah what he had announced to that king's predecessors *formerly* (viz., his brother and brother's son), of a similar bearing, and which had since come to pass; a warning to Zedekiah. Probably, in *arranging* his prophecies they were grouped for the first time in the present order, designed by the Holy Spirit to set forth the series of kings of Judah, all four alike, failing in "righteousness," followed at last by the "King," *a righteous Branch raised unto David,* in the house of Judah, "the Lord our righteousness" (ch. 23:6). The unrighteousness of Zedekiah suggested the review of his predecessors' failure in the same respects, and consequent punishment, which ought to have warned him, but did not. **1. Go down**—The temple (where Jeremiah had been prophesying) was higher than the king's palace on Mount Zion (ch. 36:10, 12; II Chron. 23:20). Hence the phrase, "Go down." **the king of Judah**—perhaps including *each of the four successive kings,* to whom it was consecutively addressed, here brought together in one picture: Shallum, vs. 11; Jehoiakim, vss. 13-18; Jeconiah, vs. 24; Zedekiah, the address to whom (ch. 21:1, 11, 12) suggests notice of the rest. **2. these gates**—of the king's palace. **3.** *Jehoiakim* is meant here especially: he, by oppression, levied the tribute imposed on him by Pharaoh-necho, king of Egypt (II Chron. 36:3), and taxed his people, and took their labor without pay, to build gorgeous palaces for himself (vss. 13-17), and shed innocent blood, e.g., that of Urijah the prophet (ch. 26:20-24; II Kings 23:35; 24:4). **4. upon the throne of David** —lit., "or David on his throne" (see *Note,* ch. 13; 13). This verse is repeated substantially from ch. 17:25. **his servants**—so the *Keri.* But *Chetib, singular,* "his servant;" i.e., distributively, "*each* with his servants;" ch. 17:25, "their princes." **5. I swear by myself**—(Heb. 6:13, 17). God swears because it seemed to them incredible that the family of David should be cast off. **this house**—the king's, where Jeremiah spake (vs. 4). **6.** Though thou art as beautiful as Gilead, and as majestic in Mine eyes (before Me) as the summit of Lebanon, *yet* surely (the *Hebrew* is a formula of swearing to express *certainly: If I do not* make thee. . . ., believe Me not ever hereafter: so "as truly as I live," Num. 14:28; "surely," Num. 14:35). The mention of Gilead may allude not only to its past beauty, but covertly also to its desolation by the judgment on Israel; a warning now to Judah and the house of David. "Lebanon" is appropriately mentioned, as the king's house was built of its noble cedars. **cities**—not other *cities,* but the different *parts* of the *city* of Jerusalem (II Sam. 12:27; II Kings 10:25) [MAURER]. **7. prepare**—lit., "sanctify," or solemnly set apart for a particular work (cf. Isa. 13:3). **thy choice cedars**—(Isa. 37:24). Thy palaces built of choice cedars (Song of Sol. 1:17). **8.** (Deut. 29:24, 25.) The Gentile nations, more intelligent than you, shall understand that which ye do not, viz., that this city is a spectacle of God's vengeance [CALVIN]. **9.** (II Kings 22:17.) **10, 11.** Weep . . . **not for**—i.e., not so much for Josiah, who was taken away by death from the evil to come (II Kings 22:20; Isa. 57:1); as for Shallum or Jehoahaz, his son (II Kings 23:30), who, after a three months' reign, was carried off by Pharaoh-necho into Egypt, never to see his native land again (II Kings 23:31-34). Dying saints are justly to be envied, while living sinners are to be pitied. The allusion is to the great weeping of the people at the death of Josiah, and on each

anniversary of it, in which Jeremiah himself took a prominent part (II Chron. 35:24, 25). The name "Shallum" is here given in irony to Jehoahaz, who reigned but three months; as if he were a second Shallum, son of Jabesh, who reigned only *one month* in Samaria (II Kings 15:13; II Chron. 36:1-4). Shallum means "retribution," a name of no good omen to him [GROTIUS]; originally the people called him *Shallom,* indicative of *peace* and prosperity. But Jeremiah applies it in irony. I Chronicles 3:15, calls Shallum the *fourth* son of Josiah. The people raised him to the throne before his brother Eliakim or Jehoiakim, though the latter was the older (II Kings 23:31, 36; II Chron. 36:1); perhaps on account of Jehoiakim's extravagance (vss. 13, 15). Jehoiakim was put in Shallum's (Jehoahaz') stead by Pharaoh-necho. Jeconiah, his son, succeeded. Zedekiah (Mattaniah), uncle of Jeconiah, and brother of Jehoiakim and Jehoahaz, was last of all raised to the throne by Nebuchadnezzar. **He shall not return**—The people perhaps entertained hopes of Shallum's return from Egypt, in which case they would replace him on the throne, and thereby free themselves from the oppressive taxes imposed by Jehoiakim. **13.** Not only did Jehoiakim tax the people (II Kings 23:35) for Pharaoh's tribute, but also took their forced labor, without pay, for building a splendid palace; in violation of Leviticus 19: 13; Deuteronomy 24:14, 15. Cf. Micah 3:10; Habakkuk 2:9; James 5:4. God will repay in justice those who will not in justice pay those whom they employ. **14. wide**—lit., a house of dimensions ("measures"). Cf. Numbers 13:32, *Margin,* "men of statures." **large**—rather, as *Margin,* "airy," from Hebrew root, "to breathe freely." Upper rooms in the East are the principal apartments. **cutteth him out windows**—The Hebrew, if a noun, is rather, "my windows"; then the translation ought to be, "and let my windows (Jehoiakim speaking) be cut out for it," i.e., in the house; or, "and let (the workman) cut out my windows for it." But the word is rather an adjective; "he cutteth it (the house) out for himself, so as to be *full of windows.*" The following words accord with this construction, "and (he makes it) ceiled with cedar," etc. [MAURER]. Retaining *English Version,* there must be understood something remarkable about the windows, since they are deemed worthy of notice. GESENIUS thinks the word *dual,* "double windows." the *blinds* being *two-leaved.* **vermilion**—*Hebrew, shashar,* called so from a people of India beyond the Ganges, by whom it is exported (PLINY, 6.19). The old vermilion was composed of sulphur and quicksilver; not of red lead, as our vermilion. **15. closest thyself**—rather, thou viest, i.e., art emulous to surpass thy forefathers in the magnificence of thy palaces. **eat and drink**—Did not Josiah, thy father, enjoy all that man *really needs* for his bodily wants? Did he need to build costly palaces to secure his throne? Nay, he *did secure* it by "judgment and justice"; whereas thou, with all thy luxurious building, sittest on a *tottering* throne. **then**—on that account, therefore. **16. was not this to know me**— viz., to show by *deeds* that one knows God's will, as was the case with Josiah (cf. John 13:17; contrast Titus 1:16). **17. thine**—as opposed to thy father, Josiah. **18. Ah my brother! . . . sister!**—addressing him with such titles of affection as one would address to a deceased friend beloved as a *brother* or *sister* (cf. I Kings 13:30). This expresses, They shall not lament him with the lamentation of *private individuals* [VATABLUS], or of *blood relatives* [GROTIUS]: as "Ah! lord," expresses *public* lamentation in the case of a king [VATABLUS], or that of *subjects* [GROTIUS]. HENDERSON thinks, "Ah! sister," refers to Jehoiakim's queen, who, though taken to Babylon and not left unburied on the way, as Jehoiakim, yet was not honored at her death with royal lamentations, such as would have been poured forth over her at Jerusalem. He notices the beauty of Jeremiah's manner in his prophecy against Jehoiakim. In vss. 13, 14 he describes him in general terms; then, in vss. 15-17, he directly addresses him without naming him; at last, in vs. 18, he names him, but in the third person, to imply that God puts him to a distance from Him. The boldness of the Hebrew prophets proves their divine mission; were it not so, their reproofs to the Hebrew kings, who held the throne by divine authority, would have been treason. **Ah his glory!**—"Alas! his majesty." **19. burial of an ass**—i.e., he shall have the same burial as an ass would get, viz., he shall be left a prey for beasts and birds [JEROME]. This is not formally narrated. But II Chronicles 36:6 states that "Nebuchadnezzar bound him in fetters to carry him to Babylon"; his treatment there is nowhere mentioned. The prophecy here, and in ch. 36:30, harmonizes these two facts. He was slain by Nebuchadnezzar, who changed his purpose of taking him to Babylon, on the way thither, and left him unburied outside Jerusalem. II Kings 24:6, "Jehoiakim slept with his fathers," does not contradict this; it simply expresses his being gathered to his fathers by *death*, not his being *buried* with his fathers (Ps. 49:19). The two phrases are found together, as expressing two distinct ideas (II Kings 15:38; 16:20). **20.** Delivered in the reign of Jehoiachin (Jeconiah or Coniah), son of Jehoiakim; appended to the previous prophecy respecting Jehoiakim, on account of the similiarity of the two prophecies. He calls on Jerusalem, personified as a mourning female, to go up to the highest points visible from Jerusalem, and lament there (ch. 3:21, *Note*) the calamity of herself, bereft of allies and of her princes, who are one after the other being cast down. **Bashan**—north of the region beyond Jordan; the mountains of Anti-libanus are referred to (Ps. 68:15). **from the passages**—viz., of the rivers (Judg. 12:6); or else the borders of the country (I Sam. 13:23; Isa. 10:29). The passes (I Sam. 14. 4). MAURER translates, "Abarim," a mountainous tract beyond Jordan, opposite Jericho, and south of Bashan; this accords with the mention of the mountains Lebanon and Bashan (Num. 27:12; 33: 47). **lovers**—the allies of Judea, especially Egypt, now unable to help the Jews, being crippled by Babylon (II Kings 24:7). **21. I** admonished thee in time. Thy sin has not been a sin of ignorance or thoughtlessness, but wilful. **prosperity**—given thee by Me; yet thou wouldest not hearken to the gracious Giver. The *Hebrew* is *plural*, to express, "In the height of thy prosperity"; so "droughts" (Isa. 58:11). **thou saidst**—not in words, but in thy conduct, virtually. **thy youth**—from the time that I brought thee out of Egypt, and formed thee into a people (ch. 7:25; 2:2; Isa. 47:12). **22. wind**—the Chaldees, as a parching wind that sweeps over rapidly and withers vegetation (ch. 4:11, 12; Ps. 103: 16; Isa. 40:7). **eat up ... pastors**—i.e., thy kings (ch. 2:8). There is a happy play on words. The *pastors*, whose office it is to feed the sheep, shall themselves be *fed on*. They who should *drive* the flock from place to place for pasture shall be *driven* into exile by the Chaldees. **23. inhabitant of Lebanon**—viz., Jerusalem, whose temple, palaces, and principal habitations were built of cedars of Lebanon. **how gracious**—irony. How graciously thou wilt be treated by the Chaldees, when they come on thee suddenly, as pangs on a woman in travail (ch. 6:24)! Nay, all thy fine buildings will win no favor for thee from them. MAURER translates, "How shalt thou be *to be pitied!*" **24. As I live**—God's most solemn formula of oath (ch. 46: 18; 4:2; Deut. 32:40; I Sam. 25:34). **Coniah**—Jeconiah or Jehoiachin. The contraction of the name is meant in contempt. **signet**—Such ring-seals were often of the greatest value (Song of Sol. 8:6; Hag. 2:23). Jehoiachin's popularity is probably here referred to. **right hand**—the hand most valued. **I would pluck thee thence**—(Cf. Obad. 4); on account of thy father's sins, as well as thine own (II Chron. 36:9). There is a change here, as often in *Hebrew* poetry, from the third to the second person, to bring the threat more directly home to him. After a three months' and ten days' reign, the Chaldees deposed him. In Babylon, however, by God's favor he was ultimately treated more kindly than other royal captives (ch. 52:31-34). But none of his direct posterity ever came to the throne. **25. give ... into ... hand**—"I will pluck thee" from "*my right hand*," and "will give thee *into the hand of them that seek thy life.*" **26. thy mother**—Nehushta, the queen dowager (II Kings 24:6, 8, 15; see ch. 13: 18). **27. they**—Coniah and his mother. He passes from the second person (vs. 26) to the third person here, to express alienation. The king is as it were put out of sight, as if unworthy of being spoken with directly. **desire**—lit., "lift up their soul" (ch. 44:14; Ps. 24:4; 25:1). Judea was the land which they in Babylon should pine after in vain. **28. broken idol**—Coniah was idolized once by the Jews; Jeremiah, therefore, in their person, expresses their astonishment at one from whom so much had been expected being now so utterly cast aside. **vessel ... no pleasure**—(Ps. 31:12; Hos. 8:8). The answer to this is given (Rom. 9:20-23; contrast II Tim. 2:21). **his seed**—(See *Note*, vs. 29). **29, 30. O earth! earth! earth!**—Jeconiah was not actually without offspring (cf. vs. 28, "his seed"; I Chron. 3:17, 18; Matt. 1:12), but he was to be "written childless," as a warning to posterity, i.e., without a lineal heir to his throne. It is with a reference to the *three* kings, Shallum, Jehoiakim, and Jeconiah, that the earth is *thrice* invoked [BENGEL]. Or, the *triple* invocation is to give intensity to the call for attention to the announcement of the end of the royal line, so far as Jehoiachin's seed is concerned. Though Messiah (Matt. 1), the heir of David's throne, was lineally descended from Jeconiah, it was only through Joseph, who, though His legal, was not His real father. Matthew gives the legal pedigree through *Solomon* down to Joseph; Luke the real pedigree, from Mary, the real parent, through *Nathan*, brother of Solomon, upwards (Luke 3:31). **no man of his seed ... upon the throne**—This explains the sense in which "childless" is used. Though the succession to the throne failed in his line, still the promise to David (Ps. 89:30-37) was revived in Zerubbabel and consummated in Christ.

CHAPTER 23

Vss. 1-40. THE WICKED RULERS TO BE SUPERSEDED BY THE KING, WHO SHOULD REIGN OVER THE AGAIN UNITED PEOPLES, ISRAEL AND JUDAH. This forms the *epilogue* to the denunciations of the four kings, in ch. 21:22. **1. pastors**—Shallum, Jehoiakim, Jeconiah, and Zedekiah (Ezek. 34:2). **2. Ye**

have not ... visited them ... I will visit upon you—just retribution. Play upon the double sense of "visit." "Visit upon," viz., in wrath (Exod. 32:34). **3, 4.** Restoration of Judah from Babylon foretold in language which in its fulness can only apply to the final restoration of *both* "Judah" and *"Israel"* (cf. vs. 6); also "out of *all* countries," in this verse and vs. 8; also, "neither shall they be lacking," i.e., none shall be missing or detached from the rest: a prophecy never yet fully accomplished. It holds good also of the spiritual Israel, the elect of both Jews and Gentiles (Mal. 3:16, 17; John 10:28; 17:12). As to the literal Israel also, see ch. 32:37; Isa. 54:13; 60:21; Ezek. 34:11-16). **shepherds ... shall feed them**—(ch. 3:15; Ezek. 34:23-31). Zerubbabel, Ezra, Nehemiah, and the Maccabees were but typical of the consummating fulfilment of these prophecies under Messiah. **5.** As Messianic prophecy extended over many years in which many political changes took place in harmony with these, it displayed its riches by a variety more effective than if it had been manifested all at once. As the moral condition of the Jews required in each instance, so Messiah was exhibited in a corresponding phase, thus becoming more and more the soul of the nation's life: so that He is represented as the antitypical Israel (Isa. 49:3). **unto David**—HENG-STENBERG observes that Isaiah dwells more on His *prophetical* and *priestly* office, which had already been partly set forth (Deut. 18:18; Ps. 110:4). Other prophets dwell more on His *kingly* office. Therefore here He is associated with "David" *the king:* but in Isaiah 11:1 with the then poor and unknown "Jesse." **righteous Branch**—"the Branch of righteousness" (ch. 33:15); "The Branch" simply (Zech. 3:8; 6:12); "The Branch of the Lord" (Isa. 4:2). **prosper**—the very term applied to Messiah's undertaking (Isa. 52:13; *Margin*; 53:10). *Righteousness* or *justice* is the characteristic of Messiah elsewhere, too, in connection with our *salvation* or *justification* (Isa. 53:11; Dan. 9:24; Zech. 9:9). So in the New Testament He is not merely "righteous" Himself, but "righteousness to us" (I Cor. 1:30), so that we become "the righteousness of God in Him" (Rom. 10:3, 4; II Cor. 5:19-21; Phil. 3:9). **execute judgment and justice in the earth**—(Ps. 72:2; Isa. 9:7; 32:1, 18). Not merely a spiritual reign in the sense in which He is "our righteousness," but a righteous reign "in the earth" (ch. 3:17, 18). In some passages He is said to come to *judge,* in others to *reign.* In Matthew 25:34, He is called "the King." Psalm 9:7 unites them. Cf. Daniel 7:22, 26, 27. **6. Judah ... Israel ... dwell safely**—Cf. ch. 33:16, where "Jerusalem" is substituted for "Israel" here. Only *Judah,* and that only in part, has as yet returned. So far are the Jews from having enjoyed, as yet, the temporal blessings here foretold as the result of Messiah's reign, that their lot has been, for eighteen centuries, worse than ever before. The accomplishment must, therefore, be still future, when both Judah and Israel in their own land shall dwell safely under a Christocracy, far more privileged than even the old theocracy (ch. 32:37; Deut. 33:28; Isa. 54:60; 65:17-25; Zech. 14:11). **shall be called, the Lord**—i.e., shall *be* (Isa. 9:6) "Jehovah," God's incommunicable name. Though when applied to created things, it expresses only some peculiar *connection* they have with Jehovah (Gen. 22:14; Exod. 17:15), yet when applied to Messiah it must express His *Godhead* manifested in justifying power *towards us* (I Tim. 3:16). **our**—marks His *manhood,* which is also implied in His being a *Branch raised unto David,* whence His

human title, "Son of David" (cf. Matt. 22:42-45). **Righteousness**—marks His *Godhead,* for God alone can justify the ungodly (cf. Rom. 4:5; Isa. 45:17, 24, 25). **7, 8.** Repeated from ch. 16:14, 15. —The prophet said the same things often, in order that his sayings might make the more impression. The same promise as in vss. 3, 4. The wide dispersion of the Jews at the Babylonish captivity prefigures their present wider dispersion (Isa. 11:11; Joel 3:6). Their second deliverance is to exceed far the former one from Egypt. But the deliverance from Babylon was inferior to that from Egypt in respect to the miracles performed and the numbers delivered. The final deliverance under Messiah must, therefore, be meant, of which that from Babylon was the earnest. **9. because of the prophets**—so the Masorites and Targum. But *Vulgate,* LXX, etc., make this the inscription of the prophecy, CONCERNING THE PROPHETS: as in ch. 46:2; 48:1; 49:1. Jeremiah expresses his horror at the so-called "prophets" not warning the people, though iniquity so fearfully abounded, soon to be followed by awful judgments. **bones shake**—(Hab. 3:16). **drunken**—God's judgments are represented as stupefying like wine. The effects of the Holy Spirit are compared to those of wine (Acts 2:17). In both cases ecstasy was produced. This accounts for the denial of wine to those likely to be inspired, Nazarites, etc. (Luke 1:15). It was necessary to put it out of men's power to ascribe inspired ecstasy to the effects of wine. **because of ... words of ... holiness**—because of Jehovah's holy words, wherewith He threatened severe penalties, soon to be inflicted, against the breakers of His law. **10. adulterers**—spiritual, i.e., forsakers of God, Israel's true Husband (Isa. 54:5) for idols, at the instigation of the false "prophets" (vss. 9, 15). *Literal* "adultery" and fornication, the usual concomitants of idolatry, are also meant. **swearing**—MAURER, etc., translate, "Because of the curse (of God on it), the land mourneth" (Deut. 27:15–26; 28:15-68; Isa. 24:6). More than usual notoriety had been given to the curses of the law, by the finding and reading of it in Josiah's time (II Kings 22:11, etc.). But Hosea 4:2, 3, favors *English Version* (cf. ch. 12:4). A drought was sent by God on the pastures ("pleasant places," oases) in the desert, on account of the "profaneness" of the priests, prophets, and people (vs. 11). **course ... evil**—They (both prophets and people) rush into wickedness (vs. 21; Isa. 59:7). **force ... not right**—Their *powers* are used not on the side of *rectitude,* but on that of falsehood. **11. profane**—(Ezek. 23:39; Zeph. 3:4). **in my house**—(ch. 7:30). They built altars to idols in the very temple (II Kings 23:12; Ezek. 8:3-16). Cf. as to covetousness under the roof of the sanctuary, Matthew 21:13; John 2:16. **12. slippery ways in ... darkness**—Their "way" is their false doctrine which proves fatal to them (ch. 13:16; Ps. 35:6; Prov. 4:19). **I will bring evil ... visitation**—still more calamities than those already inflicted. See *Note,* ch. 11:23; "visitation," viz., in wrath. **13. folly**—lit., insipidity, unsavouriness (Job 6:6), not having the salt of godliness (Col. 4:6). **in Baal**—in the name of Baal; in connection with his worship (see ch. 2:8). **caused ... to err**—(Isa. 9:16). **14.** "Jerusalem" and Judah were even worse than "Samaria" and the ten tribes; the greater were the privileges of the former, the greater was their guilt. They had the temple in their midst, which the ten tribes had not; yet in the temple itself they practised idolatry. **strengthen ... hands ... of evildoers**—(Ezek. 13:22). **as Sodom**—(Deut. 32:32; Isa. 1:10). **15. gall**—

poison (*Note*, ch. 8:14; 9:15). **16. make you vain** —They seduce you to vanity, i.e., idolatry, which will prove a vain trust to you (ch. 2:5; II Kings 17: 15; Jonah 2:8), [GESENIUS]. Rather, "they delude you with vain promises of security" (vs. 17; cf. Ps. 62:10) [MAURER]. **of . . . own heart**—of their own invention (vs. 21; ch. 14:14). **17. say still**—*Hebrew*, "say in saying," i.e., say *incessantly*. **peace**—(ch. 6: 14; Ezek. 13:10; Zech. 10:2). **imagination**—*Hebrew*, obstinacy. **no evil**—(Mic. 3:11). **18.** A reason is given why the false prophets should not be heeded: *They have not stood in the counsels of Jehovah* (an image from ministers present in a *standing* posture at councils of Eastern kings) (cf. vs. 22; Job 15:8). The spiritual man alone has the privilege (Gen. 18:17; Ps. 25:14; Amos 3:7; John 15:15; I Cor. 2:16). **19.** So far from all prosperity awaiting the people as the false prophets say (vs. 17), wrath is in store for them. **grievous**—lit., eddying, whirling itself about, a tornado. In ch. 30: 23, "continuing" is substituted for "grievous." **fall grievously**—it shall be hurled on. **20. in . . . latter days**—i.e., "the year of their visitation" (vs. 12). *Primarily* the meaning is: the Jews will not "consider" now God's warnings (Deut. 32:29); but when the prophecies shall be fulfilled in their Babylonish exile, they will consider and see, by bitter experience, their sinful folly. The *ultimate* scope of the prophecy is: the Jews, in their final dispersion, shall at last "consider" their sin and turn to Messiah "perfectly" (Hos. 3:5; Zech. 12:5, 10-14; Luke 13:35). **21. sent . . . spoken**—"sent" refers to the primary *call*: "spoken" to the subsequent *charges* given to be executed. A call is required, not only external, on the part of men, but also internal from God, that one should undertake a pastor's office [CALVIN]. **22. stood in . . . counsel**—(vs. 18). **they should have turned them from their evil way**—They would have given such counsels to the people as would have turned them from their sins (ch. 25:5; Isa. 55: 11), and so would have averted punishment. Their not teaching the law in which God's counsel is set forth proves they are not His prophets, though they boast of being so (Matt. 7:15-20). **23.** Let not the false prophets fancy that their devices (vs. 25) are unknown to Me. Are ye so ignorant as to suppose that I can only see things near Me, viz., things in heaven, and not earthly things as being too remote? **24.** (Ps. 139:7, etc.; Amos 9:2, 3.) **fill heaven and earth**—with My omniscience providence, power, and essential being (I Kings 8:27). **25. dreamed**—I have received a prophetic communication by dream (Num. 12:6; Deut. 13:1, etc.; Joel 2:28). **26. prophets**—a different *Hebrew* form from the usual one, "prophesiers." "How long," cries Jeremiah, impatient of their impious audacity, "shall these *prophecy-mongers* go on prophesying lies?" The answer is given in vss. 29-34. **27.** They "think" to make My people utterly to forget Me. But I will oppose to those dreamers my true prophets. **fathers . . . for Baal**—(Judg. 3:7; 8:33, 34). **28.** God answers the objection which might be stated, "What, then, must we do, when lies are spoken as truths, and prophets oppose prophets?" Do the same as when wheat is mixed with chaff: do not reject the wheat because of the chaff mixed with it, but discriminate between the false and the true revelations. The test is adherence to, or *forgetfulness* of, Me and My law (vs. 27). **that hath a dream**—that pretends to have a divine communication by dream, let him tell it "faithfully," that it may be compared with "my word" (II Cor. 4:2). The result will be the former (both the prophets

and their fictions) will soon be seen to be *chaff;* the latter (the true prophets and the word of God in their mouth) *wheat* (Ps. 1:4; Hos 13:3). **29.** As the "fire" consumes the "chaff," so "My word" will consume the false prophets (Matt. 3:12; Heb. 4:12). "My word" which is "wheat," i.e., food to the true prophet and his hearers, is a consuming "fire," and a crushing "hammer" (Matt. 21:44) to false prophets and their followers (II Cor. 2:16). The word of the false prophets may be known by its promising men *peace* in sin. "My word," on the contrary, burns and *breaks* the hard-hearted (ch. 20:9). The "hammer" symbolizes destructive power (ch. 50:23; Nah. 2:1, *Margin*). **30 steal my words**—a twofold plagiarism; one steals from the other, and all steal words from Jehovah's true prophets, but misapply them (see ch. 28:2; John 10:1; Rev. 22:19). **31. use** —rather, "take" their tongue: a second class (cf. vs. 30) require, in order to bring forth a revelation, nothing more than their *tongues*, wherewith they say, He (Jehovah) saith: they bungle in the very formula instead of the usual "*Jehovah* saith," being only able to say "(He) saith." **32.** Third class: inventors of lies: the climax, and worst of the three **lightness**—wanton inventions (Zeph. 3:4). **not profit**—i.e., greatly injure. **33. What is the burden**— play on the double sense of the *Hebrew*: an *oracle* and a *burden*. They scoffingly ask, Has he got any new burden (*burdensome oracle:* for all his prophecies are *disasters*) to announce (Mal. 1:1)? Jeremiah indignantly repeats their own question, Do you ask, What burden? This, then, it is, "I will forsake you." My word is burdensome in your eyes, and you long to be rid if it. You shall get your wish. There will be no more prophecy: *I will forsake you,* and that will be a far worse "burden" to you. **34. The burden**—Whoever shall in mockery call the Lord's word "a burden," shall be *visited (Margin)* in wrath. **35.** The result of My judgments shall be, ye shall address the prophet more reverentially hereafter, no longer calling his message a *burden,* but a divine *response* or *word.* "What hath the LORD *answered?*" **36. every man's word . . . his burden**—As they mockingly *call* all prophecies *burdens,* as if calamities were the sole subject of prophecy, so it shall prove to them. *God will take them at their own word.* **living God** —not lifeless as their dumb idols, ever living so as to be able to punish. **39. I will . . . forget you**— just retribution for their *forgetting* Him (Hos. 4:6). But God cannot possibly *forget* His children (Isa. 49:15). Rather for "forget" translate, "I will altogether lift you up (like a 'burden,' alluding to their mocking term for God's messages) and cast you off." God makes their wicked language fall on their own head [CALVIN]. Cf. vs. 36: "every man's word shall be his burden." **40. not be forgotten**— If we translate vs. 39 as *English Version,* the antithesis is, though *I forget you,* your *shame shall not be forgotten.*

CHAPTER 24

Vs. 1-10. THE RESTORATION OF THE CAPTIVES IN BABYLON AND THE DESTRUCTION OF THE REFRACTORY PARTY IN JUDEA AND IN EGYPT, REPRESENTED UNDER THE TYPE OF A BASKET OF GOOD, AND ONE OF BAD, FIGS. **1. Lord showed me**—Amos 7:1, 4, 7; 8:1, contains the same formula, with the addition of "thus" prefixed. **carried . . . captive Jeconiah**—(ch 22:24; II Kings 24:12, etc.; II Chron. 36:10). **carpenters . . .**—One thousand artisans were carried to

Babylon, both to work for the king there, and to deprive Jerusalem of their services in the event of a future siege (II Kings 24:16). **2. figs ... first ripe** —the boccora, or early fig (*Note,* Isa. 28:4). Baskets of figs used to be offered as first-fruits in the temple. The *good figs* represent Jeconiah and the exiles in Babylon; *the bad,* Zedekiah and the obstinate Jews in Judea. They are called *good* and *bad* respectively, not in an absolute, but a comparative sense, and in reference to the punishment of the latter. This prophecy was designed to encourage the despairing exiles, and to reprove the people at home, who prided themselves as superior to those in Babylon and abused the forbearance of God (cf. ch. 52:31-34). **5. acknowledge**—*regard with favor,* like as thou lookest on the good figs favorably. **for their good**—Their removal to Babylon saved them from the calamities which befell the rest of the nation and led them to repentance there: so God bettered their condition (II Kings 25:27-30). Daniel and Ezekiel were among these captives. **6.** (Ch. 12:15.) **not pull ... down ... not pluck ... up**—only partially fulfilled in the restoration from Babylon; antitypically and fully to be fulfilled hereafter (ch. 32:41; 33:7). **7.** (Ch. 30:22; 31:33; 32:38.) Their conversion from idolatry to the one true God, through the chastening effect of the Babylonish captivity, is here expressed in language which, in its fulness, applies to the more complete conversion hereafter of the Jews, "with their whole heart" (ch. 29:13), through the painful discipline of their present dispersion. The source of their conversion is here stated to be *God's prevenient grace.* **for they shall return**—Repentance, though not the cause of pardon, is its invariable accompaniment: it is the effect of God's *giving a heart to know Him.* **8. in ... Egypt**—Many Jews had fled for refuge to Egypt, which was leagued with Judea against Babylon. **9. removed ...**—(ch. 15:4). CALVIN translates, "I will give them up to *agitation,* in all ...." This verse quotes the curse (Deut. 28:25, 37). Cf. ch. 29:18, 22; Psalm 44:13, 14.

CHAPTER 25

Vss. 1-38. PROPHECY OF THE SEVENTY YEARS' CAPTIVITY; AND AFTER THAT THE DESTRUCTION OF BABYLON, AND OF ALL THE NATIONS THAT OPPRESSED THE JEWS. **1. fourth year of Jehoiakim**—called the *third* year in Daniel 1:1. But probably Jehoiakim was set on the throne by Pharaoh-necho on his return from Carchemish about *July,* whereas Nebuchadnezzar mounted the throne January 21, 604 B.C.; so that Nebuchadnezzar's first year was partly the *third,* partly the *fourth,* of Jehoiakim's. Here first Jeremiah gives specific dates. Nebuchadnezzar had previously entered Judea in the reign of his father Nabopolassar. **3.** From the thirteenth year of Josiah, in which Jeremiah began to prophesy (ch. 1:1), to the end of Josiah's reign, was nineteen years (II Kings 22:1); the three months (II Kings 23:31) of Jehoahaz' reign, with the not quite complete four years of Jehoiakim (vs. 1), added to the nineteen years, make up twenty-three years in all. **4. rising early**—(Ch. 7:13, *Note*). "The prophets" refer to Urijah, Zephaniah, Habakkuk, etc. It aggravates their sin, that God sent not merely one but many messengers, and those messengers, prophets; and, that during all those years specified, Jeremiah and his fellow prophets *spared no effort, late and early.* **5. Turn ... dwell**—In *Hebrew* there is expressed by sameness of sounds the correspondence

between their *turning* to God and God's turning to them to permit them to *dwell* in their land: *Shubu ... shebu,* "Return" ... so shall ye "remain." **every one from ... evil**—*Each must* separately repent and turn from *his*·own sin. None is excepted, lest they should think their guilt extenuated because the evil is general. **6.** He instances one sin, idolatry, as representative of all their sins; as nothing is dearer to God than a pure worship of Himself. **7.** Though ye provoke *Me* to anger (Deut. 32:21), yet it is not I, but *yourselves,* whom ye thereby hurt (Prov. 8:36; 20:2). **9. the north**—(*Note,* ch. 1:14, 15). The Medes and other northern peoples, confederate with Babylon, are included with the Chaldeans. **my servant**—My agent for punishing (ch. 27:6; 43:10; cf. ch. 40:2). Cf. Isaiah 44:28; Cyrus, "My shepherd." God makes even unbelievers unconsciously to fulfil His designs. A reproof to the Jews, who boasted that they were the *servants of God;* yet a heathen king is to be more the servant of God than they, and that as the agent of their punishment. **10.** (Ch. 7:34; Rev. 18:23.) The land shall be so desolated that even in the houses left standing there shall be no inhabitant; a terrible stillness shall prevail; no sound of the *hand-mill* (two circular stones, one above the other, for grinding corn, worked by two women, Exod. 11:5; Matt. 24:41; in daily use in every house, and therefore forbidden to be taken in pledge, Deut. 24:6); no *night-light,* so universal in the East that the poorest house has it, burning all night. **candle**—lamp (Job 21:17; 18:6). **11. seventy years**—(Ch. 27:7). The exact number of years of Sabbaths in 490 years, the period from Saul to the Babylonian captivity; righteous retribution for their violation of the Sabbath (Lev. 26:34, 35; II Chron. 36:21). The seventy years probably begin from the fourth year of Jehoiakim, when Jerusalem was first captured, and many captives, as well as the treasures of the temple, were carried away; they end with the first year of Cyrus, who, on taking Babylon, issued an edict for the restoration of the Jews (Ezra 1:1). Daniel's *seventy prophetic weeks* are based on the seventy years of the captivity (cf. Dan. 9:2, 24). **13. all ... written in this book, which Jeremiah ... prophesied against all ... nations**—It follows from this, that the prophecies against foreign nations (chs. 46-51) must have been already written. Hence LXX inserts here those prophecies. But if they had followed immediately (vs. 13), there would have been no propriety in the observation in the verse. The very wording of the reference shows that they existed in some other part of the book, and not in the immediate context. It was in this very year, the fourth of Jehoiakim (ch. 36:1, 2), that Jeremiah was directed to write in a regular *book* for the first time all that he had prophesied against Judah and *foreign* "nations" from the beginning of his ministry. Probably, at a subsequent time, when he completed the whole work, including chs. 46-51, Jeremiah himself inserted the clause, "all that is written in this book, which Jeremiah hath prophesied against all the nations." The prophecies in question may have been repeated, as others in Jeremiah, more than once; so in the original smaller collection they may have stood in an earlier position; and, in the fuller subsequent collection, in their later and present position. **14. serve themselves**—(ch. 27:7; 30:8; 34:10). Avail themselves of their services as slaves. **them also**—the Chaldees, who heretofore have made other nations their slaves, shall *themselves also* in their turn be slaves to them. MAURER translates, "shall impose servitude *on them, even them.*" recompense them—viz., the Chaldees and other nations against whom Jeremiah had prophesied (vs. 13), as having oppressed the Jews. **their deeds**—rather, "deed," viz., their bad treatment of the Jews (ch. 50:29; 51:6, 24; cf. II Chron. 36;17). **15. wine cup** —Cf. ch. 13:12, 13, as to this image, to express *stupefying judgments;* also ch. 49:12; 51:7. Jeremiah often embodies the imagery of Isaiah in his prophecies (Lam. 4:21; Isa. 51:17-22; Rev. 16:19; 18:6). The wine cup was not literally given by Jeremiah to the representatives of the different nations; but only in symbolical vision. **16. be moved** —reel (Nah. 3:11). **18. Jerusalem**—put first: for "judgment begins at the house of God"; they being most guilty whose religious privileges are greatest (I Pet. 4:17). **kings**—Jehoiakim, Jeconiah, and Zedekiah. **as it is this day**—The accomplishment of the curse had already begun under Jehoiakim. This clause, however, may have been inserted by Jeremiah at his final revision of his prophecies in Egypt. **19. Pharaoh**—put next after Jerusalem, because the Jews had relied most on him, and Egypt and Judea stood on a common footing (ch. 46:2, 25). **20. mingled people**—mercenary foreign troops serving under Pharaoh-hophra in the time of Jeremiah. The employment of these foreigners provoked the native Egyptians to overthrow him. Psammetichus, father of Pharaoh-necho, also had given a settlement in Egypt to Ionian and Carian adventurers (HERODOTUS, 2.152, 154). Cf. ch. 50:37; *Note,* Isaiah 19:2, 3; 20:1; Ezekiel 30:5. The term is first found in Exodus 12:38. **Uz**—in the geograph ical order here, between Egypt and the states along the Mediterranean; therefore not the "Uz" of Job 1:1 (north of Arabia Deserta), but the northern part of Arabia Petræa, between the sea and Idumea (Lam. 4:21; see Gen. 36:20, 28). **remnant of Ashdod**—called a "remnant," because Ashdod had lost most of its inhabitants in the twenty-nine years' siege by Psammetichus. Cf. also Isaiah 20:1, *Note.* Gath is not mentioned because it was overthrown in the same war. **21. Edom . . . Moab . . . Ammon** —joined together, as being related to Israel (see ch. 48:49). **22. all the kings of Tyrus**—the petty kings of the various dependencies of Tyre. **isles**—a term including all *maritime regions* (Ps. 72:10). **23. Dedan**—north of Arabia (Gen. 25:3, 4). **Tema . . . Buz**—neighboring tribes north of Arabia (Job 32:2). **all . . . in . . . utmost corners**—rather, "having the hair cut in angles," a heathenish custom (see *Note,* ch. 9:26). **24. mingled people**—not in the same sense as in vs. 20; the "motley crowd," so called in contempt (cf. ch. 49:28, 31; 50:37). By a different pointing it may be translated the "Arabs;" but the repetition of the name is not likely. BLANEY thinks there were two divisions of what we call Arabia, the west *(Araba)* and the east. The west included Arabia Petræa and the parts on the sea bordering on Egypt, the land of Cush; the east, Arabia Felix and Deserta. The latter are "the mixed race" inhabiting the desert. **25. Zimri**—perhaps the *Zabra* mentioned by PTOLEMY between Mecca and Medina. *Zimran* also, as Dedan, was one of Abraham's sons by Keturah (Gen. 25:2). **Elam**—properly, west of Persia; but used for Persia in general. **26. Sheshach**—Babylon; as the parallelism in ch. 51:41 proves. In the Cabalistic system (called *Athbash,* the first *Hebrew* letter in the alphabet being expressed by the last) *Sheshach* would exactly answer to *Babel.* Jeremiah *may* have used this system (as perhaps in ch. 51:41) for concealment at the time of this prediction, in the fourth year of Jehoiakim, while Nebuchadnezzar was before Jerusalem. In

ch. 51:41 there can be no concealment, as Babylon is expressly mentioned. MICHAELIS more simply explains the term "brazen-gated" (cf. Isa. 45:2); others, "the house of a prince." Rather, it comes from the Babylonian goddess, *Shach,* by reduplication of the first letter; from her *Misael* was named *Meshach* by the Babylonians. The term *Shace* was applied to a festival at Babylon, alluded to in ch. 51:39, 57; Isaiah 21:5. It was during this feast that Cyrus took Babylon (HERODOTUS, 1). Thus Jeremiah mystically denotes the time of its capture by this term [GLASSIUS]. **27. rise no more**—The heathen nations in question should fall to rise no more. The Jews should fall but for a time, and then rise again. Therefore, the epithet is given, "the God *of Israel.*" **28. if they refuse to take the cup**—No effort of theirs to escape destruction will avail. **29.** If I spared not Mine elect people on account of sin, much less will I spare you (Ezek. 9:6; Obad. 16; Luke 23:31; I Pet. 4:17). **be unpunished**—"be treated as innocent." **30. roar**—image from a destructive lion (Isa. 42:13; Joel 3:16). **upon his habitation**—rather, "His pasturage"; keeping up the image of a lion roaring against the flock in the pasture. The roar was first to go forth over Judea wherein were "the sheep of His pasture" (Ps. 100:3), and thence into heathen lands. **shout . . . tread . . . grapes**—(ch. 48:33; Isa. 16:9, 10). **31. controversy** —cause at issue (Mic. 6:2). **plead with all flesh**— (Isa. 66:16). God shows the whole world that He does what is altogether just in punishing. **32. from the coasts**—rather, "from the uttermost regions." Like a storm which arises in one region and then diffuses itself far and wide, so God's judgments shall pass "from nation to nation," till all has been fulfilled; no distance shall prevent the fulfilment. **33. not be lamented**—(ch. 16:4, 6). **neither gathered**— to their fathers, in their ancestral tombs (ch. 8:2). **dung**—(Ps. 83:10). **34. shepherds**—princes (ch. 22: 22). Here he returns to *the Jews* and their rulers, using the same image as in vs. 30, "pasture" (see *Note).* **wallow yourselves**—Cover yourselves as thickly with ashes, in token of sorrow, as one who rolls in them (ch. 6:26; Ezek. 27:30) [MAURER]. **principal**—leaders. LXX translates "rams," carrying out the image (cf. Isa. 14:9, *Margin;* Zech. 10:3). **days of your slaughter . . . of . . . dispersions**— rather, "your days *for* slaughter (i.e., the time of your being slain), and your dispersions (not '*of* your dispersions'), are accomplished" (are come). **pleasant vessel**—Ye were once a *precious vessel,* but ye shall *fall,* and so be a *broken vessel* (cf. ch. 22:28, *Note).* "Your past excellency shall not render you safe now. I will turn to your ignominy whatever glory I conferred on you" [CALVIN]. **35.** Lit., "Flight shall fail the shepherds . . . , escaping (shall fail) the principal . . ." (Amos 2:14). The leaders will be the first objects for slaughter; escape by flight will be out of their power. **37. habitations**—rather, carrying out the image "pastures" (vs. 30, *Note).* The pasturages where, *peaceably* and without incursion of wild beasts, the flocks have fed, shall be destroyed; i.e., the regions where, heretofore, there was *peace* and security (alluding to the name *Salem,* or Jerusalem, "possessing *peace*"). **38. his covert**—the temple, where heretofore, like a lion, as its defender, by the mere terror of His voice He warded off the foe; but now He leaves it a prey to the Gentiles [CALVIN]. **fierceness of . . . oppressor**—rather, as the *Hebrew,* for "oppressor" is an adjective *feminine,* the word *sword* is understood, which, in ch. 46:16; 50:16, is expressed (indeed, some MSS. and LXX read "sword" instead of "fierceness" here; probably interpolated from ch. 46:16), "*the oppressing* sword." The *Hebrew* for "oppressing" means also a "dove": there may be, therefore, a covert allusion to the Chaldean standard bearing a dove on it, in honor of Semiramis, the first queen, said in popular superstition to have been nourished by doves when exposed at birth, and at death to have been transformed into a dove. Her name may come from a root referring to the *cooing* of a dove. That bird was held sacred to the goddess Venus. *Vulgate* so translates "the anger of *the dove.*" his . . . anger— If the anger of Nebuchadnezzar cannot be evaded, how much less that of God (cf. vs. 37)!

CHAPTER 26

Vss. 1-24. Jeremiah Declared Worthy of Death, but by the Interposition of Ahikam Saved; the Similar Cases of Micah and Urijah Being Adduced in the Prophet's Favor. The prophecies which gave the offense were those given in detail in chs. 7, 8, 9 (cf. vs. 6 here with ch. 7:12, 14); and summarily referred to here [Maurer], probably pronounced at one of the great feasts (that of tabernacles, according to Ussher; for the inhabitants of "all the cities of Judah" are represented as present, vs. 2). See *Note*, ch. 7:1. 2. in the court—the largest court, from which he could be heard by the whole people come to worship—*Worship* is vain without *obedience* (I Sam. 15:21, 22). all the words —(Ezek. 3:10). diminish not a word—(Deut. 4:2; 12:32; Prov. 30:6; Acts 20:27; I Cor. 2:17; 4:2; Rev. 22:19). Not suppressing or softening aught for fear of giving offense; nor setting forth coldly and indirectly what can only by forcible statement do good. 3. If so be—expressed according to human conceptions; not as if God did not foreknow all contingencies, but to mark the obstinacy of the people and the difficulty of healing them; and to show His own goodness in making the offer which left them without excuse [Calvin]. 5. prophets— the inspired interpreters of the *law* (vs. 4), who adapted it to the use of the people. 6. like Shiloh —(*Note*, ch. 7:12, 14; 1 Sam. 4:10-12; Ps. 78:60). curse—(ch. 24:9; Isa. 65:15). 8. priests—The captain (or prefect) of the temple had the power of apprehending offenders in the temple with the sanction of the priests. prophets—the false prophets. The charge against Jeremiah was that of uttering falsehood in Jehovah's name, an act punishable with death (Deut. 18:20). His prophecy against the temple and city (vs. 11) might speciously be represented as contradicting God's own words (Ps. 132:14). Cf. the similar charge against Stephen (Acts 6:13, 14). 10. princes—members of the Council of State or Great Council, which took cognizance of such offenses. heard—the clamor of the popular tumult. came up—from the king's house to the temple, which stood higher than the palace. sat—as judges, in the gate, the usual place of trying such cases. new gate—originally built by Jotham (II Kings 15:35, "the higher gate") and now recently restored. 12. Lord sent me—a valid justification against any laws alleged against him. against . . . against—rather, "concerning." Jeremiah purposely avoids saying, "against," which would needlessly irritate. They had used the same *Hebrew* word (vs. 11), which ought to be translated "concerning," though they meant it in the unfavorable sense. Jeremiah takes up their word in a better sense, implying that there is still room for repentance: that his prophecies aim at the real good of the city; *for* or

concerning this house . . . city [Grotius]. 13. (Vss. 3, 19.) 14. Jeremiah's humility is herein shown, and submission to the powers that be (Rom. 13:1). 15. bring . . . upon yourselves—So far will you be from escaping the predicted evils by shedding my blood, that you will, by that very act, only incur heavier penalties (Matt. 23:35). 16. princes . . . all the people—The fickle people, as they were previously influenced by the priests to clamor for his death (vs. 8), so now under the princes' influence require that he shall not be put to death. Cf. as to Jesus, Jeremiah's antitype, the hosannas of the multitude a few days before the same people, persuaded by the priests as in this case, cried, Away with Him, crucify Him (Matt. 21 and 27:20-25). The priests, through envy of his holy zeal, were more his enemies than the princes, whose office was more secular than religious. A prophet could not legally be put to death unless he prophesied *in the name of other gods* (therefore, they say, "in the name of the Lord"), or after his prophecy had failed in its accomplishment. Meanwhile, if he foretold calamity, he might be imprisoned. Cf. Micaiah's case (I Kings 22:1-28). 17. Cf. Gamaliel's interposition (Acts 5:34, etc.). elders—some of the "princes" mentioned (vs. 16) those whose age, as well as dignity, would give weight to the precedents of past times which they adduce. 18. (Mic. 3:12.) Morasthite—called so from a village of the tribe Judah. Hezekiah—The precedent in the reign of such a good king proved that Jeremiah was not the only prophet, or the first, who threatened the city and the temple without incurring death. mountain of the house—Moriah, on which stood the temple (peculiarly called "*the house*") shall be covered with woods instead of buildings. Jeremiah, in quoting previous prophecies, never does so without alteration; he adapts the language to his own style, showing thereby his authority in his treatment of Scripture, as being himself inspired. 19. Hezekiah, so far from killing him, was led "to fear the Lord," and pray for remission of the sentence against Judah (II Chron. 32:26). Lord repented—(Exod. 32:14; II Sam. 24:16). Thus —if we kill Jeremiah. 20. As the flight and capture of Urijah must have occupied some time, "the beginning of the reign of Jehoiakim" (vs. 1) must not mean the *very* beginning, but the second or third year of his eleven years' reign. And . . . also—perhaps connected with vs. 24, as the comment of the writer, not the continuation of the speech of the elders: "And although *also* a man that prophesied . . . Urijah . . . (proving how great was the danger in which Jeremiah stood, and how wonderful the providence of God in preserving him), *nevertheless* the hand of Ahikam . . ." [Glassius]. The context, however, implies rather that the words are the continuation of the previous speech of the elders. They adduce another instance besides that of Micah, though of a different kind, viz., that of Urijah: he suffered for his prophecies, but they *imply*, though they do not venture to *express* it, that thereby sin has been added to sin, and that it has done no good to Jehoiakim, for that the notorious condition of the state at this time shows that a heavier vengeance is impending if they persevere in such acts of violence [Calvin]. 22. Jehoiakim sent . . . into Egypt—He had been put on the throne by Pharaoh of Egypt (II Kings 23:34). This explains the readiness with which he got the Egyptians to give up Urijah to him, when that prophet had sought an asylum in Egypt. Urijah was faithful in delivering his message, but faulty in leaving his work, so God permitted him to lose his life, while Jeremiah was protected in danger. The path of duty is often the path of safety. **23. graves of the common people**—lit., "sons of the people" (cf. II Kings 23:6). The prophets seem to have had a separate cemetery (Matt. 23:29). Urijah's corpse was denied this honor, in order that he should not be regarded as a true prophet. **24. Ahikan**—son of Shaphan the scribe, or royal secretary. He was one of those whom King Josiah, when struck by the words of the book of the law, sent to inquire of the Lord (II Kings 22:12, 14). Hence his interference here in behalf of Jeremiah is what we should expect from his past association with that good king. His son, Gedaliah, followed in his father's steps, so that he was chosen by the Babylonians as the one to whom they committed Jeremiah for safety after taking Jerusalem, and on whose loyalty they could depend in setting him over the remnant of the people in Judea (ch. 39:14; II Kings 25:22). **people to put him to death**—Princes often, when they want to destroy a good man, prefer it to be done by a popular tumult rather than by their own order, so as to reap the fruit of the crime without odium to themselves (Matt. 27:20).

CHAPTER 27

Vss. 1-22. THE FUTILITY OF RESISTING NEBUCHADNEZZAR ILLUSTRATED TO THE AMBASSADORS OF THE KING, DESIRING TO HAVE THE KING OF JUDAH CONFEDERATE WITH THEM, UNDER THE TYPE OF YOKES. JEREMIAH EXHORTS THEM AND ZEDEKIAH TO YIELD. **1. Jehoiakim**—The prophecy that follows was according to this reading given in the fourth year of Jehoiakim, fifteen years before it was published in the reign of Zedekiah to whom it refers; it was thus long deposited in the prophet's bosom, in order that by it he might be supported under trials in his prophetic career in the interim [CALVIN]. But "Zedekiah" *may be* the true reading. So the *Syriac* and *Arabic Versions*. Vss. 3, 12; ch. 28:1, confirm this; also, one of KENNICOTT'S MSS. The *English Version* reading *may* have originated from the first verse of ch. 26. "Son of Josiah" applies to Zedekiah as truly as to "Jehoiakim" or "Eliakim." The *fourth year* may, in a general sense here, as in ch. 28:1, be called "the beginning of his reign," as it lasted eleven years (II Kings 24:18). It was not long after the fourth year of his reign that he rebelled against Nebuchadnezzar (ch. 51:59; 52:3; II Kings 24:20), in violation of an oath before God (II Chron. 36:13). **2. bonds**—by which the yoke is made fast to the neck (ch. 5:5). **yokes**—lit., the carved piece of wood attached at both ends to the two yokes on the necks of a pair of oxen, so as to connect them. Here the *yoke* itself. The *plural* is used, as he was to wear one himself, and give the others to the ambassadors; (vs. 3; ch. 28:10, 12) proves that the symbolical act was in this instance (though not in others, ch. 25:15) actually done (cf. Isa. 20:2, etc.; Ezek. 12:3, 11, 18). **3.** Appropriate symbol, as these ambassadors had come to Jerusalem to consult as to shaking off the yoke of Nebuchadnezzar. According to Pherecydes in Clemens Alexandrinus, *Stromateis*, 567, Idanthura, king of the Scythians, intimated to Darius, who had crossed the Danube, that he would lead an army against him, by sending him, instead of a letter, *a mouse, a frog, a bird, an arrow,* and *a plough*. The task assigned to Jeremiah required great faith, as it was sure to provoke alike his own countrymen and the foreign ambassadors, and their kings, by a seeming insult, at the very time that all were full of confident hopes

grounded on the confederacy. **5.** God here, as elsewhere, connects with the symbol doctrine, which is as it were its soul, without which it would be not only cold and frivolous, but even dead [CALVIN]. God's mention of His supreme power is in order to refute the pride of those who rely on their own power (Isa. 45:12). **given it unto whom it seemed meet unto me**—(Ps. 115:15, 16; Dan. 4:17, 25, 32). Not for his merits, but of My own sole good pleasure [ESTIUS]. **6. beasts of the field**—not merely the horses to carry his Chaldean soldiers, and oxen to draw his provisions [GROTIUS]; not merely the deserts, mountains, and woods, the haunts of wild beasts, implying his unlimited extent of empire [ESTIUS]; but the beasts themselves by a mysterious instinct of nature. A reproof to men that they did not recognize God's will, which the very beasts acknowledged (cf. Isa. 1:3). As the beasts are to submit to Christ, the Restorer of the dominion over nature, lost by the first Adam (cf. Gen. 1:28; 2:19, 20; Ps. 8:6-8), so they were appointed to submit to Nebuchadnezzar, the representative of the world power and prefigurer of Antichrist; this universal power was suffered to be held by him to show the unfitness of any to wield it "until He come whose right it is" (Ezek. 21:27). **7. son . . . son's son**—(II Chron. 36:20). Nebuchadnezzar had *four* successors—Evil-merodach, his *son;* Neriglissar, husband of Nebuchadnezzar's daughter; his son, Labosodarchod; and Naboned (with whom his son, Belshazzar, was joint king), *son* of Evil-merodach. But Neriglissar and Labosodarchod were not in the *direct male line;* so that the prophecy held good to "his son and his son's son," and the intermediate two are omitted. **time of his land**—i.e., of its subjugation or its being "visited" in wrath (vs. 22; ch. 25:12; 29:10; 50:27; Dan. 5:26). **serve themselves of him**—make him their servant (ch. 25:14; Isa. 13:22). So "his day" for the destined day of his calamity (Job 18:20). **8. until I have consumed them by his hand**—until by these consuming visitations I have brought them under his power. **9. ye**—the Jews especially, for whom the address to the rest was intended. **enchanters**—augurs [CALVIN], from a root, the "eyes," i.e., lookers at the stars and other means of taking omens of futurity; or another root, a "fixed time," observers of times: forbidden in the law (Lev. 19:26; Deut. 18:10, 11, 14). **10. to remove you**—expressing the *event* which would result. The very thing they profess by their enchantments to avert, they are by them bringing on you. Better to submit to Nebuchadnezzar, and remain in your land, than to rebel, and be removed from it. **11. serve . . . till it**—The same *Hebrew* root expresses "serve" and "till," or "cultivate." *Serve* ye the king of Babylon, and the land will *serve* you [CALVIN]. **12. I spake also**—translate, "And I spake. . . ." Special application of the subject to Zedekiah. **13. Why . . . die**—by running on your own ruin in resisting Nebuchadnezzar after this warning (Ezek. 18:31). **14. lie**—(Ch. 14:14.) **15. in my name**—The devil often makes *God's name* the plea for lies (Matt. 4:6; 7:22, 23; vss. 15-20, the test whereby to know false prophets). **16.** The "vessels" had been carried away to Babylon in the reign of Jeconiah (II Kings 24:13); also previously in that of Jehoiakim (II Chron. 36:5-7). **18. at Jerusalem**—i.e., in other houses containing such vessels, besides the house of God and the king's palace. Nebuzaradan, captain of the guard under Nebuchadnezzar, carried all away (II Kings 25:13-17; II Chron. 36:18). The more costly vessels had been previously removed in the reigns of Jehoiakim and Jeconiah. **19.** (Ch. 52:

17, 20, 21.) **22. until . . . I visit them**—in wrath by Cyrus (ch. 32:5). In seventy years from the first carrying away of captives in Jehoiachin's reign (ch. 29:10; II Chron. 36:21). **restore them**—by the hand of Cyrus (Ezra 1:7). By Artaxerxes (Ezra 7:19).

CHAPTER 28

Vss. 1-17. Prophecies Immediately Following Those in Chapter 27. Hananiah Breaks the Yokes to Signify that Nebuchadnezzar's Yoke Shall Be Broken. Jeremiah Foretells that Yokes of Iron Are to Succeed Those of Wood, and that Hananiah Shall Die. **1. in the beginning of the reign of Zedekiah**—The Jews often divided any period into two halves, *the beginning* and *the end.* As Zedekiah reigned eleven years, the fourth year would be called the *beginning* of his reign, especially as during the first three years affairs were in such a disturbed state that he had little power or dignity, being a tributary; but in the fourth year he became strong in power. **Hananiah** —Another of this name was one of the three godly youths who braved Nebuchadnezzar's wrath in the fear of God (Dan. 1:6, 7; 3:12). Probably a near relation, for *Azariah* is associated with him; as *Azur* with the Hananiah here. The godly and ungodly are often in the same family (Ezek. 18:14-20). **Gibeon**—one of the cities of the priests, to which order he must have belonged. **2. broken the yoke** —*I have determined to break:* referring to Jeremiah's prophecy (ch. 27:12). **3. two full years**—lit., "years of days." So "a month of days," i.e., all its days complete (Gen. 29:14, *Margin;* 41:1). It was marvellous presumption to speak so definitely without having any divine revelation. **4. bring again—Jeconiah**—not *necessarily* implying that Hananiah wished Zedekiah to be superseded by Jeconiah. The main point intended was that the restoration from Babylon should be complete. But, doubtless, the false prophet foretold Jeconiah's return (II Kings 24:12-15), to ingratiate himself with the populace, with whom Jeconiah was a favorite (ch. 22:24, *Note*). **5. the prophet Jeremiah**—the epithet, "the prophet," is prefixed to "Jeremiah" throughout this chapter, to correspond to the same epithet before "Hananiah"; except in vs. 12, where *"the prophet"* has been inserted in *English Version.* The rival claims of the true and the false prophet are thus put in the more prominent contrast. **6. Amen**—Jeremiah prays *for* the people, though constrained to prophesy against them (I Kings 1:36). The *event* was the appointed test between contradictory predictions (Deut. 18:21, 22). "Would that what you say were true!" I prefer the safety of my country even to my own estimation. The prophets had no pleasure in announcing God's judgment, but did so as a matter of stern duty, not thereby divesting themselves of their natural feelings of sorrow for their country's woe. Cf. Exodus 32:32; Romans 9:3, as instances of how God's servants, intent only on the glory of God and the salvation of the country, forgot self and uttered wishes in a state of feeling transported out of themselves. So Jeremiah wished not to diminish aught from the word of God, though as a Jew he uttered the wish for his people [Calvin]. **8. prophets . . . before me**—Hosea, Joel, Amos, and others. **evil**—a few MSS. read *famine,* which is more usually associated with the specification of *war* and *pestilence* (ch. 15:2; 18:21; 27:8, 13). But *evil* here includes *all* the calamities flowing from *war,* not merely *famine,* but also *desolation,*

etc. *Evil,* being the more difficult reading, is less likely to be the interpolated one than *famine,* which probably originated in copying the parallel passages. **9. peace**—Hananiah had given no warning as to the need of conversion, but had foretold *prosperity* unconditionally. Jeremiah does not say that all are true prophets who foretell truths in any instance (which Deut. 13:1, 2, disproves); but asserts only the converse, viz., that whoever, as Hananiah, predicts what the event does not confirm, is a false prophet. There are two tests of prophets: (1) The event, Deuteronomy 18:22. (2) The word of God, Isaiah 8:20. **10. the yoke**—(ch. 27:2). Impious audacity to break what God had appointed as a solemn pledge of the fulfilment of His word. Hence Jeremiah deigns no reply (vs. 11; Matt. 7:6). **11. neck of all nations**—opposed to ch. 27:7. **13. Thou hast broken . . . wood . . . thou shalt make . . . iron**—Not here, "*Thou* hast broken . . . wood," and "*I* will make . . . iron" (cf. vs. 16). The same false prophets who, by urging the Jews to rebel, had caused them to throw off the then comparatively *easy* yoke of Babylon, thereby brought on them a *more severe* yoke imposed by that city. "Yokes of iron," alluding to Deuteronomy 28:48. It is better to take up a light cross in our way, than to pull a heavier on our own heads. We may escape destroying providences by submitting to humbling providences. So, spiritually, contrast the "easy yoke" of Christ with the "yoke of bondage" of the law (Acts 15:10; Gal. 5:1). **14. I have put**—Though Hananiah and those like him were secondary instruments in bringing the iron yoke on Judea, *God* was the great First Cause (ch. 27:4-7). **15. makest . . . trust in a lie**—(ch. 29:31; Ezek. 13:22.) **16. this year . . . die**—The prediction was uttered in the *fifth* month (vs. 1); Hananiah's death took place in the *seventh* month, i.e., within *two months* after the prediction, answering with awful significance to the *two years* in which Hananiah had foretold that the yoke imposed by Babylon would end. **rebellion**— opposition to God's plain direction, that all should submit to Babylon (ch. 29:32).

CHAPTER 29

Vss. 1-32. Letter of Jeremiah to the Captives in Babylon, to Counteract the Assurances Given by the False Prophets of a Speedy Restoration. **1. residue of the elders**—those still surviving from the time when they were carried to Babylon with Jeconiah; the other elders of the captives had died by either a natural or a violent death. **2. queen**— Nehushta, the queen mother, daughter of Elnathan (II Kings 24:8, 15). (Elnathan, her father, is perhaps the same as the one mentioned in ch. 26:22.) She reigned jointly with her son. **princes**—All the men of authority were taken away lest they should organize a rebellion. Jeremiah wrote his letter while the calamity was still recent, to console the captives under it. **3. Zedekiah . . . sent unto Babylon**—In ch. 51:59, Zedekiah himself goes to Babylon; *here* he *sends* ambassadors. Whatever was the object of the embassy, it shows that Zedekiah only reigned at the pleasure of the king of Babylon, who might have restored Jeconiah, had he pleased. Hence, Zedekiah permitted Jeremiah's letter to be sent, not only as being led by Hananiah's death to attach greater credit to the prophet's words, but also as the letter accorded with his own wish that the Jews should remain in Chaldea till Jeconiah's death. **Hilkiah**—the high priest who found the book of the law in the house of the Lord, and showed it to "Shaphan" the scribe (the same Shaphan probably as here), who showed it to King Josiah (II Kings 22: 8, etc.). The sons of Hilkiah and Shaphan inherited from their fathers some respect for sacred things. So in ch. 36: 25, "Gemariah" interceded with King Jehoiakim that the prophet's roll should not be burned. **5. Build . . . houses**—In opposition to the false prophets' suggestions, who told the captives that their captivity would soon cease, Jeremiah tells them that it will be of long duration, and that therefore they should build houses, as Babylon is to be for long their home. **6. that ye . . . be . . . not diminished**—It was God's will that the seed of Abraham should not fail; thus consolation is given them, and the hope, though not of an immediate, yet of an ultimate, return. **7.** (Ezra 6:10; Rom. 13:1; I. Tim. 2:2.) Not only bear the Babylonian yoke patiently, but *pray for* your masters, i.e., while the captivity lasts. God's good time was to come when they were to pray for Babylon's downfall (ch. 51:35; Ps. 137:8). They were not to forestall that time. True religion teaches patient submission, not sedition, even though the prince be an unbeliever. In all states of life let us not throw away the comfort we *may* have, because we have not all we *would* have. There is here a foretaste of gospel love towards enemies (Matt. 5:44). **8. your dreams which ye caused to be dreamed**—The Latin adage says, "The people wish to be deceived, so let them be deceived." Not mere credulity misleads men, but their own perverse "love of darkness rather than light." It was not priests who originated priest-craft, but the people's own morbid appetite to be deceived; e.g., Aaron and the golden calf (Exod. 32: 1-4). So the Jews *caused* or *made* the prophets to tell them encouraging dreams (ch. 23:25, 26; Eccles. 5:7; Zech. 10:2; John 3:19-21). **10.** (*Note,* ch. 25: 11, 12; Dan. 9:2.) This proves that the seventy years date from Jeconiah's captivity, not from the last captivity. The specification of time was to curb the impatience of the Jews lest they should hasten before God's time. **good word**—promise of a return. **11. I know**—*I* alone; not the false prophets who *know* nothing of My purposes, though they pretend to know. **thoughts . . . I think**—(Isa. 55:9.) Glancing at the Jews who had no "thoughts of peace," but only of "evil" (misfortune), because *they* could not conceive how deliverance could come to them. The moral malady of man is twofold—at one time *vain confidence;* then, when that is disappointed, *despair.* So the Jews first laughed at God's threats, confident that they should speedily return; then, when cast down from that confidence, they sank in inconsolable despondency. **expected end**—lit., "end and expectation," i.e., an end, and that such an end as you wish for. Two nouns joined by "and," standing for a noun and adjective. So in ch. 36:27, "the roll and the words," i.e., the roll of words; Genesis 3:16, "sorrow and conception," i.e., sorrow in conception. Cf. Proverbs 23: 18, where, as here "end" means "a happy issue." **12. Fulfilled** (Daniel 9:3, etc.). When God designs mercy, He puts it into the hearts of His people to pray for the mercy designed. When such a spirit of prayer is poured out, it is a sure sign of coming mercy. **go**—to the temple and other places of prayer: contrasted with their previous sloth as to going to seek God. **13.** (Lev. 26:40-42, 44, 45.) **14. to be found**—(Ps. 32:6; Isa. 55:6). **turn . . . captivity**—play upon sounds, *shabti . . . shebith.* **15. Because**—referring not to the preceding words, but to vss. 10, 11, "Jehovah saith this to you" (i.e., the prophe-

cy of the continuance of the captivity seventy years), "because ye have said, The Lord hath raised us up prophets in Babylon," viz., foretelling our *speedy* deliverance (this their prophecy is *supposed,* not *expressed;* accordingly, vss. 16-19 contradict this false hope again, vss. 8, 9, 21). He, in this 15th verse, turns his address from the godly (vss. 12-14) to the ungodly listeners, to false prophets. **16. people . . . in this city . . . not gone forth**—So far from your returning to Jerusalem soon, even *your brethren* still left dwelling there shall themselves also be cast into exile. He mentions "the throne of *David,*" lest they should think that, because David's kingdom was to be perpetual, no severe, though temporary, chastisements could interpose (Ps. 89:29-36). **17. vile figs**—*Hebrew,* "horrible," or nauseous, from a root, "to regard with loathing" (see ch. 24:8, 10). **18. removed to all . . . kingdoms**—(ch. 15:4; Deut. 28:25). **curse . . .**—(ch. 29:6; 18:16; 19:8). **21. Zedekiah**—brother of Zephaniah (vs. 25), both being sons of Maaseiah; probably of the same family as the false prophet under Ahab in Israel (I Kings 22: 11, 24). **22. shall be taken . . . a curse**—i.e., a formula of imprecation. **Lord make thee like Zedekiah**—(Cf. Gen. 48:20; Isa. 65:15). **roasted in the fire**—a Chaldean punishment (Dan. 3:6). **23. villainy**—lit., "sinful folly" (Isa. 32:6). **24-32.** A second communication which Jeremiah sent to Babylon, after the messenger who carried his first letter had brought a letter from the false prophet Shemaiah to Zephaniah, etc., condemning Jeremiah and reproving the authorities for not having apprehended him. **Nehelamite**—a name derived either from his father or from a place: alluding at the same time to the *Hebrew* meaning, "a dreamer" (cf. vs. 8). **25. in thy name**—without sanction of "the Lord of hosts, the God of Israel," which words stand in antithesis to "thy name" (John 5:43). **Zephaniah**—the second priest, or substitute (*Sagan*) of the high priest. He was one of those sent to consult Jeremiah by Zedekiah (ch. 21:1). Slain by Nebuchadnezzar at the capture of Jerusalem (II Kings 25:18-21). Zephaniah was in particular addressed, as being likely to take up against Jeremiah the prophet's prediction against his brother Zedekiah at Babylon (vs. 21). Zephaniah was to read it to the *priests,* and in the presence of *all the people,* in the temple. **26. thee . . . in the stead of Jehoiada**—Zephaniah's promotion as second priest, owing to Jehoiada's being then in exile, was unexpected. Shemaiah thus accuses him of ingratitude towards God, who had so highly exalted him before his regular time. **ye should be officers . . . for every man**—Ye should, as bearing rule in the temple (ch. 20:1, *Note*), apprehend every false prophet like Jeremiah. **mad**—Inspired prophets were often so called by the ungodly (II Kings 9:11; Acts 26:24; 2:13, 15, 17, 18). Jeremiah is in this a type of Christ, against whom the same charge was brought (John 10:20). **prison**—rather, "the stocks" (ch. 20:2, *Note*). **stocks**—from a root, "to confine"; hence rather, a narrow dungeon. According to Deuteronomy 17:8, 9, the priest was judge in such cases, but had no right to put into the stocks; this right he had assumed to himself in the troubled state of the times. **27. of Anathoth**—said contemptuously, as "Jesus *of Nazareth.*" **maketh himself**—as if *God* had not made him one, but he *himself* had done so. **28.** Referring to Jeremiah's first letter to Babylon (vs. 5). **29. Zephaniah . . . read . . . in the ears of Jeremiah**—He seems to have been less prejudiced against Jeremiah than the others; hence he reads the charge to the prophet, that he should not be condemned without a hearing. This accords with Shemaiah's imputation against Zephaniah for want of zeal against Jeremiah (vss. 26, 27). Hence the latter was chosen by King Zedekiah as one of the deputation to Jeremiah (ch. 21:1; 37:3). **30.** This resumes the thread of the sentence which began at vs. 25, but was left there not completed. Here, in vs. 30, it is completed, not however in continuity, but by a new period. The same construction occurs in Romans 5:12-15. **32. not . . . a man to dwell**–(Deut. 28:18). **not . . . behold the good**–As he despised the lawful time and wished to return before the time God had expressly announced, in just retribution he should not share in the restoration from Babylon at all. **rebellion**–going against God's revealed will as to the time (ch. 28:16).

CHAPTER 30

Vss. 1-24. RESTORATION OF THE JEWS FROM BABYLON AFTER ITS CAPTURE, AND RAISING UP OF MESSIAH. **2. Write . . . in a book**–After the destruction of Jerusalem Jeremiah is not ordered as heretofore to *speak*, but to *write* the succeeding prophecy (vs. 4, etc.), so as thereby it might be read by his countrymen wheresoever they might be in their dispersion. **3. bring again . . . captivity of . . . Israel and Judah**–the restoration not merely of the *Jews* (treated of in this ch. 30), but also of the ten tribes ("Israel"; treated in ch. 31), together forming the whole nation (vs. 18; ch. 32:44; Ezek. 39:25; Amos 9:14, 15). "Israel" is mentioned first because its exile was longer than that of Judah. *Some* captives of the Israelite ten tribes returned with those of Judah (Luke 2:36; "Aser" is mentioned). But these are only a pledge of the *full* restoration hereafter (Rom. 11:26, "*All* Israel"). Cf. ch. 16:15. This third verse is a brief statement of the subject before the prophecy itself is given. **5. We have heard . . . trembling**–God introduces the Jews speaking that which they will be reduced to at last in spite of their stubbornness. Threat and promise are combined: the former briefly; viz., the misery of the Jews in the Babylonian captivity down to their "trembling" and "fear" arising from the approach of the Medo-Persian army of Cyrus against Babylon; the promise is more fully dwelt on; viz., their "trembling" will issue in a deliverance as speedy as is the transition from a woman's labor-pangs to her joy at giving birth to a child (vs. 6). **6. Ask**–Consult all the authorities, men or books, you can, you will not find an instance. Yet in that coming day men will be seen with their hands pressed on their loins, as women do to repress their pangs. God will drive men through pain to gestures more fitting a woman than a man (ch. 4:31; 6:24). The metaphor is often used to express the previous pain followed by the sudden deliverance of Israel, as in the case of a woman in childbirth (Isa. 66:7-9). **paleness**–properly the color of herbs blasted and fading: the *green paleness* of one in jaundice: the *sickly paleness* of terror. **7. great**–marked by great calamities (Joel 2:11, 31; Amos 5:18; Zeph. 1:14). **none like it . . . but he shall be saved**–(Dan. 12:1). The partial deliverance at Babylon's downfall prefigures the final, complete deliverance of Israel, literal and spiritual, at the downfall of the mystical Babylon (Rev. 18, 19). **8. his yoke . . . thy neck**–his, i.e., Jacob's (vs. 7), the yoke imposed *on him*. The transition to the second person is frequent, God speaking *of* Jacob or Israel, at the same time addressing him directly. So "him" rightly follows; "foreigners

shall no more make him their servant" (ch. 25:14). After the deliverance by Cyrus, Persia, Alexander, Antiochus, and Rome made Judah their servant. The full of deliverance meant must, therefore, be still future. **9.** Instead of *serving strangers* (vs. 8), they shall serve the Lord, their rightful King in the theocracy (Ezek. 21:27). **David, their king**–No *king* of David's seed has held the scepter since the captivity; for Zerubbabel, though of David's line, never claimed the title of "king." The *Son of David*, Messiah, must therefore be meant; so the *Targum* (cf. Isa. 55:3, 4; Ezek. 34:23, 24; 37:24; Hos. 3:5; Rom. 11:25-32). He was appointed to the throne of David (Isa. 9:7; Luke 1:32). He is here joined with Jehovah as claiming equal allegiance. God is our "King," only when we are subject to Christ; God rules us not immediately, but through His Son (John 5:22, 23, 27). **raise up**–applied to the judges whom God *raised up* as *deliverers* of Israel out of the hand of its oppressors (Judg. 2:16; 3: 9). So Christ was *raised up* as the antitypical Deliverer (Ps. 2:6; Luke 1:69; Acts 2:30; 13:23). **10. from afar**–Be not afraid as if the distance of the places whither ye are to be dispersed precludes the possibility of return. **seed**–Though through the many years of captivity intervening, you yourselves may not see the restoration, the promise shall be fulfilled to your *seed*, primarily at the return from Babylon, fully at the final restoration. **quiet . . . none . . . make . . . afraid**–(ch. 23:6; Zech. 14:11). **11. though . . . full end of all nations . . . yet . . . not . . . of thee**–(Amos 9:8). The punishment of reprobates is final and fatal; that of God's people temporary and corrective. Babylon was utterly destroyed: Israel after chastisement was delivered. **in measure**–lit., "with judgment," i.e., moderation, not in the full rigor of justice (ch. 10:24; 46:28; Ps. 6:1; Isa. 27:8). **not . . . altogether unpunished**–(Exod. 34:7). **12.** The desperate circumstances of the Jews are here represented as an incurable wound. Their sin is so grievous that their hope of the punishment (their exile) soon coming to an end is vain (ch. 8:22; 15:18; II Chron. 36:16). **13. none to plead**–a new image from a court of justice. **bound up**–viz., with the *bandages* applied to tie up a wound. **no healing medicines**–lit., "medicines of healing," or else applications, (lit., ascensions) of medicaments. **14. lovers**–the peoples formerly allied to thee, Assyria and Egypt (cf. Lam. 1:2). **seek thee not**–have cast away all concern for thee in thy distress. **wound of an enemy**–a wound such as an enemy would inflict. God condescends to employ language adapted to human conceptions. He is incapable of "enmity" or "cruelty"; it was their grievous sin which righteously demanded a grievous punishment, *as though* He were an "enemy" (ch. 5: 6; Job 13:24; 30:21). **15. Why criest thou**–as if God's severity was excessive. Thou hast no reason to complain, for thine affliction is just. Thy cry is too late, for the time of repentance and mercy is past [CALVIN]. **16. Therefore**–connected with vs. 13, because "There is none to plead thy cause . . . *therefore*" I will plead thy cause, and heal thy wound, by overwhelming thy foes. Verse 15 is inserted to amplify what was said at the close of vs. 14. When the false ways of peace, suggested by the so-called prophets, had only ended in the people's irremediable ruin, the true prophet comes forward to announce the grace of God as bestowing repentance and healing. **devour thee . . . be devoured . . . spoil . . . be a spoil . . . prey upon . . . give for a prey**–retribution in kind (cf. *Note*, ch. 2:3; Exod. 23:22; Isa. 33:1). **17.** (Ch. 8:22; 33:6.) **Outcast**–as a wife put away by her husband (Isa. 62:4, contrasted with vs. 12). **Zion**—alluding to its *Hebrew* meaning, "dryness"; "sought after" by none, as would be the case with an *arid* region (Isa. 62:12). The extremity of the people, so far from being an obstacle to, will be the chosen opportunity of, God's grace. **18. bring again . . . captivity**—(Ch. 33:7, 11). **tents**—used to intimate that their present dwellings in Chaldea were but temporary as *tents*. **have mercy on . . . dwelling-places**—(Ps. 102:13). **own heap**—on the same hill, i.e., site, a hill being the usual site chosen for a city (cf. Josh. 11:13, *Margin*). This better answers the parallel clause, "after the manner thereof" (i.e., in the same becoming ways as formerly), than the rendering, "its own heap of *ruins*," as in ch. 49:2. **palace**—the king's, on Mount Zion. **remain**—rather, "shall be inhabited"(*Note*, ch. 17: 6, 25). This confirms *English Version,* "palace," not as others translate, "the temple" (see I Kings 16:18; II Kings 15:25). **19. thanksgiving**—The *Hebrew* word includes *confession* as well as *praise;* for, in the case of God, the highest *praises* we can bestow are only *confessing* what God really is [BENGEL], (ch. 17:26; 31:12, 13; 33:11; Isa. 35:10; 51:11). **multiply them**—(Zech. 10:8). **20. as aforetime**—as flourishing as in the time of David. **21. their nobles**—rather, "their Glorious One," or "Leader" (cf. Acts 3:15; Heb. 2:10), answering to "their Governor" in the parallel clause. **of themselves**—of their own nation, a Jew, not a foreigner; applicable to Zerubbabel, or J. Hyrcanus (hereditary high priest and governor), only as types of Christ (Gen. 49:10; Mic. 5:2; Rom. 9:5), the antitypical "David" (vs. 9). **cause him to draw near**—as the great Priest (Exod. 19:22; Lev. 21:17), through whom believers also have access to God (Heb. 10:19-22). His priestly and kingly characters are similarly combined (Ps. 110:4; Zech. 6:13). **who . . . engaged . . . heart to approach**—lit., "pledged his heart," i.e., his life; a thing unique; Messiah alone has made His life responsible as the surety (Heb. 7:22; 9:11-15), in order to gain access not only for Himself, but for us to God. *Heart* is here used for *life,* to express the *courage* which it needed to undertake such a tremendous suretyship. The question implies admiration at one being found competent by His twofold nature, as God and man, for the task. Cf. the interrogation (Isa. 63:1-3). **22. ye shall be my people . . .**—The covenant shall be renewed between God and His people through Messiah's mediation (vs. 21; ch. 31:1, 33; 32:38; Ezek. 11:20; 36:28). **23, 24.** (Ch. 23:19.) Vengeance upon God's foes always accompanies manifestations of His grace to His people. **continuing**—lit., "sojourning," abiding constantly; appropriately here in the case of Babylon, which was to be *permanently* destroyed, substituted for "whirling itself about" ("grievous" in *English Version*) (ch. 23:19, 20, see *Notes* there), where the *temporary* downfall of Judea is spoken of.

CHAPTER 31

Vss. 1-40. CONTINUATION OF THE PROPHECY IN CHAPTER 30. As in that chapter the restoration of Judah, so in this the restoration of Israel's ten tribes is foretold. **1. At the same time**—"In the latter days" (ch. 30:24). **the God of**—manifesting My *grace* to (Gen. 17:7; Matt. 22:32; Rev. 21:3). **all . . . Israel**—not the exiles of the *south* kingdom of Judah only, but also the *north* kingdom of the ten tribes; and not merely Israel in general, but "*all* the families of Israel." Never yet fulfilled (Rom. 11: 26). **2.** Upon the grace manifested to Israel "in the wilderness" God grounds His argument for renewing His favors to them *now* in their exile; because His covenant is "everlasting" (vs. 3), and changes not. The same argument occurs in Hosea 13:5, 9, 10; 14:4, 5, 8. Babylon is fitly compared to the "wilderness," as in both alike Israel was as a stranger far from his appointed "rest" or home, and Babylon is in Isaiah 40:3 called a "desert" (cf. ch. 50:12). **I went to cause him to rest**—viz., in the pillar of cloud and fire, the symbol of God's presence, which *went* before Israel to *search a resting-place* (Num. 10:33; Isa. 63:14) for the people, both a temporary one at each halt in the wilderness, and a permanent one in Canaan (Exod. 33:14; Deut. 3: 20; Josh. 21:44; Ps. 95:11; Heb. 3:11). **3.** Israel gratefully acknowledges in reply God's *past* grace; but at the same time tacitly implies by the expression "of old," that God does not appear to her *now.* "God appeared to me *of old,* but now I am forsaken!" God replies, Nay, I love thee with the same love now as of old. My love was not a momentary impulse, but *from* "everlasting" in My counsels, and *to* "everlasting" in its continuance; hence originated the covenant whereby I gratuitously adopted thee (Mal. 1:2; Rom. 11:28, 29). *Margin* translates, "from afar," which does not answer so well as "of old," to "in the wilderness" (vs. 2), which refers to the *olden* times of Israel's history. **with loving-kindness . . . drawn**—(Hos. 11: 4). Rather, "I have *drawn out continually* My loving-kindness toward thee." So Psalm 36:10, "Continue (*Margin,* Draw out at length) Thy lovingkindness." By virtue of My *everlasting* love I will *still extend* My loving-kindness to thee. So Isaiah 44:21, "O Israel, thou shalt not be forgotten of Me." **4. I will build . . . thou shalt be built**—The combination of the *active* and *passive* to express the same fact implies the infallible certainty of its accomplishment. "Build," i.e., establish in prosperity (ch. 33:7). **adorned with . . . tabrets**—(I Sam. 18:6). Or, "*adorn thyself* with thy *timbrels*"; used by damsels on occasions of public rejoicings (Exod. 15: 20; Judg. 11:34). Israel had cast away all instruments of joy in her exile (Ps. 137:4). **dances**—holy joy, not carnal mirth. **5. Samaria**—the metropolis of the ten tribes; here equivalent to *Israel.* The *mountainous* nature of their country suited the growth of the *vine.* **eat . . . as common**—lit., "shall profane," i.e., shall put to common use. For the first three years after planting, the vine was "not to be eaten of"; on the fourth year the fruit was to be "holy to praise the Lord withal"; on the fifth year the fruit was to be *eaten as common,* no longer restricted to *holy* use (Lev. 19:23-25; cf. Deut. 20:6, 28:30, *Margin*). Thus the idea here is, "The same persons who plant shall reap the fruits"; it shall no longer be that one shall plant and another reap the fruit. **6.** The watchmen, stationed on eminences (types of the preachers of the gospel), shall summon the ten tribes to go up to the annual feasts at Jerusalem ("Zion"), as they used to do before the revolt and the setting up of the idol calves at Dan and Beer-sheba (Ezek. 37:21, 22). **Mount Ephraim**—not one single mountain, but the whole mountainous region of the ten tribes. **our God**—from whom we formerly revolted, but who is now *our* God. An earnest of that good time to come is given in the partial success of the gospel in its first preaching in Samaria (John 4; Acts 8:5-25). **7.** The people are urged with praises and prayers to supplicate for their universal restoration. Jehovah is represented in the context (vss. 1, 8), as promising immediately to restore Israel. They therefore praise God for the restoration, being as certain of it as if it were actually accomplished; and at the same time *pray for* it, as prayer was a means to the desired end. Prayer does not move God to grant our wishes, but when God has determined to grant our wishes, He puts it into our hearts to pray for the thing desired. Cf. Psalm 102:13-17, as to the connection of Israel's restoration with the prayers of His people (Isa. 62:1-6). **for Jacob**—on account of Jacob; on account of his approaching deliverance by Jehovah. **among**—"for," i.e., on account of, would more exactly suit the parallelism to "*for* Jacob." **chief of the nations** —Israel: as the parallelism to "Jacob" proves (cf. Exod. 19:5; Ps. 135:4; Amos 6:1). God estimates the greatness of nations not by man's standard of material resources, but by His electing favor. **8. north**—Assyria, Media, etc. (*Note,* ch. 3:12, 18, 23: 8). **gather from . . . coasts of . . . earth**—(Ezek. 20: 34, 41, 34:13). **blind . . . lame**—Not even the most infirm and unfit persons for a journey shall be left behind, so universal shall be the restoration. **a great company**—or, they shall return "*in a great company*" [MAURER]. **9. weeping**—for their past sins which caused their exile (Ps. 126:5, 6). Although they come with weeping, they shall return with joy (ch. 50:4, 5). **supplications**—(Cf. vss. 18, 19; ch. 3:21-25; Zech. 12:10). *Margin* translates "favors," as in Joshua 11:20; Ezra 9:8; thus God's *favors* or *compassions* are put in opposition to the people's *weeping;* their tears shall be turned into joy. But *English Version* suits the parallelism best. **I will cause . . . to walk by . . . waters . . . straight way**—(Isa. 35:6-8; 43:19; 49:10, 11). God will give them waters to satisfy their thirst as in the wilderness journey from Egypt. So spiritually (Matt. 5:6; John 7:37). **Ephraim**—the ten tribes no longer severed from Judah, but forming one people with it. **my firstborn**—(Exod. 4:22; Hos. 11:1; Rom. 9:4). So the elect Church (II Cor. 6:18; Jas. 1:18). **10.** The tidings of God's interposition in behalf of Israel will arrest the attention of even the uttermost Gentile nations. **He that scattered will gather**— He who scattered knows where to find Israel; He who smote can also heal. **keep**—not only will *gather,* but *keep safely* to the end (John 13:1; 17:11). **shepherd**—(Isa. 40:11; Ezek. 34:12-14). **11. ransomed . . . from . . . hand of. . . stronger**—No strength of the foe can prevent the Lord from delivering Jacob (Isa. 49:24, 25). **12. height of Zion**—(Ezek. 17:23). **flow**—There shall be a *conflux* of worshippers to the temple on Zion (Isa. 2:2; Mic. 4:1). **to the goodness of . . . Lord**—(See vs. 14). *Beneficence,* i.e., to the Lord as the *source of all good* things (Hos. 3:5), to pray to Him and praise Him for these blessings of which He is the Fountainhead. **watered garden**—(Isa. 58:11.) Not merely for a time, but continually full of holy comfort. **not sorrow any more**—referring to the Church triumphant, as well as to literal Israel (Isa. 35:10; 65:19; Rev. 21:4). **13. young . . . old**—(Zech. 8:4, 5). **14. my goodness**—(vs. 12). **15. Ramah**—In Benjamin, east of the great northern road, two hours' journey from Jerusalem. Rachel, who all her life had pined for children (Gen. 30:1), and who died with "sorrow" in giving birth to Benjamin (Gen. 35:18, 19, *Margin;* I Sam. 10:2), and was buried at Ramah, near Bethlehem, is represented as raising her head from the tomb, and as breaking forth into "weeping" at seeing the whole land depopulated of her sons, the Ephraimites. Ramah was the place where Nebuzaradan collected all the

Jews in chains, previous to their removal to Babylon (ch. 40:1). God therefore consoles her with the promise of their restoration. Matthew 2:17, 18 quotes this as fulfilled in the massacre of the innocents under Herod. "A lesser and a greater event, of different times, may answer to the single sense of one passage of Scripture, until the prophecy is *exhausted"* [BENGEL]. Besides the temporary reference to the exiles in Babylon, the Holy Spirit foreshadowed ultimately Messiah's exile in Egypt, and the desolation caused in the neighborhood of Rachel's tomb by Herod's massacre of the children, whose mothers had "sons of sorrow" (Benoni), just as Rachel had. The return of Messiah (the representative of Israel) from Egypt, and the future restoration of Israel, both the literal and the spiritual (including the innocents), at the Lord's second advent, are antitypical of the restoration of Israel from Babylon, which is the ground of consolation held out here by Jeremiah. The clause, "They were not," i.e., were dead (Gen. 42:13), does not apply so strictly to the exiles in Babylon as it does to the history of Messiah and His people—past, present, and future. So the words, "There is hope in thine end," are to be fulfilled ultimately, when Rachel shall meet her murdered children at the resurrection, at the same time that literal Israel is to be restored. "They were not," in *Hebrew,* is *singular; each was not*: each mother at the Bethlehem massacre had but *one* child to lament, as the limitation of age in Herod's order, "two years and under," implies; this use of the *singular* distributively (the mothers weeping severally, *each for her own* child), is a coincidence between the prophecy of the Bethlehem massacre and the event, the more remarkable as not being obvious: the *singular,* too, is appropriate as to *Messiah* in His Egyptian exile, who was to be a leading object of Rachel's lamentation. **16. thy work**—thy parental weeping for thy children [ROSENMULLER]. Thine affliction in the loss of thy children, murdered for Christ's sake, shall not be fruitless to thee, as was the case in thy giving birth to the "child of thy sorrow," Benjamin. Primarily, also, thy grief shall not be perpetual: the exiles shall return, and the land be inhabited again [CALVIN]. **come again**—(Hos. 1:11). **17. hope in . . . end**—All thy calamities shall have a prosperous issue. **18. Ephraim**—representing the ten tribes. **bemoaning himself**—The spirit of penitent supplication shall at last be poured on Israel as the necessary forerunner of their restoration (Zech. 12:10-14). **Thou hast chastised me, and I was chastised**—In the first clause the chastisement itself is meant; in the second the *beneficial effect* of it in teaching the penitent true wisdom. **bullock unaccustomed to . . . yoke**— A similar image occurs in Deuteronomy 32:15. Cf. "stiff-necked," Acts 7:51; Exodus 32:9, an image from *refractory* oxen. Before my chastisement I needed the severe correction I received, as much as an untamed bullock needs the goad. Cf. Acts 9:5, where the same figure is used of Saul while unconverted. Israel has had a longer chastisement than Judah, not having been restored even at the Jews' return from Babylon. Hereafter, at its restoration, it shall confess the sore discipline was all needed to "accustom" it to God's "easy yoke" (Matt. 11:29, 30). **turn thou me**—by Thy converting Spirit (Lam. 5:21). But why does Ephraim pray for conversion, seeing that he is already converted? Because we are converted by progressive steps, and need the same power of God to carry forward, as to originate, our conversion (John 6: 44, 65; cf. with Isa. 27:3; I Pet. 1:5; Phil. 1:6). **19.**

after that I was turned, I repented—Repentance in the full sense follows, not precedes, our being turned *to* God *by* God (Zech. 12:10). The Jews' *"looking to* Him whom they pierced" shall result in their *"mourning for* Him." Repentance is the tear that flows from the eye of faith turned to Jesus. He Himself gives it: we give it not of ourselves, but must come to Him for it (Acts 5:31). **instructed**—made to learn by chastisement. God's Spirit often works through the corrections of His providence. **smote upon . . . thigh**—(Ezek. 21:12). A token of indignant remorse, shame, and grief, because of his past sin. **bear . . . reproach of . . . youth**—"because the calamities which I *bore* were the just punishment of my *scandalous wantonness* against God in *my youth*"; alluding to the idols set up at Dan and Bethel immediately after the ten tribes revolted from Judah. His sense of *shame* shows that he no longer delights in his sin. **20. Is Ephraim my dear son?** etc.—The question implies that a negative answer was to be expected. Who would have thought that one so undutiful to His heavenly Father as Ephraim had been should still be regarded by God as a "pleasant child?" Certainly he was *not* so in respect to his sin. But by virtue of God's "everlasting love" (vs. 3) on Ephraim's being "turned" to God, he was immediately welcomed as God's "dear son." This 20th verse sets forth God's readiness to welcome the penitent (vss. 18, 19), anticipating his return with prevenient grace and love. Cf. Luke 15:20: "When he was *yet a great way off,* his father saw him and had compassion . . . ." **spake against**—threatened him for his idolatry. **remember**—with favor and concern, as in Genesis 8:1; 30:22. **bowels . . . troubled for him** —(Deut. 32:36; Isa. 63:15; Hos. 11:8)—viz., with the yearnings of compassionate love. The "bowels" include the region of the heart, the seat of the affections. **21. waymarks**—*pillars* to mark the road for the returning exiles. Caravans set up *pillars,* or pointed *heaps* of stones, to mark the way through the desert against their return. So Israel is told by God to mark the way by which they went in leaving their country for exile; for by the same way they shall return. **highway**—(Isa. 35:8, 10). **22. go about**—viz., after human helps (ch. 2:18, 23, 36). Why not return immediately to me? MAURER translates, as in Song of Solomon 5:6, "How long wilt thou *withdraw thyself?*" Let thy past backslidings suffice thee now that a *new* era approaches. What God finds fault with in them is, that they looked *hither and thither,* leaning on contingencies, instead of at once trusting the word of God, which promised their restoration. To assure them of this, God promises to *create a new thing in their land, A woman shall compass a man.* CALVIN explains this: Israel, who is feeble as a woman, shall be superior to the warlike Chaldeans; the captives shall reduce their captors to captivity. HENGSTENBERG makes the "woman" the Jewish Church, and the "man" Jehovah, her husband, whose love she will again seek (Hos. 2:6, 7). MAURER, A woman shall protect (Deut. 32:10, *Margin;* Ps. 32:10) a man, i.e., You need fear no foes in returning, for all things shall be so peaceful that a *woman* would be able to take man's part, and act as his *protector.* But the Christian fathers (Augustine, etc.) almost unanimously interpreted it of *the Virgin Mary compassing Christ in her womb.* This view is favored:—(1) By the connection; it gives a reason why the exiles should desire a return to their country, viz., because Christ was conceived there. (2) The word "created" implies a divine power put

forth in the creation of a body in the Virgin's womb by the Holy Ghost for the second Adam, such as was exerted in creating the first Adam (Luke 1:35; Heb. 10:5). (3) The phrase, "a new thing," something unprecedented; a man whose like had never existed before, at once God and man; a mother out of the ordinary course of nature, at once mother and virgin. An extraordinary mode of generation; one conceived by the Holy Ghost without man. (4) The specification "in the land" (not "earth," as *English Version*), viz., of *Judah,* where probably Christ was *conceived,* in *Hebron* (cf. Luke 1:39, 41, 42, 44, with Josh. 21:11) or else in *Nazareth,* "in the territory" of *Israel,* to whom vss. 5, 6, 15, 18, 21 refer; His *birth* was at Bethlehem (Mic. 5:2; Matt. 2:5, 6). As the place of His nativity, and of His being reared (Matt. 2:23), and of His preaching (Hag. 2:7; Mal. 3:1), are specified, so it is likely the Holy Spirit designated the place of His being conceived. (5) The *Hebrew* for "woman" implies an *individual,* as the Virgin Mary, rather than a *collection of persons.* (6) The restoration of Israel is grounded on God's covenant in *Christ,* to whom, therefore, allusion is naturally made as the foundation of Israel's hope (cf. Isa. 7:14). The *Virgin* Mary's conception of Messiah in the womb answers to the "Virgin of Israel" (therefore so called, vs. 21), i.e., Israel and her sons at their final restoration, receiving Jesus as Messiah (Zech. 12:10). (7) The reference to the conception of the *child* Messiah accords with the mention of the massacre of "children" referred to in vs. 15 (cf. Matt. 2:17). (8) The *Hebrew* for "man" is properly "mighty man," a term applied to *God* (Deut. 10:17); and to Christ (Zech. 13:7; cf. Ps. 45:3; Isa. 9:6) [CALOVIUS]. **23.** Jerusalem again shall be the metropolis of the whole nation, the seat of "justice" (Ps. 122:5-8; Isa. 1:26), and of sacred worship ("holiness," Zech. 8:3) on "Mount" Moriah. **24. Judah . . . cities . . . husbandmen . . . they with flocks**—Two classes, citizens and countrymen, the latter divided into agriculturists and shepherds, all alike in security, though the latter were to be outside the protection of city walls. "Judah" here stands for the *country,* as distinguished from its *cities.* **25.** The "weary, sorrowful," and indigent state of Israel will prove no obstacle in the way of My helping them. **26.** The words of Jeremiah: *Upon this* (or, *By reason of this)* announcement of a happy restoration, "I awaked" from the prophetic *dream* vouchsafed to me (ch. 23:25) with the "sweet" impression thereof remaining on my mind. "Sleep" here means *dream,* as in Psalm 90:5. **27.** He shows how a land so depopulated shall again be peopled. God will cause both *men* and *beasts* in it to increase to a multitude (Ezek. 36:9-11; Hos. 2:23). **28.** (Ch. 44:27.) The same God who, as it were (in human language), was *on the watch* for all means to destroy, shall be as much on the watch for the means of their restoration. **29. In those days**—after their punishment has been completed, and mercy again visits them. **fathers . . . eaten . . . sour grape . . . children's teeth . . . on edge**—the proverb among the exiles' children born in Babylon, to express that they suffered the evil consequences of their fathers' sins rather than of their own (Lam. 5:7; Ezek. 18:2, 3). **30.** (Gal. 6:5, 7.) **31. the days . . . new covenant with . . . Israel . . . Judah**—The new covenant is made with literal *Israel* and *Judah,* not with the *spiritual* Israel, i.e., believers, except secondarily, and as grafted on the stock of Israel (Rom. 11:16-27). For the whole subject of chs. 30 and 31 is the restoration of the Hebrews (ch. 30:4, 7, 10, 18; 31:7, 10, 11, 23, 24,

27, 36). With the "remnant according to the election of grace" in Israel, the new covenant has already taken effect. But with regard to the *whole* nation, its realization is reserved for the last days, to which Paul refers this prophecy in an abridged form (Rom. 11:27). **32. Not . . . the covenant that I made with . . . fathers**—the Old Testament covenant, as contrasted with our gospel covenant (Heb. 8:8-12; 10:16, 17, where this prophecy is quoted to prove the abrogation of the law by the gospel), of which the distinguishing features are its securing by an adequate atonement the forgiveness of sins, and by the inworking of effectual grace ensuring permanent obedience. An earnest of this is given partially in the present eclectic or elect Church gathered out of Jews and Gentiles. But the promise here to Israel in the last days is national and universal, and effected by an extraordinary outpouring of the Spirit (vss. 33, 34; Ezek. 11:17-20), independent of any merit on their part (Ezek. 36:25-32; 37:1-28; 39:29; Joel 2:23-28; Zech. 12:10; II Cor. 3:16). **took . . . by . . . hand**—(Deut. 1:31; Hos. 11:3). **although I was an husband**—(cf. ch. 3:14; Hos. 2:7, 8). But LXX, *Syriac,* and St. Paul (Heb. 8:9) translate, "I *regarded* them not"; and GESENIUS, etc., justify this rendering of the *Hebrew* from the *Arabic.* The Hebrews *regarded not* God, so God *regarded* them *not.* **33. will be their God**—(ch. 32:38). **34.** True, specially of Israel (Isa. 54:13); secondarily, true of believers (John 6:45; I Cor. 2:10; I John 2:20). **forgive . . . iniquity . . . remember . . . no more**—(ch. 33:8; 50:20; Mic. 7:18); applying peculiarly to Israel (Rom. 11:27). Secondarily, all believers (Acts 10:43). **35. divideth . . . . sea when . . . waves . . . roar . . . Lord of hosts . . . name**—quoted from Isaiah 51:15, the genuineness of which passage is thus established on Jeremiah's authority. **36. a nation**—Israel's *national* polity has been broken up by the Romans. But their preservation as a *distinct people* amidst violent persecutions, though scattered among all nations for eighteen centuries, *unamalgamated,* whereas all other peoples under such circumstances have become incorporated with the nations in which they have been dispersed, is a perpetual standing miracle (cf. ch. 33:20; Ps. 148:6; Isa. 54:9, 10). **37.** (Cf. 33:22.) **for all that they have done**—viz., all the sins. God will regard His own covenant promise, rather than their merits. **38. tower of Hananeel**—The city shall extend beyond its former bounds (Neh. 3:1; 12:39; Zech. 14:10). **gate of . . . corner**—(II Kings 14:13; II Chron. 26:9). **39. measuring-line**—(Ezek. 40:8; Zech. 2:1). **Gareb**—from a *Hebrew* root, "to scrape"; *Syriac,* "leprosy"; the locality outside of the city, to which *lepers* were removed. **Goath**—from a root, "to toil," referring to the *toilsome* ascent there: outside of the city of David, towards the southwest, as Gareb was northwest [JUNIUS]. **40. valley of . . . dead**—Tophet, where the bodies of malefactors were cast (Isa. 30:33), south of the city. **fields . . . Kidron**—so II Kings 23:4. Fields in the suburbs reaching as far as Kidron, east of the city. **horse gate**—Through it the king's horses were led forth for watering to the brook Kidron (II Kings 11:16; Neh. 3:28). **for ever**—The city shall not only be spacious, but both "holy to the Lord," i.e., freed from all pollutions, and *everlasting* (Joel 3:17, 20; Rev. 21:2, 10, 27).

CHAPTER 32

Vss. 1-14. JEREMIAH, IMPRISONED FOR HIS PROPHECY AGAINST JERUSALEM, BUYS A PATRIMONIAL PROPERTY (HIS RELATIVE HANAMEEL'S), IN ORDER TO CERTIFY TO THE JEWS THEIR FUTURE RETURN FROM BABYLON. **1. tenth year**—The siege of Jerusalem had already begun, in the tenth month of the ninth year of Zedekiah (ch. 39:1; II Kings 25:1). **2. in . . . court of . . . prison**—i.e., in the open space occupied by the guard, from which he was not allowed to depart, but where any of his friends might visit him (vs. 12; ch. 38:13, 28). Marvellous obstinacy, that at the time when they were experiencing the truth of Jeremiah's words in the pressure of the siege, they should still keep the prophet in confinement [CALVIN]. The circumstances narrated (vss. 3-5) occurred at the beginning of the siege, when Jeremiah foretold the capture of the city (vs. 1; ch. 34:1-7; 39:1). He was at that time put into free custody in the court of the prison. At the raising of the siege by Pharaoh-hophra, Jeremiah was on the point of repairing to Benjamin, when he was cast into "the dungeon," but obtained leave to be removed again to the court of the prison (ch. 37:12-21). When there he urged the Jews, on the second advance of the Chaldeans to the siege, to save themselves by submission to Nebuchadnezzar (ch. 38:2, 3); in consequence of this the king, at the instigation of the princes, had him cast into a miry dungeon (ch. 38:4-6); again he was removed to the prison court at the intercession of a courtier (vss. 7-13), where he remained till the capture of the city (vs. 28), when he was liberated (ch. 39:11, etc.; 40:1, etc.). **4. his eyes shall behold his eyes**—i.e., only *before* reaching Babylon, which he was *not to see.* Ch. 39:6, 7 harmonizes this prophecy (ch. 32:4) with the seemingly opposite prophecy, Ezekiel 12:13, "He shall *not see.*" **5. visit him**—in a good sense (ch. 27:22); referring to the honor paid Zedekiah at his death and burial (ch. 34:4, 5). Perhaps, too, before his death he was treated by Nebuchadnezzar with some favor. **though ye fight . . . shall not prosper**—(ch. 21:4). **6. Jeremiah said**—resuming the thread of vs. 1, which was interrupted by the parenthesis (vss. 2-5). **7. son of Shallum thine uncle**—therefore, Jeremiah's first cousin. **field . . . in Anathoth**—a sacerdotal city: and so having 1000 cubits of suburban fields outside the wall attached to it (Num. 35:4, 5). The prohibition to sell these suburban fields (Lev. 25:34) applied merely to their alienating them from Levites to another tribe; so that this chapter does not contravene that prohibition. Besides, what is here meant is only the purchase of the use of the field till the year of jubilee. On the failure of the owner, the next of kin had the right of redeeming it (Lev. 25:25, etc.; Ruth 4:3-6). **8. Then I knew**—Not that Jeremiah previously doubted the reality of the divine communication, but, the effect following it, and the prophet's experimentally knowing it, confirmed his faith and was the seal to the vision. The Roman historian, FLORUS (2.6), records a similar instance: During the days that Rome was being besieged by Hannibal, the very ground on which he was encamped was put up for sale at Rome, and found a purchaser; implying the calm confidence of the ultimate issue entertained by the Roman people. **9. seventeen shekels of silver**—As the shekel was only about 50 cents, the whole would be under $10.00, a rather small sum, even taking into account the fact of the Chaldean occupation of the land, and the uncertainty of the time when it might come to Jeremiah or his heirs. Perhaps the "seven shekels," which in the *Hebrew* (see *Margin*) are distinguished from the "ten pieces of silver," were shekels *of gold* [MAURER]. **10. subscribed**—*I wrote* in the deed, "book of purchase" (vs.

12). **weighed**—coined money was not in early use; hence money was "weighed" (Gen. 23:16). **11. evidence . . . sealed . . . open**—Two deeds were drawn up in a contract of sale; the one, the original copy, witnessed and sealed with the public seal; the other not so, but open, and therefore less authoritative, being but a *copy*. GATAKER thinks that the purchaser sealed the one with *his own* seal; the other he showed to witnesses that they might write their names on the back of it and know the contents; and that some details, e.g., the conditions and time of redemption were in the *sealed* copy, which the parties might not choose to be known to the witnesses, and which were therefore not in the *open* copy. The sealed copy, when opened after the seventy years' captivity, would greatly confirm the faith of those living at that time. The "law and custom" refer, probably, not merely to the sealing up of the conditions and details of purchase, but also to the law of redemption, according to which, at the return to Judea, the deed would show that Jeremiah had bought the field by his right as next of kin (Lev. 25: 13-16), [LUDOVICUS DE DIEU]. **12. Baruch**—Jeremiah's amanuensis and agent (ch. 36:4, etc.). **before all**—In sales everything clandestine was avoided; publicity was required. So here, in the court of prison, where Jeremiah was confined, there were soldiers and others, who had free access to him, present (ch. 38:1). **14. in an earthen vessel**—that the documents might not be injured by the moisture of the surrounding earth; at the same time, being buried, they could not be stolen, but would remain as a pledge of the Jews' deliverance until God's time should come. **15.** (Cf. vss. 24, 25, 37, 43, 44.) **16.** Jeremiah, not comprehending how God's threat of destroying Judah could be reconciled with God's commanding him to purchase land in it as if in a free country, has recourse to his grand remedy against perplexities, prayer. **17. hast made . . . heaven**—Jeremiah extols God's creative power, as a ground of humility on his part as man: It is not my part to call Thee, the mighty God, to account for Thy ways (cf. ch. 12:1). **too hard**—In vs. 27 God's reply exactly accords with Jeremiah's prayer (Gen. 18:14; Zech. 8:6; Luke 1:37). **18.** Exod. 34:7; Isa. 65:6.) This is taken from the decalogue (Exod. 20: 5, 6). This is a second consideration to check hasty judgments as to God's ways: Thou art the gracious and righteous Judge of the world. **19. counsel . . . work**—devising . . . executing (Isa. 28: 29). **eyes . . . open upon all**—(Job 34:21; Prov. 5: 21). **to give . . . according to . . . ways**—(ch. 17:10). **20. even unto this day**—Thou hast given "signs" of Thy power from the day when Thou didst deliver Israel out of Egypt by mighty miracles, down to the present time [MAURER]. CALVIN explains it, "memorable even unto this day." **among other men**—not in Israel only, but among foreign peoples also. Cf. for "other" ¬understood, Psalm 73:5. **made thee a name**—(Exod. 9:16; I Chron. 17:21; Isa. 63:12). **as at this day**—*a name* of power, such as Thou hast at this day. **21.** (Ps. 136:11, 12.) **22. given . . . didst swear**—God gave it by a gratuitous covenant, not for their deserts. **23. all . . . thou commandedst . . . all this evil**—Their punishment was thus exactly commensurate with their sin. It was not fortuitous. **24. mounts**—mounds of earth raised as breastworks by the besieging army, behind which they employed their engines, and which they gradually pushed forward to the walls of the city. **behold, thou seest it**—connected with vs. 25. Thou seest all this with Thine own eyes, and yet (what seems inconsistent with it) Thou commandest me

to buy a field. **25. for the city . . .**—rather, "though . . . ." **27.** Jehovah retorts Jeremiah's own words: I am indeed, as thou sayest (vs. 17), the God and Creator of "all flesh," and "nothing is too hard for Me"; thine own words ought to have taught thee that, though Judea and Jerusalem are given up to the Chaldeans now for the sins of the Jews, yet it will not be *hard* to Me, when I please, to restore the state so that houses and lands therein shall be possessed in safety (vss. 36-44). **29. burn . . . houses upon whose roofs . . . incense unto Baal**—retribution in kind. They *burnt incense to Baal, on the houses,* so the *houses* shall be *burnt* (ch. 19:13). The god of fire was the object of their worship; so fire shall be the instrument of their punishment. **to provoke me**—indicating the *design*, not merely the *event*. They seemed to court God's "anger," and *purposely* to "provoke" Him. **30. have . . . done**—lit., "have been doing"; implying *continuous* action. **only . . . evil . . . only provoked me**—They have been doing *nothing else but* evil; their *sole* aim seems to have been to provoke Me. **their youth**—the time when they were in the wilderness, having just before come into national existence. **31. provocation of mine anger**—lit., *"for* mine anger." CALVIN, therefore, connects these words with those at the end of the verse, "this city has been to me an *object for mine anger* (viz., by reason of the provocations mentioned, vs. 30), etc., that I should remove it . . . ." Thus, there will not be the repetition of the sentiment, vs. 30, as in *English Version;* the *Hebrew* also favors this rendering. However, Jeremiah delights in repetitions. In *English Version* the words, "that I should remove it . . ." stand independently, as the result of what precedes. The time is ripe for taking vengeance on them (II Kings 23:27). **from the day that they built it**—Solomon completed the building of the city; and it was he who, first of the Jewish kings, turned to idolatry. It was originally built by the idolatrous Canaanites. **32. priests . . . prophets** —(Neh. 9:32, 34). Hence, learn, though ministers of God apostatize, we must remain faithful. **33.** (Ch. 2:27; 7:13.) **34.** (Ch. 7:30; 31; Ezek. 8:5-17.) **35. cause . . . pass through . . . fire**—By way of purification, they passed through with bare feet (Lev. 18:21). **Molech**—meaning "king"; the same as *Milcom* (I Kings 11:33). **I commanded . . . not**—This cuts off from the superstitious the plea of a good intention. All "will-worship" exposes to God's wrath (Col. 2:18, 23). **36. And now therefore**—rather, "But now, nevertheless." Notwithstanding that their guilt deserves lasting vengeance, God, for the elect's sake and for His covenant's sake, will, contrary to all that might have been expected, restore them. **ye say, It shall be delivered into . . . king of Babylon**—The reprobate pass from the extreme of self-confidence to that of despair of God's fulfilling His promise of restoring them. **37.** (*Note,* ch. 16:15.) The "all" countries implies a future restoration of Israel more universal than that from Babylon. **38.** (Ch. 30:22; 24:7.) **39. one heart**—all seeking the Lord *with one accord,* in contrast to their state when only scattered individuals sought Him (Ezek. 11:19, 20; Zeph. 3:9). **for . . . good of them**—(Ps. 34:12-15). **40.** (Ch. 31: 31, 33; Isa. 55:3.) **not depart from me**—never yet fully realized as to the Israelites. **I will not turn away from them . . . good**—(Isa. 30:21). Jehovah compares Himself to a sedulous preceptor following his pupils everywhere to direct their words, gestures. **put my fear in . . . hearts . . . not depart from me**—Both the conversion and perseverance of the saints are the work of God alone, by the operation of the

Holy Spirit. **41. rejoice over them**—(Deut. 30:9; Isa. 62:5; 65:19; Zeph. 3:17). **plant . . . assuredly**—rather, in stability, i.e., permanently, for ever (ch. 24:6; Amos 9:15). **42.** (Ch. 31:28.) The restoration from Babylon was only a slight foretaste of the grace to be expected by Israel at last through Christ. **43.** (Vs. 15.) **whereof ye say, It is desolate**—(ch. 33:10). **44.** Referring to the forms of contract (vss. 10-12). **Benjamin**—specified as Anathoth; Jeremiah's place of residence where the field lay (vs. 8), was in it.

CHAPTER 33

Vss. 1-26. PROPHECY OF THE RESTORATION FROM BABYLON, AND OF MESSIAH AS KING AND PRIEST. **1. shut up**—(ch. 32: 2, 3; II Tim. 2:9). Though Jeremiah was shut up in bondage, the word of God was "not bound." **2. maker thereof**—rather, the doer of it, viz., that which Jeremiah is about to prophesy, the restoration of Israel, an act which is thought now impossible, but which the Almighty will effect. **formed it**—viz., Jerusalem (ch. 32:44) [CALVIN]. Rather, that formed, i.e., moulds *His purpose* into due shape for execution (Isa. 37:26). **Lord . . . his name**—(Exod. 3:14, 15). **3. Call . . . I will answer**—(ch. 29:12; Ps. 91:15). Jeremiah, as the representative of the people of God, is urged by God to pray for that which God has determined to grant; viz., the restoration. God's promises are not to slacken, but to quicken the prayers of His people (Ps. 132: 13, 17; Isa. 62:6, 7). **mighty things**—*Hebrew*, "inaccessible things," i.e., incredible, hard to man's understanding [MAURER], viz., the restoration of the Jews, an event despaired of. "Hidden," or "recondite" [PISCATOR]. **thou knowest not**—Yet God had revealed those things to Jeremiah, but the unbelief of the people in rejecting the grace of God had caused him to forget God's promise, as though the case of the people admitted of no remedy. **4. houses . . . thrown down by the mounts**—viz., by the missiles cast from the besiegers' *mounds* (ch. 32:24); "and by the sword" follows properly, as, after missiles had prepared the way, the foe next advanced to close quarters "with the sword." **5. They**—the Jews; the defenders of the "houses" (vs. 4), "come forward to fight with the Chaldeans," who burst into the city through the "thrown-down houses," but all the effect that they produce "is, to fill them (the houses) with their own "dead bodies." **6.** (Ch. 30:17.) The answer to Jeremiah's mournful question (ch. 8:22). **cure**—lit., the long linen bandage employed in dressing wounds. **truth**—i.e., stability; I will bring forth for them abundant and *permanent* peace, i.e., prosperity. **7. cause . . . to return**—i.e., reverse (vs. 11; ch. 32:44). The specification, both of "Judah" and "Israel," can only apply fully to the future restoration. **as at the first**—(Isa. 1:26). **8. cleanse**—(Ezek. 36:25; Zech. 13:1; Heb. 9:13, 14). Alluding to the legal rites of purification. **all their iniquity . . . all their iniquities**—both the *principle* of sin within, and its outward manifestations in *acts*. The repetition is in order that the Jews may consider how great is the grace of God in not merely *pardoning* (as to the punishment), but also *cleansing* them (as to the pollution of guilt); not merely one iniquity, but *all* (Mic. 7:18). **9. it**—the city. **a name . . . a praise**—(ch. 13:11; Isa. 62:7). **them**—the inhabitants of Jerusalem. **they shall fear . . . for all the goodness**—(Ps. 130:4). The Gentiles shall be led to "fear" God by the proofs of His power displayed in behalf of the Jews; the ungodly among them shall "tremble" for fear of God's judgments on them;

the penitent shall reverentially fear and be converted to Him (Ps. 102:15; Isa. 60:3). **10. ye say . . . desolate**—(ch. 32:43). **11.** (Ch. 7:34; 16:9.) **Praise the Lord . . .**—the words of Psalm 136:1, which were actually used by the Jews at their restoration (Ezra 3:11). **sacrifice of praise**—(Ps. 107:22; 116: 17). This shall continue when all other sacrifices shall be at an end. **12. habitation of shepherds . . . flocks**—in contrast to vs. 10, "without man . . . *inhabitant . . . without beast*" (ch. 32:43; cf. ch. 31: 24; 50:19; Isa. 65:10). **13. pass . . . under . . . hands of him that telleth them**—Shepherds, in sending forth and bringing back their sheep to the folds, *count* them by striking each as it passes with a rod, implying the shepherd's provident care that not one should be lost (Lev. 27:32; Mic. 7:14; cf. John 10: 28, 29; 17:12). **14. perform**—"I will make to *rise*"; God's promise having for a time seemed to *lie* dead and abortive [CALVIN]. **15.** Repeated from ch. 23: 5. **the land**—the Holy Land: Israel and Judah (ch. 23:6). **16. Jerusalem**—In ch. 23:6, instead of this, it is "Israel." "*The name*" in the *Hebrew* has here to be supplied from that passage; and for "he" (Messiah, the antitypical "Israel"), the antecedent there (Isa. 49:3), we have "she" here, i.e., Jerusalem. She is called by the same name as Messiah, "The LORD our Righteousness," by virtue of the mystical oneness between her (as the literal representative of the spiritual Church) and her Lord and Husband. Thus, whatever belongs to the Head belongs also to the members (Eph. 5:30, 32). Hence, the Church is called "Christ" (Rom. 16:7; I Cor. 12:12). The Church hereby professes to draw all her righteousness from Christ (Isa. 45:24, 25). It is for the sake of Jerusalem, literal and spiritual, that God the Father gives this name (*Jehovah, Tsidkenu*, "The Lord our Righteousness") to Christ. **17.** The promises of perpetuity of the throne of David fulfilled in Messiah, the son of David (II Sam. 7:16; I Kings 2:4; Ps. 89:4, 29, 36; cf. Luke 1: 32, 33). **18.** Messiah's literal priesthood (Heb. 7:17, 21, 24-28), and His followers' spiritual priesthood and sacrifices (vs. 11; Rom. 12:1; 15:16; I Pet. 2:5, 9; Rev. 1:6), shall never cease, according to the *covenant* with Levi, broken by the priests, but fulfilled by Messiah (Num. 25:12, 13; Mal. 2:4, 5, 8). **20. covenant of the day** —i.e., covenant *with* the day: answering to "covenant *with* David" (vs. 21, also vs. 25, "*with* day"; cf. ch. 31:35, 36; Lev. 26:42; Ps. 89:34, 37). **22.** (Gen. 15:5; 22:17.) The blessing there promised belonged to *all* the tribes; here it is restricted to the family of David and the tribe of Levi, because it was on these that the welfare of the whole people rested. When the kingdom and priesthood flourish in the person of Messiah, the whole nation shall temporally and spiritually prosper. **24. this people**—certain of the Jews, especially those who spoke with Jeremiah in the court of the prison (ch. 32:12; 38:1). **the two families**—Judah and Israel. **before them**—in their judgment. They suppose that I have utterly cast off Israel so as to be no more a nation. The expression, "*My* people," of itself, shows God has not cast off Israel for ever. **25.** (Ch. 31:35, 36; Gen. 8:22; Ps. 74:16, 17.) I who have established the laws of nature am the same God who has made a covenant with the Church. **26. Isaac**—(Ps. 105: 9; Amos 7:9, 16).

CHAPTER 34

Vss. 1-22. CAPTIVITY OF ZEDEKIAH AND THE PEOPLE FORETOLD FOR THEIR DISOBEDIENCE AND PERFIDY. The prophecy (vss. 1-7) as to Zedekiah is an amplification of that in ch. 32:1-5, in consequence of which Jeremiah was then shut up in the court of the prison. The prophecy (vss. 8-22) refers to the Jews, who, afraid of the capture of the city, had, in obedience to the law, granted freedom to their servants at the end of seven years, but on the intermission of the siege forced them back into bondage. **1. Jerusalem and . . . all the cities thereof**—(*Note*, ch. 19:15). It was amazing blindness in the king, that, in such a desperate position, he should reject admonition. **3.** (Ch. 32:4.) **4, 5.** Mitigation of Zedekiah's punishment. **the burnings of thy fathers**—Thy funeral shall be honored with the same burning of aromatic spices as there was at the funerals of thy fathers (II Chron. 16:14; 21:19). The honors here mentioned were denied to Jehoiakim (ch. 22:18). **Ah, lord!**—The Hebrews in their chronology (Sederolam) mention the wailing used over him, "Alas! King Zedekiah is dead, drinking the dregs (i.e., paying the penalty for the sins) of former ages." **7. these . . . retained**—alone (cf. II Chron. 11:5,9). **8.** By the law a Hebrew, after having been a bond-servant for six years, on the seventh was to be let go free (Exod. 21:22; Deut. 15:12). **Zedekiah made a covenant**—with solemn ceremonial in the temple (vss. 15, 18, 19). **them**—bond-servants (vs. 9). **9. none . . . serve himself of a Jew**—(Lev. 25:39-46). **11.** During the interruption of the siege by Pharaoh-hophra (cf. vss. 21, 22, with ch. 37:5-10), the Jews reduced their servants to bondage again. **13.** The last year of Zedekiah was the sabbatical year. How just the retribution, that they who, against God's law and their own covenant, enslaved their brethren, should be doomed to bondage themselves: and that the bond-servants should enjoy the sabbatical freedom at the hands of the foe (ch. 52:16) which their own countrymen denied them! **14. At the end of seven years**—i.e., not on the *eighth* year, but within the limit of the seventh year, not later than the end of the seventh year (Exod. 21:2; 23:10; Deut. 15:12). So "at the end of three years" (Deut. 14:28; II Kings 18:10), and *"after three days,* I will rise again" (Matt. 27:63), i.e., on the *third day* (cf. Matt. 27:64). **15. in the house . . . called by my name**—the usual place of making such covenants (II Kings 23:3; cf. I Kings 8:31; Neh. 10:29). **16. polluted my name**—by violating your oath (Exod. 20:7). **17. not . . . proclaiming liberty**—Though the Jews had ostensibly emancipated their bond-servants, they *virtually* did not do so by revoking the liberty which they had granted. God looks not to outward appearances, but to the sincere intention. **I proclaim a liberty**—retribution answering to the offense (Matt. 7:2; 18: 32, 33; Gal. 6:7; Jas. 2:13). The Jews who would not give liberty to their brethren shall themselves receive "a liberty" calamitous to them. God will manumit them from His happy and safe service (Ps. 121:3), which is real "liberty" (Ps. 119:45; John 8:36; II Cor. 3:17), only to pass under the terrible bondage of other taskmasters, the "sword," etc. **to be removed**—The *Hebrew* expresses *agitation* (*Note*, ch. 15:4). Cf. Deuteronomy 28:25, 48, 64, 65, as to the *restless agitation* of the Jews in their ceaseless removals from place to place in their dispersion. **18. passed between the parts thereof**—The contracting parties in the "covenant" (not here the *law* in general, but their *covenant* made before God in His house to emancipate their slaves, vss. 8, 9) passed through the parts of the animal cut in two, implying that they prayed so to be cut in sunder (Matt. 24:51; *Greek*, "cut in two") if they should break the covenant (Gen. 15:10, 17). **20. I will**

even give—resuming the sentence begun, but not completed (vs. 18), "I will give," etc. **seek their life** —implacably: satisfied with nothing short of their blood; not content with booty. **dead bodies**—The breakers of the covenant shall be cut in pieces, as the calf between whose parts they passed. **21. gone up**—i.e., raised the siege in order to meet Pharaoh-hophra (ch. 37:7-10). The departure of the Chaldeans was a kind of manumission of the Jews; but as their manumission of their bond-servants was recalled, so God revoked His manumission of them from the Chaldeans. **22. I will command**—Nebuchadnezzar, impelled unconsciously by a divine instigation, returned on the withdrawal of the Egyptians.

CHAPTER 35

Vss. 1-19. PROPHECY IN THE REIGN OF JEHOIAKIM, WHEN THE CHALDEANS, IN CONJUNCTION WITH THE SYRIANS AND MOABITES, INVADED JUDEA. By the obedience of the Rechabites to their father, Jeremiah condemns the disobedience of the Jews to God their Father. The Holy Spirit has arranged Jeremiah's prophecies by the *moral* rather than the chronological connection. From the history of an event fifteen years before, the Jews, who had brought back their manumitted servants into bondage, are taught how much God loves and rewards obedience, and hates and punishes disobedience. **2. Rechabites**—a nomadic tribe belonging to the Kenites of Hemath (I Chron. 2:55), of the family of Jethro, or Hobab, Moses' father-in-law (Exod. 18:9, etc.; Num. 10:29-32; Judg. 1:16). They came into Canaan with the Israelites, but, in order to preserve their independence, chose a life in tents without a fixed habitation (I Sam. 15:6). Besides the branch of them associated with Judah and extending to Amalek, there was another section at Kadesh, in Naphtali (Judg. 4:11, 17). They seem to have been proselytes of the gate. Jonadab, son of Rechab, whose charge not to drink wine they so strictly obeyed, was zealous for God (II Kings 10:15-23). The Nabatheans of Arabia observed the same rules (Diodorus Siculus, 19.94). **bring . . . into . . . house of . . . Lord**—because there were suitable witnesses at hand there from among the priests and chief men, as also because he had the power immediately to address the people assembled there (vs. 13). It may have been also as a reproof of the priests, who drank wine freely, though commanded to refrain from it when in the discharge of their duties [CALVIN]. **chambers**—which were round about the temple, applied to various uses, e.g., to contain the vestments, sacred vessels, etc. **3. Jaazaniah**—the elder and chief of the clan. **4. man of God**—a prophet (Deut. 33:1; I Sam. 2:27; I Kings 12:22; II Kings 4:7), also "a servant of God" in general (I Tim. 6:11), one not his own, but God's; one who has parted with all right in himself to give himself wholly to God (II Tim. 3:17). He was so reverenced that none would call in question what was transacted in his chamber. **keeper of the door**— *Hebrew*, "of the vessel." Probably the office meant is that of the priest who kept in charge the capitation money paid for the use of the temple and the votive offerings, such as silver vessels, etc. There were seven such keepers [GROTIUS]. Cf. II Kings 12:9; 25:18; I Chron. 9:18, 19, which support *English Version*. **I said . . . Drink**—Jeremiah does not say, *The Lord* saith, Drink: for then they would have been bound to obey. Contrast the case in I Kings 13:7-26. **6. Jonadab . . . our father**—i.e., forefather and director, 300 years before (II Kings 10:15). They were called Rechabites, not Jonadabites, having received their name from Rechab *the father*, previously to their adopting the injunctions of Jonadab his *son*. This case affords no justification for slavish deference to the religious opinions of the Christian fathers: for Jonadab's injunction only affected matters of the present life; moreover, it was not binding on their consciences, for they deemed it not unlawful to go to Jerusalem in the invasion (vs. 11). What is praised here is not the father's injunction, but the obedience of the sons [CALVIN]. **7. tents** (Judg. 4:17). **live many days—** according to the promise connected with the fifth commandment (Exod. 20:12; Eph. 6:2, 3). **strangers**—They were not of the stock of Jacob, but sojourners in Israel. Types of the children of God, pilgrims on earth, looking for heaven as their home: having little to lose, so that losing times cost them little alarm; sitting loose to what they have (Heb. 10:34; 11:9, 10, 13-16). **8. all that he ... charged us ... all our days, we ... wives ... sons ... daughters**—unreserved obedience in all particulars, at all times, and on the part of all, without exception: in these respects Israel's obedience to God was wanting. Contrast I Samuel 15:20, 21; Psalm 78:34-37, 41, 56, 57. **11. Chaldeans ... Syrians**—when Jehoiakim revolted from Nebuchadnezzar (II Kings 24:1, 2). Necessity sets aside all other laws. This is the Rechabites' excuse for their seeming disobedience to Jonadab in temporarily settling in a city. Herein was seen the prescient wisdom of Jonadab's commands; they could at a moment's notice migrate, having no land possessions to tie them. **14. obey ... father's commandment: notwithstanding I—** (Mal. 1:6). **rising early and speaking**—*God Himself speaking* late and early by His various ways of providence and grace. **15. In vs. 15 and in II Chronicles 36:15, a distinct mode of address is alluded to, viz., *God sending His servants*. (Ch. 18:11; 25:5, 6.) I enjoined nothing unreasonable, but simply to serve Me, and I attached to the command a gracious promise, but in vain. If Jonadab's commands, which were arbitrary and not moral obligations in themselves, were obeyed, much more ought Mine, which are in themselves right. **17. because I have spoken ... not heard ... I ... called ... not answered**—(Prov. 1:24; Isa. 65:12). **19. not want a man to stand before me**—There shall always be left representatives of the clan *to worship Me* (ch. 15:1, 19); or, "before Me" means simple *existence*, for all things in existence are *in God's sight* (Ps. 89:36). The Rechabites returned from the captivity. WOLFF found traces of them in Arabia.

CHAPTER 36

Vss. 1-32. BARUCH WRITES, AND READS PUBLICLY JEREMIAH'S PROPHECIES COLLECTED IN A VOLUME. THE ROLL IS BURNT BY JEHOIAKIM, AND WRITTEN AGAIN BY BARUCH AT JEREMIAH'S DICTATION. **1. fourth year**—The command to write the roll was given in the fourth year, but it was not read publicly till the fifth year. As Isaiah subjoined to his predictions a history of events confirming his prophecies (Isa. 36, 37, 38, 39), so Jeremiah also in chs. 37, 38, 39, 40, 41, 42, 43; but he prefaces his history with the narrative of an incident that occurred some time ago, showing that he, not only by word, but in writing, and that twice, had testified all that he is about to state as having subsequently come to pass [GROTIUS]. At the end of Jehoiakim's third year,

Nebuchadnezzar enrolled an army against Jerusalem and took it in the end of the fifth or beginning of the sixth year, carrying away captive Jehoiakim, Daniel, etc. Jehoiakim returned the same year, and for three years was tributary: then he withheld tribute. Nebuchadnezzar returned and took Jerusalem, and carried off Jehoiakim, who died on the road. This harmonizes this chapter with II Kings 24: and Daniel 1. See *Note*, ch. 22:19. **2. roll of a book**—a book formed of prepared skins made into a roll. Cf. "volume of the book," i.e., the Pentateuch (Ps. 40:7). It does not follow that his prophecies were not before committed to writing; what is implied is, they were now written together in *one* volume, so as to be read continuously to the Jews in the temple. **against ... nations**—(ch. 25:15, etc.). **from ... days of Josiah**—(ch. 25:3). From Josiah's thirteenth year (ch. 1:2). **3. hear**—consider seriously. **return ... from ... evil way**—(Jonah 3:8.) **4. all ... words of ... Lord**—God specially suggesting what might otherwise have escaped his memory, and directing the choice of words, as well as the substance (John 14:26; 16:13). **5. I am shut up**—not in prison, for there is no account of his imprisonment under Jehoiakim, and vss. 19, 26 are inconsistent with it: but, "*I am prevented*," viz., by some hindrance; or, through fear of the king, to whose anger Baruch was less exposed, as not being the author of the prophecy. **6. go**—on the following year (vs. 9). **fasting day**—(See vs. 9.) An extraordinary fast, in the *ninth* month (whereas the fast on the great day of atonement was on the tenth day of the *seventh* month, Lev. 16:29; 23:27-32), appointed to avert the impending calamity, when it was feared Nebuchadnezzar, having in the year before (i.e., the fourth of Jehoiakim), smitten Pharaoh-necho at Carchemish, would attack Judea, as the ally of Egypt (II Kings 23:34, 35). The fast was likely to be an occasion on which Jeremiah would find the Jews more softened, as well as a larger number of them met together. **7. present ... supplication**—lit., "supplication shall fall"; alluding to the *prostrate attitude* of the supplicants (Deut. 9:25; Matt. 26:39), as petitioners fall at the feet of a king in the East. So *Hebrew*, ch. 38:26; Daniel 9:18, *Margin*. **9. they proclaimed ... to all the people ... to all ...**—rather, "all the people . . . all the people proclaimed a fast" [MICHAELIS]. The chiefs appointed the fast by the wish of the people. In either version the ungodly king had no share in appointing the fast. **10. chamber**—Baruch read from the window or balcony of the chamber looking into the court where the people were assembled. However, some of the chambers were large enough to contain a considerable number (Neh. 13:5). **Gemariah**—distinct from the Gemariah, son of Hilkiah, in ch. 29:3. **Shaphan** —the same person as in II Kings 22:3. **scribe**—secretary of state, or he who presided over the public records. **higher court**—that of the priests, the court of the people being lower (II Chron. 4:9). **new gate**—(ch. 26:10). The east gate. **12. scribe's chamber**—an apartment in the palace occupied by the secretary of state. **princes**—holding a counsel of state at the time. **Elnathan**—who had already been an instrument of evil in Jehoiakim's hand (ch. 26:22, 23). **Hananiah**—the false prophet (ch. 28: 10-17). **14. Jehudi**—of a good family, as appears from his pedigree being given so fully, but in a subordinate position. **come**—Instead of requiring Baruch to *come* to them, they ought to have *gone* to the temple, and there professed their penitence. But pride forbade it [CALVIN]. **16. afraid, both one and other**—*Hebrew*, fear-stricken, they turned to one another (cf. Gen. 42:28). This showed, on their part, hesitancy, and some degree of fear of God, but not enough to make them willing to sacrifice the favor of an earthly king. **We will surely tell the king**—not the language of threatening, but implying that the matter is of such moment that the king ought to be made acquainted with it, so as to seek some remedy against the divine anger. **17.** What they wished to know was, whether what Baruch had read to them was written by him from memory after hearing Jeremiah repeating his prophecies continuously, or accurately from the prophet's own dictation. **18. his mouth**—Baruch replies it was by the *oral* dictation of the prophet; vs. 2 accords with this view, rather than with the notion that Jeremiah repeated his prophecies from MSS. **ink**—his specification of the "ink" implies: I added nothing save the hand, pen, and ink. **19.** Showing that they were not altogether without better feelings (cf. vss. 16, 25). **20. chamber**—There were chambers in the king's palace round the court or great hall, as in the temple (vs. 10). The roll was "laid up" there for safekeeping, with other public records. **21. sent Jehudi**—Note how unbelievers flee from God, and yet seek Him through some kind of involuntary impulse [CALVIN]. Jehudi seems to have been the king's ready tool for evil. **22. winter-house**—(Amos 3: 15.) **ninth month**—viz., of the religious year, i.e., November or December. **fire on . . . hearth**—rather, *the stove* was burning before him. In the East neither chimneys nor ovens are used, but, in cold weather, a brazen vessel containing burning charcoal; when the wood has burned to embers, a cover is placed over the pot to make it retain the heat. **23. three or four leaves**—not distinct leaves as in a book, but the consecutive spaces on the long roll in the shape of *doors* (whence the *Hebrew* name is derived), into which the writing is divided: as the books of Moses in the synagogue in the present day are written in a long parchment rolled round a stick, the writing divided into columns, like pages. **penknife**—the writer's knife with which the reed, used as a pen, was mended. "He" refers to the king (vs. 22). As often as Jehudi read three or four columns, the king cut asunder the part of the roll read; and so he treated the whole, until all the parts read consecutively were cut and burnt; vs. 24, "*all* these words," implies that the *whole* volume was read through, not merely the first three or four columns (I Kings 22:8). **24.** The king and his "servants" were more hardened than the "princes" and councillors (vss. 12-16, *Notes*). Contrast the humble fear exhibited by Josiah at the reading of the law (II Kings 22:11). **25.** (*Note*, vs. 16.) The "nevertheless" aggravates the king's sin; though God would have drawn him back through their intercession, he persisted: judicial blindness and reprobation! **26. Hammelech**—not as *Margin*, "of the king." Jehoiakim at this time (the fifth year of his reign) had no grown-up son: Jeconiah, his successor, was then a boy of eleven (cf. II Kings 23:36, with 24:8). **hid them**—(Ps. 31:20; 83:3; Isa. 26:20). **27. roll, and . . . words**—i.e., the roll of words. **28. all the former words**—It is in vain that the ungodly resist the power of Jehovah: not one of His words shall fall to the ground (Matt. 5:18; Acts 9:5; 5:39). **29. say to Jehoiakim**—not in person, as Jeremiah was "hidden" (vs. 26), but by the written word of prophecy. **saying, Why**—This is what the king had desired to be said to Jeremiah if he should be found; kings often dislike the truth to be told them. **30. He shall have none to sit upon the throne**—fulfilled (II Kings 24:8,

etc.; 25). He had *successors,* but not directly of his posterity, *except his son Jeconiah,* whose three months' reign is counted as nothing. Zedekiah was not the son, but the uncle of Jeconiah, and was raised to the throne in contempt of him and his father Jehoiakim (ch. 22:30). **dead body . . . cast out**—(ch. 22:18, 19). **day . . . heat . . . night . . . frost**—There are often these variations of temperature in the East between night and day (Gen. 31:40). **32. added besides . . . many like words**—Sinners gain nothing but additional punishment by setting aside the word of Jehovah. The law was similarly rewritten after the first tables had been broken owing to Israel's idolatry (Exod. 32, 34).

CHAPTER 37

Vss. 1-21. HISTORICAL SECTIONS, CHAPTERS 37-44. THE CHALDEANS RAISE THE SIEGE TO GO AND MEET PHARAOH-HOPHRA. ZEDEKIAH SENDS TO JEREMIAH TO PRAY TO GOD IN BEHALF OF THE JEWS: IN VAIN, JEREMIAH TRIES TO ESCAPE TO HIS NATIVE PLACE, BUT IS ARRESTED. ZEDEKIAH ABATES THE RIGOR OF HIS IMPRISONMENT. **1. Coniah**—curtailed from Jeconiah by way of reproach. **whom**—referring to Zedekiah, not to Coniah (II Kings 24:17). **2.** Amazing stupidity, that they were not admonished by the punishment of Jeconiah [CALVIN], (II Chron. 36:12, 14)! **3. Zedekiah . . . sent**—fearing lest, in the event of the Chaldeans overcoming Pharaoh-hophra, they should return to besiege Jerusalem. See *Note* in beginning of ch. 21; that chapter chronologically comes in between chs. 37 and 38. The message of the king to Jeremiah here in ch. 37 is, however, somewhat earlier than that in ch. 21; here it is while the issue between the Chaldeans and Pharaoh was undecided; there it is when, after the repulse of Pharaoh, the Chaldeans were again advancing against Jerusalem; hence, while Zephaniah is named in both embassies, *Jehucal* accompanies him here, *Pashur* there. But, as Pashur and Jehucal are both mentioned in ch. 38:1, 2, as hearing Jeremiah's reply, which is identical with that in ch. 21:9, it is probable the two messages followed one another at a short interval; that in this ch. 37:3, and the answer, vss. 7-10, being the earlier of the two. **Zephaniah**—an abettor of rebellion against God (ch. 29:25), though less virulent than many (vs. 29; ch. 29), punished accordingly (ch. 52:24-27). **4. Jeremiah . . . not put . . . into prison**—He was no longer in the prison court, as he had been (ch. 32:2; 33:1), which passages refer to the beginning of the siege, not to the time when the Chaldeans renewed the siege, after having withdrawn for a time to meet Pharaoh. **5.** After this temporary diversion, caused by Pharaoh in favor of Jerusalem, the Egyptians returned no more to its help (II Kings 24:7). Judea had the misfortune to lie between the two great contending powers, Babylon and Egypt, and so was exposed to the alternate inroads of the one or the other. Josiah, taking side with Assyria, fell in battle with Pharaoh-necho at Megiddo (II Kings 23: 29). Zedekiah, seeking the Egyptian alliance in violation of his oath, was now about to be taken by Nebuchadnezzar (II Chron. 36:13; Ezek. 17:15, 17). **7. shall return**—without accomplishing any deliverance for you. **8.** (Ch. 34:22.) **9. yourselves**—*Hebrew,* "souls." **10. yet . . . they**—Even a few wounded men would suffice for your destruction. **11. broken up**—"gone up." **12. Benjamin**—to his own town, Anathoth. **to separate himself**—*Margin* translates, "to slip away," from a *Hebrew* root, "to be smooth," so, to slip away as a slippery thing that cannot be held. But it is not likely the prophet of God would flee in a dishonorable way; and "in the midst of the people" rather implies open departure along with others, than clandestine slipping away by mixing with the crowd of departing people. Rather, it means, *to separate himself*, or to *divide his place of residence*, so as to live partly here, partly there, without fixed habitation, going to and fro among the people [LUDOVICUS DE DIEU]. MAURER translates, "to take his portion thence," to realize the produce of his property in Anathoth [HENDERSON], or to take possession of the land which he bought from Hanameel [MAURER]. **13. ward**–i.e., the "guard," or "watch." **Hananiah**–whose death Jeremiah predicted (ch. 28:16). The grandson in revenge takes Jeremiah into custody on the charge of *deserting* ("thou fallest away," ch. 38:19; 52:15; I Sam. 29:3) to the enemy. His prophecies gave color to the charge (ch. 21:9; 38:4). **15. scribe**–one of the court secretaries; often in the East part of the private house of a public officer serves as a prison. **16. dungeon . . . cabins**–The prison consisted of a *pit* (the "dungeon") with *vaulted cells* round the sides of it. The "cabins," from a root, "to bend one's self." **17. secretly**–Zedekiah was ashamed to be seen by his courtiers consulting Jeremiah (John 12:43; 5:44; 19:38). **thou shalt be delivered**–Had Jeremiah consulted his earthly interests, he would have answered very differently. Contrast ch. 6:14; Isaiah 30:10; Ezekiel 13:10. **18. What**–In what respect have I offended? **19. Where are now your prophets**–The event has showed them to be liars; and, as surely as the king of Babylon has come already, notwithstanding their prophecy, so surely shall he return. **20. be accepted**–rather, "Let my supplication *be humbly presented*" (ch. 36: 7, *Note*), [HENDERSON]. **lest I die there**–in the subterranean dungeon (vs. 16), from want of proper sustenance (vs. 21.) The prophet *naturally* shrank from death, which makes his *spiritual* firmness the more remarkable; he was ready to die rather than swerve from his duty [CALVIN]. **21. court of the prison**–(ch. 32:2; 38:13, 28). **bakers' street**–Persons in the same business in cities in the East commonly reside in the same street. **all the bread . . . spent**–Jeremiah had bread supplied to him until he was thrown into the dungeon of Malchiah, at which time the bread in the city was spent. Cf. this verse with ch. 38:9; that time must have been very shortly before the capture of the city (ch. 52:6). God saith of His children, "In the days of famine they shall be satisfied" (Ps. 37:19; Isa. 33:16). Honest reproof (vs. 17), in the end often gains more favor than flattery (Prov. 28:23).

CHAPTER 38

Vss. 1-28. JEREMIAH PREDICTS THE CAPTURE OF JERUSALEM, FOR WHICH HE IS CAST INTO A DUNGEON, BUT IS TRANSFERRED TO THE PRISON COURT ON THE INTERCESSION OF EBED-MELECH, AND HAS A SECRET INTERVIEW WITH ZEDEKIAH. All this was subsequent to his imprisonment in Jonathan's house, and his release on his interview with Zedekiah. The latter occurred *before* the return of the Chaldeans to the siege; the similar events in this chapter occurred *after* it. **1. Jucal**–Jehucal (ch. 37:3). **Pashur**–(ch. 21: 1; cf. vs. 9 of ch. 21 with vs. 2 of this ch. 38). The deputation in ch. 21:1, to whom Jeremiah gave this reply, if not identical with the hearers of Jeremiah (ch. 38:1), must have been sent just before the latter

"heard" him speaking the same words. *Zephaniah* is not mentioned here as in ch. 21:1, but is so in ch. 37:3. *Jucal* is mentioned here and in the previous deputation (ch. 37:3), but not in ch. 21:1. *Shephatiah* and *Gedaliah* here do not occur either in ch. 21:1 or ch. 37:3. The identity of his words in both cases is natural, when uttered, at a very short interval, and one of the hearers (Pashur) being present on both occasions. **unto all the people**–They had free access to him in the court of the prison (ch. 32: 12). **2. life . . . a prey**–He shall escape with his life; though losing all else in a shipwreck, he shall carry off his life as his gain, saved by his going over to the Chaldeans. (*Note*, ch. 21:9.) **4.** Had Jeremiah not had a divine commission, he might justly have been accused of treason; but having one, which made the result of the siege certain, he acted humanely as interpreter of God's will under the theocracy, in advising surrender (cf. ch. 26:11). **5. the king is not he**–Zedekiah was a weak prince, and now in his straits afraid to oppose his princes. He hides his dislike of their overweening power, which prevented him shielding Jeremiah as he would have wished, under complimentary speeches. "It is not right that the king should deny aught to such faithful and wise statesmen"; the king is not such a one as to deny you your wishes [JEROME]. **6. dungeon**–lit., the "cistern." It was not a subterranean prison as that in Jonathan's house (ch. 37:15), but a pit or cistern, which had been full of water, but was emptied of it during the siege, so that only "mire" remained. Such empty cisterns were often used as prisons (Zech. 9:11); the depth forbade hope of escape. **Hammelech**–(ch. 36:26). His son followed in the father's steps, a ready tool for evil. **sunk in the mire**–Jeremiah herein was a type of Messiah (Ps. 69:2, 14). "I sink in deep mire . . . ." **7. Ebed-melech**–The *Hebrew* designation given this Ethiopian, meaning "king's servant." Already, even at this early time, God wished to show what good reason there was for calling the Gentiles to salvation. An Ethiopian stranger saves the prophet whom his own countrymen, the Jews, tried to destroy. So the Gentiles believed in Christ whom the Jews crucified, and Ethiopians were among the earliest converts (Acts 2:10, 41; 8:27-39). Ebed-melech probably was keeper of the royal harem, and so had private access to the king. The eunuchs over harems in the present day are mostly from Nubia or Abyssinia. **8. went forth . . . and spake**–not privately, but in public; a proof of fearless magnanimity. **9. die for hunger in the place where he is; for . . . no . . . bread in . . . . city**–(Cf. ch. 37: 21). He had heretofore got a piece of bread supplied to him. "Seeing that there is the *utmost want of bread* in the city, so that even if he were at large, there could *no more* be regularly supplied to him, much less now in a place where none remember or pity him, so that he is likely to die for hunger." "No more bread," i.e., no more left of the *public store* in the city (ch. 37:21); or, *all but* no bread left anywhere [MAURER]. **10. with thee**–*Hebrew*, "in thine hand," i.e., at "thy disposal" (I Sam. 16:2). "From hence," i.e., from the gate of Benjamin where the king was sitting (vs. 7). **thirty men**–not merely to draw up Jeremiah, but to guard Ebed-melech against any opposition on the part of the princes (vss. 1-4), in executing the king's command. Ebed-melech was rewarded for his faith, love, and courage, exhibited at a time when he might well fear the wrath of the princes, to which even the king had to yield (ch. 39:16-18). **11. cast clouts**–"torn clothes" [HENDERSON]. **rotten rags**–"worn-out garments."

God can make the meanest things His instruments of goodness to His people (I Cor. 1:27-29). **under ... armholes**—"under the joints of thine hands," i.e., where the fingers join the hand, the clothes being in order that the hands should not be cut by the cords [MAURER]. **13. court of ... prison**—Ebed-melech prudently put him there to be out of the way of his enemies. **14. third entry**—The Hebrews in determining the position of places faced the *east*, which they termed "that which is in front"; the *south* was thus called "that which is on the right hand"; the *north*, "that which is on the left hand"; the *west*, "that which is behind." So beginning with the *east* they might term it the *first* or principal entry; the *south* the *second* entry; the *north* the "*third* entry" of the outer or inner court [MAURER]. The third gate of the temple facing the palace; for through it the entrance lay from the palace into the temple (I Kings 10:5, 12). It was westward (I Chron. 26:16, 18; II Chron. 9:11) [GROTIUS]. But in the future temple it is eastward (Ezek. 46:1, 2, 8). **15. wilt thou not hearken unto me**—Zedekiah does not answer this last query; the former one he replies to in vs. 16. Rather translate, "Thou wilt not hearken to me." Jeremiah judges so from the past conduct of the king. Cf. vs. 17 with vs. 19. **16. Lord ... made us this soul**—(Isa. 57:16). Implying, "may my life (soul) be forfeited if I deceive thee" [CALVIN]. **17. princes**—(ch. 39:3). He does not say "to the king himself," for he was at Riblah, in Hamath (ch. 39:5; II Kings 25:6). "*If* thou go forth" (viz., to surrender; II Kings 24:12; Isa. 36:16), God foreknows future conditional contingencies, and ordains not only the end, but also the *means* to the end. **19. afraid of the Jews**—more than of God (Prov. 29:25; John 9:22; 12:43). **mock me**—treat me injuriously (I Sam. 31:4). **22. women**—The very evil which Zedekiah wished to escape by disobeying the command to go forth shall befall him in its worst form thereby. Not merely the Jewish deserters shall "mock" him (vs. 19), but the very "women" of his own palace and harem, to gratify their new lords, will taunt him. A noble king in sooth, to suffer thyself to be so imposed on! **Thy friends**—*Hebrew*, men of thy peace (see ch. 20:10; Ps. 41:9, *Margin*). The king's ministers and the false prophets who misled him. **sunk in ... mire**—proverbial for, Thou art involved by "thy friends' " counsels in inextricable difficulties. The phrase perhaps alludes to vs. 6; a just retribution for the treatment of Jeremiah, who literally "sank in the mire." **they are turned ... back**—Having involved thee in the calamity, they themselves shall provide for their own safety by deserting to the Chaldeans (vs. 19). **23. children**—(ch. 39:6; 41:10). "wives ... children ... thou"; an ascending climax. **24. Let no man know**—If thou wilt not tell this to the people, I will engage thy safety. **25.** Kings are often such only in title; they are really under the power of their subjects. **26. presented**—lit., "made my supplication to fall"; implying supplication with humble prostration (*Note*, ch. 36:7). **Jonathan's house**—(ch. 37:15), different from Malchiah's dungeon (vs. 6). This statement was true, though not the whole truth; the princes had no right to the information; no sanction is given by Scripture here to Jeremiah's representation of this being the cause of his having come to the king. Fear drove him to it. Cf. Genesis 20:2, 12; on the other hand, I Samuel 16:2, 5. **left off speaking with**—*Hebrew*, "were silent from him," i.e., withdrawing from him they left him quiet (I Sam. 7:8, *Margin*). **28. he was [there] when Jerusalem was taken**—These words are made the begin-

ning of ch. 39 by many; but the accents and sense support *English Version*.

CHAPTER 39

Vss. 1-18. JERUSALEM TAKEN. ZEDEKIAH'S FATE. JEREMIAH CARED FOR. EBED-MELECH ASSURED. This chapter consists of two parts: the first describes the capture of Jerusalem, the removal of the people to Babylon, and the fate of Zedekiah, and that of Jeremiah. The second tells of the assurance of safety to Ebed-melech. **1. ninth year ... tenth month**—and on the tenth day of it (ch. 52:4; II Kings 25:1-4). From vs. 2, "eleventh year ... fourth month ... ninth day," we know the siege lasted one and a half years, excepting the suspension of it caused by Pharaoh. Nebuchadnezzar was present in the beginning of the siege, but was at Riblah at its close (vss. 3, 6; cf. ch. 38:17). **3. sat**—expressing military occupation or encampment. **middle gate**—the gate from the upper city (comprehending Mount Zion) to the lower city (*north* of the former and much lower); it was into the latter (the *north* side) that the Chaldeans forced an entry and took up their position opposite the gate of the "middle" wall, between the lower and upper city. Zedekiah fled in the opposite, i.e., the south direction (vs. 4). **Nergalsharezer, Samgarnebo**—proper names formed from those of the idols, Nergal and Nebo (II Kings 17:30; Isa. 46:1). **Rab-saris**—meaning "chief of the eunuchs." **Rab-mag**—chief of the magi; brought with the expedition in order that its issue might be foreknown through his astrological skill. *Mag* is a Persian word, meaning "great," "powerful." The magi were a sacerdotal caste among the Medes, and supported the Zoroastrian religion. **4. the king's garden**—The "gate" to it from the upper city above was appropriated to the kings alone; "stairs" led down from Mount Zion and the palace to the king's garden below (Neh. 3:15). **two walls**—Zedekiah might have held the upper city longer, but want of provisions drove him to flee by the double wall south of Zion, towards the plains of Jericho (vs. 5), in order to escape beyond Jordan to Arabia Deserta. He broke an opening in the wall to get out (Ezek. 12:12). **5. Riblah**—north of Palestine (see ch. 1:14; Num. 34:11). Hamath is identified by commentators with Antioch, in Syria, on the Orontes, called Epiphania, from Antiochus Epiphanes. **gave judgment upon him**—lit., "spake judgments with him," i.e., brought him to trial as a common criminal, not as a king. He had violated his oath (Ezek. 17:13-19; II Chron. 36: 13). **6. slew ... sons ... before his eyes**—previous to his eyes being "put out" (vs. 7); lit. "dug out." The Assyrian sculptures depict the delight with which the kings struck out, often with their own hands, the eyes of captive princes. This passage reconciles ch. 32:4, "his eyes shall behold his eyes"; with Ezekiel 12:13, "he shall not see Babylon, though he shall die there." **slew all ... nobles**—(ch. 27:20). **8. burned ... the houses**—(ch. 52:12, 13). Not immediately after the taking of the city, but in the month after, viz., the fifth month (cf. vs. 2). The delay was probably caused by the princes having to send to Riblah to know the king's pleasure as to the city. **9. remnant**—excepting the poorest (vs. 10), who caused Nebuchadnezzar no apprehensions. **those ... that fell to him**—the *deserters* were distrusted; or they may have been removed at their own request, lest the people should vent their rage on them as traitors, after the departure of the Chaldeans. **rest ... that remained**—distinct from the previous "remnant"; *there* he means the remnant of those besieged in the city, whom Nebuchadnezzar spared; here, those scattered through various districts of the country which had not been besieged [CALVIN]. **10. left ... the poor ... which had nothing**—The poor have least to lose; one of the providential compensations of their lot. They who before had been stripped of their possessions by the wealthier Jews obtain, not only their own, but those of others. **11.** Jeremiah's prophecies were known to Nebuchadnezzar through deserters (vs. 9; ch. 38: 19), also through the Jews carried to Babylon with Jeconiah (cf. ch. 40:2). Hence the king's kindness to him. **12. look well to him**—*Hebrew*, set thine eyes upon him; provide for his well-being. **13. Nebuzaradan ... sent**—He was then at Ramah (ch. 40:1). **14. Gedaliah**—son of Ahikam, the former supporter of Jeremiah (ch. 26:24). Gedaliah was the chief of the deserters to the Chaldeans, and was set over the remnant in Judea as one likely to remain faithful to Nebuchadnezzar. His residence was at Mizpah (ch. 40:5). **home**—the house of Gedaliah, wherein Jeremiah might remain as in a safe asylum. As in ch. 40:1 Jeremiah is represented as "bound in chains" when he came to Ramah among the captives to be carried to Babylon, this release of Jeremiah is thought by MAURER to be distinct from that in ch. 40:5, 6. But he seems first to have been released from the court of the prison and to have been taken to Ramah, still in chains, and then committed in freedom to Gedaliah. **dwelt among the people**— i.e., was made free. **15-18.** Belonging to the time when the city was not yet taken, and when Jeremiah was still in the court of the prison (ch. 38:13). This passage is inserted here because it was now that Ebed-melech's good act (ch. 38:7-12; Matt. 25:43) was to be rewarded in his deliverance. **16. Go**—not literally, for he was in confinement, but figuratively. **16. before thee**—in thy sight. **17. the men of whom thou art afraid**—(ch. 38:1, 4-6). The courtiers and princes hostile to thee for having delivered Jeremiah shall have no power to hurt. Heretofore intrepid, he was now afraid; this prophecy was therefore the more welcome to him. **18. life ... for a prey**— (*Notes*, ch. 21:9; 38:2; 45:5). **put ... trust in me**— (ch. 38:7-9). Trust in God was the root of his fearlessness of the wrath of men, in his humanity to the prophet (I Chron. 5:20; Ps. 37:40). The "life" he thus risked was to be his reward, being spared beyond all hope, when the lives of his enemies should be forfeited ("for a prey").

CHAPTER 40

Vss. 1-16. JEREMIAH IS SET FREE AT RAMAH, AND GOES TO GEDALIAH, TO WHOM THE REMNANT OF JEWS REPAIR. JOHANAN WARNS GEDALIAH OF ISHMAEL'S CONSPIRACY IN VAIN. **1. word that came**— the heading of a new part of the book (chs. 41-44) viz., the prophecies to the Jews in Judea and Egypt after the *taking* of the city, blended with history. The prophecy does not begin till ch. 42:7, and the previous history is introductory to it. **bound in chains**—Though released from the court of the prison (*Note*, ch. 39:14), in the confusion at the burning of the city he seems to have been led away in chains with the other captives, and not till he reached Ramah to have gained full liberty. Nebuzaradan had his quarters at Ramah, in Benjamin; and there he collected the captives previous to their removal to Babylon (ch. 31:15). He in releasing Jeremiah obeyed the king's commands (ch. 39:11).

Jeremiah's "chains" for a time were due to the negligence of those to whom he had been committed; or else to Nebuzaradan's wish to upbraid the people with their perverse ingratitude in imprisoning Jeremiah [CALVIN]; hence he addresses the people (*ye ... you*) as much as Jeremiah (vss. 2, 3). **2.** The Babylonians were in some measure aware, through Jeremiah's prophecies (ch. 39:11), that they were the instruments of God's wrath on His people. **3. ye**—(*Note*, vs. 1). His address is directed to the Jews as well as to Jeremiah. God makes the very heathen testify for Him against them (Deut. 29:24, 25). **4. look well unto thee**—the very words of Nebuchadnezzar's charge (ch. 39:12). **all the land is before thee ... seemeth good**—(Gen. 20:15, *Margin*). Jeremiah alone had the option given him of staying where he pleased, when all the rest were either carried off or forced to remain there. **5. while he was not yet gone back**—parenthetical. When Jeremiah hesitated whether it would be best for him to go, Nebuzaradan proceeded to say, "Go, *then*, to Gedaliah," (not as *English Version*, "Go back, *also*"), if thou preferrest (as Nebuzaradan inferred from Jeremiah's hesitancy) to stop here rather than go with me. **victuals**—(Isa. 33:16). **reward**— **rather, a present.** This must have been a seasonable relief to the prophet, who probably lost his all in the siege. **6. Mizpah**—in Benjamin, northwest of Jerusalem (ch. 41:5, 6, 9). Not the Mizpah in Gilead, beyond Jordan (Judg. 10:17). Jeremiah showed his patriotism and piety in remaining in his country amidst afflictions and notwithstanding the ingratitude of the Jews, rather than go to enjoy honors and pleasures in a heathen court (Heb. 11:24-26). This vindicates his purity of motive in his withdrawal (ch. 37:12-14). **7. captains ... in the fields**—The leaders of the Jewish army had been "scattered" throughout the country on the capture of Zedekiah (ch. 52:8), in order to escape the notice of the Chaldeans. **8. Netophathite**—from Netophah, a town in Judah (II Sam. 23:28). **Maachathite**—from Maachathi, at the foot of Mount Hermon (Deut. 3:14). **9. Fear not**—They were afraid that they should not obtain pardon from the Chaldeans for their acts. He therefore assured them of safety by an oath. **serve**—lit., to stand before (vs. 10; ch. 52:12), i.e., to be at hand ready to execute the commands of the king of Babylon. **10. Mizpah** —lying on the way between Babylon and Judah, and so convenient for transacting business between the two countries. **As for me ... but ye**—He artfully, in order to conciliate them, represents the burden of the service to the Chaldeans as falling on *him*, while *they* may freely gather their wine, fruits, and oil. He does not now add that these very fruits were to constitute the chief part of the tribute to be paid to Babylon: which, though fruitful in corn, was less productive of grapes, figs, and olives [HERODOTUS, 1.193]. The grant of "vineyards" to the "poor" (ch. 39:10) would give hope to the discontented of enjoying the best fruits (vs. 12). **11. Jews ... in Moab**—who had fled thither at the approach of the Chaldeans. God thus tempered the severity of His vengeance that a remnant might be left. **13. in the fields**—not in the city, but scattered in the country (vs. 7). **14. Baalis**—named from the idol Baal, as was often the case in heathen names. **Ammonites**—So it was to them that Ishmael went after murdering Gedaliah (ch. 41:10). **slay**—lit., "strike thee in the soul," i.e., a deadly stroke. **Ishmael**—Being of the royal seed of David (ch. 41:1), he envied Gedaliah the presidency to which he thought himself entitled; therefore he leagued himself with the ancient heathen enemy of Judah. **believed ... not**—generous, but unwise unsuspiciousness (Eccles. 9:16). **16. thou speakest falsely**—a mystery of providence that God should permit the righteous, in spite of warning, thus to rush into the trap laid for them! Isaiah 57:1 suggests a solution.

CHAPTER 41

Vss. 1-18. ISHMAEL MURDERS GEDALIAH AND OTHERS, THEN FLEES TO THE AMMONITES. JOHANAN PURSUES HIM, RECOVERS THE CAPTIVES, AND PURPOSES TO FLEE TO EGYPT FOR FEAR OF THE CHALDEANS. **1. seventh month**—the second month after the burning of the city (ch. 52:12, 13). **and the princes**—not the nominative. And the princes *came*, for the "princes" are not mentioned either in the next verse or in II Kings 25:25: but, "Ishmael being of the seed royal and of the princes of the king" [MAURER]. But the *ten men* were the "princes of the king"; thus MAURER's objection has no weight: so *English Version*. **eat bread together**—Ishmael murdered Gedaliah, by whom he was hospitably received, in violation of the sacred right of hospitality (Ps. 41:9). **2. slew him whom the king of Babylon had made governor**—This assigns a reason for their slaying him, as well as showing the magnitude of their crime (Dan. 2:21; Rom. 13:1). **3. slew all the Jews**—namely, the attendants and ministers of Gedaliah; or, the military alone, about his person; translate, *"even* (not 'and,' as *English Version*) the men of war."* The main portion of the people with Gedaliah, including Jeremiah, Ishmael carried away captive (vss. 10, 16). **4. no man knew it**—i.e., outside Mizpah. Before tidings of the murder had gone abroad. **5. beards shaven ...**—indicating their deep sorrow at the destruction of the temple and city. **cut themselves**—a heathen custom, forbidden (Lev. 19:27, 28; Deut. 14:1). These men were mostly from Samaria, where the ten tribes, previous to their deportation, had fallen into heathen practices. **offerings**—unbloody. They do not bring sacrificial victims, but "incense," etc., to testify their piety. **house of ... Lord**—i.e., the place where the house of the Lord had stood (II Kings 25:9). The place in which a temple had stood, even when it had been destroyed, was held sacred [PAPINIAN]. Those "from Shiloh" would naturally seek the house of the Lord, since it was at Shiloh it originally was set up (Josh. 18:1). **6. weeping**—pretending to weep, as they did, for the ruin of the temple. **Come to Gedaliah**—as if he was one of Gedaliah's retinue. **7. and cast them into ... pit**—He had not killed them in the pit (cf. vs. 9); these words are therefore rightly supplied in *English Version*. **the pit**—the pit or cistern made by Asa to guard against a want of water when Baasha was about to besiege the city (I Kings 15:22). The trench or fosse round the city [GROTIUS]. Ishmael's motive for the murder seems to have been a suspicion that they were coming to live under Gedaliah. **8. treasures**—It was customary to hide grain in cavities underground in troubled times. "We have treasures," which we will give, if our lives be spared. **slew ... not**—(Prov. 13:8). Ishmael's avarice and needs overcame his cruelty. **9. because of Gedaliah**—rather, *"near* Gedaliah," viz., those intercepted by Ishmael on their way from Samaria to Jerusalem and killed *at Mizpah*, where Gedaliah had lived. So II Chronicles 17:15, "next"; Nehemiah 3:2, *Margin*, lit., as here, "at his hand." "In the reign of Gedaliah" [CALVIN]. However, *English Version* gives

a good sense: Ishmael's reason for killing them was *because* of his supposing them to be connected with Gedaliah. **10. the king's daughters**—(ch. 43:6). Zedekiah's. Ishmael must have got additional followers (whom the hope of gain attracted), besides those who had originally set out with him (vs. 1), so as to have been able to carry off all the residue of the people. He probably meant to sell them as slaves to the Ammonites (ch. 40:14, *Note*). **11. Johanan**—the friend of Gedaliah who had warned him of Ishmael's treachery, but in vain (ch. 40:8, 13). **12. the ... waters ... in Gibeon**—(II Sam. 2:13); a large reservoir or lake. **Gibeon**—on the road from Mizpah to Ammon: one of the sacerdotal cities of Benjamin, four miles northwest of Jerusalem, now *Eljib*. **13. glad**—at the prospect of having a deliverer from their captivity. **14. cast about**—came round. **16. men of war**—"The men of war," stated in vs. 3 to have been slain by Ishmael, must refer to the military about Gedaliah's person; "the men of war" here to those not so. **eunuchs**—The kings of Judah had adopted the bad practice of having harems and eunuchs from the surrounding heathen kingdoms. **17. dwelt**—for a time, until they were ready for their journey to Egypt (ch. 42). **habitation to Chimham**—his caravanserai close by Bethlehem. David, in reward for Barzillai's loyalty, took Chimham his son under his patronage, and made over to him his own patrimony in the land of Bethlehem. It was thence called the habitation of Chimham (Geruth-Chimham), though it reverted to David's heirs in the year of jubilee. Caravanserais (a compound *Persian* word, meaning "the house of a company of travellers") differ from our inns, in that there is no host to supply food, but each traveller must carry with him his own. **18. afraid**—lest the Chaldeans should suspect all the Jews of being implicated in Ishmael's treason, as though the Jews sought to have a prince of the house of David (vs. 1). Their better way towards gaining God's favor would have been to have laid the blame on the real culprit, and to have cleared themselves. A tortuous policy is the parent of fear. Righteousness inspires with boldness (Ps. 53:5; Prov. 28:1).

CHAPTER 42

Vss. 1-22. THE JEWS AND JOHANAN INQUIRE OF GOD, THROUGH JEREMIAH, AS TO GOING TO EGYPT, PROMISING OBEDIENCE TO HIS WILL. THEIR SAFETY ON CONDITION OF STAYING IN JUDEA, AND THEIR DESTRUCTION IN THE EVENT OF GOING TO EGYPT, ARE FORETOLD. THEIR HYPOCRISY IN ASKING FOR COUNSEL WHICH THEY MEANT NOT TO FOLLOW, IF CONTRARY TO THEIR OWN DETERMINATION, IS REPROVED. **2. Jeremiah**—He probably was one of the number carried off from Mizpah, and dwelt with Johanan (ch. 41:16). Hence the expression is, "came near" (vs. 1), not "sent." **Let ... supplication be accepted**—lit., "fall" (*Note*, ch. 36:7; 37:20). **pray for us**—(Gen. 20:7; Isa. 37:4; Jas. 5:16). **thy God**—(vs. 5). The Jews use this form to express their belief in the peculiar relation in which *Jeremiah* stood to God as His accredited prophet. Jeremiah in his reply reminds them that God is *their* God ("*your* God") as well as his as being the covenant people (vs. 4). They in turn acknowledge this in vs. 6, "the Lord *our* God." **few of many**—as had been foretold (Lev. 26:22). **3.** They consulted God, like many, not so much to know what was right, as wishing Him to authorize what they had already determined on, whether agreeable to

His will or not. So Ahab in consulting Micaiah (I Kings 22:13). Cf. Jeremiah's answer (vs. 4) with Micaiah's (I Kings 22:14). **4. I have heard**—i.e., I accede to your request. **your God**—Being His by adoption, ye are not your own, and are bound to whatever He wills (Exod. 19:5, 6; I Cor 6:19, 20). **answer you**—i.e., through me. **keep nothing back** —(I Sam. 3:18; Acts 20:20.) **5. Lord be a true ... witness**—(Gen. 31:50; Ps. 89:37; Rev. 1:5; 3:14; 19: 11). **6. evil**—not moral evil, which God cannot command (Jas. 1:13), but what may be *disagreeable* and *hard* to us. Piety obeys God, without questioning, at all costs. See the instance defective in this, that it obeyed only so far as was agreeable to itself (I Sam. 15:3, 9, 13-15, 20-23). **7. ten days**—Jeremiah did not speak of himself, but waited God's time and revelation, showing the reality of his inspiration. Man left to himself would have given an immediate response to the people, who were impatient of delay. The delay was designed to test the sincerity of their professed willingness to obey, and that they should have full time to deliberate (Deut. 8:2). True obedience bows to God's time, as well as His way and will. **10. If ye ... abide**— viz., under the Babylonian authority, to which God hath appointed that all should be subject (Dan. 2: 37, 38). To resist was to resist God. **build ... plant**—metaphor for, *I will firmly establish you* (ch. 24:6). **I repent ... of the evil**—(ch. 18:8; Deut. 32:36). *I am satisfied with the punishment I have inflicted on you,* if only you add not a new offense [GROTIUS]. God is said to "repent," when He alters His outward ways of dealing. **12. show mercies**— rather, I *will excite* (in him) *feelings of mercy* towards you [CALVIN]. **cause you to return**—permit you to return to the peaceable enjoyment of the possessions from which you are wishing to withdraw through fear of the Chaldeans. By departing in disobedience they should incur the very evils they wished thereby to escape; and by staying they should gain the blessings which they feared to lose by doing so. **13. if ye say ...**—avowed rebellion against God, who had often (Deut. 17:16), as now, forbidden their going to Egypt, lest they should be entangled in its idolatry. **14. where we shall see no war**—Here they betray their impiety in not believing God's promise (vss. 10, 11), as if He were a liar (I John 5:10). **15. wholly set your faces**—*firmly resolve* (Luke 9:51) in spite of all warnings (ch. 44: 12). **16. sword, which ye feared, shall overtake you** —The very evils we think to escape by sin, we bring on ourselves thereby. What our hearts are most set on often proves fatal to us. Those who think to escape troubles by changing their place will find them wherever they go (Ezek. 11:8). The "sword" here is that of Nebuchadnezzar, who fulfilled the prediction in his expedition to Africa (according to MEGASTHENES, a heathen writer), 300 B.C. **17. all the men**—excepting the "small number" mentioned (ch. 44:14, 28); viz., those who were forced into Egypt against their will, Jeremiah, Baruch, etc., and those who took Jeremiah's advice and fled from Egypt before the arrival of the Chaldeans. **18. As mine anger ...**—As ye have already, to your sorrow, found Me true to My word, so shall ye again (ch. 7:20; 18:16). **shall see this place no more**—Ye shall not return to Judea, as those shall who have been removed to Babylon. **19. I have admonished**—lit., "testified," i.e., solemnly admonished, having yourselves as My *witnesses;* so that if ye perish, ye yourselves will have to confess that it was through your own fault, not through ignorance, ye perished. **20. dissembled in your hearts**—rather, "ye have used

deceit against your (own) souls." It is not God, but yourselves, whom ye deceive, to your own ruin, by your own dissimulation (Gal. 6:7) [CALVIN]. But the words following accord best with *English Version, ye have dissembled in your hearts* (vs. 3, *Note*) towards me, *when ye sent me* to consult God for you. **21. declared it**—viz., the divine will. **I ... but ye**—antithesis. *I* have done my part; *but ye* do not yours. It is no fault of mine that ye act not rightly. **22. sojourn**—*for a time,* until they could return to their country. They expected, therefore, to be restored, in spite of God's prediction to the contrary.

CHAPTER 43

Vss. 1-13. THE JEWS CARRY JEREMIAH AND BARUCH INTO EGYPT. JEREMIAH FORETELLS BY A TYPE THE CONQUEST OF EGYPT BY NEBUCHADNEZZAR, AND THE FATE OF THE FUGITIVES. **2. Azariah**—the author of the project of going into Egypt; a very different man from the Azariah in Babylon (Dan. 1:7; 3:12-18). **proud**—Pride is the parent of disobedience and contempt of God. **3. Baruch**—He being the younger spake out the revelations which he received from Jeremiah more vehemently. From this cause, and from their knowing that he was in favor with the Chaldeans, arose their suspicion of him. Their perverse fickleness was astonishing. In ch. 42 they acknowledged the trustworthiness of Jeremiah, of which they had for so long so many proofs; yet here they accuse him of a lie. The mind of the unregenerate man is full of deceits. **5. remnant ... returned from all nations** —(ch. 40:11, 12). **6. the king's daughters**—Zedekiah's (ch. 41:10). **7. Tahpanhes**—(ch. 2:16, *Note*); Daphne on the Tanitic branch of the Nile, near Pelusium. They naturally came to it first, being on the frontier of Egypt, towards Palestine. **9. stones** —to be laid as the foundation beneath Nebuchadnezzar's throne (vs. 10). **clay**—mortar. **brick-kiln** —Bricks in that hot country are generally dried in the sun, not burned. The palace of Pharaoh was being built or repaired at this time; hence arose the mortar and brick-kiln at the entry. Of the same materials as that of which Pharaoh's house was built, the substructure of Nebuchadnezzar's throne should be constructed. By a visible symbol implying that the throne of the latter shall be raised on the downfall of the former. Egypt at that time contended with Babylon for the empire of the East. **10. my servant**—God often makes one wicked man or nation a scourge to another (Ezek. 29:18, 19, 20). **royal pavilion**—the rich tapestry (lit., ornament) which hung round the throne from above. **11. such as are for death to death**—i.e., the deadly plague. Some he shall cause to die by the plague arising from insufficient or bad food; others, by the sword; others he shall lead captive, according as God shall order it (ch. 15:2, *Note*). **12. houses of ... gods**— He shall not spare even the temple, such will be His fury. A reproof to the Jews that they betook themselves to Egypt, a land whose own safety depended on helpless idols. **burn ... carry ... captives**—*burn* the Egyptian idols of wood, *carry to* Babylon those of gold and other metals. **array himself with the land ...**—Isaiah 49:18 has the same metaphor. **as a shepherd ...**—He shall become master of Egypt as speedily and easily as a shepherd, about to pass on with his flock to another place, puts on his garment. **13. images**—statues or obelisks. **Beth-shemesh**—i.e., "the house of the sun," in *He-*

brew; called by the Greeks Heliopolis; by the Egyptians, On (Gen. 41:45); east of the Nile, and a few miles north of Memphis. Ephraim Syrus says, the statue rose to the height of sixty cubits; the base was ten cubits. Above there was a miter of 1000 pounds weight. Hieroglyphics are traced around the only obelisk remaining in the present day, sixty or seventy feet high. On the fifth year after the overthrow of Jerusalem, Nebuchadnezzar, leaving the siege of Tyre, undertook his expedition to Egypt (JOSEPHUS, *Antiquities*, 10.9, 7). The Egyptians, according to the Arabs, have a tradition that their land was devastated by Nebuchadnezzar in consequence of their king having received the Jews under his protection, and that it lay desolate forty years. But see *Note*, Ezekiel 29:2, 13. **shall he burn**—Here the act is attributed to *Nebuchadnezzar*, the instrument, which in vs. 12 is attributed to God. If even the temples be not spared, much less private houses.

CHAPTER 44

Vss. 1-30. JEREMIAH REPROVES THE JEWS FOR THEIR IDOLATRY IN EGYPT, AND DENOUNCES GOD'S JUDGMENTS ON THEM AND EGYPT ALIKE. **1. Migdol**—meaning a "tower." A city east of Egypt, towards the Red Sea (Exod. 14:2; Num. 33:7). **Noph**—Memphis, now Cairo (ch. 2:16). **Pathros**—Upper Egypt (Isa. 11:11). **2. evil...upon Jerusalem**—If I spared not My own sacred city, much less shall ye be safe in Egypt, which I loathe. **3. they went**—implying perverse assiduity: they *went out of their way* to burn incense (one species of idolatry put for all kinds), etc. **4.** (II Chron. 36:15.) **7. now**—after so many warnings. **commit...this...evil against your souls**—(ch. 7:19; Num. 16:38; Prov. 8:36). It is not God whom you injure, but yourselves. **8. in...Egypt**—where they polluted themselves to ingratiate themselves with the Egyptians. **ye be gone**—not compelled by fear, but of your own accord, when I forbade you, and when it was free to you to stay in Judea. **that ye might cut yourselves off**—They, as it were, *purposely* courted their own ruin. **9.** Have you forgotten how the *wickednesses* of your fathers were the source of the greatest calamities to you? **their wives**—The Jews' worldly queens were great promoters of idolatry (I Kings 11:1-8; 15:13; 16:31). **the land of Judah**—They defiled the land which was holy unto God. **10. They...you**—The third person puts them to a distance from God on account of their alienating themselves from Him. The second person implies that God formerly had directly addressed them. **humbled**—lit., "contrite" (Ps. 51:17). **neither...feared**—(Prov. 28:14). **11. cut off all Judah**—i.e., all the idolaters; vs. 28 shows that some returned to Judea (cf. ch. 42:17). **14. none...shall escape...that they should return,...**—The Jews had gone to Egypt *with the idea* that a return to Judea, which they thought hopeless to their brethren in Babylon, would be an easy matter to themselves in Egypt: the exact reverse should happen in the case of each respectively. The Jews whom God sent to Babylon were there weaned from idolatry, and were restored; those who went to Egypt by their perverse will were hardened in idolatry, and perished there. **have a desire**—lit., *lift up* their *soul*, i.e., their hopes (cf. ch. 22:27, *Margin*; Deut. 24:15). **none shall return but such as shall escape**—viz., the "small number" (vs. 28) who were brought by force into Egypt, as Jeremiah and Baruch, and those who, in accordance with Jeremiah's advice, should flee from Egypt before the arrival of the Chaldeans (*Note*, ch. 42:17). CALVIN less probably refers the words to the return of the exiles in Babylon, which the Jews in Egypt regarded as hopeless. **15. their wives**—The idolatry began with them (I Kings 11:4; I Tim. 2:14). Their husbands' connivance implicated them in the guilt. **16. we will not**—(ch. 6:16). **17. whatsoever...goeth...out of our...mouth**—whatever *vow* we have uttered to our gods (vs. 25; Deut. 23:23; Judg. 11:36). The source of all superstitions is that men oppose their own will and fancies to God's commands. **queen of heaven**—(*Note*, ch. 7:18); Ashtaroth or Astarte. **we...fathers...king....**—The evil was restricted to no one class: all from the highest to the lowest shared the guilt. **then had we plenty**—Fools attribute their seeming prosperity to God's connivance at their sin: but see Proverbs 1: 32; Ecclesiastes 8:11-13. In fact, God had often chastised them for their idolatry (see Judg. 2:14); but it is the curse of impiety not to perceive the hand of God in calamities. **victuals**—Men cast away the bread of the soul for the bread that perisheth (Deut. 8:3; John 6:27). So Esau (Heb. 12:16). **18.** They impute their calamities to their service of God, but these are often marks of His favor, not of wrath, to do His people good at their latter end (Deut. 8:16). **19. make...cakes to worship her**—MAURER translates, "to form her image." *Crescent-shaped cakes* were offered to the moon. *Vulgate* supports *English Version*. **without our men**—The women mentioned (vs. 15); "a great multitude" here speak: we have not engaged in secret night-orgies which might justly be regarded unfavorably by *our husbands:* our sacred rites have been open, and with their privity. They wish to show how unreasonable it is that Jeremiah should oppose himself alone to the act of all, not merely women, but *men* also. The guilty, like these women, desire to shield themselves under the complicity of others. Instead of helping one another towards heaven, husband and wife often ripen one another for hell. **21. The incense...did not the Lord remember**—Jeremiah owns that they did as they said, but in retort asks, did not God repay their own evil-doing? Their very land in its present desolation attests this (vs. 22), as was foretold (ch. 25:11, 18, 38). **23. law**—the moral precepts. **statutes**—the ceremonial. **testimonies**—the judicial (Dan. 9:11, 12). **25. Ye...have both spoken with...mouths, and fulfilled with...hand**—ironical praise. They had pleaded their obligation to fulfil their vows, in excuse for their idolatry. He answers, no one can accuse you of unsteadiness as to your idolatrous vows; but steadfastness towards God ought to have prevented you from making, or, when made, from keeping such vows. **ye will surely accomplish...vows**—Jeremiah hereby gives them up to their own fatal obstinacy. **26. I have sworn**—*I*, too have made a *vow* which I will fulfil. Since ye will not hear Me speaking and warning, hear Me *swearing*. **by my great name**—i.e., by Myself (Gen. 22:16), the greatest by whom God can swear (Heb. 6:13, 14). **my name shall no more be named**—The Jews, heretofore, amidst all their idolatry, had retained the form of appeal to the name of God and the law, the distinctive glory of their nation; God will allow this no more (Ezek. 20:39): there shall be none left there to profane His name thus any more. **27. watch over...for evil**—(ch. 1:10; Ezek. 7:6). The God, whose providence is ever solicitously watching over His people for good, shall solicitously, as it were, watch for their hurt. Contrast ch. 31:28; 32:41. **28. small number**—(*Notes*, vss. 14, 28; and ch. 42:

17; Isa. 27:13); cf. "all-consumed" (vs. 27). *A band easily counted,* whereas they were expecting to return triumphantly in large numbers. **shall know** —most of them experimentally, and to their cost. **whose words...mine, or theirs**—Hebrew, "that from Me and them." Jehovah's words are His threats of destruction to the Jews; theirs, the assertion that they expected all goods from their gods (vs. 17), etc. "Mine"; by which I predict ruin to them. "Theirs"; by which they give themselves free scope in iniquity. **shall stand** (Ps. 33:11). **29. this...sign unto you**—The calamity of Pharaoh-hophra (*Note,* vs. 30) shall be a sign to you that as he shall fall before his enemy, so you shall subsequently fall before Nebuchadnezzar (Matt. 24:8) [GROTIUS]. CALVIN makes the "sign" to be simultaneous with the event signified, not antecedent to it, as in Exodus 3:12. The Jews believed Egypt impregnable, so shut in was it by natural barriers. The Jews being "punished *in this place*" will be a sign that their view is false, and God's threat true. He calls it "a sign *unto you,*" because God's prediction is equivalent to the event, so that they may even now take it as a sign. When fulfilled it would cease to be a sign *to them:* for they would be dead. **30. Hophra**—in Herodotus called Apries. He succeeded Psammis, the successor of Pharaoh-necho, who was beaten by Nebuchadnezzar at Carchemish, on the Euphrates. Amasis rebelled against, and overcame him, in the city Sais. **them that seek his life**—HERODOTUS, in curious accordance with this, records that Amasis, after treating Hophra well at first, was instigated, by persons who thought they could not be safe unless he were put to death, to strangle him. "His enemies" refer to Amasis, etc.; the words are accurately chosen, so as not to refer to Nebuchadnezzar, who is not mentioned till the end of the verse, and in connection with Zedekiah (Ezek. 20:3; 30:21). Amasis' civil war with Hophra pioneered the way for Nebuchadnezzar's invasion in the twenty-third year of his reign (JOSEPHUS, *Antiquities,* 10.11).

CHAPTER 45

Vss. 1-5. JEREMIAH COMFORTS BARUCH. After the completion of the prophecies and histories appertaining to the Jewish people and kings, Jeremiah subjoins one referring to an individual, Baruch; even as there are subjoined to the epistles of Paul addressed to churches, epistles to individuals, some of which were prior in date to the former. Afterwards follow the prophecies referring to other nations, closing the book [GROTIUS]. The date of the events here told is eighteen years before the taking of the city; this chapter in point of time follows ch. 36. Baruch seems to have been regularly employed by Jeremiah to commit his prophecies to writing (ch. 36:1, 4, 32). **1. these words**—his prophecies from the thirteenth year of Josiah to the fourth of Jehoiakim. **3. Thou didst say...**—Jeremiah does not spare his disciple, but unveils his fault, viz., fear for his life by reason of the suspicions which he incurred in the eyes of his countrymen (cf. ch. 36: 17), as if he was in sympathy with the Chaldeans (ch. 43:3), and instigator of Jeremiah; also ingratitude in speaking of his "grief," etc., whereas he ought to deem himself highly blessed in being employed by God to record Jeremiah's prophecies. **added**—rescued from the peril of my first writing (ch. 36:26). I am again involved in a similar peril. He upbraids God as dealing harshly with him. **1**

fainted—rather, I am weary. **no rest**—no quiet resting-place. **4. that which I have built...planted I will pluck up**—(Isa. 5:5). This whole nation (the Jews) which I founded and planted with such extraordinary care and favor, I will overthrow. **5. seekest thou great things for thyself**—Thou art overfastidious and self-seeking. When My own peculiar people, a "whole" nation (vs. 4), and the temple, are being given to ruin, dost *thou* expect to be exempt from all hardship? Baruch had raised his expectations too high in this world, and this made his distresses harder to be borne. The frowns of the world would not disquiet us if we did not so eagerly covet its smiles. What folly to seek great things for ourselves here, where everything is little, and nothing certain! **all flesh**—the whole Jewish nation and even foreign peoples (ch. 25:26). **but thy life...for a prey**—Esteem it enough at such a general crisis that thy life shall be granted thee. Be content with this boon of life which I will rescue from imminent death, even as when all things are given up to plunder, if one escape with aught, he has a something saved as his "prey" (ch. 21:9). It is striking how Jeremiah, who once used such complaining language himself, is enabled now to minister the counsel requisite for Baruch when falling into the same sin (ch. 12:1-5; 15:10-18). This is part of God's design in suffering His servants to be tempted, that their temptations may adapt them for ministering to their fellow servants when tempted.

CHAPTER 46

Vss. 1-28. THE PROPHECIES, CHAPTERS 46-52, REFER TO FOREIGN PEOPLES. He begins with Egypt, being the country to which he had been removed. Chapter 46 contains two prophecies concerning it: the discomfiture of Pharaoh-necho at Carchemish by Nebuchadnezzar, and the long subsequent conquest of Egypt by the same king; also the preservation of the Jews (vss. 27, 28). **1.** General heading of the next six chapters of prophecies concerning the Gentiles; the prophecies are arranged according to nations, not by the dates. **2.** Inscription of the first prophecy. **Pharaoh-necho**—He, when going against Carchemish (Cercusium, near the Euphrates), encountered Josiah, king of Judah (the ally of Assyria), at Megiddo, and slew him there (II Kings 23:29; II Chron. 35:20-24); but he was four years subsequently overcome at Carchemish, by Nebuchadnezzar, as is foretold here; and lost all the territory which had been subject to the Pharaohs west of the Euphrates, and between it and the Nile. The prediction would mitigate the Jews' grief for Josiah, and show his death was not to be unavenged (II Kings 24:7). He is famed as having fitted out a fleet of discovery from the Red Sea, which doubled the Cape of Good Hope and returned to Egypt by the Mediterranean. **3.** Derisive summons to battle. With all your mighty preparation for the invasion of Nebuchadnezzar, when ye come to the encounter, ye shall be "dismayed" (vs. 5). Your mighty threats shall end in nothing. **buckler**—smaller, and carried by the light-armed cavalry. **shield**—of larger size, and carried by the heavily armed infantry. **4. Harness the horses**—viz., to the war-chariots, for which Egypt was famed (Exod. 14:7; 15:4). **get up, ye horsemen**—*get up* into the chariots. MAURER, because of the parallel "horses," translates, "Mount the *steeds.*" But it is rather describing the successive steps in equipping the war-chariots; first *harness* the horses to them, then let the horsemen *mount* them. **brigandines**—cuirasses, or coats of mail. **5.** (*Note*, vs. 3.) The language of astonishment, that an army so well equipped should be driven back in "dismay." The prophet sees this in prophetic vision. **fled apace**—lit., "fled a flight," i.e., flee precipitately. **look not back**—They do not even dare to look back at their pursuers. **6. Let not**—equivalent to the strongest *negation. Let not* any of the Egyptian warriors think to *escape by swiftness or by might.* **toward the north** —i.e., in respect to Egypt or Judea. In the northward region, by the Euphrates (see vs. 2). **7. as a flood**—(ch. 47:2; Isa. 8:7, 8; Dan. 11:22). The figure is appropriate in addressing Egyptians, as the ᵗᵉ, their great river, yearly overspreads their lands with a turbid, muddy flood. So their army, swelling with arrogance, shall overspread the region south of Euphrates; but it, like the Nile, shall retreat as fast as it advanced. **8.** Answer to the question in vs. 7. **waters ... moved like the rivers** —The rise of the Nile is gentle; but at the mouth it, unlike most rivers, is much agitated, owing to the sandbanks impeding its course, and so it rushes into the sea like a cataract. **9.** Ironical exhortation, as in vs. 3. The Egyptians, owing to the heat of their climate and abstinence from animal food, were physically weak, and therefore employed mercenary soldiers. **Ethiopians**—*Hebrew, Cush:* Abyssinia and Nubia. **Libyans**—*Phut,* Mauritania, west of Egypt (cf. Gen. 10:6). **shield**—The Libyans borrowed from Egypt the use of the long shield extending to the feet [XENOPHON, *Cyr.,* 6 and 7]. **Lydians**—not the Lydians west of Asia Minor (Gen. 10:22; Ezek. 30:5), but the *Ludim,* an African nation descended from Egypt (Mizraim) (Gen. 10:13; Ezek. 30:5; Nah. 3:9). **handle and bend the bow**—The employment of *two* verbs expresses the manner of bending the bow, viz., the foot being pressed on the center, and the hands holding the ends of it. **10. vengeance**—for the slaughter of Josiah (II Kings 23:29). **sword shall devour ... be ... drunk**—poetical personification (Deut. 32:42). **a sacrifice**—(Isa. 34:6; Ezek. 39:17). The slaughter of the Egyptians is represented as a sacrifice to satiate His righteous vengeance. **11. Gilead ... balm**—(*Note*, ch. 8:22); viz., for curing the wounds; but no medicine will avail, so desperate shall be the slaughter. **virgin**—Egypt is so called on account of her effeminate luxury, and as having never yet been brought under foreign yoke. **thou shalt not be cured**—lit., "there shall be no cure for thee" (ch. 30:13; Ezek. 30:21). Not that the kingdom of Egypt should cease to exist, but it should not recover its former strength; the blow should be irretrievable. **12. mighty ... stumbled against ... mighty ... fallen both together**—Their very multitude shall prove an impediment in their confused flight, one treading on the other. **13-26.** Prophecy of the invasion of Egypt by Nebuchadnezzar, which took place sixteen years after the taking of Jerusalem. Having spent thirteen years in the siege of Tyre, and having obtained nothing for his pains, he is promised by God Egypt for his reward in humbling Tyre (Ezek. 29: 17-20; 30:31). The intestine commotions between Amasis and Pharaoh-hophra prepared his way (cf. Isaiah 19:1, etc., *Notes*). **14. Declare ... publish** —as if giving sentence from a tribunal. **Migdol ... Noph ... Tahpanhes**—east, south, and north. He mentions the three other quarters, but omits the west, because the Chaldees did not advance thither. These cities, too, were the best known to the Jews, as being in their direction. **sword shall devour**

round about thee—viz., the Syrians, Jews, Moabites, and Ammonites (*Note*, ch. 48:1). The exhortation is ironical, as in vss. 4, 10. **15. thy valiant men**—MSS., the LXX, and *Vulgate* read, "thy valiant one," Apis, the bull-shaped Egyptian idol worshipped at Noph or Memphis. The contrast thus is between the palpable impotence of the idol and the *might* attributed to it by the worshippers. The *Hebrew* term, "strong," or "valiant," is applied to bulls (Ps. 22:12). Cambyses in his invasion of Egypt destroyed the sacred bull. **drive them**—(Cf. vs. 5). The *Hebrew* word is used of a sweeping rain (Prov. 28:3). **16. He**—Jehovah. **made many to fall**—lit., "multiplied the faller," i.e., fallers. **one fell upon another**—(V. 6, 12): even before the enemy strikes them (Lev. 26:37). **let us go again to our own people**—the language of the confederates and mercenaries, exhorting one another to desert the Egyptian standard, and return to their respective homes (vss. 9, 21). **from the oppressing sword**—from the cruel sword, viz., of the Chaldeans (cf. ch. 25:38). **17. there**—in their own country severally, the foreign soldiers (vs. 16) cry, "Pharaoh is ...." **but a noise**—He threatens great things, but when the need arises, he does nothing. His threats are mere "noise" (ch. I Cor. 13:1). MAURER translates, "is *ruined,*" lit. (in appropriate abruptness of language), "Pharaoh, king ... *ruin.*" The context favors English Version. His vauntings of what he would do when the time of battle should come have proved to be *empty sounds; he hath passed the time appointed* (viz., for battle with the Chaldeans). **18.** As the mountains Tabor and Carmel tower high above the other hills of Palestine, *so* Nebuchadnezzar (vs. 26) when he comes shall prove himself superior to all his foes. Carmel forms a bold promontory jutting out into the Mediterranean. Tabor is the higher of the two; therefore it is said to be "among the *mountains*"; and Carmel "by the *sea.*" **the King ... Lord of hosts**—(ch. 48:15); in contrast to "Pharaoh *king* of Egypt ... but a noise" (vs. 17). God the true "*King* ... the Lord *of hosts,*" shall cause Nebuchadnezzar to *come.* Whereas Pharaoh shall not come to battle at *the time appointed,* notwithstanding his boasts, Nebuchadnezzar *shall come* according to the prediction of the *King,* who has all *hosts* in His power, however ye Egyptians may despise the prediction. **19. furnish thyself**—lit., "make for thyself vessels" (viz., to contain food and other necessaries for the journey) for captivity. **daughter**—so in vs. 11. **dwelling in Egypt**—i.e., the *inhabitants* of Egypt, the Egyptians, represented as *the daughter of Egypt* (ch. 48:18; II Kings 19:21). "Dwelling" implies that they thought themselves to be securely fixed in their habitations beyond the reach of invasion. **20. heifer**—wanton, like a fat, untamed heifer (Hos. 10:11). Appropriate to Egypt, where Apis was worshipped under the form of a fair bull marked with spots. **destruction**—i.e., a destroyer: Nebuchadnezzar. *Vulgate* translates, "a goader," answering to the metaphor, "one who will *goad* the *heifer*" and tame her. The *Arabic* idiom favors this [ROSENMULLER]. **cometh ... cometh**—The repetition implies, it cometh surely and quickly (Ps. 96:13). **out of the north**—(*Note*, ch. 1:14; 47:2). **21.** Translate, "Also her hired men (mercenary soldiers, vss 9, 16), who are in the midst of her like fatted bullocks, even they also are turned back," i.e., shall turn their backs to flee. The same image, "heifer ... bullocks" (vss. 20, 21), is applied to Egypt's foreign mercenaries, as to *herself.* Pampered with the luxuries of Egypt, they become as enervated for battle as the natives themselves. **22.** The cry of Egypt when invaded shall be like the hissing of a serpent roused by the woodcutters from its lair. No longer shall she loudly roar like a heifer, but with a low murmur of fear, as a serpent hissing. **with axes**—the Scythian mode of armor. The Chaldeans shall come with such confidence as if not about to have to fight with soldiers, but merely to cut down trees offering no resistance. **23. her forest**—(Isa. 10:34). **though it cannot be searched** —They cut down her forest, dense and unsearchable (Job 5:9; 9:10; 36:26) as it may seem: referring to the thickly set cities of Egypt, which were at that time a thousand and twenty. The *Hebrew* particle is properly, "for," "because." **because**—the reason why the Chaldeans shall be able to cut down so dense a forest of cities as Egypt: they themselves are countless in numbers. **grasshoppers**—locusts (Judg. 6:5). **25. multitude**—*Hebrew*, "Amon" (Nah. 3:8, *Margin*, "No-Ammon"), the same as Thebes or Diospolis in Upper Egypt, where Jupiter Ammon had his famous temple. In *English Version*, "multitude" answers to "*populous* No" (Nah. 3:8; and Ezekiel 30:15). The reference to "*their gods*" which follows, makes the translation more likely, "*Ammon* of No," i.e., No and her idol Ammon; so the *Chaldee Version*. So called either from Ham, the son of Noah; or, the "nourisher," as the word means. **their kings**—the kings of the nations in league with Egypt. **26. afterward ... inhabited**— Under Cyrus forty years after the conquest of Egypt by Nebuchadnezzar, it threw off the Babylonian yoke but has never regained its former prowess (vs. 11; Ezek. 29:11-15). **27, 28.** Repeated from ch. 30:10, 11. When the Church [and literal Israel] might seem utterly consumed, there still remains hidden hope, because God, as it were, raises His people from the dead (Rom. 11:15). Whereas the godless "nations" are consumed even though they survive, as are the Egyptians after their overthrow; because they are radically accursed and doomed [CALVIN].

when the Philistines should be destroyed. **Caphtor** —the Caphtorim and Philistines both came from Mizraim (Gen. 10:13, 14). The Philistines are said to have been delivered by God from Caphtor (Amos 9:7). Perhaps before the time of Moses they dwelt near and were subjugated by the Caphtorim (Deut. 2:23) and subsequently delivered. "The remnant" means here those still left after the Egyptians had attacked Gaza and Palestine; or rather, those left of the Caphtorim after the Chaldeans had attacked them previous to their attack on the Philistines. Some identify Caphtor with Cappadocia; GESENIUS, with Crete (Ezek. 25:16, Cherethims), KITTO, Cyprus. Between Palestine and Idumea there was a city Caparorsa; and their close connection with Palestine on the one hand, and Egypt (Mizraim, Gen. 10:13, 14) on the other hand, makes this locality the most likely. **5. Baldness ... cut thyself** —Palestine is represented as a female who has torn off her hair and cut her flesh, the heathenish (Lev. 19:28) token of mourning (ch. 48:37). **their valley** —the long strip of low plain occupied by the Philistines along the Mediterranean, west of the mountains of Judea. LXX reads *Anakim*, the remains of whom were settled in those regions (Num. 13:28). Joshua dislodged them so that none were left but in Gaza, Gath, and Ashdod (Josh. 11:21, 22). But the parallel (vs. 7), "Ashkelon ... the *seashore*," established *English Version* here, "Ashkelon ... their *valley*." **6.** Jeremiah, in the person of the Philistines afflicting themselves (vs. 5), apostrophizes the "sword of the Lord," entreating mercy (cf. Deut. 32:41; Ezek. 21:3-5, 9, 10). **put up thyself**—*Hebrew*, "Gather thyself," i.e., retire or return. **7.** Jeremiah, from addressing the sword in the second person, turns to his hearers and speaks of it in the third person. **Lord ... given it a charge** —(Ezek. 14:17). **the seashore**—the strip of land between the mountains and Mediterranean, held by the Philistines: "their valley" (*Note*, vs. 5). **there hath he appointed it**—(Mic. 6:9). There hath He ordered it to rage.

CHAPTER 47

Vss. 1-7. PROPHECY AGAINST THE PHILISTINES. **1.** *Pharaoh-necho* probably smote Gaza on his return after defeating Josiah at Megiddo (II Chron. 35:20) [GROTIUS]. Or, *Pharaoh-hophra* (ch. 37:5, 7) is intended: probably on his return from his fruitless attempt to save Jerusalem from the Chaldeans, he smote Gaza in order that his expedition might not be thought altogether in vain [CALVIN], (Amos 1:6, 7). **2. waters**—(Isa. 8:7). The Chaldeans from the north are compared to the overwhelming waters of their own Euphrates. The smiting of Gaza was to be only the prelude of a greater disaster to the Philistines. Nebuzaradan was left by Nebuchadnezzar, after he had taken Jerusalem, to subdue the rest of the adjoining cities and country. **3.** (Cf. ch. 4:29.) **fathers ... not look back to ... children**—Each shall think only of his own safety, not even the fathers regarding their own children. So desperate shall be the calamity that men shall divest themselves of the natural affections. **for feebleness of hands**—The hands, the principal instruments of action, shall have lost all power; their whole hope shall be in their feet. **4. every helper**—The Philistines, being neighbors to the Phœnicians of Tyre and Sidon, would naturally make common cause with them in the case of invasion. These cities would have no *helper* left

CHAPTER 48

Vss. 1-47. PROPHECY AGAINST MOAB. It had taken part with the Chaldeans against Judea (II Kings 24:2). Fulfilled by Nebuchadnezzar five years after the destruction of Jerusalem, when also he attacked Egypt (ch. 43:8-13) and Ammon (ch. 49:1-6). [JOSEPHUS, *Antiquities*, 10.9, 7]. Jeremiah in this prophecy uses that of Isaiah 15:16, amplifying and adapting it to his purpose under inspiration, at the same time confirming its divine authority. Isaiah, however, in his prophecy refers to the devastation of Moab by the Assyrian king, *Shalmaneser;* Jeremiah refers to that by *Nebuchadnezzar*. **1. Nebo**—a mountain and town of Moab; its meaning is "that which fructifies." **Kiriathaim** —a city of Moab, *consisting of two cities*, as the word signifies; originally held by the Emim (Gen. 14:5). **Misgab**—meaning "elevation." It lay on an elevation. **2. no more praise**—(Isa. 16:14). **In Heshbon**—The foe having taken Heshbon, the chief city of Moab (vs. 45), in it *devise* evil against *Moab* ("it") saying, Come .... Heshbon was midway between the rivers Arnon and Jabbok; it was the residence of Sihon, king of the Amorites, and afterwards a Levitical city in Gad (Num. 21:26). There is a play on words in the *Hebrew*, "*Heshbon, Hashbu.*" *Heshbon* means a place of *devising* or *counsel*. The city, heretofore called the *seat of* *counsel,* shall find other *counsellors* viz., those who devise its destruction. **thou shalt be cut down . . . Madmen**—rather, by a play on words on the meaning of *madmen* (silence), *Thou shalt be brought to silence,* so as well to deserve thy name (Isa. 15:1). Thou shalt not dare to utter a sound. **3. Horonaim**—the same as the city Avara, mentioned by Ptolemy. The word means "double caves" (Neh. 2:10; Isa. 15:5). **4. little ones . . . cry**—heightening the distress of the scene. The foe does not spare even infants. **5. going up of Luhith . . . going down of Horonaim**—Horonaim lay in a plain, Luhith on a height. To the latter, therefore, the Moabites would flee with "continual *weeping,*" as a place of safety from the Chaldeans. Lit., "Weeping shall go up upon weeping." **6.** They exhort one another to flee. **heath**—or the juniper (see *Note,* ch. 17:6). MAURER translates, "Be like one *naked* in the wilderness." But the sense is, Live *in the wilderness like the heath,* or juniper; do not *"trust in" walls* (vs. 7) [GROTIUS]. (Cf. Matt. 24:16-18.) **7. thy works**—viz., fortifications built by thy work. Moab was famous for its fortresses (vs. 18). The antithesis is to vs. 6, "Be . . . in the wilderness," where there are no fortified cities. **thou . . . also**—like the rest of the surrounding peoples, Judah, etc. **Chemosh**—the tutelary god of Moab (Num. 21:29; Judg. 11:24; I Kings 11:7; II Kings 23:13). When a people were vanquished, their gods also were taken away by the victors (ch. 43:12). **8. the valley . . . shall perish**—i.e., those dwelling in the valley. **9. Give wings . . .**—(Ps. 55:6). Unless it get wings, it cannot escape the foe. "Wings," the *Hebrew* root meaning is a "flower" (Job 14:2); so the flower-like *plumage* of a bird. **10. work of . . . Lord**—the divinely appointed utter devastation of Moab. To represent how entirely this is God's will, a curse is pronounced on the Chaldeans, the instrument, if they do it *negligently* (*Margin*) or by halves (Judg. 5:23); cf. Saul's sin as to Amalek (I Sam. 15:3, 9), and Ahab's as to Syria (I Kings 20:42). **11. settled on . . . lees**— (*Note,* Isa. 25:6; Zeph. 1:12). As wine left to settle on its own lees retains its flavor and strength (which it would lose by being poured from one vessel into another), so Moab, owing to its never having been dislodged from its settlements, retains its pride of strength unimpaired. **emptied from vessel . . .**—To make it fit for use, it used to be filtered from vessel to vessel. **scent**—retaining the image: the bouquet or perfume of the wine. **12. wanderers**—rather, "pourers out," retaining the image of vs. 11, i.e., the Chaldeans who shall remove Moab from his settlements, as men pour wine from off the lees into other vessels. "His vessels" are the cities of Moab; the broken "bottles" the men slain [GROTIUS]. The *Hebrew* and the kindred *Arabic* word means, "to turn on one side," so as to empty a vessel [MAURER]. **13. ashamed**—have the shame of disappointment as to the hopes they entertained of aid from Chemosh, their idol. **Beth-el** —(I Kings 12:27, 29)—i.e., *the golden calf* set up there by Jeroboam. **15. gone up . . . gone down**—in antithesis. **out of her cities**—Rather, "Moab . . . and her cities are gone up," viz., pass away in the ascending smoke of their conflagration (Josh. 8:20, 21; Judg. 20:40). When this took place, the young warriors would *go down* from the burning citadels only to meet their own *slaughter* [GROTIUS]. *English Version* is somewhat favored by the fact that "gone out" is *singular,* and "cities" *plural.* The antithesis favors GROTIUS. **16. near**—to the prophet's eye, though probably twenty-three years elapsed between the utterance of the prophecy in the fourth

year of Jehoiakim (II Kings 24:2) and its fulfilment in the fifth year of Nebuchadnezzar. **17. bemoan** —Not that Moab deserves pity, but this mode of expression pictures more vividly the grievousness of Moab's calamities. **all ye that know his name**—those at a greater distance whom the fame of Moab's "name" had reached, as distinguished from those "about him," i.e., near. **strong staff . . . rod** —Moab is so called as striking terror into and oppressing other peoples (Isa. 9:4; 14:4, 5); also because of its dignity and power (Ps. 110:2; Zech. 11:7). (Isa. 47:1). **18. dost inhabit**—now so securely settled as if in a lasting habitation. **thirst**—Dibon, being situated on the Arnon, abounded in water (Isa. 15:9). In sad contrast with this, and with her "glory" in general, she shall be reduced not only to shame, but to the want of the commonest necessaries "(thirst") in the arid wilderness (vs. 6). **19. Aroer**—on the north bank of the Arnon, a city of Ammon (Deut. 2:36; 3:12). As it was on *"the way"* of the Moabites who fled into the desert, its inhabitants "ask" what is the occasion of Moab's flight, and so learn the lot that awaits themselves (cf. I Sam. 4:13, 16). **20.** Answer of the fleeing Moabites to the Ammonite inquirers (vs. 19; Isa. 16:2). He enumerates the Moabite cities at length, as it seemed so incredible that all should be so utterly ruined. Many of them were assigned to the Levites, while Israel stood. **in Arnon**—the north boundary between Moab and Ammon (vs. 19; Num. 21:13). **21. plain**—(vs. 8). Not only the mountainous regions, but also the plain, shall be wasted. **Holon**—(Cf. Joshua 15:51). **Jahazah**—(Num. 21: 23; Isa. 15:4). **Mephaath**—(Josh. 13:18; 21:37). **22. Beth-diblathaim**—"the house of Diblathaim": Almon-diblathaim (Num. 33:46); "Diblath" (Ezek. 6:13); not far from Mount Nebo (Num. 33:46, 47). **23. Beth-gamul**—meaning "the city of camels." **Beth-meon**—"the house of habitation": Beth-baal-meon (Josh. 13:17). Now its ruins are called Miun. **24. Kerioth**—(Josh. 15:25; Amos 2:2). **Bozrah**—(See *Note,* Isaiah 34:6); at one time under the dominion of Edom, though belonging originally to Moab (Gen. 36:33; Isa. 63:1). Others think the Bozrah in Edom distinct from that of Moab. "Bezer" (Josh. 21:36). **25. horn**—the emblem of strength and sovereignty: it is the horned animal's means of offense and defense (Ps. 75:5, 10; Lam. 2: 3). **26. drunken**—(*Note,* ch. 13:12; 25:17). Intoxicated with the cup of divine wrath, so as to be in helpless distraction. **magnified . . . against . . . Lord**—boasted arrogantly against *God's people,* that whereas Israel was fallen, Moab remained flourishing. **wallow in . . . vomit**—following up the image of a drunken man, i.e., shall be so afflicted by God's wrath as to *disgorge* all his past pride, riches, and vainglory, and *fall* in his shameful abasement. **he also . . . derision**—He in his disaster shall be an object of derision to us, as we in ours have been to him (vs. 27). Retribution in kind. **27.** (Zeph. 2:8.) **a derision**—The *Hebrew* has the article: referring to vs. 26, "Was not Israel (*the whole* nation) *the* object of derision to thee?" Therefore, Moab is to suffer as formerly for its exultation over the calamity (II Kings 17:6) of the ten tribes under the Assyrian Shalmaneser (Isa. 15:16), so now for its exultation over the fall of Judah, under the Chaldean Nebuchadnezzar. God takes up His people's cause as His own (Obad. 13-18). **was he . . . among thieves**—(Ch. 2:26). Proverbial. What did Israel do to deserve such derision? *Was he detected in theft,* that thou didst so *exult* over him *in speaking of him?* Though guilty before God, Israel was guiltless towards thee. **since**—"since ever" thou didst begin speaking of him. **skippedst for joy**—at Israel's calamity [CALVIN]; or, "thou didst *shake thy head*" in "derision" [MAURER]. **28.** Doves often have their nests in the "sides" of caverns. No longer shalt thou have cities to shelter thee: thou shalt have to flee for shelter to caves and deserts (Ps. 55:6, 8; Song of Sol. 2:14). **29. pride**—(Isa. 16:6, 7). Moab was the trumpeter of his own fame. Jeremiah adds "loftiness and arrogancy" 'to Isaiah's picture, so that Moab had not only not been bettered by the chastisement previously endured as foretold by Isaiah, but had even become worse; so that his guilt, and therefore his sentence of punishment, are increased now. Six times Moab's pride (or the synonyms) are mentioned, to show the exceeding hatefulness of his sin. **30. I know**—Moab's "proud arrogancy" (vs. 29) or "wrath," against My people, is not unknown to Me. **it shall not be so** —The result shall *not* be so as he thinks: *his lies shall not so effect* what he aims at by them. CALVIN translates, "his lies are not right (i.e., his vauntings are vain because God will not give them effect); they shall not do so" as they project in their minds, for God will set at naught their plans. **31. I will cry ...for... Moab**—Not that it deserves pity, but the prophet's "crying" for it vividly represents the greatness of the calamity. **Kir-heres**—Kir-hareseth, in Isaiah 16:7; see *Note* there. It means "the city of potters," or else "the city of the sun" [GROTIUS]. Here "the *men* of Kir-heres" are substituted for "the *foundations* of Kir-hareseth," in Isaiah 16:7. The change answers probably to the different bearing of the disaster under Nebuchadnezzar, as compared with that former one under Shalmaneser. **32. with the weeping**—with the same weeping as Jazer, now vanquished, wept with for the destruction of its vines. The same calamity shall befall thee, Sibmah, as befell Jazer. The *Hebrew* preposition here is different from that in Isaiah 16:9, for which reason MAURER translates, "with *more than* the weeping of Jazer." *English Version* understands it of the *continuation* of the weeping; after they have wept for Jazer, fresh subject of lamentation will present itself for the wasting of the vine-abounding Sibmah. **plants ... gone over ... sea of Jazer**—As LXX reads "*cities* of Jazer," and as no traces of a lake near Jazer are found, the reading of *English Version* is doubtful. Retaining the present reading, we avoid the difficulty by translating [GROTIUS], "Thy plants (i.e., *citizens:* alluding to the 'vine') are gone over the sea (i.e., shall be transported beyond the sea to Cyprus, and such distant lands subject to Babylon; and this, too, in summertime), whereas Jazer (i.e., the men of Jazer) reached the sea" (shore only, but are not transported beyond the sea); so that worse shall befall thee than befalls Jazer. **spoiler**—Nebuzaradan. **33. the plentiful field**—rather, "Carmel": as the parallel "land of Moab" requires, though in Isaiah 16:10, it is "the plentiful field." Joy is taken away as from the nearer regions (Canaan and Palestine), so from the farther "land of Moab"; what has happened to Judah shall befall Moab, too (vss. 26, 27) [MAURER]. However, Moab alone seems to be spoken of here; nor does the parallelism forbid "plentiful field" answering to "Moab." *English Version* is therefore better. **shouting**—repeated; as at the conclusion of the vintage, men sing over and over again the same cry of joy. **their shouting ... no shouting**—A shouting shall be heard, but not the joyous shouting of laborers treading the grapes, but the terrible battle cry of the foe. **34. From the cry of Heshbon...**—Those who fly from

Heshbon on its capture shall continue the cry even as far as Elealeh.... There will be continued cries in all quarters, from one end to the other, everywhere slaughter and wasting. **as an heifer of three years old**—Moab heretofore not having known foreign yoke, and in its full strength, is compared to an heifer of three years old, never yet yoked, nor as yet worn out with many birth-givings (cf. *Note*, Isa. 15:5). **waters ... of Nimrim**—i.e., the *well-watered* and therefore luxuriant *pastures* of Nimrim. **desolate**—The *Hebrew* is stronger: not merely shall be "desolate," but *desolation* itself multiplied: *plural*, "desolations." The most fertile tracts shall be dried up. **35. him that offereth**—viz., *whole burnt offerings* as the *Hebrew* requires [GROTIUS]. Cf. the awful burnt offering of the king of Moab (II Kings 3:27) **high places**—(Isa. 16:12). **36.** (*Notes*, Isa. 15:7; 16:11). **like pipes**—a plaintive instrument, therefore used at funerals and in general mourning. **riches ... gotten**—lit., *the abundance ...that which is over and above* the necessaries of life. GROTIUS translates, "They who have been left remaining shall perish"; they who have not been slain by the enemy shall perish by disease and famine. **37.** (*Note*, ch. 47:5; Isa. 15:2, 3.) **upon all ... hands**—i.e, arms, in which such cuttings used to be made in token of grief (cf. Zech. 13:6). **38. vessel ... no pleasure**—(*Note*, ch. 22:28); a vessel cast aside by the potter as refuse, not answering his design. **39. it**—Moab. **How ... how**—prodigious, yet sure to happen. **turned the back**—not daring to show her face. **derision ... dismaying to all**—a derision to some; a dismaying to others in beholding such a judgment of God, fearing a like fate for themselves. **40. he**—Nebuzaradan, the captain of Nebuchadnezzar. **as ... eagle**—not to bear them "on eagles' wings" (Exod. 19:4; Deut. 32:11, 12), as God does His people, but to pounce on them as a prey (ch. 49:22; Deut. 28:49; Hab. 1:8). **41. as ... woman in ... pangs**—(Isa. 13:8). **42.** (*Note*, vs. 26.) **43, 44.** (*Note,* Isaiah 24:17, 18.) **44.** When thou thinkest thou hast escaped one kind of danger, a fresh one will start up. **45. under ... shadow of Heshbon**—They thought that they would be safe in Heshbon. **because of the force**—i.e., "they that fled because of the force" of *the enemy*: they that fled *from* it. GLASSIUS translates, "through want of strength." So the *Hebrew* particle is translated (Ps. 109:24), "faileth of fatness," i.e., "faileth through *want* of fatness"; also Lamentations 4:9. **but a fire...**—copied in part from Sihon's hymn of victory (Num. 21:27, 28). The old "proverb" shall hold good again. As in ancient times Sihon, king of the Amorites, issued forth from his city, Heshbon, as a devouring "flame" and consumed Moab, so now the Chaldeans, making Heshbon their starting-point, shall advance to the destruction of Moab. **midst of Sihon**—i.e., the city of Sihon. **corner of Moab**—i.e., Moab from one corner to the other. **crown of ... head**—the most *elevated* points of Moab. Making some alterations, he here copies Balaam's prophecy (Num. 24:17). *Margin* there translates "princes" for corners; if so, "crown of ... head" here refers to the nobles. **tumultuous ones**— *sons of tumult;* those who have tumultuously revolted from Babylon. Heshbon passed from the Amorite to the Israelite sway. Moab had wrested it from Israel and helped the Chaldeans against the Jews; but revolting from Babylon, they brought ruin on themselves in turn. **46.** Copied from Numbers 21:29. **47.** Restoration promised to Moab, for the sake of righteous Lot, their progenitor (Gen. 19:37; Exod. 20:6; Ps. 89:30-33). Cf. as to Egypt, ch. 46:

26; Ammon, ch. 49:6; Elam, ch. 49:39. Gospel blessings, temporal and spiritual, to the Gentiles in the last days, are intended.

CHAPTER 49

Vss. 1-39. PREDICTIONS AS TO AMMON, IDUMEA, DAMASCUS, KEDAR, HAZOR, AND ELAM. The event of the prophecy as to Ammon preceded that as to Moab (*Note,* vs. 3); and in Ezekiel 21:26-28, the destruction of Ammon is subjoined to the deposition of Zedekiah. **Hath Israel . . . no heir?**—viz., to occupy the land of Gad, after it itself has been carried away captive by Shalmaneser. Ammon, like Moab, descended from Lot, lay north of Moab, from which it was separated by the river Arnon, and east of Reuben and Gad (Josh. 13:24, 25) on the same side of Jordan. It seized on Gad when Israel was carried captive. Judah was by the right of kindred the heir, not Ammon; but Ammon joined with Nebuchadnezzar against Judah and Jerusalem (II Kings 24:2) and exulted over its fall (Ps. 83:4-7, 8; Zeph. 2:8, 9). It had already, in the days of Jeroboam, in Israel's affliction, tried to "enlarge its border" (II Kings 14:26; Amos 1:1, 13). **their king**—(Amos 1:15); referring to Melchom, their tutelary idol (Zeph. 1:5); and so the LXX reads it here as a proper name (I Kings 11:5, 33; II Kings 23:13). The Ammonite god is said to do what *they* do, viz., occupy the Israelite land of Gad. To Jehovah, the theocratic "King" of Israel, the land belonged of right; so **that their Molech or Melchom was a usurper-*king*. his people**—the people of Melchom, "their king." Cf. "people of Chemosh," ch. 48:46. **2. Rabbah**—"the great," metropolis of Ammon (II Sam. 12:26-30). Its destruction is foretold also in Ezekiel 25:5; Amos 1:14, 15. **her daughters**—the towns and villages, dependencies of the metropolis (Josh. 15:45). **shall . . . be heir**—shall *possess* those who possessed him. The full accomplishment of this is still future; partially fulfilled under the Maccabees (I Maccabees 5:6). **3. Heshbon . . . Ai**—Nebuchadnezzar, coming from the north, first attacked Ammon, then its brother and neighbor, Moab. As Ai of Ammon had already suffered destruction, Heshbon of Moab being near it might well fear the same fate. **hedges**—Their cities being destroyed, the outcasts have no place of shelter save behind the "hedges" of vineyards and gardens; or else the *enclosures* of their villages. **their king**—Melchom, the idol, as the mention of "his priests" shows (cf. ch. 48:7). **4. thy flowing valley**—rather, "thy valley shall flow," viz., with the blood of the slain; in sad contrast to their "valleys" in which they had heretofore "gloried," as *flowing* with milk and honey [GROTIUS]. Or else, as *Margin,* "shall flow *away.*" **backsliding**—apostate from Jehovah, the God of their father Lot, to Molech. **treasures**—her resources for resisting the foe. **Who shall . . .**—Who *can* come . . . (ch. 21:13). **5. every man right forth**—whithersoever chance may lead him (ch. 46:5; Gen. 19:17); straight *before him,* onwards at random (Amos 4:3). **none . . . gather up him . . .**—There shall be none to *gather* together the *wandering* fugitives, so as to care for them and restore them to their own homes. **6.** (Cf. ch. 48:47.) For the sake of "righteous" Lot their progenitor. Partially fulfilled under Cyrus; in gospel times more fully. **7. Concerning Edom**—a distinct prophecy, copied in part from Obadiah, but with the freedom of one himself inspired and foretelling a later calamity. Obadiah's was fulfilled probably in Sennacherib's

time (cf. Isa. 34:5; Amos 1:11); Jeremiah's about the same time as his preceding prophecies (vs. 12; Ezek. 25:12). **wisdom**—for which the Arabs and the people of Teman (a city of Edom) in particular, were famed (Gen. 36:15; I Kings 4:30; see Job, everywhere; Obadiah 8). **vanished**—lit., "poured out," i.e., exhausted (cf. Isa. 19:3, *Margin*) [MAURER]. Or, as the kindred Ethiopic word means, "worn out" [LUDOVICUS DE DIEU]. **8. turn**—viz., your backs in flight. **dwell deep**—in deep defiles and caves [GROTIUS], which abound in Idumea. Others refer it to the Arab custom of retiring into the depth of the desert when avoiding an offended foe (vs. 30). **Dedan**—a tribe bordering on and made subject by Idumea; descended from Jokshan, son of Abraham and Keturah (Gen. 25:1-3). **Esau**—The naming of Edom's progenitor, reprobated by God, recalls the remembrance of the old curse on him for his profanity, both his sin and its punishment being perpetuated in his descendants (Heb. 12:16, 17). **9.** (Obadiah 5.) *Grape-gatherers,* yea even *thieves,* leave something behind them; but the Chaldeans will sweep Idumea clean of everything. **10.** Edom became politically extinct after the time of the Romans. **uncovered his secret places**—where he hid himself (vs. 8) and his treasures (Isa. 45:3). I have caused that nothing should be so hidden as that the conqueror should not find it. **brethren**—Ammon. **neighbours**—the Philistines. **11.** Thy fatherless and widows must rest their hope in God alone, as none of the adult males shall be left alive, so desperate will be the affairs of Edom. The verse also, besides this threat, implies a promise of mercy to Esau in God's good time, as there was to Moab and Ammon (vs. 6; ch. 48:47); the extinction of the adult males is the prominent idea (cf. vs. 12). **12.** (Cf. 25:15, 16, 29.) **they whose judgment was not to drink of the cup**—the Jews to whom, by virtue of the covenant relation, it did not belong to drink the cup. It might have been expected that they would be spared. He regards not the merits of the Jews, for they were as bad or worse than others: but the grace and adoption of God; it is just and natural ("judgment") that God should pardon His sons sooner than aliens [CALVIN]. **13. Bozrah**—(*Note,* ch. 48:24.) **14.** (Obadiah 1-3.) **ambassador . . . unto the heathen**—a messenger from God to stir up the Chaldeans against Edom. **15.** David and Joab had already humbled Edom (II Sam. 8:14). **16. terribleness**—the terror which thou didst inspire into others. **deceived thee**—rendered thee proudly confident, as if none would dare to assail thee. **dwellest in . . . rock**—Petra, the chief of Idumea, was cut in the rocks; its ruins are very remarkable. The whole south of Idumea abounds in cave-dwellings and rocks. **though . . . nest . . . eagle**—(Job 39:27; Obadiah 3, 4). The eagle builds its nest in the highest craggy eyry. **17.** (Cf. I Kings 9:8.) **18.** (Ch. 50:40; Deut. 29:23; Amos 4:11.) **no man shall abide there**—i.e., of the Idumeans. The Romans had a garrison there. **19. he**—Nebuchadnezzar, or Nebuzaradan; the name would at once suggest itself to the minds of the hearers (ch. 48:40; 46:18). **swelling**—as a lion which the overflow of the Jordan forced out of his lair on the banks, to ascend the neighboring heights [CALVIN]. See as to the translation, "pride of the Jordan," *Note,* ch. 12:5. **habitation of . . . strong**—the fastnesses of Idumea (cf. Num. 24:21). MAURER translates, "An ever verdant (lit., perennial) pasturage," i.e., Idumea heretofore having enjoyed uninterrupted tranquillity; so in vs. 20 the image is retained, the Idumeans being compared to "a flock," and their king to "a shepherd," in this verse, and the enemy to "a lion" (cf. ch. 50: 17-19). *English Version* accords more with the *Hebrew*. **suddenly**—"in the twinkling of an eye," as the *Hebrew* implies. **him . . . her**—I will make *Nebuzaradan* enter *Idumea*, and then, having in the twinkling of an eye effected the conquest, go *away speedily* elsewhere. Instead of "but," translate, "for." GROTIUS translates, "run *upon* her, or "to her," instead of "run away from her." MAURER understands it, "I will make him (the Idumean) run away from her" (i.e., from his own land); the similar change of reference of the pronouns (ch. 50:44) favors this. **who is a chosen man . . .**—God calls the *choicest* warriors to Him, to set "*over*" the work of devastating Idumea. God will surely execute His purpose, for He can call forth from all sides the agents He chooses. **who is like me?**—(Exod. 15:11). **who will appoint me the time?**—viz., for entering into a trial in judgment with Me (see *Margin*). Image from law courts (Job 9:19). **shepherd**—leader of the Idumeans; following up the previous image, "a lion"; no Idumean shepherd shall withstand the lion sent by Jehovah (Job 41:10), or save the Idumean flock. **20. least of the flock**—the weakest and humblest of the Chaldean host. Cf. ch. 6:3, where the hostile leaders and their hosts are called "shepherds and their flocks." **draw . . . out**—"shall drag them away captive" [GROTIUS]; *shall drag them to and fro*, as a lion (vs. 19) does feeble sheep [MAURER]. **with them**—i.e., the habitation which they possess. **21. was heard in**—i.e., shall be heard *at*. **Red Sea**—a considerable distance from Idumea; though the district at the Elantic bay of the Red Sea originally belonged to Idumea, and the sea itself was called from Edom, i.e., "red" (Gen. 25:30, *Margin*). Others translate, "the weedy sea" (*Margin*), and derive the name, "Red Sea," from its red weeds; the former view is preferable. **22.** (Cf. ch. 48:40, 41.) **Bozrah**—(*Note*, ch. 48:24). **23.** Prophecy as to Damascus, etc. (Isa 17:1; 10:9). The *kingdom* of Damascus was destroyed by Assyria, but the *city* revived, and it is as to the latter Jeremiah now prophesies. The fulfilment was probably about five years after the destruction of Jerusalem by Nebuchadnezzar (JOSEPHUS, 10.9, 7). **Hamath is confounded**—at the tidings of the overthrow of the neighboring Damascus. **on the sea**—i.e., at the sea; the dwellers there are alarmed. Other MSS. read, "like the sea." "There is anxiety (restless) as is the sea: they cannot quiet it," i.e., it cannot be quieted (Isa. 57:20). **It** —Whatever dwellers are there "cannot be quiet." **25. city of praise**—The prophet, in the person of a citizen of Damascus deploring its calamity, calls it "the city of praise," i.e., celebrated with praises everywhere for its beauty (ch. 33:9; 51:41). "How is it possible that such a city *has not been left* whole —has not been spared by the foe?" Cf. "left," Luke 17:35, 36. So Israel *left* standing some of the Canaanite cities (Josh. 11:13). **of my joy**—i.e., in which I delighted. **26. Therefore**—i.e., Since Damascus is doomed to fall, *therefore. . . .* **27. palaces of Ben-hadad**—that palace from which so many evils and such cruelty to Israel emanated; thus implying the *cause* of Damascus' overthrow. Not the Ben-hadad of II Kings 13:3; Amos 1:4; it was a common name of the Syrian kings (cf. I Kings 15:18; meaning "son of Hadad," the idol). **28. Kedar**—son of Ishmael (Gen. 25:13). The Kedarenes led a wandering predatory life in Arabia Petræa, as the Bedouin Arabs (II Chron. 21:16, 17; Ps. 120: 5). Kedar means "blackness" (Song of Sol. 1:5). **Hazor**—not the city in Palestine, but a district in

Arabia Petræa. "Kingdoms" refer to the several combinations of clans, each under its own sheik. **men of the east**—Kedar and Hazor were east of Judea (Judg. 6:3; Job 1:3). **29. tents**—in which they dwelt, from which they are called Scenites, i.e., tent-dwellers. **curtains**—viz., with which the tents were covered (ch. 4:20; 10:20; Ps. 104:2). **they shall cry unto them, Fear . . .**—*The foe*, on crying, Fear . . ., shall discomfit them (the Kedarenes) by their mere cry. **30.** (*Note*, vs. 8.) No conqueror would venture to follow them into the desert. **31. wealthy** —rather, "tranquil" (I Chron. 4:40). **neither gates nor bars**—The Arabs, lying out of the track of the contending powers of Asia and Africa, took no measures of defense and had neither walled cities nor gates (Ezek. 38:11). They thought their scanty resources and wilderness position would tempt no foe. **alone**—separated from other nations, without allies; and from one another scattered asunder. So as to Israel's isolation (Num. 23:9; Deut. 33:28; Mic. 7:14). **32. camels**—their chief possessions; not fields or vineyards. **in utmost . . . corners**—who seemed least likely to be dispersed. Or else, "having the hair shaven (or clipped) in angles" (ch. 9:26, 25:23) [GROTIUS]. **calamity from all sides**—which will force even those in "corners" to "scatter" themselves. **33.** (Mal. 1:3.) **34. Elam**—part of Susiana, west of Persia proper, but used to designate Persia in general. Elam proper, or Elymais, nearer Judea than Persia, is probably here meant; it had helped Nebuchadnezzar against Judea; hence its punishment. It may have been idolatrous, whereas Persia proper was mainly monotheistic. **35. bow**—Elam was famed for its bowmen (Isa. 22:6). **chief of their might**—in opposition to "bow," i.e., bowmen, who constituted their main strength. **36. four winds . . .**—Nebuchadnezzar's army containing soldiers from the four quarters. **37. consumed**—as a distinct nation (Dan. 8:2-27). Fulfilled under Alexander and his successors. **38.** I will show Myself King by My judgments there, as though My tribunal were erected there. The throne of Cyrus, God's instrument, set up over Media, of which Elam was a part, may be meant [GROTIUS]; or rather, that of Nebuchadnezzar (ch. 43:10). Then the restoration of Elam (vs. 39) will refer *partly* to that which took place on the reduction of Babylon by Cyrus, prince of Persia and Media. **39. latter days**—The *full* restoration belongs to gospel times. Elamites were among the first who heard and accepted it (Acts 2.9).

CHAPTER 50

Vss. 1-46. BABYLON'S COMING DOWNFALL; ISRAEL'S REDEMPTION. After the predictions of judgment to be inflicted on other nations by Babylon, follows this one against Babylon itself, the longest prophecy, consisting of 100 verses. The date of its utterance was the fourth year of Zedekiah, when Seraiah, to whom it was committed, was sent to Babylon (ch. 51:59, 60). The repetitions in it make it likely that it consists of prophecies uttered at different times, now collected by Jeremiah to console the Jews in exile and to vindicate God's ways by exhibiting the final doom of Babylon, the enemy of the people of God, after her long prosperity. The style, imagery, and dialogues prove its genuineness in opposition to those who deny this. It shows his faithfulness; though under obligation to the king of Babylon, he owed a higher one to God, who directed him to prophesy against Babylon. **1.** Cf. Isaiah 45; 46; 47. But as the time of fulfilment drew nearer, the prophecies are now proportionally more distinct than then. **2. Declare ... among ... nations**—who would rejoice at the fall of Babylon their oppressor. **standard**—to indicate the place of meeting to the nations where they were to hear the good news of Babylon's fall [ROSENMULLER]; or, the signal to summon the nations together against Babylon (ch. 51: 12, 27), [MAURER]. **Bel**—the tutelary god of Babylon; the same idol as the Phœnician Baal, i.e., lord, the sun (Isa. 46:1). **confounded**—because unable to defend the city under their protection. **Merodach**—another Babylonian idol; meaning in Syria "little lord"; from which Merodach-baladan took his name. **3. a nation**—the Medes, north of Babylon (ch. 51:48). The devastation of Babylon here foretold includes not only that by Cyrus, but also that more utter one by Darius, who took Babylon by artifice when it had revolted from Persia, and mercilessly slaughtered the inhabitants, hanging 4000 of the nobles; also the final desertion of Babylon, owing to Seleucia having been built close by under Seleucus Nicanor. **4.** Fulfilled only in part when some few of the ten tribes of "Israel" joined Judah in a "covenant" with God, at the restoration of Judah to its land (Neh. 9:38; 10:29). The full event is yet to come (ch. 31:9; Hos. 1:11; Zech. 12: 10). **weeping**—with joy at their restoration beyond all hope; and with sorrow at the remembrance of their sins and sufferings (Ezra 3:12, 13; Ps. 126:5, 6). **seek ... Lord**—(Hos. 3:5). **5. thitherward**—rather, "hitherward," Jeremiah's prophetical standpoint being at Zion. "Faces hitherward" implies their steadfastness of purpose not to be turned aside by any difficulties on the way. **perpetual covenant**—in contrast to the old covenant "which they brake" (ch. 31:31, etc.; 32:40). They shall return to their God first, then to their own land. **6.** (Isa. 53:6.) **on the mountains**—whereon they sacrificed to idols (ch. 2:20; 3:6, 23). **resting-place**—for the "sheep," continuing the image; *Jehovah* is the resting-place of His sheep (Matt. 11:28). They rest in His "bosom" (Isa. 40:11). Also *His temple* at Zion, their "rest," because it is His (Ps. 132:8, 14). **7. devoured**—(Ps. 79:7). "Found them" implies that they were exposed to the attacks of those whoever happened to meet them. **adversaries said**—for instance, Nebuzaradan (ch. 40:2, 3; cf. Zech. 11:5). The Gentiles acknowledged some supreme divinity. The Jews' guilt was so palpable that they were condemned even in the judgment of heathens. Some knowledge of God's peculiar relation to Judea reached its heathen invaders from the prophets (ch. 2:3; Dan. 9:16); hence the strong language they use of Jehovah here, not as worshippers of Him themselves, but as believing Him to be the tutelary God *of Judah* ("the hope of *their* fathers," Ps. 22:4; they do not say *our* hope), as each country was thought to have its *local god*, whose power extended no farther. **habitation**—(Ps. 90:1; 91:1). Alluding to the tabernacle, or, as in Ezekiel 34:14, "fold," which carries out the image in vs. 6, "resting-place" of the "sheep." But it can only mean "habitation" (ch. 31:23), which confirms *English Version* here. **hope of their fathers**—This especially condemned the Jews that their apostasy was from that God whose faithfulness their fathers had experienced. At the same time these "adversaries" unconsciously use language which corrects their own notions. The covenant with the Jews' "fathers" is not utterly set aside by their sin, as their adversaries thought; there is still "a habitation" or refuge for them with the God *of their fathers*. **8.** (Ch. 51:6, 45; Isa. 48:20; Zech. 2:6, 7; Rev. 18:4). Immediately avail yourselves of the opportunity of escape. **be as ... he-goats before ... flocks**—Let each try to be foremost in returning, animating the weak, as he-goats lead the flock; such were the companions of Ezra (Ezra 1:5, 6). **9. from thence**—i.e., from the north country. **expert**—lit., prosperous. Besides "might," "expertness" is needed, that an arrow may do execution. The *Margin* has a different *Hebrew* reading; "destroying," lit., bereaving, childless-making (ch. 15:7). LXX and *Syriac* support *English Version*. **in vain**—without killing him at whom it was aimed (II Sam. 1:22). **11.** (Isa. 47:6.) **grown fat**—and so, skip wantonly. **at grass**—fat and frisky. But there is a disagreement of gender in *Hebrew* reading thus. The *Keri* reading is better: "a heifer *threshing";* the strongest were used for threshing, and as the law did not allow their mouth to be muzzled in threshing (Deut. 25:4), they waxed wanton with eating. **bellow as bulls**—rather, "neigh as *steeds,*" lit., "strong ones," a poetical expression for *steeds* (*Note*, ch. 8:16) [MAURER]. **12. Your mother**—Babylon, the metropolis of the empire. **hindermost**—marvellous change, that Babylon, once the queen of the world, should be now the hindermost of nations, and at last, becoming "a desert," cease to be a nation! **13.** (Isa. 13. 20.) **14.** Summons to the Median army to attack Babylon. **against ... Lord**—By oppressing His people, their cause is His cause. Also by profaning His sacred vessels (Dan. 5:2). **15. Shout**—Inspirit one another to the onset with the battle cry. **given ... hand**—an idiom for, "submitted to" the conquerors (I Chron. 29:24, *Margin;* Lam. 5:6). **as she hath done, do unto her**—just retribution in kind. She had destroyed many, so must she be destroyed (Ps. 137:8). So as to spiritual Babylon (Rev. 18:6). This is right because "it is the vengeance *of the Lord";* but this will not justify *private* revenge in kind (Matt. 5:44; Rom. 12 19-21); even the Old Testament law forbade this, though breathing a sterner spirit than the New Testament (Exod. 23:4, 5; Prov. 25:21, 22). **16.** Babylon had the extent rather of a nation than of a ity. Therefore grain was grown within the city wall sufficient to last for a long siege (ARISTOTLE, *Pol.* 3.2; PLINY, 18.17). Conquerors usually spare agriculturists, but in this case *all* alike were to be "cut off." **for fear of ... oppressing sword**—because of the sword of the oppressor. **every one to his people**—from which they had been removed to Babylon from all quarters by the Chaldean conquerors (ch. 51:9; Isa. 13:14). **17. lions**—hostile kings (ch. 4:7; 49:19). **Assyria**—(II Kings 17:6, Shalmaneser; Ezra 4:2, Esar-haddon). **Nebuchadnezzar**—(II Kings 24:10, 14). **18. punish ... king of Babylon**—Nabonidus, or Labynitus. **as ... punished ... Assyrian**—Sennacherib and other kings [GROTIUS] (II Kings 19:37). **19.** (Isa. 65: 10; Ezek. 34:13, 14.) **20.** The specification of "Israel," as well as Judah, shows the reference is to times yet to come. **iniquity ... none**—not merely idolatry, which ceased among the Jews ever since the Babylonian captivity, but chiefly their rejection of Messiah. As in a cancelled debt, it shall be as if it had never been; God, for Christ's sake, shall treat them as innocent (ch. 31:34). Without cleansing away of sin, remission of punishment would be neither to the honor of God nor to the highest interests of the elect. **whom I reserve**—the elect "remnant" (Isa. 1:9). The "residue" (Zech. 14:2; 13:8, 9). **21. Merathaim**—a symbolical name for Babylon, the doubly rebellious, viz., against God. Cf. vs. 24, "thou hast striven against the Lord"; and vs. 29, "proud against the Lord." The "doubly" refers to: first, the *Assyrian's* oppression of Israel; next, the kindred *Chaldean's* oppression of Judah (cf. vss. 17-20, 33; especially vs. 18). **Pekod**—(Ezek. 23:23); a chief province of Assyria, in which Nineveh, now overthrown, once lay. But, as in Merathraim, the allusion is to the meaning of *Pekod,* viz., "visitation"; the inhabitants whose time of deserved visitation in punishment is come; not, however, without reference to the now Babylonian province, Pekod. The visitation on Babylon was a following up of that on Assyria. **after them**—even *their posterity,* and all that is still left of Babylon, until the very name is extinct [GROTIUS]. Devastate the city, *after* its inhabitants have deserted it. **all . . . I . . . commanded**—by Isaiah (Isa. 13:1, etc.). **23. hammer**—i.e., Babylon, so called because of its ponderous destructive power; just as "Martel," i.e., "a little hammer," was the surname of a king of the Franks (Isa. 14:6). **24. I**—Thou hast to do with God, not merely with men. **taken . . . not aware**—HERODOTUS relates that one half of the city was taken before those in the other half were "aware" of it. Cyrus turned the waters of the Euphrates where it was defended into a different channel, and so entered the city by the dried-up channel at night, by the upper and lower gates (Dan. 5:30, 31). **25. weapons of his indignation**—the Medes and Persians (Isa. 13:5). **26. from the utmost border**—viz., of the earth. Or, from all sides LUDOVICUS DE DIEU]. **storehouses**—or, "her houses filled with men and goods" [MICHAELIS]. When Cyrus took it, the provisions found there were enough to have lasted for many years. **as heaps**—make of the once glorious city *heaps* of ruins. Vast mounds of rubbish now mark the site of ancient Babylon. "Tread her as heaps of corn which are wont to be trodden down in the threshing-floor" [GROTIUS]. **27. bullocks**—i.e., princes and strong warriors (ch. 46:21; Ps. 22: 12; Isa. 34:7). **go down to . . . slaughter**—The slaughterhouses lay low beside the river; therefore it is said, "go down"; appropriate to Babylon on the Euphrates, the avenue through which the slaughterers entered the city. **28. declare in Zion . . . temple**—Some Jews "fleeing" from Babylon at its fall shall tell in Judea how God avenged the cause of Zion and her temple that had been profaned (ch. 52:13; Dan. 1:2; 5:2). **29. archers**—lit., very many and powerful; hence the *Hebrew* word is used of *archers* (Job 16:13) from the multitude and force of their arrows. **according to all that she hath done**—(*Note,* vs. 15). **proud against the Lord**—not merely cruel towards men (Isa. 47:10). **30.** (*Note,* ch. 49:26.) **in the streets**—The Babylonians were so discouraged by having lost some battles that they retired within their walls and would not again meet Cyrus in the field. **31. most proud**—lit., "pride"; i.e., man of pride; the king of Babylon. **visit**—punish (vs. 27). **33. Israel and . . . Judah were oppressed**—He anticipates an objection, in order to answer it: Ye have been, no doubt, "oppressed," therefore ye despair of deliverance; but, remember your "Redeemer is strong," and therefore can and will deliver you. **34. strong**—as opposed to the power of Israel's oppressor (Rev. 18:8). **plead . . . cause**—as their advocate. Image from a court of justice; appropriate as God delivers His people not by mere might, but by *righteousness.* His plea against Satan and all their enemies is His own everlasting love, reconciling mercy and justice in the Redeemer's work and person (Mic. 7:9; Zech. 3:1-5; I John 2:1). **give rest . . . disquiet**—There is a play on the similarity of sounds in the two *Hebrew* verbs to express more vividly the contrast: "that He may give quiet to the land of

Judah (heretofore disquieted by Babylon); but disquiet to the inhabitants of Babylon (heretofore quietly secure)" (Isa. 14:6-8). **35-37.** The repetition of "A sword" in the beginning of each verse, by the figure *anaphora,* heightens the effect; the reiterated judgment is universal; the same sad stroke of the sword is upon each and all connected with guilty Babylon. **wise men**—(Isa. 47:13). Babylon boasted that it was the peculiar seat of wisdom and wise men, especially in astronomy and astrology. **36. liars**—Those whom he before termed "wise men," he here calls "liars" (impostors), viz., the astrologers (cf. Isa. 44:25; Rom. 1:21-25; I Cor. 1: 20). **37. as women**—divested of all manliness (Nah. 3:13). **38. drought**—Altering the pointing, this verse will begin as the three previous verses, "A sword." However, all the pointed MSS. read, "A drought," as *English Version.* Cyrus turned off the waters of the Euphrates into a new channel and so marched through the dried-up bed into the city (ch. 51:32). Babylonia once was famed for its corn, which often yielded from one to two hundredfold [HERODOTUS]. This was due to its network of watercourses from the Euphrates for irrigation, traces of which [LAYARD] are seen still on all sides, but dry and barren (Isa. 44:27). **their idols**—lit., "terrors." They are mad after idols that are more calculated to *frighten* than to attract (ch. 51:44, 47, 52; Dan. 3:1). Mere bugbears with which to frighten children. **39. wild beasts of the desert**—wild cats, remarkable for their howl [BOCHART]. **wild beasts of the islands**—jackals (*Note,* Isa. 13:21). **owls**—rather female ostriches; they delight in solitary places. Lit., "daughters of crying." Cf. as to spiritual Babylon, Revelation 18:2. **no more inhabited for ever**—The accumulation of phrases is to express the final and utter extinction of Babylon; fulfilled not immediately, but by degrees; Cyrus took away its supremacy. Darius Hystaspes deprived it, when it had rebelled, of its fortifications. Seleucus Nicanor removed its citizens and wealth to Seleucia, which he founded in the neighborhood; and the Parthians removed all that was left to Ctesiphon. Nothing but its walls was left under the Roman emperor Adrian. **40.** (Isa. 13:19.) Repeated from ch. 49:18. **41-43.** (Cf. ch. 6:22-24.) The very language used to describe the calamities which Babylon inflicted on Zion is that here employed to describe Babylon's own calamity inflicted by the Medes. Retribution in kind. **kinds**—the allies and satraps of the various provinces of the Medo-Persian empire: Armenia, Hyrcania, Lydia, etc. **coasts**—the remote parts. **42. cruel**—the character of the Persians, and even of Cyrus, notwithstanding his wish to be thought magnanimous (Isa. 13:18). **like a man**—So orderly and united is their "array," that the whole army moves to battle as *one man* [GROTIUS]. **43. hands waxed feeble**—attempted no resistance; immediately was overcome, as HERODOTUS tells us. **44-46.** Repeated mainly from ch. 49:19-21. The identity of God's principle in His dealing with Edom, and in that with Babylon, is implied by the similarity of language as to both. **46. cry . . . among the nations**—In Edom's case it is, "at the cry the noise thereof was heard *in the Red Sea.*" The change implies the wider extent to which the crash of Babylon's downfall shall be heard.

CHAPTER 51

Vss. 1-65. CONTINUATION OF THE PROPHECY AGAINST BABYLON BEGUN IN CHAPTER 50. **1. in the**

midst of them that rise . . . against me—lit., in the heart of them . . . . Cf. Psalm 46:2, "the midst of the sea," *Margin,* "the *heart* of the seas"; Ezekiel 27:4, *Margin;* Matthew 12:40. In the center of the Chaldeans. "Against Me," because they persecute My people. The cabalistic mode of interpreting *Hebrew* words (by taking the letters in the inverse order of the alphabet, the last letter representing the first, and so on, ch. 25:26) would give the very word *Chaldeans* here; but the *mystical* method cannot be intended, as "Babylon" is plainly so called in the immediately preceding parallel clause. **wind** —God needs not warlike weapons to "destroy" His foes; a *wind* or blast is sufficient; though, no doubt, the "wind" here is the invading host of Medes and Persians (ch. 4:11; II Kings 19:7). **2. fanners**— (*Note,* ch. 15:7). The fanners separate the wheat from the chaff; so God's judgments shall sweep away guilty Babylon as chaff (Ps. 1:4). **3. Against him that bendeth**—viz., the bow; i.e., the Babylonian archer. **let the archer bend**—i.e., the Persian archer (ch. 50:4). The *Chaldean version* and JEROME, by changing the vowel points, read, "Let not him (the Babylonian) who bendeth his bow bend it." But the close of the verse is addressed to the Median invaders; therefore it is more likely that the first part of the verse is addressed to them, as in *English Version,* not to the *Babylonians,* to warn them against resistance as vain, as in the *Chaldean version.* The word "bend" is thrice repeated: "Against him that bendeth let him that bendeth bend," to imply the utmost straining of the bow. **4.** (*Notes,* ch. 49:26; 50:30, 37). **5. forsaken**—as a widow (*Hebrew*). Israel is not severed from her husband, Jehovah (Isa. 54:5-7), by a perpetual divorce. **though . . . sin**—though the land *of Israel* has been filled with sin, i.e., with *the punishment of their sin,* devastation. But, as the *Hebrew* means "for," or "and therefore," not "though," translate, "and therefore their (the Chaldeans') land has been filled with (the penal consequences of) their sin" [GROTIUS]. **6.** Warning to the Israelite captives to flee from Babylon, lest they should be involved in the punishment of her "iniquity." So as to spiritual Babylon and her captives (Rev. 18:4). **7.** Babylon is compared to a *cup,* because she was the vessel in the hand of God, to make drunken with His vengeance the other peoples (ch. 13:12; 25:15, 16). Cf. as to spiritual Babylon, Revelation 14:8; 17:4. The cup is termed "golden," to express the splendor and opulence of Babylon; whence also in the image seen by Nebuchadnezzar (Dan. 2:38) the *head* representing Babylon is of *gold* (cf. Isa. 14:4). **8, 9.** Her friends and confederates, who behold her fall, are invited to her aid. They reply, her case is incurable, and that they must leave her to her fate. **8.** (Isa. 21:9; Rev. 14:8; 18:2, 9.) **balm**—(Ch. 8:22; 46:11.) **9. We would have healed**—We attempted to heal. **her judgment**— *her crimes* provoking God's "judgments" [GROTIUS]. **reacheth unto heaven**—(Gen. 18:21; Jonah 1:2; Rev. 18:5). Even the heathen nations perceive that her awful fall must be God's judgment for her crying sins (Ps. 9:16; 64:9). **10.** Next after the speech of the confederates of Babylon, comes that of the Jews celebrating with thanksgivings the promise-keeping faithfulness of their covenant God. **brought forth . . .**—(Ps. 37:6). **our righteousness**— not the Jews' merits, but God's faithfulness to Himself and to His covenant, which constituted the "righteousness" of His people, i.e., their *justification* in their controversy with Babylon, the cruel enemy of God and His people. Cf. ch. 23:6, "The

Lord *our righteousness"*; Mic. 7:9. *Their* righteousness is *His* righteousness. **declare in Zion**— (Ps. 102:13-21). **11. Make bright**—lit., "pure." Polish and sharpen. **gather**—lit., "fill"; i.e., gather in full number, so that none be wanting. So, "gave in *full* tale" (I Sam. 18:27). GESENIUS, not so well, translates, "Fill *with your bodies* the shields" (cf. Song of Sol. 4:4). He means to tell the Babylonians, Make what preparations you will, all will be in vain (cf. ch. 46:3-6). **kings of . . . Medes**—He names the Medes rather than the Persians, because Darius, or Cyaxares, was above Cyrus in power and the greatness of his kingdom. **temple**—(ch. 50:28). **12.** With all your efforts, your city shall be taken. **standard**—to summon the defenders together to any point threatened by the besiegers. **13. waters**—(V. 32, 36; *Note,* Isa. 21:1.) The Euphrates surrounded the city and, being divided into many channels, formed islands. Cf. as to spiritual Babylon "waters," i.e., "many peoples," Revelation 17:1, 15. A large lake also was near Babylon. **measure**— lit., "cubit," which was the most common measure, and therefore is used for a *measure* in general. The time for putting a *limit* to thy covetousness [GESENIUS]. There is no *"and"* in the Hebrew: translate, "thine end, the *retribution* for thy covetousness" [GROTIUS]. MAURER takes the image to be from weaving: "the cubit where thou art to be cut off"; for the web is cut off, when the required number of cubits is completed (Isa. 38:12). **14. by himself**— lit., "by His soul" (II Sam. 15:21; Heb. 6:13). **fill . . . with caterpillars**—locusts (Nah. 3:15). Numerous as are the citizens of Babylon, the invaders shall be more numerous. **15-19.** Repeated from ch. 10: 12-16; except that "Israel" is not in the *Hebrew* of vs. 19, which ought, therefore, to be translated, "He is the Former of all things, and (therefore) of the rod of His inheritance" (i.e., of the nation peculiarly His own). In ch. 10 the contrast is between the *idols* and God; here it is between the power of populous *Babylon* and that of God: *"Thou* dwellest upon many waters" (vs. 13); but God can, by merely "uttering His voice," create "many waters" (vs. 16). The "earth" (in its *material* aspect) is the result of His "power"; the "world" (viewed in its *orderly system*) is the result of His "wisdom . . ." (vs. 15). Such an Almighty Being can be at no loss for resources to effect His purpose against Babylon. **20.** (*Note,* ch. 50:23.) "Break in pieces" refers to the "hammer" there (cf. Nah. 2:1, *Margin*). The *club* also was often used by ancient warriors. **22. old and young**—(II Chron. 36:17). **24.** The detail of particulars (vss. 20-23) is in order to express the indiscriminate slaughters perpetrated by Babylon on Zion, which, in just retribution, are all to befall her in turn (ch. 50:15, 29). **in your sight**—addressed to the Jews. **25. destroying mountain**—called so, not from its position, for it lay low (vs. 13; Gen. 11:2, 9), but from its eminence above other nations, many of which it had "destroyed"; also, because of its lofty palaces, towers, hanging gardens resting on arches, and walls, fifty royal cubits broad and two hundred high. **roll thee down from the rocks**— i.e., from thy rocklike fortifications and walls. **burnt mountain**—(Rev. 8:8.) A volcano, which, after having spent itself in pouring its "destroying" lava on all the country around, falls into the vacuum and becomes extinct, the surrounding "rocks" alone marking where the crater had been. Such was the appearance of Babylon after its destruction, and as the pumice stones of the volcano are left in their place, being unfit for building, so Babylon should never rise from its ruins. **26. corner . . . stone . . .**

foundations—The *corner-stone* was the most important one in the building, the *foundation-stones* came next in importance (Eph. 2:20). So the sense is, even as there shall be no stones useful for building left of thee, so no leading *prince*, or *governors*, shall come forth from thy inhabitants. **27.** (Ch. 50:29.) As in vs. 12 the Babylonians were told to "set up the standard," so here her foes are told to do so: the latter, to good purpose; the former, in vain. **Ararat**—Upper or Major Armenia, the regions about Mount Ararat. **Minni**—Lower or Lesser Armenia. RAWLINSON says that Van was the capital of Minni. It was conquered by Tettarrassa, the general of Tetembar II, the Assyrian king whose wars are recorded on the black obelisk now in the British Museum. **Aschenaz**—a descendant of Japhet (Gen. 10: 3), who gave his name to the sea now called the Black Sea; the region bordering on it is probably here meant, viz., Asia Minor, including places named Ascania in Phrygia and Bithynia. Cyrus had subdued Asia Minor and the neighboring regions, and from these he drew levies in proceeding against Babylon. **rough caterpillars**—The horsemen in multitude, and in appearance bristling with javelins and with crests, resemble "rough caterpillars," or locusts of the hairy-crested kind (Nah. 3: 15). **28. kings of . . . Medes**—(vs. 11). The satraps and tributary kings under Darius, or Cyaxares. **his dominion**—the king of Media's dominion. **29. land shall tremble . . . every purpose of . . . Lord shall be performed**—elegant antithesis between the *trembling* of the *land* or earth, and the stability of "every purpose of the Lord" (cf. Ps. 46:1-3). **30. forborne to fight**—for the city was not taken by force of arms, but by stratagem, according to the counsel given to Cyrus by two eunuchs of Belshazzar who deserted. **remained in . . . holds**—not daring to go forth to fight; many, with Nabonidus, withdrew to the fortified city Borsippa. **31.** (*Note*, ch. 50:24.) **One post**—*One courier* after another shall announce the capture of the city. The couriers despatched from the walls, where Cyrus enters, shall *"meet"* those sent by the king. Their confused running to and fro would result from the sudden panic at the entrance of Cyrus into the city, which he had so long besieged ineffectually; the Babylonians had laughed at his attempts and were feasting at the time without fear. **taken at one end**—which was not known for a long time to the king and his courtiers feasting in the middle of the city; so great was its extent that, when the city was already three days in the enemy's hands, the fact was not known in some parts of the city [ARISTOTLE, *Pol.* 3.2]. **32. passages are stopped**—The guarded fords of the Euphrates are occupied by the enemy (*Note*, ch. 50:38). **reeds . . . burned**—lit., "the marsh." After draining off the river, Cyrus "burned" the stockade of dense tree-like *"reeds"* on its banks, forming the outworks of the city's fortifications. The burning of these would give the appearance of the *marsh* or river itself being on "fire." **33. like a threshing-floor, it is time to thresh her**—rather, "like a threshing-floor at the time of threshing," or "at the time when it is trodden." The *treading*, or *threshing*, is here put before the *harvest*, out of the natural order, because the prominent thought is the *treading down* or destruction of Babylon. In the East the treading out of the corn took place only at harvest-time. Babylon is like a threshing-floor not trodden for a long time; but the time of harvest, when her citizens shall be trodden under foot, shall come [CALVIN]. "Like a threshing-floor full of corn, so is Babylon now full of riches, but the time of harvest shall

come, when all her prosperity shall be cut off" [LUDOVICUS DE DIEU]. GROTIUS distinguishes the "harvest" from the "threshing"; the former is the slaying of her citizens, the latter the pillaging and destruction of the city (cf. Joel 3:13; Rev. 14:15, 18). **34. me**—Zion speaks. Her groans are what bring down retribution in kind on Babylon (ch. 50:17; Ps. 102:13, 17, 20). **empty vessel**—He has drained me out. **dragon**—The serpent often "swallows" its prey whole; or a sea monster [GROTIUS]. **filled his belly . . . cast me out**—like a beast, which, having "filled" himself to satiety, "casts out" the rest [CALVIN]. After filling all his storehouses with my goods, he has *cast me out of this land* [GROTIUS]. **35. my flesh**—which Nebuchadnezzar hath "devoured" (vs. 34). Zion thus calls her *kinsmen* (Rom. 11:14) slain throughout the country or carried captives to Babylon [GROTIUS]. Or, as "my blood" follows, it and "my flesh" constitute the *whole man:* Zion, in its totality, its citizens and all its substance, have been a prey to Babylon's violence (Ps. 137:8). **36. plead . . . cause**—(ch. 50:34). **sea**—the Euphrates (vs. 13; ch. 50:38). Cf. Isaiah 19:5, "sea," i.e., the Nile (Isa. 21:1). **37.** (Ch. 50:26, 39; Rev. 18:2). **38, 39.** The capture of Babylon was effected on the night of a festival in honor of its idols. **roar . . . yell**—The Babylonians were *shouting* in drunken revelry (cf. Dan. 5:4). **39. In their heat I will make their feasts**—In the midst of their being heated with wine, I will give them "their" potions,—a very different cup to drink, but one which is *their due*, the wine-cup of My stupefying wrath (ch. 25:15; 49:12; Isa. 51:17; Lam. 4:21). **rejoice, and sleep . . . perpetual . . .**—that they may *exult*, and in the midst of their jubilant exultation sleep the sleep of death (vs. 57; Isa. 21:4, 5). **41. Sheshach**—Babylon (cf. *Note*, ch. 25:26); called so from the goddess Shach, to whom a five days' festival was kept, during which, as in the Roman Saturnalia, the most unbridled licentiousness was permitted; slaves ruled their masters, and in every house one called Zogan, arrayed in a royal garment, was chosen to rule all the rest. He calls Babylon "Sheshach," to imply that it was during this feast the city was taken [SCALIGER]. **42. The sea**—the host of Median invaders. The image (cf. ch. 47:2; Isa. 8:7, 8) is appropriately taken from the Euphrates, which, overflowing in spring, is like a "sea" near Babylon (vss. 13:32, 36). **43. Her cities**—the cities, her dependencies. So, "Jerusalem and the cities thereof" (ch. 34:1). Or, the "cities" are the inner and outer cities, the two parts into which Babylon was divided by the Euphrates [GROTIUS]. **44. Bel . . . swallowed**—in allusion to the many sacrifices to the idol which its priests pretended it swallowed at night; or rather, the precious gifts taken from other nations and offered to it (which it is said to have "swallowed"); cf. "devoured," "swallowed," vs. 34; ch. 50:17), which it should have to disgorge (cf. vs. 13; ch. 50:37). Of these gifts were the vessels of Jehovah's temple in Jerusalem (II Chron. 36:7; Dan. 1:2). The restoration of these, as foretold here, is recorded in Ezra 1:7-11. **flow**—as a river; fitly depicting the *influx* of pilgrims of all "nations" to the idol. **45, 46.** (*Note*, vs. 6.) **46. And lest**—Cf., for the same ellipsis, Genesis 3:22; Exodus 13:17; Deuteronomy 8:12. "And in order that your heart may not faint at the (first) rumor" (of war), I will give you some intimation of the time. In the first "year" there shall "come a rumor" that Cyrus is preparing for war against Babylon. "After that, in another year, shall come a rumor," viz., that Cyrus is approaching, and has already entered Assyria. Then is your time to "go out" (vs. 45). Babylon was taken the following or third year of Belshazzar's reign [GROTIUS]. **violence in the land**—of Babylon (Ps. 7:16). **ruler against ruler**—or, "ruler upon ruler," a continual change of rulers in a short space. Belshazzar and Nabonidus, supplanted by Darius or Cyaxares, who is succeeded by Cyrus. **47.** GROTIUS translates, "Because then (viz., on the third year) the time shall have come that," etc. **confounded**—at seeing their gods powerless to help them. **her slain**—in retribution for "*Israel's* slain" (vs. 49) who fell by her hand. GROTIUS translates, "her dancers," as in Judges 21:21, 23; I Samuel 18:6, the same *Hebrew* word is translated, alluding to the dancing revelry of the festival during which Cyrus took Babylon. **48. heaven . . . earth . . . sing for Babylon**—(Isa. 14:7-13; 44:23; Rev. 18:20). **49. caused . . . to fall**—lit., "has been for the falling," i.e., as Babylon made this its one aim to fill all places with the slain of Israel, so at Babylon shall all the slain *of that whole land* (not as *English Version*, "of all the *earth*") [MAURER]. HENDERSON translates, "Babylon also shall fall, ye slain of Israel. Those also of Babylon shall fall, O ye slain of all the earth." But, "in the midst of her," vs. 47, plainly answers to "at Babylon," vs. 49, *English Version*. **50. escaped . . . sword**—viz., of the Medes. So great will be the slaughter that even some of God's people shall be involved in it, as they had deserved. **afar off**—though ye are banished far off from where ye used formerly to worship God. **let Jerusalem come into your mind**—While in exile remember your temple and city, so as to prefer them to all the rest of the world wherever ye may be (Isa. 62:6). **51.** The prophet anticipates the Jews' reply; I know you will say in despair, "We are confounded . . . ." "Wherefore (God saith to you) behold, I will . . ." (vs. 52) [CALVIN]. I prefer taking vs. 51 as the *prayer* which the Jews are directed to offer in exile (vs. 50), "let Jerusalem come into your mind" (and say in prayer to God), "We are confounded." This view is confirmed by Psalm 44:15, 16; 79:4; 102:17-20; Isa. 62:6, 7. **for strangers**—The "reproach," which especially has stung us, came when they taunted us with the fact that they had burned the temple, our peculiar glory, as though our religion was a thing of naught. **52. Wherefore**—because of these sighs of the Jews directed to God (vs. 21). **I . . . judgment upon . . . images**—in opposition to the Babylonian taunt that Jehovah's religion was a thing of naught, since they had burned His temple (vs. 51): I will show that, though I have thus visited the Jews' neglect of Me, yet those gods of Babylon cannot save themselves, much less their votaries, who shall "through all her land" lie and "groan" with wounds. **53.** Cf. Obadiah 4 as to Edom (Amos 9:2). **Though . . . yet from me**—We are not to measure God's power by what seems to our perceptions natural or probable. **55. great voice**—Where once was the *great din* of a mighty city, there shall be the silence of death [VATABLUS]. Or, the "great voice" of the revellers (vss. 38, 39; Isa. 22:2). Or, the voice of *mighty boasting* [CALVIN], (cf. vs. 53). **her waves**—"when" her calamities shall cause her to give forth a widely different "voice," even such a one as the waves give that lash the shores (vs. 42) [GROTIUS]. Or, "when" is connected thus: "the great voice" in her, when her "waves . . ." (cf. vs. 13). CALVIN translates, "*their* waves," i.e., the Medes bursting on her as impetuous waves; so vs. 42. But the parallel, "a great voice," belongs to *her,* therefore the wave-like "roar" of "their voice" ought also belong to *her* (cf. vs. 54). The "great voice" of

commercial din, boasting, and feasting, is "destroyed"; but in its stead there is the wave-like roar of *her voice* in her "destruction" (vs. 54). **56. taken**—when they were least expecting it, and in such a way that resistance was impossible. **57.** (Vs. 39; Dan. 5:1, etc.). **58. broad walls**—eighty-seven feet broad [ROSENMULLER]; fifty cubits [GROTIUS]. A chariot of four horses abreast could meet another on it without collision. The walls were two hundred cubits high, and four hundred and eighty-five stadia, or sixty miles in extent. **gates**—one hundred in number, of brass; twenty-five on each of the four sides, the city being square; between the gates were two hundred and fifty towers. BEROSUS says triple walls encompassed the outer, and the same number the inner city. Cyrus caused the outer walls to be demolished. Taking the extent of the walls to be three hundred and sixty-five stadia, as DIODORUS states, it is said two hundred thousand men completed a stadium each day, so that the whole was completed in one year. **labour . . . in the fire**—The event will show that the builders of the walls have "labored" only for the "fire" in which they shall be consumed. "In the fire" answers to the parallel, "burned with fire." Translate, "*shall have labored* in vain . . . ." Cf. Job 3:14, " built desolate places for themselves," i.e., grand places, soon about to be desolate ruins. Jeremiah has in view here Habbakkuk 2:13. **59-64.** A special copy of the prophecy prepared by Jeremiah was delivered to Seraiah, to console the Jews in their Babylonian exile. Though he was to throw it into the Euphrates, a symbol of Babylon's fate, no doubt he retained the substance in memory, so as to be able orally to communicate it to his countrymen. **went with Zedekiah**—rather, "in behalf of Zedekiah"; sent by Zedekiah to appease Nebuchadnezzar's anger at his revolt [CALVIN]. **fourth year**—so that Jeremiah's prediction of Babylon's downfall was thus solemnly written and sealed by a symbolical action, six whole years before the capture of Jerusalem by the Babylonians. **quiet prince**—Cf. I Chron. 22:9, "a man of rest." Seraiah was not one of the courtiers hostile to God's prophets, but "quiet" and docile; ready to execute Jeremiah's commission, notwithstanding the risk attending it. GLASSIUS translates, "prince of Menuchah" (cf. I Chron. 2:52, *Margin*). MAURER translates, "commander of the caravan," on whom it devolved to appoint the resting-place for the night. *English Version* suits the context best. **61. read**—not in public, for the Chaldeans would not have understood *Hebrew;* but in private, as is to be inferred from his addressing himself altogether to God (vs. 62) [CALVIN]. **62. O Lord, thou**—and not merely Jeremiah or any man is the author of this prophecy; I therefore here in Thy presence embrace as true all that I read. **63. bind a stone . . .**—(Rev.ʼ 18:21). So the Phoceans in leaving their country, when about to found Marseilles, threw lead into the sea, binding themselves not to return till the lead should swim. **64. they shall be weary**—The Babylonians shall be worn out, so as not to be able to recover their strength. **Thus far . . . Jeremiah**—Hence it is to be inferred that the last chapter is not included in Jeremiah's writings but was added by some inspired man, mainly from II Kings 24:18 to ch. 25, to explain and confirm what precedes [CALVIN].

CHAPTER 52

Vss. 1-34. WRITTEN BY SOME OTHER THAN JEREMIAH (PROBABLY EZRA) AS AN HISTORICAL SUPPLE-

MENT TO THE PREVIOUS PROPHECIES (*Note*, ch. 51:
64). Jeremiah, having already (chs. 39, 40) given
the history in the proper place, was not likely to
repeat it here. Its canonical authority as inspired
is shown by its being in the LXX *version*. It contains the capture and burning of Jerusalem, etc.,
Zedekiah's punishment, and the better treatment of
Jehoiachin under Evil-merodach, down to his death.
These last events were probably subsequent to Jeremiah's time. **3. through ... anger of ... Lord ...
Zedekiah rebelled**—His "anger" against Jerusalem,
determining Him to "cast out" His people "from His
presence" heretofore manifested there, led Him to
permit Zedekiah to rebel (II Kings 23:26, 27; cf.
Exod. 9:12; 10:1; Rom. 9:18). That rebellion, being in violation of his oath "by God," was sure to
bring down God's vengeance (II Chron. 36:13; Ezek.
17:15, 16, 18). **4. forts**—rather, *towers* of wood
[KIMCHI], for watching the movements of the
besieged from the height and annoying them with
missiles. **7.** (*Note*, ch. 39:4.) **9. gave judgment
upon him**—as guilty of rebellion and perjury (vs. 3;
cf. Ezek. 23:24). **11.** Ezekiel 12:13: "I will bring
him to Babylon, yet shall he not *see it*." **prison**—
lit., the house of visitations, or punishments, i.e.,
where there was penal work enforced on the prisoners, such as grinding. Hence LXX renders it "the
house of the mill." So Samson, after his eyes were
put out, "ground" in the Philistine prison-house
(Judg. 16:21). **12. tenth day**—But in II Kings 25:8,
it is said "the *seventh* day." Nebuzaradan *started*
from Riblah on the "seventh" day and *arrived* in
Jerusalem on the "tenth" day. Seeming discrepancies, when cleared up, confirm the genuineness of
Scripture; for they show there was no collusion between the writers; as in all God's works there is
latent harmony under outward varieties. **13. all
the houses ... and all the houses of the great**—the
"and" defines what houses especially are meant,
viz., the houses of the great men. **15. poor of ...
people**—added to the account in II Kings 25:11.
"The poor of the people" are *of the city*, as distinguished from "the poor of the land," i.e., *of the
country*. **17. brake**—that they might be more
portable. Fulfilling the prophecy (ch. 27:19).
See I Kings 7:15, 23, 27, 50. Nothing is so particularly related here as the carrying away of the
articles in the temple. The remembrance of their
beauty and preciousness heightens the bitterness of
their loss and the evil of sin which caused it. **brass
... brazen**—rather "copper ... of copper." **18.**
(Exod. 27:3.) **19. of gold in gold**—implying that the
articles were of solid gold and silver respectively,
not of a different metal inside, or alloyed [GROTIUS].
Whole: not breaking them as was done to the *brass*
(vs. 17). **20. bulls ... under the bases**—But the
bulls were not "*under* the *bases*," but under the *sea*
(I Kings 7:25, 27, 38); the ten bases were not under
the sea, but under the ten lavers. In *English Version*, "bases," therefore, must mean the *lower parts
of the sea* under which the bulls were. Rather,
translate, "the bulls were *in the place of* (i.e., by
way of; so the *Hebrew*, I Sam. 14:9), bases," or
supports to the sea [BUXTORF]. So LXX. II Kings
25:16 omits the "bulls," and has "*and* the bases"; so
GROTIUS here reads "the bulls (which were) under
(the sea) *and* the bases." **21. eighteen cubits**—but
in II Chronicles 3:15, it is "thirty-five cubits." The
discrepancy is thus removed. *Each* pillar was
eighteen common cubits. The two together, deducting the base, were thirty-five, as stated in II
Chronicles 3:15 [GROTIUS]. Other ways (e.g., by
reference to the difference between the common

and the sacred cubit) are proposed: though we are
not able positively to decide now which is the true
way, at least those proposed do show that *the discrepancies are not irreconcilable*. **22. five cubits**—
so I Kings 7:16. But II Kings 25:17 has "three
cubits." There were two parts in the chapiter: the
one lower and plain, of two cubits; the other, higher
and curiously carved, of three cubits. The former
is omitted in II Kings 25:17, as belonging to the
shaft of the pillar; the latter alone is there mentioned. Here the *whole* chapter of five cubits is
referred to. **23. on a side**—lit., (on the side) *towards the air* or *wind*, i.e., the outside of the capitals
of the pillars conspicuous to the eye, opposed to the
four remaining pomegranates which were not seen
from the outside. The pomegranates here are
ninety-six; but in I Kings 7:20 they are 200 on each
chapiter, and 400 on the two (II Chron. 4:13). It
seems there were *two* rows of them, one above the
other, and in each row 100. They are here said
to be ninety-six, but immediately following 100, and
so in I Kings 7:20. *Four* seem to have been unseen
to one looking from one point; and the ninety-six
are only those that could be seen [VATABLUS]; or,
the *four* omitted here are those separating the four
sides, one pomegranate at each point of separation
(or at the four corners) between the four sides
[GROTIUS]. **24. Seraiah**—different from the Seraiah
(ch. 51:59), son of Neriah; probably son of Azariah
(I Chron. 6:14). **Zephaniah**—son of Maaseiah
(*Notes*, ch. 21:1; 29:25). **25. seven men**—but in II
Kings 25:19 it is *"five."* Perhaps two were less illustrious persons and are therefore omitted. **principal scribe of the host**—(Isa. 33:18). His office was
to preside over the levy and enroll recruits. RAW-
LINSON observes that the Assyrian records are free
from the exaggerated expressions found in the Egyptian. A minute account was taken of the spoil.
Two "scribes of the host" are seen in every bas-
relief, writing down the various objects brought to
them: the heads of the slain, the prisoners, cattle,
sheep, etc. **28. seventh year**—in II Kings 24:12,
14, 16, it is said "the *eighth year*" of Nebuchadnezzar. No doubt it was in part about the end of
the seventh year, in part about the beginning of the
eighth. Also in II Kings 24, 10000 (vs. 14), and
7000 men of might, and 1000 craftsmen (vs. 16),
are said to have been carried away, But here 3023.
Probably the latter 3023 were of the tribe of Judah,
the remaining 7000 out of the 10,000 were of the
other tribes, out of which many Israelites still had
been left in the land. The 1000 "craftsmen" were
exclusive of the 10,000, as appears, by comparing
II Kings 24:14 with vs. 16. Probably the 3023 of
Judah were first removed in the end of "the seventh
year"; the 7000 and 1000 craftsmen in the "eighth
year." This was at the first captivity under Jehoiachin. **29. eighteenth year**—when Jerusalem was
taken. But in vs. 15, and II Kings 25:8, "the nineteenth year." Probably it was at the end of the
eighteenth and the beginning of the nineteenth
[LYRA]. **eight hundred and thirty and two**—The
most illustrious persons are meant, who no doubt
were carried away first, at the end of the eighteenth
year. **30.** Not recorded in Kings or Chronicles.
Probably it took place during the commotions that
followed the death of Gedaliah (ch. 41:18; II Kings
25:26). **four thousand and six hundred**—The exact
sum-total of the numbers specified here, viz., 3023,
832, 745, not including the general multitude and
the women and children (vs. 15; ch. 39:9; II Kings
25:11). **31.** (II Kings 25:27-30.) **five and twentieth day**—but in II Kings 25:27, it is "the twenty-

seventh day." Probably on the twenty-fifth the decree for his elevation was given, and the preparations for it made by releasing him from prison; and on the twenty-seventh day it was carried into effect. **Evil-merodach**—son and successor of Nebuchadnezzar [LYRA]; and the *Hebrew* writers say that during Nebuchadnezzar's exclusion from men among beasts, Evil-merodach administered the government. When Nebuchadnezzar at the end of seven years was restored, hearing of his son's misconduct and that he had exulted in his father's calamity, he threw him into prison, where the latter met Jeconiah and contracted a friendship with him, whence arose the favor which subsequently he showed him. God, in his elevation, rewarded his having surrendered to Nebuchadnezzar (cf. ch. 38:17 with II Kings 24:12). **lifted up . . . head**—(Cf. Gen. 40:13, 20; Ps. 3:3; 27: 6). **32. set his throne above**—a mark of respect. **the kings**—The *Hebrew* text reads (the other) "kings." "*The* kings" is a Masoretic correction. **33. changed . . . garments**—gave him garments suitable to a king. **did . . . eat bread before him**—(II Sam. 9:13). **34. every day a portion**—rather, "*its* portion," *Margin* (cf. *Margin*, I Kings 8:59).

LAMENTATIONS

OF

JEREMIAH

INTRODUCTION

IN the Hebrew Bible these Elegies of Jeremiah, five in number, are placed among the *Chetuvim*, or "Holy Writings" ("the Psalms," etc., Luke 24:44), between Ruth and Ecclesiastes. But though in classification of compositions it belongs to the *Chetuvim*, it probably followed the prophecies of Jeremiah originally. For thus alone can we account for the prophetical books being enumerated by JOSEPHUS (c. *Apion*) as *thirteen:* he must have reckoned Jeremiah and Lamentations as one book, as also Judges and Ruth, the two books of Samuel, etc., Ezra and Nehemiah. The Lamentations naturally follow the book which sets forth the circumstances forming the subject of the Elegies. Similar lamentations occur in II Samuel 1:19, etc.; 3:33. The Jews read it in their synagogues on the ninth of the month Ab, which is a fast for the destruction of their holy city. As in II Chronicles 35:25, "lamentations" are said to have been "*written*" by Jeremiah on the death of Josiah, besides it having been made "an ordinance in Israel" that "singing women" should "*speak*" of that king in lamentations; JOSEPHUS (*Antiquities* 1.6), JEROME, etc., thought that they are contained in the present collection. But plainly the subject here is the overthrow of the Jewish city and people, as the LXX expressly states in an introductory verse to their version. The probability is that there is embodied in these Lamentations much of the *language* of Jeremiah's original Elegy on Josiah, as II Chronicles 35:25 states; but it is now applied to the more universal calamity of the whole state, of which Josiah's sad death was the forerunner. Thus ch. 4:20, originally applied to Josiah, was "written," in its subsequent reference, not so much of him, as of the *throne of Judah in general*, the last representative of which, Zedekiah, had just been carried away. The language, which is true of good Josiah, is too strong in favor of Zedekiah, except when viewed as representative of the crown in general. It was natural to embody the language of the Elegy on Josiah in the more general lamentations, as his death was the presage of the last disaster that overthrew the throne and state.

The title more frequently given by the Jews to these Elegies is, "How" (*Hebrew, Eechah*), from the first word, as the Pentateuch is similarly called by the first Hebrew word of Genesis 1. The LXX calls it "Lamentations," from which we derive the name. It refers not merely to the events which occurred at the capture of the city, but to the sufferings of the citizens (the penalty of national sin) from the very beginning of the siege; and perhaps from before it, under Manasseh and Josiah (II Chron. 33:11; 35:20-25); under Jehoahaz, Jehoiakim, and Zedekiah (II Chron. 36:3, 4, 6, 7, 10, 11, etc.). LOWTH says, "Every letter is written with a tear, every word the sound of a broken heart." The style is midway between the simple elevation of prophetic writing and the loftier rhythm of Moses, David, and Habakkuk. Terse conciseness marks the Hebrew original, notwithstanding Jeremiah's diffuseness in his other writings. The Elegies are grouped in stanzas as they arose in his mind, without any artificial system of arrangement as to the thoughts. The five Elegies are acrostic: each is divided into twenty-two stanzas or verses. In the first three Elegies the stanzas consist of triplets of lines (excepting Elegy 1:7, and 2:19, which contain each four lines) each beginning with the letters of the Hebrew alphabet in regular order (twenty-two in number). In three instances (Elegy 2:16, 17; 3:46-51; 4:16, 17) two letters are transposed. In the third Elegy, each line of the three forming every stanza begins with the same letter. The stanzas in the fourth and fifth Elegies consist of two lines each. The fifth Elegy, though having twenty-two stanzas (the number of letters in the Hebrew alphabet), just as the first four, yet is not alphabetical; and its lines are shorter than those of the others, which are longer than are found in other Hebrew poems, and contain twelve syllables, marked by a cæsura about the middle, dividing them into two somewhat unequal parts. The alphabetical arrangement was adopted originally to assist the memory. GROTIUS thinks the reason for the inversion of two of the Hebrew letters in Elegy 2:16, 17; 3:46-51; 4:16, 17, is that the Chaldeans, like the Arabians, used a different order from the Hebrews; in the first Elegy, Jeremiah speaks as a Hebrew, in the following ones, as one subject to the Chaldeans. This is doubtful.

CHAPTER (ELEGY) 1

Vss. 1-22. *Aleph,* א. **1. how is she ... widow! she that was great ...**—*English Version* is according to the accents. But the members of each sentence are better balanced in antithesis, thus, "how is she that was great among the nations become as a widow! (how) she who was princess among the provinces (i.e., she who ruled over the surrounding provinces from the Nile to the Euphrates, Gen. 15: 18; I Kings 4:21; II Chron. 9:26; Ezra 4:20) become tributary!" [MAURER]. **sit**—on the ground; the posture of mourners (ch. 2:10; Ezra 9:3). The coin struck on the taking of Jerusalem by Titus, representing Judea as a female sitting solitary under a palm tree, with the inscription, *Judæa Capta,* singularly corresponds to the image here; the language therefore must be prophetical of her state subsequent to Titus, as well as referring retrospectively to her Babylonian captivity. *Beth,* ב. **2. in the night**—even in the night, the period of rest and oblivion of griefs (Job 7:3). **lovers ... friends**—the heathen states allied to Judah, and their idols. The idols whom she "loved" (Jer. 2:20-25) *could* not comfort her. Her former allies *would* not: nay, some "treacherously" joined her enemies against her (II Kings 24:2, 7; Ps. 137:7). *Gimel,* ג. **3.** (Jer. 52: 27.) **because of great servitude**—i.e., in a state "of great servitude," endured from the Chaldeans. "Because" is made by VATABLUS indicative of the *cause* of her captivity; viz., her having "afflicted" and unjustly brought into "servitude" the manumitted bond-servants (Jer. 34:8-22). MAURER explains it, "Judah has *left her land* (not literally "gone into captivity") because of the yoke imposed on it by Nebuchadnezzar." **no rest**—(Deut. 28:64, 65). **overtook her between ... straits**—image from robbers, who in the East intercept travellers at the narrow passes in hilly regions. *Daleth,* ד. **4. feasts**—the passover, pentecost (or the feast of weeks), and the feast of tabernacles. **gates**—once the place of concourse. *He,* ה. **5. the chief**—rule her (Deut. 28:43, 44). **adversaries ... prosper; for the Lord**—All the foes' attempts would have failed, had not God delivered His people into their hands (Jer. 30:15). *Vau,* ו. **6. beauty ... departed**—her temple, throne, and priesthood. **harts that find no pasture**—an animal timid and fleet, especially when seeking and not able to "find pasture." *Zain,* ז. **7. remembered**—rather, "remembers," now, in her afflicted state. In the days of her prosperity she did not appreciate, as she ought, the favors of God to her. Now, awakening out of her past lethargy, she feels from what high privileges she has fallen. **when her people fell ...**—i.e., after which days of prosperity "her people fell." **mock at her sabbaths**—The heathen used to mock at the Jews' Sabbath, as showing their idleness, and term them *Sabbatarians* (MARTIAL, 4.4). Now, said they ironically, ye may keep a continuous Sabbath. So God appointed the length of the captivity (seventy years) to be exactly that of the sum of the Sabbaths in the 490 years in which the land was denied its Sabbaths (Lev. 26:33-35). MAURER translates it "ruin." But *English Version* better expresses the point of their "mocking," viz., their involuntary "Sabbaths," i.e., the *cessation* of all national movements. A fourth line is added in this stanza, whereas in all the others there are but three. So in Elegy 2:19. *Cheth,* ח. **8.** (I Kings 8:46.) **is removed**—as a woman separated from the congregation of God for legal impurity, which is a type of moral impurity. So vs. 17; Lev. 12:2; 15:19, etc. **her**

nakedness—They have treated her as contumeliously as courtesans from whom their clothes are stripped. **turneth backward**—as modest women do from shame, i.e., she is cast down from all hope of restoration [CALVIN]. *Teth,* ט. **9.** Continuation of the image in vs. 8. Her ignominy and misery cannot be concealed but are apparent to all, as if a woman were suffering under such a flow as to reach the end of her skirts. **remembereth not ... last end**—(Deut. 32:29; Isa. 47:7). She forgot how fatal must be the end of her iniquity. Or, as the words following imply: She, in despair, cannot lift herself up to lay hold of God's promises as to her "latter end" [CALVIN]. **wonderfully**—*Hebrew,* "wonders," i.e., with amazing dejection. **O Lord, behold**—Judah here breaks in, speaking for herself. **for the enemy hath magnified himself**—What might seem ground for despair, the elated insulting of the enemy, is rather ground for good hope. *Jod,* י. **10. for**—surely she hath seen .... **heathen ... command ... not enter ... congregation**—for instance, the Ammonites and Moabites (Deut. 23:3; Neh. 13:1, 2). If the heathen, as such, were not allowed to enter the sanctuary for worship, much less were they allowed to enter in order to rob and destroy. *Caph,* כ. **11.** (Jer. 37:21; 38:9; 52:6.) **given ... pleasant things for meat**—(II Kings 6:25; Job 2:4). **relieve ... soul**—lit., to cause the soul or life to return. **for I am become vile**—Her sins and consequent sorrows are made the plea in craving God's mercy. Cf. the like plea in Psalm 25:11. *Lamed,* ל. **12.** The pathetic appeal of Jerusalem, not only to her neighbors, but even to the strangers "passing by," as her sorrow is such as should excite the compassion even of those unconnected with her. She here prefigures Christ, whom the language is prophetically made to suit, more than Jerusalem. Cf. Israel, i.e., Messiah, Isaiah 49:3. Cf. with "pass by," Matthew 27:39; Mark 15:29. As to Jerusalem, Daniel 9:12. MAURER, from the *Arabic* idiom, translates, "do not go off on your way," i.e., stop, whoever ye that pass by. *English Version* is simpler. *Mem,* מ. **13. bones**—a fire which not only consumes the skin and flesh, but penetrates even to my "bones" (i.e., my vital powers). **prevaileth against**—not as ROSENMULLER, "He (Jehovah) hath *broken* them"; a sense not in the *Hebrew.* **net**—(Ezek. 12:13); image from hunting wild beasts. He has so entangled me in His judgments that I cannot escape. **turned me back**—so that I cannot go forward and get free from His meshes. *Nun,* נ. **14. yoke ... is bound by his hand**—(Deut. 28:48). Metaphor from husbandmen, who, after they have bound the yoke to the neck of oxen, hold the rein firmly twisted *round the hand.* Thus the translation will be, "*in* His hand." Or else, "the yoke of my transgressions" (i.e., of punishment for my transgressions) is held so fast fixed on me "*by*" God, that there is no loosening of it; thus *English Version,* "*by* His hand." **wreathed**—My sins are like the withes *entwined* about the neck to fasten the yoke to. **into their hands, from whom**—into the hands of those, from whom .... MAURER translates, "*before* whom I am not able to stand." *Samech,* ס. **15. trodden ...**—MAURER, from *Syriac* root, translates, "cast away"; so II Kings 23:27. But Psalm 119:118, supports *English Version.* **in ... midst of me**—They fell not on the battlefield, but in the heart of the city; a sign of the divine wrath. **assembly**—the collected forces of Babylon; a very different "assembly" from the solemn ones which once met at Jerusalem on the great feasts. The *Hebrew* means, lit., such a solemn "assembly" or feast (cf. ch. 2:22).

trodden . . . virgin . . . in a wine-press—hath forced her blood to burst forth, as the red wine from the grapes trodden in the press (Isa. 63:3; Rev. 14:19, 20; 19:15). *Ain,* **ע. 16.** (Jer. 13:17; 14:17.) Jerusalem is the speaker. mine eye, mine eye—so ch. 4:18, "our end . . . our end"; repetition for emphasis. *Pe,* **פ. 17.** Like a woman in labor-throes (Jer. 4: 31). menstruous woman—held unclean, and shunned by all; separated from her husband and from the temple (cf. vs. 8; Lev. 14:19, etc.). *Tzaddi,* **צ. 18.** The sure sign of repentance; justifying God, condemning herself (Neh. 9:33; Ps. 51:4; Dan. 9:7-14). his commandment—lit., "mouth"; His word in the mouth of the prophets. *Koph,* **ק. 19.** lovers—(vs. 2; Jer. 30:14). elders—in dignity, not merely age. sought . . . meat—Their dignity did not exempt them from having to go and seek bread (vs. 11). *Resh,* **ר. 20.** bowels . . . troubled—(Job 30:27; Isa 16:11; Jer. 4:19; 31:20). Extreme mental distress affects the bowels and the whole internal frame. heart . . . turned—(Hos. 11:8); is agitated or fluttered. abroad . . . sword . . . at home . . . as death—(Deut. 32:25; Ezek. 7:15). The "as" does not modify, but intensifies. "Abroad the sword bereaveth, at home *as it were death itself*" (personified), in the form of famine and pestilence (II Kings 25:3; Jer. 14:18; 52: 6). So Habakkuk 2:5, "as death" (MICHAELIS). *Schin,* **ש. 21.** they are glad that thou hast done it—because they thought that therefore Judah is irretrievably ruined (Jer. 40:3). the day . . . called—(but) thou wilt bring on them the day of calamity which thou hast *announced,* viz., by the prophets (Jer. 50; 48:27). like . . . me—in calamities (Ps. 137: 8, 9; Jer. 51:25, etc.). *Tau,* **ת. 22.** Such prayers against foes are lawful, if the foe be an enemy of God, and if our concern be not for our own personal feeling, but for the glory of God and the welfare of His people. come before thee—so Revelation 16:19, "Babylon *came* in remembrance *before God*" (cf. Ps. 109:15).

CHAPTER (ELEGY) 2

Vss. 1-22. *Aleph,* **א. 1.** How—The title of the collection repeated here, and in Elegy 4:1. covered . . . with a cloud—i.e., with the darkness of ignominy. cast down from heaven unto . . . earth—(Matt. 11:23); dashed down from the highest prosperity to the lowest misery. beauty of Israel—the beautiful temple (Ps. 29:2; 74:7; 96:9, *Margin;* Isa. 60:7; 64: 11). his footstool—the ark (cf. I Chron. 28:2, with Ps. 99:5; 132:7). They once had gloried more in the ark than in the God whose symbol it was; they now feel it was but His "footstool," yet that it had been a great glory to them that God deigned to use it as such. *Beth,* **ב. 2.** polluted—by delivering it into the hands of the profane foe. Cf. Psalm 89: 39, "*profaned . . . crown.*" *Gimel,* **ג. 3.** horn—worn in the East as an ornament on the forehead, and an emblem of power and majesty (I Sam. 2:10; Ps. 132:17; Jer. 48:25, *Note*). drawn back . . . right hand—(Ps. 74:11). God has withdrawn the help which He before gave them. Not as HENDERSON, "He has turned back his (*Israel's*) right hand" (Ps. 89:43). *Daleth,* **ד. 4.** (Isa. 63:10.) stood with . . . right hand—He took His stand so as to use His right hand as an adversary. HENDERSON makes the image to be that of an archer *steadying* his right hand to take aim. Not only did He *withdraw* His help, but also took arms against Israel. all . . . pleasant to . . . eye—(Ezek. 24:25). All that were conspicuous for youth, beauty, and rank. in . . . tabernacle—the dwellings of Jerusalem. *He,* **ה**

5. an enemy—(Jer. 30:14). mourning and lamentation—There is a play of similar sounds in the original, "sorrow and sadness," to heighten the effect (Job 30:3, *Hebrew; Ezek.* 35:3, *Margin*). *Vau,* **ו. 6.** tabernacle—rather, "He hath violently taken away His *hedge* (the hedge of the place sacred to Him, Ps. 80:12; 89:40; Isa. 5:5), as that of a garden" [MAURER]. CALVIN supports *English Version,* "His tabernacle (i.e., temple) as (one would take away the temporary cottage or booth) of a garden." Isaiah 1:8 accords with this (Job 27:18). places of . . . assembly—the temple and synagogues (Ps. 74:7, 8). solemn feasts—(ch. 1:4). *Zain,* **ז. 7.** they . . . made a noise in . . . house of . . . Lord, as in . . . feast—The foe's shout of triumph in the captured temple bore a resemblance (but oh, how sad a contrast as to the *occasion* of it!) to the joyous thanksgivings we used to offer in the same place at our "solemn feasts" (cf. vs. 22). *Cheth,* **ח. 8.** stretched . . . a line—The Easterns used a measuring-line not merely in building, but in destroying edifices (II Kings 21:13; Isa. 34:11); implying here the unsparing rigidness with which He would exact punishment. *Teth,* **ט. 9.** Her gates cannot oppose the entrance of the foe into the city, for they are sunk under a mass of rubbish and earth. broken . . . bars—(Jer. 51:30). her king . . . among . . . Gentiles—(Deut. 28:36). law . . . no more—(II Chron. 15:3). The civil and religious laws were one under the theocracy. "All the legal ordinances (prophetical as well as priestly) of the theocracy, are no more" (Ps. 74:9; Ezek. 7:26). *Jod,* **י. 10.** (Job 2:12, 13.) The "elders," by their example, would draw the others to violent grief. the virgins—who usually are so anxious to set off their personal appearances to advantage. *Caph,* **כ. 11.** liver is poured . . .—i.e., as the liver was thought to be the seat of the passions, *all my feelings are poured out and prostrated for . . . .* The "liver," is here put for the *bile* (see Job 16:13, "gall"; Ps. 22:14) in a bladder on the surface of the liver, copiously discharged when the passions are agitated. swoon—through faintness from the effects of hunger. *Lamed,* **ל. 12.** as the wounded—famine being as deadly as the sword (Jer. 52:6). soul . . . poured . . . into . . . mother's bosom—Instinctively turning to their mother's bosom, but finding no milk there, they *breathe out their life* as it were "into her bosom." *Mem* **מ. 13.** What thing shall I take to witness—What can I bring forward as a witness, or instance, to prove that others have sustained as grievous ills as thou? I cannot console thee as mourners are often consoled by showing that thy lot is only what others, too, suffer. The "sea" affords the only suitable emblem of thy woes, by its boundless extent and depth (ch. 1:12; Dan. 9:12). *Nun,* **נ. 14.** Thy prophets—not God's (Jer. 23:26). vain . . . for thee—to gratify thy appetite, not for truth, but for false things. not discovered thine iniquity—in opposition to God's command to the true prophets (Isa. 58:1). Lit., *They have not taken off* the veil which *was on thine iniquity,* so as to set it before thee. burdens—Their prophecies were soothing and flattering; but the result of them was *heavy* calamities to the people, worse than even what the prophecies of Jeremiah, which they in derision called "burdens," threatened. Hence he terms their pretended prophecies "false burdens," which proved to the Jews "causes of their banishment" [CALVIN]. *Samech,* **ס. 15.** clap . . . hands—in derision (Job 27: 23; 34:37). wag . . . head—(II Kings 19:21; Ps. 44: 14). perfection of beauty . . . joy of . . . earth—(Ps.

48:2; 50:2). The Jews' enemies quote their very words in scorn. *Pe*, ‌פ‌. **16, 17.** For the transposition of *Hebrew* letters (*Pe* and *Ain*) in the order of verses, see *Introduction*. **opened . . . mouth**—as ravening, roaring wild beasts (Job 16:9, 10; Ps. 22: 13). Herein Jerusalem was a type of Messiah. **gnash . . . teeth**—in vindictive malice. **we have seen it**—(Ps. 35:21). *Ain*, ‌ע‌. **17. Lord**—Let not the foe exult as if it was *their* doing. It was "the Lord" who thus fulfilled the threats uttered by His prophets for the guilt of Judea (Lev. 26:16-25; Deut. 28: 36-48, 53; Jer. 19:9). *Tzaddi*, ‌צ‌. **18. wall**—(vs. 8). Personified. "*Their* heart, i.e., the Jews'; while their heart is lifted up to the Lord in prayer, their speech is addressed to the "wall" (the part being put for *the whole city*). **let tears . . .**—(Jer. 14:17). The wall is called on to weep for its own ruin and that of the city. Cf. the similar personification (ch. 1:4). **apple**—the pupil of the eye (Ps. 17:8). *Koph*, ‌ק‌. **19. cry . . . in . . . night**—(Ps. 119:147.) **beginning of . . . watches**—i.e., the *first* of the three equal divisions (four hours each) into which the ancient Jews divided the night; viz., from sunset to ten o'clock. The second was called "the middle watch" (Judg. 7:19), from ten till two o'clock. The third, "the morning watch," from two to sunrise (Exod. 14:24; I Sam. 11:11). Afterwards, under the Romans, they had *four* watches (Matt. 14:25; Luke 12: 38). **for . . . thy . . . children**—that God, if He will not spare thee, may *at least* preserve "thy young children." **top of . . . street**—(Isa. 51:20; Nah. 3: 10). *Resh*, ‌ר‌. **20. women eat . . . fruit**—as threatened (Lev. 26:29; Deut. 28:53, 56, 57; Jer. 19:9). **children . . . span long**—or else, "children whom they carry in their arms" [MAURER]. *Schin*, ‌ש‌. **21.** (II Chron. 36:17.) **22. Thou hast called as in . . . solemn day . . . terrors**—Thou hast summoned my enemies against me from all quarters, just as multitudes used to be convened to Jerusalem, on the solemn feast-days. The objects, for which the enemies and the festal multitude respectively met, formed a sad contrast. Cf. ch. 1:15: "called an assembly against me."

CHAPTER (ELEGY) 3

Vss. 1-66. Jeremiah proposes his own experience under afflictions, as an example as to how the Jews should behave under theirs, so as to have hope of a restoration; hence the change from *singular* to *plural* (vss. 22, 40-47). The stanzas consist of three lines, each of which begins with the same Hebrew letter. *Aleph*, ‌א‌. **1-3. seen affliction**—his own in the dungeon of Malchiah (Jer. 38:6); that of his countrymen also in the siege. Both were types of that of Christ. **2. darkness**—calamity. **light**—prosperity. **3. turneth . . . hand**—to inflict again and again new strokes. "His hand," which once used to protect me. "Turned . . . turneth" implies *repeated* inflictions. *Beth*, ‌ב‌. **4-6.** (Job 16:8.) **5. builded**—mounds, as against a besieged city, so as to allow none to escape (so vss. 7, 9). **6. set me**—HENDERSON refers this to the custom of placing the dead in a sitting posture. **dark places**—sepulchers. As those "dead long since"; so Jeremiah and his people are consigned to oblivion (Ps. 88:5, 6; 143:3; Ezek. 37: 13). *Gimel*, ‌ג‌. **7-9.** **hedged**—(Job 3:23; Hos. 2:6). **chain**—lit., chain of brass. **8. shutteth out**—image from a door *shutting out* any entrance (Job 30:20). So the antitype, Christ (Ps. 22:2). **9. hewn stone**—which coheres so closely as not to admit of being broken through. **paths crooked**—thwarted our plans and efforts so that nothing went right. *Daleth*,

‌ד‌. **10-13.** (Job 10:16; Hos. 13:7, 8). **11. turned aside**—made me wander out of the right way, so as to become a prey to wild beasts. **pulled . . . in pieces**—(Hos. 6:1), as a "bear" or a "lion" (vs. 10). **12.** (Job 7:20.) *He*, ‌ה‌. **13-15. 13. arrows**—lit., *sons* of His quiver (cf. Job 6:4). **14.** (Jer. 20:7.) **their song**—(Ps. 69:12). Jeremiah herein was a type of Messiah. "All my people" (John 1:11). **15. wormwood**—(Jer. 9:15). There it is regarded as *food*, viz., the leaves: here as *drink*, viz., the juice. *Vau*, ‌ו‌. **16-18. gravel**—referring to the *grit* that often mixes with bread baked in ashes, as is the custom of baking in the East (Prov. 20:17). We fare as hardly as those who eat such bread. The same allusion is in "Covered me with ashes," viz., as bread. **17.** Not only present, but all hope of future prosperity is removed; so much so, that I am as one who never was prosperous ("I forgat prosperity"). **18. from the Lord**—i.e., my hope derived from Him (Ps. 31:22). *Zain*, ‌ז‌. **19-21.** (Jer. 9:15). **Remembering . . .**—This gives the reason why he gave way to the temptation to despair. The *Margin*, "Remember" does not suit the sense so well. **20.** As often as *my soul calls them to remembrance, it is humbled* or bowed down in me. **21. This**—viz., what follows; the view of the divine character (vss. 22, 23). CALVIN makes "this" refer to Jeremiah's infirmity. His very weakness (vss. 19, 20) gives him hope of God interposing His strength for him (cf. Ps. 25:11, 17; 42:5, 8; II Cor. 12:9, 10). *Cheth*, ‌ח‌. **22-24.** (Mal. 3:6). **23.** (Isa. 33:2.) **24.** (Num. 18:20; Ps. 16:5; 73:26; 119: 57; Jer. 10:16.) To have God for our portion is the one only foundation of hope. *Teth*, ‌ט‌. **25-27.** The repetition of "good" at the beginning of each of the three verses heightens the effect. **wait**—(Isa. 30:18). **26. quietly wait**—lit., "be in silence." Cf. vs. 28 and Psalm 39: 2, 9, i.e., to be patiently quiet under afflictions, resting in the will of God (Ps. 37: 7). So Aaron (Lev. 10:2, 3); and Job (40:4, 5). **27. yoke**—of the Lord's *disciplinary* teaching (Ps. 90:12; 119:71). CALVIN interprets it, The Lord's *doctrine* (Matt. 11:29, 30), which is to be received in a docile spirit. The earlier the better; for the old are full of prejudices (Prov. 8:17; Eccles. 12:1). Jeremiah himself received the yoke, both of doctrine and chastisement in his youth (Jer. 1:6, 7). *Jod*, ‌י‌. **28-30.** The fruit of true docility and patience. He does not fight against the yoke (Jer. 31:18; Acts 9: 5), but accommodates himself to it. **alone**—The heathen applauded magnanimity, but they looked to display and the praise of men. The child of God, in the absence of any witness, "alone," silently submits to the will of God, because he is used to bearing it on him. Rather, "because He (the Lord, vs. 26) *hath laid it on* him" [VATABLUS]. **29.** (Job 42:6.) The mouth in the dust is the attitude of supplicant and humble submission to God's dealings as righteous and loving in design (cf. Ezra 9:6; I Cor. 14:25). **if so be there may be hope**—This does not express doubt as to whether GOD be willing to receive the penitent, but the *penitent's* doubt as to himself; he whispers to himself this consolation, "Perhaps there may be hope for me." **30.** Messiah, the Antitype, fulfilled this; His practice agreeing with His precept (Isa. 50: 6; Matt. 5:39). Many take patiently afflictions from God, but when man wrongs them, they take it impatiently. The godly bear resignedly the latter, like the former, as sent by God (Ps. 17:13). *Caph*, ‌כ‌. **31-33. 31.** True repentance is never without hope (Ps. 94:14). **32.** The punishments of the godly are but for a time. **33.** He does not afflict any willingly (lit., "from His heart." i.e., as if He had any pleasure in it, Ezek. 33:11), much less the godly (Heb. 12:10). *Lamed,* ל. **34-36.** This triplet has an infinitive in the beginning of each verse, the governing finite verb being in the end of vs. 36, "the Lord approveth not," which is to be repeated in each verse. Jeremiah here anticipates and answers the objections which the Jews might start, that it was by His connivance they were "crushed under the feet" of those who "turned aside the right of a man." God approves (lit., "seeth," Hab. 1:13; so "behold," "look on," i.e., look on *with approval*) not of such unrighteous acts; and so the Jews may look for deliverance and the punishment of their foes. **35. before ...face of...most High**—Any "turning aside" of justice in court is done *before the face of God,* who is present, and "regardeth," though unseen (Eccles. 5:8). **36. subvert**—to wrong. *Mem,* מ. **37-39.** Whc is it that can (as God, Ps. 33:9) effect by a word anything, without the will of God? **38. evil... good**—*Calamity* and prosperity alike proceed from God (Job 2:10; Isa. 45:7; Amos 3:6). **39. living**— and so having a time yet given him by God for repentance. If sin were punished as it deserves, *life* itself would be forfeited by the sinner. "Complaining" (murmuring) ill becomes him who enjoys such a favor as life (Prov. 19:3). **for the punishment of his sins**—Instead of blaming God for his sufferings, he ought to recognize in them God's righteousness and the just rewards of his own sin. *Nun,* נ. **40-42. us**—Jeremiah and his fellow countrymen in their calamity. **search**—as opposed to the torpor wherewith men rest only on their outward sufferings, without attending to the cause of them (Ps. 139:23, 24). **41. heart with...hands**—the antidote to hypocrisy (Ps. 86:4; I Tim. 2:8). **42. not pardoned**—The Babylonian captivity had not yet ended. *Samech,* ס. **43-45. covered**—viz., thyself (so vs. 44), so as not to see and pity our calamities, for even the most cruel in seeing a sad spectacle are moved to pity. Cf. as to God "hiding His face," Psalm 10:11; 22:25. **44.** (Vs. 8.) The "cloud" is our sins, and God's wrath because of them (Isa. 44:22; 59:2). **45.** So the apostles were treated; but, instead of murmuring, they rejoiced at it (I Cor. 4:13). *Pe,* פ. **46-48.** *Pe* is put before *Ain,* as in Elegy 2:16, 17; 4:16, 17. **46.** (Ch. 2:16.) **47.** Like animals fleeing in fear, we fall into the snare laid for us. **48.** (Jer. 4:19.) *Ain,* ע. **49-51. without ...intermission**—or else, "because there is no intermission" [PISCATOR], viz., of my miseries. **50. Till** —His prayer is not without hope, wherein it differs from the blind grief of unbelievers. **look down...** —(Isa. 63:15). **51. eye affecteth mine heart**—i.e., causeth me grief with continual tears; or, "affecteth my *life*" (lit., "soul," *Margin*), i.e., my health [GROTIUS]. **daughters of...city**—the towns around, dependencies of Jerusalem, taken by the foe. *Tzaddi,* צ. **52-54. a bird**—which is destitute of counsel and strength. The allusion seems to be to Proverbs 1:17 [CALVIN]. **without cause**—(Ps. 69:4; 109:3, 4). Type of Messiah (John 15:25). **53. in ...dungeon**—(Jer. 37:16). **stone**—usually put at the mouth of a dungeon to secure the prisoners (Josh. 10:18; Dan. 6:17; Matt. 27:60). **54. Waters** —not literally, for there was "no water" (Jer. 38:6) in the place of Jeremiah's confinement, but emblematical of overwhelming calamities (Ps. 69:2; 124:4, 5). **cut off**—(Isa. 38:10, 11). I am abandoned by God. He speaks according to carnal

sense. *Koph,* ק. **55-57. I called...out of... dungeon**—Thus the spirit resists the flesh, and faith spurns the temptation [CALVIN], (Ps. 130:1; Jonah 2:2). **56. Thou hast heard**—viz., formerly (so in vss. 57, 58). **breathing...cry**—two kinds of prayer; the sigh of a prayer silently *breathed* forth, and the loud, earnest cry (cf. Isa. 26:16, "Prayer," *Margin,* "*secret speech,*" with Ps. 55:17, "cry aloud"). **57. Thou drewest near**—with Thy help (Jas. 4:8). *Resh,* ר. **58-60.** Jeremiah cites God's gracious answers to his prayers as an encouragement to his fellow countrymen, to trust in Him. **pleaded**—(Ps. 35:1; Mic. 7:9). **59.** God's past deliverances and His knowledge of Judah's wrongs are made the grounds of prayer for relief. **60. imaginations**—devices (Jer. 11:19). **Their vengeance**—means *their malice.* Jeremiah gives his conduct, when plotted against by his foes, as an example how the Jews should bring their wrongs at the hands of the Chaldeans before God. *Schin,* ש. **61-63. their reproach**—their reproachful language against me. **62. lips**—speeches. **63. sitting down...rising up**—whether they sit or rise, i.e., whether they be actively engaged or sedentary, and at rest "all the day" (vs. 62), I am the subject of their derisive songs (vs. 14). *Tau,* ת. **64-66.** (Jer. 11:20; II Tim. 4:14). **65. sorrow**— rather, *blindness* or *hardness;* lit., "a veil" covering their heart, so that they may rush on to their own ruin (Isa. 6:10; II Cor. 3:14, 15). **66. from under ...heavens of...Lord**—*destroy* them so that it may be seen everywhere *under heaven* that thou sittest above as Judge of the world.

CHAPTER (ELEGY) 4

Vss. 1-22. THE SAD CAPTURE OF JERUSALEM, THE HOPE OF RESTORATION, AND THE RETRIBUTION AWAITING IDUMEA FOR JOINING BABYLON AGAINST JUDEA. *Aleph,* א. **1. gold**—the splendid adornment of the temple [CALVIN] (ch. 1:10; I Kings 6:22; Jer. 52:19); or, *the principal men* of Judea [GROTIUS] (vs. 2). **stones of...sanctuary**—the gems on the breastplate of the high priest; or, metaphorically, the priests and Levites. *Beth,* ב. **2. comparable to...gold**— (Job 28:16, 19). **earthen pitchers**—(Isa. 30:14; Jer. 19:11). *Gimel,* ג. **3. sea monsters...breast**— Whales and other cetaceous monsters are mammalian. Even they suckle their young; but the Jewish women in the siege, so desperate was their misery, ate theirs (vs. 10; ch. 2:20). Others translate, "jackals." **ostriches**—see *Note,* Job 39:14-16, on their forsaking their young. *Daleth,* ד. **4. thirst** —The mothers have no milk to give through the famine. *He,* ה. **5. delicately**—on dainties. **are desolate**—or, *perish.* **in scarlet embrace dunghills** —Instead of the *scarlet* couches on which the grandees were nursed, they must lie on *dunghills.* **embrace**—They who once shrank sensitively from any soil, gladly *cling close* to heaps of filth as their only resting-place. Cf. "embrace the rock" (Job 24:8). *Vau,* ו. **6. greater than...Sodom**—(Matt. 11:23). No prophets had been sent to Sodom, as there had been to Judea; therefore the punishment of the latter was heavier than that of the former. **overthrown...in a moment**—whereas the Jews had to endure the protracted and manifold hardships of a siege. **no hands stayed on her**—No *hostile force,* as the Chaldeans in the case of Jerusalem, *continually pressed on her* before her overthrow. Jeremiah thus shows the greater severity of Jerusalem's punishment than that of Sodom. *Zain,* ז. **7. Nazarites**—lit., "separated ones" (Num. 6). They were held once in the highest estimation, but now they are degraded. God's blessing formerly caused their body not to be the less fair and ruddy for their abstinence from strong drink. Cf. the similar case of Daniel, etc. (Dan. 1:8-15). Also David (I Sam. 16:12; 17:42). Type of Messiah (Song of Sol. 5: 10). **rubies**—GESENIUS translates, "corals," from a *Hebrew* root, "to divide into branches," from the branching form of corals. **polishing**—They were like exquisitely cut and *polished sapphires.* The "sapphires" may represent the *blue* veins of a healthy person. *Cheth,* ח· **8. blacker than . . . coal**—or, "than blackness" itself (Joel 2:6; Nah. 2: 10). **like a stick**—as withered as a dry stick. *Teth,* ט· **9.** The speedy death by the sword is better than the lingering death by famine. **pine away**—lit., "flow out"; referring to the flow of blood. This expression, and "stricken through," are drawn from death by "the sword." **want of . . . fruits**—The words in italics have to be supplied in the original (Gen. 18:28; Ps. 109:24). *Jod,* י· **10.** (Ch. 2:20; Deut. 28:56, 57.) **pitiful**—naturally at other times compassionate (Isa. 49:15). JOSEPHUS describes the unnatural act as it took place in the siege under Titus. **sodden**—boiled. *Caph,* כ· **11. fire . . . devoured . . . foundations**—(Deut. 32:22; Jer. 21:14). A most rare event. Fire usually consumes only the surface; but this reached even to the *foundation,* cutting off all hope of restoration. *Lamed,* ל· **12.** Jerusalem was so fortified that all thought it impregnable. It therefore could only have been the hand of God, not the force of man, which overthrew it. *Mem,* מ· **13. prophets**—the false prophets (Jer. 23:11, 21). Supply the sense thus: "For the sins . . . *these calamities have befallen her.*" **shed the blood of the just**—(Matt. 23:31, 37). This received its full fulfilment in the slaying of Messiah and the Jews' consequent dispersion (Jas. 5:6). *Nun,* נ· **14. blind**—with mental aberration. **polluted . . . with blood**—both with blood of one another mutually shed (e.g., Jer. 2:34), and with their blood shed by the enemy [GLASSIUS]. **not touch . . . garments**—as being defiled with blood (Num. 19:16). *Samech,* ס· **15. They . . . them**—"They," i.e., "men" (vs. 14). Even the very *Gentiles,* regarded as unclean by *the Jews,* who were ordered most religiously to avoid all defilements, cried unto the *latter,* "depart," as being unclean: so universal was the defilement of the city by blood. **wandered**—As the false prophets and their followers had "wandered" blind with infatuated and idolatrous crime in the city (vs. 14), so they must now "wander" among the heathen in blind consternation with calamity. **they said**—i.e., the Gentiles said: *it was said* among the heathen, "The Jews shall no more sojourn in their own land" [GROTIUS]; or, wheresoever they go in their wandering exile, "they shall not stay long" [LUDOVICUS DE DIEU], (Deut. 28: 65). *Pe,* פ· *Ain* and *Pe* are here transposed, as in ch. 2:16, 17; 3:46-51. **16. anger**—lit., "face"; it is the countenance which, by its expression, manifests anger (Ps. 34:16). GESENIUS translates, "the *person* of Jehovah"; Jehovah present; Jehovah Himself (Exod. 33:14; II Sam. 17:11). **divided**—dispersed the Jews. **they respected not . . . priests**—This is the language of the *Gentiles.* "The Jews have no hope of a return: for *they respected not even good priests*" (II Chron. 24:19-22) [GROTIUS]. MAURER explains it, "They (the victorious foe) regard not the (Jewish) priests when imploring their pity" (ch. 5:12). The evident antithesis to "As for *us*" (vs. 17) and the language of "the heathen" at the close of vs. 15, of which vs. 16 is the continua-

tion, favor the former view. *Ain,* ע· **17. As for us**—This translation forms the best antithesis to the language of *the heathen* (vss. 15, 16). CALVIN translates, "While as *yet* we stood as a state, our eyes failed," etc. **watched for a nation that could not save us**—Egypt (II Kings 24:7; Isa. 30:7; Jer. 37:5-11). *Tzaddi,* צ· **18. They**—the Chaldeans. **cannot go**—without danger. *Koph,* ק· The last times just before the taking of the city. There was no place of escape; the foe intercepted those wishing to escape from the famine-stricken city, "on the mountains and in the wilderness." **swifter . . . than . . . eagles**—the Chaldean cavalry (Jer. 4:13). **pursued**—lit., "to be hot"; then, "to pursue hotly" (Gen. 31:36). Thus they pursued and overtook Zedekiah (Jer. 52:8, 9). *Resh,* ר· **20. breath . . . anointed of . . . Lord**—our king, with whose life ours was bound up. The original reference seems to have been to Josiah (II Chron. 35:25), killed in battle with Pharaoh-necho; but the language is here applied to Zedekiah, who, though worthless, was still lineal representative of David, and type of Messiah, the "Anointed." Viewed *personally* the language is too favorable to apply to him. **live among the heathen**—Under him we hoped to live securely, even in spite of the surrounding heathen nations [GROTIUS]. *Schin,* ש· **21. Rejoice**—at our calamities (Ps. 137:7). This is a *prophecy* that Edom should exult over the fall of Jerusalem. At the same time it is implied, Edom's joy shall be short-lived. *Ironically* she is told, Rejoice while thou mayest (*Eccles.* 11:9). **cup**—for this image of the confounding effects of God's wrath, see Jeremiah 13:12; 25:15, 16, 21; as to Edom, Jeremiah 49:7-22. *Tau,* ת· **22.** (Isa. 40:2.) Thou hast been punished enough: the end of thy punishment is at hand. **no more carry thee . . . into captivity**—i.e., by the Chaldeans. The Romans carried them away subsequently. The *full* accomplishment of this prophecy must therefore refer to the Jews' final restoration. **discover**—By the severity of His punishments on thee, God shall let men see how great was thy sin (Jer. 49:10). God "covers" sin when He forgives it (Ps. 32:1, 5). He "discovers," or "reveals," it, when He punishes it (Job 20:27). Jeremiah 49:10 shows that *Margin* is wrong, "carry captive" (this rendering is as in Nah. 2:7; cf. *Margin*).

CHAPTER (ELEGY) 5

Vss. 1-22. EPIPHONEMA, OR A CLOSING RECAPITULATION OF THE CALAMITIES TREATED IN THE PREVIOUS ELEGIES. **1.** (Ps. 89:50, 51.) **2. Our inheritance**—"Thine inheritance" (Ps. 79:1). The land given of old to us by Thy gift. **3. fatherless**—Our whole land is full of orphans [CALVIN]. Or, "we are fatherless," being abandoned by Thee our "Father" (Jer. 3:19), [GROTIUS]. **4. water for money**—The Jews were compelled to pay the enemy for the water of their own cisterns after the overthrow of Jerusalem; or rather, it refers to their sojourn in Babylon; they had to pay tax for access to the rivers and fountains. Thus, "our" means the water which we need, the commonest necessary of life. **our wood**—In Judea each one could get wood without pay; in Babylon, "our wood," the wood we need, must be paid for. **5.** Lit., "On our necks we are persecuted"; i.e., Men tread on our necks (Ps. 66:12; Isa. 51:23; cf. Josh. 10:24). The extremest oppression. The foe not merely galled the Jews' face, back, and sides, but their neck. A just retribution, as they had been stiff in neck against the yoke of God (II Chron. 30:8, *Margin;* Neh. 9:29; Isa. 48:4). **6. given ... hand to**—in token of submission (*Note,* Jer. 50:15). **to ... Egyptians**—at the death of Josiah (II Chron. 36:3, 4). **Assyrians** —i.e., the Chaldeans who occupied the empire which Assyria had held. So Jeremiah 2:18. **to be satisfied with bread**—(Deut. 28:48). **7.** (Jer. 31:29.) **borne their iniquities**—i.e., the punishment of them. The accumulated sins of our fathers from age to age, as well as our own, are visited on us. They say this as a plea why God should pity us (cf. Ezek. 18:2, etc.). **8. Servants ... ruled ... us**—Servants under the Chaldean governors ruled the Jews (Neh. 5:15). Israel, once a "kingdom of priests" (Exod. 19:6), is become like Canaan, "a servant of servants," according to the curse (Gen. 9:25). The Chaldeans were designed to be "servants" of Shem, being descended from Ham (Gen. 9:26). Now through the Jews' sin, their positions are reversed. **9. We gat our bread with ... peril**—i.e., those of us left in the city after its capture by the Chaldeans. **because of ... sword of ... wilderness**—because of the liability to attack by the robber Arabs of the wilderness, through which the Jews had to pass to get "bread" from Egypt (cf. vs. 6). **10.** As an oven is scorched with too much fire, so our skin with the hot blast of famine (*Margin,* rightly, "storms," like the hot simoom). Hunger dries up the pores so that the skin becomes like as if it were scorched by the sun (Job 30:30; Ps. 119:83). **11.** So in just retribution Babylon itself should fare in the end. Jerusalem shall for the last time suffer these woes before her final restoration (Zech. 14:2). **12. hanged ... by their hand**—a piece of wanton cruelty invented by the Chaldeans. GROTIUS translates, "Princes were hung by the hand *of the enemy";*

hanging was a usual mode of execution (Gen. 40: 19). **elders**—officials (ch. 4:16). **13. young men ... grind**—The work of the lowest *female* slave was laid on young men (Judg. 16:21; Job 31:10). **children fell under ... wood**—Mere children had to bear burdens of wood so heavy that they sank beneath them. **14.** Aged men in the East meet in the open space round the gate to decide judicial trials and to hold social converse (Job 29:7, 8). **16. The crown** —all our glory, the kingdom and the priesthood (Job 19:9; Ps. 89:39, 44). **17.** (Ch. 1:22; 2:11.) **18. foxes**—They frequent desolate places where they can freely and fearlessly roam. **19.** (Ps. 102:12.) The perpetuity of God's rule over human affairs, however He may seem to let His people be oppressed for a time, is their ground of hope of restoration. **20. for ever**—i.e., for "so long a time." **21.** (Ps. 80:3; Jer. 31:18.) "Restore us to favor with Thee, and so we shall be restored to our old position" [GROTIUS]. Jeremiah is not speaking of spiritual conversion, but of that outward turning whereby God receives men into His fatherly favor, manifested in bestowing prosperity [CALVIN]. Still, as Israel is a type of the Church, temporal goods typify spiritual blessings; and so the sinner may use this prayer for God to convert him. **22.** Rather, "Unless haply Thou hast utterly rejected us, and art beyond measure wroth against us," i.e., Unless Thou art implacable, which is impossible, hear our prayer [CALVIN]. Or, as *Margin,* "For wouldest Thou utterly reject us?" etc.—No; that cannot be. The Jews, in this book, and in Isaiah and Malachi, to avoid the ill-omen of a mournful closing sentence, repeat the verse immediately preceding the last [CALVIN].

THE BOOK OF THE PROPHET

EZEKIEL

INTRODUCTION

THE name Ezekiel means "(whom) God will strengthen" [GESENIUS]; or, "God will prevail" [ROSENMULLER]. His father was Buzi (ch. 1:3), a priest, and he probably exercised the priestly office himself at Jerusalem, previous to his captivity, as appears from the matured priestly character to be seen in his prophecies, a circumstance which much increased his influence with his captive fellow countrymen at Babylon. Tradition represents Sarera as the land of his nativity. His call to prophesy was in the fifth year from the date of his being carried away with Jehoiachin (see II Kings 24:11–15) by Nebuchadnezzar, 599 B.C. The best portions of the people seem to have been among the first carried away (ch. 11:16; Jer. 24:2–7, 8, 10). The ungodly were willing to do anything to remain in their native land; whereas the godly believed the prophets and obeyed the first summons to surrender, as the only path of safety. These latter, as adhering to the theocratic principle, were among the earliest to be removed by the Chaldeans, who believed that, if they were out of the way, the nation would fall to pieces of itself. They were despised by their brethren in the Holy Land not yet captives, as having no share in the temple sacrifices. Thus Ezekiel's sphere of labor was one happier and less impeded by his countrymen than that of Jeremiah at home. The vicinity of the river Chebar, which flows into the Euphrates near Circesium, was the first scene of his prophecies (ch. 1:1). Tel-abib there (now Thallaba) was his place of residence (ch. 3:15), whither the elders used to come to inquire as to God's messages through him. They were eager to return to Jerusalem, but he taught them that they must first return to their God. He continued to prophesy for at least twenty-two years, i.e., to the twenty-seventh year of the captivity (ch. 29:17), and probably remained with the captives by the Chebar the rest of his life. A treatise, falsely attributed to Epiphanius, states a tradition that he was killed at Babylon by a prince of his people whom he had reproved for idolatry.

He was contemporary with Jeremiah and Daniel. The former had prophesied for thirty-four years before Ezekiel, and continued to do so for six or seven years after him. The call of Ezekiel followed the very next year after the communication of Jeremiah's predictions to Babylon (Jer. 51:59), and was divinely intended as a sequel to them. Daniel's predictions are mostly later than Ezekiel's but his piety and wisdom had become proverbial in the early part of Ezekiel's ministry (ch. 14:14, 16; 28:3). They much resemble one another, especially in the visions and grotesque images. It is a remarkable proof of genuineness that in Ezekiel no prophecies against Babylon occur among those directed against the enemies of the covenant people. Probably he desired not to give needless offence to the government under which he lived. The effect of his labors is to be seen in the improved character of the people towards the close of the captivity, and their general cessation from idolatry and a return to the law. It was little more than thirty years after the close of his labors when the decree of the Jews' restoration was issued. His leading characteristic is realizing, determined energy; this admirably adapted him for opposing the "rebellious house" "of stubborn front and hard heart," and for maintaining the cause of God's Church among his countrymen in a foreign land, when the external framework had fallen to pieces. His style is plain and simple. His conceptions are definite, and the details even of the symbolical and enigmatical parts are given with lifelike minuteness. The obscurity lies in the substance, not in the form, of his communications. The priestly element predominates in his prophecies, arising from his previous training as a priest. He delights to linger about the temple and to find in its symbolical forms the imagery for conveying his instructions. This was divinely ordered to satisfy the spiritual want felt by the people in the absence of the outward temple and its sacrifices. In his images he is magnificent, though austere and somewhat harsh. He abounds in repetitions, not for ornament, but for force and weight. Poetical parallelism is not found except in a few portions, as in chs. 7, 21, 27, 28, 29–31. His great aim was to stimulate the dormant minds of the Jews. For this end nothing was better suited than the use of mysterious symbols expressed in the plainest words. The superficial, volatile, and wilfully unbelieving would thereby be left to judicial blindness (Isa. 6:10; Matt. 13:11–13, etc.); whereas the better-disposed would be awakened to a deeper search into the things of God by the very obscurity of the symbols. Inattention to this divine purpose has led the modern Jews so to magnify this obscurity as to ordain that no one shall read this book till he has passed his thirtieth year.

Rabbi Hananias is said to have satisfactorily solved the difficulties (*Mischna*) which were alleged against its canonicity. Ecclesiasticus 49:8 refers to it, and JOSEPHUS, *Antiquities* 10.5, sec. 1. It is mentioned as part of the canon in MELITO's catalogue (EUSEBIUS, H. E. 4.26); also in ORIGEN, JEROME, and the *Talmud*. The oneness of tone throughout and the repetition of favorite expressions exclude the suspicion that separate portions are not genuine. The earlier portion, chs. 1–32, which mainly treats of sin and judgment, is a key to interpret the latter portion, which is more hopeful and joyous, but remote in date. Thus a unity and an orderly progressive character are imparted to the whole. The destruction of Jerusalem is the central point. Previous to this he calls to repentance and warns against blind confidence in Egypt (ch. 17:15–17; cf. Jer. 37:7) or other human stay. After it he consoles the captives by promising them future deliverance and restoration. His prophecies against foreign nations stand between these two great divisions, and were uttered in the interval between the intimation that Nebuchadnezzar was besieging Jerusalem and the arrival of the news that he had taken it (ch. 33:21). HAVERNICK marks out nine sections:—(1) Ezekiel's call to prophesy (ch. 1–3:15). (2) Symbolical predictions of the destruction of Jerusalem (ch. 3:16–7:27). (3) A year and two months later a vision of the temple polluted by Tammuz or Adonis worship; God's consequent scattering of fire over the city and forsaking of the temple to reveal Himself to an inquiring people in exile; happier and purer times to follow (ch. 8–11). (4) Exposure of the particular sins prevalent in the several classes—priests, prophets, and princes (ch. 12–19). (5) A year later the warning of judgment for national guilt repeated with greater distinctness as the time drew nearer (ch. 20–23). (6) Two years and five months later—the very day on which Ezekiel speaks—is announced as the day of the beginning of the siege; Jerusalem shall be overthrown (ch. 24). (7) Predictions against foreign nations during the interval of his silence towards his own people; if judgment begins at the house of God, much more will it visit the ungodly world (ch. 25–32). Some of these were uttered much later than others, but they all *began* to be given after the fall of Jerusalem. (8) In the twelfth year of the captivity, when the fugitives from Jerusalem (ch. 33:21) had appeared in Chaldea, he foretells better times and the re-establishment of Israel and the triumph of God's kingdom on earth over its enemies, Seir, the heathen, and Gog (ch. 33–39). (9) After an interval of thirteen years the closing vision of the order and beauty of the restored kingdom (ch. 40–48). The particularity of details as to the temple and its offerings rather discountenances the view of this vision being only symbolical, and not at all literal. The event alone can clear it up. At all events it has not yet been fulfilled; it must be future. Ezekiel was the only *prophet* (in the strict sense) among the Jews at Babylon. Daniel was rather a *seer* than a prophet, for the spirit of prophecy was given him to qualify him, not for a spiritual office, but for disclosing future events. His position in a heathen king's palace fitted him for revelations of the *outward* relations of God's kingdom to the kingdoms of the world, so that his book is ranked by the Jews among the Hagiographa or "Sacred Writings," not among the prophetical Scriptures. On the other hand, Ezekiel was distinctively a *prophet*, and one who had to do with the *inward* concerns of the divine kingdom. As a priest, when sent into exile, his service was but transferred from the visible temple at Jerusalem to the spiritual temple in Chaldea.

CHAPTER 1

Vss. 1-28. EZEKIEL'S VISION BY THE CHEBAR. FOUR CHERUBIM AND WHEELS. **1. Now it came to pass**—rather, *And* it came. . . . As this formula in Joshua 1:1 has reference to the *written* history of previous times, so here (and in Ruth 1:1, and Esther 1:1), it refers to the *unwritten* history which was before the mind of the writer. The prophet by it,

as it were, continues the history of the preceding times. In the fourth year of Zedekiah's reign (Jer. 51:59), Jeremiah sent by Seraiah a message to the captives (Jer. 29) to submit themselves to God and lay aside their flattering hopes of a speedy restoration. This communication was in the next year, the fifth, and the fourth month of the same king (for Jehoiachin's captivity and Zedekiah's accession coincide in time), *followed up* by a prophet raised up among the captives themselves, the energetic Ezekiel. **thirtieth year**—i.e., counting from the beginning of the reign of Nabopolassar, father of Nebuchadnezzar, the era of the Babylonian empire, 625 B.C., which epoch coincides with the eighteenth year of Josiah, that in which the book of the law was found, and the consequent reformation began [SCALIGER]; or the thirtieth year of Ezekiel's life. As the Lord was about to be a "little sanctuary" (ch. 11:16) to the exiles on the Chebar, so Ezekiel was to be the ministering priest; therefore he marks his priestly relation to God and the people at the outset; the close, which describes the future temple, thus answering to the beginning. By designating himself expressly as "the priest" (vs. 3), and as having reached his thirtieth year (the regular year of priests commencing their office), he marks his office as the priest among the prophets. Thus the opening vision follows naturally as the formal institution of that spiritual temple in which he was to minister [FAIRBAIRN]. **Chebar** —the same as Chabor or Habor, whither the ten tribes had been transported by Tiglath-pileser and Shalmaneser (II Kings 17:6; I Chron. 5:26). It flows into the Euphrates near Carchemish or Circesium, 200 miles north of Babylon. **visions of God**—Four expressions are used as to the revelation granted to Ezekiel, the three first having respect to what was presented from without, to assure him of its *reality,* the fourth to his being internally made fit to receive the revelation; "the heavens were opened" (so Matt. 3:16; Acts 7:56; 10:11; Rev. 19:11); "he saw visions of God"; "the word of Jehovah came *verily* (as the meaning is rather than 'expressly,' *English Version,* vs. 3) unto him" (it was no unreal hallucination); and "the hand of Jehovah was upon him" (Isa. 8:11; Dan. 10:10, 18; Rev. 1:17; the Lord by His touch strengthening him for his high and arduous ministry, that he might be able to witness and report aright the revelations made to him). **2. Jehoiachin's captivity**—In the third or fourth year of Jehoiakim, father of Jehoiachin, the *first* carrying away of Jewish captives to Babylon took place, and among them was Daniel. The *second* was under Jehoiachin, when Ezekiel was carried away. The *third* and final one was at the taking of Jerusalem under Zedekiah. **4. whirlwind**—emblematic of God's judgments (Jer. 23:19; 25:32). **out of the north**—i.e., from Chaldea, whose hostile forces would invade Judea from a *northerly* direction. The prophet conceives himself in the temple. **fire infolding itself**—laying hold on whatever surrounds it, drawing it to itself, and devouring it. Lit., "catching itself," i.e., kindling itself [FAIRBAIRN]. The same *Hebrew* occurs in Exodus 9:24, as to the "fire *mingled with* the hail." **brightness . . . about it** —i.e., about the "cloud." **out of the midst thereof** —i.e., out of the midst of the "fire." **colour of amber**—rather, "the glancing brightness (lit., the eye, and so *the glancing appearance*) of polished brass." The *Hebrew, chasmal,* is from two roots, "smooth" and "brass" (cf. vs. 7 and Rev. 1:15) [GESENIUS]. LXX and *Vulgate* translate it, "electrum"; a brilliant metal compounded of gold and silver. **5.** Ezekiel was himself of a "gigantic nature, and thereby suited to counteract the Babylonish spirit of the times, which loved to manifest itself in gigantic, grotesque forms" [HENGSTENBERG]. **living creatures**—So the Greek ought to have been translated in the parallel passage, Revelation 4:6, not as *English Version,* "beasts"; for one of the "four" is *a man,* and man cannot be termed "beast." Ch. 10:20 shows that it is the cherubim

that are meant. **likeness of a man**—Man, the noblest of the four, is the ideal model after which they are fashioned (vs. 10; ch. 10:14). The point of comparison between him and them is the erect posture of their bodies, though doubtless including also the general mien. Also the *hands* (ch. 10:21). **6.** Not only were there four distinct living creatures, but each of the four had four faces, making sixteen in all. The four living creatures of the cherubim answer by contrast to the four world monarchies represented by four *beasts,* Assyria, Persia, Greece, and Rome (Dan. 7). The Fathers identified them with the four Gospels: Matthew the lion, Mark the ox, Luke the man, John the eagle. Two cherubim only stood over the ark in the temple; two more are now added, to imply that, while the law is retained as the basis, a new form is needed to be added to impart new life to it. The number four may have respect to the four quarters of the world, to imply that God's angels execute His commands everywhere. Each head in front had the face of a man as the primary and prominent one: on the right the face of a lion, on the left the face of an ox, above from behind the face of an eagle. The Mosaic cherubim were similar, only that the human faces were put looking towards each other, and towards the mercy seat between, being formed out of the same mass of pure gold as the latter (Exod. 25:19, 20). In Isaiah 6:2 two wings are added to cover their countenances; because there they stand by the throne, here under the throne; there God deigns to consult them, and His condescension calls forth their humility, so that they veil their faces before Him; here they execute His commands. The face expresses their intelligence; the wings, their rapidity in fulfilling God's will. The Shekinah or flame, that signified God's presence, and the written name, JEHOVAH, occupied the intervening space between the cherubim. Genesis 4:14, 16 and 3:24 ("placed"; properly, "to place in *a tabernacle*"), imply that the cherubim were appointed at the fall as symbols of God's presence in a consecrated place, and that man was to worship there. In the patriarchal dispensation when the flood had caused the removal of the cherubim from Eden, *seraphim* or *teraphim (Chaldean* dialect) were made as models of them for domestic use (Gen. 31:19, *Margin* 30). The silence of Exodus 25 and 26 as to their configuration, whereas everything else is minutely described, is because their form was so well known already to Bezaleel and all Israel by tradition as to need no detailed description. Hence Ezekiel (ch. 10:20) at once knows them, for he had seen them repeatedly in the carved work of the outer sanctuary of Solomon's temple (I Kings 6:23-29). He therefore consoles the exiles with the hope of having the same cherubim in the renovated temple which should be reared; and he assures them that the same God who dwelt between the cherubim of the temple would be still with His people by the Chebar. But they were not in Zerubbabel's temple; therefore Ezekiel's foretold temple, if literal, is yet future. The ox is selected as chief of the tame animals, the lion among the wild, the eagle among birds, and man the head of all, in his ideal, realized by the Lord Jesus, combining all the excellencies of the animal kingdom. The cherubim probably represent the ruling powers by which God acts in the natural and moral world. Hence they sometimes answer to the ministering angels; elsewhere, to the redeemed saints (the elect Church) through whom, as by the angels, God shall hereafter rule the world and proclaim the manifold wisdom of God (Matt. 19:28; I Cor. 6:2; Eph. 3:10; Rev. 3: 21; 4:6-8). The "lions" and "oxen," amidst "palms" and "open flowers" carved in the temple, were the four-faced cherubim which, being traced on a flat surface, presented only one aspect of the four. The human-headed winged bulls and eagle-headed gods found in Nineveh, sculptured amidst palms and tulip-shaped flowers, were borrowed by corrupted tradition from the cherubim placed in Eden near its fruits and flowers. So the Aaronic calf (Exod. 32: 4, 5) and Jeroboam's calves at Dan and Bethel, a schismatic imitation of the sacred symbols in the temple at Jerusalem. So the ox figures of Apis on the sacred arks of Egypt. **7. straight feet**—i.e., straight *legs*. Not protruding in any part as the legs of an ox, but straight like a man's [GROTIUS]. Or, like solid pillars; *not bending*, as man's, at the knee. They glided along, rather than walked. Their movements were all sure, right, and without effort [KITTO, *Cyclopedia*]. **sole . . . calf's foot**—HENDER- SON hence supposes that *"straight"* feet" implies that they did not project horizontally like men's feet, but vertically as calves' feet. The *solid firmness* of the round foot of a calf seems to be the point of comparison. **colour**—*the glittering appearance*, indicating God's purity. **8.** The hands of each were the hands of a man. The hand is the symbol of *active power, guided by "skilfulness"* (Ps. 78:72). **under their wings**—signifying their operations are hidden from our too curious prying; and as the "wings" signify something more than human, viz., the secret prompting of God, it is also implied that they are moved by it and not by their own power, so that they do nothing at random, but all with divine wisdom. **they four had . . . faces and . . . wings**—He returns to what he had stated already in vs. 6; this gives a reason why they had hands on their four sides, viz., because they had faces and wings on the four sides. They moved whithersoever they would, not by active energy merely, but also by knowledge (expressed by their *faces*) and divine guidance (expressed by their "wings"). **9. they**—had no occasion to turn themselves round when changing their direction, for they had a face (vs. 6) looking to each of the four quarters of heaven. They made no mistakes; and their work needed not be gone over again. Their wings were joined above in pairs (see vs. 11). **10. they . . . had the face of a man**—viz., in front. The human face was the primary and prominent one and the fundamental part of the composite whole. On its right was the lion's face; on the left, the ox's (called "cherub," ch. 10:14); at the back from above was the eagle's. **11.** The tips of the two outstretched wings reached to one another, while the other two, in token of humble awe, formed a veil for the lower parts of the body. **stretched upward**—rather, "were parted from above" (cf. *Margin*, Isa. 6:2, *Note*). The joining together of their wings above implies that, though the movements of Providence on earth may seem conflicting and confused, yet if one lift up his eyes to heaven, he will see that they admirably conspire towards the one end at last. **12.** The same idea as in vs. 9. The repetition is because we men are so hard to be brought to acknowledge the wisdom of God's doings; they seem tortuous and confused to us, but they are all tending steadily to one aim. **the spirit**—the secret impulse whereby God moves His angels to the end designed. They do not turn back or aside till they have fulfilled the office assigned them. **13. likeness . . . appearance**—not tautology. "Likeness" expresses the general form; "appearance," the particular aspect. **coals of fire**—denoting the intensely

pure and burning justice wherewith God punishes by His angels those who, like Israel, have hardened themselves against His long-suffering. So in Isaiah 6, instead of cherubim, the name "seraphim," *the burning ones,* is applied, indicating God's consuming righteousness; whence their cry to Him is, "Holy! holy! holy!" and the burning coal is applied to his lips, for the message through his mouth was to be one of judicial severance of the godly from the ungodly, to the ruin of the latter. **lamps**—torches. The fire emitted sparks and flashes of light, as torches do. **went up and down**—expressing the marvellous vigor of God's Spirit, in all His movements never resting, never wearied. **fire . . . bright**—indicating the glory of God. **out of the fire . . . lightning**— God's righteousness will at last cause the bolt of His wrath to fall on the guilty; as now, on Jerusalem. **14. ran and returned**—Incessant, restless motion indicates the plenitude of life in these cherubim; so in Revelation 4:8, "they rest not day or night" (Zech. 4:10). **flash of lightning**—rather, as distinct from "lightning" (vs. 13), "the meteor-flash," or sheet lightning [FAIRBAIRN]. **15. one wheel**—The "dreadful height" of the wheel (vs. 18) indicates the gigantic, terrible energy of the complicated revolutions of God's providence, bringing about His purposes with unerring certainty. One wheel appeared traversely without another, so that the movement might be without turning, whithersoever the living creatures might advance (vs. 17). Thus each wheel was composed of two circles cutting one another at right angles, "one" only of which appeared to touch the ground ("upon the earth)," according to the direction the cherubim desired to move in. **with his four faces**—rather, *"according* to its four faces" or sides; as there was a side or direction to each of the four creatures, so there was a wheel for each of the sides [FAIRBAIRN]. The four sides or semicircles of each composite wheel pointed, as the four faces of each of the living creatures, to the four quarters of heaven. HAVER- NICK refers "his" or "its" to *the wheels.* The cherubim and their wings and wheels stood in contrast to the symbolical figures, somewhat similar, then existing in Chaldea, and found in the remains of Assyria. The latter, though derived from the original revelation by tradition, came by corruption to symbolize the astronomical zodiac, or the sun and celestial sphere, by a circle with wings or irradiations. But Ezekiel's cherubim rise above natural objects, the gods of the heathen, to the representation of the one true God, who made and continually upholds them. **16. appearance . . . work**— their *form* and the *material* of their work. **beryl**— rather, "the glancing appearance of the Tarshish-stone"; the chrysolite or topaz, brought fron Tarshish or Tartessus in Spain. It was one of the gems in the breastplate of the high priest (Exod. 28:20; Song of Sol. 5:14; Dan. 10:6). **four had one likeness** —The similarity of the wheels to one another implies that there is no inequality in all God's works, that all have a beautiful analogy and proportion. **17. went upon their four sides**—Those faces or sides of the four wheels moved which answered to the direction in which the cherubim desired to move; while the transverse circles in each of the four composite wheels remained suspended from the ground, so as not to impede the movements of the others. **18. rings**—i.e., felloes or circumferences of the wheels. **eyes**—the multiplicity of eyes here in the wheels, and ch. 10:12, in the cherubim themselves, symbolizes the *plenitude of intelligent life,* the eye being the window through which "the spirit of the living creatures" in the wheels (vs. 20) looks forth (cf. Zech. 4:10). As the wheels signify the providence of God, so the eyes imply that He sees all the circumstances of each case, and does nothing by blind impulse. **19. went by them**—went *beside* them. **20. the spirit was to go**—i.e., their will was for going whithersoever the Spirit was for going. **over against them**—rather, *beside* or *in conjunction with them*. **spirit of the living creature**—put collectively for "the living *creatures*"; the cherubim. Having first viewed them separately, he next views them in the aggregate as the composite living *creature* in which the Spirit resided. The life intended is that connected with God, holy, spiritual life, in the plenitude of its active power. **21. over against**—rather, "along with" [HENDERSON]; or, "beside" [FAIRBAIRN]. **22. upon the heads**—rather, "above the heads" [FAIRBAIRN]. **colour**—glitter. **terrible crystal**—dazzling the spectator by its brightness. **23. straight**—erect [FAIRBAIRN]. expanded upright. **two ... two ... covered ... bodies**—not, as it might seem, contradicting vs. 11. The two wings expanded upwards, though chiefly used for flying, yet up to the summit of the figure where they were parted from each other, covered the upper part of the body, while the other two wings covered the lower parts. **24. voice of ... Almighty**—the thunder (Ps. 29:3, 4). **voice of speech**—rather, "the voice" or "sound of *tumult*," as in Jeremiah 11:16. From an *Arabic* root, meaning the "impetuous rush of heavy rain." **noise of ... host**—(Isa. 13:4; Dan. 10:6). **25. let down ... wings**—While the Almighty gave forth His voice, they reverently let their wings fall, to listen stilly to His communication. **26.** The Godhead appears in the likeness of enthroned humanity, as in Exodus 24:10. Besides the "paved work of a sapphire stone, as it were the body of heaven in clearness," there, we have here the "throne," and God "as a man," with the "appearance of fire round about." This last was a prelude of the incarnation of Messiah, but in His character as Saviour and as Judge (Rev. 19:11-16). The azure sapphire answers to the color of the sky. As others are called "sons of God," but He "the Son of God," so others are called "sons of man" (ch. 2:1, 3), but He "the Son of man" (Matt. 16:13), being the embodied representative of humanity and the whole human race; as, on the other hand, He is the representative of "the fulness of the Godhead" (Col. 2:9). While the cherubim are movable, the throne above, and Jehovah who moves them, are firmly fixed. It is good news to man, that the throne above is filled by One who even there appears as "a man." **27. colour of amber**—"the glitter of chasmal" [FAIRBAIRN]. See *Note*, vs. 4; rather, "polished brass" [HENDERSON]. Messiah is described here as in Daniel 10:5, 6; Revelation 1:14, 15. **28. the bow ... in ... rain**—the symbol of the sure covenant of mercy to God's children remembered amidst judgments on the wicked; as in the flood in Noah's days (Rev. 4:3). "Like hanging out from the throne of the Eternal a flag of peace, assuring all that the purpose of Heaven was to preserve rather than to destroy. Even if the divine work should require a deluge of wrath, still the faithfulness of God would only shine forth the more brightly at last to the children of promise, in consequence of the *tribulations* needed to prepare for the ultimate good" [FAIRBAIRN]. (Isa. 54:8-10). **I fell upon ... face**—the right attitude, spiritually, before we enter on any active work for God (ch. 2:2; 3:23, 24; Rev. 1:17). In this first chapter God gathered into one vision the substance of all that was to occupy the prophetic

agency of Ezekiel; as was done afterwards in the opening vision of the Revelation of Saint John.

CHAPTER 2

Vss. 1-10. EZEKIEL'S COMMISSION. **1. Son of man**—often applied to Ezekiel; once only to Daniel (Dan. 8:17), and not to any other prophet. The phrase was no doubt taken from Chaldean usage during the sojourn of Daniel and Ezekiel in Chaldea. But the spirit who sanctioned the words of the prophet implied by it the *lowliness and frailty* of the prophet as man "lower than the angels," though now admitted to the vision of angels and of God Himself, "lest he should be exalted through the abundance of the revelations" (II Cor. 12:7). He is appropriately so called as being type of the divine "Son of man" here revealed as "man" (*Note*, ch. 1:26). That title, as applied to Messiah, implies at once His *lowliness* and His *exaltation*, in His manifestations as *the Representative man*, at His first and second comings respectively (Ps. 8:4-8; Matt. 16:13; 20:18; and on the other hand, Dan. 7:13, 14; Matt. 26:64; John 5:27). **2. spirit entered ... when he spake**—The divine word is ever accompanied by the Spirit (Gen. 1:2, 3). **set ... upon ... feet**—He had been "upon his face" (ch. 1:28). Humiliation on our part is followed by exaltation on God's part (ch. 3:23, 24; Job 22:29; Jas. 4:6; I Pet. 5:5). "On the feet" was the fitting attitude when he was called on to wake and work for God (Eph. 5:8; 6:15). **that I heard**—rather, *"then* I heard." **3. nation**—rather, "nations"; the word usually applied to the *heathen* or *Gentiles;* here to the Jews, as being altogether *heathenized* with idolatries. So in Isaiah 1:10, they are named "Sodom" and "Gomorrah." They were now become "Lo-ammi," not the *people* of God (Hos. 1:9). **4. impudent**—lit., "hard-faced" (ch. 3:7, 9). **children**—resumptive of "they" (vs. 3); the "children" walk in their "fathers' " steps. **I ... send thee**—God opposes His command to all obstacles. Duties are ours; events are God's. **Thus saith the Lord God**—God opposes His name to the obstinacy of the people. **5. forbear**—viz., to hear. **yet shall know**—Even if they will not hear, at least they will not have ignorance to plead as the cause of their perversity (ch. 33:33). **6. briers**—not as *Margin* and GESENIUS, "rebels," which would not correspond so well to "thorns." The *Hebrew* is from a root meaning "to sting" as *nettles* do. The wicked are often so called (II Sam. 23:6; Song of Sol. 2:2; Isa. 9:18). **scorpions**—a reptile about six inches long with a deadly sting at the end of the tail. **be not afraid**—(Luke 12:4; I Peter 3:14). **7. most rebellious**—lit., "rebellion" itself: its very essence. **8. eat**—(Jer. 15:16, *Note;* Rev. 10:9, 10). The idea is to possess himself fully of the message and digest it in the mind; not literal *eating*, but such an *appropriation* of its unsavory contents that they should become, as it were, part of himself, so as to impart them the more vividly to his hearers. **9. roll**—the form in which ancient books were made. **10. within and without**—on the face and the back. Usually the parchment was written only on its *inside* when rolled up; but so full was God's message of impending woes that it was written also on the back.

CHAPTER 3

Vss. 1-27. EZEKIEL EATS THE ROLL. IS COMMISSIONED TO GO TO THEM OF THE CAPTIVITY AND GOES

TO TEL-ABIB BY THE CHEBAR: AGAIN BEHOLDS THE SHEKINAH GLORY: IS TOLD TO RETIRE TO HIS HOUSE, AND ONLY SPEAK WHEN GOD OPENS HIS MOUTH. **1. eat ... and ... speak**—God's messenger must first inwardly appropriate God's truth himself, before he "speaks" it to others (*Note*, ch. 2:8). Symbolic actions were, when possible and proper, performed outwardly; otherwise, internally and in spiritual vision, the action so narrated making the naked statement more intuitive and impressive by presenting the subject in a concentrated, embodied form. **3. honey for sweetness**—Cf. Psalm 19:10; 119:103; Revelation 10:9, where, as here in vs. 14, the "sweetness" is followed by "bitterness." The former being due to the painful nature of the message; the latter because it was the Lord's service which he was engaged in; and his eating the roll and finding it sweet, implied that, divesting himself of carnal feeling, he made God's will his will, however painful the message that God might require him to announce. The fact that God would be glorified was his greatest pleasure. **5.** See *Margin, Hebrew,* "deep of lip and heavy of tongue," i.e., men speaking an obscure and unintelligible tongue. Even they would have listened to the prophet; but the Jews, though addressed in their own tongue, will not hear him. **6. many people**—It would have increased the difficulty had he been sent, not merely to one, but to "many people" differing in tongues, so that the missionary would have needed to acquire a new tongue for addressing each. The after mission of the apostles to many peoples, and the gift of tongues for that end, are foreshadowed (cf. I Cor. 14:21 with Isa. 28:11). **had I sent thee to them, they would have hearkened** —(Matt. 11:21, 23). **7. will not hearken unto thee: for ... not ... me**—(John 15:20). Take patiently their rejection of thee, for I thy Lord bear it along with thee. **8.** Ezekiel means one "strengthened by God." Such he was in godly firmness, in spite of his people's opposition, according to the divine command to the priest tribe to which he belonged (Deut. 33:9). **9. As ... flint**—so Messiah the antitype (Isa. 50:7; cf. Jer. 1:8, 17). **10. receive in ... heart ... ears**—The transposition from the natural order, viz., first receiving with the *ears,* then in the *heart,* is designed. The preparation of the heart for God's message should precede the reception of it with the ears (cf. Prov. 16:1; Ps. 10:17). **11. thy people**—who ought to be better disposed to hearken to thee, their fellow countryman, than hadst thou been a foreigner (vss. 5, 6). **12.** (Acts 8:39.) Ezekiel's abode heretofore had not been the most suitable for his work. He, therefore, is guided by the Spirit to Tel-abib, the chief town of the Jewish colony of captives: there he sat on the ground, "the throne of the miserable" (Ezra 9:3; Lam. 1:1-3), seven days, the usual period for manifesting deep grief (Job 2:13; see Ps. 137:1), thus winning their confidence by sympathy in their sorrow. He is accompanied by the cherubim which had been manifested at Chebar (ch. 1:3, 4), after their departure from Jerusalem. They now are heard moving with the *"voice of a great rushing"* (cf. Acts 2:2), *saying,* Blessed be the glory of the Lord from His place," i.e., moving *from the place* in which it had been at Chebar, to accompany Ezekiel to his new destination (ch. 9:3); or, "from His place" may rather mean, *in His place and manifested "from"* it. Though God may seem to have forsaken His temple, He is still in it and will restore His people to it. His glory is "blessed," in opposition to those Jews who spoke evil of Him, as if He had been unjustly rigorous towards their nation [CALVIN]. **13. touched**—

lit., "kissed," i.e., closely embraced. **noise of a great rushing**—typical of great disasters impending over the Jews. **14. bitterness**—sadness on account of the impending calamities of which I was required to be the unwelcome messenger. But the "hand," or powerful impulse of Jehovah, urged me forward. **15. Tel-abib**—*Tel* means an "elevation." It is identified by MICHAELIS with *Thallaba* on the Chabor. Perhaps the name expressed the Jew's hopes of restoration, or else the fertility of the region. *Abib* means the *green ears* of corn which appeared in the month Nisan, the pledge of the harvest. **I sat ...** —This is the *Hebrew Margin* reading. The *text* is rather, "I *beheld* them sitting there" [GESENIUS]; or, "And those that were settled there," viz., the older settlers, as distinguished from the more recent ones alluded to in the previous clause. The ten tribes had been long since settled on the Chabor or Habor (II Kings 17:6) [HAVERNICK]. **17. watchman**—Ezekiel alone, among the prophets, is called a "watchman," not merely to sympathize, but to give timely warning of danger to his people where none was suspected. Habakkuk (2:1) speaks of standing upon his "watch," but it was only in order to be on the lookout for the manifestation of God's power (so Isa. 52:8; 62:6); not as Ezekiel, to act as a watchman to others. **18. warning ... speakest to warn**— The repetition implies that it is not enough to warn once in passing, but that the warning is to be inculcated continually (II Tim. 4:2, "in season, out of season"; Acts 20:31, "night and day with tears"). **save**—Ch. 2:5 had seemingly taken away all hope of salvation; but the reference there was to the mass of the people whose case was hopeless; a few individuals, however, were reclaimable. **die in ... iniquity**—(John 8:21, 24). Men are not to flatter themselves that their ignorance, owing to the negligence of their teachers, will save them (Rom. 2: 12, "As many as have sinned without law, shall also *perish* without law"). **19. wickedness ... wicked way**—*internal* wickedness of *heart,* and *external* of the *life,* respectively. **delivered thy soul**—(Isa. 49: 4, 5; Acts 20:26). **20. righteous ... turn from ... righteousness**—not one "righteous" as to the *root* and *spirit of regeneration* (Ps. 89:33; 138:8; Isa. 26:12; 27:3; John 10:28; Phil. 1:6), but as to its *outward appearance* and performances. So the "righteous" (Prov. 18:17; Matt. 9:13). As in vs. 19 the minister is required to lead the wicked to good, so in vs. 20 he is to confirm the well-disposed in their duty. **commit iniquity**—i.e., give himself up *wholly* to it (I John 3:8, 9), for even the best often fall, but not *wilfully* and *habitually*. **I lay a stumbling-block**—not that God tempts to sin (Jas. 1:13, 14), but God gives men over to judicial blindness, and to *their own* corruptions (Ps. 9:16, 17; 94:23) when they "like not to retain God in their knowledge" (Rom. 1:24, 26); just as, on the contrary, God makes "the way of the righteous plain" (Prov. 4:11, 12; 15:19), so that they do "not stumble." CALVIN refers "stumbling-block" not to the *guilt,* but to its *punishment;* "I bring *ruin* on him." The former is best. Ahab, after a kind of righteousness (I Kings 21:27-29), relapsed and consulted lying spirits in false prophets; so God permitted one of these to be his "stumbling-block," both to sin and its corresponding punishment (I Kings 22:21-23). **his blood will I require**—(Heb. 13:17). **22. hand of the Lord**—(ch. 1:3). **go ... into the plain**—in order that he might there, in a place secluded from unbelieving men, receive a fresh manifestation of the divine glory, to inspirit him for his trying work. **23. glory of the Lord**—(ch. 1:28). **24. set me upon my** feet—having been previously prostrate and unable to rise until raised by the divine power. **shut thy-self within . . . house**—implying that in the work he had to do, he must look for no sympathy from man but must be often alone with God and draw his strength from Him [FAIRBAIRN]. "Do not go out of thy house till I reveal the future to thee by signs and words," which God does in the following chapters, down to the eleventh. Thus a representation was given of the city shut up by siege [GROTIUS]. Thereby God proved the obedience of His servant, and Ezekiel showed the reality of His call by proceeding, not through rash impulse, but by the directions of God [CALVIN]. **25. put bands upon thee**—not literally, but spritually, the binding, depressing influence which their rebellious conduct would exert on his spirit. Their perversity, like bands, would repress his freedom in preaching; as in II Corinthians 6:12, Paul calls himself "straitened" because his teaching did not find easy access to them. Or else, it is said to console the prophet for being shut up; if thou wert now at once to announce God's message, they *would* rush on thee and *bind* thee with "bands" [CALVIN]. **26. I will make my tongue . . . dumb**—Israel had rejected the prophets; therefore God deprives Israel of the prophets and of His word—God's sorest judgment (I Sam. 7:2; Amos 8:11, 12). **27. when I speak . . . I will open thy mouth**—opposed to the silence imposed on the prophet, to punish the people (vs. 26). After the interval of silence has awakened their attention to the cause of it, viz., their sins, they may then hearken to the prophecies which they would not do before. **He that heareth, let him hear . . . forbear**—i.e., thou hast done thy part, whether they hear or forbear. He who shall forbear to hear, it shall be at his own peril; he who hears, it shall be to his own eternal good (cf. Rev. 22:11).

CHAPTER 4

Vss. 1-17. SYMBOLICAL VISION OF THE SIEGE AND THE INIQUITY-BEARING. **1. tile**—a sun-dried brick, such as are found in Babylon, covered with cuneiform inscriptions, often two feet long and one foot broad. **2. forth**—rather, watch-tower (Jer. 52:4) wherein the besiegers could watch the movements of the besieged [GESENIUS]. A wall of circumvallation [LXX and ROSENMULLER]. A kind of battering-ram [MAURER]. The first view is best. **a mount** —wherewith the Chaldeans could be defended from missiles. **batterings-rams**—lit., "through-borers." In ch. 21:22 the same *Hebrew* is translated, "captains." **3. iron pan**—the divine decree as to the Chaldean army investing the city. **set it for a wall of iron between thee and the city**—Ezekiel, in the person of God, represents the wall of separation between him and the people as one of iron: and the Chaldean investing army, His instrument of separating them from him, as one impossible to burst through. **set . . . face against it**—inexorably (Ps. 34:16). The exiles envied their brethren remaining in Jerusalem, but exile is better than the straitness of a siege. **4.** Another symbolical act performed at the same time as the former, in vision, not in external action, wherein it would have been only puerile: narrated as a thing ideally done, it would make a vivid impression. The second action is supplementary to the first, to bring out more fully the same prophetic idea. **left side**—referring to the *position* of the ten tribes, the *northern* kingdom, as Judah, the *southern*, answers to "the right side" (vs. 6). The Orientals, facing the east in their mode, had the north on their

left, and the south on their *right* (ch. 16:46). Also the right was more honorable than the left: so Judah, as being the seat of the temple, was more so than Israel. **bear their iniquity**—iniquity being regarded as a *burden;* so it means, "bear the *punishment* of their iniquity" (Num. 14:34). A type of Him who was the great *sin-bearer,* not in mimic show as Ezekiel, but in reality (Isa. 53:4, 6, 12). **5. three hundred and ninety days**—The 390 years of punishment appointed for Israel, and 40 for Judah, cannot refer to the siege of Jerusalem. That siege is referred to in vss. 1-3, not in a sense restricted to the literal siege, but comprehending the *whole* train of punishment to be inflicted for their sin; therefore we read here merely of its sore pressure, not of its result. The sum of 390 and 40 years is 430, a period famous in the history of the covenant people, being that of their sojourn in Egypt (Exod. 12:40, 41; Gal. 3:17). The forty alludes to the forty years in the wilderness. Elsewhere (Deut. 28:68; Hos. 9:3), God threatened to bring them back to Egypt, which must mean, not Egypt literally, but a bondage as bad as that one in Egypt. So now God will reduce them to a kind of new Egyptian bondage to the world: Israel, the greater transgressor, for a longer period than Judah (cf. ch. 20:35-38). Not the whole of the 430 years of the Egypt state is appointed to Israel; but this shortened by the forty years of the wilderness sojourn, to imply, that a way is open to their return to life by their having the Egypt state merged into that of the wilderness; i.e., by ceasing from idolatry and seeking in their sifting and sore troubles, through God's covenant, a restoration to righteousness and peace [FAIRBAIRN]. The 390, in reference to the *sin* of Israel, was also literally true, being the years from the setting up of the calves by Jeroboam (I Kings 12:20-33), i.e., from 975 to 585 B.C.: *about* the year of the Babylonian captivity; and perhaps the 40 of Judah refers to that part of Manasseh's fifty-five year's reign in which he had not repented, and which, we are expressly told, was the cause of God's removal of Judah, notwithstanding Josiah's reformation (I Kings 21:10-16; 23:26, 27). **6. each day for a year**—lit., "a day for a year, a day for a year." Twice repeated, to mark more distinctly the reference to Numbers 14:34. The picturing of the future under the image of the past, wherein the meaning was far from lying on the surface, was intended to arouse to a less superficial mode of thinking, just as the partial veiling of truth in Jesus' parables was designed to stimulate inquiry; also to remind men that God's dealings in the past are a key to the future, for He moves on the same everlasting *principles,* the *forms* alone being transitory. **7. arm . . . uncovered**—to be ready for action, which the long Oriental garment usually covering it would prevent (Isa. 52:10). **thou shalt prophesy against it** —This gesture of thine will be a tacit prophecy against it. **8. bands**—(Ch. 3:25.) **not turn from . . . side**—to imply the impossibility of their being able to shake off their punishment. **9. wheat . . . barley . . .**—Instead of simple flour used for delicate cakes (Gen. 18:6), the Jews should have a coarse mixture of six different kinds of grain, such as the poorest alone would eat. **fitches**—spelt or *dhourra*. **three hundred and ninety**—The forty days are omitted, since these latter typify the *wilderness period* when Israel stood *separate from the Gentiles* and *their pollutions,* though partially chastened by stint of bread and water (vs. 16), whereas the eating of the polluted bread in the 390 days implies a forced residence *"among the Gentiles"* who were polluted with idolatry (vs. 13). This last is said of "Israel" primarily, as being the most debased (vss. 9-15); they had *spiritually* sunk to a level with the heathen, therefore God will make their condition *outwardly* to correspond. Judah and Jerusalem fare less severely, being less guilty: they are to "eat bread by weight and with care," i.e., have a stinted supply and be chastened with the milder discipline of the wilderness period. But Judah also is secondarily referred to in the 390 days, as having fallen, like Israel, into Gentile defilements; if, then, the Jews are to escape from the exile *among Gentiles,* which is their just punishment, they must submit again to the wilderness probation (vs. 16). **10. twenty shekels**—i.e., little more than ten ounces; a scant measure to sustain life (Jer. 52:6). But it applies not only to the siege, but to their whole subsequent state. **11. sixth ... of ... hin**—about a pint and a half. **12. dung**—as fuel; so the Arabs use beasts' dung, wood-fuel being scarce. But to use human dung so implies the most cruel necessity. It was in violation of the law (Deut. 14:3; 23:12-14); it must therefore have been done only *in vision.* **13.** Implying that Israel's peculiar distinction was to be abolished and that they were to be outwardly blended with the idolatrous heathen (Deut. 28:68; Hos. 9:3). **14.** Ezekiel, as a priest, had been accustomed to the strictest abstinence from everything legally impure. Peter felt the same scruple at a similar command (Acts 10:14; cf. Isa. 65:4). *Positive precepts,* being dependent on a particular command can be set aside at the will of the divine ruler; but *moral precepts* are everlasting in their obligation because God cannot be inconsistent with His unchanging moral nature. **abominable flesh**—lit., flesh that stank from putridity. Flesh of animals three days killed was prohibited (Lev. 7:17, 18; 19:6, 7). **15. cow's dung**—a mitigation of the former order (vs. 12); no longer "the dung of man"; still the bread so baked is "defiled," to imply that, whatever partial abatement there might be for the prophet's sake, the main decree of God, as to the pollution of Israel by exile among Gentiles, is unalterable. **16. staff of bread**—bread by which life is supported, as a man's weight is by the staff he leans on (Lev. 26:26; Ps. 105:16; Isa. 3:1). **by weight, and with care**—in scant measure (vs. 10). **17. astonied one with another**—mutually regard one another with astonishment: the stupefied look of despairing want.

CHAPTER 5

Vss. 1-17. Vision of Cutting the Hairs, and the Calamities Foreshadowed Thereby. **1. knife ... razor**—the sword of the foe (cf. Isa. 7:20). This vision implies even severer judgments than the Egyptian afflictions foreshadowed in the former, for their guilt was greater than that of their forefathers. **thine head**—as representative of the Jews. The whole hair being shaven off was significant of severe and humiliating (II Sam. 10:4, 5) treatment. Especially in the case of a priest; for priests (Lev. 21: 5) were forbidden "to make baldness on their head," their hair being the token of consecration; hereby it was intimated that the ceremonial must give place to the moral. **balances**—implying the *just discrimination* with which Jehovah weighs out the portion of punishment "divided," i.e., allotted to each: the "hairs" are the Jews: the divine scales do not allow even one hair to escape accurate weighing (cf. Matt. 10:30). **2.** Three classes are described. The sword was to destroy one third of the people; famine and plague another third

("fire" in vs. 2 being explained in vs. 12 to mean pestilence and famine); that which remained was to be scattered among the nations. A few only of the last portion were to escape, symbolized by the hairs bound in Ezekiel's skirts (vs. 3; Jer. 40:6; 52: 16). Even of these some were to be thrown into the fiery ordeal again (vs. 4; Jer. 41:1, 2, etc.; 44: 14, etc.). The "skirts" being able to contain but few express that extreme limit to which God's goodness can reach. **5, 6.** Explanation of the symbols: **Jerusalem**—not the mere city, but the people of Israel generally, of which it was the center and representative. **in ... midst**—Jerusalem is regarded in God's point of view as center of the whole earth, designed *to radiate the true light over the nations in all directions.* Cf. *Margin* ("navel"), ch. 38:12; Psalm 48:2; Jeremiah 3:17. No center in the ancient heathen world could have been selected more fitted than Canaan to be a vantage-ground, whence the people of God might have acted with success upon the heathenism of the world. It lay midway between the oldest and most civilized states, Egypt and Ethiopia on one side, and Babylon, Nineveh, and India on the other, and afterwards Persia, Greece, and Rome. The Phœnician mariners were close by, through whom they might have transmitted the true religion to the remotest lands; and all around the Ishmaelites, the great *inland* traders in South Asia and North Africa. Israel was thus placed, not for its own selfish good, but to be the spiritual benefactor of the whole world. Cf. Psalm 67 throughout. Failing in this, and falling into idolatry, its guilt was far worse than that of the heathen; not that Israel *literally* went beyond the heathen in abominable idolatries. But *"corruptio optimi pessima";* the perversion of that which in itself is the best is worse than the perversion of that which is less perfect: is in fact the worst of all kinds of perversion. Therefore their punishment was the severest. So the position of the Christian professing Church now, if it be not a light to the heathen world, its condemnation will be sorer than theirs (Matt. 5:13; 11:21-24; Heb. 10:28, 29). **6. changed ... into**—rather, "hath *resisted* My judgments wickedly"; "hath *rebelled* against My ordinances for wickedness" [Buxtorf]. But see end of *Note* on vs. 7. **7. multiplied**—rather, "have been more abundantly outrageous"; lit., "to tumultuate"; to have an extravagant rage for idols. **neither have done according to the judgments of the nations**—have not been as tenacious of the true religion as the nations have been of the false. The heathen "changed" not their gods, but the Jews changed Jehovah for idols (see vs. 6, "changed My judgments into wickedness," i.e., idolatry, Jer. 2:11). The *Chaldean version* and the *Masora* support the negative. Others omit it (as it is omitted in ch. 11: 12), and translate, *"but* have done according to the judgments .... However, both ch. 11:12 and also this verse are true. They in one sense "did according to the heathen," viz., in all that was bad; in another, viz., in that which was good, zeal for religion, they did *not.* Verse 9 also proves the negative to be genuine; because in changing their religion, they have *not* done as the nations which have not changed theirs, *"I* (also) will do in thee that which I have not done." **8. I, even I**—awfully emphatic. I, even I, whom thou thinkest to be asleep, but who am ever reigning as the Omnipotent Avenger of sin, will vindicate My righteous government before the nations by judgments on thee. **9.** See *Note,* vs. 7. **that which I have not done**—worse than any former judgments (Lam. 4:6; Dan. 9:12). The prophecy includes the destruction of Jerusalem by the Romans, and the final one by Antichrist (Zech. 13:8, 9; 14:2), as well as that by Nebuchadnezzar. Their doom of evil was not exhausted by the Chaldean conquest. There was to be a germinating evil in their destiny, because there would be, as the Lord foresaw, a germinating evil in their character. As God connected Himself peculiarly with Israel, so there was to be a peculiar manifestation of God's wrath against sin in their case [FAIRBAIRN]. The higher the privileges the greater the punishment in the case of abuse of them. When God's greatest favor, the gospel, was given, and was abused by them, then "the wrath was to come on them to the uttermost" (I Thess. 2:16). **10. fathers...eat...sons**—alluding to Moses' words (Lev. 26:29; Deut. 28:53), with the additional sad feature, that "the sons should eat their fathers" (see II Kings 6:28; Jer. 19:9; Lam. 2:20; 4:10). **11. as I live**—the most solemn of oaths, pledging the self-existence of God for the certainty of the event. **defiled my sanctuary**—the climax of Jewish guilt: their defiling Jehovah's temple by introducing idols. **diminish**—lit., "withdraw," viz., Mine "eye" (which presently follows), i.e., My favors; Job 36:7 uses the *Hebrew* verb in the same way. As the Jews had *withdrawn* from God's sanctuary its sacredness by "defiling" it, so God *withdraws* His countenance from them. The significance of the expression lies in the allusion to Deuteronomy 4:2, "Ye shall not *diminish* aught from the word which I command you"; they had done so, therefore God *diminishes* them. The reading found in six MSS., "I will cut thee off," is not so good. **12.** Statement in plain terms of what was intended by the symbols (vs. 2; see ch. 6:12; Jer. 15:2; 21:9). **draw out...sword after them**—(Lev. 26:33). Skeptics object; no such thing happened under Zedekiah, as is here foretold; viz., that a third part of the nation should die by pestilence, a third part by the sword, and a third be scattered unto all winds, and a sword sent after them. But the prophecy is not restricted to Zedekiah's time. It includes all that Israel suffered, or was still to suffer, for their sins, especially those committed at that period (ch. 17:21). It only received its primary fulfilment under Zedekiah: numbers then died by the pestilence and by the sword; and numbers were scattered in all quarters and not carried to Babylonia alone, as the objectors assert (cf. Ezra 1:4; Esther 3:8; Obadiah 14). **pestilence ...and famine**—signified by the symbol "fire" (vs. 2). Cf. Isaiah 13:8; Lamentations 5:10; plague and famine burning and withering the countenance, as fire does. **13. cause my fury to rest upon them**—as on its proper and permanent *resting-place* (Isa. 30: 32, *Margin*). **I will be comforted**—expressed in condescension to man's conceptions; signifying His *satisfaction* in the vindication of His justice by His righteous judgments (Deut. 28:63; Prov. 1:26; Isa. 1:24). **they shall know**—by bitter experience. **14. reproach among the nations**—They whose idolatries Israel had adopted, instead of comforting, would only exult in their calamities brought on by those idolatries (cf. Luke 15:15). **15. instruction**—lit., "a corrective chastisement," i.e., a striking *example* to warn all of the fatal consequences of sin. For "*it* shall be"; all ancient versions have "*thou*," which the connection favors. **16. arrows of famine**—hail, rain, mice, locusts, mildew (see Deut. 32:23, 24). **increase the famine**—lit., "congregate" or "collect." When ye think your harvest safe because ye have escaped drought, mildew, etc., I will find other means [CALVIN], which I will *congregate* as the *forces of an invading army*, to bring famine on you.

17. beasts—perhaps meaning destructive conquerors (Dan. 7:4). Rather, literal "beasts," which infest *desolated* regions such as Judea was to become (cf. ch. 34:28; Exod. 23:29; Deut. 32:24; II Kings 17:25). The same threat is repeated in manifold forms to awaken the careless. **sword**—civil war.

CHAPTER 6

VSS. 1-14. CONTINUATION OF THE SAME SUBJECT. **2. mountains of Israel**—i.e., of Palestine in general. The *mountains* are addressed by personification; implying that the Israelites themselves are incurable and unworthy of any more appeals; so the prophet sent to Jeroboam did not deign to address the king, but addressed the altar (I Kings 13:2). The mountains are specified as being the scene of Jewish idolatries on "the high places" (vs. 3; Lev. 26:30). **3. rivers**—lit., the "channels" of torrents. Rivers were often the scene and objects of idolatrous worship. **4. images**—called so from a *Hebrew* root, "to wax hot," implying the mad *ardor* of Israel after idolatry [CALVIN]. Others translate it, "sun-images"; and so in vs. 6 (see II Kings 23:11; II Chron. 34:4; Isa. 17:8, *Margin*). **cast your slain men before your idols**—The foolish objects of their trust in the day of evil should witness their ruin. **5. carcasses...before...idols**—polluting thus with the dead bones of you, the worshippers, the idols which seemed to you so sacrosanct. **6. your works** —not gods, as you supposed, but the mere work of men's hands (Isa. 40:18-20). **7. ye shall know that I am the Lord**—and not your idols, lords. Ye shall know Me as the all-powerful Punisher of sin. **8.** Mitigation of the extreme severity of their punishment; still their life shall be a wretched one, and linked with exile (ch. 5:2, 12; 12:16; 14:22; Jer. 44:28). **9. they that escape of you shall remember me**—The object of God's chastisements shall at last be effected by working in them true contrition. This partially took place in the complete eradication of idolatry from the Jews ever since the Babylonian captivity. But they have yet to repent of their crowning sin, the crucifixion of Messiah; their full repentance is therefore future, after the ordeal of trials for many centuries, ending with that foretold in Zechariah 10:9; 13:8, 9; 14:1-4, 11. "They shall *remember* me in far countries" (ch. 7:16; Deut. 30:1-8). **I am broken with their whorish heart**— FAIRBAIRN translates, actively, "I will break" their whorish heart; *English Version* is better. In their exile they shall remember how long I bore with them, but was at last compelled to punish, after I was "broken" (My long-suffering wearied out) by their desperate (Num. 15:39) spiritual whorishness [CALVIN], (Ps. 78:40; 73:7; 43:24; 63:10). **loathe themselves**—(Lev. 26:39-45; Job 42:6). They shall not wait for men to condemn them but shall condemn themselves (ch. 20:43; 36:31; Job 42:6; I Cor. 11:31). **11.** Gesticulations vividly setting before the hearers the greatness of the calamity about to be inflicted. In indignation at the abominations of Israel extend thine hand towards Judea, as if about to "strike," and "stamp," shaking off the dust with thy foot, in token of how God shall "stretch out His hand upon them," and *tread* them down (vs. 14; ch. 21:14). **12. He that is far off**—viz., from the foe; those who in a distant exile fear no evil. **he that remaineth**—*he that is left* in the city; not carried away into captivity, nor having escaped into the country. Distinct from "he that is near," viz., those outside the city who are within reach of "the sword" of the foe, and so fall by it; not by "famine," as those left in the city. **14. Diblath**—another form of Diblathaim, a city in Moab (Num. 33:46; Jer. 48:22), near which, east and south of the Dead Sea, was the wilderness of Arabia Deserta.

CHAPTER 7

Vss. 1-27. LAMENTATION OVER THE COMING RUIN OF ISRAEL; THE PENITENT REFORMATION OF A REMNANT; THE CHAIN SYMBOLIZING THE CAPTIVITY. **2. An end, the end**—The indefinite "an" expresses the general fact of God bringing His long-suffering towards the whole of Judea to an end; "the," following, marks it as more definitely fixed (Amos 8:2). **4. thine abominations**—the punishment of thine abominations. **shall be in the midst of thee**—shall be manifest to all. They and thou shall recognize the fact of thine abominations by thy punishment which shall everywhere befall thee, and that manifestly. **5. An evil, an only evil**—a peculiar calamity such as was never before; unparalleled. The abruptness of the style and the repetitions express the agitation of the prophet's mind in foreseeing these calamities. **6. watcheth for thee**—rather, "waketh for thee." It awakes up from its past slumber against thee (Ps. 78:65, 66). **7. The morning**—so *Chaldean* and *Syriac* versions (cf. Joel 2:2). Ezekiel wishes to awaken them from their lethargy, whereby they were promising to themselves an uninterrupted *night* (I Thess. 5:5-7), as if they were never to be called to account [CALVIN]. The expression, "morning," refers to the fact that this was the usual time for magistrates giving sentence against offenders (cf. vs. 10, below; Ps. 101:8; Jer. 21:12). GESENIUS, less probably, translates, "the *order* of fate"; thy turn to be punished. **not the sounding again**—not an empty *echo,* such as is produced by the reverberation of *sounds* in "the mountains," but a real cry of tumult is coming [CALVIN]. Perhaps it alludes to the joyous cries of the grape-gatherers at vintage on the hills [GROTIUS], or of the idolaters in their dances on their festivals in honor of their false gods [TIRINUS]. HAVERNICK translates, "no *brightness.*" **8, 9.** Repetition of vss. 3, 4; sadly expressive of accumulated woes by the monotonous sameness. **10. rod ... blossomed, pride ... budded**—The "rod" is the Chaldean Nebuchadnezzar, the instrument of God's vengeance (Isa. 10:5; Jer. 51:20). The rod *sprouting* (as the word ought to be translated), etc., implies that God does not move precipitately, but in successive steps. He as it were has planted the ministers of His vengeance, and leaves them to grow till all is ripe for executing His purpose. "Pride" refers to the insolence of the Babylonian conqueror (Jer. 50:31, 32). The parallelism ("pride" answering to "rod") opposes JEROME's view, that "pride" refers to the *Jews* who despised God's threats; (also CALVIN's, "though the *rod* grew in Chaldea, the *root* was with the Jews"). The "rod" cannot refer, as GROTIUS thought, to the *tribe* of Judah, for it evidently refers to the "smiteth" (vs. 9) as the instrument of smiting. **11.** *Violence* (i.e., the violent foe) *is risen up as a rod of* (i.e., to punish the Jews) *wickedness* (Zech. 5:8); **theirs**—their possessions, or all that belongs to them, whether children or goods. GROTIUS translates from a different *Hebrew* root, "their nobles," lit., their *tumultuous* trains (*Margin*) which usually escorted the nobles. Thus "nobles" will form a contrast to the general "multitude." **neither ... wailing**—(Jer. 16:4-7; 25:33). GESENIUS translates, "nor

shall there be left any *beauty* among them." *English Version* is supported by the old Jewish interpreters. So general shall be the slaughter, none shall be left to mourn the dead. **12. let not ... buyer rejoice**—because he has bought an estate at a bargain price. **nor ... seller mourn**—because he has had to sell his land at a sacrifice through poverty. The Chaldeans will be masters of the land, so that neither shall the buyer have any good of his purchase, nor the seller any loss; nor shall the latter (vs. 13) return to his inheritance at the jubilee year (see Lev. 25:13). Spiritually this holds good now, seeing that "the time is short"; "they that rejoice should be as though they rejoiced not, and they that buy as though they possessed not": Paul (I Cor. 7: 30) seems to allude to Ezekiel here. Jeremiah 32: 15, 37, 43, seems to contradict Ezekiel here. But Ezekiel is speaking of the parents, and of the present; Jeremiah, of the children, and of the future. Jeremiah is addressing believers, that they should hope for a restoration; Ezekiel, the reprobate, who were excluded from hope of deliverance. **13. although they were yet alive**—although they should live to the year of jubilee. **multitude thereof**—viz., of the Jews. **which shall not return**—answering to "the seller shall not return"; not only he, but *the whole multitude,* shall not return. CALVIN omits "is" and "which": "the vision touching the whole multitude shall not return" void (Isa. 55:11). **neither shall any strengthen himself in the iniquity of his life**—No hardening of one's self in iniquity will avail against God's threat of punishment. FAIRBAIRN translates, "no one by his iniquity shall invigorate his life"; referring to the jubilee, which was regarded as a revivification of the whole commonwealth, when, its disorders being rectified, the body politic sprang up again into renewed life. That for which God thus provided by the institution of the jubilee and which is now to cease through the nation's iniquity, let none think to bring about by his iniquity. **14. They have blown the trumpet**—rather, "Blow the trumpet," or, "Let them blow the trumpet" to collect soldiers as they will, "to make all ready" for encountering the foe, it will be of no avail; none will have the courage to go to the battle (cf. Jer. 6:1), [CALVIN]. **15.** No security should anywhere be found (Deut. 32:25). Fulfilled (Lam. 1:20); also at the Roman invasion (Matt. 24:16-18). **16.** (Ch. 6:6.) **like doves**—which, though usually frequenting the valleys, mount up to the mountains when fearing the bird-catcher (Ps. 11:1). So Israel, once dwelling in its peaceful valleys, shall flee from the foe to the mountains, which, as being the scene of its idolatries, were justly to be made the scene of its flight and shame. The plaintive note of the dove (Isa. 59:11) represents the mournful repentance of Israel hereafter (Zech. 12:10-12). **17. shall be weak as water**—lit., "shall go (as) waters"; incapable of resistance (Josh. 7:5; Ps. 22:14; Isa. 13:7). **18. cover them**—as a garment. **baldness**—as a sign of mourning (Isa. 3:24; Jer. 48:37; Mic. 1:16). **19. cast ... silver in ... streets**—just retribution; they had abused their silver and gold by converting them into idols, "the stumbling-block of their iniquity" (ch. 14:3, 4, i.e., an occasion of sinning); so these silver and gold idols, so far from "being able to deliver them in the day of the Lord's wrath" (see Prov. 11:4), shall, in despair, be cast by them into the streets as a prey to the foe, by whom they shall be "removed" (GROTIUS translates as *Margin,* "shall be despised as an *unclean* thing"); or rather, as suits the parallelism, "shall be put away from them" by the Jews [CALVIN]. "They (the silver and gold) shall not satisfy their souls," i.e., their cravings of appetite and other needs. **20. beauty of his ornament**—the temple of Jehovah, the especial glory of the Jews, as a bride glories in her ornaments (the very imagery used by God as to the temple, ch. 16: 10, 11). Cf. ch. 24:21: "My sanctuary, the excellency of your strength, the desire of your eyes." **images . . . therein**—viz., in the temple (ch. 8:3-17). **set it far from them**—God had "set" the temple (their "beauty of ornament") "for His majesty"; but they had set up "abominations therein"; therefore God, in just retribution, "set it far from them," (i.e., removed them far from it, or took it away from them [VATABLUS]. *Margin* translates, "Made it unto them an *unclean thing*" (cf. *Margin* on vs. 19, "removed"); what I designed for their glory they turned to their shame, therefore I will make it turn to their ignominy and ruin. **21. strangers**—barbarous and savage nations. **22. pollute my secret place**—just retribution for the Jews' pollution of the temple. "*Robbers* shall enter and defile" the holy of holies, the place of God's manifested presence, entrance into which was denied even to the Levites and priests and was permitted to the high priest only once a year on the great day of atonement. **23. chain**—symbol of the captivity (cf. Jer. 27:2). As they enchained the land with violence, so shall they be chained themselves. It was customary to lead away captives in a row with a chain passed from the neck of one to the other. Therefore translate as the *Hebrew* requires, "*the* chain," viz., that usually employed on such occasions. CALVIN explains it, that the Jews should be dragged, whether they would or no, before God's tribunal to be tried as culprits in chains. The next words favor this: "bloody crimes," rather, "*judgment* of bloods," i.e., with blood-sheddings deserving the extreme judicial penalty. Cf. Jeremiah 51:9: "Her *judgment* reacheth unto heaven." **24. worst of the heathen**—lit., "wicked of the nations"; the giving up of Israel to their power will convince the Jews that this is a final overthrow. **pomp of . . . strong**—the *pride* wherewith men "stiff of forehead" despise the prophet. **holy places**—the sacred compartments of the temple (Ps. 68:35; Jer. 51:51) [CALVIN]. God calls it "*their* holy places," because they had so defiled it that He regarded it no longer as *His*. However, as the defilement of the temple has already been mentioned (vss. 20, 22), and "their sacred places" are introduced as a new subject, it seems better to understand this of *the places dedicated to their idols.* As they defiled God's sanctuary, He will defile their self-constituted "sacred places." **25. peace, and . . . none**—(I Thess. 5:3.) **26. Mischief . . . upon . . . mischief**—(Deut. 32:23; Jer. 4:20). This is said because the Jews were apt to fancy, at every abatement of suffering, that their calamities were about to cease; but God will accumulate woe on woe. **rumour**—of the advance of the foe, and of his cruelty (Matt. 24:6). **seek a vision**—to find some way of escape from their difficulties (Isa. 26:9). So Zedekiah consulted Jeremiah (Jer. 37:17; 38:14). **law shall perish**—fulfilled (ch. 20:1, 3; Ps. 74:9; Lam. 2:9; cf. Amos 8:11); God will thus set aside the idle boast, "The law shall not perish from the priest" (Jer. 18:18). **ancients**—the ecclesiastical rulers of the people. **27. people of the land**—the general multitude, as distinguished from the "king" and the "prince." The consternation shall pervade all ranks. The king, whose duty it was to animate others and find a remedy for existing evils, shall himself be in the utmost anxiety; a mark of the desperate state of affairs. **clothed with desolation** —Clothing is designed to keep off shame; but in this case shame shall be the clothing. **after their way**—because of their wicked ways. **deserts**—lit., "judgments," i.e., what just judgment awards to them; used to imply the exact correspondence of God's judgment with the judicial penalties they had incurred: they oppressed the poor and deprived them of liberty; therefore they shall be oppressed and lose their own liberty.

CHAPTER 8

Vss. 1-18. This eighth chapter begins a new stage of Ezekiel's prophecies and continues to the end of the eleventh chapter. The connected visions from ch. 3:12 to the end of ch. 7 comprehended Judah and Israel; but the visions (ch. 8-11) refer immediately to Jerusalem and the remnant of Judah under Zedekiah, as distinguished from the Babylonian exiles. **1. sixth year**—viz., of the captivity of Jehoiachin, as in ch. 1:2, the "fifth year" is specified. The lying on his sides 390 and 40 days (ch. 4:5, 6) had by this time been completed, at least *in vision.* That event was naturally a memorable epoch to the exiles; and the computation of years from it was to humble the Jews, as well as to show their perversity in not having repented, though so long and severely chastised. **elders**—viz., those carried away with Jehoiachin, and now at the Chebar. **sat before me**—to hear the word of God from me, in the absence of the temple and other public places of Sabbath worship, during the exile (ch. 33:30, 31). It was so ordered that they were present at the giving of the prophecy, and so left without excuse. **hand of . . . Lord God fell . . . upon me**—God's mighty operation *fell,* like a thunderbolt, *upon me* (in ch. 1:3, it is less forcible, "was upon him"); whatever, therefore, he is to utter is not his own, for he has put off the mere man, while the power of God reigns in him [CALVIN]. **2. likeness**—understand, "of a man," i.e., of Messiah, the Angel of the covenant, in the person of whom alone God manifests Himself (ch. 1:26; John 1:18). The "fire," from "His loins downward," betokens the vengeance of God kindled against the wicked Jews, while searching and purifying the remnant to be spared. The "brightness" "upward" betokens His unapproachable majesty (I Tim. 6:16). For *Hebrew,* *eesh,* "fire," LXX, etc., read *ish,* "a man." **colour of amber**—the glitter of chasmal [FAIRBAIRN], (*Note,* ch. 1:4, "polished brass"). **3.** Instead of prompting him to address directly the elders before him, the Spirit carried him away *in vision* (not in person bodily) to the temple at Jerusalem; he proceeds to report to them what he witnessed: his message thus falls into two parts: (1) The abominations reported in ch. 8. (2) The dealings of judgment and mercy to be adopted towards the impenitent and penitent Israelites respectively (ch. 9-11). The exiles looked hopefully towards Jerusalem and, so far from believing things there to be on the verge of ruin, expected a return in peace; while those left in Jerusalem eyed the exiles with contempt, as if cast away from the Lord, whereas they themselves were near God and ensured in the possessions of the land (ch. 11:15). Hence the vision here of what affected those in Jerusalem immediately was a seasonable communication to the exiles away from it. **door of the inner gate**—facing the north, the direction in which he came from Chebar, called the "altar-gate" (vs. 5); it opened into the inner court, wherein stood the altar of burnt offering; the inner court (I Kings 6: 36) was that of the priests; the outer court (ch. 10:5), that of the people, where they assembled. **seat**—the *pedestal* of the image. **image of jealousy**—Astarte, or Asheera (as the *Hebrew* for "grove" ought to be translated, II Kings 21:3, 7; 23: 4, 7), set up by Manasseh as a rival to Jehovah in His temple, and arresting the attention of all worshippers as they entered; it was the Syrian Venus, worshipped with licentious rites; the "queen of heaven," wife of Phœnician Baal. HAVERNICK thinks all the scenes of idolatry in the chapter are successive portions of the festival held in honor of Tammuz or Adonis (vs. 14). Probably, however, the scenes are separate proofs of Jewish idolatry, rather than restricted to one idol. **provoketh to jealousy**—calleth for a visitation in wrath of the "jealous God," who will not give His honor to another (cf. the second commandment, Exod. 20:5). JEROME refers this verse to a statue of Baal, which Josiah had overthrown and his successors had replaced. **4.** The Shekinah cloud of Jehovah's glory, notwithstanding the provocation of the idol, still remains in the temple, like that which Ezekiel saw "in the plain" (ch. 3:22, 23); not till ch. 10:4, 18 did it leave the temple at Jerusalem, showing the long-suffering of God, which ought to move the Jews to repentance. **5. gate or . . . altar**—the principal avenue to the altar of burnt offering; as to the *northern* position, see II Kings 16:14. Ahaz had removed the brazen altar from the front of the Lord's house to the north of the altar which he had himself erected. The locality of the idol before God's own altar enhances the heinousness of the sin. **6. that I should** [be compelled by their sin to] **go far off from my sanctuary**—(ch. 10:18); the sure precursor of its destruction. **7. door of the court**—i.e., of the inner court (vs. 3); the court of the priests and Levites, into which now others were admitted in violation of the law [GROTIUS]. **hole in . . . wall**—i.e., an aperture or window in the wall of the priests' chambers, through which he could see into the various apartments, wherein was the idolatrous shrine. **8. dig**—for it had been blocked up during Josiah's reformation. Or rather, the vision is not of an actual scene, but an ideal pictorial representation of the Egyptian idolatries into which the covenant-people had relapsed, practising them in secret places where they shrank from the light of day [FAIRBAIRN], (John 3:20). But cf, as to the *literal* introduction of idolatries into the temple, ch. 5:11; Jer. 7:30; 32:34. **10. creeping things . . . beasts**—worshipped in Egypt; still found portrayed on their chamber walls; so among the troglodytæ. **round about**—On every side they surrounded themselves with incentives to superstition. **11. seventy men**—the seventy members composing the Sanhedrim, or great council of the nation, the origination of which we find in the seventy elders, representatives of the congregation, who went up with Moses to the mount to behold the glory of Jehovah, and to witness the secret transactions relating to the establishment of the covenant; also, in the seventy elders appointed to share the burden of the people with Moses. How awfully it aggravates the national sin, that the seventy, once admitted to the Lord's secret council (Ps. 25:14), should now, "in the dark," enter "the secret" of the wicked (Gen. 49:6), those judicially bound to suppress idolatry being the ringleaders of it! **Jaazaniah**—perhaps chief of the seventy: son of Shaphan, the scribe who read to Josiah the book of the law; the spiritual privileges of the son (II Kings 22:10-14)

increased his guilt. The very name means, "Jehovah hears," giving the lie to the unbelief which virtually said (ch. 9:9), "The Lord seeth us not," etc. (cf. Ps. 10:11, 14; 50:21; 94:7, 9). The offering of incense belonged not to the elders, but to the priests; this usurpation added to the guilt of the former. **cloud of incense**—They spared no expense for their idols. Oh, that there were the same liberality toward the cause of God! **12. every man in . . . chambers of . . . imagery**—The elders ("ancients") are here the representatives of the people, rather than to be regarded literally. Mostly, the *leaders* of heathen superstitions laughed at them secretly, while publicly professing them in order to keep the people in subjection. Here what is meant is that the *people* generally addicted themselves to secret idolatry, led on by their elders; there is no doubt, also, allusion to *the mysteries,* as in the worship of Isis in Egypt, the Eleusinian in Greece, etc., to which the initiated alone were admitted. "The chambers of imagery" are their own *perverse imaginations,* answering to the *priests' chambers* in the vision, whereon the pictures were portrayed (vs. 10). **Lord . . . forsaken . . . earth**—They infer this because God has left them to their miseries, without succoring them, so that they seek help from other gods. Instead of repenting, as they ought, they bite the curb [CALVIN]. **14.** From the *secret* abominations of the chambers of imagery, the prophet's eye is turned to the *outer* court at the *north door; within* the outer court women were not admitted, but only to the *door.* **sat**—the attitude of mourners (Job 2: 13; Isa. 3:26). **Tammuz**—from a *Hebrew* root, "to melt down." Instead of weeping for the national sins, they wept for the idol. Tammuz (the *Syrian* for Adonis), the paramour of Venus, and of the same name as the river flowing from Lebanon; killed by a wild boar, and, according to the fable, permitted to spend half the year on earth, and obliged to spend the other half in the lower world. An annual feast was celebrated to him in June (hence called Tammuz in the Jewish calendar) at Byblos, when the Syrian women, in wild grief, tore off their hair and yielded their persons to prostitution, consecrating the hire of their infamy to Venus; next followed days of rejoicing for his return to the earth; the former feast being called "the disappearance of Adonis," the latter, "the finding of Adonis." This Phœnician feast answered to the similar Egyptian one in honor of Osiris. The idea thus fabled was that of the waters of the river and the beauties of spring destroyed by the summer during the half year when the sun is in the upper heat. Or else, the earth being clothed with beauty, and losing it when he departs to the lower. The name *Adonis* is not here used, as *Adon* is the appropriated title of Jehovah. **15, 16.** The next are "*greater* abominations," not in respect to the idolatry, but in respect to the place and persons committing it. In "the inner court," immediately before the door of the temple of Jehovah, between the porch and the altar, where the priests advanced only on extraordinary occasions (Joel 2:17), twenty-five men (the leaders of the twenty-four courses or orders of the priests, I Chron. 24:18, 19, with the high priest, "the princes of the sanctuary," Isa. 43: 28), representing the whole priesthood, as the seventy elders represented the people, stood with their backs turned on the temple, and their faces towards the east, making obeisance to the rising sun (contrast I Kings 8:44). Sun-worship came from the Persians, who made the sun the eye of their god Ormuzd. It existed as early as Job (Job 31:26; cf.

Deut. 4:19). Josiah could only suspend it for the time of his reign (II Kings 23:5, 11); it revived under his successors. **16. worshipped**—In the *Hebrew* a corrupt form is used to express Ezekiel's sense of the foul corruption of such worship. **17. put ... branch to ... nose**—proverbial, for "they turn up the nose in scorn," expressing their insolent security [LXX]. Not content with outraging "with their violence" the second table of the law, viz., that of duty towards one's neighbor, "they have returned" (i.e., they turn back afresh) to provoke Me by violations of the first table [CALVIN]. Rather, they held up a branch or bundle of tamarisk (called *barsom*) to their nose at daybreak, while singing hymns to the rising sun [STRABO, 1.15, p. 733]. Sacred trees were frequent symbols in idol-worship. CALVIN translates, "to their own ruin," lit., "to their nose," i.e., with the effect of rousing *My anger* (of which *the Hebrew* is "nose") to their ruin. **18. though they cry ... yet will I not hear**—(Prov. 1:28; Isa. 1:15.)

CHAPTER 9

Vss. 1-11. CONTINUATION OF THE PRECEDING VISION: THE SEALING OF THE FAITHFUL. **1. cried**—contrasted with their "cry" for mercy (ch. 8:18) is the "cry" here for vengeance, showing how vain was the former. **them that have charge**—lit., "officers"; so *officers* (Isa. 60:17), having the city in charge, not to guard, but to punish it. The angels who as "watchers" fulfil God's judgments (Dan. 4:13, 17, 23; 10:20, 21); the "princes" (Jer. 39:3) of Nebuchadnezzar's army were under their guidance. **draw near**—in the *Hebrew* intensive, "to draw near quickly." **2. clothed with linen**—(Dan. 10:5; 12:6, 7). His clothing marked his office as distinct from that of the six officers of vengeance; "linen" characterized the high priest (Lev. 16:4); emblematic of purity. The same garment is assigned to the angel of the Lord (for whom Michael is but another name) by the contemporary prophet Daniel (Dan. 10:5; 12:6, 7). Therefore the intercessory High Priest in heaven must be meant (Zech. 1:12). The six with Him are His subordinates; therefore He is said to be "among them," lit., "in the midst of them," *as their recognized Lord* (Heb. 1:6). He appears as a "man," implying His incarnation; as "one" (cf. I Tim. 2:5). Salvation is peculiarly assigned to Him, and so He bears the "inkhorn" in order to "mark" His elect (vs. 4; cf. Exod. 12:7; Rev. 7:3; 9:4; 13:16, 17; 20:4), and to write their names in His book of life (Rev. 13:8). As Oriental scribes suspend their inkhorn at their side in the present day, and as a "scribe of the host is found in Assyrian inscriptions accompanying the host" to number the heads of the slain, so He stands ready for the work before Him. "The higher gate" was probably where now the gate of Damascus is. The six with Him make up the sacred and perfect number, *seven* (Zech. 3:9; Rev. 5:6). The executors of judgment on the wicked, in Scripture teaching, are good, not bad, angels; the bad have permitted to them the trial of the pious (Job 1:12; II Cor. 12:7). The judgment is executed by Him (ch. 10:2, 7; John 5:22, 27) through the six (Matt. 13:41; 25:31); so beautifully does the Old Testament harmonize with the New Testament. The seven come "from the way of the north"; for it was there the idolatries were seen, and from the same quarter must proceed the judgment (Babylon lying northeast of Judea). So Matthew

24:28. **stood**—the attitude of waiting reverently for Jehovah's commands. **brazen altar**—the altar of burnt offerings, not the altar of incense, which was *of gold*. They "stood" there to imply reverent obedience; for there God gave His answers to prayer [CALVIN]; also as being about to slay victims to God's justice, they stand where sacrifices are usually slain [GROTIUS], (ch. 39:17; Isa. 34:6; Jer. 12:3; 46: 10). **3. glory of ... God**—which had heretofore, as a bright cloud, rested on the mercy seat between the cherubim in the holy of holies (II Sam. 6:2; Ps. 80: 1); its departure was the presage of the temple being given up to ruin; its going from the inner sanctuary to the threshold without, towards the officers standing at the altar outside, was in order to give them the commission of vengeance. **4. midst of ... city ... midst of Jerusalem**—This twofold designation marks more emphatically the scene of the divine judgments. **a mark**—lit., the Hebrew letter *Tau*, the last in the alphabet, used as a *mark* (Job 31:35, *Margin*, "my sign"); lit., *Tau*; originally written in the form of a *cross*, which TERTULLIAN explains as referring to the badge and only means of salvation, the cross of Christ. But nowhere in Scripture are the words which are now employed as names of letters used to denote the letters themselves or their figures [VITRINGA]. The noun here is cognate to the verb, *"mark a mark."* So in Revelation 7:3 no particular mark is specified. We *seal* what we wish to guard securely. When all things else on earth are confounded, God will secure His people from the common ruin. God gives the *first* charge as to their safety before He orders the punishment of the rest (Ps. 31:20; Isa. 26:20, 21). So in the case of Lot and Sodom (Gen. 19:22); also the Egyptian firstborn were not slain till Israel had time to sprinkle the blood-mark, ensuring their safety (cf. Rev. 7:3; Amos 9:9). So the early Christians had Pella provided as a refuge for them, before the destruction of Jerusalem. **upon the foreheads**—the most conspicuous part of the person, to imply how their safety would be manifested to all (cf. Rev. 15:11; 39: 11-18). It was customary thus to mark worshippers (Rev. 13:16; 14:1, 9) and servants. So the Church of England marks the forehead with the sign of the cross in baptizing. At the exodus the mark was on the *houses*, for then it was families; here, it is on the *foreheads*, for it is individuals whose safety is guaranteed. **sigh and ... cry**—similarly sounding verbs in *Hebrew*, as in *English Version*, expressing the prolonged sound of their grief. "Sigh" implies their *inward grief* ("groanings which cannot be uttered," Rom. 8:26); "cry," the outward expression of it. So Lot (II Pet. 2:7, 8). Tenderness should characterize the man of God, not harsh sternness in opposing the ungodly (Ps. 119:53, 136; Jer. 13:17; II Cor. 12:21); at the same time zeal for the honor of God (Ps. 69:9, 10; I John 5:19). **5. the others**—the six officers of judgment (vs. 2). **6. come not near any ... upon whom ... mark**—(Rev. 9:4). It may be objected that Daniel, Jeremiah, and others were carried away, whereas many of the vilest were left in the land. But God does not promise believers exemption from all suffering, but only from what will prove really and lastingly hurtful to them. His sparing the ungodly turns to their destruction and leaves them without excuse [CALVIN]. However, the prophecy waits a fuller and final fulfilment, for Revelation 7:3-8, in ages long after Babylon, foretells, as still future, the same sealing of a remnant (144,000) of Israel previous to the final outpouring of wrath on the rest of the nation; the correspondence is exact; the same pouring of fire from the altar follows the marking of the remnant in both (cf. Rev. 8:5, with ch. 10:2). So Zechariah 13:9 and 14:2, distinguish the remnant from the rest of Israel. **begin at . . . sanctuary**—For in it the greatest abominations had been committed; it had lost the reality of consecration by the blood of victims sacrificed to idols; it must, therefore, lose its semblance by the dead bodies of the slain idolaters (vs. 7). God's heaviest wrath falls on those who have sinned against the highest privileges; these are made to feel it first (I Pet. 4:17, 18). He hates sin most in those nearest to Him; e.g., the priests, etc. **ancient men**—the seventy elders. **8. I was left**—lit., "there was left I." So universal seemed the slaughter that Ezekiel thought himself the only one left [CALVIN]. He was the only one left *of the priests* "in the sanctuary." **fell upon my face**—to intercede for his countrymen (so Num. 16:22). **all the residue**—a plea drawn from God's covenant promise to save the elect *remnant*. **9. exceeding**—lit., "very, very"; doubled. **perverseness**—"apostasy" [GROTIUS]; or, "wresting aside of justice." **Lord . . . forsaken . . . earth . . . seeth not**—The order is reversed from ch. 8:12. There they speak of His neglect of His people in their misery; here they go farther and deny His providence (Ps. 10:11), so that they may sin fearlessly. God, in answer to Ezekiel's question (vs. 8), leaves the difficulty unsolved; He merely vindicates His justice by showing it did not exceed their sin: He would have us humbly acquiesce in His judgments, and wait and trust. **10. mine eye**—to show them their mistake in saying, "The Lord *seeth* not." **recompense their way upon their head**—(Prov. 1:31). Retribution in kind. **11. I have done as thou hast commanded**—The characteristic of Messiah (John 17:4). So the angels (Ps. 103:21); and the apostles report their fulfilment of their orders (Mark 6:30).

CHAPTER 10

Vss. 1-22. VISION OF COALS OF FIRE SCATTERED OVER THE CITY: REPETITION OF THE VISION OF THE CHERUBIM. **1.** The throne of Jehovah appearing in the midst of the judgments implies that whatever intermediate agencies be employed, He controls them, and that the whole flows as a necessary consequence from His essential holiness (ch. 1:22, 26). **cherubim**—in ch. 1:5, called "living creatures." The repetition of the vision implies that the judgments are approaching nearer and nearer. These two visions of Deity were granted in the beginning of Ezekiel's career, to qualify him for witnessing to God's glory amidst his God-forgetting people and to stamp truth on his announcements; also to signify the removal of God's manifestation from the visible temple (vs. 18) for a long period (ch. 43:2). The feature (vs. 12) mentioned as to the cherubim that they were "full of eyes," though omitted in the former vision, is not a difference, but a more specific detail observed by Ezekiel now on closer inspection. Also, here, there is no rainbow (the symbol of *mercy* after the flood of wrath) as in the former; for here *judgment* is the prominent thought, though the *marking* of the remnant in ch. 9:4, 6 shows that there was mercy in the background. The cherubim, perhaps, represent redeemed humanity combining in and with itself the highest forms of subordinate creaturely life (cf. Rom. 8:20). Therefore they are associated with the twenty-four elders and are distinguished from the angels (Rev. 5). They

stand on the mercy seat of the ark, and *on that ground* become the habitation of God from which His glory is to shine upon the world. The different forms symbolize the different phases of the Church. So the quadriform Gospel, in which the incarnate Saviour has lodged the revelation of Himself in a fourfold aspect, and from which His glory shines on the Christian world, answers to the emblematic throne from which He shone on the Jewish Church. **2. he**—Jehovah; He who sat on the "throne." **the man**—the Messenger of mercy becoming the Messenger of judgment (*Note*, ch. 9:2). Human agents of destruction shall fulfil the will of "the Man," who is Lord of men. **wheels** —*Hebrew, galgal,* implying *quick* revolution; so *the impetuous onset of the foe* (cf. ch. 23:24; 26:10); whereas "*ophan*," in ch. 1:15, 16 implies mere revolution. **coals of fire**—the wrath of God about to *burn the city*, as His sword had previously *slain* its guilty inhabitants. This "fire," how different from *the fire on the altar never going out* (Lev. 6:12, 13), whereby, in type, peace was made with God! Cf. Isaiah 33:12, 14. It is therefore not taken from the altar of reconciliation, but from between the wheels of the cherubim, representing the providence of God, whereby, and not by chance, judgment is to fall. **3. right . . . of . . . house**—The scene of the locality whence judgment emanates is the temple, to mark God's vindication of His holiness injured there. The cherubim here are not those in the holy of holies, for the latter had not "wheels." They stood on "the right of the house," i.e., the south, for the Chaldean power, guided by them, had already advanced from the north (the direction of Babylon), and had destroyed *the men in the temple*, and was now proceeding to destroy the *city*, which lay south and west. **the cherubim . . . the man**—There was perfect concert of action between the cherubic representative of the angels and "the Man," to minister to whom they "stood" there (vs. 7). **cloud**—emblem of God's displeasure; as the "glory" or "brightness" (vs. 4) typifies His majesty and clearness in judgment. **4.** The court outside was full of the Lord's *brightness*, while it was only the *cloud* that filled the *house inside*, the scene of idolatries, and therefore of God's displeasure. God's throne was *on the threshold*. The temple, once filled with brightness, is now darkened with cloud. **5. sound of . . . wings**—prognostic of great and awful changes. **voice of . . . God**—the thunder (Ps. 29:3, etc.). **6. went in**—not into the temple, but between the cherubim. Ezekiel sets aside the Jews' boast of the presence of God with them. The cherubim, once the ministers of grace, are now the ministers of vengeance. When "commanded," He without delay obeys (Ps. 40:8; Heb. 10:7). **7.** See vs. 3, *Note*. **one cherub**—one of the four cherubim. **his hand**—(ch. 1:8). **went out**—to burn the city. **8.** "wings" denote alacrity, the "hands" efficacy and aptness, in executing the functions assigned to them. **9. wheels**—(*Note*, ch. 1:15, 16). The things which, from vs. 8 to the end of the chapter, are repeated from ch. 1 are expressed more decidedly, now that he gets a nearer view: the words "as it were," and "as if," so often occurring in ch. 1, are therefore mostly omitted. The "wheels" express the manifold changes and revolutions in the world; also that in the chariot of His providence God transports the Church from one place to another and everywhere can preserve it; a truth calculated to alarm the people in Jerusalem and to console the exiles [POLANUS]. **10. four had one likeness**—In the wonderful variety of God's works there is the greatest harmony:—

"In human works, though labored on with pain,
One thousand movements scarce one purpose gain;
In God's one single doth its end produce,
Yet serves to second, too, some other use."

(*See note*, ch. 1:16.) **wheel ... in ... a wheel**—cutting one another at right angles, so that the whole might move in any of the four directions or quarters of the world. God's doings, however involved they seem to us, cohere, so that lower causes subserve the higher. **11.** (*Note*, ch. 1:17). **turned not**—without accomplishing their course (Isa. 55:11) [GROTIUS]. Rather, "they moved *straight on* without turning" (so ch. 1:9). Having a face towards each of the four quarters, they needed not to turn around when changing their direction. **whither ... head looked**—i.e., "whither the head" of the animal cherub-form, belonging to and directing each wheel, "looked," thither the wheel "followed." The wheels were not guided by some external adventitious impetus, but by some secret divine impulse of the cherubim themselves. **12. body**—lit., flesh, because a body consists of flesh. **wheels ... full of eyes**—The description (ch. 1:18) attributes eyes to the "*wheels*" alone; here there is added, on closer observation, that the *cherubim* themselves had them. The "eyes" imply that God, by His wisdom, beautifully reconciles seeming contrarieties (cf. II Chron. 16:9; Prov. 15:3; Zech. 4:10). **13. O wheel**—rather, "they were called, whirling," i.e., they were *most rapid in their revolutions* [MAURER]; or, better, "It was cried unto them, The whirling" [FAIRBAIRN]. *Galgal* here used for "wheel," is different from *ophan*, the simple word for "wheel." *Galgal* is the whole *wheelwork* machinery with its *whirlwind-like rotation*. Their being so addressed is in order to call them immediately to put themselves in rapid motion. **14. cherub**—but in ch. 1:10 it is *an ox*. The chief of the four cherubic forms was not the *ox, but man*. Therefore "cherub" cannot be synonymous with "ox." Probably Ezekiel, standing in front of one of the cherubim (viz., that which handed the coals to the man in linen), saw of him, not merely the ox-form, but the *whole fourfold* form, and therefore calls him simply "cherub"; whereas of the other three, having only a side view, he specifies the form of each which met his eye [FAIRBAIRN]. As to the likelihood of the lower animals sharing in "the restoration of all things," see Isaiah 11:6; 65:25; Romans 8:20, 21; this accords with the animal forms combined with the human to typify redeemed man. **15.** The repeated declaration of the identity of the vision with that at the Chebar is to arouse attention to it (vs. 22; ch. 3:23). **the living creature**—used collectively, as in vss. 17, 20; ch. 1:20. **16.** (*Note*, vs. 11; ch. 1:19). **lifted up ... wings**—to depart, following "the glory of the Lord" which was on the point of departing (vs. 18). **17.** (Ch. 1:12, 20, 21). **stood**—God never *stands* still (John 5:17), therefore neither do the angels; but to human perceptions He seems to do so. **18.** The departure of the symbol of God's presence from the temple preparatory to the destruction of the city. Foretold in Deuteronomy 31:17. Woe be to those from whom God departs (Hos. 9:12)! Cf. I Sam. 28:15, 16; 4:21: "I-chabod, Thy glory is departed." Successive steps are marked in His departure; so slowly and reluctantly does the merciful God leave His house. First He leaves the sanctuary (ch. 9:3); He elevates His throne above the threshold of the house (vs. 1); leaving the cherubim He sits on the throne (vs. 4); He and the cherubim, after *standing* for a time *at the*

door of the east gate (where was the exit to the lower court of the people), leave the house altogether (vss. 18, 19), not to return till ch. 43:2. **20. I knew ... cherubim**—By the second sight of the cherubim, he learned to identify them with the angelic forms situated above the ark of the covenant in the temple, which as a priest, he "knew" about from the high priest. **21.** The repetition is in order that the people about to live without the temple might have, instead, the knowledge of the temple mysteries, thus preparing them for a future restoration of the covenant. So perverse were they that they would say, "Ezekiel fancies he saw what has no existence." He, therefore, repeats it over and over again. **22. straight forward**—intent upon the object they aimed at, not deviating from the way nor losing sight of the end (Luke 9:52).

CHAPTER 11

Vss. 1-25. PROPHECY OF THE DESTRUCTION OF THE CORRUPT "PRINCES OF THE PEOPLE;" PELATIAH DIES; PROMISE OF GRACE TO THE BELIEVING REMNANT; DEPARTURE OF THE GLORY OF GOD FROM THE CITY; EZEKIEL'S RETURN TO THE CAPTIVES. **1. east gate**—to which the glory of God had moved itself (ch. 10:19), the chief entrance of the sanctuary; the portico or porch of Solomon. The Spirit moves the prophet thither, to witness, in the presence of the divine glory, a new scene of destruction. **five and twenty men**—The same as the twenty-five (i.e., twenty-four heads of courses, and the high priest) sun-worshippers seen in ch. 8:16. The leading *priests* were usually called "princes of the sanctuary" (Isa. 43:28) and "chiefs of the priests" (II Chron. 36:14); but here two of them are called "princes of the people," with irony, as using their priestly influence to be ringleaders of the people in sin (vs. 2). Already the wrath of God had visited the *people* represented by the *elders* (ch. 9:6); also the glory of the Lord had left its place in the holy of holies and, like the cherubim and flaming sword in Eden, had occupied the gate into the deserted sanctuary. The judgment on the representatives of the *priesthood* naturally follows here, just as the *sin* of the priests had followed in the description (ch. 8:12, 16) after the sin of the elders. **Jaazaniah**—signifying "God hears." **son of Azur**—different from Jaazaniah the son of Shaphan (ch. 8:11). Azur means "help." He and Pelatiah ("God delivers"), son of Benaiah ("God builds"), are singled out as Jaazaniah, son of Shaphan, in the case of the seventy elders (ch. 8:11, 12), because their names ought to have reminded them that "God" would have "heard" had they sought His "help" to "deliver" and "build" them up. But, neglecting this, they incurred the heavier judgment by the very relation in which they stood to God [FAIRBAIRN]. **2. he**—the Lord sitting on the cherubim (ch. 10:2). **wicked counsel**—in opposition to the prophets of God (vs. 3). **3. It is not near**—viz., the destruction of the city; therefore "let us build houses," as if there was no fear. But the *Hebrew* opposes *English Version*, which would require the infinitive absolute. Rather, "Not at hand is the building of houses." They sneer at Jeremiah's letter to the captives, among whom Ezekiel lived (Jer. 29:5). "*Build* ye *houses*, and dwell in them," i.e., do not fancy, as many persuade you, that your sojourn in Babylon is to be short; it will be for seventy years (Jer. 25:11, 12; 29:10); therefore build houses and settle quietly there. The scorners in Jerusalem reply, Those far off in exile may build if they please, but it is *too remote* a concern for us to trouble ourselves about [FAIRBAIRN], (cf. ch. 12:22, 27; II Pet. 3:4). **this city . . . caldron . . . we . . . flesh**—sneering at Jer. 1:13, when he compared the city to a caldron with its mouth towards the north. "Let Jerusalem be so if you will, and we the flesh, exposed to the raging foe from the north, still its fortifications will secure us from the flame of war outside; the city must stand for our sakes, just as the pot exists for the safety of the flesh in it." In opposition to this God says (vs. 11), "This city shall not be your caldron, to defend you *in* it from the foe *outside*: nay, ye shall be driven out of your imaginary sanctuary and slain *in the border of the land*." "But," says God, in vs. 7, "your slain are the flesh, and this city the caldron; but (not as you fancy shall ye be kept safe *inside*) I will bring you forth *out of the midst of it*"; and again, in ch. 24:3, "Though not a caldron in *your* sense, Jerusalem shall be so in the sense of its being exposed to a consuming foe, and you yourselves in it and with it." **4. prophesy . . . prophesy**—The repetition marks emphatic earnestness. **5. Spirit . . . fell upon me**—stronger than "entered into me" (ch. 2:2; 3:24), implying the zeal of the Spirit of God roused to immediate indignation at the contempt of God shown by the scorners. **I know**—(Ps. 139:1-4). Your scornful jests at My word escape not My notice. **6. your slain**—those on whom you have brought ruin by your wicked counsels. Bloody crimes within the city brought on it a bloody foe from without (ch. 7:23, 24). They had made it a caldron in which to boil the flesh of God's people (Mic. 3:1-3), and eat it by unrighteous oppression; therefore God will make it a caldron in a different sense, one not wherein they may be safe in their guilt, but "out of the midst of" which they shall be "brought forth" (Jer. 34:4, 5). **7. The city** is a caldron to them, but it shall not be so to you. Ye shall meet your doom on the frontier. **8. The** Chaldean sword, to escape which ye abandoned your God, shall be brought on you by God because of that very abandonment of Him. **9. out of the midst thereof**—i.e., of the city, as captives led into the open plain for judgment. **10. in the border of Israel**—on the frontier: at Riblah, in the land of Hamath (cf. II Kings 25:19-21, with I Kings 8:65). **ye shall know that I am the Lord**—by the judgments I inflict (Ps. 9:16). **11.** (*Note*, vs. 3). **12.** (Deut. 12: 30, 31). **13. Pelatiah**—probably the ringleader of the scorners (vs. 1). His being stricken dead (like Ananias, Acts 5:5) was an earnest of the destruction of the rest of the twenty-five, as Ezekiel had foretold, as also of the general ruin. **fell . . . upon . . . face**—(*Note*, ch. 9:8). **wilt thou make a full end of the remnant**—Is Pelatiah's destruction to be the token of the destruction of all, even of the remnant? The people regarded Pelatiah as a mainstay of the city. His name (derived from a *Hebrew* root, "a remnant," or else "God delivers") suggested hope. Is that hope, asks Ezekiel, to be disappointed? **15. thy brethren . . . brethren**—The repetition implies, "Thy real brethren" are no longer the priests at Jerusalem with whom thou art connected by the *natural* ties of blood and common temple service, but thy fellow exiles on the Chebar, and the house of Israel whosoever of them belong to the remnant to be spared. **men of thy kindred**—lit., "of thy redemption," i.e., the nearest relatives, whose duty it was to do the part of Goel, or vindicator and redeemer of a forfeited inheritance (Lev. 25:25). Ezekiel, seeing the priesthood doomed to destruction, as a priest, felt anxious to vindicate their cause, as if they were his nearest kinsmen and he their Goel. But he is told

to look for his true kinsmen in those, his fellow exiles, whom his natural kinsmen at Jerusalem despised, and he is to be their vindicator. Spiritual ties, as in the case of Levi (Deut. 33:9), the type of Messiah (Matt. 12:47-50) are to supersede natural ones where the two clash. The hope of better days was to rise from the despised exiles. The gospel principle is shadowed forth here, that the despised of men are often the chosen of God and the highly esteemed among men are often an abomination before Him (Luke 16:15; I Cor. 1:26-28). "No door of hope but in the valley of Achor" ("trouble," Hos. 2:15), [FAIRBAIRN]. **Get you far . . . unto us is this land**—the contemptuous words of those left still in the city at the carrying away of Jeconiah to the exiles, "However far ye be outcasts from the Lord and His temple, *we* are secure in our possession of the land." **16. Although**—anticipating the objection of the priests at Jerusalem, that the exiles were "cast far off." Though this be so, and they are far from the outer temple at Jerusalem, I will be their asylum or sanctuary instead (Ps. 90:1; 91:9; Isa. 8:14). My shrine is the humble heart: a preparation for gospel catholicity when the local and material temple should give place to the spiritual (Isa. 57:15; 66:1; Mal. 1:11; John 4:21-24; Acts 7: 48, 49). The trying discipline of the exile was to chasten the outcasts so as to be meet recipients of God's grace, for which the carnal confidence of the priests disqualified them. The dispersion served the end of spiritualizing and enlarging the views even of the better Jews, so as to be able to worship God *everywhere* without a material temple; and, at the same time, it diffused some knowledge of God among the greatest Gentile nations, thus providing materials for the gathering in of the Christian Church among the Gentiles; so marvellously did God overrule a present evil for an ultimate good. Still more does all this hold good in the present much longer dispersion which is preparing for a more perfect and universal restoration (Isa. 2:2-4; Jer. 3:16-18). Their long privation of the temple will prepare them for appreciating the more, but without Jewish narrowness, the temple that is to be (chs. 40-44). **a little**—rather, "for a little season"; No matter how long the captivity may be, the seventy years will be but as a little season, compared with their long subsequent settlement in their land. This holds true only partially in the case of the first restoration; but as in a few centuries they were dispersed again, the full and permanent restoration is yet future (Jer. 24:6). **17.** (Ch. 28:25; 34:13; 36: 24.) **18.** They have eschewed every vestige of idolatry ever since their return from Babylon. But still the Shekinah glory had departed, the ark was not restored, nor was the second temple strictly inhabited by God until He came who made it more glorious than the first temple (Hag. 2:9); even then His stay was short, and ended in His being rejected; so that the full realization of the promise must still be future. **19. I will give them**—lest they should claim to *themselves* the praise given them in vs. 18, God declares it is to be *the free gift of His Spirit*. **one heart**—not *singleness*, i.e., uprightness, but *oneness* of heart in all, *unanimously* seeking Him in contrast to their state at that time, when only single scattered individuals sought God (Jer. 32:39; Zeph. 3:9) [HENGSTENBERG]. Or, "content with *one God*," not distracted with "the many detestable things" (vs. 18; I Kings 18:21; Hos. 10:2) [CALVIN]. **new spirit** —(Ps. 51:10; Jer. 31:33). Realized fully in the "new creature" of the New Testament (II Cor. 5:17); having new motives, new rules, new aims. **stony**

heart—like "adamant" (Zech. 7:12); the natural heart of every man. **heart of flesh**—impressible to what is good, tender. **20. walk in my statutes**—Regeneration shows itself by its fruits (Gal. 5:22, 25). **they ... my people, ... I ... their God**—(Ch. 14:11; 36: 28; 37:27; Jer. 24:7). In its fullest sense still future (Zech. 13:9). **21. whose heart ... after ... heart of ... detestable things**—The repetition of "heart" is emphatic, signifying that the heart of those who so obstinately clung to idols, impelled itself to fresh superstitions in one continuous tenor [CALVIN]. Perhaps it is implied that they and their idols are much alike in character (Ps. 115:8). The *heart* walks astray first, the feet follow. **recompense ... way upon ... heads**—They have abandoned Me, so will I abandon them; they profaned My temple, so will I profane it by the Chaldeans (ch. 9:10). **23.** The Shekinah glory now moves from the east gate (ch. 10:4, 19) to the Mount of Olives, altogether abandoning the temple. The mount was chosen as being the height whence the missiles of the foe were about to descend on the city. So it was from it that Jesus ascended to heaven when about to send His judgments on the Jews; and from it He predicted its overthrow before His crucifixion (Matt. 24:3). It is also to be the scene of His return in person to deliver His people (Zech. 14:4), when He shall come by the same way as He went, "the way of the east" (ch. 43:2). **24. brought me in a vision**—not in actual fact, but in ecstatic vision. He had been as to the outward world all the time before the elders (ch. 8:3) in Chaldea; he now reports what he had witnessed with the inner eye. **25. things ... showed me**—lit., "words"; an appropriate expression; for the word communicated to him was not simply a word, but one clothed with outward symbols "shown" to him as in the sacrament, which Augustine terms "the visible word" [CALVIN].

CHAPTER 12

Vss. 1-28. EZEKIEL'S TYPICAL MOVING TO EXILE: PROPHECY OF ZEDEKIAH'S CAPTIVITY AND PRIVATION OF SIGHT: THE JEWS' UNBELIEVING SURMISE AS TO THE DISTANCE OF THE EVENT REPROVED. **1, 2. eyes to see, and see not, ... ears to hear, and hear not**—fulfilling the prophecy of Deuteronomy 29:4, here quoted by Ezekiel (cf. Isa. 6:9; Jer. 5:21). Ezekiel needed often to be reminded of the people's perversity, lest he should be discouraged by the little effect produced by his prophecies. Their "not seeing" is the result of perversity, not incapacity. They are wilfully blind. The persons most interested in this prophecy were those dwelling at Jerusalem; and it is among them that Ezekiel was transported in spirit, and performed in vision, not outwardly, the typical acts. At the same time, the symbolical prophecy was designed to warn the exiles at Chebar against cherishing hopes, as many did in opposition to God's revealed word, of returning to Jerusalem, as if that city was to stand; externally living afar off, their hearts dwelt in that corrupt and doomed capital. **3. stuff for removing**—rather, "an exile's outfit," the articles proper to a person going as an exile, a staff and knapsack, with a supply of food and clothing; so in Jeremiah 46:19, *Margin*, "instruments of captivity," i.e., the needful equipments for it. His simple announcements having failed, he is symbolically to give them an ocular demonstration conveyed by a word-painting of actions performed in vision. **consider**—(Deut. 32:29). **4. by day**—in broad daylight, when all can see thee. **at even**—not

contradicting the words "by day." The baggage was to be sent before *by day*, and Ezekiel was to follow *at nightfall* [GROTIUS]; or, the preparations were to be made by day, the actual departure was to be effected at night [HENDERSON]. **as they that go forth into captivity**—lit., as the goings forth of the captivity, i.e., of the captive band of exiles, viz., amid the silent darkness: typifying Zedekiah's flight by night on the taking of the city (Jer. 39:4; 52:7). **5. Dig**—as Zedekiah was to escape like one digging through a wall, furtively to effect an escape (vs. 12). **carry out**—viz., "thy stuff" (vs. 4). **thereby**—by the opening in the wall. Zedekiah escaped "by the gate betwixt the two walls" (Jer. 39:4). **6. in ... twilight**—rather, "in the dark." So in Genesis 15:17, "it" refers to "thy stuff." **cover thy face**—as one who muffles his face, afraid of being recognized by anyone meeting him. So the Jews and Zedekiah should make their exit stealthily and afraid to look around, so hurried should be their flight [CALVIN]. **sign**—rather, a portent, viz., for evil. **9. What doest thou?** —They ask not in a docile spirit, but making a jest of his proceedings. **10. burden**—i.e., weighty oracle. **the prince**—The very man Zedekiah, in whom they trust for safety, is to be the chief sufferer. JOSEPHUS (*Antiquities*, 10.7) reports that Ezekiel sent a copy of this prophecy to Zedekiah. As Jeremiah had sent a letter to the captives at the Chebar, which was the means of calling forth at first the agency of Ezekiel, so it was natural for Ezekiel to send a message to Jerusalem confirming the warnings of Jeremiah. The prince, however, fancying a contradiction between ch. 12:13; "he shall not see Babylon," and Jeremiah 24:8, 9, declaring he should be carried to Babylon, believed neither. Seeming discrepancies in Scripture on deeper search prove to be hidden harmonies. **11. sign**—*portent of evil* to come (ch. 24:27; Zech. 3:8, *Margin*). Fulfilled (II Kings 25: 1-7; Jer. 52:1-11). **12. prince ... among them**—lit., that is in the midst of them, i.e., on whom the eyes of all are cast, and "under whose shadow" they hope to live (Lam. 4:20). **shall bear**—viz., his "stuff for removing"; his equipments for his journey. **cover his face, that he see not the ground**—*Note*, vs. 6; the symbol in vs. 6 is explained in this verse. He shall muffle his face so as not to be recognized: a humiliation for a king! **13. My net**—the Chaldean army. He shall be inextricably entangled in it, as in the meshes of a net. It is *God's* net (Job 19:6). Babylon was God's instrument (Isa. 10:5). Called "a net" (Hab. 1:14-16). **bring him to Babylon ...;** yet shall he not see it—because he should be deprived of sight before he arrived there (Jer. 52:11). **14. all ... about him**—his satellites: his bodyguard. **bands**—lit., the wings of an army (Isa. 8:8). **draw out ... sword after them**—(*Note*, ch. 5:2, 12). **16. I will leave a few ... that they may declare ... abominations**—God's purpose in scattering a remnant of Jews among the Gentiles; viz., not only that they themselves should be weaned from idolatry (see vs. 15), but that by their own *word*, as also *by their whole state as exiles,* they should make God's righteousness manifest among the Gentiles, as vindicated in their punishment for their sins (cf. Isa. 43:10; Zech. 8:13). **18.** Symbolical representation of the famine and fear with which they should eat their scanty morsel, in their exile, and especially at the siege. **19. people of the land**—the Jews "in the land" of Chaldea who thought themselves miserable as being exiles and envied the Jews left in Jerusalem as fortunate. **land of Israel**—contrasted with "the people in the land" of Chaldea. So far from being fortunate as the exiles in Chaldea regarded them, the Jews in Jerusalem are truly miserable, for the worst is before them, whereas the exiles have escaped the miseries of the coming siege. **land ... desolate from all that is therein**—lit., "that the land (viz., Judea) may be despoiled of the fulness thereof"; emptied of the inhabitants and abundance of flocks and corn with which it was filled. **because of ... violence**—(Ps. 107:34). **20. the cities**—left in Judea after the destruction of Jerusalem. **22. proverb**—The infidel scoff, that the threatened judgment was so long in coming, it would not come at all, had by frequent repetition come to be a "proverb" with them. This skeptical habit contemporary prophets testify to (Jer. 17:15; 20:7; Zeph. 1:12). Ezekiel, at the Chebar, thus sympathizes with Jeremiah and strengthens his testimony at Jerusalem. The *tendency* to the same scoff showed itself in earlier times, but had not then developed into a settled "proverb" (Isa. 5:19; Amos 5:18). It shall again be the characteristic of the last times, when "faith" shall be regarded as an antiquated thing (Luke 18:8), seeing that it remains stationary, whereas worldly arts and sciences progress, and when the "continuance of all things from creation" will be the argument against the possibility of their being suddenly brought to a standstill by the coming of the Lord (Isa. 66:5; II Pet. 3:3, 4). The very long-suffering of God, which ought to lead men to repentance, is made an argument against His word (Eccles. 8:11; Amos 6:3). **days ... prolonged ... vision faileth**—their twofold argument: (1) The predictions shall not come to pass till long after our time. (2) They shall fail and prove vain shadows. God answers both in vss. 23, 25. **23. effect**—lit., "the word," viz., fulfilled; i.e., the effective fulfilment of whatever the prophets have spoken is at hand. **24. no more ... vain vision ... flattering divination**—All those false prophets (Lam. 2:14), who "flattered" the people with promises of peace and safety, shall be detected and confounded by the event itself. **25. word ... shall come to pass**—in opposition to their scoff "the vision faileth" (vs. 22). The repetition, "I will speak ... speak ..." (or as FAIRBAIRN, "For I, Jehovah, will speak whatever word I shall speak, and it shall be done") implies that whenever God speaks, the effect must follow; for God, who speaks, is not divided in Himself (vs. 28; Isa. 55:11; Dan. 9:12; Luke 21:33). **no more prolonged**—in opposition to the scoff (vs. 22), "The days are prolonged." **in your days**—while you are living (cf. Matt. 24:34). **27.** Not a mere repetition of the scoff (vs. 22); there the *scoffers* asserted that the evil was so often threatened and postponed, it must have no reality; here *formalists* do not go so far as to deny that a day of evil is coming, but assert it is still far off (Amos 6:3). The transition is easy from this carnal security to the gross infidelity of the former class.

CHAPTER 13

Vss. 1-23. DENUNCIATION OF FALSE PROPHETS AND PROPHETESSES; THEIR FALSE TEACHINGS, AND GOD'S CONSEQUENT JUDGMENTS. **1.** As ch. 12 denounced the false expectations of the people, so this denounces the false leaders who fed those expectations. As an independent witness, Ezekiel confirms at the Chebar the testimony of Jeremiah (ch. 29:21, 31) in his letter from Jerusalem to the captive exiles, against the false prophets; of these some were conscious knaves, others fanatical dupes of their own frauds; e.g., Ahab, Zedekiah, and Shemaiah. Hananiah must have believed his own lie, else he

would not have specified so *circumstantial* details (Jer. 28:2-4). The conscious knaves gave only *general* assurances of peace (Jer. 5:31; 6:14; 14:13). The language of Ezekiel has plain references to the similar language of Jeremiah (e.g., Jeremiah 23:9-38); the bane of false prophecy, which had its stronghold in Jerusalem, having in some degree extended to the Chebar; this chapter, therefore, is primarily intended as a message to those still in the Jewish metropolis; and, secondarily, for the good of the exiles at the Chebar. **2. that prophesy**—viz., a speedy return to Jerusalem. **out of ... own hearts**—alluding to the words of Jeremiah (Jer. 23:16, 26); i.e., what they prophesied was what they and the people *wished*; the wish was father to the thought. The people *wished* to be deceived, and so were deceived. They were inexcusable, for they had among them true prophets (who spoke not *their own* thoughts, but as they were moved by the Holy Ghost, II Peter 1:21), whom they might have known to be such, but they did not wish to know (John 3:19). **3. foolish**—though vaunting as though exclusively possessing "wisdom" (I Cor. 1:19-21); the fear of God being the only beginning of wisdom (Ps. 111:10). **their own spirit**—instead of the Spirit of God. A threefold distinction lay between the false and the true prophets: (1) The source of their messages respectively; of the false, "their own hearts"; of the true, an object presented to the spiritual sense (named from the noblest of the senses, a *seeing*) by the Spirit of God as from without, not produced by their own natural powers of reflection. The word, the body of the thought, presented itself not audibly to the natural sense, but directly to the spirit of the prophet; and so the perception of it is properly called a *seeing*, he perceiving that which thereafter forms itself in his soul as the cover of the external word [DELITZSCH]; hence the peculiar expression, *seeing the word of God* (Isa. 2:1; 13:1; Amos 1:1; Mic. 1:1). (2) The point aimed at; the false "walking after their own spirit"; the true, after the Spirit of God. (3) The result; the false saw nothing, but spake as if they had seen; the true had a vision, not subjective, but objectively real [FAIRBAIRN]. A refutation of those who set the *inward* word above the *objective*, and represent the Bible as flowing subjectively from the inner light of its writers, not from the revelation of the Holy Ghost from without. "They are impatient to get possession of the kernel without its fostering shell—they would have Christ without the Bible" [BENGEL]. **4. foxes**—which cunningly "spoil the vines" (Song of Sol. 2:15), Israel being the vineyard (Ps. 80:8-15; Isa. 5:1-7; 27:2; Jer. 2:21); their duty was to have guarded it from being spoiled, whereas they themselves spoiled it by corruptions. **in ... deserts**—where there is nothing to eat; whence the foxes become so ravenous and crafty in their devices to get food. So the prophets wander in Israel, a moral desert, unrestrained, greedy of gain which they get by craft. **5. not gone up into ... gaps**—metaphor from *breaches* made in a wall, to which the defenders ought to betake themselves in order to repel the entrance of the foe. The breach is that made in the theocracy through the nation's sin; and, unless it be made up, the vengeance of God will break in through it. Those who would advise the people to repentance are the restorers of the breach (ch. 22:30; Ps. 106:23, 30). **hedge**—the law of God (Ps. 80:12; Isa. 5:2, 5); by violating it, the people stripped themselves of the *fence* of God's protection and lay exposed to the foe. The false prophets did not try to repair the evil by bringing back the people to the law with good counsels, or by checking the bad with reproofs. These two duties answer to the double office of defenders in case of a breach made in a wall: (1) To repair the breach from within; (2) To oppose the foe from without. **to stand**— i.e., that the city may "stand." **in . . . day of . . . Lord** —In the day of the battle which God wages against Israel for their sins, ye do not try to stay God's vengeance by prayers, and by leading the nation to repentance. **6. made others to hope . . .**—rather, "they *hoped*" to confirm (i.e., make good) their word, by the event corresponding to their prophecy. The *Hebrew* requires this [HÄVERNICK]. Also the parallel clause, "they have *seen* vanity," implies that they believed their own lie (II Thess. 2:11). Subjective revelation is false unless it rests on the objective. **8. I am against you**—rather understand, "I *come* against you," to punish your wicked profanation of My name (cf. Rev. 2:5, 16). **9. mine hand**—My power in vengeance. **not . . . in . . . assembly**—rather, the "council"; "They shall not occupy the honorable office of *councillors* in the senate of elders after the return from Babylon" (Ezra 2:1, 2). **neither . . . written in . . . Israel**— They shall not even have a place in the *register* kept of all *citizens'* names; they shall be erased from it, just as the names of those who died in the year, or had been deprived of citizenship for their crimes. were at the annual revisal erased. Cf. Jeremiah 17:13; Luke 10:20; Revelation 3:5, as to those *spiritually* Israelites; John 1:47, and those not so. Literally fulfilled (Ezra 2:59, 62; cf. Neh. 7:5; Ps. 69:28). **neither . . . enter . . . land**—They shall not so much as be allowed to come back at all to their country. **10. Because, even because**—The repetition heightens the emphasis. **Peace**—*safety* to the nation. Ezekiel confirms Jeremiah 6:14; 8:11. **one**—lit., "this one"; said contemptuously, as in II Chronicles 28:22. **a wall**—rather, a loose wall. Ezekiel had said that the false prophets did not "go up into the gaps, or make up the breaches" (vs. 5), as good architects do; now he adds that they make a bustling show of anxiety about repairing the wall; but it is without right mortar, and therefore of no use. **one . . . others**—besides *individual* effort, they *jointly co-operated* to delude the people. **daubed . . . with untempered mortar**—as sand without lime, mud without straw [GROTIUS]. FAIRBAIRN translates, "plaster it with whitewash." But besides the hypocrisy of merely *outwardly* "daubing" to make the wall look fair (Matt. 23:27, 29; Acts 23:3), there is implied the unsoundness of the wall from the absence of *true uniting cement;* the "untempered cement" answering to *the lie* of the prophets, who say, *in support of their prophecies,* "Thus saith the Lord, when the Lord hath not spoken" (ch. 22:28). **11. overflowing**—*inundating;* such as will at once wash away the mere clay mortar. The three most destructive agents shall co-operate against the wall —wind, rain, and hailstones. These last in the East are more out of the regular course of nature and are therefore often particularly specified as the instruments of God's displeasure against His foes (Exod. 9:18; Josh. 10:11; Job 38:22; Ps. 18:12, 13; Isa. 28:2; 30:30; Rev. 16:21). The *Hebrew* here is, lit., "stones of ice." They fall in Palestine at times an inch thick with a destructive velocity. The personification heightens the vivid effect, "O ye hailstones." The Chaldeans will be the violent agency whereby God will unmask and refute them, overthrowing their edifice of lies. **12. shall it not be said**—Your vanity and folly shall be so manifested that it shall pass into a proverb, "Where is the daub-

ing?" **13.** God repeats, *in His own name,* as the Source of the coming calamity, what had been expressed generally in vs. 11. **14.** The repetition of the same threat is to awaken the people out of their dream of safety by the *certainty* of the event. **foundation**—As the "wall" represents the security of the nation, so the "foundation" is *Jerusalem,* on the fortifications of which they rested their confidence. GROTIUS makes the "foundation" refer to *the false principles* on which they rested; vs. 16 supports the former view. **16. prophesy concerning Jerusalem**— With all their "seeing visions of peace for her," they cannot ensure peace or safety to themselves. **17. set thy face**—put on a bold countenance, fearlessly to denounce them (ch. 3:8, 9; Isa. 50:7). **daughters** —the false prophetesses; alluded to only here; elsewhere the guilt specified in the women is the active share they took in maintaining idolatry (ch. 8:14). It was only in extraordinary emergencies that God bestowed prophecy on women, e.g. on Miriam, Deborah, Huldah (Exod. 15:20; Judg. 4:4; II Kings 22: 14); so in the last days to come (Joel 2:28). The rareness of such instances enhanced their guilt in pretending inspiration. **18. sew pillows to . . . armholes**—rather, *elbows and wrists,* for which the false prophetesses made cushions to lean on, as a symbolical act, typifying the perfect tranquility which they foretold to those consulting them. Perhaps they made their dupes rest on these cushions in a fancied state of ecstasy after they had made them at first *stand* (whence the expression, "every *stature,*" is used for "men of every *age*"). As the men are said to have built a wall (vs. 10), so the women are said to sew pillows, etc., both alike typifying the "peace" they promised the impenitent. **make kerchiefs**—magical *veils,* which they put over the heads of those consulting them, as if to fit them for receiving a response, that they might be rapt in spiritual trance above the world. **head of every stature**—"men of every age," old and young, great and small, if only these had pay to offer them. **hunt souls**—eagerly trying to allure them to the love of yourselves (Prov. 6:26; II Pet. 2:14), so as unwarily to become your prey. **will ye save . . . souls . . . that come unto you**—Will ye haul after souls, and when they are yours ("come unto you"), will ye *promise them life?* "Save" is explained (vs. 22), "*promising* life" [GROTIUS]. CALVIN explains, "Will ye hunt My people's souls and yet will ye save *your own* souls"; I, the Lord God, will not allow it. But "save" is used (vs. 19) of the false prophetesses *promising life* to the impenitent, so that *English Version* and GROTIUS explain it best. **19. handfuls**—expressing the paltry gain for which they bartered immortal souls (cf. Mic. 3:5, 11; Heb. 12: 16). **They** "polluted" God by making His name the cloak under which they uttered falsehoods. **among my people**—an aggravation of their sin, that they committed it "among the people" whom God had chosen as peculiarly *His own,* and among whom He had His temple. It would have been a sin to have done so even among the Gentiles, who knew not God; much more so among the people of God (cf. Prov. 28:21). **slay . . . souls that should not die, . . .**—to *predict* the slaying or perdition of the godly whom I will save. As true ministers are said to save and slay their hearers, according to the spirit respectively in which these receive their message (II Cor. 2:15, 16), so false ministers imitate them; but they promise safety to those on the broad way to ruin and predict ruin to those on the narrow way of God. **my people that hear your lies**—who are therefore *wilfully* deceived, so that their guilt lies at their own door (John 3:19). **20. I am against your pillows**—i.e., against your lying ceremonial tricks by which ye cheat the people. **to make them fly**—viz., into their snares, as fowlers disturb birds so as to be suddenly caught in the net spread for them. "Fly" is peculiarly appropriate as to those lofty spiritual *flights* to which they pretended to raise their dupes when they veiled their heads with kerchiefs and made them rest on luxurious arm-cushions (vs. 18). **let . . . souls go**—"Ye make them fly" in order to destroy them; "I will let them go" in order to save them (Ps. 91:3; Prov. 6:5; Hos. 9:8). **21. in your hand**—in your power. "My people" are the elect remnant of Israel to be saved. **ye shall know**—by the judgments which ye shall suffer. **22. ye have made . . . the righteous sad**—by *lying* predictions of calamities impending over the godly. **strengthened . . . wicked**—(Jer. 23:14). **heart of . . . righteous . . . hands of . . . wicked**—*Heart* is applied to the righteous because the terrors foretold penetrated to their inmost feelings; *hands,* to the wicked because they were so hardened as not only to despise God in their minds, but also to manifest it in their whole *acts,* as if avowedly waging war with Him. **23. ye shall see no more vanity**—The event shall confute your lies, involving yourselves in destruction (vs. 9; ch. 14:8; 15:7; Mic. 3:6).

CHAPTER 14

Vss. 1-23. HYPOCRITICAL INQUIRERS ARE ANSWERED ACCORDING TO THEIR HYPOCRISY. THE CALAMITIES COMING ON THE PEOPLE; BUT A REMNANT IS TO ESCAPE. **1. elders**—persons holding that dignity among the exiles at the Chebar. GROTIUS refers this to Seraiah and those sent with him *from Judea* (Jer. 51:59). The prophet's reply, first, reflecting on the character of the inquirers, and, secondly, foretelling the calamities coming on Judea, may furnish an idea of the subject of their inquiry. **sat before me**—not at once able to find a beginning of their speech; indicative of anxiety and despondency. **3. heart . . . face**—The *heart* is first corrupted, and then the *outward manifestation* of idol-worship follows; they set their idols *before their eyes.* With all their pretense of consulting God now, they have not even put away their idols *outwardly;* implying gross contempt of God. **"Set up," lit., "raised** aloft"; implying that their idols had gained the supreme *ascendancy* over them. **stumbling block of . . . iniquity**—See Proverbs 3:21, 23, "Let not them (God's laws) depart *from thine eyes,* then . . . thy foot shall not *stumble."* Instead of God's law, which (by being kept before their eyes) would have saved them from stumbling, they set up their idols before their eyes, which proved a stumbling block, causing them to stumble (ch. 7:19). **inquired of at all**—lit., "should I with inquiry be inquired of" by such hypocrites as they are? (Ps. 66:18; Prov. 15:29; 28:9). **4. and cometh**—*and yet* cometh, feigning himself to be a true worshipper of Jehovah. **him that cometh**—so the *Margin Hebrew* reads. But the *text Hebrew* reading is, *"according to it,* according to the multitude of his idols"; the anticipative clause with the pronoun not being pleonastic, but increasing the emphasis of the following clause with the noun. "I will answer," lit., reflexively, "I will Myself (or *for Myself*) answer him." **according to . . . idols**—thus, "answering a fool according to his folly"; making the sinner's sin his punishment; retributive justice (Prov. 1:31; 26:5). **5. That I may take**—i.e., unveil and *overtake with punishment* the

dissimulation and impiety of Israel hid *in their own heart.* Or, rather, "That I may punish them by answering them *after their own hearts";* corresponding to "according to the multitude of his idols" (*Note,* vs. 4); an instance is given in vs. 9; Rom. 1:28; II Thess. 2:11, God giving them up in wrath to their own lie. **idols**—though pretending to "inquire" of Me, "in their hearts" they are "estranged from Me," and love "idols." **6.** Though God so threatened the people for their idolatry (vs. 5), yet He would rather they should avert the calamity by "repentance." **turn** *yourselves*—CALVIN translates, "turn *others"* (viz., the stranger proselytes in the land). As ye have been the advisers of others (see vs. 7, "the stranger that sojourneth in Israel") to idolatry, so bestow at least as much pains in turning them to the truth; the surest proof of repentance. But the parallelism to vss. 3, 4 favors *English Version.* Their sin was twofold: (1) "In their *heart"* or *inner* man; (2) "Put before their *face,"* i.e., exhibited *outwardly.* So their repentance is generally expressed by "repent," and is then divided into: (1) "Turn *yourselves* (inwardly) from your idols"; (2) "Turn away your *faces* (outwardly) from all your abominations." It is not likely that an exhortation to convert others should come *between* the two affecting themselves. **7. stranger**—the proselyte, tolerated in Israel only on condition of worshipping no God but Jehovah (Lev. 17:8, 9). **inquire of him concerning me**—i.e., concerning My will. **by myself**—not by word, but by deed, i.e., by *judgments, marking My hand and direct agency;* instead of answering him through the prophet he consults. FAIRBAIRN translates, as it is the same *Hebrew* as in the previous clause, "concerning Me," it is natural that God should use *the same expression* in His reply as was used in the consultation of Him. But the *sense,* I think, is the same. The hypocrite inquires of the prophet *concerning God;* and God, instead of replying through the prophet, replies for Himself *concerning Himself.* **8. make him a sign**—lit., "I will destroy him so as to become a sign"; it will be no ordinary destruction, but such as will make him be an object pointed at with wonder by all, as Korah, etc. (Num. 26:10; Deut. 28:37). **9. I the Lord have deceived that prophet**—not directly, but through Satan and his ministers; not merely permissively, but by overruling their evil to serve the purposes of *His righteous judgment,* to be a touchstone to separate the precious from the vile, and to "prove" His people (Deut. 13:3; I Kings 22:23; Jer. 4:10; II Thess. 2:11, 12). Evil comes not from God, though God overrules it to serve His will (Job 12:16; Jas. 1:3). This declaration of God is intended to answer their objection, "Jeremiah and Ezekiel are but two opposed to the many prophets who announce 'peace' to us." "Nay, deceive not yourselves, those prophets of yours are deluding you, and I permit them to do so as a righteous judgment on your wilful blindness." **10.** As they dealt deceitfully with God by seeking answers of peace without repentance, so God would let them be dealt with deceitfully by the prophets whom they consulted. God would chastise their sin with a corresponding sin; as they rejected the safe directions of the true light, He would send the pernicious delusions of a false one; prophets would be given them who should re-echo the deceitfulness that already wrought in their own bosom, to their ruin [FAIRBAIRN]. The people had themselves alone to blame, for they were long ago forewarned how to discern and to treat a false prophet (Deut. 13:3); the very existence of such deceivers among them was a sign of God's judicial displeasure (cf. in Saul's case, I Sam. 16:14; 28:6, 7). They and the prophet, being dupes of a common delusion, should be involved in a common ruin. **11.** Love was the spring of God's very judgments on His people, who were incurable by any other process (ch. 11:20; 37:27). **12.** The second part of the chapter: the effect which the presence of a few righteous persons was to have on the purposes of God (cf. Gen. 18:24-32). God had told Jeremiah that the guilt of Judah was too great to be pardoned even for the intercession of Moses and Samuel (Ps. 99:6; Jer. 14:2; 15:1), which had prevailed formerly (Exod. 32:11-14; Num. 14:13-20; I Sam. 7:8-12), implying the extraordinary heinousness of their guilt, since in *ordinary* cases "the effectual fervent prayer of a righteous man [for others] availeth much" (Jas. 5:16). Ezekiel supplements Jeremiah by adding that not only those two once successful *intercessors,* but not even the three pre-eminently *righteous* men, Noah, Daniel, and Job, could stay God's judgments by their righteousness. **13. staff of ... bread**—on which man's existence is supported as on a staff (ch. 4:16; 5:16; Lev. 26:26; Ps. 104:15; Isa. 3:1). I will send a famine. **14. Noah, Daniel ... Job**—specified in particular as having been saved from overwhelming calamities for their personal righteousness. Noah had the members of his family alone given to him, amidst the general wreck. Daniel saved from the fury of the king of Babylon the three youths (Dan. 2:17, 18, 48, 49). Though his *prophecies* mostly were later than those of Ezekiel, his *fame for piety and wisdom* was already established, and the events recorded in Daniel 1, 2 had transpired. The Jews would naturally, in their fallen condition, pride themselves on one who reflected such glory on his nation at the heathen capital, and would build vain hopes (here set aside) on his influence in averting ruin from them. Thus the objection to the authenticity of Daniel from this passage vanishes. "Job" forms the climax (and is therefore put out of chronological order), having not even been left a son or a daughter, and having had himself to pass through an ordeal of suffering before his final deliverance, and therefore forming the most simple instance of the righteousness of God, which would save the righteous themselves alone in the nation, and that after an ordeal of suffering, but not spare even a son or daughter for their sake (vss. 16, 18, 20; cf. Jer. 7:16; 11:14; 14:11). **deliver ... souls by ... righteousness**—(Prov. 11:4); not the righteousness of works, but that of grace, a truth less clearly understood under the law (Rom. 4:3). **15-21.** The argument is cumulative. He first puts the case of the land sinning so as to fall under the judgment of a famine (vs. 13); then (vs. 15) "noisome beasts" (Lev. 26:22); then "the sword"; then, worst of all, "pestilence." The three most righteous of men should deliver only themselves in these several four cases. In vs. 21 he concentrates the whole in one mass of condemnation. If Noah, Daniel, Job, could not deliver the land, when deserving only *one* judgment, "how much more" when all *four* judgments combined are justly to visit the land for sin, shall these three righteous men not deliver it. **19. in blood**—not literally. In *Hebrew,* "blood" expresses every premature kind of death. **21. How much more**—lit., "Surely shall it be so now, when I send ...." If none could avert *the one only* judgment incurred, *surely now,* when all four are incurred by sin, *much more* impossible it will be to deliver the land. **22. Yet ... a remnant**—not of righteous persons, but some of the guilty who should "come forth" from the destruction of Jerusalem to Babylon, to lead a life of hopeless exile there. The reference here is to judgment, not mercy, as vs. 23 shows. **ye shall see their ... doings; and ... be comforted**—Ye, the exiles at the Chebar, who now murmur at God's judgment about to be inflicted on Jerusalem as harsh, when ye shall see the wicked "ways" and character of the escaped remnant, shall acknowledge that both Jerusalem and its inhabitants deserved their fate; his recognition of the righteousness of the judgment will reconcile you to it, and so ye shall be "comforted" under it [CALVIN]. Then would follow mercy to the elect remnant, though *that* is not referred to here, but in ch. 20:43. **23. they shall comfort you**—not in words, but by your recognizing in their manifest guilt, that God had not been unjustly severe to them and the city.

CHAPTER 15

Vss. 1-8. THE WORTHLESSNESS OF THE VINE AS WOOD ESPECIALLY WHEN BURNT, IS THE IMAGE OF THE WORTHLESSNESS AND GUILT OF THE JEWS, WHO SHALL PASS FROM ONE FIRE TO ANOTHER. This chapter represents, in the way of a brief introduction, what ch. 16 details minutely. **2, 3.** What has the vine-*wood* to make it pre-eminent above other forest-*wood?* Nothing. Nay, the reverse. Other trees yield useful timber, but vine-wood is soft, brittle, crooked, and seldom large; not so much as a "pin" (the large wooden peg used inside houses in the East to hang household articles on, Isa. 22:23-25) can be made of it. Its sole excellency is that it should bear fruit; when it does not bear fruit, it is not only not better, but inferior to other trees: so if God's people lose their distinctive excellency by not bearing fruits of righteousness, they are more unprofitable than the worldly (Deut. 32:32), for they are the vine; the sole end of their being is to bear fruit to His glory (Ps. 80:8, 9; Isa. 5:1, etc.; Jer. 2:21; Hos. 10:1; Matt. 21:33). In all respects, except in their being planted by God, the Jews were inferior to other nations, as Egypt, Babylon, etc., e.g., in antiquity, extent of territory, resources, military power, attainments in arts and sciences. **2.** or than **a branch**—rather, in apposition with "the vine tree." Omit "*or than.*" What superiority has the vine *if it be but a branch among the trees of the forest,* i.e., if, as having no fruit, it lies cut down among other woods of trees? **4. cast into ... fire**—(John 15:6). **both the ends**—the north kingdom having been already overturned by Assyria under Tiglath-pileser; the south being pressed on by Egypt (II Kings 23:29-35). **midst of it is burned**—rather, "is on flame"; viz., Jerusalem, which had now caught the flame by the attack of Nebuchadnezzar. **Is it meet for any work**—"it," i.e., the scorched part still remaining. **5.** If useless before, much more so when almost wholly burnt. **6.** So will I give the inhabitants of Jerusalem, as being utterly unprofitable (Matt. 21:33-41; 25:30; Mark 11:12-14; Luke 13:6-9) in answering God's design that they should be witnesses for Jehovah before the heathen (Matt. 3:10; 5:13). **7. from one fire ... another**—(Cf. Isa. 24:18). "Fire" means here every kind of calamity (Ps. 66:12). The Jewish fugitives shall escape from the ruin of Jerusalem, only to fall into some other calamity. **8. trespass**—rather, "they have perversely fallen into perverse rebellion." The Jews were not merely *sinners* as the other nations, but *revolters* and *apostates.* It is one thing to neglect what we know not, but quite another thing to despise what we profess to worship [JEROME], as the Jews did towards God and the law.

CHAPTER 16

Vss. 1-63. DETAILED APPLICATION OF THE PARABOLICAL DELINEATION OF CHAPTER 15 TO JERUSALEM PERSONIFIED AS A DAUGHTER. 1. Taken up by God's gratuitous favor from infancy (vss. 1-7); 2. and, when grown up, joined to Him in spiritual marriage (vss. 8-14); 3. her unfaithfulness, her sin (vss. 15-34); 4. the judgment (vss. 35-52); 5. her unlooked-for restoration (vss. 53 to the close). **2. cause Jerusalem to know**—Men often are so blind as not to perceive their guilt which is patent to all. "Jerusalem" represents the whole kingdom of Judah. **3. birth ... nativity**—thy origin and birth; lit., "thy diggings" (cf. Isa. 51:1) "and thy bringings forth." **of ... Canaan**—in which Abraham, Isaac, and Jacob sojourned before going to Egypt, and from which thou didst derive far more of thy innate characteristics than from the virtues of those thy progenitors (ch. 21:30). **an Amorite ... an Hittite** —These, being the most powerful tribes, stand for the whole of the Canaanite nations (cf. Josh. 1:4; Amos 2:9), which were so abominably corrupt as to have been doomed to utter extermination by God (Lev. 18:24, 25, 28; Deut. 18:12). Translate rather, *"the* Amorite ... *the* Canaanite," i.e., these two tribes personified; their wicked characteristics, respectively, were concentrated in the parentage of Israel (Gen. 15:16). "The Hittite" is made their "mother"; alluding to Esau's wives, daughters of *Heth,* whose ways vexed Rebekah (Gen. 26:34, 35; 27:46), but pleased the degenerate descendants of Jacob, so that these are called, in respect of morals, children of the Hittite (cf. vs. 45). **4.** Israel's helplessness in her first struggling into national existence, under the image of an infant (Hos. 2:3) cast forth without receiving the commonest acts of parental regard. Its very life was a miracle (Exod. 1:15-22). **navel ... not cut**—Without proper attention to the navel cord, the infant just born is liable to die. **neither ... washed in water to supple thee**—i.e., to make the skin soft. Rather, "for purification"; from an *Arabic* root [MAURER]. GESENIUS translates as *Margin,* "that thou mightest (be presented to thy parents to) be *looked* upon," as is customary on the birth of a child. **salted**—Anciently they rubbed infants with salt to make the skin firm. **5. cast ... in ... open field**—The exposure of infants was common in ancient times. **to the loathing of thy person** —referring to the unsightly aspect of the exposed infant. FAIRBAIRN translates, "With contempt (or disdainful indifference) of thy *life.*" **6. when I passed by**—as if a traveller. **polluted in ... blood**—but PISCATOR, "ready to be trodden on." **I said**—In contrast to Israel's helplessness stands God's omnipotent word of grace which bids the outcast little one "live." **in thy blood**—Though thou wast foul with blood, I said, "Live" [GROTIUS]. "Live in thy blood," i.e., Live, but live a life exposed to many deaths, as was the case in the beginnings of Israel's national existence, in order to magnify the grace of God [CALVIN]. The former view is preferable. Spiritually, till the sinner is made sensible of his abject helplessness, he will not appreciate the provisions of God's grace. **7. caused ... to multiply**— lit., "I ... made thee a myriad." **bud of ... field**— the produce of the field. In 250 years they increased from seventy-five persons to eight hundred thousand (Acts 7:14) [CALVIN]. But see Exodus 12: 37, 38. **excellent ornaments**—lit., "ornament of ornaments." **naked ... bare**—(Hos. 2:3). Lit., "nakedness ... bareness" itself; more emphatic. **8. thy time of love**—lit., "loves" (cf. Song of Sol. 2:10-13). Thou wast of marriageable age, but none was willing to marry thee, naked as thou wast. I then regarded thee with a look of grace when the full time of thy deliverance was come (Gen. 15:13, 14; Acts 7:6, 7). It is not she that makes the advance to God, but God to her; she has nothing to entitle her to such notice, yet He regards her not with mere benevolence, but with *love,* such as one cherishes to the person of his wife (Song of Sol. 1:3-6; Jer. 31:3; Mal. 1:2). **spread my skirt over thee**—the mode of espousals (Ruth 3:9). I betrothed thee (Deut. 4: 37; 10:15; Hos. 11:1). The cloak is often used as a bed coverlet in the East. God explains what He means, "I entered into ... covenant with thee," i.e., at Sinai. So Israel became "the wife of God's covenant" (Isa. 54:5; Jer. 3:14; Hos..2:19, 20); Mal. 2:14). **thou ... mine**—(Exod. 19:5; Jer. 2:2). **9. washed I thee**—as brides used to pass through a preparatory purification (Esther 2:12). So Israel, before the giving of the law at Sinai (Exod. 19:14); "Moses sanctified the people, and they washed their clothes." So believers (I Cor. 6:11). **oil**—emblem of the Levitical priesthood, the type of Messiah (Ps. 45:7). **10.** Psalm 45:13, 14, similarly describes the Church (Israel, the appointed mother of Christendom) adorned as a bride (so Isa. 61:10). It is Messiah who provides the wedding garment (Rev. 3:18; 19:8). **badgers' skin**—*tahash;* others translate, "seal skins." They formed the over-covering of the tabernacle, which was, as it were, the nuptial tent of God and Israel (Exod. 26:14), and the material of the shoes worn by the Hebrews on festival days. **fine linen**—used by the priests (Lev. 6:10); emblem of purity. **11.** The marriage gifts to Rebekah (Gen. 24:22, 47). **12. jewel on thy forehead**—rather, "a ring in thy nose" (Isa. 3:21). **a crown**—at once the badge of a bride, and of her being made a queen, as being consort of the King; the very name *Israel* meaning "a prince of God." So they are called "a *kingdom* of priests" (Exod. 19:6; cf. Rev. 1:6). Though the external blessings bestowed on Israel were great, yet not these, but the internal and spiritual, form the main reference in the kingly marriage to which Israel was advanced. **13. flour ... honey ... oil**—These three mixed form the sweetest cakes; not dry bread and leeks as in Egypt. From raiment He passes to food (Deut. 32:13, 14). **exceeding beautiful**—Psalm 48:2, the city; also, Psalm 29:2, the temple. **prosper into a kingdom**—exercising empire over surrounding nations. **14. thy renown ... among ... heathen**—The theocracy reached its highest point under Solomon, when distant potentates heard of his "fame" (I Kings 10:1, etc), e.g., the queen of Sheba, Hiram, etc. (Lam. 2:15). **my comeliness**—It was not thine own, but imparted by Me. **15.** Instead of attributing the glory of her privileges and gifts to God, Israel prided herself on them as her own (Deut. 32:15; Jer. 7:4; Mic. 3:11), and then wantonly devoted them to her idols (Hos. 2:8; cf. Luke 15:12, 13). **playedst ... harlot because of thy renown**—"didst play the wanton upon thy name" [FAIRBAIRN], viz., by allowing thy renown to lead thee into idolatry and leagues with idolaters (Isa. 1:21; 57:8; Jer. 3:2, 6). *English Version* is better, "because of thy renown," i.e., relying on it; answering to "thou didst *trust in* thine own beauty." **his it was**—Thy beauty was yielded up to every passer-by. Israel's zest for the worship of foul idols was but an anxiety to have the approbation of heaven for their carnal lusts, of which the idols were the personification; hence, too, their tendency to wander from Jehovah, who was a restraint on corrupt nature. **16. deckedst ... with divers colours**—or, "didst make ... of divers colors" [FAIRBAIRN]; the metaphor and the literal are here mixed. The high places whereon they sacrificed to Astarte are here compared to *tents of divers colors,* which an impudent harlot would spread to show her house was open to all [CALVIN]. Cf. as to "woven hangings for Astarte" (the right translation for "grove") II Kings 23:7. **the like ... shall not come, neither shall ... be**—rather, "have not come, nor shall be." These thy doings are unparalleled in the past, and shall be so in the future. **17. my gold ... my silver** —(Hag. 2:8). **images of men**—rather, "of the *phallus,*" the Hindoo *lingam,* or membrum virile [HAVERNICK], deified as the emblem of fecundity; man making his lust his god. *English Version,* however, is appropriate; Israel being represented as a *woman* playing the harlot with *"male* images," i.e., images of male gods, as distinguished from female deities. **18. tookest thy ... garments ... coveredst them**—i.e., the idols, as if an adulteress were to cover her paramours with garments which she had received from the liberality of her husband. **my oil**—the holy anointing oil sacred to God (Exod. 30:22-25). Also that used in sacrifices (Lev. 2:1, 2). **19. My meat ... I gave**—(Hos. 2:83). **set it before them**—as a *minchah* or "meat offering" (Lev. 2:1). **a sweet savour**—lit., "a savor of rest," i.e., whereby they might be propitiated, and be at peace ("rest") with you; how ridiculous to seek to propitiate gods of wood! **thus it was**—The fact cannot be denied, for I saw it, and say it was so, saith Jehovah. **20, 21. sons and ... daughters borne unto me**—Though "thy children," yet they belong "unto Me," rather than to thee, for they were born under the immutable covenant with Israel, which even Israel's sin could not set aside, and they have received the sign of adoption as Mine, viz., circumcision. This aggravates the guilt of sacrificing them to Molech. **to be devoured**—not merely to *pass through* the fire, as sometimes children were made to do (Lev. 18: 21) *without hurt,* but to pass through so as to be made *the food* of the flame in honor of idols (Isa. 57:5; Jer. 7:31; 19:5; 32:35, *Notes*). **Is this of thy whoredoms a small matter, that thou hast slain my children**—rather, "Were thy whoredoms a small matter (i.e., not enough, but) that thou hast slain (i.e., must also slay)," etc. As if thy unchastity was not enough, thou hast added this unnatural and sacrilegious cruelty (Mic. 6:7). **22. not remembered ... youth**—Forgetfulness of God's love is the source of all sins. Israel forgot her deliverance by God in the infancy of her national life. See vs. 43, to which vs. 60 forms a lovely contrast (Jer. 2:2, Hos. 11:1). **23. woe, woe unto thee ...**—This parenthetical exclamation has an awful effect coming like a lightning flash of judgment amidst the black clouds of Israel's guilt. **24. eminent place**—rather, "a fornication-chamber," often connected with the impure rites of idolatry; spiritual fornication, on "an eminent place," answering to "fornication-chamber," is mainly meant, with an allusion also to the literal fornication associated with it (Jer. 2:20; 3:2). **25. at every head of the way**—in the most frequented places (Prov. 9:14). **thy beauty ... abhorred, ... opened ... feet to every one**—The wanton advances were all on Israel's part; the idolatrous nations yielded to her nothing in return. She had yielded so much that, like a worn-out prostitute, her tempt-

ers became weary of her. When the Church lowers her testimony for God to the carnal tastes of the world, with a view to conciliation, she loses everything and gains nothing. **26. fornication with ... Egyptians**—alliances with Egypt, cemented by sharing their idolatries. **great of flesh**—of powerful virile parts; fig. for the gross and lustful religion of Egypt (e.g., Isis, etc.), which alone could satisfy the abominable lust of Israel (ch. 20:7, 8; 23:19, 20, 21). **to provoke me**—wantonly and purposely. **27.** The consequent judgments, which, however, proved of no avail in reforming the people (Isa. 9:13; Jer. 5: 3). **delivered thee unto ... Philistines**—(II Kings 16:6; II Chron. 28:18, 19). **ashamed of thy lewd way**—The Philistines were less wanton in idolatry, in that they did not, like Israel, adopt the idols of every foreign country but were content with their own (vs. 57; Jer. 2:11). **28. unsatiable**—Not satisfied with whoredoms with neighbors, thou hast gone off to the distant Assyrians, i.e., hast sought a league with them, and with it adopted their idolatries. **29. multiplied ... fornication in ... Canaan unto Chaldea**—Thou hast multiplied thy idolatries "in Canaan" by sending "unto Chaldea" to borrow from thence the Chaldean rites, to add to the abominations already practised "in Canaan," before the carrying away of Jehoiachin to Chaldea. The name "Canaan" is used to imply that they had made Judea as much the scene of abominations as it was in the days of the corrupt Canaanites. The land had become utterly Canaanitish (ch. 23:14, etc.). **30. weak ... heart**—Sin weakens the *intellect* ("heart") as, on the contrary, "the way of the Lord is strength to the upright" (Prov. 10:29). **31.** Repetition of vs. 24. **not ... as ... harlot ... thou scornest hire**—Unlike an ordinary harlot thou dost prostitute thy person gratis, merely to satisfy thy lust. JEROME translates, "Thou hast not been as a harlot in scorning (i.e., who ordinarily scorns) a hire offered," *in order to get a larger one:* nay, thou hast offered hire thyself to thy lovers (vss. 33, 34). But these verses show *English Version* to be preferable, for they state that Israel prostituted herself, not merely for *any small reward without demanding more,* but for "no reward." **32. instead of her husband**—referring to Numbers 5:19, 20, 29. FAIRBAIRN translates, "whilst under her husband." **33, 34.** Israel hired her paramours, instead of being, like other harlots, hired by them; she also followed them without their following her. **35.** Here begins the threat of wrath to be poured out on her. **36. filthiness**—lit., brass; metaphor for *the lowest part of the person* [CALVIN]. *English Version* is better: thy filthy lewdness is poured out without restraint (cf. Jer. 13:27). As silver is an emblem of purity, *brass* typifies "filthiness," because it easily contracts rust. HENDERSON explains it, "Because thy *money* was lavished on thy lovers (vss. 31, 33, 34). **blood of thy children**—(vs. 20; Jer. 2:34). **37. thy lovers**—the Chaldeans and the Assyrians. The law of retribution is the more signally exemplified by God employing, as His instruments of judgment on Israel, those very nations whose alliance and idols Israel had so eagerly sought, besides giving her up to those who had been always her enemies. "God will make him, who leaves God for the world, disgraced even in the eyes of the world, and indeed the more so the nearer he formerly stood to Himself" [HENGSTENBERG], (Isa. 47:3; Jer. 13:26; Hos. 2:12; Nah. 3:5). **all ... thou hast hated**—the Edomites and Philistines; also Moab and Ammon especially (Deut. 23:3). **I ... will discover thy nakedness**—punishment in kind, as she had "discovered her nakedness through whoredoms" (vs. 36); the sin and its penalty corresponded. I will expose thee to public infamy. **38-40. judge thee, as women that break wedlock**–(Lev. 20:10; cf. vs. 2). In the case of *individual* adulteresses, *stoning* was the penalty (John 8:4, 5). In the case of *communities*, the *sword*. Also apostasy (Deut. 13:10) and sacrificing children to Molech (Lev. 20:1-5) incurred stoning. Thus the penalty was doubly due to Israel; so the other which was decreed against an apostate city (Deut. 13:15, 16) is added, "they shall stone thee with stones and thrust thee through with ... swords." The Chaldeans hurled *stones* on Jerusalem at the siege and slew with the *sword* on its capture. **shed blood ... judged**–(Gen. 9:6). **jealousy**–image taken from the fury of a husband in jealousy shedding the blood of an unfaithful wife, such as Israel had been towards God, her husband spiritually. Lit., "I will *make thee* (to become) *blood* of fury and jealousy." **39. thine eminent place**–lit., "fornication-chamber" (*Note*, vs. 24), the temple which Israel had converted into a place of spiritual fornication with idols, to please the Chaldeans (ch. 23:14-17). **strip thee of ... clothes**–(Ch 23:26; Hos. 2:3). They shall *dismantle* thy city of its walls. **fair jewels**–lit., "vessels of thy fairness" or beauty; the vessels of the temple [GROTIUS]. All the gifts wherewith God hath adorned thee [CALVIN]. **40.** (Ch. 23:10, 47.) Cf. as to the destruction under Titus, Luke 19:43, 44. **41.** The result of the awful judgment shall be, when divine vengeance has run its course, it shall cease. **burn**–(Deut. 13:16; II Kings 25:9). **women**–the surrounding Gentile nations to whom thou shalt be an object of mocking (Ps. 137:7). **I will cause thee to cease ... harlot**–(Ch. 23:27). Thou shalt *no longer be able* to play the harlot *through My judgments*. **thou ... shalt give ... no hire ... any more**–Thou shalt have none to give. **42. my fury ... rest**–when My justice has exacted the full penalty commensurate with thy awful guilt (*Note*, ch. 5:13). It is not a mitigation of the penalty that is here foretold, but such an utter destruction of *all* the guilty that there shall be no need of further punishment [CALVIN]. **43.** (Vs. 22; Ps. 78:42.) In gratitude for God's favors to her in her early history. **fretted me**–(Isa. 63:10; Eph. 4:30). **thou shalt not commit this lewdness above all thine abominations**–i.e., this the wickedness (cf. Zech. 5:8), peculiarly hateful to God, viz., spiritual unchastity or idolatry, over and "above" (i.e., besides) all thine other abominations. I will put it out of thy power to commit it by cutting thee off. FAIRBAIRN translates, "I will not do what is scandalous (viz., encouraging thee in thy sin by letting it pass with impunity) upon all thine abominations"; referring to Leviticus 19:29, the conduct of a father who encouraged his daughter in harlotry. *English Version* is much better. **44. As ... mother ... her daughter**–"*Is*," and "so is," are not in the original; the ellipsis gives the proverb (but two words in the *Hebrew*) epigrammatic brevity. Jerusalem proved herself a true daughter of the Hittite mother in sin (vs. 3). **45. mother's ... that loatheth her husband**–i.e., God (haters of God," Rom. 1:30); therefore the knowledge of the true God had originally been in Canaan, handed down from Noah (hence we find Melchizedek, king of Salem, in Canaan, "priest of the most high God," Gen. 14:18), but Canaan apostatized from it; this was what constituted the blackness of the Canaanites' guilt. **loathed ... children**–whom she put to death in honor of Saturn; a practice common among the Phœnicians. **sister of thy sisters**–Thou art akin in guilt to Samaria and Sodom, to which thou art akin

by birth. Moab and Ammon, the incestuous children of Lot, nephew of Abraham, Israel's progenitor, had their origin from Sodom; so Sodom might be called Judah's sister. Samaria, answering to the ten tribes of Israel, is, of course, sister tu Judah. **46. elder sister ... Samaria ...** *older* than Sodom, to whom Judah was *less nearly related by kindred* than she was to Samaria. Sodom is therefore called her *younger* sister; Samaria, her "elder sister" [GROTIUS]. Samaria is called the "elder," because *in a moral respect more nearly related* to Judah [FAIRBAIRN]. Samaria had made the calves at Dan and Bethel in imitation of the cherubim. **her daughters**–the inferior towns subject to Samaria (cf. Num. 21:25, *Margin*). **left**–The Orientals faced the east in marking the directions of the sky; thus the north was "left," the south "right." **Sodom ... daughters**–Ammon and Moab, offshoots from Sodom; also the towns subject to it. **47. their abominations**–Milcom and Chemosh, the "abominations of Ammon and Moab" (I Kings 11:5, 7). **corrupted more than they**–So it is expressly recorded of Manasseh (II Kings 21:9). **48. Sodom**–(Matt. 11:24). Judah's guilt was not positively, but *relatively*, greater than Sodom's; because it was in the midst of such higher privileges, and such solemn warnings; *a fortiori*, the guilt of unbelievers in the midst of the highest of all lights, viz., the Gospel, is the greatest. **49. pride**–inherited by Moab, her offspring (Isa. 16:6; Jer. 48:26), and by Ammon (Jer. 49:4). God, the heart-searcher, here specifies as Sodom's sin, not merely her notorious lusts, but the secret spring of them, "pride" flowing from "fullness of bread," caused by the fertility of the soil (Gen. 13: 10), and producing "idleness." **abundance of idleness**–lit., "the secure carelessness of ease" or idleness. **neither did she strengthen ... the poor**–Pride is always cruel; it arrogates to itself all things, and despises brethren, for whose needs it therefore has no feeling; as Moab had not for the outcast Jews (Isa. 16:3, 4; Jer. 48:27; Luke 16:19-21; Jas. 5:1-5). **50. haughty**–puffed up with prosperity. **abomination before me**–"sinners *before the Lord*" (Gen. 13: 13); said of those whose sin is so heinous as to cry out to God for immediate judgments; presumptuous sins, daring God *to the face* (Gen. 18:20; 19:5). **I took them away**–(Gen. 19:24). **as I saw good**–rather, "according to what I saw"; referring to Genesis 18:21, where God says, "I will go down, and *see* whether they have done altogether *according* to the cry of it which is come unto Me." **51. Samaria**–the kingdom of the ten tribes of Israel less guilty than Judah; for Judah betrayed greater ingratitude, having greater privileges, viz., the temple, the priesthood, and the regular order of kings. **justified thy sisters**–made them appear almost innocent by comparison with thy guilt (Jer. 3:11; Matt. 12:41, 42). **52. Thou ... which hast judged ... bear thine own** –(Matt. 7:1, 2; Rom. 2:1, 17-23). Judah had judged Sodom (representing the heathen nations) and Samaria (Israel), saying they were justly punished, as if she herself was innocent (Luke 13:2). **thy shame**–ignominious punishment. **53.** Here follows a promise of restoration. Even the sore chastisements coming on Judah would fail to reform its people; God's returning goodness alone would effect this, to show how entirely of grace was to be their restoration. The restoration of her erring sisters is mentioned before hers, even as their punishment preceded hers; so all self-boasting is excluded [FAIRBAIRN]. "Ye shall, indeed, at some time or other return, but Moab and Ammon shall return with you, and some of the ten tribes" [GROTIUS]. **bring again . . . captivity**–i.e., change the affliction into prosperity (so Job 42:10). Sodom itself was not so restored (Jer. 20:16), but Ammon and Moab (her representatives, as sprung from Lot who dwelt in Sodom) were (Jer. 48:47; 49: 6); probably most of the ten tribes and the adjoining nations, Ammon and Moab, etc., were in part restored under Cyrus; but the full realization of the restoration is yet future; *the heathen nations* to be brought to Christ being typified by "Sodom," whose sins they now reproduce (Deut. 32:32). **captivity of thy captives**–lit., "of thy captivities." However, the gracious promise rather begins with the "nevertheless" (vs. 60), not here; for vs. 59 is a threat, not a promise. The sense here thus is, Thou shalt be restored when Sodom and Samaria are, but not till then (vs. 55), i.e., *never.* This applies to the guilty who should be utterly destroyed (vss. 41, 42); but it does not contradict the subsequent promise of restoration to their posterity (Num. 14:29-33), and to the elect remnant of grace [CALVIN]. **54. bear thine own shame**–by being put on a level with those whom thou hast so much despised. **thou art a comfort unto them**–since they see thee as miserable as themselves. It is a kind of melancholy "comfort" to those chastised to see others as sorely punished as themselves (ch. 14:22, 23). **55.** (*Note,* vs. 53.) **56. Sodom was not mentioned**–lit., "was not for a report." Thou didst not deign to mention her name as if her case could possibly apply as a warning to thee, but it did apply (II Pet. 2:6). **57. Before thy wickedness was discovered**–manifested to all, viz., by the punishment inflicted on thee. **thy reproach of . . . Syria and . . . Philistines**–the indignity and injuries done thee by Syria and the Philistines (II Kings 16:5; II Chron. 28:18; Isa. 9: 11, 12). **58. borne thy lewdness**–i.e., the punishment of it (ch. 23:49). I do not treat thee with excessive rigor. Thy sin and punishment are exactly commensurate. **59. the oath**–the covenant between God and Israel (Deut. 29:12, 14). As thou hast despised it, so will I despise thee. No covenant is one-sided; where Israel broke faith, God's promise of favor ceased. **60.** The promise here bursts forth unexpectedly like the sun from the dark clouds. With all her forgetfulness of God, God still remembers her; showing that her redemption is altogether of grace. Contrast "I will remember," with "thou hast not remembered" (vss. 22, 43); also "*My* covenant," with "*Thy* covenant" (vs. 61; Ps. 106:45); then the effect produced on her is (vs. 63) "that thou mayest remember." God's promise was one of *promise* and of *grace.* The law, *in its letter,* was *Israel's* ("thy") *covenant,* and in this restricted view was long subsequent (Gal. 3:17). Israel interpreted it as a covenant of works, which she while boasting of, failed to fulfil, and so fell under its condemnation (II Cor. 3:3, 6). The law, *in its spirit,* contains the germ of the Gospel; the New Testament is the full development of the Old, the husk of the outer form being laid aside when the inner spirit was fulfilled in Messiah. God's covenant with Israel, in the person of Abraham, was the reason why, notwithstanding all her guilt, mercy was, and is, in store for her. Therefore the heathen or Gentile nations must come to her for blessings, not she to them. **everlasting covenant**–(ch. 37:26; II Sam. 23:5; Isa. 55:3). The temporary forms of the law were to be laid aside, that in its permanent and "everlasting" spirit it might be established (Jer. 31:31-37; 32:40; 50:4, 5; Heb. 8:8-13). **61. thou shalt remember**–It is God who first remembers her before she remembers Him and her own ways before Him (vs. 60; ch. 20:43; 36:31). **ashamed**–the fruit of repentance (II Cor. 7:10, 11). None please God unless those who displease themselves; a foretaste of the Gospel (Luke 18:9-14). **I will give them unto thee for daughters**–(Isa. 54:1; 60:3, 4; Gal. 4:26, etc.). All the heathen nations, not merely Sodom and Samaria, are meant by "thy sisters, elder and younger." In Jerusalem first, *individual* believers were gathered into the elect Church. From Jerusalem the Gospel went forth to gather in *individuals* of the Gentiles; and Judah with Jerusalem shall also be the first *nation* which, as such, shall be converted to Christ; and to her the other *nations* shall attach themselves as believers in Messiah, Jerusalem's King (Ps. 110:2; Isa. 2:2, 3). "The king's daughter" in Psalm 45:12-14 is Judah; her "companions," as "the daughter of Tyre," are the nations given to her as converts, here called "daughters." **not by thy covenant**–This does not set aside the Old Testament in its spirit, but in its mere letter on which the Jews had rested, while they broke it: the latter ("thy covenant") was to give place to *God's* covenant of grace and promise in Christ who "fulfilled" the law. God means, "not that thou on thy part hast stood to the covenant, but that 'I am the Lord, I change not' (Mal. 3:6) from My original love to thee in thy youth" (see Rom. 3:3). **62.** (Hos. 2:19, 20.) **thou shalt know that I am the Lord**–not, as elsewhere, by the judgments falling on thee, but by My so marvellously restoring thee through grace. **63. never open thy mouth**–in vindication, or even palliation, of thyself, or expostulation with God for His dealings (Rom. 3: 19), when thou seest thine own exceeding unworthiness, and My superabounding grace which has so wonderfully overcome with love thy sin (Rom. 5: 20). "If we would judge ourselves, we should not be judged" (I Cor. 11:31). **all that thou hast done** –enhancing the grace of God which has pardoned so many and so great sins. Nothing so melts into love and humility as the sense of the riches of God's pardoning grace (Luke 7:47).

CHAPTER 17

Vss. 1-24. PARABLE OF THE TWO GREAT EAGLES, AND THE CROPPING OF THE CEDAR OF LEBANON. JUDAH IS TO BE JUDGED FOR REVOLTING FROM BABYLON, WHICH HAD SET UP ZEDEKIAH INSTEAD OF JEHOIACHIN, TO EGYPT; GOD HIMSELF, AS THE RIVAL OF THE BABYLONIAN KING, IS TO PLANT THE GOSPEL CEDAR OF MESSIAH. The date of the prophecy is between the sixth month of Zedekiah's sixth year of reign and the fifth month of the seventh year after the carrying away of Jehoiachin, i.e., five years before the destruction of Jerusalem [HENDERSON]. **2. riddle** –a continued allegory, expressed enigmatically, requiring more than common acumen and serious thought. The *Hebrew* is derived from a root, "sharp," i.e., calculated to stimulate attention and whet the intellect. Distinct from "fable," in that it teaches not fiction, but fact. Not like the ordinary riddle, designed to puzzle, but to instruct. The "riddle" is here identical with the "parable," only that the former refers to the obscurity, the latter to the likeness of the figure to the thing compared. **3. eagle**–the king of birds. The literal *Hebrew* is, "*the* great eagle." The symbol of the Assyrian supreme god, *Nisroch;* so applied to "the great king" of Babylon, his vicegerent on earth (Jer. 48:40; 49:22). His "wings" are his great forces. Such symbols were familiar to the Jews, who saw them portrayed on the great buildings of Babylon; such as are now seen in the Assyrian remains. **long-winged** —implying the wide extent of his empire. **full of feathers**—when they have been renewed after moulting; and so in the full freshness of renovated youth (Ps. 103:5; Isa. 40:31). Answering to the many peoples which, as tributaries, constituted the strength of Babylon: **divers colours**—the golden eagle, marked with starlike spots, supposed to be the largest of eagles [BOCHART]. Answering to the variety of languages, habits, and costumes of the peoples subject to Babylon. **came unto Lebanon**— continuing the methaphor: as the eagle frequents mountains, not cities. The temple at Jerusalem was called "Lebanon" by the Jews [EUSEBIUS], because its woodwork was wholly of cedars of Lebanon. "The mountain of the Lord's house" (Isa. 2:2). *Jerusalem*, however, is chiefly meant, the chief seat of civil honor, as Lebanon was of external elevation. **took the highest branch**—King Jeconiah, then but eighteen years old, and many of the chiefs and people with him (II Kings 24:8, 12-16). The *Hebrew* for "highest branch" is, properly, the *fleecelike tuft* at the top of the tree. (So in ch. 31:3-14.) The cedar, as a tall tree, is the symbol of kingly elevation (cf. Dan. 4:10-12). **4. land of traffic ... merchants**—Babylon (II Kings 24:15, 16), famous for its transport traffic on the Tigris and Euphrates. Also, by its connection with the Persian Gulf, it carried on much commerce with India. **5. seed of the land**—not a foreign production, but one native in the region; a son of the soil, not a foreigner: Zedekiah, uncle of Jehoiachin, of David's family. **in a fruitful field**—lit., a "field of seed"; i.e., fit for propagating and continuing the seed of the royal family. **as a willow**—derived from a *Hebrew* root, "to overflow," from its fondness for water (Isa. 44:4). Judea was "a land of brooks of *water* and fountains" (Deut. 8:7-9; cf. John 3:23). **6. vine of low stature**—not now, as before, a stately "cedar"; the kingdom of Judah was to be prosperous, but not elevated. **branches turned toward him**—expressing the fealty of Zedekiah as a vassal looking up to Nebuchadnezzar, to whom Judah owed its peace and very existence as a separate state. The "branches" mean his sons and the other princes and nobles. **The roots ... under him**—The stability of Judah depended on Babylon. The repetition "branches" and "springs" is in order to mark the ingratitude of Zedekiah, who, not content with moderate prosperity, revolted from him to whom he had sworn allegiance. **7. another ... eagle**—the king of Egypt (vs. 15). The "long-winged" of vs. 3 is omitted, as Egypt had not such a wide empire and large armies as Babylon. **vine ... bend ... roots towards him**—lit., "thirsted after him with its roots"; expressing the longings after Egypt in the Jewish heart. Zedekiah sought the alliance of Egypt, as though by it he could throw off his dependence on Babylon (II Kings 24:7, 20; II Chron. 36:13; Jer. 37:5, 7). **water it by ... furrows of ... plantation**—i.e., *in* the garden beds (Judea) wherein (the vine) it was planted. Rather, "*by*" or "*out of* the furrows." It refers to the waters of Egypt, the Nile being made to water the fields by means of small canals or "furrows"; these waters are the figure of the auxiliary forces wherewith Egypt tried to help Judah. See the same figure, Isaiah 8:7. But see *Note,* vs. 10, "furrows *where it grew.*" **8. It was planted in a good soil**— It was not want of the necessaries of life, nor oppression on the part of Nebuchadnezzar, which caused Zedekiah to revolt: it was gratuitous ambition, pride, and ingratitude. **9. Shall it prosper?**— Could it be that gratuitous treason should prosper?

God will not allow it. "It," i.e., the vine. **he ... pull up**—i.e., the first eagle, or Nebuchadnezzar. **in all ... leaves of her spring**—i.e., all its springing (sprouting) leaves. **without great power or many**— It shall not need all the forces of Babylon to destroy it; a small division of the army will suffice because God will deliver it into Nebuchadnezzar's hand (Jer. 37:10). **10 being planted**—i.e., *though* planted, **east wind**—The east wind was noxious to vegetation in Palestine; a fit emblem of Babylon, which came from the northeast. **wither in ... furrows where it grew**—Zedekiah was taken at Jericho, on Jewish soil (Jer. 52:8). "It shall wither, although it has furrows from which it expects continual waterings" [CALVIN], (ch. 19:12; Hos. 13:15). **12. Know ye not**—He upbraided them with moral, leading to intellectual, stupidity. **hath taken the king**—Jeconiah or Jehoiachin (II Kings 24:11, 12-16). **13. the king's seed**— Zedekiah, Jeconiah's uncle. **taken ... oath of him** —swearing fealty as a vassal to Nebuchadnezzar (II Chron. 36:13). **also taken the mighty**—as hostages for the fulfilment of the covenant; whom, therefore, Zedekiah exposed to death by his treason. **14. That the kingdom might be base**—i.e., low as to national elevation by being Nebuchadnezzar's dependent; but, at the same time, safe and prosperous, if faithful to the "oath." Nebuchadnezzar dealt sincerely and openly in proposing conditions, and these moderate ones; therefore Zedekiah's treachery was the baser and was a counterpart to their treachery towards God. **15. he rebelled**—God permitted this because of His wrath against Jerusalem (II Kings 24: 20). **horses**—in which Egypt abounded and which were forbidden to Israel to seek from Egypt, or indeed to "multiply" at all (Deut. 17:16; Isa. 31:1, 3; cf. Isa. 36:9). DIODORUS SICULUS (1.45) says that the whole region from Thebes to Memphis was filled with royal stalls, so that 20,000 chariots with two horses in each could be furnished for war. **Shall he prosper?**—The third time this question is asked, with an indignant denial understood (vss. 9, 10). Even the heathen believed that breakers of an oath would not "escape" punishment. **16. in the place where the king dwelleth**—righteous retribution. He brought on himself in the worst form the evil which, in a mild form, he had sought to deliver himself from by perjured treachery, viz., vassalage (ch. 12: 13; Jer. 32:5; 34:3; 52:11). **17. Pharaoh**—Pharaoh-hophra (Jer. 37:7; 44:30), the successor of Necho (II Kings 23:29). **Neither ... make for him**—lit., "*effect* (anything) *with* him," i.e., be of any avail to Zedekiah. Pharaoh did not *act in concert with* him, for he was himself compelled to retire to Egypt. **by casting up mounts ...**—So far from Pharaoh doing so *for* Jerusalem, this was what Nebuchadnezzar did *against* it (Jer. 52:4). CALVIN, MAURER, etc., refer it to *Nebuchadnezzar,* "when Nebuchadnezzar shall cast up mounts." **18. given his hand**—in ratification of the oath (II Kings 10:15; Ezra 10:19), and also in token of subjection to Nebuchadnezzar (I Chron. 29: 24, *Margin;* II Chron. 30:8, *Margin;* Lam. 5:6). **19. mine oath**—The "covenant" being sworn in God's name was really *His* covenant; a new instance in relation to man of the treacherous spirit which had been so often betrayed in relation to God. God Himself must therefore avenge the violation of *His covenant* "on the head" of the perjurer (cf. Ps. 7:16). **20. my net**—(ch. 12:13; 32:3). God entraps him as he had tried to entrap others (Ps. 7:15). This was spoken at least upwards of three years before the fall of Jerusalem (cf. ch. 8:1, with ch. 20:1). **21. all his fugitives**—the soldiers that accompany him in his flight. **22. When the state of Israel shall seem** past recovery, Messiah, Jehovah Himself, will unexpectedly appear on the scene as Redeemer of His people (Isa. 63:5). **I . . . also**—God opposes Himself to Nebuchadnezzar: *"He* took of the seed of the land and planted it (vss. 3, 5), so will *I,* but with better success than he had. The branch he plucked (Zedekiah) and planted, flourished but for a time, to perish at last; *I* will plant a scion of the same tree, the house of David, to whom the kingdom belongs by an everlasting covenant, and it shall be the shelter of the whole world, and shall be for ever." **branch** —the peculiar title of Messiah (Zech. 3:8; 6:12; Isa. 11:1; 4:2; Jer. 23:5; 33:15). **a tender one**—Zerubbabel never reigned as a universal (vs. 23) king, nor could the great things mentioned here be said of him, except as a type of Messiah. Messiah alone can be meant: originally "a *tender* plant and root out of a dry ground" (Isa. 53:2); the beginning of His kingdom being humble, His reputed parents of lowly rank, though King David's lineal representatives; yet, even then, God here calls Him, in respect to His everlasting purpose, "the highest . . . of the high" (Ps. 89:27). **I . . . will plant it upon an high mountain**—Zion; destined to be the *moral* center and eminence of grace and glory shining forth to the world, outtopping all mundane elevation. The kingdom, typically begun at the return from Babylon, and the rebuilding of the temple, fully began with Christ's appearing, and shall have its highest manifestation at His reappearing to reign on Zion, and thence over the whole earth (Ps. 2:6, 8; Isa. 2:2, 3; Jer. 3:17). **23. under it . . . all fowl**—the Gospel "mustard tree," small at first, but at length receiving all under its covert (Matt. 13:32); the antithesis to Antichrist, symbolized by Assyria, of which the same is said (ch. 31:6), and Babylon (Dan. 4:12). Antichrist assumes in mimicry the universal power really belonging to Christ. **24. I . . . brought down the high**—the very attribute given to God by the virgin mother of Him, under whom this was to be accomplished. **high . . . low tree**—i.e., princes elevated . . . lowered. All the empires of the world, represented by Babylon, once flourishing ("green"), shall be brought low before the once depressed ("dry"), but then exalted, kingdom of Messiah and His people, the head of whom shall be Israel (Dan. 2:44).

CHAPTER 18

Vss. 1-32. THE PARABLE OF THE SOUR GRAPES REPROVED. Vindication of God's moral government as to His retributive righteousness from the Jewish imputation of injustice, as if they were suffering, not for their own sin, but for that of their fathers. As in ch. 17 he foretold Messiah's happy reign in Jerusalem, so now he warns them that its blessings can be theirs only upon their individually turning to righteousness. **2. fathers . . . eaten sour grapes, . . . children's teeth . . . set on edge**—Their unbelieving calumnies on God's justice had become so common as to have assumed a proverbial form. The sin of Adam in eating the forbidden fruit, visited on his posterity, seems to have suggested the peculiar form; noticed also by Jeremiah (31:29); and explained in Lamentations 5:7, "Our fathers have sinned, and are not; and we have borne their iniquities." They mean by "the children" *themselves,* as though they were innocent, whereas they were far from being so. The partial reformation effected since Manasseh's wicked reign, especially among the exiles at Chebar, was their ground for thinking so; but the improvement was only superficial and only

fostered their self-righteous spirit, which sought anywhere but in themselves the cause of their calamities; just as the modern Jews attribute their present dispersion, not to their own sins, but to those of their forefathers. It is a universal mark of corrupt nature to lay the blame, which belongs to ourselves, on others and to arraign the justice of God. Cf. Genesis 3:12, where Adam transfers the blame of his sin to Eve, and even to God, "The *woman* whom *thou* gavest to be with me, she gave me of the tree, and I did eat." **3. ye shall not have occasion any more to use this proverb**—because I will let it be seen by the whole world in the very fact that you are not righteous, as ye fancy yourselves, but wicked, and that you suffer only the just penalty of your guilt; while the elect righteous remnant alone escapes. **4. all souls are mine**—Therefore I can deal with all, being My own creation, as I please (Jer. 18:6). As the Creator of all alike I can have no reason, but the principle of equity, according to men's works, to make any difference, so as to punish some, and to save others (Gen. 18:25). "The soul that sinneth it shall die." The curse descending from father to son assumes guilt shared in by the son; there is a natural tendency in the child to follow the sin of his father, and so he shares in the father's punishment: hence the principles of God's government, involved in Exodus 20:5 and Jeremiah 15.4, are justified. The sons, therefore (as the Jews here), cannot complain of being unjustly afflicted by God (Lam. 5:7); for they filled up the guilt of their fathers (Matt. 23:32, 34-36). The same God who "recompenses the iniquity of the fathers into the bosom of their children," is immediately after set forth as "giving to every man according to his ways" (Jer. 32:18, 19). In the same law (Exod. 20:5) which "visited the iniquities of the fathers upon the children unto the third and fourth generation" (where the explanation is added, "of them that *hate me,*" i.e., the *children hating God,* as well as their fathers: the former being too likely to follow their parents, sin going down with cumulative force from parent to child), we find (Deut. 24:16), "the fathers shall not be put to death for the children, neither the children for the fathers: every man shall be put to death for his own sin." The inherited guilt of sin in infants (Rom. 5:14) is an awful *fact,* but one met by the atonement of Christ; but it is of adults that he speaks here. Whatever penalties fall on *communities* for connection with sins of their fathers, *individual* adults who repent shall escape (II Kings 23:25, 26). This was no new thing, as some misinterpret the passage here; it had been *always* God's principle to punish only the guilty, and not also the innocent, for the sins of their fathers. God does not here change the principle of His administration, but is merely about to *manifest* it so personally to each that the Jews should no longer throw on God and on their fathers the blame which was their own. **soul that sinneth, it shall die**—and it *alone* (Rom. 6:23); not also the innocent. **5.** Here begins the illustration of God's impartiality in a series of supposed cases. The first case is given in vss. 5-9, the just man. The excellencies are selected in reference to the prevailing sins of the age, from which such a one stood aloof; hence arises the omission of some features of righteousness, which, under different circumstances, would have been desirable to be enumerated. Each age has *its own* besetting temptations, and the just man will be distinguished by his guarding against the peculiar defilements, inward and outward, of his age. **just . . . lawful . . . right**—the duties of the second table of the law, which flow from the fear of God. Piety is the root of all charity; to render to each his own, as well to our neighbor, as to God. **6. not eaten upon** . . . . **mountains**—the high places, where altars were reared. A double sin: sacrificing elsewhere than at the temple, where only God sanctioned sacrifice (Deut. 12:13, 14); and this to idols instead of to Jehovah. "Eaten" refers to the feasts which were connected with the sacrifices (see Exod. 32:6; Deut. 32:38; Judg. 9:27; I Cor. 8:4, 10; 10:7). **lifted** . . . **eyes to**—viz., in adoration (Ps. 121:1). The superstitious are compared to harlots; their eyes go eagerly after spiritual lusts. The righteous man not merely refrains from the act, but from the *glance* of spiritual lust (Job 31:1; Matt. 5:28). **idols of** . . . **Israel**—not merely those of the Gentiles, but even those of Israel. The fashions of his countrymen could not lead him astray. **defiled** . . . **neighbour's wife**—Not only does he shrink from spiritual, but also from carnal, adultery (cf. I Cor. 6:18). **neither** . . . **menstruous woman**—Leprosy and elephantiasis were said to be the fruit of such a connection [JEROME]. Chastity is to be observed even towards one's own wife (Lev. 18:19; 20:18). **7. restored** . . . **pledge**—that which the poor debtor absolutely needed; as his raiment, which the creditor was bound to restore before sunset (Exod. 22:26, 27), and his millstone, which was needed for preparing his food (Deut. 24:6, 10-13). **bread to** . . . **hungry** . . . **covered** . . . **naked**—(Isa. 58:7; Matt. 25:35, 36). After duties of justice come those of benevolence. It is not enough to refrain from doing a wrong to our neighbor, we must also do him good. The bread owned by a man, though "his," is given to him, not to keep to himself, but to impart to the needy. **8. usury**—lit., "biting." The law forbade the Jew to take interest from brethren but permitted him to do so from a foreigner (Exod. 22:25; Deut. 23:19, 20; Neh. 5:7; Ps. 15:5). The letter of the law was restricted to the Jewish polity, and is not binding now; and indeed the principle of taking interest was even then sanctioned, by its being allowed in the case of a foreigner. The *spirit* of the law still binds us, that we are not to take advantage of our neighbor's necessities to enrich ourselves, but be satisfied with moderate, or even no, interest, in the case of the needy. **increase**—in the case of *other* kinds of wealth; as "usury" refers to *money* (Lev. 25:36). **withdrawn** . . . **hand** . . .—Where he has the opportunity and might find a plausible plea for promoting his own gain at the cost of a wrong to his neighbor, he keeps back his hand from what selfishness prompts. **judgment**—justice. **9. truly**—with integrity. **surely live**—lit., "live in life." Prosper in this life, but still more in the life to come (Prov. 3:1, 2; Amos 5:4). **10-13.** The second case is that of an impious son of a pious father. His pious parentage, so far from excusing, aggravates his guilt. **robber**—or lit., "a breaker," viz., through all constraints of right. **doeth the like to any one**—The *Hebrew* and the parallel (vs. 18) require us to translate rather, "doeth to his *brother* any of these things," viz., the things which follow in vs. 11, etc. [MAURER]. **11. those duties**—which his father did (vss. 5, 9). **12. oppressed the poor**—an aggravation to his oppressions, that they were practised against *the poor;* whereas in vs. 7 the expression is simply "oppressed *any*." **abomination**—singular number referring to the particular one mentioned at the end of vs. 6. **13. shall he** . . . **live?** —because of the merits of his father; answering, by contrast, to "die for the iniquity of his father" (vs. 17). **his blood shall be upon him**—The cause of his bloody death shall rest with himself; God is not to

blame, but is vindicated as just in punishing him. **14-18.** The third case: a son who walks not in the steps of an unrighteous father, but in the ways of God; e.g., Josiah, the pious son of guilty Amon; Hezekiah, of Ahaz (II Kings 16:18, 21, 22). **seeth** . . . **and considereth**—The same *Hebrew* stands for both verbs, "seeth . . . yea, seeth." The repetition implies the attentive observation needed, in order that the son may not be led astray by his father's bad example; as sons generally are blind to parents' sins, and even imitate them as if they were virtues. **17. taken off his hand from the poor**—i.e., *abstained* from oppressing the poor, when he had the opportunity of doing so with impunity. The different sense of the phrase in ch. 16:49, in reference to *relieving* the poor, seems to have suggested the reading followed by FAIRBAIRN, but not sanctioned by the *Hebrew*, "hath *not* turned his hand from . . . ." But ch. 20:22 uses the phrase in a somewhat similar sense to *English Version* here, *abstained from hurting.* **19.** Here the Jews object to the prophet's word and in their objection seem to seek a continuance of that very thing which they had originally made a matter of complaint. Therefore translate, "Wherefore doth not the son bear the iniquity of his father?" It now would seem a consolation to them to think the son might suffer for his father's misdeeds; for it would soothe their self-love to regard themselves as innocent sufferers for the guilt of others and would justify them in their present course of life, which they did not choose to abandon for a better. In reply, Ezekiel reiterates the truth of each being dealt with according to his own merits [FAIRBAIRN]. But GROTIUS supports *English Version,* wherein the Jews contradict the prophet, "Why (sayest thou so) doth not the son (often, as in our case, though innocent) bear (i.e., suffer for) the iniquity of their father?" Ezekiel replies, It is not as you say, but as I in the name of God say: "When the son hath done . . . ." *English Version* is simpler than that of FAIRBAIRN. **20. son shall not bear** . . . **iniquity of** . . . **father**—(Deut. 24:16; II Kings 14:6). **righteousness** . . . **wickedness**—i.e., the reward for righteousness . . . the punishment of wickedness. "Righteousness" is not used as if any were *absolutely* righteous; but, of such as have it *imputed* to them for Christ's sake, though not under the Old Testament themselves understanding the ground on which they were regarded as righteous, but sincerely seeking after it in the way of God's appointment, so far as they then understood this way. **21-24.** Two last cases, showing the equity of God: (1) The penitent sinner is dealt with according to his new obedience, not according to his former sins. (2) The righteous man who turns from righteousness to sin shall be punished for the latter, and his former righteousness will be of no avail to him **21. he shall surely live**—Despair drives men into hardened recklessness; God therefore allures men to repentance by holding out hope [CALVIN].

To threats the stubborn sinner oft is hard,
Wrapt in his crimes, against the storm prepared,
But when the milder beams of mercy play,
He melts, and throws the cumbrous cloak away.

Hitherto the cases had been of a change from bad to good, or vice versa, in one generation compared with another. Here it is such a change in one and the same individual. This, as practically affecting the persons here addressed, is properly put last. So far from God laying on men the penalty of others' sins, He will not even punish them for their own, if they turn from sin to righteousness; but if they turn from righteousness to sin, they must expect in justice that their former goodness will not atone for subsequent sin (Heb. 10:38, 39; II Pet. 2: 20-22). The exile in Babylon gave a season for repentance of those sins which would have brought death on the perpetrator in Judea while the law could be enforced; so it prepared the way for the Gospel [GROTIUS]. **22. in his righteousness ... he shall live**—*in* it, not *for* it, as if that atoned for his former sins; but *"in his righteousness"* he shall live, as the *evidence* of his being already in favor with God through the merit of Messiah, who was to come. The Gospel clears up for us many such passages (I Pet. 1:12), which were dimly understood at the time, while men, however, had light enough for salvation. **23.** (I Tim. 2:4; II Pet. 3:9). If men perish, it is because they *will not* come to the Lord for salvation; not that the Lord is not willing to save them (John 5:40). They trample on not merely justice, but mercy; what farther hope can there be for them, when even mercy is against them? (Heb. 10:26-29). **24. righteous**—one *apparently* such; as in Matt. 9:13, "I came not to call the righteous ...," i.e., those who fancy themselves righteous. Those alone are true saints who by the grace of God persevere (Matt. 24:13; I Cor. 10:12; John 10:28, 29). **turneth away from ... righteousness**—an utter apostasy; not like the exceptional offenses of the godly through infirmity or heedlessness, which they afterwards mourn over and repent of. **not be mentioned**—not be taken into account so as to save them. **his trespass**—utter apostasy. **25.** Their plea for saying, "The way of the Lord is not equal," was that God treated different classes in a different way. But it was really their way that was unequal, since living in sin they expected to be dealt with as if they were righteous. God's way was invariably to deal with different men according to their deserts. **26-28.** The two last instances repeated in inverse order. God's emphatic statement of His principle of government needs no further proof than the simple statement of it. **26. in them**—in the actual *sins*, which are the manifestations of the principle of "iniquity," mentioned just before. **27. he shall save his soul**—i.e., he shall have it saved upon his repentance. **28. considereth**—the first step to repentance; for the ungodly do not consider either God or themselves (Deut. 32:29; Ps. 119:59, 60; Luke 15:17, 18). **29.** Though God's justice is so plainly manifested, sinners still object to it because they do not wish to see it (Mic. 2:7; Matt. 11:18, 19). **30-32.** As God is to judge them "according to their ways" (Prov. 1:31), their only hope is to "repent"; and this is a sure hope, for God takes no delight in judging them in wrath, but graciously desires their salvation on repentance. **30. I will judge you**—Though ye cavil, it is a sufficient answer that I, your Judge, declare it so, and will judge you according to My will; and then your cavils must end. **Repent** —*inward* conversion (Rev. 2:5). In the *Hebrew* there is a play of like sounds, *"Turn* ye and *return."* **turn** *yourselves ... —*the *outward* fruits of repentance. Not as *Margin,* "turn *others";* for the parallel clause (vs. 31) is, "cast away from *you* all *your* transgressions." Perhaps, however, the omission of the object after the verb in the *Hebrew* implies that *both* are included: Turn alike *yourselves* and *all whom you can influence.* **from all . . . transgressions**—not as if believers are perfect; but they sincerely *aim* at perfection, so as to be habitually and wilfully on terms with no sin (I John 3:6-9). **your ruin**—lit., "your snare," entangling you in ruin. **31.**

Cast away from you—for the cause of your evil rests with yourselves; your sole way of escape is to be reconciled to God (Eph. 4:22, 23). **make you a new heart**—This shows, not what men *can* do, but what they *ought* to do: what God requires of us. God alone can make us a new heart (ch. 11:19; 36: 26, 27). The command to do what men cannot themselves do is designed to drive them (instead of laying the blame, as the Jews did, elsewhere rather than on themselves) to feel their own helplessness, and to seek God's Holy Spirit (Ps. 51:11, 12). Thus the outward exhortation is, as it were, the organ or instrument which God uses for conferring grace. So we may say with AUGUSTINE, "Give what thou requirest, and (then) require what thou wilt." Our strength (which is weakness in itself) shall suffice for whatever He exacts, if only He gives the supply [CALVIN]. **spirit**—the *understanding:* as the "heart" means *the will and affections.* The root must be changed before the fruit can be good. **why will ye die**—bring on your own selves your ruin. God's decrees are secret to us; it is enough for us that He invites all, and will reject none that seek Him. **32.** (Lam. 3:33; II Pet. 3:9). God is "slow to anger"; punishment is "His strange work" (Isa. 28:21).

CHAPTER 19

Vss. 1-14. ELEGY OVER THE FALL OF DAVID'S HOUSE. There is a tacit antithesis between this lamentation and that of the Jews for their own miseries, into the causes of which, however, they did not inquire. **1. princes of Israel**—i.e., Judah, whose "princes" alone were recognized by prophecy; those of the ten tribes were, in respect to the theocracy, usurpers. **2. thy mother**—the mother of Jehoiachin, the representative of David's line in exile with Ezekiel. The "mother" is Judea: "a lioness," as being fierce in catching prey (vs. 3), referring to her heathenish practices. Jerusalem was called Ariel (the lion of God) in a good sense (Isa. 29:1); and Judah "a lion's whelp ... a lion ... an old lion" (Gen. 49: 9), to which, as also to Numbers 23:24; 24:9, this passage alludes. **nourished ... among young lions** —She herself had "lain" among lions, i.e., had intercourse with the corruptions of the surrounding heathen and had brought up the royal young ones similarly: utterly degenerate from the stock of Abraham. **Lay down**—or "couched," is appropriate to the lion, the Arab name of which means "the coucher." **3. young lion**—Jehoahaz, son of Josiah, carried captive from Riblah to Egypt by Pharaoh-necho (II Kings 23:33). **4. The nations**—Egypt, in the case of Jehoahaz, who probably provoked Pharaoh by trying to avenge the death of his father by assailing the bordering cities of Egypt (II Kings 23:29, 30). **in their pit**—image from the *pitfalls* used for catching wild beasts (Jer. 22:11, 12). **chains**—or hooks, which were fastened in the noses of wild beasts (see *Note,* vs. 9). **5. saw that she had waited, and her hope was lost**—i.e., that her long-waited-for hope was disappointed, Jehoahaz not being restored to her from Egypt. **she took another of her whelps**—Jehoiakim, brother of Jehoahaz, who was placed on the throne by Pharaoh (II Kings 23:34), according to the wish of Judah. **6. went up and down among the lions**—imitated the recklessness and tyranny of the surrounding kings (Jer. 22:13-17). **catch ... prey**—to do evil, gratifying his lusts by oppression (II Kings 23:37). **7. knew ... desolate palaces**—i.e., *claimed as his own* their palaces, which he then proceeded to "desolate." The *Hebrew,* literally "wid-

ows"; hence *widowed palaces* (Isa. 13:22). VATA-
BLUS (whom FAIRBAIRN follows) explains it, "He
knew (carnally) the widows of those whom he devoured" (vs. 6). But thus the metaphor and the
literal reality would be blended: the *lion* being represented as *knowing widows*. The reality, however, often elsewhere thus breaks through the veil.
fulness thereof—all that it contained; its inhabitants.
8. the nations—the Chaldeans, Syrians, Moab, and
Ammon (II Kings 24:2). **9. in chains**—(II Chron.
36:6; Jer. 22:18). *Margin,* "hooks"; perhaps referring to the hook often passed through the nose of
beasts; so, too, through that of captives, as seen in
the Assyrian sculptures (see *Note,* vs. 4). **voice**—
i.e., his roaring. **no more be heard upon the
mountains**—carrying on the metaphor of the lion,
whose roaring on the mountains frightens all the
other beasts. The insolence of the prince, not at all
abated though his kingdom was impaired, was now
to cease. **10.** A new metaphor taken from the
vine, the chief of the fruit-bearing trees, as the *lion*
is of the beasts of prey (see ch. 17:6). **in thy blood**
—"planted when thou wast in thy blood," i.e., in thy
very infancy; as in ch. 16:6, when thou hadst just
come from the womb, and hadst not yet the blood
washed from thee. The Jews from the first were
planted in Canaan to take root there [CALVIN]. GRO-
TIUS translates as *Margin,* "in thy quietness," i.e.,
in the period when Judah had not yet fallen into her
present troubles. *English Version* is better. GLAS-
SIUS explains it well, retaining the metaphor, which
CALVIN's explanation breaks, "in the blood of thy
grapes," i.e., in her full strength, as the red wine is
the strength of the grape. Genesis 49:11 is evidently
alluded to. **many waters**—the well-watered land of
Canaan (Deut. 8:7-9). **11.** **strong rods**—princes of
the royal house of David. The vine shot forth her
branches like so many scepters, not creeping lowly
on the ground like many vines, but trained aloft on
a tree or wall. The mention of their former royal
dignity, contrasting sadly with her present sunken
state, would remind the Jews of their sins whereby
they had incurred such judgments. **stature**—(Dan.
4:11). **among the thick branches**—i.e., the central
stock or trunk of the tree shot up highest "among
its own branches" or offshoots, surrounding it. Emblematic of the numbers and resources of the people.
HENGSTENBERG translates, "among the clouds." But
ch. 31:3, 10, 14, supports *English Version.* **12.**
plucked up—not *gradually* withered. The *sudden*
upturning of the state was designed to awaken the
Jews out of their torpor to see the hand of God in
the national judgment. **east wind**—(*Note,* ch. 17:
10). **13. planted**—i.e., transplanted. Though already "dried up" in regard to the nation generally,
the vine is said to be "transplanted" as regards God's
mercy to the remnant in Babylon. **dry . . . ground**
—Chaldea was well watered and fertile; but it is the
condition of the captive people, not that of the land,
which is referred to. **14. fire . . . out of a rod of her
branches**—The Jews' disaster was to be ascribed, not
so much to the Chaldeans as to *themselves;* the "fire
out of the rod" is *God's wrath* kindled by the perjury of Zedekiah (ch. 17:18). "The anger of the
Lord" against Judah is specified as the cause why
Zedekiah was permitted to rebel against Babylon (II
Kings 24:20; cf. Judg. 9:15), thus bringing Nebuchadnezzar against Jerusalem. **no strong rod . . .
sceptre to rule**—No more kings of David's stock
are now to rule the nation. Not at least until "the
Lord shall send the rod of His strength (Messiah,
Ps. 110:2; Isa. 11:1) out of Zion," to reign first as a
spiritual, then hereafter as a literal king. **is . . . and**

shall be for a lamentation—Part of the lamentation
(that as to Jehoahaz and Jehoiakim) was matter of
history as already accomplished; part (as to Zedekiah) was yet to be fulfilled; or, this prophecy both
is a subject for lamentation, and shall be so to
distant posterity.

CHAPTER 20

VSS. 1-49. REJECTION OF THE ELDERS' APPLICA-
TION TO THE PROPHET: EXPOSURE OF ISRAEL'S PRO-
TRACTED REBELLIONS, NOTWITHSTANDING GOD'S
LONG-SUFFERING GOODNESS: YET WILL GOD RE-
STORE HIS PEOPLE AT LAST. **1. seventh year . . .**—
viz., from the carrying away of Jeconiah (ch. 1:2; 8:
1). This computation was calculated to make them
cherish the more ardently the hope of the restoration promised them in seventy years; for, when
prospects are hopeless, years are not computed
[CALVIN]. **elders . . . came to inquire**—The object
of their inquiry, as in ch. 14:1, is not stated; probably it was to ascertain the cause of the national calamities and the time of their termination, as their
false prophets assured them of a speedy restoration.
3. The chapter falls into two great parts: vss. 1-32,
the recital of the people's rebellions during five distinct periods: in Egypt, the wilderness, on the borders of Canaan when a new generation arose, in Canaan, and in the time of the prophet. **I will not be
inquired of by you**—because their moral state pre-
cluded them from capability of knowing the will of
God (Ps. 66:18; Prov. 28:9; John 7:17). **4. Wilt
thou judge? . . . judge**—The emphatical repetition expresses, "Wilt thou *not* judge? yes, judge them.
There is a loud call for immediate judgment." The
Hebrew interrogative here is a *command,* not a prohibition]MAURER[. Instead of spending time in
teaching them, tell them of the abomination of their
fathers, of which their own are the complement and
counterpart, and which call for *judgment.* **5, 6.** The
thrice lifting up of God's hand (the sign of His *oath,*
Rev. 10:5, 6; Exod. 6:8, *Margin;* Num. 14:30; to
which passages the form of words here alludes) implies the solemn earnestness of God's purpose of
grace to them. **made myself known unto them**—
proving Myself faithful and true by the actual fulfilment of My promises (Exod. 4:31; 6:3); revealing
Myself as "Jehovah," i.e., not that the *name* was unknown before, but that then first the *force* of that
name was manifested in the promises of God then
being realized in performances. **6. espied for them**
—as though God had spied out all other lands, and
chose Canaan as the best of all lands (Deut. 8:7, 8).
See Daniel 8:9; 11:16, 41, "the glorious land"; see
Margin, "land of delight or *ornament";* Zechariah 7:
14, "the pleasant land," or land of desire. **glory of
all lands**—i.e., *Canaan* was "the beauty of all lands";
the most lovely and delightful land; "milk and honey" are not the antecedents to "which." **7.** Moses
gives no formal statement of idolatries practised by
Israel in Egypt. But it is implied in their readiness
to worship the golden calf (resembling the Egyptian ox, Apis) (Exod. 32), which makes it likely
they had worshipped such idols in Egypt. Also, in
Leviticus 17:7, "They shall *no more* offer their sacrifices unto devils (lit., *seirim,* 'he-goats,' the symbol of the false god, Pan), after whom they have
gone a-whoring." The call of God by Moses was
as much to them to separate from idols and follow
Jehovah, as it was to Pharaoh to let them go forth.
Exodus 6:6, 7 and Joshua 24:14, expressly mention
their idolatry "in Egypt." Hence the need of their

being removed out of the contagion of Egyptian idolatries by the exodus. **every man**—so universal was the evil. **of his eyes**—It was not fear of their Egyptian masters, but their own *lust of the eye* that drew them to idols (ch. 6:9; 18:6). **8, 9. then I said, I will ... But ...**—i.e., (God speaking in condescension to human modes of conception) their spiritual degradation *deserved* I should destroy them, "but I wrought (viz., the deliverance 'out of ... Egypt') for My name's sake"; not for their merits (a rebuke to their national pride). God's "name" means the sum-total of His perfections. To manifest these, His gratuitous mercy abounding above their sins, yet without wrong to His justice, and so to set forth His glory, was and is the ultimate end of His dealings (vss. 14, 22; II Sam. 7:23; Isa. 63:12; Rom. 9: 17). **11. which if a man do, he shall ... live in them** —not "*by* them," as though they could justify a man, seeing that man cannot render the faultless obedience required (Lev. 18:5; Gal. 3:12). "By them" is the expression indeed in Romans 10:5; but there the design is to show that, *if man could* obey all God's laws, he would be justified "by them" (Gal. 3:21); but he cannot; he therefore needs to have justification by "the Lord our righteousness" (Jer. 23;6); then, having thus received life, he "lives," i.e., maintains, enjoys, and exercises this life only in so far as he walks "*in*" the laws of God. So Deuteronomy 30:15, 16. The Israelites, *as a nation*, had life already freely given to them by God's covenant of promise; the laws of God were designed to be the means of the outward expression of their spiritual life. As the natural life has its healthy manifestation in the full exercise of its powers, so their spiritual being as a nation was to be developed in vigor, or else decay, according as they did, or did not, walk in God's laws. **12. sabbaths, ... a sign between me and them**—a kind of sacramental pledge of the covenant of adoption between God and His people. The Sabbath is specified as a sample of the whole law, to show that the law is not merely precepts, but privileges, of which the Sabbath is one of the highest. Not that the Sabbath was first instituted at Sinai, as if it were an exclusively Jewish ordinance (Gen. 2:2, 3), but it was then more formally enacted, when, owing to the apostasy of the world from the original revelation, one people was called out (Deut. 5:15) to be the covenant people of God. **sanctify them**—The observance of the Sabbath contemplated by God was not a mere *outward* rest, but a *spiritual* dedication of the day to the glory of God and the good of man. Otherwise it would not be, as it is made, the pledge of universal *sanctification* (Exod. 31:13-17; Isa. 58:13, 14). Virtually it is said, all sanctity will flourish or decay, according as this ordinance is observed in its full spirituality or not. **13. in the wilderness**—They "rebelled" in the very place where death and terror were on every side and where they depended on My miraculous bounty every moment! **15. I swore** against them (Ps. 95:11; 106:26) that I would not permit the generation that came out of Egypt to enter Canaan. **16.** The *special* reason is stated by Moses (Num. 13, 14) to be that they, through fear arising from the false report of the spies, wished to return to Egypt; the *general* reasons are stated here which lay at the root of their rejection of God's grace; viz., contempt of God and His laws, and love of idols. **their heart**—The fault lay in it (Ps. 78:37). **17. Nevertheless**—How marvellous that God should spare such sinners! His everlasting covenant explains it, His long-suffering standing out in striking contrast to their rebellions (Ps. 78:38; Jer. 30:11).

18. I said unto their children—being unwilling to speak any more to the fathers as being incorrigible. **Walk ye not in ... statutes of ... fathers**—The traditions of the fathers are to be carefully weighed, not indiscriminately followed. He forbids the imitation of not only their gross sins, but even their plausible statutes [CALVIN]. **19.** It is an indirect denial of God, and a robbing Him of His due, to add man's inventions to His precepts. **20.** (Jer. 17:22). **21.** Though warned by the judgment on their fathers, the next generation also rebelled against God. The "kindness of Israel's youth and love of her espousals in the wilderness" (Jer. 2:2, 3) were only comparative (the corruption in later times being more general), and confined to the minority; as a whole, Israel at no time fully served God. The "children" it was that fell into the fearful apostasy on the plains of Moab at the close of the wilderness sojourn (Num. 25:1, 2; Deut. 31:27). **23.** It was to that generation the threat of dispersion was proclaimed (Deut. 28:64; cf. ch. 29:4). **25. I gave them ... statutes ... not good**—Since they would not follow My statutes that were good, "I gave them" their own (vs. 18) and their fathers' "which were not good"; statutes spiritually corrupting, and, finally, as the consequence, destroying them. Righteous retribution (Ps. 81:12; Hos. 8:11; Rom. 1:24; II Thess. 2:11). Verse 39 proves this view to be correct (cf. Isa. 63:17). Thus on the plains of Moab (Num. 25), in chastisement for the secret unfaithfulness to God in their hearts, He permitted Baal's worshippers to tempt them to idolatry (the ready success of the tempters, moreover, proving the inward unsoundness of the tempted); and this again ended necessarily in punitive judgments. **26. I polluted them**—not directly; "but I judicially *gave them up* to pollute themselves." A just retribution for their "polluting My sabbaths" (vs. 24). This vs. 26 is explanatory of vs. 25. Their own sin I made their punishment. **caused to pass through** *the fire*— FAIRBAIRN translates, "In their *presenting* (lit., the causing to pass over) all their first-born," viz., *to the Lord;* referring to the command (Exod. 13:12, *Margin*, where the very same expression is used). The lustration of children by passing through the fire was *a later abomination* (vs. 31). The evil here spoken of was the admixture of heathenish practices with Jehovah's worship, which made Him regard all as "polluted." Here, "to the Lord" is omitted purposely, to imply, "They kept up the outward service indeed, but I did not own it as done unto Me, since it was mingled with such *pollutions.*" But *English Version* is supported by the similar phraseology in vs. 31, where see *Note*. They made all their children pass through the fire; but he names the *first-born*, in aggravation of their guilt; i.e., "I had willed that the first-born should be redeemed as being Mine, but they imposed on themselves the cruel rites of offering them to Molech" (Deut. 18:10). **might know ... the Lord**—that they may be compelled to know Me as a powerful Judge, since they were unwilling to know Me as a gracious Father. **27-29.** The next period, viz., that which followed the settlement in Canaan: the fathers of the generation existing in Ezekiel's time walked in the same steps of apostasy as the generation in the wilderness. **Yet in this**—Not content with past rebellions, and not moved with gratitude for God's goodness, "yet in this" *still further* they rebelled. **blasphemed**— "have insulted me" [CALVIN]. Even those who did not sacrifice to heathen gods have offered "their sacrifices" (vs. 28) in forbidden places. **28. provocation of their offering**—an offering as it were purposely made to provoke God. **sweet savour**—What ought to have been *sweet* became offensive by their corruptions. He specifies the various kinds of offerings, to show that in *all* alike they violated the law. **29. What is the high place whereunto ye go?** —What is the meaning of this name? For My *altar* is not so called. What excellence do ye see in it, that ye go there, rather than to My temple, the only lawful place of sacrificing? The very name, "high place," convicts you of sinning, not from ignorance but perverse rebellion. **is called . . . unto this day**—whereas this name ought to have been long since laid aside, along with the custom of sacrificing on high places which it represents, being borrowed from the heathen, who so called their places of sacrifice (the Greeks, for instance, called them by a cognate term, *Bomoi*), whereas I call mine *Mizbeaach*, "altar." The very name implies the place is not that sanctioned by Me, and therefore your sacrifices even to ME there (much more those you offer to idols) are only a "provocation" to Me (vs. 28; Deut. 12:1-5). David and others, it is true, sacrificed to God on high places, but it was under exceptional circumstances, and before the altar was set up on Mount Moriah. **30.** The interrogation implies a strong affirmation, as in vs. 4, "Are ye *not* polluted . . . ? Do ye *not* commit . . .?" Or, connecting this verse with vs. 31, "Are ye thus polluted . . ., and yet (do ye expect that) I shall be inquired of by you?" **31. through the fire**—As "the fire" is omitted in vs. 26, FAIRBAIRN represents the generation here referred to (viz., that of Ezekiel's day) as attaining the climax of guilt (see *Note*, vs. 26), in making their children pass through the fire, which that former generation did not. The reason, however, for the omission of "the fire" in vs. 26 is, perhaps, that there it is implied the children only "*passed through* the fire" for purification, whereas here they are actually *burnt to death* before the idol; and therefore "the fire" is specified in the latter, not in the former case (cf. II Kings 3:27). **32. We will be as the heathen**—and so escape the odium to which we are exposed, of having a peculiar God and law of our own. "We shall live on better terms with them by having a similar worship. Besides, we get from God nothing but threats and calamities, whereas the heathen, Chaldeans, etc., get riches and power from their idols." How literally God's words here ("that . . . shall not be at all") are fulfilled in the modern Jews! Though the Jews seemed so likely (had Ezekiel spoken as an uninspired man) to have blended with the rest of mankind and laid aside their distinctive peculiarities, as was their wish at that time, yet they have remained for eighteen centuries dispersed among all nations and without a home, but still distinct: a standing witness for the truth of the prophecy given so long ago. **33.** Here begins the second division of the prophecy. Lest the covenant people should abandon their distinctive hopes and amalgamate with the surrounding heathen, He tells them that, as the wilderness journey from Egypt was made subservient to discipline and also to the taking from among them the rebellious, so a severe discipline (such as the Jews are now for long actually undergoing) should be administered to them during the next exodus for the same purpose (vs. 38), and so to prepare them for the restored possession of their land (Hos. 2:14, 15). This was only partially fulfilled before, and at the return from Babylon: its full and final accomplishment is future. **with a mighty hand, . . . will I rule over you**—I will assert My right over you in spite of your resistance (vs. 32), as a master would in the case of his slave, and I will not let you be wrested from Me, because of My regard to My covenant. **34.** The Jews in exile might think themselves set free from the "rule" of God (vs. 33); therefore, He intimates, He will reassert His right over them by chastening judgments, and these, with an ultimate view, not to destroy, but to restore them. **people**—rather, "peoples." **35. wilderness of the people**—rather, "peoples," the various *peoples* among whom they were to be scattered, and about whom God saith (vs. 34), "I will bring you out." In contrast to the literal "wilderness of Egypt" (vs. 36), "the wilderness of the peoples" is their *spiritual* wilderness period of trial, discipline, and purification while exiled among the nations. As the state when they are "brought into the wilderness of the peoples" and that when they were among the peoples "from" which God was to "bring them out" (vs. 34) are distinguished, the wilderness state probably answers partially to the transition period of discipline from the first decree for their restoration by Cyrus to the time of their complete settlement in their land, and the rebuilding of Jerusalem and temple. But the full and final fulfilment is future; the wilderness state will comprise not only the transition period of their restoration, but the beginning of their occupancy of Palestine, a time in which they shall endure the sorest of all their chastisements, to "purge out the rebels" (vs. 38; Dan. 12:1); and then the remnant (Zech. 13:8, 9; 14:2, 3) shall "all serve God in the land" (vs. 40). Thus the wilderness period does not denote *locality*, but their *state* intervening between their rejection and future restoration. **plead**—bring the matter in debate between us to an issue. Image is from a plaintiff in a law court meeting the defendant "face to face." Appropriate, as God in His dealings acts not arbitrarily, but in most *righteous justice* (Jer. 2:9; Mic. 6:2). **36.** (Num. 14:21-29.) Though God saved them out of Egypt, He afterwards destroyed in the wilderness them that believed not (Jude 5); so, though He brought the exiles out of Babylon, yet their wilderness state of chastening discipline continued even after they were again in Canaan. **37. pass under the rod**—metaphor from a shepherd who makes his sheep *pass under his rod* in counting them (Lev. 27:32; Jer. 33:13). Whether you will or not, ye shall be counted as Mine, and so shall be subjected to My chastening discipline (Mic. 7:14), with a view to My ultimate saving of the chosen remnant (cf. John 10:27-29). **bond of . . . covenant**—I will constrain you by sore chastisements to submit yourselves to the *covenant* to which ye are lastingly *bound*, though now you have cast away God's bond from you. Fulfilled in part, Nehemiah 9:8, 26, 32-38; 10:1-39; fully hereafter (Isa. 54:10-13; 52:1, 2). **38.** (Zech. 13:9; 14:2.) **purge out**—or, "separate." *Hebrew, barothi,* forming a designed alliteration with "*berith,*" *the covenant;* not a promise of grace, but a threat against those Jews who thought they could in exile escape the observation and "rule" of God. **land of Israel**—Though brought out of the country of their sojourn or exile (Babylon formerly, and the various lands of their exile hereafter) into the literal land of *Palestine*, even it shall be to them an exile state, "they shall not enter into the land of *Israel*," i.e., the spiritual state of restored favor of God to His covenant people, which shall only be given to the remnant to be saved (Zech. 13:8, 9). **39.** Equivalent to, "I would rather have you open idolaters than hypocrites, fancying you can worship Me and yet at the same time serve idols" (Amos 5:21, 22, 25, 26; cf. I Kings 18:21; II Kings 17:41; Matt. 6:24;

Rev. 3:15, 16). **Go ye, serve**—This is not a *command* to serve idols, but a judicial declaration of God's giving up of the half-idol, half-Jehovah worshippers to utter idolatry, if they will not serve Jehovah alone (Ps. 81:12; Rev. 22:11). **hereafter also**—God anticipates the same apostasy *afterwards*, as *now.* **40. For**—Though ye, the rebellious portion, withdraw from My worship, others, even the believing remnant, will succeed after you perish, and will serve Me purely. **in mine holy mountain**—(Isa. 2:2, 3). Zion, or Moriah, "the height of Israel" (pre-eminent above all mountains because of the manifested presence of God there with *Israel*), as opposed to their "high places," the worship on which was an abomination to God. **all**—not merely individuals, such as constitute the elect Church now; but the whole *nation*, to be followed by the conversion of the Gentile *nations* (Isa. 2:2, "*all* nations"; Rom. 11:26; Rev. 11:15). **with**—rather, "*in* all your holy things" [MAURER]. **41. with**—i.e., in respect to your sweet savor (lit., "savor of rest," *Note*, ch. 16: 19). Or, I will accept you (your worship) "*as* a sweet savor" [MAURER], (Eph. 5:2; Phil. 4:18). God first accepts the *person* in Messiah, then the *offering* (vs. 40; Gen. 4:4). **bring . . . out from . . . . people . . .**—the same words as in vs. 34; but there applied to the bringing forth of the hypocrites, as well as the elect; here restricted to the saved remnant, who alone shall be at last restored literally and spiritually in the fullest sense. **sanctified in you before . . . heathen**—(Jer. 33:9). All the nations will acknowledge My power displayed in restoring you, and so shall be led to seek Me (Isa. 66:18; Zech. 14:16-19). **43. there**—not merely in exile when suffering punishment which makes even reprobates sorry for sin, but when received into favor *in your own land.* **remember**—(ch. 16:61, 63). The humiliation of Judah (Neh. 9) is a type of the future penitence of the whole nation (Hos. 5:15; 6:1; Zech. 12:10-14). God's goodness realized by the sinner is the only thing that leads to true repentance (Hos. 3:5; Luke 7:37, 38). **44.** The *English Version* chapter ought to have ended here, and ch. 21 begun with "Moreover . . . ," as in the *Hebrew* Bible. **for my name's sake**—(ch. 36:22). Gratuitously; according to My compassion, not your merits. After having commented on this verse, CALVIN was laid on his deathbed, and his commentary ended. **45-49.** An introductory brief description in enigma of the destruction by fire and sword, detailed more explicitly in ch. 21. **46. south . . . south . . . south**—three different *Hebrew* words, to express the certainty of the divine displeasure resting on the region specified. The third term is from a root meaning "dry," referring to the sun's heat in the south; representing the burning judgments of God on the southern parts of Judea, of which Jerusalem was the capital. **set thy face**—determinately. The prophets used to turn themselves towards those who were to be the subjects of their prophecies. **drop**—as the rain, which *flows* in a continuous stream, sometimes gently (Deut. 32:2), sometimes violently (Amos 7:16; Mic. 2:6, *Margin*), as here. **forest**—the densely populated country of Judea; trees representing people. **47. fire**—every kind of judgment (ch. 19:12; 21:3, "my sword"; Jer. 21:14). **green tree . . . dry**—fit and unfit materials for fuel alike; "the righteous and the wicked," as explained in ch. 21:3, 4; Luke 23: 31. Unsparing universality of the judgment! **flaming flame**—one continued and unextinguished flame. "The glowing flame" [FAIRBAIRN]. **faces**—persons; here the metaphor is merged in the reality. **49.** Ezekiel complains that by this parabolical form of

prophecy he only makes himself and it a jest to his countrymen. God therefore in ch. 21 permits him to express the same prophecy more plainly.

CHAPTER 21

Vss. 1-32. PROPHECY AGAINST ISRAEL AND JERUSALEM, AND AGAINST AMMON. **2. the holy places**—the three parts of the temple: the courts, the holy place, and the holiest. If "synagogues" existed before the Babylonian captivity, as Psalm 74:8 seems to imply, they and the *proseuchæ*, or oratories, may be included in the "holy places" here. **3. righteous . . . wicked**—not contradictory to ch. 18:4, 9 and Genesis 18:23. Ezekiel here views the mere *outward* aspect of the indiscriminate universality of the national calamity. But *really* the same captivity to the "righteous" would prove a blessing as a wholesome discipline, which to the "wicked" would be an unmitigated punishment. The godly were sealed with a mark (ch. 9:4), not for outward exemption from the common calamity, but as marked for the secret interpositions of Providence, overruling even evil to their good. The godly were by comparison so few, that not their salvation but the universality of the judgment is brought into view here. **4.** The "sword" did not, literally, *slay* all; but the *judgments* of God by the foe swept through the land "from the south to the north." **6. with the breaking of thy loins**—as one afflicted with pleurisy; or as a woman, in labor-throes, clasps her loins in pain, and heaves and sighs till *the girdle of the loins is broken* by the violent action of the body (Jer. 30:6). **7.** The abrupt sentences and mournful repetitions imply violent emotions. **9. sword**—viz., of God (Deut. 32:41). The Chaldeans are His instrument. **10. to make a sore slaughter**—lit., "that killing it may kill." **glitter**—lit., "glitter as the lightning-flash": flashing terror into the foe. **should we . . . make mirth**—It is no time for levity when such a calamity is impending (Isa. 22:12, 13). **it contemneth the rod of my son . . .**—The sword has no more respect to the trivial "rod" or scepter of Judah (Gen. 49:10) than if it were any common "tree." "Tree" is the image retained from ch. 20:47; explained in ch. 21:2, 3. God calls Judah "My son" (cf. Exod. 4:22; Hos. 11:1). FAIRBAIRN arbitrarily translates, "Perchance the scepter of My son rejoiceth; it (the sword) despiseth every tree." **11. the slayer**—the Babylonian king in this case; in general, *all* the instruments of God's wrath (Rev. 19:15). **12. terrors by reason of the sword . . .**—rather, "they (the princes of Israel) are *delivered up to* the sword together with My people" [GLASSIUS]. **smite . . . upon . . . thigh**—a mark of grief (Jer. 31: 19). **13. it is a trial**—rather, "There is a trial" being made: the sword of the Lord will subject all to the ordeal. "What, then, if it contemn even the rod" (scepter of Judah)? Cf. as to a similar scourge of unsparing trial, Job 9:23. **it shall be no more**—the scepter, i.e., *the state,* must necessarily then come to an end. Fulfilled in part at the overthrow of Judah by Nebuchadnezzar, but fully at the time of "Shiloh's" (Messiah's) coming (Gen. 49:10), when Judea became a Roman province. **14. smite . . . , hands together**—(Num. 24:10), indicative of the indignant fury with which God will "smite" the people. **sword . . . doubled the third time**—referring to the threefold calamity:—1. The taking of Zedekiah (to whom the "rod," or scepter, may refer); 2. the taking of the city; 3. the removal of all those who remained with Gedaliah. "Doubled" means "multiplied" or "repeated." The stroke shall be doubled and even trebled. **of the slain**—i.e., by which many are slain. As the *Hebrew* is *singular*, FAIRBAIRN makes it refer to the king, "the sword of the great one that is slain," or "pierced through." **entereth . . . privy chambers**—(Jer. 9:21). The sword shall overtake them, not merely in the open battlefield, but in the chambers whither they flee to hide themselves (I Kings 20:30; 22:25). MAURER translates, "which *besieged* them"; FAIRBAIRN, "which penetrates to them." *English Version* is more literal. **15. point**—"the *whirling glance* of the sword" [FAIRBAIRN]. "The *naked* (bared) sword" [HENDERSON]. **ruins**—lit., "stumbling blocks." Their own houses and walls shall be stumbling blocks in their way, whether they wish to fight or flee. **made bright**—made to glitter. **wrapped . . .**—viz., in the hand of him who holds the hilt, or in its scabbard, that the edge may not be blunt when it is presently drawn forth to strike. GESENIUS, translates, "sharpened . . . ." **16.** Apostrophe to the sword. **Go . . . one way**—or, "Concentrate thyself"; "*Unite* thy forces on the right hand" [GROTIUS]. The sword is commanded to take the nearest route for Jerusalem, "whither their face was set,' whether south or north ("right hand or left"), according to where the several parts of the Chaldean host may be. **or other, . . . on the left**—rather "*set thyself* on the left." The verbs are well chosen. The main "*concentration*" of forces was to be on "the right hand," or *south*, the part of Judea in which Jerusalem was, and which lay south in marching from Babylon, whereas the Chaldean forces advancing on Jerusalem from Egypt, of which Jerusalem was north, were fewer, and therefore "set thyself" is the verb used. **17.** Jehovah Himself smites His hands together, doing what He had commanded Ezekiel to do (*Note*, vs. 14), in token of His smiting Jerusalem; cf. the similar symbolical action (II Kings 13:18, 19). **cause . . . fury to rest**—give it full vent, and so satisfy it (ch. 5:13). **19. two ways**—The king coming from Babylon is represented in the graphic style of Ezekiel as reaching the point where the road branched off in two ways, one leading by the south, by Tadmor or Palmyra, to Rabbath of Ammon, east of Jordan; the other by the north, by Riblah in Syria, to Jerusalem—and hesitating which way to take. Ezekiel is told to "appoint the two ways" (as in ch. 4:1); for Nebuchadnezzar, though knowing no other control but his own will and superstition, had really this path "appointed" for him by the all-ruling God. **out of one land**—viz., Babylon. **choose . . . a place**—lit., "a hand." So it is translated by FAIRBAIRN, "make a *finger-post*," viz., at the head of the two ways, the hand-post pointing Nebuchadnezzar to the way to Jerusalem as the way he should select. But MAURER rightly supports *English Version*. Ezekiel is told to "choose the place" where Nebuchadnezzar should do as is described in vss. 20, 21; so entirely does God order by the prophet every particular of place and time in the movements of the invader. **20. Rabbath of the Ammonites**—distinct from Rabbah in Judah (II Sam. 12:26). Rabbath is put first, as it was from her that Jerusalem, that doomed city, had borrowed many of her idols. **to Judah in Jerusalem**—instead of simply putting "Judah," to imply the sword was to come not merely to Judah, but to its people *within* Jerusalem, defended though it was; its defenses on which the Jews relied so much would not keep the foe out. **21. parting**—lit., "mother of the way." As "head of the two ways" follows, which seems tautology after "parting of the

way," HAVERNICK translates, according to *Arabic* idiom, "the highway," or principal road. *English Version* is not tautology, "head of the two ways" defining more accurately "parting of the way." **made . . . bright**—rather, "shook," from an *Arabic* root. **arrows**—Divination by arrows is here referred to: they were put into a quiver marked with the names of particular places to be attacked, and then *shaken* together; whichever came forth first intimated the one selected as the first to be attacked [JEROME]. The same usage existed among the Arabs, and is mentioned in the Koran. In the Nineveh sculptures the king is represented with a cup in his right hand, his left resting on a bow; also with two arrows in the right, and the bow in the left, probably practising divination. **images**—*Hebrew*. "teraphim"; household gods, worshipped as family talismans, to obtain direction as to the future and other blessings. First mentioned in Mesopotamia, whence Rachel brought them (Gen. 31:19, 34); put away by Jacob (Gen. 35:4); set up by Micah as household gods (Judg. 17:5); stigmatized as idolatry (I Sam. 15:23, *Hebrew*; cf. Zech. 10:2, *Margin*). **liver**—They judged of the success, or failure, of an undertaking by the healthy, or unhealthy, state of the liver and entrails of a sacrifice. **22.** Rather, "*In* his right hand was [is] the divination," i.e., he holds up in his right hand the arrow marked for "Jerusalem," to encourage his army to march for it. **captains**—The *Margin*, "battering-rams," adopted by FAIRBAIRN, is less appropriate, for "battering-rams" follow presently after [GROTIUS]. **open the mouth in . . . slaughter**—i.e., commanding slaughter: raising the war cry of death. Not as GESENIUS, "to open the mouth *with the war shout*." **23.** Unto *the Jews,* though credulous of divinations when in their favor, Nebuchadnezzar's divination "shall be [seen] as false." **unto them . . .**—This gives the reason which makes the Jews fancy themselves safe from the Chaldeans, viz., that they "have sworn" to the latter "oaths" of allegiance, forgetting that they had violated them (ch. 17:13, 15, 16, 18). **but he . . .**—Nebuchadnezzar will remember in consulting his idols that he swore to Zedekiah by them, but that Zedekiah broke the league [GROTIUS]. Rather, *God* will remember against them (Rev. 16:19) their violating their oath sworn by the true God, whereas Nebuchadnezzar kept his oath sworn by a false god; vs. 24 confirms this. **24.** Their unfaithfulness to Nebuchadnezzar was a type of their general unfaithfulness to their covenant God. **with the hand**—viz., of the king of Babylon. **25. profane**—as having desecrated by idolatry and perjury his office as the Lord's anointed. HAVERNICK translates, as in vs. 14, "slain," i.e., not literally, but virtually; to Ezekiel's idealizing view Zedekiah was the grand victim "pierced through" by God's sword of judgment, as his sons were slain before his eyes, which were then put out, and he was led a captive in chains to Babylon. *English Version* is better: so GESENIUS (II Chron. 36:13; Jer. 52:2). **25. when iniquity shall have an end**—(vs. 29). When thine iniquity, having reached its last stage of guilt, shall be put an end to by judgment (ch. 35:5). **26. diadem**—rather, "the miter" of the holy priest (Exod. 28:4; Zech. 3:5). His priestly emblem as representative of the priestly people. Both this and "the crown," the emblem of the kingdom, were to be removed, until they should be restored and united in the Mediator, Messiah (Ps. 110:2, 4; Zech. 6:13), [FAIRBAIRN]. As, however, King Zedekiah alone, not the high priest also, is referred to in the context, *English Version* is supported by GENESIUS. **this shall not be**

the same—The diadem shall not be as it was [ROSENMULLER]. Nothing shall remain what it was [FAIRBAIRN]. **exalt ... low, ... abase ... high**—not the general truth expressed (Prov. 3:34; Luke 1:52; Jas. 4:6; I Pet. 5:5); but specially referring to Messiah and Zedekiah contrasted together. The "tender plant ... out of the dry ground" (Isa. 53:2) is to be "exalted" in the end (vs. 27); the now "high" representative on David's throne, Zedekiah, is to be "abased." The *outward* relations of things shall be made to change places in just retaliation on the people for having so perverted the *moral* relations of things [HENGSTENBERG]. **27.** Lit., "An over-turning, overturning, overturning, will I make it." The threefold repetition denotes the awful *certainty* of the event; not as ROSENMULLER explains, the overthrow of the *three*, Jehoiakim, Jeconiah, and Zedekiah; for Zedekiah alone is referred to. **it shall be no more, until he come whose right it is**—strikingly parallel to Genesis 49:10. Nowhere shall there be rest or permanence; all things shall be in fluctuation until He comes who, as the rightful Heir, shall restore the throne of David that fell with Zedekiah. The *Hebrew* for "right" is "judgment"; it perhaps includes, besides the *right* to rule, the idea of His rule being one in *righteousness* (Ps. 72:2; Isa. 9:6, 7; 11:4; Rev. 19:11). Others (Nebuchadnezzar, etc.), who held the rule of the earth delegated to them by God, abused it by unrighteousness, and so forfeited the "right." He both has the truest "right" to the rule, and exercises it in "right." It is true the *tribal* "scepter" continued with Judah "till Shiloh came" (Gen. 49:10); but there was no *kingly* scepter till Messiah came, as the *spiritual* King then (John 18:36, 37); this spiritual kingdom being about to pass into the *literal, personal* kingdom over Israel at His second coming, when, and not before, this prophecy shall have its exhaustive fulfilment (Luke 1:32, 33; Jer. 3:17; 10:7; "To thee doth it appertain"). **28.** Lest Ammon should think to escape because Nebuchadnezzar had taken the route to Jerusalem, Ezekiel denounces judgment against Ammon, without the prospect of a restoration such as awaited Israel. Jeremiah 49:6, it is true, speaks of a "bringing again of its captivity," but this probably refers to its *spiritual* restoration under Messiah; or, if referring to it *politically*, must refer to but a partial restoration at the downfall of Babylon under Cyrus. **their reproach**—This constituted a leading feature in their guilt; they treated with proud contumely the covenant people after the taking of Jerusalem by Nebuchadnezzar (ch. 25:3, 6; Zeph. 2:9, 10), and appropriated Israel's territory (Jer. 49:1; Amos 1:13-15). **furbished, to consume**—MAURER punctuates thus, "Drawn for the slaughter, it is furbished to devour ('consume'), to glitter." *English Version*, "to consume because of the glittering," means, "to consume *by reason of the lightning, flash-like rapidity* with which it falls." Five years after the fall of Jerusalem, Ammon was destroyed for aiding Ishmael in usurping the government of Judea against the will of the king of Babylon (II Kings 25: 25; Jer. 41:15) [GROTIUS]. **29. see vanity ... divine a lie**—Ammon, too, had false diviners who flattered them with assurances of safety; the only result of which will be to "bring Ammon upon the necks ...," i.e., to add the Ammonites to the *headless trunks* of the slain of Judah, whose bad example Ammon followed, and "whose day" of visitation for their guilt "is come." **when their iniquity shall have an end**—See *Note*, vs. 25. **30. Shall I cause it to return into his sheath**—viz., without first destroying Ammon. Certainly not (Jer.

47:6, 7). Others, as *Margin*, less suitably read it imperatively, "Cause it to return," i.e., after it has done the work appointed to it. **in the land of thy nativity**—Ammon was not to be carried away captive as Judah, but to perish in his own land. **31. blow against thee in ...**—rather, "blow upon thee with the fire ...." Image from smelting metals (ch. 22: 20, 21). **brutish**—ferocious. **skilful to destroy**—lit., "artificers of destruction"; alluding to Isaiah 54:16. **32. thy blood shall be**—i.e., shall flow. **be no more remembered**—be consigned as a nation to oblivion.

CHAPTER 22

Vss. 1-31. GOD'S JUDGMENT ON THE SINFULNESS OF JERUSALEM. Repetition of the charges in ch. 20; only that there they were stated in an historical review of the *past* and present; here the *present* sins of the nation exclusively are brought forward. **2.** See ch. 20:4; i.e., "Wilt thou *not* judge ... ?" (cf. ch. 23:36). **the bloody city**—lit., "the city of bloods"; so called on account of murders perpetrated in her, and sacrifices of children to Molech (vss. 3, 4, 6, 9; ch. 24:6, 9). **3. sheddeth blood ... that her time may come**—Instead of deriving advantage from her bloody sacrifices to idols, she only thereby brought on herself "the time" of her punishment. **against herself**—(Prov. 8:36). **4. thy days**—the shorter period, viz., that of the *siege*. **thy years**—the longer period of the *captivity*. The "days" and "years" express that she is ripe for punishment. **5. infamous**—They mockingly call thee, "Thou polluted one in name (*Margin*), and full of confusion" [FAIRBAIRN], (referring to the tumultuous violence prevalent in it). Thus the nations "far and near" mocked her as at once sullied in character and in actual fact lawless. What a sad contrast to the Jerusalem once designated "the holy city!" **6.** Rather, "The princes ... each according to his power, were in thee, to shed blood" (as if this was the only object of their existence). "Power," lit., "arm"; they, who ought to have been patterns of justice, made their own arm of might their only law. **7. set light by**—Children have made light of, disrespected, father ... (Deut. 27:16). From vs. 7 to vs. 12 are enumerated the sins committed in violation of Moses' law. **9. men that carry tales**—informers, who by misrepresentations cause innocent blood to be shed (Lev. 19:16). Lit., "one who goes to and fro as a *merchant*." **10. set apart for pollution**—i.e., set apart *as unclean* (Lev. 18:19). **12. forgotten me**—(Deut. 32:18; Jer. 2:32; 3:21). **13. smitten mine hand**—in token of the indignant vengeance which I will execute on thee (*Note*, ch. 21:17). **14.** (Ch. 21:7.) **15. consume thy filthiness out of thee**—the object of God in scattering the Jews. **16. take thine inheritance in thyself**—Formerly thou wast Mine inheritance; but now, full of guilt, thou art no longer Mine, but *thine own inheritance to thyself;* "in the sight of the heathen," i.e., even they shall see that, now that thou hast become a captive, thou art no longer owned as Mine [VATABLUS]. FAIRBAIRN and others needlessly take the *Hebrew* from a different root, "thou shalt be *polluted by* ('in' [HENDERSON]) *thyself ...;*" the heathen shall regard thee as a polluted thing, who hast brought thine own reproach on thyself. **18. dross ... brass**—Israel has become a worthless compound of the dross of silver (implying not merely corruption, but *degeneracy* from good to bad, Isa. 1:22, especially offensive) and of the baser metals. Hence the people must be thrown into the furnace of judgment, that the bad may be consumed, and the good separated (Jer. 6:29, 30). **23.** From this verse to the end he shows the general corruption of all ranks. **24. land . . . not cleansed**—not cleared or cultivated; all a scene of desolation; a fit emblem of the moral wilderness state of the people. **nor rained upon**—a mark of divine "indignation"; as the early and latter rain, on which the productiveness of the land depended, was one of the great covenant blessings. Joel (2:23) promises the return of the former and latter rain, with the restoration of God's favor. **25. conspiracy**—The false prophets have conspired both to propagate error and to oppose the messages of God's servants. *They* are mentioned first, as their bad influence extended the widest. **prey**—Their aim was greed of gain, "treasure, and precious things" (Hos. 6:9; Zeph. 3:3, 4; Matt. 23:14). **made . . . many widows**—by òccasioning, through false prophecies, the war with the Chaldeans in which the husbands fell. **26. Her priests**—whose "lips should have kept knowledge" (Mal. 2:7). **violated**—not simply *transgressed;* but, *have done violence to* the law, by wresting it to wrong ends, and putting wrong constructions on it. **put no difference between the holy and profane . . .** —made no distinction between the clean and unclean (Lev. 10:10), the Sabbath and other days, sanctioning violations of that holy day. "Holy" means, *what is dedicated to God;* "profane," *what is in common use;* "unclean," *what is forbidden to be eaten;* "clean," *what is lawful to be eaten.* **I am profaned among them**—They abuse My name to false or unjust purposes. **27. princes**—who should have employed the influence of their position for the people's welfare, made "gain" their sole aim. **wolves**—notorious for fierce and ravening cruelty (Mic. 3:2, 3, 9-11; John 10:12). **28.** Referring to the false assurances of peace with which the prophets flattered the people, that they should not submit to the king of Babylon (*Note,* ch. 13:10; 21:29; Jer. 6:14; 23:16, 17; 27:9, 10). **29. The people**—put last, after the mention of those in office. Corruption had spread downwards through the whole community. **wrongfully**—i.e., "without cause," gratuitously, without the stranger proselyte giving any just provocation; nay, he of all others being one who ought to have been won to the worship of Jehovah by kindness, instead of being alienated by oppression; especially as the Israelites were commanded to remember that they themselves had been "strangers in Egypt" (Exod. 22:21; 23:9). **30. the hedge**—the wall (*Note,* ch. 13:5); image for *leading the people to repentance.* **the gap**—the breach (Ps. 106:23); image for *interceding between the people and God* (Gen. 20:7; Exod. 32:11; Num. 16:48). **I found none**— (Jer. 5:1)—not that literally there was not a righteous man in the city. For Jeremiah, Baruch, etc., were still there; but Jeremiah had been forbidden to pray for the people (Jer. 11:14), as being doomed to wrath. None now, of the godly, knowing the desperate state of the people, and God's purpose as to them, was *willing* longer to interpose between God's wrath and them. And none "among them," i.e., among those just enumerated as guilty of such sins (vss. 25-29), was morally *able* for such an office. **31. their own way . . . recompensed upon their heads**—(ch. 9:10; 11:21; 16:43; Prov. 1:31; Isa. 3:11; Jer. 6:19).

CHAPTER 23

Vss. 1-49. Israel's and Judah's Sin and Punishment Are Parabolically Portrayed under the

Names Aholah and Aholibah. The imagery is similar to that in ch. 16; but here the reference is not as there so much to the breach of the spiritual marriage covenant with God by the people's *idolatries,* as by their *worldly spirit,* and their trusting to alliances with the heathen for safety, rather than to God. **2. two . . . of one mother**—Israel and Judah, one nation by birth from the same ancestress, Sarah. **3.** Even so early in their history as their Egyptian sojourn, they committed idolatries (*Notes,* ch. 20: 6-8; Josh. 24:14). **in their youth**—an aggravation of their sin. It was at the very time of their receiving extraordinary favors from God (ch. 16:6, 22). **they bruised**—viz., the Egyptians. **4. Aholah**—i.e., *"Her* tent" (put for *worship,* as the first worship of God in Israel was in a *tent* or tabernacle), as contrasted with Aholibah, i.e., *"My* tent in her." The Bethel worship of Samaria was of *her own* devising, not of God's appointment; the temple-worship of Jerusalem was expressly *appointed by Jehovah,* who "dwelt" there, "setting up His tabernacle among the people as His" (Exod. 25:8; Lev. 26:11, 12; Josh. 22: 19; Ps. 76:2). **the elder**—Samaria is called "the elder" because she preceded Judah in her apostasy and its punishment. **they were mine**—Previous to apostasy under Jeroboam, Samaria (Israel, or the ten tribes), equally with Judah, worshipped the true God. God therefore never renounced the right over Israel, but sent prophets, as Elijah and Elisha, to declare His will to them. **5. when . . . mine**—lit., "under Me," i.e., subject to Me as her lawful husband. **neighbours**—On the northeast the kingdom of Israel bordered on that of Assyria; for the latter had occupied much of Syria. Their neighborhood in locality was emblematical of their being near in corruption of morals and worship. The *alliances* of Israel with Assyria, which are the chief subject of reprobation here, tended to this (II Kings 15:19; 16:7, 9; 17:3; Hos. 8:9). **6. blue**—rather, "purple" [FAIRBAIRN]. As a lustful woman's passions are fired by showy dress and youthful appearance in men, so Israel was seduced by the pomp and power of Assyria (cf. Isa. 10:8). **horsemen**—cavaliers. **7. all their idols**—There was nothing that she refused to her lovers. **8. whoredoms brought from Egypt** —the calves set up in Dan and Bethel by Jeroboam, answering to the Egyptian bull-formed idol Apis. Her *alliances* with Egypt *politically* are also meant (Isa. 30:2, 3; 31:1). The ten tribes probably resumed the Egyptian rites, in order to enlist the Egyptians against Judah (II Chron. 12:2-4). **9.** God, in righteous retribution, turned their objects of trust into the instruments of their punishment: Pul, Tiglath-pileser, Esar-haddon, and Shalmaneser (II Kings 15:19, 29; 17:3, 6, 24; Ezra 4:2, 10). "It was their sin to have sought after such lovers, and it was to be their punishment that these lovers should become their destroyers" [FAIRBAIRN]. **10. became famous**—lit., "she became a name," i.e., as notorious by her punishment as she had been by her sins, so as to be quoted as a *warning* to others. **women** i.e., neighboring peoples. **11.** Judah, the southern kingdom, though having the "warning" (*Note,* vs. 10) of the northern kingdom before her eyes, instead of profiting by it, went to even greater lengths in corruption than Israel. Her greater spiritual privileges made her guilt the greater (ch. 16:47, 51; Jer. 3:11). **12.** (Vss. 6, 23.) **most gorgeously**—lit., "to perfection." GROTIUS translates, "wearing a crown," or "chaplet," such as lovers wore in visiting their mistresses. **13. one way**—both alike forsaking God for heathen confidences. **14. vermilion**—the peculiar color of the Chaldeans, as purple was of the Assyrians. In striking agreement with this verse is the fact that the Assyrian sculptures lately discovered have painted and colored bas-reliefs in red, blue, and black. The Jews (for instance Jehoiakim, Jer. 22:14) copied these (cf. ch. 8:10). **15. exceeding in dyed attire**—rather, "in ample dyed *turbans*"; lit., "redundant with dyed turbans." The Assyrians delighted in ample, flowing, and richly colored tunics, scarfs, girdles, and head-dresses or turbans, varying in ornaments according to the rank. **Chaldea, . . . land of their nativity**—between the Black and Caspian Seas (*Note*, Isa. 23:13). **princes**—lit., a first-rate military class that fought by threes in the chariots, one guiding the horses, the other two fighting. **16. sent messengers . . . into Chaldea**—(ch. 16: 29). It was she that solicited the Chaldeans, not they her. Probably the occasion was when Judah sought to strengthen herself by a Chaldean alliance against a menaced attack by Egypt (cf. II Kings 23: 29-35; 24:1-7). God made the object of their sinful desire the instrument of their punishment. Jehoiakim, probably by a stipulation of tribute, enlisted Nebuchadnezzar against Pharaoh, whose tributary he previously had been; failing to keep his stipulation, he brought on himself Nebuchadnezzar's vengeance. **17. alienated from them**—viz., from the Chaldeans: turning again to the Egyptians (vs. 19), trying by their help to throw off her solemn engagements to Babylon (cf. Jer. 37:5, 7; II Kings 24:7). **18. my mind was alienated from her**—lit., "was broken off from her." Just retribution for "her mind being alienated (broken off) from the Chaldeans" (vs. 17), to whom she had sworn fealty (ch. 17:12-19). "Discovered" implies the open shamelessness of her apostasy. **19.** Israel first "called" her lusts, practised when in Egypt, "to her (fond) *remembrance*," and then actually returned to them. Mark the danger of suffering the memory to dwell on the pleasure felt in past sins. **20. their paramours**—i.e., her paramours *among them* (the Egyptians); she doted upon their persons as her paramours (vss. 5, 12, 16). **flesh**—the membrum virile (very large in the ass). Cf. Leviticus 15:2, *Margin;* Ezekiel 16:26. **issue of horses**—the seminal issue. The horse was made by the Egyptians the hieroglyphic for a lustful person. **21. calledst to remembrance**—"didst repeat" [MAURER]. **in bruising**—in suffering . . . to be bruised. **22. lovers . . . alienated**—(vs. 17). Illicit love, soon or late, ends in open hatred (I Sam. 13:15). The Babylonians, the objects formerly of their God-forgetting love, but now, with characteristic fickleness, objects of their hatred, shall be made by God the instruments of their punishment. **23. Pekod . . .**—(Jer. 50:21). Not a geographical name, but descriptive of Babylon. "Visitation," peculiarly the *land of "judgment"*; in a double sense: *actively,* the inflicter of judgment on Judah; *passively,* as about to be afterwards herself the object of judgment. **Shoa . . . Koa**—"rich . . . noble"; descriptive of Babylon in her prosperity, having all the world's wealth and dignity at her disposal. MAURER suggests that, as descriptive appellatives are subjoined to the proper name, "all the Assyrians" in the second hemistich of the verse (as the verse ought to be divided at "Koa"), so Pekod, Shoa, and Koa must be appellatives descriptive of "The Babylonians and . . . Chaldeans" in the first hemistich; "Pekod" meaning "prefects"; Shoa . . . Koa, "rich . . . princely." **desirable young men**—strong irony. Alluding to vs. 12, these "desirable young men" whom thou didst so "dote upon" for their manly vigor of appearance, shall by that very vigor be the better able

to chastise thee. **24. with chariots**—or, "with armaments"; so LXX; "axes" [MAURER]; or, joining it with "wagons," translate, "with *scythe-armed* wagons," or "chariots" [GROTIUS]. **weels**—The unusual height of these increased their formidable appearance (ch. 1:16-20). **their judgments**—which awarded barbarously severe punishments (Jer. 52:9; 29:22). **25. take away thy nose . . . ears**—Adulteresses were punished so among the Egyptians and Chaldeans. Oriental beauties wore ornaments in the ear and nose. How just the retribution, that the features most bejewelled should be mutilated! So, allegorically as to Judah, the spiritual adulteress. **26. strip . . . of . . . clothes**—whereby she attracted her paramours (ch. 16:39). **27. Thus . . . make . . . lewdness to cease**—The captivity has made the Jews ever since abhor idolatry, not only on their return from Babylon, but for the last nineteen centuries of their dispersion, as foretold (Hos. 3:4). **28.** (Vss. 17, 18; ch. 16:37.) **29. take away . . . thy labour**—i.e., the fruits of thy labor. **leave thee naked**—as captive females are treated. **31. her cup** —of punishment (Ps. 11:6; 75:8; Jer. 25:15, etc.). Thy guilt and that of Israel being alike, your punishment shall be alike. **34. break . . . sherds**—So greedily shalt thou suck out every drop like one drinking to madness (the effect invariably ascribed to drinking God's cup of wrath, Jer. 51:7; Hab. 2: 16) that thou shalt crunch the very shreds of it; i.e., there shall be no evil left which thou shalt not taste. **pluck off thine own breasts**—enraged against them as the ministers to thine adultery. **35. forgotten me**—(Jer. 2:32; 13:25). **cast me behind thy back**— (I Kings 14:9; Neh. 9:26). **bear . . . thy lewdness**— i.e., its penal consequences (Prov. 1:31). **36-44.** A summing up of the sins of the two sisters, especially those of Judah. **36.** Wilt thou (not) judge (*Note,* ch. 20:4)? **38. the same day**—On the very day that they had burned their children to Molech in the valley of Gehenna, they shamelessly and hypocritically presented themselves as worshippers in Jehovah's temple (Jer. 7:9, 10). **40. messenger was sent**—viz., by Judah (vs. 16; Isa. 57:9). **paintedst . . . eyes**—(II Kings 9:30, *Margin;* Jer. 4:30). Black paint was spread on the eyelids of beauties to make the white of the eye more attractive by the contrast, so Judah left no seductive art untried. **41. bed**—divan. While men reclined at table, women sat, as it seemed indelicate for them to lie down (Amos 6:4), [GROTIUS]. **table**—i.e., the idolatrous altar. **mine incense**—which I had given thee, and which thou oughtest to have offered to Me (ch. 16: 18, 19; Hos. 2:8; cf. Prov. 7:17). **42. Sabeans**—Not content with the princely, handsome Assyrians, the sisters brought to themselves the rude robber hordes of *Sabeans* (Job 1:15). The *Keri,* or *Margin,* reads "drunkards." **upon their hands**—upon the hands of the sisters, i.e., they allured Samaria and Judah to worship their gods. **43. Will they . . .**—Is it possible that paramours will desire any longer to commit whoredoms with so worn-out an old adulteress? **45. the righteous men**—the Chaldeans; the executioners of God's righteous vengeance (ch. 16:38), not that they were "righteous" in themselves (Hab. 1:3, 12, 13). **46. a company**—properly, "a council of judges" passing sentence on a criminal [GROTIUS]. The "removal" and "spoiling" by the Chaldean army is the execution of the judicial sentence of God. **47. stones**—the legal penalty of the adulteress (ch. 16:40, 41; John 8:5). Answering to the *stones* hurled by the Babylonians from engines in besieging Jerusalem. **houses . . . fire**—fulfilled (II Chron. 36: 17, 19). **48.** (Vs. 27.) **that all . . . may be taught**

not to do...–(Deut. 13:11). **49. bear the sins of your idols**–i.e., the punishment of your idolatry. **know that I am the Lord God**–i.e., know it to your cost ... by bitter suffering.

CHAPTER 24

Vss. 1-27. VISION OF THE BOILING CALDRON, AND OF THE DEATH OF EZEKIEL'S WIFE. **1, 2.** Ezekiel proves his divine mission by announcing the very day ("this same day") of the beginning of the investment of the city by Nebuchadnezzar; "the ninth year," viz., of Jehoiachin's captivity, "the tenth day of the tenth month"; though he was 300 miles away from Jerusalem among the captives at the Chebar (II Kings 25:1; Jer. 39:1). **set himself**–*laid siege;* "lay against." **3. pot**–caldron. Alluding to the self-confident proverb used among the people, ch. 11:3 (see my *Note*), "This city is the caldron and we be the flesh"; your proverb shall prove awfully true, but in a different sense from what you intend. So far from the city proving an iron, caldron-like defense from the fire, it shall be as a caldron set on the fire, and the people as so many pieces of meat subjected to boiling heat. See Jeremiah 1:13. **4. pieces thereof**–those which properly *belong to it, as its own.* **every good piece...choice bones**–i.e., the most distinguished of the people. The "choice bones" *in* the pot have flesh adhering to them. The "bones" *under* the pot (vs. 5) are those having no flesh and used as fuel, answering to the poorest who suffer first, and are put out of pain sooner than the rich who endure what answers to the slower process of boiling. **5. burn...bones**–rather, "*pile* the bones." Lit., "Let there be a *round* pile of the bones." **therein**–lit., "in the midst of it." **6. scum**–not ordinary, but *poisonous scum,* i.e., the people's all-pervading wickedness. **bring it out piece by piece**–"it," the contents of the pot; its flesh, i.e., "I will destroy the people of the city, not all at the same time, but by a series of successive attacks." Not as FAIRBAIRN, "on its every piece let it (the poisonous scum) go forth." **let no lot fall upon it**–i.e., no lot, such as is sometimes cast, to decide who are to be destroyed and who saved (II Sam. 8:2; Joel 3:3; Obadiah 11; Nah. 3:10). In former carryings away of captives, lots were cast to settle who were to go, and who to stay, but now all alike are to be cast out without distinction of rank, age, or sex. **7. upon the top of a rock**–or, "the dry, bare, exposed rock," so as to be conspicuous to all. Blood poured on a rock is not so soon absorbed as blood poured on the earth. The law ordered the blood even of a beast or fowl to be "covered with the dust" (Lev. 17:13); but Jerusalem was so shameless as to be at no pains to cover up the blood of innocent men slain in her. *Blood,* as the consummation of all sin, presupposes every other form of guilt. **8. That it might cause**–God *purposely* let her so shamelessly pour the blood on the bare rock, "*that it might*" the more loudly and openly cry for vengeance from on high; and that the connection between the guilt and the punishment might be the more palpable. The blood of Abel, though the ground received it, still cries to heaven for vengeance (Gen. 4:10, 11); much more blood shamelessly exposed on the bare rock. **set her blood**–She *shall* be paid back in kind (Matt. 7:2). She openly shed blood, and her blood shall openly be shed. **9. the pile for fire**–the hostile materials for the city's destruction. **10. spice it well**–that the meat may be the more palatable, i.e., I will make the foe delight in its de-

struction as much as one delights in well-seasoned, savory meat. GROTIUS, needlessly departing from the obvious sense, translates, "Let it be boiled down to a compound." **11. set it empty...that...brass ...may burn,...that...scum...may be consumed**–Even the consumption of the contents is not enough; the caldron itself which is infected by the poisonous scum must be destroyed, i.e., the city itself must be destroyed, not merely the inhabitants, just as the very house infected with leprosy was to be destroyed (Lev. 14:34-45). **12.** *herself*–rather, "she hath wearied *Me* out with lies"; or rather "with vain labors" on My part to purify her without being obliged to have recourse to judgments (cf. Isa. 43:24; Mal. 2:17) [MAURER]. However, *English Version* gives a good sense (cf. Isa. 47:13; 57: 10). **13. lewdness**–determined, deliberate wickedness; from a *Hebrew* root, "to purpose." **I have purged thee**–i.e., I have left nothing untried which would tend towards purging thee, by sending prophets to invite thee to repentance, by giving thee the law with all its promises, privileges, and threats. **thou shalt not be purged...any more**–i.e., by My gracious interpositions; thou shalt be left to thine own course to take its fatal consequences. **14. go back**–desist; relax [FAIRBAIRN]. **15.** Second part of the vision; announcement of the death of Ezekiel's wife, and prohibition of the usual signs of mourning. **16. desire of...eyes**–his wife: representing the sanctuary (vs. 21) in which the Jews so much gloried. The energy and subordination of Ezekiel's whole life to his prophetic office is strikingly displayed in this narrative of his wife's death. It is the only memorable event of his personal history which he records, and this only in reference to his soul-absorbing work. His natural tenderness is shown by that graphic touch, "the desire of thine eyes." What amazing subjection, then, of his individual feeling to his prophetic duty is manifested in the simple statement (vs. 18), "So I spake ... in the morning; and at even my wife died; and I did in the morning as I was commanded." **stroke**–a sudden visitation. The suddenness of it enhances the self-control of Ezekiel in so entirely merging individual feeling, which must have been especially acute under such trying circumstances, in the higher claims of duty to God. **17. Forbear to cry**–or, "Lament in silence"; not forbidding sorrow, but the *loud expression* of it [GROTIUS]. **no mourning**–typical of the universality of the ruin of Jerusalem, which would preclude mourning, such as is usual where calamity is but partial. "The dead" is purposely put in the *plural,* as referring ultimately to the *dead* who should perish at the taking of Jerusalem; though the *singular* might have been expected, as Ezekiel's wife was the immediate subject referred to: "make no mourning" *such as is usual* "for *the dead,* and such as shall be hereafter in Jerusalem" (Jer. 16:5-7). **tire of thine head**–thy headdress [FAIRBAIRN]. JEROME explains, "Thou shalt retain the hair which is usually cut in mourning." The fillet, binding the hair about the temples like a chaplet, was laid aside at such times. Uncovering the head was an ordinary sign of mourning in priests; whereas others covered their heads in mourning (II Sam. 15:30). The reason was, the priests had their headdress of fine twined linen given them for ornament, and as a badge of office. The high priest, as having on his head the holy anointing oil, was forbidden in *any* case to lay aside his headdress. But the priests might do so in the case of the death of the nearest relatives (Lev. 21:2, 3, 10). They then put on inferior attire, sprinkling also on their heads dust and ashes (cf. Lev. 10:6, 7). **shoes upon thy feet**—whereas mourners went "barefoot" (II Sam. 15:30). **cover not ... lips**—rather, the "upper lip," with the moustache (Lev. 13:45; Mic. 3:7). **bread of men**—the bread usually brought to mourners by friends in token of sympathy. So the "cup of consolation" brought (Jer. 16:7). "Of men" means such as is usually furnished *by men.* So Isaiah 8:1, "a *man's* pen"; Revelation 21:17, "the measure *of a man.*" **19. what these things are to us**—The people perceive that Ezekiel's strange conduct has a symbolical meaning as to themselves; they ask, "What is that meaning?" **21. excellency of your strength**—(cf. Amos 6:8). The object of your pride and confidence (Jer. 7:4, 10, 14). **desire of ... eyes**—(Ps. 27:4). The antitype to Ezekiel's wife (vs. 16). **pitieth**—loveth, as pity is akin to love: "yearned over." **Profane**—an appropriate word. They had profaned the temple with idolatry; God, in just retribution, will profane it with the Chaldean sword, i.e., lay it in the dust, as Ezekiel's wife. **sons ... daughters ... left**—the children *left* behind in Judea, when the parents were carried away. **22.** (Jer. 16:6, 7.) So general shall be the calamity, that all ordinary usages of mourning shall be suspended. **23. ye shall not mourn ... but ... pine away for your iniquities**—The Jews' not mourning was to be not the result of insensibility, any more than Ezekiel's not mourning for his wife was not from want of feeling. They could not in their exile manifest publicly their lamentation, but they would privately "mourn *one to another.*" Their "iniquities" would then be their chief sorrow ("pining away"), as feeling that these were the cause of their sufferings (cf. Lev. 26:39; Lam. 3:39). The fullest fulfilment is still future (Zech. 12:10-14). **24. sign**—a typical representative in his own person of what was to befall them (Isa. 20:3). **when this cometh**—alluding probably to their taunt, as if God's word spoken by His prophets would never come to pass. "Where is the word of the Lord? Let it *come* now" (Jer. 17:15). When the prophecy is fulfilled, "ye shall know (to your cost) that I am the Lord," who thereby show My power and fulfil My word spoken by My prophet (John 13:19; 14:29). **25, 26.** "The day" referred to in these verses is the day of the overthrow of the temple, when the fugitive "escapes." But "that day," in vs. 27, is the day on which the fugitive brings the sad news to Ezekiel, at the Chebar. In the interval the prophet suspended his prophecies *as to the Jews,* as was foretold. Afterwards his mouth was "opened," and no more "dumb" (ch. 3:26, 27; cf. vs. 27 here in ch. 24; and ch. 33:21, 22).

CHAPTER 25

Vss. 1-17. Appropriately in the Interval of Silence as to the Jews in the Eight Chapters, 25-32, Ezekiel Denounces Judgments on the Heathen World Kingdoms. If Israel was not spared, much less the heathen utterly corrupt, and having no mixture of truth, such as Israel in its worst state possessed (I Pet. 4:17, 18). Their ruin was to be utter: Israel's but temporary (Jer. 46:28). The nations denounced are *seven,* the perfect number; implying that God's judgments would visit, not merely these, but *the whole round* of the heathen foes of God. Babylon is excepted, because she is now for the present viewed as the rod of God's retributive justice, a view too much then lost sight of by those who fretted against her universal supremacy. **3.** (Jer. 49:1). **when ... profaned; ... when**

... desolate; ... when ... captivity—rather, "for ... for ... for": the *cause* of the insolent exultation of Ammon over Jerusalem. They triumphed especially over the fall of the "sanctuary," as the triumph of heathenism over the rival claims of Jehovah. In Jehoshaphat's time, when Psalm 83 was written (Ps. 83:4, 7, 8, 12, "Ammon ... *holpen the children of Lot,*" who were, therefore, the *leaders* of the unholy conspiracy, "Let us take to ourselves the *houses of God* in possession"), we see the same profane spirit. Now at last their wicked wish seems accomplished in the fall of Jerusalem. Ammon, descended from Lot, held the region east of Jordan, separated from the Amorites on the north by the river Jabbok, and from Moab on the south by the Arnon. They were auxiliaries to Babylon in the destruction of Jerusalem (II Kings 24:2). **4. men of ... east**—lit., "children of the East," the nomad tribes of Arabia Deserta, east of the Jordan and the Dead Sea. **palaces**—their nomadic encampments or folds, surrounded with mud walls, are so called in irony. Where thy "palaces" once stood, there shall their very different "palaces" stand. Fulfilled after the ravaging of their region by Nebuchadnezzar, shortly after the destruction of Jerusalem (cf. ch. 21:22; Jer. 49:1-28). **5. Rabbah**—meaning "the Great," Ammon's metropolis. Under the Ptolemies it was rebuilt under the name Philadelphia; the ruins are called *Amman* now, but there is no dwelling inhabited. **Ammonites**—i.e., the Ammonite *region* is to be a "couching-place for flocks," viz., of the Arabs. The "camels," being the chief beast of burden of the Chaldeans, are put first, as their invasion was to prepare the Ammonite land for the Arab "flocks." Instead of busy men, there shall be "still and couching flocks." **6, 7.** "Because *thou* hast clapped *thine* hands," exulting over the downfall of Jerusalem, "*I* also will stretch out *Mine* hand upon thee" (to which ch. 21:17 also may refer, "I will smite Mine hands together"). **hands ... feet ... heart**—with the whole inward feeling, and with every outward indication. *Stamping with the foot* means *dancing for joy.* **7. a spoil**—so Hebrew *Margin* or *Keri,* for the text or *Chetib,* "meat" (so ch. 26:5; 34:28). Their *goods* were to be a "spoil to the foe"; their *state* was to be "cut off," so as to be no more a "people"; and they were as *individuals,* for the most part, to be "destroyed." **8.** Moab, Seir, and Ammon were contiguous countries, stretching in one line from Gilead on the north to the Red Sea. They therefore naturally acted in concert, and in joint hostility to Judea. **Judah is like ... all ... heathen**—The Jews fare no better than others: it is of no use to them to serve Jehovah, who, they say, is the only true God. **9, 10. open ... from the cities**—*I will open up the side,* or border *of Moab* (metaphor from a man whose side is open to blows), *from the* direction of *the cities* on his northwest border beyond the Arnon, once assigned to Reuben (Josh. 13:15-21), but now in the hands of their original owners; and the "men of the east," the wandering Bedouin hordes, shall enter through these cities into Moab and waste it. Moab accordingly was so wasted by them, that long before the time of Christ it had melted away among the hordes of the desert. For "cities," Grotius translates the *Hebrew* as proper names, the *Ar* and *Aroer,* on the Arnon. Hence the *Hebrew* for "cities," "Ar" is repeated twice (Num. 21:28; Deut. 2:36; Isa. 15:1). **glory of the country**—The region of Moab was richer than that of Ammon; it answers to the modern Belka, the richest district in South Syria, and the scene in consequence of many a contest among the Bedouins.

Hence it is called here a "glorious land" (lit., "a glory," or "ornament of a land") [FAIRBAIRN]. Rather, "the glory of the country" is in apposition with "cities" which immediately precedes, and the names of which presently follow. **Beth-jeshimoth** —meaning "the city of desolations"; perhaps so named from some siege it sustained; it was towards the west. **Baal-meon**—called also "Beth-meon" (Jer. 48:23), and "Beth-baal-meon" (Josh. 13:17, called so from the worship of Baal), and "Bajith," simply (Isa. 15:2). **Kiriathaim**—"the double city." The strength of these cities engendered "the pride" of Moab (Isa. 16:6). **10. with the Ammonites**— FAIRBAIRN explains and translates, *"upon* the children of Ammon" (elliptically for, "I will open Moab to the men of the east, who, having overrun the children of Ammon, shall then fall on Moab"). MAURER, as *English Version*, *"with* the Ammonites," i.e., Moab, *"together with* the land of Ammon," is to be thrown "open to the men of the east," to enter and take possession (Jer. 49). **12. taking vengeance** —lit., "revenging with revengement," i.e., the most unrelenting vengeance. It was not simple hatred, but deep-brooding, implacable revenge. The grudge of Edom or Esau was originally for Jacob's robbing him of Isaac's blessing (Gen. 25:23; 27:27-41). This purpose of revenge yielded to the extraordinary kindness of Jacob, through the blessing of Him with whom Jacob wrestled in prayer; but it was revived as an hereditary grudge in the posterity of Esau when they saw the younger branch rising to the pre-eminence which they thought of right belonged to themselves. More recently, for David's subjugation of Edom to Israel (II Sam. 8:14). They therefore gave vent to their spite by joining the Chaldeans in destroying Jerusalem (Ps. 137:7; Lam. 4:22; Obadiah 10-14), and then intercepting and killing the fugitive Jews (Amos 1:11) and occupying part of the Jewish land as far as Hebron. **13. Teman...they of Dedan**—rather, "I will make it desolate from Teman (in the south) *even to* Dedan" (in the northwest) [GROTIUS], (Jer. 49:8), i.e., the whole country from north to south, stretching from the south of the Dead Sea to the Elanitic gulf of the Red Sea. **14. by...my people Israel**—viz., by Judas Maccabeus. The Idumeans were finally, by compulsory circumcision, incorporated with the Jewish state by John Hyrcanus (see Isa. 34:5; 63:1, etc.; I Maccabees 5:3). So complete was the amalgamation in Christ's time, that the Herods of Idumean origin, as Jews, ruled over the two races as one people. Thus the ancient prophecy was fulfilled (Gen. 25:23), "The elder shall serve the younger." **15.** (I Sam. 13, 14; II Chron. 28:18.) The "old hatred" refers to their continual enmity to the covenant people. They lay along Judea on the seacoast at the opposite side from Ammon and Moab. They were overthrown by Uzziah (II Chron. 26:6), and by Hezekiah (II Kings 18:8). Nebuchadnezzar overran the cities on the seacoast on his way to Egypt after besieging Tyre (Jer. 47). God will take vengeance on those who take the avenging of themselves out of His hands into their own (Rom. 12:19-21; Jas. 2:13). **16. cut off the Cherethims**—There is a play on similar sounds in the *Hebrew, hichratti cherethim,* "I will slay the slayers." The name may have been given to a section of the Philistines from their warlike disposition (I Sam. 30:14; 31:3). They excelled in archery, whence David enrolled a bodyguard from them (II Sam. 8:18; 15:18; 20:7). They sprang from Caphtor, identified by many with Crete. which was famed for archery, and to which the name *Cher-*

ethim seems akin. Though in emigration, which mostly tended westwards, Crete seems more likely to be colonized from Philistia than Philistia from Crete, a *section* of Cretans may have settled at Cherethim in South Philistia, while the Philistines, *as a nation,* may have come originally from the east (cf. Deut. 2:23; Jer. 47:4; Amos 9:7; Zeph. 2:5). In Genesis 10:14 the Philistines are made *distinct from the Caphtorim,* and are said to come from the Casluhim; so that the Cherethim were but *a part* of the Philistines, which I Samuel 30:14 confirms. **remnant of**—i.e., "on the seacoast" of the Mediterranean: those left *remaining* after the former overthrows inflicted by Samuel, David, Hezekiah, and Psammetichus of Egypt, father of Pharaoh-necho (Jer. 25:20). **17. know...vengeance**—They shall know Me, not in mercy, but by My vengeance on them (Ps. 9:16).

CHAPTER 26

Vss. 1-21. THE JUDGMENT ON TYRE THROUGH NEBUCHADNEZZAR (CHS. 26-28). In ch. 26, Ezekiel sets forth:—1. Tyre's sin; 2. its doom; 3. the instruments executing it; 4. the effects produced on other nations by her downfall. In ch. 27, a lamentation over the fall of such earthly splendor. In ch. 28, an elegy addressed to the king, on the humiliation of his sacrilegious pride. Ezekiel, in his prophecies as to the heathen, exhibits *the dark side only;* because he views them simply in their hostility to the people of God, who shall outlive them all. Isaiah (Isa. 23), on the other hand, at the close of judgments, holds out the prospect of blessing, when Tyre should turn to the Lord. **1.** The specification of the date, which had been omitted in the case of the four preceding objects of judgment, marks the greater weight attached to the fall of Tyre. **eleventh year**—viz., after the carrying away of Jehoiachin, the year of the fall of Jerusalem. The number of the month is, however, omitted, and the day only given. As the month of the *taking* of Jerusalem was regarded as one of particular note, viz., *the fourth month,* also *the fifth,* on which it was actually *destroyed* (Jer. 52: 6, 12, 13), RABBI-DAVID reasonably supposes that Tyre uttered her taunt at the close of the fourth month, as her nearness to Jerusalem enabled her to hear of its fall very soon, and that Ezekiel met it with his threat against herself on "the first day" *of the fifth month.* **2. Tyre**—(Josh. 19:29; II Sam. 24: 7), lit., meaning "the rock-city," *Zor;* a name applying to the *island Tyre,* called New Tyre, rather than *Old Tyre* on the *mainland.* They were half a mile apart. New Tyre, a century and a half before the fall of Jerusalem, had successfully resisted Shalmaneser of Assyria, for five years besieging it (MENANDER, from the Tyrian archives, quoted by JOSEPHUS, *Antiquities,* 9. 14. 2). It was the stronger and more important of the two cities, and is the one chiefly, though not exclusively, here meant. Tyre was originally a colony of Zidon. Nebuchadnezzar's siege of it lasted thirteen years (ch. 29:18; Isa. 23). Though no profane author mentions his having succeeded in the siege, JEROME states he read the fact in Assyrian histories. **Aha!**—exultation over a fallen rival (Ps. 35:21, 25). **she...that was the gates**—i.e., the single gate composed of two folding doors. Hence the verb is *singular.* "Gates" were the place of resort for traffic and public business: so here it expresses *a mart of commerce* frequented by merchants. Tyre regards Jerusalem not as an open enemy, for her territory being the **nar-**

row, long strip of land north of Philistia, between Mount Lebanon and the sea, her interest was to cultivate friendly relations with the Jews, on whom she was dependent for corn (ch. 27:17; I Kings 5:9; Acts 12:20). But Jerusalem had intercepted some of the inland traffic which she wished to monopolize to herself; so, in her intensely selfish wordly-mindedness, she exulted heartlessly over the fall of Jerusalem as her own gain. Hence she incurred the wrath of God as pre-eminently the world's representative in its ambition, selfishness, and pride, in defiance of the will of God (Isa. 23:9). **she is turned unto me**—i.e., the mart of corn, wine, oil, balsam, etc. which she once was, is transferred to me. The caravans from Palmyra, Petra, and the East will no longer be intercepted by the market ("the gates") of Jerusalem, but will come to me. **3, 4. nations ... as the sea ... waves**—In striking contrast to the boasting of Tyre, God threatens to bring against her Babylon's army levied from "many nations," even as the Mediterranean waves that dashed against her rock-founded city on all sides. **scrape her dust ... make her ... top of ... rock**—or, "a bare rock" ʳGROTI-US]. The soil which the Tyrians had brought together upon the rock on which they built their city, I will scrape so clean away as to leave no dust, but only the bare rock as it was. An awful contrast to her expectation of filling herself with *all* the wealth of the East now that Jerusalem has fallen. **5. in the midst of the sea**—plainly referring to New Tyre (ch. 27:32). **6. her daughters ... in the field**—The surrounding villages, dependent on her in the open country, shall share the fate of the mother city. **7. from the north**—the original locality of the Chaldeans; also, the direction by which they entered Palestine, taking the route of Riblah and Hamath on the Orontes, in preference to that across the desert between Babylon and Judea. **king of kings**—so called because of the many kings who owned allegiance to him II Kings 18:28). God had delegated to him the universal earth-empire which is His (Dan. 2:47). The Son of God alone has the right and title inherently, and shall assume it when the world-kings shall have been fully proved as abusers of the trust (I Tim. 6:15; Rev. 17:12-14; 19:15, 16). Ezekiel's prophecy was not based on conjecture from the past, for Shalmaneser, with all the might of the Assyrian empire, had failed in his siege of Tyre. Yet Nebuchadnezzar was to succeed. JOSEPHUS tells us that Nebuchadnezzar began the siege in the seventh year of Ithobal's reign, king of Tyre. **9. engines of war**—lit., "an apparatus for *striking*." "He shall apply *the stroke* of the battering-ram *against* thy walls." HAVERNICK translates, "His enginery of destruction;" lit., the *"destruction* (not merely the *stroke*) of his enginery." **axes**—lit., "swords." **10. dust**—So thick shall be the "dust" stirred up by the immense numbers of "horses," that it shall "cover" the whole city as a cloud. **horses ... chariots**—As in vss. 3-5, *New Tyre* on the insular rock in the sea (cf. Isa. 23:2, 4, 6) is referred to; so here, in vss. 9-11, *Old Tyre* on the mainland. *Both* are included in the prophecies under one name. **wheels**—FAIRBAIRN thinks that here, and in ch. 23:24, as "the wheels" are distinct from the "chariots," some wheelwork for riding on, or for the operations of the siege, are meant. **11. thy strong garrisons**—lit., "the statutes of thy strength"; so *the forts* which are "monuments of thy strength." MAURER understands, in stricter agreement with the literal meaning, "the statues" or "obelisks erected in honor of the idols, the tutelary gods of Tyre," as Melecarte, answering to the Grecian Hercules, whose temple

stood in Old Tyre (cf. Jer. 43:13, *Margin*). **12. lay thy stones ... timber ... in ... midst of ... water**—referring to the insular New Tyre (vss. 3, 5; ch. 27: 4, 25, 26). When its lofty buildings and towers fall, surrounded as it was with the sea which entered its double harbor and washed its ramparts, the "stones ...timbers...and dust" appropriately are described as thrown down "in the midst of the water." Though Ezekiel attributes the capture of Tyre to Nebuchadnezzar (*Note*, ch. 29:18), yet it does not follow that the *final* destruction of it described is attributed by him to the same monarch. The overthrow of Tyre by Nebuchadnezzar was the first link in the long chain of evil—the first deadly blow which prepared for, and was the earnest of, the final doom. The change in this verse from the individual conqueror "he," to the general "they," marks that what he did was not the whole, but only paved the way for others to complete the work begun by him. It was to be a progressive work until she was utterly destroyed. Thus the words here answer exactly to what Alexander did. With the "stones, timber," and rubbish of Old Tyre, he built a causeway in seven months to New Tyre on the island and so took it [QUINT. CURT., 4, 2], 322 B.C. **13.** Instead of the joyousness of thy prosperity, a deathlike silence shall reign (Isa. 24:8; Jer. 7:34). **14.** He concludes in nearly the same words as he began (vss. 4, 5). **built no more**—fulfilled as to the mainland Tyre, under Nebuchadnezzar. The insular Tyre recovered partly, after seventy years (Isa. 23:17, 18), but again suffered under Alexander, then under Antigonus, then under the Saracens at the beginning of the fourteenth century. Now its harbors are choked with sand, precluding all hope of future restoration, "not one entire house is left, and only a few fishermen take shelter in the vaults" [MAUNDRELL]. So accurately has God's word come to pass. **15-21.** The impression which the overthrow of Tyre produced on other maritime nations and upon her own colonies, e.g., Utica, Carthage, and Tartessus or Tarshish in Spain. **15. isles** —maritime lands. Even mighty Carthage used to send a yearly offering to the temple of Hercules at Tyre: and the mother city gave high priests to her colonies. Hence the consternation at her fall felt in the widely scattered dependencies with which she was so closely connected by the ties of religion, as well as commercial intercourse. **shake**—metaphorically: "be agitated" (Jer. 49:21). **16. come down from their thrones...upon the ground**—"the throne of the mourners" (Job 2:13; Jonah 3:6). **princes of the sea**—are the merchant rulers of Carthage and other colonies of Tyre, who had made themselves rich and powerful by trading on the sea (Isa. 23:8). **clothe ... with trembling**—*Heb.* "tremblings." Cf. ch. 7:27, "clothed with desolation"; Psalm 132:18. In a public calamity the garment was changed for a mourning garb. **17. inhabited of seafaring men**—i.e., which was frequented by merchants of various sea-bordering lands [GROTIUS]. FAIRBAIRN translates with Peschito, "Thou inhabitant of the seas" (the *Hebrew* literal meaning). Tyre rose as it were *out of* the seas as if she got thence her inhabitants, being peopled so closely down to the waters. So Venice was called "the bride of the sea." **strong in the sea**—through her insular position. **cause their terror to be on all that haunt it**—viz., the sea. The *Hebrew* is rather, "they put their terror upon all *her* (the city's) inhabitants," i.e., they make the name of every Tyrian to be feared [FAIRBAIRN]. **18. thy departure**—Isaiah 23:6, 12 predicts that the Tyrians, in consequence of the siege, should pass over the Mediterranean to the lands bordering on it ("Chittim,"

"Tarshish," etc.). So Ezekiel here. Accordingly JEROME says that he read in Assyrian histories that, "when the Tyrians saw no hope of escaping, they *fled* to Carthage or some islands of the Ionian and Ægean Seas" [BISHOP NEWTON]. (See my *Note* on ch. 29:18.) GROTIUS explains "departure," i.e., "in the day when hostages shall be *carried away* from thee to Babylon." The parallelism to "thy *fall*" makes me think "departure" must mean "thy end" in general, but with an *included* allusion to the "departure" of most of her people to her colonies at *the fall* of the city. **19. great waters**—appropriate metaphor of the Babylonian hosts, which literally, by breaking down insular Tyre's ramparts, caused the sea to "cover" part of her. **20. the pit**—Tyre's disappearance is compared to that of *the dead placed in their sepulchers* and no more seen among the living (cf. ch. 32:18, 23; Isa. 14:11, 15, 19). **I shall set glory in the land**—In contrast to Tyre consigned to the "pit" of *death,* I shall set glory (i.e., My presence symbolized by the Shekinah cloud, the antitype to which shall be Messiah, "the *glory* as of the only-begotten of the Father," John 1:14; Isa. 4:2, 5; Zech. 6:13) in Judah. **of the living**—as opposed to Tyre consigned to the "pit" of death. Judea is to be the land of national and spiritual *life,* being restored after its captivity (ch. 47:9). FAIRBAIRN loses the antithesis by applying the negative to both clauses, "and that thou be *not* set as a glory in the land of the living." **21. terror**—an example of judgment calculated to terrify all evildoers. **thou shalt be no more**—Not that there was to be no more *a* Tyre, but she was no more to be *the* Tyre that once was: her glory and name were to be no more. As to Old Tyre, the prophecy was literally fulfilled, not a vestige of it being left.

CHAPTER 27

Vss. 1-36. TYRE'S FORMER GREATNESS, SUGGESTING A LAMENTATION OVER HER SAD DOWNFALL. 2. lamentation—a funeral dirge, eulogizing her great attributes, to make the contrast the greater between her former and her latter state. **3. situate at the entry of the sea**—lit., plural, "entrances," i.e., ports or havens; referring to the double port of Tyre, at which vessels entered round the north and south ends of the island, so that ships could find a ready entrance from whatever point the wind might blow (cf. ch. 28:2). **merchant of ... people for many isles**—i.e., a mercantile emporium of the peoples of many seacoasts, both from the east and from the west (Isa. 23:3), "a mart of nations." **of perfect beauty**—(ch. 28:12). **4.** Tyre, in consonance with her seagirt position, separated by a strait of half a mile from the mainland, is described as a ship built of the best material, and manned with the best mariners and skilful pilots, but at last wrecked in tempestuous seas (vs. 26). **5. Senir**—the Amorite name of Hermon, or the southern height of Anti-libanus (Deut. 3:9); the Sidonian name was *Sirion.* "All thy ... boards"; dual in *Hebrew,* "double-boards," viz., placed in a double order on the two sides of which the ship consisted [VATABLUS]. Or, referring to the two sides or the two ends, the prow and the stern, which every ship has [MUNSTER]. **cedars**—most suited for "masts," from their height and durability. **6. Bashan**—celebrated for its oaks, as Lebanon was for its cedars. **the company of ... Ashurites**—the most skilful workmen summoned from Assyria. Rather, as the *Hebrew* orthography requires, "They have made thy (rowing) benches of

ivory inlaid *in the daughter of cedars*" [MAURER], or, *the best boxwood.* FAIRBAIRN, with BOCHART, reads the *Hebrew* two words as *one:* "Thy plankwork (*deck:* instead of 'benches,' as the *Hebrew* is *singular*) they made ivory *with boxes."* **English Version,** with MAURER'S correction, is simpler. **Chittim**—Cyprus and Macedonia, from which, PLINY tells us, the best boxwood came [GROTIUS]. **7. broidered ... sail**—The ancients embroidered their sails often at great expense, especially the Egyptians, whose linen, still preserved in mummies, is of the finest texture. **Elishah**—Greece; so called from Elis, a large and ancient division of Peloponnesus. Pausanias says that the best of linen was produced in it, and in no other part of Greece; called by Homer, *Alisium.* **that which covered thee**—thy awning. **8. Arvad**—a small island and city near Phœnicia, now *Ruad:* its inhabitants are still noted for seafaring habits. **thy wise men, O Tyrus ... thy pilots**—While the men of Arvad, once thy equals (Gen. 10:18), and the Sidonians, once thy superiors, were employed by thee in subordinate positions as "mariners," thou madest thine own skilled men alone to be commanders and pilots. Implying the political and mercantile superiority of Tyre. **9. Gebal**—a Phœnician city and region between Beirut and Tripolis, famed for skilled workmen (*Margin,* I Kings 5:18; Ps. 83:7). **calkers**—*stoppers of chinks* in a vessel: carrying on the metaphor as to Tyre. **occupy thy merchandise**—i.e., to exchange merchandise with thee. **10. Persia ... Phut**—warriors from the extreme east and west. **Lud**—the Lydians of Asia Minor, near the Meander, famed for archery (Isa. 66:19); rather than those of Ethiopia, as the Lydians of Asia Minor form a kind of intermediate step between Persia and Phut (the Libyans about Cyrene, shielded warriors, Jer. 46:9, descended from Phut, son of Ham). **hanged ... shield ... comeliness**—Warriors hanged their accoutrements on the walls for ornament. Divested of the metaphor, it means that it was an honor to thee to have so many nations supplying thee with hired soldiers. **11. Gammadims**—rather, as the Tyrians were Syro-Phœnicians, from a *Syriac* root, meaning *daring,* "men of daring" [LUDOVICUS DE DIEU]. It is not likely the keeping of watch "in the towers" would have been entrusted to foreigners. Others take it from a *Hebrew* root, "a dagger," or short sword (Judg. 3:16), "short-swordsmen." **12. Tarshish**—Tartessus in Spain, a country famed for various metals, which were exported to Tyre. Much of the "tin" probably was conveyed by the Phœnicians from Cornwall to Tarshish. **traded in thy fairs**—"did barter with thee" [FAIRBAIRN]; from a root, "to leave," something *left* in barter for something else. **13. Javan**—the Ionians or *Greeks:* for the *Ionians* of Asia Minor were the first Greeks with whom the Asiatics came in contact. **Tubal ... Meshech**—the Tibareni and Moschi, in the mountain region between the Black and Caspian Seas. **persons of men**—i.e., as slaves. So the Turkish harems are supplied with female slaves from Circassia and Georgia. **vessels**—all kinds of *articles.* Superior weapons are still manufactured in the Caucasus region. **14. Togarmah**—Armenia: descended from Gomer (Gen. 10:3). Their mountainous region south of the Caucasus was celebrated for horses. **horsemen**—rather, "riding-horses," as distinct from "horses" for chariots [FAIRBAIRN]. **15. Dedan**—near the Persian Sea: thus an avenue to the commerce of India. Not the Dedan in Arabia (vs. 20), as the names in the context here prove, but the Dedan sprung from Cush [BOCHART], (Gen. 10:7). **merchandise of thine hand**—i.e., were dependent on thee for trade [FAIRBAIRN]; came to buy *the produce of thy hands* [GROTIUS]. **a present**–lit., "a reward in return"; a price paid for merchandise. **horns of ivory**–Ivory is so termed from its resemblance to *horns*. The *Hebrew* word for "ivory" means "tooth"; so that they cannot have mistaken ivory as if *coming from the horns* of certain animals, instead of from the tusks of the elephant. **16.** "Syria was thy mart for the multitude . . . ." For "Syria" the LXX reads "Edom." But the Syrians were famed as merchants. **occupied**–old English for "traded"; so in Luke 19:13. **agate**–Others translate, "ruby," "chalcedony," or "pearls." **17. Minnith . . . Pannag**–names of places in Israel famed for good wheat, wherewith Tyre was supplied (I Kings 5:9, 11; Ezra 3:7; Acts 12:20); Minnith was formerly an Ammonite city (Judg. 11:33). "Pannag" is identified by GROTIUS with "Phenice," the Greek name for "Canaan". "They traded . . . wheat," i.e., they supplied thy market with wheat. **balm**–or, "balsam." **18. Helbon**–or Chalybon, in Syria, now Aleppo; famed for its wines; the Persian monarchs would drink no other. **19. Dan also**–None of the other places enumerated commence with the copula ("also"; *Hebrew, ve*). Moreover, the products specified, "cassia, calamus," apply rather to places in Arabia. Therefore, FAIRBAIRN translates, "Vedan"; perhaps the modern Aden, near the straits of Bab-el-mandeb. GROTIUS refers it to Dana, mentioned by Ptolemy. **Javan**–not the Greeks of *Europe* or *Asia Minor*, but of a Greek settlement in *Arabia*. **going to and fro**–rather, as *Hebrew* admits, "from *Uzal*." This is added to "Javan," to mark *which* Javan is meant" (Gen. 10:27). The metropolis of Arabia Felix, or Yemen; called also Sanaa [BOCHART]. *English Version* gives a good sense, thus: All peoples, whether near as the Israelite "Dan," or far as the Greeks or "Javan," who were wont to "go to and fro" from their love of traffic, frequented thy marts, bringing bright iron, etc., these products not being necessarily represented as those of Dan or Javan. **bright iron**–Yemen is still famed for its sword blades. **calamus**–aromatic cane. **20. Dedan**–in Arabia; distinct from the Dedan in vs. 15 (see *note*). Descended from Abraham and Keturah (Gen. 25:3) [BOCHART]. **precious clothes**–splendid coverlets. **21. Arabia**–the nomadic tribes of Arabia, among which Kedar was pre-eminent. **occupied with thee**–lit., "of thy hand," i.e., they *traded* with thee for wares, the product *of thy hand* (see *Notes*, vss. 15, 16). **22. Sheba . . . Raamah**–in Arabia. **spices . . .**–obtained from India and conveyed in caravans to Tyre. **chief of . . . spices**–i.e., *best* spices (Deut. 33:15). **23. Haran**–the dwelling-place of Abraham in Mesopotamia, after he moved from Ur (Gen. 11:31). **Canneh**–Calneh, an Assyrian city on the Tigris; the Ctesiphon of the Greeks (Gen. 10:10). **Eden**–probably a region in Babylonia (see Gen. 2:8). **Chilmad**–a compound; the place designated by Ptolemy "Gaala of Media." The *Chaldee version* interprets it of Media. HENDERSON refers it to Carmanda, which Xenophon describes as a large city beyond the Euphrates. **24. all sorts of things**–*Hebrew*, "perfections"; exquisite articles of finery [GROTIUS]. **clothes**–rather, "mantles" or "cloaks"; lit., "wrappings." For "blue," HENDERSON translates, purple." **chests of rich apparel, bound with cords**–treasures or repositories of damask stuffs, consisting of variegated threads woven together in figures [HENDERSON]. **cedar**–The "chests" were made of *cedar*, in order to last the longer; and it also keeps off decay and has a sweet odor. **25. sing of thee**–personification; thy great merchant ships were palpable

proofs of thy greatness. Others translate from a different *Hebrew* root, "were thy (mercantile) travellers." FAIRBAIRN translates, "Were thy walls." But the parallelism to "thou wast glorious" favors *English Version*, "sing of thee." **26.** In contrast to her previous greatness, her downfall is here, by a sudden transition, depicted under the image of a vessel foundering at sea. **east wind**–blowing from Lebanon, the most violent wind in the Mediterranean (Ps. 48:7). A Levanter, as it is called. Nebuchadnezzar is meant. The "sea" is the war with him which the "rowers," or rulers of the state vessel, had "brought" it into, to its ruin. **27.** The detailed enumeration implies the *utter completeness* of the ruin. **and in all thy company**–"even with all thy collected multitude" [HENDERSON]. **28. The suburbs**–the buildings of Tyre on the adjoining continent. **29.** So on the downfall of spiritual Babylon (Rev. 18:17, etc.). **shall stand upon . . . land**–being cast out of their ships in which heretofore they prided themselves. **30. against thee**–rather, "concerning thee." **31. utterly bald**–lit., "bald with baldness." The Phœnician custom in mourning; which, as being connected with heathenish superstitions, was forbidden to Israel (Deut. 14:1). **32. take up**–lift up. **the destroyed**–a destroyed one. Lit., (as opposed to its previous bustle of thronging merchants and mariners, vs. 27), "one brought to death's stillness." **in . . . midst of . . . sea**–insular Tyre. **33. out of the seas**–brought on shore *out of* the ships. **filledst**–didst supply plentifully with wares. **enrich . . . kings**–with the custom dues levied on the *wares*. **34. In the time when . . . shalt . . . shall**–*Now* that thou *art* broken (wrecked) . . ., thy merchandise . . . are fallen [MAURER]. **35. isles** –seacoasts. **36. hiss**–with astonishment; as in I Kings 9:8.

CHAPTER 28

Vss. 1-26. PROPHETICAL DIRGE ON THE KING OF TYRE, AS THE CULMINATION AND EMBODIMENT OF THE SPIRIT OF CARNAL PRIDE AND SELF-SUFFICIENCY OF THE WHOLE STATE. THE FALL OF ZIDON, THE MOTHER CITY. THE RESTORATION OF ISRAEL IN CONTRAST WITH TYRE AND ZIDON. **2. Because . . .**–repeated resumptively in vs. 6. The apodosis begins at vs. 7. "The prince of Tyrus" at the time was Ithobal, or Ithbaal II; the name implying his close connection with Baal, the Phœnician supreme god, whose representative he was. **I am a god, I sit in . . . seat of God . . . the seas**–As God sits enthroned in His heavenly citadel exempt from all injury, so I sit secure in my impregnable stronghold amidst the stormiest elements, able to control them at will, and make them subserve my interests. The language, though primarily here applied to the king of Tyre, as similar language is to the king of Babylon (Isa. 14:13, 14), yet has an ulterior and fuller accomplishment in Satan and his embodiment in Antichrist (Dan. 7:25; 11:36, 37; II Thess. 2:4; Rev. 13:6). This feeling of superhuman elevation in the king of Tyre was fostered by the fact that the island on which Tyre stood was called "the holy island" [SANCONIATHON], being sacred to Hercules, so much so that the colonies looked up to Tyre as the mother city of their religion, as well as of their political existence. The *Hebrew* for "God" is *El*, i.e., "the Mighty One." yet . . .–keen irony. **set thine heart as . . . heart of God**–Thou thinkest of thyself as if thou wert God. **3.** Ezekiel ironically alludes to Ithbaal's overweening opinion of the wisdom of himself and the Tyrians, as though superior to that of

Daniel, whose fame had reached even Tyre as eclipsing the Chaldean sages. "Thou art wiser," viz., in thine own opinion (Zech. 9:2). **no secret**—viz., forgetting riches (vs. 4). **that they can hide**—i.e., that can be hidden. **5.** (Ps. 62:10.) **6. Because . . .**—resumptive of vs. 2. **7. therefore**—apodosis. **strangers . . . terrible of the nations**—the Chaldean foreigners noted for their ferocity (ch. 30:11; 31: 12). **against the beauty of thy wisdom**—i.e., against thy beautiful possessions acquired by thy wisdom on which thou pridest thyself (vss. 3-5). **defile thy brightness**—obscure the brightness of thy kingdom. **8. the pit** i.e., the bottom of the sea; the image being that of one conquered in a sea-fight. **the deaths**—*plural*, as various kinds of deaths are meant (Jer. 16: 4). **of them . . . slain**—lit., "pierced through." Such deaths as those pierced with many wounds die. **9. yet say**—i.e., still say; referring to vs. 2. **but . . .**—But thy blasphemous boastings shall be falsified, and thou shalt be shown to be but man, and not God, in the hand (at the mercy) of Him. **10. deaths of . . . uncircumcised**—i.e., such a death as the uncircumcised or godless heathen *deserve;* and perhaps, also, such as the uncircumcised *inflict,* a great ignominy in the eyes of a Jew (I Sam. 31:4); a fit retribution on him who had scoffed at the circumcised Jews. **12. sealest up the sum**—lit., "Thou art the one sealing the sum of perfection." A thing is *sealed* when *completed* (Dan. 9:24). "The sum" implies *the full measure of beauty,* from a *Hebrew* root, "to measure." The normal man—one formed after accurate rule. **13. in Eden**—The king of Tyre is represented in his former high state (contrasted with his subsequent downfall), under images drawn from the primeval man in Eden, the type of humanity in its most Godlike form. **garden of God** —the model of ideal loveliness (ch. 31:8, 9; 36:35). In the person of the king of Tyre a new trial was made of humanity with the greatest earthly advantages. But as in the case of Adam, the good gifts of God were only turned into ministers to pride and self. **every precious stone**—so in Eden (Gen. 2:12), "gold, bdellium, and the onyx stone." So the king of Tyre was arrayed in jewel-bespangled robes after the fashion of Oriental monarchs. The nine precious stones here mentioned answer to nine of the twelve (representing the twelve tribes) in the high priest's breastplate (Exod. 39:10-13; Rev. 21:14, 19-21). Of the four rows of three in each, the third is omitted in the *Hebrew,* but is supplied in the LXX. In this, too, there is an ulterior reference to Antichrist, who is blasphemously to arrogate the office of our divine High Priest (Zech. 6:13). **tabrets**—tambourines. **pipes**—lit., "holes" in musical pipes or flutes. **created**—i.e., in *the day of thine accession to the throne.* Tambourines and all the marks of joy were ready prepared for thee ("in thee," i.e., with and for thee). Thou hadst not, like others, to work thy way to the throne through arduous struggles. No sooner created than, like Adam, thou wast surrounded with the gratifications of Eden. FAIRBAIRN, for "pipes," translates, "females" (having reference to Gen. 1:27), i.e., musician-women. MAURER explains the *Hebrew* not as to music, but as to the *setting* and *mounting* of the gems previously mentioned. **14. anointed cherub**—GESENIUS translates from an *Aramaic* root, "extended cherub." *English Version,* from a *Hebrew* root, is better. "The cherub consecrated to the Lord by the anointing oil" [FAIRBAIRN]. **covereth**—The imagery employed by Ezekiel as a priest is from the Jewish temple, wherein the cherubim overshadowed the

mercy seat, as the king of Tyre, a demi-god in his own esteem, extended his protection over the interests of Tyre. The cherub—an ideal compound of the highest kinds of aimal existence and the type of redeemed man in his ultimate state of perfection —is made the image of the king of Tyre, as if the beau ideal of humanity. The pretensions of Antichrist are the ulterior reference, of whom the king of Tyre is a type. Cf. "As God . . . in the *temple* of God" (II Thess. 2:4). **I have set thee**—not *thou* set thyself (Prov. 8:16; Rom. 13:1). **upon the holy mountain of God**—Zion, following up the image. **in . . . midst of . . . stones of fire**—In ambitious imagination he stood in the place of God, "under whose feet was, as it were, a pavement of sapphire," while His glory was like "devouring fire" (Exod. 24:10, 17). **15. perfect**—prosperous [GROTIUS], and having no defect. So Hiram was a sample of the Tyrian monarch in his early days of wisdom and prosperity (I Kings 5:7, etc.). **till iniquity . . . in thee**—Like the primeval man thou hast fallen by abusing God's gifts, and so hast provoked God's wrath. **16. filled the midst of thee**—i.e., they have filled *the midst of the city;* he as the head of the state being involved in the guilt of the state, which he did not check, but fostered. **cast thee as profane**—no longer treated as sacred, but driven out of the place of sanctity (see vs. 14) which thou hast occupied (cf. Ps. 89:39). **17. brightness**—thy splendor. **lay thee before kings**—as an example of God's wrath against presumptuous pride. **18. thy sanctuaries**—i.e., the holy places, attributed to the king of Tyre in vs. 14, as his ideal position. As he "profaned" it, so God will "profane" him (vs. 16). **fire . . . devour**—As he abused his supposed elevation amidst "the stones of fire" (vs. 16), so God will make His "fire" to "devour" him. **21. Zidon**—famous for its fishery (from a root, *Zud,* "to fish"); and afterwards for its wide extended commerce; its artistic elegance was proverbial. Founded by Canaan's first-born (Gen. 10:15). Tyre was an offshoot from it, so that it was involved in the same overthrow by the Chaldeans as Tyre. It is mentioned separately, because its idolatry (Ashtaroth, Tammuz, or Adonis) infected Israel more than that of Tyre did (ch. 8; Judg. 10:6; I Kings 11:33). The notorious Jezebel was a daughter of the Zidonian king. **22. shall be sanctified in her**—when all nations shall see that I am the Holy Judge in the vengeance that I will inflict on her for sin. **24. no more . . . brier . . . unto . . . Israel**—as the idolatrous nations left in Canaan (among which Zidon is expressly specified in the limits of Asher, Judg. 1:31) had been (Num. 33:55; Josh. 23:13). "A brier," first ensnaring the Israelites in sin, and then being made the instrument of punishing them. **pricking** —lit., "causing *bitterness."* The same *Hebrew* is translated "fretting" (Lev. 13:51, 52). The wicked are often called "thorns" (II Sam. 23:6). **25, 26.** Fulfilled in part at the restoration from Babylon, when Judaism, so far from being merged in heathenism, made inroads by conversions on the idolatry of surrounding nations. The full accomplishment is yet future, when Israel, under Christ, shall be the center of Christendom; of which an earnest was given in the woman from the coasts of Tyre and Sidon who sought the Saviour (Matt. 15:21, 24, 26-28; cf. Isa. 11:12). **dwell safely**—(Jer. 23:6).

CHAPTER 29

Vss. 1-21. THE JUDGMENT ON EGYPT BY NEBUCHADNEZZAR; THOUGH ABOUT TO BE RESTORED AFTER

FORTY YEARS, IT WAS STILL TO BE IN A STATE OF DEGRADATION. This is the last of the world kingdoms against which Ezekiel's prophecies are directed, and occupies the largest space in them, viz., the next four chapters. Though farther off than Tyre, it exercised a more powerful influence on Israel. **2. Pharaoh**—a common name of all the kings of Egypt, meaning "the sun"; or, as others say, a "crocodile," which was worshipped in parts of Egypt (cf. vs. 3). Hophra or Apries was on the throne at this time. His reign began prosperously. He took Gaza (Jer. 47:1) and Zidon and made himself master of Phœnicia and Palestine, recovering much that was lost to Egypt by the victory of Nebuchadnezzar at Carchemish (II Kings 24:7; Jer. 46:2), in the fourth year of Jehoiakim [WILKINSON'S *Ancient Egypt*, 1. 169]. So proudly secure because of his successes for twenty-five years did he feel, that he said not even a god could deprive him of his kingdom [HERODOTUS, 2. 169]. Hence the appropriateness of the description of him in vs. 3. No mere human sagacity could have enabled Ezekiel to foresee Egypt's downfall in the height of its prosperity. There are four divisions of these prophecies; the first in the tenth year of Ezekiel's captivity; the last in the twelfth. Between the first and second comes one of much later date, not having been given till the twenty-seventh year (ch. 29:17; 30:19), but placed there as appropriate to the subject matter. Pharaoh-hophra, or Apries, was dethroned and strangled, and Amasis substituted as king, by Nebuchadnezzar (cf. Jer. 44:30). The Egyptian priests, from national vanity, made no mention to HERODOTUS of the Egyptian loss of territory in Syria through Nebuchadnezzar, of which JOSEPHUS tells us, but attributed the change in the succession from Apries to Amasis solely to the Egyptian soldiery. The civil war between the two rivals no doubt lasted several years, affording an opportunity to Nebuchadnezzar of interfering and of elevating the usurper Amasis, on condition of his becoming tributary to Babylon [WILKINSON]. Cf. Jeremiah 43:10-12, and my *Note*, vs. 13, for another view of the grounds of interference of Nebuchadnezzar. **3. dragon**—*Hebrew, tanim,* any large aquatic animal, here the crocodile, which on Roman coins is the emblem of Egypt. **lieth**—restest proudly secure. **his rivers**—the mouths, branches, and canals of the Nile, to which Egypt owed its fertility. **4. hooks in thy jaws**—(Isa. 37:29; cf. Job 41:1, 2). Amasis was the "hook." In the Assyrian sculptures prisoners are represented with a hook in the underlip, and a cord from it held by the king. **cause ...fish...stick unto...scales**—Pharaoh, presuming on his power as if he were God (vs. 3, "I have made it"), wished to stand in the stead of God as defender of the covenant people, his motive being, not love to them, but rivalry with Babylon. He raised the siege of Jerusalem, but it was only for a time (cf. vs. 6; Jer. 37:5, 7-10); ruin overtook not only them, but himself. As the fish that clung to the horny scales of the crocodile, the lord of the Nile, when he was caught, shared his fate, so the adherents of Pharaoh, lord of Egypt, when he was overthrown by Amasis, should share his fate. **5. wilderness**—captivity beyond thy kingdom. The expression is used perhaps to imply retribution in kind. As Egypt pursued after Israel, saying, "The *wilderness* hath shut them in" (Exod. 14:3), so she herself shall be brought into a *wilderness state*. **open fields**—lit., "face of the field." **not be brought together**—As the crocodile is not, when caught, restored to the river, so no remnant of thy routed

army shall be brought together, and rallied, after its defeat in the wilderness. Pharaoh led an army against Cyrene in Africa, in support of Aricranes, who had been stripped of his kingdom by the Cyrenians. The army perished and Egypt rebelled against him [JUNIUS]. But the reference is mainly to the defeat by Nebuchadnezzar. **beasts... fowls** —hostile and savage men. **6. staff of reed to ... Israel**—alluding to the reeds on the banks of the Nile, which broke if one leaned upon them (*Note*, vs. 4; Isa. 36:6). All Israel's dependence on Egypt proved hurtful instead of beneficial (Isa. 30:1-5). **7. hand**—or handle of the reed. **rend...shoulder** —by the splinters on which the shoulder or arm would fall, on the support failing the hand. **madest ...loins...at a stand**—i.e., made them to be disabled. MAURER somewhat similarly (referring to a kindred *Arabic* form), "Thou hast stricken both their loins." FAIRBAIRN, not so well, "Thou lettest all their loins stand," i.e., by themselves, bereft of the support which they looked for from thee. **8. a sword**—Nebuchadnezzar's army (vs. 19). Also Amasis and the Egyptian revolters who after Pharaoh-hophra's discomfiture in Cyrene dethroned and strangled him, having defeated him in a battle fought at Memphis [JUNIUS]. **9. I am the Lord**—in antithesis to the blasphemous boast repeated here from vs. 3, "The river is mine, and I have made it." **10. from the tower of Syene**—GROTIUS translates, "from Migdol (a fortress near Pelusium on the north of Suez) to Syene" (in the farthest south); i.e., from one end of Egypt to the other. So in ch. 30:6, *Margin.* However, *English Version* rightly refers Syene to Seveneh, i.e., Sebennytus, in the eastern delta of the Nile, the capital of the Lower Egyptian kings. The Sebennyte Pharaohs, with the help of the Canaanites, who, as shepherds or merchants, ranged the desert of Suez, extended their borders beyond the narrow province east of the delta, to which they had been confined by the Pharaohs of Upper Egypt. The defeated party, in derision, named the Sebennyte or Lower Egyptians *foreigners* and *shepherd kings* (a shepherd being an abomination in Egypt, Genesis 46:34). They were really a *native* dynasty. Thus, in *English Version*, "Ethiopia" in the extreme south is rightly contrasted with Sebennytus or Syene in the north. **11. forty years** —answering to the forty years in which the Israelites, their former bondsmen, wandered in "the wilderness" (cf. *Note*, vs. 5). JEROME remarks the number *forty* is one often connected with affliction and judgment. The rains of the flood in forty days brought destruction on the world. Moses, Elias, and the Saviour fasted forty days. The interval between Egypt's overthrow by Nebuchadnezzar and the deliverance by Cyrus, was about forty years. The *ideal* forty years' wilderness state of social and political degradation, rather than a *literal* non passing of man or beast for that term, is mainly intended (so ch. 4:6; Isa. 19:2, 11). **12.** As Israel passed through a term of wilderness discipline (cf. ch. 20: 35, etc.), which was in its essential features to be repeated again, so it was to be with Egypt [FAIRBAIRN]. Some Egyptians were to be carried to Babylon, also many "scattered" in Arabia and Ethiopia through fear; but mainly the "scattering" was to be the *dissipation of their power*, even though the people still remained in their own land. **13.** (Jer. 46:26). **14. Pathros**—the Thebaid, or Upper Egypt, which had been especially harassed by Nebuchadnezzar (Nah. 3:8, 10). The oldest part of Egypt as to civilization and art. The Thebaid was anciently called "Egypt" [ARISTOTLE]. Therefore it is called the "land of the Egyptians' *birth*" (*Margin*, for "habitation"). **base kingdom**—Under Amasis it was made dependent on Babylon; humbled still more under Cambyses; and though somewhat raised under the Ptolemies, never has it regained its ancient pre-eminence. **16.** Egypt, when restored, shall be so circumscribed in power that it shall be no longer an object of confidence to Israel, as formerly; e.g., as when, relying on it, Israel broke faith with Nebuchadnezzar (ch. 17:13, 15, 16). **which bringeth their iniquity to remembrance, when they shall look after them**—rather, "while they (the Israelites) look to (or, *turn after*) them" [HENDERSON]. Israel's looking to Egypt, rather than to God, causes their iniquity (unfaithfulness to the covenant) to be remembered by God. **17.** The departure from the chronological order occurs here only, among the prophecies as to foreign nations, in order to secure greater unity of subject. **18. every head ... bald, ... shoulder ... peeled**—with carrying baskets of earth and stones for the siege-works. **no wages ... for the service**—i.e., *in proportion to* it and the time and labor which he expended on the siege of Tyre. Not that he actually failed in the siege (JEROME expressly states, from Assyrian histories, that Nebuchadnezzar succeeded); but, so much of the Tyrian resources had been exhausted, or transported to her colonies in ships, that little was left to compensate Nebuchadnezzar for his thirteen year's siege. **19. multitude**—not as FAIRBAIRN, "store"; but, he shall take away a *multitude of captives* out of Egypt. The success of Nebuchadnezzar is implied in Tyre's receiving a king from Babylon, probably one of her captives there, Merbal. **take her spoil ... prey**—lit., "spoil her spoil, prey her prey," i.e., as she spoiled other nations, so shall she herself be a spoil to Babylon. **20. because they wrought for me**—the Chaldeans, fulfilling My will as to Tyre (cf. Jer. 25:9). **21.** In the evil only, not in the good, was Egypt to be parallel to Israel. The very downfall of Egypt will be the signal for the rise of Israel, because of God's covenant with the latter. **I cause the horn of ... Israel to bud**—(Ps. 132:17). I will cause its ancient glory to revive: an earnest of Israel's full glory under Messiah, the son of David (Luke 1:69). Even in Babylon an earnest was given of this in Daniel (Dan. 6:2) and Jeconiah (Jer. 52:31). **I will give thee ... opening of ... mouth**—When thy predictions shall have come to pass, thy words henceforth shall be more heeded (cf. ch. 24:27).

CHAPTER 30

Vss. 1-26. CONTINUATION OF THE PROPHECIES AGAINST EGYPT. Two distinct messages: (1) From vs. 1 to vs. 9, a repetition of ch. 29:1-16, with fuller details of lifelike distinctness. The date is probably not long after that mentioned in ch. 29:17, on the eve of Nebuchadnezzar's march against Egypt after subjugating Tyre. (2) A vision relating directly to Pharaoh and the overthrow of his kingdom; communicated at an earlier date, the seventh of the first month of the eleventh year. Not a year after the date in ch. 29:1, and three months before the taking of Jerusalem by Nebuchadnezzar. **2. Woe worth the day!**—i.e., Alas for the day! **3. the time of the heathen**—viz., for taking vengeance on them. The judgment on Egypt is the beginning of a world-wide judgment on all the heathen enemies of God (Joel 1: 15; 2:1, 2; 3; Obadiah 15). **4. pain**—lit., "pangs with trembling as of a woman in childbirth." **5. the mingled people**—the mercenary troops of Egypt

from various lands, mostly from the interior of Africa (cf. ch. 27:10; Jer. 25:20, 24; 46:9, 21). **Chub**—the people named *Kufa* on the monuments [HAVERNICK], a people considerably north of Palestine [WILKINSON]; *Coba* or *Chobat*, a city of Mauritania [MAURER]. **men of the land that is in league**—too definite an expression to mean merely, "men in league" with Egypt; rather, "*sons* of the land *of the covenant*," i.e., the *Jews* who migrated to Egypt and carried Jeremiah with them (Jer. 42-44). Even they shall not escape (Jer. 42:22; 44:14). **6. from the tower of Syene**—(see *Note*, ch. 29:10). **7. in the midst of ... countries ... desolate**—Egypt shall fare no better than they (ch. 29:10). **9. messengers ... in ships to ... Ethiopians** (Isa. 18:1, 2). The cataracts interposing between them and Egypt should not save them. Egyptians "fleeing from before Me" in My execution of judgment, as "messengers" in "skiffs" ("vessels of bulrushes," Isa. 18:2) shall go up the Nile as far as navigable, to announce the advance of the Chaldeans. **as in the day of Egypt**—The day of Ethiopia's "pain" shall come shortly, as Egypt's day came. **10. the multitude**—the large population. **12. rivers**—the artificial canals made from the Nile for irrigation. The drying up of these would cause scarcity of grain, and so prepare the way for the invaders (Isa. 19:5-10). **13. Noph**—Memphis, the capital of Middle Egypt, and the stronghold of "idols." Though no record exists of Nebuchadnezzar's "destroying" these, we know from HERODOTUS and others, that Cambyses took Pelusium, the key of Egypt, by placing before his army dogs, cats, etc., all held sacred in Egypt, so that no Egyptian would use any weapon against them. He slew Apis, the sacred ox, and burnt other idols of Egypt. **no more a prince**—referring to the anarchy that prevailed in the civil wars between Apries and Amasis at the time of Nebuchadnezzar's invasion. There shall no more be a prince of the land of Egypt, ruling the whole country; or, no *independent* prince. **14. Pathros**—Upper Egypt, with "No" or Thebes its capital (famed for its stupendous buildings, of which grand ruins remain), in antithesis to Zoan or Tanis, a chief city in Lower Egypt, within the Delta. **15. Sin**—i.e., Pelusium, the frontier fortress on the northeast, therefore called "the strength (i.e., the key) of Egypt." It stands in antithesis to No or Thebes at the opposite end of Egypt; i.e., I will afflict Egypt from one end to the other. **16. distresses daily**—MAURER translates, "enemies during the day," i.e., open enemies who do not wait for the covert of night to make their attacks (cf. Jer. 6:4; 15:8). However, the *Hebrew*, though rarely, is sometimes rendered (see Ps. 13:2) as in *English Version*. **17. Aven**—meaning "vanity" or "iniquity": applied, by a slight change of the *Hebrew* name, to On or Heliopolis, in allusion to its idolatry. Here stood the temple of the sun, whence it was called in *Hebrew*, *Beth-shemesh* (Jer. 43:13). The Egyptian hieroglyphics call it, *Re Athom*, the sun, the father of the gods, being impersonate in *Athom* or *Adam*, the father of mankind. **Pi-beseth**—i.e., Bubastis, in Lower Egypt, near the Pelusiac branch of the Nile: notorious for the worship of the goddess of the same name (*Coptic, Pasht*), the granite stones of whose temple still attest its former magnificence. **these cities**—rather, as LXX, "the women," viz., of Aven and Pi-beseth, in antithesis to "the young men." So in vs. 18, "*daughters* shall go into captivity" [MAURER]. **18. Tehaphnehes**—called from the queen of Egypt mentioned in I Kings 11:19. The same as Daphne, near Pelusium, a royal residence of the Pharaohs (Jer. 43:7, 9). Called

Hanes (Isa. 30:4). **break ... the yokes of Egypt**—i.e., the tyrannical supremacy which she exercised over other nations. Cf. "bands of their yoke" (ch. 34:7). **a cloud**—viz., of calamity. **20.** Here begins the earlier vision, not long after that in ch. 29, about three months before the taking of Jerusalem, as to Pharaoh and his kingdom. **21. broken ... arm of Pharaoh**—(Ps. 37:17; Jer. 48:25). Referring to the defeat which Pharaoh-hophra sustained from the Chaldeans, when trying to raise the siege of Jerusalem (Jer. 37:5, 7); and previous to the deprivation of Pharaoh-necho of all his conquests from the river of Egypt to the Euphrates (II Kings 24:7; Jer. 46:2); also to the Egyptian disaster in Cyrene. **22. arms**—Not only the "one arm" broken already (vs. 21) was not to be healed, but the other two should be broken. Not a corporal wound, but a *breaking of the power* of Pharaoh is intended. **cause ... sword to fall out of ... hand**—deprive him of the resources of making war.

CHAPTER 31

Vss. 1-18. THE OVERTHROW OF EGYPT ILLUSTRATED BY THAT OF ASSYRIA. Not that Egypt was, like Assyria, utterly to cease to be, but it was, like Assyria, to lose its prominence in the empire of the world. **1. third month**—two months later than the prophecy delivered in ch. 30:20. **2. Whom art thou like**—The answer is, Thou art like the haughty king of Assyria; as he was overthrown by the Chaldeans, so shalt thou be by the same. **3.** He illustrates the pride and the consequent overthrow of the Assyrian, that Egypt may the better know what she must expect. **cedar in Lebanon**—often eighty feet high, and the diameter of the space covered by its boughs still greater: the symmetry perfect. Cf. the similar image (ch. 17:3; Dan. 4:20-22). **with a shadowing shroud**—with an overshadowing thicket. **top ... among ... thick boughs**—rather [HENGSTENBERG], "among the clouds." But *English Version* agrees better with the *Hebrew*. The *top*, or *topmost shoot,* represents the king; the *thick boughs,* the large resources of the empire. **4. waters ... little rivers**—the Tigris with its branches and "rivulets," or "conduits" for irrigation, the source of Assyria's fertility. "The deep" is the ever flowing water, never dry. Metaphorically, for Assyria's resources, as the "conduits" are her colonies. **5. when he shot forth**—because of the abundant moisture which nourished him in shooting forth. But see *Margin.* **6. fowls ... made ... nests in ... boughs**—so ch. 17: 23; Daniel 4:12. The gospel kingdom shall gather all under its covert, for their good and for the glory of God, which the world kingdoms did for evil and for self-aggrandizement (Matt. 13:32). **8. cedars ... could not hide him**—could not outtop him. No other king eclipsed him. **were not like**—were not comparable to. **garden of God**—As in the case of Tyre (ch. 28:13), the imagery, that is applied to the Assyrian king, is taken from Eden; peculiarly appropriate, as Eden was watered by rivers that afterwards watered Assyria (Gen. 2:10-14). This cedar seemed to revive in itself all the glories of paradise, so that no tree there outtopped it. **9. I ... made him**—It was all due to *My* free grace. **10. thou ... he**—The change of persons is because the language refers partly to the cedar, partly to the person signified by the cedar. **11.** Here the literal supersedes the figurative. **shall surely deal with him**—according to his own pleasure, and according to the Assyrian's (Sardanapalus) desert. Nebuchadnezzar is

called "the mighty one" (*El,* a name of God), because he was God's representative and instrument of judgment (Dan. 2:37, 38). **12. from his shadow**—*under* which they had formerly *dwelt* as their covert (vs. 6). **13.** Birds and beasts shall insult over his fallen trunk. **14. trees by the waters**—i.e., that are plentifully supplied by the waters: nations abounding in resources. **stand up in their height**—i.e., trust in their height: *stand upon* it as their ground of confidence. FAIRBAIRN points the *Hebrew* differently, so as for "their trees," to translate, "(And that none that drink water may stand) *on themselves,* (because of their greatness)." But the usual reading is better, as Assyria and the confederate states throughout are compared to strong trees. The clause, "All that drink water," marks the ground of the trees' confidence "in their height," viz., that they have ample sources of supply. MAURER, retaining the same *Hebrew,* translates, "that neither their *terebinth trees* may stand up in their height, nor all (the other trees) that drink water." **to ... nether ... earth ... pit**—(ch. 32:18; Ps. 82:7). **15. covered the deep**—as mourners cover their heads in token of mourning, "I made the deep that watered the cedar" to wrap itself in mourning for him. The waters of the deep are the tributary peoples of Assyria (Rev. 17:15). **fainted**—lit., were "faintness" (itself); more forcible than the verb. **16. hell**—Sheol or Hades, the unseen world: equivalent to, "I cast him into oblivion" (cf. Isa. 14:9-11). **shall be comforted**—because so great a king as the Assyrian is brought down to a level with them. It is a kind of consolation to the wretched to have companions in misery. **17. his arm, that dwelt under his shadow**—those who were the helpers or tool of his tyranny, and therefore enjoyed his protection (e.g., Syria and her neighbors). These were sure to share her fate. Cf. the same phrase as to the Jews living under the protection of their king (Lam. 4:20); both alike "making flesh their arm, and in heart departing from the Lord" (Jer. 17:5). **18.** Application of the parabolic description of Assyria to the parallel case of Egypt. "All that has been said of the Assyrian consider as said to thyself. To whom art thou so like, as thou art to the Assyrian? To none." The lesson on a gigantic scale of Eden-like privileges abused to pride and sin by the Assyrian, as in the case of the first man in Eden, ending in ruin, was to be repeated in Egypt's case. For the unchangeable God governs the world on the same unchangeable principles. **thou shalt lie in ... uncircumcised**—As circumcision was an object of mocking to thee, ʰthou shalt lie in the midst of the uncircumcised, slain by their sword [GROTIUS]. Retribution in kind (ch. 28: 10). **This is Pharaoh**—Pharaoh's end shall be the same humiliating one as I have depicted the Assyrian's to have been. "This" is demonstrative, as if he were pointing with the finger to Pharaoh lying prostrate, a spectacle to all, as on the shore of the Red Sea (Exod. 14:30, 31).

CHAPTER 32

Vss. 1-32. TWO ELEGIES OVER PHARAOH, ONE DELIVERED ON THE FIRST DAY (vs. 1), THE OTHER ON THE FIFTEENTH DAY OF THE SAME MONTH, THE TWELFTH OF THE TWELFTH YEAR. **1.** The twelfth year from the carrying away of Jehoiachin; Jerusalem was by this time overthrown, and Amasis was beginning his revolt against Pharaoh-hophra. **2. Pharaoh**—"Phra" in Burmah, signifies the king, high priest, and idol. **whale**—rather, any monster of the waters; here, the crocodile of the Nile. Pharaoh is as a lion on dry land, a crocodile in the waters; i.e., an object of terror everywhere. **camest forth with thy rivers** "breakest forth" [FAIRBAIRN]. The antithesis of "seas" and "rivers" favors GROTIUS' rendering, "Thou camest forth from the sea *into* the rivers"; i.e., from thy own empire into other states. However, *English Version* is favored by the "thy": thou camest forth with *thy* rivers (i.e., with thy forces) and with thy feet didst fall irrecoverably; so Israel, once desolate, troubles the waters (i.e., neighboring states). **3. with a company of many people**—viz., the Chaldeans (ch. 29:3, 4; Hos. 7:12). **my net**—for they are My instrument. **4. leave thee upon the land**—as a fish drawn out of the water loses all its strength, so Pharaoh (in vs. 3, compared to a water monster) shall be (ch. 29:5). **5. thy height**—thy hugeness [FAIRBAIRN]. The great heap of corpses of thy forces, on which thou pridest thyself. "Height" may refer to *mental elevation*, as well as bodily [VATABLUS]. **6. land wherein thou swimmest**—Egypt: the land watered by the Nile, the the source of its fertility, wherein thou swimmest (carrying on the image of the crocodile, i.e., wherein thou dost exercise thy wanton power at will). Irony. The land shall still afford seas to swim in, but they shall be seas of blood. Alluding to the plague (Exod. 7:19; Rev. 8:8). HAVERNICK translates, "I will water the land with *what flows from thee,* even thy blood, reaching to the mountains": "with thy blood *overflowing* even to the mountains." Perhaps this is better. **7. put thee out**—extinguish thy light (Job 18:5). Pharaoh is represented as a bright star, at the extinguishing of whose light in the political sky the whole heavenly host is shrouded in sympathetic darkness. Here, too, as in vs. 6, there is an allusion to the supernatural darkness sent formerly (Exod. 10:21-23). The heavenly bodies are often made images of earthly dynasties (Isa. 13:10; Matt. 24:29). **9. thy destruction**—i.e., tidings of thy destruction (lit., "thy breakage") carried by captive and dispersed Egyptians "among the nations" [GROTIUS]; or, *thy broken people,* resembling one great *fracture,* the ruins of what they had been [FAIRBAIRN]. **10. brandish my sword before them**—lit., "in their faces," or sight. **13.** (See *Note* on ch. 29:11.) The picture is ideally true, not to be interpreted by the letter. The political ascendency of Egypt was to cease with the Chaldean conquest [FAIRBAIRN]. Henceforth Pharaoh must figuratively no longer *trouble the waters by man or beast,* i.e., no longer was he to flood other peoples with his overwhelming forces. **14. make their waters deep**—rather, "make . . . to subside"; lit., "sink" [FAIRBAIRN]. **like oil**—emblem of *quietness.* No longer shall they descend violently on other countries as the overflowing Nile, but shall be still and sluggish in political action. **16.** As in ch. 19:14. This is a prophetical lamentation; yet so it shall come to pass [GROTIUS]. **17.** The second lamentation for Pharaoh. This funeral dirge in imagination accompanies him to the unseen world. Egypt personified in its political head is ideally represented as undergoing the change by death to which man is liable. Expressing that Egypt's supremacy is no more, a thing of the past, never to be again. **the month**—the twelfth month (vs. 1); fourteen days after the former vision. **18. cast them down**—i.e., predict that they shall be *cast down* (so Jer. 1:10). The prophet's word was God's, and carried with it its own fulfilment. **daughters of . . . nations**—i.e., the nations with their peoples. Egypt is to share the fate of other ancient nations

once famous, now consigned to oblivion: Elam (vs. 24), Meshech, etc. (vs. 26), Edom (vs. 29), Zidon (vs. 30). **19. Whom dost thou pass in beauty?**—Beautiful as thou art, thou art not more so than other nations, which nevertheless have perished. **go down** . . .—to the nether world, where all "beauty" is speedily marred. **20. she is delivered to the sword**—viz., by God. **draw her**—as if addressing her executioners: drag her forth to death. **21.** (Ch. 31:16.) Ezekiel has before his eyes Isaiah 14:9, etc. **shall speak to him**—with "him" join "with them that help him"; *shall speak to him and his helpers* with a taunting welcome, as now one of themselves. **22. her . . . his**—The abrupt change of gender is, because Ezekiel has in view at one time the *kingdom* (feminine), at another the *monarch.* "Asshur," or Assyria, is placed first in punishment. as being first in guilt. **23. in the sides of the pit**—Sepulchers in the East were caves hollowed out of the rock, and the bodies were laid in niches formed at the sides. MAURER needlessly departs from the ordinary meaning, and translates, "extremities" (cf. Isa. 14:13, 15). **which caused terror**—They, who alive were a terror to others, are now, in the nether world, themselves a terrible object to behold. **24. Elam**—placed next, as having been an auxiliary to Assyria. Its territory lay in Persia. In Abraham's time an independent kingdom (Gen. 14:1). Famous for its bowmen (Isa. 22:6). **borne their shame**—the just retribution of their lawless *pride.* Destroyed by Nebuchadnezzar (Jer. 49:34-38). **25. a bed**—a sepulchral niche. **all . . . slain by . . . sword,** . . .—(vss. 21, 23, 24). The very monotony of the phraseology gives to the dirge an awe-inspiring effect. **26. Meshech, Tubal**—northern nations: the Moschi and Tibareni, between the Black and Caspian Seas. HERODOTUS, 3. 94, mentions them as a subjugated people, tributaries to Darius Hystaspes (see ch. 27:13). **27. they shall not lie with the mighty**—i.e., they shall not have separate tombs such as mighty conquerors have: but shall all be heaped together in one pit, as is the case with the vanquished [GROTIUS]. HAVERNICK reads it interrogatively, "Shall they not lie with the mighty that are fallen?" But *English Version* is supported by the parallel (Isa. 14:18, 19), to which Ezekiel refers, and which represents them as *not* lying as mighty kings lie in a grave, but cast out of one, as a carcass trodden under foot. **with . . . weapons of war**—alluding to the custom of burying warriors with their arms (I Maccabees 13:29). Though honored by the laying of "their swords under their heads," yet the punishment of "their iniquities shall be upon their bones." Their swords shall thus attest their shame, not their glory (Matt. 26:52), being the instruments of their violence, the penalty of which they are paying. **28. Yea, thou**—Thou, too, Egypt, like them, shalt lie as one vanquished. **29. princes**—Edom was not only governed by kings, but by subordinate "princes" or "dukes" (Gen. 36:40). **with their might**—notwithstanding their might, they shall be brought down (Isa. 34:5, 10-17; Jer. 49:7, 13-18). **lie with the uncircumcised**—Though Edom was circumcised, being descended from Isaac, he shall lie with the uncircumcised; much more shall Egypt, who had no hereditary right to circumcision. **30. princes of the north**—Syria, which is still called by the Arabs the north; or the Tyrians, north of Palestine, conquered by Nebuchadnezzar (chs. 26, 27, 28), [GROTIUS]. **Zidonians**—who shared the fate of Tyre (ch. 28:21). **with their terror they are ashamed of their might**—i.e., notwithstanding the terror which they inspired in their contemporaries. "Might" is connected by

MAURER thus, "Notwithstanding the terror *which resulted from* their might." **31. comforted**—with the melancholy satisfaction of not being alone, but of having other kingdoms companions in his downfall. This shall be his only comfort—a very poor one! **32. my terror**—the reading of the *Margin* or *Keri*. The *Hebrew* text or *Chetib* is *"his terror,"* which gives good sense (vss. 25, 30). *"My terror"* implies that God puts *His* terror on Pharaoh's multitude, as they put "their terror" on others, e.g., under Pharaoh-necho on Judea. As "the land of the living" was the scene of "their terror," so it shall be God's; especially in Judea, He will display His glory to the terror of Israel's foes (ch. 26:20). In Israel's case the judgment is temporary, ending in their future restoration under Messiah. In the case of the world kingdoms which flourished for a time, they fall to rise no more.

CHAPTER 33

Vss. 1-33. RENEWAL OF EZEKIEL'S COMMISSION, NOW THAT HE IS AGAIN TO ADDRESS HIS COUNTRYMEN, AND IN A NEW TONE. Heretofore his functions had been chiefly threatening; from this point, after the evil had got to its worst in the overthrow of Jerusalem, the consolatory element preponderates. **2. to the children of thy people**—whom he had been forbidden to address from ch. 24:26, 27, till Jerusalem was overthrown, and the "escaped" came with tidings of the judgment being completed. So now, in vs. 21, the tidings of the fact having arrived, he opens his heretofore closed lips to the Jews. In the interval he had prophesied as to foreign nations. The former part of the chapter, from vs. 2 to vs. 20, seems to have been imparted to Ezekiel on the evening previous (vs. 22), being a preparation for the latter part (vss. 23-33) imparted after the tidings had come. This accounts for the first part standing without intimation of the date, which was properly reserved for the latter part, to which the former was the anticipatory introduction [FAIRBAIRN]. **watchman**—The first nine verses exhibit Ezekiel's office as a spiritual watchman; so in ch. 3:16-21; only here the duties of the earthly watchman (cf. II Sam. 18:24, 25; II Kings 9:17) are detailed first, and then the application is made to the spiritual watchman's duty (cf. Isa. 21:6-10; Hos. 9:8; Hab. 2:1). "A man of their coasts" is a man specially chosen for the office *out of their whole number.* So Judges 18:2, "five men *from their coasts*"; also the *Hebrew* of Genesis 47:2; implying the care needed in the choice of the watchman, the spiritual as well as the temporal (Acts 1:21, 22, 24-26; I Tim. 5:22). **3. the sword**—invaders. An appropriate illustration at the time of the invasion of Judea by Nebuchadnezzar. **4. blood . . . upon his own head**—metaphor from sacrificial victims, on the heads of which they used to lay their hands, praying that their guilt should be upon the victims. **6. his iniquity**—his negligence in not maintaining constant watchfulness, as they who are in warfare ought to do. The thing signified here appears from under the image. **7. I have set thee a watchman**—application of the image. Ezekiel's appointment to be a watchman spiritually is far more solemn, as it is derived from God, not from the people. **8. thou shalt surely die**—by a violent death, the earnest of everlasting death; the qualification being supposed, "if thou dost not repent." **9.** Blood had by this time been shed (vs. 21), but Ezekiel was clear. **10. be upon us**—i.e., their guilt remain on us. **pine**

away in them—if we suffer the penalty threatened for them in ch. 24:23, according to the law (Lev. 26:39). **how should we . . . live?**—as Thou dost promise in vs. 5 (cf. ch. 37:11; Isa. 49:14). **11. To** meet the Jews' cry of despair in vs. 10, Ezekiel here cheers them by the assurance that God has no pleasure in their death, but that they should repent and live (II Pet. 3:9). A yearning tenderness manifests itself here, notwithstanding all their past sins; yet with it a holiness that abates nothing of its demands for the honor of God's authority. God's righteousness is vindicated as in ch. 3:18-21 and ch. 18, by the statement that each should be treated with the closest adaptation of God's justice to his particular case. **12. not fall . . . in the day that he turneth**—(II Chron. 7:14; see ch. 3:20; 18:24). **15. give again that he had robbed**—(Luke 19:8). **statutes of life**—in the obeying of which life is promised (Lev. 18:5). If the law has failed to give life to man, it has not been the fault of the law, but of man's sinful inability to keep it (Rom. 7:10, 12; Gal. 3:21). It becomes life-giving through Christ's righteous obedience to it (II Cor. 3:6). **17. The way of the Lord**—The Lord's way of dealing in His moral government. **21. twelfth year . . . tenth month**—a year and a half after the capture of the city (Jer. 39:2; 52:5, 6), in the eleventh year and fourth month. The one who escaped (as foretold, ch. 24:26) may have been so long on the road through fear of entering the enemy's country [HENDERSON]; or, the *singular* is used for the *plural* in a collective sense, "the escaped remnant." Cf. similar phrases, "the escaped of Moab," Isaiah 15:9; "He that escapeth of them," Amos 9:1. Naturally the reopening of the prophet's mouth for consolation would be deferred till the number of the escaped remnant was complete: the removal of such a large number would easily have occupied seventeen or eighteen months. **22. in the evening**—(see *Note,* vs. 2). Thus the capture of Jerusalem was known to Ezekiel by revelation before the messenger came. **my mouth . . . no more dumb**—i.e., to my countrymen; as foretold (ch. 24:27), He spake (vss. 2-20) in the evening before the tidings came. **24. they that inhabit . . . wastes of . . . Israel**—marking the blindness of the fraction of Jews under Gedaliah who, though dwelling amidst regions laid waste by the foe, still cherished hopes of deliverance, and this without repentance. **Abraham was one . . . but we are many**—If God gave the land for an inheritance to Abraham, who was but one (Isa. 51:2), much more it is given to us, who, though reduced, are still many. If he, with 318 servants, was able to defend himself amid so many foes, much more shall we, so much more numerous, retain our own. The grant of the land was not for his sole use, but for his numerous posterity. **inherited the land**—not actually possessed it (Acts 7:5), but had the right of dwelling and pasturing his flocks in it [GROTIUS]. The Jews boasted similarly of their Abrahamic descent in Matthew 3:9 and John 8:39. **25. eat with the blood**—in opposition to the law (Lev. 19:26; cf. Gen. 9:4). They did so as an idolatrous rite. **26. Ye stand upon your sword**—Your dependence is, not on right and equity, but on force and arms. **every one**—Scarcely anyone refrains from adultery. **27. shall fall by the sword**—The very object of their confidence would be the instrument of their destruction. Thinking to "stand" by it, by it they shall "fall." Just retribution! Some fell by the sword of Ishmael; others by the Chaldeans in revenge for the murder of Gedaliah (Jer. 40:44). **caves**—(Judg. 6:2; I Sam. 13:6). In the hilly parts of Judea there were caves almost inaccessible, as having only crooked and extremely narrow paths of ascent, with rock in front stretching down into the valleys beneath perpendicularly (JOSEPHUS, *Jew. War*, 1. 16. 4). **28. most desolate**— (Jer. 4:27; 12:11). **none . . . pass through**—from fear of wild beasts and pestilence [GROTIUS].∗ **30.** Not only the remnant in Judea, but those at the Chebar, though less flagrantly, betrayed the same unbelieving spirit. **talking against thee**—Though going to the prophet to hear the word of the Lord, they criticised, *in an unfriendly spirit*, his peculiarities of manner and his enigmatical style (ch. 20:49); making these the excuse for their impenitence. Their talking was not directly *"against"* Ezekiel, for they professed to like his ministrations; but God's word speaks of things as they really are, not as they appear. **by the walls**—in the public haunts. In the East groups assemble under the walls of their houses in winter for conversation. **in the doors**—privately. **what is the word**—Their motive was curiosity, seeking pastime and gratification of the ear (II Tim. 4: 3); not reformation of the heart. Cf. Johanan's consultation of Jeremiah, to hear the word of the Lord without desiring to *do* it (Jer. 42:43). **31. as the people cometh**—i.e., in crowds, as disciples flock to their teacher. **sit before thee**—on lower seats at thy feet, according to the Jewish custom of pupils (Deut. 33:3; II Kings 4:38; Luke 10:39; Acts 22:3). **as my people**—though they are not. **hear . . . not do** —(Matt. 13:20, 21; Jas. 1:23, 24). **they show much love**—lit., "make love," i.e., act the part of lovers. Profess love to the Lord (Matt. 7:21). GESENIUS translates, according to *Arabic* idiom, "They do the delights of God," i.e., all that is agreeable to God. *Vulgate* translates, "They turn thy words into a song of their mouths." **heart goeth after . . . covetousness**—the grand rival to the love of God; therefore called "idolatry," and therefore associated with impure carnal love, as both alike transfer the heart's affection from the Creator to the creature (Matt. 13:22; Eph. 5:5, I Tim. 6:10). **32. very lovely song**—lit., a "song of loves": a lover's song. They praise thy eloquence, but care not for the subject of it as a real and personal thing; just as many do in the modern church [JEROME]. **play well on an instrument**—Hebrew singers accompanied the "voice" with the harp. **33. when this cometh to pass**—when My predictions are verified. **lo, it will come**—rather, "lo it *is* come" (see vs. 22). **know**—experimentally, and to their cost.

CHAPTER 34

Vss. 1-31. REPROOF OF THE FALSE SHEPHERDS; PROMISE OF THE TRUE AND GOOD SHEPHERD. Having in chapter 33 laid down repentance as the necessary preliminary to happier times for the people, He now promises the removal of the false shepherds as preparatory to the raising up of the Good Shepherd. **2.** Jeremiah 23:1 and Zechariah 11:17 similarly make the removal of the false shepherds the preliminary to the interposition of Messiah the Good Shepherd in behalf of His people Israel. The "shepherds" are not prophets or priests, but *rulers* who sought in their government their own selfish ends, not the good of the people ruled. The term was appropriate, as David, the first king and the type of the true David (vss. 23, 24), was taken from being a shepherd (II Sam. 5:2; Ps. 78:70, 71); and the office, like that of a shepherd for his flock, is to guard and provide for his people. The choice of a *shepherd* for the first king was therefore designed to

suggest this thought, just as Jesus' selection of *fishermen* for apostles was designed to remind them of their spiritual office of catching men (cf. Isa. 44: 28; Jer. 2:8; 3:15; 10:21; 23:1, 2). **3. fat**—or, by differently pointing the *Hebrew*, "milk" [LXX]. Thus the repetition "fat" and "fed" is avoided: also the eating of "fat" would not probably be put before the "killing" of the sheep. The eating of sheep's or goats' milk as food (Deut. 32:14; Prov. 27:27) was unobjectionable, had not these shepherds milked them too often, and that without duly "feeding" them [BOCHART], (Isa. 56:11). The rulers levied exorbitant tributes. **kill . . . fed**—kill the rich by false accusation so as to get possession of their property. **feed not . . . flock**—take no care of the people (John 10:12). **4. The diseased**—rather, those *weak* from the effects of "disease," as "strengthened" (i.e., with due nourishment) requires [GROTIUS]. **broken**—i.e., fractures from wounds inflicted by the wolf. **brought again . . . driven away**— (Exod. 23:4). Those "driven away" by the enemy into foreign lands through God's judgments are meant (Jer. 23:3). A spiritual reformation of the state by the rulers would have turned away God's wrath, and "brought again" the exiles. The rulers are censured as *chiefly* guilty (though the people, too, were guilty), because they, who ought to have been foremost in checking the evil, promoted it. **neither . . . sought . . . lost**—Contrast the Good Shepherd's love (Luke 15:4). **with force . . . ruled** —(Exod. 1:13, 14). With an Egyptian bondage. The very thing forbidden by the law they did (Lev. 25:43; cf. I Pet. 5:3). **5. scattered, because . . . no shepherd**—i.e., none worthy of the name, though there were some *called* shepherds (I Kings 22:17; Matt. 9:36). Cf. Matt. 26:31, where the sheep were scattered when the true Shepherd was smitten. God calls them *"My* sheep"; for they were not, as the shepherds treated them, *their* patrimony whereby to "feed themselves." **meat to all . . . beasts**— They became a prey to the Syrians, Ammon, Moab, and Assyria. **6. every high hill**—the scene of their idolatries sanctioned by the rulers. **search . . . seek** —rather, "seek" . . . "search." The former is the part of the superior rulers *to inquire after: to search out* is the duty of the subordinate rulers [JUNIUS]. **10. I will require my flock**—(Heb. 13:17), rather, *"I require . . . ,"* for God already had begun to do so, punishing Zedekiah and the other princes severely (Jer. 52:10). **11. . . . will . . . search**—doing that which the so-called shepherds had failed to do, I being the rightful owner of the flock. **12. in the day that he is among**—*in the midst of* (*Hebrew*) His sheep that had been scattered. Referring to Messiah's second advent, when He shall be "the glory *in the midst of* Israel" (Zech. 2:5). **in the cloudy . . . day**—the day of the nation's calamity (Joel 2:2). **13.** (Ch. 28:25; 36:24; 37:21, 22; Isa. 65:9, 10; Jer. 23:3.) **14. good pasture**—(Ps. 23:2). **high mountains of Israel**—In chs. 17:23 and 20:40, the phrase is "the mountain of the height of Israel" in the *singular* number. The reason for the difference is: *there* Ezekiel spoke of the central seat of the kingdom, Mount Zion, where the people met for the worship of Jehovah; *here* he speaks of the kingdom of Israel at large, all the parts of which are regarded as possessing a moral elevation. **16.** In contrast to the unfaithful shepherds (vs. 4). The several duties neglected by *them I* will faithfully discharge. **fat . . . strong**—i.e., those rendered wanton by prosperity (Deut. 32:15; Jer. 5:28), who use their strength to oppress the weak. Cf. vs. 20, "the fat cattle" (Isa. 10:16). The image is from fat cattle that wax refractory. **with judgment**—i.e., justice and equity, as contrasted with the "force" and "cruelty" with which the unfaithful shepherds ruled the flock (vs. 4). **17. you, ... my flock**—passing from the rulers to the people. **cattle and cattle**—rather, "sheep and sheep"; *Margin,* "small cattle," or "flocks of lambs and kids," i.e., I judge between one class of citizens and another, so as to award what is right to each. He then defines the class about to be punitively "judged," viz., "the rams and he goats," or great he goats (cf. Isa. 14:9, *Margin;* Zech. 10:3; Matt. 25:32, 33). They answer to "the fat and strong," as opposed to the "sick" (vs. 16). The rich and ungodly of the people are meant, who imitated the bad rulers in oppressing their poorer brethren, as if it enhanced their own joys to trample on others' rights (vs. 18). **18, 19.** Not content with appropriating to their own use the goods of others, they from mere wantonness spoiled what they did not use, so as to be of no use to the owners. **deep waters**—i.e., "limpid," as deep waters are generally *clear.* GROTIUS explains the image as referring to the usuries with which the rich ground the poor (ch. 22:12; Isa. 24:2). **they eat**—scantily. **they drink**—sorrowfully. **20. fat ... lean**—the rich oppressors ... the humble poor. **21. scattered them abroad**—down to the time of the carrying away to Babylon [GROTIUS]. **22.** After the restoration from Babylon, the Jews were delivered in some degree from the oppression, not only of foreigners, but also of their own great people (Neh. 5:1-19). The full and final fulfilment of this prophecy is future. **23. set up**—i.e., raise up by divine appointment; alluding to the declaration of God to David, "I will *set up* thy seed after thee" (II Sam. 7:12); and, "Yet have I *set* My king on My holy hill of Zion" (Ps. 2:6; cf. Acts 2:30; 13:23). **one shepherd**—lit., "a Shepherd, one": singularly and pre-eminently *one:* the only one of His kind, to whom none is comparable (Song of Sol. 5:10). The Lord Jesus refers to this prophecy (John 10:14), "I am THE Good Shepherd." Also "one" as uniting in one the heretofore divided kingdoms of Israel and Judah, and also "gathering together in one all things in Christ, both which are in heaven and on earth" (Eph. 1:10); thus healing worse breaches than that between Israel and Judah (Col. 1:20). "God by Him reconciling all things unto Himself, whether things in earth or in heaven." **David**—the antitypical David, Messiah, of the seed of David, which no other king after the captivity was: who was *fully,* what David was only in a degree, "the man after God's own heart." Also, David means *beloved:* Messiah was truly God's *beloved* Son (Isa. 42:1; Matt. 3:17). Shepherd means *King,* rather than religious instructor; in this pre-eminently He was the true David, who was the *Shepherd King* (Luke 1:32, 33). Messiah is called "David" in Isaiah 55:3, 4; Jeremiah 30:9; Hosea 3:5. **24. my servant**—implying fitness for ruling in the name of God, not pursuing a self-chosen course, as other kings, but acting as the faithful administrator of the will of God; Messiah realized fully this character (Ps. 40:7, 8; Isa. 42:1; 49:3, 6; 53:11; Phil. 2:7), which David typically and partially represented (Acts 13:36); so He is the fittest person to wield the world scepter, abused by all the world kings (Dan. 2:34, 35, 44, 45). **25. covenant of peace ... evil beasts ... to cease ... dwell safely**—The original promise of the law (Lev. 26:6) shall be realized for the first time fully under Messiah (Isa. 11:6-9; 35:9; Hos. 2:18). **26. them and the places round about my hill**—The Jews, and Zion, God's hill (Ps. 2:6), are to be sources of blessing, not merely to themselves, but to the sur-

rounding heathen (Isa. 19:24; 56:6, 7; 60:3; Mic. 5: 7; Zech. 8:13). The literal fulfilment is, however, the primary one, though the spiritual also is designed. In correspondence with the settled reign of righteousness internally, all is to be prosperity externally, fertilizing showers (according to the promise of the ancient covenant, Lev. 26:4; Ps. 68: 9; Mal. 3:10), and productive trees and lands (vs. 27). Thus shall they realize the image of vs. 14; viz., a flock richly pastured by God Himself. **27. served themselves of them**—availed themselves of their services, as if the Jews were their slaves (Jer. 22:13; 25:14; cf. Gen. 15:13; Exod. 1:14). **28. dwell safely**—(Jer. 23:6). **29. plant of renown**—Messiah, the "Rod" and "Branch" (Isa. 11:1), the "righteous Branch" (Jer. 23:5), who shall obtain for them "renown." FAIRBAIRN less probably translates, "A plantation for a name," i.e., a flourishing condition, represented as a garden (alluding to Eden, Gen. 2:8-11, with its various trees, good for food and pleasant to the sight), the planting of the Lord (Isa. 60:21; 61:3), and an object of "renown" among the heathen. **31. ye my flock ... are men**—not merely an explanation of the image, as JEROME represents. But as God had promised many things which mere "men" could not expect to realize, He shows that it is not from *man's* might their realization is to be looked for, but from GOD, who would perform them for His covenant people, "*His* flock" [ROSENMULLER]. When we realize most our weakness and God's power and faithfulness to His covenant, we are in the fittest state for receiving His blessings.

CHAPTER 35

Vss. 1-15. JUDGMENT ON EDOM. Another feature of Israel's prosperity; those who exulted over Israel's humiliation, shall themselves be a "prey." Already stated in ch. 25:12-14; properly repeated here in full detail, as a commentary on vs. 28 of last chapter. The Israelites "shall be no more a prey"; but Edom, the type of their most bitter foes, shall be destroyed irrecoverably. **2. Mount Seir**—i.e., Idumea (Gen. 36:9). Singled out as badly pre-eminent in its bitterness against God's people, to represent all their enemies everywhere and in all ages. So in Isaiah 34:5, and 63:1-4, Edom, the region of the greatest enmity towards God's people, is the ideal scene of the final judgments of all God's foes. "Seir" means "shaggy," alluding to its rugged hills and forests. **3. most desolate**—lit., "desolation and desolateness" (Jer. 49:17, etc.). It is only in their national character of foes to God's people, that the Edomites are to be utterly destroyed. A *remnant* of Edom, as of the other heathen, is to be "called by the name of God" (Amos 9:12). **5. perpetual hatred**—(Ps. 137:7; Amos 1:11; Obad. 10-16). Edom perpetuated the hereditary hatred derived from Esau against Jacob. **shed the blood of ...** —The lit., translation is better. "Thou hast poured out the children of Israel"; viz., like water. So Psalm 22:14; 63:10, *Margin;* Jeremiah 18:21. Cf. II Samuel 14:14. **by the force of the sword**—lit., "by" or "upon the hands of the sword"; the sword being personified as a devourer whose "hands" were the instruments of destruction. **in the time that their iniquity had an end**—i.e., had its consummation (ch. 21:25, 29). Edom consummated his guilt when he exulted over Jerusalem's downfall, and helped the foe to destroy it (Ps. 137: 7; Obad. 11). **6. I will prepare thee unto blood**—I will expose thee to slaughter. **sith**—old English for "seeing that" or "since." **thou hast not hated blood**—The *Hebrew* order is, "thou hast hated not—blood"; i.e., thou couldst not bear to live without bloodshed [GROTIUS]. There is a play on similar sounds in the *Hebrew; Edom* resembling *dam*, the *Hebrew* for "blood"; as Edom means "red," the transition to "blood" is easy. Edom, akin to blood in name, so also in nature and acts; "blood therefore shall pursue thee." The measure which Edom meted to others should be meted to himself (Ps. 109: 17; Matt. 7:2; 26:52). **7. cut off . . . him that passeth**—i.e., every passer to and fro; "the highways shall be unoccupied" (ch. 29:11; Judg. 5:6). **9. shall not return**—to their former state (ch. 16:55); shall not be restored. The *Hebrew* text (*Chetib*) reads, "shall not *be inhabited*" (cf. ch. 26:20; Mal. 1:3, 4). **10.** So far from being allowed to enter on Israel's vacated inheritance, as Edom hoped (ch. 36:5; Ps. 83:4, 12; Obad. 13), it shall be that he shall be deprived of his own; and whereas Israel's humiliation was temporary, Edom's shall be perpetual. **Lord was there**—(ch. 48:35; Ps. 48:1, 3; 132:13, 14). Jehovah claimed Judea as His own, even when the Chaldeans had overthrown the state; they could not remove Him, as they did the idols of heathen lands. The broken sentences express the excited feelings of the prophet at Edom's wicked presumption. The transition from the "two nations and two countries" to "it" marks that the two are regarded as one whole. The last clause, "and Jehovah was there," bursts in, like a flash of lightning, reproving the wicked presumption of Edom's thought. **11. according to thine anger**—(Jas. 2:13). As thou in anger and envy hast injured them, so I will injure thee. **I will make myself known among them**—viz., the Israelites. I will manifest My favor to them, after I have punished thee. **12, 13. blasphemies . . . against . . . Israel . . . against me**—God regards what is done against His people as done against Himself (Matt. 25:45; Acts 9:2, 4, 5). Edom *implied,* if he did not express it, in his taunts against Israel, that God had not sufficient power to protect His people. A type of the spirit of all the foes of God and His people (I Sam. 2:3; Rev. 13:6). **14.** (Isa. 65:13, 14.) "The whole earth" refers to *Judea and the nations that submit themselves to Judea's God;* when these rejoice, the foes of God and His people, represented by Edom *as a nation,* shall be desolate. Things shall be completely reversed; Israel, that now for a time mourns, shall then rejoice and for ever. Edom, that now rejoices over fallen Israel, shall then, when elsewhere all is joy, mourn, and for ever (Isa. 65:17-19; Matt. 5:4; Luke 6:25). HAVERNICK loses this striking antithesis by translating, "According to the joy of the whole land (of Edom), so I will make thee desolate"; which would make the next verse a mere repetition of this. **15.** (Obadiah 12, 15.)

CHAPTER 36

Vss. 1-38. ISRAEL AVENGED OF HER FOES, AND RESTORED, FIRST TO INWARD HOLINESS, THEN TO OUTWARD PROSPERITY. The distinction between Israel and the heathen (as Edom) is: Israel has a covenant relation to God ensuring restoration after chastisement, so that the heathen's hope of getting possession of the elect people's inheritance must fail, and they themselves be made desolate (vss. 1-15). The reason for the chastisement of Israel was Israel's sin and profanation of God's name (vss. 16-21). God has good in store for Israel, for His own name's sake, to revive His people; first, by a spirit-

ual renewal of their hearts, and, next, by an external restoration to prosperity (vss. 22-33). The result is that the heathen shall be impressed with the power and goodness of God manifested so palpably towards the restored people (vss. 34-38). **1, 2. mountains of Israel**—in contrast to *"Mount Seir"* of the previous prophecy. They are here personified; Israel's elevation is moral, not merely physical, as Edom's. Her hills are "the everlasting hills" of Jacob's prophecy (Gen. 49:26). "The enemy" (Edom, the singled-out representative of all God's foes), with a shout of exultation, "Aha!" had claimed, as the nearest kinsman of Israel (the brother of their father Esau), his vacated inheritance; as much as to say, the so-called "everlasting" inheritance of Israel and of the "hills," which typified the unmoved perpetuity of it (Ps. 125:1, 2), has come to an end, in spite of the promise of God, and has become "ours" (cf. Deut. 32:13; 33:15). **3.** Lit., "Because, even because." **swallowed you up**—lit., "panted after" you, as a beast after its prey; implying the greedy cupidity of Edom as to Israel's inheritance (Ps. 56:1, 2). **lips of talkers**—lit., "lips of *the tongue,*" i.e., of the slanderer, the man of tongue. Edom slandered Israel because of the connection of the latter with Jehovah, as though He were unable to save them. Deuteronomy 28:37, and Jeremiah 24:9 had foretold Israel's reproach among the heathen (Dan. 9:16). **4.** Inanimate creatures are addressed, to imply that the creature also, as it were, groans for deliverance from the bondage of corruption into the glorious liberty of the children of God (Rom. 8:19-21) [POLANUS]. The completeness of the renewed blessedness of all parts of the land is implied. **derision**—(Ps. 79:4). **5. to cast it out for a prey**—i.e., to take the land for a prey, its inhabitants being cast out. Or the land is compared to a prey cast forth to wild beasts. FAIRBAIRN needlessly alters the *Hebrew* pointing and translates, "that they may plunder its pasturage." **6. the shame of the heathen**—viz., the shame with which the heathen cover you (Ps. 123:3, 4). **7. lifted . . . mine hand**—in token of an oath (ch. 20:5; Gen. 14:22). **they shall bear their shame**—a *perpetual* shame; whereas the "shame" which Israel bore from these heathen was only for a time. **8. they are at hand to come**—i.e., the Israelites are soon about to return to their land. This proves that the primary reference of the prophecy is to the return from Babylon, which was "at hand," or comparatively near. But this only in part fulfilled the prediction, the full and final blessing in future, and the restoration from Babylon was an earnest of it. **10. wastes . . . builded**—Isaiah 58:12; 61:4; Amos 9:11, 12, 14, where, as here (ch. 34:23, 24), the names of David, Messiah's type, and Edom, Israel's foe, are introduced in connection with the coming restoration. **11. do better . . . than at your beginnings**—as in the case of Job (Job 42:12). Whereas the heathen nations fall irrevocably, Israel shall be more than restored; its last estate shall exceed even its first. **12. to walk upon you**—O mountains of Israel (vs. 8)! **thee . . . thou**—change from *plural* to *singular*: O hill of Zion, singled out from the other mountains of Israel (ch. 34:26); or land. **thou shalt no more . . . bereave them** *of men*—Thou shalt no more provoke God to bereave them *of children* (so the ellipsis ought to be supplied, as Ezekiel probably alludes to Jer. 15:7, "I will bereave them *of children*"). **13. Thou land devourest up men**—alluding to the words of the spies (Num. 13:32). The land personified is represented as doing that which was done in it. Like an unnatural mother it devoured, i.e., it was the grave of its people; of the Canaanites, its former possessors, through mutual wars, and finally by the sword of Israel; and now, of the Jews, through internal and external ills; e.g., wars, famine (to which vs. 30, "reproach of *famine* among the heathen," implies the allusion here is). **14. bereave**—so the *Keri* or *Hebrew Margin* reads, to correspond to "bereave" in vs. 13; but "cause to fall" or "stumble," in the *Hebrew* text or *Chetib*, being the more difficult reading, is the one least likely to come from a corrector; also, it forms a good transition to the next subject, viz., the moral *cause* of the people's calamities, viz., their *falls*, or *stumblings* through sin. The latter ceasing, the former also cease. So the same expression follows in vs. 15, "Neither shalt thou cause thy nations to *fall* any more." **17. removed woman**—(Lev. 15:19, etc.). **18, 19.** The reason for their removal was their sin, which God's holiness could not let pass unpunished; just as a woman's legal uncleanness was the reason for her being *separated* from the congregation. **20. profaned my holy name, when they**—the heathen—**said to them**—the Israelites. **These . . .** —The Israelites gave a handle of reproach to the heathen against God, who would naturally say, These who take usury, oppress, commit adultery, etc., and who, in such an abject plight, are "gone forth" as exiles "out of His land," are specimens of what Jehovah can or will effect, for His people, and show what kind of a God this so-called holy, omnipotent, covenant-keeping God must be! (Isa. 52:5; Rom. 2:24). **21. I had pity for mine holy name**—i.e., I felt pity for it; God's own name, so dishonored, was the primary object of His pitying concern; then His people, secondarily, through His concern for it [FAIRBAIRN]. **22. not . . . for your sakes**—i.e., not for any merit in you; for, on the contrary, on your part, there is everything to call down continued severity (cf. Deut. 9:5, 6). The sole and sure ground of hope was God's regard to "His own name," as the God of covenant grace (Ps. 106:45), which He must vindicate from the dishonor brought on it by the Jews, before the heathen. **23. sanctify**—vindicate and manifest as holy, in opposition to the heathen reproaches of it brought on by the Jews' sins and their punishment (*Note,* vs. 20). **sanctified in you**—i.e., in respect of you; I shall be regarded in their eyes as the Holy One, and righteous in My dealings towards you (ch. 20:41; 28:22). **24.** Fulfilled primarily in the restoration from Babylon; ultimately to be so in the restoration "from all countries." **25.** The *external* restoration must be preceded by an *internal* one. The change in their condition must not be superficial, but must be based on a radical renewal of the heart. Then the heathen, understanding from the regenerated lives of God's people how holy God is, would perceive Israel's past troubles to have been only the necessary vindications of His righteousness. Thus God's name would be "sanctified" before the heathen, and God's people be prepared for outward blessings. **sprinkle . . . water**—phraseology taken from the law; viz., the water mixed with the ashes of a heifer sprinkled with a hyssop on the unclean (Num. 19:9-18); the thing signified being the cleansing blood of Christ sprinkled on the conscience and heart (Heb. 9:13, 14; 10:22; cf. Jer. 33:8; Eph. 5:26). **from all your idols**—Literal idolatry has ceased among the Jews ever since the captivity; so far, the prophecy has been already fulfilled; but "cleansing from *all*

their idols," e.g., covetousness, prejudices against Jesus of Nazareth, is yet future. **26. new heart**—mind and will. **spirit**—motive and principle of action. **stony heart**—unimpressible in serious things; like the "stony ground" (Matt. 13), unfit for receiving the good seed so as to bring forth fruit. **heart of flesh**—not "carnal" in opposition to "spiritual"; but impressible and docile, fit for receiving the good seed. In ch. 18:31 they are commanded, "*Make you* a new heart, and a new spirit." Here God says, "A new heart will *I* give you, and a new spirit will *I put* within you." Thus the responsibility of man, and the sovereign grace of God, are shown to be coexistent. Man cannot make himself a new heart unless God gives it (Phil. 2:12, 13). **27. my spirit**—(ch. 11:19; Jer. 32:39). The partial reformation at the return from Babylon (Ezra 10:6, etc.; Neh. 8, 9) was an earnest of the full renewal hereafter under Messiah. **28. ye . . . my people, . . . I . . . your God**—(ch. 11:20; Jer. 30:22). **29. save . . . from all . . . uncleannesses**—the province of Jesus, according to the signification of His name (Matt. 1:21). To be specially exercised in behalf of the Jews in the latter days (Rom. 11:26). **call for . . . corn**—as a master "calls for" a servant; all the powers and productions of nature are the servants of Jehovah (Ps. 105:16; Matt. 8:8, 9). Cf. as to the subordination of all the intermediate agents to the Great First Cause, who will give "corn" and all good things to His people, Hos. 2: 21, 22; Zech. 8:12. **30. no more reproach of famine among the heathen**—to which their taunt (vs. 13), "Thou land devourest up men," in part referred. **31. remember your . . . evil ways**—with shame and loathing. The unexpected grace and love of God, manifested in Christ to Israel, shall melt the people into true repentance, which mere legal fear could not (ch. 16:61, 63; Ps. 130:4; Zech. 12:10; cf. Jer. 33:8, 9). **35. they shall say**—The heathen, who once made Israel's desolation a ground of reproach against the name of Jehovah Himself (vss. 20, 21); but now He so vindicates its sanctity (vss. 22, 23) that these same heathen are constrained to acknowledge Israel's more than renewed blessedness to be God's own work, and a ground for glorifying His name (vs. 36). **Eden**—as Tyre (the type of the world powers in general: so Assyria, a cedar "in the garden of God, Eden," ch. 31:8, 9), in original advantages, had been compared to "Eden, the garden of God" (ch. 28:13), from which she had fallen irrecoverably; so Israel, once desolate, is to be as "the garden of Eden" (Isa. 51:3), and is to be so unchangeably. **36. Lord . . . spoken . . . do it**—(Num. 23:19). **37. I will yet for this be inquired of**—so as to grant it. On former occasions He had refused to be inquired of by Israel because the inquirers were not in a fit condition of mind to receive a blessing (ch. 14:3; 20:3). But hereafter, as in the restoration from Babylon (Neh. 8, 9; Dan. 9:3-20, 21, 23), God will prepare His people's hearts (vs. 26) to pray aright for the blessings which He is about to give (Ps. 102:13-17, 20; Zech. 12:10-14; 13:1). **like a flock** —resuming the image (ch. 34:23, 31). **38. As the holy flock**—the great flock of choice animals for sacrifice, brought up to Jerusalem at the three great yearly festivals, the passover, pentecost, and feast of the tabernacles.

CHAPTER 37

Vss. 1-28. THE VISION OF DRY BONES REVIVIFIED, SYMBOLIZING ISRAEL'S DEATH AND RESURREC-

TION. Three stages in Israel's revival present themselves to the prophet's eye. 1. The new awakening of the people, the resurrection of the dead (ch. 37:1-14). 2. The reunion of the formerly hostile members of the community, whose contentions had affected the whole (ch. 37:15-28). 3. The community thus restored is strong enough to withstand the assault of Gog, etc. (chs. 38, 29) [EWALD]. 1. carried ... in the spirit—The matters transacted, therefore, were not literal, but in vision. the valley—probably that by the Chebar (ch. 3:22). The valley represents Mesopotamia, the scene of Israel's sojourn in her state of national deadness. 2. dry—bleached by long exposure to the atmosphere. 3. can these bones live? ...thou knowest—implying that, humanly speaking, they could not; but faith leaves the question of possibility to rest with God, with whom nothing is impossible (Deut. 32: 39). An image of Christian faith which believes in the coming general resurrection of the dead, in spite of all appearances against it, because God has said it (John 5:21; Rom. 4:17; II Cor. 1:9). 4. Prophesy—Proclaim God's quickening word to them. On account of this innate power of the divine word to effect its end, prophets are said to *do* that which they *prophesy as about to be done* (Jer. 1:10). 5. I ... cause breath to enter into you —So Isaiah 26:19, containing the same vision, refers *primarily* to Israel's restoration. Cf. as to God's renovation of the earth and all its creatures hereafter by His breath, Psalm 104:30. ye shall live—come to life *again*. 6. ye shall know that I am the Lord—by the actual proof of My divinity which I will give in reviving Israel. 7. noise—of the bones when coming in mutual collision. Perhaps referring to the decree of Cyrus, or the noise of the Jews' exultation at their deliverance and return. bones came together—lit., "*ye* bones came together"; as in Jeremiah 49:11 (*Hebrew*), "*ye* widows of thine shall trust in Me." The second person puts the scene vividly before one's eyes, for the whole resurrection scene is a *prophecy in action* to render more palpably to the people the prophecy in word (vs. 21). 8. So far, they were only cohering in order as unsightly skeletons. The next step, that of covering them successively with sinews, skin, and flesh, gives them beauty; but still "no breath" of life in them. This may imply that Israel hereafter, as at the restoration from Babylon was the case in part, shall return to Judea unconverted at first (Zech. 13:8, 9). Spiritually: a man may assume all the semblances of spiritual life, yet have none, and so be dead before God. 9. wind— rather, *the spirit* of life or *life-breath* (*Margin*). For it is distinct from "the four *winds*" from which it is summoned. from the four winds—implying that Israel is to be gathered from the four quarters of the earth (Isa. 43:5, 6; Jer. 31:8), even as they were "scattered into all the winds" (ch. 5:10; 12:14; 17:21; cf. Rev. 7:1, 4). 10. Such honor God gives to the divine word, even in the mouth of a man. How much more when in the mouth of the Son of God! (John 5:25-29). Though this chapter does not *directly* prove the resurrection of the dead, it does so *indirectly;* for it takes for granted the future fact as one recognized by believing Jews, and so made the image of their national restoration (so Isa. 25:8; 26:19; Dan. 12:2; Hos. 6:2; 13:14; cf. *Note,* vs. 12). 11. Our bones are dried—(Ps. 141: 7), explained by "our hope is lost" (Isa. 49:14); our national state is as hopeless of resuscitation, as marrowless bones are of reanimation. cut off for our parts—i.e., so far as we are concerned. There

is nothing in us to give hope, like a withered branch "cut off" from a tree, or a limb from the body. 12. my people—in antithesis to "for our parts" (vs. 11). The hope that is utterly gone, if looking at *themselves,* is sure for them in *God,* because He regards them as *His* people. Their covenant relation to God ensures His not letting death permanently reign over them. Christ makes the same principle the ground on which the literal resurrection rests. God had said, "I am the God of Abraham," etc.; God, by taking the patriarchs as *His,* undertook to do for them all that Omnipotence can perform: He, being the ever living God, is necessarily the God of, not dead, but living persons, i.e., of those whose bodies His covenant love binds Him to raise again. He can—and because He can—He will—He must [FAIRBAIRN]. He calls them "*My* people" when receiving them into favor; but "*thy* people," in addressing His servant, as if He would put them away from Him (ch. 13:17; 33:2; Exod. 32:7). out of your graves—out of your politically dead state, primarily in Babylon, finally hereafter in all lands (cf. ch. 6:8; Hos. 13:14). The Jews regarded the lands of their captivity and dispersion as their "graves"; their restoration was to be as "life from the dead" (Rom. 11:15). Before, the bones were in the open plain (vss. 1, 2); now, in the graves, i.e., some of the Jews were in the graves of actual captivity, others at large but dispersed. Both alike were nationally dead. 16. stick—alluding to Numbers 17:2, the tribal rod. The union of the two rods was a prophecy in action of the brotherly union which is to reunite the ten tribes and Judah. As their severance under Jeroboam was fraught with the greatest evil to the covenant people, so the first result of both being joined by the spirit of life to God is that they become joined to one another under the one covenant King, Messiah-David. Judah, and ... children of Israel his companions—i.e., Judah and, besides Benjamin and Levi, those who had joined themselves to him of Ephraim, Manasseh, Simeon, Asher, Zebulun, Issachar, as having the temple and lawful priesthood in his borders (II Chron. 11:12, 13, 16; 15:9; 30:11, 18). The latter became identified with Judah after the carrying away of the ten tribes, and returned with Judah from Babylon, and so shall be associated with that tribe at the future restoration. For Joseph, the stick of Ephraim—Ephraim's posterity took the lead, not only of the other descendants of Joseph (cf. vs. 19), but of the ten tribes of Israel. For 400 years, during the period of the judges, with Manasseh and Benjamin, its dependent tribes, it had formerly taken the lead: Shiloh was its religious capital; Shechem, its civil capital. God had transferred the birthright from Reuben (for dishonoring his father's bed) to Joseph, whose representative, Ephraim, though the younger, was made (Gen. 48:19; I Chron. 5:1). From its pre-eminence "Israel" is attached to it as "companions." The "all" in this case, not in that of Judah, which has only attached as "companions" the children of Israel" (i.e., some of them, viz., those who followed the fortunes of Judah), implies that the *bulk* of the ten tribes did not return at the restoration from Babylon, but are distinct from Judah, until the coming union with it at the restoration. 18. God does not explain the symbolical prophecy until the Jews have been stimulated by the type to consult the prophet. 19. The union effected at the restoration from Babylon embraced but comparatively few of Israel; a future complete fulfilment must therefore be looked for. stick of Joseph ... in the

hand of Ephraim—Ephraim, of the descendants of Joseph, had exercised the rule among the ten tribes: that rule, symbolized by the "stick," was now to be withdrawn from him, and to be made one with the other, Judah's rule, in God's hand. **them**—the "*stick* of Joseph," would strictly require "it"; but Ezekiel expresses the sense, viz., the ten tribes who were subject to it. **with him**—i.e., Judah; or "it," i.e., the stick of Judah. **22. one nation**—(Isa. 11: 13; Jer. 3:18; Hos. 1:11). **one king**—not Zerubbabel, who was not a king either in fact or name, and who ruled over but a few Jews, and that only for a few years; whereas the King here reigns for ever. MESSIAH is meant (ch. 34:23, 24). The union of Judah and Israel under King Messiah symbolizes the union of Jews and Gentiles under Him, partly now, perfectly hereafter (vs. 24; John 10:16). **23.** (Ch. 36:25.) **out of ... their dwelling-places**—(Ch. 36:28, 33). I will remove them from the scene of their idolatries to dwell in their own land, and to serve idols no more. **24. David** —Messiah (*Notes*, ch. 34:23, 24). **25. for ever**— (Isa. 60:21; Joel 3:20; Amos 9:15). **26. covenant of peace**—better than the old legal covenant, because an unchangeable covenant of grace (ch. 34: 25; Isa. 55:3; Jer. 32:40). **I will place them**—set them in an established position; no longer unsettled as heretofore. **my sanctuary**—the temple of God; spiritual in the heart of all true followers of Messiah (II Cor. 6:16); and, in some literal sense, in the restored Israel (chs. 40-44). **27. My tabernacle ... with them**—as foretold (Gen. 9:27); John 1:14, "The Word ... *dwelt* among us" (lit., "tabernacled"); first, in humiliation; hereafter, in manifested glory (Rev. 21:3). **28.** (Ch. 36:23.) **sanctify Israel**—set it apart as holy unto Myself and inviolable (Exod. 19:5, 6).

CHAPTER 38

Vss. 1-23. THE ASSAULT OF GOG, AND GOD'S JUDGMENT ON HIM. The objections to a *literal* interpretation of the prophecy are—1. The ideal nature of the name Gog, which is the root of Magog, the only kindred name found in Scripture or history. 2. The nations congregated are selected from places most distant from Israel, and from one another, and therefore most unlikely to act in concert (Persians and Libyans, etc.). 3. The whole spoil of Israel could not have given a handful to a tithe of their number, or maintained the myriads of invaders a single day (ch. 38:12, 13). 4. The wood of their invaders' weapons was to serve for fuel to Israel for seven years! And *all* Israel were to take seven months in burying the dead! Supposing a million of Israelites to bury each two corpses a day, the aggregate buried in the 180 working days of the seven months would be 360 millions of corpses! Then the pestilential vapors from such masses of victims before they were all buried! What Israelite could live in such an atmosphere? 5. The scene of the Lord's controversy here is different from that in Isaiah 34:6, Edom, which creates a discrepancy. (But probably a different judgment is alluded to.) 6. The gross carnality of the representation of God's dealings with His adversaries is inconsistent with Messianic times. It therefore requires a non-literal interpretation. The prophetical delineations of the divine principles of government are thrown into the familiar forms of Old Testament relations. The final triumph of Messiah's truth over the most distant and barbarous nations is represented as a literal conflict on a gigantic scale, Israel being the battlefield, ending in the complete triumph of Israel's anointed King, the Saviour of the world. It is a *prophetical parable* [FAIRBAIRN]. However, though the *details* are not literal, the distinctiveness in this picture, characterizing also parallel descriptions in writers less idealy picturesque than Ezekiel, gives probability to a more definite and *generally* literal interpretation. The awful desolations caused in Judea by Antiochus Epiphanes, of Syria (I Maccabees; and PORPHYRY, quoted by JEROME on Ezekiel), his defilement of Jehovah's temple by sacrificing swine and sprinkling the altar with the broth, and setting up the altar of Jupiter Olympius, seem to be an earnst of the final desolations to be caused by Antichrist in Israel, previous to His overthrow by the Lord Himself, coming to reign (cf. Dan. 8:10-26; 11:21-45; 12:1; Zech. 13:9; 14:2, 3). GROTIUS explains Gog as a name taken from Gyges, king of Lydia; and Magog as Syria, in which was a city called Magag (PLINY 5. 28). What Ezekiel stated more generally, Revelation 20:7-9 states more definitely as to the antiChristian confederacy which is to assail the beloved city. **2. Gog**—the prince of the land of Magog. The title was probably a common one of the kings of the country, as "Pharaoh" in Egypt. Chakan was the name given by the Northern Asiatics to their king, and is still a title of the Turkish sultan: "Gog" may be a contraction of this. In Ezekiel's time a horde of northern Asiatics, termed by the Greeks "Scythians," and probably including the Moschi and Tibareni, near the Caucasus, here ("Meshech ... Tubal") undertook an expedition against Egypt (HERODOTUS, 1. 103-106). These names might be adopted by Ezekiel from the historical fact familiar to men at the time, as ideal titles for the great last anti-Christian confederacy. **1. Magog**—(Gen. 10:2; I Chron. 1:5). The name of a land belonging to Japheth's posterity. *Maha*, in Sanscrit, means "land." Gog is the ideal political head of the region. In Revelation 20:8, Gog and Magog are two peoples. **the chief prince**— rather, "prince of *Rosh*," or "*Rhos*" [LXX]. The Scythian Tauri in the Crimea were so called. The Araxes also was called "Rhos." The modern Russians may have hence *assumed* their name, as Moscow and Tobolsk from Meshech and Tubal, though their *proper* ancient name was *Slavi*, or *Wends*. HENGSTENBERG supports *English Version*, as "Rosh" is not found in the Bible. "Magog was Gog's original kingdom, though he acquired also Meshech and Tubal, so as to be called their *chief prince*." 3. His high sounding titles are repeated to imply the haughty selfconfidence of the invader as if invincible. **4. turn thee back**—as a refractory wild beast, which thinks to take its own way, but is bent by a superior power to turn on a course which must end in its destruction. Satan shall be, by overruling Providence, permitted to deceive them to their ruin (Rev. 20:7, 8). **hooks into thy jaws**—(ch. 29:4; II Kings 19:28). **5. Persia ... Libya**—expressly specified by APPIAN as supplying the ranks of Antiochus' army. **6. Gomer**—the Celtic Cimmerians of Crim-Tartary. **Togarmah**—the Armenians of the Caucasus, south of Iberia. **7.** Irony. Prepare thee and all thine with all needful accoutrements for war —that ye may perish together. **be .. a guard unto them**—i.e., *if thou canst*. **8. thou shalt be visited** —in wrath, by God (Isa. 29:6). Probably there is allusion to Isaiah 24:21, 22, "The host of the high ones ... shall be gathered ... as prisoners ... in the pit, ... and *after many days shall they be visited*."

I therefore prefer *English Version* to GROTIUS' rendering, "Thou shalt get *the command*" of the expedition. The "after many days" is defined by "in the latter years," i.e., in the times just before the coming of Messiah, viz., under Antiochus, before His first coming; under Antichrist, before His second coming. **the mountains of Israel . . . always waste**—i.e., waste during the long period of the captivity, the earnest of the much longer period of Judea's present desolation (to which the language "always waste" more fully applies). This marks the impious atrocity of the act, to assail God's people, who had only begun to recover from their protracted calamities. **but it is brought . . . and they shall dwell**—rather, "And they (the Israelites) were brought . . . dwelt safely" [FAIRBAIRN]. *English Version* means, "Against Israel, which has been waste, but which (i.e., whose people) is now (at the time of the invasion) brought forth out of the nations where they were dispersed, and shall be found by the invader dwelling securely, so as to seem an easy prey to him." **9. cloud to cover the land**—with the multitude of thy forces. **10. an evil thought**—as to attacking God's people in their defenseless state. **11. dwell safely**—i.e., securely, without fear of danger (cf. Esther 9:19). Antiochus, the type of Antichrist, took Jerusalem without a blow. **12. midst of the land**—lit., "the navel" of the land (Judg. 9:37, *Margin*). So, in ch. 5:5, Israel is said to be set "in the midst of the nations"; not physically, but morally, a central position for being a blessing to the world: so (as the favored or "beloved city," Rev. 20:9) an object of envy. GROTIUS translates, "In the *height* of the land" (so vs. 8), "the mountains of Israel," Israel being morally elevated above the rest of the world. **13. Sheba . . .** —These mercantile peoples, though not taking an active part against the cause of God, are well pleased to see others do it. Worldliness makes them ready to deal in the ill-gotten spoil of the invaders of God's people. Gain is before godliness with them (I Maccabees 3:41). **young lions**—daring princes and leaders. **14. shalt thou not know it?**—to thy cost, being visited with punishment, while Israel dwells safely. **16. I will bring thee against my land, that the heathen may know me**—So in Exodus 9:16, God tells Pharaoh, "For this cause have I raised thee up, for to show in thee My power; and that My name may be declared throughout all the earth." **17. thou he of whom I have spoken in old time**—Gog, etc. are here identified with the enemies spoken of in other prophecies (Num. 24:17-24; Isa. 27:1; cf. Isa. 26:20, 21; Jer. 30:23, 24; Joel 3:1; Mic. 5:5, 6; Isa. 14:12-14; 59: 19). God is represented as addressing Gog at the time of his assault; therefore, the "old time" is the time long prior, when Ezekiel uttered these prophecies; so, he also, as well as Daniel (11) and Zechariah (14) are included among "the prophets of Israel" here. **many years**—ago. **18. fury shall come up in my face**—lit., "nose"; in *Hebrew*, the idiomatic expression for *anger*, as men in anger breathe strongly through the nostrils. Anthropopathy: God stooping to human modes of thought (Ps. 18: 8). **19. great shaking**—an earthquake: physical agitations after accompanying social and moral revolutions. Foretold also in Joel 3:16; (cf. Hag. 2: 6, 7; Matt. 24:7, 29; Rev. 16:18). **20. fishes**—disturbed by the fleets which I will bring. **fowls . . .** frightened at the sight of so many men: an ideal picture. **mountains**—i.e., the fortresses on the mountains. **steep places**—lit., "stairs" (Song of Sol. 2:14); steep terraces for vines on the sides of hills,

to prevent the earth being washed down by the rains. **every wall**—of towns. **21. every man's sword . . . against his brother**—I will destroy them partly by My people's sword, partly by their swords being turned against one another (cf. II Chron. 20: 23). **22. plead**—a forensic term; because God in His inflictions acts on the principles of His own immutable *justice*, not by arbitrary impulse (Isa. 66: 16; Jer. 25:31). **blood . . . hailstones, fire**—(Rev. 8: 7; 16:21). The imagery is taken from the destruction of Sodom and the plagues of Egypt (cf. Ps. 11: 6). Antiochus died by "pestilence" (II Maccabees 9:5).

CHAPTER 39

VSS. 1-29. CONTINUATION OF THE PROPHECY AGAINST GOG. **1.** Repeated from ch. 38:3, to impress the prophecy more on the mind. **2. leave but the sixth part of thee**—*Margin*, "strike thee with six plagues" (viz., pestilence, blood, overflowing rain, hailstones, fire, brimstone, ch. 38:22); or, "draw thee back with a hook of six teeth" (ch. 38:4), the six teeth being those six plagues. Rather, "lead thee about" [LUDOVICUS DE DIEU and LXX]. As Antiochus was led (to his ruin) to leave Egypt for an expedition against Palestine, so shall the last great enemy of God be. **north parts**—from the extreme north [FAIRBAIRN]. **3. bow**—in which the Scythians were most expert. **4, 5.** (Cf. vss. 17-20.) **upon the mountains of Israel**—The scene of Israel's preservation shall be that of the ungodly foe's destruction. **6. carelessly**—in self-confident security. **the isles**—Those dwelling in maritime regions, who had helped Gog with fleets and troops, shall be visited with the fire of God's wrath in their own lands. **7. not let them pollute my holy name**—by their sins bringing down judgments which made the heathen think that I was unable or unwilling to save My people. **8. it is come . . . it is done**—The prediction of the salvation of My people, and the ruin of their enemy, is come to pass—is done: expressing that the event foretold is as certain as if it were already accomplished. **9, 10.** The burning of the foe's weapons implies that nothing belonging to them should be left to pollute the land. The *seven* years (*seven* being the sacred number) spent on this work, implies the completeness of the cleansing, and the people's zeal for purity. How different from the ancient Israelites, who left not merely the arms, but the heathen themselves, to remain among them [FAIRBAIRN], (Judg. 1:27, 28; 2:2, 3; Ps. 106:34-36). The desolation by Antiochus began in the one hundred and forty-first year of the Seleucidæ. From this date to 148, a period of six years and four months ("2300 days," Dan. 8:14), when the temple worship was restored (I Maccabeees 4:52), God vouchsafed many triumphs to His people; from this time to the death of Antiochus, early in 149, a period of seven months, the Jews had rest from Antiochus, and purified their land, and on the twenty-fifth day of the ninth month celebrated the Encænia, or feast of dedication (John 10:22) and purification of the temple. The whole period, in round numbers, was seven years. Mattathias was the patriotic Jewish leader, and his third son, Judas, the military commander under whom the Syrian generals were defeated. He retook Jerusalem and purified the temple. Simon and Jonathan, his brothers, succeeded him: the independence of the Jews was secured, and the crown vested in the Asmonean family, in which it continued till Herod the Great. **11. place . . . of graves**—Gog found only a grave where he had expected the spoils of conquest. **valley**—So vast were to be the masses that nothing but a deep valley would suffice for their corpses. **the passengers on the east of the sea**—those travelling on the high road, east of the Dead Sea, from Syria to Petra and Egypt. The publicity of the road would cause many to observe God's judgments, as the stench (as *English Version* translates) or the multitude of graves (as HENDERSON translates, "it shall *stop the passengers*") would arrest the attention of passersby. Their grave would be close to that of their ancient prototypes, Sodom and Gomorrah in the Dead Sea, both alike being signal instances of God's judgments. **13. I . . . glorified**—in destroying the foe (ch. 28:22). **14. with the passengers**—The men employed continually in the burying were to be helped by those happening to pass by; all were to combine. **after the end of seven months shall they search**—to see if the work was complete [MUNSTER]. **15.** First *"all"* the people of the land" engaged in the burying for seven months; then special men were employed, at the end of the seven months, to search for any still left unburied. The passersby helped them by setting up a mark near any such bones, in order to keep others from being defiled by casually touching them, and that the buriers might come and remove them. Denoting the minute care to put away every relic of heathen pollution from the Holy Land. **16.** A city in the neighborhood was to receive the name Hamonah, "multitude," to commemorate the overthrow of the multitudes of the foe [HENDERSON]. The multitude of the slain shall give a name to the city of Jerusalem after the land shall have been cleansed [GROTIUS]. Jerusalem shall be famed as the conqueror of multitudes. **17.** (Rev. 19:17.) **sacrifice**—Anciently worshippers feasted on the sacrifices. The birds and beasts of prey are invited to the sacrificial feast provided by God (cf. Isa. 18:6; 34:6; Zeph. 1:7; Mark 9:49). Here this sacrifice holds only a subordinate place in the picture, and so is put last. Not only shall their bones lie long unburied, but they shall be stripped of the flesh by beasts and birds of prey. **18. rams . . . lambs . . . goats**—By these various animal victims used in sacrifices are meant various ranks of men, princes, generals, and soldiers (cf. Isa. 34:6). **fatlings of Bashan**—ungodly men of might (Ps. 22:12). Bashan, beyond Jordan, was famed for its fat cattle. Fat implies prosperity which often makes men refractory towards God (Deut. 32:14, 15). **20. my table**—the field of battle on the mountains of Israel (ch. 38:8, 20). **chariots**—i.e., charioteers. **22. So the house of Israel shall know . . . Lord**—by My interposition for them. So, too, the heathen shall be led to fear the name of the Lord (Ps. 102:15). **23. hid I my face**—(Deut. 31: 17; Isa. 59:2). **25. bring again the captivity**—restore **from calamity to prosperity. the whole house of Israel**—so *"all"* Israel" (Rom. 11:26). The restorations of Israel heretofore have been partial; there must be one yet future that is to be *universal* (Hos. 1:11). **26. After that they have borne their shame**—the punishment of their sin: after they have become sensible of their guilt, and ashamed of it (ch. 20:43; 36:31). **27. sanctified in them**—vindicated as holy in My dealings with them. **28.** The Jews, having no dominion, settled country, or fixed property to detain them, may return at any time without difficulty (cf. Hos. 3:4, 5). **29. poured out my Spirit upon . . . Israel**—the sure forerunner of their conversion (Joel 2:28; Zech. 12:10). The pouring out of His Spirit is a pledge that He will hide His face no more (II Cor. 1:22; Eph. 1:14; Phil. 1:6).

CHAPTER 40

Vss. 1-49. THE REMAINING CHAPTERS, 40-48. GIVE AN IDEAL PICTURE OF THE RESTORED JEWISH TEMPLE. The arrangements as to the land and the temple are, in many particulars, different from those subsisting before the captivity. There are things in it so improbable physically as to preclude a *purely* literal interpretation. The general truth seems to hold good that, as Israel served the nations for his rejection of Messiah, so shall they serve him in the person of Messiah, when he shall acknowledge Messiah (Isa. 60:12; Zech. 14:17-19; cf. Ps. 72:11). The ideal temple exhibits, under Old Testament forms (used as being those then familiar to the men whom Ezekiel, a priest himself, and one who delighted in sacrificial images, addresses), not the precise literal outline, but *the essential character* of the worship of Messiah as it shall be when He shall exercise sway in Jerusalem among His own people, the Jews, and thence to the ends of the earth. The very fact that the whole is a vision (vs. 2), not an oral face-to-face communication such as that granted to Moses (Num. 12:6-8), implies that the directions are not to be understood so precisely literally as those given to the Jewish lawgiver. The description involves things which, taken literally, almost involve natural impossibilities. The square of the temple, in ch. 42:20, is six times as large as the circuit of the wall enclosing the old temple, and larger than all the earthly Jerusalem. Ezekiel gives three and a half miles and 140 yards to his temple square. The boundaries of the ancient city were about two and a half miles. Again, the city in Ezekiel has an area between three or four thousand square miles, including the holy ground set apart for the prince, priests, and Levites. This is nearly as large as the whole of Judea west of the Jordan. As Zion lay in the center of the ideal city, the onehalf of the sacred portion extended to nearly thirty miles south of Jerusalem, i.e., covered nearly the whole southern territory, which reached only to the Dead Sea (ch. 47:19), and yet five tribes were to have their inheritance on that side of Jerusalem, *beyond* the sacred portion (ch. 48:23-28). Where was land to be found for them there? A breadth of but four or five miles apiece would be left. As the boundaries of the land are given the same as under Moses, these incongruities cannot be explained away by supposing physical changes about to be effected in the land such as will meet the difficulties of the purely literal interpretation. The distribution of the land is in equal portions among the twelve tribes, without respect to their relative numbers, and the parallel sections running from east to west. There is a difficulty also in the supposed separate existence of the twelve tribes, such separate tribeships no longer existing, and it being hard to imagine how they could be restored as distinct tribes, mingled as they now are. So the stream that issued from the east threshold of the temple and flowed into the Dead Sea, in the rapidity of its increase and the quality of its waters, is unlike anything ever known in Judea or elsewhere in the world. Lastly, the catholicity of the Christian dispensation, and the spirituality of its worship, seem incompatible with a return to the local narrowness and "beggarly elements" of the Jewish ritual and carnal ordinances, disannulled "because of the unprofitableness thereof" [FAIRBAIRN], (Gal. 4:3, 9; 5: 1; Heb. 9:10; 10:18). "A temple with sacrifices now would be a denial of the all-sufficiency of the sacrifice of Christ. He who sacrificed before confessed the Messiah. He who should sacrifice now would solemnly deny Him" [DOUGLAS]. These difficulties, however, may be all *seeming*, not real. Faith accepts God's Word as it is, waits for the event, sure that it will clear up all such difficulties. Perhaps, as some think, the beau ideal of a sacred commonwealth is given according to the then existing pattern of temple services, which would be the imagery most familiar to the prophet and his hearers at the time. The minute particularizing of details is in accordance with Ezekiel's style, even in describing purely ideal scenes. The old temple embodied in visible forms and rites spiritual truths affecting the people even when absent from it. So this ideal temple is made in the absence of the outward temple to serve by description the same purpose of symbolical instruction as the old literal temple did by forms and acts. As in the beginning God promised to be a "sanctuary" (ch. 11:16) to the captives at the Chebar, so now at the close is promised a complete restoration and realization of the theocratic worship and polity under Messiah in its noblest ideal (cf. Jer. 31:38-40). In Revelation 21:22 "no temple" is seen, as in the perfection of the new dispensation the accidents of place and form are no longer needed to realize to Christians what Ezekiel imparts to Jewish minds by the imagery familiar to them. In Ezekiel's temple holiness stretches over the entire temple, so that in this there is no longer a distinction between the different parts, as in the old temple: parts left undeterminate in the latter obtain now a divine sanction, so that all arbitrariness is excluded. So that it is be a perfect manifestation of the love of God to His covenant people (chs. 40-43:12); and from it, as from a new center of religious life, there gushes forth the fulness of blessings to them, and so to all people (ch. 47) [FAIRBAIRN and HAVERNICK]. The temple built at the return from Babylon can only very partially have realized the model here given. The law is seemingly opposed to the gospel (Matt. 5:21, 22, 27, 28, 33, 34). It is not really so (cf. Matt. 5:17, 18; Rom. 3:31; Gal. 3:21, 22). It is true Christ's sacrifice superseded the law sacrifices (Heb. 10:12-18). Israel's province may hereafter be to show the essential identity, even in the minute details of the temple sacrifices, between the law and gospel (Rom. 10:8). The ideal of the theocratic temple will then first be realized. **1. beginning of the year**—the ecclesiastical year, the first month of which was Nisan. **the city . . . thither**—Jerusalem, the center to which all the prophet's thoughts tended. **2. visions of God**—divinely sent visions. **very high mountain**—Moriah, very high, as compared with the plains of Babylon, still more so as to its *moral* elevation (ch. 17:22; 20:40). **by which**—Ezekiel coming from the north is set down *at* (as the *Hebrew* for "upon" may be translated) Mount Moriah, and sees the city-like frame of the temple stretching *southward*. In vs. 3, "God brings him thither," i.e., close up to it, so as to inspect it minutely (cf. Rev. 21:10). In this closing vision, as in the opening one of the book, the divine hand is laid on the prophet, and he is borne away in the visions of God. But the scene there was by the Chebar, Jehovah having forsaken Jerusalem; now it is the mountain of God, Jehovah having returned thither; there, the vision was calculated to inspire terror; here, hope and assurance. **3. man**—The Old Testament manifestations of heavenly beings as *men* prepared men's minds for the coming incarnation. **brass**—resplendent. **line**—used for longer measurements (Zech. 2:1). **reed**—used in measuring houses (Rev. 21:15). It marked

the straightness of the walls. **5. Measures** were mostly taken from the human body. The *greater cubit*, the length from the elbow to the end of the middle finger, a little more than two feet: exceeding the ordinary *cubit* (from the elbow to the wrist) by an hand-breadth, i.e., twenty-one inches in all. Cf. ch. 43:13, with ch. 40:5. The *palm* was the full breadth of the hand, three and a half inches. **breadth of the building**—i.e., the boundary wall. The imperfections in the old temple's boundary wall were to have no place here. The buildings attached to it had been sometimes turned to common uses; e.g., Jeremiah was imprisoned in one (Jer. 20:2; 29: 26). But now all these were to be holy to the Lord. The gates and doorways to the city of God were to be imprinted in their architecture with the idea of the exclusion of everything defiled (Rev. 21:27). The east gate was to be especially sacred, as it was through it the glory of God had departed (ch. 11:23), and through it the glory was to return (ch. 43:1, 2; 44:2, 3). **6. the stairs**—seven in number (vs. 26). **threshold**—the sill [FAIRBAIRN]. **other threshold**—FAIRBAIRN considers there is but one threshold, and translates, "even the one threshold, one rod broad." But there is another threshold mentioned in vs. 7. The two thresholds here seem to be the upper and the lower. **7. chamber**—These chambers were for the use of the Levites who watched at the temple gates; *guard-chambers* (II Kings 22:4; I Chron. 9:26, 27); also used for storing utensils and musical instruments. **9. posts**—projecting column-faced fronts of the sides of the doorway, opposite to one another. **12. space**—rather, "the boundary." **16. narrow**—latticed [HENDERSON]. The ancients had no glass, so they had them latticed, narrow in the interior of the walls, and widening at the exterior. "Made fast," or "firmly fixed in the chambers" [MAURER]. **arches**—rather, "porches." **17. pavement**—tesselated mosaic (Esther 1:6). **chambers**—serving as lodgings for the priests on duty in the temple, and as receptacles of the tithes of salt, wine, and oil. **18.** The higher pavement was level with the entrance of the gates, the lower was on either side of the raised pavement thus formed. Whereas Solomon's temple had an outer court open to alterations and even idolatrous innovations (II Kings 23:11, 12; I Chron. 20:5), in this there was to be no room for human corruptions. Its compass was exactly defined, 100 cubits; and the fine pavement implied it was to be trodden only by clean feet (cf. Isa. 35:8). **20-27.** The different approaches corresponded in plan. In the case of these two other gates, however, no mention is made of a building with thirty chambers such as was found on the east side. Only one was needed, and it was assigned to the east as being the sacred quarter, and that most conveniently situated for the officiating priests. **23. and toward the east**—an elliptical expression for "The gate of the inner court was over against the (outer) gate toward the north (just as the inner gate was over against the outer gate) toward the east." **28-37.** The inner court and its gates. **28. according to these measures**—viz., the measures of the outer gate. The figure and proportions of the inner answered to the outer. **30.** This verse is omitted in the LXX, the Vatican MS., and others. The dimensions here of the inner gate do not correspond to the outer, though vs. 28 asserts that they do. HAVERNICK, retaining the verse, understands it of another porch looking inwards toward the temple. **arches**—the porch [FAIRBAIRN]; the columns on which the arches rest [HENDERSON]. **31. eight steps**—The outer porch had only *seven* (vs. 26). **37. posts**—LXX and *Vul-*

gate read, "the porch," which answers better to vss. 31-34. "The arches" or "porch" [MAURER]. **38. chambers . . . entries**—lit., "a chamber and its door." **by the posts**—i.e., *at* or *close by* the posts or *colums*. **where they washed the burnt offering**—This does not apply to all the gates but only to the north gate. For Leviticus 1:11 directs the sacrifices to be killed north of the altar; and ch. 8:5 calls the north gate, "the gate of the altar." And vs. 40 particularly mentions the *north gate*. **43. hooks**—cooking apparatus for cooking the flesh of the sacrifices that fell to the priests. The hooks were "fastened" in the walls within the apartment, to hang the meat from, so as to roast it. The *Hebrew* comes from a root "fixed" or "placed." **44. the chambers of the singers**—two in number, as proved by what follows: "and their prospect (i.e., the prospect of *one*) was toward the south, (and) one toward the north." So LXX. **46. Zadok**—lineally descended from Aaron. He had the high priesthood conferred on him by Solomon, who had set aside the family of Ithamar because of the part which Abiathar had taken in the rebellion of Adonijah (I Kings 1:7; 2:26, 27). **47. court, an hundred cubits . . . foursquare**—not to be confounded with the inner court, or court of Israel, which was open to all who had sacrifices to bring, and went round the three sides of the sacred territory, 100 cubits broad. This court was 100 cubits square, and had the altar in it, in front of the temple. It was the court of the priests, and hence is connected with those who had charge of the altar and the music. The description here is brief, as the things connected with this portion were from the first divinely regulated. **48, 49.** These two verses belong to ch. 41, which treats of the temple itself. **twenty . . . eleven cubits**—in Solomon's temple (I Kings 6:3) "twenty . . . *ten* cubits." The breadth perhaps was ten *and a half;* I Kings 6:3 designates the number by the *lesser* next round number, "ten"; Ezekiel here, by the *larger* number, "eleven" [MENOCHIUS]. LXX reads "twelve." **he brought me by the steps**—They were *ten* in number [LXX].

CHAPTER 41

Vss. 1-26. THE CHAMBERS AND ORNAMENTS OF THE TEMPLE. **1. tabernacle**—As in the measurement of the outer porch he had pointed to Solomon's *temple*, so here in the edifice itself, he points to the old *tabernacle*, which being eight boards in breadth (each one and a half cubits broad) would make in all twelve cubits, as here. On the interior it was only ten cubits. **2. length thereof**—viz., of the holy place [FAIRBAIRN]. **3. inward**—towards the most holy place. **4. thereof**—of the holy of holies. **before the temple**—i.e., before, or in front of the most holy place (so "temple" is used in I Kings 6:3). The angel went in and measured it, while Ezekiel stood in front, in the only part of the temple accessible to him. The dimensions of the two apartments are the same as in Solomon's temple, since being fixed originally by God, they are regarded as finally determined. **5. side chamber**—the singular used collectively for the plural. These chambers were appendages attached to the outside of the temple, on the west, north, and south; for on the east side, the principal entrance, there were no chambers. The narrowness of the chambers was in order that the beams could be supported without needing pillars. **6. might . . . hold, but . . . not hold in . . . wall of the house**—I Kings 6:6 tells us there were rests made in the walls of the temple for supports to the side chambers; but the temple walls did not thereby become part of this side building; they stood separate from it. "They entered," viz., the beams of the chambers, which were three-storied and thirty in consecutive order, entered into the wall, i.e., were made to lean on rests projecting from the wall. **7. the breadth . . . so increased from the lowest . . . to the highest**—i.e., the breadth of the interior space above was greater than that below. **8. foundations . . . six . . . cubits**—the substructure, on which the foundations rested, was a full reed of six cubits. **great**—lit., "to the extremity" or root, viz., of the hand [HENDERSON]. "To the joining," or point, where the foundation of one chamber ceased and another began [FAIRBAIRN]. **9. that which was left**—There was an unoccupied place within chambers that belonged to the house. The buildings in this unoccupied place, west of the temple, and so much resembling it in size, imply that no place was to be left which was to be held, as of old, not sacred. Manasseh (II Kings 23:11) had abused these "suburbs of the temple" to keeping horses sacred to the sun. All excuse for such abominations was henceforth to be taken away, the Lord claiming every space, and filling up this also with sacred erections [FAIRBAIRN]. **10. the chambers**—i.e., of the priests in the court: between these and the side chambers was the wideness, etc. While long details are given as to the chambers, etc., no mention is made of the ark of the covenant. FAIRBAIRN thus interprets this: In future there was to be a perfect conformity to the divine idea, such as there had not been before. The dwellings of His people should all become true sanctuaries of piety. Jehovah Himself, in the full display of the divine Shekinah, shall come in the room of the ark of the covenant (Jer. 3:16, 17). The interior of the temple stands empty, waiting for His entrance to fill it with His glory (ch. 43:1-12). It is the same temple, but the courts of it have become different to accommodate a more numerous people. The entire compass of the temple mount has become a holy of holies (ch. 43:12). **12-15.** Sum of the measures of the temple, and of the buildings behind and on the side of it. **15. galleries**—terrace buildings. On the west or back of the temple, there was a separate place occupied by buildings of the same external dimensions as the temple, i.e., one hundred cubits square in the entire compass [FAIRBAIRN]. **16. covered**—being the highest windows they were "covered" from the view below. Or else "covered" *with lattice-work*. **17. by measure**—Measurements were taken [FAIRBAIRN]. **21. appearance of the one as the appearance of the other**—The appearance of the sanctuary or holy of holies was similar to that of the temple. They differed only in magnitude. **22. table . . . before the Lord**—the altar of incense (ch. 44:16). At it, not at the table of shewbread, the priests daily ministered. It stood in front of the veil, and is therefore said to be "before the Lord." It is called a table, as being that at which the Lord will take delight in His people, as at a feast. Hence its dimensions are larger than that of old—three cubits high, two broad, instead of two and one. **25. thick planks**—a thick-plank work at the threshold.

CHAPTER 42

Vss. 1-20. CHAMBERS OF THE PRIESTS: MEASUREMENTS OF THE TEMPLE. **2. Before the length of an hundred cubits**—i.e., before "the separate place," which was that length (ch. 41:13). He had before spoken of chambers for the officiating priests on the north and south gates of the inner court (ch. 40:44-46). He now returns to take a more exact view of them. **5. shorter**—i.e., the building became *narrower* as it rose in height. The chambers were many: so "in My Father's house are many mansions" (John 14:2); and besides these there was much "room" still left (cf. Luke 14:22). The chambers, though private, were near the temple. Prayer in our chambers is to prepare us for public devotions, and to help us in improving them. **16. five hundred reeds**—LXX substitutes "cubits" for "reeds," to escape the immense compass assigned to the whole, viz., a square of 500 rods or 3000 cubits (two feet each; ch. 40:5), in all a square of one and one-seventh miles, i.e., more than all ancient Jerusalem; also, there is much space thus left unappropriated. FAIRBAIRN rightly supports *English Version*, which agrees with the *Hebrew*. The vast extent is another feature marking the ideal character of the temple. It symbolizes the great enlargement of the kingdom of God, when Jehovah-Messiah shall reign at Jerusalem, and from thence to the ends of the earth (Isa. 2:2-4; Jer. 3:17; Rom. 11:12, 15). **20. wall... separation between... sanctuary and... profane**—No longer shall the wall of partition be to separate the Jew and the Gentile (Eph. 2:14), but to separate the sacred from the profane. The lowness of it renders it unfit for the purpose of defense (the object of the wall, Rev. 21:12). But its square form (as in the city, Rev. 21:16) is the emblem of the kingdom that cannot be shaken (Heb. 12:28), resting on prophets and apostles, Jesus Christ being the chief cornerstone.

CHAPTER 43

Vss. 1-27. JEHOVAH'S RETURN TO THE TEMPLE. Everything was now ready for His reception. As the Shekinah glory was the peculiar distinction of the old temple, so it was to be in the new in a degree as much more transcendent as the proportions of the new exceeded those of the old. The fact that the Shekinah glory was not in the second temple proves that it cannot be that temple which is meant in the prophecy. **2. the way of the east**—the way whereby the glory had departed (ch. 11:22, 23), and rested on Mount Olivet (cf. Zech. 14:4). **his voice ... like ... many waters**—So *English Version* rightly, as in ch. 1:24, "voice of the Almighty"; Revelation 1:15; 14:2, prove this. Not as FAIRBAIRN translates, "its noise." **earth his glory**—(Rev. 18:1). **3. when I came to destroy the city**—i.e., to pronounce God's word for its destruction. So completely did the prophets identify themselves with Him in whose name they spake. **6. the man**—who had been measuring the buildings (ch. 40:3). **7. the place**—i.e., *behold* the place of My throne... —the place on which your thoughts have so much dwelt (Isa. 2:1-3; Jer. 3:17; Zech. 14:16-20; Mal. 3:1). God from the first claimed to be their King politically as well as religiously: and He had resisted their wish to have a human king, as implying a rejection of Him as the proper Head of the state. Even when He yielded to their wish, it was with a protest against their king ruling except as His vicegerent. When Messiah shall reign at Jerusalem, He shall then first realize the original idea of the theocracy, with its at once divine and human king reigning in righteousness over a people all righteous (vs. 12; Isa. 52:1; 54:13; 60:21). **9. carcasses of their kings**—It is supposed that some of their idolatrous kings were buried within the bounds of Solomon's temple [HENDERSON]. Rather, "the carcasses of their *idols*," here called "kings," as having had lordship over them in past times (Isa. 26:13); but henceforth Jehovah, alone their rightful lord, shall be their king, and the idols that had been their "king" would appear but as "carcasses." Hence these defunct kings are associated with the "high places" in vs. 7 [FAIRBAIRN]. Leviticus 26:30 and Jeremiah 16:18, confirm this. Manasseh had built altars in the courts of the temple to the host of heaven (II Kings 21:5; 23:6). **I will dwell in the midst... for ever**—(Rev. 21:3). **10. show the house ... that they may be ashamed of their iniquities**—When the spirituality of the Christian scheme is *shown* to men by the Holy Ghost, it makes them "ashamed of their iniquities." **12. whole... most holy**—This superlative, which had been used exclusively of the holy of holies (Exod. 26:34), was now to characterize the entire building. This all-pervading sanctity was to be "*the* law of the (whole) house," as distinguished from the Levitical law, which confined the peculiar sanctity to a single apartment of it. **13-27.** As to the altar of burnt offering, which was the appointed means of access to God. **15. altar**—*Hebrew, Harel,* i.e., "mount of God"; denoting the high security to be imparted by it to the restored Israel. It was a high place, but a high place *of God,* not of idols. **from the altar**—lit., "the lion of God," *Ariel* (in Isa. 29:1, "Ariel" is applied to Jerusalem). MENOCHIUS supposes that on it four animals were carved; the lion perhaps was the uppermost, whence the horns were made to issue. GESENIUS regards the two words as expressing the "hearth" or fireplace of the altar. **16. square in the four squares**—square on the four sides of its squares [FAIRBAIRN]. **17. settle**—ledge [FAIRBAIRN]. **stairs**—rather, "the ascent," as "steps" up to God's altar were forbidden in Exodus 20:26. **18-27.** The sacrifices here are not mere commemorative, but propitiatory ones. The expressions, "blood" (vs. 18), and "for a sin offering (vss. 19, 21, 22), prove this. In the *literal* sense they can only apply to the second temple. Under the Christian dispensation they would directly oppose the doctrine taught in Hebrews 10:1-18, viz., that Christ has by one offering for ever atoned for sin. However, it is *possible* that they might exist with a *retrospective* reference to Christ's sufferings, as the Levitical sacrifices had a *prospective* reference to them; not propitiatory in themselves, but memorials to keep up the remembrance of His propitiatory sufferings, which form the foundation of His kingdom, lest they should be lost sight of in the glory of that kingdom [DE BURGH]. The particularity of the directions make it unlikely that they are to be understood in a merely vague spiritual sense. **20. cleanse**—lit., "make expiation for." **21. burn it... without the sanctuary**—(Heb. 13:11). **26. consecrate themselves**—lit., "fill their hands," viz., with offerings; referring to the mode of consecrating a priest (Exod. 29:24, 35). **26. Seven days**—referring to the original directions of Moses for seven days' purification services of the altar (Exod. 29:37). **27. I will accept you**—(Ch. 20:40, 41; Rom. 12:1; I Pet. 2:5).

CHAPTER 44

Vss. 1-31. ORDINANCES FOR THE PRINCE AND THE PRIESTS. **2. shut... not be opened**—(Job 12:14; Isa. 22:22; Rev. 3:7). "Shut" to the people (Exod.

19:21, 22), but open to "the prince" (vs. 3), he holding the place of God in political concerns, as the priests do in spiritual. As a mark of respect to an Eastern monarch, the gate by which he enters is thenceforth shut to all other persons (cf. Exod. 19: 24). **3. the prince**—not King Messiah, as He never would offer a burnt offering for Himself, as the prince is to do (ch. 46:4). The prince must mean the civil ruler under Messiah. His connection with the east gate (by which the Lord had returned to His temple) implies, that, as ruling under God, he is to stand in a place of peculiar nearness to God. He represents Messiah, who entered heaven, the true sanctuary, by a way that none other could, viz., by His own holiness; all others must enter as sinners by faith in His blood, through grace. **eat bread before the Lord**—a custom connected with sacrifices (Gen. 31:54; Exod. 18:12; 24:11; I Cor. 10:18). **4-6.** Directions as to the priests. Their acts of desecration are attributed to "the house of Israel" (vss. 6, 7), as the sins of the priesthood and of the people acted and reacted on one another; "like people, like priest" (Jer. 5:31; Hos. 4:9). **7. uncircumcised in heart**—Israelites circumcised outwardly, but wanting the true circumcision of the heart (Deut. 10:16; Acts 7:51). **uncircumcised in flesh**—not having even the outward badge of the covenant people. **8. keepers . . . for yourselves**—such as you yourselves thought fit, not such as I approve of. Or else, "Ye have not *yourselves* kept the charge of My holy things, but have set *others as* keepers of My charge in My sanctuary for yourselves" [MAURER]. **10, 11. Levites . . . shall . . . bear** —viz., the punishment of—**their iniquity . . . Yet they shall be ministers**—So Mark, a *Levite*, nephew of Barnabas (Acts 4:36), was punished by Paul for losing an opportunity of bearing the cross of Christ, and yet was afterwards admitted into his friendship again, and showed his zeal (Acts 13:13; 15:37; Col. 4:10; II Tim. 4:11). One may be a believer, and that too in a distinguished place, and yet lose some special honor—be acknowledged as pious, yet be excluded from some dignity [BENGEL]. **charge at the gates**—Better to be "a doorkeeper in the house of God, than to dwell in the tents of wickedness" (Ps. 84:10). Though standing as a mere doorkeeper, it is in the *house* of God, which hath foundations: whereas he who *dwells* with the wicked, dwells in but shifting *tents*. **15. Zadok**—The priests of the line of Ithamar were to be discharged from ministrations in the temple, because of their corruptions, following in the steps of Eli's sons, against whom the same denunciation was uttered (I Sam. 2:32, 35). Zadok, according to his name (which means "righteous") and his line, were to succeed (I Kings 2:35; I Chron. 24:3), as they did not take part in the general apostasy to the same degree, and perhaps [FAIRBAIRN] the prophet, referring to their original state, speaks of them as they appeared when first chosen to the office. **17. linen**—symbolical of purity. Wool soon induces perspiration in the sultry East and so becomes uncleanly. **18. bonnets** —turbans. **19. not sanctify the people with their garments**—viz., those peculiarly priestly vestments in which they ministered in the sanctuary. **20. Neither . . . shave . . . heads**—as mourners do (Lev. 21:1-5). The worshippers of the Egyptian idols Serapis and Isis shaved their heads; another reason why Jehovah's priests are not to do so. **nor suffer . . . locks to grow long**—as the luxurious, barbarians, and soldiers in warfare did [JEROME]. **21. Neither . . . wine**—lest the holy enthusiasm of their devotion should be mistaken for inebriation, as in Peter's case

(Acts 2:13, 15, 18). **28. I am their inheritance**— (Num. 18:20; Deut. 10:9; 18:1; Josh. 13:14, 32). **30. give . . . priest the first . . . that he may cause the blessing to rest**—(Prov. 3:9, 10; Mal. 3:10).

CHAPTER 45

Vss. 1-25. ALLOTMENT OF THE LAND FOR THE SANCTUARY, THE CITY, AND THE PRINCE. **1. offer an oblation**—from a *Hebrew* root to "heave" or "raise"; when anything was offered to God, the offerer raised the hand. The special territorial division for the tribes is given in chapters 47, 48. Only Jehovah's portion is here subdivided into its three parts: (1) that for the sanctuary (vss. 2, 3); (2) that for the priests (vs. 4); (3) that for the Levites (vs. 5). Cf. ch. 48:8-13. **five and twenty thousand** *reeds . . .*— So *English Version* rightly fills the ellipsis (cf. *Note*, ch. 42:16). Hence "cubits" are mentioned in vs. 2, not here, implying that *there alone* cubits are meant. Taking each reed at twelve feet, the area of the whole would be a square of sixty miles on each side. The whole forming a square betokens the settled stability of the community and the harmony of all classes. "An holy portion of the land" (vs. 1) comprised the whole length, and only two-fifths of the breadth. The outer territory in its distribution harmonizes with the inner and more sacred arrangements of the sanctuary. No room is to be given for *oppression* (see vs. 8), all having ample provision made for their wants and comforts. All will mutually co-operate without constraint or contention. **7.** The prince's possession is to consist of two halves, one on the west, the other on the east, of the sacred territory. The prince, as head of the holy community, stands in closest connection with the sanctuary; his possession, therefore, on both sides must adjoin that which was peculiarly the Lord's [FAIRBAIRN]. **12.** The standard weights were lost when the Chaldeans destroyed the temple. The threefold enumeration of shekels (twenty, twenty-five, fifteen) probably refers to coins of different value, representing respectively so many shekels, the three collectively making up a *maneh*. By weighing these together against the *maneh*, a test was afforded whether they severally had their proper weight: sixty shekels in all, containing one coin a fourth of the whole (fifteen shekels), another a third (twenty shekels), another a third and a twelfth (twenty-five shekels) [MENOCHIUS]. LXX reads, *"fifty shekels shall be your maneh."* **13-15.** In these oblations there is a progression as to the relation between the kind and the quantity: of the corn, the sixth of a tenth, i.e., a sixtieth part of the quantity specified; of the oil, the tenth of a tenth, i.e., an hundredth part; and of the flock, one from every 200. **18.** The year is to begin with a consecration service, not mentioned under the Levitical law; but an earnest of it is given in the feast of dedication of the second temple, which celebrated its purification by Judas Maccabeus, after its defilement by Antiochus. **20. for him that is simple**—for sins of ignorance (Lev. 4:2, 13, 27). **21.** As a new solemnity, the feast of consecration is to prepare for the passover; so the passover itself is to have different sacrifices from those of the Mosaic law. Instead of one ram and seven lambs for the daily burnt offering, there are to be seven bullocks and seven rams. So also whereas the feast of tabernacles had its own offerings, which diminished as the days of the feast advanced, here the same are appointed as on the passover. Thus it is implied that the letter of the law is to give place to its spirit, those outward rites of Judaism having no intrinsic efficacy, but symbolizing the spiritual truths of Messiah's kingdom, as for instance the perfect holiness which is to characterize it. Cf. I Corinthians 5:7, 8, as to our spiritual "passover," wherein, at the Lord's supper, we feed on Christ by faith, accompanied with "the unleavened bread of sincerity and truth." Literal ordinances, though not slavishly bound to the letter of the law, will set forth the catholic and eternal verities of Messiah's kingdom.

CHAPTER 46

Vss. 1-24. Continuation of the Ordinances for the Prince and for the People in Their Worship. **2.** The prince is to go through the east gate without (open on the Sabbath only, to mark its peculiar sanctity) to the entrance of the gate of the inner court; he is to go no further, but "stand by the post" (cf. I Kings 8:14, 22, Solomon standing before the altar of the Lord in the presence of the congregation; also II Kings 11:14; 23:3, "by a pillar": the customary place), the court within belonging exclusively to the priests. There, as representative of the people, in a peculiarly near relation to God, he is to present his offerings to Jehovah, while at a greater distance, the people are to stand worshipping at the outer gate of the same entrance. The offerings on Sabbaths are larger than those of the Mosaic law, to imply that the worship of God is to be conducted by the prince and people in a more munificent spirit of self-sacrificing liberality than formerly. **9.** The worshippers were on the great feasts to pass from one side to the other, through the temple courts, in order that, in such a throng as should attend the festivals, the ingress and egress should be the more unimpeded, those going out not being in the way of those coming in. **10. prince in the midst** —not isolated as at other times, but joining the great throng of worshippers, at their head, after the example of David (Ps. 42:4, "I had gone with the multitude . . . to the house of God, with the voice of joy and praise, with a multitude that kept holy day"); the highest in rank animating the devotions of the rest by his presence and example. **12-15.** Not only is he to perform *official* acts of worship on holy days and feasts, but in "voluntary" offerings daily he is to show his individual zeal, surpassing all his people in liberality, and so setting them a princely example. **16-18.** The prince's possession is to be inalienable, and any portion given to a servant is to revert to his sons at the year of jubilee, that he may have no temptation to spoil his people of their inheritance, as formerly (cf. Ahab and Naboth, I Kings 21). The mention of the year of jubilee implies that there is something literal meant, besides the spiritual sense. The jubilee year was restored after the captivity [Josephus, *Antiquities,* 14. 10, 6; I Maccabees 6:49]. Perhaps it will be restored under Messiah's coming reign. Cf. Isaiah 61:2, 3, where "the acceptable year of the Lord" is closely connected with the comforting of the mourners in Zion, and "the day of vengeance" on Zion's foes. The mention of the prince's *sons* is another argument against Messiah being meant by "the prince." **19-24.** Due regard is to be had for the sanctity of the officiating priests' food, by cooking-courts being provided close to their chambers. One set of apartments for cooking was to be at the corners of the *inner* court, reserved for the flesh of the sin offerings, to be eaten only by the priests whose perquisite it was (Lev. 6:25; 7:7), before com-

ing forth to mingle again with the people; another set at the corners of the *outer* court, for cooking the flesh of the peace offerings, of which the people partook along with the priests. All this implies that no longer are the common and unclean to be confounded with the sacred and divine, but that in even the least things, as eating and drinking, the glory of God is to be the aim (I Cor. 10:31). **22. courts joined**—Fairbairn translates, "roofed" or "vaulted." But these cooking apartments seem to have been uncovered, to let the smoke and smell of the meat the more easily pass away. They were "joined" or "attached" to the walls of the courts at the corners of the latter [Menochius]. **23. boiling-places**—boilers. **under the rows**—At the foot of the rows, i.e., in the lowest part of the *walls,* were the places for boiling made.

CHAPTER 47

Vss. 1-23. Vision of the Temple Waters. Borders and Division of the Land. The happy fruit to the earth at large of God's dwelling with Israel in holy fellowship is that the blessing is no longer restricted to the one people and locality, but is to be diffused with comprehensive catholicity through the whole world. So the plant from the cedar of Lebanon is represented as gathering under its shelter "all fowl of every wing" (ch. 17:23). Even the desert places of the earth shall be made fruitful by the healing waters of the Gospel (cf. Isa. 35:1). **1. waters**—So Revelation 22:1, represents "the water of life as proceeding out of the throne of God and of the Lamb." His throne was set up in the temple at Jerusalem (ch. 43:7). Thence it is to flow over the earth (Joel 3:18; Zech. 13:1; 14:8). Messiah is the temple and the door; from His pierced side flow the living waters, ever increasing, both in the individual believer and in the heart. The fountains in the vicinity of Moriah suggested the image here. The waters flow eastward, i.e., towards the Kedron, and thence towards the Jordan, and so along the Ghor into the Dead Sea. The main point in the picture is the rapid augmentation from a petty stream into a mighty river, not by the influx of side streams, but by its own self-supply from the sacred miraculous source in the temple [Henderson]. (Cf. Ps. 36:8, 9; 46:4; Isa. 11:9; Hab. 2:14). Searching into the things of God, we find some easy to understand, as the water up to the ankles; others more difficult, which require a deeper search, as the waters up to the knees or loins; others beyond our reach, of which we can only adore the depth (Rom. 11:33). The *healing* of the waters of the Dead Sea here answers to "there shall be no more curse" (Rev. 22:3; cf. Zech. 14:11). **7. trees**— not merely *one* tree of life as in Paradise (Gen. 2), but many: to supply immortal food and medicine to the people of God, who themselves also become "trees of righteousness" (Isa. 61:3) planted by the waters and (Ps. 1:3) bearing fruit unto holiness. **8. the desert**—or "plain," *Hebrew, Arabah* (Deut. 3:17; 4:49; Josh. 3:16), which is the name still given to the valley of the Jordan and the plain south of the Dead Sea, and extending to the Elanitic gulf of the Red Sea. **the sea**—the Dead Sea. *"The sea"* noted as covering with its waters the guilty cities of the plain, Sodom and Gomorrah. In its bituminous waters no vegetable or animal life is said to be found. But now death is to give place to life in Judea, and throughout the world, as symbolized by the healing of these death-pervaded waters covering the doomed cities. Cf. as to "the sea" in general, regarded as a symbol of the troubled powers of nature, disordered by the fall, henceforth to rage no more, Revelation 21:1. **9. rivers**—in *Hebrew, "two* rivers." Hence *Hebrew* expositors think that the waters from the temple were divided into two branches, the one emptying itself into the eastern or Dead Sea, the other into the western or Mediterranean. So Zechariah 14:8. However, though this probably is covertly implied in the *Hebrew dual,* the flowing of the waters into the *Dead Sea only* is expressed. Cf. vs. 8, "waters . . . healed," which can apply only to it, not to the Mediterranean: also vs. 10, "fish as the fish of the great sea"; the Dead Sea, when healed, containing fish, as the Mediterranean does. **10. En-gedi . . . En-eglaim**—En-gedi (meaning "fountain of the kid"), anciently, Hazazon-Tamar, now Ain-Jidy; west of the Dead Sea; David's place of refuge from Saul. En-eglaim means "fountain of two calves," on the confines of Moab, over against En-gedi, and near where Jordan enters the Dead Sea (Isa. 15:8). These two limits are fixed on, to comprise between them the whole Dead Sea. **fish . . . according to their kinds**—JEROME quotes an ancient theory that "there are 153 kinds of fishes," all of which were taken by the apostles (John 21:11), and not one remained uncaptured; signifying that both the noble and baseborn, the rich and the poor, and every class, are being drawn out of the sea of the world to salvation. Cf. Matthew 14:47, the gospel net; the apostles being fishermen, at first literally, afterwards spiritually (Matt. 4:19). **11. marshes**—marshy places. The region is known to have such pits and marshes. The Arabs take the salt collected by evaporation in these pits for their own use, and that of their flocks. **not be healed**—Those not reached by the healing waters of the Gospel, through their sloth and earthly-mindedness, are given over (Rev. 22:11) to their own bitterness and barrenness (as "saltness" is often employed to express, Deut. 29:23; Ps. 107:34; Zeph. 2:9); and awful example to others in the punishment they suffer (II Peter 2:6). **12.** Instead of the "vine of Sodom and grapes of Gomorrah" (Deut. 32:32), nauseous and unwholesome, trees of life-giving and life-restoring virtue shall bloom similar in properties to, and exceeding in number, the tree of life in Eden (Rev. 2:7; 22:2, 14). **leaf . . . not fade**—expressing not only the unfailing character of the heavenly medicine of the tree of life, but also that the graces of the believer (as a tree of righteousness), which are the *leaves,* and his deeds, which are the fruits that flow from those graces, are immortal (Ps. 1:3; Jer. 17:8; Matt. 10:42; I Cor. 15:58). **new fruit**—lit., "firstlings," or first fruit. They are still, each month afresh, as it were, yielding their first fruit [FAIRBAIRN]. The *first-born* of a thing, in *Hebrew* idiom, means *the chiefest.* As Job 18:13, "the first-born of death," i.e., *the most fatal* death. **13.** *The redivision of the land: the boundaries.* The latter are substantially the same as those given by Moses in Numbers 34; they here begin with the north, but in Numbers 34 they begin with the south. It is only Canaan proper, exclusive of the possession of the two and a half tribes beyond Jordan, that is here divided. **Joseph . . . two portions**—according to the original promise of Jacob (Gen. 48:5, 22). Joseph's sons were given the birthright forfeited by Reuben, the first-born (I Chron. 5:1). Therefore the former is here put first. His *two* sons having distinct portions make up the whole number *twelve* portions, as he had just before specified "*twelve* tribes of Israel"; for Levi had no

separate inheritance, so that he is not reckoned in the twelve. **15. Zedad**—on the north boundary of Canaan. **16. Hamath**—As Israel was a separate people, so their land was a separate land. On no scene could the sacred history have been so well transacted as on it. On the east was the sandy desert. On the north and south, mountains. On the west, an inhospitable seashore. But it was not always to be a separate land. Between the parallel ranges of Lebanon is the long valley of El-Bekaa, leading to "the entering in of Hamath" on the Orontes, in the Syrian frontier. Roman roads, and the harbor made at Cæsarea, opened out doors through which the Gospel should go from it to all lands. So in the last days, when all shall flock to Jerusalem as the religious center of the world. **Berothah**—a city in Syria conquered by David (II Sam. 8:8); meaning "wells." **Hazar-hatticon**—meaning "the middle village." **Hauran**—a tract in Syria, south of Damascus; Auranitis. **17. Hazar-enan**—a town in the north of Canaan, meaning "village of fountains." **18. east sea**—the Dead Sea. The border is to go down straight to it by the valley of the Jordan. So Numbers 34:11, 12. **19. Tamar**—not Tadmor in the desert, but Tamar, the last town of Judea, by the Dead Sea. Meaning "palm tree"; so called from palm trees abounding near it. **22. to the strangers**—It is altogether unprecedented under the old covenant, that "strangers" should have "inheritance" among the tribes. There would not be room locally within Canaan for more than the tribes. The literal sense must therefore be modified, as expressing that Gentiles are not to be excluded from settling among the covenant people, and that spiritually their privileges are not to be less than those of Israel (Rom. 10:12; Gal. 3:28; Eph. 3:6; Col. 3:11; Rev. 7:9, 10). Still, "sojourneth," in vs. 23, implies that in Canaan, the covenant people are regarded as *at home,* the strangers as *settlers.*

CHAPTER 48

Vss. 1-35. ALLOTMENT OF THE LAND TO THE SEVERAL TRIBES. **1. Dan**—The lands are divided into portions of ideal exactness, running alongside of each other, the whole breadth from west to east, standing in a common relation to the temple in the center: seven tribes' portions on the north, five in the smaller division in the south. The portions of the city, the temple, the prince, and the priesthood, are in the middle, not within the boundaries of any tribe, all alike having a common interest in them. Judah has the place of honor next the center on the north, Benjamin the corresponding place of honor next the center on the south; because of the adherence of these two to the temple ordinances and to the house of David for so long, when the others deserted them. Dan, on the contrary, so long locally and morally semi-heathen (Judg. 18), is to have the least honorable place, at the extreme north. For the same reason, St. John (Rev. 7:5-8) omits Dan altogether. **3. Asher**—a tribe of which no one of note is mentioned in the Old Testament. In the New Testament one is singled out of it, the prophetess Anna. **4. Manasseh**—The intercourse and unity between the two and a half tribes east of the Jordan, and the nine and a half west of it, had been much kept up by the splitting of Manasseh, causing the visits of kinsmen one to the other from both sides of the Jordan. There shall be no need for this in the new order of things. **5. Ephraim**—This tribe, within its two dependent tribes, Manasseh and

Benjamin, for upwards of 400 years under the judges held the pre-eminence. **6. Reuben**—doomed formerly for incest and instability "not to excel" (Gen. 49:4). So no distinguished prophet, priest, or king had come from it. Of it were the notorious Dathan and Abiram, the mutineers. A pastoral and Bedouin character marked it and Gad (Judg. 5:16). **15-17.** The 5000 rods, apportioned to the city out of the 25,000 square, are to be laid off in a square of 4500, with the 250 all around for suburbs. **profane**—i.e., not strictly sacred as the sacerdotal portions, but applied to secular uses. **24. Benjamin** —Cf. Jacob's prophecy (Gen. 49:27; Deut. 33:12). It alone with Judah had been throughout loyal to the house of David, so its prowess at the "night" of the national history was celebrated as well as in the

"morning." **25. Simeon**—omitted in the blessing of Moses in Deuteronomy 33 perhaps because of the Simeonite "prince," who at Baal-peor led the Israelites in their idolatrous whoredoms with Midian (Num. 25:14). **26. Issachar**—Its ancient portion had been on the plain of Esdraelon. Compared (Gen. 49:14) to "a strong ass crouching between two burdens," i.e., tribute and tillage; never meddling with wars except in self-defense. **31. gates**—(Rev. 21:12, etc.). The twelve gates bear the names of the twelve tribes to imply that all are regarded as having an interest in it. **35. Lord is there**—*Jehovah-Shammah*. Not that the city will be called so in mere name, but that the reality will be best expressed by this descriptive title (Jer. 3:17; 33:16; Zech. 2:10; Rev. 21:3; 22:3).

THE BOOK OF

DANIEL

INTRODUCTION

DANIEL, i.e., "God is my judge"; probably of the blood royal (cf. ch. 1:3, with I Chron. 3:1, where *a son of David* is named so). Jerusalem may have been his birthplace (though ch. 9:24, "thy holy city," does not *necessarily* imply this). He was carried to Babylon among the Hebrew captives brought thither by Nebuchadnezzar at the first deportation in the fourth year of Jehoiakim. As he and his three companions are called (ch. 1:4) "children," he cannot have been more than about twelve years old when put in training, according to Eastern etiquette, to be a courtier (ch. 1:3, 6). He then received a new name, by which it was usual to mark a change in one's condition (II Kings 23:34; 24:17; Ezra 5:14; Esther 2:7), Belteshazzar, i.e., "a prince favored by Bel." His piety and wisdom were proverbial among his countrymen at an early period; probably owing to that noble proof he gave of faithfulness, combined with wisdom, in abstaining from the food sent to him from the king's table, as being polluted by the idolatries usual at heathen banquets (ch. 1:8–16). Hence Ezekiel's reference to him (Ezekiel 14:14, 20; 28:3) is precisely of that kind we should expect; a coincidence which must be undesigned. Ezekiel refers to him not as a *writer*, but as exhibiting a character righteous and wise in discerning secrets, in those circumstances now found in his book, which are *earlier* than the time when Ezekiel wrote. As Joseph rose in Egypt by interpreting Pharaoh's dreams, so Daniel, by interpreting Nebuchadnezzar's, was promoted to be governor of Babylonia, and president of the Magian priest-caste. Under Evil-merodach, Nebuchadnezzar's successor, as a change of officers often attends the accession of a new king, Daniel seems to have had a lower post, which led him occasionally to be away from Babylon (ch. 8:2, 27). Again he came into note when he read the mystic writing of Belshazzar's doom on the wall on the night of that monarch's impious feast. BEROSUS calls the last Babylonian king Nabonidus and says he was not killed, but had an honorable abode in Carmania assigned to him, after having surrendered voluntarily in Borsippa. RAWLINSON has cleared up the discrepancy from the Nineveh inscription. Belshazzar was joint king with his father, Evil-merodach or Nabonidus (called Minus in the inscriptions), to whom he was subordinate. He shut himself up in Babylon, while the other king took refuge elsewhere, viz., in Borsippa. BEROSUS gives the Chaldean account, which suppresses all about Belshazzar, as being to the national dishonor. Had Daniel been a *late* book, he would no doubt have taken up the later account of BEROSUS. If he gave a history differing from that current in Babylonia, the Jews of that region would not have received it as true. Darius the Mede, or Cyaxares II, succeeded and reigned two years. The mention of this monarch's reign, almost unknown to profane history (being eclipsed by the splendor of Cyrus) is an incidental proof that Daniel wrote as a contemporary historian of events which he knew, and did not borrow from others. In the third year of Cyrus he saw the visions (chs. 10–12) relating to his people down to the latest days and the coming resurrection. He must have been about eighty-four years old at this time. Tradition represents Daniel as having died and been buried at Shushan. Though his advanced age did not allow him to be among those who returned to Palestine, yet he never ceased to have his people's interests nearest to his heart (chs. 9 and 10:12).

AUTHENTICITY OF THE BOOK OF DANIEL. Chs. 7:1, 28; 8:2; 9:2; 10:1, 2; 12:4, 5, testify that it was composed by Daniel himself. He does not mention himself in the first six chapters, which are *historical;* for in these it is not the author, but the *events* which are the prominent point. In the last six, which are *prophetical,* the author makes himself known, for here it was needed, prophecy being a revelation of *words* to particular men. It holds a third rank in the *Hebrew* canon: not among *the prophets,* but in the Hagiographa (Chetubim), between Esther and Ezra, books like it relating to the captivity; because he did not strictly belong to those who held exclusively the *profession* of "prophets" in the theocracy, but was rather a "seer," having the *gift,* but not the *office* of prophet. Were the book an interpolated one, it doubtless would have been placed among the prophets. Its present position is a proof of its genuineness, as it was *deliberately* put in a position different from that where most would expect to find it. Placed between Esther, and Ezra and Nehemiah, it separated the historical books of the time after the captivity. Thus, Daniel was, as BENGEL calls him, the politician, chronologer, and historian among the prophets. The Psalms also, though many are prophetical, are ranked with the Hagiographa, not with the prophets; and the Revelation of John is separated from his Epistles, as Daniel is from the Old Testament prophets. Instead of writing in the midst of the covenant people, and making them the foreground of his picture, he writes in a heathen court, the world kingdoms occupying the foreground, and the kingdom of God, though ultimately made the most significant, the background. His peculiar position in the heathen court is reflected in his peculiar position in the canon. As the "prophets" in the Old Testament, so the epistles of the apostles in the New Testament were written by divinely commissioned persons for their contemporaries. But Daniel and John were not in immediate contact with the congregation, but isolated and alone with God, the one in a heathen court, the other on a lonely isle (Rev. 1:9). PORPHYRY, the assailant of Christianity in the third century, asserted that the Book of Daniel was a forgery of the time of the Maccabees (170–164 B.C.), a time when *confessedly* there were no prophets, written after the events as to Antiochus Epiphanes, which it professes to *foretell;* so accurate are the details. A conclusive proof of Daniel's inspiration, if his prophecies can be shown to have been *before* the events. Now we know, from JOSEPHUS, that the Jews in Christ's days recognized Daniel as in the canon. Zechariah, Ezra, and Nehemiah, centuries before Antiochus, refer to it. Jesus refers to it in His characteristic designation, "Son of man," Matthew 24:30 (Dan. 7:13); also expressly by name, and as a "prophet," in Matthew 24:15 (cf. Matt. 24:21, with Dan. 12:1, etc.); and in the moment that decided His life (Matthew 26:64) or death, when the high priest adjured him by the living God. Also, in Luke 1:19–26, "Gabriel" is mentioned, whose name occurs nowhere else in Scripture, save in ch. 8:16; 9:21. Besides the references to it in Revelation, Paul confirms the prophetical part of it, as to the blasphemous king (Dan. 7:8, 25; 11:36), in I Corinthians 6:2; II Thessalonians 2:3, 4; the narrative part, as to the miraculous deliverances from "the lions" and "the fire," in Hebrews 11:33, 34. Thus the book is expressly attested by the New Testament on the three points made the stumbling block of neologists—the predictions, the narratives of miracles, and the manifestations of angels. An objection has been started to the unity of the book, viz., that Jesus quotes no part of the first half of Daniel. But Matthew 21:44 would be an enigma if it were not a reference to the "stone that smote the image" (Dan. 2:34, 35, 44, 45). Thus the New Testament sanctions chs. 2, 3, 6, 7, and 11. The design of the miracles in the heathen courts where Daniel was, as of those of Moses in Egypt, was to lead the world power, which seemed to be victorious over the theocracy, to see the essential inner superiority of the seemingly fallen kingdom of God to itself, and to show prostrate Israel that the power of God was the same as of old in Egypt. The first book of Maccabees (cf. I Maccabees 1:24; 9:27, 40, with Dan. 12:1; 11:26, of LXX) refers to Daniel as an accredited book, and even refers to the LXX Alexandrian version of it. The fact of Daniel having a place in the LXX shows it was received by the Jews at large prior to the Maccabean times. The LXX version so arbitrarily deviated from the *Hebrew* Daniel, that Theodotius' version was substituted for it in the early Christian Church. JOSEPHUS (*Antiquities*, 7.11, 8) mentions that Alexander the Great had designed to punish the Jews for their fidelity to Darius, but that Jaddua (332 B.C.), the high priest, met him at the head of a procession and averted his wrath by showing him Daniel's prophecy that a Grecian monarch should overthrow Persia. Certain it is, Alexander favored the Jews, and JOSEPHUS' statement gives an explanation of the fact; at least it shows that the Jews in JOSEPHUS' days *believed* that Daniel was extant in Alexander's days, long before the Maccabees. With Jaddua (high priest from 341–322 B.C.) the Old Testament history ends (Neh. 12:11). (The register of the priests and Levites was not written by Nehemiah, who died about 400 B.C., but was inserted with divine sanction by the collectors of the canon subsequently.) An objection to Daniel's authenticity has been rested on a few Greek words found in it. But these are mostly names of Greek musical instruments, which were imported by Greece from the East, rather than vice versa. Some of the words are derived from the common Indo-Germanic stock of both Greek and Chaldee: hence their appearance in both tongues. And one or two may have come through the Greeks of Asia Minor to the Chaldee. The fact that from the fourth verse of the second chapter to the end of the seventh, the language is Chaldee, but the rest Hebrew, is not an argument against, but for, its authenticity. So in Ezra the two languages are found. The work, if that of one author, must have been composed by someone in the circumstances of Daniel, i.e., by one familiar with both languages. No native-born Hebrew who had not lived in Chaldea would know Chaldee so well as to use it with the same idiomatic ease as his native tongue; the very impurities in Daniel's use of both are just such as were *natural* to one in his circumstances, but *unnatural* to one in a later age, or to one not half Hebrew, half Chaldean in residence as Daniel was. Those parts of Daniel which concern the whole world are mostly Chaldee, then the language of the world empire. So Greek was made the language of the New Testament, which was designed for the whole world. Those affecting the Jews, mostly Hebrew; and this not so impure as that of Ezekiel. His Chaldee is a mixture of Hebrew and Aramaic. Two predictions alone are enough to prove to us that Daniel was a true prophet. (1) That his prophecies reach beyond Antiochus; viz., he foretells the rise of *the four great monarchies*, Babylon, Medo-Persia, Greece, and Rome (the last not being in Daniel's time known beyond the precincts of Italy, or rather of Latium), and that no other earthly kingdom would subvert the fourth, but that it would divide into parts. All this has come to pass. No *fifth* great earthly monarchy has arisen, though often attempted, as by Charlemagne, Charles V, and Napoleon. (2) The time of Messiah's advent, as dated from a certain decree, His being cut off, and the destruction of the city. "He who denies Daniel's prophecies," says Sir Isaac Newton, "undermines Christianity, which is founded on Daniel's prophecies concerning Christ."

CHARACTERISTICS OF DANIEL. The *vision mode of revelation* is the exception in other prophets, the rule in Daniel. In Zechariah (1–6), who lived after Daniel, the same mode appears, but the other form from the seventh chapter to the end. The Revelation of St. John alone is perfectly parallel to Daniel, which may be called the

Old Testament Apocalypse. In the *contents* too there is the difference above noticed, that he views the kingdom of God from the standpoint of the world kingdoms, the development of which is his great subject. This mode of viewing it was appropriate to his own position in a heathen court, and to the relation of subjection in which the covenant people then stood to the world powers. No longer are single powers of the world incidentally introduced, but the *universal monarchies* are the chief theme, in which the worldly principle, opposed to the kingdom of God, manifests itself fully. The near and distant are not seen in the same perspective, as by the other prophets, who viewed the whole future from the eschatological point; but in Daniel the historical *details* are given of that development of the world powers which must precede the advent of the kingdom [AUBERLEN].

SIGNIFICANCE OF THE BABYLONIAN CAPTIVITY. The exile is the historical basis of Daniel's prophecies, as Daniel implies in the first chapter, which commences with the beginning, and ends with the termination, of the captivity (ch. 1:1, 21; cf. ch. 9:1, 2). A new stage in the theocracy begins with the captivity. Nebuchadnezzar made three incursions into Judah. The first under Jehoiakim (606 B.C.), in which Daniel was carried away, subjected the theocracy to the Babylonian world power. The second (598 B.C.) was that in which Jehoiachin and Ezekiel were carried away. In the third (588 B.C.), Nebuchadnezzar destroyed Jerusalem and carried away Zedekiah. Originally, Abraham was raised out of the "sea" (Dan. 7:2) of the nations, as an island holy to God, and his seed chosen as God's mediator of His revelations of love to mankind. Under David and Solomon, the theocracy, as opposed to the heathen power, attained its climax in the Old Testament, not only being independent, but lord of the surrounding nations; so that the period of these two kings was henceforth made the type of the Messianic. But when God's people, instead of resting on Him, seek alliance with the world power, that very power is made the instrument of their chastisement. So Ephraim (722 B.C.) fell by Assyria; and Judah also, drawn into the sphere of the world's movements from the time of Ahaz, who sought Assyrian help (740 B.C.; Isa. 7) at last fell by Babylon, and thenceforth has been more or less dependent on the world monarchies, and so, till Messiah, was favored with no revelations from the time of Malachi (400 years). Thus, from the beginning of the exile, the theocracy, in the strict sense, ceased on earth; the rule of the world powers superseding it. But God's covenant with Israel remains firm (Rom. 11:29); therefore, a period of blessing under Messiah's kingdom is *now* foretold as about to follow their long chastisement. The exile thus is the turning point in the history of the theocracy, which Roos thus divides: (1) From Adam to the exodus out of Egypt. (2) From the exodus to the beginning of the Babylonian captivity. (3) From the captivity to the millennium. (4) From the millennium to the end of the world. *The position of Daniel* in the Babylonian court was in unison with the altered relations of the theocracy and the world power, which new relation was to be the theme of his prophecy. Earlier prophets, from the standpoint of Israel, treated of Israel in its relation to the world powers; Daniel, from Babylon, the center of the then world power, treats of the world powers in their relation to Israel. His seventy years' residence in Babylon, and his high official position there, gave him an insight into the world's politics, fitting him to be the recipient of political revelations; while his spiritual experiences, gained through Nebuchadnezzar's humiliation, Belshazzar's downfall, and the rapid decay of the Babylonian empire itself, as well as the miraculous deliverances of himself and his friends (chs. 3–6), all fitted him for regarding things from the spiritual standpoint, from which the world's power appears transient, but the glory of God's kingdom eternal. As his political position was the *body*, the school of magicians in which he had studied for three years (ch. 1:4, 5) was the *soul;* and his mind strong in faith and nourished by the earlier prophecies (ch. 9:2), the *spirit* of his prophecy, which only waited for the spirit of revelation from above to kindle it. So God fits His organs for their work. AUBERLEN compares Daniel to Joseph: the one at the beginning, the other at the end of the Jewish history of revelation; both representatives of God and His people at heathen courts; both interpreters of the dim presentiments of truth, expressed in God-sent dreams, and therefore raised to honor by the powers of the world: so representing Israel's calling to be a royal priesthood among the nations; and types of Christ, the true Israel, and of Israel's destination to be a light to lighten the whole Gentile world, as Romans 11:12, 15 foretells. As Achilles at the beginning, and Alexander at the end, of Grecian history are the mirrors of the whole life of the Hellenic people, so Joseph and Daniel of Israel.

CONTENTS OF THE BOOK. Historical and biographical *introduction* in *the first chapter*. Daniel, a captive exile, is representative of his nation in its servitude and exile: while his heavenly insight into dreams, far exceeding that of the magi, represents the divine superiority of the covenant people over their heathen lords. The high dignities, even in the world, which he thereby attained, typify the giving of the earth-kingdom at last "to the people of the saints of the Most High" (ch. 7:27). Thus Daniel's personal history is the typical foundation of his prophecy. The prophets had to experience in themselves, and in their age, something of what they foretold about future times; just as David felt much of Christ's sufferings in his own person (cf. Hos. 1:2–9, 10, 11; 2:3). So Jonah 1, etc. [Roos]. Hence biographical notices of Daniel and his friends are inserted among his prophecies. Chs. 2–12 contain the substance of the book, and consist of *two parts*. The first (chs. 2–7) represents the development of the world powers, viewed from a historical point. The second (chs. 8–12), their development in relation to Israel, especially in the future preceding Christ's first advent, foretold in the ninth chapter. But prophecy looks beyond the immediate future to the complete fulfilment in the last days, since the individual parts in the organic history of salvation cannot be understood except in connection with the whole. Also Israel looked forward to the Messianic time, not only for spiritual salvation, but also for the visible restoration of the kingdom which even now we too expect. The prophecy which they needed ought therefore to comprise both, and so much of the history of the world as would elapse before the final consummation. The period of Daniel's prophecies, therefore, is that from the downfall of the theocracy at the captivity till its final restoration, yet future—the period of the dominion of the world powers, not set aside by Christ's first coming (John 18:36; for, to have taken the earth-kingdom *then*, would have been to take it from Satan's hands, Matt. 4; 8–10), but to be superseded by His universal and everlasting kingdom at His second coming (Rev. 11:15). Thus the general survey of the development and final destiny of the world powers (chs. 2–7) fittingly precedes the disclosures as to the immediate future (chs. 8–12). Daniel marks the division by writing the first part in Chaldee, and the second, and the introduction, in Hebrew; the former, referring to the powers of the world, in the language of the then dominant world power under which he lived; the latter, relating to the people of God, in their own language. An interpolator in a later age would have used Hebrew, the language of the ancient prophets throughout, or if anywhere Aramaic, so as to be understood by his contemporaries, he would have used it in the second rather than in the first part as having a more immediate reference to his own times [AUBERLEN].

CHAPTER 1

Vss. 1-21. THE BABYLONIAN CAPTIVITY BEGINS; DANIEL'S EDUCATION AT BABYLON, etc. **1. third year** —cf. Jeremiah 25:1, "the *fourth* year; Jehoiakim came to the throne at the *end* of the year, which Jeremiah reckons as the *first* year, but which Daniel leaves out of count, being an incomplete year: thus, in Jeremiah, it is "the *fourth* year"; in Daniel, "the *third*" [JAHN]. However, Jeremiah (25:1; 46:2) merely says, the fourth year of Jehoiakim concided with the first of Nebuchadnezzar, when the latter *conquered the Egyptians at Carchemish*; not that the *deportation of captives from Jerusalem* was in the fourth year of Jehoiakim: this probably took place in the end of the third year of Jehoiakim, shortly *before* the battle of Carchemish [FAIRBAIRN]. Nebuchadnezzar took away the captives as hostages for the submission of the Hebrews. *Historical* Scripture gives no positive account of this first deportation, with which the Babylonian captivity, i.e., Judah's subjection to Babylon for seventy years (Jer. 29:10), begins. But II Chronicles 36:6, 7, states that Nebuchadnezzar had intended "to carry Jehoiakim to Babylon," and that he "carried off the vessels of the house of the Lord" thither. But Jehoiakim died at Jerusalem, before the conqueror's intention as to him was carried into effect (Jer. 22: 18, 19; 36:30), and his dead body, as was foretold, was dragged out of the gates by the Chaldean besiegers, and left unburied. The second deportation under Jehoiachin was eight years later. **2. Shinar** —the old name of Babylonia (Gen. 11:2; 14:1; Isa. 11:11; Zech. 5:11). Nebuchadnezzar took only "part of the vessels," as he did not intend wholly to overthrow the state, but to make it tributary, and to leave such vessels as were absolutely needed for the public worship of Jehovah. Subsequently all were taken away and were restored under Cyrus (Ezra 1:7). **his god**—Bel. His temple, as was often the case among the heathen, was made "treasure-house" of the king. **3. master of . . . eunuchs**—called in Turkey the *kislar aga*. **of the king's seed**—cf. the prophecy, II Kings 20:17, 18. **4. no blemish** —A handsome form was connected, in Oriental ideas, with mental power. "Children" means youths of twelve or fourteen years old. **teach . . . tongue of . . . Chaldeans**—their language and literature, the Aramaic-Babylonian. That the heathen lore was not altogether valueless appears from the Egyptian magicians who opposed Moses; the Eastern Magi who sought Jesus, and who may have drawn the tradition as to the "King of the Jews" from Daniel 9:24, etc., written in the East. As Moses was trained in the learning of the Egyptian sages, so Daniel in that of the Chaldeans, to familiarize his mind with mysterious lore, and so develop his heaven-bestowed gift of understanding in visions (vss. 4, 5, 17). **5. king's meat**—It is usual for an Eastern king to entertain, from the food of his table, many retainers and royal captives (Jer. 52:33, 34). The *Hebrew* for "meat" implies *delicacies*. **stand before the king**—as attendant courtiers; not as eunuchs. **6. children of Judah**—the most noble tribe, being

that to which the "king's seed" belonged (cf. vs. 3). **7. gave names**—designed to mark their new relation, that so they might forget their former religion and country (Gen. 41:45). But as in Joseph's case (whom Pharaoh called Zaphnath-paaneah), so in Daniel's, the name indicative of his relation to a heathen court ("Belteshazzar," i.e., "Bel's prince"), however flattering to him, is not the one retained by Scripture, but the name marking his relation to God ("Daniel," *God my Judge,* the theme of his prophecies being *God's judgment* on the heathen world powers). **Hananiah**—i.e., "whom Jehovah hath favored." **Shadrach**—from *Rak,* in Babylonian, "the King," i.e., "the Sun"; the same root as in *Abrech* (*Margin,* Gen. 41:43), inspired or illumined by the Sun-god." **Mishael**—i.e., "who is what God is?" *Who is comparable to God?* **Meshnach** —The Babylonians retained the first syllable of Mishael, the *Hebrew* name; but for *El,* i.e., GOD, substituted *Shak,* the Babylonian goddess, called Sheshach (Jer. 25:26; 51:41), answering to the Earth, or else Venus, the goddess of love and mirth; it was during her feast that Cyrus took Babylon. **Azariah**—i.e., "whom Jehovah helps." **Abednego** —i.e., "servant of the shining fire." Thus, instead of to Jehovah, these His servants were dedicated by the heathen to their four leading gods [HERODOTUS, *Clio*]; Bel, the Chief-god, the Sun-god, Earth-god, and Fire-god. To the last the three youths were consigned when refusing to worship the golden image (ch. 3). The *Chaldee version* translates "Lucifer," in Isaiah 14:12, *Nogea,* the same as *Nego.* The names thus at the outset are significant of the seeming triumph, but sure downfall, of the heathen powers before Jehovah and His people. **8. Daniel . . . would not defile himself with . . . king's meat**— Daniel is specified as being the leader in the "purpose" (the word implies a *decided* resolution) to abstain from defilement, thus manifesting a character already formed for prophetical functions. The other three youths, no doubt, shared in his purpose. It was the custom to throw a small part of the viands and wine upon the earth, as an initiatory offering to the gods, so as to consecrate to them the whole entertainment (cf. Deut. 32:38). To have partaken of such a feast would have been to sanction idolatry, and was forbidden even after the legal distinction of clean and unclean meats was done away (I Cor. 8:7, 10; 10:27, 28). Thus the faith of these youths was made instrumental in overruling the evil foretold against the Jews (Ezek. 4:13; Hos. 9:3), to the glory of God. Daniel and his three friends, says AUBERLEN, stand out like an oasis in the desert. Like Moses, Daniel "chose rather to suffer affliction with the people of God, than to enjoy the pleasures of sin for a season" (see ch. 9). He who is to interpret divine revelations must not feed on the dainties, nor drink from the intoxicating cup, of this world. This made him as dear a name to his countrymen as Noah and Job, who also stood alone in their piety among a perverse generation (Ezek. 14:14; 28:3). **requested**—While decided in principle, we ought to seek our object by gentleness, rather than by an ostentatious testimony, which, under the plea of faithfulness, courts opposition. **9. God . . . brought Daniel into favour**—The favor of others towards the godly is the doing of God. So in Joseph's case (Gen. 39:21). Especially towards Israel (Ps. 106: 46; cf. Prov. 16:7). **10. worse liking**—looking less healthy. **your sort**—of *your age,* or *class; lit.,* "circle." **endanger my head**—An arbitrary Oriental despot could, in a fit of wrath at his orders having been disobeyed, command the offender to be instantly decapitated. **11. Melzar**—rather, the steward, or chief butler, entrusted by Ashpenaz with furnishing the daily portion to the youths [GESENIUS]. The word is still in use in Persia. **12. pulse**—The *Hebrew* expresses any vegetable grown from *seeds,* i.e., vegetable food in general [GESENIUS]. **13-15.** Illustrating Deuteronomy 8:3, "Man doth not live by bread only, but by every word that proceedeth out of the mouth of the Lord." **17. God gave them knowledge**—(Exod. 31:2, 3; I Kings 3:12; Job. 32:8; Jas. 1:5, 17). **Daniel had understanding in . . . dreams**—God thus made one of the despised covenant people eclipse the Chaldean sages in the very science on which they most prided themselves. So Joseph in the court of Pharaoh (Gen. 40:5; 41:1-8). Daniel, in these praises of his own "understanding," speaks not through vanity, but by the direction of God, as one transported out of himself. See my *Introduction,* "CONTENTS OF THE BOOK." **18. brought them in**—i.e., not only Daniel and his three friends, but other youths (vs. 3; and vs. 19, "among *them all*). **19. stood . . . before the king**—i.e., were advanced to a position of favor near the throne. **20. ten times**—lit., "ten hands." **magicians**—properly, "sacred scribes, skilled in the sacred writings, a class of Egyptian priests" [GESENIUS]; from a *Hebrew* root, "a pen." The word in our *English Version,* "magicians," comes from *mag,* i.e., "a priest." The Magi formed one of the six divisions of the Medes. **astrologers**—*Hebrew,* "enchanters," from a root, "to conceal," practisers of the occult arts. **21. Daniel continued . . . unto . . . first year of Cyrus**—(II Chron. 36:22; Ezra 1:1). Not that he did not continue *beyond* that year, but the expression is designed to mark the fact that he who was one of the first captives taken to Babylon, lived to see the end of the captivity. See my *Introduction,* "SIGNIFICANCE OF THE BABYLONIAN EXILE." In ch. 10:1 he is mentioned as living "in the third year of Cyrus." See *Margin Note,* on the use of "till," (Ps. 110:1, 112:8).

CHAPTER 2

Vss. 1-49. NEBUCHADNEZZAR'S DREAM: DANIEL'S INTERPRETATION OF IT, AND ADVANCEMENT. **1. second year of . . . Nebuchadnezzar**—Ch. 1:5 shows that "three years" had elapsed since Nebuchadnezzar had taken Jerusalem. The solution of this difficulty is: Nebuchadnezzar first ruled as subordinate to his father Nabopolassar, to which time ch. 1 refers; whereas "the second year" in ch. 2 is dated from his sole sovereignty. The very difficulty is a proof of genuineness; all was clear to the writer and the original readers from *their* knowledge of the circumstances, and so he adds no explanation. A forger would not *introduce* difficulties; the author did not *then* see any difficulty in the case. Nebuchadnezzar is called "king" (ch. 1:1), *by anticipation.* Before he left Judea, he became actual king by the death of his father, and the Jews always called him "king," as commander of the invading army. **dreams**—It is significant that not to Daniel, but to the-then-world-ruler, Nebuchadnezzar, the dream is vouchsafed. It was from the first of its repre-

sentatives who had conquered the theocracy, that the world power was to learn its doom, as about to be in its turn subdued, and for ever, by the kingdom of God. As this vision opens, so that in ch. 7 developing the same truth more fully, closes the first part. Nebuchadnezzar, as vicegerent of God (vs. 37; cf. Jer. 25:9; Ezek. 28:12-15; Isa. 44:28; 45:1; Rom. 13:1), is honored with the revelation in the form of a dream, the appropriate form to one outside the kingdom of God. So in the cases of Abimelech, Pharaoh, etc. (Gen. 20 and 41), especially as the heathen attached such importance to dreams. Still it is not he, but an Israelite, who interprets it. Heathendom is passive, Israel active, in divine things, so that the glory redounds to "the God of heaven." **2. Chaldeans**—here, a certain order of priest-magicians, who wore a peculiar dress, like that seen on the gods and deified men in the Assyrian sculptures. Probably they belonged exclusively to the Chaldeans, the original tribe of the Babylonian nation, just as the Magians were properly Medes. **3. troubled to know the dream**—He awoke in alarm, remembering that something solemn had been presented to him in a dream, without being able to recall the form in which it had clothed itself. His thoughts on the unprecedented greatness to which his power had attained (vs. 29) made him anxious to know what the issue of all this should be. God meets this wish in the way most calculated to impress him. **4.** Here begins the Chaldee portion of Daniel, which continues to the end of ch. 7. In it the course, character, and crisis of the Gentile power are treated; whereas, in the other parts, which are in Hebrew, the things treated apply more particularly to the Jews and Jerusalem. **Syriac**—the Aramean Chaldee, the vernacular tongue of the king and his court; the prophet, by mentioning it here, hints at the reason of his own adoption of it from this point. **live for ever**—a formula in addressing kings, like our "Long live the king!" Cf. I Kings 1:31. **5. The thing**—i.e., The dream, "is gone from me." GESENIUS translates, "The *decree* is gone forth from me," irrevocable (cf. Isa. 45:23); viz., that you shall be executed, if you do not tell both the dream and the interpretation. *English Version* is simpler, which supposes the king himself to have forgotten the dream. Pretenders to supernatural knowledge often bring on themselves their own punishment. **cut in pieces**—(I Sam. 15:33). **houses . . . dunghill**—rather, "a morass heap." The Babylonian houses were built of sun-dried bricks; when demolished, the rain dissolves the whole into a mass of mire, in the wet land, near the river [STUART]. As to the consistency of this cruel threat with Nebuchadnezzar's character, see ch. 4:17, "basest of men"; Jeremiah 39:5, 6; 52:9-11. **6. rewards**—lit., "presents *poured out in* lavish profusion." **8. gain . . . time**—lit., "buy." Cf. Ephesians 5:16; Colossians 4:5, where the sense is somewhat different. **the thing is gone from me**—(See *Note,* vs. 5). **9. one decree**—There can be no second one reversing the first (Esther 4:11). **corrupt**—deceitful. **till the time be changed**—till a new state of things arrive, either by my ceasing to trouble myself about the dream, or by a change of government (which perhaps the agitation caused by the dream made Nebuchadnezzar to forebode, and so to suspect the Chaldeans of plotting). **tell . . . dream, and I shall know . . . ye can show . . . interpretation**—If ye cannot tell the past, a dream actually presented to me, how can ye know, and show, the future events prefigured in it? **10. There is not a man . . . that can show**—God makes the heathen, out of their own mouth, condemn their impotent pretensions to supernatural knowledge, in order to bring out in brighter contrast His power to reveal secrets to His servants, though but "men upon the earth" (cf. vss. 22, 23). **therefore . . .**—i.e., If such things could be done by men, other absolute princes would have required them from their magicians; as they have not, it is proof such things cannot be done and cannot be reasonably asked from us. **11. gods, whose dwelling is not with flesh**—answering to "no man *upon the earth*"; for there were, in their belief, "men *in heaven*," viz., men deified; e.g., Nimrod. The *supreme* gods are referred to here, who alone, in the Chaldean view, could solve the difficulty, but who do not communicate with men. The *inferior* gods, intermediate between men and the supreme gods, are unable to solve it. Contrast with this heathen idea of the utter severance of God from man, John 1:14, "The Word was made *flesh,* and *dwelt* among us"; Daniel was in this case made His representative. **12, 13.** Daniel and his companions do not seem to have been actually numbered among the Magi or Chaldeans, and so were not summoned before the king. Providence ordered it so that all mere human wisdom should be shown vain before His divine power, through His servant, was put forth. Verse 24 shows that the decree for slaying the wise men had not been actually executed when Daniel interposed. **14. captain of the king's guard**—commanding the executioners (see *Margin;* and Gen. 37:36, *Margin*). **15. Why is the decree so hasty**—Why were not all of us consulted before the decree for the execution of all was issued? **the thing**—the agitation of the king as to his dream, and his abortive consultation of the Chaldeans. It is plain from this that Daniel was till now ignorant of the whole matter. **16. Daniel went in**—perhaps not in person, but by the mediation of some courtier who had access to the king. His first direct interview seems to have been verse 25 [BARNES]. **time**—The king granted "time" to Daniel, though he would not do so to the Chaldeans because they betrayed their lying purpose by requiring him to tell the dream, which Daniel did not. Providence doubtless influenced his mind, already favorable (ch. 1:19, 20), to show special favor to Daniel. **17.** Here appears the reason why Daniel sought "time" (vs. 16), viz., he wished to engage his friends to join him in prayer to God to reveal the dream to him. **18.** An illustration of the power of united prayer (Matt. 18:19). The same instrumentality rescued Peter from his peril (Acts 12:5-12). **19. revealed . . . in . . . night vision**—(Job 33:15, 16). **20. answered**—responded to God's goodness by praises. **name of God**—*God in His revelation of Himself* by acts of love, "wisdom, and might" (Jer. 32:19). **21. changeth . . . times . . . seasons**— "He herein gives a general preparatory intimation, that the dream of Nebuchadnezzar is concerning the changes and successions of kingdoms" [JEROME]. The "times" are the *phases* and periods of *duration* of empires (cf. ch. 7:25; I Chron. 12:32; 29:30; the "seasons" the *fitting* times for their culmination, decline, and fall (Eccles. 3:1; Acts 1:7; I Thess. 5:1). The vicissitudes of states, with their times and seasons, are not regulated by chance or fate, as the heathen thought, but by God. **removed kings**—(Job 12:18; Ps. 75:6, 7; Jer. 27:5; cf. I Sam. 2:7, 8). **giveth wisdom**—(I Kings 3:9-12; Jas. 1:5). **22. revealeth**—(Job 12:22). So spiritually (Eph. 1:17, 18). **knoweth what is in . . . darkness**—(Ps. 139: 11, 12; Heb. 4:13). **light . . . him**—(Jas. 1:17; I John 1:4). *Apocalypse* (or "revelation") signifies a di-

vine, *prophecy* a human, activity. Cf. I Corinthians 14:6, where the two are distinguished. The prophet is connected with the outer world, addressing to the congregation the words with which the Spirit of God supplies him; he *speaks* in the Spirit, but the apocalyptic seer *is in* the Spirit in his whole person (Rev. 1:10; 4:2). The form of the apocalyptic revelation (the very term meaning that the *veil* that hides the invisible world is *taken off*) is subjectively either the *dream,* or, higher, the *vision.* The interpretation of Nebuchadnezzar's dream was a preparatory education to Daniel himself. By gradual steps, each revelation preparing him for the succeeding one, God fitted him for disclosures becoming more and more special. In chs. 2 and 4 he is but an interpreter of Nebuchadnezzar's dreams; then he has a dream himself, but it is only a vision in a dream of the night (ch. 7:1, 2); then follows a vision in a waking state (ch. 8:1-3); lastly, in the two final revelations (chs. 9 and 10-12) the ecstatic state is no longer needed. The progression in the *form* answers to the progression in the *contents* of his prophecy; at first general *outlines,* and these afterwards filled up with minute chronological and historical *details,* such as are not found in the Revelation of John, though, as became the New Testament, the form of revelation is the highest, viz., clear waking visions [AUBERLEN]. **23. thee . . . thee**—He ascribes all the glory to God. **God of my fathers**—Thou hast shown Thyself the same God of grace to me, a captive exile, as Thou didst to Israel of old and this on account of the *covenant* made with our "fathers" (Luke 1:54, 55; cf. Ps. 106:45). **given me wisdom and might**—Thou being the fountain of both; referring to vs. 20. Whatever *wise ability* I have to stay the execution of the king's cruel decree, is Thy gift. **me . . . we . . . us**—The revelation was given to Daniel, as "me" implies; yet with just modesty he joins his friends with him; because it was to their joint prayers, and not to his individually, that he owed the revelation from God. **known . . . the king's matter**—the very words in which the Chaldeans had denied the *possibility* of *any man on earth* telling the dream ("not a man upon the earth can show *the king's matter,*" (vs. 10). Impostors are compelled by the God of truth to eat up their own words. **24. Therefore**—because of having received the divine communication. **bring me in before the king**—implying that he had not previously been in person before the king (*Note,* vs. 16). **25. I have found a man**—Like all courtiers, in announcing agreeable tidings, he ascribes the merit of the discovery to himself [JEROME]. So far from it being a discrepancy, that he says nothing of the previous understanding between him and Daniel, or of Daniel's application to the king (vss. 15, 16), it is just what we should expect. Arioch would not dare to tell an absolute despot that he had stayed the execution of his sanguinary decree, on his own responsibility; but would, in the first instance, secretly stay it until Daniel had got, by application from the king, the time required, without Arioch seeming to know of Daniel's application as the cause of the respite; then, when Daniel had received the revelation, Arioch would in trembling haste bring him in, as if then for the first time he had "found" him. The very difficulty when cleared up is a proof of genuineness, as it never would be *introduced* by a forger. **27. cannot**—Daniel, being learned in all the lore of the Chaldeans (ch. 1:4), could authoritatively declare the *impossibility* of mere man solving the king's difficulty. **soothsayers**—from a root, "to cut off"; referring to their *cutting* the heavens into divisions, and so guessing at men's destinies from the place of the stars at one's birth. **28. God** —in contrast to "the wise men," etc. (vs. 27). **revealeth secrets**—(Amos 3:7; 4:13). Cf. Genesis 41: 45, *Zaphnath-paaneah,* "revealer of secrets," the title given to Joseph. **the latter days**—lit., "in the after days" (vs. 29); "hereafter" (Gen. 49:1). It refers to the whole future, including the Messianic days, which is the final dispensation (Isa. 2:2). **visions of thy head**—conceptions formed in the brain. **29.** God met with a revelation Nebuchadnezzar, who had been meditating on 'the future destiny of his vast empire. **30. not . . . for any wisdom that I have**—not *on account of* any previous wisdom which I may have manifested (ch. 1:17, 20). The specially-favored servants of God in all ages disclaim merit in themselves and ascribe all to the grace and power of God (Gen. 41:16; Acts 3:12). The "as for me," disclaiming extraordinary merit, contrasts elegantly with "as for thee," whereby Daniel courteously, but without flattery, implies, that God honored Nebuchadnezzar, as His vicegerent over the world kingdoms, with a revelation on the subject uppermost in his thoughts, the ultimate destinies of those kingdoms. **for their sakes that shall make known . . .**—a Chaldee idiom for, "to the intent that the interpretation may be made known to the king." **the thoughts of thy heart**—thy subject of thought before falling asleep. Or, perhaps the *probation of Nebuchadnezzar's character* through this revelation may be the meaning intended (cf. II Chron. 32:31; Luke 2:35). **31.** The world power in its totality appears as a colossal human form: Babylon the head of gold, Medo-Persia the breast and *two* arms of silver, Græco-Macedonia the belly and *two* thighs of brass, and Rome, with its Germano-Slavonic offshoots, the legs of iron and feet of iron and clay, the fourth still existing. Those kingdoms only are mentioned which stand in some relation to the kingdom of God; of these none is left out; the final establishment of that kingdom is the aim of His moral government of the world. The colossus of metal stands on weak feet, of clay. All man's glory is as ephemeral and worthless as chaff (cf. I Pet. 1:34). But the kingdom of God, small and unheeded as a "stone" on the ground is compact in its homogeneous unity; whereas the world power, in its heterogeneous constituents successively supplanting one another, contains the elements of decay. The relation of the stone to the mountain is that of the kingdom of the cross (Matt. 16:23; Luke 24:26) to the kingdom of glory, the latter beginning, and the former ending when the kingdom of God breaks in pieces the kingdoms of the world (Rev. 11:15). Christ's contrast between the two kingdoms refers to this passage. **a great image** —lit., "*one* image that was great." Though the kingdoms were different, it was essentially *one* and the same world power under different phases, just as the image was *one,* though the parts were of different metals. **32.** On ancient coins states are often represented by human figures. The head and higher parts signify the earlier times; the lower, the later times. The metals become successively baser and baser, implying the growing degeneracy from worse to worse. Hesiod, 200 years before Daniel, had compared the four ages to the four metals in the same order; the idea is sanctioned here by Holy Writ. It was perhaps one of those fragments of revelation among the heathen, derived from the tradition as to the fall of man. The metals lessen in *specific gravity,* as they go downwards; silver is not so heavy as gold, brass not so heavy as silver, and

iron not so heavy as brass, the *weight* thus being arranged in the reverse of stability [TREGELLES]. Nebuchadnezzar derived his authority from God, not from man, nor as responsible to man. But the Persian king was so far dependent on others that he could not deliver Daniel from the princes (ch. 6:14, 15); contrast ch. 5:18, 19, as to Nebuchadnezzar's power from God, whom he would he slew, and whom he would he kept alive" (cf. Ezra 7:14; Esther 1:13-16). Græco-Macedonia betrays its deterioration in its divisions, not united as Babylon and Persia. Iron is stronger than brass, but inferior in other respects; so Rome hardy and strong to tread down the nations, but less kingly and showing its chief deterioration in its last state. Each successive kingdom incorporates its predecessor (cf. ch. 5:28). Power that in Nebuchadnezzar's hands was a God-derived (vss. 37, 38) autocracy, in the Persian king's was a rule resting on his nobility of person and birth, the nobles being his equals in rank, but not in office; in Greece, an aristocracy not of birth, but individual influence, in Rome, lowest of all, dependent entirely on popular choice, the emperor being appointed by popular military election. **33.** As the two arms of silver denote the kings of the Medes and Persians [JOSEPHUS]; and the two thighs of brass the Seleucidæ of Syria and Lagidæ of Egypt, the two leading sections into which Græco-Macedonia parted, so the two legs of iron signify the two Roman consuls [NEWTON]. The clay, in verse 41, "potter's clay," verse 43, "miry clay," means "earthenware," hard but brittle (cf. Ps. 2:9; Rev. 2:27, where the same image is used of the same event); the feet are stable while bearing only direct pressure, but easily broken to pieces by a blow (vs. 34), the iron intermixed not retarding, but hastening, such a result. **34. stone**—Messiah and His kingdom (Gen. 49:24; Ps. 118:22; Isa. 28:16). In its relations to Israel, it is a "stone of stumbling" (Isa. 8:14; Acts 4:11; I Pet. 2:7, 8) on which both houses of Israel are broken, not destroyed (Matt. 21:32). In its relation to the Church, the same stone which destroys the image is the foundation of the Church (Eph. 2:20). In its relation to the Gentile world power, the stone is its destroyer (vss. 35, 44; cf. Zech. 12:3). Christ saith (Matt. 21:44, referring to Isa. 8:14, 15), "Whosoever shall fall on this stone [i.e., stumble, and be offended, at Him, as the *Jews* were, from whom, therefore, He says, 'The kingdom shall be taken'] shall be *broken;* but [referring to vss. 34, 35] on whomsoever it shall fall [referring to *the world power* which had been the instrument of *breaking* the Jews], it will [not merely *break,* but] *grind him to powder*" (I Cor. 15:24). The falling of the stone of the feet of the image cannot refer to Christ at His first advent, for the fourth kingdom was not then as yet divided—no toes were in existence (see *Note,* vs. 44). **cut out**—viz., from "the mountain" (vs. 45); viz., Mount Zion (Isa. 2:2), and antitypically, the heavenly mount of the Father's glory, from whom Christ came. **without hands**—explained in vs. 44, "The *God of heaven* shall set up a kingdom," as contrasted with the image which was made *with hands* of man. Messiah not created by human agency, but conceived by the Holy Ghost (Matt. 1:20; Luke 1:35; cf. Zech. 4:6; Mark 14:58; Heb. 9:11, 24). So "not made with hands," i.e., "heavenly," II Corinthians 5:1; *spiritual,* Colossians 2:11. The world kingdoms were reared by *human* ambition: but this is the "kingdom of *heaven*"; "not of this world" (John 18:36). As the fourth kingdom, or Rome, was represented in a twofold state, first strong, with legs of iron, then weak, with toes part of iron, part of clay; so this fifth kingdom, that of Christ, is seen conversely, first insignificant as a "stone," then as a "mountain" filling the whole earth. The ten toes are the ten lesser kingdoms into which the Roman kingdom was finally to be divided; this tenfold division here hinted at is not specified in detail till the seventh chapter. The fourth empire originally was bounded in Europe pretty nearly by the line of the Rhine and Danube; in Asia by the Euphrates. In Africa it possessed Egypt and the north coasts; South Britain and Dacia were afterwards added but were ultimately resigned. The ten kingdoms do not arise until a deterioration (by mixing clay with the iron) has taken place; they are in existence when Christ comes in glory, and then are broken in pieces. The ten have been sought for in the invading hosts of the fifth and sixth century. But though many provinces were then severed from Rome as independent kingdoms, the dignity of emperor still continued, and the imperial power was exercised over Rome itself for two centuries. So the tenfold divisions cannot be looked for before A.D. 731. But the East is not to be excluded, five toes being on each foot. Thus no point of time before the overthrow of the empire at the taking of Constantinople by the Turks (A.D. 1453) can be assigned for the division. It seems, therefore, that the definite ten will be the ultimate development of the Roman empire just before the rise of Antichrist, who shall overthrow three of the kings, and, after three and a half years, he himself be overthrown by Christ in person. Some of the ten kingdoms will, doubtless, be the same as some past and present divisions of the old Roman empire, which accounts for the *continuity* of the connection between the toes and legs, a gap of centuries not being interposed, as is objected by opponents of the futurist theory. The lists of the ten made by the latter differ from one another; and they are set aside by the fact that they include countries which were never Roman, and exclude one whole section of the empire, viz., the East [TREGELLES]. **upon his feet**—the last state of the Roman empire. Not "upon his *legs*." Cf. "in the days of these kings" (*Note*, vs. 44). **35. broken ... together**—excluding a contemporaneous existence of the kingdom of the world and the kingdom of God (in its *manifested*, as distinguished from its *spiritual*, phase). The latter is not gradually to wear away the former, but to destroy it at once, and utterly (II Thess. 1:7-10; 2:8). However, the *Hebrew* may be translated, "in one discriminate mass." **chaff**—image of the ungodly, as they shall be dealt with in the judgment (Ps. 1:4, 5; Matt. 3:12). **summer threshing-floors**—Grain was winnowed in the East on an elevated space in the open air, by throwing the grain into the air with a shovel, so that the wind might clear away the chaff. **no place ... found for them**—(Rev. 20:11; cf. Ps. 37:10, 36; 103:16). **became ... mountain**—cut out of the mountain (vs. 45) originally, it ends in *becoming a mountain*. So the kingdom of God, coming from heaven originally, ends in heaven being established on earth (Rev. 21:1-3). **filled ... earth**—(Isa. 11:9; Hab. 2:14). It is to do so in connection with Jerusalem as the mother Church (Ps. 80:9; Isa. 2:2, 3). **36. we**—Daniel and his three friends. **37. Thou ... art a king of kings**—The committal of power in fullest plenitude belongs to Nebuchadnezzar personally, as having made Babylon the mighty empire it was. In twenty-three years after him the empire was ended: with him its greatness is identified (ch. 4:30), his

successors having done nothing notable. Not that he actually ruled every part of the globe, but that God granted him illimitable dominion *in whatever direction his ambition led him,* Egypt, Nineveh, Arabia, Syria, Tyre, and its Phœnician colonies (Jer. 27:5-8). Cf. as to Cyrus, Ezra 1:2. **38. men ... beasts ... fowls**—the dominion originally designed for man (Gen. 1:28; 2:19, 20), forfeited by sin; temporarily delegated to Nebuchadnezzar and the world powers; but, as they abuse the trust for self, instead of for God, to be taken from them by the Son of man, who will exercise it for God, restoring in His person to man the lost inheritance (Ps. 8:4-6). **Thou art ... head of gold**—alluding to the riches of Babylon, hence called "the golden city" (Isa. 14:4; Jer. 51:7; Rev. 18:16). **39.** That Medo-Persia is the second kingdom appears from ch. 5:28 and 8:20. Cf. II Chronicles 36:20; Isaiah 21:2. **inferior**—"The kings of Persia were the worst race of men that ever governed an empire" [PRIDEAUX]. Politically (which is the main point of view here) the power of the central government in which the nobles shared with the king, being weakened by the growing independence of the provinces, was inferior to that of Nebuchadnezzar, whose sole word was law throughout his empire. **brass**—The Greeks (the third empire, ch. 8:21; 10:20; 11:2-4) were celebrated for the *brazen* armor of their warriors. JEROME fancifully thinks that the brass, as being a *clear-sounding* metal, refers to the *eloquence* for which Greece was famed. The "belly," in verse 32, may refer to the drunkenness of Alexander and the luxury of the Ptolemies [TIRINUS]. **over all the earth**—Alexander commanded that he should be called "king of all the world" [JUSTIN, 12. sec. 16. 9; ARRIAN, Exp. Alex. 7. sec. 15]. The four successors (*diadochi*) who divided Alexander's dominions at his death, of whom the Seleucidæ in Syria and the Lagidæ in Egypt were chief, held the same empire. **40. iron**—This vision sets forth the *character* of the Roman power, rather than its territorial extent [TREGELLES]. **breaketh in pieces**—So, in righteous retribution, itself will at last be *broken in pieces* (vs. 44) by the kingdom of God (Rev. 13:10). **41-43. feet ... toes ... part ... clay ... iron**—explained presently, "the kingdom shall be partly strong, partly broken" (rather, "brittle," as earthenware); and verse 43, "they shall mingle ... with the seed of men," i.e., there will be power (in its deteriorated form, *iron*) mixed up with that which is wholly of man, and therefore brittle; power in the hands of the people having no internal stability, though something is left of the strength of the iron [TREGELLES]. NEWTON, who understands the Roman empire to be parted into the ten kingdoms already (whereas TREGELLES makes them *future*), explains the "clay" mixture as the blending of barbarous nations with Rome by intermarriages and alliances, in which there was no stable amalgamation, though the ten kingdoms retained much of Rome's strength. The "mingling with the seed of men" (vs. 44) seems to refer to Genesis 6:2, where the marriages of the seed of godly Seth with the daughters of ungodly Cain are described in similar words. The reference, therefore, seems to be to the blending of the Christianized Roman empire with the pagan nations, a deterioration being the result. Efforts have been often made to reunite the parts into one great empire, as by Charlemagne and Napoleon, but in vain. Christ alone shall effect that. **44. in the days of these kings**—in the days of these kingdoms, i.e., of the last of the four. So Christianity was set up when Rome had become mistress of

Judea and the world (Luke 2:1, etc.) [NEWTON]. Rather, "in the days of these kings," answers to "upon his feet" (vs. 34); i.e., the ten *toes* (vs. 42), or ten kings, the final state of the Roman empire. For "these kings" cannot mean the four successional monarchies, as they do not *coexist* as the holders of power; if the fourth had been meant, the *singular,* not the *plural,* would be used. The falling of the stone on the image must mean, *destroying judgment* on the fourth Gentile power, not gradual evangelization of it by grace; and the destroying judgment cannot be dealt by Christians, for they are taught to submit to the powers that be, so that it must be dealt by Christ Himself at His coming again. We live under the divisions of the Roman empire which began 1400 years ago, and which at the time of His coming shall be definitely *ten.* All that had failed in the hand of man shall then pass away, and that which is kept in His own hand shall be introduced. Thus the second chapter is the alphabet of the subsequent prophetic statements in Daniel [TREGELLES]. **God of heaven . . . kingdom**—hence the phrase, "the kingdom of heaven" (Matt. 3:2). **not . . . left to other people**—as the Chaldees had been forced to leave their kingdom to the Medo-Persians, and these to the Greeks, and these to the Romans (Mic. 4:7; Luke 1:32, 33). **break . . . all**—(Isa. 60: 12; I Cor. 15:24). **45. without hands**—(*Note,* vs. 35). **46. fell upon . . . face, and worshipped Daniel** —worshipping God in the person of Daniel. Symbolical of the future prostration of the world power before Messiah and His kingdom (Phil. 2:10). As other servants of God refused such honors (Acts 10: 25, 26; 14:13-15; Rev. 22:8, 9), and Daniel (ch. 1:8) would not taste defiled food, nor give up prayer to God at the cost of his life (ch. 6), it seems likely that Daniel rejected the proffered divine honors. The word "answered" (vs. 47) implies that Daniel had objected to these honors; and in compliance with his objection, "the king *answered,* Of a truth, your God is a God of gods." Daniel had disclaimed all personal merit in vs. 30, giving GOD all the glory (cf. vs. 45). **commanded . . . sweet odours** —divine honors (Ezra 6:10). It is not said his command was executed. **47. Lord of kings**—The world power shall at last have to acknowledge this (Rev. 17:14; 19:16); even as Nebuchadnezzar, who had been the God-appointed "king of kings" (vs. 37), but who had abused the trust, is constrained by God's servant to acknowledge that God is the true "Lord of kings." **48.** One reason for Nebuchadnezzar having been vouchsafed such a dream is here seen; viz., that Daniel might be promoted, and the captive people of God be comforted: the independent state of the captives during the exile and the alleviation of its hardships, were much due to Daniel. **49. Daniel requested**—Contrast this honorable remembrance of his humble friends in his elevation with the spirit of the children of the world in the chief butler's case (Gen. 40:23; Eccles. 9:15, 16; Amos 6:6). **in the gate**—the place of holding courts of justice and levees in the East (Esther 2:19; Job 29:7). So "the Sublime *Porte,*" or "Gate," denotes the sultan's government, his counsels being formerly held in the entrance of his palace. Daniel was a chief counsellor of the king, and president over the governors of the different orders into which the Magi were divided.

CHAPTER 3

Vss. 1-30. NEBUCHADNEZZAR'S IDOLATROUS IMAGE; SHADRACH, MESHACH, AND ABED-NEGO ARE DE-LIVERED FROM THE FURNACE. Between the vision of Nebuchadnezzar in the second chapter and that of Daniel in the seventh, four narratives of Daniels and his friends' personal history are introduced. As chapters 2 and 7 go together, so chapters 3 and 6 (the deliverance from the lions' den), and chapters 4 and 5. Of these last two pairs, the former shows God's nearness to save His saints when faithful to Him, at the very time they seem to be crushed by the world power. The second pair shows, in the case of the two kings of the first monarchy, how God can suddenly humble the world power in the height of its insolence. The latter advances from mere self-glorification, in the fourth chapter, to open opposition to God in the fifth. Nebuchadnezzar demands homage to be paid to his image (ch. 3), and boasts of his power (ch. 4). But Belshazzar goes further, blaspheming God by polluting His holy vessels. There is a similar progression in the conduct of God's people. Shadrach, Meshach, and Abednego refuse *positive* homage to the image of the world power (ch. 3); Daniel will not yield it even a *negative* homage, by omitting for a time the worship of God (ch. 6). Jehovah's power manifested for the saints against the world in individual histories (ch. 3-6) is exhibited in chapters 2 and 7, in worldwide prophetical pictures; the former heightening the effect of the latter. The miracles wrought in behalf of Daniel and his friends were a manifestation of God's glory in Daniel's person, as the representative of the theocracy before the Babylonian king, who deemed himself almighty, at a time when God could not manifest it in His people as a body. They tended also to secure, by their impressive character, that respect for the covenant people on the part of the heathen powers which issued in Cyrus' decree, not only restoring the Jews, but ascribing honor to the God of heaven, and commanding the building of the temple (Ezra 1:1-4) [AUBERLEN]. **1. image**—Nebuchadnezzar's confession of God did not prevent him being a worshipper of. idols, besides. Ancient idolaters thought that each nation had its own gods, and that, in addition to these, foreign gods might be worshipped. The Jewish religion was the only exclusive one that claimed *all* homage for Jehovah as the *only* true God. Men will in times of trouble confess God, if they are allowed to retain their favorite heart-idols. The image was that of Bel, the Babylonian tutelary god; or rather, Nebuchadnezzar *himself,* the personification and representative of the Babylonian empire, as suggested to him by the dream (ch. 2:38), "*Thou* art this head *of gold.*" The interval between the dream and the event here was about nineteen years. Nebuchadnezzar had just returned from finishing the Jewish and Syrian wars, the spoils of which would furnish the means of rearing such a colossal statue [PRIDEAUX]. The colossal size makes it likely that the frame was wood, overlaid with gold. The "height," 60 cubits, is so out of proportion with the "breadth," exceeding it ten times, that it seems best to suppose the *thickness* from breast to back to be intended, which is exactly the right proportion of a well-formed man [AUGUSTINE, *De Civitate Dei,* 15. 20]. PRIDEAUX thinks the 60 cubits refer to *the image and pedestal together,* the image being 27 cubits high, or 40 feet, the pedestal 33 cubits, or 50 feet. HERODOTUS (1. 183) confirms this by mentioning a *similar* image, 40 *feet* high, in the temple of Belus at Babylon. It was not the *same* image, for the one here was on the plain of Dura, not in the city. **2. princes**—"satraps" of provinces [GESENIUS]. **captains**—*rulers*, not exclusively military. **sheriffs**—men learned in the law, like the Arab *mufti* [GESENIUS]. **3. stood before the image**—in an attitude of devotion. Whatever the king approved of, they all approve of. There is no stability of principle in the ungodly. **4.** The arguments of the persecutor are in brief, Turn or burn. **5. cornet**—A wind instrument, like the French horn, is meant. **flute**—a pipe or pipes, not blown transversely as our "flute," but by mouthpieces at the end. **sackbut**—a triangular stringed instrument, having short strings, the sound being on a high sharp key. **psaltery**—a kind of harp. **dulcimer**—a bagpipe consisting of two pipes, thrust through a leathern bag, emitting a sweet plaintive sound. *Chaldee sumponya,* the modern Italian *zampogna,* Asiatic *zambonja.* **fall down**—that the recusants might be the more readily detected. **6.** No other nation but the Jews would feel this edict oppressive; for it did not prevent them worshipping their own gods *besides.* It was evidently aimed at the Jews by those jealous of their high position in the king's court, who therefore induced the king to pass an edict as to all recusants, representing their refusal of homage as an act of treason to Nebuchadnezzar as civil and religious "head" of the empire. So the edict under Darius (6th ch.) was aimed against the Jews by those jealous of Daniel's influence. The literal image of Nebuchadnezzar is a typical prophecy of "the image of the beast," connected with mystical Babylon, in Revelation 13:14. The second mystical beast there causeth the earth, and them that dwell therein, to worship the first beast, and that as many as would not, should be killed (Rev. 13:12, 15). **furnace**—a common mode of punishment in Babylon (Jer. 29:22). It is not necessary to suppose that the furnace was made for the occasion. Cf. "brick kiln," II Samuel 12:31. Any furnace for common purposes in the vicinity of Dura would serve. CHARDIN, in his travels (A.D. 1671-1677), mentions that in Persia, to terrify those who took advantage of scarcity to sell provisions at exorbitant prices, the cooks were roasted over a slow fire, and the bakers cast into a burning oven. **7.** None of the Jews seem to have been present, except the *officers,* summoned specially. **8. accused the Jews**—lit., "ate the rent limbs," or flesh of the Jews (cf. Job 31:31; Ps. 14:4; 27:2; Jer. 10:25). Not probably in general, but as verse 12 states, Shadrach, Meshach, and Abednego. Why Daniel was not summoned does not appear. Probably he was in some distant part of the empire on state business, and the general summons (vs. 2) had not time to reach him before the dedication. Also, the Jews' enemies found it more politic to begin by attacking Shadrach, Meshach, and Abed-nego, who were nearer at hand, and had less influence, before they proceeded to attack Daniel. **9. live for ever**—A preface of flattery is closely akin to the cruelty that follows. So Acts 24:2, 3, etc., Tertullus in accusing Paul before Felix. **12. serve not thy gods**—not only not the golden image, but also *not any of* Nebuchadnezzar's *gods.* **13. bring**—Instead of commanding their immediate execution, as in the case of the Magi (ch. 2:12), Providence inclined him to command the recusants to be *brought* before him, so that their noble "testimony" for God might be given before the world powers "against them" (Matt. 10:18), to the edification of the Church in all ages. **14. Is it true**—rather, as *Margin* [THEODOTION], "Is it *purposely* that . . . ?" Cf. the *Hebrew,* Numbers 35:20, 22. Notwithstanding his "fury," his past favor for them disposes him to give them the

opportunity of excusing themselves on the ground that their disobedience had not been *intentional;* so he gives them another trial to see whether they would still worship the image. **15. who is that God** —so Sennacherib's taunt (II Kings 18:35), and Pharaoh's (Exod. 5:2). **16. not careful to answer thee** —rather, "We have *no need* to answer thee"; thou art determined on thy side, and our mind is made up not to worship the image: there is therefore no use in our arguing as if we could be shaken from our principles. Hesitation, or parleying with sin, is fatal; unhesitating decision is the only safety, where the path of duty is clear (Matt. 10:19, 28). **17. If it be so**—VATABLUS translates, "Assuredly." *English Version* agrees better with the original. The sense is, *If it be* our lot to be cast into the furnace, *our God* (quoted from Deut. 6:4) is able to deliver us (a reply to Nebuchadnezzar's challenge, "Who is that God that shall deliver you?"); and He will deliver us (either *from* death, or *in* death, II Tim. 4:17, 18). He will, *we trust,* literally deliver us, but certainly He will do so spiritually. **18. But if not . . .**—connected with vs. 18. "Whether our God deliver us, as He is able, or do not, we will not serve thy gods." Their service of God is not mercenary in its motive. Though He slay them, they will still trust in Him (Job 13:15). Their deliverance from sinful compliance was as great a miracle in the kingdom of grace, as that from the furnace was in the kingdom of nature. Their youth, and position as captives and friendless exiles, before the absolute world potentate and the horrid death awaiting them if they should persevere in their faith, all enhance the grace of God, which carried them through such an ordeal. **19. visage . . . changed**—He had shown forbearance (vss. 14, 15) as a favor to them, but now that they despise even his forbearance, anger "fills" him, and is betrayed in his whole countenance. **seven times more than it was wont**—lit., "than it was (ever) *seen* to be heated." *Seven* is the perfect number; i.e., it was made *as hot as possible.* Passion overdoes and defeats its own end, for the hotter the fire, the sooner were they likely to be put out of pain. **21. coats . . . hosen . . . hats**—HERODOTUS (1. 195) says that the Babylonian costume consisted of three parts: 1. wide, long pantaloons; 2. a woollen shirt; 3. an outer *mantle* with a girdle round it. So these are specified [GESENIUS], "their pantaloons, inner tunics (*hosen,* or stockings, are not commonly worn in the East), and outer mantles." Their being cast in so hurriedly, with all their garments on, enhanced the miracle in that not even the smell of fire passed on their clothes, though of delicate, inflammable material. **22. flame . . . slew those men** —(ch. 6:24; Ps. 7:16). **23. fell down**—not *cast down;* for those who brought the three youths to the furnace, perished by the flames themselves, and so could not *cast* them in. Here follows an addition in LXX, *Syrian, Arabic,* and *Vulgate versions.* "The Prayer of Azarias," and "The Song of the Three Holy Children." It is not in the *Chaldee.* The hymn was sung throughout the whole Church in their liturgies, from the earliest times (RUFINUS *in Symb. Ap.,* and ATHANASIUS). The "astonishment" of Nebuchadnezzar in verse 24 is made an argument for its genuineness, as if it explained the cause of his astonishment, viz., "they walked in the midst of the fire praising God, but the angel of the Lord came down into the oven" (vs. 1 and vs. 27 of the Aprocryphal addition). But verse 25 of *English Version* explains his astonishment, without need of any addition. **24. True, O king**—God extorted this confession from His enemies' own mouths. **25. four**

—whereas but three had been cast in. **loose**—whereas they had been cast in "bound." Nebuchadnezzar's question, in verse 24, is as if he can scarcely trust his own memory as to a fact so recent, now that he sees through an aperture in the furnace what seems to contradict it. **walking in . . . midst of . . . fire**—image of the godly unhurt, and at large (John 8:36), "in the midst of trouble" (Ps. 138:7; cf. Ps. 23:3, 4). They walked up and down in the fire, not leaving it, but waiting for God's time to bring them out, just as Jesus waited in the tomb as God's prisoner, till God should let Him out (Acts 2:26, 27). So Paul (II Cor. 12:8, 9). So Noah waited in the ark, after the flood, till God brought him forth (Gen. 8:12-18). **like the Son of God**—Unconsciously, like Saul, Caiaphas (John 11:49-52), and Pilate, he is made to utter divine truths. "Son of God" in *his* mouth means only an "angel" from heaven, as verse 28 proves. Cf. Job 1:6; 38:7; Psalm 34:7, 8; and the probably heathen centurion's exclamation (Matthew 27:54). The Chaldeans believed in *families* of gods: Bel, the supreme god, accompanied by the goddess Mylitta, being the father of the gods; thus the expression *he* meant: *one sprung from and sent by the gods. Really* it was the "messenger of the covenant," who herein gave a prelude to His incarnation. **26. the most high God**—He acknowledges Jehovah to be supreme above other gods (not that he ceased to believe in these); so he returns to his original confession, "your God is a God of gods" (ch. 2:47), from which he had swerved in the interim, perhaps intoxicated by his success in taking Jerusalem, whose God he therefore thought unable to defend it. **27. nor . . . an hair**—(Luke 12:7; 21:18). **fire had no power**—fulfilling Isaiah 43:2; cf. Hebrews 11:34. God alone is a "consuming fire" (Heb. 12:29). **nor . . . smell of fire**—cf. spiritually, I Thess. 5:22. **28.** In giving some better traits in Nebuchadnezzar's character, Daniel agrees with Jeremiah 39:11; 42:12. **changed the king's word**—have made the king's attempt to coerce into obedience vain. Have set aside his word (so "alter . . . word," Ezra 6:11) from regard to God. Nebuchadnezzar now admits that God's law should be obeyed, rather than his (Acts 5:29). **yielded . . . bodies**—viz., to the fire. **not serve**—by sacrificing. **nor worship**—by prostration of the body. Decision for God at last gains the respect even of the worldly (Prov. 16:7). **29.** This decree promulgated throughout the vast empire of Nebuchadnezzar must have tended much to keep the Jews from idolatry in the captivity and thenceforth (Ps. 76:10).

CHAPTER 4

Vss. 1-37. Edict of Nebuchadnezzar Containing His Second Dream, Relating to Himself. Punished with insanity for his haughtiness, he sinks to the level of the beasts (illustrating Ps. 49:6, 12). The opposition between bestial and human life, set forth here, is a key to interpret the symbolism in the seventh chapter concerning the beasts and the Son of man. After his conquests, and his building in fifteen days a new palace, according to the heathen historian, Abydenus (268 b.c.), whose account confirms Daniel, he ascended upon his palace roof (see vs. 29, *Margin*), whence he could see the surrounding city which he had built, and seized by some deity, he predicted the Persian conquest of Babylon, adding a prayer that the Persian leader might on his return be borne where there is no path of men,

and where the wild beasts graze (*language* evidently derived by tradition from vss. 32, 33, though the *application* is different). In his insanity, his excited mind would naturally think of the coming conquest of Babylon by the Medo-Persians, already foretold to him in ch. 2. **1. Peace**—the usual salutation in the East, *shalom,* whence "salaam." The primitive revelation of the fall, and man's alienation from God, made "peace" to be felt as the first and deepest want of man. The Orientals (as the East was the cradle of revelation) retained the word by tradition. **2. I thought it good**—"It was seemly before me" (Ps. 107:2-8). **signs**—tokens significant of God's omnipotent agency. The *plural* is used, as it comprises the marvellous dream, the marvellous interpretation of it, and its marvellous issue. **4. I was . . . at rest**—my wars over, my kingdom at peace. **flourishing**—"green." Image from a tree (Jer. 17:8). Prosperous (Job 15:32). **6.** It may seem strange that Daniel was not first summoned. But it was ordered by God's providence that he should be reserved to the last, in order that all mere human means should be proved vain, before God manifested His power through His servant; thus the haughty king was stripped of all fleshly confidences. The Chaldees were the king's recognized interpreters of dreams; whereas Daniel's interpretation of the one in ch. 2 had been a peculiar case, and very many years before; nor had he been consulted on such matters since. **8. Belteshazzar**—called so from the god Bel or Belus (see *Note,* ch. 1:7). **9. spirit of the holy gods**—Nebuchadnezzar speaks as a heathen, who yet has imbibed some notions of the true God. Hence he speaks of "gods" in the *plural* but gives the epithet "holy," which applies to Jehovah alone, the heathen gods making no pretension to purity, even in the opinion of their votaries (Deut. 32:31; cf. Isa. 63:11). "I know" refers to his knowledge of Daniel's skill many years before (ch. 2); hence he calls him "master of the magicians." **troubleth**—gives thee difficulty in explaining it. **10. tree**—So the Assyrian is compared to a "cedar" (Ezek. 31:3; cf. Ezek. 17:24). **in the midst of the earth**—denoting its conspicuous position as the center whence the imperial authority radiated in all directions. **12. beasts . . . shadow under it**—implying that God's purpose in establishing empires in the world is that they may be as trees affording men "fruits" for "meat," and a "shadow" for rest (cf. Lam. 4:20). But the world powers abuse their trust for self; therefore Messiah comes to plant the tree of His gospel kingdom, which alone shall realize God's purpose (Ezek. 17:23; Matt. 13:32). Herodotus (7. 19) mentions a dream (probably suggested by the tradition of this dream of Nebuchadnezzar in Daniel) which Xerxes had; viz., that he was crowned with olive, and that the branches of the olive filled the whole earth, but that afterwards the crown vanished from his head: signifying his universal dominion soon to come to an end. **13. watcher and an holy one**—rather, "even an holy one." Only *one* angel is intended, and he not one of the bad, but of the *holy* angels. Called a "watcher," because ever on the watch to execute God's will [Jerome], (Ps. 103:20, 21). Cf. as to their watchfulness, Revelation 4:8, "*full of eyes* within . . . they rest not day *and night.*" Also they watch good men committed to their charge (Ps. 34:7; Heb. 1:14); and watch over the evil to record their sins, and at God's bidding at last punish them (Jer. 4:16, 17), "watchers" applied to *human* instruments of God's vengeance. As to God (ch. 9:14; Job 7:12; 14:16; Jer. 44:27). In a good sense (Gen. 31:49; Jer. 31:28).

The idea of heavenly "watchers" under the supreme God (called in the *Zendavesta* of the Persian Zoroaster, *Ormuzd*) was founded on the primeval revelation as to evil angels having *watched* for an opportunity until they succeeded in tempting man to his ruin, and good angels ministering to God's servants (as Jacob, Gen. 28:15; 32:1, 2). Cf. the watching over Abraham for good, and over Sodom for wrath after long watching in vain for good men it, for whose sake He would spare it, Genesis 18; and over Lot for good, Genesis 19. Daniel fitly puts in Nebuchadnezzar's mouth the expression, though not found elsewhere in Scripture, yet substantially sanctioned by it (II Chron. 16:9; Prov. 15:3, Jer. 32:19), and natural to him according to Oriental modes of thought. **14. Hew down**—(Matt. 3:10; Luke 13:7). The holy (Jude 14) one incites his fellow angels to God's appointed work (cf. Rev. 14:15, 18). **beasts get away from under it**—It shall no longer afford them shelter (Ezek. 31:12). **15. stump**—The kingdom is still reserved secure for him at last, as a tree stump secured by a hoop of brass and iron from being split by the sun's heat, in the hope of its growing again (Isa. 11:1; cf. Job 14:7-9). BARNES refers it to the chaining of the royal maniac. **16. heart**—understanding (Isa. 6:10). **times**—i.e., "years" (ch. 12:7). "Seven" is the perfect number: a week of years: a complete revolution of time accompanying a complete revolution in his state of mind. **17. demand**—i.e., determination; viz., as to the change to which Nebuchadnezzar is to be doomed. A solemn council of the heavenly ones is supposed (cf. Job 1: 6; 2:1), over which God presides supreme. His "decree" and "word" are therefore said to be theirs (cf. vs. 24, "decree of the Most High"); "the decree of the watchers," "the word of the holy ones." For He has placed particular kingdoms under the administration of angelic beings, subject to Him (ch. 10:13, 20; 12:1). The word "demand," in the second clause, expresses a distinct idea from the first clause. Not only as members of God's council (ch. 7:10; I Kings 22:19; Ps. 103:21; Zech. 1:10) do they subscribe to His "decree," but that decree is in answer to their prayers, wherein they *demand* that every mortal who tries to obscure the glory of God shall be humbled [CALVIN]. Angels are grieved when God's prerogative is in the least infringed. How awful to Nebuchadnezzar to know that angels plead against him for his pride, and that the decree has been passed in the high court of heaven for his humiliation in answer to angels' *demands!* The conceptions are moulded in a form peculiarly adapted to Nebuchadnezzar's modes of thought. **the living**—not as distinguished from the dead, but from the inhabitants of heaven, who "know" not that which the men of the world need to the taught (Ps. 9:16); the ungodly confess there is a God, but would gladly confine Him to heaven. But, saith Daniel, God ruleth not merely there, but "in the kingdom of men." **basest**—the lowest in condition (I Sam. 2:8; Luke 1:52). It is not one's talents, excellency, or noble birth, but God's will, which elevates to the throne. Nebuchadnezzar abased to the dunghill, and then restored, was to have in himself an experimental proof of this (vs. 37). **19. Daniel . . . Belteshazzar**—The use of the Hebrew as well as the Chaldee name, so far from being an objection, as some have made it, is an undesigned mark of genuineness. In a proclamation to "*all* people," and one designed to honor the God of the Hebrews, Nebuchadnezzar would naturally use the Hebrew name (derived from *El,* "God," the name by which the prophet was best

known among his countrymen), as well as the Gentile name by which he was known in the Chaldean empire. **astonied**—overwhelmed with awe at the terrible import of the dream. **one hour**—the original means often "a moment," or "short time," as in ch. 3:6, 15. **let not the dream . . . trouble thee** —Many despots would have punished a prophet who dared to foretell his overthrow. Nebuchadnezzar assures Daniel he may freely speak out. **the dream be to them that hate thee**—We are to desire the prosperity of those under whose authority God's providence has placed us (Jer. 29:7). The wish here is not so much against others, as for the king: a common formula (II Sam. 18:32). It is not the language of uncharitable hatred. **20.** The *tree* is the king. The *branches,* the princes. The *leaves,* the soldiers. The *fruits,* the revenues. The *shadow,* the protection afforded to dependent states. **22. It is thou**—He speaks pointedly, and without circumlocution (II Sam. 12:7). While pitying the king, he uncompromisingly pronounces his sentence of punishment. Let ministers steer the mean between, on the one hand, fulminations against sinners under the pretext of zeal, without any symptom of compassion; and, on the other, flattery of sinners under the pretext of moderation. **to the end of the earth**—(Jer. 27:6:8). To the Caspian, Euxine, and Atlantic seas. **24. decree of the Most High**—What was termed in vs. 17 by Nebuchadnezzar, "the decree *of the watchers,*" is here more accurately termed by Daniel, "the decree *of the Most High.*" They are but His ministers. **25. they shall drive thee**—a Chaldee idiom for "thou shalt be driven." Hypochondriacal madness was his malady, which "drove" him under the fancy that he was a beast, to "dwell with the beasts"; verse 34 proves this, "mine understanding returned." The regency would leave him to roam in the large beast-abounding parks attached to the palace. **eat grass**—i.e., vegetables, or herbs in general (Gen. 3:18). **they shall wet thee**—i.e., thou shalt be wet. **till thou know . . .**—(Ps. 83: 17, 18; Jer. 27:5). **26. thou shalt have known . . .** —a promise of spiritual grace to him, causing the judgment to humble, not harden, his heart. **heavens do rule**—The plural is used, as addressed to Nebuchadnezzar, the head of an organized earthly kingdom, with various principalities under the supreme ruler. So "the kingdom of heaven" (Matt. 4:17; *Greek,* "kingdom of the *heavens*") is a *manifold* organization, composed of various orders of angels, under the Most High (Eph. 1:20, 21; 3:10; Col. 1:16). **27. break off**—as a galling yoke (Gen. 27:40); sin is a heavy load (Matt. 11:28). LXX and *Vulgate* translate not so well, "redeem," which is made an argument for Rome's doctrine of the expiation of sins by meritorious works. Even translate it so, it can only mean; Repent and show the reality of thy repentance by works of justice and charity (cf. Luke 11:41); so God will remit thy punishment. The trouble will be longer before it comes, or shorter when it does come. Cf. the cases of Hezekiah, Isa. 38:1-5; Nineveh, Jonah 3:5-10; Jeremiah 18:7, 8. The change is not in God, but in the sinner who repents. As the king who had provoked God's judgments by sin, so he might avert it by a return to righteousness (cf. Ps. 41:1, 2; Acts 8:22). Probably, like most Oriental despots, Nebuchadnezzar had oppressed the poor by forcing them to labor in his great public works without adequate remuneration. **if . . . lengthening of . . . tranquillity**—if haply thy present prosperity shall be prolonged. **29. twelve months**—This respite was granted to him to leave him without excuse. So the 120 years granted before the flood (Gen. 6:3). At the first announcement of the coming judgment he was alarmed, as Ahab (I Kings 21:27), but did not thoroughly repent; so when judgment was not executed at once, he thought it would never come, and so returned to his former pride (Eccles. 8:11). **in the palace**—rather, upon the (flat) palace roof, whence he could contemplate the splendor of Babylon. So the heathen historian, ABYDENUS, records. The palace roof was the scene of the fall of another king (II Samuel 11:2). The outer wall of Nebuchadnezzar's new palace embraced six miles; there were two other embattled walls within, and a great tower, and three brazen gates. **30. Babylon, that I have built**—HERODOTUS ascribes the building of Babylon to Semiramis and Nitocris, his informant under the *Persian* dynasty giving him the Assyrian and Persian account. BEROSUS and ABYDENUS give the *Babylonian* account, viz., that Nebuchadnezzar added much to the old city, built a splendid palace and city walls. HERODOTUS, the so-called "father of history," does not even mention Nebuchadnezzar. (Nitocris, to whom he attributes the beautifying of Babylon, seems to have been Nebuchadnezzar's wife.) Hence infidels have doubted the Scripture account. But the latter is proved by thousands of bricks on the plain, the inscriptions of which have been deciphered, each marked "Nebuchadnezzar, the son of Nabopolassar." "Built," i.e., restored and enlarged (II Chron. 11:5, 6). It is curious, all the bricks have been found with the stamped face downwards. Scarcely a figure in stone, or tablet, has been dug out of the rubbish heaps of Babylon, whereas Nineveh abounds in them; fulfilling Jer. 51:37, "Babylon shall become *heaps*." The *"I"* is emphatic, by which he puts himself in the place of God; so the "my . . . my." He impiously opposes *his* might to God's, as though God's threat, uttered a year before, could never come to pass. He would be more than man; God, therefore, justly, makes him less than man. An acting over again of the fall; Adam, once lord of the world and the very beasts (Gen. 1:28; so Nebuchadnezzar ch. 2:38), would be a god (Gen. 3:5); therefore he must die like the beasts (Ps. 82:6; 49:12). The second Adam restores the forfeited inheritance (Ps. 8:4-8). **31. While . . .**—in the very act of speaking, so that there could be no doubt as to the connection between the crime and the punishment. So Luke 12:19, 20. **O king . . . to thee it is spoken**—Notwithstanding thy *kingly* power, to thee thy doom *is* now *spoken,* there is to be no further respite. **33. driven from men**—as a maniac fancying himself a wild beast. It is possible, a conspiracy of his nobles may have co-operated towards his having been "driven" forth as an outcast. **hairs . . . eagles' feathers**—matted together, as the hair-like, thick plumage of the ossifraga eagle. The "nails," by being left uncut for years, would become like "claws." **34. lifted up mine eyes unto heaven**—whence the "voice" had issued (vs. 31) at the beginning of his visitation. Sudden mental derangement often has the effect of annihilating the whole interval, so that, when reason returns, the patient remembers only the event that immediately preceded his insanity. Nebuchadnezzar's looking up towards heaven was the first symptom of his "understanding" having "returned." Before, like the beasts, his eyes had been downward to the earth. Now, like Jonah's (Jonah 2:1, 2, 4) out of the fish's belly, they are lifted up to heaven in prayer. He turns to Him that smiteth him (Isa. 9:13), with the faint glimmer of reason left to him, and owns God's justice in punishing him.

praised . . . him—Praise is a sure sign of a soul spiritually healed (Ps. 116:12, 14; Mark 5:15, 18, 19). **I . . . honoured him**—implying that the cause of his chastisement was that he had before robbed God of His honor. **everlasting dominion**—not temporary or mutable, as a human king's dominion. **35. all . . . as nothing**—(Isa. 40:15, 17). **according to his will in . . . heaven**—(Ps. 115:3; 135:6; Matt. 6:10; Ephesians 1:11). **army**—the heavenly hosts, angels and starry orbs (cf. Isa. 24:21). **none . . . stay his hand**—lit., "strike His hand." Image from striking the hand of another, to check him in doing anything (Isa. 43:13; 45:9). **What doest thou**—(Job 9:12; Rom. 9:20). **36.** An inscription in the East India Company's Museum is read as describing the period of Nebuchadnezzar's insanity [G. V. SMITH]. In the so-called standard inscription read by Sir H. Rawlinson, Nebuchadnezzar relates that during four (?) years he ceased to lay out buildings, or to furnish with victims Merodach's altar, or to clear out the canals for irrigation. No other instance in the cuneiform inscriptions occurs of a king recording his own inaction. **my counsellors . . . sought unto me**—desired to have me, as formerly, to be their head, wearied with the anarchy which prevailed in my absence (cf. *Note,* vs. 33); the likelihood of a conspiracy of the nobles is confirmed by this verse. **majesty was added**—My authority was greater than ever before (Job 42:12; Prov. 22:4; Matt. 6:33, "added"). **37. praise . . . extol . . . honour**—He heaps word on word, as if he cannot say enough in praise of God. **all whose works . . . truth . . . judgment**—i.e., are true and just (Rev. 15: 3; 16:7). God has not dealt unjustly or too severely with me; whatever I have suffered, I deserved it all. It is a mark of true contrition to condemn one's self, and justify God (Ps. 51:4). **those that walk in pride . . . abase**—exemplified in me. He condemns himself before the whole world, in order to glorify God.

CHAPTER 5

Vss. 1-31.　BELSHAZZAR'S IMPIOUS FEAST; THE HANDWRITING ON THE WALL INTERPRETED BY DANIEL OF THE DOOM OF BABYLON AND ITS KING. **1. Belshazzar**—RAWLINSON, from the Assyrian inscriptions, has explained the seeming discrepancy between Daniel and the heathen historians of Babylon, BEROSUS and ABYDENUS, who say the last king (Nabonidus) surrendered in Borsippa, after Babylon was taken, and had an honorable abode in Caramania assigned to him. *Belshazzar was joint king with his father* (called *Minus* in the inscriptions), *but subordinate to him;* hence the *Babylonian* account suppresses the facts which cast discredit on Babylon, viz., that Belshazzar shut himself up in that city and fell at its capture; while it records the surrender of the principal king in Borsippa (see my *Introduction* to Daniel). The heathen XENOPHON's description of Belshazzar accords with Daniel's; he calls him "impious," and illustrates his cruelty by mentioning that he killed one of his nobles, merely because, in hunting, the noble struck down the game before him; and unmanned a courtier, Gadates, at a banquet, because one of the king's concubines praised him as handsome. Daniel shows none of the sympathy for him which he had for Nebuchadnezzar. XENOPHON confirms Daniel as to Belshazzar's end. WINER explains the "shazzar" in the name as meaning "fire." **made . . . feast**—heaven-sent infatuation when his city was at the time being besieged by Cyrus. The fortifications and abundant provisions in the city made the king despise the besiegers. It was a festival-day among the Babylonians [XENO-PHON]. **drank ... before the thousand**—The king, on this extraordinary occasion, departed from his usual way of feasting apart from his nobles (cf. Esther 1:3). **2. whiles he tasted the wine**—While under the effects of wine, men will do what they dare not do when sober. **his father Nebuchadnezzar**—i.e., his forefather. So "Jesus ... the *son* of David, the *son* of Abraham." Daniel does not say that the other kings mentioned in other writers did not reign between Belshazzar and Nebuchadnezzar, viz., Evil-merodach (Jer. 52:31), Neriglissar, his brother-in-law, and Laborasoarchod (nine months). BERO-SUS makes Nabonidus, the last king, to have been *one of the people,* raised to the throne by an insurrection. As the inscriptions show that Belshazzar was distinct from, and joint king with, him, this is not at variance with Daniel, whose statement that Belshazzar was *son* (grandson) *of Nebuchadnezzar* is corroborated by Jeremiah (Jer. 27:7). Their joint, yet independent, testimony, as contemporaries, and having the best means of information, is more trustworthy than any of the heathen historians, if there were a discrepancy. Evilmerodach, son of Nebuchadnezzar (according to BEROSUS), reigned but a short time (one or two years), having, in consequence of his bad government, been dethroned by a plot of Neriglissar, his sister's husband; hence Daniel does not mention him. At the elevation of Nabonidus as supreme king, Belshazzar, the grandson of Nebuchadnezzar, was doubtless suffered to be subordinate king and successor, in order to conciliate the legitimate party. Thus the seeming discrepancy becomes a confirmation of genuineness when cleared up, for the real harmony must have been undesigned. **wives ... concubines**—not usually present at feasts in the East, where women of the harem are kept in strict seclusion. Hence Vashti's refusal to appear at Ahasuerus' feast (Esther 1). But the Babylonian court, in its reckless excesses, seems not to have been so strict as the Persian. XENOPHON (*Cyrop.* 5.2, 28) confirms Daniel, representing a feast of Belshazzar where the concubines are present. At the beginning "the lords" (vs. 1), for whom the feast was made, alone seem to have been present; but as the revelry advanced, the women were introduced. Two classes of them are mentioned, those to whom belonged the privileges of "wives," and those strictly concubines (II Sam. 5:13; I Kings 11:3; Song of Sol. 6:8). **3.** This act was not one of necessity, or for honor's sake, but in reckless profanity. **4. praised**—sang and shouted praises to "gods," which being of gold, "are their own witnesses" (Isa. 44:9), confuting the folly of those who fancy such to be gods. **5. In the same hour**—that the cause of God's visitation might be palpable, viz., the profanation of His vessels and His holy name. **fingers of ... hand**—God admonishes him, not by a dream (as Nebuchadnezzar had been warned), or by a voice, but by "fingers coming forth," the invisibility of Him who moved them heightening the awful impressiveness of the scene, the hand of the Unseen One attesting his doom before the eyes of himself and his guilty fellow revellers. **against the candlestick**—the candelabra; where the mystic characters would be best seen. BARNES makes it the candlestick taken from the temple of Jerusalem, the nearness of the writing to it intimating that the rebuke was directed against the sacrilege. **upon the plaster of the wall of the king's palace**—Written in cuneiform letters on slabs on the walls, and on the very bricks, are found the

perpetually recurring recital of titles, victories, and exploits, to remind the spectator at every point of the regal greatness. It is significant, that on the same wall on which the king was accustomed to read the flattering legends of his own magnificence, he beholds the mysterious inscription which foretells his fall (cf. Prov. 16:18; Acts 12:21-23). **part of the hand**—the anterior part, viz., the fingers. **6. countenance**—lit., "brightness," i.e., his bright look. **joints of his loins**—"the vertebræ of his back" [GESENIUS]. **7.** He calls for the magicians, who more than once had been detected in imposture. He neglects God, and Daniel, whose fame as an interpreter was then well established. The world wishes to be deceived and shuts its eyes against the light [CALVIN]. The Hebrews think the words were Chaldee, but in the old Hebrew character (like that now in the Samaritan Pentateuch). **third ruler**—The first place was given to the king; the second, to the son of the king, or of the queen; the third, to the chief of the satraps. **8.** The words were in such a character as to be illegible to the Chaldees, God reserving this honor to Daniel. **10. queen**—the queen mother, or *grandmother,* Nitocris, had not been present till now. She was wife either of Nebuchadnezzar or of Evil-merodach; hence her acquaintance with the services of Daniel. She completed the great works which the former had begun. Hence HERODOTUS attributes them to her alone. This accounts for the deference paid to her by Belshazzar. (See *Note,* ch. 4:36.) Cf. similar rank given to the queen mother among the Hebrews (I Kings 15:13). **11. spirit of the holy gods**—She remembers and repeats Nebuchadnezzar's language (ch. 4:8, 9, 18). As Daniel was probably, according to Oriental custom, deprived of the office to which Nebuchadnezzar had promoted him, as "master of the magicians" (ch. 4:9), at the king's death, Belshazzar might easily be ignorant of his services. **the king ... thy father the king ... thy father**—The repetition marks with emphatic gravity both the excellencies of Daniel, and the fact that Nebuchadnezzar, whom Belshazzar is bound to reverence as his father, had sought counsel from him in similar circumstances. **13. the captivity of Judah**—the captive Jews residing in Babylon. **17.** Not inconsistent with verse 29. For here he declares his interpretation of the words is not from the *desire* of reward. The honors in verse 29 were doubtless *urged* on him, without his wish, in such a way that he could not with propriety refuse them. Had he refused them after announcing the doom of the kingdom, he might have been suspected of cowardice or treason. **18. God gave**—It was not his own birth or talents which gave him the vast empire, as he thought. To make him unlearn his proud thought was the object of God's visitation on him. **majesty**—in the eyes of his subjects. **glory**—from his victories. **honour**—from the enlargement and decoration of the city. **19.** A purely absolute monarchy (Jer. 27:7). **21. heart was made like ... beasts**—lit., "he made his heart like the beasts," i.e., he desired to dwell with them. **22.** Thou hast erred not through ignorance, but through deliberate contempt of God, notwithstanding that thou hadst before thine eyes the striking warning given in thy grandfather's case. **23. whose are all thy ways**—(Jer. 10:23). **24. Then**—When thou liftedst up thyself against the Lord. **the part of the hand**—the fore part, the fingers. **was ... sent from him**—i.e., from God. **25. Mene, Mene, Tekel, Up-harsin**—lit., "numbered, weighed, and dividers." **26.** God hath fixed the number of years of thine empire, and that number is now complete. **27.**

weighed in the balances—The Egyptians thought that Osiris weighed the actions of the dead in a literal balance. The Babylonians may have had the same notion, which would give a peculiar appropriateness to the image here used. **found wanting** —too light before God, the weigher of actions (I Sam. 2:3; Ps. 62:9). Like spurious gold or silver (Jer. 6:30). **28. Peres**—the explanation of "dividers" (vs. 25), the *active participle plural* there being used for the *passive participle singular*, "dividers" for "divided." The word *Peres* alludes to the similar word "Persia." **divided**—viz., among the Medes and Persians [MAURER]; or, "severed" from thee [GROTIUS]. **29. Belshazzar . . . clothed Daniel with scarlet**—To come from the presence of a prince in a dress presented to the wearer as a distinction is still held a great honor in the East. Daniel was thus restored to a similar rank to what he had held under Nebuchadnezzar (ch. 2:48). Godly fidelity which might be expected to bring down vengeance, as in this case, is often rewarded even in this life. The king, having promised, was ashamed before his courtiers to break his word. He perhaps also affected to despise the prophecy of his doom, as an idle threat. As to Daniel's reasons for now accepting what at first he had declined, cf. *Note*, vs. 17. The insignia of honor would be witnesses for God's glory to the world of his having by God's aid interpreted the mystic characters. The *cause* of his elevation too would secure the favor of the new dynasty (ch. 6:2) for both himself and his captive countrymen. As the capture of the city by Cyrus was not till near daylight, there was no want of *time* in that eventful night for accomplishing all that is here recorded. The capture of the city so immediately after the prophecy of it (following Belshazzar's sacrilege), marked most emphatically to the whole world the connection between Babylon's sin and its punishment. **30.** HERODOTUS and XENOPHON confirm Daniel as to the *suddenness* of the event. Cyrus diverted the Euphrates into a new channel and, guided by two deserters, marched by the dry bed into the city, while the Babylonians were carousing at an annual feast to the gods. See also Isaiah 21:5; 44:27; and Jer. 50:38, 39; and 51:36. As to Belshazzar's being slain, cf. Isaiah 14:18-20; 21:2-9; Jeremiah 50:29-35; 51:57. **31. Darius the Median**—i.e., Cyaxares II, the son and successor of Astyages, 569-536 B.C. Though Koresh, or Cyrus, was leader of the assault, yet all was done in the name of Darius; therefore, he alone is mentioned here; but ch. 6:28 shows Daniel was not ignorant of *Cyrus'* share in the capture of Babylon. Isaiah 13:17 and 21:2, confirm Daniel in making the *Medes* the leading nation in destroying Babylon. So also Jeremiah 51:11, 28. HERODOTUS, on the other hand, omits mentioning Darius, as that king, being weak and sensual, gave up all the authority to his energetic nephew, Cyrus (XENOPHON, *Cyrop*. 1.5; 8.7). **threescore and two years old**—This agrees with XENOPHON, Cyrop. 8.5, 19, as to Cyaxares II.

CHAPTER 6

Vss. 1-28. DARIUS' DECREE: DANIEL'S DISOBEDIENCE, AND CONSEQUENT EXPOSURE TO THE LION'S: HIS DELIVERANCE BY GOD, AND DARIUS' DECREE. **1. Darius**—GROTEFEND has read it in the cuneiform inscriptions at Persepolis, as *Darheush*, i.e., "Lord-King," a name applied to many of the Medo-Persian kings in common. Three of that name occur: Darius Hystaspes, 521 B.C., in whose reign the decree

was carried into effect for rebuilding the temple (Ezra 4:5; Hag. 1:1); Darius Codomanus, 336 B.C., whom Alexander overcame, called "the Persian" (Neh. 12:22), an expression used after the rule of Macedon was set up; and Darius Cyaxares II, between Astyages and Cyrus (ÆSCHYLUS, Pers. 762, 763). **hundred and twenty**—satraps; set over the conquered provinces (including Babylon) by Cyrus (XENOPHON, *Cyrop*. 8. 6. 1). No doubt Cyrus acted *under Darius,* as in the capture of Babylon; so that Daniel rightly attributes the appointment to *Darius.* **3. Daniel was preferred**—probably because of his having so wonderfully foretold the fall of Babylon. Hence the very expression used by the queen mother on that occasion (ch. 5:12) is here used, "because *an excellent spirit was in him."* **king thought to set him over the whole realm**—Agreeing with Darius' character, weak and averse to business, which he preferred to delegate to favorites. God overruled this to the good both of Daniel and, through him, of His people. **4. occasion . . . concerning the kingdom**—pretext for accusation in his administration (Eccles. 4:4). **5.** It is the highest testimony to a godly man's walk, when his most watchful enemies can find no ground of censure save in that he walks according to the law of God even where it opposes the ways of the world. **6. assembled together**—lit., "assembled hastily and tumultuously." Had they come more deliberately, the king might have refused their grant; but they gave him no time for reflection, representing that their *test-decree* was necessary for the safety of the king. **live for ever**— ARRIAN (4) records that Cyrus was the first before whom prostration was practised. It is an undesigned mark of genuineness that Daniel should mention no prostration before Nebuchadnezzar or Darius (see *Note*, ch. 3:9). **7.** The Persian king was regarded as representative of the chief god, Ormuzd; the seven princes near him represented the seven Amshaspands before the throne of Ormuzd; hence Mordecai (Esther 3:4) refused such homage to Haman, the king's prime minister, as inconsistent with what is due to God alone. A weak despot, like Darius, much under the control of his princes, might easily be persuaded that such a decree would test the obedience of the Chaldeans just conquered, and tame their proud spirits. So absolute is the king in the East, that he is regarded not merely as the ruler, but the owner, of the people. **All . . . governors . . . counsellors . . .**—Several functionaries are here specified, not mentioned in verses 4, 6. They evidently exaggerated the case of the weak king, as if *their* request was that of *all* the officers in the empire. **den of lions**—an underground cave or pit, covered with a stone. It is an undesigned proof of genuineness, that the "fiery furnace" is not made the means of punishment here, as in ch. 3; for the Persians were *fire-worshippers,* which the Babylonians were not. **8. decree**—or, "interdict." **that it be not changed**—(Esther 1:19; 8:8). This immutability of the king's commands was peculiar to the Medes and Persians: it was due to their regarding him as infallible as the representative of Ormuzd; it was not so among the Babylonians. **Medes and Persians**—The order of the names is an undesigned mark of genuineness. Cyrus the Persian reigned subordinate to Darius the Mede as to dignity, though exercising more real power. After Darius' death, the order is "the Persians and Medes" (Esther 1:14, 19, etc.). **9.** Such a despotic decree is quite explicable by remembering that the king, as the incarnation of Ormuzd, might demand such an act of religious obedience as a *test of loyalty.*

Persecuting laws are always made on false pretenses. Instead of bitter complaints against men, Daniel prays to God. Though having vast business as a ruler of the empire, he finds time to pray thrice a day. Daniel's three companions (ch. 3), are not alluded to here, nor any other Jew who conscientiously may have disregarded the edict, as the conspirators aimed at Daniel alone (vs. 5). **10. when Daniel knew...writing...signed**—and that, therefore, the power of advising the king against it was taken from him. **went into his house**—withdrawing from the God-dishonoring court. **windows... open**—not in vainglory, but that there might be no obstruction to his view of the direction in which Jerusalem, the earthly seat of Jehovah under the Old Testament, lay; and that the sight of heaven might draw his mind off from earthly thoughts. To Christ in the heavenly temple let us turn our eyes in prayer, from this land of our captivity (I Kings 8:44, 48; II Chron. 6:29, 34, 38; Ps. 5:7). **chamber**—the upper room, where prayer was generally offered by the Jews (Acts 1:13). Not on the housetop (Acts 10:9), where he would be conspicuous. **upon his knees**—Humble attitudes in prayer become humble suppliants. **three times a day**—(Ps. 55:17). The third, sixth, and ninth hour; our nine, twelve, and three o'clock (Acts 2:15; 10:9; 3:1; 10:30; cf. ch. 9:21). **as...aforetime**—not from contempt of the king's command. **11. assembled**—as in vs. 6, "assembled" or "ran hastily," so as to come upon Daniel suddenly and detect him in the act. **12.** They preface their attack by alleging the king's edict, so as to get him again to confirm it unalterably, before they mention *Daniel's* name. Not to break a wicked promise, is not firmness, but guilty obstinacy (Matt. 14:9; Mark 6:26). **13. That Daniel**—contemptuously. **of...captivity of Judah**—recently a captive among thy servants, the Babylonians—one whom humble obedience most becomes. Thus they aggravate his guilt, omitting mention of his being prime minister, which might only remind Darius of Daniel's state services. **regardeth not thee**—because he regarded God (Acts 4:19; 5:29). **14. displeased with himself**—for having suffered himself to be entrapped into such a hasty decree (Prov. 29:20). On the one hand he was pressed by the immutability of the law, fear that the princes might conspire against him, and desire to consult for his own reputation, not to seem fickle; on the other, by regard for Daniel, and a desire to save him from the effects of his own rash decree. **till...going down of...sun**—The king took this time to deliberate, thinking that after sunset Daniel would be spared till morning, and that meanwhile some way of escape would turn up. But (vs. 15) the conspirators "assembled tumultuously" (lit.) to prevent this delay in the execution, lest the king should meantime change his decree. **16. Thy God...will deliver thee**—The heathen believed in the interposition of the gods at times in favor of their worshippers. Darius recognized Daniel's God as a god, but not *the only true* God. He had heard of the deliverance of the three youths in ch. 3 and hence augurs Daniel's deliverance. I am not my own master, and cannot deliver thee, however much I wish it. "Thy God will." Kings are the slaves of their flatterers. Men admire piety to God in others, however disregarding Him themselves. **17. stone...sealed**—typical of Christ's entombment under a seal (Matt. 27:66). Divinely ordered, that the deliverance might be the more striking. **his own signet, and...of his lords**—The *concurrence* of the lords was required for making laws. In this, king-

ly power had fallen since it was in Nebuchadnezzar's hands. The Median king is a puppet in his lords' hands; they take the security of their own seal as well as his, that he should not release Daniel. The king's seal guaranteed Daniel from being killed by them, should he escape the lions. **18. neither were instruments of music...**—GESENIUS translates, "concubines." Daniel's mentioning to us as an extraordinary thing of Darius, that he neither approached his table nor his harem, agrees with XENOPHON's picture of him as devoted to wine and women, vain, and without self-control. He is sorry for the evil which he himself had caused, yet takes no steps to remedy it. There are many such halters between good and bad, who are ill at ease in their sins, yet go forward in them, and are drawn on by others. **19.** His grief overcame his fear of the nobles. **20. living God**—having life Himself, and able to preserve thy life; contrasted with the lifeless idols. Darius borrowed the phrase from Daniel; God extorting from an idolater a confession of the truth. **thou servest continually**—in times of persecution, as well as in times of peace. **is thy God... able**—the language of doubt, yet hope. **21.** Daniel might have indulged in anger at the king, but does not; his sole thought is, God's glory has been set forth in his deliverance. **22. his angel**—the instrument, not the author, of his deliverance (Ps. 91:11; 34:7). **shut...lions' mouths**—(Heb. 11:33). So spiritually, God will shut the roaring lion's mouth (I Pet. 5:8) for His servants. **forasmuch as before him innocency**—not absolutely (in ch. 9:7, 18 he disclaims such a plea), but relatively to this case. God has attested the justice of my cause in standing up for His worship, by delivering me. Therefore, the "forasmuch" does not justify Rome's doctrine of works meriting salvation. **before thee**—Obedience to God is in strictest compatibility with loyalty to the king (Matt. 22:21; I Pet. 2:17). Daniel's disobedience to the king was seeming, not real, because it was not from contempt of the king, but from regard to the King of kings (cf. Acts 24:16). **23. because he believed**—"Faith" is stated in Hebrews 11:33 to have been his actuating principle: a prelude to the Gospel. His belief was not with a view to a miraculous deliverance. He shut his eyes to the event, committing the keeping of his soul to God, in well-doing, as unto a faithful Creator (I Pet. 4:19), sure of deliverance in a better life, if not in this. **24.** (Deut. 19:19; Prov. 19:5.) **accused**—lit., "devoured the bones and flesh." It was just that they who had torn Daniel's character, and sought the tearing of his person, should be themselves given to be torn in pieces (Prov. 11:8). **their children**—Among the Persians, all the kindred were involved in the guilt of one culprit. The Mosaic law expressly forbade this (Deut. 24:16; II Kings 14:6). **or ever**—i.e., "before ever." The lions' sparing Daniel could not have been because they were full, as they showed the keenness of their hunger on the accusers. **26.** Stronger than the decree (ch. 3:29). That was negative; this, positive; not merely men must say "nothing amiss of," but must "fear before God." **28.** It was in the third year of Cyrus that Daniel's visions (ch. 10-12) were given. Daniel "prospered" because of his prophecies (Ezra 1:1, 2).

CHAPTER 7

Vss. 1-28. VISION OF THE FOUR BEASTS. This chapter treats of the same subject as the second chapter. But there the four kingdoms, and Messiah's final kingdom, were regarded according to their *external* political aspect, but here according to the mind of God concerning them, and their *moral* features. The outward political history had been shown in its general features to the world ruler, whose position fitted him for receiving such a revelation. But God's prophet here receives disclosures as to the characters of the powers of the world, in a religious point of view, suited to *his* position and receptivity. Hence in the second chapter the images are taken from the inanimate sphere; in the seventh chapter they are taken from the animate. Nebuchadnezzar saw superficially the world power as a splendid human figure, and the kingdom of God as a mere stone at the first. Daniel sees the world kingdoms in their inner essence as of an *animal* nature lower than human, being estranged from God; and that only in the kingdom of God ("the Son of *man*," the representative-man) is the true dignity of man realized. So, as contrasted with Nebuchadnezzar's vision, the kingdom of God appears to Daniel, *from the very first*, superior to the world kingdom. For though in *physical* force the beasts excel man, man has essentially *spiritual* powers. Nebuchadnezzar's colossal image represents mankind in its own strength, but only the outward man. Daniel sees man spiritually degraded to the beast level, led by blind impulses, through his alienation from God. It is only from above that the perfect Son of man comes, and in His kingdom man attains his true destiny. Cf. Psalm 8 with Genesis 1:26-28. Humanity is impossible without divinity: it sinks to bestiality (Ps. 32:9; 49:20; 73:22). Obstinate heathen nations are compared to "bulls" (Ps. 68:30); Egypt to the dragon in the Nile (Isa. 27:1; 51:9; Ezek. 29:3). The animal with all its sagacity looks always to the ground, without consciousness of relation to God. What elevates man is communion with God, in willing subjection to Him. The moment he tries to exalt himself to independence of God, as did Nebuchadnezzar (ch. 4: 30), he sinks to the beast's level. Daniel's acquaintance with the animal colossal figures in Babylon and Nineveh was a psychological preparation for his animal visions. Hosea 13:7, 8 would occur to him while viewing those ensigns of the world power. Cf. Jeremiah 2:15; 4:7; 5:6. **1. Belshazzar**—Good *Hebrew* MSS. have "Belshazzar"; meaning "Bel is to be burnt with hostile fire" (Jer. 50:2; 51:44). In the *history* he is called by his ordinary name; in the *prophecy*, which gives his true destiny, he is called a corresponding name, by the change of a letter. **visions of his head**—not *confused* "dreams," but distinct images seen *while his mind was collected.* **sum**—a "summary." In predictions, generally, details are not given so fully as to leave no scope for free agency, faith, and patient waiting for God manifesting His will in the event. He "wrote" it for the Church in all ages; he "told" it for the comfort of his captive fellow countrymen. **2. the four winds**—answering to the "four beasts"; their several *conflicts in the four quarters or directions of the world.* **strove**—burst forth (from the abyss) [MAURER]. **sea**—The world powers rise out of the agitations of the political *sea* (Jer. 46:7, 8; Luke 21:25; cf. Rev. 13:1; 17:15; 21:1); the kingdom of God and the Son of man from the *clouds of heaven* (vs. 13; cf. John 8:23). TREGELLES takes "the great sea" to mean, as always elsewhere in Scripture (Josh. 1:4; 9:1), *the Mediterranean*, the center territorially of the four kingdoms of the vision, which all border on it, and have Jerusalem subject to them. *Babylon*

did not border on the Mediterranean, nor rule Jerusalem, till Nebuchadnezzar's time, when both things took place simultaneously. *Persia* encircled more of this sea, viz., from the Hellespont to Cyrene. *Greece* did not become a monarchy before Alexander's time, but then, succeeding to Persia, it became mistress of Jerusalem. It surrounded still more of the Mediterranean, adding the coasts of Greece to the part held by Persia. *Rome*, under Augustus, realized three things at once—it became a monarchy; it became mistress of the last of the four parts of Alexander's empire (symbolized by the four heads of the third beast), and of Jerusalem; it surrounded *all* the Mediterranean. **3. beasts**—not *living animals*, as the cherubic four in Revelation 4: 7 (for the original is a different word from "beasts," and ought to be there translated, "living animals"). The cherubic *living animals* represent redeemed man, combining in himself the highest forms of animal life. But the "beasts" here represent the world powers, in their beastlike, grovelling character. It is on the fundamental harmony between nature and spirit, between the three kingdoms of nature, history, and revelation, that Scripture symbolism rests. The selection of symbols is not arbitrary, but based on the essence of things. **4. lion**—the symbol of *strength and courage;* chief among the kingdoms, as the lion among the beasts. Nebuchadnezzar is called "the lion" (Jer. 4:7). **eagle's wings**—denoting a widespread and rapidly acquired (Isa. 46:11; Jer. 4:13; Lam. 4:19; Hab. 1:6) empire (Jer. 48:40). **plucked**—Its ability for widespread conquests passed away under Evil-merodach, etc. [GROTIUS]; rather, during Nebuchadnezzar's privation of his throne, while deranged. **it was lifted up from the earth**—i.e., from its grovelling bestiality. **made stand . . . as a man**—So long as Nebuchadnezzar, in haughty pride, relied on his own strength, he forfeited the true dignity of man, and was therefore degraded to be with the beasts. Ch. 4:16: "Let his *heart* be changed from *man's*, and let a beast's *heart* be given unto him." But after he learned by this sore discipline that "the Most High ruleth in the kingdom of men" (ch. 4:35, 36), the change took place in him, "a *man's* heart is given to him; instead of his former beast's heart, he attains man's true position, viz., to be consciously dependent on God." Cf. Psalm 9:20. **5. bear**—symbolizing the austere life of the Persians in their mountains, also their cruelty (Isa. 13:17, 18; Cambyses, Ochus, and other of the Persian princes were notoriously cruel; the Persian laws involved, for one man's offense, the whole kindred and neighborhood in destruction, ch. 6:24) and rapacity. "A bear is an *all-devouring* animal" [ARISTOTLE, 8. 5], (Jeremiah 51:48, 56). **raised . . . itself on one side**—but the *Hebrew*, "It raised up one dominion." The Medes, an ancient people, and the Persians, a modern tribe, formed *one united sovereignty* in contrast to the third and fourth kingdoms, each originally one, afterwards divided. *English Version* is the result of a slight change of a *Hebrew* letter. The idea then would be, "It lay on one of its fore feet, and stood on the other"; a figure still to be seen on one of the stones of Babylon (MUNTER, *Relig. Babyl.,* 112); denoting a kingdom that had been at rest, but is now rousing itself for conquest. Media is the lower side, passiveness; Persia, the upper, active element [AUBERLEN]. The three ribs in its mouth are *Media, Lydia, and Babylon,* brought under the Persian sway. Rather, *Babylon, Lydia, and Egypt,* not properly parts of its body, but seized by Medo-Persia [SIR I. NEWTON]. Called "ribs" because they strengthened the Medo-Persian empire.

"Between its teeth," as being much grinded by it. **devour much flesh**—i.e., subjugate many nations. **6. leopard**—smaller than the lion; swift (Hab. 1:8); cruel (Isa. 11:6), the opposite of tame; springing suddenly from its hiding-place on its prey (Hos. 13:7); spotted. So Alexander, a small king, of a small kingdom, Macedon, attacked Darius at the head of the vast empire reaching from the Ægean Sea to the Indies. In twelve years he subjugated part of Europe, and all Asia from Illyricum and the Adriatic to the Ganges, not so much fighting as conquering [JEROME]. Hence, whereas Babylon is represented with *two* wings, Macedon has *four*, so rapid were his conquests. The various spots denote the various nations incorporated into his empire [BOCHART]; or Alexander's own variation in character, at one time mild, at another cruel, now temperate, and now drunken and licentious. **four heads**—explained in chapter 8:8, 22; the four kingdoms of the *Diadochi* or "successors" into which the Macedonian empire was divided at the death of Alexander, viz., Macedon and Greece under Cassander, Thrace and Bithynia under Lysimachus, Egypt under Ptolemy, and Syria under Seleucus. **dominion . . . given to it**—by God; not by Alexander's own might. For how unlikely it was that 30,000 men should overthrow several hundreds of thousands! JOSEPHUS (*Antiquities*, 11.6) says that Alexander adored the high priest of Jerusalem, saying that he at Dium in Macedonia had seen a vision of God so habited, inviting him to go to Asia, and promising him success. **7.** As Daniel lived under the kingdom of the first beast, and therefore needed not to describe it, and as the second and third are described fully in the second part of the book, the chief emphasis falls on the fourth. Also prophecy most dwells on the *end,* which is the consummation of the preceding series of events. It is in the fourth that the world power manifests fully its God-opposing nature. Whereas the three former kingdoms were designated respectively, as a lion, bear, and leopard, no particular beast is specified as the image of the fourth; for Rome is so terrible as to be not describable by any one, but combines in itself all that we can imagine inexpressibly fierce in all beasts. Hence *thrice* (vss. 7, 19, 23) it is repeated, that the fourth was "diverse from all" the others. The formula of introduction, "I saw in the night visions," occurs here, as at vs. 2, and again at vs. 13, thus dividing the whole vision into three parts—the first embracing the three kingdoms, the second the fourth and its overthrow, the third Messiah's kingdom. The first three together take up a few centuries; the fourth, thousands of years. The whole lower half of the image in ch. 2 is given to it. And whereas the other kingdoms consist of only one material, this consists of two, iron and clay (on which much stress is laid, ch. 2:41-43); the *"iron teeth"* here allude to one material in the fourth kingdom of the image. **ten horns**—It is with the *crisis,* rather than the *course,* of the fourth kingdom that this seventh chapter is mainly concerned. The ten *kings* (vs. 24, the "horns" representing *power*), i.e., *kingdoms,* into which Rome was divided on its incorporation with the Germanic and Slavonic tribes, and again at the Reformation, are thought by many to be here intended. But the variation of the list of the ten, and their ignoring the eastern half of the empire altogether, and the existence of the Papacy *before* the breaking up of even the *Western* empire, instead of being the "little horn" springing up *after* the other ten, are against this view. The Western Roman empire continued

till A.D. 731, and the Eastern, till A.D. 1453. The ten kingdoms, therefore, prefigured by the ten "toes" (ch. 2:41; cf. Rev. 13:1; 17:12), are the ten kingdoms into which Rome shall be found finally divided when Antichrist shall appear [TREGELLES]. These, probably, are prefigured by the number *ten* being the prevalent one at the chief turning points of Roman history. **8. little horn**—*little* at first, but afterwards waxing greater than all others. He must be sought "among them," viz., the ten horns. The Roman empire did not represent itself as a continuation of Alexander's; but the Germanic empire calls itself "the holy Roman empire." Napoleon's attempted universal monarchy was avowedly Roman: his son was called king of Rome. The czar (*Cæsar*) also professes to represent the eastern half of the Roman empire. The Roman civilization, church, language, and law are the chief elements in Germanic civilization. But the Romanic element seeks universal empire, while the Germanic seeks individualization. Hence the universal monarchies attempted by the Papacy, Charlemagne, Charles V, and Napoleon have failed, the iron not amalgamating with the clay. In the king symbolized by "the little horn," the God-opposing, haughty spirit of the world, represented by the fourth monarchy, finds its intensest development. "The man of sin," "the son of perdition" (II Thess. 2). Antichrist (I John 2: 18, 22; 4:3). It is the complete evolution of the evil principle introduced by the fall. **three of the first horns plucked up**—the exarchate of Ravenna, the kingdom of the Lombards and the state of Rome, which constituted the Pope's dominions at the first; obtained by Pope Zachary and Stephen II in return for acknowledging the usurper Pepin lawful king of France [NEWTON]. See TREGELLES' objections, vs. 7, "ten horns," *Note.* The "little horn," in his view, is to be Antichrist rising three and a half years before Christ's second advent, having first overthrown three of the ten contemporaneous kingdoms, into which the fourth monarchy, under which we live, shall be finally divided. Popery seems to be *a* fulfilment of the prophecy in many particulars, the Pope claiming to be God on earth and above all earthly dominions; but the spirit of Antichrist prefigured by Popery will probably culminate in ONE *individual,* to be destroyed by Christ's coming; He will be the product of the political *world* powers, whereas Popery which prepares His way, is a *Church* become worldly. **eyes of man**—Eyes express intelligence (Ezek. 1:18); so (Gen. 3:5) the serpent's promise was, man's "eyes should be opened," if he would but rebel against God. Antichrist shall consummate the self-apotheosis, begun at the fall, high intellectual culture, independent of God. The metals representing Babylon and Medo-Persia, gold and silver, are more precious than brass and iron, representing Greece and Rome; but the latter metals are more useful to civilization (Gen. 4:22). The clay, representing the Germanic element, is the most plastic material. Thus there is a progress in *culture;* but this is not a progress *necessarily* in man's truest dignity, viz., union and likeness to God. Nay, it has led him farther from God, to self-reliance and world-love. The beginnings of civilization were among the children of Cain (Gen. 4:17-24; Luke 16:8). Antiochus Epiphanes, the first Antichrist, came from civilized Greece, and loved art. As Hellenic civilization produced the *first,* so modern civilization under the fourth monarchy will produce the *last* Antichrist. The "mouth" and "eyes" are those of a man, while the symbol is otherwise brutish, i.e., it will assume man's true dignity, viz., wear the guise of the kingdom of God (which comes as the "Son of *man*" from above), while it is really bestial, viz., severed from God. Antichrist promises the same things as Christ, but in an opposite way: a caricature of Christ, offering a regenerated world without the cross. Babylon and Persia in their religion had more reverence for things divine than Greece and Rome in the imperial stages of their history. Nebuchadnezzar's human *heart,* given him (ch. 4:16) on his repentance, contrasts with the human *eyes* of Antichrist, the pseudo son of man, viz., intellectual culture, while heart and mouth blaspheme God. The deterioration politically corresponds: the first kingdom, an organic unity; the second, divided into Median and Persian; the third branches off into four; the fourth, into ten. The two eastern kingdoms are marked by nobler metals; the two western, by baser; individualization and division appear in the latter, and it is they which produce the two Antichrists. **9. I beheld till**–I continued looking till. **thrones ... cast down**–rather, "thrones were *placed*" [*Vulgate* and LUTHER], viz., for the saints and elect angels to whom "judgment is given" (vs. 22), as assessors with the Judge. Cf. vs. 10, "thousand thousands ministered unto Him" (Matt. 19:28; Luke 22:30; I Cor. 6:2, 3; I Tim. 5:21; Rev. 2:26; 4:4). In *English Version* the thrones *cast down* are those of the previously mentioned kings who give place to Messiah. **Ancient of days**–"The everlasting Father" (Isa. 9:6). HE is the Judge here, as THE SON does not judge in His own cause, and it is His cause which is the one at issue with Antichrist. **sit**–the attitude of a judge about to pass sentence. **white**–The judicial purity of the Judge, and of all things round Him, is hereby expressed (Rev 1:14). **wheels** –as Oriental thrones move on wheels. Like the rapid flame, God's judgments are most swift in falling where He wills them (Ezek. 1:15, 16). The judgment here is not the last judgment, for *then* there will be no beast, and heaven and earth shall have passed away; but it is that on Antichrist (the last development of the fourth kingdom), typical of the last judgment: "Christ coming to substitute the millennial kingdom of *glory* for that of *the cross*" (Rev. 17:12-14; 19:15-21; 11:15). **10 thousand ... ministered unto him**–so at the giving of the law (Deut. 33:2; Ps. 68:17; Heb. 12:22; Jude 14). **ten ... thousand before him**–image from the Sanhedrin, in which the father of the consistory sat with his assessors on each side, in the form of a semicircle, and the people standing before him. **judgment was set**–The judges sat (Rev. 20:4). **books ... opened**–(Rev. 20:12). Forensic image; all the documents of the cause at issue, connected with the condemnation of Antichrist and his kingdom, and the setting up of Messiah's kingdom. *Judgment* must pass on the world as being under the curse, before the glory comes; but Antichrist offers glory without the cross, a renewed world without the world being *judged.* **11.** Here is set forth the execution on earth of the judgment pronounced in the unseen heavenly court of judicature (vss. 9, 10). **body ... given to ... flame**–(Rev. 19:20). **12.** "The rest of the beasts," i.e., the three first, had passed away not by *direct* destroying judgments, such as consumed the little horn, as being the finally matured evil of the fourth beast. They had continued to exist, but their *"dominion* was taken away"; whereas the fourth beast shall cease utterly, superseded by Messiah's kingdom. **for a season ... time**–Not only the triumph of the beasts over the godly, but their very

existence is limited to a *definite time,* and that time the *exactly suitable* one (cf. Matt. 24:22). Probably a definite period is meant by a "season and time" (cf. vs. 25; Rev. 20:3). It is striking, the fourth monarchy, though Christianized for 1500 years past, is not distinguished from the previous heathen monarchies, or from its own heathen portion. Nay, it is represented as the most God-opposed of all, and culminating at last in blasphemous Antichrist. The reason is: Christ's kingdom *now* is not of this world (John 18:36); and only at the second advent of Christ does it become an external power of the world. Hence Daniel, whose province it was to prophesy of the world powers, does not treat of Christianity until it becomes a world power, viz., at the second advent. The kingdom of God is a hidden one till Jesus comes again (Rom. 8:17; Col. 3:2, 3; II Tim. 2:11, 12). Rome was worldly while heathen, and remains worldly, though Christianized. So the New Testament views the present æon or age of the world as essentially heathenish, which we cannot love without forsaking Christ (Rom. 12:2; I Cor. 1:20; 2:6, 8; 3:18; 7: 31; II Cor. 4:4; Gal. 1:4; Eph. 2:2; II Tim. 4:10; cf. I John 2:15, 17). The object of Christianity is not so much to Christianize the present world as to save souls out of it, so as not to be condemned with the world (I Cor. 11:32), but to rule with Him in His millennium (Matt. 5:5; Luke 12:32; 22:28-30; Rom. 5:17; I Cor. 6:2; Rev. 1:6; 2:26-28; 3:21; 20: 4). This is to be our *hope,* not to reign in the present world course (I Cor. 4:8; II Cor. 4:18; Phil. 3: 20; Heb. 13:14). There must be a "regeneration" of the world, as of the individual, a death previous to a resurrection, a *destruction* of the world kingdoms, before they rise anew as the kingdoms of Christ (Matt. 19:28). Even the millennium will not perfectly eradicate the world's corruption; another apostasy and judgment will follow (Rev. 20:7-15), in which the world of *nature* is to be destroyed and renewed, as the world of *history* was before the millennium (II Pet. 3:8-13); then comes the perfect earth and heaven (Rev. 21:1). Thus there is an onward progress, and the Christian is *waiting* for the consummation (Mark 13:33-37; Luke 12:35, 36, 40-46; I Thess. 1:9, 10), as His Lord also is "expecting" (Heb. 10:13). **13. Son of man**–(See *Note,* Ezek. 2:1). Not merely Son of David, and King of Israel, but Head of restored *humanity* (corresponding to the world-wide horizon of Daniel's prophecy); the seed of the woman, crushing Antichrist, the seed of the serpent, according to the Protevangel in Paradise (Gen. 3). The Representative Man shall then realize the original destiny of man as Head of the creation (Gen. 1:26, 28); the center of unity to Israel and the Gentiles. The beast, which taken conjointly represents the four beasts, ascends from the sea (ch. 7:2; Rev. 13:1); the Son of man descends *from* "*heaven.*" Satan, as the serpent, is the representative head of all that is bestial; man, by following the serpent, has become bestial. God must, therefore, become man, so that man may cease to be beastlike. Whoever rejects the incarnate God will be judged by the Son of man just because He is the Son of man (John 5:27). This title is always associated with His coming again, because the kingdom that then awaits Him is that which belongs to Him as the Saviour of man, the Restorer of the lost inheritance. "Son of man" expresses His VISIBLE state, formerly in His humiliation, hereafter in His exaltation. He "comes to the Ancient of days" to be invested with the kingdom. Cf. Psalm 110:2: "The Lord shall send the rod of thy strength [Messiah] out of Zion." This investiture was at His ascension "with the clouds of heaven" (Acts 1:9; 2:33, 34; Ps. 2:6-9; Matt. 28:18), which is a pledge of His return "in like manner" in the clouds" (Acts 1:11; Matt. 26:64), and "with clouds" (Rev. 1:7). The kingdom then was given to Him in *title* and *invisible* exercise; at His second coming it shall be in *visible* administration. He will vindicate it from the misrule of those who received it to hold for and under God, but who ignored His supremacy. The Father will assert His right by the Son, the heir, who will hold it for Him (Ezek. 1:27; Heb. 1:2; Rev. 19:13-16). TREGELLES thinks the investiture here *immediately precedes* Christ's coming forth; because He sits at God's right hand *until* His enemies are made His footstool, *then* the kingdom is given to the Son in actual investiture, and He comes to crush His so prepared footstool under His feet. But the words, "with the clouds," and the universal power actually, though invisibly, given Him then (Eph. 1:20-22), agree best with His investiture at the ascension, which, in the prophetic view that overleaps the interval of ages, is the precursor of His coming visibly to reign; no event of equal moment taking place in the interval. **15. body**—lit., "sheath": the body being the "sheath" of the soul. **17. kings**—i.e., kingdoms. Cf. vs. 23, "fourth kingdom"; ch. 2: 38; 8:20-22. Each of the four kings represents a dynasty. Nebuchadnezzar, Alexander, Antiochus, and Antichrist, though *individually* referred to, are representatives of characteristic tendencies. **18. the Most High**—the emphatic title of God in this prophecy, who delegates His power first to Israel; then to the Gentiles (ch. 2:37, 38) when Israel fails to realize the idea of the theocracy; lastly, to Messiah, who shall rule truly for God, taking it from the Gentile world powers, whose history is one of continual degeneracy culminating in the last of the kings, Antichrist. Here, in the interpretation, "the saints," but in the vision (vss. 13, 14), "the Son of man," takes the kingdom; for Christ and His people are one in suffering, and one in glory. TREGELLES translates, "most high places" (Eph. 1:3; 2:6). Though oppressed by the beast and little horn, they belong not to the earth from which the four beasts arise, but to the most high places. **19.** Balaam, an Aramean, dwelling on the Euphrates, at the beginning of Israel's independent history, and Daniel at the close of it, prophetically exhibit to the hostile world powers Israel as triumphant over them at last, though the world powers of the East (Asshur) and the West (Chittim) carry all before them and afflict Eber (Israel) for a time (Num. 23:8-10, 28; 24:2, 7-9, 22-24). To Balaam's "Asshur" correspond Daniel's two eastern kingdoms, Babylon and Medo-Persia; to "Chittim," the two western kingdoms, Greece and Rome (cf. Gen. 10:4, 11, 22). In Babel, Nimrod the hunter (revolter) founds the first kingdom of the world (Gen. 10:8-13). The Babylonian world power takes up the thread interrupted at the building of Babel, and the kingdom of Nimrod. As at Babel, so in Babylon the world is united against God; Babylon, the first world power, thus becomes the type of the God-opposed world. The fourth monarchy consummates the evil; it is "diverse" from the others only in its more unlimited universality. The three first were not in the full sense universal monarchies. The fourth is; so in it the God-opposed principle finds its full development. All history moves within the Romanic, Germanic, and Slavonic nations; it shall continue so to Christ's second advent. The fourth monarchy

represents universalism externally; Christianity, internally. Rome is Babylon fully developed. It is the world power corresponding in contrast to Christianity, and therefore contemporary with it (Matt. 13:38; Mark 1:15; Luke 2:1; Gal. 4:4). **20. look ... more stout than ... fellows**—viz., than that of the other horns. **21. made war with the saints**—persecuted the Church (Rev. 11:7; 13:7). **prevailed** —but not ultimately. The limit is marked by "until" (vs. 22). The little horn continues, *without intermission,* to persecute up to Christ's second advent (Rev. 17:12, 14; 19:19, 20). **22. Ancient of days came**—The title applied to the Father in vs. 13 is here applied to the Son; who is called "the everlasting Father" (Isa. 9:6). The Father is never said to "come"; it is the Son who *comes.* **judgment was given to ... saints**—*Judgment* includes *rule;* "kingdom" in the end of this verse (I Cor. 6:2; Rev. 1:6, 5:10; 20:4). Christ first receives "judgment" and the "kingdom," then the saints with Him (vss. 13, 14). **24. ten horns**—answering to the ten "toes" (ch. 2:41). **out of this kingdom**—It is *out of the* fourth kingdom that ten others arise, whatever exterior territory any of them possess (Rev. 13:1; 17: 12). **rise after them**—yet contemporaneous with them; the ten are contemporaries. Antichrist rises after their rise, at first "little" (vs. 8); but after destroying three of the ten, he becomes greater than them all (vss. 20, 21). The three being gone, he is the eighth (cf. Rev. 17:11); a distinct head, and yet "of the seven." As the previous world kingdoms had their representative heads (Babylon, Nebuchadnezzar; Persia, Cyrus; Greece, Alexander), so the fourth kingdom and its Antichrists shall have their evil concentrated in the one final Antichrist. As Antiochus Epiphanes, the Antichrist of the third kingdom in ch. 8, was the personal enemy of God, so the final Antichrist of the fourth kingdom, his antitype. The Church has endured a pagan and a papal persecution; there remains for her an infidel persecution, general, purifying, and cementing [CECIL]. He will not merely, as Popery, *substitute* himself for Christ *in Christ's name,* but *"deny the* Father and the Son" (I John 2:22). The persecution is to continue *up to Christ's second coming* (vss. 21, 22); the horn of blasphemy cannot therefore be past; for now there is almost a general cessation of persecution. **25.** Three attributes of Antichrist are specified: (1) The highest worldly wisdom and civilization. (2) The uniting of the whole civilized world under his dominion. (3) Atheism, antitheism, and autotheism in its fullest development (I John 2:22). Therefore, not only is power taken from the fourth beast, as in the case of the other three, but God destroys it and the world power in general by a final judgment. The present external Christianity is to give place to an almost universal apostasy. **think**—lit., "carry within him as it were the burden of the thought." **change times**—the prerogative of God alone (ch. 2:21); blasphemously assumed by Antichrist. The "times and laws" here meant are those of religious ordinance; *stated times of feasts* [MAURER]. Perhaps there are included the *times assigned by God to the duration of kingdoms.* He shall set Himself above all that is called God (II Thess. 2:4), putting his own "will" above God's times and laws (ch. 11:36, 37). But the "times" of His wilfulness are limited for the elect's sake (Matt. 24:22). **they**—the saints. **given into his hand**—to be persecuted. **time ... times and ... dividing of time**—one year, two years, and half a year: 1260 days (Rev. 12:6, 14); forty-two months (Rev. 11:2, 3). That literally three and a half years are to be the term of Antichrist's persecution is favored by ch. 4:16, 23, where the year-day theory would be impossible. If the Church, moreover, had been informed that 1260 years must elapse before the second advent, the attitude of expectancy which is inculcated (Luke 12:38; I Cor. 1:7; I Thess. 1:9, 10; II Pet. 3:12) on the ground of the uncertainty of the time, would be out of place. The original word for "time" denotes *a stated period* or *set feast;* or the interval from one set feast to its recurrence, i.e., a year [TREGELLES]; Leviticus 23:4, "seasons"; Leviticus 23:44, "feasts." The passages in favor of the year-day theory are Ezekiel 4:6, where each day of the forty during which Ezekiel lay on his right side is defined by God as meaning a year. Cf. Numbers 14:34, where a year of wandering in the wilderness was appointed for each day of the forty during which the spies searched Canaan; but the days were, in these two cases, merely the type or reason for the years, which were *announced as they were to be fulfilled.* In the prophetic part of Numbers 14:34 *years* are literal. If the year-day system was applied to them, they would be 14,400 years! In Ezekiel 4:4-6, if *day* meant *year,* Ezekiel would have lain on his right side forty years! The context here in vss. 24, 25, is not symbolical. Antichrist is no longer called a horn, but a *king* subduing three out of ten *kings* (no longer horns. vss. 7, 8). So in ch. 12:7, where "time, times, and half a time," again occurs, nothing symbolic occurs in the context. So that there is no reason why the three and a half years should be so. For the first four centuries the "days" were interpreted literally; a mystical meaning of the 1260 days then began. WALTER BRUTE first suggested the year-day theory in the end of the fourteenth century. The *seventy years* of the Babylonian captivity foretold by Jeremiah (Jer. 25:12; 29:10) were understood by Daniel (ch. 9:2) as literal years, not symbolical, which would have been 25,200 years! [TREGELLES]. It is possible that the year-day and day-day theories are *both* true. The seven (symbolical) times of the Gentile monarchies (Lev. 26:24) during Israel's casting off will end in the seven years of Antichrist. The 1260 years of papal misrule in the name of Christ may be represented by three and a half years of open Antichristianity and persecution before the millennium. Witnessing churches may be succeeded by witnessing individuals, the former occupying the longer, the latter the shorter period (Rev. 11:3). The beginning of the 1260 years is by ELLIOTT set at A.D. 529 or 533, when Justinian's edict acknowledged Pope John II to be head of the Church; by LUTHER, at 606, when Phocas confirmed Justinian's grant. But 752 is the most likely date, when the *temporal* dominion of the popes began by Pepin's grant to Stephen II (for Zachary, his predecessor's recognition of his title to France), confirmed by Charlemagne. For it was then first that the little horn plucked up three horns, and so became the prolongation of the fourth *secular* kingdom [NEWTON]. This would bring us down to about A.D. 2000, or the seventh thousand millenary from creation. But CLINTON makes about 1862 the seventh millenary, which may favor the dating from A.D. 529. **26. consume ... destroy**—a twofold operation. Antichrist is to be *gradually* "consumed," as the Papacy has been consuming for 400 years past, and especially of late years. He is also to be "destroyed" *suddenly* by Christ at His coming; the fully developed man of sin (II Thess. 2:3) or false prophet making a last desperate effort in confederacy with the "beast" (Rev. 16:13, 14, 16) or

secular power of the Roman empire (some conjecture Louis Napoleon): destroyed at Armageddon in Palestine. **27. greatness of the kingdom under ... whole heaven**—The power, which those several kingdoms had possessed, shall all be conferred on Messiah's kingdom. "Under ... heaven," shows it is a kingdom *on earth*, not in heaven. **people of ... saints of ... Most High**—"the people of the saints, or holy ones" (*Margin*, ch. 8:24): the Jews, the people to whom the saints stand in a peculiar relation. The saints are gathered out of Jews and Gentiles, but the stock of the Church is Jewish (Rom. 9:24; 11:24); God's faithfulness to this election Church is thus virtually faithfulness to Israel, and a pledge of their future national blessing. Christ confirms this fact, while withholding the date (Acts 1:6, 7). **everlasting kingdom**—If *everlasting,* how can the kingdom here refer to the millennial one? Answer: Daniel saw the whole time of future blessedness as *one period.* The clearer light of the New Testament distinguishes, in the whole period, the millennium and the time of the new heaven and new earth (cf. Rev. 20:4 with 21:1 and 22:5). Christ's kingdom is "everlasting." Not even the last judgment shall end it, but only give it a more glorious appearance, the new Jerusalem coming down from God out of heaven, with the throne of God and the Lamb in it (cf. Rev. 5:9, 10; 11:15). **28. cogitations ... troubled me**—showing that the Holy Spirit intended much more to be understood by Daniel's words than Daniel himself understood. We are not to limit the significance of prophecies to what the prophets themselves understood (I Pet. 1: 11, 12).

CHAPTER 8

Vss. 1-27. VISION OF THE RAM AND HE-GOAT: THE 2300 DAYS OF THE SANCTUARY BEING TRODDEN DOWN. With this chapter the Hebrew part of the book begins and continues to be the language of the remainder; the visions relating wholly to the Jews and Jerusalem. The scene here narrows from world-wide prophecies to those affecting the one covenant people in the five centuries between the exile and the advent. Antichrist, like Christ, has a more immediate future, as well as one more remote. The vision, ch. 8, begins, and that, chs. 10-12, concludes, the account of the Antichrist of the third kingdom. Between the two visions ch. 9 is inserted, as to Messiah and the covenant people at the end of the half millennium (seventy weeks of years). **1. vision**—a higher kind of revelation than a dream. **after that ... at the first**—that in ch. 7:1. **2. Shushan**—Susa. Though then comparatively insignificant, it was destined to be the capital of Persia after Cyrus' time. Therefore Daniel is transported into it, as being the capital of the kingdom signified by the two-horned ram (Neh. 1:1; Esther 1:2-5). **Elam**—west of Persia proper, east of Babylonia, south of Media. Daniel was not present there personally, but *in vision*. **Ulai**—called in Pliny Eulœus; by the Greeks, Choaspes. Now Kerah, or Karasu. So in ch. 10:4 he receives a vision near another river, the Hiddekel. So Ezekiel (Ezek. 1:1) at the Chebar. Perhaps because synagogues used to be built near rivers, as before praying they washed their hands in the water [ROSENMULLER], (Ps. 137:1). **3. two horns**—The *"two"* ought not to be in italics, as if it were not in the original; for it is expressed by the *Hebrew* dual. "Horn" in the East is the symbol of power and royalty. **one ... high-**

er than ... other ... the higher came up last—Persia, which was of little note till Cyrus' time, became then ascendant over Media, the more ancient kingdom. Darius was sixty-two years old (ch. 5:31) when he began to reign; during his short reign of two years, being a weak king (ch. 6), the government was almost entirely in Cyrus' hands. Hence HERODOTUS does not mention Darius; but XENOPHON does under the name of Cyaxares II. The "ram" here corresponds to the "bear" (ch. 7:5), symbolizing *clumsy firmness.* The king of Persia wore a jewelled ram's head of gold instead of a diadem, such as are seen on the pillars at Persepolis. Also the *Hebrew* for "ram" springs from the same root as "Elam," or Persia [NEWTON]. The "one horn higher than the other" answers to the bear "raising itself *on one side*" (cf. *Note,* ch. 7:5). **4. ram pushing westward**—Persia conquered westward Babylon, Mesopotamia, Syria, Asia Minor. **northward**—Colchis, Armenia, Iberia, and the dwellers on the Caspian Sea. **southward**—Judea, Egypt, Ethiopia, Libya; also India, under Darius. He does not say *eastward,* for the Persians themselves came from the east (Isa. 46:11). **did according to his will**—(Ch. 11:3, 16; cf. ch. 5:19). **5. he-goat**—Græco-Macedonia. **notable horn**—Alexander. "Touched not ... ground," implies the incredible swiftness of his conquests; he overran the world in less than twelve years. The he-goat answers to the leopard (ch. 7:6). Caranus, the first king of Macedonia, was said to have been led by *goats* to Edessa, which he made the seat of his kingdom, and called Æge, i.e., "goat-city." **6. standing before the river**—Ulai. It was at the "river" Granicus that Alexander fought his first victorious battle against Darius, 334 B.C. **7. moved with choler**—Alexander represented the concentrated wrath of Greece against Persia for the Persian invasions of Greece; also for the Persian cruelties to Greeks, and Darius' attempts to seduce Alexander's soldiers to treachery [NEWTON]. **stamped upon him**—In 331 B.C. he defeated Darius Codomanus, and in 330 B.C. burned Persepolis and completed the conquest of Persia. **none ... could deliver**—Not the immense hosts of Persia could save it from the small army of Alexander (Ps. 33:16). **8. when he was strong ... great horn was broken**—The empire was in full strength at Alexander's death by fever at Babylon, and seemed then least likely to fall. Yet it was then "broken." His natural brother, Philip Aridœus, and his two sons, Alexander Ægus and Hercules, in fifteen months were murdered. **four ... toward ... four winds**—Seleucus, in the east, obtained Syria, Babylonia, Media, etc.; Cassander, in the west, Macedon Thessaly, Greece; Ptolemy, in the south, Egypt, Cyprus, etc.; Lysimachus, in the north, Thrace, Cappadocia, and the north parts of Asia Minor. **9. little horn**—not to be confounded with the little horn of the fourth kingdom in ch. 7:8. The little horn in ch. 7 comes as an eleventh horn after ten preceding horns. In ch. 8 it is not an independent fifth horn, after the four previous ones, but it arises out of one of the four existing horns. This horn is explained (vs. 23) to be "a king of fierce countenance," etc. Antiochus Epiphanes is meant. Greece with all its refinement produces the first, i.e., the Old Testament Antichrist. Antiochus had an extraordinarily love of art, which expressed itself in grand temples. He wished to substitute Zeus Olympius for Jehovah at Jerusalem. Thus first heathen civilization from below, and revealed religion from above, came into collision. Identifying himself with Jupiter, his aim was to make *his own* worship universal (cf. vs. 25 with ch. 11:36);

so mad was he in this that he was called Epimanes (maniac) instead of Epiphanes. None of the previous world rulers, Nebuchadnezzar (ch. 4:31-34), Darius (ch. 6:27, 28), Cyrus (Ezra 1:2-4), Artaxerxes Longimanus (Ezra 7:12), had systematically opposed the Jews' religious worship. Hence the need of prophecy to prepare them for Antiochus. The struggle of the Maccabees was a fruit of Daniel's prophecy (I Maccabees 2:59). He is the forerunner of the final Antichrist, standing in the same relation to the first advent of Christ that Antichrist does to His second coming. The sins in Israel which gave rise to the Greek Antichrist were that some Jews adopted Hellenic customs (cf. ch. 11:30, 32), erecting theaters, and regarding all religions alike, sacrificing to Jehovah, but at the same time sending money for sacrifices to Hercules. Such shall be the state of the world when ripe for Antichrist. At vs. 9 and vs. 23 the description passes from the literal Antiochus to features which, though partially attributed to him, hold good in their fullest sense only of his antitype, the New Testament Antichrist. The Mohammedan Antichrist may also be included; answering to the Euphratean (Turk) horsemen (Rev. 9:14-21), loosed "an hour, a day, a month, a year" (391 years, in the year-day theory), to scourge corrupted idolatrous Christianity. In A.D. 637 the Saracen Moslem mosque of Omar was founded on the site of the temple, "treading under foot the sanctuary" (vss. 11 -13); and there it still remains. The first conquest of the Turks over Christians was in A.D. 1281; and 391 years after they reached their zenith of power and began to decline, Sobieski defeating them at Vienna. Mohammed II, called "the conqueror," reigned A.D. 1451-1481, in which period Constantinople fell; 391 years after brings us to our own day, in which Turkey's fall is imminent. **waxed ... great; toward ... south**—(ch. 11:25). Antiochus fought against Ptolemy Philometer and Egypt, i.e., the south. **toward the east**—He fought against those who attempted a change of government in Persia. **toward the pleasant land**—Judea, "the glorious land" (ch. 11:16, 41, 45; cf. Ps. 48:2; Ezek. 20:6, 15). Its chief *pleasantness* consists in its being God's chosen land (Ps. 132:13; Jer. 3:19). Into it Antiochus made his inroad after his return from Egypt. **10. great, even to ... host of heaven**—explained in vs. 24, "the mighty and holy people," i.e., the Jews (ch. 7:21) and their priests (cf. Isa. 24:21). The Levites' service is called "a *warfare*" (*Margin,* Num. 8:24, 25). Great civil and religious powers are symbolized by "stars" (Matt. 24:29). See I Maccabees 1:25, etc.; 2:35, etc.; 5:2, 12, 13. TREGELLES refers "stars" to those Jews whose portion from God is heavenly glory (ch. 12:3), being believers in Him who is above at God's right hand: not the blinded Jews. **cast ... stars to the ground**—So Babel, as type of Antichrist, is described (Isa. 14: 13, 14), "I will exalt my throne above the stars of God." Cf. Revelation 12:4; II Maccabees 9:10, as to Antiochus. **11. to the prince of the host**—i.e., God Himself, the Lord of Sabaoth, the hosts in heaven and earth, stars, angels, and earthly ministers. So vs. 25, he shall stand up against the *Prince of princes";* "against the God of gods" (ch. 11:36; cf. ch. 7:8). He not only opposes God's ancient people, but also God Himself. **daily sacrifice** —offered morning and evening (Exod. 29:38, 39). **taken away**—by Antiochus (I Maccabees 1:20-50). **sanctuary ... cast down**—Though robbed of its treasures, it was not strictly "cast down" by Antiochus. So that a fuller accomplishment is future.

Antiochus took away the daily sacrifice for a few years; the Romans, for many ages, and "cast down" the temple; and Antichrist, in connection with Rome, the fourth kingdom, shall do so again after the Jews in their own land, still unbelieving, shall have rebuilt the temple, and restored the Mosaic ritual: God giving them up to him "by reason of transgression" (vs. 12), i.e., not owning the worship so rendered [Tregelles]; and then the opposition of the horn to the "truth" is especially mentioned. **12. an host**—rather, "*the* host was given *up* to him," i.e., *the holy people* were given into his hands. So in vs. 10 "the host" is used; and again in vs. 13, where also "give" is used as here for "*giving up*" for destruction (cf. ch. 11:6) [Maurer]. **against ... daily sacrifice**—rather (the host was given up for him to tread upon), "*together* with the daily sacrifice" (cf. vs. 13). **by reason of transgression**—I Maccabees 1:11-16 traces all the calamities suffered under Antiochus to the *transgression* of certain Jews who introduced heathen customs into Jerusalem just before. But *transgression* was not *at the full* (vs. 23) under Antiochus; for Onias the high priest administered the laws in godliness at the time (II Maccabees 3:1). Therefore the "transgression" must refer to that of the Jews hereafter restored to Palestine in unbelief. **the truth**—the worship of the true God. Isaiah 59:14, "Truth is fallen in the street." **practised, and prospered**—Whatever he undertook succeeded (vs. 4; ch. 11:28, 36). **13. that certain saint**—Daniel did not know the names of these two holy angels, but saw only that one was speaking to the other. **How long shall be the vision concerning ... daily sacrifice**—How long shall the daily sacrifice be suspended? **transgression of desolation—lit.**, "making desolate," i.e., Antiochus' *desolating profanation* of the temple (ch. 11:31; 12: 11). Cf. as to Rome and the last Antichrist, Matthew 24:15. **14. unto me**—The answer is to *Daniel*, not to the inquirer, for the latter had asked in Daniel's name; as vice versa the saint or angel (Job 15:15; Ps. 89:6, 7) speaks of the vision granted to Daniel, as if it had been granted to himself. For holy men are in Scripture represented as having attendant angels, with whom they are in a way identified in interests. If the conversation had been limited to the angels, it could have been of no use to us. But God conveys it to prophetical men, for our good, through the ministry of angels. **two thousand ... three hundred days**—lit., "mornings and evenings," specified in connection with the *morning and evening* sacrifice. Cf. Genesis 1:5. Six years and 110 days. This includes not only the three and a half years during which the daily sacrifice was *forbidden* by Antiochus (Josephus, B. J. 1. 1. sec. 1), but the whole series of events whereby it was practically interrupted: beginning with the "little horn waxing great toward the pleasant land," and "casting down some of the host" (vss. 9, 10); viz., when in 171 B.C., or the month Sivan in the year 142 of the era of the Seleucidæ, the sacrifices began to be neglected, owing to the high priest Jason introducing at Jerusalem Grecian customs and amusements, the palæstra and gymnasium; ending with the death of Antiochus, 165 B.C., or the month Shebath, in the year 148 of the Seleucid era. Cf. I Maccabees 1:11-15; II Maccabees 4:9, etc. The reason for the greater minuteness of historical facts and dates, given in Daniel's prophecies, than in those of the New Testament, is that Israel, not having yet the clear views which Christians have of immortality and the heavenly inheritance, could only be directed to the earthly future: for it was on earth the looked-for Messiah was to appear, and the sum and subject of Old Testament prophecy was *the kingdom of God upon earth*. The minuteness of the revelation of Israel's earthly destiny was to compensate for the absence, in the Old Testament, of views of heavenly glory. Thus, in ch. 9, the times of Messiah are foretold to the very year; in ch. 8 the times of Antiochus, even to the day; and in ch. 11 the Syro-Egyptian struggles in most minute detail. Tregelles thinks the 2300 days answer to the week of years (ch. 9:27), during which the destroying prince (ch. 9:26) makes a covenant, which he breaks in the midst of the week (viz., at the end of three and a half years). The seven years exceed the 2300 days by considerably more than a half year. This period of the seven years' excess above the 2300 days may be allotted to the preparations needed for setting up the temple worship, with Antichrist's permission to the restored Jews, according to his "covenant" with them; and the 2300 days may date from the actual setting up of the worship. But, says Auberlen, the more accurate to a day the dates as to Antiochus are given, the less should we say the 1290, or 1335 days (ch. 12:11, 12) correspond to the half week (roughly), and the 2300 to the whole. The event, however, may, in the case of Antichrist, show a correspondence between the days here given and ch. 9:27, such as is not yet discernible. The term of 2300 days cannot refer to 2300 years of the treading down of Christianity by Mohammedanism, as this would leave the greater portion of the time yet future; whereas, Mohammedanism is fast waning. If the 2300 *days* mean *years*, dating from Alexander's conquests, 334 B.C. to 323, we should arrive at about the close of the sixth thousand years of the world, just as the 1260 years (ch. 7:25) from Justinian's decree arrive at the same terminus. The Jews' tradition represents the seventh thousand as the millennium. Cumming remarks, 480 B.C. is the date of the waning of the Persian empire before Greece; deducting 480 from 2300, we have 1820; and in 1821, Turkey, the successor of the Greek empire, began to wane, and Greece became a separate kingdom. See *Note*, ch. 12:11. **cleansed**—lit., "justified," vindicated from profanation. Judas Maccabeus celebrated the feast of dedication after the cleansing, on the twenty-fifth of the ninth month, Kisleu (I Maccabees 4:51-58; II Maccabees 10:1-7; John 10:22). As to the antitypical dedication of the new temple, see Ezekiel 43, etc.; also Amos 9:11, 12. **16. Gabriel**—meaning, "the strength of God." **17. the time of the end**—so vs. 19; ch. 11:35, 36, 40. The event being to take place at "the time of the end" makes it likely that the Antichrist ultimately referred to (besides the immediate reference to Antiochus) in this chapter, and the one in ch. 7:8, are one and the same. The objection that the one in ch. 7 springs out of the ten divisions of the Roman earth, the fourth kingdom, the one in ch. 8 and ch. 11 from one of the four divisions of the third kingdom, Greece, is answered thus: The four divisions of the Grecian empire, having become parts of the Roman empire, shall at the end form four of its ten final divisions [Tregelles]. However, the origin from one of the four parts of the third kingdom may be *limited to Antiochus*, the immediate subject of ch. 8 and ch. 11, while the ulterior typical reference of these chapters (viz., Antichrist) may belong to one of the ten Roman divisions, not *necessarily* one formerly of the four of the third kingdom. The event will tell. "Time of the end" may apply to the time of Antiochus. For it is the prophetic phrase for the time of fulfilment, seen always at the end of the prophetic horizon (Gen. 49:1; Num. 24:14). **19. the last end of the indignation**—God's displeasure against the Jews for their sins. For their comfort they are told, the calamities about to come are not to be for ever. The "time" is limited (ch. 9:27; 11:27, 35, 36; 12:7; Hab. 2:3). **21. the first king**—Philip was king of Macedon before Alexander, but the latter was the first who, as a generalissimo of Greece, subdued the Persian empire. **22. not in his power**—not with the power which Alexander possessed [MAURER]. An empire united, as under Alexander, is more powerful than one divided, as under the four Diadochi. **23. transgressors are come to the full**—This does not hold good of the times of Antiochus, but of the closing times of the Christian era. Cf. Luke 18:8, and II Timothy 3: 1-9, as to the wickedness of the world in general just before Christ's second coming. *Israel's* guilt, too, shall then be at the full, when they who rejected Christ shall receive Antichrist; fulfilling Jesus' words, "I am come in My Father's name, and ye receive Me not; if another shall come in his own name, him ye will receive" (cf. Gen. 15:16; Matt. 23:32; I Thess. 2:16). **of fierce countenance**—(Deut. 28:50); one who will spare neither old nor young. **understanding dark sentences**—rather, "artifices" [GESENIUS]. Antiochus made himself master of Egypt and Jerusalem successively by *craft* (I Maccabees 1:30, etc.; II Maccabees 5:24, etc.). **24. not by his own power**—which in the beginning was "little" (vs. 9; ch. 7:8); but by gaining over others through craft, the once *little* horn became "mighty" (cf. vs. 25; ch. 11:23). To be fully realized by Antichrist. He shall act by the power of Satan, who shall then be permitted to work through him in unrestricted license, such as he has not now (Rev. 13:2; hence the ten kingdoms shall give the beast their power (II Thess. 2:9-12; Rev. 17:13). **prosper and practise**—prosper in all that he attempts (vs. 12). **holy people**—His persecutions are especially directed against the *Jews*. **25. by peace**—by pretending "peace" and friendship; *in the midst of security* [GESENIUS], suddenly striking his blow (cf. *Note,* Jer. 15:8). "A spoiler *at noon-day.*" **also . . . against the Prince of princes**—not merely against the Jews (vs. 11; ch. 11:36). **broken without hand** —by God's special visitation. The stone "cut out of the mountain without hands," i.e., Christ is to smite the world-power image *on his feet* (ch. 2:34), i.e., in its last development (cf. ch. 7:11). Antiochus' horrible death by worms and ulcers, when on his way to Judea, intending to take vengeance for the defeat of his armies by the Maccabees, was a primary fulfilment, foreshadowing God's judgment on the last enemy of the Jewish Church. **26. shut . . . up . . . vision**—implying the vision was *not to be understood* for the present. In Revelation 22:10 it is said, *"Seal not the vision, for the time is at hand."* What in Daniel's time was hidden was more fully explained in Revelation, and as the time draws nearer, it will be clearer still. **it shall be for many days**—It refers to remote times (Ezek. 12:27). **27. I . . . was sick**—through grief at the calamities coming on my people and the Church of God (cf. Ps. 102:14). **afterward I . . . did the king's business**— He who holds nearest communion with heaven can best discharge the duties of common life. **none understood it**—He had heard of kings, but knew not their names; He foresaw the events, but not the time when they were to take place; thereupon he could only feel "astonished," and leave all with the omniscient God [JEROME].

CHAPTER 9

Vss. 1-27. DANIEL'S CONFESSION AND PRAYER FOR JERUSALEM: GABRIEL COMFORTS HIM BY THE PROPHECY OF THE SEVENTY WEEKS. The world powers here recede from view; Israel, and the salvation by Messiah promised to it, are the subject of revelation. Israel had naturally expected salvation at the end of the captivity. Daniel is therefore told, that, after the seventy years of the captivity, seventy times seven must elapse, and that even then Messiah would not come in glory as the Jews might through misunderstanding expect from the earlier prophets, but by dying would put away sin. This ninth chapter (Messianic prophecy) stands between the two visions of the Old Testament Antichrist, to comfort "the wise." In the interval between Antiochus and Christ, no further revelation was needed; therefore, as in the first part of the book, so in the second, Christ and Antichrist in connection are the theme. **1. first year of Darius**—Cyaxares II, in whose name Cyrus, his nephew, son-in-law, and successor, took Babylon, 538 B.C. The date of this chapter is therefore 537 B.C., a year before Cyrus permitted the Jews to return from exile, and sixty-nine years after Daniel had carried captive at the beginning of the captivity, 606 B.C. **son of Ahasuerus**—called Astyages by XENOPHON. Ahasuerus was a name common to many of the kings of Medo-Persia. **made king**—The phrase implies that Darius owed the kingdom not to his own prowess, but to that of another, viz., Cyrus. **2. understood by books**— rather, letters, i.e., Jeremiah's letter (Jer. 29:10) to the captives in Babylon; also Jeremiah 25:11, 12; cf. II Chronicles 36:21; Jeremiah 30:18; 31:38. God's promises are the ground on which we should, like Daniel, rest sure hope; not so as to make our prayers needless, but rather to encourage them. **3. prayer . . . supplications**—lit., "intercessions . . . entreaties *for mercy.*" Praying for *blessings,* and deprecating evils. **4. my confession**—according to God's promises in Leviticus 26:39-42, that if Israel in exile for sin should repent and *confess,* God would remember for them His covenant with Abraham (cf. Deut. 30:1-5; Jer. 29:12-14; Jas. 4:10). God's promise was absolute, but prayer also was ordained as about to precede its fulfilment, this too being the work of God *in* His people, as much as the *external* restoration which was to follow. So it shall be at Israel's final restoration (Ps. 102:13-17). Daniel takes his countrymen's place of confession of sin, identifying himself with them, and, as their representative and intercessory priest, "accepts the punishment of their iniquity." Thus he typifies Messiah, the Sin-bearer and great Intercessor. The prophet's own life and experience form the fit starting point of the prophecy concerning the sin-atonement. He prays for Israel's restoration as associated in the prophets (cf. Jer. 31:4, 11, 12, 31, etc.) with the hope of Messiah. The revelation, now granted, analyzes into its successive parts that which the prophets, in prophetical perspective, heretofore saw together in one; viz., the redemption from captivity, and the full Messianic redemption. God's servants, who, like Noah's father (Gen. 5:29), hoped many a time that now the Comforter of their afflictions was at hand, had to wait from age to age, and to view preceding fulfilments only as pledges of the coming of Him whom they so earnestly desired to see (Matt. 13:17); as now also Christians, who believe that the Lord's second coming is nigh, are expected to continue waiting. So Daniel is informed of a long period of seventy prophetic weeks before Messiah's coming, instead of seventy years, as *he* might have expected (cf. Matt. 18:21, 22) [AUBERLEN]. **great and dreadful God**—as we know to our cost by the calamities we suffer. The *greatness* of God and His *dreadful* abhorrence of sin should prepare sinners for reverent, humble acknowledgment of the justice of their punishment. **keeping ... covenant and mercy**—i.e., the covenant of Thy mercy, whereby Thou hast promised to deliver us, not for our merits, but of Thy mercy (Ezek. 36:22, 23). So weak and sinful is man that any covenant for good on God's part with him, to take effect, must depend solely on His grace. If He be a God to be *feared* for His justice, He is one to be *trusted* for His "mercy." **love ... keep his commandments**—Keeping His commandments is the only sure test of love to God (John 14:15). **5.** Cf. Nehemiah's confession (Nehemiah 9). **sinned ... committed iniquity ... done wickedly ... rebelled**—a climax. Erred in *ignorance* ... sinned by *infirmity* ... *habitually and wilfully* done wickedness ... as *open and obstinate rebels* set ourselves against God. **6. prophets ... spake ... to our kings ... to all the people**—They fearlessly warned all without respect of persons. **7. confusion of faces, as at this day**—Shame at our guilt, betrayed in our countenance, is what belongs to us; as our punishment "at this day" attests. **near, and ... far off**—the chastisement, however varied, some Jews not being cast off so far from Jerusalem as others, all alike were sharers in the guilt. **9. mercies**—The *plural* intensifies the force; mercy manifold and exhibited in countless ways. As it is humbling to recollect "*righteousness* belongeth unto God," so it is comforting, that "*mercies* belong to the Lord OUR God." **though we have rebelled**—rather, "since ..." [*Vulgate*], (Ps. 25:11). Our punishment is not inconsistent with His "mercies," *since* we have rebelled against Him. **10. set before us**—not ambiguously, but plainly, so that we were without excuse. **11. all**—(Ps. 14:3; Rom. 3:12). **the curse ... and ... oath ... in ... law**—the *curse* against Israel, if disobedient, which God ratified by *oath* (Lev. 26:14-39; Deut. 27:15-26; 28:15-68; 29). **12. confirmed his words**—showed by the punishments we suffer, that His words were no idle threats. **under ... heaven hath not been done as ... upon Jerusalem**—(Lam. 1:12). **13. yet made we not our prayer before**—lit., "soothed not the face of." Not even our chastisement has taught us penitence (Isa. 9:13; Jer. 5:3; Hos. 7:10). Diseased, we spurn the healing medicine. **that we might turn ...**—Prayer can only be accepted when joined with the desire to *turn* from sin to God (Ps. 66:18; Prov. 28:9). **understand thy truth**—"attentively regard Thy faithfulness" in fulfilling Thy promises, and also Thy threats [CALVIN]. *Thy law* (ch. 8:12), [MAURER]. **14. watched upon the evil**—expressing ceaseless vigilance that His people's sins might not escape His judgment, as a watchman on guard night and day (Job 14:16; Jer. 31:28; 44:27). God *watching* upon the Jews' punishment forms a striking contrast to the Jews' slumbering in their sins. **God is righteous**—True penitents "justify" God, "ascribing righteousness to Him," instead of complaining of their punishment as too severe (Neh. 9:33; Job 36:3; Ps. 51:4; Lam. 3:39-42). **15. brought thy people ... out of ... Egypt**—a proof to all ages that the seed of Abraham is Thy covenant people. That ancient benefit gives us hope that Thou wilt confer a like one on us now under similar circumstances (Ps. 80:8-14; Jer. 32:21; 23:7, 8). **as at this day**—is known. **16. thy righteousness**—not stern *justice* in punishing, but Thy

faithfulness to Thy promises of mercy to them who trust in Thee (Ps. 31:1; 143:1). **thy city**—chosen as *Thine* in the election of grace, which changes not. **for ... iniquities of ... fathers**—(Exod. 20:5). He does not impugn God's justice in this, as did the murmurers (Ezek. 18:2, 3; cf. Jer. 31:29). **thy people ... a reproach**—which brings reproach on Thy name. "All the nations that are about us" will say that Thou, Jehovah, wast not able to save Thy peculiar people. So vs. 17, "for the Lord's sake"; vs. 19, "for Thine own sake" (Isa. 48:9, 11). **17. cause thy face to shine**—metaphor from the sun, which gladdens all that it beams upon (Num. 6:25; Mal. 4:2). **18. present ... supplications**—lit., "cause to fall ..." (cf. *Note,* Jer. 36:7). **19.** The short broken ejaculations and repetitions show the intense fervor of his supplications. **defer not**—He implies that the seventy years are now all but complete. **thine own sake**—often repeated, as being the strongest plea (Jer. 14:21). **20. whiles I was speaking**—repeated in vs. 21; emphatically marking that the answer was given before the prayer was completed, as God promised (Isa. 30:19; 65:24; cf. Ps. 32:5). **21. I had seen in the vision at the beginning**—viz., in the former vision by the river Ulai (ch. 8:1, 16). **fly swiftly**—lit., "with weariness," i.e., move swiftly as one breathless and wearied out with quick running [GESENIUS]. *English Version* is better (Isa. 6:2; Ezek. 1:6; Rev. 14:6). **time of ... evening oblation**—the ninth hour, three o'clock (cf. I Kings 18:36). As formerly, when the temple stood, this hour was devoted to sacrifices, so now to prayer. Daniel, during the whole captivity to the very last, with pious patriotism never forgot God's temple-worship, but speaks of its rites long abolished, as if still in use. **22. to give thee ... understanding**—Ch. 8:16; vs. 26 in that chapter shows that the symbolical vision had not been understood. God therefore now gives "information" directly, instead of by symbol, which required interpretation. **23. At the beginning of thy supplications ...**—The promulgation of the divine decree was made in heaven to the angels as soon as Daniel began to pray. **came forth**—from the divine throne; so vs. 22. **thou art greatly beloved**—lit., "a man of desires" (cf. Ezek. 23:6,12); the object of God's delight. As the apocalyptic prophet of the New Testament was "the disciple whom Jesus loved," so the apocalyptic prophet of the Old Testament was "greatly beloved" of God. **the vision**—the further revelation as to Messiah in connection with Jeremiah's prophecy of seventy years of the captivity. The charge to "understand" is the same as in Matthew 24:15, where Rome primarily, and Antichrist ultimately, is referred to (cf. *Note*, vs. 27, below). **24. Seventy weeks**—viz., of years; lit., Seventy sevens"; seventy heptads or hebdomads; 490 years; expressed in a form of "*concealed* definiteness" [HENGSTENBERG], a usual way with the prophets. The Babylonian captivity is a turning point in the history of the kingdom of God. It terminated the free Old Testament theocracy. Up to that time Israel, though oppressed at times, was, as a rule, free. From the Babylonian captivity the theocracy never recovered its full freedom down to its entire suspension by Rome; and this period of Israel's subjection to the Gentiles is to continue till the millennium (Rev. 20), when Israel shall be restored as head of the New Testament theocracy, which will embrace the whole earth. The free theocracy ceased in the first year of Nebuchadnezzar, and the fourth of Jehoiakim; the year of the world 3338, the point at which the seventy years of the captivity begin. Heretofore Israel had a right, if subjugated by a foreign king, to shake off the yoke (Judg. 4 and 5; II Kings 18:7) as an unlawful one, at the first opportunity. But the prophets (Jer. 27:9-11) declared it to be *God's will* that they should submit to Babylon. Hence every effort of Jehoiakim, Jeconiah, and Zedekiah to rebel was vain. The period of the world-times, and of Israel's depression, from the Babylonian captivity to the millennium, though abounding more in afflictions (e.g., the two destructions of Jerusalem, Antiochus' persecution, and those which Christians suffered), contains all that was good in the preceding ones, summed up in Christ, but in a way visible only to the eye of faith. Since He came as a servant, He chose for His appearing the period darkest of all as to His people's temporal state. Always fresh persecutors have been rising, whose end is destruction, and so it shall be with the last enemy, Antichrist. As the Davidic epoch is the point of the covenant people's highest glory, so the captivity is that of their lowest humiliation. Accordingly, the people's sufferings are reflected in the picture of the suffering Messiah. He is no longer represented as the theocratic King, the Antitype of David, but as the Servant of God and Son of man; at the same time the cross being the way to glory (cf. ch. 9 with ch. 2:34, 35, 44, and ch. 12:7). In the second and seventh chapters, Christ's first coming is not noticed, for Daniel's object was to prophesy to his nation as to the whole period from the destruction to the re-establishment of *Israel;* but this ninth chapter minutely predicts Christ's first coming, and its effects on the covenant people. *The seventy weeks date thirteen years before the rebuilding of Jerusalem;* for then the re-establishment of the theocracy began, viz., at *the return of Ezra to Jerusalem,* 457 B.C. So Jeremiah's seventy years of the captivity begin 606 B.C., eighteen years before the destruction of Jerusalem, for then Judah ceased to exist as an independent theocracy, having fallen under the sway of Babylon. Two periods are marked in Ezra: (1) The return from the captivity under Jeshua and Zerubbabel, and rebuilding of the *temple,* which was the first anxiety of the theocratic nation. (2) The return of Ezra (regarded by the Jews as a second Moses) from Persia to Jerusalem, the restoration of *the city, the nationality,* and the law. Artaxerxes, in the *seventh* year of his reign, gave him the commission which virtually includes permission to rebuild the city, afterwards confirmed to, and carried out by, Nehemiah in the *twentieth* year (Ezra 9:9; 7, 11, etc.); vs. 25, "from the going forth of the commandment *to build Jerusalem,"* proves that the second of the two periods is referred to. The words in verse 24 are not, "are determined upon the holy city," but *"upon thy people* and thy holy city"; thus the restoration of the religious *national polity* and the law (the inner work fulfilled by Ezra the priest), and the rebuilding of the *houses and walls* (the outer work of Nehemiah, the governor), are both included in vs. 25, "restore and build Jerusalem." "Jerusalem" represents both the city, the body, and the congregation, the soul of the state. Cf. Psalms 46, 48, 87. The starting point of the seventy weeks dated from eighty-one years after Daniel received the prophecy: the object being not to fix *for him* definitely the time, but for the Church: the prophecy taught *him* that the Messianic redemption, which he thought near, was separated from him by at least a half millennium. Expectation was sufficiently kept alive by the *general* conception of the time; not only the Jews, but many Gentiles looked for some great Lord of the earth to spring from Judea *at that very time* (TACITUS, *Hist.* 5.13; SUETONIUS, *Vesp.* 4). Ezra's placing of Daniel in the canon immediately before his own book and Nehemiah's was perhaps owing to his feeling that he himself brought about the beginning of the fulfilment of the prophecy (ch. 9) [AUBERLEN]. **determined**—*lit.,* "cut out," viz., from the whole course of time, for God to deal in a particular manner with Jerusalem. **thy...thy**—Daniel had in his prayer often spoken of Israel as *"Thy* people, *Thy* holy city"; but Gabriel, in reply, speaks of them as *Daniel's* ("thy" ... "thy") people and city, God thus intimating that until the "everlasting righteousness" should be brought in by Messiah, He could not fully own them as *His* [TREGELLIS] (cf. Exod. 32:7). Rather, as God is wishing to console Daniel and the godly Jews, "the people whom *thou* art so anxiously praying for"; such weight does God give to the intercessions of the righteous (Jas. 5:16-18). **finish**—*lit.,* "shut up"; remove from God's sight, i.e., abolish (Ps. 51:9) [LENGKERKE]. The seventy years' exile was a punishment, but not a full atonement, for the sin of the people; this would come only after seventy prophetic weeks, through Messiah. **make an end of**—The *Hebrew* reading, "to steal," i.e., to hide out of sight (from the custom of *sealing* up things to be concealed, cf. Job 9:7), is better supported. **make reconciliation for**—*lit.,* "to cover," to overlay (as with pitch, Gen. 6:14). Cf. Psalm 32:1. **bring in everlasting righteousness**—viz., the restoration of the normal state between God and man (Jer. 23:5, 6); to continue eternally (Heb. 9: 12; Rev. 14:6). **seal up...vision...prophecy**—lit., "prophet." To give the seal of confirmation to the prophet and his vision by the fulfilment. **anoint the Most Holy**—primarily, to "anoint," or to *consecrate* after its pollution "the Most Holy" *place* but mainly *Messiah,* the antitype to the Most Holy place (John 2:19-22). The propitiatory in the temple (the same Greek word expresses *the mercy seat* and *propitiation,* Rom. 3:25), which the Jews looked for at the restoration from Babylon, shall have its true realization only in Messiah. For it is only when sin is "made an end of" that God's presence can be perfectly manifested. As to "anoint," cf. Exodus 40:9, 34. Messiah was *anointed* with the Holy Ghost (Acts 4:27; 10:38). So hereafter, God-Messiah will "anoint" or consecrate with His presence the holy place at Jerusalem (Jer. 3:16, 17; Ezek. 37:27, 28), after its pollution by Antichrist, of which the feast of dedication after the pollution by Antiochus was a type. **25. from the going forth of the commandment**—viz., the command from God, whence originated the command of the Persian king (Ezra 6:14). AUBERLEN remarks, there is but one Apocalypse in each Testament. Its purpose in each is to sum up all the preceding prophecies, previous to the "troublous times" of the Gentiles, in which there was to be no revelation. Daniel sums up all the previous Messianic prophecy, separating into its individual phases what the prophets had seen in one and the same perspective, the temporary deliverance from captivity and the antitypical final Messianic deliverance. The seventy weeks are separated (vss. 25-27) into three unequal parts, seven, sixty-two, one. The seventieth is the consummation of the preceding ones, as the Sabbath of God succeeds the working days; an idea suggested by the division into *weeks.* In the sixty-nine weeks Jerusalem is restored, and so a place is prepared for Messiah wherein to accomplish His sabbatic work (vss. 25, 26) of "confirming the covenant" (vs. 27). The Messianic time is the Sabbath of Israel's history, in which it had the offer of all God's mercies, but in which it was cut off for a time by its rejection of them. As the seventy weeks end with seven years, or a week, so they begin with seven times seven, i.e., seven weeks. As the seventieth week is separated from the rest *as a period of revelation,* so it may be with the seven weeks. The number *seven* is associated with revelation; for the *seven* spirits of God are the mediators of all His revelations (Rev. 1:4; 3:1; 4:5). *Ten* is the number of what is human; e.g., the world power issues in *ten heads* and *ten horns* (ch. 2:42; 7:7). *Seventy* is *ten* multiplied by *seven,* the human moulded by the divine. The *seventy* years of exile symbolize the triumph of the world power over Israel. In the seven times seventy years the world number ten is likewise contained, i.e., God's people is still under the power of the world ("troublous times"); but the number of the divine is multiplied by itself; seven times seven years, at the beginning a period of Old Testament revelation to God's people by Ezra, Nehemiah, and Malachi, whose labors extend over about half a century, or *seven weeks,* and whose writings are last in the canon; and in the end, seven years, the period of New Testament revelation in Messiah. The commencing seven weeks of years of Old Testament revelation are hurried over, in order that the chief stress might rest on the Messianic week. Yet the seven weeks of Old Testament revelation are marked by their separation from the sixty-two, to be above those sixty-two wherein there was to be none. **Messiah the Prince**—Hebrew, *Nagid. Messiah* is Jesus' title in respect to *Israel* (Ps. 2:2; Matt. 27:37, 42). *Nagid,* as Prince of the *Gentiles* (Isa. 55:4). *Nagid* is applied to Titus, only as representative of Christ, who designates the Roman destruction of Jerusalem as, in a sense, His coming (Matt. 24; John 11:22). *Messiah* denotes His calling; *Nagid,* His power. He is to "be cut off, and there shall be nothing for Him." (So the *Hebrew* for "not for Himself," vs. 26, ought to be translated). Yet He is "the Prince" who is to "come," by His representative at first, to inflict judgment, and at last in person. **wall**—the "trench" or "scarped rampart" [TREGELLES]. The **street and trench** include the complete restoration of the city externally and internally, which was during the sixty-nine weeks. **26. after threescore and two weeks**—rather, *the* threescore and two, etc. In this verse, and in verse 27, Messiah is made the prominent subject, while the fate of the city and sanctuary are secondary, being mentioned only in the second halves of the verses. Messiah appears in a twofold aspect, salvation to believers, judgment on unbelievers (Luke 2:34; cf. Mal. 3:1-6; 4:1-3). He repeatedly, in Passion week, connects His being "cut off" with *the destruction of the city,* as cause and effect (Matt. 21:37-41; 23:37, 38; Luke 21:20-24; 23:28-31). Israel might naturally expect Messiah's kingdom of glory, if not after the seventy years' captivity, at least at the end of the sixty-two weeks; but, instead of that, shall be His death, and the consequent destruction of Jerusalem. **not for himself**—rather, "there shall be nothing to Him" [HENGSTENBERG]; not that the real object of His first coming (His *spiritual* kingdom) should be frustrated; but the *earthly* kingdom anticipated by the Jews should, for the present, *come to naught,* and not *then* be realized. TREGELLES refers the title, "the Prince" (vs. 25), to the time of His entering Jerusalem on an ass's colt, His only appearance as a king, and six days afterwards put to death as

"King of the Jews." **the people of the prince**—the Romans, led by Titus, the representative of the world power, ultimately to be transferred to Messiah, and so called by Messiah's title, "the Prince"; as also because sent by Him, as His instrument of judgment (Matt. 22:7). **end thereof**—of the sanctuary. TREGELLES takes it, "the end of the Prince," the last head of the Roman power, Antichrist. **with a flood**—viz., of war (Ps. 90:5; Isa. 8:7, 8; 28:18). Implying the completeness of the catastrophe, "not one stone left on another." **unto the end of the war**—rather, "unto the end *there* is war." **determined**—by God's decree (Isa. 10:23; 28:22). **27. he shall confirm the covenant**—Christ. The confirmation of the covenant is assigned to Him also elsewhere. Isaiah 42:6, "I will give thee for a *covenant* of the people" (i.e., He in whom the covenant between Israel and God is personally expressed); cf. Luke 22:20, "The new testament in My blood"; Malachi 3:1, "the angel of the covenant"; Jeremiah 31:31-34, describes the Messianic covenant in full. Contrast ch. 11:30, 32, "forsake the covenant," "do wickedly against the covenant." The prophecy as to Messiah's *confirming the covenant with many* would comfort the faithful in Antiochus' times, who suffered partly from persecuting enemies, partly from false friends (ch. 11:33-35). Hence arises the similarity of the language here and in ch. 11:30, 32, referring to Antiochus, the type of Antichrist. **with many**—(Isa. 53:11; Matt. 20:28; 26:28; Rom. 5:15, 19; Heb. 9:28). **in ... midst of ... week**—The seventy weeks extend to A.D. 33. Israel was not actually destroyed till A.D. 79, but it was so virtually, A.D. 33, about three or four years after Christ's death, during which the Gospel was preached exclusively to the Jews. When the Jews persecuted the Church and stoned Stephen (Acts 7), the respite of grace granted to them was at an end (Luke 13:7-9). Israel, having rejected Christ, was rejected by Christ, and henceforth is counted dead (cf. Gen. 2:17 with 5:5; Hos. 13:1, 2), its actual destruction by Titus being the consummation of the removal of the kingdom of God from Israel to the Gentiles (Matt. 21:43), which is not to be restored until Christ's second coming, when Israel shall be at the head of humanity (Matt. 23:39; Acts 1:6, 7; Rom. 11:25-31; 15). The interval forms for the covenant people a great parenthesis. **he shall cause the sacrifice ... oblation to cease**—distinct from the temporary *"taking away"* of "the daily" (sacrifice) by Antiochus (ch. 8:11; 11:31). Messiah was to cause all sacrifices and oblations in general to *"cease"* utterly. There is here an *allusion* only to Antiochus' act; to comfort God's people when sacrificial worship was to be trodden down, by pointing them to the Messianic time when salvation would fully come and yet temple sacrifices cease. This is the same consolation as Jeremiah and Ezekiel gave under like circumstances, when the destruction of Jerusalem by Nebuchadnezzar was impending (Jer. 3:16; 31:31; Ezek. 11:19). Jesus died in the middle of the last week, A.D. 30. His prophetic life lasted three and a half years; the very time in which "the saints are given into the hand" of Antichrist (ch. 7:25). Three and a half does not, like ten, designate the power of the world in its fulness, but (while opposed to the divine, expressed by *seven*) broken and defeated in its seeming triumph; for immediately after the three and a half times, judgment falls on the victorious world powers (ch. 7:25, 26). So Jesus' death seemed the triumph of the world, but was really its defeat (John 12:31). The rending of the veil marked the cessation of sacrifices through

Christ's death (Lev. 4:6, 17; 16:2, 15; Heb. 10:14-18). There cannot be a covenant without sacrifice (Gen. 8:20; 9:17; 15:9, etc.; Heb. 9:15). Here the old covenant is to be confirmed, but in a way peculiar to the New Testament, viz., by the one sacrifice, which would terminate all sacrifices (Ps. 40:6, 11). Thus as the Levitical rites approached their end, Jeremiah, Ezekiel, and Daniel, with ever increasing clearness, oppose the spiritual new covenant to the transient earthly elements of the old. **for the overspreading of abominations**—*On account of the abominations* committed by the unholy people against the Holy One, He shall not only destroy the city and sanctuary (vs. 25), but shall continue its desolation until the time of the consummation "determined" by God (the phrase is quoted from Isa. 10:22, 23), when at last the world power shall be judged and dominion be given to the saints of the Most High (ch. 7:26, 27). AUBERLEN translates, "On account of the desolating *summit* of abominations (cf. ch. 11:31; 12:11; thus the repetition of the same thing as in vs. 26 is avoided), and till the consummation which is determined, it (the curse, vs. 11, foretold by Moses) will pour on the desolated." Israel reached the summit of abominations, which drew down desolation (Matt. 24:28), nay, which is the desolation itself, when, after murdering Messiah, they offered sacrifices, Mosaic indeed in form, but heathenish in spirit (cf. Isa. 1:13; Ezek. 5:11). Christ refers to this passage (Matt. 24:15), "When ye see the abomination of desolation, spoken of by Daniel the prophet, stand *in the holy place*" (the latter words being *tacitly implied* in "abominations" as being such as are committed *against the sanctuary*). TREGELLES translates, "upon the *wing* of abominations shall be that which causeth desolation"; viz., an idol set up on a wing or pinnacle of the temple (cf. Matt. 4:5) by Antichrist, who makes a covenant with the restored Jews for the last of the seventy weeks of years (fulfilling Jesus' words, "If another shall come in his own name, him ye will receive"), and for the first three and a half years keeps it, then in the midst of the week breaks it, causing the daily sacrifices to cease. TREGELLES thus identifies the last half week with the time, times, and a half of the persecuting little horn (ch. 7:25). But thus there is a gap of at least 1830 years put between the sixty-nine weeks and the seventieth week. SIR ISAAC NEWTON explains the wing ("overspreading") of abominations to be the Roman ensigns (eagles) brought to the east gate of the temple, and there sacrificed to by the soldiers; the war, ending in the destruction of Jerusalem, lasted from spring A.D. 67 to autumn A.D. 70, i.e., just three and a half years, or the last half week of years (JOSEPHUS, *B.J.* 6. 6). **poured upon the desolate**—TREGELLES translates, "the *causer* of desolation," viz., Antichrist. Cf. "abomination *that maketh* desolate" (ch. 12:11). Perhaps *both* interpretations of the whole passage may be in part true; the Roman desolator, Titus, being a type of Antichrist, the final desolator of Jerusalem. BACON (*Adv. Learn.* 2. 3) says, "Prophecies are of the nature of the Author, with whom a thousand years are as one day; and therefore are not fulfilled punctually at once, but have a springing and germinant accomplishment through many years, though the height and fulness of them may refer to one age."

CHAPTER 10

Vss. 1-21. DANIEL COMFORTED BY AN ANGELIC VISION. Chapters 10 through 12 more fully describe the vision in chapter 8 by a second vision on the same subject, just as the vision in the seventh chapter explains more fully that in the second. The tenth chapter is the prologue; the eleventh, the prophecy itself; and the twelfth, the epilogue. The tenth chapter unfolds the spiritual worlds as the background of the historical world (Job 1:7; 2:1, etc.; Zech. 3:1, 2; Rev. 12:7), and angels as the ministers of God's government of men. As in the world of nature (John 5:4; Rev. 7:1-3), so in that of history here; Michael, the champion of Israel, and with him another angel, whose aim is to realize God's will in the heathen world, resist the God-opposed spirit of the world. These struggles are not merely symbolical, but real (I Sam. 16:13-15; I Kings 22:22; Eph. 6:12). **1. third year of Cyrus**—two years after Cyrus' decree for the restoration of the Jews had gone forth, in accordance with Daniel's prayer in ch. 9. This vision gives not merely general outlines, or symbols, but minute details of the future, in short, anticipative history. It is the expansion of the vision in ch. 8. That which then "none understood," he says here, "he understood"; the messenger being sent to him for this (vss. 11, 14), to make him understand it. Probably Daniel was no longer in office at court; for in ch. 1:21, it is said, "Daniel continued even unto the first year of King Cyrus"; not that he *died* then. See *Note* there. **but the time appointed was long**—rather, "it (i.e., the prophecy) referred to *great calamity*" [MAURER]; or, "long and calamitous warfare" [GESENIUS]. Lit., "host going to war"; hence, warfare, calamity. **2. mourning**—i.e., afflicting myself by fasting from "pleasant bread, flesh and wine" (vs. 3), as a sign of sorrow, not for its own sake. Cf. Matthew 9:14, "fast," answering to "mourn" (vs. 15). Cf. I Corinthians 8:8; I Timothy 4:3, which prove that "fasting" is not an indispensable Christian obligation; but merely an outward expression of sorrow, and separation from ordinary worldly enjoyments, in order to give one's self to prayer (Acts 13:2). Daniel's mourning was probably for his countrymen, who met with many obstructions to their building of the temple, from their adversaries in the Persian court. **3. no pleasant bread**—"unleavened bread, even the bread of affliction" (Deut. 16:3). **anoint**—The Persians largely used unguents. **4. first month**—Nisan, the month most suited for considering Israel's calamity, being that in which the feast of unleavened bread reminded them of their Egyptian bondage. Daniel mourned not merely for the *seven* days appointed (Exod. 12:18), from the evening of the fourteenth to the twenty-first of Nisan, but *thrice seven* days, to mark extraordinary sorrow. His mourning ended on the twenty-first day, the closing day of the passover feast; but the vision is not till the twenty-fourth, because of the opposition of "the prince of Persia" (vs. 13). **I was by . . . the . . . river**—in waking reality, not a trance (vs. 7); when younger, he saw the future in images, but now when old, he receives revelations from angels in common language, i.e., in the *apocalyptic mode*. In the patriarchal period God often appeared *visibly*, i.e., theophany. In the *prophets*, next in the succession, the *inward* character of revelation is prominent. The consummation is when the seer looks up from earth into the unseen world, and has the future shown to him by angels, i.e., apocalypse. So in the New Testament there is a parallel progression: God in the flesh, the spiritual activity of the apostles and the apocalypse [AUBERLEN]. **Hiddekel**—the Tigris. **5. lifted up mine eyes**—from the ground on which they had been fixed in his mourning. **certain man**—lit., "one man." An angel of the highest order; for in ch. 8:16 he commands Gabriel to make Daniel to understand the vision, and in ch. 12:6 one of the two angels inquires of him how long it would be till the end predicted. **linen** —the raiment of priests, being the symbol of sanctity, as more pure than wool (Exod. 28:42); also of *prophets* (Jer. 13:1); and of *angels* (Rev. 15: 6). **girded with ... gold**—i.e., with a girdle interwoven with gold (Rev. 1:13). **6. beryl**—lit., "Tarshish," in Spain. The beryl, identical with the chrysolite or topaz, was imported into the East from Tarshish, and therefore is called "the Tarshish stone." **7. they fled**—terrified by the presence of the angel. **8. comeliness**—lit., "vigor," i.e., lively expression and color. **into corruption**— "deadliness," i.e., death-like paleness (ch. 5:6; 7:28). **9. voice of his words**—the *sound* of his words. **was I in a deep sleep**—"I *sank* into a deep sleep" [LENGKERKE]. **10. an hand**—viz., of Gabriel, who interpreted other revelations to Daniel (ch. 8:16) [THEODORET]. **set me upon my knees**—GESENIUS translates, "cause me to reel on my knees ...." **11. man ... beloved**—(ch. 9:23, *Note*). **understand**—"attend to." See ch. 8:17, 18. **12. Fear not**—Be not affrighted at my presence. **didst set thine heart to understand**—what shall come to pass to thy people at the last times (cf. vs. 14). **chasten thyself**—(vss. 2, 3). **thy words were heard**—(Acts 10:4). Prayer is heard at once in heaven, though the sensible answer may *seem* to be delayed. God's messenger was detained on the way (vs. 13) by the opposition of the powers of darkness. If in our prayers amidst long protracted sorrows we believed God's angel is on his way to us, what consolation it would give us! **for thy words**—because of thy prayers. **13. prince of ... Persia**—the angel of darkness that represented the Persian world power, to which Israel was then subject. This verse gives the reason why, though Daniel's "words were heard from the first day" (vs. 12), the good angel did not come to him until more than three weeks had elapsed (vs. 4). **one and twenty days**—answering to the three weeks of Daniel's mourning (vs. 2). **Michael**—i.e., "Who is like God?" Though an archangel, "one of the chief princes," Michael was not to be compared to God. **help me**—Michael, as patron of Israel before God (vs. 21; 12:1), "helped" to influence the Persian king to permit the Jews' return to Jerusalem. **I remained**—*I was detained* there with the kings of Persia, i.e., with the angel of the Persian rulers, with whom I had to contend, and from whom I should not have got free, but for the help of Michael. GESENIUS translates, "I obtained the ascendency," i.e., I gained my point against the adverse angel of Persia, so as to influence the Persian authorities to favor Israel's restoration. **14. what shall befall thy people in the latter days**—an intimation that the prophecy, besides describing the doings of Antiochus, reaches to the concluding calamities of Israel's history, prior to the nation's full restoration at Christ's coming—calamities of which Antiochus' persecutions were the type. **vision is for many days**—i.e., extends far into the future. **15. face toward the ground**—in humble reverence (Gen. 19:1). **dumb**—with overwhelming awe. **16. touched my lips**—the same significant action wherewith the Son of man accompanied His healing of the dumb (Mark 7:33). He alone can give spiritual utterance (Isa. 6:6, 7; Eph. 6:19), enabling one to "open the mouth boldly." The same one who makes dumb (vs. 15) opens the mouth. **sorrows**—lit., "writhings" as of a woman in travail.

17. this ... this my lord—to avoid the tautology in *English Version,* join rather "this," with *servant,* "How can *this servant* of my lord (i.e., how can I who am *so feeble*) talk with this my lord (who is *so majestic*)?" Thus Daniel gives the reason why he is so overwhelmed with awe [MAURER]. **18. again ... touched me**—It was gradually that Daniel recovered his strength. Hence there was need of the second touch, that he might hear the angel with composure. **19. peace be unto thee**—God is favorable to thee and to thy people Israel. See Judges 13:21, 22, as to the fear of some evil resulting from a vision of angels. **20. Knowest thou wherefore**—The angel asks, after Daniel had recovered from his fright, whether he has understood what was revealed (vs. 13). On Daniel, by his silence, intimating that he did understand, the angel declares he will return to renew the fight with the evil angel, the prince of Persia. This points to new difficulties to the Jews' restoration which would arise in the Persian court, but which would be counteracted by God, through the ministry of angels. **prince of Grecia shall come**—Alexander the Great, who conquered Persia, and favored the Jews [CALVIN]. Rather, as the prince of Persia is an angel, representing the hostile world power, so the prince of Grecia is a fresh angelic adversary, representing Greece. When I am gone forth from conquering the Persian foe, a fresh one starts up, viz., the world power that succeeds Persia, Greece; Antiochus Epiphanes, and his antitype Antichrist; but him, too, with the help of Michael, Israel's champion, I shall overcome [GEJER]. **21. noted in the scripture of truth**—in the secret book of God's decrees (Ps. 139: 16; Rev. 5:1), which are truth, i.e., the things which shall most surely come to pass, being determined by God (cf. John 17:17). **none ... but Michael**— To him alone of the angels the office of protecting Israel, in concert with the angelic speaker, was delegated; all the world powers were against Israel.

CHAPTER 11

Vss. 1-45. This chapter is an enlargement of the eighth: THE OVERTHROW OF PERSIA BY GRECIA: THE FOUR DIVISIONS OF ALEXANDER'S KINGDOM: CONFLICTS BETWEEN THE KINGS OF THE SOUTH AND OF THE NORTH, THE PTOLEMIES AND SELEUCIDÆ: ANTIOCHUS EPIPHANES. **1. I**—the angel (ch. 10:18). **first year of Darius**—Cyaxares II; the year of the conquest of Babylon (ch. 5:31). Cyrus, who wielded the real power, though in name subordinate to Darius, in that year promulgated the edict for the restoration of the Jews, which Daniel was at the time praying for (ch. 9:1, 2, 21, 23). **stood**—implying promptness in helping (Ps. 94:16). **strengthen him**—viz., Michael; even as Michael (ch. 10:21, "*strengtheneth* himself with me") helped the angel, both joining their powers in behalf of Israel [ROSENMULLER]. Or, *Darius,* the angel "confirming him" in his purpose of kindness to Israel. **2. three kings in Persia**—Cambyses, Pseudo-Smerdis, and Darius Hystaspes. (Ahasuerus, Artaxerxes, and Darius, in Ezra 4:6, 7, 24.) The Ahasuerus of *Esther* (see *Note,* ch. 9:1) is identified with Xerxes, both in Greek history and in Scripture, appearing proud, self-willed, careless of contravening Persian customs, amorous, facile, and changeable (vs. 2). **fourth ... riches ... against ... Grecia**—Xerxes, whose riches were proverbial. Persia reached its climax and showed its greatest power in his invasion of Greece, 480 B.C. After his overthrow at Salamis,

Persia is viewed as politically dead, though it had an *existence*. Therefore, the third verse, without noticing Xerxes' successors, proceeds at once to Alexander, under whom, first, the third world kingdom, Grecia, reached its culmination, and assumed an importance as to the people of God. **stir up all** —Four years were spent in gathering his army out of all parts of his vast empire, amounting to two millions six hundred and forty-one thousand men. [PRIDEAUX, *Connex*. 1. 4. 1. 410]. **3. mighty king ... do according to his will**—answering to the he-goat's "notable horn" (ch. 8:6, 7, 21). Alexander invaded Persia 334 B.C., to avenge the wrongs of Greece on Persia for Xerxes' past invasion (as Alexander said in a letter to Darius Codomanus, ARRIAN, *Alex*. 2. 14. 7). **4. kingdom ... divided toward ... four winds**—the fourfold division of Alexander's kingdom at his death (ch. 8:8, 22), after the battle of Ipsus, 301 B.C. **not to his posterity**— (*Notes*, ch. 8:8, 22). **nor according to his dominion** —None of his successors had so wide a dominion as Alexander himself. **others besides those**—besides *Alexander's sons*, Hercules by Barsine, Darius' daughter, and Alexander by Roxana, who were both slain [MAURER]. Rather, besides *the four successors* to the four chief divisions of the empire, there will be other lesser chiefs who shall appropriate smaller fragments of the Macedonian empire [JEROME]. **5.** Here the prophet leaves Asia and Greece and takes up Egypt and Syria, these being in continual conflict under Alexander's successors, entailing misery on Judea, which lay between the two. Holy Scripture handles external history only so far as it is connected with God's people, Israel [JEROME]. TREGELLES puts a chasm between vs. 4 and vs. 5, making the transition to the final Antichrist here, answering to the chasm (in his view) at ch. 8:22, 23. **king of ... south**—lit., "of midday": Egypt (vss. 8, 42), Ptolemy Soter, son of Lagus. He took the title "king," whereas Lagus was but "governor." **one of his princes**—Seleucus, at first a satrap of Ptolemy Lagus, but from 312 B.C. king of the largest empire after that of Alexander (Syria, Babylon, Media, etc.), and called therefore *Nicator*, i.e., "conqueror." Connect the words thus, "And one of his (Ptolemy's) princes, *even* he (Seleucus) shall be strong above him" (above Ptolemy, his former master). **6. in ... end of years**—when the predicted time shall be consummated (vs. 13, *Margin*; ch. 8:17; 12:13). **king's daughter of the south** —Berenice, daughter of Ptolemy Philadelphus of Egypt. The latter, in order to end his war with Antiochus Theus, "king of the north" (lit., "midnight": the prophetical phrase for the region whence came affliction to Israel, Jer. 1:13-15; Joel 2:20), i.e., Syria, gave Berenice to Antiochus, who thereupon divorced his former wife, Laodice, and disinherited her son, Seleucus Callinicus. The designation, "king of the north" and "of the south," is given in relation to Judea, as the standpoint. Egypt is mentioned by name (vss. 8, 42), though Syria is not; because the former was in Daniel's time a flourishing kingdom, whereas Syria was *then* a mere dependency of Assyria and Babylon: an undesigned proof of the genuineness of the Book of Daniel. **agreement**—lit., "rights," i.e., to put things to rights between the belligerents. **she shall not retain the power of the arm**—She shall not be able to effect the purpose of the alliance, viz., that she should be the *mainstay* of peace. Ptolemy having died, Antiochus took back Laodice, who then poisoned him, and caused Berenice and her son to be put to death, and raised her own son, Seleucus Nicator, to the

throne. **neither shall he stand**—The king of Egypt shall not gain his point of setting his line on the throne of Syria. **his arm**—that on which he relied. Berenice and her offspring. **they that brought her**— her attendants from Egypt. **he that begat her**—rather as *Margin*, "the child *whom she brought forth*" [EWALD]. If *English Version* (which MAURER approves) be retained, as Ptolemy died a natural death, "given up" is not in his case, as in Berenice's, to be understood of giving up *to death*, but in a general sense, of his plan proving abortive. **he that strengthened her in these times**—Antiochus Theus, who is to *attach himself to her* (having divorced Laodice) at the times predicted [GEJER]. **7. a branch of her roots ... in his estate**—Ptolemy Euergetes, brother of Berenice, succeeding *in the place* (see *Margin*) of Philadelphus, avenged her death by overrunning Syria, even to the Euphrates. **deal against them**—He shall deal with the Syrians at his own pleasure. He slew Laodice. **8. carry ... into Egypt their gods ...**—Ptolemy, on hearing of a sedition in Egypt, returned with 40,000 talents of silver, precious vessels, and 2400 images, including Egyptian idols, which Cambyses had carried from Egypt into Persia. The idolatrous Egyptians were so gratified, that they named him Euergetes, or "benefactor." **continue more years**—Ptolemy survived Seleucus four years, reigning in all forty-six years. MAURER translates, "Then he for several years shall *desist from* (contending with) the king of the north" (cf. vs. 9). **9. come into his kingdom**— Egypt: not only with impunity, but with great spoil. **10. his sons**—the two sons of the king of the north, Seleucus Callinicus, upon his death by a fall from his horse, viz., Seleucus Ceraunus and Antiochus the Great. **one shall ... come**—Ceraunus having died, Antiochus alone prosecuted the war with Ptolemy Philopater, Euergetes' son, until he had recovered all the parts of Syria subjugated by Euergetes. **pass through**—like an "overflowing" torrent (vss. 22, 26, 40; Isa. 8:8). Antiochus penetrated to Dura (near Cæsarea), where he gave Ptolemy a four months' truce. **return**—renew the war at the expiration of the truce (so vs. 13). **even to his fortress**—Ptolemy's; Raphia, a border-fortress of Egypt against incursions by way of Edom and Arabia Petræa, near Gaza; here Antiochus was vanquished. **11. the king of the south ... moved with choler**—at so great losses, Syria having been wrested from him, and his own kingdom imperilled, though otherwise an indolent man, to which his disasters were owing, as also to the odium of his subjects against him for having murdered his father, mother, and brother, whence in irony they called him *Philopater*, "father-lover." **he shall set forth a great multitude**—Antiochus, king of Syria, whose force was 70,000 infantry and 5000 cavalry. **but ... multitude ... given into his hand**—into Ptolemy's hands; 10,000 of Antiochus' army were slain, and 4000 made captives. **12. when he hath taken away**—i.e., *subdued* "the multitude" of Antiochus. **heart ... lifted up**—instead of following up his victory by making himself master of the whole of Syria, as he might, he made peace with Antiochus, and gave himself up to licentiousness [POLYB. 87; JUSTIN. 30.4], and *profaned the temple of God* by entering the holy place [GROTIUS]. **not be strengthened by it**—He shall lose the power gained by his victory through his luxurious indolence. **13. return** —renew the war. **after certain years**—*fourteen years* after his defeat at Raphia. Antiochus, after successful campaigns against Persia and India, made war with Ptolemy Epiphanes, son of Philopater, a mere child. **14. many stand up against the king of the south**—Philip, king of Macedon, and rebels in Egypt itself, combined with Antiochus against Ptolemy. **robbers of thy people**—i.e., factious men of the Jews shall exalt themselves, so as to revolt from Ptolemy, and join themselves to Antiochus; the Jews helped Antiochus' army with provisions, when on his return from Egypt he besieged the Egyptian garrison left in Jerusalem (JOSEPHUS, *Antiquities*, 12.3.3). **to establish the vision**—Those turbulent Jews unconsciously shall help to fulfil the purpose of God, as to the trials which await Judea, according to this vision. **but they shall fall**—Though helping to fulfil the vision, they shall fail in their aim, of making Judea independent. **15. king of ... north**—Antiochus the Great. **take ... fenced cities**—Scopas, the Egyptian general, met Antiochus at Paneas, near the sources of the Jordan, and was defeated, and fled to Sidon, a strongly "fenced city," where he was forced to surrender. **chosen people**—Egypt's choicest army was sent under Eropus, Menocles, ana Damoxenus, to deliver Scopas, but in vain [JEROME]. **16. he that cometh against him**—Antiochus coming against Ptolemy Epiphanes. **glorious land**—Judea (vss. 41, 45; ch. 8:9; Ezek. 20:6, 15). **by his hand shall be consumed**—lit., "perfected," i.e., completely brought under his sway. JOSEPHUS (*Antiquities*, 12. 3. 3) shows that the meaning is not, that the Jews should be utterly consumed: for Antiochus favored them for taking his part against Ptolemy, but that their land should be *subjected* to him [LENGKERKE]. GROTIUS translates, "shall be perfected by him," i.e., shall flourish under him. *English Version* gives a good sense; viz., that Judea was much "*consumed*" or *desolated* by being the arena of conflict between the combatants, Syria and Egypt. TREGELLES refers (vs. 14), "robbers of thy people," to the Gentiles, once oppressors, attempting to restore the Jews to their land by mere human effort, whereas this is to be effected only by divine interposition: their attempt is frustrated (vs. 16) by the wilful king, who makes Judea the scene of his military operations. **17. set his face**—*purpose* steadfastly. Antiochus' purpose was, however, turned from open assault to wile, by his war with the Romans in his endeavor to extend his kingdom to the limits it had under Seleucus Nicator. **upright one**—*Jasher*, or *Jeshurun* (Deut. 32:15; Isa. 44:2); the epithet applied by the Hebrews to their nation. It is here used not in praise; for in vs. 14 (see *Note*) they are called "robbers," or "men of violence, factious": it is the general designation of Israel, as *having God for their God*. Probably it is used to rebuke those who ought to have been God's "upright ones" for confederating with godless heathen in acts of *violence* (the contrast to the term in vs. 14 favors this). **thus shall he do**—Instead of at once invading Ptolemy's country with his "whole strength," he prepares his way for doing so by the following plan: he gives to Ptolemy Epiphanes his daughter Cleopatra in marriage, promising Cœlo-Syria and Judea as a dowry, thus securing his neutrality in the war with Rome: he hoped through his daughter to obtain Syria, Cilicia, and Lycia, and even Egypt itself at last; but Cleopatra favored her husband rather than her father, and so defeated his scheme [JEROME]. "She shall not stand on his side." **18. isles**—He "took many" of the isles in the Ægean in his war with the Romans, and crossed the Hellespont. **prince for his own behalf shall cause the reproach ... to cease**—Lucius Scipio Asiaticus, the Roman general, by routing Antiochus at Magnesia (190 B.C.), caused

the reproach which he offered Rome by inflicting injuries on Rome's allies, to cease. He did it *for his own glory*. **without his own reproach**—with untarnished reputation. **19. Then he shall turn ... toward ... his own land**—Compelled by Rome to relinquish all his territory west of the Taurus, and defray the expenses of the war, he garrisoned the cities left to him. **stumble ... not be found**—Attempting to plunder the temple of Jupiter at Elymais by night, whether through avarice, or the want of money to pay the tribute imposed by Rome (a thousand talents), he was slain with his soldiers in an insurrection of the inhabitants [JUSTIN 32. 2]. **20. in his estate**—in Antiochus' stead: his successor, Seleucus Philopater, his son. **in the glory of the kingdom**—i.e., inheriting it by hereditary right. MAURER translates, "one who shall cause the taxgatherer (Heliodorus) to pass through the glory of the kingdom," i.e., *Judea*, "the glorious land" (vss. 16, 41; ch. 8:9). Simon, a Benjamite, in spite against Onias III, the high priest, gave information of the treasures in the Jewish temple; and Seleucus having reunited to Syria Cœlo-Syria and Palestine, the dowry formerly given by Antiochus the Great to Cleopatra, Ptolemy's wife, sent Heliodorus to Jerusalem to plunder the temple. This is narrated in II Maccabees 3:4, etc. Contrast Zechariah 9:8, "No oppressor shall pass through ... any more." **within few days ... destroyed**—after a reign of twelve years, which were "few" compared with the thirty-seven years of Antiochus' reign. Heliodorus, the instrument of Seleucus' sacrilege, was made by God the instrument of his punishment. Seeking the crown, in the absence at Rome of Seleucus' only son and heir, Demetrius, he poisoned Seleucus. But Antiochus Epiphanes, Seleucus' brother, by the help of Eumenes, king of Pergamos, succeeded to the throne, 175 B.C. **neither in anger, nor in battle**—not in a popular outbreak, nor in open battle. **21. vile**—Antiochus called Epiphanes, i.e., "the illustrious," for vindicating the claims of the royal line against Heliodorus, was nicknamed, by a play of sounds, Epimanes, i.e., "the madman," for his mad freaks beneath the dignity of a king. He would carouse with the lowest of the people, bathe with them in the public baths, and foolishly jest and throw stones at passers-by [POLYB. 26. 10]. Hence, as also for his crafty supplanting of Demetrius, the rightful heir, from the throne, he is termed "vile." **they shall not give ... kingdom: but ... by flatteries**—The nation shall not, by a public act, confer the kingdom on him, but he shall obtain it by artifice, "flattering" Eumenes and Attalus of Pergamos to help him, and, as he had seen candidates at Rome doing, canvassing the Syrian people high and low, one by one, with embraces [LIVY, 41. 20]. **22. shall they be overflown ... before him**—Antiochus Epiphanes shall invade Egypt with overwhelming forces. **prince of the covenant**—Ptolemy Philometer, the son of Cleopatra, Antiochus' sister, who was joined in covenant with him. Ptolemy's guardians, while he was a boy, sought to recover from Epiphanes Cœlo-Syria and Palestine, which had been promised by Antiochus the Great as Cleopatra's dowry in marrying Ptolemy Epiphanes. Hence arose the war. Philometer's generals were vanquished, and Pelusium, the key of Egypt, taken by Antiochus, 171 B.C. **23.** TREGELLES notes three divisions in the history of the "vile person," which is continued to the end of the chapter: (1) His rise (vss. 21, 22). (2) The time from his making the covenant to the taking away of the daily sacrifice and setting up of the abomination of desolation (vss. 23-31). (3) His career of blasphemy, to his destruction (vss. 32-45); the latter two periods answering to the "week" of years of his "covenant with many" (viz., in Israel) (ch. 9:27), and the last being the closing half week of ch. 9. But the context so accurately agrees with the relations of Antiochus to Ptolemy that the primary reference seems to be to the "league" between them. *Antitypically,* Antichrist's relations towards *Israel* are probably delineated. Cf. ch. 8:11, 25, with vs. 22 here, "prince of the covenant." **work deceitfully**—Feigning friendship to young Ptolemy, as if he wished to order his kingdom for him, he took possession of Memphis and all Egypt ("the fattest places," vs. 34) as far as Alexandria. **with a small people**—At first, to throw off suspicion, his forces were small. **24. peaceably**—lit., "unexpectedly"; under the guise of friendship he seized Ptolemy Philometer. **he shall do that which his fathers have not done**—His predecessors, kings of Syria, had always coveted Egypt, but in vain: he alone made himself master of it. **scatter among them . . . prey**—among his followers (I Maccabees 1: 19). **forecast his devices against . . . strongholds**—He shall form a studied scheme for making himself master of the Egyptian fortresses. He gained them all except Alexandria, which successfully resisted him. Retaining to himself Pelusium, he retired to Judea, where, in revenge for the joy shown by the Jews at the report of his death, which led them to a revolt, he subdued Jerusalem by storm or stratagem. **for a time**—His rage shall not be for ever; it is but for a time limited by God. CALVIN makes "for a time" in antithesis to "unexpectedly," in the beginning of the verse. He *suddenly* mastered the weaker cities: he had to "forecast his plans" more *gradually* ("for a time") as to how to gain the stronger fortresses. **25.** A fuller detail of what was summarily stated (vss. 22-24). This is the first of Antiochus' three (vs. 29) open invasions of Egypt. **against the king of the south**—against Ptolemy Philometer. Subsequently, Ptolemy Physcon (the Gross), or Euergetes II, was made king by the Egyptians, as Ptolemy Philometer was in Antiochus' hands. **great army**—as distinguished from the "small people" (vs. 23) with which he first came. This was his first *open* expedition; he was emboldened by success to it. Antiochus "entered Egypt with an overwhelming multitude, with chariots, elephants, and cavalry" (I Maccabees 1:17). **stirred up**—by the necessity, though naturally indolent. **not stand**—Philometer was defeated. **they shall forecast . . .**—*His own nobles* shall frame treacherous "devices" against him (see vs. 26). Eulœus and Lenœus maladministered his affairs. Antiochus, when checked at last at Alexandria, left Ptolemy Philometer at Memphis as king, pretending that his whole object was to support Philometer's claims against the usurper Physcon. **26. they that feed of . . . his meat**—those from whom he might naturally have looked for help, his intimates and dependents (Ps. 41:9; John 13:18); his ministers and guardians. **his army shall overflow**—Philometer's army shall be dissipated as water. The phrase is used of overflowing *numbers,* usually in a victorious sense, but here in the sense of *defeat,* the very numbers which ordinarily ensure victory, hastening the defeat through mismanagement. **many shall fall down slain**—(I Maccabees 1:18, "many fell wounded to death"). Antiochus, when he might have slain all in the battle near Pelusium, rode around and ordered the enemy to be taken alive, the fruit of which policy was, he soon gained Pelusium and all Egypt [DIODORUS SICULUS, 26.77]. **27. both . . . to**

do mischief—each to the other. **speak lies at one table**—They shall, under the semblance of intimacy, at Memphis try to deceive one another (*Notes,* vss. 3, 25). **it shall not prosper**—Neither of them shall carry his point at this time. **yet the end shall be**—"the end" of the contest between them is reserved for "the time appointed" (vss. 29, 30). **28.** (I Maccabees 1:19, 20, etc.). **against the holy covenant**—On his way back to Syria, he attacked Jerusalem, the metropolis of Jehovah's covenant people, slew 80,000, took 40,000 prisoners, and sold 40,000 as slaves (II Maccabees 5:5-14). **he shall do exploits**—He shall effect his purpose. Guided by Menelaus, the high priest, he entered the sanctuary with blasphemies, took away the gold and silver vessels, sacrificed swine on the altar, and sprinkled broth of the flesh through the temple (II Maccabees 5:15-21). **29. At the time appointed**—"the time" spoken of in vs. 27. **return**—his second open invasion of Egypt. Ptolemy Philometer, suspecting Antiochus' designs with Physcon, hired mercenaries from Greece. Whereupon Antiochus advanced with a fleet and an army, demanding the cession to him of Cyprus, Pelusium, and the country adjoining the Pelusiac mouth of the Nile. **it shall not be as the former**—not successful as the former expedition. Popilius Lœnas, the Roman ambassador, met him at Eleusis, four miles from Alexandria, and presented him the decree of the senate; on Antiochus replying that he would consider what he was to do, Popilius drew a line round him with a rod and said, "I must have a reply to give to the senate before you leave this circle." Antiochus submitted, and retired from Egypt; and his fleets withdrew from Cyprus. **or as the latter**—that mentioned in vss. 42, 43 [TREGELLES]. Or, making this the *third* expedition, the sense is "not as the first or as the second" expeditions [PISCATOR]. Rather "not as the former, *so* shall be *this* latter" expedition [GROTIUS]. **30. ships of Chittim**—the Roman ambassadors arriving in *Macedonian Grecian* vessels (see *Note,* Jer. 2:10). *Chittim,* properly *Cyprian,* so called from a Phœnician colony in Cyprus; then the islands and coasts of the Mediterranean in general. **grieved**—humbled and dispirited through fear of Rome. **indignation against the holy covenant**—Indignant that meantime God's worship had been restored at Jerusalem, he gives vent to his wrath at the check given him by Rome, on the Jews. **intelligence with them that forsake the . . . covenant**—viz., with the apostates in the nation (I Maccabees 1:11-15). Menelaus and other Jews instigated the king against their religion and country, learning from Greek philosophy that all religions are good enough to keep the masses in check. These had cast off circumcision and the religion of Jehovah for Greek customs. Antiochus, on his way home, sent Apollonius (167 B.C.) with 22,000 to destroy Jerusalem, two years after its capture by himself. Apollonius slew multitudes, dismantled and pillaged the city. They then, from a fortress which they built commanding the temple, fell on and slew the worshippers; so that the temple service was discontinued. Also, Antiochus decreed that all, on pain of death, should conform to the Greek religion, and the temple was consecrated to Jupiter Olympus. Identifying himself with that god, with fanatical haughtiness he wished to make his own worship universal (I Maccabees 1:41; II Maccabees 6:7). This was the gravest peril which ever heretofore threatened revealed religion, the holy people, and the theocracy on earth, for none of the previous world rulers had interfered with the religious worship of the covenant people, when subject to them (ch. 4:31-34; 6:27, 28; Ezra 1:2, 4; 7:12; Neh. 2:18). Hence arose the need of such a forewarning of the covenant people as to him—so accurate, that PORPHYRY, the adversary of revelation, saw it was hopeless to deny its correspondence with history, but argued from its accuracy that it must have been written *subsequent* to the event. But as Messianic events are foretold in Daniel, the Jews, the adversaries of Jesus, would never have forged the prophecies which confirm His claims. The ninth chapter was to comfort the faithful Jews, in the midst of the "abominations" against "the covenant," with the prospect of Messiah who would "confirm the covenant." He would show by bringing salvation, and yet abolishing sacrifices, that the temple service which they so grieved after, was not absolutely necessary; thus the correspondence of phraseology would suggest comfort (cf. ch. 9:27 with ch. 11:30, 31). **31. arms**—viz., of the human body; not *weapons;* human forces. **they**—Antiochus' hosts confederate with the apostate Israelites; these latter attain the climax of guilt, when they not only, as before, "*forsake* the covenant" (vs. 30), but "*do wickedly against*" it (vs. 32), turning complete heathens. Here Antiochus' actings are described in language which reach beyond him the type to Antichrist the antitype [JEROME] (just as in Ps. 72 many things are said of Solomon the type, which are only applicable to Christ the Antitype); including perhaps Rome, Mohammed, and the final personal Antichrist. SIR ISAAC NEWTON refers the rest of the chapter from this verse to the Romans, translating, "*after him* arms (i.e., the Romans) shall stand up"; at the very time that Antiochus left Egypt, the Romans conquered Macedon, thus finishing the reign of Daniel's third beast; so here the prophet naturally proceeds to the fourth beast. JEROME'S view is simpler; for the narrative seems to continue the history of Antiochus, though with features only in type applicable to him, fully to Antichrist. **sanctuary of strength**—not only naturally a place of strength, whence it held out to the last against the besiegers, but chiefly the *spiritual* stronghold of the covenant people (Ps. 48:1-3, 12-14). Apollonius "polluted" it with altars to idols and sacrifices of swine's flesh, after having "taken away the daily sacrifice" (see *Note,* ch. 8:11). **place . . . abomination that maketh desolate**—i.e., that pollutes the temple (ch. 8:12, 13). Or rather, "the abomination *of the desolater,*" Antiochus Epiphanes (I Maccabees 1:29, 37-49). Cf. ch. 9:27, wherein the antitypical *desolating abomination* of Rome (the eagle standard, the bird of Jupiter, sacrificed to by Titus' soldiers within the sacred precincts, at the destruction of Jerusalem; and of Mohammed and of the final Antichrist, is foretold. I Maccabees 1:54, uses the very phrase, "the fifteenth day of the month Casleu, in the 145th year, they set up the *abomination of desolation* on the altar"; viz., an idol-altar and image of Jupiter Olympius, erected upon Jehovah's altar of burnt offerings. "Abomination" is the common name for an *idol* in the Old Testament. The Roman emperor Adrian's erection of a temple to Jupiter Capitolinus where the temple of God had stood, A.D. 132; also the erection of the Mohammedan mosque of Omar in the same place (it is striking, Mohammedanism began to prevail in A.D. 610, only about three years of the time when Popery assumed the temporal power); and the idolatry of the Church of Rome in the spiritual temple, and the final blasphemy of the personal Antichrist in the literal temple (II Thess. 2) may all

be antitypically referred to here under Antiochus the type, and the Old Testament Antichrist. **32.** (I Maccabees 1:52.) **corrupt**—seduce to apostasy. **by flatteries**—promises of favor. **people that . . . know their God**—the Maccabees and their followers (I Maccabees 1:62, 63). **33. they that understand**—who know and keep the truth of God (Isa. 11:2). **instruct many**—in their duty to God and the law, not to apostatize. **yet they shall fall**—as Eleazar (II Maccabees 6:18, etc.). They shall be sorely persecuted, even to death (Heb. 11:35, 36, 37; II Maccabees 6, 7). Their enemies took advantage of the Sabbath to slay them on the day when they would not fight. TREGELLES thinks, from comparison with vs. 35, it is *the people* who "fall," not *those of understanding.* But vs. 35 makes *the latter* "fall," not an unmeaning repetition; in vs. 33 they fall (die) by persecution; in vs. 35 they fall (spiritually) for a time by their own weakness. **flame**—in caves, whither they had retired to keep the Sabbath. Antiochus caused some to be roasted alive (II Maccabees 7:3-5). **many days**—rather, "*certain days,*" as in ch. 8:27. JOSEPHUS (*Antiquities,* 12. 7. 6, 7) tells us the persecution lasted for three years (I Maccabees 1:59; 4:54; II Maccabees 10:1-7). **34. a little help**—The liberty obtained by the Maccabean heroes for the Jews was of but short duration. They soon fell under the Romans and Herodians, and ever since every attempt to free them from Gentile rule has only aggravated their sad lot. The period of the world times (Gentile rule) is the period of depression of the theocracy, extending from the exile to the millennium [ROOS]. The more immediate reference seems to be, the forces of Mattathias and his five sons were originally *few* (I Maccabees 2). **many shall cleave to them**—as was the case under Judas Maccabeus, who was thus able successfully to resist Antiochus. **with flatteries**—Those who had deserted the Jewish cause in persecution, now, when success attended the Jewish arms, joined the Maccabean standard, (e.g., Joseph, the son of Zecharias, Azarias, etc. (I Maccabees 5:55-57; II Maccabees 12:40; 13:21). MAURER explains it, of those who through fear of the Maccabees' severity against apostates joined them, though ready, if it suited their purpose, to desert them (I Maccabees 2:44; 3:58). **35. to try them**—the design of affliction. Image from *metals* tried with fire. **to purge** —Even in the elect there are dregs which need to be purged out (I Pet. 1:7). Hence they are allowed to fall for a time; not finally (II Chron. 32:31; Luke 22:31). Image from wheat cleared of its chaff by the wind. **make . . . white**—image from cloth (Rev. 7:9). **to . . . time of . . . end**—God will not suffer His people to be persecuted without limitation (I Cor. 10:13). The godly are to wait patiently for "the end" of "the time" of trial; "for it is (to last) yet for a time appointed" by God. **36.** The wilful king here, though primarily Antiochus, is antitypically and mainly Antichrist, the seventh head of the seven-headed and ten-horned beast of Revelation 13, and the "beast" of Armageddon (Rev. 16:13, 16; 19:19). Some identify him with the revived French emperorship, the eighth head of the beast (Rev. 17:11), who is to usurp the kingly, as the Pope has the priestly, dignity of Christ—the false Messiah of the Jews, who will "plant his tabernacle between the seas in the holy mountain," "exalting himself above every god" (II Thess. 2:4; Rev. 13:5, 6). This last clause only in part holds good of Antiochus; for though he assumed divine honors, identifying himself with Jupiter Olympius, yet it was for that god he claimed them; still it applies to him

as *the type*. **speak marvellous things against . . .
God of gods**—so ch. 7:25, as to the "little horn,"
which seemingly identifies the two (cf. ch. 8:25).
Antiochus forbade the worship of Jehovah by a
decree "marvellous" for its wickedness: thus he was
a type of Antichrist. Cf. ch. 7:8, "a mouth speaking great things." **indignation . . . accomplished**—
God's visitation of wrath on the Jews for their sins
(ch. 8:19). **that . . . determined**—(ch. 9:26, 27; 10:
21). **37. Neither . . . regard . . . the desire of wom-
en**—(Cf. Ezek. 24:16, 18). The wife, as the *desire*
of man's eyes, is the symbol of the tenderest relations (II Samuel 1:26). Antiochus would set at
naught even their entreaties that he should cease
from his attack on Jehovah's worship [POLANUS].
MAURER refers it to Antiochus' attack on the temple
of *the Syrian Venus, worshipped by women* (I Maccabees 6:1, etc.; II Maccabees 1:13). NEWTON refers it to Rome's "forbidding to marry." ELLIOTT
rightly makes the antitypical reference be to *Messiah*. Jewish women desired to be mothers with a
view to Him, the promised seed of the woman
(Gen. 30:23; Luke 1:25, 28). **nor regard any god**
—(II Thess. 2:4). **38. God of forces**—probably
Jupiter Capitolinus, to whom Antiochus began to
erect a temple at Antioch [LIVY 41. 20]. Translate,
"He shall honor the god of *fortresses on his basis*,"
i.e., the base of the statue. NEWTON translates,
"And the god 'Mahuzzim' (*guardians*, i.e., saints
adored as *'protectors'* in the Greek and Roman
churches) shall he honor." **honour with gold . . .**
—Cf. Revelation 17:4 as to Antiochus' antitype, Antichrist. **39.** NEWTON translates, "*to be defenders
of Mahuzzim* (the monks and priests who uphold
saint-worship), together with the strange god whom
he shall acknowledge, he shall multiply honor."
English Version is better: He shall do (exploits) in
the most strongholds (i.e., shall succeed against
them) with a strange god (under the auspices of a
god which he worshipped not before, viz., Jupiter
Capitolinus, whose worship he imported into his
empire from Rome). Antiochus succeeded against
Jerusalem, Sidon, Pelusium, Memphis. **cause them**
—Antiochus "caused" his *followers and the apostates* "to rule over many" Jews, having "divided their
land" (Judea), "for gain" (i.e., as a *reward* for their
compliance). **40.** The difficulty of reconciling this
with Antiochus' history is that no historian but
PORPHYRY mentions an expedition of his into *Egypt*
towards the close of his reign. This vs. 40, therefore, may be a recapitulation summing up the facts
of the first expedition to Egypt (171-170 B.C., in
vss. 22, 25; and vs. 41, the former invasion of
Judea, in vs. 28; vss. 42, 43, the second and
third invasions of Egypt (169 and 168 B.C.) in vss.
23, 24, 29, 30. AUBERLEN takes rather PORPHYRY's
statement, that Antiochus, in the eleventh year of
his reign (166-165 B.C.), invaded Egypt again, and
took Palestine on his way. The "tidings" (vs. 44)
as to the revolt of tributary nations then led him to
the East. PORPHYRY's statement that Antiochus
starting from Egypt took Arad in Judah, and devastated all Phœnicia, agrees with vs. 45; then he turned
to check Artaxias, king of Armenia. He died in
the Persian town Tabes, 164 B.C., as both POLYBIUS
and PORPHYRY agree. Doubtless, antitypically, the
final Antichrist, and its predecessor Mohammed, are
intended, to whom the language may be more fully
applicable than to Antiochus the type. The Saracen Arabs "of the south" "pushed at" the Greek
emperer Heraclius, and deprived him of Egypt and
Syria. But the Turks of "the north" not merely
pushed at, but destroyed the Greek empire; there-

fore more is said of them than of the Saracens.
Their "horsemen" are specfied, being their chief
strength. Their standards still are *horse tails*. Their
"ships," too, often gained the victory over Venice, the great naval power of Europe in that day.
They "overflowed" Western Asia, and then "passed
over" into Europe, fixing their seat of empire at
Constantinople under Mohammed II [NEWTON]. **41.**
Antiochus, according to PORPHYRY, marching against
Ptolemy, though he turned from his course to
wreak his wrath on the Jews, did not meddle with
Edom, Moab, and Ammon on the side of Judea.
In I Maccabees 4:61; 5:3 etc., it is stated that he
used their help in crushing the Jews, of whom they
were the ancient enemies. Cf. Isaiah 11:14, as to
Israel's future retribution, just as the Maccabees
made war on them as the friends of Antiochus (I
Maccabees 5). Antitypically, the Turks under Se-
lim entered Jerusalem on their way to Egypt, and
retain "the glorious land" of Palestine to this day.
But they never could conquer the Arabs, who are
akin to Edom, Moab, and Ammon (Gen. 16:12).
So in the case of the final Antichrist. **42, 43. Egypt
. . . Libyans . . . Ethiopians**—The latter two, being
the allies of the first, served under Antiochus when
he conquered Egypt. Antitypically, Egypt, though
it held out long under the Mamelukes, in A.D. 1517
fell under the Turks. Algiers, Tunis, and other
parts of Africa, are still under them. **at his steps**—
following him (*Margin*, Exod. 11:8; Judg. 4:10).
44. tidings out of the east and out of the north—Artaxias, king of Armenia, his vassal, had revolted in
the north, and Arsaces, leader of the Parthians, in
the east (I Maccabees 3:10, etc., 37; TACITUS, *H.* 5.
8). In 147 B.C. Antiochus went on the expedition
against them, on the return from which he died.
great fury—at the Jews, on account of their successes under Judas Maccabeus, whence he desired to
replenish his treasury with means to prosecute the
war with them; also at Artaxias and Arsaces, and
their respective followers. DE BURGH makes the
"tidings" which rouse his fury, to be concerning the
Jews' restoration; such may be the antitypical reference. **45. plant . . . between the seas**—the Dead Sea
and the Mediterranean. **tabernacles of . . . palace**—
his palace-like military tents, such as Oriental
princes travel with. See *Note*, vs. 40, as to the
time of Antiochus' attack on Judea, and his subsequent "end" at Tabes, which was caused by chagrin both at hearing that his forces under Lysias
were overcome by the Jews, and at the failure of his
expedition against the temple of Elymais (II Maccabees 9:5). **holy mountain**—Jerusalem and Mount
Zion. The desolation of the sanctuary by Antiochus, and also the desecration of the consecrated
ground round Jerusalem by the idolatrous Roman
ensigns, as also by the Mohammedan mosque, and,
finally, by the last Antichrist, are referred to. So
the last Antichrist is to sit upon "the *mount* of the
congregation" (Isa. 14:13), but "shall be brought
down to hell" (cf. *Note*, ch. 7:26; II Thess. 2:8).

CHAPTER 12

Vss. 1-13. CONCLUSION OF THE VISION (chs. 10-
12) AND EPILOGUE TO THE BOOK. Cf. vss. 4, 13; as
vss. 6, 7 refer to ch. 7:25, i.e., to the time of Antichrist, so the subsequent vss. 8-12 treat of the time
of Antiochus (cf. vs. 11 with ch. 11:31), thus putting together in one summary view the two great
periods of distress. The political resurrection of
the Jews under the Maccabees is the starting point

of transition to the literal resurrection about to follow the destruction of Antichrist by Christ's coming in glory. The language passes here from the nearer to the more remote event, to which alone it is fully applicable. **1. at that time**—*typically*, towards the close of Antiochus' reign; *antitypically*, the time when Antichrist is to be destroyed at Christ's coming. **Michael**—the guardian angel of Israel ("thy people"), (ch. 10:13). The transactions on earth affecting God's people have their correspondences in heaven, in the conflict between good and bad angels; so at the last great contest on earth which shall decide the ascendency of Christianity (Rev. 12:7-10). An archangel, not the Lord Jesus; for he is distinguished from "the Lord" in Jude 9. **there shall be**—rather, "it shall be." **time of trouble, such as never was**—partially applicable to the time of Antiochus, who was the first subverter of the Jews' religion, and persecutor of its professors, which no other world power had done. Fully applicable to the last times of Antichrist, and his persecutions of Israel restored to Palestine. Satan will be allowed to exercise an unhindered, unparalleled energy (Isa. 26:20, 21; Jer. 30:7; Matt. 24:21; cf. ch. 8:24, 25; 11:36). **thy people shall be delivered**—(Rom. 11:26). The same deliverance of Israel as in Zechariah 13:8, 9, "the third part . . . brought through the fire . . . refined as silver." The remnant in Israel spared, as not having joined in the Antichristian blasphemy (Rev. 14:9, 10); not to be confounded with those who have confessed Christ before His coming, "the remnant according to the election of grace" (Rom. 11:5), part of the Church of the first-born who will share His millennial reign in glorified bodies; the spared remnant (Isa. 10:21) will only know the Lord Jesus when they see Him, and when the spirit of grace and supplication is poured out on them [TREGELLES]. **written in the book**—viz., of God's secret purpose, as destined for deliverance (Ps. 56:8; 69:28; Luke 10:20; Rev. 20: 15; 21:27). Metaphor from a muster-roll of citizens (Neh. 7:5). **2. many . . . that sleep**—"many *from among* the sleepers . . . *these* shall be unto everlasting life; but *those* (the rest of the sleepers who do not awake at this time) shall be unto shame" [TREGELLES]. Not the *general* resurrection, but that of those who share in the first resurrection; the rest of the dead being not to rise till the end of the thousand years (Rev. 20:3, 5, 6; cf. I Cor. 15:23; I Thess. 4:16). Israel's national resurrection, and the first resurrection of the elect Church, are similarly connected with the Lord's coming forth out of His place to punish the earth in Isaiah 26:19, 21; 27:6. Cf. Isaiah 25:6-9. The Jewish commentators support TREGELLES. AUBERLEN thinks the sole purpose for which the resurrection is introduced in this verse is an incitement to faithful perseverance in the persecutions of Antiochus; and that there is no *chronological* connection between the time of trouble in vs. 1 and the resurrection in vs. 2; whence the phrase, "at that time," twice occurs in vs. 1, but no fixing of time in vss. 2, 3; II Maccabees 7:9, 14, 23, shows the fruit of this prophecy in animating the Maccabean mother and her sons to brave death, while confessing the resurrection in words like those here. Cf. Hebrews 11:35. NEWTON'S view that "many" means *all*, is not so probable; for Romans 5:15, 19, which he quotes, is not in point, since the *Greek* is "*the* many," i.e., all, but there is no article in the *Hebrew* here. Here only *in the Old Testament* is "everlasting life" mentioned. **3. wise**—(Prov. 11:30). Answering to "they that understand" (ch. 11:33, 35), the same *Hebrew, Maskilim;*

Israelites who, though in Jerusalem when wickedness is coming to a head, are found intelligent witnesses against it. As *then* they appeared worn out with persecutions (typically, of Antiochus; antitypically, of Antichrist); so *now* in the resurrection they "shine as the brightness of the firmament." The design of past afflictions here appears "to make them white" (Matt. 13:43; Rev. 7:9, 14). **turn . . . to righteousness**—lit., "justify," i.e., convert many to justification through Christ (Jas. 5:20). **stars**—(I Cor. 15:41, 42). **4. shut up . . . seal the book**—John, on the contrary, is told (Rev. 22:10) not to seal his visions. Daniel's prophecy refers to a *distant* time, and is therefore obscure for the immediate future, whereas John's was to be *speedily* fulfilled (Rev. 1:1, 3; 22:6). *Israel,* to whom Daniel prophesied after the captivity, with premature zeal sought after signs of the predicted period: Daniel's prophecy was designed to restrain this. The *Gentile* Church, on the contrary, for whom John wrote, needs to be impressed with the shortness of the period, as it is, owing to its Gentile origin, apt to conform to the world, and to forget the coming of the Lord (cf. Matt. 25:13, 19; Mark 13:32-37; II Pet. 3:8, 12; Rev. 22:20). **run to and fro**—not referring to the modern rapidity of locomotion, as some think, nor to Christian missionaries going about to preach the Gospel to the world at large [BARNES]; but, whereas now but few care for this prophecy of God, "at the time of the end," i.e., near its fulfilment, "many shall run to and fro," i.e., scrutinize it, running through every page. Cf. Habakkuk 2:2 [CALVIN]: it is thereby that "*the* knowledge (viz., of God's purposes as revealed in prophecy) shall be increased." This is probably being now fulfilled. **5.** A vision of two other angels, one on one side of the Hiddekel or Tigris, the other on the other side, implying that on all sides angels attend to execute God's commands. The angel addressing Daniel had been *over* the river "from above" (vs. 6, *Margin*). **6. one**—viz., of the two (vs. 5). **man . . . in linen**—who had spoken up to this point. God impelled the angel to ask in order to waken us out of our torpor, seeing that the very "angels desire to look into" the things affecting man's redemption (I Pet. 1:12), as setting forth the glory of their Lord and ours (Eph. 3:10). **How long . . . to the end of these wonders**—This question of the angel refers to the final dealings of God in general, Antichrist's overthrow, and the resurrection. Daniel's question (vs. 8) refers to the more immediate future of his nation [AUBERLEN]. **7. held up . . . right . . . and . . . left hand**—Usually the right hand was held up in affirmation as an appeal to heaven to attest the truth (Deut. 32:40; Rev. 10:5, 6). Here *both* hands are lifted up for the fuller confirmation. **time, times, and a half**—(See *Note,* ch. 7:25). NEWTON, referring this prophecy to the Eastern apostasy, Mohammedanism, remarks that the same period of three and a half years, or 1260 prophetic days, is assigned to it as the Western apostasy of the little horn (ch. 7:25); and so, says PRIDEAUX, Mohammed began to forge his imposture, retiring to his cave, A.D. 606, the very year that Phocas made the grant to the bishop of Rome, whence he assumed the title, The Universal Pastor; Antichrist thus setting both his feet on Christendom together, the one in the East, and the other in the West. Three and a half is the time of the world power, in which the earthly kingdoms rule over the heavenly [AUBERLEN]. "Three and a half" represents *the idea of spiritual trial;* (besides this certain *symbolical* meaning, there is doubtless an accurate *chronological* meaning, which is as yet to us uncertain): it is half of "seven," the complete number, so a semi-perfect state, one of probation. The holy city is trodden by the Gentiles forty-two months (Rev. 11:2), so the exercise of the power of the beast (Rev. 13:5). The two witnesses preach in sackcloth 1260 days, and remained unburied *three days and a half:* so the woman in the wilderness: also the same for a "time, times, and a half" (Rev. 11:3, 9, 11; 12:6, 14). *Forty-two* connects the Church with Israel, whose haltings in the wilderness were *forty-two* (Num. 33: 1-50). The famine and drought on Israel in Elijah's days were for "three years and six months" (Luke 4:25; Jas. 5:17); there same period as Antiochus' persecution: so the ministry of the Man of Sorrows, which ceased in the midst of a week (ch. 9:27) [WORDSWORTH, *Apocalypse*]. **scatter ... holy people**—"accomplished" here answers to "the consummation" (ch. 9:27), viz., the "pouring out" of the last dregs of the curse on the "desolated holy people." Israel's lowest humiliation (the utter "scattering of her power") is the precursor of her exaltation, as it leads her to seek her God and Messiah (Matt. 23:39). **8. understood not**—Daniel "understood" the main features of the vision as to Antiochus (ch. 10:1, 14), but not as to the *times.* I Peter 1:10-12 refers mainly to Daniel: for it is he who foretells "the sufferings of Christ and the glory that should follow"; it is he who prophesies "not unto himself, but unto us"; it is he who "searched what, or what manner of *time* the Spirit of Christ in him did signify." **9.** Daniel's desire of knowing more is thus deferred "till the time of the end." John's Revelation in part reveals what here is veiled (*Note*, vs. 4, and ch. 8:26). **10.** There is no need of a fuller explanation as to the *time;* for when the predictions so far given shall have come to pass, the godly shall be "purified" by the foretold trials and shall understand that the end is at hand; but the wicked shall not understand, and so shall rush on to their own ruin (ch. 11:33-35) [MAURER]. The "end" is primarily, of Antiochus' persuasion; antitypically, the end of Antichrist's. It is the very clearness in the main which renders necessary the obscurity. The fulfilment of God's decree is not a mere arithmetical problem which the profane may understand by arithmetical calculations, but a holy enigma to stimulate to a faithful observance of God's ways, and to a diligent study of the history of God's people [AUBERLEN]. To this Christ refers (Matt. 24: 15), "Whose readeth, let him *understand.*" **11. from ... sacrifice ... taken way ... abomination**— (ch. 11:31). As to this epoch, which probably is prophetically germinant and manifold; the profanation of the temple *by Antiochus* (in the month Ijar of the year 145 B.C., till the restoration of the wor-

ship by Judas Maccabeus on the twenty-fifth day of the ninth month (Chisleu) of 148 B.C., according to the Seleucid era, 1290 days; forty-five days more elapsed before Antiochus' death in the month Shebat of 148 B.C., so ending the Jews' calamities [MAURER]); *by pagan Rome,* after Christ's death; *by Mohammed; by Antichrist,* the culmination of apostate Rome. The "abomination" must reach its climax (see AUBERLEN's translation, "summit," ch. 9:27), and the measure of iniquity be full, before Messiah comes. **thousand two hundred and ninety days**—a month beyond the "time, times, and a half" (vs. 7). In vs. 12, forty-five days more are added, in all 1335 days. TREGELLES thinks Jesus at His coming will deliver the Jews. An interval elapses, during which their consciences are awakened to repentance and faith in Him. A second interval elapses in which Israel's outcasts are gathered, and then the united blessing takes place. These stages are marked by the 1260, 1290, and 1335 days. CUMMING thinks the 1260 years begin when Justinian in A.D. 533 subjected the Eastern churches to John II, bishop of Rome; ending in 1792, when the Code Napoleon was established and the Pope was dishonored. 1290 reach to 1822, about the time of the waning of the Turkish power, the successor to Greece in the empire of the East. Forty-five years more end in 1867, the end of "the times of the Gentiles." See Leviticus 26:24, "seven times," i.e., 7×360, or 2520 years: 652 B.C. is the date of Judah's captivity, beginning under Manasseh; 2520 from this date end in 1868, thus nearly harmonizing with the previous date, 1867. See *Note,* also ch. 8:14. The seventh millenary of the world [CLINTON] begins in 1862. Seven years to 1869 (the date of the second advent) constitute the reign of the personal Antichrist; in the last three and a half, the period of final tribulation, Enoch (or else Moses) and Elijah, the two witnesses, prophesy in sackcloth. This theory is very dubious (cf. Matt. 24:36; Acts 1:7; I Thess. 5:2; II Pet. 3:10); still the event alone can tell whether the chronological coincidences of such theories are fortuitous, or solid data on which to fix the future times. HALES makes the periods 1260, 1290, 1335, begin with the Roman destruction of Jerusalem and end with the precursory dawn of the Reformation, the preaching of Wycliffe and Huss. **13. rest**—in the grave (Job 3:17; Isa. 57:2). He, like his people Israel, was to wait patiently and confidently for the blessing till God's time. He "received not the promise," but had to wait until the Christian elect saints should be brought in, at the first resurrection, that he and the older Old Testament saints "without us should not be made perfect" (Heb. 11:40). **stand** —implying *justification* unto life, as opposed to condemnation (Ps. 1:5). **thy lot**—image from the *allotment* of the earthly Canaan.

THE BOOK OF

HOSEA

INTRODUCTION

THE first of the twelve minor prophets in the order of the canon (called "minor," not as less in point of inspired authority, but simply in point of size). The twelve are first mentioned by Jesus, the son of Sirach

(Ecclesiasticus 49:10). St. Stephen, in Acts 7:42 (in referring to Amos 5:27), quotes them as forming one collective body of writings, "the book of the prophets." So JEROME and MELITO, the first Greek father who has left us a catalogue of these books. The collection of the sacred books is by Jewish tradition attributed to the great synagogue of learned scribes formed by Ezra. Many think Nehemiah completed this collection by adding to the books already in the canon those of his own times. Malachi, the last in the series, probably aided him in determining with infallible authority what books were entitled to be ranked in the inspired canon. The chronological order differs from the canonical. Joel, about 810 B.C.; Jonah, about 810 B.C., or, as others, *first*, 862 B.C.; Amos, about 790 B.C.; Hosea, about 784 B.C. Hosea, the contemporary of Isaiah, Micah, and Amos, seems to have entered on his prophetical office in the last years of Jeroboam (contemporary in part with Uzziah), and to have ended it in the beginning of Hezekiah's reign, 722 B.C., i.e., about *sixty* years in all, from 784 B.C. to 722 B.C. The prophets, however, were not uninterruptedly engaged in prophesying. Considerable intervals elapsed, though their office as divinely-commissioned public teachers was never wholly laid aside. The Book of Hosea which we have constitutes only that portion of his public teachings which the Holy Spirit saw fit to preserve for the benefit of the Church. The cause of his being placed first of the twelve was, probably, the length, the vivid earnestness, and patriotism of his prophecies, as well as their closer resemblance to those of the greater prophets. His style is abrupt, sententious, and unrounded; the connecting particles are few; there are changes of person, and anomalies of gender, number, and construction. His name means *Salvation*. He was son of Beeri, of the tribe of Issachar, born in Beth-shemesh [JEROME]. His mention, in the inscription, of Uzziah, Jotham, Ahaz, and Hezekiah, kings of Judah, is no proof that he belonged to Judah: for the prophets in Israel regarded its separation from Judah, *civil* as well as religious, as an apostasy from God, who promised the dominion of the theocracy to the line of David. Hence Elijah in Israel took *twelve* stones to represent Judah, as well as Israel (I Kings 18:31). Hence Hosea dates from Judah's kings, as well as from Jeroboam of Israel, though he belonged to Israel, with whose sins and fate his book is chiefly occupied. He, however, makes incidental references to Judah. His first prophecy foretells the overthrow of Jehu's house, fulfilled on the death of Jeroboam, Jehu's great-grandson (II Kings 15:12), in Zachariah, Jeroboam's son, the fourth and last from Jehu, conspired against by Shallum. This first prediction was doubtless in Jeroboam's life, as Zachariah, his son, was only suffered to reign six months; thus the inscription is verified that "the word of the Lord came unto him in the days of Jeroboam." Again, in ch. 10:14, Shalmaneser's expedition against Israel is alluded to as *past*, i.e., the first inroad against King Hoshea, who began to reign in the twelfth year of Ahaz; so that as Ahaz' whole reign was sixteen years, the prophecy seems to have been given about the beginning of Hezekiah's reign. Thus the inscription is confirmed that the exercise of his prophetical functions was of such a protracted duration.

Hosea (ch. 11:1) is quoted in Matthew 2:15; also ch. 6:6 in Matthew 9:13; 12:7; cf. Romans 9:25, 26, quoting ch. 1:10; 2:1, 23; I Corinthians 15:55, quoting ch. 13:14; I Peter 2:10, quoting ch. 1:9, 10; 2:23. Messianic references are not frequent; but the predictions of the future conversion of Israel to the Lord their God, and David their king, and of the fulfilment of the promise to Abraham that his spiritual seed should be as the sand of the sea (ch. 1:10; 3:5), clearly refer to the New Testament dispensation.

The first and third chapters are in prose, the rest of the book is rhythmical.

CHAPTER 1

Vss. 1-11. INSCRIPTION. Spiritual whoredom of Israel set forth by symbolical acts; Gomer taken to wife at God's command: Jezreel, Lo-ruhamah, and Lo-ammi, the children. Yet a promise of Judah and Israel's restoration. **1.** See *Introduction*. **Jeroboam**—the second; who died in the fifteenth year of Uzziah's forty-one years' reign. From his time forth *all* Israel's kings worshipped false gods: Zachariah (II Kings 15:9), Menahem (II Kings 15:18), Pekahiah (II Kings 15:24), Pekah (II Kings 15:28), Hoshea (II Kings 17:2). As Israel was most flourishing externally under Jeroboam II, who recovered the possessions seized on by Syria, Hosea's prophecy of its downfall at that time was the more striking as it could not have been foreseen by mere human sagacity. Jonah the prophet had promised success to Jeroboam II from God, not for the king's merit, but from God's mercy to Israel; so the coast of Israel was restored by Jeroboam II from the entering of Hamath to the sea of the plain (II Kings 14:23-27). **2. beginning**—not of the prophet's predictions generally, but of those spoken by *Hosea*. **take . . . wife of whoredoms**—not externally acted, but internally and in vision, as a pictorial illustration of Israel's unfaithfulness [HENGSTENBERG]. Cf. Ezekiel 16:8, 15, etc. Besides the loathsomeness of such a marriage, if an external act, it would require years for the birth of three children, which would weaken the symbol (cf. Ezek. 4:4). HENDERSON ob-

jects that there is no hint of the transaction being fictitious: Gomer fell into lewdness *after* her union with Hosea, not before; for thus only she was a fit symbol of Israel, who lapsed into spiritual whoredom *after* the marriage contract with God on Sinai, and made even before at the call of the patriarchs of Israel. Gomer is called "a wife of whoredoms," anticipatively. **children of whoredoms**—The kingdom collectively is viewed as a *mother*; the individual subjects of it are spoken of as her *children*. "Take" being applied to both implies that they refer to the same thing viewed under different aspects. The "children" were not the prophet's own, but born of adultery, and presented to him as his [KITTO, *Biblical Cyclopædia*]. Rather, "children of whoredoms" means that the children, like their mother, fell into spiritual fornication. Cf. "bare *him* a son" (see ch. 2:4, 5). Being children of a spiritual whore, they naturally fell into her whorish ways. **3. Gomer . . . daughter of Diblaim** —symbolical names; lit., "completion, daughter of grape-cakes"; the dual expressing the double layers in which these dainties were baked. So, *one completely given up to sensuality*. MAURER explains "Gomer" as lit., "a burning coal." Cf. Proverbs 6: 27, 29, as to an adulteress; Job 31:9, 12. **4. Jezreel** —i.e., "God will scatter" (cf. Zech. 10:9). It was the royal city of Ahab and his successors, in the tribe of Issaschar. Here Jehu exercised his greatest cruelties (II Kings 9:16, 25, 33; 10:11, 14, 17). There is in the name an allusion to "Israel" by a play of letters and sounds. **5. bow**—the prowess (Jer. 49:35; cf. Gen. 49:24). **valley of Jezreel**—afterwards called Esdraelon, extending ten miles in breadth, and in length from Jordan to the Mediterranean near Mount Carmel, the great battlefield of Palestine (Judg. 6:33; I Sam. 29:1). **6. Lo-ruhamah**—i.e., "not an object of mercy or gracious favor." **take ... away**—Israel, as a kingdom, was never restored from Assyria, as Judah was from Babylon after seventy years. MAURER translates according to the primary meaning, "No more will I have mercy on the house of Israel, so as to *pardon* them." **7.** *Judah* is only incidentally mentioned to form a contrast to *Israel*. **by the Lord their God**—more emphatic than "by Myself"; by that Jehovah (Me) whom they worship as *their God*, whereas ye despise Him. **not ... by bow**—on which ye Israelites rely (vs. 5, "the bow of Israel"); Jeroboam II was famous as a warrior (II Kings 14:25). Yet it was not by their warlike power Jehovah would save Judah (I Sam. 17:47; Ps. 20:7). The deliverance of Jerusalem from Sennacherib (II Kings 19:35), and the restoration from Babylon, are herein predicted. **8. weaned**—said to complete the symbolical picture, not having any special signification as to Israel [HENDERSON]. Israel was bereft of all the privileges which were as needful to them as milk is to infants (cf. Ps. 131:2; I Pet. 2:2) [VATABLUS]. Israel was *not suddenly,* but *gradually* cast off; God bore with them with long-suffering, until they were incurable [CALVIN]. But as it is not God, but *Gomer* who weans Loruhamah, the weaning may imply the lust of Gomer, who was hardly weaned when she is again pregnant [MANGER]. **9. Lo-ammi**—once "My people," but henceforth *not* so (Ezek. 16:8). The intervals between the marriage and the successive births of the three children, imply that three successive generations are intended. Jezreel, the first child, represents the dynasty of Jeroboam I and his successors, ending with Jehu's shedding the blood of Jeroboam's line in Jezreel; it was there that Jezebel was slain, in vengeance for Naboth's blood shed in the same Jezreel (I Kings 16:1; II Kings 9: 21, 30). The scenes of Jezreel were to be enacted over again on Jehu's degenerate race. At Jezreel Assyria routed Israel [JEROME]. The child's name associates past sins, intermediate punishments, and final overthrow. Lo-ruhamah ("not pitied"), the second child, is a *daughter,* representing the effeminate period which followed the overthrow of the first dynasty, when Israel was at once abject and impious. Lo-ammi ("not my people"), the third child, a *son,* represents the vigorous dynasty (II Kings 14:25) of Jeroboam II; but, as prosperity did not bring with it revived piety, they were still *not God's people.* **10.** Literally fulfilled *in part* in the return from Babylon, in which many Israelites joined with Judah. Spiritually, the believing seed of Jacob or Israel, Gentiles as well as Jews, numerous "as the sand" (Gen. 32:12); the Gentiles, once not God's people, becoming His "sons" (John 1:12; Rom. 9:25, 26; I Pet. 2:10; I John 3:1). To be fulfilled in its literal *fulness* hereafter in Israel's restoration (Rom. 11:26); the **living God**—opposed to their *dead* idols. **11. Judah ... Israel ... together**—(Isa. 11:12, 13; Jer. 3:18; Ezek. 34:23; 37:16-24). **one head**—Zerubbabel typically; Christ antitypically, under whom alone Israel and Judah are joined, the "Head" of the Church (Eph. 1:22; 5:23), and of the hereafter united kingdom of Judah and Israel (Jer. 34:5, 6; Ezek. 34:23). Though "appointed" by the Father (Ps. 2:6), Christ is in another sense "appointed" as their Head by His people, when they

accept and embrace Him as such. **out of the land**—of the Gentiles among whom they sojourn. **the day of Jezreel**—"The day of one" is the time of God's special visitation of him, either in wrath or in mercy. Here "Jezreel" is in a different sense from that in vs. 4, "God will sow," not "God will scatter"; they shall be *the seed of God,* planted by God again in their own land (Jer. 24:6; 31:28; 32: 41; Amos 9:15).

CHAPTER 2

VSS. 1-23. APPLICATION OF THE SYMBOLS IN CHAPTER I. Israel's spiritual fornication, and her threatened punishment: yet a promise of God's restored favor, when chastisements have produced their designed effect. **1. Say ... unto ... brethren, Ammi ...** —i.e., When the prediction (ch. 1:11) shall be accomplished, then ye will call one another, as *brothers* and *sisters* in the family of God, Ammi and Ruhamah. **2. Plead**—expostulate. **mother**—i.e., the nation *collectively.* The address is to "her children," i.e., to the *individual* citizens of the state (cf. Isa. 50:1). **for she is not my wife**—She has deprived herself of her high privilege by spiritual adultery. **out of her sight**—rather, "from her face." Her very countenance unblushingly betrayed her lust, as did also her exposed "breasts." **3. set her as in the day ... born**—(Ezek. 16:4; 23:25, 26, 28, 29). The day of her political "birth" was when God delivered her from the bondage of Egypt, and set up the theocracy. **make her as a wilderness**—(Jer. 6:8; Zeph. 2:13). Translate, "make her as the wilderness," viz., that in which she passed forty years on her way to her goodly possession of Canaan. With this agrees the mention of "thirst" (cf. Jer. 2:6). **4. her children**—Not even her *individual* members shall escape the doom of the nation collectively, for they are individually guilty. **5. I will go after**—The *Hebrew* expresses a *settled determination.* **lovers**—the idols which Israel fancied to be the givers of all their goods, whereas God gave all these goods (vss. 8-13; cf. Jer. 44:17-19). **bread and ... water**— the *necessaries* of life in food. **wool ... flax**—clothing. **oil ... drink**—perfumed unguents and palatable drinks: the *luxuries* of Hebrew life. **6, 7. thorns ... wall**—(Job 19:8; Lam. 3:7, 9). The hindrances which the captivity interposed between Israel and her idols. As she attributes all her temporal blessings to idols, I will reduce her to straits in which, when she in vain has sought help from false gods, she will at last seek Me as her only God and Husband, as at the first (Isa. 54:5; Jer. 3:14; Ezek. 16:8). **then**—before Israel's apostasy, under Jeroboam. The way of duty is hedged *about* with thorns; it is the way of sin that is hedged *up* with thorns. Crosses in an evil course are God's hedges to turn us from it. Restraining grace and restraining providences (even sicknesses and trials) are great blessings when they stop us in a course of sin. Cf. Luke 15:14-18, "I will arise, and go to my father." So here, "I will go, and return ..."; crosses in the both cases being sanctified to produce this effect. **8. she did not know that I**—not the idols, as she thought: the "lovers" alluded to in vs. 5. **which they prepared for Baal**—i.e., of which they made images of Baal, or at least the plate-covering of them (ch. 8:4). Baal was the Phœnician sun-god: answering to the female Astarte, the moon-goddess. The name of the idol is found in the Phœnician Hannibal, Hasdrubal. Israel borrowed it from the Tyrians. **9. my corn ... my wool ... my flax**—in contrast to "*my* bread

... my wool *... my* flax," (vs. 5). Cf. also vss. 21-23, on God as the great First Cause giving these through secondary instruments in nature. "Return, and take away," is equivalent to, "I will take back again," viz., by sending storms, locusts, Assyrian enemies, etc. "Therefore," i.e., because she did not acknowledge Me as the Giver. **in the time thereof** —in the harvest time. **10. lewdness**—rather, "the shame of her nakedness"; laying aside the figure, "I will expose her in *her state, bereft of every necessary,* before her lovers," i.e., the idols (personified, as if they could see), who, nevertheless, can give her no help. "Discover" is appropriate to stripping off the self-flatteries of her hypocrisy. **11. her feast days**—of Jeroboam's appointment, distinct from the Mosaic (I Kings 12:32). However, most of the Mosaic feasts, "new moons" and "sabbaths" to Jehovah, remained, but to degenerate Israel worship was a weariness; they cared only for the carnal indulgence on them (Amos 8:5). **12. my rewards**—my hire as a harlot (Isa. 23:17, 18). **lovers**—idols. **destroy ... vines ... make ... forest**— (Isa. 5:6; 7:23, 24). Fulfilled in the overthrow of Israel by Assyria (ch. 9:4, 5). **13. days of Baalim** —the days consecrated to the Baals, or various images of Baal in different cities, whence the names *Baal-gad, Baal-hermon,* etc. **decked herself with ... earrings**—rather, "nose-rings" (Isa. 3:21; *Margin,* Ezek. 16:12), with which harlots decked themselves to attract admirers: answering to the ornaments in which the Israelites decked themselves on the idols' feasts. **forgat me**—worse than the nations which had never known God. Israel *wilfully apostatized* from Jehovah, whom she had known. **14. Therefore** —rather, "Nevertheless" [HENDERSON]. *English Version* gives a more lovely idea of God. That which would provoke all others to unappeasable wrath, Israel's perversity and consequent punishment, is made a reason why God should at last have mercy on her. As the "therefore" (vs. 9) expresses Israel's punishment as the *consequence* of Israel's guilt, so "therefore" here, as in vs. 6, expresses, that when that punishment has effected its designed end, the hedging up her way with thorns so that she returns to God, her first love, the *consequence* in God's wondrous grace is, He "speaks comfortably" (lit., "speaks to her heart"; cf. Judg. 19:8; Ruth 2: 13). So obstinate is she that God has to "allure her," i.e., so to temper judgment with unlooked-for grace as to *win* her to His ways. For this purpose it was necessary to "bring her into the wilderness" (i.e., into temporal want and trials) first, to make her sin hateful to her by its bitter fruits, and God's subsequent grace the more precious to her by the contrast of the "wilderness." JEROME makes the "bringing into the wilderness" to be rather a *deliverance from her enemies,* just as ancient Israel was brought into the wilderness from the bondage of Egypt; to this the phrase here alludes (cf. vs. 15). The wilderness sojourn, however, is not literal, but moral: while still in the land of their enemies *locally,* by the discipline of the trial rendering the word of God sweet to them, they are to be brought *morally* into the wilderness state, i.e., into a state of preparedness for returning to their temporal and spiritual privileges in their own land; just as the literal wilderness prepared their fathers for Canaan: thus the bringing of them into the *wilderness state* is *virtually* a deliverance from their enemies. **15. from thence**—returning from the wilderness. God gives Israel a fresh grant of Canaan, which she had forfeited; so of her vineyards, etc. (vss. 9, 12). **Achor**—i.e. "trouble." As formerly Israel, after

their tedious journey through the wilderness, met with the *trouble* resulting from Achan's crime in this valley, on the very threshold of Canaan, and yet that *trouble* was presently turned into *joy* at the great victory at Ai, which threw all Canaan into their hands (Josh. 7, 8); so the very trouble of Israel's wilderness state will be the "door of hope" opening to better days. The valley of Achor, near Jericho, was specially fruitful (Isa. 65:10); so "trouble" and "hope" are rightly blended in connection with it. **sing ... as ... when she came ... out of ... Egypt**—It shall be a second exodus song, such as Israel sang after the deliverance at the Red Sea (Exod. 15; cf. Isa. 11:15, 16); and "the song of Moses" (Rev. 15:2, 3) sung by those who through the Lamb overcome the beast, and so stand on the sea of glass mingled with fire, emblems of fiery trial, such as that of Israel at the Red Sea. **16. Ishi ... no more Baali**—"my *Husband ...* no more my *Lord.*" *Affection* is the prominent idea in "Husband"; *rule,* in "Lord." The chief reason for the substitution of *Husband* for *Lord appears* in the next verse; viz., *Baali,* the *Hebrew* for *my Lord,* had been perverted to express the images of Baal, whose name ought not to be taken on their lips (Exod. 23:13; Zech. 13:2). **17. Baalim**—*plural,* expressing the various images of Baal, which, according to the places of their erection, received various names, Baal-gad, Baal-ammon, etc. **18. for them**— for their benefit. **covenant ... with the beasts**— not to hurt them (Job 5:23). They shall fulfil the original law of their creation by becoming subject to man, when man fulfils the law of his being by being subject to God. To be realized fully in millennial times (Isa. 11:6-9). **break the bow ... out of the earth**—rather, "out of the *land*"; i.e., I will break *and remove* war out of the earth (Ps. 46:9); and "out of the *land*" *of Israel* first (Isa. 2:4; Ezek. 39:9, 10; Zech. 9:9, 10). **lie down**—A reclining posture is the usual one with Orientals when not in action. **safely**—(Jer. 23:6). **19, 20. "Betroth"** is *thrice* repeated, implying the intense love of God to His people; and perhaps, also, *the three Persons* of the *Triune God,* severally engaging to make good the betrothal. The marriage covenant will be as it were renewed from the beginning, on a different footing; not for a time only, as before, through the apostasy of the people, but "forever" through the grace of God writing the law on their hearts by the Spirit of Messiah (Jer. 31:31-37). **righteousness ... judgment**—in rectitude and truth. **lovingkindness ...**—Hereby God assures Israel, who might doubt the possibility of their restoration to His favor; low, sunk, and unworthy as thou art. I will restore thee from a regard to My own "lovingkindness," not thy merits. **30. faithfulness**—to My new covenant of grace with thee (I Thess. 5:24; Heb. 10:23). **21. in that day**—of grace to Israel. **heavens ... hear the earth**—personification. However many be the intermediate instruments, God is the Great First Cause of all nature's phenomena. God had threatened (vs. 9) He would *take back His corn, His wine, etc.* Here, on the contrary, God promises to *hearken to the skies,* as it were, supplicating Him to fill them with rain to pour on the earth; and that the skies again would hearken to the earth begging for a supply of the rain it requires; and again, that the earth would hearken to the corn, wine, and oil, begging it to bring them forth; and these again would hear Jezreel, i.e., would fulfil Israel's prayers for a supply of them. Israel is now no longer "Jezreel" in the sense, *God will* SCATTER (ch. 1:4), but in the sense, "*God will* PLANT" (ch. 1:11). **23. I will sow her**—referring to the meaning of *Jezreel* (vs. 22).

CHAPTER 3

Vss. 1-5. ISRAEL'S CONDITION IN THEIR PRESENT DISPERSION, SUBSEQUENT TO THEIR RETURN FROM BABYLON, SYMBOLIZED. The prophet is to take back his wife, though unfaithful, as foretold in ch. 1:2. He purchases her from her paramour, stipulating she should wait for a long period before she should be restored to her conjugal rights. So Israel is to live for a long period without her ancient rites of religion, and yet be free from idolatry; then at last she shall acknowledge Messiah, and know Jehovah's goodness restored to her. **1. Go yet**—"Go *again*," referring to ch. 1:2 [HENDERSON]. **a woman**—purposely indefinite, for *thy wife*, to express the *separation* in which Hosea had lived from Gomer for her unfaithfulness. **beloved of her friend**—used for "her *husband*," on account of the estrangement between them. She was still beloved of her husband, though an adulteress; just as God still loved Israel, though idolatrous (Jer. 3:20). Hosea is told, not as in ch. 1:2, "*take a wife*," but "*love*" her, i.e., renew thy conjugal kindness to her. **who look to other gods**—i.e., have done so heretofore, but henceforth (from the return from Babylon) shall do so no more (vs. 4). **flagons of wine**—rather, pressed cakes of dried grapes, such as were offered to idols (Jer. 7:18) [MAURER]. **2. I bought her**—The price paid is too small to be a probable dowry wherewith to buy *a wife* from her parents; but it is just half the price of a female *slave*, in money, the rest of the price being made up in grain (Exod. 21:32). Hosea pays this for the redemption of his wife, who has become the *slave of her paramour*. The price being *half grain* was because the latter was the allowance of food for the slave, and of the coarsest kind, not *wheat*, but *barley*. Israel, as *committing sin*, was the *slave of sin* (John 8:34; Rom. 6:16-20; II Pet. 2:19). The low price expresses Israel's *worthlessness*. **3. abide for me**—separate from intercourse with any other man, and *remaining* for me who have redeemed thee (cf. Deut. 21:13). **so will I also be for thee**—*remain for thee*, not taking any other consort. As Israel should long *remain* without serving other gods, yet separate from Jehovah; so Jehovah on His part, in this long period of estrangement, would form no marriage covenant with any other people (cf. vs. 4). He would not *immediately* receive her to marriage privileges, but would test her repentance and discipline her by the long probation; still the marriage covenant would hold good, she was to be kept separated for but a time, not divorced (Isa. 50:1); in God's good time she shall be restored. **4.** The long period here foretold was to be one in which Israel should have no civil polity, king, or prince, no sacrifice to Jehovah, and yet no idol, or false god, no ephod, or teraphim. Exactly describing their state for the last nineteen centuries, separate from idols, yet without any legal sacrifice to Jehovah, whom they profess to worship, and without being acknowledged by Him as His Church. So KIMCHI, a Jew, explains it. The ephod was worn by the high priest above the tunic and robe. It consisted of two finely wrought pieces which hung down, the one in front over the breast, the other on the back, to the middle of the thigh; joined on the shoulders by golden clasps set in onyx stones with the names of the twelve tribes, and fastened round the waist by a girdle (Exod. 28:6-12). The *common* ephod worn by the lower priests, Levites, and any person performing sacred rites, was of linen (II Sam. 6:14; I Chron. 15:27). In the breast were the Urim and Thummim by which God gave responses to the Hebrews. The latter was one of the five things which the second temple lacked, and which the first had. It, as representing the divinely constituted priesthood, is opposed to the idolatrous "teraphim," as "sacrifice" (to Jehovah) is to "an [idolatrous] image." "Abide" answers to "thou shalt *abide* for me" (vs. 3). *Abide* in solitary isolation, as a separated wife. The teraphim were tutelary household gods, in the shape of human busts, cut off at the waist (as the root of the *Hebrew* word implies) [MAURER], (Gen. 31:19, 30-35). They were supposed to give responses to consulters (II Kings 23: 24; *Margin*, Ezek. 21:21; Zech. 10:2). Saul's daughter, Michal, putting one in a bed, as if it were David, proves the shape to have been that of a man. **5. Afterward**—after the long period ("many days," vs. 4) has elapsed. **return**—from their idols to "their God," from whom they had wandered. **David their king**—Israel had forsaken the worship of Jehovah at the same time that they forsook their allegiance to David's line. Their repentance towards God is therefore to be accompanied by their return to the latter. So Judah and Israel shall be one, and under "one head," as is also foretold (ch. 1:11). That representative and antitype of David is Messiah. "David" means "the beloved." Cf. as to Messiah, Matthew 3:17; Ephesians 1:6. Messiah is called David (Isa. 55:3, 4; Jer. 30:9; Ezek. 34:23, 24; 37: 24, 25). **fear the Lord and his goodness**—i.e., tremblingly flee to the Lord, to escape from the wrath to come; and to His goodness," as manifested in Messiah, which attracts them to Him (Jer. 31:12). The "fear" is not that which "hath torment" (I John 4:18), but *reverence* inspired by His goodness realized in the soul (Ps. 130:4). **the latter days**—those of Messiah [KIMCHI].

CHAPTER 4

Vss. 1-19. HENCEFORTH THE PROPHET SPEAKS PLAINLY AND WITHOUT SYMBOL, IN TERSE, SENTENTIOUS PROPOSITIONS. In this chapter he reproves the people and priests for their sins in the interregnum which followed Jeroboam's death; hence there is no mention of the king or his family; and in vs. 2 bloodshed and other evils usual in a civil war are specified. **1. Israel**—the ten tribes. **controversy**—judicial ground of complaint (Isa. 1:18; Jer. 25:31; Mic. 6:2). **no ... knowledge of God**—exhibited in practice (Jer. 22:16). **2. they break out**—bursting through every restraint. **blood toucheth blood**—lit., "bloods." One act of bloodshed follows another without any interval between (see II Kings 15:8-16, 25; Mic. 7:2). **3. land ... languish**—(Isa. 19:8; 24:4; Joel 1:10, 12). **sea**—including all bodies of water, as pools and even rivers (*Note*, Isa. 19:5). A general drought, the greatest calamity in the East, is threatened. **4. let no man ... reprove**—Great as is the sin of Israel, it is hopeless to reprove them; for their presumptuous guilt is as great as that of one who refuses to obey the priest when giving judgment in the name of Jehovah, and who therefore is to be put to death (Deut. 17:12). They rush on to their own destruction as wilfully as such a one. **thy people**—the ten tribes of Israel; distinct from Judah (vs. 1). **5. fall in the day**—in broad *daylight*, a time when an attack would not be expected (*Notes*, Jer. 6:4, 5; 15:8). **in ... night**—No time, night or day, shall be free from the slaughter of individuals of the people, as well as of the false prophets. **thy mother**—the Israelitish state, of which the citizens are the children (ch. 2:2). **6. lack of knowledge**—"of God" (vs. 1), i.e., lack of piety. Their ignorance was wilful, as the epithet, *"My people,"* implies; they *ought* to have known, having the opportunity, as the people of God. **thou**—O priest, so called. Not regularly constituted, but still bearing the name, while confounding the worship of Jehovah and of the calves in Beth-el (I Kings 12:29, 31). **I will . . . forget thy children**—Not only those who then were alive should be deprived of the priesthood, but their children who, in the ordinary course would have succeeded them, should be set aside. **7. As they were increased**—in numbers and power. Cf. vs. 6, "thy children," to which their "increase" in *numbers* refers. **so they sinned**—(Cf. ch. 10:1 and 13:6). **will I change their glory into shame**—i.e., I will strip them of all they now *glory* in (their numbers and power), and give them *shame* instead. A just retribution: as they changed their glory into shame, by idolatry (Ps. 106:20; Jer. 2:11; Rom. 1: 23; Phil. 3:19). **8. eat . . . sin of my people**—i.e., the sin offerings (Lev. 6:26; 10:17). The priests greedily devoured them. **set their heart on their iniquity**—lit., "lift up the animal soul to lust after," or strongly desire. Cf. *Margin,* Deuteronomy 24: 15; Psalm 24:4; Jeremiah 22:27. The priests set *their own* hearts on the iniquity *of the people,* instead of trying to suppress it. For the more the people sinned, the more sacrificial victims in atonement for sin the priests gained. **9. like people, like priest**—They are one in guilt; therefore they shall be one in punishment (Isa. 24:2). **reward them their doings**—in homely phrase, "pay them back in their own coin" (Prov. 1:31). **10. eat, and not have enough**—just retribution on those who "eat up [greedily] the sin of My people" (vs. 8; Mic. 6:14; Hag. 1:6). **whoredom, and . . . not increase**—lit., "break forth"; used of *giving birth to children* (Gen. 28:14, *Margin;* cf. Gen. 38:29). Not only their wives, but their concubines, shall be barren. To be childless was considered a great calamity among the Jews. **11.** A moral truth applicable to all times. The special reference here is to the licentious orgies connected with the Syrian worship, which lured Israel away from the pure worship of God (Isa. 28:1, 7; Amos 4:1). **take away the heart**—i.e., the understanding; make men blind to their own true good (Eccles. 7:7). **12.** Instances of their understanding ("heart") being "taken away." **stocks**—wooden idols (Jer. 2:27; Hab. 2:19). **staff**—alluding to divination by rods (*Notes,* Ezek. 21:21, 22). The diviner, says ROSENMULLER, threw a rod from him, which was stripped of its bark on one side, not on the other: if the bare side turned uppermost, it was a good omen; if the side with the bark, it was a bad omen. The Arabs used two rods, the one marked *God bids,* the other, *God forbids;* whichever came out first, in drawing them out of a case, gave the omen for, or against, an undertaking. **declareth**—i.e., is consulted to inform them of future events. **spirit of whoredoms**—a general *disposition* on the part of all *towards idolatry* (ch. 5:4). **err**—go astray from the true God. **from under their God**—They have gone away from God *under* whom they were, as a wife is under the dominion of her husband. **13. upon . . . mountains**—High places were selected by idolaters on which to sacrifice, because of their greater nearness to the heavenly hosts which they worshipped (Deut. 12:2). **elms**—rather, "terebinths" [MAURER]. **shadow . . . good**—screening the

lascivious worshippers from the heat of the sun. **daughters . . . commit whoredom . . . spouses . . . adultery**—in the polluted worship of Astarte, the Phœnician goddess of love. **14. I will not punish . . . daughters**—I will visit with the heaviest punishments "not" the unchaste "daughters and spouses," but the fathers and husbands; for it is these who "themselves" have set the bad example, so that as compared with the punishment of the latter, that of the former shall seem as nothing [MUNSTER]. **separated with whores**—withdrawn from the assembly of worshippers to some receptacle of impurity for carnal connection with *whores.* **sacrifice with harlots**—They commit lewdness with *women* who *devote their persons* to be violated in honor of Astarte. (So the *Hebrew* for "harlots" means, as distinguished from "whores.") Cf. Numbers 25:1-3; and the prohibition, Deuteronomy 23:18. **not understand**—(Isa. 44:18; 45:20). **shall fall**—shall be cast down. **15.** Though *Israel's* ten tribes indulge in spiritual harlotry, at least thou, *Judah,* who hast the legal priesthood, and the temple rites, and Jerusalem, do not follow her bad example. **Gilgal** —situated between Jordan and Jericho on the confines of Samaria; once a holy place to Jehovah (Josh. 5:10-15; I Sam. 10:8; 15:21); afterwards desecrated by idol-worship (ch. 9:15; 12:11; Amos 4:4; 5:5; cf. Judg. 3:19, *Margin*). **Beth-aven**—i.e., "house of vanity" or idols: a name substituted in contempt for *Beth-el,* "the house of God"; once sacred to Jehovah (Gen. 28:17, 19; 35:7), but made by Jeroboam the seat of the worship of the calves (I Kings 12:28-33; 13:1; Jer. 48:13; Amos 3:14; 7:13). "Go *up*" refers to the fact that Beth-el was on a hill (Josh. 16:1). **nor swear, The Lord liveth**—This formula of oath was appointed by God Himself (Deut. 6:13; 10:20; Jer. 4:2). It is therefore here forbidden not absolutely, but in conjunction with idolatry and falsehood (Isa. 48:1; Ezek. 20:39; Zeph. 1:5). **16. backsliding**—Translate, "Israel is refractory, as a refractory heifer," viz., one that throws the yoke off her neck. Israel had represented God under the form of "calves" (I Kings 12:28); but it is she herself who is one. **lamb in a large place**—not in a good sense, as in Isaiah 30:23. Here there is irony: lambs like a large pasture; but it is not so safe for them as a small one, duly fenced from wild beasts. God will "feed" them, but it shall be with the "rod" (Mic. 7:14). It shall be no longer in the narrow territory of Israel, but "in a large place," viz., they shall be scattered in exile over the wide realm of Assyria, a prey to their foes; as lambs, which are timid, gregarious, and not solitary, are a prey when scattered asunder to wild beasts. **17. Ephraim**—the ten tribes. Judah was at this time not so given to idolatry as afterwards. **joined to idols**—closely and voluntarily; identifying themselves with them as a whoremonger becomes one flesh with the harlot (Num. 25:3; I Cor. 6:16, 17). **idols**—The *Hebrew* means also "sorrows," "pains," implying the pain which idolatry brings on its votaries. **let him alone** —Leave him to himself. Let him reap the fruits of his own perverse choice; his case is desperate; say nothing to him (cf. Jer. 7:16). Here vs. 15 shows the address is to *Judah,* to avoid the contagion of Israel's bad example. He is bent on his own ruin; leave him to his fate, lest, instead of saving him, thou fall thyself (Isa. 48:20; Jer. 50:8; 51:6, 45; II Cor. 6:17). **18. Their drink is sour**—metaphor for *utter degeneracy* of principle (Isa. 1:22). Or, *unbridled licentiousness;* not mere ordinary sin, but as abandoned as drunkards who vomit and smell sour with wine potations [CALVIN]. MAURER not so well translates, "When their drinking *is over,* they commit whoredoms," viz., in honor of Astarte (vss. 13, 14). **her rulers**—Israel's; lit., "shields" (cf. Ps. 47:9). **with shame . . . love, Give ye**—(Prov. 30:15). No remedy could be effectual against their corruptions since the very rulers sold justice for gifts [CALVIN]. MAURER translates, "The rulers are marvelously enamored of shame." *English Version* is better. **19.** Israel shall be swept away from her land (vs. 16) suddenly and violently as if by "the wings of the wind" (Ps. 18:10; 104:3; Jer. 4:11, 12). **ashamed . . . of their sacrifices**—disappointed to their shame in their hope of help through their sacrifices to idols.

CHAPTER 5

Vss. 1-5. GOD'S JUDGMENTS ON THE PRIESTS, PEOPLE, AND PRINCES OF ISRAEL FOR THEIR SINS. Judah, too, being guilty shall be punished; nor shall Assyria, whose aid they both sought, save them; judgments shall at last lead them to repentance. **1. the king**—probably Pekah; the contemporary of Ahaz, king of Judah, under whom idolatry was first carried so far in Judah as to call for the judgment of the joint Syrian and Israelite invasion, as also that of Assyria. **judgment is towards you**—i.e., threatens you from God. **ye have been a snare on Mizpah . . . net . . . upon Tabor**—As hunters spread their net and snares on the hills, Mizpah and Tabor, so ye have snared the people into idolatry and made them your prey by injustice. As *Mizpah* and *Tabor* mean a "watch tower," and a "lofty place," a fit scene for hunters, playing on the words, the prophet implies, in the lofty place in which I have set you, whereas ye ought to have been the *watchers* of the people, guarding them from evil, ye have been as *hunters entrapping* them into it [JEROME]. These two places are specified, Mizpah in the east and Tabor in the west, to include the *high places* throughout the *whole* kingdom, in which Israel's rulers set up idolatrous altars. **2. revolters** —apostates. **profound**—*deeply* rooted [CALVIN] and sunk to the lowest depths, *excessive* in their idolatry (ch. 9:9; Isa. 31:6) [HENDERSON]. From the antithesis (vs. 3), "not hid from me," I prefer explaining, *profoundly cunning* in their idolatry. Jeroboam thought it a *profound* piece of policy to set up golden calves to represent God in Dan and Beth-el, in order to prevent Israel's heart from turning again to David's line by going up to Jerusalem to worship. So Israel's subsequent idolatry was grounded by their leaders on various pleas of state expediency (cf. Isa. 29:15). **to . . . slaughter**—He does not say "to *sacrifice*," for their so-called sacrifices were *butcheries* rather than sacrifices; there was nothing sacred about them, being to idols instead of to the holy God. **though**—MAURER translates, "*and* [in spite of their hope of safety through their slaughter of victims to idols] *I will be* a chastisement to them all." *English Version* is good sense: They have deeply revolted, *notwithstanding* all my prophetical warnings. **3. Ephraim**—the tribe so called, as distinguished from "Israel" here, the other nine tribes. It was always foremost of the tribes of the northern kingdom. For 400 years in early history, it, with Manasseh and Benjamin, its two dependent tribes, held the pre-eminence in the whole nation. Ephraim is here addressed as foremost in idolatry. **I know . . . not hid from me**—notwithstanding their supposed *profound* cunning (vs. 2; Rev. 2:2, 9, 13, 19). **now**—"though I have been a rebuker of all them" (vs. 2) who *commit* such spiritual *whoredoms,*

thou art *now* continuing in them. **4. They**—Turning from a direct address to Ephraim, he uses the third person *plural* to characterize the people in general. The *Hebrew* is against the *Margin,* their doings will not suffer *them*" the omission of "them" in the *Hebrew* after the verb being unusual. The sense is, they are incurable, for they will not *permit* (as the *Hebrew* lit. means) their doings to be framed so as to turn unto God. Implying that they *resist* the Spirit of God, not *suffering* Him to renew them; and give themselves up to "the spirit of whoredoms" (in antithesis to "the Spirit of God" implied in "suffer" or "permit") (ch. 4:12; Isa. 63:10; Ezek. 16:43; Acts 7:51). **5. the pride of Israel**—wherewith they reject the warnings of God's prophets (vs. 2), and prefer their idols to God (ch. 7:10; Jer. 13:17). **testify to his face**—openly *to his face* he shall be convicted of the pride which is so palpable in him. Or, "*in* his face," as in Isaiah 3:9. **Judah . . . shall fall with them**—This prophecy is later than ch. 4:15, when Judah had not gone so far in idolatry; now her imitation of Israel's bad example provokes the threat of her being doomed to share in Israel's punishment. **6. with . . . flocks**—to propitiate Jehovah (Isa. 1:11-15). **seek . . . not find**—because it is slavish fear that leads them to seek Him; and because it then shall be too late (Prov. 1:28; John 7: 34). **7. treacherously**—as to the marriage covenant (Jer. 3:20). **strange children**—alluding to "children of whoredoms" (ch. 1:2; 2:4). "Strange" or *foreign* implies that their idolatry was imported from abroad [HENDERSON]. Or rather, "regarded by God as strangers, not His," as being reared in idolatry. The case is desperate, when not only the existing, but also the rising, generation is reared in apostasy. **a month**—*a very brief space of time* shall elapse, and then punishment shall overtake them (Zech. 11:8). The allusion seems to be to money loans, which were *by the month,* not as with us by the year. You cannot put it off; the time of your destruction is immediately and suddenly coming on you; just as the debtor must meet the creditor's demand at the expiration of the month. The prediction is of the invasion of Tiglath-pileser, who carried away Reuben, Gad, Naphtali, and the half tribe of Manasseh. **portions**—i.e., possessions. Their resources and garrisons will not avail to save them. HENDERSON explains from Isaiah 57:6, "portions" as *their idols;* the context favors this, "the Lord" the true "*portion* of His people" (Deut. 32:9), being in antithesis to "their portions," the idols. **8.** The arrival of the enemy is announced in the form of an injunction to *blow an alarm.* **cornet . . . trumpet**—The "cornet" was made of the curved horn of animals and was used by shepherds. The "trumpet" was of brass or silver, straight, and used in wars and on solemn occasions. The *Hebrew* is *hatzotzerah,* the sound imitating the trumpet note (ch. 8:1; Num. 10:2; Jer. 4:5; Joel 2:1). **Gibeah . . . Ramah** —both in Benjamin (Isa. 10:29). **Beth-aven**—in Benjamin; not as in ch. 4:15; *Beth-el,* but a town east of it (Josh. 7:2). "Cry aloud," viz., to raise the alarm. "Benjamin" is put for the whole southern kingdom of Judah (cf. vs. 5), being the first part of it which would meet the foe advancing from the north. "After thee, O Benjamin," implies the position of Beth-aven, *behind* Benjamin, at the borders of Ephraim. When the foe is at Beth-aven, he is at Benjamin's rear, close upon thee, O Benjamin (Judg. 5:14). **9, 10.** Israel is referred to in vs. 9, Judah in vs. 10. **the day of rebuke**—the day when I shall chastise him. **among the tribes of Israel have I made known**—proving that the scene of Hosea's labor was among the ten tribes. **that which shall surely be**—viz., the coming judgment here foretold. It is no longer a conditional decree, leaving a hope of pardon on repentance; it is absolute, for Ephraim is hopelessly impenitent. **remove the bound**—(Deut. 19:14; 27:17; Job 24:2; Prov. 22:28; 23:10). Proverbial for the rash setting aside of the ancestral laws by which men are kept to their duty. Ahaz and his courtiers ("the princes of Judah"), setting aside the ancient ordinances of God, removed the borders of the bases and the laver and the sea and introduced an idolatrous altar from Damascus (II Kings 16:10-18); also he burnt his children in the valley of Hinnom, after the abominations of the heathen (II Chron. 28:3). **11. broken in judgment**—viz., the "judgment" of God on him (vs. 1). **walked after the commandment**—Jeroboam's, to worship the calves (II Kings 10:28-33). Cf. Micah 6:16, "the *statutes* of Omri," viz., idolatrous statutes. We ought to obey God rather than men (Acts 5:29). Jerome reads "filthiness." LXX gives the sense, not the literal translation: "after *vanities.*" **12. as a moth**—consuming a garment (Job 13:28; Ps. 39:11; Isa. 50:9). **Judah . . . rottenness**—Ephraim, or the ten tribes, are as a *garment* eaten by the moth; Judah as the *body* itself consumed by rottenness (Prov. 12:4). Perhaps alluding to the superiority of the latter in having the house of David, and the temple, the religious center of the nation [Grotius]. As in vss. 13, 14, the violence of the calamity is prefigured by the "wound" which "a lion" inflicts, so here its long protracted duration, and the certainty and completeness of the destruction from small unforeseen beginnings, by the images of a slowly but surely consuming *moth* and *rottenness.* **13. wound**—lit., "bandage"; hence a *bandaged wound* (Isa. 1:6; Jer. 30:12). "Saw," i.e., felt its weakened state politically, and the dangers that threatened it. It aggravates their perversity, that, though aware of their unsound and calamitous state, they did not inquire into the cause or seek a right remedy. **went . . . to the Assyrian**—First, Menahem (II Kings 15:19) applied to Pul; again, Hoshea to Shalmaneser (II Kings 17:3). **sent to King Jareb**—Understand *Judah* as the nominative to "sent." Thus, as "Ephraim saw his sickness" (the first clause) answers in the parallelism to "Ephraim went to the Assyrian" (the third clause), so "Judah saw his wound" (the second clause) answers to (*Judah*) "sent to King Jareb" (the fourth clause). *Jareb* ought rather to be translated, "their *defender*," lit., "avenger" [Jerome]. The Assyrian "king," ever ready, for his own aggrandizement, to mix himself up with the affairs of neighboring states, professed to *undertake* Israel's and Judah's *cause;* in Judges 6:32, *Jerub,* in Jerub-baal is so used, viz., "*plead* one's cause." Judah, under Ahaz, applied to Tiglath-pileser for aid against Syria and Israel (II Kings 16:7, 8; II Chron. 28:16-21); the Assyrian "distressed him, but strengthened him not," fulfiling the prophecy here, "he could not heal your, nor cure. you of your wound. **14. lion**—The *black lion* and the *young lion* are emblems of strength and ferocity (Ps. 91:13). **I, even I**—emphatic; when I, even I, the irresistible God, tear in pieces (Ps. 50: 22), no Assyrian power can rescue. **go away**—as a lion stalks leisurely back with his prey to his lair. **15. return to my place**—i.e., withdraw My favor. **till they acknowledge their offence**—The *Hebrew* is, "till they suffer the penalty of their guilt." Probably "*accepting* the punishment of their guilt" (cf. Zech. 11:5) is included in the idea, as *English Version* translates. Cf. Leviticus 26:40, 41; Jeremiah

29:12, 13; Ezekiel 6:9; 20:43; 36:31. **seek my face** —i.e., seek My favor (Prov. 29:26, *Margin*). **in . . . affliction . . . seek me early**—i.e., diligently; rising up before dawn to seek Me (Ps. 119:147; cf. Ps. 78:34).

CHAPTER 6

Vss. 1-11. The Israelites' Exhortation to One Another to Seek the Lord. At vs. 4 a new discourse, *complaining of them,* begins; for vss. 1-3 evidently belong to vs. 15, of ch. 5, and form the *happy* termination of Israel's *punishment:* primarily, the return from Babylon; ultimately, the return from their present long dispersion. The eighth verse perhaps refers to the murder of Pekahiah; the discourse cannot be later than Pekah's reign, for it was under it that *Gilead* was carried into captivity (II Kings 15:29). **1. let us return**—in order that God who has "returned to His place" may return to us (ch. 5:15). **torn, and . . . heal**—(Deut. 32:39; Jer. 30:17). They ascribe their punishment not to fortune, or man, but to God, and acknowledge that none (not the Assyrian, as they once vainly thought, ch. 5:13) but God can heal their wound. They are at the same time persuaded of the mercy of God, which persuasion is the starting-point of true repentance, and without which men would not seek, but hate and flee from God. Though our wound be severe, it is not past hope of recovery; there is room for grace, and a hope of pardon. He hath smitten us, but not so badly that He cannot heal us (Ps. 130:4). **2.** Primarily, in type, Israel's national revival, *in a short period* ("*two or three*" being used to denote a *few* days, Isa. 17:6; Luke 13:32, 33); antitypically the language is so framed as to refer in its *full accuracy* only to Messiah, the ideal Israel (Isa. 49:3; cf. Matt. 2:15, with ch. 11:1), raised on the third day (John 2:19; I Cor. 15.4; cf. Isa. 53:10). "He shall *prolong* His *days.*" Cf. the similar use of Israel's political resurrection as the type of the general resurrection of which "Christ is the first fruits" (Isa. 26:19; Ezek. 37:1-14; Dan. 12:2). **live in his sight**—enjoy His countenance shining on us, as of old; in contrast to ch. 5:6, 15, "Withdrawn Himself from them." **3. know, if we follow on to know the Lord**—The result of His recovered favor (vs. 2) will be onward growth in saving knowledge of God, as the result of perseverance in following after Him (Ps. 63:8; Isa. 54:13). "Then" implies the consequence of the revival in vs. 2. The "if" is not so much *conditional*, as expressive of the *means* which God's grace will sanctify to the full enlightenment of Israel in the knowledge of Him. As want of "knowledge of God" has been the source of all evils (ch. 4:1; 5:4), so the knowledge of Him will bring with it all blessings; yea, it is "life" (John 17: 3). This knowledge is practice, not mere theory (Jer. 22:15, 16). Theology is life, not science; realities, not words. This onward progress is illustrated by the light of "morning" increasing more and more "unto the perfect day" (Prov. 4:18). **prepared**—"is sure," lit., "fixed," ordered in His everlasting purposes of love to His covenant people. Cf. "prepared of God" (*Margin,* Gen. 41:32; Rev. 12:6). Jehovah shall surely come to the relief of His people after their dark night of calamity. **as the morning**—(II Sam. 23:4). **as the rain . . . latter . . . former** —(Job 29:23; Joel 2:23). First, "the rain" generally is mentioned; then the two rains (Deut. 11:14) which caused the fertility of Palestine, and the absence of which was accounted the greatest calamity: "the latter rain" which falls in the latter half of February, and during March and April, just before the harvest whence it takes its name, from a root meaning "*to gather*"; and "the former rain," lit., "the darting rain," from the middle of October to the middle of December. As the rain fertilizes the otherwise barren land, so God's favor will restore Israel long nationally lifeless. **4. what shall I do unto thee**—to bring thee back to piety. What more could be done that I have not done, both in mercies and chastenings (Isa. 5:4)? At this verse a new discourse begins, resuming the threats (ch. 5:14). See opening remarks on this chapter. **goodness**—godliness. **morning cloud**—soon dispersed by the sun (ch. 13:3). There is a tacit contrast here to the promise of God's grace to Israel hereafter, in vs. 3. *His* going forth is "as the morning," shining more and more unto the perfect day; *your* goodness is "as a morning cloud," soon vanishing. His coming to His people is "as the [fertilizing] latter and former rains"; your coming to Him "as the early dew goeth away." **5. I hewed them by the prophets**—i.e., I *announced* by the prophets that they should be hewn asunder, like trees of the forest. God identifies His act with that of His prophets; the word being His instrument for executing His will (Jer. 1:10; Ezek. 43:3). **by ... words of my mouth**—(Isa. 11:4; Jer. 23:29; Heb. 4:12). **thy judgments**—the judgments which I will inflict on thee, Ephraim and Judah (vs. 4). So "*thy* judgments," i.e., those inflicted *on thee* (Zeph. 3:15). **are as the light ...**—like the light, palpable to the eyes of all, as coming from God, the punisher of sin. HENDERSON translates, "lightning" (cf. *Margin*, Job 37:3, 15). **6. mercy**—put for *piety* in general, of which *mercy* or *charity* is a branch. **not sacrifice**—i.e., "*rather than* sacrifice." So "not" is merely comparative (Exod. 16:8; Joel 2:13; John 6:27; I Tim. 2:14). As God Himself instituted sacrifices, it cannot mean that He desired them not absolutely, but that even in the Old Testament, He valued *moral obedience* as the only end for which *positive* ordinances, such as sacrifices, were instituted—as of more importance than a mere external ritual obedience (I Sam. 15:22; Ps. 50:8, 9; 51:16; Isa. 1:11, 12; Mic. 6:6-8; Matt. 9:13; 12:7). **knowledge of God**—experimental and practical, not merely theoretical (vs. 3; Jer. 22:16; I John 2:3, 4). "Mercy" refers to the *second* table of the law, our duty to our fellow man; "the knowledge of God" to the *first* table, our duty to God, including inward spiritual worship. The second table is put first, not as superior in dignity, for it is secondary, but in the order of our understanding. **7. like men**—the common sort of men (Ps. 82:7). Not as *Margin*, "like Adam," Job 31:33. For the *expression* "covenant" is not found elsewhere applied to Adam's relation to God; though the *thing* seems implied (Rom. 5:12-19). Israel "transgressed the covenant" of God as lightly as men break everyday compacts with their fellow men. **there**—in the northern kingdom, Israel. **8. Gilead ... city**—probably Ramoth-gilead, metropolis of the hilly region beyond Jordan, south of the Jabbok, known as "Gilead" (I Kings 4:13; cf. Gen. 31:21-25). **work iniquity**—(ch. 12:11). **polluted with blood**—"marked with blood traces [MAURER]. Referring to Gilead's complicity in the regicidal conspiracy of Pekah against Pekahiah (II Kings 15:25). See *Note*, on vs. 1. Many homicides were there, for there were beyond Jordan more cities of refuge, in proportion to the extent of territory, than on this side of Jordan (Num. 35:14; Deut. 4:41-43; Josh. 20:8). Ramoth-gilead was one. **9. company**—"association" or guild of priests. **murder ... by**

consent—lit., "with one shoulder" (cf. Zeph. 3:9, *Margin*). The image is from oxen putting their *shoulders together* to pull the same yoke [RIVETUS]. MAURER translates, "in the way *towards Shechem*." It was a city of refuge between Ebal and Gerizim; on Mount Ephraim (Josh. 20:7; 21:21), long the civil capital of Ephraim, as Shiloh was the religious capital; now called Naploos; for a time the residence of Jeroboam (I Kings 12:25). The priests there became so corrupted that they waylaid and murdered persons fleeing to the asylum for refuge [HENDERSON]; the sanctity of the place enhanced the guilt of the priests who abused their priestly privileges, and the right of asylum to perpetrate murders themselves, or to screen those committed by others [MAURER]. **commit lewdness**—deliberate crime, presumptuous wickedness, from an *Arabic* root, "to form a deliberate purpose." **10. horrible thing**—(Jer. 5:30; 18:13; 23:14). **whoredom**—idolatry. **11. an harvest**—viz., of judgments (as in Jer. 51:33; Joel 3:13; Rev. 14:15). Called a "harvest" because it is the fruit of the seed which Judah herself had sown (ch. 8:7; 10:12; Job 4:8; Prov. 22:8). Judah, under Ahaz, lost 120,000 "slain in one day (by Israel under Pekah), because they had forsaken the Lord God of their fathers." **when I returned the captivity of my people**—when I, by Oded My prophet, caused 200,000 women, sons, and daughters, of Judah to be restored from captivity by Israel (II Chron. 28:6-15). This prophecy was delivered under Pekah [LUDOVICUS DE DIEU]. MAURER explains, When Israel shall have been exiled for its sins, and has been subsequently restored by Me, thou, Judah, also shalt be exiled for thine. But as Judah's punishment was not at the time *when* God restored Israel, LUDOVICUS DE DIEU's explanation must be taken. GROTIUS translates, "When I *shall have returned to make captive* (i.e., when I shall have again made captive) My people." The first captivity of Israel under Tiglath-pileser was followed by a *second* under Shalmaneser. Then came the siege of Jerusalem, and the capture of the fenced cities of Judah, by Sennacherib, the forerunner of other attacks, ending in Judah's captivity. But the *Hebrew* is elsewhere used of *restoration*, not *renewed punishment* (Deut. 30:3; Ps. 14:7).

CHAPTER 7

Vss. 1-16. REPROOF OF ISRAEL. Probably delivered in the interregn and civil war at Pekah's death; for vs. 7, "all their kings ... fallen," refers to the murder of Zechariah, Shallum, Menahem, Pekahiah, and Pekah. In vs. 8 the reference seems to be to Menahem's payment of tribute to Pul, in order to secure himself in the usurped throne, also to Pekah's league with Rezin of Syria, and to Hoshea's connection with Assyria during the interregnum at Pekah's death [MAURER]. **1. I would have healed Israel**—Israel's restoration of the 200,000 Jewish captives at God's command (II Chron. 28:8-15) gave hope of Israel's reformation [HENDERSON]. Political, as well as moral, healing is meant. When I would have healed Israel in its calamitous state, then their iniquity was discovered to be so great as to preclude hope of recovery. Then he enumerates their wickedness: "The thief cometh in [indoors stealthily], and the troop of robbers spoileth without" (out-of-doors with open violence). **2. consider not in their hearts**—lit., "say not to ..." (Ps. 14:1). **that I remember**—and will punish. **their own doings have beset them about**—

as so many witnesses against them (Ps. 9:16; Prov. 5:22). **before my face**—(Ps. 90:8). **3.** Their princes, instead of checking, "have pleasure in them that do" such crimes (Rom. 1:32). **4. who ceaseth from raising**—rather, "heating" it, from an *Arabic* root, "to be hot." So LXX. Their adulterous and idolatrous lust is inflamed as the oven of a baker who has it at such a heat that he ceaseth from heating it only from the time that he hath kneaded the dough, until it be leavened; he only needs to omit feeding it during the short period of the fermentation of the bread. Cf. II Peter 2:14, "that cannot cease from sin" [HENDERSON]. **5. the day of our king**—his birthday or day of inauguration. **have made** *him* **sick**—viz., the king. MAURER translates, "make themselves sick." **with bottles of wine**—drinking not merely glasses, but *bottles.* MAURER translates, "owing to the heat of wine." **he stretched out his hand with scorners**—the gesture of revellers in holding out the cup and in drinking to one another's health. Scoffers were the king's boon companions. **6. they have made ready**—rather, "they make their heart approach," viz., their king, in going to drink with him. **like an oven**—following out the image in vs. 4. As it conceals the lighted fire all night while the baker sleeps but in the morning burns as a flaming fire, so they brood mischief in their hearts while conscience is lulled asleep, and their wicked designs wait only for a fair occasion to break forth [HORSLEY]. Their heart is the oven, their baker the ringleader of the plot. In vs. 7 their plots appear, viz., the intestine disturbances and murders of one king after another, after Jeroboam II. **7. all hot**—All burn with eagerness to cause universal disturbance (II Kings 15). **devoured their judges**—magistrates; as the fire of the oven devours the fuel. **all their kings . . . fallen**—See *Notes* at the beginning of this chapter. **none . . . calleth unto me**—Such is their perversity that amid all these national calamities, none seeks help from Me (Isa. 9:13; 64:7). **8. mixed . . . among the people**—by leagues with idolaters, and the adoption of their idolatrous practices (vss. 9, 11; Ps. 106:35). **Ephraim . . . cake not turned**—a cake burnt on one side and unbaked on the other, and so uneatable; an image of the *worthlessness* of Ephraim. The Easterners bake their bread on the ground, covering it with embers (I Kings 19:6), and *turning* it every ten minutes, to bake it thoroughly without burning it. **9.** **Strangers**—foreigners: the Syrians and Assyrians (II Kings 13:7; 15:19, 20; 17:3-6). **gray hairs**—i.e., symptoms of approaching national dissolution. **are here and there upon**—lit., "are sprinkled on" him. **yet he knoweth not**—Though old age ought to bring with it wisdom, he neither knows of his senile decay, nor has the true knowledge which leads to reformation. **10.** Repetition of ch. 5:5. **not return to . . . Lord . . . for all this**—notwithstanding all their calamities (Isa. 9:13). **11. like a silly dove**—a bird proverbial for simplicity: easily deceived. **without heart**—i.e., understanding. **call to Egypt**—Israel lying between the two great rival empires Egypt and Assyria, sought each by turns to help her against the other. As this prophecy was written in the reign of Hoshea, the allusion is probably to the alliance with So or Sabacho II (of which a record has been found on the clay cylindrical seals in Koyunjik), which ended in the overthrow of Hoshea and the deportation of Israel (II Kings 17:3-6). As the dove betrays its foolishness by fleeing in alarm from its nest only to fall into the net of the fowler, so Israel, though warned that foreign alliances would be their ruin,

rushed into them. **12. When they shall go**—to seek aid from this or that foreign state. **spread my net upon them**—as on birds taken on the ground (Ezek. 12:13), as contrasted with *"bringing them down* as the fowls *of the heavens,* viz., by the use of missiles. **as their congregation hath heard**—viz., by My prophets through whom I threatened "chastisement" (ch. 5:9; II Kings 17:13-18). **13. fled**—as birds from their nest (Prov. 27:8; Isa. 16:2). **me**—who both could and would have healed them (vs. 1), had they applied to Me. **redeemed them**—from Egypt and their other enemies (Mic. 6:4). **lies**—(Ps. 78:36; Jer. 3:10). Pretending to be My worshippers, when they all the while worshipped idols (vs. 14; ch. 12:1); also defrauding Me of the glory of their deliverance, and ascribing it and their other blessings to idols [CALVIN]. **14. not cried unto me**—but unto other gods [MAURER], (Job 35:9, 10). Or, they did indeed cry unto Me, but not "with their heart": answering to "lies," vs. 13 (see *Note*). **when they howled upon their beds**—sleepless with anxiety; image of *deep affliction.* Their cry is termed "howling," as it is the cry of anguish, not the cry of repentance and faith. **assemble . . . for corn . . .**—viz., in the temples of their idols, to obtain from them a good harvest and vintage, instead of coming to Me, the true Giver of these (ch. 2:5, 8, 12), proving that their cry to God was "not with their heart." **rebel against me**—lit., "withdraw themselves *against* Me," i.e., not only withdraw *from* Me, but also rebel *against* Me. **15. I . . . bound**—when I saw their arms as it were relaxed with various disasters, I bound them so as to strengthen their sinews; image from surgery [CALVIN]. MAURER translates, "I *instructed* them" to war (Ps. 18:34; 144:1), viz., under Jeroboam II (II Kings 14:25). GROTIUS explains, "Whether I chastised them *(Margin)* or strengthened their arms, they imagined mischief against Me." *English Version* is best. **16. return, but not to the Most High**—or, "to one who is *not the Most High,*" one very different from Him, a stock or a stone. So LXX. **deceitful bow**—(Ps. 78:57). A bow which, from its faulty construction, shoots wide of the mark. So Israel pretends to seek God, but turns aside to idols. **for the rage of their tongue**—their boast of safety from Egyptian aid, and their "lies" (vs. 13), whereby they pretended to serve God, while worshipping idols; also their perverse defense for their idolatries and blasphemies against God and His prophets (Ps. 73:9; 120:2, 3). **their derision in . . . Egypt**—Their "fall" shall be the subject of "derision" to Egypt, to whom they had applied for help (ch. 9:3, 6; II Kings 17:4).

CHAPTER 8

VSS. 1-14. PROPHECY OF THE IRRUPTION OF THE ASSYRIANS, IN PUNISHMENT FOR ISRAEL'S APOSTASY, IDOLATRY, AND SETTING UP OF KINGS WITHOUT GOD'S SANCTION. In vs. 14, *Judah* is said to multiply fenced cities; and in vss. 7-9, Israel, to its great hurt, is said to have gone up to Assyria for help. This answers best to the reign of Menahem. For it was then that Uzziah of Judah, his contemporary, built fenced cities (II Chron. 26:6, 9, 10). Then also Israel turned to Assyria and had to pay for their sinful folly a thousand talents of silver (II Kings 15:19) [MAURER]. **1. Set the trumpet . . .**—to give warning of the approach of the enemy: "To thy *palate* (i.e., "mouth," Job 31:30, *Margin*) the trumpet"; the abruptness of expression indicates the suddenness of the attack. So ch. 5:8. **as . . . eagle**—the Assyrian

(Deut. 28:49; Jer. 48:40; Hab. 1:8). **against ... house of ... Lord**—not the temple, but Israel viewed as *the family of God* (ch. 9:15; Num. 12:7; Zech. 9:8; Heb. 3:2; I Tim. 3:15; I Pet. 4:17). **2. My God, we know thee**—the singular, "My," is used distributively, each one so addressing God. They, in their hour of need, plead their knowledge of God as the covenant people, while in their *acts* they acknowledge Him not (cf. Matt. 7:21, 22; Titus 1:16; also Isa. 29:13; Jer. 7:4). The *Hebrew* joins "Israel," not as *English Version*, with "shall cry," but "*We, Israel,* know thee"; God denies the claim thus urged on the ground of their descent from Israel. **3. Israel** —God repeats the name in opposition to *their* use of it (vs. 2). **the thing that is good**—JEROME translates, "God" who is good and doing good (Ps. 119: 68). He is the chief object rejected, but with Him also all that is good. **the enemy shall pursue him** —in just retribution from God. **4. kings ... not by me**—not with My sanction (I Kings 11:31; 12:20). Israel set up Jeroboam and his successors, whereas God had appointed the house of David as the rightful kings of the whole nation. **I knew it not**—I *approved* it not (Ps. 1:6). **of ... gold ... idols**— (Ch. 2:8; 13:2). **that they may be cut off**—i.e., though warned of the consequences of idolatry, as it were with open eyes they rushed on their own destruction. So Jeremiah 27:10, 15; 44:8. **5. hath cast thee off**—As the ellipsis of *thee* is unusual, MAURER translates, "thy calf *is abominable*." But the antithesis to vs. 3 establishes *English Version,* "Israel *hath cast off* the thing that is good"; therefore, in just retribution, "thy calf hath *cast thee off,*" i.e., is made by God the cause of thy being cast off (ch. 10:15). Jeroboam, during his sojourn in Egypt, saw Apis worshipped at Memphis, and Mnevis at Heliopolis, in the form of an ox; this, and the temple cherubim, suggested the idea of the calves set up at Dan and Beth-el. **how long ... ere they attain to innocency?**—How long will they be incapable of bearing innocency? [MAURER]. **6. from Israel was it**—i.e., the calf originated with them, not from Me. "It also," as well as their "kings set up" by them, "but not by Me" (vs. 4). **7. sown ... reap**—(Prov. 22:8; Gal. 6:7). "Sow ... wind," i.e., to make the vain show of worship, while faith and obedience are wanting [CALVIN]. Rather, to offer senseless supplications to the calves for good harvests (cf. ch. 2: 8); the result being that God will make them "reap no stalk," i.e., "standing corn." Also, the phraseology proverbially means that all their undertakings shall be profitless (Prov. 11:29; Eccles. 5:16). **the bud**—or, "growth." **strangers**—foreigners (ch. 7: 9). **8. vessel wherein is no pleasure**—(Ps. 41:12; Jer. 22:28; 48:38). **9. gone ... to Assyria**—referring to Menahem's application for Pul's aid in establishing him on the throne (cf. ch. 5:13; 7:11). Menahem's name is read in the inscriptions in the southwest palace of Nimrod, as a tributary to the Assyrian king in his eighth year. The dynasty of Pul, or Phalluka, was supplanted at Nineveh by that of Tiglath-pileser, about 768 (or 760) B.C. Semiramis seems to have been Pul's wife, and to have withdrawn to Babylon in 768; and her son, Nabonassar, succeeding after a period of confusion, originated "the era of Nabonassar," 747 B.C. [G. V. SMITH]. Usually foreigners coming to Israel's land were said to go *up*"; here it is the reverse, to intimate Israel's *sunken* state, and Assyria's superiority. **wild ass**—a figure of Israel's headstrong perversity in following her own bent (Jer. 2:24). **alone by himself**—characteristic of Israel in all ages: "lo, the people shall dwell alone" (Num. 23:9; cf. Job 39:

5-8). **hired lovers**—reversing the ordinary way, viz., that lovers should hire her (Ezek. 16:33, 34). **10. will I gather them**—viz., the *nations* (Assyria, etc.) against Israel, instead of their assisting her as she had wished (Ezek. 16:37). **a little**—rather, "in a little" [HENDERSON]. *English Version* gives good sense: They shall sorrow *a little* at the imposition of the tribute; God suspended yet the *great* judgment, viz., their deportation by Assyria. **the burden of the king of princes**—the tribute imposed on Israel (under Menahem) by the Assyrian king Pul, (II Kings 15:19-22), who had many "princes" under his sway (Isa. 10:8). **11.** God in righteous retribution gives them up to their own way; the sin becomes its own punishment (Prov. 1:31). **many altars**—in opposition to God's law (Deut. 12:5, 6, 13, 14). **to sin ... to sin**—Their altars which were "sin" (whatever religious intentions they might plead) should be treated as such, and be the source of their punishment (I Kings 12:30; 13:34). **12. great things of ... law**—(Deut. 4:6, 8; Ps. 19:8; 119:18, 72; 147:19, 20). MAURER not so well translates, "*the many* things of My law." **my law**—as opposed to their inventions. This reference of Hosea to the Pentateuch alone is against the theory that some earlier written prophecies have not come down to us. **strange thing**—as if a thing with which they had nothing to do. **13. sacrifices of mine offerings**—i.e., which they offer to Me. **eat it**—Their own carnal gratification is the object which they seek, not My honor. **now**—i.e., "speedily." **shall return to Egypt**—(ch. 9:3, 6; 11: 11). The same threat as in Deuteronomy 28:68. They fled thither to escape from the Assyrians (cf. as to *Judah,* Jer. 42-44), when these latter had overthrown their nation. But see *Note,* ch. 9:3. **14. forgotten ... Maker**—(Deut. 32:18). **temples**—to idols. **Judah ... fenced cities**—Judah, though less idolatrous than Israel, betrayed lack of faith in Jehovah by trusting more to its fenced cities than to Him; instead of making peace with God, Judah multiplied human defenses (Isa. 22:8; Jer. 5:17; Mic. 5:10, 11). **I will send ... fire upon ... cities** —Sennacherib burned all Judah's fenced cities except Jerusalem (II Kings 18:13). **palaces thereof**— viz., of the land. Cf. as to Jerusalem, Jeremiah 17:27.

CHAPTER 9

Vss. 1-17. WARNING AGAINST ISRAEL'S JOY AT PARTIAL RELIEF FROM THEIR TROUBLES: THEIR CROPS SHALL FAIL, AND THE PEOPLE LEAVE THE LORD'S LAND FOR EGYPT AND ASSYRIA, WHERE THEY CANNOT, IF SO INCLINED, SERVE GOD ACCORDING TO THE ANCIENT RITUAL: FOLLY OF THEIR FALSE PROPHETS. **1. Rejoice not ... for joy**—lit., "to exultation." Thy exultation at the league with Pul, by which peace seems secured, is out of place: since thy idolatry will bring ruin on thee. **as other people**— the Assyrians for instance, who, unlike thee, are in the height of prosperity. **loved a reward upon every corn-floor**—Thou hast desired, in *reward* for thy homage to idols, abundance of corn on every threshing-floor (ch. 2:12). **2.** (Ch. 2:9, 12.) **fail**— disappoint her expectation. **3. return to Egypt**— (*Note,* ch. 8:13). As in ch. 11:5 it is said, "He shall *not* return into ... Egypt." FAIRBAIRN thinks it is not the exact country that is meant, but the *bondage state* with which, from past experience, Egypt was identified in their minds. Assyria was to be a second Egypt to them. Deuteronomy 28:68, though threatening a return to Egypt, speaks (vs. 36) of their being brought to a nation which *neither they nor* *their fathers had known,* showing that it is not the literal Egypt, but a second Egypt-like bondage that is threatened. **eat unclean things in Assyria**—reduced by necessity to eat meats pronounced unclean by the Mosaic law (Ezek. 4:13). See II Kings 17: 6. **4. offer wine offerings**—lit., "pour as a libation (Exod. 30:9; Lev. 23:13). **neither shall they be pleasing unto him**—as being offered on a profane soil. **sacrifices ... as the bread of mourners**—which was unclean (Deut. 26:14; Jer. 16:7; Ezek. 24:17). **their bread for their soul**—their offering for the expiation of their soul [Calvin], (Lev. 17:11). Rather, "their bread for their sustenance ('soul' being often used for *the animal life,* Gen. 14:21, *Margin*) shall not come into the Lord's house"; it shall only subserve their own uses, not My worship. **5.** (Ch. 2: 11.) **6. because of destruction**—to escape from the devastation of their country. **Egypt shall gather them up**—i.e., into its sepulchres (Jer. 8:2; Ezek. 29: 5). Instead of returning to Palestine, they should die in Egypt. **Memphis**—famed as a necropolis. **the pleasant** *places* **for their silver**—i.e., their desired treasuries for their money. Or, "whatever precious thing they have of silver" [Maurer]. **nettles**—the sign of desolation (Isa. 34:13). **7. visitation**—vengeance: punishment (Isa. 10:3). **Israel shall know it**—to her cost experimentally (Isa. 9:9). **the prophet is a fool**—The false prophet who foretold prosperity to the nation shall be convicted of folly by the event. **the spiritual man**—the man pretending to inspiration (Lam. 2:14; Ezek. 13:3; Mic. 3: 11; Zeph. 3:4). **for the multitude of thine iniquity ...**—Connect these words with, "the days of visitation ... are come"; "the prophet ... is mad," being parenthetical. **the great hatred**—or, "the great provocation" [Henderson]; or, (thy) "great apostasy" [Maurer]. *English Version* means Israel's *"hatred"* of God's prophets and the law. **8. The watchman ... was with my God**—The spiritual watchmen, the true prophets, formerly consulted my God (Jer. 31:6; Hab. 2:1); but their so-called *prophet* is a snare, entrapping Israel into idolatry. **hatred**—rather, (a cause of) "apostasy" (see vs. 7) [Maurer]. **house of his God**—i.e., the state of Ephraim, as in ch. 8:1 [Maurer]. Or, "the house of his (false) god," the calves [Calvin]. Jehovah, *"my* God," seems contrasted with *"his* God." Calvin's view is therefore preferable. **9. as in the days of Gibeah**—as in the day of the perpetration of the atrocity of Gibeah, narrated in Judges 19:16-22, etc. **10.** As the traveller in a wilderness is delighted at finding grapes to quench his thirst, or the early fig (esteemed a great delicacy in the East, Isa. 28:4; Jer. 24:2; Mic. 7:1); so it was My delight to choose your fathers as My peculiar people in Egypt (ch. 2:15). **at her first time**—when the first fruits of the tree become ripe. **went to Baal-peor**—(Num. 25:3): the Moabite idol, in whose worship young women prostituted themselves; the very sin Israel latterly was guilty of. **separated themselves**—consecrated themselves. **unto that shame**—to that shameful or foul idol (Jer. 11:13). **their abominations were according as they loved**—rather, as *Vulgate,* "they became abominable like the object of their love" (Deut. 7:26; Ps. 115:8). *English Version* gives good sense, "their abominable idols they followed after, according as their lusts prompted them" (*Margin,* Amos 4:5). **11. their glory shall fly away**—fit retribution to those who "separated themselves unto that *shame"* (vs. 10). Children were accounted the *glory* of parents; sterility, a reproach. "Ephraim" means "fruitfulness" (Gen. 41:52); this its name shall cease to be its characteristic. **from the birth**

... womb ... conception—Ephraim's children shall perish in a threefold gradation; (1) From the time of birth. (2) From the time of pregnancy. (3) From the time of their first conception. **12.** Even though they should rear their children, yet will I bereave them (the Ephraimites) of them (Job 27:14). **woe ... to them when I depart**—Yet the ungodly in their madness desire God to depart from them (Job 21:14; 22:17; Matt. 8:34). At last they know to their cost how awful it is when God has departed (Deut. 31:17; I Sam. 28:15, 16; cf. vs. 11, and I Sam. 4:21). **13. Ephraim, as I saw Tyrus ... in a pleasant place**—i.e., in looking towards Tyrus (on whose borders Ephraim lay) I saw Ephraim beautiful in situation like her (Ezek. 26, 27 and 28). **is planted**—as a *fruitful* tree; image suggested by the meaning of "Ephraim" (vs. 11). **bring forth his children to the murderer**—(vs. 16; ch. 13:16). With all his fruitfulness, his children shall only be brought up to be slain. **14. what wilt thou give?**—As if overwhelmed by feeling, he deliberates with God what is most desirable. **give ... a miscarrying womb**—Of two evils he chooses the least. So great will be the calamity, that barrenness will be a blessing, though usually counted a great misfortune (Job 3:3; Jer. 20:14; Luke 23:29). **15. All their wickedness**—i.e., their chief guilt. **Gilgal**—(see *Note,* ch. 4:15). This was the scene of their first contumacy in rejecting God and choosing a king (I Sam. 11:14, 15; cf. I Sam. 8:7), and of their subsequent idolatry. **there I hated them**—not with the human passion, but holy hatred of their sin, which required punishment to be inflicted on themselves (cf. Mal. 1:3). **out of mine house**—as in ch. 8:1: out of the land holy unto me. Or, as "love" is mentioned immediately after, the reference may be to the Hebrew mode of divorce, the husband (God) putting the wife (Israel) out of the house. **princes ... revolters**—*"Sarim ... Sorerim" (Hebrew),* a play on similar sounds. **16.** The figures "root," "fruit," are suggested by the word "Ephraim," i.e., *fruitful"* (*Notes,* vss. 11, 12). "Smitten," viz., with a blight (Ps. 102:4). **17. My God**—"My," in contrast to "them," i.e., the people, whose God Jehovah no longer is. Also Hosea appeals to God as supporting his authority against the whole people. **wanderers among ... nations**—(II Kings 15:29; I Chron. 5:26).

CHAPTER 10

Vss. 1-15. Israel's Idolatry, the Source of Perjuries and Unlawful Leagues, Soon Destined to Be the Ruin of the State, Their King and Their Images Being About to Be Carried Off; a Just Chastisement, the Reaping Corresponding to the Sowing. The prophecy was uttered between Shalmaneser's first and second invasions of Israel. Cf. vs. 14; also vs. 6, referring to Hoshea's calling So of Egypt to his aid; also vss. 4, 13. **1. empty**—stripped of its fruits [Calvin], (Nah. 2:2); compelled to pay tribute to Pul (II Kings 15:20). Maurer translates, "A *widespreading* vine"; so LXX. Cf. Genesis 49:22; Psalm 80:9-11; Ezekiel 17:6. **bringeth forth fruit unto himself**—not unto Me. **according to ... multitude of ... fruit ... increased ... altars**—In proportion to the abundance of their prosperity, which called for fruit unto God (cf. Rom. 6:22), was the abundance of their idolatry (ch. 8:4, 11). **2. heart ... divided**—(I Kings 18:21; Matt. 6:24; Jas. 4:8). **now**—i.e., soon. **he**—Jehovah. **break down**—"cut off," viz., the heads of the victims. Those altars, which were the scene of *cut-*

ting off the victims' heads, shall be themselves cut off. **3. now** . . . —Soon they, deprived of their king, shall be reduced to say, We have no king (vss. 7, 15), for Jehovah deprived us of him, because of our not fearing God. What then (seeing God is against us) should a king be able to do for us, if we had one? As they rejected the heavenly King, they were deprived of their earthly king. **4. words**—mere empty words. **swearing falsely in making a covenant**—breaking their engagement to Shalmaneser (II Kings 17:4), and making a covenant with So, though covenants with foreigners were forbidden. **judgment . . . as hemlock**—i.e., divine judgment shall spring up as rank, and as deadly, as hemlock in the furrows (Deut. 29:18; Amos 5:7; 6:12). GESENIUS translates, "poppy." GROTIUS, "darnel." **5. fear because of the calves**—i.e., shall fear *for* them. **Beth-aven**—substituted for Beth-el in contempt (ch. 4:15). **it**—*singular,* the *one* in Beth-el; after the pattern of which the other "calves" (*plural*) were made. "Calves" in the *Hebrew* is *feminine,* to express contempt. **priests**—The *Hebrew* is only used of *idolatrous priests* (II Kings 23:5; Zeph. 1:4), from a root meaning either "the black garment" in which they were attired; or, "to resound," referring to their howling cries in their sacred rites [CALVIN]. *that* **rejoiced on it**—because it was a source of gain to them. MAURER translates, "Shall leap in trepidation on account of it"; as Baal's priests did (I Kings 18:26). **the glory thereof**—the magnificence of its ornaments and its worship. **6. It . . . also**—The calf, so far from saving its worshippers from deportation, itself shall be carried off; hence "Israel shall be ashamed" of it. **Jareb**—(*Note,* ch. 5:13). "A present to the king (whom they looked to as) their *defender,*" or else *avenger,* whose wrath they wished to appease, viz., Shalmaneser. The minor states applied this title to the Great King, as the avenging Protector. **his own counsel**—the calves, which Jeroboam set up as a stroke of policy to detach Israel from Judah. Their severance from Judah and Jehovah proved now to be not politic, but fatal to them. **7.** (Vss. 3, 15.) **foam**—denoting short-lived existence and speedy dissolution. As the foam, though seeming to be eminent raised on the top of the water, yet has no solidity, such is the throne of Samaria. MAURER translates, "a chip" *or broken branch* that cannot resist the current. **8. Aven**—i.e., Beth-aven. **the sin**—i.e., the occasion of sin (Deut. 9:21; I Kings 12:30). **they shall say to . . . mountains, Cover us**—So terrible shall be the calamity, that men shall prefer death to life (Luke 23:30; Rev. 6:16; 9:6). Those very hills on which were their idolatrous altars (one source of their confidence, as their "king," vs. 7, was the other), so far from helping them, shall be called on by them to overwhelm them. **9. Gibeah**—(ch. 9:9; Judg. 19 and 20). They are singled out as a specimen of the whole nation. **there they stood**—The Israelites have, as there and then, so ever since, *persisted* in their sin [CALVIN]. Or, better, "they stood their ground," i.e., did not perish then [MAURER]. **the battle . . . did not overtake them**—Though God spared you then, He will not do so now; nay, the battle whereby God punished the Gibeonite "children of iniquity," shall the more heavily visit you for your continued impenitence. Though "they stood" then, it shall not be so now. The change from "thou" to "they" marks God's alienation from them; they are, by the use of the third person, put to a greater distance from God. **10. my desire . . . chastise**—expressing God's *strong inclination* to vindicate His justice against sin, as be-

ing the infinitely holy God (Deut. 28:63). **the people**—*Foreign invaders* "shall be gathered against them." **when they shall bind themselves in their two furrows**—image from two oxen ploughing together side by side, in two contiguous furrows: so the Israelites shall join themselves, to unite their powers against all dangers, but it will not save them from My destroying them [CALVIN]. Their "two furrows" may refer to their *two places of setting up the calves,* their ground of confidence, Dan and Beth-el; or, the two divisions of the nation, *Israel and Judah,* "in their two furrows," i.e., in their respective two places of habitation; vs. 11, which specifies the two, favors this view. HENDERSON prefers the *Keri* (*Hebrew Margin*) reading, "for their two *iniquities*"; and translates, "when they are bound" in captivity. *English Version* is best, as the image is carried out in vs. 11; only it is perhaps better to translate, "the people (the invaders) *binding them,*" i.e., making them captives; and so vs. 11 alludes to the yoke being put on the neck of Ephraim and Judah. **11. taught**—i.e., accustomed. **loveth to tread out . . . corn**—a far easier and more self-indulgent work than ploughing. In treading corn, cattle were not bound together under a yoke, but either trod it singly with their feet, or drew a threshing sledge over it (Isa. 28:27, 28): they were free to eat some of the corn from time to time, as the law required they should be unmuzzled (Deut. 25: 4), so that they grew fat in this work. An image of Israel's freedom, prosperity, and self-indulgence heretofore. But now God will put the Assyrian yoke upon her, instead of freedom, putting her to servile work. **I passed over upon**—I put the yoke upon. **make . . . to ride**—as in Job 30:22; i.e., *hurry* Ephraim *away* to a distant region [CALVIN]. LYRA translates, "I will make (the Assyrian) to ride upon Ephraim." MAURER, "I will make Ephraim to carry," viz., a charioteer. **his clods**—"the clods before him." **12.** Continuation of the image in vs. 11 (Prov. 11:18). Act righteously and ye shall reap the reward; a reward not of debt, but of grace. **in mercy**—according to the measure of the divine "mercy," which over and above repays the *goodness* or "mercy" which we show to our fellow man (Luke 6:38). **break . . . fallow ground**—Remove your superstitions and vices, and be renewed. **seek . . . Lord, till he come**—Though not answered immediately, persevere unceasingly "*till* He come." **rain**—send down as a copious shower. **righteousness**—the reward of righteousness, i.e., *salvation,* temporal and spiritual (I Sam. 26:23; cf. Joel 2:23). **13. reaped iniquity**—i.e., the *fruit* of iniquity; as "righteousness" (vs. 12) is "the *fruit* of righteousness" (Job 4:8; Prov. 22:8; Gal. 6:7, 8). **lies**—false and spurious worship. **trust in thy way**—thy perverse way (Isa. 57:10; Jer. 2:23), thy worship of false gods. This was their internal safeguard, as their external was "the multitude of their mighty men." **14. tumult**—a tumultuous war. **among thy people**—lit., "peoples": the war shall extend to the whole people of Israel, through all the tribes, and the peoples allied to her. **Shalman spoiled Beth-arbel**—i.e., Shalmaneser, a compound name, in which the part common to it and the names of three other Assyrian kings, is omitted; Tiglath-pileser, Esar-haddon, Shar-ezer. So Jeconiah is abbreviated to Coniah. Arbel was situated in Naphtali in Galilee, on the border nearest Assyria. Against it Shalmaneser, at his first invasion of Israel (II Kings 17:3), vented his chief rage. God threatens Israel's fortresses with the same fate as Arbel suffered "in the day [on the occasion] of the battle" then well known, though not mentioned elsewhere (cf. II Kings 18:34). This event, close on the reign of Hezekiah, shows the inscription of Hosea (ch. 1:1) to be correct. **15. So shall Beth-el do unto you**—Your idolatrous calf at Beth-el shall be the cause of a like calamity befalling you. **your great wickedness**—lit., "the wickedness of your wickedness." **in a morning**—speedily as quickly as the dawn is put to flight by the rising sun (ch. 6:4; 13:3; Ps. 30:5). **king**—Hoshea.

CHAPTER 11

Vss. 1-12. GOD'S FORMER BENEFITS, AND ISRAEL'S INGRATITUDE RESULTING IN PUNISHMENT, YET JEHOVAH PROMISES RESTORATION AT LAST. Verse 5 shows this prophecy was uttered after the league made with Egypt (II Kings 17:4). **1. Israel ... called my son out of Egypt**—BENGEL translates, "*From* the time that he [Israel] was *in* Egypt, I called him My son," which the parallelism proves. So ch. 12:9 and 13:4 use "from ... Egypt," for "from the time that thou didst sojourn *in* Egypt." Exodus 4:22 also shows that Israel was called by God, "My son," from the time of his Egyptian sojourn (Isa. 43:1). God is always said to have led or *brought forth*, not to have "called," Israel from Egypt. Matthew 2: 15, therefore, in quoting this prophecy (typically and primarily referring to Israel, antitypically and fully to Messiah), applies it to Jesus' sojourn *in* Egypt, not His return *from* it. Even from His infancy, partly spent in Egypt, God called Him His son. God included Messiah, and Israel for Messiah's sake, in one common love, and therefore in one common prophecy. Messiah's people and Himself are one, as the Head and the body. Isaiah 49:3 calls Him "Israel." The same general reason, danger of extinction, caused the infant Jesus, and Israel in its national infancy (cf. Gen. 42:3; 45:18; 46:3, 4; Ezek. 16:4-6; Jer. 31:20) to sojourn in Egypt. So He, and His spiritual Israel, are already called "God's sons" while yet in the Egypt of the world. **2. As they called them**—"they," viz., monitors sent by Me. "Called," in vs. 1, suggests the idea of the many subsequent calls by the prophets. **went from them**—turned away in contempt (Jer. 2: 27). **Baalim**—images of Baal, set up in various places. **3. taught ... to go**—lit., "to use his feet." Cf. a similar image, Deuteronomy 1:31; 8:2, 5, 15; 32:10, 11; Nehemiah 9:21; Isaiah 63:9; Amos 2:10. God bore them as a parent does an infant, unable to supply itself, so that it has no anxiety about food, raiment, and its going forth. Acts 13:18, which probably refers to this passage of Hosea; He took them by the arms, to guide them that they might not stray, and to hold them up that they might not stumble. **knew not that I healed them**—i.e., that My design was to restore them spiritually and temporally (Exod. 15:26). **4. cords of a man**—parallel to "bands of love"; not such cords as oxen are led by, but *humane methods,* such as men employ when inducing others, as for instance, a father drawing his child, by leading-strings, teaching him to go (vs. 1). **I was ... as they that take off the yoke on their jaws ... I laid meat**—as the humane husbandman occasionally loosens the straps under the jaws by which the yoke is bound on the neck of oxen and lays food before them to eat. An appropriate image of God's deliverance of Israel from the Egyptian yoke, and of His feeding them in the wilderness. **5. He shall not return into ... Egypt**

—viz., to seek help against Assyria (cf. ch. 7:11), as Israel lately had done (II Kings 17:4), after having revolted from Assyria, to whom they had been tributary from the times of Menahem (II Kings 15: 19). In a *figurative* sense, "he *shall* return to Egypt" (ch. 9:3), i.e., to Egypt-like bondage; also many Jewish fugitives were literally to *return* to Egypt, when the Holy Land was to be in Assyrian and Chaldean hands. **Assyrian shall be his king**—instead of having kings of their own, and Egypt as their auxiliary. **because they refused to return**—just retribution. They would not return (spiritually) to God, therefore they shall not return (corporally) to Egypt, the object of their desire. **6. abide**—or, "fall upon" [CALVIN]. **branches**—villages, which are the branches or dependencies of the cities [CALVIN]. GROTIUS translates, "his bars" (so Lam. 2:9), i.e., the warriors who were the bulwarks of the state. Cf. ch. 4:18, "rulers" (*Margin*), "shields" (Ps. 47:9). **because of their own counsels**—in worshipping idols, and relying on Egypt (cf. ch. 10: 6). **7. bent to backsliding**—Not only do they *backslide,* and that too *from* ME, their "chief good," but they are *bent upon* it. Though they (the prophets) called them (the Israelites) to the Most High (from their idols), "none would exalt (i.e., extol or honor) Him." To exalt God, they must cease to be "*bent on* backsliding," and *must* lift themselves upwards. **8. as Admah ... Zeboim**—among the cities, including Sodom and Gomorrah, irretrievably overthrown (Deut. 29:23). **heart is turned within me**—with the deepest compassion, so as not to execute My threat (Lam. 1:20; cf. Gen. 43:30; I Kings 3:26). So the phrase is used of a new turn given to the feeling (Ps. 105:25). **repentings**—God speaks according to *human* modes of thought (Num. 23:19). God's *seeming* change is in accordance with His secret everlasting purpose of love to His people, to magnify His grace after their desperate rebellion. **9. I will not return to destroy Ephraim**—i.e., I will no more, as in past times, destroy Ephraim. The destruction primarily meant is probably that by Tiglath-pileser, who, as the Jewish king Ahaz' ally against Pekah of Israel and Rezin of Syria, deprived Israel of Gilead, Galilee, and Naphtali (II Kings 15: 29). The ulterior reference is to the long dispersion hereafter, to be ended by God's covenant mercy restoring His people, not for their merits, but of His grace. **God, ... not man**—not dealing as man would, with implacable wrath under awful provocation (Isa. 55:7-9; Mal. 3:6). I do not, like man, change when once I have made a covenant of everlasting love, as with Israel (Num. 23:19). We measure God by the human standard, and hence are slow to credit fully His promises; these, however, belong to the faithful remnant, not to the obstinately impenitent. **in the midst of thee**—as peculiarly thy God (Exod. 19:5, 6). **not enter into the city**—as an enemy: as I entered Admah, Zeboim, and Sodom, utterly destroying them, whereas I will not utterly destroy thee. Somewhat similarly JEROME: "I am *not one such as human dwellers in a city,* who take cruel vengeance; I save those whom I correct." Thus "not man," and "in the midst of thee," are parallel to "into the city." Though I am in the midst of thee, it is not as man entering a rebellious city to destroy utterly. MAURER needlessly translates, "I will not come *in wrath.*" **10. he shall roar like a lion**—by awful judgments on their foes (Isa. 31:4; Jer. 25:26-30; Joel 3:16), calling His dispersed "children" from the various lands of their dispersion. **shall tremble**—shall flock in eager agitation of haste. **from the west**—(Zech. 8:7). Lit., "the sea." Probably the Mediterranean, including its "isles of the sea," and maritime coast. Thus as vs. 11 specifies regions of Africa and Asia, so here Europe. Isaiah 11:11-16, is parallel, referring to the very same regions. On "children," see ch. 1:10. **11. tremble**—flutter in haste. **dove**—no longer "a silly dove" (ch. 7:11), but as "doves flying to their windows" (Isa. 60:8). **in their houses**—(Ezek. 28: 26). Lit., "upon," for the Orientals live almost as much *upon* their flat-roofed houses as *in* them. **12.** MAURER joins this verse with ch. 12. But as this verse praises Judah, whereas ch. 12:2 censures him, it must belong rather to ch. 11 and a new prophecy begins at ch. 12. To avoid this, MAURER translates this verse as a censure, "Judah wanders with God," i.e., though having the true God, he wanders after false gods. **ruleth with God**—to serve God is to reign. Ephraim wished to rule *without God* (cf. I Cor. 4:8); nay, even, in order to rule, cast off God's worship [RIVETUS]. In Judah was the legitimate succession of kings and priests. **with the saints**— the holy priests and Levites [RIVETUS]. With the fathers and prophets who handed down the pure worship of God. Israel's apostasy is the more culpable, as he had before him the good example of Judah, which he set at naught. The parallelism ("with GOD") favors *Margin*, "With THE MOST HOLY ONE."

CHAPTER 12

Vss. 1-14. REPROOF OF EPHRAIM AND JUDAH: THEIR FATHER JACOB OUGHT TO BE A PATTERN TO THEM. This prophecy was delivered about the time of Israel's seeking the aid of the Egyptian king So, in violation of their covenant with Assyria (see vs. 1). He exhorts them to follow their father Jacob's persevering prayerfulness, which brought God's favor upon him. As God is unchangeable, He will show the same favor to Jacob's posterity as He did to Jacob, if, like him, they seek God. **1. feedeth on wind**—(Prov. 15:14; Isa. 44:20). Followeth after vain objects, such as alliances with idolaters and their idols (cf. ch. 8:7). **east wind**—the simoon, blowing from the desert east of Palestine, which not only does not benefit, but does injury. Israel follows not only things vain, but things pernicious (cf. Job 15:2). **increaseth lies**—accumulates lie upon lie, i.e., impostures wherewith they deceive themselves, forsaking the truth of God. **desolation** —*violent oppressions* practised by Israel [MAURER]. Acts which would prove the *cause* of Israel's own *desolation* [CALVIN]. **covenant with ... Assyrians** —(ch. 5:13; 7:11). **oil ... into Egypt**—as a present from Israel to secure Egypt's alliance (Isa. 30:6; 57: 9; cf. II Kings 17:4). Palestine was famed for oil (Ezek. 27:17). **2. controversy with Judah**—(ch. 4:1; Mic. 6:2). Judah, under Ahaz, had fallen into idolatry (II Kings 16:3, etc.). **Jacob**—i.e., the ten tribes. If Judah, the favored portion of the nation, shall not be spared, much less degenerate Israel. **3. He**—Jacob, contrasted with his degenerate descendants, called by his name, Jacob (vs. 2; cf. Mic. 2:7). *He* took Esau by the heel in the womb in order to obtain, if possible, the privileges of the first-born (Gen. 25:22-26), whence he took his name, Jacob, meaning "supplanter"; and again, by his strength, prevailed in wrestling with God for a blessing (Gen. 32:24-29); whereas ye disregard My promises, putting your confidence in idols and foreign alliances. *He* conquered God, *ye* are the slaves of idols. Only have Jehovah on your side, and ye are stronger than Edom, or even Assyria. So the spiritual Is-

rael lays hold of the heel of Jesus, "the First-born of many brethren," being born again of the Holy Spirit. Having no right in themselves to the inheritance, they lay hold of the bruised heel, the humanity of Christ crucified, and let not go their hold of Him who is not, as Esau, a curse (Heb. 12: 16, 17), but, by becoming a curse for us, is a blessing to us. **power with God**—referring to his name, "Israel," *prince of God,* acquired on that occasion (cf. Matt. 11:12). As the promised Canaan had to be gained forcibly by Israel, so heaven by the faithful (Rev. 3:21; cf. Luke 13:24). "Strive," lit., "as in the agony of a contest." So the Canaanitess (Matt. 15:22). **his strength**—which lay in his conscious weakness, whence, when his thigh was put out of joint by God, he *hung upon Him.* To seek strength was his object; to grant it, God's. Yet God's mode of procedure was strange. In human form He tries as it were to throw Jacob down. When simple wrestling was not enough, He does what seems to ensure Jacob's fall, dislocating his thigh joint, so that he could no longer stand. Yet it was then that Jacob prevailed. Thus God teaches us the irresistible might of conscious weakness. For when weak in ourselves, we are strong by His strength put in us (Job 23:6; Isa. 27:5; II Cor. 12:9, 10). **4. the angel**—the uncreated Angel of the Covenant, as God the Son appears in the Old Testament (Mal. 3:1). **made supplication**—Genesis 32:26; I will not let thee go, except thou bless me. **he found him**—The angel found Jacob, when he was fleeing from Esau into Syria: the Lord appearing to him "in Beth-el" (Gen. 28:11-19; 35:1). What a sad contrast, that in this same Beth-el now Israel worships the golden calves! **there he spake with us** —"with *us,*" as being in the loins of our progenitor Jacob (cf. Ps. 66:6, "They ... *we*"; Heb. 7:9, 10). What God there spoke to Jacob appertains to us. God's promises to him belong to all his posterity who follow in the steps of his prayerful faith. **5. Lord God**—JEHOVAH, a name implying His *immutable constancy to His promises.* From the *Hebrew* root, meaning "existence." "He that is, was, and is to be," always the same (Heb. 13:8; Rev. 1:4, 8; cf. Exod. 3:14, 15; 6:3). As He was unchangeable in His favor to Jacob, so will He be to His believing posterity. **of hosts**—which Israel foolishly worshipped. Jehovah has all the hosts (*saba*) or powers of heaven and earth at His command, so that He is as all-powerful, as He is faithful, to fulfil His promises (Ps. 135:6; Amos 5:27). **memorial**—the name expressive of the character in which God was ever to be remembered (Ps. 135:13). **6. thou**—who dost wish to be a true descendant of Jacob. **to THY God**—who is therefore bound by covenant to hear thy prayers. **keep mercy and judgment**—(Mic. 6: 8). These two include the second-table commandments, duty towards one's neighbor, the most visible test of the sincerity on one's repentance. **wait on thy God**—alone, not on thy idols. Including all the duties of the first table (Ps. 37:3, 5, 7; 40:1). **7. merchant**—a play on the double sense of the *Hebrew,* "Canaan," i.e., a Canaanite and a "merchant" Ezekiel 16:3: "Thy birth is ... of Canaan." They who naturally were descendants of pious *Jacob* had become virtually *Canaanites,* who were proverbial as cheating *merchants* (cf. Isa. 23:11, *Margin*), the greatest reproach to Israel, who despised Canaan. The Phœnicians called themselves *Canaanites* or *merchants* (Isa. 23:8). **oppress**—*open* violence: as the "balances of deceit" imply *fraud.* **8. And**—i.e., Notwithstanding. **Yet I am ... rich**—I regard not what the prophets say: I am content with my state, as I am rich (Rev. 3:17). Therefore, in just retribution, this is the very language of the enemy in being the instrument of Israel's punishment. Zechariah 11:5: "They that sell them say ... *I am rich.*" Far better is poverty with honesty, than riches gained by sin. **my labours**—my gains by labor. **they shall find none**—i.e., none, shall find any. **iniquity ... that were sin**—iniquity that would bring down the penalty of sin. Ephraim argues, My success in my labors proves that I am not a guilty sinner as the prophets assert. Thus sinners pervert God's long-suffering goodness (Matt. 5:45) into a justification of their impenitence (cf. Eccles. 8:11-13). **9. And**—rather, "And yet." Though Israel deserves to be cast off for ever, yet I am still what I have been from the time of My delivering thee out of Egypt, their covenant God; therefore, "I will yet make thee to dwell in tabernacles," i.e., to keep the feast of tabernacles again in remembrance of a new deliverance out of bondage. Fulfilled primarily at the return from Babylon (Neh. 8:17). Fully and antitypically to be fulfilled at the final restoration from the present dispersion (Zech. 14:16; cf. Lev. 23:42, 43). **10. by ... the prophets**—lit., "upon," i.e., My spirit resting *on* them. I deposited *with them* My instructions which ought to have brought you to the right way. An aggravation of your guilt, that it was not through ignorance you erred, but in defiance of God and His prophets [CALVIN]. Ahijah the Shilonite, Shemaiah, Iddo, Azariah, Hanani, Jehu, Elijah, Elisha, Micaiah, Joel, and Amos were "the prophets" before Hosea. **visions ... similitudes**—I adopted such modes of communication, adapted to man's capacities, as were calculated to arouse attention: I left no means untried to reform you. Chs. 1, 2, 3 contain examples of "similitudes." **11. Is there iniquity in Gilead?**—He asks the question, not as if the answer was doubtful, but to strengthen the affirmation: "Surely they are vanity"; or as MAURER translates, "They are *nothing but* iniquity." *Iniquity,* especially idolatry, in Scripture is often termed "vanity." Proverbs 13:11: "Wealth gotten by *vanity,*" i.e., iniquity. Isaiah 41:29: "They are all *vanity ... images.*" "Gilead" refers to Mizpah-gilead, a city representing the region beyond Jordan (ch. 6:8; Judg. 11:29); as "Gilgal," the region on this side of Jordan (ch. 4:15). In all quarters alike they are utterly vile. **their altars are as heaps in the furrows**—i.e., as numerous as such heaps: viz., the heaps of stones cleared out of a stony field. An appropriate image, as at a distance they look like altars (cf. ch. 10:1, 4, and 8:11). As the third member in the parallelism answers to the first, "Gilgal" to "Gilead," so the fourth to the second, "altars" to "vanity." The word "heaps" alludes to the name "Gilgal," meaning "a heap of stones." The very scene of the general circumcision of the people, and of the solemn passover kept after crossing Jordan, is now the stronghold of Israel's idolatry. **12. Jacob fled ... served**—Though ye pride yourselves on the great name of "Israel," forget not that your progenitor was the same Jacob who was a fugitive, and who served for Rachel fourteen years. *He* forgot not ME who delivered him when fleeing from Esau, and when oppressed by Laban (Gen. 28:5; 29:20, 28; Deut. 26:5). *Ye,* though delivered from Egypt (vs. 13), and loaded with My favors, are yet unwilling to return to Me. **country of Syria**—the champaign region of Syria, the portion lying between the Tigris and Euphrates, hence called Mesopotamia. Padan-aram means the same, i.e., "Low Syria," as opposed to Aramea (meaning

the "high country") or Syria (Gen. 48:7). **13. by a prophet**—Moses (Num. 12:6-8; Deut. 18:15, 18). **preserved**—Translate, "kept"; there is an allusion to the same *Hebrew* word in vs. 12, "*kept* sheep"; Israel was *kept* by God as *His flock,* even as *Jacob kept* sheep (Ps. 80:1; Isa. 63:11). **14. provoked him**—i.e., God. **leave his blood upon him**—not take away the guilt and penalty of the innocent blood shed by Ephraim in general, and to Molech in particular. **his reproach shall his Lord return unto him** Ephraim's dishonor to God in worshipping idols, God will repay to him. That God is "*his* Lord" by right redemption and special revelation to Ephraim only aggravates his guilt, instead of giving him hope of escape. God does not give up His claim to them as *His,* however they set aside His dominion.

CHAPTER 13

Vss. 1-16. EPHRAIM'S SINFUL INGRATITUDE TO GOD, AND ITS FATAL CONSEQUENCE; GOD'S PROMISE AT LAST. This chapter and chapter 14 probably belong to the troubled times that followed Pekah's murder by Hoshea (cf. ch. 13:11; II Kings 15:30). The subject is the idolatry of Ephraim, notwithstanding God's past benefits, destined to be his ruin. **1. When Ephraim spake trembling**—rather, "When Ephraim [the tribe most powerful among the twelve in Israel's early history] spake [authoritatively] there was trembling"; all reverentially feared him [JEROME], (cf. Job 29:8, 9, 21). **offended in Baal**—i.e., *in respect to* Baal, by worshipping him (I Kings 16:31), under Ahab; a more heinous offense than even the calves. Therefore it is at this climax of guilt that Ephraim "died." Sin has, in the sight of God, within itself the germ of death, though that death may not visibly take effect till long after. Cf. Romans 7:9, "Sin revived, and I *died.*" So Adam in the day of his sin was to die, though the sentence was not visibly executed till long after (Gen. 2:17; 5:5). Israel is similarly represented as politically dead in Ezekiel 37. **2. according to their own understanding**—i.e., their arbitrary devising. Cf. "will-worship," Colossians 2:23. Men are not to be "wise above that which is written," or to follow their own understanding, but God's command in worship. **kiss the calves**—an act of adoration to the golden calves (cf. I Kings 19:18; Job 31:27; Ps. 2:12). **3. they shall be as the morning cloud ... dew**—(ch. 6:4). As their "goodness" soon vanished like the morning cloud and dew, so they shall perish like them. **the floor**—the threshing-floor, generally an open area, on a height, exposed to the winds. **chimney**—generally in the East an orifice in the wall, at once admitting the light, and giving egress to the smoke. **4.** (Ch. 12:9; Isa. 43:11.) **no saviour** [temporal as well as spiritual] besides me—(Isa. 45:21). **5. I did know thee**—did acknowledge thee as Mine, and so took care of thee (Ps. 144:3; Amos 3:2). As *I knew* thee as Mine, so *thou* shouldest *know* no God but Me (vs. 4). **in ... land of ... drought**—(Deut. 8:15). **6.** Image from cattle, waxing wanton in abundant pasture (cf. ch. 2:5, 8; Deut. 32:13-15). In proportion as I fed them to the full, they were so satiated that "their heart was exalted"; a sad contrast to the time when, by God's blessing, Ephraim truly "exalted himself in Israel" (vs. 1). **therefore have they forgotten me**—the very reason why men should remember God (viz., prosperity, which comes from Him) is the cause often of their forgetting Him. God had warned them of this danger (Deut. 6:11, 12). **7.** (Ch. 5, 14; Lam. 3:10). **leopard**—The *Hebrew* comes from a root meaning "spotted" (cf. Jer. 13:23). Leopards lurk in thickets and thence spring on their victims. **observe**—i.e., *lie in wait* for them. Several MSS., LXX, *Vulgate, Syriac,* and *Arabic* read, by a slight change of the *Hebrew* vowel pointing, "by the way *of Assyria,*" a region abounding in leopards and lions. *English Version* is better. **8.** "Writers on the natures of beasts say that none is more savage than a *she bear,* when *bereaved of her whelps*" [JEROME]. **caul of . . . heart**—the membrane enclosing it: the pericardium. **there**—"by the way" (vs. 7). **9. thou . . . in me**—in contrast. **hast destroyed thyself**—i.e., thy destruction is of thyself (Prov. 6:32; 8:36). **in me is thine help**—lit., "in thine help" (cf. Deut. 33: 26). Hadst thou rested thy hope *in Me,* I would have been always ready at hand *for thy help* [GROTIUS]. **10. I will be thy king; where**—rather, as *Margin* and LXX, *Syriac, Vulgate,* "Where now is thy king?" [MAURER]. *English Version* is, however, favored both by the *Hebrew,* by the antithesis between Israel's self-chosen and *perishing kings,* and God, Israel's *abiding King* (cf. ch. 3:4, 5). **where . . . Give me a king**—Where now is the king whom ye substituted in My stead? Neither Saul, whom the whole nation begged for, not contented with Me their true king (I Sam. 8:5, 7, 19, 20; 10:19), nor Jeroboam, whom subsequently the ten tribes chose instead of the line of David My anointed, can save thee now. They had expected from their kings what is the prerogative of God alone, viz., the power of saving them. **judges**—including all civil authorities under the king (cf. Amos 2:3). **11. I gave . . . king in. . . anger . . . took . . . away in . . . wrath**—true both of Saul (I Sam. 15:22, 23; 16:1) and of Jeroboam's line (II Kings 15:30). Pekah was taken away through Hoshea, as he himself took away Pekahiah; and as Hoshea was soon to be taken away by the Assyrian king. **12. bound up . . . hid**—Treasures, meant to be kept, are bound up and hidden; i.e., do not flatter yourselves, because of the delay, that I have forgotten your sin. Nay (ch. 9: 9), Ephraim's iniquity is kept as it were safely sealed up, until the due time comes for bringing it forth for punishment (Deut. 32:34; Job 14:17; 21:19; cf. Rom. 2:5). Opposed to "blotting out the handwriting against" the sinner (Col. 2:14). **13. sorrows of a travailing woman**—calamities sudden and agonizing (Jer. 30:6). **unwise**—in not foreseeing the impending judgment, and averting it by penitence (Prov. 22:3). **he should not stay long in the place of the breaking forth of children**—When Israel might deliver himself from calamity by the pangs of penitence, he brings ruin on himself by so long deferring a new birth unto repentance, like a child whose mother has not strength to bring it forth, and which therefore remains so long in the passage from the womb as to run the risk of death (II Kings 19:3; Isa. 37:3; 66:9). **14.** Applying primarily to God's restoration of Israel from Assyria partially, and, in times yet future, fully from all the lands of their present long-continued dispersion, and political *death* (cf. ch. 6:2; Isa. 25:8; 26:19; Ezek. 37:12). God's power and grace are magnified in quickening what to the eye of flesh seems dead and hopeless (Rom. 4:17, 19). As Israel's history, past and future, has a representative character in relation to the Church, this verse is expressed in language alluding to Messiah's (who is the ideal Israel) grand victory over the grave and death, the first fruits of His own resurrection, the full harvest to come at the general resurrection; hence the simi-

larity between this verse and Paul's language as to the latter (I Cor. 15:55). That similarity becomes more obvious by *translating* as LXX, from which Paul plainly quotes; and as the same *Hebrew* word is translated in vs. 10, "O death, *where* are thy plagues (paraphrased by LXX, 'thy victory')? O grave, where is thy destruction" (rendered by LXX, 'thy sting')?" The question is that of one triumphing over a foe, once a cruel tyrant, but now robbed of all power to hurt. **repentance shall be hid from mine eyes**—i.e., I will not change My purpose of fulfilling My promise by delivering Israel, on the condition of their return to Me (cf. ch. 14:2-8; Num. 23:19; Rom. 11:29). **15. fruitful**—referring to the meaning of "Ephraim," from a *Hebrew* root, "to be fruitful" (Gen. 41:52). It was long the most numerous and flourishing of the tribes (Gen. 48:19). **wind of the Lord**—i.e., sent by the Lord (cf. Isa. 40: 7), who has His instruments of punishment always ready. The Assyrian, Shalmaneser, etc., is meant (Jer. 4:11; 18:17; Ezek. 19:12). **from the wilderness**—i.e., the desert part of Syria (I Kings 19:15), the route from Assyria into Israel. **he**—the Assyrian invader. Shalmaneser began the siege of Samaria in 723 B.C. Its close was in 721 B.C., the first year of Sargon, who seems to have usurped the throne of Assyria while Shalmaneser was at the siege of Samaria. Hence, while II Kings 17:6 states, "the *king of Assyria* took Samaria," II Kings 18:10 says, "at the end of three years *they* took it." In Sargon's magnificent palace at Khorsabad, inscriptions mention the number—27,280—of Israelites carried captive from Samaria and other places of Israel by the founder of the palace [G. V. SMITH]. **16.** This verse and vs. 15 foretell the calamities about to befall Israel before her restoration (vs. 14), owing to her impenitence. **her God**—the greatest aggravation of her rebellion, that it was against *her* God (vs. 4). **infants . . . dashed in pieces . . .**—(II Kings 8:12; 15:16; Amos 1:13).

CHAPTER 14

Vss. 1-9. GOD'S PROMISE OF BLESSING, ON THEIR REPENTANCE: THEIR ABANDONMENT OF IDOLATRY FORETOLD: THE CONCLUSION OF THE WHOLE, THE JUST SHALL WALK IN GOD'S WAYS, BUT THE TRANSGRESSOR SHALL FALL THEREIN. **1. fallen by thine iniquity**—(ch. 5:5; 13:9). **2. Take with you words**—instead of sacrifices, viz., the words of penitence here put in your mouths by God. "Words," in *Hebrew,* mean "realities," there being the same term for "words" and "things"; so God implies, He will not accept empty professions (Ps. 78:36; Isa. 29:13). He does not ask costly sacrifices, but *words* of heartfelt penitence. **receive us graciously**—lit. (for) "good." **calves of our lips**—i.e., instead of sacrifices of *calves,* which we cannot offer to Thee in exile, we present the praises of our *lips.* Thus the exile, wherein the temple service ceased, prepared the way for the gospel time when the types of the animal sacrifices of the Old Testament being realized in Christ's perfect sacrifice once for all, "the sacrifice of praise to God continually that is *the fruit of our lips*" (Heb. 13:14) takes their place in the New Testament. **3.** Three besetting sins of Israel are here renounced, trust in Assyria, application to Egypt for its cavalry (forbidden, Deut. 17:16; cf. ch. 7:11; 11:5; 12:1; II Kings 17:4; Ps. 33:17; Isa. 30:2, 16; 31:1), and idolatry. **fatherless**—descriptive of the *destitute* state of Israel, when severed from God, their true Father. We shall henceforth trust in none but Thee, the only Father of the fatherless, and Helper of the destitute (Ps. 10:14; 68:5); our nation has experienced Thee such in our helpless state in Egypt, and now in a like state again our only hope is Thy goodness. **4.** God's gracious reply to their self-condemning prayer. **backsliding**— —*apostasy;* not merely occasional backslidings. God can heal the most desperate sinfulness [CALVIN]. **freely**—with a gratuitous, unmerited, and abundant love (Ezek. 16:60-63). So as to the spiritual Israel (John 15:16; Rom. 3:24; 5:8; I John 4:10). **5. as the dew**—which falls copiously in the East, taking the place of the more frequent rains in other regions. God will not be "as the early dew that goeth away," but constant (ch. 6:3, 4; Job 29:19; Prov. 19:12). **the lily**—No plant is more productive than the lily, one root often producing fifty bulbs [PLINY, H. N. 21. 5]. The common lily is white, consisting of six leaves opening like bells. The royal lily grows to the height of three or four feet; Matthew 6:29 alludes to the beauty of its flowers. **roots as Lebanon**—i.e., as the trees of Lebanon (especially the cedars), which cast down their roots as deeply as is their height upwards; so that they are immovable [JEROME], (Isa. 10:34). Spiritual growth consists most in the growth of the root which is out of sight. **6. branches**—shoots, or suckers. **beauty . . . as the olive**—which never loses its verdure. One plant is not enough to express the graces of God's elect people. The *lily* depicts its lovely growth; but as it wants duration and firmness, the deeply rooted cedars of Lebanon are added; these, however, are fruitless, therefore the fruitful, peace-bearing, fragrant, ever green *olive* is added. **smell as Lebanon**—which exhaled from it the fragrance of odoriferous trees and flowers. So Israel's name shall be in good savor with all (Gen. 27:27; Song of Sol. 4:11). **7.** *They that* used to *dwell under* Israel's *shadow* (but who shall have been forced to leave it), shall *return,* i.e., be restored (Ezek. 35:9). Others take *"His"* shadow" to mean *Jehovah's* (cf. Ps. 17:8; 91:1; Isa. 4:6), which vss. 1, 2 ("*return* unto *the Lord . . ."*) favor. But the "his" in vs. 6 refers to Israel, and therefore must refer to the same here. **revive as . . . corn**—As the corn long buried in the earth springs up, with an abundant produce, so shall they revive from their calamities, with a great increase of offspring (cf.

John 12:24). **scent thereof**—i.e., Israel's *fame.* Cf. vs. 6, "His smell as Lebanon"; Song of Solomon 1:3: "Thy *name* is as ointment poured forth." LXX favors *Margin,* "memorial." **as the wine of Lebanon**—which was most celebrated for its aroma, flavor, and medicinal restorative properties. **8. Ephraim** *shall say*—being brought to penitence by God's goodness, and confessing and abhorring his past madness. **I have heard . . . and observed him** —I Jehovah have *answered* and *regarded* him *with favor;* the opposite of God's "hiding His face from" one (Deut. 31:17). It is the experience of God's favor, in contrast to God's wrath heretofore, that leads Ephraim to abhor his past idolatry. Jehovah *heard* and answered: whereas the idols, as Ephraim now sees, could not *hear,* much less answer. **I am . . . a green fir**—or cypress; ever green, winter and summer alike; the leaves not falling off in winter. **From me is thy fruit found**—"From Me," as the root. Thou needest go no farther than Me for the supply of all thy wants; not merely the *protection* implied by the *shadow* of the cypress, but that which the cypress has not, viz., *fruit,* all spiritual and temporal blessings. It may be also implied, that whatever spiritual graces Ephraim seeks for or may have, are not of themselves, but of God (Ps. 1:3; John 15:4, 5, 8; Jas. 1:17). God's promises to us are more our security for mortifying sin than our promises to God (Isa. 27:9). **9.** EPILOGUE, summing up the whole previous teaching. Here alone Hosea uses the term "righteous," so rare were such characters in his day. There is enough of saving truth clear in God's Word to guide those humbly seeking salvation, and enough of difficulties to confound those who curiously seek them out, rather than practically seek salvation. **fall**—stumble and are offended at difficulties opposed to their prejudices and lusts, or above their self-wise understanding (cf. Prov. 10:29; Mic. 2:7; Matt. 11:19; Luke 2: 34; John 7:17; I Pet. 2:7, 8). To him who sincerely seeks the *agenda,* God will make plain the *credenda.* Christ is the foundation-stone to some: a stone of stumbling and rock of offense to others. The same sun softens wax and hardens clay. But their fall is the most fatal who fall in the ways of God, split on the Rock of ages, and suck poison out of the Balm of Gilead.

THE BOOK OF

JOEL

INTRODUCTION

JOEL (meaning "one to whom Jehovah is God," i.e. worshipper of Jehovah) seems to have belonged to Judah, as no reference occurs to Israel; whereas he speaks of Jerusalem, the temple, the priests, and the ceremonies, as if he were intimately familiar with them (cf. ch. 1:14; 2:1, 15, 32; 3:1, 2, 6, 16, 17, 20, 21). His predictions were probably delivered in the early days of Joash 870–865 B.C.; for no reference is made in them to the Babylonian, Assyrian, or even the Syrian invasion; and the only enemies mentioned are the Philistines, Phœnicians, Edomites, and Egyptians (ch. 3:4, 19). Had he lived after Joash, he would doubtless have mentioned the Syrians among the enemies whom he enumerates since they took Jerusalem and carried off immense spoil to Damascus (II Chron. 24:23, 24). No idolatry is mentioned; and the temple services, the priesthood, and other institutions of the theocracy, are represented as flourishing. This all answers to the state of things under the high priesthood of Jehoiada, through whom Joash had been placed on the throne and who lived in the early years of Joash (II Kings 11:17, 18; 12:2–16; II Chron. 24, 4–14). He was the son of Pethuel.
The first chapter describes the desolation caused by an inroad of locusts—one of the instruments of divine

judgment mentioned by Moses (Deut. 28:38, 39) and by Solomon (I Kings 8:37). The second chapter (vss. 1–11): the appearance of them, under images of a hostile army suggesting that the locusts were symbols and fore-runners of a more terrible scourge, viz., foreign enemies who would consume all before them. (The absence of mention of *personal* injury to the inhabitants is not a just objection to the figurative interpretation; for the figure is consistent throughout in attributing to the locusts only injury to *vegetation*, thereby injuring indirectly man and beast.) Ch. 2:12–17: exhortation to repentance, the result of which will be: God will deliver His people, the former and latter rains shall return to fertilize their desolated lands, and these shall be the pledge of the spiritual outpouring of grace beginning with Judah, and thence extending to "all flesh." Ch. 2:18–32; ch. 3: God's judgments on Judah's enemies, whereas Judah shall be established for ever.

Joel's style is pre-eminently pure. It is characterized by smoothness and fluency in the rhythms, roundness in the sentences, and regularity in the parallelisms. With the strength of Micah it combines the tenderness of Jeremiah, the vividness of Nahum, and the sublimity of Isaiah. As a specimen of his style take ch. 2, wherein the terrible aspect of the locusts, their rapidity, irresistible progress, noisy din, and instinct-taught power of marshalling their forces for their career of devastation, are painted with graphic reality.

CHAPTER 1

Vss. 1-20. The Desolate Aspect of the Coun-try through the Plague of Locusts; the People Admonished to Offer Solemn Prayers in the Temple; for This Calamity Is the Earnest of a Still Heavier One. **1. Joel**—meaning, "Jehovah is God." **son of Pethuel**—to distinguish Joel the prophet from others of the name. Persons of emi-nence also were noted by adding the father's name. **2, 3.** A spirited introduction calling attention. **old men**—the best judges in question concerning the past (Deut. 32:7; Job 32:7). **Hath this been . . .**— i.e., Hath any *so grievous* a calamity *as this* ever been before? No such plague of locusts had been since the ones *in Egypt*. Exodus 10:14 is not at variance with this verse, which refers to *Judea,* in which Joel says there had been no such devastation before. **3. Tell ye your children**—in order that they may be admonished by the severity of the punish-ment to fear God (Ps. 78:6-8; cf. Exod. 13:8; Josh. 4:7). **4.** This verse states the subject on which he afterwards expands. Four species or stages of locusts, rather than four different insects, are meant (cf. Lev. 11:22). Lit., (1) the *gnawing* locust; (2) the *swarming* locust; (3) the *licking* locust; (4) the *consuming* locust; forming a climax to the most destructive kind. The last is often three inches long, and the two antennæ, each an inch long. The two hinder of its six feet are larger than the rest, adapting it for leaping. The first "kind" is that of the locust, having just emerged from the egg in spring, and without wings. The second is when at the end of spring, still in their first skin, the lo-custs put forth little ones without legs or wings. The third, when after their third casting of the old skin, they get small wings, which enable them to leap the better, but not to fly. Being unable to go away till their wings are matured, they devour all before them, grass, shrubs, and bark of trees: trans-lated "rough caterpillars" (Jer. 51:27). The fourth kind, the matured winged locusts (see *Note,* Nah. 3:16). In ch. 2:25 they are enumerated in the re-verse order, where the restoration of the devasta-tions caused by them is promised. The Hebrews make the first species refer to Assyria and Babylon; the second species, to Medo-Persia; the third, to Greco-Macedonia and Antiochus Epiphanes; the fourth, to the Romans. Though the primary refer-ence be to literal locusts, the Holy Spirit doubt-less had in view the successive empires which as-sailed Judea, each worse than its predecessor, Rome being the climax. **5. Awake**—out of your ordinary state of drunken stupor, to realize the cutting off from you of your favorite drink. Even the drunk-ards (from a *Hebrew* root, "any strong drink") shall

be forced to "howl," though usually laughing in the midst of the greatest national calamities, so palpably and universally shall the calamity affect all. **wine . . . new wine**—"New" or "fresh wine," in *Hebrew,* is the unfermented, and therefore unintoxicating, *sweet juice* extracted by pressure from grapes or other fruit, as *pomegranates* (Song of Sol. 8:2). "Wine" is the produce of the grape alone, and is intoxicating (see *Note,* vs. 10). **6. nation**—applied to the locusts, rather than "people" (Prov. 30:25, 26), to mark not only their *numbers,* but also their *savage hostility;* and also to prepare the mind of the hearer for the transition to the figurative lo-custs in ch. 2, viz., the "nation" or *Gentile* foe com-ing against Judea. (cf. ch. 2:2). **my land**—i.e., Je-hovah's; which never would have been so devasta-ted were *I* not pleased to inflict punishment (ch. 2: 18; Isa. 14:25; Jer. 16:18; Ezek. 36:5; 38:16). **strong**—as irresistibly sweeping away before its compact body the fruits of man's industry. **with-out number**—so Judges 6:5; 7:12, "like grasshop-pers (or "locusts") for multitude" (Jer. 46:23; Nah. 3:15). **teeth . . . lion**—i.e., the locusts are as de-structive as a lion; there is no vegetation that can resist their bite (cf. Rev. 9:8). Pliny says "they gnaw even the doors of houses." **7. barked**—Bo-chart, with LXX and *Syriac,* translates, from an *Arabic* root, "hath broken," viz., the topmost shoots, which locusts most feed on. Calvin supports *Eng-lish Version.* **my vine . . . my fig tree**—being in "My land," i.e., Jehovah's (vs. 6). As to the vine-abounding nature of ancient Palestine, see Numbers 13:23, 24. **cast it away**—down to the ground. **branches . . . white**—both from the bark being stripped off (Gen. 30:37), and from the branches drying up through the trunk, both bark and wood being eaten up below by the locusts. **8. Lament**—O "my land" (vs. 6; Isa. 24:4). **virgin . . . for the hus-band**—A virgin betrothed was regarded as married (Deut. 22:23; Matt. 1:19). The *Hebrew* for "hus-band" is "lord" or "possessor," the husband being considered the master of the wife in the East. **of her youth**—when the affections are strongest and when sorrow at bereavement is consequently keen-est. Suggesting the thought of what Zion's grief ought to be for her separation from Jehovah, the betrothed husband of her early days (Jer. 2:2; Ezek. 16:8; Hos. 2:7; cf. Prov. 2:17; Jer. 3:4). **9.** The greatest sorrow to the mind of a religious Jew, and what ought to impress the whole nation with a sense of God's displeasure, is the cessation of the usual temple worship. **meat offering**—*Hebrew, mincha;* "meat" not in the English sense "flesh," but the un-bloody offering made of flour, oil, and frankincense. As it and the drink offering or libation *poured out* ac-companied every sacrificial *flesh* offering, the latter is included, though not specified, as being also "cut off," owing to there being no food left for man or beast. **priests . . . mourn**—not for their own loss of sacrificial perquisites (Num. 18:8-15), but because they can no longer offer the appointed offerings to Jehovah, to whom they minister. **10. field . . . land** differing in that "field" means the open, unenclosed country; "land," the rich *red* soil (from a root "to be red") fit for cultivation. Thus, "a man of the field," in *Hebrew,* is a hunter; a "man of the ground" or "land," an agriculturist (Gen. 25:27). "Field" and "land" are here personified. **new wine**—from a *Hebrew* root implying that it *takes possession* of the brain, so that a man is not master of himself. So the *Arabic* term is from a root "to hold captive." It is already fermented, and so intoxicating, unlike the *sweet fresh wine,* in vs. 5, called also "new wine," though a different *Hebrew* word. It and "the oil" stand for the vine and the olive tree, from which the "wine" and "oil" are obtained (vs. 12). **dried up**—not "ashamed," as *Margin,* as is proved by the parallelism to "languisheth," i.e., droopeth. **11. Be . . . ashamed**—i.e., Ye shall have the *shame* of disappointment on account of the failure of "the wheat" and "barley" "harvest." **howl . . . vine dressers**—The semicolon should follow, as it is the "husbandmen" who are to be "ashamed" "for the wheat." The reason for the "vine dressers" being called to "howl" does not come till vs. 12, "The vine is dried up." **12. pomegranate**—a tree straight in the stem growing twenty feet high; the fruit is of the size of an orange, with blood-red colored pulp. **palm tree**—The dates of Palestine were famous. The palm is the symbol of Judea on coins under the Roman emperor Vespasian. It often grows a hundred feet high. **apple tree**—The *Hebrew* is generic, including the orange, lemon, and pear tree. **joy is withered away**—such as is felt in the harvest and the vintage seasons (Ps. 4:7; Isa. 9:3). **13. Gird yourselves**—viz., with sackcloth; as in Isaiah 32:11, the ellipsis is supplied (cf. Jer. 4:8). **lament, ye priests**—as it is your duty to set the example to others; also as the guilt was greater, and a greater scandal was occasioned, by your sin to the cause of God. **come**—LXX, "enter" *the house of God* (cf. vs. 14). **lie all night in sackcloth**—so Ahab (I Kings 21:27). **ministers of my God**—(I Cor. 9: 13). Joel claims authority for his doctrine; it is *in God's name and by His mission* I speak to you. **14. Sanctify . . . a fast**—Appoint a solemn fast. **solemn assembly**—lit., a "day of restraint" or cessation from work, so that all might give themselves to supplication (ch. 2:15, 16; I Sam. 7:5, 6; II Chron. 20:3-13). **elders**—The contrast to "children" (ch. 2:16) requires age to be intended, though probably elders in *office* are included. Being the people's leaders in guilt, they ought to be their leaders also in repentance. **15. day of the Lord**—(ch. 2:1, 11); i.e., the day of His anger (Isa. 13:9; Obad. 15; Zeph. 1:7, 15). It will be a foretaste of the coming day of the Lord as Judge of all men, whence it receives the same name. Here the transition begins from the plague of locusts to the worse calamities (ch. 2) from invading armies about to come on Judea, of which the locusts were the prelude. **16. Cf. vs. 9,** and latter part of vs. 12. **joy**—which prevailed at the annual feasts, as also in the ordinary sacrificial offerings, of which the offerers ate before the Lord with gladness and thanksgivings (Deut. 12:6, 7, 12; 16:11, 14, 15). **17. is rotten**—"is dried up," "vanishes away," from an *Arabic* root [MAURER]. "Seed," lit., "grains." The drought causes the seeds to lose all their vitality and moisture. **garners**—

granaries; generally underground, and divided into separate receptacles for the different kinds of grain. **18. cattle . . . perplexed**—implying the restless gestures of the dumb beasts in their inability to find food. There is a tacit contrast between the sense of the brute creation and the insensibility of the people. **yea, the . . . sheep**—*Even the sheep,* which are content with less rich pasturage, cannot find food. **are made desolate**—lit., "suffer punishment." The innocent brute shares the *punishment* of guilty man (Exod. 12:29; Jonah 3:7; 4:11). **19. to thee will I cry**—Joel here interposes, As this people is insensible to shame or fear and will not hear, I will leave them and address myself directly to Thee (cf. Isa. 15:5; Jer. 23:9). **fire**—i.e., the parching heat. **pastures**—"grassy places"; from a *Hebrew* root "to be pleasant." Such places would be selected for "habitations." But the *English Version* rendering is better than *Margin.* **20. beasts . . . cry . . . unto thee**—i.e., look up to heaven with heads lifted up, as if their only expectation was from God (Job 38:41; Ps. 104:21; 145:15; 147:9; cf. Ps. 42:1). They tacitly reprove the deadness of the Jews for not even now invoking God.

CHAPTER 2

Vss. 1-32. THE COMING JUDGMENT A MOTIVE TO REPENTANCE. PROMISE OF BLESSINGS IN THE LAST DAYS. A more terrific judgment than that of the locusts is foretold, under imagery drawn from that of the calamity then engrossing the afflicted nation. He therefore exhorts to repentance, assuring the Jews of Jehovah's pity if they would repent. Promise of the Holy Spirit in the last days under Messiah, and the deliverance of all believers in Him. **1. Blow . . . trumpet**—to sound an alarm of coming war (Num. 10; Hos. 5:8; Amos 3:6); the office of the priests. Ch. 1:15 is an anticipation of the fuller prophecy in this chapter. **2. darkness . . . gloominess . . . clouds . . . thick darkness**—accumulation of synonyms, to intensify the picture of *calamity* (Isa. 8:22). Appropriate here, as the swarms of locusts intercepting the sunlight suggested *darkness* as a fit image of the coming visitation. **as the morning spread upon the mountains: a great people**—Substitute a comma for a colon after mountains: As the morning light spreads itself over the mountains, so a people *numerous* [MAURER] and strong shall spread themselves. The *suddenness* of the rising of the morning light, which gilds the mountain tops first, is less probably thought by others to be the point of comparison to the sudden inroad of the foe. MAURER refers it to the *yellow splendor* which arises from the reflection of the sunlight on the wings of the immense hosts of locusts as they approach. This is likely; understanding, however, that the locusts are only the symbols of human foes. The immense Assyrian host of invaders under Sennacherib (cf. Isa. 37:36) destroyed by God (vss. 18, 20, 21), may be the primary objects of the prophecy; but ultimately the last antichristian confederacy, destroyed by special divine interposition, is meant (*Note,* ch. 3:2). **there hath not been ever the like**—(Cf. ch. 1:2 and Exod. 10:14). **3. before . . . behind**—i.e., *on every side* (I Chron. 19:10). **fire . . . flame**—destruction . . . desolation (Isa. 10:17). **as . . . Eden . . . wilderness**—conversely (Isa. 51:3; Ezek. 36: 35). **4. appearance . . . of horses**—(Rev. 9:7). Not literal, but figurative locusts. The fifth trumpet, or first woe, in the parallel passage (Rev. 9), cannot be literal: for in Revelation 19:11 it is said, "they had a king over them, the angel of the bottomless pit—in the *Hebrew, Abaddon* ("destroyer"), but in the *Greek, Apollyon*—and (Rev. 9:7) "on their heads were as it were *crowns* like gold, and their faces were as the faces of *men*." Cf. vs. 11, "the day of the Lord ... great and very terrible"; implying their ultimate reference to be connected with Messiah's second coming in judgment. The locust's head is so like that of a horse that the Italians call it *cavalette.* Cf. Job 39:20, "the horse ... as the grasshopper," or *locust.* **run**—The locust *bounds,* not unlike the horse's gallop, raising and letting down together the two front feet. **5. Like the noise of chariots**—referring to the loud sound caused by their wings in motion, or else the movement of their hind legs. **on the tops of mountains**—Maurer connects this with "they," i.e., the locusts, which first occupy the higher places, and thence descend to the lower places. It may refer (as in *English Version*) to "chariots," which make most noise in crossing over rugged heights. **6. much pained**—viz., with terror. The Arab proverb is, "More terrible than the locusts." **faces shall gather blackness**—(Isa. 13:8; Jer. 30:6; Nah. 2:10). Maurer translates, "withdraw their brightness," i.e., wax pale, lose color (cf. vs. 10 and ch. 3:15). **7-9.** Depicting the regular military order of their advance, "One locust not turning a nail's breadth out of his own place in the march" [Jerome]. Cf. Proverbs 30:27, "The locusts have no king, yet go they forth all of them *by bands.*" **8. Neither shall one thrust another**—i.e., press upon so as to thrust his next neighbor out of his place, as usually occurs in a large multitude. **when they fall upon the sword**—i.e., among *missiles.* **not be wounded**—because they are protected by defensive armor [Grotius]. Maurer translates, "Their (the locusts') ranks are *not broken* when they rush among missiles" (cf. Dan. 11:22). **9. run to and fro in the city**—greedily seeking what they can devour. **the wall**—surrounding each house in Eastern buildings. **enter in at the windows**—though barred. **like a thief**—(John 10:1; cf. Jer. 9:21). **10. earth ... quake before them**—i.e., the inhabitants of the earth quake with fear of them. **heavens ... tremble**—i.e., the powers of heaven (Matt. 24:29); its illumining powers are disturbed by the locusts which intercept the sunlight with their dense flying swarms. These, however, are but the images of revolutions of states caused by such foes as were to invade Judea. **11. Lord ... his army**—So among Mohammedans, "Lord of the locusts" is a title of God. **his voice**—His word of command to the locusts, and to the antitypical human foes of Judea, as "His army." **strong that executeth his word**—(Rev. 18:8). **12.** With such judgments impending over the Jews, Jehovah Himself urges them to repentance. **also now**—*Even now,* what none could have hoped or believed possible, God still invites you to the hope of salvation. **fasting ... weeping ... mourning**—Their sin being most heinous needs extraordinary humiliation. The outward marks of repentance are to signify the depth of their sorrow for sin. **13. Let there be the inward sorrow of heart, and not the mere outward manifestation of it by "rending the garment" (Josh. 7:6). the evil**—the calamity which He had threatened against the impenitent. **14. leave ... a meat offering and a drink offering**—i.e., give plentiful harvests, out of the first fruits of which we may offer the meat and drink offering, now "cut off" through the famine (ch. 1:9, 13, 16). "Leave behind Him": as God in visiting His people now has left behind Him a curse, so He will, on returning to visit them, leave behind Him a blessing. **15. Blow**

the **trumpet**—to convene the people (Num. 10:3). Cf. ch. 1:14. The nation was guilty, and therefore there must be a national humiliation. Cf. Hezekiah's proceedings before Sennacherib's invasion (II Chron. 30). **16. sanctify the congregation**—viz., by expiatory rites and purification with water [Calvin], (Exod. 19:10, 22). Maurer translates, "appoint a solemn assembly," which would be a tautological repetition of vs. 15. **elders ... children**—No age was to be excepted (II Chron. 20:13). **bridegroom** —ordinarily exempted from public duties (Deut. 24: 5; cf. I Cor. 7:5, 29). **closet**—or, nuptial bed, from a *Hebrew* root "to cover," referring to the canopy over it. **17. between the porch and ... altar**—the porch of Solomon's temple on the east (I Kings 6:3); the altar of burnt offerings in the court of the priests, before the porch (II Chron. 8:12; cf. Ezek. 8:16; Matt. 23:35). The suppliants thus were to stand with their backs to the altar on which they had nothing to offer, their faces towards the place of the Shekinah presence. **heathen should rule over them** —This shows that not locusts, but human foes, are intended. The *Margin* translation, "use a byword against them," is not supported by the *Hebrew.* **wherefore should they say ..., Where is their God?** —i.e., do not for thine own honor's sake, let the heathen sneer at the God of Israel, as unable to save His people (Ps. 79:10; 115:2). **18. Then**—when God sees His people penitent. **be jealous for his land**— as a husband *jealous* of any dishonor done to the wife whom he loves, as if done to himself. The *Hebrew* comes from an *Arabic* root, "to be flushed in face" through indignation. **19. corn ... wine ... oil**—rather, as *Hebrew,* "*the* corn ... *the* wine ... *the* oil," viz., which the locusts have destroyed [Henderson]. Maurer not so well explains, "the corn, etc., necessary for your sustenance." "The Lord will *answer,*" viz., the prayers of His people, priests, and prophets. Cf. in the case of Sennacherib, II Kings 19:20, 21. **20. the northern army** —The *Hebrew* expresses that the *north* in relation to Palestine is not merely the quarter whence the invader comes, but is his native land, "the Northlander"; viz., the Assyrian or Babylonian (cf. Jer. 1:14, 15; Zeph. 2:13). The locust's native country is not the *north,* but the *south,* the deserts of Arabia, Egypt, and Libya. Assyria and Babylon are the type and forerunner of all Israel's foes (Rome, and the final Antichrist), from whom God will at last deliver His people, as He did from Sennacherib (II Kings 19:35). **face ... hinder part**—more applicable to a human army's *van* and *rear,* than to locusts. The northern invaders are to be dispersed in every other direction but that from which they had come: "a land barren and desolate," i.e., Arabia Deserta: "the eastern (or *front*) sea," i.e., the Dead Sea: "the utmost (or *hinder*) sea," i.e., the Mediterranean. *In front* and *behind* mean east and west; as, in marking the quarters of the world, they *faced* the east, which was therefore "in front"; the west was *behind* them; the south was on their *right,* and the north on their *left.* **stink**—metaphor from *locusts,* which perish when blown by a storm into the sea or the desert, and emit from their putrefying bodies such a stench as often breeds a pestilence. **because he hath done great things**—i.e., because the invader hath *haughtily magnified himself in his doings.* Cf. as to Sennacherib, II Kings 19:11-13, 22, 28. This is quite inapplicable to the locusts, who merely seek food, not self-glorification, in invading a country. **21-23.** In an ascending gradation, the *land* destroyed by the enemy, *the beasts of the field,* and the *children of Zion,* the land's inhabitants, are addressed, the former two by personification. **Lord will do great things**—In contrast to the "great things" done by the haughty foe (vs. 20) to the hurt of Judah stand the "great things" to be done by Jehovah for her benefit (cf. Ps. 126:2, 3). **22.** (Zech. 8:12). As before (ch. 1:18, 20) he represented the beasts as *groaning* and *crying* for want of food in the "pastures," so now he reassures them by the promise of *springing pastures*. **23. rejoice in the Lord**—not merely *in the springing pastures,* as the brute "beasts" which cannot raise their thoughts higher (Isa. 61:10; Hab. 3:18). **former rain . . . the rain . . . the former . . . the latter rain**—The autumnal, or "former rain," from the middle of October to the middle of December, is put first, as Joel prophesies in summer when the locusts' invasion took place, and therefore looks to the time of early sowing in autumn, when the autumnal rain was indispensably required. Next, "the rain," *generically,* lit., "the showering" or "heavy rain." Next, the two species of the latter, "the former and the latter rain" (in March and April). The repetition of the "former rain" implies that He will give it not merely for the exigence of that particular season when Joel spake, but also for the future in the regular course of nature, the autumn and the spring rain; the former being put first, in the order of nature, as being required for the sowing in autumn, as the latter is required in spring for maturing the young crop. The *Margin,* "a teacher of righteousness," is wrong. For the same *Hebrew* word is translated "former rain" in the next sentence, and cannot therefore be differently translated here. Besides, Joel begins with the inferior and temporal blessings, and not till vs. 28 proceeds to the higher and spiritual ones, of which the former are the pledge. **moderately**—rather, "in due measure," as much as the land requires; lit., "according to right"; neither too much nor too little, either of which extremes would hurt the crop (cf. Deut. 11:14; Prov. 16:15; Jer. 5:24; *Note,* Hos. 6:3). The phrase, "in due measure," in this clause is parallel to "in the first month," in the last clause (i.e., *"in the month* when *first* it is needed," each rain in its proper season). Heretofore the *just* or *right* order of nature has been interrupted through your sin; now God will restore it. See my *Introduction* to Joel. **24.** The effect of the seasonable rains shall be abundance of all articles of food. **25. locust . . . cankerworm . . . caterpiller . . . palmer worm**—the reverse order from ch. 1:4, where (see *Note*) God will restore not only what has been lost by the full-grown *consuming locust,* but also what has been lost by the less destructive *licking locust,* and *swarming locust,* and *gnawing locust.* **26. never be ashamed**—shall no longer endure the "reproach of the heathen (vs. 17), [MAURER]; or rather, "shall not bear the shame of disappointed hopes," as the husbandmen had heretofore (ch. 1: 11). So spiritually, waiting on God, His people shall not have the shame of disappointment in their expectations from Him (Rom. 9:33). **27. know that I am in the midst of Israel**—As in the Old Testament dispensation God was present by the Shekinah, so in the New Testament first, for a brief time by the Word made flesh dwelling among us (John 1:14), and to the close of this dispensation by the Holy Spirit in the Church (Matt. 28:20), and probably in a more perceptible manner with Israel when restored (Ezek. 37:26-28). **never be ashamed**—not an unmeaning repetition from vs. 26. The twice-asserted truth enforces its unfailing certainty. As the "shame" in vs. 26 refers to temporal blessings, so in this verse it refers to the spiritual blessings

flowing from the presence of God with His people (cf. Jer. 3:16, 17; Rev. 21:3). **28. afterward**—"in the last days" (Isa. 2:2) under Messiah *after* the invasion and deliverance of Israel from the *northern army*. Having heretofore stated the outward blessings, he now raises their minds to the expectation of extraordinary spiritual blessings, which constitute the true restoration of God's people (Isa. 44:3). Fulfilled in earnest (Acts 2:17) on Pentecost; among the Jews and the subsequent election of a people among the Gentiles; hereafter more fully at the restoration of Israel (Isa. 54:13; Jer. 31:9, 34; Ezek. 39:29; Zech. 12:10) and the consequent conversion of the whole world (Isa. 2:2; 11:9; 66:18-23; Mic. 5:7; Rom. 11:12, 15). As the Jews have been the seedmen of the elect Church gathered out of Jews and Gentiles, the first Gospel preachers being Jews from Jerusalem, so they shall be the harvest-men of the coming world-wide Church, to be set up at Messiah's appearing. That the promise is not *restricted* to the first Pentecost appears from Peter's own words: "The promise is [not only] unto you and to your children, [but also] to *all that are afar off* [both in space and in time], even as many as the Lord our God shall call" (Acts 2:39). So here "upon *all* flesh." I will *pour out*—under the new covenant: not merely, *let fall drops,* as under the Old Testament (John 7:39). **my spirit**—the Spirit "proceeding from the Father and the Son," and at the same time one with the Father and the Son (cf. Isa. 11:2). **sons . . . daughters . . . old . . . young**—not merely on a privileged few (Num. 11:29) as the prophets of the Old Testament, but men of all ages and ranks. See Acts 21:9, and I Corinthians 11: 5, as to "daughters," i.e., women, prophesying. **dreams . . . visions**—(Acts 9:10; 16:9). The "dreams" are attributed to the "old men," as more in accordance with their years; "visions" to the "young men," as adapted to their more lively minds. The three modes whereby God revealed His will under the Old Testament (Num. 12:6), "prophecy, dreams, and visions," are here made the symbol of the full manifestation of Himself to all His people, not only in miraculous gifts to some, but by His indwelling Spirit to all in the New Testament (John 14:21, 23; 15:15). In Acts 16:9, and 18:9, the term used is "vision," though in the night, not a *dream*. No other dream is mentioned in the New Testament save those given to Joseph in the very beginning of the New Testament, before the full Gospel had come; and to the wife of Pilate, a *Gentile* (Matt. 1:20; 2:13; 27:19). "Prophesying" in the New Testament is applied to all speaking under the enlightenment of the Holy Spirit, and not merely to foretelling events. All true Christians are "priests" and "ministers" of our God (Isa. 61:6), and have the Spirit (Ezek. 36:26, 27). Besides this, probably, a special gift of prophecy and miracle-working is to be given at or before Messiah's coming again. **29. And also**—"And even." The very slaves by becoming the Lord's servants are His freemen (I Cor. 7:22; Gal. 3:28; Col. 3:11; Philemon 16). Therefore, in Acts 2:18 it is quoted, *"My* servants" and *"My* handmaidens"; as it is only by becoming *the Lord's* servants they are spiritually free, and partake of the same spirit as the other members of the Church. **30, 31.** As Messiah's manifestation is full of joy to believers, so it has an aspect of wrath to unbelievers, which is represented here. Thus when the Jews received Him not in His coming of grace, He came in judgment on Jerusalem. Physical prodigies, massacres, and conflagrations preceded its destruction [JOSEPHUS, J. B.]. To these the language here may allude; but the figures chiefly symbolize political revolutions and changes in the ruling powers of the world, prognosticated by previous disasters (Amos 8:9; Matt. 24:29; Luke 21:25-27), and convulsions such as preceded the overthrow of the Jewish polity. Such shall probably occur in a more appalling degree before the final destruction of the ungodly world ("the great and terrible day of Jehovah," cf. Mal. 4:5), of which Jerusalem's overthrow is the type and earnest. **32. call on ... name of ... Lord**—*Hebrew*, JEHOVAH. Applied to Jesus in Romans 10:13 (cf. Acts 9:14; I Cor. 1:2). Therefore, Jesus is JEHOVAH; and the phrase means, "Call on Messiah in His divine attributes." **shall be delivered**—as the Christians were, just before Jerusalem's destruction, by retiring to Pella, warned by the Saviour (Matt. 24:16); a type of the spiritual deliverance of all believers, and of the last deliverance of the elect "remnant" of Israel from the final assault of Antichrist. "In Zion and Jerusalem" the Saviour first appeared; and there again shall He appear as the *Deliverer* (Zech. 14:1-5). **as the Lord hath said**—Joel herein refers, not to the other prophets, but to his own words preceding. **call**—metaphor from an invitation to a feast, which is an act of gratuitous kindness (Luke 14:16). So the remnant called and saved is according to the election of grace, not for man's merits, power, or efforts (Rom. 11:5).

CHAPTER 3

Vss. 1-21. GOD'S VENGEANCE ON ISRAEL'S FOES IN THE VALLEY OF JEHOSHAPHAT. HIS BLESSING ON THE CHURCH. **1. bring again the captivity**—i.e., reverse it. The Jews restrict this to the return from Babylon. Christians refer it to the coming of Christ. But the prophet comprises the whole redemption, beginning from the return out of Babylon, then continued from the first advent of Christ down to the last day (His second advent), when God will restore His Church to perfect felicity [CALVIN]. **2.** Parallel to Zechariah 14:2, 3, 4, where the "Mount of Olives" answers to the "Valley of Jehoshaphat" here. The latter is called "the valley of blessing (*Berachah*) (II Chron. 20:26). It lies between Jerusalem and the Mount of Olives and has the Kedron flowing through it. As Jehoshaphat overthrew the confederate foes of Judah, viz., Ammon, Moab, etc. (Ps. 83:6-8), in this valley, so God was to overthrow the Tyrians, Zidonians, Philistines, Edom, and Egypt, with a similar utter overthrow (vss. 4, 19). This has been long ago fulfilled; but the ultimate event shadowed forth herein is still future, when God shall specially interpose to destroy Jerusalem's last foes, of whom Tyre, Zidon, Edom, Egypt, and Philistia are the types. As "Jehoshaphat" means "the judgment of Jehovah," *the valley of Jehoshaphat* may be used as a *general* term for the theater of God's final judgments on Israel's foes, with an allusion to the judgment inflicted on them by Jehoshaphat. The definite mention of the Mount of Olives in Zechariah 14, and the fact that this was the scene of the ascension, makes it likely the same shall be the scene of Christ's coming again: cf. "this same Jesus ... shall so come in *like manner* as ye have seen Him go into heaven" (Acts 1:11). **all nations**—viz., which have maltreated Judah. **plead with them**—(Isa. 66:16; Ezek. 38:22). **my heritage Israel**—(Deut. 32:9; Jer. 10:16). Implying that the source of Judah's redemption is God's free love, wherewith He chose Israel as *His peculiar heritage,* and at the

same time assuring them, when desponding because of trials, that He would plead their cause as His own, and as if He were injured in their person. **3. cast lots for my people**—i.e., divided among themselves My people as their captives by lot. Cf. as to the distribution of captives by lot (Obad. 11; Nah. 3:10). **given a boy for ... harlot**—Instead of paying a harlot for her prostitution in money, they gave her a Jewish captive boy as a slave. **girl for wine**—So valueless did they regard a Jewish girl that they would sell her for a draught of wine. **4. what have ye to do with me**—Ye have no connection with Me (i.e., with My people: God identifying Himself with Israel; I (i.e., My people) have given you no cause of quarrel, why then do ye trouble Me (i.e., My people)? (Cf. the same phrase, Josh. 22: 24; Judg. 11:12; II Sam. 16:10; Matt. 8:29). **Tyre ... Zidon ... Palestine**—(Amos 1:6, 9). **if ye recompense me**—If *ye injure Me* (My people), *in revenge* for fancied wrongs (Ezek. 25:15-17), I will requite you in your own coin swiftly and speedily. **5. my silver ... my gold**—i.e., the gold and silver of My people. The Philistines and Arabians had carried off all the treasures of King Jehoram's house (II Chron. 21:16, 17). Cf. also I Kings 15:18; II Kings 12:18; 14:14, for the spoiling of the treasures of the temple and the king's palace in Judah by Syria. It was customary among the heathen to hang up in the idol temples some of the spoils of war as presents to their gods. **6. Grecians**—lit., Javanites, i.e., the Ionians, a Greek colony on the coast of Asia Minor who were the first Greeks known to the Jews. The Greeks themselves, however, in their *original descent* came from Javan (Gen. 10:2, 4). Probably the germ of Greek civilization in part came through the Jewish slaves imported into Greece from Phœnicia by traffickers. Ezekiel 27:13 mentions *Javan* and Tyre as trading in the persons of men. **far from their border**—far from Judea; so that the captive Jews were cut off from all hope of return. **7. raise them**—i.e., I will *rouse* them. Neither sea nor distance will prevent My bringing them back. Alexander, and his successors, restored to liberty many Jews in bondage in Greece (JOSEPHUS 13.5; J. B. 9, 2). **8. sell them to ... Sabeans**—The Persian Artaxerxes Mnemon and Darius Ochus, and chiefly the Greek Alexander, reduced the Phœnician and Philistine powers. Thirty thousand Tyrians after the capture of Tyre by the last conqueror, and multitudes of Philistines on the taking of Gaza, were sold as slaves. The Jews are here said to do that which the God of Judah does in vindication of their wrong, viz., sell the Phœnicians who sold them, to a people "far off," as was Greece, whither the Jews had been sold. The Sabeans at the most remote extremity of Arabia Felix are referred to (cf. Jer. 6:20; Matt. 12:42). **9.** The nations hostile to Israel are summoned by Jehovah to "come up" (this phrase is used because Jerusalem was on a *hill*) against Jerusalem, not that they may destroy it, but to be destroyed by the Lord (Ezek. 38:7-23; Zech. 12:2-9; 14:2, 3). **Prepare war**—lit., *sanctify* war: because the heathen always began war with religious ceremonies. The very phrase used of Babylon's *preparations* against Jerusalem (Jer. 6:4) is now used of the final foes of Jerusalem. As Babylon was then desired by God to advance against her for her destruction, so now all her foes, of whom Babylon was the type, are desired to advance against her for *their own* destruction. **10. Beat your ploughshares into swords**—As the foes are desired to "beat their *ploughshares into swords, and their pruning hooks into spears,*" that so they may perish in their unhallowed attack on Judah and Jerusalem, so these latter, and the nations converted to God by them, after the overthrow of the antichristian confederacy, shall, on the contrary, "beat their *swords into ploughshares,* and their *spears into pruning hooks,"* when under Messiah's coming reign there shall be war no more (Isa. 2:4; Hos. 2:18; Mic. 4:3). **let the weak say, I am strong**—So universal shall be the rage of Israel's foes for invading her, that even the *weak* among them will fancy themselves *strong* enough to join the invading forces. Age and infirmity were ordinarily made valid excuses for exemption from service, but so mad shall be the fury of the world against God's people, that even the feeble will not desire to be exempted (cf. Ps. 2:1-3). **11. Assemble**—"Hasten" [MAURER]. **thither**—to the valley of Jehoshaphat. **thy mighty ones**—the warriors who fancy themselves "mighty ones," but who are on that very spot to be overthrown by Jehovah [MAURER]. Cf. "the mighty men" (vs. 9). Rather, Joel speaks of God's really "mighty ones" in contrast to the self-styled "mighty men" (vs. 9; Ps. 103:20; Isa. 13:3; cf. Dan. 10:13). AUBERLEN remarks: One prophet supplements the other, for they all prophesied only "in part." What was obscure to one was revealed to the other; what is briefly described by one is more fully so by another. Daniel calls Antichrist a king, and dwells on his worldly conquests; John looks more to his spiritual tyranny, for which reason he adds a second beast, wearing the semblance of spirituality. Antichrist *himself* is described by Daniel. Isaiah (Isa. 29), Joel (ch. 3), and Zechariah (Zech. 12, 13 and 14) describe *his army* of heathen followers coming up against Jerusalem, but not Antichrist himself. **12.** See vs. 2. **judge all the heathen round about**—i.e., all the nations from all parts of the earth which have maltreated Israel; not merely, as HENDERSON supposes, the nations *round about* Jerusalem (cf. Ps. 110:6; Isa. 2:4; Mic. 4:3, 11-13; Zeph. 3:15-19; Zech. 12:9; 14:3-11; Mal. 4:1-3). **13.** Direction to the ministers of vengeance to execute God's wrath, as the enemy's wickedness is come to its full maturity. God does not cut off the wicked at once, but waits till their guilt is at its *full* (so as to the Amorites' iniquity, Gen. 15:16), to show forth His own long-suffering, and the justice of their doom who have so long abused it (Matt. 13:27-30, 38, 40; Rev. 14:15-19). For the image of a harvest to be threshed, cf. Jeremiah 51:33; and a wine press, Isaiah 63:3 and Lamentations 1:15. **14.** The prophet in vision seeing the immense array of nations congregating, exclaims, "Multitudes, multitudes!" a Hebraism for *immense multitudes.* **valley of decision**—i.e., the valley in which they are to meet their *determined doom.* The same as "the valley of Jehoshaphat," i.e., "the valley *of judgment"* (*Note,* vs. 2). Cf. vs. 12, "there will I sit to *judge,"* which confirms *English Version* rather than *Margin,* "threshing." The repetition of "valley of decision" heightens the effect and pronounces the awful *certainty* of their doom. **15.** (*Notes,* ch. 2:10, 31).

16. (Cf. Ezek. 38:18-22.) The victories of the Jews over their cruel foe Antiochus, under the Maccabees, may be a reference of this prophecy; but the ultimate reference is to the last Antichrist, of whom Antiochus was the type. Jerusalem being the central seat of the theocracy (Ps. 132:13), it is from thence that Jehovah discomfits the foe. **roar**—as a lion (Jer. 25:30; Amos 1:2; 3:8). Cf. as to Jehovah's voice thundering, Psalm 18:13; Habakkuk 3: 10, 11. **Lord ... the hope of his people**—or, "their refuge" (Ps. 46:1). **17. shall ye know**—experimentally by the proofs of favors which I shall vouchsafe to you. So "know" (Isa. 60:16; Hos. 2:20). **dwelling in Zion**—as peculiarly *your God.* **holy ... no strangers pass through**—to attack, or to defile, the holy city (Isa. 35:8; 52:1; Zech. 14:21). *Strangers,* or Gentiles, shall come to Jerusalem, but it shall be in order to worship Jehovah there (Zech. 14: 16). **18. mountains ... drop ... wine**—figurative for *abundance of vines,* which were cultivated in terraces of earth between the rocks on the sides of the hills of Palestine (Amos 9:13). **hills ... flow with milk**—i.e., they shall abound in flocks and herds yielding milk plentifully, through the richness of the pastures. **waters**—the great desideratum for fertility in the parched East (Isa. 30:25). **fountain ... of ... house of ... Lord ... water ... valley of Shittim**—The blessings, temporal and spiritual, issuing from Jehovah's house at Jerusalem, shall extend even to Shittim, on the border between Moab and Israel, beyond Jordan (Num. 25:1; 33:49; Josh. 2:1; Mic. 6:5). Shittim means "acacias," which grow only in arid regions: implying that even *the arid desert* shall be fertilized by the blessing from Jerusalem. So Ezekiel 47:1-12 describes the waters issuing from the threshold of the house as flowing into the Dead Sea, and purifying it. Also in Zechariah 14:8 the waters flow on one side into the Mediterranean, on the other side into the Dead Sea, near which latter Shittim was situated (cf. Ps. 46: 4; Rev. 22:1). **19. Edom**—It was subjugated by David, but revolted under Jehoram (II Chron. 21: 8-10); and at every subsequent opportunity tried to injure Judah. Egypt under Shishak spoiled Jerusalem under Rehoboam of the treasures of the temple and the king's house; subsequently to the captivity, it inflicted under the Ptolemies various injuries on Judea. Antiochus spoiled Egypt (Dan. 11:40-43). Edom was made "desolate" under the Maccabees (JOSEPHUS 12.11, 12). The low condition of the two countries for centuries proves the truth of the prediction (cf. Iša. 19:1, etc. Jer. 49:17; Obad. 10). So shall fare all the foes of Israel, typified by these two (Isa. 63:1, etc.). **20. dwell for ever**—(Amos 9:15), i.e., be established as a flourishing state. **21. cleanse ... blood ... not cleansed**—I will purge away from Judah the extreme guilt (represented by "blood," the shedding of which was the climax of her sin, Isa. 1:15) which was for long not purged away, but visited with judgments (Isa. 4:4). Messiah saves from guilt, in order to save from punishment (Matt. 1:21).

THE BOOK OF

AMOS

INTRODUCTION

AMOS (meaning in *Hebrew* "a burden") was (ch. 1:1) a shepherd of Tekoa, a small town of Judah, six miles southeast from Bethlehem, and twelve from Jerusalem, on the borders of the great desert (II Chron. 20:20; cf. 11:6, *ibid*). The region being sandy was more fit for pastoral than for agricultural purposes. Amos therefore owned and tended flocks, and collected sycamore figs; not that the former was a menial office, kings themselves, as Mesha of Moab (II Kings 3:4), exercising it. Amos, however (from ch. 7:14, 15), seems to have been of humble rank.

Though belonging to Judah, he was commissioned by God to exercise his prophetical function in Israel; as the latter kingdom abounded in impostors, and the prophets of God generally fled to Judah through fear of the kings of Israel, a true prophet from Judah was the more needed in it. His name is not to be confounded with that of Isaiah's father, Amoz.

The time of his prophesying was in the reigns of Uzziah king of Judea, and Jeroboam II, son of Joash, king of Israel (ch. 1:1), i.e., in part of the time in which the two kings were contemporary; probably in Jeroboam's latter years, after that monarch had recovered from Syria "the coast of Israel from the entering of Hamath to the sea of the plain" (II Kings 14:25-27); for Amos foretells that these same coasts, "from the entering in of Hamath unto the river of the wilderness," should be the scene of Israel's being afflicted (ch. 6:14); also his references to the state of luxurious security then existing (ch. 6:1, 4, 13), and to the speedy termination of it by the Assyrian foe (ch. 1:5; 3:12, 15; 5:27; 8:2), point to the latter part of Jeroboam's reign, which terminated in 784 B.C., the twenty-seventh year of Uzziah's reign, which continued down to 759 B.C.

He was contemporary with Hosea, only that the latter continued to prophesy in reigns subsequent to Uzziah (Hos. 1:1); whereas Amos ceased to prophesy in the reign of that monarch. The scene of his ministry was Beth-el, where the idol calves were set up (ch. 7:10-13). There his prophecies roused Amaziah, the idol priest, to accuse him of conspiracy and to try to drive him back to Judah.

The first six chapters are without figure; the last three symbolical, but with the explanation subjoined. He first denounces the neighboring peoples, then the Jews, then Israel (from ch. 3 to the end), closing with the promise or restoration under Messiah (ch. 9:11-15). His style is thought by JEROME to betray his humble origin; but though not sublime, it is regular, perspicuous, and energetic; his images are taken from the scenes in nature with which he was familiar; his rhythms are flowing, his parallelisms exact, and his descriptions minute and graphic. Some peculiar expressions occur: "cleanness of teeth," i.e., *want of bread* (ch. 4:6); "the excellency of Jacob" (ch. 6:8; 8:7); "the high places of Isaac" (ch. 7:9); "the house of Isaac" (ch. 7:16); "he that createth the wind" (ch. 4:13).

HENGSTENBERG draws an able argument for the genuineness of the Mosaic records from the evidence in Amos, that the existing institutions in Israel as well as Judah (excepting the calves of Jeroboam), were framed according to the Pentateuch rules.

Two quotations from Amos occur in the New Testament (cf. Acts 7:42, 43, with ch. 5:25, 26; and Acts 15:16, 17, with ch. 9:11).

PHILO, JOSEPHUS, MELITO's catalogue, JEROME, JUSTIN MARTYR (sec. 22, quoting the fifth and six chapters of Amos as "one of the twelve minor prophets"), and the 60th canon of the Laodicean council support the canonicity of the book of Amos.

CHAPTER 1

Vss. 1-15. GOD'S JUDGMENTS ON SYRIA, PHILISTIA, TYRE, EDOM, AND AMMON. **1. The words of Amos**—i.e., Amos' *oracular communications*. A heading found only in Jeremiah 1:1. **among the herdmen**—rather, "shepherds"; both owning and tending sheep; from an *Arabic* root, "to mark with pricks," viz., to select the best among a species of sheep and goats *ill-shapen and short-footed* (as others explain the name from an *Arabic* root), but distinguished by their wool [MAURER]. God chooses "the weak things of the world to confound the mighty," and makes a humble shepherd reprove the arrogance of Israel and her king arising from prosperity (cf. I Sam. 17:40). **which he saw**—in supernatural *vision* (Isa. 1:1). **two years before the earthquake**—mentioned in Zechariah 14:5. The earthquake occurred in Uzziah's reign, at the time of his being stricken with leprosy for usurping the priest's functions [JOSEPHUS, *Antiquities* 9. 10. 4].

This clause must have been inserted by Ezra and the compilers of the Jewish canon. **2. will roar**—as a lion (Joel 3:16). Whereas Jehovah is there represented roaring in Israel's behalf, here He roars against her (cf. Ps. 18:13; Jer. 25:30). **from Zion ... Jerusalem**—the seat of the theocracy, from which ye have revolted; not from Dan and Beth-el, the seat of your idolatrous worship of the calves. **habitations ... mourn**—poetical personification. Their *inhabitants* shall mourn, imparting a sadness to the very *habitations*. **Carmel**—the mountain promontory north of Israel, in Asher, abounding in rich pastures, olives, and vines. The name is the symbol of *fertility*. When Carmel itself "withers," how utter the desolation! (Song of Sol. 7:5; Isa. 33:9; 35:2; Jer. 50:19; Nah. 1:4). **3.** Here begins a series of threatenings of vengeance against six other states, followed by one against Judah, and ending with one against Israel, with whom the rest of the prophecy is occupied. The eight predictions are in symmetrical stanzas, each prefaced by "Thus saith the Lord." Beginning with the sin of others, which Israel would be ready enough to recognize, he proceeds to bring home to Israel her own guilt. Israel must not think hereafter, because she sees others visited similarly to herself, that such judgments are matters of chance; nay, they are divinely foreseen and foreordered, and are confirmations of the truth that God will not clear the guilty. If God spares not the nations that know not the truth, how much less Israel that sins wilfully (Luke 12:47, 48; Jas. 4:17)! **for three transgressions...and for four**—If Damascus had only sinned once or twice, I would have spared them, but since, after having been so often pardoned, they still persevere *so continually,* I will no longer *"turn away" their punishment.* The *Hebrew* is simply, "I will not reverse *it,"* viz., the sentence of punishment which follows; the negative expression implies more than it expresses; i.e., "I will *most surely execute* it"; God's fulfilment of His threats being more awful than human language can express. "Three and four" imply sin *multiplied on sin* (cf. Exod. 20:5; Prov. 30:15, 18, 21; "six and seven," Job 5:19; "once and twice," Job 33:14; "twice and thrice," *Margin;* "oftentimes," *English Version,* Job 33:29; "seven and also eight," Eccles. 11:2). There may be also a reference to *seven,* the product of *three* and *four* added; *seven* expressing the *full completion* of the measure of their guilt (Lev. 26: 18, 21, 24; cf. Matt. 23:32). **threshed**—the very term used of the Syrian king Hazael's oppression of Israel under Jehu and Jehoahaz (II Kings 10:32, 33; 13:7). The victims were thrown before the threshing-sledges, the teeth of which tore their bodies. So David to Ammon (II Sam. 12:31; cf. Isa. 28:27). **4. Hazael ... Ben-hadad**—A black marble obelisk found in the central palace of Nimroud, and now in the British Museum, is inscribed with the names of Hazael and Ben-hadad of Syria, as well as Jehu of Israel, mentioned as tributaries of "Shalmanubar," king of Assyria. The kind of tribute from Jehu is mentioned: gold, pearls, precious oil, etc. [G. V. Smith]. The Ben-hadad here is the son of Hazael (II Kings 13:3), not the Ben-hadad supplanted and slain by Hazael (II Kings 8:7, 15). The phrase, "I will send a fire," i.e., the flame of war (Ps. 78:63), occurs also in vss. 7, 10, 12, 14, and ch. 2:2, 5; Jeremiah 49:27; Hosea 8:14. **5. bar of Damascus**—i.e., the bar of its gates (cf. Jer. 51:30). **the inhabitant**—*singular* for *plural,* "inhabitants." Henderson, because of the parallel, "him that holdeth the scepter," translates, "the ruler." But the parallelism is that of one clause complementing the other, "the inhabitant" or *subject* here answering to "him that holdeth the scepter" or *ruler* there, both ruler and subject alike being cut off. **Aven**—the same as *Oon* or *Un,* a delightful valley, four hours' journey from Damascus, towards the desert. Proverbial in the East as a place of delight [Josephus Abassus]. It is here parallel to "Eden," which also means "pleasantness"; situated at Lebanon. As Josephus Abassus is a doubtful authority, perhaps the reference may be rather to the valley between Lebanon and Anti-Lebanon, called *El-Bekaa,* where are the ruins of the Baalbek temple of the sun; so the LXX renders it *On,* the same name as the city in Egypt bears, dedicated to the sun-worship (Gen. 41:45; *Margin,* Ezek. 30:17, *Heliopolis,* "the city of the sun"). It is termed by Amos "the valley of Aven," or "vanity," from the worship of idols in it. **Kir**—a region subject to Assyria (Isa. 22:6) in Iberia, the same as that called now in *Armenian Kur,* lying by the river Cyrus

which empties itself into the Caspian Sea. Tiglath-pileser fulfilled this prophecy when Ahaz applied for help to him against Rezin king of Syria, and the Assyrian king took Damascus, slew Rezin, and carried away its people captive to Kir. **6. Gaza**—the southernmost of the five capitals of the five divisions of Philistia, and the key to Palestine on the south: hence put for the whole Philistine nation. Uzziah commenced the fulfilment of this prophecy (see II Chron. 26:6). **because they carried away ...the whole captivity**—i.e., they left none. Cf. with the phrase here, Jeremiah 13:19, "Judah... carried captive *all* of it ... *wholly* carried away." Under Jehoram already the Philistines had carried away all the substance of the king of Judah, and his wives and his sons, "so that there was never a son left to him, save Jehoahaz"; and after Amos' time (if the reference includes the *future,* which to the prophet's eye is as if already done), under Ahaz (II Chron. 28:18), they seized on all the cities and villages of the low country and south of Judah. **to deliver them up to Edom**—Judah's bitterest foe; as slaves (vs. 9; cf. Joel 3:1, 3, 6). Grotius refers it to the fact (Isa. 16:4) that on Sennacherib's invasion of Judah, many fled for refuge to neighboring countries; the Philistines, instead of hospitably sheltering the refugees, sold them, as if captives in war, to their enemies, the Idumeans. **7. fire**—i.e., the flame of war (Num. 21:28; Isa. 26:11). Hezekiah fulfilled the prophecy, smiting the Philistines unto Gaza (II Kings 18:8). Foretold also by Isaiah 14: 29, 31. **8. Ashdod...**—Gath alone is not mentioned of the five chief Philistine cities. It had already been subdued by David; and it, as well as Ashdod, was taken by Uzziah (II Chron. 26:6). Gath perhaps had lost its position as one of the five primary cities before Amos uttered this prophecy, whence arose his omission of it. So Zephaniah 2:4, 5. Cf. Jeremiah 47:4; Ezekiel 25:16. Subsequently to the subjugation of the Philistines by Uzziah, and then by Hezekiah, they were reduced by Psammetichus of Egypt, Nebuchadnezzar, the Persians, Alexander, and lastly the Asmoneans. **9. Tyrus ... delivered up the ... captivity to Edom**—the same charge as against the Philistines (vs. 6). **remembered not the brotherly covenant**—the league of Hiram of Tyre with David and Solomon, the former supplying cedars for the building of the temple and king's house in return for oil and corn (II Sam. 5:11; I Kings 5: 2-6; 9:11-14, 27; 10-22; I Chron. 14:1; II Chron. 8: 18; 9:10). **10. fire**—(Cf. vss. 4, 7; *Notes,* Isa. 23: Ezek. 26, 27, and 28). Many parts of Tyre were burnt by fiery missiles of the Chaldeans under Nebuchadnezzar. Alexander of Macedon subsequently overthrew it. **11. Edom ... did pursue his brother**—(Isa. 34:5). The chief aggravation to Edom's violence against Israel was that they both came from the same parents, Isaac and Rebekah (cf. Gen. 25:24-26; Deut. 23:7, 8; Obad. 10, 12; Mal. 1:2). **cast off all pity**—lit., "destroy compassions," i.e., did suppress all the natural feeling of pity for a brother in distress. **his wrath for ever**—As Esau kept up his grudge against Jacob, for having twice supplanted him, viz., as to the birthright and the blessing (Gen. 27:41), so Esau's posterity against Israel (Num. 20:14, 21). Edom first showed his spite in not letting Israel pass through his borders when coming from the wilderness, but threatening to "come out against him with the sword"; next, when the Syrians attacked Jerusalem under Ahaz (cf. II Chron. 28:17, with II Kings 16:5); next, when Nebuchadnezzar assailed Jerusalem (Ps. 137:7, 8). In each case Edom chose the day of Israel's calamity for venting his grudge. This is the point of Edom's guilt dwelt on in Obadiah 10-13. God punishes the children, not for the sin of their fathers, but for their own filling up the measure of their fathers' guilt, as children generally follow in the steps of, and even exceed, their fathers' guilt (cf. Exod. 20:5). **12. Teman**—a city of Edom, called from a grandson of Esau (Gen. 36:11, 15; Obad. 8, 9); situated five miles from Petra; south of the present Wady Musa. Its people were famed for wisdom (Jer. 49:7). **Bozrah**—a city of Edom (Isa. 63:1). Selah or Petra is not mentioned, as it had been overthrown by Amaziah (II Kings 14:7). **13. Ammon**—The Ammonites under Nahash attacked Jabesh-gilead and refused to accept the offer of the latter to save them, unless the Jabesh-gileadites would put out all their right eyes (I Sam. 11:1, etc.). Saul rescued Jabesh-gilead. The Ammonites joined the Chaldeans in their invasion of Judea for the sake of plunder. **ripped up ... women with child**—as Hazael of Syria also did (II Kings 8:12; cf. Hos. 13:16). Ammon's object in this cruel act was to leave Israel without "heir," so as to seize on Israel's inheritance (Jer. 49:1). **14. Rabbah**—the capital of Ammon: meaning "the Great." Distinct from Rabbah of Moab. Called *Philadelphia,* afterwards, from Ptolemy Philadelphus. **tempest**—i.e., with an onset swift, sudden, and resistless as a *hurricane.* **day of the whirlwind**—parallel to "the day of battle"; therefore meaning "the day of the foe's *tumultuous assault."* **15. their king ... princes**—or else, "their Molech [the idol of Ammon] and his priests" [Grotius and LXX]. Isaiah 43:28 so uses "princes" for *priests.* So ch. 5:26, "your Molech"; and Jeremiah 49:3, *Margin.* English Version, however, is perhaps preferable both here and in Jeremiah 49:3; see *Notes* there.

CHAPTER 2

Vss. 1-16. Charges against Moab, Judah, and Lastly Israel, the Chief Subject of Amos' Prophecies. **1. burned ... bones of ... king of Edom into lime**—When Jehoram of Israel, Jehoshaphat of Judah, and the king of Edom, combined against Mesha king of Moab, the latter failing in battle to break through to the king of Edom, took the oldest son of the latter and offered him as a burnt offering on the wall (II Kings 3:27) [Michaelis]. Thus, *"king* of Edom" is taken as *the heir to the throne of Edom.* But "his son" is rather the *king of Moab's own son,* whom the father offered to Molech [Josephus, *Antiquities,* 9. 3]. Thus the reference here in Amos is not to that fact, but to the revenge which probably the king of Moab took on the king of Edom, when the forces of Israel and Judah had retired after their successful campaign against Moab, leaving Edom without allies. The Hebrew tradition is that Moab in revenge tore from their grave and burned the bones of the king of Edom, the ally of Jehoram and Jehoshaphat, who was already buried. Probably the "burning of the bones" means, "he burned the king of Edom alive, reducing his very bones to lime" [Maurer]. **2. Kirioth**—the chief city of Moab, called also Kir-Moab (Isa. 15:1). The form is *plural* here, as including both the acropolis and town itself (see Jer. 48:24, 41, *Margin*). **die with tumult**—i.e., amid the tumult of battle (Hos. 10:14). **3. the judge**—the chief magistrate, the supreme source of justice. "King" not being used, it seems likely a change of government had been before this time substituted for

kings, supreme *judges.* **4. From foreign kingdoms** he passes to Judah and Israel, lest it should be said, he was strenuous in denouncing sins abroad, but connived at those of his own nation. Judah's guilt differs from that of all the others, in that it was directly against God, not merely against man. Also because Judah's sin was wilful and wittingly against light and knowledge. **law**—the Mosaic code in general. **commandments**—or *statutes,* the ceremonies and civil laws. **their lies**—their lying idols (Ps. 40:4; Jer. 16:19), from which they drew false hopes. The order is to be observed. The Jews first cast off the divine *law,* then fall into *lying errors;* God thus visiting them with a righteous retribution (Rom. 1:25, 26, 28; II Thess. 2:11, 12). The pretext of a *good intention* is hereby refuted: the "lies" that mislead them are *"their* [own] lies" [Calvin]. **after ... which their fathers ... walked**—We are not to follow the fathers in error, but must follow the word of God alone. It was an aggravation of the Jews' sin that it was not confined to preceding generations; the sins of the sons rivalled those of their fathers (Matt. 23:32; Acts 7:51) [Calvin]. **5. a fire** —Nebuchadnezzar. **6. Israel**—the ten tribes, the main subject of Amos' prophecies. **sold the righteous**—Israel's judges for a bribe are induced to condemn in judgment him who has a righteous cause; in violation of Deuteronomy 16:19. **the poor for a pair of shoes**—lit., "sandals" of wood, secured on the foot by leather straps; less valuable than shoes. Cf. the same phrase, for "the most paltry bribe," ch. 8:6; Ezekiel 13:19; Joel 3:3. They were not driven by poverty to such a sin; beginning with suffering themselves to be tempted by a large bribe, they at last are so reckless of all shame as to prostitute justice for the merest trifle. Amos convicts them of injustice, incestuous unchastity, and oppression first, as these were so notorious that they could not deny them, before he proceeds to reprove their contempt of God, which they would have denied on the ground that they worshipped God in the form of the calves. **7. pant after ... dust of ... earth on ... head of ... poor**—i.e., eagerly thirst for this object, by their oppression to prostrate the poor so as to cast the dust on their heads in mourning on the earth (cf. II Sam. 1:2; Job 2:12; Ezek. 27:30). **turn aside ... way of ... meek**—pervert their cause (ch. 5:12; Job 24:4 [Grotius]; Isa. 10:2). **a man and his father**—a crime "not so much as named among the Gentiles" (I Cor. 5:1). When God's people sin in the face of light, they often fall lower than even those who know not God. **go in unto the same maid**—from vs. 8 it seems likely "the damsel" meant is one of the prostitutes attached to the idol Astarte's temple: prostitution being part of her filthy worship. **to profane my ... name**—Israel in such abominations, as it were, *designedly* seeks to insult God. **8. lay themselves ... upon clothes laid to pledge**—the *outer garment,* which Exodus 22:25-27 ordered to be restored to the poor man before sunset, as being his only covering. It aggravated the crime that they lay on these clothes in an idol temple. **by every altar**—They partook in a recumbent posture of their idolatrous feasts; the ancients being in the habit of reclining at full length in eating, the upper part of the body resting on the left elbow, not sitting as we do. **drink ... wine of the condemned**—i.e., wine bought with the money of those whom they unjustly fined. **9. Yet** —My former benefits to you heighten your ingratitude. **the Amorite**—the most powerful of all the Canaanite nations, and therefore put for them all (Gen. 15:16; 48:22; Deut. 1:20; Josh. 7:7).

height . . . like . . . cedars–(Num. 13:32, 33). **destroyed his fruit. . . above . . . roots . . . beneath**–i.e., destroyed him *utterly* (Job 18:16; Ezek. 17:9; Mal. 4:1). **10. brought you up from . . . Egypt**–"brought up" is the phrase, as Egypt was low and flat, and Canaan hilly. **to possess the land of the Amorite** –The Amorites strictly occupied both sides of the Jordan and the mountains afterward possessed by Judah; but they here, as in vs. 9, stand for *all* the Canaanites. God kept Israel forty years in the wilderness, which tended to discipline them in His statutes, so as to be the better fitted for entering on the possession of Canaan. **11.** Additional obligations under which Israel lay to God; the *prophets* and *Nazarites,* appointed by Him, to furnish religious instruction and examples of holy self-restraint. **of your young men**–It was a specimen of Israel's highly favored state, that, of the class most addicted to pleasures, God chose those who by a solemn vow bound themselves to abstinence from all produce of the vine, and from all ceremonial and moral defilement. The Nazarite was not to shave (Num. 6:2, etc.). God left nothing undone to secure the purity of their worship and their faithfulness to it (Lam. 4:7). The same comes from a *Hebrew* root, *nazar,* "to set apart." Samson, Samuel, and John the Baptist were Nazarites. **Is it not even thus**–Will any of you dare to deny it is so? **12.** Ye so despised these My favors, as to tempt the Nazarite to break his vow; and forbade the prophets prophesying (Isa. 30:10). So Amaziah forbade Amos (ch. 7:12, 13, 14). **13. I am pressed under you**–so CALVIN (cf. Isa. 1:14). *Margin* translates actively, "I will depress your place," i.e., "I will make it narrow," a metaphor for *afflicting* a people; the opposite of *enlarging,* i.e., relieving (Ps. 4:1; Prov. 4:12). MAURER translates, "I will press you *down*" (not as *Margin,* "your place"; so the *Hebrew,* Job 40:12; or vs. 7 in *Hebrew* text). Amos, as a shepherd, appropriately draws his similes from rustic scenes. **14. flight shall perish from . . . swift** –Even the swift shall not be able to escape. **strong shall not strengthen his force**–i.e., shall not be able to use his strength. **himself**–lit., "his life." **16. flee . . . naked**–If any escape, it must be with the loss of accoutrements, and all that would impede rapid flight. They must be content with saving their life alone.

CHAPTER 3

Vss. 1-15. GOD'S EXTRAORDINARY LOVE, BEING REPAID BY ISRAEL WITH INGRATITUDE, OF NECESSITY CALLS FOR JUDGMENTS, WHICH THE PROPHETS ANNOUNCE, NOT AT RANDOM, BUT BY GOD'S COMMISSION, WHICH THEY CANNOT BUT FULFIL. THE OPPRESSION PREVALENT IN ISRAEL WILL BRING DOWN RUIN ON ALL SAVE A SMALL REMNANT. **1. children of Israel**–not merely the ten tribes, but "the *whole family* brought up from Egypt"; all the descendants of Jacob, including Judah and Benjamin. Cf. Jeremiah 8:3, and Micah 2:3, on "family" for the nation However, as the prophecy following refers to the ten tribes, *they* must be chiefly, if not solely, meant: they were the majority of the nation; and so Amos concedes what they so often boasted, that they were the elect people of God [CALVIN], *but* implies that this only heightens their sins. **2. You only have I known**–i.e., acknowledged as My people, and treated with peculiar favor (Exod. 19:5; Deut. 4:20). Cf. the use of "know," Psalm 1:6; 144:3; John 10:14; II Timothy 2:19. **therefore I will punish**–the

greater the privileges, the heavier the punishment for the abuse of them; for to the other offenses there is added, in this case, ingratitude. When God's people do not glorify Him, He glorifies Himself by punishing them. **3.** Here follow several questions of a parable-like kind, to awaken conviction in the people. **Can two walk together, except they be agreed?**–Can God's prophets be so unanimous in prophesying against you, if God's Spirit were not joined with them, or if their prophecies were false? The Israelites were "at ease," not believing that God was with the prophets in their denunciations of coming ruin to the nation (ch. 6:1, 3; cf. I Kings 22:18, 24, 27; Jer. 43:2). This accords with vss. 7, 8. So "I will be with thy mouth" (Exod. 4:12; Jer. 1:8; Matt. 10:20). If the prophets and God were not agreed, the former could not predict the future as they do. In ch. 2:12 He had said, the Israelites forbade the prophets prophesying; therefore, in vss. 3, 8, He asserts the agreement between the prophets and God who spake by them against Israel [ROSENMULLER]. Rather, I once walked with you (Lev. 26:12) as a Father and Husband (Isa. 54:5; Jer. 3:14); but now your way and Mine are utterly diverse; there can therefore be no fellowship between us such as there was (vs. 2); I will walk with you only to "punish you"; as a "lion" walks with his "prey" (vs. 4), as a bird-catcher with a bird [TARNOVIUS]. The prophets, and all servants of God, can have no fellowship with the ungodly (Ps. 119:63; II Cor. 6:16, 17; Eph. 5:11; Jas. 4:4). **4.** The same idea as in Matthew 34:28. Where a corrupt nation is, there God's instruments of punishment are sure also to be. The lion roars loudly only when he has prey in sight. **Will a young lion cry out . . . if he**–the "lion," not the "young lion"– **have taken nothing?**–The young lion just weaned lies silent, until the old lion brings the prey near; then the scent rouses him. So, the prophet would not speak against Israel, if God did not reveal to him Israel's sins as requiring punishment. **5.** When a bird trying to fly upwards is made to fall upon the earth-snare, it is a plain proof that the snare is there; so, Israel, now that thou art falling, infer thence, that it is in the snare of the divine judgment that thou art entangled [LUDOVICUS DE DIEU]. **shall one take up a snare from the earth, and have taken nothing**–The bird-catcher does not remove his snare off the ground till he has caught some prey; so God will not withdraw the Assyrians, etc., the instruments of punishment, until they have had the success against you which God gives them. The foe corresponds to the "snare," suddenly *springing* from the ground and enclosing the bird on the latter touching it; the *Hebrew* is lit., "Shall the snare *spring* from the earth?" Israel entangled in judgments answers to the bird "taken." **6.** When the sound of alarm is trumpeted by the watchman in the city, the people are sure to *run to and fro in alarm (Hebrew* lit.). Yet Israel is not alarmed, though God threatens judgments. **shall there be evil in a city, and the Lord hath not done it?**–This is the explanation of the preceding similes: God is the Author of all the calamities which come upon you, and which are foretold by His prophets. The evil of sin is from ourselves; the evil of trouble is from God, whoever be the instruments. **7. his secret**–viz., His purpose hidden from all, until it is revealed to His prophets (cf. Gen. 18:17). In a wider sense, God's will is revealed to all who love God, which it is not to the world (Ps. 25:14; John 15:15; 17:25, 26). **unto his servants**–who being *servants* cannot but obey their Lord in setting forth His purpose (viz., that of judgment against Israel) (Jer. 20:9; Ezek. 9: 11). Therefore the fault which the ungodly find with them is groundless (I Kings 18:17). It aggravates Israel's sin, that God is not about to inflict judgment, without having fully warned the people, if haply they might repent. **8.** As when "the lion roars" (cf. ch. 1:2; and vs. 4 above), none can help but "fear," so when Jehovah communicates His awful message, the prophet cannot but prophesy. Find not fault with me for prophesying; I must obey God. In a wider sense true of all believers (Acts 4:20; 5:29). **9. Publish in ... palaces**—as being places of greatest resort (cf. Matt. 10:27); and also as it is the sin of *princes* that he arraigns, he calls on princes (the occupants of the "palaces") to be the witnesses. **Ashdod**—put for all Philistia. Convene the Philistine and the Egyptian magnates, from whom I have on various occasions rescued Israel. (The opposite formula to "Tell it not in Gath," viz., lest the heathen should glory over Israel). Even these idolaters, in looking on your enormities, will condemn you; how much more will the holy God? **upon the mountains of Samaria**—on the hills surrounding and commanding the view of Samaria, the metropolis of the ten tribes, which was on a lower hill (ch. 4:1; I Kings 16:24). The mountains are to be the tribunal on which the Philistines and Egyptians are to sit aloft to have a view of your crimes, so as to testify to the justice of your punishment (vs. 13). **tumults**—caused by the violence of the princes of Israel in "oppressions" of the poor (Job 35:9; Eccles. 4:1). **10. know not to do**—Their moral corruption blinds their power of discernment so that they cannot do right (Jer. 4:22). Not simple intellectual ignorance; the defect lay in the heart and will. **store up violence and robbery**—i.e., treasures obtained by "violence and robbery" (Prov. 10:2). **11.** Translate, "An adversary [the abruptness produces a startling effect]! *and that too,* from every side of the land." So in the fulfilment, II Kings 17:5: "The king of Assyria [Shalmaneser] came up *throughout all the land,* and went up to Samaria, and besieged it three years." **bring down thy strength from thee**—i.e., bring thee down from thy strength (the strength on which thou didst boast thyself): all thy resources (Prov. 10:15). **palaces shall be spoiled**—a just retribution in kind (vs. 10). *The palaces* in which spoils of *robbery* were *stored up,* "shall be spoiled." **12. shepherd**—a pastoral image, appropriately used by Amos, a shepherd himself. **piece of ... ear**—brought by the shepherd to the owner of the sheep, so as not to have to pay for the loss (Gen. 31:39; Exod. 22:13). So if aught of Israel escapes, it shall be a miracle of God's goodness. It shall be but a scanty remnant. There is a kind of goat in the East the ears of which are a foot long, and proportionally broad. Perhaps the reference is to this. Cf. on the image I Samuel 17:34, 35; II Timothy 4:17. **that dwell in Samaria in the corner of a bed**—i.e., that live luxuriously in Samaria (cf. ch. 6:1, 4). "A bed" means here the Oriental divan, a raised part of the room covered with cushions. **in Damascus in a couch**—Jeroboam II had lately restored Damascus to Israel (II Kings 14:25, 28). So the Israelites are represented as not merely in "the corner of a bed," as in Samaria, but "in a [whole] couch," at Damascus, living in luxurious ease. Of these, now so luxurious, soon but a remnant shall be left by the foe. The destruction of Damascus and that of Samaria shall be conjoined; as here their luxurious lives, and subsequently under Pekah and Rezin their inroads on Judah, were combined (Isa. 7:1-8; 8:4, 9; 17:3). The parallelism

of "Samaria" to "Damascus," and LXX favor *English Version* rather than Gesenius: "on a *damask* couch." The *Hebrew* pointing, though generally expressing *damask,* may express the city "Damascus"; and many MSS. point it so. Cf. for Israel's overthrow, II Kings 17:5, 6; 18:9-12. **13. testify in the house ...**—i.e., *against* the house of Jacob. God calls on the same persons as in vs. 9, viz., the heathen Philistines and the Egyptians to witness with their own eyes Samaria's corruptions above described, so that none may be able to deny the justice of Samaria's punishment [Maurer]. **God of hosts**—having all the powers of heaven and earth at His command, and therefore One calculated to strike terror into the hearts of the guilty whom He threatens. **14. That**—rather, "since," or "for." This verse is not, as *English Version* translates, the thing which the witnesses cited are to "testify" (vs. 13), but the reason why God calls on the heathen to witness Samaria's guilt; viz., in order to justify the punishment which He declares He will inflict. **I will also visit ... Beth-el**—the golden calves which were the source of all "the transgressions of Israel" (I Kings 12:32; 13:2; II Kings 23:15, 16), though Israel thought that by them their transgressions were atoned for and God's favor secured. **horns of the altar**—which used to be sprinkled with the blood of victims. They were horn-like projecting points at the corners of ancient altars. The *singular,* "altar," refers to the great altar erected by Jeroboam to the calves. The "altars," *plural,* refer to the lesser ones made in imitation of the great one (II Chron. 34:5, cf. with I Kings 13:2; Hos. 8: 11;; 10:1). **15. winter ... summer house**—(Judg. 3: 20; Jer. 36:22). Winter houses of the great were in sheltered positions facing the south to get all possible sunshine, summer houses in forests and on hills, facing the east and north. **houses of ivory**—having their walls, doors, and ceilings inlaid with ivory. So Ahab's house (I Kings 22:39; Ps. 45:8).

CHAPTER 4

Vss. 1-13. Denunciation of Israel's Nobles for Oppression; and of the Whole Nation for Idolatry; and for Their Being Unreformed Even by God's Judgments: Therefore They Must Prepare for the Last and Worst Judgment of All. 1. kine of Bashan—fat and wanton cattle such as the rich pasture of Bashan (east of Jordan, between Hermon and Gilead) was famed for (Deut. 32:14; Ps. 22:12; Ezek. 39:18). Figurative for those luxurious nobles mentioned, ch. 3:9, 10, 12, 15. The feminine, *kine,* or *cows,* not *bulls,* expresses their effeminacy. This accounts for masculine forms in the *Hebrew* being intermixed with feminine; the latter being figurative, the former the real persons meant. **say to their masters**—i.e., to *their king,* with whom the princes indulged in potations (Hos. 7:5), and whom here they importune for more wine. "Bring" is *singular,* in the *Hebrew* implying that *one* "master" alone is meant. **2. The Lord**—the same *Hebrew* as "masters" (vs. 1). Israel's nobles say to their master or lord, Bring us drink: but "the Lord" of him and them "hath sworn ...." **by his holiness**—which binds Him to punish the guilty (Ps. 89:35). **he will take you away**—i.e., God by the instrumentality of the enemy. **with hooks**—lit., "thorns" (cf.II Chron. 33:11). As fish are taken out of the water by hooks, so the Israelites are to be taken out of their cities by the enemy (Ezek. 29: 4; cf. Job 41:1, 2; Jer. 16:16; Hab. 1:15). The image is the more appropriate, as anciently captives were led by their conquerors by a hook made to pass through the nose (II Kings 19:28), as is to be seen in the Assyrian remains. **3. go out at the breaches**—viz., of the city walls broken by the enemy. **every** cow at that which is **before her**—figurative for *the once luxurious nobles* (cf. vs. 1, "kine of Bashan") shall go out *each one right before her; not through the gates, but each at the breach before him,* not turning to the right or left, apart from one another. **ye shall cast** them **into the palace**—"them," i.e., "your posterity," from vs. 2. You yourselves shall escape through the breaches, after having cast your little children into the palace, so as not to see their destruction, and to escape the more quickly. Rather, "ye shall cast *yourselves* into the palace," so as to escape from it out of the city [CALVIN]. The palace, the scene of the princes' riots (ch. 3:10, 15; 4:1), is to be the scene of their ignominious flight. Cf. in the similar case of *Jerusalem's* capture, the king's escape by way of the palace, through a breach in the wall (Ezek. 12:5, 12). GESENIUS translates, "Ye shall be cast [as captives] into the [enemy's] stronghold"; in this view, the enemy's stronghold is called "palace," in retributive contrast to the "palaces" of Israel's nobles, the *store houses* of their *robberies* (ch. 3:10). **4.** God gives them up to their self-willed idolatry, that they may see how unable their idols are to save them from their coming calamities. So Ezekiel 20: 39. **Beth-el**—(ch. 3:14). **Gilgal**—(Hos. 4:15; 9:15; 12:11). **sacrifices every morning**—as commanded in the law (Num. 28:3, 4). They imitated the letter, while violating by calf worship the spirit, of the Jerusalem temple worship. **after three years**—every third year; lit., "after three [years of] days" (i.e., the fullest complement of days, or *a year*); "after three *full* years." Cf. Leviticus 25:20; Judges 17:10, and "the days" for the *years,* Joel 1:2. So *a month of days* is used for *a full month,* wanting no day to complete it (*Margin,* Gen. 29:14; Num. 11:20, 21). The Israelites here also kept to the letter of the law in bringing in the tithes of their increase every third year (Deut. 14:28; 26:12). **5. offer**—lit., "burn incense"; i.e., "offer a sacrifice of thanksgiving with *burnt incense* and with leavened bread." The frankincense was laid on the meat offering, and taken by the priest from it to burn on the altar (Lev. 2:1, 2, 8-11). Though *unleavened cakes* were to accompany the peace offering sacrifice of animals, *leavened bread* was also commanded (Lev. 7:12, 13), but not as a "meat offering" (Lev. 2:11). **this liketh you**—i.e., this is what ye like. **6-11.** Jehovah details His several chastisements inflicted with a view to reclaiming them: but adds to each the same sad result, "yet have ye not returned unto Me" (Isa. 9:13; Jer. 5:3; Hos. 7:10); the monotonous repetion of the same burden marking their pitiable obstinacy. **cleanness of teeth**—explained by the parallel, "want of bread." The famine alluded to is that mentioned in II Kings 8:1 [GROTIUS]. Where there is no food to masticate, the teeth are free from uncleanness, but it is the cleanness of want. Cf. Proverbs 14:4, "Where no oxen are, the crib is clean." So spiritually, where all is outwardly smooth and clean, it is often because there is no solid religion. Better fighting and fears with real piety, than peace and respectable decorum without spiritual life. **7. withholden . . . rain . . . three months to . . . harvest** —the time when rain was most needed, and when usually "the latter rain" fell, viz., in spring, the latter half of February, and the whole of March and April (Hos. 6:3; Joel 2:23). The drought meant is that

mentioned in I Kings 17:1 [GROTIUS]. **rain upon one city . . . not . . . upon another**—Any rain that fell was only partial. **8. three cities wandered**—i.e., *the inhabitants of* three cities (cf. Jer. 14:1-6). GROTIUS explains this verse and vs. 7, "The rain fell on neighboring countries, but not on Israel, which marked the drought to be, not accidental, but the special judgment of God." The Israelites were obliged to leave their cities and homes to seek water at a distance [CALVIN]. **9. blasting**—the blighting influence of the east wind on the corn (Gen. 41:6). **when . . . gardens . . . increased**—In vain ye multiplied your gardens, etc., for I destroyed their produce. BOCHART supports *Margin,* "the *multitude* of your gardens." **palmer worm**—A species of *locust* is here meant, hurtful to fruits of trees, not to herbage or corn. The same east wind which brought the drought, blasting, and mildew, brought also the locusts into Judea [BOCHART], (Exod. 10:13). **10. pestilence after the manner of Egypt**—such as I formerly sent on the Egyptians (Exod. 9:3, 8, etc.; 12:29; Deut. 28:27, 60). Cf. the same phrase, Isaiah 10:24. **have taken away your horses**—lit., "accompanied with the captivity of your horses"; I have given up your young men to be slain, and their horses to be taken by the foe (cf. II Kings 13:7). **stink of your camps**—i.e., of your slain men (cf. Isa. 34:3; Joel 2:20). **to come up unto your nostrils**—The *Hebrew* is more emphatic, "to come up, *and that* unto your nostrils." **11. some of you**—some parts of your territory. **as God overthrew Sodom** —(Deut. 29:23; Isa. 13:19; Jer. 49:18; 50:40; II Peter 2:6; Jude 7). "God" is often repeated in *Hebrew* instead of *"I."* The earthquake here apparently alluded to is not that in the reign of Uzziah, which occurred "two years" later (ch. 1:1). Traces of earthquakes and volcanic agency abound in Palestine. The allusion here is to some of the effects of these in previous times. Cf. the prophecy, Deuteronomy 28:15-68, with vss. 6-11 here. **as a firebrand plucked out of . . . burning**—(Cf. Isa. 7:4; Zech. 3:2). The phrase is proverbial for a narrow escape from utter extinction. Though Israel revived as a nation under Jeroboam II, it was but for a time, and that after an almost utter destruction previously (II Kings 14:26). **12. Therefore**—as all chastisements have failed to make thee "return unto Me." **thus will I do unto thee**—as I have threatened (vss. 2, 3). **prepare to meet thy God**—God is about to inflict the last and worst judgment on thee, the extinction of thy nationality; consider then what preparation thou canst make for encountering Him as thy foe (Jer. 46:14; Luke 14:31, 32). But as that would be madness to think of (Isa. 27:4; Ezek. 22: 14; Heb. 10:31), see what can be done towards mitigating the severity of the coming judgment, by penitence (Isa. 27:5; I Cor. 11:31). This latter exhortation is followed up in ch. 5:4, 6, 8, 14, 15. **13.** The God whom Israel is to "prepare to meet" (vs. 12) is here described in sublime terms. **wind**—not as *Margin,* "spirit." The God with whom thou hast to do is the Omnipotent Maker of things *seen,* such as the stupendous mountains, and of things *too subtle* to be seen, though of powerful agency, as the "wind." **declareth unto man . . . his thought**—(Ps. 139:2). Ye think that your secret thoughts escape My cognizance, but I am the searcher of hearts. **maketh . . . morning darkness**—(ch. 5:8; 8:9). Both literally turning the sunshine into darkness, and figuratively turning the prosperity of the ungodly into sudden adversity (Ps. 73:12, 18, 19; cf. Jer. 13: 16). **treadeth upon . . . high places**—God treadeth down the proud of the earth. He subjects to Him all things however high they be (Mic. 1:3). Cf. Deuteronomy 32:13; 33:29, where the same phrase is used of God's people, elevated by God above every other human height.

CHAPTER 5

Vss. 1-27. ELEGY OVER THE PROSTRATE KINGDOM: RENEWED EXHORTATIONS TO REPENTANCE: GOD DECLARES THAT THE COMING DAY OF JUDGMENT SHALL BE TERRIBLE TO THE SCORNERS WHO DESPISE IT: CEREMONIAL SERVICES ARE NOT ACCEPTABLE TO HIM WHERE TRUE PIETY EXISTS NOT: ISRAEL SHALL THEREFORE BE REMOVED FAR EASTWARD. **1. lamentation**—an elegy for the destruction coming on you. Cf. Ezekiel 32:2, "take up," viz., as a mournful *burden* (Ezek. 19:1; 27:2). **2. virgin of Israel**—the Israelite state heretofore unsubdued by foreigners. Cf. Isaiah 23:12; Jeremiah 18:13; 31:4, 21; Lamentations 2:13; may be interpreted, Thou who wast once the "virgin daughter of Zion." Rather, "virgin" as applied to a state implies its beauty, and the delights on which it prides itself, its luxuries, power, and wealth [CALVIN]. **no more rise**—in the existing order of things: in the Messianic dispensation it is to rise again, according to many prophecies. Cf. II Kings 6:23; 24:7, for the restricted sense of "no more." **forsaken upon her land**—or, "prostrated upon . . ." (cf. Ezek. 29:5; 32:4) [MAURER]. **3. went out by a thousand**—i.e., "the city from which there used to go out a thousand" equipped for war. "City" is put for "the inhabitants of the city," as in ch. 4:8. **shall leave ... hundred**—shall have only a hundred left, the rest being destroyed by sword and pestilence (Deut. 28:62). **4. Seek ye me, and ye shall live**—lit., "Seek...Me, and live." The second imperative expresses the *certainty* of "life" (escape from judgment) resulting from obedience to the precept in the first imperative. If they perish, it is their own fault; God would forgive, if they would repent (Isa. 55:3, 6). **5. seek not Beth-el**—i.e., the calves at Beth-el. **Gilgal**—(*Note*, ch. 4:4). **Beer-sheba**—in Judah on the southern frontier towards Edom. Once "the well of the oath" by Jehovah, ratifying Abraham's covenant with Abimelech, and the scene of his calling on "the Lord, the everlasting God" (Gen. 21:31, 33), now a stronghold of idolatry (ch. 8:14). **Gilgal shall surely go into captivity**—a play on similar sounds in the *Hebrew, Gilgal, galoh, yigleh:* "Gilgal (the place of *rolling*) shall rolling be rolled away." **Beth-el shall come to naught**—Beth-el (i.e., the "house of God"), called because of its vain idols Beth-aven (i.e., "the house of vanity," or "naught," Hos. 4:15; 10:5, 8), shall indeed "come to naught." **6. break out like fire**—bursting through everything in His way. God is "a consuming fire" (Deut. 4:24; Isa. 10:17; Lam. 2:3). **the house of Joseph**—the kingdom of Israel, of which the tribe of Ephraim, Joseph's son, was the chief tribe (cf. Ezek. 37:16). **none to quench it in Beth-el**—i.e., none in Beth-el to quench it; none of the Beth-el idols on which Israel so depended, able to remove the divine judgments. **7. turn judgment to wormwood**—i.e., pervert it to most bitter wrong. As justice is sweet, so injustice is bitter to the injured. "Wormwood" is from a *Hebrew* root, to "execrate," on account of its noxious and bitter qualities. **leave on righteousness in ... earth**—MAURER translates, "*cast* righteousness *to the ground*," as in Isaiah 28:2; Daniel 8:12. **8. the seven stars**—lit., the *heap* or cluster of *seven* larger stars and others smaller (Job 9:9; 38:31). The

former whole passage seems to have been in Amos' mind. He names the stars well known to shepherds (to which class Amos belonged), Orion as the precursor of the tempests which are here threatened, and the Pleiades as ushering in spring. **shadow of death**—Hebraism for *the densest darkness.* **calleth for the waters of the sea**—both to send *deluges* in judgment, and the ordinary *rain* in mercy (I Kings 18:44). **9. strengtheneth the spoiled**—lit., "spoil" or "devastation": hence the "person spoiled." WINER, MAURER, and the best modern critics translate, "*maketh devastation* (or *destruction*) *suddenly to arise,*" lit., maketh it to gleam forth like the dawn. Ancient versions support *English Version.* The *Hebrew* is elsewhere used, *to make, to shine, to make glad:* and as *English Version* here (Ps. 39:13), "recover *strength.*" **the spoiled shall come**—"devastation," or "destruction shall come upon" [MAURER]. *English Version* expresses that, strong as Israel fancies herself after the successes of Jeroboam II (I Kings 14:25), even the *weakest* can be made by God to prevail against the strong. **10. him that rebuketh in the gate**—the *judge* who condemns their iniquity *in the place of judgment* (Isaiah 29:21). **abhor him that speaketh uprightly**—the *prophet* telling them the unwelcome truth: answering in the parallelism to the *judge* "that rebuketh in the gate" (cf. I Kings 22:8; Prov. 9:8; 12:1; Jer. 36:23). **11. burdens of wheat**—*burdensome taxes* levied in kind from the *wheat* of the needy, to pamper the lusts of the great [HENDERSON]. Or wheat advanced in time of scarcity, and exacted again at a burdensome interest [RABBI SALOMON]. **built houses ... but not dwell in them ... vineyards, ... but not drink wine of them**—according to the original prophecy of Moses (Deut. 28:30, 38, 39). The converse shall be true in restored Israel (ch. 9:14; Isa. 65:21, 22). **12. they afflict ... they take**—rather, "(ye) who afflict... take." **bribe**—lit., a *price* with which one who has an unjust cause *ransoms* himself from your sentence (I Sam. 12:3, *Margin;* Prov. 6:35). **turn aside the poor in the gate**—refuse them their right *in the place of justice* (ch. 2:7; Isa. 29:21). **13. the prudent**—the spiritually wise. **shall keep silence**—not mere silence of tongue, but the prudent shall keep himself quiet from taking part in any public or private affairs which he can avoid: as it is "an evil time," and one in which all law is set at naught. Ephesians 5:16 refers to this. Instead of impatiently agitating against irremediable evils, the godly wise will not cast pearls before swine, who would trample these, and rend the offerers (Matt. 7:6), but will patiently wait for God's time of deliverance in silent submission (Ps. 39:9). **14. and so**—on condition of your "seeking good." **shall be with you, as ye have spoken**—as ye have boasted; viz., that God is with you, and that you are His people (Mic. 3:11). **15. Hate ... evil ... love ... good**—(Isa. 1:16, 17; Rom. 12:9). **judgment in the gate**—*justice* in the place where causes are tried. **it may be that the Lord ... will be gracious**—so, "peradventure" (Exod. 32:30). Not that men are to come to God with an *uncertainty* whether or no He will be gracious: the expression merely implies the difficulty in the way, because of the want of true repentance on man's part, so as to stimulate the zealous earnestness of believers in seeking God (cf. Gen. 16:2; Joel 2:14; Acts 8:22). **the remnant of Joseph**—(see vs. 6). Israel (represented by "Ephraim," the leading tribe, and descendant of Joseph) was, as compared to what it once was, now but a remnant, Hazael of Syria having smitten all the coasts from Jordan eastward, Gilead and Bashan, Gad, Reuben, and Manasseh (II Kings 10:32, 33) [HENDERSON]. Rather, "the remnant of Israel that shall have been left after the wicked have been destroyed" [MAURER]. **16. Therefore**—resumed from vs. 13. God foresees they will not obey the exhortation (vss. 14, 15), but will persevere in the unrighteousness stigmatized (vss. 7, 10, 12). **the Lord** [JEHOVAH], **the God of hosts, the Lord**—an accumulation of titles, of which His lordship over all things is the climax, to mark that from His judgment there is no appeal. **streets . . . highways**—the *broad open spaces* and the *narrow streets* common in the East. **call the husbandman to mourning**—The citizens shall call the inexperienced *husbandmen* to act the part usually performed by professional mourners, as there will not be enough of the latter for the universal mourning which prevails. **such as are skilful of lamentation**—professional mourners hired to lead off the lamentations for the deceased; alluded to in Ecclesiastes 12:5; generally women (Jer. 9:17-19). **17. in all vineyards . . . wailing**—where usually songs of joy were heard. **pass through thee**—taking vengeance (Exod. 12:12, 23; Nah. 1:12). "Pass *over*" and "pass by," on the contrary, are used of God's *forgiving* (Exod. 12:23; Mic. 7:18; cf. ch. 7:8). **18.** Woe unto you who do not scruple to say in irony, "We desire that the day of the Lord would come," i.e., "Woe to you who treat it as if it were a mere dream of the prophets" (Isa. 5:19; Jer. 17:15; Ezek. 12:22). **to what end is it for you!**—Amos taking their ironical words in earnest: for God often takes the blasphemer at his own word, in righteous retribution making the scoffer's jest a terrible reality against himself. Ye have but little reason to desire the day of the Lord; for it will be to you calamity, and not joy. **19. As if a man did flee . . . a lion, and a bear met him**—Trying to escape one calamity, he falls into another. This perhaps implies that in vs. 18 their ironical desire for the day of the Lord was as if it would be an escape from existing calamities. The coming of the day of the Lord would be good news to us, if true: for we have served God (i.e., the golden calves). So do hypocrites flatter themselves as to death and judgment, as if these would be a relief from existing ills of life. The lion may from generosity spare the prostrate, but the *bear* spares none (cf. Job 20:24; Isa. 24:18). **leaned . . . on the wall**—on the side wall of the house, to support himself from falling. Snakes often hid themselves in fissures in a wall. Those not reformed by God's judgments will be pursued by them: if they escape one, another is ready to seize them. **21. I hate, I despise**—The two verbs joined without a conjunction express God's strong abhorrence. **your feast days**—*yours;* not *Mine;* I do not acknowledge them: unlike those in Judah, yours are of human, not divine institution. **I will not smell**—i.e., I will take *no delight in* the sacrifices offered (Gen. 8:21; Lev. 26:31). **in your solemn assemblies**—lit., "days of restraint." Isaiah 1:10-15 is parallel. Isaiah is fuller; Amos, more condensed. Amos condemns Israel not only on the ground of their thinking to satisfy God by sacrifices without obedience (the charge brought by Isaiah against the Jews), but also because even their external ritual was a mere corruption, and unsanctioned by God. **22. meat offerings**—flour, etc. Unbloody offerings. **peace offerings**—offerings for obtaining from God peace and prosperity. *Hebrew,* "thank offerings." **23. Take . . . away from me**—lit., "Take away, *from upon* Me"; the idea being that of a *burden* pressing *upon* the bearer. So Isaiah 1:14, "They are a trouble unto Me (lit., a

burden *upon* Me): I am weary to bear them." **the noise of thy songs**—The hymns and instrumental music on sacred occasions are to Me nothing but a disagreeable *noise*. **I will not hear**—Isaiah substitutes "prayers" (Isa. 1:15) for the "songs" and "melody" here; but, like Amos, closes with "I will not hear." **24. judgment**—justice. **run down**—lit., "roll," i.e., flow abundantly (Isa. 48:18). Without the desire to fulfil righteousness in the offerer, the sacrifice is hateful to God (I Sam. 15:22; Ps. 66:18; Hos. 6:6; Mic. 6:8). **25, 26. Have ye offered . . .**—Yes: ye have. "But (all the time with strange inconsistency) ye have borne (aloft in solemn pomp) the tabernacle (i.e., the portable shrine, or model *tabernacle:* small enough not to be detected by Moses; cf. Acts 19:24) of your Molech" (that idol is *"your"* god; I am not, though ye go through the form of presenting offerings to Me). The question, "Have ye," is not a denial (for they *did* offer in the wilderness to Jehovah sacrifices of the cattle which they took with them in their nomad life there, Exodus 24:4; Numbers 7 and 9:1, etc.), but a strong affirmation (cf. I Sam. 2:27, 28; Jer. 31:20; Ezek. 20:4). The sin of Israel in Amos' time is the very sin of their forefathers, mocking God with worship, while at the same time worshipping idols (cf. Ezek. 20:39). It was clandestine in Moses' time, else he would have put it down; he was aware generally of their unfaithfulness, though not knowing the particulars (Deut. 31:21, 27). **Molech . . . Chiun**—Molech means "king" answering to *Mars* [BENGEL]; *the Sun* [JABLONSKI]; *Saturn,* the same as "Chiun" [MAURER]. The LXX translates "Chiun" into *Remphan,* as Stephen quotes it (Acts 7:42, 43). The same god often had different names. *Molech* is the Ammonite name; *Chiun,* the Arabic and Persian name, written also *Chevan.* In an Arabic lexicon *Chiun* means "austere"; so astrologers represented *Saturn* as a planet baleful in his influence. Hence the Phœnicians offered human sacrifices to him, children especially; so idolatrous Israel also. *Rimmon* was the Syrian name (II Kings 5:18); pronounced as *Remvan,* or "Remphan," just as *Chiun* was also *Chevan.* Molech had the form of a king; Chevan, or Chiun, of a star [GROTIUS]. Remphan was the Egyptian name for *Saturn:* hence the LXX translator of Amos gave the Egyptian name for the Hebrew, being an Egyptian. [HODIUS II: *Bibl.* 4. 115.] The same as the Nile, of which the Egyptians made the star *Saturn* the representative [HARENBERG]. BENGEL considers *Remphan* or *Rephan* akin to *Teraphim* and *Remphis,* the name of a king of Egypt. The Hebrews became infected with Sabeanism,the oldest form of idolatry, the worship of the *Saba* or starry hosts, in their stay in the Arabian desert, where Job notices its prevalence (Job 31: 26); in opposition, in vs. 27, Jehovah declares Himself "the God of *hosts.*" **the star of your god**—R. ISAAC CARO says all the astrologers represented Saturn as *the star of Israel.* Probably there was a figure of a star on the head of the image of the idol, to represent the planet Saturn; hence "images" correspond to "star" in the parallel clause. A star in hieroglyphics represents God (Num. 24:17). "Images" are either a Hebraism for "image," or refer to the many images made to represent Chiun. **27. beyond Damascus**—In Acts 7:43 it is "beyond *Babylon,"* which includes *beyond Damascus.* In Amos' time, Damascus was the object of Israel's fear because of the Syrian wars. Babylon was not yet named as the place of their captivity. Stephen supplies this name. Their place of exile was in fact, as he states, *"beyond* Babylon," in Halah and

Habor by the river Gozan, and in the cities of the Medes (II Kings 17:6; cf. here ch. 1:5; 4:3; 6:14). The road to Assyria lay through "Damascus." It is therefore specified, that not merely shall they be carried captives to Damascus, as they had been by Syrian kings (II Kings 10:32, 33; 13:7), but, beyond that, to a region whence a return was not so possible as from Damascus. They were led captive by Satan into idolatry, therefore God caused them to go captive among idolaters. Cf. II Kings 15:29; 16:9; Isa. 8:4, whence it appears Tiglath pileser attacked Israel and Damascus at the same time at Ahaz' request (Amos 3:11).

CHAPTER 6

Vss. 1-14. DENUNCIATION OF BOTH THE SISTER NATIONS (ESPECIALLY THEIR NOBLES) FOR WANTON SECURITY—ZION, AS WELL AS SAMARIA: THREAT OF THE EXILE: RUIN OF THEIR PALACES AND SLAUGHTER OF THE PEOPLE: THEIR PERVERSE INJUSTICE. **1. named chief of the nations**—i.e., you nobles, so eminent in influence, that your names are celebrated among the chief nations [LUDOVICUS DE DIEU]. *Hebrew,* "Men designated by name among the first fruits of the nations," i.e., men of note in Israel, the people chosen by God as first of the nations (Exod. 19:5; cf. Num. 24:20) [PISCATOR]. **to whom ... Israel came**—i.e., the princes to whom the Israelites used to repair for the decision of controversies, recognizing their authority [MAURER]. I prefer to refer "which" to the antecedent "Zion" and "Samaria"; these were esteemed "chief" strongholds among the heathen nations "to whom ... Israel came" when it entered Canaan; vs. 2 accords with this. **2. Calneh**—on the east bank of the Tigris. Once powerful, but recently subjugated by Assyria (Isa. 10:9; about 794 B.C.). **Hameth**—subjugated by Jeroboam II (II Kings 14:25). Also by Assyria subsequently (II Kings 18:34). Cf. vs. 14, below. **Gath**—subjugated by Uzziah (II Chron. 26:6). **be they better**—no. Their so recent subjugation renders it needless for Me to tell you they *are* not. And yet they *once were;* still they could not defend themselves against the enemy. How vain, then, *your* secure confidence in the strength of Mounts Zion and Samaria! He takes cities respectively east, north, south, and west of Israel (cf. Nah. 3:8). **3.** Ye persuade yourselves that "the evil day" foretold by the prophets is "far off," though they declare it near (Ezek. 12:22, 27). Ye in your imagination put it far off, and therefore bring near *violent oppression,* suffering it to *sit enthroned,* as it were, among you (Ps. 94:20). The notion of judgment being far off has always been an incentive to the sinner's recklessness of living (Eccles. 8:12, 13; Matt. 24:48). Yet that very recklessness brings near the evil day which he puts far off. "Ye bring on fever by your intemperance, and yet would put it far off" [CALVIN]. **4.** (See ch. 2:8.) **beds of ivory**—i.e., adorned, or inlaid, with ivory (ch. 3:15). **stretch themselves**—in luxurious self-indulgence. **lambs out of the flock** —picked out as the choicest, for their owners' selfish gratification. **5. chant**—lit., "mark distinct sounds and tones." **viol**—the lyre, or lute. **invent ... instruments ... like David**—They fancy they equal David in musical skill (I Chron. 23:5; Neh. 12:36). They defend their luxurious passion for music by his example: forgetting that *he* pursued this study when at peace and free from danger, and that for the praise of God; but *they* pursue for their own self-gratification, and that when God is angry

and ruin is imminent. **6. drink ... in bowls**—in the *large vessels* or basins in which wine was mixed; not satisfied with the smaller *cups* from which it was ordinarily drunk, after having been poured from the large mixer. **chief ointments**—i.e., the most costly: not for health or cleanliness, but wanton luxury. **not grieved for the affliction of Joseph**—lit., "the breach," i.e., the national wound or calamity (Ps. 60:2; Ezek. 34:4) of the house of *Joseph* (ch. 5:6); resembling in this the heartlessness of their forefathers, the sons of Jacob, towards Joseph, "eating bread" while their brother lay in the pit, and then selling him to Ishmaelites. **7. Therefore ... shall they go captive with the first**—As they were first among the people in rank (vs. 1), and anointed themselves "with the chief ointments" (vs. 6), so shall they be among the foremost in going into captivity. **banquet**—lit., the "merry-making shout of revellers"; from an *Arabic* root, "to cry out." In the *Hebrew, marzeach;* here, there is an allusion to *mizraqu,* "bowls" (vs. 6). **them that stretched themselves**—on luxurious couches (vs. 4). **8. the excellency of Jacob**—(Ps. 47:4). The *sanctuary* which was the great glory of the covenant people [VATABLUS], (Ezek. 24:21). The priesthood, and kingdom, and dignity, conferred on them by God. These, saith God, are of no account in My eyes towards averting punishment [CALVIN]. **hate his palaces**—as being the storehouses of "robbery" (ch. 3:10, 15). How sad a change from God's *love* of Zion's gates (Ps. 87:2) and palaces (Ps. 48:3, 13), owing to the people's sin! **the city**—collectively: both Zion and Samaria (vs. 1). **all that is therein**—lit., "its fulness"; the *multitude* of men and of riches in it (cf. Ps. 24:1). **9.** If as many as *ten* (Lev. 26:26; Zech. 8:23) remain in a house (a rare case, and only in the scattered villages, as there will be scarcely a house in which the enemy will leave any), they shall all, to a man, die of the plague, a frequent concomitant of war in the East (Jer. 24:10; 44:13; Ezek. 6:11). **10. a man's uncle**—The nearest relatives had the duty of burying the dead (Gen. 25: 9; 35:29; Judg. 16:31). No nearer relative was left of this man than an *uncle.* **and he that burneth him**—the uncle, who is *also* at the same time the one that burneth him (one of the "ten," vs. 9). Burial was the usual Hebrew mode of disposing of their dead. But in cases of necessity, as when the men of Jabesh-gilead took the bodies of Saul and his three sons from the walls of Beth-shan and burned them to save them from being insulted by the Philistines, burning was practised. So in this case, to prevent contagion. **the bones**—i.e., the dead *body* (Gen. 50:25). Perhaps here there is an allusion in the phrase to the *emaciated* condition of the body, which was little else but skin and bones. **say unto him that is by the sides of the house**—i.e., to the only one left of the ten *in the interior of the house* [MAURER] (cf. *Note,* Isa. 14:13). **Hold thy tongue ... we may not ... mention ... the Lord**—After receiving the reply, that none is left besides the one addressed, when the man outside fancies the man still surviving inside to be on the point, as was customary, of expressing devout gratitude to God who spared him, the man outside interrupts him, "Hold thy tongue! for there is not now cause for mentioning with praise (Josh. 23:7) the name of Jehovah"; for *thou* also must die; as all the ten are to die to the last man (vs. 9; cf. ch. 8:3). Formerly ye boasted in the name of Jehovah, as if ye were His peculiar people; now ye shall be silent and shudder at His name, as hostile to you, and as one from whom ye wish to be hidden (Rev. 6:16), [CALVIN]. **11. commandeth, and he will** smite—His word of command, when once given, cannot but be fulfilled (Isa. 55:11). His mere word is enough to smite with destruction. **great house ... little house**—He will spare none, great or small (ch. 3:15). JEROME interprets "the great house" as Israel, and "the small house" as Judah: the former being reduced to branches or ruins, lit., "small drops"; the latter, though injured with "clefts" or rents, which threaten its fall, yet still permitted to stand. **12.** In turning "judgment [justice] into gall [poison], and ... righteousness into hemlock" [or wormwood, bitter and noxious], ye act as perversely as if one were to make "horses run upon the rock" or to "plough with oxen there" [MAURER]. As horses and oxen are useless on a rock, so ye are incapable of fulfilling justice [GROTIUS]. Ye impede the course of God's benefits, because ye are as it were a hard rock on which His favor cannot run. "Those that will not be tilled as fields, shall be abandoned as rocks" [CALVIN]. **13. rejoice in a thing of naught**—i.e., in your vain and fleeting riches. **Have we not taken to us horns**—i.e., acquired power, so as to conquer our neighbors (II Kings 14:25). *Horns* are the Hebrew symbol of *power*, being the instrument of strength in many animals (Ps. 75:10). **14. from the entering in of Hamath**—the point of entrance for an invading army (as Assyria) into Israel from the north; specified here, as Hamath had been just before subjugated by Jeroboam II (vs. 2). Do not glory in your recently acquired city, for it shall be the starting-point for the foe to afflict you. How sad the contrast to the feast of Solomon attended by a congregation *from* this same *Hamath*, the most northern boundary of Israel, *to* the Nile, the *river of Egypt*, the most southern boundary! **unto the river of the wilderness**—i.e., to Kedron, which empties itself into the north bay of the Dead Sea below Jericho (II Chron. 28:15), the southern boundary of the ten tribes (II Kings 14:25, "from the entering of Hamath unto the sea of the plain") [MAURER]. *To the river Nile*, which skirts the Arabian wilderness and separates Egypt from Canaan [GROTIUS]. If this verse includes Judah, as well as Israel (cf. vs. 1, "Zion" and "Samaria"), GROTIUS' view is correct; and it agrees with I Kings 8:65.

CHAPTER 7

Vss. 1-9. Chapters 7, 8, 9, contain VISIONS, WITH THEIR EXPLANATIONS. Ch. 7 consists of two parts. First (vss. 1-9): PROPHECIES ILLUSTRATED BY THREE SYMBOLS: (1) A vision of *grasshoppers* or young locusts, which devour the grass, but are removed at Amos' entreaty; (2) *Fire* drying up even the deep, and withering part of the land, but removed at Amos' entreaty; (3) A *plumb-line* to mark the buildings for destruction. Secondly (vss. 10-17): NARRATIVE OF AMAZIAH'S INTERRUPTION OF AMOS IN CONSEQUENCE OF THE FOREGOING PROPHECIES, AND PREDICTION OF HIS DOOM. **1. showed ... me; and, behold**—The same formula prefaces the three visions in this chapter, and the fourth in ch. 8:1. **grasshoppers**—rather, "locusts" in the caterpillar state, from a *Hebrew* root, "to creep forth." In the autumn the eggs are deposited in the earth; in the spring the young come forth [MAURER]. **the latter growth**—viz., of grass, which comes up after the mowing. They do not in the East mow their grass and make hay of it, but cut it off the ground as they require it. **the king's mowings**—the first fruits of the mown grass, tyrannically exacted by the king from the people. The literal locusts, as in

Joel, are probably symbols of human foes: thus the "growth" of grass "after the king's mowings" will mean the political revival of Israel under Jeroboam II (II Kings 14:25), after it had been mown down, as it were, by Hazael and Ben-hadad of Syria (II Kings 13:3), [GROTIUS]. **2. by whom shall Jacob arise?**—If Thou, O God, dost not spare, how can *Jacob maintain his ground*, reduced as he is by repeated attacks of the Assyrians, and erelong about to be invaded by the Assyrian Pul (II Kings 15:19, 20)? Cf. Isaiah 51:19. The mention of "Jacob" is a plea that God should "remember for them His covenant" with their forefather, the patriarch (Ps. 106:45). **he is small**—reduced in numbers and in strength. **3. repented for this**—i.e., of this. The change was not in the mind of God (Num. 2:19; Jas. 1:17), but in the effect outwardly. God unchangeably does what is just; it is just that He should hear intercessory prayer (Jas. 5:16-18), as it would have been just for Him to have let judgment take its course at once on the guilty nation, but for the prayer of one or two righteous men in it (cf. Gen. 18:23-33; I Sam. 15:11; Jer. 42:10). The repentance of the sinner, and God's regard to His own attributes of mercy and covenanted love, also cause God outwardly to deal with him as if he repented (Jonah 3:10), whereas the change in outward dealing is in strictest harmony with God's own unchangeableness. **It shall not be**—Israel's utter overthrow now. Pul was influenced by God to accept money and withdraw from Israel. **4. called to contend**—i.e., with Israel judicially (Job 9:3; Isa. 66:16; Ezek. 38:22). He ordered to come at His call the infliction of punishment by "fire" on Israel, i.e., drought (cf. ch. 4:6-11), [MAURER]. Rather, *war* (Num. 21:28), viz., Tiglath-pileser [GROTIUS]. **devoured the ... deep**—i.e., a great part of Israel, whom he carried away. *Waters* are the symbol for *many people* (Rev. 17:15). **did eat up a part**—viz., all the *land* (cf. ch. 4:7) of Israel east of Jordan (I Chron. 5:26; Isa. 9:1). This was a worse judgment than the previous one: the locusts ate up the grass: the fire not only affects the surface of the ground, but burns up the very roots and reaches even to the deep. **7. wall made by a plumb-line**—viz., perpendicular. **8. plumb-line in ... midst of ... Israel**—No longer are the symbols, as in the former two, stated generally; this one is expressly applied to Israel. God's long-suffering is worn out by Israel's perversity: so Amos ceases to intercede (cf. Gen. 18:33). The plummet-line was used not only in building, but in destroying houses (II Kings 21:13; Isa. 28:17; 34:11; Lam. 2:8). It denotes that God's judgments are measured out by the most exact rules of justice. Here it is placed "in the midst" of Israel, i.e., the judgment is not to be confined to an outer part of Israel, as by Tiglath-pileser; it is to reach the very center. This was fulfilled when Shalmaneser, after a three years' siege of Samaria, took it and carried away Israel captive finally to Assyria (II Kings 17:3, 5, 6, 23). **not ... pass by ... any more**—not forgive them any more (ch. 8:2; Prov. 19:11; Mic. 7:18). **9. high places**—dedicated to idols. **of Isaac**—They boasted of their following the example of their forefather Isaac, in erecting high places at Beer-sheba (ch. 5:5; cf. Gen. 26:23, 24; 46:1); but he and Abraham erected them before the temple was appointed at Jerusalem—and to God; whereas they did so, after the temple had been fixed as the only place for sacrifices—and to idols. In the *Hebrew* here "Isaac" is written with *s*, instead of the usual *ts*; both forms mean "laughter"; the change of spelling perhaps expresses that their "high places of Isaac" may be well so called, but not as they meant by the name; for they are only fit to be *laughed at* in scorn. Probably, however, the mention of "Isaac" and "Israel" simply expresses that these names, which their degenerate posterity boasted in as if ensuring their safety, will not save them and their idolatrous "sanctuaries" on which they depended from ruin (cf. ch. 8:14). **house of Jeroboam with . . . sword**—fulfilled in the extinction of Zachariah, son of Jeroboam II, the last of the descendants of Jeroboam I, who had originated the idolatry of the calves (II Kings 15:8-10). **10-17.** AMAZIAH'S CHARGE AGAINST AMOS: HIS DOOM FORETOLD. **10. priest of Beth-el**—chief priest of the royal sanctuary to the calves at Beth-el. These being a device of state policy to keep Israel separate from Judah. Amaziah construes Amos' words against them as treason. So in the case of Elijah and Jeremiah (I Kings 18:17; Jer. 37:13, 14). So the antitype Jesus was charged (John 19:12); political expediency being made in all ages the pretext for dishonoring God and persecuting His servants (John 11:48-50). So in the case of Paul (Acts 17:6, 7; 24:5). **in the midst of . . . Israel**—probably alluding to Amos' own words, "in the midst of . . . Israel" (vs. 8), foretelling the state's overthrow *to the very center*. Not secretly, or in a corner, but openly, in *the very center of the state*, so as to upset the whole utterly. **land is not able to bear all his words**—They are so many and so intolerable. A sedition will be the result. The mention of his being "priest of Beth-el" implies that it was for his own priestly gain, not for the king or state, he was so keen. **11. Jeroboam shall die . . .**—Amos had not said this: but that "the *house* of Jeroboam" should fall "with the sword" (vs. 9). But Amaziah exaggerates the charge, to excite Jeroboam against him. The king, however, did not give ear to Amaziah, probably from religious awe of the prophet of Jehovah. **12. Also**—Besides informing the king against Amos, lest that course should fail, as it did, Amaziah urges the troublesome prophet himself to go back to his own land Judah, pretending to advise him in friendliness. **seer**—said contemptuously in reference to Amos' visions which precede. **there eat bread**—You can earn a livelihood there, whereas remaining here you will be ruined. He judges of Amos by his own selfishness, as if regard to one's own safety and livelihood are the paramount considerations. So the false prophets (Ezek. 13:19) were ready to say whatever pleased their hearers, however false, for "handfuls of barley and pieces of bread." **13. prophesy not again**—(ch. 2:12). **at Beth-el**—Amaziah wants to be let alone at least in his own residence. **the king's chapel**—Beth-el was preferred by the king to Dan, the other seat of the calf worship, as being nearer Samaria, the capital, and as hallowed by Jacob of old (Gen. 28:16, 19; 35:6, 7). He argues by implication against Amos' presumption, as a private man, in speaking against the worship sanctioned by the king, and that in the very place consecrated to it for the king's own devotions. **king's court**—i.e., residence: the seat of empire, where the king holds his court, and which thou oughtest to have reverenced. Samaria was the usual king's residence: but for the convenience of attending the calf worship, a royal palace was at Beth-el also. **14. I was no prophet**—in answer to Amaziah's insinuation (vs. 12), that he discharged the prophetical office to earn his "bread" (like Israel's mercenary prophets). So far from being rewarded, Jehovah's prophets had to expect imprison-

ment and even death as the result of their prophesying in Samaria or Israel: whereas the prophets of Baal were maintained at the king's expense (cf. I Kings 18:19). I was not, says Amos, of the order of prophets, or educated in their schools, and deriving a livelihood from exercising the public functions of a prophet. I am a *shepherd* (cf. vs. 15, "flock"; the *Hebrew* for "herdsman" includes the meaning, *shepherd*, cf. ch. 1:1) in humble position, who did not even think of prophesying among you, until a divine call impelled me to it. **prophet's son**—i.e., disciple. Schools of prophets are mentioned first in I Samuel; in these youths were educated to serve the theocracy as public instructors. Only in the kingdom of the ten tribes is the continuance of the schools of the prophets mentioned. They were missionary stations near the chief seats of superstition in Israel, and associations endowed with the Spirit of God; none were admitted but those to whom the Spirit had been previously imparted. Their spiritual fathers travelled about to visit the training schools, and cared for the members and even their widows (II Kings 4:1, 2). The pupils had their common board in them, and after leaving them still continued members. The offerings which in Judah were given by the pious to the Levites, in Israel went to the schools of the prophets (II Kings 4:42). Prophecy (e.g., Elijah and Elisha) in Israel was more connected with extraordinary events than in Judah, inasmuch as, in the absence of the legal hierarchy of the latter, it needed to have more palpable divine sanction. **sycamore**—abounding in Palestine. The fruit was like the fig, but inferior; according to PLINY, a sort of compound, as the name expresses, of the fig and the mulberry. It was only eaten by the poorest (cf. I Kings 10:27). **gatherer**—one occupied with their cultivation [MAURER]. To cultivate it, an incision was made in the fruit when of a certain size, and on the fourth day afterwards it ripened (PLINY, H. N. 13. 7, 14). GROTIUS from JEROME says, if it be not plucked off and "gathered" (which favors *English Version*), it is spoiled by gnats. **15. took me as I followed the flock**—So David was taken (II Sam. 7:8; Ps. 78: 70, 71). Messiah is the antitypical *Shepherd* (Ps. 23; John 10). **unto my people**—"against" [MAURER]; so vs. 16. Jehovah claims them still as *His* by right, though slighting His authority. God would recover them to His service by the prophet's ministry. **16. drop**—distil as the refreshing drops of rain (Deut. 32:2; Ezek. 21:2; cf. Mic. 2:6, 11). **17. Thy wife shall be an harlot in the city**—i.e., shall be forced by the enemy, while thou art looking on, unable to prevent her dishonor (Isa. 13:16; Lam. 5:11). The words, "saith the LORD," are in striking opposition to "*Thou* sayest (vs. 16). **divided by line**—among the foe. **a polluted land**—Israel regarded every foreign land as that which really her own land was now, "polluted" (Isa. 24:5; Jer. 2:7).

CHAPTER 8

Vss. 1-14. VISION OF A BASKET OF SUMMER FRUIT SYMBOLICAL OF ISRAEL'S END. RESUMING THE SERIES OF SYMBOLS INTERRUPTED BY AMAZIAH, AMOS ADDS A FOURTH. THE AVARICE OF THE OPPRESSORS OF THE POOR: THE OVERTHROW OF THE NATION: THE WISH FOR THE MEANS OF RELIGIOUS COUNSEL, WHEN THERE SHALL BE A FAMINE OF THE WORD. **1. summer fruit**—*Hebrew, kitz.* In vs. 2 "end" is in *Hebrew, keetz.* The similarity of sounds implies that, as the *summer* is the *end* of the year and the time of the ripeness of fruits, so Israel is *ripe* for her *last* punishment, *ending* her national existence. As the fruit is plucked when ripe from the tree, so Israel from her land. **2. end**—(Ezek. 7:2, 6). **3. songs of ... temple**—(ch. 5:23). The joyous hymns in the temple of Judah (or rather, in the *Beth-el* "royal temple," ch. 7:13; for the allusion is to *Israel,* not Judah, throughout this chapter) shall be changed into "howlings." GROTIUS translates, "palace"; cf. ch. 6:5, as to the songs there. But ch. 5:23, and 7:13, favor *English Version.* **they shall cast them forth with silence**—not as *Margin,* "be silent." It is an adverb, "silently." There shall be such great slaughter as even to prevent the bodies being buried [CALVIN]. There shall be none of the usual professional mourners (ch. 5: 16), but the bodies will be cast out in silence. Perhaps also is meant that terror, both of God (cf. ch. 6:10) and of the foe, shall close their lips. **4. Hear** —The nobles needed to be urged thus, as hating to *hear* reproof. **swallow up the needy**—or, "gape after," i.e., pant for their goods; so the word is used, Job 7:2, *Margin.* **to make the poor ... to fail** —"that they (themselves) may be placed alone in the midst of the earth" (Isa. 5:8). **5.** So greedy are they of unjust gain that they cannot spare a single day, however sacred, from pursuing it. They are strangers to God and enemies to themselves, who love market days better than sabbath days; and they who have lost piety will not long keep honesty. The new moons (Num. 10:10) and sabbaths were to be kept without working or trading (Neh. 10:31). **set forth wheat**—lit., "open out" stores of wheat for sale. **ephah**—containing three seahs, or above three pecks. **making ... small**—making it below the just weight to purchasers. **shekel great**—taking from purchasers a greater weight of money than was due. Shekels used to be *weighed out* in payments (Gen. 23:16). Thus they committed a double fraud against the law (Deut. 25:13, 14). **6. buy ... poor for silver ... pair of shoes**—i.e., that we may compel the needy for money, or any other thing of however little worth, to sell themselves to us as bondmen, in defiance of Leviticus 25:39; the very thing which brings down God's judgment (ch. 2:6). **sell the refuse of ... wheat**—which contains no nutriment, but which the poor eat at a low price, being unable to pay for flour. **7. Lord hath sworn by the excellency of Jacob**—i.e., by Himself, in whom Jacob's seed glory [MAURER]. Rather, by the spiritual privileges of Israel, the adoption as His peculiar people [CALVIN], the temple, and its Shekinah symbol of His presence. Cf. ch. 6:8, where it means Jehovah's *temple* (cf. ch. 4:2). **never forget**—not *pass by* without punishing (vs. 2; Hos. 8:13; 9:9). **8. the land ... rise up wholly as a flood**—The land will, as it were, be wholly turned into a flooding river (a flood being the image of overwhelming calamity, Dan. 9:26). **cast out and drowned ...**— swept away and overwhelmed, as the land adjoining the Nile is by it, when flooding (ch. 9:5). The Nile rises generally twenty feet. The waters then "cast out" mire and dirt (Isa. 57:20). **9.** "Darkness" made to rise "at noon" is the emblem of great calamities (Jer. 15:9; Ezek. 32:7-10). **10. baldness**—a sign of mourning (Isa. 15:2; Jer. 48:37; Ezek. 7:18). **I will make it as ... mourning of an only son**—"it," i.e., "the earth" (vs. 9). I will reduce the land to such a state that there shall be the same occasion for mourning as when parents mourn for an only son (Jer. 6:26; Zech. 12:10). **11. famine of ... hearing the words of the Lord**—a just retribution on those who now will not hear the Lord's prophets, nay

even try to drive them away, as Amaziah did (ch. 7:12); they shall look in vain, in their distress, for divine counsel, such as the prophets now offer (Ezek. 7:26; Mic. 3:7). Cf. as to the Jews' rejection of Messiah, and their consequent rejection by Him (Matt. 21:43); and their desire for Messiah too late (Luke 17:22; John 7:34; 8:21). So, the prodigal when he had sojourned awhile in the "far-off country, began to be in want" in the "mighty famine" which arose (Luke 15:14; cf. I Sam. 3:1; 7: 2). It is remarkable that the Jews' religion is almost the only one that *could* be abolished *against the will of the people themselves,* on account of its being dependent on a particular *place,* viz., the temple. When that was destroyed, the Mosaic ritual, which could not exist without it, necessarily ceased. Providence designed it, that, as the law gave way to the Gospel, so all men should perceive it was so, in spite of the Jews' obstinate rejection of the Gospel. **12. they shall wander from sea to sea** —i.e., from the Dead Sea to the Mediterranean, from east to west. **from ... north ... to ... east**— where we might expect "from north to south." But so alienated was Israel from Judah, that no Israelite even then would think of repairing *southward,* i.e., to Jerusalem for religious information. The circuit is traced as in Numbers 34:3, etc., except that the south is omitted. Their "seeking the word of the Lord" would not be from a sincere desire to obey God, but under the pressure of punishment. **13. faint for thirst**—viz., thirst for hearing the words of the Lord, being destitute of all other comfort. If even the young and strong faint, how much more the infirm (Isa. 40:30, 31)! **14. swear by the sin of Samaria**—viz., the calves (Deut. 9:21; Hos. 4:15). "Swear by" means to *worship* (Ps. 63:11). **The manner**—i.e., as "the way" is used (Ps. 139:24; Acts 9:2), *the mode of worship.* **Thy god, O Dan**—the other golden calf at Dan (I Kings 22:26-30). **liveth ... liveth**—rather, "May thy god ... live ... may the manner ... live." Or, "As (surely as) thy god, O Dan, liveth." This is their formula when they swear; not "May Jehovah live!" or, "As Jehovah liveth!"

CHAPTER 9

Vss. 1-15. FIFTH AND LAST VISION. *None can escape the coming judgment in any hiding-place: for God is omnipresent and irresistible (vss. 1-6). As a kingdom, Israel shall perish as if it never was in covenant with Him: but as individuals the house of Jacob shall not utterly perish, nay, not one of the least of the righteous shall fall, but only all the sinners (vss. 7-10). Restoration of the Jews finally to their own land after the re-establishment of the fallen tabernacle of David; consequent conversion of all the heathen (vss. 11-15).* **1. Lord ... upon the altar**—viz., in the idolatrous temple at Beth-el; the calves which were spoken of in the verse just preceding, of ch. 8. Hither they would flee for protection from the Assyrians, and would perish in the ruins, with the vain object of their trust [HENDERSON]. Jehovah stands here to direct the destruction of it, them, and the idolatrous nation. He demands many victims on the altar, but they are to be human victims. CALVIN and FAIRBAIRN, and others, make it in the *temple at Jerusalem.* Judgment was to descend both on Israel and Judah. As the services of both alike ought to have been offered on the Jerusalem temple-altar, it is there that Jehovah ideally stands, as if the whole people were assembled there, their abominations lying unpardoned there, and crying for vengeance, though in fact committed elsewhere (cf. Ezek. 8:1-18). This view harmonizes with the similarity of the vision in Amos to that in Isaiah 6, *at Jerusalem.* Also with the end of this chapter (vss. 11-15), which applies both to *Judah* and Israel: "the tabernacle of David," viz., at Jerusalem. His attitude, "standing," implies fixity of purpose. **lintel**—rather, the spherelike *capital* of the column [MAURER]. **posts**—rather, thresholds, as in Isaiah 6:4, *Margin.* The temple is to be smitten below as well as above, to ensure utter destruction. **cut them in the head**—viz., with the broken fragments of the capitals and columns (cf. Ps. 68:21; Hab. 3:13). **slay the last of them**—their posterity [HENDERSON]. The survivors [MAURER]. Jehovah's directions are addressed to His angels, ministers of judgment (cf. Ezek. 9). **he that fleeth . . . shall not flee away**—He who fancies himself safe and out of reach of the enemy shall be taken (ch. 2: 14). **2. Though they dig into hell**—though they hide ever so deeply in the earth (Ps. 139:8). **though they climb up to heaven**—though they ascend the greatest heights (Job 20:6, 7; Jer. 51:53; Obad. 4). **3. Carmel**—where the forests, and, on the west side, the caves, furnished hiding-places (ch. 1:2; Judg. 6:2; I Sam. 13:6). **the sea**—the Mediterranean, which flows at the foot of Mount Carmel; forming a strong antithesis to it. **command the serpent**—the sea-serpent, a term used for any great water-monster (Isa. 27:1). The symbol of *cruel and oppressive kings* (Ps. 74:13, 14). **4. though they go into captivity**—hoping to save their lives by voluntarily surrendering to the foe. **5.** As Amos had threatened that nowhere should the Israelites be safe from the divine judgments, he here shows God's omnipotent ability to execute His threats. So in the case of the threat in ch. 8:8, God is here stated to be the first cause of the mourning of "all that dwell" in the land, and of its rising "like a flood," and of its being "drowned, as by the flood of Egypt." **6. stories**—lit., "ascents," i.e., upper chambers, to which the ascent is by steps [MAURER]; evidently referring to the words in Psalm 104:3, 13. GROTIUS explains it, *God's royal throne,* expressed in language drawn from Solomon's throne, to which the ascent was by steps (cf. I Kings 10:18, 19). **founded his troop**—viz., all animate creatures, which are God's *troop,* or *host* (Gen. 2:1), doing His will (Ps. 103:20, 21; Joel 2:11). MAURER translates, "His *vault,*" i.e., the vaulted sky, which seems to rest on the earth supported by the horizon. **7. unto me**—however great ye seem *to yourselves.* Do not rely on past privileges, and on My having delivered you from Egypt, as if therefore I never would remove you from Canaan. I make no more account of you than of "the Ethiopian" (cf. Jer. 13:23). "Have not I (who) brought you out of Egypt," done as much for other peoples? For instance, did I not bring "the Philistines (*Notes,* Isa. 14:29, etc.) from Caphtor (cf. Deut. 2:23; *Note,* Jer. 47:4), where they had been bond-servants, and the Syrians from Kir?" It is appropriate, that as the Syrians migrated into Syria from Kir (cf. *Note,* Isa. 22:6), so they should be carried back captive into the same land (*Note,* ch. 1:15; II Kings 16:9), just as elsewhere Israel is threatened with a return to Egypt whence they had been delivered. The "Ethiopians," *Hebrew,* "Cushites," were originally akin to the race that founded Babylon: the cuneiform inscriptions in this confirming independently the Scripture statement (Gen. 10: 6, 8, 10). **8. eyes . . . upon the sinful kingdom**—i.e., I am watching all its sinful course in order to punish it (cf. vs. 4; Ps. 34:15, 16). **not utterly destroy the house of Jacob**—Though as a "kingdom" the nation is now utterly to perish, a remnant is to be spared for "Jacob," their forefather's sake (cf. Jer. 30:11); to fulfil the covenant whereby "the seed of Israel" is hereafter to be "a nation for ever" (Jer. 31:36). **9. sift**—I will cause the Israelites to be tossed about through all nations as corn is shaken about in a sieve, in such a way, however, that while the chaff and dust (the wicked) fall through (perish), all the solid grains (the godly elect) remain (are preserved), (Rom. 11:26; cf. *Note,* Jer. 3:14). So spiritual Israel's final safety is ensured (Luke 22:32; John 10:28; 6:39). **10. All the sinners**—answering to the chaff in the image in vs. 9, which falls on the earth, in opposition "to the grain" that does not "fall." **overtake . . . us**—"come on us from behind" [MAURER]. **11. In that day**—quoted by James (Acts 15: 16, 17), "After this," i.e., in the dispensation of Messiah (Gen. 49:10; Hos. 3:4, 5; Joel 2:28; 3:1). **tabernacle of David**—not "the *house* of David," which is used of his affairs when prospering (II Sam. 3:1), but the *tent* or *booth,* expressing the low condition to which his kingdom and family had fallen in Amos' time, and subsequently at the Babylonian captivity before the restoration; and secondarily, in the last days preceding Israel's restoration under Messiah, the antitype to David (Ps. 102:13, 14; *Note,* Isa. 12:1; Jer. 30:9; Ezek. 34:24; 37:24). The type is taken from architecture (Eph. 2:20). The restoration under Zerubbabel can only be a partial, temporary fulfilment; for it did not include Israel, which nation is the main subject of Amos' prophecies, but only Judah; also Zerubbabel's kingdom was not independent and settled; also all the prophets end their prophecies with Messiah, whose advent is the cure of all previous disorders. "Tabernacle" is appropriate to Him, as His human nature is the tabernacle which He assumed in becoming Immanuel, "God with us" (John 1:14). "Dwelt," lit., *tabernacled* "among us" (cf. Rev. 21: 3). Some understand "the tabernacle of David" as that which David pitched for the ark in Zion, after bringing it from Obededom's house. It remained there all his reign for thirty years, till the temple of Solomon was built, whereas the "tabernacle of the congregation" remained at Gibeon (II Chron. 1:3), where the priests ministered in sacrifices (I Chron. 16:39). Song and praise was the service of David's attendants before the ark (Asaph, etc.): a type of the gospel separation between the sacrificial service (*Messiah's* priesthood now *in heaven*) and the access of *believers on earth* to the presence of God, apart from the former (cf. II Sam. 6:12-17; I Chron. 16: 37-39; II Chron. 1:3). **breaches thereof**—lit., "of them," i.e., of the *whole* nation, Israel as well as Judah. **as in . . . days of old**—as it was formerly in the days of David and Solomon, when the kingdom was in its full extent and undivided. **12. That they may possess . . . remnant of Edom, and of all the heathen**—"Edom," the bitter foe, though the brother, of Israel; therefore to be punished (ch. 1:11, 12). Israel shall be lord of the "remnant" of Edom left after the punishment of the latter. James quotes it, "That *the residue of men* might *seek after the Lord, and all the Gentiles . . . .*" For "all the heathen" nations stand on the same footing as *Edom:* Edom is the representative of them all. The *residue* or *remnant* in both cases expresses those left after great antecedent calamities (Rom. 9:27; Zech. 14: 16). Here the conversion of *all* nations (of which the earnest was given in James's time) is represented as only to be realized on the re-establishment of the theocracy under Messiah, the Heir of the throne of

David (vs. 11). The possession of the heathen nations by Israel is to be spiritual, the latter being the ministers to the former for their conversion to Messiah, King of the Jews; just as the first conversions of pagans were through the ministry of the apostles, who were Jews. Cf. Isaiah 54:3, "thy seed shall *inherit the Gentiles*" (cf. Isa. 49:8; Rom. 4:13). A remnant of Edom became Jews under John Hyrcanus, and the rest amalgamated with the Arabians, who became Christians subsequently. **which are called by my name**—i.e., who belong to Me, whom I claim as Mine (Ps. 2:8); in the purposes of electing grace, God terms them already *called by His name*. Cf. the title, "the children," applied by anticipation, Hebrews 2:14. Hence as an act of sovereign grace, fulfilling His promise, it is spoken of God. Proclaim His title as sovereign, "the Lord that doeth this" ("all these things," Acts 15:17, viz., all these and such like acts of sovereign love). **13.**

the days come—at the future restoration of the Jews to their own land. **ploughman shall overtake . . . reaper . . . treader of grapes him that soweth**—fulfilling Leviticus 26:5. Such shall be the abundance that the harvest and vintage can hardly be gathered before the time for preparing for the next crop shall come. Instead of the greater part of the year being spent in war, the whole shall be spent in sowing and reaping the fruits of earth. Cf. Isaiah 65:21-23, as to the same period. **soweth seed**—lit., "draweth it forth," viz., from the sack in order to sow it. **mountains . . . drop sweet wine**—an appropriate image, as the vines in Palestine were trained on *terraces at the sides of the hills*. **14. build the waste cities**—(Isa. 61:4; Ezek. 36:33-36). **15. plant them . . . no more be pulled up**—(Jer. 32:41). **thy God**—Israel's; this is the ground of their restoration, God's original choice of them as His.

THE BOOK OF

OBADIAH

INTRODUCTION

THIS is the shortest book in the Old Testament. The name means "servant of Jehovah." Obadiah stands fourth among the minor prophets according to the Hebrew arrangement of the canon, the fifth according to the Greek. Some consider him to be the same as the Obadiah who superintended the restoration of the temple under Josiah, 627 B.C. (II Chron. 34:12). But vss. 11-16, 20 imply that Jerusalem was by this time overthrown by the Chaldeans, and that he refers to the cruelty of Edom towards the Jews on that occasion, which is referred to also in Lamentations 4:21, 22; Ezekiel 25:12-14, and 35; Psalm 137:7. From comparing vs. 5 with Jeremiah 49:9; vs. 6 with Jeremiah 49:10; vs. 8 with Jeremiah 49:7, it appears that Jeremiah embodied in his prophecies part of Obadiah's, as he had done in the case of other prophets also (cf. Isa. 15 and 16 with Jer. 48). The reason for the present position of Obadiah before other of the minor prophets anterior in date is: Amos at the close of his prophecies foretells the subjugation of Edom hereafter by the Jews; the arranger of the minor prophets in one volume, therefore, placed Obadiah next, as being a fuller statement, and, as it were, a commentary on the foregoing briefer prophecy of Amos as to Edom [MAURER], (cf. Amos 1:11). The date of Obadiah's prophecies was probably immediately after the taking of Jerusalem by Nebuchadnezzar, 588 B.C. Five years afterwards (583 B.C.) Edom was conquered by Nebuchadnezzar. Jeremiah must have incorporated part of Obadiah's prophecies with his own immediately after they were uttered, thus stamping its canonicity.

JEROME makes him contemporary with Hosea, Joel, and Amos. It is an argument in favor of this view that Jeremiah would be more likely to insert in his prophecies a portion from a preceding prophet than from a contemporary. If so, the allusion in vss. 11-14 will be to one of the former captures of Jerusalem: by the Egyptians under Rehoboam (I Kings 14:25, 26; II Chron. 12:2, etc.), or that by the Philistines and Arabians in the reign of Joram (II Chron. 21:16, 17); or that by Joash, king of Israel, in the reign of Amaziah (II Chron. 25:22, 23); or that in the reign of Jehoiakim (II Kings 24:1, etc.); or that in the reign of Jehoiachin (II Kings 24:8-16). On all occasions the Idumeans were hostile to the Jews; and the terms in which that enmity is characterized are not stronger in Obadiah than in Joel 3:19 (cf. Obad. 10; Amos 1:11, 12). The probable capture of Jerusalem alluded to by Obadiah is that by Joash and the Israelites in the reign of Amaziah. For as, a little before, in the reign of the same Amaziah, the Jews had treated harshly the Edomites after conquering them in battle (II Chron. 25:11-23), it is probable that the Edomites, in revenge, joined the Israelites in the attack on Jerusalem [JAEGER].

This book may be divided into two parts: (1) vss. 1-6 set forth Edom's violence toward his brother Israel in the day of the latter's distress, and his coming destruction with the rest of the foes of Judah; (2) vss. 17-21, the coming re-establishment of the Jews in their own possessions, to which shall be added those of the neighboring peoples, and especially those of Edom.

Vss.1-21. DOOM OF EDOM FOR CRUELTY TO JUDAH, EDOM'S BROTHER; RESTORATION OF THE JEWS. **1. Obadiah**—i.e., servant of Jehovah; same as *Abdeel* and *Arabic Abd-allah*. **We**—I and my people. **heard**—(Isa. 21:10). **and an ambassador is sent**—Yea, an ambassador is *already* sent, viz., an angel,

to stir up the Assyrians (and afterwards the Chaldeans) against Edom. The result of the ambassador's message on the heathen is, they simultaneously exclaim, "Arise ye, and let us [with united strength] rise . . . ." Jeremiah 49:14 quotes this. **2. I have made thee small**—Thy reduction to insignificance is *as sure as if it were already accomplished;* therefore the past tense is used [MAURER]. Edom then extended from Dedan of Arabia to Bozrah in the north (Jer. 49:8, 13). CALVIN explains it, "Whereas thou wast made by Me an insignificant people, why art thou so *proud*" (vs. 3)? But if so, why should the heathen peoples be needed to subdue one so insignificant? Jeremiah 49:15, confirms MAURER'S view. **3. clefts of . . . rock**–(Song of Sol. 2:14; Jer. 48:28). The cities of Edom, and among them Petra (*Hebrew, sela,* meaning "rock," II Kings 14:7, *Margin*), the capital, in the Wady Musa, consisted of houses mostly cut in the rocks. **4. exalt *thyself***– or supply from the second clause, "thy nest" [MAURER] (cf. Job 20:6; Jer. 49:16; Amos 9:2). **set . . . nest among . . . stars**–viz., on the loftiest hills which seem to reach the very stars. Edom is a type of Antichrist (Isa. 14:13; Dan. 8:10; 11:37). **thence will I bring thee down**–in spite of thy boast (vs. 3), "*Who* shall bring me down?" **5.** The spoliation which thou shalt suffer shall not be such as that which thieves cause, bad as that is, for these when they have seized enough, or all they can get in a hurry, leave the rest–nor such as grape-gatherers cause in a vineyard, for they, when they have gathered most of the grapes, leave gleanings behind –but it shall be utter, so as to leave thee nothing. The exclamation, "How art thou cut off!" bursting in amidst the words of the image, marks strongly excited feeling. The contrast between Edom where no gleanings shall be left, and Israel where at the worst a gleaning is left (Isa. 17:6; 24:13), is striking. **6. How are** *the things of* **Esau searched out!**–by hostile soldiers seeking booty. Cf. with vss. 5, 6 here, Jer. 49:9, 10. **hidden things**–or *places.* Edom abounded in such hiding-places, as caves, clefts in the rock, etc. None of these would be left unexplored by the foe. **7. Men of thy confederacy**–i.e., thy confederates. **brought thee . . . to the border**–i.e., when Idumean ambassadors shall go to confederate states seeking aid, these latter shall conduct them with due ceremony to their border, giving them empty compliments, but not the aid required [DRUSIUS]. This view agrees with the context, which speaks of false friends *deceiving* Edom: i.e., failing to give help in need (cf. Job 6:14, 15). CALVIN translates, "have driven," i.e., *shall drive thee;* shall help to drive thee *to thy border* on thy way into captivity in foreign lands. **the men that were at peace with thee**–lit., "the men of thy peace." Cf. Psalm 41:9; Jeremiah 38:22 (*Margin*), where also the same formula occurs, "prevailed against thee." **they that eat thy bread**–the poorer tribes of the desert who subsisted on the bounty of Edom. Cf. again Psalm 41:9, which seems to have been before Obadiah's mind, as his words were before Jeremiah's. **have laid a wound under thee**– "laid" implies that their intimacy was used as a SNARE *laid* with a view to wound; also, these guest friends of Edom, instead of the cushions ordinarily *laid* under guests at table, *laid* snares to wound, i.e., had a secret understanding with Edom's foe for that purpose. MAURER translates, "a snare." But *English Version* agrees with the *Hebrew,* which means, lit., "a bandage for a wound." **none understanding**–none of the wisdom for which Edom was famed (see vs. 8) to extricate him from his perilous position. **in him**–instead of "in thee." The change implies the alienation of God from Edom: Edom has so estranged himself from God, that He speaks now *of* him, not *to* him. **8.** (Isa. 49:7; cf. Job 5:12, 13; Isa. 19:3; Jer. 19:7). **in that day . . . even destroy**– Heretofore Edom, through its intercourse with Baby-

lon and Egypt, and from its means of information through the many caravans passing to and fro between Europe and India, has been famed for knowledge; but in that day *at last* ("even") I will destroy its wise men. **mount of Esau**–i.e., Idumea, which was a mountainous region. **9. cut off by slaughter**– MAURER translates, "on account of the slaughter," viz., that inflicted on Judea by Edom (cf. vs. 14). LXX, *Syriac,* and *Vulgate* connect these words with vs. 10, "for the slaughter, for the violence (of which thou art guilty) against thy brother Jacob." *English Version,* "cut off *by slaughter*" (i.e., an *utter* cutting off), answers well to "cut off *for ever*" (vs. 10). However, the arrangement of LXX gives a better parallelism in vs. 10. "For the *slaughter*" (1) being balanced in just retribution by "thou shalt be *cut off* for ever" (4); as "For thy *violence* (not so bad as *slaughter*) against thy brother Jacob" (2) is balanced by "*shame* (not so bad as being *cut off*) shall cover thee" (3). Shame and extinction shall repay violence and slaughter (Matt. 26:52; Rev. 13: 10). Cf. as to Edom's violence, Ps. 137:7; Ezek. 25:12; Amos 1:11. **10. against thy brother**–This aggravates the sin of Esau, that it was against him who was his brother by birth and by circumcision. The posterity of Esau followed in the steps of their father's hatred to Jacob by violence against Jacob's seed (Gen. 27:41). **Jacob**–not merely his own brother, but his *twin* brother; hence the name *Jacob,* not Israel, is here put emphatically. Cf. Deuteronomy 23:7 for the opposite feeling which Jacob's seed was commanded to entertain towards Edom's. **shame . . . cover thee**–(Ps. 35:26; 69:7). **for ever** –(Isa. 34:10; Ezek. 35:9; Mal. 1:4). Idumea, *as a nation,* should be "cut off for ever," though the land should be again inhabited. **11. thou stoodest on the other side**–in an attitude of hostility, rather than the sympathy which became a brother, feasting thine eyes (see vs. 12) with the misery of Jacob, and eagerly watching for his destruction. So Messiah, the antitype to Jerusalem, abandoned by His kinsmen (Ps. 38:11). **strangers**–the Philistines, Arabians in the reign of Jehoram, etc. (II Chron. 21:16); the Syrians in the reign of Joash of Judah (II Chron. 24:24); the Chaldeans (II Chron. 36). **carried . . . captive his forces**–his "host" (vs. 20): the multitude of Jerusalem's inhabitants. **cast lots upon Jerusalem**–(Joel 3:3). So Messiah, Jerusalem's antitype, had lots cast for His only earthly possessions (Ps. 22:18). **12. looked on**–with malignant pleasure, and a brutal stare. So the antitypes, Messiah's foes (Ps. 22:17). MAURER translates, as *Margin,* "thou shouldest not look" any more. *English Version* agrees with the context better. **the day of thy brother**–his day of calamity. **became a stranger**–i.e., was banished as an alien from his own land. God sends heavy calamities on those who rejoice in the calamities of their enemies (Prov. 17:5; 24:17, 18). Contrast the opposite conduct of David and of the divine Son of David in a like case (Ps. 35:13-15). **spoken proudly**–lit., "made great the mouth"; proudly insulting the fallen (Ezek. 35:13, *Margin;* cf. I Sam. 2:8 Rev. 13:6). **13. substance**–translated "forces" in vs. 11. **14. stood in the crossway, to cut off those of his** [Judah's] **that did escape**–The Jews naturally fled by the crossways. (MAURER translates, "narrow mountain passes") well known to them, to escape to the desert, and through Edom to Egypt; but the Edomites stood ready to intercept the fugitives and either kill or "deliver them up" to the foe. **15. For**– resumptive in connection with vs. 10, wherein Edom was threatened with *cutting off for ever.* **the day of** the Lord—the day in which He will manifest Himself as the Righteous Punisher of the ungodly peoples (Joel 3:14). The "all" shows that the fulfilment is not exhausted in the punishment inflicted on the surrounding nations by the instrumentality of Nebuchadnezzar; but, as in Joel 3:14, and Zechariah 12:3, that the last judgment to come on the nations confederate against Jerusalem is referred to. **as thou hast done, it shall be done unto thee**—the righteous principle of retribution in kind (Lev. 24:17; Matt. 7:2; cf. Judg. 1:6, 7; 8:19; Esther 7:10). **thy reward**—the reward of thy deed (cf. Isa. 3:9-11). **16. ye . . . upon my holy mountain**—a periphrasis for, "ye Jews" [MAURER], whom Obadiah now by a sudden apostrophe addresses. The clause, "upon My holy mountain," expresses the reason of the vengeance to be taken on Judah's foes; viz., that Jerusalem is God's holy mountain, the seat of His temple, and Judah His covenant people. Jeremiah 49:12, which is copied from Obadiah, establishes this view (cf. I Pet. 4:17). **as ye have drunk . . .**—viz., the cup of wrath, being dispossessed of your goods and places as a nation, by Edom and all the heathen; so shall all the heathen (Edom included) drink the same cup (Ps. 60:3; Isa. 51:17, 22; Jer. 13:12, 13; 25:15-33; 49:12; 51:7; Lam 4:21, 22; Nah. 3:11; Hab. 2:16). **continually**—whereas Judah's calamity shall be temporary (vs. 17). The foes of Judah shall never regain their former position (vs. 18, 19). **swallow down**—so as not to leave anything in the cup of calamity; not merely "drink" (Ps. 75:8). **be as though they had not been**—not a trace left of their national existence (Job 10:19; Ps. 37:36; Ezek. 26:21). **17. upon . . . Zion . . . deliverance**—both in the literal sense and spiritual sense (Joel 2:32; Isa. 46:16; 59:20; Rom. 11:26). MAURER as *Margin* explains it, "there shall be a remnant that shall escape." Cf. Isaiah 37:32; to the deliverance from Sennacherib there described GROTIUS thinks Obadiah here refers. "Jerusalem shall not be taken, and many of the neighboring peoples also shall find deliverance there." Unlike Judah's heathen foes of whom no remnant shall escape (vss. 9, 16), a remnant of Jews shall escape when the rest of the nation has perished, and shall regain their ancient "possessions." **there shall be holiness**—i.e., Zion shall be sacrosanct or inviolable: no more violated by foreign invaders (Isa. 42:1; Joel 3:17). **18. fire**—See the same figure, Numbers 21:28; Isaiah 5:24; 10:17. **house of Jacob . . . Joseph**—i.e., the two kingdoms, Judah and Ephraim or Israel [JEROME]. The two shall form one kingdom, their former feuds being laid aside (Isa. 11:12, 13; 37:22-28; Jer. 3:18; Hos. 1:11). The Jews returned with some of the Israelites from Babylon; and, under John Hyrcanus, so subdued and, compelling them to be circumcised, incorporated the Idumeans with themselves that they formed part of the nation [JOSEPHUS, 13. 17, and 12. 11]. This was but an earnest of the future union of Israel and Judah in the possession of the enlarged land as one kingdom (Ezek. 37:16, etc.). **stubble**—(Mal. 4:1). **19. they of the south**—The Jews who in the coming time are to occupy the south of Judea shall possess, in addition to their own territory, the adjoining *mountainous region of Edom.* **they of the plain**—The Jews who shall occupy the low country along the Mediterranean, south and southwest of Palestine, shall possess, in addition to their own territory, the land of "the Philistines," which runs as a long strip between the hills and the sea. **and they shall possess the fields of Ephraim**—i.e., the rightful owners

shall be restored, the Ephraimites to the fields of Ephraim. **Benjamin shall possess Gilead**—i.e., the region east of Jordan, occupied formerly by Reuben, Gad, and half Manasseh. Benjamin shall possess besides its own territory the adjoining territory eastward, while the two and a half tribes shall in the redistribution occupy the adjoining territory of Moab and Ammon. **20. the captivity of this host**—i.e., the captives of this multitude of Israelites. **shall possess that of the Canaanites**—MAURER translates, "the captives . . . whom the Canaanites (carried away captive into Phœnicia) even unto Zarephath, shall possess the south," viz., Idumea as well as the south (vs. 19). HENDERSON, similarly, "the captives that are among the Canaanites . . . ." But the corresponding clauses of the parallelism are better balanced in *English Version*, "the ten tribes of Israel shall possess the territory of the Canaanites," viz., Western Palestine and Phœnicia (Judg. 3:3). "And the captives of Jerusalem (and Judah) shall possess the southern cities," viz., Edom, etc. Each has the region respectively assigned to it; Israel has the western Canaanite region; Judah, the southern. **even unto Zarephath**—near Zidon; called Sarepta in Luke 4:26. The name implies it was a place for smelting metals. From this quarter came the "woman of Canaan" (Matt. 15:21, 22). Captives of the Jews had been carried into the coasts of Palestine or Canaan, about Tyre and Zidon (Joel 3:3, 4; Amos 1:9). The Jews when restored shall possess the territory of their ancient oppressors. **in Sepharad**—i.e., the Bosphorus [JEROME, *from his Hebrew instructor*]. Sephar, according to others (Gen. 10:30). Palæography confirms JEROME. In the cuneiform inscription containing a list of the tribes of Persia [NIEBUHR, *Tab.* 31.1], before Ionia and Greece, and after Cappadocia, comes the name CPaRaD. It was therefore a district of Western Asia Minor, about Lydia, and near the Bosphorus. It is made an appellative by MAURER. "The Jerusalem captives *of the dispersion*" (cf. Jas. 1:1), wherever they be dispersed, shall return and possess the southern cities. Sepharad, though literally the district near the Bosphorus, represents the Jews' far and wide dispersion. JEROME says the name in Assyrian means a *boundary,* i.e., "the Jews scattered in all boundaries and regions." **21. saviours**—There will be in the kingdom yet to come no king, but a prince; the sabbatic period of the judges will return (cf.the phrase so frequent in Judges, only once found in the times of the kings, II Chronicles 14:1, "the land had *rest*"), when there was no visible king, but God reigned in the theocracy. Israelites, not strangers, shall dispense justice to a God-fearing people (Isa. 1:26; Ezek. 45). The judges were not such a burden to the people as the kings proved afterwards (I Sam. 8:11-20). In their time the people more readily repented than under the kings (cf. II Chron. 15:17), [Roos]. Judges were from time to time raised up as *saviours* or *deliverers* of Israel from the enemy. These, and the similar deliverers in the long subsequent age of Antiochus, the Maccabees, who conquered the *Idumeans* (as here foretold, cf. II Maccabees 10:15, 23), were types of the peaceful period yet to come to Israel. **to judge . . . Esau**—*to punish* (so "judge," I Sam. 3:13) . . . Edom (cf. vss. 1-9, 15-19). Edom is the type of Israel's and God's last foes (Isa. 63:1-4). **kingdom shall be the Lord's**—under Messiah (Dan. 2:44; 7:14, 27; Zech. 14:9; Luke 1:33; Rev. 11:15; 19:6).

THE BOOK OF

JONAH

INTRODUCTION

JONAH was the son of Amittai, of Gath-hepher in Zebulun (called Gittah-hepher in Josh. 19:10-13), so that he belonged to the kingdom of the ten tribes, not to Judah. His date is to be gathered from II Kings 14:25-27, "He (Jeroboam II) restored the coast of Israel from the entering of Hamath unto the sea of the plain, according to the word of the Lord God of Israel, which He spake by the hand of His servant Jonah, the son of Amittai, the prophet, which was of Gath-hepher. For the Lord saw the affliction of Israel, that it was very bitter: for there was not any shut up, nor any left, nor any helper for Israel. And the Lord said not that He would blot out the name of Israel from under heaven: but He saved them by the hand of Jeroboam the son of Joash." Now as this prophecy of Jonah was given at a time when Israel was at the lowest point of depression, when "there was not any shut up or left," i.e., confined or left at large, none to act as a helper for Israel, it cannot have been given in Jeroboam's reign, which was marked by prosperity, for in it Syria was worsted in fulfilment of the prophecy, and Israel raised to its former greatness. It must have been, therefore, in the early part of the reign of Joash, Jeroboam's father, who had found Israel in subjection to Syria, but had raised it by victories which were followed up so successfully by Jeroboam. Thus Jonah was the earliest of the prophets, and close upon Elisha, who died in Joash's reign, having just before his death given a token prophetical of the thrice defeat of Syria (II Kings 13:14-21). Hosea and Amos prophesied also in the reign of Jeroboam II, but towards the closing part of his forty-one years' reign. The transactions in the Book of Jonah probably occurred in the latter part of his life; if so, the book is not much older than part of the writings of Hosea and Amos. The use of the third person is no argument against Jonah himself being the writer: for the sacred writers do in mentioning themselves do so in the third person (cf. John 19:26). Nor is the use of the past tense (ch. 3:3, "Now Nineveh *was* an exceeding great city") a proof that Nineveh's greatness was past when the Book of Jonah was being written; it is simply used to carry on the negative uniformly,—"the word of the Lord *came* to Jonah— so Jonah *arose*—now Nineveh *was*," etc. The mention of its *greatness* proves rather that the book was written at an early date, *before* the Israelites had that intimate knowledge of it which they must have had soon afterwards through frequent Assyrian inroads.

As early as Julian and Porphyry, pagans ridiculed the credulity of Christians in believing the deliverance of Jonah by a fish. Some infidels have derived it from the heathen fable of the deliverance of Andromeda from a sea monster by Perseus (APOLLOD. 2. 4, 3); or from that of Arion the musician thrown into the sea by sailors, and carried safe to shore on a dolphin (HERODOTUS, 1. 24); or from that of Hercules, who sprang into the jaws of a sea monster, and was three days in its belly, when he undertook to save Hesione (DIODORUS SICULUS, 4. 42; *Iliad*, 20. 145; 21. 442). Probably the heathen fables are, vice versa, corruptions of the sacred narrative, if there be any connection. JEROME states that near Joppa lay rocks, pointed out as those to which Andromeda was bound when exposed to the sea monster. This fable implies the likelihood of the story of Jonah having passed through the Phœnicians in a corrupted form to Greece. That the account of Jonah is history, and not parable (as rationalists represent), appears from our Lord's reference to it, in which the *personal existence*, *miraculous fate*, and *prophetical office* of Jonah are explicitly asserted: "No sign shall be given but the *sign* of the prophet Jonas: for, as Jonas was three days and three nights in the whale's belly, so shall the Son of man be three days and three nights in the heart of the earth." The Lord recognizes his being in the belly of the fish as a "sign," i.e., a real miracle, typical of a similar event in His own history; and assumes the execution of the prophet's commission to Nineveh, "The men of Nineveh . . . repented at the preaching of Jonas; and behold, a greater than Jonas is here" (Matt. 12:39-41).

It seemed strange to Kimchi, a Jew himself, that the Book of Jonah is among the Scriptures, as the only prophecy in it concerns Nineveh, a heathen city, and makes no mention of Israel, which is referred to by every other prophet. The reason seems to be: a tacit reproof of Israel is intended; a heathen people were ready to repent at the first preaching of the prophet, a stranger to them; but Israel, who boasted of being God's elect, repented not, though warned by their own prophets at all seasons. This was an anticipatory streak of light before the dawn of the full "light to lighten the Gentiles." Jonah is himself a strange paradox: a prophet of God, and yet a runaway from God: a man drowned, and yet alive: a preacher of repentance, yet one that repines at repentance. Yet Jonah, saved from the jaws of death himself on repentance, was the fittest to give a hope to Nineveh, doomed though it was, of a merciful respite on its repentance. The patience and pity of God stand in striking contrast with the selfishness and hard-heartedness of man.

Nineveh in particular was chosen to teach Israel these lessons, on account of its being capital of the then world-kingdom, and because it was now beginning to make its power felt by Israel. Our Lord (Matt. 12:41) makes Nineveh's repentance a reproof of the Jews' impenitence in His day, just as Jonah provoked Israel to jealousy (Deut. 32:21) by the same example. Jonah's mission to Nineveh implied that a heathen city afforded as legitimate a field for the prophet's labors as Israel, and with a more successful result (cf. Amos 9:7).

The book is prose narrative throughout, except the prayer of thanksgiving in ch. 2. The Chaldæisms in the original do not prove spuriousness, or a later age, but were natural in the language of one living in Zebulun on the borders of the north, whence Aramaic peculiarities would readily arise; moreover, his message to Nineveh implies acquaintance with Assyrian. Living as Jonah did in a part of Israel exposed to Assyrian invasions, he probably stood in the same relation to Assyria as Elijah and Elisha had stood to Syria. The purity of the language implies the antiquity of the book, and the likelihood of its being Jonah's own writing. Indeed, none but Jonah could have written or dictated such peculiar details, known only to himself.

The tradition that places the tomb of Jonah opposite to Mosul, and names it "Nebbi Junus" (i.e., prophet Jonah), originated probably in the spot having been occupied by a Christian church or convent dedicated to him [LAYARD]. A more ancient tradition of JEROME's time placed the tomb in Jonah's native village of Gath-hepher.

CHAPTER 1

Vss. 1-17. JONAH'S COMMISSION TO NINEVEH, FLIGHT, PUNISHMENT, AND PRESERVATION BY MIRACLE. **1. Jonah**—meaning in *Hebrew*, "dove." Cf. Genesis 8:8, 9, where the dove in vain seeks rest after flying from Noah and the ark: so Jonah. GROTIUS not so well explains it, "one sprung from Greece" or Ionia, where there were prophets called *Amythaonidæ*. **Amittai**—*Hebrew* for "truth," "truth-telling"; appropriate to a prophet. **2. to Nineveh**—east of the Tigris, opposite the modern Mosul. The only case of a prophet being sent to the heathen. Jonah, however, is sent to Nineveh, not solely for Nineveh's good, but also to shame *Israel*, by the fact of a heathen city repenting at the first preaching of a single stranger, Jonah, whereas God's people will not repent, though preached to by their many national prophets, late and early. Nineveh means "the residence of Ninus," i.e., Nimrod. Genesis 10:11, where the translation ought to be, "*He* [Nimrod] went forth *into* Assyria and builded Nineveh." Modern research into the cuneiform inscriptions confirms the Scripture account that Babylon was founded earlier than Nineveh, and that both cities were built by descendants of Ham, encroaching on the territory assigned to Shem (Gen. 10:5, 6, 8, 10, 25). **great city**—480 stadia in circumference, 150 in length, and 90 in breadth (DIODORUS SICULUS, 2. 3). Taken by Arbaces the Mede, in the reign of Sardanapalus, about the seventh year of Uzziah; and a second time by Nabopolassar of Babylon and Cyaxares the Mede in 625 B.C. See my *Note*, ch. 3:3. **cry**—(Isa. 40:6; 58:1). **come up before me**—(Gen. 4:10; 6:13; 18:21; Ezra 9:6; Rev. 18:5); i.e., their wickedness is so great as to require My open interposition for punishment. **3. flee**—Jonah's motive for flight is hinted at in ch. 4:2: fear that after venturing on such a dangerous commission to so powerful a heathen city, his prophetical threats should be set aside by God's "repenting of the evil," just as God had so long spared Israel notwithstanding so many provocations, and so he should seem a false prophet. Besides, he may have felt it beneath him to discharge a commission to a foreign idolatrous nation, whose destruction he desired rather than their repentance. This is the only case of a prophet, charged with a prophetical message, concealing it. **from the presence of the Lord**—(Cf. Gen. 4:16). Jonah thought in fleeing from the land of Israel, where Jehovah was peculiarly present, that he should escape from Jehovah's prophecy-inspiring influence. He probably knew the truth stated in Psalm 139:7-10, but virtually ignored it (cf. Gen. 3:8-10; Jer. 23:24). **went down**—appropriate in going from land to the sea (Ps. 107:23). **Joppa**—now Jaffa, in the region of Dan; a harbor as early as Solomon's time (II Chron. 2: 16). **Tarshish**—Tartessus in Spain; in the farthest west at the greatest distance from Nineveh in the east. **4. sent out**—lit., *caused* a wind *to burst forth*. COVERDALE translates, "hurled a greate wynde into the see." **5. mariners were afraid**—though used to storms; the danger therefore must have been extreme. **cried every man unto his god**—The idols proved unable to save them, though each, according to Phœnician custom, called on his tutelary god. But Jehovah proved able: and the heathen sailors owned it in the end by sacrificing to Him (vs. 16). **into the sides**—i.e., the interior recesses (cf. I Sam. 24:3; Isa. 14:13, 15). Those conscious of guilt shrink from the presence of their fellow man into concealment. **fast asleep**—Sleep is no necessary proof of innocence; it may be the fruit of carnal security and a seared conscience. How different was Jesus' sleep on the Sea of Galilee! (Mark 4:37-39). Guilty Jonah's indifference to fear contrasts with the unoffending mariners' alarm. The original therefore is in the nominative absolute: "But *as for Jonah*, he. . . ." Cf. spiritually, Ephesians 5: 14. **6. call upon thy God**—The ancient heathen in dangers called on foreign gods, besides their national ones (cf. Ps. 107:28). MAURER translates the preceding clause, "What is the reason that thou sleepest?" **think upon us**—for good (cf. Gen. 8:1; Exod. 2:25; 3:7, 9; Ps. 40:17). **7. cast lots**—God sometimes sanctioned this mode of deciding in difficult cases. Cf. the similar instance of Achan, whose guilt involved Israel in suffering, until God revealed the offender, probably by the casting of lots (Prov. 16:33; Acts 1:26). Primitive tradition and natural conscience led even the heathen to believe that one guilty man involves all his associates, though innocent, in punishment. So CICERO (*Nat. Deorum*, 3. 37) mentions that the mariners sailing with Diagoras, an atheist, attributed a storm that overtook them to his presence in the ship (cf. *Hor. Od.* 3. 2. 26). **8.** The guilty individual being discovered is interrogated so as to make full confession with his own mouth. So in Achan's case (Josh. 7:19). **9. I am an Hebrew**—He does not say "an Israelite." For this was the name used among themselves; "Hebrew," among foreigners (Gen. 40:15; Exod. 3:18). **I fear the Lord**—in profession: his practice belied his profession: his profession aggravated his guilt. **God . . . which . . . . made the sea**—appropriately expressed, as accounting for the tempest sent on the *sea*. The heathen had distinct gods for the "heaven," the "sea," and the "land." Jehovah is the one and only true God of all alike. Jonah at last is awakened by the violent remedy from his lethargy. Jonah was but the reflection of Israel's backsliding from God, and so must bear the righteous punishment. The guilt of the minister is the result of that of the people, as in Moses' case (Deut. 4:21). This is what makes Jonah a suitable type of Messiah, who bore the *imputed* sin of the people. **10.** "The men were exceedingly afraid," when made aware of the wrath of so powerful a God at the flight of Jonah. **Why hast thou done this?**—If professors of religion do wrong, they will hear of it from those who make no such profession. **11. What shall we do unto thee?**—They ask this, as Jonah himself must best know how his God is to be appeased. "We would gladly save thee, if we can do so, and yet be saved ourselves" (vss. 13, 14). **12. cast me . . . into the sea**—Herein Jonah is a type of Messiah, the one man who offered Himself to die, in order to allay the stormy flood of God's wrath (cf. Ps. 69:1, 2, as to Messiah), which otherwise must have engulfed all other men. So Caiaphas by the Spirit declared it expedient that one man should die, and that the whole nation should not perish (John 11:50). Jonah also herein is a specimen of true repentance, which leads the penitent to "accept the punishment of his iniquity" (Lev. 26:41, 43), and to be more indignant at his sin than at his suffering. **13. they could not**—(Prov. 21:30). Wind and tide—God's displeasure and God's counsel—were against them. **14. for this man's life**—i.e., for taking this man's life. **innocent blood**—Do not punish us as Thou wouldst punish the shedders of innocent blood (cf. Deut. 21: 8). In the case of the Antitype, Pontius Pilate washed his hands and confessed Christ's *innocence,* "I am innocent of the blood of this *just* person." But whereas Jonah the victim was guilty and the sailors innocent, Christ our sacrificial victim was innocent and Pontius Pilate and all of us men were guilty. But by *imputation* of our guilt to Him and His righteousness to us, the spotless Antitype exactly corresponds to the guilty type. **thou ... Lord, hast done as it pleased thee**—That Jonah has embarked in this ship, that a tempest has arisen, that he has been detected by casting of lots, that he has passed sentence on himself, is all Thy doing. We reluctantly put him to death, but it is Thy pleasure it should be so. **15. sea ceased ... raging**—so at Jesus' word (Luke 8:24). God spares the prayerful penitent, a truth illustrated now in the case of the sailors, presently in that of Jonah, and thirdly, in that of Nineveh. **16. offered a sacrifice**—They offered some sacrifice of thanksgiving at once, and vowed more when they should land. GLASSIUS thinks it means only, "They *promised* to offer a sacrifice." **17. prepared a great fish**—not *created* specially for this purpose, but appointed in His providence, to which all creatures are subservient. The fish, through a mistranslation of Matthew 12:40, was formerly supposed to be a whale; there, as here, the original means "a great fish." The whale's neck is too narrow to receive a man. BOCHART thinks, the *dogfish,* the stomach of which is so large that the body of a man in armor was once found in it (HIEROZO. 2. 5. 12). Others, the *shark* [JEBB]. The *cavity in the whale's throat,* large enough, according to Captain SCORESBY, to hold a ship's jolly-boat full of men. A *miracle* in any view is needed, and we have no data to speculate further. A "sign" or miracle it is expressly called by our Lord in Matthew 12. Respiration in such a position could only be by miracle. The miraculous interposition was not without a sufficient reason; it was calculated to affect not only Jonah, but also Nineveh and Israel. The life of a prophet was often marked by experiences which made him, through sympathy, best suited for discharging the prophetical function to his hearers and his people. The infinite resources of God in mercy as well as judgment are prefigured in the devourer being transformed into Jonah's preserver. Jonah's condition under punishment, shut out from the outer world, was rendered as much as possible the emblem of death, a present type to Nineveh and Israel, of the death in sin, as his deliverance was of the spiritual resurrection on repentance; as also, a future type of Jesus' literal death for sin, and resurrection by the Spirit of God. **three days and three nights**—probably, like the Antitype, Christ, Jonah was cast forth on the land on the *third* day (Matt. 12:40); the Hebrew counting the first and third parts of days as whole twenty-four hour days.

CHAPTER 2

VSS. 1-10. JONAH'S PRAYER OF FAITH AND DELIVERANCE. **1. his God**—"his" still, though Jonah had fled from Him. Faith enables Jonah now to feel this; just as the returning prodigal says of the Father, from whom he had wandered, "I will arise and go to *my* Father" (Luke 15:18). **out of the fish's belly**—Every place may serve as an oratory. No place is amiss for prayer. Others translate, "when (delivered) out of the fish's belly." *English Version* is better. **2.** His prayer is partly descriptive and precatory, partly eucharistical. Jonah incorporates with his own language inspired utterances familiar to the Church long before in vs. 2, Psalm 120:1; in vs. 3, Psalm 42:7; in vs. 4, Psalm 31:22; in vs. 5, Psalm 69:1; in vs. 7, Psalm 142:3, and 18:6; in vs. 8, Psalm 31:6; in vs. 9, Psalm 116:17, 18, and 3:8. Jonah, an inspired man, thus attests both the antiquity and inspiration of the Psalms. It marks the spirit of faith, that Jonah identifies himself with the saints of old, appropriating their experiences as recorded in the Word of God (Ps. 119:50). Affliction opens up the mine of Scripture, before seen only on the surface. **out of the belly of hell**—*Sheol,* the unseen world, which the belly of the fish resembled. **3. thou hadst cast ... thy billows ... thy waves**—Jonah recognizes the source whence his sufferings came. It was no mere chance, but *the hand of God* which sent them. Cf. Job's similar recognition of God's hand in calamities, Job 1:21; 2:10; and David's, II Samuel 16:5-11. **4. cast out from thy sight**—i.e., from Thy favorable regard. A just retribution on one who had fled *"from the presence* of the Lord" (ch. 1:3). Now that he has got his desire, he feels it to be his bitterest sorrow to be deprived of God's presence, which once he regarded as a burden, and from which he desired to escape. He had turned his back on God; so God turned His back on him, making his sin his punishment. **toward thy holy temple**—In the confidence of faith he anticipates yet to see the temple at Jerusalem, the appointed place of worship (I Kings 8:38), and there to render thanksgiving [HENDERSON]. Rather, I think, "Though cast out of Thy sight, I will still *with the eye of faith* once more *look in prayer* towards Thy temple at Jerusalem, whither, as Thy earthly throne, Thou hast desired Thy worshippers to direct their prayers." **5. even to the soul**—i.e., threatening to extinguish the *animal life.* **weeds**—He felt as if the seaweeds through which he was dragged were wrapped about his head. **6. bottoms of ... mountains**—their *extremities* where they *terminate* in the hidden depths of the sea. Cf. Psalm 18:7, "the foundations of the hills" (Ps. 18:15). **earth with her bars was about me**—Earth, the land of the living, is (not "was") shut against me. **for ever**—so far as any effort of *mine* can deliver me. **yet hast thou brought up my life from corruption**—rather, "Thou bringest ... from the pit" [MAURER]. As in the previous clauses he expresses the hopelessness of his state, so in this, his sure hope of deliverance through Jehovah's infinite resources. "Against hope he believes in hope," and speaks as if the deliverance were actually being accomplished. Hezekiah seems to have incorporated Jonah's very words in his prayer (Isa. 38:17), just as Jonah appropriated the language of the Psalms. **7. soul fainted ... I remembered the Lord**—beautifully exemplifying the triumph of spirit over flesh, of faith over sense (Ps. 73:26; 42:6). For a time troubles shut out hope; but faith revived when Jonah "remembered the Lord," what a gracious God He is, and how now He still preserves his life and consciousness in his dark prison house. **into thine holy temple**—the temple at Jerusalem (vs. 4). As there he looks in believing prayer towards it, so here he regards his prayer as already heard. **8. observe lying vanities** —regard or reverence idols, powerless to save (Ps. 31:6). **mercy**—Jehovah, the very idea of whom is identified now in Jonah's mind with mercy and loving-kindness. As the Psalmist (Ps. 144:2) styles Him, "my goodness"; God who is to me all benefi-cence. Cf. Psalm 59:17, "the God of my mercy," lit., "my kindness-God." Jonah had "forsaken His own mercy," God, to flee to heathen lands where "lying vanities" (idols) were worshipped. But now, taught by his own preservation in conscious life in the fish's belly, and by the inability of the mariners' idols to lull the storm (ch. 1:5), estrangement from God seems estrangement from his own happiness (Jer. 2:13; 17:13). Prayer has been restrained in Jonah's case, so that he was "fast asleep" in the midst of danger, heretofore; but now prayer is the sure sign of his return to God. **9. I will sacrifice ... thanksgiving**—In the believing anticipation of sure deliverance, he offers thanksgivings already. So Jehoshaphat (II Chron. 20:21) appointed singers to *praise* the Lord in front of the army before the battle with Moab and Ammon, as if the victory was already gained. God honors such confidence in Him. There is also herein a mark of sanctified af-fliction, that he vows amendment and thankful obedience (Ps. 119:67). **10. upon the dry land**— probably on the coast of Palestine.

CHAPTER 3

Vss. 1-10. JONAH'S SECOND COMMISSION TO NINE-VEH: THE NINEVITES REPENT OF THEIR EVIL WAY: SO GOD REPENTS OF THE EVIL THREATENED. **2. preach ... the preaching**—lit., "proclaim the proc-lamation." On the former occasion the specific object of his commission to Nineveh was declared; here it is indeterminate. This is to show how freely he yields himself, in the spirit of unconditional obe-dience, to speak whatever God may please. **3. arose and went**—like the son who was at first dis-obedient to the father's command, "Go work in my vineyard," but who afterwards "repented and went" (Matt. 21:28, 29). Jonah was thus the fittest in-strument for proclaiming judgment, and yet hope of mercy on repentance to Nineveh, being himself a living exemplification of both—judgment in his en-tombment in the fish, mercy on repentance in his deliverance. Israel professing to obey, but not obeying, and so doomed to exile in the same Nine-veh, answers to the son who said, "I go, sir, and went not." In Luke 11:30 it is said that Jonas was not only a sign to the men in Christ's time, but also "unto the Ninevites." On the latter occasion (Matt. 16:1-4) when the Pharisees and Sadducees tempted Him, asking a sign *from heaven,* He answered, "No sign shall be given, but the sign of the prophet Jo-nas." Thus the sign had a *twofold* aspect, a direct bearing on the Ninevites, an indirect bearing on the Jews in Christ's time. To the Ninevites he was not merely a prophet, but himself a wonder in the earth, as one who had tasted of death, and yet had not seen corruption, but had now returned to witness among them for God. If the Ninevites had in-dulged in a captious spirit, they never would have inquired and so known Jonah's wonderful history; but being humbled by God's awful message, they learned from Jonah himself that it was the previous

concealing in his bosom of the same message of their own doom that caused him to be entombed as an outcast from the living. Thus he was a "sign" to them of wrath on the one hand, and, on the other, of mercy. Guilty Jonah saved from the jaws of death gives a ray of hope to guilty Nineveh. Thus God, who brings good from evil, made Jonah in his fall, punishment, and restoration, a sign (an *em-bodied lesson* or *living symbol*) through which the Ninevites were roused to hear and repent, as they would not have been likely to do, had he gone on the first commission before his living entombment and resurrection. To do evil that good may come, is a policy which can only come from Satan; but from evil already done to extract an instrument against the kingdom of darkness, is a triumphant display of the grace and wisdom of God. To the Pharisees in Christ's time, who, not content with the many signs exhibited by Him, still demanded a sign *from heaven,* He gave a sign in the opposite quarter, viz., Jonah, who came "out of the belly of *hell*" (the unseen region). They looked for a Messiah glo-riously coming in the clouds of *heaven;* the Messiah, on the contrary, is to pass through a like, though a deeper, humiliation than Jonah; He is to lie "in the heart of *the earth."* Jonah and his Antitype alike appeared low and friendless among their hearers; both victims to death for God's wrath against sin, both preaching repentance. Repentance derives all its efficacy from the death of Christ, just as Jo-nah's message derived its weight with the Ninevites from his entombment. The Jews stumbled at Christ's death, the very fact which ought to have led them to Him, as Jonah's entombment attracted the Ninevites to his message. As Jonah's restoration gave hope of God's placability to Nineveh, so Christ's resurrection assures us God is fully recon-ciled to man by Christ's death. But Jonah's en-tombment only had the effect of a *moral suasive*; Christ's resurrection assures us God is fully recon-ciliation between God and man [FAIRBAIRN]. **Nin-eveh was an exceeding great city**—lit., "great to God," i.e., before God. All greatness was in the Hebrew mind associated with GOD; hence arose the idiom (cf. Ps. 36:6; 80:10), "great mountains," *Mar-gin,* "mountains of God"; "goodly cedars," *Margin,* "cedars of God," Genesis 10:9, "a mighty hunter *before the Lord."* **three days' journey**—i.e., about sixty miles, allowing about twenty miles for a day's journey. Jonah's statement is confirmed by hea-then writers, who describe Nineveh as 480 stadia in circumference [DIODORUS SICULUS, 2. 3]. HERODO-TUS defines a day's journey to be 150 stadia; so three days' journey will not be much below DIODORUS' estimate. The parallelogram in Central Assyria covered with remains of buildings has Khorsabad northeast; Koyunjik and Nebbi Yunus near the Ti-gris, northwest; Nimroud, between the Tigris and the Zab, southwest; and Karamless, at a distance inward from the Zab, southeast. From Koyunjik to Nimroud is about eighteen miles; from Khorsa-bad to Karamless, the same; from Koyunjik to Khorsabad, thirteen or fourteen miles; from Nim-roud to Karamless, fourteen miles. The length thus was greater than the breadth; cf. vs. 4, "a day's journey," which is confirmed by heathen writers and by modern measurements. The walls were 100 feet high, and broad enough to allow three chariots abreast, and had moreover 1500 lofty towers. The space between, including large parks and arable ground, as well as houses, was Nineveh in its full extent. The oldest palaces are at Nimroud, which was probably the original site. LAYARD latterly has thought that the name Nineveh belonged originally to Koyunjik, rather than to Nimroud. Jonah (ch. 4:11) mentions the children as numbering 120,000, which would give about a million to the whole population. Existing ruins show that Nineveh acquired its greatest extent under the kings of the second dynasty, i.e., the kings mentioned in Scripture; it was then that Jonah visited it, and the reports of its magnificence were carried to the west [LAYARD]. **4. a day's journey**—not going straight forward without stopping: for the city was but eighteen miles in length; but stopping in his progress from time to time to announce his message to the crowds gathering about him. **Yet forty days, and Nineveh shall be overthrown**—The commission, given indefinitely at his setting out, assumes now on his arrival a definite form, and that severer than before. It is no longer a cry against the sins of Nineveh, but an announcement of its ruin in forty days. This number is in Scripture associated often with humiliation. It was forty days that Moses, Elijah, and Christ fasted. Forty years elapsed from the beginning of Christ's ministry (the antitype of Jonah's) to the destruction of Jerusalem. The more definite form of the denunciation implies that Nineveh has now almost filled up the measure of her guilt. The change in the form which the Ninevites would hear from Jonah on anxious inquiry into his history, would alarm them the more, as implying the increasing nearness and certainty of their doom, and would at the same time reprove Jonah for his previous guilt in delaying to warn them. The very solitariness of the one message announced by the stranger thus suddenly appearing among them, would impress them with the more awe. Learning from him, that so far from lightly prophesying evil against them, he had shrunk from announcing a less severe denunciation, and therefore had been cast into the deep and only saved by miracle, they felt how imminent was their peril, threatened as they now were by a prophet whose fortunes were so closely bound up with theirs. In Noah's days 120 years of warning were given to men, yet they repented not till the flood came, and it was too late. But in the case of Nineveh, God granted a double mercy: first, that its people should repent immediately after threatening; second, that pardon should immediately follow their repentance. **5. believed God**—gave credit to Jonah's message from God; thus recognizing Jehovah as the true God. **fast ... sackcloth**—In the East outward actions are often used as symbolical expressions of inward feelings. So fasting and clothing in sackcloth were customary in humiliation. Cf. in Ahab's case, parallel to that of Nineveh, both receiving a *respite* on penitence (I Kings 21:27; 20:31, 32; Joel 1:13). **from the greatest ... to the least**—The penitence was not partial, but pervading all classes. **6. in ashes**—emblem of the deepest humiliation (Job 2:8; Ezek. 27:30). **7. neither .. beast ... taste any thing**—The brute creatures share in the evil effects of man's sin (ch. 4:11; Rom. 8:20, 22); so they here according to Eastern custom, are made to share in man's outward indications of humiliation. "When the Persian general Masistias was slain, the horses and mules of the Persians were shorn, as well as themselves" [NEWCOME from PLUTARCH; also HERODOTUS, 9.24]. **8. cry ... turn**—Prayer without reformation is a mockery of God (Ps. 66:18; Isa. 58: 6). Prayer, on the other hand, must precede true reformation, as we cannot turn to God from our evil way unless God first turns us (Jer. 31:18, 19). **9. Who can tell**—(Cf. Joel 2:14). Their acting on

a vague possibility of God's mercy, without any special ground of encouragement, is the more remarkable instance of faith, as they had to break through long-rooted prejudices in giving up idols to seek Jehovah at all. The only ground which their ready faith rested on, was the fact of God sending one to warn them, instead of destroying them at once; this suggested the thought of a possibility of pardon. Hence they are cited by Christ as about to condemn in the judgment those who, with much greater light and privileges, yet repent not (Matt. 12:41). **11. God repented of the evil**—When the message was sent to them, they were so ripe for judgment that a purpose of destruction to take effect in forty days was the only word God's righteous abhorrence of sin admitted of as to them. But when they repented, the position in which they stood towards God's righteousness was altered. So God's mode of dealing with them must alter accordingly, if God is not to be inconsistent with His own immutable character of dealing with men according to their works and state of heart, taking vengeance at last on the hardened impenitent, and delighting to show mercy on the penitent. Cf. Abraham's reasoning, Gen. 18:25; Ezek. 18:21-25; Jer. 18:7-10. What was really a change *in them* and in God's corresponding dealings is, in condescension to human conceptions, represented as a change in God (cf. Exod. 32:14), who, in His essential righteousness and mercy, changeth not (Num. 23:19; I Sam. 15:29; Mal. 3:6; Jas. 1:17). The reason why the announcement of destruction was made absolute, and not dependent on Nineveh's continued impenitence, was that this form was the only one calculated to rouse them; and at the same time it was a *truthful* representation of God's purpose towards Nineveh under its existing state, and of Nineveh's due. When that state ceased, a new relation of Nineveh to God, not contemplated in the message, came in, and room was made for the word to take effect, "the curse causeless shall not come" [FAIRBAIRN]. Prophecy is not merely for the sake of proving God's omniscience by the verification of predictions of the future, but is mainly designed to vindicate God's justice and mercy in dealing with the impenitent and penitent respectively (Rom. 11: 22). The Bible ever assigns the first place to the eternal principles of righteousness, rooted in the character of God, subordinating to them all divine arrangements. God's sparing Nineveh, when in the jaws of destruction, on the first dawn of repentance encourages the timid penitent, and shows beforehand that Israel's doom, soon after accomplished, is to be ascribed, not to unwillingness to forgive on God's part, but to their own obstinate impenitence.

CHAPTER 4

Vss. 1-11. JONAH FRETS AT GOD'S MERCY TO NINEVEH: IS REPROVED BY THE TYPE OF A GOURD. **1. angry**—lit., "hot," probably, with *grief* or *vexation*, rather than *anger* [FAIRBAIRN]. How sad the contrast between God's feeling on the repentance of Nineveh towards Him, and Jonah's feeling on the repentance of God towards Nineveh. Strange in one who was himself a monument of mercy on his repentance! We all, like him, need the lesson taught in th parable of the unforgiving, though forgiven, debtor (Matt. 18:23-35). Jonah was grieved because Nineveh's preservation, after his denunciation, made him seem a false prophet [CALVIN]. But it would make Jonah a demon, not a man, to have preferred the destruction of 600,000 men rather than that his prophecy should be set aside through God's mercy triumphing over judgment. And God in that case would have severely chastised, whereas he only expostulates mildly with him, and by a mode of dealing, at once gentle and condescending, tries to show him his error. Moreover, Jonah himself, in apologizing for his vexation, does not mention *the failure of his prediction* as the cause: but solely the thought of God's *slowness to anger.* This was what led him to flee to Tarshish at his first commission; not the likelihood *then* of his prediction being falsified; for in fact his commission then was not to foretell Nineveh's downfall, but simply to "cry against" Nineveh's "wickedness" as having "come up before God." Jonah could hardly have been so vexed for the letter of his prediction failing, when the end of his commission had virtually been gained in leading Nineveh to repentance. This then cannot have been regarded by Jonah as the *ultimate* end of his commission. If Nineveh had been the prominent object with him, he would have rejoiced at the result of his mission. But Israel was the prominent aim of Jonah, as a prophet of the elect people. Probably then he regarded the destruction of Nineveh as fitted to be an example of God's judgment at last suspending His long forbearance so as to startle Israel from its desperate degeneracy, heightened by its new prosperity under Jeroboam II at that very time, in a way that all other means had failed to do. Jonah, despairing of anything effectual being done for God in Israel, unless there were first given a striking example of severity, thought when he proclaimed the downfall of Nineveh in forty days, that now at last God is about to give such an example; so when this means of awakening Israel was set aside by God's mercy on Nineveh's repentance, he was bitterly disappointed, not from pride or mercilessness, but from hopelessness as to anything being possible for the reformation of Israel, now that his cherished hope is baffled. But GOD's plan was to teach Israel, by the example of Nineveh, how inexcusable is their own impenitence, and how inevitable their ruin if they persevere. Repenting Nineveh has proved herself more worthy of God's favor than apostate Israel; the children of the covenant have not only fallen down to, but actually below, the level of a heathen people; Israel, therefore, must go down, and the heathen rise above her. Jonah did not know the important lessons of hope to the penitent, and condemnation to those amidst outward privileges impenitent, which Nineveh's preservation on repentance was to have for aftertimes, and to all ages. He could not foresee that Messiah Himself was thus to apply that history. A lesson to us that if we *could* in any particular alter the plan of Providence, it would not be for the better, but for the worse [FAIRBAIRN]. **2. my saying**—my thought, or feeling. **fled before**—*I anticipated by fleeing,* the disappointment of my design through Thy long-suffering mercy. **gracious . . . and merciful . . .**—Jonah here has before his mind Exodus 34: 6; as Joel (Joel 2:13) in his turn quotes from Jonah. **3.** Jonah's impatience of life under disappointed hopes of Israel's reformation through the destruction of Nineveh, is like that of Elijah at his plan for reforming Israel (I Kings 18) failing through Jezebel (I Kings 19:4). **4. Doest thou well to be angry?**—or *grieved;* rather as *Margin,* "Art thou *much* angry," or "grieved?" [FAIRBAIRN with LXX and *Syriac*]. But *English Version* suits the spirit of the passage, and is quite tenable in the *Hebrew*

[GESENIUS]. **5. made him a booth**—i.e., a temporary hut of branches and leaves, so slightly formed as to be open to the wind and sun's heat. **see what would become of the city**—The term of forty days had not yet elapsed, and Jonah did not know that anything more than a suspension, or mitigation, of judgment had been granted to Nineveh. Therefore, not from sullennesss, but in order to watch the event from a neighboring station, he lodged in the booth. As a stranger, he did not know the depth of Nineveh's repentance; besides, from the Old Testament standpoint he knew that chastening judgments often followed, as in David's case (II Sam. 12:10-12, 14), even where sin had been repented of. To show him what he knew not, the largeness and completeness of God's mercy to penitent Nineveh, and the reasonableness of it, God made his booth a school of discipline to give him more enlightened views. **6. gourd**—*Hebrew, kikaion;* the Egyptian *kiki,* the "ricinus" or castor-oil plant, commonly called "palm-christ" (*palma christi*). It grows from eight to ten feet high. Only one leaf grows on a branch, but that leaf being often more than a foot large, the collective leaves give good shelter from the heat. It grows rapidly, and fades as suddenly when injured. **to deliver him from his grief** —It was therefore *grief,* not selfish anger, which Jonah felt (*Note,* vs. 1). Some external comforts will often turn the mind away from its sorrowful bent. **7. a worm**—of a particular kind, deadly to the ricinus. A small worm at the root destroys a large gourd. So it takes but little to make our creature comforts wither. It should silence discontent to remember, that when our gourd is gone, our God is not gone. **the next day**—after Jonah was so "exceeding glad" (cf. Ps. 80:7). **8. vehement** —rather, "scorching"; *Margin, silent,* expressing sultry *stillness,* not *vehemence.* **9.** (*Note,* vs. 4). **I do well to be angry, even unto death**—"I am very much grieved, even to death" [FAIRBAIRN]. So the Antitype (Matt. 26:38). **10, 11.** The main lesson of the book. If Jonah so pities a plant which cost him no toil to rear, and which is so short lived and valueless, much more must Jehovah pity those hundreds of thousands of immortal men and women in great Nineveh whom He has made with such a display of creative power, especially when many of them repent, and seeing that, if all in it were destroyed, "more than six score thousand" of *unoffending* children, besides "much cattle," would be involved in the common destruction. Cf. the same argument drawn from God's justice and mercy in Genesis 18:23-33. A similar illustration from the insignificance of a plant, which "to-day is and to-morrow is cast into the oven," and which, nevertheless, is clothed by God with surpassing beauty, is given by Christ to prove that God will care for the infinitely more precious bodies and souls of men who are to live for ever (Matt. 6:28-30). One soul is of more value than the whole world; surely, then, one soul is of more value than many gourds. The point of comparison spiritually is the *need* which Jonah, for the time being, had of the foliage of the gourd. However he might dispense with it at other times, now it was necessary for his comfort, and almost for his life. So now that Nineveh, as a city, fears God and turns to Him, God's cause needs it, and would suffer by its overthrow, just as Jonah's material well-being suffered by the withering of the gourd. If there were any hope of Israel's being awakened by Nineveh's destruction to fulfil her high destination of being a light to surrounding heathenism, then there would not have been the same need to God's cause of Nineveh's preservation, (though there would have always been need of saving the penitent). But as Israel, after judgments, now with returning prosperity turns back to apostasy, the means *needed* to vindicate God's cause, and provoke Israel, if possible, to jealousy, is the example of the great capital of heathendom suddenly repenting at the first warning, and consequently being spared. Thus Israel would see the kingdom of heaven transplanted from its ancient seat to another which would willingly yield its spiritual fruits. The tidings which Jonah brought back to his countrymen of Nineveh's repentance and rescue, would, if believingly understood, be far more fitted than the news of its overthrow to recall Israel to the service of God. Israel failed to learn the lesson, and so was cast out of her land. But even this was not an unmitigated evil. Jonah was a type, as of Christ, so also of Israel. Jonah, though an outcast, was highly honored of God in Nine-

veh; so Israel's outcast condition would prove no impediment to her serving God's cause still, if only she was faithful to God. Ezekiel and Daniel were so at Babylon; and the Jews, scattered in all lands as witnesses for the one true God, pioneered the way for Christianity, so that it spread with a rapidity which otherwise was not likely to have attended it [FAIRBAIRN]. **that cannot discern between their right hand and their left**—children under three of four years old (Deut. 1:39). *Six score thousand* of these, allowing them to be a fifth of the whole, would give a *total* population of 600,000. **much cattle**—God cares even for the brute creatures, of which man takes little account. These in wonderful powers and in utility are far above the shrub which Jonah is so concerned about. Yet Jonah is reckless as to their destruction and that of innocent children. The abruptness of the close of the book is more strikingly suggestive than if the thought had been followed out in detail.

THE BOOK OF

MICAH

INTRODUCTION

MICAH was a native of Moresheth, not the same as Mareshah in ch. 1:15, but the town called Moreshethgath (ch. 1:14), which lay near Eleutheropolis, west of Jerusalem, on the border of the Philistine country; so called to distinguish it from Moresheth of Judah. His full name is *Micaiah* (not the Micaiah mentioned I Kings 22:8, the son of Imlah), signifying, *Who is like Jehovah?* The time of his prophesying is stated in the introduction to be in the reigns of Jotham. Ahaz, and Hezekiah, i.e., between 757 and 699 B.C. Jeremiah (Jer. 26:18) quotes ch. 3:12, as delivered in the reign of Hezekiah. He was thus a contemporary of Isaiah and Hosea. The idolatries practised in the reign of Ahaz accord with Micah's denunciations of such gross evils, and confirm the truth of the time assigned ch. 1:1. His prophecies are partly against Israel (Samaria), partly against Judah. As Samaria, Israel's metropolis, was taken first, and Jerusalem, the capital of Judah, subsequently, in the introductory heading, ch. 1:1, *Samaria* is put first, then *Jerusalem*. He prophesies the capture of both; the Jews' captivity and restoration; and the coming and reign of Messiah. His style is full, round, and perspicuous; his diction pure, and his parallelisms regular. His description of Jehovah (ch. 7:18, 19) is not surpassed by any elsewhere in Scripture. The similarity between Isaiah and Micah in some passages (cf. ch. 4:1–3, with Isa. 2:2–4) is to be accounted for by their being contemporaries, acquainted with each other's inspired writings, and having the same subjects for their theme. HENGSTENBERG maintains that the passage in Micah is the original. Isaiah was somewhat the older, being a prophet in the reign of Uzziah, Jotham's predecessor, whereas Micah began his prophecies under Jotham.

The book consists of two parts: (1) ch. 1–5; (2) chs. 6, 7, a dialogue or contestation between Jehovah and His people, in which He reproaches them with their unnatural and ungrateful conduct, and threatens judgment for their corruptions, but consoles them with the promise of restoration from captivity.

Micah stands sixth among the minor prophets in the *Hebrew* canon, but third in the LXX.

CHAPTER 1

Vss. 1-16. GOD'S WRATH AGAINST SAMARIA AND JUDAH; THE FORMER IS TO BE OVERTHROWN; SUCH JUDGMENTS IN PROSPECT CALL FOR MOURNING. **2. all that therein is**—*Hebrew*, "whatever fills it." Micaiah, son of Imlah, begins his prophecy similarly, "Hearken, O people, every one of you." Micah designedly uses the same preface, implying that his ministrations are a continuation of his predecessor's of the same name. Both probably had before their mind Moses' similar attestation of heaven and earth in a like case (Deut. 31:28; 32:1; cf. Isa. 1:2). **God be witness against you**—viz., that none of you can say, when the time of your punishment shall come, that you were not forewarned. The punishment

denounced is stated in vs. 3, etc. **from his holy temple**—i.e., heaven (I Kings 8:30; Ps. 11:4; Jonah 2:7; cf. Rom. 1:18). **3. tread upon the high places of the earth**—He shall destroy the fortified heights (cf. Deut. 32:13; 33:29) [GROTIUS]. **4.** Imagery from earthquakes and volcanic agency, to describe the terrors which attend Jehovah's coming in judgment (cf. Judg. 5:5). Neither men of high degree, as the mountains, nor men of low degree, as the valleys, can secure themselves or their land from the judgments of God. **as wax**—(Ps. 97:5; cf. Isa. 64: 1-3). The third clause, "as wax . . . ," answers to the first in the parallelism, "the mountains shall be molten"; the fourth, "as the waters . . . ," to the second, "the valleys shall be cleft." As wax melts by fire, so the mountains before God, at His approach; and as waters poured down a steep cannot stand but are diffused abroad, so the valleys shall be cleft before Jehovah. **5. For the transgression of Jacob is all this**—All these terrors attending Jehovah's coming are caused by the sins of Jacob or Israel, i.e., the whole people. **What is the transgression of Jacob?**—Taking up the question often in the mouths of the people when reproved, "What is our transgression?" (cf. Mal. 1:6,7), He answers, Is it not Samaria? Is not that city (the seat of the calf worship) the cause of Jacob's apostasy (I Kings 14: 16; 15:26, 34; 16:13, 19, 25, 30)? **and what are the high places of Judah?**—What city is the cause of the idolatries on the high places of Judah? Is it not Jerusalem (cf. II Kings 18:4)? **6.** Samaria's punishment is mentioned first, as it was to fall before Jerusalem. **as an heap of the field**—(ch. 3:12). Such a heap of stones and rubbish as is gathered out of fields, to clear them (Hos. 12:11). Palestine is of a soil abounding in stones, which are gathered out before the vines are planted (Isa. 5:2). **as plantings of a vineyard**—as a place where vines are planted. Vineyards were cultivated on the sides of hills exposed to the sun. The hill on which Samaria was built by Omri, had been, doubtless, planted with vines originally; now it is to be reduced again to its original state (I Kings 16:24). **pour down**—*dash down* the stones of the people of the city into the valley beneath. A graphic picture of the present appearance of the ruins, which is as though "the buildings of the ancient city had been thrown down from the brow of the hill" [SCOTTISH MISSION OF INQUIRY, pp. 293, 294]. **discover the foundations**—destroy it so utterly as to lay bare its foundations (Ezek. 13:14). Samaria was destroyed by Shalmaneser. **7. all the hires**—the wealth which Israel boasted of receiving from her idols as the "rewards" or "hire" for worshipping them (Hos. 2:5, 12). **idols . . . will I . . . desolate**—i.e., give them up to the foe to strip off the silver and gold with which they are overlaid. **she gathered it of the hire of an harlot, and they shall return to the hire of an harlot**—Israel gathered (made for herself) her idols from the gold and silver received from false gods, as she thought, the "hire" of her worshipping them; and they shall again become what they had been before, the hire of spiritual harlotry, i.e., the prosperity of the foe, who also being worshippers of idols will ascribe the acquisition to their idols [MAURER]. GROTIUS explains it, *The offerings sent to Israel's temple by the Assyrians,* whose idolatry Israel adopted, shall go back to the Assyrians, her teachers in idolatry, as the hire or *fee for having taught it.* The image of a *harlot's hire* for the supposed temporal reward of spiritual fornication, is more common in Scripture (Hos. 9: 1). **8. Therefore I will wail**—The prophet first shows how the coming judgment affects himself, in order that he might affect the minds of his countrymen similarly. **stripped**—i.e., *of shoes,* or *sandals,* as the LXX translates. Otherwise "naked" would be a tautology. "Naked" means *divested of the upper garment* (Isa. 20:2). "Naked and barefoot," the sign of mourning (II Sam. 15:30). The prophet's upper garment was usually rough and coarse-haired (II Kings 1:8; Zech. 13:4). **like the dragons**—so JEROME. Rather, "the wild dogs," jackals or wolves, which wail like an infant when in distress or alone [MAURER]. (See *Note,* Job 30: 29.) **owls**—rather, "ostriches," which give a shrill and long-drawn, sigh-like cry, especially at night. **9. wound . . . incurable**—Her case, politically and morally, is desperate (Jer. 8:22). **it is come**—the wound, or impending calamity (cf. Isa. 10:28). **he**

is come . . . even to Jerusalem—The evil is no longer limited to Israel. The prophet foresees Sennacherib coming even "to the gate" of the principal city. The use of "it" and "he" is appropriately distinct. "It," the calamity, "came unto" Judah, many of the inhabitants of which suffered, but did not reach the citizens of Jerusalem, "the gate" of which the foe ("he") "came unto," but did not enter (Isa. 36:1; 37:33-37). **10. Declare ye it not at Gath**—on the borders of Judea, one of the five cities of the Philistines, who would exult at the calamity of the Hebrews (II Sam. 1:20). Gratify not those who exult over the falls of the Israel of God. **weep ye not at all**—Do not betray your inward sorrow by outward weeping, within the cognizance of the enemy, lest they should exult at it. RELAND translates, "Weep not *in Acco,*" i.e., Ptolemais, now St. Jean d'Acre, near the foot of Mount Carmel; allotted to Asher, but never occupied by that tribe (Judg. 1:31); Acco's inhabitants would, therefore, like Gath's, rejoice at Israel's disaster. Thus the parallelism is best carried out in all the three clauses of the verse, and there is a similar play on sounds in each, in the *Hebrew Gath,* resembling in sound the *Hebrew* for "declare"; *Acco,* resembling the *Hebrew* for "weep"; and *Aphrah,* meaning "dust." While the Hebrews were not to expose their misery to foreigners, they ought to bewail it in their own cities, e.g., Aphrah or Ophrah (Josh. 18:23; I Sam. 13:17), in the tribe of Benjamin. To "roll in the dust" marked deep sorrow (Jer. 6:26; Ezek. 27:30). **11. Pass ye away**—i.e., Thou shalt go into captivity. **inhabitant of Saphir**—a village amidst the hills of Judah, between Eleutheropolis and Ascalon, called so, from the *Hebrew* word for "beauty". Though thy name be "beauty," which heretofore was thy characteristic, thou shalt have thy "shame" made "naked." This city shall be dismantled of its walls, which are the garments, as it were, of cities; its citizens also shall be hurried into captivity, with persons exposed (Isa. 47:3; Ezek. 16:37; Hos. 2:10). **the inhabitant of Zaanan came not forth**—Its inhabitants did not come forth to console the people of Beth-ezel in their mourning, because the calamity was universal; none was exempt from it (cf. Jer. 6:25). "Zaanan" is the same as Zenan, in Judah (Josh. 15:37), meaning the "place of flocks." The form of the name used is made like the *Hebrew* for "came forth." Though in name seeming to imply that thou dost *come forth,* thou "camest not forth." **Beth-ezel**—perhaps Azal (Zech. 14:5), near Jerusalem. It means a "house on the side," or "near." Though *so near,* as its name implies, to Zaanan, Beth-ezel received no succor or sympathy from Zaanan. **he shall receive of you his standing**—"he," i.e., the foe; "his standing," i.e., his sustenance [PISCATOR]. Or, "he shall be caused a delay by you, Zaanan." He shall be brought to a stand for a time in besieging you; hence it is said just before, "Zaanan came not forth," i.e., shut herself up within her walls to withstand a siege. But it was only for a time. She, too, fell like Beth-ezel before her [VATABLUS]. MAURER construes thus: "The inhabitant of Zaanan came not forth; the mourning of Beth-ezel *takes away from* you her shelter." Though Beth-ezel be *at your side* (i.e., near), according to her name, yet as she also mourns under the oppression of the foe, she cannot give you shelter, or be *at your side* as a helper (as her name might lead you to expect), if you come forth and be intercepted by him from returning to Zaanan. **12. Maroth**—possibly the same as Maarath (Josh. 15:59). Perhaps a different town, lying between the previously mentioned towns and the capital, and one of those plundered by Rabshakeh on his way to it. **waited carefully for good**—i.e., for better fortune, but in vain [CALVIN]. GESENIUS translates, "*is grieved* for her goods" *taken away* from her. This accords with the meaning of Maroth, "bitterness," to which allusion is made in "is grieved." But the antithesis favors *English Version*, "waited carefully (i.e., anxiously) for *good*; but *evil* came down." **from the Lord**—not from *chance*. **unto the gate of Jerusalem**—after the other cities of Judah have been taken. **13.** "Bind the chariot to the swift *steed*," in order by a hasty flight to escape the invading foe. Cf. *Note,* Isaiah 36:2, on "Lachish," at which Sennacherib fixed his headquarters (II Kings 18:14, 17; Jer. 34:7). **she is the beginning of the sin to ... Zion**—Lachish was the first of the cities of Judah, according to this passage, to introduce the worship of false gods, imitating what Jeroboam had introduced in Israel. As lying near the border of the north kingdom, Lachish was first to be infected by its idolatry, which thence spread to Jerusalem. **14. shalt thou give presents to Moresheth-gath**—that its inhabitants may send thee help. MAURER explains it, "thou shalt give a writing of renunciation to Moresheth-gath," i.e., thou shalt renounce all claim to it, being compelled to yield it up to the foe. "Thou," i.e., Judah. "Israel" in this verse is used for the kingdom of *Judah,* which was the chief representative of the whole nation of Israel. Moresheth-gath is so called because it had fallen for a time under the power of the neighboring Philistines of *Gath.* It was the native town of Micah (vs. 1). **Achzib**—meaning "lying." Achzib, as its name implies, shall prove a "lie to ... Israel," i.e., shall disappoint Israel's hopes of succor from her (cf. Job 6:15-20; Jer. 15:18). Achzib was in Judah between Keilah and Mareshah (Josh. 15:44). Perhaps the same as Chezib (Gen. 38:5). **15. Yet will I bring an heir unto thee**—rather, "*the* heir." As thou art now occupied by possessors who expelled the former inhabitants, so will I bring "yet" again *the* new *possessor,* viz., the Assyrian foe. Other heirs will supplant us in every inheritance but that of heaven. There is a play upon the meaning of Mareshah, "an inheritance": there shall come the new *heir* of the *inheritance.* **Adullam the glory of Israel**—so called as being superior in situation; when it and the neighboring cities fell, Israel's glory was gone. MAURER, as *Margin,* translates, "the glory of Israel" (her chief citizens: answering to "thy delicate children," vs. 16) "shall come in flight to Adullam." *English Version* better preserves the parallelism, "the heir" in the first clause answering to "he" in the second. **16. Make thee bald, ...**—a token of deep mourning (Erza 9:3; Job 1:20). Mourn, O land, for thy darling children. **poll**—shave off thy hair. **enlarge thy baldness**—Mourn grievously. The land is compared to a mother weeping for her children. **as the eagle**—the bald eagle, or the dark-winged vulture. In the moulting season all eagles are comparatively bald (cf. Ps. 103:5).

CHAPTER 2

Vss. 1-13. DENUNCIATION OF THE EVILS PREVALENT: THE PEOPLE'S UNWILLINGNESS TO HEAR THE TRUTH: THEIR EXPULSION FROM THE LAND THE FITTING FRUIT OF THEIR SIN: YET JUDAH AND ISRAEL ARE HEREAFTER TO BE RESTORED. **1. devise ... work ... practise**—They do evil not merely on a sudden impulse, but with deliberate design. As in the former chapter sins against the first table are reproved, so in this chapter sins against the second

table. A gradation: "devise" is the *conception* of the evil purpose; "work" (Ps. 58:2), or "fabricate," the *maturing* of the scheme; "practise," or "effect," the *execution* of it. **because it is in the power of their hand**—for the phrase see Genesis 31:29; Proverbs 3:27. Might, not right, is what regulates their conduct. Where they can, they commit oppression; where they do not, it is because they cannot. **2.** Parallelism, "Take by violence," answers to "take away"; "fields" and "houses," to "house" and "heritage" (i.e., one's land). **3. against this family** —against the nation, and especially against those reprobates in vss. 1, 2. **I devise an evil**—a happy antithesis between God's dealings and the Jews' dealings (vs. 1). Ye "devise evil" against your fellow countrymen; I devise evil against you. Ye devise it wrongfully, I by righteous retribution in kind. **from which ye shall not remove your necks** —as ye have done from the law. The yoke I shall impose shall be one which ye cannot shake off. They who will not bend to God's "easy yoke" (Matt. 11:29, 30), shall feel His iron yoke. **go haughtily**— (Cf. *Note,* Jer. 6:28). Ye shall not walk as now with neck haughtily uplifted, for the yoke shall press down your "neck." **this time is evil**—rather, "for *that* time shall be an evil time," viz., the time of the carrying away into captivity (cf. Amos 5:13; Eph. 5:16). **4. one take up a parable against you**— i.e., Some of your foes shall do so, taking in derision from your own mouth your "lamentation," viz., "We be spoiled ...." **lament with a doleful lamentation**—lit., "lament with a lamentation of lamentations." *Hebrew, naha, nehi, nihyah,* the repetition representing the continuous and monotonous wail. **he hath changed the portion of my people**— a charge of injustice against Jehovah. He transfers to other nations the sacred territory assigned as the rightful portion of our people (ch. 1:15). **turning away he hath divided our fields**—Turning away from us to the enemy, He hath divided among them our fields. CALVIN, as *Margin,* explains, "*Instead of restoring* our territory, He hath divided our fields among our enemies, each of whom henceforward will have an interest in keeping what he hath gotten: so that we are utterly shut out from hope of restoration." MAURER translates as a noun, "He hath divided our fields *to a rebel,*" i.e., to the foe who is a rebel against the true God, and a worshipper of idols. So "backsliding," i.e., backslider (Jer. 49:4). *English Version* gives a good sense; and is quite tenable in the *Hebrew.* **5. Therefore**—resumed from vs. 3. On account of your crimes described in vss. 1, 2. **thou**—the ideal individual ("me," vs. 4), representing the guilty people in whose name he spake. **none that ... cast a cord by lot**—none who shall have any possession *measured out.* **in the congregation of the Lord**—among the people consecrated to Jehovah. By covetousness and violence (vs. 2) they had forfeited "the portion of Jehovah's people." This is God's implied answer to their complaint of injustice (vs. 4). **6. Prophesy ye not, say they**—viz., the Israelites say to the true prophets, when announcing unwelcome truths. Therefore God judicially abandons them to their own ways: "The prophets, by whose ministry they might have been saved from *shame* (ignominious captivity), shall not (i.e., no longer) prophesy to them" (Isa. 30:10; Amos 2:12; 7:16). MAURER translates the latter clause, "they shall not prophesy *of such things*" (as in vss. 3-5, these being rebellious Israel's words); "let them not prophesy"; "they never cease from insult" (from prophesying insults to us). *English Version* is supported by the parallelism: wherein the similarity of sound and word implies how exactly God makes their punishment answer to their sin, and takes them at their own word. "Prophesy," lit., "drop" (Deut. 32:2; Ezek. 21:2). **7. O thou ... named the house of Jacob**—priding thyself on the *name*, though having naught of the spirit, of thy progenitor. Also, bearing the name which ought to remind thee of God's favors granted to thee because of His covenant with Jacob. **is the Spirit of the Lord straitened?**—Is His *compassion* contracted within narrower limits now than formerly, so that He should delight in your destruction (cf. Ps. 77:7-9; Isa. 59:1, 2)? **are these his doings?**—i.e., Are such threatenings His delight? Ye dislike the prophets' threatenings (vs. 6): but who is to blame? Not God, for He delights in blessing, rather than threatening; but yourselves (vs. 8) who provoke His threatenings [GROTIUS]. CALVIN translates, "Are your doings such as are prescribed by Him?" Ye boast of being God's peculiar people: Do ye then conform your lives to God's law? **do not my words do good to him that walketh uprightly**—Are not My words good to the upright? If your ways were upright, My words would not be threatening (cf. Ps. 18:26; Matt. 11:19; John 7:17). **8.** Your ways are not such that I can deal with you as I would with the upright. **Even of late**—lit., "yesterday," "long ago." So "of old." *Hebrew*, "yesterday" (Isa. 30:33); "heretofore," *Hebrew*, "since yesterday" (Josh. 3:4). **my people is risen up as an enemy**—i.e., has rebelled against My precepts; also has become *an enemy* to the unoffending passers-by. **robe with the garment**—Not content with the outer "garment," ye greedily rob passers-by of the ornamental "robe" fitting the body closely and flowing down to the feet [LUDOVICUS DE DIEU] (Matt. 5:40). **as men averse from war**—in antithesis to (*My people*) "as an enemy." Israel treats the innocent passers-by, though "averse from war," as an enemy" would treat captives in his power, stripping them of their habiliments as lawful spoils. GROTIUS translates, "as men *returning* from war," i.e., as captives over whom the right of war gives the victors an absolute power. *English Version* is supported by the antithesis. **9. The women of my people**—i.e., the *widows* of the men slain by you (vs. 2) ye cast out from their homes which had been their delight, and seize on them for yourselves. **from their children**—i.e., from the orphans of the widows. **taken away my glory**—viz., their substance and raiment, which, being the fruit of God's blessing on the young, reflected *God's glory*. Thus Israel's crime was not merely robbery, but sacrilege. Their sex did not save the women, nor their age the children from violence. **for ever**—There was no repentance. They persevered in sin. The pledged garment was to be restored to the poor before sunset (Exod. 22:26, 27); but these *never* restored their unlawful booty. **10. Arise ye, and depart**—not an exhortation to the children of God to depart out of an ungodly world, as it is often applied; though that sentiment is a scriptural one. This world is doubtless not our "rest," being "polluted" with sin: it is our passage, not our portion; our aim, not our home (II Cor. 6:17; Heb. 13:14). The imperatives express the *certainty* of the *future* event *predicted*. "Since such are your doings (cf. vss. 7, 8, etc.), My sentence on you is irrevocable (vss. 4, 5), however distasteful to you (vs. 6); ye who have *cast out* others from their homes and possessions (vss. 2, 8, 9) must *arise, depart*, and be cast out of your own (vss. 4, 5): *for this is not your rest*" (Num. 10:33; Deut. 12:9; Ps. 95:11). Canaan was designed to be a *rest* to

them after their wilderness fatigues. But it is to be so no longer. Thus God refutes the people's self-confidence, as if God were bound to them inseparably. The promise (Ps. 132:14) is quite consistent with temporary withdrawal of God from Israel for their sins. **it shall destroy you**—*The land* shall spew you out, because of the defilements wherewith ye "polluted" it (Lev. 18:25, 28; Jer. 3:2; Ezek. 36:12-14). **11. walking in the spirit**—The *Hebrew* means also "wind." "If a man professing to have the 'spirit' of inspiration (Ezek. 13:3; so 'man of the spirit,' i.e., one claiming inspiration, Hos. 9:7), but really walking in 'wind' (prophecy void of nutriment for the soul, and unsubstantial as the *wind*) and falsehood, do lie, saying (that which ye like to hear), I will prophesy....," even such a one, however false his prophecies, since he flatters your wishes, shall be your prophet (cf. vs. 6; Jer. 5:31). **prophesy ... of wine**—i.e., of an abundant supply of wine. **12.** A sudden transition from threats to the promise of a glorious restoration. Cf. a similar transition in Hos. 1:9, 10. Jehovah, too, prophesies of good things to come, but not like the false prophets, "of wine and strong drink" (vs. 11). After I have sent you into captivity as I have just threatened, I will thence assemble you again (cf. ch. 4:6, 7). **all of thee**—The restoration from Babylon was partial. Therefore that here meant must be still future, when "*all* Israel shall be saved" (Rom. 11:26). The restoration from "Babylon" (specified ch. 4:10) is the type of the future one. **Jacob ... Israel**—the ten tribes' kingdom (Hos. 12:2) and Judah (II Chron. 19:8; 21:2, 4). **remnant**—the elect remnant, which shall survive the previous calamities of Judah, and from which the nation is to spring into new life (Isa. 6:13; 10:20-22). **as the sheep of Bozrah**—a region famed for its rich pastures (cf. II Kings 3:4). GESENIUS for Bozrah translates, "sheepfold." But thus there will be tautology unless the next clause be translated, "in the midst of their *pasture*." *English Version* is more favored by the *Hebrew*. **13. The breaker**—Jehovah Messiah, who *breaks* through every obstacle in the way of their restoration: not as formerly *breaking forth* to destroy them for transgression (Exod. 19:22; Judg. 21:15), but breaking a way for them through their enemies. **they**—the returning Israelites and Jews. **passed through the gate**—i.e., through the gate of the foe's city in which they had been captives. So the image of the resurrection (Hos. 13:14) represents Israel's restoration. **their king**—"the Breaker," peculiarly "*their* king" (Hos. 3: 5; Matt. 27:37). **pass before them**—as He did when they went up out of Egypt (Exod. 13:21; Deut. 1:30, 33). **the Lord on the head of them**—Jehovah at their head (Isa. 52:12). Messiah, the second person, is meant (cf. Exod. 23:20; 33:14; Isa. 63:9).

CHAPTER 3

Vss. 1-12. THE SINS OF THE PRINCES, PROPHETS, AND PRIESTS: THE CONSEQUENT DESOLATION OF ZION. **1. princes**—magistrates or judges. **Is it not for you?** —Is it not your special function (Jer. 5:4, 5)? **judgment**—justice. Ye sit in judgment on others; surely then ye ought to know the judgment for injustice which awaits yourselves (Rom. 2:1). **2. pluck off their skin ... flesh**—rob their fellow countrymen of all their substance (Ps. 14:4; Prov. 30:14). **3. pot ... flesh within ... caldron**—manifold species of cruel oppressions. Cf. Ezekiel 24:3, etc., containing, as to the coming punishment, the same figure as is here used of the sin: implying that the sin and punishment exactly correspond. **4. Then**—at the time of judgment, which Micah takes for granted, so certain is it (cf. ch. 2:3). **they cry. . . . but he will not hear**—just as those oppressed by them had formerly cried, and they would not hear. Their prayer shall be rejected, because it is the mere cry of nature for deliverance from pain, not that of repentance for deliverance from sin. **ill in their doings**—Men cannot expect to do ill and fare well. **5.** Here he attacks the false prophets, as before he had attacked the "princes." **make my people err**—knowingly mislead My people by not denouncing their sins as incurring judgment. **bite with . . . teeth, and cry, Peace**—i.e., who, so long as they are supplied with food, promise *peace* and prosperity in their prophecies. **he that putteth not into their mouths, they . . . prepare war against him**—Whenever they are not supplied with food, they foretell war and calamity. **prepare war**—lit., "sanctify war," i.e., proclaim it as a *holy* judgment of God because they are not fed (*Note,* Jer. 6:4; cf. Isa. 13:3; Joel 1:14). **6 night . . . dark**—Calamities shall press on you so overwhelming as to compel you to cease pretending to *divine* (Zech. 13:4). Darkness is often the image of calamity (Isa. 8:22; Amos 5:18; 8:9). **7. cover their lips**—The Orientals prided themselves on the moustache and beard (*Margin*, "upper lip"). To *cover* it, therefore, was a token of shame and sorrow (Lev. 13:45; Ezek. 24:17, 22). "They shall be so ashamed of themselves as *not to dare to open their mouths* or boast of the name of prophet" [CALVIN]. **there is no answer of God**—They shall no more profess to have responses from God, being struck dumb with calamities (vs. 6). **8. I**—in contrast to the false prophets (vss. 5, 7). **full of power**—that which "the Spirit of Jehovah" imparts for the discharge of the prophetical function (Luke 1:17; 24:49; Acts 1:8). **judgment**—a sense of *justice* [MAURER]; as opposed to the false prophets' speaking to please men, not from a regard to truth. Or, "judgment" to discern between graver and lighter offenses, and to denounce punishments accordingly [GROTIUS]. **might**—moral *intrepidity* in speaking the truth at all costs (II Tim. 1:7). **to declare unto Jacob his . . . sin**—(Isa. 58:1). Not to flatter the sinner as the false prophets do with promises of peace. **9. Hear** —resumed from vs. 1. Here begins the leading subject of the prophecy: a demonstration of his assertion that he is "full of power by the Spirit of Jehovah" (vs. 8). **10. They**—change of person from "ye" (vs. 9); the third person puts them to a greater distance as estranged from Him. It is, lit., "*Whosoever* builds," *singular*. **build up Zion with blood** —build on it stately mansions with wealth obtained by the condemnation and murder of the innocent (Jer. 22:13; Ezek. 22:27; Hab. 2:12). **11. heads thereof**—the princes of Jerusalem. **judge for reward**—take bribes as judges (ch. 7:3). **priests teach for hire**—It was their duty to teach the law and to decide controversies gratuitously (Lev. 10:11; Deut. 17:11; Mal. 2:7; cf. Jer. 6:13; Jude 11). **prophets . . . divine**—i.e., false prophets. **Is not the Lord among us?**—viz., in the temple (Isa. 48:2; Jer. 7:4, 8-11). **12.** Jeremiah 26:18 quotes this verse. The Talmud and Maimonides record that at the destruction of Jerusalem by the Romans under Titus, Terentius Rufus, who was left in command of the army, with a ploughshare tore up the foundations of the temple. **mountain of the house**—the height on which the temple stands. **as the high places of the forest**—shall become as heights in a forest overrun with wild shrubs and brushwood.

CHAPTER 4

Vss. 1-13. Transition to the Glory, Peace, Kingdom, and Victory of Zion. **1-3.** Almost identical with Isaiah 2:2-4. **the mountain of the house of the Lord**—which just before (ch. 3:12) had been doomed to be a wild forest height. Under Messiah, its elevation is to be not that of situation, but of moral dignity, as the seat of God's universal empire. **people shall flow into it**—In Isaiah it is "all nations": a more universal prophecy. **3. rebuke**—convict of sin (John 16:8, 9); and subdue with judgments (Ps. 2:5, 9; 110:5, 6; Rev. 2:27; 12:5). **many people . . . strong nations afar off**—In Isaiah 2:4 it is "the nations . . . many people." **4. sit every man under his vine . . .**—i.e., enjoy the most prosperous tranquillity (I Kings 4:25; Zech. 3:10). The "vine" and "fig tree" are mentioned rather than a *house,* to signify, there will be no need of a covert; men will be safe even in the fields and open air. **Lord of hosts hath spoken it**—Therefore it must come to pass, however unlikely now it may seem. **5. For**—rather, *Though it be that* all people walk after their several gods, yet we (the Jews in the dispersion) will walk in the name of the Lord. So the *Hebrew* particle means in *Margin,* Genesis 8:21; Exodus 13:17; Joshua 17:18. The resolution of the exile Jews is: As Jehovah gives us hope of so glorious a restoration, notwithstanding the overthrow of our temple and nation, we must in confident reliance on His promise persevere in the true worship of Him, however the nations around, our superiors now in strength and numbers, walk after their gods [ROSENMULLER]. As the Jews were thoroughly weaned from idols by the Babylonian captivity, so they shall be completely cured of unbelief by their present long dispersion (Zech. 10:8-12). **6. assemble her that halteth**—feminine for neuter in *Hebrew* idiom, "*whatever* halteth": metaphor from sheep wearied out with a journey: all the suffering exiles of Israel (Ezek. 34:16; Zeph. 3:19). **her . . . driven out**—all Israel's outcasts. Called "the Lord's flock' (Jer. 13:17; Ezek. 34:13; 37:21). **7. I will make her that halted a remnant**—I will cause a remnant to remain which shall not perish. **Lord shall reign . . . in . . . Zion**—David's kingdom shall be restored in the person of Messiah, who is the seed of David and at the same time Jehovah (Isa. 24:23). **for ever**—(Isa. 9:6, 7; Dan. 7:14, 27; Luke 1:33; Rev. 11:15). **8. tower of the flock**—following up the metaphor of *sheep* (*Note,* vs. 6). Jerusalem is called the "tower," from which the King and Shepherd observes and guards His flock: both the spiritual Jerusalem, the Church now whose tower-like elevation is that of doctrine and practice (Song of Sol. 4:4, "Thy neck is like the *tower* of David"), and the literal hereafter (Jer. 3:17). In large pastures it was usual to erect a high wooden tower, so as to oversee the flock. JEROME takes the *Hebrew* for "flock," *Eder* or *Edar,* as a proper name, viz., a village near Bethlehem, for which it is put, Bethlehem being taken to represent the *royal stock of David* (ch. 5:2; cf. Gen. 35:21). But the explanatory words, "the stronghold of the daughter of Zion," confirm *English Version.* **stronghold**—*Hebrew,* "Ophel"; an impregnable height on Mount Zion (II Chron. 27:3; 33:14; Neh. 3:26, 27). **unto thee shall . . . come . . . the first dominion**—viz., the dominion formerly exercised by thee shall come back to thee. **kingdom shall come to the daughter of Jerusalem**—rather, "the kingdom *of* the daughter of Jerusalem shall come (again)"; such as it was under David, before its being weakened by the secession of the ten tribes. **9.** Addressed to the daughter of Zion, in her consternation at the approach of the Chaldeans. **is there no king in thee?**—asked tauntingly. There *is* a king in her; but it is the same as if there were none, so helpless to devise means of escape are he and his counsellors [MAURER]. Or, Zion's pains are because her king *is* taken away from her (Jer. 52:9; Lam. 4:20; Ezek. 12:13) [CALVIN]. The former is perhaps the preferable view (cf. Jer. 49:7). The latter, however, describes better Zion's kingless state during her present long dispersion (Hos. 3:4, 5). **10. Be in pain, and labour**—carrying on the metaphor of a pregnant woman. Thou shalt be affected with bitter sorrows before thy deliverance shall come. I do not forbid thy grieving, but I bring thee consolation. Though God cares for His children, yet they must not expect to be exempt from trouble, but must prepare for it. **go forth out of the city**—on its capture. So "come out" is used II Kings 24:12; Isaiah 36:16. **dwell in the field**—viz., in the open country, defenseless, instead of their fortified *city*. Beside the Chebar (Ps. 137:1; Ezek. 3:15). **Babylon**—Like Isaiah, Micah looks beyond the existing Assyrian dynasty to the Babylonian, and to Judah's captivity under it, and restoration (Isa. 39:7; 43:14; 48:20). Had they been, as rationalists represent, merely sagacious politicians, they would have restricted their prophecies to the sphere of the existing *Assyrian* dynasty. But their seeing into the far-off future of *Babylon's* subsequent supremacy, and Judah's connection with her, proves them to be inspired prophets. **there … there**—emphatic repetition. The very scene of thy calamities is to be the scene of thy deliverance. In the midst of enemies, where all hope seems cut off, *there* shall Cyrus, the deliverer, appear (cf. Judg. 14:14). Cyrus again being the type of the greater Deliverer, who shall finally restore Israel. **11. many nations**—the subject peoples composing Babylon's armies: and also Edom, Ammon, etc., who exulted in Judah's fall (Lam. 2:16; Obad. 11-13). **defiled**—metaphor from a virgin. Let her be defiled (i.e., outraged by violence and bloodshed), and let our eye gaze insultingly on her shame and sorrow (ch. 7:10). Her foes desired to feast their *eyes* on her calamities. **12. thoughts of the Lord**—Their *unsearchable wisdom,* overruling seeming disaster to the final good of His people, is the very ground on which the restoration of Israel hereafter (of which the restoration from Babylon is a type) is based in Isaiah 55:8; cf. with vss. 3, 12, 13, which prove that *Israel,* not merely the Christian Church, is the ultimate subject of the prophecy; also in Romans 11:13. God's counsel is to discipline His people for a time with the foe as a scourge; and then to destroy the foe by the hands of His people. **gather them as … sheaves**—them who "gathered" themselves for Zion's destruction (vs. 11) the Lord "shall gather" for destruction by Zion (vs. 13), like *sheaves gathered to be threshed* (cf. Isa. 21:10; Jer. 51:33). The *Hebrew* is *singular,* "sheaf." However great the numbers of the foe, they are all but as *one sheaf* ready to be threshed [CALVIN]. Threshing was done by treading with the feet: hence the propriety of the image for treading under foot and breaking asunder the foe. **13. thresh**—destroy thy foes "gathered" by Jehovah as "sheaves" (Isa. 41:15, 16). **thine horn**—Zion being compared to an ox treading corn, and an ox's strength lying in the horns, her *strength* is implied by giving her a *horn of iron* (cf. Kings 22:11). **beat in pieces many**—(Dan. 2:44). **I will consecrate their gain unto the Lord**—God subjects the nations

to Zion, not for her own selfish aggrandizement, but for His glory (Isa. 60:6, 9; Zech. 14:20, with which cf. Isa. 23:18) and for their ultimate good; therefore He is here called, not merely God of Israel, but "Lord of the whole earth."

CHAPTER 5

Vss. 1-15. THE CALAMITIES WHICH PRECEDE MESSIAH'S ADVENT. HIS KINGDOM, CONQUEST OF JACOB'S FOES, AND BLESSING UPON HIS PEOPLE. **1. gather thyself in troops**—i.e., thou shalt do so, to resist the enemy. Lest the faithful should fall into carnal security because of the previous promises, he reminds them of the calamities which are to precede the prosperity. **daughter of troops**—Jerusalem is so called on account of her numerous *troops.* **he hath laid siege**—*the enemy* hath. **they shall smite the judge of Israel with a rod upon the cheek**—the greatest of insults to an Oriental. Zedekiah, the judge (or *king,* Amos 2:3) of Israel, was loaded with insults by the Chaldeans; so also the other princes and judges (Lam. 3:30). HENGSTENBERG thinks the expression, "the judge," marks a time when no king of the house of David reigned. The smiting on the cheek of other judges of Israel was a type of the same indignity offered to Him who nevertheless is the Judge, not only of Israel, but also of the world, and who is "from everlasting" (vs. 2; Isa. 50:6; Matt. 26:67; 27:30). **2. Beth-lehem Ephratah**—(Gen. 48: 7), or, Beth-lehem Judah; so called to distinguish it from Beth-lehem in Zebulun. It is a few miles southwest of Jerusalem. Beth-lehem means "the house of bread"; *Ephratah* means "fruitful": both names referring to the fertility of the region. **though thou be little among**—*though thou be scarcely large enough to be reckoned among* …. It was insignificant in size and population; so that in Joshua 15:21, etc., it is not enumerated among the cities of Judah; nor in the list in Nehemiah 11:25, etc. Under Rehoboam it became a city: II Chronicles 11:6, "He *built* Beth-lehem." Matthew 2:6 seems to contradict Micah, "thou art *not* the least." But really he, by an independent testimony of the Spirit, confirms the prophet, Little in *worldly* importance, thou art not least (i.e., far from least, yea, *the very greatest*) among the thousands, of princes of Judah, in the spiritual significance of being the birthplace of Messiah (John 7:42). God chooses the little things of the world to eclipse in glory its greatest things (Judg. 6:15; John 1:46; I Cor. 1:27, 28). The low state of David's line when Messiah was born is also implied here. *thousands*—Each tribe was divided into *clans* or "thousands" (each thousand containing a thousand families), which had their several heads or "princes"; hence in Matthew 2:6 it is quoted "princes," substantially the same as in Micah, and authoritatively explained in Matthew. It is not so much this thousand that is preferred to the other thousands of Judah, but the Governor or Chief Prince out of it, who is preferred to the governors of all the other thousands. It is called a "town" (rather in the *Greek,* "village"), John 7:42; though scarcely containing a thousand inhabitants, it is ranked among the "thousands" or larger divisions of the tribe, because of its being the cradle of David's line, and of the Divine Son of David. Moses divided the people into thousands, hundreds, fifties, and tens, with their respective "rulers" (Exod. 18:25; cf. I Sam. 10:19). **unto me**—unto God the Father (Luke 1:32): to fulfil all the Father's will and purpose from eternity. So the Son declares

(Ps. 2:7; 40:7, 8; John 4:34); and the Father confirms it (Matt. 3:17; 12:18, cf. with Isa. 42:1). God's glory is hereby made the ultimate end of redemption. **ruler**–the "Shiloh," "Prince of peace," "on whose shoulders the government is laid" (Gen. 49: 10; Isa. 9:6). In II Samuel 23:3, "*He that ruleth over men must be just*," the same *Hebrew* word is employed; Messiah alone realizes David's ideal of a ruler. Also in Jeremiah 30:21, "*their governor shall proceed from the midst of them*"; answering closely to "out of thee shall come forth *the ruler*," here (cf. Isa. 11:1-4). **goings forth ... from everlasting**–The plain antithesis of this clause, to "come forth out of thee" (*from Beth-lehem*), shows that the eternal generation of the Son is meant. The terms convey the strongest assertion of infinite duration of which the *Hebrew* language is capable (cf. Ps. 90:2; Prov. 8:22, 23; John 1:1). Messiah's generation as man coming forth unto God to do His will on earth is *from Beth-lehem;* but as Son of God, His goings forth are *from everlasting.* The promise of the Redeemer at first was vaguely general (Gen. 3:15). Then the Shemitic division of mankind is declared as the quarter in which He was to be looked for (Gen. 9:26, 27); then it grows clearer, defining the race and nation whence the Deliverer should come, viz., the seed of Abraham, the Jews (Gen. 12:3); then the particular tribe, Judah (Gen. 49:10); then the family, that of David (Ps. 89:19, 20); then the very town of His birth, here. And as His coming drew nigh, the very parentage (Matt. 1; Luke 1 and 2); and then all the scattered rays of prophecy concentrate in Jesus, as their focus (Heb. 1:1, 2). **3.** "*Therefore* (because of His settled plan) *will* God *give up* to their foes His people Israel, *until* . . . ." **she which travaileth hath brought forth** –viz., "the virgin" mother, mentioned by Micah's contemporary, Isaiah 7:14. *Zion* "in travail" (ch. 4:9, 10) answers to the *virgin* in travail of Messiah. Israel's deliverance from her long travail pains of sorrow will synchronize with the appearance of Messiah as her Redeemer (Rom. 11:26) in the last days, as the Church's spiritual deliverance synchronized with the virgin's giving birth to Him at His first advent. The ancient *Church's* travail-like waiting for Messiah is represented by *the virgin's* travail. Hence, *both* may be meant. It cannot be *restricted* to the Virgin Mary: for Israel is still "given up," though Messiah has been "brought forth" almost two thousand years ago. But the Church's throes are included, which are only to be ended when Christ, having been preached for a witness to all nations, shall at last appear as the Deliverer of Jacob, and when the times of the Gentiles shall be fulfilled, and Israel as a nation shall be born in a day (Isa. 66:7-11; Luke 21:24; Rev. 12:1, 2, 4: cf. Rom. 8:22). **the remnant of his brethren shall return unto the children of Israel**– (Cf. ch. 4:7). The remainder of the Israelites dispersed in foreign lands shall return to join their countrymen in Canaan. The *Hebrew* for "unto" is, lit, "upon," implying superaddition to those already gathered. **4. he shall stand**–i.e., persevere: implying the endurance of His kingdom [CALVIN]. Rather, His sedulous care and pastoral circumspection, as a shepherd *stands* erect to survey and guard His flock on every side (Isa. 61:5) [MAURER]. **feed**–i.e., rule: as the Greek word similarly in Matthew 2:6 (*Margin*), means both "feed" and "rule" (Isa. 40:11; 49:10; Ezek. 34:23; cf. II Sam. 5:2; 7:8). **in the majesty of the name of the Lord**–possessing the majesty of all Jehovah's *revealed attributes* ("name") (Isa. 11:2; Phil. 2:6, 9; Heb. 2:7-9). **his**

God–God is "*His* God" in a oneness of relation distinct from the sense in which God is *our* God (John 20:17). **they shall abide**–the Israelites ("they," viz., the *returning remnant* and the "children of Israel" previously in Canaan) shall *dwell in permanent security and prosperity* (ch. 4:4; Isa. 14:30). **unto the ends of the earth**–(ch. 4:1; Ps. 72:8; Zech. 9:10). **5. this man**–in *Hebrew* simply "This." The One just mentioned; He and He alone. Emphatical for Messiah (cf. Gen. 5:29). **the peace**–the fountainhead of peace between God and man, between Israel and Israel's justly offended God (Gen. 49:10; Isa. 9:6; Eph. 2:14, 17; Col. 1:20), and, as the consequence, the fountain of "peace on earth," where heretofore all is strife (ch. 4:3; Hos. 2:18; Zech. 9: 10; Luke 2:14). **the Assyrian**–Being Israel's most powerful foe at that time, Assyria is made the representative of all the foes of Israel in all ages, who shall receive their final destruction at Messiah's appearing (Ezek. 38). **seven shepherds, and eight**– "Seven" expresses perfection; "seven and eight" is an idiom for *a full and sufficient number* (Job 5:19; Prov. 6:16; Eccles. 11:2). **principal men**–lit., "anointed (humble) men" (Ps. 62:9), such as the apostles were. Their anointing, or consecration and qualification to office, was by the Holy Spirit [CALVIN] (I John 2:20, 27). "Princes" also were anointed, and they are mentioned as under Messiah (Isa. 32:1). *English Version* therefore gives the probable sense. **6. waste**–lit., "eat up": following up the metaphor of "shepherds" (cf. Num. 22:4; Jer. 6:3). **land of Nimrod**–Babylon (ch. 4:10; Gen. 10: 10); or, including Assyria also, to which he extended his borders (Gen. 10:11). **in the entrances**–the passes into Assyria (II Kings 3:21). The *Margin* and JEROME, misled by a needless attention to the parallelism, "with the sword," translate, "with her own naked swords"; as in Psalm 55:21 the *Hebrew* is translated. But "in the entrances" of Assyria, answers to, "within our borders." As the Assyrians invade *our borders,* so shall *their own* borders or "entrances" be invaded. **he ... he**– *Messiah* shall deliver us, when the *Assyrian* shall come. **7. remnant of Jacob**–already mentioned in vs. 3. It in comparative smallness stands in antithesis to the "many people." Though Israel be but a remnant amidst many nations after her restoration, yet she shall exercise the same blessed influence in quickening them spiritually that the small imperceptible dew exercises in refreshing the grass (Deut. 32:2; Ps. 72: 6; 110:3). The influence of the Jews restored from Babylon in making many Gentile proselytes is an earnest of a larger similar effect hereafter (Isa. 66: 19; Zech. 8:13). **from the Lord**–Israel's restoration and the consequent conversion of the Gentiles are solely of grace. **tarrieth not for man**–entirely God's work, as independent of human contrivance as the dew and rains that fertilize the soil. **8. as a lion**–In vs. 7 Israel's benignant influence on the nations is described; but here her vengeance on the godless hosts who assail her (Isa. 66:15, 16, 19, 24; Zech. 12:3, 6, 8, 9; 14:17, 18). Judah will be "as as lion," not in respect to its cruelty, but in its power of striking terror into all opponents. Under the Maccabees, the Jews acquired Idumea, Samaria, and parts of the territory of Ammon and Moab [GROTIUS]. But this was only the earnest of their future glory on their coming restoration. **9. Thine hand shall be lifted up**–In Isaiah 26:11 it is *Jehovah's* hand that is lifted up; here *Israel's* as vs. 8 implies, just as "Zion" is addressed and directed to "beat in pieces many people" (ch. 4:13; cf. Isa. 54: 15, 17). For Israel's foes are Jehovah's foes.

When her hand is said to be lifted up, it is Jehovah's hand that strikes the foe by her (cf. Exod. 13:9, with 14:8). **10. cut off thy horses ... chariots**—viz., those used for the purposes of war. Israel had been forbidden the use of cavalry, or to go to Egypt for horses (Deut. 17:16), lest they should trust in worldly forces, rather than in God (Ps. 20:7). Solomon had disregarded this command (I Kings 10:26, 28). Hereafter, saith God, I will remove these impediments to the free course of My grace: horses, chariots, etc., on which ye trust. The Church will never be safe, till she is stripped of all creature-trusts, and rests on Jehovah alone [CALVIN]. The universal peace given by God shall cause warlike instruments to be needless. He will *cut* them *off* from Israel (Zech. 9:10); as she will cut them off from Babylon, the representative of the nations (Jer. 50:37; 51:21). **11. cut off ... cities ... strongholds**—such as are fortified for war. In that time of peace, men shall live in unwalled villages (Ezek. 38:11; cf. Jer. 23:6; 49:31; Zech. 2:8). **12. witchcrafts out of thine hand**—i.e., which thou now usest. **13. graven images ... cut off**—(Cf. Isa. 2:8, 18-21; 30:22; Zech. 13:2). **standing images**—statues. **14. groves ... cities**—The "groves" are the idolatrous symbol of Astarte (Deut. 16:21; II Kings 21:7). "Cities" being parallel to "groves," must mean cities in or near which such idolatrous groves existed. Cf. "city of the house of Baal" (II Kings 10:25), i.e., a portion of the city sacred to Baal. **15. vengeance ... such as they have not heard**—or, as the *Hebrew order* favors, "the *nations* that have not hearkened to My warnings." So LXX (Ps. 149:7).

CHAPTER 6

Vss. 1-16. APPEAL BEFORE ALL CREATION TO THE ISRAELITES TO TESTIFY, IF THEY CAN, IF JEHOVAH EVER DID AUGHT BUT ACTS OF KINDNESS TO THEM FROM THE EARLIEST PERIOD: GOD REQUIRES OF THEM NOT SO MUCH SACRIFICES, AS REAL PIETY AND JUSTICE: THEIR IMPIETIES AND COMING PUNISHMENT. **1. contend thou**—Israel is called by Jehovah to plead with Him in controversy. Ch. 5:11-13 suggested the transition from those happy times described in ch. 4 and 5, to the prophet's own degenerate times and people. **before the mountains**—in their presence; personified as if witnesses (cf. ch. 1: 2; Deut. 32:1; Isa. 1:2). Not as *Margin*, "with"; as God's controversy is with Israel, not *with* them. **2. Lord's controversy**—How great is Jehovah's condescension, who, though the supreme Lord of all, yet wishes to prove to worms of the earth the equity of His dealings (Isa. 5:3; 43:26). **3. my people**—the greatest aggravation of their sin, that God always treated them, and still treats them, as *His people*. **what have I done unto thee?**—save kindness, that thou revoltest from Me (Jer. 2:5, 31). **wherein have I wearied thee?**—What commandments have I enjoined that should have wearied thee as irksome (I John 5:3)? **4. For**—*On the contrary*, so far from doing anything harsh, I did thee every kindness from the earliest years of thy nationality. **Miriam**—mentioned, as being the prophetess who led the female chorus who sang the song of Moses (Exod. 15:20). God sent Moses to give the best laws; Aaron to pray for the people; Miriam as an example to the women of Israel. **5. what Balak ... consulted**—how Balak plotted to destroy thee by getting Balaam to curse thee (Num. 22:5). **what Balaam ... answered**—how the avaricious prophet was constrained against his own will, to bless Israel

whom he had desired to curse for the sake of Balak's reward (Num. 24:9-11) [MAURER]. GROTIUS explains it, "how Balaam *answered*, that the only way to injure thee was by tempting thee to idolatry and whoredom" (Num. 31:16). The mention of "Shittim" agrees with this: as it was the scene of Israel's sin (Num. 25:1-5; II Pet. 2:15; Rev. 2:14). **from Shittim unto Gilgal**—not that Balaam accompanied Israel from Shittim *to Gilgal*: for he was slain in Midian (Num. 31:8). But the clause, "from Shittim," alone applies to Balaam. "Remember" God's kindnesses "from Shittim," the scene of Balaam's wicked counsel taking effect in Israel's sin, whereby Israel merited utter destruction but for God's sparing mercy, "to Gilgal," the place of Israel's first encampment in the promised land between Jericho and Jordan, where God renewed the covenant with Israel by circumcision (Josh. 5:2-11). **know the righteousness**—Recognize that, so far from God having treated thee harshly (vs. 3), His dealings have been kindness itself (so "righteous acts" for *gracious* Judg. 5:11; Ps. 24:5, 112:9). **6. Wherewith shall I come before the Lord?**—The people, convicted by the previous appeal of Jehovah to them, ask as if they knew not (cf. vs. 8) what Jehovah requires of them to appease Him, adding that they are ready to offer an immense heap of sacrifices, and those the most costly, even to the fruit of their own body. **burnt offerings**—(Lev. 1). **calves of a year old**—which used to be offered for a priest (Lev. 9:2, 3). **7. rivers of oil**—used in sacrifices (Lev. 2:1, 15). Will God be appeased by my offering so much oil that it shall flow in myriads of torrents? **my firstborn**—(II Kings 3:27). As the king of Moab did. **fruit of my body**—*my children*, as an atonement (Ps. 132:11). The Jews offered human sacrifices in the valley of Hinnom (Jer. 19:5; 32:35; Ezek. 23:27). **8. He**—Jehovah. **hath showed thee**—long ago, so that thou needest not ask the question as if thou hadst never heard (vs. 6; cf. Deut. 10:12; 30:11-14). **what is good**—"the good things to come" under Messiah, of which "the law had the shadow." The Mosaic sacrifices were but suggestive foreshadowings of His *better* sacrifice (Heb. 9:23; 10:1). To have this "good" first "showed," or *revealed* by the Spirit, is the only basis for the superstructure of the moral requirements which follow. Thus the way was prepared for the Gospel. The banishment of the Jews from Palestine is designed to preclude the possibility of their looking to the Mosaic rites for redemption, and shuts them up to Messiah. **justly ... mercy**—preferred by God to sacrifices. For the latter being *positive* ordinances, are only *means* designed with a view to the former, which being *moral* duties are the *ends*, and of everlasting obligation (I Sam. 15:22; Hos. 6:6; 12:6; Amos 5:22, 24). Two duties towards *man* are specified—*justice*, or strict equity; and *mercy*, or a kindly abatement of what we might justly demand, and a hearty desire to do good to others. **to walk humbly with thy God**—passive and active obedience towards God. The three moral duties here are summed up by our Lord (Matt. 23:23), "judgment, mercy, and faith" (in Luke 11:42, "the love of God"). Cf. James 1: 27. *To walk with God* implies constant prayer and watchfulness, familiar yet "humble" *converse* with God (Gen. 5:24; 17:1). **9. unto the city**—Jerusalem. *the man of wisdom*—As in Proverbs 13: 6, *Hebrew*, "sin" is used for "*a man of* sin," and in Psalm 109:4, "prayer" for "*a man of* prayer"; so here "wisdom" for "*the man of* wisdom." **shall see thy name**—shall regard Thee, in Thy revelations of Thyself. Cf. the end of ch. 2, vs. 7. God's "name" expresses the sum total of His revealed attributes. Contrast with this Isaiah 26:10, "will not behold the majesty of the Lord." Another reading is adopted by LXX, *Syriac,* and *Vulgate,* "there is deliverance for those who *fear* Thy name." *English Version* is better suited to the connection; and the rarity of the *Hebrew* expression, as compared with the frequency of that in the other reading, makes it less likely to be an interpolation. **hear ... the rod ...**—Hear what punishment (cf. vs. 13, etc.; Isa. 9:3; 10:5, 24) awaits you, and from whom. I am but a man, and so ye may disregard me; but remember my message is not mine, but God's. Hear the rod when it is come, and you feel its smart. Hear what counsels, what cautions it speaks. **appointed it**—(Jer. 47:7). **10. Are there yet**—notwithstanding all My warnings. Is there to be no end of acquiring treasures by wickedness? Jehovah is speaking (vs. 9). **scant measure ... abominable**—(Prov. 11:1; Amos 8:5). **11. Shall I count them pure**—lit., "Shall I be pure with ...?" *With the pure God shows Himself pure;* but *with the froward God shows Himself froward* (Ps. 18:26). Men often are changeable in their judgments. But God, in the case of the impure who use "wicked balances," cannot be pure, i.e., cannot deal with them as He would with the pure. VATABLUS and HENDERSON make the "I" to be "any one"; "Can I (i.e., one) be innocent with wicked balances?" But as "I," in vs. 13, refers to Jehovah, it must refer to Him also here. **the bag**—in which weights used to be carried, as well as money (Deut. 25:13; Prov. 16:11). **12. For**—rather, "Inasmuch as"; the conclusion "therefore ...," following in vs. 13. **thereof**—of Jerusalem. **13. make** *thee* **sick in smiting**—(Lev. 26:16, to which perhaps the allusion here is, as in vs. 14; Ps. 107:17, 18; Jer. 13:13). **14. eat ... not be satisfied**—fulfilling the threat, Leviticus 26:26. **thy casting down shall be in the midst of thee**—Thou shalt be cast down, not merely on My borders, but in the midst of thee, thy metropolis and temple being overthrown [TIRINUS]. Even though there should be no enemy, yet thou shalt be consumed with intestine evils [CALVIN]. MAURER translates as from an *Arabic* root, "there shall be *emptiness* in thy belly." Similarly GROTIUS, "there shall be a sinking of thy belly (once filled with food), through hunger." This suits the parallelism to the first clause. But *English Version* maintains the parallelism sufficiently. The casting down in the midst of the land, including the failure of food, through the invasion thus answering to, "Thou shalt eat, and not be satisfied." **thou shalt take hold, but ... not deliver**—Thou shalt take hold (with thine arms), in order to save [CALVIN] thy wives, children and goods. MAURER, from a different root, translates, "thou shalt remove them," in order to save them from the foe. But thou shalt fail in the attempt to deliver them (Jer. 50:37). **that which thou deliverest**—If haply thou dost rescue aught, it will be for a time: I will give it up to the foe's sword. **15. sow ... not reap**—fulfilling the threat (Lev. 26:16; Deut. 28:38-40; Amos 5:11). **16. statutes of Omri**—the founder of Samaria and of Ahab's wicked house; and a supporter of Jeroboam's superstitions (I Kings 16:16-28). This verse is a recapitulation of what was more fully stated before, Judah's sin and consequent punishment. Judah, though at variance with Israel on all things else, imitated her impiety. **works of ... Ahab** (I Kings 21:25, 26). **ye walk in their counsels**—Though these superstitions were the fruit of their king's "counsels" as a master stroke of state policy, yet these pretexts were no excuse for setting at naught

the counsels and will of God. **that I should make thee a desolation**—Thy conduct is framed so, as if it was thy set purpose "that I should make thee a desolation." **inhabitants thereof**—viz., of Jerusalem. **hissing**—(Lam. 2:15). **the reproach of my people**—The very thing ye boast of, viz., that ye are "My people," will only increase the severity of your punishment. The greater My grace to you, the greater shall be your punishment for having despised it, Your being God's people in name, while walking in His love, was an honor; but now the name, without the reality, is only a "reproach" to you.

CHAPTER 7

VSS. 1-20. THE UNIVERSALITY OF THE CORRUPTION; THE CHOSEN REMNANT, DRIVEN FROM EVERY HUMAN CONFIDENCE, TURNS TO GOD; TRIUMPHS BY FAITH OVER HER ENEMIES; IS COMFORTED BY GOD'S PROMISES IN ANSWER TO PRAYER, AND BY THE CONFUSION OF HER ENEMIES, AND SO BREAKS FORTH INTO PRAISES OF GOD'S CHARACTER. **1. I am as when ...**—It is the same with me as with one seeking fruits after the harvest, grapes after the vintage. "There is not a cluster" to be found: no "first-ripe fruit" (or early fig. *Note,* Isa. 28:4) which "my soul desireth" [MAURER]. So I look in vain for any good men left (vs. 2). **2.** (Ps. 12:1). **good man**—The *Hebrew* expresses "one *merciful and good* in relation to man," rather than to God. **3. That they may do evil with both hands earnestly**—lit., "Their hands are for evil that they may do it well" (i.e., cleverly and successfully). **the great man, he**—emphatic repetition. *As for the great man, he* no sooner has expressed his bad desire (lit., the "mischief or lust of his soul"), than the venal judges are ready to wrest the decision of the case according to his wish. **so they wrap it up**—The *Hebrew* is used of *intertwining cords together.* The "threefold cord is not quickly broken" (Eccles. 4:12); here the "prince," the "judge," and the "great man" are the three in guilty complicity. "They wrap it up," viz., they conspire to carry out the great man's desire at the sacrifice of justice. **4. as a brier**—or *thorn;* pricking with injury all who come in contact with them (II Sam. 23:6, 7; Isa. 55:13; Ezek. 2:6). **the day of thy watchmen**—the day foretold by thy (true) prophets, as the time of "thy visitation" in wrath [GROTIUS]. Or, "the day of thy *false* prophets being punished"; they are specially threatened as being not only blind themselves, but leading others blindfold [CALVIN]. **now**—at the time foretold, "at that time"; the prophet transporting himself into it. **perplexity**—(Isa. 22:5). They shall not know whither to turn. **5. Trust ye not in a friend**—Faith is kept nowhere: all to a man are treacherous (Jer. 9:2-6). When justice is perverted by the great, faith nowhere is safe. So, in gospel times of persecution, "a man's foes are they of his own household" (Matt. 10:35, 36; Luke 12:53). **guide**—a counsellor [CALVIN] able to help and advise (cf. Ps. 118:8, 9; 146:3). *The head of your family,* to whom all the members of the family would naturally repair in emergencies. Similarly the *Hebrew* is translated in Joshua 22:14 and "chief friends" in Proverbs 16:28 [GROTIUS]. **her that lieth in thy bosom**—thy wife (Deut. 13:6). **6. son dishonoureth the father**—The state of unnatural lawlessness in all relations of life is here described which is to characterize the last times, before Messiah comes to punish the ungodly and save Israel (cf. Luke 21:16; II Tim. 3:1-3). **7. Therefore I will look unto the Lord**—as if no one else were before mine eyes. We must not only "look *unto* the Lord," but also "wait *for* Him." Having no hope from man (vss. 5, 6), Micah speaks in the name of Israel, who herein, taught by chastisement (vs. 4) to feel her sin (vs. 9), casts herself on the Lord as her only hope," in patient waiting (Lam. 3:26). She did so under the Babylonian captivity; she shall do so again hereafter when the spirit of grace shall be poured on her (Zech. 12:10-13). **8. Rejoice not**—at my fall. **when I fall, I shall arise**—(Ps. 37:24; Prov. 24:16). **when I sit in darkness, the Lord shall be a light**—Israel reasons as her divine representative, Messiah, reasoned by faith in His hour of darkness and desertion (Isa. 50:7, 8, 10). Israel addresses Babylon, her triumphant foe (or Edom), as *a female;* the type of her last and worst foes (Ps. 137:7, 8). "Mine enemy," in *Hebrew,* is feminine. **9. bear**—patiently. **the indignation of the Lord**—His punishment inflicted on me (Lam. 3:39). The true penitent "accepts the punishment of his iniquity" (Lev. 26:41, 43); they who murmur against God, do not yet know their guilt (Job 40:4, 5). **execute judgment for me**—against my foe. God's people plead guilty before God; but, in respect to their human foes, they are innocent and undeserving of their foes' injuries. **bring me forth to the light**—to the temporal and spiritual redemption. **I shall behold his righteousness**—His gracious faithfulness to His promises (Ps. 103:17). **10. shame shall cover her** —in seeing how utterly mistaken she was in supposing that I was utterly ruined. **Where is . . . thy God**—(Ps. 42:3, 10). If He be *"thy* God," as thou sayest, let Him come now and deliver thee. So as to Israel's representative, Messiah (Matt. 27:43). **mine eyes shall behold her**—a just retribution in kind upon the foe who had said, "Let our *eye look upon* Zion." Zion shall behold her foe prostrate, not with the carnal joy of revenge, but with spiritual joy in God's vindicating His own righteousness (Isa. 66:24; Rev. 16:5-7). **shall she be trodden down**—herself, who had trodden down me. **11. thy walls . . . be built**—under Cyrus, after the seventy years' captivity; and again, hereafter, when the Jews shall be restored (Amos 9:11; Zech. 12:6). **shall the decree be far removed**—viz., thy tyrannical decree or rule of Babylon shall be put away from thee, "the statutes that were not good" (Ezek. 20:25) [Calvin]. Psalm 102:13-16; Isaiah 9:4. The *Hebrew* is against Maurer's translation, "the boundary of the city shall be *far extended,"* so as to contain the people flocking into it from all nations (vs. 12; Isa. 49:20; 54:2). **12. In that day also**—rather, an answer to the supposed question of Zion, When shall my walls be built? "The day (of thy walls being built) is the day when he (i.e., many) shall come to thee from Assyria . . ." [Ludovicus de Dieu]. The Assyrians (including the Babylonians) who spoiled thee shall come. **and from the fortified cities**—rather, to suit the parallelism, "from Assyria *even to Egypt."* (*Matzor* may be so translated.) So Assyria and Egypt are contrasted in Isaiah 19:23 [Maurer]. Calvin agrees with *English Version,* "from all fortified cities." **from the fortress even to the river**—"from *Egypt* even to the river" Euphrates (answering in parallelism to "Assyria") [Maurer]. Cf. Isaiah 11:15, 16; 19:23-25; 27:13; Hosea 11:11; Zechariah 10:10. **13.** However glorious the prospect of restoration, the Jews are not to forget the visitation on their "land" which is to intervene for the "fruit of (evil caused by) their doings" (cf. Prov. 1:31; Isa. 3:10, 11; Jer. 21:14).

14. Feed thy people—Prayer of the prophet, in the name of his people to God, which, as God fulfils believing prayer, is prophetical of what God *would* do. When God is about to deliver His people, He stirs up their friends to pray for them. **Feed**—including the idea of both pastoral *rule* and care over His people (*Margin,* ch. 5:4), regarded as a flock (Ps. 80:1; 100:3). Our calamity must be fatal to the nation, unless Thou of Thy unmerited grace, remembering Thy covenant with "Thine heritage" (Deut. 4:20; 7:6; 32:9), shalt restore us. **thy rod**— the shepherd's rod, wherewith He directs the flock (Ps. 23:4). No longer the rod of punishment (ch. 6:9). **which dwell solitarily in the wood, in . . . Carmel**—Let Thy people who have been dwelling as it were in a solitude of woods (*in* the world, but not *of* it), scattered among various nations, dwell in Carmel, i.e., where there are fruit-bearing lands and vineyards [Calvin]. Rather, "which are about to dwell (i.e., that they may dwell) separate in the wood, in . . . Carmel" [Maurer], which are to be no longer mingled with the heathen, but are to dwell as a distinct people in their own land. Micah has here Balaam's prophecy in view (cf. ch. 6:5, where also Balaam is referred to). "Lo, the people shall dwell *alone*" (Num. 23:9; cf. Deut. 33:28). To "feed in the wood in Carmel," is to feed in the rich pastures among its woods. To "sleep in the woods," is the image of *most perfect security* (Ezek. 34:25). So that the Jews' *security,* as well as their *distinct nationality,* is here foretold. Also Jeremiah 49:31. **Bashan**—famed for its cattle (Ps. 22:12; Amos 4:1). Parallel to this passage is Jeremiah 50:19. Bashan and Gilead, east of Jordan, were chosen by Reuben, Gad, and half Manasseh, as abounding in pastures suited for their many cattle (Num. 32; Deut. 3:12-17). **15. thy . . . him**—both referring to Israel. So in vs. 19 the person is changed from the first to the third, "us . . . our . . . their." Jehovah here answers Micah's prayer in vs. 14, assuring him, that as He delivered His people from Egypt by miraculous power, so He would again "show" it in their behalf (Jer. 16:14, 15). **16. shall see**—the "marvellous things" (vs. 15; Isa. 26: 11). **confounded at all their might**—having so suddenly proved unavailing: that might wherewith they had thought that there is nothing which they could not effect against God's people. **lay . . hand upon . . . mouth**—the gesture of silence (Job 21:5; 40:4; Ps. 107:42; Isa. 52:15). They shall be struck dumb at Israel's marvellous deliverance, and no longer boast that God's people is destroyed. **ears . . . deaf** —They shall stand astounded so as not to hear what shall be said [Grotius]. Once they had eagerly drunk in all rumors as so many messages of victories; but then they shall be afraid of hearing them, because they continually fear new disasters, when they see the God of Israel to be so powerful [Calvin]. They shall close their ears so as not to be compelled to hear of Israel's successes. **17. lick the dust**—in abject prostration as suppliants (Ps. 72: 9; cf. Isa. 49:23; 65:25). **move out of their holes**— As reptiles from their holes, they shall come forth from their hiding-places, or fortresses (Ps. 18:45), to give themselves up to the conquerors. More lit., "they shall tremble from," i.e., tremblingly come forth from their coverts. **like worms**—reptiles or crawlers (Deut. 32:24). **they shall be afraid of the Lord**—or, they shall in *fear turn with haste to* the Lord. Thus the antithesis is brought out. They shall tremble forth *from* their holes: they shall in trepidation turn *to* the Lord for salvation (cf. *Note,* Hos. 3:5, and Jer. 33:9). **fear because of thee**—

shall fear Thee, Jehovah [and so fear Israel as under Thy guardianship]. There is a change here from speaking of God to speaking to God [MAURER]. Or rather, "shall fear thee, Israel" [HENDERSON]. **18.** Grateful at such unlooked-for grace being promised to Israel, Micah breaks forth into praises of Jehovah. **passeth by the transgression**—not conniving at it, but forgiving it; leaving it unpunished, as a traveller *passes by* what he chooses not to look into (Prov. 19:11). Contrast Amos 7: 8, and "*mark* iniquities," Ps. 130:3. **the remnant**—who shall be permitted to survive the previous judgment: the elect remnant of grace (ch. 4:7; 5:3, 7, 8). **retaineth not ... anger**—(Ps. 103:9). **delighteth in mercy**—God's forgiving is founded on His nature, which delights in loving-kindness, and is averse from wrath. **19. turn again**—to us, from having been turned away from us. **subdue our iniquities**—lit., "tread under foot," as being hostile and deadly to us. Without subjugation of our bad propensities, even pardon could not give us peace. When God takes away the guilt of sin that it may not condemn us, He takes away also the power of sin that it may not rule us. **cast ... into ... depths of the sea**—never to rise again to view, buried out of sight in eternal oblivion: not merely at the shore side, where they may rise again. **our ... their**—change of person. Micah in the first case identifying himself and his sins with his people and their sins; in the second, speaking of them and their sins. **20. perform the truth**—the faithful promise. **to Jacob ... Abraham**—Thou shalt make good to their posterity the promise made to the patriarchs. God's promises are called "mercy," because they flow slowly from grace; "truth," because they will be surely performed (Luke 1:72, 73; I Thess. 5:24). **sworn unto our fathers**—(Ps. 105:9, 10). The promise to Abraham is in Genesis 12:2; to Isaac, in Genesis 26:24; to Jacob, in Genesis 28:13. This unchangeable promise implied an engagement that the seed of the patriarchs should never perish, and should be restored to their inheritance as often as they turned wholly to God (Deut. 30:1, 2).

THE BOOK OF

NAHUM

INTRODUCTION

NAHUM means "consolation" and "vengeance"; symbolizing the "consolation" in the book for God's people, and the "vengeance" coming on their enemies. In the first chapter the two themes alternate; but as the prophet advances, vengeance on the capital of the Assyrian foe is the predominant topic. He is called "the Elkoshite" (ch. 1:1), from *Elkosh*, or Elkesi, a village of Galilee, pointed out to JEROME (*Preface in Nahum*) as a place of note among the Jews, having traces of ancient buildings. The name *Capernaum*, i.e., "village of Nahum," seems to take its name from Nahum having resided in it, though born in Elkosh in the neighborhood. There is another Elkosh east of the Tigris, and north of Mosul, believed by Jewish pilgrims to be the birthplace and burial place of the prophet. But the book of Nahum in its allusions shows a particularity of acquaintance with Palestine (ch. 1:4), and only a more general knowledge as to Nineveh (ch. 2:4–6; 3:2, 3).

His graphic description of Sennacherib and his army (ch. 1:9–12) makes it not unlikely that he was in or near Jerusalem at the time: hence the number of phrases corresponding to those of Isaiah (cf. ch. 1:8, 9, with Isa. 8:8; 10:23; ch. 2:10, with Isa. 24:1, and 21:3; ch. 1:15, with Isa. 52:7). The prophecy in ch. 1:14 probably refers to the murder of Sennacherib twenty years after his return from Palestine (Isa. 37:38). The date of his prophecies, thus, seems to be about the former years of Hezekiah. So JEROME thinks. He plainly writes while the Assyrian power was yet unbroken (ch. 1:12; 2:11–13; 3:15–17). The correspondence between the sentiments of Nahum and those of Isaiah and Hezekiah, as recorded in II Kings and Isaiah, proves the likelihood of Nahum's prophecies belonging to the time when Sennacherib was demanding the surrender of Jerusalem, and had not yet raised the siege (cf. ch. 1:2, etc., with II Kings 19:14, 15; ch. 1:7, with II Kings 18:22; 19:19, 31; II Chron. 32:7, 8; ch. 1:9, 11, with II Kings 19:22, 27, 28; ch. 1:14, with II Kings 19:6, 7; ch. 1:15, and 2:1, 2, with II Kings 19:32, 33; ch. 2:13, with II Kings 19:22, 23). The historical data in the book itself are the humiliation of Israel and Judah by Assyria (ch. 1:9, 11); the invasion of Judah (ch. 1:9, 11); and the conquest of No-ammon, or Thebes, in Upper Egypt (ch. 3:8–10). Tiglath-pileser and Shalmaneser had carried away Israel. The Jews were harassed by the Syrians, and impoverished by Ahaz' payments to Tiglath-pileser (II Chron. 28; Isa. 7:9). Sargon, Shalmaneser's successor, after the reduction of Phœnicia by the latter, fearing lest Egypt should join Palestine against him, undertook an expedition to Africa (Isa. 20), and took Thebes; the latter fact we know only from Nahum, but the *success* of the expedition in general is corroborated in Isaiah 20. Sennacherib, Sargon's successor, made the last Assyrian attempt against Judea, ending in the destruction of his army in the fourteenth year of Hezekiah (713–710 B.C.). As Nahum refers to this in part prophetically, in part as matter of history (ch. 1:9–13; 2:13), he must have lived about 720–714 B.C., that is, almost 100 years before the event foretold, viz., the overthrow of Nineveh by the joint forces of Cyaxares and Nabopolassar in the reign of Chyniladanus, 625 or 603 B.C.

The prophecy is remarkable for its unity of aim. Nahum's object was to inspire his countrymen, the Jews, with the assurance that, however alarming their position might seem, exposed to the attacks of the mighty Assyrian, who had already carried away the ten tribes, yet that not only should the Assyrian (Sennacherib) fail in his attack on Jerusalem, but Nineveh, his own capital, be taken and his empire overthrown; and this, not by an arbitrary exercise of Jehovah's power, but for the iniquities of the city and its people.

His position in the canon is seventh of the minor prophets in both the Hebrew and Greek arrangement. He is seventh in point of date.

His style is clear, elegant, and forcible. Its most striking characteristic is the power of representing several phases of an idea in the briefest sentences, as in the majestic description of God in the commencement, the conquest of Nineveh, and the destruction of No-ammon [EICHORN] DE WETTE calls attention to his variety of manner in presenting ideas, as marking great poetic talent. "Here there is something sonorous in his language there something murmuring; with both these alternates something that is soft, delicate, and melting, as the subject demands." Excepting two alleged Assyrian words (ch. 3:17), *English Version* "crowned," or *princes*, and *English Version*, "captains," or *satraps* (used by Jer. 51:27), the language is pure. These two, doubtless, came to be known in Judea from the intercourse with Assyria in the eighth and seventh centuries B.C.

CHAPTER 1

Vss. 1-15. JEHOVAH'S ATTRIBUTES AS A JEALOUS JUDGE OF SIN, YET MERCIFUL TO HIS TRUSTING PEOPLE, SHOULD INSPIRE THEM WITH CONFIDENCE. HE WILL NOT ALLOW THE ASSYRIANS AGAIN TO ASSAIL THEM, BUT WILL DESTROY THE FOE. **1. burden of Nineveh**—the *prophetic doom* of Nineveh. Nahum prophesied against that city 150 years after Jonah. **2. jealous**—In this there is sternness, yet tender affection. We are jealous only of those we love: a husband, of a wife; a king, of his subjects' loyalty. God is jealous of men because He loves them. God will not bear a rival in His claims on them. His burning jealousy for His own wounded honor and their love, as much as His justice, accounts for all His fearful judgments: the flood, the destruction of Jerusalem, that of Nineveh. His jealousy will not admit of His friends being oppressed, and their enemies flourishing (cf. Exod. 20:5; I Cor. 16: 22; II Cor. 11:2). *Burning zeal* enters into the idea in "jealous" here (cf. Num. 25:11, 13; I Kings 19: 10). **the Lord revengeth . . . Lord revengeth**—The repetition of the incommunicable name JEHOVAH, and of His *revenging*, gives an awful solemnity to the introduction. **furious**—lit., "a master of fury." So *a master of the tongue*, i.e., "eloquent." "One who, if He pleases, can most readily give effect to His fury" [GROTIUS]. Nahum has in view the provocation to fury given to God by the Assyrians, after having carried away the ten tribes, now proceeding to invade Judea under Hezekiah. **reserveth wrath for his enemies**—*reserves it* against His own appointed time (II Pet. 2:9). After long waiting for their repentance in vain, at length punishing them. A wrong estimate of Jehovah is formed from His suspending punishment: it is not that He is insensible or dilatory, but He reserves wrath for His own fit time. In the case of the penitent, He does not *reserve* or retain His anger (Ps. 103:9; Jer. 3:5, 12; Mic. 7:18). **3. slow to anger, and great in power**—i.e., *but* great in power, so as to be able in a moment, if He pleases, to destroy the wicked. His long-suffering is not from want of power to punish (Exod. 34:6, 7). **not at all acquit**—lit., "will not acquitting acquit," or treat as innocent. **Lord hath his way in the whirlwind**—From this to vs. 5, inclusive, is a description of His power exhibited in the phenomena of nature, especially when He is wroth. His vengeance shall sweep away the Assyrian foe like a whirlwind (Prov. 10:25). **clouds are the dust of his feet**—Large as they are, He treads on them, as a man would on the small dust; He is Lord of the clouds, and uses them as He pleases. **4. rebuketh the sea**—as Jesus did (Matt. 8:26), proving Himself God (cf. Isa. 50:2). **Bashan languisheth**—through drought; ordinarily it was a region famed for its rich pasturage (Joel 1:10). **flower of Lebanon**—*its bloom;* all that blooms so luxuriantly on Lebanon (Hos. 14:7). As Bashan was famed

for its pastures, Carmel for its cornfields and vineyards, so Lebanon for its forests (Isa. 33:9). There is nothing in the world so blooming that God cannot change it when He is wroth. **5. earth is burned** —so GROTIUS. Rather, "lifts itself," i.e., "heaveth" [MAURER]: as the *Hebrew* is translated in Psalm 89: 9; Hosea 13:1; cf. *Margin*, II Samuel 5:21. **6. fury is poured out like fire**—like the liquid fire poured out of volcanoes in all directions (see Jer. 7:20) **rocks are thrown down**—or, "are burnt asunder"; the usual effect of volcanic fire (Jer. 51:25, 56). As Hannibal burst asunder the Alpine rocks by fire to make a passage for his army [GROTIUS]. **7. Here** Nahum enters on his special subject, for which the previous verses have prepared the way, viz., to assure his people of safety in Jehovah under the impending attack of Sennacherib (vs. 7), and to announce the doom of Nineveh, the capital of the Assyrian foe (vs. 8). The contrast of vss. 7 and 8 heightens the force. **he knoweth**—recognizes as His own (Hos. 13:5; Amos 3:2); and so, cares for and guards (Ps. 1:6; II Tim. 2:19). **8. with an overrunning flood**—i.e., with irresistible might which *overruns* every barrier like a flood. This image is often applied to overwhelming *armies* of invaders. Also of *calamity* in general (Ps. 32:6; 42:7; 90:5). There is, perhaps, a special allusion to the mode of Nineveh's capture by the Medo-Babylonian army; viz., through a *flood* in the river which broke down the wall twenty furlongs (see *Note*, ch. 2:6; Isa. 8: 8; Dan. 9:26; 11:10, 22:40). **end of the place thereof**—Nineveh is personified as a queen; and *"her* place" of residence (the *Hebrew* for "thereof" is feminine) is *the city itself* (ch. 2:8), [MAURER]. Or, He shall so utterly destroy Nineveh that its place cannot be found; ch. 3:17 confirms this (cf. Ps. 37:36; Dan. 2:35; Rev. 12:8 and 20:11). **darkness**—the severest calamities. **9. What do ye imagine against the Lord?**—abrupt address to the Assyrians. How mad is your attempt, O Assyrians, to resist so powerful a God! What can ye do against such an adversary, successful though ye have been against all other adversaries? Ye *imagine* ye have to *do* merely with mortals and with a weak people, and that so you will gain an easy victory; but you have to encounter God, the protector of His people. Parallel to Isaiah 37:23-29; cf. Psalm 1:1. **he will make an utter end**—The utter overthrow of Sennacherib's host, soon about to take place, is an earnest of the "utter end" of Nineveh itself. **affliction shall not rise up the second time**—Judah's "affliction" caused by the invasion shall never rise again. So vs. 12. But CALVIN takes the "affliction" to be that of *Assyria*: "There will be no need of His inflicting on you a second blow: He will make an utter end of you once for all" (I Sam. 3:12; 26:8; II Sam. 20:10). If so, this verse, in contrast to vs. 12, will express, Affliction shall visit the Assyrian no more, in a sense very different from that in which God will afflict Judah no more. In the Assyrian's case, because the blow will be fatally final; the latter, because God will make lasting blessedness in Judah's case succeed temporary chastisement. But it seems simpler to refer "affliction" here, as in vs. 12, to Judah; indeed *destruction,* rather than *affliction,* applies to the Assyrian. **10. while they are folden together as thorns** —lit., "*to the same degree* as thorns" (cf. *Margin,* I Chron. 4:27). As thorns, so folded together and entangled that they cannot be loosed asunder without trouble, are thrown by the husbandmen all in a mass into the fire, so the Assyrians shall all be given together to destruction. Cf. II Samuel 23:6, 7, where also "thorns" are the image of the wicked. As this image represents the speediness of their destruction *in a mass,* so that of "drunkards," their rushing as it were *of their own accord* into it; for drunkards fall down without any one pushing them [KIMCHI]. CALVIN explains, *Although* ye be *dangerous to touch* as thorns (i.e., full of rage and violence), yet the Lord can easily consume you. But "although" will hardly apply to the next clause. *English Version* and KIMCHI, therefore, are to be preferred. The comparison to drunkards is appropriate. For drunkards, though exulting and bold, are weak and easily thrown down by even a finger touching them. So the insolent self-confidence of the Assyrians shall precipitate their overthrow by God. The *Hebrew* is "*soaked,*" or "drunken as with their own wine." Their drunken revelries are perhaps *alluded to,* during which the foe (according to DIODORUS SICULUS, 2) broke into their city, and Sardanapalus *burned* his palace; though the main and ultimate destruction of Nineveh referred to by Nahum was long subsequent to that under Sardanapalus. **11.** The cause of Nineveh's overthrow: Sennacherib's plots against Judah. **out of thee**—O Nineveh. From thyself shall arise the source of thy own ruin. Thou shalt have only thyself to blame for it. **imagineth evil**—Sennacherib carried out the *imaginations* of his countrymen (vs. 9) against the Lord and His people (II Kings 19:22, 23). **a wicked counsellor** —lit., "a counsellor of Belial." Belial means "without profit," worthless, and so bad (I Sam. 25:25; II Cor. 6:15). **12-14.** The same truths repeated as in vss. 9-11, Jehovah here being the speaker. He addresses Judah, prophesying good to it, and evil to the Assyrian. **Though they be quiet**—i.e., without fear, and tranquilly secure. So *Chaldee* and CALVIN. Or, "entire," "complete"; "Though their power be *unbroken* [MAURER], and though they be *so many, yet even so* they shall be cut down" (lit., "shorn"; as *hair shaved off closely by a razor,* Isa. 7:20). As the Assyrian was a razor shaving others, so shall he be shaven himself. Retribution in kind. In the height of their pride and power, they shall be clean cut off. The same *Hebrew* stands for "likewise" and "yet thus." So *many* as they are, *so* many shall they perish. **when he shall pass through** —or, "and he shall pass away," viz., "the wicked counsellor" (vs. 11), Sennacherib. The change of number to the *singular* distinguishes *him* from *his host. They* shall be cut down, *he* shall pass away home (II Kings 19:35, 36) [HENDERSON]. *English Version* is better, "they shall be cut down, *when* He [Jehovah] shall pass through," destroying by one stroke the Assyrian host. This gives the reason why they with all their numbers and power are to be so utterly cut off. Cf. "pass through," i.e., in destroying power (Ezek. 12:12, 23; Isa. 8:8; Dan. 11:10). **Though I have afflicted thee**—Judah, "I will afflict thee no more" (Isa. 40:1, 2; 52:1, 2). The

contrast is between "they," the Assyrians, and "thee," Judah. *Their* punishment is fatal and final. Judah's was temporary and corrective. **13. will I break his yoke**—the Assyrian's yoke, viz., the tribute imposed by Sennacherib on Hezekiah (II Kings 18: 14). **from off thee**—O Judah (Isa. 10:27). **14. that no more of thy name be sown**—that no more of thy seed, bearing thy name, as kings of Nineveh, be propagated; that thy dynasty become extinct, viz., on the destruction of Nineveh here foretold; "thee" means the *king of Assyria.* **will I cut off ... graven image**—The Medes under Cyaxares, the joint destroyers of Nineveh with the Babylonians, hated idolatry, and would delight in destroying its idols. As the Assyrians had treated the gods of other nations, so their own should be treated (II Kings 19:18). The Assyrian palaces partook of a sacred character [LAYARD]; so that "house of thy gods" *may* refer to the *palace.* At Khorsabad there is remaining a representation of a man cutting an idol to pieces. **I will make thy grave**—rather, "I will make it (viz., 'the house of thy gods,' i.e., Nisroch) thy grave" (II Kings 19:37; Isa. 37:38). Thus, by Sennacherib's being slain in it, Nisroch's house should be defiled. Neither thy gods, nor thy temple, shall save thee; but the latter shall be thy sepulchre. **thou art vile**—or, thou art lighter than due weight (Dan. 5:27; cf. Job 31:6) [MAURER]. **15.** This verse is joined in the *Hebrew* text to ch. 2. It is nearly the same as Isaiah 52:7, referring to the similar deliverance from Babylon. **him that bringeth good tidings**—announcing the overthrow of Sennacherib and deliverance of Jerusalem. The "mountains" are those round Jerusalem, on which Sennacherib's host had so lately encamped, preventing Judah from keeping her "feasts," but on which messengers now speed to Jerusalem, publishing his overthrow with a loud voice where lately they durst not have opened their mouths. A type of the far more glorious spiritual deliverance of God's people from Satan by Messiah, heralded by ministers of the Gospel (Rom. 10:15). **perform thy vows**— which thou didst promise if God would deliver thee from the Assyrian. **the wicked**—lit., "Belial"; the same as the "counsellor of Belial" (*Margin,* ch. 1: 11); viz., Sennacherib.

CHAPTER 2

VSS. 1-13. THE ADVANCE OF THE DESTROYING FORCES AGAINST NINEVEH, AFTER IT WAS USED AS GOD'S ROD FOR A TIME TO CHASTISE HIS PEOPLE: THE CAPTURE OF THAT LION'S DWELLING, ACCORDING TO THE SURE WORD OF JEHOVAH. **1. He that dasheth in pieces**—God's "battle-axe," wherewith He "breaks in pieces" His enemies. Jeremiah 51: 20 applies the same *Hebrew* term to Nebuchadnezzar (cf. Prov. 25:18; Jer. 50:23, "the hammer of the whole earth"). Here the Medo-Babylonian army under Cyaxares and Nabopolassar, that destroyed Nineveh, is prophetically meant. **before thy face** —before Nineveh. *Openly,* so that the work of God may be manifest. **watch the way**—by which the foe will attack, so as to be ready to meet him. Ironical advice; equivalent to a prophecy, Thou shalt have need to use all possible means of defense; but use what thou wilt, all will be in vain. **make thy loins strong**—The loins are the seat of strength; to gird them up is to prepare all one's strength for conflict (Job 40:7). Also gird on thy sword (II Sam. 20:8; II Kings 4:29). **2. For the Lord hath turned away the excellency of Jacob**—i.e., the time for Nineveh's overthrow is ripe, because Jacob (Judah) and Israel (the ten tribes) have been sufficiently chastised. The Assyrian rod of chastisement, having done its work, is to be thrown into the fire. If God chastised Jacob and Israel with all their "excellency" (Jerusalem and the temple, which was their pre-eminent excellency above all nations in God's eyes, Ps. 47:4; 87:2; Ezek. 24:21; *Note,* Amos 6:8), how much more will He punish fatally Nineveh, an alien to Him, and idolatrous? MAURER, not so well, translates, "restores," or "will restore the excellency of Jacob." emptiers—the Assyrian spoilers. have emptied them out—have spoiled the Israelites and Jews (Hos. 10:1). Cf. Psalm 80:8-16, on "vine branches," as applied to Israel. 3. his mighty men—the Medo-Babylonian general's *mighty men* attacking Nineveh. made red—The ancients dyed their bull's-hide shields *red,* partly to strike terror into the enemy, chiefly lest the blood from wounds which they might receive should be perceived and give confidence to the foe [CALVIN]. G. V. SMITH conjectures that the reference is to the red reflection of the sun's rays from shields of bronze or copper, such as are found among the Assyrian remains. in scarlet—or *crimson* military tunics (cf. Matt. 27:28). Xenophon mentions that the Medes were fond of this color. The Lydians and Tyrians extracted the dye from a particular worm. chariots . . . with flaming torches—i.e, the chariots shall be like flaming torches, their wheels in lightning-like rapidity of rotation flashing light and striking sparks from the stones over which they pass (cf. Isa. 5:28). *English Version* supposes a transposition of the *Hebrew* letters. It is better to translate the *Hebrew* as it is, "the chariots (shall be furnished) with fire-flashing *scythes"* (lit., "with the fire," or glitter, *of iron weapons*). Iron scythes were fixed at right angles to the axles and turned down, or parallel to it, inserted into the felly of the wheel. The Medes, perhaps, had such chariots, though no traces of them are found in Assyrian remains. On account of the latter fact, it may be better to translate, "the chariots (shall come) with the glitter of *steel weapons"* [MAURER and G. V. SMITH]. in the day of his preparation—JEHOVAH'S (Isa. 13:3). Or, *"Medo-Babylonian commander's* day of preparation for the attack" (vs. 1). "He" confirms this, and "his" in this verse. the fir trees —their fir-tree lances. terribly shaken—branded so as to strike terror. Or, "shall be tremulous with being brandished" [MAURER]. 4. rage—are driven in furious haste (Jer. 46:9). justle one against another—run to and fro [MAURER]. in the broad ways—(II Chron. 32:6). Large open spaces in the suburbs of Nineveh. they shall seem like torches —lit., "their (feminine in *Hebrew*) appearance" (is): viz., the appearance of *the broad places* is like that of torches, through the numbers of chariots in them flashing in the sun (*Margin,* Prov. 8:26). run like the lightnings—with rapid violence (Matt. 24:27; Luke 10:18). 5. The Assyrian preparations for defense. He—the Assyrian king. shall recount his worthies—(ch. 3:18). *Review,* or *count over in his mind,* his nobles, choosing out the bravest to hasten to the walls and repel the attack. But in vain; for "they shall stumble in their *advance"* through fear and hurry. the defence shall be prepared—rather, *the covering machine used by besiegers* to protect themselves in advancing to the wall. Such sudden transitions, as here from the besieged to the besiegers, are frequent (cf. Ezek. 4:2), [MAURER]. Or, used *by the besieged Assyrians* [CALVIN]. 6. The gates of the rivers . . . opened—The river wall on the

Tigris (the west defense of Nineveh) was 4,530 yards long. On the north, south, and east sides, there were large moats, capable of being easily filled with water from the Khosru. Traces of dams ("gates," or sluices) for regulating the supply are still visible, so that the whole city could be surrounded with a water barrier (vs. 8). Besides, on the east, the weakest side, it was further protected by a lofty double rampart with a moat 200 feet wide between its two parts, cut in the rocky ground. The moats or canals, flooded by the Ninevites before the siege to repel the foe, were made a dry bed to march into the city, by the foe turning the waters into a different channel: as Cyrus did in the siege of Babylon [MAURER]. In the earlier capture of Nineveh by Arbaces the Mede, and Belesis the Babylonian, DIODORUS SICULUS, *l.* 2. 80, states that there was an old prophecy that it should not be taken till the river became its enemy; so in the third year of the siege, the river by a flood broke down the walls twenty furlongs, and the king thereupon burnt himself and his palace and all his concubines and wealth together, and the enemy entered by the breach in the wall. Fire and water were doubtless the means of the second destruction here foretold, as of the first. dissolved—by the inundation [HENDERSON]. Or, those in the palace shall melt with fear, viz., the king and his nobles [GROTIUS]. 7. Huzzab—the name of the queen of Nineveh, from a *Hebrew* root implying that she *stood by* the king (Ps. 45:9), [VATABLUS]. Rather, Nineveh personified as a queen. She who had long *stood* in the most supreme prosperity. Similarly CALVIN. MAURER makes it not a proper name, and translates, "It is established," or "determined" (cf. Gen. 41:32). *English Version* is more supported by the parallelism. led away captive—The *Hebrew* requires rather, "she *is laid bare"*; brought forth from the apartments where Eastern women remained secluded, and is stripped of her ornamental attire. Cf. Isaiah 47:2, 3, where the same image of a woman with face and legs exposed is used of a city captive and dismantled (cf. ch. 3:5), [MAURER]. brought up—Her people shall be *made to go up* to Babylon. Cf. the use of "go up" for *moving from* a place in Jeremiah 21:2. her maids . . . as . . . doves—As Nineveh is compared to a queen dethroned and dishonored, so she has here assigned to her in the image *handmaids attending her with dove-like plaints* (Isa. 38:14; 59:11. The image implies *helplessness and grief suppressed, but at times breaking out).* The minor cities and dependencies of Nineveh may be meant, or her captive women [JEROME]. GROTIUS and MAURER translate, for "lead *her," "moan,"* or *"sigh."* tabering—*beating* on their breasts *as on a tambourine.* 8. But— rather, "Though" [G. V. SMITH]. of old—rather, *"from the days* that she hath been"; from the earliest period of her existence. Alluding to Nineveh's antiquity (Gen. 10:11). "Though Nineveh has been of old defended by water surrounding her, yet her inhabitants shall flee away." GROTIUS, less probably (cf. ch. 3:8-12), interprets, the "waters" of her *numerous population* (Isa. 8:7; Jer. 51:13; Rev. 17:15). Stand, stand, *shall they cry*—i.e., the few patriotic citizens *shall cry* to their *fleeing* countrymen; "but none looketh back," much less stops in flight, so panic-stricken are they. 9. silver . . . gold —The conquerors are summoned to plunder the city. Nineveh's riches arose from the annual tribute paid by so many subject states, as well as from its extensive merchandise (ch. 3:16; Ezek. 27:23, 24). store—accumulated by the plunder of subject nations. It is remarkable, that while small articles of value (bronze inlaid with gold, gems, seals, and alabaster *vases*) are found in the ruins of Nineveh, there are none of *gold* and *silver*. These, as then foretold, were "taken for spoil" before the palaces were set on fire. **glory out of all the pleasant furniture**—or, "there is abundance of precious vessels of every kind" [MAURER]. **10.** Lit., "emptiness, and emptiedness, and devastation." The accumulation of substantives without a verb (as in ch. 3:2), the two first of the three being derivatives of the same root, and like in sound, and the number of syllables in them increasing in a kind of climax, intensify the gloomy effectiveness of the expression. *Hebrew, Bukah, Mebukah, Mebullakah* (cf. Isa. 24:1, 3, 4; Zeph. 1:15). **faces of all gather blackness**—(*Note,* Joel 2:6). CALVIN translates, "withdraw (lit., 'gather up') their glow," or flush, i.e. grow pale. This is probably the better rendering. So MAURER. **11. dwelling of ... lions**—Nineveh, the seat of empire of the rapacious and destructive warriors of various ranks, typified by the "lions," "young lions," "old lion" (or *lioness* [MAURER]), "the lion's whelp." The image is peculiarly appropriate, as lions of every form, winged, and sometimes with the head of a man, are frequent in the Assyrian sepulchres. It was as full of spoils of all nations as a lion's den is of remains of its prey. The question, "Where ..." implies that Jehovah "would make an utter end of *the place,*" so that its very site could not be found (ch. 1:8). It is a question expressing wonder, so incredible did it then seem. **12. prey ... ravin**—different kinds of prey. Cf. Isaiah 3:1, "the stay and the staff." **13. burn ... in the smoke**—or (so as to pass) "*into* smoke," i.e., "entirely" [MAURER], (Ps. 37:20; 46:9). CALVIN, like *English Version,* explains, As soon as the flame catches, and the fire smokes, by the mere smoke I will burn her chariots. **cut off thy prey from the earth**—Thou shalt no more carry off prey from the nations of the earth. **the voice of thy messengers ... no more ... heard**—No more shall thy emissaries be heard throughout thy provinces conveying thy king's commands, and exacting tribute of subject nations.

CHAPTER 3

Vss. 1-19. REPETITION OF NINEVEH'S DOOM, WITH NEW FEATURES; THE CAUSE IS HER TYRANNY, RAPINE, AND CRUELTY: NO-AMMON'S FORTIFICATIONS DID NOT SAVE HER; IT IS VAIN, THEREFORE, FOR NINEVEH TO THINK HER DEFENSES WILL SECURE HER AGAINST GOD'S SENTENCE. **1. the bloody city!** —lit., "city of blood," viz., shed by Nineveh; just so now her own blood is to be shed. **robbery**—violence [MAURER]. Extortion [GROTIUS]. **the prey departeth not**—Nineveh never ceases to live by rapine. Or, the *Hebrew* verb is transitive, "she (Nineveh) does not make the prey depart"; she ceases not to plunder. **2.** The reader is transported into the midst of the fight (cf. Jer. 47:3). The "noise of the whips" urging on the horses (in the chariots) is heard, and of "the rattling of the wheels" of war-chariots, and the "horses" are seen "prancing," and the "chariots jumping," etc. **3. horseman**—distinct from "the horses" (in the chariots, vs. 2). **lifteth up**—denoting readiness for fight [EWALD]. GESENIUS translates, "lifteth up (lit., makes to ascend) his horse." Similarly MAURER, "makes his horse to rise up on his hind feet." *Vulgate* translates, "ascending," i.e., making his horse to advance up to the assault. This last is perhaps better than Eng-

lish *Version.* **the bright sword and the glittering spear**—lit., "the glitter of the sword and the flash of the spear!" This, as well as the translation, "the horseman advancing up," more graphically presents the battle scene to the eye. **they stumble upon their corpses**—The *Medo-Babylonian* enemy stumble upon the *Assyrian* corpses. **4. Because of the multitude of the whoredoms**—This assigns the reason for Nineveh's destruction. **whoredoms of the well-favoured harlot**—As Assyria was not a worshipper of the true God, "whoredoms" cannot mean, as in the case of Israel, apostasy to the worship of false gods; but, her *harlot-like artifices* whereby she allured neighboring states so as to subject them to herself. As the unwary are allured by the "well-favored harlot's" looks, so Israel, Judah (e.g., under Ahaz, who, calling to his aid Tiglath-pileser, was made tributary by him, II Kings 16:7-10), and other nations, were tempted by the plausible professions of Assyria, and by the lure of commerce (Rev. 18:2, 3), to trust her. **witchcrafts**—(Isa. 47:9, 12). Alluding to the love incantations whereby harlots tried to dement and ensnare youths; answering to the subtle machinations whereby Assyria attracted nations to her. **selleth**—deprives of their liberty; as slaves used to be *sold:* and in other property also *sale* was a usual mode of transfer. MAURER understands it of depriving nations of their freedom, and literally *selling* them as slaves to distant peoples (Joel 3:2, 3, 6-8). But elsewhere there is no evidence that the Assyrians did this. **families**—peoples. **5. I will discover thy skirts upon thy face**—i.e., discover thy nakedness by *throwing up thy skirts upon thy face* (the greatest possible insult), pulling them up as as high as thy head (Jer. 13:22; Ezek. 16:37-41). I will treat thee not as a matron, but as a harlot whose shame is exposed; her gaudy finery being lifted up off her (Isa. 47:2, 3). So Nineveh shall be stripped of all her glory and defenses on which she prides herself. **6. cast abominable filth upon thee**—as infamous harlots used to be treated. **gazing-stock**—exposed to public ignominy as a warning to others (Ezek. 28:17). **7. all ... that look upon thee**—when thou hast been made "a gazing-stock" (vs. 6). **shall flee from thee**—as a thing horrible to look upon. Cf. "standing *afar off,*" Rev. 18:10. **whence shall I seek comforters for thee?**—Cf. Isaiah 51:19, which Nahum had before his mind. **8. populous No**—rather, as *Hebrew,* "No-ammon," the Egyptian name for Thebes in Upper Egypt; meaning the *portion* or *possession of Ammon,* the Egyptian Jupiter (whence the Greeks called the city Diospolis), who was especially worshipped there. The Egyptian inscriptions call the god *Amon-re,* i.e., "*Amon the Sun*"; he is represented as a human figure with a ram's head, seated on a chair (Jer. 46:25; Ezek. 30:14-16). The blow inflicted on No-ammon, described in vs. 10, was probably by the Assyrian Sargon (cf. *Notes* on Isa. 18 and 20). As Thebes, with all her resources, was overcome by Assyria, so Assyrian Nineveh, notwithstanding all her might, in her turn, shall be overcome by Babylon. *English Version,* "populous," if correct, implies that No's large population did not save her from destruction. **situate among the rivers**—probably the *channels* into which the Nile here divides (cf. Isa. 19:6-8). Thebes lay on both sides of the river. It was famed in Homer's time for its hundred gates (*Illiad,* 9.381). Its ruins still describe a circumference of twenty-seven miles. Of them the temples of Luxor and Karnak, east of the river, are most famous. The colonnade of the former, and the grand hall of the latter, are of stupendous dimensions. One wall still represents the expedition of Shishak against Jerusalem under Rehoboam (I Kings 14:25; II Chron. 12:2-9). **whose ... wall was from the sea**—i.e., *rose up* "from the sea." MAURER translates, "whose wall consisted *of the sea.*" But this would be a mere repetition of the former clause. The Nile is called a *sea,* from its appearance in the annual flood (Isa. 19:5). **9. Ethiopia**—*Hebrew, Cush.* Ethiopia is thought at this time to have been mistress of Upper Egypt. **Egypt** —Lower Egypt. **her strength**—her safeguard as an ally. **it was infinite**—The resources of these, her allies, were endless. **Put**—or Phut (Gen. 10:6); descended from Ham (Ezek. 27:10). From a root meaning a *bow;* as they were famed as archers [GESENIUS]. Probably west of Lower Egypt. JOSEPHUS (*Antiquities,* 1. 6. 2) identifies it with Mauritania (cf. *Margin,* Jer. 46:9; Ezek. 38:5). **Lubim**—the Libyans, whose capital was Cyrene; extending along the Mediterranean west of Egypt (II Chron. 12:3; 16:8; Acts 2:10). As, however, the *Lubim* are always connected with the Egyptians and Ethiopians, they are perhaps distinct from the *Libyans.* The Lubim were probably at first wandering tribes, who afterwards were settled under Carthage in the region of Cyrene, under the name Libyans. **thy**—No's. **helpers**—lit., "in thy help," i.e., among thy auxiliaries. **10.** Notwithstanding all her might, she was overcome. **cast lots for her honourable men**—They divided them among themselves by lot, as slaves (Joel 3:3). **11. drunken**—made to drink of the cup of Jehovah's wrath (Isa. 51:17, 21; Jer. 25:15). **hid**—covered out of sight: a prediction remarkably verified in the state in which the ruins of Nineveh have been found [G. V. SMITH]. But as "hid" precedes "seek strength . . . ," it rather refers to Nineveh's state when attacked by her foe: "Thou who now so vauntest thyself, shalt be compelled to seek a hiding-place from the foe" [CALVIN]; or, shalt be neglected and slighted by all [MAURER]. **seek strength because of the enemy**—Thou too, like Thebes (vs. 9), shalt have recourse to other nations for help against thy Medo-Babylonian enemy. **12. thy strongholds**—on the borders of Assyria, protecting the approaches to Nineveh: "the gates of thy land" (vs. 13). **fig trees with the first ripe figs**—expressing the rapidity and ease of the capture of Nineveh (cf. Isa. 28.4; Rev. 6.13). **13. thy people**—thy soldiers. **women**—unable to fight for thee (Isa. 19:16; Jer. 50:37; 51:30). **gates on thy land**—the fortified passes or entrances to the region of Nineveh (cf. Jer. 15:7). Northeast of Nineveh there were hills affording a natural barrier against an invader; the guarded passes through these are probably "the gates of the land" meant. **fire shall devour thy bars**—the "bars" of the fortresses at the passes into Assyria. So in Assyrian remains the Assyrians themselves are represented as setting fire to the gates of a city [BONOMI, *Nin.* pp. 194, 197]. **14.** Ironical exhortation to Nineveh to defend herself. **Draw ... waters**—so as not to be without water for drinking, in the event of being cut off by the besiegers from the fountains. **make strong the brick-kiln**—or "repair" [MAURER]; so as to have a supply of bricks formed of kiln-burnt clay, to repair breaches in the ramparts, or to build

new fortifications inside when the outer ones are taken by the foe. **15. There**—in the very scene of thy great preparations for defense; and where thou now art so secure. **fire**—even as at the former destruction; Sardanapalus (Pul?) perished with all his household in the conflagration of his palace, having in despair set it on fire, the traces of which are still remaining. **cankerworm**—"the licking locust" [HENDERSON]. **make thyself many as the locusts**—"the swarming locusts" [HENDERSON]; i.e., however "many" be thy forces, like those of "the swarming locusts," or the "licking locusts," yet the foe shall consume thee as the "licking locust" licks up all before it. **16. multiplied thy merchants**—(Ezek. 27: 23, 24). Nineveh, by large canals, had easy access to Babylon; and it was one of the great routes for the people of the west and northwest to that city; lying on the Tigris it had access to the sea. The Phœnicians carried its wares everywhere. Hence its merchandise is so much spoken of. **the cankerworm spoileth, and fleeth away**—i.e., spoiled *thy merchants.* The "cankerworm," or licking locust, answers to the Medo-Babylonian invaders of Nineveh [G. V. SMITH]. CALVIN explains less probably, "Thy merchants spoiled many regions; but the same shall befall them as befalls locusts, they in a moment shall be scattered and flee away." MAURER, somewhat similarly, "The licking locust puts off (the envelope in which his wings had been folded), and fleeth away" (ch. 2:9; cf. Joel 1:4). The *Hebrew* has ten different names for the locust, so destructive was it. **17. Thy crowned**—Thy princes (Rev. 9:7). The king's nobles and officers wore the tiara, as well as the king; hence they are called here "thy crowned ones." **as the locusts**—as many as *the swarming locusts.* **thy captains**—*Tiphsar,* an Assyrian word; found also in Jeremiah 51:27, meaning *satraps* [MICHAELIS]; or rather, "military leaders" [MAURER]. The last syllable, *sar* means a "prince," and is found in *Belshaz-zar, Nabopolas-sar, Nebuchadnez-zar.* **as the great grasshoppers**—lit., as the locust of locusts, i.e., the largest locust. MAURER translates, "as many as *locusts upon locusts,*" i.e., swarms of locusts. *Hebrew* idiom favors *English Version.* **in the hedges in the cold**—Cold deprives the locust of the power of flight; so they alight in cold weather and at night, but when warmed by the sun soon "flee away." So shall the Assyrian multitudes suddenly disappear, not leaving a trace behind (cf. PLINY *Hist. Nat.* 11. 29). **18. Thy shepherds**—i.e., Thy leaders. **slumber**—are carelessly secure [MAURER]. Rather, "lie in death's sleep, having been slain" [JEROME] (Exod. 15:16; Ps. 76:6). **shall dwell** *in the dust* (Ps. 7:5; 94:17). **thy people is scattered**—the necessary consequence of their leaders being laid low (I Kings 22:17). **19. bruit**—the report. **clap the hands**—with joy at thy fall. The sole descendants of the ancient Assyrians and Babylonians in the whole country are the Nestorian Christians, who speak a Chaldean language [LAYARD]. **upon whom hath not thy wickedness passed continually?**—implying God's long forbearance, and the consequent enormity of Assyria's guilt, rendering her case one that admitted no hope of restoration.

THE BOOK OF

HABAKKUK

INTRODUCTION

HABAKKUK, from a *Hebrew* root meaning to "embrace," denoting a "favorite" (viz., of God) and a "struggler" (for his country's good). Some ancient authors represent him as belonging to the tribe of Levi; others (PSEUDO EPIPHANIUS), to that of Simeon. The inscription to Bel and the dragon in the LXX asserts the former; and ch. 3:19 perhaps favors this. EUSEBIUS states that in his time Habakkuk's tomb was shown at Celia in Palestine.

The time seems to have been about 610 B.C. For the Chaldeans attacked Jerusalem in the ninth month of the fifth year of Jehoiakim, 605 B.C. (II Kings 24:1; II Chron. 36:6; Jer. 46:2 and 36:9). And Habakkuk (ch. 1:5, 6, etc.) speaks of the Chaldeans as about to invade Judah, but not as having actually done so. In ch. 2 he proceeds to comfort his people by foretelling the humiliation of their conquerors, and that the vision will soon have its fulfilment. In ch. 3 the prophet in a sublime ode celebrates the deliverances wrought by Jehovah for His people in times past, as the ground of assurance, notwithstanding all their existing calamities, that He will deliver them again; vs. 16 shows that the invader is still coming, and not yet arrived; so that the whole refers to the invasion in Jehoiakim's times, not those under Jehoiachin and Zedekiah. The Apocryphal appendix to Daniel states that he lived to see the Babylonian exile (588 B.C.), which accords with his prophesying early in Jehoiakim's reign, about 610 B.C.

The position of the book immediately after Nahum is appropriate; as Nahum treated of the judgments of the Lord on Assyria, for its violence against Israel, so Habakkuk, those inflicted by, and on, the Chaldeans for the same reason.

The style is poetical and sublime. The parallelisms are generally regular. Borrowed ideas occur (cf. ch. 3:19, with Ps. 18:33; ch. 2:6, with Isa. 14:4; ch. 2:14, with Isa. 11:9).

The ancient catalogues imply that his book is part of the canon of Scripture. In the New Testament, Romans 1:17 quotes Habakkuk 2:4 (though not naming him); cf. also Galatians 3:11; Hebrews 10:38. Acts 13:40, 41 quotes Habakkuk 1:5. One or two *Hebrew* words peculiar to Habakkuk occur (ch. 1:9; 2:6, 16).

CHAPTER 1

Vss. 1-17. HABAKKUK'S EXPOSTULATION WITH JE-HOVAH ON ACCOUNT OF THE PREVALENCE OF INJUSTICE: JEHOVAH SUMMONS ATTENTION TO HIS PURPOSE OF SENDING THE CHALDEANS AS THE AVENGERS. THE PROPHET COMPLAINS, THAT THESE ARE WORSE THAN THOSE ON WHOM VENGEANCE WAS TO BE TAKEN. **1. burden**—the prophetic sentence. **2, 3. violence ... Why dost thou show me iniquity?**—Similar language is used of the Chaldeans (vss. 9, 13), as here is used of the Jews: implying, that as the Jews sinned by *violence* and *injustice,* so they should be punished by *violence* and *injustice* (Prov. 1:31). Jehoiakim's reign was marked by injustice, treachery, and bloodshed (Jer. 22:3, 13-17). Therefore the Chaldeans should be sent to deal with him and his nobles according to their dealings with others (vss. 6, 10, 11, 17). Cf. Jeremiah's expostulation with Jehovah, Jeremiah 12:1; 20:8; and Job 19:7, 8. **3. cause me to behold grievance**—MAURER denies that the *Hebrew* verb is ever *active;* he translates," (Wherefore) dost Thou behold (without doing aught to check) grievance?" The context favors *English Version.* **there are that raise up strife and contention**—so CALVIN. But MAURER, not so well, translates, "There is strife, and contention raises *itself.*" **4. Therefore**—because Thou dost suffer such crimes to go unpunished. **law is slacked**—is chilled. It has no authority and secures no respect. **judgment**—justice. **wrong judgment proceedeth**—Decisions are given contrary to right. **5. Behold ... marvellously ... a work**—(Cf. Isa. 29:14). Quoted by Paul (Acts 13:41). **among the heathen**—In Acts 13:41, "ye despisers," from the LXX. So the *Syriac* and *Arabic* versions; perhaps from a different *Hebrew* reading. In the *English Version* reading of Habakkuk, God, in reply to the prophet's expostulation, addresses the Jews as about to be punished, "Behold ye *among the heathen* (with whom ye deserve to be classed, and by whom ye shall be punished, as despisers; the sense *implied,* which Paul *expresses*): learn from them what ye refused to learn from Me!" For "wonder marvellously," Paul, in Acts 13:41, has, "wonder *and perish,*" which gives the *sense,* not the literal wording, of the *Hebrew,* "Wonder, wonder," i.e., be overwhelmed in wonder. The despisers are to be given up to their own stupefaction, and so perish. The Israelite unbelievers would not credit the prophecy as to the fearfulness of the destruction to be wrought by the Chaldeans, nor afterwards the deliverance promised from that nation. So analogously, in Paul's day, the Jews would not credit the judgment coming on them by the Romans, nor the salvation proclaimed through Jesus. Thus the same Scripture applied to both. **ye will not believe, though it be told you**—i.e,, ye will not believe *now that I foretell it.* **6. I raise up**—not referring to God's having brought the Chaldeans from their original seats to Babylonia (*Note,* Isa. 23:13), for they had already been upwards of twenty years (since Nabopolassar's era) in political power there; but to His being about now to raise them up as the instruments of God's "work" of judgment on the Jews (II Chron. 36:6). The *Hebrew* is *future,* "I will raise up." **bitter**—i.e., cruel (Jer. 50:42; cf. *Margin,* Judg. 18:25; I Sam. 17:8). **hasty**—not *passionate,* but "impetuous." **7. their judgment and ... dignity ... proceed of themselves** —i.e., they recognize no *judge* save themselves, and they get for themselves and keep their own "dignity" without needing others' help. It will be vain for the Jews to complain of their tyrannical *judgments;* for whatever the Chaldeans decree they will do according to their own will, they will not brook anyone attempting to interfere. **8. swifter than the** leopards—OPPIAN (*Cyneg.* 3. 76), says of the leopard, "It runs most swiftly straight on: you would fancy it was flying through the air." **more fierce**—rather, "more keen"; lit., "sharp." **evening wolves**—wolves famished with fasting all day and so most keen in attacking the fold under covert of the approaching night (Jer. 5:6; Zeph. 3:3; cf. Gen. 49:27). Hence "twilight" is termed in *Arabic* and *Persian* "the wolf's tail"; and in French, *entre chien et loup.* **spread themselves**—proudly; as in Jeremiah 50:11, and Malachi 4:2, it implies *strength* and *vigor.* So also the *Arabic* cognate word [MAURER]. **their horsemen . . . come from far**—and yet are not wearied by the long journey. **9. all for violence**—The sole object of all is not to establish just rights, but to get all they can by violence. **their faces shall sup up as the east wind**—i.e., they shall, as it were, *swallow up* all before them; so the horse in Job 39: 24 is said to "*swallow* the ground with fierceness and rage." MAURER takes it from an *Arabic* root, "the *desire* of their faces," i.e., the eager desire expressed by their faces. HENDERSON, with SYMMACHUS and *Syriac,* translates, "the aspect." **as the east wind**—the simoon, which spreads devastation wherever it passes (Isa. 27:8). GESENIUS translates, "(is) forwards." The rendering proposed, *eastward,* as if it referred to the Chaldeans' return home *eastward* from Judea, laden with spoils, is improbable. Their "gathering the sand" accords with the simoon being meant, as it carries with it whirlwinds of sand collected in the desert. **10. scoff at . . . kings**—as unable to resist them. **they shall heap dust, and take it**—"they shall heap" earth mounds outside, and so "take every stronghold" (cf. II Sam. 20:15; II Kings 19:32) [GROTIUS]. **11. Then**—when elated by his successes. **shall his mind change**—He shall lose whatever of reason or moderation ever was in him, with pride. **he shall pass over**—all bounds and restraints: his pride preparing the sure way for his destruction (Prov. 16:18). The language is very similar to that describing Nebuchadnezzar's "change" from man's heart (understanding) to that of a beast, because of pride (Dan. 4:16, 30-34; see *Notes* there). An undesigned coincidence between the two sacred books written independently. *imputing* this his power unto his god—(Dan. 5:4). Sacrilegious arrogance, in ascribing to his idol Bel the glory that belongs to God [CALVIN]. GROTIUS explains, "(saying that) his power is his own as one who is a god to himself" (cf. vs. 10, and Dan. 3). So MAURER, "He shall offend as one to whom his power is his god" (Job 12:6; *Note,* Mic. 2:1). **12.** In opposition to the impious deifying of the Chaldeans' power as their god (MAURER, or, as *English Version,* their attributing of their successes to their idols), the prophet, in an impassioned address to Jehovah, vindicates His being "from everlasting," as contrasted with the Chaldean so-called "god." **my God, mine Holy One**—Habakkuk speaks in the name of his people. God was "the Holy One of *Israel,*" against whom the Chaldean was setting up himself (Isa. 37:23). **we shall not die**—Thou, as being *our* God, wilt not permit the Chaldeans utterly to destroy us. This reading is one of the eighteen called by the Hebrews "the appointment of the scribes"; the Rabbis think that Ezra and his colleagues corrected the old reading, "*Thou shalt not die.*" **thou hast ordained them for judgment**—i.e., to execute Thy judgments. **for correction**—to chastise transgressors (Isa. 10:5-7). But not that they may deify their own power (vs. 11, for their power is from Thee, and but for a time); nor that they may destroy utterly Thy people. The *Hebrew*

for "mighty God" is *Rock* (Deut. 32:4). However the world is shaken, or man's faith wavers, God remains unshaken as the Rock of Ages (*Margin,* Isa. 26:4). **13. purer . . . than to behold evil**—without being displeased at it. **canst not look on iniquity**—unjust injuries done to Thy people. The prophet checks himself from being carried too far in his expostulatory complaint, by putting before himself honorable sentiments of God. **them that deal treacherously**—the Chaldeans, once allies of the Jews, but now their violent oppressors. Cf. "treacherous dealers," (Isa. 21:2; 24:16). Instead of speaking evil against God, he goes to God Himself for the remedy for his perplexity (Ps. 73:11-17). **devoureth the man that is more righteous**—The Chaldean oppresses the Jew, who with all his faults, is better than his oppressor (cf. Ezek. 16:51, 52). **14. And**—i.e., And *so,* by suffering oppressors to go unpunished, "Thou makest men as the fishes . . . that have no ruler"; i.e., no defender. All may fish in the sea with impunity; so the Chaldeans with impunity afflict Thy people, as these have no longer the God of the theocracy, their King, to defend them. Thou reducest men to such a state of anarchy, by wrong going unpunished, as if there were no God. He compares the world to the *sea;* men to *fishes;* Nebuchadnezzar to a *fisherman* (vss. 15-17). **15. they take up all of them**—all kinds of fishes, i.e., *men,* as captives, and all other prey that comes in their way. **with the angle**—i.e., the hook. Some they take up as with the hook, one by one; others in shoals, as in a "net" and "drag" or enclosing net. **therefore**—because of their successes. **they rejoice** —They glory in their crimes because attended with success (cf. vs. 11). **16. sacrifice unto their net**—i.e., their arms, power, and military skill, wherewith they gained their victories; instead of to God. Cf. vs. 11, MAURER's interpretation. They idolize themselves for their own cleverness and might (Deut. 8:17; Isa. 10:13; 37:24, 25). **by them**—by their net and dragnet. **their portion**—image from a banquet: the prey which they have gotten. **17. Shall they . . . empty their net?**—Shall they be allowed without interruption to enjoy the fruits of their violence? **therefore**—seeing that they attribute all their successes to themselves, and not to Thee. The answer to the prophet's question, he by inspiration gives himself in ch. 2.

CHAPTER 2

VSS. 1-20. THE PROPHET, WAITING EARNESTLY FOR AN ANSWER TO HIS COMPLAINTS (ch. 1), RECEIVES A REVELATION, WHICH IS TO BE FULFILLED, NOT IMMEDIATELY, YET IN DUE TIME, AND IS THEREFORE TO BE WAITED FOR IN FAITH: THE CHALDEANS SHALL BE PUNISHED FOR THEIR CRUEL RAPACITY, NOR CAN THEIR FALSE GODS AVERT THE JUDGMENT OF JEHOVAH, THE ONLY TRUE GOD. **1. stand upon . . . watch**—i.e., watch-post. The prophets often compare themselves, awaiting the revelations of Jehovah with earnest patience, to watchmen on an eminence watching with intent eye all that comes within their view (Isa. 21:8, 11; Jer. 6:17; Ezek. 3: 17; 33:2, 3; cf. Ps. 5:3; 85:8). The "watch-post" is the withdrawal of the whole soul from earthly, and fixing it on heavenly, things. The accumulation of synonyms, "stand open . . . watch . . . set me upon . . . tower . . . watch to see" implies persevering fixity of attention. **what he will say unto me**—in answer to my complaints (ch. 1:13). Lit., "in me," God speaking, not to the prophet's outward ear, but *inwardly.* When we have prayed to God, we must observe what answers God gives by His word, His Spirit, and His providences. **what I shall answer when I am reproved**—what answer I am to make to the *reproof* which I anticipate from God on account of the liberty of my expostulation with Him. MAURER translates, "What I am to answer in respect to my complaint against Jehovah" (ch. 1:12-17). **2. Write the vision**—which I am about to reveal to thee. **make it plain**—(Deut. 27:8). In large legible characters. **upon tables**—boxwood tables covered with wax, on which national affairs were engraved with an iron pen, and then hung up in public, at the prophets' own houses, or at the temple, that those who passed might read them. Cf. Luke 1:63, "writing-table," i.e., tablet. **that he may run that readeth it**—commonly explained, "so intelligible as to be easily read by any one running past"; but then it would be, "that he that runneth may read it." The true sense is, "so legible *that whoever readeth it, may run* to tell all whom he can the good news of the foe's coming doom, and Judah's deliverance." Cf. Daniel 12:4, "many shall *run* to and fro," viz., with the explanation of the prophecy, then unsealed; also, Revelation 22:17, "let him that heareth [the good news] say [to every one within his reach], Come." "Run" is equivalent to *announce the divine revelation* (Jer. 23:21); as everyone who becomes informed of a divine message is bound to *run,* i.e., use all despatch to make it known to others [HENDERSON]. GROTIUS, LUDOVICUS DE DIEU, and MAURER interpret it: "Run" is not literal *running,* but "that he who reads it may run through it," i.e., read it *at once without difficulty.* **3. for**—assigning the cause why it ought to be *committed to writing: because* its fulfilment belongs to the future. **the vision is yet for an appointed time**—(Dan. 10:14; 11:27, 35). Though the time appointed by God for the fulfilment be yet future, it should be enough for your faith that God hath spoken it (Lam. 3:26). **at the end it shall speak**—MAURER translates, "it *pants for* the end." But the antithesis between, "it shall *speak,*" and "not be silent," makes *English Version* the better rendering. So the *Hebrew* is translated in Proverbs 12:17. Lit., "breathe out words," "break forth as a blast." **though it tarry, wait for it**—(Gen. 49:18). **4. his soul which is lifted up**—the Chaldean's [MAURER]. The unbelieving Jew's [HENDERSON]. **is not upright in him**—i.e., is not accounted upright in God's sight; in antithesis to "shall live." So Hebrew 10:38, which with inspired authority applies the general sense to the particular case which Paul had in view, "If any man *draw back* (one result of being "lifted up" with overweening arrogancy), *my soul shall have no pleasure in him."* **the just shall live by his faith**—the *Jewish nation,* as opposed to the unbelieving Chaldean (cf. vs. 5, etc.; ch. 1:6, etc., 13) [MAURER]. HENDERSON's view is that the *believing* Jew is meant, as opposed to the unbelieving Jew (cf. Rom. 1:17; Gal. 3:11). The believing Jew, though God's promise tarry, will wait for it; the unbelieving "draws back," as Hebrews 10:38 expresses it. The sense, in MAURER's view, which accords better with the context (vs. 5, etc.) is: the Chaldean, though for a time seeming to prosper, yet being lifted up with haughty unbelief (ch. 1:11, 16), is not upright; i.e., has *no right* stability of soul resting on God, to ensure permanence of prosperity; hence, though for a time executing God's judgments, he at last becomes "lifted up" so as to attribute to his own power what is the work of God, and in this sense "draws back" (Heb. 10:38), becoming thereby a type of all backsliders

who thereby incur God's displeasure; as the believing Jew is of all who *wait* for God's promises with patient *faith,* and so "live" (stand accepted) before God. The *Hebrew* accents induce BENGEL to translate, "he who is just by his faith shall live." Other MSS. read the accents as *English Version,* which agrees better with *Hebrew* syntax. **5. Yea also, because**—additional reason why the Jews may look for God punishing their Chaldean foe, viz., *because . . . he is* **a proud man**—rather, this clause continues the reason for the Jews expecting the punishment of the Chaldeans, "because he transgresseth by wine (a besetting sin of Babylon, cf. Dan. 5, and CURTIUS, 5.1), *being* a proud man." Love of wine often begets a *proud* contempt of divine things, as in Belshazzar's case, which was the immediate cause of the fall of Babylon (Dan. 5:2-4, 30; cf. Prov. 20:1; 30:9; 31:5). **enlargeth his desire as hell**—the grave, or the unseen world, which is "never full" (Prov. 27: 20; 30:16; Isa. 5:14). The Chaldeans under Nebuchadnezzar were filled with an insatiable desire of conquest. Another reason for their punishment. **6. Shall not all these**—the "nations" and "peoples" (vs. 5) "heaped unto him" by the Chaldean. **take up a parable**—a derisive song. Habakkuk follows Isaiah (Isa. 14:4) and Micah (Mic. 2:4) in the phraseology. **against him**—when dislodged from his former eminence. **Woe**—The "derisive song" here begins, and continues to the end of the chapter. It is a symmetrical whole, and consists of five stanzas, the first three consisting of three verses each, the fourth of four verses, and the last of two. Each stanza has its own subject, and all except the last begin with "Woe"; and all have a closing verse introduced with "for," "because," or "but." **how long?**—*how long* destined to retain his ill-gotten gains? But for a short time, as his fall now proves [MAURER]. "Covetousness is the greatest bane to men. For they who invade others' goods, often lose even their own" [MENANDER]. CALVIN makes "how long?" to be the cry of those groaning under the Chaldean oppression while it still lasted: How long shall such oppression be permitted to continue? But it is plainly part of the *derisive song,* after the Chaldean tyranny had passed away. **ladeth himself with thick clay**—viz., gold and silver dug out of the "clay," of which they are a part. The covetous man in heaping them together is only lading himself with a clay burden, as he dares not enjoy them, and is always anxious about them. LEE and FULLER translate the *Hebrew* as a reduplicated single noun, and not two words, "an accumulation of pledges" (Deut. 24:10-13). The Chaldean is compared to a harsh usurer, and his ill-gotten treasures to heaps of pledges in the hands of a usurer. **7. suddenly**—the answer to the question, "How long?" (vs. 6). **bite**—often used of *usury;* so favoring LEE's rendering (vs. 6). As the Chaldean, like a usurer, oppressed others, so other nations shall, like usurers, *take pledges of,* i.e., spoil, him. **8. the remnant of the people**—Those remaining of the peoples spoiled by thee, though but a remnant, will suffice to inflict vengeance on thee. **the violence of the land . . . city**—i.e., on account of *thy violent oppression of the lands and cities* of the earth [GROTIUS] (cf. vss. 5, 6, 12). The same phrase occurs in vs. 17, where the "land" and "city" are Judea and Jerusalem. **9. coveteth an evil covetousness**—i.e., a covetousness so surpassingly evil as to be fatal to himself. **to his house**—greedily seizing enormous wealth, not merely for himself, but for his family, to which it is destined to be fatal. The very same "evil covetousness" that was the cause of Jehoiakim's being given up to the Chaldean oppressor (Jer. 22:13) shall be the cause of the Chaldean's own destruction. **set his nest on high**—(Num. 24: 21; Jer. 49:16; Obad. 4). The image is from an eagle (Job 39:27). The *royal citadel* is meant. The Chaldean built high towers, like the Babel founders, to "be delivered from the power of evil" (Gen. 11: 4). **10. Thou hast consulted shame . . . by cutting off many**—MAURER, more lit., "Thou hast consulted shame . . . to destroy many," i.e., in consulting (determining) to cut off many, thou hast consulted shame to thy house. **sinned against thy soul**—i.e., against thyself; thou art the guilty cause of thine own ruin (Prov. 8:36; 20:2). They who wrong their neighbors, do much greater wrong to their own souls. **11. stone . . . cry out**—personification. The very stones of thy palace built by rapine shall testify against thee (Luke 19:40). **the beam out of the timber**—the crossbeam or main rafter connecting the timbers in the walls. **shall answer it**—viz., the stone. The stone shall begin and the crossbeam continue the cry against thy rapine. **12. buildeth a town with blood**—viz., Babylon rebuilt and enlarged by blood-bought spoils (cf. Dan. 4:30). **13. is it not of the Lord of hosts**—JEHOVAH, who has at His command all the *hosts* of heaven and earth, is the righteous author of Babylon's destruction. "Shall not God have His turn, when cruel rapacious men have triumphed so long, though He seem now to be still?" [CALVIN]. **people . . . labour in the . . . fire . . . weary themselves for . . . vanity**—The Chaldeans labor at what is to be food for the fire, viz., their city and fortresses which shall be burnt. Jeremiah 51:58 adopts the same phraseology to express the vanity of the Chaldean's labor on Babylon, as doomed to the flames. **14.** Adapted from Isaiah 11:9. Here the sense is, "The Jews shall be restored and the temple rebuilt, so that God's glory in saving His people, and punishing their Chaldean foe, shall be manifested throughout the world," of which the Babylonian empire formed the greatest part; a type of the ultimate full manifestation of His glory in the final salvation of Israel and His Church, and the destruction of all their foes. **waters cover the sea**—viz., the bottom of the sea; the sea-bed. **15. giveth . . . neighbour drink . . . puttest . . . bottle to him**—lit., "skin," as the Easterns use "bottles" of skin for wine. MAURER, from a different *Hebrew* root, translates, "that pourest in thy *wrath.*" *English Version* keeps up the metaphor better. It is not enough for thee to be "drunken" thyself, unless thou canst lead others into the same state. The thing meant is, that the Chaldean king, with his insatiable desires (a kind of *intoxication*), allured neighboring states into the same mad thirst for war to obtain booty, and then at last exposed them to loss and shame (cf. Isa. 51:17; Obad. 16). An appropriate image of Babylon, which at last fell during a drunken revel (Dan. 5). **that thou mayest look on their nakedness!**—with light, like Ham of old (Gen. 9:22). **16. art filled**—now that thou art fallen. "Thou art filled" indeed (though so insatiable), but it is "with shame." **shame for glory**—instead of thy former glory (Hos. 4:7). **drink thou also**—The cup of sorrow is now in thy turn to pass to thee (Jer. 25:15-17; Lam. 4:21). **thy foreskin**—expressing in Hebrew feeling the most utter contempt. So of Goliath (I Sam. 17:36). It is not merely thy "nakedness," as in vs. 15, that shall be "uncovered," but the foreskin, the badge of thy being an uncircumcised alien from God. The same shall be done to thee, as thou didst to others, and worse. **cup . . . shall be turned unto thee**—lit., shall

turn itself, viz., from the nations whom thou hast made to drink it. "Thou shalt drink it *all,* so that it may be *turned* as being drained" [GROTIUS]. **shameful spewing**—i.e., vomiting; viz., that of the king of Babylon, compelled to disgorge the spoil he had swallowed. It expresses also the ignominious state of Babylon in its calamity (Jer. 25:27). "Be drunken, spew, and fall." Less appropriately it is explained *of the foe* spewing in the face of the Babylonian king. **17. the violence of Lebanon**—thy "violence" against "Lebanon," i.e., Jerusalem (Isa. 37:24; Jer. 22:23; Ezek. 17:3, 12; for Lebanon's cedars were used in building the temple and houses of Jerusalem; and its beauty made it a fit type of the metropolis), shall fall on thine own head. **cover**—i.e., *completely* overwhelm. **the spoil of beasts, which made them afraid**—MAURER explains, *"the spoiling* inflicted on *the beasts* of Lebanon (i.e., on the people of Jerusalem, of which city 'Lebanon' is the type), *which made them afraid* (shall cover thee)." But it seems inappropriate to compare the elect people to "beasts." I therefore prefer explaining, "the spoiling of beasts," i.e., such as is inflicted on beasts caught in a net, and "which makes them afraid" (shall cover thee). Thus the Babylonians are compared to wild beasts terrified at being caught suddenly in a net. In cruel rapacity they resembled wild beasts. The ancients read, "the spoiling of wild beasts *shall make* THEE *afraid.*" Or else explain, "the spoiling of beasts (the Medes and Persians) which (*inflicted by thee*) made them afraid (shall in turn cover thyself—revert on thyself from them)." This accords better with the parallel clause, "the violence of Lebanon," i.e., inflicted by thee on Lebanon. As thou didst hunt men as wild beasts, so shalt thou be hunted thyself as a wild beast, which thou resemblest in cruelty. **because of men's blood**—shed by thee; repeated from vs. 8. But here the "land" and "city" are used of *Judea* and *Jerusalem:* not of the *earth* and cities *generally,* as in vs. 8. **the violence of the land . . .**—i.e., inflicted *on* the land by thee. **18.** The powerlessness of the idols to save Babylon from its doom is a fitting introduction to the last stanza (vs. 19), which, as the former four, begins with "Woe." **teacher of lies**—its priests and prophets uttering lying oracles, as if from it. **make dumb idols**—Though men can "make" idols, they cannot *make them speak.* **19. Awake**—Arise to my help. **it shall teach!**—rather, An exclamation *of the prophet,* implying an ironical question to which a negative answer must be given. What! "It teach?" Certainly not [MAURER]. Or, "It (the idol itself) shall (i.e., ought to) teach you that it is deaf, and therefore no God" [CALVIN]. Cf. "they are their own witnesses" (Isa. 44:9). **Behold**—The *Hebrew* is nominative, "There it is" [HENDERSON]. **it is laid over with gold . . . no breath . . . in the midst**—Outside it has some splendor, within none. **20. But the Lord**—JEHOVAH; in striking contrast with the idols. **in his holy temple**—"His place" (Isa. 26:21); heaven (Ps. 11:4; Jonah 2:7; Mic. 1:2). The temple at Jerusalem is a type of it, and there God is to be worshipped. He does not lie hid under gold and silver, as the idols of Babylon, but reigns in heaven and fills heaven, and thence succors His people. **keep silence**—in token of reverent submission and subjection to His judgments (Job 40:4; Ps. 76:8; Zeph. 1:7; Zech. 2:13).

CHAPTER 3

Vss. 1-19. HABAKKUK'S PRAYER TO GOD: GOD'S GLORIOUS REVELATION OF HIMSELF AT SINAI AND AT

GIBEON, A PLEDGE OF HIS INTERPOSING AGAIN IN BEHALF OF ISRAEL AGAINST BABYLON, AND ALL OTHER FOES; HENCE THE PROPHET'S CONFIDENCE AMID CALAMITIES. This sublime ode begins with an exordium (vss. 1, 2), then follows the main subject, then the peroration (vss. 16-19), a summary of the practical truth, which the whole is designed to teach. (Deut. 33:2-5; Ps. 77:13-20 are parallel odes). This was probably designed by the Spirit to be a fit formula of prayer for the people, first in their Babylonian exile, and now in their dispersion, especially towards the close of it, just before the great Deliverer is to interpose for them. It was used in public worship, as the musical term, Selah! (vss. 3, 9, 13), implies. **1. prayer**—the only strictly called prayers are in vs. 2. But all devotional addresses to God are called "prayers" (Ps. 72:20). The *Hebrew* is from a root "to apply to a judge for a favorable decision." *Prayers* in which *praises* to God for deliverance, anticipated in the sure confidence of faith, are especially calculated to enlist Jehovah on His people's side (II Chron. 20:20-22, 26). **upon Shigionoth**—a musical phrase, "after the manner of elegies," or mournful odes, from an *Arabic* root [LEE]; the phrase is *singular* in Psalm 7, title. More simply, from a *Hebrew* root to "err," "on account of *sins of ignorance.*" Habakkuk thus teaches his countrymen to confess not only their more grievous sins, but also their *errors* and *negligences*, into which they were especially likely to fall when in exile away from the Holy Land [CALVIN]. So *Vulgate* and AQUILA, and SYMMACHUS. "For voluntary transgressors" [JEROME]. Probably the subject would regulate the kind of music. DELITZSCH and HENDERSON translate, "With triumphal music," from the same root "to err," implying its enthusiastic irregularity. **2. I have heard thy speech**—Thy revelation to me concerning the coming chastisement of the Jews [CALVIN], and the destruction of their oppressors. This is Habakkuk's reply to God's communication [GROTIUS]. MAURER translates, "the report of Thy coming," lit., "Thy report." **and was afraid**—reverential fear of God's judgments (vs. 16). **revive thy work**—Perfect the *work* of delivering *Thy* people, and do not let Thy promise lie as if it were dead, but *give it new life* by performing it [MENOCHUS]. CALVIN explains "thy work" to be *Israel;* called "the work of My hands" (Isa. 45:11). God's elect people are peculiarly His work (Isa. 43:1), pre-eminently illustrating His power, wisdom, and goodness. "Though we seem, as it were, dead nationally, *revive* us" (Ps. 85:6). However (Ps. 64:9), where "the work of God" refers to *His judgment on their enemies*, favors the former view (Ps. 90:16, 17; Isa. 51:9, 10). **in the midst of the years**—viz., of calamity in which we live. Now that our calamities are at their height; during our seventy years' captivity. CALVIN more fancifully explains it, in the midst of the years of Thy people, extending from Abraham to Messiah; if they be cut off before His coming, they will be cut off as it were *in the midst of their years*, before attaining their maturity. So BENGEL makes *the midst of the years* to be the middle point of the years of the world. There is a strikingly similar phrase (Dan. 9:27), *"In the midst of the week."* The parallel clause, "in wrath" (i.e., *in the midst* of wrath), however, shows that "in the midst of the years" means "in the years of our present exile and calamity." **make known**—Made *it* (*Thy* work) known by experimental proof; show in very deed, that this is Thy work. **3. God**—*singular* in the *Hebrew*, "Eloah," instead of "Elohim," *plural*, usually employed. The sin-

gular is not found in any other of the minor prophets, or Jeremiah, or Ezekiel; but it is in Isaiah, Daniel, Job, and Deuteronomy. **from Teman**—the country south of Judea and near Edom, in which latter country Mount Paran was situated [HENDERSON]. "Paran" is the desert region, extending from the south of Judah to Sinai. Seir, Sinai, and Paran are adjacent to one another, and are hence associated together, in respect to God's giving of the law (Deut. 33:2). Teman is so identified with Seir or *Edom,* as here to be substituted for it. Habakkuk appeals to God's glorious manifestations to His people at Sinai, as the ground for praying that God will "revive His work" (vs. 2) now. For He is the same God now as ever. **Selah**—a musical sign, put at the close of sections and strophes, always at the end of a verse, except thrice; viz., here, and vs. 9. and Psalm 55:19; 57:3, where, however, it closes the hemistich. It implies a change of the modulation. It comes from a root to "rest" or "pause" [GESENIUS]; implying a cessation of the chant, during an instrumental interlude. The solemn pause here prepares the mind for contemplating the glorious description of Jehovah's manifestation which follows. **earth . . . full of his praise**—i.e., of His glories which were calculated to call forth universal *praise;* the parallelism to "glory" proves this to be the sense. **4. as the light**—viz., of the sun (Job 37:21; Prov. 4:18). **horns**—the emblem of *power* wielded by "His hand" [LUDOVICUS DE DIEU]. "Rays" emanating from "His hand," compared by the Arabs to the horns of the gazelle (cf. "hind of the morning," Ps. 22, title, *Margin*). The *Hebrew* verb for to "emit rays," is from the root meaning "horns" (Exod. 34:29, 30, 35) [GROTIUS]. The rays are His *lightnings* (Ps. 18:8), [MAURER]. **there**—*in that "brightness." In it,* notwithstanding its brilliancy, there was but the veil ("*the hiding*) of His power." Even "light," God's "garment," covers, instead of revealing fully, His surpassing glory (Ps. 104:2) [HENDERSON]. Or, *on Mount Sinai* [DRUSIUS]. (Cf. Exod. 24:17.) LXX and *Syriac* versions read for "there," *He* made a hiding, etc.; He hid Himself with clouds. *English Version* is better, which CALVIN explains, there is said to be "a hiding of God's power," because God did not reveal it indiscriminately to all, but specially to His people (Ps. 31:20). The contrast seems to me to be between the "horns" or *emanations* out of His power ("hand"), and that "power" itself. The latter was *hidden*, whereas the "horns" or *emanations* alone were manifested. If the mere scintillations were so awfully overwhelming, how much more so the hidden power itself! This was especially true of His manifestation at Sinai (Ps. 18:11; cf. Isa. 45:15, 17). **5. pestilence**—to destroy His people's foes (I Sam. 5:9, 11). As Jehovah's advent is glorious to His people, so it is terrible to His foes. **burning coals**—Psalm 18:8 favors *English Version.* But the parallelism requires, as *Margin* translates, "burning disease" (cf. Deut. 32:24; Ps. 91:6). **went . . . at his feet**—i.e., after Him, as His attendants (Judg. 4:10). **6. He stood, and measured the earth**—Jehovah, in His advance, is represented as stopping suddenly, and *measuring* the earth with His all-seeing glance, whereat there is universal consternation. MAURER, from a different root, translates, "rocked the earth"; which answers better to the parallel "drove asunder"; the *Hebrew* for which latter, however, may be better translated, "made to tremble." **everlasting mountains**—which have ever been remembered as retaining the same place and form from the foundation of the world. **did bow**—as it were, in reverent submission. **his ways are everlasting**—His marvellous ways of working for the salvation of His people mark His everlasting character: such as He was in His workings for them formerly, such shall He be now. **7. the tents**—i.e, the dwellers. **Cushan** the same as *Cush;* made Cush-*an* to hamonize with Midi-*an* in the parallel clause. So *Lotan* is found in the *Hebrew* of Genesis for *Lot.* BOCHART therefore considers it equivalent to Midian, or a part of Arabia. So in Numbers 12:1, Moses' Midianite wife is called an Ethiopian (*Hebrew, Cushite*). MAURER thinks *the dwellers on both sides of the Arabian Gulf,* or *Red Sea,* are meant; for in the preceding verse God's *everlasting* or ancient *ways* of delivering His people are mentioned; and in the following verse, the *dividing* of the Red Sea for them. Cf. Miriam's song as to the *fear* of Israel's foes far and near caused thereby (Exod. 15:14-16). Hebrew expositors refer it to Cushan-rishathaim, king of Mesopotamia, or Syria, the first oppressor of Israel (Judg. 3:8, 10), from whom Othniel delivered them. Thus the second hemistich of the verse will refer to the deliverance of Israel from Midian by Gideon (Judg. 6 and 7) to which vs. 11 plainly refers. Whichever of these views be correct, the general reference is to God's interpositions against Israel's foes of old. **in affliction**—rather, "*under affliction*" (regarded) as a heavy burden. Lit., "vanity" or "iniquity," hence the *punishment* of it (cf. Num. 25:17, 18). **curtains**—the coverings of their tents; the shifting habitations of the nomad tribes, which resembled the modern Bedouins. **tremble**—viz., at Jehovah's terrible interposition for Israel against them. **8. Was the Lord displeased against the rivers?**—"Was the cause of His dividing the Red Sea and Jordan His displeasure against these waters?" The answer to this is tacitly implied in "Thy chariots *of salvation.*" "Nay; it was not displeasure against the waters, but His pleasure in interposing for His people's *salvation*" (cf. vs. 10). **thy chariots**—in antithesis to Thy foe, *Pharaoh's* chariots," which, notwithstanding their power and numbers, were engulfed in the waters of *destruction.* God can make the most unlikely means work for His people's salvation (Exod. 14:7, 9, 23, 25-28; 15: 3-8, 19). Jehovah's chariots are His angels (Ps. 68:17), or the cherubim, or the ark (Josh. 3:13 and 4:7; cf. Song of Solomon 1:9). **9. bow . . . made . . . naked**—i.e., was drawn forth from its cover, in which bows usually were cased when not in use. Cf. Isaiah 22:6, "Kir uncovered the shield." *according* **to the oaths of the tribes** *even thy word*—i.e., Thy *oaths* of promise to *the tribes* of Israel (Ps. 77:8; Luke 1:73, 74). Habakkuk shows that God's miraculous interpositions for His people were not limited to one time, but that God's *oaths* to His people are sure ground for their always expecting them. The mention of the *tribes,* rather than *Abraham* or Moses, is in order that they may not doubt that to them belongs this grace of which Abraham was the depository [CALVIN and JEROME]. MAURER translates, "The spears were glutted with blood, the triumphal song!" i.e., no sooner did Jehovah begin the battle by baring His bow, than the spears were glutted with blood and the triumphal song sung. **Thou didst cleave the earth with rivers**—the result of the earthquake caused by God's approach [MAURER]. GROTIUS refers it to the bringing forth water from the rock (Exod. 17:6; Num. 20:10, 11; Ps. 78: 15, 16; 105:4). But the context implies not the giving of water to His people to drink, but the fearful physical phenomena attending Jehovah's attack on Israel's foes. **10. The mountains**—repetition with

increased emphasis of some of the tremendou: phenomena mentioned in vs. 6. **overflowing of the water passed by**—viz., of the Red Sea; and again, o: the Jordan. God marked His favor to His people in all the elements, causing every obstacle, whethe: mountains or waters, which impeded their progress to *pass away* [CALVIN]. MAURER, not so well, translates, "torrents (rains) of water rush down." **lifted . . . hands on high**—viz., its billows *lifted on high* by the tempest. Personification. As men signify by *voice* or gesture of *hand* that they will do what they are commanded, so these parts of nature testified their obedience to God's will (Exod. 14:22; Josh. 3: 16; Ps. 77:17, 18; 114:4). **11. sun . . . moon stood still**—at Joshua's command (Josh. 10:12, 13). MAURER wrongly translates, "stand" (*withdrawn,* or *hidden from view,* by the clouds which covered the sky during the thunders). **light of thine arrows**—hail mixed with lightnings (Josh. 10:10, 11). **they went**— The *sun* and *moon* "went," not as always heretofore, but according to the light and direction of Jehovah's arrows, viz., His lightnings hurled in defense of His people; astonished at these they stood still [CALVIN]. MAURER translates, "At the light of Thine arrows (which) went" or flew. **12. march**—implying Jehovah's majestic and irresistible progress before His people (Judg. 5:4; Ps. 68:7). Israel would not have dared to attack the nations, unless Jehovah had gone before. **thresh**—(Mic. 4:13). **13. with thine anointed** —with Messiah; of whom Moses, Joshua, and David, God's anointed leaders of Israel, were the types (Ps. 89:19, 20, 38). God from the beginning delivered His people in person, or by the hand of a Mediator (Isa. 63:11). Thus Habakkuk confirms believers in the hope of their deliverance, as well because God is always the same, as also because the same anointed Mediator is ready now to fulfil God's will and interpose for Israel, as of old [CALVIN]. MAURER translates to suit the parallelism, "for salvation to Thine anointed," viz., Israel's *king* in the abstract, answering to the "people" in the former clause (cf. Ps. 28:8; Lam. 4:20). Or Israel is meant, the *anointed,* i.e., consecrated people of Jehovah (Ps. 105:15). **woundedst the head out of the house of the wicked**—probably an allusion to Psalm 68:21. Each *head person* sprung from and belonging to *the house of* Israel's *wicked* foes; such as Jabin, whose city Hazor was "the head of all the kingdoms" of Canaan (Josh. 11:10; cf. Judg. 4:2, 3, 13). **discovering the foundation**—Thou destroyedst high and low. As the *head* of the house" means the prince, so the "foundation" means the general *host* of the enemy. **unto the neck**—image from a flood reaching *to the* neck (Isa. 8:8; 30:28). So God, by His wrath overflowing on the foe, caused their princes' *necks* to be trodden under foot by Israel's leaders (Josh. 10:24; 11:8, 12). **14. strike . . . with his staves**—with the "wicked" (vs. 13) foe's own sword (MAURER translates, "spears") (Judg. 7: 22). **head of his villages**—Not only kings were overthrown by God's hand, but His vengeance passed through the foe's *villages* and dependencies. A just retribution, as the foe had made "the inhabitants of Israel's villages to cease" (Judg. 5:7). GROTIUS translates, "of his warriors"; GESENIUS, "the chief of his captains." **to scatter me**—Israel, with whom Habakkuk identifies himself (cf. ch. 1:12). **rejoicing . . . to devour the poor secretly**—"The poor" means the *Israelites,* for whom in their helpless state the foe lurks *in his lair,* like a wild beast, to pounce on and *devour* (Ps. 10:9; 17:12). **15. Thou didst walk through the sea with thine horses** —(*V.* 8). No obstacle could prevent Thy progress when leading Thy people in safety to their inheritance, whether the Red Sea, Jordan, or the figurative waves of foes raging against Israel (Ps. 65:7; 77:19). **16. When I heard ... trembled**–viz., at the judgments which God had declared (ch. 1) were to be inflicted on Judea by the Chaldeans. **belly**–The *bowels* were thought by the Hebrews to be the seat of yearning compassion (Jer. 31:20). Or "heard" may refer to vs. 2 of this ch. 3, "When I *heard* as to Jehovah's coming interposition for Israel against the Chaldeans being still at some distance" (ch. 2:3); so also the voice" [MAURER]. **at the voice**–of the divine threatenings (ch. 1:6). The faithful tremble at the *voice* alone of God before He inflicts punishment. Habakkuk speaks in the person of all the faithful in Israel. **trembled in myself**–i.e., I trembled all over [GROTIUS]. **that I might rest in the day of trouble**–The true and only path to *rest* is through such fear. Whoever is securely torpid and hardened towards God, will be tumultuously agitated in the day of affliction, and so will bring on himself a worse destruction; but he who in time meets God's wrath and trembles at His threats, prepares the best *rest* for himself in the day of affliction [CALVIN]. HENDERSON translates, "Yet I shall have rest." Habakkuk thus consoling his mind, Though trembling at the calamity coming, yet I shall have rest in God (Isa. 26:3). But that sentiment does not seem to be directly asserted till vs. 17, as the words following at the close of this verse imply. **when he cometh up unto the people, he will invade**–rather (as *English Version* is a mere truism), connected with the preceding clause, "that I might rest ... when he (the Chaldean foe) cometh up unto the people (the Jews), *that he may cut them off*" [CALVIN]. The *Hebrew* for "invade" means, *to rush upon, or to attack and cut off with congre-*

gated troops. **17.** Destroy the "vines" and "fig trees" of the carnal heart, and his mirth ceases. But those who when full enjoyed God in all, when emptied can enjoy all in God. They can sit down upon the heap of ruined creature comforts, and rejoice in Him as the "God of their salvation." Running in the way of His commandments, we outrun our troubles. Thus Habakkuk, beginning his prayer with trembling, ends it with a song of triumph (Job 13:15; Ps. 4:7; 43:3, 5). **labour of the olive**–i.e., the *fruit* expected from the olive. **fail**–lit., "lie", i.e., disappoint the hope (*Margin,* Isa. 58:11). **fields**–from a *Hebrew* root meaning "to be yellow"; as they look at harvest-time. **meat** –food, grain. **cut off**–i.e., cease. **18. yet I will rejoice**–The prophet speaks in the name of his people. **19. hinds' feet ... walk upon ... high places**–Habakkuk has here before his mind Psalm 18:33, 34; Deuteronomy 32:13. "Hinds' (gazelles' feet" imply the *swiftness* with which God enables him (the prophet and his people) to escape from his enemies, and return to his native land. The "high places" are called "mine," to imply that Israel shall be restored to *his own* land, a land of hills which are places of safety and of eminence (cf. Gen. 19:17, and Matt. 24:16). Probably not only the *safety,* but the *moral elevation,* of Israel above all the lands of the earth is implied (Deut. 33:29). **on my stringed instruments**–*neginoth.* This is the prophet's direction to the *precentor* ("chief singer") as to how the preceding ode (ch. 3) is to be performed (cf. Ps. 4 and 6, titles). The prophet had in mind a certain form of stringed instrument adapted to certain numbers and measures. This formula at the end of the ode, directing the kind of instrument to be used, agrees with that in the beginning of it, which directs the kind of melody (cf. Isa. 38:20).

THE BOOK OF

ZEPHANIAH

INTRODUCTION

ZEPHANIAH, ninth in order of the minor prophets, prophesied "in the days of Josiah" (ch. 1:1), i.e., between 642 and 611 B.C. The name means "Jehovah hath guarded," lit., "hidden" (Ps. 27:5; 83:3). The specification in the introductory heading, of not only his father, but also his grandfather, and great-grandfather, and great-great-grandfather, implies that the latter were persons of note, or else the design was to distinguish him from another Zephaniah of note at the time of the captivity. The Jews' supposition, that persons recorded as a prophet's ancestors were themselves endowed with the prophetic spirit, seems groundless. There is no impossibility of the Hezekiah, who was Zephaniah's great-great-grandfather, being King Hezekiah as to the number of generations; for Hezekiah's reign of twenty-nine years, and his successor's reign of fifty-five years, admit of *four* generations interposing between. Yet the omission of the designation, "king of Judah," is fatal to the theory (cf. Prov. 25:1; Isa. 38:9).

He must have flourished in the earlier part of Josiah's reign. In ch. 2:13–15 he foretells the doom of Nineveh, which happened in 625 B.C.; and in ch. 1:4 he denounces various forms of idolatry, and specially that of Baal. Now Josiah's reformation began in the twelfth and was completed in the eighteenth year of his reign. Zephaniah, therefore, in denouncing Baal worship, co-operated with that good king in his efforts, and so must have prophesied somewhere between the twelfth and eighteenth years of his reign. The silence of the historical books is no argument against this, as it would equally apply against Jeremiah's prophetical existence at the same time. Jewish tradition says that Zephaniah had for his colleagues Jeremiah, whose sphere of labor was the thoroughfares and market places, and Huldah the prophetess, who exercised her vocation in the college in Jerusalem.

The prophecy begins with the nation's sin and the fearful retribution coming at the hands of the Chaldeans. These are not mentioned by name, as in Jeremiah; for the prophecies of the latter, being nearer the fulfilment, become more explicit than those of an earlier date. The second chapter dooms the persecuting states in the neighborhood as well as Judea itself. The third chapter denounces Jerusalem, but concludes with the promise of her joyful re-establishment in the theocracy.

The style, though not generally sublime, is graphic and vivid in details (cf. ch. 1:4–12). The language is pure, and free from Aramaisms. There are occasional coincidences with former prophets (cf. ch. 2:14, with Isa. 34:11; ch. 2:15, with Isa. 47:8; ch. 3:10, with Isa. 18:1; ch. 2:8, with Isa. 16:6; also ch. 1:5, with Jer. 8:2; ch. 1:12, with Jer. 48:11). Such coincidences in part arise from the phraseology of Hebrew prophetic poetry being the common language of the inspired brotherhood. The New Testament, at Romans 15:6, seems to refer to Zephaniah 3:9.

CHAPTER 1

Vss. 1-18. GOD'S SEVERE JUDGMENT ON JUDAH FOR ITS IDOLATRY AND NEGLECT OF HIM: THE RAPID APPROACH OF THE JUDGMENT, AND THE IMPOSSIBILITY OF ESCAPE. **1. days of Josiah**—Had their idolatries been under former kings, they might have said, Our kings have forced us to this and that. But under Josiah, who did all in his power to reform them, they have no such excuse. **son of Amon**—the idolater, whose bad practices the Jews clung to, rather than the good example of Josiah, his son; so incorrigible were they in sin. **Judah**—Israel's ten tribes had gone into captivity before this. **2. utterly consume**—from a root to "sweep away," or "scrape off utterly." See the *Margin*, Jeremiah 8:13, and here. **from off the land**—of Judah. **3.** Enumeration in detail of the "all things" (vs. 2; cf. Jer. 9:10; Hos. 4:3). **the stumbling blocks**—idols which cause Judah to offend or stumble (Ezek. 14:3, 4, 7). **with the wicked**—The idols and their worshippers shall be involved in a common destruction. **4. stretch out mine hand**—indicating some remarkable and unusual work of vengeance (Isa. 5:25; 9:12, 17, 21). **Judah**—including Benjamin. These two tribes are to suffer, which thought themselves perpetually secure, because they escaped the captivity in which the ten tribes were involved. **Jerusalem**—the fountain-head of the evil. God begins with His sanctuary (Ezek. 9:6), and those who are nigh Him (Lev. 10:3). **the remnant of Baal**—the remains of Baal-worship, which as yet Josiah was unable utterly to eradicate in remote places. Baal was the Phœnician tutelary god. From the time of the Judges (Judg. 2:13), Israel had fallen into this idolatry; and Manasseh lately had set up this idol within Jehovah's temple itself (II Kings 21:3, 5, 7). Josiah began his reformation in the twelfth year of his reign (II Chron. 34:4, 8), and in the eighteenth had as far as possible completed it. **Chemarims**—idol priests, who had not reached the age of puberty; meaning "ministers of the gods" (SERVIUS on *Æneid*, 11), the same name as the Tyrian *Camilli*, *r* and *l* being interchangeable (cf. *Margin*, Hos. 10:5). Josiah is expressly said (*Margin*, II Kings 23:5) to have "put down the Chemarim." The *Hebrew* root means "black" (from the *black garments* which they wore or the *marks* which they branded on their foreheads); or "zealous," from their idolatrous fanaticism. The very "name," as well as themselves, shall be forgotten. **the priests**—of Jehovah, of Aaronic descent, who ought to have used all their power to eradicate, but who secretly abetted, idolatry (cf. ch. 3:4; Ezek. 8; 22:26; 44:10). From the *priests* Zephaniah passes to the *people*. **5. worship the host of heaven**—*Saba:* whence, in contrast to Sabeanism, Jehovah is called Lord of Sabaoth. **upon the housetops**—which were flat (II Kings 23:5, 6, 12; Jer. 19:13; 32:29). **swear by the Lord**—rather, "swear *to* JEHOVAH" (II Chron. 15:14); solemnly dedicating themselves to Him (cf. Isa. 48:1; Hos. 4:15). **and**—"*and yet* (with strange inconsistency, I Kings 18:21; Ezek. 20:39; Matt. 6:24) swear by

Malcham," i.e., "*their king*" [MAURER]: the same as Molech (*Note*, Amos 5:26), and "Milcom the god of . . . Ammon" (I Kings 11:33). If Satan have half the heart, he will have all; if the Lord have but half offered to Him, He will have none. **6. This** verse describes more comprehensively those guilty of defection from Jehovah in any way (Jer. 2:13, 17). **7. Hold thy peace at the presence of the Lord** —(Hab. 2:20). Let the *earth* be silent at His approach [MAURER]. Or, "Thou whosoever hast been wont to speak against God, as if He had no care about earthly affairs, cease thy murmurs and self-justifications; submit thyself to God, and repent in time" [CALVIN]. **Lord . . .prepared a sacrifice**— viz., a slaughter of the guilty Jews, the victims due to His justice (Isa. 34:6; Jer. 46:10; Ezek. 39:17). **bid his guests**—lit., "sanctified His called ones" (cf. Isa. 13:3). It enhances the bitterness of the judgment that the heathen Chaldeans should be *sanctified,* or consecrated as it were, by God as His priests, and be *called* to eat the flesh of the elect people; as on feast days the priests used to feast among themselves on the remains of the sacrifices [CALVIN]. *English Version* takes it not of the *priests,* but the *guests bidden,* who also had to "sanctify" or purify themselves before coming to the sacrificial feast (I Sam. 9:13, 22; 16:5). Nebuchadnezzar was *bidden* to come to take vengeance on guilty Jerusalem (Jer. 25:9). **8. the princes**—who ought to have been an example of good to others, but were ringleaders in all evil. **the king's children** —fulfilled on Zedekiah's children (Jer. 39:6); and previously, on Jehoahaz and Eliakim, the sons of Josiah (II Kings 23:31, 36; II Chron. 36:6; cf. also II Kings 20:18; 21:13). Huldah the prophetess (II Kings 22:20) intimated that which Zephaniah now more expressly foretells. **all such as are clothed with strange apparel**—the *princes* or *courtiers* who attired themselves in costly garments, imported from abroad; partly for the sake of luxury, and partly to ingratiate themselves with foreign great nations whose costume as well as their idolatries they imitated, [CALVIN]; whereas in costume, as in other respects, God would have them to be separate from the nations. GROTIUS refers the "strange apparel" to garments forbidden by the law, e.g., men's garments worn by women, and vice versa, a heathen usage in the worship of Mars and Venus (Deut. 22: 5). **9. those that leap on the threshold**—the servants of the princes, who, after having gotten prey (like hounds) for their masters, leap exultingly on their masters' thresholds; or, on the thresholds of the houses which they break into [CALVIN]. JEROME explains it of those *who walk up the steps into the sanctuary with haughtiness.* ROSENMULLER translates, "Leap *over* the threshold"; viz., in imitation of the Philistine custom of not treading on the threshold, which arose from the head and hands of Dagon being broken off on the threshold before the ark (I Sam. 5:5). Cf. Isa. 2:6, "thy people . . . are soothsayers *like the Philistines.*" CALVIN'S view agrees best with the latter clause of the verse. **fill . . . masters' houses with violence . . .**—i.e., with goods obstained *with violence.* . . . **10. fish gate**— (II Chron. 33:14; Neh. 3:3; 12:39). Situated on the east of the lower city, north of the sheep gate [MAURER]: near the stronghold of David in Milo, between Zion and the lower city, towards the west [JEROME]. This verse describes the state of the city when it was besieged by Nebuchadnezzar. It was through the fish gate that he entered the city. It received its name from the fish market which was near it. Through it passed those who used to bring fish from the lake of Tiberias and Jordan. It answers to what is now called the Damascus gate [HENDERSON]. **the second**—viz., the gate which was *second* in dignity [CALVIN]. Or, *the second* or lower part of the city. Appropriately, the fish gate, or extreme end of the lower part of the city, first resounds with the cries of the citizens as the foe approaches; then, as he advances further, that part of the city itself, viz., its inner part; lastly, when the foe is actually come and has burst in, the hills, the higher ones, especially Zion and Moriah, on which the upper city and temple were founded [MAURER]. The *second*, or lower city, answers to Akra, north of Zion, and separated from it by the valley of Tyropœon running down to the pool of Siloam [HENDERSON]. The *Hebrew* is translated "college," II Kings 22:14; so VATABLUS would translate here. **hills**—not here those outside, but those within the walls: Zion, Moriah, and Ophel. **11. Maktesh**—rather, "the mortar," a name applied to the valley of Siloam from its hollow shape [JEROME]. The valley between Zion and Mount Olivet, at the eastern extremity of Mount Moriah, where the merchants dwelt. Zechariah 14:21, "The Canaanite," viz., merchant [*Chaldee Version*]. The Tyropœon (i.e., *cheese-makers'*) valley below Mount Akra [ROSENMULLER]. Better *Jerusalem itself*, so called as lying in the midst of hills (Isa. 22:1; Jer. 21:13) and as doomed to be the scene of its people being destroyed as corn or drugs are pounded in a *mortar* (Prov. 27:22) [MAURER]. Cf. the similar image of a "pot" (Ezek. 24:3, 6). The reason for the destruction is subjoined, viz., its *merchant people's* greediness of gain. **all the merchant people**— lit., the "Canaanite people": irony: all the merchant people of Jerusalem are very *Canaanites* in greed for gain and in idolatries (*Note,* Hos. 12:7). **all ...that bear silver**—loading themselves with that which will prove but a *burden* (Hab. 2:6). **12. search ... with candles**—or lamps; so as to leave no dark corner in it wherein sin can escape the punishment, of which the Chaldeans are My instruments (cf. vs. 13; Luke 15:8). **settled on their lees**— "hardened" or crusted; image from the crust formed at the bottom of wines long left undisturbed (Jer. 48:11). The effect of *wealthy undisturbed ease* ("lees") on the ungodly is *hardening*: they become stupidly secure (cf. Ps. 55:19; Amos 6:1). **Lord will not do good ... evil**—They deny that God regards human affairs, or renders good to the good; or evil to the evil, but that all things go haphazard (Ps. 10: 4; Mal. 2:17). **13.** Fulfilling the prophecy in Deuteronomy 28:30, 39 (cf. Amos 5:11). **14. voice of ...day of ...Lord**—i.e., Jehovah ushering in that day with a roar of vengeance against the guilty (Jer. 25:30; Amos 1:2). They who will not now heed (vs. 12) His voice by His prophets, must heed it when uttered by the avenging foe. **mighty ... shall cry ... bitterly**—in hopeless despair; the might on which Jerusalem now prides itself, shall then fail utterly. **15. wasteness...desolation**—The *Hebrew* terms by their similarity of sounds, *Shoah, Umeshoah,* express the dreary monotony of desola-

tion (cf. *Note,* Nah. 2:10). **16. the trumpet**—viz., of the besieging enemy (Amos 2:2). **alarm**—the war shout [MAURER]. **towers**—lit., "angles"; for city walls used not to be built in a direct line, but with sinuous curves and angles, so that besiegers advancing might be assailed not only in front, but on both sides, caught as it were in a cul-de-sac; towers were built especially at the angles. So TACITUS describes the walls of Jerusalem (*Hist.* 5. 11. 7). **17. like blind men**—unable to see whither to turn themselves so as to find an escape from existing evils. **flesh**—*Hebrew,* "bread"; so the *Arabic* term for "bread" is used for "flesh" (Matt. 26:26). **18. Neither ... silver nor ... gold shall ... deliver them ...**—(Prov. 11:4). **fire of his jealousy**—(Ezek. 38:19); His wrath jealous for His honor consuming the guilty like fire. **make even a speedy riddance of all**—rather, a consummation (complete destruction: "full end," Jer. 46:28; Ezek. 11:13) *altogether sudden* [MAURER]. "A consummation, *and that* a sudden one" [CALVIN].

CHAPTER 2

Vss. 1-15. EXHORTATION TO REPENT BEFORE THE CHALDEAN INVADERS COME. DOOM OF JUDAH'S FOES, THE PHILISTINES, MOAB, AMMON, WITH THEIR IDOLS, AND ETHIOPIA AND ASSYRIA. **1. Gather yourselves** —*to a religious assembly,* to avert the judgment by prayers (Joel 2:16) [GROTIUS]. Or, so as not to be dissipated "as chaff" (vs. 2). The *Hebrew* is akin to a root meaning "chaff." Self-confidence and corrupt desires are the dissipation from which they are exhorted to *gather themselves* [CALVIN]. The foe otherwise, like the wind, will scatter you "as the chaff." Repentance is the *gathering of themselves* meant. **nation not desired**—(Cf. II Chron. 21:20), i.e., not desirable; unworthy of the grace or favor of God; and yet God so magnifies that grace as to be still solicitous for their safety, though they had destroyed themselves and forfeited all claims on His grace [CALVIN]. *Margin* from *Chaldee Version* has, "not desirous," viz., of returning to God. MAURER and GESENIUS translate, "Not waxing pale," i.e., dead to shame. *English Version* is best. **2. Before the decree bring forth**—i.e., Before God's decree against you announced by me (ch. 1) *have its fulfilment.* As the embryo lies hid in the womb, and then emerges to light in its own due time, so though God for a time hides His vengeance, yet He *brings* it *forth* at the proper season. **before the day pass as the chaff**—i.e., before *the day* for repentance *pass,* and with it you, the ungodly, pass away *as the chaff* (Job 21:18; Ps. 1:4). MAURER puts it parenthetically, "the day (i.e., time) passes as the chaff" (i.e., most quickly). CALVIN, "before the decree bring forth" (the predicted vengeance), (then) the chaff (the Jews) shall pass in a day, i.e., in a moment, though they thought that it would be long before they could be overthrown. *English Version* is best; the latter clause being explanatory of the former, and so the *before* being understood, not expressed. **3.** As in vs. 1 (cf *Note,* ch. 1:12) he had warned the hardened among the people to humble themselves, so now he admonishes "the meek" to proceed in their right course, that so they may escape the general calamity (Ps. 76:9). The *meek* bow themselves under God's chastisements to God's will, whereas the ungodly become only the more hardened by them. **Seek ye the Lord**—in contrast to those that "sought not the Lord" (ch. 1: 6). The *meek* are not to regard what the multitudes do, but seek God at once. **his judgment**—i.e., law. The true way of "seeking the Lord" is to "work judgment," not merely to be zealous about outward ordinances. **seek meekness**—not perversely murmuring against God's dealings, but patiently submitting to them, and composedly waiting for deliverance. **it may be ye shall be hid**—(Isa. 26:20; Amos 5:6). This phrase does not imply doubt of the deliverance of the godly, but expresses the difficulty of it, as well that the ungodly may see the certainty of their doom, as also that the faithful may value the more the grace of God in their case (I Pet. 4:17-19) [CALVIN]. Cf. II Kings 25:12. **4. For**—He makes the punishment awaiting the neighboring states an argument why the ungodly should repent (vs. 1) and the godly persevere, viz., that so they may escape from the general calamity. **Gaza shall be forsaken**—In the *Hebrew* there is a play of similar sounds, *Gaza Gazubah;* Gaza shall be forsaken, as its name implies. So the *Hebrew* of the next clause, *Ekron teeakeer*. **at the noonday**—when on account of the heat Orientals usually sleep, and military operations are suspended (II Sam. 4:5). Hence an attack *at noon* implies one sudden and unexpected (Jer. 6:4, 5; 15:8). **Ekron**—*Four* cities of the Philistines are mentioned, whereas *five* was the normal number of their leading cities. Gath is omitted, being at this time under the Jews' dominion. David had subjugated it (I Chron. 18:1). Under Joram the Philistines almost regained it (II Chron. 21:16), but Uzziah (II Chron. 26:6) and Hezekiah (II Kings 18:8) having conquered them, it remained under the Jews. Amos 1:6, Zechariah 9:5, 6, Jeremiah 25:20, similarly mention only *four* cities of the Philistines. **5. inhabitants of the seacoast**—the Philistines dwelling on the strip of seacoast southwest of Canaan. Lit., the "cord" or "line" of sea (cf. Jer. 47:7; Ezek. 25:16). **the Cherethites**—the Cretans, a name applied to the Philistines as sprung from Crete (Deut. 2:23; Jer. 47:4; Amos 9:7). *Philistine* means "an emigrant." **Canaan . . . land of the Philistines**—They occupied the southwest of *Canaan* (Josh. 13:2, 3); a name which hints that they are doomed to the same destruction as the early occupants of the land. **6. dwellings** *and* **cottages for shepherds**—rather, "dwellings with cisterns" (i.e., water-tanks *dug* in the earth) *for shepherds.* Instead of a thick population and tillage, the region shall become a pasturage for nomad shepherds' flocks. The *Hebrew* for "dug cisterns," *Ceroth,* seems a play on sounds, alluding to their name Cherethites (vs. 5): Their land shall become what their national name implies, a land of *cisterns.* MAURER translates, "*Feasts* for shepherds' (flocks)," i.e., one wide pasturage. **7. remnant of . . . Judah**—those of the Jews who shall be left after the coming calamity, and who shall return from exile. **feed thereupon**—viz., in the pastures of that seacoast region (vs. 6). **visit**—in mercy (Exod. 4:31). **8. I have heard**—A seasonable consolation to Judah when wantonly assailed by Moab and Ammon with impunity: God saith, "I have heard it all, though I might seem to men not to have observed it because I did not immediately inflict punishment." **magnified themselves**—acted haughtily, invading the territory of Judah (Jer. 48:29; 49:1; cf. vs. 10; Ps. 35:26; Obad. 12). **9. the breeding of nettles**—or, *the overspreading* of nettles, i.e., a place overrun with them. **salt pits**—found at the south of the Dead Sea. The water overflows in the spring, and salt is left by the evaporation. Salt land is barren (Judg. 9:45; *Margin,* Ps. 107:34). **possess them**—i.e., their land; in retribution for their having occupied Ju-

dah's land. **10.** (Cf. vs. 8.) **their pride**—in antithesis to the *meek* (vs. 3). **11. famish**—bring low by taking from the idols their former fame; as beasts are famished by their food being withheld. Also by destroying the kingdoms under the tutelage of idols (Ps. 96:4; Isa. 46:1). **gods of the earth**—who have their existence only *on earth,* not in heaven as the true God. **every one from his place** —each *in his own* Gentile *home,* taught by the Jews in the true religion: not in Jerusalem alone shall men worship God, but everywhere (Ps. 68:29, 30; Mal. 1:11; John 4:21; I Cor. 1:2; I Tim. 2:8). It does not mean, as in Isaiah 2:2; Micah 4:1, 2; Zechariah 8:22; 14:16 that they shall come *from* their several *places* to Jerusalem to worship [MAURER]. **all . . . isles of . . . heathen**—i.e., all the maritime regions, especially the west, now being fulfilled in the gathering in of the Gentiles to Messiah. **12.** Fulfilled when Nebuchadnezzar (God's *sword,* Isa. 10: 5) conquered Egypt, with which Ethiopia was closely connected as its ally (Jer. 46:2-9; Ezek. 30:5-9). **Ye**—lit., "They." The third person expresses estrangement; while doomed before God's tribunal in the second person, they are spoken of in the third as aliens from God. **13.** Here he passes suddenly to the north. Nineveh was destroyed by Cyaxares and Nabopolassar, 625 B.C. The Scythian hordes, by an inroad into Media and thence in the southwest of Asia (thought by many to be the forces described by Zephaniah, as the invaders of Judea, rather than the Chaldeans), for a while interrupted Cyaxares' operations; but he finally succeeded. Arbaces and Belesis previously subverted the Assyrian empire under Sardanapalus (i.e., Pul?), 877 B.C. **14. flocks**—of sheep; answering to "beasts" in the parallel clause. Wide pastures for sheep and haunts for wild beasts shall be where once there was a teeming population (cf. vs. 6). MAURER, needlessly for the parallelism, makes it "flocks *of savage animals."* **beasts of the nations**—i.e., beasts of the earth (Gen. 1:24). Not as ROSENMULLER, "all kinds of beasts that form a nation," i.e., gregarious beasts (Prov. 30:25, 26). **cormorant**—rather, the pelican (so Ps. 102:6; *Margin,* Isa. 34:11). **bittern**—(Isa. 14:23). MAURER translates, "the hedgehog"; HENDERSON, "the porcupine." **upper lintels** —rather, "*the capitals* of her columns," viz., in her temples and palaces [MAURER]. Or, "on the pomegranate-like knops at the tops of the houses" [GROTIUS]. **their voice shall sing in the windows**—The desert-frequenting birds' "voice in the windows" implies desolation reigning in the upper parts of the palaces, answering to "desolation . . . in the thresholds," i.e., in the lower. **he shall uncover the cedar work**—laying the cedar wainscoting on the walls, and beams of the ceiling, bare to wind and rain, the roof being torn off, and the windows and doors broken through. All this is designed as a consolation to the Jews that they may bear their calamities patiently, knowing that God will avenge them. **15.** Nothing then seemed more improbable than that the capital of so vast an empire, a city sixty miles in compass, with walls 100 feet high, and so thick that three chariots could go abreast on them, and with 1500 towers, should be so totally destroyed that its site is with difficulty discovered. Yet so it is, as the prophet foretold. **there is none beside me**—This peculiar phrase, expressing self-gratulation as if peerless, is plainly adopted from Isaiah 47:8. The later prophets, when the spirit of prophecy was on the verge of departing, leaned more on the predictions of their predecessors. **hiss** —in astonishment at a desolation so great and sudden (I Kings 9:8); also in derision (Job 27:23; Lam. 2:15; Ezek. 27:36).

CHAPTER 3

Vss. 1-20. Resumption of the Denunciation of Jerusalem, as Being Unreformed by the Punishment of Other Nations: After Her Chastisement Jehovah Will Interpose for Her against Her Foes; His Worship Shall Flourish in All Lands, Beginning at Jerusalem, Where He Shall Be in the Midst of His People, and Shall Make Them a Praise in All the Earth. 1. filthy—Maurer translates from a different root, "rebellious," "contumacious." But the following term, "polluted," refers rather to her inward moral *filth*, in spite of her outward ceremonial purity [Calvin]. Grotius says, the *Hebrew* is used of women who have prostituted their virtue. There is in the *Hebrew Moreah*; a play on the name *Moriah,* the hill on which the temple was built; implying the glaring contrast between their *filthiness* and the holiness of the worship on Moriah in which they professed to have a share. oppressing—viz., the poor, weak, widows, orphans and strangers (Jer. 22:3). 2. received not correction—Jerusalem is incurable, obstinately rejecting salutary admonition, and refusing to be reformed by "correction" (Jer. 5:3). trusted not in ... Lord—Distrust in the Lord as if He were insufficient, is the parent of all superstitions and wickednesses [Calvin]. drew not near to her God—Though God was specially near to her (Deut. 4:7) as "her God," yet she drew not near to Him, but gratuitously estranged herself from Him. 3. roaring—for prey (Prov. 28:15; Ezek. 22:27; Amos 3:4; Mic. 2:2). evening wolves—which are most ravenous at evening after being foodless all day (Jer. 5:6; Hab. 1:8). they gnaw not the bones till the morrow—rather, "they put not off till tomorrow to gnaw the bones"; but devour all at once, bones and flesh, so ragingly ravenous are they [Calvin]. 4. light—in whose life and teaching there is no truth, gravity, or steadiness. treacherous—false to Jehovah, whose prophets they profess to be (Jer. 23:32; Ezek. 22:28). polluted ... sanctuary—by their profane deeds. 5-7. The Jews regard not God's justice manifested in the midst of them, nor His judgments on the guilty nations around. 5. The just Lord—Why then are ye so unjust? is in the midst thereof—He retorts on them their own boast, "Is not the Lord among us" (Mic. 3:11)? True He is, but it is for another end from what ye think [Calvin]; viz., to lead you *by the example of His righteousness* to be righteous. Leviticus 19:2, "Ye shall be holy: for I the Lord your God am holy" [Maurer]. But Calvin, "That ye may feel His hand to be the nearer *for taking vengeance for your crimes:* 'He will not do iniquity' by suffering your sins to go unpunished" (Deut. 32:4). every morning—lit., "morning by morning." The time in the sultry East for dispensing justice. bring ... to light—publicly and manifestly by the teaching of His prophets, which aggravates their guilt; also by samples of His judgments on the guilty. he faileth not—He is continually setting before you samples of His justice, sparing no pains. Cf. Isaiah 5:4; 50:4, "he wakeneth *morning by morning.*" knoweth no shame—The unjust Jews are not shamed by His justice into repentance. 6. I had hoped that My people by My judgments on other nations would be led to amendment; but they are not, so blinded by sin are they. towers—lit., "angles" or "cor-

ners"; hence the *towers* built at the angles of their city walls. Under Josiah's long and peaceful reign the Jews were undisturbed, while the great incursion of Scythians into Western Asia took place. The judgment on the ten tribes in a former reign also is here alluded to. 7. I said, Surely ...—God speaks after the manner of men in condescension to man's infirmity; not as though God was ignorant of the future contingency, but in their sense, *Surely one might have expected* ye would under such circumstances repent: but no! thou—at least, O Jerusalem! Cf. *"thou, even thou,* at least in this thy day" (Luke 19:42). their dwelling—the *sanctuary* [Buxtorf]. Or, the *city.* Cf. Jesus' words (Luke 13: 35), "Behold, *your house* is left unto you desolate" (Lev. 26:31, 32; Ps. 69:25); and used as to *the temple* (Mic. 3:12). "Their" is used instead of "thy"; this change of person implies that God puts them to a greater distance. howsoever I punished them —Howsoever I might have punished them, I would not have *cut off their dwelling.* Calvin, "Howsoever I had marked them out for punishment" because of their provocations, still, if even then they had repented, taught by My corrections, I was ready to have pardoned them. Maurer, "Altogether in accordance with what I had long ago decreed (ordained) concerning you" (Deut. 28:1-14, and, on the other hand, 15-68; 27:15-26). *English Version,* or Calvin's view, is better. rose early, and corrupted ...—Early morning is in the East the best time for transacting serious business, before the relaxing heat of midday comes on. Thus it means, With the greatest earnestness they set themselves to "corrupt *all* their doings" (Gen. 6:12; Isa. 5:11; Jer. 11:7; 25: 3). 8. wait ye upon me—Here Jehovah turns to the pious Jews. Amidst all these judgments on the Jewish nation, look forward to the glorious time of restoration to be ushered in by God's precious outpouring of wrath on all nations, Isaiah 30:18-33; where the same phrase, "blessed are all they that *wait for* Him," is used as to the same great event. Calvin erroneously makes this verse an address to the ungodly; and so Maurer, "Ye shall not have to wait for Me in vain"; I will presently come armed with indignation: I will no longer contend with you by My prophets. until the day—i.e., waiting for the day (Hab. 2:3). rise up to the prey—like a savage beast rising from his lair, greedy for the prey (cf. Matt. 24:28). Or rather, as a warrior leading Israel to *certain victory,* which is expressed by "the prey," or *booty,* which is the reward of victory. LXX and *Syriac* versions read the *Hebrew,* "I rise up as a *witness"* (cf. Job 16:8; Mal. 3:5). Jehovah being in this view *witness,* accuser, and judge. *English Version* is better (cf. Isa. 33:23). gather the nations—against Jerusalem (Zech. 14:2), to pour out His indignation upon them there (Joel 3:2; Zech. 12:2, 3). 9. For—The blessed things promised in this and vs. 10 are the immediate results of the punishment inflicted on the nations, mentioned in vs. 8 (cf. vs. 19). turn to the people a pure language— i.e., *changing* their impure language I will *give* to them again *a pure language* (lit., "lip"). Cf. for this *Hebrew* idiom, *Margin,* I Samuel 10:9. The confusion of languages was of the penalty sin, probably idolatry at Babel (*Margin,* Gen. 11:1-6, where also "lip" expresses *language,* and perhaps also *religion;* vs. 4, "a tower whose top *may reach* unto heaven," or rather, *points to heaven,* viz., dedicated to *the heavens* idolized, or Bel); certainly, of rebellion against God's will. An earnest of the removal of this penalty was the gift of tongues on pentecost (Acts 2). The full restoration of the earth's unity of language and of worship is yet future, and is connected with the restoration of the Jews, to be followed by the conversion of the world. Cf. Isaiah 19:18; Zechariah 14:9; Romans 15:6, "with one mind and *one mouth* glorify God." The Gentiles' *lips* have been rendered impure through being the instruments of calling on idols and dishonoring God (cf. Ps. 16:4; Hos. 2:17). Whether Hebrew shall be the one universal language or not, the God of the Hebrews shall be the one only object of worship. Until the Holy Ghost purify the *lips*, we cannot rightly call upon God (Isa. 6:5-7). **serve him with one consent**—lit., "shoulder" or "back"; metaphor from a yoke, or burden, borne between two (Num. 13:23); helping one another with conjoint effort. If one of the two bearers of a burden, laid on both conjointly, give way, the burden must fall to the earth [CALVIN]. Christ's rule is called a *burden* (Matt. 11:30; Acts 15:28; Rev. 2:24; cf. II Cor. 6:14 for the same image). **10. From beyond . . . Ethiopia my suppliants**—lit., "burners of incense" (cf. Ps. 141:2; Rev. 5:8, and 8:3, 4). The Israelites are meant, called "the daughter of My dispersed," a *Hebrew* idiom for *My dispersed people.* "The rivers of Ethiopia" are those which enclose it on the north. In the west of Abyssinia there has long existed a people called *Falashas,* or "emigrants" (akin to the synonym "Philistine"). These trace their origin to Palestine and profess the Jewish religion. In physical traits they resemble the Arabs. When Bruce was there, they had a Jewish king, Gideon, and his queen, Judith. Probably the Abyssinian Christians were originally in part converted Jews. They are here made the representatives of all Israel which is to be restored. **shall bring mine offering**—i.e., the *offering* that is *My right.* I prefer, with DE WETTE and *Chaldee Version,* making "suppliants" the objective case, not the nominative. The *peoples* (vss. 8, 9), brought to fear Me by My judgments, "shall bring as Mine offering My suppliants (an appropriate term for the Jews, on whom then there shall have been poured the spirit of *supplications,* Zech. 12:10), the daughter of My dispersed." So Isaiah 66:20, "they shall bring all your brethren for an *offering* unto the Lord." Cf. HORSLEY'S view of Isaiah 18:1, 2, 7. England in this view may be the naval power to restore Israel to Palestine (Isa. 60:9). The *Hebrew* for Ethiopia is *Cush,* which may include not only Ethiopia, but also the region of the Tigris and Babylon, where Nimrod, Cush's son (Gen. 10:8-12), founded Nineveh and acquired Babylon, and where the ten tribes are mentioned as being scattered (I Peter 1:1; 5:13; cf. Isa. 11:11). The restoration under Cyrus of the Jews transported under Pharaohnecho to Egypt and Ethiopia, was an earnest of the future restoration under Christ. **11. shalt thou not be ashamed**—Thou shalt then have no cause to be ashamed; for I will then *take away out of the midst of thee* those who by their sins gave thee cause for shame (vs. 7). **them that rejoice in thy pride**—those priding themselves *on that which thou boastest of,* thy temple ("My holy mountain"), thy election as God's people, etc., in the Pharisaic spirit (Jer. 7:4; Mic. 3:11; Matt. 3:9). Cf. Jeremiah 13:17, "mine eyes shall weep for *your pride.*" The converted remnant shall be of a humble spirit (vs. 12; Isa. 66:

2, 10). **12. afflicted . . . they shall trust in . . . Lord**—the blessed effect of sanctified affliction on the Jewish remnant. Entire trust in the Lord cannot be, except where all cause for boasting is taken away (Isa. 14:32; Zech. 11:11). **13. nor speak lies**—worshipping God in truth, and towards man having love without dissimulation. The characteristic of the 144,000 *sealed of Israel.* **none shall make them afraid**—either foreign foe, or unjust prince (vs. 3), prophet, or priest (vs. 4). **14.** The prophet in mental vision sees the joyful day of Zion present, and bids her rejoice at it. **15.** The cause for joy: "The Lord hath taken away thy judgments," viz., those sent by Him upon thee. After the taking away of sin (vs. 13) follows the taking away of trouble. When the cause is removed, the effect will cease. Happiness follows in the wake of holiness. **the Lord is in the midst of thee**—Though He seemed to desert thee for a time, He is now present as thy safeguard (vs. 17). **not see evil any more**—Thou shalt not *experience* it (Jer. 5:12; 44:17). **16. Let not thine hands be slack**—(Heb. 12:12). Do not faint in the work of the Lord. **17. he will rest in his love**—content with it as His supreme delight (cf. Luke 15:7, 10) [CALVIN], (Isa. 62:5; 55:19). Or, *He shall be silent,* viz. as to thy faults, not imputing them to thee [MAURER] (Ps. 32:2; Ezek. 33:16). I prefer explaining it of that calm *silent* joy in the possession of the object of one's love, too great for words to express: just as God after the six days of creation *rested* with silent satisfaction in His work, for "behold it was very good" (Gen. 1:31; 2:2). So the parallel clause by contrast expresses the joy, not kept silent as this, but uttered in "singing." **18. sorrowful for the solemn assembly**—pining after the solemn assembly which they cannot celebrate in exile (Lam. 1:4; 2:6). **who are of thee**—i.e., of thy true citizens; and whom therefore I will restore. **to whom the reproach of it was a burden**—i.e., to whom *thy* reproach ("the reproach of My people," Mic. 6:16; their ignominious captivity) was a burden. "Of it" is put of *thee,* as the person is often changed. Those who shared in the burden of reproach which fell on My people. Cf. Isaiah 25:8, "the rebuke of His people shall He take away from off all the earth." **19. undo**—MAURER translates, "I will deal with," i.e., as they deserve. Cf. Ezek. 23:25, where the *Hebrew* is similarly translated. The destruction of Israel's foes precedes Israel's restoration (Isa. 66:15, 16). **her that halteth**—all that are helpless. Their weakness will be no barrier in the way of My restoring them. So in Psalm 35:15 (*Margin*), "halting" is used for *adversity.* Also Ezekiel 34:16; Micah 4:6, 7. **I will get them praise . . .**—lit., "I will make them (to become) a praise and a name. . . ." **shame**—(Ezek. 34:29). **20. make you a name . . . praise**—make you to become celebrated and praised. **turn back your captivity**—bring back your captives [MAURER]. The *Hebrew* is *plural,* "captivities"; to express the captivities of different ages of their history, as well as the diversity of places in which they were and are dispersed. **before your eyes**—Incredible as the event may seem, *your own eyes* with delight shall see it. You will scarcely believe it for joy, but the testimony of your own eyes shall convince you of the delightful reality (cf. Luke 24:41).

THE BOOK OF

HAGGAI

INTRODUCTION

THE name *Haggai* means "my feast"; given, according to COCCEIUS, in anticipation of the joyous return from exile. He probably was one of the Jewish exiles (of the tribes Judah, Benjamin, and Levi) who returned under Zerubbabel, the civil head of the people, and Joshua, the high priest, 536 B.C., when Cyrus (actuated by the striking prophecies as to himself, Isa. 44:28; 45:1) granted them their liberty, and furnished them with the necessaries for restoring the temple (II Chron. 36:23; Ezra 1:1; 2:2). The work of rebuilding went on under Cyrus and his successor Cambyses (called Ahasuerus in Ezra 4:6) in spite of opposition from the Samaritans, who, when their offers of help were declined, began to try to hinder it. These at last obtained an interdict from the usurper Smerdis the Magian (called Artaxerxes in Ezra 4:7-23), whose suspicions were easy to rouse. The Jews thereupon became so indifferent to the work that when Darius came to the throne (521 B.C.), virtually setting aside the prohibitions of the usurper, instead of recommencing their labors, they pretended that as the prophecy of *the seventy years* applied to the temple as well as to the captivity in Babylon (ch. 1:2), they were only in the sixty-eighth year of it [HENDERSON]; so that, the proper time not having yet arrived, they might devote themselves to building splendid mansions for themselves. Haggai and Zechariah were commissioned by Jehovah (ch. 1:1) in the second year of Darius (Hystaspes), 520 B.C., sixteen years after the return under Zerubbabel, to rouse them from their selfishness to resume the work which for fourteen years had been suspended. Haggai preceded Zechariah in the work by two months.

The dates of his four distinct prophecies are accurately given: (1) The first (ch. 1), on the first day of the sixth month of the second year of Darius, 520 B.C., reproved the people for their apathy in allowing the temple to lie in ruins and reminded them of their ill success in everything because of their not honoring God as to His house. The result was that twenty-four days afterwards they commenced building under Zerubbabel (ch. 1:12-15). (2) The second, on the twenty-first day of the seventh month (ch. 2:1-9), predicts that the glory of the new temple would be greater than that of Solomon's, so that the people need not be discouraged by the inferiority in outward splendor of the new, as compared with the old temple, which had so moved to tears the elders who had remembered the old (Ezra 3:12, 13). Isaiah, Jeremiah, and Ezekiel had implied the same prediction, whence some had doubted whether they ought to proceed with a building so inferior to the former one; but Haggai shows wherein the superior glory was to consist, viz., in the presence of Him who is the "desire of all nations" (vs. 7). (3) The third, on the twenty-fourth day of the ninth month (ch. 10:19), refers to a period when building materials had been collected, and the workmen had begun to put them together, from which time forth God promises His blessing; it begins with removing their past error as to the efficacy of mere outward observances to cleanse from the taint of disobedience as to the temple building. (4) The fourth (ch. 2:20-23), on the same day as the preceding, was addressed to Zerubbabel, as the representative of the theocratic people, and as having asked as to the national revolutions spoken of in the second prophecy (ch. 2:7).

The prophecies are all so brief as to suggest the supposition that they are only a summary of the original discourses. The space occupied is but three months from the first to the last.

The Jews' adversaries, on the resumption of the work under Zerubbabel, Haggai, and Zechariah, tried to set Darius against it; but that monarch confirmed Cyrus' decree and ordered all help to be given to the building of the temple (Ezra 5:3, &c.; 6:1, etc.). So the temple was completed in the sixth year of Darius' reign 516-515 B.C. (Ezra 6:14).

The style of Haggai is consonant with his messages: pathetic in exhortation, vehement in reproofs, elevated in contemplating the glorious future. The repetition of the same phrases (e.g., "saith the Lord," or "the Lord of hosts," ch. 1:2, 5, 7; and thrice in one verse, ch. 2:4; so "the spirit," thrice in one verse, ch. 1:14) gives a simple earnestness to his style, calculated to awaken the solemn attention of the people, and to awaken them from their apathy, to which also the interrogatory form, often adopted, especially tends. Chaldæisms occur (ch. 2:3; 2:6; 2:16), as might have been expected in a writer who was so long in Chaldea. Parts are purely prose history; the rest is somewhat rhythmical, and observant of poetic parallelism.

Haggai is referred to in Ezra 5:1; 6:14; and in the New Testament (Heb. 12:26; cf. ch. 2, 6, 7, 22).

CHAPTER 1

Vss. 1-15. HAGGAI CALLS THE PEOPLE TO CONSIDER THEIR WAYS IN NEGLECTING TO BUILD GOD'S HOUSE: THE EVIL OF THIS NEGLECT TO THEMSELVES: THE HONOR TO GOD OF ATTENDING TO IT: THE PEOPLE'S PENITENT OBEDIENCE UNDER ZERUBBABEL FOLLOWED BY GOD'S GRACIOUS ASSURANCE. **1. second year of Darius**—Hystaspes, the king of Medo-Persia, the second of the world-empires, Babylon having been overthrown by the Persian Cyrus. The Jews having no king of their own, dated by the reign of the world-kings to whom they were sub-ject. Darius was a common name of the Persian kings, as Pharaoh of those of Egypt, and Cæsar of those of Rome. The name in the cuneiform inscriptions at Persepolis is written *Daryawus*, from the root *Darh*, "to preserve," the *Conservator* [LASSEN]. HERODOTUS, 6.98, explains it *Coercer*. Often opposite attributes are assigned to the same god; in which light the Persians viewed their king. Erza 4:24 harmonizes with Haggai in making this year the date of the resumption of the building. **sixth month**—of the Hebrew year, not of Darius' reign (cf. Zech. 1:7; 7:1, 3; 8:19). Two months later (the eighth month," Zech. 1:1) Zechariah began to prophesy, seconding Haggai. **the Lord**—*Hebrew,* JEHOVAH: God's covenant title, implying His unchangeableness, the guarantee of His faithfulness in keeping His promises to His people. **by Haggai**—*Hebrew,* "in the hand of Haggai"; God being the real speaker, His prophet but the instrument (cf. Acts 7:35; Gal. 3:19). **Zerubbabel**—called also Shesh-bazzar in Ezra 1:8; 5:14, 16, where the same work is attributed to Shesh-bazzar that in ch. 3:8 is attributed to Zerubbabel. Shesh-bazzar is probably his Chaldean name; as Belteshazzar was that of Daniel. Zerubbabel, his *Hebrew* name, means "one born in Babylon." **son of Shealtiel**—or Salathiel. But I Chronicles 3:17, 19 makes Pedaiah his father. Probably he was adopted by his *uncle* Salathiel, or Shealtiel, at the death of his father (cf. Matt. 1:12; Luke 3:27). **governor of Judah**—to which office Cyrus had appointed him. The *Hebrew Pechah* is akin to the original of the modern Turkish *Pasha;* one ruling a region of the Persian empire of less extent than that under a satrap. **Joshua**—called Jeshua (Ezra 2:2); so the son of Nun in Nehemiah 8:17. **Josedech**—or Jehozadak (I Chron. 6:15), one of those carried captive by Nebuchadnezzar. Haggai addresses the civil and the religious representatives of the people, so as to have them as his associates in giving God's commands; thus priest, prophet, and ruler jointly testify in God's name. **2. the Lord of hosts**—Jehovah, Lord of the powers of heaven and earth, and therefore requiring implicit obedience. **This people**—"This" sluggish and selfish "people." He does not say, *My* people, since they had neglected the service of God. **The time**—the proper time for building the temple. Two out of the seventy predicted years of captivity (dating from the destruction of the temple, 558 B.C., (II Kings 25:9) were yet unexpired; this they make their plea for delay [HENDERSON]. The seventy years of captivity were completed long ago in the first year of Cyrus, 536 B.C. (Jer. 29:10); dating from 606 B.C., Jehoiakim's captivity (II Chron. 36:6). The seventy years to the completion of the temple (Jer. 25:12) were completed this very year, the second of Darius [VATABLUS]. Ingenious in excuses, they pretended that the interruption in the work caused by their enemies proved it was *not yet the proper time;* whereas their real motive was selfish dislike of the trouble, expense, and danger from enemies. "God," say they, "hath interposed many difficulties to punish our rash haste" [CALVIN]. Smerdis' interdict was no longer in force, now that Darius the rightful king was on the throne; therefore they had no real excuse for not beginning at once to build. AUBERLEN denies that by "Artaxerxes" in Ezra 4:7-22 is meant Smerdis. Whether Smerdis or Artaxerxes Longimanus be meant, the interdict referred only to the rebuilding of the *city,* which the Persian kings feared might, if rebuilt, cause them trouble to subdue; not to the rebuilding of the *temple.* But the Jews were easily turned aside from the work. Spiritually, like the Jews, men do not say they will never be religious, but, It is not time yet. So the great work of life is left undone. **4. Is it time**—It is not time (vs. 2), ye say, to build Jehovah's house; yet how is it that ye make it a fit time not only to *build,* but to "dwell" at ease in your own houses? **you, O ye**—rather, for "you, you"; the repetition marking the shameful contrast between their concern for *themselves,* and their unconcern for God [MAURER]. Cf. a similar repetition in I Samuel 25:24; Zechariah 7:5. **ceiled**—rather, "wainscoted," or "paneled," referring to the walls as well as the ceilings; furnished

not only with comfort but luxury, in sad contrast to God's house not merely unadorned, but the very walls not raised above the foundations. How different David's feelings (II Sam. 7:2)! **5. Consider your ways**—lit., "Set your heart" on your ways. The *plural* implies, Consider both what ye have done (actively, Lam. 3:40) and what ye have suffered (passively) [JEROME]. Ponder earnestly whether ye have gained by seeking self at the sacrifice of God. **6.** Nothing has prospered with you while you neglected your duty to God. The punishment corresponds to the sin. They thought to escape poverty by not building, but keeping their money to themselves; God brought it on them *for* not building (Prov. 13:7; 11:24; Matt. 6:33). Instead of cheating God, they had been only cheating themselves. **ye clothe . . . but . . . none warm**—through insufficiency of clothing; as ye are unable through poverty from failure of your crops to purchase sufficient clothing. The verbs are infinitive, implying a *continued state:* "Ye have sown, and *been bringing in* but little; ye have *been eating,* but not to *being satisfied;* ye have *been drinking,* but not to *being filled;* ye have been *putting* on clothes, but not to *being warmed*" [MOORE]. Careful consideration of God's dealings with us will indicate God's will regarding us. The events of life are the hieroglyphics in which God records His feelings towards us, the key to which is found in the Bible [MOORE]. **wages . . . put . . . into a bag with holes**—proverbial for labor and money spent profitlessly (Zech. 8:10; cf. Isa. 55:2; Jer. 2:13). Contrast, spiritually, the "bags that wax not old, the treasure in heaven that faileth not" (Luke 12:33). Through the high cost of necessaries, those who wrought for a day's wages parted with them at once, as if they had put them into a bag with holes. **8. Go up to the mountain**—Moriah [ROSENMULLER]; Lebanon [HENDERSON]. Rather, generally, *the mountains* around, now covered with wood, the growth of the long period of the captivity. So Nehemiah 8:15, "Go forth unto *the mount,*" i.e., the neighboring hills [MAURER]. **wood**—Haggai specifies this as being the first necessary; not to the exclusion of other materials. *Stones* also were doubtless needed. That the old walls were not standing, as the Hebrew interpreters quoted by JEROME state, or the new walls partly built, appears from ch. 2: 18, where express mention is made of *laying the foundations.* **I will take pleasure in it, and I will be glorified**—I will be propitious to suppliants in it (I Kings 8:30), and shall receive the honor due to Me which has been withheld. In neglecting the temple, which is the mirror of My presence, ye dishonor Me [CALVIN]; in its being built, ye shall glorify Me. **9. Ye looked for much**—lit., "looked" so as to turn your eyes "to much." The *Hebrew* infinitive here expresses *continued* looking. Ye hoped to have your store made "much" by neglecting the temple. The greater was your greediness, the more bitter your disappointment in being poorer than ever. **when ye brought it home, I did blow upon it**—even the little crop brought into your barns I *dissipated.* "I did blow upon," i.e., I scattered and caused to perish with My mere breath, as scattered and blighted corn. **mine house . . . his own house**—in emphatic antithesis. **ye run**—expressing the keenness of everyone of them in pursuing their own selfish interests. Cf. "run," Psalm 119:32; Proverbs 1:16, contrasted with their apathy about God's house. **10. heaven . . . is stayed from dew**—lit., stays itself. Thus heaven or the sky is personified; implying that inanimate nature obeys Jehovah's will; and, shocked at His people's disobedience, withholds its goods from them (cf. Jer. 2:12, 13). **11. I called**–what the "heaven" and "earth," the second causes, were said to do (vs. 10), being the *visible* instruments, Jehovah, in this verse, the invisible first cause, declares to be His doing. He "calls for" famine, etc., as instruments of His wrath (II Kings 8:1; Ps. 105:16). The contrast is striking between the prompt obedience of these material agencies, and the slothful disobedience of living men, His people. **drought**– *Hebrew, Choreb,* like in sound to *Chareeb,* "waste" (vss. 4, 9), said of God's house; implying the correspondence between the sin and its punishment. Ye have let My house be *waste,* and I will send on all that is yours a *wasting drought.* This would affect not merely the "corn," etc., but also "men" and "cattle," who must perish in the absence of the "corn," etc., lost by the drought. **labour of the hands**–all the fruits of lands, gardens, and vineyards, obtained by labor of the hands (Deut. 28:33; Ps. 78:46). **12. remnant of the people**–all those who have returned from the exile (Zech. 8:6). **as . . . God sent him**–according to all that Jehovah had enjoined him to speak. But as it is not till vs. 14 after Haggai's second message (vs. 13) that the people actually *obeyed,* MAURER translates here, "*hearkened to* the voice of the Lord," and instead of "as," "*because* the Lord had sent him." However, *English Version* rightly represents their *purpose* of obedience as obedience in God's eyes already, though not carried into effect till vs. 14. **13. the Lord's messenger**–so the priests (Mal. 2:7) are called (cf. Gal. 4:14; II Pet. 1:21). **in the Lord's message**–by the Lord's authority and commission: on the Lord's embassage. **I** *am* **with you**–(Matt. 28:20). On the people showing the mere disposition to obey, even before they actually set to work, God passes at once from the reproving tone to that of tenderness. He hastens as it were to forget their former unfaithfulness, and to assure them, when obedient, that He *both is and will be* with them: *Hebrew,* "I with you!" God's presence is the best of blessings, for it includes all others. This is the sure guarantee of their success no matter how many their foes might be (Rom. 8:31). Nothing more inspirits men and rouses them from torpor, than, when relying on the promises of divine aid, they have a sure hope of a successfull issue [CALVIN]. **14. Lord stirred up the spirit of . . .**–God gave them alacrity and perseverance in the good work, though slothful in themselves. Every good impulse and revival of religion is the direct work of God by His Spirit. **came and did work**–collected the wood and stones and other materials (cf. vs. 8) for the work. Not actually built or "laid the (secondary) foundations" of the temple, for this was not done till three months after, viz., the twenty-fourth day of the *ninth* month (ch. 2:18) [GROTIUS]. **15. four and twentieth day**–twenty-three days after the first message of Haggai (vs. 1).

CHAPTER 2

Vss. 1-9. SECOND PROPHECY. *The people, discouraged at the inferiority of this temple to Solomon's, are encouraged nevertheless to persevere, because God is with them, and this house by its connection with Messiah's kingdom shall have a glory far above that of gold and silver.* **1. seventh month** –of the Hebrew year; in the second year of Darius' reign (ch. 1:1); not quite a month after they had begun the work (ch. 1:15). This prophecy was very shortly before that of Zechariah. **3. Who is left . . . that saw . . . first glory**–Many elders present at the laying of the foundation of the second temple who had seen the first temple (Ezra 3:12, 13) in all its glory, wept at the contrast presented by the rough and unpromising appearance of the former in its beginnings. From the destruction of the first temple to the second year of Darius Hystaspes, the date of Haggai's prophecy, was a space of seventy years (Zech. 1:12); and to the first year of Cyrus, or the end of the captivity, fifty-two years; so that the elders might easily remember the first temple. The Jews note five points of inferiority: The absence from the second temple of (1) the sacred fire; (2) the Shekinah; (3) the ark and cherubim; (4) the Urim and Thummim; (5) the spirit of prophecy. The connection of it with Messiah more than counterbalanced all these; for He is the antitype to all the five (vs. 9). **how do ye see it now?**–God's estimate of things is very different from man's (Zech. 8:6; cf. I Sam. 16:7). However low their estimate of the present temple ("it") from its outward inferiority, God holds it superior (Zech. 4:10; I Cor. 1:27, 28). **4. be strong . . . for I am with you** –The greatest *strength* is to have Jehovah *with* us as our strength. Not in man's "might," but in that of God's Spirit (Zech. 4:6). **5. *According to* the word that**–lit., "(I am with you) the word (or *thing*) which I covenanted"; i.e., I am with you as I covenanted with you when ye came out of Egypt (Exod. 19:5, 6; 34:10, 11). The *covenant* promise of God to the elect people at Sinai is an additional motive for their persevering. The *Hebrew* for to "covenant" is lit. "to cut," alluding to the sacrificial victims *cut* in ratification of a covenant. **so**–or, "and." **my Spirit remaineth among you**–to strengthen you for the work (ch. 1:14; Zech. 4:6). The inspiration of Haggai and Zechariah at this time was a specimen of the presence of God's *Spirit* remaining still *with* His people, as He had been with Moses and Israel of old (Ezra 5:1; Isa. 63:11). **6. Yet once, it** *is* **a little while**–or, "(it is) yet *a* little while." The *Hebrew* for "once" expresses the indefinite article "a" [MAURER]. Or, "it is yet *only* a little while"; lit., one little, i.e., a single brief space till a series of movements is to begin; viz., the shakings of nations soon to begin which are to end in the advent of Messiah, "the desire of all nations" [MOORE]. The *shaking of nations* implies judgments of wrath on the foes of God's people, to precede the reign of the Prince of peace (Isa. 13:13). The kingdoms of the world are but the scaffolding for God's spiritual temple, to be thrown down when their purpose is accomplished. The transitoriness of all that is earthly should lead men to seek "peace" in Messiah's everlasting kingdom (vs. 9; Heb. 12:27, 28) [MOORE]. The Jews in Haggai's times hesitated about going forward with the work, through dread of the world power, Medo-Persia, influenced by the craft of Samaria. The prophet assures them this and all other world powers are to fall before Messiah, who is to be associated with this temple; therefore they need fear naught. So Hebrews, 12:26, which quotes this passage; the apostle compares the heavier punishment which awaits the disobedient under the New Testament with that which met such under the Old Testament. At the establishment of the Sinaitic covenant, only the earth was shaken to introduce it, but now heaven and earth and all things are to be shaken, i.e., along with prodigies in the world of nature, all kingdoms that stand in the way of Messiah's kingdom, "which cannot be shaken," are to be upturned

(Dan. 2:35, 44; Matt. 21:44). Hebrews 12:27, "Yet *once more*," favors *English Version.* Paul condenses together the two verses of Haggai (vss. 6, 7, and vss. 21, 22), implying that it was one and the same shaking, of which the former verses of Haggai denote the beginning, the latter the end. The shaking began introductory to the first advent; it will be finished at the second. Concerning the former, cf. Matthew 3:17; 27:51; 28:2; Acts 2:2; 4: 31; concerning the latter, Matthew 24:7; Revelation 16:20; 18:20; 20:11 [BENGEL]. There is scarcely a prophecy of Messiah in the Old Testament which does not, to some extent at least, refer to His second coming [SIR I. NEWTON]. Psalm 68:8 mentions the *heavens* dropping near the mountain (Sinai); but Haggai speaks of the whole created heavens: "Wait only *a little while*, though the promised event is not apparent yet; for soon will God change things for the better: do not stop short with these preludes and fix your eyes on the present state of the temple [CALVIN]. God shook the *heaven* by the lightnings at Sinai; the *earth*, that it should give forth waters; the *sea*, that it should be divided asunder. In Christ's time God *shook the heaven*, when He spake from it; the *earth*, when it quaked; the *sea*, when He commanded the winds and waves [GROTIUS]. CICERO records at the time of Christ the silencing of the heathen oracles; and DIO, the fall of the idols in the Roman capitol. **7. shake**—not *convert*; but cause that agitation which is to precede Messiah's coming as the healer of the nations' agitations. The previous shaking shall cause the yearning *"desire"* for the Prince of peace. MOORE and others translate "the beauty," or "the desirable things (the precious gifts) of all nations shall come" (Isa. 60:5, 11; 61:6). He brings these objections to applying "the desire of all nations" to Messiah: (1) The *Hebrew* means the *quality*, not the *thing* desired, viz., its *desirableness* or beauty, But the abstract is often put for the concrete. So "a man of desires," i.e., *one desired* or *desirable* (*Margin*, Dan. 9:23; 10:3, 11). (2) Messiah was not desired by all nations, but "a root out of a dry ground," having "no beauty that we should *desire* Him" (Isa. 53:2). But what is implied is not that the nations definitely desired *Him*, but that He was the only one to satisfy the yearning desires which all felt unconsciously for a Saviour, shown in their painful rites and bloody sacrifices. Moreover, while the Jews as a nation desired Him not (to which people Isa. 53:2 refers), the Gentiles, who are plainly pointed out by "all nations," accepted Him; and so to them He was peculiarly desirable. (3) The verb, "shall come," is *plural*, which requires the noun to be understood in the *plural*, whereas if Messiah be intended, the noun is *singular*. But when two nouns stand together, of which one is governed by the other, the verb agrees sometimes *in number* with the latter, though it really has the former as its nominative, i.e., the *Hebrew* "come" is made *in number* to agree with "nations," though really agreeing with "the desire." Besides, Messiah may be described as realizing in Himself at His coming *"the desires* (the noun expressing collectively the *plural*) of all nations"; whence the verb is *plural*. So in Song of Solomon, 5:16, "He is altogether lovely," in the *Hebrew* the same word as here, "all *desires*," i.e., altogether desirable, or the object of desires. (4) Verse 8, "The silver is mine..." accords with the translation, "the choice things of all nations" shall be brought in. But the eighth verse harmonizes quite as well with *English Version* of vs. 7, as the *Note* on vs. 8 will show. (5) LXX and *Syriac* versions agree with MOORE'S translation. But *Vulgate* confirms *English Version.* So also early Jewish Rabbis before JEROME'S time. PLATO, *Alcibiades* 2, shows the yearning of the Gentiles after a spiritual deliverer: "It is therefore necessary," says Alcibiades on the subject of acceptable worship, "to wait until One teach us how we ought to behave towards the gods and men." Alcibiades replies, "When shall that time arrive, and who shall that Teacher be? For most glad would I be to see such a man." The "good tidings of great joy" were "to all people" (Luke 2:10). The Jews, and those in the adjoining nations instructed by them, looked for *Shiloh* to *come unto whom the gathering of the people was to be,* from Jacob's prophecy (Gen. 49:10). The early patriarchs, Job (Job 19:25-27; 33:23-26) and Abraham (John 8:56), *desired Him.* **fill this house with glory**—(vs. 9). As the first temple was filled with the cloud of glory, the symbol of God (I Kings 8:11; II Chron. 5:14), so this second temple was filled with the "glory" of God (John 1:14) *veiled* in the flesh (as it were in the cloud) at Christ's first coming, when He entered it and performed miracles there (Matt. 21:12-14); but that "glory" is to be *revealed* at His second coming, as this prophecy in its ulterior reference foretells (Mal. 3:1). The Jews before the destruction of Jerusalem all expected Messiah would appear in the second temple. Since that time they invent various forced and false interpretations of such plain Messianic prophecies. **8. The silver is mine**—(Job 41:11; Ps. 50:12). Ye are disappointed at the absence of these precious metals in the adorning of this temple, as compared with the first temple: If I pleased I could adorn this temple with them, but I will adorn it with a "glory" (vss. 7, 9) far more precious; viz., with the presence of My divine Son in His veiled glory first, and at His second coming with His revealed glory, accompanied with outward adornment of gold and silver, of which the golden covering within and without put on by Herod is the type. Then shall the nations bring offerings of those precious metals which ye now miss so much (Isa. 2:3; 60:3, 6, 7; Ezek. 43:2, 4, 5; 44:4). The heavenly Jerusalem shall be similarly adorned, but shall need "no temple" (Rev. 21:10-22). Cf. I Corinthians 3:12, where *gold* and *silver* represent the most precious things (Zech. 2:5). The inward glory of New Testament redemption far exceeds the outward glory of the Old Testament dispensation. So, in the case of the individual poor believer, God, if He pleased, could bestow gold and silver, but He bestows far better treasures, the possession of which might be endangered by that of the former (Jas. 2:5). **9. The glory of this latter house ... greater than of the former**—viz., through the presence of Messiah, *in* whose *face is given the light of the knowledge of the glory of God* (II Cor. 4:6; cf. Heb. 1:2), and who said of Himself, "in this place is one greater than the temple" (Matt. 12:6), and who "sat daily teaching in it" (Matt. 26:55). Though Zerubbabel's temple was taken down to the foundations when Herod rebuilt the temple, the latter was considered, in a religious point of view, as not a *third* temple, but virtually the second temple. **in this place ... peace**—viz., at Jerusalem, the metropolis of the kingdom of God, whose seat was the temple: where Messiah "made peace through the blood of His cross" (Col. 1:20). Thus the "glory" consists in this "peace." This peace begins by the removal of the difficulty in the way of the just God accepting the guilty (Ps. 85:8, 10; Isa. 9:6, 7; 53:5; Zech. 6:13; II Cor. 5:18, 19); then it creates peace in the sinner's own heart (Isa. 57:19; Acts 10:36; Rom. 5: 1; 14:17; Eph. 2:13-17; Phil. 4:7); then peace in the whole earth (Mic. 5:5; Luke 2:14). First *peace* between God and man, then between man and God, then between man and man (Isa. 2:4; Hos. 2:18; Zech. 9:10). As "Shiloh" (Gen. 49:10) means *peace,* this verse confirms the view that vs. 7, "the desire of all nations," refers to Shiloh or Messiah, foretold in Gen. 49:10.

10-19. THIRD PROPHECY. *Sacrifices without obedience (in respect to God's command to build the temple) could not sanctify. Now that they are obedient, God will bless them, though no sign is seen of fertility as yet.* **10. four and twentieth day ... ninth month**—three days more than two months from the second prophecy (vs. 1); in the month Chisleu, the lunar one about the time of our December. The Jews seem to have made considerable progress in the work in the interval (vss. 15-18). **11. Ask ... the priests**—Propose this question to them on the law. The priests were the authorized expounders of the law (Lev. 10:11; Deut. 33:10; Ezek. 44:23; Mal. 2:7). **12.** "Holy flesh" (i.e., the flesh of a sacrifice, Jer. 11:15), indeed, makes holy the "skirt" in which it is carried; but that "skirt" cannot impart its sanctity to any thing beyond, as "bread," etc. (Lev. 6:27). This is cited to illustrate the principle, that a sacrifice, holy, as enveloping divine things (just as the "skirt" is "holy" which envelops "holy" flesh), cannot by its inherent or *opus operatum* efficacy make holy a person whose disobedience, as that of the Jew while neglecting God's house, made him unholy. **13.** On the other hand, a legally "unclean" person imparts his uncleanness to any thing, whereas a legally holy thing cannot confer its sanctity on an "unclean" person (Num. 19:11, 13, 22). Legal sanctity is not so readily communicated as legal impurity. So the paths to sin are manifold: the paths to holiness one, and that one of difficult access [GROTIUS]. One drop of filth will defile a vase of water: many drops of water will not purify a vase of filth [MOORE]. **14. Then answered Haggai**—rather, "Then Haggai answered (in rejoinder to the priests' answer) and said" [MAURER]. **so is this people**—heretofore not in such an obedient state of mind as to deserve to be called *My* people (Titus 1:15). Here he applies the two cases just stated. By the first case, "this people" is not made "holy" by their offerings "there" (viz., on the altar built in the open air, under Cyrus, Ezra 3:3); though the ritual sacrifice can ordinarily sanctify outwardly so far as it reaches (Heb. 9:13), as the "holy flesh" sanctified the "skirt," yet it cannot make the offerers in their persons and all their works acceptable to God, because lacking the spirit of obedience (I Sam. 15:22) so long as they neglected to build the Lord's house. On the contrary, by the second case, they made "unclean" their very *offerings* by being unclean through "dead works" (disobedience), just as the person unclean by contact with a dead body imparted his uncleanness to all that he touched (cf. Heb. 9:14). This all applies to them as they had been, not as they are now that they have begun to obey; the design is to guard them against falling back again. The "there" points to the altar, probably in view of the audience which the prophet addressed. **15. consider**—lit., "lay it to heart." Ponder earnestly, retracing the past *upward* (i.e., backward), comparing what evils heretofore befell you before ye set about this work, with the present time when you have again commenced it, and when in consequence I now engage to "bless you." Hence ye may perceive the evils of disobedience and the blessing of obedience. **16. Since those** *days* **were** —from the time that those days of your neglect of the temple work have been. **when** *one* **came to an heap of twenty** *measures*—i.e., to a heap *which he had expected would be one* of twenty measures, there were but ten. **fifty** *vessels* **out of the press**— As LXX translates "measure," and *Vulgate* "a flagon," and as we should rather expect *vat* than *press.* MAURER translates (omitting *vessels,* which is not in the original), "*purahs,*" or "wine-measures." **17.** Appropriated from Amos 4:9, whose canonicity is thus sealed by Haggai's inspired authority; in the last clause, "*turned,*" however, has to be supplied, its omission marking by the elliptical abruptness ("yet ye not to Me!") God's displeasure. Cf. *(let him come)* unto Me!" Moses in excitement omitting the bracketed words (Exod. 32:26). "Blasting" results from excessive drought; "mildew," from excessive moisture. **18.** Resumed from vs. 15 after vss. 16, 17, that the blessing in vs. 19 may stand in the more marked contrast with the curse in vss. 16, 17. Affliction will harden the heart, if not referred to God as its author [MOORE]. **even from the day that the foundation of ... temple was laid**—The first foundation beneath the earth had been long ago laid in the second year of Cyrus, 535 B.C. (Ezra 3:10, 11); the foundation now laid was the secondary one, which, above the earth, was laid on the previous work [TIRINUS]. Or, translate, "From this day on which the temple is being *begun,*" viz., on the foundations long ago laid [GROTIUS]. MAURER translates, "Consider ... from the four and twentieth day ... *to* (the time which has elapsed) from the day on which the foundation ... was laid." The *Hebrew* supports *English Version.* **19. Is the seed yet in the barn?**—implying, It is *not.* It has been already sown this month, and there are no more signs of its bearing a good crop, much less of its being safely stored *in the barn,* than there were in the past season, when there was such a failure; yet I promise to you *from this day* (emphatically marking by the repetition the connection of the blessing with *the day* of their obedience) a *blessing* in an abundant harvest. So also the vine, etc., which heretofore have borne little or nothing, shall be *blessed* with productiveness. Thus it will be made evident that the blessing is due to Me, not to nature. We may trust God's promise to bless us, though we see no visible sign of its fulfilment (Hab. 2:3).

20-23. FOURTH PROPHECY. *God's promise through Zerubbabel to Israel of safety in the coming commotions.* **20. the month**—the ninth in the second year of Darius. The same date as Prophecy III (vs. 10). **21. to Zerubbabel**—Perhaps Zerubbabel had asked as to the convulsions foretold (vss. 6, 7). This is the reply: The Jews had been led to fear that these convulsions would destroy their national existence. *Zerubbabel,* therefore, as their civil leader and representative is addressed, not Joshua, their religious leader. Messiah is the antitypical Zerubbabel, their national Representative and King, with whom God the Father makes the covenant wherein they, as identified with Him, are assured of safety in God's electing love (cf. vs. 23, "will make thee as a signet"; "I have chosen thee"). **shake ... heavens**—*(Note,* vss. 6, 7); violent political convulsions accompanied with physical prodigies (Matt. 24:7, 29). **22.** All other world kingdoms are to be overthrown to make way for Christ's universal kingdom (Dan. 2:44). War chariots are to give place to His reign of peace (Mic. 5:10; Zech. 9:10). **23. take** thee—under My protection and to promote thee and thy people to honor (Ps. 78:70). **a signet**—(Song of Sol. 8:6; Jer. 22:24). A ring with a seal on it; the legal representative of the owner; generally of precious stones and gold, etc., and much valued. Being worn on the finger, it was an object of constant regard. In all which points of view the theocratic people, and their representative, Zerubbabel the type, and Messiah his descendant the Antitype, are regarded by God. The safety of Israel to the end is guaranteed in Messiah, in whom God hath chosen them as His own (Isa. 42:1; 43:10; 44:1; 49: 3). So the spiritual Israel is sealed in their covenant head by His Spirit (II Cor. 1:20, 22; Eph. 1:4, 13, 14). All is ascribed, not to the merits of Zerubbabel, but to God's gratuitous *choice*. Christ is the "signet" on God's hand: always in the Father's presence, ever pleasing in his sight. The signet of an Eastern monarch was the sign of *delegated authority;* so Christ (Matt. 28:18; John 5:22, 23).

THE BOOK OF

ZECHARIAH

INTRODUCTION

THE name *Zechariah* means *one whom Jehovah remembers:* a common name, four others of the same name occurring in the Old Testament. Like Jeremiah and Ezekiel, he was a priest as well as a prophet, which adapts him for the sacerdotal character of some of his prophecies (ch. 6:13). He is called "the son of Berechiah the son of Iddo" (ch. 1:1); but simply "the son of Iddo" in Ezra 5:1; 6:14. Probably his father died when he was young; and hence, as sometimes occurs in Jewish genealogies, he is called "the son of Iddo," his grandfather. Iddo was one of the priests who returned to Zerubbabel and Joshua from Babylon (Neh. 12:4).

Zechariah entered early on his prophetic functions (ch. 2:4); only two months later than Haggai, in the second year of Darius' reign, 520 B.C. The design of both prophets was to encourage the people and their religious and civil leaders, Joshua and Zerubbabel, in their work of rebuilding the temple, after the interruption caused by the Samaritans (*see Introduction* to Haggai). Zechariah does so especially by unfolding in detail the glorious future in connection with the present depressed appearance of the theocracy, and its visible symbol, the temple. He must have been very young in leaving Babylonia, where he was born. The Zechariah, son of Barachias, mentioned by our Lord (Matt. 23:35) as slain between the porch and the altar, must have been the one called the son of *Jehoiada* in II Chron. 24:21, who so perished: the same person often had two names; and our Lord, in referring to the *Hebrew* Bible, of which II Chronicles is the last book, would naturally mention the last martyr in the *Hebrew* order of the canon, as He had instanced Abel as the first. Owing to Matthew 27:9 quoting Zechariah 11:12, 13 as the words of *Jeremiah,* MEDE doubts the authenticity of chs. 9, 10, 11, 12, 13, 14, and ascribes them to *Jeremiah:* he thinks that these chapters were not found till after the return from the captivity, and being approved by Zechariah, were added to his prophecies, as Agur's Proverbs were added to those of Solomon. All the oldest authorities, except two MSS. of the old Italian or Pre-vulgate version, read "Jeremiah" in Matthew 27:9. The quotation there is not to the letter copied from Zechariah, Jeremiah 18:1, 2; 32:6-12, may also have been in the mind of Matthew, and perhaps in the mind of Zechariah, whence the former mentions *Jeremiah.* HENGSTENBERG similarly thinks that Matthew names *Jeremiah,* rather than *Zechariah,* to turn attention to the fact that Zechariah's prophecy is but a reiteration of the fearful oracle in Jeremiah 18 and 19, to be fulfilled in the destruction of the Jewish nation. Jeremiah had already, by the image of a potter's vessel, portrayed their ruin in Nebuchadnezzar's invasion; and as Zechariah virtually repeats this threat, to be inflicted again under Messiah for the nation's rejection of Him, Matthew, virtually, by mentioning *Jeremiah,* implies that the "field of blood," now bought by "the reward of iniquity" in the valley of Hinnom, was long ago a scene of prophetic doom in which awful disaster had been symbolically predicted: that the present purchase of that field with the traitor's price renewed the prophecy and revived the curse—a curse pronounced of old by Jeremiah, and once fulfilled in the Babylonian siege—a curse reiterated by Zechariah, and again to be verified in the Roman desolation. LIGHTFOOT (referring to B. BATHRA and KIMCHI) less probably thinks the third division of Scripture, the prophets, began with Jeremiah, and that the whole body of prophets is thus quoted by the name "Jeremiah." The mention of "Ephraim" and "Israel" in these chapters as distinct from Judah, does not prove that the prophecy was written while the ten tribes existed as a separate kingdom. It rather implies that hereafter not only Judah, but the ten tribes also, shall be restored, the earnest of which was given in the numbers out of the ten tribes who returned with their brethren the Jews from captivity under Cyrus. There is nothing in these characters to imply that a king reigned in Judah at that time. The editor of the *Hebrew* canon joined these chapters to Zechariah, not to Jeremiah; the LXX, 300 years B.C., confirms this.

The prophecy consists of four parts: (1) Introductory, ch. 1:1-6. (2) Symbolical, ch. 1:7, to the end of ch. 6, containing nine visions; all these were vouchsafed in one night, and are of a symbolical character. (3) Didactic, chs. 7 and 8 containing an answer to a query of the Bethelites concerning a certain feast. And (4) Prophetic, ch. 9 to the end. These six last chapters predict Alexander's expedition along the west coast of Palestine to Egypt; God's protection of the Jews, both at that time and under the Maccabees; the advent, sufferings, and reign of Messiah; the destruction of Jerusalem by Rome, and dissolution of the Jews' polity; their conversion and restoration; the overthrow of the wicked confederacy which assailed them in Canaan; and the Gentiles' joining in their holy worship [HENDERSON]. The difference in style between the former and the latter chapters is due to the difference of subject; the first six chapters being of a symbolical and peculiar character, while the poetical style of the concluding chapters is adapted admirably to the subjects treated. The titles (ch. 9:1; 12:1) accord with the prophetic matter which follows; nor is it necessary for unity of authorship that the introductory formulas occurring in the first eight chapters should occur in the last six. The non-reference in the last six chapters to the completion of the temple and the Jews' restoration after the captivity is just what we should expect, if, as seems likely, these chapters were written long after the completion of the temple and the restoration of the Jews' polity after the captivity, in circumstances different from those which engaged the prophet when he wrote the earlier chapters.

The style varies with the subject: at one time conversational, at another poetical. His symbols are enigmatical and are therefore accompanied with explanations. His prose is like that of Ezekiel, diffuse, uniform, and repetitious. The rhythm is somewhat unequal, and the parallelisms are not altogether symmetrical. Still, there is found often much of the elevation met with in the earlier prophets, and a general congruity between the style and the subjects. Graphic vividness is his peculiar merit. Chaldæisms occur occasionally. Another special characteristic of Zechariah is his introduction of spiritual beings into his prophetic scenes.

CHAPTER 1

Vss. 1-17. INTRODUCTORY EXHORTATION TO REPENTANCE. THE VISIONS—*The man among the myrtles: Comforting explanation by the angel, an encouragement to the Jews to build the city and temple: The four horns and four artificers.* **1.** See *Introduction*. **2.** God fulfilled His threats against your fathers; beware, then, lest by disregarding His voice by me, as they did in the case of former prophets, ye suffer like them. The special object Zechariah aims at is that they should awake from their selfish negligence to obey God's command to rebuild His temple (Hag. 1:4-8). **sore displeased**—*Hebrew*, "displeased with a displeasure," i.e., vehemently, with no common displeasure, exhibited in the destruction of the Jews' city and in their captivity. **3. saith the Lord of hosts**—a phrase frequent in Haggai and Zechariah, implying God's boundless resources and universal power, so as to inspire the Jews with confidence to work. **Turn ye unto me ... and I will turn**—i.e., *and then,* as the sure consequence, "I will turn unto you" (Mal. 3:7; Jas. 4:8; cf. also Jer. 3:12; Ezek. 18:30; Mic. 7:19). Though God hath brought you back from captivity, yet this state will not last long unless ye are really converted. God has heavier scourges ready, and has begun to give symptoms of displeasure [CALVIN]. (Hag. 1:6). **4. Be ye not as your fathers**—The Jews boasted of their *fathers;* but he shows that their fathers were refractory, and that ancient example and long usage will not justify disobedience (II Chron. 36:15, 16). **the former prophets**—those who lived before the captivity. It aggravated their guilt that, not only had they the law, but they had been often called to repent by God's *prophets.* **5. Your fathers ... and the prophets, do they live for ever?**—In contrast to "*My* words" (v. 6), which "endure for ever" (I Pet. 1:25). "Your fathers have perished, as was foretold; and their fate ought to warn you. But you may say, The prophets too are dead. I grant it, but still My words do not die: though dead, their prophetical words from Me, fulfilled against *your fathers,* are not dead with them. Beware, then, lest ye share their fate." **6. statutes**—My determined purposes to punish for sin. **which I commanded my servants**—viz., to announce to your fathers. **did they not take hold**—i.e., overtake, as a foe overtakes one fleeing. **they returned**—*Turning* from their former self-satisfaction, they recognized their punishment as that which God's prophets had foretold. **thought to do**—i.e., decreed to do. Cf. with this verse Lamentations 2:17. **our ways**—evil ways (Jer. 4:18; 17:10; 23:2). **7.** The general plan of the nine following visions (ch. 1:8 to end of ch. 6) is first to present the symbol; then, on a question

being put, to subjoin the interpretation. Though the visions are distinct, they form one grand whole, presented in one night to the prophet's mind, two or three months after the prophet's first commission (vs. 1). **Sebat**—the eleventh month of the Jewish year, from the new moon in February to the new moon in March. The term is Chaldee, meaning a "shoot," viz., the month when trees begin to shoot or bud. **8. by night**—The Jews begin their day with sunset; therefore the night which preceded the twenty-fourth day of the month is meant (vs. 7). **a man**—Jehovah, the second person of the Trinity, manifested in *man's* form, an earnest of the incarnation; called the "angel of Jehovah" (vss. 11, 12), "Jehovah the angel of the covenant" (Mal. 3: 1; cf. Gen. 16:7 with vs. 13; 22:11 with vs. 12; Exodus 3:2 with vs. 4). Being at once divine and human, He must be God and man in one person. **riding**—implying swiftness in executing God's will in His providence; hastening to help His people. **red horse**—the color that represents *bloodshed:* implying vengeance to be inflicted on the foes of Israel (cf. II Kings 3:22; Isa. 63:1, 2; Rev. 6:4); also *fiery zeal.* **among the myrtle trees**—symbol of the Jewish Church: not a stately cedar, but a lowly, though fragrant, myrtle. It was its depressed state that caused the Jews to despond; this vision is designed to cheer them with better hopes. The uncreated angel of Jehovah's presence *standing* (as His abiding-place, Ps. 122:14) *among* them, is a guarantee for her safety, lowly though she now be. **in the bottom**—in a low place or bottom of a river; alluding to Babylon near the rivers Euphrates and Tigris, the scene of Judah's captivity. The myrtle delights in low places and the banks of waters [PEMBELLUS]. MAURER translates, from a different root, "in a *shady* place." **red horses**—i.e., *horsemen* mounted on *red horses;* vss. 10, 11, confirm this view. **speckled ... white**—The "white" implies triumph and victory for Judah; "speckled" (from a root "to intertwine"), a combination of the two colors *white* and *red* (bay [MOORE]), implies a state of things mixed, partly prosperous, partly otherwise [HENDERSON]; or, the connection of the wrath (answering to the "red") about to fall on the Jews' foes, and triumph (answering to the "white") to the Jews themselves in God's arrangements for His people [MOORE]. Some angels ("the red horses") exercised offices of vengeance; others ("the white"), those of joy; others ("the speckled"), those of a mixed character (cf. ch. 6:2, 3). God has ministers of every kind for promoting the interests of His Church. **9. the angel that talked with me**—not the "man upon the red horse," as is evident from the tenth verse, where he (the Divine Angel) is distinguished from the "angel that talked with me" (the phrase used of him, vs. 13, 14; ch. 2:3; 4:1, 4, 5; 5:5, 10; 6:4), i.e., the interpreting angel. The *Hebrew* for *"with me,"* or, *"in me"* (Num. 12:8), implies *internal, intimate* communication [JEROME]. **show thee**—reveal to thy mental vision. **10. answered**—The "angel of the covenant" here gives the reply instead of the interpreting angel, to imply that all communications through the interpreting angel come from Him as their source. **Lord hath sent to walk to and fro through the earth**—If "Satan walks to and fro in the earth" (implying *restless activity*) on errands of mischief to God's people (Job 1:7), the Lord *sends* other angels to "walk to and fro" with unceasing activity everywhere to counterwork Satan's designs, and to defend His people (Ps. 34:7; 91:11; 103:20, 21; Heb. 1:41). **11.** The attendant angels report to the Lord of angels, "the earth . . . is at rest." The flourishing state of the heathen "earth," while Judah was desolate and its temple not yet restored, is the powerful plea in the Divine Angel's intercession with God the Father in vs. 12. When Judah was depressed to the lowest point, and the heathen elated to the highest, it was time for Jehovah to work for His people. **sitteth still**—dwells surely. **12.** Not only does Messiah *stand among* His people (the "myrtles," vs. 8), but intercedes for them with the Father ("Lord," or "Jehovah of hosts") effectively (vs. 13; Heb. 7:25). Cf. Psalm 102:13-20; Isaiah 62:6, 7, as to Judah's restoration in answer to prayer. **answered and said**—said *in continuation* of the discourse: *proceeded to say*. **how long**—Messiah's people pray similarly to their Head. Revelation 6:10, "How long. . . ." Heretofore it was vain to pray, but now that the divinely appointed "threescore and ten years" (Jer. 25:11; 29:10) are elapsed, it is time to pray to Thee for the fulfilment of Thy promise, seeing that Thy grace is not yet fully manifested, nor Thy promise fulfilled. God's promises are not to make us slothful, but to quicken our prayers. HENDERSON, dating the seventy years from the destruction of Jerusalem (588 B.C.), supposes two years of the seventy had yet to run (520 B.C.). **13. the Lord**—JEHOVAH, called "the angel of the Lord (Jehovah)" (vs. 12). **good words** *and* **comfortable words**—lit., "words, consolations." The subject of these consolatory words is stated in vs. 14, etc.; the promise of full re-establishment, Jeremiah 29:10, 11 (cf. Isa. 57: 18; Hos. 11:8). **14. Cry**—Proclaim so as to be heard clearly by all (Isa. 40:6; 58:1). **I am jealous for Jerusalem**—As a husband jealous for his wife, wronged by others, so Jehovah is for Judah, who has been injured wantonly by the heathen (ch. 8:2; Num. 25:11, 13; I Kings 19:10; Joel 2:18). **15. very sore displeased with the heathen**—in contrast with "I was *but a little* displeased" with My people. God's displeasure with His people is temporary and for their chastening; with the heathen oppressors, it is final and fatal (Jer. 30:11). God's instruments for chastising His people, when He has done with them, He casts into the fire. **are at ease**—carnally secure. A stronger phrase than "is at rest" (vs. 11). They are "at ease," but as I am "sore displeased" with them, their ease is accursed. Judah is in "affliction," but as I love her and am jealous for her, she has every reason to be encouraged in prosecuting the temple work. **helped forward the affliction**—afflicted My people more than I desired. The heathen sought the utter extinction of Judah to gratify their own ambition and revenge (Isa. 47:6; Ezek. 25:3, 6; Obad. 10-17). **16. I am returned**—whereas in anger I had before

withdrawn from her (Hos. 5:15). **with mercies**—not merely of one kind, nor once only, but repeated mercies. **my house shall be built**—which at this time (the second year of Darius, ch. 1:1) had only its foundations laid (Hag. 2:18). It was not completed till the sixth year of Darius (Ezra 6:15). **line**—(Job 38:5). The measuring-line for building, not hastily, but with measured regularity. Not only the temple, but *Jerusalem* also was to be rebuilt (Neh. 2:3, etc.; cf. ch. 2:1, 2). Also, as to the future temple and city, Ezekiel 41:3; 42; 43; 44; 45:6. **17. yet**—though heretofore lying in abject prostration. **My cities**—not only Jerusalem, but the subordinate *cities* of Judah. God claims them all as peculiarly *His,* and therefore will restore them. **through prosperity . . . spread abroad**—or *overflow;* metaphor from an overflowing vessel or fountain (cf. Prov. 5:16) [PEMBELLUS]. Abundance of fruits of the earth, corn and wine, and a large increase of citizens, are meant; also spiritual prosperity. **comfort Zion**—(Isa. 40:1, 2; 51:3). **choose**—(ch. 2:12; 3:2; Isa. 14:1). Here meaning, *"show by acts of loving-kindness* that He has chosen." His immutable *choice* from everlasting is the fountain whence flow all such particular acts of love.

18-21. SECOND VISION. *The power of the Jews' foes shall be dissipated.* **18. four horns**—To a pastoral people like the Jews the *horns* of the strongest in the herd naturally suggested a symbol of *power* and *pride* of conscious strength: hence *the ruling powers of the world* (Rev. 17:3, 12). The number *four* in Zechariah's time referred to the four cardinal points of the horizon. Wherever God's people turned, there were foes to encounter (Neh. 4:7); the Assyrian, Chaldean, and Samaritan on the north; Egypt and Arabia on the south; Philistia on the west; Ammon and Moab on the east. But the Spirit in the prophet looked farther; viz., to the *four* world powers, the only ones which were, or are, to rise till the kingdom of Messiah, the fifth, overthrows and absorbs all others in its universal dominion. Babylon and Medo-Persia alone had as yet risen, but soon Græco-Macedonia was to succeed (as ch. 9:13 foretells), and Rome the fourth and last, was to follow (Daniel, chs. 2 and 7). The fact that the repairing of the evils caused to Judah and Israel by *all four* kingdoms is spoken of here, proves that the exhaustive fulfilment is yet future, and only the earnest of it given in the overthrow of the two world powers which up to Zechariah's time had "scattered" Judah (Jer. 51:2; Ezek. 5:10, 12). That only two of the four had as yet risen, is an argument having no weight with us, as we believe God's Spirit in the prophets regards the future as present; we therefore are not to be led by Rationalists who on such grounds deny the reference here and in ch. 6:1 to the four world kingdoms. **19. Judah, Israel**—Though some of the ten tribes of *Israel* returned with *Judah* from Babylon, the full return of the former, as of the latter, is here foretold and must be yet future. **20. four carpenters**—or "artificers." The several instrumentalities employed, or to be employed, in crushing the "Gentile" powers which "scattered" Judah, are hereby referred to. For every one of the *four horns* there was a cleaving "artificer" to beat it down. For every enemy of God's people, God has provided a counteracting power adequate to destroy it. **21. These are the horns**—rather, *Those . . .* viz., the horns being distinguished from the "carpenters," or destroying workmen ("skilful to destroy," Exod. 21: 31), intended in the "these" of the question. **no man . . . lift up his head**—so depressed were they with a heavy weight of evils (Job 10:15). **to fray** —to strike terror into them (Ezek. 30:9). **lifted up ... horn**—in the haughtiness of conscious strength (Ps. 75:4, 5) tyrannizing over Judah (Ezek. 34:21).

CHAPTER 2

Vss. 1-13. THIRD VISION. *The man with the measuring line.* The city shall be fully restored and enlarged (vss. 2-5). Recall of the exiles (vss. 6, 7). Jehovah will protect His people and make their foes a spoil unto them (vss. 8, 9). The nations shall be converted to Jehovah, as the result of His dwelling manifestly amidst His people (vss. 10-13). **1. man with a measuring-line**—the same image to represent the same future fact as in Ezekiel 40:3; 41, 42. The "man" is Messiah (*Note*, ch. 1:8), who, by measuring Jerusalem, is denoted as the Author of its coming restoration. Thus the Jews are encouraged in Zechariah's time to proceed with the building. Still more so shall they be hereby encouraged in the future restoration. **2. To measure Jerusalem**—(Cf. Rev. 11:1; 21:15, 16). **to see what** *is* **the breadth ... what** *is* **the length**—rather, what *is to be the due* breadth and length. **3. angel that talked with me ... another angel**—The interpreting angel is met by another angel sent by the measuring Divine Angel to "run" to Zechariah (vs. 4). Those who perform God's will must not merely creep, nor walk, but *run* with alacrity. **went forth**—viz., from me (Zechariah). **went out**—from the measuring angel. **4. this young man**—So Zechariah is called as being still a *youth* when prophetically inspired [GROTIUS]. Or, he is so called in respect to his *ministry* or *service* (cf. Num. 11:27; Josh. 1:1) [VATABLUS]. Naturally the "angel that talked with" Zechariah is desired to "speak to" him the further communications to be made from the Divine Being. **towns without walls for the multitude ... cattle**—So many shall be its inhabitants that all could not be contained within the walls, but shall spread out in the open country around (Esther 9:19); and so secure shall they be as not to need to shelter themselves and their cattle behind walls. So hereafter Judea is to be "the land of unwalled villages" (Ezek. 38:11). Spiritually, now the Church has extended herself beyond the walls (Eph. 2:14, 15) of Mosaic ordinances and has spread from cities to country villages, whose inhabitants gave their Latin name (*pagani*) to *pagans,* as being the last in parting with heathenism. **5. I ... wall of fire round**—Cf. vs. 4. Yet as a city needs some wall, I JEHOVAH will act as one of fire which none durst approach (ch. 9:8; Isa. 26:1). **glory in the midst**—not only a defense from foes outside, but a *glory* within (Isa. 60:19; Rev. 21:23). The same combination of "glory and defense" is found in Isaiah 4: 5, alluding to the pillar of cloud and fire which defended and enlightened Israel in the desert. Cf. Elisha in Dothan (II Kings 6:17). As God is to be her "glory," so she shall be His "glory" (Isa. 62:3). **6. flee from the land of the north**—i.e., from Babylon: a type of the various Gentile lands, from which the Jews are to be recalled hereafter; hence "the four winds of heaven" are specified, implying that they are to return from all quarters (Deut. 28:64; Jer. 16:15; Ezek. 17:21). The reason why they should flee from Babylon is: (1) because of the blessings promised to God's people in their own land; (2) because of the evils about to fall on their foe (vss. 7-9). Babylon was soon to fall before Darius, and its inhabitants to endure fearful calamities (Isa. 48:

20; Jer. 50:8; 51:6, 45). Many of the Jews in Zechariah's time had not yet returned to Judea. Their tardiness was owing to (1) unbelief; (2) their land had long lain waste, and was surrounded with bitter foes; (3) they regarded suspiciously the liberty of return given by Cyrus and Darius, as if these monarchs designed suddenly to crush them; (4) their long stay in Babylon had obliterated the remembrance of their own land; (5) the wealth and security there contrasted with Judea, where their temple and city were in ruins. All this betrayed foul ingratitude and disregard of God's extraordinary favor, which is infinitely to be preferred to all the wealth of the world [CALVIN and PEMBELLUS]. **for I have spread you abroad**—The reasoning is: I who scattered you from your land to all quarters, can also gather you again to it. **7. O Zion ... daughter of Babylon**—Thou whose only sure dwelling is "Zion," inseparably connected with the temple, art altogether out of thy place in "dwelling with the daughter of Babylon" (i.e., Babylon and her people, Ps. 137:8; Isa. 1:8). **After the glory**—*After* restoring the "glory" (vs. 5; Isa. 4:5; Rom. 9:4) of Jehovah's presence to Jerusalem, He (God the Father) hath commissioned ME (God the Son, Isa. 48:16, the Divine Angel: God thus being at once the Sender and the Sent) to visit in wrath "the nations which spoiled you." Messiah's twofold office from the Father is: (1) to glorify His Church; (2) to punish its foes (II Thess. 1:7-10). Both offices manifest His *glory* (Prov. 16:4). **toucheth ... the apple of his eye**—viz., of Jehovah's eye (Deut. 32:10; Ps. 17:8; Prov. 7:2). The pupil, or aperture, through which rays pass to the retina, is the tenderest part of the eye; the member which we most sedulously guard from hurt as being the dearest of our members; the one which feels most acutely the slightest injury, and the loss of which is irreparable. **9. shake ... hand**—A mere wave of God's hand can prostrate all foes (cf. Ruth 1:13; Job 31:21; Isa. 11:15; 19:16; Acts 13:11). **a spoil to their servants** —to the Jews whom they had once as their slaves (cf. Isa. 14:2). As the Jews' state between the return from Babylon and Christ's coming was checkered with much adversity, this prophecy can only have its fulfilment under Christ. **sent me**— (Isa. 48:16; 61:1; John 10:36). **10. I will dwell in ... midst of thee**—primarily at Messiah's first advent (Ps. 40:7; John 1:14; Col. 2:9; I Tim. 3:16); more fully at His second advent (Isa. 40:10). So ch. 9:9 where see the *Note* (Isa. 12:6; Ezek. 37:27; Zeph. 3:14). Meanwhile God dwells spiritually in His people (II Cor. 6:16). **11. many nations ... joined to the Lord in that day**—The result of the Jews' exile in Babylon was that, at their subsequent return, through the diffusion of knowledge of their religion, many Gentiles became proselytes, worshipping in the court of the Gentiles (I Kings 8:41). Cyrus, Darius, Alexander, Ptolemy Philadelphus, Augustus, and Tiberius, paid respect to the temple by sending offerings [GROTIUS]. But all this is but a shadow of the future conversion of the Gentiles which shall result from Jehovah dwelling in Jerusalem (Ps. 102:15, 16; Phil. 2:10, 11). **sent me unto thee**—"unto thee" is here added to the same formula (vs. 9). Zion first shall "know (generally) that Jehovah of hosts hath sent" Messiah, by the judgments inflicted by Him on her foes. Subsequently, she shall know experimentally the particular *sending* of Messiah *unto her.* Jehovah here says, "*I* will dwell," and then that JEHOVAH of hosts sent Him; therefore Jehovah the Sender and Jehovah the Sent must be One. **12. Judah his portion in the**

holy land—Lest the joining of the Gentile "nations to Jehovah" (vs. 11) should lead the Jews to fear that their peculiar relation to Him (Deut. 4:20; 9: 29; 32:9) as "His inheritance" should cease, this verse is added to assure them of His making them so hereafter "again." **choose Jerusalem again**—The course of God's grace was interrupted for a time, but His covenant was not set aside (Rom. 11:28, 29); the election was once for all, and therefore shall hold good for ever. **13. Be silent, O all flesh**—(Hab. 2:20.) "Let all in silent awe and reverence await the Lord's coming interposition in behalf of His people!" The address is both to the Gentile foes, who prided themselves on their power as if irresistible, and to the unbelieving Jews, who distrusted God's promises as incredible. Three reasons why they must be silent are implied: (1) they are but "flesh," weak and ignorant; (2) He is JEHOVAH, all-wise and all-powerful; (3) He is already "raised up out of His place," and who can stand before Him? [PEMBELLUS], (Ps. 76:8, 9). **he is raised up out of his holy habitation**—i.e., out of *heaven* (Deut. 26:15; II Chron. 30:27; Isa. 63:15), to judge and avenge His people (Isa. 26:21); or, "out of His holy" *temple*, contemptible and incomplete as it looked then when Zechariah urged them to rebuild it [CALVIN]. But the call to all to "be silent" is rather when God has come forth from heaven where so long He has dwelt unseen, and is about to inflict vengeance on the foe, *before* taking up His dwelling in Zion and the temple. However, Psalm 50:1, 2 ("Out of Zion"), 3 (cf. Hab. 2:3), 4, favors CALVIN's view. God is now "silent" while the Gentile foe speaks arrogance against His people; but "our God shall come and *no longer keep silence*"; then in turn must all flesh "be silent" before Him.

CHAPTER 3

Vss. 1-10. FOURTH VISION. *Joshua the high priest before the angel of Jehovah; accused by Satan, but justified by Jehovah through Messiah the coming Branch.* **1.** Joshua as high priest (Hag. 1:1) represents "Jerusalem" (vs. 2), or the elect people, put on its trial, and "plucked" narrowly "out of the fire." His attitude, "standing before the Lord," is that of a high priest ministering before the altar erected previously to the building of the temple (Ezra 3:2, 3, 6; Ps. 135:2). Yet, in this position, by reason of his own and his people's sins, he is represented as on his and their trial (Num. 35:12). **he showed me**—"He" is *the interpreting angel.* Jerusalem's (Joshua's) "filthy garments" (vs. 3) are its sins which had hitherto brought down God's judgments. The "change of raiment" implies its restoration to God's favor. Satan suggested to the Jews that so consciously polluted a priesthood and people could offer no acceptable sacrifice to God, and therefore they might as well desist from the building of the temple. Zechariah encourages them by showing that their demerit does not disqualify them for the work, as they are accepted in the righteousness of another, their great High Priest, the Branch (vs. 8), a scion of their own royal line of David (Isa. 11:1). The full accomplishment of Israel's justification and of Satan the accuser's being "rebuked" finally, is yet future (Rev. 12:10). Cf. Revelation 11:8, wherein "Jerusalem," as here, is shown to be meant primarily, though including the whole Church in general (cf. Job 1:9). **Satan**—the *Hebrew* term meaning "adversary" in a law court: as *devil* is the *Greek* term, meaning *accuser*. Mes-

siah, on the other hand, is "advocate" for His people in the court of heaven's justice (I John 2:1). **standing at his right hand**—the usual position of a *prosecutor* or *accuser* in court, as the left hand was the position of the defendant (Ps. 109:6). The "angel of the Lord" took the same position just before another high priest was about to beget the forerunner of Messiah (Luke 1:11), who supplants Satan from his place as accuser. Some hence explain Jude 9 as referring to this passage: "the body of Moses" being thus *the Jewish Church*, for which Satan contended as his by reason of its sins; just as the "body of Christ" is *the Christian Church*. However, Jude 9 plainly speaks of the literal body of Moses, the resurrection of which at the transfiguration Satan seems to have opposed on the ground of Moses' error at Meribah; the same divine rebuke, "the Lord rebuke thee," checked Satan in contending for judgment against Moses' body, as checked him when demanding judgment against the Jewish Church, to which Moses' body corresponds. **2. the Lord**—JEHOVAH, hereby identified with the "angel of the Lord (Jehovah)" (vs. 1). **rebuke thee**—twice repeated to express the certainty of Satan's accusations and machinations against Jerusalem being frustrated. Instead of lengthened argument, Jehovah *silences* Satan by the one plea, viz., God's *choice.* **chosen Jerusalem**—(Rom. 9:16; 11:5). The conclusive answer. If the issue rested on Jerusalem's merit or demerit, condemnation must be the award; but Jehovah's "choice" (John 15:16) rebuts Satan's charge against Jerusalem (ch. 1:17; 2:16; Rom. 8:33, 34, 37), represented by Joshua (cf. in the great atonement, Lev. 16:6-20, etc.), not that she may continue in sin, but be freed from it (vs. 7). **brand plucked out of ... fire**—(Amos 4:11; I Pet. 4:18; Jude 23). Herein God implies that His acquittal of Jerusalem is not that He does not recognize her sin (vss. 3, 4, 9), but that having punished her people for it with a seventy years' captivity, He on the ground of His *electing* love has delivered her from the fiery ordeal; and when once He has begun a deliverance, as in this case, He will perfect it (Ps. 89:30-35; Phil. 1:6). **3. filthy garments**—symbol of sin (Prov. 30:12; Isa 4:4; 64:6); proving that it is not on the ground of His people's righteousness that He accepts them. Here primarily the "filthy garments" represent the abject state temporally of the priesthood and people at the return from Babylon. Yet he "stood before the angel." Abject as he was, he was *before Jehovah's eye,* who graciously accepts His people's services, though mixed with sin and infirmity. **4. those that stood before him**—the ministering angels (cf. the phrase in I Kings 10:8; Dan. 1:5). **Take away the filthy garments**—In vs. 9 it is "remove the iniquity of *that land*"; therefore Joshua represents the land. **from him**—lit., "from upon him"; pressing upon him as an overwhelming burden. **change of raiment**—festal robes of the high priest, most costly and gorgeous; symbol of Messiah's imputed righteousness (Matt. 22:11). The restoration of the glory of the priesthood is implied: first, partially, at the completion of the second temple; fully realized in the great High Priest *Jesus,* whose name is identical with *Joshua* (Heb. 4:8), the Representative of Israel, the "kingdom of priests" (Exod. 19:6); once clad in the filthy garments of our vileness, but being the chosen of the Father (Isa. 42:1; 44:1; 49:1-3), He hath by death ceased from sin, and in garments of glory entered the heavenly holy place as our High Priest (Heb. 8:1; 9:24). Then, as the consequence (I Pet. 2:5), realized in the Church generally (Luke

5:22; Rev. 19:8), and in Israel in particular (Isa. 1:10, cf. 3:6; 66:21). **5. And I said**—Here the prophet, rejoicing at the change of raiment so far made, interposes to ask for the crowning assurance that the priesthood would be fully restored, viz., me putting *the miter* or priestly turban on Joshua: is *fair* color symbolizing the official purity of the order restored. He does not command, but prays; not "Set," but "Let them set." *Vulgate* and *Syriac* version read it, *"He* then said," which is the easier reading; but the very difficulty of the present *Hebrew* reading makes it less likely to come from a modern corrector of the text. **angel of . . . Lord stood by**—the Divine Angel had been sitting (the posture of a judge, Dan. 7:9); now He "stands" to see that Zechariah's prayer be executed, and then to give the charge (vss. 6, 7). **6. protested**—proceeded *solemnly to declare.* A forensic term for an affirmation on oath (Heb. 6:17, 18). God thus solemnly states the end for which the priesthood is restored—the people, His own glory in their obedience and pure worship, and their consequent promotion to heavenly honor. **7.** God's *choice* of Jerusalem (vs. 2) was unto its sanctification (John 15:16; Rom. 1:29); hence the charge here which connects the promised blessing with obedience. **my charge**—the ordinances, ritual and moral (Num. 3:28, 31, 32, 38; Josh. 1:7-9; I Kings 2:3; Ezek. 44:16). **judge my house**—Thou shalt long preside over the temple ceremonial as high priest (Lev. 10:10; Ezek. 44:23; Mal. 2:7) [GROTIUS]. Or, rule over My house, i.e., My people [MAURER] (Num. 12:7; Hos. 8:1). We know from Deuteronomy 17:9 that the priest judged cases. He was not only to obey the Mosaic institute himself, but to see that it was obeyed by others. God's people are similarly to exercise judgment hereafter, as the reward of their present faithfulness (Dan. 7:18, 22; Luke 19:17; I Cor. 6:2); by virtue of their royal priesthood (Rev. 1:6). **keep my courts**—guard My house from profanation. **places to walk**—free ingress and egress (I Sam. 18:16; I Kings 3:7; 15:17), so that thou mayest go through these ministering angels who stand by Jehovah (ch. 4:14; 6:5; I Kings 23:19) into His presence, discharging thy priestly function. In Ezekiel 42:4 the same *Hebrew* word is used of a *walk* before the priests' chambers in the future temple. Zechariah probably refers here to such a *walk* or *way;* Thou shalt not merely walk among priests like thyself, as in the old temple *walks,* but among the very angels as thine associates. HENGSTENBERG translates, "I will give thee *guides* (from) among these . . . ." But there is no "from" in the *Hebrew; English Version* is therefore better. Priests are called *angels* or "messengers" (Mal. 2:7); they are therefore thought worthy to be associated with heavenly angels. So these latter are present at the assemblies of true Christian worshippers (1 Cor. 11:10; cf. Eccles. 5:6; Eph. 3:10; Rev. 22:9). **8. Hear**—On account of the magnitude of what He is about to say, He at once demands solemn attention. **thy fellows that sit before thee**—thy subordinate colleagues in the priesthood; not that they were actually then *sitting before him;* but their usual posture in consultations was on chairs or benches before him, while he sat on an elevated seat as their president. **they are**—From speaking to Joshua He passes to speaking *of him and them,* in the third person, to the attendant angels (cf. vs. 9). **men wondered at**—*Hebrew,* "men of wonder," i.e., having a typical character (Isa. 8:18; 20:3; Ezek. 12:11; 24:24). Joshua the high priest typifies Messiah, as Joshua's "fellows" typify believers whom Messiah admits to share His Priesthood (I Pet. 2:5; Rev. 5:10). This, its typical character, then, is a pledge to assure the desponding Jews that the priesthood shall be preserved till the great Antitype comes. There may be also an indirect reproof of the unbelief of the multitude who "wonder" at God's servants and even at God's Son incredulously (Ps. 71:7; Isa. 8:18; 53:1, etc.). **behold**—marking the greatness of what follows. **my servant**—the characteristic title of Messiah (Isa. 42:1; 49:3; 50:10; 52:13; 53:11; Ezek. 34:23, 24). **the Branch**—Messiah, a tender branch from the almost extinct royal line of David (ch. 6:12; Isa. 4:2; 11:1; Jer. 23:5; 33:15). Luke 1:78, where for "day spring," "branch" may be substituted (Mal. 4:2, however, favors *English Version*). The reference cannot be to Zerubbabel (as GROTIUS thinks), for *he* was then in the full discharge of his office, whereas "the Branch" here is regarded as future. **9. For**—expressing the ground for encouragement to the Jews in building the temple: I (Jehovah) have laid the (foundation) stone as the chief architect, before (in the presence of) Joshua, by "the hand of Zerubbabel" (ch. 4:10; Ezra 3:8-13), so that your labor in building shall not be vain. Antitypically, the (foundation) stone alluded to is Christ, before called "the Branch." Lest any should think from that term that His kingdom is weak, He now calls it "the stone," because of its solidity and strength whereby it is to be the foundation of the Church, and shall crush all the world kingdoms (Ps. 118:22; cf. Isa. 28:16; Dan. 2:45; Matt. 21:42; I Cor. 3:11; I Pet. 2:6, 7). The angel pointing to the chief stone lying before Him, intimates that a deeper mystery than the material temple is symbolized. MOORE thinks the "stone" is *the Jewish Church,* which Jehovah engages watchfully to guard. *The temple,* rather, is that symbolically. But the antitype of the foundation *stone* is Messiah. **upon one stone shall be seven eyes**—viz., the watchful "eyes" of Jehovah's care ever fixed "upon" it (ch. 4:10) [MAURER]. The eye is the symbol of *Providence:* "seven," of *perfection* (Rev. 5:6; cf. II Chron. 16:9; Ps. 32:8). Antitypically, "the seven eyes upon the stone" are the eyes of all angels (I Tim. 3:16), and of all saints (John 3:14, 15; 12:32), and of the patriarchs and prophets (John 8:56; I Pet. 1:10, 11), fixed on Christ; above all, the eyes of the Father ever rest with delight on Him. CALVIN (perhaps better) considers *the seven eyes* to be *carved on the stone,* i.e., not the eyes of the Father and of angels and saints ever *fixed on* Him, but *His own* sevenfold (perfect) fullness of grace, and of gifts of the Spirit (Isa. 11:2, 3; John 1:16; 3:34; Col. 1:19; 2:9), and *His* watchful providence now for the Jews in building the temple, and always for His Church, His spiritual temple. Thus the "stone" is not as other stones senseless, but *living* and full of eyes of perfect intelligence (I Pet. 2:4, "a *living* stone"), who not only attracts the eyes (John 12:32) of His people, but emits illumination so as to direct them to Him. **engrave . . . graving**—implying Messiah's exceeding beauty and preciousness; alluding to the polished stones of the temple: Christ excelled them, as much as God who "prepared His body" (Heb. 10:5; cf. John 2:21) is superior to all human builders. **remove . . . iniquity of that land in one day**—i.e., the iniquity and its consequences, viz., the punishment to which the Jews heretofore had been subjected (Hag. 1:6, 9-11). The remission of sin is the fountain of every other blessing. The "one day" of its *removal* is primarily the day of national atonement celebrated after the completion of the

temple (Lev. 23:27) on the tenth day of the seventh
month. Antitypically, the atonement by Messiah
for all men, *once for all* ("one day") offered, needing
no repetition like the Mosaic sacrifices (Heb. 10:10,
12, 14). **10. under . . . vine . . . fig tree**—emblem
of tranquil prosperity (I Kings 4:25). Type of spiritual *peace* with God through Christ (Rom. 5:1);
and of millennial blessedness (Mic. 4:4).

CHAPTER 4

Vss. 1-14. FIFTH VISION. *The golden candlestick and the two olive trees. The temple shall be
completed by the aid of God's Spirit.* **1. waked
me**—The prophet was lying in a state of ecstatic
slumber with astonishment at the previous vision.
"Came again, and waked me," does not imply that
the angel had departed and now returned, but is an
idiom for "waked me again." **2. candlestick**—
symbolizing the Jewish theocracy; and ultimately,
the Church of which the Jewish portion is to be the
head: the *light-bearer* (so the original is of "lights,"
Matt. 5:14, 16; Phil. 2:15) to the world. **all . . .
gold**—all pure in doctrine and practice, precious and
indestructible; such is the true ideal of the Church;
such she shall be (Ps. 45:13). **bowl upon the top**—
In the candlestick of the tabernacle the *plural* is
used, *bowls* (Exod. 25-31). The *Hebrew* implies
that it was the *fountain* of supply of oil to the lamps.
Christ at the head ("on the top") of the Church is
the true fountain, *of* whose *fulness of the Spirit all
we receive grace* (John 1:16). **his seven lamps**—
united in one stem; so in Exodus 25:32. But in
Revelation 1:12 the seven candlesticks are separate.
The Gentile churches will not realize their unity
till the Jewish Church as the stem unites all the
lamps in one candlestick (Rom. 11:16-24). The
"seven lamps," in Revelation 4:5, are the "seven
Spirits of God." **seven pipes**—feeding tubes, seven
apiece from the "bowl" to each lamp (see *Margin*)
[MAURER and CALVIN]; lit., "seven and seven":
forty-nine in all. The greater the number of oil-
feeding pipes, the brighter the light of the lamps.
The explanation in vs. 6 is, that man's power by itself can neither retard nor advance God's work, that
the real motive-power is God's *Spirit*. The seven
times seven imply the manifold modes by which
the Spirit's grace is imparted to the Church in her
manifold work of enlightening the world. **3. two
olive trees**—supplying oil to the bowl. The Holy
Ghost, who fills with His fulness Messiah (the
anointed: the "bowl"), from whom flow supplies of
grace to the Church. **by it**—lit., "upon it," i.e.,
growing so as somewhat to overtop it. For the
explanation of the "two" see vss. 12, 14. **4. The**
prophet is instructed in the truths meant, that we
may read them with the greater reverence and attention [CALVIN]. **5. Knowest thou not . . .**—Not a
reproof of his ignorance, but a stimulus to reflection
on the mystery. **No, my lord**—ingenious confession of ignorance; as a little child he casts himself
for instruction at the feet of the Lord. **6. Not by
might . . . but by my Spirit**—As the lamps burned
continually, supplied with oil from a source (the
living olive trees) which man did not make, so
Zerubbabel need not be disheartened because of
his weakness; for as the work is one to be effected
by the living Spirit (cf. Hag. 2:5) of God, man's
weakness is no obstacle, for God's might will perfect strength out of weakness (Hos. 1:7; II Cor. 12:
10; Heb. 11:34). "Might and power" express human strength of every description, physical, mental,

moral. Or, "might" is the strength *of many* (an
"army,"); "power," that *of one man* [PEMBELLUS].
God can save, "whether with many, or with them
that have no power" (II Chron. 14:11; cf. I Sam.
14:6). So in the conversion of sinners (I Cor. 3:6;
II Cor. 10:4). "Zerubbabel" is addressed as the
chief civil authority in directing the work. **7.** All
mountain-like obstacles (Isa. 40:4; 49:11) in *Zerubbabel's* way shall be removed, so that the crowning
topstone shall be put on, and the completion of the
work be acknowledged as wholly of "grace." Antitypically, the antichristian last foe of Israel, the
obstacle preventing her establishment in Palestine,
about to be crushed before Messiah, is probably
meant (Jer. 51:25; Dan. 2:34, 44; Matt. 21:44).
bring forth the headstone—Primarily, bring it forth
from the place where it was chiselled and give it to
the workmen to put on the top of the building. It
was customary for chief magistrates to lay the
foundation, and also the crowning top-stone (cf.
Ezra 3:10). Antitypically, the reference is to the
time when the full number of the spiritual Church
shall be completed, and also when "all Israel shall
be saved" (cf. Rom. 11:26; Heb. 11:40; 12:22, 23;
Rev. 7:4—9). **Grace, grace**—The repetition expresses, *Grace* from first to last (*Margin*, Isa. 26:
3). Thus the Jews are urged to pray perseveringly and earnestly that the same grace which completed it may always preserve it. "Shoutings" of acclamation accompanied the foundation of the literal
temple (Ezra 3:11, 13). So shoutings of "Hosanna" greeted the Saviour in entering Jerusalem
(Matt. 21:9), when about to complete the purchase
of salvation by His death: His Body being the second
temple, or place of God's inhabitation (John 2:20,
21). So when the full number of the saints and of
Israel is complete, and God shall say, "It is done,"
then again shall "a great voice of much people in
heaven" attribute all to the "grace" of God, saying,
"Alleluia! Salvation, and glory, and honor, and
power, unto the Lord our God" (Rev. 19:1, 6).
Psalm 118:22 regards Him as "the headstone of the
corner," i.e., the *foundation*-stone. Cf. the angels'
acclamations at His birth, Luke 2:14. Here it is
the *top-stone*. Messiah is not only the "Author,"
but also the Finisher (Heb. 12:2). "Grace" is
ascribed "unto it," i.e. the stone, Messiah. Hence
the benediction begins, "The *grace* of the Lord Jesus
Christ" (II Cor. 13:14). **9. Zerubbabel . . . shall
. . . finish it**—(Ezra 6:15) in the sixth year of Darius'
reign. **Lord . . . sent me unto you**—(ch. 2:9). The
Divine Angel announces that in what He has just
spoken, He has been commissioned by God the
Father. **10. who . . . despised . . . small things**—He
reproves their ungrateful unbelief, which they felt
because of the humble beginning, compared with
the greatness of the undertaking; and encourages
them with the assurance that their progress in the
work, though small, was an earnest of great and
final success, because Jehovah's eye is upon Zerubbabel and the work, to support Him with His favor.
Contrast, "great is *the day* of Jezreel" (Hos. 1:11)
with "the day of *small* things" here. **they shall rejoice . . . with those seven; they** *are* **the eyes of the
Lord**—rather, "they, *even* those seven eyes of the
Lord (cf. ch. 3:9), which . . . shall rejoice and see
(i.e., rejoicingly see) the plummet (lit., the "stone
of tin") in the hand of Zerubbabel" [MOORE]; the
plummet in his hand indicating that the work is going forward to its completion. The *Hebrew*
punctuation, however, favors *English Version*, of
which the sense is, They who incredulously "despised" such "small" beginnings of the work as are

made now, shall rejoicingly see its going on to completion under Zerubbabel, "with (*the aid of*) those seven," viz., the "seven eyes upon one stone" (ch. 3:9): which are explained, "They are the eyes of the Lord which . . . " [PEMBELLUS]. So differently do men and Jehovah regard the "small" beginnings of God's work (Ezra 3:12; Hag. 2:3). Men "despised" the work in its early stage: God rejoicingly regards it, and shall continue to do so. **run to and fro . . .** —Nothing in the whole earth escapes the eye of Jehovah, so that He can ward off all danger from His people, come from what quarter it may, in prosecuting His work (Prov. 15:3; I Cor. 16:9). **11, 12.** Zechariah three times (vss. 4, 11, 12) asks as to the two olives before he gets an answer; the question becomes more minute each time. What he at first calls "two olive trees," he afterwards calls "branches," as on closer looking he observes that the "branches" of the trees are the channels through which a continual flow of oil dropped into the bowl of the lamps (vs. 2), and that this is the purpose for which the two olive trees stand beside the candlestick. Primarily, the "two" refer to Joshua and Zerubbabel. God, says AUBERLEN, at each of the transition periods of the world's history has sent great men to guide the Church. So the two witnesses shall appear before the destruction of Antichrist. Antitypically, "the two anointed ones" (vs. 14) are the twofold supports of the Church, the civil power (answering to Zerubbabel) and the ecclesiastical (answering to Joshua, the high priest), which in the restored Jewish polity and temple shall "stand by," i.e., minister to "the Lord of the whole earth," as He shall be called in the day that He sets up His throne in Jerusalem (ch. 14:9; Dan. 2:44; Rev. 11: 15). Cf. the description of the offices of the "priests" and the "prince" (Isa. 39:23 and Ezek. 44, 45, 46). As in Revelation 11:3, 4, the "two witnesses" are identified with the two olive trees and the two candlesticks. WORDSWORTH explains them to mean the Law and the Gospel: the two Testaments that *witness* in the Church for the truth of God. But this is at variance with the sense here, which requires Joshua and Zerubbabel to be primarily meant. So Moses (the prophet and lawgiver) and Aaron (the high priest) ministered to the Lord among the covenant people at the exodus; Ezekiel (the priest) and Daniel (a ruler) in the Babylonian captivity; so it shall be in restored Israel. Some think Elijah will appear again (cf. the transfiguration, Matt. 17:3, 11, with Mal. 4:4, 5; John 1:21) with Moses. Revelation 11:6, which mentions the very miracles performed by Elijah and Moses (shutting heaven so as not to rain, and turning water into blood), favors this (cf. Exod. 7:19; I Kings 17:1; Luke 4:25; Jas. 5:16, 17). The period is the same, "three years and six months"; the scene also is in Israel (Rev. 11:8), "where our Lord was crucified." It is supposed that for the first three and a half years of the hebdomad (Dan. 9), God will be worshipped in the temple; in the latter three and a half years, Antichrist will break the covenant (Dan. 9:27), and set himself up in the temple to be worshipped as God (II Thess. 2:4). The witnesses prophesy the former three and a half years, while corruptions prevail and faith is rare (Luke 18:8); then they are slain and remain dead three and a half years. Probably, besides individual witnesses and literal years, there is a fulfilment in long periods and general witnesses, such as the Church and the Word, the civil and religious powers so far as they have witnessed for God. So "the

beast" in Revelation answers to the civil power of the apostasy; "the false prophet" to the spiritual power. Man needs the *priest* to atone for guilt, and the *prophet king* to teach holiness with kingly authority. These two typically united in Melchisedek were divided between two till they meet in Messiah, the Antitype. Zechariah 6:11-13 accords with this. The Holy Spirit in this His twofold power of applying to man the grace of the *atonement,* and that of *sanctification,* must in one point of view be meant by the two olive trees which supply the bowl at the top of the candlestick (i.e., Messiah at the head of the Church); for it is He who filled Jesus with all the fulness of His unction (John 3:34). But this does not exclude the primary application to *Joshua and Zerubbabel,* "anointed" (vs. 14) with grace to minister to the Jewish Church: and so applicable to the twofold supports of the Church which are anointed with the Spirit, the *prince* and the *priest,* or *minister.* **through**—lit., "by the hand of," i.e., by the agency of. **branches** —lit., "ears"; so the olive branches are called, because as ears are full of grain, so the olive branches are full of olives. **golden** *oil*—lit., "gold," i.e., gold-like liquor. **out of themselves**—Ordinances and ministers are channels of grace, not the grace itself. The supply comes not from a dead reservoir of oil, but through living olive trees (Ps. 52:8; Rom. 12:1) fed by God. **13. Knowest thou not**—God would awaken His people to zeal in learning His truth. **14. anointed ones**—lit., "sons of oil" (*Margin,* Isa. 5:1). Joshua the high priest, and Zerubbabel the civil ruler, must first be anointed with grace themselves, so as to be the instruments of furnishing it to others (cf. I John 2:20, 27).

CHAPTER 5

Vss. 1-4. SIXTH VISION. THE FLYING ROLL. *The fraudulent and perjuring transgressors of the law shall be extirpated from Judea.* **1. flying roll**— of papyrus, or dressed skins, used for writing on when paper was not known. It was inscribed with the words of the curse (Deut. 27:15-26; 28:15-68). Being written implied that its contents were beyond all escape or repeal (Ezek. 2:9). Its "flying" shows that its curses were ready swiftly to visit the transgressors. It was unrolled, or else its dimensions could not have been seen (vs. 2). Being open to all, none could say in excuse he knew not the law and the curses of disobedience. As the previous visions intimated God's favor in restoring the Jewish state, so this vision announces judgment, intimating that God, notwithstanding His favor, did not approve of their sins. Being written on both sides, "on this and on that side" (vs. 3), VATABLUS connects it with the two tables of the law (Exod. 32: 15), and implies its comprehensiveness. One side denounced "him that sweareth falsely (vs. 4) by God's name," according to the third commandment of *the first table,* duty to God; the other side denounced *theft,* according to the eighth commandment, which is in *the second table,* duty to one's neighbor. **2. length . . . twenty cubits . . . breadth . . . ten cubits**—thirty feet by fifteen, the dimensions of the temple porch (I Kings 6:3), where the law was usually read, showing that it was divinely authoritative in the theocracy. Its large size implies the great number of the curses contained. The *Hebrew* for "roll" or "volume" is used of the law (Ps. 40:7). **3. curse . . . earth**—(Mal. 4:6). The Gentiles are amenable to the curse of the law, as they have its substance, so far as they have not seared and corrupted conscience, written on their hearts (Rom. 2:15). cut off—lit., "cleared away." as on this side . . . as on that side—both sides of the *roll* [VATABLUS]. From this place . . . from this place (repeated twice, as "the house" is repeated in vs. 4) [MAURER]; so "hence" is used, Gen. 37:17 (or, "on this and on that side," i.e., *on every side*) [HENDERSON]. None can escape, sin where he may: for God from one side to the other shall call all without exception to judgment [CALVIN]. God will not spare even "this place," Jerusalem, when it sins [PEMBELLUS]. *English Version* seems to take VATABLUS' view. according to it—according as it is written. 4. The "theft" immediately meant is similar sacrilege to that complained of in Nehemiah 13:10; Malachi 3:8. They robbed God by neglecting to give Him His due in building His house, while they built their own houses, forswearing their obligations to Him; therefore, the "houses" they build shall be "consumed" with God's "curse." Probably literal theft and perjury accompanied their virtual theft and perjury as to the temple of God (Mal. 3:5). Stealing and perjury go together; for the covetous and fraudulent perjure themselves by God's name without scruple (see Prov. 30:9). enter . . . the house—In vain they guard and shut themselves up who incur the curse; it will inevitably enter even when they think themselves most secure. consume . . . timber . . . stones—not leaving a vestige of it. So the "stones" and "timber" of the house of a leper (type of the sinner) were to be utterly removed (Lev. 14:15; cf. I Kings 18:38).

5-11. SEVENTH VISION. THE WOMAN IN THE EPHAH. *Wickedness and idolatry removed from the Holy Land to Babylon, there to mingle with their kindred elements.* The "ephah" is the Hebrew dry measure containing about 37 quarts. Alluding to the previous vision as to theft and perjury: the ephah which, by falsification of the measure, they made the instrument of defrauding, shall be made the instrument of their punishment [GROTIUS]. Cf. "this is their resemblance" (vs. 6), i.e., this is a representation of what the Jews have done, and what they shall suffer. Their total dispersion ("the land of Shinar" being the emblem of the various Gentile lands of their present dispersion) is herein foretold, when the *measure* (to which the ephah alludes) of their sins should be full. The former vision denounces judgment on individuals; this one, on the whole state: but enigmatically, not to discourage their present building [PEMBELLUS]. Rather, the vision is consolatory after the preceding one [CALVIN]. Idolatry and its kindred sins, covetousness and fraud (denounced in the vision of the roll), shall be removed far out of the Holy Land to their own congenial soil, never to return (so ch. 3: 9; Isa. 27:9; 52:1; 60:21; Jer. 50:20; Zeph. 3:13). For more than 2000 years, ever since the Babylonian exile, the Jews have been free from *idolatry;* but the full accomplishment of the prophecy is yet future, when *all* sin shall be purged from Israel on their return to Palestine, and conversion to Christ. 5. went forth—The interpreting angel had withdrawn after the vision of the roll to receive a fresh revelation from the Divine Angel to communicate to the prophet. 6. This is their resemblance— lit., "eye" (cf. Ezek. 1:4, 5, 16). HENGSTENBERG translates, "Their (the people's) eye" was all directed to evil. But *English Version* is better. "This is the appearance (i.e., an image) of the Jews in all *the land*" (not as *English Version,* "in all *the earth*"), i.e., of the wicked Jews. This—Here used of what

was *within* the ephah, not the ephah itself. 7. lifted up—The cover is lifted off the ephah to let the prophet see the female personification of "wickedness" within, about to be removed from Judea. The cover being "of lead," implies that the "woman" cannot escape from the ponderous load which presses her down. talent—lit., "a round piece": hence a talent, a weight of 125 pounds troy. woman—cf. for comparison of "wickedness" to a *woman,* Proverbs 2:16; 5:3, 4. In personifying abstract terms, the feminine is used, as the idea of giving birth to life is associated with woman. 8. wickedness—lit., *the* wickedness: implying wickedness in its peculiar development. Cf. "*the* man of sin," II Thessalonians 2:3. cast it—i.e., her, Wickedness, who had moved more freely while the heavy lid was partially lifted off. weight—lit., "stone," i.e., round mass. 9. The agents to carry away the "woman," are, consistently with the image, "women." God makes the wicked themselves the agents of punishing and removing wickedness. "Two" are employed, as one is not enough to carry such a load [MAURER]. Or, the Assyrians and Babylonians, who carried away idolatry in the persons, respectively, of Israel and Judah [HENDERSON]. As two "anointed ones" (ch. 4:14) stand by the Lord as His ministers, so *two* winged women execute His purpose here in removing the embodiment of "wickedness": answering to the "mystery of iniquity" (the LXX here in Zechariah uses the same words as Paul and "the man of sin," whom the Lord shall destroy with the spirit of His mouth and the brightness of His coming, II Thess. 2:3, 7, 8). Their "wings" express velocity. The "stork" has long and wide wings, for which reason it is specified; also it is a migratory bird. The "wind" helps the rapid motion of the wings. The being "lifted up between heaven and earth" implies open execution of the judgment before the eyes of all. As the "woman" here is removed to Babylon as her own dwelling, so the woman in the Apocalypse of St. John is Babylon (Rev. 17:3-5). 11. To build . . . house in . . . Shinar—Babylonia (Gen. 10:10), the capital of the God-opposed world kingdoms, and so representing in general the seat of irreligion. As the "building of houses" in Babylon (Jer. 29:5, 28) by the Jews themselves expressed their long exile there, so the building of an house for "wickedness" there implies its permanent stay. set . . . upon her own base—fixed there as in its proper place. "Wickedness" being cast out of Judah, shall for ever dwell with the antichristian apostates (of whom Babylon is the type), who shall reap the fruit of it, which they deserve.

CHAPTER 6

Vss. 1-8. EIGHTH VISION. THE FOUR CHARIOTS. 1. four chariots—symbolizing the various dispensations of Providence towards the Gentile nations which had been more or less brought into contact with Judea; especially in punishing Babylon. Cf. vs. 8 ("the north country," i.e., Babylon); ch. 1:15; 2:6. The number "four" is specified not merely in reference to the four quarters of the horizon (implying *universal* judgments), but in allusion to the *four* world kingdoms of Daniel. from between two mountains—the valley of Jehoshaphat, between Moriah and Mount Olivet [MOORE]; or the valley between Zion and Moriah, where the Lord is (ch. 2:10), and whence He sends forth His ministers of judgment on the heathen [MAURER]. The temple on Mount Moriah is the symbol of the theocracy; hence the nearest spot accessible to chariots in the valley below is the most suitable for a vision affecting Judah in relation to the Gentile world powers. The chariot is the symbol of war, and so of judgments. **of brass**—the metal among the ancients representing hard solidity; so the immovable and resistless firmness of God's people (cf. Jer. 1:18). CALVIN explains the "two mountains" thus: The secret purpose of God from eternity does not come forth to view before the execution, but is hidden and kept back irresistibly till the fit time, as it were *between* lofty *mountains; the chariots* are the various changes wrought in nations, which, as swift heralds, announce to us what before we knew not. The "two" may thus correspond to the number of the "olive trees" (ch. 4:3); the *allusion* to the "two mountains" near the temple is not necessarily excluded in this view. HENDERSON explains them to be the Medo-Persian kingdom, represented by the "two horns" (Dan. 8:3, 4), now employed to execute God's purpose in punishing the nations; but the prophecy reaches far beyond those times. **2. red**—implying carnage. **black**—representing sorrow; also famine (Rev. 6:5, 6; cf. ch. 1:8). **3. white**—implying joy and victory [CALVIN]. **grizzled**—piebald. Implying a *mixed* dispensation, partly prosperity, partly adversity. All four dispensations, though various in character to the Gentile nation, portended alike good to God's people. **bay**—rather, "strong" or "fleet"; so *Vulgate* [GESENIUS]. The horses have this epithet, whose part it was to "walk to and fro through the earth" (vs. 7). However, LXX and *Chaldee* agree with *English Version* in referring the *Hebrew* to *color,* not strength. **4.** The prophet humbly and teachably seeks instruction from God, and therefore seeks not in vain. **5. four spirits of the heavens**—heavenly spirits who "stand before Jehovah" to receive God's commands (ch. 4:14; I Kings 22:19; Job 2:1; Luke 1:19) in heaven (of which Zion is the counterpart on earth, *Note,* vs. 1), and proceed with chariot speed (II Kings 6:17; Ps. 68:17) to execute them on earth in its four various quarters (Ps. 104: 4; Heb. 1:7, 14) [PEMBELLUS]. Or, the secret impulses of God which emanate from His counsel and providence; the prophet implies that all the revolutions in the world are from the Spirit of God and are as it were, His messengers or spirits [CALVIN]. **6. north country**—Babylon (*Note,* Jer. 1:14). The north is the quarter specified in particular whence Judah and Israel are hereafter to return to their own land (ch. 2:6; Jer. 3:18). "The black horses" go to Babylon, primarily to represent the awful desolation with which Darius visited it in the fifth year of his reign (two years after this prophecy) for revolting [HENDERSON]. The "white" go after the "black" horses to the same country; *two* sets being sent to it because of its greater cruelty and guilt in respect to Judea. The white represent Darius' triumphant subjugation of it [MOORE]. Rather, I think, the white are sent to victoriously subdue Medo-Persia, the second world kingdom, lying in the same quarter as Babylon, viz., north. **grizzled ... toward the south**—i.e., to Egypt, the other great foe of God's people. It, being a part of the Græco-Macedonian kingdom, stands for the whole of it, the third world kingdom. **7. bay**—rather the "fleet" (or "strong"). As the "red" are not otherwise mentioned, the epithet "fleet" (as the *Hebrew* for "bay" ought to be translated) in vs. 3 seems to apply to all four, and here especially to the "red." Their office is to complete hereafter the work al-

ready in part executed by the previous three who have stilled Babylon, Medo-Persia, and Græco-Macedonia; viz., to punish finally the last great foe of Israel, the final form assumed by the fourth world kingdom, Rome, which is to continue down to the second advent of Christ. Hence they "walk to and fro through the earth," counterworking Satan's "going to and fro in the earth" (Job 1:7; II Thess. 2:8, 9; I Tim. 4:1), in connection with the last awful development of the fourth world kingdom. Their "fleetness" is needed to counteract his restless activity; their red color implies the final great carnage (Ezek. 39; Rev. 19:17, 18, 21). **8. north ... quieted ... my spirit**—i.e., caused My *anger* to rest (*Margin,* Judg. 8:3; Eccles. 10:4; Ezek. 5:13; 16:42). Babylon alone of the four great world kingdoms had in Zechariah's time been finally punished; therefore, in its case alone does God now say His anger is satisfied; the others had as yet to expiate their sin; the fourth has still to do so.

9-15. NINTH VISION. THE CROWNING OF JOSHUA. The double crown is placed on Joshua's head, symbolizing that the true priesthood and the kingdom shall be conferred on the one Messiah. Cf. Hebrews 6:20; 7:1-21, on Melchizedek, who similarly combined the kingdom and priesthood as type of Messiah. **10. Take of** *them of* **the captivity**—Take *silver and gold* (vs. 11) *from* them. The three named came from Babylon (where some of the exiled Jews still were left) to present gifts of silver and gold towards the building of the temple. But in vss. 11, 14, "crowns" are directed to be made of them, then to be set on Joshua's head, and to be deposited in the temple as a memorial of the donors, until Messiah shall appear. **Heldai**—meaning "robust." Called *Helem* below. **Tobijah**—i.e., "the goodness of God." **Jedaiah**—i.e., "God knows." **which are come from Babylon**—This clause in the *Hebrew* comes after "Josiah son of Zephaniah." Therefore, MOORE thinks Josiah as well as the three "came from Babylon." But as he has a "house" at Jerusalem, he is plainly a resident, not a visitor. Therefore *English Version* is right; or MAURER, "Josiah son of Zephaniah, to *whom* they are come (as guests) from Babylon." **the same day**—No time was to be lost to mark the significancy of their coming from afar to offer gifts to the temple, typifying, in the double crown made of their gifts and set on Joshua's head, the gathering in of Israel's outcasts to Messiah hereafter, who shall then be recognized as the true king and priest. **11.** The high priest wore a crown above the miter (ch. 3:5; Lev. 8:9). Messiah shall wear many *crowns,* one surmounting the other (Rev. 19:12). It was a thing before unknown in the Levitical priesthood that the same person should wear at once the crown of a king and that of a high priest (Ps. 110:4; Heb. 5:10). Messiah shall be revealed fully in this twofold dignity when He shall "restore the kingdom to Israel" (Acts 1:6). **12. Behold, the man**—viz., shall arise. Pilate unconsciously spake God's will concerning Him, "*Behold* the man" (John 19:5). The sense here is, "Behold in Joshua a remarkable shadowing forth of Messiah." It is not for his own sake that the crown is placed on him, but as type of Messiah about to be at once king and priest. Joshua could not personally be crowned king, not being of the royal line of David, but only in his *representative* character. **Branch**—(*Note,* ch. 3:8; Isa. 4:2; Jer. 23:5; 33:15). **he shall grow up out of his place**—retaining the image of a "Branch"; "He shall sprout up from His place," i.e., the place peculiar to Him: not merely from Bethlehem or Nazareth, but by His own power, without man's aid, in His miraculous conception [HENDERSON]; a sense brought out in the original, "from under Himself," or "from (of) Himself" [CALVIN]. MOORE makes it refer to His growing lowly *in His place* of obscurity, "as a tender plant and a root out of a dry ground" (Isa. 53:2), for thirty years unknown except as the son of a carpenter. MAURER translates, "Under Him there shall be growth (in the Church)." *English Version* accords better with the *Hebrew* (cf. Exod. 10:23). The idea in a Branch is that Christ's glory is growing, not yet fully manifested as a full-grown tree. Therefore men reject Him now. **build the temple** —The promise of the future true building of the spiritual temple by Messiah (Matt. 16:18; I Cor. 3:17; II Cor. 6:16; Eph. 2:20-22; Heb. 3:3) is an earnest to assure the Jews, that the material temple will be built by Joshua and Zerubbabel, in spite of all seeming obstacles. It also raises their thoughts beyond the material to the spiritual temple, and also to the future glorious temple, to be reared in Israel under Messiah's superintendence (Ezek. 40, 41, 42, 43). The repetition of the same clause (vs. 13) gives emphasis to the statement as to Messiah's work. **13. bear the glory**—i.e., wear the insignia of the kingly glory, "the crowns" (Ps. 21:5; 102:16; Isa. 52:13). *He himself* shall bear the glory, not thou, Joshua, though thou dost bear the crowns. The Church's dignity is in her head alone, Christ. So Eliakim, type of Messiah, was to have "all the glory of his father's house hung upon him" (Isa. 22:24). **sit**—implying security and permanence. **priest . . . throne**—(Gen. 14:18; Ps. 110:4; Heb. 5:6, 10; 6:20; 7). **counsel of peace . . . between . . . both** —Joshua and Zerubbabel, the religious and civil authorities co-operating in the temple, typify the *peace*, or harmonious union, *between both* the kingly and priestly offices. The kingly majesty shall not depress the priestly dignity, nor the priestly dignity the kingly majesty [JEROME]. The peace of the Church, formerly sought for in the mutual "counsels" of the kings and the priests, who had been always distinct, shall be perfectly ensured by the concurrence of the two offices in the one Messiah, who by His mediatorial priesthood purchases it, and by His kingly rule maintains it. VITRINGA takes *"His"* throne" to be Jehovah the Father's. Thus it will be, "there shall be . . . peace between the Branch and Jehovah" [LUDOVICUS DE DIEU]. The other view is better, viz., *"Messiah's* throne." As Priest He expiates sin; as King, extirpates it. *"Counsel* of peace," implies that it is the plan of infinite "wisdom," whence Messiah is called "Counsellor" (Isa. 9:6; Eph. 1:8, 11; Heb. 6:17). Peace between the kingly and priestly attributes of Messiah implies the harmonizing of the conflicting claims of God's justice as a King, and His love as a Father and Priest. Hence is produced peace to man (Luke 2:14; Acts 10:36; Eph. 2:13-17). It is only by being pardoned through His atonement and ruled by His laws, that we can find "peace." The royal "throne" was always connected with the "temple," as is the case in the Apocalypse (Rev. 7: 15), because Christ is to be a king on His throne and a priest, and because the people, whose "king" the Lord is, cannot approach Him except by a priestly mediation [ROOS]. Jesus shall come to effect, by His presence (Isa. 11:4; Dan. 7:17), that which in vain is looked for, in His absence, by other means. He shall exercise His power mediatorially as priest on His throne (vs. 13); therefore His reign is for a limited period, which it could not be if it were the final and everlasting state of glory. But being for

a special purpose, to reconcile all things in this world, now disordered by sin, and so present it to God the Father that He may again for the first time since the fall come into direct connection with His creatures; therefore it is limited, forming the dispensation in the fulness of times (Eph. 1:10), when God shall gather in one all things in Christ, the final end of which shall be, "God all in all" (I Cor. 15:24-28). **14. the crowns shall be to Helem . . . a memorial**—deposited in the temple, to the honor of the donors; a memorial, too, of the coronation of Joshua, to remind all of Messiah, the promised antitypical king-priest, soon to come. Helem, the same as Heldai above. So Hen (i.e., "favor") is another name for Josiah (i.e., "God founds") above. The same person often had two names. **15. they . . . far off shall . . . build**—The reason why the crowns were made of gold received from afar, viz., from the Jews of Babylon, was to typify the conversion of the Gentiles to Messiah, King of Israel. This, too, was included in the "peace" spoken of in vs. 13 (Acts 2:39; Eph. 2:12-17). Primarily, however, the return of the dispersed Israelites "from afar" (Isa. 60:9) to the king of the Jews at Jerusalem is intended, to be followed, secondly, by the conversion of the Gentiles from "far off" (ch. 2:11; 8:22, 23; Isa. 60:10; 57:19). **build in the temple**—Christ "builds the temple" (vss. 12, 13; Heb. 3:3, 4): His people "build in the temple." Cf. Hebrews 3:2, "Moses *in* His house." **ye shall know . . .** —when the event corresponds to the prediction (ch. 2:9; 4:9). **this shall come to pass, if ye . . . obey . . .**—To the Jews of Zechariah's day a stimulus is given to *diligent* prosecution of the temple building, the work which it was meanwhile their duty to fulfil, relying on the hope of the Messiah afterwards to glorify it. The completion of the temple shall "come to pass," if ye diligently on your part "obey the Lord." It is not meant that their unbelief could set aside God's gracious purpose as to Messiah's coming. But there is, secondarily, meant, that Messiah's glory as priest-king of Israel shall not be manifested to the Jews till they turn to Him with obedient penitence. They meanwhile are cast away "branches" until they be grafted in again on the Branch and their own olive tree (ch. 38; 12:10-12; Matt. 23:39; Rom. 11:16-24).

CHAPTER 7

Vss. 1-14. II. DIDACTIC PART, CHAPS. 7, 8. OBEDIENCE, RATHER THAN FASTING, ENJOINED: ITS REWARD. **1. fourth year of . . . Darius**—two years after the previous prophecies (ch. 1:1, etc.). **Chisleu**—meaning "torpidity," the state in which nature is in November, answering to this month. **2. they . . . sent unto . . . house of God**—*The Jews* of the country sent to the house of God or congregation at Jerusalem. The altar was long since reared (Ezra 3:3), though the temple was not completed till two years afterwards (Ezra 6:15). The priests' duty was to give decision on points of the law (Deut. 17:9; Matt. 2:4). *Beth-el* is here used instead of *Beth-Jehovah,* because the religious authorities, rather than the house itself (designated Beth-Jehovah in next verse), are intended. The old Beth-el had long ceased to be the seat of idol worship, so that the name had lost its opprobrious meaning. "The house of the Lord" is used for the congregation of worshippers headed by their priests (ch. 3:7; Hos. 8:1). MAURER makes the "house of God" nominative to "sent." HENDERSON makes "Beth-el" so. **Sherezer**—an Assyrian name meaning, "Prefect of the treasury." **Regemmelech**—meaning, "The king's official." These names perhaps intimate the semi-heathen character of the inquirers, which may also be implied in the name "Beth-el" (*Hebrew* for "house of God"), so notorious once for its calf worship. They sent to *Jehovah's house* as their forefathers sent to old *Beth-el*, not in the spirit of true obedience. **pray before the Lord**—lit., "to entreat the face of," i.e., to offer sacifices, the accompaniment of prayers, to conciliate His favor (I Sam. 13:12). **3. Should I weep in the fifth month**—"I" represents here the people of God (cf. ch. 8:21). This rather favors MAURER'S view, taking "the house of God," *the congregation,* as nominative to "sent." Their hypocrisy appeared because they showed more concern about a ceremony of human institution (not improper in itself) than about moral obedience. If, too, they had trusted God's promise as to the restoration of Church and State, the fast would have now given place to joy, for which there was more cause than for grief [PEMBELLUS]. **to the prophets**—Haggai and Zechariah especially. *The tenth day of the fifth month* was kept a fast, being the anniversary of the destruction of Jerusalem (Jer. 52:12-14). They ask, Should the fast *be continued,* now that the temple and city are being restored? **separating myself**—sanctifying myself by separation, not only from food, but from all defilements (cf. Joel 2:16) as was usual in a solemn fast. **5. Speak unto all**—The question had been asked in the name of the people in general by Sherezer and Regemmelech. The self-imposed fast they were tired of, not having observed it in the spirit of true religion. **seventh month**—This fast was in memory of the murder of Gedaliah and those with him at Mizpah, issuing in the dispersion of the Jews (II Kings 25: 25, 26; Jer. 41:1-3). **did ye ... fast unto me?**—No; it was to gratify yourselves in hypocritical will-worship. If it had been "unto *Me*," ye would have "separated yourselves" not only from food, but from your sins (Isa. 58:3-7). They falsely made the fast an end intrinsically meritorious in itself, not a means towards God's glory in their sanctification. The true principle of piety, *reference to God,* was wanting: hence the emphatic repetition of "unto Me." Before settling questions as to the outward forms of piety (however proper, as in this case), the great question was as to piety itself; that being once settled, all their outward observances become sanctified, being "unto the Lord" (Rom. 14:6). **6. did not ye eat** *for yourselves*?—lit., "Is it not ye who eat?" i.e., it is not unto Me and My glory. It tends no more to My glory, your feasting than your fasting. **7. Should ye not hear the words**—rather, "Should ye not *do* the words," as their question naturally was as to what they should do (vs. 3); "hearing" is not mentioned till vs. 12. The sense is, It is not fasts that Jehovah requires of you, but that ye should keep His precepts given to you at the time when Jerusalem was in its integrity. Had ye done so then, ye would have had no occasion to institute fasts to commemorate its destruction, for it would never have been destroyed (vss. 9-14) [MAURER]. Or, as *Margin,* "*Are* not *these* the words" of the older prophets (Isa. 58:3; Jer. 14:12) which threatened a curse for disobedience, which the event has so awfully confirmed. If ye follow them in sin, ye must follow them in suffering. *English Version* is good sense: Ye inquire anxiously about the fasts, whereas ye ought to be anxious about *hearing* the lesson taught by the former prophets and verified in the nation's punishment; peni-

tence and obedience are required rather than fasts. **the plain**—southwest of Jerusalem. They then inhabited securely the region most unguarded. **9. speaketh**—implying that these precepts addressed to their ancestors were the requirements of Jehovah not merely then, but *now.* We must not only not hurt, but we must help our fellow men. God is pleased with such loving obedience, rather than with empty ceremonies. **10. imagine evil**—i.e., devise evil. LXX takes it, Harbor not the desire of revenge (Lev. 19:18). "Devise evil against one another" is simpler (Ps. 36:4; Mic. 2:1). **11. pulled away the shoulder**—lit., "presented a refractory shoulder"; an image from beasts refusing to bear the yoke (*Margin,* Neh. 9:29). **stopped ... ears**—(Isa. 6:10; Jer. 7:26; Acts 7:57). **12. hearts ... adamant**—(Ezek. 3:9; 11:19). **Lord ... sent in his Spirit by ... prophets**—i.e., sent by the former prophets *inspired with His Spirit.* **therefore ... great wrath**—(II Chron. 36:16). As they pushed from them the yoke of obedience, God laid on them the yoke of oppression. As they made their heart hard as adamant, God brake their hard hearts with judgments. Hard hearts must expect hard treatment. The harder the stone, the harder the blow of the hammer to break it. **3. he cried**—by His prophets. **they cried**—in their calamities. **I ... not hear**—retribution in kind (Prov. 1:24-26; Isa. 1:15; Mic. 3:4) **14. whirlwind**—of wrath (Nah. 1:3). **nations whom they knew not**—foreign and barbarous. **desolate after them**—after their expulsion and exile. It was ordered remarkably by God's providence, that no occupants took possession of it, but that during the Jews' absence it was reserved for them against their return after seventy years. **they laid ... desolate**—The Jews did so by their sins. The blame of their destruction lay with themselves, rather than with the Babylonians (II Chron. 36:21). **pleasant land**—Canaan. Lit., "the land of desire" (Jer. 3:19).

CHAPTER 8

Vss. 1-23. CONTINUATION OF THE SUBJECT IN CHAP. 7. *After urging them to obedience by the fate of their fathers, he urges them to it by promises of coming prosperity.* **2. jealous for Zion**—(ch. 1:14). **with great fury**—against her oppressors. **3. I am returned**—i.e., I am determined to return. My decree to that effect is gone forth. **Jerusalem ... city of truth**—i.e., faithful to her God, who is the God of truth (Isa. 1:21, 26; John 17:17). Never yet fully fulfilled, therefore still to be so. **the mountain of the Lord**—(Isa. 2:2, 3). **holy mountain**—(Jer. 31:23). **4.** So tranquil and prosperous shall the nation be that wars shall no longer prematurely cut off the people: men and women shall reach advanced ages. The promise of long life was esteemed one of the greatest blessings in the Jewish theocracy with its temporal rewards of obedience (Exod. 20:12; Deut. 4:40). Hence this is a leading feature in millennial blessedness (Isa. 65:20, 22). **for very age**—lit., "for multitude of days." **5. boys and girls playing**—implying security and a numerous progeny, accounted a leading blessing among the Jews. Contrast Jeremiah 6:11; 9:21. **6.** However impossible these things just promised by Me seem to you, they are not so with God. The "remnant" that had returned from the captivity, beholding the city desolate and the walls and houses in ruins, could hardly believe what God promised. The expression "remnant" glances at their ingratitude in rating so low God's power, though they had experienced it so "marvellously" displayed in their restoration. A great source of unbelief is, men "limit" God's power by their own (Ps. 78:19, 20, 41). **these days**—"of small things" (ch. 4:10), when such great things promised seemed incredible. MAURER, after JEROME, translates, "in *those* days"; i.e., if the thing which I promised to do in *those* days, seems "marvellous . . . ." **7. save my people from . . . east . . . west**—i.e., from every region (cf. Ps. 50:1; the "West" is lit., "the going down of the sun") to which they are scattered; they are now found especially in countries west of Jerusalem. The dispersion under Nebuchadnezzar was only to the east, viz., to Babylonia. The restoration, including a spiritual return to God (vs. 8), here foretold, must therefore be still future (Isa. 11:11, 12; 43:5, 6; Ezek. 37:21; Amos 9:14, 15; also ch. 13:9; Jer. 30:22; 31:1, 33). **8. in truth**—in good faith, both on their side and Mine: God being faithful to His everlasting covenant and enabling them by His Spirit to be faithful to Him. **9-13.** All adversities formerly attended them when neglecting to build the temple: but now God promises all blessings, as an encouragement to energy in the work. **hands . . . strong**—be of courageous mind (II Sam. 16:21), not merely in building, but in general, as having such bright prospects (vs. 13, etc.). **these days**—the time that had elapsed between the prophet's having spoken "these words" and the time (vs. 10; cf. Hag. 2:15-19) when they set about in earnest restoring the temple. **the prophets**—Haggai and Zechariah himself (Ezra 5:1, 2). The same prophets who promised prosperity at the foundation of the temple, now promised still greater blessings hereafter. **10. before these days**—before the time in which ye again proceeded with the building of the temple (vs. 9), viz., at the time that the temple lay neglected. **no hire for man . . . beast**—i.e., no produce of the field to repay the labor of man and beast on it (Hag. 1:6, 9, 10; 2:16). **neither . . . peace to him that went out or came in**—(II Chron. 15:5). No one could in safety do his business at home or abroad, in the city or in the country, whether going or returning. **because of the affliction**—so *sorely pressed* were they by the foe outside. MAURER translates, "Because of *the foe*" (Ezra 4:1). **every one against . . . neighbour**—There was internal discord, as well as foes from without. **11.** "But now that the temple has been built, I will not do as I had formerly done to those who returned from Babylon" [JEROME]. Henceforth I will bless you. **12. seed . . . prosperous**—i.e., shall not fail to yield abundantly (Hos. 2: 21,22; Hag. 2:19). Contrast with this verse Haggai 1:6, 9-11; 2:16. **dew**—especially beneficial in hot countries where rain is rare. **13. a curse**—As the heathen have made you another name for "a curse," wishing to your foes as bad a lot as yours (Jer. 24:9; 29:18); so your name shall be a formula of blessing, so that men shall say to their friend, May thy lot be as happy as that of Judah (Gen. 48:20). Including also the idea of the Jews being a source of blessing to the Gentile nations (Mic. 5:7; Zeph. 3: 20). The distinct mention of "Judah" and "Israel" proves that the prophecy has not yet had its full accomplishment, as *Israel* (the ten tribes) has never yet been restored, though *individuals* of Israel returned with Judah. **14. I thought**—I determined. **you**—i.e., your fathers, with whom ye are one; the Jewish Church of all ages being regarded as an organic whole (cf. Hag. 2:5; Matt. 23:31, 32). **repented not**—I changed not My purpose, because they changed not their mind (II Chron. 36:16). With the froward God shows Himself froward (Ps.

18:26). If the threatened punishment has been so unchangeably inflicted, much more will God surely give the promised blessing, which is so much more consonant to His nature (Jer. 31:28). **16, 17.** The promised blessings are connected with obedience. God's covenanted grace will lead those truly blessed by it to holiness, not licentiousness. **truth to . . . neighbour**—not that the truth should not be spoken to foreigners too; but He makes it an aggravation of their sin, that they spared not even their brethren. Besides, and above all outward ordinances (ch. 7:3), God requires truth and justice. **judgment of . . . peace**—Equitable decisions tend to allay feuds and produce peace. **gates**—the place where courts of judicature in the East were held. **17. all these . . . I hate**—therefore ye too ought to hate them. Religion consists in conformity to God's nature, that we should love what God loves and hate what God hates. **18, 19.** The prophet answers the query (ch. 7:3) as to the fast in the fifth month, by a reply applying to all their fasts: these are to be turned into days of rejoicing. So Jesus replied to His disciples when similarly consulting Him as to why fasting was not imposed by Him, as it was by John the Baptist. When the Sun of righteousness shines, tears are dried up (Matt. 9:15). So hereafter (Isa. 35:10). **fast of . . . fourth month**—On the fourth month of the eleventh year of Zedekiah's reign, on the ninth day, Jerusalem was taken (Jer. 39:2; 52:6, 7). It was therefore made a fast day. **fifth . . . seventh**—(*Notes*, ch. 7:3-5). **tenth**—On the tenth month and tenth day, in the ninth year of Zedekiah, the siege began (Jer. 52:4). **therefore love the truth**—or, "*only* love." *English Version* is better. God's blessing covenanted to Israel is not made to depend on Israel's goodness: but Israel's goodness should follow as the consequence of God's gracious promises (vss. 16, 17; ch. 7:9, 10). God will bless, but not those who harden themselves in sin. **20.** (Isa. 2:3; Mic. 4:2.) **Thus saith the Lord of hosts**—a preface needed to assure the Jews, now disheartened by the perils surrounding them, and by the humble aspect of the temple. "Unlikely as what follows may seem to you, *Jehovah of hosts*, boundless in resources, *saith* it, therefore it shall be so." Just before Christ's coming, a feeling grew up among the heathen of the unsatisfactoriness of their systems of religion and philosophy; this disposed them favorably towards the religion of the Jew, so that proselytes embraced the worship of Jehovah from various parts of Asia; these again were predisposed to embrace Christianity when it was preached to them (Acts 2:9-12, 41). But the full accomplishment of the conversion of the Gentiles foretold here is reserved till "Jerusalem" (vs. 22) becomes the center of Christianized Jewry (Rom. 11:12, 15). **21. Let us . . . I**—manifesting zeal and love: converted themselves, they seek the conversion of others (Song of Sol. 1:4). To exhortation in *general* ("Let us go"), they add *individual* example ("I will go"). Or, the change from *plural* to *singular* implies that the *general* consent in religious earnestness leads *each individual* to decide for God. **go speedily**—lit., "go, going"; implying intense earnestness. **pray**—*Hebrew, entreat the face* (ch. 7:2); entreat His favor and grace. **22. many . . . strong nations . . . in Jerusalem**—In contrast to the few and weak Jews now building the temple and city, then such shall be their influence that *many and strong nations* shall come to worship Jehovah their God in Jerusalem (Isa. 60: 3; 66:23). **23. ten**—a definite number for an indefinite. So in Leviticus 22:26; Numbers 14:22. **of all languages of the nations**—i.e., of nations of all languages (cf. Isa. 66:18; Rev. 7:9). **take hold of the skirt**—a gesture of suppliant entreaty as to a superior. Cf. Isa. 3:6; 4:1, on a different occasion. The Gentiles shall eagerly seek to share the religious privileges of the Jew. The skirt with a fringe and blue ribbon upon it (Num. 15:38; Deut. 22:12) was a distinguishing badge of a Jew. **God is with you** —the effect produced on unbelievers in entering the assemblies of the Church (I Cor. 14:25). But primarily, that produced on the nations in witnessing the deliverance of the Jews by Cyrus. Finally, that to be produced on the nations by the future grand interposition of Messiah in behalf of His people.

CHAPTER 9

Vss. 1-17. CHAPS. 9 TO 14 ARE PROPHETICAL. Written long after the previous portions of the book, whence arise the various features which have been made grounds for attacking their authenticity, notwithstanding the testimony of the LXX and of the compilers of the Jewish canon in their favor. See *Introduction.* ALEXANDER'S CONQUESTS IN SYRIA (vss. 1-8). GOD'S PEOPLE SAFE BECAUSE HER KING COMETH LOWLY, BUT A SAVIOUR (vss. 9-10). THE MACCABEAN DELIVERANCE A TYPE THEREOF (vss. 11-17). **1. in … Hadrach**—rather, *concerning* or *against* Hadrach (cf. Isa. 21:13). "Burden" means *a prophecy* BURDENED *with wrath against the guilty.* MAURER, not so well, explains it, *What is taken up and uttered, the utterance, a solemn declaration.* **Hadrach**—a part of Syria, near Damascus. As the name is not mentioned in ancient histories, it probably was the less-used name of a region having two names (Hadrach and Bikathaven, *Margin,* Amos 1: 5); hence it passed into oblivion. An ancient RABBI JOSE is, however, stated to have expressly mentioned it. Ant Arab, Jos. Abassi, in 1768 also declared to MICHAELIS that there was then a town of that name, and that it was capital of the region Hadrach. The name means "enclosed" in Syrian, i.e., the west interior part of Syria, *enclosed* by hills, the Cœlo-Syria of Strabo [MAURER]. JEROME considers Hadrach to be the metropolis of Cœlo-Syria, as Damascus was of the region about that city. HENGSTENBERG regards Hadrach as a symbolical name of Persia, which Zechariah avoids designating by its proper name so as not to offend the government under which he lived. But the context seems to refer to the Syrian region. GESENIUS thinks that the name is that of a Syrian king, which might more easily pass into oblivion than that of a region. Cf. the similar "land of Sihon," Nehemiah 9:22. **Damascus … rest thereof**—i.e., the place on which the "burden" of the Lord's wrath shall rest. It shall permanently settle on it until Syria is utterly prostrate. Fulfilled under Alexander the Great, who overcame Syria [CURTIUS, B. 3 and 4]. **eyes of man, as of all … Israel … toward the Lord**—The eyes of men in general, and of all Israel in particular, through consternation at the victorious progress of Alexander, shall be directed to Jehovah. The Jews, when threatened by him because of Jaddua the high priest's refusal to swear fealty to him, prayed earnestly to the Lord, and so were delivered (II Chron. 20:12; Ps. 23:2). Typical of the effect of God's judgments hereafter on all men, and especially on the Jews in turning them to Him. MAURER, PEMBELLUS and others, less probably translate, "The eyes of the Lord are upon man, as they are upon all Israel," viz., to punish the ungodly and to protect His people. He, who has chastised His

people, will not fail to punish men for their sins severely. The "all," I think, implies that whereas men's attention generally (whence "man" is the expression) was directed to Jehovah's judgments, *all* Israel especially looks to Him. **2. Hamath**—a Syrian kingdom with a capital of the same name, north of Damascus. **shall border thereby**—shall be joined to Damascus in treatment, as it is in position; shall share in the burden of wrath of which Damascus is the resting-place. MAURER understands "which"; "Hamath, which borders on Damascus, also *shall be the resting-place of Jehovah's wrath*" (the latter words being supplied from vs. 1). Riblah, the scene of the Jews' sufferings from their foe, was there: it therefore shall suffer (II Kings 23: 33; 25:6, 7, 20, 21). **Tyrus … Zidon**—lying in the conqueror's way on his march along the Mediterranean to Egypt (cf. Isa. 23). Zidon, the older city, surrendered, and Abdolonymus was made its viceroy. **very wise**—in her own eyes. Referring to Tyre: vs. 3 shows wherein her *wisdom* consisted, viz., in *building a stronghold,* and *heaping up gold and silver* (Ezek. 38:3, 5, 12, 17). On Alexander's expressing his wish to sacrifice in Hercules' temple in New Tyre on the island, she showed her wisdom in sending a golden crown, and replying that the true and ancient temple of Hercules was at Old Tyre on the mainland. With all her wisdom she cannot avert her doom. **3.** The heathen historian, DIODORUS SICULUS (17. 40), confirms this. "Tyre had the greatest confidence owing to her insular position and fortifications, and the abundant stores she had prepared." New Tyre was on an island 700 paces from the shore. As Isaiah's and Ezekiel's (Ezekiel 27) prophecies were directed against Old Tyre on the mainland and were fulfilled by Nebuchadnezzar, so Zechariah's are against New Tyre, which was made seemingly impregnable by a double wall 150 feet high, as well as the sea on all sides. **4.** (Ezek. 26:4, 12; 27:27). **cast her out**—*Hebrew,* "dispossess her," i.e., will cast her inhabitants into exile [GROTIUS]. Alexander, though without a navy, by incredible labor constructed a mole of the ruins of Old Tyre (fulfilling Ezek. 26:4-12, etc., by "scraping her dust from her," and "laying her stones, timber, and dust in the midst of the water"), from the shore to the island, and, after a seven months' siege, took the city by storm, slew with the sword about 8000, enslaved 13,000, crucified 2000, and set the city on "fire," as here foretold [CURTIUS, B. 4]. **smite her power in the sea**— situated though she be *in the sea,* and so seeming impregnable (cf. Ezek. 28:2, "I sit in the seat of God, *in the midst of the sea*"). "Her power" includes not only her fortifications, but her fleet, all of which Alexander sank *in the sea* before her very walls [CURTIUS, B. 4]. Ezekiel 26:17 corresponds, "How art thou destroyed which wast strong in the sea!" **5.** Ashkelon …—Gath alone is omitted, perhaps as being somewhat inland, and so out of the route of the advancing conqueror. **Ekron … expectation … ashamed**—Ekron, the farthest north of the Philistine cities, had *expected* Tyre would withstand Alexander, and so check his progress southward through Philistia to Egypt. This hope being confounded ("put to *shame*"), Ekron shall "fear." **king shall perish from Gaza**—Its government shall be overthrown. In literal fulfilment of this prophecy, after a two month's siege, Gaza was taken by Alexander, 10,000 of its inhabitants slain, and the rest sold as slaves. Betis the satrap, or petty "king," was bound to a chariot by thongs thrust through the soles of his feet, and dragged round the city. **6. bastard**—not the rightful heir; vile and low men, such as are bastards (Deut. 23:2) [GROTIUS]. *An alien*; so LXX; implying the desolation of the region wherein men shall not settle, but sojourn in only as aliens passing through [CALVIN]. **7. take . . . his blood out of . . . mouth**—*Blood* was forbidden as food (Gen. 9:4; Lev. 7:26). **abominations**—things sacrificed to idols and then partaken of by the worshippers (Num. 25:2; Acts 15:29). The sense is, "I will cause the Philistines to cease from the worship of idols." **even he** *shall be* **for our God**—"even he," like Hamath, Damascus, Tyre, etc., which, these words imply, shall also be converted to God (Isa. 56:3. "son of the stranger joined himself to the Lord") [ROSENMULLER]. The "even," however, may mean, *Besides the Hebrews,* "even" the Philistine shall worship Jehovah (so Isa. 56:8) [MAURER]. **he shall be as a governor in Judah**—On the conversion of the Philistine prince, he shall have the same dignity "in Judah as a governor"; there shall be no distinction [HENDERSON]. The Philistine princes with their respective states shall equally *belong to the Jews' communion, as if they were* among the "governors" of states "in Judah" [MAURER]. **Ekron as a Jebusite**—The Jebusites, the original inhabitants of Jerusalem, who, when subjugated by David, were incorporated with the Jews (II Sam. 24:16, etc.), and enjoyed their privileges: but in a subordinate position *civilly* (I Kings 9:20, 21). The Jebusites' condition under Solomon being that of bond-servants and tributaries, CALVIN explains the verse differently: "I will rescue the Jew *from the teeth* of the Philistine foe (image from wild beasts rending their prey with their *teeth*), who would have devoured him, as he would devour *blood* or flesh of his *abominable* sacrifices to idols: and *even he,* the seemingly ignoble remnant of the Jews, shall be sacred to *our God* (consecrated by His favor); and though so long bereft of dignity, I will make them to be *as governors* ruling others, and Ekron shall be a tributary bond-servant as the Jebusite." Thus the antithesis is between the Jew *that remaineth* (the elect remnant) and the Ekronite. **8. encamp about**—(Ps. 34:7). **mine house**—viz., the Jewish people (ch. 3:7; Hos. 8:1) [MAURER]. Or, *the temple:* reassuring the Jews engaged in building, who might otherwise fear their work would be undone by the conqueror [MOORE]. The Jews were, in agreement with this prophecy, uninjured by Alexander, though he punished the Samaritans. Typical of their final deliverance from every foe. **passeth by . . . returneth**—Alexander, when advancing against Jerusalem, was arrested by a dream, so that neither in "passing by" to Egypt, nor in "returning," did he injure the Jews, but conferred on them great privileges. **no oppressor . . . . pass through . . . any more**—The prophet passes from the immediate future to the final deliverance to come (Isa. 60:18; Ezek. 28:24). **seen with mine eyes**—viz., how Jerusalem has been oppressed by her foes [ROSENMULLER] (Exod. 3:7; 2:25). God is said *now* to have *seen,* because He now begins to bring the foe to judgment, and manifests to the world His sense of His people's wrongs. **9.** From the coming of the Grecian conqueror, Zechariah makes a sudden transition, by the prophetical law of suggestion, to the coming of King Messiah, a very different character. **daughter of Zion**—The theocratic people is called to "rejoice" at the coming of her King (Ps. 2:11). **unto thee**—He comes not for His own gain or pleasure, as earthly kings come, but for the sake of His Church: especially for the Jews' sake, at His

second coming (Rom. 11:26). **he is just**—*righteous:* an attribute constantly given to Messiah (Isa. 45:21; 53:11; Jer. 23:5, 6) in connection with *salvation.* He does not merely pardon by conniving at sin, but He *justifies* by becoming the Lord our righteousness-fulfiller, so that not merely mercy, but justice, requires the justification of the sinner who by faith becomes one with Christ. God's justice is not set aside by the sinner's salvation, but is magnified and made honorable by it (Isa. 42:1, 21). His future *reign* "in righteousness," also, is especially referred to (Isa. 32:1). **having salvation**—not passively, as some interpret it, "saved," which the context, referring to a "king" coming to reign, forbids; also the old versions, LXX, *Syriac,* and *Vulgate,* give *Saviour.* The *Hebrew* is reflexive in sense, "showing Himself a Saviour;" "having salvation in Himself" for us. Endowed with a salvation which He bestows as a king. Cf. *Margin,* "saving Himself." Cf. Matthew 1:21, in the *Greek,* "*Himself* shall save His people"; i.e., not by any other, but by Himself shall He save [PEARSON *on the Creed*]. His "having salvation" for others manifested that He had in Himself that righteousness which was indispensable for the justification of the unrighteous (I Cor. 1:30; II Cor. 5:21; I John 2:1). This contrasts beautifully with the haughty Grecian conqueror who came to destroy, whereas Messiah came to save. Still, Messiah shall come to take "just" vengeance on His foes, previous to His reign of peace (Mall. 4:1, 2). **lowly**—mild, gentle: corresponding to His "riding on an ass" (not a despised animal, as with us; nor a badge of humiliation, for princes in the East rode on asses, as well as low persons, Judg. 5:10), i.e., coming as "Prince of *peace*" (vs. 10; Isa. 9:6); the "horse," on the contrary is the emblem of *war,* and shall therefore be "cut off." Perhaps the *Hebrew* includes both the "lowliness" of His *outward* state (which applies to His first coming) and His "meekness" *of disposition, as* Matt. 21:5 quotes it (cf. Matt. 11:29), which applies to both His comings. Both adapt Him for loving sympathy with us men; and at the same time are the ground of His coming manifested exaltation (John 5:27; Phil. 2:7-9). **colt**—untamed, "whereon yet never man sat" (Luke 19:30). The symbol of a triumphant conqueror and judge (Judg. 5:10; 10:4; 12:14). **foal of an ass**—lit., "asses": in *Hebrew* idiom, the indefinite *plural* for *singular* (so Gen. 8:4, "*mountains* of Ararat," for *one* of the mountains). The dam accompanied the colt (Matt. 21:2). The entry of Jesus into Jerusalem at His first coming is a pledge of the full accomplishment of this prophecy at His second coming. It shall be "the day of the Lord" (Ps. 118:24), as that first Palm *Sunday* was. The Jews shall then *universally* (Ps. 118:26) say, what *some* of them said then, "Blessed is He that cometh in the name of the Lord" (cf. Matt. 21:9, with 23:39); also "Hosanna," or "Save now, I beseech thee." "Palms," the emblem of triumph, shall then also be in the hands of His people (cf. John 12:13, with Rev. 7:9, 10). Then also, as on His former entry, shall be the feast of tabernacles (at which they used to draw water from Siloam, quoting Isaiah 12:3). Cf. Psalm 118:15, with ch. 14:16. **10.** (Isa. 2:4; Hos. 2:18; Mic. 5:10). **Ephraim . . . Jerusalem**—the ten tribes, and Judah and Benjamin; both alike to be restored hereafter. **speak peace**—command it authoritatively. **dominion . . . from sea . . . river . . . ends of . . . earth**—fulfilling Genesis 15:18; Exodus 23:31; and Psalm 72:8. "Sea . . . sea," are the Red Sea and Mediterranean. The "river" is the Euphrates. Jerusalem and the Holy Land, extended to the limits promised to Abraham, are to be the center of His future dominion; whence it will extend to the remotest parts of the earth. **11. As for thee also**—i.e., the daughter of Zion," or "Jerusalem" (vs. 9): the theocracy. The "thee also," in contradistinction to *Messiah* spoken of in vs. 10, implies that besides *cutting off the battle-bow* and extending MESSIAH's "dominion to the ends of the earth," God would *also* deliver *for* her *her* exiled people from their foreign captivity. **by the blood of thy covenant**—i.e., according to the covenant vouchsafed to thee on Sinai, and ratified by the blood of sacrifices (Exod. 24:8; Heb. 9:18-20). **pit wherein . . . no water**—Dungeons were often pits without water, miry at the bottom, such as Jeremiah sank in when confined (Gen. 37:24; Jer. 38:6). An image of the misery of the Jewish exiles in Egypt, Greece, etc., under the successors of Alexander, especially under Antiochus Epiphanes, who robbed and profaned the temple, slew thousands, and enslaved more. God delivered them by the Maccabees. A type of the future deliverance from their last great persecutor hereafter (Isa. 51:14; 60:1). **12. stronghold**—in contrast to the "pit" (vs. 11); lit., "a place *cut off* from access." MAURER thinks, "*a height*" (Ps. 18: 33). An image for the *security* which the returning Jews shall have in Messiah (vs. 8) *encamped about* His people (Ps. 46:1, 5; cf. Isa. 49:9; Prov. 18:10). **prisoners of hope**—i.e., who in spite of afflictions (Job 13:15; Ps. 42:5, 11) maintain hope in the covenant-keeping God; in contrast to unbelievers, who say, "There is no hope" (Jer. 2:25; 18:12). Especially those *Jews* who believe God's word to Israel (Jer. 31:17), "there is hope in the end, that thy children shall come again to their own border," and do not say, as in Ezekiel 37:11, "Our hope is lost." Primarily, the Jews of Zechariah's time are encouraged not to be dispirited in building by their trials; secondarily, the Jews before the coming restoration are encouraged to look to Messiah for deliverance from their last oppressors. **even to-day**—when your circumstances seem so unpromising; in contrast with the "day of the Lord," when Zion's King shall come to her deliverance (vs. 9). **I will render double**—Great as has been thy adversity, thy prosperity shall be *doubly* greater (Isa. 61:7). **13. bent Judah**—made Judah as it were My bow, and "filled" it "with Ephraim," as My arrow, wherewith to overcome the successor of the Grecian Alexander, Antiochus Epiphanes (cf. *Notes,* Dan. 8 and 11:32; I Maccabees 1:62; 2:41-43), the oppressor of Judah. Having spoken (vss. 1-8) of Alexander's victories, after the parenthesis (vss. 9, 10) as to Messiah the infinitely greater King coming, he passes to the victories which God would enable Judah to gain over Alexander's successor, after his temporary oppression of them. **O Zion . . . O Greece**—God on one hand addresses Zion, on the other Greece, showing that He rules all people. **14.** Another image: "Jehovah shall be seen (conspicuously manifesting His power) over them" (i.e., in behalf of the Jews and against their foes), as formerly He appeared in a cloud over the Israelites against the Egyptians (Exod. 14:19, 24). **his arrow . . . as . . . lightning**—flashing forth instantaneous destruction to the foe (Ps. 18:14). **blow . . . trumpet**—to summon and incite His people to battle for the destruction of their foe. **go with whirlwinds of the south**—i.e., go forth in the most furious storm, such as is one from the south (Isa. 21:1). Alluding, perhaps, to Jehovah's ancient miracles at Sinai coming "from Teman" ("*the south*," in *Margin*). **15. devour**—the flesh of

their foes. **drink**—the blood of their foes; i.e., utterly destroy them. Image (as Jer. 46:10) from a sacrifice, wherein part of the flesh was eaten, and the blood poured in libation (cf. Isa. 63:1, etc.). **subdue with sling-stones**—or, "tread under foot the sling-stones" hurled by the foe at them; i.e., will contemptuously trample on the hostile missiles which shall fall harmless under their feet (cf. Job 41:28). Probably, too, it is implied that *their foes* are as impotent as the common *stones* used in *slinging* when they have fallen under foot: in contrast to the people of God (vs. 16), "the (precious) stones of a crown" (cf. I Sam. 25:29) [MAURER]. *English Version* is good sense: The Jews shall subdue the foe *at the first onset,* with the mere *slingers* who stood in front of the line of battle and began the engagement. Though armed with but sling-stones, like David against Goliath, they shall subdue the foe (Judg. 20:16; I Chron. 12:2) [GROTIUS]. **noise** —the battle shout. **through wine**—(Ch. 10:7). The Spirit of God fills them with triumph (Eph. 5:18). **filled**—with blood. **like bowls**—the bowls used to receive the blood of the sacrifices. **as . . . corners** —or "horns" of the altar, which used to be sprinkled with blood from the bowls (Exod. 29:12; Lev. 4:18). **16. save them . . . as the flock of his people**—as the flock of His people ought to be saved (Ps. 77:20). Here the image of *war* and *bloodshed* (vs. 15) is exchanged for the *shepherd* and *flock,* as God will give not only victory, but afterwards safe and lasting peace. In contrast to the worthless *sling-stones* trodden under foot stand the (gems) "stones of the crown (Isa. 62:3; Mal. 3:17), lifted up as an ensign," that all may flock to the Jewish Church (Isa. 11: 10, 12; 62:10). **17. his goodness . . . his beauty**—the goodness and beauty which Jehovah Messiah bestows on His people. Not as MAURER thinks, the goodness, etc., of *His land* or *His people* (Ps. 31:19; Jer. 31:12). **make . . . cheerful**—lit., *make it grow.* **new wine the maids**—supply, "shall make . . . to grow." *Corn* and *wine* abundant indicate peace and plenty. The new wine gladdening the maids is peculiar to this passage. It confutes those who interdict the use of wine as food. The Jews, heretofore straitened in provisions through pressure of the foe, shall now have abundance to cheer, not merely the old, but even the youths and maidens [CALVIN].

CHAPTER 10

Vss. 1-12. PRAYER AND PROMISE. Call to prayer to Jehovah, as contrasted with the idol worship which had brought judgments on the princes and people. Blessings promised in answer to prayer: (1) rulers of themselves; (2) conquest of their enemies; (3) restoration and establishment of both Israel and Judah in their own land in lasting peace and piety. **1. Ask . . . rain**—on which the abundance of "corn" promised by the Lord (ch. 9:17) depends. Jehovah alone can give it, and will give it on being asked (Jer. 10:13; 14:22). **rain in . . . time of . . . latter rain**—i.e., the latter rain in its due time, viz., in spring, about February or March (Job 29:23; Joel 2:23). The latter rain ripened the grain, as the former rain in October tended to fructify the seed. Including *all* temporal blessings; these again being types of spiritual ones. Though God has begun to bless us, we are not to relax our prayers. The former rain of conversion may have been given, but we must also ask for the latter rain of ripened sanctification. Though at Pentecost there was a former rain on the Jewish Church, a latter rain is still to be looked for, when the full harvest of the nation's conversion shall be gathered in to God. The spirit of prayer in the Church is an index at once of her piety, and of the spiritual blessings she may expect from God. When the Church is full of prayer, God pours out a full blessing. **bright clouds**—rather, "lightnings," the precursors of rain [MAURER]. **showers of rain**—lit., "rain of heavy rain." In Job 37:6 the same words occur in inverted order [HENDERSON]. **grass**—a general term, including both *corn* for men and *grass* for cattle. **2. idols**—lit., "the teraphim," the household gods, consulted in divination (*Note,* Hos. 3:4). Derived by GESENIUS from an *Arabic* root, "comfort," indicating them as the givers of comfort. Or an Ethiopian root, "relics." Herein Zechariah shows that the Jews by their own idolatry had stayed the grace of God heretofore, which otherwise would have given them all those blessings, temporal and spiritual, which they are now (vs. 1) urged to "ask" for. **diviners**—who gave responses to consulters of the teraphim: opposed to Jehovah and His true prophets. **seen a lie**—pretending to see what they saw not in giving responses. **comfort in vain**—lit., "give *vapor* for comfort"; i.e., give comforting promises to consulters which are sure to come to naught (Job 13:4; 16:2; 21:34). **therefore they went their way**—i.e., Israel and Judah were led away captive. **as a flock . . . no shepherd**—As sheep wander and are a prey to every injury when without a shepherd, so the Jews had been while they were without Jehovah, the true shepherd; for the false prophets whom they trusted were no shepherds (Ezek. 34:5). So now they are scattered, while they know not Messiah their shepherd; typified in the state of the disciples, when they had forsaken Jesus and fled (Matt. 26:56; cf. ch. 13:7). **3. against the shepherds**—the civil rulers of Israel and Judah who abetted idolatry. **punished** —lit., "visited *upon.*" The same word "visited," without the "upon," is presently after used in a good sense to heighten the contrast. **goats**—he-goats. As "shepherds" described what they *ought* to have been, so "he-goats" describes what they *were,* the emblem of headstrong wantonness and offensive lust (*Margin,* Isa. 14:9; Ezek. 34:17; Dan. 8:5; Matt. 25: 33). The he-goats head the flock. They who are first in crime will be first in punishment. **visited**— in mercy (Luke 1:68). **as his goodly horse**—In ch. 9:13 they were represented under the image of *bows and arrows,* here under that of their commander-in-chief, Jehovah's *battle horse* (Song of Sol. 1:9). God can make His people, timid though they be as sheep, courageous as the charger. The general rode on the most beautiful and richly caparisoned, and had his horse tended with the greatest care. Jehovah might cast off the Jews for their vileness, but He regards His election or adoption of them: whence He calls them here "*His* flock," and therefore saves them. **4. Out of him**—Judah is to be no more subject to foreigners, but *from itself* shall come its rulers. **the corner**—stone, Messiah (Isa. 28:16). "Corners" simply express *governors* (*Margin,* I Sam. 14:38; *Margin,* Isa. 19:13). The Maccabees, Judah's governors and deliverers from Antiochus the oppressor, are primarily meant; but Messiah is the Antitype. Messiah supports and binds together the Church, Jews and Gentiles. **the nail**— (Judg. 4:21; Isa. 22:23). The large peg inside an Oriental tent, on which is hung most of its valuable furniture. On Messiah hang all the glory and hope of His people. **bow**—(ch. 9:13). Judah shall

not need foreign soldiery. Messiah shall be her battle bow (Ps. 45:4, 5; Rev. 6:2). **every oppressor** —rather, in a good sense, *ruler,* as the kindred Ethiopic term means. So "exactor," in Isaiah 60:17, viz., one who exacts the tribute from the nations made tributary to Judah [LUDOVICUS DE DIEU]. **5. riders on horses**—viz., the enemy's horsemen. Though the Jews were forbidden by the law to multiply horses in battle (Deut. 17:16), they are made Jehovah's war horse (vs. 3; Ps. 20:7), and so tread down on foot the foe with all his cavalry (Ezek. 38:4; Dan. 11:40). Cavalry was the chief strength of the Syro-Grecian army (I Maccabees 3: 39). **6. Judah . . . Joseph**—i.e., the ten tribes. The distinct mention of both Judah and Israel shows that there is yet a more complete restoration than that from Babylon, when Judah alone and a few Israelites from the other tribes returned. The Maccabean deliverance is here connected with it, just as the painter groups on the same canvas objects in the foreground and hills far distant; or as the comparatively near planet and the remote fixed star are seen together in the same firmament. Prophecy ever hastens to the glorious final consummation under Messiah. **bring them again to place them**— viz., securely in their own land. The *Hebrew* verb is compounded of two, "I will bring again," and "I will place them" (Jer. 32:37) MAURER, from a different form, translates, "I will make them to dwell." **7. like a mighty man**—in the battle with the foe (vss. 3, 5). **rejoice**—at their victory over the foe. **children shall see it**—who are not yet of age to serve. To teach patient waiting for God's promises. If ye do not at present see the fulfilment, your *children* shall, and their joy shall be complete. **rejoice in the Lord**—the Giver of such a glorious victory. **8. hiss for them**—Keepers of bees by a whistle call them together. So Jehovah by the mere word of His call shall gather back to Palestine His scattered people (vs. 10; Isa. 5:26; Ezek. 36:11). The multitudes mentioned by JOSEPHUS (B. 3. ch. 3:2), as peopling Galilee 200 years after this time, were a pledge of the future more perfect fulfilment of the prophecy. **for I have redeemed them**—viz., in My covenant purpose "redeemed" both temporally and spiritually. **as they have increased**—in former times. **9. sow them among . . . people**—Their dispersion was with a special design. Like seed sown far and wide, they shall, when quickened themselves, be the fittest instruments for quickening others (cf. Mic. 5:7). The slight hold they have on every soil where they now live, as also the commercial and therefore cosmopolitan character of their pursuits, making a change of residence easy to them, fit them peculiarly for missionary work [MOORE]. The wide dispersion of the Jews just before Christ's coming prepared the way similarly for the apostles' preaching in the various Jewish synagogues throughout the world; everywhere some of the Old Testament seed previously sown was ready to germinate when the New Testament light and heat were brought to bear on it by Gospel preachers. Thus the way was opened for entrance among the Gentiles. "*Will sow*" is the *Hebrew* future, said of that which has been done, is being done, and may be done afterwards [MAURER], (cf. Hos. 2:23). **shall remember me in far countries**— (Deut. 30:1; II Chron. 6:37). Implying the Jews' return to a right mind in "all the nations" where they are scattered simultaneously. Cf. Luke 15:17, 18, with Psalm 22:27, "All the ends of the world *remembering* and turning unto the Lord," preceded by the "seed of Jacob . . . Israel . . . fearing and glorifying Him"; also Psalm 102:13-15. **live**—in political and spiritual life. **10. Egypt . . . Assyria**—the former the first, the latter among the last of Israel's oppressors (or *representing the four great world kingdoms,* of which it was the first): types of the present *universal* dispersion, Egypt being south, Assyria north, opposite ends of the compass. MAURER *conjectures* that many Israelites fled to "Egypt" on the invasion of Tiglath-pileser. But Isaiah 11: 11 and this passage rather accord with the view of the *future* restoration. **Gilead . . . Lebanon**—The whole of the Holy Land is described by two of its boundaries, the eastern ("Gilead" beyond Jordan) and the northern ("Lebanon"). **place shall not be found for them**—i.e., there shall not be room enough for them through their numbers (Isa. 49:20; 54:3). **11. pass . . . sea with affliction**—Personifying the "sea"; He shall afflict the sea, i.e., cause it to cease to be an obstacle to Israel's return to Palestine (Isa. 11:15, 16). *Vulgate* translates, "The strait of the sea." MAURER, "He shall *cleave and* smite." *English Version* is best (Ps. 114:3). As Jehovah smote the Red Sea to make a passage for His people (Exod. 14:16, 21), so hereafter shall He make a way through every obstacle which opposes Israel's restoration. **the river**—the Nile (Amos 8:8; 9:5), or the Euphrates. Thus the Red Sea and the Euphrates in the former part of the verse answer to "Assyria" and "Egypt" in the latter. **sceptre of Egypt . . . depart**—(Ezek. 30:13). **12. I . . . strengthen them in . . . Lord**—(Hos. 1:7). I, the Father, will strengthen them in the name, i.e., the manifested power, of the Lord, Messiah, the Son of God. **walk . . . in his name**—i.e., live everywhere and continually under His protection, and according to His will (Gen. 5:22; Ps. 20:1, 7; Mic. 4:5).

CHAPTER 11

VSS. 1-17. DESTRUCTION OF THE SECOND TEMPLE AND JEWISH POLITY FOR THE REJECTION OF MESSIAH. **1. Open thy doors, O Lebanon**—i.e., the temple so called, as being constructed of cedars of Lebanon, or as being lofty and conspicuous like that mountain (cf. Ezek. 17:3; Hab. 2:17). Forty years before the destruction of the temple, the tract called "Massecheth Joma" states, its doors of their own accord opened, and Rabbi Johanan in alarm said, I know that thy desolation is impending according to Zechariah's prophecy. CALVIN supposes Lebanon to refer to *Judea,* described by its north boundary: "Lebanon," the route by which the Romans, according to JOSEPHUS, gradually advanced towards Jerusalem. MOORE, from HENGSTENBERG, refers the passage to the civil war which caused the calling in of the Romans, who, like a storm sweeping through the land from Lebanon, deprived Judea of its independence. Thus the passage forms a fit introduction to the prediction as to Messiah born when Judea became a Roman province. But the weight of authority is for the former view. **2. fir tree . . . cedar**—if even the *cedars* (the highest in the state) are not spared, how much less the *fir trees* (the lowest)! **forest of . . . vintage**—As the vines are stripped of their grapes in the vintage (cf. Joel 3:13), so the forest of Lebanon "is come down," stripped of all its beauty. Rather, "*the fortified*" or "*inaccessible* forest" [MAURER]; i.e., Jerusalem dense with houses as a thick forest is with trees, and "fortified" with a wall around. Cf. Micah. 3:12, where its desolate state is described as a forest. **3. shepherds**—the Jewish rulers. **their glory** –*their* wealth and

magnificence; or that *of the temple,* "their glory" (Mark 13:1; Luke 21:5). **young lions**—the princes, so described on account of their cruel rapacity. **pride of Jordan**—its thickly wooded banks, the lair of "lions" (Jer. 12:5; 49:19). Image for Judea "spoiled" of the magnificence of its rulers ("the young lions"). The valley of the Jordan forms a deeper gash than any on the earth. The land at Lake Merom is on a level with the Mediterranean Sea; at the Sea of Tiberias it falls 650 feet below that level, and to double that depression at the Dead Sea, i.e., in all, 1950 feet below the Mediterranean; in twenty miles' interval there is a fall of from 3000 to 4000 feet. **4.** The prophet here proceeds to show the cause of the destruction just foretold, viz., the rejection of Messiah. **flock of . . . slaughter**—(Ps. 44:22). God's people doomed to slaughter by the Romans. Zechariah here represents typically Messiah, and performs in vision the actions enjoined: hence the language is in part appropriate to him, but mainly to the Antitype, Messiah. A million and a half perished in the Jewish war, and one million one hundred thousand at the fall of Jerusalem. "Feed" implies that the Jews could not plead ignorance of God's will to execute their sin. Zechariah and the other prophets had by God's appointment "fed" them (Acts 20:28) with the word of God, teaching and warning them to escape from coming wrath by repentance: the type of Messiah, the chief Shepherd, who receives the commission of the Father, with whom He is one (vs. 4); and Himself says (vs. 7), "*I* will feed the flock of slaughter." Zechariah did not live to "feed" literally the "flock of slaughter"; Messiah alone "fed" those who, because of their rejection of Him, were condemned to slaughter. Jehovah-Messiah is the speaker. It is He who threatens to inflict the punishments (vss. 6, 8). The typical breaking of the staff, performed in vision by Zechariah (vs. 10), is fulfilled in His breaking the covenant with Judah. It is He who was sold for thirty pieces of silver (vss. 12, 13). **5. possessors**—The *buyers* [MAURER], their Roman oppressors, contrasted with "they that sell men." The instruments of God's righteous judgment, and therefore "not holding themselves guilty" (Jer. 50:7). It is meant that they *might* use this plea, not that they actually used it. Judah's adversaries felt no compunction in destroying them; and God in righteous wrath against Judah allowed it. **they that sell them**—(Cf. vs. 12). The rulers of Judah, who by their avaricious rapacity and selfishness (John 11:48, 50) virtually sold their country to Rome. Their covetousness brought on Judea God's visitation by Rome. The climax of this was the sale of the innocent Messiah for thirty pieces of silver. They thought that Jesus was thus sold and their selfish interest secured by the delivery of Him to the Romans for crucifixion; but it was themselves and their country that they thus sold to the Roman "possessors." **I am rich**—by selling the sheep (Deut. 29:19; Hos. 12:8). In short-sighted selfishness they thought they had gained their object, covetous self-aggrandizement (Luke 16:14), and hypocritically "thanked" God for their wicked gain (cf. Luke 18:11). **say . . . pity**—In *Hebrew* it is *singular:* i.e., *each* of those that sell them *saith:* Not *one* of their own shepherds *pitieth* them. An emphatical mode of expression by which each individual is represented as doing, or not doing, the action of the verb [HENDERSON]. HENGSTENBERG refers the *singular* verbs to JEHOVAH, the true actor; the wicked shepherds being His unconscious instruments. Cf. vs. 6, "For *I* will no more pity," with the *Hebrew* "*pitieth* not" here. **6.** Jehovah, in vengeance for their rejection of Messiah, gave them over to intestine feuds and Roman rule. The Zealots and other factious Jews expelled and slew one another by turns at the last invasion by Rome. **his king**—Vespasian or Titus: they themselves (John 19: 15) had said, unconsciously realizing Zechariah's words, identifying Rome's king with Judah's ("his") king, "We have no king but Cæsar." God took them at their word, and gave them the Roman king, who "smote (lit., dashed in pieces) their land," breaking up their polity, when they rejected their true King who would have saved them. **7. And**—rather, *Accordingly:* implying the motive cause which led Messiah to assume the office, viz., the will of the Father (vss. 4, 5), who pitied the sheep without any true shepherd. **I will feed**—"I fed" [CALVIN], which comes to the same thing, as the past tense must in Zechariah's time have referred to the event of Messiah's advent then future: the prophets often speaking of the future in vision as already present. It was not My fault, Jehovah implies, that these sheep were not fed; the fault rests solely with you, because ye rejected the grace of God [CALVIN]. **even you, O poor of the flock**—rather, "in order that (I might feed, i.e., save) the poor (humble; cf. vs. 11; Zeph. 3:12; Matt. 5:3) of the flock"; lit., (not "*you*," but), "*therefore* (I will feed)" [MOORE]. See *Margin*, "*Verily* the poor." It is for the sake of the believing remnant that Messiah took charge of the flock, though He would have saved all, if they would have come to Him. They would not come; therefore, *as a nation,* they are "the flock of (i.e., doomed to) slaughter." **I took...two staves**—i.e., shepherds' staves or rods (Ps. 23:4). Symbolizing His assumption of the pastor's office. **Beauty**—The Jews' peculiar *excellency* above other nations (Deut. 4:7), God's special manifestation to them (Ps. 147: 19, 20), the glory of the temple ("the *beauty* of holiness," Ps. 29:2; cf. Ps. 27:4, and 90:17; II Chron. 20:21), the "pleasantness" of their land (Gen. 49: 15; Dan. 8:9; 11:16), "the glorious land." **Bands**—implying the *bond* of "brotherhood" between Judah and Israel. "Bands," in Psalm 119:61 (*Margin*), is used for confederate *companies:* The Easterns in making a confederacy often tie a cord or band as a symbol of it, and untie it when they dissolve the confederacy [LUDOVICUS DE DIEU]. Messiah would have joined Judah and Israel in the *bonds* of a common faith and common laws (vs. 14), but they would not; therefore in just retribution He broke "His covenant which He had made with all the people." Alexander, Antiochus Epiphanes, and Pompey were all kept from marring utterly the distinctive "beauty" and "brotherhood" of Judah and Israel, which subsisted more or less so long as the temple stood. But when Jehovah brake the staves, not even Titus could save the temple from his own Roman soldiery, nor was Jurian able to restore it. **8. Three shepherds...I cut off**—lit., to cause to disappear, to destroy so as not to leave a vestige of them. The three shepherds whom Messiah removes are John, Simon, and Eleazar, three leaders of factions in the Jewish war [DRUSIUS]. Or, as Messiah, the Antitype, was at once *prophet, priest, and king,* so He by the destruction of the Jewish polity destroyed these *three* orders for the unbelief of both the rulers and people [MOORE]. If they had accepted Messiah, they would have had all three combined in Him, and would have been themselves spiritually prophets, priests, and kings to God. Refusing Him, they lost all three, in every sense. **one month**—a brief

and fixed space of time (Hos. 5:7). Probably alluding to the last period of the siege of Jerusalem, when all authority within the city was at an end [HENDERSON]. **loathed them**—lit., "was straitened" as to them; instead of being *enlarged* towards them in love (II Cor. 6:11, 12). The same *Hebrew* as in Numbers 21:4, *Margin.* No room was left by them for the grace of God, as His favors were rejected [CALVIN]. The mutual distaste that existed between the holy Messiah and the guilty Jews is implied. **9. Then said I**—at last when all means of saving the nation had been used in vain (John 8:24). **I will not**—i.e., *no more* feed you. The last rejection of the Jews is foretold, of which the former under Nebuchadnezzar, similarly described, was the type (Jer. 15:1-3; 34:17; 43:11; Ezek. 6:12). Perish those who are doomed to perish, since they reject Him who would have saved them! Let them rush on to their own ruin, since they will have it so. **eat...flesh of another**—Let them madly perish by mutual discords. JOSEPHUS attests the fulfilment of this prophecy of *threefold calamity:* pestilence and famine ("dieth...die"), war ("cut off...cut off"), intestine discord ("eat...one...another"). **10. covenant which I made with all the people**—The covenant made with the *whole nation* is to hold good no more except to the elect remnant. This is the force of the clause, not as MAURER, and others translate. The covenant which I made with all the *nations* (not to hurt My elect people, Hos. 2:18). But the *Hebrew* is the term for the *elect people* (*Ammim*), not that for the *Gentile nations* (*Goiim*). The *Hebrew plural* expresses the great numbers of the Israelite people formerly (I Kings 4:20). The article is, in the *Hebrew,* all *the* or *those* peoples. His cutting in sunder the staff "Beauty," implies the setting aside of the outward symbols of the Jews' distinguishing excellency above the Gentiles (*Note,* vs. 7) as God's own people. **11. poor...knew**—The humble, godly remnant knew by the event the truth of the prediction and of Messiah's mission. He had, thirty-seven years before the fall of Jerusalem, forewarned His disciples when they should see the city compassed with armies, to "flee unto the mountains." Accordingly, Cestius Gallus, when advancing on Jerusalem, unaccountably withdrew for a brief space, giving Christians the opportunity of obeying Christ's words by fleeing to Pella. **waited upon me**—looked to the hand of God in all these calamities, not blindly shutting their eyes to the true cause of the visitation, as most of the nation still do, instead of referring it to their own rejection of Messiah. Isaiah 30:18-21 refers similarly to the Lord's return in mercy to the remnant that "wait for Him" and "cry" to Him (Zeph. 3:12, 13). **12. I said**—The prophet here represents the person of Jehovah-Messiah. **If ye think good**—lit., "If it be good in your eyes." Glancing at their self-sufficient pride in not *deigning* to give Him that return which His great love in coming down to them from heaven merited, viz., their love and obedience. "My price"; my reward for pastoral care, both during the whole of Israel's history from the Exodus, and especially the three and a half years of Messiah's ministry. He speaks as their "servant," which He was to them in order to fulfil the Father's will (Phil. 2:7). **if not, forbear**—They withheld that which He sought as His only reward, their love; yet He will not force them, but leave His cause with God (Isa. 49:4, 5). Cf. the type Jacob cheated of his wages by Laban, but leaving his cause in the hands of God (Gen. 31:41, 42). **So ...thirty pieces of silver**—*thirty shekels.* They not only refused Him His due, but added insult to injury by giving for Him the price of a gored bondservant (Exod. 21:32; Matt. 26:15). A freeman was rated at twice that sum. **13. Cast it unto the potter**—proverbial: Throw it to the temple-potter, the most suitable person to whom to cast the despicable sum, plying his trade as he did in the polluted valley (II Kings 23:10) of Hinnom, because it furnished him with the most suitable clay. This same valley, and the potter's shop, were made the scene of symbolic actions by Jeremiah (ch. 18 and 19) when prophesying of this very period of Jewish history. Zechariah connects his prophecy here with the older one of Jeremiah: showing the further application of the same divine threat against his unfaithful people in their destruction under Rome, as before in that under Nebuchadnezzar. Hence Matthew 27:9, in *English Version,* and in the oldest authorities, quotes Zechariah's words as *Jeremiah's,* the latter being the original author from whom Zechariah derived the groundwork of the prophecy. Cf. the parallel case of Mark 1:2, 3 in the oldest MSS. (though not in *English Version*), quoting Malachi's words as those of "Isaiah," the original source of the prophecy. Cf. my *Introduction* to Zechariah. The "potter" is significant of God's absolute power over the clay framed by His own hands (Isa. 45:9; Jer. 18:6; Rom. 9:20,21). **in the house of the Lord**—The thirty pieces are thrown down *in the temple,* as the house of Jehovah, the fit place for the money of Jehovah-Messiah being deposited, in the treasury, and the very place accordingly where Judas "cast them down." The thirty pieces were cast "to the potter," because it was to him they were "appointed by the Lord" ultimately to go, as a worthless price (cf. Matt. 27:6, 7, 10). For "I took," "I threw," here Matthew has *"they took,"* *"they* gave them"; because their (the Jews' and Judas') act was all His *"appointment"* (which Matthew also expresses), and therefore is here attributed to Him (cf. Acts 2:23; 4:28). It is curious that some old translators translate, for "to the potter," *"to the treasury"* (so MAURER), agreeing with Matthew 27:6. But *English Version* agrees better with *Hebrew* and Matthew 27:10. **14.** The breaking of the bond of union between Judah and Israel's ten tribes under Rehoboam is here the image used to represent the *fratricidal discord of factions* which raged within Jerusalem on the eve of its fall, while the Romans were thundering at its gates without. See JOSEPHUS, J. B. Also the continued *severance of the tribes* till their coming reunion (Rom. 11:15). **15. yet**—"take *again*"; as in vs. 7 previously he had taken other implements. **instruments**—the accoutrements, viz., the shepherd's crook and staff, wallet, etc. Assume the character of a bad ("foolish" in Scripture is synonymous with *wicked,* Ps. 14:1) shepherd, as before thou assumedst that of a good shepherd. Since the Jews would not have Messiah, "the Good Shepherd" (John 10:11), they were given up to Rome, heathen and papal, both alike their persecutor, especially the latter, and shall be again to Antichrist, the "man of sin," the instrument of judgment by Christ's permission. Antichrist will first make a covenant with them as their ruler, but then will break it, and they shall feel the iron yoke of his tyranny as the false Messiah, because they rejected the light yoke of the true Messiah (Dan. 11:35-38; 12:1; 9:27; II Thess. 2:3-12). But at last he is to perish utterly (vs. 17), and the elect remnant of Judah and Israel is to be saved gloriously. **16. in the land**—Antichrist will probably be a Jew, or at least one in Judea. **not visit . . . neither . . .**

seek . . . heal . . . broken, nor feed . . . but . . . eat . . . flesh . . . tear—Cf. similar language as to the unfaithful shepherds of Israel in Ezekiel 34: 2-4. This implies, they shall be paid in kind. Such a shepherd in the worst type shall "tear" them for a limited time. **those . . . cut off**— "those perishing" [LXX], i.e., those sick unto death, as if already cut off. **the young**—The *Hebrew* is always used of human youths, who are really referred to under the image of the young of the flock. Ancient expositors [*Chaldee Version,* JEROME, etc.] translate, *"the straying,"* "the dispersed"; so GESENIUS. **broken**—the wounded. **standeth still** —with faintness lagging behind. **tear . . . claws**— expressing cruel voracity; tearing off the very hoofs (cf. Exod. 10:26), giving them excruciating pain, and disabling them from going in quest of pasture. **17. the idol**—The *Hebrew* expresses both *vanity* and *an idol.* Cf. Isaiah 14:13; Daniel 11:36; II Thessalonians 2:4; Revelation 13:5, 6, as to the idolatrous and blasphemous claims of Antichrist. The "idol shepherd *that leaveth the flock"* cannot apply to Rome, but to some ruler among the Jews themselves, at first cajoling, then "leaving" them, nay, destroying them (Dan. 9:27; 11:30-38). God's sword shall descend on his "arm," the instrument of his tyranny towards the sheep (II Thess. 2:8); and on his "right eye," wherewith he ought to have watched the sheep (John 10:12, 13). However, Antichrist shall *destroy,* rather than *"leave* the flock." Perhaps, therefore, the reference is to the shepherds who *left the flock* to Antichrist's rapacity, and who, in just retribution, shall feel his "sword" on their "arm," which ought to have protected the flock but did not, and on their "eye," which had failed duly to watch the sheep from hurt. The blinding of "the *right* eye" has attached to it the notion of ignominy (I Sam. 11:2).

CHAPTER 12

Vss. 1-14. JERUSALEM THE INSTRUMENT OF JUDGMENT ON HER FOES HEREAFTER; HER REPENTANCE AND RESTORATION. **1. burden**—"weighty prophecy"; fraught with destruction to Israel's foes; the expression may also refer to the distresses of Israel *implied* as about to precede the deliverance. **for Israel**—*concerning* Israel [MAURER]. **stretcheth forth**—present; *now,* not merely *"hath* stretched forth," as if God only created and then left the universe to itself (John 5:17). To remove all doubts of unbelief as to the possibility of Israel's deliverance, God prefaces the prediction by reminding us of His creative and sustaining power. Cf. a similar preface in Isaiah 42:5; 43:1; 65:17, 18. **formeth . . . spirit of man**—(Num. 16:22; Heb. 12:9). **2. cup of trembling**—a cup causing those who drink it to *reel* (from a *Hebrew* root "to reel"). Jerusalem, who drank the "cup of trembling" herself, shall be so to her foes (Isa. 51:17, 22; Jer. 13:13). CALVIN with LXX translates, *"threshold of destruction,"* on which they shall stumble and be crushed when they attempt to cross it. *English Version* is better. **both against Judah**—The *Hebrew* order of words is lit., "And also against Judah shall he (the foe) be in the siege against Jerusalem"; implying virtually that Judah, as it shares the invasion along with Jerusalem, so it shall, like the metropolis, prove a cup of trembling to the invaders. MAURER with JEROME translates, "Also upon Judah shall be (the cup of trembling); i.e., some Jews forced by the foe shall join in the assault on Jerusalem, and shall share the overthrow with the besiegers. But vss. 6, 7 show that Judah escapes and proves the scourge of the. foe. **3.** (Cf. 14:4, 6-9, 13.) JEROME states it was a custom in Palestine to test the strength of youths by their lifting up a massive stone; the phrase, "burden themselves with it," refers to this custom. Cf. Matthew 21:44: The Jews "fell" on the rock of offense, Messiah, and were "broken"; but the rock shall fall on Antichrist, who "burdens himself with it" by his assault on the restored Jews, and "grind him to powder." **all ... people of ... earth**—The Antichristian confederacy against the Jews shall be almost universal. **4. I will smite ... horse**—The arm of attack especially formidable to Judah, who was unprovided with cavalry. So in the overthrow of Pharaoh (Exod. 15:19, 21). **open mine eyes upon ... Judah**—to watch over Judah's safety. Heretofore Jehovah seemed to have shut His eyes, as having no regard for her. **blindness**—so as to rush headlong on to their own ruin (cf. ch. 14:12, 13). **5. shall say**—when they see the foe divinely smitten with "madness." **Judah ... Jerusalem**—here distinguished as the country and the metropolis. Judah recognizes her "strength" to be "Jerusalem and its inhabitants" as the instrument, and "Jehovah of hosts their God" (dwelling especially there) as the author of all power (Joel 3:16). My strength is the inhabitants of Jerusalem, who have the Lord their God as their help. The repulse of the foe by the metropolis shall assure the Jews of the country that the same divine aid shall save them. **6.** On "governors of Judah," see *Note,* ch. 9:7. **hearth**—or pan. **torch ... in a sheaf**—Though small, it shall consume the many foes around. One prophet supplements the other. Thus Isaiah 29, Joel 3, and Zechariah 12, 13, 14, describe more Antichrist's *army* than himself. Daniel represents him as a horn growing out of the fourth beast or fourth kingdom; St. John, as a separate beast having an individual existence. Daniel dwells on his worldly conquests as a king; St. John, more on his spiritual tyranny, whence he adds a second beast, the false prophet coming in a semblance of spirituality. What is briefly described by one is more fully prophesied by the other [ROOS]. **7.** Judah is to be "first saved," because of her meek acknowledgment of dependence on Jerusalem, subordinate to Jehovah's aid. **tents**—shifting and insecure, as contrasted with the solid fortifications of Judah. But God chooses the weak to confound the mighty, that all human glorying may be set aside. **8.** Jerusalem, however, also shall be specially strengthened against the foe. **feeble ... shall be as David**—to the Jew, the highest type of strength and glory on earth (II Sam. 17:8; 18:3; Joel 3:10). **angel of the Lord before them**—the divine angel that went "before them" through the desert, the highest type of strength and glory in heaven (Exod. 23:20; 32:34). "The house of David" is the "prince," and his family sprung from David (Ezek. 45:7, 8). David's house was then in a comparatively weak state. **9. I will seek to destroy**—I will set Myself with determined earnestness to destroy ... (Hag. 2:22). **10.** Future conversion of the Jews is to flow from an extraordinary outpouring of the Holy Spirit (Jer. 31:9, 31-34; Ezek. 39:29). **spirit of grace ... supplications**—"spirit" is here not the spirit produced, but THE HOLY SPIRIT *producing* a "*gracious*" disposition, and inclination for "*supplications.*" CALVIN explains "spirit of grace" as *the grace of God* itself (whereby He "pours" out His bowels of mercy), "conjoined with the sense of it in man's heart." The "spirit of supplications" is the mercury whose

rise or fall is an unerring test of the state of the Church [MOORE]. In *Hebrew,* "grace" and "supplications" are kindred terms; translate, therefore, "*gracious* supplications." The *plural* implies suppliant prayers "without ceasing." Herein not merely external help against the foe, as before, but internal grace is promised subsequently. **look upon me**—with profoundly earnest regard, as the Messiah whom they so long denied. **pierced**—implying Messiah's humanity: as "*I* will pour ... spirit" implies His divinity. **look ... mourn**—True repentance arises from the sight by faith of the crucified Saviour. It is the tear that drops from the eye of faith looking on Him. Terror only produces remorse. The true penitent weeps over his sins in love to Him who in love has suffered for them. **me ... him**—The change of person is due to Jehovah-Messiah speaking *in His own person* first, then the prophet speaking *of Him.* The Jews, to avoid the conclusion that He whom they have "pierced" is Jehovah-Messiah, who says, "I will pour out ... spirit," altered "me" into "him," and represent the "pierced" one to be Messiah Ben (son of) Joseph, who was to suffer in the battle with Gog, before Messiah Ben David should come to reign. But *Hebrew, Chaldee, Syriac,* and *Arabic* oppose this; and the ancient Jews interpreted it of Messiah. Psalm 22:16 also refers to His being "pierced." So John 19:37; Revelation 1:7. The actual piercing of His side was the culminating point of all their insulting treatment of Him. The act of the Roman soldier who pierced Him was their act (Matt. 27:25), and is so accounted here in Zechariah. The *Hebrew* word is always used of a literal piercing (so ch. 13:3); not of a metaphorical *piercing,* "insulted," as MAURER and other Rationalists (from the LXX) represent. **as one mourneth for ... son** —(Jer. 6:26; Amos 8:10). A proverbial phrase peculiarly forcible among the Jews, who felt childlessness as a curse and dishonor. Applied with peculiar propriety to mourning for Messiah, "the *first-born* among many brethren" (Rom. 8:29). **11.** As in vs. 10 the bitterness of their mourning is illustrated by a private case of mourning, so in this verse by a public one, the greatest recorded in Jewish history, that for the violent death in battle with Pharaoh-necho of the good King Josiah, whose reign had been the only gleam of brightness for the period from Hezekiah to the downfall of the state; lamentations were written by Jeremiah for the occasion (II Kings 23:29, 30; II Chron. 35:22-27). **Hadad-rimmon**—a place or city in the great plain of Esdraelon, the battlefield of many a conflict, near Megiddo; called so from the Syrian idol Rimmon. the Syrians (MACROB, *Saturnalia,* 1.23). **12-14.** A Hadad also was the name of the sun, a chief god of universal and an individual mourning at once. **David ... Nathan**—representing the highest and lowest of the royal order. Nathan, not the prophet, but a younger son of David (II Sam. 5:14; Luke 3:31). **apart**—Retirement and seclusion are needful for deep personal religion. **wives apart**—Jewish females worship separately from the males (Exod. 15:1, 20). **13. Levi ... Shimei**—the highest and lowest of the priestly order (Num. 3:18, 21). Their example and that of the royal order would of course influence the rest. **14. All ... that remain**—after the fiery ordeal, in which two-thirds fall (ch. 13: 8, 9).

CHAPTER 13

Vss. 1-9. CLEANSING OF THE JEWS FROM SIN; ABOLITION OF IDOLATRY; THE SHEPHERD SMITTEN;

THE PEOPLE OF THE LAND CUT OFF, EXCEPT A THIRD PART REFINED BY TRIALS. **1.** Connected with the close of ch. 12. The mourning penitents are here comforted. **fountain opened**—It has been long opened, but then first it shall be so *"to the house of David ..."* (representing all Israel) after their long and weary wanderings. Like Hagar in the wilderness they remain ignorant of the refreshment near them, until God *"opens their eyes"* (Gen. 21:19) [MOORE]. It is not the fountain, but their eyes that need to be opened. It shall be a "fountain" ever flowing; not a laver needing constantly to be replenished with water, such as stood between the tabernacle and altar (Exod. 30:18). **for sin ... uncleanness**—i.e., judicial guilt and moral impurity. Thus justification and sanctification are implied in this verse as both flowing from the blood of Christ, not from ceremonial sacrifices (I Cor. 1:30; Heb. 9:13, 14; I John 1:7; cf. Ezek. 36:25). *Sin* in *Hebrew* is literally *a missing the mark* or *way.* **2.** Consequences of pardon; not indolence, but the extirpation of sin. **names of ... idols**—Their very names were not to be mentioned; thus the Jews, instead of Mephi-baal, said Mephibosheth (*Bosheth* meaning a contemptible thing) (Exod. 23:13; Deut. 12:3; Ps. 16:4). **out of the land**—Judea's two great sins, idolatry and false prophecy, have long since ceased. But these are types of all sin (e.g., covetousness, Eph. 5:5, a besetting sin of the Jews now). Idolatry, combined with the "spirit" of "Satan," is again to be incarnated in "the man of sin," who is to arise in Judea (II Thess. 2:3-12), and is to be "consumed with the Spirit of the Lord's mouth." Cf. as to Antichrist's papal precursor, "seducing spirits ... doctrines of devils," etc., I Timothy 4:1-3; II Peter 2:1. **the unclean spirit**—*Hebrew, spirit of uncleanness* (cf. Rev. 16:13); opposed to "the Spirit of holiness" (Rom. 1:4), "spirit of error" (I John 4:6). One assuming to be divinely inspired, but in league with Satan. **3.** The form of phraseology here is drawn from Deuteronomy 13:6-10; 18:20. The substantial truth expressed is that false prophecy shall be utterly abolished. If it were possible for it again to start up, the very parents of the false prophet would not let parental affection interfere, but would be the first to thrust him through. Love to Christ must be paramount to the tenderest of natural ties (Matt. 10:37). Much as the godly love their children, they love God and His honor more. **4. prophets ... ashamed**—of the false prophecies which they have uttered in times past, and which the event has confuted. **rough garment**—sackcloth. The badge of a prophet (II Kings 1:8; Isa. 20:2), to mark their frugality alike in food and attire (Matt. 3:4); also, to be consonant to the mournful warnings which they delivered. It is not the dress that is here condemned, but the purpose for which it was worn, viz., to conceal wolves under sheep's clothing [CALVIN]. The monkish hair-shirt of Popery, worn to inspire the multitude with the impression of superior sanctity, shall be then cast aside. **5, 6.** The detection of one of the false prophets dramatically represented. He is seized by some zealous vindicator of the law, and in fear cries out, "I am no prophet." **man**—i.e., one. **taught me to keep cattle**—As "keeping cattle" is not the same as to be "an husbandman," translate rather, "Has used (or 'appropriated') me as a servant," viz., *in husbandry* [MAURER]. However, husbandry and keeping cattle might be regarded as jointly the occupation of the person questioned: then Amos 7:14, "herdman," will accord with *English Version.* A *Hebrew* kindred word means "cattle." Both occupations,

the respondent replies, are inconsistent with my being a "prophet." **6. wounds in thine hand**—The interrogator still suspects him: "If so, if you have never pretended to be a prophet, whence come those wounds?" The *Hebrew* is literally, *"between* thine hands." The hands were naturally held up to ward off the blows, and so were "thrust through" (vs. 3) "between" the bones of the hand. *Stoning* was the usual punishment; "thrusting through" was also a fit retribution on one who tried to "thrust Israel away" from the Lord (Deut. 13:10); and perfects the type of Messiah, condemned as a false prophet, and pierced with "wounds *between* His hands." Thus the transition to the direct prophecy of Him (vs. 7) is natural, which it would not be if He were not indirectly and in type alluded to. **wounded in ... house of my friends**—an implied admission that he had pretended to prophecy, and that his friends had wounded him for it in zeal for God (vs. 3). The Holy Spirit in Zechariah alludes indirectly to Messiah, the Antitype, wounded by those whom He came to befriend, who ought to have been His "friends," who were His kinsmen (cf. vs. 3, as to the false prophet's friends, with Mark 3:21, "His friends," *Margin,* "kinsmen"; John 7:5; "His own," John 1:11; *the Jews,* "of whom as concerning the flesh He came," Rom. 9:5), but who wounded Him by the agency of the Romans (ch. 12:10). **7.** Expounded by Christ as referring to Himself (Matt. 26: 31, 32). Thus it is a resumption of the prophecy of His betrayal (ch. 11:4, 10, 13, 14), and the subsequent punishment of the Jews. It explains the mystery why He, who came to be a blessing, was cut off while bestowing the blessing. God regards sin in such a fearful light that He spared not His own co-equal Son in the one Godhead, when that Son bore the sinner's guilt. **Awake**—Cf. a similar address to the sword of justice personified (Jer. 46:6, 7). For "smite" (imperative), Matthew 26:31 has "I will smite." The act of the sword, it is thus implied, is GOD's act. So the prophecy in Isaiah 6:9, "Hear ye," is imperative; the fulfilment as declared by Jesus is future (Matt. 13:14), "ye shall hear." **sword**—the symbol of judicial power, the highest exercise of which is to take away the life of the condemned (Ps. 17:13; Rom. 13:4). Not merely a show, or expression, of justice (as Socinians think) is distinctly implied here, but an actual execution of it on Messiah the shepherd, the substitute for the sheep, by God as judge. Yet God in this shows His love as gloriously as His justice. For God calls Messiah *"My* shepherd," i.e., provided (Rev. 13:8) for sinners by My love to them, and ever the object of My love, though judicially smitten (Isa. 53:4) for their sins (Isa. 42:1; 59:16). **man that is my fellow**—lit., *the "man of my union."* The *Hebrew* for "man" is "a mighty man," one peculiarly man in his noblest ideal. "My fellow," i.e., "my associate." "My equal" ([DE WETTE]; a remarkable admission from a Rationalist). "My nearest kinsman" [HENGSTENBERG], (John 10:30; 14: 10, 11; Phil. 2:6). **sheep shall be scattered**—The scattering of Christ's disciples on His apprehension was the partial fulfilment (Matt. 26:31), a pledge of the dispersion of the Jewish nation (once the Lord's *sheep,* Ps. 100:3) consequent on their crucifixion of Him. The Jews, though "scattered," are still the Lord's "sheep," awaiting their being "gathered' 'by Him (Isa. 40:9, 11). **I will turn ... hand upon ... little ones**—i.e., I will interpose in favor of (cf. the phrase in a good sense, Isa. 1:25) "the little ones," viz., the humble followers of Christ from the Jewish Church, despised by the world: "the poor of the flock" (ch. 11:7, 11); comforted after His crucifixion at the resurrection (John 20:17-20); saved again by a special interposition from the destruction of Jerusalem, having retired to Pella when Cestius Gallus so unaccountably withdrew from Jerusalem. Ever since there has been a Jewish "remnant" of "the little ones" "according to the election of grace." The hand of Jehovah was laid in wrath on the Shepherd that His *hand might be turned* in grace *upon the little ones.* **8, 9.** Two-thirds of the Jewish nation were to perish in the Roman wars, and a third to survive. Probably from the context (ch. 14:2-9), which has never yet been fulfilled, the destruction of the two-thirds (lit., "the proportion of two," or "portion of two") and the saving of the remnant, the one-third, are still future, and to be fulfilled under Antichrist. **9. through ... fire**—of trial (Ps. 66:10; Amos 4:11; I Cor. 3:15; I Peter 1: 6, 7). It hence appears that the Jews' conversion is not to precede, but to follow, their external deliverance by the special interposition of Jehovah; which latter shall be the main cause of their conversion, combined with a preparatory inward shedding abroad in their hearts of the Holy Spirit (ch. 12:10-14); and here, "they shall call on My name," in their trouble, which brings Jehovah to their help (Ps. 50: 15). **my people**—(Jer. 30:18-22; Ezek. 11:19, 20; Hos. 2:23).

CHAPTER 14

Vss. 1-21. LAST STRUGGLE WITH THE HOSTILE WORLD POWERS: MESSIAH-JEHOVAH SAVES JERUSALEM AND DESTROYS THE FOE, OF WHOM THE REMNANT TURNS TO THE LORD REIGNING AT JERUSALEM. 1. day of the Lord—in which He shall vindicate His justice by punishing the wicked and then saving His elect people (Joel 2:31; 3:14; Mal. 4:1, 5). **thy spoil ... divided in the midst of thee**—by the foe; secure of victory, they shall not divide the spoil taken from thee in their camp outside, but "in the midst" of the city itself. **2. gather all nations ...**—The prophecy seems literal (cf. Joel 3:2). If Antichrist be the leader of the nations, it seems inconsistent with the statement that he will at this time be sitting in the temple as God at Jerusalem (II Thess. 2:4); thus Antichrist outside would be made to besiege Antichrist within the city. But difficulties do not set aside revelations: the event will clear up seeming difficulties. Cf. the complicated movements, Daniel 11. **half ... the residue**—In ch. 13: 8, 9, it is "two-thirds" that perish, and "the *third*" escapes. There, however, it is "in *all the land*"; here it is "half *of the city.*" Two-thirds of the *whole people* perish, one-third survives. One-half of the *citizens* are led captive, the residue are not cut off. Perhaps, too, we ought to translate, "a (not 'the') residue." **3. Then**—In Jerusalem's extremity. **as ... in ... day of battle**—as when Jehovah fought for Israel against the Egyptians at the Red Sea (Exod. 14:14; 15:3). As He then made a way through the divided sea, so will He now divide in two "the Mount of Olives" (vs. 4). **4.** The object of the cleaving of the mount in two by a fissure or valley (a prolongation of the valley of Jehoshaphat, and extending from Jerusalem on the west towards Jordan, eastward) is to open a way of escape to the besieged (ch. Joel 3:12, 14). Half the divided mount is thereby forced northward, half southward; the valley running between. The place of His departure at His ascension shall be the place of His return: and the "manner" of His return shall also be

similar (Acts 1:11). He shall probably "come from the east" (Matt. 24:27). He so made His triumphal entry into the city from the Mount of Olives from the east (Matt. 21:1-10). This was the scene of His agony: so it shall be the scene of His glory. Cf. Ezekiel 11:23, with 43:2, "from the way of the east.' **5. ye shall flee** *to* **the valley**—rather *"through* the valley," as in II Samuel 2:29. The valley made by the cleaving asunder of the Mount of Olives (vs. 4) is designed to be their way of escape, not their place of refuge [MAURER]. JEROME is on the side of *English Version.* If it be translated so, it will mean, Ye shall flee *to* the valley, not to hide there, but as the passage through which an escape may be effected. The same divinely sent earthquake which swallows up the foe, opens out a way of escape to God's people. The earthquake in Uzziah's days is mentioned (Amos 1:1) as a recognized epoch in Jewish history. Cf. also Isaiah 6:1: perhaps the same year that Jehovah held His heavenly court and gave commission to Isaiah for the Jews, an earthquake in the physical world, as often happens (Matt. 24:7), marked momentous movements in the unseen spiritual world. **of the mountains**—rather, "of *My* mountains," viz., Zion and Moriah, peculiarly sacred to Jehovah [MOORE]. Or, the mountains formed by *My* cleaving Olivet into two [MAURER]. **Azal**—the name of a place *near* a gate east of the city. The *Hebrew* means "adjoining" [HENDERSON]. Others give the meaning, "departed," "ceased." The valley reaches up to the city gates, so as to enable the fleeing citizens to betake themselves immediately to it on leaving the city. **Lord my God ... with thee**—The mention of the "Lord my God" leads the prophet to pass suddenly to a direct address to Jehovah. It is as if "lifting up his head" (Luke 21:28), he suddenly sees in vision the Lord coming, and joyfully exclaims, "All the saints with Thee!" So Isaiah 25:9. **saints**—*holy angels* escorting the returning King (Matt. 24:30, 31; Jude 14); and redeemed men (I Cor. 15:23; I Thess. 3:13; 4: 14). Cf. the similar mention of the "saints" and "angels" at His coming on Sinai (Deut. 32:2, 3; Acts 7:53; Gal. 3:19; Heb. 2:2). PHILLIPS thinks Azal is Ascalon on the Mediterranean. An earthquake beneath Messiah's tread will divide Syria, making from Jerusalem to Azal a valley which will admit the ocean waters from the west to the Dead Sea. The waters will rush down the valley of Arabah, the old bed of the Jordan, clear away the sand-drift of 4000 years, and cause the commerce of Petra and Tyre to center in the holy city. The Dead Sea rising above its shores will overflow by the valley of Edom, completing the straits of Azal into the Red Sea. Thus will be formed the great pool of Jerusalem (cf. vs. 8; Ezek. 47:1, etc.; Joel·3:18). Euphrates will be the north boundary, and the Red Sea the south. Twenty-five miles north and twenty-five miles south of Jerusalem will form one side of the fifty miles square of the Lord's Holy Oblation (Ezek. 48). There are seven spaces of fifty miles each from Jerusalem northward to the Euphrates, and five spaces of fifty miles each southward to the Red Sea. Thus there are thirteen equal distances on the breadth of the future promised land, one for the oblation and twelve for the tribes, according to Ezekiel 48. That the Euphrates north, Mediterranean west, the Nile and Red Sea south, are to be the future boundaries of the holy land, which will include Syria and Arabia, is favored by Genesis 15:8; Exodus 23:31; Deuteronomy 11:24; Joshua 1: 4; I Kings 4:21; II Chronicles 9:26; Isaiah 27:12; all which was partially realized in Solomon's reign, shall be antitypically so hereafter. The theory, if true, will clear away many difficulties in the way of the literal interpretation of this chapter and Ezekiel 48. **6. light . . . not . . . clear . . . dark**—JEROME, *Chaldee, Syriac,* and LXX *translate,* "There shall not be light, but cold and ice"; i.e., a day full of horror (Amos 5:18). But the *Hebrew* for "clear" does not mean "cold," but "precious," "splendid" (cf. Job 31:26). CALVIN translates, "The light shall not be clear, *but* dark" (lit., "condensation," i.e., thick mist); like a dark day in which you can hardly distinguish between day and night. *English Version* accords with vs. 7: "There shall not be altogether light nor altogether darkness," but an intermediate condition in which sorrows shall be mingled with joys. **7. one day**—a day altogether *unique,* different from all others [MAURER]. Cf. "one," i.e., unique (Song of Sol. 6:9; Jer. 30:7). Not as HENDERSON explains, "One continuous day, without night" (Rev. 22:5, 25); the millennial period (Rev. 20:3-7). **known to . . . Lord**—This truth restrains man's curiosity and teaches us to wait the Lord's own time (Matt. 24:36). **not day, nor night**—answering to "not . . . clear nor . . . dark" (vs. 6); not altogether daylight, yet not the darkness of night. **at evening . . . shall be light**—Towards the close of this twilight-like time of calamity, "light" shall spring up (Ps. 97:11; 112:4; Isa. 30:26; 60:19, 20). **8. living waters**—(Ezek. 47:1; Joel 3:18). **former sea**—i.e., the *front,* or east, which Orientalists face in taking the points of the compass; the Dead Sea. **hinder sea**—the west or Mediterranean. **summer . . . winter**—neither dried up by heat, nor frozen by cold; ever flowing. **9. king over all . . . earth**—Isaiah 54:5 implies that this is to be the consequence of Israel being again recognized by God as His own people (Dan. 2:44; Rev. 11:15). **one Lord . . . name one**—Not that He is not so already, but He shall then be *recognized by all unanimously* as "One." Now there are "gods many and lords many." Then Jehovah alone shall be worshipped. The *manifestation* of the unity of the Godhead shall be simultaneous with that of the unity of the Church. Believers are one in spirit already, even as God is one (Eph. 4:3-6). But externally there are sad divisions. Not until these disappear, shall God reveal fully His unity to the world (John 17:21, 23). Then shall there be "a pure language, that all may call upon the name of the Lord with one consent" (Zeph. 3:9). The Son too shall at last give up His mediatorial kingdom to the Father, when the purposes for which it was established shall have been accomplished, "that God may be all in all" (I Cor. 15:24). **10. turned**—or, "changed round about": lit., "to make a circuit." The whole hilly land *round* Jerusalem, which would prevent the free passage of the living waters, shall be *changed* so as to be "as a [or *the*] plain" (Isa. 40:4). **from Geba to Rimmon**—Geba (II Kings 23:8) in Benjamin, the north border of Judah. Rimmon, in Simeon (Josh. 15:32), the south border of Judah; not the Rimmon northeast of Michmash. "*The* plain from Geba to Rimmon" (i.e., from one boundary to the other) is the Arabah or plain of the Jordan, extending from the Sea of Tiberias to the Elanitic Gulf of the Red Sea. **it shall be lifted up**—viz., Jerusalem shall be exalted, the hills all round being lowered (Mic. 4:1). **inhabited in her place**—(ch. 12:6). **from Benjamin's gate**—leading to the territory of Benjamin. The same as Ephraim's gate, the north boundary of the city (II Kings 14:13). **the first gate**—west of the city [GROTIUS]. "The place ot . . ." implies that the gate itself was then not in existence. "The old gate"

(Neh. 3:6). **the corner gate**—east of the city [GROTIUS]. Or the "corner" joining the north and west parts of the wall [VILLALPANDUS]. GROTIUS thinks "corners" refers to the *towers* there built (cf. *Margin,* Zeph. 3:6). **tower of Hananeel**—south of the city, near the sheep gate (Neh. 3:1; 12:39; Jer. 31:38) [GROTIUS]. **king's winepresses**—(Song of Sol. 8:11). In the interior of the city, at Zion [GROTIUS]. **11. no more utter destruction**—(Jer. 31:40). Lit., "no more *curse*" (Rev. 22:3; cf. Mal. 4:6), for there will be no more sin. Temporal blessings and spiritual prosperity shall go together in the millennium: long life (Isa. 65:20-22), peace (Isa. 2:4), honor (Isa. 60:14-16), righteous government (Isa. 54:14; 60:18). Judgment, as usual, begins at the house of God, but then falls fatally on Antichrist, whereon the Church obtains perfect liberty. The last day will end everything evil (Rom. 8:21) [AUBERLEN]. **12.** Punishment on the foe, the last Antichristian confederacy (Isa. 59:18; 66:24; Ezek. 38, 39; Rev. 19:17-21). A living death: the *corruption* (Gal. 6:8) of death combined in ghastly union with the conscious sensibility of life. Sin will be felt by the sinner in all its loathsomeness, inseparably clinging to him as a festering, putrid body. **13. tumult**—consternation (ch. 12:4; I Sam. 14:15, 20). **lay hold . . . on . . . hand of . . . neighbour**—instinctively grasping it, as if thereby to be safer, but in vain [MENOCHIUS]. Rather, in order to assail "his neighbor" [CALVIN], (Ezek. 38:21). Sin is the cause of all quarrels on earth. It will cause endless quarrels in hell (Jas. 3:15, 16). **14. Judah . . . fight at Jerusalem**—viz., against the foe: not against Jerusalem, as MAURER translates in variance with the context. As to the spoil gained from the foe, cf. Ezekiel 39:10, 17. **15.** The plague shall affect the very beasts belonging to the foe. A typical foretaste of all this befell Antiochus Epiphanes and his host at Jerusalem (I Maccabees 13:49; II Maccabees 9:5). **16. every one . . . left**—(Isa. 66:19, 23). God will conquer all the foes of the Church. Some He will destroy; others He will bring into willing subjection. **from year to year**—lit., "from the sufficiency of a year in a year." **feast of tabernacles**—The other two great yearly feasts, passover and pentecost, are not specified, because, their antitypes having come, the types are done away with. But the feast of tabernacles will be commemorative of the Jews' sojourn, not merely forty years in the wilderness, but for almost 2000 years of their dispersion. So it was kept on their return from the Babylonian dispersion (Neh. 8:14-17). It was the feast on which Jesus made His triumphal entry into Jerusalem (Matt. 21:8); a pledge of His return to His capital to reign (cf. Lev. 23:34, 39, 40, 42; Rev. 7:9; 21:3). A feast of peculiar joy (Ps. 118:15; Hos. 12:9). The feast on which Jesus gave the invitation to the living waters of salvation ("Hosanna," *save us now,* was the cry, Matt. 21:9; cf. Ps. 118:25, 26) (John 7:2, 37). To the Gentiles, too, it will be significant of perfected salvation after past wanderings in a moral wilderness, as it originally commemorated the ingathering of the harvest. The seedtime of tears shall then have issued in the harvest of joy [MOORE]. "All the nations" could not possibly in person go up to the feast, but they may do so by representatives. **17. no rain**—including every calamity which usually follows in the East from want of rain, viz., scarcity of provisions, famine, pestilence, etc. Rain is the symbol also of God's favor (Hos. 6:3). That there shall be unconverted men under the millennium appears from the outbreak of God and Magog at the end of it

(Rev. 20:7-9); but they, like Satan their master, shall be restrained during the thousand years. Note, too, from this verse that the Gentiles shall come up to Jerusalem, rather than the Jews go as missionaries to the Gentiles (Isa. 2:2; Mic. 5:7). However, Isaiah 66:19 *may* imply the converse. **18. if . . . Egypt go not up**—specified as Israel's ancient foe. If Egypt go not up, and so there be no rain on them (a judgment which Egypt would condemn, as depending on the Nile's overflow, not on rain), there shall be the plague . . . . Because the guilty are not affected by one judgment, let them not think to escape, for God has other judgments which shall plague them. MAURER translates, "If Egypt go not up, upon them also there shall be none" (no rain). Psalm 105:32 mentions "rain" in Egypt. But it is not their main source of fertility. **19. punishment**—lit., "sin"; i.e., "punishment for sin." **20. shall there be upon the bells**—viz., this inscription, "Holiness to the Lord," the same as was on the miter of the high priest (Exod. 28:36). This implies that all things, even the most common, shall be sacred to Jehovah, and not merely the things which under the law had peculiar sanctity attached to them. The "bells" were metal plates hanging from the necks of horses and camels as ornaments, which *tinkled* (as the *Hebrew* root means) by striking against each other. Bells attached to horses are found represented on the walls of Sennacherib's palace at Koyunjik. **pots . . . like . . . bowls**—the vessels used for boiling, for receiving ashes, etc., shall be as holy as the bowls used for catching the blood of the sacrificial victims (*Note*, ch. 9:15; I Sam. 2:14). The priesthood of Christ will be explained more fully both by the Mosaic types and by the New Testament in that temple of which Ezekiel speaks. Then the Song of Solomon, now obscure, will be understood, for the marriage feast of the Lamb will be celebrated in heaven (Rev. 19), and on earth it will be a Solomonic period, peaceful, glorious, and nuptial. There will be no king but a prince; the sabbatic period of the judges will return, but not with the Old Testament, but New Testament glory (Isa. 1:26; Ezek. 45) [Roos]. **21. every pot**—even in private houses, as in the temple, shall be deemed holy, so universal shall be the consecration of all things and persons to Jehovah. **take of them**—as readily as they would take of the pots of the temple itself, whatever number they wanted for sacrifice. **no . . . Canaanite**—no unclean or ungodly person (Isa. 35:8; 52:1; Joel 3:17). Cf. as to the final state subsequent to the millennium, Revelation 21:27; 22:15. MAURER not so well translates "merchant" here, as in Proverbs 31:24. If a man would have the beginnings of heaven, it must be by absolute consecration of everything to God on earth. Let his life be a liturgy, a holy service of acted worship [MOORE].

THE BOOK OF

MALACHI

INTRODUCTION

MALACHI forms the transition link between the two dispensations, the Old and the New, "the skirt and boundary of Christianity" [TERTULLIAN], to which perhaps is due the abrupt earnestness which characterizes his prophecies. His very name is somewhat uncertain. Malachi is the name of an office, rather than a person, "My messenger," and as such is found in ch. 3:1. LXX favors this view in ch. 1:1; translate, not "by Malachi," but "by the hand of His messenger" (cf. Hag 1:13). Malachi is the last inspired messenger of the Old Testament, announcing the advent of the Great Messenger of the New Testament. The *Chaldee* paraphrase identifies him with Ezra wrongly, as Ezra is never called a prophet but a scribe, and Malachi never a scribe but a prophet. Still it hence appears that Malachi was by some old authorities not regarded as a proper name. The analogy of the headings of other prophets, however, favors the common view that Malachi is a proper name. As Haggai and Zechariah, the contemporary prophets, supported Joshua and Zerubbabel in the building of the temple, so he at a subsequent period supported the priest Ezra and the governor Nehemiah. Like that ruler, he presupposes the temple to have been already built (ch. 1:10; 3:1–10). Both alike censure the abuses still unreformed (Neh. 13:5, 15–22, 23–30), the profane and mercenary character of the priests, the people's marriages contracted with foreigners, the non-payment of the tithes, and want of sympathy towards the poor on the part of the rich. Nehemiah 6:7 implies that Nehemiah was supported by prophets in his work of reformation. The date thus will be about 420 B.C., or later. Both the periods after the captivity (that of Haggai and Zechariah, and that of Malachi) were marked by royal, priestly, and prophetic men at the head of God's people. The former period was that of the building of the temple; the latter, that of the restoration of the people and rebuilding of the city. It is characteristic of the people of God that the first period after the restoration was exclusively devoted to the rebuilding of the temple; the political restoration came secondarily. Only a colony of 50,000 settled with Joshua and Zerubbabel in Palestine (Ezra 2:64). Even these became intermingled with the heathen around during the sixty years passed over by Ezra in silence (Ezra 9:6–15; Nehemiah 1:3). Hence a second restoration was needed which should mould the national life into a Jewish form, re-establishing the holy law and the holy city—a work effected by Ezra and Nehemiah, with the aid of Malachi, in a period of about half a century, ending with the deaths of Malachi and Nehemiah in the last ten years of the fifth century B.C.; i.e., the "seven weeks" (Daniel 9:25) put in the beginning of the "seventy" by themselves, to mark the fundamental difference between them, the last period of Old Testament revelation, and the period which followed without any revelation (the sixty-two weeks), preceding the final week standing out in unrivalled dignity by itself as the time of Messiah's appearing. The seventy weeks thus begin with the seventh year of Artaxerxes who allowed Ezra to go to Jerusalem, 457 B.C., in accordance with the commandment which then went forth from God. Ezra the priest performed the inner work of purifying the nation from heathenish elements and reintroducing the law; while Nehemiah did the outer work of rebuilding the city and restoring the national polity [AUBERLEN]. VITRINGA makes the date of Malachi's prophecies to be about the second return of Nehemiah from Persia, not later than 424 B.C., the date of Artaxerxes' death (Neh. 13:6). About this time Socrates was teaching the only approach to a pure morality which corrupt Athens ever knew. MOORE distinguishes six portions: (1) Charge against Israel for insensibility to God's love, which so distinguished Israel above Edom (ch. 1:1–5). (2) The priests are reproved for neglect and profanation (ch. 1:6 to ch. 2:9). (3) Mixed marriages, and the wrongs done to Jewish wives, are reproved (ch. 2:10–16). (4) Coming of Messiah and His forerunners (ch. 2:17 to ch. 3:6). (5) Reproof for tithes withheld (ch. 3:7–12). (6) Contrast between the godly and the ungodly at the present time, and in the future judgment; exhortation, therefore, to return to the law (ch. 3:13 to ch. 4:6).

The style is animated, but less grand, and the rhythm less marked, than in some of the older prophets.

The canonicity of the book is established by the references to it in the New Testament (Matt. 11:10; 17:12; Mark 1:2; 9:11, 12; Luke 1:17; Rom. 9:13).

CHAPTER 1

Vss. 1-14. GOD'S LOVE: ISRAEL'S INGRATITUDE: THE PRIESTS' MERCENARY SPIRIT: A GENTILE SPIRITUAL PRIESTHOOD SHALL SUPERSEDE THEM. **1. burden**—heavy sentence. **to Israel**—represented now by the two tribes of Judah and Benjamin, with individuals of the ten tribes who had returned with the Jews from Babylon. So "Israel" is used, Ezra 7:10. Cf. II Chronicles 21:2, "Jehoshaphat king of *Israel*," where Judah, rather than the ten tribes, is regarded as the truest representative of Israel (cf. II Chronicles 12:6; 28:19). **Malachi**—see *Introduction*. God sent no prophet after him till John the Baptist, the forerunner of Christ, in order to enflame His people with the more ardent desire for Him, the great antitype and fulfiller of prophecy. **2. I have loved you**—above other men; nay, even above the other descendants of Abraham and Isaac. Such gratuitous love on My part called for love on yours. But the return ye make is sin and dishonor to Me. This which is to be supplied is left unexpressed, sorrow as it were breaking off the sentence [MENOCHIUS], (Deut. 7:8; Hos. 11:1). **Wherein hast thou loved us?**—In painful contrast to the tearful tenderness of God's love stands their insolent challenge. The root of their sin was insensibility to God's *love,* and to their own wickedness. Having had prosperity taken from them, they imply they have no tokens of God's love; they look at what God had taken, not at what God had left. God's love is often least acknowledged where it is most manifested. We must not infer God does not love us because He afflicts us. Men, instead of referring their sufferings to their proper cause, their own sin, impiously accuse God of indifference to their welfare [MOORE]. Thus the four first verses form a fit introduction to the whole prophecy. **Was not Esau Jacob's brother?**—and so, as far as dignity went, as much entitled to God's favor as Jacob. My adoption of Jacob, therefore, was altogether by gratuitous favor (Rom. 9:13). So God has passed by our elder brethren, the angels who kept not their first estate, and yet He has provided salvation for man. The perpetual rejection of the fallen angels, like the perpetual desolations of Edom, attests God's severity to the lost, and goodness to those gratuitously saved. The sovereign eternal purpose of God is the only ground on which He bestows on one favors withheld from another. There are difficulties in referring salvation to the election of God, there are greater in referring it to the election of man [MOORE]. Jehovah illustrates His condescension and patience in arguing the case with them. **3. hated**—not positively, but relatively; i.e., did not

choose him out to be the object of gratuitous favor, as I did Jacob (cf. Luke 14:26, with Matt. 10:37; Gen. 29:30, 31; Deut. 21:15, 16). **laid his mountains . . . waste**—i.e., his territory which was generally mountainous. Israel was, it is true, punished by the Chaldeans, but Edom has been utterly destroyed; viz., either by Nebuchadnezzar [ROSENMULLER], or by the neighboring peoples, Egypt, Ammon, and Moab [JOSEPHUS, *Antiquities*, 10.9, 7; MAURER], (Jer. 49:18). **dragons**—jackals [MOORE] (cf. Isa. 34:13). MAURER translates, "*Abodes* of the wilderness," from an *Arabic* root "*to stop*," or "to abide." *English Version* is better. **4. Whereas**—*But if* Edom say [MAURER]. Edom may strive as she may to recover herself, but it shall be in vain, for I doom her to perpetual desolation, whereas I restore Israel. This Jehovah states, to illustrate His gratuitous love to Israel, rather than to Edom. **border of wickedness**—a region given over to the curse of reprobation [CALVIN]. For a time Judea seemed as desolate as Idumea; but though the latter was once the highway of Eastern commerce, now the lonely rock-houses of Petra attest the fulfilment of the prophecy. It is still "the border of wickedness," being the resort of the marauding tribes of the desert. Judea's restoration, though delayed, is yet certain. **the Lord hath indignation**—"the people of My curse" (Isa. 34:5). **5. from the border of Israel**—Ye, restored to your own "borders" in Israel, "from" them shall raise your voices to "magnify the Lord," acknowledging that Jehovah has shown to you a gratuitous favor not shown to Edom, and so ought to be especially "magnified from the borders of Israel." **6.** Turning from the people to the priests, Jehovah asks, whereas His love to the people was so great, where was their love towards Him? If the priests, as they profess, regard Him as their Father (Isa. 63:16) and Master, let them show the reality of their profession by *love and reverential fear* (Exod. 20:12; Luke 6:46). He addresses the priests because they ought to be leaders in piety to the rest of the people, whereas they are foremost in "despising His name." **Wherein have we despised . . .**—The same captious spirit of self-satisfied insensibility as prompted their question (vs. 2), "Wherein hast Thou loved us?" They are blind alike to God's love and their own guilt. **7. ye offer . . .**—God's answer to their challenge (vs. 6), "Wherein have we despised?" **polluted bread**—viz., blemished sacrifices (vss. 8, 13, 14; Deut. 15:21). So "the *bread* of thy God" is used for "*sacrifices* to God" (Lev. 21:8). **polluted thee**—i.e., offered to thee "polluted bread." **table of the Lord**—i.e., the altar (Ezek. 41:22) (not the table of shewbread). Just as the sacrificial *flesh* is called "bread."

contemptible—(vss. 12, 13). Ye sanction the niggardly and blemished offerings of the people on the altar, to gain favor with them. Darius, and probably his successors, had liberally supplied them with victims for sacrifice, yet they presented none but the worst. A cheap religion, costing little, is rejected by God, and so is worth nothing. It costs more than it is worth, for it is worth nothing, and so proves really dear. God despises not the widow's mite, but he does despise the miser's mite [MOORE]. 8. Your earthly ruler would feel insulted, if offered by you the offering with which ye put off God (see Lev. 22:22, 24). **is it not evil?**—MAURER translates, "There is no evil," in your opinion, in such an offering; it is quite good enough for such a purpose. 9. **now ... beseech God that he will be gracious**—Ironical. Think you that God will be persuaded by such polluted gifts to be gracious to you? Far from it. **this hath been by your means**—lit., "hand." These contemptible offerings are your doing, as being the priests mediating between God and the people; and think you, will God pay any regard to you (cf. vss. 8, 10)? "Accept thy person" ("face"), vs. 8, answers to "regard your persons," in this verse. 10. **Who ... for naught**—Not one even of the least priestly functions (as shutting the doors, or kindling a fire on the altar) would ye exercise without pay, therefore ye ought to fulfil them faithfully (I Cor. 9:13). DRUSIUS and MAURER translate, "Would that there were absolutely some one of you who would shut the doors of the temple (i.e., of the inner court, in which was the altar of burnt offerings), and that ye would not kindle fire on My altar in vain!" Better no sacrifices than vain ones (Isa. 1:11-15). It was the duty of some of the priests to stand at the doors of the court of the altar of burnt offerings, and to have excluded blemished victims [CALVIN]. 11. **For**—Since ye Jewish priests and people "despise My name" (vs. 6), I shall find others who will magnify it (Matt. 3:9). Do not think I shall have no worshippers because I have not you; for from the east to the west My name shall be great among the Gentiles (Isa. 66:19, 20), those very peoples whom ye look down upon as abominable. **pure offering** —not "the blind, the lame, and the sick," such as ye offer (vs. 8). "In every place," implies the catholicity of the Christian Church (John 4:21, 23; I Tim. 2:8). The "incense" is figurative of *prayers* (Ps. 141:2; Rev. 8:3). "Sacrifice" is used metaphorically (Ps. 51:17; Heb. 13:10, 15, 16; I Pet. 2:5, 12). In this sense the reference to the Lord's Supper, maintained by many of the fathers, may be admitted; it, like prayer, is a spiritual offering, accepted through the literal offering of the "Lamb without blemish," once for all slain. 12. Renewal of the charge in vs. 7. **fruit ... meat**—the offerings of the people. The "fruit" is the *produce* of the altar, on which the priests subsisted. They did not literally say, The Lord's table is contemptible; but their *acts* virtually said so. They did not act so as to lead the people to reverence, and to offer their best to the Lord on it. The people were poor, and put off God with the worst offerings. The priests let them do so, for fear of offending the people, and so losing all gains from them. 13. **what a weariness is it!**—Ye regard God's service as irksome, and therefore try to get it over by presenting the most worthless offerings. Cf. Micah 6:3, where God challenges His people to show wherein is the "weariness" or hardship of His service. Also Isaiah 43:22-24, wherein He shows that it is they who have "wearied" Him, not He who has wearied them. **snuffed at**—de-

spised. **it**—the table of the Lord, and the meat on it (vs. 12). **torn**—viz., by beasts, which it was not lawful to eat, much less to offer (Exod. 22:31). **thus ... offering**—*Hebrew*, "mincha"; the *unbloody offering* of flour, etc. Though this may have been of ordinary ingredients, yet the *sacrifices* of blemished animals accompanying it rendered it unacceptable. 14. **deceiver**—hypocrite. Not poverty, but avarice was the cause of their mean offerings. **male**—required by law (Lev. 1:3, 10). **great King**—(Ps. 48:2; Matt. 5:35). **my name ... dreadful among ... heathen**—Even the heathen dread Me because of My judgments; what a reproach this is to you, My people, who fear Me not (vs. 6)! Also it may be translated, "*shall be* feared among ...," agreeing with the prophecy of the call of the Gentiles (vs. 11).

CHAPTER 2

Vss. 1-17. REPROOF OF THE PRIESTS FOR VIOLATING THE COVENANT; AND THE PEOPLE ALSO FOR MIXED MARRIAGES AND UNFAITHFULNESS 1. **for you**—The priests in particular are reproved, as their part was to have led the people aright, and reproved sin, whereas they encouraged and led them into sin. Ministers cannot sin or suffer alone. They drag down others with them if they fall [MOORE]. 2. **lay ... to heart**—My commands. **send a curse**—rather, as *Hebrew*, "*the* curse"; viz., that denounced in Deuteronomy 27:15-26; 28:15-68. **curse your blessings**—turn the blessings you enjoy into curses (Ps. 106:15). **cursed them**—*Hebrew, them severally;* i.e., I have cursed each one of your blessings. 3. **corrupt ...**—lit., "rebuke," answering to the opposite prophecy of blessing (ch. 3:11), "I will *rebuke* the devourer." To rebuke the seed is to forbid its growing. **your**—lit., "*for you*"; i.e., to your hurt. **dung of ... solemn feasts**—The dung in the maw of the victims sacrificed on the feast days; the maw was the perquisite of the priests (Deut. 18:3), which gives peculiar point to the threat here. You shall get the dung of the maw as your perquisite, instead of the maw. **one shall take you away with it**—i.e., ye shall be taken away with it; it shall cleave to you wherever ye go [MOORE]. Dung shall be thrown on your faces, and ye shall be taken away as dung would be, dung-begrimed as ye shall be (I Kings 14:10; cf. Jer. 16:4; 22:19). 4. **ye shall know**—by bitter experience of consequences, that it was with this design I admonished you, in order "that My covenant with Levi might be" maintained; i.e., that it was for your own good (which would be ensured by your maintaining the Levitical command) I admonished you, that ye should return to your duty [MAURER] (cf. vss. 5, 6). Malachi's function was that of a reformer, leading back the priests and people to the law (ch. 4:4). 5-9. He describes the promises, and also the conditions of the covenant; Levi's observance of the conditions and reward (cf. Num. 25:11-13, Phinehas' zeal); and on the other hand the violation of the conditions, and consequent punishment of the present priests. "Life" here includes the *perpetuity* implied in Numbers 25:13, "everlasting priesthood." "Peace" is specified both here and there. MAURER thus explains it; the *Hebrew* is, lit., "My covenant was with him, *life* and *peace* (to be given him on My part), and I gave them to him: (and on his part) fear (i.e., reverence), and he did fear Me ....." The former portion of the verse expresses the *promise,* and Jehovah's fulfilment of it; the latter, the *condition,* and Levi's steadfastness to it (Deut. 33:8, 9). The Jewish priests self-deceivingly claimed the privileges of the covenant, while neglecting the conditions of it, as if God were bound by it to bless them, while they were free from all the obligation which it imposed to serve Him. The covenant is said to be not merely *"of life and peace,"* but "life and peace"; for the keeping of God's law is its own reward (Ps. 19:11). **6. law of truth was in his mouth**—He taught the people the truths of the law in all its fulness (Deut. 33:10). The priest was the ordinary expounder of the law; the prophets were so only on special occasions. **iniquity . . . not found**—no injustice in his judicial functions (Deut. 17:8, 9; 19:17). **walked with me** —by faith and obedience (Gen. 5:22). **in peace**— viz., the "peace" which was the fruit of obeying the covenant (vs. 5). Peace with God, man, and one's own conscience, is the result of "walking with God" (cf. Job 22:21; Isa. 27:5; Jas. 3:18). **turn many . . . from iniquity**—both by positive precept and by tacit example "walking with God" (Jer. 23:22; Dan. 12: 3; Jas. 5:20). **7.** In doing so (vs. 6) he did his duty as a priest, "for . . . ." **knowledge**—of the law, its doctrines, and positive and negative precepts (Lev. 10:10, 11; Deut. 24:8; Jer. 18:18; Hag. 2:11). **the law**—i.e., its true sense. **messenger of . . . Lord**— the interpreter of His will; cf. as to the prophets, Haggai 1:13. So ministers are called "ambassadors of Christ" (II Cor. 5:20); and the bishops of the seven churches in Revelation, "angels" or messengers (cf. Gal. 4:14). **8. out of the way**—i.e., from the covenant. **caused many to stumble**—By scandalous example, the worse inasmuch as the people look up to you as ministers of religion (I Sam. 2:17; Jer. 18:15; Matt. 18:6; Luke 17:1). **at the law**— i.e., in respect to the observances of the law. **corrupted . . . covenant**—made it of none effect, by not fulfilling its conditions, and so forfeiting its promises (Zech. 11:10; Neh. 13:29). **9.** Because ye do not keep the condition of the covenant, I will not fulfil the promise. **partial in the law**—having respect to persons rather than to truth in the interpretation and administration of the law (Lev. 19:15). **10-16.** Reproof of those who contracted marriages with foreigners and repudiated their Jewish wives. **10. Have we not all one father?**—Why, seeing we all have one common origin, "do we deal treacherously against *one another*" ("His brother" being a general expression implying that all are "brethren" and sisters as children of the same Father above, II Thess. 4:6 and so including the *wives* so injured)? viz., by putting away our Jewish wives, and taking foreign women to wife (cf. vs. 14 and vs. 11; Ezra 9:1-9), and so violating "the covenant" made by Jehovah with "our fathers," by which it was ordained that we should be a people separated from the other peoples of the world (Exod. 19:5; Lev. 20:24, 26; Deut. 7:3). To intermarry with the heathen would defeat this purpose of Jehovah, who was the common Father of the Israelites in a peculiar sense in which He was not Father of the heathen. The "one Father" is Jehovah (Job 31:15; I Cor. 8:6; Eph. 4:6). "Created us": not merely physical creation, but "created us" to be His peculiar and chosen people (Ps. 102:18; Isa. 43:1; 45:8; 60:21; Eph. 2:10), [CALVIN]. How marked the contrast between the honor here done to the female sex, and the degradation to which Oriental women are generally subjected! **11. dealt treacherously**—viz., in respect to the Jewish wives who were put away (vs. 14; also vss. 10, 15, 16). **profaned the holiness of . . . Lord** —by ill-treating the Israelites (viz., the wives), who were set apart as a people *holy unto the Lord:* "the holy seed" (Ezra 9:2; cf. Jer. 2:3). Or, "the holi-

ness of the Lord" means His holy ordinance and covenant (Deut. 7:3). But "which He loved," seems to refer to *the holy people,* Israel, whom God so gratuitously loved (ch. 1:2), without merit on their part (Ps. 47:4). **married . . .**—(Ezra 9:1, 2; 10: 2; Neh. 13:23, etc.). **daughter of a strange god**— women worshipping idols: as the worshipper in Scripture is regarded in the relation of a child to a father (Jer. 2:27). **12. master and . . . scholar**—lit., "him that watcheth and him that answereth." So "wakeneth" is used of *the teacher* or "master" (Isa. 50:4); masters are *watchful* in guarding their scholars. The reference is to the priests, who ought to have taught the people piety, but who led them into evil. "Him that answereth" is the *scholar* who has to answer the questions of his teacher (Luke 2: 47) [GROTIUS]. The Arabs have a proverb, "None calling and none answering," i.e., there being *not one alive.* So GESENIUS explains it of the Levite watches in the temple (Ps. 134:1), one *watchman* calling and another *answering.* But the scholar is rather the *people,* the pupils of the priests "in doing this," viz., forming unions with foreign wives. "Out of the tabernacles of Jacob" proves it is not the priests alone. God will spare neither priests nor people who act so. **him that offereth**—His offerings will not avail to shield him from the penalty of his sin in repudiating his Jewish wife and taking a foreign one. **13. done again**—"a second time": an aggravation of your offense (Neh. 13:23-31), in that it is a relapse into the sin already checked once under Ezra (Ezra 9:10) [HENDERSON]. Or, "the second time" means this: Your first sin was your blemished offerings to the Lord: now "again" is added your sin towards your wives [CALVIN]. **covering . . . altar . . . with tears**—shed by your unoffending wives, repudiated by you that ye might take foreign wives. CALVIN makes the "tears" to be those of all the people on perceiving their sacrifices to be sternly rejected by God. **14. Wherefore?** —Why does God reject our offerings? **Lord . . . witness between thee and . . . wife**—(so Gen. 31:49, 50). **of thy youth**—The Jews still marry very young, the husband often being but thirteen years of age, the wife younger (Prov. 5:18; Isa. 54:6). **wife of thy covenant**—not merely joined to thee by the marriage covenant generally, but by *the covenant between God and Israel,* the covenant people, whereby a sin against a wife, a daughter of Israel, is a sin against God [MOORE]. Marriage also is called "the covenant of God" (Prov. 2:17), and to it the reference may be (Gen. 2:24; Matt. 19:6; I Cor. 7:10). **15.** MAURER and HENGSTENBERG explain the verse thus: The Jews had defended their conduct by the precedent of Abraham, who had taken Hagar to the injury of Sarah, his lawful wife; to this Malachi says now, "No one (ever) did so in whom there was a residue of intelligence (discriminating between good and evil); and what did the one (Abraham, to whom you appeal for support) do, seeking a godly seed?" His object (viz., not to gratify passion, but to obtain the seed promised by God) makes the case wholly inapplicable to defend your position. MOORE (from FAIRBAIRN) better explains, in accordance with vs. 10, "Did not He make (us Israelites) one? Yet He had the residue of the Spirit (i.e., His isolating us from other nations was not because there was no residue of the Spirit left for the rest of the world). And wherefore (i.e., *why then* did He thus isolate us as) the one (people; the *Hebrew* is *'the* one')? In order that He might seek a godly seed"; i.e., that He might have "a seed of God," a nation the repository of the covenant, and the stock of the Messiah, and the witness for the one God amidst the surrounding polytheisms. Marriage with foreign women, and repudiation of the wives wedded in the Jewish covenant, utterly set aside this divine purpose. CALVIN thinks "the one" to refer to the conjugal one body formed by the original pair (Gen. 2). God might have joined many wives as one with the one husband, for He had no lack of spiritual being to impart to others besides Eve; the design of the restriction was to secure a pious offspring: but cf. *Note*, vs. 10. One object of the marriage relation is to raise a seed for God and for eternity. **16. putting away**—i.e., divorce. **for one covereth violence with . . . garment**—MAURER translates, "And (Jehovah hateth him who) covereth his garment (i.e., his *wife*, in *Arabic* idiom; cf. Genesis 20:16, 'He is to thee *a covering* of thy eyes'; the husband was so to the wife, and the wife to the husband; also Deuteronomy 22:30; Ruth 3:9; Ezekiel 16:8) with injury." The *Hebrew* favors "garment," being accusative of the *thing covered*. Cf. with *English Version*, Psalm 73:6, "violence covereth them as a garment." Their "violence" is the putting away of their wives; the "garment" with which they try to cover it is the plea of Moses' permission (Deut. 24:1; cf. Matt. 19:6-9). **17. wearied . . . Lord**—(Isa. 43:24). This verse forms the transition to ch. 3:1, etc. The Jewish skeptics of that day said virtually, God delighteth in evil-doers (inferring this from the prosperity of the surrounding heathen, while they, the Jews, were comparatively not prosperous: forgetting that their attendance to minor and external duties did not make up for their neglect of the weightier duties of the law; e.g., the duty they owed their wives, just previously discussed); or (if not) Where (is the proof that He is) the God of judgment? To this the reply (ch. 3:1) is, "The Lord whom ye seek, and whom as messenger of the covenant (i.e., divine ratifier of God's covenant with Israel) ye delight in (thinking He will restore Israel to its proper place as first of the nations), shall suddenly come," not as a Restorer of Israel temporally, but as a consuming *Judge* against Jerusalem (Amos 5:18, 19, 20). The "suddenly" implies the unpreparedness of the Jews, who, to the last of the siege, were expecting a temporal deliverer, whereas a destructive judgment was about to destroy them. So skepticism shall be rife before Christ's second coming. He shall suddenly and unexpectedly come then also as a consuming Judge to unbelievers (II Pet. 3:3, 4). Then, too, they shall affect to seek His coming, while really denying it (Isa. 5:19; Jer. 17:15; Ezek. 12:22, 27).

CHAPTER 3

Vss. 1-18. MESSIAH'S COMING, PRECEDED BY HIS FORERUNNER, TO PUNISH THE GUILTY FOR VARIOUS SINS, AND TO REWARD THOSE WHO FEAR GOD. **1. Behold**—Calling especial attention to the momentous truths which follow. Ye unbelievingly ask, Where is the God of judgment (ch. 2:7)? "Behold," therefore, "I send . . . " Your unbelief will not prevent My keeping My covenant, and bringing to pass in due time that which ye say will never be fulfilled. **I will** *send* **. . .** *he shall* **come**—The Father *sends* the Son: the Son *comes*. Proving the distinctness of personality between the Father and the Son. **my messenger**—John the Baptist; as Matthew 3:3; 11:10; Mark 1:2, 3; Luke 1:76; 3:4; 7:26, 27; John 1:23, prove. This passage of Malachi evidently rests on that of Isaiah his predecessor (Isa. 40:3-5). Per-

haps also, as HENGSTENBERG thinks, "messenger" includes *the long line of prophets* headed by *Elijah* (whence his name is put in ch. 4:5 as a representative name), and terminating in John, the last and greatest of the prophets (Matt. 11:9-11). John as the representative prophet (the forerunner of Messiah the representative God-man) gathered in himself all the scattered lineaments of previous prophecy (hence Christ terms him "much more than a prophet," Luke 7:26), reproducing all its awful and yet inspiriting utterances: his coarse garb, like that of the old prophets, being a visible exhortation to repentance; the wilderness in which he preached symbolizing the lifeless, barren state of the Jews at that time, politically and spiritually; his topics sin, repentance, and salvation, presenting for the last time the condensed epitome of all previous teachings of God by His prophets; so that he is called pre-eminently God's "messenger." Hence the oldest and true reading of Mark 1:2 is, "as it is written in *Isaiah* the prophet"; the difficulty of which is, How can the prophecy of Malachi be referred to Isaiah? The explanation is: the passage in Malachi rests on that in Isaiah 40:3, and therefore the *original source* of the prophecy is referred to in order to mark this dependency and connection. **the Lord**—*Ha-Adon* in *Hebrew*. The article marks that it is JEHOVAH (Exod. 23:17; 34:23; cf. Josh. 3:11, 13). Cf. Daniel 9:17, where the Divine Son is meant by "for THE *Lord's* sake." God the speaker makes "the Lord," the "messenger of the covenant," one with Himself: "I will send . . . before Me," adding, "THE LORD . . . shall . . . come"; so that *the Lord* must be one with the "Me," i.e., He must be GOD, "before" whom John was *sent*. As the divinity of the Son and His oneness with the Father are thus proved, so the distinctness of personality is proved by "I send" and He "shall come," as distinguished from one another. He also comes to the temple as "His temple": marking His divine lordship *over* it, as contrasted with all creatures, who are but "servants *in*" it (Hag. 2:7; Heb. 3:2, 5, 6). **whom ye seek . . . whom ye delight in**—(see *Note*, ch. 2:17). At His first coming they "sought" and "delighted in" the hope of a *temporal* Saviour: not in what He then was. In the case of those whom Malachi in his time addresses, "whom ye seek . . . delight in," is ironical. They unbelievingly asked, When will He come at last? Ch. 2:17, "Where is the God of judgment" (Isa. 5:19; Amos 5:18; II Pet. 3:3, 4)? In the case of the godly the desire for Messiah was sincere (Luke 2:25, 28). He is called "Angel of God's presence" (Isa. 63:9), also Angel of Jehovah. Cf. His appearances to Abraham (Gen. 18:1, 2, 17, 33), to Jacob (Gen. 31:11; 48:15, 16), to Moses in the bush (Exod. 3:2-6); He went before Israel as the Shekinah (Exod. 14:19), and delivered the law at Sinai (Acts 7:38). **suddenly**—This epithet marks the second coming, rather than the first; the earnest of that unexpected coming (Luke 12:38-46; Rev. 16:15) to judgment was given in the judicial expulsion of the money-changing profaners from the temple by Messiah (Matt. 21:12, 13), where also as here He calls the temple *His temple*. Also in the destruction of Jerusalem, most unexpected by the Jews, who to the last deceived themselves with the expectation that Messiah would suddenly appear as a temporal Saviour. Cf. the use of "suddenly" in Numbers 12:4-10, where He appeared in wrath. **messenger of the covenant**—viz., of the ancient covenant with Israel (Isa. 63:9) and Abraham, in which the promise to the Gentiles is ultimately included (Gal. 4:16, 17). The gospel at the first advent began with Israel, then embraced the Gentile world: so also it shall be at the second advent. All the manifestations of God in the Old Testament, the Shekinah and human appearances, were made in the person of the Divine Son (Exod. 23:20, 21; Heb. 11:26; 12:26). He was the messenger of the old covenant, as well as of the new. **2.** (Ch. 4:1; Rev. 6:16, 17.) The Messiah would come, not, as they expected, to flatter the theocratic nation's prejudices, but to subject their principles to the fiery test of His heart-searching truth (Matt. 3:10-12), and to destroy Jerusalem and the theocracy after they had rejected Him. His mission is here regarded as a whole from the first to the second advent: the process of refining and separating the godly from the ungodly beginning during Christ's stay on earth, going on ever since, and about to continue till the final separation (Matt. 25:31-46). The refining process, whereby a third of the Jews is refined as silver of its dross, while two-thirds perish, is described, Zechariah 13:8, 9 (cf. Isa. 1:25). **3. sit**—The purifier *sits* before the crucible, fixing his eye on the metal, and taking care that the fire be not too hot, and keeping the metal in, only until he knows the dross to be completely removed by his seeing his own image reflected (Rom. 8:29) in the glowing mass. So the Lord in the case of His elect (Job 23:10; Ps. 66:10; Prov. 17:3; Isa. 48:10; Heb. 12:10; I Pet. 1:7). He will *sit* down to the work, not perfunctorily, but with patient love and unflinching justice. The Angel of the Covenant, as in leading His people out of Egypt by the pillar of cloud and fire, has an aspect of terror to His foes, of love to His friends. The same separating process goes on in the world as in each Christian. When the godly are completely separated from the ungodly, the world will end. When the dross is taken from the gold of the Christian, he will be for ever delivered from the furnace of trial. The purer the gold, the hotter the fire now; the whiter the garment, the harder the washing [MOORE]. **purify...sons of Levi**—of the sins specified above. The very Levites, the ministers of God, then needed cleansing, so universal was the depravity. **that they may offer...in righteousness**—as originally (ch. 2:6), not as latterly (ch. 1:7-14). So believers, the spiritual priesthood (I Pet. 2:5). **4. as in the days of old**—(ch. 1:11; 2:5, 6). The "offering" (*Mincha, Hebrew*) is not expiatory, but prayer, thanksgiving, and self-dedication (Rom. 12:1; Heb. 13:15; I Pet. 2:5). **5. I... come near...to judgment**—*I* whom ye challenged, saying, "Where is the God of judgment?" (ch. 2:17). I whom ye think far off, and to be slow in judgment, am "near," and will come as a "swift witness"; not only a judge, but also an eye-*witness* against sorcerers; for Mine eyes see every sin, though ye think I take no heed. Earthly judges need witnesses to enable them to decide aright: I alone need none (Ps. 10:11; 73:11; 94:7, etc.). **sorcerers**—a sin into which the Jews were led in connection with their foreign idolatrous wives. The Jews of Christ's time also practised sorcery (Acts 8:9; 13:6; Gal. 5: 20; JOSEPHUS, *Antiquities,* 20. 6; B. Jud. 2; 12.23). It shall be a characteristic of the last Antichristian confederacy, about to be consumed by the brightness of Christ's coming (Matt. 24:24; II Thess. 2:9; Rev. 13:13, 14; 16:13, 14; also 9:21; 18:23; 21:8; 22:15). Romanism has practised it; an order of *exorcists* exists in that Church. **adulterers**—(ch. 2:15, 16). **fear not me**—the source of all sins. **6. the Lord**—Jehovah: a name implying His immutable faithfulness in fulfilling His promises: the covenant name of God to the Jews (Exod. 6:3), called here "the sons of Jacob," in reference to God's covenant with that patriarch. **I change not**—Ye are mistaken in inferring that, because I have not yet executed judgment on the wicked, I am changed from what I once was, viz., a God of judgment. **therefore ye...are not consumed**—Ye yourselves being "not consumed," as ye have long ago deserved, are a signal proof of My unchangeableness. Romans 11:29: cf. the whole chapter, in which God's mercy in store for Israel is made wholly to flow from God's unchanging faithfulness to His own covenant of love. So here, as is implied by the phrase "sons of *Jacob*" (Gen. 28:13; 35:12). They are spared because I am JEHOVAH, and they *sons of Jacob;* while I spare them, I will also punish them; and while I punish them, I will not wholly consume them. The unchangeableness of God is the sheet-anchor of the Church. The perseverance of the saints is guaranteed, not by their unchangeable love to God, but by His unchangeable love to them, and His eternal purpose and promise in Christ Jesus [MOORE]. He upbraids their ingratitude that they turn His very long-suffering (Lam. 3:22) into a ground for skeptical denial of His coming as a Judge at all (Ps. 50: 1, 3, 4, 21; Eccles. 8:11, 12; Isa. 57:11; Rom. 2: 4-10). **7-12.** Reproof for the non-payment of tithes and offerings, which is the cause of their national calamities, and promise of prosperity on their paying them. **7. from...days of your fathers**—Ye live as your fathers did when they brought on themselves the Babylonian captivity, and ye wish to follow in their steps. This shows that nothing but God's unchanging long-suffering had prevented their being long ago "consumed" (vs. 6). **Return unto me**—in penitence. **I will return unto you**—in blessings. **Wherein...**—(*V.* 16). The same insensibility to their guilt continues: they speak in the tone of injured innocence, as if God calumniated them. **8. rob**—lit., "cover": hence, defraud. Do ye call defrauding God no sin to be "returned" from (vs. 7)? Yet ye have done so to Me in respect to the tithes due to Me, viz., the tenth of all the remainder after the first fruits were paid, which tenth was paid to the Levites for their support (Lev. 27:30-33): a tenth paid by the Levites to the priests (Num. 18:26-28): a second tenth paid by the people for the entertainment of the Levites, and their own families, at the tabernacle (Deut. 12:18): another tithe every third year for the poor, etc. (Deut. 14:28, 29). **offerings**—the first fruits, not less than onesixtieth part of the corn, wine, and oil (Deut. 18:4; Neh. 13:10, 12). The priests had this perquisite also, the tenth of the tithes which were the Levites' perquisite. But they appropriated all the tithes, robbing the Levites of their due nine-tenths; as they did also, according to JOSEPHUS, before the destruction of Jerusalem by Titus. Thus doubly God was defrauded, the priests not discharging aright their sacrificial duties, and robbing God of the services of the Levites, who were driven away by destitution [GROTIUS]. **9. cursed**—(ch. 2:2). As ye despoil Me, so I despoil you, as I threatened I would, if ye continued to disregard Me. In trying to defraud God we only defraud ourselves. The eagle who robbed the altar set fire to her nest from the burning coal that adhered to the stolen flesh. So men who retain God's money in their treasuries will find it a losing possession. No man ever yet lost by serving God with a whole heart, nor gained by serving Him with a half one. We may compromise with conscience for half the price, but God will not endorse the compromise; and, like Ananias and Sapphira, we shall lose not only what we thought we had purchased so cheaply, but also the price we paid for it. If we would have God "open" His treasury, we must open ours. One cause of the barrenness of the Church is the parsimony of its members [MOORE]. **10.** (Prov. 3:9, 10.) **storehouse**—(*Margin*, II Chron. 31:11; cf. I Chron. 26:20; Neh. 10:38; 13:5, 12). **prove me . . . herewith**—with this; by doing so. Test Me whether I will keep My promise of blessing you, on condition of your doing your part (II Chron. 31:10). **pour . . . out**—lit., "empty out": image from a vessel completely emptied of its contents: no blessing being kept back. **windows of heaven**—(II Kings 2:7). **that . . . not . . . room enough . . .**—lit., "even to not . . . sufficiency," i.e., either, as *English Version*. Or, even so as that there should be *"not merely"* "sufficiency" but *superabundance* [JEROME, MAURER]. GESENIUS not so well translates, "Even to a failure of sufficiency," which in the case of God could never arise, and therefore means *for ever, perpetually:* so Psalm 72: 5, "as long as the sun and moon endure"; lit., "until a failure of the sun and moon," which is never to be; and therefore means, *for ever.* **11. I will rebuke**—(*Note*, ch. 2:3). I will no longer "rebuke [*English Version*, 'corrupt'] the seed," but will rebuke every agency that could hurt it (Amos 4:9). **12.** Fulfilling the blessing (Deut. 33:29; Zech. 8:13). **delightsome land**—(Dan. 8:9). **13-18.** He notices the complaint of the Jews that it is of no profit to serve Jehovah, for that the ungodly proud are happy; and declares He will soon bring the day when it shall be known that He puts an everlasting distinction between the godly and the ungodly. **words . . . stout**—*Hebrew*, "hard"; so "the *hard* speeches which ungodly sinners have spoken against Him" (Jude 15) [HENDERSON]. **have we spoken**—The *Hebrew* expresses at once their *assiduity* and *habit* of speaking against God [VATABLUS]. The niphal form of the verb implies that these things were said, not directly *to* God, but *of* God, to one another (Ezek. 33:20) [MOORE]. **14. what profit . . . that we . . . kept . . .**—(*Note*, ch. 2:17). They here resume the same murmur against God. Job 21:14, 15; 22:17 describe a further stage of the same skeptical spirit, when the skeptic has actually ceased to keep God's service. Psalm 73:1-14 describes the temptation to a like feeling in the saint when seeing the really godly suffer and the ungodly prosper in worldly goods now. The Jews here mistake utterly the nature of God's service, converting it into a mercenary bargain; they attended to outward observances, not from love to God, but in the hope of being well paid for in outward prosperity; when this was withheld, they charged God with being unjust, forgetting alike that God requires very different motives from theirs to accompany outward observances, and that God rewards even the true worshipper not so much in this life, as in the life to come. **his ordinance**—lit., what He requires to be kept, "His observances." **walked mournfully**—*in mournful garb*, sackcloth and ashes, the emblems of penitence; they forget Isaiah 58:3-8, where God, by showing what is true fasting, similarly rebukes those who then also said, Wherefore have we fasted and Thou seest not? etc. They mistook the outward show for real humiliation. **15. And now**—Since we who serve Jehovah are not prosperous and "the proud" heathen flourish in prosperity, we must pronounce them the favorites of God (ch. 2:17; Ps. 73:12). **set up**—lit., "built up": metaphor from architecture (Prov. 24:3; cf. *Margin*, Gen. 16:2; *Margin*, 30:3).

tempt God—dare God to punish them, by breaking His laws (Ps. 95:9). **16.** "Then," when the ungodly utter such blasphemies against God, the godly hold mutual converse, defending God's righteous dealings against those blasphemers (Heb. 3:13). The "often" of *English Version* is not in the *Hebrew*. There has been always in the darkest times a remnant that feared God (I Kings 19: 18; Rom. 11:4). **feared the Lord**—reverential and loving fear, not slavish terror. When the fire of religion burns low, true believers should draw the nearer together, to keep the holy flame alive. Coals separated soon go out. **book of remembrance . . . for them**—for their advantage, against the day when those found faithful among the faithless shall receive their final reward. The kings of Persia kept a record of those who had rendered services to the king, that they might be suitably rewarded (Esther 6:1, 2; cf. Esther 2:23; Ezra 4:15; Ps. 56:8; Isa. 65:6; Dan. 7:10; Rev. 20:12). CALVIN makes the fearers of God to be those awakened from among the ungodly mass (before described) to true repentance; the *writing* of the book thus will imply that some were reclaimable among the blasphemers, and that the godly should be assured that, though no hope appeared, there would be a door of penitence opened for them *before* God. But there is nothing in the context to support this view. **17. jewels**—(Isa. 62:3). Lit., "My peculiar treasure" (Exod. 19: 5; Deut. 7:6; 14:2; 26:18; Ps. 135:4; Titus 2:14; I Pet. 2:9; cf. Eccles. 2:8). CALVIN translates more in accordance with *Hebrew* idiom, "They shall be My peculiar treasure *in the day in which I will do it"* (i.e., fulfil My promise of gathering My completed Church; or, "make" those things come to pass foretold in vs. 5 above [GROTIUS]); so in ch. 4:3 "do" is used absolutely, "in the day that I shall do *this.*" MAURER, not so well, translates, "in the day which I shall make," i.e., appoint as in Psalm 118:24. **as . . . man spareth . . . son**—(Ps. 103:18). **18. Then shall ye . . . discern**—Then shall ye see the falseness of your calumny against God's government (vs. 15), that the "proud" and wicked prosper. Do not judge before the time till My work is complete. It is in part to test your disposition to trust in God in spite of perplexing appearances, and in order to make your service less mercenary, that the present blended state is allowed; but at last *all* ("ye," both godly and ungodly) shall see the eternal difference there really is "between him that serveth God and him that serveth Him not" (Ps. 58:11). **return**—Ye shall turn to a better state of mind on this point.

CHAPTER 4

Vss. 1-6. GOD'S COMING JUDGMENT: TRIUMPH OF THE GODLY: RETURN TO THE LAW THE BEST PREPARATION FOR JEHOVAH'S COMING: ELIJAH'S PREPARATORY MISSION OF REFORMATION. **1. the day cometh . . . burn**—(ch. 3:2; II Peter 3:7). Primarily is meant the judgment coming on Jerusalem; but as this will not exhaust the meaning, without supposing what is inadmissible in Scripture—exaggeration—the final and full accomplishment, of which the former was the earnest, is the day of general judgment. This principle of interpretation is not double, but *successive fulfilment.* The language is abrupt, "Behold, the day cometh! It burns like a furnace." The abruptness imparts terrible reality to the picture, as if it suddenly burst on the prophet's view. **all the proud**—in opposition to the cavil above (ch. 3:15), "now we call the *proud* (haughty despisers of

God) happy." **stubble**—(Obad. 18; Matt. 3:12). As Canaan, the inheritance of the Israelites, was prepared for their possession by purging out the heathen, so judgment on the apostates shall usher in the entrance of the saints upon the Lord's inheritance, of which Canaan is the type—not heaven, but earth to its utmost bounds (Ps. 2:8) purged of all things that offend (Matt. 13:41), which are to be "gathered *out of His kingdom*," the scene of the judgment being that also of the kingdom. The present dispensation is a spiritual kingdom, parenthetical between the Jews' literal kingdom and its antitype, the coming literal kingdom of the Lord Jesus. **neither root nor branch**— proverbial for *utter* destruction (Amos 2:9). **2.** The effect of the judgment on the righteous, as contrasted with its effect on the wicked (vs. 1). To the wicked it shall be as an oven that consumes the stubble (Matt. 6:30); to the righteous it shall be the advent of the gladdening Sun, not of condemnation, but "of righteousness"; not destroying, but "healing" (Jer. 23:6). **you that fear my name**—The same as those in ch. 3:16, who confessed God amidst abounding blasphemy (Isa. 66:5; Matt. 10:32). The spiritual blessings brought by Him are summed up in the two, "righteousness" (I Cor. 1:30) and spiritual "healing" (Ps. 103:3; Isa. 57:19). Those who walk in the dark now may take comfort in the certainty that they shall walk hereafter in eternal light (Isa. 50:10). **in his wings**—implying the *winged swiftness* with which He shall appear (cf. "suddenly," ch. 3:1) for the relief of His people. The *beams* of the Sun are His "wings." Cf. "wings of the morning," Psalm 139:9. The "Sun" gladdening the righteous is suggested by the previous "day" of terror consuming the wicked. Cf. as to Christ, II Sam. 23:4; Ps. 84:11; Luke 1:78; John 1:9; 8:12; Eph. 5:14; and in His second coming, II Peter 1:19. The Church is the *moon* reflecting His light (Rev. 12:1). The righteous shall by His righteousness "shine as the Sun in the kingdom of the Father" (Matt. 13:43). **ye shall go forth**—from the straits in which you were, as it were, held captive. An earnest of this was given in the escape of the Christians to Pella before the destruction of Jerusalem. **grow up**—rather, "leap" as frisking calves [CALVIN]; lit., "spread," "take a wide range." **as calves of the stall**—which when set free from the stall disport with joy (Acts 8:8; 13:52; 20:24; Rom. 14:17; Gal. 5:22; Phil. 1:4, I Pet. 1:8). Especially the godly shall rejoice at their final deliverance at Christ's second coming (Isa. 61:10). **3.** Solving the difficulty (ch. 3:15) that the wicked often now prosper. Their prosperity and the adversity of the godly shall soon be reversed. Yea, the righteous shall be the army attending Christ in His final destruction of the ungodly (I Sam. 22:43; Ps. 49:14; 47:3; Mic. 7:10; Zech. 10:5; I Cor. 6:2 Rev. 2:26, 27; 19:14, 15). **ashes**—after having been burnt with the fire of judgment (vs. 1). **4. Remember . . . law**—"The law and all the prophets" were to be in force until John (Matt. 11:13), no prophet intervening after Malachi; therefore they are told, "Remember the law," for in the absence of living prophets, they were likely to forget it. The office of Christ's forerunner was to bring them back to the law, which they had too much forgotten, and so "to make ready a people prepared for the Lord" at His coming (Luke 1:17). God withheld prophets for a time that men might seek after Christ with the greater desire [CALVIN]. The history of human advancement is marked by periods of rest, and again progress. So in Revelation: it is given for a time; then during its

suspension men live on the memories of the past. After Malachi there was a silence of 400 years; then a harbinger of light in the wilderness, ushering in the brightest of all the lights that had been manifested, but short-lived; then eighteen centuries during which we have been guided by the light which shone in that last manifestation. The silence has been longer than before, and will be succeeded by a more glorious and awful revelation than ever. John the Baptist was to "restore" the defaced image of "the law," so that the original might be recognized when it appeared among men [HINDS]. Just as "Moses" and "Elias" are here connected with the Lord's coming, so at the transfiguration they converse with Him, implying that the law and prophets which had prepared His way were now fulfilled in Him. **statutes . . . judgments**—*ceremonial* "statutes": "judgments" in civil questions at issue. "The law" refers to *morals* and *religion*. **5. I send you Elijah**—as a means towards your "remembering the law" (vs. 4). **the prophet**—emphatical; not "the Tishbite"; for it is in his official, not his personal capacity, that his coming is here predicted. In this sense, John the Baptist was *an* Elijah in spirit (Luke 1:16, 17), but not *the literal* Elijah; whence when asked, "Art thou Elias?" (John 1:21), He answered, "I am not." "Art thou that prophet?" "No." This implies that John, though knowing from the angel's announcement to his father that he was referred to by Malachi 4:5 (Luke 1:17), whence he wore the costume of Elijah, yet knew by inspiration that he did not exhaustively fulfil *all* that is included in this prophecy: that there is a further fulfilment (cf. *Note*, ch. 3:1). As Moses in vs. 4 represents the law, so Elijah represents the prophets. The Jews always understood it of the literal Elijah. Their saying is, "Messiah must be anointed by Elijah." As there is another consummating advent of Messiah Himself, so also of His forerunner Elijah; perhaps in person, as at the transfiguration (Matt. 17:3; cf. 11). He in his appearance at the transfiguration in that body on which death had never passed is the forerunner of the saints who shall be found alive at the Lord's second coming. Revelation 11:3 may refer to the same witnesses as at the transfiguration, Moses and Elijah; Revelation 11:6 identifies the latter (cf. I Kings 17:1; Jas. 5:17). Even after the transfiguration Jesus (Matt. 17:11) speaks of Elijah's coming "to restore all things" as still future, though He adds that Elijah (in the person of John the Baptist) is come already *in a sense* (cf. Acts 3:21). However, the future forerunner of Messiah at His second coming may be a prophet or number of prophets clothed with Elijah's power, who, with zealous upholders of "the law" clothed in the spirit of "Moses," may be the forerunning witnesses alluded to here and in Revelation 11:2-12. The words "before the . . . *dreadful* day of the Lord," show that John cannot be exclusively meant; for he came before the day of Christ's coming in grace, not before His coming in terror, of which last the destruction of Jerusalem was the earnest (vs. 1; Joel 2:31). **6. turn . . . heart of . . . fathers to . . . children . . .**—Explained by some, that John's preaching should restore harmony in families. But Luke 1:16, 17 substitutes for "the heart of the children to the fathers," "the disobedient to the wisdom of the just," implying that the reconciliation to be effected was that between the unbelieving disobedient children and the believing ancestors, Jacob, Levi, "Moses," and "Elijah" (just mentioned) (cf. ch. 1:2; 2:4, 6; 3:3, 4). The threat here is that, if this restoration were not effected, Messiah's coming would prove "a curse" to the "earth," not a blessing. It proved so to guilty Jerusalem and the "earth," i.e., the *land* of Judea when it rejected Messiah at His first advent, though He brought blessings (Gen. 12:3) to those who accepted Him (John 1:11-13). Many were delivered from the common destruction of the nation through John's preaching (Rom. 9:29; 11:5). It will prove so to the disobedient at His second advent, though He comes to be glorified in His saints (II Thess. 1:6-10). **curse**—*Hebrew, Cherem,* "a ban"; the fearful term applied by the Jews to the extermination of the guilty Canaanites. Under this ban Judea has long lain. Similar is the awful curse on all of Gentile churches who love not the Lord Jesus now (I Cor. 16:22). For if God spare not the natural branches, the Jews, much less will He spare unbelieving professors of the Gentiles (Rom. 11:20, 21). It is deeply suggestive that the last utterance from heaven for 400 years before Messiah was the awful word "curse." Messiah's first word on the mount was "Blessed" (Matt. 5:3). The law speaks wrath; the Gospel, blessing. Judea is now under the "curse" because it rejects Messiah; when the spirit of Elijah, or a literal Elijah, shall bring the Jewish children back to the Hope of their "fathers," blessing shall be theirs, whereas the apostate "earth" shall be "smitten with the curse" previous to the coming restoration of all things (Zech. 12:13, 14).

May the writer of this Commentary and his readers have grace "to take heed to the sure word of prophecy as unto a light shining in a dark place, until the day dawn!" To the triune Jehovah be all glory ascribed for ever!

THE NEW TESTAMENT

THE GOSPEL ACCORDING TO
MATTHEW

INTRODUCTION

THE *author* of this Gospel was a publican or tax-gatherer, residing at Capernaum, on the western shore of the Sea of Galilee. As to his identity with the "Levi" of the second and third Gospels, and other particulars, see on Matthew 9:9. Hardly anything is known of his apostolic labors. That, after preaching to his countrymen in Palestine, he went to the East, is the general testimony of antiquity; but the precise scene or scenes of his ministry cannot be determined. That he died a natural death may be concluded from the belief of the best-informed of the Fathers—that of the apostles only three, James the Greater, Peter, and Paul, suffered martyrdom. That the first Gospel was written by this apostle is the testimony of all antiquity.

For the *date* of this Gospel we have only internal evidence, and that far from decisive. Accordingly, opinion is much divided. That it was the first issued of all the Gospels was universally believed. Hence, although in the order of the Gospels, those by the two apostles were placed first in the oldest MSS. of the old Latin version, while in all the Greek MSS., with scarcely an exception, the order is the same as in our Bibles, the Gospel according to Matthew is *in every case* placed first. And as this Gospel is of all the four the one which bears the most evident marks of having been prepared and constructed with a special view to the Jews—who certainly first required a written Gospel, and would be the first to make use of it—there can be no doubt that it was issued before any of the others. That it was written before the destruction of Jerusalem is equally certain; for as HUG observes (*Introduction to the New Testament*, p. 316, Fosdick's translation), when he reports our Lord's prophecy of that awful event, on coming to the warning about "the abomination of desolation" which they should "see standing in the holy place," he interposes (contrary to his invariable practice, which is to *relate* without *remark*) a call to his readers to read intelligently — "Whoso readeth, let him understand" (Matt. 24:15)—a call to attend to the divine signal for flight which could be intended only for those who lived before the event. But how long before that event this Gospel was written is not so clear. Some internal evidences seem to imply a very early date. Since the Jewish Christians were, for five or six years, exposed to persecution from their own countrymen—until the Jews, being persecuted by the Romans, had to look to themselves—it is not likely (it is argued) that they should be left so long without some written Gospel to reassure and sustain them, and Matthew's Gospel was eminently fitted for that purpose. But the digests to which Luke refers in his Introduction (see on Luke 1:1-4) would be sufficient for a time, especially as the living voice of the "eye-witnesses and ministers of the Word" was yet sounding abroad. Other considerations in favor of a very early date—such as the tender way in which the author seems studiously to speak of Herod Antipas, as if still reigning, and his writing of Pilate apparently as if still in power—seem to have no foundation in fact, and cannot therefore be made the ground of reasoning as to the date of this Gospel. Its Hebraic structure and hue, though they prove, as we think, that this Gospel must have been published at a period considerably anterior to the destruction of Jerusalem, are no evidence in favor of so early a date as A.D. 37 or 38—according to some of the Fathers, and, of the moderns, TILLEMONT, TOWNSON, OWEN, BIRKS, TREGELLES. On the other hand, the date suggested by the statement of Irenæus (3:1), that Matthew put forth his Gospel while Peter and Paul were at Rome preaching and founding the Church—or after A.D. 60—though probably the majority of critics are in favor of it, would seem rather too late, especially as the second and third Gospels, which were doubtless published, as well as this one, before the destruction of Jerusalem, had still to be issued. Certainly, such statements as the following, "Wherefore that field is called the field of blood *unto this day*"; "And this saying is commonly reported among the Jews *until this day*" (Matt. 27:8 and 28:15), bespeak a date considerably later than the events recorded. We incline, therefore, to a date intermediate between the earlier and the later dates assigned to this Gospel, without pretending to greater precision.

We have adverted to the strikingly Jewish character and coloring of this Gospel. The facts which it selects, the points to which it gives prominence, the cast of thought and phraseology, all bespeak the Jewish point of view *from* which it was written and *to* which it was directed. This has been noticed from the beginning, and is universally acknowledged. It is of the greatest consequence to the right interpretation of it; but the tendency among some even of the best of the Germans to infer, from this special design of the first Gospel, a certain laxity on the part of the Evangelist in the treatment of his facts, must be guarded against.

But by far the most interesting and important point connected with this Gospel is the *language* in which it was written. It is believed by a formidable number of critics that this Gospel was originally written in what is loosely called Hebrew, but more correctly *Aramaic*, or *Syro-Chaldaic*, the native tongue of the country at the time of our Lord; and that the Greek Matthew which we now possess is a translation of that work, either by the Evangelist himself or some unknown hand. The evidence on which this opinion is grounded is wholly external, but it has been deemed conclusive by GROTIUS, MICHAELIS (and his translator), MARSH, TOWNSON, CAMPBELL, OLSHAUSEN, CRESWELL, MEYER, EBRARD, LANGE, DAVIDSON, CURETON, TREGELLES, WEBSTER and WILKINSON, etc. The evidence referred to cannot be given here, but will be found, with remarks on its unsatisfactory character, in the "Introduction to the Gospels" prefixed to our larger Commentary, pp. 28-31.

But how stand the facts as to our Greek Gospel? We have not a title of historical evidence that it is a *translation*, either by Matthew himself or anyone else. All antiquity refers to it as the work of Matthew the publican and apostle, just as the other Gospels are ascribed to their respective authors. This Greek Gospel was from the first received by the Church as an integral part of the one quadriform *Gospel*. And while the Fathers often advert to the two Gospels which we have from apostles, and the two which we have from men not apostles—in order to show that as that of Mark leans so entirely on Peter, and that of Luke on Paul, these are really no less apostolical than the other two—though we attach less weight to this circumstance than they did, we cannot but think it striking that, in thus speaking, they never drop a hint that the full apostolic authority of the Greek Matthew had ever been questioned on the ground of its not being the *original*. Further, not a trace can be discovered in this Gospel itself of its being a translation. MICHAELIS tried to detect, and fancied that he had succeeded in detecting, one or two such. Other Germans since, and DAVIDSON and CURETON among ourselves, have made the same attempt. But the entire failure of all such attempts is now generally admitted, and candid advocates of a Hebrew original are quite ready to own that none such are to be found, and that but for external testimony no one would have imagined that the Greek was not the original. This they regard as showing how perfectly the translation has been executed; but those who know best what translating from one language into another is will be the readiest to own that this is tantamount to giving up the question. This Gospel proclaims its own originality in a number of striking points; such as its manner of quoting from the Old Testament, and its phraseology in some peculiar cases. But the close *verbal coincidences* of our Greek Matthew with the next two Gospels must not be quite passed over. There are but two possible ways of explaining this. Either the translator, sacrificing verbal fidelity in his version, intentionally conformed certain parts of his author's work to the second and third Gospels—in which case it can hardly be called Matthew's Gospel at all—or our Greek Matthew is itself the original.

Moved by these considerations, some advocates of a Hebrew original have adopted the theory of *a double original*; the external testimony, they think, requiring us to believe in a Hebrew original, while internal evidence is decisive in favor of the originality of the Greek. This theory is espoused by GUERICKS, OLSHAUSEN, THIERSCH, TOWNSON, TREGELLES, etc. But, besides that this looks too like an artificial theory, invented to solve a difficulty, it is utterly void of historical support. There is not a vestige of testimony to support it in Christian antiquity. This ought to be decisive against it.

It remains, then, that our Greek Matthew is the original of that Gospel, and that no other original ever existed. It is greatly to the credit of Dean ALFORD, that after maintaining, in the first edition of his "Greek Testament" the theory of a Hebrew original, he thus expresses himself in the second and subsequent editions: "On the whole, then, I find myself constrained to abandon the view maintained in my first edition, and to adopt that of a Greek original."

One argument has been adduced on the other side, on which not a little reliance has been placed; but the determination of the main question does not, in our opinion, depend upon the point which it raises. It has been very confidently affirmed that the Greek language was not sufficiently understood by the Jews of Palestine when Matthew published his Gospel to make it at all probable that he would write a Gospel, for their benefit in the first instance, in that language. Now, as this merely alleges the improbability of a Greek original, it is enough to place against it the evidence already adduced, which is positive, in favor of the sole originality of our Greek Matthew. It is indeed a question how far the Greek language was understood in Palestine at the time referred to. But we advise the reader not to be drawn into that question as essential to the settlement of the other one. It is an element in it, no doubt, but not an essential element. There are extremes on both sides of it. The old idea, that our Lord hardly ever spoke anything but Syro-Chaldaic, is now pretty nearly exploded. Many, however, will not go the length, on the other side, of HUG (in his *Introduction*, pp. 326, etc.) and ROBERTS ("Discussions," etc. pp. 25, etc.). For ourselves, though we believe that our Lord, in all the more public scenes of His ministry, spoke in Greek, all we think it necessary here to say is that there is no ground to believe that Greek was so little understood in Palestine as to make it improbable that Matthew would write his Gospel exclusively in that language—so improbable as to outweigh the evidence that he did so. And when we think of the number of digests or short narratives of the principal facts of our Lord's history which we know from Luke (1:1-4) were floating about for some time before he wrote his Gospel, of which he speaks by no means disrespectfully, and nearly all of which would be in the mother tongue, we can have no doubt that the Jewish Christians and the Jews of Palestine generally would have from the first reliable written matter sufficient to supply every necessary requirement until the publican-apostle should leisurely draw up the first of the four Gospels in a language to them not a strange tongue, while to the rest of the world it was *the* language in which the entire quadriform Gospel was to be for all time enshrined. The following among others hold to this view of the sole originality of the Greek Matthew: ERASMUS, CALVIN, BEZA, LIGHTFOOT, WETSTEIN, LARDNER, HUG, FRITZSCHE, CREDNER, DE WETTE, STUART, DA COSTA, FAIRBAIRN, ROBERTS.

On two other questions regarding this Gospel it would have been desirable to say something, had not our available space been already exhausted: The *characteristics*, both in language and matter, by which it is distinguished from the other three, and its *relation to the second and third Gospels*. On the latter of these topics —whether one or more of the Evangelists made use of the materials of the other Gospels, and, if so, which of the Evangelists drew from which—the opinions are just as numerous as the possibilities of the case, every conceivable way of it having one or more who plead for it. The most popular opinion until recently—and perhaps the most popular still—is that the second Evangelist availed himself more or less of the materials of the first Gospel, and the third of the materials of both the first and second Gospels. Here we can but state our own belief, that each of the first three Evangelists wrote independently of both the others; while the fourth, familiar with the first three, wrote to supplement them, and, even where he travels along the same line, wrote quite independently of them. This judgment we express, with all deference for those who think otherwise, as the result of a close study of each of the Gospels in immediate juxtaposition and comparison with the others. On the former of the two topics noticed, the linguistic peculiarities of each of the Gospels have been handled most closely and ably by CREDNER (*Einleitung*), of whose results a good summary will be found in DAVIDSON'S *Introduction*. The other peculiarities of the Gospels have been most felicitously and beautifully brought out by DA COSTA in his *Four Witnesses*, to which we must simply refer the reader, though it contains a few things in which we cannot concur.

CHAPTER 1

Vss. 1-17. GENEALOGY OF CHRIST. (–Luke 3:23-38). **1. The book of the generation**–an expression purely Jewish; meaning, "table of the genealogy." In Genesis 5:1 the same expression occurs in this sense. We have here, then, the title, not of this whole Gospel of Matthew, but only of the first seventeen verses. **of Jesus Christ**–For the meaning of these glorious words, see on vss. 16, 21. "Jesus," the name given to our Lord at His circumcision (Luke 2:21), was that by which He was familiarly known while on earth. The word "Christ"–though applied to Him as a proper name by the angel who announced His birth to the shepherds (Luke 2:11), and once or twice used in this sense by our Lord Himself (ch. 23:8, 10; Mark 9: 41)–only began to be so used by others about the very close of His earthly career (ch. 26:68; 27:17). The full form, "Jesus Christ," though once used by Himself in His Intercessory Prayer (John 17:3), was never used by others till after His ascension and the formation of churches in His name. Its use, then, in the opening words of this Gospel (and in vss. 17, 18) is in the style of the late period when our Evangelist wrote, rather than of the events he was going to record. **the son of David, the son of Abraham**–As Abraham was the *first* from whose family it was predicted that Messiah should spring (Gen. 22:18), so David was the *last*. To a Jewish reader, accordingly, these behooved to be the two great starting-points of any true genealogy of the promised Messiah; and thus this opening verse, as it stamps the first Gospel as one peculiarly Jewish, would at once tend to conciliate the writer's people. From the nearest of those two fathers came that familiar name of the promised Messiah, "the son of David" (Luke 20:41), which was applied to Jesus, either in devout acknowledgment of His rightful claim to it (ch. 9:27; 20:31), or in the way of insinuating inquiry whether such were the case (see on John 4:29; ch. 12:23). **2. Abraham begat Isaac; and Isaac begat Jacob; and Jacob begat Judas and his brethren**–Only the fourth son of Jacob is here named, as it was from his loins that Messiah was to spring (Gen. 49:10). **3. And Judas begat Phares and Zara of Thamar; and Phares begat Esrom; and Esrom begat Aram; 4. And Aram begat Aminadab; and Aminadab begat Naásson; and Naasson begat Salmon; 5. And Salmon begat Booz of Rachab; and Booz begat Obed of Ruth; and Obed begat Jesse; 6. And Jesse begat David the king; and David the king begat Solomon of her of Urias**–Four women are here introduced; two of them Gentiles by birth–*Rachab* and *Ruth;* and three of them with a blot at their names in the Old Testament–*Thamar, Rachab,* and *Bath-sheba.* This feature in the present genealogy–herein differing from that given by Luke–comes well from him who styles himself in his list of the Twelve, what none of the other lists do, "Matthew *the publican";* as if thereby to hold forth, at the very outset, the unsearchable riches of that grace which could not only fetch in "them that are afar off," but reach down even to "publicans and harlots," and raise them to "sit with the princes of his people." David is here twice emphatically styled "David the king," as not only the first of that royal line from which Messiah was to descend, but the one king of all that line from which the throne that Messiah was to occupy took its name–"the throne of David." The angel Gabriel, in announcing Him to His virgin-mother, calls it "the throne of David His father," sinking all the intermediate kings of

that line, as having no importance save as links to connect the first and the last king of Israel as father and son. It will be observed that Rachab is here represented as the great-grandmother of David (see Ruth 4:20-22; and I Chron. 2:11-15)–a thing not beyond possibility indeed, but extremely improbable, there being about four centuries between them. There can hardly be a doubt that one or two intermediate links are omitted. **7. And Solomon begat Roboam; and Roboam begat Abia; and Abia begat Asa; 8. And Asa begat Josaphat; and Josaphat begat Joram; and Joram begat Ozias** [or Uzziah]–Three kings are here omitted–*Ahaziah, Joash,* and *Amaziah* (I Chron. 3:11, 12). Some omissions behooved to be made, to compress the whole into three fourteens (vs. 17). The reason why these, rather than other names, are omitted, must be sought in *religious* considerations–either in the connection of those kings with the house of Ahab (as LIGHTFOOT, EBRARD, and ALFORD view it); in their slender right to be regarded as true links in the theocratic chain (as LANGE takes it); or in some similar disqualification. **11. And Josias begat Jechonias and his brethren**–Jeconiah was Josiah's grandson, being the son of Jehoiakim, Josiah's second son (I Chron. 3:15); but Jehoiakim might well be sunk in such a catalogue, being a mere puppet in the hands of the king of Egypt (II Chron. 36:4). The "brethren" of Jechonias here evidently mean his uncles–the chief of whom, Mattaniah or Zedekiah, who came to the throne (II Kings 24:17), is, in II Chronicles 36:10, as well as here, called "his brother." **about the time they were carried away to Babylon**–lit., "of their migration," for the Jews avoided the word "captivity" as too bitter a recollection, and our Evangelist studiously respects the national feeling. **12. And after they were brought to** [after the migration of] **Babylon, Jechonias begat Salathiel**–So I Chron. 3:17. Nor does this contradict Jeremiah 22:30, Thus saith the Lord, Write ye this man [Coniah, or Jeconiah] childless"; for what follows explains in what sense this was meant–"for no man of his seed shall prosper, sitting upon the throne of David." He *was* to have seed, but no *reigning* child. **and Salathiel** [or Shealtiel] **begat Zorobabel** –So Ezra 3:2; Nehemiah 12:1; Haggai 1:1. But it would appear from I Chronicles 3:19 that Zerubbabel was Salathiel's grandson, being the son of Pedaiah, whose name, for some reason unknown, is omitted. **13-15. And Zorobabel begat Abiud . . .** –None of these names are found in the Old Testament; but they were doubtless taken from the public or family registers, which the Jews carefully kept, and their accuracy was never challenged. **16. And Jacob begat Joseph, the husband of Mary, of whom was born Jesus**–From this it is clear that the genealogy here given is not that of Mary, but of Joseph; nor has this ever been questioned. And yet it is here studiously proclaimed that Joseph was not the natural, but only the legal father of our Lord. His birth of a virgin was known only to a few; but the acknowledged descent of his legal father from David secured that the descent of Jesus Himself from David should never be questioned. See on vs. 20. **who is called Christ**–signifying "anointed." It is applied in the Old Testament to the *kings* (I Sam. 24:6, 10); to the *priests* (Lev. 4:5, 16, etc.); and to the *prophets* (I Kings 19:16)–these all being anointed with oil, the symbol of the needful spiritual gifts to consecrate them to their respective offices; and it was applied, in its most sublime and comprehensive sense, to the promised Deliverer, inasmuch as He was to be consecrated to an office embracing all three by the immeasurable anointing of the Holy Ghost (Isa. 61:1; cf. John 3:34). **17. So all the generations from Abraham to David are fourteen generations; and from David until the carrying away** [or migration] **into Babylon are fourteen generations; and from the carrying away into** [the migration of] **Babylon unto Christ are fourteen generations**—that is, the whole may be conveniently divided into three fourteens, each embracing one marked era, and each ending with a notable event, in the Israelitish annals. Such artificial aids to memory were familiar to the Jews, and much larger gaps than those here are found in some of the Old Testament genealogies. In Ezra 7:1-5 no fewer than six generations of the priesthood are omitted, as will appear by comparing it with I Chronicles 6:3-15. It will be observed that the last of the three divisions of fourteen appears to contain only thirteen distinct names, including Jesus as the last. LANGE thinks that this was meant as a tacit hint that *Mary* was to be supplied, as the thirteenth link of the last chain, as it is impossible to conceive that the Evangelist could have made any mistake in the matter. But there is a simpler way of accounting for it. As the Evangelist himself (vs. 17 reckons David twice—as the last of the first fourteen and the first of the second—so, if we reckon the second fourteen to end with Josiah, who was coeval with the "carrying away into captivity" (vs. 11), and the third to begin with Jeconiah, it will be found that the last division, as well as the other two, embraces fourteen names, including that of our Lord.

13-25. BIRTH OF CHRIST. 18. Now the birth of Jesus Christ was on this wise [or, thus]: **When as his mother Mary was espoused** [rather, betrothed] **to Joseph, before they came together, she was found** [discovered to be] **with child of the Holy Ghost**—It was, of course, the fact only that was discovered; the explanation of the fact here given is the Evangelist's own. That the Holy Ghost is a living conscious Person is plainly implied here, and is elsewhere clearly taught (Acts 5:3, 4, etc.): and that, in the unity of the Godhead, He is distinct both from the Father and the Son, is taught with equal distinctness (Matt. 28:19; II Cor. 13:14). On the miraculous conception of our Lord, see on Luke 1:35. **19. Then Joseph her husband**—Cf. vs. 20, "Mary, thy wife." Betrothal was, in Jewish law, valid marriage. In giving Mary up, therefore, Joseph had to take legal steps to effect the separation. **being a just man, and not willing to make her a public example** to expose her (see Deut. 22: 23, 24) **was minded to put her away privily**—i.e., privately by giving her the required writing of divorcement (Deut. 24:1), in presence of only two or three witnesses, and without cause assigned, instead of having her before a magistrate. That some communication had passed between him and his betrothed, directly or indirectly, on the subject, after she returned from her three months' visit to Elizabeth, can hardly be doubted. Nor does the purpose to divorce her necessarily imply disbelief, on Joseph's part, of the explanation given him. Even supposing him to have yielded to it some reverential assent—and the Evangelist seems to convey as much, by ascribing the proposal to screen her to the *justice* of his character—he might think it altogether unsuitable and incongruous in such circumstances to follow out the marriage. **20. But while he thought on these things**—Who would not feel for him after receiving such intelligence, and before receiving any light from above? As he brooded over the matter alone, in the stillness of the night,

his domestic prospects darkened and his happiness blasted for life, his mind slowly making itself up to the painful step, yet planning how to do it in the way least offensive—at the last extremity the Lord Himself interposes. **behold, the angel of the Lord appeared to him in a dream, saying, Joseph thou son of David**—This style of address was doubtless advisedly chosen to remind him of what all the families of David's line so early coveted, and thus it would prepare him for the marvellous announcement which was to follow. **fear not to take unto thee Mary thy wife**—Though a dark cloud now overhangs this relationship, it is unsullied still. **for that which is conceived in her is of the Holy Ghost. 21. And she shall bring forth a son**—Observe, it is not said, "she shall bear *thee* a son," as was said to Zacharias of his wife Elizabeth (Luke 1:13). **and thou** [as his legal father] **shalt call his name JESUS** from the *Hebrew* meaning "Jehovah the Saviour"; in *Greek* JESUS—to the awakened and anxious sinner sweetest and most fragrant of all names, expressing so melodiously and briefly His whole saving office and work! **for he shall save**—The "He" is here emphatic—He it is that shall save; He personally, and by personal acts (as WEBSTER and WILKINSON express it). **his people**—the lost sheep of the house of Israel, in the first instance; for they were the only people He then had. But, on the breaking down of the middle wall of partition, the saved people embraced the "redeemed unto God by His blood out of every kindred and people and tongue and nation." **from their sins**—in the most comprehensive sense of salvation from sin (Rev. 1:5; Eph. 5:25-27). **22. Now all this was done, that it might be fulfilled which was spoken of the Lord by the prophet** [Isa. 7:14], **saying, 23. Behold, a virgin**—It should be "*the* virgin" meaning that particular virgin destined to this unparalleled distinction. **shall be with child, and shall bring forth a son, and they shall call his name Emmanuel, which, being interpreted, is, God with us**—Not that He was to have this for a proper name (like "Jesus"), but that He should come to be known *in this character,* as God manifested in the flesh, and the living bond of holy and most intimate fellowship between God and men from henceforth and for ever. **24. Then Joseph, being raised from sleep** [and all his difficulties now removed], **did as the angel of the Lord had bidden him, and took unto him his wife**—With what deep and reverential joy would this now be done on his part; and what balm would this minister to his betrothed one, who had till now lain under suspicions of all others the most trying to a chaste and holy woman—suspicions, too, arising from what, though to her an honor unparalleled, was to all around her wholly unknown! **25. And knew her not till she had brought forth her first-born son: and he called his name JESUS**—The word "till" does not necessarily imply that they lived on a different footing afterwards (as will be evident from the use of the same word in I Sam. 15:35; II Sam. 6:23; Matt. 12:20); nor does the word "first-born" decide the much-disputed question, whether Mary had any children to Joseph after the birth of Christ; for, as LIGHTFOOT says, "The law, in speaking of the first-born, regarded not whether any were born *after* or no, but only that none were born before." (See on ch. 13:55, 56).

CHAPTER 2

Vss. 1-12. VISIT OF THE MAGI TO JERUSALEM AND BETHLEHEM. *The Wise Men Reach Jerusalem*—

The Sanhedrim, on Herod's Demand, Pronounce Bethlehem to Be Messiah's Predicted Birthplace (vss. 1-6). **1. Now when Jesus was born in Bethlehem of Judea**—so called to distinguish it from another Bethlehem in the tribe of Zebulun, near the Sea of Galilee (Josh. 19:15); called also *Beth-le-hem-judah*, as being in that tribe (Judg. 17:7); and *Ephrath* (Gen. 35:16); and combining both, *Beth-lehem Ephratah* (Mic. 5:2). It lay about six miles southwest of Jerusalem. But how came Joseph and Mary to remove thither from Nazareth, the place of their residence? Not of their own accord, and certainly not with the view of fulfilling the prophecy regarding Messiah's birthplace; nay, they stayed at Nazareth till it was almost too late for Mary to travel with safety; nor would they have stirred from it at all, had not an order which left them no choice forced them to the appointed place. A high hand was in all these movements. (See on Luke 2:1-6.) **in the days of Herod the king**—styled the Great; son of Antipater, an *Edomite*, made king by the Romans. Thus was "the sceptre departing from Judah" (Gen. 49:10), a sign that Messiah was now at hand. As Herod is known to have died in the year of Rome 750, in the fourth year before the commencement of our Christian era, the birth of Christ must be dated four years before the date usually assigned to it, even if He was born within the year of Herod's death, as it is next to certain that He was. **there came wise men**—lit., "Magi" or "Magians," probably of the learned class who cultivated astrology and kindred sciences. Balaam's prophecy (Num. 24:17), and perhaps Daniel's (ch. 9:24, etc.), might have come down to them by tradition; but nothing definite is known of them. **from the east**—but whether from Arabia, Persia, or Mesopotamia is uncertain. **to Jerusalem**—as the Jewish metropolis. **2. Saying, Where is he that is born King of the Jews?**—From this it would seem they were not themselves Jews. (Cf. the language of the Roman governor, John 18:33, and of the Roman soldiers, ch. 27:29, with the very different language of the Jews themselves, ch. 27:42, etc.). The Roman historians, SUETONIUS and TACITUS, bear witness to an expectation, prevalent in the East, that out of Judea should arise a sovereign of the world. **for we have seen his star in the east**—Much has been written on the subject of this star; but from all that is here said it is perhaps safest to regard it as simply a luminous meteor, which appeared under special laws and for a special purpose. **and are come to worship him**—to do Him homage, as the word signifies; the nature of that homage depending on the circumstances of the case. That not civil but religious homage is meant here is plain from the whole strain of the narrative, and particularly vs. 11. Doubtless these simple strangers expected all Jerusalem to be full of its new-born King, and the time, place, and circumstances of His birth to be familiar to every one. Little would they think that the first announcement of His birth would come from themselves, and still less could they anticipate the startling, instead of transporting, effect which it would produce—else they would probably have sought their information regarding His birthplace in some other quarter. But God overruled it to draw forth a noble testimony to the predicted birthplace of Messiah from the highest ecclesiastical authority in the nation. **3. When Herod the king had heard these things, he was troubled**—viewing this as a danger to his own throne: perhaps his guilty conscience also suggested other grounds of fear. **and all Jerusalem with him**—from a dread of revolutionary commotions, and perhaps also of Herod's rage. **4. And when he had gathered all the chief priests and scribes of the people together**—The class of the "chief priests" included the high priest for the time being, together with all who had previously filled this office; for though the then head of the Aaronic family was the only rightful high priest, the Romans removed them at pleasure, to make way for creatures of their own. In this class probably were included also the heads of the four-and-twenty courses of the priests. The "scribes" were at first merely transcribers of the law and synagogue-readers; afterwards interpreters of the law, both civil and religious, and so both lawyers and divines. The first of these classes, a proportion of the second, and "the elders"—that is, as LIGHTFOOT thinks, "those elders of the laity that were not of the Levitical tribe"—constituted the supreme council of the nation, called the *Sanhedrim*, the members of which, at their full complement, numbered seventy-two. That this was the council which Herod now convened is most probable, from the solemnity of the occasion; for though the elders are not mentioned, we find a similar omission where all three were certainly meant (cf. ch. 26:59; 27:1). As MEYER says, it was all the theologians of the nation whom Herod convened, because it was a theological response that he wanted. **he demanded of them**—as the authorized interpreters of Scripture. **where Christ**—the Messiah. **should be born**—according to prophecy. **5. And they said unto him, In Bethlehem of Judea**—a prompt and involuntary testimony from the highest tribunal; which yet at length condemned Him to die. **for thus it is written by the prophet**—(Mic. 5:2). **6. And thou, Bethlehem, [in] the land of Juda**—the "in" being familiarly left out, as we say, "London, Middlesex." **art not the least among the princes of Juda: for out of thee shall come a Governor . . .**—This quotation, though differing verbally, agrees substantially with the *Hebrew* and LXX. For says the prophet, "Though thou be little, yet out of thee shall come the Ruler"—this honor more than compensating for its natural insignificance; while our Evangelist, by a lively turn, makes him say, "Thou art *not the least*: for out of thee shall come a Governor"—this distinction lifting it from the lowest to the highest rank. The "thousands of Juda," in the prophet, mean the subordinate divisions of the tribe: our Evangelist, instead of these, merely names the "princes" or heads of these families, including the districts which they occupied **that shall rule**—or "feed," as in the margin. **my people Israel**—In the Old Testament, kings are, by a beautiful figure, styled "shepherds" (Ezek. 31, etc.). The classical writers use the same figure. The pastoral rule of Jehovah and Messiah over His people is a representation pervading all Scripture, and rich in import. (See Ps. 23; Isa 40:11; Ezek. 37:24; John 10:11; Rev. 7:17). That this prophecy of Micah referred to the Messiah, was admitted by the ancient Rabbins.

The Wise Men, Despatched to Bethlehem by Herod to See the Babe, and Bring Him Word, Make a Religious Offering to the Infant King, but Divinely Warned, Return Home by another Way (vss. 7-12). **7. Then Herod, when he had privily called the wise men**—Herod has so far succeeded in his murderous design: he has tracked the spot where lies his victim, an unconscious babe. But he has another point to fix—the date of His birth—without which he might still miss his mark. The one he had got from the Sanhedrim; the other he will have from the sages; but secretly, lest his object should be suspected and defeated. So he **inquired of them diligently**—rather, "precisely." **what time the star appeared**—presuming that this would be the best clue to the age of the child. The unsuspecting strangers tell him all. And now he thinks he is succeeding to a wish, and shall speedily clutch his victim; for at so early an age as they indicate, He would not likely have been removed from the place of His birth. Yet he is wary. He sends them as messengers from himself, and bids them come to *him,* that he may follow their pious example. **8. And he sent them to Bethlehem, and said, Go and search diligently**—"Search out carefully." **for the young child; and when ye have found him, bring me word again, that I may come and worship him also**—The cunning and bloody hypocrite! Yet this royal mandate would meantime serve as a safe-conduct to the strangers. **9. When they had heard the king, they departed**—But where were ye, O Jewish ecclesiastics, ye chief priests and scribes of the people? Ye could tell Herod where Christ should be born, and could hear of these strangers from the far East that the Desire of all nations had actually come; but I do not see you trooping to Bethlehem —I find these devout strangers journeying thither all alone. Yet God ordered this too, lest the news should be blabbed, and reach the tyrant's ears, before the Babe could be placed beyond his reach. Thus are the very errors and crimes and cold indifferences of men all overruled. **and, lo, the star, which they saw in the east**—implying apparently that it had disappeared in the interval. **went before them, and stood over where the young child was**—Surely this could hardly be but by a luminous meteor, and not very high. **10. When they saw the star, they rejoiced with exceeding great joy**—The language is very strong, expressing exuberant transport. **11. And when they were come into the house** —not the stable; for as soon as Bethlehem was emptied of its strangers, they would have no difficulty in finding a dwelling-house. **they saw**—The received text has "found"; but here our translators rightly depart from it, for it has no authority. **the young child with Mary his mother**—The blessed Babe is naturally mentioned first, then the mother; but Joseph, though doubtless present, is not noticed, as being but the head of the house. **and fell down and worshipped him**—Clearly this was no civil homage to a petty Jewish king, whom these starguided strangers came so far, and inquired so eagerly, and rejoiced with such exceeding joy, to pay, but a lofty spiritual homage. The next clause confirms this. **and when they had opened their treasures they presented**—rather, "offered." **unto him gifts** —This expression, used frequently in the Old Testament of the oblations presented to God, is in the New Testament employed seven times, and always in *a religious* sense of *offerings to God.* Beyond doubt, therefore, we are to understand the presentation of these gifts by the Magi as *a religious offering.* **gold, frankincense, and myrrh**—Visits were seldom paid to sovereigns without a present (I Kings 10:2, etc.); cf. Ps. 72:10, 11, 15; Isa. 60:3, 6). "Frankincense" was an aromatic used in sacrificial offerings: "myrrh" was used in perfuming ointments. These, with the "gold" which they presented, seem to show that the offerers were persons in affluent circumstances. That the gold was presented to the infant King in token of His royalty; the frankincense in token of His divinity, and the myrrh, of His sufferings; or that they were designed to express His divine and human natures; or that the prophetical, priestly, and kingly offices

of Christ are to be seen in these gifts; or that they were the offerings of three individuals respectively, each of them kings, the very names of whom tradition has handed down—all these are, at the best, precarious suppositions. But that the feelings of these devout givers are to be seen in the richness of their gifts, and that the gold, at least, would be highly serviceable to the parents of the blessed Babe in their unexpected journey to Egypt and stay there —that much at least admits of no dispute. **12. And being warned of God in a dream that they should not return to Herod, they departed** [or, withdrew] **to their own country another way**—What a surprise would this vision be to the sages, just as they were preparing to carry the glad news of what they had seen to the *pious* king! But the Lord knew the bloody old tyrant better than to let him see their face again.

13-25. The Flight into Egypt—The Massacre at Bethlehem—The Return of Joseph and Mary with the Babe, after Herod's Death, and Their Settlement at Nazareth. (= Luke 2:39). *The Flight into Egypt* (vss. 13-15). **13. And when they were departed, behold, the angel of the Lord appeareth to Joseph in a dream, saying, Arise, and take the young child and his mother**—Observe this form of expression, repeated in the next verse—another indirect hint that Joseph was no more than the Child's *guardian.* Indeed, personally considered, Joseph has no spiritual significance, and very little place at all, in the Gospel history. **and flee into Egypt**—which, being near, as Alford says, and a Roman province independent of Herod, and much inhabited by Jews, was an easy and convenient refuge. Ah! blessed Saviour, on what a checkered career hast Thou entered here below! At Thy birth there was no room for Thee in the inn; and now all Judea is too hot for Thee. How soon has the sword begun to pierce through the Virgin's soul (Luke 2:35)! How early does she taste the reception which this mysterious Child of hers is to meet with in the world! And whither is He sent? To "the house of bondage?" Well, it once was that. But Egypt was a house of refuge before it was a house of bondage, and now it has but returned to its first use. **and be thou there until I bring thee word; for Herod will seek the young child to destroy** him—Herod's murderous purpose was formed before the Magi had reached Bethlehem. **14. When he arose, he took the young child and his mother by night**—doubtless the same night. **and departed into Egypt; 15. And was there until the death of Herod** —which took place not very long after this of a horrible disease; the details of which will be found in Josephus (*Antiquities,* 17. 6. 1, 5, 7, 8). **that it might be fulfilled which was spoken of the Lord by the prophet, saying** [Hos. 11:1], **Out of Egypt have I called my son**—Our Evangelist here quotes directly from the *Hebrew,* warily departing from the LXX, which renders the words, "From Egypt have I recalled his children," meaning Israel's children. The prophet is reminding his people how dear Israel was to God in the days of his youth; how Moses was bidden to say to Pharaoh, "Thus saith the Lord, Israel is My *son,* My first-born; and I say unto thee, Let *My* son go, that he may serve Me; and if thou refuse to let him go, behold, I will slay *thy* son, even thy first-born" (Exod. 4:22, 23); how, when Pharaoh refused, God having slain all *his* first-born, "called His own son out of Egypt," by a stroke of high-handed power and love. Viewing the words in this light, even if our Evangelist had not applied them to the recall from Egypt of God's own beloved, Only-begotten Son, the application would have been irresistibly made by all who have learnt to pierce beneath the surface to the deeper relations which Christ bears to His people, and both to God; and who are accustomed to trace the analogy of God's treatment of each respectively. **16. Then Herod . . .**—As Deborah sang of the mother of Sisera: "She looked out at a window, and cried through the lattice, Why is his chariot so long in coming? why tarry the wheels of his chariots? Have they not sped?" so Herod wonders that his messengers, with pious zeal, are not hastening with the news that all is ready to receive him as a worshipper. What can be keeping them? Have they missed their way? Has any disaster befallen them? At length his patience is exhausted. He makes his inquiries and finds they are already far beyond his reach on their way home. **when he saw that he was mocked** [was trifled with] **of the wise men**—No, Herod, thou art not mocked of the wise men, but of a Higher than they. He that sitteth in the heavens doth laugh at thee; the Lord hath thee in derision. He disappointeth the devices of the crafty, so that their hands cannot perform their enterprise. He taketh the wise in their own craftiness, and the counsel of the froward is carried headlong (Ps. 2:4; Job 5:12, 13). That blessed Babe shall die indeed, but not by thy hand. As He afterwards told that son of thine—as cunning and as unscrupulous as thyself—when the Pharisees warned Him to depart, for *Herod would seek to kill Him*—"Go ye, and tell that *fox*, Behold, I cast out devils, and I do cures to-day and to-morrow, and the third day I shall be perfected. Nevertheless I must walk to-day, and to-morrow, and the day following: for it cannot be that a prophet perish out of Jerusalem" (Luke 13:32, 33). Bitter satire! **was exceeding wroth**—To be made a fool of is what none like, and proud kings cannot stand. Herod burns with rage and is like a wild bull in a net. So he **sent forth** [a band of hired murderers], **and slew all the** [male] **children that were in Bethlehem, and in all the coasts** [environs] **thereof, from two years old and under, according to the time which he had diligently** [carefully] **inquired of the wise men**—In this ferocious step Herod was like himself—as crafty as cruel. He takes a large sweep, not to miss his mark. He thinks this will surely embrace his victim. And so it had, if He had been there. But He is gone. Heaven and earth shall sooner pass away than thou shalt have that Babe into thy hands. Therefore, Herod, thou must be content to want Him: to fill up the cup of thy bitter mortifications, already full enough—until thou die not less of a broken heart than of a loathsome and excruciating disease. Why, ask skeptics and skeptical critics, is not this massacre, if it really occurred, recorded by JOSEPHUS, who is minute enough in detailing the cruelties of Herod? To this the answer is not difficult. If we consider how small a town Bethlehem was, it is not likely there would be many male children in it from two years old and under; and when we think of the number of fouler atrocities which JOSEPHUS has recorded of him, it is unreasonable to make anything of his silence on this. **17. Then was fulfilled that which was spoken by Jeremy the prophet, saying**—(Jer. 31:15, from which the quotation differs but verbally). **18. In Rama was there a voice heard, lamentation, and weeping, and great mourning, Rachel weeping for her children, and would not be comforted, because they are not**—These words, as they stand in Jeremiah, undoubtedly relate to the Babylonish captivity. Rachel,

the mother of Joseph and Benjamin, was buried in the neighborhood of Bethlehem (Gen. 35:19), where her sepulchre is still shown. She is figuratively represented as rising from the tomb and uttering a double lament for the loss of her children—first, by a bitter captivity, and now by a bloody death. And a foul deed it was. O ye mothers of Bethlehem! methinks I hear you asking why your innocent babes should be the ram caught in the thicket, while Isaac escapes. I cannot tell you, but one thing I know, that ye shall, some of you, live to see a day when that Babe of Bethlehem shall be Himself the Ram, caught in another sort of thicket, in order that your babes may escape a worse doom than they now endure. And if these babes of yours be now in glory, through the dear might of that blessed Babe, will they not deem it their honor that the tyrant's rage was exhausted upon themselves instead of their infant Lord? **19. But when Herod was dead**—Miserable Herod! Thou thoughtest thyself safe from a dreaded Rival; but it was He only that was safe from thee; and thou hast not long enjoyed even this fancied security. See on vs. 15. **behold, an angel of the Lord**—Our translators, somewhat capriciously, render the same expression "*the* angel of the Lord," ch. 1:20; 2:13; and "*an* angel of the Lord," as here. As the same angel appears to have been employed on all these high occasions—and most likely he to whom in Luke is given the name of "Gabriel," ch. 1:19, 26—perhaps it should in every instance except the first, be rendered "*the* angel." **appeareth in a dream to Joseph in Egypt, 20. Saying, Arise, and take the young child and his mother, and go into the land of Israel**—not to the land of Judea, for he was afterward expressly warned not to settle there, nor to Galilee, for he only went thither when he found it unsafe to settle in Judea but to "the land of Israel," in its most general sense; meaning the Holy Land at large—the particular province being not as yet indicated. So Joseph and the Virgin had, like Abraham, to "go out, not knowing whither they went," till they should receive further direction. **for they are dead which sought the young child's life**—a common expression in most languages where only one is meant, who here is Herod. But the words are taken from the strikingly analogous case in Exodus 4:19, which probably suggested the plural here; and where the command is given to Moses to return *to* Egypt for the same reason that the greater than Moses was now ordered to be brought back *from* it—the death of him who sought his life. Herod died in the seventieth year of his age, and thirty-seventh of his reign. **21. And he arose, and took the young child and his mother, and came into the land of Israel**—intending, as is plain from what follows, to return to Bethlehem of Judea, there, no doubt, to rear the Infant King, as at His own royal city, until the time should come when they would expect Him to occupy Jerusalem, "the city of the Great King." **22. But when he heard that Archelaus did reign in Judea in the room of his father Herod**—Archelaus succeeded to Judea, Samaria, and Idumea; but Augustus refused him the title of *king* till it should be seen how he conducted himself; giving him only the title of *ethnarch* [JOSEPHUS, *Antiquities*, 17., 11, 4]. Above this, however, he never rose. The people, indeed, recognized him as his father's successor; and so it is here said that he "*reigned*" in the room of his father Herod." But, after ten years' defiance of the Jewish law and cruel tyranny, the people lodged heavy complaints against him, and the emperor banished him to Vienne in Gaul, reducing Judea again to a Roman province. Then the "scepter" clean "departed from Judah." **he was afraid to go thither**—and no wonder, for the reason just mentioned. **notwithstanding** [or more simply, "but"] **being warned of God in a dream, he turned aside** [withdrew] **into the parts of Galilee,** or the Galilean parts. The whole country west of the Jordan was at this time, as is well known, divided into three provinces—GALILEE being the northern, JUDEA the southern, and SAMARIA the central province. The province of Galilee was under the jurisdiction of Herod Antipas, the brother of Archelaus, his father having left him that and Perea, on the east side of the Jordan, as his share of the kingdom, with the title of *tetrarch,* which Augustus confirmed. Though crafty and licentious, according to JOSEPHUS —precisely what the Gospel history shows him to be (see on Mark 6:14-30, and on Luke 13:31-35)—he was of a less cruel disposition than Archelaus; and Nazareth being a good way off from the seat of government, and considerably secluded, it was safer to settle there. **23. And he came and dwelt in a city called Nazareth**—a small town in Lower Galilee, lying in the territory of the tribe of Zebulun, and about equally distant from the Mediterranean Sea on the west and the Sea of Galilee on the east. N.B. —If, from Luke 2:39, one would conclude that the parents of Jesus brought Him straight back to Nazareth after His presentation in the temple—as if there had been no visit of the Magi, no flight to Egypt, no stay there, and no purpose on returning to settle again at Bethlehem—one might, from our Evangelist's way of speaking here, equally conclude that the parents of our Lord had never been at Nazareth until now. Did we know exactly the sources from which the matter of each of the Gospels was drawn up, or the mode in which these were used, this apparent discrepancy would probably disappear at once. In neither case is there any inaccuracy. At the same time it is difficult, with these facts before us, to conceive that either of these two Evangelists wrote his Gospel with that of the other before him—though many think this a precarious inference. **that it might be fulfilled which was spoken by the prophets, He shall be called a Nazarene**—better, perhaps, "Nazarene." The best explanation of the origin of this name appears to be that which traces it to the word *netzer* in Isaiah 11: 1—the small *twig, sprout,* or sucker, which the prophet there says, "shall come forth from the stem (or rather, 'stump') of Jesse, the branch which should fructify from his roots." The little town of Nazareth, mentioned neither in the Old Testament nor in JOSEPHUS, was probably so called from its insignificance: a weak twig in contrast to a stately tree; and a special contempt seemed to rest upon it —"Can any good thing come out of Nazareth?" (John 1:46)—over and above the general contempt in which all Galilee was held, from the number of Gentiles that settled in the upper territories of it, and, in the estimation of the Jews, debased it. Thus, in the providential arrangement by which our Lord was brought up at the insignificant and opprobrious town called *Nazareth,* there was involved, first, a local humiliation; next, an allusion to Isaiah's prediction of His lowly, twig-like upspringing from the branchless, dried-up stump of Jesse; and yet further, a standing memorial of that humiliation which the prophets," in a number of the most striking predictions, had attached to the Messiah.

CHAPTER 3

Vss. 1-12. PREACHING AND MINISTRY OF JOHN. (= Mark 1:1-8; Luke 3:1-18.) For the proper introduction to this section, we must go to Luke 3:1, 2. Here, as BENGEL well observes, the curtain of the New Testament is, as it were, drawn up, and the greatest of all epochs of the Church commences. Even our Lord's own age is determined by it (vs. 23). No such elaborate chronological precision is to be found elsewhere in the New Testament, and it comes fitly from him who claims it as the peculiar recommendation of his Gospel, that "he had traced down all things with precision from the very first" (ch. 1: 3). Here evidently commences his proper narrative. Vs. 1: "Now in the fifteenth year of the reign of Tiberius Cæsar"—not the fifteenth from his full accession on the death of Augustus, but from the period when he was associated with him in the government of the empire, three years earlier, about the end of the year of Rome 779, or about four years before the usual reckoning. "Pontius Pilate being governor of Judea." His proper title was *procurator,* but with more than the usual powers of that office. After holding it for about ten years, he was summoned to Rome to answer to charges brought against him; but ere he arrived, Tiberius died (A.D. 35), and soon after miserable Pilate committed suicide. "And Herod being tetrarch of Galilee [see on Mark 6:14], and his brother Philip" —a very different and very superior Philip to the one whose name was *Herod Philip,* and whose wife, Herodias, went to live with Herod Antipas (see on Mark 6:17)—"tetrarch of Iturea"—lying to the northeast of Palestine, and so called from *Itur* or *Jetur,* Ishmael's son (I Chron. 1:31), and anciently belonging to the half-tribe of Manasseh. "and of the region of Trachonitis"—lying farther to the northeast, between Iturea and Damascus; a rocky district infested by robbers, and committed by Augustus to Herod the Great to keep in order. "and Lysanias the tetrarch of Abilene"—still more to the northeast; so called, says ROBINSON, from *Abila,* eighteen miles from Damascus. Vs. 2: "Annas and Caiaphas being the high priests." The former, though deposed, retained much of his influence, and, probably, as *sagan* or deputy, exercised much of the power of the high priesthood along with Caiaphas, his son-in-law (John 18:13; Acts 4:6). In David's time both Zadok and Abiathar acted as high priests (II Sam. 15:35), and it seems to have been the fixed practice to have two (II Kings 25:18). "the word of God came unto John the son of Zacharias in the wilderness." Such a way of speaking is never once used when speaking of Jesus, because He was Himself *The Living Word;* whereas to all merely creature-messengers of God, the word they spoke was a foreign element. See on John 3:31. We are now prepared for the opening words of Matthew. **1. In those days**—of Christ's secluded life at Nazareth, where the last chapter left Him. **came John the Baptist, preaching**—about six months before his Master. **in the wilderness of Judea**—the desert valley of the Jordan, thinly peopled and bare in pasture, a little north of Jerusalem. **2. And saying, Repent ye**—Though the word strictly denotes a *change of mind,* it has respect here (and wherever it is used in connection with salvation) primarily to that *sense of sin* which leads the sinner to flee from the wrath to come, to look for relief only from above, and eagerly to fall in with the provided remedy. **for the kingdom of heaven is at hand**—This sublime phrase, used in none of the other Gospels, occurs in this peculiarly Jewish Gospel nearly thirty times; and being suggested by Daniel's grand vision of the Son of man coming in the clouds of heaven to the Ancient of days, to receive His investiture in a world-wide kingdom (Dan. 7:13, 14), it was fitted at once both to meet the national expectations and to turn them into the right channel. A kingdom for which *repentance* was the proper preparation behooved to be essentially spiritual. Deliverance from sin, the great blessing of Christ's kingdom (ch. 1:21), can be valued by those only to whom sin is a burden (ch. 9:12). John's great work, accordingly, was to awaken this feeling and hold out the hope of a speedy and precious remedy. **3. For this is he that was spoken of by the prophet Esaias** [ch. 11:3], **saying. The voice of one crying in the wilderness**—(see on Luke 3:2); the scene of his ministry corresponding to its rough nature. **Prepare ye the way of the Lord, make his paths straight** —This prediction is quoted in all the four Gospels, showing that it was regarded as a great outstanding one, and the predicted forerunner as the connecting link between the old and the new economies. Like the great ones of the earth, the Prince of peace was to have His immediate approach proclaimed and His way prepared; and the call here—taking it generally —is a call to put out of the way whatever would obstruct His progress and hinder His complete triumph, whether those hindrances were public or personal, outward or inward. In Luke (3:5, 6) the quotation is thus continued: "Every valley shall be filled, and every mountain and hill shall be brought low; and the crooked shall be made straight, and the rough ways shall be made smooth; and all flesh shall see the salvation of God." Levelling and smoothing are here the obvious figures whose sense is conveyed in the first words of the proclamation—"*Prepare ye the way of the Lord*." The idea is that every obstruction shall be so removed as to reveal to the whole world the salvation of God in Him whose name is the "Saviour." (Cf. Ps. 98:3; Isa. 11: 10; 49:6; 52:10; Luke 2:31, 32; Acts 13:47.) **4. And the same John had his raiment of camel's hair** [woven of it] **and a leathern girdle about his loins**— the prophetic dress of Elijah (II Kings 1:8; and see Zech. 13:4). **and his meat was locusts**—the great, well-known Eastern locust, a food of the poor (Lev. 11:22). **and wild honey**—made by wild bees (I Sam. 14:25, 26). This dress and diet, with the shrill cry in the wilderness, would recall the stern days of Elijah. **5. Then went out to him Jerusalem, and all Judea, and all the region round about Jordan**—From the metropolitan center to the extremities of the Judean province the cry of this great preacher of repentance and herald of the approaching Messiah brought trooping penitents and eager expectants. **6. And were baptized of him in Jordan, confessing** [probably confessing aloud] **their sins**—This baptism was at once a public seal of their felt need of deliverance from sin, of their expectation of the coming Deliverer, and of their readiness to welcome Him when He appeared. The baptism itself startled, and was intended to startle, them. They were familiar enough with the *baptism of proselytes* from heathenism; but this *baptism of Jews* themselves was quite new and strange to them. **7. But when he saw many of the Pharisees and Sadducees come to his baptism, he said unto them** [astonished at such a spectacle]; **O generation of vipers**—"Viperbrood," expressing the deadly influence of both sects alike upon the community. Mutually and entirely antagonistic as were their religious principles and spirit, the stern prophet charges both alike

with being the poisoners of the nation's religious principles. In ch. 12:34, and 23:33, this strong language of the Baptist is anew applied by the faithful and true Witness to the Pharisees specifically—the only party that had zeal enough actively to diffuse this poison. **who hath warned you** [given you the hint, as the idea is] **to flee from the wrath to come?**—"What can have brought *you* hither?" John more than suspected it was not so much their own spiritual anxieties as the popularity of his movement that had drawn them thither. What an expression is this, "The wrath to come!" God's "wrath," in Scripture, is His righteous displeasure against sin, and consequently against all in whose skirts sin is found, arising out of the essential and eternal opposition of His nature to all moral evil. This is called "the *coming* wrath," not as being wholly future—for as a merited sentence it lies on the sinner already, and its effects, both inward and outward, are to some extent experienced even now— but because the impenitent sinner will not, until "the judgment of the great day," be concluded under it, will not have sentence publicly and irrevocably passed upon him, will not have it discharged upon him and experience its effects without mixture and without hope. In this view of it, it is a wrath *wholly* to come, as is implied in the noticeably different form of the expression employed by the apostle in I Thessalonians 1:10. Not that even true penitents came to John's baptism with all these views of "the wrath to come." But what he says is that this was the *real import of the step itself*. In this view of it, how striking is the word he employs to express that step—*fleeing* from it—as of one who, beholding a tide of fiery wrath rolling rapidly towards him, sees in instant flight his only escape! **8. Bring forth therefore fruits** [the true reading clearly is "fruit"] **meet for repentance**—that is, such fruit as *befits* a true penitent. John now being gifted with a knowledge of the human heart, like a true minister of righteousness and lover of souls here directs them how to evidence and carry out their repentance, supposing it genuine; and in the following verses warns them of their danger in case it were not. **9. And think not to say within yourselves, We have Abraham to our father**—that pillow on which the nation so fatally reposed, that rock on which at length it split. **for I say unto you, that God is able of these stones to raise up children unto Abraham**— i.e., "Flatter not yourselves with the fond delusion that God stands in need of you, to make good His promise of a seed to Abraham; for I tell you that, though you were all to perish, God is able to raise up a seed to Abraham out of *those stones as He was* to take Abraham himself out of the rock whence he was hewn, out of the hole of the pit whence he was digged" (Isa. 51:1). Though the stern speaker may have pointed as he spoke to the pebbles of the bare clay hills that lay around (so STANLEY's *Sinai and Palestine*), it was clearly the calling of the *Gentiles* at that time stone-dead in their sins, and quite as unconscious of it—into the room of unbelieving and disinherited Israel that he meant thus to indicate (see ch. 21:43; Rom. 11:20, 30). **10. And now also** [And even already] **the axe is laid unto** [lieth at] **the root of the trees**—as it were ready to strike: an expressive figure of impending judgment, only to be averted in the way next described. **therefore every tree which bringeth not forth good fruit is hewn down, and cast into the fire**—Language so personal and individual as this can scarcely be understood of any national judgment like the approaching destruction of Jerusalem, with the breaking up of the

Jewish polity and the extrusion of the chosen people from their peculiar privileges which followed it; though this would serve as the dark shadow, cast before, of a more terrible retribution to come. The "fire," which in another verse is called "unquenchable," can be no other than that future "torment" of the impenitent whose "smoke ascendeth up for ever and ever," and which by the Judge Himself is styled "everlasting punishment" (Matt. 25:48). What a strength, too, of just indignation is in that word "cast" or "flung into the fire!" The third Gospel here adds the following important particulars in Luke 3:10-16. Vs. 10: "And the people [the multitudes] asked him, saying, What shall we do then?"—that is, to show the sincerity of our repentance. Vs. 11: "He answereth and saith unto them, He that hath two coats, let him impart to him that hath none; and he that hath meat [provisions, victuals] let him do likewise." This is directed against the reigning avarice and selfishness. (Cf. the corresponding precepts of the Sermon on the Mount, ch. 5:40-42.) Vs. 12: "Then came also the publicans to be baptized, and said unto him, Master [Teacher] what shall we do?"—In what special way is the genuineness of our repentance to be manifested? Vs. 13: "And he said unto them, Exact no more than that which is appointed you." This is directed against that extortion which made the publicans a byword. (See on ch. 5:46; and on Luke 15:1.) Vs. 14: "And the soldiers [rather, 'And soldiers'—the word means 'soldiers on active duty'] likewise demanded [asked] of him, saying, And what shall we do? And he said unto them, Do violence to [Intimidate] no man." The word signifies to "shake thoroughly," and refers probably to the extorting of money or other property. "neither accuse any falsely"—by acting as informers vexatiously on frivolous or false pretexts—"and be content with your wages," or "rations." We may take this, say WEBSTER and WILKINSON, as a warning against mutiny, which the officers attempted to suppress by largesses and donations. And thus the "fruits" which would evidence their repentance were just resistance to the reigning sins—particularly of the *class* to which the penitent belonged—and the manifestation of an opposite spirit. Vs. 15: "And as the people were in expectation"—in a state of excitement, looking for something new—"and all men mused in their hearts of John, whether he were the Christ, or not"—rather, "whether he himself might be the Christ." The structure of this clause implies that they could hardly think it, but yet could not help asking themselves whether it might not be; showing both how successful he had been in awakening the expectation of Messiah's immediate appearing, and the high estimation and even reverence, which his own character commanded. Vs. 16: "John answered,"—either to that deputation from Jerusalem, of which we read in John 1:19, etc., or on some other occasion, to remove impressions derogatory to his blessed Master, which he knew to be taking hold of the popular mind—"saying unto them all"—in solemn protestation: (We now return to the first Gospel). **11. I indeed baptize you with water unto repentance** [see on vs. 6]: **but he that cometh after me is mightier than I**—In Mark and Luke this is more emphatic—"But there cometh the Mightier than I," **whose shoes** [sandals] **I am not worthy to bear**—The sandals were tied and untied, and borne about by the meanest servants. **he shall baptize you**—the emphatic "He": "He it is," to the exclusion of all others, "that shall baptize you." **with the Holy Ghost**—"So far from entertaining such a

thought as laying claim to the honors of Messiahship, the meanest services I can render to that "Mightier than I that is coming after me" are too high an honor for me; I am but the servant, but the Master is coming; I administer but the outward symbol of purification; His it is, as His sole prerogative, to dispense the inward reality. Beautiful spirit, distinguishing this servant of Christ throughout! **and with fire**—To take this as a distinct baptism from that of the Spirit—a baptism of the impenitent with hell-fire—is exceedingly unnatural. Yet this was the view of ORIGEN among the Fathers; and among moderns, of NEANDER, MEYER, DE WETTE, and LANGE. Nor is it much better to refer it to the fire of the great day, by which the earth and the works that are therein shall be burned up. Clearly, as we think, it is but the *fiery* character of the Spirit's operations upon the soul—searching, consuming, refining, sublimating—as nearly all good interpreters understand the words. And thus, in two successive clauses, the two most familiar emblems—*water* and *fire*—are employed to set forth the same purifying operations of the Holy Ghost upon the soul. **12. Whose** [winnowing] **fan is in his hand** —ready for use. This is no other than the preaching of the Gospel, even now beginning, the effect of which would be to separate the solid from the spiritually worthless, as wheat, by the winnowing fan, from the chaff. (Cf. the similar representation in Mal. 3:1-3.) **and he will throughly purge his** [threshing] **floor**—that is, the visible Church. **and gather his wheat**—His true-hearted saints; so called for their solid worth (cf. Amos 9:9; Luke 22:31). **into the garner**—"the kingdom of their Father," as this "garner" or "barn" is beautifully explained by our Lord in the parable of the wheat and the tares (ch. 13:30, 43). **but he will burn up the chaff**— empty, worthless professors of religion, void of all solid religious principle and character (see Ps. 1:4). **with unquenchable fire**—Singular is the strength of this apparent contradiction of figures:—to be burnt up, but with a fire that is unquenchable; the one expressing the *utter destruction* of all that constitutes one's true life, the other the *continued consciousness of existence* in that awful condition. Luke adds the following important particulars (3: 18-20): Vs. 18: "And many other things in his exhortation preached he unto the people," showing that we have here but an abstract of his teaching. Besides what we read in John 1: 29, 33, 34; 3:27-36, the incidental allusion to his having taught his disciples to pray (Luke 11:1)—of which not a word is said elsewhere—shows how varied his teaching was. Vs. 19: "But Herod the tetrarch, being reproved by him for Herodias his brother Philip's wife, and for all the evils which Herod had done." In this last clause we have an important fact, here only mentioned, showing how *thoroughgoing* was the fidelity of the Baptist to his royal hearer, and how strong must have been the workings of conscience in that slave of passion when, notwithstanding such plainness, he "did many things, and heard John gladly" (Mark 6:20). Vs. 20: "Added yet this above all, that he shut up John in prison." This imprisonment of John, however, did not take place for some time after this; and it is here recorded merely because the Evangelist did not intend to recur to his history till he had occasion to relate the message which he sent to Christ from his prison at Machærus (Luke 7:18, etc.).

13-17. BAPTISM OF CHRIST, AND DESCENT OF THE SPIRIT UPON HIM IMMEDIATELY THEREAFTER. (= Mark 1:9-11; Luke 3:21, 22; John 1:31-34.) *Bap-*

tism of Christ (vss. 13-15). **13. Then cometh Jesus from Galilee to Jordan unto John, to be baptized of him**—Moses rashly anticipated the divine call to deliver his people, and for this was fain to flee the house of bondage, and wait in obscurity for forty years more (Exod. 2:11, etc.). Not so this greater than Moses. All but thirty years had He now spent in privacy at Nazareth, gradually ripening for His public work, and calmly awaiting the time appointed of the Father. Now it had arrived; and this movement from Galilee to Jordan is the step, doubtless, of deepest interest to all heaven since that first one which brought Him into the world. Luke (3:21) has this important addition—"Now *when all the people were baptized*, it came to pass, that Jesus being baptized, ..."—implying that Jesus waited till all other applicants for baptism that day had been disposed of, ere He stepped forward, that He might not seem to be merely one of the crowd. Thus, as He rode into Jerusalem upon an ass "whereon yet never man sat" (Luke 19:30), and lay in a sepulchre "wherein was never man yet laid" (John 19:41), so in His baptism, too. He would be "separate from sinners." **14. But John forbade him**—rather, "was [in the act of] hindering him," or "attempting to hinder him." **saying, I have need to be baptized of thee, and comest thou to me?**—(How John came to recognize Him, when he says he knew Him not, see on John 1:31-34). The emphasis of this most remarkable speech lies all in the pronouns: "What! Shall the Master come for baptism to the servant—the sinless Saviour to a sinner?" That thus much is in the Baptist's words will be clearly seen if it be observed that he evidently regarded Jesus as *Himself needing no purification* but rather *qualified to impart it to those who did.* And do not all his other testimonies to Christ fully bear out this sense of the words? But it were a pity if, in the glory of this testimony to Christ, we should miss the beautiful spirit in which it was borne—"Lord, must *I* baptize *Thee?* Can I bring myself to do such a thing?"—reminding us of Peter's exclamation at the supper table, "Lord, dost Thou wash my feet?" while it has nothing of the false humility and presumption which dictated Peter's next speech. "Thou shalt never wash my feet" (John 13:6, 8). **15. And Jesus answering said unto him, Suffer it to be so now**—"Let it pass for the present"; i.e., "Thou recoilest, and no wonder, for the seeming incongruity is startling; but in the present case do as thou art bidden." **for thus it becometh us**—"us," not in the sense of me and thee," or "men in general," but as in John 3:11. **to fulfil all righteousness**—If this be rendered, with SCRIVENER, "every ordinance," or, with CAMPBELL, "every institution," the meaning is obvious enough; and the same sense is brought out by "all righteousness," or compliance with everything enjoined, baptism included. Indeed, if this be the meaning, our version perhaps best brings out the force of the opening word "Thus." But we incline to think that our Lord meant more than this. The import of circumcision and of baptism seems to be radically the same. And if our remarks on the circumcision of our Lord (on Luke 2:21-24) are well founded, He would seem to have said, "Thus do I impledge Myself to the whole righteousness of the Law—thus symbolically do enter on and engage to fulfil it all." Let the thoughtful reader weigh this. **Then he suffered him**—with true humility, yielding to higher authority than his own impressions of propriety. *Descent of the Spirit upon the Baptized Redeemer* (vss. 16, 17). **16. And Jesus when he was baptized, went up straightway out of** [rather, "from"] the

water. Mark has "out of the water." "and"—adds Luke (3:21), "while He was praying"; a grand piece of information. Can there be a doubt about the burden of that prayer; a prayer sent up, probably, while yet in the water—His blessed head suffused with the baptismal element; a prayer continued likely as He stepped out of the stream, and again stood upon the dry ground; the work before Him, the needed and expected Spirit to rest upon Him for it, and the glory He would then put upon the Father that sent Him—would not these fill His breast, and find silent vent in such form as this?—"Lo, I come; I delight to do Thy will, O God. Father, glorify Thy name. Show Me a token for good. Let the Spirit of the Lord God come upon Me, and I will preach the Gospel to the poor, and heal the broken-hearted, and send forth judgment unto victory." While He was yet speaking—**lo, the heavens were opened**—Mark says, sublimely, "He saw the heavens cleaving." **and he saw the Spirit of God descending**—that is, He only, with the exception of His honored servant, as he tells us himself (John 1:32-34); the bystanders apparently seeing nothing. **like a dove, and lighting upon him**—Luke says, "in a bodily shape" (3:22); that is, the blessed Spirit, assuming the corporeal form of a dove, descended thus upon His sacred head. But why in this form? The Scripture use of this emblem will be our best guide here. "My dove, *my undefiled* is one," says the Song of Solomon (6:9). This is chaste purity. Again, "Be ye *harmless* as doves," says Christ Himself (Matt. 10:16). This is the same thing, in the form of inoffensiveness towards men. "A conscience void of offense toward God and toward men" (Acts 24:16) expresses both. Further, when we read in the Song (2:14), "O my dove, that art in the *clefts* of the rocks, in the *secret places* of the stairs (see Isaiah 60:8), let me see thy countenance, let me hear thy voice; for sweet is thy voice, and thy countenance is comely"—it is shrinking modesty, meekness, gentleness, that is thus charmingly depicted. In a word—not to allude to the historical emblem of the dove that flew back to the ark, bearing in its mouth the olive leaf of *peace* (Gen. 8:11)—when we read (Ps. 68:13), "Ye shall be as the wings of a dove covered with silver, and her feathers with yellow gold," it is *beauteousness* that is thus held forth. And was not such that "holy, harmless, undefiled One," the "separate from sinners"? "Thou art fairer than the children of men; grace is poured into Thy lips; therefore God hath blessed Thee for ever!" But the fourth Gospel gives us one more piece of information here, on the authority of one who saw and testified of it: "John bare record, saying, I saw the Spirit descending from heaven like a dove, and IT ABODE UPON HIM." And lest we should think that this was an accidental thing, he adds that this last particular was expressly given him as part of the sign by which he was to recognize and identify Him as the Son of God: "And I knew Him not: but He that sent me to baptize with water, the same said unto me, Upon whom thou shalt see the Spirit descending AND REMAINING ON HIM, the same is He which baptizeth with the Holy Ghost. And I saw and bare record that this is the Son of God" (John 1:32-34). And when with this we compare the predicted descent of the Spirit upon Messiah (Isa. 11:2), "And *the Spirit of the Lord shall rest upon Him*," we cannot doubt that it was this permanent and perfect resting of the Holy Ghost upon the Son of God—now and henceforward in His *official* capacity—that was here visibly manifested. **17. And lo a voice from heav-**

en, saying, **This is**—Mark and Luke give it in the direct form, "Thou art." **my beloved Son, in whom I am well pleased**—The verb is put in the aorist to express absolute complacency, once and for ever felt towards Him. The English here, at least to modern ears, is scarcely strong enough. "I delight" comes the nearest, perhaps, to that ineffable *complacency* which is manifestly intended; and this is the rather to be preferred, as it would immediately carry the thoughts back to that august Messianic prophecy to which the voice from heaven plainly alluded (Isa. 42:1), "Behold My Servant, whom I uphold; Mine Elect, IN WHOM MY SOUL DELIGHTETH." Nor are the words which follow to be overlooked, "I have put My Spirit upon Him; He shall bring forth judgment to the Gentiles." (The LXX perverts this, as it does most of the Messianic predictions, interpolating the word "Jacob," and applying it to the Jews.) Was this voice heard by the bystanders? From Matthew's form of it, one might suppose it so designed; but it would appear that it was not, and probably John only heard and saw anything peculiar about that great baptism. Accordingly, the words, "Hear ye Him," are not added, as at the Transfiguration.

CHAPTER 4

Vss. 1-11. TEMPTATION OF CHRIST. (= Mark 1:12, 13; Luke 4:1-13.) **1. Then**—an indefinite note of sequence. But Mark's word (1:12) fixes what we should have presumed was meant, that it was "immediately" after His baptism; and with this agrees the statement of Luke (4:1). **was Jesus led up**—i.e., from the low Jordan valley to some more elevated spot. **of the Spirit**—that blessed Spirit immediately before spoken of as descending upon Him at His baptism, and abiding upon Him. Luke, connecting these two scenes, as if the one were but the sequel of the other, says, "Jesus, being full of the Holy Ghost, returned from Jordan, and was led . . . ." Mark's expression has a startling sharpness about it—"Immediately the Spirit driveth Him," "putteth," or "hurrieth Him forth," or "impelleth Him." (See the same word in Mark 1:43; 5:40; Matt. 9:25; 13:52; John 10:4.) The thought thus strongly expressed is the mighty constraining impulse of the Spirit under which He went; while Matthew's more gentle expression, "was led up," intimates how purely voluntary on His own part this action was. **into the wilderness**—probably the wild Judean desert. The particular spot which tradition has fixed upon has hence got the name of *Quarantana* or *Quarantaria*, from the forty days, —"an almost perpendicular wall of rock twelve or fifteen hundred feet above the plain" [ROBINSON'S *Palestine*]. The supposition of those who incline to place the temptation amongst the mountains of Moab is, we think, very improbable. **to be tempted** —The *Greek* word (*peirazein*) means simply to *try* or make proof of; and when ascribed to God in His dealings with men, it means, and can mean no more than this. Thus, Genesis 22:1, "It came to pass that God did tempt Abraham," or put his faith to a severe proof. (See Deut. 8:2.) But for the most part in Scripture the word is used in a bad sense, and means to entice, solicit, or provoke to sin. Hence the name here given to the wicked one—"the tempter" (vs. 3). Accordingly "to be tempted" here is to be understood both ways. The Spirit conducted Him into the wilderness simply to have His faith *tried;* but as the agent in this trial was to be the

wicked one, whose whole object would be to seduce Him from His allegiance to God, it was a *temptation* in the bad sense of the term. The unworthy inference which some would draw from this is energetically repelled by an apostle (Jas. 1:13-17). **of the devil.** The word signifies a slanderer—one who casts imputations upon another. Hence that other name given him (Rev. 12:10), "The accuser of the brethren, who accuseth them before our God day and night." Mark (1:13) says, "He was forty days tempted of Satan," a word signifying an *adversary*, one who lies in wait for, or sets himself in opposition to another. These and other names of the same fallen spirit point to different features in his character or operations. What was the high design of this? First, as we judge, to give our Lord a taste of what lay before Him in the work He had undertaken; next, to make trial of the glorious equipment for it which He had just received; further, to give Him encouragement, by the victory now to be won, to go forward spoiling principalities and powers, until at length He should make a show of them openly, triumphing over them in His cross: that the tempter, too, might get a taste, at the very outset, of the new kind of material in *man* which he would find he had here to deal with; finally, that He might acquire experimental ability "to succor them that are tempted" (Heb. 2:18). The temptation evidently embraced two stages: the one continuing throughout the forty days' fast; the other, at the conclusion of that period. FIRST STAGE: **2. And when he had fasted forty days and forty nights**— Luke says, "When they were quite ended." **he was afterward an hungered**—evidently implying that the sensation of hunger was unfelt during all the forty days; coming on only at their close. So it was apparently with Moses (Exod. 34:28) and Elijah (1 Kings 19:8) for the same period. A supernatural power of endurance was of course imparted to the body, but this probably operated through a natural law—the absorption of the Redeemer's Spirit in the dread conflict with the tempter. (See on Acts 9:9.) Had we only this Gospel, we should suppose the temptation did not begin till after this. But it is clear, from Mark's statement, that "He was in the wilderness forty days tempted of Satan," and Luke's, "being forty days tempted of the devil," that there was a forty days' temptation *before* the three specific temptations afterwards recorded. And this is what we have called the First Stage. What the precise nature and object of the forty days' temptation were is not recorded. But two things seem plain enough. First, the tempter had utterly failed of his object, else it had not been renewed; and the terms in which he opens his second attack imply as much. But further, the tempter's whole object during the forty days evidently was to get Him to distrust the heavenly testimony borne to Him at His baptism as THE SON OF GOD—to persuade Him to regard it as but a splended illusion—and, generally, to dislodge from His breast the consciousness of His Sonship. With what plausibility the events of His previous history from the beginning would be urged upon Him in support of this temptation it is easy to imagine. And it makes much in support of this view of the forty days' temptation that the particulars of it are not recorded; for how the details of such a purely internal struggle could be recorded it is hard to see. If this be correct, how naturally does the SECOND STAGE of the temptation open! In Mark's brief notice of the temptation there is one expressive particular not given either by Matthew or by Luke—that "He was with the wild beasts," no doubt to add terror to solitude, and aggravate the horrors of the whole scene. **3. And when the tempter came to him**—Evidently we have here a new scene. **he said, if thou be the Son of God, command that these stones be made bread**—rather, "loaves," answering to "stones" in the plural; whereas Luke, having said, "Command this stone," in the singular, "that it be made bread," in the singular. The sensation of hunger, unfelt during all the forty days, seems now to have come on in all its keenness—no doubt to open a door to the tempter, of which he is not slow to avail himself; "Thou still clingest to that vainglorious confidence that Thou art the Son of God, carried away by those illusory scenes at the Jordan. Thou wast born in a stable; but Thou art the Son of God! hurried off to Egypt for fear of Herod's wrath; but Thou art the Son of God! a carpenter's roof supplied Thee with a home, and in the obscurity of a despicable town of Galilee Thou hast spent thirty years, yet still Thou art the Son of God! and a voice from heaven, it seems, proclaimed it in Thine ears at the Jordan! Be it so; but after *that,* surely Thy days of obscurity and trial should have an end. Why linger for weeks in this desert, wandering among the wild beasts and craggy rocks, unhonored, unattended, unpitied, ready to starve for want of the necessaries of life? Is this befitting "the Son of God"? At the bidding of "the Son of God" surely those stones shall all be turned into loaves, and in a moment present an abundant repast." **4. But he answered and said, It is written**—(Deut. 8:3). **Man shall not live by bread alone**—more emphatically, as in the *Greek,* "Not by bread alone shall man live." **but by every word that proceedeth out of the mouth of God**—Of all passages in Old Testament Scripture, none could have been pitched upon more apposite, perhaps not one so apposite, to our Lord's purpose. "The Lord ... led thee [said Moses to Israel, at the close of their journeyings] these forty years in the wilderness, to humble thee, and to prove thee, to know what was in thine heart, whether thou wouldest keep His commandments, or no. And He humbled thee, and suffered thee to hunger, and fed thee with manna, which thou knewest not, neither did thy fathers know; that He might make thee know that man doth not live by bread only ...", "Now, if Israel spent, not forty days, but forty years in a waste, howling wilderness, where there were no means of human subsistence, not starving, but divinely provided for, on purpose to prove to every age that human support depends not upon bread, but upon God's unfailing word of promise and pledge of all needful providential care, am I, distrusting this word of God, and despairing of relief, to take the law into My own hand? True, the Son of God is able enough to turn stones into bread: but what the Son of God is able to do is not the present question, but what is *man's duty* under want of the necessaries of life. And as Israel's condition in the wilderness did not justify their unbelieving murmurings and frequent desperation, so neither would Mine warrant the exercise of the power of the Son of God in snatching despairingly at unwarranted relief. As man, therefore, I will await divine supply, nothing doubting that at the fitting time it will arrive." The *second* temptation in this Gospel is in Luke's the *third.* That Matthew's order is the right one will appear, we think, quite clearly in the sequel. **5. Then the devil taketh him up**—rather, "conducteth Him." **into the holy city**—so called (as in Isa. 48:2; Neh. 11:1) from its being "the city of the Great King," the seat of the

temple, the metropolis of all Jewish worship. **and setteth him on a pinnacle** [rather, the pinnacle] **of the temple**—a certain well-known projection. Whether this refers to the highest summit of the temple, which bristled with golden spikes (JOSEPHUS, *Antiquities,* 5. 5, 6); or whether it refers to another peak, on Herod's royal portico, overhanging the ravine of Kedron, at the valley of Hinnom—an immense tower built on the very edge of this precipice, from the top of which dizzy height JOSEPHUS says one could not look to the bottom (*Antiquities,* 15. 11, 5)—is not certain; but the latter is probably meant. **6. And saith unto him, If thou be the Son of God**—As this temptation starts with the same point as the first—our Lord's determination not to be disputed out of His Sonship—it seems to us clear that the one came directly after the other; and as the remaining temptation shows that the hope of carrying that point was abandoned, and all was staked upon a desperate venture, we think that remaining temptation is thus shown to be the last; as will appear still more when we come to it. **cast thyself down**—"from hence" (Luke 4:9). **for it is written**—(Ps. 91:11, 12). "But what is this I see?" exclaims stately BISHOP HALL—"Satan himself with a Bible under his arm and a text in his mouth!" Doubtless the tempter, having felt the power of God's Word in the former temptation, was eager to try the effect of it from his own mouth (II Cor. 11: 14). **He shall give his angels charge concerning thee: and in** [rather, on] **their hands they shall bear thee up, lest at any time thou dash thy foot against a stone**—The quotation is precisely as it stands in the *Hebrew* and LXX, save that after the first clause the words, "to keep thee in all thy ways," are here omitted. Not a few good expositors have thought that this omission was intentional, to conceal the fact that this would *not* have been one of "His ways," i.e., of duty. But as our Lord's reply makes no allusion to this, but seizes on the great principle involved in the promise quoted, so when we look at the promise itself, it is plain that the sense of it is precisely the same whether the clause in question be inserted or not. **7. Jesus said unto him, It is written again**—(Deut. 6:16), q.d., "True, it is so written, and on that promise I implicitly rely; but in using it there is another Scripture which must not be forgotten. **Thou shalt not tempt the Lord thy God**—Preservation in danger is divinely pledged: shall I then *create* danger, either to put the promised security skeptically to the proof, or wantonly to demand a display of it? That were "to tempt the Lord my God," which, being expressly forbidden, would forfeit the right to expect preservation." **8. Again, the devil taketh him up** ["conducteth him," as before] **into** [or unto] **an exceeding high mountain, and showeth him all the kingdoms of the world, and the glory of them**—Luke (4:5) adds the important clause, "in a moment of time"; a clause which seems to furnish a key to the true meaning. That a scene was presented to our Lord's natural eye seems plainly expressed. But to limit this to the most extensive scene which the natural eye could take in, is to give a sense to the expression, "all the kingdoms of the world," quite violent. It remains, then, to gather from the expression, "in a moment of time"—which manifestly is intended to intimate some supernatural operation—that it was permitted to the tempter to extend preternaturally for a moment our Lord's range of vision, and throw a "glory" or glitter over the scene of vision: a thing not inconsistent with the analogy of other scriptural statements regarding the permitted operations of the wicked one. In this case, the "exceeding height" of the "mountain" from which this sight was beheld would favor the effect to be produced. **9. And saith unto him, All these things will I give thee**—"and the glory of them," adds Luke. But Matthew having already said that this was "showed Him," did not need to repeat it here. Luke (4:6) adds these other very important clauses, here omitted—"for that is," or "has been," "delivered unto me, and to whomsoever I will I give it." Was this wholly false? That were not like Satan's unusual policy, which is to insinuate his lies under cover of some truth. What truth, then, is there here? We answer, Is not Satan thrice called by our Lord Himself, "the prince of this world" (John 12:31; 14:30; 16:11)? Does not the apostle call him "the god of this world" (II Corinthians 4:4)? And still further, is it not said that Christ came to destroy by His death "him that *hath the power of death,* that is, the devil" (Heb. 2:14)? No doubt these passages only express men's voluntary subjection to the rule of the wicked one while they live, and his power to surround death to them, when it comes, with all the terrors of the wages of sin. But as this is a real and terrible sway, so all Scripture represents men as righteously sold under it. In this sense he speaks what is not devoid of truth, when he says, "All this is delivered unto me." But how does he deliver this "to whomsoever he will?" As employing whomsoever he pleases of his willing subjects in keeping men under his power. In this case his offer to our Lord was that of a *deputed* supremacy commensurate with his own, though as *his gift* and for *his ends.* **if thou wilt fall down and worship me**—This was the sole but monstrous condition. No Scripture, it will be observed, is quoted now, because none could be found to support so blasphemous a claim. In fact, he has ceased now to present his temptations under the mask of piety, and he stands out unblushingly as the rival of God Himself in his claims on the homage of men. Despairing of success as an angel of light, he throws off all disguise, and with a splended bribe solicits divine honor. This again shows that we are now at the last of the temptations, and that Matthew's order is the true one. **10. Then saith Jesus unto him, Get thee hence, Satan**—Since the tempter has now thrown off the mask, and stands forth in his true character, our Lord no longer deals with him as a pretended friend and pious counsellor, but calls him by his right name—His knowledge of which from the outset He had carefully concealed till now—and orders him off. This is the final and conclusive evidence, as we think, that Matthew's must be the right order of the temptations. For who can well conceive of the tempter's returning to the assault after this, in the pious character again, and hoping still to dislodge the consciousness of His Sonship, while our Lord must in that case be supposed to quote Scripture to one He had called the devil to his face—thus throwing His pearls before worse than swine? **for it is written**—(Deut. 6:13). Thus does our Lord part with Satan on the rock of Scripture. **Thou shalt worship**—In the *Hebrew* and LXX it is, "Thou shalt *fear*"; but as the sense is the same, so "worship" is here used to show emphatically that what the tempter claimed was precisely what God had forbidden. **the Lord thy God, and him only shalt thou serve**—The word "serve" in the second clause, is one never used by the LXX of any but *religious* service; and in this sense exclusively is it used in the New Testament, as we find it here. Once more the word "only," in the second clause—not expressed in the *Hebrew* and LXX—is here added to bring out emphatically the *negative* and *prohibitory* feature of the command. (See Gal. 3:10 for a similar supplement of the word "all" in a quotation from Deut. 27:26). **11. Then the devil leaveth him**—Luke says, "And when the devil had exhausted"—or "quite ended," as in Luke 4:2—"every [mode of] temptation, he departed from him till a season." The definite "season" here indicated is expressly referred to by our Lord in John 14:36 and Luke 22:52, 53. **and, behold, angels came and ministered unto him**—or supplied Him with food, as the same expression means in Mark 1:31 and Luke 8:3. Thus did angels to Elijah (I Kings 19:5-8). Excellent critics think that they ministered, not food only, but supernatural support and cheer also. But this would be the natural *effect* rather than the direct *object* of the visit, which was plainly what we have expressed. And after having refused to claim the *illegitimate* ministration of angels in His behalf, oh, with what deep joy would He accept their services when sent, unasked, at the close of all this temptation, direct from Him whom He had so gloriously honored! What "angels' food" would this repast be to Him! and as He partook of it, might not a Voice from heaven be heard again, by any who could read the Father's mind, "Said I not well, This is my beloved Son, in whom I am well pleased?"

12-25. CHRIST BEGINS HIS GALILEAN MINISTRY —CALLING OF PETER AND ANDREW, JAMES AND JOHN —HIS FIRST GALILEAN CIRCUIT. (= Mark, 1:14-20, 35-39; Luke 4:14, 15). *There is here a notable gap in the history,* which but for the fourth Gospel we should never have discovered. From the former Gospels we should have been apt to draw three inferences, which from the fourth one we know to be erroneous: First, that our Lord awaited the close of John's ministry, by his arrest and imprisonment, before beginning His own; next, that there was but a brief interval between the baptism of our Lord and the imprisonment of John; and further, that our Lord not only opened His work in Galilee, but never ministered out of it, and never visited Jerusalem at all nor kept a passover till He went thither to become "our Passover, sacrificed for us." The fourth Gospel alone gives the true succession of events; not only recording those important openings of our Lord's public work which preceded the Baptist's imprisonment—extending to the end of the third chapter—but so specifying the passover which occurred during our Lord's ministry as to enable us to line off, with a large measure of certainty, the events of the first three Gospels according to the successive passover which they embraced. EUSEBIUS, the ecclesiastical historian, who, early in the fourth century, gave much attention to this subject, in noticing these features of the Evangelical Records, says (3:24) that John wrote his Gospel at the entreaty of those who knew the important materials he possessed, and filled up what is wanting in the first three Gospels. Why it was reserved for the fourth Gospel, published at so late a period, to supply such important particulars in the life of Christ, it is not easy to conjecture with any probability. It may be, that though not unacquainted with the general facts, they were not furnished with reliable details. But one thing may be affirmed with tolerable certainty, that as our Lord's teaching at Jerusalem was of a depth and grandeur scarcely so well adapted to the prevailing character of the first three Gospels, but altogether congenial to the fourth; and as the bare mention of the successive passovers, without any account of the transactions and discourses they gave rise to, would have served little purpose in the first three Gospels, there may have been no way of preserving the unity and consistency of each Gospel, so as to furnish by means of them all the precious information we get from them, save by the plan on which they are actually constructed.

Entry into Galilee (vss. 12-17). **12. Now when Jesus had heard that John was cast into prison**—more simply, "was delivered up", as recorded in ch. 14:3-5; Mark 6:17-20; Luke 3:19, 20. **he departed**—rather, "withdrew." **into Galilee**—as recorded, in its proper place, in John 4:1-3. **13. And leaving Narazeth**—The prevalent opinion is that this refers to a *first* visit to Nazareth after His baptism, whose details are given by Luke (4:16, etc.); a *second* visit being that detailed by our Evangelist (ch. 13:54-58), and by Mark (ch. 6:1-6). But to us there seem all but insuperable difficulties in the supposition of two visits to Nazareth after His baptism; and on the grounds stated in Luke 4:16, etc., we think that the *one only visit* to Nazareth is that recorded by Matthew (13), Mark (6), and Luke (4). But how, in that case, are we to take the word *"leaving* Nazareth" here? We answer, just as the same word is used in Acts 21:3, "Now when we had sighted Cyprus, and *left* it on the left, we sailed into Syria,"—i.e., without entering Cyprus at all, but merely "sighting" it, as the nautical phrase is, they steered southeast of it, leaving it on the northwest. So here, what we understand the Evangelist to say is, that Jesus, on His return to Galilee, did not, as might have been expected, make Nazareth the place of His stated residence, but, "leaving [or passing by] Nazareth," **he came and dwelt in Capernaum, which is upon the seacoast**—maritime Capernaum, on the northwest shore of the Sea of Galilee; but the precise spot is unknown. (See on ch. 11:23). Our Lord seems to have chosen it for several reasons. Four or five of the Twelve lived there; it had a considerable and mixed population, securing some freedom from that intense bigotry which even to this day characterizes all places where Jews in large numbers dwell nearly alone; it was centrical, so that not only on the approach of the annual festivals did large numbers pass through it or near it, but on any occasion multitudes could easily be collected about it; and for crossing and recrossing the lake, which our Lord had so often occasion to do, no place could be more convenient. But one other high reason for the choice of Capernaum remains to be mentioned, the only one specified by our Evangelist. **in the borders of Zabulon and Nephthalim**—the one lying to the west of the Sea of Galilee, the other to the north of it; but the precise boundaries cannot now be traced out. **14. That it might be fulfilled which was spoken by Esaias the prophet**—(ch. 9:1, 2 or, as in *Hebrew*, ch. 8:23, and 9:1). **saying, 15. The land of Zabulon, and the land of Nephthalim,** [by] **the way of the sea**—the coast skirting the Sea of Galilee westward—beyond Jordan—a phrase commonly meaning eastward of Jordan; but here and in several places it means westward of the Jordan. The word seems to have got the general meaning of "the other side"; the nature of the case determining which side that was. **Galilee of the Gentiles**—so called from its position, which made it the frontier between the Holy Land and the external world. While Ephraim and Judah, as STANLEY says, were separated from the world by the Jordan valley on one side and the hostile Philistines on another, the northern tribes were in the

direct highway of all the invaders from the north, in unbroken communication with the promiscuous races who have always occupied the heights of Lebanon, and in close and peaceful alliance with the most commercial nation of the ancient world, the Phœnicians. Twenty of the cities of Galilee were actually annexed by Solomon to the adjacent kingdom of Tyre, and formed, with their territory, the "boundary" or "offscouring" (*Gebul* or *Cabul*) of the two dominions—at a later time still known by the general name of "the boundaries (coasts or borders) of Tyre and Sidon." In the first great transportation of the Jewish population, Naphtali and Galilee suffered the same fate as the transjordanic tribes before Ephraim or Judah had been molested (II Kings 15:29). In the time of the Christian era this original disadvantage of their position was still felt; the speech of the Galileans "bewrayed them" by its uncouth pronunciation (Matt. 26:73); and their distance from the seats of government and civilization at Jerusalem and Cæsarea gave them their character for turbulence or independence, according as it was viewed by their friends or their enemies. **16. The people which sat in darkness saw great light; and to them which sat in the region and shadow of death light is sprung up.** The prophetic strain to which these words belong commences with Isaiah 7, to which ch. 6 is introductory, and goes down to the end of ch. 12, which hymns the spirit of that whole strain of prophecy. It belongs to the reign of Ahaz and turns upon the combined efforts of the two neighboring kingdoms of Syria and Israel to crush Judah. In these critical circumstances Judah and her king were, by their ungodliness, provoking the Lord to sell them into the hands of their enemies. What, then, is the burden of this prophetic strain, on to the passage here quoted? First, Judah shall not, cannot perish, because IMMANUEL, the Virgin's Son, is to come forth from his loins. Next, one of the invaders shall soon perish, and the kingdoms of neither be enlarged. Further, while the Lord will be the Sanctuary of such as confide in these promises and await their fulfilment, He will drive to confusion, darkness, and despair the vast multitude of the nation who despised His oracles, and, in their anxiety and distress, betook themselves to the lying oracles of the heathen. This carries us down to the end of the eighth chapter. At the opening of the ninth chapter a sudden light is seen breaking in upon one particular part of the country, the part which was to suffer most in these wars and devastations—"the land of Zebulon, and the land of Naphtali, the way of the sea, beyond Jordan, Galilee and the Gentiles." The rest of the prophecy stretches over both the Assyrian and the Chaldean captivities and terminates in the glorious Messianic prophecy of ch. 11 and the choral hymn of ch. 12. Well, this is the point seized on by our Evangelist. By Messiah's taking up His abode in those very regions of Galilee, and shedding His glorious light upon them, this prediction, He says, of the Evangelical prophet was now fulfilled; and if it was not thus fulfilled, we may confidently affirm it was not fulfilled in any age of the Jewish ceremony, and has received no fulfilment at all. Even the most rationalistic critics have difficulty in explaining it in any other way. **17. From that time Jesus began to preach, and to say, Repent; for the kingdom of heaven is at hand**—Thus did our Lord not only take up the strain, but give forth the identical summons of His honored forerunner. Our Lord sometimes speaks of the new kingdom as already come—in His own Person and ministry; but the *economy* of it was only "at hand" until the blood of the cross was shed, and the Spirit on the day of Pentecost opened the fountain for sin and for uncleanness to the world at large.

Calling of Peter and Andrew, James and John (vss. 18-22). **18. And Jesus, walking**—The word "Jesus" here appears not to belong to the text, but to have been introduced from those portions of it which were transcribed to be used as church lessons; where it was naturally introduced as a connecting word at the commencement of a lesson. **by the Sea of Galilee, saw two brethren, Simon called Peter**—for the reason mentioned in ch. 16:18. **and Andrew his brother, casting a net into the sea; for they were fishers. 19. And he saith unto them, Follow me**—rather, as the same expression is rendered in Mark, "Come ye after Me." **and I will make you fishers of men**—raising them from a lower to a higher *fishing*, as David was from a lower to a higher *feeding* (Ps. 78:70-72). **20. And they straightway left their nets, and followed him. 21. And going on from thence, he saw other two brethren, James the son of Zebedee, and John his brother, in a ship**—rather, "in the ship," their fishing boat. **with Zebedee their father, mending their nets: and he called them. 22. And they immediately left the ship and their father**—Mark adds an important clause: "They left their father Zebedee in the ship with the *hired servants*"; showing that the family were in easy circumstances. **and followed him**—Two harmonistic questions here arise: *First*, Was this the same calling as that recorded in John 1:35-42? Clearly not. For, (1) That call was given while Jesus was yet in Judea: this, after His return to Galilee. (2) Here, Christ calls Andrew: there, Andrew solicits an interview with Christ. (3) Here, Andrew and Peter are called together: there, Andrew having been called, with an unnamed disciple, who was clearly the beloved disciple (see on John 1:40), goes and fetches Peter his brother to Christ, who then calls him. (4) Here, John is called along with James his brother: there, John is called along with Andrew, after having at their own request had an interview with Jesus; no mention being made of James, whose call, if it then took place, would not likely have been passed over by his own brother. Thus far nearly all are agreed. But on the *next* question opinion is divided: Was this the same calling as that recorded in Luke 5:1-11? Many able critics think so. But the following considerations are to us decisive against it. First here, the four are called separately, in pairs: in Luke, all together. Next, in Luke, after a glorious miracle: here, the one pair are casting their net, the other are mending theirs. Further, here, our Lord had made no public appearance in Galilee, and so had gathered none around Him; He is walking solitary by the shores of the lake when He accosts the two pairs of fishermen: in Luke, the multitude are pressing upon Him, and hearing the word of God, as He stands by the Lake of Gennesaret—a state of things implying a somewhat advanced stage of His early ministry, and some popular enthusiasm. Regarding these successive callings, see on Luke 5:1.

First Galilean Circuit (vss. 23-35). **23. And Jesus went about all Galilee, teaching in their synagogues**—These were houses of local worship. It cannot be proved that they existed before the Babylonish captivity; but as they began to be erected soon after it, probably the idea was suggested by the religious inconveniences to which the captives had been subjected. In our Lord's time, the rule was to have one wherever ten learned men or professed students of the law resided; and they extended to Syria, Asia Minor, Greece, and most places of the dispersion. The larger towns had several, and in Jerusalem the number approached 500. In point of officers and mode of worship, the Christian congregations are modelled after the synagogue. **and preaching the gospel** [proclaiming the glad tidings] **of the kingdom, and healing all manner of sickness** [every disease] **and all manner of disease** [every complaint] —The word means any incipient malady causing "softness"—among the people. **24. And his fame went throughout all Syria**—reaching first to the part of it adjacent to Galilee, called Syro-phœnicia (Mark 7:26), and thence extending far and wide. **and they brought unto him all sick people**—all that were ailing or unwell [those] **that were taken**—for this is a distinct class, not an explanation of the "unwell" class, as our translators understood it. **with divers diseases and torments**—i.e., acute disorders. **and those which were possessed with devils**—that were demonized or possessed with demons. **and those which were lunatic**—moon-struck. **and those that had the palsy**—paralytics, a word not naturalized when our version was made. **and he healed them**—These healings were at once His credentials and illustrations of "the glad tidings" which He proclaimed. After reading this account of our Lord's first preaching tour, can we wonder at what follows? **25. And there followed him great multitudes of people from Galilee, and from Decapolis**—a region lying to the east of the Jordan, so called as containing ten cities, founded and chiefly inhabited by Greek settlers. **and from Jerusalem, and from beyond Jordan**—meaning from Perea. Thus not only was all Palestine upheaved, but all the adjacent regions. But the more immediate object for which this is here mentioned is, to give the reader some idea both of the vast concourse and of the varied complexion of eager attendants upon the great Preacher, to whom the astonishing discourse of the next three chapters was addressed. On the importance which our Lord Himself attached to this first preaching circuit, and the preparation which He made for it, see on Mark 1:35-39.

CHAPTERS 5-8

SERMON ON THE MOUNT

That this is the *same Discourse* as that in Luke 6: 17-49—only reported more fully by Matthew, and less fully, as well as with considerable variation, by Luke—is the opinion of many very able critics (of the Greek commentators; of CALVIN, GROTIUS, MALDONATUS—who stands almost alone among Romish commentators; and of most moderns, as THOLUCK, MEYER, DE WETTE, TISCHENDORF, STIER, WIESELER, ROBINSON). The prevailing opinion of these critics is that Luke's is the original form of the discourse, to which Matthew has added a number of sayings, uttered on other occasions, in order to give at one view the great outlines of our Lord's ethical teaching. But that they are *two distinct discourses*—the one delivered about the close of His first missionary tour, and the other after a second such tour and the solemn choice of the Twelve—is the judgment of others who have given much attention to such matters (of most Romish commentators, including ERASMUS; and among the moderns, of LANGE, GRESWELL, BIRKS, WEBSTER *and* WILKINSON. The question is left undecided by ALFORD). AUGUSTINE'S opinion

—that they were both delivered on one occasion, Matthew's on the mountain, and to the disciples; Luke's in the plain, and to the promiscuous multitude—is so clumsy and artificial as hardly to deserve notice. To us the weight of argument appears to lie with those who think them two separate discourses. It seems hard to conceive that Matthew should have put this discourse before his own calling, if it was not uttered till long after, and was spoken in his own hearing as one of the newly chosen Twelve. Add to this, that Matthew introduces his discourse amidst very definite markings of time, which fix it to our Lord's first preaching tour; while that of Luke, which is expressly said to have been delivered immediately after the choice of the Twelve, could not have been spoken till long after the time noted by Matthew. It is hard, too, to see how either discourse can well be regarded as the expansion or contraction of the other. And as it is beyond dispute that our Lord repeated some of His weightier sayings in different forms, and with varied applications, it ought not to surprise us that, after the lapse of perhaps a year—when, having spent a whole night on the hill in prayer to God, and set the Twelve apart, He found Himself surrounded by crowds of people, few of whom probably had heard the Sermon on the Mount, and fewer still remembered much of it—He should go over its principal points again, with just as much sameness as to show their enduring gravity, but at the same time with that difference which shows His exhaustless fertility as the great Prophet of the Church.

CHAPTER 5

Vss. 1-16. The Beatitudes, and Their Bearing upon the World. **1. And seeing the multitudes** —those mentioned in ch. 4:25—**he went up into a mountain**—one of the dozen mountains which ROBINSON says there are in the vicinity of the Sea of Galilee, any one of them answering about equally well to the occasion. So charming is the whole landscape that the descriptions of it, from JOSEPHUS downwards (*J. W.*, 4. 10, 8), are apt to be thought a little colored. **and when he was set** [had sat or seated Himself] **his disciples came unto him**—already a large circle, more or less attracted and subdued by His preaching and miracles, in addition to the smaller band of devoted adherents. Though the latter only answered to the subjects of His kingdom, described in this discourse, there were drawn from time to time into this inner circle souls from the outer one, who, by the power of His matchless word, were constrained to forsake their all for the Lord Jesus. **2. And he opened his mouth**—a solemn way of arousing the reader's attention, and preparing him for something weighty (Job 9:1; Acts 8: 35; 10:34). **and taught them, saying, 3. Blessed . . .** —Of the two words which our translators render "blessed," the one here used points more to what is *inward*, and so might be rendered "happy," in a lofty sense; while the other denotes rather what comes to us *from without* (as Matt. 25:34). But the distinction is not always clearly carried out. One Hebrew word expresses both. On these precious Beatitudes, observe that though eight in number, there are here but *seven* distinct features of character. The eighth one—the "persecuted for righteousness' sake"—denotes merely the possessors of the seven preceding features, on account of which it is that they are persecuted (II Tim. 3:12). Ac-

cordingly, instead of any distinct promise to this class, we have merely a repetition of the first promise. This has been noticed by several critics, who by the *sevenfold* character thus set forth have rightly observed that a *complete* character is meant to be depicted, and by the *sevenfold* blessedness attached to it, a *perfect* blessedness is intended. Observe, again, that the language in which these Beatitudes are couched is purposely fetched from the Old Testament, to show that the new kingdom is but the old in a new form; while the characters described are but the varied forms of that *spirituality* which was the essence of real religion all along, but had well-nigh disappeared under corrupt teaching. Further, the things here promised, far from being mere arbitrary rewards, will be found in each case to grow out of the characters to which they are attached, and in their completed form are but the appropriate coronation of them. Once more, as "the kingdom of heaven," which is the first and the last thing here promised, has two stages—a present and a future, an initial and a consummate stage—so the fulfilment of each of these promises has two stages—a present and a future, a partial and a perfect stage. **3. Blessed are the poor in spirit**—All familiar with Old Testament phraseology know how frequently God's true people are styled "the poor" (the "oppressed," "afflicted," "miserable") or "the needy" —or both together (as in Ps. 40:17; Isa. 41:17). The explanation of this lies in the fact that it is generally "the poor of this world" who are "rich in faith" (Jas. 2:5; cf. II Cor. 6:10, and Rev. 2:9); while it is often "the ungodly" who "prosper in the world" (Ps. 73:12). Accordingly, in Luke (6:20, 21). it seems to be this class—the literally "poor" and "hungry"—that are specially addressed. But since God's people are in so many places styled "the poor" and "the needy," with no evident reference to their temporal circumstances (as in Ps. 68: 10; 69:29-33; 132:15; Isa. 61:1; 66:2), it is plainly a *frame of mind* which those terms are meant to express. Accordingly, our translators sometimes render such words "the humble" (Ps. 10:12, 17), "the meek" (Ps. 22:26), "the lowly" (Prov. 3:34), as having no reference to outward circumstances. But here the explanatory words, "in spirit," fix the sense to "those who in their deepest consciousness realize their entire need" (cf. the *Greek* of Luke 10: 21; John 11:33; 13:21; Acts 20:22; Rom. 12:11; I Cor. 5:3; Phil. 3). This self-emptying conviction, that "before God we are void of everything," lies at the foundation of all spiritual excellence, according to the teaching of Scripture. Without it we are inaccessible to the riches of Christ; with it we are in the fitting state for receiving all spiritual supplies (Rev. 3:17, 18; Matt. 9:12, 13). **for theirs is the kingdom of heaven.** (See on ch. 3:2). The poor in spirit not only shall have—they already have—the kingdom. The very sense of their poverty is begun riches. While others "walk in a vain show" —"in a shadow," "an image"—in an unreal world, taking a false view of themselves and all around them—the poor in spirit are rich in the knowledge of their real case. Having courage to look this in the face, and own it guilelessly, they feel strong in the assurance that "unto the upright there ariseth light in the darkness" (Ps. 112:4); and soon it breaks forth as the morning. God wants nothing from us as the price of His saving gifts; we have but to feel our universal destitution, and cast ourselves upon His compassion (Job 33:27, 28; I John 1:9). So the poor in spirit are enriched with the fulness of Christ, which is the kingdom in substance; and when

He shall say to them from His great white throne, "Come, ye blessed of My Father, inherit the kingdom *prepared for you*," He will invite them merely to the full enjoyment of an already possessed inheritance. **4. Blessed are they that mourn: for they shall be comforted**—This "mourning" must not be taken loosely for that feeling which is wrung from men under pressure of the ills of life, nor yet strictly for sorrow on account of committed sins. Evidently it is that entire feeling which the sense of our spiritual poverty begets; and so the second beatitude is but the complement of the first. The one is the intellectual, the other the emotional aspect of the same thing. It is poverty of spirit that says, "I am undone"; and it is the mourning which this causes that makes it break forth in the form of a lamentation—"Woe is me! for I am undone." Hence this class are termed "mourners *in Zion*," or, as we might express it, religious mourners, in sharp contrast with all other sorts (Isa. 61:1-3; 66:2). Religion, according to the Bible, is neither a set of intellectual convictions nor a bundle of emotional feelings, but a compound of both, the former giving birth to the latter. Thus closely do the first two beatitudes cohere. The mourners shall be "comforted." Even now they get beauty for ashes, the oil of joy for mourning, the garment of praise for the spirit of heaviness. Sowing in tears, they reap even here in joy. Still, all present comfort, even the best, is partial, interrupted, short-lived. But the days of our mourning shall soon be ended, and then God shall wipe away all tears from our eyes. Then, in the fullest sense, shall the mourners be "comforted." **5. Blessed are the meek: for they shall inherit the earth**—This promise to the meek is but a repetition of Psalm 37:11; only the word which our Evangelist renders "the meek," after the LXX, is the same which we have found so often translated "the poor," showing how closely allied these two features of character are. It is impossible, indeed, that "the poor in spirit" and "the mourners" in Zion should not at the same time be "meek"; that is to say, persons of a lowly and gentle carriage. How fitting, at least, it is that they should be so, may be seen by the following touching appeal: "Put them in mind to be subject to principalities and powers, to obey magistrates, to be ready to every good work, to speak evil of no man, to be no brawlers, *but gentle, showing all meekness unto all men:* FOR WE OURSELVES WERE ONCE FOOLISH, disobedient, deceived, serving divers lusts and pleasures . . . But after that the kindness and love of God our Saviour toward man appeared: . . . according to His mercy He saved us . . ." (Titus 3:1-7). But He who had no such affecting reasons for manifesting this beautiful carriage, said, nevertheless, of Himself, "Take My yoke upon you, and learn of Me; for I am meek and lowly in heart: and ye shall find rest unto your souls" (Matt. 11:29); and the apostle besought one of the churches by "the meekness and gentleness of Christ" (II Cor. 10:1). In what esteem this is held by Him who seeth not as man seeth, we may learn from I Peter 3:4, where the true adorning is said to be that of "a meek and quiet spirit, which in the sight of God is of great price." Towards men this disposition is the opposite of high-mindedness, and a quarrelsome and revengeful spirit; it "rather takes wrong, and suffers itself to be defrauded" (I Cor. 6:7); it "avenges not itself, but rather gives place unto wrath" (Rom. 12:19); like the meek One, "when reviled, it reviles not again; when it suffers, it threatens not: but commits itself to Him that judgeth righteously" (I Pet. 2:19-22).

"The earth" which the meek are to inherit might be rendered "the land"—bringing out the more immediate reference to Canaan as the promised land, the secure possession of which was to the Old Testament saints the evidence and manifestation of God's favor resting on them, and the ideal of all true and abiding blessedness. Even in the Psalm from which these words are taken the promise to the meek is not held forth as an arbitrary reward, but as having a kind of natural fulfilment. When they delight themselves in the Lord, He gives them the desires of their heart: when they commit their way to Him, He brings it to pass; bringing forth their righteousness as the light, and their judgment as the noonday: the little that they have, even when despoiled of their rights, is better than the riches of many wicked (Ps. 37). All things, in short, are theirs—in the possession of that favor which is life, and of those rights which belong to them as the children of God—whether the world, or life, or death, or things present, or things to come; all are theirs (I Cor. 3:21, 22); and at length, overcoming, they "inherit all things" (Rev. 21:7). Thus are the meek the only rightful occupants of a foot of ground or a crust of bread here, and heirs of all coming things. **6. Blessed are they which do hunger and thirst after righteousness: for they shall be filled**—"shall be saturated." "From this verse," says THOLUCK, "the reference to the Old Testament background ceases." Surprising! On the contrary, none of these beatitudes is more manifestly dug out of the rich mine of the Old Testament. Indeed, how could any one who found in the Old Testament "the poor in spirit," and "the mourners in Zion," doubt that he would also find those same characters also *craving* that righteousness which they feel and mourn their want of? But what is the precise meaning of "righteousness" here? Lutheran expositors, and some of our own, seem to have a hankering after that more restricted sense of the term in which it is used with reference to the sinner's justification before God. (See Jer. 23:6; Isa. 45:24; Rom. 4:6; II Cor. 5:21). But, in so comprehensive a saying as this, it is clearly to be taken —as in vs. 10 also—in a much wider sense, as denoting that spiritual and entire conformity to the law of God, under the want of which the saints groan, and the possession of which constitutes the only true saintship. The Old Testament dwells much on this righteousness, as that which alone God regards with approbation (Ps. 11:7; 23:3; 106:3; Prov. 12:28; 16:31; Isa. 64:5, etc.). As hunger and thirst are the keenest of our appetites, our Lord, by employing this figure here, plainly means "those whose deepest cravings are after spiritual blessings." And in the Old Testament we find this craving variously expressed: "Hearken unto Me, ye that follow after righteousness, ye that seek the Lord" (Isa. 51:1); "I have waited for Thy salvation, O Lord," exclaimed dying Jacob (Gen. 49:18); "My soul," says the sweet Psalmist, "breaketh for the longing that it hath unto Thy judgments at all times" (Ps. 119:20): and in similar breathings does he give vent to his deepest longings in that and other Psalms. Well, our Lord just takes up here this blessed frame of mind, representing it as the surest pledge of the coveted supplies, as it is the best preparative, and indeed itself the beginning of them. "They shall be saturated," He says; they shall not only have what they so highly value and long to possess, but they shall have their fill of it. Not here, however. Even in the Old Testament this was well understood. "Deliver me," says the Psalmist, in language which, beyond all doubt, stretches beyond the present scene, "from men of the world, which have their portion in this life: as for me, I shall behold Thy face in righteousness: I shall be satisfied, when I awake, with Thy likeness" (Ps. 17:13-15). The foregoing beatitudes—the first four—represent the saints rather as *conscious of their need of salvation*, and acting suitably to that character, than as possessed of it. The next three are of a different kind —representing the saints as *having now found salvation*, and conducting themselves accordingly. **7. Blessed are the merciful: for they shall obtain mercy.** Beautiful is the connection between this and the preceding beatitude. The one has a natural tendency to beget the other. As for the words, they seem directly fetched from Psalm 18:25, "With the merciful Thou wilt show Thyself merciful." Not that our mercifulness comes absolutely first. On the contrary, our Lord Himself expressly teaches us that God's method is to awaken in us compassion towards our fellow men by His own exercise of it, in so stupendous a way and measure, towards ourselves. In the parable of the unmerciful debtor, the servant to whom his lord forgave ten thousand talents was naturally expected to exercise the small measure of the same compassion required for forgiving his fellow servant's debt of a hundred pence; and it is only when, instead of this, he relentlessly imprisoned him till he should pay it up, that his lord's indignation was roused, and he who was designed for a vessel of mercy is treated as a vessel of wrath (ch. 18:23-35; and see ch. 5:23, 24; 6:15; Jas. 2:13). "According to the view given in Scripture," says TRENCH most justly, "the Christian stands in a middle point, between a mercy received and a mercy yet needed." Sometimes the first is urged upon him as an argument for showing mercy—"forgiving one another, as Christ forgave you" (Col. 3:13; Eph. 4:32): sometimes the last—"Blessed are the merciful: for they shall obtain mercy"; "Forgive, and ye shall be forgiven" (Luke 6:37; Jas. 5: 9). And thus, while he is ever to look back on the mercy received as the source and motive of the mercy which he shows, he also looks forward to the mercy which he yet needs, and which he is assured that the merciful—according to what BENGEL beautifully calls the *benigna talio* (the gracious requital) of the kingdom of God—shall receive, as a new provocation to its abundant exercise. The foretastes and beginnings of this judicial recompense are richly experienced here below: its perfection is reserved for that day when, from His great white throne, the King shall say, "Come, ye blessed of My Father, inherit the kingdom prepared for you from the foundation of the world; for I was an hungered, and thirsty, and a stranger, and naked, and sick, and in prison, and ye ministered unto Me." Yes, thus He acted towards us while on earth, even laying down His life for us; and He will not, He cannot disown, in the merciful, the image of Himself. **8. Blessed are the pure in heart: for they shall see God.** Here, too, we are on Old Testament ground. There the difference between outward and inward purity, and the acceptableness of the latter only in the sight of God, are everywhere taught. Nor is the "vision of God" strange to the Old Testament; and though it was an understood thing that this was not possible in the present life (Exod. 33:20; and cf. Job 19:26, 27; Isa. 6:5), yet spiritually it was known and felt to be the privilege of the saints even here (Gen. 5: 24; 6:9; 17:1; 48:15; Ps. 27:4; 36:9; 63:2; Isa. 38:3, 11, etc.). But oh, with what grand simplicity, brevity, and power is this great fundamental

truth here expressed! And in what striking contrast would such teaching appear to that which was then current, in which exclusive attention was paid to ceremonial purification and external morality! This heart-purity begins in a "heart sprinkled from an evil conscience," or a "conscience purged from dead works" (Heb. 10:22; 9:14; and see Acts 15:9); and this also is taught in the Old Testament (Ps. 32:1, 2; cf. Rom. 4:5-8; and Isa. 6:5-8). The conscience thus purged—the heart thus sprinkled—there is light within wherewith to see God. "If we say that we have fellowship with Him, and walk in darkness, we lie, and do not the truth: but if we walk in the light, as He is in the light, we have fellowship one with the other"—He with us and we with Him—"and the blood of Jesus Christ His Son cleanseth us"—us who have this fellowship, and who, without such continual cleansing, would soon lose it again—"from all sin" (I John 1:6, 7). "Whosoever sinneth hath not seen Him, neither known Him" (I John 3:6); "He that doeth evil hath not seen God" (III John 11). The inward vision thus clarified, and the whole inner man in sympathy with God, each looks upon the other with complacency and joy, and we are "changed into the same image from glory to glory." But the full and beatific vision of God is reserved for that time to which the Psalmist stretches his views—"As for me, I shall behold Thy face in righteousness: I shall be satisfied, when I awake, with Thy likeness" (Ps. 17:15). Then shall His servants serve Him: and they shall see His face; and His name shall be in their foreheads (Rev. 22:3, 4). They shall see Him as He is (I John 3:2). But, says the apostle, expressing the converse of this beatitude—"Follow holiness, without which no man shall see the Lord" (Heb. 12:14). **9. Blessed are the peacemakers**—who not only study peace, but diffuse it—**for they shall be called the children** [shall be called sons] **of God**—Of all these beatitudes this is the only one which could hardly be expected to find its definite ground in the Old Testament; for that most glorious character of God, the likeness of which appears in the peacemakers, had yet to be revealed. His glorious name, indeed—as "The Lord, the Lord God, merciful and gracious, longsuffering, and abundant in goodness and truth, forgiving iniquity and transgression and sin"—had been proclaimed in a very imposing manner (Exod. 34: 6), and manifested in action with affecting frequency and variety in the long course of the ancient economy. And we have undeniable evidence that the saints of that economy felt its transforming and ennobling influence on their own character. But it was not till Christ "made peace by the blood of the cross" that God could manifest Himself as "the God of peace, that brought again from the dead our Lord Jesus, that great Shepherd of the sheep, through the blood of the everlasting covenant" (Heb. 13:20)—could reveal Himself as "in Christ reconciling the world unto Himself, not imputing their trespasses unto them," and hold Himself forth in the astonishing attitude of beseeching men to be "reconciled to Himself" (II Cor. 5:19, 20). When this reconciliation actually takes place, and one has "peace with God through our Lord Jesus Christ"—even "the peace of God which passeth all understanding"—the peace-receivers become transformed into peace-diffusers. God is thus seen reflected in them; and by the family likeness these peacemakers are recognized as the children of God. In now coming to the eighth, or supplementary beatitude, it will be seen that all that the saints are *in themselves* has been already described, in seven features of character; that number indicating *completeness* of delineation. The last feature, accordingly, is a passive one, representing the treatment that the characters already described may expect from the world. He who shall one day fix the destiny of all men here pronounces certain characters "blessed"; but He ends by forewarning them that the world's estimation and treatment of them will be the reserve of His. **10. Blessed are they which are persecuted for righteousness' sake ...**—How entirely this final beatitude has its ground in the Old Testament, is evident from the concluding words, where the encouragement held out to endure such persecutions consists in its being but a continuation of what was experienced by the Old Testament servants of God. But how, it may be asked, could such beautiful features of character provoke persecution? To this the following answers should suffice: "Every one that doeth evil hateth the light, neither cometh to the light, lest his deeds should be reproved." "The world cannot hate you; but Me it hateth, because I testify of it, that the works thereof are evil." "If ye were of the world, the world would love his own: but because ye are not of the world, but I have chosen you out of the world, therefore the world hateth you." "There is yet one man (said wicked Ahab to good Jehoshaphat) by whom we may inquire of the Lord: but I hate him; for he never prophesied good unto me, but always evil" (John 3: 20; 7:7; 15:19; II Chron. 18:7). But more particularly, the seven characters here described are all in the teeth of the spirit of the world, insomuch that such hearers of this discourse as breathed that spirit must have been startled, and had their whole system of thought and action rudely dashed. Poverty of spirit runs counter to the pride of men's heart; a pensive disposition, in the view of one's universal deficiencies before God, is ill relished by the callous, indifferent, laughing, self-satisfied world; a meek and quiet spirit, taking wrong, is regarded as pusillanimous, and rasps against the proud, resentful spirit of the world; that craving after spiritual blessings rebukes but too unpleasantly the lust of the flesh, the lust of the eye, and the pride of life; so does a merciful spirit the hardheartedness of the world; purity of heart contrasts painfully with painted hypocrisy; and the peacemaker cannot easily be endured by the contentious, quarrelsome world. Thus does "righteousness" come to be "persecuted." But blessed are they who, in spite of this, dare to be righteous. **for theirs is the kingdom of heaven** —As this was the reward promised to the poor in spirit—the leading one of these seven beatitudes—of course it is the proper portion of such as are persecuted for exemplifying them. **11. Blessed are ye when men shall revile you**—or abuse you to your face, in opposition to backbiting. (See Mark 15: 32). **and persecute you, and shall say all manner of evil against you, falsely, for my sake.** Observe this. He had before said, "for righteousness' sake." Here He identifies Himself and His cause with that of righteousness, binding up the cause of righteousness in the world with the reception of Himself. Would Moses, or David, or Isaiah, or Paul have so expressed themselves? Never. Doubtless they suffered for righteousness' sake. But to have called this "their sake," would, as every one feels, have been very unbecoming. Whereas He that speaks, being Righteousness incarnate (see Mark 1: 24; Acts 3:14; Rev. 3:7), when He so speaks, speaks only like Himself. **12. Rejoice, and be exceeding glad**—"exult." In the corresponding passage of

Luke (6:22, 23), where every indignity trying to flesh and blood is held forth as the probable lot of such as were faithful to Him, the word is even stronger than here: "leap," as if He would have their inward transport to overpower and absorb the sense of all these affronts and sufferings; nor will anything else do it. **for great is your reward in heaven: for so persecuted they the prophets which were before you:**—i.e., "You do but serve yourselves heirs to their character and sufferings, and the reward will be common." **13-16.** We have here the practical application of the foregoing principles to those disciples who sat listening to them, and to their successors in all time. Our Lord, though He began by pronouncing certain *characters* to be blessed—without express reference to any of His hearers—does not close the beatitudes without intimating that such characters were in existence, and that already they were before Him. Accordingly, from characters He comes to *persons* possessing them, saying, "Blessed are ye when men shall revile you ..." And now, continuing this mode of direct personal address, He startles those humble, unknown men by pronouncing them the exalted benefactors of their whole species. **13. Ye are the salt of the earth**—to preserve it from corruption, to season its insipidity, to freshen and sweeten it. The value of salt for these purposes is abundantly referred to by classical writers as well as in Scripture; and hence its symbolical significance in the religious offerings as well of those without as of those within the pale of revealed religion. In Scripture, mankind, under the unrestrained workings of their own evil nature, are represented as entirely corrupt. Thus, before the flood (Gen. 6:11, 12); after the flood (Gen. 8:21); in the days of David (Ps. 14:2, 3); in the days of Isaiah (Isa. 1:5, 6); and in the days of Paul (Eph. 2:1-3; see also Job 14:4; 15:15, 16; John 3:6; compared with Rom. 8:8; Titus 3:2, 3). The remedy for this, says our Lord here, is the active presence of His disciples among their fellows. The character and principles of Christians, brought into close contact with it, are designed to arrest the festering corruption of humanity and season its insipidity. But how, it may be asked, are Christians to do this office for their fellow men, if their righteousness only exasperate them, and recoil, in every form of persecution, upon themselves? The answer is: That is but the first and partial effect of their Christianity upon the world: though the great proportion would dislike and reject the truth, a small but noble band would receive and hold it fast; and in the struggle that would ensue, one and another even of the opposing party would come over to His ranks, and at length the Gospel would carry all before it. **but if the salt have lost his savour**—"become unsavory" or "insipid"; losing its saline or salting property. The meaning is: If that Christianity on which the health of the world depends, does in any age, region, or individual, exist only in *name,* or if it contain not those *saving elements* for want of which the world languishes, **wherewith shall it be salted?**—How shall the salting qualities be restored it? (Cf. Mark 9:50.) Whether salt ever does lose its saline property—about which there is a difference of opinion—is a question of no moment here. The point of the case lies in the supposition—that *if it should lose it,* the consequence would be as here described. So with Christians. The question is not: Can, or do, the saints ever totally lose that grace which makes them a blessing to their fellow men? But, What is to be the issue of that Christianity which is found wanting in those elements which can alone stay the corruption and season the tastelessness of an all-pervading carnality? The restoration or non-restoration of *grace,* or true living Christianity, to those who have lost it, has, in our judgment, nothing at all to do here. The question is not, If a man lose his grace, how shall *that* grace be restored to him? but, Since living Christianity is the only "salt of the earth," if men lose that, *what else* can supply its place? What follows is the appalling answer to this question. **it is thenceforth good for nothing, but to be cast out**—a figurative expression of indignant exclusion from the kingdom of God (cf. ch. 8:12; 22:13; John 6:37; 9:34). **and to be trodden under foot of men**—expressive of contempt and scorn. It is not the mere want of a certain character, but the want of it in those whose *profession* and *appearance* were fitted to beget expectation of finding it. **14. Ye are the light of the world**—This being the distinctive title which our Lord appropriates to Himself (John 8:12; 9:5; and see John 1:4, 9; 3:19; 12:35, 36)—a title expressly said to be unsuitable even to the highest of all the prophets (John 1:8)—it must be applied here by our Lord to His disciples only as they shine with His light upon the world, in virtue of His Spirit dwelling in them, and the same mind being in them which was also in Christ Jesus. Nor are Christians anywhere else so called. Nay, as if to avoid the august title which the Master has appropriated to Himself, Christians are said to "shine"—not as "lights," as our translators render it, but—"as *luminaries* in the world" (Phil. 2:15); and the Baptist is said to have been "the burning and shining"—not "light," as in our translation, but "*lamp*" of his day (John 5:35). Let it be observed, too, that while the two figures of salt and sunlight both express the same function of Christians—their blessed influence on their fellow men—they each set this forth under a different aspect. Salt operates *internally*, in the mass with which it comes in contact; the sunlight operates *externally*, irradiating all that it reaches. Hence Christians are warily styled "the salt of the *earth*"—with reference to the masses of mankind with whom they are expected to mix; but "the light of the *world*"—with reference to the vast and variegated surface which feels its fructifying and gladdening radiance. The same distinction is observable in the second pair of those seven parables which our Lord spoke from the Galilean Lake—that of the "mustard seed," which grew to be a great overshadowing tree, answering to the sunlight which invests the world, and that of the "leaven," which a woman took and, like the salt, *hid* in three measures of meal, till the whole was leavened (ch. 13:31-33). **A city that is set on an hill cannot be hid**—nor can it be supposed to have been so built except to be seen by many eyes. **15. Neither do men light a candle** [or, lamp] **and put it under a bushel** [a dry measure] **but on a candlestick**—rather, under the bushel, but on the lampstand." The article is inserted in both cases to express the familiarity of everyone with those household utensils. **and it giveth light** [shineth] **unto all that are in the house. 16. Let your light so shine before men, that they may see your good works, and glorify your Father which is in heaven**—As nobody lights a lamp only to cover it up, but places it so conspicuously as to give light to all who need light, so Christians, being the light of the world, instead of hiding their light, are so to hold it forth before men that they may see what a life the disciples of Christ lead, and seeing this, may glorify their Father for so redeeming, transforming, and

ennobling earth's sinful children, and opening to themselves the way to like redemption and transformation.

17-48. IDENTITY OF THESE PRINCIPLES WITH THOSE OF THE ANCIENT ECONOMY, IN CONTRAST WITH THE REIGNING TRADITIONAL TEACHING. *Exposition of Principles* (vss. 17-20). 17. Think not that I am come [that I came] **to destroy the law, or the prophets**—i.e., "the authority and principles of the Old Testament." (On the phrase, see ch. 7:12; 22:40; Luke 16:16; Acts 13:15). This general way of taking the phrase is much better than understanding "the law" and "the prophets" separately, and inquiring, as many good critics do, in what sense our Lord could be supposed to meditate the subversion of each. To the various classes of His hearers, who might view such supposed abrogation of the law and the prophets with very different feelings, our Lord's announcement would, in effect, be such as this—"Ye who tremble at the word of the Lord, *fear* not that I am going to sweep the foundation from under your feet: Ye restless and revolutionary spirits, *hope* not that I am going to head any revolutionary movement: And ye who hypocritically affect great reverence for the law and the prophets, *pretend* not to find anything in My teaching derogatory to God's living oracles." **I am not come to destroy, but to fulfil**—Not to subvert, abrogate, or annul, but to establish the law and the prophets—to unfold them, to embody them in living form, and to enshrine them in the reverence, affection, and character of men, am I come. **18. For verily I say unto you**—Here, for the first time, does that august expression occur in our Lord's recorded teaching, with which we have grown so familiar as hardly to reflect on its full import. It is the expression manifestly, of *supreme legislative authority;* and as the subject in connection with which it is uttered is the Moral Law, no higher claim to an authority *strictly divine* could be advanced. For when we observe how jealously Jehovah asserts it as His exclusive prerogative to give law to men (Lev. 18:1-5; 19:37; 26:1-4; 13-16, etc.), such language as this of our Lord will appear totally unsuitable, and indeed abhorrent, from any creature-lips. When the Baptist's words—"I say unto you" (ch. 3:9)—are compared with those of his Master here, the difference of the two cases will be at once apparent. **Till heaven and earth pass**—Though even the Old Testament announces the ultimate "perdition of the heavens and the earth," in contrast with the immutability of Jehovah (Ps. 102:24-27), the prevalent representation of the heavens and the earth in Scripture, when employed as a popular figure, is that of their *stability* (Ps. 119:89-91; Eccles. 1:4; Jer. 33:25, 26). It is the enduring stability, then, of the great truths and principles, moral and spiritual, of the Old Testament revelation which our Lord thus expresses. **one jot**—the smallest of the Hebrew letters. **one tittle**—one of those little strokes by which alone some of the Hebrew letters are distinguished from others like them. **shall in no wise pass from the law, till all be fulfilled**—The meaning is that "not so much as the smallest loss of authority or vitality shall ever come over the law." The expression, "till all be fulfilled," is much the same in meaning as "it *shall* be had in undiminished and enduring honor, from its greatest to its least requirements." Again, this general way of viewing our Lord's words here seems far preferable to that *doctrinal* understanding of them which would require us to determine the different kinds of "fulfilment" which the *moral* and the *ceremonial* parts of it were to have. **19. Whosoever therefore shall break**—rather, dissolve, annul, or make invalid. **one of these least commandments**—an expression equivalent to "one of the least of these commandments." **and shall teach men so**—referring to the Pharisees and their teaching, as is plain from the next verse, but of course embracing all similar schools and teaching in the Christian Church. **he shall be called the least in the kingdom of heaven**—As the thing spoken of is not the practical breaking, or disobeying, of the law, but annulling or enervating its obligation by a vicious system of interpretation, and teaching others to do the same; so the thing threatened is not exclusion from heaven, and still less the lowest place in it, but a degraded and contemptuous position in the present stage of the kingdom of God. In other words, they shall be reduced by the retributive providence that overtakes them, to the same condition of dishonor to which, by their system and their teaching, they have brought down those eternal principles of God's law. **but whosoever shall do and teach them**—whose principles and teaching go to exalt the authority and honor of God's law, in its lowest as well as highest requirements. **the same shall be called great in the kingdom of heaven**—shall, by that providence which watches over the honor of God's moral administration, be raised to the same position of authority and honor to which they exalt the law. **20. For I say unto you, That except your righteousness shall exceed the righteousness of the scribes and Pharisees**—The superiority to the Pharisaic righteousness here required is plainly in *kind*, not *degree;* for all Scripture teaches that entrance into God's kingdom, whether in its present or future stage, depends, not on the degree of our excellence in anything, but solely on our having the character itself which God demands. Our righteousness, then—if it is to contrast with the *outward* and *formal* righteousness of the scribes and Pharisees—must be *inward, vital, spiritual*. Some, indeed, of the scribes and Pharisees themselves might have the very righteousness here demanded; but our Lord is speaking, not of persons, but of the *system* they represented and taught. **ye shall in no case enter into the kingdom of heaven**—If this refer, as in the preceding verse, rather to the earthly stage of this kingdom, the meaning is that without a righteousness exceeding that of the Pharisees, we cannot be members of it at all, save in name. This was no new doctrine (Rom. 2:28, 29; 9:6; Phil. 3:3). But our Lord's teaching here stretches beyond the present scene, to that everlasting stage of the kingdom, where without "purity of heart" none "shall see God."

The Spirituality of the True Righteousness, in Contrast with That of the Scribes and Pharisees, Illustrated from the Sixth Commandment (vss. 21-26). **21. Ye have heard that it was said by them of old time**—or, as in the margin, "to them of old time." Which of these translations is the right one has been much controverted. Either of them is grammatically defensible, though the latter—"*to* the ancients"—is more consistent with New Testament usage (see the *Greek* of Rom. 9:12, 26; Rev. 6:11; 9:4); and most critics decide in favor of it. But it is not a question of Greek only. Nearly all who would translate "to the ancients" take the speaker of the words quoted to be *Moses in the law;* "the ancients" to be *the people* to whom Moses gave the law; and the intention of our Lord here to be to contrast His own teaching, more or less, with that of Moses; either as opposed to it—as some go the

length of affirming—or at least as modifying, enlarging, elevating it. But who can reasonably imagine such a thing, just after the most solemn and emphatic proclamation of the perpetuity of the law, and the honor and glory in which it was to be held under the new economy? To us it seems as plain as possible that our Lord's one object is to contrast the traditional perversions of the law with the true sense of it as expounded by Himself. A few of those who assent to this still think that "to the ancients" is the only legitimate translation of the words; understanding that our Lord is reporting what had been said to the ancients, not by Moses, but by the perverters of his law. We do not object to this; but we incline to think (with BEZA, and after him with FRITZSCHE, OLSHAUSEN, STIER, and BLOOMFIELD) that "by the ancients" must have been what our Lord meant here, referring to the corrupt teachers rather than the perverted people. **Thou shalt not kill:**—i.e., This being all that the law requires, whosoever has imbrued his hands in his brother's blood, but he only, is guilty of a breach of this commandment. **and whosoever shall kill shall be in danger of** [liable to] **the judgment**—i.e., of the sentence of those inferior courts of judicature which were established in all the principal towns, in compliance with Deuteronomy 16:16. Thus was this commandment reduced, from a holy law of the heart-searching God, to a mere outward statute, taking cognizance only of outward actions, such as that which we read in Exodus 21:12; Leviticus 24:17. **22. But I say unto you**—Mark the authoritative tone in which—as Himself the Lawgiver and Judge —Christ now gives the true sense, and explains the deep reach, of the commandment. **That whosoever is angry with his brother without a cause shall be in danger of the judgment; and whosoever shall say to his brother, Raca! shall be in danger of the council; but whosoever shall say, Thou fool! shall be in danger of hell fire**—It is unreasonable to deny, as ALEXANDER does, that three degrees of punishment are here meant to be expressed, and to say that it is but a threefold expression of one and the same thing. But Romish expositors greatly err in taking the first two—"the judgment" and "the council"—to refer to degrees of *temporal* punishment with which lesser sins were to be visited under the Gospel, and only the last—"hell fire"—to refer to the future life. All three clearly refer to *divine retribution,* and that alone, for breaches of this commandment; though this is expressed by an *allusion* to Jewish tribunals. The "judgment," as already explained, was the lowest of these; the "council," or "Sanhedrim,"—which sat at Jerusalem—was the highest; while the word used for "hell fire" contains an allusion to the "valley of the son of Hinnom" (Josh. 18:16). In this valley the Jews, when steeped in idolatry, went the length of burning their children to Molech "on the high places of Tophet"—in consequence of which good Josiah defiled it, to prevent the repetition of such abominations (II Kings 23:10); and from that time forward, if we may believe the Jewish writers, a fire was kept burning in it to consume the carrion and all kinds of impurities that collected about the capital. Certain it is, that while the final punishment of the wicked is described in the Old Testament by allusions to this valley of Tophet or Hinnom (Isa. 30:33; 66:24), our Lord Himself describes the same by merely quoting these terrific descriptions of the evangelical prophet (Mark 9:43-48). What precise degrees of unholy feeling towards our brothers are indicated by the words "Raca" and "fool" it would be as useless as it is vain to inquire. Every age and every country has its modes of expressing such things; and no doubt our Lord seized on the then current phraseology of unholy disrespect and contempt, merely to express and condemn the different degrees of such feeling when brought out in words, as He had immediately before condemned the feeling itself. In fact, so little are we to make of mere *words,* apart from the feeling which they express, that as *anger* is expressly said to have been borne by our Lord towards His enemies though mixed with "grief for the hardness of their hearts" (Mark 3:5), and as the apostle teaches us that there is an anger which is not sinful (Eph. 4:26); so in the Epistle of James (2:20) we find the words, "O vain [or, empty] man"; and our Lord Himself applies the very word "fools" twice in one breath to the blind guides of the people (ch. 23:17, 19)—although, in both cases, it is to *false reasoners* rather than persons that such words are applied. The spirit, then, of the whole statement may be thus given: "For ages ye have been taught that the sixth commandment, for example, is broken only by the murderer, to pass sentence upon whom is the proper business of the recognized tribunals. But I say unto you that it is broken even by causeless anger, which is but hatred in the bud, as hatred is incipient murder (I John 3:15); and if by the feelings, much more by those *words* in which all ill feeling, from the slightest to the most envenomed, are wont to be cast upon a brother: and just as there are gradations in human courts of judicature, and in the sentences which they pronounce according to the degrees of criminality, so will the judicial treatment of all the breakers of this commandment at the divine tribunal be according to their real criminality before the heart-searching Judge." Oh, what holy teaching is this! **23. Therefore**—to apply the foregoing, and show its paramount importance. **if thou bring thy gift to the altar, and there rememberest that thy brother hath aught** [of just complaint] **against thee; 24. Leave there thy gift before the altar, and go thy way; first be reconciled to thy brother**—The meaning evidently is—not, "dismiss from thine own breast all ill feeling, "but" get thy brother to dismiss from his mind all grudge against thee." **and then come and offer thy gift**—"The picture," says Tholuck," is drawn from life. It transports us to the moment when the Israelite, having brought his sacrifice to the court of the Israelites, awaited the instant when the priest would approach to receive it at his hands. He waits with his gift at the rails which separate the place where he stands from the court of the priests, into which his offering will presently be taken, there to be slain by the priest, and by him presented upon the altar of sacrifice." It is at this solemn moment, when about to cast himself upon divine mercy, and seek in his offering a seal of divine forgiveness, that the offerer is supposed, all at once, to remember that some brother has a just cause of complaint against him through breach of this commandment in one or other of the ways just indicated. What then? Is he to say, As soon as I have offered this gift I will go straight to my brother, and make it up with him? Nay; but before another step is taken—even before the offering is presented—this reconciliation is to be sought, though the gift have to be left unoffered before the altar. The converse of the truth here taught is very strikingly expressed in Mark 11:25, 26: "And *when ye stand praying* [in the very act], forgive, if ye have aught [of just complaint] against any; that your Father also which is in heaven may forgive you

your trespasses. But if ye do not forgive, neither will your Father which is in heaven forgive you . . ." Hence the beautiful practice of the early Church, to see that all differences amongst brethren and sisters in Christ were made up, in the spirit of love, before going to the Holy Communion; and the Church of England has a rubrical direction to this effect in her Communion service. Certainly, if this be the highest act of worship on earth, such reconciliation—though obligatory on all other occasions of worship—must be peculiarly so then. **25. Agree with thine adversary**—thine opponent in a matter cognizable by law. **quickly, whiles thou art in the way with him** —"to the magistrate," as in Luke 12:58. **lest at any time**—here, rather, "lest at all," or simply "lest." **the adversary deliver thee to the judge, and the judge** [having pronounced thee in the wrong] **deliver thee to the officer**—the official whose business it is to see the sentence carried into effect. **26. Verily I say unto thee, Thou shalt by no means come out thence, till thou hast paid the uttermost farthing**— a fractional Roman coin, worth about half a cent. That our Lord meant here merely to give a piece of prudential advice to his hearers, to keep out of the hands of the law and its officials by settling all disputes with one another privately, is not for a moment to be supposed, though there are critics of a school low enough to suggest this. The concluding words—"Verily I say unto thee, Thou shalt by no means come out . . ."—manifestly show that though the *language* is drawn from human disputes and legal procedure, He is dealing with a higher than any human quarrel, a higher than any human tribunal, a higher than any human and temporal sentence. In this view of the words—in which nearly all critics worthy of the name agree—the spirit of them may be thus expressed: "In expounding the sixth commandment, I have spoken of offenses between man and man; reminding you that the offender has another party to deal with besides him whom he has wronged on earth, and assuring you that all worship offered to the Searcher of hearts by one who knows that a brother has just cause of complaint against him, and yet takes no steps to remove it, is vain: But I cannot pass from this subject without reminding you of One whose cause of complaint against you is far more deadly than any that man can have against man: and since with that Adversary you are already on the way to judgment, it will be your wisdom to make up the quarrel without delay, lest sentence of condemnation be pronounced upon you, and then will execution straightway follow, from the effects of which you shall never escape as long as any remnant of the offense remains unexpiated." It will be observed that as the *principle* on which we are to "agree" with this "Adversary" is not here specified, and the precise *nature* of the retribution that is to light upon the despisers of this warning is not to be gathered from the mere use of the word "prison"; so, the *remedilessness* of the punishment is not in so many words expressed, and still less is its actual *cessation* taught. The language on all these points is designedly general; but it may safely be said that the *unending duration* of future punishment—elsewhere so clearly and awfully expressed by our Lord Himself, as in vss. 29 and 30, and Mark 9:43, 48—is the only doctrine with which His language here quite naturally and fully accords. (Cf. ch. 18:30, 34).

The Same Subject Illustrated from the Seventh Commandment (vss. 27-32). **27. Ye have heard that it was said**—The words by," or "to them of old time," in this verse are insufficiently supported, and probably were not in the original text. **Thou shalt not commit adultery**—Interpreting this seventh, as they did the sixth commandment, the traditional perverters of the law restricted the breach of it to *acts* of criminal intercourse between, or with, married persons exclusively. Our Lord now dissipates such delusions. **28. But I say unto you, That whosoever looketh on a woman to lust after her**—with the intent to do so, as the same expression is used in ch. 6:1; or, with the full consent of his will, to feed thereby his unholy desires. **hath committed adultery with her already in his heart**—We are not to suppose, from the word here used—"adultery"—that our Lord means to restrict the breach of this commandment to married persons, or to criminal intercourse with such. The expressions, *"whosoever* looketh," and "looketh upon a *woman,"* seem clearly to extend the range of this commandment to all forms of impurity, and the counsels which follow—as they most certainly were intended for all, whether married or unmarried—seem to confirm this. As in dealing with the sixth commandment our Lord first expounds it, and then in the four following verses applies His exposition, so here He first expounds the seventh commandment, and then in the four following verses applies His exposition. **29. And if thy right eye**—the readier and the dearer of the two. **offend thee**—be a "trap-spring," or as in the New Testament, be "an occasion of stumbling" to thee. **pluck it out and cast it from thee**—implying a certain indignant promptitude, heedless of whatever cost to feeling the act may involve. Of course, it is not *the eye simply* of which our Lord speaks—as if execution were to be done upon the bodily organ—though there have been fanatical ascetics who have both advocated and practiced this, showing a very low apprehension of spiritual things—but *the offending eye,* or the eye considered as the occasion of sin; and consequently, only the *sinful exercise* of the organ which is meant. For as one might put out his eyes without in the least quenching the lust to which they ministered, so, "if thine eye be single, thy whole body shall be full of light," and, when directed by a holy mind, becomes an "instrument of righteousness unto God." At the same time, just as by cutting off a hand, or plucking out an eye, the *power* of acting and of seeing would be destroyed, our Lord certainly means that we are to *strike at the root* of such unholy dispositions, as well as cut off the occasions which tend to stimulate them. **for it is profitable for thee that one of thy members should perish, and not that thy whole body should be cast into hell**—He who despises the warning to cast from him, with indignant promptitude, an offending member, will find his whole body "cast," with a retributive promptitude of indignation, "into hell." Sharp language, this, from the lips of Love incarnate! **30. And if thy right hand** [the organ of *action,* to which the eye excites] **offend thee. cut it off, and cast it from thee; for it is profitable . . .**—See on vs. 29. The repetition, in identical terms, of such stern truths and awful lessons seems characteristic of our Lord's manner of teaching. Cf. Mark 9:43-48. **31. It hath been said**—This shortened form was perhaps intentional, to mark a transition from the commandments of the Decalogue to a civil enactment on the subject of divorce, quoted from Deuteronomy 24:1. The law of divorce—according to its strictness or laxity—has so intimate a bearing upon purity in the married life, that nothing could be more natural than to pass from the seventh com-

mandment to the loose views on that subject then current. **Whosoever shall put away his wife, let him give her a writing of divorcement**—a legal check upon reckless and tyrannical separation. The one legitimate ground of divorce allowed by the enactment just quoted was "some uncleanness"—in other words, conjugal infidelity. But while one school of interpreters (that of Shammai) explained this quite correctly, as prohibiting divorce in every case save that of adultery, another school (that of Hillel) stretched the expression so far as to include everything in the wife offensive or disagreeable to the husband—a view of the law too well fitted to minister to caprice and depraved inclination not to find extensive favor. And, indeed, to this day the Jews allow divorces on the most frivolous pretexts. It was to meet this that our Lord uttered what follows: **32. But I say unto you, That whosoever shall put away his wife, saving for the cause of fornication, causeth her to commit adultery**—i.e., drives her into it in case she marries again. **and whosoever shall marry her that is divorced** [for anything short of conjugal infidelity] **committeth adultery**—for if the commandment is broken by the one party, it must be by the other also. But see on ch. 19:4-9. Whether the innocent party, after a just divorce, may lawfully marry again, is not treated of here. The Church of Rome says, No; but the Greek and Protestant Churches allow it.

Same Subject Illustrated from the Third Commandment (vss. 33-37). **33. Again, ye have heard that it hath been said by them of old time, Thou shalt not forswear thyself**—These are not the precise words of Exodus 20:7; but they express all that it was currently understood to condemn, viz., false swearing (Lev. 19:12, etc.). This is plain from what follows. **But I say unto you, Swear not at all**—That this was meant to condemn swearing of every kind and on every occasion—as the Society of Friends and some other ultra-moralists allege—is not for a moment to be thought. For even Jehovah is said once and again to have sworn by Himself; and our Lord certainly answered upon oath to a question put to Him by the high priest; and the apostle several times, and in the most solemn language, takes God to witness that he spoke and wrote the truth; and it is inconceivable that our Lord should here have quoted the precept about not forswearing ourselves, only performing to the Lord our oaths, only to give a precept of His own directly in the teeth of it. Evidently, it is swearing in common intercourse and on frivolous occasions that is here meant. Frivolous oaths were indeed severely condemned in the teaching of the times. But so narrow was the circle of them that a man might swear, says LIGHTFOOT, a hundred thousand times and yet not be guilty of vain swearing. Hardly anything was regarded as an oath if only the name of God were not in it; just as among ourselves, as TRENCH well remarks, a certain lingering reverence for the name of God leads to cutting off portions of His name, or uttering sounds nearly resembling it, or substituting the name of some heathen deity, in profane exclamations or asseverations. Against all this our Lord now speaks decisively; teaching His audience that every oath carries an appeal to God, whether named or not. **neither by heaven; for it is God's throne: 35. Nor by the earth; for it is his footstool** [quoting Isa. 66:1]; **neither by Jerusalem; for it is the city of the great King** [quoting Ps. 48:2]. **36. Neither shalt thou swear by thy head, because thou canst not make one hair white or black**—In the other oaths specified,

God's name was profaned quite as really as if His name had been uttered, because it was instantly *suggested* by the mention of His "throne," His "footstool," His "city." But in swearing by our own *head* and the like, the objection lies in their being "beyond our control," and therefore profanely assumed to have a stability which they have not. **37. But let your communication**—"your word," in ordinary intercourse, be, **Yea, yea; Nay, nay**—Let a simple *Yes* and *No* suffice in affirming the truth or the untruth of anything. (See Jas 5:12, and II Cor. 1:17, 18). **for whatsoever is more than these cometh of evil**—not "of the evil one"; though an equally correct rendering of the words, and one which some expositors prefer. It is true that all evil in our world is originally of the devil, that it forms a kingdom at the head of which he sits, and that, in every manifestation of it he has an active part. But any reference to this here seems unnatural, and the allusion to this passage in the Epistle of James (5:12) seems to show that this is not the sense of it: "Let your yea be yea; and your nay, nay; *lest ye fall into condemnation.*" The untruthfulness of our corrupt nature shows itself not only in the tendency to deviate from the strict truth, but in the disposition to suspect others of doing the same; and as this is not diminished, but rather aggravated, by the habit of confirming what we say by an oath, we thus run the risk of having all reverence for God's holy name, and even for strict truth, destroyed in our hearts, and so "fall into condemnation." The practice of going beyond Yes and No in affirmations and denials —as if our word for it were not enough, and we expected others to question it—springs from that vicious root of untruthfulness which is only aggravated by the very effort to clear ourselves of the suspicion of it. And just as swearing to the truth of what we say begets the disposition it is designed to remove, so the love and reign of truth in the breasts of Christ's disciples reveals itself so plainly even to those who themselves cannot be trusted, that their simple Yes and No come soon to be more relied on than the most solemn asseverations of others. Thus does the grace of our Lord Jesus Christ, like a tree cast into the bitter waters of human corruption, heal and sweeten them.

Same Subject—Retaliation (vss. 38-42). We have here the converse of the preceding lessons. They were *negative*: these are *positive*. **38. Ye have heard that it hath been said** [Exod. 21:23-25; Lev. 24:19, 20; Deut. 19:21], **An eye for an eye, and a tooth for a tooth**—i.e., whatever penalty was regarded as a proper equivalent for these. This law of retribution—designed to take vengeance out of the hands of private persons, and commit it to the magistrate—was abused in the opposite way to the commandments of the Decalogue. While they were reduced to the level of civil enactments, this judicial regulation was held to be a warrant for taking redress into their own hands, contrary to the injunctions of the Old Testament itself (Prov. 20:22; 24:29). **39. But I say unto you, That ye resist not evil; but whosoever shall smite thee on thy right cheek, turn to him the other also**—Our Lord's own meek, yet dignified bearing, when smitten rudely on the cheek (John 18:22, 23), and *not* literally presenting the other, is the best comment on these words. It is the preparedness, after one indignity, not to invite but to submit meekly to another, without retaliation, which this strong language is meant to convey. **40. And if any man will sue thee at the law, and take away thy coat**—the inner garment; in pledge for a debt (Exod. 22:26, 27). **let him have**

thy cloak also—the outer and more costly garment. This overcoat was not allowed to be retained over night as a pledge from the poor because they used it for a bed-covering. **41. And whosoever shall compel thee to go a mile, go with him twain**—an allusion, probably, to the practice of the Romans and some Eastern nations, who, when government despatches had to be forwarded, obliged the people not only to furnish horses and carriages, but to give personal attendance, often at great inconvenience, when required. But the thing here demanded is a readiness to submit to unreasonable demands of whatever kind, rather than raise quarrels, with all the evils resulting from them. What follows is a beautiful extension of this precept. **42. Give to him that asketh thee**—The sense of *unreasonable* asking is here implied (cf. Luke 6:30). **and from him that would borrow of thee turn not thou away** —Though the word signifies classically "to have money lent to one on security," or "with interest," yet as this was not the original sense of the word, and as usury was forbidden among the Jews (Exod. 22:25, etc.), it is doubtless simple borrowing which our Lord here means, as indeed the whole strain of the exhortation implies. This shows that such counsels as "Owe no man anything" (Rom. 13:8), are not to be taken absolutely; else the Scripture commendations of the righteous for "lending" to his necessitous brother (Ps. 37:36; 112:5; Luke 6: 37) would have no application. **turn not thou away** —a graphic expression of unfeeling refusal to relieve a brother in extremity.

Same Subject—Love to Enemies (vss. 43-48). **43. Ye have heard that it hath been said**—(Lev. 19:18). **Thou shalt love thy neighbour**—To this the corrupt teachers added, **and hate thine enemy**—as if the one were a legitimate inference from the other, instead of being a detestable gloss, as BENGEL indignantly calls it. LIGHTFOOT quotes some of the cursed maxims inculcated by those traditionists regarding the proper treatment of all Gentiles. No wonder that the Romans charged the Jews with hatred of the human race. **44. But I say unto you, Love your enemies**—The word here used denotes *moral* love, as distinguished from the other word, which expresses *personal* affection. Usually, the former denotes "complacency in the character" of the person loved; but here it denotes the benignant, compassionate outgoings of desire for anothers' good. **bless them that curse you, do good to them that hate you, and pray for them which despitefully use you, and persecute you**—The best commentary on these matchless counsels is the bright example of Him who gave them. (See I Pet. 2:21-24; and cf. Rom. 12:20, 21; I Cor. 4:12; I Pet. 3:9). But though such precepts were never before expressed—perhaps not even conceived—with such breadth, precision, and sharpness as here, our Lord is here only the incomparable Interpreter of the law in force from the beginning; and this is the only satisfactory view of the entire strain of this discourse. **45. That ye may be the children [sons] of your Father which is in heaven**—The meaning is, "that ye may show yourselves to be such by *resembling* Him" (cf. vs. 9 and Eph. 5:1). **for he maketh his sun**—"your Father's sun." Well might BENGEL exclaim, "Magnificent appellation!"—**to rise on the evil and on the good, and sendeth rain on the just and on the unjust**—rather (without the article) "on evil and good, and on just and unjust." When we find God's own procedure held up for imitation in the law, and much more in the prophets (Lev. 19:2; 20:26; and cf. I Pet. 1:15, 16), we may see that the principle of this surprising verse was nothing new: but the form of it certainly is that of One who spake as never man spake. **46. For if ye love them which love you, what reward have ye? do not even the publicans the same?**—The publicans, as collectors of taxes due to the Roman government, were ever on this account obnoxious to the Jews, who sat uneasy under a foreign yoke, and disliked whatever brought this unpleasantly before them. But the extortion practiced by this class made them hateful to the community, who in their current speech ranked them with "harlots." Nor does our Lord scruple to speak of them as others did, which we may be sure He never would have done if it had been calumnious. The meaning, then, is, "In loving those who love you, there is no evidence of superior principle; the worst of men will do this: even a publican will go that length." **47. And if ye salute your brethren only**—of the same nation and religion with yourselves. **what do ye more [than others]?**—what do ye uncommon or extraordinary? i.e, wherein do ye *excel*? **do not even the publicans so?**—The true reading here appears to be, "Do not even the heathens the same?" Cf. ch. 18:17, where the excommunicated person is said to be "as an heathen man and a publican." **48. Be ye therefore**—rather, "Ye shall therefore be," or "Ye are therefore to be," as My disciples and in My kingdom—**perfect**, or complete. Manifestly, our Lord here speaks, not of *degrees* of excellence, but of the *kind* of excellence which was to distinguish His disciples and characterize His kingdom. When therefore He adds, **even as your Father which is in heaven is perfect,** He refers to that fullorbed glorious completeness which is in the great Divine Model, "their Father which is in heaven."

CHAPTER 6

SERMON ON THE MOUNT—*continued*. Vss. 1-18. FURTHER ILLUSTRATION OF THE RIGHTEOUSNESS OF THE KINGDOM—ITS UNOSTENTATIOUSNESS. *General Caution against Ostentation in Religious Duties* (vs. 1). **1. Take heed that ye do not your alms**—But the true reading seems clearly to be "your righteousness." The external authority for both readings is pretty nearly equal; but internal evidence is decidedly in favor of "righteousness." The subject of the second verse being "almsgiving" that word—so like the other in Greek—might easily be substituted for it by the copyist: whereas the opposite would not be so likely. But it is still more in favor of "righteousness," that if we so read the first verse, it then becomes a general heading for this whole section of the discourse, inculcating unostentatiousness in *all* deeds of righteousness—Almsgiving, Prayer, and Fasting being, in that case, but selected examples of this righteousness; whereas, if we read, "Do not your *alms* ...", this first verse will have no reference but to that one point. By "righteousness," in this case, we are to understand that same righteousness of the kingdom of heaven, whose leading features—in opposition to traditional perversions of it—it is the great object of this discourse to open up: that righteousness of which the Lord says, "Except your righteousness shall exceed the righteousness of the scribes and Pharisees, ye shall in no case enter into the kingdom of heaven" (ch. 5:20). To "*do*" this righteousness, was an old and well-understood expression. Thus, "Blessed is he that doeth righteousness at all times" (Ps. 106:3). It refers to the *actings* of righteousness in the life—the outgoings of the gracious nature—of which our

Lord afterwards said to His disciples, "Herein is My Father glorified, that ye bear much fruit; so shall ye be My disciples" (John 15:8). **before men, to be seen of them**—with the view or intention of being beheld of them. See the same expression in ch. 5:28. True, He had required them to let their light so shine before men that they might see their good works, and glorify their Father which is in heaven (ch. 5:16). But this is quite consistent with not making a display of our righteousness for self-glorification. In fact, the doing of the former necessarily implies our *not* doing the latter. **otherwise ye have no reward of your Father which is in heaven**—When all duty is done to God—as primarily enjoining and finally judging of it—He will take care that it be duly recognized; but when done purely for ostentation, God cannot own it, nor is His judgment of it even thought of—God accepts only what is done to Himself. So much for the general principle. Now follow three illustrations of it.

Almsgiving (vss. 2-4). **2. Therefore, when thou doest thine alms, do not sound a trumpet before thee**—The expression is to be taken figuratively for *blazoning* it. Hence our expression to "trumpet." **as the hypocrites do**—This word—of such frequent occurrence in Scripture, signifying primarily "one who acts a part"—denotes one who either *pretends* to be what he is not (as here), or *dissembles* what he really is (as in Luke 12:1, 2). **in the synagogues and in the streets**—the places of religious and secular resort. **that they may have glory of men. Verily I say unto you**—In such august expressions, it is the Lawgiver and Judge Himself that we hear speaking to us. **They have their reward**—All they wanted was human applause, and they have it—and with it, all they will ever get. **3. But when thou doest alms, let not thy left hand know what thy right hand doeth**—So far from making a display of it, dwell not on it even in thine own thoughts, lest it minister to spiritual pride. **4. That thine alms may be in secret, and thy Father which seeth in secret [himself] shall reward thee openly**—The word "Himself" appears to be an unauthorized addition to the text, which the sense no doubt suggested. (See I Tim. 5:25; Rom. 2:16; I Cor. 4:5).

Prayer (vss. 5, 6). **5. And when thou prayest, thou shalt** [or, preferably, when ye pray ye shall] **not be as the hypocrites are: for they love to pray standing in the synagogues and in the corners of the streets** [see on vs. 2], **that they may be seen of men. Verily I say unto you, They have ...**—The *standing* posture in prayer was the ancient practice, alike in the Jewish and in the early Christian Church. But of course this conspicuous posture opened the way for the ostentatious. **6. But thou, when thou prayest, enter into thy closet** [a place of retirement] **and when thou hast shut thy door, pray to thy Father which is in secret; and thy Father which seeth in secret shall reward thee openly**—Of course, it is not the simple publicity of prayer which is here condemned. It may be offered in any circumstances, however open, if not prompted by the spirit of ostentation, but dictated by the great ends of prayer itself. It is the *retiring* character of true prayer which is here taught.

Supplementary Directions, and Model Prayer (vss. 7-15). **7. But when ye pray, use not vain repetitions**—"Babble not" would be a better rendering, both for the form of the word—which in both languages is intended to imitate the sound—and for the sense, which expresses not so much the repetition of the same words as a senseless multiplication of them; as appears from what follows. **as the heathen do: for they think that they shall be heard for their much speaking**—This method of heathen devotion is still observed by Hindoo and Mohammedan devotees. With the Jews, says LIGHT-FOOT, it was a maxim, that "Every one who multiplies prayer is heard." In the Church of Rome, not only is it carried to a shameless extent, but, as THOLUCK justly observes, the very prayer which our Lord gave as an antidote to vain repetitions is the most abused to this superstitious end; the number of times it is repeated counting for so much more merit. Is not this just that characteristic feature of heathen devotion which our Lord here condemns? But praying much, and using at times the same words, is *not* here condemned, and has the example of our Lord Himself in its favor. **8. Be not ye therefore like unto them: for your Father knoweth what things ye have need of before ye ask him**—and so needs not to be *informed* of our wants, any more than to be *roused* to attend to them by our incessant speaking. What a view of God is here given, in sharp contrast with the gods of the heathen! But let it be carefully noted that it is not as *the general Father of mankind* that our Lord says, "Your Father" knoweth what ye need before ye ask it; for it is not men, as such, that He is addressing in this discourse, but His own disciples—the poor in spirit, the mourners, the meek, hungry and thirsty souls, the merciful, the pure in heart, the peacemakers, who allow themselves to have all manner of evil said against them for the Son of man's sake—in short, the newborn children of God, who, making their Father's interests their own, are here assured that their Father, in return, makes their interests His, and needs neither to be told nor to be reminded of their wants. Yet He will have His children pray to Him, and links all His promised supplies to their petitions for them; thus encouraging us to draw near and keep near to Him, to talk and walk with Him, to open our every case to Him, and assure ourselves that thus asking we shall receive—thus seeking we shall find—thus knocking it shall be opened to us. **9. After this manner** [more simply "Thus"] **therefore pray ye**—The "ye" is emphatic here, in contrast with the heathen prayers. That this matchless prayer was given not only as a *model*, but as a *form*, might be concluded from its very nature. Did it consist only of hints or directions for prayer, it could only be used as a directory; but seeing it is an actual prayer—designed, indeed, to show how much real prayer could be compressed into the fewest words, but still, as a prayer, only the more incomparable for that—it is strange that there should be a doubt whether we ought to pray that very prayer. Surely the words with which it is introduced, in the second utterance and varied form of it which we have in Luke 11:2, ought to set this at rest: "When ye pray, *say*, Our Father." Nevertheless, since the second form of it varies considerably from the first, and since no example of its actual use, or express quotation of its phraseology, occurs in the sequel of the New Testament, we are to guard against a superstitious use of it. How early this began to appear in the church services, and to what extent it was afterwards carried, is known to every one versed in Church History. Nor has the spirit which bred this abuse quite departed from some branches of the Protestant Church, though the opposite and equally condemnable extreme is to be found in other branches of it.

Model Prayer (vss. 9-13). According to the Latin fathers and the Lutheran Church, the petitions of the Lord's Prayer are *seven* in number; according to the Greek fathers, the Reformed Church and the Westminster divines, they are only *six;* the two last being regarded—we think, less correctly—as one. The first three petitions have to do exclusively with God: "*Thy* name be hallowed"—"*Thy* kingdom come"—"*Thy* will be done." And they occur in a *descending* scale—from Himself down to the manifestation of Himself in His kingdom; and from His kingdom to the entire subjection of its subjects, or the complete doing of His will. The remaining four petitions have to do with OURSELVES: "Give *us* our daily bread"—"Forgive *us* our debts"—"Lead *us* not into temptation"—"Deliver *us* from evil." But these latter petitions occur in an *ascending* scale—from the bodily wants of every day up to our final deliverance from all evil.

Invocation: **Our Father which art in heaven.** In the former clause we express His nearness to us; in the latter, His distance from us. (See Eccles. 5:2; Isa. 66:1). Holy, loving familiarity suggests the one; awful reverence the other. In calling Him "Father" we express a relationship we have all known and felt surrounding us even from our infancy; but in calling Him our Father "who art in heaven," we contrast Him with the fathers we all have here below, and so raise our souls to that "heaven" where He dwells, and that Majesty and Glory which are there as in their proper home. These first words of the Lord's Prayer—this invocation with which it opens—what a brightness and warmth does it throw over the whole prayer, and into what a serene region does it introduce the praying believer, the child of God, as he thus approaches Him! It is true that the paternal relationship of God to His people is by no means strange to the Old Testament. (See Deut. 32:6; Ps. 103: 13; Isa. 63:16; Jer. 3:4, 19; Mal. 1:6; 2:10.) But these are only glimpses—the "back parts" (Exod. 33:23), if we may so say, in comparison with the "open face" of our Father revealed in Jesus. (See on II Cor. 3:18). Nor is it too much to say, that the view which our Lord gives, throughout this His very first lengthened discourse, of "our Father in heaven," beggars all that was ever taught, even in God's own Word, or conceived before by His saints, on this subject.

First Petition: **Hallowed be**—i.e., "Be held in reverence"; *regarded* and *treated* as holy. **thy name** —God's name means "Himself as revealed and manifested." Everywhere in Scripture God defines and marks off the faith and love and reverence and obedience He will have from men by the disclosures which He makes to them of what He is; both to shut out false conceptions of Him, and to make all their devotion take the shape and hue of His own teaching. Too much attention cannot be paid to this.

Second Petition: **10. Thy kingdom come**—The kingdom of God is that moral and spiritual kingdom which the God of grace is setting up in this fallen world, whose subjects consist of as many as have been brought into hearty subjection to His gracious scepter, and of which His Son Jesus is the glorious Head. In the inward reality of it, this kingdom existed ever since there were men who "walked with God" (Gen. 5:24), and "waited for His salvation" (Gen. 49:18); who were "continually with Him, holden by His right hand" (Ps. 73:23), and who, even in the valley of the shadow of death, feared no evil when He was with them (Ps. 23:4). When Messiah Himself appeared, it was, as a visible kingdom, "at hand." His death laid the deep foundations of it. His ascension on high, "leading captive and receiving gifts for men, yea, for the rebellious, that the Lord God might dwell among them," and the Pentecostal effusion of the Spirit, by which those gifts for men descended upon the rebellious, and the Lord God was beheld, in the persons of thousands upon thousands, "dwelling" among men—was a glorious "coming" of this kingdom. But it is still to come, and this petition, "Thy kingdom come," must not cease to ascend so long as one subject of it remains to be brought in. But does not this prayer stretch further forward—to "the glory to be revealed," or that stage of the kingdom called "the everlasting kingdom of our Lord and Saviour Jesus Christ" (II Peter 1:11)? Not directly, perhaps, since the petition that follows this —"Thy will be done in earth, as it is in heaven"— would then bring us back to this present state of imperfection. Still, the mind refuses to be so bounded by stages and degrees, and in the act of praying, "Thy kingdom come," it irresistibly stretches the wings of its faith, and longing, and joyous expectation out to the final and glorious consummation of the kingdom of God.

Third Petition: **Thy will be done in earth, as it is in heaven**—or, as the same words are rendered in Luke, "as in heaven, so upon earth"—as *cheerfully,* as *constantly,* as *perfectly.* But some will ask, Will this ever be? We answer, If the "new heavens and new earth" are to be just our present material system purified by fire and transfigured, of course it will. But we incline to think that the aspiration which we are taught in this beautiful petition to breathe forth has no direct reference to any such *organic* fulfilment, and is only the spontaneous and resistless longing of the renewed soul—put into words—to see the whole inhabited earth in entire conformity to the will of God. It asks not if ever it shall be—or if ever it can be—in order to pray this prayer. It *must* have its holy yearnings breathed forth, and this is just the bold yet simple expression of them. Nor is the Old Testament without prayers which come very near to this (Ps. 7:9; 67; 72:19, etc.).

Fourth Petition: **11. Give us this day our daily bread**—The compound word here rendered "daily" occurs nowhere else, either in classical or sacred Greek, and so must be interpreted by the analogy of its component parts. But on this critics are divided. To those who would understand it to mean, "Give us this day the bread of to-morrow"— as if the sense thus slid into that of Luke "Give us *day by day*" (as Bengel, Meyer, etc.)—it may be answered that the sense thus brought out is scarcely intelligible, if not something less; that the expression "bread of to-morrow" is not at all the same as bread "from day to day," and that, so understood, it would seem to contradict vs. 34. The great majority of the best critics (taking the word to be compounded of *ousia,* "*substance,*" or "*being*") understand by it the "staff of *life,*" the bread of *subsistence,* and so the sense will be, "Give us this day the bread which this day's necessities require." In this case, the rendering of our authorized version (after the *Vulgate,* Luther and some of the best modern critics)—"our daily bread"—is, in sense, accurate enough. (See Prov. 30:8.) Among commentators, there was early shown an inclination to understand this as a prayer for the heavenly bread, or spiritual nourishment; and in this they have been followed by many superior expositors, even down to our own times. But as this is quite unnatural, so it deprives the Christian of one of the sweetest of his privileges—to cast his bodily wants in this short prayer, by one simple petition, upon his heavenly Father. No doubt the spiritual mind will, from "the meat that perisheth," naturally rise in thought to "that meat which endureth to everlasting life." But let it be enough that the petition about bodily wants irresistibly *suggests* a higher petition; and let us not rob ourselves—out of a morbid spirituality—of our one petition in this prayer for that bodily provision which the immediate sequel of this discourse shows that our heavenly Father has so much at heart. In limiting our petitions, however, to provision *for the day,* what a spirit of childlike dependence does the Lord both demand and beget!

Fifth Petition: **12. And forgive us our debts**—A vitally important view of sin, this—as an offense against God demanding reparation to His dishonored claims upon our absolute subjection. As the debtor in the creditor's hand, so is the sinner in the hands of God. This idea of sin had indeed come up before in this discourse—in the warning to agree with our adversary quickly, in case of sentence being passed upon us, adjudging us to payment of the last farthing, and to imprisonment till then (ch. 5:25, 26). And it comes up once and again in our Lord's subsequent teaching—as in the parable of the creditor and his two debtors (Luke 7: 41, etc.), and in the parable of the unmerciful debtor (ch. 18:23, etc.). But by embodying it in this brief model of acceptable prayer, and as the first of three petitions more or less bearing upon sin, our Lord teaches us, in the most emphatic manner conceivable, to regard this view of sin as the primary and fundamental one. Answering to this is the "forgiveness" which it directs us to seek—not the removal from our own hearts of the stain of sin, nor yet the removal of our just dread of God's anger, or of unworthy suspicions of His love, which is all that some tell us we have to care about—but the removal from God's own mind of His displeasure against us on account of sin, or, to retain the figure, the wiping or crossing out from His "book of remembrance" of all entries against us on this account. **as we forgive our debtors**—the same view of sin as before; only now transferred to the region of offenses given and received between man and man. After what has been said on ch. 5:7, it will not be thought that our Lord here teaches that our exercise of forgiveness towards our offending fellow men absolutely precedes and is the proper ground of God's forgiveness of us. His whole teaching, indeed—as of all Scripture—is the reverse of this. But as no one can reasonably imagine himself to be the object of divine forgiveness who is deliberately and habitually unforgiving towards his fellow men, so it is a beautiful provision to make our right to ask and expect daily forgiveness of our daily shortcomings and our final absolution and acquittal at the great day of admission into the kingdom, dependent upon our consciousness of a forgiving disposition towards our fellows, and our preparedness to protest before the Searcher of hearts that we do actually forgive them. (See Mark 11:25, 26). God sees His own image reflected in His forgiving children; but to ask God for what we ourselves refuse to men, is to insult Him. So much stress does our Lord put upon this, that immediately after the close of this prayer, it is the one point in it which He comes back upon (vss. 14, 15), for the purpose of solemnly assuring us that the divine procedure in this matter of forgiveness will be exactly what our own is.

Sixth Petition: **13. And lead us not into temptation**—He who honestly seeks, and has the assurance of, forgiveness for past sin, will strive to avoid committing it for the future. But conscious that "when we would do good evil is present with us," we are taught to offer this sixth petition, which comes naturally close upon the preceding, and flows, indeed, instinctively from it in the hearts of all earnest Christians. There is some difficulty in the form of the petition, as it is certain that God does bring His people—as He did Abraham, and Christ Himself—into circumstances both fitted and designed to try them, or test the strength of their faith. Some meet this by regarding the petition as simply an humble expression of self-distrust and instinctive shrinking from danger; but this seems too weak. Others take it as a prayer against yielding to temptation, and so equivalent to a prayer for support and deliverance when we are tempted; but this seems to go beyond the precise thing intended. We incline to take it as a prayer against being *drawn* or sucked, *of our own will,* into temptation, to which the word here used seems to lend some countenance—"Introduce us not." This view, while it does not put into our mouths a prayer against being tempted—which is more than the divine procedure would seem to warrant—does not, on the other hand, change the sense of the petition into one for support *under* temptation, which the words will hardly bear; but it gives us a subject for prayer, in regard to temptation, most *definite,* and of all others most *needful.* It was precisely this which Peter needed to ask, but did not ask, when—of his own accord, and in spite of difficulties—he pressed for entrance into the palace-hall of the high priest, and where, once sucked into the scene and atmosphere of temptation, he fell so foully. And if so, does it not seem pretty clear that this was exactly what our Lord meant His disciples to pray against when He said in the garden—"Watch and pray, that ye *enter not into* temptation?" (ch. 26:41).

Seventh Petition: **But deliver us from evil**—We can see no good reason for regarding this as but the second half of the sixth petition. With far better ground might the second and third petitions be regarded as one. The "but" connecting the two petitions is an insufficient reason for regarding them as one, though enough to show that the one thought naturally follows close upon the other. As the expression "from evil" may be equally well rendered "from the evil one," a number or superior critics think the devil is intended, especially from its following close upon the subject of "temptation." But the comprehensive character of these brief petitions, and the place which this one occupies, as that on which all our desires die away, seems to us against so contracted a view of it. Nor can there be a reasonable doubt that the apostle, in some of the last sentences which he penned before he was brought forth to suffer for his Lord, alludes to this very petition in the language of calm assurance—"And the Lord shall deliver me from every evil work [cf. the *Greek* of the two passages], and will preserve me unto his heavenly kingdom" (II. Tim. 4:18). The final petition, then, is only rightly grasped when regarded as a prayer for deliverance from all evil of whatever kind—not only from sin, but from all its consequences—fully and finally. Fitly, then, are our prayers ended with this. For what can we desire which this does not carry with it? **For thine is the kingdom, and the power, and the glory, for ever. Amen**—If any reliance is to be placed on external evidence, this doxology, we think, can hardly be considered part of the original text. It is wanting in all the most ancient MSS.; it is wanting in the *Old Latin* version and in the *Vulgate:* the former mounting up to about the middle of the second century, and the latter being a revision of it in the fourth century by JEROME, a most reverential and conservative as well as able and impartial critic. As might be expected from this, it is passed by in silence by the earliest Latin fathers; but even the Greek commentators, when expounding this prayer, pass by the doxology. On the other hand, it is found in a majority of MSS., though not the oldest; it is found in all the Syriac versions, even the *Peshito*—dating probably as early as the second century—although this version lacks the "Amen," which the doxology, if genuine, could hardly have wanted; it is found in the *Sahidic* or *Thebaic* version made for the Christians of Upper Egypt, possibly as early as the Old Latin; and it is found in perhaps most of the later versions. On a review of the evidence, the strong probability, we think, is that it was no part of the original text. **14. For if ye forgive men ... 15. But if ye forgive not ...**—See on vs. 12.

Fasting (vss. 16-18). Having concluded His supplementary directions on the subject of prayer with this Divine Pattern, our Lord now returns to the subject of *Unostentatiousness* in our deeds of righteousness, in order to give one more illustration of it, in the matter of fasting. **16. Moreover, when ye fast**—referring, probably, to private and voluntary fasting, which was to be regulated by each individual for himself; though in spirit it would apply to any fast—**be not, as the hypocrites, of a sad countenance: for they disfigure their faces**—lit., "make unseen"; very well rendered "disfigure." They went about with a slovenly appearance, and ashes sprinkled on their head. **that they may appear unto men to fast**—It was not the *deed,* but *reputation* for the deed which they sought; and with this view those hypocrites multiplied their fasts. And are the exhausting fasts of the Church of Rome, and of Romanizing Protestants, free from this taint? **Verily I say unto you, They have their reward. 17. But thou, when thou fastest, anoint thine head, and wash thy face**—as the Jews did, except when mourning (Dan. 10:3); so that the meaning is, "Appear as usual"—appear so as to attract no notice. **18. That thou appear not unto men to fast, but unto thy Father which is in secret: and thy Father, which seeth in secret, shall reward thee [openly]**—The "openly" seems evidently a later addition to the text of this verse from vss. 4, 7, though of course the idea is implied.

19-34. CONCLUDING ILLUSTRATIONS OF THE RIGHTEOUSNESS OF THE KINGDOM—HEAVENLY-MINDEDNESS AND FILIAL CONFIDENCE. **19. Lay not up for ourselves** [hoard not] **treasures upon earth, where moth**—a "clothes-moth." Eastern treasures, consisting partly in costly dresses stored up (Job 27:16), were liable to be consumed by moths (Job 13:28; Isa. 50:9; 51:8). In James 5:2 there is an evident reference to our Lord's words here. **and rust**—any "eating into" or "consuming"; here, probably, "wear-and-tear." **doth corrupt**—cause to disappear. By this reference to moth and rust our Lord would teach how *perishable* are such earthly treasures. **and where thieves break through and steal**—Treasures these, how *precarious*! **20. But lay up for yourselves treasures in heaven**—The language in Luke (12:33) is very bold—"Sell that ye have, and give alms; provide yourselves bags which wax not old, a treasure in the heavens that faileth not ...

where neither moth nor rust doth corrupt, and where thieves do not break through nor steal—Treasures these, *imperishable* and *unassailable!* (Cf. Col. 3:2). **21. For where your treasure is** [that which ye value most] **there will your heart be also**—"Thy treasure—thy heart" is probably the true reading here: "your," in Luke 12:34, from which it seems to have come in here. Obvious though this maxim be, by what multitudes who profess to bow to the teaching of Christ is it practically disregarded! "What a man loves," says LUTHER, quoted by THOLUCK, "that is his God. For he carries it in his heart, he goes about with it night and day, he sleeps and wakes with it; be it what it may—wealth or pelf, pleasure or renown." But because "laying up" is not in itself sinful, nay, in some cases enjoined (II Cor. 12:14), and honest industry and sagacious enterprise is usually rewarded with prosperity, many flatter themselves that all is right between them and God, while their closest attention, anxiety, zeal, and time are exhausted upon these earthly pursuits. To put this right, our Lord adds what follows, in which there is profound practical wisdom. **22. The light** [the lamp] **of the body is the eye: if therefore thine eye be single**—simple, clear. As applied to the outward eye, this means general soundness; particularly, not looking two ways. Here, as also in classical Greek, it is used figuratively to denote the simplicity of the mind's eye, singleness of purpose, looking right at its object, as opposed to having two ends in view. (See Prov. 4:25-27.) **thy whole body shall be full of light**—illuminated. As with the bodily vision, the man who looks with a good, sound eye, walks in light, seeing every object clear; so a simple and persistent purpose to serve and please God in everything will make the whole character consistent and bright. **23. But if thine eye be evil**—distempered, or, as we should say, If we have got a *bad* eye—**thy whole body shall be full of darkness**—darkened. As a vitiated eye, or an eye that looks not straight and full at its object, sees nothing as it is, so a mind and heart divided between heaven and earth is all dark. **If therefore the light that is in thee be darkness, how great is that darkness!**—As the conscience is the regulative faculty, and a man's inward purpose, scope, aim in life, determines his character—if these be not simple and heavenward, but distorted and double, what must all the other faculties and principles of our nature be which take their direction and character from these, and what must the whole man and the whole life be but a mass of darkness? In Luke (11: 36) the converse of this statement very strikingly expresses what pure, beautiful, broad perceptions the *clarity of the inward eye* imparts: "If thy whole body therefore be full of light, having no part dark, the whole shall be full of light, as when the bright shining of a candle doth give thee light." But now for the application of this. **24. No man can serve**—The word means to "belong wholly and be entirely under command to." **two masters: for either he will hate the one, and love the other; or else he will hold to the one, and despise the other**—Even if the two masters be of one character and have but one object, the servant must *take law* from one or the other: though he may do what is agreeable to both, he cannot, in the nature of the thing, be *servant* to more than one. Much less if, as in the present case, their interests are quite different, and even conflicting. In this case, if our affections be in the service of the one—if we "love the one"—we must of necessity "hate the other"; if we determine resolutely to "hold to the one," we must at the same

time disregard, and (if he insist on his claims upon us) even "despise the other." **Ye cannot serve God and mammon**—The word "*mamon*"—better written with one *m*—is a foreign one, whose precise derivation cannot certainly be determined, though the most probable one gives it the sense of "what one trusts in." Here, there can be no doubt it is used for *riches*, considered as an idol master, or god of the heart. The service of this god and the true God together is here, with a kind of indignant curtness, pronounced impossible. But since the teaching of the preceding verses might seem to endanger our falling short of what is requisite for the present life, and so being left destitute, our Lord now comes to speak to that point. **25. Therefore I say unto you, Take no thought**—"Be not solicitous." The English word "thought," when our version was made, expressed this idea of "solicitude," "anxious concern"—as may be seen in any old English classic; and in the same sense it is used in I Samuel 9:5, etc. But this sense of the word has now nearly gone out, and so the mere English reader is apt to be perplexed. *Thought* or forethought, for temporal things—in the sense of reflection, consideration—is required alike by Scripture and common sense. It is that anxious solicitude, that oppressive care, which springs from unbelieving doubts and misgivings, which alone is here condemned. (See Phil. 4:6). **for your life, what ye shall eat, or what ye shall drink; nor yet for your body, what ye shall put on**—In Luke (12:29) our Lord adds, "neither be ye unsettled"—not "of doubtful mind," as in our version. When "careful (or 'full of care') about nothing," but committing all in prayer and supplication with thanksgiving unto God, the apostle assures us that "the peace of God, which passeth all understanding, shall keep our hearts and minds in Christ Jesus" (Phil. 4:6, 7); i.e., shall guard both our feelings and our thoughts from undue agitation, and keep them in a holy calm. But when we commit our whole temporal condition to the wit of our own minds, we get into that "unsettled" state against which our Lord exhorts His disciples. **Is not the life more than meat** [food] **and the body than raiment?**—If God, then, gives and keeps up the greater—the life, the body—will He withhold the less, food to sustain life and raiment to clothe the body? **26. Behold the fowls of the air**—in vs. 28, "observe well," and in Luke 12:24, "consider"—so as to learn wisdom from them. **for they sow not, neither do they reap, nor gather into barns; yet your heavenly Father feedeth them. Are ye not much better than they?**—nobler in yourselves and dearer to God. The argument here is from the greater to the less; but how rich in detail! The brute creation—void of reason—are incapable of sowing, reaping, and storing: yet your heavenly Father suffers them not helplessly to perish, but sustains them without any of those processes. Will He see, then, His own children using all the means which reason dictates for procuring the things needful for the body—looking up to Himself at every step—and yet leave them to starve? **27. Which of you, by taking thought** [anxious solicitude]—**can add one cubit unto his stature?**—"Stature" can hardly be the thing intended here: first, because the subject is the *prolongation of life,* by the supply of its necessaries of food and clothing: and next, because no one would dream of adding a cubit—or a foot and a half—to his stature, while in the corresponding passage in Luke (12:25, 26) the thing intended is represented as "that thing which is *least*." But if we take the word in its primary sense of "*age*" (for "stature" is but a secondary sense) the idea will be this, "Which of you, however anxiously you vex yourselves about it, can add so much as a step to the length of your life's journey?" To compare the length of life to measures of this nature is not foreign to the language of Scripture (cf. Ps. 39:5; II Tim. 4:7, etc.). So understood, the meaning is clear and the connection natural. In this the best critics now agree. **28. And why take ye thought for raiment? Consider** [observe well] **the lilies of the field, how they grow: they toil not**—as men, planting and preparing the flax. **neither do they spin**—as women. **29. And yet I say unto you, That even Solomon in all his glory was not arrayed like one of these**—What incomparable teaching!—best left in its own transparent clearness and rich simplicity. **30. Wherefore, if God so clothe the grass**—the "herbage." **of the field, which to-day is, and to-morrow is cast into the oven**—wild flowers cut with the grass, withering by the heat, and used for fuel. (See Jas 1: 11). **shall He not much more clothe you, O ye of little faith?**—The argument here is something fresh. Gorgeous as is the array of the flowers that deck the fields, surpassing all artificial human grandeur, it is for but a brief moment; you are ravished with it to-day, and tomorrow it is gone; your own hands have seized and cast it into the oven: Shall, then, God's children, so dear to Him, and instinct with a life that cannot die, be left naked? He does not say, Shall they not be more beauteously arrayed? but, Shall He not much more *clothe* them? that being all He will have them regard as secured to them (cf. Heb. 13:5). The expression, "Littlefaithed ones," which our Lord applies once and again to His disciples (ch. 8:26; 14:31; 16:8), can hardly be regarded as rebuking any actual manifestations of unbelief at that early period, and before such an audience. It is His way of gently chiding the *spirit* of unbelief, so natural even to the best, who are surrounded by a world of sense, and of kindling a generous desire to shake it off. **31. Therefore take no thought** [solicitude], **saying, What shall we eat? or, What shall we drink? or, Wherewithal shall we be clothed? 32. (For after all these things do the Gentiles seek)**—rather, "pursue." Knowing nothing definitely beyond the present life to kindle their aspirations and engage their supreme attention, the heathen naturally pursue present objects as their chief, their only good. To what an elevation above these does Jesus here lift His disciples! **for your heavenly Father knoweth that ye have need of all these things**—How precious this word! Food and raiment are pronounced *needful* to God's children; and He who could say, "No man knoweth the Father but the Son, and he to whomsoever the Son will reveal Him" (ch. 11:27), says with an authority which none but Himself could claim, "Your heavenly Father *knoweth* that ye have need of all these things." Will not that suffice you, O ye needy ones of the household of faith? **33. But seek ye first the kingdom of God, and his righteousness; and all these things shall be added unto you**—This is the great summing up. Strictly speaking, it has to do only with the subject of the present section—the right state of the heart with reference to heavenly and earthly things; but being couched in the form of a brief general directory, it is so comprehensive in its grasp as to embrace the whole subject of this discourse. And, as if to make this the more evident, the two keynotes of this great sermon seem purposely struck in it—"the KINGDOM" and "the RIGHTEOUSNESS" of the kingdom—as the grand objects, in the supreme pursuit of which all things

needful for the present life will be added to us. The precise sense of every word in this golden verse should be carefully weighed. "*The kingdom of God*" is the primary subject of the Sermon on the Mount—that kingdom which the God of heaven is erecting in this fallen world, within which are all the spiritually recovered and inwardly subject portion of the family of Adam, under Messiah as its Divine Head and King. "*The righteousness thereof*" is the character of all such, so amply described and variously illustrated in the foregoing portions of this discourse. The "*seeking*" of these is the making them the object of supreme choice and pursuit; and the seeking of them "*first*" is the seeking of them before and above all else. The "*all these things*" which shall in that case be added to us are just the "all these things" which the last words of the preceding verse assured us "our heavenly Father knoweth that we have need of"; i.e., all we require for the present life. And when our Lord says they shall be "*added*," it is implied, as a matter of course, that the seekers of the kingdom and its righteousness shall have these' as their proper and primary portion: the rest being their gracious reward for *not* seeking them. (See an illustration of the principle of this in II Chron. 1:11, 12.) What follows is but a reduction of this great general direction into a practical and ready form for daily use. **34. Take therefore no thought** [anxious care] **for the morrow: for the morrow shall take thought for the things of itself**—(or, according to other authorities, "for itself")—shall have its own causes of anxiety. **Sufficient unto the day is the evil thereof**—An admirable practical maxim, and better rendered in our version than in almost any other, not excepting the preceding English ones. Every day brings its own cares; and to anticipate is only to double them.

CHAPTER 7

SERMON ON THE MOUNT—*concluded*

Vss. 1-12. MISCELLANEOUS SUPPLEMENTARY COUNSELS. That these verses are entirely supplementary is the simplest and most natural view of them. All attempts to make out any evident connection with the immediately preceding context are, in our judgment, forced. But, though supplementary, these counsels are far from being of subordinate importance. On the contrary, they involve some of the most delicate and vital duties of the Christian life. In the vivid form in which they are here presented, perhaps they could not have been introduced with the same effect under any of the foregoing heads; but they spring out of the same great principles, and are but other forms and manifestations of the same evangelical "righteousness."

Censorious Judgment (vss. 1-5). **1. Judge not, that ye be not judged**—To "judge" here does not exactly mean to pronounce condemnatory judgment, nor does it refer to simple judging at all, whether favorable or the reverse. The context makes it clear that the thing here condemned is that disposition to look unfavorably on the character and actions of others, which leads invariably to the pronouncing of rash, unjust, and unlovely judgments upon them. No doubt it is the judgments so pronounced which are here spoken of; but what our Lord aims at is the spirit out of which they spring.

Provided we eschew this unlovely spirit, we are not only warranted to sit in judgment upon a brother's character and actions, but in the exercise of a necessary discrimination are often constrained to do so for our own guidance. It is the violation of the law of love involved in the exercise of a censorious disposition which alone is here condemned. And the argument against it—"that ye be not judged"—confirms this: "that your own character and actions be not pronounced upon with the like severity"; i.e., at the great day. **2. For with what judgments ye judge, ye shall be judged: and with what measure ye mete** [whatever standard of judgment ye apply to others] **it shall be measured to you again**—This proverbial maxim is used by our Lord in other connections—as in Mark 4:24, and with a slightly different application in Luke 6:38—as a great principle in the divine administration. Unkind judgment of others will be judicially returned upon ourselves, in the day when God shall judge the secrets of men by Jesus Christ. But, as in many other cases under the divine administration, such harsh judgment gets self-punished even here. For people shrink from contact with those who systematically deal out harsh judgment upon others—naturally concluding that they themselves may be the next victims—and feel impelled in self-defense, when exposed to it, to roll back upon the assailant his own censures. **3. And why beholdest thou the mote**—"splinter," here very well rendered "mote," denoting any small fault. **that is in thy brother's eye, but considerest not the beam that is in thine own eye?**—denoting the much greater fault which we overlook in ourselves. **4. Or how wilt thou say to thy brother, Let me pull out the mote out of thine eye; and, behold, a beam is in thine own eye? 5. Thou hypocrite** [Hypocrite] **—first cast out the beam out of thine own eye; and then shalt thou see clearly to cast out the mote out of thy brother's eye**—Our Lord uses a most hyperbolical, but not unfamiliar figure, to express the monstrous inconsistency of this conduct. The "hypocrisy" which, not without indignation, He charges it with, consists in the pretense of a zealous and compassionate charity, which cannot possibly be real in one who suffers worse faults to lie uncorrected in himself. He only is fit to be a reprover of others who jealously and severely judges himself. Such persons will not only be slow to undertake the office of censor on their neighbors, but, when constrained in faithfulness to deal with them, will make it evident that they do it with *reluctance* and not satisfaction, with *moderation* and not exaggeration, with *love* and not harshness.

Prostitution of Holy Things (vs. 6): The opposite extreme to that of censoriousness is here condemned—want of discrimination of character. **6. Give not that which is holy unto the dogs**—savage or snarling haters of truth and righteousness. **neither cast ye your pearls before swine**—the impure or coarse, who are incapable of appreciating the priceless jewels of Christianity. In the East, dogs are wilder and more gregarious, and, feeding on carrion and garbage, are coarser and fiercer than the same animals in the West. Dogs and swine, besides being ceremonially unclean, were peculiarly repulsive to the Jews, and indeed to the ancients generally. **lest they trample them under their feet**—as swine do—**and turn again and rend you**—as dogs do. Religion is brought into contempt, and its professors insulted, when it is forced upon those who cannot value it and will not have it. But while the indiscriminately zealous have need of this caution, let us be on our guard against too readily setting our neighbors down

as dogs and swine, and excusing ourselves from endeavoring to do them good on this poor plea.

Prayer (vss. 7-11). Enough, one might think, had been said on this subject in ch. 6:5-15. But the difficulty of the foregoing duties seems to have recalled the subject, and this gives it quite a new turn. "How shall we ever be able to carry out such precepts as these, of tender, holy, yet discriminating love?" might the humble disciple inquire. "Go to God with it," is our Lord's reply; but He expresses this with a fulness which leaves nothing to be desired, urging now not only confidence, but importunity in prayer. **7. Ask, and it shall be given you; seek, and ye shall find; knock, and it shall be opened unto you**—Though there seems evidently a climax here, expressive of more and more importunity, yet each of these terms used presents what we desire of God in a different light. We *ask* for what we *wish;* we *seek* for what we *miss;* we *knock* for that from which we feel ourselves *shut out.* Answering to this threefold representation is the triple assurance of success to our believing efforts. "But ah!" might some humble disciple say, "I cannot persuade myself that *I* have any interest with God." To meet this, our Lord repeats the triple assurance He had just given, but in such a form as to silence every such complaint. **8. For every one that asketh receiveth; and he that seeketh findeth; and to him that knocketh it shall be opened**—Of course, it is presumed that he asks aright—i.e., in faith—and with an honest purpose to make use of what he receives. "If any of you lack wisdom, let him ask of God. But let him ask in faith, nothing wavering [undecided whether to be altogether on the Lord's side]. For he that wavereth is like a wave of the sea driven with the wind and tossed. For *let not that man think that he shall receive any thing of the Lord*" (Jas 1:5-7). Hence, "Ye ask, and receive not, because ye ask amiss, that ye may consume it upon your lusts" (Jas. 4:3). **9. Or what man is there of you, whom if his son ask bread** [a loaf] **will he give him a stone?**—round and smooth like such a loaf or cake as was much in use, but only to mock him. **10. Or if he ask a fish, will he give him a serpent?**—like it, indeed, but only to sting him. **11. If ye then, being evil, know how to give good gifts unto your children, how much more shall your Father which is in heaven give good things to them that ask him!**—Bad as our fallen nature is, the *father* in us is not extinguished. What a heart, then, must the Father of all fathers have towards His pleading children! In the corresponding passage in Luke (see on 11:13), instead of "good things," our Lord asks whether He will not much more give *the Holy Spirit* to them that ask Him. At this early stage of His ministry, and before such an audience, He seems to avoid such sharp doctrinal teaching as was more accordant with His plan at the riper stage indicated in Luke, and in addressing His own disciples exclusively.

Golden Rule (vs. 12). **12. Therefore**—to say all in one word. **all things whatsoever ye would that men should do to you, do ye even so** [the same thing and in the same way] **to them: for this is the law and the prophets**—"This is the substance of all relative duty; all Scripture in a nutshell." Incomparable summary! How well called "the royal law!" (Jas. 2:8; cf. Rom. 13:9). It is true that similar maxims are found floating in the writings of the cultivated Greeks and Romans, and naturally enough in the Rabbinical writings. But so expressed as it is here—in immediate connection with, and as the sum of *such* duties as has been just enjoined, and such principles as had been before taught—it is to be found nowhere else. And the best commentary upon this fact is, that never till our Lord came down thus to teach did men effectually and widely exemplify it in their practice. The precise sense of the maxim is best referred to common sense. It is not, of course, what—in our wayward, capricious, grasping moods—we should *wish* that men would do to us, that we are to hold ourselves bound to do to them; but only what—in the exercise of an impartial judgment, and putting ourselves in their place—we consider it reasonable that they should do to us, that we are to do to them.

13-29. CONCLUSION AND EFFECT OF THE SERMON ON THE MOUNT. We have here the application of the whole preceding discourse. *Conclusion of the Sermon on the Mount* (vss. 13-27). "The righteousness of the kingdom," so amply described, both in principle and in detail, would be seen to involve *self-sacrifice* at every step. Multitudes would never face this. But it must be faced, else the consequences will be fatal. This would divide all within the sound of these truths into two classes: the many, who will follow the path of ease and self-indulgence—end where it might; and the few, who, bent on eternal safety above everything else, take the way that leads to it—at whatever cost. This gives occasion to the two opening verses of this application. **13. Enter ye in at the strait gate**—as if hardly wide enough to admit one at all. This expresses the difficulty of the first right step in religion, involving, as it does, a triumph over all our natural inclinations. Hence the still stronger expression in Luke (13:24), "Strive to enter in at the strait gate." **for wide is the gate** [easily entered] **and broad is the way** [easily trodden] **that leadeth to destruction, and** [thus lured] **many there be which go in thereat: 14. Because strait is the gate, and narrow is the way, which leadeth unto life**—In other words, the whole course is as difficult as the first step; and (so it comes to pass that)—**few there be that find it.** The recommendation of the broad way is the ease with which it is trodden and the abundance of company to be found in it. It is sailing with a fair wind and a favorable tide. The natural inclinations are not crossed, and fears of the issue, if not easily hushed, are in the long run effectually subdued. The one disadvantage of this course is its end—it "leadeth to destruction." The great Teacher says it, and says it as "One having authority." To the supposed injustice or harshness of this He never once adverts. He leaves it to be inferred that such a course righteously, naturally, necessarily so ends. But whether men see this or no, here He lays down the law of the kingdom, and leaves it with us. As to the other way, the disadvantage of it lies in its narrowness and solicitude. Its very first step involves a revolution in all our purposes and plans for life, and a surrender of all that is dear to natural inclination, while all that follows is but a repetition of the first great act of self-sacrifice. No wonder, then, that few find and few are found in it. But it has one advantage—it "leadeth unto life." Some critics take "the gate" here, not for the first, but the last step in religion; since gates seldom open into roads, but roads usually terminate in a gate, leading straight to a mansion. But as this would make our Lord's words to have a very inverted and unnatural form as they stand, it is better, with the majority of critics, to view them as we have done. But since such teaching would be as unpopular as the way itself, our Lord next forewarns His hearers that preachers of smooth things—the true heirs and representatives

of the false prophets of old—would be rife enough in the new kingdom. **15. Beware [But beware] of false prophets**—i.e., of teachers coming as authorized expounders of the mind of God and guides to heaven. (See Acts 20:29, 30; II Pet. 2:1, 2). **which come to you in sheep's clothing**—with a bland, gentle, plausible exterior; persuading you that the gate is not strait nor the way narrow, and that to teach so is illiberal and bigoted—precisely what the old prophets did (Ezek. 13:1-10, 22). **but inwardly they are ravening wolves**—bent on devouring the flock for their own ends (II Cor. 11:2, 3, 13-15). **16. Ye shall know them by their fruits**—not their doctrines—as many of the elder interpreters and some later ones explain it—for that corresponds to the tree itself; but the practical effect of their teaching, which is the proper fruit of the tree. **Do men gather grapes of thorns** [any kind of prickly plant] **or figs of thistles?**—a threepronged variety. The general sense is obvious—Every tree bears its own fruit. **17. Even so every good tree bringeth forth good fruit: but a corrupt tree bringeth forth evil fruit. 18. A good tree cannot bring forth evil fruit, neither can a corrupt tree bring forth good fruit**—Obvious as is the truth here expressed in different forms—that the heart determines and is the only proper interpreter of the actions of our life—no one who knows how the Church of Rome makes a merit of actions, quite apart from the motives that prompt them, and how the same tendency manifests itself from time to time even among Protestant Christians, can think it too obvious to be insisted on by the teachers of divine truth. Here follows a wholesome digression. **19. Every tree that bringeth not forth good fruit is hewn down, and cast into the fire**—See on ch. 3:10. **20. Wherefore by their fruits ye shall know them**—i.e., But the point I now press is not so much the end of such, as the means of detecting them; and this, as already said, is their fruits. The hypocrisy of teachers now leads to a solemn warning against religious hypocrisy in general. **21. Not every one that saith unto me, Lord, Lord**—the reduplication of the title "Lord" denoting zeal in according it to Christ (see Mark 14:45). Yet our Lord claims and expects this of all His disciples, as when He washed their feet: "Ye call me Master and Lord: and ye say well; for so I am" (John 13:13). **shall enter into the kingdom of heaven; but he that doeth the will of my Father which is in heaven**—that will which it had been the great object of this discourse to set forth. Yet our Lord says warily, not "the will of *your* Father," but "of *My* Father"; thus claiming a relationship to His Father with which His disciples might not intermeddle, and which He never lets down. And He so speaks here to give authority to His asseverations. But now He rises higher still—not formally *announcing* Himself as the Judge, but intimating what men will say to Him, and He to them, *when* He sits as their final judge. **22. Many will say to me in that day**—What day? It is emphatically unnamed. But it is the day to which He had just referred, when men shall "enter" or not enter "into the kingdom of heaven." (See a similar way of speaking of "that day" in II Tim. 1:12; 4:8). **Lord, Lord**—The reiteration denotes surprise. "What, Lord? How is this? Are *we* to be disowned?" **have we not prophesied**—or, "publicly taught." As one of the special gifts of the Spirit in the early Church, it has the sense of "inspired and authoritative teaching," and is ranked next to the apostleship. (See I Cor. 12:28; Eph. 4:11.) In this sense it is used here, as appears from what follows. **in thy name**—or, "to thy name," and so in the two following clauses—"having reference to Thy name as the sole power in which we did it." **and in thy name have cast out devils? and in thy name done many wonderful works**—or, miracles. These are selected as three examples of the highest services rendered to the Christian cause, and through the power of Christ's own name, invoked for that purpose; He Himself, too, responding to the call. And the threefold repetition of the question, each time in the same form, expresses in the liveliest manner the astonishment of the speakers at the view now taken of them. **23. And then will I profess unto them**—or, openly proclaim—tearing off the mask. **I never knew you**—What they claimed intimacy with Christ, is just what He repudiates, and with a certain scornful dignity. "Our acquaintance was not broken off —there never was any." **depart from me**—(Cf. ch. 25:41). The connection here gives these words an awful significance. They claimed intimacy with Christ, and in the corresponding passage, Luke 13: 26, are represented as having gone out and in with Him on familiar terms. "So much the worse for you," He replies: "I bore with that long enough; but now—begone!" **ye that work iniquity**—not "that *wrought* iniquity"; for they are represented as fresh from the scenes and acts of it as they stand before the Judge. (See on the almost identical, but even more vivid and awful, description of the scene in Luke 13:24-27.) That the apostle alludes to these very words in II Tim. 2:19 there can hardly be any doubt—"Nevertheless the foundation of God standeth sure, having this seal, The Lord *knoweth* them that are His. And, Let every one that nameth the *name* of Christ depart from iniquity." **24. Therefore**—to bring this discourse to a close. **whosoever heareth these sayings of mine, and doeth them**—see James 1:22, which seems a plain allusion to these words; also Luke 11:28; Romans 2:13; I John 3:7— **I will liken him unto a wise man**—a shrewd, prudent, provident man. **which built his house upon a rock** —the rock of true discipleship, or genuine subjection to Christ. **25. And the rain** [from above] **descended, and the floods** [from below] **came, and the winds** [sweeping across] **blew, and** [thus from every direction] **beat upon that house; and it fell not; for it was founded upon a rock**—See I John 2:17. **26. And every one that heareth these sayings of mine**—in the attitude of discipleship—**and doeth them not, shall be likened unto a foolish man, which built his house upon the sand**—denoting a loose foundation— that of an empty profession and mere external services. **27. And the rain descended, and the floods came, and the winds blew, and beat upon** [struck against] **that house; and it fell: and great was the fall of it**—terrible the ruin! How lively must this imagery have been to an audience accustomed to the fierceness of an Eastern tempest, and the suddenness and completeness with which it sweeps everything unsteady before it!

Effect of the Sermon on the Mount. (vss. 28, 29). **28. And it came to pass, when Jesus had ended these sayings, the people were astonished at his doctrine** —rather, "His teaching," for the reference is to the manner of it quite as much as the matter, or rather more so. **29. For he taught them as [one] having authority**—The word "one," which our translators have here inserted, only weakens the statement. **and not as the scribes**—The consciousness of divine authority, as Lawgiver, Expounder and Judge, so beamed through His teaching, that the scribes' teaching could not but appear drivelling in such a light.

CHAPTER 8

Vss. 1-4. HEALING OF A LEPER. (= Mark 1:40-45; Luke 5:12-16). The time of this miracle seems too definitely fixed here to admit of our placing it where it stands in Mark and Luke, in whose Gospels no such precise note of time is given. **1. When he was come down from the mountain, great multitudes followed him. 2. And, behold, there came a leper** —"a man full of leprosy," says Luke 5:12. Much has been written on this disease of leprosy, but certain points remain still doubtful. All that needs be said here is that it was a cutaneous disease, of a loathsome, diffusive, and, there is reason to believe, when thoroughly pronounced, incurable character; that though in its distinctive features it is still found in several countries—as Arabia, Egypt, and South Africa—it prevailed, in the form of what is called white leprosy, to an unusual extent, and from a very early period, among the Hebrews; and that it thus furnished to the whole nation a familiar and affecting symbol of SIN, considered as (1) *loathsome*, (2) *spreading*, (3) *incurable*. And while the ceremonial ordinances for detection and cleansing prescribed in this case by the law of Moses (Lev. 13, 14) held forth a coming remedy "for sin and for uncleanness" (Ps. 51:7; II Kings 5:1, 7, 10, 13, 14), the numerous cases of leprosy with which our Lord came in contact, and the glorious cures of them which He wrought, were a fitting manifestation of the work which He came to accomplish. In this view, it deserves to be noticed that the first of our Lord's miracles of healing recorded by Matthew is this cure of a leper. **and worshipped him**—in what sense we shall presently see. Mark says (1:40), he came, "beseeching and kneeling to Him," and Luke says (5:12), "he fell on his face." **saying, Lord, if thou wilt, thou canst make me clean**—As this is the only cure of leprosy recorded by all the three first Evangelists, it was probably the first case of the kind; and if so, this leper's faith in the power of Christ must have been formed in him by what he had heard of His other cures. And how striking a faith is it! He does not say he *believed* Him able, but with a brevity expressive of a confidence that knew no doubt, he says simply, "Thou canst." But of Christ's willingness to heal him he was not so sure. It needed more knowledge of Jesus than he could be supposed to have to assure him of that. But one thing he was sure of, that He had but to "will" it. This shows with what "worship" or Christ this leper fell on his face before Him. Clear theological knowledge of the Person of Christ was not then possessed even by those who were most with Him and nearest to Him. Much less could full insight into all that we know of the Only-begotten of the Father be expected of this leper. But he who at that moment felt and owned that to heal an incurable disease needed but the *fiat* of the Person who stood before him, had assuredly that very faith in the germ which now casts its crown before Him that loved us, and would at any time die for His blessed name. **3. And Jesus**—or "He," according to another reading,—"moved with compassion," says Mark (1:41); a precious addition. **put forth his hand, and touched him**—Such a touch occasioned ceremonial defilement (Lev. 5:3); even as the leper's coming near enough for contact was against the Levitical regulations (Lev. 13:46). But as the man's faith told him there would be no case for such regulations if the cure he hoped to experience should be accomplished, so He who had healing in His wings transcended all such statutes.

is the different senses—a higher and a lower—in
which the same word "dead" is used: There are two
kingdoms of God in existence upon earth; the kingdom of nature, and the kingdom of grace: To the
one kingdom all the children of this world, even the
most ungodly, are fully alive; to the other, only the
children of light: The reigning irreligion consists not
in indifference to the common humanities of social
life, but to things spiritual and eternal: Fear not,
therefore, that your father will in your absence be
neglected, and that when he breathes his last there
will not be relatives and friends ready enough to do
to him the last offices of kindness. Your wish to
discharge these yourself is natural, and to be allowed to do it a privilege not lightly to be fore-
gone. But the kingdom of God lies now all neglected and needy: Its more exalted character few
discern; to its paramount claims few are alive: and
to "preach" it fewer still are qualified and called:
But thou art: The Lord therefore hath need of thee:
Leave, then, those claims of nature, high though
they be, to those who are dead to the still higher
claims of the kingdom of grace, which God is now
erecting upon earth—Let the dead bury their dead;
but go thou and preach the kingdom of God. And
so have we here the genuine, but Procrastinating or
Entangled Disciple. The next case is recorded only
by Luke:

III. *The Irresolute or Wavering Disciple* (Luke 9:
61, 62). Vs. 61: "And another also said, Lord, I
will follow thee; but let me first go bid them farewell which are at home at my house. Vs. 62: And
Jesus said unto him, No man, having put his hand
to the plough, and looking back, is fit for the kingdom of God." But for the very different replies
given, we should hardly have discerned the difference between this and the second case: the one
man called, indeed, and the other volunteering, as
did the first; but both seemingly alike willing, and
only having a difficulty in their way just at that
moment. But, by help of what is said respectively
to each, we perceive the great difference between the
two cases. From the warning given against "looking back," it is evident that this man's discipleship
was not yet *thorough*, his separation from the world
not entire. It is not a case of *going* back, but of
looking back; and as there is here a manifest reference to the case of "Lot's wife" (Gen. 19:26; and
see on Luke 17:32), we see that it is not *actual return*
to the world that we have here to deal with, but a
reluctance to break with it. The figure of putting
one's hand to the plough and looking back is an
exceedingly vivid one, and to an agricultural people
most impressive. As ploughing requires an eye intent on the furrow to be made, and is marred the
instant one turns about, so will they come short
of salvation who prosecute the work of God with
a distracted attention, a divided heart. The reference may be chiefly to ministers; but the application at least is general. As the image seems plainly
to have been suggested by the case of Elijah and
Elisha, a difficulty may be raised, requiring a moment's attention. When Elijah cast his mantle
about Elisha, which the youth quite understood to
mean appointing him his successor, he was ploughing with twelve yoke of oxen, the last pair held by
himself. Leaving his oxen, he ran after the prophet, and said, "Let me, I pray thee, kiss my father
and my mother, and [then] I will follow thee." Was
this said *in the same spirit* with the same speech uttered by our disciple? Let us see. "And Elijah
said unto him, Go back again: for what have I done
to thee." Commentators take this to mean that

Elijah had really done nothing to hinder him from
going on with all his ordinary duties. But to us it
seems clear that Elijah's intention was to try what
manner of spirit the youth was of:—"Kiss thy father
and mother? And why not? By all means, go
home and stay with them; for what have I done to
thee? I did but throw a mantle about thee; but
what of that?" If this was his meaning, Elisha
thoroughly apprehended and nobly met it. "He
returned back from him, and took a yoke of oxen,
and slew them, and boiled their flesh with the instruments of the oxen [the wood of his ploughing
implements], and gave unto the people, and they
did eat: then he arose, and went after Elijah, and
ministered unto him" (I Kings 19:19-21). We
know not if even his father and mother had time to
be called to this hasty feast. But this much is plain,
that, though in affluent circumstances, he gave up
his lower calling, with all its prospects, for the
higher and at that time perilous, office to which he
was called. What now is the bearing of these two
cases? Did Elisha do wrong in bidding them farewell with whom he was associated in his early calling? Or, if not, would this disciple have done
wrong if he had done the same thing, and in the
same spirit, with Elisha? Clearly not. Elisha's
doing it proved that he could *with safety* do it; and
our Lord's warning is not against bidding them
farewell which were at home at his house, but
against the probable *fatal consequences* of that step;
lest the embraces of earthly relationship should
prove too strong for him, and he should never return to follow Christ. Accordingly, we have called
this the Irresolute or Wavering Disciple.

23-27. Jesus, Crossing the Sea of Galilee,
Miraculously Stills a Tempest. (=Mark 4:35-
41; Luke 8:22-25). For the exposition, see on Mark
4:35-41.

28-34. Jesus Heals the Gergesene Demoniacs.
(= Mark 5:1-20; Luke 8:26-39). For the exposition, see on Mark 5:1-20.

CHAPTER 9

Vss. 1-8. Healing of a Paralytic. (= Mark
2:1-12; Luke 5:17-26.) This incident appears to
follow next in order of time to the cure of the leper
(ch. 8:1-4). For the exposition, see on Mark 2:1-12.

9-13. Matthew's Call and Feast. (= Mark
2:14-17; Luke 5:27-32.) *The call of Matthew*
(vs. 9). **9. And as Jesus passed forth from thence**—
i.e., from the scene of the paralytic's cure in Capernaum, towards the shore of the Sea of Galilee, on
which that town lay. Mark, as usual, pictures the
scene more in detail, thus (2:13): "And He went
forth again by the seaside; and all the multitude
resorted unto Him, and He taught them"—or, "kept
teaching them." "And as He passed by" **he saw a
man, named Matthew**—the writer of this precious
Gospel, who here, with singular modesty and
brevity, relates the story of his own calling. In
Mark and Luke he is called *Levi,* which seems to
have been his family name. In their lists of the
twelve apostles, however, Mark and Luke give him
the name of Matthew, which seems to have been the
name by which he was known as a disciple. While
he himself sinks his family name, he is careful not
to sink his occupation, the obnoxious associations
with which he would place over against the grace
that called him from it, and made him an apostle.
(See on ch. 10:3.) Mark alone tells us (2:14) that
he was "the son of Alphaeus"—the same, probably,
with the father of James the Less. From this and

saying, **I will; be thou clean**—How majestic those two words! By not assuring the man of His *power* to heal him, He delightfully sets His seal to the man's previous confession of that power; and by assuring him of the one thing of which he had any doubt, and for which he waited—His *will* to do it—He makes a claim as divine as the cure which immediately followed it. **And immediately his leprosy was cleansed**—Mark, more emphatic, says (1: 42), "And as soon as He had spoken, immediately the leprosy departed from him, and he was cleansed"—as perfectly as instantaneously. What a contrast this to modern pretended cures! **4. And Jesus** ["straitly charged him, and forthwith sent him away," Mark 1:43, and] **saith unto him, See thou tell no man**—A hard condition this would seem to a grateful heart, whose natural language, in such a case, is "Come, hear, all ye that fear God, and I will declare what He hath done for my soul" (Ps. 66:16). We shall presently see the reason for it. **but go thy way, show thyself to the priest, and offer the gift that Moses commanded** [Lev. 14] **for a testimony unto them**—a palpable witness that the Great Healer had indeed come, and that "God had visited His people." What the sequel was, our Evangelist Matthew does not say; but Mark thus gives it (1:45): "But he went out, and began to publish it much, and to blaze abroad the matter, insomuch that Jesus could no more openly enter into the city, but was without in desert places: and they came to Him from every quarter." Thus—by an over-zealous, though most natural and not very culpable, infringement of the injunction to keep the matter quiet—was our Lord, to some extent, thwarted in His movements. As His whole course was sublimely noiseless (ch. 12:19), so we find Him repeatedly taking steps to prevent matters prematurely coming to a crisis with Him. (But see on Mark 5:19, 20). "And He withdrew Himself," adds Luke (5:16), "into the wilderness, and prayed"; retreating from the popular excitement into the secret place of the Most High, and thus coming forth as dew upon the mown grass, and as showers that water the earth (Ps. 72:6). And this is the secret both of strength and of sweetness in the servants and followers of Christ in every age.

5-13. HEALING OF THE CENTURION'S SERVANT. (= Luke 7:1-10.) This incident belongs to a later stage. For the exposition, see on Luke 7:1-10.

14-17. HEALING OF PETER'S MOTHER-IN-LAW, AND MANY OTHERS. (= Mark. 1:29-34; Luke 4: 38-41). For the exposition, see on Mark 1:29-34.

18-22. INCIDENTS ILLUSTRATIVE OF DISCIPLESHIP. (= Luke 9:57-62). The incidents here are two: in the corresponding passage of Luke they are three. Here they are introduced before the mission of the Twelve: in Luke, when our Lord was making preparation for His final journey to Jerusalem. But to conclude from this, as some good critics do (as BENGEL, ELLICOTT, etc.) that one of these incidents at least occurred twice—which led to the mention of the others at the two different times—is too artificial. Taking them, then, as one set of occurrences, the question arises. Are they recorded by Matthew or by Luke in their proper place? NEANDER, SCHLEIERMACHER, and OLSHAUSEN adhere to Luke's order; while MEYER, DE WETTE, and LANGE prefer that of Matthew. Probably the first incident is here in its right place. But as the command, in the second incident, to preach the kingdom of God, would scarcely have been given at so early a period, it is likely that it and the third incident have their

true place in Luke. Taking these three here then we have—

I. *The Rash or Precipitate Disciple* (**19. And a certain scribe came, and sai Master, I will follow thee whithersoeve 20. And Jesus saith unto him, The foxes and the birds of the air have nests; bu man hath not where to lay his head**—F were of the scribes who attached thems sus. it would appear, from his calling Hi that this one was a "disciple" in that of the word in which it is applied to the d flocked after Him, with more or less con His claims were well founded. But fr swer which he received we are led to infe was more of transient emotion—of temp pulse—than of intelligent principle in t The preaching of Christ had riveted an him; his heart had swelled; his enthusiasm kindled; and in this state of mind he wi where with Him, and feels impelled to te "Wilt thou?" replies the Lord Jesus. thou whom thou art pledging thyself to fe whither haply He may lead thee? No wa no downy pillow has He for thee: He has for Himself. The foxes are not without th nor do the birds of the air lack their nest Son of man has to depend on the hospi others, and borrow the pillow whereon H head." How affecting is this reply! An rejects not this man's offer, nor refuses him erty to follow Him. Only He will ha know what he is doing, and "count the cos will have him weigh well the real nature strength of his attachment, whether it be will abide in the day of trial. If so, he will welcome, for Christ puts none away. But i too plain that in this case that had not beer And so we have called this the Rash or Pre Disciple.

II. *The Procrastinating or Entangled Discip* 21, 22). As this is more fully given in Lu must take both together. "And He said another of His disciples, Follow Me. But he "**Lord, suffer me first to go and bury my f But Jesus said unto him, Follow me; and le dead bury their dead**—or, as more definitely in l "Let the dead bury their dead: but go thou preach the kingdom of God." This disciple not, like the former, volunteer his services, b called by the Lord Jesus, not only to follow, bu preach Him. And he is quite willing; only he is ready just yet. "Lord, I *will*; but"—"There is a ficulty in the way just now; but that once remov I am Thine." What now is this difficulty? his father actually dead—lying a corpse—having o to be buried? Impossible. As it was the practi as noticed on Luke 7:12, to bury on the day death, it is not very likely that this disciple wou have been here at all if his father had just breath his last; nor would the Lord, if He was there, hav hindered him discharging the last duties of a son to father. No doubt it was the common case of a so having a frail or aged father, not likely to live long whose head he thinks it his duty to see under th ground ere he goes abroad. "This aged father o mine will soon be removed; and if I might but delay till I see him decently interred, I should then be free to preach the kingdom of God wherever duty might call me." This view of the case will explain the curt reply, "Let the dead bury their dead: but go thou and preach the kingdom of God." Like all the other paradoxical sayings of our Lord, the key to other considerations it is pretty certain that he must at least have heard of our Lord before this meeting. Unnecessary doubts, even from an early period, have been raised about the identity of Levi and Matthew. No capable jury, with the evidence before them which we have in the Gospels, would hesitate in giving a unanimous verdict of identity. **sitting at the receipt of custom**—as a publican, which Luke (5:27) calls him. It means the place of receipt, the toll-house or booth in which the collector sat. Being in this case by the seaside, it might be the ferry tax for the transit of persons and goods across the lake, which he collected. (See on ch. 5:46.) **and he saith unto him, Follow me**—Witching words these, from the lips of Him who never employed them without giving them resistless efficacy in the hearts of those they were spoken to. **And he** ["left all" (Luke 5:28)] **arose and followed him.**

The Feast (vss. 10-13). **10. And it came to pass, as Jesus sat at meat in the house**—The modesty of our Evangelist signally appears here. Luke says (vs. 29) that "Levi made Him *a great feast,*" or "reception," while Matthew merely says, "He sat at meat"; and Mark and Luke say that it was in Levi's "own house," while Matthew merely says, "He sat at meat *in the house.*" Whether this feast was made now, or not till afterwards, is a point of some importance in the order of events, and not agreed among harmonists. The probability is that it did not take place till a considerable time afterwards. For Matthew, who ought surely to know what took place while his Lord was speaking at his own table, tells us that the visit of Jairus, the ruler of the synagogue, occurred at that moment (vs. 18). But we know from Mark and Luke that this visit of Jairus did not take place till after our Lord's return, at a later period from the country of the Gadarenes. (See Mark 5:21, etc., and Luke 8:40, etc.). We conclude, therefore, that the feast was not made in the novelty of his discipleship, but after Matthew had had time to be somewhat established in the faith; when returning to Capernaum, his compassion for old friends, of his own calling and character, led him to gather them together that they might have an opportunity of hearing the gracious words which proceeded out of His Master's mouth, if haply they might experience a like change. **behold, many publicans and sinners**—Luke says, "a great company" (vs. 29)—**came and sat down with him and his disciples.** In all such cases the word rendered "sat" is "reclined," in allusion to the ancient mode of lying on couches at meals. **11. And when the Pharisees**—"and scribes," add Mark and Luke. **saw it, they**—"murmured" or "muttered," says Luke (5: 30). **said unto his disciples**—not venturing to put their question to Jesus Himself. **Why eateth your Master with publicans and sinners?**—(See on Luke 15:2.) **12. But when Jesus heard** [that], **he said unto them**—to the Pharisees and scribes; addressing Himself to them, though they had shrunk from addressing Him. **They that be whole need not a physician, but they that are sick**—i.e., "Ye deem yourselves whole; My mission, therefore, is not to you: The physician's business is with the sick; therefore eat I with publicans and sinners." Oh, what myriads of broken hearts, of sin-sick souls, have been bound up by this matchless saying! **13. But go ye and learn what that meaneth** (Hos. 6:6), **I will have mercy, and not sacrifice**—i.e., the one rather than the other. "Sacrifice," the chief part of the ceremonial law, is here put for a religion of literal adherence to mere rules; while "mercy" expresses

such compassion for the fallen as seeks to lift them up. The duty of keeping aloof from the polluted, in the sense of "having no fellowship with the unfruitful works of darkness," is obvious enough; but to understand this as prohibiting such intercourse with them as is necessary to their recovery, is to abuse it. This was what these pharisaical religionists did, and this is what our Lord here exposes. **for I am not come to call the righteous, but sinners** [to repentance]—The words enclosed in brackets are of doubtful authority here, and more than doubtful authority in Mark 2:17; but in Luke 5:32 they are undisputed. We have here just the former statement stripped of its figure. "The righteous" are the whole; "sinners," the sick. When Christ "called" the latter, as He did Matthew, and probably some of those publicans and sinners whom he had invited to meet Him, it was to heal them of their spiritual maladies, or save their souls: "The righteous," like those miserable self-satisfied Pharisees, "He sent empty away."

14-17. DISCOURSE ON FASTING. See on Luke 5: 33-39.

18-26. THE WOMAN WITH THE ISSUE OF BLOOD HEALED.—THE DAUGHTER OF JAIRUS RAISED TO LIFE. (= Luke 8: 40-56; Mark 5:21-43.) For the exposition, see on Mark 5:21-43.

27-34. TWO BLIND MEN, AND A DUMB DEMONIAC HEALED. These two miracles are recorded by Matthew alone. *Two Blind Men Healed* (vss. 27-31). **27. And when Jesus departed thence, two blind men followed him** [hearing, doubtless, as in a later case is expressed, "that Jesus passed by" (ch. 20:30)] **crying, and saying, Thou son of David, have mercy on us.** It is remarkable that in the only other recorded case in which the blind applied to Jesus for their sight, and obtained it, they addressed Him, over and over again, by this one Messianic title, so well known—"Son of David" (ch. 20:30). Can there be a doubt that their faith fastened on such great Messianic promises as this, "Then the eyes of the blind shall be opened . . ." (Isa. 35:5)? and if so, this appeal to Him, as the Consolation of Israel, to do His predicted office, would fall with great weight upon the ears of Jesus. **28. And when he was come into the house**—To try their faith and patience, He seems to have made them no answer. But the blind men came to Him [which, no doubt, was what He desired] **and Jesus saith unto them, Believe ye that I am able to do this? they said unto him, Yea, Lord**—Doubtless our Lord's design was not only to put their faith to the test by this question, but to deepen it, to raise their expectation of a cure, and so prepare them to receive it; and the cordial acknowledgment, so touchingly simple, which they immediately made to Him of His power to heal them, shows how entirely that object was gained. **29. Then touched he their eyes, saying, According to your faith be it unto you**—not, Receive a cure *proportioned* to your faith. but, Receive this cure as *granted to* your faith. Thus would they carry about with them, in their restored vision, a gracious seal of the faith which drew it from their compassionate Lord. **30. And their eyes were opened: and Jesus straitly charged them**—The expression is very strong, denoting great earnestness. **31. But they, when they were departed, spread abroad his fame in all that country**—(See on ch. 8:4.)

A Dumb Demoniac Healed (vss. 32-34). **32. As they went out, behold, they brought to him a dumb man possessed with a devil**—"demonized." The dumbness was not natural, but was the effect of the possession. **33. And when the devil** [demon] **was**

cast out, the dumb spake—The particulars in this case are not given; the object being simply to record the instantaneous restoration of the natural faculties on the removal of the malignant oppression of them, the form which the popular astonishment took, and the very different effect of it upon another class. **and the multitudes marvelled, saying, It was never so seen in Israel**—referring, probably, not to this case only, but to all those miraculous displays of healing power which seemed to promise a new era in the history of Israel. Probably they meant by this language to indicate, as far as they thought it safe to do so, their inclination to regard Him as the promised Messiah. **34. But the Pharisees said, He casteth out devils through the prince of the devils**—"the demons through the prince of the demons." This seems to be the first muttering of a theory of such miracles which soon became a fixed mode of calumniating them—a theory which would be ridiculous if it were not melancholy as an outburst of the darkest malignity. (See on ch. 12:24, etc.)

35–ch. 10:5. Third Galilean Circuit—Mission of the Twelve Apostles. As the Mission of the Twelve supposes the previous choice of them—of which our Evangelist gives no account, and which did not take place till a later stage of our Lord's public life—it is introduced here out of its proper place, which is after what is recorded in Luke 6: 12-19.

Third Galilean Circuit (vs. 35)—and probably the last. **35. And Jesus went about all the cities and villages, teaching in their synagogues, and preaching the gospel of the kingdom, and healing every sickness and every disease [among the people]**—The bracketed words are of more than doubtful authority here, and were probably introduced here from ch. 4:23. The language here is so identical with that used in describing the first circuit (ch. 4:23), that we may presume the work done on both occasions was much the same. It was just a further preparation of the soil, and a fresh sowing of the precious seed. (See on ch. 4:23.) To these fruitful journeyings of the Redeemer, "with healing in His wings," Peter no doubt alludes, when, in his address to the household of Cornelius, he spoke of "How God anointed Jesus of Nazareth with the Holy Ghost and with power: who *went about* doing good, and healing all that were oppressed of the devil: for God was with Him" (Acts 10:38).

Jesus, Compassionating the Multitudes, Asks Prayer for Help (vss. 36-38). He had now returned from His preaching and healing circuit, and the result, as at the close of the first one, was the gathering of a vast and motley multitude around Him. After a whole night spent in prayer, He had called His more immediate disciples, and from them had solemnly chosen the twelve; then, coming down from the mountain, on which this was transacted, to the multitudes that waited for Him below, He had addressed to them—as we take it—that discourse which bears so strong a resemblance to the Sermon on the Mount that many critics take it to be the same. (See on Luke 6:12-49; and on ch. 5, Introductory Remarks.) Soon after this, it should seem, the multitudes still hanging on Him, Jesus is touched with their wretched and helpless condition, and acts as is now to be described. **36. But when he saw the multitudes, he was moved with compassion on them, because they fainted**—This reading, however, has hardly any authority at all. The true reading doubtless is, "were harassed." **and were scattered abroad**—rather, "lying about," "abandoned," or "neglected." **as sheep, having no shep-**

herd—their pitiable condition as wearied under bodily fatigue, a vast disorganized mass, being but a faint picture of their wretchedness as the victims of pharisaic guidance; their souls uncared for, yet drawn after and hanging upon Him. This moved the Redeemer's compassion. **37. Then saith he unto his disciples, The harvest truly is plenteous**—His eye doubtless rested immediately on the Jewish field, but this he saw widening into the vast field of "the world" (ch. 13:38), teeming with souls having to be gathered to Him. **but the labourers**—men divinely qualified and called to gather them in. **38. Pray ye therefore the Lord of the harvest**—the great Lord and Proprietor of all. Cf. John 15:1, "I am the true vine, and My Father is the husbandman." **that he will send forth labourers into his harvest**—The word properly means "thrust forth"; but this emphatic sense disappears in some places, as in vs. 25, and John 10:4—"When He *putteth forth* His own sheep." (See on ch. 4:1.)

CHAPTER 10

Vss. 1-5. Mission of the Twelve Apostles. (= Mark 6:7-13; Luke 9:1-6.) The last three verses of ch. 9 form the proper introduction to the Mission of the Twelve, as is evident from the remarkable fact that the Mission of the Seventy was prefaced by the very same words. (See on Luke 10:2.) **1. And when he had called unto him his disciples, he gave them power**—The word signifies both "power," and "authority" or "right." Even if it were not evident that here both ideas are included, we find both words expressly used in the parallel passage of Luke (9:1)—"He gave them power and authority"—in other words, He both *qualified* and *authorized* them. **against**—or "over." **2. Now the names af the twelve apostles are these**—The other Evangelists enumerate the twelve in immediate connection with their appointment (Mark 3:13-19; Luke 6:13-16). But our Evangelist, not intending to record the appointment, but only the Mission of the Twelve, gives their names here. And as in the Acts (1:13) we have a list of the Eleven who met daily in the upper room with the other disciples after their Master's ascension until the day of Pentecost, we have four catalogues in all for comparison. **The first, Simon, who is called Peter**—(See on John 1:42). **and Andrew his brother; James [the son] of Zebedee, and John his brother**—named after James, as the younger of the two. **3. Philip and Bartholomew**—That this person is the same with "Nathanael of Cana in Galilee" is justly concluded for the three following reasons: First, because Bartholomew is not so properly an individual's name as a family surname; next, because not only in this list, but in Mark's and Luke's, he follows the name of "Philip," who was the instrument of bringing Nathanael first to Jesus (John 1:45); and again, when our Lord, after His resurrection, appeared at the Sea of Tiberias, "Nathanael of Cana in Galilee" is mentioned along with six others, all of them apostles, as being present (John 21:2). **Matthew the publican**—In none of the four lists of the Twelve is this apostle so branded but in his own, as if he would have all to know how deep a debtor he had been to his Lord. (See on ch. 1:3, 5, 6; 9:9.) **James the son of Alphaeus**—the same person apparently who is called *Cleopas* or *Clopas* (Luke 24:18; John 19:25); and, as he was the husband of Mary, sister to the Virgin, James the Less must have been our Lord's cousin. **and Lebbaeus, whose surname was Thaddaeus**—the same, without doubt, as "Judas the

brother of James," mentioned in both the lists of
Luke (6:16; Acts 1:13), while no one of the name
of Lebbaeus or Thaddaeus is so. It is he who in
John (14:22) is sweetly called "Judas, not Iscariot."
That he was the author of the Catholic Epistle of
"Jude," and not "the Lord's brother" (ch. 13:55),
unless these be the same, is most likely. **4. Simon
the Canaanite;** rather "Kananite," but better still,
"the Zealot," as he is called in Luke 6:15, where the
original term should not have been retained as in
our version ("Simon, called Zelotes"), but rendered
"Simon, called the Zealot." The word "Kananite"
is just the Aramaic, or Syro-Chaldaic, term for
"Zealot." Probably before his acquaintance with
Jesus, he belonged to the sect of the Zealots, who
bound themselves, as a sort of voluntary ecclesiastical police, to see that the law was not broken with
impunity. **and Judas Iscariot**—i.e., Judas of Kerioth, a town of Judah (Josh. 15:25); so called to
distinguish him from "Judas the brother of James"
(Luke 6:16). **who also betrayed him**—a note of
infamy attached to his name in all the catalogues
of the Twelve.

5-42. THE TWELVE RECEIVE THEIR INSTRUC-
TIONS. This directory divides itself into three
distinct parts. The *first* part—extending from vs. 5
to vs. 15—contains directions for the brief and
temporary mission on which they were now going
forth, with respect to the places they were to go to,
the works they were to do, the message they were
to bear, and the manner in which they were to conduct themselves. The *second* part—extending from
vs. 16 to vs. 23—contains directions of no such
limited and temporary nature, but opens out into
the permanent exercise of the Gospel ministry.
The *third* part—extending from vs. 24 to vs. 42—is
of wider application still, reaching not only to the
ministry of the Gospel in every age, but to the
service of Christ in the widest sense. *It is a strong
confirmation of this threefold division, that each
part closes with the words,* "VERILY I SAY UNTO
YOU (vss. 15, 23, 42).

Directions for the Present Mission (vss. 5-15).
**5. These twelve Jesus sent forth, and commanded
them, saying, Go not into the way of the Gentiles,
and into any city of the Samaritans enter ye not**—
The Samaritans were Gentiles by blood; but being
the descendants of those whom the king of Assyria
had transported from the East to supply the place of
the ten tribes carried captive, they had adopted the
religion of the Jews, though with admixtures of
their own: and, as the nearest neighbors of the Jews,
they occupied a place intermediate between them
and the Gentiles. Accordingly, when this prohibition was to be taken off, on the effusion of the Spirit
at Pentecost, the apostles were told that they should
be Christ's witnesses first "in Jerusalem, and in all
Judea," then "in Samaria," and lastly, "unto the
uttermost part of the earth" (Acts 1:8). **6. But go
rather to the lost sheep of the house of Israel**—Until
Christ's death, which broke down the middle wall
of Partition (Eph. 2:14), the Gospel commission was
to the Jews only, who, though the visible people of
God, were "lost sheep," not merely in the sense
which all sinners are (Isa. 53:6; I Pet. 2:25; cf. with
Luke 19:10), but as abandoned and left to wander
from the right way by faithless shepherds (Jer. 50:6,
17; Ezek. 34:2-6, etc.). **7. And as ye go, preach,
saying, The kingdom of heaven is at hand**—(See on
ch. 3:2). **8. Heal the sick, cleanse the lepers, [raise
the dead,] cast out devils**—(The bracketed clause—
"raise the dead"—is wanting in many MSS.). Here
we have the first communication of supernatural

power by Christ Himself to His followers—thus anticipating the gifts of Pentecost. And right royally
does He dispense it. **freely ye have received, freely
give**—Divine saying, divinely said! (Cf. Deut. 15:
10, 11; Acts 3:6)—an apple of gold in a setting of
silver (Prov. 25:11.) It reminds us of that other
golden saying of our Lord, rescued from oblivion
by Paul, "It is more blessed to give than to receive"
(Acts 20:35). Who can estimate what the world
owes to such sayings, and with what beautiful foliage and rich fruit such seeds have covered, and will
yet cover, this earth! **9. Provide neither gold, nor
silver, nor brass in**—for—**your purses**—lit., "your
belts," in which they kept their money. **10. Nor
scrip for your journey**—the bag used by travelers for
holding provisions. **neither two coats**—or tunics,
worn next the skin. The meaning is, Take no
change of dress, no additional articles. **neither
shoes**—i.e., change of them. **nor yet staves**—The
received text here has "a staff," but our version follows another reading, "staves," which is found in
the received text of Luke (9:3). The true reading,
however, evidently is "a staff"—meaning, that they
were not to procure even that much expressly for
this missionary journey, but to go with what they
had. No doubt it was the misunderstanding of this
that gave rise to the reading "staves" in so many
MSS. Even if this reading were genuine, it could
not mean "more than one"; for who, as ALFORD
well asks, would think of taking a spare staff? **for
the workman is worthy of his meat**—his "food" or
"maintenance"; a principle which, being universally
recognized in secular affairs, is here authoritatively
applied to the services of the Lord's workmen, and
by Paul repeatedly and touchingly employed in his
appeals to the churches (Rom. 15:27; I Cor. 9:11;
Gal. 6:6), and once as "scripture" (I Tim. 5:18).
11. And into whatsoever city or town—town or village. **ye shall enter** [carefully] **inquire who in it is
worthy**—or "meet" to entertain such messengers;
not in point of rank, of course, but of congenial
disposition. **and there abide till ye go thence**—not
shifting about, as if discontented, but returning the
welcome given with a courteous, contented, accommodating disposition. **12. And when ye come into
an house**—or "the house," but it means not the
worthy house, but the house ye first enter, to try if
it be worthy. **salute it**—show it the usual civilities.
13. And if the house be worthy—showing this by
giving you a welcome—**let your peace come upon it**
—This is best explained by the injunction to the
Seventy, "And into whatsoever house ye enter, first
say, Peace be to this house" (Luke 10:5). This was
the ancient salutation of the East, and it prevails
to this day. But from the lips of Christ and His
messengers, it means something far higher, both in
the gift and the giving of it, than in the current
salutation. (See on John 14:27.) **but if it be not
worthy, let your peace return to you**—If your peace
finds a shut, instead of an open, door in the heart of
any household, take it back to yourselves, who know
how to value it; and it will taste the sweeter to you
for having been offered, even though rejected. **14.
And whosoever shall not receive you, nor hear your
words, when ye depart out of that house or city**—
for possibly a whole town might not furnish one
"worthy." **shake off the dust of your feet**—"for a
testimony against them," as Mark and Luke add.
By this symbolical action they vividly shook themselves from all *connection* with such, and all
responsibility for the guilt of rejecting them and their
message. Such symbolical actions were common in
ancient times, even among others than the Jews,

as strikingly appears in Pilate (ch. 27:24). And even to this day it prevails in the East. **15. Verily I say unto you, It shall be more tolerable**—more bearable—**for Sodom and Gomorrah in the day of judgment, than for that city**—Those Cities of the Plain, which were given to the flames for their loathsome impurities, shall be treated as less criminal, we are here taught, than those places which, though morally respectable, reject the Gospel message and affront those that bear it.

Directions for the Future and Permanent Exercise of the Christian Ministry (vss. 16-23). **16. Behold, I send you forth**—The "I" here is emphatic, holding up Himself as the Fountain of the Gospel ministry, as He is also the Great Burden of it. **as sheep**—defenseless—**in the midst of wolves**—ready to make a prey of us (John 10:12). To be left exposed, as sheep to wolves, would have been startling enough; but that the sheep should be *sent* among the wolves would sound strange indeed. No wonder this announcement begins with the exclamation, "Behold." **be ye therefore wise as serpents, and harmless as doves**—Wonderful combination this! Alone, the wisdom of the serpent is mere cunning, and the harmlessness of the dove little better than weakness: but in combination, the wisdom of the serpent would save them from unnecessary exposure to danger; the harmlessness of the dove, from sinful expedients to escape it. In the apostolic age of Christianity, how harmoniously were these qualities displayed! Instead of the fanatical thirst for martyrdom, to which a later age gave birth, there was a manly combination of unflinching zeal and calm discretion, before which nothing was able to stand. **17. But beware of men; for they will deliver you up to the councils**—the local courts, used here for civil magistrates in general. **and they will scourge you in their synagogues**—By this is meant persecution at the hands of the ecclesiastics. **18. And ye shall be brought before governors**—provincial rulers—**and kings**—the highest tribunals—**for my sake, for a testimony against them**—rather, "to them," in order to bear testimony to the truth and its glorious effects. **and [to] the Gentiles**—a hint that their message would not long be confined to the lost sheep of the house of Israel. The Acts of the Apostles are the best commentary on these warnings. **19. But when they deliver you up, take no thought**—be not solicitous or anxious. (See on ch. 6:25.) **how or what ye shall speak**—i.e., either in what *manner* ye shall make your defense, or of what *matter* it shall consist—**for it shall be given you in that same hour what ye shall speak**—(See Exod. 4:12; Jer. 1:7). **20. For it is not ye that speak, but the Spirit of your Father which speaketh in you**—How remarkably this has been verified, the whole history of persecution thrillingly proclaims—from the Acts of the Apostles to the latest martyrology. **21. And the brother shall deliver up the brother to death, and the father the child: and the children shall rise up against their parents, and cause them to be put to death**—for example, by lodging information against them with the authorities. The deep and virulent hostility of the old nature and life to the new—as of Belial to Christ—was to issue in awful wrenches of the dearest ties; and the disciples, in the prospect of their cause and themselves being launched upon society, are here prepared for the worst. **22. And ye shall be hated of all men for my name's sake**—The universality of this hatred would make it evident to them, that since it would not be owing to any temporary excitement, local virulence, or personal prejudice, on the part of their enemies, so no

amount of discretion on their part, consistent with entire fidelity to the truth, would avail to stifle that enmity—though it might soften its violence, and in some cases avert the outward manifestations of it. **but he that endureth to the end shall be saved**—a great saying, repeated, in connection with similar warnings, in the prophecy of the destruction of Jerusalem (ch. 24:13); and often reiterated by the apostle as a warning against "drawing back unto perdition" (Heb. 3:6, 13; 6:4-6; 10:23, 26-29, 38, 39; etc.). As "drawing back unto perdition" is merely the palpable evidence of the want of "root" from the first in the Christian profession (Luke 8:13), so "enduring to the end" is just the proper evidence of its reality and solidity. **23. But when they persecute you in this city, flee ye into another**—"into the other." This, though applicable to all time, and exemplified by our Lord Himself once and again, had special reference to the brief opportunities which Israel was to have of "knowing the time of His visitations." **for verily I say unto you**—what will startle you, but at the same time show you the solemnity of your mission, and the need of economizing the time for it. **Ye shall not have gone over**—Ye shall in nowise have completed—**the cities of Israel, till the Son of man be come**—To understand this—as LANGE and others do—in the first instance, of Christ's own peregrinations, as if He had said, "Waste not your time upon hostile places, for I Myself will be after you ere your work be over"—seems almost trifling. "The coming of the Son of man" has a fixed doctrinal sense, here referring immediately to the crisis of Israel's history as the visible kingdom of God, when Christ was to come and judge it; when "the wrath would come upon it to the uttermost"; and when, on the ruins of Jerusalem and the old economy, He would establish His own kingdom. This, in the uniform language of Scripture, is more immediately "the coming of the Son of man," "the day of vengeance of our God" (ch. 16:28; 24:27, 34; cf. with Heb. 10:25; Jas. 5:7-9)—but only as being such a lively anticipation of His second coming for vengeance and deliverance. So understood, it is parallel with ch. 24:14 (on which see).

Directions for the Service of Christ in Its Widest Sense (vss. 24-42). **24. The disciple is not above his master**—teacher. **nor the servant above his lord**—another maxim which our Lord repeats in various connections (Luke 6:40; John 13:16; 15:20). **25. It is enough for the disciple that he be as his master, and the servant as his lord. If they have called the master of the house Beelzebub**—All the Greek MSS. write "Beelzebul," which undoubtedly is the right form of this word. The other reading came in no doubt from the Old Testament "Baalzebub," the god of Ekron (II Kings 1:2), which it was designed to express. As all idolatry was regarded as devil worship (Lev. 17:7; Deut. 32:17; Ps. 106:37; I Cor. 10:20), so there seems to have been something peculiarly satanic about the worship of this hateful god, which caused his name to be a synonym of Satan. Though we nowhere read that our Lord was actually called "Beelzebul," He was charged with being in league with Satan under that hateful name (ch. 12:24, 26), and more than once Himself was charged with "having a devil" or "demon" (Mark 3:30; John 7:20; 8:48). Here it is used to denote the most opprobrious language which could be applied by one to another. **how much more shall they call them of his household**—"the inmates." Three relations in which Christ stands to His people are here mentioned: He is their Teacher—they His disciples; He is their Lord—they His servants; He is the Master of the household—they its inmates. In all these relations, He says here, He and they are so bound up together that they cannot look to fare better than He, and should think it enough if they fare no worse. **26. Fear them not therefore: for there is nothing covered, that shall not be revealed; and hid, that shall not be known** i.e., There is no use, and no need, of concealing anything; right and wrong, truth and error, are about to come into open and deadly collision; and the day is coming when all hidden things shall be disclosed, everything seen as it is, and every one have his due (I Cor. 4:5). **27. What I tell you in darkness**—in the privacy of a teaching for which men are not yet ripe—**that speak ye in the light**—for when ye go forth all will be ready—**and what ye hear in the ear, that preach ye upon the housetops**—Give free and fearless utterance to all that I have taught you while yet with you. *Objection:* But this may cost us our life? *Answer:* It may, but there their power ends: **28. And fear not them which kill the body, but are not able to kill the soul**—In Luke 12:4, "and after that have no more that they can do." **but rather fear him**—In Luke this is peculiarly solemn, "I will forewarn you whom ye shall fear," even Him—**which is able to destroy both soul and body in hell**—A decisive proof this that there is a hell for the body as well as the soul in the eternal world; in other words, that the torment that awaits the lost will have elements of suffering adapted to the *material* as well as the spiritual part of our nature, both of which, we are assured, will exist for ever. In the corresponding warning contained in Luke, Jesus calls His disciples "My friends," as if He had felt that such sufferings constituted a bond of peculiar tenderness between Him and them. **29. Are not two sparrows sold for a farthing?**—In Luke (12:6) it is "five sparrows for two farthings"; so that, if the purchaser took two farthings' worth, he got one in addition—of such small value were they. **and one of them shall not fall on the ground**—exhausted or killed—**without your Father**—"Not one of them is forgotten before God," as it is in Luke. **30. But the very hairs of your head are all numbered**—See Luke 21:18 (and cf. for the language I Sam. 14:45; Acts 27:34). **31. Fear ye not therefore, ye are of more value than many sparrows**—Was ever language of such simplicity felt to carry such weight as this does? But here lies much of the charm and power of our Lord's teaching. **32. Whosoever therefore shall confess me before men**—despising the shame—**him will I confess also before my Father which is in heaven**—I will not be ashamed of him, but will own him before the most august of all assemblies. **33. But whosoever shall deny me before men, him will I also deny before my Father which is in heaven**—before that same assembly: "He shall have from Me his own treatment of Me on the earth." (But see on ch. 16:27.) **34. Think not that I am come to send peace on earth: I came not to send peace, but a sword**—strife, discord, conflict; deadly opposition between eternally hostile principles, penetrating into and rending asunder the dearest ties. **35. For I am come to set a man at variance against his father, and the daughter against her mother, and the daughter-in-law against her mother-in-law**—(See on Luke 12:51-53). **36. And a man's foes shall be they of his own household**—This saying, which is quoted, as is the whole verse, from Micah 7:6, is but an extension of the Psalmist's complaint (Ps. 41:9; 55: 12-14), which had its most affecting illustration in the treason of Judas against our Lord Himself (John 13:18; Matt. 26:48-50). Hence would arise the

necessity of a choice between Christ and the nearest relations, which would put them to the severest test. **37. He that loveth father or mother more than me, is not worthy of me; and he that loveth son or daughter more than me, is not worthy of me**—(Cf. Deut. 33:9). As the preference of the one would, in the case supposed, necessitate the abandonment of the other, our Lord here, with a sublime, yet awful self-respect, asserts His own claims to supreme affection. **38. And he that taketh not his cross, and followeth after me, is not worthy of me**—a saying which our Lord once and again emphatically reiterates (ch. 16:24; Luke 9:23; 14:27). We have become so accustomed to this expression—"taking up one's cross"—in the sense of "being prepared for trials in general for Christ's sake," that we are apt to lose sight of its primary and proper sense here—"a preparedness to go forth even to crucifixion," as when our Lord had to bear His own cross on His way to Calvary—a saying the more remarkable as our Lord had not as yet given a hint that He would die this death, nor was crucifixion a Jewish mode of capital punishment. **39. He that findeth his life shall lose it: and he that loseth his life for my sake shall find it**—another of those pregnant sayings which our Lord so often reiterates (ch. 16:25; Luke 17:33; John 12:25). The pith of such paradoxical maxims depends on the double sense attached to the word "life"—a lower and a higher, the natural and the spiritual, the temporal and eternal. An entire sacrifice of the lower, with all its relationships and interests—or, a willingness to make it which is the same thing—is indispensable to the preservation of the higher life; and he who cannot bring himself to surrender the one for the sake of the other shall eventually lose both. **40. He that receiveth**—entertaineth—**you, receiveth me; and he that receiveth me, receiveth him that sent me**—As the treatment which an ambassador receives is understood and regarded as expressing the light in which he that sends him is viewed, so, says our Lord here, "Your authority is Mine, as Mine is My Father's." **41. He that receiveth a prophet**—one divinely commissioned to deliver a message from heaven. Predicting future events was no necessary part of a prophet's office, especially as the word is used in the New Testament. **in the name of a prophet**—for his office' sake and love to his master. (See II Kings 4:9, 10.) **shall receive a prophet's reward**—What an encouragement to those who are not prophets! (See John 3:5-8.) **and he that receiveth a righteous man in the name of a righteous man**—from sympathy with his character and esteem for himself as such—**shall receive a righteous man's reward**—for he must himself have the seed of righteousness who has any real sympathy with it and complacency in him who possesses it. **42. And whosoever shall give to drink unto one of these little ones**—Beautiful epithet! Originally taken from Zechariah 13:7. The reference is to their lowliness in spirit, their littleness in the eyes of an undiscerning world, while high in Heaven's esteem. **a cup of cold water only**—meaning, the smallest service. **in the name of a disciple**—or, as it is in Mark (9:41), because ye are Christ's: from love to Me, and to him from his connection with Me. **verily I say unto you, he shall in no wise lose his reward**—There is here a descending climax—"a prophet," "a righteous man," "a little one"; signifying that however low we come down in our services to those that are Christ's, all that is done for His sake, and that bears the stamp of love to His blessed name, shall be divinely appreciated and owned and rewarded.

CHAPTER 11

Vss. 1-19. The Imprisoned Baptist's Message to his Master—The Reply, and Discourse, on the Departure of the Messengers, Regarding John and His Mission. (=Luke 7:18-35). **1. And it came to pass, when Jesus had made an end of commanding his**—rather, "the"—**twelve disciples, he departed thence to teach and to preach in their cities** —This was scarcely a fourth circuit—if we may judge from the less formal way in which it was expressed —but, perhaps, a set of visits paid to certain places, either not reached at all before, or too rapidly passed through, in order to fill up the time till the return of the Twelve. As to their labors, nothing is said of them by our Evangelist. But Luke (9:6) says, "They departed, and went through, the towns," or "villages," "preaching the Gospel, and healing everywhere." Mark (6:12, 13), as usual, is more explicit: "And they went out, and preached that men should repent. And they cast out many devils [demons], and anointed with oil many that were sick, and healed them." Though this "anointing with oil" was not mentioned in our Lord's instructions—at least in any of the records of them—we know it to have been practiced long after this in the apostolic Church (see Jas. 5:14, and cf. Mark 6:12, 13)—not *medicinally,* but as a sign of the healing virtue which was communicated by their hands, and a symbol of something still more precious. It was *unction,* indeed, but, as BENGEL remarks, it was something very different from what Romanists call *extreme* unction. He adds, what is very probable, that they do not appear to have carried the oil about with them, but, as the Jews used oil as a medicine, to have employed it just as they found it with the sick, in their own higher way. **2. Now when John had heard in the prison**—For the account of this imprisonment, see on Mark 6:17-20. **the works of Christ, he sent . . .**—On the whole passage, see on Luke 7:18-35.

20-30. Outburst of Feeling, Suggested to the Mind of Jesus by the Result of his Labors in Galilee. The connection of this with what goes before it and the similarity of its tone make it evident, we think, that it was delivered on the same occasion, and that it is but a new and more comprehensive series of reflections in the same strain. **20. Then began he to upbraid the cities wherein most of his mighty works were done, because they repented not. 21. Woe unto thee, Chorazin!**—not elsewhere mentioned, but it must have lain near Capernaum. **woe unto thee, Bethsaida**—"fishing-house," a fishing station—on the western side of the Sea of Galilee, and to the north of Capernaum; the birthplace of three of the apostles—the brothers Andrew and Peter, and Philip. These two cities appear to be singled out to denote the whole region in which they lay—a region favored with the Redeemer's presence, teaching, and works above every other. **for if the mighty works** —the miracles—**which were done in you had been done in Tyre and Sidon**—ancient and celebrated commercial cities, on the northeastern shores of the Mediterranean Sea, lying north of Palestine, and the latter the northernmost. As their wealth and prosperity engendered luxury and its concomitant evils —irreligion and moral degeneracy—their overthrow was repeatedly foretold in ancient prophecy, and once and again fulfilled by victorious enemies. Yet they were rebuilt, and at this time were in a flourishing condition. **they would have repented long ago in sackcloth and ashes**—remarkable language, showing that they had done less violence to conscience, and so, in God's sight, were less criminal than the region here spoken of. **22. But I say unto you, It shall be more tolerable**—more endurable—**for Tyre and Sidon at the day of judgment, than for you. 23. And thou, Capernaum**—(see on ch. 4:13)—**which art exalted unto heaven**—Not even of Chorazin and Bethsaida is this said. For since at Capernaum Jesus had His stated abode during the whole period of His public life which He spent in Galilee, it was *the most favored spot upon earth,* the most exalted in privilege. **shall be brought down to hell: for if the mighty works, which have been done in thee, had been done in Sodom**—destroyed for its pollutions—**it would have remained until this day**—having done no such violence to conscience, and so incurred speakably less guilt. **24. But I say unto you, That it shall be more tolerable for the land of Sodom in the day of judgment, than for thee**—"It has been indeed," says Dr. STANLEY, "more tolerable, in one sense, in the day of its earthly judgment, for the land of Sodom than for Capernaum; for the name, and perhaps even the remains of Sodom are still to be found on the shores of the Dead Sea; while that of Capernaum has, on the Lake of Gennesareth, been utterly lost." But the judgment of which our Lord here speaks is still future; a judgment not on material cities, but their responsible inhabitants—a judgment final and irretrievable. **25. At that time Jesus answered and said** —We are not to understand by this, that the previous discourse had been concluded, and that this is a record only of something said about the same period. For the connection is most close, and the word "answered"—which, when there is no one to answer, refers to something just before said, or rising in the mind of the speaker in consequence of something said—confirms this. What Jesus here "answered" evidently was the melancholy results of His ministry, lamented over in the foregoing verses. It is as if He had said, "Yes; but there is a brighter side to the picture; even in those who have rejected the message of eternal life, it is the pride of their own hearts only which has blinded them, and the glory of the truth does but the more appear in their inability to receive it. Nor have all rejected it even here; souls thirsting for salvation have drawn water with joy from the wells of salvation; the weary have found rest; the hungry have been filled with good things, while the rich have been sent empty away." **I thank thee**—rather, "I assent to thee." But this is not strong enough. The idea of *"full"* or "cordial" concurrence is conveyed by the preposition. The thing expressed is adoring acquiescence, holy satisfaction with that law of the divine procedure about to be mentioned. And as, when He afterwards uttered the same words, He "exulted in spirit" (see on Luke 10:21), probably He did the same now, though not recorded. **O Father, Lord of heaven and earth**—He so styles His Father here, to signify that from Him of right emanates all such high arrangements. **because thou hast hid these things**— the knowledge of these saving truths. **from the wise and prudent**—The former of these terms points to the men who pride themselves upon their speculative or philosophical attainments; the latter to the men of worldly shrewdness—the clever, the sharp-witted, the men of affairs. The distinction is a natural one, and was well understood. (See I Cor. 1: 19, etc.) But why had the Father hid from such the things that belonged to their peace, and why did Jesus so emphatically set His seal to this arrangement? Because it is not for the offending and revolted to speak or to speculate, but to listen to Him from whom we have broken loose, that we may learn whether there be any recovery for us at all; and if there be, on what principles—of what nature —to what ends. To bring our own "wisdom and prudence" to such questions is impertinent and presumptuous; and if the truth regarding them, or the glory of it, be "hid" from us, it is but a fitting retribution, to which all the right-minded will set their seal along with Jesus. **hast revealed them unto babes**—to babelike men; men of unassuming docility, men who, conscious that they know nothing, and have no right to sit in judgment on the things that belong to their peace, determine simply to "hear what God the Lord will speak." Such are well called "babes." (See Heb. 5:13; I Cor. 13:11; 14:20, etc.) **26. Even so, Father; for so it seemed good**—the emphatic and chosen term for expressing any object of divine complacency; whether Christ Himself (see on ch. 3:17), or God's gracious eternal arrangements (see on Phil. 2:13)—**in thy sight**—This is just a sublime echo of the foregoing words; as if Jesus, when He uttered them, had paused to reflect on it, and as if the glory of it—not so much in the light of its own reasonableness as of God's absolute will that so it should be—had filled His soul. **27. All things are delivered unto me of my Father**—He does not say, They are *revealed*—as to one who knew them not, and was an entire stranger to them save as they were discovered to Him—but, They are "delivered over," or "committed," to Me of My Father; meaning the whole administration of the kingdom of grace. So in John 3:35, "The Father loveth the Son, and hath given all things into His hand" (see on that verse). But though the "all things" in both these passages refer properly to the kingdom of grace, they of course include all things necessary to the full execution of that trust—that is, *unlimited* power. (So ch. 28:18; John 17:2; Eph. 1:22). **and no man knoweth the Son, but the Father; neither knoweth any man the Father, save the Son, and he to whomsoever the Son will**—willeth —**to reveal him**—What a saying is this, that "the Father and the Son are mutually and exclusively known to each other!" A higher claim to equality with the Father cannot be conceived. Either, then, we have here one of the revolting assumptions ever uttered, or the proper divinity of Christ should to Christians be beyond dispute. "But, alas for me!" may some burdened soul, sighing for relief, here exclaim. If it be thus with us, what can any poor creature do but lie down in passive despair, unless he could dare to hope that *he* may be one of the favored class "to whom the Son is willing to reveal the Father." But nay. This testimony to the sovereignty of that gracious "will," on which alone men's salvation depends, is designed but to reveal the source and enhance the glory of it when once imparted—not to paralyze or shut the soul up in despair. Hear, accordingly, what follows: **28. Come unto me, all ye that labour and are heavy laden, and I will give you rest**—Incomparable, ravishing sounds these—if ever such were heard in this weary, groaning world! What gentleness, what sweetness is there in the very style of the invitation—"Hither to Me"; and in the words, "All ye that toil and are burdened," the universal wretchedness of man is depicted, on both its sides—the *active* and the *passive* forms of it. **29. Take my yoke upon you**—the yoke of subjection to Jesus—**and learn of me; for I am meek and lowly in heart: and ye shall find rest unto your souls**—As Christ's willingness to empty Himself to the uttermost of His Father's requirements was the spring of

ineffable repose to His own Spirit, so in the same track does He invite all to follow Him, with the assurance of the same experience. **30. For my yoke is easy, and my burden is light**—Matchless paradox, even among the paradoxically couched maxims in which our Lord delights! That rest which the soul experiences when once safe under Christ's wing makes all yokes easy, all burdens light.

CHAPTER 12

Vss. 1-8. PLUCKING CORN-EARS ON THE SABBATH DAY. (=Mark. 2:23-28; Luke 6:1-5.) The season of the year when this occurred is determined by the event itself. Ripe corn-ears are found in the fields only just before harvest. The barley harvest seems clearly intended here, at the close of our March and beginning of our April. It coincided with the Passover season, as the wheat harvest with Pentecost. But in Luke (6:1) we have a still more definite note of time, if we could be certain of the meaning of the peculiar term which he employs to express it. "It came to pass [he says] on the sabbath, which was the *first-second*," for that is the proper rendering of the word, and not "the second sabbath after the first," as in our version. Of the various conjectures what this may mean, that of SCALIGER is the most approved, and, as we think, the freest from difficulty, viz., the first sabbath after the second day of the Passover; i.e., the first of the seven sabbaths which were to be reckoned from the second day of the Passover, which was itself a sabbath, until the next feast, the feast of Pentecost (Lev. 23:15, 16; Deut. 16:9, 10). In this case, the day meant by the Evangelist is the first of those seven sabbaths intervening between Passover and Pentecost. And if we are right in regarding the "feast" mentioned in John 5:1 as a *Passover,* and consequently the second during our Lord's public ministry (see on that passage), this plucking of the ears of corn must have occurred immediately after the scene and the discourse recorded in John 5, which, doubtless, would induce our Lord to hasten His departure for the north, to avoid the wrath of the Pharisees, which He had kindled at Jerusalem. Here, accordingly, we find Him in the fields—on His way probably to Galilee. **1. At that time Jesus went on the sabbath day through the corn**—"the cornfields" (Mark 2:23; Luke 6:1). **and his disciples were an hungered**—not as one may be before his regular meals; but evidently from shortness of provisions: for Jesus defends their plucking the corn-ears and eating them on the plea of *necessity.* **and began to pluck the ears of corn, and to eat**—"rubbing them in their hands" (Luke 6:1). **2. But when the Pharisees saw it, they said unto him, Behold, thy disciples do that which is not lawful to do upon the sabbath day**—The act itself was expressly permitted (Deut. 23:25). But as being "servile work," which was prohibited on the sabbath day, it was regarded as sinful. **3. But he said unto them, Have ye not read**—or, as Mark has it, "Have ye never read." **what David did** (1 Sam. 21:1-6)—**when he was an hungered, and they that were with him; 4. How he entered into the house of God, and did eat the showbread, which was not lawful for him to eat, neither for them which were with him, but only for the priests?**—No example could be more apposite than this. The man after God's own heart, of whom the Jews ever boasted, when suffering in God's cause and straitened for provisions, asked and obtained from the high priest what, according to the law, it was illegal for anyone save the priests to touch. Mark (2:26) says this occurred "in the days of Abiathar the high priest." But this means not during his high priesthood—for it was under that of his father Ahimelech—but simply, in his time. Ahimelech was soon succeeded by Abiathar, whose connection with David, and prominence during his reign, may account for his name, rather than his father's, being here introduced. Yet there is not a little confusion in what is said of these priests in different parts of the Old Testament. Thus he is called both the son of the father of Ahimelech (I Sam. 22:20; II Sam. 8:17); and Ahimelech is called Ahiah (I Sam. 14:3), and Abimelech (I Chron. 18:16). **5. Or have ye not read in the law, how that on the sabbath days the priests in the temple profane the sabbath**—by doing "servile work"—**and are blameless?**—The double offerings required on the sabbath day (Num. 28:9) could not be presented, and the new-baked showbread (Lev. 24:5; I Chron. 9:32) could not be prepared and presented every sabbath morning, without a good deal of servile work on the part of the priests; not to speak of circumcision, which, when the child's eighth day happened to fall on a sabbath, had to be performed by the priests on that day. (See on John 7:22, 23). **6. But I say unto you, That in this place is one greater than the temple**—or rather, according to the reading which is best supported, "something greater." The argument stands thus: "The ordinary rules for the observance of the sabbath give way before the requirements of the temple; but there are rights here before which the temple itself must give way." Thus indirectly, but not the less decidedly, does our Lord put in His own claims to consideration in this question—claims to be presently put in even more nakedly. **7. But if ye had known what this meaneth, I will have mercy, and not sacrifice**—(Hos. 6:6; Mic. 6:6-8, etc.). See on ch. 9:13. **ye would not have condemned the guiltless**—i.e., Had ye understood the great principle of all religion, which the Scripture everywhere recognizes—that ceremonial observances must give way before moral duties, and particularly the necessities of nature—ye would have refrained from these captious complaints against men who in this matter are blameless. But our Lord added a specific application of this great principle to the law of the sabbath, preserved only in Mark: "And he said unto them, the sabbath was made for man, and not man for the sabbath" (Mark 2:27). A glorious and far-reaching maxim, alike for the permanent establishment of the sabbath and the true freedom of its observance. **8. For the Son of man is Lord even of the sabbath day**—In what sense now is the Son of man Lord of the sabbath day? Not surely to abolish it—that surely were a strange lordship, especially just after saying that it was made or instituted for MAN—but to *own* it, to *interpret* it, to *preside over* it, and to *ennoble* it, by merging it in the "Lord's Day" (Rev. 1:10), breathing into it an air of liberty and love necessarily unknown before, and thus making it the nearest resemblance to the eternal sabbatism.

9-21. THE HEALING OF A WITHERED HAND ON THE SABBATH DAY, AND RETIREMENT OF JESUS TO AVOID DANGER. (=Mark 3:1-12; Luke 6:6-11). *Healing of a Withered Hand* (vss. 9-14). **9. And when he was departed thence**—but "on another sabbath" (Luke 6:6)—**he went into their synagogue**—and taught," He had now, no doubt, arrived in Galilee; but this, it would appear, did not occur at Capernaum, for after it was over, He "withdrew Himelf," it is said "*to the sea*" (Mark 3:7), whereas Capernaum was *at* the sea. **And, behold, there was a man which had his hand withered**—disabled by

paralysis (as in I Kings 13:4). It was his right hand, as Luke graphically notes. **And they asked him, saying, Is it lawful to heal on the sabbath days? that they might accuse him**—Matthew and Luke say they "watched Him whether He would heal on the sabbath day." They were now come to the length of dogging His steps, to collect materials for a charge of impiety against Him. It is probable that it was to their *thoughts* rather than their words that Jesus addressed Himself in what follows. **11. And he said unto them, What man shall there be among you that shall have one sheep, and if it fall into a pit on the sabbath day, will he not lay hold on it, and lift it out? 12. How much then is a man better than a sheep?**—Resistless appeal! "A righteous man regardeth the life of his beast" (Prov. 12:10), and would instinctively rescue it from death or suffering on the sabbath day; how much more his nobler fellow man! But the reasoning, as given in the other two Gospels, is singularly striking: "But He knew their thoughts, and said to the man which had the withered hand, Rise up, and stand forth in the midst. And he arose and stood forth. Then said Jesus unto them, I will ask you one thing: Is it lawful on the sabbath days to do good, or to do evil? to save life or to destroy it?" (Luke 6:8, 9), or as in Mark (3:4), "to kill?" He thus shuts them up to this startling alternative: "Not to do good, when it is in the power of our hand to do it, is to do evil; not to save life, when we can, is to kill"—and must the letter of the sabbath rest be kept at this expense? This unexpected thrust shut their mouths. By this great ethical principle our Lord, we see, held Himself bound, as man. But here we must turn to Mark, whose graphic details make the second Gospel so exceedingly precious. "When He had looked round about on them with anger, being grieved for the hardness of their hearts, He saith unto the man" (Mark 3:5). This is one of the very few passages in the Gospel history which reveal our Lord's *feelings*. How holy this anger was appears from the "grief" which mingled with it at "the hardness of their hearts." **13. Then saith he to the man, Stretch forth thine hand. And he stretched it forth**—the power to obey going forth with the word of command. **and it was restored whole, like as the other**—The poor man, having faith in this wonderful Healer—which no doubt the whole scene would singularly help to strengthen—disregarded the proud and venomous Pharisees, and thus gloriously put them to shame. **14. Then the Pharisees went out, and held a council against him, how they might destroy him**—This is the first explicit mention of their murderous designs against our Lord. Luke (6:11) says, they were filled with madness, and communed one with another what they might do to Jesus." But their doubt was not, *whether* to get rid of Him, but *how* to compass it. Mark (3:6), as usual, is more definite: "The Pharisees went forth, and straightway took counsel with the Herodians against Him, how they might destroy Him." These Herodians were supporters of Herod's dynasty, created by Cæsar—a political rather than religious party. The Pharisees regarded them as untrue to their religion and country. But here we see them combining together against Christ as a common enemy. So on a subsequent occasion (ch. 22:15, 16).

Jesus Retires to Avoid Danger (vss. 15-21). **15. But when Jesus knew it, he withdrew himself from thence**—whither, our Evangelist says not; but Mark (3:7) says "it was *to the sea*"—to some distance, no doubt, from the scene of the miracle, the madness, and the plotting just recorded. **and great multitudes followed him, and he healed them all**—Mark gives the following interesting details: "A great multitude from Galilee followed Him, and from Judea and from Jerusalem, and from Idumea, and from beyond Jordan; and they about Tyre and Sidon, a great multitude, when they had heard what great things He did, came unto Him. And He spake to His disciples, that a small ship should wait on Him because of the multitude, lest they should throng Him. For He had healed many; insomuch that they pressed upon Him for to touch Him, as many as had plagues. And unclean spirits, when they saw Him, fell down before Him, and cried, saying, Thou art the Son of God. And He straitly charged them that they should not make Him known" (Mark 3:7-12). How glorious this extorted homage to the Son of God! But as this was not the time, so neither were they the fitting preachers, as BENGEL says. (See on Mark 1:25, and cf. Jas. 2:19.) Coming back now to our Evangelist: after saying, "He healed them all," he continues: **16. And charged them**—the healed—**that they should not make him known**—(See on ch. 8:4). **17. That it might be fulfilled which was spoken by Esaias the prophet, saying** (Isa. 42:1). **18. Behold my servant, whom I have chosen; my beloved, in whom my soul is well pleased: I will put my Spirit upon him, and he shall show judgment to the Gentiles. 19. He shall not strive nor cry; neither shall any man hear his voice in the streets. 20. A bruised reed shall he not break, and smoking flax shall he not quench, till he send forth judgment unto victory**—"unto truth," says the Hebrew original, and the LXX also. But our Evangelist merely seizes the spirit, instead of the letter of the prediction in this point. The grandeur and completeness of Messiah's victories would prove, it seems, not more wonderful than the unobtrusive noiselessness with which they were to be achieved. And whereas one rough touch will break a bruised reed, and quench the flickering, smoking flax, His it should be, with matchless tenderness, love, and skill, to lift up the meek, to strengthen the weak hands and confirm the feeble knees, to comfort all that mourn, to say to them that are of a fearful heart, Be strong, fear not. **21. And in his name shall the Gentiles trust**—Part of His present audience were Gentiles—from Tyre and Sidon—first fruits of the great Gentile harvest contemplated in the prophecy.

22-37. A BLIND AND DUMB DEMONIAC HEALED, AND REPLY TO THE MALIGNANT EXPLANATION PUT UPON IT. (=Mark 3:20-30; Luke 11:14-23.) The precise time of this section is uncertain. Judging from the statements with which Mark introduces it, we should conclude that it was when our Lord's popularity was approaching its zenith, and so before the feeding of the five thousand. But, on the other hand, the advanced state of the charges brought against our Lord, and the plainness of His warnings and denunciations in reply, seem to favor the later period at which Luke introduces it. "And the multitude," says Mark (3:20, 21), "cometh together again," referring back to the immense gathering which Mark had before recorded (ch. 2:2)—"so that they could not so much as eat bread. And when His friends"—or rather, "relatives," as appears from vs. 31, and see on ch. 12:46—"heard of it, they went out to lay hold on Him; for they said, He is beside Himself." Cf. II Corinthians 5:13, "For whether we be beside ourselves, it is *to God*. **22. Then was brought unto him one possessed with a devil**—"a

demonized person—**blind and dumb, and he healed him, insomuch that the blind and the dumb both spake and saw. 23. And all the people were amazed, and said, Is not this the son of David?**—The form of the interrogative requires this to be rendered, "Is this the Son of David?" And as questions put in this form (in *Greek*) suppose doubt, and expect rather a negative answer, the meaning is, "Can it possibly be?"—the people thus indicating their secret impression that this must be He; yet saving themselves from the wrath of the ecclesiastics, which a direct assertion of it would have brought upon them. (See on a similar question in John 4:29; and on the phrase, "Son of David," on ch. 9:27.) **24. But when the Pharisees heard it**—Mark (3:22) says, "the scribes which came down from Jerusalem"; so that this had been a hostile party of the ecclesiastics, who had come all the way from Jerusalem to collect materials for a charge against Him. (See on vs. 14.) **they said, This fellow**—an expression of contempt—**doth not cast out devils, but by Beelzebub**—rather, Beelzebul (see on ch. 10:25)—**the prince of the devils**—Two things are here implied—first, that the bitterest enemies of our Lord were unable to deny the reality of His miracles; and next, that they believed in an *organized internal kingdom of evil,* under one chief. This belief would be of small consequence, had not our Lord set His seal to it; but this He immediately does. Stung by the unsophisticated testimony of "all the people," they had no way of holding out against His claims but the desperate shift of ascribing His miracles to Satan. **25. And Jesus knew their thoughts**—"called them" (Mark 3:23). **and said unto them, Every kingdom divided against itself is brought to desolation; and every city or house**—household—**divided against itself shall not stand. 26. And if Satan cast out Satan, he is divided against himself; how shall then his kingdom stand?**—The argument here is irresistible. "No organized society can stand—whether kingdom, city, or household—when turned against itself; such intestine war is suicidal: But the works I do are destructive of Satan's kingdom: That I should be in league with Satan, therefore, is incredible and absurd." **27. And if I by Beelzebub cast out devils, by whom do your children**—"your sons," meaning here the "disciples" or pupils of the Pharisees, who were so termed after the familiar language of the Old Testament in speaking of the sons of the prophets (I Kings 20:35; II Kings 2:3, etc.). Our Lord here seems to admit that such works were wrought by them; in which case the Pharisees stood self-condemned, as expressed in Luke (11:19), "Therefore shall they be your judges." **28. But if I cast out devils by the Spirit of God**—In Luke (11:20) it is, "with [or 'by'] the finger of God." This latter expression is just a figurative way of representing the *power* of God, while the former tells us the *living Personal Agent* was made use of by the Lord Jesus in every exercise of that power. **then**—"no doubt" (Luke 11:20). **the kingdom of God is come unto you**—rather "upon you," as the same expression is rendered in Luke: —i.e., "If this expulsion of Satan is, and can be, by no other than the Spirit of God, then is his Destroyer already in the midst of you, and that kingdom which is destined to supplant his is already rising on its ruins." **29. Or else how can one enter into a**—or rather, "the"—**strong man's house, and spoil his goods, except he first bind the strong man? and then he will spoil his house. 30. He that is not with me is against me; and he that gathereth not with me scattereth abroad**—On this important parable, in connection with the corresponding one (vss. 43-45), see on Luke 11:21-26. **31. Wherefore I say unto you, All manner of sin and blasphemy shall be forgiven unto men**—The word "blasphemy" properly signifies "detraction," or "slander." In the New Testament it is applied, as it is here, to vituperation directed against God as well as against men; and in this sense it is to be understood as an aggravated form of sin. Well, says our Lord, all sin—whether in its ordinary or its more aggravated forms—shall find forgiveness with God. Accordingly, in Mark (3:28) the language is still stronger: "All sin shall be forgiven unto the sons of men, and blasphemies wherewith soever they shall blaspheme." There is no sin whatever, it seems, of which it may be said. "That is not a pardonable sin." This glorious assurance is not to be limited by what follows; but, on the contrary, what follows is to be explained by this. **but the blasphemy against the Holy Ghost shall not be forgiven unto men. 32. And whosoever speaketh a word against the Son of man, it shall be forgiven him: but whosoever speaketh against the Holy Ghost, it shall not be forgiven him, neither in this world, neither in the world to come**—In Mark the language is awfully strong, "hath never forgiveness, but is in danger of eternal damnation" —or rather, according to what appears to be the preferable though very unusual reading, "in danger of eternal guilt"—a guilt which he will underlie for ever. Mark has the important addition (vs. 30), "Because they said, He hath an unclean spirit." (See on ch. 10:25.) What, then, is this sin against the Holy Ghost—the unpardonable sin? One thing is clear: Its unpardonableness cannot arise from anything in the nature of sin itself; for that would be a naked contradiction to the emphatic declaration of vs. 31, that all manner of sin is pardonable. And what is this but the fundamental truth of the Gospel? (See Acts 13:38, 39; Rom. 3:22, 24; I John 1:7, etc.). Then, again when it is said (vs. 32), that to speak against or blaspheme the Son of man is pardonable, but the blasphemy against the Holy Ghost is not pardonable, it is not to be conceived that this arises from any greater sanctity in the one blessed Person than the other. These remarks so narrow the question that the true sense of our Lord's words seem to disclose themselves at once. It is a contrast between slandering "the Son of man" *in His veiled condition and unfinished work*—which might be done "ignorantly, in unbelief" (I Tim. 1:13), and slandering the same blessed Person after the blaze of glory which *the Holy Ghost* was soon to throw around His claims, and in the full knowledge of all that. This would be to slander Him with eyes open, or to do it "presumptuously." To blaspheme Christ in the former condition—when even the apostles stumbled at many things—left them still open to conviction on fuller light: but to blaspheme Him in the latter condition would be to hate the light the clearer it became, and resolutely to shut it out; which, of course, precludes salvation. (See on Heb. 10:26-29). The Pharisees had not as yet done this; but in charging Jesus with being in league with hell they were displaying beforehand a malignant determination to shut their eyes to all evidence, and so, *bordering upon*, and *in spirit* committing, the unpardonable sin. **33. Either make the tree good . . . 34. O generation of vipers**—(See on ch. 3:7). **how can ye, being evil, speak good things? for out of the abundance of the heart the mouth speaketh**—a principle obvious enough, yet of deepest significance and vast application. In Luke 6:45 we find it uttered as part of the discourse delivered after

the choice of the apostles. **35. A good man, out of the good treasure of the heart, bringeth**—or, putteth—**forth good things: and an evil man, out of the evil treasure, bringeth**—or putteth—**forth evil things** —The word "putteth" indicates the spontaneity of what comes from the heart; for it is out of the abundance of the heart that the mouth speaketh. We have here a new application of a former saying (see on ch. 7:16-20). Here, the sentiment is, "There are but two kingdoms, interests, parties—with the proper workings of each: If I promote the one, I cannot belong to the other; but they that set themselves in wilful opposition to the kingdom of light openly proclaim to what other kingdom they belong. As for you, in what ye have now uttered, ye have but revealed the venomous malignity of your hearts." **36. But I say unto you, That every idle word that men shall speak, they shall give account thereof in the day of judgment**—They might say, "It was nothing: we meant no evil; we merely threw out a supposition, as one way of accounting for the miracle we witnessed; if it will not stand, let it go; why make so much of it, and bear down with such severity for it?" Jesus replies, "It was not nothing, and at the great day will not be treated as nothing: Words, as the index of the heart, however idle they may seem, will be taken account of, whether good or bad, in estimating character in the day of judgment."

38-50. A SIGN DEMANDED, AND THE REPLY—HIS MOTHER AND BRETHREN SEEK TO SPEAK WITH HIM, AND THE ANSWER. (=Luke 11:16, 24-36; Mark 3: 31-35; Luke 8:19-21.) *A Sign Demanded, and the Reply* (vss. 38-45). The occasion of this section was manifestly the same with that of the preceding. **38. Then certain of the scribes and of the Pharisees answered, saying, Master**—"Teacher," equivalent to "Rabbi." **we would see a sign from thee**—"a sign from heaven" (Luke 11:16); something of an immediate and decisive nature, to show, not that His miracles were *real*—that they seemed willing to concede—but that they were from above, not from beneath. These were not the same class with those who charged Him with being in league with Satan (as we see from Luke 11:15, 16); but as the spirit of both was similar, the tone of severe rebuke is continued. **39. But he answered and said unto them** —"when the people were gathered thick together" (Luke 11:29). **An evil and adulterous generation**—This latter expression is best explained by Jeremiah 3:20, "Surely as a wife treacherously departeth from her husband, so have ye dealt treacherously with Me, O house of Israel, saith the Lord." For this was the relationship in which He stood to the covenant people—"I am married unto you" (Jer. 3:14). **seeketh after a sign**—In the eye of Jesus this class were but the spokesmen of their generation, the exponents of the reigning spirit of unbelief. **and there shall no sign be given to it, but the sign of the prophet Jonas. 40. For as Jonas was**—"a sign unto the Ninevites, so shall also the Son of man be to this generation" (Luke 11:30). For as Jonas was **three days and three nights in the whale's belly**—(Jonah 1:17),—**so shall the Son of man be three days and three nights in the heart of the earth**—This was the second public announcement of His resurrection three days after His death. (For the first, see John 2:19.) Jonah's case was analogous to this, as being a signal judgment of God; reversed in three days; and followed by a glorious mission to the Gentiles. The expression "in the heart of the earth," suggested by the expression of Jonah with respect to the sea (2:3, in LXX), means simply the grave, but this considered as the most emphatic expression of real and total entombment. The period during which He was to lie in the grave is here expressed in round numbers, according to the Jewish way of speaking, which was to regard any part of a day, however small, included within a period of days, as a full day. (See I Sam. 30:12, 13; Esther 4:16; 5:1; ch. 27:63, 64, etc.). **41. The men of Nineveh shall rise in judgment with this generation, . . .**–The Ninevites, though heathens, repented at a man's preaching; while they, God's covenant people, repented not at the preaching of the Son of God–whose supreme dignity is rather implied here than expressed. **42. The queen of the south shall rise up in the judgment with this generation . . .**–The queen of Sheba (a tract in Arabia, near the shores of the Red Sea) came from a remote country, "south" of Judea, to hear the wisdom of a mere man, though a gifted one, and was transported with wonder at what she saw and heard (I Kings 10:1-9). They, when a Greater than Solomon had come *to them,* despised and rejected, slighted and slandered Him. **43-45. When the unclean spirit is gone out of a man, . . .**–On this important parable, in connection with the corresponding one (vs. 29) see on Luke 11:21-26. A charming little incident, given only in Luke 11:27, 28, seems to have its proper place here. "And it came to pass, as He spake these things, a certain woman of the company [out of the crowd] lifted up her voice and said unto Him, Blessed is the womb that bare Thee, and the paps which Thou hast sucked." With true womanly feeling she envies the mother of such a wonderful Teacher. And a higher and better than she had said as much before her (see on Luke 1:28). 42. How does our Lord, then, treat it? He is far from condemning it. He only holds up as "blessed rather" another class: "But he said, Yea rather, blessed are they that hear the word of God, and keep it"–in other words, the humblest real saint of God. How utterly alien is this sentiment from the teaching of the Church of Rome, which would doubtless excommunicate any one of its members that dared to talk in such a strain!

His Mother and Brethren Seek to Speak with Him, and the Answer (vss. 46-50). **46. While he yet talked to the people, behold, his mother and his brethren**–(see on ch. 13:55, 56)–**stood without, desiring to speak with him**–"and could not come at Him for the press" (Luke 8:19). For what purpose these came, we learn from Mark 3:20, 21. In His zeal and ardor He seemed indifferent both to food and repose, and "they went to lay hold of Him" as one "beside Himself." Mark says graphically, "And the multitude sat about Him"–or "around Him." **47. Then one said unto him, Behold, thy mother and thy brethren stand without, desiring to speak with thee,...**–Absorbed in the awful warnings He was pouring forth, He felt this to be an unseasonable interruption, fitted to dissipate the impression made upon the large audience–such an interruption as duty to the nearest relatives did not require Him to give way to. But instead of a direct rebuke, He seizes on the incident to convey a sublime lesson, expressed in a style of inimitable condescension. **49. And he stretched forth his hand toward his disciples**–How graphic is this! It is the language evidently of an eye-witness. **and said, Behold my mother and my brethren! 50. For whosoever shall do the will of my Father which is in heaven, the same is my brother, and sister, and mother**–i.e., "There stand here the members of a family transcending and surviving this of earth: Filial subjection to the will of My Father in heaven is the indissoluble bond of union between Me and all its members; and whosoever enters this hallowed circle becomes to Me brother, and sister, and mother!"

CHAPTER 13

Vss. 1-52. JESUS TEACHES BY PARABLES. (= Mark 4:1-34; Luke 8:4-18; 13:18-20.) *Introduction* (vss. 1-3). **1. The same day went Jesus out of the house, and sat by the seaside. 2. And great multitudes were gathered together unto him, so that he went into a ship**–the article in the received text lacks authority–**and sat; and the whole multitude stood on the shore**–How graphic this picture!–no doubt from the pen of an eyewitness, himself impressed with the scene. It was "the same day" on which the foregoing solemn discourse was delivered, when His kindred thought Him "beside Himself" for His indifference to food and repose–that same day retiring to the seashore of Galilee; and there seating Himself, perhaps for coolness and rest, the crowds again flock around Him, and He is fain to push off from them, in the boat usually kept in readiness for Him; yet only to begin, without waiting to rest, a new course of teaching by parables to the eager multitudes that lined the shore. To the parables of our Lord there is nothing in all language to be compared, for simplicity, grace, fulness, and variety of spiritual teaching. They are adapted to all classes and stages of advancement, being understood by each according to the measure of his spiritual capacity. **3. And he spake many things unto them in parables, saying, . . .**–These parables are SEVEN in number; and it is not a little remarkable that while this is the *sacred number,* the first FOUR of them were spoken to the mixed multitude, while the remaining THREE were spoken to the Twelve in private–these divisions, *four* and *three,* being themselves notable in the symbolical arithmetic of Scripture. Another thing remarkable in the structure of these parables is, that while the first of the Seven–that of the Sower –is of the nature of an Introduction to the whole, the remaining Six consist of *three pairs*–the Second and Seventh, the Third and Fourth, and the Fifth and Sixth, corresponding to each other; each pair setting forth the same general truths, but with a certain diversity of aspect. All this can hardly be accidental.

First Parable: THE SOWER (vss. 3-9, 18-23). This parable may be entitled, THE EFFECT OF THE WORD DEPENDENT ON THE STATE OF THE HEART. For the exposition of this parable, see on Mark 4:1-9, 14-20.

Reason for Teaching in Parables (vss . 10-17). **10. And the disciples came, and said unto him**– "they that were with Him, when they were alone" (Mark 4:10). **Why speakest thou to them in parables?**–Though before this He had couched some things in the parabolic form, for more vivid illustration, it would appear that He now, for the first time, formally employed this method of teaching. **11. He answered and said unto them, Because it is given unto you to know the mysteries of the kingdom of heaven**–The word "mysteries" in Scripture is not used in its classical sense–of religious secrets, nor yet of things incomprehensible, or in their own nature difficult to be understood–but in the sense of things of purely divine revelation, and, usually, things darkly announced under the ancient economy, and during all that period darkly understood, but fully published under the Gospel (I Cor. 2:6-10;

Eph. 3:3-6, 8, 9). "The mysteries of the kingdom of heaven," then, mean those glorious Gospel truths which at that time only the more advanced disciples could appreciate, and they but partially. **but to them it is not given**—(See on ch. 11:25). Parables serve the double purpose of *revealing* and *concealing;* presenting "the mysteries of the kingdom" to those who know and relish them, though in never so small a degree, in a new and attractive light; but to those who are insensible to spiritual things yielding only, as so many tales, some temporary entertainment. **12. For whosoever hath**—i.e., keeps; as a thing which he values. **to him shall be given, and he shall have more abundance**—He will be rewarded by an increase of what he so much prizes. **but whosoever hath not**—who lets this go or lie unused, as a thing on which he sets no value. **from him shall be taken away even that he hath**—or as it is in Luke (8:18), "what he seemeth to have," or, thinketh he hath. This is a principle of immense importance, and, like other weighty sayings, appears to have been uttered by our Lord on more than one occasion, and in different connections. (See on ch. 25:9.) As a great ethical principle, we see it in operation everywhere, under the general law of *habit;* in virtue of which moral principles become stronger by exercise, while by disuse, or the exercise of their contraries, they wax weaker, and at length expire. The same principle reigns in the intellectual world, and even in the animal—if not in the vegetable also—as the facts of physiology sufficiently prove. Here, however, it is viewed as a divine ordination, as a judicial retribution in continual operation under the divine administration. **13. Therefore speak I to them in parables**—which our Lord, be it observed, did not begin to do till His miracles were malignantly ascribed to Satan. **because they seeing, see not**—They "saw," for the light shone on them as never light shone before; but they "saw not," for they closed their eyes. **and hearing, they hear not; neither do they understand**—They "heard," for He taught them who "spake as never man spake"; but they "heard not," for they took nothing in, apprehending not the soul-penetrating, life-giving words addressed to them. In Mark and Luke, what is here expressed as a human fact is represented as the fulfilment of a divine purpose—"that seeing they may see, and not perceive . . . ." The explanation of this lies in the statement of the foregoing verse—that, by a fixed law of the divine administration, the duty men voluntarily refuse to do, and in point of fact do not do, they at length become morally incapable of doing. **14. And in them is fulfilled**—rather, is fulfilling, or is receiving its fulfilment. **the prophecy of Esaias, which saith**—(Isa. 6:9, 10—here quoted according to the LXX). **By hearing ye shall hear, and shall not understand, . . .**—They were thus judicially sealed up under the darkness and obduracy which they deliberately preferred to the light and healing which Jesus brought nigh to them. **16. But blessed are your eyes, for they see; and your ears, for they hear**—i.e., "Happy ye, whose eyes and ears, voluntarily and gladly opened, are drinking in the light divine." **17. For verily I say unto you, That many prophets and righteous men have desired**—rather, 'coveted'—**to see those things which ye see, and have not seen them; and to hear those things which ye hear, and have not heard them**—Not only were the disciples blessed above the blinded just spoken of, but favored above the most honored and the best that lived under the old economy, who had but glimpses of the things of the new kingdom, just sufficient to kindle in them

desires not to be fulfilled to any in their day. In Luke 10:23, 24, where the same saying is repeated on the return of the Seventy—the words, instead of "many prophets and righteous men," are "many prophets *and kings'';* for several of the Old Testament saints were kings.

Second and Seventh Parables, or *First Pair:* THE WHEAT AND THE TARES, and THE GOOD AND BAD FISH (vss. 24-30; vss. 36-43; and vss. 47-50). The subject of both these parables—which teach the same truth, with a slight diversity of aspect—is: THE MIXED CHARACTER OF THE KINGDOM IN ITS PRESENT STATE, AND THE FINAL ABSOLUTE SEPARATION OF THE TWO CLASSES.

The Tares and the Wheat (vss. 24-30, 36-43). **24. Another parable put he forth unto them, saying, The kingdom of heaven is likened unto a man which sowed good seed in his field**—Happily for us, these exquisite parables are, with like charming simplicity and clearness, expounded to us by the Great Preacher Himself. Accordingly, we pass to: **36-38. Then Jesus sent the multitude away, and went into the house: and his disciples came unto him, saying, Declare unto us the parable of the tares of the field, . . .**—In the parable of the Sower, "the seed is the word of God" (Luke 8:11). But here that word has been received into the heart, and has converted him that received it into a new creature, a "child of the kingdom," according to that saying of James (1: 18), "Of His own will begat He us with the word of truth, that we should be a kind of first fruits of His creatures." It is worthy of notice that this vast field of the world is here said to be *Christ's own*—"His field," says the parable. (See Psalm 2:8.) **25. But while men slept, his enemy came and sowed tares among the wheat, and went his way. 38. The tares are the children of the wicked one**—As this sowing could only be "while men slept," no blame seems intended, and certainly none is charged upon "the servants"; it is probably just the dress of the parable. **39. The enemy that sowed them is the devil**—emphatically *"His"* enemy (vs. 25). (See Gen. 3:15; I John 3:8.) By "tares" is meant, not what in our husbandry is so called, but some noxious plant, probably *darnel.* "The tares are the children of the wicked one"; and by their being sown "among the wheat" is meant their being deposited within the territory of the visible Church. As they resemble the children of the kingdom, so they are produced, it seems, by a similar process of "sowing"—the seeds of evil being scattered and lodging in the soil of those hearts upon which falls the seed of the world. The enemy, after sowing his "tares," "went his way" —his dark work soon done, but taking time to develop its true character. **26. But when the blade was sprung up, and brought forth fruit, then appeared the tares also**—the growth in both cases running parallel, as antagonistic principles are seen to do. **27. So the servants of the householder came**— i.e., Christ's ministers—**and said unto him, Sir, didst not thou sow good seed in thy field? from whence then hath it tares?**—This well expresses the surprise, disappointment, and anxiety of Christ's faithful servants and people at the discovery of "false brethren" among the members of the Church. **28. He said unto them, An enemy hath done this**—Kind words these from a good Husbandman, honorably clearing His faithful servants of the wrong done to his field. **The servants said unto him, Wilt thou then that we go and gather them up?**—Cf. with this the question of James and John (Luke 9:54), "Lord, wilt Thou that we command fire to come down from heaven and consume" those Samaritans? In this kind of zeal there is usually a large mixture of carnal heat. (See Jas. 1:20.) **29. But he said, Nay** —"It will be done in due time, but not now, nor is it your business." **lest, while ye gather up the tares, ye root up also the wheat with them**—Nothing could more clearly or forcibly teach the difficulty of distinguishing the two classes, and the high probability that in the attempt to do so these will be confounded. **30, 39. Let both grow together**—i.e., in the visible Church. **until the harvest**—till the one have ripened for full salvation, the other for destruction. **The harvest is the end of the world**—the period of Christ's second coming, and of the judicial separation of the righteous and the wicked. Till then, no attempt is to be made to effect such separation. But to stretch this so far as to justify allowing openly scandalous persons to remain in the communion of the Church, is to wrest the teaching of this parable to other than its proper design, and go in the teeth of apostolic injunctions (I Cor. 5). **and in the time of harvest I will say to the reapers. And the reapers are the angels**—But whose angels are they? "The Son of man shall send forth His angels (vs. 41). Cf. I Peter 3:22, "Who is gone into heaven, and is on the right hand of God; angels and authorities and powers being made subject unto him." **Gather ye together first the tares, and bind them in bundles to burn them**—"in the fire" (vs. 40) —**but gather the wheat into my barn**—Christ, as the Judge, will separate the two classes (as in ch. 25:32). It will be observed that the tares are burned *before* the wheat is housed; in the exposition of the parable (vss. 41, 43) the same order is observed: and the same in ch. 25:46—as if, in some literal sense, "with thine eyes shalt thou behold and see the reward of the wicked" (Ps. 91:8). **41. The Son of man shall send forth his angels, and they shall gather out of his kingdom**—to which they never really belonged. They usurped their place and name and outward privileges; but "the ungodly shall not stand in the judgment, nor sinners [abide] in the congregation of the righteous" (Ps. 1:5). **all things that offend**— all those who have proved a stumbling block to others—**and them which do iniquity**—The former class, as the worst, are mentioned first. **42. And shall cast them into a**—rather, "the"—**furnace of fire: there shall be wailing and gnashing of teeth**— What terrific strength of language—the "casting" or "flinging" expressive of indignation, abhorrence, contempt (cf. Ps. 9:17; Dan. 12:2): "the furnace of fire" denoting the fierceness of the torment: the "wailing" signifying the anguish this causes; while the "gnashing of teeth" is a graphic way of expressing the despair in which its remedilessness issues (see on ch. 8:12)! **43. Then shall the righteous shine forth as the sun in the kingdom of their Father** —as if they had been under a cloud during their present association with ungodly pretenders to their character, and claimants of their privileges, and obstructors of their course. **Who hath ears to hear, let him hear**—(See on Mark 4:9).

The Good and Bad Fish (vss. 47-50). The object of this brief parable is the same as that of the Tares and Wheat. But as its details are fewer, so its teaching is less rich and varied. **47. Again, the kingdom of heaven is like unto a net, that was cast into the sea, and gathered of every kind**—The word here rendered "net" signifies a large *drag-net,* which draws everything after it, suffering nothing to escape, as distinguished from a *casting-net* (Mark 1:16, 18). The far-reaching efficacy of the Gospel is thus denoted. This Gospel net "gathered of every kind," meaning every variety of character.

48. Which, when it was full, they drew to shore— for the separation will not be made till the number of the elect is accomplished. **and sat down**—expressing the deliberateness with which the judicial separation will at length be made. **and gathered the good into vessels, but cast the bad away**—lit., 'the rotten,' but here meaning, 'the foul' or 'worthless' fish: corresponding to the "tares" of the other parable. **49. So shall it be at the end of the world . . .**—(See on vs. 42). We have said that each of these two parables holds forth the same truth under a slight diversity of aspect. What is that diversity? First, the *bad,* in the former parable, are represented as vile seed sown among the wheat by the enemy of souls; in the latter, as foul fish drawn forth out of the great sea of human beings by the Gospel net itself. Both are important truths— that the Gospel draws within its pale, and into the communion of the visible Church, multitudes who are Christians only in name; and that the injury thus done to the Church on earth is to be traced to the wicked one. But further, while the former parable gives chief prominence to the present mixture of good and bad, in the latter, the prominence is given to the future separation of the two classes.

Third and Fourth Parables, or *Second Pair:* THE MUSTARD SEED and THE LEAVEN (vss. 31-33). The subject of both these parables, as of the first pair, is the same, but under a slight diversity of aspect, namely—

THE GROWTH OF THE KINGDOM FROM THE SMALLEST BEGINNINGS TO ULTIMATE UNIVERSALITY.

The Mustard Seed (vss. 31, 32). **31. Another parable put he forth unto them, saying, The kingdom of heaven is like to a grain of mustard seed, which a man took, and sowed in his field; 32. Which indeed is the least of all seeds**—not absolutely, but popularly and proverbially, as in Luke 17:6, "If ye had faith as a grain of mustard seed," i.e., 'never so little faith.' **but when it is grown, it is the greatest among herbs**—not absolutely, but in relation to the small size of the seed, and in warm latitudes proverbially great. **and becometh a tree, so that the birds of the air come and lodge in the branches thereof**—This is added, no doubt, to express the *amplitude* of the tree. But as this seed has a hot, fiery vigor, gives out its best virtues when bruised, and is grateful to the taste of birds, which are accordingly attracted to its branches both for shelter and food, is it straining the parable, asks TRENCH, to suppose that, besides the wonderful *growth* of His kingdom, our Lord selected this seed to illustrate further the *shelter, repose* and *blessedness* it is destined to afford to the nations of the world?

The Leaven (vs. 33). **33. Another parable spake he unto them; The kingdom of heaven is like unto leaven, which a woman took and hid in three measures of meal, till the whole was leavened**—This parable, while it teaches the same general truth as the foregoing one, holds forth, perhaps, rather the *inward* growth of the kingdom, while "the Mustard Seed" seems to point chiefly to the *outward.* It being a woman's work to knead, it seems a refinement to say that "the woman" here represents *the Church,* as the instrument of depositing the leaven. Nor does it yield much satisfaction to understand the "three measures of meal" of that threefold division of our nature into "spirit, soul, and body," alluded to in 1 Thessalonians 5:23, or of the threefold partition of the world among the three sons of Noah (Gen. 10:32), as some do. It yields more real satisfaction to see in this brief parable just the *all-penetrating* and *assimilating* quality of the Gospel, by virtue of which it will yet mould all institutions and tribes of men, and exhibit over the whole earth one "kingdom of our Lord and of His Christ." **34. All these things spake Jesus unto the multitude in parables; and without a parable spake he not unto them**—i.e., on this occasion; refraining not only from all naked discourse, but even from all interpretation of these parables to the mixed multitude. **35. That it might be fulfilled which was spoken by the prophet, saying**—(Ps. 78:2, nearly as in LXX)— **I will open my mouth in parables ...**—Though the Psalm seems to contain only a summary of Israelitish *history,* the Psalmist himself calls it "a parable," and "dark sayings from of old"—as containing, *underneath the history,* truths for all time, not fully brought to light till the Gospel day.

Fifth and Sixth Parables, or *Third Pair:* THE HIDDEN TREASURE and THE PEARL OF GREAT PRICE (vss. 44-46). The subject of this last pair, as of the two former, is the same, but also under a slight diversity of aspect: namely—

THE PRICELESS VALUE OF THE BLESSINGS OF THE KINGDOM. And while the one parable represents the Kingdom as *found without seeking,* the other holds forth the Kingdom as *sought and found.*

The Hidden Treasure (vs. 44). **44. Again, the kingdom of heaven is like unto treasure hid in a field**—no uncommon thing in unsettled and half-civilized countries, even now as well as in ancient times, when there was no other way of securing it from the rapacity of neighbors or marauders. (Jer. 41:8; Job 3:21; Prov. 2:4.) **the which when a man hath found**—i.e., unexpectedly found. **he hideth, and for joy thereof**—on perceiving what a treasure he had lighted on, surpassing the worth of all he possessed. **goeth and selleth all that he hath, and buyeth that field**—in which case, by Jewish law, the treasure would become his own.

The Pearl of Great Price (vss. 45, 46). **45. Again, the kingdom of heaven is like unto a merchantman, seeking goodly pearls. 46. Who, when he had found one pearl of great price, went and sold all that he had, and bought it**—The one pearl of great price, instead of being found by accident, as in the former case, is found by one whose *business* it is to seek for such, and who finds it just in the way of *searching* for such treasures. But in both cases the surpassing value of the treasure is alike recognized, and in both all is parted with for it. **51. Jesus saith unto them**—i.e., to the Twelve. He had spoken the first *four* in the hearing of the mixed multitude: the last *three* He reserved till, on the dismissal of the mixed audience, He and the Twelve were alone (vs. 36, etc.). **Have ye understood all these things? They say unto him, Yea, Lord. 52. Then said he unto them, Therefore**—or as we should say, Well, then. **every scribe**—or Christian teacher: here so called from that well-known class among the Jews. (See ch. 23:34). **which is instructed unto the kingdom of heaven**— himself taught in the mysteries of the Gospel which he has to teach to others. **is like unto a man that is an householder which bringeth forth**—"turneth" or "dealeth out." **out of his treasure**—his store of divine truth. **things new and old**—old truths in ever new forms, aspects, applications, and with ever new illustrations.

53-58. HOW JESUS WAS REGARDED BY HIS RELATIVES. (= Mark 6:1-6; Luke 4:16-30.) **53. And it came to pass, that, when Jesus had finished these parables, he departed thence. 54. And when he was come into his own country**—i.e., Nazareth; as is plain from Mark 6:1. See on John 4:43, where also the same phrase occurs. This, according to the majority of Harmonists, was the *second* of *two* visits which our Lord paid to Nazareth during His public ministry; but in our view it was His *first* and *only* visit to it. See on ch. 4:13; and for the reasons, see on Luke 4:16-30. **Whence hath this man this wisdom, and these mighty works?**—"these miracles." These surely are not like the questions of people who had asked precisely the same questions before, who from astonishment had proceeded to rage, and in their rage had hurried Him out of the synagogue, and away to the brow of the hill whereon their city was built, to thrust Him down headlong, and who had been foiled even in that object by His passing through the midst of them, and going His way. But see on Luke 4:16, etc. **55. Is not this the carpenter's son?**—In Mark (6:3) the question is, "Is not this the carpenter?" In all likelihood, our Lord, during His stay under the roof of His earthly parents, wrought along with His legal father. **is not his mother called Mary?**—'Do we not know all about His parentage? Has He not grown up in the midst of us? Are not all His relatives our own townsfolk? Whence, then, such wisdom and such miracles?' These particulars of our Lord's *human* history constitute the most valuable testimony, first, to His true and real humanity—for they prove that during all His first thirty years His townsmen had discovered nothing about Him different from other men; secondly, to the divine character of His mission—for these Nazarenes proclaim both the unparalleled character of His teaching and the reality and glory of His miracles, as transcending human ability; and thirdly, to His wonderful humility and self-denial—in that when He was such as they now saw Him to be, He yet never gave any indications of it for thirty years, because "His hour was not yet come." **And his brethren, James, and Joses, and Simon, and Judas? 56. And his sisters, are they not all with us? Whence then hath this man all these things?** An exceedingly difficult question here arises—What were these "brethren" and "sisters" to Jesus? Were they, *First,* His full brothers and sisters? or, *Secondly,* Were they His step-brothers and step-sisters, children of Joseph by a former marriage? or, *Thirdly,* Were they His cousins, according to a common way of speaking among the Jews respecting persons of collateral descent? On this subject an immense deal has been written, nor are opinions yet by any means agreed. For the second opinion there is no ground but a vague tradition, arising probably from the wish for some such explanation. The first opinion undoubtedly suits the text best in all the places where the parties are certainly referred to (ch. 12:46; and its parallels, Mark 3:31, and Luke 8:19; our present passage, and its parallels, Mark 6:3; John 2:12; 7:3, 5, 10; Acts 1:14). But, in addition to other objections, many of the best interpreters, thinking it in the last degree improbable that our Lord, when hanging on the cross, would have committed His mother to John if He had had full brothers of His own then alive, prefer the third opinion; although, on the other hand, it is not to be doubted that our Lord might have good reasons for entrusting the guardianship of His doubly widowed mother to the beloved disciple in preference even to full brothers of His own. Thus dubiously we prefer to leave this vexed question, encompassed as it is with difficulties. As to the names here mentioned, the *first* of them, "JAMES," is afterwards called "the Lord's brother" (see on Galatians 1:19), but is perhaps not to be confounded with "James the son of Alpheus," one of the Twelve, though many think their identity beyond dispute. This question also is one of considerable difficulty, and not without importance; since the James who occupies so prominent a place in the Church of Jerusalem, in the latter part of the Acts, was apparently the apostle, but is by many regarded as "the Lord's brother," while others think their identity best suits all the statements. The *second* of those here named, "Joses" (or Joseph), must not be confounded with "Joseph called Barsabas, who was surnamed Justus" (Acts 1:23); and the *third* here named, "Simon," is not to be confounded with Simon the Kananite or Zealot (see on ch. 10:4). These three are nowhere else mentioned in the New Testament. The *fourth* and last-named, "Judas," can hardly be identical with the apostle of that name—though the brothers of both were of the name of "James"—nor (unless the two be identical, was this Judas) with the author of the catholic Epistle so called. **58. And he did not many mighty works there, because of their unbelief**—"save that He laid His hands on a few sick folk, and healed them" (Mark 6:5). See on Luke 4:16-30.

CHAPTER 14

Vss. 1-12. Herod Thinks Jesus a Resurrection of the Murdered Baptist—Account of His Imprisonment and Death. (=Mark 6:14-29; Luke 9:7-9.) The time of this alarm of Herod Antipas appears to have been during the mission of the Twelve, and shortly after the Baptist—who had been in prison for probably more than a year—had been cruelly put to death.

Herod's Theory of the Works of Christ (vss. 1, 2). **1. At that time Herod the tetrarch**—Herod Antipas, one of the three sons of Herod the Great, and own brother of Archelaus (ch. 2:22), who ruled as *ethnarch* over Galilee and Perea. **heard of the fame of Jesus**—"for His name was spread abroad" (Mark 6:14). **2. And said unto his servants**—his counsellors or court-ministers. **This is John the Baptist: he is risen from the dead . . .**—The murdered prophet haunted his guilty breast like a specter and seemed to him alive again and clothed with unearthly powers in the person of Jesus.

Account of the Baptist's Imprisonment and Death (vss. 3-12). For the exposition of this portion, see on Mark 6:17-29.

12-21. Hearing of the Baptist's Death, Jesus Crosses the Lake with Twelve and Miraculously Feeds Five Thousand. (= Mark 6:30-44; Luke 9: 10-17; John 6:1-14.) For the exposition of this section—one of the very few where all the four Evangelists run parallel—see on Mark 6:30-44.

22-36. Jesus Crosses to the Western Side of the Lake, Walking on the Sea—Incidents on Landing. (= Mark 6:45; John 6:15-24.) For the exposition, see on John 6:15-24.

CHAPTER 15

Vss. 1-20. Discourse on Ceremonial Pollution. (= Mark 7:1, 23.) The time of this section was after that Passover which was nigh at hand when our Lord fed the five thousand (John 6:4)—the third Passover, as we take it, since His public ministry began, but which He did not keep at Jerusalem for the reason mentioned in John 7:1. **1.**

Then came to Jesus scribes and Pharisees, which were of—or "from"—**Jerusalem**—Mark says they "came from" it: a deputation probably sent from the capital expressly to watch Him. As He had not come to them at the last Passover, which they had reckoned on, they now come to Him. "And," says Mark, "when they saw some of His disciples eat bread with defiled, that is to say, with unwashen hands"—hands not ceremonially cleansed by washing—"they found fault. For the Pharisees, and all the Jews, except they wash their hands oft"—lit., "in" or "with the fist"; i.e., probably washing the one hand by the use of the other—though some understand it, with our version, in the sense of 'diligently,' 'sedulously'—"eat not, holding the tradition of the elders"; acting religiously according to the custom handed down to them. "And when they come from the market"—"And after market": after any common business, or attending a court of justice, where the Jews, as Webster and Wilkinson remark, after their subjection to the Romans, were especially exposed to intercourse and contact with heathens—"except they wash, they eat not. And many other things there be, which they have received to hold, as the washing of cups and pots, brazen vessels and tables"—rather, "couches," such as were used at meals, which probably were merely *sprinkled* for ceremonial purposes. "Then the Pharisees and scribes asked Him," **saying, 2. Why do thy disciples transgress the tradition of the elders? for they wash not their hands when they eat bread. 3. But he answered and said unto them, Why do ye also transgress the commandment of God by your tradition?**—The charge is retorted with startling power: "The tradition they transgress is but *man's*, and is itself the occasion of heavy transgression, undermining the authority of *God's law*." **4. For God commanded, saying, Honour thy father and mother** Deut. 5:16; **and, He that curseth father or mother, let him die the death**—(Exod. 21:17). **5. But ye say, Whosoever shall say to his father or his mother, It is a gift**—or simply, "A gift!" In Mark it is, "*Corban!*" i.e., "An oblation!" meaning, any unbloody offering or gift dedicated to sacred uses. **by whatsoever thou mightest be profited by me; 6. And honour not his father or his mother, [he shall be free]**—i.e., It is true, father—mother—that by giving to thee this, which I now present, thou mightest be profited by me; but I have gifted it to pious uses, and therefore, at whatever cost to thee, I am not now at liberty to alienate any portion of it. "And," it is added in Mark, "ye suffer him no more to do aught for his father or his mother." To dedicate property to God is indeed lawful and laudable, but not at the expense of filial duty. **Thus have ye made the commandment of God of none effect**—cancelled or nullified it—**by your tradition. 7. Ye hypocrites, well did Esaias prophesy of you, saying**—(Isa. 29:13)—**8. This people draweth nigh unto me with their mouth, . . .**—By putting the commandments of men on a level with the divine requirements, *their whole worship was rendered vain*—a principle of deep moment in the service of God. "For," it is added in Mark 7:8, "laying aside the commandment of God, ye hold the tradition of men, as the washing of pots and cups; and many other such like things ye do." The drivelling nature of their multitudinous observances is here pointedly exposed, in contrast with the manly observance of "the commandment of God"; and when our Lord says, "Many other such like things ye do," it is implied that He had but given a specimen of the hideous treatment which the divine law received, and the grasping disposition which, under the mask of piety, was manifested by the ecclesiastics of that day. **10. And he called the multitude, and said unto them**—The foregoing dialogue, though in the people's hearing, was between Jesus and the pharisaic cavilliers, whose object was to disparage Him with the people. But Jesus, having put them down, turns to the multitude, who at this time were prepared to drink in everything He said, and with admirable plainness, strength, and brevity, lays down the great principle of real pollution, by which a world of bondage and uneasiness of conscience would be dissipated in a moment, and the sense of sin be reserved for deviations from the holy and eternal law of God. **Hear and understand: 11. Not that which geeth into the mouth defileth a man; but that which cometh out of the mouth, this defileth a man**—This is expressed even more emphatically in Mark (17:15, 16), and it is there added, "If any man have ears to hear, let him hear." As in ch. 13:9, this so oft-repeated saying seems designed to call attention to the *fundamental* and *universal* character of the truth it refers to. **12. Then came his disciples, and said unto him, Knowest thou that the Pharisees were offended, after they heard this saying?**—They had given vent to their irritation, and perhaps threats, not to our Lord Himself, from whom they seem to have slunk away, but to some of the disciples, who report it to their Master. **13. But he answered and said, Every plant, which my heavenly Father hath not planted, shall be rooted up**—They are offended, are they? Heed it not: their corrupt teaching is already doomed: the garden of the Lord upon earth, too long cumbered with their presence, shall yet be purged of them and their accursed system: yea, and whatsoever is not of the planting of My heavenly Father, the great Husbandman (John 15:1), shall share the same fate.' **14. Let them alone: they are blind leaders of the blind. And if the blind lead the blind, both shall fall into the ditch**—Striking expression of the ruinous effects of erroneous teaching! **15. Then answered Peter and said unto him**—"when He was entered into the house from the people," says Mark. **Declare unto us this parable. 16. And Jesus said, Are ye also yet without understanding?**—Slowness of spiritual apprehension in His genuine disciples grieves the Saviour: from others He expects no better (ch. 13: 11). **17, 18. Do not ye yet understand that whatsoever entereth in at the mouth, . . .**—Familiar though these sayings have now become, what freedom from bondage to outward things do they proclaim, on the one hand; and on the other, how searching is the truth which they express—that nothing which enters from without can really defile us; and that only the evil that is in the heart, that is allowed to stir there, to rise up in thought and affection, and to flow forth in voluntary action, really defiles a man! **19. For out of the heart proceed evil thoughts**—"evil reasonings"; referring here more immediately to those corrupt reasonings which had stealthily introduced and gradually reared up that hideous fabric of tradition which at length practically nullified the unchangeable principles of the moral law. But the statement is far broader than this; viz., that the first shape which the evil that is in the heart takes, when it begins actively to stir, is that of "considerations" or "reasonings" on certain suggested actions. **murders, adulteries, fornications, thefts, false witness, blasphemies**—detractions, whether directed against God or man; here the reference seems to be to the latter. Mark adds, "covetousnesses"—or desires after more; "wicked-

nesses"—here meaning, perhaps, malignities of various forms; "deceit, lasciviousness"—meaning, excess or enormity of any kind, though by later writers restricted to lewdness; "an evil eye"—meaning, all looks or glances of envy, jealousy, or ill-will towards a neighbor; "pride, foolishness"—in the Old Testament sense of "folly"; i.e., criminal senselessness, the folly of the *heart*. How appalling is this black catalogue! **20. These are the things which defile a man: but to eat with unwashen hands defileth not a man**—Thus does our Lord sum up this whole searching discourse.

21-28. The Woman of Canaan and Her Daughter. For the exposition, see on Mark 7:24-30.

29-39. Miracles of Healing—Four Thousand Miraculously Fed. For the exposition, see on Mark 7:31; 8:10.

CHAPTER 16

Vss. 1-12. A Sign from Heaven Sought and Refused—Caution against the Leaven of the Pharisees and Sadducees. For the exposition, see on Mark 8:11-21.

13-28. Peter's Noble Confession of Christ, and the Benediction Pronounced upon Him—Christ's First Explicit Announcement of His Approaching Sufferings, Death, and Resurrection—His Rebuke of Peter and Warning to All the Twelve. (= Mark 8:27; 9:1; Luke 9:18-27.) The time of this section—which is beyond doubt, and will presently be mentioned—is of immense importance, and throws a touching interest around the incidents which it records. *Peter's Confession, and the Benediction Pronounced upon Him* (vss. 13-20). **13. When Jesus came into the coasts**—"the parts," i.e., the territory or region. In Mark (8:27) it is "the towns" or "villages." **of Caesarea Philippi**—It lay at the foot of Mount Lebanon, near the sources of the Jordan, in the territory of Dan, and at the northeast extremity of Palestine. It was originally ealled *Panium* (from a cavern in its neighborhood dedicated to the god *Pan*) and *Paneas*. Philip, the tetrarch, the only good son of Herod the Great, in whose dominions Paneas lay, having beautified and enlarged it, changed its name to *Caesarea*, in honor of the Roman emperor, and added *Philippi* after his own name, to distinguish it from the other *Caesarea* (Acts 10:1) on the northeast coast of the Mediterranean Sea. (Josephus, *Antiquities*, 15:10, 3; 18:2, 1.) This quiet and distant retreat Jesus appears to have sought with the view of talking over with the Twelve the fruit of His past labors, and breaking to them for the first time the sad intelligence of His approaching death. **he asked his disciples**—"by the way," says Mark (8: 27), and "as He was alone praying," says Luke (9: 18). **saying, Whom**—or more grammatically, "Who"—**do men say that I the Son of man am?**—(or, "that the Son of man is"—the recent editors omitting here the *me* of Mark and Luke; though the evidence seems pretty nearly balanced)—i.e., 'What are the views generally entertained of Me, the Son of man, after going up and down among them so long?' He had now closed the first great stage of His ministry, and was just entering on the last dark one. His spirit, burdened, sought relief in retirement, not only from the multitude, but even for a season from the Twelve. He retreated into "the secret place of the Most High," pouring out His soul "in supplications and prayers, with strong crying and tears" (Heb. 5:7). On rejoining His disciples, and as they were pursuing their quiet journey, He asked them this question. **14. And they said, Some say that thou art John the Baptist**—risen from the dead. So that Herod Antipas was not singular in his surmise (ch. 14:1, 2). **some, Elias**—(Cf. Mark 6:15). **and others, Jeremias**—Was this theory suggested by a supposed resemblance between the "Man of Sorrows" and "the weeping prophet"? **or one of the prophets**—or, as Luke (9: 8) expresses it, "that one of the old prophets is risen again." In another report of the popular opinions which Mark (6:15) gives us, it is thus expressed, "That it is a prophet [or], as one of the prophets": in other words, That He was a prophetical person, resembling those of old. **15. He saith unto them, But whom**—rather, "who"—**say ye that I am?**—He had never put this question before, but the crisis He was reaching made it fitting that He should now have it from them. We may suppose this to be one of those moments of which the prophet says, in His name, "Then I said, I have labored in vain; I have spent my strength for naught, and in vain" (Isa. 49:4): Lo, these three years I come seeking fruit on this fig tree; and what is it? As the result of all, I am taken for John the Baptist, for Elias, for Jeremias, for one of the prophets. Yet some there are that have beheld My glory, the glory as of the Only-begotten of the Father, and I shall hear their voice, for it is sweet. **16. And Simon Peter answered and said, Thou art the Christ, the Son of the living God**—He does not say, "Scribes and Pharisees, rulers and people, are all perplexed; and shall we, unlettered fishermen, presume to decide?" But feeling the light of his Master's glory shining in his soul, he breaks forth—not in a tame, prosaic acknowledgment, "*I believe that Thou art . . .*"—but in the language of adoration—such as one uses in worship, "THOU ART THE CHRIST, THE SON OF THE LIVING GOD!" He first owns Him the promised *Messiah* (see on ch. 1:16); then he rises higher, echoing the voice from heaven—"This is My beloved Son, in whom I am well pleased"; and in the important addition—"Son of the LIVING GOD"—he recognizes the essential and eternal life of God as in this His Son—though doubtless without that distinct perception afterwards vouchsafed. **17. And Jesus answered and said unto him, Blessed art thou**—Though it is not to be doubted that Peter, in this noble testimony to Christ, only expressed the conviction of all the Twelve, yet since he alone seems to have had clear enough apprehensions to put that conviction in proper and suitable words, and courage enough to speak them out, and readiness enough to do this at the right time—so he only, of all the Twelve, seems to have met the present want, and communicated to the saddened soul of the Redeemer at the critical moment that balm which was needed to cheer and refresh it. Nor is Jesus above giving indication of the deep satisfaction which this speech yielded Him, and hastening to respond to it by a signal acknowledgment of Peter in return. **Simon-Barjona**—or, "son of Jona" (John 1:42), or "Jonas" (John 21:15). This name, denoting his humble fleshly extraction, seems to have been purposely here mentioned, to contrast the more vividly with the spiritual elevation to which divine illumination had raised him. **for flesh and blood hath not revealed it unto thee**—"This is not the fruit of human teaching." **but my Father which is in heaven**—In speaking of God, Jesus, it is to be observed, never calls Him, "our Father" (see on John 20:17), but either "your Father"—when He would encourage His timid believing ones with the assurance that He was theirs, and teach themselves to call Him so—or, as here, "My Father," to signify some peculiar action or aspect of Him as "the God and Father of our Lord Jesus Christ." **18. And I say also unto thee**—i.e., "As thou hast borne such testimony to Me, even so in return do I to thee." **That thou art Peter**—At his first calling, this new name was announced to him as an honor afterwards to be conferred on him (John 1:43). Now he gets it, with an explanation of what it was meant to convey. **and upon this rock**—As "Peter" and "Rock" are one word in the dialect familiarly spoken by our Lord—the Aramaic or Syro-Chaldaic, which was the mother tongue of the country—this exalted *play upon the word* can be fully seen only in languages which have one word for both. Even in the Greek it is imperfectly represented. In French, as WEBSTER and WILKINSON remark, it is perfect, *Pierre —pierre*. **I will build my Church**—not on the man Simon Barjona; but on him as the heavenly-taught confessor of a faith. "My Church," says our Lord, calling the Church HIS OWN; a magnificent expression regarding Himself, remarks BENGEL—nowhere else occurring in the Gospel. **and the gates of hell** —"of Hades," or, the unseen world; meaning, the gates of Death: in other words, "It shall never perish." Some explain it of "the assaults of the powers of darkness"; but though that expresses a glorious truth, probably the former is the sense here. **19. And I will give unto thee the keys of the kingdom of heaven**—the kingdom of God about to be set up on earth—**and whatsoever thou shalt bind on earth shall be bound in heaven: and whatsoever thou shalt loose on earth shall be loosed in heaven**—Whatever this mean, it was soon expressly *extended to all the apostles* (ch. 18:18); so that the claim of supreme authority in the Church, made for Peter by the Church of Rome, and then arrogated to themselves by the popes as the legitimate successors of St. Peter, is baseless and impudent. As first in confessing Christ, Peter got this commission before the rest; and with these "keys," on the day of Pentecost, he first "opened the door of faith" to the *Jews,* and then, in the person of Cornelius, he was honored to do the same to the *Gentiles.* Hence, in the lists of the apostles, Peter is always first named. See on ch. 18:18. One thing is clear, that not in all the New Testament is there the vestige of any authority either claimed or exercised by Peter, or conceded to him, above the rest of the apostles—a thing conclusive against the Romish claims in behalf of that apostle. **20. Then charged he his disciples that they should tell no man that he was Jesus the Christ**—Now that He had been so explicit, they might naturally think the time come for giving it out openly; but here they are told it had not.

Announcement of His Approaching Death, and Rebuke of Peter (vss. 21-28). The occasion here is evidently the same. **21. From that time forth began Jesus to show unto his disciples**—i.e., with an *explicitness and frequency* He had never observed before—**how that he must go unto Jerusalem and suffer many things** "and be rejected," (Matthew and Mark)—**of the elders and chief priests and scribes**—not as before, merely by not receiving Him, but by formal deeds. **and be killed, and be raised again the third day**—Mark (8:32) adds, that "He spake that saying openly"—"explicitly," or "without disguise." **22. Then Peter took him**—aside, apart from the rest; presuming on the distinction just conferred on him; showing how *unexpected* and *distasteful* to them all was the announcement. **and began to rebuke him**—affectionately, yet with a certain generous indignation, to chide Him. **saying, Be it far from thee: this shall not be unto thee**—i.e., 'If I can help it': the same spirit that prompted him in the garden to draw the sword in His behalf (John 18:10). **23. But he turned, and said**—in the hearing of the rest; for Mark (8:33) expressly says, "When He had turned about and looked on His disciples, He rebuked Peter"; perceiving that he had but boldly uttered what others felt, and that the check was needed by them also. **Get thee behind me, Satan**—the same words as He had addressed to the Tempter (Luke 4:8); for He felt in it a satanic lure, a whisper from hell, to move Him from His purpose to suffer. So He shook off the Serpent, then coiling around Him, and "felt no harm" (Acts 28:5). How quickly has the "rock" turned to a devil! The fruit of divine teaching the Lord delighted to honor in Peter; but the mouth-piece of hell, which he had in a moment of forget-fulness become, the Lord shook off with horror. **thou art an offence**—a stumbling block—**unto me:** 'Thou playest the Tempter, casting a stumbling block in My way to the Cross. Could it succeed, where wert thou? and how should the Serpent's head be bruised?' **for thou savourest not**—thou thinkest not—**the things that be of God, but those that be of men**—"Thou art carried away by human views of the way of setting up Messiah's kingdom, quite contrary to those of God." This was kindly said, not to take off the sharp edge of the rebuke. but to explain and justify it, as it was evident Peter knew not what was in the bosom of his rash speech. **24. Then said Jesus unto his disciples**—Mark (8:34) says, "When He had called the people unto Him, with His disciples also, He said unto them"—turning the rebuke of one into a warning to all. **If any man will come after me, let him deny himself, and take up his cross, and follow me. 25. For whosoever will save**—is minded to save, or bent on saving—**his life shall lose it, and whosoever will lose his life for my sake shall find it**—See on ch. 10:38, 39. "A suf-fering and dying Messiah liketh you ill; but what if His servants should meet the same fate? They may not; but who follows Me must be prepared for the worst." **26. For what is a man profited, if he shall gain the whole world, and lose**—or forfeit—**his own soul? or what shall a man give in exchange for his soul?**—Instead of these weighty words, which we find in Mark also, it is thus expressed in Luke: "If he gain the whole world, and lose himself, or be cast away," or better, "If he gain the whole world, and destroy or forfeit himself." How awful is the stake as here set forth! If a man makes the present world —in its various forms of riches, honors, pleasures, and such like -the object of supreme pursuit, be it that he gains the world; yet along with it he forfeits his own soul. Not that any ever did, or ever will gain the whole world—a very small portion of it, in-deed, falls to the lot of the most successful of the world's votaries—but to make the extravagant con-cession, that by giving himself entirely up to it, a man gains the whole world; yet, setting over against this gain the forfeiture of his soul—necessarily fol-lowing the surrender of his whole heart to the world —what is he profited? But, if not the whole world, yet possibly something else may be conceived as an equivalent for the soul. Well, what is it?—"Or what shall a man give in exchange for his soul?" Thus, in language the weightiest, because the sim-plest, does our Lord shut up His hearers, and all who shall read these words to the end of the world, to the priceless value to every man of his own soul. In Mark and Luke the following words are added: "Whosoever therefore shall be ashamed of Me and of My words [shall be ashamed of belonging to Me, and ashamed of My Gospel] in this adulterous and sinful generation" (see on ch. 12:39), "of him shall the Son of man be ashamed when He cometh in the glory of His Father, with the holy angels" (Mark 8: 38; Luke 9:26). He will render back to that man his own treatment, disowning him before the most august of all assemblies, and putting him to "*shame and everlasting contempt*" (Dan. 12:2). "O shame," exclaims BENGEL, "to be put to shame before God, Christ, and angels!" The sense of *shame* is founded on our love of *reputation*, which causes instinctive aversion to what is fitted to lower it, and was given us as a preservative from all that is properly *shame-ful*. To be *lost to shame* is to be nearly past hope. (Zeph. 3:5; Jer. 6:15; 3:3.) But when Christ and "His words" are unpopular, the same instinctive desire to *stand well with others* begets that tempta-tion to be ashamed of Him which only the expulsive power of a higher affection can effectually counter-act. **27. For the Son of man shall come in the glory of his Father with his angels**—in the splendor of His Father's authority and with all His angelic ministers, ready to execute His pleasure. **and then he shall reward . . . 28. Verily I say unto you, There be some standing here**—"some of those stand-ing here." **which shall not taste of death, till they see the Son of man coming in his kingdom**—or, as in Mark (9:1), "till they see the kingdom of God come with power"; or, as in Luke (9:27), more simply still, "till they see the kingdom of God." The reference, beyond doubt, is to the firm establish-ment and victorious progress, in the lifetime of some then present, of that new kingdom of Christ, which was destined to work the greatest of all changes on this earth, and be the grand pledge of His final com-ing in glory.

CHAPTER 17

Vss. 1-13. JESUS IS TRANSFIGURED—CONVERSA-TION ABOUT ELIAS. (=Mark 9:2-13; Luke 9:28-36.) For the exposition, see on Luke 9:28-36.

14-23. HEALING OF A DEMONIAC BOY—SECOND EXPLICIT ANNOUNCEMENT BY OUR LORD OF HIS AP-PROACHING DEATH AND RESURRECTION. (=Mark 9: 14-32; Luke 9:37-45.) The time of this section is sufficiently denoted by the events which all the nar-ratives show to have immediately preceded it—the first explicit announcement of His death, and the transfiguration—both being between His third and His fourth and last Passover.

Healing of the Demoniac and Lunatic Boy (vss. 14-21). For the exposition of this portion, see on Mark 9:14-32.

Second Announcement of His Death (vss. 22, 23). **22. And while they abode in Galilee, Jesus said unto them**—Mark (9:30), as usual, is very precise here: "And they departed thence"—i.e., from the scene of the last miracle—"and passed through Galilee; and He would not that any man should know it." So this was not a preaching, but a private, journey through Galilee. Indeed, His public ministry in Galilee was now all but concluded. Though He sent out the Seventy after this to preach and heal, He Himself was little more in public there, and He was soon to bid it a final adieu. Till this hour ar-rived, He was chiefly occupied with the Twelve, preparing them for the coming events. **The Son of man shall be betrayed into the hands of men . . . And they were exceeding sorry**—Though the shock would not be so great as at the first announcement (ch. 16:21, 22), their "sorrow" would not be the less, but probably the greater, the deeper the intelligence went down into their hearts, and a new wave dashing upon them by this repetition of the heavy tidings. Accordingly, Luke (9:43, 44), connecting it with the scene of the miracle just recorded, and the teaching which arose out of it—or possibly with all His recent teaching—says our Lord forewarned the Twelve that they would soon stand in need of all that teaching: "But while they wondered every one at all things which Jesus did, He said unto His disciples, Let these sayings sink down into your ears; for the Son of man shall be delivered . . .": 'Be not carried off your feet by the grandeur you have lately seen in Me, but remember what I have told you, and now tell you again, that that Sun in whose beams ye now rejoice is soon to set in midnight gloom.' Remarkable is the antithesis in those words of our Lord preserved in all the three narratives—"The son of *man* shall be betrayed into the hands of *men.*" Luke adds (vs. 45) that "they understood not this saying, and it was hid from them, that they perceived it not"—for the plainest statements, when they encounter long-continued and obstinate prejudices, are seen through a distorting and dulling medium—"and were afraid to ask Him"; deterred partly by the air of lofty sadness with which doubtless these sayings were uttered, and on which they would be reluctant to break in, and partly by the fear of laying themselves open to rebuke for their shallowness and timidity. How artless is all this!

24-27. THE TRIBUTE MONEY. The time of this section is evidently in immediate succession to that of the preceding one. The brief but most pregnant incident which it records is given by Matthew alone —for whom, no doubt, it would have a peculiar interest, from its relation to his own town and his own familiar lake. **24. And when they were come to Capernaum, they that received tribute money**— the double drachma; a sum equal to two Attic drachmas, and corresponding to the Jewish "half-shekel," payable, towards the maintenance of the temple and its services, by every male Jew of twenty years old and upward. For the origin of this annual tax, see Exodus 30:13, 14; II Chronicles 24:6, 9. Thus, it will be observed, it was not a civil, but an ecclesiastical tax. The tax mentioned in the next verse was a civil one. The whole teaching of this very remarkable scene depends upon this distinction. **came to Peter**—at whose house Jesus probably resided while at Capernaum. This explains several things in the narrative. **and said, Doth not your master pay tribute?**—The question seems to imply that the payment of this tax was *voluntary,* but *expected;* or what, in modern phrase, would be called a 'voluntary assessment.' **25. He saith, yes**—i.e., "To be sure He does"; as if eager to remove even the suspicion of the contrary. If Peter knew—as surely he did—that there was at this time no money in the bag, this reply must be regarded as a great act of faith in his Master. **And when he was come into the house**—Peter's—**Jesus prevented him**—anticipated him; according to the old sense of the word "prevent." **saying, What thinkest thou, Simon?**—using his family name for familiarity. **of whom do the kings of the earth take custom**—meaning custom on goods exported or imported—**or tribute**—meaning the poll-tax, payable to the Romans by everyone whose name was in the census. This, therefore, it will be observed, was strictly a *civil* tax. **of their own children, or of strangers**—This cannot mean 'foreigners,' from

whom sovereigns certainly do not raise taxes, but those who are not of their own family, i.e., their subjects. **26. Peter saith unto him, Of strangers**— "of those not their children." **Jesus saith unto him, Then are the children free**—By "the children" our Lord cannot here mean Himself and the Twelve together, in some loose sense of their near relationship to God as their common Father. For besides that our Lord never once mixes Himself up with His disciples in speaking of their relation to God, but ever studiously keeps His relation and theirs apart (see, for example, on the last words of this chapter)—this would be to teach the right of believers to exemption from the dues required for sacred services, in the teeth of all that Paul teaches and that He Himself indicates throughout. He can refer here, then, only to Himself; using the word "children" evidently in order to express the general principle observed by sovereigns, who do not draw taxes from their own children, and thus convey the truth respecting His own exemption the more strikingly:—viz., "If the sovereign's own family be exempt, you know the inference in My case"; or to express it more nakedly than Jesus thought needful and fitting: "This is a tax for upholding My Father's House. As His Son, then, that tax is not due by Me—I AM FREE." **27. Notwithstanding, lest we should offend**—stumble—**them** all ignorant as they are of My relation to the Lord of the Temple, and should misconstrue a claim to exemption into indifference to His honor who dwells in it. **go thou to the sea**—Capernaum, it will be remembered, lay on the Sea of Galilee. **and cast an hook, and take up the fish that first cometh up; and when thou hast opened his mouth, thou shalt find a piece of money**—a stater. So it should have been rendered, and not indefinitely, as in our version, for the coin was an Attic silver coin equal to two of the afore-mentioned "didrachms" of half a shekel's value, and so, was the exact sum required for both. Accordingly, the Lord adds—**that take, and give unto them for me and thee**—lit., "instead of Me and thee"; perhaps because the payment was a *redemption of the person* paid for (Exod. 30:12)—in which view Jesus certainly was "free." If the house was Peter's, this will account for payment being provided on this occasion, not for all the Twelve, but only for him and His Lord. Observe, our Lord does not say "for us," but "for Me and thee"; thus distinguishing the Exempted One and His non-exempted disciple.

CHAPTER 18

Vss. 1-9. STRIFE AMONG THE TWELVE WHO SHOULD BE GREATEST IN THE KINGDOM OF HEAVEN, WITH RELATIVE TEACHING. (=Mark 9:33-50; Luke 9:46-50.) For the exposition, see on Mark 9:33-50.

10-35. FURTHER TEACHING ON THE SAME SUBJECT, INCLUDING THE PARABLE OF THE UNMERCIFUL DEBTOR.

Same Subject (vss. 10-20). **10. Take heed that ye despise**—stumble—**not one of these little ones; for I say unto you, That in heaven their angels do always behold the face of my Father which is in heaven**—A difficult verse; but perhaps the following may be more than an illustration:—Among men, those who nurse and rear the royal children, however humble in themselves, are allowed free entrance with their charge, and a degree of familiarity which even the highest state ministers dare not assume. Probably our Lord means that, in virtue of their charge over His disciples (Heb. 1:13; John 1:51), the angels have *errands* to the throne, a *welcome* there, and a *dear familiarity* in dealing with "His Father which is in heaven," which on their own matters they could not assume. **11. For the Son of man is come to save that which was** —or "is"—**lost**—A golden saying, once and again repeated in different forms. Here the connection seems to be, "Since the whole object and errand of the Son of man into the world is to save the lost, take heed lest, by causing offenses, ye lose the saved." That this is the idea intended we may gather from vs. 14. **12, 13. How think ye? If a man have an hundred sheep, and one of them be gone astray, . . .**—This is another of those pregnant sayings which our Lord uttered more than once. See on the delightful parable of the lost sheep in Luke 15:4-7. Only the object *there* is to show what the good Shepherd will do, when even one of His sheep is lost, to *find* it; *here* the object is to show, when found, how reluctant He is to *lose* it. Accordingly, it is added—vs. 14. **Even so it is not the will of your Father which is in heaven that one of these little ones should perish**—How, then, can He but visit for those "offenses" which endanger the souls of these little ones? **15. Moreover, if thy brother shall trespass against thee, go and tell him his fault between thee and him alone: if he shall hear thee, thou hast gained thy brother, . . .**—Probably our Lord had reference still to the late dispute, Who should be the greatest? After the rebuke—so gentle and captivating, yet so dignified and divine—under which they would doubtless be smarting, perhaps each would be saying, It was not *I* that began it, it was not I that threw out unworthy and irritating insinuations against my brethren. Be it so, says our Lord; but as such things will often arise, I will direct you how to proceed. *First,* Neither harbor a grudge against your offending brother, nor break forth upon him in presence of the unbelieving; but take him aside, show him his fault, and if he own and make reparation for it, you have done more service to him than even justice to yourself. *Next,* If this fail, take two or three to witness how just your complaint is, and how brotherly your spirit in dealing with him. *Again,* If this fail, bring him before the Church or congregation to which both belong. *Lastly,* If even this fail, regard him as no longer a brother Christian, but as one "without"—as the Jews did Gentiles and publicans. **18. Verily I say unto you, Whatsoever ye shall bind on earth shall be bound in heaven; and whatsoever ye shall loose on earth shall be loosed in heaven**—Here, what had been granted but a short time before to Peter only (see on ch. 16:19) is plainly extended to all the Twelve; so that whatever it means, it means nothing peculiar to Peter, far less to his pretended successors at Rome. It has to do with admission to and rejection from the membership of the Church. But see on John 20:23. **19. Again I say unto you, That if two of you shall agree on earth as touching anything that they shall ask, it shall be done for them of my Father which is in heaven. 20. For where two or three are gathered together in**—or "unto"—**my name, there am I in the midst of them**—On this passage—so full of sublime encouragement to Christian union in action and prayer—observe, first, the connection in which it stands. Our Lord had been speaking of church meetings before which the obstinate perversity of a brother was in the last resort to be brought, and

whose decision was to be final—such honor does the Lord of the Church put upon its lawful assemblies. But not these assemblies only does He deign to countenance and honor. For even two uniting to bring any matter before Him shall find that they are not alone, for My Father is with them, says Jesus. Next, observe the *premium here put upon union in prayer.* As this cannot exist with fewer than two, so by letting it down so low as that number, He gives the utmost conceivable encouragement to union in this exercise. But what kind of union? Not an agreement merely to pray in concert, but to pray *for some definite thing.* "As touching anything which they shall ask," says our Lord—anything they shall agree to ask in concert. At the same time, it is plain He had certain things at that moment in His eye, as most fitting and needful subjects for such concerted prayer. The Twelve had been "falling out by the way" about the miserable question of precedence in their Master's kingdom, and this, as it stirred their corruptions, had given rise—or at least was in danger of giving rise—to "offenses" perilous to their souls. The Lord Himself had been directing them how to deal with one another about such matters. "But now shows He unto them a more excellent way." Let them bring all such matters—yea, and everything whatsoever by which either their own loving relationship to each other, or the good of His kingdom at large, might be affected—to their Father in heaven; and if they be but agreed in petitioning Him about that thing, it shall be done for them of His Father which is in heaven. But further, it is not merely union in prayer for the same thing—for that might be with very jarring ideas of the thing to be desired—but it is to symphonious prayer, the prayer by kindred spirits, members of one family, servants of one Lord, constrained by the same love, fighting under one banner, cheered by assurances of the same victory; a living and loving union, whose voice in the divine ear is as the sound of many waters. Accordingly, what they ask "*on earth*" is done for them, says Jesus, "of My Father which is *in heaven.*" Not for nothing does He say, "of MY FATHER"—not "YOUR FATHER"; as is evident from what follows: "For where two or three are gathered together *unto My name*"—the "My" is emphatic, "*there am I* in the midst of them." As His name would prove a spell to draw together many clusters of His dear disciples, so if there should be but two or three, that will attract Himself down into the midst of them; and related as He is to both the parties, the petitioners and the Petitioned—to the one on earth by the tie of His assumed flesh, and to the other in heaven by the tie of His eternal Spirit—their symphonious prayers on earth would thrill upward through Him to heaven, be carried by Him into the holiest of all, and so reach the Throne. Thus will He be the living Conductor of the prayer upward, and the answer downward.

Parable of the Unmerciful Debtor (vss. 21-35). **21. Then came Peter to him, and said, Lord, how oft shall my brother sin against me, and I forgive him?**—In the recent dispute, Peter had probably been an object of special envy, and his forwardness in continually answering for all the rest would likely be cast up to him—and if so, probably by Judas—notwithstanding his Masters' commendations. And as such insinuations were perhaps made once and again, he wished to know how often and how long he was to stand it. **till seven times?** —This being the sacred and complete number, perhaps his meaning was, Is there to be a limit at which the needful forbearance will be *full*? **22. Jesus saith unto him, I say not unto thee, Until seven times; but, Until seventy times seven**—i.e., so long as it shall be needed and sought: you are never to come to the point of refusing forgiveness sincerely asked. (See on Luke 17:3, 4). **23. Therefore**—'with reference to this matter'—**is the kingdom of heaven likened unto a certain king, which would take account of his servants**—or, would scrutinize the accounts of his revenue-collectors. **24. And when he had begun to reckon, one was brought unto him, which owed him ten thousand talents**—If *Attic* talents are here meant, 10,000 of them would amount to above $ 7,500,000; if Jewish talents, to a much larger sum. **25. But forasmuch as he had not to pay, his lord commanded him to be sold, and his wife and children, and all that he had, and payment to be made**—(See II Kings 4:1; Neh. 5:8; Lev. 25:39). **26. The servant therefore fell down, and worshipped him**—or did humble obeisance to him—**saying, Lord, have patience with me, and I will pay thee all**—This was just an acknowledgment of the justice of the claim made against him, and a piteous imploration of mercy. **27. Then the lord of that servant was moved with compassion, and loosed him, and forgave him the debt**—Payment being hopeless, the master is first moved with compassion; next, liberates his debtor from prison; and then cancels the debt freely. **28. But the same servant went out, and found one of his fellow servants**—Mark the difference here. The first case is that of master and servant; in this case, both are on a footing of equality. (See vs. 33, below.) **which owed him an hundred pence**—If Jewish money is intended, this debt was to the other less than *one to a million.* **and he laid hands on him, and took him by the throat**—he seized and throttled him. **saying, Pay me that thou owest**—Mark the mercilessness even of the tone. **29. And his fellow servant fell down at his feet, and besought him, saying, Have patience with me, and I will pay thee all**—The same attitude, and the sam words which drew compassion from his master, are here employed towards himself by his fellow servant. **30. And he would not; but went and cast him into prison, till he should pay the debt, . . .**—Jesus here vividly conveys the intolerable injustice and impudence which even the servants saw in this act on the part of one so recently laid under the heaviest obligation to their common master. **32, 33. Then his lord, after that he had called him, said unto him, O thou wicked servant, . . .**—Before bringing down his vengeance upon him, he calmly points out to him how shamefully unreasonable and heartless his conduct was; which would give the punishment inflicted on him a double sting. **34. And his lord was wroth, and delivered him to the tormentors**—more than *jailers*; denoting the severity of the treatment which he thought such a case demanded. **till he should pay all that was due unto him. 35. So likewise**—in this *spirit*, or on this principle—**shall my heavenly Father do also unto you, if ye from your hearts forgive not every one his brother their trespasses.**

CHAPTER 19

Vss. 1-12. FINAL DEPARTURE FROM GALILEE— DIVORCE. (=Mark 10:1-12; Luke 9:51.)
Farewell to Galilee. **1. And it came to pass, that when Jesus had finished these sayings, he de-** **parted from Galilee**—This marks a very solemn period in our Lord's public ministry. So slightly is it touched here, and in the corresponding passage of Mark (10:1), that few readers probably note it as the Redeemer's *Farewell to Galilee,* which however it was. See on the sublime statement of Luke (9:51), which relates to the same transition stage in the progress of our Lord's work. **and came into the coasts**—or, boundaries—**of Judea beyond Jordan**—i.e., to the further, or east side of the Jordan, into Perea, the dominions of Herod Antipas. But though one might conclude from our Evangelist that our Lord went straight from the one region to the other, we know from the other Gospels that a considerable time elapsed between the departure from the one and the arrival at the other, during which many of the most important events in our Lord's public life occurred—probably a large part of what is recorded in Luke 9:51, onward to ch. 18:15, and part of John 7:2-11, 54. **2. And great multitudes followed him; and he healed them there** —Mark says further (10:1), that "as He was wont, He taught them there." What we now have on the subject of divorce is some of that teaching.

Divorce (vss. 3-12). **3. Is it lawful for a man to put away his wife for every cause?**—Two rival schools (as we saw on ch. 5:31) were divided on this question—a delicate one, as DE WETTE pertinently remarks, in the dominions of Herod Antipas. **4. And he answered and said unto them, Have ye not read, that he which made them at the beginning made them male and female**—or better, perhaps, "He that made them made them from the beginning a male and a female." **5. And said, For this cause**—to follow out this divine appointment. **shall a man leave father and mother, and shall cleave to his wife: and they twain shall be one flesh?**—Jesus here sends them back to the original constitution of man as one pair, a male and a female; to their marriage, as such, by divine appointment; and to the purpose of God, expressed by the sacred historian, that in all time one man and one woman should by marriage become one flesh— so to continue as long as both are in the flesh. This being *God's* constitution, let not *man* break it up by causeless divorces. **7. They say unto him, Why did Moses then command to give a writing of divorcement, and to put her away? 8. He saith unto them, Moses**—as a civil lawgiver. **because of**—or "having respect to." **the hardness of your hearts** —looking to your low moral state, and your inability to endure the strictness of the original law. **suffered you to put away your wives**—tolerated a relaxation of the strictness of the marriage bond— not as approving of it, but to prevent still greater evils. **But from the beginning it was not so**—This is repeated, in order to impress upon His audience the temporary and purely civil character of this Mosaic relaxation. **9. And I say unto you, Whosoever shall put away his wife, except . . .**—See on ch. 5:31. **10. His disciples say unto him, If the case of the man be so with his wife, it is not good to marry**—i.e., "In this view of marriage, surely it must prove a snare rather than a blessing, and had better be avoided altogether." **11. But he said unto them, All men cannot receive this saying, save they to whom it is given**—i.e., "That the unmarried state is better, is a saying not for everyone, and indeed only for such as it is divinely intended for." But who are these? they would naturally ask; and this our Lord proceeds to tell them in three particulars. **12. For there are some eunuchs which were so born from their mother's womb**—persons constitutionally either incapable of or indisposed to marriage. **and there are some eunuchs which were made eunuchs of men**—persons rendered incapable by others. **and there be eunuchs which have made themselves eunuchs for the kingdom of heaven's sake**—persons who, to do God's work better, deliberately choose this state. Such was Paul (I Cor. 7:7). **He that is able to receive it, let him receive it**—"He who feels this to be his proper vocation, let him embrace it"; which, of course, is as much as to say—"he only." Thus, all are left free in this matter.

13-15. LITTLE CHILDREN BROUGHT TO CHRIST. (=Mark 10:13-16; Luke 18:15-17.) For the exposition, see on Luke 18:15-17.

16-30. THE RICH YOUNG RULER. (=Mark 10: 17-31; Luke 18:18-30.) For the exposition, see on Luke 18:18-30.

CHAPTER 20

Vss. 1-16. PARABLE OF THE LABORERS IN THE VINEYARD. This parable, recorded only by Matthew, is closely connected with the end of ch. 19, being spoken with reference to Peter's question as to how it should fare with those who, like himself, had left all for Christ. It is designed to show that while *they* would be richly rewarded, a certain equity would still be observed towards *later* converts and workmen in His service. **1. For the kingdom of heaven is like unto a man that is an householder,...**—The figure of a vineyard, to represent the rearing of souls for heaven, the culture required and provided for that purpose, and the care and pains which God takes in that whole matter, is familiar to every reader of the Bible. (Ps. 80:8-16; Isa. 5:1-7; Jer. 2:21; Luke 20:9-16; John 15:1-8.) At vintage-time, as WEBSTER and WILKINSON remark, labor was scarce, and masters were obliged to be early in the market to secure it. Perhaps the pressing nature of the work of the Gospel, and the comparative paucity of laborers, may be incidentally suggested, ch. 9:37, 38. The "laborers," as in ch. 9:38, are first, the *official* servants of the Church, but after them and along with them *all* the servants of Christ, whom He has laid under the weightiest obligation to work in His service. **2. And when he had agreed with the labourers for a penny**—a usual day's hire. **he sent them into his vineyard. 3. And he went out about the third hour**—about nine o'clock, or after a fourth of the working day had expired: the day of twelve hours was reckoned from six to six. **and saw others standing idle**—unemployed. **in the market-place. 4. And said unto them, Go ye also into the vineyard; and whatsoever is right**—just, equitable, in proportion to their time. **I will give you. And they went their way. 5. Again he went out about the sixth and ninth hour**—about noon, and about three o'clock in the afternoon. **and did likewise**—hiring and sending into his vineyard fresh laborers each time. **6. And about the eleventh hour**—but one hour before the close of the working day; a most unusual hour both for offering and engaging **and found others standing idle, and saith, Why stand ye here all the day idle?**—Of course they had not been there, or not been disposed to offer themselves at the proper time; but as they were now willing, and the day was not over, and "yet there was room," they also are engaged, and on similar terms with all the rest. **8. So when even was come**—i.e., the reckoning time

between masters and laborers (see Deut. 24:15); pointing to the day of final account—**the lord of the vineyard saith unto his steward**—answering to Christ Himself, represented "as a Son over His own house" (Heb. 3:6; see ch. 11:27; John 3:35; 5:27). **Call the labourers and give them their hire, beginning from the last unto the first**—Remarkable direction this—last hired, first paid. **9. And when they came that were hired about the eleventh hour, they received every man a penny**—a full day's wages. **10. But when the first came, they supposed that they should have received more**—This is that calculating, mercenary spirit which had peeped out —though perhaps very slightly—in Peter's question (ch. 19:27), and which this parable was designed once for all to put down among the servants of Christ. **11. And when they had received it, they murmured against the goodman of the house**—rather, "the householder," the word being the same as in vs. 1. **12. Saying, These last have wrought but one hour, and thou hast made them equal unto us, which have borne the burden and heat**—the burning heat—**of the day**—who have wrought not only longer but during a more trying period of the day. **13. But he answered one of them**—doubtless the spokesman of the complaining party. **and said, Friend, I do thee no wrong: didst not thou agree with me for a penny?... 15. Is it not lawful for me to do what I will with mine own? Is thine eye evil, because I am good?**—i.e., "You appeal to *justice*, and by that your mouth is shut; for the sum you agreed for is paid you. Your case being disposed of, with the terms I make with other laborers you have nothing to do; and to grudge the benevolence shown to others, when by your own admission you have been honorably dealt with, is both unworthy envy of your neighbor, and discontent with the goodness that engaged and rewarded you in his service at all." **16. So the last shall be first, and the first last**—i.e., "Take heed lest by indulging the spirit of these murmurers at the penny given to the last hired, ye miss your own penny, though first in the vineyard; while the consciousness of having come in so late may inspire these last with such a humble frame, and such admiration of the grace that has hired and rewarded them at all, as will put them into the foremost place in the end." **for many be called, but few chosen** —This is another of our Lord's terse and pregnant sayings, more than once uttered in different connections. (See ch. 19:30; 22:14.) The "calling" of which the New Testament almost invariably speaks is what divines call *effectual* calling, carrying with it a supernatural operation on the will to secure its consent. But that cannot be the meaning of it here; the "called" being emphatically distinguished from the "chosen." It can only mean here the "invited." And so the sense is, Many receive the invitations of the Gospel whom God has never "chosen to salvation through sanctification of the Spirit and belief of the truth" (II Thess. 2:13). But what, it may be asked, has this to do with the subject of our parable? Probably this— to teach us that men who have wrought in Christ's service all their days may, by the spirit which they manifest at the last, make it too evident that, as between God and their own souls, they never were chosen workmen at all.

17-28. THIRD EXPLICIT ANNOUNCEMENT OF HIS APPROACHING SUFFERINGS, DEATH, AND RESURRECTION—THE AMBITIOUS REQUEST OF JAMES AND JOHN, AND THE REPLY. (=Mark 10:32-45; Luke 18:31-34.) For the exposition, see on Mark 10:32-45.

29-34. Two Blind Men Healed. (=Mark 10: 46-52; Luke 18:35-43). For the exposition, see on Luke 18:35-43.

CHAPTER 21

Vss. 1-9. Christ's Triumphal Entry into Jerusalem on the First day of the Week. (=Mark 11:1-11; Luke 19:29-40; John 12:12-19). For the exposition of this majestic scene—recorded, as will be seen, by all the Evangelists—see on Luke 19:29-40.

10-22. Stir about Him in the City—Second Cleansing of the Temple, and Miracles There—Glorious Vindication of the Children's Testimony—The Barren Fig Tree Cursed, with Lessons from It. (=Mark 11:11-26; Luke 19:45-48.) For the exposition, see Luke 19 after vs. 44; and on Mark 11:12-26.

23-46. The Authority of Jesus Questioned, and the Reply—The Parables of the Two Sons, and of the Wicked Husbandman. (=Mark 11: 27-12; 12; Luke 20:1-19.) Now commences, as Alford remarks, that series of parables and discourses of our Lord with His enemies, in which He develops, more completely than ever before, His hostility to their hypocrisy and iniquity: and so they are stirred up to compass His death.

The Authority of Jesus Questioned, and the Reply (vss. 23-27). **23. By what authority doest thou these things!**—referring particularly to the expulsion of the buyers and sellers from the temple. **and who gave thee this authority? 24. And Jesus answered and said unto them, I also will ask you one thing . . . 25. The baptism of John**—meaning his whole mission and ministry, of which baptism was the proper character. **whence was it? from heaven, or of men?**—What wisdom there was in this way of meeting their question will best appear by their reply. **If we shall say, From heaven; he will say unto us, Why did ye not then believe him?** —"Why did ye not believe the testimony which he bore to Me, as the promised and expected Messiah?" for that was the burden of John's whole testimony. **26. But if we shall say, Of men; we fear the people**—rather the multitude. In Luke (20:6) it is, "all the people will stone us." **for all hold John as a prophet**—Crooked, cringing hypocrites! No wonder Jesus gave you no answer. **27. And they answered Jesus, and said, We cannot tell**—Evidently their difficulty was, how to answer, so as neither to shake their determination to reject the claims of Christ nor damage their reputation with the people. For the truth itself they cared nothing whatever. **Neither tell I you by what authority I do these things**—What composure and dignity of wisdom does our Lord here display, as He turns their question upon themselves, and, while revealing His knowledge of their hypocrisy, closes their mouths! Taking advantage of the surprise, silence, and awe produced by this reply, our Lord followed it up immediately by the two following parables.

Parable of the Two Sons (vss. 28-32.) **28. But what think ye? A certain man had two sons; and he came to the first and said, Son, go work to-day in my vineyard**—for true religion is a practical thing, a "bringing forth fruit unto God." **29. He answered and said, I will not**—Trench notices the rudeness of this answer, and the total absence of any attempt to excuse such disobedience, both characteristic; representing careless, reckless sinners resisting God to His face. **30. And he came** to the second, and said likewise. **And he answered and said, I [go], sir**—"I, sir." The emphatic "I," here, denotes the self-righteous complacency which says, "God, I thank thee that *I* am not as other men" (Luke 18:11). **and went not**—*He* did not "afterward repent" and refuse to go; for there was here no *intention* to go. It is the class that "say and do not" (ch. 23:3)—a falseness more abominable to God, says Stier, than any "I will not." **31. Whether of them twain did the will of his Father? They say unto him, The first**—Now comes the application. **Jesus saith unto them, Verily I say unto you, That the publicans and the harlots go**—or, "are going"; even now entering, while ye hold back—**into the kingdom of God before you**—The publicans and the harlots were the first son, who, when told to work in the Lord's vineyard, said, I will not; but afterwards repented and went. Their early life was a flat and flagrant refusal to do what they were commanded; it was one continued rebellion against the authority of God. The chief priests and the elders of the people, with whom our Lord was now speaking, were the second son, who said, I go, sir, but went not. They were early called, and all their life long professed obedience to God, but never rendered it; their life was one of continued disobedience. **32. For John came unto you in the way of righteousness**—i.e., calling you to repentance; as Noah is styled "a preacher of righteousness" (II Pet. 2:5), when like the Baptist he warned the old world to "flee from the wrath to come." **and ye believed him not**—They did not reject him; nay, they "were willing for a season to rejoice in his light" (John 5:35); but they would not receive his testimony to Jesus. **but the publicans and the harlots believed him**—Of the publicans this is twice expressly recorded, Luke 3: 12; 7:29. Of the harlots, then, the same may be taken for granted, though the fact is not expressly recorded. These outcasts gladly believed the testimony of John to the coming Saviour, and so hastened to Jesus when He came. See Luke 7:37; 15:1, etc. **and ye, when ye had seen it, repented not afterward, that ye might believe him**—Instead of being "provoked to jealousy" by their example, ye have seen them flocking to the Saviour and getting to heaven, unmoved.

Parable of the Wicked Husbandmen (vss. 33-46). **33. Hear another parable: There was a certain householder, which planted a vineyard**—See on Luke 13:6. **and hedged it round about, and digged a winepress in it, and built a tower**—These details are taken, as is the basis of the parable itself, from that beautiful parable of Isaiah 5:1-7, in order to fix down the application and sustain it by Old Testament authority. **and let it out to husbandmen**—These are just the ordinary spiritual guides of the people, under whose care and culture the fruits of righteousness are expected to spring up. **and went into a far country**—"for a long time" (Luke 20:9), leaving the vineyard to the laws of the spiritual husbandry during the whole time of the Jewish economy. On this phraseology, see on Mark 4:26. **34. And when the time of the fruit drew near, he sent his servants to the husbandmen** —By these "servants" are meant the prophets and other extraordinary messengers, raised up from time to time. See on ch. 23:37. **that they might receive the fruits of it**—See again on Luke 13:6. **35. And the husbandmen took his servants, and beat one**—see Jeremiah 37:15; 38:6. **and killed another**—see Jeremiah 26:20-23. **and stoned another**—see II Chronicles 24:21. Compare with this whole verse ch. 23:37, where our Lord reiterates these charges in the most melting strain. **36. Again, he sent other servants more than the first; and they did unto them likewise**—see II Kings 17: 13; II Chronicles 36:16, 18; Nehemiah 9:26. **37. But last of all he sent unto them his son, saying, They will reverence my son**—In Mark (12:6) this is most touchingly expressed: "Having yet therefore one son, His well-beloved, He sent Him also last unto them, saying, They will reverence My Son." Luke's version of it too (20:13) is striking: "Then said the lord of the vineyard, What shall I do? I will send My beloved Son: it may be they will reverence Him when they see Him." Who does not see that our Lord here severs Himself, by the sharpest line of demarkation, from all merely *human* messengers, and claims for Himself *Sonship* in its loftiest sense? (Cf. Heb. 3:3-6.) The expression, "*It may be* they will reverence My Son," is designed to teach the almost unimaginable guilt of *not* reverentially welcoming God's Son. **38. But when the husbandmen saw the son, they said among themselves**—Cf. Genesis 37:18-20; John 11:47-53. **This is the heir**—Sublime expression this of the great truth, that God's inheritance was destined for, and in due time is to come into the possession of, His own Son *in our nature* (Heb. 1:2). **come, let us kill him, and let us seize on his inheritance**—that so, from mere *servants,* we may become *lords.* This is the deep aim of the depraved heart; this is emphatically "the root of all evil." **39. And they caught him, and cast him out of the vineyard**—cf. Hebrews 13:11-13 ("without the gate—without the camp"); I Kings 21:13; John 19:17. **and slew him. 40. When the lord therefore of the vineyard cometh**—This represents 'the settling time,' which, in the case of the Jewish ecclesiastics, was that judicial trial of the nation and its leaders which issued in the destruction of their whole state. **what will he do unto those husbandmen? 41. They say unto him, He will miserably destroy those wicked men**—an emphatic alliteration not easily conveyed in English: "He will badly destroy those bad men," or "miserably destroy those miserable men," is something like it. **and will let out his vineyard unto other husbandmen, which shall render him the fruits in their seasons**—If this answer was given by the Pharisees, to whom our Lord addressed the parable, they thus unwittingly pronounced their own condemnation: as did David to Nathan the prophet (II Sam. 12:5-7), and Simon the Pharisee to our Lord (Luke 7:43, etc.). But if it was given, as the two other Evangelists agree in representing it, by our Lord Himself, and the explicitness of the answer would seem to favor that supposition, then we can better explain the exclamation of the Pharisees which followed it, in Luke's report—"And when they heard it, they said, God forbid"—His whole meaning now bursting upon them. **42. Jesus saith unto them. Did ye never read in the scriptures,**—(Ps. 118:22, 23)—**The stone which the builders rejected ...** A bright Messianic prophecy, which reappears in various forms (Isa. 28:16, etc), and was made glorious use of by Peter before the Sanhedrim (Acts 4:11). He recurs to it in his first epistle (I Pet. 2:4-6). **43. Therefore say I unto you, The kingdom of God**—God's visible Kingdom, or Church, upon earth, which up to this time stood in the seed of Abraham. **shall be taken from you, and given to a nation bringing forth the fruits thereof**—i.e., the great evangelical community of the faithful, which, after the extrusion of the Jewish nation, would consist chiefly of Gentiles,

until "all Israel should be saved" (Rom. 11:25, 26). This vastly important statement is given by Matthew only. **44. And whosoever shall fall on this stone shall be broken: but on whomsoever it shall fall, it will grind him to powder**—The Kingdom of God is here a Temple, in the erection of which a *certain stone,* rejected as unsuitable by the spiritual builders, is, by the great Lord of the House, made the keystone of the whole. On that Stone the builders were now "falling" and being "broken" (Isa. 8:15). They were sustaining great spiritual hurt; but soon that Stone should "fall upon *them*" and "grind them to powder" (Dan. 2:34, 35; Zech. 12:2)—in their *corporate* capacity, in the tremendous destruction of Jerusalem, but *personally,* as unbelievers, in a more awful sense still. **45. And when the chief priests and Pharisees had heard his parables**—referring to that of the Two Sons and this one of the Wicked Husbandmen—**they perceived that he spake of them. 46. But when they sought to lay hands on him**—which Luke (20:19) says they did "the same hour," hardly able to restrain their rage. **they feared the multitude**—rather, 'the multitudes'—**because they took him for a prophet**—just as they feared to say John's baptism was of men, because the masses took him for a prophet (vs. 26). Miserable creatures! So, for this time, "they left Him and went their way" (Mark 12:12).

CHAPTER 22

Vss. 1-14. PARABLE OF THE MARRIAGE OF THE KING'S SON. This is a different parable from that of the Great Supper, in Luke 14:15, etc., and is recorded by Matthew alone. **2. The kingdom of heaven is like unto a certain king, which made a marriage for his son**—"In this parable," as TRENCH admirably remarks, "we see how the Lord is revealing Himself in ever clearer light as the central Person of the kingdom, giving here a far plainer hint than in the last parable of the nobility of His descent. There He was indeed the Son, the only and beloved one (Mark 12:6), of the Householder; but here His race is royal, and He appears as Himself at once the King and the King's Son (Ps. 72:1). The last was a parable of the Old Testament history; and Christ is rather the last and greatest of the line of its prophets and teachers than the founder of a new kingdom. In that, God appears *demanding* something *from* men; in this, a parable of grace, God appears more as *giving* something *to* them. Thus, as often, the two complete each other: this taking up the matter where the other left it." The "marriage" of Jehovah to His people Israel was familiar to Jewish ears; and in Psalm 45 this marriage is seen consummated in the Person of Messiah "THE KING," Himself addressed as "GOD" and yet as anointed by "HIS GOD" with the oil of gladness above His fellows. These apparent contradictions (see on Luke 20:41-44) are resolved in this parable; and Jesus, in claiming to be this King's Son, *serves Himself Heir to all that the prophets and sweet singers of Israel held forth as to Jehovah's ineffably near and endearing union to His people.* But observe carefully, that THE BRIDE does not come into view in this parable; its design being to teach certain truths under the figure of *guests* at a wedding *feast,* and the want of a wedding *garment,* which would not have harmonized with the introduction of the Bride. **3. and sent forth his servants**—representing all preachers of the Gospel. **to call them that were

bidden—here meaning the Jews, who were "bidden," from the first choice of them onwards through every summons addressed to them by the prophets to hold themselves in readiness for the appearing of their King. **to the wedding**—or the marriage festivities, when the preparations were all concluded. **and they would not come**—as the issue of· the whole ministry of the Baptist, our Lord Himself, and His apostles thereafter, too sadly showed. **4. my oxen and my fatlings are killed, and all things are ready; come unto the marriage**—This points to those Gospel calls *after* Christ's death, resurrection, ascension, and effusion of the Spirit, to which the parable could not directly allude, but when only it could be said, with strict propriety, "that all things were ready." Cf. I Corinthians 5:7, 8, "Christ our Passover is sacrificed for us; therefore, let us keep the feast"; also John 6:51, "I am the living bread which came down from heaven: if any man eat of this bread, he shall live for ever: and the bread which I will give is My flesh, which I will give for the life of the world." **5. But they made light of it, and went their ways, one to his farm, another to his merchandise: 6. And the remnant took his servants, and entreated them spitefully**—insulted them—**and slew them**—These are two different classes of unbelievers: the one simply *indifferent;* the other absolutely *hostile*—the one, contemptuous *scorners;* the other, bitter *persecutors.* **7. But when the king**—the Great God, who is the Father of our Lord Jesus Christ. **heard thereof, he was wroth**—at the affront put both on His Son, and on Himself who had deigned to invite them. **and he sent forth his armies**—The *Romans* are here styled God's armies, just as the Assyrian is styled "the rod of His anger" (Isa. 10:5), as being the executors of His judicial vengeance. **and destroyed those murderers**—and in what vast numbers did they do it! **and burned up their city**—Ah! Jerusalem, once "the city of the Great King" (Ps. 48:2), and even up almost to this time (ch. 5:35); but now it is *"their"* city—just as our Lord, a day or two after this, said of the temple, where God had so long dwelt, "Behold *your* house is left unto you desolate" (ch. 23:38)! Cf. Luke 19:43, 44. **8. The wedding is ready, but they which were bidden were not worthy**—for how should those be deemed worthy to sit down at His table who had affronted Him by their treatment of His gracious invitation? **9. Go ye therefore into the highways**—the great outlets and thoroughfares, whether of town or country, where human beings are to be found. **and as many as ye shall find, bid to the marriage**—i.e., just as they are. **10. So those servants went out into the highways, and gathered together all as many as they found, both bad and good**—i.e., without making any distinction between open sinners and the morally correct. The Gospel call fetched in Jews, Samaritans, and outlying heathen alike. Thus far the parable answers to that of 'the Great Supper' (Luke 14:16, etc.). But the distinguishing feature of our parable is what follows: **11. And when the king came in to see the guests**—Solemn expression this, of that *omniscient inspection of every professed disciple of the Lord Jesus* from age to age, in virtue of which his true character will hereafter be judicially proclaimed! **he saw there a man**—This shows that it is the judgment of *individuals* which is intended in this latter part of the parable: the first part represents rather *national* judgment. **which had not on a wedding garment**—The language here is drawn from the following remarkable passage in Zephaniah 1:7, 8:—"Hold thy peace at the presence of the Lord God; for the day of the Lord is at hand: for the Lord

hath prepared a sacrifice, He hath bid His guests. And it shall come to pass in the day of the Lord's sacrifice, that I will punish the princes, and the king's children, and all such as are clothed with strange apparel." The custom in the East of presenting festival garments (see Gen. 45:22; II Kings 5:22), even though not clearly proved, is certainly presupposed here. It undoubtedly means something which they bring not of their own—for how could they have any such dress who were gathered in from the highways indiscriminately?— but which they *receive* as their appropriate dress. And what can that be but what is meant by "putting on the Lord Jesus," as "THE LORD OUR RIGHTEOUS-NESS?" (See Ps. 45:13, 14.) Nor could such language be strange to those in whose ears had so long resounded those words of prophetic joy: "I will greatly rejoice in the Lord, my soul shall be joyful in my God; for He hath clothed me with the garments of salvation, He hath covered me with the robe of righteousness, as a bridegroom decketh himself with ornaments, and as a bride adorneth herself with her jewels" (Isa. 61:10). **12. Friend, how camest thou in hither, not having a wedding garment? And he was speechless**—being self-condemned. **13. Then said the king to the servants**— the angelic ministers of divine vengeance (as in ch. 13:41)—**Bind him hand and foot**—putting it out of his power to resist. **and take him away, and cast him into outer darkness**—So ch. 8:12; 25:30. The expression is emphatic—"the darkness which is outside." To be *"outside"* at all—or, in the language of Revelation 22:15, to be *"without"* the heavenly city, excluded from its joyous nuptials and gladsome festivities—is sad enough of itself, without anything else. But to find themselves not only excluded from the brightness and glory and joy and felicity of the kingdom above, but thrust into a region of "darkness," with all its horrors, this is the dismal retribution here announced, that awaits the unworthy at the great day. **there**—in that region and condition. **shall be weeping and gnashing of teeth.** See on ch. 13:42. **14. For many are called, but few are chosen** —So ch. 19:30. See on ch. 20:16.

15-40. ENTANGLING QUESTIONS ABOUT TRIBUTE, THE RESURRECTION, AND THE GREAT COMMANDMENT, WITH THE REPLIES. (= Mark 12:13-34; Luke 20: 20-40.) For the exposition, see on Mark 12:13-34.

41-46. CHRIST BAFFLES THE PHARISEES BY A QUESTION ABOUT DAVID AND MESSIAH. (= Mark 12:35-37; Luke 20:41-44.) For the exposition, see on Mark 12:35-37.

CHAPTER 23

Vss. 1-39. DENUNCIATION OF THE SCRIBES AND PHARISEES—LAMENTATION OVER JERUSALEM, AND FAREWELL TO THE TEMPLE. (= Mark 12:38-40; Luke 20:45-47.) For this long and terrible discourse we are indebted, with the exception of a few verses in Mark and Luke, to Matthew alone. But as it is only an extended repetition of denunciations uttered not long before at the table of a Pharisee, and recorded by Luke (11:37-54), we may take both together in the exposition.

Denunciation of the Scribes and Pharisees (vss. 1-36). The first twelve verses were addressed more immediately to the disciples, the rest to the scribes and Pharisees. **1. Then spake Jesus to the multitude**—to the multitudes. **and to his disciples. 2. Saying, The scribes and the Pharisees sit**—The Jewish teachers *stood* to read, but *sat* to expound the

Scriptures, as will be seen by comparing Luke 4:16 with vs. 20—**in Moses' seat**—i.e., as interpreters of the law given by Moses. **3. All therefore**—i.e., all which, as *sitting in that seat* and teaching *out of that law*. **they bid you observe, that observe and do**—The word "therefore" is thus, it will be seen, of great importance, as limiting those injunctions which He would have them obey to what they fetched from the law itself. In requiring implicit obedience to such injunctions, He would have them to recognize the authority with which they taught over and above the obligations of the law itself—an important principle truly; but He who denounced the traditions of such teachers (ch. 15:3) cannot have meant here to throw His shield over these. It is remarked by WEBSTER and WILKINSON that the warning to *beware* of the scribes is given by Mark and Luke without any qualification: the charge to *respect* and *obey* them being reported by Matthew alone, indicating for whom this Gospel was especially written, and the writer's desire to conciliate the Jews. **4. For they bind heavy burdens and grievous to be borne, and lay them on men's shoulders; but they themselves will not move them**—"touch them not" (Luke 11:46)—**with one of their fingers**—referring not so much to the irksomeness of the legal rites, though they were irksome enough (Acts 15:10), as to the heartless rigor with which they were enforced, and by men of shameless inconsistency. **5. But all their works they do for to be seen of men**—Whatever good they do, or zeal they show, has but one motive—human applause. **they make broad their phylacteries**—strips of parchment with Scripture-texts on them, worn on the forehead, arm, and side, in time of prayer. **and enlarge the borders of their garments**—fringes of their upper garments (Num. 15: 37-40). **6. And love the uppermost rooms**—The word "room" is now obsolete in the sense here intended. It should be "the uppermost place," i.e., the place of highest honor. **at feasts, and the chief seats in the synagogues.** See on Luke 14:7, 8. **7. And greetings in the markets, and to be called of men, Rabbi, Rabbi**—It is the spirit rather than the *letter* of this that must be pressed; though the violation of the letter, springing from spiritual pride, has done incalculable evil in the Church of Christ. The reiteration of the word "Rabbi" shows how it tickled the ear and fed the spiritual pride of those ecclesiastics. **8. But be not ye called Rabbi; for one is your Master**—your Guide, your Teacher. **9. And call no man your father upon the earth: for one is your Father, which is in heaven, . . .**—To construe these injunctions into a condemnation of every title by which Church rulers may be distinguished from the flock which they rule, is virtually to condemn that rule itself; and accordingly the same persons do both—but against the whole strain of the New Testament and sound Christian judgment. But when we have guarded ourselves against these extremes, let us see to it that we retain the full spirit of this warning against that itch for ecclesiastical superiority which has been the bane and the scandal of Christ's ministers in every age. (On the use of the word "Christ" here, see on ch. 1:1.) **11. But he that is greatest among you shall be your servant**—This plainly means, "shall show that he is so by becoming your servant"; as in ch. 20:27, compared with Mark 10:44. **12. And whosoever shall exalt himself shall be abased**—See on Luke 18:14. What follows was addressed more immediately to the scribes and Pharisees. **13. But woe unto you, scribes and Pharisees, hypocrites! for ye shut up the kingdom of heaven against men**—Here they are charged with *shutting heaven* against men: in Luke 11:52 they are charged with what was worse, *taking away the key*—"the key of knowledge"—which means, not the key to open knowledge, but knowledge as the only key to open heaven. A right knowledge of God's revealed word is eternal life, as our Lord says (John 17:3 and 5:39); but this they took away from the people, substituting for it their wretched traditions. **14. Woe unto you, scribes and Pharisees, hypocrites! for ye devour widows' houses . . .**—Taking advantage of the helpless condition and confiding character of "widows," they contrived to obtain possession of their property, while by their "long prayers" they made them believe they were raised far above "filthy lucre." So much "the greater damnation" awaits them. What a lifelike description of the Romish clergy, the true successors of those scribes! **15. Woe unto you, scribes and Pharisees, hypocrites! for ye compass sea and land to make one proselyte**—from heathenism. We have evidence of this in JOSEPHUS. **and when he is made, ye make him twofold more the child of hell than yourselves**—condemned, for the hypocrisy he would learn to practice, both by the religion he left and that he embraced. **16. Woe unto you, ye blind guides**—Striking expression this of the ruinous effects of erroneous teaching. Our Lord, here and in some following verses, condemns the subtle distinctions they made as to the sanctity of oaths—distinctions invented only to promote their own avaricious purposes. **which say, Whosoever shall swear by the temple, it is nothing**—He has incurred no debt. **but whosoever shall swear by the gold of the temple**—meaning not the gold that adorned the temple itself, but the *Corban*, set apart for sacred uses (see on ch. 15:5). **he is a debtor!**—i.e., it is no longer his own, even though the necessities of the parent might require it. We know who the successors of these men are. **but whosoever sweareth by the gift that is upon it, he is guilty**—It should have been rendered, "he is a debtor," as in vs. 16. **19. Ye fools, and blind! for whether is greater, the gift, or the altar that sanctifieth the gift?**—(See Exod. 29:37.) **20-22. Whose therefore shall swear by the altar . . .**—See on ch. 5:33-37. **23. Woe unto you, scribes and Pharisees, hypocrites! for ye pay tithe of mint and anise**—rather, "dill," as in margin—**and cummin**—In Luke (11:42) it is "and rue, and all manner of herbs." They grounded this practice on Leviticus 27:30, which they interpreted rigidly. Our Lord purposely names the most trifling products of the earth as examples of what they punctiliously exacted the tenth of. **and have omitted the weightier matters of the law, judgment, mercy, and faith**—In Luke (11: 42) it is "judgment, mercy, and the love of God"—the expression being probably varied by our Lord Himself on the two different occasions. In both His reference is to Micah 6:6-8, where the prophet makes all acceptable religion to consist of three elements—"doing justly, loving mercy, and walking humbly with our God"; which third element presupposes and comprehends both the "faith" of Matthew and the "love" of Luke. See on Mark 12:29, 32, 33. The same tendency to merge greater duties in less besets even the children of God; but *it is the characteristic of hypocrites*. **these ought ye to have done, and not to leave the other undone**—There is no need for one set of duties to jostle out another; but it is to be carefully noted that of the *greater* duties our Lord says, "Ye ought to have done" them, while of the *lesser* He merely says, "Ye ought not to leave them undone." **24. Ye blind guides, which strain at a gnat**—The proper rendering—as in the older English translations, and perhaps our own as it came from the translators' hands—evidently is, "strain out." It was the custom, says TRENCH, of the stricter Jews to strain their wine, vinegar, and other potables through linen or gauze, lest unawares they should drink down some little unclean insect therein and thus transgress (Lev. 11:20, 23, 41, 42) —just as the Buddhists do now in Ceylon and Hindustan—and to this custom of theirs our Lord here refers. **and swallow a camel**—the largest animal the Jews knew, as the "gnat" was the smallest; both were by the law *unclean*. **25. within they are full of extortion**—In Luke (11:39) the same word is rendered "ravening," i.e., "rapacity." **26. Thou blind Pharisee, cleanse first that which is within the cup and platter, that the outside of them may be clean also**—In Luke (11:40) it is, "Ye fools, did not He that made that which is without make that which is within also?"—"He to whom belongs the outer life, and of right demands its subjection to Himself, is the inner man less His?" A remarkable example this of our Lord's power of drawing the most striking illustrations of great truths from the most familiar objects and incidents in life. To these words, recorded by Luke, He adds the following, involving a principle of immense value: "But rather give alms of such things as ye have, and behold, all things are clean unto you" (Luke 11:41). As the greed of these hypocrites was one of the most prominent features of their character (Luke 16:14), our Lord bids them exemplify the opposite character, and then their *outside*, ruled by this, would be beautiful in the eye of God, and their meals would be eaten with clean hands, though much fouled with the business of this everyday world. (See Eccles. 9:7.) **27. Woe unto you, scribes and Pharisees, hypocrites! for ye are like whited**—or, white-washed—**sepulchres** —(cf. Acts 23:3). The process of white-washing the sepulchres, as LIGHTFOOT says, was performed on a certain day every year, not for ceremonial cleansing, but, as the following words seem rather to imply, to beautify them. **which indeed appear beautiful outward, but are within full of dead men's bones, and of all uncleanness**—What a powerful way of conveying the charge, that with all their fair show their hearts were full of corruption! (Cf. Ps. 5:9; Rom. 3:13.) But our Lord, stripping off the figure, next holds up their iniquity in naked colors. **Wherefore ye be witnesses unto yourselves, that ye are the children of them which killed the prophets**—i.e., "ye be witnesses that ye have inherited, and voluntarily served yourselves heirs to, the truth-hating, prophet-killing, spirit of your fathers." Out of pretended respect and honor, they repaired and beautified the sepulchres of the prophets, and with whining hypocrisy said, "If we had been in their days, how differently should we have treated these prophets?" While all the time they were witnesses to themselves that they were the children of them that killed the prophets, convicting themselves daily of as exact a resemblance in spirit and character to the very classes over whose deeds they pretended to mourn, as child to parent. In Luke 11:44 our Lord gives another turn to this figure of a grave: "Ye are as graves which appear not, and the men that walk over them are not aware of them." As one might unconsciously walk over a grave concealed from view, and thus contract ceremonial defilement, so the plausible exterior of the Pharisees kept people from perceiving the pollution they contracted from coming in contact with such corrupt characters. **33. Ye serpents, ye generation of vipers, how can ye escape the damnation of hell?**—In thus, at the end of

His ministry, recalling the words of the Baptist at the outset of his, our Lord would seem to intimate that the only difference between their condemnation now and then was, that now they were ripe for their doom, which they were not then. **34. Wherefore, behold, I send unto you prophets, and wise men, and scribes**—The *I* here is emphatic: "I am sending," i.e., "am about to send." In Luke 11:49 the variation is remarkable: "Therefore also, said the wisdom of God, I will send them . . . ." What precisely is meant by "the wisdom of God" here, is somewhat difficult to determine. To us it appears to be simply an announcement of a purpose of the Divine Wisdom, in the high style of ancient prophecy, to send a last set of messengers whom the people would reject, and rejecting, would fill up the cup of their iniquity. But, whereas in Luke it is "I, the Wisdom of God, will send them," in Matthew it is "I, Jesus, am sending them"; language only befitting the one sender of all the prophets, the Lord God of Israel now in the flesh. They are evidently evangelical messengers, but called by the familiar Jewish names of "prophets, wise men, and scribes," whose counterparts were the inspired and gifted servants of the Lord Jesus; for in Luke (11:49) it is "prophets and apostles." **unto the blood of Zacharias son of Barachias, whom ye slew between the temple and the altar**—As there is no record of any fresh murder answering to this description, probably the allusion is not to any recent murder, but to II Chronicles 24: 20-22, as the *last recorded* and most suitable case for illustration. And as Zacharias' last words were, "The Lord *require it*," so they are here warned that of that generation it should be *required*. **36. Verily I say unto you, All these things shall come upon this generation**—As it was only in the last generation of them that "the iniquity of the Amorites was full" (Gen. 15:16), and then the abominations of ages were at once completely and awfully avenged, so the iniquity of Israel was allowed to accumulate from age to age till in that generation it came to the full, and the whole collected vengeance of heaven broke at once over its devoted head. In the first French Revolution the same awful principle was exemplified, and *Christendom has not done with it yet*.

Lamentation over Jerusalem, and Farewell to the Temple (vss. 37-39). **37. O Jerusalem, Jerusalem, thou that killest the prophets, and stonest them which are sent unto thee, . . .**—How ineffably grand and melting is this apostrophe! It is the very heart of God pouring itself forth through human flesh and speech. It is this incarnation of the innermost life and love of Deity, pleading with men, bleeding for them, and ascending only to open His arms to them and win them back by the power of this story of matchless love, that has conquered the world, that will yet "draw all men unto Him," and beautify and ennoble Humanity itself! "Jerusalem" here does not mean the mere city or its inhabitants; nor is it to be viewed merely as the metropolis of the *nation*, but as the *center of their religious life*—"the city of their solemnities, whither the tribes went up, to give thanks unto the name of the Lord"; and at this moment it was full of them. It is the whole family of God, then, which is here apostrophized by a name dear to every Jew, recalling to him all that was distinctive and precious in his religion. The intense feeling that sought vent in this utterance comes out first in the redoubling of the opening word—"Jerusalem, Jerusalem!" but, next, in the picture of it which He draws—"that killest the prophets, and stonest them which are sent unto thee!"—not content with spurning God's messages of mercy, that canst not suffer even the messengers to live! When He adds, "How often would I have gathered thee!" He refers surely to something beyond the six or seven times that He visited and taught in Jerusalem while on earth. No doubt it points to "the prophets," whom they "killed," to "them that were sent unto her," whom they "stoned." But whom would He have gathered so often? "Thee," truth-hating, mercy-spurning, prophet-killing Jerusalem—how often would I have gathered *thee!* Compare with this that affecting clause in the great ministerial commission, "that repentance and remission of sins should be preached in His name among all nations, *beginning at Jerusalem!*" (Luke 24:47). What encouragement to the heartbroken at their own long-continued and obstinate rebellion! But we have not yet got at the whole heart of this outburst. I would have gathered thee, He says, "even as a hen gathereth her chickens under her wings." Was ever imagery so homely invested with such grace and such sublimity as this, at our Lord's touch? And yet how exquisite the figure itself—of protection, rest, warmth, and all manner of conscious well-being in those poor, defenseless, dependent little creatures, as they creep under and feel themselves overshadowed by the capacious and kindly wing of the mother-bird! If, wandering beyond hearing of her peculiar call, they are overtaken by a storm or attacked by an enemy, what can they do but in the one case droop and die, and in the other submit to be torn in pieces? But if they can reach in time their place of safety, under the mother's wing, in vain will any enemy try to drag them thence. For rising into strength, kindling into fury, and forgetting herself entirely in her young, she will let the last drop of her blood be shed out and perish in defense of her precious charge, rather than yield them to an enemy's talons. How significant all this of what Jesus is and does for men! Under His great Mediatorial wing would He have "gathered" Israel. For the figure, see Deuteronomy 32:10-12; Ruth 2:12; Psalm 17:8; 36:7; 61:4; 63:7; 91:4; Isaiah 31:5; Malachi 4:2. The ancient rabbins had a beautiful expression for proselytes from the heathen—that they had "come under the wings of the Shekinah." For this last word, see on vs. 38. But what was the result of all this tender and mighty love? The answer is, "And ye would not." O mysterious word! mysterious the resistance of such patient Love-mysterious the liberty of self-undoing! The awful dignity of the *will*, as here expressed, might make the ears to tingle. **38. Behold, your house**—the temple, beyond all doubt; but *their* house now, not *the Lord's*. See on ch. 22:7. **is left unto you desolate**—deserted, i.e., of its Divine Inhabitant. But who is that? Hear the next words: **39. For I say unto you**—and these were *His last words* to the impenitent nation, see opening remarks on Mark 13.—**Ye shall not see me henceforth**—What? Does Jesus mean that He was Himself the Lord of the temple, and that it became "deserted" when HE finally left it? It is even so. Now is thy fate sealed, O Jerusalem, for the glory is departed from thee! That glory, once visible in the holy of holies, over the mercy seat, when on the day of atonement the blood of typical expiation was sprinkled on it and in front of it—called by the Jews the *Shekinah,* or the *Dwelling,* as being the visible pavilion of Jehovah—that glory, which Isaiah (ch. 6) saw in vision, the beloved disciple says was *the glory of Christ* (John 12:41). Though it was never visible in the second temple, Haggai foretold that "*the glory of that latter house*

should be greater than of the former" (ch. 2:9) because "the Lord whom they sought was suddenly to come to His temple" (Mal. 3:1), not in a mere bright cloud, but enshrined in living humanity! Yet brief as well as "sudden" was the manifestation to be: for the words He was now uttering were to be His VERY LAST within its precincts. **till ye shall say, Blessed is he that cometh in the name of the Lord**—i.e., till those "Hosannas to the Son of David" with which the multitude had welcomed Him into the city—instead of "sore displeasing the chief priests and scribes" (ch. 21:15)—should break forth from the whole nation, as their glad acclaim to their once pierced, but now acknowledged, Messiah. That such a time will come is clear from Zechariah 12:10; Romans 11:26; II Corinthians 3:15, 16, etc. In what sense they shall then "see Him" may be gathered from Zechariah 2:10-13; Ezekiel 37:23-28; 39:28, 29, etc.

CHAPTER 24

Vss. 1-51. CHRIST'S PROPHECY OF THE DESTRUCTION OF JERUSALEM, AND WARNINGS SUGGESTED BY IT TO PREPARE FOR HIS SECOND COMING. (= Mark 13:1-37; Luke 21:5-36.) For the exposition, see on Mark 13:1-37.

CHAPTER 25

Vss. 1-13. PARABLE OF THE TEN VIRGINS. This and the following parable are in Matthew alone. **1. Then**—at the time referred to at the close of the preceding chapter, the time of the Lord's Second Coming to reward His faithful servants and take vengeance on the faithless. *Then* **shall the kingdom of heaven be likened unto ten virgins, which took their lamps, and went forth to meet the bridegroom**—This supplies a key to the parable, whose object is, in the main, the same as that of the last parable—to illustrate *the vigilant and expectant attitude of faith,* in respect of which believers are described as "they that look for Him" (Heb. 9:28), and "love His appearing" (II Tim. 4:8). In the last parable it was that of servants waiting for their absent Lord; in this it is that of virgin attendants on a Bride, whose duty it was to go forth at night with lamps, and be ready on the appearance of the Bridegroom to conduct the Bride to his house, and go in with him to the marriage. This entire and beautiful change of figure brings out the lesson of the former parable in quite a new light. But let it be observed that, just as in the parable of the Marriage Supper, so in this—the *Bride* does not come into view at all in this parable; the *Virgins* and the *Bridegroom* holding forth all the intended instruction: nor could believers be represented both as Bride and Bridal Attendants without incongruity. **2. And five of them were wise, and five were foolish**—They are not distinguished into good and bad, as TRENCH observes, but into "wise" and "foolish"—just as in ch. 7:25-27 those who reared their house for eternity are distinguished into "wise" and "foolish builders"; because in both cases a certain degree of goodwill towards the truth is assumed. To make anything of the equal number of both classes would, we think, be precarious, save to warn us how large a portion of those who, up to the last, so nearly resemble those that love Christ's appearing will be disowned by Him when He comes. **3. They that were foolish took their lamps, and took no oil with**

them: 4. But the wise took oil in their vessels with their lamps—What are these "lamps" and this "oil"? Many answers have been given. But since the foolish as well as the wise took their lamps and went forth with them to meet the Bridegroom, these lighted lamps and this advance a certain way in company with the wise, must denote that Christian profession which is common to all who bear the Christian name; while the insufficiency of this without something else, of which they never possessed themselves, shows that "the foolish" mean those who, with all that is common to them with real Christians, *lack the essential preparation for meeting Christ.* Then, since the wisdom of "the wise" consisted in their taking with their lamps a supply of oil in their vessels, keeping their lamps burning till the Bridegroom came, and so fitting them to go in with Him to the marriage, this supply of oil must mean that *inward reality of grace* which alone will stand when He appears whose eyes are as a flame of fire. But this is too general; for it cannot be for nothing that this inward grace is here set forth by the familiar symbol of *oil,* by which the *Spirit of all grace* is so constantly represented in Scripture. Beyond all doubt, this was what was symbolized by that precious anointing oil with which Aaron and his sons were consecrated to the priestly office (Exod. 30:23-25, 30); by "the oil of gladness above His fellows" with which Messiah was to be anointed (Ps. 45:7; Heb. 1:9), even as it is expressly said, that "God giveth not the Spirit by measure unto Him" (John 3:34); and by the bowl full of golden oil, in Zechariah's vision, which, receiving its supplies from the two olive trees on either side of it, poured it through seven golden pipes into the golden lampstand to keep it continually burning bright (Zech. 4) —for the prophet is expressly told that it was to proclaim the great truth, "Not by might, nor by power, but by My Spirit, saith the Lord of hosts [shall this temple be built]. Who art thou, O great mountain [of opposition to this issue]? Before Zerubbabel thou shalt become a plain [or, be swept out of the way], and he shall bring forth the head-stone [of the temple], with shoutings [crying], Grace, grace unto it." This supply of oil, then, representing that inward grace which distinguishes the wise, must denote, more particularly, that "supply of the Spirit of Jesus Christ," which, as it is the source of the new spiritual life at the first, is the secret of its *enduring* character. Everything *short of this* may be possessed by "the foolish"; while it is the possession of this that makes "the wise" to be "ready" when the Bridegroom appears, and fit to "go in with Him to the marriage." Just so in the parable of the Sower, the stony-ground hearers, "having no deepness of earth" and "no root in themselves," though they spring up and get even into ear, never ripen, while they in the good ground bear the precious grain. **5. While the bridegroom tarried**—So in ch. 24:48, "My Lord delayeth His coming"; and so Peter says sublimely of the ascended Saviour, "Whom the heaven must receive until the times of restitution of all things" (Acts 3:21, and cf. Luke 19:11, 12). Christ "tarries," among other reasons, to try the faith and patience of His people. **they all slumbered and slept**—the wise as well as the foolish. The world "slumbered" signifies, simply, "nodded," or, "became drowsy"; while the world "slept" is the usual word for lying down to sleep, denoting two stages of spiritual declension—first, that half-involuntary lethargy or drowsiness which is apt to steal over one who falls into inactivity; and then a conscious, deliberate yielding to it, after a

little vain resistance. Such was the state alike of the wise and the foolish virgins, even till the cry of the Bridegroom's approach awoke them. So likewise in the parable of the Importunate Widow: "When the Son of man cometh, shall He find faith on the earth?" (Luke 18:8). **6. And at midnight**—i.e., the time when the Bridegroom will be least expected; for "the day of the Lord so cometh as a thief in the night" (I Thess. 5:2). **there was a cry made, Behold, the Bridegroom cometh; go ye out to meet him**—i.e., Be ready to welcome Him. **7. Then all those virgins arose, and trimmed their lamps**—the foolish virgins as well as the wise. How very long do both parties seem the same—almost to the moment of decision! Looking at the mere form of the parable, it is evident that the folly of "the foolish" consisted not in having no oil at all; for they must have had oil enough in their lamps to keep them burning up to this moment: their folly consisted in not making provision against its *exhaustion,* by taking with their lamp an *oil-vessel* wherewith to replenish their lamp from time to time, and so have it burning until the Bridegroom should come. Are we, then—with some even superior expositors—to conclude that the foolish virgins must represent true Christians as well as do the wise, since only true Christians have the Spirit, and that the difference between the two classes consists only in the one having the necessary watchfulness which the other wants? Certainly not. Since the parable was designed to hold forth the prepared and the unprepared to meet Christ at His coming, and how the unprepared might, up to the very last, be confounded with the prepared—the structure of the parable behooved to accommodate itself to this, by making the lamps of the foolish to burn, as well as those of the wise, up to a certain point of time, and only then to discover their inability to burn on for want of a fresh supply of oil. But this is evidently just a *structural device;* and the real difference between the two classes who profess to love the Lord's appearing is a *radical one*—the possession by the one class of *an enduring principle of spiritual life,* and the want of it by the other. **8. And the foolish said unto the wise, Give us of your oil; for our lamps are gone out**—rather, as in the margin, "are going out"; for oil will not light an extinguished lamp, though it will keep a burning one from going out. Ah! now at length they have discovered not only their own folly, but the wisdom of the other class, and they do homage to it. They did not perhaps despise them before, but they thought them righteous overmuch; now they are forced, with bitter mortification, to wish they were like them. **9. But the wise answered, Not so; lest there be not enough for us and you**—The words "Not so," it will be seen, are not in the original, where the reply is very elliptical—"In case there be not enough for us and you." A truly wise answer this. "And what, then, if we shall share it with you? Why, both will be undone." **but go ye rather to them that sell, and buy for yourselves**—Here again it would be straining the parable beyond its legitimate design to make it teach that men may get salvation even after they are supposed and required to have it already gotten. It is merely a friendly way of reminding them of the proper way of obtaining the needed and precious article, with a certain reflection on them for having it now to seek. Also, when the parable speaks of "selling" and "buying" that valuable article, it means simply, "Go, get it in the only legitimate way." And yet the word "buy" is significant; for we are elsewhere bidden, "buy wine and milk without money and without price," and "buy of Christ gold tried in the fire," (Isa. 55:1; Rev. 3:18). Now, since what we pay the demanded price for becomes thereby *our own property*, the salvation which we thus take gratuitously at God's hands, being bought in His own sense of that word, becomes ours thereby in inalienable possession. (Cf. for the language, Prov. 23:23; ch. 13:44.) **10. And while they went to buy, the Bridegroom came; and they that were ready went in with him to the marriage: and the door was shut**—They are sensible of their past folly; they have taken good advice: they are in the act of getting what alone they lacked: a very little more, and they also are ready. But the Bridegroom comes; the ready are admitted; "the door is shut," and they are undone. How graphic and appalling this picture of one *almost saved—but lost!* **11. Afterward came also the other virgins, saying, Lord, Lord, open to us**—In ch. 7:22 this reiteration of the name was an exclamation rather of surprise; here it is a piteous cry of urgency, bordering on despair. Ah! now at length their eyes are wide open, and they realize all the consequences of their past folly. **12. But he answered and said, Verily I say unto you, I know you not**—The attempt to establish a difference between "I know you not" here, and "I never knew you" in ch. 7:23—as if this were gentler, and so implied a milder fate, reserved for "the foolish" of this parable—is to be resisted, though advocated by such critics as OLSHAUSEN, STIER, and ALFORD. Besides being inconsistent with the general tenor of such language, and particularly the solemn moral of the whole (vs. 13), it is a *kind* of criticism which tampers with some of the most awful warnings regarding the future. If it be asked why unworthy guests were admitted to the marriage of the King's Son, in a former parable, and the foolish virgins are excluded in this one, we may answer, in the admirable words of GERHARD, quoted by TRENCH, that those festivities are celebrated in this life, in the Church militant; these at the last day, in the Church triumphant; to those, even they are admitted who are not adorned with the wedding garment; but to these, only they to whom it is granted to be arrayed in fine linen clean and white, which is the righteousness of saints (Rev. 19:8); to those, men are called by the trumpet of the Gospel; to these by the trumpet of the Archangel; to those, who enters may go out from them, or be cast out; who is once introduced to these never goes out, nor is cast out, from them any more: wherefore it is said, "The door is shut." **13. Watch therefore; for ye know neither the day nor the hour wherein the Son of man cometh**—This, the moral or practical lesson of the whole parable, needs no comment.

14-30. PARABLE OF THE TALENTS. This parable, while closely resembling it, is yet a different one from that of THE POUNDS, in Luke 19:11-27; though CALVIN, OLSHAUSEN, MEYER, and others identify them—but not DE WETTE and NEANDER. For the difference between the two parables, see the opening remarks on that of The Pounds. While, as TRENCH observes with his usual felicity, "the virgins were represented as *waiting* for their Lord, we have the servants *working* for Him; there the *inward spiritual life* of the faithful was described; here his *external activity*. It is not, therefore, without good reason that they appear in their actual order—that of the Virgins first, and of the Talents following—since it is the sole condition of a profitable outward activity for the kingdom of God, that the life of God be diligently maintained within the heart." **14. For [the kingdom of heaven is] as**

a man—The ellipsis is better supplied by our translators in the corresponding passage of Mark (13: 34), "[For the Son of man is] as a man . . . **travelling into a far country**—or more simply, "going abroad." The idea of long "tarrying" is certainly implied here, since it is expressed in vs. 19. **who called his own servants, and delivered unto them his goods**—Between master and slaves this was not uncommon in ancient times. Christ's "servants" here mean all who, by their Christian profession, stand in the relation to Him of entire subjection. His "goods" mean all their gifts and endowments, whether original or acquired, natural or spiritual. As all that slaves have belongs to their master, so Christ has a claim to everything which belongs to His people, everything which may be turned to good, and He demands its appropriation to His service, or, viewing it otherwise, they first offer it up to Him; as being "not their own, but bought with a price" (I Cor. 6:19, 20), and He "delivers it to them" again to be put to use in His service. **15. And unto one he gave five talents, to another two, and to another one**—While the *proportion of gifts* is different in each, the same *fidelity is* required of all, and equally rewarded. And thus there is perfect equity. **to every man according to his several ability**—his natural capacity as enlisted in Christ's service, and his opportunities in providence for employing the gifts bestowed on him. **and straightway took his journey**—Cf. ch. 21:33, where the same departure is ascribed to God, after setting up the ancient economy. In both cases, it denotes the leaving of men to the action of all those spiritual laws and influences of Heaven under which they have been graciously placed for their own salvation and the advancement of their Lord's kingdom. **16. Then he that had received the five talents went and traded with the same**—expressive of the activity which he put forth and the labor he bestowed. **and made them other five talents. 17. And likewise he that had received two he also gained other two**—each doubling what he received, and therefore *both equally faithful*. **18. But he that had received one went and digged in the earth, and hid his lord's money**—not misspending, but simply making no use of it. Nay, his action seems that of one anxious that the gift should not be misused or lost, but ready to be returned, just as he got it. **19. After a long time the lord of those servants cometh and reckoneth with them**—That any one—within the lifetime of the apostles at least—with such words before them, should think that Jesus had given any reason to expect His Second Appearing within that period, would seem strange, did we not know the tendency of enthusiastic, ill-regulated love of His appearing ever to take this turn. **20. Lord, thou deliveredst unto me five talents; behold, I have gained besides them five talents more**—How beautifully does this illustrate what the beloved disciple says of "boldness in the day of judgment," and his desire that "when He shall appear we may have confidence, and not be ashamed before Him at His coming!" (I John 4:17; 2:28). **21. His lord said unto him, Well done**—a single word, not of bare satisfaction, but of warm and delighted commendation. And from what Lips!—**thou hast been faithful over a few things, I will make thee ruler over many things . . . 22.** He also that had received two talents came . . . **good and faithful servant: thou hast been faithful over a few things, I will make thee ruler over many things**—*Both are commended in the same terms, and the reward of both is precisely the same.* (See on vs. 15.) Observe also the contrasts: "Thou hast been faithful as a *servant;* now be a *ruler*—thou hast been *entrusted* with a *few* things; now have *dominion* over *many* things." **enter thou into the joy of thy lord**—thy Lord's own joy. (See John 15:11; Heb. 12:2.) **24. Then he which had received the one talent came and said, Lord, I knew thee that thou art an hard man**—harsh. The word in Luke (19:21) is "austere."—**reaping where thou hast not sown, and gathering where thou hast not strawed**—The sense is obvious: "I knew thou wast one whom it was impossible to serve, one whom nothing would please: exacting what was impracticable, and dissatisfied with what was attainable." Thus do men secretly think of God as a hard Master, and virtually throw on Him the blame of their fruitlessness. **25. And I was afraid**—of making matters worse by meddling with it at all. **and went and hid thy talent in the earth**—This depicts the conduct of all those who shut up their gifts from the active service of Christ, without actually prostituting them to unworthy uses. Fitly, therefore, may it, at least, comprehend those, to whom TRENCH refers, who, in the early Church, pleaded that they had enough to do with their own souls, and were afraid of losing them in trying to save others; and so, instead of being the salt of the earth, thought rather of keeping their own saltness by withdrawing sometimes into caves and wildernesses, from all those active ministries of love by which they might have served their brethren. **Thou wicked and slothful servant**—"Wicked" or "bad" means "falsehearted," as opposed to the others, who are emphatically styled *"good"* servants." The addition of "slothful" is to mark the precise nature of his wickedness: it consisted, it seems, not in his doing anything *against,* but simply *nothing for* his master. **Thou knewest that I reap where I sowed not, and gather where I have not strawed**—He takes the servant's own account of his demands, as expressing graphically enough, not the *hardness* which he had basely imputed to him, but simply his demand of *a profitable return for the gift entrusted.* **27. thou oughtest therefore to have put my money to the exchangers**—the banker. **and then at my coming I should have received mine own with usury**—interest. **29. For unto every one that hath shall be given . . .**—See on ch. 13:12. **30. And cast ye**—cast ye out. **the unprofitable servant**—the useless servant, that does his Master no service. **into outer darkness**—the darkness which is outside. On this expression see on ch. 22:13. **there shall be weeping and gnashing of teeth**—See on ch. 13:42.

31-46. THE LAST JUDGMENT. The close connection between this sublime scene—peculiar to Matthew—and the two preceding parables is too obvious to need pointing out. **31. When the Son of man shall come in his glory**—His *personal* glory—**and all the holy angels with him**—See Deuteronomy 33:2; Daniel 7:9, 10; Jude 14; with Hebrews 1:6; I Peter 3:22—**then shall he sit upon the throne of his glory**—the glory of His *judicial authority.* **32. And before him shall be gathered all nations**—or, "all the nations." That this should be understood to mean the *heathen nations,* or all *except* believers in Christ, will seem amazing to any simple reader. Yet this is the exposition of OLSHAUSEN, STIER, KEIL, ALFORD (though latterly with some diffidence), and of a number, though not all, of those who hold that Christ will come the second time before the millennium, and that the saints will be caught up to meet Him in the air before His appearing. Their chief argument is, the impossibility of any

that ever knew the Lord Jesus wondering, at the Judgment Day, that they should be thought to have done—or left undone—anything "unto Christ." To that we shall advert when we come to it. But here we may just say, that if this scene does not describe a personal, public, final judgment on men, according to the treatment they have given to Christ—and consequently men within the Christian pale—we shall have to consider again whether our Lord's teaching on the greatest themes of human interest does indeed possess that incomparable simplicity and transparency of meaning which, by universal consent, has been ascribed to it. If it be said, But how can this be the general judgment, if only those within the Christian pale be embraced by it?—we answer, What is here described, as it certainly does not meet the case of all the family of Adam, is of course *so far* not general. But we have no right to conclude that the whole "judgment of the great day" will be limited to the point of view here presented. Other explanations will come up in the course of our exposition. **and he shall separate them**—now for the first time; the two classes having been mingled all along up to this awful moment. **as a shepherd divideth his sheep from the goats**—(see Ezek. 34:17). **33. And he shall set the sheep on his right hand**—the side of honor (I Kings 2:19; Ps. 45:9; 110:1, etc.). **but the goats on the left**—the side consequently of dishonor. **34. Then shall the King**—Magnificent title, here for the first and only time, save in parabolical language, given to Himself by the Lord Jesus, and that on the eve of His deepest humiliation! It is to intimate that in then addressing the heirs of the kingdom, *He will put on all His regal majesty.* **say unto them on his right hand, Come**—the same sweet word with which He had so long invited all the weary and heavy laden to come unto Him for rest. Now it is addressed exclusively to such as *have* come and found rest. It is still, "Come," and to "rest" too; but to rest in a higher style, and in another region. **ye blessed of my Father, inherit the kingdom prepared for you from the foundation of the world**—The whole story of this their blessedness is given by the apostle, in words which seem but an expression of these: "Blessed be the God and Father of our Lord Jesus Christ, who hath blessed us with all spiritual blessings in heavenly places in Christ; according as He hath chosen us in Him before the foundation of the world, that we should be holy and without blame before Him in love." They were chosen from everlasting to the possession and enjoyment of all spiritual blessings in Christ, and so chosen in order to be holy and blameless in love. This is the holy love whose practical manifestations the King is about to recount in detail; and thus we see that their whole life of love to Christ is the fruit of an eternal purpose of love to them in Christ. **35. For I was an hungered . . . thirsty . . . a stranger . . . 36. Naked . . . sick . . . prison, and ye came unto me. 37-39. Then shall the righteous answer him . . . 40. And the King shall answer and say unto them, Verily I say unto you, . . .**—Astonishing dialogue is this between the King, from the Throne of His glory, and His wondering people! "I was an hungered, and ye gave Me meat . . ."—"Not we," they reply. "We never did that, Lord: We were born out of due time, and enjoyed not the privilege of ministering unto Thee." "But ye did it to these My brethren, now beside you, when cast upon your love." "Truth, Lord, but was that doing it to Thee? Thy name was indeed dear to us, and we thought it a great honor to suffer shame for it. When among the destitute and distressed we discerned any of the household of faith, we will not deny that our hearts leapt within us at the discovery, and when their knock came to our dwelling, our bowels were moved, as though 'our Beloved Himself had put in His hand by the hole of the door.' Sweet was the fellowship we had with them, as if we had 'entertained angels unawares'; all difference between giver and receiver somehow melted away under the beams of that love of Thine which knit us together; nay, rather, as they left us with gratitude for our poor givings, we seemed the debtors—not they. But, Lord, were we all that time in company with Thee?" "Yes, that scene was all with Me," replies the King—"Me in the disguise of My poor ones. The door shut against Me by others was opened by you—'Ye took Me in.' Apprehended and imprisoned by the enemies of the truth, ye whom the truth had made free sought Me out diligently and found Me; visiting Me in My lonely cell at the risk of your own lives, and cheering My solitude; ye gave Me a coat, for I shivered; and then I felt warm. With cups of cold water ye moistened My parched lips; when famished with hunger ye supplied Me with crusts, and my spirit revived— "YE DID IT UNTO ME." What thoughts crowd upon us as we listen to such a description of the scenes of the Last Judgment! And in the light of this view of the heavenly dialogue, how bald and wretched, not to say unscriptural, is that view of it to which we referred at the outset, which makes it a dialogue between Christ and *heathens* who never heard of His name, and of course never felt any stirrings of His love in their hearts! To us it seems a poor, superficial objection to the *Christian* view of this scene, that Christians could never be supposed to ask such questions as the "blessed of Christ's Father" are made to ask here. If there were any difficulty in explaining this, the difficulty of the other view is such as to make *it*, at least, insufferable. But there is no real difficulty. The surprise expressed is not at their being told that they acted from love to Christ, but that *Christ Himself* was the *Personal Object* of all their deeds: that they found *Him* hungry, and supplied *Him* with food: that they brought water to *Him*, and slaked His thirst; that seeing *Him* naked and shivering, they put warm clothing upon *Him*, paid *Him* visits when lying in prison for the truth, and sat by *His* bedside when laid down with sickness. This is the astonishing interpretation which Jesus says "the King" will give to them of their own actions here below. And will any Christian reply, "How could this astonish them? Does not every Christian know that He does these very things, when He does them at all, just as they are here represented?" Nay, rather, is it conceivable that they should *not* be astonished, and almost doubt their own ears, to hear such an account of their own actions upon earth from the lips of the Judge? And remember, that Judge has come in His glory, and now sits upon the throne of His glory, and all the holy angels are with Him; and that it is from those glorified Lips that the words come forth, "Ye did all this unto ME." Oh, can we imagine such a word addressed to *ourselves,* and then fancy ourselves replying, "Of course we did—To whom else did we anything? It must be others than we that are addressed, who never knew, in all their good deeds, what they were about?" Rather, can we imagine ourselves not overpowered with astonishment, and scarcely able to credit the testimony borne to us

by the King? **41. Then shall he say also unto them on the left hand, Depart from me, ye cursed . . .**— As for you on the left hand, ye did nothing for Me. I came to you also, but ye knew Me not: ye had neither warm affections nor kind deeds to bestow upon Me: I was as one despised in your eyes." "In *our* eyes, Lord? We never saw Thee before, and never, sure, behaved we so to Thee." "But thus ye treated these little ones that believe in Me and now stand on My right hand. In the disguise of these poor members of Mine I came soliciting your pity, but ye shut up your bowels of compassion from Me: I asked relief, but ye had none to give Me. Take back therefore your own coldness, your own contemptuous distance: Ye bid Me away from your presence, and now I bid you from Mine—*Depart from Me, ye cursed!"* **46. And these shall go away** —these "cursed" ones. Sentence, it should seem, was first *pronounced*—in the hearing of the wicked —upon the *righteous,* who thereupon sit as assessors in the judgment upon the wicked (I Cor. 6:2); but sentence is first *executed,* it should seem, upon the *wicked,* in the sight of the righteous—whose glory will thus not be beheld by the wicked, while *their* descent into "their own place" will be witnessed by the righteous, see on BENGEL notes. **into everlasting punishment**—or, as in vs. 41, "everlasting fire, prepared for the devil and his angels." Cf. ch. 13:42; II Thessalonians 1:9, etc. This is said to be "prepared for the devil and his angels," because they were "first in transgression." But both have one doom, because one unholy character. **but the righteous into life eternal**—i.e., "life everlasting." The word in both clauses, being in the original the same, should have been the same in the translation also. Thus the decisions of this awful day will be final, irreversible, unending.

CHAPTER 26

Vss. 1-16. CHRIST'S FINAL ANNOUNCEMENT OF HIS DEATH, AS NOW WITHIN TWO DAYS, AND THE SIMULTANEOUS CONSPIRACY OF THE JEWISH AUTHORITIES TO COMPASS IT—THE ANOINTING AT BETHANY —JUDAS AGREES WITH THE CHIEF PRIESTS TO BETRAY HIS LORD. (=Mark 14:1-11; Luke 22:1-6; John 12:1-11.) For the exposition, see on Mark 14:1-11.
17-30. PREPARATION FOR AND LAST CELEBRATION OF THE PASSOVER, ANNOUNCEMENT OF THE TRAITOR, AND INSTITUTION OF THE SUPPER. (=Mark 14:12-26; Luke 22:7-23; John 13:1-3, 10, 11, 18-30.) For the exposition, see on Luke 22:7-23.
31-35. THE DESERTION OF JESUS BY HIS DISCIPLES, AND THE DENIAL OF PETER FORETOLD. (= Mark 14:27-31; Luke 22:31-38; John 13:36-38.) For the exposition, see on Luke 22:31-38.
36-46. THE AGONY IN THE GARDEN. (=Mark 14:32-42; Luke 22:39-46.) For the exposition, see on Luke 22:39-46.
47-56. BETRAYAL AND APPREHENSION OF JESUS— FLIGHT OF HIS DISCIPLES. (=Mark 14:43-52; Luke 22:47-54; John 18:1-12). For the exposition, see on John 18:1-12.
57-75. JESUS ARRAIGNED BEFORE THE SANHEDRIM, CONDEMNED TO DIE, AND SHAMEFULLY ENTREATED—THE DENIAL OF PETER. (=Mark 14:53-72; Luke 22:54-71; John 18:13-18, 24-27.) For the exposition, see on Mark 14:53-72.

CHAPTER 27

Vss. 1-10. JESUS LED AWAY TO PILATE—REMORSE AND SUICIDE OF JUDAS. (= Mark 15:1; Luke 23:1; John 18:28).

Jesus Led Away to Pilate (vss. 1, 2). For the exposition of this portion, see on John 18:28, etc.

Remorse and Suicide of Judas (vss. 3-10). This portion is peculiar to Matthew. On the progress of guilt in the traitor, see on Mark 14:1-11; and on John 13:21-30. **3. Then Judas, which had betrayed him, when he saw that he was condemned**—The condemnation, even though not unexpected, might well fill him with horror. But perhaps this unhappy man expected, that, while he got the bribe, the Lord would miraculously escape, as He had once and again done before, out of His enemies' power: and if so, his remorse would come upon him with all the greater keenness. **repented himself**—but, as the issue too sadly showed, it was "the sorrow of the world, which worketh death" (II Cor. 7:10)—**and brought again the thirty pieces of silver to the chief priests and elders**—A remarkable illustration of the power of an awakened conscience. A short time before, the promise of this sordid pelf was temptation enough to his covetous heart to outweigh the most overwhelming obligations of duty and love; now, the possession of it so lashes him that he cannot use it, cannot even keep it! **4. Saying, I have sinned in that I have betrayed the innocent blood**—What a testimony this to Jesus! Judas had been with Him in all circumstances for three years; his post, as treasurer to Him and the Twelve (John 12:6), gave him peculiar opportunity of watching the spirit, disposition, and habits of his Master; while his covetous nature and thievish practices would incline him to dark and suspicious, rather than frank and generous, interpretations of all that He said and did. If, then, he could have fastened on one questionable feature in all that he had so long witnessed, we may be sure that no such speech as this would ever have escaped his lips, nor would he have been so stung with remorse as not to be able to keep the money and survive his crime. **And they said, What is that to us? see thou to that**—"Guilty or innocent is nothing to us: We have Him now—begone!" Was ever speech more hellish uttered? **5. And he cast down the pieces of silver**—The sarcastic, diabolical reply which he had got, in place of the sympathy which perhaps he expected, would deepen his remorse into an agony —**in the temple**—the temple proper, commonly called "the sanctuary," or "the holy place," into which only the priests might enter. How is this to be explained? Perhaps he flung the money in after them. But thus were fulfilled the words of the prophet—"I cast them to the potter in the house of the Lord" (Zech. 11:13)—**and departed, and went and hanged himself**—See, for the details, on Acts 1:18. **6. And the chief priests took the silver pieces, and said, It is not lawful for to put them into the treasury**—"the *Corban*," or chest containing the money dedicated to sacred purposes (see on ch. 15:5). **because it is the price of blood**—How scrupulous now! But those punctilious scruples made them unconsciously fulfil the Scripture. **9. Then was fulfilled that which was spoken by Jeremy the prophet, saying**—(Zech. 11:12, 13). Never was a complicated prophecy, otherwise hopelessly dark, more marvellously fulfilled. Various conjectures have been formed to account for Matthew's ascribing to Jeremiah a prophecy found in the book of Zechariah. But since with this book he was plainly familiar, having quoted one of its most remarkable prophecies of Christ but a few chapters before (ch. 21:4, 5), the question is one more of critical interest than real importance. Perhaps the true explanation is the following, from

LIGHTFOOT: "Jeremiah of old had the first place among the prophets, and hereby he comes to be mentioned above all the rest in ch. 16:14; because he stood first in the volume of the prophets [as he proves from the learned DAVID KIMCHI] therefore he is first named. When, therefore, Matthew produceth a text of Zechariah under the name of Jeremy, he only cites the words of the volume of the prophets under his name who stood first in the volume of the prophets. Of which sort is that also of our Saviour (Luke 24:41), "All things must be fulfilled which are written of Me in the Law, and the Prophets, and the Psalms," or the Book of Hagiographa, in which the Psalms were placed first."

11-26. JESUS AGAIN BEFORE PILATE—HE SEEKS TO RELEASE HIM, BUT AT LENGTH DELIVERS HIM TO BE CRUCIFIED. (=Mark 15:1-15; Luke 23:1-25; John 18:28-40). For the exposition, see on Luke 23:1-25, and on John 18:28-40.

27-33. JESUS, SCORNFULLY AND CRUELLY ENTREATED OF THE SOLDIERS, IS LED AWAY TO BE CRUCIFIED. (=Mark 15:16-22; Luke 23:26-31; John 19:2, 17.) For the exposition, see on Mark 15:16-22.

34-50. CRUCIFIXION AND DEATH OF THE LORD JESUS. (=Mark 15:25-37; Luke 23:33-46; John 19:18-30). For the exposition, see on John 19:18-30.

51-66. SIGNS AND CIRCUMSTANCES FOLLOWING THE DEATH OF THE LORD JESUS—HE IS TAKEN DOWN FROM THE CROSS, AND BURIED—THE SEPULCHRE IS GUARDED. (=Mark 15:38-47; Luke 23:47-56; John 19:31-42).

The Veil Rent (vs. 51). **51. And, behold, the veil of the temple was rent in twain from the top to the bottom**—This was the thick and gorgeously wrought veil which was hung between the "holy place" and the "holiest of all," shutting out all access to the presence of God as manifested "from above the mercy seat and from between the cherubim"—"the Holy Ghost this signifying, that the way into the holiest of all was *not yet* made manifest" (Heb. 9:8). Into this holiest of all none might enter, not even the high priest, save once a year, on the great day of atonement, and then only with the blood of atonement in his hands, which he sprinkled "upon and before the mercy seat seven times" (Lev. 16:14)—to signify that *access for sinners to a holy God is only through atoning blood*. But as they had only the blood of bulls and of goats, which could not take away sins (Heb. 10:4), during all the long ages that preceded the death of Christ the thick veil remained; the blood of bulls and of goats continued to be shed and sprinkled; and once a year access to God through an atoning sacrifice was vouchsafed—*in a picture*, or rather, was *dramatically represented*, in those symbolical actions—nothing more. But *now*, the one atoning Sacrifice being provided in the precious blood of Christ, access to this holy God could no longer be denied; and so the moment the Victim expired on the altar, that thick veil which for so many ages had been the dread symbol of *separation between God and guilty men* was, without a hand touching it, mysteriously "rent in twain from top to bottom" —"the Holy Ghost this signifying, that the way into the holiest of all was NOW made manifest!" How emphatic the statement, "*from top to bottom*"; as if to say, Come boldly now to the Throne of Grace; *the veil is clean gone*; the mercy seat stands open to the gaze of sinners, and the way to it is sprinkled with the blood of Him—"who through the eternal

Spirit hath offered Himself without spot to God!" Before, it was death *to go in,* now it is *death to stay out.* See more on this glorious subject on Hebrews 10:19-22.

An Earthquake—The Rocks Rent—The Graves Opened, that the Saints Which Slept in Them Might Come Forth after Their Lord's Resurrection (vss. 51-53). **51. and the earth did quake**—From what follows it would seem that this earthquake was local, having for its object the rending of the rocks and the opening of the graves—**and the rocks rent**—"were rent"—the physical creation thus sublimely proclaiming, at the bidding of its Maker, the *concusssion* which at that moment was taking place in the moral world at the most critical moment of its history. Extraordinary rents and fissures have been observed in the rocks near this spot. **52. And the graves were opened; and many bodies of the saints which slept arose**—These sleeping saints (see on I Thess. 4:14) were Old Testament believers, who—according to the usual punctuation in our version—were quickened into resurrection-life at the moment of their Lord's death, but lay in their graves till His resurrection, when they came forth. But it is far more natural, as we think, and consonant with other Scriptures, to understand that only the graves were opened, probably by the earthquake, at our Lord's death, and this only in preparation for the subsequent exit of those who slept in them, when the Spirit of life should enter into them from their risen Lord, and along with Him they should come forth, trophies of His victory over the grave. Thus, in the opening of the graves at the moment of the Redeemer's expiring, there was a glorious symbolical proclamation that the death which had just taken place had "swallowed up death in victory"; and whereas the saints that slept in them were awakened only by their risen Lord, to accompany Him out of the tomb, it was fitting that "the Prince of Life" "should be *the First* that should rise from the dead" (Acts 26: 23; I Cor. 15:20, 23; Col. 1:18; Rev. 1:5). **and went into the holy city**—that city where He, in virtue of whose resurrection they were now alive, had been condemned. **and appeared unto many**—that there might be undeniable evidence of their own resurrection first, and through it of their Lord's. Thus, while it was not deemed fitting that He Himself should appear again in Jerusalem, save to the disciples, provision was made that the fact of His resurrection should be left in no doubt. It must be observed, however, that the resurrection of these sleeping saints was not like those of the widow of Nain's son, of Jairus' daughter, of Lazarus, and of the man who "revived and stood upon his feet," on his dead body touching the bones of Elisha (II Kings 13:21)—which were mere temporary recallings of the departed spirit to the *mortal* body, to be followed by a final departure of it "till the trumpet shall sound." But this was a resurrection *once for all, to life everlasting;* and so there is no room to doubt that they went to glory with their Lord, as bright trophies of His victory over death.

The Centurion's Testimony (vs. 54). **Now when the centurion**—the military superintendent of the execution. **and they that were with him watching Jesus, saw the earthquake**—or felt it and witnessed its effects. **and those things that were done** —reflecting upon the entire transaction. **they feared greatly**—convinced of the presence of a Divine Hand. **saying, Truly this was the Son of God**— There cannot be a reasonable doubt that this expression was used in the Jewish sense, and that it

points to the claim which Jesus made to be the Son of God, and on which His condemnation expressly turned. The meaning, then, clearly is that He must have been what He professed to be; in other words, that He was no impostor. There was no medium between those two. See, on the similar testimony of the penitent thief—"This man hath done nothing amiss"—on Luke 23:41.

The Galilean Women (vss. 55, 56). **55. And many women were there beholding afar off, which followed Jesus**—The sense here would be better brought out by the use of the pluperfect, "which had followed Jesus." **from Galilee, ministering unto him**—As these dear women had ministered to Him during His glorious missionary tours *in* Galilee (see on Luke 8:1-3), so from this statement it should seem that they accompanied him and ministered to His wants *from* Galilee on His final journey to Jerusalem. **56. Among which was Mary Magdalene**—(see on Luke 8:2). **and Mary the mother of James and Joses**—the wife of Cleophas, or rather Clopas, and sister of the Virgin (John 19:25). See on ch. 13:55, 56. **and the mother of Zebedee's children**—i.e., Salome: cf. Mark 15:40. All this about the women is mentioned for the sake of what is afterwards to be related of their purchasing spices to anoint their Lord's body.

The Taking Down from the Cross and the Burial (vss 57-60). For the exposition of this portion, see on John 19:38-42.

The Women Mark the Sacred Spot, that They Might Recognize It on Coming Thither to Anoint the Body (vs. 61). **61. And there was Mary Magdalene, and the other Mary**—"the mother of James and Joses," mentioned before (vs. 56)—**sitting over against the sepulchre**—See on Mark 16:1.

The Sepulchre Guarded (vss. 62-66). **62. Now the next day, that followed the day of the preparation**—i.e., after six o'clock of our *Saturday* evening. The crucifixion took place on the *Friday* and all was not over till shortly before sunset, when the Jewish sabbath commenced; and "that sabbath day was an high day" (John 19:31), being the first day of the feast of unleavened bread. That day being over at six on Saturday evening, they hastened to take their measures. **63. Saying, Sir, we remember that that deceiver**—Never, remarks Bengel, will you find the heads of the people calling Jesus by His own name. And yet here there is betrayed a certain uneasiness, which one almost fancies they only tried to stifle in their own minds, as well as crush in Pilate's, in case he should have any lurking suspicion that he had done wrong in yielding to them. **said, while he was yet alive**—Important testimony this, from the lips of His bitterest enemies, to *the reality of Christ's death*; the cornerstone of the whole Christian religion. **After three days**—which, according to the customary Jewish way of reckoning, need signify no more than "after the commencement of the third day." **I will rise again**— "I rise," in the present tense, thus reporting not only the *fact* that this prediction of His had reached their ears, but that they understood Him to look forward *confidently* to its occurring on the very day named. **64. Command therefore that the sepulchre be made sure**—by a Roman guard. **until the third day**—after which, if He still lay in the grave, the imposture of His claims would be manifest to all. **and say unto the people, he is risen from the dead.** —Did they really fear this? **so the last error shall be worse than the first**—the imposture of His pretended resurrection worse than that of His pretended Messiahship. **65. Pilate said unto them,**

Ye have a watch—The guards had already acted under orders of the Sanhedrim, with Pilate's consent; but probably they were not clear about employing them as a night-watch without Pilate's express authority. **go your way, make it as sure as ye can**—as ye know how, or in the way ye deem securest. Though there may be no irony in this speech, it evidently insinuated that *if* the event should be contrary to their wish, it would not be for want of sufficient human appliances to prevent it. **66. So they went, and made the sepulchre sure, sealing the stone**—which Mark (16:4) says was "very great." **and setting a watch**—to guard it. What more could man do? But while they are trying to prevent the resurrection of the Prince of Life, God makes use of their precautions for His own ends. Their stone-covered, sealsecured sepulchre shall preserve the sleeping dust of the Son of God free from all indignities, in undisturbed, sublime repose; while their watch shall be His guard of honor until the angels shall come to take their place.

CHAPTER 28

Vss. 1-15. Glorious Angelic Announcement on the First Day of the Week, that Christ Is Risen—His Appearance to the Women—The Guards Bribed to Give a False Account of the Resurrection. (=Mark 16:1-8; Luke 24:1-8; John 20:1).

The Resurrection Announced to the Women (vss. 1-8). **1. In the end of the sabbath, as it began to dawn**—after the Sabbath, as it grew toward daylight. **toward the first day of the week**—Luke (24:1) has it, "very early in the morning"—properly, "at the first appearance of daybreak"; and corresponding with this, John (20:1) says, "when it was yet dark." See on Mark 16:2. Not an hour, it would seem, was lost by those dear lovers of the Lord Jesus. **came Mary Magdalene, and the other Mary**—"the mother of James and Joses" (see on ch. 27:56, 61). **to see the sepulchre**—with a view to the anointing of the body, for which they had made all their preparations. (See on Mark 16:1, 2). **And, behold, there was**—i.e., there had been, before the arrival of the women. **a great earthquake; for the angel of the Lord descended from heaven...**—And this was the state of things when the women drew near. Some judicious critics think all this was transacted while the women were approaching; but the view we have given, which is the prevalent one, seems the more natural. All this august preparation—recorded by Matthew alone—bespoke the grandeur of the exit which was to follow. The angel sat upon the huge stone, to overawe, with the lightning-luster that darted from him, the Roman guard, and do honor to his rising Lord. **3. His countenance**—appearance—**was like lightning, and his raiment white as snow**—the one expressing the *glory,* the other the *purity* of the celestial abode from which he came. **4. And for fear of him the keepers did shake, and became as dead men**—Is the sepulchre "sure" now, O ye chief priests? He that sitteth in the heavens doth laugh at you. **5. And the angel answered and said unto the women, Fear not ye**—The "ye" here is emphatic, to contrast their case with that of the guards. "Let those puny creatures, sent to keep the Living One among the dead, for fear of Me shake and become as dead men (vs. 4); but ye that have come hither on another errand, fear not ye." **for I know that ye seek Jesus, which was crucified**—Jesus the Cruci-

fied. **6. He is not here; for he is risen, as he said**—See on Luke 24:5-7. **Come**—as in ch. 11:28. **see the place where the Lord lay.** Charming invitation! "Come, see the spot where the Lord of glory lay: now it is an empty grave: He lies not here, but He *lay* there. Come, feast your eyes on it!" But see on John 20:12. **7. And go quickly, and tell his disciples**—For a precious addition to this, see on Mark 16:7. **that he is risen from the dead; and, behold, he goeth before you into Galilee**—to which those women belonged (ch. 27:55). **there shall ye see him**—This must refer to those more public manifestations of Himself to large numbers of disciples at once, which He vouchsafed only in Galilee; for individually He was seen of some of those very women almost immediately after this (vss. 9, 10). **Lo, I have told you**—Behold, ye have this word from the world of light! **8. And they departed quickly**—Mark (16:8) says "they fled." **from the sepulchre with fear and great joy**—How natural this combination of feelings! See on a similar statement of Mark 16:11. **and did run to bring his disciples word**—"Neither said they anything to any man [by the way]; for they were afraid" (Mark 16:8).

Appearance to the Women (vss. 9,:10). This appearance is recorded only by Matthew. **9. And as they went to tell his disciples, behold, Jesus met them, saying, All hail!**—the usual salute, but from the lips of Jesus bearing a higher signification. **And they came and held him by the feet**—How truly womanly! **10. Then said Jesus unto them, Be not afraid**—What dear associations would these familiar words—now uttered in a higher style, but by the same Lips—bring rushing back to their recollection! **go tell my brethren that they go into Galilee, and there shall they see me**—The brethren here meant must have been His brethren after the flesh (cf. 13:55); for His brethren in the higher sense (see on John 20:17) had several meetings with Him at Jerusalem *before* He went to Galilee, which they would have missed if they had been the persons ordered to Galilee to meet Him.

The Guards Bribed (vss. 11-15). The whole of this important portion is peculiar to Matthew. **11. Now when they were going**—while the women were on their way to deliver to His brethren the message of their risen Lord. **some of the watch came into the city, and showed unto the chief priests all the things that were done**—Simple, unsophisticated soldiers! How could ye imagine that such a tale as ye had to tell would not at once commend itself to your scared employers? Had they doubted this for a moment, would they have ventured to go near them, knowing it was death to a Roman soldier to be proved asleep when on guard? and of course that was the only other explanation of the case. **12. And when they were assembled with the elders**—But Joseph at least was absent: Gamaliel probably also; and perhaps others. **and had taken counsel, they gave large money unto the soldiers**—It would need a good deal; but the whole case of the Jewish authorities was now at stake. With what contempt must these soldiers have regarded the Jewish ecclesiastics! **13. Saying, Say ye, His disciples came by night, and stole him away while we slept**—which, as we have observed, was a capital offense for soldiers on guard. **14. And if this come to the governor's ears**—rather, "If this come before the governor"; i.e., not in the way of mere report, but for judicial investigation—**we will persuade him, and secure you**—The "we" and the "you" are emphatic here—"we shall [take care to] persuade him and keep you from trouble," or "save you harmless." The grammatical form of this clause implies that the thing supposed was expected to happen. The meaning then is, "If this come before the governor—as it likely will—we shall see to it that . . . ." The "persuasion" of Pilate meant, doubtless, quieting him by a bribe, which we know otherwise he was by no means above taking (like Felix afterwards, Acts 24:26). **15. So they took the money, and did as they were taught**—thus consenting to brand themselves with infamy. **and this saying is commonly reported among the Jews until this day**—to the date of the publication of this Gospel. The wonder is that so clumsy and incredible a story lasted so long. But those who are resolved *not* to come to the light will catch at straws. JUSTIN MARTYR, who flourished about A.D. 170, says, in his *Dialogue with Trypho the Jew,* that the Jews dispersed the story by means of special messengers sent to every country.

16-20. JESUS MEETS WITH THE DISCIPLES ON A MOUNTAIN IN GALILEE, AND GIVES FORTH THE GREAT COMMISSION. **16. Then the eleven disciples went away into Galilee**—but certainly not before the second week after the resurrection, and probably somewhat later. **into a mountain where Jesus had appointed them**—It should have been rendered "the mountain," meaning some certain mountain which He had named to them—probably the night before He suffered, when He said, "After I am risen, I will go before you into Galilee" (ch. 26:32; Mark 14:28). What it was can only be conjectured; but of the two between which opinions are divided—the Mount of the Beatitudes or Mount Tabor—the former is much the more probable, from its nearness to the Sea of Tiberias, where last before this the Narrative tells us that He met and dined with seven of them. (John 21:1, etc.). That the interview here recorded was the same as that referred to in one place only—I Corinthians 15:6—when "He was seen of above five hundred brethren at once; of whom the greater part remained unto that day, though some were fallen asleep," is now the opinion of the ablest students of the evangelical history. Nothing can account for such a number as five hundred assembling at one spot but the expectation of some promised manifestation of their risen Lord: and the promise before His resurrection, twice repeated after it, best explains this immense gathering. **17. And when they saw him, they worshipped him; but some doubted**—certainly none of "the Eleven," after what took place at previous interviews in Jerusalem. But if the five hundred were now present, we may well believe this of some of them. **19. Go ye therefore, and teach all nations**—rather, "make disciples of all nations"; for "teaching," in the more usual sense of that word, comes in afterwards, and is expressed by a different term. **baptizing them in the name**—It should be, "into the name"; as in I Corinthians 10:2, "And were all baptized unto (or rather '*into*') Moses"; and Galatians 3:27, "For as many of you as have been baptized *into* Christ." **of the Father, and of the Son, and of the Holy Ghost; 20. Teaching them**—This is teaching in the more usual sense of the term; or instructing the converted and baptized disciples. **to observe all things whatsoever I have commanded you: and, lo, I**—The "I" here is emphatic. It is enough that *I*—**am with you alway** —"all the days"; i.e., till making converts, baptizing, and building them up by Christian instruction, shall

be no more. **even unto the end of the world. Amen**—This glorious Commission embraces two primary departments, the *Missionary* and the *Pastoral,* with two sublime and comprehensive *Encouragements* to undertake and go through with them.

First, The MISSIONARY department (vs. 18): "Go, make disciples of all nations." In the corresponding passage of Mark (16:15) it is, "Go ye into all the world, and preach the Gospel to every creature." The only difference is, that in this passage the *sphere,* in its worldwide compass and its universality of *objects,* is more fully and definitely expressed; while in the former the great *aim* and certain *result* is delightfully expressed in the command to "make disciples of all nations." "Go, conquer the world for Me; carry the glad tidings into all lands and to every ear, and deem not this work at an end till all nations shall have embraced the Gospel and enrolled themselves My disciples." Now, Was all this meant to be done by the Eleven men nearest to Him of the multitude then crowding around the risen Redeemer? Impossible. Was it to be done even in their lifetime? Surely not. In that little band Jesus virtually addressed Himself to all who, in every age, should take up from them the same work. Before the eyes of the Church's risen Head were spread out, in those Eleven men, all His servants of every age; and one and all of them received His commission at that moment. Well, what next? Set the seal of visible discipleship upon the converts, by "baptizing them into the name," i.e., into the whole fulness of the grace "of the Father, and of the Son, and of the Holy Ghost," as belonging to them who believe. (See on II Cor. 13:14.) This done, the Missionary department of your work, which in its own nature is temporary, must merge in another, which is permanent. This is—

Second, The PASTORAL department (vs. 20): "Teach them"—teach these baptized members of the Church visible—"to observe all things whatsoever I have commanded you," My apostles, during the three years ye have been with Me.

What must have been the feelings which such a Commission awakened? "WE who have scarce conquered our own misgivings—we, fishermen of Galilee, with no letters, no means, no influence over the humblest creature, conquer the world for Thee, Lord? Nay, Lord, do not mock us." "I mock you not, nor send you a warfare on your own charges. For"—Here we are brought to—

Third, The ENCOURAGEMENTS to undertake and go through with this work. These are two; one in the van, the other in the rear of the Commission itself.

First Encouragement: "All power in *heaven*"— the whole power of Heaven's love and wisdom and strength, "and all power in *earth*"—power over all persons, all passions, all principles, all movements —to bend them to this one high object, the evangelization of the world: All this "is *given unto Me,*" as the risen Lord of all, to be *by Me placed at your command*—"Go ye therefore." But there remains a—

Second Encouragement: "And lo! I am with you all the days"—not only to perpetuity, but without one day's interruption, "even to the end of the world," The "Amen" is of doubtful genuineness in this place. If, however, it belongs to the text, it is the Evangelist's own closing word.

THE GOSPEL ACCORDING TO

MARK

INTRODUCTION

THAT the Second Gospel was written by Mark is universally agreed, though by what Mark, not so. The great majority of critics take the writer to be "John whose surname was Mark," of whom we read in the Acts, and who was "sister's son to Barnabas" (Col. 4:10). But no reason whatever is assigned for this opinion, for which the tradition, though ancient, is not uniform; and one cannot but wonder how it is so easily taken for granted by WETSTEIN, HUG, MEYER, EBRARD, LANGE, ELLICOTT, DAVIDSON, TREGELLES, etc. ALFORD goes the length of saying it "has been universally believed that he was the same person with the John Mark of the Gospels." But GROTIUS thought differently, and so did SCHLEIERMACHER, CAMPBELL, BURTON, and DA COSTA; and the grounds on which it is concluded that they were two different persons appear to us quite unanswerable. "Of John, surnamed Mark," says CAMPBELL, in his Preface to this Gospel, "one of the first things we learn is, that he attended Paul and Barnabas in their apostolical journeys, when these two travelled together (Acts 12:25; 13:5). And when afterwards there arose a dispute between them concerning him, insomuch that they separated, Mark accompanied his uncle Barnabas, and Silas attended Paul. When Paul was reconciled to Mark, which was probably soon after, we find Paul again employing Mark's assistance, recommending him, and giving him a very honorable testimony (Col. 4:10; II Tim. 4:11; Philemon 24). But we hear not a syllable of his attending Peter as his minister, or assisting him in any capacity." And yet, as we shall presently see, no tradition is more ancient, more uniform, and better sustained by internal evidence, than that Mark, in his Gospel, was but "the interpreter of Peter," who, at the close of his first Epistle speaks of him as "Marcus my son" (I Peter 5:13), that is, without doubt, his son in the Gospel—converted to Christ through his instrumentality. And when we consider how little the Apostles Peter and Paul were together—how seldom they even met—how different were their tendencies, and how separate their spheres of labor, is there not, in the absence of all evidence of the fact, something approaching to violence in the supposition that the same Mark was the intimate associate of both? "In brief," adds CAMPBELL, "the accounts given of Paul's attendant, and those of Peter's interpreter, concur in nothing but the name, Mark or Marcus; too slight a circumstance to conclude the sameness of the person from, especially when we consider how common the name was at Rome, and how customary it was for the Jews in that age to assume some Roman name when they went thither."

Regarding the Evangelist Mark, then, as another person from Paul's companion in travel, all we know of his personal history is that he was a convert, as we have seen, of the Apostle Peter. But as to his Gospel, the tradition regarding Peter's hand in it is so ancient, so uniform, and so remarkably confirmed by internal evidence, that we must regard it as an established fact. "Mark," says PAPIAS (according to the testimony of EUSEBIUS, *Ecclesiastical History*, 3:39), "becoming *the interpreter of Peter*, wrote accurately, though not in order, whatever he remembered of what was either said or done by Christ; for he was neither a hearer of the Lord nor a follower of Him, but afterwards, as I said, [he was a follower] of Peter, who arranged the discourses for use, but not according to the order in which they were uttered by the Lord." To the same effect IRENÆUS (*adverses* HÆRESES, 3:1): "Matthew published a Gospel while Peter and Paul were preaching and founding the Church at Rome; and after their departure (or decease), Mark, *the disciple and interpreter of Peter*, he also gave forth to us in writing the things which were preached by Peter." And CLEMENT of Alexandria is still more specific, in a passage preserved to us by EUSEBIUS (*Ecclesiastical History*, 6:14): "Peter having publicly preached the word at Rome, and spoken forth the Gospel by the Spirit, many of those present exhorted Mark, as *having long been a follower of his*, and remembering what he had said, to write what had been spoken; and that having prepared the Gospel, he delivered it to those who had asked him for it; which, when Peter came to the knowledge of, he neither decidedly forbade nor encouraged him." EUSEBIUS' own testimony, however, from other accounts, is rather different: that Peter's hearers were so penetrated by his preaching that they gave Mark, as being *a follower of Peter*, no rest till he consented to write his Gospel, as a memorial of his oral teaching; and "that the apostle, when he knew by the revelation of the Spirit what had been done, was delighted with the zeal of those men, and sanctioned the reading of the writing (that is, of this Gospel of Mark) in the churches" (*Ecclesiastical History*, 2:15). And giving in another of his works a similar statement, he says that "Peter, from excess of humility, did not think himself qualified to write the Gospel; but Mark, his acquaintance and pupil, is said to have recorded his relations of the actings of Jesus. And Peter testifies these things of himself; for all things that are recorded by Mark are said to be memoirs of Peter's discourses." It is needless to go farther—to ORIGEN, who says Mark composed his Gospel "as Peter guided" or "directed him, who, in his Catholic Epistle, calls him his son," etc.; and to JEROME, who but echoes EUSEBIUS.

This, certainly, is a remarkable chain of testimony; which, confirmed as it is by such striking internal evidence, may be regarded as establishing the fact that the Second Gospel was drawn up mostly from materials furnished by Peter. In DA COSTA's *Four Witnesses* the reader will find this internal evidence detailed at length, though all the examples are not equally convincing. But if the reader will refer to our remarks on Mark 16:7, and John 18:27, he will have convincing evidence of a *Petrine* hand in this Gospel.

It remains only to advert, in a word or two, to the *readers* for whom this Gospel was, in the first instance, designed, and the *date* of it. That it was not for *Jews* but *Gentiles*, is evident from the great number of explanations of Jewish usages, opinions, and places, which to a Jew would at that time have been superfluous, but were highly needful to a Gentile. We can here but refer to chs. 2:18; 7:3, 4; 12:18; 13:3; 14:12; 15:42, for examples of these. Regarding the date of this Gospel—about which nothing certain is known—if the tradition reported by IRENÆUS can be relied on that it was written at Rome, "after the departure of Peter and Paul," and if by that word "departure" we are to understand their *death*, we may date it somewhere between the years 64 and 68; but in all likelihood this is too late. It is probably nearer the truth to date it eight or ten years earlier.

CHAPTER 1

Vss. 1-8. THE PREACHING AND BAPTISM OF JOHN. (=Matthew 3:1-12; Luke 3:1-18.) **1. The beginning of the gospel of Jesus Christ, the Son of God** —By the "Gospel" of Jesus Christ here is evidently meant the blessed Story which our Evangelist is about to tell of His Life, Ministry, Death, Resurrection, and Glorification, and of the begun Gathering of Believers in His Name. The abruptness with which he announces his subject, and the energetic brevity with which, passing by all preceding events, he hastens over the ministry of John and records the Baptism and Temptation of Jesus—as if impatient to come to the Public Life of the Lord of glory—have often been noticed as characteristic of this Gospel—a Gospel whose direct, practical, and singularly vivid setting imparts to it a preciousness peculiar to itself. What strikes every one is, that though the briefest of all the Gospels, this is in some of the principal scenes of our Lord's history the fullest. But what is not so obvious is, that wherever the finer and subtler feelings of humanity, or the deeper and more peculiar hues of our Lord's character were brought out, these, though they should be lightly passed over by all the other Evangelists, are sure to be found here, and in touches of such quiet delicacy and power, that though scarce observed by the cursory reader, they leave indelible impressions upon all the thoughtful and furnish a key to much that is in the other Gospels. These few opening words of the Second Gospel are enough to show, that though it was the purpose of this Evangelist to record chiefly the outward and palpable facts of our Lord's public life, he recognized in Him, in common with the Fourth Evangelist, the glory of the Only-begotten of the Father. **2. As it is written in the prophets,**—(Mal. 3:1; Isa. 40:3)—**Behold, I send my messenger before thy face, which shall prepare thy way before thee. 3. The voice of one crying in the wilderness, Prepare ye the way of the Lord, make his paths straight**—The second of these quotations is given by Matthew and Luke in the same connection, but they reserve the former quotation till they have occasion to return to the Baptist, after his imprisonment (Matt. 11:10; Luke 7: 27). (Instead of the words, "as it is written in the Prophets," there is weighty evidence in favor of the following reading: "As it is written in Isaiah the prophet." This reading is adopted by all the latest critical editors. If it be the true one, it is to be explained thus—that of the two quotations, the one from Malachi is but a later development of the great primary one in Isaiah, from which the whole prophetical matter here quoted takes its name. But the received text is quoted by IRENAEUS, before the end of the second century, and the evidence in its favor is greater in *amount*, if not in weight. The chief objection to it is, that if this was the true reading, it is difficult to see how the other one could have got in at all; whereas, if it be not the true reading, it is very easy to see how it found its way into the text, as it removes the startling difficulty of a prophecy beginning with the words of Malachi being ascribed to Isaiah). For

the exposition, see on Matthew 3:1-6, 11.

9-11. BAPTISM OF CHRIST, AND DESCENT OF THE SPIRIT UPON HIM IMMEDIATELY THEREAFTER. (= Matt. 3:13-17; Luke 3:21, 22.) See on Matthew 3:13-17.

12, 13. TEMPTATION OF CHRIST. (=Matt. 4:1-11; Luke 4:1-13.) See on Matthew 4:1-11.

14-20. CHRIST BEGINS HIS GALILEAN MINISTRY —CALLING OF SIMON AND ANDREW, JAMES AND JOHN. See on Matthew 4:12-22.

21-39. HEALING OF A DEMONIAC IN THE SYNAGOGUE OF CAPERNAUM, AND THEREAFTER OF SIMON'S MOTHER-IN-LAW AND MANY OTHERS—JESUS, NEXT DAY, IS FOUND IN A SOLITARY PLACE AT MORNING PRAYERS, AND IS ENTREATED TO RETURN, BUT DECLINES, AND GOES FORTH ON HIS FIRST MISSIONARY CIRCUIT. (=Luke 4:31-44; Matt. 8:14-17; 4:23-25.) **21. And they went into Capernaum**—(See on Matthew 4:13). **and straightway on the sabbath day he entered into the synagogue, and taught**— This should have been rendered, "straightway on the sabbaths He entered into the synagogue and taught," or "continued to teach." The meaning is, that as He began this practice on the very first sabbath after coming to settle at Capernaum, so He continued it regularly thereafter. **22. And they were astonished at his doctrine**—or "teaching" —referring quite as much to the manner as the matter of it. **for he taught them as one that had authority, and not as the scribes**—See on Matthew 7:28, 29. **23. And there was in their synagogue a man with**—lit., "in"—**an unclean spirit**—i.e., so entirely under demoniacal power that his personality was sunk for the time in that of the spirit. The frequency with which this character of "impurity" is ascribed to evil spirits—some twenty times in the Gospels—is not to be overlooked. **and he cried out, 24.** Saying, Let us alone—or rather, perhaps, "ah!" expressive of mingled *astonishment* and *terror*. **what have we to do with thee**—an expression of frequent occurrence in the Old Testament (I Kings 17:18; II Kings 3:13; II Chron. 35:21, etc.). It denotes *entire separation of interests:*—i.e., "Thou and we have nothing in common; we want not Thee; what wouldst Thou with us?" For the analogous application of it by our Lord to His mother, see on John 2:4. **thou Jesus of Nazareth**—"Jesus, Nazarene!" an epithet originally given to express contempt, but soon adopted as the current designation by those who held our Lord in honor (Luke 18:37; ch. 16:6; Acts 2:22). **art thou come to destroy us?** —In the case of the Gadarene demoniac the question was, "Art Thou come hither to torment us before the time?" (Matt. 8:29). Themselves tormentors and destroyers of their victims, they discern in Jesus their own destined tormentor and destroyer, anticipating and dreading what they know and feel to be awaiting them! Conscious, too, that their power was but permitted and temporary, and perceiving in Him, perhaps, the woman's Seed that was to bruise the head and destroy the works of the devil, they regard His approach to them on this occasion as a signal to let go their grasp of this miserable victim. **I know thee who thou art, the Holy One of God**—This and other even more glorious testimonies to our Lord were given, as we know, with no good will, but in hope that, by the acceptance of them, He might appear to the people to be in league with evil spirits—a calumny which His enemies were ready enough to throw out against Him. But a Wiser than either was here, who invariably rejected and silenced the testimonies that came to Him from beneath, and thus was able to rebut the imputations of His enemies against Him (Matt. 12:24-30). The expression, "Holy One of God," seems evidently taken from that Messianic Psalm (16:10), in which He is styled "Thine Holy One." **25. And Jesus rebuked him, saying, Hold thy peace, and come out of him**—A glorious word of command. BENGEL remarks that it was only the testimony borne to Himself which our Lord meant to silence. That he should afterwards cry out for fear or rage (vs. 26) He would right willingly permit. **26. And when the unclean spirit had torn him**—Luke (4:35) says, "When he had thrown him in the midst," Malignant cruelty—just showing what he *would* have done, if permitted to go farther: it was a last fling! **and cried with a loud voice**—the voice of enforced submission and despair. **he came out of him**—Luke (4:35) adds, "and hurt him not." Thus impotent were the malignity and rage of the impure spirit when under the restraint of "the Stronger than the strong one armed" (Luke 11: 21, 22). **27. What thing is this? what new doctrine**—teaching—**is this?**—The audience, rightly apprehending that the miracle was wrought to illustrate the teaching and display the character and glory of the Teacher, begin by asking what novel kind of teaching this could be, which was so marvellously attested. **28. And immediately his fame spread abroad throughout all the region round about Galilee**—rather, "the whole region of Galilee"; though some, as MEYER and ELLICOTT, explain it of the country surrounding Galilee. **29. And forthwith, when they were come out of the synagogue**—so also in Luke 4:38. **they entered into the house of Simon and Andrew, with James and John**—The mention of these four—which is peculiar to Mark —is the first of those traces of Peter's hand in this Gospel, of which we shall find many more. The house being his, and the illness and cure so nearly affecting himself, it is interesting to observe this minute specification of the number and names of the witnesses; interesting also as the first occasion on which the sacred triumvirate of Peter and James and John are selected from among the rest, to be a threefold cord of testimony to certain events in their Lord's life (see on ch. 5:37)—Andrew being present on this occasion, as the occurrence took place in his own house. **30. But Simon's wife's mother lay sick of a fever**—Luke, as was natural in "the beloved *physician*" (Col. 4:14), describes it professionally; calling it a "great fever," and thus distinguishing it from that lighter kind which the Greek physicians were wont to call "small fevers," as GALEN, quoted by WETSTEIN, tells us. **and anon**—immediately. **they tell him of her**—naturally hoping that His compassion and power towards one of His own disciples would not be less signally displayed than towards the demonized stranger in the synagogue. **31. And he came and took her by the hand**—rather, "And advancing, He took her . . ." The beloved physician again is very specific: "And He stood over her." **and lifted her up**—This act of condescension, most felt doubtless by Peter, is recorded only by Mark. **and immediately the fever left her, and she ministered unto them**—preparing their sabbath-meal: in token both of the perfectness and immediateness of the cure, and of

her gratitude to the glorious Healer. **32. And at even, when the sun did set**—so Matthew 8:16. Luke (4:40) says it was setting. **they brought unto him all that were diseased, and them that were possessed with devils**—the demonized. From Luke 13:14 we see how unlawful they would have deemed it to bring their sick to Jesus for a cure during the sabbath hours. They waited, therefore, till these were over, and then brought them in crowds. Our Lord afterwards took repeated occasion to teach the people by example, even at the risk of His own life, how superstitious a straining of the sabbath-rest this was. **33. And all the city was gathered together at the door**—of Peter's house; i.e., the sick, and those who brought them, and the wondering spectators. This bespeaks the presence of an eye-witness, and is one of those lively examples of word-painting so frequent in this Gospel. **34. And he healed many that were sick of divers diseases, and cast out many devils**—In Matthew 8:16 it is said, "He cast out the spirits with His word"; or rather, "with a word"—a word of command. **and suffered not the devils to speak, because they knew him**—Evidently they *would* have spoken, if permitted, proclaiming His Messiahship in such terms as in the synagogue; but once in one day, and that testimony immediately silenced, was enough. See on vs. 24. After this account of His miracles of healing, we have in Matthew 8:17 this pregnant quotation, "That it might be fulfilled which was spoken by Esaias the prophet, saying [53:4], Himself took our infirmities, and bare our sicknesses." **35. And in the morning**—i.e., of the day after this remarkable sabbath; or, *on the first day of the week*. His choosing this day to inaugurate a new and glorious stage of His public work, should be noted by the reader. **rising up a great while before day**—"while it was yet night," or long before daybreak. **he went out**—all unperceived from Peter's house, where He slept. **and departed into a solitary place, and there prayed**—or, "continued in prayer." He was about to begin His first preaching and healing circuit; and as on similar solemn occasions (Luke 5:16; 6:12; 9:18, 28, 29; ch. 6:46), He spent some time in special prayer, doubtless with a view to it. What would one not give to have been, during the stillness of those grey morning-hours, within hearing—not of His "strong crying and tears," for He had scarce arrived at the stage for that—but of His calm, exalted anticipations of the work which lay immediately before Him, and the outpourings of His soul about it into the bosom of Him that sent Him! He had doubtless enjoyed some uninterrupted hours of such communings with His heavenly Father ere His friends from Capernaum arrived in search of Him. As for them, they doubtless expected, after such a day of miracles, that the next day would witness similar manifestations. When morning came, Peter, loath to break in upon the repose of his glorious Guest, would await His appearance beyond the usual hour; but at length, wondering at the stillness, and gently coming to see where the Lord lay, he finds it—like the sepulchre afterwards—empty! Speedily a party is made up to go in search of Him, Peter naturally leading the way. **36. And Simon and they that were with him followed after him**—rather, "pressed after Him." Luke (4:42) says, "The multitudes sought after Him"; but this would be a party from the town. Mark, having his information from Peter himself, speaks only of what related directly to him. "They that were with him" would probably be Andrew his brother, James and John, with a few other choice brethren. **37. And when they had found him—**evidently after some search. **they said unto him, All men seek for thee—**By this time, "the multitudes" who, according to Luke, "sought after Him" —and who, on going to Peter's house, and there learning that Peter and a few more were gone in search of Him, had set out on the same errand—would have arrived, and "came unto Him and stayed Him, that He should not depart from them" (Luke 4:42); all now urging His return to their impatient townsmen. **38. And he said unto them, Let us go—**or, according to another reading, "Let us go elsewhere." **into the next towns—**rather, "unto the neighboring village-towns"; meaning those places intermediate between towns and villages, with which the western side of the Sea of Galilee was studded. **that I may preach there also; for therefore came I forth—**not from Capernaum, as DE WETTE miserably interprets, nor from His privacy in the desert place, as MEYER, no better; but from the Father. Cf. John 16:28, "I came forth from the Father, and am come into the world . . ."—another proof, by the way, that the lofty phraseology of the Fourth Gospel was not unknown to the authors of the others, though their design and point of view are different. The language in which our Lord's reply is given by Luke (4:43) expresses the high necessity under which, in this as in every other step of His work, He acted—"I must preach the kingdom of God to other cities also; for therefore"—or, "to this end"—"am I sent." An act of self-denial it doubtless was, to resist such pleadings to return to Capernaum. But there were overmastering considerations on the other side.

40-45. HEALING OF A LEPER. (=Matt. 8:1-4; Luke 5:12-16.) See on Matthew 8:1-4.

CHAPTER 2

Vss. 1-12. HEALING OF A PARALYTIC. (=Matt. 9:1-8; Luke 5:17-26.) This incident, as remarked on Matthew 9:1, appears to follow next in order of time after the cure of the leper (ch. 1:40-45). **1. And again he entered into Capernaum—**"His own city" (Matt. 9:1). **and it was noised that he was in the house—**no doubt of Simon Peter (ch. 1:29). **2. And straightway many were gathered together, insomuch that there was no room to receive them, no, not so much as about the door—**This is one of Mark's graphic touches. No doubt in this case, as the scene occured at his informant's own door, these details are the vivid recollections of that honored disciple. **and he preached the word unto them—**i.e., indoors; but in the hearing, doubtless, of the multitude that pressed around. Had He gone forth, as He naturally would, the paralytic's faith would have had no such opportunity to display itself. Luke (5:17) furnishes an additional and very important incident in the scene—as follows: "And it came to pass on a certain day, as He was teaching, that there were Pharisees and doctors of the law sitting by, which were come out of every town," or village, "of Galilee, and Judea, and Jerusalem." This was the highest testimony yet borne to our Lord's growing influence, and the necessity increasingly felt by the ecclesiastics throughout the country of coming to some definite judgment regarding Him. "And the power of the Lord was [present] to heal them"—or, "was [efficacious] to heal them," i.e., the sick that were brought before Him. So that the miracle that is now to be de-

scribed was among the most glorious and worthy to be recorded of many then performed; and what made it so was doubtless the faith which was manifested in connection with it, and the proclamation of the forgiveness of the patient's sins that immediately preceded it. **3. And they come unto him—**i.e., towards the house where He was. **bringing one sick of the palsy—**"lying on a bed" (Matt. 9: 2). **which was borne of four—**a graphic particular of Mark only. **4. And when they could not come nigh unto him for the press—**or, as in Luke, "when they could not find by what way they might bring him in because of the multitude," they "went upon the housetop"—the flat or terrace-roof, universal in Eastern houses. **they uncovered the roof where he was: and when they had broken it up, they let down the bed—**or portable couch—**wherein the sick of the palsy lay—**Luke says, they "let him down through the tilling with his couch into the midst before Jesus." Their whole object was to *bring the patient into the presence of Jesus;* and this not being possible in the ordinary way, because of the multitude that surrounded Him, they took the very unusual method here described of accomplishing their object, and succeeded. Several explanations have been given of the way in which this was done; but unless we knew the precise plan of the house, and the part of it from which Jesus taught—which may have been a quadrangle or open court, within the buildings of which Peter's house was one, or a gallery covered by a veranda—it is impossible to determine precisely how the thing was done. One thing, however, is clear, that we have both the accounts from an eye-witness. **5. When Jesus saw their faith—**It is remarkable that all the three narratives call it *"their* faith" which Jesus saw. That the patient himself had faith, we know from the proclamation of his forgiveness, which Jesus made before all; and we should have been apt to conclude that his four friends bore him to Jesus merely out of benevolent compliance with the urgent entreaties of the poor sufferer. But here we learn, not only that his bearers had the same faith with himself, but that Jesus marked it as a faith which was not to be defeated—a faith victorious over all difficulties. This was the faith for which He was ever on the watch, and which He never saw without marking, and, in those who needed anything from Him, richly rewarding. **he said unto the sick of the palsy, Son—**"be of good cheer" (Matt. 9:2). **thy sins be forgiven thee—**By the word "be," our translators perhaps meant "are," as in Luke (5:20). For it is not a command to his sins to depart, but an authoritative proclamation of the man's pardoned state as a believer. And yet, as the Pharisees understood our Lord to be *dispensing* pardon by this saying, and Jesus not only acknowledges that they were right, but founds His whole argument upon the correctness of it, we must regard the saying as a royal proclamation of the man's forgiveness by Him to whom it belonged to dispense it; nor could such a style of address be justified on any lower supposition. (See on Luke 7:41, etc.). **6. But there were certain of the scribes—**"and the Pharisees" (Luke 5:21)—**sitting there—**those Jewish ecclesiastics who, as Luke told us, "were come out of every village of Galilee, and Judea, and Jerusalem," to make their observations upon this wonderful Person, in anything but a teachable spirit, though as yet their venomous and murderous feeling had not showed itself. **and reasoning in their hearts. 7. Why doth this man thus speak blasphemies? who can forgive sins but**

God only?—In this second question they expressed a great truth. (See Isa. 43:25; Mic. 7:18; Ex. 34: 6, 7, etc.). Nor was their first question altogether unnatural, though in our Lord's sole case it was unfounded. That a man, to all appearances like one of themselves, should claim authority and power to forgive sins, they could not, on the first blush of it, but regard as in the last degree startling; nor were they entitled even to weigh such a claim, as worthy of a hearing, save on supposition of resistless evidence afforded by Him in support of the claim. Accordingly, our Lord deals with them as men entitled to such evidence, and supplies it; at the same time chiding them for rashness, in drawing harsh conclusions regarding Himself. **8. Why reason ye these things**—or, as in Matthew, "Wherefore think ye evil." **in your hearts? 9. Whether is it easier to say to the sick of the palsy, Thy sins be**—or "are"—**forgiven thee; or to say, Arise, and take up thy bed and walk?**—"Is it easier to command away disease than to bid away sin? If, then, I do the one which you can see, know thus that I have done the other, which you cannot see." **10. But that ye may know that the Son of man hath power on earth to forgive sins**—that forgiving power dwells in the Person of this Man, and is exercised by Him while on this earth and going out and in with you. **(he saith to the sick of the palsy), 11. I say unto thee, Arise, and take up thy bed, and go thy way into thine house**—This taking up the portable couch, and walking home with it, was designed to prove the completeness of the cure. **12. And immediately he arose, took up the bed**—"Sweet saying!" says BENGEL: "The bed had borne the man: now the man bore the bed." **and went forth before them all**—proclaiming by that act to the multitude, whose wondering eyes would follow him as he pressed through them, that He who could work such a glorious miracle of healing, must indeed "have power on earth to forgive sins." **We never saw it on this fashion**—"never saw it thus," or, as we say, "never saw the like." In Luke (5:26) it is, "We have seen strange [unexpected] things to-day" —referring both to the miracles wrought and the forgiveness of sins pronounced by Human Lips. In Matthew (9:8) it is, "They marvelled, and glorified God, which had given such power unto men." At forgiving power they wondered not, but that a man, to all appearance like one of themselves, should possess it!

13-17. LEVI'S (OR MATTHEW'S) CALL AND FEAST. (=Mat. 9:9-13; Luke 5:27-32). See on Matthew 9:9-13.

18-22. DISCOURSE ON FASTING. (=Matt. 9:14-17; Luke 5:33-39). See on Luke 5:33-39.

23-28. PLUCKING CORN-EARS ON THE SABBATH DAY. (=Matt. 12:1-8; Luke 6:1-5.) See on Matthew 12: 1-8.

CHAPTER 3

Vss. 1-12. THE HEALING OF A WITHERED HAND ON THE SABBATH DAY, AND RETIREMENT OF JESUS TO AVOID DANGER. (=Matt. 12:9-21; Luke 6:6-11.) See on Matthew 12:9-21.

13-19. THE TWELVE APOSTLES CHOSEN. See on Luke 6:12-19.

20-30. JESUS IS CHARGED WITH MADNESS AND DEMONIACAL POSSESSION—HIS REPLY. (=Matt. 12: 22-37; Luke 11:14-26.) See on Matthew 12:22-37, and on Luke 11:21-26.

31-35. HIS MOTHER AND BRETHREN SEEK TO SPEAK WITH HIM, AND THE REPLY. (=Matt. 12:46-50; Luke 8:19-21.) See on Matthew 12:46-50.

CHAPTER 4

Vss. 1-34. PARABLE OF THE SOWER—REASON FOR TEACHING IN PARABLES—PARABLES OF THE SEED GROWING WE KNOW NOT HOW, AND OF THE MUSTARD SEED. (=Matt. 13:1-23, 31, 32; Luke 8:4-18.) **1. And he began again to teach by the seaside: and there was gathered unto him a great multitude**—or, according to another well-supported reading, "a mighty" or "immense multitude." **so that he entered into a ship**—rather, "the ship," meaning the one mentioned in ch. 3:9. (See on Matt. 12:15). **and sat in the sea; and the whole multitude was by the sea on the land**—crowded on the seashore to listen to Him. (See on Matt. 13:1,2.) **2. And he taught them many things by parables, and said unto them in his doctrine**—or "teaching."

Parable of the Sower (vss. 3-9, 13-20). After this parable is recorded, the Evangelist says: **vs. 10. And when he was alone, they that were about him with the twelve**—probably those who followed Him most closely and were firmest in discipleship, next to the Twelve. **asked of him the parable**—The reply would seem to intimate that this parable of the sower was of that fundamental, comprehensive, and introductory character which we have assigned to it (see on Matt. 13:1). **13. Know ye not this parable? and how then will ye know all parables?** —Probably this was said not so much in the spirit of rebuke, as to call their attention to the exposition of it which He was about to give, and so train them to the right apprehension of His future parables. As in the parables which we have endeavored to explain in Matthew 13, we shall take this parable and the Lord's own exposition of the different parts of it together.

THE SOWER, THE SEED, AND THE SOIL. **3. Hearken; Behold, there went out a sower to sow**—What means this? **14. The sower soweth the word**—or, as in Luke (8:11), "Now the parable is this: The seed is *the word of God.*" But who is "the sower"? This is not expressed here because if "the word of God" be the seed, every scatterer of that precious seed must be regarded as a sower. It is true that in the parable of the tares it is said, "He that soweth the good seed is the Son of man," as "He that soweth the tares is the devil" (Matt. 13:37, 38). But these are only the great unseen parties, struggling in this world for the possession of man. Each of these has his agents among men themselves; and Christ's agents in the sowing of the good seed are the *preachers* of the word. Thus, as in all the cases about to be described, the sower is the same, and the seed is the same; while the result is entirely different, the whole difference must lie in the *soils,* which mean the *different states of the human heart.* And so, the great general lesson held forth in this parable of the sower is, that however faithful the preacher, and how pure soever his message, *the effect of the preaching of the word depends upon the state of the hearer's heart.* Now follow the cases.

First Case: THE WAYSIDE. **4. And it came to pass, as he sowed, some fell by the wayside**—by the side of the hard path through the field, where the soil was not broken up. **and the fowls [of the air] came and devoured it up**—Not only could the seed not get beneath the surface, but "it was trodden down" (Luke 8:5), and afterwards picked up and devoured by the fowls. What means this? **15. And these are they by the wayside, where the word is sown; but, when they have heard...**—or, more fully (Matt. 13:19), "When any one heareth the word of the kingdom, and understandeth it not, then cometh the wicked one, and catcheth away that which was sown in his heart." The great truth here taught is, that *hearts all unbroken and hard are no fit soil for saving truth.* They apprehend it not (Matt. 13:19) as God's means of restoring them to Himself; it penetrates not, makes no impression, but lies loosely on the surface of the heart, till the wicked one–afraid of losing a victim by his "believing to salvation" (Luke 8:12) –finds some frivolous subject by whose greater attractions to draw off the attention, and straightway it is gone. Of how many hearers of the word is this the graphic but painful history!

Second Case: THE STONY, or rather, ROCKY GROUND. **5. And some fell on stony ground, where it had not much earth**–"the rocky ground"; in Matthew (13:5), "the rocky places"; in Luke, "the rock." The thing intended is, not ground with stones in it which would not prevent the roots striking downward, but ground where a quite thin surface of earth covers a rock. What means this? **16. And these are they likewise which are sown on stony ground . . .**–"Immediately" the seed in such a case "springs up"–all the quicker from the shallowness of the soil–"because it has no depth of earth." But the sun, beating on it, as quickly scorches and withers it up, "because it has no root" (vs. 6), and "lacks moisture" (Luke 8:6). The great truth here taught is that *hearts superficially impressed are apt to receive the truth with readiness, and even with joy* (Luke 8:13); *but the* heat *of tribulation or persecution because of the word, or the trials which their new profession brings upon them quickly dries up their relish for the truth, and withers all the hasty promise of fruit which they showed.* Such disappointing issues of a faithful and awakening ministry–alas, how frequent are they!

Third Case: THE THORNY GROUND. **7. And some fell among thorns, and the thorns grew up, and choked it, and it yielded no fruit**–This case is that of ground not thoroughly cleaned of the thistles, etc.; which, rising above the good seed, "choke" or "smother" it, excluding light and air, and drawing away the moisture and richness of the soil. Hence it "becomes unfruitful" (Matt. 13:22); it grows, but its growth is checked, and it never ripens. The evil here is neither a hard nor a shallow soil–there is *softness* enough, and *depth* enough; but it is the existence in it of what draws all the moisture and richness of the soil away to itself, and so *starves the plant.* What now are these "thorns?" **18. And these are they which are sown among thorns; such as hear the word, 19. And the cares of this world, and the deceitfulness of riches, and the lusts of other things entering in**–or "the pleasures of this life" (Luke 8:14)–**choke the word, and it becometh unfruitful.** First, "The cares of this world" –anxious, unrelaxing attention to the business of this present life; second, "The deceitfulness of riches"–of those riches which are the fruit of this worldly "care"; third, "The pleasures of this life," or "the lusts of other things entering in"–the enjoyments in themselves may be innocent, which worldly prosperity enables one to indulge. These "*choke*" or "*smother*" the word; drawing off so much of one's attention, absorbing so much of one's interest, and using up so much of one's time, that only the dregs of these remain for spiritual things, and a fagged, hurried, and heartless formalism is at length all the religion of such persons. What a vivid picture is this of the mournful con-

dition of many, especially in great commercial countries, who once promised much fruit! "They bring no fruit *to perfection*" (Luke 8:14); indicating how much *growth* there may be, in the early stages of such a case, and *promise* of fruit–which after all never *ripens.*

Fourth Case: THE GOOD GROUND. **8. And other fell on good ground, and did yield fruit . . .**–The goodness of this last soil consists in its qualities being precisely the reverse of the other three soils: from its softness and tenderness, receiving and cherishing the seed; from its depth, allowing it to take firm root, and not quickly losing its moisture; and from its cleanness, giving its whole vigor and sap to the plant. In such a soil the seed "brings forth fruit," in all different degrees of profusion, according to the measure in which the soil possesses those qualities. **20. And these are they which are sown on good ground; such as hear the word, and receive it, and bring forth fruit, some thirtyfold, some sixty, and some an hundred**–A heart soft and tender, stirred to its depths on the great things of eternity, and jealously guarded from worldly engrossments, such only is the "honest and good heart" (Luke 8:15), which "keeps," i.e., "retains" the seed of the word, and bears fruit just in proportion as it is such a heart. Such "bring forth fruit with *patience*" (vs. 15), or continuance, "enduring to the end"; in contrast with those in whom the word is "choked" and brings no fruit *to perfection.* The "thirtyfold" is designed to express the *lowest* degree of fruitfulness; the "hundredfold" the *highest*; and the "sixtyfold" the *intermediate* degrees of fruitfulness. As a hundredfold," though not unexampled (Gen. 26:12), is a rare return in the natural husbandry, so the highest degrees of spiritual fruitfulness are too seldom witnessed. The closing words of this introductory parable seem designed to call attention to the *fundamental* and *universal* character of it. **9. And he said unto them, He that hath ears to hear, let him hear.**

Reason for Teaching in Parables (vss. 11, 12). **11, 12. And he said unto them, Unto you it is given to know the mystery of the kingdom of God: but unto them . . .**–See on Matthew 13:10-17. **21. And he said unto them, Is a candle**–or "lamp"–**brought to be put under a bushel, or under a bed? and not to be set on a candlestick?**–"that they which enter in may see the light" (Luke 8:16). See on Matthew 5:15, of which this is nearly a repetition. **22. For there is nothing hid which shall not be manifested . . .**–See on Matthew 10:26, 27; but the connection there and here is slightly different. Here the idea seems to be this–'I have privately expounded to you these great truths, but only that ye may proclaim them publicly; and if ye will not, others will. For these are not designed for secrecy. They are imparted to be diffused abroad, and they shall be so; yea, a time is coming when the most hidden things shall be brought to light.' **23. If any man have ears to hear, let him hear**–This for the second time on the same subject (see on vs. 9). **24. And he saith unto them, Take heed what ye hear**–In Luke (8:18) it is, "Take heed how ye hear." The one implies the other, but both precepts are very weighty. **with what measure ye mete, it shall be measured to you**–See on Matthew 7:2. **and unto you that hear**–i.e., thankfully, teachably, profitably. **shall more be given. 25. For he that hath, to him shall be given; and he that hath not, from him shall be taken even that which he hath** –or "seemeth to have," or "thinketh he hath."

(See on Matt. 13:12.) This "having" and "thinking he hath" are not different; for when it hangs loosely upon him, and is not appropriated to its proper ends and uses, it both *is* and *is not* his.

Parable of the Seed Growing We Know not How (vss. 26-29). This beautiful parable is peculiar to Mark. Its design is to teach the *Imperceptible Growth* of the word sown in the heart, from its earliest stage of development to the ripest fruits of practical righteousness. **26. So is the kingdom of God, as if a man should cast seed into the ground; 27. And should sleep, and rise night and day**—go about his other ordinary occupations, leaving it to the wellknown laws of vegetation under the genial influences of heaven. This is the sense of "the earth bringing forth fruit *of herself*," in the next verse. **28. For the earth bringeth forth fruit of herself; first the blade, then the ear, after that the full corn in the ear**—beautiful allusion to the succession of similar stages, though not definitely marked periods, in the Christian life, and generally in the kingdom of God. **29. But when the fruit is brought forth**—to maturity—**immediately he putteth in the sickle, because the harvest is come**—This charmingly points to the transition from the earthly to the heavenly condition of the Christian and the Church.

Parable of the Mustard Seed (vss. 30-32). For the exposition of this portion, see on Matthew 13: 31, 32.

33. And with many such parables spake he the word unto them, as they were able to hear it—Had this been said in the corresponding passage of Matthew, we should have concluded that what that Evangelist recorded was but a specimen of other parables spoken on the same occasion. But Matthew (13:34) says, "All *these* things spake Jesus unto the multitude in parables"; and as Mark records only some of the parables which Matthew gives, we are warranted to infer that the "many such parables" alluded to here mean no more than the full complement of them which we find in Matthew. **34. But without a parable spake he not unto them**—See on Matthew 13:34. **and when they were alone, he expounded all things to his disciples**—See on vs. 22.

35-ch. 5:20. JESUS, CROSSING THE SEA OF GALILEE, MIRACULOUSLY STILLS A TEMPEST—HE CURES THE DEMONIAC OF GADARA. (=Matt. 8:23-34; Luke 8:22-39.) The time of this section is very definitely marked by our Evangelist, and by him alone, in the opening words.

Jesus Stills a Tempest on the Sea of Galilee (vss. 35-41). **35. And the same day**—on which He spoke the memorable parables of the preceding section, and of Matthew 13. **when the even was come**—See on ch. 6:35. This must have been the earlier evening—what we should call the afternoon—since after all that passed on the other side, when He returned to the west side, the people were waiting for Him in great numbers (vs. 21; Luke 8:40). **he saith unto them, Let us pass over unto the other side**—to the east side of the lake, to grapple with a desperate case of possession, and set the captive free, and to give the Gadarenes an opportunity of hearing the message of salvation, amid the wonder which that marvellous cure was fitted to awaken and the awe which the subsequent events could not but strike into them. **36. And when they had sent away the multitude, they took him even as he was in the ship**—i.e., without any preparation, and without so much as leaving the vessel, out of which He had been all day teaching. **And there were also with him other little ships**—with passengers, probably, wishing to accompany Him. **37. And there arose a great storm of wind**—"a tempest of wind." To such sudden squalls the Sea of Galilee is very liable from its position, in a deep basin, skirted on the east by lofty mountain ranges, while on the west the hills are intersected by narrow gorges through which the wind sweeps across the lake, and raises its waters with great rapidity into a storm. **and the waves beat into the ship**—kept beating or pitching on the ship. **so that it was now full**—rather, "so that it was already filling." In Matthew (8:24), "insomuch that the ship was covered with the waves"; but this is too strong. It should be, "so that the ship was getting covered by the waves." So we must translate the word used in Luke (8:23)—not as in our version—"And there came down a storm on the lake, and they were filled [with water]"—but "they were getting filled," i.e., those who sailed; meaning, of course, that their ship was so. **38. And he was in the hinder**—or stern—**part of the ship, asleep on a pillow**—either a place in the vessel made to receive the head, or a cushion for the head to rest on. It was evening; and after the fatigues of a busy day of teaching under the hot sun, having nothing to do while crossing the lake, He sinks into a deep sleep, which even this tempest raging around and tossing the little vessel did not disturb. **and they awake him, and say unto him, Master**—or "Teacher." In Luke (8: 24) this is doubled—in token of their life-and-death earnestness—"Master, Master." **carest thou not that we perish?**—Unbelief and fear made them sadly forget their place, to speak so. Luke has it, "Lord, save us, we perish." When those accustomed to fish upon that deep thus spake, the danger must have been imminent. They say nothing of what would become of *Him*, if they perished; nor think, whether, if He could not perish, it was likely He would let this happen to them; but they hardly knew what they said. **39. And he arose, and rebuked the wind**—"and the raging of the water" (Luke 8:24). **and said unto the sea, Peace, be still**—two sublime words of command, from a Master to His servants, the elements. **And the wind ceased, and there was a great calm**—The sudden hushing of the wind would not at once have calmed the sea, whose commotion would have settled only after a considerable time. But the word of command was given to both elements at once. **40. And he said unto them, Why are ye so fearful?**—There is a natural apprehension under danger; but there was unbelief in their fear. It is worthy of notice how considerately the Lord defers this rebuke till He had first removed the danger, in the midst of which they would not have been in a state to listen to anything. **how is it that ye have no faith?**—next to none, or none in present exercise. In Luke it is, "Why are ye fearful, O ye of little faith?" *Faith* they had, for they applied to Christ for relief: but *little,* for they were afraid, though Christ was in the ship. Faith dispels fear, but only in proportion to its strength. **41. And they feared exceedingly**—were struck with deep awe. **and said one to another, What manner of man is this, that even the wind and the sea obey him?**—'What is this? Israel has all along been singing of JEHOVAH, 'Thou rulest the raging of the sea: when the waves thereof arise, Thou stillest them!' 'The Lord on high is mightier than the noise of many waters, yea, than the mighty waves of the sea!' (Ps. 89:9; 93:4). But, lo, in this very boat of ours is One of our own flesh and blood, who with His word of command hath done the same! Exhausted with the fatigues of the day, He was but a moment ago in a deep sleep, undisturbed by the howling tempest, and we had to waken Him with the cry of our terror; but rising at our call, His majesty was felt by the raging elements, for they were instantly hushed—'WHAT MANNER OF MAN IS THIS?' "

CHAPTER 5

Glorious Cure of the Gadarene Demoniac (vss. 1-20). **1. And they came over unto the other side of the sea, into the country of the Gadarenes. 2. And when he was come out of the ship, immediately**—(see vs. 6)—**there met him a man with an unclean spirit**—"which had devils [demons] long time" (Luke 8:27). In Matthew (8:28), "there met him two men possessed with devils." Though there be no discrepancy between these two statements—more than between two witnesses, one of whom testifies to something done by one person, while the other affirms that there were two—it is difficult to see how the principal details here given could apply to more than one case. **3. Who had his dwelling among the tombs**—Luke says, "He ware no clothes, neither abode in any house." These tombs were hewn out of the rocky caves of the locality, and served for shelters and lurking-places (Luke 8:26). **4. Because that he had been often bound with fetters and chains ...**—Luke says (8:29) that "oftentimes it [the unclean spirit] had caught him"; and after mentioning how they had vainly tried to bind him with chains and fetters, because, "he brake the bands," he adds, "and was driven of the devil [demon] into the wilderness." The dark tyrant-power by which he was held clothed him with superhuman strength and made him scorn restraint. Matthew (8:28) says he was "exceeding fierce, so that no man might pass by that way." He was the terror of the whole locality. **5. And always, night and day, he was in the mountains, and in the tombs, crying, and cutting himself with stones**—Terrible as he was to others, he himself endured untold misery, which sought relief in tears and self-inflicted torture. **6. But when he saw Jesus afar off, he ran and worshipped him**—not with the spontaneous alacrity which says to Jesus, "Draw me, we will *run* after thee," but inwardly compelled, with terrific rapidity, before the Judge, to receive sentence of expulsion. **7. What have I to do with thee, Jesus, Son of the most high God? I adjure thee by God, that thou torment me not**—or, as in Matthew 8:29, "Art Thou come to torment us before the time?" (See on ch. 1:24.) Behold the *tormentor* anticipating, dreading, and entreating exemption from *torment!* In Christ they discern their destined Tormentor; the time, they know, is fixed, and they feel as if it were come already! (Jas. 2:19.) **8. For he said unto him**—i.e., before the unclean spirit cried out. **Come out of the man, unclean spirit!** —Ordinarily, obedience to a command of this nature was immediate. But here, a certain delay is permitted, the more signally to manifest the power of Christ and accomplish His purposes. **9. And he asked him, What is thy name?**—The object of this question was to extort an acknowledgment of the virulence of demoniacal power by which this victim was enthralled. **And he answered, saying, My name is Legion: for we are many**—or, as in Luke, "because many devils [demons] were entered into him." A legion, in the Roman army, amounted, at its full complement, to six thousand; but here the

word is used, as such words with us, and even this one, for an indefinitely large number—large enough however to rush, as soon as permission was given, into two thousand swine and destroy them. **10. And he besought him much that he would not send them away out of the country**—The entreaty, it will be observed, was made by *one spirit*, but in behalf of *many*—"*he* besought Him not to send *them* ..." —just as in the former verse, "*he* answered *we* are many." But what do they mean by entreating so earnestly not to be ordered out of the country? Their next petition (vs. 12) will make that clear enough. **11. Now there was there, nigh unto the mountains**—rather, "to the mountain," according to what is clearly the true reading. In Matthew 8:30, they are said to have been "a good way off." But these expressions, far from being inconsistent, only confirm, by their precision, the minute accuracy of the narrative. **a great herd of swine feeding**—There can hardly be any doubt that the owners of these were Jews, since to them our Lord had now come to proffer His services. This will explain what follows. **12. And all the devils besought him, saying** —"if thou cast us out" (Matt. 8:31)—**Send us into the swine, that we may enter into them**—Had they spoken out all their mind, perhaps this would have been it: "If we must quit our hold of this man, suffer us to continue our work of mischief in another form, that by entering these swine, and thus destroying the people's property, we may steel their hearts against Thee!" **13. And forthwith Jesus gave them leave**—In Matthew this is given with majestic brevity—"Go!" The owners, if Jews, drove an illegal trade; if heathens, they insulted the national religion: in either case the permission was just. **And the unclean spirits went out**—of the man —**and entered into the swine: and the herd ran violently**—rushed—**down a steep place**—down the hanging cliff—**into the sea (they were about two thousand)**—The number of them is given by this graphic Evangelist alone. **and were choked in the sea**—"perished in the waters" (Matt. 8:32). **14. And they that fed the swine fled, and told it**—"told everything, and what was befallen to the possessed of the devils" (Matt. 8:33)—**in the city, and in the country. And they went out to see what it was that was done**—Thus had they the evidence, both of the herdsmen and of their own senses, to the reality of both miracles. **15. And they come to Jesus**—Matthew (8:34) says, "Behold, the whole city came out to meet Jesus." **and see him that was possessed with the devil**—the demonized person—**and had the legion, sitting**—"at the feet of Jesus," adds Luke (8:35); in contrast with his former *wild* and *wandering* habits. **and clothed**—As our Evangelist had not told us that he "ware no clothes," the meaning of this statement could only have been conjectured but for "the beloved physician" (Luke 8:27), who supplies the missing piece of information here. This is a striking case of what are called *Undesigned Coincidences* amongst the different Evangelists; one of them taking a thing for granted, as familiarly known at the time, but which we should never have known but for one or more of the others, and without the knowledge of which some of their statements would be unintelligible. The clothing which the poor man would feel the want of the moment his consciousness returned to him, was doubtless supplied to him by some of the Twelve. **and in his right mind**—but now, oh, in what a lofty sense! (Cf. an analogous, though a different kind of case, Dan. 4:34-37.) **and they were afraid**—Had this been *awe* only, it had been natural enough; but other feelings, alas! of a darker kind, soon showed themselves. **16. And they that saw it told them how it befell to him that was possessed with the devil** ('the demonized person') **and also concerning the swine**—Thus had they the double testimony of the herdsmen and their own senses. **17. And they began to pray him to depart out of their coasts**—Was it the owners only of the valuable property now lost to them that did this? Alas, no! For Luke (8:37) says, "Then the whole multitude of the country of the Gadarenes round about besought Him to depart from them; for they were taken with great fear." The evil spirits had thus, alas! their object. Irritated, the people could not suffer His presence; yet awe-struck, they dared not order Him off: so they entreat Him to withdraw, and—He takes them at their word. **18. he that had been possessed with the devil prayed him that he might be with him**—the grateful heart, fresh from the hand of demons, clinging to its wondrous Benefactor. How exquisitely natural! **19. Howbeit, Jesus suffered him not, . . .**—To be a missionary for Christ, in the region where he was so well known and so long dreaded, was a far nobler calling than to follow Him where nobody had ever heard of him, and where other trophies not less illustrious could be raised by the same power and grace. **20. And he departed, and began to publish**—not only among his friends, to whom Jesus immediately sent him, but—**in Decapolis**—so called, as being a region of ten cities. (See on Matt. 4:25.) **how great things Jesus had done for him: and all men did marvel**—Throughout that considerable region did this monument of mercy proclaim his new-found Lord; and some, it is to be hoped, did more than "marvel."

21-43. THE DAUGHTER OF JAIRUS RAISED TO LIFE —THE WOMAN WITH AN ISSUE OF BLOOD HEALED. (= Matt. 9:18-26; Luke 8:41-56.) The occasion of this scene will appear presently.

Jairus' Daughter (vss. 21-24). **21. And when Jesus was passed over again by ship unto the other side**—from the Gadarene side of the lake, where He had parted with the healed demoniac, to the west side, at Capernaum. **much people gathered unto him**—who "gladly received Him; for they were all waiting for Him" (Luke 8:40). The abundant teaching earlier that day (ch. 4:1, etc., and Matthew 13) had only whetted the people's appetite: and disappointed, as would seem, that He had left them in the evening to cross the lake, they remain hanging about the beach, having got a hint, probably through some of His disciples, that He would be back the same evening. Perhaps they witnessed at a distance the sudden calming of the tempest. The tide of our Lord's popularity was now fast rising. **and he was nigh unto the sea. 22. And, behold, there cometh one of the rulers of the synagogue**—of which class there were but few who believed in Jesus (John 7:48). One would suppose from this that the ruler had been with the multitude on the shore, anxiously awaiting the return of Jesus, and immediately on His arrival had accosted Him as here related. But Matthew (9:18) tells us that the ruler came to Him while He was in the act of speaking at His own table on the subject of fasting; and as we must suppose that this converted publican ought to know what took place on that memorable occasion when he made a feast to his Lord, we conclude that here the right order is indicated by the First Evangelist alone. **Jairus by name**—or "Jaeirus." It is the same name as *Jair*, in the Old Testament (Num. 32:41; Judg. 10:3; Esther 2:5). **and when he saw him, he fell at his feet**—in Mat-

thew (9:18), "worshipped Him." The meaning is the same in both. **23. And besought him greatly, saying, My little daughter**—Luke (8:42) says, "He had one only daughter, about twelve years of age." According to a well-known rabbin, quoted by LIGHTFOOT, a daughter. till she had completed her twelfth year, was called "little," or "a little maid"; after that, "a young woman." **lieth at the point of death**—Matthew gives it thus: "My daughter is even now dead"—"has just expired." The news of her death reached the father after the cure of the woman with the issue of blood: but Matthew's brief account gives only the *result,* as in the case of the centurion's servant (Matt. 8:5, etc.). **come and lay thy hands on her, that she may be healed; and she shall live**—or, "that she may be healed and live," according to a fully preferable reading. In one of the class to which this man belonged, so steeped in prejudice, such faith would imply more than in others.

The Woman with an Issue of Blood Healed (vss. 23-34). **24. And Jesus went with him; and much people followed him, and thronged him**—The word in Luke is stronger—"choked," "stifled Him." **26. And had suffered many things of many physicians**—The expression perhaps does not necessarily refer to the suffering she endured under medical treatment, but to the much varied treatment which she underwent. **and had spent all that she had, and was nothing bettered, but rather grew worse**—pitiable case, and affectingly aggravated; emblem of our natural state as fallen creatures (Ezek. 16:5, 6), and illustrating the worse than vanity of all human remedies for spiritual maladies (Hos. 5:13). The higher design of all our Lord's miracles of healing irresistibly suggests this way of viewing the present case, the propriety of which will still more appear as we proceed. **27. When she had heard of Jesus, came**—This was the right experiment at last. What had she "heard of Jesus?" No doubt it was His marvellous cures she had heard of; and the hearing of these, in connection with her bitter experience of the vanity of applying to any other, had been blessed to the kindling in her soul of a firm confidence that He who had so willingly wrought such cures on others was able and would not refuse to heal her also. **in the press behind**—shrinking, yet seeking. **touched his garment**—According to the ceremonial law, the touch of anyone having the disease which this woman had would have defiled the person touched. Some think that the recollection of this may account for her stealthily approaching Him in the crowd behind, and touching but the hem of His garment. But there was an instinct in the faith which brought her to Jesus, which taught her, that if that touch could set her free from the defiling disease itself, it was impossible to communicate defilement to Him, and that this wondrous Healer must be above such laws. **28. For she said**—"within herself" (Matt. 9:21). **If I may touch but his clothes, I shall be whole**—i.e., if I may but *come in contact* with this glorious Healer *at all.* Remarkable faith this! **29. And straightway the fountain of her blood was dried up**—Not only was her issue of blood stanched (Luke 8:44), but the cause of it was thoroughly removed, insomuch that by her bodily sensations she immediately knew herself perfectly cured. **30. And Jesus immediately knowing in himself that virtue**—or "efficacy." **had gone out of him**—He was conscious of the forthgoing of His healing power, which was not—as in prophets and apostles—something *foreign to Himself* and imparted merely, but what He had *dwelling within Him* as "His own fulness." **turned him about in the press**—crowd. **and said, Who touched my clothes? 31. And his disciples said unto him**—Luke says (8:45), "When all denied, Peter and they that were with Him said, Master"—**Thou seest the multitude thronging thee, and sayest thou, Who touched me?**—"Askest thou, Lord, who touched Thee? Rather ask who touched Thee *not* in such a throng." "And Jesus said, Somebody hath touched Me"—a certain person has touched Me"—"for I perceive that virtue is gone out of Me" (Luke 8:46). Yes, the multitude *"thronged* and *pressed* Him"—they *jostled against* Him, but all *involuntarily;* they were merely *carried along;* but one, one only—"a certain person—TOUCHED HIM," with the conscious, voluntary, dependent touch of faith, reaching forth its hand expressly to have contact with Him. This and this only Jesus acknowledges and seeks out. Even so, as AUGUSTINE long ago said, *multitudes still come similarly close to Christ in the means of grace, but all to no purpose, being only sucked into the crowd.* The voluntary, living contact of faith is that electric conductor which alone draws virtue out of Him. **32. And he looked round about to see her that had done this thing**—not for the purpose of summoning forth a culprit, but, as we shall presently see, to obtain from the healed one a testimony to what He had done for her. **33. But the woman, fearing and trembling, knowing what was done in her**—alarmed, as a humble, shrinking female would naturally be, at the necessity of so public an exposure of herself, yet conscious that she had a tale to tell which would speak for her. **came and fell down before him, and told him all the truth**—In Luke (8:47) it is, "When the woman saw that she was not hid, she came trembling, and falling down before Him, she declared unto Him before all the people for what cause she had touched Him, and how she was healed immediately." This, though it tried the modesty of the believing woman, was just what Christ wanted in dragging her forth, her public testimony to the facts of her case—the disease, with her abortive efforts at a cure, and the instantaneous and perfect relief which her touching the Great Healer had brought her. **34. And he said unto her, Daughter**—"be of good comfort" (Luke 8:48). **thy faith hath made thee whole; go in peace, and be whole of thy plague**—Though healed as soon as she believed, it seemed to her a stolen cure—she feared to acknowledge it. Jesus therefore sets His royal seal upon it. But what a glorious dismissal from the lips of Him who is "our Peace" is that, "Go in peace!"

Jairus' Daughter Raised to Life (vss. 35-43). **35. Thy daughter is dead; why troublest thou the Master**—the Teacher—**any further? 36. he saith unto the ruler of the synagogue, Be not afraid, only believe**—Jesus, knowing how the heart of the agonized father would sink at the tidings, and the reflections at the *delay* which would be apt to rise in his mind, hastens to reassure him, and in His accustomed style: "Be not afraid, only believe"—words of unchanging preciousness and power! How vividly do such incidents bring out Christ's knowledge of the human heart and tender sympathy! (Heb. 4:15.) **37. And he suffered no man to follow him, save Peter, and James, and John the brother of James**—See on ch. 1:29. **38. And he cometh**—rather, "they come." **to the house of the ruler of the synagogue, and seeth the tumult, and them that wept and wailed greatly**—"the minstrels and the people making a noise" (Matt. 9:23)—lamenting for the dead. (See II Chron. 35:25; Jer. 9:20; Amos 5:16.) **39. And when he was come in, he saith unto them, Why make ye this ado, and weep? the damsel is not dead, but sleepeth**—so brief her state of death as to be more like a short sleep. **40. And they laughed him to scorn**—rather, simply, "laughed at Him"—"knowing that she was dead" (Luke 8:53); an important testimony this to the reality of her death. **But when he had put them all out**—The word is strong—"turned them all out"; meaning all those who were making this noise, and any others that may have been there from sympathy, that only those might be present who were most nearly concerned, and those whom He had Himself brought as witnesses of the great act about to be done. **he taketh the father and the mother of the damsel, and them that were with him**—Peter, and James, and John. **and entereth in where the damsel was lying. 41. And he took the damsel by the hand**—as He did Peter's mother-in-law (ch. 1:31). **and said unto her, Talitha cumi**—The words are Aramaic, or Syro-Chaldaic, the then language of Palestine. Mark loves to give such wonderful words just as they were spoken. See ch. 7:34; 14:36. **42. And straightway the damsel**—The word here is different from that in vss. 39, 40, 41, and signifies "young maiden," or "little girl." **arose, and walked**—a vivid touch evidently from an eyewitness. **And they were astonished with a great astonishment**—The language here is the strongest. **43. And he charged them straitly**—strictly—**that no man should know it**—The only reason we can assign for this is His desire not to let the public feeling regarding Him come too precipitately to a crisis. **and commanded that something should be given her to eat**—in token of perfect restoration.

CHAPTER 6

Vss. 1-6. CHRIST REJECTED AT NAZARETH. (= Matt. 13:54-58; Luke 4:16-30.) See on Luke 4: 16-30.

7-13. MISSION OF THE TWELVE APOSTLES. (= Matt. 10:1, 5-15; Luke 9:1-6.) See on Matthew 10:1, 5-15.

14-29. HEROD THINKS JESUS A RESURRECTION OF THE MURDERED BAPTIST—ACCOUNT OF HIS DEATH. (= Matt. 14:1-12; Luke 9:7-9.)

Herod's View of Christ (vss. 14-16). **14. And King Herod**—i.e., Herod Antipas, one of the three sons of Herod the Great, and own brother of Archelaus (Matt. 2:22), who ruled as *ethnarch* over Galilee and Perea. **heard of him; (for his name was spread abroad); and he said**—"unto his servants" (Matt. 14:2), his councillors or courtministers. **That John the Baptist was risen from the dead**—The murdered prophet haunted his guilty breast like a specter, and seemed to him alive again and clothed with unearthly powers, in the person of Jesus. **15. Others said, That it is Elias. And others, That it is a prophet, or as one of the prophets**—See on Matthew 16:14. **16. But when Herod heard thereof, he said, It is John, whom I beheaded; he is risen from the dead**—"himself has risen"; as if the innocence and sanctity of his faithful reprover had not suffered that he should lie long dead.

Account of the Baptist's Imprisonment and Death (vss. 17-29). **17. For Herod himself had sent forth, and laid hold upon John, and bound him in prison**—in the castle of Machærus, near the southern extremity of Herod's dominions, and adjoining the Dead Sea [JOSEPHUS, *Antiquities*, 18:5,

2]. **for Herodias' sake**—She was the granddaughter of Herod the Great. **his brother Philip's wife**—and therefore the niece of both brothers. This Philip, however, was not the tetrarch of that name mentioned in Luke 3:1 (see there), but one whose distinctive name was "Herod Philip," another son of Herod the Great—who was disinherited by his father. Herod Antipas' own wife was the daughter of Aretas, king of Arabia; but he prevailed on Herodias, his half-brother Philip's wife, to forsake her husband and live with him, on condition, says JOSEPHUS (*Antiquities,* 18:5, 1), that he should put away his own wife. This involved him afterwards in war with Aretas, who totally defeated him and destroyed his army, from the effects of which he was never able to recover himself. **18. For John had said unto Herod, It is not lawful for thee to have thy brother's wife**—Noble fidelity! It was not lawful because Herod's wife and Herodias husband were both living; and further, because the parties were within the forbidden degrees of consanguinity (see Lev. 20:21); Herodias being the daughter of Aristobulus, the brother of both Herod and Philip [JOSEPHUS, 18:5, 4]. **19. Therefore Herodias had a quarrel against him**—rather, as in the margin, "had a grudge against him." Probably she was too proud to speak to him; still less would she quarrel with him. **and would have killed him; but she could not. 20. For Herod feared John**—but, as BENGEL notes, John feared not Herod. **knowing that he was a just man and an holy**—Cf. the ease of Elijah with Ahab, after the murder of Naboth (I Kings 21:20). **and observed him**—rather, as in the margin, "kept" or "saved him"; i.e., from the wicked designs of Herodias, who had been watching for some pretext to get Herod entangled and committed to despatch him. **and when he heard him, he did many things**—many good things under the influence of the Baptist on his conscience. **and heard him gladly**—a striking statement this, for which we are indebted to our graphic Evangelist alone, illustrating the working of contrary principles in the slaves of passion. But this only shows how far Herodias must have wrought upon him, as Jezebel upon Ahab, that he should at length agree to what his awakened conscience kept him long from executing. **21. And when a convenient day**—for the purposes of Herodias—**was come, that Herod**—rather, A convenient day being come, when Herod—**on his birthday, made a supper to his lords, high captains, and chief [estates] of Galilee**—This graphic minuteness of detail adds much to the interest of the tragic narrative. **22. And when the daughter of the said Herodias**—i.e.,—her daughter by her proper husband, Herod Philip: Her name was Salome [JOSEPHUS, *ibid.*]. **came in and danced, and pleased Herod and them that sat with him, the king said unto the damsel**—"the girl" (See on ch. 5:42). **Ask of me whatsoever thou wilt, and I will give it thee. 23. And he**—the king, so called, but only by courtesy (see on vs. 14). **sware unto her Whatsoever thou shalt ask of me, unto the half of my kingdom**—Those in whom passion and luxury have destroyed self-command will in a capricious moment say and do what in their cool moments they bitterly regret. **24. And she said, The head of John the Baptist**—Abandoned women are more shameless and heartless than men. The Baptist's fidelity marred the pleasures of Herodias, and this was too good an opportunity of getting rid of him to let slip. **25. I will that thou give me by and by**—rather, "at once" —**in a charger**—large, flat trencher—**the head of John the Baptist. 26. And the king was exceeding**

sorry--With his feelings regarding John, and the truths which so told upon his conscience from that preacher's lips, and after so often and carefully saving him from his paramour's rage, it must have been very galling to find himself at length entrapped by his own rash folly. **yet for his oath's sake**—See how men of no principle, but troublesome conscience, will stick at breaking a rash oath, while yielding to the commission of the worst crimes! **and for their sakes which sat with him**—under the influence of that false shame, which could not brook being thought to be troubled with religious or moral scruples. To how many has this proved a fatal snare! **he would not reject her. 27. And immediately the king sent an executioner**—one of the guards in attendance. The word is Roman, denoting one of the Imperial Guard. **and commanded his head to be brought: and he went and beheaded him in the prison**—after, it would seem, more than twelve months' imprisonment. Blessed martyr! Dark and cheerless was the end reserved for thee: but now thou hast thy Master's benediction, "Blessed is he whosoever shall not be offended in Me" (Matt. 11:6), and hast found the life thou gavest away (Matt. 10:39). But where are they in whose skirts is found thy blood? **28. And brought his head in a charger, and gave it to the damsel: and the damsel gave it to her mother**—Herodias did not shed the blood of the stern reprover; she only got it done, and then gloated over it, as it streamed from the trunkless head. **29. And when his disciples heard of it**—i.e., the Baptist's own disciples. **they came and took up his corpse, and laid it in a tomb** —"and went and told Jesus" (Matt. 14:12). If these disciples had, up to this time, stood apart from Him, as adherents of John (Matt. 11:2), perhaps they now came to Jesus, not without some secret reflection on Him for His seeming neglect of their master; but perhaps, too, as orphans, to cast in their lot henceforth with the Lord's disciples. How Jesus felt, or what He said, on receiving this intelligence, is not recorded; but He of whom it was said, as He stood by the grave of His friend Lazarus, "Jesus wept," was not likely to receive such intelligence without deep emotion. And one reason why He might not be unwilling that a small body of John's disciples should cling to him to the last, might be to provide some attached friends who should do for his precious body, on a small scale, what was afterwards to be done for His own.

30-56. THE TWELVE, ON THEIR RETURN, HAVING REPORTED THE SUCCESS OF THEIR MISSION, JESUS CROSSES THE SEA OF GALILEE WITH THEM, TEACHES THE PEOPLE, AND MIRACULOUSLY FEEDS THEM TO THE NUMBER OF FIVE THOUSAND—HE SENDS HIS DISCIPLES BY SHIP AGAIN TO THE WESTERN SIDE, WHILE HE HIMSELF RETURNS AFTERWARDS WALKING ON THE SEA—INCIDENTS ON LANDING. (= Matt. 14:13-36; Luke 9:10-17; John 6:1-24.) Here, for the first time, all the four streams of sacred text run parallel. The occasion and all the circumstances of this grand section are thus brought before us with a vividness quite remarkable.

Five Thousand Miraculously Fed (vss. 30-44). **30. And the apostles gathered themselves together**—probably at Capernaum, on returning from their mission (vss. 7-13). **and told him all things, both what they had done, and what they had taught**—Observe the various reasons He had for crossing to the other side. First, Matthew (14:13) says, that "when Jesus heard" of the murder of His faithful forerunner—from those attached disciples of his who had taken up his body and laid it in a sepulchre (see on vs. 29)—"He departed by ship into a desert place apart"; either to avoid some apprehended consequences to Himself, arising from the Baptist's death (Matt. 10:23), or more probably to be able to indulge in those feelings which that affecting event had doubtless awakened, and to which the bustle of the multitude around Him was very unfavorable. Next, since He must have heard the report of the Twelve with the deepest interest, and probably with something of the emotion which He experienced on the return of the Seventy (see on Luke 10:17-22), He sought privacy for undisturbed reflection on this begun preaching and progress of His kingdom. Once more, He was wearied with the multitude of "comers and goers"—depriving Him even of leisure enough to take His food—and wanted *rest:* "Come ye yourselves apart into a desert place, and rest a while . . . ." Under the combined influence of all these considerations, our Lord sought this change. **32. And they departed into a desert place by ship privately**—"over the Sea of Galilee, which is the Sea of Tiberias," says John (6:1), the only one of the Evangelists who so fully describes it; the others having written when their readers were supposed to know something of it, while the last wrote for those at a greater distance of time and place. This "desert place" is more definitely described by Luke (9:10) as "belonging to the city called Bethsaida." This must not be confounded with the town so called on the western side of the lake (see on Matt. 11:21). This town lay on its northeastern side, near where the Jordan empties itself into it: in Gaulonitis, out of the dominions of Herod Antipas, and within the dominions of Philip the Tetrarch (Luke 3:1), who raised it from a village to a city, and called it *Julias,* in honor of Julia, the daughter of Augustus [JOSEPHUS, *Antiquities,* 18:2, 1]. **33. And the people**—the multitudes—**saw them departing, and many knew him**—The true reading would seem to be: "And many saw them departing, and knew or recognized [them]. **and ran afoot**—Here, perhaps, it should be rendered "by land"—running round by the head of the lake, and taking one of the fords of the river, so as to meet Jesus, who was crossing with the Twelve by ship. **thither out of all cities, and outwent them**—got before them —**and came together unto him**—How exceedingly graphic is this! every touch of it betokening the presence of an eye-witness. John (6:3) says, that "Jesus went up into a mountain"—somewhere in that hilly range, the green tableland which skirts the eastern side of the lake. **34. And Jesus, when he came out of the ship**—having gone on shore—**saw much people**—a great multitude—**and was moved with compassion toward them, because they were as sheep not having a shepherd**—At the sight of the multitudes who had followed Him by land and even got before Him, He was so moved, as was His wont in such cases, with compassion, because they were like shepherdless sheep, as to forego both privacy and rest that He might minister to them. Here we have an important piece of information from the Fourth Evangelist (John 6:4), "And the passover, a feast of the Jews, was nigh"—rather, "Now the passover, the feast of the Jews, was nigh." This accounts for the multitudes that now crowded around Him. They were on their way to keep that festival at Jerusalem. But Jesus did not go up to this festival, as John expressly tells us, (ch. 7:1)—remaining in Galilee, because the ruling Jews sought to kill Him. **35. And when the day was now far spent**—"began to wear away" or "decline," says Luke (9:12). Matthew (14:15) says,

"when it was evening"; and yet he mentions a later evening of the same day (vs. 23). This earlier evening began at three P.M.; the latter began at sunset. **36. Send them away, that they may go into the country round about, and into the villages, and buy themselves bread: for they have nothing to eat**—John tells us (6:5, 6) that "Jesus said to Philip, Whence shall we buy bread, that these may eat? (And this He said to prove him: for He Himself knew what He would do.)" The subject may have been introduced by some remark of the disciples; but the precise order and form of what was said by each can hardly be gathered with precision, nor is it of any importance. **37. He answered and said unto them**—"They need not depart" (Matt. 14:10). **Give ye them to eat**—doubtless said to prepare them for what was to follow. **And they say unto him, Shall we go and buy two hundred pennyworth of bread, and give them to eat?**—"Philip answered Him, Two hundred pennyworth of bread is not sufficient for them, that every one of them may take a little" (John 6:7). **38. He saith unto them, How many loaves have ye? go and see. And when they knew, they say, Five, and two fishes**—John is more precise and full: "One of His disciples, Andrew, Simon Peter's brother, saith unto Him, There is a lad here which hath five barley loaves and two small fishes: but what are they among so many?" (John 6:8, 9.) Probably this was the whole stock of provisions then at the command of the disciples —no more than enough for one meal to them—and entrusted for the time to this lad. "He said, Bring them hither to me" (Matthew 14:18). **39. And he commanded them to make all sit down by companies upon the green grass**—or "green hay"; the rank grass of those bushy wastes. For, as John (6:10) notes, "there was much grass in the place." **40. And they sat down in ranks, by hundreds, and by fifties**—Doubtless this was to show at a glance the number fed, and to enable all to witness in an orderly manner this glorious miracle. **41. And when he had taken the five loaves and the two fishes, he looked up to heaven**—Thus would the most distant of them see distinctly what He was doing. **and blessed**—John says, "And when he had given thanks." The sense is the same. This thanksgiving for the meal, and benediction of it as the food of thousands, was the crisis of the miracle. **and brake the loaves, and gave them to his disciples to set before them**—thus virtually holding forth these men as His future ministers. **and the two fishes divided he among them all. 42. And they did all eat, and were filled**—All the four Evangelists mention this: and John (6:11) adds, "and likewise of the fishes, as much as they would"—to show that vast as was the multitude, and scanty the provisions, the meal to each and all of them was a plentiful one. "When they were filled, He said unto His disciples, Gather up the fragments that remain, that nothing be lost" (John 6:12). This was designed to bring out the whole extent of the miracle. **43. And they took up twelve baskets full of the fragments, and of the fishes**—"Therefore (says John 6:13), they gathered them together, and filled twelve baskets with the fragments of the five barley loaves, which remained over and above unto them that had eaten." The article here rendered "baskets" in all the four narratives was part of the luggage taken by Jews on a journey—to carry, it is said, both their provisions and hay to sleep on, that they might not have to depend on Gentiles, and so run the risk of ceremonial pollution. In this we have a striking corroboration of the truth of the four narratives.

Internal evidence renders it clear, we think, that the first three Evangelists wrote independently of each other, though the fourth must have seen all the others. But here, each of the first three Evangelists uses the same word to express the apparently insignificant circumstance that the baskets employed to gather up the fragments were of the kind which even the Roman satirist, JUVENAL, knew by the name of *cophinus*, while in both the narratives of the feeding of the Four Thousand the baskets used are expressly said to have been of the kind called *spuris*. (See on ch. 8:19, 20.) **44. And they that did eat of the loaves were about five thousand men** —"besides women and children" (Matt. 14:21). Of these, however, there would probably not be many; as only the males were obliged to go to the approaching festival.

Jesus Recrosses to the Western side of the Lake, Walking on the Sea (vss. 45-56). One very important particular given by John alone (6:15) introduces this portion: "When Jesus therefore perceived that they would take Him by force, to make Him a king, He departed again into a mountain Himself alone." **45. And straightway he constrained his disciples to get into the ship, and to go to the other side before**—Him—**unto Bethsaida** —Bethsaida of Galilee (John 12:21). John says they "went over the sea towards Capernaum"—the wind, probably, occasioning this slight deviation from the direction of Bethsaida. **while he sent away the people**—"the multitude." His object in this was to put an end to the misdirected excitement in His favor (John 6:15), into which the disciples themselves may have been somewhat drawn. The word "constrained" implies reluctance on their part, perhaps from unwillingness to part with their Master and embark at night, leaving Him alone on the mountain. **46. And when he had sent them away, he departed into a mountain to pray**—thus at length getting that privacy and rest which He had vainly sought during the earlier part of the day; opportunity also to pour out His soul in connection with the extraordinary excitement in His favor that evening—which appears to have marked the zenith of His reputation, for it began to decline the very next day; and a place whence He might watch the disciples on the lake, pray for them in their extremity, and observe the right time for coming to them, in a new manifestation of His glory, on the sea. **47. And when even was come**—the later evening (see on vs. 35). It had come even when the disciples embarked (Matt. 14:23; John 6:16). **the ship was in the midst of the sea, and he alone on the land**—John says (6:17), "It was now dark, and Jesus was not come to them." Perhaps they made no great effort to push across at first, having a lingering hope that their Master would yet join them, and so allowed the darkness to come on. "And the sea arose" (adds the beloved disciple, 6: 18), "by reason of a great wind that blew." **48. And he saw them toiling in rowing; for the wind was contrary unto them**—putting forth all their strength to buffet the waves and bear on against a head wind, but to little effect. He "saw" this from His mountain-top, and through the darkness of the night, for His heart was all with them: yet would He not go to their relief till His own time came. **and about the fourth watch of the night**— The Jews, who used to divide the night into three watches, latterly adopted the Roman division into four watches, as here. So that, at the rate of three hours to each, the fourth watch, reckoning from six P.M., would be three o'clock in the morning.

"So when they had rowed about five and twenty or thirty furlongs" (John 6:19)—rather more than halfway across. The lake is about seven miles broad at its widest part. So that in eight or nine hours they had only made some three and a half miles. By this time, therefore, they must have been in a state of exhaustion and despondency bordering on despair; and now at length, having tried them long enough—**he cometh unto them, walking upon the sea**—"and draweth nigh unto the ship" (John 6:19). **and would have passed by them** —but only in the sense of Luke 24:28; Genesis 32: 26; cf. Genesis 18:3, 5; 42:7. **49. But when they saw him walking upon the sea, they supposed it had been a spirit, and cried out**—"for fear" (Matt. 14:26). He would appear to them at first like a dark moving speck upon the waters; then as a human figure; but in the dark tempestuous sky, and not dreaming that it could be their Lord, they take it for a spirit. Cf. Luke 24:37. **50. For they all saw him, and were troubled. And immediately he talked with them, and saith unto them, Be of good cheer: It is I; be not afraid**—There is something in these two little words—given by Matthew, Mark and John—" 'Tis I," which from the mouth that spake it and the circumstances in which it was uttered, passes the power of language to express. Here were they in the midst of a raging sea, their little bark the sport of the elements, and with just enough of light to descry an object on the waters which only aggravated their fears. But Jesus deems it enough to dispel all apprehension to let them know that *He was there*. From other lips that "I am" would have merely meant that the person speaking was such a one and not another person. That, surely, would have done little to calm the fears of men expecting every minute, it may be, to go to the bottom. But spoken by One who at that moment was "treading upon the waves of the sea," and was about to hush the raging elements with His word, what was it but the Voice which cried of old in the ears of Israel, even from the days of Moses, "I AM"; "I, EVEN I, AM HE!" Cf. John 18:5, 6; 8:58. Now, that Word is "made flesh, and dwells among us," uttering itself from beside us in dear familiar tones—"It is the Voice of my Beloved!" How far was this apprehended by these frightened disciples? There was one, we know, in the boat who outstripped all the rest in susceptibility to such sublime appeals. It was not the deep-toned writer of the Fourth Gospel, who, though he lived to soar beyond all the apostles, was as yet too young for prominence, and all unripe. It was Simon-Barjonas. Here follows a very remarkable and instructive episode, recorded by Matthew alone:

Peter Ventures to Walk upon the Sea (Matt. 14: 28-32). 28. "And Peter answered Him, and said, Lord, If it be Thou, bid me come unto Thee on the water"; not "*let* me," but "give me the word of *command*"—"command," or "order me to come unto Thee upon the waters." 29. "And He said, Come." Sublime word, issuing from One conscious of power over the raging element, to bid it serve both Himself and whomsoever He pleased! "And when Peter was come down out of the ship, he walked upon the water"—"waters"— "to come to Jesus." "It was a bold spirit," says BISHOP HALL, "that could wish it; more bold that could act it—not fearing either the softness or the roughness of that uncouth passage." 30. "But when he saw the wind boisterous, he was afraid; and beginning to sink, he cried, saying, Lord, save me." The wind was as boisterous before, but Peter "*saw*" it not, seeing only the power of Christ, in the lively exercise of faith. Now he "*sees*" the fury of the elements, and immediately the power of Christ to bear him up fades before his view, and this makes him "afraid"—as how could he be otherwise, without any *felt* power to keep him up? He then "begins to sink"; and finally, conscious that his experiment had failed, he casts himself, in a sort of desperate confidence, upon his "Lord" for deliverance! 31. "And immediately Jesus stretched forth His hand, and caught him, and said unto him, O thou of little faith, wherefore didst thou doubt?" *This rebuke was not administered while Peter was sinking, nor till Christ had him by the hand:* first reinvigorating his faith, and then with it enabling him again to walk upon the crested wave. Useless else had been this loving reproof, which owns the *faith* that had ventured on the deep upon the bare word of Christ, but asks why that *distrust* which so quickly marred it. 32. "And when they [Jesus and Peter] were come into the ship, the wind ceased." **51. And he went up unto them into the ship**—John (6:21) says, "Then they willingly received him into the ship"—or rather, "Then were they willing to receive Him" (with reference to their previous terror); but implying also a glad welcome, their first fears now converted into wonder and delight. "And immediately," adds the beloved disciple, "they were at the land whither they went," or "were bound." This additional miracle, for as such it is manifestly related, is recorded by the fourth Evangelist alone. As the storm was suddenly calmed, so the little bark—propelled by the secret power of the Lord of nature now sailing in it—glided through the now unruffled waters, and, while they were wrapt in wonder at what had happened, not heeding their rapid motion, *was found* at port, to their still further surprise.

> Then are they glad, because at rest
>   And quiet now they be;
> So to the haven He them brings
>   Which they desired to see.

Matthew (14:33) says, "Then they that were in the ship came [i.e., ere they got to land] and worshipped him, saying, Of a truth Thou art the Son of God." But our Evangelist is wonderfully striking. **and the wind ceased and they were sore amazed in themselves beyond measure, and wondered**—The Evangelist seems hardly to find language strong enough to express their astonishment. **52. For they considered not the miracle of the loaves; for their heart was hardened**—What a singular statement! The meaning seems to be that if they had but "considered [reflected upon] the miracle of the loaves," wrought but a few hours before, they would have *wondered at nothing* which He might do within the whole circle of power and grace. *Incidents on Landing* (vss. 53-56). The details here are given with a rich vividness quite peculiar to this charming Gospel. **53. And when they had passed over, they came into the land of Gennesaret**—from which the lake sometimes takes its name, stretching along its western shore. Capernaum was their landing-place (John 6:24, 25). **and drew to the shore**—a nautical phrase, nowhere else used in the New Testament. **54. And when they were come out of the ship, straightway they knew him**—"immediately they recognized Him"; i.e., the people did. **55. and began to carry about in beds those that were sick, where they heard he was**—At this period of our Lord's ministry the popular enthusiasm in His favor was at its height. **56. and besought him that they might touch if it were but the border of his garment**—having heard, no doubt, of what the woman with the issue of blood experienced on doing so (ch. 5:25-29), and perhaps of other unrecorded cases of the same nature. **and as many as touched him**—or "it"—the border of His garment—**were made whole**—All this they *continued* to do and to experience while our Lord was in that region. The *time* corresponds to that mentioned (John 7:1), when He "walked in Galilee," instead of appearing in Jerusalem at the passover, "because the Jews," i.e., *the rulers,* "sought to kill Him"—while *the people* sought to enthrone Him!

CHAPTER 7

Vss. 1-23. Discourse on Ceremonial Pollution. (=Matt. 15:1-20). See on Matthew 15:1-20.

24-37. The Syrophoenician Woman and Her Daughter—A Deaf and Dumb Man Healed. (= Matt. 15:21-31).

The Syrophoenician Woman and Her Daughter (vss. 24-30). The first words of this narrative show that the incident followed, in point of time, immediately on what precedes it. **24. And from thence he arose, and went into**—or "unto". **borders of Tyre and Sidon**—the two great Phœnician seaports, but here denoting the territory generally, to the frontiers of which Jesus now came. But did Jesus actually enter this heathen territory? The whole narrative, we think, proceeds upon the supposition that He did. His immediate object seems to have been to avoid the wrath of the Pharisees at the withering exposure He had just made of their traditional religion. **and entered into an house, and would have no man know it**—because He had not come there to minister to heathens. But though not "*sent* but to the lost sheep of the house of Israel" (Matt. 15:24), He hindered not the lost sheep of the vast Gentile world from coming to Him, nor put them away when they did come—as this incident was designed to show. **but he could not be hid**—Christ's fame had early spread from Galilee into this very region (ch. 3:8; Luke 6:17). **25. For a certain woman, whose young daughter had an unclean spirit**—or, as in Matthew, "was badly demonized." **heard of him**—One wonders how; but distress is quick of hearing. **26. The woman was a Greek**—i.e., "a Gentile," as in the margin. **a Syrophœnician by nation**—so called as inhabiting the Phœnician tract of Syria. Juvenal uses the same term, as was remarked by Justin Martyr and Tertullian. Matthew calls her "a woman of Canaan"—a more intelligible description to his Jewish readers (cf. Judg. 1:30, 32, 33). **and she besought him that he would east forth the devil out of her daughter**—"She cried unto Him, saying, Have mercy on me, O Lord, Son of David: my daughter is grievously vexed with a devil" (Matt. 15:22). Thus, though no Israelite herself, she salutes Him as Israel's promised Messiah. Here we must go to Matthew 15:23-25 for some important links in the dialogue omitted by our Evangelist. 23. "But he answered her not a word." The design of this was first, perhaps, to show that He was not *sent* to such as she. He had said expressly to the Twelve, "Go not into the way of the Gentiles" (Matt. 10:5); and being now among them Himself, He would, for consistency's sake, let it be seen that He had not gone thither for *missionary* purposes. Therefore He not only kept silence, but had actually left the house, and—as will presently appear—was proceeding on His way back, when this woman accosted Him. But another reason for keeping silence plainly was to try and whet her faith, patience, and perseverance. And it had the desired effect: "She *cried after them*," which shows that He was already on His way from the place. "And His disciples came and besought Him, saying, Send her away; for she crieth after us." They thought her troublesome with her importunate cries, just as they did the people who brought young children to be blessed of Him, and they ask their Lord to "send her away," i.e., to grant her request and be rid of her; for we gather from His reply that they meant to solicit favor for her, though not for her sake so much as their own. 24. "But He answered and said, I am not sent but unto the lost sheep of the house of Israel"— a speech evidently intended for the disciples themselves, to satisfy them that, though the grace He was about to show to this Gentile believer was *beyond His strict* commission, He had not gone *spontaneously* to dispense it. Yet did even this speech open a gleam of hope, could she have discerned it. For thus might she have spoken: "I am not SENT, did He say? Truth, Lord, Thou comest not hither in quest of *us,* but I come in quest of *Thee;* and must I go empty away? So did not the woman of Samaria, whom when Thou foundest her on Thy way to Galilee, Thou sentest away to make many rich!' But this our poor Syrophœnician could not attain to. What, then, can she answer to such a speech? Nothing. She has reached her lowest depth, her darkest moment: she will just utter her last cry: 25. "Then came she and worshipped Him, saying, Lord, help me!" This appeal, so artless, wrung from the depths of a believing heart, and reminding us of the publican's "God be merciful to me a sinner," moved the Redeemer at last to break silence—but in what style? Here we return to our own Evangelist. 27. **But Jesus said unto her, Let the children first be filled** —"Is there hope for me here?" "Filled FIRST?" "Then my turn, it seems, *is* coming!"—but then, "The CHILDREN first?" "Ah! when, on that rule, shall my turn ever come!" But ere she has time for these ponderings of His word, another word comes to supplement it. **for it is not meet to take the children's bread, and to cast it unto the dogs**— Is this the death of her hopes? Nay, rather it is life from the dead. Out of the eater shall come forth meat (Judg. 14:14). "At evening-time, it shall be light" (Zech. 14:7). "Ah! I have it now. Had He kept silence, what could I have done but go unblest? but He hath spoken, and the victory is mine." 28. **And she answered and said unto him, Yes, Lord**—or, as the same word is rendered in Matthew 15:27. "Truth, Lord." **yet the dogs eat of the children's crumbs**—which fall from their master's table" (Matt. 15:27). "I thank Thee, O blessed One, for that word! That's my whole case. Not of the children? True. A dog? True also: *Yet* the dogs under the table are allowed to eat of the children's crumbs—the droppings from their master's full table: Give me that, and I am content: One crumb of power and grace from Thy table shall cast the devil out of my daughter." Oh, what lightning-quickness, what reach of instinctive ingenuity, do we behold in this heathen woman! 29. **And he said unto her**—"O woman, great is thy

faith" (Matt. 15:28). As BENGEL beautifully remarks, Jesus "marvelled" only at two things—*faith* and *unbelief* (see on Luke 7:9). **For this saying go thy way; the devil is gone out of thy daughter**— That moment the deed was done. **30. And when she was come to her house, she found the devil gone out, and her daughter laid upon the bed**—But Matthew is more specific; "And her daughter was made whole from that very hour." The wonderfulness of this case in all its features has been felt in every age of the Church, and the balm it has administered, and will yet administer, to millions will be known only in that day that shall reveal the secrets of all hearts.

Deaf and Dumb Man Healed (vss. 31-37). **31. And again, departing from the coasts of Tyre and Sidon, he came unto the Sea of Galilee**—or, according to what has very strong claims to be regarded as the true text here, "And again, departing from the coasts of Tyre, He came through Sidon to the Sea of Galilee." The MSS. in favor of this reading, though not the most numerous, are weighty, while the versions agreeing with it are among the most ancient; and all the best critical editors and commentators adopt it. In this case we must understand that our Lord, having once gone out of the Holy Land the length of Tyre, proceeded as far north as Sidon, though without ministering, so far as appears, in those parts, and then bent His steps in a southeasterly direction. There is certainly a difficulty in the supposition of so long a *detour* without any missionary object: and some may think this sufficient to cast the balance in favor of the received reading. Be this as it may, on returning from these coasts of Tyre, He passed **through the midst of the coasts**—frontiers—**of Decapolis**—crossing the Jordan, therefore, and approaching the lake on its east side. Here Matthew, who omits the details of the cure of this deaf and dumb man, introduces some particulars, from which we learn that it was only one of a great number. "And Jesus," says that Evangelist (15:29-31), "departed from thence, and came nigh unto the Sea of Galilee, and went up into a mountain"—the mountain range bounding the lake on the northeast, in Decapolis: "And great multitudes came unto Him, having with them lame, blind, dumb, maimed"—not "mutilated," which is but a secondary sense of the word, but "deformed"—"and many others, and cast them down at Jesus' feet; and He healed them: insomuch that the multitude [multitudes] wondered, when they saw the dumb to speak, the maimed to be whole, the lame to walk, and the blind to see; and they glorified the God of Israel"—who after so long and dreary an absence of visible manifestation, had returned to bless His people as of old (cf. Luke 7: 16). Beyond this it is not clear from the Evangelist's language that the people saw into the claims of Jesus. Well, of these cases Mark here singles out one, whose cure had something peculiar in it. **32. And they bring unto him one that was deaf … and they beseech him to put his hand upon him**— In their eagerness they appear to have been somewhat too officious. Though usually doing as here suggested, He will deal with this case in His own way. **33. And he took him aside from the multitude**—As in another case He "took the blind man by the hand and led him out of the town" (ch. 8: 23), probably to fix his undistracted attention on Himself, and, by means of certain actions He was about to do, to awaken and direct his attention to the proper source of relief. **and put his fingers into his ears**—As his indistinct articulation arose from his deafness, our Lord addresses Himself to this first. To the impotent man He said, "Wilt thou be made whole?" to the blind men, "What will ye that I shall do unto you?" and "Believe ye that I am able to do this?" (John 5:6; Matt. 20:32; 9: 28.) But as this patient could *hear* nothing, our Lord substitutes symbolical actions upon each of the organs affected. **and he spit and touched his tongue**—moistening the man's parched tongue with saliva from His own mouth, as if to lubricate the organ or facilitate its free motion; thus indicating the source of the healing virtue to be His own person. (For similar actions, see ch. 8:23; John 9:6.) **34. And looking up to heaven**—ever acknowledging His Father, even while the healing was seen to flow from Himself (see on John 5:19). **he sighed**—"over the wreck," says TRENCH, "which sin had brought about, and the malice of the devil in deforming the fair features of God's original creation." But, we take it, there was a yet more painful impression of that "evil thing and bitter" whence all our ills have sprung, and which, when "Himself took our infirmities and bare our sicknesses" (Matt. 8:17), became mysteriously His own.

> In thought of these his brows benign,
> Not even in healing, cloudless shine.
>   KEBLE

and saith unto him, Ephphatha, that is, Be opened—Our Evangelist, as remarked on ch. 5:41, loves to give such wonderful words just as they were spoken. **35. And straightway his ears were opened**—This is mentioned first as the source of the other derangement. **and the string of his tongue was loosed, and he spake plain**—The cure was thus alike instantaneous and perfect. **36. And he charged them that they should tell no man**—Into this very region He had sent the man out of whom had been cast the legion of devils, to proclaim "what the Lord had done for him" (ch. 5:19). Now He will have them "tell no man." But in the former case there was no danger of obstructing His ministry by "blazing the matter" (ch. 1:45), as He Himself had left the region; whereas now He was sojourning in it. **but the more he charged them, so much the more a great deal they published it**—They could not be restrained; nay, the prohibition seemed only to whet their determination to publish His fame. **37. And were beyond measure astonished, saying, He hath done all things well**—reminding us, says TRENCH, of the words of the first creation (Gen. 1: 31, LXX), upon which we are thus not unsuitably thrown back, for Christ's work is in the truest sense "a new creation," **he maketh both the deaf to hear and the dumb to speak**—"and they glorified the God of Israel" (Matt. 15:31). See on vs. 31 of this chapter.

CHAPTER 8

Vss. 1-26. FOUR THOUSAND MIRACULOUSLY FED —A SIGN FROM HEAVEN SOUGHT AND REFUSED—THE LEAVEN OF THE PHARISEES AND SADDUCEES—A BLIND MAN AT BETHSAIDA RESTORED TO SIGHT. (= Matt. 15:32 to 16:12.) This section of miscellaneous matter evidently follows the preceding one in point of time, as will be seen by observing how it is introduced by Matthew.
Feeding of the Four Thousand (vss. 1-9). **1. In those days the multitude being very great... 2. I have compassion on the multitude**—an expres-

sion of that deep emotion in the Redeemer's heart which always preceded some remarkable interposition for relief. (See Matt. 14:14; 20:34; Mark 1: 41; Luke 7:13; also Matt. 9:36, before the mission of the Twelve; cf. Judg. 2:18; 10:16.) **because they have now been with me**—in constant attendance— **three days, and have nothing to eat: 3. And if I send them away fasting to their own houses, they will faint by the way**—In their eagerness they seem not to have thought of the need of provisions for such a length of time; but the Lord thought of it. In Matt. (15:32) it is, "I will not send them away fasting"—or rather, "To send them away fasting I am unwilling." **4. From whence can a man satisfy these men with bread here in the wilderness?**—Though the question here is the same as when He fed the five thousand, they evidently *now* meant no more by it than that *they* had not the means of feeding the multitude; modestly leaving the Lord to decide what was to be done. And this will the more appear from His not now trying them, as before, by saying, "They need not depart, give ye them to eat"; but simply asking what they had, and then giving His directions. **5. And he asked them. How many loaves have ye? And they said, Seven** —It was important in this case, as in the former, that the precise number of the loaves should be brought out. Thus also does the distinctness of the two miracles appear. **9. And they that had eaten about four thousand: and he sent them away**—Had not our Lord distinctly referred, in this very chapter and in two successive sentences, to the feeding of the five thousand and of the four thousand as two distinct miracles, many critics would have insisted that they were but two different representations of one and the same miracle, as they do of the two expulsions of the buyers and sellers from the temple, at the beginning and end of our Lord's ministry. But even in spite of what our Lord says, it is painful to find such men as NEANDER endeavoring to identify the two miracles. The localities, though both on the eastern side of the lake, were different; the time was different; the preceding and following circumstances were different; the period during which the people continued fasting was different—in the one case not even one entire day, in the other three days; the number fed was different —five thousand in the one case, in the other four thousand; the number of the loaves was different— five in the one case, in the other seven; the number of the fishes in the one case is definitely stated by all the four Evangelists—two; in the other case both give them indefinitely—"a few small fishes"; in the one case the multitude were commanded to sit down "upon the green grass"; in the other "on the ground"; in the one case the number of the baskets taken up filled with the fragments was twelve, in the other seven; but more than all, perhaps, because apparently quite incidental, in the one case the name given to the kind of baskets used is the same in all the four narratives—the *cophinus* (see on ch. 6:43); in the other case the name given to the kind of baskets used, while it is the same in both the narratives, is quite different—the *spuris,* a basket large enough to hold a man's body, for Paul was let down in one of these from the wall of Damascus (Acts 9:25). It might be added, that in the one case the people, in a frenzy of enthusiasm, would have taken Him by force to make Him a king; in the other case no such excitement is recorded. In view of these things, who could have believed that these were one and the same miracle, even if the Lord Himself had not expressly distinguished them?

Sign from Heaven Sought (vss. 10-13). **10. And straightway he entered into a ship,**—"into the ship," or "embarked." **with his disciples, and came into the parts of Dalmanutha**—In Matthew (15:39) it is "the coasts of Magdala." Magdala and Dalmanutha were both on the western shore of the lake, and probably not far apart. From the former the surname "Magdalene" was probably taken, to denote the residence of Mary Magdalene. Dalmanutha may have been a village, but it cannot now be identified with certainty. **11. seeking of him a sign from heaven, tempting him**—not in the least desiring evidence for their conviction, but hoping to entrap Him. The first part of the answer is given in Matthew alone (16:2, 3): "He answered and said unto them, When it is evening, ye say, It will be fair weather; for the sky is red. And in the morning, It will be foul weather to-day: for the sky is red and lowering [sullen, gloomy]. Hypocrites! ye can discern the face of the sky; but can ye not discern the signs of the times?" The same simplicity of purpose and careful observation of the symptoms of approaching events which they showed in common things would enable them to "discern the signs of the times"—or rather "seasons," to which the prophets pointed for the manifestation of the Messiah. The scepter had departed from Judah; Daniel's seventy weeks were expiring, etc.; and many other significant indications of the close of the old economy, and preparations for a freer and more comprehensive one, might have been discerned. But all was lost upon them. **12. And he sighed deeply in his spirit**—The language is very strong. These glimpses into the interior of the Redeemer's heart, in which our Evangelist abounds, are more precious than rubies. The state of the Pharisaic heart, which prompted this desire for a fresh sign, went to His very soul. **and saith, Why doth this generation**—"this wicked and adulterous generation" (Matt. 16:4)—**seek after a sign?**—when they have had such abundant evidence already. **There shall no sign be given unto this generation**—lit., "If there shall be given to this generation a sign"; a Jewish way of expressing a solemn and peremptory determination to the contrary (cf. Heb. 4:5; Ps. 95:11, *Margin*). "A generation incapable of appreciating such demonstrations shall not be gratified with them." In Matthew 16:4 He added, "but the sign of the prophet Jonas." (See on Matthew 12:39, 40.) **13. And he left them**—no doubt with tokens of displeasure.

The Leaven of the Pharisees and Sadducees (vss. 14-21). **14. Now the disciples had forgotten to take bread, neither had they in the ship with them more than one loaf**—This is another example of that graphic circumstantiality which gives such a charm to this briefest of the four Gospels. The circumstance of the "one loaf" only remaining, as WEBSTER and WILKINSON remark, was more suggestive of their Master's recent miracles than the entire absence of provisions. **15. And he charged them, saying, Take heed, beware of the leaven of the Pharisees**—"and of the Sadducees" (Matt. 16:6). **and of the leaven of Herod**—The teaching or "doctrine" (Matt. 16:12) of the Pharisees and of the Sadducees was quite different, but both were equally pernicious; and the Herodians, though rather a political party, were equally envenomed against our Lord's spiritual teaching. See on Matthew 12:14. The *penetrating* and *diffusive* quality of leaven, for good or bad, is the ground of the comparison. **16. And they reasoned among themselves, saying, It is because we have no bread**—But a little while ago He was tried with the obduracy of the Pharisees; now He is tried with the obtuseness of His own disciples. The *nine* questions following each other in rapid succession (vss. 17-21) show how deeply He was hurt at this want of spiritual apprehension, and worse still, their low thoughts of Him, as if He would utter so solemn a warning on so petty a subject. It will be seen, however, from the very form of their conjecture, "It is because *we* have no bread," and our Lord's astonishment that they should not by that time have known better with what He took up His attention—that He ever left *the whole care for His own temporal wants to the Twelve:* that He did this so entirely, that finding they were reduced to their last loaf they felt as if unworthy of such a trust, and could not think but that the same thought was in their Lord's mind which was pressing upon their own; but that in this they were so far wrong that it hurt His feelings—sharp just in proportion to His love—that such a thought of Him should have entered their minds! Who that, like angels, "desire to look into these things" will not prize such glimpses above gold? **17. have ye your heart yet hardened?**—How strong an expression to use of true-hearted disciples! See on ch. 6:52. **18. Having eyes, see ye not? and having ears, hear ye not?**—See on Matthew 13:13. **and do ye not remember? 19. When I brake the five loaves among**—the—**five thousand, how many baskets full of fragments took ye up?** ... **21. How is it that ye do not understand?**—"do not understand that the warning I gave you could not have been prompted by any such petty consideration as the want of loaves in your scrip." Profuse as were our Lord's miracles, we see from this that they were not wrought at random, but that He carefully noted their minutest details, and desired that this should be done by those who witnessed, as doubtless by all who read the record of them. Even the different kind of baskets used at the two miraculous feedings, so carefully noted in the two narratives, are here also referred to; the one smaller, of which there were twelve, the other much larger, of which there were seven.

Blind Man at Bethsaida Restored to Sight (vss. 22-26). **22. And he cometh to Bethsaida**—Bethsaida-Julias, on the northeast side of the lake, whence after this He proceeded to Cæsarea Philippi (vs. 27). **and they bring a blind man unto him, and besought him to touch him**—See on ch. 7:32. **23. And he took the blind man by the hand, and led him out of the town**—Of the deaf and dumb man it is merely said that "He took him aside" (ch. 7:33); but this blind man He *led by the hand* out of the town, doing it Himself rather than employing another—great humility, exclaims BENGEL—that He might gain his confidence and raise his expectation. **and when he had spit on his eyes**—the organ affected—see on ch. 7:33. **and put his hands upon him, he asked him if he saw aught. 24. And he looked up, and said, I see men as trees, walking**—This is one of the cases in which one edition of what is called the received text differs from another. That which is decidedly the best supported, and has also internal evidence on its side is this: "I see men; for I see [them] as trees walking"—i.e., he could distinguish them from trees only by their motion; a minute mark of truth in the narrative, as ALFORD observes, describing how human objects had appeared to him during that gradual failing of sight which had ended in blindness. **25. After that he put his hands again upon his eyes, and made him look up; and he was** restored, and saw every man clearly—Perhaps the one operation perfectly restored the *eyes,* while the other imparted immediately the *faculty of using them.* It is the only recorded example of a *progressive* cure, and it certainly illustrates similar methods in the spiritual kingdom. Of the four recorded cases of sight restored, all the patients save one either *came* or *were brought* to the Physician. In the case of the man born blind, *the Physician came* to the patient. So some seek and find Christ; of others He is found who seek Him not. **26. Neither go into the town, nor tell it to any in the town**—Besides the usual reasons against going about "blazing the matter," retirement in this case would be salutary to himself.

27-38. PETER'S NOBLE CONFESSION OF CHRIST— OUR LORD'S FIRST EXPLICIT ANNOUNCEMENT OF HIS APPROACHING SUFFERINGS, DEATH, AND RESURRECTION—HIS REBUKE OF PETER, AND WARNING TO ALL THE TWELVE. (= Matt. 16:13-27; Luke 9:18-26.) For the exposition, see on Matthew 16:13-28.

CHAPTER 9

Vss. 1-13. JESUS IS TRANSFIGURED—CONVERSATION ABOUT ELIAS. (= Matt. 16:28-17:13; Luke 9: 27-36.) See Luke 9:27-36.

14-32. HEALING OF A DEMONIAC BOY—SECOND EXPLICIT ANNOUNCEMENT OF HIS APPROACHING DEATH AND RESURRECTION. (= Matt. 17:14-23; Luke 9:37-45.)

Healing of the Demoniac Boy (vss. 14-29). **14. And when he came to his disciples, he saw a great multitude about them, and the scribes questioning with them**—This was "on the next day, when they were come down from the hill" (Luke 9:37). The Transfiguration appears to have taken place at night. In the morning, as He came down from the hill on which it took place—with Peter, and James, and John—on approaching the other nine, He found them surrounded by a great multitude, and the scribes disputing or discussing with them. No doubt these cavillers were twitting the apostles of Jesus with their inability to cure the demoniac boy of whom we are presently to hear, and insinuating doubts even of their Master's ability to do it; while they, zealous for their Master's honor, would no doubt refer to His past miracles in proof of the contrary. **15. And straightway all the people**—the multitude. **when they beheld him, were greatly amazed**—were astounded. **and running to him saluted him**—The singularly strong expression of surprise, the sudden arrest of the discussion, and the rush of the multitude towards Him, can be accounted for by nothing less than something amazing in His appearance. There can hardly be any doubt that *His countenance still retained traces of His transfiguration-glory.* (See Exod. 34:29, 30.) So BENGEL, DE WETTE, MEYER, TRENCH, ALFORD. No wonder, if this was the case, that they not only ran to Him, but saluted Him. Our Lord, however, takes no notice of what had attracted them, and probably it gradually faded away as He drew near; but addressing Himself to the scribes, He demands the subject of their discussion, ready to meet them where they had pressed hard upon His half-instructed and as yet timid apostles. **16. And he asked the scribes, What question ye with them?**—Ere they had time to reply, the father of the boy, whose case had occasioned the dispute, himself steps forward and answers the question; telling a piteous tale of deaf-

ness, and dumbness, and fits of epilepsy—ending with this, that the disciples, though entreated, could not perform the cure. **17. And one of the multitude answered, and said, Master, I have brought unto thee my son**—"mine only child" (Luke 9:38). **which hath a dumb spirit**—a spirit whose operation had the effect of rendering his victim speechless, and deaf also (vs. 25). In Matthew's report of the speech (17:15), the father says "he is lunatic"; this being another and most distressing effect of the possession. **18. And wheresoever he taketh him, he teareth him; and he foameth, and gnasheth with his teeth, and pineth away**—rather, "becomes withered," "dried up," or "paralyzed"; as the same word is everywhere else rendered in the New Testament. Some additional particulars are given by Luke, and by our Evangelist below. "Lo," says he in Luke 9: 39, "a spirit taketh him, and he suddenly crieth out; and it teareth him that he foameth again, and bruising him hardly [or with difficulty] departeth from him." **and I spake to thy disciples that they should cast him out; and they could not**—Our Lord replies to the father by a severe rebuke to the disciples. As if wounded at the exposure before such a multitude, of the weakness of His disciples' faith, which doubtless He felt as a reflection on Himself, He puts them to the blush before all, but in language fitted only to raise expectation of what He Himself would do. **19. He answereth him, and saith, O faithless generation**—"and perverse," or "perverted" (Matt. 17:17; Luke 9:41). **how long shall I be with you? how long shall I suffer you?**—language implying that it was a shame to them to want the faith necessary to perform this cure, and that it needed some patience to put up with them. It is to us surprising that some interpreters, as CHRYSOSTOM and CALVIN, should represent this rebuke as addressed, not to the disciples at all, but to the scribes who disputed with them. Nor does it much, if at all, mend the matter to view it as addressed to both, as most expositors seem to do. With BENGEL, DE WETTE, and MEYER, we regard it as addressed directly to the nine apostles who were unable to expel this evil spirit. And though, in ascribing this inability to their "want of faith" and the "perverted turn of mind" which they had drunk in with their early training, the rebuke would undoubtedly apply, with vastly greater force, to those who twitted the poor disciples with their inability, it would be to change the whole nature of the rebuke to suppose it addressed to those who had *no faith at all,* and were *wholly perverted.* It was because faith sufficient for curing this youth was to be expected of the disciples, and because they should by that time have got rid of the perversity in which they had been reared, that Jesus exposes them thus before the rest. And who does not see that this was fitted, more than anything else, to impress upon the bystanders the severe loftiness of the training He was giving to the Twelve, and the unsophisticated footing He was on with them? **Bring him unto me**— The order to bring the patient to Him was instantly obeyed; when, lo! as if conscious of the presence of his Divine Tormentor, and expecting to be made to quit, the foul spirit rages and is furious, determined to die hard, doing all the mischief he can to this poor child while yet within his grasp. **20. And they brought him unto him: and when he saw him, straightway the spirit tare him**—Just as the man with the legion of demons, "when he *saw* Jesus, ran and worshipped Him" (ch. 5:6), so this demon, *when he saw Him,* immediately "tare him." The feeling of terror and rage was the same in both cases. **and he fell on the ground, and wallowed foaming**—Still Jesus does nothing, but keeps conversing with the father about the case—partly to have its desperate features told out by him who knew them best, in the hearing of the spectators; partly to let its virulence have time to show itself; and partly to deepen the exercise of the father's soul, to draw out his faith, and thus to prepare both him and the bystanders for what He was to do. **21. And he asked his father, How long is it ago since this came unto him? And he said, Of a child . . .**—Having told briefly the affecting features of the case, the poor father, half dispirited by the failure of the disciples and the aggravated virulence of the malady itself in presence of their Master, yet encouraged too by what he had heard of Christ, by the severe rebuke He had given to His disciples for not having faith enough to cure the boy, and by the dignity with which He had ordered him to be brought to Him—in this mixed state of mind, he closes his description of the case with these touching words: **27. but if thou canst do anything, have compassion on us, and help us**—"us," says the father; for it was a sore family affliction. Cf. the language of the Syrophœnician woman regarding her daughter, "Lord, help *me*." Still nothing is done: the man is but *struggling into faith:* it must come a step farther. But he had to do with Him who breaks not the bruised reed, and who knew how to inspire what He demanded. The man had said to Him, "*If Thou canst do.*" **23. Jesus said unto him, If thou canst believe**—The man had said, "If Thou canst do *anything.*" Jesus replies. **all things are possible to him that believeth**—"My doing all depends on thy believing." To impress this still more, He redoubles upon the believing: "If thou canst believe, all things are possible to him that believeth." Thus the Lord helps the birth of faith in that struggling soul; and now, though with pain and sore travail, it comes to the birth, as TRENCH, borrowing from OLSHAUSEN, expresses it. Seeing the case stood still, waiting not upon the Lord's power but his own faith, the man becomes immediately conscious of conflicting principles, and rises into one of the noblest utterances on record. **24. And straightway the father of the child cried out, and said with tears, Lord, I believe: help thou mine unbelief**—i.e., " 'Tis useless concealing from Thee, O Thou mysterious, mighty Healer, the unbelief that still struggles in this heart of mine; but that heart bears me witness that I do believe in Thee; and if distrust still remains, I disown it, I wrestle with it, I seek help from Thee against it." Two things are very remarkable here: First, *The felt and owned presence of unbelief,* which only the strength of the man's faith could have so revealed to his own consciousness. Second, *His appeal to Christ for help against his felt unbelief*—a feature in the case quite unparalleled, and showing, more than all protestations could have done, the insight he had attained into the existence of *a power in Christ more glorious than any he had besought for his poor child.* The work was done; and as the commotion and confusion in the crowd was now increasing, Jesus at once, as Lord of spirits, gives the word of command to the dumb and deaf spirit to be gone, never again to return to his victim. **26. And the spirit cried, and rent him sore, and came out of him; and he was as one dead; insomuch that many said, He is dead**—The malignant, cruel spirit, now conscious that his time was come, gathers up his whole strength, with intent by a last stroke to kill his victim, and had nearly succeeded.

But the Lord of life was there; the Healer of all maladies, the Friend of sinners, the Seed of the woman, "the Stronger than the strong man armed," was there. The very faith which Christ declared to be enough for everything being now found, it was not possible that the serpent should prevail. Fearfully is he permitted to bruise the *heel,* as in this case; but his own *head* shall go for it—his works shall be destroyed (I John 3:8). **27. But Jesus took him by the hand, and lifted him up; and he arose. 28. Why could not we cast him out? 29. And he said unto them, This kind can come forth by nothing but by prayer and fasting**—i.e., as nearly all good interpreters are agreed, "this kind of evil spirits cannot be expelled," or "so desperate a case of demoniacal possession cannot be cured, but by prayer and fasting." But since the Lord Himself says that His disciples could not fast while He was with them, perhaps this was designed, as ALFORD hints, for their after-guidance—unless we take it as but a definite way of expressing the general truth, that great and difficult duties require special preparation and self-denial. But the answer to their question, as given in Matthew 17 is fuller: "And Jesus said unto them, Because of your unbelief. For verily I say unto you, If ye have faith as a grain of mustard seed, ye shall say unto this mountain, Remove hence to yonder place, and it shall remove; and nothing shall be impossible unto you" (vs. 20). See on ch. 11:23. "Howbeit this kind goeth not out but by prayer and fasting" (vs. 21). i.e., though nothing is impossible to faith, yet such a height of faith as is requisite for such triumphs is not to be reached either in a moment or without effort–either with God in prayer or with ourselves in self-denying exercises. Luke (9:43) adds, "And they were all amazed at the mighty power of God" —"at the majesty" or "mightiness of God," in this last miracle, in the Transfiguration, etc.; or, at the *divine grandeur* of Christ rising upon them daily.

Second Explicit Announcement of His Approaching Death and Resurrection (vss. 30-32). **30. And they departed thence, and passed**—were passing along. **through Galilee; and he would not that any man should know it**—By comparing Matthew 17:22, 23 and Luke 9:43, 44 with this, we gather, that as our Lord's reason for going through Galilee more privately than usual on this occasion was to reiterate to them the announcement which had so shocked them at the first mention of it, and thus familiarize them with it by little and little, so this was His reason for enjoining silence upon them as to their present movements. **31. For he taught his disciples, and said unto them**—"Let these sayings sink down into your ears" (Luke 9:44); not what had been passing between them as to His grandeur, but what He was now to utter. **The Son of man is delivered**—The use of the present tense expresses how near at hand He would have them to consider it. As BENGEL says, steps were already in course of being taken to bring it about. **into the hands of men**—This remarkable antithesis, "the Son of *man* shall be delivered into the hands of *men,*" it is worthy of notice, is in all the three Evangelists. **and they shall kill him**—i.e., "Be not carried off your feet by all that grandeur of Mine which ye have lately witnessed, but bear in mind what I have already told you and now distinctly repeat, that that Sun in whose beams ye now rejoice is soon to set in midnight gloom." **and after he is killed, he shall rise the third day. 32. But they understood not that saying**—"and it was hid from them, [so] that they preceived it not" (Luke 9:45). **and were** afraid to ask him—Their most cherished ideas were so completely dashed by such announcements, that they were afraid of laying themselves open to rebuke by asking Him any questions. But "they were exceeding sorry" (Matt. 17:23). While the other Evangelists, as WEBSTER and WILKINSON remark, notice their ignorance and their fear, Matthew, who was one of them, retains a vivid recollection of their sorrow.

33-50. STRIFE AMONG THE TWELVE WHO SHOULD BE GREATEST IN THE KINGDOM OF HEAVEN, WITH RELATIVE TEACHING—INCIDENTAL REBUKE OF JOHN FOR EXCLUSIVENESS. (= Matt. 18:1-9; Luke 9:46-50.)

Strife among the Twelve, with Relative Teaching (vss. 33-37). **33. What was it that ye disputed among yourselves by the way?**—From this we gather that after the painful communication He had made to them, the Redeemer had allowed them to travel so much of the way by themselves; partly, no doubt, that He might have privacy for Himself to dwell on what lay before Him, and partly that they might be induced to weigh together and prepare themselves for the terrible events which He had announced to them. But if so, how different was their occupation! **34. But they held their peace: for by the way they had disputed among themselves, who should be the greatest**—From Matthew 18:1 we should infer that the subject was introduced, not by our Lord, but by the disciples themselves, who came and asked Jesus who should be greatest. Perhaps one or two of them first referred the matter to Jesus, who put them off till they should all be assembled together at Capernaum. He had all the while "perceived the thought of their heart" (Luke 9:47); but now that they were all together "in the house," He questions them about it, and they are put to the blush, conscious of the *temper* towards each other which it had kindled. This raised the whole question afresh, and at this point our Evangelist takes it up. The subject was suggested by the recent announcement of the Kingdom (Matt. 16:19-28), the transfiguration of their Master, and especially the preference given to three of them at that scene. **35. If any man desire to be first, the same shall be last of all, and servant of all**—i.e., "let him be" such: he must be prepared to take the last and lowest place. See on ch. 10:42-45. **36. And he took a child**—"a little child" (Matt. 18:2); but the word is the same in both places, as also in Luke 9:47. **and set him in the midst of them: and when he had taken him in his arms**—This beautiful trait is mentioned by our Evangelist alone. **he said unto them**—Here we must go to Matthew (18:3, 4) for the first of this answer: "Verily I say unto you, except ye be converted, and become as little children, ye shall not enter into the kingdom of Heaven:" i.e., "Conversion must be thorough; not only must the heart be turned to God in general, and from earthly to heavenly things, but in particular, except ye be converted from that carnal ambition which still rankles within you, into that freedom from all such feelings which ye see in this child, ye have neither part nor lot in the kingdom at all; and he who in this feature has most of the child, is highest there." Whosoever, therefore, shall "humble himself as this little child, the same is greatest in the kingdom of heaven": "for he that is [willing to be] least among you all, the same shall be great" (Luke 9:48). **37. Whosoever shall receive one of such children**—so manifesting the spirit unconsciously displayed by this child. **in my name**—from love to Me. **re-**

ceiveth me; and whosoever shall receive me, receiveth not me, but Him that sent me—See on Matthew 10:40.

Incidental Rebuke of John for Exclusiveness (vss. 38-41). **38. And John aswered him, saying, Master, we saw one casting out devils in thy name, and he followeth not us: and we forbade him, because he followeth not us**—The link of connection here with the foregoing context lies, we apprehend, in the emphatic words which our Lord had just uttered, "in My name." "Oh," interposes John—young, warm, but not sufficiently apprehending Christ's teaching in these matters—"that reminds me of something that we have just done, and we should like to know if we did right. We saw one casting out devils "in *Thy name,*" and we forbade him, because he followeth not us. Were we right, or were we wrong?" Answer—"Ye were wrong." "But we did it because he followeth not us." "No matter." **39. But Jesus said, Forbid him not: for there is no man which shall do a miracle in my name, that can lightly**—soon, i.e., readily—**speak evil of me. 40. For he that is not against us is on our part**—Two principles of immense importance are here laid down: "First, No one will readily speak evil of Me who has the faith to do a miracle in My name; and second, If such a person cannot be supposed to be *against* us, ye are to consider him *for* us." Let it be carefully observed that our Lord does not say this man should *not* have "followed them," nor yet that it was indifferent whether he did or not; but simply teaches how such a person was to be regarded, *although he did not*—viz., as a reverer of His name and a promotor of His cause. **41. For whosoever shall give you a cup of water to drink in my name, because ye belong to Christ, verily I say unto you, he shall not lose his reward**—See on Matthew 10:42.

Continuation of Teaching Suggested by the Disciple's Strife (vss. 42-50). What follows appears to have no connection with the incidental reproof of John immediately preceding. As that had interrupted some important teaching, our Lord hastens back from it, as if no such interruption had occurred. **42. For whosoever shall offend one of these little ones that believe in me**—or, shall cause them to stumble; referring probably to the effect which such unsavory disputes as they had held would have upon the inquiring and hopeful who came in contact with them, leading to the belief that after all they were no better than others. **it is better for him that a millstone were hanged about his neck**—The word here is simply "millstone," without expressing of which kind. But in Matthew 18:6 it is the "ass-turned" kind, far heavier than the small hand-mill turned by female slaves, as in Luke 17:35. It is of course the same which is meant here. **and he were cast into the sea**—meaning, that if by such a death that stumbling were prevented, and so its eternal consequences averted, it would be a happy thing for them. Here follows a striking verse in Matthew 18:7, "Woe unto the world because of offences!" (There will be stumblings and falls and loss of souls enough from the world's treatment of disciples, without any addition from you: dreadful will be its doom in consequence; see that ye share not in it.) "For it must needs be that offences come; but woe to that man by whom the offence cometh!" (The struggle between light and darkness will inevitably cause stumblings, but not less guilty is he who wilfully makes any to stumble.) **43. And if thy hand offend thee, cut it off: it is better for thee to enter** into life maimed, than having two hands to go into hell—See Matthew 5:29, 30. The only difference between the words there and here is that there they refer to impure inclinations; here, to an ambitious disposition, an irascible or quarrelsome temper, and the like: and the injunction is to strike at the root of such dispositions and cut off the occasions of them. **47. And if thine eye offend thee, pluck it out: it is better for thee to enter into the kingdom of God with one eye, than having two eyes to be cast into hell-fire; 48. Where their worm dieth not, and the fire is not quenched**—See on Matthew 5:30; and on the words "hell" and "hell-fire," or "the hell of fire," see on Matthew 5:22. The "unquenchableness" of this fire has already been brought before us (see on Matt. 3:12); and the awfully vivid idea of an undying worm, everlastingly consuming an unconsumable body, is taken from the closing words of the evangelical prophet (Isa. 66:24), which seem to have furnished the later Jewish Church with its current phraseology on the subject of future punishment (see LIGHTFOOT). **49. For every one shall be salted with fire, and every sacrifice shall be salted with salt**—A difficult verse, on which much has been written—some of it to little purpose. "Every one" probably means "Every follower of mine"; and the "fire" with which he "must be salted" probably means "a fiery trial" to season him. (Cf. Mal. 3:2, etc.) The reference to salting the sacrifice is of course to that maxim of the Levitical law, that every acceptable sacrifice must be sprinkled with salt, to express symbolically its soundness, sweetness, wholesomeness, acceptability. But as it had to be *roasted* first, we have here the further idea of a salting with fire. In this case, "every sacrifice," in the next clause, will mean, "Every one who would be found an acceptable offering to God"; and thus the whole verse may perhaps be paraphrased as follows: "Every disciple of Mine shall have a fiery trial to undergo, and everyone who would be found an odor of a sweet smell, a sacrifice acceptable and well-pleasing to God, must have such a *salting*, like the Levitical sacrifices." Another, but, as it seems to us, far-fetched as well as harsh, interpretation—suggested first, we believe, by MICHAELIS, and adopted by ALEXANDER—takes the "every sacrifice which must be salted with fire" to mean those who are "cast into hell," and the *preservative* effect of this salting to refer to the preservation of the lost not only *in* but *by means of* the fire of hell. Their reason for this is that the other interpretation changes the meaning of the "fire," and the characters too, from the lost to the saved, in these verses. But as our Lord confessedly ends His discourse with the case of His own true disciples, the transition to them in the preceding verse is perfectly natural; whereas to apply the preservative salt of the sacrifice to the preserving quality of hell-fire, is equally contrary to the symbolical sense of salt and the Scripture representations of future torment. Our Lord has still in His eye the unseemly jarrings which had arisen among the Twelve, the peril to themselves of allowing any indulgence to such passions, and the severe self-sacrifice which salvation would cost them. **50. Salt is good; but if the salt have lost his saltness**—its power to season what it is brought into contact with. **wherewith will ye season it?**—How is this property to be restored? See on Matthew 5:13. **Have salt in yourselves**—See to it that ye retain in yourselves those precious qualities that will make you a blessing to one another, and to all around you. **and**—with respect to the miserable strife out of which all this discourse has sprung, in one concluding word—**have peace one with another**—This is repeated in I Thessalonians 5:13.

CHAPTER 10

Vss. 1-12. FINAL DEPARTURE FROM GALILEE—DIVORCE. (=Matt. 19:1-12; Luke 9:51.) See on Matthew 19:1-12.

13-19. LITTLE CHILDREN BROUGHT TO CHRIST. (=Matt. 19:13-15; Luke 18:15-17.) See on Luke 18:15-17.

17-31. THE RICH YOUNG RULER. (=Matt. 19:16-30; Luke 18:18-30.) See on Luke 18:18-30.

32-45. THIRD EXPLICIT AND STILL FULLER ANNOUNCEMENT OF HIS APPROACHING SUFFERINGS, DEATH, AND RESURRECTION—THE AMBITIOUS REQUEST OF JAMES AND JOHN, AND THE REPLY. (= Matt. 20:17-28; Luke 18:31-34.)

Third Announcement of His approaching Sufferings, Death, and Resurrection (vss. 32-34). **32. And they were in the way**—on the road. **going up to Jerusalem**—in Perea, and probably somewhere between Ephraim and Jericho, on the farther side of the Jordan, and to the northeast of Jerusalem. **and Jesus went before them**—as GROTIUS says, in the style of an intrepid Leader. **and they were amazed**—or "struck with astonishment" at His courage in advancing to certain death. **and as they followed, they were afraid**—for their own safety. These artless, lifelike touches—not only from an eye-witness, but one whom the noble carriage of the Master struck with wonder and awe—are peculiar to Mark, and give the second Gospel a charm all its own; making us feel as if we ourselves were in the midst of the scenes it describes. Well might the poet exclaim—

> The Saviour, what a noble flame
> Was kindled in His breast,
> When, hasting to Jerusalem,
> He march'd before the rest!
> COWPER

And he took again the twelve—referring to His previous announcements on this sad subject. **and began to tell them what things should happen unto him**—were going to befall Him." The word expresses something already begun but not brought to a head, rather than something wholly future. **33. Saying, Behold, we go up to Jerusalem**—for the last time, and—"all things that are written by the prophets concerning the Son of man shall be accomplished" (Luke 18:31). **the Son of man shall be delivered unto the chief priests and unto the scribes; and they shall condemn him to death, and shall deliver him to the Gentiles**—This is the first express statement that the Gentiles would combine with the Jews in His death; the two grand divisions of the human race for whom He died thus taking part in crucifying the Lord of Glory, as WEBSTER and WILKINSON observe. **34. And they shall mock him, and shall scourge him, and shall spit upon him, and shall kill him: and the third day he shall rise again**—Singularly explicit as this announcement was, Luke (18:34) says "they understood none of these things; and this saying was hid from them, neither knew they the things which were spoken." The meaning of the words they could be at no loss to understand, but their import in relation to His Messianic kingdom they could not penetrate; the whole prediction being right in the teeth of their preconceived notions. That they should have clung so tenaciously to the popular notion of an *un*suffering Messiah, may surprise us; but it gives inexpressible weight to their after-testimony to a suffering and dying Saviour.

Ambitious Request of James and John—The Reply (vss. 35-45). **35. And James and John, the sons of Zebedee, come unto him, saying**—Matthew (20:20) says their "mother came to Him with her sons, worshipping Him and desiring . . ." (Cf. Matt. 27:56, with ch. 15:40.) Salome her name (ch. 16:1). We cannot be sure with which of the parties the movement originated; but as our Lord, even in Matthew's account, addresses Himself to James and John, taking no account of the mother, it is likely the mother was merely set on by them. The thought was doubtless suggested to her sons by the recent promise to the Twelve of "thrones to sit on, when the Son of man should sit on the throne of His glory" (Matt. 19:28); but after the reproof so lately given them (ch. 9:33, etc.) they get their mother to speak for them. **Master, we would that thou shouldest do for us whatsoever we shall desire**—thus cautiously approaching the subject. **36. And he said unto them, What would ye that I should do for you?**—Though well aware what was in their mind and their mother's, our Lord will have the unseemly petition uttered before all. **37. Grant unto us that we may sit, one on thy right hand, and the other on thy left hand, in thy glory**—i.e., Assign to us the two places of highest honor in the coming kingdom. The semblance of a plea for so presumptuous a request might possibly have been drawn from the fact that one of the two usually leaned on the breast of Jesus, or sat next Him at meals, while the other was one of the favored three. **38. But Jesus said unto them, Ye know not what ye ask**—How gentle the reply to such a request, preferred at such a time, after the sad announcement just made! **can ye drink of the cup that I drink of?**—To "drink of a cup" is in Scripture a figure for getting one's fill either of good (Ps. 16:5; 23:5; 116:13; Jer. 16:7) or of ill (Ps. 75:8; John 18:11; Rev. 14:10). Here it is the cup of suffering. **and be baptized with the baptism that I am baptized with**—(Cf. for the language, Ps. 42:7). The object of this question seems to have been to try how far those two men were *capable* of the dignity to which they aspired and this on the principle that he who is able to suffer most for His sake will be the nearest to Him in His kingdom. **39. And they said unto him, We can**—Here we see them owning their mother's petition for them as their own; and doubtless they were perfectly sincere in professing their willingness to follow their Master to any suffering He might have to endure. As for James, he was the first of the apostles who was honored, and showed himself able to be baptized with his Master's baptism of blood (Acts 12:1, 2); while *John,* after going through all the persecutions to which the infant Church was exposed from the Jews, and sharing in the struggles and sufferings occasioned by the first triumphs of the Gospel among the Gentiles, lived to be the victim, after all the rest had got to glory, of a bitter persecution in the evening of his days, for the word of God and for the testimony of Jesus Christ. Yes, they were dear believers and blessed men, in spite of this unworthy ambition, and their Lord knew it; and perhaps the foresight of what they would have to pass through, and the courageous testimony He would yet receive from them, was the cause of that gentleness which we cannot but wonder at in His

reproof. **And Jesus said unto them, Ye shall indeed drink of the cup that I drink of; and with the baptism that I am baptized withal shall ye be baptized**—No doubt this prediction, when their sufferings at length came upon them, cheered them with the assurance, not that they would sit on His right and left hand—for of that thought they would be heartily ashamed—but that "if they suffered with Him, they should be also glorified together." **40. But to sit on my right hand and on my left hand in not mine to give; but it shall be given to them for whom it is prepare**d—"of My Father" (Matt. 20:23). The supplement which our translators have inserted is approved by some good interpreters, and the proper sense of the word rendered "but" is certainly in favor of it. But besides that it makes the statement too elliptical—leaving too many words to be supplied—it seems to make our Lord repudiate the right to assign to each of His people his place in the kingdom of glory; a thing which He nowhere else does, but rather the contrary. It is true that He says their place is "prepared for them by His Father." But that is true of their admission to heaven at all; and yet from His great white throne Jesus will Himself adjudicate the kingdom, and authoritatively invite into it those on His right hand, calling them the "blessed of His Father"; so little inconsistency is there between the eternal choice of them by His Father, and that public adjudication of them, not only to heaven in general, but each to his own position in it, which all Scripture assigns to Christ. The true rendering, then, of this clause, we take it, is this: "But to sit on My right hand and on My left hand is not Mine to give, save to them for whom it is prepared." When therefore He says, "It is not Mine to give," the meaning is, "I cannot give it as a *favor* to whomsoever I *please,* or on a principle of *favoritism;* it belongs exclusively to those for whom it is prepared," etc. And if this be His meaning, it will be seen how far our Lord is from disclaiming the right to assign to each his proper place in His Kingdom; that on the contrary, He expressly asserts it, merely announcing that the principle of distribution is quite different from what these petitioners supposed. Our Lord, it will be observed, does not *deny* the petition of James and John, or say they shall *not* occupy the place in His kingdom which they now improperly sought:—for aught we know, *that may be their true place.* All we are sure of is, that their asking it was displeasing to Him "to whom all judgment is committed," and so was not fitted to gain their object, but just the reverse. (See what is taught in Luke 14:8-11.) One at least of these brethren, as ALFORD strikingly remarks, saw on the right and on the left hand of their Lord, as He hung upon the tree, the crucified thieves; and bitter indeed must have been the remembrance of this ambitious prayer at that moment. **41. And when the ten heard it, they began to be much displeased with James and John**—or "were moved with indignation," as the same word is rendered in Matthew 20:24. The expression *"began* to be," which is of frequent occurrence in the Gospels, means that more passed than is expressed, and that we have but the result. And can we blame the ten for the indignation which they felt? Yet there was probably a spice of the old spirit of rivalry in it, which in spite of our Lord's recent lengthened, diversified, and most solemn warnings against it, had not ceased to stir in their breasts. **42. But Jesus called them to him, and saith unto them, Ye know that they which are ac-**

counted to rule—are recognized or acknowledged as rulers. **over the Gentiles exercise lordship over them: and their great ones exercise authority upon them**—as superiors exercising an acknowledged authority over inferiors. **43. But so shall it not be among you: but whosoever will be great among you, shall be your minister**—a subordinate servant. **44. And whosoever of you will be the chiefest**—or "first." **shall be**—i.e., "let him be, or "shall be he who is prepared to be." **servant of all**—one in the lowest condition of service. **45. For even the Son of man came not to be ministered unto, but to minister, and to give his life a ransom for.** instead of—**many**—i.e., "In the kingdom about to be set up, this principle shall have no place. All My servants shall there be equal; and the only greatness known to it shall be the greatness of humility and devotedness to the service of others. He that goes down the deepest in these services of self-denying humility shall rise the highest and hold the chiefest place in that kingdom; even as the Son of man, whose abasement and self-sacrifice for others, transcending all, gives Him of right a place above all!" As "the Word in the beginning with God," He *was* ministered unto; and as the risen Redeemer in our nature He now *is* ministered unto, "angels and authorities and powers being made subject unto Him" (I Pet. 3:22); but not for this came He hither. The Served of all came to be the Servant of all; and His last act was the grandest Service ever beheld by the universe of God—"HE GAVE HIS LIFE A RANSOM FOR MANY!" "Many" is here to be taken, not in contrast with *few* or with *all,* but in opposition to *one*—the one Son of man for the many sinners.

46-52. BLIND BARTIMEUS HEALED. (=Matt. 20:29-34; Luke 18:35-43.) See on Luke 18:35-43.

CHAPTER 11

Vss. 1-11. CHRIST'S TRIUMPHAL ENTRY INTO JERUSALEM, ON THE FIRST DAY OF THE WEEK. (= Matt. 21:1-9; Luke 19:29-40; John 12:12, 19.) See on Luke 19:29-40.

11-26. THE BARREN FIG TREE CURSED, WITH LESSONS FROM IT—SECOND CLEANSING OF THE TEMPLE, ON THE SECOND AND THIRD DAYS OF THE WEEK. (=Matt. 21:12-22; Luke 19:45-48.) **11. And Jesus entered into Jerusalem, and into the temple: and when he had looked round about upon**—surveyed—**all things, and now the eventide was come, he went out into Bethany with the twelve**—Thus briefly does our Evangelist dispose of this His first day in Jerusalem, after the triumphal entry. Nor do the Third and Fourth Gospels give us more light. But from Matthew (21:10, 11, 14-16) we learn some additional and precious particulars, for which see on Luke 19:45-48. It was not now safe for the Lord to sleep in the city, nor, from the day of His Triumphal Entry, did He pass one night in it, save the last fatal one.

The Barren Fig Tree Cursed (vss. 12-14). **12. And on the morrow**—The Triumphal Entry being on the first day of the week, this following day was Monday. **when they were come from Bethany**—"in the morning" (Matt. 21:18). **he was hungry**—How was that? Had he stolen forth from that dear roof at Bethany to the "mountain to pray, and continued all night in prayer to God?" (Luke 6:12); or, "in the morning," as on a former occasion, "risen up a great while before day, and departed into a solitary place, and there prayed"

(ch. 1:35); not breaking His fast thereafter, but bending His steps straight for the city, that He might "work the works of Him that sent Him while it was day"? (John 9:4). We know not, though one lingers upon and loves to trace out the every movement of that life of wonders. One thing, however we are sure of—it was *real bodily hunger* which He now sought to allay by the fruit of this fig tree, "if haply He might find any thing thereon"; not a mere *scene* for the purpose of teaching a lesson, as some early heretics maintained, and some still seem virtually to hold. **13. And seeing a fig tree**—(In Matt. 21:19, it is "one fig tree," but the sense is the same as here, "a certain fig tree," as in Matt. 8:19, etc.) Bethphage, which adjoined Bethany, derives his name from its being a *fig region*—"House of figs." **afar off having leaves**—and therefore promising fruit, which in the case of figs come before the leaves. **he came, if haply he might find any thing thereon: and when he came to it, he found nothing but leaves; for the time of figs was not yet**—What the precise import of this explanation is, interpreters are not agreed. Perhaps all that is meant is, that as the proper fig season had not arrived, no fruit would have been expected even of this tree but for the leaves which it had, which were in this case prematurely and unnaturally developed. **14. And Jesus answered and said unto it, No man eat fruit of thee hereafter for ever**—That word did not *make* the tree barren, but sealed it up in its own barrenness. See on Matthew 13:13-15. **And his disciples heard it**—and marked the saying. This is introduced as a connecting link, to explain what was afterwards to be said on the subject, as the narrative has to proceed to the other transactions of this day.

Second Cleansing of the Temple (vss. 15-18). For the exposition of this portion, see on Luke 19:45-48.

Lessons from the Cursing of the Fig Tree (vss. 20-26). **20. And in the morning**—of Tuesday, the third day of the week: He had slept, as during all this week, at Bethany. **as they passed by**—going into Jerusalem again. **they saw the fig tree dried up from the roots**—no partial blight, leaving life in the root; but it was now dead, root and branch. In Matthew 21:19 it is said it withered away as soon as it was cursed. But the full blight had not appeared probably at once; and in the dusk perhaps, as they returned to Bethany, they had not observed it. The precision with which Mark distinguishes the days is not observed by Matthew, intent only on holding up the truths which the incident was designed to teach. In Matthew the whole is represented as taking place at once, just as the two stages of Jairus' daughter—dying and dead—are represented by him as one. The only difference is between a mere summary and a more detailed narrative, each of which only confirms the other. **21. And Peter calling to remembrance saith unto him**—satisfied that a miracle so very peculiar —a miracle, not of *blessing,* as all His other miracles, but of *cursing*—could not have been wrought but with some higher reference, and fully expecting to hear something weighty on the subject. **Master, behold, the fig tree which thou cursedst is withered away**—so connecting the two things as to show that he traced the death of the tree entirely to the curse of his Lord. Matthew (21:20) gives this simply as a general exclamation of surprise by the disciples "how soon" the blight had taken effect. **22. And Jesus answering saith unto them, Have**

faith in God. 23. For verily I say unto you, That whosoever shall say unto this mountain, Be thou removed ... he shall have whatsoever he saith— Here is the lesson now. From the nature of the case supposed—that they might wish a mountain removed and cast into the sea, a thing far removed from anything which they could be thought actually to desire—it is plain that not physical but moral obstacles to the progress of His kingdom were in the Redeemer's view, and that what He designed to teach was the great lesson, that *no obstacle should be able to stand before a confiding faith in God.* **24. Therefore I say unto you, What things soever ye desire, when ye pray, believe that ye receive them, and ye shall have them—**This verse only *generalizes* the assurance of the former verse; which seems to show that it was designed for the special encouragement of *evangelistic* and *missionary* efforts, while this is a directory for prevailing *prayer in general.* **25. And when ye stand praying, forgive, if ye have aught against any; that your Father also which is in heaven may forgive you your trespasses ...—**This is repeated from the Sermon on the Mount (see on Matt. 6:14, 15); to remind them that if this was necessary to the acceptableness of *all* prayer, much more *when great things were to be asked and confidently expected.*

27-33. The Authority of Jesus Questioned— His Reply. (=Matt. 21:23-27; Luke 20:1-8.) See on Matthew 21:23-27.

CHAPTER 12

Vss. 1-12. Parable of the Wicked Husbandmen. (=Matt. 21:33-46; Luke 20:9-18.) See on Matthew 21:33-46.

13-40. Entangling Questions about Tribute, the Resurrection, and the Great Commandment, with the Replies—Christ Baffles the Pharisees by a Question about David, and Denounces the Scribes. (=Matt. 22:15-46; Luke 20:20-47). The time of this section appears to be still the third day (Tuesday) of Christ's last week. Matthew introduces the subject by saying (22:15), "Then went the Pharisees and took counsel how they might entangle Him in His talk." **13. And they send unto him certain of the Pharisees—**"their disciples," says Matthew; probably young and zealous scholars in that hardening school. **and of the Herodians** —See on Matthew 22:16. In Luke 20:20 these willing tools are called "spies, which should feign themselves just [righteous] men, that they might take hold of His words, that so they might deliver Him unto the power and authority of the governor." Their plan, then, was to entrap Him into some expression which might be construed into disaffection to the Roman government; the Pharisees themselves being notoriously discontented with the Roman yoke.

Tribute to Cæsar (vss. 14-17). **14. And when they were come, they say unto him, Master—**Teacher—**we know that thou art true, and carest for no man; for thou regardest not the person of men, but teachest the way of God in truth—**By such flattery—though they said only the truth—they hoped to throw Him off His guard. **Is it lawful to give tribute to Cæsar, or not?—**It was the civil poll-tax paid by all enrolled in the "census." See on Matthew 17:25. **15. Shall we give, or shall we not give? But he, knowing their hypocrisy—**"their wickedness" (Matt. 22:18); "their craftiness" (Luke 20:23). The malignity of their hearts took the

form of craft, pretending what they did not feel—an anxious desire to be guided aright in a matter which to a scrupulous few might seem a question of some difficulty. Seeing perfectly through this, He **said unto them, Why tempt ye me?—hypocrites!" bring me a penny that I may see it—**"the tribute money" (Matt. 22:19). **16. And they brought it. And he saith unto them, Whose is this image—**stamped upon the coin. **and superscription?—**the words encircling it on the obverse side. **And they said unto him, Cæsar's. 17. And Jesus answering said unto them, Render to Cæsar the things that are Cæsar's—**Putting it in this general form, it was imposible for sedition itself to dispute it, and yet it dissolved the snare. **and to God the things that are God's—**How much is there in this profound but to them startling addition to the maxim, and how incomparable is the whole for fulness, brevity, clearness, weight! **and they marvelled at him—** "at His answer, and held their peace" (Luke 20:26), "and left Him, and went their way" (Matt. 22:22).

The Resurrection (vss. 18-27). **18. Then come unto him the Sadducees, which say there is no resurrection—**"neither angel nor spirit" (Acts 23:7). They were the materialists of the day. See on Acts 23:7. **and they asked him, saying, 19-22. Master, Moses wrote unto us—**(Deut. 25:5)—**If a man's brother die, and leave his wife behind him ... And the seven had her, and left no seed: last of all the woman died also. 23. In the resurrection therefore when they shall rise ... 24. Do ye not therefore err, because ye know not the scriptures—**regarding the future state. **neither the power of God?—**before which a thousand such difficulties vanish. **25. For when they shall rise from the dead, they neither marry, nor are given in marriage** —"neither can they die any more" (Luke 20:36). Marriage is ordained to perpetuate the human family; but as there will be no breaches by death in the future state, this ordinance will cease. **but are as the angels which are in heaven—**In Luke it is "equal unto the angels." But as the subject is death and resurrection, we are not warranted to extend the equality here taught beyond the one point—the *immortality* of their nature. A beautiful clause is added in Luke—"and are the children of God"—not in respect of *character,* which is not here spoken of, but of *nature*—"being the children of the resurrection," as rising to an undecaying existence (Rom. 8:21, 23), and so being the children of their Father's immortality (I Tim. 6:16). **26. And as touching the dead, that they rise: have ye not read in the book of Moses—**"even Moses" (Luke 20:37), whom they had just quoted for the purpose of entangling Him. **how in the bush God spake unto him—**either "at the bush," as the same expression is rendered in Luke 20:37, i.e., when he was there; or "in the (section of his history regarding the) bush." The structure of our verse suggests the latter sense, which is not unusual. **saying—**(Exod. 3:6)—**I am the God of Abraham, and the God of Isaac, and the God of Jacob? 27. He is not the God of the dead, but the God of the living—**not "the God of dead but [the God] of living persons." The word in brackets is almost certainly an addition to the genuine text, and critical editors exclude it. "For all live unto Him" Luke 20:28—"in His view," or "in His estimation." This last statement—found only in Luke—though adding nothing to the argument, is an important additional illustration. It is true, indeed, that to God no human being is dead or ever will be, but all mankind sustain an abiding conscious relation to Him; but the "all" here means "those who shall be accounted worthy to obtain that world." These sustain a gracious covenant relation to God which cannot be dissolved. (Cf. Rom. 6:10, 11.) In this sense our Lord affirms that for Moses to call the Lord the "God" of His patriarchal servants, if at that moment they had no existence, would be unworthy of Him. He "would be *ashamed* to be called their God, if He had not prepared for them a city" (Heb. 11:16). It was concluded by some of the early Fathers, from our Lord's resting His proof of the Resurrection on such a passage as this, instead of quoting some much clearer testimonies of the Old Testament, that the Sadducees, to whom this was addressed, acknowledged the authority of no part of the Old Testament but the Pentateuch; and this opinion has held its ground even till now. But as there is no ground for it in the New Testament, so JOSEPHUS is silent upon it; merely saying that they rejected the Pharisaic traditions. It was because the Pentateuch was regarded by all classes as the fundamental source of the Hebrew religion, and all the succeeding books of the Old Testament but as developments of it, that our Lord would show that even there the doctrine of the Resurrection was taught. And all the rather does He select this passage, as being not a bare annunciation of the doctrine in question, but as expressive of that glorious truth *out of which the Resurrection springs.* "And when the multitude heard this" (says Matt. 22:23), "they were astonished at His doctrine." "Then," adds Luke 20:39, 40, "certain of the scribes answering said, Master, thou hast well said"—enjoying His victory over the Sadducees. "And after that they durst not ask Him any [question at all]"—neither party could; both being for the time utterly foiled.

The Great Commandment (vss. 28-34). "But when the Pharisees had heard that He had put the Sadducees to silence, they were gathered together" (Matthew 22:34). **28. And one of the scribes**—"a lawyer," says Matthew (22:35); i.e., teacher of the law. **came, and having heard them reasoning together, and perceiving that he had answered them well, asked him**—manifestly in no bad spirit. When Matthew therefore says he came "tempting," or "trying him," as one of the Pharisaic party who seemed to enjoy the defeat He had given to the Sadducees, we may suppose that though somewhat priding himself upon his insight into the law, and not indisposed to measure his knowledge with One in whom he had not yet learned to believe, he was nevertheless an honest-hearted, fair disputant. **Which is the first commandment of all?**—first in importance; the primary, leading commandment, the most fundamental one. This was a question which, with some others, divided the Jewish teachers into rival schools. Our Lord's answer is in a strain of respect very different from what He showed to cavillers—ever observing His own direction, "Give not that which is holy to the dogs, neither cast ye your pearls before swine; lest they trample them under their feet, and turn again and rend you" (Matt. 7:6). **29. And Jesus answered him, The first of all the commandments is**—The readings here vary considerably. TISCHENDORF and TREGELLES read simply, "the first is"; and they are followed by MEYER and ALFORD. But though the authority for the precise form of the received text is slender, a form almost identical with it seems to have most weight of authority. Our Lord here gives His explicit sanction to the distinction between commandments of a more *fundamental* and

primary character, and commandments of a more *dependent* and *subordinate* nature; a distinction of which it is confidently asserted by a certain class of critics that the Jews knew nothing, that our Lord and His apostles nowhere lay down, and which has been invented by Christian divines. (Cf. Matt. 23: 23.) **Hear, O Israel; the Lord our God is one Lord**—This every devout Jew recited twice every day, and the Jews do it to this day; thus keeping up the great ancient national protest against the polytheisms and pantheisms of the heathen world: it is the great utterance of the national faith in One Living and Personal God—"ONE JEHOVAH!" **30. And thou shalt**—We have here the language of *law,* expressive of God's *claims.* What then are we here bound down to do? One word is made to express it. And what a word! Had the essence of the divine law consisted in *deeds,* it could not possibly have been expressed in a single word; for no one deed is comprehensive of all others embraced in the law. But as it consists in *an affection of the soul,* one word suffices to express it—but only one. *Fear,* though due to God and enjoined by Him, is *limited* in its sphere and *distant* in character. *Trust, hope,* and the like, though essential features of a right state of heart towards God, are called into action only by *personal necessity,* and so are—in a good sense, it is true, but still are properly—*selfish* affections; that is to say, they have respect to *our own well-being.* But LOVE is an *all-inclusive* affection, embracing not only every other affection proper to its object, but all that is proper to be *done* to its object; for as love spontaneously seeks to please its object, so, in the case of men to God, it is the native well-spring of a voluntary obedience. It is, besides, the most *personal* of all affections. One may fear an *event,* one may hope for an *event,* one may rejoice in an *event;* but one can love only a *Person.* It is the *tenderest,* the most *unselfish,* the most *divine* of all affections. Such, then, is the affection in which the essence of the divine law is declared to consist. **Thou shalt love**—We now come to the glorious Object of that demanded affection. Thou shalt love the **Lord, thy God**—i.e., Jehovah, the Self-Existent One, who has revealed Himself as the "I AM," and there is *"none else";* who, though by His name JEHOVAH apparently at an unapproachable distance from His finite creatures, yet bears to *thee* a real and definite relationship, out of which arises *His claim* and *thy duty*—of LOVE. But with what are we to love Him? Four things are here specified. First, "Thou shalt love the Lord thy God" **with thy heart**—This sometimes means "the whole inner man"(as Prov. 4:23); but that cannot be meant here; for then the other three particulars would be superfluous. Very often it means "our emotional nature"—the seat of *feeling* as distinguished from our intellectual nature or the seat of *thought,* commonly called the "mind" (as in Phil. 4:7). But neither can this be the sense of it here; for here the heart is distinguished both from the "mind" and the "soul." The "heart," then, must here mean the *sincerity* of both the thoughts and the feelings; in other words, *uprightness* or *trueheartedness,* as opposed to a *hypocritical* or *divided* affection. But next, "Thou shalt love the Lord thy God" with thy soul. This is designed to command our emotional nature: Thou shalt put *feeling* or *warmth* into thine affection. Further, "Thou shalt love the Lord thy God" **with thy mind** —This commands our intellectual nature: Thou shalt put *intelligence* into thine affection—in opposition to a blind devotion, or mere devoteeism.

Lastly, "Thou shalt love the Lord thy God" **with thy strength**—This commands our energies: Thou shalt put *intensity* into thine affection—"Do it with thy might" (Eccles. 9:10). Taking these four things together, the command of the Law is, "Thou shalt love the Lord thy God *with all thy powers*—with a *sincere*, a *fervid*, an *intelligent*, an *energetic* love." But this is not all that the Law demands. God will have all these qualities in their most perfect exercise. "Thou shalt love the Lord thy God," says the Law, "with *all* thy heart," or, with perfect sincerity; "Thou shalt love the Lord thy God with *all* thy soul," or, with the utmost fervor; "Thou shalt love the Lord thy God with *all* thy mind," or, in the fullest exercise of an enlightened reason; and "Thou shalt love the Lord thy God with *all* thy strength," or, with the whole energy of our being! So much for the First Commandment. **31. And the second is like**—"unto it" (Matt. 22:39); as demanding the same affection, and only the extension of it, in its proper measure, to the creatures of Him whom we thus love—our *brethren* in the participation of the same nature, and *neighbors*, as connected with us by ties that render each dependent upon and necessary to the other. **Thou shalt love thy neighbour as thyself**—Now, as we are not to love ourselves supremely, this is virtually a command, in the first place, *not* to love our neighbor with all our heart and soul and mind and strength. And thus it is a condemnation of the idolatry of the creature. Our supreme and uttermost affection is to be reserved for God. But as *sincerely* as ourselves we are to love all mankind, and with *the same readiness to do and suffer for them* as we should reasonably desire them to show to us. The golden rule (Matt. 7:12) is here our best interpreter of the nature and extent of these claims. **There is none other commandment greater than these**—or, as in Matthew 22:40, "On these two commandments hang all the law and the prophets" (see on Matt. 5:17). It is as if He had said, "This is all Scripture in a nutshell; the whole law of human duty in a portable, pocket form." Indeed, it is so *simple* that a child may understand it, so *brief* that all may remember it, so *comprehensive* as to embrace all possible cases. And from its very nature it is *unchangeable*. It is inconceivable that God should require from his rational creatures anything *less*, or in substance anything *else*, under any *dispensation*, in any *world*, at any *period* throughout eternal duration. He cannot but claim this—all this—alike in *heaven*, in *earth*, and in *hell!* And this incomparable summary of the divine law belonged to the *Jewish religion!* As it shines in its own self-evidencing splendor, so it reveals its own true source. The religion from which the world has received it could be none other than a *Godgiven religion!* **32. And the scribe said unto him, Well, Master**—Teacher—**thou hast said the truth: for there is one God; and there is none other but he**—The genuine text here seems clearly to have been, "There is one," without the word "God"; and so nearly all critical editors and expositors read. **33. And to love him with all the heart . . . and to love his neighbour as himself, is more than all whole burnt offerings and sacrifices**—more, i.e., than all positive institutions; thereby showing insight into the essential difference between what is *moral* and in its own nature *unchangeable*, and what is obligatory only *because enjoined*, and only *so long as enjoined*. **34. And when Jesus saw that he answered discreetly**—rather, "intelligently," or "sensibly"; not only in a good spirit, but with a promising

measure of insight into spiritual things. **he said unto him, Thou art not far from the kingdom of God**—for he had but *to follow out a little further* what he seemed sincerely to own, to find his way into the kingdom. He needed only the experience of another eminent scribe who at a later period said, "We know that *the law is spiritual*, but *I am carnal*, sold under sin": who exclaimed, "O wretched man that I am! Who shall deliver me?" but who added, "I thank God through Jesus Christ!" (Rom. 7:14, 24, 25). Perhaps among the "great company of the priests" and other Jewish ecclesiastics who "were obedient to the faith," almost immediately after the day of Pentecost (Acts 6:7), this upright lawyer was one. But for all his nearness to the Kingdom of God, it may be he never entered it. **And no man after that durst ask any question**—all feeling that they were no match for Him, and that it was vain to enter the lists with Him.

Christ Baffles the Pharisees regarding David (vss. 35-37). **35. And Jesus answered and said, while he taught in the temple**—and "while the Pharisees were gathered together" (Matt. 22:41). **How say the scribes that Christ is the son of David?**—How come they to give it out that Messiah is to be the son of David? In Matthew, Jesus asks them, "What think ye of Christ?" or of the promised and expected Messiah? "Whose son is He [to be]? They say unto Him, The son of David." The sense is the same. "He saith unto them, How then doth David in spirit call Him Lord?" (Matt. 22:42, 43.) **36. For David himself said by the Holy Ghost, The Lord said to my Lord, Sit thou on my right hand, till I make thine enemies thy footstool**—(Ps. 110:1). **37. David therefore himself calleth him Lord; and whence is he then his son?**—There is but one solution of this difficulty. Messiah is at once inferior to David as his son according to the flesh, and superior to him as the Lord of a kingdom of which David is himself a subject, not the sovereign. The human and divine natures of Christ, and the spirituality of His kingdom—of which the highest earthly sovereigns are honored if they be counted worthy to be its subjects—furnish the only key to this puzzle. **And the common people**—the immense crowd. **heard him gladly** "And no man was able to answer Him a word; neither durst any man from that day forth ask Him any more questions" (Matthew 22: 46).

The Scribes Denounced (vss. 38-40). **38. And he said unto them in his doctrine**—rather, "in His teaching"; implying that this was but a specimen of an extended discourse, which Matthew gives in full (ch. 23). Luke says (20:45) this was "in the audience of all the people said unto His disciples." **Beware of the scribes, which love**—or like—**to go in long clothing**—(see on Matt. 23:5). **and [love] salutations in the market-places, 39. And the chief seats in the synagogues, and the uppermost rooms**—or positions—**at feasts**—See on this love of distinction, Luke 14:7; and on Matthew 6:5. **40. Which devour widows' houses, and for a pretence make long prayers: these shall receive greater damnation**—They took advantage of their helpless condition and confiding character to obtain possession of their property, while by their "long prayers" they made them believe they were raised far above "filthy lucre." So much the "greater damnation" awaited them. (Cf. Matt. 23:33.) A lifelike description this of the Romish clergy, the true successors of "the scribes."

41-44. THE WIDOW'S TWO MITES. (=Luke 21: 1-4.) See on Luke 21:1-4.

CHAPTER 13

Vss. 1-37. Christ's Prophecy of the Destruction of Jerusalem, and Warnings Suggested by It to Prepare for His Second Coming. (=Matt. 24:1-51; Luke 21:5-36.) Jesus had uttered all His mind against the Jewish ecclesiastics, exposing their character with withering plainness, and denouncing, in language of awful severity, the judgments of God against them for that unfaithfulness to their trust which was bringing ruin upon the nation. He had closed this His last public discourse (Matt. 23) by a passionate lamentation over Jerusalem, and a solemn farewell to the temple. "And," says Matt. 24:1, "Jesus went out and departed from the temple"—never more to re-enter its precincts, or open His mouth in public teaching. *With this act ended His public ministry.* As He withdrew, says Olshausen, the gracious presence of God left the sanctuary; and the temple, with all its service, and the whole theocratic constitution, was given over to destruction. What immediately followed is, as usual, most minutely and graphically described by our Evangelist. **1. And as he went out of the temple, one of his disciples saith unto him**—The other Evangelists are less definite. "As some spake," says Luke; "His disciples came to Him," says Matthew. Doubtless it was the speech of one, the mouthpiece, likely, of others. **Master**—Teacher —see what manner of stones and what buildings are here—wondering probably, how so massive a pile could be overthrown, as seemed implied in our Lord's last words regarding it. Josephus, who gives a minute account of the wonderful structure, speaks of stones forty cubits long (*Jewish War*, v. 5. 1.) and says the pillars supporting the porches were twenty-five cubits high, all of one stone, and that of the whitest marble (*ibid.*, v. 5.2). Six days' battering at the walls, during the siege, made no impression upon them (*ibid.*, vi. 4. 1). Some of the underbuilding, yet remaining, and other works, are probably as old as the first temple. **2. And Jesus answering said unto him, Seest thou these great buildings?**—"Ye call My attention to these things? I have seen them. Ye point to their massive and durable appearance: now listen to their fate." **there shall not be left**—"left here" (Matt. 24:2). **one stone upon another, that shall not be thrown down**—Titus ordered the whole city and temple to be demolished [Josephus, *J. W.*, vii. 1. 1]; Eleazar wished they had all died before seeing that holy city destroyed by enemies' hands, and before the temple was so profanely *dug up* (*ibid.*, vii. 8. 7). **3. And as he sat upon the Mount of Olives, over against the temple**—On their way from Jerusalem to Bethany they would cross Mount Olivet; on its summit He seats Himself, over against the temple, having the city all spread out under His eye. How graphically is this set before us by our Evangelist! **Peter and James and John and Andrew asked him privately**—The other Evangelists tell us merely that "the disciples" did so. But Mark not only says that it was four of them, but names them; and they were the first *quarternion* of the Twelve. **4. Tell us, when shall these things be? and what shall be the sign when all these things shall be fulfilled?**— "and what shall be the sign of Thy coming, and of the end of the world?" They no doubt looked upon the date of all these things as one and the same, and their notions of the things themselves were as confused as of the times of them. Our Lord takes His own way of meeting their questions. *Prophecies of the Destruction of Jerusalem* (vss. 5-31). **5. And Jesus answering them began to say, Take heed lest any man deceive you: 6. For many shall come in my name, saying, I am Christ**—(see Matt. 24:5)—"and the time draweth nigh" (Luke 21:8); that is, the time of the kingdom in its full splendor. **and shall deceive many**—"Go ye not therefore after them" (Luke 21:8). The reference here seems not to be to pretended Messiahs, deceiving those who rejected the claims of Jesus, of whom indeed there were plenty—for our Lord is addressing His own genuine disciples—but to persons pretending to be Jesus Himself, returned in glory to take possession of His kingdom. This gives peculiar force to the words, "Go ye not therefore after them." **7. And when ye shall hear of wars and rumours of wars, be ye not troubled**—see on vs. 13, and compare Isaiah 8:11-14. **for such things must needs be; but the end shall not be yet**—In Luke (21:9), "the end is not by and by," or "immediately." Worse must come before all is over. **8. These are the beginnings of sorrows**—"of travail-pangs," to which heavy calamities are compared. (See Jer. 4: 31, etc.). The annals of Tacitus tell us how the Roman world was convulsed, before the destruction of Jerusalem, by rival claimants of the imperial purple. **9. But take heed to yourselves: for**—"before all these things" (Luke 21:12); i.e., before these public calamities come. **they shall deliver you up to councils; and in the synagogues ye shall be beaten** —These refer to *ecclesiastical* proceedings against them. **and ye shall be brought before rulers and kings**—before *civil* tribunals next. **for my sake, for a testimony against them**—rather "unto them"—to give you an opportunity of bearing testimony to Me before them. In the Acts of the Apostles we have the best commentary on this announcement. (Cf. Matt. 10:17, 18.) **10. And the gospel must first be published among all nations**—"for a witness, and then shall the end come" (Matt. 24:14). God never sends judgment without previous warning; and there can be no doubt that the Jews, already dispersed over most known countries, had nearly all heard the Gospel "as a witness," before the end of the Jewish state. The same principle was repeated and will repeat itself to "*the* end." **11. But when they shall lead you, and deliver you up, take no thought beforehand**—"Be not anxious beforehand." **what ye shall speak, neither do ye premeditate**—"Be not filled with apprehension, in the prospect of such public appearances for Me, lest ye should bring discredit upon My name, nor think it necessary to prepare beforehand what ye are to say." **but whatsoever shall be given you in that hour, that speak ye: for it is not ye that speak, but the Holy Ghost**—(See on Matt. 10:19, 20). **13. And ye shall be hated of all men for my name's sake**—Matthew (24:12) adds this important intimation: "And because iniquity shall abound, the love of many"—'of the many,' or 'of the most', i.e., of the generality of professed disciples—"shall wax cold." Sad illustrations of the effect of abounding iniquity in cooling the love even of faithful disciples we have in the *Epistle of James*, written about the period here referred to, and too frequently ever since. **but he that shall endure unto the end, the same shall be saved**—See on Matthew 10:21, 22; and cf. Hebrews 10:38, 39, which is a manifest allusion to these words of Christ; also Revelation 2:10. Luke adds these reassuring words: "But there shall not an hair of your heads perish" (21:18). Our Lord had just said (Luke 21: 16) that they should be *put to death;* showing that this precious promise is far above immunity from mere bodily harm, and furnishing a key to the right interpretation of Psalm 91 and such like. **14. But when ye shall see**—"Jerusalem compassed by armies"—by encamped armies; in other words, when ye shall see it *besieged,* and—**the abomination of desolation, spoken of by Daniel the prophet, standing where it ought not**—i.e., as explained in Matthew (24:15), "standing in the holy place." **(let him that readeth**—readeth that prophecy—**understand.**) That "the abomination of desolation" here alluded to was intended to point to the Roman ensigns, as the symbols of an idolatrous, and so unclean pagan power, may be gathered by comparing what Luke says in the corresponding verse (21:20); and commentators are agreed on it. It is worthy of notice, as confirming this interpretation, that in I Maccabees 1:54—which, though aprocryphal *Scripture,* is authentic *history*—the expression of Daniel is applied to the idolatrous profanation of the Jewish altar by Antiochus Epiphanes. **then let them that be in Judea flee to the mountains**—The ecclesiastical historian, EUSEBIUS, early in the fourth century, tells us that the Christians fled to *Pella,* at the northern extremity of Perea, being "prophetically directed"—perhaps by some prophetic intimation more explicit than this, which would be their chart —and that thus they escaped the predicted calamities by which the nation was overwhelmed. **15. And let him that is on the housetop not get down into the house, neither enter therein, to take any thing out of his house**—i.e., let him take the outside flight of steps from the roof to the ground; a graphic way of denoting the extreme urgency of the case, and the danger of being tempted, by the desire to save his property, to delay till escape should become impossible. **16. And let him that is in the field not turn back again for to take up his garment. 17. But woe to them**—or, "alas for them"—**that are with child, and to them that give suck in those days**—in consequence of the aggravated suffering which those conditions would involve. **18. And pray ye that your flight be not in the winter**—making escape perilous, or tempting you to delay your flight. Matthew (24:20) adds, "neither on the sabbath day," when, from fear of a breach of its sacred rest, they might be induced to remain. **19. For in those days shall be affliction, such as was not from the beginning of the creation which God created unto this time, neither shall be**—Such language is not unusual in the Old Testament with reference to tremendous calamities. But it is matter of literal fact that there was crowded into the period of the Jewish war an amount and complication of suffering perhaps unparalleled; as the narrative of JOSEPHUS, examined closely and arranged under different heads, would show. **20. And except that the Lord had shortened those days, no flesh**—i.e., no human life—**should be saved: but for the elect's sake, whom he hath chosen, he hath shortened the days**—But for this merciful "shortening," brought about by a remarkable concurrence of causes, the whole nation would have perished, in which there yet remained a remnant to be afterwards gathered out. This portion of the prophecy closes, in Luke, with the following vivid and important glance at the subsequent fortunes of the chosen people: "And they shall fall by the sword, and shall be led away captive into all nations: and Jerusalem shall be trodden down of the Gentiles, until the times of the Gentiles be fulfilled" (Luke 21:24). The language as well as the idea of this remarkable statement is taken from Daniel 8: 10, 13. What, then, is its import here? It implies, first, that a time is coming when Jerusalem shall cease to be "trodden down of the Gentiles"; which

it was then by pagan, and since and till now is by Mohammedan unbelievers: and next, it implies that the period when this treading down of Jerusalem by the Gentiles is to cease will be when "the times of the Gentiles are fulfilled" or "completed." But what does this mean? We may gather the meaning of it from Romans 11 in which the divine purposes and procedure towards the chosen people from first to last are treated in detail. In vs. 25 of that chapter these words of our Lord are thus reproduced: "For I would not, brethren, that ye should be ignorant of this mystery, lest ye should be wise in your own conceits; that blindness in part is happened to Israel, until the fulness of the Gentiles be come in." See the exposition of that verse, from which it will appear that "till the fulness of the Gentiles be come in"—or, in our Lord's phraseology, "till the times of the Gentiles be fulfilled"—does not mean "till the general conversion of the world to Christ," but "till the Gentiles have had their *full time* of that place in the Church which the Jews had before them." After that period of *Gentilism,* as before of *Judaism,* "Jerusalem" and Israel, no longer "trodden down by the Gentiles," but "grafted into their own olive tree," shall constitute, with the believing Gentiles, one Church of God, and fill the whole earth. What a bright vista does this open up! **21. And then, if any man shall say to you, Lo, here is Christ; or, lo he is there; believe him not**— So Luke 17:23. No one can read JOSEPHUS' account of what took place before the destruction of Jerusalem without seeing how strikingly this was fulfilled. **to seduce, if it were possible, even the elect** —implying that this, though all *but* done, will prove impossible. What a precious assurance! (Cf. II Thess. 2:9-12.) **23. But take ye heed; behold, 1 have foretold you all things**—He had just told them that the seduction of the elect would prove impossible; but since this would be all but accomplished, He bids them be on their guard, as the proper means of averting that catastrophe. In Matthew (24:26-28) we have some additional particulars: "Wherefore, if they shall say unto you, Behold, He is in the desert; go not forth: behold, He is in the secret chambers; believe it not. For as the lightning cometh out of the east, and shineth even unto the west; so shall also the coming of the Son of man be." See on Luke 17:23, 24. "For wheresoever the carcass is, there will the eagles be gathered together." See on Luke 17:37. **24. But in those days, after that tribulation**—"Immediately after the tribulation of those days" (Matt. 24:29). **the sun shall be darkened, and the moon shall not give her light. 25. And the stars of heaven shall fall**—"and upon the earth distress of nations, with perplexity; the sea and the waves roaring; men's hearts failing them for fear, and for looking after those things which are coming on the earth" (Luke 21:25, 26). **and the powers that are in heaven shall be shaken**— Though the grandeur of this language carries the mind over the head of all periods but that of Christ's Second Coming, nearly every expression will be found used of the Lord's coming in terrible national judgments: as of Babylon (Isa. 13:9-13); of Idumea (Isa. 34:1, 2, 4, 8-10); of Egypt (Ezek. 32:7, 8); compare also Psalm 18:7-15; Isaiah 24:1, 17-19; Joel 2:10, 11, etc. We cannot therefore consider the mere strength of this language a proof that it refers exclusively or primarily to the precursors of the final day, though of course in *"that day"* it will have its most awful fulfilment. **26. And then shall they see the Son of man coming in the clouds with great power and glory**—In Matthew 24:30, this is given most fully: "And then shall appear the sign of the Son of man in heaven; and then shall all the tribes of the earth mourn, and they shall see the Son of man . . ." That this language finds its highest interpretation in the Second Personal Coming of Christ, is most certain. But the question is, whether that be the primary sense of it as it stands here? Now if the reader will turn to Daniel 7:13, 14, and connect with it the preceding verses, he will find, we think, the true key to our Lord's meaning here. There the powers that oppressed the Church —symbolized by rapacious wild beasts—are summoned to the bar of the Great God, who as the Ancient of days seats Himself, with His assessors, on a burning Throne: thousand thousands ministering to Him, and ten thousand times ten thousand standing before Him. "The judgment is set, and the books are opened." Who that is guided by the *mere words* would doubt that this is a description of the Final Judgment? And yet nothing is clearer than that it is *not,* but a description of a vast *temporal* judgment, upon organized bodies of men, for their incurable hostility to the kingdom of God upon earth. Well, after the doom of these has been pronounced and executed, and room thus prepared for the unobstructed development of the kingdom of God over the earth, what follows? "I saw in the night visions, and behold, one like THE SON OF MAN came with the clouds of heaven, and came to the Ancient of days, and they (the angelic attendants) brought Him near before Him." For what purpose? To receive investiture in the kingdom, which, as Messiah, of right belonged to Him. Accordingly, it is added, "And there was given Him dominion, and glory, and a kingdom, that all peoples, nations, and languages should serve Him: His dominion is an everlasting dominion, which shall not pass away, and His kingdom that which shall not be destroyed." Comparing this with our Lord's words, He seems to us, by "the Son of man [on which phrase, see on John 1:51] coming in the clouds with great power and glory," to mean, that when judicial vengeance shall once have been executed upon Jerusalem, and the ground thus cleared for the unobstructed establishment of His own kingdom, His true regal claims and rights would be visibly and gloriously asserted and manifested. See on Luke 9:28 (with its parallels in Matthew and Mark), in which nearly the same language is employed, and where it can hardly be understood of anything else than *the full and free estabishment of the kingdom of Christ on the destruction of Jerusalem.* But what is that "sign of the Son of man in heaven?" Interpreters are not agreed. But as before Christ came to destroy Jerusalem some appalling portents were seen in the air, so before His Personal appearing it is likely that something *analogous* will be witnessed, though of what nature it would be vain to conjecture. **27. And then shall he send his angels**—"with a great sound of a trumpet" (Matt. 24:31). **and shall gather together his elect . . .**—As the tribes of Israel were anciently gathered together by sound of trumpet (Exod. 19:13, 16, 19; Lev. 23:24; Ps. 81:3-5), so any mighty gathering of God's people, by divine command, is represented as collected by sound of trumpet (Isa. 27:13; cf. Rev. 11:15); and the ministry of angels, employed in all the great operations of Providence, is here held forth as the agency by which the present assembling of the elect is to be accomplished. LIGHTFOOT thus explains it: "When Jerusalem shall be reduced to ashes, and that wicked nation cut off and rejected, then shall the Son of man send His ministers with

the trumpet of the Gospel, and they shall gather His elect of the several nations, from the four corners of heaven: so that God shall not want a Church, although that ancient people of His be rejected and cast off: but that ancient Jewish Church being destroyed, a new Church shall be called out of the Gentiles." But though something like this appears to be the primary sense of the verse, in relation to the destruction of Jerusalem, no one can fail to see that the language swells beyond any gathering of a human family into a Church upon earth, and forces the thoughts onward to that gathering of the Church "at the last trump," to meet the Lord in the air, which is to wind up the present scene. Still, this is not, in our judgment, the *direct* subject of the prediction; for the next verse limits the whole prediction to the generation then existing. **28. Now learn a parable of the fig tree**—"Now from the fig tree learn the parable," or the high lesson which this teaches. **When her branch is yet tender, and putteth forth leaves**—"its leaves." **29. So ye, in like manner, when ye shall see these things come to pass**—rather, 'coming to pass'—**know that it**—"the kingdom of God" (Luke 21:31)—**is nigh, even at the doors**—that is, the full manifestation of it; for till then it admitted of no full development. In Luke (21:28) the following words precede these: "And when these things begin to come to pass, then look up, and lift up your heads; for your redemption draweth nigh"—their redemption, in the first instance certainly, from Jewish oppression (I Thess. 2:14-16; Luke 11:52): but in the highest sense of these words, redemption from all the oppressions and miseries of the present state at the second appearing of the Lord Jesus. **30. Verily I say unto you, that this generation shall not pass till all these things be done**—or "fulfilled" (Matt. 24:34; Luke 21:32). Whether we take this to mean that the whole would be fulfilled within the limits of the generation then current, or, according to a usual way of speaking, that the generation then existing would not pass away without seeing a *begun* fulfilment of this prediction, the facts entirely correspond. For either the whole was fulfilled in the destruction accomplished by Titus, as many think; or, if we stretch it out, according to others, till the thorough dispersion of the Jews a little later, under Adrian, every requirement of our Lord's words seems to be met. **31. Heaven and earth shall pass away; but my words shall not pass away**—the strongest possible expression of the divine authority by which He spake; not as Moses or Paul might have said of their own inspiration, for such language would be unsuitable in any merely human mouth.

Warnings to Prepare for the Coming of Christ Suggested by the Foregoing Prophecy (vss. 32-37). It will be observed that, in the foregoing prophecy, as our Lord approaches the crisis of the day of vengeance on Jerusalem and redemption for the Church—at which stage the analogy between that and the day of final vengeance and redemption waxes more striking—His language rises and swells beyond all temporal and partial vengeance, beyond all earthly deliverances and enlargements, and ushers us resistlessly into the scenes of the final day. Accordingly, in these six concluding verses it is manifest that preparation for "THAT DAY" is what our Lord designs to inculcate. **32. But of that day and that hour**—i.e., the precise time. **knoweth no man**—lit., no one—**no, not the angels which are in heaven, neither the Son, but the Father**—This very remarkable statement regarding "the Son" is peculiar to Mark. Whether it means that the Son was *not at that time in possession of the knowledge* referred to, or simply that it was not *among the things which He had received to communicate*—has been matter of much controversy even among the firmest believers in the proper Divinity of Christ. In the latter sense it was taken by some of the most eminent of the ancient Fathers, and by LUTHER, MELANCTHON, and most of the older Lutherans; and it is so taken by BENGEL, LANGE, WEBSTER and WILKINSON. CHRYSOSTOM and others understood it to mean that *as man* our Lord was ignorant of this. It is taken literally by CALVIN, GROTIUS, DE WETTE, MEYER, FRITZSCHE, STIER, ALFORD, and ALEXANDER. **33. Take ye heed, watch and pray; for ye know not when the time is. 34. For the Son of man is as a man taking a far journey . . .**—The idea thus far is similar to that in the opening part of the parable of the talents (Matt. 25:14, 15). **and commanded the porter**—the gatekeeper—**to watch**—pointing to the official duty of the ministers of religion to give warning of approaching danger to the people. **35. Watch ye therefore; for ye know not when the master of the house cometh, at even, or at midnight, or at the cock-crowing, or in the morning**—an allusion to the four Roman watches of the night. **36. Lest, coming suddenly, he find you sleeping**—See on Luke 12:35-40, 42-46. **37. And what I say unto you**—this discourse, it will be remembered, was delivered in private. **I say unto all, Watch**—anticipating and requiring the diffusion of His teaching by them among all His disciples, and its perpetuation through all time.

CHAPTER 14

Vss. 1-11. THE CONSPIRACY OF THE JEWISH AUTHORITIES TO PUT JESUS TO DEATH—THE SUPPER AND THE ANOINTING AT BETHANY—JUDAS AGREES WITH THE CHIEF PRIESTS TO BETRAY HIS LORD. (=Matt. 26:1-16; Luke 22:1-6; John 12:1-11.) The events of this section appeared to have occurred on the fourth day (*Wednesday*) of the Redeemer's Last Week.

Conspiracy of the Jewish Authorities to Put Jesus to Death (vss. 1, 2). **1. After two days was the feast of the passover, and of unleavened bread**—The meaning is, that two days after what is about to be mentioned the passover would arrive; in other words, what follows occurred two days *before* the feast. **and the chief priests and the scribes sought how they might take him by craft, and put him to death**—From Matthew's fuller account (ch. 26) we learn that our Lord announced this to the Twelve as follows, being the first announcement to them of the precise time: "And it came to pass, when Jesus had finished all these sayings"—referring to the contents of chs. 24, 25, which He delivered to His disciples; His public ministry being now closed: from His *prophetical* He is now passing into His *priestly* office, although all along He Himself took our infirmities and bare our sicknesses—"He said unto His disciples, Ye know that after two days is [the feast of] the passover, and the Son of man is betrayed to be crucified."The *first* and the *last* steps of His final sufferings are brought together in this brief announcement of all that was to take place. The *passover* was the first and the chief of the three great annual festivals, commemorative of the redemption of God's people from Egypt, through the sprinkling of the blood of a lamb divinely appointed to be slain for that end; the destroying

angel, "when he saw the blood, *passing over*" the Israelitish houses, on which that blood was seen, when he came to destroy all the first-born in the land of Egypt (Exod. 12)—bright typical foreshadowing of the great Sacrifice, and the Redemption effected thereby. Accordingly, "by the determinate counsel and foreknowledge of God, who is wonderful in counsel and excellent in working," it was so ordered that precisely at the passover season, "Christ our Passover should be sacrificed for us." On the day following the passover commenced "the feast of unleavened bread," so called because for seven days only unleavened bread was to be eaten (Exod. 12:18-20). See on I Corinthians 5:6-8. We are further told by Matthew (26:3) that the consultation was held in the palace of Caiaphas the high priest, between the chief priests, [the scribes], and the elders of the people, how "they might take Jesus by subtlety and kill Him." **2. But they said, Not on the feast day**—rather, not during the feast; not until the seven days of unleavened bread should be over—**lest there be an uproar of the people**—In consequence of the vast influx of strangers, embracing all the male population of the land who had reached a certain age, there were within the walls of Jerusalem at this festival some two million people; and in their excited state, the danger of tumult and bloodshed among "the people," who for the most part took Jesus for a prophet, was extreme. (See JOSEPHUS, *Antiquities*, xx. 5. 3.) What plan, if any, these ecclesiastics fixed upon for seizing our Lord, does not appear. But the proposal of Judas being at once and eagerly gone into, it is probable they were till then at some loss for a plan sufficiently quiet and yet effectual. So, just at the feast-time shall it be done; the unexpected offer of Judas relieving them of their fears. Thus, as BENGEL remarks, did the divine counsel take effect.

The Supper and the Anointing at Bethany Six Days before the Passover (vss. 3-9). The time of this part of the narrative is *four days before* what has just been related. Had it been part of the regular train of events which our Evangelist designed to record, he would probably have inserted it in its proper place, before the conspiracy of the Jewish authorities. But having come to the treason of Judas, he seems to have gone back upon this scene as what probably gave immediate occasion to the awful deed. **3. And being in Bethany, in the house of Simon the leper, as he sat at meat, there came a woman**—It was "Mary," as we learn from John 12:3. **having an alabaster box of ointment of spikenard**—pure *nard*, a celebrated aromatic—(See Song of Sol. 1:12). **very precious**—"very costly" (John 12:3). **and she brake the box, and poured it on his head**—"and anointed," adds John, "the feet of Jesus, and wiped His feet with her hair: and the house was filled with the odor of the ointment." The only use of this was to refresh and exhilarate —a grateful compliment in the East, amid the closeness of a heated atmosphere, with many guests at a feast. Such was the form in which Mary's love to Christ, at so much cost to herself, poured itself out. **4. And there were some that had indignation within themselves and said**—Matthew says (26:8), "But when His disciples saw it, they had indignation, saying . . ." The spokesman, however, was none of the true-hearted Eleven—as we learn from John (12:4): "Then saith one of His disciples, Judas Iscariot, Simon's son, which should betray Him." Doubtless the thought stirred first in his breast, and issued from his base lips; and some of the rest, ignorant of his true character and feelings, and carried away by his plausible speech, might for the moment feel some chagrin at the apparent waste. **Why was this waste of the ointment made? 5. For it might have been sold for more than three hundred pence**—about $50 in our currency. **and have been given to the poor. And they murmured against her**—"This he said," remarks John, and the remark is of exceeding importance, "not that he cared for the poor but because he was a thief, and had the bag"—the scrip or treasure-chest—"and bare what was put therein"—not 'bare it off' by theft, as some understand it. It is true that he did this; but the expression means simply that he had charge of it and its contents, or was treasurer to Jesus and the Twelve. What a remarkable arrangement was this, by which an avaricious and dishonest person was not only taken into the number of the Twelve, but entrusted with the custody of their little property! The purposes which this served are obvious enough; but it is further noticeable, that the remotest hint was never given to the Eleven of his true character, nor did the disciples most favored with the intimacy of Jesus ever suspect him, till a few minutes before he voluntarily separated himself from their company—for ever! **6. And Jesus said, Let her alone; why trouble ye her? she hath wrought a good work on me**—It was good in itself, and so was acceptable to Christ; it was eminently seasonable, and so more acceptable still; and it was "what she could," and so most acceptable of all. **7. For ye have the poor with you always**—referring to Deuteronomy 15:11. **and whensoever ye will ye may do them good: but me ye have not always**—a gentle hint of His approaching departure, by One who knew the worth of His own presence. **8. She hath done what she could**—a noble testimony, embodying a principle of immense importance. **she is come aforehand to anoint my body to the burying**—or, as in John (12:7), "Against the day of my burying hath she kept this." Not that she, dear heart, thought of His burial, much less reserved any of her nard to anoint her dead Lord. But as the time was so near at hand when that office would have to be performed, *and she was not to have that privilege even after the spices were brought for the purpose* (ch. 16:1), He lovingly *regards it as done now*. "In the act of love done to Him," says OLSHAUSEN beautifully, "she has erected to herself an eternal monument, as lasting as the Gospel, the eternal Word of God. From generation to generation this remarkable prophecy of the Lord has been fulfilled; and even we, in explaining this saying of the Redeemer, of necessity contribute to its accomplishment." "Who but Himself, asks STIER, "had the power to ensure to any work of man, even if resounding in His own time through the whole earth, an imperishable remembrance in the stream of history? Behold once more here the majesty of His royal judicial supremacy in the government of the world, in this, 'Verily I say unto you.' " **10. And Judas Iscariot, one of the twelve, went unto the chief priests, to betray him unto them**—i.e., to make his proposals, and to bargain with them, as appears from. Matthew's fuller statement (ch. 26: 14, 15) which says, he "went unto the chief priests, and said, What will ye give me, and I will deliver Him unto you? And they covenanted with him for thirty pieces of silver." The thirty pieces of silver were thirty shekels, the fine paid for man-or maid-servant acidentally killed (Exod. 21:32), and equal to about $25 in our currency—"a *goodly* price that I was prized at of them!" (Zech. 11:13). **11. And when they heard it, they were glad, and**

promised to give him money—Matthew alone records the precise sum, because a remarkable and complicated prophecy, which he was afterwards to refer to, was fulfilled by it. **And he sought how he might conveniently betray him**—or, as more fully given in Luke (22:6), "And he promised, and sought opportunity to betray Him unto them in the absence of the multitude." That he should avoid an "uproar" or "riot" among the people, which probably was made an essential condition by the Jewish authorities, was thus assented to by the traitor; into whom, says Luke (22:3), "Satan entered," to put him upon this hellish deed.

12-26. PREPARATION FOR, AND LAST CELEBRATION OF, THE PASSOVER—ANNOUNCEMENT OF THE TRAITOR—INSTITUTION OF THE SUPPER. (=Matt. 26: 17-30; Luke 22:7-23, 39; John 13:21-30.) See on Luke 22:7-23, 39; and on John 13:10, 11, 18, 19, 21-30.

27-31. THE DESERTION OF JESUS BY HIS DISCIPLES, AND THE FALL OF PETER, FORETOLD. (=Matt. 26:31-35; Luke 22:31-38; John 13:36-38.) See on Luke 22:31-46.

32-42. THE AGONY IN THE GARDEN. (=Matt. 26:36-46; Luke 22:39-46). See on Luke 22:39-46.

43-52. BETRAYAL AND APPREHENSION OF JESUS—FLIGHT OF HIS DISCIPLES. (=Matt. 26:47-56; Luke 22:47-53; John 18:1-12.) See on John 18: 1-12.

53-72. JESUS ARRAIGNED BEFORE THE SANHEDRIM, CONDEMNED TO DIE, AND SHAMEFULLY ENTREATED—THE FALL OF PETER. (=Matt. 26:57-75; Luke 22:54-71; John 18:13-18, 24-27.) Had we only the first three Gospels, we should have concluded that our Lord was led immediately to Caiaphas, and had before the Council. But as the Sanhedrim could hardly have been brought together at the dead hour of night—by which time our Lord was in the hands of the officers sent to take Him—and as it was only "as soon as it was day" that the Council met (Luke 22:66), we should have had some difficulty in knowing what was done with Him during those intervening hours. In the Fourth Gospel, however, all this is cleared up, and a very important addition to our information is made (John 18:13, 14, 19-24). Let us endeavor to trace the events in the true order of succession, and in the detail supplied by a comparison of all the four streams of text.

Jesus Is Brought Privately before Annas, the Father-in-Law of Caiaphas (John 18:13, 14). **13.** "And they led Him away to Annas first; for he was father-in-law to Caiaphas, which was the high priest that same year." This successful Annas, as ELLICOT remarks, was appointed high priest by Quirinus, A.D. 12, and after holding the office for several years, was deposed by Valerius Gratius, Pilate's predecessor in the procuratorship of Judea [JOSEPHUS, *Antiquities*, xviii. 2. 1, etc.]. He appears, however, to have possessed vast influence, having obtained the high priesthood, not only for his son Eleazar, and his son-in-law Caiaphas, but subsequently for four other sons, under the last of whom James, the brother of our Lord, was put to death (*ibid* xx. 9. 1). It is thus highly probable that, besides having the title of "high priest" merely as one who had filled the office, he to a great degree retained the powers he had formerly exercised, and came to be regarded practically as a kind of rightful high priest. **14.** "Now Caiaphas was he which gave counsel to the Jews, that it was expedient that one man should die for the people." See on John 11:50. What passed between Annas and our Lord during this interval the beloved disciple reserves till he has related the beginning of Peter's fall. To this, then, as recorded by our own Evangelist, let us meanwhile listen.

Peter Obtains Access within the Quadrangle of the High Priest's Residence, and Warms Himself at the Fire (vss. 53,54). **53. And they led Jesus away to the high priest: and with him were assembled—**or rather, "there gathered together unto him"—**all the chief priests and the elders and the scribes**—it was then a full and formal meeting of the Sanhedrim. Now, as the first three Evangelists place all Peter's denials of his Lord after this, we should naturally conclude that they took place *while our Lord stood before the Sanhedrim.* But besides that the natural impression is that the scene around the fire took place *overnight,* the *second crowing of the cock,* if we are to credit ancient writers, would occur about the beginning of the fourth watch, or between three and four in the morning. By that time, however, the Council had probably convened, being warned, perhaps, that they were to prepare for being called at any hour of the morning, should the Prisoner be successfully secured. If this be correct, it is fairly certain that only the *last* of Peter's three denials would take place while our Lord was under trial before the Sanhedrim. One thing more may require explanation. If our Lord had to be transferred from the residence of Annas to that of Caiaphas, one is apt to wonder that there is no mention of His being marched from the one to the other. But the building, in all likelihood, was one and the same; in which case He would merely have to be taken perhaps across the court, from one chamber to another. **54. And Peter followed him afar off, even into**—or "from afar, even to the interior of"—**the palace of the high priest**—"An Oriental house," says Robinson, "is usually built around a quadrangular interior court; into which there is a passage (sometimes arched) through the front part of the house, closed next the street by a heavy folding gate, with a smaller wicket for single persons, kept by a porter. The interior court, often paved or flagged, and open to the sky, is the *hall,* which our translators have rendered 'palace,' where the attendants made a fire; and the passage beneath the front of the house, from the street to this court, is the *porch.* The place where Jesus stood before the high priest may have been an open room, or place of audience on the ground-floor, in the rear or on one side of the court; such rooms, open in front, being customary. It was close upon the court, for Jesus heard all that was going on around the fire, and turned and looked upon Peter (Luke 22:61). **and he sat with the servants, and warmed himself at the fire**—The graphic details, here omitted, are supplied in the other Gospels. John 18:18, "And the servants and officers stood there" that is, in the hall, within the quadrangle, open to the sky, "who had made a fire of coals," or charcoal (in a brazier probably), "for it was cold." John alone of all the Evangelists mentions the *material,* and the *coldness* of the night, as Webster and Wilkinson remark. The elevated situation of Jerusalem, observes Tholuck, renders it so cold about Easter as to make a watch fire at night indispensable. "And Peter stood with them and warmed himself." "He went in," says Matthew (26:58), "and sat with the servants *to see the end.*" These two minute statements throw an interesting light on each other. His wishing to "see the end," or issue of these proceedings, was what led him into the palace, for he evidently feared the

worst. But once in, the serpent-coil is drawn closer; it is a cold night, and why should not he take advantage of the fire as well as others? Besides, in the talk of the crowd about the all-engrossing topic he may pick up something which he would like to hear. Poor Peter! But now, let us leave him warming himself at the fire, and listening to the hum of talk about this strange case by which the subordinate officials, passing to and fro and crowding around the fire in this open court, would while away the time; and, following what appears the order of the Evangelical Narrative, let us turn to Peter's Lord.

Jesus Is Interrogated by Annas—His Dignified Reply—Is Treated with Indignity by One of the Officials—His Meek Rebuke (John 18:19-23). We have seen that it is only the Fourth Evangelist who tells us that our Lord was sent to Annas first, overnight, until the Sanhedrim could be got together at earliest dawn. We have now, in the same Gospel, the deeply instructive scene that passed during this non-official interview. 19. "The high priest [Annas] then asked Jesus of His disciples and of His doctrine"—probably to entrap Him into some statements which might be used against Him at the trial. From our Lord's answer it would seem that "His disciples" were understood to be some secret party. 20. "Jesus answered him, I spake openly to the world"—cf. ch. 7:4. He speaks of His public teaching as now a past thing—as now all over. "I ever taught in the synagogue and in the temple, whither the Jews always resort," courting publicity, though with sublime noiselessness, "and in secret have I said nothing"—rather, 'spake I nothing'; that is, nothing different from what He taught in public: all His private communications with the Twelve being but explanations and developments of His public teaching. (Cf. Isa. 45:19; 48:16). 21. "Why askest thou Me? ask them which heard Me what I have said to them"—rather, what I said unto them; "behold, they know what I said." From this mode of replying, it is evident that our Lord saw the attempt to draw Him into self-crimination, and resented it by falling back upon the right of every accused party to have some charge laid against Him by competent witnesses. 22. "And when He had thus spoken, one of the officers which stood by struck Jesus with the palm of his hand, saying, Answerest Thou the high priest so?" (see Isa. 50:6). It would seem from Acts 23:2 that this summary and undignified way of punishment what was deemed insolence in the accused had the sanction even of the high priests themselves. 23. "Jesus answered him, If I have spoken evil"—rather, 'If I spoke evil,' in reply to the high priest, "bear witness of the evil; but if well, why smitest thou Me?" He does not say 'if *not* evil,' as if His reply had been merely unobjectionable; but "if *well,*" which seems to challenge something altogether fitting in the remonstrance. He had addressed to the high priest. From our Lord's procedure here, by the way, it is evident enough that His own precept in the Sermon on the Mount—that when smitten on the one cheek we are to turn to the smiter the other also (Matt. 5:39)—is not to be taken to the letter.

Annas Sends Jesus to Caiaphas (John 18:24). 24. "Now Annas had sent Him bound unto Caiaphas the high priest." On the meaning of this verse there is much diversity of opinion; and according as we understand it it will be the conclusion we come to, whether there was but *one hearing* of our Lord before Annas and Caiaphas together, or whether, according to the view we have given above, there were *two hearings*—a preliminary and informal one before Annas, and a formal and official one before Caiaphas and the Sanhedrim. If our translators have given the right sense of the verse, there was but one hearing before Caiaphas; and then this 24th verse is to be read as a *parenthesis*, merely supplementing what was said in vs. 13. This is the view of CALVIN, BEZA, GROTIUS, BENGEL, DE WETTE, MEYER, LUCKE, THOLUCK. But there are decided objections to this view. First: We cannot but think that the *natural* sense of the whole passage, embracing vss. 13, 14 and 19-24, is that of a preliminary non-official hearing before "Annas first," the particulars of which are accordingly recorded; and then of a transference of our Lord from Annas to Caiaphas. Second: On the other view, it is not easy to see why the Evangelist should not have inserted vs. 24 immediately after vs. 13; or rather, how he could well have done otherwise, As it stands, it is not only quite out of its proper place, but comes in most perplexingly. Whereas, if we take it as a simple statement of fact, that after Annas had finished his interview with Jesus, as recorded in vss. 19-23, he transferred Him to Caiaphas to be formally tried, all is clear and natural. Third: The pluperfect sense *"had sent"* is in the translation only; the sense of the original word being simply "sent." And though there are cases where the aorist here used has the sense of an English pluperfect, this sense is not to be put upon it unless it be obvious and indisputable. Here that is so far from being the case, that the pluperfect "had sent" is rather an unwarrantable *interpretation* than a simple *translation* of the word: informing the reader that, *according to the view of our translators,* our Lord "had been" sent to Caiaphas *before* the interview just recorded by the Evangelist; whereas, if we translate the verse literally—"Annas *sent* Him bound unto Caiaphas the high priest"—we get just the information we expect, that Annas, having merely *"precognosced"* the prisoner, hoping to draw something out of Him, "sent Him to Caiaphas" to be formally tried before the proper tribunal. This is the view of CHRYSOSTOM and AUGUSTINE among the Fathers; and of the moderns, of OLSHAUSEN, SCHLEIERMACHER, NEANDER, EBRARD, WIESELER, LANGE, LUTHARDT. This brings us back to the text of our second Gospel, and in it to—

The Judicial Trial and Condemnation of the Lord Jesus by the Sanhedrim (vss. 55-64). But let the reader observe, that though this is introduced by the Evangelist before any of the denials of Peter are recorded, we have given reasons for concluding that probably the *first two denials* took place while our Lord was with Annas, and the last only during the trial before the Sanhedrim. **55. And the chief priests and all the council sought for witness against Jesus to put him to death**—Matthew (26:59) says they "sought *false* witness." They knew they could find nothing valid; but having their Prisoner to bring before Pilate, they behooved to *make a case.* **and found none**—none that would suit their purpose, or make a decent ground of charge before Pilate. **56. For many bare false witness against him**—From their debasing themselves to *"seek"* them, we are led to infer that they were *bribed* to bear false witness; though there are never wanting sycophants enough, ready to sell themselves for naught, if they may but get a smile from those above them: see a similar scene in Acts 6:11-14. How is one reminded here of that complaint, "False witnesses did rise up: they laid to my charge things that I knew not" (Ps. 31:11)!—**but their wit-**

ness agreed not together—If even *two* of them had been agreed, it would have been greedily enough laid hold of, as all that the law insisted upon even in capital cases (Deut. 17:6). But even in this they failed. One cannot but admire the providence which secured this result; since, on the one hand, it seems astonishing that those unscrupulous prosecutors and their ready tools should so bungle a business in which they felt their whole interests bound up; and, on the other hand, if they *had* succeeded in making even a plausible case, the effect on the progress of the Gospel might for a time have been injurious. But at the very time when His enemies were saying, "God hath forsaken Him; persecute and take Him; for there is none to deliver Him" (Ps. 71:11), He whose Witness He was and whose work He was doing was keeping Him as the apple of His eye, and while He was making the wrath of man to praise Him, was restraining the remainder of that wrath (Ps. 76:10). **57. And there arose certain, and bare false witness against him**—Matthew (26:60) is more precise here: *"At the last came two false witnesses."* As no two had before agreed in anything, they felt it necessary to secure a duplicate testimony to something, but they were long of succeeding. And what was it, when at length it was brought forward? **saying, 58. We heard him say, I will destroy this temple that is made with hands, and within three days I will build another made without hands**—On this charge, observe, first, that eager as His enemies were to find criminal matter against our Lord, they had to go back to the outset of His ministry, His first visit to Jerusalem, more than three years before this. In all that He said and did after that, though ever increasing in boldness, they could find nothing. Next, that even then, they fix only on one speech, of two or three words, which they dared to adduce against Him. Further, they most manifestly pervert the speech of our Lord. We say not this because in Mark's form of it, it differs from the report of the words given by the Fourth Evangelist (John 2:18-22)—the only one of the Evangelists who reports it all, or mentions even any visit paid by our Lord to Jerusalem before His last—but because the one report bears truth, and the other falsehood, on its face. When our Lord said on that occasion, "Destroy this temple, and in three days I will raise it up," they *might,* for a moment, have understood Him to refer to the temple out of whose courts He had swept the buyers and sellers. But *after* they had expressed their astonishment at His words, in that sense of them, and reasoned upon the time it had taken to rear the temple as it then stood, since *no answer* to this appears to have been given by our Lord, it is hardly conceivable that they should continue in the persuasion that this was really His meaning. But finally, even if the more ignorant among them had done so, it is next to certain that *the ecclesiastics,* who were *the prosecutors* in this case, *did not believe that this was His meaning.* For in less than three days after this they went to Pilate, saying, "Sir, we remember that that deceiver said, while he was yet alive, *after three days I will rise again"* (Matt. 27:63). Now what utterance of Christ known to His enemies, *could* this refer to, if not to this very saying about destroying and rearing up the temple? And if so, it puts it beyond a doubt that by this time, at least, they were perfectly aware that our Lord's words referred to *His death by their hands and His resurrection by His own.* But this is confirmed by the next verse. **59. But neither so did their witness agree together**—i.e., not even as to so brief a speech, consisting of but a few words, was there such a concurrence in their mode of reporting it as to make out a decent case. In such a charge *everything depended on the very terms alleged to have been used.* For every one must see that a very slight turn, either way, given to such words, would make them either something like *indictable matter,* or else a *ridiculous ground for a criminal charge*—would either give them a colorable pretext for the charge of impiety which they were bent on making out, or else make the whole saying appear, on the worst view that could be taken of it, as merely some mystical or empty boast. **60. Answerest thou nothing? what is it which these witness against thee?**—Clearly, they felt that *their case had failed,* and by this artful question the high priest hoped to get *from His own mouth* what they had in vain tried to obtain from their false and contradictory witnesses. But in this, too, they failed. **61. But he held his peace, and answered nothing**—This must have nonplussed them. But they were not to be easily baulked of their object. **Again the high priest**—arose (Matt. 26:62), matters having now come to a crisis. **asked him, and said unto him, Art thou the Christ, the Son of the Blessed?**—Why our Lord should have answered this question, when He was silent as to the former, we might not have quite seen, but for Matthew, who says (26:63) that the high priest *put Him upon solemn oath,* saying, "I adjure Thee by the living God, that Thou tell us whether Thou be the Christ, the Son of God." Such an adjuration was understood to render an answer legally necessary (Lev. 5:1). **62. And Jesus said, I am**—or, as in Matthew 26:64, "Thou hast said [it]." In Luke, however (22:70), the answer, "Ye say that I am," should be rendered—as DE WETTE, MEYER, ELLICOTT, and the best critics agree that the preposition requires —"Ye say [it], for I am [so]." Some words, however, were spoken by our Lord before giving His answer to this solemn question. These are recorded by Luke alone (22:67, 68): "Art Thou the Christ [they asked]? tell us. And He said unto them, If I tell you, ye will not believe: and if I also ask [interrogate] "you, ye will not answer Me, nor let Me go." This seems to have been uttered before giving His direct answer, as a calm remonstrance and dignified protest against the prejudgment of His case and the unfairness of their mode of procedure. But now let us hear the rest of the answer, in which the conscious majesty of Jesus breaks forth from behind the dark cloud which overhung Him as He stood before the Council. **and**—in that character—**ye shall see the Son of man sitting on the right hand of power, and coming in the clouds of heaven**—In Matthew (26:64) a slightly different but interesting turn is given to it by one word: "Thou hast said [it]: nevertheless"—We prefer this sense of the word to "besides," which some recent critics decide for—"I say unto you, Hereafter shall ye see the Son of man sit on the right hand of power, and coming in the clouds of heaven." The word rendered "hereafter" means, not "at some future time" (as today "hereafter commonly does), but what the English word originally signified, "after here," "after now," or "from this time." Accordingly, in Luke 22:69, the words used mean "from now." So that though the reference we have given it to the day of His glorious Second Appearing is too obvious to admit of doubt, He would, by using the expression, "From this time," convey the important thought which He had before expressed, immediately after the traitor left the supper-table to do his dark work, *"Now* is the Son of man glorified" (John 13:31). At this moment, and by this speech, did He "witness *the* good confession" emphatically and properly, as the apostle says in I Timothy 6:13. Our translators render the words there, "Who *before* Pontius Pilate witnessed"; referring it to the admission of His being a *King,* in the presence of Cæsar's own chief representative. But it should be rendered, as LUTHER renders it, and as the best interpreters now understand it, "Who *under* Pontius Pilate witnessed . . . In this view of it, the apostle is referring not to what our Lord confessed *before* Pilate—which, though noble, was not of such primary importance—but to that sublime confession which, under Pilate's administration, He witnessed before the only competent tribunal on such occasions, the Supreme Ecclesiastical Council of God's chosen nation, that He was THE MESSIAH, and THE SON OF THE BLESSED ONE; in the former word owning His Supreme *Official,* in the latter His Supreme *Personal,* Dignity. **63. Then the high priest rent his clothes**—On this expression of *horror of blasphemy,* see II Kings 18: 37—**and saith, What need we any further witnesses? 64. Ye have heard the blasphemy**—(See John 10: 33). In Luke (22:71), "For we ourselves have heard of His own mouth"—an affectation of religious horror. **what think ye?**—'Say what the verdict is to be.' **they all condemned him to be guilty of death**—or of a capital crime, which *blasphemy* against God was according to the Jewish law (Lev. 24:16). Yet *not absolutely all; for Joseph* of Arimathea, "a good man and a just," was one of that Council, and *"he was not a consenting party* to the counsel and deed of them," for that is the strict sense of the words of Luke 23:50, 51. Probably he absented himself, and *Nicodemus* also, from this meeting of the Council, the temper of which they would know too well to expect their voice to be listened to; and in that case, the words of our Evangelist are to be taken strictly, that, without one dissentient voice, "all [present] condemned him to be guilty of death."

The Blessed One Is Now Shamefully Entreated (vs. 65). Every word here must be carefully observed, and the several accounts put together, that we may lose none of the awful indignities about to be described. **65. some began to spit on him**—or, as in Matthew 26:67, "to spit in [into] His face." Luke (22:63) says in addition, "And the men that held Jesus mocked him"—or cast their jeers at Him. **to cover his face**—or "to blindfold him" (as in Luke 22:64). **to buffet him**—Luke's word, which is rendered "smote Him" (22:63), is a stronger one, conveying an idea for which we have an exact equivalent in English, but one too colloquial to be inserted here—**began to say unto him, Prophesy**— In Matthew 26:68 this is given more fully: "Prophesy unto us, thou Christ, Who is he that smote Thee?" The sarcastic fling at Him as *the Christ,"* and the demand of Him in this character to name the unseen perpetrator of the blows inflicted on Him, was in them as infamous as to Him it must have been, and was intended to be, stinging. **and the servants did strike him with the palms of their hands**—or "struck Him on the face" (Luke 22:64). Ah! Well did He say prophetically, in that Messianic prediction which we have often referred to, "I gave My back to the smiters, and My cheeks to them that plucked off the hair: I hid not My face from shame and spitting!" (Isa. 50:6). "And many other things blasphemously spake they against Him" (Luke 22:65). This general statement is important, as showing that virulent and varied as were the *recorded* affronts put upon Him, they are but a *small specimen* of what He endured on that dark occasion.

Peter's FIRST DENIAL *of His Lord* (vss. 66-68). **66. And as Peter was beneath in the palace**—This little word *"beneath"*—one of our Evangelist's graphic touches—is most important for the right understanding of what we may call the topography of the scene. We must take it in connection with Matthew's word (26:69): "Now Peter sat *without* in the palace"—or quadrangular court, in the center of which the fire would be burning; and crowding around and buzzing about it would be the menials and others who had been admitted within the court. At the upper end of this court, probably, would be the memorable chamber in which the trial was held—*open to the court*, likely, and *not far from the fire* (as we gather from Luke 22:61), but *on a higher level*; for (as our verse says) the court, with Peter in it, was "beneath" it. The ascent to the Council chamber was perhaps by a short flight of steps. If the reader will bear this explanation in mind, he will find the intensely interesting details which follow more intelligible. **there cometh one of the maids of the high priest**—"the damsel that kept the door" (John 18:17). The Jews seem to have employed women as porters of their doors (Acts 12:13). **67. And when she saw Peter warming himself, she looked upon him**—Luke (22:56) is here more graphic; "But a certain maid beheld him as he sat by the fire"—lit., 'by the *light*,' which, shining full upon him, revealed him to the girl—"and earnestly looked upon him"—or, 'fixed her gaze upon him.' His demeanor and timidity, which must have attracted notice, as so generally happens, leading," says OLSHAUSEN, "to the recognition of him." **and said, And thou also wast with Jesus of Nazareth**—"with Jesus the Nazarene," or, "with Jesus of Galilee" (Matthew 26:69). The *sense* of this is given in John's report of it (18:17), "Art not thou also one of this man's disciples?" i.e., thou as well as "that other disciple," whom she knew to be one, but did not challenge, perceiving that he was a privileged person. In Luke (22:56) it is given as a remark made by the maid to one of the bystanders—this man was also with Him." If so expressed in Peter's hearing—drawing upon him the eyes of every one that heard it (as we know it did, Matt. 26:70), and compelling him to answer to it—that would explain the different forms of the report naturally enough. But in such a case this is of no real importance. **68. But he denied**—"before all" (Matt. 26:70). **saying, I know not, neither understand I what thou sayest**—in Luke, "I know Him not." **And he went out into the porch**—the vestibule leading to the street—no doubt finding the fire-place too *hot* for him; possibly also with the hope of escaping—but that was not to be, and perhaps he dreaded that, too. Doubtless by this time his mind would be getting into a sea of commotion, and would fluctuate every moment in its resolves. AND THE COCK CREW. See on Luke 22:34. This, then, was the First Denial.

Peter's SECOND DENIAL *of His Lord* (vss. 69, 70). There is here a verbal difference among the Evangelists, which without some information which has been withheld, cannot be quite extricated. **69. And a maid saw him again**—or, "a girl." It might be rendered "the girl"; but this would not necessarily mean the same one as before, but might, and probably does, mean just the female who had charge of the door or gate near which Peter now

was. Accordingly, in Matthew 26:71, she is expressly called "another [maid]." But in Luke it is a *male* servant: "And after a little while (from the time of the first denial) another"—i.e., as the word signifies, "another male" servant. But there is no real difficulty, as the challenge, probably, after being made by one was reiterated by another. Accordingly, in John, it is, "*They* said therefore unto him . . .," as if more than one challenged him at once. **and began to say to them that stood by, This is one of them**—or, as in Matthew 26:71—"This [fellow] was also with Jesus the Nazarene. **70. And he denied it again**—In Luke, "Man, I am not." But worst of all in Matthew—"And again he denied with an oath, I do not know the man" (26:72). This was the Second Denial, more vehement, alas! than the first.

Peter's THIRD DENIAL *of His Lord*. (vss. 70-72). **70. And a little after**—"about the space of one hour after" (Luke 22:59). **they that stood by said again to Peter, Surely thou art one of them: for thou art a Galilean, and thy speech agreeth thereto**—"bewrayeth (or "discovereth") thee" (Matt. 26:73). In Luke it is, "Another confidently affirmed, saying, Of a truth this [fellow] also was with him: for he is a Galilean." The Galilean dialect had a more *Syrian* cast than that of Judea. *If Peter had held his peace*, this peculiarity had not been observed; but hoping, probably, to put them off the scent by joining in the *fireside talk*, he was thus discovered. The Fourth Gospel is particularly interesting here: "One of the servants of the high priest, being his kinsman (or kinsman to him) whose ear Peter cut off, saith, Did not I see thee in the garden with Him?" (John 18:26.) No doubt his relationship to Malchus drew his attention to the man who had smitten him, and this enabled him to identify Peter. "Sad reprisals!" exclaims BENGEL. Poor Peter! Thou art caught in thine own toils; but like a wild bull in a net, thou wilt toss and rage, filling up the measure of thy terrible declension by one more denial of thy Lord, and that the foulest of all. **71. But he began to curse**—'anathematize,' or wish himself accursed if what he was now to say was not true. **and to swear**—or to take a solemn oath. **saying, I know not this man of whom ye speak. 72. And the second time the cock crew.** The other three Evangelists, who mention but one crowing of the cock—and that not the first, but the second and last one of Mark—all say the cock crew "immediately," but Luke says, "Immediately, while he yet spake, the cock crew" (22:60). Alas!—But now comes the wonderful sequel.

The Redeemer's Look upon Peter, and Peter's Bitter Tears (vs. 72; Luke 22:61, 62). It has been observed that while the beloved disciple is the only one of the four Evangelists who does not record the repentance of Peter, he is the only one of the four who records the affecting and most beautiful scene of his complete restoration (John 21:15-17). Luke 22:61: "And the Lord turned and looked upon Peter." How? it will be asked. We answer, From the chamber in which the trial was going on, in the direction of the court where Peter then stood —in the way already explained. See on vs. 66. Our Second Evangelist makes no mention of this look, but dwells on the warning of his Lord about the double crowing of the cock, which would announce his triple fall, as what rushed stingingly to his recollection and made him dissolve in tears. **And Peter called to mind the word that Jesus said unto him, Before the cock crow twice, thou shalt deny me thrice. And when he thought thereon, he**

wept—To the same effect is the statement of the First Evangelist (Matt. 26:75), save that like "the beloved physician," he notices the "bitterness" of the weeping. The most precious link, however, in the whole chain of circumstances in this scene is beyond doubt that "look" of deepest, tenderest import reported by Luke alone. Who can tell what lightning flashes of wounded love and piercing reproach shot from that "look" through the eye of Peter into his heart! "And Peter remembered the word of the Lord, how He had said unto him, Before the cock crow, thou shalt deny Me thrice. And Peter went out and wept bitterly." How different from the sequel of Judas' act! Doubtless the hearts of the two men towards the Saviour were perfectly different from the first; and the treason of Judas was but the consummation of the wretched man's resistance of the blaze of light in the midst of which he had lived for three years, while Peter's denial was but a momentary obscuration of the heavenly light and love to his Master which ruled his life. But the immediate cause of the blessed revulsion which made Peter "weep bitterly" was, beyond all doubt, this heart-piercing "look" which his Lord gave him. And remembering the Saviour's own words at the table, "Simon, Simon, Satan hath desired to have you, that he may sift you as wheat; *but I prayed for thee, that thy faith fail not,*" may we not say that *this prayer fetched down all that there was in that "look"* to pierce and break the heart of Peter, to keep it from despair, to work in it "repentance unto salvation not to be repented of," and at length, under other healing touches, to "restore his soul?" (See on Mark 16:7.)

CHAPTER 15

Vss. 1-20. Jesus Is Brought before Pilate—At a Second Hearing, Pilate, after Seeking to Release Him, Delivers Him Up—After Being Cruelly Entreated, He Is Led Away to Be Crucified. (=Matt.26:1, 2, 11-31; Luke 23:1-6, 13-25; John 18:28-19:16.) See on John 18:28-19; 16.

21-37. Crucifixion and Death of the Lord Jesus. (=Matt. 27:32-50; Luke 23:26-46; John 19:17-30.) See on John 19:17-30.

38-47. Signs and Circumstances following the Death of The Lord Jesus.—He Is Taken Down from the Cross and Buried—The Sepulchre Is Guarded. (=Matt. 27:51-66; Luke 23:45, 47-56; John 19:31-42). See on Matthew 27:51-56; and on John 19:31-42.

CHAPTER 16

Vss. 1-20. Angelic Announcement to the Women on the First Day of the Week, that Christ Is Risen—His Appearances after His Resurrection—His Ascension—Triumphant Proclamation of His Gospel. (=Matt. 28:1-10, 16-20; Luke 24:1-51; John 20:1, 2, 11-29.)

The Resurrection Announced to the Women (vss. 1-8). **1. when the sabbath was past**—that is, at sunset of our Saturday. **Mary Magdalene**—see on Luke 8:2. **Mary the mother of James**—James the Less (see on ch. 15:40). **and Salome**—the mother of Zebedee's sons (cf. ch. 15:40 with Matt. 27:56). **had bought sweet spices, that they might come and anoint him**—The word is simply "bought." But our translators are perhaps right in rendering it here "had bought," since it would appear, from

Luke 23:56, that they had purchased them immediately after the Crucifixion, on the *Friday* evening, during the short interval that remained to them before sunset, when the sabbath rest began; and that they had only deferred using them to anoint the body till the sabbath rest should be over. On this "anointing," see on John 19:40. **2. very early in the morning**—see on Matthew 28:1. **the first day of the week, they came unto the sepulchre at the rising of the sun**—not quite literally, but "at earliest dawn"; according to a way of speaking not uncommon, and occurring sometimes in the Old Testament. Thus our Lord rose on the third day; having lain in the grave part of Friday, the whole of Saturday, and part of the following First day. **3. they said among themselves**—as they were approaching the sacred spot. **Who shall roll us away the stone from the door of the sepulchre? . . . for it was very great**—On reaching it they find their difficulty gone—the stone already rolled away by an unseen hand. *And are there no others who, when advancing to duty in the face of appalling difficulties, find their stone also rolled away?* **5. entering into the sepulchre, they saw a young man**—In Matthew 28:2 he is called "the angel of the Lord"; but here he is described as he appeared to the eye, in the bloom of a life that knows no decay. In Matthew he is represented as sitting on the stone *outside* the sepulchre; but since even there he says, "*Come,* see the place where the Lord lay" (28:6), he seems, as Alford says, to have gone in with them from without; only awaiting their arrival to accompany them into the hallowed spot, and instruct them about it. **sitting on the right side**—having respect to the position in which His Lord had lain there. This trait is peculiar to Mark; but cf. Luke 1:11. **clothed in a long white garment**—On its *length,* see Isaiah 6:1; and on its *whiteness,* see on Matthew 28:3. **and they were affrighted. 6. he saith unto them, Be not affrighted**—a stronger word than "Fear not" in Matthew. **Ye seek Jesus of Nazareth, which was crucified**—"the Nazarene, the Crucified," **he is risen; he is not here**—See on Luke 24:5, 6. **behold the place where they laid him**—See on Matthew 28:6. **7. But go your way, tell his disciples and Peter**—This Second Gospel, being drawn up—as all the earliest tradition states—*under the eye of Peter,* or from materials chiefly furnished by him, there is something deeply affecting in the preservation of this little phrase by Mark alone. **that he goeth before you into Galilee; there shall ye see him, as he said unto you**—See on Matthew 28:7. **8. And they went out quickly, and fled from the sepulchre: for they trembled and were amazed**—"for tremor and amazement seized them." **neither said they anything to any man; for they were afraid**—How intensely natural and simple is this!

Appearances of Jesus after His Resurrection (vss. 9-18). **9. Now when Jesus was risen early the first day of the week, he appeared first to Mary Magdalene, out of whom he had cast seven devils**—There is some difficulty here, and different ways of removing it have been adopted. She had gone with the other women to the sepulchre (vs. 1), parting from them, perhaps, before their interview with the angel, and on finding Peter and John she had come with them back to the spot; and it was at this second visit, it would seem, that Jesus appeared to this Mary, as detailed in John 20:11-18. *To a woman was this honor given to be the first that saw the risen Redeemer, and that woman was* not *his virgin-mother.* **11. they, when they had heard that he** was alive, and had been seen of her, believed not— This, which is once and again repeated of them all, is most important in its bearing on their subsequent testimony to His resurrection at the risk of life itself. **12. After that he appeared in another form**—(cf. Luke 24:16). **unto two of them as they walked, and went into the country**—The reference here, of course, is to His manifestation to the two disciples going to Emmaus, so exquisitely told by the Third Evangelist (see on Luke 24:13, etc.). **13. they went and told it unto the residue: neither believed they them.** . . . **15. he said unto them, Go ye into all the world, and preach the Gospel to every creature**—See on John 20:19-23; and on Luke 24: 36-49. **16. He that believeth and is baptized**— Baptism is here put for the external signature of the inner faith of the heart, just as "confessing with the mouth" is in Romans 10:10; and there also as here this *outward* manifestation, once mentioned as the proper fruit of faith, is not repeated in what follows (Romans 10:11)—**shall be saved; but he that believeth not shall be damned**—These awful issues of the reception or rejection of the Gospel, though often recorded in other connections, are given in this connection only by Mark. **17. these signs shall follow them that believe . . . 18. They shall take up serpents . . .**—These two verses also are peculiar to Mark.

The Ascension and Triumphant Proclamation of the Gospel Thereafter (vss. 19-20). **19. So then after the Lord**—an epithet applied to Jesus by this Evangelist only in the two concluding verses, when He comes to His glorious Ascension and its subsequent fruits. It is most frequent in Luke. **had spoken unto them, he was received up into heaven** —See on Luke 24:50, 51. **and sat on the right hand of God**—This great truth is here only related as a fact in the Gospel history. In that exalted attitude He appeared to Stephen (Acts 7:55, 56); and it is thereafter perpetually referred to as His proper condition in glory. **20. they went forth, and preached everywhere, the Lord working with them, and confirming the word with signs following. Amen.**—We have in this closing verse a most important link of connection with the Acts of the Apostles, where He who directed all the movements of the infant Church is perpetually styled "THE LORD"; thus illustrating His own promise for the founding and building up of the Church, "Lo, I AM WITH YOU alway!"

THE GOSPEL ACCORDING TO

LUKE

INTRODUCTION

THE writer of this Gospel is universally allowed to have been Lucas (an abbreviated form of Lucanus, as Silas of Silvanus), though he is not expressly named either in the Gospel or in the Acts. From Colossians 4:14 we learn that he was a "physician"; and by comparing that verse with vss. 10, 11—in which the apostle enumerates all those of the circumcision who were then with him, but does not mention Luke, though he immediately afterwards sends a salutation from him—we gather that Luke was not a born Jew. Some have thought he was a freed-man (*libertinus*), as the Romans devolved the healing art on persons of this class and on their slaves, as an occupation beneath themselves. His intimate acquaintance with Jewish customs, and his facility in Hebraic Greek, seem to show that he was an early convert to the Jewish faith; and this is curiously confirmed by Acts 21:27-29, where we find the Jews enraged at Paul's supposed introduction of Greeks into the temple, because they had seen "Trophimus the Ephesian" with him; and as we know that Luke was with Paul on that occasion, it would seem that they had taken him for a Jew, as they made no mention of him. On the other hand, his fluency in classical Greek confirms his Gentile origin. The time when he joined Paul's company is clearly indicated in the Acts by his changing (at ch. 16:10) from the third person singular ("he") to the first person plural ("we"). From that time he hardly ever left the apostle till near the period of his martyrdom (II Tim. 4:11). EUSEBIUS makes him a native of Antioch. If so, he would have every advantage for cultivating the literature of Greece and such medical knowledge as was then possessed. That he died a natural death is generally agreed among the ancients; GREGORY NAZIANZEN alone affirming that he died a martyr.

The *time* and *place* of the publication of his Gospel are alike uncertain. But we can approximate to it. It must at any rate have been issued before the Acts, for there the 'Gospel' is expressly referred to as the same author's "former treatise" (Acts 1:1). Now the Book of the Acts was not published for two whole years after Paul's arrival as a prisoner at Rome, for it concludes with a reference to this period; but probably it was published soon after that, which would appear to have been early in the year 63. Before that time, then, we have reason to believe that the Gospel of Luke was in circulation, though the majority of critics make it later. If we date it somewhere between A.D. 50 and 60, we shall probably be near the truth; but nearer it we cannot with any certainty come. Conjectures as to the place of publication are too uncertain to be mentioned here.

That it was addressed, in the first instance, to Gentile *readers*, is beyond doubt. This is no more, as DAVIDSON remarks (*Introduction*, p. 186), than was to have been expected from the companion of an "apostle of the Gentiles," who had witnessed marvellous changes in the condition of many heathens by the reception of the Gospel. But the explanations in his Gospel of things known to every Jew, and which could only be intended for Gentile readers, make this quite plain—see chs. 1:26; 4:31; 8:26; 21:37; 22:1; 24:13. A number of other minute particulars, both of things inserted and of things omitted, confirm the conclusion that it was Gentiles whom this Evangelist had in the first instance in view.

We have already adverted to the classical *style* of Greek which this Evangelist writes—just what might have been expected from an educated Greek and travelled physician. But we have also observed that along with this he shows a wonderful flexibility of style, so much so, that when he comes to relate transactions wholly Jewish, where the speakers and actors and incidents are all Jewish, he writes in such Jewish Greek as one would do who had never been out of Palestine or mixed with any but Jews. In DA COSTA's *Four Witnesses* will be found some traces of "the beloved *physician*" in this Gospel. But far more striking and important are the traces in it of his intimate connection with the apostle of the Gentiles. That one who was so long and so constantly in the society of that master-mind has in such a work as this shown no traces of that connection, no stamp of that mind, is hardly to be believed. Writers of Introductions seem not to see it, and take no notice of it. But those who look into the interior of it will soon discover evidences enough in it of a *Pauline* cast of mind. Referring for a number of details to DA COSTA, we notice here only two examples: In I Corinthians 11:23, Paul ascribes to an express revelation from Christ Himself the account of the Institution of the Lord's Supper which he there gives. Now, if we find this account differing in small yet striking particulars from the accounts given by Matthew and Mark, but agreeing to the letter with Luke's account, it can hardly admit of a doubt that the one had it from the other; and in that case, of course, it was Luke that had it from Paul. Now Matthew and Mark both say of the Cup, "This is my blood of the New Testament"; while Paul and Luke say, in identical terms, "This cup is the New Testament in My blood." Further, Luke says, "Likewise also the cup *after supper*, saying . . ."; while Paul says, "After the same manner He took the cup *when He had supped*, saying . . ."; whereas neither Matthew nor Mark mention that this was after supper. But still more striking is another point of coincidence in this case. Matthew and Mark both say of the Bread merely this: "Take, eat; this is My body"; whereas Paul says, "Take, eat, this is My body, *which is broken for you*," and Luke, "This is My body, *which is given for you.*" And while Paul adds the precious clause, "*This do in remembrance of Me*," Luke does the same, in identical terms. How can one who reflects on this resist the conviction of a Pauline stamp in this Gospel? The other proof of this to which we ask the reader's attention is in the fact that Paul, in enumerating the parties by whom Christ was seen after His resurrection," begins, singularly enough, with Peter—"And that He rose again the third day according to the Scriptures and that He was seen of Cephas, then of the Twelve" (I Cor. 15:4, 5)—coupled with the remarkable fact, that Luke is the only one of the Evangelists who mentions that Christ appeared to Peter at all. When the disciples had returned from Emmaus to tell their brethren how the Lord had appeared to them in the way, and how He had made Himself known to them in the breaking of bread, they were met, as Luke relates, ere they had time to utter a word, with this wonderful piece of news, "The Lord is risen indeed, and hath appeared to Simon" (Luke 24:34).

Other points connected with this Gospel will be adverted to in the Commentary.

CHAPTER 1

Vss. 1-4. It appears from the Acts of the Apostles, and the Apostolic Epistles, that the earliest preaching of the Gospel consisted of a brief summary of the facts of our Lord's earthly history, with a few words of pointed application to the parties addressed. Of these astonishing facts, notes would naturally be taken and *digests* put into circulation. It is to such that Luke here refers; and in terms of studied respect, as narratives of what was "believed surely," or "on sure grounds" among Christians, and drawn up from the testimony of "eye-witnesses and ministering servants of the word." But when he adds that "it seemed good to him also to write in order, having traced down all things with exactness from their first rise," it is a virtual claim for his own Gospel to supersede these "many" narratives. Accordingly, while not one of them has survived the wreck of time, this and the other canonical Gospels live, and shall live, the only fitting vehicles of those life-bringing facts which have made all things new. Apocryphal or spurious gospels, upheld by parties unfriendly to the truths exhibited in the canonical Gospels, have *not* perished; but those well-meant and substantially correct narratives here referred to, used only while better were not to be had, were by tacit consent allowed to merge in the four peerless documents which from age to age, and with astonishing unanimity, have been accepted as the written charter of all Christianity. **1. set forth in order**—more simply, to draw up a narrative. **2. from the beginning**—that is, of His public ministry, as is plain from what follows. **3. from the very first**—that is, from the very earliest events; referring to those precious details of the birth and early life, not only of our Lord, but of His forerunner, which we owe to Luke alone. **in order**—or "consecu-

tively"—in contrast, probably, with the disjointed productions to which he had referred. But this must not be pressed too far; for, on comparing it with the other Gospels, we see that in some particulars the strict chronological order is not observed in this Gospel. **most excellent**—or "most noble"—a title of rank applied by this same writer twice to Felix and once to Festus (Acts 22:26; 24:3; 26:25). It is likely, therefore, that "Theophilus" was chief magistrate of some city in Greece or Asia Minor [WEBSTER and WILKINSON]. **4. that thou mightest know**—"know thoroughly." **hast been instructed**—orally instructed—lit., "catechized" or "catechetically taught," at first as a catechumen or candidate for Christian baptism.

5-25. ANNOUNCEMENT OF THE FORERUNNER. **5. Herod**—(See on Matt. 2:1). **course of Abia**—or Abijah; the eighth of the twenty-four orders of courses into which David divided the priests (see I Chron. 24:1, 4, 10). Of these courses only four returned after the captivity (Ezra 2:34-39), which were again subdivided into twenty-four—retaining the ancient name and order of each. They took the whole temple service for a week each. **his wife was of the daughters of Aaron**—The priests might marry into any tribe, but "it was most commendable of all to marry one of the priests' line" [LIGHTFOOT]. **6. commandments and ordinances**—The one expressing their *moral*—the other their *ceremonial*—obedience [CALVIN and BENGEL], (Cf. Ezek. 11:20; Heb. 9:1). It has been denied that any such distinction was known to the Jews and New Testament writers. But Mark 12:33, and other passages, put this beyond all reasonable doubt. **7. So with Abraham and Sarah, Isaac and Rebekah, Elkanah and Hannah, Manoah and his wife. 9. his lot was to burn incense**—The part assigned to each priest in his week of service was decided by lot. Three were employed at the offering of incense—to remove the ashes of the former service; to bring in and place on the golden altar the pan filled with hot burning coals taken from the altar of burnt offering; and to sprinkle the incense on the hot coals; and, while the smoke of it ascended, to make intercession for the people. This was the most distinguished part of the service (Rev. 8:3), and this was what fell to the lot of Zacharias at this time [LIGHTFOOT]. **10. praying without**—outside the court in front of the temple, where stood the altar of burnt offering; the men and women in separate courts, but the altar visible to all. **the time of incense**—which was offered along with the morning and evening sacrifice of every day; a beautiful symbol of the acceptableness of the *sacrifice* offered on the altar of burnt offering, with coals from whose altar the incense was burnt (Lev. 16:12, 13). This again was a symbol of the "living sacrifice" of themselves and their services offered daily to God by the worshippers. Hence the language of Psalm 141:2; Revelation 8:3. But that the acceptance of this daily offering depended on the *expiatory virtue* presupposed in the burnt offering, and pointing to the one "sacrifice of a sweet-smelling savor" (Eph. 5:2), is evident from Isaiah 6:6, 7. **11. right side**—the south side, between the altar and the candlestick, Zacharias being on the north side, in front of the altar, while offering incense [WEBSTER and WILKINSON]. But why there? The right was the favorable side (Matt. 25:33) [SCHOTTGEN and WETSTEIN in MEYER]; cf. Mark 16:5. **13. thy prayer is heard**—doubtless for *offspring*, which by some presentiment he even yet had not despaired of. **John**—the same as "Johanan," so frequent in the Old Testament, meaning "Jehovah's gracious gift." **14. shall rejoice**—so they did (vss. 58, 66); but the meaning rather is, "shall have cause to rejoice"—it would prove to many a joyful event. **15. great in the sight of the Lord**—nearer to Him in official standing than all the prophets. (See on Matt. 11: 10, 11.) **drink neither wine ...**—i.e., shall be a *Nazarite*, or "a separated one" (Num. 6:2, etc.). As the leper was the living symbol of *sin*, so was the Nazarite of *holiness;* nothing inflaming was to cross his lips; no razor to come on his head; no ceremonial defilement to be contracted. Thus was he to be "holy to the Lord [ceremonially] all the days of his separation." This separation was in ordinary cases temporary and voluntary: only *Samson* (Judg. 13:7), *Samuel* (I Sam. 1:11), and *John Baptist* were Nazarites from the womb. It was fitting that the utmost severity of legal consecration should be seen in Christ's forerunner. HE was the REALITY and PERFECTION of the Nazarite without the symbol, which perished in that living realization of it: "Such an High Priest became us, who was SEPARATE FROM SINNERS" (Heb. 7:26). **filled with the Holy Ghost, from ... womb**—a holy vessel for future service. **16, 17.** A religious and moral *reformer,* Elijah-like, he should be (Mal. 4:6, where the "turning of the people's heart to the Lord" is borrowed from I Kings 18:37). In both cases their success, though great, was *partial*—the *nation* was not gained. **17. before him**—before "the Lord their God" (vs. 16). By comparing this with Malachi 3:1 and Isaiah 40:3, it is plainly "Jehovah" in the flesh of Messiah [CALVIN and OLSHAUSEN] before whom John was to go as a *herald* to announce His approach, and a *pioneer* to prepare His way. **in the spirit**—after the model. **and power of Elias**—not his miraculous power, for "John did no miracle" (John 10:41), but his power in "turning the heart," or with like success in his

ministry. Both fell on degenerate times; both witnessed fearlessly for God; neither appeared much save in the direct exercise of their ministry; both were at the head of schools of disciples; the success of both was similar. **fathers to the children**—taken *literally,* this denotes the *restoration of parental fidelity* [MEYER and others], the decay of which is the beginning of religious and social corruption—one prominent feature of the coming revival being put for the whole. But what follows, explanatory of this, rather suggests a *figurative* sense. If "the disobedient" be "the children," and to "the fathers" belongs "the wisdom of the just" [BENGEL], the meaning will be, "he shall bring back the ancient spirit of the nation into their degenerate children" [CALVIN, etc.]. So Elijah invoked *"the God of Abraham, Isaac, and Israel,"* when seeking to "turn their heart back again" (I Kings 18:36, 37). **to make ready ...**—more clearly, "to make ready for the Lord a prepared people," to have in readiness a people prepared to welcome Him. Such preparation requires, in every age *and every soul,* an operation corresponding to the Baptist's ministry. **18. whereby ...**—Mary believed what was far harder without a sign. Abraham, though older, and doubtless Sarah, too, when the same promise was made to him, "staggered not at the promise of God through unbelief, but was strong in faith, giving glory to God." This was that in which Zacharias failed. **19. Gabriel**—signifying "man of God," the same who appeared to Daniel at the time of incense (Dan. 9:21) and to Mary (vs. 26). **stand, ...**—as his attendant (cf. I Kings 17:1). **20. dumb**—speechless. **not able**—deprived of the power of speech (vs. 64). He asked a *sign,* and now he got it. **until the day ...**—See on vs. 64. **21. waited**—to receive from him the usual benediction (Num. 6:23-27). **tarried so long**—It was not usual to tarry long, lest it should be thought vengeance had stricken the people's representative for something wrong [LIGHTFOOT]. **22. speechless**—dumb, and deaf also (see vs. 62). **24. hid five months**—till the event was put beyond doubt and became apparent.

26-38. ANNUNCIATION OF CHRIST. (See on Matt. 1:18-21.) **26. sixth month**—of Elisabeth's time. **Joseph, of the house of David**—(See on Matthew 1: 16). **28. highly favoured**—a word only once used elsewhere (Eph. 1:6, "made accepted"): cf. vs. 30, "Thou hast found favour with God." The mistake of the *Vulgate's* rendering, "full of grace," has been taken abundant advantage of by the Romish Church. As the mother of our Lord, she was the most "blessed among women" in external distinction; but let them listen to the Lord's own words. "Nay, rather blessed are they that hear the word of God and keep it." (See on ch. 11:27.) **31. The** angel purposely conforms his language to Isaiah's famous prophecy (ch. 7:14) [CALVIN]. **32, 33.** This is but an echo of the sublime prediction in Isaiah 9:6, 7. **34. How ...**—not the unbelief of Zacharias, "Whereby shall I know this?" but, taking the fact for granted, *"How is it to be,* so contrary to the unbroken law of human birth?" Instead of reproof, therefore, her question is answered in mysterious detail. **35. Holy Ghost**—(See on Matthew 1:18). **power of the highest**—the immediate energy of the Godhead conveyed by the Holy Ghost. **overshadow**—a word suggesting how gentle, while yet efficacious, would be this Power [BENGEL]; and its mysterious secrecy, withdrawn, as if by a cloud, from human scrutiny [CALVIN]. **that holy thing born of thee**—that holy Offspring of thine. **therefore ... Son of God**—That Christ is the Son of God in His divine and eternal nature is clear from all the New Testament; yet here we see that Sonship efflorescing into human and palpable manifestation by His being born, through "the power of the Highest," an Infant of days. We must neither think of a *double* Sonship, as some do, harshly and without all ground, nor deny what is here plainly expressed, the connection between His human birth and His proper personal Sonship. **36. thy cousin**—"relative," but how near the word says not. **conceived . . .**—This was to Mary an *unsought* sign, in reward of her faith. **37. For . . .**—referring to what was said by the angel to Abraham in like case (Gen. 18:14), to strengthen her faith. **38.** Marvellous faith in *such* circumstances!

39-56. **VISIT OF MARY TO ELISABETH. 39. hill country**—the mountainous tract running along the middle of Judea, from north to south [WEBSTER and WILKINSON]. **with haste**—transported with the announcement to herself and with the tidings, now first made known to her, of Elisabeth's condition. **a city of Juda**—probably Hebron (see Josh. 20:7; 21:11). **40. saluted Elisabeth**—now returned from her seclusion (vs. 24). **41. babe leaped**—From vs. 44 it is plain that this maternal sensation was something extraordinary—a sympathetic emotion of the unconscious babe, at the presence of the mother of his Lord. **42-44.** What beautiful superiority to *envy* have we here! High as was the distinction conferred upon herself, Elisabeth loses sight of it altogether, in presence of one more honored still; upon whom, with her unborn Babe, in an ecstasy of inspiration, she pronounces a benediction, feeling it to be a wonder unaccountable that the mother of her Lord should come to *her*." "Turn this as we will, we shall never be able to see the propriety of calling an unborn child "Lord," but by supposing Elisabeth, like the prophets of old, enlightened to perceive the Messiah's *Divine nature*" [OLSHAUSEN]. "The mother of *my Lord*"—but not *"My Lady"* (cf. ch. 20:42; John 20:28) [BENGEL]. **45.** An additional benediction on the Virgin for her implicit faith, in tacit and delicate contrast with her own husband. **for . . .**—rather, as in the margin, "that." **46-55.** A magnificent canticle, in which the strain of Hannah's ancient song, in like circumstances, is caught up, and just slightly modified and sublimed. Is it unnatural to suppose that the spirit of the blessed Virgin had been drawn beforehand into mysterious sympathy with the ideas and the tone of this hymn, so that when the life and fire of inspiration penetrated her whole soul it spontaneously swept the chorus of this song, enriching the Hymnal of the Church with that spirit-stirring canticle which has resounded ever since from its temple walls? In both songs, those holy women, filled with wonder to behold "the proud, the mighty, the rich," passed by, and, in their persons the lowliest chosen to usher in the greatest events, sing of this as no capricious movement, but *a great law of the kingdom of God,* by which He delights to *"put down the mighty from their seats and exalt them of low degree."* In both songs the strain dies away under CHRIST; in Hannah's under the name of "Jehovah's King"—to whom, through all His line, from David onwards to Himself, He will "give strength"; His "Anointed," whose horn He will exalt (I Sam. 2:10); in the Virgin's song, it is as the "Help" promised to Israel by all the prophets. **My soul . . . my spirit**—"all that is within me" (Ps. 103:1). **47. my Saviour**—Mary, poor heart, never dreamt, we see, of her own "immaculate conception"—in the offensive language of the Romanists—any more than of her

own immaculate life. **54. holpen**—Cf. Psalm 89:19, "I have laid *help* on One that is mighty." **55. As he spake to our fathers**—*The sense requires this clause to be read as a parenthesis.* (Cf. Mic. 7:20; Ps. 98:3.) **for ever**—the perpetuity of Messiah's kingdom, as expressly promised by the angel (vs. 33). **56. abode with her about three months**—What an honored roof was that which, for such a period, overarched these cousins! and yet not a trace of it is now to be seen, while the progeny of those two women—the one but the honored pioneer of the other—have made the world new. **returned to her own house**—at Nazareth, *after which took place what is recorded in* Matthew 1:18-25.

57-80. **BIRTH AND CIRCUMCISION OF JOHN—SONG OF ZACHARIAS, AND PROGRESS OF THE CHILD. 59. eighth day**—The law (Gen. 17:12) was observed, even though the eighth day after birth should be a sabbath (John 7:23; and see Phil. 3:5). **called him**—lit., "were calling"—i.e., (as we should say) "were for calling." The *naming* of children at baptism has its origin in the Jewish custom at circumcision (Gen. 21:3, 4); and the names of Abram and Sarai were changed at its first performance (Gen. 17:5, 15). **62. made signs**—showing he was deaf, as well as dumb. **63. marvelled all**—at his giving the same name, not knowing of any communication between them on the subject. **64. mouth opened immediately**—on thus palpably showing his full faith in the vision, for disbelieving which he had been struck dumb (vss. 13, 20). **65. fear**—religious awe; under the impression that God's hand was specially in these events (cf. ch. 5:26; 7:16; 8:37). **66. hand of the Lord was with him**—by special tokens marking him out as one destined to some great work (I Kings 18:46; II Kings 3:15; Acts 11:21). **68-79.** There is not a word in this noble burst of divine song about his own child; like Elisabeth losing sight entirely of self, in the glory of a Greater than both. **Lord God of Israel**—the ancient covenant God of the peculiar people. **visited and redeemed**—i.e., in order to redeem: returned after long absence, and broken His long silence (see on Matt. 15:31). In the Old Testament, God is said to "visit" chiefly for *judgment,* in the New Testament for *mercy.* Zacharias would, as yet, have but imperfect views of such "visiting and redeeming," "saving from and delivering out of the hand of enemies" (vss. 71, 74). But this Old Testament phraseology, used at first with a *lower* reference, is, when viewed in the light of a loftier and more comprehensive kingdom of God, equally adapted to express the most spiritual conceptions of the redemption that is in Christ Jesus. **69. horn of salvation**—i.e., "strength of salvation," or "mighty Salvation," meaning the Saviour Himself, whom Simeon calls "Thy Salvation" (ch. 2:30). The metaphor is taken from those animals whose *strength* is in their *horns* (Ps. 18:2; 75:10; 132:17). **house of . . . David**—This shows *that Mary must have been known to be of the royal line,* independent of Joseph; of whom Zacharias, if he knew anything, could not know that after this he would recognize Mary. **70. since the world began**—or, "from the earliest period." **72. the mercy promised . . . his holy covenant . . . 73. the oath . . . to . . . Abraham**—The whole work and kingdom of Messiah is represented as a mercy pledged on oath to Abraham and his seed, to be realized at an appointed period; and at length, in "the fulness of the time," gloriously made good. Hence, not only *"grace,"* or the *thing* promised; but *"truth,"* or *fidelity* to the promise, are said to "come by Jesus Christ" (John 1:17). **74. that he would** grant us... How comprehensive is the view here given! (1) The *purpose* of all redemption—"that we should *serve* Him"—i.e., "the Lord God of Israel" (vs. 68). The word signifies *religious* service distinctively—"the *priesthood* of the New Testament" [BENGEL]. (2) The *nature* of this service— "in holiness and righteousness before Him"—or, as in His presence (cf. Ps. 56:13). (3) Its *freedom*— "being delivered out of the hand of our enemies." (4) Its *fearlessness*—"might serve Him without fear." (5) Its *duration*—"all the days of our life." **76-79.** Here are the dying echoes of this song; and very beautiful are these closing notes—like the setting sun, shorn indeed of its noontide radiance, but skirting the horizon with a wavy and quivering light—as of molten gold—on which the eye delights to gaze, till it disappears from the view. The song passes not here from Christ to John, but only from Christ direct to Christ as heralded by His forerunner. **76. thou child**—not "my son"—this child's relation to himself being lost in his relation to a Greater than either. **prophet of the Highest; for thou shalt go before him**—i.e., "the Highest." As "the Most High" is an epithet in Scripture only of *the supreme God,* it is inconceivable that inspiration should apply this term, as here undeniably, to Christ, unless He were "God over all blessed for ever" (Rom. 9:5). **77. to give knowledge of salvation**—To sound the note of a *needed* and *provided* "salvation" was the noble office of John, above all that preceded him; as it is that of all subsequent ministers of Christ; but infinitely loftier was it to be the "Salvation" itself (vs. 69 and ch. 2:30). **by the remission of... sins**—This stamps at once the *spiritual* nature of the salvation here intended, and explains vss. 71, 74. **78. Through the tender mercy...**—the sole spring, necessarily, of all salvation for sinners. **dayspring from on high...**—either *Christ Himself,* as the "Sun of righteousness" (Mal. 4:2), arising on a dark world [BEZA, GROTIUS, CALVIN, DE WETTE, OLSHAUSEN, etc.], or the light which He sheds. The sense, of course, is one. **79.** (Cf. Isa. 9:2; Matt. 4:13-17.) "That St. Luke, of all the Evangelists, should have obtained and recorded these inspired utterances of Zacharias and Mary—is in accordance with his character and habits, as indicated in vss. 1-4" [WEBSTER and WILKINSON]. **80. And the child...**—"a concluding paragraph, indicating, in strokes full of grandeur, the bodily and mental development of the Baptist; and bringing his life up to the period of his public appearance" [OLSHAUSEN]. **in the deserts**—probably "the wilderness of Judea" (Matt. 3:1), whither he had retired early in life, in the *Nazarite* spirit, and where, free from rabbinical influences and alone with God, his spirit would be educated, like Moses in the desert, for his future high vocation. **his showing unto Israel**—the presentation of himself before his nation, as Messiah's forerunner.

CHAPTER 2

Vss. 1-7. BIRTH OF CHRIST. **1. Cæsar Augustus** —the first of the Roman emperors. **all the world**— so the vast Roman Empire was termed. **taxed**— enrolled, or register themselves. **2. first... when Cyrenius...**—a very perplexing verse, inasmuch as Cyrenius, or Quirinus, appears not to have been governor of Syria for about ten years after the birth of Christ, and the "taxing" under his administration was what led to the insurrection mentioned in

Acts 5:37. That there *was* a taxing, however, of the whole Roman Empire under Augustus, is now admitted by all; and candid critics, even of skeptical tendency, are ready to allow that there is not likely to be any real inaccuracy in the statement of our Evangelist. Many superior scholars would render the words thus, "This registration was *previous* to Cyrenius being governor of Syria"—as the word "first" is rendered in John 1:15; 15:18. In this case, of course, the difficulty vanishes. But it is perhaps better to suppose, with others, that the registration may have been ordered with a view to the taxation, about the time of our Lord's birth, though the taxing itself—an obnoxious measure in Palestine—was not carried out till the time of Quirinus. **3. went.. to his own city**—the city of his *extraction,* according to the Jewish custom, not of his *abode,* which was the usual Roman method. **4, 5.** Not only does Joseph, who was of the royal line, go to Bethlehem (I Samuel 16:1), but Mary too—not from choice surely in her condition, but, probably, for personal enrolment, as herself an heiress. **5. espoused wife**—now, without doubt, taken home to him, as related in Matthew 1:18; 25: 6. **6. while... there...**—Mary had up to this time been living at the wrong place for Messiah's birth. A little longer stay at Nazareth, and the prophecy would have failed. But lo! with no intention certainly on her part, much less of Cæsar Augustus, to fulfil the prophecy, she is brought from Nazareth to Bethlehem, and at that nick of time her period arrives, and her Babe is born (Ps. 118:23). "Every creature walks blindfold; only He that dwells in light knows whether they go" [BISHOP HALL]. **7. first-born**—So Matthew 1:25, 26; yet the law, in speaking of the first-born, regardeth not whether any were born *after* or no, but only that none were born *before* [LIGHTFOOT]. **wrapt him... laid him** —The mother herself did so. Had she then none to help her? It would seem so (II Cor. 8:9). **a manger**—the manger, the bench to which the horses' heads were tied, on which their food could rest [WEBSTER and WILKINSON]. **no room in the inn**— a square erection, open inside, where travellers put up, and whose rear parts were used as stables. The ancient tradition, that our Lord was born in a grotto or cave, is quite consistent with this, the country being rocky. In Mary's condition the journey would be a slow one, and ere they arrived, the inn would be fully occupied—affecting anticipation of the reception He was throughout to meet with (John 1:11).

> Wrapt in His swaddling-bands,
> And in His manger laid,
> The hope and glory of all lands
> Is come to the world's aid.
> No peaceful home upon His cradle smiled,
> Guests rudely went and came where slept the
> royal Child.
> KEBLE

But some "guests went and came" *not* "rudely," but reverently. God sent visitors of His own to pay court to the newborn King.
8-20. ANGELIC ANNUNCIATION TO THE SHEPHERDS —THEIR VISIT TO THE NEWBORN BABE. **8. abiding in the fields**—staying there, probably in huts or tents. **watch... by night**—or, night watches, taking their turn of watching. From about passover-time in April until autumn, the flocks pastured constantly in the open fields, the shepherds lodging there all that time. (From this it seems plain that the period

of the year usually assigned to our Lord's birth is too late.) Were these shepherds chosen to have the first sight of the blessed Babe without any respect of their own state of mind? That, at least, is not God's way. "No doubt, like Simeon (vs. 25), they were among the waiters for the Consolation of Israel" [OLSHAUSEN]; and, if the simplicity of their rustic minds, their quiet occupation, the stillness of the midnight hours, and the amplitude of the deep blue vault above them for the heavenly music which was to fill their ear, pointed them out as fit recipients for the first tidings of an Infant Saviour, the congenial meditations and conversations by which, we may suppose, they would beguile the tedious hours would perfect their preparation for the unexpected visit. Thus was Nathanael engaged, all alone but not unseen, under the fig tree, in unconscious preparation for his first interview with Jesus. (See on John 1:48.) So was the rapt seer on his lonely rock "in the spirit on the Lord's Day," little thinking that this was his preparation for hearing behind him the trumpet-voice of the Son of man (Rev. 1:10, etc.). But if the shepherds in His immediate neighborhood had the *first,* the sages from afar had the *next* sight of the newborn King. Even so still, simplicity first, science next, finds its way to Christ, whom

In quiet ever and in shade
Shepherds and Sage may find—
They, who have bowed untaught to Nature's sway,
And they, who follow Truth along her star-pav'd
way.
KEBLE

9. glory of the Lord—"the brightness or glory which is represented as encompassing all heavenly visions" [OLSHAUSEN]. **sore afraid**—So it ever was (Dan. 10:7, 8; Luke 1:12; Rev. 1:17). Men have never felt easy with the invisible world laid suddenly open to their gaze. It was never meant to be permanent; a momentary purpose was all it was intended to serve. **10. to all people**—"to the whole people," i.e., of Israel; to be by them afterwards opened up to the whole world. (See on vs. 14.) **11. unto you is born . . .**—you shepherds, Israel, mankind [BENGEL]. Cf. Isaiah 9:6, "Unto us a Child is born." It is a *birth*—"The Word is *made flesh.*" When? *"This day."* Where? *"In the city of David"*—in the right *line* and at the right *spot;* where prophecy bade us look for Him, and faith accordingly expected Him. How dear to us should be these *historic moorings* of our faith! With the loss of them, all substantial Christianity is lost. By means of them how many have been kept from making shipwreck, and attained to a certain external admiration of Him, ere yet they have fully "beheld His glory." **a Saviour**—not One who *shall* be a Saviour, but *"born a Saviour."* **Christ the Lord**—"magnificent appellation!" [BENGEL]. "This is the only place where these words come together; and I see no way of understanding this "Lord" but as corresponding to the Hebrew JEHOVAH" [ALFORD]. **12. a sign**—"the sign." **the babe**—"a Babe." **a manger**—"the manger." The sign was to consist, it seems, solely in the overpowering *contrast* between the things just said of Him and the lowly condition in which they would find Him— Him whose goings forth have been from of old, from everlasting, "ye shall find a Babe"; whom the heaven of heavens cannot contain, "wrapt in swaddling-bands"; the "Saviour, Christ the Lord," lying in a manger! Thus early were these amazing

contrasts, which are His chosen style, held forth. (See II Cor. 8:9.) **13. suddenly**—as if only waiting till their fellow had done. **with the angel**—who retires not, but is joined by others, come to seal and to celebrate the tidings he has brought. **heavenly host**—or "army," an *army* celebrating *peace!* [BENGEL] "transferring the occupation of their exalted station to this poor earth, which so seldom resounds with the pure praise of God" [OLSHAUSEN]; to let it be known how this event is regarded in *heaven* and should be regarded on *earth.* **14. Glory . . .**—brief but transporting hymn—not only in articulate human speech, for our benefit, but in tunable measure, in the form of a Hebrew parallelism of two complete clauses, and a third one only amplifying the second, and so without a connecting "and." The *"glory to God,"* which the newborn "Saviour" was to bring, is the first note of this sublime hymn: to this answers, in the second clause, the *"peace on earth,"* of which He was to be "the Prince" (Isa. 9:6)—probably sung responsively by the celestial choir; while quickly follows the glad echo of this note, probably by a third detachment of the angelic choristers—*"good will to men."* "They say not, glory to God in *heaven,* where angels are, but, using a rare expression, *"in the highest* [heavens]," whither angels aspire not," (Heb. 1:3, 4) [BENGEL]. "Peace" with God is the grand necessity of a fallen world. To bring in this, and all other peace in its train, was the prime errand of the Saviour to this earth, and, along with it, Heaven's whole "good will to men"—the divine complacency—descends to rest upon men, as upon the Son Himself, in whom God is "well-pleased." (Matt. 3:17, the same word as here.) **15. Let us go . . .**—lovely simplicity of devoutness and faith this! They are not taken up with the angels, the glory that invested them, and the lofty strains with which they filled the air. Nor do they say, Let us go and see *if this be true*—they have no misgivings. But "Let us go and see this thing *which is come to pass,* which *the Lord hath made known unto us."* Does not this confirm the view given on vs. 8 of the spirit of these humble men? **16. with haste**—Cf. ch. 1:39; Matthew 28:8 ("did *run*"); John 4:28 ("left her water-pot," as they do their flocks, in a transport). **found Mary . . .**— "mysteriously guided by the Spirit to the right place through the obscurity of the night" [OLSHAUSEN]. **a manger**—*"the* manger," as before. **17. made known abroad**—before their return (vs. 20), and thus were the first evangelists [BENGEL]. **20. glorifying and praising God . . .**—The latter word, used of the song of the angels (vs. 13), and in ch. 19:37, and ch. 24: 53, leads us to suppose that theirs was a song too, probably some canticle from the Psalter—meet vehicle for the swelling emotions of their simple hearts at what "they had *heard* and *seen."*

21. CIRCUMCISION OF CHRIST—Here only recorded, and even here merely alluded to, for the sake of the name then given to the holy Babe, "JESUS," or SAVIOUR (Matt. 1:21; Acts 13:23). Yet in this naming of Him "Saviour," in the act of circumcising Him, which was a symbolical and bloody removal of the body of sin, we have a tacit intimation that they "had need"—as John said of His Baptism— rather to be circumcised by Him "with the circumcision made without hands, in the putting off of the body [of the sins] of the flesh by the circumcision of Christ" (Col. 2:11), and that He only "suffered it to be so, because thus it became Him to fulfil all righteousness" (Matt. 3:15). Still the circumcision of Christ had a profound bearing on His own work

—by few rightly apprehended. For since "he that is circumcised is a *debtor to do the whole law*" (Gal. 5:3), Jesus thus bore about with Him in His very flesh the seal of a voluntary obligation to do the whole law—by Him only possible in the flesh since the fall. And as He was "made under the law" for no ends of His own, but only *"to redeem them that were under the law,*" that we might receive the adoption of sons" (Gal. 4:4, 5), the obedience to which His circumcision pledged Him was a *redeeming obedience*—that of a "Saviour." And, finally, as "Christ hath redeemed us from the curse of the law" by "being made *a curse* for *us*" (Gal. 3:13), we must regard Him, in His circumcision, as brought under a palpable pledge to be *"obedient unto death, even the death of the cross"* (Phil. 2:8). 22-40. PURIFICATION OF THE VIRGIN—PRESENTATION OF THE BABE IN THE TEMPLE—SCENE THERE WITH SIMEON AND ANNA. **22, 24 her purification** —Though the most and best copies read "their," it was the mother only who needed purifying from the legal uncleanness of child-bearing. "The days" of this purification for a male child were forty in all (Lev. 12:2, 4), on the expiry of which the mother was required to offer a lamb for a burnt offering, and a turtledove or a young pigeon for a sin offering. If she could not afford a lamb, the mother had to bring another turtledove or young pigeon; and, if even this was beyond her means, then a portion of fine flour, but without the usual fragrant accompaniments of oil and frankincense, as it represented a sin offering (Lev. 12:6-8; 5:7-11). From the intermediate offering of "a pair of turtledoves or two young pigeons," we gather that Joseph and the Virgin were in poor circumstances (II Cor. 8:9), though not in abject poverty. Being a firstborn male, they "bring him to Jerusalem, to present him to the Lord." All such had been claimed as "holy to the Lord," or set apart to sacred uses, in memory of the deliverance of the first-born of Israel from destruction in Egypt, through the sprinkling of blood (Exod. 13:2). In lieu of these, however, one whole tribe, that of Levi, was accepted, and set apart to occupations exclusively sacred (Num. 3:11-38); and whereas there were 273 fewer Levites than first-born of all Israel on the first reckoning, each of these first-born was to be redeemed by the payment of five shekels, yet not without being *"presented* (or brought) *unto the Lord,*" in token of His rightful claim to them and their service (Num. 3:44-47; 18:15, 16). It was in obedience to this "law of Moses," that the Virgin presented her babe unto the Lord, "in the east gate of the court called Nicanor's Gate, where she herself would be sprinkled by the priest with the blood of her sacrifice [LIGHTFOOT]. By that Babe, in due time, we were to be redeemed, "not with corruptible things as silver and gold, but with the precious blood of Christ" (I Pet. 1:18, 19), and the consuming of the mother's burnt offering, and the sprinkling of her with the blood of her sin offering, were to find their abiding realization in the "living sacrifice" of the Christian mother herself, in the fulness of a "heart sprinkled from an evil conscience," by "the blood which cleanseth from all sin." **25. just**—upright in his moral character. **devout**—of a religious frame of spirit. **waiting for the consolation of Israel**—a beautiful title of the coming Messiah, here intended. **the Holy Ghost was**—supernaturally—**upon him**—Thus was the Spirit, after a dreary absence of nearly 400 years, returning to the Church, to quicken expectation, and prepare for coming events. **26. revealed by the Holy Ghost**—

implying, beyond all doubt, the personality of the Spirit. **should see not death till he had seen**—"sweet antithesis!" [BENGEL]. How would the one sight gild the gloom of the other! He was, probably, by this time, advanced in years. **27, 28.** The Spirit guided him to the temple at the very moment when the Virgin was about to present Him to the Lord. **28. took him up in his arms**—immediately recognizing in the child, with unhesitating certainty, the promised Messiah, without needing Mary to inform him of what had happened to her. [OLSHAUSEN]. The remarkable act of taking the babe in his arms must not be overlooked. It was as if he said, "This is all my salvation and all my desire" (II Sam. 23:5). **29. Lord**—"Master," a word rarely used in the New Testament, and selected here with peculiar propriety, when the aged saint, feeling that his last object in wishing to live had now been attained, only awaited his Master's word of command to "depart." **now lettest...**—more clearly, "now Thou art releasing Thy servant"; a patient yet reverential mode of expressing a desire to depart. **30. seen thy salvation**—Many saw this child, nay, the full-grown "man, Christ Jesus," who never saw in Him "God's Salvation." This estimate of an object of sight, an unconscious, helpless babe, was pure faith. He "beheld His glory" (John 1:14). In another view it was *prior faith* rewarded by *present sight*. **31, 32. all people**—all the peoples, mankind at large. **a light to the Gentiles**—then in thick darkness. **glory of thy people Israel**—already Thine, and now, in the believing portion of it, to be so more gloriously than ever. It will be observed that this "swanlike song, bidding an eternal farewell to this terrestrial life" [OLSHAUSEN], takes a more comprehensive view of the kingdom of Christ than that of Zacharias, though the kingdom they sing of is one. **34, 35. set**—appointed. **fall and rising again of many in Israel, and for a sign spoken against**—Perhaps the former of these phrases expresses the two stages of temporary "fall of many in Israel" through unbelief, during our Lord's earthly career, and the subsequent "rising again" of *the same persons* after the effusion of the Spirit at pentecost threw a new light to them on the whole subject; while the latter clause describes the determined enemies of the Lord Jesus. Such opposite views of Christ are taken from age to age. **35. Yea, ...**—"Blessed as thou art among women, thou shalt have thine own deep share of the struggles and sufferings which this Babe is to occasion"—pointing not only to the continued obloquy and rejection of this Child of hers, those agonies of His which she was to witness at the cross, and her desolate condition thereafter, but to dreadful alternations of faith and unbelief, of hope and fear regarding Him, which she would have to pass through. **that the thoughts...**—Men's views and decisions regarding Christ are a mirror in which the very "thoughts of their hearts" are seen. **36, 37. Anna**—or, Hannah. **a prophetess**—another evidence that "the last times" in which God was to "pour out His Spirit upon all flesh" were at hand. **of the tribe of Aser**—one of the ten tribes, of whom many were not carried captive, and not a few reunited themselves to Judah after the return from Babylon. The distinction of tribes, though practically destroyed by the captivity, was well enough known up to their final dispersion (Rom. 11:1; Heb. 7:14); nor is it now entirely lost. **lived...**—she had lived seven years with her husband, and been a widow eighty-four years; so that if she married at the earliest marriageable age, twelve years, she could not at this time be less than 103 years old. **37. departed not from the temple**—was found there at all stated hours of the day, and even during the night services of the temple watchmen (Ps. 134:1, 2), "serving God with fastings and prayer." (See I Tim. 5:5, suggested by this.) **38. coming in**— "presenting herself." She had been there already but now is found "standing by," as Simeon's testimony to the blessed Babe died away, ready to take it up "in turn" (as the word rendered "likewise" here means). **to all them . . .**—the sense is, "to all them in Jerusalem that were looking for redemption"—saying in effect, In that Babe are wrapt up all your expectations. If this was at the hour of prayer, when numbers flocked to the temple, it would account for her having such an audience as the words imply [ALFORD]. **39.** Nothing is more difficult than to fix the precise order in which the visit of the Magi, with the flight into and return from Egypt (Matt. 2), are to be taken, in relation to the circumcision and presentation of Christ in the temple, here recorded. It is perhaps best to leave this in the obscurity in which we find it, as the result of two independent, though if we knew all, easily reconcilable narratives. **40.** His mental development kept pace with His bodily, and "the grace of God," the divine favor, rested manifestly and increasingly upon Him. See vs. 52.

41-52. FIRST CONSCIOUS VISIT TO JERUSALEM. "Solitary flowered out of the wonderful enclosed garden of the thirty years, plucked precisely there where the swollen bud, at a *distinctive crisis* (at twelve years of age), bursts into flower. To mark that is assuredly the design and the meaning of this record" [STIER]. **42. went up**—"were wont to go." Though males only were required to go up to Jerusalem at the three annual festivals (Exod. 23:14-17), devout women, when family duties permitted, went also, as did Hannah (I Sam. 1:7), and, as we here see, the mother of Jesus. **when twelve years old**—At this age every Jewish boy was styled "a son of the law," being put under a course of instruction and trained to fasting and attendance on public worship, besides being set to learn a trade. At this age accordingly our Lord is taken up for the first time to Jerusalem, at the passover season, the chief of the three annual festivals. But oh, with what thoughts and feelings must this Youth have gone up! Long ere He beheld it, He had doubtless "loved the habitation of God's house and the place where His honor dwelt" (Ps. 26:8), a love nourished, we may be sure, by that "word hid in His heart," with which in afterlife He showed so perfect a familiarity. As the time for His first visit approached, could one's ear have caught the breathings of His young soul, he might have heard Him whispering, "As the hart panteth after the water brooks, so panteth my soul after Thee, O God. The Lord loveth the gates of Zion more than all the dwellings of Jacob. I was glad when they said unto me, Let us go unto the house of the Lord. Our feet shall stand within thy gates, O Jerusalem!" (Ps. 42:1; 87:2; 122:1, 2). On catching the first view of "the city of their solemnities," and high above all in it, "the place of God's rest," we hear Him saying to Himself, "Beautiful for situation, the joy of the whole earth, is Mount Zion, on the sides of the north, the city of the great King: Out of Zion, the perfection of beauty, God doth shine" (Ps. 48:2; 50:2). Of His feelings or actions during all the eight days of the feast not a word is said. As a devout child, in company with its parents, He would go through the services, keeping His thoughts

to Himself. But methinks I hear Him, after the sublime services of that feast, saying to Himself, "He brought me to the banqueting-house, and his banner over me was love. I sat down under his shadow with great delight, and his fruit was sweet to my taste" (Song of Sol. 2:3, 4). **43. as they returned**—If the duties of life must give place to worship, worship, in its turn, must give place to them. *Jerusalem* is good, but *Nazareth* is good, too; let him who neglects the one, on pretext of attending to the other, ponder this scene. **tarried behind . . . Joseph and his mother knew not**—Accustomed to the discretion and obedience of the lad [OLSHAUSEN], they might be thrown off their guard. **44. sought him among their kinsfolk and acquaintances** —On these sacred journeys, whole villages and districts travelled in groups together, partly for protection, partly for company; and as the well-disposed would beguile the tediousness of the way by good discourse, to which the child Jesus would be no silent listener, they expect to find Him in such a group. **45, 46.** After three sorrowing days, they find Him still in Jerusalem, not gazing on its architecture, or surveying its forms of busy life, but in the temple—not the "sanctuary" (as in ch. 1:9), to which only the priests had access, but in some one of the enclosures around it, where the rabbins, or "doctors," taught their scholars. **46. hearing . . . asking**—The method of question and answer was the customary form of rabbinical teaching; teacher and learner becoming by turns questioner and answerer, as may be seen from their extant works. This would give full scope for all that "astonished them in His understanding and answers." Not that He assumed the office of *teaching*—"His hour" for that "was not yet come," and His equipment for that was not complete; for He had yet to "increase in wisdom" as well as "stature" (vs. 52). In fact, the beauty of Christ's example lies very much in His never at one stage of His life anticipating the duties of another. All would be in the style and manner of a learner, "opening His mouth and panting." "His soul breaking for the longing that it had unto God's judgments at all times" (Ps. 119:20), and now more than ever before, when finding Himself for the first time in His Father's house. Still there would be in *His questions* far more than in *their answers*; and if we may take the frivolous interrogatories with which they afterwards plied Him, about the woman that had seven husbands and such like, as a specimen of their present drivelling questions, perhaps we shall not greatly err, if we suppose that "the questions" which He now "asked them" in return were just the germs of those pregnant questions with which He astonished and silenced them in after years: *"What think ye of Christ? Whose Son is He? If David call Him Lord, how is He then his Son?" "Which is the first and great commandment?" "Who is my neighbour?"* **49. about my Father's businesss**—lit., "in" or "at My Fathers," i.e., either "about My Father's *affairs*," or "in My Father's *courts*"—where He dwells and is to be found—*about His hand*, so to speak. This latter shade of meaning, which includes the former, is perhaps the true one, Here He felt Himself *at home*, breathing His own proper air. His words convey a gentle rebuke of their obtuseness in requiring Him to *explain this*. "Once here, thought ye I should so readily hasten away? Let ordinary worshippers be content to keep the feast and be gone; but is this all ye have learnt of Me?" Methinks we are here let into the holy privacies of Nazareth; for what He says they *should* have known, He must have given them *ground* to know. She tells Him of the sorrow with which *His father* and she had sought Him. He speaks of *no Father but one,* saying, in effect, My Father has *not* been seeking Me; I have been with Him all this time; "the King hath brought me into His chambers . . . His left hand is under my head, and His right hand doth embrace me" (Song of Sol. 1:4; 2: 6). How is it that ye do not understand? (Mark 8:21.) **50, 51. understood not**—probably He had never expressly *said* as much, and so confounded them, though it was but the true interpretation of many things which they had seen and heard from Him at home. (See on John 14:4, 5.) But lest it should be thought that now He threw off the filial yoke, and became His own Master henceforth, and theirs too, it is purposely added, "And He went down *with them,* and was *subject unto them.*" The marvel of this condescension lies in its coming after such a scene, and such an assertion of His higher Sonship; and the words are evidently meant to convey this. "From this time we have *no more mention of Joseph.* The next we hear is of his "mother and brethren" (John 2:12); whence it is inferred, that between this time and the commencement of our Lord's public life, *Joseph died*" [ALFORD], having now served the double end of being the protector of our Lord's Virgin-mother, and affording Himself the opportunity of presenting a matchless pattern of subjection to both parents. **52.** See on vs. 40. **stature**—or better, perhaps, as in the margin, "age," which implies the other. This is all the record we have of the next eighteen years of that wondrous life. What seasons of tranquil meditation over the lively oracles, and holy fellowship with His Father; what inlettings, on the one hand, of light, and love, and power from on high, and outgoings of filial supplication, freedom, love, and joy on the other, would these eighteen years contain! And would they not seem "but a few days" if they were so passed, however ardently He might long to be more directly "about His Father's business?"

CHAPTER 3

Vss. 1-20. PREACHING, BAPTISM, AND IMPRISONMENT OF JOHN. See on Matthew 3:1-12; Mark 6: 17, etc. **1, 2.** Here the curtain of the New Testament is, as it were, drawn up, and the greatest of all epochs of the Church commences. Even our Lord's own age ˈ(vs. 23) is determined by it [BENGEL]. No such elaborate chronological precision is to be found elsewhere in the New Testament, and it comes fitly from him who claims it as the peculiar recommendation of his Gospel, that he had "accurately traced down all things from the first" (ch. 1:3). Here, evidently, commences his proper narrative. **the fifteenth year of Tiberius**—reckoning from the period when he was admitted, three years before Augustus' death, to a share of the empire [WEBSTER and WILKINSON], about the end of the year of Rome 779, or about four years before the usual reckoning. **Pilate . . . governor of Judea**—His proper title was *Procurator,* but with more than the usual powers of that office. After holding it about ten years he was ordered to Rome, to answer to charges brought against him, but ere he arrived Tiberius died (A.D. 35), and soon after Pilate committed suicide. **Herod**—(See on Mark 6:14). **Philip**—a different and very superior Philip to the one whose wife Herodias went to live with Herod Antipas. (See Mark 6:17.) **Iturea**—to the

northeast of Palestine; so called from Ishmael's son *Itur* or *Jetur* (I Chron. 1:31), and anciently belonging to the half tribe of Manasseh. **Trachonitis**—farther to the northeast, between Iturea and Damascus; a rocky district, infested by robbers, and committed by Augustus to Herod the Great to keep in order. **Abilene**—still more to the northeast, so called from *Abila,* eighteen miles from Damascus [ROBINSON]. **7. Annas and Caiaphas . . . high priests** —the former, though deposed, retained much of his influence, and, probably, as *sagan* or deputy, exercised much of the power of the high priesthood along with Caiaphas (John 18:13; Acts 4:6). Both Zadok and Abiathar acted as high priests in David's time (II Sam. 15:35), and it seems to have become the fixed practice to have two (II Kings 25: 18). **word of God came unto John**—*Such formulas, of course, are never used when speaking of Jesus,* because the divine nature manifested itself in Him not at certain isolated moments of His life. *He was the one everlasting manifestation of the Godhead*—THE WORD [OLSHAUSEN]. **5. every valley . . .** —*levelling* and *smoothing,* obvious figures, the sense of which is in the first words of the proclamation, *"Prepare ye the way of the Lord."* **6. all flesh . . .**—(quoted literally from the Septuagint of Isa. 40:5). The idea is that every obstruction shall be so removed as to reveal to the whole world the Salvation of God in Him whose name is the "Saviour" (cf. Ps. 98:3; Isa. 11:10; 49:6; 52:10; Luke 2:31, 32; Acts 13:47). **10-14. What shall we do then?**—to show the sincerity of our repentance. **11. two coats . . .**—directed against the reigning *avarice.* **12. publicans . . . 13. Exact no more . . .** —directed against that *extortion* which made the publicans a byword. (See on ch. 19:2, 8.) **14. soldiers . . . Do violence to none**—The word signifies to "shake thoroughly," and so to "intimidate," probably in order to extort money or other property. **accuse . . . falsely**—acting as informers vexatiously, on frivolous or false grounds. **content with your wages**—"rations." We may take this as a warning against mutiny, which the officers attempted to suppress by largesses and donations [WEBSTER and WILKINSON]. And thus the "fruits" which would evidence their repentance were just resistance to the reigning sins, particularly of the *class* to which the penitent belonged, and the manifestation of an opposite spirit. **15-17. whether he were the Christ**—showing both how successful he had been in awakening the expectation of Messiah's immediate appearing, and the high estimation, and even reverence, which his own character commanded. **16. John answered . . .**—either to the deputation from Jerusalem (see John 1:19, etc.), or on some other occasion, simply to remove impressions derogatory to his blessed Master which he knew to be taking hold of the popular mind. **saying unto them all, . . .**—in solemn protestation. So far from entertaining such a thought as laying claim to the honors of Messiahship, the meanest services I can render to that "Mightier than I that is coming after me," are too high an honor for me. Beautiful spirit, distinguishing this servant of Christ throughout! **one mightier than I**—"the Mighter than I." **18. many other things, . . .**—such as we read in John 1:29, 33, 34; 3:27-36. **19, 20. but Herod . . .**—See on Mark 6:14, etc. **and for all the evils which Herod had done**—important fact here only mentioned, showing how *thoroughgoing* was the fidelity of the Baptist to his royal hearer, and how strong must have been the workings of conscience in that slave of passion when, notwithstanding such plainness, he "did many things and heard John gladly" (Mark 6:20, 26).

21, 22. BAPTISM OF AND DESCENT OF THE SPIRIT UPON JESUS. See on Matthew 3:13-17. **21. when all the people were baptized**—that He might not seem to be merely one of the crowd. Thus, as He rode into Jerusalem upon an ass, *"whereon yet never man sat"* (ch. 19:30), and lay in a sepulchre *"wherein was never man yet laid"* (John 19:41), so in His baptism He would be *"separate from sinners."*

23-38. GENEALOGY OF JESUS. **23. he began to be about thirty**—i.e., "was about entering on His thirtieth year." So our translators have taken the word [and so CALVIN, BEZA, BLOOMFIELD, WEBSTER and WILKINSON, etc.]: but "was about thirty years of age when He began (His ministry)," makes better Greek, and is probably the true sense [BENGEL, OLSHAUSEN, DE WETTE, MEYER, ALFORD, etc.]. At this age the priests entered on their office (Num. 4: 3). **being, as was supposed, the son of Joseph . . .** —Have we in this genealogy, as well as in Matthew's, the line of *Joseph?* or is this the line of *Mary?*—a point on which there has been great difference of opinion and much acute discussion. Those who take the *former* opinion contend that it is the natural sense of this verse, and that no other would have been thought of but for its supposed improbability and the uncertainty which it seems to throw over our Lord's real descent. But it is liable to another difficulty; viz., that in this case Matthew makes *"Jacob,"* while Luke makes *"Heli,"* to be Joseph's father; and though the same man had often more than one name, we ought not to resort to that supposition, in such a case as this, without necessity. And then, though the descent of Mary from David would be liable to no real doubt, even though we had no table of her line preserved to us (see, for example, ch. 1:2-32, and on ch. 2:5), still it does seem unlikely—we say not incredible—that two genealogies of our Lord should be preserved to us, neither of which gives his *real* descent. Those who take the *latter* opinion, that we have here the line of *Mary*, as in Matthew that of *Joseph*—here His *real*, there His *reputed* line—explain the statement about Joseph, that he was *"the son* of Heli," to mean that he was his *son-in-law,* as the husband of his daughter Mary (as in Ruth 1:11, 12), and believe that Joseph's name is only introduced instead of Mary's, in conformity with the Jewish custom in such tables. Perhaps this view is attended with fewest difficulties, as it certainly is the best supported. However we decide, it is a satisfaction to know that not a doubt was thrown out by the bitterest of the early enemies of Christianity as to *our Lord's real descent from David.* On comparing the two genealogies, it will be found that Matthew, writing more immediately for *Jews,* deemed it enough to show that the Saviour was sprung from Abraham and David; whereas Luke, writing more immediately for *Gentiles,* traces the descent back to Adam, the parent stock of the whole human family, thus showing Him to be the promised "Seed of the woman." "The possibility of constructing such a table, comprising a period of thousands of years, in an uninterrupted line from father to son, of a family that dwelt for a long time in the utmost retirement, would be inexplicable, had not the members of this line been endowed with *a thread* by which they could extricate themselves from the many families into which every tribe and branch was again subdivided, and thus hold fast and know *the* member that was destined to con-

tinue the lineage. This thread was the hope that Messiah would be born of the race of Abraham and David. The ardent desire to behold Him and be partakers of His mercy and glory suffered not the attention to be exhausted through a period embracing thousands of years. Thus the member destined to continue the lineage, whenever doubtful, became easily distinguishable, awakening the hope of a final fulfilment, and keeping it alive until it was consummated" [OLSHAUSEN]. **24-30. son of Matthat, . . .**—(See on Matt. 1:13-15). In vs. 27, Salathiel is called the *son,* while in Matthew 1:12, he is called the *father* of Zerubbabel. But they are probably different persons. **38. son of God**—Cf. Acts 17:28.

CHAPTER 4

Vss. 1-13. TEMPTATION OF CHRIST.—See on Matthew 4:1-11.

14-32. JESUS, ENTERING ON HIS PUBLIC MINISTRY, MAKES A CIRCUIT OF GALILEE—REJECTION AT NAZARETH. *N.B.*—A large gap here occurs, embracing the important transactions in Galilee and Jerusalem which are recorded in John 1:29 to 4:54, and which occurred *before* John's imprisonment (John 3:24); whereas the transactions here recorded occurred (as appears from Matt. 4:12, 13) *after* that event. The visit to Nazareth recorded in Matthew 13:54-58 (and Mark 6:1-6) we take to be not a later visit, but the same with this first one; because we cannot think that the Nazarenes, after being so enraged at His *first* display of wisdom as to attempt His destruction, should, on a *second* display of the same, wonder at it and ask how He came by it, as if they had never witnessed it before. **16. as his custom was**—Cf. Acts 17:2. **stood up for to read**—Others besides rabbins were allowed to address the congregation. (See Acts 13:15.) **18, 19.** To have fixed on any passage announcing His *sufferings* (as Isaiah 53), would have been unsuitable at that early stage of His ministry. But He selects a passage announcing the sublime object of His whole mission, its divine character, and His special endowments for it; expressed in the first person, and so singularly adapted to *the first opening of the mouth* in His prophetic capacity, that it seems as if made expressly for this occasion. It is from the well-known section of Isaiah's prophecies whose burden is that mysterious "SERVANT OF THE LORD," despised of man, abhorred of the nation, but before whom kings on seeing Him are to arise, and princes to worship; in visage more marred than any man and His form than the sons of men, yet sprinkling many nations; laboring seemingly in vain, and spending His strength for naught and in vain, yet Jehovah's Servant to raise up the tribes of Jacob and be His Salvation to the ends of the earth (Isa. 49, etc.). The quotation is chiefly from the Septuagint version, used in the synagogues. **19. acceptable year**—an allusion to the jubilee year (Lev. 25:10), a year of universal *release* for person and property. (See also Isa. 49:8; II Cor. 6:2.) As the maladies under which humanity groans are here set forth under the names of *poverty, brokenheartedness, bondage, blindness, bruisedness* (or *crushedness*), so, as the glorious HEALER of all these maladies, Christ announces Himself in the act of reading it, stopping the quotation just before it comes to "the day of vengeance," which was only to come on the rejecters of His message (John 3: 17). The first words, "THE SPIRIT OF THE LORD is upon ME," have been noted since the days of the Church Fathers, as an illustrious example of *Father, Son, and Holy Ghost* being exhibited as in distinct yet harmonious action in the scheme of salvation. **20. the minister**—the *chazan* or synagogue-officer. **all eyes ... fastened on Him**—astounded at His putting in such claims. **21. began to say ...**—His whole address was just a detailed application to Himself of this and perhaps other like prophecies. **22. gracious words**—"the words of grace," referring both to the richness of His matter and the sweetness of His manner (Ps. 45:2). **Is not this ...**—(See on Matt. 13:54-56). They knew He had received no rabbinical education, and anything *supernatural* they seemed incapable of conceiving. **23. this proverb**—like our "Charity begins at home." **whatsoever ...**—"Strange rumors have reached our ears of Thy doings at Capernaum; but if such power resides in Thee to cure the ills of humanity, why has none of it yet come nearer home, and why is all this alleged power reserved for strangers?" His choice of Capernaum as a place of residence since entering on public life was, it seems, already well known at Nazareth; and when He did come thither, to give no displays of His power when distant places were ringing with His fame, wounded their pride. He had indeed "laid his hands on a few sick folk and healed them" (Mark 6:5); but this seems to have been done quite privately the general unbelief precluding anything more open. **24. And he said ...**—Her replies to the one proverb by another, equally familiar, which we express in a rougher form—"Too much familiarity breeds contempt." Our Lord's long residence in Nazareth merely as a townsman had made Him *too common*, incapacitating them for appreciating Him as others did who were *less familiar with His everyday demeanor in private life*. A most important principle, to which the wise will pay due regard. (See also Matt. 7:6, on which our Lord Himself ever acted.) **25-27. But I tell you ...**—falling back for support on the well-known examples of Elijah and Elisha (Eliseus), whose miraculous power, passing by those who were *near*, expended itself on those *at a distance*, yea on *heathens*, "the two great prophets who stand at the commencement of prophetic antiquity, and whose miracles strikingly prefigured those of our Lord. As He intended like them to feed the poor and cleanse the lepers, He *points to these miracles of mercy*, and not to the *fire* from heaven and the *bears* that tore the mockers" [STIER]. **three years and six months**—So James 5:17, including perhaps the six months *after the last fall of rain*, when there would be little or none at any rate; whereas in I Kings 18:1, which says the rain returned "in the third year," that period is probably not reckoned. **26, 27. save ... saving**—"but only." (Cf. Mark 13: 32, *Greek*.) **Sarepta**—"Zarephath" (I Kings 17:9), a heathen village between Tyre and Sidon. (See Mark 7:24.) **28, 29. when they heard these things** —these allusions to the *heathen*, just as afterwards with Paul (Acts 22:21, 22). **rose up**—broke up the service irreverently and rushed forth. **thrust him** —with violence, as a prisoner in their hands. **brow ...**—Nazareth, though not built on the ridge of a hill, is in part surrounded by one to the west, having several such precipices. (See II Chron. 25:12; II Kings 9:33.) It was a mode of capital punishment not unusual among the Romans and others. This was the first insult which the Son of God received, and it came from "them of His own household!" (Matt. 10:36.) **30. passing through the**

midst ...—evidently in a miraculous way, though perhaps quite noiselessly, leading them to wonder afterwards what spell could have come over them, that they allowed Him to escape. (Similar escapes, however, in times of persecution, are not unexampled.) **31. down to Capernaum**—It lay on the Sea of Galilee (Matt. 4:13), whereas Nazareth lay high.

33-37. DEMONIAC HEALED. unclean—The frequency with which this character of *impurity* is applied to evil spirits is worthy of notice. **cried out ...**—(See on Matt. 8:29; Mark 3:11). **35. rebuked them ...**—(see on vs. 41). **thrown him ...** —see on Mark 9:20. **36. What a word**—a word from the *Lord of spirits*.

38-41. PETER'S MOTHER-IN-LAW, AND MANY OTHERS, HEALED. See on Matt. 8:14-17. **41. suffered them not to speak**—The marginal reading here is wrong. Our Lord ever refused testimony from devils, *for the very reason why they were eager to give it*, because He and they would thus seem to be one interest, as His enemies actually alleged. (See on Matt. 12:24, etc.; see also Acts 16:16-18.)

42-44. JESUS, SOUGHT OUT AT MORNING PRAYER, AND ENTREATED TO STAY, DECLINES FROM THE URGENCY OF HIS WORK. See on Mark 1:35-39, where we learn how early He retired, and how He was engaged in solitude when they came seeking Him. **47. stayed him**—"were staying Him," or sought to do it. What a contrast to the Gadarenes! The nature of His mission required Him to keep moving, that all might hear the glad tidings (Matt. 8:34). **43. I must ...**—but duty only could move Him to deny entreaties so grateful to His spirit.

CHAPTER 5

Vss. 1-11. MIRACULOUS DRAUGHT OF FISHES— CALL OF PETER, JAMES, AND JOHN. Not their *first* call, however, recorded in John 1:35-42; nor their *second*, recorded in Matthew 4:18-22; but their *third* and last before their appointment to the apostleship. That these calls were all distinct and *progressive*, seems quite plain. (Similar stages are observable in other eminent servants of Christ.) **3. taught ... out of the ship**—See on Matthew 13: 2). **4. for a draught**—munificent recompense for the use of his boat. **5. Master**—betokening not surely a first acquaintance, but a relationship already formed. **all night**—the usual time of fishing then (John 21:3), and even now Peter, as a fisherman, knew how hopeless it was to "let down his net" again, save as a mere act of faith, "at His word" of command, which carried in it, as it ever does, assurance of success. (This shows he must have been already and for some time a follower of Christ.) **6. net brake**—rather "was breaking," or "beginning to break," as in vs. 7, "beginning to sink." **8. Depart ...**—Did Peter then wish Christ to leave him? Verily no. His all was wrapt up in Him (John 6:68). "Twas rather, Woe is me, Lord! How shall I abide this blaze of glory? A sinner such as I am is not fit company for Thee." (Cf. Isa. 6:5.) **10. Simon, fear not**—This shows how the Lord read Peter's speech. *The more highly they deemed Him, ever the more grateful it was to the Redeemer's spirit. Never did they pain Him by manifesting too lofty conceptions of Him.* **from henceforth**—marking a new stage of their connection with Christ. The last was simply, "I will make you fishers." **fishers of men**—"What wilt thou think, Simon, overwhelmed by this draught of fishes, when I shall bring to thy net what will beggar all this glory?" (See on Matt. 4:18.) **11. forsook all**—They did this before (Matt. 4:20); now they do it again; and yet after the Crucifixion they are at their boats once more (John 21:3). In such a business this is easily conceivable. After pentecost, however, they appear to have finally abandoned their secular calling.

12-16. LEPER HEALED. (See on Matt. 8:2-4.) **15. But so . . .**—(See on Mark 1:45).

17-26. PARALYTIC HEALED. (See on Matt. 9:1-8.) **17. Pharisees and doctors . . . sitting by**—the highest testimony yet borne to our Lord's growing influence, and the necessity increasingly felt by the ecclesiastics throughout the country of coming to some definite judgment regarding Him. **power of the Lord . . . present**—with Jesus. **to heal them**—the sick people. **19. housetop**—the flat roof. **through the tiling . . . before Jesus**—(See on Mark 2:2). **24. take up thy couch**—"sweet saying! The bed had borne the man; now the man shall bear the bed!" [BENGEL].

27-32. LEVI'S CALL AND FEAST. (See on Matt. 9:9-13; and Mark 2:14.) **30. their scribes**—a mode of expression showing that Luke was writing for *Gentiles.*

33-39. FASTING. (See on Matt. 9:14-17.) The *incongruities* mentioned in vss. 36-38 were intended to illustrate the difference between the *genius* of the old and new economies, and the danger of *mixing up* the one with the other. As in the one case supposed, "the rent is made worse," and in the other, "the new wine is spilled," *so by a mongrel mixture of the ascetic ritualism of the old with the spiritual freedom of the new economy, both are disfigured and destroyed.* The additional parable in vs. 39, which is peculiar to Luke, has been variously interpreted. But the "new wine" seems plainly to be the evangelical freedom which Christ was introducing; and the old, the opposite spirit of Judaism: men long accustomed to the latter could not be expected "straightway"—all at once—to take a liking for the former; i.e., "These inquiries about the difference between My disciples and the Pharisees," and even John's, are not surprising; they are the effect of *a natural revulsion against sudden change,* which time will cure; *the new wine will itself in time become old, and so acquire all the added charms of antiquity.* What lessons does this teach, on the one hand, to those who unreasonably cling to what is getting antiquated; and, on the other, to hasty reformers who have no patience with the timidity of their weaker brethren!

CHAPTER 6

Vss. 1-5. PLUCKING CORN EARS ON THE SABBATH. (See on Matt. 12:1-8; and Mark 2:23-28.) **1. second sabbath after the first**—an obscure expression, occurring here only, generally understood to mean, the first sabbath after the second day of unleavened bread. The reasons cannot be stated here, nor is the opinion itself quite free from difficulty. **5. Lord also**—rather "even" (as in Matt. 12:8). **of the sabbath**—as naked a claim to *all the authority of Him who gave the law at Mount Sinai* as could possibly be made; i.e., "I have said enough to vindicate the men ye carp at on My account: *but in this place is the Lord of the law, and they have HIS sanction.*" (See on Mark 2:28.)

6-11. WITHERED HAND HEALED. (See on Matthew 12:9-15; and Mark 3:1-7). **7. watched whether . . .**—In Matthew this is put as an ensnaring question of theirs to our Lord, who accordingly speaks to *the state of their hearts* (vs. 9), just as if they had spoken it out. **9. good, or . . . evil, save . . . or destroy**—By this novel way of putting His case, our Lord teaches the great ethical principle, that *to neglect any opportunity of doing good is to incur the guilt of doing evil;* and by this law He bound His own spirit. (See on Mark 3:4.) **11. filled with madness**—The word denotes senseless rage at the confusion to which our Lord had put them, both by word and deed. **what . . . do to Jesus**—not so much *whether* to get rid of Him, but *how* to compass it. (See on Matt. 3:6.)

12-19. THE TWELVE APOSTLES CHOSEN—GATHERING MULTITUDES—GLORIOUS HEALING. **12, 13.** **went out**—probably from Capernaum. **all night in prayer . . . and when . . . day, he called . . .**—The work with which the next *day* began shows what had been the burden of this *night's* devotions. As He directed His disciples to pray for "laborers" just before sending themselves forth (see on Matt. 9:37; 10:1), so here we find the Lord Himself in prolonged communion with His Father in preparation for the solemn appointment of those men who were to give birth to His Church, and from whom the world in all time was to take a new mould. How instructive is this! **13-16.** (See on Matt. 10:2-4.) **17. in the plain**—by some rendered "on a level place," i.e., a piece of high tableland, by which they understand the same thing, as "on the mountain," where our Lord delivered the sermon recorded by Matthew (5:1), of which they take this following discourse of Luke to be but an abridged form. But as the sense given in our version is the more accurate, so there are weighty reasons for considering the discourses different. This one contains little more than a fourth of the other; it has *woes* of its own, as well as the beatitudes common to both; but above all, that of Matthew was plainly delivered a good while *before,* while this was spoken *after* the choice of the twelve; and as we know that our Lord delivered some of His weightiest sayings more than once, there is no difficulty in supposing this to be one of His more extended repetitions; nor could anything be more worthy of it. **19. healed**—kept healing, denoting successive acts of mercy till it went over "*all*" that needed. There is something unusually grand and pictorial in this touch of description. **20, 21.** In the Sermon on the Mount the benediction is pronounced upon the "poor *in spirit*" and those who "hunger and thirst *after righteousness*" (Matt. 5:3, 6). Here it is simply on the "poor" and the "hungry now." In this form of the discourse, then, our Lord seems to have had in view "*the poor of this world,* rich in faith, and heirs of the kingdom which God hath promised to them that love Him," as these very beatitudes are paraphrased by James (2:5). **21. laugh**—How charming is the liveliness of this word, to express what in Matthew is called being "comforted"! **22. separate you**—whether from their *Church,* by excommunication, or from their society; both hard to flesh and blood. **for the Son of man's sake**—Cf. Matthew 5:11, "for MY SAKE"; and immediately before, "for *righteousness*' sake" (vs. 10). Christ thus *binds up the cause of righteousness in the world with the reception of Himself.* **23. leap for joy**—a livelier word than "be exceeding glad" of "exult" (Matt. 5:12). **24, 25. rich . . . full . . . laugh**—who have all their good things and joyous feelings *here and now*, in perishable objects. **received your consolation**—(see on ch. 16:25). **shall hunger**—their inward craving strong as ever, but the materials of satisfaction forever gone. **26. all ... speak well of you**—alluding to the court paid to the false prophets of old (Mic. 2:11). For the principle of this woe, and its proper limits, see John 15:19. **27-36.** (See on Matt. 5:44-48; 7:12; and 14:12-14.) **37, 38.** See on Matt. 7:1, 2; but this is much fuller and more graphic. **39. Can the blind ...**—not in the Sermon on the Mount, but recorded by Matthew in another and very striking connection (ch. 15:14). **40. The disciple ...** i.e., "The disciple aims to come up to his master, and he thinks himself complete when he does so: if you then be blind leaders of the blind, the perfection of one's training under you will only land him the more certainly in one common ruin with yourselves." **41-49.** (See on Matt. 7:3-5, 16-27.)

CHAPTER 7

Vss. 1-10. CENTURION'S SERVANT HEALED. (See on Matt. 8:5-13.) **4. he was worthy ...**—a testimony most precious, coming from those who probably were strangers to the principle from which he acted (Eccles. 7:1). **5. loved our nation**—Having found that "salvation was of the Jews," he loved them for it. **built ...**—His love took this practical and appropriate form.

11-17. WIDOW OF NAIN'S SON RAISED TO LIFE. (In Luke only.) **11. Nain**—a small village not elsewhere mentioned in Scripture, and only this once probably visited by our Lord; it lay a little to the south of Mount Tabor, about twelve miles from Capernaum. **12. carried out**—"was being carried out." Dead bodies, being ceremonially unclean, were not allowed to be buried within the cities (though the kings of David's house were buried in the city of David), and the funeral was usually on the same day as the death. **only son ...**—affecting particulars, told with delightful simplicity. **13, 14. the Lord**—"This sublime appellation is more usual with Luke and John than Matthew; Mark holds the mean" [BENGEL]. **saw her, he had compassion ...**—What consolation to thousands of the bereaved has this single verse carried from age to age! **14, 15.** What mingled majesty and grace shines in this scene! The Resurrection and the Life in human flesh, with a word of command, bringing back life to the dead body; Incarnate Compassion summoning its absolute power to dry a widow's tears! **16. visited his people**—more than bringing back the days of Elijah and Elisha (I Kings 17:17-24; II Kings 4:32-37; and see on Matt. 15:31).

18-35. THE BAPTIST'S MESSAGE, THE REPLY, AND CONSEQUENT DISCOURSE. (See on Matt. 11:2-14.) **29, 30. And all the people that heard**—"on hearing (this)." These are the observations of *the Evangelist*, not of our Lord. **and the publicans**—a striking clause. **justified God, being baptized ...**—rather, "having been baptized." The meaning is, They acknowledged the divine wisdom of such a preparatory ministry as John's, in leading them to Him who now spake to them (see ch. 1:16, 17); whereas the Pharisees and lawyers, true to themselves in refusing the baptism of John, set at naught also the merciful design of God in the Saviour Himself, to their own destruction. **31-35. the Lord said ...**—As cross, capricious children, invited by their playmates to join them in their amusements, will play with them neither at weddings nor funer-

als (juvenile imitations of the joyous and mournful scenes of life), so that generation rejected both John and his Master: the one because he was too unsocial—more like a demoniac than a rational man; the other, because He was too much the reverse, given to animal indulgences, and consorting with the lowest classes of society. But the children of Wisdom recognize and honor her, whether in the austere garb of the Baptist or in the more attractive style of his Master, whether in the Law or in the Gospel, whether in rags or in royalty, for *"the full soul loatheth an honeycomb,"* but *to the hungry soul every bitter thing is sweet"* (Prov. 27:7).

36-50. CHRIST'S FEET WASHED WITH TEARS. **37, 38. a sinner**—one who had led a profligate life. *N.B.—There is no ground whatever for the popular notion that this woman was Mary Magdalene,* nor do we know what her name was. (See on ch. 8:2.) **an alabaster box of ointment**—a perfume-vessel, in some cases very costly (John 12:5). "The ointment has here a peculiar interest, as the offering by a penitent of what had been an accessory in her unhallowed work of sin" [ALFORD]. **38. at his feet behind him**—the posture at meals being a reclining one, with the feet out behind. **began to wash ...**—to "water with a shower." The tears, which were quite *involuntary*, poured down in a flood upon His naked feet, as she bent down to kiss them; and deeming them rather fouled than washed by this, she hastened to wipe them off with the only towel she had, the long tresses of her own hair, "with which slaves were wont to wash their masters' feet" [STIER]. **kissed**—The word signifies "to kiss fondly, to caress," or to "kiss again and again," which vs. 45 shows is meant here. What prompted this? *Much love, springing from a sense of much forgiveness.* So says He who knew her heart (vs. 47). Where she had met with Christ before, or what words of His had brought life to her dead heart and a sense of divine pardon to her guilty soul, we know not. But probably she was of the crowd of "publicans and *sinners"* whom Incarnate Compassion drew so often around Him, and heard from His lips some of those words such as never man spake, "Come unto Me, all ye that labour .... No personal interview had up to this time taken place between them; but she could keep her feelings no longer to herself, and having found her way to Him (and entered along with him, vs. 45), they burst forth in this surpassing yet most artless style, as if her whole soul would go out to Him. **39. the Pharisee**—who had formed no definite opinion of our Lord, and invited Him apparently to obtain materials for a judgment. **spake within himself ...**—"Ha! I have Him now; He plainly knows nothing of the person He allows to touch Him; and so, He can be no prophet." Not so fast, Simon; thou hast not seen through thy Guest yet, but He hath seen through thee. **40-43.** Like Nathan with David, our Lord conceals His home-thrust under the veil of a parable, and makes His host himself pronounce upon the case. The two debtors are the woman and Simon; the criminality of the one was *ten times* that of the other (in the proportion of "500" to "50"); but both being equally insolvent, both are with equal frankness forgiven; and Simon is made to own that the greatest debtor to forgiving mercy will cling to her Divine Benefactor with the deepest gratitude. Does our Lord then admit that Simon was a forgiving man? Let us see. **44-47. I entered ... no water**—a compliment to guests. Was this "much love?" Was it *any*? **45. no kiss**

—of salutation. How much love was here? *Any at all?* **46. with oil ... not anoint**—even common *olive oil* in contrast with the woman's "ointment" or *aromatic balsam*. What evidence was thus afforded of any feeling which forgiveness prompts? Our Lord speaks this with delicate politeness, as if *hurt* at these inattentions of His host, which though not *invariably* shown to guests, were the customary marks of studied respect and regard. The inference is plain—*only one of the debtors was really forgiven,* though in the first instance, to give room for the play of withheld feelings, the forgiveness of both is supposed in the parable. **47. Her sins which are many**—"Those many sins of hers," our Lord, who admitted how much more she owed than the Pharisee, now proclaims in naked terms the forgiveness of her guilt. **for**—not *because,* as if love were the cause of forgiveness, but "inasmuch as," or "in proof of which." The latter clause of the verse, and the whole structure of the parable, plainly show this to be the meaning. **little forgiven ... loveth little**—delicately ironical intimation of *no love* and *no forgiveness* in the present case. **48. said unto her ...**—an unsought assurance, usually springing up unexpected in the midst of active duty and warm affections, while often it flies from those who mope and are paralyzed for want of it. **49, 50. they that sat ... Who is this ... ?**—No wonder they were startled to hear One who was reclining at the same couch, and partaking of the same hospitalities with themselves, assume the awful prerogative of "even forgiving sins." But so far from receding from this claim, or softening it down, our Lord only repeats it, with two precious additions: one, announcing what was the one secret of the "forgiveness" she had experienced, and which carried "salvation" in its bosom; the other, a glorious dismissal of her in that "peace" which she had already felt, but is now assured she has His full warrant to enjoy! This wonderful scene teaches two very weighty truths: (1) *Though there be degrees of guilt, insolvency, or inability to wipe out the dishonor done to God, is common to all sinners.* (2) *As Christ is the Great Creditor to whom all debt, whether great or small, contracted by sinners is owing, so to Him belongs the prerogative of forgiving it.* This latter truth is brought out in the structure and application of the present parable as it is nowhere else. Either then Jesus was a blaspheming deceiver, or He is God manifest in the flesh.

CHAPTER 8

Vss. 1-3. A GALILEAN CIRCUIT, WITH THE TWELVE AND CERTAIN MINISTERING WOMEN. (In Luke only.) **went**—travelled, made a progress. **throughout every city and village**—through town and village. **preaching ...**—the Prince of itinerant preachers scattering far and wide the seed of the Kingdom. **2. certain women ... healed ...**—on whom He had the double claim of having brought healing to their bodies and new life to their souls. Drawn to Him by an attraction more than magnetic, they accompany Him on this tour as His *almoners*—ministering unto Him of their substance. Blessed Saviour! It melts us to see Thee living upon the love of Thy ransomed people. That they bring Thee their poor offerings we wonder not. Thou hast sown unto them spiritual things, and they think it, as well they might, a small thing that Thou shouldst reap their material things (I Cor. 9:

11). But dost Thou take it at their hand, and subsist upon it? "Oh, the depth of the riches"—of this poverty of His! **Mary Magdalene**—i.e., probably, of *Magdala* (on which see Matt. 15:39). **went**—rather "had gone." **seven devils**—(Mark 16:9). It is a great wrong to this honored woman to identify her with the once profligate woman of ch. 7:37, and to call all such penitents *Magdalenes.* The mistake has arisen from confounding unhappy demoniacal possession with the conscious entertainment of diabolic impurity, or supposing the one to have been afflicted as a punishment for the other —for which there is not the least scriptural ground. **3. Joanna, wife of Chuza, Herod's steward**—If the steward of such a godless, cruel, and licentious wretch as Herod Antipas (see on Mark 6:14, etc.) differed greatly from himself, his post would be no easy or enviable one. That he was a disciple of Christ is very improbable, though he might be favorably disposed towards Him. But what we know not of him, and may fear he lacked, we are sure his wife possessed. Healed either of "evil spirits" or of some one of the "infirmities" here referred to—the ordinary diseases of humanity—she joins in the Saviour's train of grateful, clinging followers. Of "Susanna," next mentioned, we know nothing but the name, and that here only. But her services on this memorable occasion have immortalized her name. "Wheresoever this gospel shall be preached throughout the whole world, this also that she hath done," in ministering to the Lord of her substance on His Galilean tour, "shall be spoken of as a memorial of her" (Mark 14:9). **many others**—i.e., many other *healed women.* What a train! and all ministering unto Him of their substance, and He allowing them to do it and subsisting upon it! "He who was the support of the spiritual life of His people disdained not to be supported by them in the body. He was not ashamed to penetrate so far into the depths of poverty as to live upon the alms of love. He only fed others miraculously; for Himself, He lived upon the love of His people. He gave all things to men, His brethren, and received all things from them, enjoying thereby the pure blessing of love: which is then only perfect when it is at the same time both giving and receiving. Who could invent such things as these? *"It was necessary to live in this manner that it might be so recorded"* [OLSHAUSEN]. 4-18. PARABLE OF THE SOWER. (See on Mark 4:3-9, 14-20.) **16. No man ...**—(see on Matt. 5:15, of which this is nearly a repetition). **17. For nothing ...**—(see on ch. 12:2. **18. how ye**—in Mark 4: 24, *"what ye hear."* The one implies the other. The precept is very weighty. **seemeth to have**—or, "thinketh that he hath" (*Margin*). The "having" of Matthew 13:12 (on which see), and this "thinking he hath," are not different. Hanging loosely on him, and not appropriated, it *is* and *is not* his. 19-21. HIS MOTHER AND BRETHREN DESIRE TO SPEAK WITH HIM. (See on Mark 12:46-50.) 22-25. JESUS, CROSSING THE LAKE, STILLS THE STORM. (See on Matt. 8:23-27, and Mark 4:35-41.) **23. filled**—lit., "were getting filled," i.e., those who sailed; meaning that their ship was so. 26-39. DEMONIAC OF GADARA HEALED. (See on Matt. 8:28-34; and Mark 5:1-20.) 40-56. JAIRUS' DAUGHTER RAISED, AND ISSUE OF BLOOD HEALED. (See on Matthew 9:18-26; and Mark 5:21-43.) **40. gladly received him, for ... all waiting for him**—The abundant teaching of that day (in Matt. 13: and see Mark 4:36), had only whetted the people's appetite; and disappointed, as would seem, that He had left them in the evening to cross the lake, they remain hanging about the beach, having got a hint, probably through some of His disciples, that He would be back the same evening. Perhaps they witnessed at a distance the sudden calming of the tempest. Here at least they are, watching for His return, and welcoming Him to the shore. The tide of His popularity was now fast rising. **45. Who touched me?**—"Askest Thou, Lord, who touched Thee? Rather ask who touched Thee *not* in such a throng." **46. Somebody hath touched**—yes, the multitude *"thronged* and *pressed* Him—"they *jostled against* Him," but all *involuntarily;* they were merely *carried along; but one, one only*—"Somebody TOUCHED" HIM, with the conscious, voluntary, dependent touch of faith, reaching forth its hands expressly to have contact with Him. This and this only Jesus acknowledges and seeks out. Even so, as the Church Father AUGUSTINE long ago said, *multitudes still come similarly close to Christ in the means of grace, but all to no purpose, being only sucked into the crowd.* The voluntary, living contact of faith is that electric conductor which alone draws virtue out of Him. **47. declared ... before all**—This, though a great trial to the shrinking modesty of the believing woman, was just what Christ wanted in dragging her forth, her public testimony to the facts of her case—both her disease, with her abortive efforts at a cure, and the instantaneous and perfect relief which her touch of the Great Healer had brought her. **55. give her meat**—(see on Mark 5:43).

CHAPTER 9

Vss. 1-6. MISSION OF THE TWELVE APOSTLES. (See on Matt. 10:1-15.) **1. power and authority**—He both *qualified* and *authorized* them.

7-9. HEROD TROUBLED AT WHAT HE HEARS OF CHRIST, DESIRES TO SEE HIM. (See on Mark 6:14-30.) **7. perplexed**—at a loss, embarrassed. **said of some, that John was risen**—Among many opinions, this was the one which Herod himself adopted, for the reason, no doubt, mentioned on Mark 6:14. **9. desired to see him**—but did not, till as a prisoner He was sent to him by Pilate just before His death, as we learn from ch. 23:8.

10-17. ON THE RETURN OF THE TWELVE, JESUS RETIRES WITH THEM TO BETHSAIDA, AND THERE MIRACULOUSLY FEEDS FIVE THOUSAND. (See on Mark 6:31-44.)

18-27. PETER'S CONFESSION OF CHRIST—OUR LORD'S FIRST EXPLICIT ANNOUNCEMENT OF HIS APPROACHING DEATH, AND WARNINGS ARISING OUT OF IT. (See on Matt. 16:13-28; and Mark 8:34.) **24. will save**—"is minded to save," bent on saving. The pith of this maxim depends—as often in such weighty sayings (for example, "Let the *dead* bury the *dead,*" Matt. 8:22)—on the double sense attached to the word "life," a lower and a higher, the natural and the spiritual, temporal and eternal. An entire sacrifice of the lower, or a willingness to make it, is indispensable to the preservation of the higher life; and he who cannot bring himself to surrender the one for the sake of the other shall eventually lose both. **26. ashamed of me, and of my words**—The sense of *shame* is one of the strongest in our nature, one of the social affections founded on our love of *reputation,* which causes instinctive aversion to what is fitted to lower it, and was given us as a preservative from all that is properly *shameful.* When one is, in this sense

of it, *lost to shame,* he is nearly past hope (Zech. 3:5; Jer. 6:15; 3:3). But when Christ and "His words"—Christianity, especially in its more spiritual and uncompromising features—are unpopular, the same instinctive desire to *stand well with others* begets the temptation to be ashamed of Him, which only the 'expulsive power' of a higher affection can effectually counteract. **Son of man be ashamed when he cometh ...**—He will render to that man his own treatment; He will disown him before the most august of all assemblies, and put him to *"shame"* and everlasting *contempt"* (Dan. 12:2). "Oh shame, to be put to shame before God, Christ, and angels!" [BENGEL]. **27. not taste of death till they see the kingdom of God**—"see it come with power" (Mark 9:1); or see "the Son of man coming in His kingdom" (Matt. 16:28). The reference, beyond doubt, is to the firm establishment and victorious progress, in the lifetime of some then present, of that new Kingdom of Christ, which was destined to work the greatest of all changes on this earth, and be the grand pledge of His final coming in glory.

28-36. JESUS TRANSFIGURED. **28. an eight days after these sayings**—including the day on which this was spoken and that of the Transfiguration. Matthew and Mark say "after six days," *excluding* these two days. As the "sayings" so definitely connected with the transfiguration scene are those announcing His *death*—at which Peter and all the Twelve were so startled and scandalized—so this scene was designed to show to the eyes as well as the heart how *glorious* that death was in the view of Heaven. **Peter, James, and John**—partners before in secular business; now sole witnesses of the resurrection of Jairus' daughter (Mark 5:37), the transfiguration, and the agony in the garden (Mark 14:33). **a mountain**—not *Tabor,* according to long tradition, with which the facts ill comport, but some one near the lake. **to pray**—for the period He had now reached was a critical and anxious one. (See on Matt. 16:13.) But who can adequately translate those "strong cryings and tears?" Methinks, as I steal by His side, I hear from Him these plaintive sounds, Lord, who hath believed Our report? I am come unto Mine own and Mine own receive Me not; I am become a stranger unto My brethren, an alien to My mother's children: Consider Mine enemies, for they are many, and they hate Me with cruel hatred. Arise, O Lord, let not man prevail. Thou that dwellest between the cherubim, shine forth: Show Me a token for good: Father, glorify Thy name." **29. as he prayed, the fashion ...**—Before He cried He was answered, and while He was yet speaking He was heard. Blessed interruption to prayer this! Thanks to God, transfiguring manifestations are not quite strangers here. Ofttimes in the deepest depths, out of groanings which cannot be uttered, God's dear children are suddenly transported to a kind of heaven upon earth, and their soul is made as the chariots of Amminadab. Their prayers fetch down such light, strength, holy gladness, as make their face to shine, putting a kind of celestial radiance upon it (II Corinthians 3:18, with Exod. 34:29-35). **raiment white ...**—Matthew says, "His face did shine as the sun" (17:2), and Mark says "His raiment became shining, exceeding white as snow, so as no fuller on earth can white them" (9:2). The light, then, it would seem, shone not *upon* Him *from without,* but *out of* Him *from within;* He was all irradiated, was in one blaze of celestial glory. What a contrast to that "visage more marred than men, and His form than the sons of men!" (Isa. 52:14). **30, 31. there talked with him two men ... Moses and Elias ... appeared in glory**—"Who would have believed these were not *angels* had not their *human* names been subjoined?" [BENGEL]. (Cf. Acts 1:10; Mark 16:5.) Moses represented "the law," Elijah "the prophets," and both together the whole testimony of the Old Testament Scriptures, and the Old Testament saints, to Christ; now not borne in a *book*, but by *living men*, not to a *coming*, but a *come* Messiah, *visibly*, for they "appeared," and *audibly*, for they "spake." **spake**—"were speaking." **of his decease**—"departure"; beautiful euphemism (softened term) for *death*, which Peter, who witnessed the scene, uses to express his own expected death, and the use of which single term seems to have recalled the whole by a sudden rush of recollection, and occasioned that delightful allusion to this scene which we find in II Peter 1:15-18. **which he should accomplish**—"was to fulfil." **at Jerusalem**—Mark the *historical character* and *local features* which Christ's death assumed to these glorified men—as important as it is charming—and see on ch. 2:11. What now may be gathered from this statement? (1) *That a dying Messiah is the great article of the true Jewish theology.* For a long time the Church had fallen clean away from the faith of this article, and even from a preparedness to receive it. But here we have that jewel raked out of the dunghill of Jewish traditions, and by the true representatives of the Church of old made the one subject of talk with Christ Himself. (2) *The adoring gratitude of glorified men for His undertaking to accomplish such a decease; their felt dependence upon it for the glory in which they appeared; their profound interest in the progress of it; their humble solaces and encouragements to go through with it; and their sense of its peerless and overwhelming glory.* "Go, matchless, adored One, a Lamb to the slaughter! rejected of men, but chosen of God and precious; dishonored, abhorred, and soon to be slain by men, but worshipped by cherubim, ready to be greeted by all heaven. In virtue of that decease we are here; our all is suspended on it and wrapped up in it. Thine every step is watched by us with ineffable interest; and though it were too high an honor to us to be permitted to drop a word of cheer into that precious but now clouded spirit, yet, as the first fruits of harvest; the very joy set before Him, we cannot choose but tell Him that what is the depth of shame to Him is covered with glory in the eyes of Heaven, that the Cross to Him is the Crown to us, that that 'decease' is all our salvation and all our desire." And who can doubt that such a scene *did* minister deep cheer to that spirit? 'Tis said they "talked" not *to Him*, but "*with Him*"; and if they told *Him* how glorious His decease was, might He not fitly reply, "I know it, but your voice, as messengers from heaven come down to tell it Me, is music in Mine ears." **32. and when they were awake**—so, certainly, the most commentators: but if we translate literally, it should be "*but having kept awake*" [MEYER, ALFORD]. Perhaps "*having roused themselves up*" [OLSHAUSEN] may come near enough to the literal sense; but from the word used we can gather no more than that they *shook off their drowsiness*. It was night, and the Lord seems to have spent the whole night on the mountain (vs. 37). **saw his glory ...**—The emphasis lies on "*saw*," qualifying them to become "*eye-witnesses*" of His majesty" (II Pet. 1:16). **33. they departed**—Ah! bright manifestations in this vale of tears are always "departing" manifestations. **34, 35. a**

cloud—not one of our watery clouds, but the Shekinah-cloud (see on Matt. 23:39), the pavilion of the manifested presence of God with His people, what Peter calls "the excellent" of "magnificent glory" (II Pet. 1:17). **a voice**—"*such* a voice," says Peter emphatically; "and this voice [he adds] we heard, when we were with Him in the holy mount" (II Pet. 1:17, 18). **35. my beloved Son ... hear him**—*reverentially, implicitly, alone.* **36. Jesus was found alone**—Moses and Elias are gone. Their work is done, and they have disappeared from the scene, feeling no doubt with their fellow servant the Baptist, "He must increase, but I must decrease." The cloud too is gone, and the naked majestic Christ, braced in spirit, and enshrined in the reverent affection of His disciples, is left—to suffer! **kept it close**—feeling, for once at least, that such things were unmeet as yet for the general gaze.

37-45. DEMONIAC AND LUNATIC BOY HEALED—CHRIST'S SECOND EXPLICIT ANNOUNCEMENT OF HIS DEATH AND RESURRECTION. (See on Mark 9:14-32). **43-45. the mighty power of God**—"the majesty" or "mightiness" of God in this last miracle, the transfiguration, etc.: the *divine grandeur* of Christ rising upon them daily. By comparing Matthew 17:22, and Mark 9:30, we gather that this had been the subject of conversation between the Twelve and their Master as they journeyed along. **44. these sayings**—not what was passing between them about His grandeur [MEYER, etc.], but what He was now to repeat for the second time about His sufferings [DE WETTE, STIER, ALFORD, etc.]; i.e., "Be not carried off your feet by all this grandeur of Mine, but bear in mind what I have already told you, and now distinctly repeat, that that Sun in whose beams ye now rejoice is soon to set in midnight gloom." "The Son of *man*," says Christ, "into the hands of *men*"—a remarkable antithesis (also in Matt. 17:22, and Mark 9:31). **45. and they feared**—"insomuch that they feared." Their most cherished ideas were so completely dashed by such announcements, that they were afraid of laying themselves open to rebuke by asking Him any questions.

46-48. STRIFE AMONG THE TWELVE, WHO SHOULD BE GREATEST—JOHN REBUKED FOR EXCLUSIVENESS. 46-48. (See on Matt. 18:1-5.) **49, 50. John answered ...**—The link of connection here with the foregoing context lies in the words "in My name" (vs. 48). "Oh, as to that," said John, young, warm, but not sufficiently apprehending Christ's teaching in these things, "we saw one casting out devils in Thy name, and we forbade him: Were we wrong?" "Ye were wrong." "But we did because he followeth not us,'" "No matter. For (1) There is no man which shall do a miracle in My name that can lightly [soon] speak evil of Me' [Mark 9:39]. And (2) If such a person cannot be supposed to be '*against* us,' you are to consider him '*for* us.'" Two principles of immense importance. Christ does not say this man should *not* have followed "with them," but simply teaches how he was to be regarded *though he did not*—as a reverer of His name and a promoter of His cause. Surely this condemns not only those horrible attempts *by force* to shut up all within one visible pale of discipleship, which have deluged Christendom with blood in Christ's name, but the same spirit in its milder form of proud ecclesiastic scowl upon all who "after the form which they call *a sect* (as the word signifies, Acts 24:14), do so worship the God of their fathers." Visible unity in Christ's Church is devoutly to be sought, but this is not the way to it.

See the noble spirit of Moses (Num. 11:24-29).

51-56. THE PERIOD OF HIS ASSUMPTION APPROACHING, CHRIST TAKES HIS LAST LEAVE OF GALILEE—THE SAMARITANS REFUSE TO RECEIVE HIM. **51. the time was come**—rather, "the days were being fulfilled," or approaching their fulfilment—**that he should be received up**—"of His assumption," meaning His exaltation to the Father; a sublime expression, taking the sweep of His whole career, as if at one bound He was about to vault into glory. The work of Christ in the flesh is here divided into *two great stages;* all that preceded this belonging to the one, and all that follows it to the other. During the one, He formally *"came to His own,"* and *"would have gathered them";* during the other, the awful consequences of *"His own receiving Him not"* rapidly revealed themselves. **he steadfastly set his face**—the "He" here is emphatic—"He Himself then." See His own prophetic language, "I have set my face like a flint" (Isa. 50:7). **go to Jerusalem**—as His *goal,* but including His preparatory visits to it at the feasts of tabernacles and of dedication (John 7:2, 10; and 10:22, 23), and all the intermediate movements and events. **52. messengers before his face ... to make ready for him**—He had not done this before; but now, instead of avoiding, He seems to court publicity—all now hastening to maturity. **53. did not receive him, because ...**—The Galileans, in going to the festivals at Jerusalem, usually took the Samaritan route [JOSEPHUS, *Antiquities,* 20. 6. 1], and yet seem to have met with no such inhospitality. But if they were asked to prepare quarters *for the Messiah,* in the person of one whose "face was as though He would go *to Jerusalem,*" their national prejudices would be raised at so marked a slight upon their claims. (See on John 4:20.) **54. James and John** not *Peter,* as we should have expected, but those *"sons of thunder"* (Mark 3:17), who afterwards wanted to have all the highest honors of the Kingdom to themselves, and the younger of whom had been rebuked already for his exclusiveness (vss. 49, 50). Yet this was "the disciple whom Jesus loved," while the other willingly drank of His Lord's bitter cup. (See on Mark 10:38-40 and Acts 12:2.) That same fiery zeal, in a mellowed and hallowed form, in the beloved disciple, we find in II John 5: 10 and III John 10. **fire ... as Elias**—a plausible case, occurring also in *Samaria* (II Kings 1:10-12). **55, 56. know not what ... spirit** The thing ye demand, though in keeping with the *legal,* is unsuited to the genius of the *evangelical* dispensation. The sparks of *unholy* indignation would seize readily enough on this example of Elias, though our Lord's rebuke (as is plain from vs. 56) is directed to the *principle* involved rather than the animal heat which doubtless prompted the reference. "It is a golden sentence of Tillotson, Let us never do anything for religion which is contrary to religion" [WEBSTER and WILKINSON]. **56. for the Son of man ...**—a saying truly divine, of which all His miracles—for salvation, never destruction—were one continued illustration. **went to another**—illustrating His own precept (Matt. 10:23).

57-62. INCIDENTS ILLUSTRATIVE OF DISCIPLESHIP. **57, 58.** The PRECIPITATE disciple. (See on Matt. 8:19, 20.) **59, 60.** The PROCRASTINATING disciple. (See on Matt. 8:21, 22.) **61, 62.** The IRRESOLUTE disciple. **I will follow ... but**—The second disciple had a "but" too—a difficulty in the way just then. Yet the different *treatment* of the two cases shows how different was the *spirit* of the two, and to that our Lord addressed Himself. The

case of Elisha (I Kings 19:19-21), though *apparently* similar to this, will be found quite different from the "looking back" of this case, the best illustration of which is that of *those Hindoo converts of our day who, when once persuaded to leave their spiritual fathers in order to "bid them farewell which are at home at their house," very rarely return to them.* **62. No man ...**—As ploughing requires an eye intent on the furrow to be made, and is marred the instant one turns about, so will they come short of salvation who prosecute the work of God with a distracted attention, a divided heart. Though the reference seems chiefly to ministers, the application is general. The expression "looking back" has a manifest reference to "Lot's wife" (Gen. 19:26; and see on ch. 17:32). It is not *actual return* to the world, but a *reluctance to break with it.*

CHAPTER 10

Vss. 1-24. MISSION OF THE SEVENTY DISCIPLES, AND THEIR RETURN. As our Lord's end approaches, the preparations for the establishment of the coming Kingdom are quickened and extended. **1. the Lord**—a becoming title here, as this appointment was an act truly *lordly* [BENGEL]. **other seventy also**—rather, "others (also in number), 70"; probably with allusion to the seventy elders of Israel on whom the Spirit descended in the wilderness (Num. 11:24, 25). The mission, unlike that of the Twelve, was evidently quite *temporary.* All the instructions are in keeping with a brief and hasty *pioneering* mission, intended to supply what of general preparation for coming events the Lord's own visit afterwards to the same "cities and places" (vs. 1) would not, from want of time, now suffice to accomplish; whereas the instructions to the Twelve, besides embracing all those to the Seventy, contemplate *worldwide* and *permanent* effects. Accordingly, after their return from this single missionary tour, we never again read of the Seventy. **2. the harvest ...**—(See on Matt. 9:37, 38). **3-12.** (See on Matt. 10: 7-16.) **10. son of peace**—inwardly prepared to embrace your message of peace. See note on "worthy," (Matt. 10:13). **12-15.** (See on Matt. 11:20-24). **12. for Sodom**—Tyre and Sidon were ruined by commercial prosperity; Sodom sank through its vile pollutions: but the doom of otherwise correct persons who, amidst a blaze of light, reject the Saviour, shall be *less endurable* than that of any of these. **16. He that ...**—(See on Matt. 10:40). **17. returned**—evidently not long away. **Lord ...**—"Thou hast exceeded Thy promise, for '*even the devils ...*'." The possession of such power, not being expressly in their commission, as in that to the Twelve (ch. 9:1), filled them with more astonishment and joy than all else. **through thy name**—taking no credit to themselves, but feeling lifted into a region of unimagined superiority to the powers of evil simply through their connection with Christ. **18. I beheld**—As much of the force of this glorious statement depends on the nice shade of sense indicated by the *imperfect tense* in the original, it should be brought out in the translation: "I was beholding Satan as lightning falling from heaven"; i.e., "I followed you on your mission, and watched its triumphs; while you were wondering at the subjection to you of devils in My name, a grander spectacle *was opening* to My view; sudden as the darting of lightning from heaven to earth, lo! Satan was beheld falling from heaven!" How remarkable is this, that by that law of association which connects a part with the whole, those feeble triumphs of the Seventy seem to have not only brought vividly before the Redeemer the whole ultimate result of His mission, but compressed it into a moment and quickened it into the rapidity of lightning! *N. B.*—The word rendered *"devils,"* is always used for those spiritual agents employed in *demoniacal possessions*—never for the ordinary agency of Satan in rational men. When therefore the Seventy say, "the *devils* [demons] are subject to us," and Jesus replies, "Mine eye was beholding *Satan falling,"* it is plain that He meant to raise their minds not only from the *particular* to the *general*, but from a very *temporary* form of satanic operation to *the entire kingdom of evil.* (See John 12: 31; and cf. Isa. 14:12). **19. Behold, I give you . . .** —not for any renewal of their mission, though probably many of them afterwards became ministers of Christ; but simply as disciples. **serpents and scorpions**—the latter more venomous than the former: literally, in the first instance (Mark 16:17, 18; Acts 28:5); but the next words, *"and over all the power of the enemy, and nothing shall by any means hurt you,"* show that the glorious power of faith to "overcome the world" and "quench all the fiery darts of the wicked one," by the communication and maintenance of which to His people He makes them *innocuous,* is what is meant (I John 5:4; Eph. 6:16). **20. rejoice not, . . .**—i.e., not so much. So far from forbidding it, He takes occasion here to tell them what had been passing in His own mind. But as power over demons was after all intoxicating, He gives them a higher joy to *balance* it, the joy of having their names in Heaven's register (Phil. 4:3). **21, 22. Jesus . . . said . . . .**—The very same sublime words were uttered by our Lord on a former similar occasion (Matt. 11:25-27, on which see *Note*); but (1) There we are merely told that He "answered and said" thus; here, He *"rejoiced in spirit* and said . . ." (2) There it was merely "at that time" (or season) that He spoke thus, meaning with a general reference to the rejection of His gospel by the self-sufficient; here, *"In that hour* Jesus said," with express reference probably to the humble class from which He had to draw the Seventy, and the similar class that had chiefly welcomed their message. "Rejoice" is too weak a word. It is "exulted in spirit"—evidently giving visible expression to His unusual emotions; while, at the same time, the words "in spirit" are meant to convey to the reader the *depth* of them. This is one of those rare cases in which the veil is lifted from off the Redeemer's inner man, that, angel-like, we may "look into it" for a moment (I Pet. 1:12). Let us gaze on it with reverential wonder, and as we perceive what it was that produced that mysterious ecstasy, we shall find rising in our hearts a still rapture— "Oh, the depths!" **23, 24.**—(See on Matt. 13:16, 17).

25-37. QUESTION OF A LAWYER, AND PARABLE OF THE GOOD SAMARITAN. **25. tempted him**—"tested him"; in no hostile spirit, yet with no tender anxiety for light on that question of questions, but just to see what insight into this great Galilean teacher had. **26. What is written in the law**—apposite question to a doctor of the *law,* and putting him in turn to the test [BENGEL]. **27. Thou shalt . . .**—the answer Christ Himself gave to another lawyer. (See on Mark 12:29-33). **28. he said . . .**—"Right; THIS do, and life is thine"—laying such emphasis on "this" as to indicate, without expressing it, *where the real difficulty to a sinner lay*, and thus nonplussing the

questioner himself. **29. willing**—"wishing," to get himself out of the difficulty, by throwing on Jesus the definition of "neighbor," which the Jews interpreted very narrowly and technically, as excluding Samaritans and Gentiles [ALFORD]. **30. A certain man**—a Jew. **from Jerusalem to Jericho**—a distance of nineteen miles northeast, a deep and very fertile hollow—"the *Temple* of Judea" [TRENCH]. **thieves** —"robbers." The road, being rocky and desolate, was a notorious haunt of robbers, then and for ages after, and even to this day. **31, 32. came down a . . . priest . . . and a Levite**—Jericho, the second city of Judea, was a city of the priests and Levites, and thousands of them lived there. The two here mentioned are supposed, apparently, to be returning from *temple duties,* but they "had not learnt what that meaneth, 'I will have mercy and not sacrifice' [TRENCH]. **saw him**—It was not *inadvertently* that he acted. **came and looked**—a further aggravation. **passed by**—although the law expressly required the opposite treatment even of the *beast* not only of their *brethren,* but of their *enemy* (Deut. 22:4; Exod. 23.4, 5. Cf. Isa. 58:7). **33. Samaritan**—one excommunicated by the Jews, a byword among them, synonymous with heretic and devil (John 8:48; See on ch. 17:18). **had compassion**—His best is mentioned first; for "He who gives outward things gives something *external to himself,* but he who imparts compassion and tears gives him something *from his very self"* [GREGORY the Great, in TRENCH]. No doubt the priest and Levite had their excuses—'Tisn't safe to be lingering here; besides, he's past recovery; and then, mayn't suspicion rest upon ourselves? So might the Samaritan have reasoned, *but did not* [TRENCH]. Nor did he say, He's a Jew, who would have had no dealings with me (John 4:9), and why should I with him? **34. oil and wine**—the remedies used in such cases all over the East (Isa. 1:6), and elsewhere; the *wine* to cleanse the wounds, the *oil* to assuage their smartings. **on his own beast**—himself going on foot. **35. two pence**—equal to two day's wages of a laborer, and enough for several days' support. **36. Which . . . was neighbour?**—a most dexterous way of putting the question: (1) Turning the question from, "Whom am I to love as my neighbour?" to "Who is the man that shows that love?" (2) Compelling the lawyer to give a reply very different from what he would like—not only condemning his own nation, but those of them who should be the most exemplary. (3) Making him commend one of a deeply hated race. And he does it, but it is almost extorted. For he does not answer, "The Samaritan"—that would have sounded heterodox, heretical —but"He that showed mercy on him." It comes to the same thing, no doubt, but the circumlocution is significant. **37. Go . . .**—O exquisite, matchless teaching! What new fountains of charity has not this opened up in the human spirit—rivers in the wilderness, streams in the desert! What noble Christian institutions have not such words founded, all undreamed of till that wondrous One came to bless this heartless world of ours with His incomparable love—first in words, and then in deeds which have translated His words into flesh and blood, and poured the life of them through that humanity which He made His own! Was this parable, now, designed to magnify the law of love, and to show who fulfils it and who not? And who did this as never man did it, as our Brother Man, "our Neighbor?" The priests and Levites had not strengthened the diseased, nor bound up the broken (Ezek. 34:4), while He bound up the brokenhearted (Isa.

61:1), and poured into all wounded spirits the balm of sweetest consolation. All the Fathers saw through the thin veil of this noblest of stories, *the* Story of love, and never wearied of tracing the analogy (though sometimes fancifully enough) [TRENCH]. "He hungered," exclaims GREGORY of Nazianzen (in the fourth century), "but He fed thousands; He was weary, but He is the Rest of the weary; He is saluted 'Samaritan' and 'Demoniac,' but He *saves him that went down from Jerusalem and fell among thieves,*" etc.

38-42. MARTHA AND MARY. **38. certain village** —Bethany (John 11:1), which Luke so speaks of, having no farther occasion to notice it. **received him . . . her house**—The house belonged to her, and she appears throughout to be the older sister. **39. which also**—"who for her part," in contrast with Martha. **sat**—"seated herself." From the custom of sitting *beneath* an instructor, the phrase "sitting at one's feet" came to mean being a disciple of any one (Acts 22:3). **heard**—rather, "kept listening" to His word. **40. cumbered**—"distracted." **came to him**—"presented herself before Him," as from another apartment, in which her sister had "*left* her to serve (or make preparation) *alone.*" **carest thou not . . . my sister . . .**—"Lord, here am I with everything to do, and this sister of mine will not lay a hand to anything; thus I miss something from Thy lips, and Thou from our hands." **bid her . . .**—She presumes not to stop Christ's teaching by calling her sister away, and thus leaving Him without His one auditor, nor did she hope perhaps to succeed if she had tried. **41. Martha, Martha**—emphatically redoubling upon the name. **careful and cumbered** —the one word expressing the inward *worrying anxiety* that her preparations should be worthy of her Lord; the other, the outward *bustle* of those preparations. **many things**—"much service" (vs. 40); too elaborate preparation, which so engrossed her attention that she missed her Lord's teaching. **42. one thing . . .**—The idea of "Short work and little of it suffices for Me" is not so much the *lower sense* of these weighty words, as *supposed* in them, as the basis of something far loftier than any precept on economy. Underneath that idea is couched another, as to the littleness both of elaborate preparation for the present life and *of that life itself,* compared with another. **chosen the good part**—not in the general sense of Moses' choice (Heb. 11:25), and Joshua's (Josh. 24:15), and David's (Ps. 119:30); i.e., of good in opposition to *bad;* but, of two good ways of serving and pleasing the Lord, choosing *the better.* Wherein, then, was Mary's better than Martha's? Hear what follows. **not be taken away** —Martha's choice would be taken from her, for *her services would die with her*; Mary's *never,* being spiritual and eternal. Both were true-hearted disciples, but the one was absorbed in the higher, the other in the lower of two ways of honoring their common Lord. Yet neither despised, or would willingly neglect, the other's occupation. The one represents the *contemplative,* the other the *active* style of the Christian character. A Church full of Marys would perhaps be as great an evil as a Church full of Marthas. Both are needed, each to be the complement of the other.

CHAPTER 11

Vss. 1-13. THE DISCIPLES TAUGHT TO PRAY. **1. one . . .**—struck with either the matter or the manner of our Lord's prayers. **as John . . .**—From this reference to John, it is possible that disciple had not heard the Sermon on the Mount. Nothing of John's *inner* teaching (to his own disciples) has been preserved to us, but we may be sure he never taught his disciples to say, "Our Father." **2-4.** (See on Matt. 6:9-13). **3. day by day . . .**—an extension of the petition in Matthew for "*this day's*" supply, to every successive day's necessities. The closing doxology, wanting here, is wanting also in all the best and most ancient copies of Matthew's Gospel. Perhaps our Lord purposely left that part *open:* and as the grand Jewish doxologies were ever resounding, and passed immediately and naturally, in all their hallowed familiarity into the Christian Church, probably this prayer was never used in the Christian assemblies but in its present form, as we find it in Matthew, while in Luke it has been allowed to stand as originally uttered. **5-8. at midnight . . . for a friend is come**—The heat in warm countries makes evening preferable to day for travelling; but "midnight" is everywhere a most *unseasonable* hour of call, and for that very reason it is here selected. **1. Trouble me not**—the *trouble* making him insensible both to the urgency of the case and the claims of friendship. **I cannot**—without exertion which he would not make. **8. importunity**—The word is a strong one—"shamelessness"; persisting in the face of all that seemed reasonable, and refusing to take a denial. **as many . . .**—His reluctance once overcome, all the claims of friendship and necessity are felt to the full. The sense is obvious: If the churlish and self-indulgent—deaf both to friendship and necessity—can after a positive refusal, be won over, by sheer persistency, to do all that is needed, *how much more* may the same determined perseverance in prayer be expected to prevail with Him whose very nature is "*rich* unto all that call upon Him" (Rom. 10:12). **9-13.** (See on Matt. 7:7-11.) **13. the Holy Spirit**—in Matthew (7:11), "good gifts"; the former, the Gift of gifts descending on the Church through Christ, and comprehending the latter.

14-36. BLIND AND DUMB DEMONIAC HEALED— CHARGE OF BEING IN LEAGUE WITH HELL, AND REPLY—DEMAND OF A SIGN, AND REPLY. (See on Matt. 12:22-45). **14. dumb**—blind also (Matthew 12:22). **20. the finger of God**—"the Spirit of God" (Matt. 12:28); the former figuratively denoting the *power* of God, the latter the *living Personal Agent* in every exercise of it. **21, 22. strong man**—meaning *Satan.* **armed**—pointing to all the subtle and varied methods by which he wields his dark power over men. **keepeth**—"guardeth." **his palace**— man whether viewed more largely or in individual souls—how significant of what men are to Satan! **in peace**—undisturbed, secure in his possession. **22. a stronger than he**—*Christ:* Glorious title, in relation to Satan! **come upon him and overcome him**— sublimely expressing the Redeemer's approach, as the Seed of the woman, to bruise the Serpent's head. **taketh from him all his armour**—"his panoply," "his complete armor." Vain would be the victory, were not the *means of regaining* his lost power wrested from him. It is this that completes the triumph and ensures the final overthrow of his kingdom. The parable that immediately follows (vss. 24-26) is just the *reverse of this.* (See on Matt. 12:43-35.) In the one case, Satan is *dislodged by Christ,* and so finds, in all future assaults, the house *preoccupied;* in the other, he merely goes out and comes in again, finding the house "EMPTY" (Matt. 12:44) of any rival, and all ready to welcome him back. This explains the important saying that comes in *between the two parables* (vs. 23). *Neutrality in religion there is none.* The absence of positive attachment to Christ involves hostility to Him. **23. gathereth . . . scattereth**—referring probably to gleaners. The meaning seems to be, Whatever in religion is disconnected from Christ comes to nothing. **27, 28. as he spake these things, a . . . woman of the company**—of the multitude, the crowd. A charming little incident and profoundly instructive. With true womanly feeling, she envies the mother of such a wonderful Teacher. Well, and higher and better than she had said as much before her (ch. 1:28. 42); and our Lord is far from condemning it. He only holds up—as *"blessed rather"*—the hearers and keepers of God's word; in other words, *the humblest real saint of God.* (See on Matt. 12:49, 50). How utterly alien is this sentiment from the teaching of the Church of Rome, which would excommunicate any one of its members who dared to talk in the spirit of this glorious saying! **29-32.** (See on Matt. 12:39-42.) **33-36.** (See on Matt. 5:14-16; 6:22, 23.) But vs. 36 here is peculiarly vivid, expressing what pure, beautiful, broad perceptions *the clarity of the inward eye* imparts.

37-54. DENUNCIATION OF THE PHARISEES. **38. marvelled . . .**—(See on Mark 7:2-4). **39-41. cup and platter**—remarkable example of our Lord's way of drawing the most striking illustrations of great truths from the most familiar objects and incidents of life. **ravening**—rapacity. **40. that which is without . . .**—i.e., He to whom belongs the outer life, and right to demand its subjection to Himself —is the inner man less His? **41. give alms . . . and . . . all . . . clean**—a principle of immense value. As the greed of these hypocrites was one of the most prominent features of their character (ch. 16:14; Matt. 23:14), our Lord bids them exemplify the opposite character, and then their *outside,* ruled by this, would be beautiful in the eye of God, and their meals would be eaten with clean hands, though never so fouled with the business of this worky world. (See Eccles. 9:7.) **42. mint . . . rue . . .**—founding on Leviticus 27:30, which they interpreted rigidly. Our Lord purposely names the most trifling products of the earth, as examples of what they punctiliously exacted the tenth of. **judgment and the love of God**—in Matthew 23:25, "judgment, mercy, and *faith."* The reference is to Micah 6:6-8, whose third element of all acceptable religion, "walking humbly with God," comprehends both "love" and "faith." (See on Mark 12:29, 32, 33.) The same tendency to merge greater duties in less besets us still, *but it is the characteristic of hypocrites.* **these ought ye . . .**—There is no need for one set of duties to jostle out another; but of the *greater,* our Lord says, "Ye *ought to have done"* them; of the *lesser,* only "ye ought *not to leave them undone.*) **43. uppermost seats**—See on ch. 14:7-11. **greetings**—(See on Matt. 23:7-10). **44. appear not . . .**—As one might unconsciously walk over a grave concealed from view, and thus contract ceremonial defilement, so the plausible exterior of the Pharisees kept people from perceiving the pollution they contracted from coming in contact with such corrupt characters. (See Ps. 5:9; Rom. 3:13; a different illustration from Matt. 23:27.) **46. burdens grievous . . .**—referring not so much to the irksomeness of the legal rites (though they were irksome, Acts 15:10), as to the heartless rigor with which they were enforced, and by men of shameless inconsistency. **47, 48. ye build . . .**—Out of

pretended respect and honor, they repaired and beautified the sepulchres of the prophets, and with whining hypocrisy said, "If we had been in the days of our fathers, we should not have been partakers with them in the blood of the prophets," while all the time they "were witnesses to themselves that they were the children of them that killed the prophets" (Matt. 23:29, 30); convicting themselves daily of as exact a resemblance in spirit and character to the very classes over whose deeds they pretended to mourn, as child to parent. **49-51. said the wisdom . . . .**—a remarkable variation of the words in Matthew 23:34, "Behold *I* SEND." As there seems plainly an allusion to ancient warnings of what God would do with so incorrigible a people, so here Christ, stepping majestically into the place of God, so to speak, says, "Now I am going to carry all that out." *Could this be other than the Lord of Israel in the flesh?* **50. all . . . required of this generation**—As it was only in the last generation of them that "the iniquity of the Amorites was full" (Gen. 15:16), and then the abominations of ages were at once completely and awfully avenged, so the iniquity of Israel was allowed to accumulate from age to age till in that generation it came to the full, and the whole collected vengeance of Heaven broke at once over its devoted head. In the first French Revolution the same awful principle was exemplified, and *Christendom has not done with it yet.* **prophets**—in the New Testament sense (Matt. 23:34; see I Cor. 12:28). **51. blood of Zacharias**—Probably the allusion is not to any recent murder, but to II Chronicles 24:20-22, as *the last recorded* and most suitable case for illustration. And as Zacharias' last words were, "The Lord *require it,"* so they are warned that "of that generation it should be *required."* **52. key of knowledge**—not the key to open knowledge, but knowledge, the only key to open heaven. In Matthew 23:13, they are accused of *shutting heaven;* here of *taking away the key,* which was worse. A right knowledge of God's Word is eternal life (John 17:3); but this they took away from the people, substituting for it their wretched traditions. **53, 54.** Exceedingly vivid and affecting. They were stung to the quick—and can we wonder?—yet had not materials for the charge they were preparing against Him. **provoke him . . .**—"to harass Him with questions."

CHAPTER 12

Vss. 1-12. WARNING AGAINST HYPOCRISY. **1-3. meantime**—in close connection, probably, with the foregoing scene. Our Lord had been *speaking out* more plainly than ever before, as matters were coming to a head between Him and His enemies, and this seems to have suggested to His own mind the warning here. He had just Himself illustriously exemplified His own precepts. **his disciples first of all**—afterwards to "the multitudes" (vs. 54). **covered**—from the view. **2. hid**—from knowledge. "'Tis no use concealing anything, for all will one day come out. Give free and fearless utterance then to all the truth." (Cf. I Cor. 4:3, 5). **4, 5. I say . . .**—You will say, That may cost us our life. Be it so; but, "My friends,' there their power ends." He calls them "my friends" here, not in any loose sense, but, as we think, from the feeling He then had that in this "killing of the body" *He and they* were going to be affectingly one with each other. **Fear Him . . .–Fear Him**–how striking the repetition here! *Only the one fear would effectually expel the other.* **after he hath killed . . .**–Learn here –(1) To play false with one's convictions to save one's life, may fail of its end after all, for God can inflict a violent death in some other and equally formidable way. (2) There is a *hell*, it seems, for the body as well as the soul; consequently, sufferings adapted to the one as well as the other. (3) *Fear of hell* is a divinely authorized and needed motive of action even to Christ's "friends." (4) As Christ's meekness and gentleness were not compromised by such harsh notes as these, so those servants of Christ lack their Master's spirit who soften down all such language to please ears 'polite.' (See on Mark 9:43-48.) **6, 7. five . . . for two farthings**–In Matthew 10:29 it is two for one farthing"; so if one took two farthings' worth, he got one in addition–of such small value were they. **than many sparrows**–not "than millions of sparrows"; the charm and power of our Lord's teaching is very much in this simplicity. **8, 9. confess . . . deny . . .** –The point lies in doing it "before men," because one has to do it "despising the *shame*." But when done, the Lord holds Himself bound to repay it *in kind* by confessing such "before the angels of God." For the rest, see on ch. 9:26. **10. Son of man . . . Holy Ghost**–(See on Matt. 12:31, 32).

13-53. COVETOUSNESS–WATCHFULNESS–SUPERIORITY TO EARTHLY TIES. **13. Master . . .**–i.e., "Great Preacher of righteousness, help; there is need of Thee in this rapacious world; here am I the victim of injustice, and that from my own brother, who withholds from me my rightful share of the inheritance that has fallen to us." In this most inopportune intrusion upon the solemnities of our Lord's teaching, there is a mixture of the absurd and the irreverent, the one, however, occasioning the other. The man had not the least idea that his case was not of as urgent a nature, and as worthy the attention of our Lord, as anything else He could deal with. **14. Man, . . .**–*Contrast this style of address with* "my friends," (vs. 4). **who . . .** –a question literally repudiating the office which Moses assumed (Exod. 2:14). *The influence of religious teachers in the external relations of life has ever been immense, when only the* INDIRECT *effect of their teaching; but whenever they intermeddle* DIRECTLY *with secular and political matters, the spell of that influence is broken.* **15. unto them** –the multitude around Him (vs. 1). **of covetousness**–The best copies have "all," i.e., "every kind of covetousness"; because as this was one of the more plausible forms of it, so He would strike at once at the *root* of the evil. **a man's life . . .**–a singularly weighty maxim, and not less so because its meaning and its truth are equally evident. **16-19. a certain rich man . . .**–Why is this man called a "fool?" (1) Because he deemed a life of secure and abundant earthly enjoyment the summit of human felicity. (2) Because, possessing the means of this, through prosperity in his calling, he flattered himself that he had a long lease of such enjoyment, and nothing to do but give himself up to it. Nothing else is laid to his charge. **20, 21. this night . . .** –This sudden cutting short of his career is designed to express not only the folly of building securely upon the future, but of throwing one's whole soul into what may at any moment be gone. "Thy *soul* shall be required of thee" is put in opposition to his own treatment of it, "I will say to my *soul, Soul, . . .*" **whose shall those things be . . .**–Cf.

Psalm 39:6, "He heapeth up riches and *knoweth not who shall gather them.*" **21. So is he . . .**– Such is a picture of his folly here, and of its awful issue. **is not rich . . .**–lives to amass and enjoy riches which terminate on *self,* but as to the riches of God's favor, which is life (Ps. 30:5), of "precious" faith (II Peter 1:1; Jas. 2:5), of good works (I Tim. 6:18), of wisdom which is better than rubies (Prov. 8:11)–lives and dies *a beggar!* **22-31.**–(See on Matthew 6:25-33.) **25, 26. which of you . . .**– Corroding solicitude will not bring you the least of the things ye fret about, though it may double the evil of wanting them. And if not the least, why vex yourselves about things of more consequence? **29. of doubtful . . .**–unsettled mind. put off your balance. **32. little flock . . .**–How sublime and touching a contrast between this tender and pitying appellation, "Little flock" (in the original a double diminutive, which in German can be expressed, but not in English)–and the "good pleasure" of the Father to give them the Kingdom; the one recalling the insignificance and helplessness of that then literal handful of disciples, the other holding up to their view the eternal love that encircled them, the everlasting arms that were underneath them, and the high inheritance awaiting them!–"the kingdom"; grand word; then why not "bread" (vs. 31 [BENGEL]. Well might He say, "Fear not!" **33, 34. Sell . . .**–This is but a more vivid expression of Matthew 6:19-21 (see *Note* there). **35-40. loins . . . girded**–to fasten up the long outer garment, always done before travel and work (II Kings 4:29; Acts 12:8). The meaning is, Be in readiness. **lights . . .**(See on Matt. 25:1). **return from the wedding** not come to it, as in the parable of the virgins. Both have their spiritual significance; but *preparedness for Christ's coming* is the prominent idea. **37. gird himself . . .**–"a promise the most august of all: Thus will the Bridegroom entertain his friends [nay, servants] on the solemn Nuptial Day" [BENGEL]. **38. second . . . third watch**–To find them ready to receive Him at any hour of day or night, when one might least of all expect Him, is peculiarly blessed. A servant may be truly faithful, even though taken so far unawares that he has not everything in *such* order and readiness for his master's return as he thinks is due to him, and both could and would have had if he had had notice of the time of his coming, and so may not be willing to open to him "*immediately*," but fly to preparation, and let his master knock again ere he admit him, and even then *not with full joy.* A too common case this with Christians. But if the servant have himself and all under his charge in such a state that at any hour when his master knocks, he can open to him "immediately," and hail his "return"–that is the most enviable, "blessed" servant of all. **41-48. unto us or even to all?**–us the Twelve, or all this vast audience? **42. Who then . . .**–answering the question indirectly by another question, from which they were left to gather what it would be:– To you certainly in the first instance, representing the "stewards" of the "household" I am about to collect, and generally to all "servants" in My house. **faithful and wise**–*Fidelity* is the first requisite in a servant, *wisdom* (discretion and judgment in the exercise of his functions), the next. **steward**– house-steward, whose it was to distribute to the servants their allotted portion of food. **shall make** –will deem fit to be made. **44. make him ruler over all he hath**–will advance him to the highest post, referring to the world to come. (See Matt. 25:21, 23.) **45. begin to beat . . .**–In the confidence

that his Lord's return will not be speedy, he throws off the role of servant and plays the master, maltreating those faithful servants who refuse to join him, seizing on and revelling in the fulness of his master's board; intending, when he has got his fill, to resume the mask of fidelity ere his master appear. **46. cut him in sunder**—a punishment not unknown in the East; cf. Hebrews 11:37, "sawn asunder" (I Sam. 15:33; Dan. 2:5). **the unbelievers**—the unfaithful, those unworthy of trust (Matt. 24:51), "the hypocrites," falsely calling themselves "servants." **48. knew not**—i.e., knew but *partially;* for *some* knowledge is presupposed both in the name "servant" of Christ, and his being liable to punishment at all. **many ... few stripes**—degrees of future punishment proportioned to the knowledge sinned against. Even heathens are not without knowledge enough for future judgment; but the reference here is not to such. It is a solemn truth, and though *general,* like all other revelations of the future world, discloses a tangible and momentous principle in its awards. **49-53. to send**—cast. **fire** —"the higher spiritual element of life which Jesus came to introduce into this earth (cf. Matt. 3:11), with reference to its mighty effects in quickening all that is akin to it and *destroying all that is opposed.* To cause this element of life to take up its abode on earth, and wholly to pervade human hearts with its warmth, was the lofty destiny of the Redeemer" [OLSHAUSEN: so CALVIN, STIER, ALFORD, etc.]. **what will I ...**—an obscure expression, uttered under deep and half-smothered emotion. In its general import all are agreed; but the nearest to the precise meaning seems to be, "And what should I have to desire if it were once already kindled?" [BENGEL and BLOOMFIELD]. **50. But ... a baptism ....**—clearly, His own bloody baptism, first to take place. **how ... straitened**—not, "how do I long for its accomplishment," as many understand it, thus making it but a repetition of the former verse; but "what a pressure of spirit is upon Me." **till it be accomplished**—till it be over. Before a promiscuous audience, such obscure language was fit on a theme like this; but oh, what surges of mysterious emotion in the view of what was now so near at hand does it reveal! **51. peace . . . .?** **Nay**—the reverse of peace, *in the first instance.* (See on Matt. 10:34-36.) The connection of all this with the foregoing warnings about hypocrisy, covetousness, and watchfulness, is deeply solemn: "My conflict hasten apace; Mine over, yours begins; and then, let the servants tread in their Master's steps, uttering their testimony entire and fearless, neither loving nor dreading the world, anticipating awful wrenches of the dearest ties in life, but looking forward, as I do, to the completion of their testimony, when, reaching the haven after the tempest, they shall enter into the joy of their Lord."
54-59. NOT DISCERNING THE SIGNS OF THE TIME. **54. to the people**—"the multitude," a word of special warning to the thoughtless crowd, before dismissing them. (See on Matt. 16:2, 3). **56. how ... not discern ...**—unable to perceive what a critical period that was for the Jewish Church. **57. why even of yourselves ...**—They might say, To do this requires more knowledge of Scripture and providence than we possess; but He sends them to their own conscience, as enough to show them who He was, and win them to immediate discipleship. **58. When thou goest ...**—(See on Matt. 5:25, 26). The *urgency of the case with them, and the necessity, for their own safety, of immediate decision,* was the object of these striking words.

CHAPTER 13

Vss. 1-9. THE LESSON, "REPENT OR PERISH," SUGGESTED BY TWO RECENT INCIDENTS, AND ILLUSTRATED BY THE PARABLE OF THE BARREN FIG TREE. **1-3. Galileans**—possibly the followers of Judas of Galilee, who, some twenty years before this, taught that Jews should not pay tribute to the Romans, and of whom we learn, from Acts 5:37, that he drew after him a multitude of followers, who on his being slain were all dispersed. About this time that party would be at its height, and if Pilate caused this detachment of them to be waylaid and put to death as they were offering their sacrifices at one of the festivals, that would be "mingling their blood with their sacrifices" [GROTIUS, WEBSTER and WILKINSON, but doubted by DE WETTE, MEYER, ALFORD, etc.]. News of this being brought to our Lord, to draw out His views of such, and whether it was not a judgment of Heaven, He simply points them to the practical view of the matter: "These men are not signal examples of divine vengeance, as ye suppose; but every impenitent sinner—*ye yourselves, except ye repent*—shall be like monuments of the judgment of Heaven, and in a more awful sense." The reference here to the impending destruction of Jerusalem is far from exhausting our Lord's weighty words; they manifestly point to a "perdition" of a more awful kind—*future, personal, remediless.* **4, 5. tower in Siloam**—probably one of the towers of the city wall, near the pool of Siloam. Of its fall nothing is known. **6-9. fig tree**—Israel, as the visible witness of God in the world, but generally all within the pale of the visible Church of God; a familiar figure (cf. Isa. 5:1-7; John 15:1-8, etc.). **vineyard**—a spot selected for its fertility, separated from the surrounding fields, and cultivated with special care, with a view solely to *fruit.* **came and sought fruit**—a heart turned to God; the fruits of righteousness; cf. Matthew 21:33, 34, and Isaiah 5:2, "He *looked* that it should bring forth fruit"; He has a *right* to it, and will *require* it. **7. three years**—a long enough trial for a fig tree, and so denoting probably just a *sufficient* period of culture for spiritual fruit. The supposed allusion to the duration of our Lord's ministry is precarious. **cut it down**—indignant language. **cumbereth**—not only doing no good, but wasting ground. **8. He answering ...**—Christ, as Intercessor, loath to see it cut down so long as there was any hope (see vs. 34). **dig ...**—loosen the earth about it and enrich it with manure; pointing to changes of method in the divine treatment of the impenitent, in order to freshen spiritual culture. **9. if fruit, well**—Genuine repentance, however late, avails to save (Ch. 23:42, 43). **after that ...**—The final perdition of such as, after the utmost limits of reasonable forbearance, are found fruitless, will be pre-eminently and confessedly just (Prov. 1:24-31; Ezek. 24:13).
10-17. WOMAN OF EIGHTEEN YEAR'S INFIRMITY HEALED ON THE SABBATH. **11. spirit of infirmity**—Cf. vs. 17, "whom *Satan* hath bound." From this it is probable, though not certain, that her protracted infirmity was the effect of some milder form of *possession;* yet she was "a daughter of Abraham," in the same gracious sense, no doubt, as Zaccheus, after his conversion, was "a son of Abraham" (ch. 19:9). **12, 13. said ... Woman ... and laid**—both at once. **14. with indignation**—not so much at the sabbath violation as at the glorification of Christ. (Cf. Matt. 21:15) [TRENCH]. **said to the people**—"Not daring directly to find fault with the Lord, he seeks circuitously to reach Him through the people,

who were more under his influence, and whom he feared less" [TRENCH]. **15. the Lord**–(See on ch. 10:1). **hypocrite!**–How "the faithful and true Witness" tears off the masks which men wear! **his ox . . .**–(see on Matt. 12:9-13; and ch. 6:9). **16. ought not . . .**–How gloriously the Lord vindicates the superior claims of this woman, in consideration of the sadness and long duration of her suffering, and of her dignity notwithstanding, as an heir of the promise!

18-30.   MISCELLANEOUS TEACHINGS.   **18-21. mustard seed . . . leaven**–See on Mark 4:30-32). The parable of the "Leaven" sets forth, perhaps, rather the *inward* growth of the kingdom, while "the Mustard Seed" seems to point chiefly to the *outward*. It being a woman's work to knead, it seems a refinement to say that "the woman" here represents *the Church*, as the instrument of depositing the leaven. Nor does it yield much satisfaction to understand the "three measures of meal" of that threefold division of our nature into "spirit, soul, and body," (alluded to in I Thess. 5:23) or of the threefold partition of the world among the three sons of Noah (Gen. 10:32), as some do. It yields more real satisfaction to see in this brief parable just the *all-penetrating* and *assimilating* quality of the Gospel, by virtue of which it will yet mould all institutions and tribes of men, and exhibit over the whole earth one "Kingdom of our Lord and of His Christ." (See on Rev. 11:15.) **23. Lord . . .**–one of those curious questions by talking of which some flatter themselves they are *religious*. **said unto them**– the multitude; taking no notice of the man or his question, save as furnishing the occasion of a solemn warning not to trifle with so momentous a matter as "salvation." **24. Strive**–The word signifies to "contend" as for the mastery, to "struggle," expressive of the *difficulty* of being saved, as if one would have to *force his way in*. **strait gate** –another figure of the same. (See *Note* on Matt. 7:13, 14). **for many . . . will seek**–*desire*, i.e., with a mere wish or slothful endeavor. **and shall not be able**–because it must be made a *life-and-death struggle*. **25. master of the house is risen up and hath shut to the door**–awfully sublime and vivid picture! At present he is represented as in a *sitting* posture, as if calmly looking on to see who will "strive," while entrance is practicable, and who will merely "seek" to enter in. But this is to have an end, by the great Master of the house Himself rising and shutting the door, after which there will be *no admittance*. **Lord, Lord**–emphatic reduplication, expressive of the earnestness *now* felt, but too late. (See on Matt. 7:21, 22). **26, 27.** See on the similar passage (Matt. 7:22, 23). **eaten and drunk . . .**–We have sat with Thee at the same table. **taught in our streets**–Do we not remember listening in our own streets to Thy teaching? Surely *we* are not to be denied admittance? **But he shall say . . .**–*No nearness of external communion with Christ will avail at the great day, in place of that "holiness without which no man shall see the Lord."* Observe the *style* which Christ intimates that He will then assume, that of absolute Disposer of men's eternal destinies, and contrast it with His "despised and rejected" condition at that time. **28, 29.** (See on Matt. 8:11, 12.)

31-35.   MESSAGE TO HEROD.   **31. and depart hence**–and "go forward," *push on*. He was on His way out of Perea, east of Jordan, and in Herod's dominions, "journeying towards Jerusalem" (vs. 22). Haunted by guilty fears, probably, Herod wanted to get rid of Him (see on Mark 6:14), and

seems, from our Lord's answer, to have sent these Pharisees, under pretense of a friendly hint, to persuade Him that the sooner He got beyond Herod's jurisdiction the better it would be for His own safety. Our Lord saw through both of them, and sends the cunning ruler a message couched in dignified and befitting irony. **32. that fox**–that crafty, cruel enemy of God's innocent servants. **Behold, I cast out devils and I do cures**–i.e., "Plot on and ply thy wiles; I also have My plans; My works of mercy are nearing completion, but some yet remain; I have work for to-day and to-morrow too, and the third day; by that time I shall be where his jurisdiction reaches not; the guilt of My blood shall not lie at his door; that dark deed is reserved for others." He does not say, I preach the Gospel–that would have made little impression upon Herod–in the light of the *merciful* character of Christ's *actions* the *malice* of Herod's snares is laid bare [BENGEL]. **to-day, to-morrow, the third day**–remarkable language expressive of *successive steps* of His work yet remaining, the calm *deliberateness* with which He meant to go through with them, one after another, to the last, unmoved by Herod's threat, yet the *rapid march* with which they were now hastening to completion. (Cf. John 22:18.) **I shall be perfected**–I finish my course, I attain completion. **33. it cannot be that a prophet . . .**–"*It would never do* that . . .*"*–awful severity of satire this upon "the bloody city!" "He seeks to kill me, does he? Ah! I must be out of Herod's jurisdiction for that. Go tell him I neither fly from him nor fear him, but Jerusalem is the prophets' slaughter-house." **34, 35. O Jerusalem . . .**–(See on Matt. 23:37, 39).

CHAPTER 14

Vss. 1-24.   HEALING OF A DROPSICAL MAN, AND MANIFOLD TEACHINGS AT A SABBATH FEAST.   **2. man before him**–not one of the company, since this was apparently *before* the guests sat down, and probably the man came in hope of a cure, though not expressly soliciting it [DE WETTE]. **3-6.** (See on Matt. 12:11, 12.) **7-11. a parable**–showing that His design was not so much to inculcate mere politeness or good manners, as *underneath* this to teach something *deeper* (vs. 11). **chief rooms**– principal seats, in the middle part of the couch on which they reclined at meals, esteemed the most honorable. **8. wedding**–and seating thyself at the wedding *feast*. Our Lord avoids the appearance of personality by this delicate allusion to a *different* kind of entertainment than this of his host [BENGEL]. **9. the lowest**–not a *lower* merely [BENGEL]. **with shame**–"To be lowest is only ignominious to him who affects the highest" [BENGEL]. **10. Friend**– said to the *modest* guest only, not the proud one (vs. 9) [BENGEL]. **worship**–honor. The whole of this is but a reproduction of Proverbs 25:6, 7. But it was reserved for the matchless Teacher to *utter articulately*, and *apply to the regulation of the minutest features of social life, such great laws of the Kingdom of God* as that of vs. 11. **"whosoever . . ."**–couching them in a chaste simplicity and proverbial terseness of style which makes them "apples of gold in a setting of silver." (See on ch. 18:14.) **12-14. call not thy friends**–Jesus certainly did not mean us to dispense with the duties of ordinary fellowship, but, remitting these to their proper place, inculcates what is better [BENGEL]. **lest . . . a recompense be given thee**–a fear the world is not afflicted with [BENGEL]. The meaning, however, is that no *exercise of principle* is involved in it, as selfishness itself will suffice to prompt to it (Matt. 5:46, 47). **13. call the poor**—"Such God Himself calls" (vs. 21) [BENGEL]. **14. blessed**—acting from disinterested, god-like compassion for the wretched. **15-24. when one . . . heard . . . he said, Blessed . . .**—As our Lord's words seemed to hold forth the future "recompense" under the idea of a great Feast, the thought passes through this man's mind, how blessed they would be who should be honored to sit down to it. Our Lord's reply is in substance this: "The great Feast is prepared already; the invitations are issued, *but declined;* the feast, notwithstanding, shall not want abundance of guests; but not one of its present contemners—who shall yet come to sue for admission—shall be allowed to taste of it." This shows what was lacking in the seemingly pious exclamation of this man. It was Balaam's, "Let me *die the death* of the righteous, and let my *last end* be like his" (Num. 23:10), without any anxiety about *living his life;* fondly wishing that all were right with him *at last,* while all heedless of the precious *present.* **16. a great supper**—(Cf. Isa. 25:6). **bade many**—*historically,* the Jews (see on Matt. 22:3); generally, those within the pale of professed discipleship. **17. supper-time . . . all now ready**—pointing undoubtedly to the now ripening preparations for the great Gospel call. (See on Matt. 22:4.) **18. all began to make excuse**—(Cf. Matthew 22:5). Three excuses, given as specimens of the rest, answer to "the *care of this world*" (vs. 18), "the *deceitfulness of riches*" (vs. 19), and "the *pleasures of this life*" (vs. 20), which "choke the word" (Matt. 13:22 and ch. 8:14). Each differs from the other, and each has its own plausibility, but *all come to the same result:* "We have other things to attend to, more pressing just now." Nobody is represented as saying, I *will not* come; nay, all the answers imply that *but for* certain things they *would* come, and when these are out of the way they *will* come. So it certainly is in the case intended, for the last words clearly imply that the *refusers* will one day become *petitioners.* **21. came and told . . .**—saying as in Isaiah 53:1. "It is the part of ministers to report to the Lord in their prayers the compliance or refusal of their hearers" [BENGEL]. **angry**—in one sense a *gracious* word, showing how sincere he was in issuing his invitations (Ezek. 33:11). But it is the *slight* put upon him, the sense of which is intended to be marked by this word. **streets and lanes**—*historically,* those within the same pale of "the city" of God as the former class, but the despised and outcasts of the nation, the "publicans and sinners" [TRENCH]; generally, all similar classes, usually overlooked in the first provision for supplying the means of grace to a community, half heathen in the midst of revealed light, and in every sense miserable. **22. yet there is room**—implying that these classes *had* embraced the invitation (Matt. 21:32; Mark 12:37; last clause; John 7:48, 49); and beautifully expressing the longing that should fill the hearts of ministers to see their Master's table filled. **23. highways and hedges**—outside the city altogether; *historically,* the heathen, sunk in the lowest depths of spiritual wretchedness, as being beyond the pale of all that is revealed and saving, "without Christ, strangers from the covenant of promise, having no hope, and without God in the world" (Eph. 2:12); generally, all such still. Thus, this parable *prophetically* contemplates the extension of the kingdom of God to the whole world; and *spiritually,* directs the Gospel

invitations to be carried to the lowest strata, and be brought in contact with the outermost circles, of human society. **compel them to come in**—not as if they would make the "excuses" of the first class, but because it would be hard to get them over two difficulties: (1) "We are not fit company for such a feast." (2) "We have no proper dress, and are ill in order for such a presence." How fitly does this represent the difficulties and fears of the *sincere!* How is this met? "Take no excuse—make them come as they are—bring them along with you." What a directory for ministers of Christ! **that my house may be filled**—"Grace no more than nature will endure a vacuum" [BENGEL]. **24. I say unto you, That none**—Our Lord here appears to throw off the veil of the parable, and proclaim the Supper *His own,* intimating that when transferred and transformed into its final glorious form, and the refusers themselves would give all for another opportunity, *He* will not allow one of them to taste it. (*N.B.*—This parable must not be confounded with that of Prov. 1:24-33; *The Marriage Supper,* Matt. 22:2-14.)

25-35. ADDRESS TO GREAT MULTITUDES TRAVELLING WITH HIM. 25. great multitudes with him —on His final journey to Jerusalem. The "great multitudes" were doubtless people going to the passover, who moved along in clusters (ch. 2:44), and who on this occasion falling in with our Lord had formed themselves into one mass about Him. **26, 27. If any man . . .**—(See on Matt. 10:34-36, and Mark 8:34, 35). **28-33. which of you . . .**—Common sense teaches men not to *begin* any costly work without first seeing that they have wherewithal to *finish.* And he who does otherwise exposes himself to general ridicule. Nor will any wise potentate enter on a war with any hostile power without first seeing to it that, despite formidable odds (two to one), he be able to stand his ground; and if he has no hope of this, he will feel that nothing remains for him but to make the best terms he can. *"Even so,"* says our Lord, "in the warfare you will each have to wage as My disciples, despise not your enemy's strength, for the odds are all against you; and you had better see to it that, despite every disadvantage, you still have wherewithal to hold out and win the day, or else not begin at all, and make the best you can in such awful circumstances." In this simple sense of the parable (STIER, ALFORD, etc., go wide of the mark here in making the enemy to be *God,* because of the "conditions of peace," vs. 32), two things are taught: (1) Better not begin (Rev. 3:15), than begin and not finish. (2) Though the contest for salvation be on our part an awfully unequal one, the *human will,* in the exercise of that "faith which overcometh the world" (I John 5:4), and nerved by power from above, which "out of *weakness* makes it *strong*" (Heb. 11:34; I Pet. 1:5), becomes heroical and will come off "more than conqueror." But without *absolute surrender of self* the contest is hopeless (vs. 33). **34. 35. salt . . .**—(See on Matt. 5:13-16; and Mark 9:50).

CHAPTER 15

Vss. 1-32. PUBLICANS AND SINNERS WELCOMED BY CHRIST—THREE PARABLES TO EXPLAIN THIS. **1. drew near . . . all the publicans and sinners . . .**—drawn around Him by the extraordinary adaptation of His teaching to their case, who, till He appeared—at least His forerunner—might well say, "No man careth for my soul." **2. murmured, say-**

ing . . .–took it ill, were scandalized at Him, and insinuated (on the principle that a man is known by the company he keeps) that He must have some secret sympathy with their *character*. But oh, what a truth of unspeakable preciousness do their lips, as on other occasions, unconsciously utter: Now follow three parables representing the sinner: (1) *in his stupidity;* (2) as *all-unconscious of his lost condition;* (3) *knowingly and willingly estranged from God* [BENGEL]. The first two set forth the *seeking* love of God; the last, His *receiving* love [TRENCH]. **3-7. I. THE LOST SHEEP**–occurring again (Matt. 18:12-14); but there to show how precious one of His sheep is to the Good Shepherd; here, to show that the shepherd, though the sheep stray never so widely, will seek it out, and when he hath found, will rejoice over it. **4. leave the ninety and nine**–bend all His attention and care, as it were, to the one object of recovering the lost sheep; not saying. " 'Tis but one; let it go; enough remain." **go after . . . until . . .**–pointing to all the diversified means which God sets in operation for recovering sinners. **6. Rejoice with me . . .**–The principle here is, that one feels *exuberant joy* to be almost too much for himself to bear alone, and is positively relieved by having others to *share it with him.* (See on vs. 10.) **7. ninety-nine just . . . needing no repentance**–not *angels,* whose place in these parables is very different from this; but those represented by the *prodigal's wellbehaved brother,* who have "served their Father" many years and not at any time transgressed His commandment (in the outrageous sense of the prodigal). (See on vss. 29, 31.) In other words, *such as have grown up from childhood* in the fear of God and as the sheep of His pasture. Our Lord does not *say* "the Pharisees and scribes" were such; but as there *was* undoubtedly such a class, while "the publicans and sinners" were confessedly the strayed sheep and the prodigal children, He leaves them to fill up the place of the other class, *if they could.* **8-10. II. THE LOST COIN. sweep the house**–"not done without *dust* on man's part" [BENGEL]. **10. Likewise**–on the same principle. **joy . . .**–Note carefully the language here–not "joy *on the part,*" but "joy *in the presence* of the angels of God." True to the idea of the parables. The Great Shepherd. The Great Owner Himself, is He *whose the joy properly is over His own recovered property;* but so vast and exuberant is it (Zech. 8:17), that as if He could not keep it to Himself, He "calleth His friends and neighbors together"–His whole celestial family–saying, "Rejoice WITH ME, for I have found *My* sheep-My-piece," etc. In this sublime sense it is "joy," *before "or in the presence* of the angels"; they only "catch the flying joy," sharing it *with Him!* The application of this to the reception of those publicans and sinners that stood around our Lord is grand in the extreme: "Ye turn from these lost ones with disdain, and because I do not the same, ye murmur at it: but a very different feeling is cherished in heaven. There, the recovery of even one such outcast is watched with interest and hailed with joy; nor are they left to come home of themselves or perish; for lo! even now the great Shepherd is going after His lost sheep, and the Owner is making diligent search for the lost property; and He is finding it, too, and bringing it back with joy, and all heaven is full of it." (Let the reader mark what sublime claims Himself our Lord covertly puts in here–as if in Him they beheld, all unknown to themselves, nothing less than heaven in the habili-

ments of earth, the Great Shepherd above, clothed in a garment of flesh, come "to seek and to save that which was lost")! **11-32. III. THE PRODIGAL SON.** **12. the younger**–as the more thoughtless. **said . . .**–weary of restraint, panting for independence, unable longer to abide the check of a father's eye. *This is man* impatient of divine control, desiring to be independent of God, seeking to be his own master; that "sin of sins, in which all subsequent sins are included as in their germ, for they are but the unfolding of this one" [TRENCH]. **he divided . . .**–Thus "God, when His service no longer appears a perfect freedom, and man promises himself something far better elsewhere, allows him to make the trial; and he shall discover, if need be by saddest proof, that to depart from Him is not to throw off the yoke, but to exchange a light yoke for a heavy one, and one gracious Master for a thousand imperious tyrants and lords" [TRENCH]. **13. not many days**–intoxicated with his new-found resources, and eager for the luxury of using them at will. **a far country**–beyond all danger of interference from home. **wasted . . .**–So long as it lasted, the inward monitor (Isa. 55:2) would be silenced (Isa. 9:10; 57:10; Amos 4:6-10). **riotous living**–(vs. 30), "with harlots." Ah! but this reaches farther than the sensualist; for "in the deep symbolical language of Scripture fornication is the standing image of idolatry; they are in fact ever spoken of as one and the same sin, considered now in its fleshly, now in its spiritual aspect" (Jer. 3; Ezek. 16 and 17), [TRENCH]. **14. when he had spent all . . . a mighty famine**–a mysterious providence holding back the famine till he was in circumstances to feel it in all its rigor. Thus, like Jonah, whom the storm did not overtake till on the mighty deep at the mercy of the waves, does the sinner feel as if "the stars in their courses were fighting against" him (Judg. 5:20). **in want**–the first stage of his bitter experience, and preparation for a change. **15. joined himself . . .**–his pride not yet humbled, unable to brook the shame of a return. **to feed swine**–glad to keep life anyhow, behold the son sank into a swineherd–among the Jews, on account of the prohibition of swine's flesh, emphatically vile!" "He who begins by using the world as a servant, to minister to his pleasure, ends by reversing the relationship" [TRENCH]. **16. would fain have filled**–rather, "was fain to fill," ate greedily of the only food he could get. **the husks**–"the hulls of a leguminous plant which in the East is the food of cattle and swine, and often the nourishment of the poorest in times of distress" [STIER]. **no man gave . . . him**–not this food, for that he had, but *anything better* (Jer. 30:14). This was his lowest depth–*perishing unpitied, alone in the world,* and *ready to disappear from it unmissed!* But this is just the blessed turning-point; midnight before dawn of day (II Chron. 12:8; 33:11-13; Jer. 2:19). **17. came to himself**–Before, he had been "beside himself" (Eccles. 9:3), in what sense will presently appear. **how many hired . . .**–What a testimony to the *nature* of the home he had left! But did he not know all this ere he departed and every day of his voluntary exile? He did, and he did not. His heart being wholly estranged from home and steeped in selfish gratification, his father's house never came within the range of his vision, or but as another name for bondage and gloom. Now empty, desolate, withered, perishing, *home,* with all its peace, plenty, freedom, dignity, starts into view, fills all his visions as a warm and living reality, and breaks his heart. **18. I will arise and**

go to my FATHER—The change has come at last, and what a change!—couched in terms of such exquisite simplicity and power as if expressly framed for all heart-broken penitents. **Father ...**—Mark the term. Though "no more *worthy* to be called his son," the prodigal sinner is taught to claim the *defiled,* but *still existing* relationship, asking not to be made a servant, but *remaining a son* to be made "*as* a servant," willing to take the lowest place and do the meanest work. Ah! and is it come to this? Once it was, "Any place rather than home." Now, "Oh, that home! Could I but dare to hope that the door of it would not be closed against me, how gladly would I take any place and do any work, happy only to be there at all." Well, *that is conversion*—nothing absolutely new, yet all new; old familiar things seen in a new light and for the first time as realities of overwhelming magnitude and power. *How this is brought about the parable says not.* (We have that abundantly elsewhere, Phil. 2: 13, etc.). Its one object is to paint the *welcome home* of the greatest sinners, when (no matter for the present *how*) they "arise and go *to their* Father." **20. a great way off**—Oh yes, when but the face is turned *homeward,* though as yet far, far away, our Father recognizes His own child in us, and bounds to meet us—not saying, Let him come to Me and sue for pardon first, but Himself taking the first step. **fell on his neck and kissed him**—What! In all his filth? Yes. In all his rags? Yes. In all his haggard, shattered wretchedness? Yes. "Our Father who art in heaven," is this Thy portraiture? It is even so (Jer. 31:20). And because it is so, I wonder not that such incomparable teaching hath made the world new. **21. Father, I have sinned ...**—"This confession is uttered *after the kiss of reconciliation*" (Ezek. 16:63) [TRENCH]. **22. But the Father said ...**—The son has not said all he purposed, not so much, because the father's demonstrations had rekindled the filial, and swallowed up all servile feeling [TRENCH] (see on the word "Father," vs. 18), but because the father's heart is made to appear too full to listen, at that moment, to more in this strain. **the best robe**—Cf. Zech. 3:4, 5, "Take away the filthy garments from him; behold I have clothed thee with change of raiment; and they clothed him with garments" (Isa. 61:10; Rev. 3:18). **a ring**—(Cf. Gen. 41:42; Jas. 2:2). **shoes**—Slaves went barefoot. Thus, we have here a threefold symbol of *freedom* and *honor,* restored, as the fruit of *perfect reconciliation.* **23. the fatted calf**—kept for festive occasions. **24. my son**—now *twice* is my son. **dead ... lost**—to *me;* to *himself*—to my service, my satisfaction; to his own dignity, peace, profit. **alive again ... found**—to all these. **merry**—(See on vs. 10). **25. in the field**—engaged in his father's business: cf. vs. 29, "These many years do I *serve* thee." **28. came his father out, and entreated him**—"Like as a father pitieth his children, so the Lord pitieth them that fear Him" (Ps. 103:13). As it is the elder brother who now errs, so it is *the same paternal compassion* which had fallen on the neck of the younger that comes forth and pleads with the elder. **29. these many years ... neither transgressed I at any time ...**—The words are not to be pressed too far. He is merely contrasting *his constancy of love and service* with the conduct of his brother; just as Job, resenting the charge of *hypocrisy* by his friends, speaks as if nothing could be laid to his charge (Job 23:10-12), and David too (Ps. 18:20-24). *The father attests the truth of all he says.* **never ... a kid**—I say not a *calf,* but not even a kid.

that I might make merry with my friends—Here lay his misapprehension. It was no entertainment for the gratification of the prodigal: it was a *father's* expression of the joy *he* felt at his recovery. **thy son ... thy living**—How unworthy a reflection on the common father of both, for the one not only to disown the other, but fling him over upon his father, as if he should say, Take him, and have joy of him! **31. Son ...**—The father resents not the insult—how could he, after the largeness of heart which had kissed the returning prodigal? He calmly expostulates with him, "Son, listen to reason. What need for special, exuberant joy over thee? Didst thou say, 'Lo, these many years do I serve thee?' In that saidst thou truly; but *just for that reason* do I not set the whole household a-rejoicing over thee. For thee is reserved *what is higher still*—a tranquil lifelong satisfaction in thee, as a true-hearted faithful son in thy father's house, nor of the inheritance reserved for thee is aught alienated by this festive and fitting joy over the once foolish but now wise and newly recovered one." **32. It was meet**—Was it possible he should simply take his long vacant place in the family without one special sign of wonder and delight at the change? Would that have been *nature?* But *this* being the meaning of the festivity, it would for that very reason be *temporary.* In time, the dutifulness of even the younger son would become the *law* and not the *exception;* he too at length might venture to say, "Lo, these many years do I serve thee"; and of him the father would say, "Son, thou art ever with me." In that case, therefore, it would *not* be "meet that they should make merry and be glad." The lessons are obvious, but how beautiful! (1) The deeper sunk and the longer estranged any sinner is, the more exuberant is the joy which his recovery occasions. (2) Such joy is *not* the portion of those whose whole lives have been spent in the service of their Father in heaven. (3) Instead of grudging the want of this, they should deem it the highest testimony to their lifelong fidelity, that something better is reserved for them—the deep, abiding complacency of their Father in heaven.

CHAPTER 16

Vss. 1-31. PARABLES OF THE UNJUST STEWARD AND OF THE RICH MAN AND LAZARUS, OR, THE RIGHT USE OF MONEY. **1. steward**—manager of his estate. **accused**—informed upon. **had wasted**—rather, "was wasting." **3. cannot dig ... to beg, ashamed**—therefore, when dismissed, shall be in utter want. **4. may receive me ...**—Observe his one object—*when cast out of one home to secure another.* This is the key to the parable, on which there have been many differing views. **5-7. fifty ... fourscore**—deducting a half from the debt of the one, and a fifth from that of the other. **8. the lord**—evidently the steward's lord, so called in vss. 3, 5. **commended ...**—not for his "injustice," but "because he had done *wisely,*" or prudently; with commendable *foresight* and *skilful adaptation of means to end.* **children of this world**—so ch. 20:34; cf. Psalm 17:14 ("their portion in this life"); Philippians 3:19 ("mind earthly things"); Psalm 4:6, 7. **in**—or "for"—**their generation**—i.e., for the purposes of the "world" they are "of." The greater wisdom (or shrewdness) of the one, in *adaptation of means to ends,* and in energetic, determined prosecution of them, is none of it for *God* and *eternity*—a region they were never in, an atmosphere they never breathed, an undiscovered world, an unborn existence to them—but all for the purposes of their own grovelling and fleeting generation. **children of light**—(so John 12:36; Eph. 5:8; I Thess. 5:5). Yet this is only "as night-birds see better in the dark than those of the day—owls than eagles" [CAJETAN and TRENCH]. But we may learn lessons from them, as our Lord now shows, and "be wise as *serpents*." **9. Make . . . friends of**—Turn to your advantage; i.e., as the steward did, "by showing mercy to the poor" (Dan. 4:27; cf. 12:33; 14:13, 14). **mammon of unrighteousness**—treacherous, precarious. (See on Matt. 6:24.) **ye fail**—in respect of life. **they may receive you**—not generally, "ye may be received" (as ch. 6:38, "shall *men* give"), but "those ye have relieved may rise up as witnesses for you" at the great day. Then, like the steward, when turned out of one home shall ye secure another; but better than he, a heavenly for an earthly, an everlasting for a temporary habitation. Money is not here made the key to heaven, more than "the deeds done in the body" in general, according to which, as a test of character—but not by the merit of which—men are to be judged (II Cor. 5:10, and see Matt. 25:34-40). **10. He . . .**—a maxim of great pregnancy and value; rising from the *prudence* which the steward had to the *fidelity* which he had not, the "*harmlessness* of the dove, to which the serpent" with all his "*wisdom*" is a total stranger. Fidelity depends not on the *amount entrusted*, but on the *sense of responsibility*. He that feels this in little will feel it in much, and conversely. **11, 12. unrighteous mammon**—To the whole of this He applies the disparaging term "what is least," in contrast with "the true riches." **12. another man's . . . your own**—an important turn to the subject. Here all we have is *on trust* as stewards, who have an account to render. Hereafter, what the faithful have will be *their own property,* being no longer on probation, but in secure, undisturbed, rightful, everlasting possession and enjoyment of all that is graciously bestowed on us. Thus money is neither to be *idolized* nor *despised;* we must sit loose to it and use it for God's glory. **13. can serve**—be *entirely at the command* of; and this is true even where the services are not opposed. **hate . . . love**—showing that the two *here intended* are in uncompromising hostility to each other: an awfully searching principle! **14-18. covetous . . . derided him**—sneered at Him; their master-sin being too plainly struck at for them to relish. But it was easier to *run down* than to *refute* such teaching. **15. justify yourselves**—make a show of righteousness. **highly esteemed among men**—generally carried away by plausible appearances. (See I Sam. 16:7; and ch. 14:11.) **16. The law . . .**—(See on Matt. 11:13). **every man presseth . . .**—Publicans and sinners, all indiscriminately, are eagerly pressing into it; and ye, interested adherents of the mere forms of an economy which is passing away, "discerning not the signs of this time," will allow the tide to go past you and be found a stranded monument of blindness and obstinacy. **17. it is easier . . .**—(See on Matt. 5:17, 18). **18. putteth away his wife . . .**—(See on Matt. 19:3-9). Far from intending to weaken the force of the law, in these allusions to a new economy, our Lord, in this unexpected way, sends home its high requirements with a pungency which the Pharisees would not fail to feel. **19. purple and fine linen . . .**—(Cf. Esther 8:15; Rev. 18:12); wanting nothing which taste and appetite craved and money could

procure. **20, 21. laid**—having to be carried and put down. **full of sores**—open, running, "not closed, nor bound up, nor mollified with ointment" (Isa. 1:6). **21. desiring to be fed with**—but was not [GROTIUS, BENGEL, MEYER, TRENCH, etc.]. The words may mean indeed "was fain to feed on," or "gladly fed on," as in ch. 15:16 [ALFORD, WEBSTER and WILKINSON, etc.]. But the context rather favors the former. **licked . . .**—a touching act of brute pity, in the absence of human relief. It is a case of heartless indifference, amidst luxuries of every kind, to one of God's poorest and most afflicted ones, presented daily before the eye. **22. died**—His burial was too unimportant to mention; while "the rich man died and *was buried*"—his carcass carried in pomp to its earthly restingplace. **in to Abraham's bosom**—as if seen reclining next to Him at the heavenly feast (Matt. 8:11). **23. in hell**—not the final place of the lost (for which another word is used), but as we say "the unseen world." But as the object here is certainly to depict the *whole torment* of the one and the *perfect bliss* of the other, it comes in this case to much the same. **seeth Abraham**—not God, to whom therefore he cannot cry [BENGEL]. **24. Father Abraham** —a well-founded, but unavailing, claim of natural descent (ch. 3:8; John 8:37). **mercy on me**—who never showed any (Jas. 2:3). **send Lazarus**—the pining victim of his merciless neglect. **that he may** —take me hence? No; that he dares not to ask. **dip . . . tongue**—i.e., the *least* conceivable and the *most momentary* abatement of his torment; that is all. But even this he is told is (1) *unreasonable.* **25, 26. Son**—stinging acknowledgment of the claimed relationship. **thou . . . Lazarus . . .**—As it is a great law of God's kingdom, that *the nature of our present desires shall rule that of our future bliss,* so by that law, he whose "good things," craved and enjoyed, were all bounded by time, could look for none after his connection with time had come to an end (ch. 6:24). But by this law, he whose "evil things," all crowded into the present life, drove him to seek, and find, consolation in a life beyond the grave, is by death released from all evil and ushered into unmixed and uninterrupted good (ch. 6:21). (2) It is *impossible.* **26. besides all this**—independently of this consideration. **a great gulf fixed**—*By an irrevocable decree* there has been placed a vast impassable abyss between the two states, and the occupants of each. **27-31. Then he said**—now abandoning all hope for himself—**send him to my father's house . . .**—no waking up of good in the heart of the lost, but bitter reproach against God and the old economy, as not warning him sufficiently [TRENCH]. The answer of Abraham is, They *are* sufficiently warned. **30. Nay**—giving the lie to Abraham. **if . . .**—a principle of awful magnitude and importance. The greatest miracle will have no effect on those who are determined not to believe. A *real* Lazarus soon "rose from the dead," but the sight of him by crowds of people, inclined thereby to Christ, only crowned the unbelief and hastened the murderous plots of the Pharisees against the Lord of glory; nor has His own resurrection, far more overpowering, yet won over that "crooked and perverse nation."

CHAPTER 17

Vss. 1-10. OFFENSES—FAITH—HUMILITY. **1, 2.** (See on Matt. 18:6, 7.) **3, 4.** (See on Matt. 18:15-17, 21, 22.) **seven times**—not a *lower* measure of the forgiving spirit than the "seventy times seven" enjoined on Peter, which was occasioned by his asking if he was to *stop* at seven times. "No," is the virtual answer, "though it come to seventy times that number, if only he ask forgiveness in sincerity." **5. Lord**—(See on ch. 10:1). **increase our faith**—moved by the difficulty of avoiding and forgiving "offenses." This is the only instance in which *a spiritual operation upon their souls* was solicited of Christ by the Twelve; but a kindred and higher prayer had been offered before, by one with far fewer opportunities. (See on Mark 9:24.) **6. sycamine**—mulberry. (See on Mark 11:22-24.) **7-10. say unto him by and by**—The "by and by" (or rather "directly") should be joined not to the *saying* but the *going:* "Go directly." The connection here is: "But when your faith *has* been so increased as both to avoid and forgive offenses, and do things impossible to all but faith, be not puffed up as though you had laid the Lord under any obligations to you." **9. I trow not**—or, as we say, when much more is meant, "I should think not." **10. unprofitable**—a word which, though usually denoting the *opposite* of profit, is here used simply in its *negative* sense. "We have not, as his servants, profited or benefited God at all." (Cf. Job 22:2, 3; Rom. 11:35.)

11-19. TEN LEPERS CLEANSED. **11-13. through the midst of Samaria and Galilee**—probably on the *confines* of both. **12. stood afar off**—(Cf. Lev. 13: 45, 46). **13. they lifted up**—their common misery drawing these poor outcasts together (II Kings 7:3), nay, making them forget the fierce national antipathy of Jew and Samaritan [TRENCH]. **Jesus...** —(Cf. Matt. 20:30-33). How quick a teacher is felt misery, even though as here the teaching may be soon forgotten! **14. show yourselves**—as cleansed persons. (See on Matt. 8:4.) Thus too would the Samaritan be taught that "salvation is of the Jews" (John 4:22). **as they went, were cleansed**—In how many different ways were our Lord's cures wrought, and this different from all the rest. **17, 18. Were there not ten cleansed**—rather, were not *the ten* cleansed? i.e., the whole of them—an example (by the way) of Christ's omniscience [BENGEL]. **18. this stranger**—"this alien" (literally, "of another race"). The language is that of wonder and admiration, as is expressly said of another exhibition of Gentile faith (Matt. 8:10). **19. Arise**—for he had "fallen down on his face at His feet" (vs. 16) and there lain prostrate. **faith made thee whole**—not as the others, merely in body, but in that higher spiritual sense with which His constant language has so familiarized us.

20-37. COMING OF THE KINGDOM OF GOD AND OF THE SON OF MAN. **20-25. when...**—To meet the erroneous views not only of the Pharisees, but of the disciples themselves, our Lord addresses both, announcing the coming of the kingdom under different aspects. "It cometh not with observation"—with watching or lying in wait, as for something outwardly imposing and at once revealing itself. **21. Lo here!...lo there!**—shut up within *this* or *that* sharply defined and visible geographical or ecclesiastical limit. **within you**—is of an internal and *spiritual* character (as contrasted with their *outside* views of it). But it has its *external* side too. **22. The days**—rather "Days." **will come**—as in ch. 19: 43, when, amidst calamities, etc., you will anxiously look for a deliverer, and deceivers will put themselves forward in this character. **one of the days of the Son of man**—Himself again among them but for one day; as we say when all seems to be

going wrong and the one person who could keep them right is removed [NEANDER in STIER, etc.]. "This is said to guard against the mistake of supposing that His visible presence would accompany the manifestation and establishment of His kingdom" [WEBSTER and WILKINSON]. **23. they shall say, See here...go not...**—a warning to all so-called expositors of prophecy and their followers, who cry, Lo there and see here, every time that war breaks out or revolutions occur. **24. as lightning...so...the Son of man**—i.e., it will be as manifest. The Lord speaks here of His coming and manifestation in a prophetically indefinite manner, and in these preparatory words *blends into one the distinctive epochs* [STIER]. When the whole polity of the Jews, civil and ecclesiastical alike, was broken up at once, and its continuance rendered impossible by the destruction of Jerusalem, it became as manifest to all as the lightning of heaven that the kingdom of God had ceased to exist in its old, and had entered on a new and perfectly different form. So it may be again, ere its final and greatest change at the personal coming of Christ, and of which the words in their highest sense are alone true. **But first...suffer...**—This shows that the more immediate reference of previous verse is to an event *soon* to follow the death of Christ. It was designed to withdraw the attention of "His disciples" from the *glare* in which His foregoing words had invested the approaching establishment of His kingdom. **26-30. eat...married...planted...**—all the ordinary occupations and enjoyments of life. Though the antediluvian world and the cities of the plain were awfully wicked, it is not their *wickedness,* but their *worldliness,* their unbelief and indifference to the future, their *unpreparedness,* that is here held up as a warning. *N.B.*—These recorded events of Old Testament history—denied or explained away nowadays by not a few—are referred to here as *facts.* **31-33. to take it away...Remember...**—a warning against that *lingering reluctance to part with present treasures* which induces some to remain in a burning house, in hopes of saving this and that precious article till consumed and buried in its ruins. The cases here supposed, though different, are similar. **Lot's wife**—her "*look back,*" for that is all that is said of her, and her recorded *doom.* Her heart was in Sodom still, and the "look" just said, "And must I bid it adieu?" **Whosoever...**—(See on ch. 9:23-27). **34. two in one bed**—the prepared and unprepared mingled in closest intercourse together in the ordinary walks and fellowships of life, when the moment of severance arrives. Awful truth! realized before the destruction of Jerusalem, when the Christians found themselves forced by their Lord's directions (ch. 21:21) at once and for ever away from their old associates; but most of all when the second coming of Christ shall burst upon a heedless world. **37. Where**—shall this occur? **Wheresoever...**—"As birds of prey scent out the carrion, so wherever is found a mass of incurable moral and spiritual corruption, there will be seen alighting the ministers of divine judgment," a proverbial saying terrifically verfied at the destruction of Jerusalem, and many times since, though its most tremendous illustration will be at the world's final day.

CHAPTER 18

Vss. 1-8. PARABLE OF THE IMPORTUNATE WIDOW. **1-5. always**—Cf. vs. 7, "night and day." **faint**—

lose heart, or slacken. **2. feared not . . . neither regarded**–defying the vengeance of God and despising the opinion of men. **widow**–weak, desolate, defenseless (I Tim. 5:5, which is taken from this). **3. came**–kept coming. See vs. 5, "her continual coming." **Avenge me**–i.e., rid me of the oppression of. **5. continual coming**–coming for ever. **6-8. the Lord**–a name expressive of the *authoritative* style in which He interprets His own parable. **7. shall not God**–not unjust, but the infinitely righteous Judge. **avenge**–redeem from oppression. **his own elect**–not like this widow, the object of indifference and contempt, but dear to Him as the apple of the eye (Zech. 2:8). **cry day and night**–whose every cry enters into the ears of the Lord of Sabaoth (Jas. 5:4), and how much more their incessant and persevering cries! **bear long with them**–rather, "in their case," or "on their account" (as Jas. 5:7, "for it"), [GROTIUS, DE WETTE, etc.]. **8. speedily**–as if pained at the long delay, impatient for the destined moment to interpose. (Cf. Prov. 29:1.) **Nevertheless . . .**–i.e., Yet ere the Son of man will come to redress the wrongs of His Church, so low will the hope of relief sink, through the length of the delay, that one will be fain to ask, Will He find any faith of a coming avenger left on the earth? From this we learn: (1) That the *primary* and *historical* reference of this parable is to the Church in its *widowed,* desolate, oppressed, defenseless condition during the present absence of her Lord in the heavens; (2) That in these circumstances importunate, persevering prayer for deliverance is the Church's fitting exercise; (3) That notwithstanding every encouragement to this, so long will the answer be delayed, while the need of relief continues the same, and all hope of deliverance will have nearly died out, and "faith" of Christ's coming scarcely to be found. But the application of the parable to *prayer in general* is so obvious as to have nearly hidden its more direct reference, and so precious that one cannot allow it to disappear in any public and historical interpretation.

9-14. PARABLE OF THE PHARISEE AND THE PUBLICAN. **11, 12. stood**–as the Jews in prayer (Mark 11:25). **God . . .**–To have been kept from gross iniquities was undoubtedly a just cause of thankfulness to God; but instead of the devoutly humble, admiring frame which this should inspire, the Pharisee arrogantly severs himself from the rest of mankind, as quite above them, and, with a contemptuous look at the poor publican, thanks God that he has not to stand afar off like him, to hang down his head like a bulrush and beat his breast like him. But these are only his *moral* excellencies. His *religious* merits complete his grounds for congratulation. Not confining himself to the one divinely prescribed annual fast (Lev. 16:29), he was not behind the most rigid, who fasted on the second and fifth days of every week [LIGHTFOOT], and gave the tenth not only of what the law laid under tithing, but of "all his gains." Thus, besides doing *all his duty,* he did *works of supererogation;* while sins to confess and spiritual wants to be supplied he seems to have felt none. What a picture of the Pharisaic character and religion! **13. standing afar off**–as unworthy to draw near; but that was the way *to get* near (Ps. 34:18; Isa. 57:15). **would not lift up**–blushing and ashamed to do so (Ezra 9:6). **smote . . .**–kept smiting; for anguish (ch. 23:48), and self-reproach (Jer. 31:19). **be merciful**–"be propitiated," a very unusual word in such a sense, only once else used in the New Testament, in the

sense of "making reconciliation" by sacrifice (Heb. 2:17). There *may* therefore, be some allusion to this here, though not likely. **a sinner**–literally, "*the* sinner"; i.e., "If ever there was one, I am he." **14. rather than the other**–The meaning is, "and not the other"; for the Pharisee was not seeking justification, and felt no need of it. This great law of the Kingdom of God is, in the teaching of Christ, inscribed, as in letters of gold, over its entrance gate. And in how many different forms is it repeated (Ps. 138:6; 147:6; ch. 1:53). To be *self-emptied,* or, "poor in spirit," is the fundamental and indispensable preparation for the reception of the "grace which bringeth salvation": wherever this exists, the "mourning" for it which precedes "comfort" and the earnest "hungerings and thirstings after righteousness" which are rewarded by the "fulness" of it, will, as we see here, be surely found. Such, therefore, and such only, are the justified ones (Job 33:27, 28; Ps. 34:18; Isa. 57:15).

15-17. LITTLE CHILDREN BROUGHT TO CHRIST. **infants**–showing that some, at least, of those called in Matthew (19:13) and Mark (10:13) simply "little" or "young children," were literally "*babes.*" **touch them**–or, as more fully in Matthew, "put His hands on them and *pray,*" or invoke a "blessing" on them (Mark 10:16), according to venerable custom (Gen. 48:14, 15). **rebuked them**–Repeatedly the disciples thus interposed to save annoyance and interruption to their Master; but, as the result showed, *always against the mind of Christ* (Matt. 15:23; ch. 18:39, 40). Here, it is plain from our Lord's reply, that they thought the intrusion a useless one, as *infants* were not capable of receiving anything from Him. His ministrations were for *grown people.* **16. But Jesus**–*much displeased,"* says Mark (10:14); and invaluable addition. **said**–"SUFFER THE LITTLE CHILDREN TO COME UNTO ME"–"AND FORBID THEM NOT," is the important addition of Matthew (19:14) and Mark (10:14). What words are these from the lips of Christ! The price of them is above rubies. But the *reason* assigned, "FOR OF SUCH IS THE KINGDOM OF GOD," or "of heaven," as in Matthew 19:14, completes the previous information here conveyed; especially as interpreted by what immediately follows: "AND HE TOOK THEM UP IN HIS ARMS, PUT HIS HANDS UPON THEM, AND BLESSED THEM" (Mark 10:16). It is surely not to be conceived that all our Lord meant was to inform us, that seeing *grown people* must become childlike in order to be capable of the Kingdom of God, therefore they should not hinder *infants* from coming to Him, and therefore He took up and blessed *the infants themselves.* Was it not just the grave mistake of the disciples that infants should not be brought to Christ, because only grown people could profit by Him, which "much displeased" our Lord? And though He took the irresistible opportunity of lowering their pride of reason, by informing them that, in order to enter the Kingdom, "*instead of the children first becoming like them, they must themselves become like the children*" [RICHTER in STIER], this was but by the way; and, returning to the *children themselves,* He took them up in His gracious arms, put His hands upon them and blessed them, for no conceivable reason but to show that *they were thereby made capable,* AS INFANTS, *of the Kingdom of God.* And if so, then "*Can any man forbid water that these should not be baptized which have received the Holy Ghost as well as we?*" (Acts 10:47). But such application of the baptismal water can have no warrant here, save where the infants have been *previously brought to Christ Himself* for His benediction, and only as the *sign and seal* of that benediction.

18-30. THE RICH YOUNG RULER, AND DISCOURSE THEREON. This case presents some remarkable points. (1) The man was of irreproachable moral character; and this amidst all the temptations of *youth*, for he was a "young man" (Matt. 19:22), and *wealth*, for "he was very rich" (vs. 23; Mark 10:22). (2) But restless notwithstanding, his heart craves eternal life. (3) Unlike the "rulers," to whose class he belonged (vs. 18), he so far believed in Jesus as to be persuaded He could authoritatively direct him on this vital point. (4) So earnest is he that he comes "running" and even "kneeling before Him," and that when He was gone forth *into the war* (Mark 10:17)—the high-road, by this time crowded with travellers to the passover; undeterred by the virulent opposition of the class he belonged to as a "ruler" and by the shame he might be expected to feel at broaching such a question in the hearing of a crowd and on the open road. **19. Why . . .**—Did our Lord mean then to teach that God only ought to be called "good"? Impossible, for that had been to contradict all Scripture teaching, and His own, too (Ps. 112:5; Matt. 25:21; Titus 1:8). Unless therefore we are to ascribe captiousness to our Lord, He could have had but one object — *to raise the youth's ideas of Himself*, as not to be classed merely with other "good masters," and declining to receive this title *apart from* the "One" who is essentially and only "good." This indeed is but distantly hinted; but unless this is seen in *the background* of our Lord's words, nothing worthy of Him can be made out of them. (Hence, *Socinianism*, instead of having any support here, is only baffled by it.) **20. Thou knowest . . .**—Matthew is more complete here: "but if thou wilt enter into life, keep the commandments. He saith unto him, Which?"—as if he had said, Point me out one of them which I have not kept?—"Jesus said, Thou shalt . . ." (Matt. 19: 17, 18). Our Lord purposely confines Himself to the *second* table, which He would consider easy to keep, enumerating them all—for in Mark (10:19), "Defraud not" stands for the *tenth* (else the eighth is twice repeated). In Matthew the *sum* of this second table of the law is added, "Thou shalt love thy neighbor as thyself," as if to see if he would venture to say he had kept *that*. **21. All these . . .** —"what lack I yet?" adds Matthew. Ah! this gives us a glimpse of his heart. Doubtless he was perfectly sincere; but something within whispered to him that *his* keeping of the commandments was *too easy* a way of getting to heaven. He felt something beyond this to be necessary; after keeping all the commandments he was at a loss to know what that could be; and he came to Jesus just upon that point. "Then," says Mark (10:21), "Jesus beholding him loved him," or "looked lovingly upon him." His sincerity, frankness, and nearness to the kingdom of God, in themselves most winning qualities, won our Lord's regard even though he turned his back upon Him—a lesson to those who can see nothing lovable save in the regenerate. **22. lackest . . . one thing**—Ah! but that a fundamental, fatal lack. **sell . . .**—As riches were his idol, our Lord, who knew if from the first, lays His great authoritative grasp at once upon it, saying, "Now give Me up that, and all is right." No general direction about the disposal of riches, then, is here given, save that we are to sit loose to them and lay them at the feet of Him who gave them. He who does this with all he has, whether rich or poor, is a true

heir of the kingdom of heaven. **23-25. was very sorrowful**—Matthew more fully, "*went away* sorrowful"; Mark still more, "was sad" or "sullen" at that saying, and "went away grieved." Sorry he was, very sorry, to part with Christ; but to part with his riches would have cost him a pang more. When Riches or Heaven, on Christ's terms, were the alternative, the result showed to which side the balance inclined. Thus was he shown to lack the one all-comprehensive requirement of the law—the *absolute subjection of the heart to God*, and this want vitiated all his other obediences. **24. when Jesus saw** —Mark says, He "looked round about"—as if first following the departing youth with His eye—"and saith unto His disciples." **how hardly . . .**—with what difficulty. In Mark an explanation is added, "How hard is it for them that *trust* in riches . . ."—i.e., with what difficulty is this idolatrous trust conquered, without which they cannot enter; and this is introduced by the word "children"—sweet diminutive of affection and pity (John 21:5). **easier for a camel . . .**—a proverbial expression denoting literally a thing impossible, but figuratively, very difficult. **26, 27. For . . .**—"At that rate none can be saved": "Well, it does pass *human* power, but not *divine*. **28-30. Lo . . .**—in the simplicity of his heart (as is evident from the reply), conscious that the required surrender had been made, and generously taking in his brethren with him—"*we*"; not in the spirit of the young ruler. "All these have I kept," **left all**—"The workmen's little is as much his 'all' as the prince's much [BENGEL]. In Matthew (19:27) he adds, "What shall we have therefore?" How shall it fare with us? **29. There is no man . . .**—graciously acknowledging at once the completeness and the acceptableness of the surrender as a thing already made. **house . . .**—The specification is still more minute in Matthew and Mark, to take in *every* form of self-sacrifice. **for the kingdom of God's sake**—in Mark, "for MY sake and the Gospel's." See on ch. 6:22. **30. manifold more in this present time** in Matthew (19:29) "an hundredfold," to which Mark (10:30) gives this most interesting addition, "Now in this present time, houses, and brethren, and sisters, and mothers, and children, and lands, with persecutions." We have here the blessed promise of a *reconstruction of all human relationships and affections on a Christian basis and in a Christian state, after being sacrificed, in their natural form, on the altar of love to Christ*. This He calls "manifold more"—"an hundredfold more"—than what they sacrificed. Our Lord was Himself the first to exemplify this *new adjustment of His own relationships*. (See on Matt. 12:49, 50; and on II Cor. 6:14-18.) But this "with persecutions"; for how could such a transfer take place without the most cruel wrenches to flesh and blood? but the persecution would haply follow them into their new and higher circle, breaking that up too! But best of all, "in the world to come life everlasting." And

> When the shore is won at last
> Who will count the billows past?
>   KEBLE

These promises are for *every one* who forsakes his all for Christ. But in Matthew (19:28) this is prefaced by a special promise to *the Twelve*: "Verily I say unto you, That ye which have followed Me in the Regeneration, when the Son of man shall sit in the throne of His glory, ye also shall sit on twelve thrones judging the twelve tribes of Israel." Ye who have now adhered to Me shall, in the new kingdom, rule, or give law to, the great Christian world, here set forth in Jewish dress as the twelve tribes, presided over by the twelve apostles on so many judicial thrones. In this sense certainly the promise has been illustriously fulfilled [CALVIN, GROTIUS, LIGHTFOOT, etc.]. But if the promise refers to the yet future glory (as may be thought from ch. 22:28-30, and as most take it), it points to the highest personal distinction of the first founders of the Christian Church.

31-34. FULLER ANNOUNCEMENT OF HIS APPROACHING DEATH AND RESURRECTION. (See on Mark 10:32-34). **31. all written by the prophets concerning the Son of man ... be accomplished**—showing how Christ Himself read, and would have us to read, the Old Testament, in which some otherwise evangelical interpreters find no prophecies, or *virtually* none, of the sufferings of the Son of man. **34. understood none ...**—The Evangelist seems unable to say strongly enough how entirely hidden from them at that time was the *sense* of these exceeding plain statements: no doubt to add weight to their subsequent testimony, which from this very circumstance was prodigious, and with all the simple-hearted irresistible.

35-43. BLIND MAN HEALED. In Matthew 20: 29-34, they are *two,* as in the case of the Demoniac of Gadara. In Matthew and Mark (10:46-52) the occurrence is connected with Christ's *departure from* Jericho; in Luke with His *approach to it.* Many ways of accounting for these slight divergences of detail have been proposed. Perhaps, *if we knew all the facts,* we should see no difficulty; but that we have been left so far in the dark shows that the thing is of no moment any way. One thing is plain, there could have been no collusion among the authors of these Gospels, else they would have taken care to remove these "spots on the sun." **38. son of David ...**—(See on Matthew 12:23). **39. rebuked ...**—(See on vs. 15). **so much the more**—that *importunity* so commended in the Syrophœnician woman, and so often enjoined (ch. 11:5-13; 18:1-8). **40. commanded ...**—Mark has this interesting addition: "And they call the blind man, saying unto him, Be of good comfort, rise, He calleth thee"—just as one earnestly desiring an interview with some exalted person, but told by one official after another that it is vain to wait, as he will not succeed (they know it), yet persists in waiting for some answer to his suit, and at length the door opens, and a servant appears, saying, "You will be admitted—he has called you." *And are there no other suitors to Jesus who sometimes fare thus?* "And he, casting away his garment"—how lively is this touch, evidently of an eye-witness, expressive of his earnestness and joy—"came to Jesus" (Mark 10:49, 50). **41-43. What wilt thou ...**—to try them; to deepen their present consciousness of need; and to draw out their faith in Him. **Lord** "*Rabboni*" (Mark 10:51); an emphatic and confiding exclamation. (See on John 9.)

CHAPTER 19

Vss. 1-10. ZACCHEUS THE PUBLICAN. The name is Jewish. **2-4. chief among the publicans**—farming a considerable district, with others under him. **rich**—Illgotten riches some of it certainly was. (See on vs. 8). **3. who he was**—what sort of person. *Curiosity* then was his only motive, though his determination not to be baulked was overruled for

more than he sought. **4. sycamore**—the Egyptian fig, with leaves like the mulberry. **5, 6. looked up ...**—in the full knowledge of who was in the tree, and preparatory to addressing him. **Zaccheus ...** whom he had never seen in the flesh, nor probably heard of. "He calleth His own sheep *by name* and leadeth them out" (John 10:3). **make haste, and come down**—to which he literally responded—"he made haste and came down." **for to-day ...**—Our Lord *invites Himself,* and in *royal* style, which waits not for invitations, but as the honor is done to the subject, not the sovereign, announces the purpose of royalty to partake of the subject's hospitalities. Manifestly our Lord speaks as knowing how the privilege would be appreciated. **to-day ... abide**—(Cf. John 1:39), probably over night. **6. joyfully**—Whence this so sudden "joy" in the cold bosom of an avaricious publican? The internal revolution was as perfect as instantaneous. "He spake and it was done." "Then shall the lame man leap as an hart, and the tongue of the dumb sing" (Isa. 35:6). **7. to be guest**—or *lodge:* something more than "eating with" such (ch. 15:2). **a sinner**—that *was* one but a minute ago, but now is not. This mighty change, however, was all unknown to them. But they shall know it presently. "Sinner" would refer both to his office, vile in the eyes of a Jew, and to his character, which it is evident was not good. **8-10. stood**—before all. **said unto the Lord, Behold, Lord**—Mark how frequently Luke uses this title, and always where lordly *authority, dignity,* or *power* is intended. **if I have** —i.e., "so far as I have," for evidently the "if" is so used (as in Philippians 4:8). **taken by false accusation**—defrauded, overcharged (ch. 3:12, 13). **fourfold**—The Roman law required this; the Jewish law, but the principal and a fifth more (Num. 5: 7). There was no *demand* made for either; but, as if to revenge himself on his hitherto reigning sin (see on John 20:28), and to testify the change he had experienced, besides surrendering the half of his *fair* gains to the poor, he voluntarily determines to give up all that was ill-gotten, quadrupled. He gratefully addressed this to the "Lord," to whom he owed the wonderful change. **9. Jesus said unto him**—but also before all. **This day ...**—memorable saying! Salvation already come, but not a day old. **to this house**—so expressed probably to meet the taunt, "He is gone to be guest ..." The house is no longer polluted; it is now fit to receive Me. But *salvation to a house* is an exceedingly precious idea, expressing the new air that would henceforth breathe in it, and the new impulses from its head which would reach its members (Ps. 118:15; Acts 16:15, 16, 31). **son of Abraham**—He was that by birth, but here it means a partaker of his *faith,* being mentioned as the sufficient explanation of *salvation* having come to him. **10. lost**—and such "lost" ones as this Zaccheus. (See on ch. 15:32). What encouragement is there in this narrative to hope for unexpected conversions!

11-27. PARABLE OF THE POUNDS. A different parable from that of the Talents (Matt. 25:14-30). For, (1) This parable was spoken "when He was *nigh* to Jerusalem" (vs. 11); that one, some days after entering it, and from the Mount of Olives. (2) This parable was spoken to the promiscuous crowd; that, to the Twelve alone. Accordingly, (3) Besides the "servants" in this parable, who profess subjection to Him, there is a class of "citizens" who refuse to own Him, and who are treated differently, whereas in the parable of the talents, spoken to the *former* class alone, this latter class is omitted. (4) In the Talents, each servant receives a different number of them (5, 2, 1); in the Pounds all receive the same one pound, which is but about the 60th part of a talent; also, in the talents, each shows the same fidelity by doubling what he received (the 5 are made 10, the 2, 4); in the Pounds, each receiving the same, render a *different* return (one making his pound 10, another 5). Plainly, therefore, the intended lesson is different; the one illustrating *equal fidelity with different degrees of advantage;* the other, *different degrees of improvement of the same opportunities;* yet with all this difference, the parables are remarkably similar. **12. a far country**—said to put down the notion that He was just on His way to set up His kingdom, and to inaugurate it by His personal presence. **to receive . . . a kingdom**—be invested with royalty; as when Herod went to Rome and was there made king; a striking expression of what our Lord went away for and received, "sitting down at the right hand of the Majesty on high." **to return**—at His second coming. **13. Occupy**—"negotiate," "do business," with the resources entrusted. **14. his citizens**—His proper subjects; meaning the Jews, who expressly repudiating our Lord's claims said, "We have no king but Caesar" (John 19:15). In Christendom, these correspond to infidel rejecters of Christianity, as distinguished from professed Christians. **15-26.** (See on Matt. 25:19-29). **ten . . . five cities**—different degrees of future gracious reward, proportioned to the measure of present fidelity. **27. bring hither . . .**—(Cf. I Sam. 15:32, 33). Referring to the awful destruction of Jerusalem, but pointing to the final destruction of all that are found in open rebellion against Christ.

28-44. CHRIST'S TRIUMPHANT ENTRY INTO JERUSALEM, AND TEARS OVER IT. (See on Matt. 21:1-11). **29-38. Bethphage**—"house of figs," a village which with Bethany lay along the further side of Mount Olivet, east of Jerusalem. **30. whereon . . .** (See on John 19:41). **31. the Lord hath need . . .** —He both knew all and had the key of the human heart. (See on vs. 5.) Perhaps the owner was a disciple. **35. set Jesus on**—He allowing this, as befitting the *state* He was for the first and only time assuming. **37. whole multitude . . .**—The language here is very grand, intended to express a burst of admiration far wider and deeper than ever had been witnessed before. **38. Blessed be the King . . .**—Mark more fully, "Hosanna," i.e., *"Save now,"* the words of Psalm 118:25, which were understood to refer to Messiah; and so they add, "to the Son of David, blessed is He that cometh in the name of the Lord (Ps. 118:26), Hosanna in the highest." This was the very loftiest style in which He could be saluted as the promised Deliverer. **peace . . .**—(See on ch. 2:13, 14). **40. the stones . . .**—Hitherto the Lord had discouraged all demonstrations in His favor; latterly He had *begun* an opposite course; on this one occasion He seems to yield His whole soul to the wide and deep acclaim with a mysterious satisfaction, regarding it as *so necessary* a part of the regal dignity in which as Messiah He for this last time entered the city, that if not offered by the vast multitude, it would have been *wrung out of the stones* rather than be withheld (Hab. 2:11). **41-44. when beheld . . . wept,**—Cf. Lamentations 3:51, "Mine eye affecteth mine heart"; the heart again affecting the eye. Under this sympathetic law of the relation of mind and body, Jesus, in His beautiful, tender humanity, was constituted even as we. What a contrast to the immediately preceding profound joy! He yielded Himself alike freely to both.

(See on Matt. 23:37. **42. at least in this . . .**—even at this moving moment. (See on ch. 13:9). **thy peace**—thinking perhaps of the name of the city (Heb. 7:2) [WEBSTER and WILKINSON]. How much is included in this word! **now . . . hid**—It was His among His *last* open efforts to "gather them," but their eyes were judicially closed. **43. a trench** —a rampart; first of wood, and when this was burnt, a built wall, four miles in circuit, built in three days—so determined were they. This "cut off all hope of escape," and consigned the city to unparalleled horrors. (See JOSEPHUS, *Jewish Wars,* vss. 6: 2; 12:3, 4.) All here predicted was with dreadful literality fulfilled.

45-48. SECOND CLEANSING OF THE TEMPLE, AND SUBSEQUENT TEACHING. **45, 46.** As the first cleansing was on His *first* visit to Jerusalem (John 2:13-22), so this second cleansing was on His last. **den of thieves**—banded together for plunder, reckless of principle. The mild term "house of merchandise,' used on the former occasion, was now unsuitable. **47. sought**—continued seeking, i.e., daily, as He taught. **48. were very attentive to hear him**—hung upon His words.

CHAPTER 20

Vss. 1-19. THE AUTHORITY OF JESUS QUESTIONED, AND HIS REPLY—PARABLE OF THE WICKED HUSBANDMEN. (See on Matthew 21:23.) **2. these things**—particularly the clearing of the temple. **4. baptism of John**—his whole ministry and mission, of which baptism was the seal. **5. Why then believed ye him not?**—i.e., in his testimony to Jesus, the sum of his whole witness. **7. could not tell**—crooked, cringing hypocrites! No wonder Jesus gave you no answer (Matt. 7:6). But what dignity and composure does our Lord display as He turns their question upon themselves! **9-13. vineyard**—(See on ch. 13:6). In Matthew 21:33 additional points are given, taken literally from Isaiah 5:2, to fix down the application and sustain it by Old Testament authority. **husbandmen**—the ordinary spiritual guides of the people, under whose care and culture the fruits of righteousness might be yielded. **went . . .**—leaving it to the laws of the spiritual husbandry during the whole length of the Jewish economy. (See on Mark 4:26.) **10. beat . . .**—(Matt. 21:35); i.e., the prophets, extraordinary messengers raised up from time to time. (See on Matt. 23:37.) **13. my beloved son**—Mark (12:6) still more affectingly, "Having yet therefore one son, his well-beloved"; our Lord thus severing Himself from all merely *human* messengers, and claiming Sonship in its loftiest sense. (Cf. Heb. 3:3-6.) **it may be**—"surely"; implying the almost unimaginable guilt of *not* doing so. **14. reasoned among themselves . . .**—(Cf. Genesis 37:18-20; John 11:47-53). **the heir**—sublime expression of the great truth, that God's inheritance was destined for, and in due time to come into the possession of, His Son *in our nature* (Heb. 1:2). **inheritance . . . ours**—and so from mere *servants* we may become *lords;* the deep aim of the depraved heart, and literally *"the root of all evil."* **15. cast him out of the vineyard**—(Cf. Hebrews 13:11-13; I Kings 21:13; John 19:17). **16. He shall come . . .**—This answer was given by the Pharisees themselves (Matt. 21: 41), thus pronouncing their own righteous doom. Matthew alone (21:43) gives the naked application, that "the kingdom of God should be taken from them, and given to a nation bringing forth the fruits thereof"—the great evangelical community of the faithful, chiefly Gentiles. **God forbid**—His whole meaning now bursting upon them. **17-19. written** —(in Ps. 118:22, 23. See on ch. 19:38). The Kingdom of God is here a Temple, in the erection of which *a certain stone,* rejected as unsuitable by the spiritual builders, is, by the great Lord of the House, made the keystone of the whole. On that Stone the builders were now "falling" and being "broken" (Isa. 8:15), "sustaining great spiritual hurt; but soon that Stone should fall upon *them* and grind them to powder" (Dan. 2:34, 35; Zech. 12:3)—in their *corporate* capacity in the tremendous destruction of Jerusalem, but *personally,* as unbelievers, in a more awful sense still. **19. the same hour**—hardly able to restrain their rage.

20-40. ENTANGLING QUESTIONS ABOUT TRIBUTE AND THE RESURRECTION—THE REPLIES. **20-26. sent forth**—after consulting (Matt. 22:15) on the best plan. **spies**—"of the Pharisees and Herodians" (Mark 12:13). See on Mark 3:6. **21. we know ...**— hoping by flattery to throw Him off His guard. **22. tribute**—(See on Matt. 17:24). **25. things which be Caesar's**—Putting it in this general form, it was impossible for sedition itself to dispute it, and yet it dissolved the snare. **and unto God**—How much there is in this profound but to them startling addition to the maxim, and how incomparable is the whole for fulness, brevity, clearness, weight! **27-34. no resurrection**—"nor angel nor spirit" (Acts 23:8); the *materialists* of the day. **34. said unto them**—In Matthew 22:29, the reply begins with this important statement:—"Ye do err, not knowing the Scriptures," regarding the future state, "nor the power of God," before which a thousand such difficulties vanish (also Mark 12:24). **36. neither ... die any more**—Marriage is ordained to perpetuate the human family; but as there will be no breaches by death in the future state, this ordinance will cease. **equal**—or "like." **unto the angels**—i.e., in the *immortality* of their nature. **children of God**— not in respect of *character* but *nature;* "being the children of the resurrection" to an undecaying existence (Rom. 8:21, 23). And thus the children of their Father's immortality (I Tim. 6:16). **37, 38. even Moses**—whom they had just quoted to entangle Him. **not ... of the dead, ... for all ...** —To God, no human being is dead, or ever will be; but all sustain an abiding conscious relation to Him. But the "all" here meant "those who shall be accounted worthy to obtain that world." These *sustain a gracious covenant relation to God, which cannot be dissolved.* In this sense our Lord affirms that for Moses to call the Lord the "God" of His patriarchal servants if at that moment they had no existence, would be unworthy of Him. He "would be *ashamed* to be called their God, if He had not prepared for them a city" (Heb. 11:16). How precious are these glimpses of the *resurrection state!* **39. scribes ... well said**—enjoying His victory over the Sadducees. **they durst not**— neither party, both for the time utterly foiled.

41-47. CHRIST BAFFLES THE PHARISEES BY A QUESTION ABOUT DAVID AND MESSIAH, AND DENOUNCES THE SCRIBES. **41. said ...**—"What think ye of Christ [the promised and expected Messiah]? Whose son is He [to be]? They say unto Him, The son of David. He saith unto them, How then doth David in spirit [by the Holy Ghost, Mark 12: 36] call Him LORD?" (Matt. 22:42, 43). The difficulty can only be solved by the *higher* and *lower* —the *divine* and *human* natures of our Lord (Matt. 1:23). Mark the testimony here given to the *inspiration* of the Old Testament (cf. ch. 24:44).

46, 47. Beware ...—(See on Matt. 23:5; and on ch. 14:7). **devour ...**—taking advantage of their helpless condition and confiding character, to obtain possession of their property, while by their "long prayers" they made them believe they were raised far above "filthy lucre." So much "the greater damnation" awaits them. What a lifelike description of the Romish clergy, the true successors of "the scribes!"

CHAPTER 21

Vss. 1-4. THE WIDOW'S TWO MITES. **looked up**—He had "sat down over against the treasury" (Mark 12:41), probably to rest, for He had continued long standing as he taught in the temple-court (Mark 11:27), and "looking up He saw"—as in Zaccheus' case, not quite casually. **the rich ...** —"the people," says Mark 12:41 "cast money into the treasury, and many rich cast in much"; i.e., into chests deposited in one of the courts of the temple to receive the offerings of the people towards its maintenance (II Kings 12:9; John 8:20). **2. two mites**—"which make a farthing" (Mark 12:42), the smallest Jewish coin. "She might have kept one" [BENGEL]. **3. And he said**—"to His disciples," whom He "called to Him" (Mark 12:43), to teach from it a great future lesson. **more than ... all**— in proportion to her means, which is God's standard (II Cor. 8:12). **4. of their abundance**—their *superfluity;* what they had to spare," or beyond what they needed. **of her penury**—or "want" (Mark 12:44)—her *deficiency,* of what was *less* than her own wants required, "all the living she had." Mark still more emphatically, "all that she had— her whole subsistence." Note: (1) *As temple offerings are needed still for the service of Christ at home and abroad, so "looking down" now, as then "up," Me "sees" who "cast in," and how much.* (2) *Christ's standard of commendable offering is not our superfluity, but our deficiency*—not what will never be missed, but what costs us some real sacrifice, and just in proportion to the relative amount of that sacrifice. (See II Cor. 8:1-3.)

5-38. CHRIST'S PROPHECY OF THE DESTRUCTION OF JERUSALEM, AND WARNINGS TO PREPARE FOR HIS SECOND COMING, SUGGESTED BY IT—HIS DAYS AND NIGHTS DURING HIS LAST WEEK. **5-7.** (See on Matt. 24:1-3.) **8. the time**—of the Kingdom, in its full glory. **go ... not ... after them**—"I come not so very soon" (II Thess. 2:1, 2) [STIER]. **9-11. not terrified**—(See vs. 19; Isa. 8:11-14). **end not by and by**—or immediately, not yet (Matt. 24:6; Mark 13:7): i.e., "Worse must come before all is over." **10. Nation ...**—Matthew and Mark add, "All these are the beginning of sorrows," or travailpangs, to which heavy calamities are compared (Jer. 4:31, etc.). **12. brought before ...**—The book of Acts verifies all this. **13. for a testimony**—an opportunity of bearing testimony. **18. not a hair ... perish**—He had just said (vs. 16) they should be *put to death;* showing that this precious promise is far above immunity from mere bodily harm, and furnishing a key to the right interpretation of Psalm 91, and such like. Matthew adds the following: "And because iniquity shall abound, the love of many," the many or the most—the generality of professed disciples—"shall wax cold." But he that endureth to the end shall be saved. Sad illustrations of the effect of abounding iniquity in cooling the love of faithful disciples we have in the *Epistle of James,* written about this period referred to, and too frequently ever since (Heb. 10:38, 39;

Rev. 2:10). "And this gospel of the kingdom shall be preached in all the world for a witness, and then shall the end come" (Matt. 24:14). God never sends judgment without previous warning; and there can be no doubt that the Jews, already dispersed over most known countries, had nearly all heard the Gospel "as a witness," before the end of the Jewish state. The same principle was repeated and will repeat itself to *the* end. **20, 21. by armies**—encamped armies, i.e., besieged: "the abomination of desolation" (meaning the Roman ensigns, as the symbols of an idolatrous, pagan, unclean power) "spoken of by Daniel the prophet" (Dan. 9:27) "standing where it ought not" (Mark 13:14). "Whoso readeth [that prophecy] let him understand" (Matt. 24:15). **Then ... flee ...**—EUSEBIUS says the Christians fled to *Pella,* at the north extremity of Perea, being "prophetically directed"; perhaps by some prophetic intimation still more explicit than this, which still would be their *chart.* **23. woe unto**—"alas for." **with child ...**—from the greater suffering it would involve; as also "flight in winter, and on the sabbath," which they were to "pray" against (Matt. 24:20), the one as more trying to the body, the other to the soul. "For then shall be tribulation such as was not since the beginning of the world, nor ever shall be"—language not unusual in the Old Testament for tremendous calamities, though of this it may perhaps be literally said, "And except those days should be shortened, there should no flesh be saved, but for the elect's sake those days shall be shortened" (Matt. 24:21, 22). But for this merciful "shortening," brought about by a remarkable concurrence of causes, the whole nation would have perished, in which there yet remained a remnant to be afterwards gathered out. Here in Matthew and Mark are some particulars about "false Christs," who should, *"if possible"*—a precious clause—"deceive the very elect." (Cf. II Thess. 2:9-11; Rev. 13:13.) **24. Jerusalem ... trodden down ... until ...**—Implying (1) that one day Jerusalem shall cease to be "trodden down by the *Gentiles*" (Rev. 11:2), as then by pagan so now by Mohammedan unbelievers; (2) that this shall be at the "completion" of "the times of the Gentiles," which from Romans 11:25 (taken from this) we conclude to mean till the Gentiles have had their *full time* of that place in the Church which the Jews in *their time* had before them—after which, the Jews being again "graffed into their own olive tree," one Church of Jew and Gentile together shall fill the earth (Rom. 11). What a vista this opens up! **25-28. signs ...**—Though the grandeur of this language carries the mind over the head of all periods but that of Christ's second coming, nearly every expression will be found used of the Lord's coming in terrible national judgments, as of Babylon, etc.; and from vss. 28, 32, it seems undeniable that its *immediate* reference was to the destruction of Jerusalem, though its *ultimate* reference beyond doubt is to Christ's final coming. **28. redemption**—from the oppression of ecclesiastical despotism and legal bondage by the total subversion of the Jewish state and the firm establishment of the evangelical kingdom (vs. 31). But the words are of far wider and more precious import. Matthew (24:30) says, "And then shall appear *the sign* of the Son of man in heaven," evidently something distinct from Himself, mentioned immediately after. What this was intended to mean, interpreters are not agreed. But as before Christ came to destroy Jerusalem, some appalling portents were

seen in the air, so before His personal appearing it is likely that something *analogous* will be witnessed, though of what nature it is vain to conjecture. **32. This generation**—not "this nation," as some interpret it, which, though admissible in itself, seems very unnatural here. It is rather as in ch. 9:27. **34-37. surfeiting, and drunkenness**—All animal excesses, quenching spirituality. **cares of this life**—(See on Mark 4:7, 19). **36. Watch ... pray ...**—the two great duties which in prospect of trial are constantly enjoined. These warnings, suggested by the need of preparedness for the tremendous calamities approaching, and the total wreck of the existing state of things, are the *general improvement* of the whole discourse, carrying the mind forward to Judgment and Vengeance of another kind and on a grander and more awful scale—not ecclesiastical or political but personal, not temporal but eternal—when all safety and blessedness will be found to lie in being able to "STAND BEFORE THE SON OF MAN" in the glory of His personal appearing. **37, 38. in the daytime**—of this His last week. **abode in the mount**—i.e., at Bethany (Matt. 21:17).

CHAPTER 22

Vss. 1-6. CONSPIRACY OF THE JEWISH AUTHORITIES TO PUT JESUS TO DEATH—COMPACT WITH JUDAS. **1, 2.** (See on Matt. 26:1-5.) **3. Then entered Satan ...**—but not yet in the full sense. The awful stages of it were these: (1) *Covetousness* being his master-passion, the Lord let it reveal itself and gather strength by entrusting him with "the bag" (John 12:6), as treasurer to Himself and the Twelve. (2) In the discharge of that most sacred trust he became "a thief," appropriating its contents from time to time to his own use. Satan, seeing this door into his heart standing wide open, determines to enter by it, but cautiously (II Cor. 2:11); first merely *"putting it into his heart* to betray Him" (John 13:2), suggesting the thought to him that by this means he might enrich himself. (3) This thought was probably converted into a settled purpose by what took place in Simon's house at Bethany. (See on Matt. 26:6, and John 12:4-8.) (4) Starting back, perhaps, or mercifully held back, for some time, the determination to carry it into immediate effect was not consummated till, sitting at the paschal supper, *"Satan entered into him"* (see on John 13:27), and conscience, effectually stifled, only rose again to be his tormentor. What lessons in all this for every one (Eph. 4:27; Jas. 4:7; I Pet. 5:8, 9)! **5. money**—"thirty pieces of silver" (Matt. 26:15); thirty shekels, the fine payable for man-or maidservant accidentally killed (Exod. 21:32), and equal to $25 in our money—"a *goodly price* that I was priced at of them" (Zech. 11:13). (See on John 19:16.) **6. in the absence, ...**—(See on Matt. 26:5).

7-38. LAST PASSOVER—INSTITUTION OF THE SUPPER—DISCOURSE AT THE TABLE. **7. the day of unleavened bread**—strictly the 15th Nisan (part of our March and April) *after* the paschal lamb was killed; but here, the 14th (Thursday). Into the difficult questions raised on this we cannot here enter. **10-13. when ye are entered the city**—He Himself probably stayed at Bethany during the day. **there shall a man ...**—(See on ch. 19:29-32). **14-18. the hour**—about 6 P.M. Between three and this hour the lamb was killed (Exod. 12:6, *Margin*). **15. With desire ... desired**—"earnestly have I longed" (as Gen. 31:30, "sore longedst"). Why?

It was to be His *last* "before He suffered"—and so became *"Christ our Passover sacrificed for us"* (I Cor. 5:7), when it was *"fulfilled* in the Kingdom of God," the typical ordinance thenceforth disappearing. **17. took the cup**—the first of several partaken of in this service. **divide it among . . .**—i.e., It is to be *your* last as well as Mine, "until the Kingdom of God come," or as it is beautifully given in Matthew 26:29, "until that day when I shall drink it new with you in my Father's kingdom." It was *the point of transition between two economies and their two great festivals,* the one about to close for ever, the other immediately to open and run its majestic career until from earth it be transferred to heaven. **21, 22.** (See on John 13:21, etc.) **24-30. there was**—or "had been," referring probably to some symptoms of the former strife which had reappeared, perhaps on seeing the whole paschal arrangements committed to two of the Twelve. (See on Mark 10:42-45.) **25. benefactors**—a title which the vanity of princes eagerly coveted. **26. But ye . . . not**—Of how little avail has this condemnation of "lordship" and vain titles been against the vanity of Christian ecclesiastics? **28. continued . . .**—affecting evidence of Christ's tender susceptibility to human sympathy and support! (See on John 6:66, 67; 16:32.) **29. I appoint . . .**—Who is this that dispenses kingdoms, nay, the Kingdom of kingdoms, within an hour or two of His apprehension, and less than a day of His shameful death? These sublime contrasts, however, perpetually meet and entrance us in this matchless history. **30. eat and drink . . .**—(See on vs. 16, and on ch. 18:28, etc.). **31-34. Simon, Simon**—(See on ch. 10:41). **desired to have**—rather, "hath obtained you," properly "asked and obtained"; alluding to Job (1:6-12; 2:1-6), whom he solicited and obtained that he might sift him as wheat, insinuating as "the accuser of the brethren" (Rev. 12:10), that he would find chaff enough in his religion, if indeed there was any wheat at all. **to have you**—not Peter only, but them *all.* **32. But I have prayed**—have been doing it already. **for thee**—as most in danger. (See on vss. 61, 62.) **fail not**—i.e., entirely; for partially it did fail. **converted**—brought back afresh as a penitent disciple. **strengthen . . .**—i.e., make use of thy bitter experience for the fortifying of thy tempted brethren. **33. I am ready . . .**—honest-hearted, warmly-attached disciple, thinking thy present feelings immovable as a rock, thou shalt find them in the hour of temptation unstable as water: "I have been praying for thee," therefore thy faith shall not perish; but thinking this superfluous, thou shalt find that "he that trusteth in his own heart is a fool" (Prov. 28:26). **34. cock . . . crow**—"twice" (Mark 14:30). **35-38. But now**—that you are going forth not as before on a temporary mission, provided for without purse or scrip, but into scenes of continued and severe trial, your *methods* must be different; for purse and scrip will now be needed for support, and the usual means of defense. **37. the things concerning me**—decreed and written. **have an end**—are rapidly drawing to a close. **38. two swords . . . enough**—they thinking He referred to present defense, while His answer showed He meant something else.

39-46. AGONY IN THE GARDEN. **39. as . . . wont**—(See John 18:2). **40. the place**—the Garden of Gethsemane, on the west or city side of the mount. Comparing all the accounts of this mysterious scene, the facts appear to be these: (1) He bade nine of the Twelve remain "here" while He went and prayed "yonder." (2) He "took the other three,

Peter, James, and John, and began to be sore amazed [appalled], sorrowful, and very heavy [oppressed], and said, My soul is exceeding sorrowful even unto death"—'I feel as if nature would sink under this load, as if life were ebbing out, and death coming before its time'—"tarry ye here, and watch with Me"; not, 'Witness for Me,' but, 'Bear Me company.' It did Him good, it seems, to have them beside Him. (3) But soon even they were too much for Him: He must be alone. "He was withdrawn from them about a stone's-cast"—though near enough for them to be competent witnesses—and kneeled down, uttering that most affecting prayer (Mark 14:36), that if possible "the cup," of His approaching *death,* "might pass from Him, but if not, His Father's will be done": implying that *in itself* it was so purely revolting that only its being the Father's will would induce Him to taste it, but that *in that view* of it He was perfectly prepared to drink it. It is no struggle between a reluctant and a compliant will, but between two views of one event—an *abstract* and a *relative* view of it, in the one of which it was *revolting,* in the other *welcome.* By signifying how it felt in the *one* view, He shows His beautiful oneness with ourselves in nature and feeling; by expressing how He regarded it in the other light, He reveals His absolute obediential subjection to His Father. (4) On this, having a momentary relief, for it came upon Him, we imagine, by surges, He returns to the three, and finding them sleeping, He addresses them affectingly, particularly *Peter,* as in Mark 14:37, 38. He then (5) goes back, not now to kneel, but fell on His face on the ground, saying the same words, but with this turn, "If this cup *may not pass . . .*" (Matt. 26:42)—i.e., 'Yes, I understand this mysterious silence (Ps. 22:1-6); it may not pass; I am to drink it, and I will'—"Thy will be done!" (6) Again, for a moment relieved, He returns and finds them "sleeping for sorrow," warns them as before, but puts a loving construction upon it, separating between the "willing spirit" and the **"weak flesh."** (7) Once more, returning to His solitary spot, the surges rise higher, beat more tempestuously, and seem ready to overwhelm Him. To fortify Him for this, "there appeared an angel unto Him from heaven strengthening Him"—not to minister light or comfort (He was to have none of that, and they were not needed nor fitted to convey it), but purely to sustain and brace up sinking nature for a yet hotter and fiercer struggle. And now, He is "in an agony, and prays more earnestly"—even Christ's prayer, it seems, admitted of and now demanded such increase—"and His sweat was as it were great drops [literally clots] of blood falling down to the ground." What was this? *Not His proper sacrificial offering,* though essential to it. It was just the internal struggle, apparently hushing itself before, but now swelling up again, convulsing His whole inner man, and this so affecting His animal nature that the sweat oozed out from every pore in thick drops of blood, falling to the ground. It was just *shuddering nature* and *indomitable will* struggling together. But again the cry, If it must be, *Thy will be done,* issues from His lips, and all is over. "The bitterness of death is past." He has anticipated and rehearsed His final conflict, and won the victory—now on the theater of an *invincible will,* as then on the arena of the Cross. 'I *will* suffer,' is the grand result of Gethsemane: "It is finished" is the shout that bursts from the Cross. The Will without the Deed had been all in vain; but His work was consummated when He carried the now manifested Will into the palpable Deed, *"by the which* WILL *we are sanctified* THROUGH THE OFFERING OF THE BODY OF JESUS CHRIST ONCE FOR ALL" (Heb. 10:10). (8) At the close of the whole scene, finding them still sleeping (worn out with continued sorrow and racking anxiety), He bids them, with an irony of deep emotion, "sleep on now and take their rest, the hour is come, the Son of man is betrayed into the hands of sinners, rise, let us be going, the traitor is at hand." And while He spoke, Judas approached with his armed band. Thus they proved "miserable comforters," broken reeds; and thus in His whole work He was *alone,* and "of the people there was none with Him."

47-54. BETRAYAL AND APPREHENSION OF JESUS—FLIGHT OF HIS DISCIPLES.

55-62. JESUS BEFORE CAIAPHAS—FALL OF PETER. The particulars of these two sections require a combination of all the narratives, for which see on John 18:1-27.

63-71. JESUS CONDEMNED TO DIE AND SHAMEFULLY ENTREATED. (See on Mark 14:53-63; John 18:19, etc.; and on vss. 55-62.)

CHAPTER 23

Vss. **1-5.** JESUS BEFORE PILATE. (See on Mark 15:1-5; and John 18:28-19:22.)

6-12. JESUS BEFORE HEROD. (See on Mark 15:6). **7. sent him to Herod**—hoping thus to escape the dilemma of an unjust condemnation or an unpopular release. **at Jerusalem ... at that time**—to keep the passover. **8. some miracle**—Fine sport thou expectedst, as the Philistines with Samson (Judg. 16:25), O coarse, crafty, cruel tyrant! But thou hast been baulked before (see on ch. 13:31-33), and shalt be again. **9. answered ... nothing**—(See Matt. 7:6). **10. stood and vehemently accused him**—no doubt both of *treason* before the *king,* and of *blasphemy,* for the king was a *Jew.* **11. his men of war**—his bodyguard. **set him at naught ...**—stung with disappointment at His refusal to amuse him with miracles or answer any of his questions. **gorgeous robe**—bright robe. If this mean (as sometimes) of shining white, this being the royal color among the Jews, it may have been in derision of His claim to be "King of the Jews." But if so, "He in reality honored Him, as did Pilate with His true title blazoned on the cross" [BENGEL]. **sent him again to Pilate**—instead of releasing him as he ought, having established nothing against Him (vss. 14, 15). "Thus he implicated himself with Pilate in all the guilt of His condemnation, and with him accordingly he is classed" (Acts 4:27) [BENGEL]. **at enmity**—perhaps about some point of disputed jurisdiction, which this exchange of the Prisoner might tend to heal.

13-38. JESUS AGAIN BEFORE PILATE—DELIVERED UP—LED AWAY TO BE CRUCIFIED. (See on Mark 15:6-15; and John 19:2-17.) **26. Cyrenian**—of Cyrene, in Libya, on the north coast of Africa, where were many Jews who had a synagogue at Jerusalem (Acts 6:9, and see 2:10). He was "the father of Alexander and Rufus" (Mark 15:21), probably better known afterwards than himself, as disciples. (See Rom. 16:13.) **out of the country**—and casually drawn into that part of the crowd. **laid the cross**—"Him they compel to bear his cross," (Matt. 27:32)—sweet compulsion, if it issued in him or his sons *voluntarily* "taking up *their* cross!" It would appear that our Lord had first to bear His own cross (John 19:17), but being from exhaustion unable to proceed, it was laid on another

to bear it "after Him." **27-31. women**—not the precious Galilean women (vs. 49), but part of the crowd. **28. not for me ...**—noble spirit of compassion, rising above His own dread endurances, in tender commiseration of sufferings yet in the distance and far lighter, but *without His supports and consolations!* **30. mountains ... hills ...**—(Hos. 10:8), flying hither and thither as they did in despair for shelter, during the siege; a very slight premonition of cries of another and more awful kind (Isa. 2:10, 19, 21; Rev. 6:16, 17). **31. green tree**—that naturally resists the fire. **the dry**—that attracts the fire, being its proper fuel. The proverb here plainly means: "If such sufferings alight upon the innnocent One, the very Lamb of God, what must be in store for those who are provoking the flames?"

32-38, 44-46. CRUCIFIXION AND DEATH OF THE LORD JESUS. (See on John 19:17-30.)

39-43. THE TWO THIEVES. **39. railed on him**—catching up the universal derision, but with a turn of his own. Jesus, "reviled, reviles not again"; but another voice from the cross shall nobly wipe out this dishonor and turn it to the unspeakable glory of the dying Redeemer. **40. Dost not thou**—"thou" is emphatic: 'Let others jeer, but dost *thou?'* **fear God**—Hast thou no fear of meeting Him so soon as thy righteous Judge? Thou art within an hour or two of eternity, and dost thou spend it in reckless disregard of coming judgment? **in the same condemnation**—He has been condemned to die, but is it better with thee? Doth even a common lot kindle no sympathy in thy breast? **41. we ... justly ...**—He owns the worst of his crimes and deserts, and would fain shame his fellow into the same. **nothing amiss**—lit., "out of place"; hence "unnatural"; a striking term here. Our Lord was not charged with *ordinary crime,* but only with laying claim to office and honors which amounted to blasphemy. The charge of treason had not even a show of truth, as Pilate told His enemies. In this defense then there seems more than meets the eye. 'He made Himself the promised Messiah, the Son of God; but in this He "did nothing amiss"; He ate with publicans and sinners, and bade all the weary and heavy laden come and rest under His wing; but in this He "did nothing amiss": He claimed to be Lord of the Kingdom of God, to shut it at will, but also to open it at pleasure even to such as we are; but in this He "did nothing amiss!" ' Does His next speech imply *less* than this? Observe: (1) His frank confession and genuine selfcondemnation. (2) His astonishment and horror at the very different state of his fellow's mind. (3) His anxiety to bring him to a better mind while yet there was hope. (4) His noble testimony, not only to the innocence of Jesus, but to all that this implied of the rightfulness of His claims. **42. said to Jesus ...**—Observe here (1) The "kingdom" referred to was one *beyond the grave;* for it is inconceivable that he should have expected Him to come down from the cross to erect any *temporal* kingdom. (2) This he calls Christ's own (Thy) kingdom. (3) As such, he sees in Christ the absolute right to dispose of that kingdom to whom He pleased. (4) He does not presume to *ask* a place in that kingdom, though that is what he means, but with a humility quite affecting, just says, "Lord, *remember me* when...." Yet was there mighty faith in that word. If Christ will but "think upon him" (Neh. 5:19), at that august moment when He "cometh into His kingdom," it will do. 'Only assure me that then Thou wilt not forget such a wretch as I, that once hung by Thy side, and I am content.' Now contrast with this bright act of faith the darkness even of the apostles' minds, who could hardly be got to believe that their Master would die at all, who now were almost despairing of Him, and who when dead had almost buried their hopes in His grave. Consider, too, the man's previous *disadvantages* and *bad life*. And then mark how his faith comes out—not in protestations, 'Lord, I cannot doubt, I am firmly persuaded that Thou art Lord of a kingdom, that death cannot disannul Thy title nor impede the assumption of it in due time,' etc.—but as having no shadow of doubt, and rising above it as a question altogether, he just says, "Lord, remember me *when* Thou comest . . ." Was ever faith like this exhibited upon earth? It looks as if the brightest crown had been reserved for the Saviour's head at His darkest moment! **43. Jesus said . . .**—The dying Redeemer speaks as if He Himself viewed it in this light. It was a "song in the night." It ministered cheer to His spirit in the midnight gloom that now enwrapt it. **Verily I say unto thee**—'Since thou speakest as to the king, with kingly authority speak I to thee.' **to-day**—"Thou art prepared for a long delay before I come into My kingdom, but not a day's delay shall there be for thee; thou shalt not be parted from Me even for a moment, but together we shall go, and with Me, ere this day expire, shalt thou be in Paradise" (future bliss, II Cor. 12:4; Rev. 2:7). Learn (1) How "One is taken and another left"; (2) How easily divine teaching can raise the rudest and worst above the best instructed and most devoted servants of Christ; (3) How *presumption* and *despair* on a death hour are equally discountenanced here, the one in the impenitent thief, the other in his penitent fellow.

47-56. Signs and Circumstances Following His Death—His Burial. (See on Matt. 27:51-56, 62-66; John 19:31-42.)

CHAPTER 24

Vss. 1-12. Angelic Announcement to the Women that Christ Is Risen—Peter's Visit to the Empty Sepulchre. (See on Mark 16:1-8; and Matt. 28:1-5.) **5. Why . . .**—Astonishing question! not "the *risen*," but "*the Living One*" (cf. Rev. 1: 18); and the surprise expressed in it implies an *incongruity* in His being there at all, as if, though He might *submit* to it, "it was impossible He should be *holden* of it" (Acts 2:24). **6. in Galilee**—to which these women themselves belonged (ch. 23: 55). **7. saying . . .**—How remarkable it is to hear angels quoting a whole sentence of Christ's to the disciples, mentioning where it was uttered, and wondering it was not fresh in their memory, as doubtless it was in theirs! (I Tim. 3:16, "seen of angels," and I Pet. 1:12.) **10. Joanna**—(See on ch. 8:1-3). **12. Peter . . .**—(See on John 20:1-10).

13-35. Christ Appears to the Two Going to Emmaus. **13. two of them**—One was *Cleopas* (vs. 18); who the other is mere conjecture. **Emmaus**—about seven and a half miles from Jerusalem. They probably lived there and were going home after the Passover. **14-16. communed and reasoned**—exchanged views and feelings, weighing afresh all the facts, as detailed in vss. 18-24. **drew near**—coming up behind them as from Jerusalem. **eyes holden**—Partly He was "in another form" (Mark 16:12), and partly there seems to have been an operation on their own vision; though certainly, as they did not believe that He was alive, His

company as a fellow traveller was the last thing they would expect. **17-24. communication . . .**— The words imply the earnest discussion that had appeared in their manner. **18. knowest not . . .**— If he knew not the events of the last few days in Jerusalem, he must be a mere sojourner; if he did, how could he suppose they would be talking of anything else? How artless all this! **19. Concerning Jesus . . .**—As if feeling it a relief to have someone to unburden his thoughts and feelings to, this disciple goes over the main facts in his own desponding style, and this was just what our Lord wished. **21. we trusted . . .**—They expected the promised Deliverance at His hand, but in the current sense of it, not by His death. **besides all this** —not only did His death seem to give the fatal blow to their hopes, but He had been two days dead already, and this was the third. It is true, they add, some of our women gave us a surprise, telling us of a vision of angels they had at the empty grave this morning that said He was alive, and some of ourselves who went thither confirmed their statement; but then Himself they saw not. A doleful tale truly, told out of the deepest despondency. **25-27. fools**—senseless, without understanding. **26. Ought not Christ**—"the Christ," "the Messiah." **to suffer . . . and enter**—i.e., through the gate of suffering (and suffering "*these things*," or *such a death*) to enter into His glory. 'Ye believe in the glory; but these very sufferings are the predicted gate of entrance into it.' **27. Moses and all the prophets . . .**—Here our Lord both teaches us the reverence due to Old Testament Scripture, and the great burden of it—"Himself." **28-31. made as though . . .**—(Cf. Mark 6:48; Gen. 18:3, 5; 32:24-26). **29. constrained . . .**—But for this, the whole design of the interview had been lost, but *it was not to be lost,* for He who only wished to be constrained had kindled a longing in the hearts of His travelling companions which was not to be so easily put off. And does not this still repeat itself in the interviews of the Saviour with His loving, longing disciples? Else why do they say,

> Abide with me from morn to eve,
> For without Thee I cannot live;
> Abide with me when night is nigh,
> For without Thee I cannot die.
>
> Keble

30-31. he took . . . and blessed . . and their eyes were opened—The stranger first startles them by taking the place of master at their own table, but on proceeding to that act which reproduced the whole scene of the last Supper, a rush of associations and recollections disclosed their guest, and He stood confessed before their astonished gaze—their risen Lord! They were going to gaze on Him, perhaps embrace Him, but that moment He is gone! It was enough. **32-34.** They now tell each to the other how their hearts burned—were fired—within them at His talk and His expositions of Scripture. 'Ah! this accounts for it: We could not understand the glow of self-evidencing light, love, glory that ravished our hearts; but now we do.' They cannot rest—how could they?—they must go straight back and tell the news. They find the eleven, but ere they have time to tell their tale, their ears are saluted with the thrilling news, "The Lord is risen indeed, and hath appeared to *Simon*." Most touching and precious intelligence this. The only one of the Eleven to whom He appeared *alone* was he, it seems, who had so shamefully denied Him.

What passed at that interview we shall never know here. Probably it was too sacred for disclosure. (See on Mark 16:7.) The two from Emmaus now relate what had happened to them, and while thus comparing notes of their Lord's appearances, lo! Christ Himself stands in the midst of them. What encouragement to doubting, dark, true-hearted disciples! **36-53.** JESUS APPEARS TO THE ASSEMBLED DISCIPLES—HIS ASCENSION. **36. Jesus . . . stood**—(See on John 20:19). **37, 38. a spirit**—the ghost of their dead Lord, but not Himself in the body (Acts 12:15; Matt. 14:26). **thoughts**—rather, reasonings; i.e., whether He were risen or no, and whether this was His very self. **39-43. Behold . . .**—lovingly offering them both *ocular* and *tangible* demonstration of the reality of His resurrection. **a spirit hath not**—an important statement regarding "spirits." **flesh and bones**—He says not "flesh and *blood*"; for the blood is the life of the animal and corruptible body (Gen. 9:4), which "cannot inherit the kingdom of God" (I Cor. 15:50; but "flesh and bones," implying the *identity*, but w*ith diversity of laws*, of the resurrection-body. (See on John 20:24-28.) **44. believed not for joy . . .**—They did believe, else they had not rejoiced [BENGEL]. But it seemed *too good* to be true (Ps. 126:1, 2). **42. honeycomb**—common frugal fare, anciently. **43. eat before them**—i.e., let them see Him doing it: not for His own necessity, but their conviction. **44-49. These are the words . . .**—i.e., "Now you will understand what seemed so dark to you when I told you about the Son of man being put to death and rising again (ch. 18:31-34). **while . . . yet with you**—a striking expression, implying that He was now, as the dead and risen Saviour, virtually dissevered from this scene of mortality, and from all ordinary intercourse with His mortal disciples. **law . . . prophets . . . psalms**—the three Jewish divisions of the Old Testament Scriptures. **45. Then opened he . . .**—a statement of unspeakable value; expressing, on the one hand, Christ's *immediate access to the human spirit* and *absolute power over it,* to the adjustment of its vision, and permanent rectification for spiritual discernment (than which it is impossible to conceive a stronger evidence of His proper divinity); and, on the other hand, making it certain that the *manner of interpreting the Old Testament which the apostles afterwards employed* (see the Acts and Epistles), *has the direct sanction of Christ Himself.* **46. behoved Christ**—(See on vs. 26.) **47. beginning at Jerusalem**—(1) As the metropolis and heart of the then existing kingdom of God:—"to the Jew first" (Rom. 1:16; Acts 13:46; Isa. 2:3, see on Matt. 10:6). (2) As the great reservoir and laboratory of all the sin and crime of the nation, thus proclaiming for all time that there is mercy in Christ for the chief of sinners. (See on Matt. 23: 37.) **48. witnesses**—(Cf. Acts 1:8, 22). **49. I send** —the present tense, to intimate its nearness. **promise of my Father**—i.e., what My Father hath promised; the Holy Ghost, of which Christ is the authoritative Dispenser (John 14:7; Rev. 3:1, 5:6). **endued**—invested, or clothed with; implying, as the parallels show (Rom. 13:14; I Cor. 15:53; Gal. 3: 27; Col. 3:9, 10), their being *so penetrated and acted upon by conscious supernatural "power"* (in the full sense of that word) *as to stamp with divine authority the whole exercise of their apostolic office,* including, of course, their *pen* as well as their *mouth*. **50-53. to Bethany**—not to the village itself, but on the *descent* to it from Mount Olivet. **51. while he blessed . . . parted . . .**—Sweet intimation! Incarnate Love, Crucified Love, Risen Love, now on the wing for heaven, waiting only those odorous gales which were to waft Him to the skies, goes away in benedictions, that in the character of Glorified, Enthroned Love, He might continue His benedictions, but in yet higher form, until He come again! And oh, if angels were so transported at His birth into this scene of tears and death, what must have been their ecstasy as they welcomed and attended Him "far above all heavens" into the presence-chamber, and conducted Him to the right hand of the Majesty on High! Thou hast an everlasting right, O my Saviour, to that august place. The brightness of the Father's glory, enshrined in our nature, hath won it well; for He poured out His soul unto death, and led captivity captive, receiving gifts for men, yea for the rebellious, that the Lord God might dwell among them. Thou art the King of glory, O Christ. Lift up your heads, O ye gates, be lifted up, ye everlasting doors, that the King of glory may come in! Even so wilt Thou change these vile bodies of ours, that they may be like unto Thine own glorious body; and then with gladness and rejoicing shall they be brought, they shall enter into the King's palace! **52. worshipped him**—certainly in the strictest sense of adoration. **returned to Jerusalem**—as instructed to do: but not till after gazing, as if entranced, up into the blue vault in which He had disappeared, they were gently checked by two shining ones, who assured them He would come again to them in the like manner as He had gone into heaven. (See on Acts 1:10, 11.) This made them return, not with disappointment at His removal, but "with great joy." **53. were continually in the temple**—i.e., every day at the regular hours of prayer till the day of Pentecost.

THE GOSPEL ACCORDING TO

JOHN

INTRODUCTION

THE author of the Fourth Gospel was the younger of the two sons of Zebedee, a fisherman on the Sea of Galilee, who resided at Bethsaida, where were born Peter and Andrew his brother, and Philip also. His mother's name was Salome, who, though not without her imperfections (Matt. 20:20-28), was one of those dear and honored women who accompanied the Lord on one of His preaching circuits through Galilee, ministering to His bodily wants; who followed Him to the cross, and bought sweet spices to anoint Him after His burial, but, on bringing them to the grave, on the morning of the First Day of the week, found their loving services gloriously superseded by His resurrection ere they arrived. His father, Zebedee, appears to have been in good circumstances, owning a vessel of his own and having hired servants (Mark 1:20). Our Evangelist, whose occupation was that of a fisherman with his father, was beyond doubt a disciple of the Baptist, and one of the two who had the first interview with Jesus. He was called while engaged at his secular occupation (Matt. 4:21, 22), and again on a memorable occasion (Luke 5:1-11), and finally chosen as one of the Twelve Apostles (Matt. 10:2). He was the youngest of the Twelve—the "Benjamin," as DA COSTA calls him—and he and James his brother were named in the native tongue by Him who knew the heart, "Boanerges," which the Evangelist Mark (3:17) explains to mean "Sons of thunder"; no doubt from their natural *vehemence* of *character*. They and Peter constituted that select triumvirate of whom see on Luke 9:28. But the highest honor bestowed on this disciple was his being admitted to the bosom-place with his Lord at the table, as "the disciple whom Jesus loved" (John 13:23; 20:2; 21:7, 20:24), and to have committed to him by the dying Redeemer the care of His mother (19:26,27). There can be no reasonable doubt that this distinction was due to a sympathy with His own spirit and mind on the part of John which the all-penetrating Eye of their common Master beheld in none of the rest; and although this was probably never seen either in his life or in his ministry by his fellow apostles, it is brought out wonderfully in his writings, which, in Christlike spirituality, heavenliness, and love, surpass, we may freely say, all the other inspired writings.

After the effusion of the Spirit on the day of Pentecost, we find him in constant but silent company with Peter, the great spokesman and actor in the infant Church until the accession of Paul. While his love to the Lord Jesus drew him spontaneously to the side of His eminent servant, and his chastened vehemence made him ready to stand courageously by him, and suffer with him, in all that his testimony to Jesus might cost him, his modest humility, as the youngest of all the apostles, made him an admiring listener and faithful supporter of his brother apostle rather than a speaker or separate actor. Ecclesiastical history is uniform in testifying that John went to Asia Minor; but it is next to certain that this could not have been till after the death both of Peter and Paul; that he resided at Ephesus, whence, as from a center, he superintended the churches of that region, paying them occasional visits; and that he long survived the other apostles. Whether the mother of Jesus died before this, or went with John to Ephesus, where she died and was buried, is not agreed. One or two anecdotes of his later days have been handed down by tradition, one at least bearing marks of reasonable probability. But it is not necessary to give them here. In the reign of Domitian (A.D. 81–96) he was banished to "the isle that is called Patmos" (a small rocky and then almost uninhabited island in the Ægean Sea), "for the word of God and for the testimony of Jesus Christ" (Rev. 1:9). Irenæus and Eusebius say that this took place about the end of Domitian's reign. That he was thrown into a cauldron of boiling oil, and miraculously delivered, is one of those legends which, though reported by Tertullian and Jerome, is entitled to no credit. His return from exile took place during the brief but tolerant reign of Nerva; he died at Ephesus in the reign of Trajan [EUSEBIUS, *Ecclesiastical History*, 3, 23], at an age above 90, according to some; according to others, 100; and even 120, according to others still. The intermediate number is generally regarded as probably the nearest to the truth.

As to the *date* of this Gospel, the arguments for its having been composed before the destruction of Jerusalem (though relied on by some superior critics) are of the slenderest nature; such as the expression in ch. 5:2, "there *is* at Jerusalem, by the sheep-gate, a pool . . ."; there being no allusion to Peter's martyrdom as having occurred according to the prediction in ch. 21:18-a thing too well known to require mention. That it was composed long after the destruction of Jerusalem, and after the decease of all the other apostles, is next to certain, though the precise time cannot be determined. Probably it was before his banishment, however; and if we date it between the years 90 and 94, we shall probably be close to the truth.

As to the *readers* for whom it was more immediately designed, that they were Gentiles we might naturally presume from the lateness of the date; but the multitude of explanations of things familiar to every Jew puts this beyond all question.

No doubt was ever thrown upon the genuineness and authenticity of this Gospel till about the close of the eighteenth century; nor were these embodied in any formal attack upon it till BRETSCHNEIDER, in 1820, issued his famous treatise (Probabilia . . .), the conclusions of which he afterwards was candid enough to admit had been satisfactorily disproved. To advert to these would be as painful as unnecessary; consisting as they mostly do of assertions regarding the Discourses of our Lord recorded in this Gospel which are revolting to every spiritual mind. The Tubingen school did their best, on their peculiar mode of reasoning, to galvanize into fresh life this theory of the post-Joannean date of the Fourth Gospel; and some Unitarian critics still cling to it. But to use the striking language of VAN OOSTERZEE regarding similar speculations on the Third Gospel, "Behold, the feet of them that shall carry it out dead are already at the door" (Acts 5:9). Is there one mind of the least elevation of spiritual discernment that does not see in this Gospel marks of historical truth and a surpassing glory such as none of the other Gospels possess, brightly as they too attest their own verity; and who will not be ready to say that if not historically true, and true *just as it stands*, it never could have been by mortal man composed or conceived?

Of the peculiarities of this Gospel, we note here only two. The one is its *reflective* character. While the others are purely *narrative*, the Fourth Evangelist "pauses, as it were, at every turn," as DA COSTA says (*Four Witnesses*, p. 234), "at one time to give a reason, at another to fix the attention, to deduce consequences, or make applications, or to give utterance to the language of praise." See chs. 2:20, 21, 23–25; 4:1, 2; 7:37–39; 11:12, 13, 49–52; 21:18, 19, 22, 23. The other peculiarity of this Gospel is its *supplementary* character. By this, in the present instance, we mean something more than the studiousness with which he omits many most important particulars in our Lord's history, for no conceivable reason but that they were already familiar as household words to all his readers, through the three preceding Gospels, and his substituting in place of these an immense quantity of the richest matter not found in the other Gospels. We refer here more particularly to the *nature* of the additions which distinguish this Gospel; particularly the notices of the different Passovers which occurred during our

Lord's public ministry, and the record of His teaching at Jerusalem, without which it is not too much to say that we could have had but a most imperfect conception either of the duration of His ministry or of the plan of it. But another feature of these additions is quite as noticeable and not less important. "We find," to use again the words of DA COSTA (pp. 238, 239), slightly abridged, "only six of our Lord's miracles recorded in this Gospel, but these are all of the most remarkable kind, and surpass the rest in depth, specialty of application, and fulness of meaning. Of these six we find only one in the other three Gospels—the multiplication of the loaves. That miracle chiefly, it would seem, on account of the important instructions of which it furnished the occasion (ch. 6), is here recorded anew. The five other tokens of divine power are distinguished from among the many recorded in the three other Gospels by their furnishing a still higher display of power and command over the ordinary laws and course of nature. Thus we find recorded here the first of all the miracles that Jesus wrought—the changing of water into wine (ch. 2), the cure of the nobleman's son *at a distance* (ch. 4); of the numerous cures of the lame and the paralytic by the word of Jesus, only one—of the man impotent for *thirty and eight years* (ch. 5); of the many cures of the blind, one only—of the man *born blind* (ch. 9); the restoration of Lazarus, not from a deathbed, like Jairus' daughter, nor from a bier, like the widow of Nain's son, but *from the grave,* and after lying there four days, and there sinking into corruption (ch. 11); and lastly, after His resurrection, the miraculous draught of fishes on the Sea of Tiberias (ch. 21). But these are all recorded chiefly to give occasion for the record of those astonishing discourses and conversations, alike with friends and with foes, with His disciples and with the multitude which they drew forth."

Other illustrations of the peculiarities of this Gospel will occur, and other points connected with it be adverted to, in the course of the Commentary.

CHAPTER 1

Vss. 1-14. THE WORD MADE FLESH. **1. In the beginning**—of all time and created existence, for this Word gave it being (vss. 3, 10); therefore, "before the world was" (ch. 17:5, 24); or, from all eternity. **was the Word**—He *who is to God what man's word is to himself, the manifestation or expression of himself to those without him.* (See on vs. 18.) On the *origin* of this most lofty and now for ever consecrated title of Christ, this is not the place to speak. It occurs only in the writings of this seraphic apostle. **was with God**—having a conscious personal existence *distinct from God* (as one is from the person he is "with"), but *inseparable from Him* and *associated with Him* (vs. 18; ch. 17:5; I John 1:2), where "THE FATHER" is used in the same sense as "GOD" here. **was God**—in substance and essence GOD; or was possessed of essential or proper divinity. Thus, each of these brief but pregnant statements is the complement of the other, correcting any misapprehensions which the others might occasion. Was the Word *eternal?* It was *not* the eternity of "the Father," but of a conscious personal existence *distinct from Him and associated with Him.* Was the Word thus "with God?" It was not the distinctness and the fellowship of *another being,* as if there were *more Gods than one,* but of One who was *Himself God*— in such sense that the *absolute unity* of the Godhead, the great principle of all religion, is only transferred from the region of shadowy abstraction to the region of essential life and love. But why all this definition? Not to give us any *abstract information* about certain mysterious distinctions in the Godhead, but solely to let the reader know *who it was that* in the fulness of time "*was made flesh.*" After each verse, then, the reader must say, "It was He who is thus, and thus, and thus described, who was made flesh." **2. The same . . .**—See what property of the Word the stress is laid upon—His *eternal distinctness,* in unity, from God—the Father (John 1:2). **3. All things . . .**—all things *absolutely* (as is evident from vs. 10; I Cor. 8:6; Col. 1:16, 17; but put beyond question by what follows). "Without Him was *not one thing* made [brought into being] that was made." This is a denial of the *eternity* and *non-creation* of matter, which was held by the whole thinking world *outside of Judaism and Christianity:* or rather, its proper *crea-*

tion was never so much as dreamt of save by the children of *revealed religion.* **4. In Him was life**— essentially and originally, as the previous verses show to be the meaning. Thus He is *the Living Word,* or, as He is called in I John 1:1,2, "the Word of Life." **the life . . . the light of men**—All that in men which is *true light*—knowledge, integrity, intelligent, willing subjection to God, love to Him and to their fellow creatures, wisdom, purity, holy joy, rational happiness—all this "light of men" has its fountain in the essential original "life" of "the Word" (I John 1:5-7; Ps. 36:9). **5. shineth in darkness . . .**—in this dark, fallen world, or in mankind "sitting in darkness and the shadow of death," *with no ability to find the way either of truth or of holiness.* In this thick darkness, and consequent intellectual and moral obliquity, "the light of the Word" shineth—*by all the rays whether of natural or revealed teaching which men* (apart from the Incarnation of the Word) *are favored with.* **the darkness comprehended it not**—*did not take it in,* a brief summary of the effect of all the strivings of this *unincarnate* Word throughout this wide world from the beginning, and a hint of the necessity of His putting on *flesh,* if any recovery of men was to be effected (I Cor. 1:21). **6-9.** The Evangelist here *approaches* his grand thesis, so paving his way for the full statement of it in vs. 14, that we may be able to bear the bright light of it, and take in its length and breadth and depth and height. **7. through him**—John. **8. not that Light**—(See on ch. 5:35). What a testimony to John to have to explain that "he was *not* that Light!" Yet was he but a foil to set it off, his night-taper dwindling before the Dayspring from on high (ch. 3:30). **9. lighteth every man . . .**—rather, "which, coming into the world, enlighteneth every man"; or, is "the Light of the world" (ch. 9:5). "Coming into the world" is a superfluous and quite unusual description of "every man"; but it is of all descriptions of Christ amongst the most familiar, especially in the writings of this Evangelist (ch. 12:46; 16:28; 18:37; I John 4:9; I Tim. 1:15, etc.). **10-13. He was in the world . . .**—The language here is nearly as wonderful as the thought. Observe its compact simplicity, its sonorousness—"the world" resounding in each of its three members—and the enigmatic form in which it is couched, startling the reader and setting his ingenuity a-working to solve the stupendous enigma of *Christ ignored in His* *own world.* "The world," in the first two clauses, plainly means the *created* world, *into* which *He* came, says vs. 9; "*in* it He was," says this verse. By His Incarnation, He became *an inhabitant of it,* and bound up with it. Yet it "was made by Him" (vss. 3, 4, 5). Here, then, it is merely alluded to, in contrast partly with His being *in* it, but still more with the reception He met with from it. "The world that knew Him not" (I John 3:1) is of course the intelligent world of mankind. (See on vss. 11, 12.) Taking the first two clauses as one statement, we try to apprehend it by thinking of the infant Christ conceived in the womb and born in the arms of His own creature, and of the Man Christ Jesus breathing His own air, treading His own ground, supported by substances to which He Himself gave being, and the Creator of the very men whom He came to save. But the most vivid commentary on this entire verse will be got by tracing (in His matchless history) Him of whom it speaks walking amidst all the elements of nature, the diseases of men and death itself, the secrets of the human heart, and "the rulers of the darkness of this world" in all their number, subtlety, and malignity, not only with absolute ease, as their conscious Lord, but, as we might say, with full consciousness on their part of the presence of their Maker, whose will to one and all of them was law. And this is He of whom it is added, "the world knew Him not!" **11. his own**—"His own" (property or possession), for the word is in the *neuter* gender. It means His own land, city, temple, Messianic rights and possessions. **and his own**—"His own" (people); for now the word is *masculine.* It means the Jews, as the "peculiar people." Both *they* and their *land,* with all that this included, were "HIS OWN," not so much as part of "the world which was made by Him," but as "THE HEIR" of the inheritance (Luke 20:14; see also on Matt. 22:1). **received him not**—*nationally,* as God's chosen witnesses. **12. But as many**—*individuals,* of the "disobedient and gainsaying people." **gave he power**—The word signifies both *authority* and *ability,* and both are certainly meant here. **to become**—Mark these words: Jesus is the Son of God; He is never said to have become such. **the sons**—or more simply, "sons of God," in *name* and in *nature.* **believe on his name**—*a phrase never used in Scripture of any mere creature,* to express the credit given to human testimony, even of prophets or apostles, inasmuch it carries with it the idea of *trust* proper only towards GOD. In this sense of *supreme faith,* as due to Him who "gives those that *believe in Himself* power to become sons of God," it is manifestly used here. **13. Which were born**—a sonship therefore not of mere title and privilege, but of *nature,* the soul being made conscious of the vital capacities, perceptions, and emotions of *a child of God,* before unknown. **not of blood . . .**—not of superior human descent, not of human generation at all, not of man in any manner of way. By this elaborate threefold denial of the *human* source of this sonship, immense force is given to what follows—"*but of God.*" Right royal gift, and He who confers must be absolutely divine. For who would not worship Him who can bring him into the family, and evoke within him the very life, of the sons of God? **14. And the Word . . .**—*To raise the reader to the altitude of this climax were the thirteen foregoing verses written.* **was made flesh**—BECAME MAN, in man's present frail, mortal condition, denoted by the word "flesh" (Isa. 40:6; I Pet. 1:24). It is directed probably against the *Docetæ,* who held that Christ was not really

but only *apparently* man; against whom this gentle spirit is vehement in his Epistles (I John 4:3; II John 7:10, 11), [LUCKE, etc.]. Nor could He be too much so, for with the verity of the Incarnation all substantial Christianity vanishes. But now, married to our nature, henceforth He is as *personally conscious of all that is strictly human as of all that is properly divine;* and our nature is in His Person redeemed and quickened, ennobled and transfigured. **and dwelt**—tabernacled or pitched his tent; a word peculiar to John, who uses it four times, all in the sense of *a permanent stay* (Rev. 7:15; 12:12; 13:6; 21:3). For ever wedded to our *"flesh,"* He has entered this tabernacle to "go no more out." The allusion is to that tabernacle where dwelt the *Shekinah* (see on Matt. 23:38, 39), or manifested "GLORY OF THE LORD," and with reference to God's *permanent dwelling among His people* (Lev. 26:11; Ps. 68:18; 132:13, 14; Ezek. 37:27). This is put almost beyond doubt by what immediately follows, **"And we beheld His glory"** [LUCKE, MEYER, DE WETTE, which last critic, rising higher than usual, says that thus were perfected all former partial manifestations of God in *an essentially Personal and historically Human* manifestation]. **full of grace and truth**—So it should read. "He dwelt among us full of grace and truth"; or, in Old Testament phrase, "Mercy and truth," denoting the whole fruit of God's purposes of love towards sinners of mankind, which until now existed only in *promise,* and the *fulfilment* at length of that promise in Christ; in one great word, *"the* SURE MERCIES *of David"* (Isa. 55:3; Acts 13:34; cf. II Sam. 23:5). In His Person all that Grace and Truth which had been floating so long in shadowy forms, and darting into the souls of the poor and needy its broken beams, took everlasting possession of human flesh and filled it full. By this Incarnation of Grace and Truth, the teaching of thousands of years was at once transcended and beggared, and the family of God sprang into Manhood. **and we beheld his glory**—not by the eye of *sense,* which saw in Him only "the carpenter." His glory was "spiritually discerned" (I Cor. 2:7-15; II Cor. 3:18; 4:4, 6; 5:16)—the glory of surpassing grace, love, tenderness, wisdom, purity, spirituality; majesty and meekness, richness and poverty, power and weakness, meeting together in unique contrast; ever attracting and at times ravishing the "babes" that followed and forsook all for Him. **the glory as of the only begotten of the Father**—(See on Luke 1:35); not *like,* but "such as (belongs to)," such as *became* or was *befitting* the only begotten of the Father [CHRYSOSTOM in LUCKE, CALVIN, etc.], according to a wellknown use of the word "as."

15. A SAYING OF THE BAPTIST CONFIRMATORY OF THIS. **after me**—in *official manifestation.* **before me**—*in rank and dignity.* **for he was before me**—in *existence;* "His goings forth being from of old, from everlasting" (Mic. 5:2). (Anything lower than this His words cannot mean); i.e., "My Successor is my Superior, for He was my Predecessor." This enigmatic play upon the different senses of the words "before" and "after" was doubtless employed by the Baptist to arrest attention, and rivet the thought; and the Evangelist introduces it just to clinch his own statements.

16-18. SAME SUBJECT CONTINUED. **of his fulness**—of "grace and truth," resuming the thread of vs. 14. **grace for grace**—i.e., grace upon grace (so all the best interpreters), in successive communications and larger measures, as each was able to take it in. Observe, the word "truth" is here dropped.

"Grace" being the chosen New Testament word for the whole fulness of the new covenant, all that dwells in Christ for men. **17. For . . .**—The Law elicits the consciousness of sin and the need of redemption; it only typifies the reality. The Gospel, on the contrary, actually communicates reality and power from above (cf. Rom. 6:14). Hence Paul terms the Old Testament "shadow," while he calls the New Testament "substance" (Col. 2:17), [OLSHAUSEN]. **18. No man**—"No one," in the widest sense. **hath seen God**—by immediate gaze, or direct intuition. **in the bosom of the Father**—A remarkable expression, used only here, presupposing *the Son's conscious existence distinct from the Father,* and expressing *His immediate and most endeared access to, and absolute acquaintance with, Him.* **he**—emphatic; *q.d.,* "He and He only hath declared Him," because He only *can.*

19-36. THE BAPTIST'S TESTIMONY TO CHRIST. **19. record**—testimony. **the Jews**—i.e., the heads of the nation, the members of the Sanhedrim. *In this peculiar sense our Evangelist seems always to use the term.* **20. confessed . . .**—i.e., While many were ready to hail him as the Christ, he neither gave the slightest ground for such views, nor the least entertainment to them. **21. Elias**—in His own proper person. **that prophet**—announced in Deuteronomy 18:15, etc., about whom they seem not to have been agreed whether he were the same with the Messiah or no. **25. Why baptizest thou, if not . . .**—Thinking he disclaimed any special connection with Messiah's kingdom, they demand his right to gather disciples by baptism. **26. there standeth**—This must have been spoken after the baptism of Christ, and possibly just after His temptation (see on vs. 29). **28. Bethabara**—Rather, Bethany (according to nearly all the best and most ancient MSS.); not the Bethany of Lazarus, but another of the same name, and distinguished from it as lying "beyond Jordan," on the east. **29. seeth Jesus**—fresh, probably, from the scene of the temptation. **coming unto him**—as to congenial company (Acts 4:23), and to receive from him His first greeting. **and saith**—catching a sublime inspiration at the sight of Him approaching. **the Lamb of God**—the one God-ordained, God-gifted sacrificial offering. **that taketh away**—*taketh up* and *taketh away.* The word signifies both, as does the corresponding Hebrew word. Applied to sin, it means to *be chargeable with the guilt of it* (Exod. 28:38; Lev. 5:1; Ezek. 18:20), and to *bear it away* (as often). In the Levitical victims both ideas met, as they do in Christ, the people's guilt being viewed as *transferred* to them, *avenged* in their death, and so *borne away* by them (Lev. 4:15; 16:15, 21, 22; and cf. Isa. 53:6-12; II Cor. 5:21). **the sin**—The *singular* number being used to mark the *collective burden* and *all-embracing efficacy.* **of the world**—not of Israel only, for whom the typical victims were exclusively offered. Wherever there shall live a sinner throughout the wide world, sinking under that burden too heavy for him to bear, he shall find in this "Lamb of God," a shoulder equal to the weight. The right note was struck at the first—balm, doubtless, to Christ's own spirit; nor was ever after, or ever will be, a more glorious utterance. **31-34. knew him not**—Living mostly apart, the one at Nazareth, the other in the Judean desert—to prevent all appearance of collusion, John only knew that at a definite time after his own call, his Master would show Himself. As He drew near for baptism one day, the last of all the crowd, the spirit of the Baptist heaving under a divine presenti-

ment that the moment had at length arrived, and an air of unwonted serenity and dignity, not without traits, probably, of the family features, appearing in this Stranger, the Spirit said to him as to Samuel of his youthful type, "Arise, anoint Him, for this is He!" (I Sam. 16:12). But *the* sign which he was told to expect was the visible descent of the Spirit upon Him as He emerged out of the baptismal water. *Then,* catching up the voice from heaven, "he saw and bare record that this is the Son of God." **35. John stood**—"was standing," at his accustomed place. **36. looking**—having fixed his eyes, with significant gaze, on Jesus. **as he walked** —but not now *to him.* To have done this once (see on vs. 29) was humility enough [BENGEL]. **Behold . . .**—The repetition of that wonderful proclamation, in identical terms and without another word, could only have been meant as a gentle hint to go after Him—as they did.

37-51. FIRST GATHERING OF DISCIPLES—JOHN, ANDREW, SIMON, PHILIP, NATHANAEL. **38. What seek ye**—gentle, winning question, remarkable as the Redeemer's *first public utterance.* (See on Matt. 12:18-20.) **where dwellest thou**—i.e., "That is a question we cannot answer in a moment; but had we Thy company for a calm hour in private, gladly should we open our burden." **39. Come and see**—His *second utterance,* more winning still. **tenth hour**—not 10 A.M. (as some), according to *Roman,* but 4 P.M., according to *Jewish* reckoning, which John follows. The hour is mentioned to show why they stayed out the day with him—because little of it remained. **40. One . . . was Andrew**—The other was doubtless our Evangelist himself. His great sensitiveness is touchingly shown in his representation of this first contact with the Lord; the circumstances are present to him in the minutest details; he still remembers the very hour. But "he reports no particulars of those discourses of the Lord by which he was bound to Him for the whole of His life; he allows everything personal to retire" [OLSHAUSEN]. **Peter's brother**—and the elder of the two. **41. have found the Messias**—The previous preparation of their simple hearts under the Baptist's ministry, made quick work of this blessed conviction, while others hesitated till doubt settled into obduracy. *So it is still.* **42. brought him to Jesus**—Happy brothers that thus do to each other! **beheld him**—fixed his eyes on him, with significant gaze (as vs. 36). **Cephas . . . stone**—(See on Matt. 16:18). **43. would go . . . into Galilee**—for from His baptism He had sojourned in *Judea* (showing that the calling at the Sea of Galilee (Matt. 4:18) was a *subsequent* one; see on Luke 5:1). **Follow me**—the first express call given, the former three having come to Him spontaneously. **44. the city of Andrew and Peter**—of their *birth* probably, for they seem to have *lived* at Capernaum (Mark 1:29). **45. Nathanael**—(See on Matt. 10:3). **Moses** —(See ch. 5:46). **son of Joseph**—the current way of speaking. (See Luke 3:23.) **46. any good out of Nazareth**—remembering Bethlehem, perhaps, as Messiah's predicted birthplace, and Nazareth having no *express* prophetic place at all, besides being in no repute. The question sprang from mere dread of mistake in a matter so vital. **Come and see**—Noble remedy against preconceived opinions [BENGEL]. Philip, though he could not perhaps solve his difficulty, could show him how to get rid of it. (See on ch. 6:68.) **47. an Israelite indeed . . . no guile**—not only no hypocrite, but with a guileless simplicity not always found even in God's own people, ready to follow wherever truth might lead him, saying, Samuel-like, "Speak, Lord, for Thy servant heareth." **48. Whence knowest thou me**—conscious that his very heart had been read, and at this critical moment more than ever before. **Before Philip called thee**—showing He knew all that passed between Philip and him at a distance. **when ... under the fig tree ...**—where retirement for meditation and prayer was not uncommon [LIGHTFOOT]. Thither, probably—hearing that his master's Master had at length appeared, and heaving with mingled eagerness to behold Him and dread of deception—he had retired to pour out his guileless heart for light and guidance, ending with such a prayer as this, "Show me a token for good!" (See on Luke 2:8.) Now he has it, 'Thou guileless one, that fig tree scene, with all its heaving anxieties, deep pleadings and tremulous hopes—I saw it all.' The first words of Jesus had astonished, but this quite overpowered and won him. **49. Son of God ... King of Israel**—the one denoting His person, the other His office. How much loftier this than anything Philip had said to him! But just as the earth's vital powers, the longer they are frost-bound, take the greater spring when at length set free, so souls, like Nathanael and Thomas (see on ch. 20:28), the outgoings of whose faith are hindered for a time, take the start of their more easy-going brethren when loosed and let go. **50, 51. Because I said ...**—"So quickly convinced, and on this evidence only?"—an expression of admiration. **Hereafter ...**—The key to this great saying is Jacob's vision (Gen. 28:12-22), to which the allusion plainly is. To show the patriarch that though alone and friendless on earth his interests were busying all heaven, he was made to see "heaven opened and the angels of God ascending and descending upon a" mystic "*ladder* reaching from heaven to earth." 'By and by,' says Jesus here, 'ye shall see this communication between heaven and earth thrown wide open, and *the Son of man the real Ladder of this intercourse.*'

CHAPTER 2

Vss. 1-12. FIRST MIRACLE, WATER MADE WINE —BRIEF VISIT TO CAPERNAUM. **1. third day**—He would take two days to reach Galilee, and this was the third. **mother there**—it being probably some relative's marriage. *John never names her* [BENGEL]. **3. no wine**—evidently expecting some display of His glory, and hinting that now was His time. **4, 5. Woman**—no term of disrespect in the language of that day (ch. 19:26). **what ... to do with thee**—i.e., 'In my Father's business I have to do with Him only." 'Twas a gentle rebuke for *officious interference,* entering a region from which all creatures were excluded (cf. Acts 4:19, 20). **mine hour ...**—hinting that He *would* do something, but at His own time; and so she understood it (vs. 5). **6. firkins**—about seven and a half gallons in Jewish, or nine in Attic measure; each of these huge water jars, therefore, holding some twenty or more gallons, for washings at such feasts (Mark 7:4). **7, 8. Fill ... draw ... bear ...**—directing all, but Himself touching nothing, to prevent all appearance of collusion. **9, 10. well drunk**—"drunk abundantly" (as Song of Sol. 5:1), speaking of the general practice. **the good ... till now**—thus testifying, while ignorant of the source of supply, not only that it was real wine, but better than any at the feast. **11. manifested forth his glory**—Nothing in the least like this is said of the miracles of prophet or apostle, nor could without manifest blasphemy be said of any mere creature. Observe, (1) At a marriage Christ made His first public appearance in any company, and at a marriage He wrought His first miracle—the noblest sanction that could be given to that God-given institution. (2) As the miracle did not make *bad good,* but *good better,* so Christianity only redeems, sanctifies, and ennobles the beneficent but abused institution of marriage; and Christ's whole work only turns the water of earth into the wine of heaven. Thus "this beginning of miracles" exhibited the character and "manifested forth the glory" of His entire Mission. (3) As Christ countenanced our seasons of *festivity,* so also that greater *fulness* which befits such; so far was He from encouraging that *asceticism* which has since been so often put for all religion. (4) The character and authority ascribed by Romanists to the Virgin is directly in the teeth of this and other scriptures. **12. Capernaum**—on the Sea of Galilee. (See on Matt. 9:1.) **his mother and his brethren**—(See on Luke 2:51, and Matt. 13:54-56).

13-25. CHRIST'S FIRST PASSOVER—FIRST CLEANSING OF THE TEMPLE. **14-17. in the temple**—not the temple itself, as vs. 19-21, but the *temple-court.* **sold oxen ...**—for the convenience of those who had to offer them in sacrifice. **changers of money**—of Roman into Jewish money, in which the temple dues (see on Matt. 17:24) had to be paid. **15. small cords**—likely some of the rushes spread for bedding, and when twisted used to tie up the cattle there collected. "Not by this slender whip but by divine majesty was the ejection accomplished, the whip being but a sign of the scourge of divine anger" [GROTIUS]. **poured out ... overthrew ...**—thus expressing the mingled indignation and authority of the impulse. **16. my Father's house**—How close the resemblance of these remarkable words to Luke 2:49; the same *consciousness of intrinsic relation to the temple*—as the seat of His Father's most august worship, and so the symbol of all that is due to Him on earth—dictating both speeches. Only, when but a youth, *with no authority,* He was simply "a SON IN His own house"; now He was "a SON OVER His own house" (Hebrews 3:6), the proper Representative, and in flesh "the Heir," of his Father's rights. **house of merchandise**—There was nothing wrong in the merchandise; but to bring it, for their own and others' convenience, into that most sacred place, was a high-handed profanation which the eye of Jesus could not endure. **17. eaten me up**—a glorious feature in the predicted character of the suffering Messiah (Ps. 69:9), and rising high even in some not worthy to loose the latchet of His shoes. (Exod. 32:19 etc.). **18-22. What sign ...**—Though the *act* and the *words* of Christ, taken together, were sign enough, they were unconvinced: yet they were *awed,* and though at His very next appearance at Jerusalem they "sought to kill Him" for speaking of "His Father" just as He did now (ch. 5:18), they, at this early stage, only ask a sign. **19. Destroy this temple ...**—(See on Mark 14:58, 59). **20. Forty-six years**—From the eighteenth year of Herod till then was just forty-six years [JOSEPHUS, *Antiquities,* xv. 11. 1]. **21. temple of his body**—in which was enshrined the glory of the eternal Word. (See on ch. 1:14.) By its resurrection the true Temple of God upon earth was reared up, of which the stone one was but a shadow; so that the allusion is not *quite* exclusively to Himself, but takes in that Temple of which He is the foundation, and all believers are the "lively stones." (I Pet. 2:4, 5.) **22. believed the scripture**—on this subject; i.e., what was meant, which was hid from them till then. Mark (1) *The act by which Christ signalized His first public appearance in the Temple.* Taking "His fan in His hand, He purges His floor," not thoroughly indeed, but enough to *foreshadow His last act* towards that faithless people—*to sweep them out of God's house.* (2) The sign of His authority to do this is the announcement, at this first outset of His ministry, of that coming death by their hands, and resurrection by His own, which were to pave the way for their judicial ejection. **23-25. in the feast day**—the foregoing things occurring probably before the feast began. **many believed**—superficially, struck merely by "the miracles He did." Of these we have no record. **24. did not commit**—"entrust," or let Himself down familiarly to them, as to His genuine disciples. **25. knew what was in man**—It is impossible for language more clearly to assert of Christ what in Jeremiah 17:9, 10, and elsewhere, is denied of all mere creatures.

CHAPTER 3

Vss. 1-21. NIGHT INTERVIEW OF NICODEMUS WITH JESUS. **1, 2. Nicodemus**—In this member of the Sanhedrim sincerity and timidity are seen struggling together. One of those superficial "believers" mentioned in ch. 2:23, 24, yet inwardly craving further satisfaction, he comes to Jesus in quest of it, but comes "by night" (see ch. 19:38, 39; 12:42); he avows his conviction that He was "come from God"—*an expression never applied to a merely human messenger,* and probably meaning more here—but only as "a *teacher*," and in His miracles he sees a proof merely that "God is with Him." Thus, while unable to repress his convictions, he is afraid of committing himself too far. **3. Except ...**—This blunt and curt reply was plainly meant to shake the whole edifice of the man's religion, in order to lay a deeper and more enduring foundation. Nicodemus probably thought he had gone a long way, and expected, perhaps, to be complimented on his candor. Instead of this, he is virtually told that he has raised a question which he is not in a capacity to solve, and that before approaching it, *his spiritual vision required to be rectified by an entire revolution on his inner man.* Had the man been less sincere, this would certainly have repelled him; but with persons in his mixed state of mind—to which Jesus was no stranger (ch. 2:25)—such methods speed better than more honeyed words and gradual approaches. **a man**—not *a Jew* merely; the necessity is a universal one. **born again**—or, as it were, *begin life anew* in relation to God; his manner of thinking, feeling, and acting, with reference to spiritual things, undergoing *a fundamental and permanent revolution.* **cannot see**—can have no part in (just as one is said to "see life," "see death," etc.). **the kingdom of God**—whether in its beginnings here (Luke 16:16), or its consummation hereafter (Matt. 25:34; Eph. 5:5). **4. How ...**—The figure of the new birth, if it had been meant only of *Gentile proselytes* to the Jewish religion, would have been intelligible enough to Nicodemus, being quite in keeping with the language of that day; but that *Jews themselves* should need a new birth was to him incomprehensible. **5. of water and of the Spirit**—A twofold explanation of the "new birth," so startling to Nicodemus. To a Jewish ecclesiastic, so familiar with the symbolical application of water, in every variety of way and form of expression, this language was fitted to show that the thing intended was no other

than a *thorough spiritual purification by the operation of the Holy Ghost.* Indeed, element of *water* and operation of *the Spirit* are brought together in a glorious evangelical prediction of Ezekiel (36:25-27), which Nicodemus might have been reminded of had such spiritualities not been almost lost in the reigning formalism. Already had the symbol of water been embodied in an initiatory ordinance, in the baptism of the Jewish expectants of Messiah by the Baptist, not to speak of the baptism of Gentile proselytes before that; and in the Christian Church it was soon to become the great visible door of entrance into "the kingdom of God," *the reality being the sole work of the Holy Ghost* [Titus 3:5]. **6-8. That which is born ...**—A great universal proposition; "That which is begotten carries within itself the nature of that which begat it" [OLSHAUSEN]. **flesh**—Not the mere material body, but all that comes into the world by birth, *the entire man;* yet not humanity simply, but in its corrupted, depraved condition, *in complete subjection to the law of the fall* (Rom. 8:1-9). So that though a man "*could enter a second time into his mother's womb and be born*," he would be no nearer this "new birth" than before (Job 14:4; Ps. 51:5). **is spirit**—*partakes of and possesses His spiritual nature.* **7. Marvel not ...**—If a spiritual nature only can see and enter the kingdom of God; if all we bring into the world with us be the reverse of spiritual; and if this spirituality be solely of the Holy Ghost, no wonder a new birth is indispensable. **Ye must**—"*Ye,* says Jesus, not *we*" [BENGEL]. After those universal propositions, about what "*a man*" must be, to "enter the kingdom of God,"—this is remarkable, showing that our Lord meant to hold Himself forth as "*separate from sinners*." **8. The wind ...**—*Breath* and *spirit* (one word both in Hebrew and Greek) are constantly brought together in Scripture as analogous (Job 27:3; 33:4; Ezek. 37:9-14). **canst not tell ...**—The laws which govern the motion of the *winds* are even yet but partially discovered; but the risings, fallings, and change in direction many times in a day, of those *gentle breezes* here referred to, will probably ever be a mystery to us: So of the operation of the Holy Ghost in the new birth. **9, 10. How ...**—Though the subject still confounds him, the necessity and possibility of the new birth is no longer the point with him, but the nature of it and how it is brought about [LUTHARDT]. "From this moment Nicodemus *says nothing more,* but has sunk unto a disciple who has found his true teacher. *Therefore* the Saviour now graciously advances in His communications of truth, and once more solemnly brings to the mind of this teacher in Israel, now become a learner, his own not guiltless *ignorance,* that He may then proceed to utter, out of the fulness of His divine knowledge, such farther testimonies both of earthly and heavenly things as his docile scholar may to his own profit receive" [STIER]. **master**—"teacher." The question clearly implies that *the doctrine of regeneration is so far disclosed in the Old Testament that Nicodemus was culpable in being ignorant of it.* Nor is it merely as something that should be experienced *under the* Gospel that the Old Testament holds it forth—as many distinguished critics allege, denying that there was any such thing as regeneration before Christ. For our Lord's proposition is universal, that no fallen man is or can be spiritual without a regenerating operation of the Holy Ghost, and the necessity of a *spiritual obedience* under whatever name, in opposition to mere mechanical services, is proclaimed throughout all the Old Testament. **11-13. We speak that we know, and ... have seen**—i.e., by *absolute* knowledge and *immediate* vision of God, which "the only-begotten Son in the bosom of the Father" claims as exclusively His own (ch. 1:18). The "we" and "our" are here used, though Himself only is intended, in emphatic contrast, probably, with the opening words of Nicodemus, "Rabbi, *we* know ...." **ye receive not ...**—referring to the *class* to which Nicodemus belonged, but from which he was beginning to be separated in spirit. **12. earthly things**—such as *regeneration,* the gate of entrance to the kingdom of God *on earth,* and which Nicodemus should have understood better, as a truth even of that more *earthly* economy to which he belonged. **heavenly things**—the things of the new and more heavenly evangelical economy, only to be fully understood after the effusion of the Spirit from heaven through the exalted Saviour. **13. no man hath ascended ...**—There is something paradoxical in this language—'No one has gone up but He that came down, even He who is at once both up and down.' Doubtless it was intended to startle and constrain His auditor to think that there must be mysterious elements in His Person. The old Socinians, to subvert the doctrine of the pre-existence of Christ, seized upon this passage as teaching that the man Jesus was secretly caught up to heaven to receive His instructions, and then "came down from heaven" to deliver them. But the sense manifestly is this: 'The perfect knowledge of God is not obtained by any man's going up from earth to heaven to receive it—no man hath so ascended—but He whose *proper habitation,* in His essential and eternal nature, is heaven, hath, by taking human flesh, descended as the "Son of man" to disclose the Father, whom He knows by immediate gaze alike in the flesh as before He assumed it, being essentially and unchangeably "in the bosom of the Father" ' (ch. 1:18). **14-16. And as Moses ...**—Here now we have the "heavenly things," as before the "earthly," but under a veil, for the reason mentioned in vs. 12. The crucifixion of Messiah is twice after this veiled under the same lively term—"*uplifting,*" ch. 8:28; 12:32, 33. Here it is still further veiled—though to us who know what it means, rendered vastly more instructive—by reference to the brazen serpent. The venom of the fiery serpents, shooting through the veins of the rebellious Israelites, was spreading death through the camp—lively emblem of the perishing condition of men by reason of sin. In both cases the remedy was divinely provided. In both the way of cure strikingly resembled that of the disease. Stung by serpents, by a serpent they are healed. By "fiery serpents" bitten—serpents, probably, with skin spotted fiery-red (KURTZ)—the instrument of cure is a serpent of brass or copper, having at a distance *the same appearance.* So in redemption, as by man came death, by Man also comes life—Man, too, "*in the likeness of sinful flesh,*" differing in nothing *outward and apparent* from those who, pervaded by the poison of the serpent, were ready to perish. But as the uplifted serpent had none of the venom of which the serpent-bitten people were dying, so while the whole human family were perishing of the deadly wound inflicted on it by the old serpent, "the Second Man," who arose over humanity with healing in His wings, was without spot or wrinkle, or any such thing. In both cases the remedy is *conspicuously displayed;* in the one case on a pole, in the other on the cross, to "draw all men unto Him"

(ch. 12:32). In both cases it is by *directing the eye to the uplifted Remedy* that the cure is effected; in the one case the bodily eye, in the other the gaze of the soul by "believing in Him," as in that glorious ancient proclamation—"*Look* unto me and be ye saved, all the ends of the earth ..." (Isa. 45:22). Both methods are stumbling to human reason. What, to any thinking Israelite, could seem more unlikely than that a deadly poison should be dried up in his body by simply looking on a reptile of brass? Such a stumbling block to the Jews and to the Greeks foolishness was faith in the crucified Nazarene as a way of deliverance from eternal perdition. Yet was the warrant in both cases to expect a cure equally rational and well grounded. As the serpent was *God's ordinance* for the cure of every bitten Israelite, so is Christ for the salvation of every perishing sinner—the one however a purely *arbitrary* ordinance, the other divinely *adapted* to man's complicated maladies. In both cases the efficacy is the same. As one simple look at the serpent, however distant and however weak, brought an instantaneous cure, even so, real faith in the Lord Jesus, however tremulous, however distant—be it but *real* faith—brings certain and instant healing to the perishing soul. In a word, the consequences of disobedience are the same in both. Doubtless many bitten Israelites, galling as their case was, would *reason* rather than *obey,* would *speculate* on the absurdity of expecting the bite of a living serpent to be cured by looking at a piece of dead metal in the shape of one—speculate thus *till they died.* Alas! is not salvation by a crucified Redeemer subjected to like treatment? Has the offense of the cross yet ceased? (Cf. II Kings 5:12). **16. For God so loved ...**—What proclamation of the Gospel has been so oft on the lips of missionaries and preachers in every age since it was first uttered? What has sent such thrilling sensations through millions of mankind? What has been honored to bring such multitudes to the feet of Christ? What to kindle in the cold and selfish breasts of mortals the fires of selfsacrificing love to mankind, as these words of transparent simplicity, yet overpowering majesty? The picture embraces several distinct compartments: "THE WORLD"—in its widest sense—*ready* "*to perish*"; the immense "LOVE OF GOD" *to that perishing world,* measurable only, and conceivable only, by the gift which it drew forth from Him; THE GIFT itself—"He *so* loved the world that He *gave His* only begotten Son," or, in the language of Paul, "*spared not* His own Son" (Rom. 8:32), or in that addressed to Abraham when ready to offer Isaac on the altar, "*withheld not* His Son, His only Son, whom He loved" (Gen. 22:16); the FRUIT of this stupendous gift—not only *deliverance from* impending "*perdition,*" but *the bestowal of everlasting life;* and the MODE in which all takes effect—by "*believing*" on the Son. How would Nicodemus' narrow Judaism become invisible in the blaze of this Sun of righteousness seen rising on "the world" with healing in His wings! **17-21. not to condemn ...**—A statement of vast importance. Though "condemnation" is to many the *issue* of Christ's mission (vs. 19), it is not the *object* of His mission, which is purely a *saving* one. **18. is not condemned**—Having, immediately on his believing, "passed from death unto life" (ch. 5:24). **condemned already**—Rejecting the one way of deliverance from that "condemnation" which God gave His Son to *remove,* and so wilfully *remaining* condemned. **19. this is the condemnation ...**—emphatically so, *revealing* the condemnation already existing, and *sealing up* under it those who will not be delivered from it. **light is come into the world**—in the Person of Him to whom Nicodemus was listening. **loved darkness...**—This can only be known by the deliberate rejection of Christ, but that *does* fearfully reveal it. **20. reproved**—by detection. **21. doeth truth**—whose only object in life is to be and do what will bear the light. Therefore he loves and "comes to the light," that all he is and does, being thus thoroughly tested, may be seen to have nothing in it but what is divinely wrought and divinely approved. This is the "Israelite, indeed, in whom is no guile."

22-36. JESUS IN THE NEIGHBORHOOD OF THE BAPTIST—HIS NOBLE TESTIMONY TO HIS MASTER. 22-24. land of Judea—the rural parts of that province, the foregoing conversation being held in the capital. **baptized**—in the sense explained in ch. 4:2. **23. Ænon...Salim**—on the west of Jordan. (Cf. vs. 26 with ch. 1:28.) **24. John not yet cast into prison**—Hence it is plain that our Lord's ministry did not *commence* with the imprisonment of John, though, but for this, we should have drawn that inference from Matthew 4:12 and Mark's (1: 14) express statement. **25, 26. between some of**—rather, "on the part of." **and the Jews**—rather (according to the best MSS.), "and a Jew," **about purifying**—i.e., baptizing, the symbolical meaning of washing with water being put (as in ch. 2:6) for the act itself. As John and Jesus were the only teachers who baptized Jews, discussions might easily arise between the Baptist's disciples and such Jews as declined to submit to that rite. **26. Rabbi...**—'Master, this man tells us that He to whom thou barest such generous witness beyond Jordan is requiting thy generosity by drawing all the people away to Himself. At this rate, thou shalt soon have no disciples at all.' The reply to this is one of the noblest and most affecting utterances that ever came from the lips of man. **27-30. A man...**—'I do my heaven-prescribed work, and that is enough for me. Would you have me mount into my Master's place? Said I not unto you, I am not the Christ? The Bride is not mine, why should the people stay with me? Mine it is to point the burdened to the Lamb of God that taketh away the sin of the world, to tell them there is Balm in Gilead, and a Physician there. And shall I grudge to see them, in obedience to the call, flying as a cloud, and as doves to their windows? Whose is the Bride but the Bridegroom's? Enough for me to be the Bridegroom's *friend*, sent by Him to negotiate the match, privileged to bring together the Saviour and those He is come to seek and to save, and rejoicing with joy unspeakable if I may but "stand and hear the Bridegroom's voice," witnessing the blessed espousals. Say ye, then, they go from me to Him? Ye bring me glad tidings of great joy. He must increase, but I must decrease; this, my joy, therefore is fulfilled.' **A man can receive...**—can assume nothing, i.e., lawfully and with any success; i.e., Every man has his work and sphere appointed him from above. Even Christ Himself came under this law (Heb. 5:4). **31-34. He that...**—Here is the reason why He must increase while all human teachers must decrease. The Master "cometh from above"—descending from *His proper element*, the region of those "heavenly things" which He came to reveal, and so, although mingling with men and things on the earth, is not "of the earth," either in Person or Word. The servants, on the contrary, springing of earth, are of the earth, and their tes-

timony, even though divine in authority, partakes necessarily of their own earthiness. (So strongly did the Baptist feel this contrast that the last clause just repeats the first.) It is impossible for a sharper line of distinction to be drawn between Christ and all human teachers, even when divinely commissioned and speaking by the power of the Holy Ghost. And who does not perceive it? The words of prophets and apostles are undeniable and most precious truth; but in the words of Christ we hear a voice as from the excellent Glory, the Eternal Word making Himself heard in our own flesh. **32. what he hath seen and heard**—(See on vs. 11 and ch. 1:18). **no man receiveth...**—John's disciples had said, "*All* come to Him" (vs. 26). The Baptist here virtually says, Would it were so, but alas! they are next to "*none*" [BENGEL]. They were far readier to receive himself, and obliged him to say, I am not the Christ, and he seems pained at this. **33. hath set to His seal...**—gives glory to God whose words Christ speaks, not as prophets and apostles by a partial communication of the Spirit to them. **34. for God giveth not the Spirit by measure**—Here, again, the sharpest conceivable line of distinction is drawn between Christ and all human-inspired teachers: 'They have the Spirit in a *limited* degree; but God giveth not [to Him] the Spirit *by measure.*' It means the entire fulness of divine life and divine power. The present tense *"giveth,"* very aptly points out the permanent communication of the Spirit by the Father to the Son, so that a constant flow and reflow of living power is to be understood (Cf. ch. 1:15) [OLSHAUSEN]. **35, 36. The Father loveth...**—See on Matthew 11:27, where we have the *"delivering over"* of all things into the hands of the Son," while here we have the deep spring of that august act in the Father's ineffable *"love of the Son."* **36. hath everlasting life**—already has it. (See on vs. 18 and ch. 5:24). **shall not see**—The contrast here is striking: The one has already a life that will endure for ever—the other not only has it not now, but shall never have it—never see it. **abideth on him**—It was on Him before, and not being *removed* in the only possible way, by "believing on the Son," it necessarily *remaineth* on him! N.B.—How flatly does this contradict the teaching of many in our day, that there neither was, nor is, anything *in God* against sinners which needed to be removed by Christ, but only *in men* against God!

CHAPTER 4

Vss. 1-42. CHRIST AND THE WOMAN OF SAMARIA —THE SAMARITANS OF SYCHAR. **1-4. the Lord knew** —not by report, but in the sense of ch. 2:25, for which reason He is here styled "the Lord." **2. Jesus baptized not**—John being a servant baptized with his own hand; Christ as the Master, "baptizing with the Holy Ghost," administered the outward symbol only through His disciples. **3. left Judea** —to avoid persecution, which at that early stage would have marred His work. **departed into Galilee**—by which time John had been cast into prison (Mark 1:14). **4. must needs go through Samaria**—for a geographical reason, no doubt, as it lay straight in his way, but certainly not without a higher design. **5. cometh...to**—i.e., as far as: for He remained at some distance from it. **Sychar**—the "Shechem" of the Old Testament, about thirty-four miles from Jerusalem, afterwards called "Neapolis," and now "Nablous." **6-8. wearied...sat thus**--

i.e., "as you might fancy a weary man would"; an instance of the graphic style of St. John [WEBSTER and WILKINSON]. In fact, this is perhaps the most *human* of all the scenes of our Lord's earthly history. We seem to be beside Him, overhearing all that is here recorded, nor could any painting of the scene on canvas, however perfect, do other than lower the conception which this exquisite narrative conveys to the devout and intelligent reader. But with all that is *human*, how much also of the *divine* have we here, both blended in one glorious manifestation of the majesty, grace, pity, patience with which "the Lord" imparts light and life to this unlikeliest of strangers, standing midway between Jews and heathens. **the sixth hour**—*noonday*, reckoning from 6 A.M. From Song of Solomon 1: 7 we know, as from other sources, that the very flocks "rested at noon." But Jesus, whose maxim was, "I must work the works of Him that sent Me while it is day" (ch. 9:4), seems to have denied Himself that repose, at least on this occasion, probably that He might reach this well when He knew the woman would be there. Once there, however, He accepts ... the grateful ease of a seat on the patriarchal stone. But what music is that which I hear from His lips, "Come unto Me, all ye that labor and are heavy laden, and I will give you rest" (Matt. 11:28). **7. Give me to drink**—for the heat of a noonday sun had parched His lips. But "in the last, that great day of the feast," Jesus stood and cried, saying, "If any man thirst let him come unto Me and *drink*" (ch. 7:37). **9-12. How is it that thou**—not altogether refusing, yet wondering at so unusual a request from a Jew, as His dress and dialect would at once discover Him to be, to a Samaritan. **For ...**—It is this national antipathy that gives point to the parable of the good Samaritan (Luke 10:30-37), and the thankfulness of the Samaritan leper (Luke 17:16, 18). **10. If thou knewest ...**—i.e., 'In Me thou seest only a petitioner to thee but if thou knewest who that Petitioner is, and the Gift that God is giving to men, thou wouldst have changed places with Him, gladly suing of Him living water—nor shouldst thou have sued in vain" (gently reflecting on her for not immediately meeting His request). **12. Art thou greater ...**—already perceiving in this Stranger a claim to some mysterious greatness. **our father Jacob**—for when it went well with the Jews, they claimed kindred with them, as being descended from Joseph; but when misfortunes befell the Jews, they disowned all connection with them [JOSEPHUS, 9. 14, 3]. **13, 14. thirst again ... never thirst ...**—The contrast here is fundamental and all comprehensive. "This water" plainly means 'this natural water and *all satisfactions of a like earthly and perishable nature.*' Coming to us *from without*, and reaching only the *superficial* parts of our nature, they are soon spent, and need to be anew supplied as much as if we had never experienced them before, while the deeper wants of our being are not reached by them at all; whereas the "water" that Christ gives—*spiritual life*—is struck out of the very depths of our being, making the soul not a *cistern*, for holding water *poured into* it *from without*, but a *fountain* (the word had been better so rendered, to distinguish it from the word rendered "well" in vs. 11), springing, gushing, bubbling up and flowing forth *within* us, ever fresh, ever living. *The indwelling of the Holy Ghost as the Spirit of Christ* is the secret of this life with all its enduring energies and satisfactions, as is expressly said (ch. 7:37-39). "Never thirsting," then, means simply that such souls have

the supplies *at home*. **into everlasting life**—carrying the thoughts up from the eternal freshness and vitality of these waters to the great ocean in which they have their confluence. "Thither may I arrive!" [BENGEL]. **15-18. give me this water ...**—This is not obtuseness—that is giving way—it expresses a wondering desire after she scarce knew what from this mysterious Stranger. **16. call thy husband**—now proceeding to arouse her slumbering conscience by laying bare the guilty life she was leading, and by the minute details which that life furnished, not only bringing her sin vividly up before her, but preparing her to receive in His true character that wonderful Stranger to whom her whole life, in its minutest particulars, evidently lay open. **19, 20. Sir I perceive ...**—Seeing herself all revealed, does she now break down and ask what hopes there might be for one so guilty? Nay, her convictions have not reached that point yet. She ingeniously shifts the subject from a personal to a public question. It is not, "Alas, what a wicked life am I leading!" but "Lo, what a wonderful prophet I got into conversation with! He will be able to settle that interminable dispute between us and the Jews. Sir, you must know all about such matters—our fathers hold to this mountain here," pointing to *Gerizim* in Samaria, "as the divinely consecrated place of worship, but ye Jews say that *Jerusalem* is the proper place—which of us is right?" How slowly does the human heart submit to *thorough* humiliation! (Compare the *prodigal;* see on Luke 15:15). Doubtless our Lord saw through the fetch; but does He say, "That question is not the point just now, but have you been living in the way described, yea or nay? Till this is disposed of I cannot be drawn into theological controversies." The Prince of preachers takes another method: He humors the poor woman, letting her take her own way, allowing her to lead while He follows—but thus only the more effectually gaining His object. He answers her question, pours light into her mind on the *spirituality* of all true worship, as of its glorious Object, and so brings her insensibly to the point at which He could disclose to her wondering mind whom she was all the while speaking to. **21-24. Woman ...** Here are three weighty pieces of information: (1) The point raised will very soon cease to be of any moment, for a total change of dispensation is about to come over the Church. (2) The Samaritans are wrong, not only as to the *place*, but the whole *grounds* and *nature* of their worship, while in all these respects the truth lies with the Jews. (3) As God is a *Spirit*, so He both *invites* and *demands* a *spiritual worship*, and already all is in preparation for a *spiritual economy*, more in harmony with the true nature of acceptable service than the ceremonial worship by consecrated *persons, place*, and *times*, which God for a time has seen meet to keep up till fulness of the time should come. **neither in this mountain nor yet at Jerusalem**—i.e., *exclusively* (Mal. 1:11; I Tim. 2:8). **worship the Father**—She had talked simply of "worship"; our Lord brings up before her the great OBJECT of all acceptable worship—"THE FATHER." **22. Ye worship ye know not what**—without any *revealed authority*, and so very much in the dark. In this sense, the Jews *knew what they were about*. But the most glorious thing here is the reason assigned, *"For salvation is of the Jews,"* intimating to her that *Salvation* was not a thing left to be reached by any one who might vaguely desire it of a God of mercy, but something that had been *revealed, prepared, deposited with a par-*

ticular people, and must be sought *in connection with, and as issuing from them;* and that people "the Jews." **23. hour cometh, and now is**—evidently meaning her to understand that this new economy was in some sense being set up while He was talking to her, a sense which would in a few minutes so far appear, when He told her plainly He was *the Christ.* **25, 26. I know Messias cometh ... when He is come ...**—If we take our Lord's immediate disclosure of Himself, in answer to this, as the proper key to its meaning to *His ear,* we can hardly doubt that the woman was already *all but prepared for even this startling announcement,* which indeed she seems (from vs. 29) to have already begun to suspect by His revealing her to herself. Thus quickly, under so matchless a Teacher, was she brought up from her sunken condition to a frame of mind and heart capable of the noblest revelations. **tell us all things**—an expectation founded probably on Deuteronomy 18:15. **26. I that speak .. am he**—He scarce ever said anything like this to His own people, the Jews. He had magnified them to the woman, and yet to themselves He is to the last far more reserved than to her—*proving* rather than plainly *telling* them He was the Christ. But what would not have been *safe* among them was safe enough with her, whose *simplicity* at this stage of the conversation appears from the sequel to have become perfect. What now will the woman say? We listen, the scene has changed, a new party arrives, the disciples have been to Sychar, at some distance, to buy bread, and on their return are astonished at the company their Lord has been holding in their absence. **27. marvelled that he talked with the woman**—It never probably occurred to them to marvel that He talked with *themselves;* yet in His eye, as the sequel shows, He was quite as nobly employed. How poor, if not false, are many of our most plausible estimates! **no man said ... What? ... Why?**—awed by the spectacle, and thinking there must be something under it. **28-30. left her water-pot**—How exquisitely natural! The presence of strangers made her feel that it was time for her to withdraw, and He who knew what was in her heart, and what she was going to the city to do, let her go without exchanging a word with her in the hearing of others. Their interview was too sacred, and the effect on the woman too overpowering (not to speak of His own deep emotion) to allow of its being continued. But this one artless touch—that she "left her water-pot"—speaks volumes. The living water was already beginning to spring up within her; she found that man doth not live by bread nor by water only, and that there was a water of wondrous virtue that raised people above meat and drink, and the vessels that held them, and all human things. In short, she was transported, forgot everything but One, and her heart running over with the tale she had to tell, she hastens home and pours it out. **29. is not this the Christ**—The *form* of the question (in the *Greek*) is a distant, modest way of only half *insinuating* what it seemed hardly fitting for her to *affirm;* nor does she refer to what He said of Himself, but solely to His disclosure to her of the particulars of her own life. **30. they went out ...**—How different from the Jews! and richly was their openness to conviction rewarded. **31-38. meantime**—i.e., while the woman was away. **Master, eat**—*Fatigue* and *thirst* we saw He felt; here is revealed another of our common infirmities to which the Lord was subject—*hunger.* **32. meat ye know not of**—What spirituality of mind! 'I *have* been

eating all the while, and such food as ye dream not of.' What can that be? they ask each other; have any supplies been brought Him in our absence? He knows what they are saying though He hears it not. **34. My meat is ...**—'A Servant here to fulfil a prescribed work, to *do* and to *finish,* that is "meat" to Me; and of this, while you were away, I have had My fill.' And of what does He speak thus? Of the condescension, pity, patience, wisdom He had been laying out upon *one soul*—a very humble woman, and in some respects repulsive too! But He had gained her, and through her was going to gain more, and lay perhaps the foundations of a great work in the country of Samaria; and this filled His whole soul and raised Him above the sense of natural hunger (Matt. 4:4). **35. yet four months, and then harvest**—i.e., 'In current speech, ye say thus at this season; but lift up your eyes and look upon those fields in the light of *another* husbandry, for lo! *in that sense,* they are even now white to harvest, ready for the sickle.' The simple beauty of this language is only surpassed by the glow of holy emotion in the Redeemer's own soul which it expresses. It refers to the *ripeness* of these Sycharites for accession to Him, and the joy of this great Lord of the reapers over the anticipated ingathering. Oh, could we but *so,* "lift up our eyes and look" upon many fields abroad and at home, which to dull sense appear unpromising, as *He* beheld those of Samaria, what movements, as yet scarce in embryo, and accessions to Christ, as yet seemingly far distant, might we not discern as quite near at hand, and thus, amidst difficulties and discouragements too much for nature to sustain, be cheered—*as our Lord Himself was* in circumstances far more overwhelming—with "songs in the night!" **36. he that reapeth ...**—As our Lord could not mean that the reaper only, and not the sower, received "wages," in the sense of *personal reward* for his work, the "wages" here can be no other than the joy of having such a harvest to gather in—the joy of "gathering fruit unto life eternal." **rejoice together**—The blessed issue of the whole ingathering is the interest alike of the sower as of the reaper; it is no more the fruit of the last operation than of the first; and just as there can be no reaping without previous sowing, so have those servants of Christ, to whom is assigned the pleasant task of merely reaping the spiritual harvest, no work to do, and no joy to taste, that has not been prepared to their hand by the toilsome and often thankless work of their predecessors in the field. *The joy, therefore, of the great harvest festivity will be the common joy of all who have taken any part in the work from the first operation to the last.* (See Deut. 16:11, 14; Ps. 126:6; Isa. 9:3.) What encouragement is here for those "fishers of men" who "have toiled all the night" of their official life, and, to human appearance, "have taken nothing!" **38. I sent you ...**—The *I* is emphatic—I, the Lord of the whole harvest: "sent you," points to their *past* appointment to the apostleship, though it has reference only to their *future* discharge of it, for they had nothing to do with the present ingathering of the Sycharites. **ye bestowed no labour**—meaning that much of their future success would arise from the *preparation already made* for them. (See on vs. 42.) **others laboured**—Referring to the Old Testament laborers, the Baptist, and *by implication* Himself, though He studiously keeps this in the background, *that the line of distinction between Himself and all His servants might not be lost sight of.* "Christ represents Himself as the Husbandman [rather the Lord of the laborers], who has the direction both of the sowing and of the harvest, who commissions *all* the agents–those of the Old Testament as well as of the New–and therefore does not stand on a level with either the sowers or the reapers" [OLSHAUSEN]. **39-42. many ... believed ...**–The truth of vs. 35 begins to appear. These Samaritans were the foundation of the Church afterwards built up there. No miracle appears to have been wrought there [but unparalleled supernatural knowledge displayed]: "*we have heard Him ourselves*" sufficed to raise their faith to a point never attained by the Jews, and hardly as yet by the disciples–that He was "the Saviour of *the world*" [ALFORD]. "This incident is further remarkable as a rare instance of the Lord's ministry producing *an awakening on a large scale*" [OLSHAUSEN]. **40. abode two days**–Two precious days, surely, to the Redeemer Himself! Unsought, He had come to His own, yet His own received Him not: now those who were not His own had come to Him, been won by Him, and invited Him to their town that others might share with them in the benefit of His wonderful ministry. Here, then, would He solace His already wounded spirit and have in this outfield village triumph of His grace, a sublime foretaste of the inbringing of the whole Gentile world into the Church.

43-54. SECOND GALILEAN MIRACLE–HEALING OF THE COURTIER'S SON. 43, 44. after two days–lit., the two days of His stay at Sychar. **For Jesus testified ...**–This verse had occasioned much discussion. For it seems strange, if "His own country" here means *Nazareth,* which was in Galilee, that it should be said He came to Galilee *because* in one of its towns He expected no good reception. But all will be simple and natural if we fill up the statement thus: 'He went into the region of Galilee, but not, as might have been expected, to that part of it called "His own country," Nazareth (see Mark 6:4; Luke 4:24), *for* He acted on the maxim which He oft repeated, that a prophet ... **45. received**–welcomed Him. **having seen ... at the feast**–proud, perhaps, of their Countryman's wonderful works at Jerusalem, and possibly won by this circumstance to regard His claims as at least worthy of respectful investigation. Even this our Lord did not despise, for saving conversion often begins in less than this (so Zaccheus, Luke 19:3-10). **for they also went**–i.e., it was their practice to go up to the feast. **46, 47. nobleman**–courtier, king's servant, or one connected with a royal household; such as Chuza (Luke 8:3), or Manaen (Acts 13:1). **heard that Jesus was come out of Judea**–"where he had doubtless seen or heard what things Jesus had done at Jerusalem" (vs. 45), [BENGEL]. **come down**–for Capernaum was down on the northwest shore of the Sea of Galilee. **48-54. Except ye see signs ...**–He *did* believe, both as his coming and his urgent entreaty show; but how imperfectly we shall see; and our Lord would deepen his faith by such a blunt and seemingly rough answer as He made to Nicodemus. **49. come down ere my child die**–'While we talk, the case is at its crisis, and if Thou come not instantly, all is over. This was faith, but partial, and our Lord would perfect it. The man cannot believe the cure could be wrought without the Physician coming to the patient–the thought of such a thing evidently never occurred to him. But Jesus will in a moment bring him up to this. **50. Go thy way; thy son liveth**–Both effects instantaneously followed:–"The man believed the word," and the cure, shooting quicker

than lightning from Cana to Capernaum, was felt by the dying youth. In token of faith, the father takes his leave of Christ–in the circumstances this evidenced full faith. The servants hasten to convey the joyful tidings to the anxious parents, whose faith now only wants one confirmation. "*When began he to amend?*" "Yesterday, at the seventh hour, the fever left him"–the very hour in which was uttered that great word, "Thy son liveth!" So "himself believed and his whole house." He *had* believed before this, first very imperfectly; then with assured confidence of Christ's word; but now with a faith crowned by "sight." And the wave rolled from the head to the members of his household. "To-day is salvation come to this *house*" (Luke 19:9); and no mean house this! **second miracle Jesus did**–i.e., in Cana; done "after He came out of Judea," as the former before.

CHAPTER 5

VSS. 1-47. THE IMPOTENT MAN HEALED–DISCOURSE OCCASIONED BY THE PERSECUTION ARISING THEREUPON. **1. a feast of the Jews**–*What feast?* No question has more divided the Harmonists of the Gospels, and the duration of our Lord's ministry may be said to hinge on it. For if, as the majority have thought (until of late years) it was a *Passover,* His ministry lasted three and a half years; if not, probably a year less. Those who are dissatisfied with the Passover-view all differ among themselves what other feast it was, and some of the most acute think there are no grounds for deciding. In our judgment the evidence is in favor of its being a *Passover,* but the reasons cannot be stated here. **2, 3. sheep [market]**–The supplement should be (as in *Margin*) 'sheep [gate]', mentioned in Nehemiah 3:1, 32. **Bethesda**–i.e., 'house (place) of mercy,' from the cures wrought there. **five porches**–for shelter to the patients. **3. impotent**–infirm. **4. an angel ...**–This miracle differed in two points from all other miracles recorded in Scripture: (1) It was not one, but a succession of miracles periodically wrought: (2) As it was only wrought "when the waters were troubled," so only upon one patient at a time, and that the patient "who first stepped in after the troubling of the waters." But this only the more undeniably fixed its miraculous character. We have heard of many waters having a medicinal virtue; but what water was ever known to cure *instantaneously* a single disease? And who ever heard of any water curing all, even the most diverse diseases–"blind, halt, withered"–alike? Above all, who ever heard of such a thing being done "only at a certain season," and most singularly of all, doing it only to the first person who stepped in after the moving of the waters? Any of these peculiarities–much more all taken together–must have proclaimed the supernatural character of the cures wrought. (If the text here be genuine, there can be no doubt of the miracle, as there were multitudes living when this Gospel was published who, from their own knowledge of Jerusalem, could have exposed the falsehood of the Evangelist, if no such cure had been known there. The want of vs. 4 and part of vs. 3 in some good MSS., and the use of some unusual words in the passage, are more easily accounted for than the evidence in their favor if they were not originally in the text. Indeed vs. 7 is unintelligible without vs. 4. The *internal* evidence brought against it is merely the *unlikelihood* of such a miracle–a principle which will carry us a great deal farther if we allow it to weigh against positive evidence). **5-9. thirty-eight years** —but not all that time at the pool. This was probably the most pitiable of all the cases, and *therefore selected.* **6. saw him lie and knew . . .**—As He doubtless visited the spot just to perform this cure, so He knows where to find His patient, and the whole previous history of his case (ch. 2:25). **Wilt thou be made whole?**—Could anyone doubt that a sick man would like to be made whole, or that the patients came thither, and this man had returned again and again, just in hope of a cure? But our Lord asked the question. (1) To fasten attention upon Himself; (2) By making him detail his case to deepen in him the feeling of entire helplessness; (3) By so singular a question to beget in his desponding heart the hope of a cure. (Cf. Mark 10: 51.) **Sir, I have no man . . .**—Instead of *saying* he wished to be cured, he just tells with piteous simplicity how fruitless had been all his efforts to obtain it, and how *helpless* and all but *hopeless* he was. Yet not quite. For here he is at the pool, waiting on. It seemed of no use; nay, only tantalizing—"While I am coming, another steppeth down before me"—the fruit was snatched from his lips. Yet he will not go away. He may get nothing by staying, he may drop into his grave ere he get into the pool; but by going from the appointed, divine way of healing, he can get nothing. Wait therefore he will, wait he does, and when Christ comes to heal him, lo! he is waiting his turn. *What an attitude for a sinner* at Mercy's gate! The man's hopes seemed low enough ere Christ came to him. He might have said, just before "Jesus passed by that way," 'This is no use; I'll never get in; let me die at home.' Then all had been lost. But he *held on,* and his perseverance was rewarded with a glorious cure. Probably some rays of hope darted into his heart as he told his tale before those Eyes whose glance measured his whole case. But the word of command consummates his preparation to receive the cure, and instantaneously works it. **8. Rise, take up thy bed . . .**—"Immediately" he did so. "He *spake* and it was *done.*" The slinging of his portable couch over his shoulders was designed to show the perfection of the cure. **9. the same day was the sabbath**—Beyond all doubt this was intentional, as in so many other healings, in order that when opposition arose on this account men might be compelled to listen to His claims and His teaching. **10-16. The Jews**—i.e., *those in authority.* (See on ch. 1:19.) **it is not lawful to carry thy bed** —a glorious testimony to the cure, as *instantaneous* and *complete,* from the lips of the most prejudiced! (And what a contrast does it, as all our Lord's miracles, present to the bungling miracles of the Church of Rome!) In *ordinary* circumstances, the rulers had the law on their side (Neh. 13:15; Jer. 17:21). But when the man referred them to "Him that had made him whole" as his authority, the argument was resistless. Yet they ingeniously parried the thrust, asking him, not who had "made him whole"—that would have condemned themselves and defeated their purpose—but who had bidden him "take up his bed and walk," in other words, who had dared to order a breach of the sabbath? Tis time we were looking after Him—thus hoping to shake the man's faith in his Healer. **13. he that was healed wist not . . .**—That some one, with unparelleled generosity, tenderness and power, had done it, the man knew well enough: but as he had never heard of Him before, so he disappeared too quickly for any inquiries. **conveyed himself away**

—slipped out of the crowd that had gathered, to avoid both hasty popularity and precipitate hatred (Matt. 12:14-19). **14. findeth him in the temple**— saying, perhaps, "I will go into Thy house with burnt offerings, I will pay my vows which my lips have uttered and my mouth hath spoken when I was in trouble" (Ps. 66:13, 14). Jesus, there Himself for His own ends, "findeth him there"—*not all accidentally,* be assured. **sin no more . . .**—a glimpse this of the reckless life he had probably led *before* his thirty-eight years' infirmity had come upon him, and which not improbably had brought on, in the just judgment of God, his chronic complaint. Fearful illustration this of "the severity of God," but glorious manifestation of our Lord's insight into "what was in man." **15. The man departed and told . . .**—little thinking how unwelcome his grateful and eager testimony would be. "The darkness received not the light which was pouring its rays upon it" (John 1:5, 11), [OLSHAUSEN]. **16. because he had done these things on the sabbath day** —What to these hypocritical religionists was the doing of the most glorious and beneficent miracles, compared with the atrocity of doing them on the sabbath day! Having given them this handle, on purpose to raise the first public controversy with them, and thus open a fitting opportunity of laying His claims before them, He rises at once to the whole height of them, in a statement which for grandeur and terseness exceeds almost anything that ever afterwards fell from Him, at least to His enemies. **17, 18. My Father worketh hitherto and I work**—The "*I*" is emphatic; 'The creative and conservative activity of My Father has known no sabbath-cessation from the beginning until now, *and that is the law of My working.*' **God was his Father**—lit., "His own [or peculiar] Father," (as in Rom. 8:32). The addition is their own, but a very proper one. **making himself equal with God**— rightly gathering this to be His meaning, not from the mere words "My Father," but from His claim of right to act as His Father did in the like high sphere, and by the same law of ceaseless activity in that sphere. And as, instead of instantly disclaiming any such meaning—as He must have done if it was false—He positively sets His seal to it in the following verses, merely explaining how consistent such claim was with the prerogatives of His Father, it is beyond all doubt that we have here an assumption of *peculiar personal Sonship,* or participation in the Father's essential nature. **19, 20. the Son can do nothing of himself**—i.e., *apart from* and *in rivalry of* the Father, as they supposed. The meaning is, 'The Son can have no separate *interest* or *action* from the Father.' **for what things . . .** 'On the contrary, whatever the Father doeth that same doeth the Son,' likewise—'in the like manner.' What claim to absolute equality with the Father could exceed this: not only to do *the same things,* but to do them *as the Father does them*? **20. Father loveth . . . and showeth him all . . .**—As love has no concealments, so it results from the perfect fellowship and mutual endearment of the Father and the Son (see on ch. 1:1, 18), whose interests are one, even as their nature, that the Father communicates to the Son all His counsels, and what has been thus shown to the Son is by Him executed in His mediatorial character. "With the Father, *doing* is *willing;* it is only the Son who *acts in Time*" [ALFORD]. Three things here are clear: (1) The *personal distinctions* in the Godhead. (2) Unity of *action* among the Persons results from unity of *nature*. (3) Their oneness of interest is no unconscious or involuntary thing, but a thing of glorious *consciousness, will,* and *love,* of which the Persons themselves are the proper Objects. **show him greater things . . .**—referring to what He goes on to mention (vss. 21-31), comprised in two great words, LIFE and JUDGMENT, which STIER beautifully calls God's *Regalia.* Yet these, Christ says, the Father and He do in common. **21-23. raiseth the dead and quickeneth them**—one act in two stages. This is His absolute prerogative as God. **so the Son quickeneth**—i.e., raiseth up and quickeneth. **whom he will**—not only *doing the same divine act,* but doing it *as the result of His own will,* even as the Father does it. This statement is of immense importance in relation to the miracles of Christ, distinguishing them from similar miracles of prophets and apostles, who as *human instruments* were employed to perform super-natural actions, while Christ did all as the Father's *commissioned Servant* indeed, but *in the exercise of His own absolute right of action.* **22. For the Father judgeth no man . . .**—rather, "For neither doth the Father judge any man," implying that the same "thing was meant in the former verse of the quickening of the dead"—both acts being done, not by the Father *and* the Son, as though twice done, but by the Father *through* the Son as His voluntary Agent. **all judgment**—judgment in its most comprehensive sense, or as we should say, all *administration.* **23. honour the Son as . . . the Father**—As he who believes that Christ in the foregoing verses has given a true account of His relation to the Father must of necessity hold Him entitled to the same *honor* as the Father, so He here adds that it was the Father's express intention in making over all judgment to the Son, that men *should* thus honor Him. **honoureth not the Father . . .**—does not do it in fact, whatever he may imagine, and will be held as not doing it by the Father Himself, who will accept no homage which is not accorded to His own Son. **24. believeth on him that sent me**—i.e., believeth in Him as having sent Me. I have spoken of the Son's right not only to heal the sick but to raise from the dead, and quicken whom He will: And now I say unto you, *That life-giving operation has already passed upon all who receive My words as the Sent of the Father* on the great errand of mercy. **hath everlasting life**—immediately on his believing (cf. ch. 3:18; I John 5:12, 13). **is passed**—'hath passed over' "from death unto life." What a transition! (Cf. I John 3:14). **25-29. The hour cometh**—in its whole fulness, at Pentecost. **and now is**—in its beginnings. **the dead**—the *spiritually* dead, as is clear from vs. 28. Here He rises from the calmer phrase "hearing *his word*" (vs. 24), to the grander expression, "hearing *the voice of the Son of God,*" to signify that as it finds men in a *dead* condition, so it carries with it a *resurrection-power.* **shall live**—in the sense of vs. 24. **26. given to the Son . . .**—Does this refer to the essential life of the Son before all time (ch. 1:4) [as most of the Fathers, and OLSHAUSEN, STIER, ALFORD, etc., among the moderns], or to the purpose of God that this essential life should reside in the Person of the Incarnate Son, and be manifested thus to the world? [CALVIN, LUCKE, LUTHARDT, etc.] The question is as difficult as the subject is high. But as all that Christ says of His *essential* relation to the Father is intended to explain and exalt His *mediatorial* functions, so the one seems in our Lord's own mind and language mainly the starting-point of the other. **27. because he is the Son of man**—This seems to confirm the last remark, that what Christ had properly in view was the indwelling of the Son's essential life in *humanity* as the great *theater* and *medium* of divine display, in both the great departments of His work—*lifegiving and judgment.* The appointment of *a Judge in our own nature* is one of the most beautiful arrangements of divine wisdom in redemption. **28. Marvel not at this**—this committal of all judgment **to *the*** *Son of man.* **for the hour is coming**—He adds not in this case (as in vs. 25), "and now is," because this was not to be till the close of the whole dispensation of mercy. **29. resurrection of life**—i.e., to life everlasting (Matt. 25:46). **of damnation**—It would have been harsh to say 'the resurrection of death,' though that is meant, for sinners rise *from death to death* [BENGEL]. The resurrection of both classes is an exercise of *sovereign authority;* but in the one case it is an act of *grace,* in the other of *justice.* (Cf. Dan. 12:2, from which the language is taken.) How awfully grand are these unfoldings of His dignity and authority from the mouth of Christ Himself! And they are all in the *third person;* in what follows He resumes the *first person.* **30-32. of mine own self do nothing**—i.e., apart from the Father, or in any interest than My own. (See on vs. 19.) **as I hear**—i.e., "My judgments are all *anticipated* in the bosom of My Father, to which I have immediate access, and by Me only *responded* to and *reflected.* They cannot therefore err, as I live for one end only, to carry into effect the will of Him that sent Me." **31. If I . . . witness of myself**—standing alone, and setting up any separate interest. **32. There is another**—i.e., *the Father,* as is plain from the connection. How brightly the distinction of the Persons shines out here! **and I know that the witness . . .**—"This is the Son's testimony to the Father's truth (see ch. 7:28; 8:26, 55). It testifies to the full consciousness on the part of the Son, even in the days of His humiliation, of the righteousness of the Father" [ALFORD]. And thus He cheered His spirit under the cloud of human opposition which was already gathering over His head. **33-35. Ye sent unto John**—(See ch. 1:19, etc.). **receive not testimony . . . from man**—i.e., depend not on human testimony. **but . . . that ye might be saved**—'I refer to him merely to aid your salvation.' **35. He was a burning and a shining light**—lit., "*the* burning and shining lamp" (or torch):—i.e., 'the great light of his day.' Christ is never called by the humble word here applied to John—a *light-bearer*—studiously used to distinguish him from his Master, but ever *the Light* in the most absolute sense. (See on ch. 1:6.) **willing for a season**—i.e., till they saw that it pointed whither they were not prepared to go. **to rejoice in his light**—There is a play of irony here, referring to the hollow delight with which his testimony tickled them. **36-38. I have greater witness**—rather, The witness which I have is greater. **the works . . . bear witness of me**—not simply as *miracles* nor even as a miracle of *mercy,* but these miracles, *as He did them,* with a *will* and a *power,* a *majesty* and a *grace* manifestly *His own.* **37. the Father himself . . . hath borne witness of me**—not referring, probably, to the voice of His baptism, but (as seems from what follows) to the testimony of the Old Testament Scripture [CALVIN, LUCKE, MEYER, LUTHARDT, etc.]. **neither heard his voice . . .**—never recognized Him in this character. (The words are "designedly mysterious, like many others which our Lord uttered" [STIER]. **38. not his word abiding in you**—passing now from the *Witness* to the *testimony* borne by Him in "the lively oracles": both were alike strangers to their breasts, as was evidenced by their rejecting Him to whom all that witness was borne. **39-42. Search the scriptures ...** —'In the Scriptures ye find your charter of eternal life; go search them then, and you will find that I am the Great Burden of their testimony; yet ye will not come to Me for that life eternal which you profess to find there, and of which they tell you I am the appointed Dispenser.' (Cf. Acts 17:11, 12.) How touching and gracious are these last words! Observe here (I) The honor which Christ gives to the Scriptures, as a record which all *have a right* and *are bound* to search—the reverse of which the Church of Rome teaches; (2) The opposite extreme is, resting in the mere *Book* without *the living Christ,* to direct the soul to whom is its main use and chiefest glory. **41. I receive not honour from men**—contrasting His own end with theirs, which was to obtain *human applause.* **42. not the love of God in you**—which would inspire you with a single desire to know His mind and will, and yield yourselves to it, in spite of prejudice and regardless of consequences. **42-47. if another shall come ...** —How strikingly has this been verified in the history of the Jews! "From the time of the true Christ to our time, sixty-four false Christs have been reckoned by whom they have been deceived" [BENGEL]. **How can ye believe ...**—(See on vss. 40, 41). The *"will not"* of vs. 40, and *"cannot"* here are just different features of the same awful state of the human heart. **45. Do not think I will accuse you**—'My errand hither is not to collect evidence to condemn you at God's bar.' **one that judgeth you, Moses ...**—'Alas! that will be too well done by another, and him the object of all your religious boastings—Moses,' here put for *"the Law,"* the basis of the Old Testament Scriptures. **46. he wrote of me**—"an important testimony to the subject of the whole Pentateuch—'of Me'" [ALFORD]. **47. If ye believe not ...**—(See on Luke 16:31). **his writings ... my words**—a remarkable contrast, not *absolutely* exalting Old Testament Scripture above His own words, but pointing to the office of those venerable documents to *prepare* Christ's way, to the necessity universally felt for *documentary* testimony in revealed religion, and perhaps (as STIER adds) to the relation which the comparative *"letter"* of the Old Testament holds to the more flowing "words" of "spirit and life" which characterize the New Testament.

CHAPTER 6

Vss. 1-13. FIVE THOUSAND MIRACULOUSLY FED. (See on Mark 6:31-44.) **3. a mountain**—somewhere in that hilly range which skirts the east side of the lake. **4. passover ... was nigh**—but for the reason mentioned (ch. 7:1), Jesus kept away from it, remaining in Galilee.

14-21. JESUS WALKS ON THE SEA. (See also on Mark 6:45-56.) **14, 15. that prophet**—(See on ch. 1:21). **15. departed ... to a mountain himself alone**—(1) to *rest,* which He came to this "desert place" on purpose to do before the miracle of the loaves, but could not for the multitude that followed Him (see on Mark 6:31); and (2) *"to pray"* (Matt. 14:23; Mark 6:46). But from His mountain-top He kept watching the ship (see on vs. 18), and doubtless prayed both for them, and with a view to the new manifestation which He was to give them of His glory. **16, 17. when even was come**—(See on Mark 6:35). **entered into a ship**—*"constrained"* to

do so by their Master (Matt. 14:22; Mark 6:45), in order to put an end to the misdirected excitement in His favor (vs. 15), into which the disciples themselves may have been somewhat drawn. The word "constrained" implies reluctance on their part, perhaps from unwillingness to part with their Master and embark at night, leaving Him alone on the mountain. **went**—rather, "were proceeding." **toward Capernaum**—Mark says (6:45), "unto Bethsaida," meaning "Bethsaida of Galilee" (ch. 12:21), on the west side of the lake. The place they left was of the same name (see on Mark 6:31). **Jesus was not come to them**—They probably lingered in hopes of His still joining them, and so let the darkness come on. **18, 19. sea arose ...**—and they were "now in the midst of it" (Matt. 14:24). Mark adds the graphic and touching particular, "He saw them toiling in rowing" (6:48), putting forth all their strength to buffet the waves and bear on against a head wind, but to little effect. He *saw* this from His mountain-top, and through the darkness of the night, for His heart was all with them; yet would He not go to their relief till His own time came. **19. they see Jesus**—"about the fourth watch of the night" (Matt. 14:25; Mark 6:48), or between three and six in the morning. **walking on the sea**—What Job (9:8) celebrates as the distinguishing prerogative of GOD, "WHO ALONE spreadeth out the heavens, and TREADETH UPON THE WAVES OF THE SEA"—what AGUR challenges as GOD's unapproachable prerogative, to "GATHER THE WIND IN HIS FISTS, and BIND THE WATERS IN A GARMENT" (Prov. 30:4)—lo! this is here done *in flesh,* by "THE SON OF MAN." **drawing nigh to the ship**—yet as though He *"would have passed by them,"* Mark 6:48 (cf. Luke 24:28; Gen. 18:3:5; 32:24-26). *they were afraid*—"cried out for fear" (Matt. 14:26), "supposing it had been a spirit" (Mark 6:49). He would appear to them at first like a dark moving speck upon the waters; then as a human figure, but—in the dark tempestuous sky, and not dreaming that it could be their Lord—they take it for a spirit. (How often thus we miscall our chiefest mercies—not only thinking them distant when they are near, but thinking the best the worst!) **20. It is I; be not afraid**—Matthew and Mark give before these exhilarating words, that to them well-known one, "Be of good cheer!" **21. willingly received him into the ship**—their first fears being now converted into wonder and delight. **and immediately the ship was at the land**—This additional miracle, for as such it is manifestly related, is recorded here alone. Yet all that is meant seems to be that as the storm was suddenly calmed, so the little bark—propelled by the secret power of the Lord of Nature now sailing in it—glided through the now unruffled waters, and while they were wrapt in wonder at what had happened, not heeding their rapid motion, *was found* at port, to their still further surprise.

22-71. JESUS, FOLLOWED BY THE MULTITUDES TO CAPERNAUM, DISCOURSES TO THEM IN THE SYNAGOGUE OF THE BREAD OF LIFE—EFFECT OF THIS ON TWO CLASSES OF THE DISCIPLES. **22-24.** These verses are a little involved, from the Evangelist's desire to mention every circumstance, however minute, that might call up the scene as vividly to the reader as it stood before his own view. **The day following**—the miracle of the loaves, and the stormy night; the day on which they landed at Capernaum. **the people which stood on the other side of the sea**—not the whole multitude that had been fed, but only such of them as remained over night about the shore, i.e., on the *east* side of the lake; for we are supposed to have come, with Jesus and His disciples in the ship, to the *west* side, to Capernaum. **saw that there was none other boat there** ...—The meaning is, the people had observed that there had been only one boat on the east side where they were; namely, the one in which the disciples had crossed at night to the other, the west side, and they had also observed that Jesus had not gone on board that boat, but His disciples had put off without Him: "Howbeit," adds the Evangelist, in a lively parenthesis, "there came other boats from Tiberias" (which lay near the southwest coast of the lake), whose passengers were part of the multitude that had followed Jesus to the east side, and been miraculously fed; these boats were fastened somewhere (says the Evangelist) "nigh unto the place where they did eat bread, after that the Lord had given thanks"—thus he refers to the glorious "miracle of the loaves"—and now they were put in requisition to convey the people back again to the west side. For when "the people saw that Jesus was not there, neither His disciples, they also took shipping [in these boats] and came to Capernaum, seeking for Jesus." **25. when they had found him on the other side**—at Capernaum—**they said** ...—astonished at His *being* there, and wondering *how* He could have accomplished it, whether by land or water, and *when* He came; for being quite unaware of His having walked upon the sea and landed with the disciples in the ship, they could not see how, unless He had travelled all night round the head of the lake alone, He could have reached Capernaum, and even then, how He could have arrived before themselves. **26. Ye seek me** ...—Jesus does not put them through their difficulty, says nothing of His treading on the waves of the sea, nor even notices their question, but takes advantage of the favorable moment for pointing out to them how forward, flippant, and superficial were their views, and how low their desires. "Ye seek Me not because ye saw the miracles"—lit., 'the *signs*,' i.e., supernatural tokens of a higher presence, and a divine commission, "but because ye did eat of the loaves and were filled." From this He proceeds at once to that *other Bread,* just as, with the woman of Samaria, to that *other Water* (ch. 4). We should have supposed all that follows to have been delivered by the wayside, or wherever they happened first to meet. But from vs. 59 we gather that they had probably met about the door of the synagogue—"for that was the day in which they assembled in their synagogues" [LIGHTFOOT]—and that on being asked, at the close of the service, if He had any word of exhortation to the people, He had taken the two breads, the *perishing* and the *living* bread, for the subject of His profound and extraordinary discourse. **27. which the Son of man**—taking that title of Himself which denoted His incarnate life. **shall give unto you**—in the sense of vs. 51. **him hath God the Father sealed** —marked out and authenticated for that transcendent office, to impart to the world the bread of an everlasting life, and this in the character of "the Son of *man.*" **28-31. What shall we do ... the works of God**—such works as God will approve. Different answers may be given to such a question, according to the *spirit* which prompts the inquiry. (See Hos. 6:6-8; Luke 3:12-14.) Here our Lord, knowing whom He had to deal with, shapes His reply accordingly. **29. This is the work of God** ... —That lies at the threshold of all acceptable obedience, being not only the prerequisite to it, but

the proper spring of it—in that sense, the work of works, emphatically *"the* work of God." **30. What sign showest thou** ...—But how could they ask "a sign," when many of them scarce a day before had witnessed such a "sign" as had never till then been vouchsafed to men; when after witnessing it, they could hardly be restrained from making Him a king; when they followed Him from the one side of the lake to the other; and when, in the opening words of this very discourse, He had chided them for seeking Him, "not because they *saw the signs,"* but for the loaves? The truth seems to be that they were confounded by the *novel claims* which our Lord had just advanced. In proposing to make Him a king, it was for far other purposes than dispensing to the world the bread of an everlasting life; and when He seemed to raise His claims even higher still, by representing it as the grand "work of God," that they should believe *on Himself* as His Sent One, they saw very clearly that He was making a demand upon them beyond anything they were prepared to accord to Him, and beyond all that man had ever before made. Hence their question, "What dost Thou *work?"* **31. Our fathers did eat manna** ...—insinuating the inferiority of Christ's miracle of the loaves to those of Moses: 'When Moses claimed the confidence of the fathers, "he gave them bread from heaven to eat"—not for a few thousands, but for millions, and not once only, but daily throughout their wilderness journey.' **32, 33. Moses gave you not** ...—'It was not Moses that gave you the manna, and even it was but from the lower heavens; "but *My Father* giveth you *the true bread,"* and that *"from heaven."* ' **33. the bread of God is he** ...—This verse is perhaps best left in its own transparent grandeur—holding up the Bread Itself as *divine, spiritual,* and *eternal;* its ordained Fountain and essential Substance, *"Him who came down from heaven to give it"* (that Eternal Life which was with the Father and was manifested unto us, I John 1:2); and its designed objects, *"the* world." **34. Lord, evermore give us this bread**—speaking now with a certain reverence (as at vs. 25), the perpetuity of the manna floating perhaps in their minds, and much like the Samaritan woman, when her eyes were but half opened, "Sir, give Me this water ..." (ch. 4:15). **35. I am the bread of life**—Henceforth the discourse is all *in the first person,* "I," "Me," which occur in one form or other, as STIER reckons, thirty-five times. **he that cometh to me**—to obtain what the soul craves, and as the only all-sufficient and ordained source of supply. **hunger ... thirst** —shall have conscious and abiding satisfaction. **36. But ... ye have seen me, and believe not**—seen Him not in His mere bodily presence, but in all the majesty of His life, His teaching, His works. **37-40. All that** ...—This comprehensive and very grand passage is expressed with a peculiar artistic precision. The opening general statement (vs. 37) consists of two members: (1) "ALL THAT THE FATHER GIVETH ME SHALL COME TO ME"—i.e., 'Though ye, as I told you, have no faith in Me, My errand into the world shall in no wise be defeated; for all that the Father giveth Me shall infallibly come to Me.' Observe, what is *given* Him by the Father is expressed in the *singular* number and *neuter* gender—lit., 'everything'; while those who *come to* Him are put in the *masculine* gender and *singular* number—'every one.' The *whole mass,* so to speak, is gifted by the Father to the Son as a *unity,* which the Son evolves, one by one, in the execution of His trust. So ch. 17:2, "that He should give eternal life to *all that which* Thou hast given Him" [BENGEL]. This "*shall*" expresses the glorious *certainty* of it, the Father being pledged to see to it that the gift be no empty mockery. (2) "AND HIM THAT COMETH TO ME I WILL IN NO WISE CAST OUT." As the former was the *divine*, this is just the *human* side of the same thing. True, the "coming" ones of the second clause are just the "given" ones of the first. But had our Lord merely said, "*When those* that have been given Me of My Father shall come to Me, I will receive them"—besides being very flat, the impression conveyed would have been quite different, sounding as if there were *no other laws in operation*, in the movement of sinners to Christ, but such as are wholly *divine* and *inscrutable* to us; whereas, though He does speak of it as a sublime certainty which men's *refusals* cannot frustrate, He speaks of that certainty as taking effect only by men's *voluntary advances* to Him and acceptance of Him —"Him that cometh to Me," "whosoever will," throwing the door wide open. Only it is not the simply *willing*, but the actually *coming*, whom He will not cast out; for the word here employed usually denotes *arrival*, as distinguished from the ordinary word, which rather expresses the *act of coming* (see ch. 8:42, *Greek*), [WEBSTER and WILKINSON]. "In no wise" is an emphatic negative, to meet the fears of the timid (as in Rev. 21:27, to meet the presumption of the hardened). These, then, being the two members of the general opening statement, what follows is meant to take in both, "For I came down from heaven not to do Mine own will"—to play an independent part—"but [in respect to both the foregoing things, the *divine* and the *human* side of salvation] the will of Him that sent Me." What this twofold will of Him that sent Me is, we are next sublimely told (vss. 39, 40): "And this"—in the *first* place—"is the will of Him that sent Me, that of all [everything] which He hath given Me (taking up the identical words of vs. 37), I should lose nothing, but should raise it up at the last day." The meaning is not, of course, that He is charged to keep the objects entrusted to Him *as He received them*, so as they should merely suffer nothing in His hands. For as they were just "perishing" *sinners* of Adam's family, to let "nothing" of such "be lost," but "raise them up at the last day," must involve, *first*, giving His flesh for them" (vs. 51), that they "might not perish, but have everlasting life"; and *then*, after "keeping them from falling," raising their sleeping dust in incorruption and glory, and presenting them, body and soul, perfect and entire, wanting nothing, to Him who gave them to Him, saying, "Behold I and the children which God hath given Me." So much for the *first* will of Him that sent Him, the *divine* side of man's salvation, whose every stage and movement is inscrutable to us, but infallibly certain. "And this"—in the *second* place—"is the will of Him that sent Me, that every one which seeth the Son and believeth [seeing the Son believeth] on Him, may have everlasting life, and I will raise him up at the last day." This is the *human* side of the same thing as in the foregoing verse, and answering to "*Him that cometh unto Me I will in no wise cast out*"; i.e., I have it expressly in charge that everyone that *so* "beholdeth [so vieweth] the Son as to believe on Him shall have everlasting life; and, that *none* of Him be lost, "I will raise him up at the last day." (See on vs. 54.) **41-46. Jews murmured**—muttered, not in our Lord's hearing, but He knew it (vs. 43;

ch. 2:25). **he said, I am the bread . . .**—Missing the sense and glory of this, and having no relish for such sublimities, they harp upon the "Bread from heaven." 'What *can* this mean? Do we not know all about Him—where, when, and of whom He was born? And yet He says He came down from heaven!' **43. Murmur not . . . 44. No man**—i.e., Be not either startled or stumbled at these sayings; for it needs divine teaching to understand them, divine drawing to submit to them. **can come to me**—in the sense of vs. 35. **except the Father which hath sent me**—i.e., the Father *as the Sender of Me* and *to carry out the design of My mission*. **draw him**—by an *internal* and *efficacious* operation; though by all the means of rational conviction, and in a way altogether consonant to their moral nature (Song of Sol. 1:4; Jer. 31:3; Hos. 11:3, 4). **raise him up . . .**—See on vs. 54. **45. written in the prophets**—in Isaiah 54:13; Jeremiah 31:33, 34; other similar passages may also have been in view. Our Lord thus falls back upon Scripture authority for this seemingly hard saying. **all taught of God** —not by *external* revelation merely, but by *internal illumination*, corresponding to the "drawing" of vs. 44. **Every man therefore . . .**—i.e., who hath been thus efficaciously taught of Him. **cometh unto me**—*with absolute certainty*, yet in the sense above given of "drawing'; i.e., 'As none can come to Me but as divinely drawn, so none thus drawn shall fail to come.' **Not that any man hath seen . . .**—Lest they should confound that "hearing and learning of the Father," to which believers are admitted by divine *teaching*, with His own immediate access to Him, He here throws in a parenthetical explanation; stating, as explicitly as words could do it, how totally different the two cases were, and that only He who is "from God" **hath this naked**, immediate access to the Father. (See ch. 1:18). **47-51. He that believeth . . .**—(See on ch. 3:36; 5: 24). **48. I am the bread of life . . .**—'As he that believeth in Me hath everlasting life, so I am Myself the everlasting *Sustenance* of that life.' (Repeated from vs. 35.) **49. Your fathers**—of whom ye spake (vs. 31); not "*ours*," by which He would hint that *He* had a higher descent, of which they dreamt not [BENGEL]. **did eat manna . . . and are dead**—recurring to their own point about the manna, as one of the noblest of the *ordained* preparatory illustrations of His own office: 'Your fathers, ye say, ate manna in the wilderness; and ye say well, for so they did, *but they are dead*—even they whose carcasses fell in the wilderness did eat of that bread; the Bread whereof I speak cometh down from heaven, which the manna never did, that men, eating of it, may *live for ever*.' **51. I am . . .**— Understand, it is of MYSELF I now speak as the Bread from heaven; of ME if a man eat he shall live for ever; and "THE BREAD WHICH I WILL GIVE IS MY FLESH, WHICH I WILL GIVE FOR THE LIFE OF THE WORLD." Here, for the first time in this high discourse, our Lord explicitly introduces His sacrificial *death*—for only rationalists can doubt this— not only as that which constitutes Him the Bread of life to men, but as THAT very element IN HIM WHICH POSSESSES THE LIFE-GIVING VIRTUE.—"From this time we hear no more (in this discourse) of 'Bread'; this figure is dropped, and the reality takes its place" [STIER]. The words "I will *give*" may be compared with the words of institution at the Supper, "This is My body which is *given* for you" (Luke 22:19), or in Paul's report of it, "*broken* for you" (I Cor. 11:24). **52. Jews strove among themselves**—arguing the point together. **How can . . .**—

i.e., Give us His flesh to eat? Absurd. **53-58. Except ye eat the flesh ... and drink the blood ... no life ...**—The harshest word He had yet uttered in their ears. They asked how it was *possible* to eat His flesh. He answers, with great solemnity, "It is *indispensable*." Yet even here a thoughtful hearer might find something to temper the harshness. He says they must not only "eat His *flesh*" but "drink His *blood*," which could not but suggest the idea of His *death*—implied in the separation of one's flesh from his blood. And as He had already hinted that it was to be something very different from a *natural* death, saying, "My flesh I will give for the life of the world" (vs. 51), it must have been pretty plain to candid hearers that He meant something above the gross idea which the bare terms expressed. And farther, when He added that they "had no *life* in them unless they thus ate and drank," it was impossible they should think He meant that the *temporal* life they were then living was dependent on their eating and drinking, in this gross sense, His flesh and blood. Yet the whole statement was certainly confounding, and beyond doubt was meant to be so. Our Lord had told them that in spite of all they had "seen" in Him, they "did not believe" (vs. 36). For *their* conviction therefore he does not here lay Himself out; but having the ear not only of them but of the more *candid and thoughtful* in the crowded synagogue, and the miracle of the loaves having led up to the most exalted of all views of His Person and Office, He takes advantage of their very difficulties and objections to announce, for all time, those most profound truths which are here expressed, regardless of the disgust of the unteachable, and the prejudices even of the most sincere, which His language would seem only designed to deepen. The *truth* really conveyed here is no other than that expressed in vs. 51, though in more emphatic terms —that He Himself, in the virtue of His sacrificial death, is the spiritual and eternal life of men; and that unless men voluntarily appropriate to themselves this death, in its sacrificial virtue, so as to become the very life and nourishment of their inner man, they have no spiritual and eternal life at all. Not as if His death were the *only* thing of value, but it is what gives all else in Christ's Incarnate Person, Life, and Office, their whole value *to us sinners*. **54. Whoso eateth ... hath ...**—The former verse said that *unless* they partook of Him they had no life; this adds, that *whoever* does so "hath eternal life." **And I will raise him up at the last day**—For the *fourth* time this is repeated (see vss. 39, 40, 44)—showing most clearly that the "eternal life" which such a man "*hath*" cannot be the same with the *future* resurrection-life from which it is carefully distinguished each time, but a life communicated *here below* immediately on believing (ch. 3:36; 5:24, 25); and giving to *the resurrection of the body* as that which consummates the redemption *of the entire man,* a prominence which in the current theology, it is to be feared, it has seldom had. (See Rom. 8:23; I Cor. 15, throughout.) **56. He that eateth ... dwelleth in me and I in him**—As our food becomes incorporated with ourselves, so Christ and those who eat His flesh and drink His blood become spiritually *one life,* though *personally* distinct. **57. As the living Father hath sent me**—to communicate His own life. **and I live by the Father**—lit., "because of the Father"; My life and His being one, and Mine that of a *Son,* whose it is to be "*of* the Father." (See ch. 1:18; 5:26.) **he that eateth me, ... shall live by**

me—lit., 'because of Me.' So that though *one spiritual* life with Him, "the Head of every man is Christ, as the head of Christ is God" (I Cor. 11:3; 3:23). **58. This is that bread ...**—a sort of summing up of the whole discourse, on which let this one further remark suffice—that as our Lord, instead of softening down His figurative sublimities, or even putting them in naked phraseology, leaves the great truths of His Person and Office, and our participation of Him and it, enshrined for all time in those glorious forms of speech, so when we attempt to strip the truth of these figures, figures though they be, it goes away from us, like water when the vessel is broken, and our wisdom lies in raising our own spirit, and attuning our own ear, to our Lord's chosen modes of expression. (It should be added that although this discourse has nothing to do with the Sacrament of the Supper, the Sacrament has everything to do with it, as *the visible embodiment* of these figures, and, to the believing partaker, a *real,* yea, and the most lively and affecting participation of His flesh and blood, and nourishment thereby of the spiritual and eternal life, here below.) **59. These things said he in the synagogue** —which seems to imply that what follows took place after the congregation had broken up. **60-65. Many ... of his disciples**—His pretty constant followers, though an outer circle of them. **hard saying**—not merely harsh, but insufferable, as the word often means in the Old Testament. **who can hear**—submit to listen to it. **61. Doth this offend... What and if ...**—i.e., 'If ye are stumbled at what I *have* said, how will ye bear what I *now* say?' Not that His ascension itself would stumble them more than His death, but that after recoiling from the *mention* of the one, they would not be in a state of mind to take in the other. **the flesh profiteth nothing**—Much of His discourse was *about* "flesh"; but flesh as such, mere flesh, could profit nothing, much less impart that *life* which the Holy Spirit alone communicates to the soul. **the words that I speak ... are spirit and ... life**—The whole burden of the discourse is *"spirit,"* not mere flesh, and *"life"* in its highest, not its lowest sense, and the words I have employed are to be interpreted solely in that sense. **64. But there are some ...**—i.e., "But it matters little to some of you in what sense I speak, for ye believe not." This was said, adds the Evangelist, not merely of the outer but of the inner circle of His disciples; for He knew the traitor, though it was not yet time to expose him. **65. Therefore said I ...**—i.e., "That was why I spoke to you of the necessity of divine teaching which some of you are strangers to." **except it were given him**—plainly showing that by the Father's "drawing" (vs. 44) was meant an *internal* and *efficacious* operation, for in recalling the statement here He says, it must be *"given* to a man to come" to Christ. **66-71. From that time ...**—or, in consequence of this. Those last words of our Lord seemed to have given them the finishing stroke— they could not stand it any longer. **walked no more**—Many a journey, it may be, they had taken with Him, but now they gave Him up finally! **67. the twelve**—the first time they are thus mentioned in this Gospel. **Will ye also go away?**—Affecting appeal! Evidently Christ *felt* the desertion of Him even by those miserable men who could not abide His statements; and seeing a disturbance even of the *wheat* by the violence of the wind which blew away the *chaff* (not yet visibly showing itself, but open to His eyes of fire), He would *nip it in the bud* by this home question. **68. Then Simon Peter**

—whose forwardness in this case was noble, and to the wounded spirit of His Lord doubtless very grateful. **Lord, to whom...**—i.e., 'We cannot deny that *we* have been staggered as well as they, and seeing so many go away who, as we thought, might have been retained by teaching a little less hard to take in, our own endurance has been severely tried, nor have we been able to stop short of the question, Shall *we* follow the rest, and give it up? But when it came to this, our light returned, and our hearts were reassured. For as soon as we thought of going away, there arose upon us that awful question, "To WHOM shall we go?" To the lifeless formalism and wretched traditions of the elders? to the gods many and lords many of the heathen around us? or to blank unbelief? Nay, Lord, we are shut up. *They* have none of that "ETERNAL LIFE" to offer us whereof Thou hast been discoursing, in words rich and ravishing as well as in words staggering to human wisdom. That life we cannot want; that life we have learnt to crave as a necessity of the deeper nature which Thou hast awakened: "*the words* of that eternal life" (the authority to *reveal* it and the power to confer it). Thou hast: Therefore will we stay with Thee—"we *must*." **69. And we believe...**—(See on Matt. 16:16). Peter seems to have added this not merely—probably not so much—as an assurance *to his Lord* of his heart's belief in Him, as for the purpose of fortifying *himself* and his faithful brethren against that *recoil* from his Lord's harsh statements which he was probably struggling against with difficulty at that moment. N.B.— There are seasons when one's faith is tried to the utmost, particularly by speculative difficulties; the spiritual eye then swims, and all truth seems ready to depart from us. At such seasons, a clear perception that to abandon the faith of Christ is *to face black desolation, ruin and death;* and on recoiling from this, to be able to fall back, not merely on *first principles and immovable foundations,* but on *personal experience of a Living Lord in whom all truth is wrapt up and made flesh for our very benefit*—this is a relief unspeakable. Under that blessed Wing taking shelter, until we are again fit to grapple with the questions that have staggered us, we at length either find our way through them, or attain to a calm satisfaction in the discovery that they lie beyond the limits of present apprehension. **70. Have not I chosen... and one of you is a devil:**—'Well said, Simon-Barjonas, but that "we" embraces not so wide a circle as in the simplicity of thine heart thou thinkest; for though I have chosen you but twelve, one even of these is a "devil" ' (the temple, the tool of that wicked one).

CHAPTER 7

Vss. 1-53. CHRIST AT THE FEAST OF TABERNACLES. **1, 2. After these things**—i.e., *all that is recorded after ch.* 5:18. **walked in Galilee**—continuing His labors there, instead of going to Judea, as might have been expected. **sought to kill him ...**—referring back to ch. 5:18. *Hence it appears that our Lord did not attend the Passover mentioned in* ch. 6:4—being the *third* since His ministry began, if the feast mentioned in ch. 5:1 was a Passover. **2. feast of tabernacles... at hand**—This was the last of the three annual festivals, celebrated on the 15th of the 7th month (September). (See Lev. 23:33, etc.; Deut. 16:13, etc.; Neh. 8:14-18). **3-5. His brethren said**—(See on Matt. 13:54-56). **Depart... into Judea...**—In vs. 5 this speech is as-

cribed to their *unbelief*. But as they were in the "upper room" among the one hundred and twenty disciples who waited for the descent of the Spirit after the Lord's ascension (Acts 1:14), they seem to have had their prejudices removed, perhaps after His resurrection. Indeed here their language is more that of strong prejudice and suspicion (*such as near relatives, even the best, too frequently show in such cases*), than from unbelief. There was also, probably, a tincture of *vanity* in it. 'Thou hast many disciples in Judea; here in Galilee they are fast dropping off; it is not like one who advances the claims Thou dost to linger so long here, away from the city of our solemnities, where surely "the kingdom of our father David" is to be set up: "seeking," as Thou dost, "to be known openly," those miracles of Thine ought not to be confined to this distant corner, but submitted at headquarters to the inspection of "the world." ' (See Ps. 69:8, "I am become a stranger to *my brethren*, an alien unto *my mother's children!*") **6-10. My time is not yet come**—i.e., for showing Myself to the world. **your time is always ready**—i.e., 'It matters little when we go up, for ye have no great plans in life, and nothing hangs upon your movements. With Me it is otherwise; on every movement of Mine there hangs what ye know not. The world has no quarrel with you, for ye bear no testimony against it, and so draw down upon yourselves none of its wrath; but I am here to lift up My voice against its hypocrisy, and denounce its abominations; therefore it cannot endure Me, and one false step might precipitate its fury on its Victim's head before the time. Away, therefore, to the feast as soon as it suits you; I follow at the fitting moment, but "My time is not yet full come." ' **10. then went he... not openly**—not "in the (caravan) company" [MEYER]. See on Luke 2:44.) **as it were in secret**—rather, in a manner secretly; perhaps by some other route, and in a way not to attract notice. **11-13. Jews** —the rulers—**sought him**—for no good end. Where is He?—He had not been at Jerusalem for probably *a year and a half.* **12. much murmuring**—buzzing. **among the people**—the multitudes; the natural expression of a Jewish writer, indicating without design the crowded state of Jerusalem at this festival [WEBSTER and WILKINSON]. **a good man ...Nay...deceiveth...**—the two opposite views of His claims, that they were *honest,* and that they were an *imposture.* **none spake openly of him**— i.e., in His favor, "for fear of the [*ruling*] Jews." **14, 15. about the midst of the feast**—the fourth or fifth day of the eight, during which it lasted. **went up into the temple and taught**—The word denotes *formal* and *continuous teaching,* as *distinguished* from mere casual sayings. This was probably the *first time* that He did so thus openly in Jerusalem. He had kept back till the feast was half through, to let the stir about Him subside, and entering the city unexpectedly, had begun His "teaching" at the temple, and created a certain awe, before the wrath of the rulers had time to break it. **15. How knoweth...letters**—learning (Acts 26:24). **having never learned**—at any rabbinical school, as Paul under Gamaliel. These rulers knew well enough that He had not *studied* under any human teacher —an important admission against ancient and modern attempts to trace our Lord's wisdom to human sources [MEYER]. Probably His teaching on this occasion was *expository,* manifesting that unrivalled faculty and depth which in the Sermon on the Mount had excited the astonishment of all. **16-18. doctrine...not mine...**—i.e., from Myself unauthorized; I am here by commission. **17. If any man will do his will . . .**—'is willing,' or 'wishes to do.' **whether . . . of God or . . . of myself**—from above or from beneath; is divine or an imposture of Mine. A principle of immense importance, showing, on the one hand, that *singleness of desire to please God is the grand inlet to light on all questions vitally affecting one's eternal interests,* and on the other, that *the want of his,* whether perceived or not, *is the chief cause of infidelity amidst the light of revealed religion.* **18. seeketh his own glory . . .**—(See on ch. 5:41-44). **19, 20. Did not Moses . . .**—i.e., In opposing Me ye pretend zeal for Moses, but to the spirit and end of that law which he gave ye are total strangers, and in "going about to kill Me" ye are its greatest enemies. **20. The people answered, Thou hast a devil: who goeth about to kill thee?**—This was said by *the multitude,* who as yet had no bad feeling to Jesus, and were not in the secret of the plot hatching, as our Lord knew, against Him. **21-24. I have done one work . . .**—Taking no notice of the popular appeal, as there were those there who knew well enough what He meant, He recalls His cure of the impotent man, and the murderous rage it had kindled (ch. 5:9, 16, 18). It may seem strange that He should refer to an event a year and a half old, as if but newly done. But their present attempt "to kill Him" brought up the past scene vividly, not only to Him, but without doubt to them, too, if indeed they had ever forgotten it; and by this fearless reference to it, exposing their hypocrisy and dark designs, He gave His position great moral strength. **22. Moses . . . gave you circumcision . . .**—Though servile work was forbidden on the sabbath, the circumcision of males on that day (which certainly was a servile work) was counted no infringement of the Law. How much less ought fault to be found with One who had made a man "every whit whole"—or rather, 'a man's entire body whole'—on the sabbath-day? What a testimony to the reality of the miracle, none daring to meet the bold appeal. **24. Judge not . . .**—i.e., Rise above the *letter* into the *spirit* of the law. **25-27. some of them of Jerusalem**—the citizens, who, knowing the long-formed purpose of the rulers to put Jesus to death, wondered that they were now letting Him teach openly. **26. Do the rulers know . . .**—Have they got some new light in favor of His claims? **27. Howbeit we know this man . . .**—This seems to refer to some current opinion that Messiah's origin would be mysterious (not *altogether* wrong), from which they concluded that Jesus could not be He, since they knew all about His family at Nazareth. **28, 29. cried Jesus**—in a louder tone, and more solemn, witnessing style than usual. **Ye both . . .**—i.e., 'Yes, ye know both Myself and My local parentage, "and (*yet*) I am not come of Myself." **he that sent me is true . . .**—Probably the meaning is, 'He that sent Me is the only *real* Sender of any one.' **30-32. sought to take . . . none laid hands**—their *impotence* being equal to their *malignity.* **31. When Christ cometh, will he . . .**—i.e., If this be not the Christ, what can the Christ do, when He does come, which has not been anticipated and eclipsed by this man? This was evidently the language of friendly persons, overborne by their spiteful superiors, but unable to keep quite silent. **32. heard that the people murmured**—that mutterings to this effect were going about, and thought it high time to stop Him if He was not to be allowed to carry away the people. **33, 34. Yet a little while . . .**—i.e., 'Your desire to

be rid of Me will be for you all too soon fulfilled. Yet a little while and we part company—for ever; for I go whither ye cannot come: nor, even when ye at length seek Him whom ye now despise, shall ye be able to find Him'—referring not to any penitential, but to purely selfish cries in their time of desperation. **35, 36. Whither will he go . . .**—They cannot comprehend Him, but seem awed by the solemn grandeur of His warning. He takes no notice, however, of their questions. **37-39. the last day, that great day of the feast**—the eigthth (Lev. 23:39). It was a sabbath, the last feast day of the year, and distinguished by very remarkable ceremonies. "The generally joyous character of this feast broke out on this day into loud jubilation, particularly at the solemn moment when the priest, as was done on every day of this festival, brought forth, in golden vessels, water from the stream of Siloah, which flowed under the temple-mountain, and solemnly poured it upon the altar. Then the words of Isaiah 12:3 were sung, "With joy shall ye draw water out of the wells of Salvation," and thus the symbolical reference of this act, intimated in vs. 39, was expressed" [OLSHAUSEN]. So ecstatic was the joy with which this ceremony was performed—accompanied with sound of trumpets—that it used to be said, "Whoever had not witnessed it had never seen rejoicing at all" [LIGHTFOOT]. On this high occasion, then, He who had already drawn all eyes upon Him by His supernatural power and unrivalled teaching—"JESUS stood," probably in some elevated position, "and cried," as if making proclamation in the audience of all the people, "IF ANY MAN THIRST, LET HIM COME UNTO ME AND DRINK!" What an offer! The deepest cravings of the human spirit are here, as in the Old Testament, expressed by the figure of "*thirst,*" and the eternal satisfaction of them by "*drinking.*" To the woman of Samaria He had said almost the same thing, and in the same terms (John 4:13, 14). But what to her was simply affirmed to her as a *fact,* is here turned into a world-wide *proclamation;* and whereas there, the *gift* by Him of the living water is the most prominent idea—in contrast with her hesitation to give Him the perishable water of Jacob's well—here, the prominence is given to *Himself* as the Well-spring of all satisfaction. He had in Galilee invited all the WEARY AND HEAVYLADEN of the human family to come under His wing and they should find REST (Matt. 11:28), which is just the same deep want, and the same profound relief of it, under another and equally grateful figure. He had in the synagogue of Capernaum (ch. 6) announced Himself, in every variety of form, as "the BREAD of Life," and as both able and authorized to appease the "HUNGER," and quench the "THIRST," of all that apply to Him. There is, and there can be, nothing beyond that here. But what was on all those occasions uttered in private, or addressed to a provincial audience, is here sounded forth in the streets of the great religious metropolis, and in language of surpassing majesty, simplicity, and grace. *It is just Jehovah's ancient proclamation now sounding forth through human flesh,* "Ho, EVERY ONE THAT THIRSTETH, COME YE TO THE WATERS, AND HE THAT HATH NO MONEY . . . !" (Isa. 55:1). In this light we have but two alternatives; either to say with Caiaphas of Him that uttered such words, "*He is guilty of death,*" or falling down before Him to exclaim with Thomas, "MY LORD AND MY GOD!" **38. as the scripture hath said**—These words belong to what follows, "Out of his belly, as the scripture hath said, shall flow . . ." referring not to any particular passage, but to such as Isaiah 58:11; Joel 3: 18; Zechariah 14:8; Ezekiel 47:1-12; in most of which the idea is that of waters issuing from beneath the temple, to which our Lord compares Himself and those who believe in Him. **out of his belly**—i.e., his inner man, his soul, as in Proverbs 20:27. **rivers of living water**—(See on ch. 4:13, 14). It refers primarily to the *copiousness,* but indirectly also to the *diffusiveness,* of this living water to the good of others. **39. This spake he of the Spirit** —who, by His direct personal agency, opens up this spring of living waters in the human spirit (ch. 3: 6), and by His indwelling in the renewed soul ensures their *unfailing flow.* **they that believe . . .**— As the Holy Ghost is, in the rendemption of man, entirely *at the service of Christ,* as His Agent, so it is *only in believing connection with Christ* that any one "receives" the Spirit. **for the Holy Ghost was not yet [given]**—Beyond all doubt the word "given," or some similar word, is the right supplement. In ch. 16:7 the Holy Ghost is represented not only as the *gift of Christ,* but a gift the communication of which was *dependent upon His own departure to the Father.* Now as Christ was *not yet gone,* so the Holy Ghost *was not yet given.* **Jesus not yet glorified**—The word *"glorified"* is here used advisedly, to teach the reader not only that the *departure* of Christ to the Father was *indispensable* to the giving of the Spirit, but that this illustrious Gift, direct from the hands of the ascended Saviour, was God's intimation to the world that He whom it had cast out, crucified, and slain, was "His Elect, in whom His soul delighted," and that it was through the smiting of that Rock that the waters of the Spirit—for which the Church was waiting, and with pomp at the feast of tabernacles proclaiming its expectation—had gushed forth upon a thirsty world. **40-43. Many . . . when they heard this . . . said, Of a truth . . .**—The only wonder is they did not all say it. "But their minds were blinded." **Others, This is the Christ**—(See on ch. 1:21). **Shall Christ come out of Galilee . . . scripture said . . . of the seed of David and out of . . . Bethlehem . . .**—We accept this spontaneous testimony to our David-descended, Bethlehemborn Saviour. Had those who gave it made the inquiry which the case demanded, they would have found that Jesus "came out of Galilee" and "out of Bethlehem" both, alike in fulfilment of prophecy as in point of fact. (Matt. 2:23; 4:13-16.) **44-49. would have taken him, but . . .**—(See on vs. 30). **45. Then came the officers**—"sent to take him" (vs. 32). **Why . . . not brought him?**—already thirsting for their Victim, and thinking it an easy matter to seize and bring Him. **46. Never man spake like this man**—Noble testimony of unsophisticated men! Doubtless they were strangers to the profound intent of Christ's teaching, but there was that in it which by its mysterious grandeur and transparent purity and grace, held them spellbound. No doubt it was of God that they should so feel, that their arm might be paralyzed, as Christ's hour was not yet come; but even in human teaching there has sometimes been felt such a divine power, that men who came to kill them (e.g., ROWLAND HISS) have confessed to all that they were unmanned. **47. ye also deceived**—In their own servants this seemed intolerable. **48. any of the rulers or . . . Pharisees believed**—"Many of them" did, including Nicodemus and Joseph, but not one of these had openly "confessed Him" (ch. 12:42), and this appeal must have stung such of them as heard it to the quick. **49. But this people**—lit., "multitude," meaning the

ignorant rabble. It is a pity that these important distinctions, so marked in the orginal of this Gospel, should not be also in our version.) **knoweth not the law**—i.e., by school learning, which only subverted it by human traditions. **are cursed**—a cursed set (a kind of swearing at them, out of mingled rage and scorn). **50-53. Nicodemus**—reappearing to us after nearly three years' absence from the history, as a member of the council, probably then sitting. **51. Doth our law . . .**—a very proper, but all too tame rejoinder, and evidently more from pressure of conscience than any design to pronounce *positively* in the case. "The feebleness of his defense of Jesus has a strong contrast in the flerceness of the rejoinders of the Pharisees" [WEBSTER and WILKINSON]. **52. thou of Galilee**—in this taunt expressing their scorn of the party. Even a word of caution, or the gentlest proposal to inquire before condemning, was with them equivalent to an espousal of the hated One. **Search . . . out of Galilee . . . no prophet**—Strange! For had not *Jonah* (of Gathhepher) and even Elijah (of Thisbe) arisen out of Galilee? And there it may be more, of whom we have no record. But rage is blind, and deep prejudice distorts all facts. Yet it looks as if they were afraid of losing Nicodemus, when they take the trouble to reason the point at all. It was just *because* he had "searched," as they advised him, that he went the length even that he did. **53. every man went unto his own home**—*finding their plot could not at that time be carried into effect.* Is your rage thus impotent, ye chief priests?

CHAPTER 8

VSS. 1-11. THE WOMAN TAKEN IN ADULTERY. **1, 2. Jesus went unto the Mount of Olives**—This should have formed the last verse of the foregoing chapter. "The return of the people to the inert quiet and security of their *dwellings* (ch. 7:53), at the close of the feast, is designedly contrasted with our Lord's *homeless* way, so to speak, of spending the short night, who is early in the morning on the scene again. One cannot well see why what is recorded in Luke 21:37, 38 may not even thus early have taken place; it might have been the Lord's ordinary custom from the beginning to leave the brilliant misery of the city every night, that so He might compose His sorrowful and interceding heart, and collect His energies for new labors of love; preferring for His resting-place Bethany, and the *Mount of Olives,* the scene thus consecrated by many preparatory prayers for His final humiliation and exaltation" [STIER]. **3-6. scribes and Pharisees**—foiled in their yesterday's attempt, and hoping to succeed better in this. **4. woman . . . in adultery . . . 5. Moses . . . commanded . . . should be stoned**—simply put to death (Deut. 22:22), but in aggravated cases, at least in later times, this was probably by stoning (Ezek. 16:40). **but what sayest thou**—hoping, whatever He might answer, to put Him in the wrong:—if He said, Stone her, that would seem a stepping out of His province; if He forbade it, that would hold Him up as a relaxer of the public morals. But these cunning hypocrites were overmatched. **6. stooped down**—It will be observed He was *sitting* when they came to Him. **with his finger wrote on the ground**—The words of our translators in italics ("as though He heard them not") have hardly improved the sense, for it is scarcely probable He could wish that to be thought. Rather He wished to show them His aversion to enter on the subject. But as this did not suit them, they "continue asking Him," pressing for an answer. At last, raising Himself He said. **7. He that is without sin**—not meaning sinless altogether; nor yet, guiltless of a literal breach of the Seventh Commandment; but probably, he whose conscience acquits him of *any such* sin. **cast a stone**—"*the* stone," meaning the first one (Deut. 17:7). **8. again he stooped down and wrote** —The design of this second stooping and writing on the ground was evidently to give her accusers an opportunity to slink away unobserved *by Him,* and so avoid an exposure to His eye which they could ill have stood. Accordingly it is added. **9. they ...convicted...went out one by one...Jesus was left alone**—i.e., without one of her accusers remaining; for it is added—**the woman in the midst**—i.e., of the remaining audience. While the trap failed to catch Him for whom it was laid, it caught those who laid it. Stunned by the unexpected home-thrust, they immediately made off—which makes the impudence of those impure hypocrites in dragging such a case before the public eye the more disgusting. **10. Woman...**—What inimitable tenderness and grace! Conscious of her own guilt, and till now in the hands of men who had talked of stoning her, wondering at the *skill* with which her accusers had been dispersed, and the *grace* of the few words addressed to herself, she would be disposed to listen, with a reverence and teachableness before unknown, to our Lord's admonition. "And Jesus said unto her, Neither do I condemn thee, go and sin no more." He pronounces no pardon upon the woman (such as, "Thy sins are forgiven thee" —"Go in peace"), much less does He say that she had done nothing condemnable; He simply leaves the matter where it was. He meddles not with the magistrate's office, nor acts the *Judge* in any sense (ch. 12:47). But in saying, "Go and sin no more," which had been before said to one who undoubtedly believed (ch. 5:14), more is probably implied than expressed. If brought suddenly to conviction of sin, admiration of her Deliverer, and a willingness to be admonished and guided by Him, this call to begin a new life may have carried with it what would ensure and naturally bring about a permanent change. (This whole narrative is wanting in some of the earliest and most valuable MSS., and those which have it vary to some extent. The internal evidence in its favor is almost overpowering. It is easy to account for its *omission,* though genuine; but if not so, it is next to impossible to account for its *insertion*).

12-59. FURTHER DISCOURSES OF JESUS—AT-TEMPT TO STONE HIM. 12. I am the light of the world—As the former references to *water* (chs. 4 and 7) and to *bread* (ch. 6) were occasioned by outward occurrences, so this one to *light.* In "the treasury" where it was spoken (see on vs. 20) stood two colossal golden lamp-stands, on which hung a multitude of lamps, lighted after the evening sacrifice (probably every evening during the feast of tabernacles), diffusing their brilliancy, it is said, over all the city. Around these the people danced with great rejoicing. Now, as amidst the festivities of the *water* from Siloam Jesus cried, saying, "If any man thirst, let him come unto me and drink," so now amidst the blaze and the joyousness of this illumination, He proclaims, "I AM THE LIGHT OF THE WORLD"—plainly in the most *absolute* sense. For though He gives His disciples the same title, they are only "light *in the Lord*" (Eph. 5:8); and though He calls the Baptist "the burning and shin-

ing light" (or "*lamp*" of his day, ch. 5:35), yet "he was *not that Light,* but was sent to bear witness of that Light: that was THE TRUE LIGHT which, coming into the world, *lighteth every man*" (ch. 1:8, 9). Under this magnificent title Messiah was promised of old (Isa. 42:6; Mal. 4:2, etc.). **he that followeth me**—as one does a light going before him, and as the Israelites did the pillar of bright cloud in the wilderness. **but shall have the light of life**—the light, as of a new world, a newly awakened spiritual and eternal life. **13-19. bearest record of thyself; thy record is not true**—How does He meet this specious cavil? Not by disputing the wholesome human maxim that "self-praise is no praise," but by affirming that He was *an exception to the rule,* or rather, that *it had no application to Him.* **14. for I know whence I came, and whither I go...**— (See on ch. 7:28, 29). **15. Ye judge after the flesh** —with no spiritual apprehension. **I judge no man. 16. And yet if I judge, my judgment is true...**—Ye not only *form* your carnal and warped judgments of Me, but are bent on carrying them into effect; I, though I form and utter My judgment of you, am not here to carry this into execution—that is reserved to a future day; yet the judgment I now pronounce and the witness I now bear is not Mine only as ye suppose, but His also that sent Me. (See on ch. 5:31, 32.) And these are the two witnesses to any fact which your law requires. **20. These words spake Jesus in the treasury**—a division, so called, of the fore-court of the temple, part of the court of the women [JOSEPHUS, *Antiquities,* xix. 6. 2, etc.), which may confirm the genuineness of vss. 2-11, as the place where the woman was brought. **no man laid hands on him...**—(See on ch. 7:30). In the dialogue that follows, the conflict waxes sharper on both sides, till rising to its climax, they take up stones to stone him. **21-25. Then said Jesus again unto them, I go my way...**—(See on ch. 7:34). **22. Then said the Jews, Will he kill himself?**—seeing something more in His words than before (ch. 7:35), but their question more malignant and scornful. **23. Ye are from beneath; I am from above**—contrasting Himself, not as in ch. 3:31, simply with *earthborn messengers of God,* but *with men sprung from and breathing an opposite element* from His, which rendered it impossible that He and they should have any present fellowship, or dwell eternally together. (See again on ch. 7:34: also vs. 44.) **24. if ye believe not that I am he, ye shall die in your sins**—They knew well enough what He meant (Mark 13:6, *Gr.;* cf. Matt. 24:5). But He would not, by speaking it out, give them the materials for a charge for which they were watching. At the same time, one is irresistibly reminded by such language, so far transcending what is becoming in *men,* of those ancient declarations of the God of Israel, "I AM HE" (Deut. 32:39; Isa. 43:10, 13; 46:4; 48:12). See on ch. 6:20. **25. Who art thou?**—hoping thus to extort an explicit answer; but they are disappointed. **26, 27. I have many things to say and to judge of you; but he that sent me is true...** —i.e., I could, and at the fitting time, will say and judge many things of you (referring perhaps to the work of the Spirit which is for *judgment* as well as *salvation,* ch. 16:8); but what I do say is just the message My Father hath given Me to deliver. **28-30. When ye have lifted up the Son of man**— The plainest intimation He had yet given *in public* of *the manner* and the *authors* of His death. **then shall ye know that I am he...**—i.e., *find out,* or have sufficient evidence, how true was all He said, though they would be far from owning it. **29. the**

Father hath not left me alone; for I do always those things that please him...—i.e., To you, who gnash upon Me with your teeth, and frown down all open appearance for Me, I seem to stand uncountenanced and alone; but I have a sympathy and support transcending all human applause; I came hither to do My Father's will, and in the doing of it have not ceased to please Him; therefore is He ever by Me with His approving smile, His cheering words, His supporting arm. **30. As he spake these words, many believed on him**—Instead of wondering at this, the wonder would be if words of such unearthly, surpassing grandeur *could* be uttered without captivating *some* that heard them. And just as "all that sat in the council" to try Stephen "*saw his face*" —though expecting nothing but death—"*as it had been the face of an angel*" (Acts 6:15), so may we suppose that, full of the sweet supporting sense of His Father's presence, amidst the rage and scorn of the rulers, a divine benignity beamed from His countenance, irradiated the words that fell from Him, and won over the candid "many" of His audience. **31-33. Then said Jesus to those Jews who believed, If ye continue in my word, then are ye my disciples indeed**...—The impression produced by the last words of our Lord may have become visible by some decisive movement, and here He takes advantage of it to press on them "*continuance*" in the faith, since then only were they His real disciples (cf. ch. 15:3-8), and then should they *experimentally* "know the truth," and "by the truth be made (*spiritually*) free." **33. They answered him, We are Abraham's seed, and were never in bondage to any man**...—Who said this? Not surely the very class just spoken of as won over by His divine words, and exhorted to continue in them. Most interpreters seem to think so; but it is hard to ascribe such a petulant speech to the newly gained disciples, even in the lowest sense, much less persons *so* gained as they were. It came, probably, from persons mixed up with them in the same part of the crowd, but of a very different spirit. The *pride* of the Jewish nation, even now after centuries of humiliation, is the most striking feature of their character. 'Talk of freedom to *us*? Pray when or to whom were we ever in bondage?' This bluster sounds almost ludicrous from such a nation. Had they forgotten their long and bitter bondage in Egypt? their dreary captivity in Babylon? their present bondage to the Roman yoke, and their restless eagerness to throw it off? But probably they saw that our Lord pointed to something else—freedom, perhaps, from the leaders of sects or parties —and were not willing to allow their subjection even to these. Our Lord, therefore, though He knew what slaves they were in this sense, drives the ploughshare somewhat deeper than this, to a bondage they little dreamt of. **34, 35. Whosoever committeth sin**—i.e., *liveth in the commission* of it— (Cf. I John 3:8; Matt. 7:23). **is the servant of sin** —i.e., the *bond-servant*, or *slave* of it; for the question is not about free service, but who are in *bondage*. (Cf. II Pet. 2:19; Rev. 6:16.) The great truth here expressed was not unknown to heathen moralists; but it was applied only to *vice*, for they were total strangers to what in revealed religion is called *sin*. The thought of *slaves* and *freemen* in the house suggests to our Lord a wider idea. **35. And the servant abideth not in the house for ever, but the Son abideth ever**—i.e., 'And if your connection with the family of God be that of BOND-SERVANTS, ye have no *natural tie* to the house; your tie is essentially *uncertain* and *precarious*. But the

SON'S relationship to the FATHER is a *natural and essential* one; it is an indefeasible tie; His abode in it is *perpetual* and *of right:* That is My relationship, My tie: If, then, ye would have your connection with God's family made *real, rightful, permanent*, ye must by the Son be *manumitted* and *adopted* as sons and daughters of the Lord Almighty.' In this sublime statement there is no doubt a *subordinate* allusion to Genesis 21:10, "*Cast out* this *bondwoman and her son*, for *the son of this bondwoman shall not be heir with my son*, with Isaac." (Cf. Gal. 4:22-30.) **37-41. ye seek to kill me**—He had said this to their face before: He now repeats it, and they do not deny it; yet are they held back, as by some marvellous spell —it was the awe which His combined dignity, courage, and benignity struck into them. **because my word hath no place in you**—When did ever *human prophet* so speak of His words? They tell us of "the word of the Lord" coming to them. But here is One who holds up "His word" as that which ought to find entrance and abiding room for itself in the souls of all who hear it. **38. my Father...your father**—(See on vs. 23). **39. If ye were Abraham's children, ye would do the works of Abraham**—He had just said He "knew they were Abraham's children," i.e., according to the *flesh;* but the children of his *faith and holiness* they were not, but the reverse. **40. this did not Abraham**—In so doing ye act in direct opposition to him. **41. We be not born of fornication...we have one Father, God** —meaning, as is generally allowed, that they were not an illegitimate race in point of *religion*, pretending only to be God's people, but were descended from His own chosen Abraham. **42, 43. If God were your Father, ye would love me**—'If ye had anything of His moral image, as children have their father's likeness, ye would love Me, for I am immediately of Him and directly from Him. But "My speech" (meaning His peculiar style of expressing Himself on these subjects) is unintelligible to you because ye cannot take in the truth which it conveys. **44. Ye are of your father the devil**— "This is one of the most decisive testimonies to the *objective* (outward) *personality* of the devil. It is quite impossible to suppose an accommodation to Jewish views, or a metaphorical form of speech, in so solemn an assertion as this" [ALFORD]. **the lusts of your father**—his impure, malignant, ungodly propensities, inclinations, desires. **ye will do**—are willing to do; not of any *blind necessity of nature*, but of *pure natural inclination*. **He was a murderer from the beginning**—The reference is not to *Cain* [as LOCKE, DE WETTE, ALFORD, etc.], but to *Adam* [GROTIUS, CALVIN, MEYER, LUTHARDT, etc.]. The death of the human race, in its widest sense, is ascribed to the murderous seducer of our race. **and abode not in the truth**—As, strictly speaking, the word means "abideth," it has been denied that the *fall* of Satan from a former holy state is here expressed [LOCKE, etc.], and some superior interpreters think it only *implied* [OLSHAUSEN, etc.]. But though the *form* of the thought is present—not past —this is to express the important idea, that his whole character and activity are just *a continual aberration from his own original truth or rectitude;* and thus his fall is not only the *implied basis* of the thought, but *part of the statement itself*, properly interpreted and brought out. **no truth in him**— void of all that holy, transparent rectitude which, as His creature, he originally possessed. **When he speaketh a lie, he speaketh of his own**—perhaps his own resources, treasures (Matt. 12:35) [ALFORD].

(The word is *plural*.) It means that he has no temptation to it *from without;* it is purely *self-begotten,* springing from a nature which is nothing but obliquity. **the father of it**—i.e., of lying: all the falsehood in the world owes its existence to him. What a verse is this! It holds up the devil (1) as the murderer of the human race; but as this is meant here in the more profound sense of *spiritual* death, it holds him up, (2) as the spiritual parent of this fallen human family, communicating to his offspring his own evil passions and universal obliquity, and stimulating these into active exercise. But as there is "a stronger than he," who comes upon him and overcomes him (Luke 11:21, 22), it is only such as "love the darkness," who are addressed as children of the devil (Matt. 13:38; I John 3:8-10). **45-47. And because I tell you the truth, ye believe me not**—not *although,* but just *because* He did so, for the reason given in the former verse. Had He been *less* true they would have hailed Him more readily. **46. Which of you convinceth me of sin**—"Convicteth," bringeth home a charge of sin. Glorious dilemma! 'Convict Me of sin, and reject Me: If not, why stand ye out against My claims?' Of course, they could only be supposed to impeach His *life*; but in One who had already passed through unparalleled complications, and had continually to deal with friends and foes of every sort and degree, such a challenge thrown wide among His bitterest enemies, can amount to nothing short of a claim to *absolute sinlessness.* **48-51. Say we not well that thou art a Samaritan, and hast a devil?**—What intense and virulent scorn! (See Heb. 12:3.) The "say we not well" refers to ch. 7:20. "A Samaritan" means more than "no Israelite at all"; it means one who *pretended, but had no manner of claim* to the title—retorting perhaps, this denial of their *true* descent from Abraham. **49. Jesus answered, I have not a devil**—What calm dignity is here! Verily, "when reviled, He reviled not again" (I Pet. 2:23). Cf. Paul (Acts 26:25), "I am not mad..." He adds not, "Nor am I a Samaritan," that He might not even seem to partake of their contempt for a race that had already welcomed Him as the Christ, and began to be blessed by Him. **I honour my Father, and ye do dishonour me**—the language of *wounded feeling.* But the *interior* of His soul at such moments is only to be seen in such prophetic utterances as these, "For thy sake I have borne reproach; shame hath covered my face; I am become a *stranger* unto my brethren, an *alien* unto my mother's children. For the zeal of thine house hath eaten me up, and *the reproaches of them that* reproached thee are fallen upon me" (Ps. 69:7-9.) **50. I seek not mine own glory: there is one that seeketh**—i.e., evidently, *'that seeketh My glory';* requiring "all men to honor the Son even as they honor the Father"; judicially *treating* him "who honoreth not the Son as honoring not the Father that hath sent Him" (ch. 5:23; and cf. Matt. 17:5); but giving to Him (ch. 6:37) such as will yet cast their crowns before His throne, in whom He "shall see of the travail of his soul, and be satisfied" (Isa. 53:11). **51. If a man keep my saying, he shall never see death**—Partly thus vindicating His lofty claims as Lord of the kingdom of life everlasting, and, at the same time, holding out even to His revilers the scepter of grace. The word *"keep"* is in harmony with vs. 31, "If ye *continue* in My word," expressing the permanency, as a living and paramount principle, of that faith to which He referred: *"never see death,"* though virtually uttered before (ch. 5:24; 6:40, 47, 51), is the strongest and most

naked statement of a very glorious truth yet given. (In ch. 11:26 it is repeated in nearly identical terms.) **52, 53. Then said the Jews unto him, Now we know that thou hast a devil...**—'Thou art now self-convicted; only a demoniac could speak so; the most illustrious of our fathers are dead, and Thou promisest exemption from death to anyone who will keep *Thy saying!* pray, who art Thou?' **54-56. If I honour myself, my honour is nothing...**—(See on ch. 5:31, etc.). **I shall be a liar like unto you**—now rising to the summit of holy, naked severity, thereby to draw this long dialogue to a head. **56. Abraham rejoiced to see my day...**—exulted, or exceedingly rejoiced that he should see, he exulted to see it, i.e., by *anticipation.* Nay, **he saw it and was glad**—he *actually* beheld it, to his joy. If this mean no more than that he had a prophetic foresight of the gospel-day—the second clause just repeating the first—how could the Jews understand our Lord to mean that He "had seen Abraham"? And if it mean that Abraham was *then beholding,* in his disembodied spirit, the incarnate Messiah [STIER, ALFORD, etc.], the words seem very unsuitable to express it. It expresses something *past* —"he *saw* My day, and *was* glad," i.e., surely *while he lived.* He seems to refer to the familiar intercourse which Abraham had with *God,* who is once and again in the history called *"the Angel of the Lord,"* and whom Christ here identifies with Himself. On those occasions, Abraham "saw ME" [OLSHAUSEN, though he thinks the reference is to some unrecorded scene]. If this be the meaning, all that follows is quite natural. **57-59. Then said the Jews unto him, Thou art not yet fifty years old**—"No inference can be drawn from this as to the age of our Lord at the time as man. Fifty years was with the Jews the completion of manhood" [ALFORD]. **and hast thou seen Abraham?**—He had said Abraham saw *Him,* as being his peculiar privilege. They give the opposite turn to it—"Hast Thou seen *Abraham?*" as an honor too great for Him to pretend to. **58. Before Abraham was, I am**—The words rendered "was" and "am" are quite different. The one clause means, 'Abraham was *brought into being';* the other, *'I exist.'* The statement therefore is not that *Christ came into existence before Abraham did* (as Arians affirm is the meaning), but that He never *came* into being at all, but *existed* before Abraham had a being; in other words, existed before *creation,* or *eternally* (as ch. 1:1). *In that sense the Jews plainly understood Him,* since "then took they up stones to cast at Him," *just as they had before done when they saw that He made Himself equal with God* (ch. 5:18). **hid himself**—(See on Luke 4:30).

CHAPTER 9

Vss. 1-41. THE OPENING OF THE EYES OF ONE BORN BLIND, AND WHAT FOLLOWED ON IT. **1-5. as Jesus passed by, he saw a man which was blind from birth**—and who "sat begging" (vs. 8). **2. who did sin, this man or his parents, that he was born blind** —not in a former state of existence, in which, as respects the wicked, the Jews did not believe; but, perhaps, expressing loosely that sin *somewhere* had surely been the cause of this calamity. **3. Neither ... this man ...**—The cause was neither in himself nor his parents, but, in order to the manifestation of "the works of God," in his cure. **4. I must work the works of him that sent me ...**—a most interesting statement from the mouth of Christ; intimating,

(1) that He had a precise work to do upon earth, with every particular of it arranged and laid out to Him; (2) that all He did upon earth was just "the works of God"—particularly "going about *doing good*," though not exclusively by miracles; (3) that each work had its precise *time* and *place* in His programme of instructions, so to speak; hence, (4) that as His period for work had definite termination, so by letting any one service pass by its alotted time, the whole would be disarranged, marred, and driven beyond its destined period for completion; (5) that He acted ever under the impulse of these considerations, as man—"the night cometh when no man [or no one] can work." What lessons are here for others, and what encouragement from such Example! **5. As long as I am in the world, I am the light of the world**—not as if He would cease, after that, to be so; but that He must make full proof of His fidelity while His earthly career lasted by displaying His glory. "As before the raising of Lazarus (ch. 11:25), He announces Himself as *the Resurrection and the Life,* so now He sets Himself forth as the source of the archetypal spiritual light, of which the natural, now about to be conferred, is only a derivation and symbol" [AL-FORD]. **6, 7. he spat on the ground, and made clay ... and he anointed the eyes of the blind man ...** —These operations were not so incongruous in their nature as might appear, though it were absurd to imagine that they contributed in the least degree to the effect which followed. (See on Mark 6:13; and 7:33, 34). **7. Go, wash in Siloam which is ..., Sent ...**—(See II Kings 5:10, 14). As the prescribed action was purely symbolical in its design, so in connection with it the Evangelist notices the symbolical name of the pool as in this case bearing testimony to him who was *sent* to do what it only *symbolized.* (See Isa. 8:6, where this same pool is used figuratively to denote "the streams that make glad the city of God," and which, humble though they be, betoken *a present God of Israel.*) **8-15. The neighbours therefore ... said, Is not this he that sat and begged**—Here are a number of details to identify the newly seeing with the long-known blind beggar. **13. They brought to the Pharisees** —sitting probably in council, and chiefly of that sect (ch. 7:47, 48). **16, 17. This man is not of God ...**—(See on ch. 5:9, 16). **Others said ...**—such as Nicodemus and Joseph. **the blind man ... said, He is a prophet**—rightly viewing the miracle as but a "sign" of His prophetic commission. **18-23. the Jews did not believe ... he had been born blind ... till they called the parents of him that had received his sight**—Foiled by the testimony of the young man himself, they hope to throw doubt on the fact by close questioning his parents, who, perceiving the snare laid for them, ingeniously escape it by testifying simply to the identity of their son, and his birth-blindness, leaving it to himself, as a competent witness, to speak as to the cure. They prevaricated, however, in saying they "knew not who had opened his eyes," for "they feared the Jews," who had come to an understanding (probably after what is recorded (ch. 7:50, etc.) but by this time well known), that whoever owned Him as the Christ would be put out of the synagogue—i.e., not simply *excluded,* but *excommunicated.* **24-34. Give God the praise; we know that this man is a sinner** —not wishing him to own, even to the praise of God, that a miracle had been wrought upon him, but to show more regard to the honor of God than ascribe any such act to one who was a sinner. **25. He answered and said, Whether a sinner or no ...**

—Not that the man meant to insinuate any doubt in his own mind on the point of His being "a sinner," but as his *opinion* on such a point would be of no consequence to others, he would speak only to what he *knew* as *fact* in his *own case.* **26. Then said they ... again, What did he to thee ...**— hoping by repeated questions to ensnare him, but the youth is more than a match for them. **27. I have told you already ... will ye also be his disciples?**—In a vein of keen irony he treats their questions as those of anxious inquirers, almost ready for discipleship! Stung by this, they retort upon *him* as the disciple (and here they plainly were not wrong); for themselves, they fall back upon Moses; about *him* there could be no doubt; but who knew about this upstart? **30. The man answered, Herein is a marvellous thing, that ye know not from whence he is, and yet he hath opened mine eyes**—He had no need to say another word; but waxing bolder in defense of his Benefactor, and his views brightening by the very courage which it demanded, he puts it to them how they could pretend inability to tell whether one who opened the eyes of a man born blind was "of God" or "a sinner"—from above or from beneath—and proceeds to argue the case with remarkable power. So irresistible was his argument that their rage burst forth in a speech of intense Pharisaism, 'Thou wast altogether born in sins, and dost thou teach us?— *thou,* a base-born, uneducated, impudent youth, teach *us,* the trained, constituted, recognized guides of the people in the things of God! Out upon thee! **31. they cast him out**—judicially, no doubt, as well in fact. The allusion to his being "born in sins" seems a tacit admission of his being blind from birth—the very thing they had been so unwilling to own. But rage and enmity to truth are seldom consistent in their outbreaks. The friends of this excommunicated youth, crowding around him with their sympathy, would probably express surprise that One who could work such a cure should be unable to protect his patient from the persecution it had raised against him, or should possess the power without using it. Nor would it be strange if such thoughts should arise in the youth's own mind. But if they did, it is certain, from what follows, that they made no lodgment there, conscious as he was that "wheras he was blind, now he saw," and satisfied that if his Benefactor "were not of God, He could do nothing" (vs. 33). There was a word for him too, which, if whispered in his ear from the oracles of God, would seem expressly designed to describe his case, and prepare him for the coming interview with his gracious Friend. "Hear the word of the Lord, ye that tremble at His word. *Your brethren that hated you, that cast you out for My name's sake, said, Let the Lord be glorified;* BUT HE SHALL APPEAR TO YOUR JOY, *and they shall be ashamed*" (Isa. 66:5). But how was *He* engaged to whom such noble testimony had been given, and for whom such persecution had been borne? Uttering, perhaps, in secret, "with strong crying and tears," the words of the prophetic psalm, "Let not them that wait on Thee, O Lord God of hosts, be ashamed for my sake; let none that seek Thee be confounded for my sake, O God of Israel; because for Thy sake I have borne reproach ... and the reproaches of them that reproached Thee are fallen upon me" (Ps. 69:6, 7, 9). **35-38. Jesus heard**—i.e., by intelligence brought Him. **that they had cast him out; and when he had found him**—by accident? Not very likely. Sympathy in that breast could not long keep aloof from its object. **he said unto him, Dost thou believe on the Son of God?**—A question stretching purposely beyond his present attainments, in order the more quickly to lead him—in his present teachable frame—into the highest truth. **36. He answered and said, Who is he, Lord, that I may believe on him?**—"His reply is affirmative, and believing by anticipation, promising faith as soon as Jesus shall say who He is" [STIER]. **37. Jesus said unto him, Thou hast both seen him**—the new sense of sight having at that moment its highest exercise, in gazing upon "the Light of the world." **38. he said, Lord, I believe: and he worshipped him**—a *faith* and a *worship*, beyond doubt, meant to express far more than he would think proper to any human "prophet" (vs. 17)—the unstudied, resistless expression, probably of SUPREME faith and adoration, though without the full understanding of what that implied. **39-41. Jesus said**—perhaps at the same time, but after a crowd, including some of the skeptical and scornful rulers, had, on seeing Jesus talking with the healed youth, hastened to the spot. **that they which see not might see . . .**—rising to that *sight* of which the natural vision communicated to the youth was but the symbol. (See on vs. 5, and cf. Luke 4:18.) **that they which see might be made blind**—judicially incapable of apprehending and receiving the truth, to which they have wilfully shut their eyes. **40. Are we blind also?**—We, the constituted, recognized guides of the people in spiritual things? pride and rage prompting the question. **41. If ye were blind**—wanted light to discern My claims, and only waited to receive it—**ye should have no sin**—none of the guilt of shutting out the light. **ye say, We see; therefore your sin remaineth**—Your claim to possess light, while rejecting Me, is that which seals you up in the guilt of unbelief.

CHAPTER 10

Vss. 1-21. THE GOOD SHEPHERD. This discourse seems plainly to be a continuation of the closing verses of ch. 9. The figure was familiar to the Jewish ear (from Jer. 23; Ezek. 34; Zech. 11, etc.). "This simple creature [the sheep] has this special note among all animals, that it quickly hears the voice of the shepherd, follows no one else, depends entirely on him, and seeks help from him alone—cannot help itself, but is shut up to another's aid" [LUTHER in STIER]. **1, 2. He that entereth not by the door**—the legitimate way (without saying what that was, as yet). **into the sheepfold**—the sacred enclosure of God's true people. **climbeth up some other way**—not referring to the assumption of ecclesiastical office without an external call, for those Jewish rulers, specially aimed at, had this (Matt. 23:2), but to the want of a true spiritual commission, the seal of heaven going along with the outward authority; it is the assumption of the spiritual guidance of the people *without this* that is meant. **2. he that entereth in by the door is the shepherd of the sheep**—a true, divinely recognized shepherd. **3. To him the porter openeth**—i.e., *right of free access* is given, by order of Him to whom the sheep belong; for it is better not to give the allusion a more specific interpretation [CALVIN, MEYER, LUTHARDT]. **and the sheep hear his voice**—This and all that follows, though it admits of important *application* to every faithful shepherd of God's flock, is in its direct and highest sense true only of "the great Shepherd of the sheep," who in the first five verses seems

plainly, under the simple character of a true shepherd, to be drawing His own portrait [LAMPE, STIER, etc.]. **7-14. I am the door of the sheep**—i.e., *the way in* to the fold, with all blessed privileges, both for shepherds and sheep (cf. ch. 14:6; Eph. 2: 18). **8. All that ever came before me**—the false prophets; not as claiming the prerogatives of Messiah, but as perverters of the people from the way of life, all pointing to Him [OLSHAUSEN]. **the sheep did not hear them**—the instinct of their divinely taught hearts preserving them from seducers, and attaching them to the heaven-sent prophets, of whom it is said that "the Spirit of Christ was in them" (I Peter 1:11). **9. by me if any man enter in**—whether shepherd or sheep. **shall be saved**—the great object of the pastoral office, as of all the divine arrangements towards mankind. **and shall go in and out and find pasture**—*in*, as to a place of *safety* and *repose*; *out*, as to "green pastures and still waters" (Ps. 23:2) for nourishment and refreshing, and all this only transferred to another clime, and enjoyed in another manner, at the close of this earthly scene (Rev. 7:17). **10. I am come that they might have life, and . . . more abundantly**—not merely to *preserve* but *impart* LIFE, and communicate it in rich and unfailing exuberance. What a claim! Yet it is only an echo of all His teaching; and He who uttered these and like words must be either a blasphemer, all worthy of the death He died, or "God with us"—there can be no middle course. **11. I am the good shepherd**—emphatically, and, in the sense intended, exclusively so (Isa. 40:11; Ezek. 34:23; 37:24; Zech. 13:7). **the good shepherd giveth his life for the sheep**—Though this may be said of literal shepherds, who, even for their brute flock, have, like David, encountered "the lion and the bear" at the risk of their own lives, and still more of faithful pastors who, like the early bishops of Rome, have been the foremost to brave the fury of their enemies against the flock committed to their care; yet here, beyond doubt, it points to the struggle which was to issue in the willing surrender of the Redeemer's own life, to save His sheep from destruction. **12. an hireling . . . whose own the sheep are not**—who has no *property* in them. By this He points to His own peculiar relation to the sheep, the same as His Father's, the great Proprietor and Lord of the flock, who styles Him "My Shepherd, *the Man that is My Fellow*" (Zech. 13:7), and though faithful undershepherds are so in their Master's interest, that they feel a measure of His own concern for their charge, the language is strictly applicable only to "the Son over His own house" (Heb. 3:6). **seeth the wolf coming**—not *the devil* distinctively, as some take it [STIER, ALFORD, etc.], but generally whoever comes upon the flock with hostile intent, in whatever form: though the wicked one, no doubt, is *at the bottom* of such movements [LUTHARDT]. **14. I am the good shepherd, and know my sheep**—in the peculiar sense of II Timothy 2:19. **am known of mine**—the soul's response to the voice that has inwardly and efficaciously called it; for of this mutual loving acquaintance ours is the *effect* of His. "The Redeemer's knowledge of us is the *active* element, penetrating us with His power and life; that of believers is the *passive* principle, the reception of His life and light. In this reception, however, an assimilation of the soul to the sublime Object of its knowledge and love takes place; and thus an activity, though a derived one, is unfolded, which shows itself in obedience to His commands" [OLSHAUSEN]. From this mutual knowledge Jesus rises to another and loftier reciprocity of knowledge. **15-18. As the Father knoweth me, even so know I the Father**—What claim to absolute equality with the Father could exceed this? (See on Matt. 11:27.) **and I lay down my life for the sheep**—How sublime this, immediately following the lofty claim of the preceding clause! 'Tis the riches and the poverty of "the Word made flesh"—one glorious Person reaching at once up to the Throne and down even to the dust of death, "that we might live through Him." A candid interpretation of the words, *"for the sheep,"* ought to go far to establish the special relation of the vicarious death of Christ to the Church. **16. other sheep I have . . . not of this fold: them also I must bring**—He means the perishing Gentiles, *already His "sheep"* in the love of His heart and the purpose of His grace to *"bring them"* in due time. **they shall hear my voice**—*This is not the language of mere foresight that they would believe, but the expression of a purpose to draw them to Himself by an inward and efficacious call, which would infallibly issue in their spontaneous accession to Him.* **and there shall be one fold**—rather "one flock" (for the word for "fold," as in the foregoing verses, is quite different). **17. Therefore doth my Father love me, because I lay down my life . . .**—As the highest act of the Son's love to the Father was the laying down of His life for the sheep at His "commandment," so the Father's love to Him as His *incarnate* Son reaches its consummation, and finds its highest justification, in that sublimest and most affecting of all acts. **that I might take it again**—His resurrection-life being indispensable to the accomplishment of the fruit of His death. **18. No man taketh it from me, but I lay it down myself: I have power to lay it down, and I have power to take it again**—It is impossible for language more plainly and emphatically to express the *absolute voluntariness* of Christ's death, such a voluntariness as it would be manifest presumption in any mere *creature* to affirm of his own death. It is beyond all doubt the language of One who was conscious that *His life was His own* (which no creature's is), and therefore His to surrender or retain *at will.* Here lay the glory of His sacrifice, that it was *purely* voluntary. The claim of "power to take it again" is no less important, as showing that His resurrection, though ascribed to the Father, in the sense we shall presently see, was nevertheless *His own assertion of His own right to life* as soon as the purposes of His voluntary death were accomplished. **This commandment**—to "lay down His life, that He might take it again." **have I received of my Father**—So that Christ died at once by "command" of His Father, and by such a voluntary obedience to that command as has made Him (so to speak) infinitely dear to the Father. The *necessity* of Christ's death, in the light of these profound sayings, must be manifest to all but the superficial student. **19-21. There was a division . . . again among the Jews for these sayings**—the light and the darkness revealing themselves with increasing clearness in the separation of the teachable from the obstinately prejudiced. The one saw in Him only "a devil and a madman"; the other revolted at the thought that *such words* could come from one possessed, and sight be given to the blind by a demoniac; showing clearly that a deeper impression had been made upon them than their words expressed.

22-42. DISCOURSE AT THE FEAST OF DEDICATION —FROM THE FURY OF HIS ENEMIES JESUS ESCAPES

BEYOND JORDAN, WHERE MANY BELIEVE ON HIM. **22, 23. it was . . . the feast of the dedication**—celebrated rather more than *two months* after the feast of tabernacles, during which intermediate period our Lord seems to have remained in the neighborhood of Jerusalem. It was instituted by Judas Maccabeus, to commemorate the purification of the temple from the profanations to which it had been subjected by Antiochus Epiphanes 165 B.C., and kept for eight days, from the 25th Chisleu (December), the day on which Judas began the first joyous celebration of it (I Maccabees 4:52, 56, 59; and JOSEPHUS, *Antiquities*, xii. 7. 7). **it was winter**—implying some *inclemency.* Therefore **Jesus walked . . . in Solomon's porch**—for shelter. This portico was on the east side of the temple, and Josephus says it was part of the original structure of Solomon [*Antiquities*, xx. 9. 7]. **24. Then came the Jews**—*the rulers.* (See on ch. 1:19.) **How long dost thou make us to doubt**—"hold us in suspense" (*marg.*). **If thou be the Christ, tell us plainly**—But when the plainest *evidence* of it was resisted, what weight could a mere *assertion* of it have? **25, 26. Jesus answered them, I told you**—i.e., in substance, what I am (e.g. ch. 7:37, 38; 8: 12, 35, 36, 58). **26. ye believe not, because ye are not of my sheep, as I said**—referring to the whole strain of the Parable of the Sheep, (vs. 1, etc.). **27-30. My sheep hear my voice . . .**—(See on vs. 8.) **I give unto them eternal life**—not "will give them"; for it is a present gift. (See on ch. 3: 36; 5:24.) It is a very grand utterance, couched in the language of majestic authority. **29. My Father, which gave them me**—(See on ch. 6:37-39). **is greater than all**—with whom no adverse power can contend. It is a general expression of an admitted truth, and what follows shows for what purpose it was uttered, "and none is able to pluck them out of My Father's hand." The impossibility of true believers being lost, in the midst of all the temptations which they may encounter, does not consist in their fidelity and decision, but is founded upon the *power of God.* Here the doctrine of predestination is presented in its sublime and sacred aspect; there is a predestination of the holy, which is taught from one end of the Scriptures to the other; not, indeed, of such a nature that an "irresistible grace" *compels* the opposing will of man (of course not), but so that that will of man which receives and loves the commands of God is *produced* only by God's grace [OLSHAUSEN—a testimony all the more valuable, given in spite of *Lutheran* prejudice]. **30. I and my Father are one** —Our language admits not of the precision of the original in this great saying. *"Are"* is in the *masculine* gender—"we (two persons) are"; while *"one"* is *neuter*—*"one thing."* Perhaps *"one interest"* expresses, as nearly as may be, the purport of the saying. There seemed to be some contradiction between His saying they had been given by His Father into *His own* hands, out of which they could not be plucked, and then saying that none could pluck them out of *His Father's* hands, as if they had not been given *out of* them. 'Neither *have they,*' says He; 'though He has given them to Me, they are as much in His own almighty hands as ever—they *cannot be,* and when given to Me they *are not,* given away from Himself; for HE AND I HAVE ALL IN COMMON.' Thus it will be seen, that, though *oneness of essence* is not the precise thing here affirmed, that truth is *the basis of what is affirmed,* without which it would not be true. And Augustine was right in saying the *"We are"* condemns the *Sabellians* (who denied the *distinction of Persons* in the Godhead), while the *"one"* (as explained) condemns the *Arians* (who denied the unity of their essence). **31. Then the Jews took up stones again to stone Him**—and for precisely the same thing as before (ch. 8:58, 59). **32. Many good works have I showed you**—i.e., works of pure benevolence (as in Acts 10:38, "Who went about doing good . . ."; see Mark 7:37). **from my Father**—not so much by His power, but as directly *commissioned by Him to do them*. This He says to meet the imputation of unwarrantable assumption of the divine prerogatives [LUTHARDT]. **for which of those works do ye stone me?**—"are ye stoning (i.e., going to stone) me?" **33. for a blasphemy**—whose legal punishment was stoning (Lev. 24:11-16). **thou, being a man**—i.e., a man only. **makest thyself God**—Twice before they understood Him to advance the same claim, and both times they prepared themselves to avenge what they took to be the insulted honor of God, as here, in the way directed by their law (ch. 5:18; 8:59). **34-36. Is it not written in your law**—in Psalm 82:6, respecting judges or magistrates. **Ye are gods**—being the *official representatives* and *commissioned agents* of God. **If he called them gods unto whom the word of God came . . . Say ye of him whom the Father hath sanctified and sent into the world, Thou blasphemest**—The whole force of this reasoning, which has been but in part seized by the commentators, lies in what is said of the two parties compared. The *comparison* of Himself with mere men, divinely commissioned, is intended to show [as NEANDER well expresses it] that the idea of a communication of the Divine Majesty to human nature was by no means foreign to the revelations of the Old Testament; but there is also a *contrast* between Himself and all merely human representatives of God—the one *"sanctified by the Father and sent into the world";* the other, *"to whom the word of God [merely] came,"* which is expressly designed to prevent His being massed up with them as only one of many human officials of God. *It is never said of Christ* that "the word of the Lord came to Him"; whereas this is the well-known formula by which the divine commission, even to the highest of *mere men*, is expressed, as John the Baptist (Luke 3:2). The reason is that given by the Baptist himself (see on ch. 3:31). The contrast is between those "to whom the word of God came"—men of the earth, earthy, who were merely privileged to get a divine *message* to utter (if prophets), or a divine *office* to discharge (if judges)—and "Him whom (not being of the earth at all) *the Father sanctified* (or set apart), and *sent into the world,"* an expression *never used of any merely human messenger of God, and used only of Himself*. **because, I said, I am the Son of God**—It is worthy of special notice that our Lord *had not said*, in so many words, that He was the Son of God, on this occasion. But He had said what beyond doubt amounted to it—namely, that He gave His sheep eternal life, and none could pluck them out of His hand; that He had got them from His Father, in whose hands, though given to Him, they still remained, and out of whose hand none could pluck them; and that they were *the indefeasible property of both*, inasmuch as "He and His Father were one." Our Lord considers all this as just saying of Himself, "I am the Son of God"—*one nature* with Him, yet mysteriously *of Him*. The parenthesis (vs. 35), "and the Scripture cannot be broken," referring to the terms used of magistrates in the 82d Psalm, has an important

bearing on the *authority* of the living oracles. "The Scripture, as the expressed will of the unchangeable God, is itself unchangeable and indissoluble" [OLSHAUSEN]. (Cf. Matt. 5:17.) **37-39. though ye believe not me, believe the works**—There was in Christ's words, independently of any miracles, a self-evidencing truth, majesty and grace, which those who had any spiritual susceptibility were unable to resist (ch. 7:46; 8:30). But, for those who wanted this, "the works" were a mighty help. When these failed, the case was desperate indeed. **that ye may know and believe that the Father is in me, and I in him**—thus reiterating His claim to essential *oneness with the Father*, which He had only *seemed* to soften down, that He might calm their rage and get their ear again for a moment. **39. Therefore they sought again to take him**—true to their original understanding of His words, for they saw perfectly well that He *meant* to "make Himself God" throughout all this dialogue. **he escaped out of their hand**—(See on Luke 4:30; ch. 8:59). **40-42. went away again beyond Jordan . . . the place where John at first baptized**—(See on ch. 1:28). **41. many resorted to him**—on whom the ministry of the Baptist had left permanent impressions. **John did no miracle, but all things John spake of this man were true**—what they now heard and saw in Jesus only confirming in their minds the divinity of His forerunner's mission, though unaccompanied by any of His Master's miracles. And thus, "many believed on Him there."

CHAPTER 11

Vss. 1-46. LAZARUS RAISED FROM THE DEAD—THE CONSEQUENCES OF THIS. **1. of Bethany**—at the east side of Mount Olivet. **the town of Mary and her sister Martha**—thus distinguishing it from the other Bethany, "beyond Jordan." (See on ch. 1: 28; 10:40.) **2. It was that Mary who anointed the Lord with ointment . . .**—This, though not recorded by our Evangelist till ch. 12:3, was so well known in the teaching of all the churches, according to our Lord's prediction (Matt. 26:13), that it is here alluded to by anticipation, as the most natural way of identifying her; and she is first named, though the younger, as the more distinguished of the two. She "anointed THE LORD," says the Evangelist—led doubtless to the use of this term here, as he was about to exhibit Him illustriously as the *Lord of Life*. **3-5. his sisters sent unto him, saying, Lord, he whom thou lovest is sick**—a most womanly appeal, yet how reverential, to the known affection of her Lord for the patient. (See vss. 5, 11.) "Those whom Christ loves are no more exempt than others from their share of earthly trouble and anguish: rather are they bound over to it more surely" [TRENCH]. **4. When Jesus heard that, he said, This sickness is not unto death**—to *result* in death—**but for the glory of God, that the Son of God may be glorified thereby**—i.e., by this glory of God. (See *Gr.*) Remarkable language this, which from creature lips would have been intolerable. It means that the glory of GOD manifested in the resurrection of dead Lazarus would be shown to be the glory, *personally* and immediately, of THE SON. **5. Jesus loved Martha and her sister and Lazarus**—what a picture!—one that in every age has attracted the admiration of the whole Christian Church. No wonder that those miserable skeptics who have carped at the ethical system of the Gospel, as not embracing private friendships in the list of its virtues, have been referred to the Saviour's peculiar regard for this family as a triumphant refutation, if such were needed. **6. When he heard he was sick, he abode two days still ... where he was**—at least twenty-five miles off. Beyond all doubt this was just to let things come to their worst, in order to display His glory. But how trying, meantime, to the faith of his friends, and how unlike the way in which love to a dying friend usually shows itself, on which it is plain that Mary reckoned. But the ways of *divine* are not as the ways of *human* love. Often they are the reverse. When His people are sick, in body or spirit; when their case is waxing more and more desperate every day; when all hope of recovery is about to expire—just then and therefore it is that "*He abides two days still in the same place where He is.*" Can they still hope against hope? Often they do not; but "this is their infirmity." For it is His chosen style of acting. We have been well taught it, and should not *now* have the lesson to learn. From the days of Moses was it given sublimely forth as the character of His grandest interpositions, that "the Lord will judge His people and repent Himself for His servants"—*when He seeth that their power is gone* (Deut. 32:36). **7-10. Let us go into Judea again**—He was now in Perea, "beyond Jordan." **8. His disciples say unto him, Master, the Jews of late sought ...**—lit., 'were (just) now seeking' "to stone thee" (ch. 10:31). **goest thou thither again?**—*to certain death,* as vs. 16 shows they thought. **9. Jesus answered, Are there not twelve hours in the day?**—(See on ch. 9:4). Our Lord's day had now reached its eleventh hour, and having till now "walked in the day," He would not *mistime* the remaining and more critical part of His work, which would be as fatal, He says, as omitting it altogether; for "if *a man* (so He speaks, putting Himself under the same great law of duty as all other men—if a man) walk in the night, he stumbleth, because there is no light in him." **11-16. Our friend Lazarus sleepeth; but I go that I may wake him out of sleep**—Illustrious title! "*Our friend* Lazarus." To *Abraham only* is it accorded in the Old Testament, and not till *after his death,* (II Chron. 20:7; Isa. 41:8, to which our attention is called in the New Testament (Jas. 2:23). When Jesus came in the flesh, His forerunner applied this name, in a certain sense, to himself (ch. 3:29); and into the same fellowship the Lord's chosen disciples are declared to have come (ch. 15: 13-15). "The phrase here employed, 'our friend Lazarus,' means more than 'he whom *Thou* lovest' in vs. 3, for it implies that Christ's affection was *reciprocated* by Lazarus" [LAMPE]. Our Lord had been told only that Lazarus was "sick." But the change which his two days' delay had produced is here tenderly alluded to. Doubtless, His spirit was all the while with His dying, and now dead "friend." The symbol of "sleep" for *death* is common to all languages, and familiar to us in the Old Testament. In the New Testament, however, a higher meaning is put into it, in relation to believers in Jesus (see on I Thess. 4:14), a sense hinted at, and clearly, in Psalm 17:15 [LUTHARDT]; and the "awaking out of sleep" acquires a corresponding sense far transcending bare resuscitation. **12. if he sleep, he shall do well**—lit., "be preserved"; i.e., recover. 'Why then go to Judea?' **14. Then said Jesus unto them plainly, Lazarus is dead**—'Sleep [says BENGEL, beautifully] is the death of the saints, in the language of heaven; but this language the disciples

here understood not; incomparable is the generosity of the divine manner of discoursing, but such is the slowness of men's apprehension that Scripture often has to descend to the more miserable style of human discourse; cf. Matthew 16:11.' **15. I am glad for your sakes I was not there**—This certainly implies that if He had been present, Lazarus would not have died; not because He could not have resisted the importunities of the sisters, but because, in presence of the personal Life, death could not have reached His friend [LUTHARDT]. "It is beautifully congruous to the divine decorum that in presence of the Prince of Life no one is ever said to have died" [BENGEL]. **that ye may believe**—This is added to explain His "gladness"' at not having been present. His friend's death, as such, could not have been to Him "joyous"; the sequel shows it was "grievous"; but *for them* it was safe. Phil. 3:1). **16. Thomas, ... called Didymus**—or "the twin." **Let us also go, that we may die with him**—lovely spirit, though tinged with some sadness, such as reappears at ch. 14:5, showing the tendency of this disciple to take the *dark* view of things. On a memorable occasion this tendency opened the door to downright, though but momentary, unbelief (ch. 20:25). Here, however, though alleged by many interpreters there is nothing of the sort. He perceives clearly how this journey to Judea will end, as respects his Master, and not only sees in it peril to themselves, as they all did, but feels as if he could not and cared not to survive his Master's sacrifice to the fury of His enemies. It was that kind of affection which, living only in the light of its Object, cannot contemplate, or has no heart for life, without it. **17-19. when Jesus came, he found that he had lain in the grave four days**—If he died on the day the tidings came of his illness—and was, according to the Jewish custom, buried the same day (see JAHN's *Archæology,* and vs. 39; Acts 5:5, 6, 10)—and if Jesus, after two days' farther stay in Perea, set out on the day following for Bethany, some ten hours' journey, that would make out the four days; the first and last being incomplete [MEYER]. **18. Bethany was nigh Jerusalem, about fifteen furlongs**—rather less than two miles; mentioned to explain the visits of sympathy noticed in the following words, which the proximity of the two places facilitated. **19. many of the Jews came to Martha and Mary to comfort them**—Thus were provided, in a most natural way, so many witnesses of the glorious miracle that was to follow, as to put the fact beyond possible question. **20-22. Martha, as soon as she heard that Jesus was coming, went and met him**—true to the *energy* and *activity* of her character, as seen in Luke 10:38-42. (See *Notes* there.) **but Mary sat ... in the house**—equally true to her *placid* character. These undesigned touches not only charmingly illustrate the minute *historic fidelity* of both narratives, but their *inner harmony.* **21. Then said Martha ... Lord, if thou hadst been here, my brother had not died**—As Mary afterwards said the same thing (vs. 32), it is plain they had made this very natural remark to each other, perhaps many times during these four sad days, and not without having their confidence in His love at times overclouded. Such trials of faith, however, are not peculiar to them. **22. But I know that even now ...**—Energetic characters are usually sanguine, the rainbow of hope peering through the drenching cloud. **whatsoever thou wilt ask of God, God will give it thee**—i.e., 'even to the restoration of my dead brother to life,' for that plainly is her meaning, as the sequel shows. **23-27. Jesus saith unto her, Thy brother shall rise again**—purposely expressing Himself in general terms, to draw her out. **24. Martha said,... I know that he shall rise again ... at the last day**—'But are we never to see him in life till then?' **25. Jesus said, I am the resurrection and the life**—*'The whole power to restore, impart, and maintain* life, resides in Me.' (See on ch. 1:4; 5:21.) What higher claim to supreme divinity than this grand saying can be conceived? **he that believeth in me, though ... dead ... shall he live**—i.e., The believer's death shall be swallowed up in life, and his life shall never sink into death. As death comes by sin, it is His to dissolve it; and as life flows through His righteousness, it is His to communicate and eternally maintain it (Rom. 5:21). The temporary separation of soul and body is here regarded as not even interrupting, much less impairing, the new and everlasting life imparted by Jesus to His believing people. **Believest thou this?**—Canst thou take this in? **27. Yea,... I believe that thou art the Christ, the Son of God ...**—i.e., And having *such* faith in Thee, I can believe all which that comprehends. While she had a glimmering perception that Resurrection, in every sense of the word, belonged to the Messianic office and Sonship of Jesus, she means, by this way of expressing herself, to cover much that she felt her ignorance of—as no doubt belonging to Him. **28-32. The Master is come and calleth for thee**—The narrative does not give us this interesting detail, but Martha's words do. **29. As soon as she heard that, she arose quickly**—affection for her Lord, assurance of His sympathy, and His hope of interposition, putting a spring into her distressed spirit. **31. The Jews ... followed her ... to the grave**—Thus *casually* were provided witnesses of the glorious miracle that followed, *not prejudiced,* certainly, *in favor* of Him who wrought it. **to weep there**—according to Jewish practice, for some days after burial. **fell at his feet**—more impassioned than her sister, though her words were fewer. (See on vs. 21.) **33-38. When Jesus ... saw her weeping, and the Jews ... weeping ..., he groaned in the spirit**—the tears of Mary and her friends acting sympathetically upon Jesus, and drawing forth His emotions. What a vivid and beautiful outcoming of His *real* humanity! The word here rendered "groaned" does not mean "sighed" or "grieved," but rather "powerfully checked his emotion"—made a visible effort to restrain those tears which were ready to gush from His eyes. **and was troubled**—rather, "troubled himself" (*Margin*); referring probably to this visible difficulty of repressing His emotions. **34. Where have ye laid him? ... Lord, come and see**—Perhaps it was to retain composure enough to ask this question, and on receiving the answer to proceed with them to the spot, that He checked Himself. **35. Jesus wept**—This beautifully conveys the sublime brevity of the two original words; else "*shed tears*" might have better conveyed the difference between the word here used and that twice employed in vs. 33, and there properly rendered "weeping," denoting the loud wail for the dead, while that of Jesus consisted of *silent tears*. Is it for nothing that the Evangelist, some *sixty years* after it occurred, holds up to all ages with such touching brevity the sublime spectacle of *the Son of God in tears?* What a seal of His perfect oneness with us in the most redeeming feature of our stricken humanity! But was there nothing in those tears beyond sorrow for human suffering and

death? Could these *effects* move Him without suggesting the *cause?* Who can doubt that in His ear every feature of the scene proclaimed that stern law of the Kingdom, "*The wages of sin is death,*" and that this element in His visible emotion underlay all the rest? **36. Then said the Jews, Behold how he loved him!**—We thank you, O ye visitors from Jerusalem, for this spontaneous testimony to the *human* tenderness of the Son of God. **37. And**—rather "But"—**some ... said, Could not this man, which opened the eyes of the blind, have caused that this man should not have died?**—The former exclamation came from the better-feeling portion of the spectators; this betokens a measure of suspicion. It hardly goes the length of attesting the miracle on the blind man; but 'if (as everybody says) He did that, why could He not also have kept Lazarus alive?' As to the restoration of the dead man to life, they never so much as thought of it. But *this disposition to dictate to divine power, and almost to peril our confidence in it upon its doing our bidding, is not confined to men of no faith.* **38. Jesus again groaning in himself**—i.e., as at vs. 33, checked or repressed His rising feelings, in the former instance, of sorrow, here of righteous indignation at their unreasonable unbelief; (cf. Mark 3:5) [WEBSTER and WILKINSON]. But here, too, struggling emotion was deeper, now that His eye was about to rest on the spot where lay, in the still horrors of death, His *friend.* **a cave**—the cavity, natural or artificial, of a rock. This, with the number of condoling visitors from Jerusalem, and the costly ointment with which Mary afterwards anointed Jesus at Bethany, all go to show that the family was in good circumstances. **39-44. Jesus said, Take ye away the stone**—spoken to the attendants of Martha and Mary; for it was a work of no little labor [GROTIUS]. According to the Talmudists, it was forbidden to open a grave after the stone was placed upon it. Besides other dangers, they were apprehensive of legal impurity by contact with the dead. Hence they avoided coming nearer a grave than four cubits [MAIMONIDES in LAMPE]. But He who touched the leper, and the bier of the widow of Nain's son, rises here also above these Judaic memorials of evils, every one of which He had come to roll away. *Observe here what our Lord did Himself, and what He made others do.* As Elijah himself repaired the altar on Carmel, arranged the wood, cut the victim, and placed the pieces on the fuel, but made the bystanders fill the surrounding trench with water, that no suspicion might arise of fire having been secretly applied to the pile (I Kings 18:30-35); so our Lord would let the most skeptical see that, without laying a hand on the stone that covered His friend, He could recall him to life. But what could be done by human hand He orders to be done, reserving only to Himself what transcended the ability of all creatures. **Martha, the sister of ... the dead**—and as such the proper guardian of the precious remains; the relationship being *here* mentioned to account for her venturing gently to remonstrate against his exposure, in a state of decomposition, to eyes that had loved him so tenderly in life. **Lord, by this time he stinketh, for he hath been dead four days**—(See on vs. 17). It is wrong to suppose from this [as LAMPE and others do] that, like the bystanders, she had not thought of his restoration to life. But the glimmerings of hope which she cherished from the first (vs. 22), and which had been brightened by what Jesus said to her (vss. 23-27), had suffered a momentary eclipse on the proposal to expose the now sightless corpse. *To such fluctuations all real faith is subject in dark hours.* (See, for example, the case of Job.) **40. Jesus saith unto her, Said I not unto thee, that if thou wouldest believe, thou shouldest see the glory of God?**—He had not said those very words, but this was the scope of all that He had uttered to her about His life-giving power (vss. 23, 25, 26); a gentle yet emphatic and most instructive rebuke: 'Why doth the restoration of life, even to a decomposing corpse, seem hopeless in the presence of the Resurrection and the Life? Hast thou yet to learn that "if thou canst believe, all things are possible to him that believeth?"' (Mark 9:23). **41. Jesus lifted up his eyes**—an expression marking His calm solemnity. (Cf. ch. 17:1.) **Father, I thank thee that thou hast heard me**—rather, "heardest Me," referring to a specific prayer offered by Him, probably on intelligence of the case reaching Him (vss. 3,4); for His living and loving oneness with the Father was maintained and manifested in the flesh, not merely by the spontaneous and uninterrupted outgoing of Each to Each in spirit, but by specific actings of faith and exercises of prayer about each successive case as it emerged. He prayed [says LUTHARDT well] not for what He wanted, but for the manifestation of what He had; and having the bright consciousness of the answer in the felt liberty to ask it, and the assurance that it was at hand, He gives thanks for this with a grand simplicity before performing the act. **42. And**—rather "Yet"—**I knew that thou hearest me always, but because of the people that stand by I said it, that they might believe that thou hast sent me**—Instead of praying now, He simply gives thanks for answer to prayer offered ere He left Perea, and adds that His doing even this, in the audience of the people, was not from any doubt of the prevalency of His prayers in any case, but to show the people that *He did nothing without His Father, but all by direct communication with Him.* **43, 44. and when he had thus spoken, he cried with a loud voice**—On one other occasion only did He this—on the *cross.* His last utterance was a "loud cry" (Matt. 27:50). "He shall not cry," said the prophet, nor, in His ministry, did He. What a sublime contrast is this "loud cry" to the magical "whisperings" and "mutterings" of which we read in Isaiah 8:19; 29:4 [as GROTIUS remarks]! It is second only to the grandeur of that voice which shall raise all the dead (ch. 5:28, 29; I Thess. 4:16). **44. Jesus saith unto them, Loose him and let him go**—Jesus will no more do this Himself than roll away the stone. The one was the necessary *preparation* for resurrection, the other the necessary *sequel* to it. THE LIFE-GIVING ACT ALONE HE RESERVES TO HIMSELF. So *in the quickening of the dead to spiritual life, human instrumentality is employed first to prepare the way, and then to turn it to account.* **45, 46. many . . . which . . . had seen . . . believed. . . . But some . . . went . . . to the Pharisees and told them what Jesus had done**—the two classes which continually reappear in the Gospel history; nor is there ever any great work of God which does not produce both. "It is remarkable that on each of the three occasions on which our Lord raised the dead, a large number of persons was assembled. In two instances, the resurrection of the widow's son and of Lazarus, these were all witnesses of the miracle; in the third (of Jairus' daughter) they were necessarily cognizant of it. Yet this important circumstance is in each case only incidentally noticed by the historians, not

put forward or appealed to as a proof of their veracity. In regard to this miracle, we observe a greater degree of preparation, both in the provident arrangement of events, and in our Lord's actions and words than in any other. The preceding miracle (cure of the man born blind) is distinguished from all others by the open and formal investigation of its facts. And both these miracles, the most public and best attested of all, are related by John, who wrote long after the other Evangelists" [WEBSTER and WILKINSON]. **47-54. What do we? for this man doeth many miracles.**—'While we trifle, "this man," by His "many miracles," will carry all before Him; the popular enthusiasm will bring on a revolution, which will precipitate the Romans upon us, and our all will go down in one common ruin.' What a testimony to the reality of our Lord's miracles, and their resistless effect, from His bitterest enemies! **Caiaphas . . . prophesied that Jesus should die for that nation.**—He meant nothing more than that the way to prevent the apprehended ruin of the nation was to make a sacrifice of the Disturber of their peace. But in giving utterance to this suggestion of political expediency, he was so guided as to give forth a divine prediction of deep significance; and God so ordered it that it should come from the lips of the high priest for that memorable year, the recognized head of God's visible people, whose ancient office, symbolized by the Urim and Thummim, was to decide in the last resort, all vital questions as the oracle of the divine will. **and not for that nation only . . .**—These are the Evangelist's words, not Caiaphas'. **53. they took council together to put him to death**—Caiaphas but expressed what the party was secretly wishing, but afraid to propose. **Jesus . . . walked no more openly among the Jews**—How could He, unless He had wished to die before His time? **near to the wilderness**—of Judea. **a city called Ephraim**—between Jerusalem and Jericho. **55-57. passover . . . at hand . . . many went . . . up . . . before the passover, to purify themselves**—from any legal uncleanness which would have disqualified them from keeping the feast. This is mentioned to introduce the graphic statement which follows. **56. sought they for Jesus, and spake among themselves, as they stood in the temple**—giving forth the various conjectures and speculations about the probability of His coming to the feast. **that he will not come**—The form of this question implies the opinion that He *would* come. **57. chief priests and the Pharisees had given a commandment that if any knew where he were, he should show it, that they might take him**—This is mentioned to account for the conjectures whether He would come, in spite of this determination to seize Him.

CHAPTER 12

Vss. 1-11. THE ANOINTING AT BETHANY. (See on Matt. 26:6-13.) **1-8. six days before the passover**—i.e., on the sixth day before it; probably after sunset on *Friday* evening, or the commencement of the Jewish *sabbath* preceding the passover. **2. Martha served**—This, with what is afterwards said of Mary's way of honoring her Lord, is so true to the character in which those two women appear in Luke 10:38-42, as to constitute one of the strongest and most delightful confirmations of the truth of both narratives. (See also on ch. 11:20.) **Lazarus**

... **sat at the table**—*"Between the raised Lazarus and the healed leper* [Simon, Mark 14:3], *the Lord probably sits as between two trophies of His glory"* [STIER]. **3. spikenard**—or pure *nard,* a celebrated aromatic (Song of Sol. 1:12). **anointed the feet of Jesus**—and "poured it on His head" (Matt. 26:7; Mark 14:3). The only use of this was to refresh and exhilarate—a grateful compliment in the East, amidst the closeness of a heated atmosphere, with many guests at a feast. Such was the form in which Mary's love to Christ, at so much cost to herself, poured itself out. **4. Judas ... who should betray him**—For the reason why this is here mentioned, see on Matthew 26:6. **5. three hundred pence**—about $50. **6. had the bag**—the purse. **bare what was put therein**—not, bare it off by theft, though that he did; but simply, had charge of its contents, was treasurer to Jesus and the Twelve. How worthy of notice is this arrangement, by which an avaricious and dishonest person was not only taken into the number of the Twelve, but entrusted with the custody of their little property! The purposes which this served are obvious enough; but it is further noticeable, that the remotest hint was never given to the eleven of His true character, nor did the disciples most favored with the intimacy of Jesus ever suspect him, till a few minutes before he voluntarily separated himself from their company—for ever! **7. said Jesus, Let her alone, against the day of my burying hath she done this**—not that she thought of His burial, much less reserved any of her nard to anoint her dead Lord. But as the time was so near at hand when that office would have to be performed, *and she was not to have that privilege even after the spices were brought for the purpose* (Mark 16:1), He lovingly *regards it as done now.* **8. the poor always ... with you**—referring to Deuteronomy 15:11. **but me ... not always**—a gentle hint of His approaching departure. He adds (Mark 14:8), *"She hath done what she could,"* a noble testimony, embodying a principle of immense importance. "Verily, I say unto you, Wheresoever this Gospel shall be preached in the whole world, there shall also this, that this woman hath done, be told for a memorial of her" (Matt. 26:13; Mark 14:9). "In the act of love done to Him she had erected to herself an eternal monument, as lasting as the Gospel, the eternal word of God. From generation to generation this remarkable prophecy of the Lord has been fulfilled; and even we, in explaining this saying of the Redeemer, of necessity contribute to its accomplishment" [OLSHAUSEN]. "Who but Himself had the power to ensure to any work of man, even if resounding in his own time through the whole earth, an imperishable remembrance in the stream of history? Behold once more here, the majesty of His royal judicial supremacy in the government of the world, in this, Verily I say unto you" [STIER]. Beautiful are the lessons here: (1) *Love to Christ transfigures the humblest services.* All, indeed, who have themselves a heart value its least outgoings beyond the most costly mechanical performances; but how does it endear the Saviour to us to find Him endorsing the principle as His own standard in judging of character and deeds!

What though in poor and humble guise
　Thou here didst sojourn, cottage-born,
Yet from Thy glory in the skies
　Our earthly gold Thou didst not scorn.
For Love delights to bring her best,
And where Love is, that offering evermore is blest.

Love on the Saviour's dying head
　Her spikenard drops unblam'd may pour,
May mount His cross, and wrap Him dead
　In spices from the golden shore.
　　　　　　　　KEBLE

(2) Works of *utility* should never be set in opposition to the promptings of self-sacrificing *love,* and the sincerity of those who do so is to be suspected. Under the mask of concern for the poor at home, how many excuse themselves from all care of the perishing heathen abroad. (3) Amidst conflicting duties, that which our "hand (*presently*) findeth to do" is to be preferred, and even a less duty *only to be done now* to a greater *that can be done at any time.* (4) "If there be first a willing mind, it is accepted according to that a man hath, and not according to that he hath not" (II Cor. 8:12).—"She hath done what she could." (5) As Jesus beheld in spirit the universal diffusion of His Gospel, while His lowest depth of humiliation was only approaching, so He regards *the facts of His earthly history* as constituting *the substance of this Gospel,* and the relation of them as just the "preaching of this Gospel." Not that preachers are to confine themselves to a bare narration of these facts, but that they are to make their whole preaching turn upon them as its grand center, and derive from them its proper vitality; all that goes before this in the Bible being but the *preparation* for them, and all that follows but the *sequel.* **9-11.** Crowds of the Jerusalem Jews hastened to Bethany, not so much to see Jesus, whom they knew to be there, as to see dead Lazarus alive; and this, issuing in their accession to Christ, led to a plot against the life of Lazarus also, as the only means of arresting the triumphs of Jesus (see vs. 19)—to such a pitch had these chief priests come of diabolical determination to shut out the light from themselves, and quench it from the earth!

12-19. CHRIST'S TRIUMPHAL ENTRY INTO JERUSALEM. (See on Matt. 21:1-9; and Luke 19:29-36. **12. On the next day**—the Lord's day, or Sunday (see on vs. 1); the tenth day of the Jewish month Nisan, on which the paschal lamb was set apart to be "kept up until the 14th day of the same month, when the whole assembly of the congregation of Israel were to kill it in the evening" (Exod. 12:3, 6). Even so, from the day of this solemn entry into Jerusalem, "Christ our Passover" was virtually set apart to be "sacrificed for us" (I Cor. 5:7). **16. when Jesus was glorified, then remembered they that these things were written of him ...**—The Spirit, descending on them from the glorified Saviour at Pentecost, opened their eyes suddenly to the true sense of the Old Testament, brought vividly to their recollection this and other Messianic predictions, and to their unspeakable astonishment showed them that they, and all the actors in these scenes, had been unconsciously fulfilling those predictions.

20-36. SOME GREEKS DESIRE TO SEE JESUS—THE DISCOURSE AND SCENE THEREUPON. **20-22. Greeks**—Not Grecian Jews, but Greek proselytes to the Jewish faith, who were wont to attend the annual festivals, particularly this primary one, the Passover. **The same came therefore to Philip ... of Bethsaida**—possibly as being from the same quarter. **saying, Sir, we would see Jesus**—certainly in a far better sense than Zaccheus (Luke 19:3). Perhaps He was then in that part of the temple court to which Gentile proselytes had no access. "These men from the *west* represent, at the end of Christ's life, what the wise men from the *east* represented at its beginning; but those come to the cross of the King, even as these to His manger" [STIER]. **22. Philip . . . telleth Andrew**—As follow townsmen of Bethsaida (ch. 1:44), these two seem to have drawn to each other. **Andrew and Philip tell Jesus**—The minuteness of these details, while they add to the graphic force of the narrative, serves to prepare us for something important to come out of this introduction. **23-26. Jesus answered them, The hour is come that the Son of man should be glorified**—i.e., They would see Jesus, would they? Yet a little moment, and they shall see Him so as now they dream not of. The middle wall of partition that keeps them out from the commonwealth of Israel is on the eve of breaking down, "and I, if I be lifted up from the earth, shall draw all men unto Me"; I see them "flying as a cloud, and as doves to their cotes"—a glorious event that will be for the Son of man, by which this is to be brought about. It is His *death* He thus sublimely and delicately alluded to. Lost in the scenes of triumph which this desire of the Greeks to see Him called up before His view, He gives no direct answer to their petition for an interview, but sees the cross which was to bring them gilded with glory. **24. Except a corn of wheat fall into the ground and die, it abideth alone; but if it die, it bringeth forth much fruit**—The *necessity* of His death is here brightly expressed, and its proper operation and fruit—*life springing forth out of death*—imaged forth by a beautiful and deeply significant law of the vegetable kingdom. For a double reason, no doubt, this was uttered—to explain what he had said of His death, as the hour of His own glorification, and to sustain His own Spirit under the agitation which was mysteriously coming over it in the view of that death. **25. He that loveth his life in this world shall lose it; and he that hateth his life in this world shall keep it unto life eternal**—(See on Luke 9:24) Did our Lord mean to exclude Himself from the operation of the great principle here expressed—*selfrenunciation the law of self-preservation*; and its converse, *self-preservation the law of self-destruction?* On the contrary, as He became Man to exemplify this fundamental law of the Kingdom of God in its most sublime form, so the very utterance of it on this occasion served to sustain His own Spirit in the double prospect to which He had just alluded. **26. If any man serve me, let him follow me; and where I am, there shall also my servant be: If any man serve me, him will my Father honour**—*Jesus here claims the same absolute subjection to Himself, as the law of men's exaltation to honor, as He yielded to the Father.* **27, 28. Now is my soul troubled**—He means at the prospect of His death, just alluded to. Strange view of the Cross this, immediately after representing it as the hour of His glory! (vs. 23.) But the two views naturally meet, and blend into one. It was the Greeks, one might say, that troubled Him. Ah! they shall see Jesus, but *to Him* it shall be a costly sight. **and what shall I say?**—He is in a strait betwixt two. The death of the cross was, and could not but be, appalling to His spirit. But to shrink from absolute subjection to the Father, was worse still. In asking Himself, "What shall I say?" He seems as if thinking aloud, feeling His way between two dread alternatives, looking both of them sternly in the face, measuring, weighing them, in order that the choice actually made might be seen, *and even by himself the more vividly felt*, to be a profound, deliberate, spontaneous election. **Father, save me from this hour**—

To take this as a question—"Shall I say, Father, save me . . ."—as some eminent editors and interpreters do, is unnatural and jejune. It is a real petition, like that in Gethsemane, "Let this cup pass from Me"; only whereas *there* He prefaces the prayer with an "If it be possible," *here* He follows it up with what is tantamount to that—"Nevertheless for this cause came I unto this hour." The sentiment conveyed, then, by the prayer, in both cases, is twofold: (1) that only one thing could reconcile Him to the death of the cross—its being His Father's will He should endure it—and (2) that in this view of it He yielded Himself freely to it. *What He recoils from is not subjection to His Father's will: but to show how tremendous a self-sacrifice that obedience involved,* He first asks the Father to save Him from it, and then signifies how perfectly He knows that He is there for the very purpose of enduring it. Only by letting these mysterious words speak their full meaning do they become intelligible and consistent. As for those who see *no bitter elements in the death of Christ*—nothing beyond mere dying—what can they make of such a scene? and when they place it over against the feelings with which thousands of His adoring followers have welcomed death for His sake, how can they hold Him up to the admiration of men? **28. Father, glorify thy name**—by a present testimony. **I have both glorified it**—referring specially to the voice from heaven at His *baptism*, and again at His *transfiguration.* **and will glorify it again**—i.e., in the yet future scenes of His still deeper necessity; although this promise was a present and sublime testimony, which would irradiate the clouded spirit of the Son of man. **29-33. The people therefore that stood by, said, It thundered; others, An angel spake to him**—some hearing only a sound, others an articulate, but to them unintelligible voice. **30. Jesus . . . said, This voice came not because of me, but for your sakes**—i.e., probably, to correct the unfavorable impressions which His momentary agitation and mysterious prayer for deliverance may have produced on the bystanders. **31. Now is the judgment of this world**—the world that "crucified the Lord of glory" (I Cor. 2:8), considered as a vast and complicated kingdom of Satan, breathing his spirit, doing his work, and involved in his doom, which Christ's death by its hands irrevocably sealed. **now shall the prince of this world be cast out**—How differently is that fast-approaching "hour" regarded in the kingdoms of darkness and of light! "The hour of relief; from the dread Troubler of our peace—how near it is! Yet a little moment, and the day is ours!" So it was calculated and felt in the one region. "Now shall the prince of this world be cast out," is a somewhat different view of the same event. We know who was right. Though yet under a veil, He sees the triumphs of the Cross in unclouded and transporting light. **32. And I, if I be lifted up from the earth, will draw all men unto me**—The "I" here is emphatic—I, taking the place of the world's ejected prince. "If lifted up," means not only *after that I have been lifted up*, but, *through the virtue of that uplifting.* And truly, the death of the Cross, in all its significance, revealed in the light, and borne in upon the heart, by the power of the Holy Ghost, possesses an attraction over the wide world—to civilized and savage, learned and illiterate, alike—which breaks down all opposition, assimilates all to itself, and forms out of the most heterogeneous and discordant materials a kingdom of surpassing glory, whose uniting principle is adoring subjection "to Him that loved them." "Will draw all men 'UNTO ME,'" says He. What lips could venture to utter such a word but His, which "dropt as an honeycomb," whose manner of speaking was evermore in the same spirit of conscious equality with the Father? **33. This he said, signifying what death he should die**—i.e., "by being lifted up from the earth" on "the accursed tree" (ch. 3:14; 8:28). **34. We have heard out of the law**—the scriptures of the Old Testament (referring to such places as Ps. 89:28, 29; 110:4; Dan. 2:44; 7:13, 14). **that Christ**—the Christ "endureth for ever." **and how sayest thou, The Son of Man must be lifted up...**—How can that consist with this "uplifting?" They saw very well both that He was holding Himself up as *the Christ* and *a Christ to die a violent death;* and as that ran counter to all their ideas of the Messianic prophecies, they were glad to get this seeming advantage to justify their unyielding attitude. **35, 36. Yet a little while is the light with you. Walk while ye have the light,...**—Instead of answering their question, He warns them, with mingled majesty and tenderness, against trifling with their last brief opportunity, and entreats them to let in the Light while they have it in the midst of them, that they themselves might be "light in the Lord." In this case, all the clouds which hung around His Person and Mission would speedily be dispelled, while if they continued to hate the light, bootless were all His answers to their merely speculative or captious questions. (See on Luke 13:23.) **36. These things spake Jesus, and departed, and did hide himself from them**—He who spake as never man spake, and immediately after words fraught with unspeakable dignity and love, had to "hide Himself" from His auditors! What then must *they* have been? He retired, probably to Bethany. (The parallels are: Matt. 21:17; Luke 21:37.) **37-41.** It is the manner of this Evangelist alone to record his own reflections on the scenes he describes; but here, having arrived at what was virtually the close of our Lord's public ministry, he casts an affecting glance over the fruitlessness of His whole ministry on the bulk of the now doomed people. **37. though he had done so many miracles**—The word used suggests their *nature* as well as *number*. **38. That the saying of Esaias... might be fulfilled.** This unbelief did not at all set aside the purposes of God, but, on the contrary, fulfilled them. **39-40. Therefore they could not believe, because Esaias said again, He hath blinded their eyes, that they should not see...** That this expresses *a positive divine act,* by which those who wilfully close their eyes and harden their hearts against the truth are judicially *shut up* in their unbelief and impenitence, is admitted by all candid critics [as OLSHAUSEN], though many of them think it necessary to contend that this is in no way inconsistent with the liberty of the human will, which of course it is not. **41. These things said Esaias, when he saw his glory, and spake of him**—a key of immense importance to the opening of Isaiah's vision (Isa. 6), and all similar Old Testament representations. "THE SON is the King Jehovah who rules in the Old Testament and appears to the elect, as in the New Testament. THE SPIRIT, the invisible Minister of the Son, is the Director of the Church and the Revealer in the sanctuary of the heart" [OLSHAUSEN]. **42, 43. among the chief rulers also**—rather, even of the rulers; such as Nicodemus and Joseph. **because of the Pharisees**—i.e., the *leaders* of the sects; for they were of it themselves. **put out of the synagogue**—See on ch. 9:22, 34. **43. they loved the praise of men more than the praise**

of God—"a severe remark, considering that several at least of these persons afterwards boldly confessed Christ. It indicates the displeasure with which God regarded their conduct at this time, and with which He continues to regard similar conduct" [WEBSTER and WILKINSON]. **44-50. Jesus cried**—in a loud tone, and with peculiar solemnity. (Cf. ch. 7:37.) **and said, He that believeth...**—This seems to be a supplementary record of some weighty proclamations, for which there had been found no natural place before, and introduced here as a sort of *summary and winding up* of His whole testimony.

CHAPTER 13

Vss. 1-20. AT THE LAST SUPPER JESUS WASHES THE DISCIPLES' FEET—THE DISCOURSE ARISING THEREUPON. **1. when Jesus knew that his hour was come that he should depart out of this world unto the Father**—On these beautiful euphemisms, see on Luke 9:31, 51. **having loved his own which were in the world, he loved them unto the end**—The meaning is, that on the very edge of His last sufferings, when it might have been supposed that He would be absorbed in His own awful prospects, He was so far from forgetting "His own," who were to be left struggling "in the world" after He had "departed out of it to the Father" (ch. 17:11), that in His care for them He seemed scarce to think of Himself save in connection with them: "Herein is love," not only "enduring to the end," but most affectingly manifested when, judging by a human standard, least to be expected. **2. supper being ended**—rather, being prepared, being served, or, going on; for that it was not "ended" is plain from vs. 26. **the devil having now**—or, "already"—**put into the heart of Judas... to betray him**—referring to the agreement he had *already* made with the chief priests (Luke 22:3-6). **3. Jesus knowing that the Father had given all things into his hands...**—This verse is very sublime, and as a preface to what follows, were we not familiar with it, would fill us with inexpressible surprise. An unclouded perception of His relation to the Father, the commission He held from Him, and His approaching return to Him, possessed His soul. **4, 5. He riseth from supper, and laid aside his**—outer—**garments**—which would have impeded the operation of washing. **and took a towel and girded himself**—assuming a servant's dress. **5. began to wash**—proceeded to wash. *Beyond all doubt the feet of Judas were washed,* as of all the rest. **6-11. Peter saith... Lord, dost thou wash my feet?**—Our language cannot bring out the intensely vivid contrast between the *"Thou"* and the *"my,"* which, by bringing them together, the original expresses, for it is not good English to say, "Lord, *Thou my* feet dost wash?" But *every word* of this question is emphatic. Thus far, and in the question itself, there was nothing but the most profound and beautiful astonishment at a condescension to him quite incomprehensible. Accordingly, though there can be no doubt that already Peter's heart rebelled against it as a thing not to be tolerated, Jesus ministers no rebuke as yet, but only bids him wait a little, and he should understand it all. **7. Jesus answered and said...,, What I do thou knowest not now**—i.e., Such condescension *does* need explanation; it *is* fitted to astonish. **but thou shalt know hereafter**—afterwards, meaning *presently;* though viewed as a general maxim, applicable to all dark sayings in God's

Word, and dark doings in God's providence, these words are full of consolation. **8. Peter saith unto him, Thou shalt never wash . . .**—more emphatically, 'Never shalt Thou wash my feet': i.e., 'That is an incongruity to which I can never submit.' How like the man! **If I wash thee not, thou hast no part with me**—What Peter could not submit to was, that the Master should serve His servant. But *the whole saving work of Christ was one continued series of such services, ending with and consummated by the most self-sacrificing and transcendent of all services:* THE SON OF MAN CAME *not to be ministered unto, but* TO MINISTER, AND TO GIVE HIS LIFE A RANSOM FOR MANY. (See on Mark 10:45.) If Peter then could not submit to let his Master go down so low as to wash his feet, *how should he suffer himself to be served by Him at all?* This is couched under the one pregnant word "wash," which though applicable to the *lower* operation which Peter resisted, is the familiar scriptural symbol of that *higher* cleansing, which Peter little thought he was at the same time virtually putting from him. *It is not humility to refuse what the Lord deigns to do for us, or to deny what He has done,* but it is self-willed presumption—*not rare, however, in those inner circles of lofty religious profession and traditional spirituality, which are found wherever Christian truth has enjoyed long and undisturbed possession.* The truest humility is to receive reverentially, and thankfully to own, the gifts of grace. **9. Lord, not my feet only, but also my hands and my head**—i.e., 'To be severed from Thee, Lord, is death to me: If that be the meaning of my speech, I tread upon it; and if to be washed of Thee have such significance, then not my feet only, but hands, head, and all, be washed!' This artless expression of clinging, life-and-death attachment to Jesus, and felt dependence upon Him for his whole spiritual wellbeing, compared with the similar saying in ch. 6:68, 69 (on which see *Notes*), furnishes such evidence of *historic verity* such as no thoroughly honest mind can resist. **10. He that is washed**—in this *thorough* sense, to express which the word is carefully changed to one meaning to wash *as in a bath*. **needeth not**—to be *so* washed any more. **save to wash his feet**—needeth to do no more than wash his feet (and here the former word is resumed, meaning to wash *the hands or feet*). **but is clean every whit**—as a whole. This sentence is singularly instructive. Of the *two cleansings,* the one points to that which takes place at the *commencement* of the Christian life, embracing *complete absolution from sin as a guilty state,* and *entire deliverance from it as a polluted life* (Rev. 1:5; I Cor. 6:11)—or, in the language of theology, *Justification* and *Regeneration.* This cleansing is effected *once for all,* and is never repeated. The other cleansing, described as that of "the feet," is *such as one walking from a bath quite cleansed still needs, in consequence of his contact with the earth.* (Cf. Exod. 30:18, 19.) It is the *daily* cleansing which we are taught to seek, when in the spirit of adoption we say, "Our Father which art in heaven—*forgive us our debts*"; and, when burdened with the sense of manifold shortcomings—as what tender spirit of a Christian is not?—is it not a relief to be permitted thus to wash our feet after a day's contact with the earth? This is not to call in question the completeness of our past justification. Our Lord, while graciously insisting on washing Peter's feet, refuses to extend the cleansing farther, that the symbolical instruction intended to be conveyed might not be marred. **and**

ye are clean—in the first and *whole* sense. **but not all**—important, as showing that Judas, instead of being as true-hearted a disciple as the rest at first, and merely *falling away* afterwards—as many represent it—*never experienced that cleansing at all which made the others what they were.* **12-15. Know ye what I have done?**—i.e., its intent. The question, however, was put merely to summon their attention to His own answer. **13. Ye call me Master**—Teacher—**and Lord**—*learning* of Him in the one capacity, *obeying* Him in the other. **and ye say well, for so I am**—The conscious dignity with which this claim is made is remarkable, following immediately on His laying aside the towel of service. Yet what is this whole history but a succession of such astonishing contrast from first to last? **14. If I then**—the Lord—**have washed your feet**—the servants'—**ye**—but fellow servants—**ought to wash one another's feet**—not in the narrow sense of a literal washing, profanely caricatured by popes and emperors, but by the very humblest *real* services one to another. **16, 17. The servant is not greater than his lord . . .**—an oft-repeated saying (Matt. 10: 24, etc.). **If ye know these things, happy are ye if ye do them**—a hint that even among real Christians the *doing* of such things would come lamentably short of the *knowing.* **18, 19. I speak not of you all**—the "happy *are* ye," of vs. 17, being on no supposition applicable to Judas. **I know whom I have chosen**—in the *higher* sense. **But that the scripture may be fulfilled**—i.e., one has been added to your number, by no accident or mistake, who is none of Mine, but just that he might fulfil his predicted destiny. **He that eateth bread with me**—"did eat of *my bread*" (Ps. 41:9), as one of My family; admitted to the nearest familiarity of discipleship and of social life. **hath lifted up his heel against me**—turned upon Me, adding *insult* to injury. (Cf. Heb. 10:29.) In the Psalm the immediate reference is to Ahithophel's treachery against David (II Sam. 17), one of those scenes in which the parallel of his story with that of His great Antitype is exceedingly striking. "The eating bread derives a fearful meaning from the participation in the sacramental supper, a meaning which must be applied for ever to all unworthy communicants, as well as to all betrayers of Christ who eat the bread of His Church" [STIER, with whom, and others, we agree in thinking that Judas partook of the Lord's Supper.] **19. I tell you before . . . that when it comes to pass, ye may believe**—and it came to pass when they deeply needed such confirmation. **20. He that receiveth whomsoever I send, receiveth me . . .**—(See on Matt. 10: 40). The connection here seems to be that despite the dishonor done to Him by Judas, and similar treatment awaiting themselves, they were to be cheered by the assurance that their office, even as His own, was divine.

21-30. THE TRAITOR INDICATED—HE LEAVES THE SUPPER ROOM. **21. When Jesus had thus said, he was troubled in spirit, and testified, and said, Verily, verily, I say unto you, One of you shall betray me**—The announcement of vs. 18 seems not to have been plain enough to be quite apprehended, save by the traitor himself. He will therefore speak it out in terms not to be misunderstood. But how much it cost Him to do this, appears from the "trouble" that came over His "spirit"—visible emotion, no doubt—before He got it uttered. What wounded susceptibility does this disclose, and what exquisite delicacy in His social intercourse with the Twelve, to whom He cannot, without an effort, break the subject! **22. the disciples looked one on another, doubting of whom he spake**—Further intensely interesting particulars are given in the other Gospels: (1) "They were exceeding sorrowful" (Matt. 26:22). (2) "They began to inquire among themselves which of them it was that should do this thing" (Luke 22:23). (3) "They began to say unto Him one by one, Is it I, and another, Is it I?" (Mark 14:19). Generous, simple hearts! They abhorred the thought, but, instead of putting it on others, each was only anxious to purge *himself,* and know if *he* could be the wretch. Their putting it at once to Jesus Himself, as knowing doubtless who was to do it, was the best, as it certainly was the most spontaneous and artless evidence of their innocence. (4) Jesus, apparently while this questioning was going on, added, "The Son of man goeth as it is written of Him, but woe unto that man by whom the Son of man is betrayed! It had been good for that man if he had not been born" (Matt. 26:24). (5) "Judas," *last of all,* "answered and said, *Lord, is it I*?" evidently feeling that when all were saying this, if he held his peace, that of itself would draw suspicion upon him. To prevent this the question is wrung out of him, but perhaps, amidst the stir and excitement at the table, in a half-suppressed tone as we are inclined to think the answer also was—"Thou hast said" (Matt. 26:25), or possibly by little more than a sign; for from vs. 28 it is evident that till the moment when he went out, he was not openly discovered. **23-26. there was leaning on Jesus' bosom one of his disciples, whom Jesus loved**—Thus modestly does our Evangelist denote himself, as reclining next to Jesus at the table. **Peter ... beckoned to him to ask who it should be of whom he spake**—reclining probably at the corresponding place on the other side of Jesus. **25. He then lying**—rather leaning over on Jesus' bosom—**saith**—*in a whisper,* "Lord, who is it?" **26. Jesus answered**—*also inaudibly,* the answer being communicated to Peter perhaps from behind—**He ... to whom I shall give a sop when I have dipped it**—a piece of the bread soaked in the wine or the sauce of the dish; one of the ancient ways of testifying peculiar regard; cf. vs. 18, "*he that eateth bread with Me.*" **And when he had dipped ... he gave it to Judas ...**—Thus the sign of Judas' treachery was an affecting expression, and the last, of the Saviour's wounded love! **27-30. after the sop Satan entered into him**—Very solemn are these brief hints of the successive steps by which Judas reached the climax of his guilt. "The devil had already put it into his heart to betray his Lord." Yet who can tell what struggles he went through ere he brought himself to carry that suggestion into effect? Even after this, however, his compunctions were not at an end. With the thirty pieces of silver already in his possession, he seems still to have quailed—and can we wonder? When Jesus stooped to wash his feet, it may be the last struggle was reaching its crisis. But that word of the Psalm, about "one that ate of his bread who would lift up his heel against Him," probably all but turned the dread scale, and the still more explicit announcement, that one of those sitting with Him at the table should betray Him, would beget the thought, "I am detected; it is now too late to draw back." At that moment the sop is given; offer of friendship is once more made—and how affectingly! But already "Satan has *entered into him,*" and though the Saviour's act might seem enough to recall him even yet, hell is now in his bosom, and he says within himself, "The die is cast; now let me go through

with it; fear, begone!" (See on Matt. 12:43-45.) Then said Jesus unto him, That thou doest, do quickly—i.e., Why linger here? Thy presence is a restraint, and thy work stands still; thou hast the wages of iniquity, go work for it! **28-29. no man ... knew for what intent he spake this unto him ... some thought ... Jesus ... said ..., But what we need ... or, ... give ... to the poor**—a very important statement, as showing how carefully Jesus had kept the secret, and Judas his hypocrisy, to the last. **30. He then, having received the sop, went immediately out**—severing himself *for ever* from that holy society with which he never had any spiritual sympathy. **and it was night**—but far blacker night in the soul of Judas than in the sky over his head.

31-38. DISCOURSE AFTER THE TRAITOR'S DEPARTURE—PETER'S SELF-CONFIDENCE—HIS FALL PREDICTED. **31. when he was gone out, Jesus said, Now is the Son of man glorified**—These remarkable words plainly imply that up to this moment our Lord had spoken *under a painful restraint,* the presence of a traitor within the little circle of His holiest fellowship on earth preventing the free and full outpouring of His heart; as is evident, indeed, from those oft-recurring clauses, "Ye are not all clean," "I speak not of you all," etc. "Now" the restraint is removed, and the embankment which kept in the mighty volume of living waters having broken down, they burst forth in a torrent which only ceases on His leaving the supper room and entering on the next stage of His great work—the scene in the Garden. But with what words is the silence first broken on the departure of Judas? By no reflections on the traitor, and, what is still more wonderful, by no reference to the dread character of His own approaching sufferings. He does not even name them, save by announcing, as with a burst of triumph, that the hour of His *glory* has arrived! And what is very remarkable, in five brief clauses He repeats this word "glorify" *five times,* as if to His view a coruscation of glories played at that moment about the Cross. (See on ch. 12:23.) **God is glorified in him**—the glory of Each reaching its zenith in the Death of the Cross! **32. If God be glorified in him, God shall also**—in return and reward of this highest of all services ever rendered to Him, or capable of being rendered—**glorify him in himself, and ... straightway glorify him**—referring now to the Resurrection and Exaltation of Christ *after* this service was over, including all the honor and glory then put upon Him, and that will for ever encircle Him as Head of the new creation. **33-35. Little children**—From the height of His own glory He now descends, with sweet pity, to His "little children," *all now His own.* This term of endearment, nowhere else used in the Gospels, and once only employed by Paul (Gal. 4: 19), is appropriated by the beloved disciple himself, who no fewer than seven times employs it in his first Epistle. **Ye shall seek me**—feel the want of Me. **as I said to the Jews**—ch. 7:34; 8:21. But oh in what a different sense! **34. a new commandment I give unto you, That ye love one another; as I have loved you, that ye also love one another**—This was the *new* feature of it. Christ's love to His people in giving His life a ransom for them was altogether new, and consequently as a Model and Standard for theirs to one another. It is not, however, something transcending the great moral law, which is "the *old* commandment" (I John 2:7, and see on Mark 12:28-33), but that law *in a new and peculiar form.* Hence it is said to be both *new* and *old* (I John 2:7, 8). **35. By this shall all men know that ye are my disciples**—the disciples of Him who laid down His life for those He loved. **if ye have love one to another**—for My sake, and as one in Me; for to *such* love men outside the circle of believers know right well they are entire strangers. Alas, how little of it there is even within this circle! **36-38. Peter said**—seeing plainly in these directions how to behave themselves, that He was indeed going from them. **Lord, whither goest thou?**—having hardly a glimmer of the real truth. **Jesus answered, . . . thou canst not follow me now, but thou shalt follow me afterwards**—How different from what He said to the Jews: "Whither I go *ye cannot come*" (ch. 8:21). **37. why not . . . now? I will lay down my life for thy sake**—He seems now to see that it was *death* Christ referred to as what would sever Him from them, but is not staggered at following Him thither. Jesus answered, **38. Wilt thou lay down thy life for my sake?**—In this repetition of Peter's words there is deep though affectionate irony, and this Peter himself would feel for many a day after his recovery, as he retraced the painful particulars. **Verily . . . The cock . . .**—See on Luke 22:31-34.

CHAPTER 14

Vss. 1-31. Discourse at the Table, after Supper. We now come to that portion of the evangelical history which we may with propriety call its *Holy of Holies.* Our Evangelist, like a consecrated priest, alone opens up to us the view into this sanctuary. It is the record of the last moments spent by the Lord in the midst of His disciples before His passion, when words full of heavenly thought flowed from His sacred lips. All that His heart, glowing with love, had still to say to His friends, was compressed into this short season. At first (from ch. 13:31) the intercourse took the form of conversation; sitting at table, they talked familiarly together. But when (14:31) the repast was finished, the language of Christ assumed a loftier strain; the disciples, assembled around their Master, listened to the words of life, and seldom spoke a word (only ch. 16:17, 29). At length, in the Redeemer's sublime intercessory prayer, His full soul was poured forth in express petitions to His heavenly Father on behalf of those who were His own. It is a peculiarity of these last chapters, that they treat almost exclusively of the most profound relations—as that of the Son to the Father, and of both to the Spirit, that of Christ to the Church, of the Church to the world, and so forth. Moreover, a considerable portion of these sublime communications surpassed the point of view to which the disciples had at that time attained; hence the Redeemer frequently repeats the same sentiments in order to impress them more deeply upon their minds, and, because of what they still did not understand, points them to the Holy Spirit, who would remind them of all His sayings, and lead them into all truth (14:26)" [OLSHAUSEN]. **1. Let not your heart be troubled . . .**—What myriads of souls have not these opening words cheered, in deepest gloom, since first they were uttered! **ye believe in God**—absolutely. **believe also in me**—i.e., Have the *same trust* in Me. What less, and what else, can these words mean? And if so, what a demand to make by one sitting familiarly with them at the supper table! Cf. the saying in ch. 5:17, for which

the Jews took up stones to stone Him, as "making himself equal with God" (vs. 18). But it is no *transfer of our trust from its proper Object;* it is but *the concentration of our trust in the Unseen and Impalpable One upon His Own Incarnate Son,* by which that trust, instead of the distant, unsteady, and too often cold and scarce real thing it otherwise is, acquires a conscious reality, warmth, and power, which makes all things new. *This is Christianity in brief.* **2. In my Father's house are many mansions** —and so room for all, and a place for each. **if not, I would have told you**—i.e., I would tell you so at once; I would not deceive you. **I go to prepare a place for you**—to obtain for you a right to be there, and to possess your "place." **3. I will come again and receive you unto myself**—*strictly,* at His Personal appearing; but in a secondary and comforting sense, to each individually. Mark again the claim made:—to come again to receive His people *to Himself,* that where *He is* there they may be also. *He thinks it ought to be enough to be assured that they shall be where He is and in His keeping.* **4-7. whither I go ye know . . . Thomas saith, Lord, we know not whither thou goest . . ., Jesus saith, I am the way . . .**—By saying this, He meant rather to draw out their inquiries and reply to them. Christ is "THE WAY" to the Father—"no man cometh unto the Father but by Me"; He is "THE TRUTH" of all we find in the Father when we get to Him, "For in Him dwelleth all the fulness of the Godhead bodily" (Col. 2:9), and He is all "THE LIFE" that shall ever flow to us and bless us from the Godhead thus approached and thus manifested in Him—"this is the true God and eternal life" (I John 5:20). **7. from henceforth**—now, or from this time, understand. **8-12.** The substance of this passage is that the Son is the ordained and perfect manifestation of the Father, that His own word for this ought to His disciples to be enough; that if any doubts remained His words ought to remove them (see on ch. 10:37, 38); but yet that these works of His were designed merely to aid weak faith, and would be repeated, nay exceeded, by His disciples, in virtue of the power He would confer on them after His departure. His miracles the apostles wrought, though wholly in His name and by His power, and the "greater" works—not in degree but in kind—were the conversion of thousands in a day, by His Spirit accompanying them. **13, 14. whatsoever ye . . . ask in my name**—as Mediator—**that will I do**—as Head and Lord of the kingdom of God. This comprehensive promise is emphatically repeated in vs. 14. **15-17. If ye love me, keep my commandments. And I will pray the Father . . .**—This connection seems designed to teach that the proper temple for the indwelling Spirit of Jesus is a heart filled with that love to Him which lives actively for Him, and so this was the fitting preparation for the promised gift. **he shall give you another Comforter**—a word used only by John; in his *Gospel* with reference to the Holy Spirit, in his *First Epistle* (2:1), with reference to Christ Himself. Its proper sense is an "advocate," "patron," "helper." In this sense it is plainly meant of Christ (I John 2:1), and in this sense it comprehends all the *comfort* as well as *aid* of the Spirit's work. The Spirit is here promised as One who would *supply Christ's own place* in His absence. **that he may abide with you for ever**—never go away, as Jesus was going to do in the body. **17. whom the world cannot receive . . .**—(See I Cor. 2:14). **he dwelleth with you, and shall be in you**—Though the proper fulness of both these was yet future, our Lord, by using both the present and the future, seems plainly to say that they *already* had the germ of this great blessing. **18-20. I will not leave you comfortless**—in a bereaved and desolate condition; or (as *Margin*) "orphans." **I will come to you**—"I come" or "am coming" to you; i.e., plainly *by the Spirit*, since it was to make His departure to be *no bereavement*. **19. world seeth**—beholdeth—**me no more, but ye see** —behold—**me**—His bodily presence, being all the sight of Him which "the world" ever had, or was capable of, it "beheld Him no more" after His departure to the Father; but by the coming of the Spirit, the presence of Christ was not only *continued* to His spiritually enlightened disciples, but rendered *far more efficacious and blissful* than His bodily presence had been *before* the Spirit's coming. **because I live**—not '*shall* live,' only when raised from the dead; for it is His unextinguishable, divine life of which He speaks, in view of which His *death and resurrection* were but as shadows passing over the sun's glorious disk. (Cf. Luke 24: 5; Rev. 1:18, "the Living One"). And this grand saying Jesus uttered *with death immediately in view*. What a brightness does this throw over the next clause, "ye shall live also!" "Knowest thou not," said LUTHER to the King of Terrors, "that thou didst devour the Lord Christ, but wert obliged to give Him back, and wert devoured of Him? So thou must leave me undevoured because I abide in Him, and live and suffer for His name's sake. Men may hunt me out of the world—that I care not for—but I shall not on that account abide in death. I shall live with my Lord Christ, since I know and believe that *He liveth!*" [quoted in STIER]. **20. At that day** —of the Spirit's coming. **ye shall know that I am in my Father, ye in me, I in you**—(See on ch. 17: 22, 23). **21. He that hath my commandments and keepeth them . . .**—(See on vss. 15, 16). **my Father and I will love him**—Mark the sharp line of distinction here, not only between the Divine Persons but the actings of love in Each respectively, towards true 'disciples. **22. Judas saith . . . , not Iscariot**— Beautiful parenthesis this! The traitor being no longer present, we needed not to be told that this question came not from *him*. But it is as if the Evangelist had said, "A very different Judas from the traitor, and a very different question from any that he would have put. Indeed [as one in STIER says], we never read of Iscariot that he entered in any way into his Master's words, or ever put a question even of rash curiosity (though it may be he did, but that nothing from *him* was deemed fit for immortality in the Gospels but his name and treason). **"how . . . manifest thyself to us, and not to the world**—a most natural and proper question, founded on vs. 19, though interpreters speak against it as *Jewish*. **23. we will come and make our abode with him**—Astonishing statement! In the Father's "coming" He "refers to the revelation of Him *as a Father* to the soul, which does not take place till the Spirit comes into the heart, teaching it to cry, *Abba*, Father" [OLSHAUSEN]. The "abode" means a permanent, eternal stay! (Cf. Lev. 26:11, 12: Ezek. 37:26, 27; II Cor. 6:16; and *contrast* Jer. 14: 8). **25, 26. he shall teach you all things, and bring all to . . . remembrance, whatsoever I have said unto you**—(See on vss. 16, 17). As the Son came in *the Father's* name, so the Father shall send the Spirit "*in My name*," says Jesus, i.e., with like divine *power* and *authority* to reproduce in their souls what Christ taught them, "bringing to living consciousness what lay like slumbering germs in their minds" [OLSHAUSEN]. *On this rests the credibility*

and ultimate divine authority of THE GOSPEL HISTORY. The whole of what is here said of THE SPIRIT is decisive of His divine *personality*. "He who can regard all the *personal* expressions, applied to the Spirit in these three chapters ("teaching," "reminding," "testifying," "coming,'" "convincing,'" "guiding," "speaking," "hearing," "prophesying," "taking") as being no other than a long drawnout figure, deserves not to be recognized even as an interpreter of intelligible words, much less an expositor of Holy Scripture" [STIER]. **27. Peace I leave with you, my peace I give unto you**—If the two preceding verses sounded like a note of preparation for drawing the discourse to a close, this would sound like a farewell. But oh, how different from ordinary adieus! It *is* a parting word, but of richest import, the customary "peace" of a parting friend sublimed and transfigured. As "the Prince of Peace" (Isa. 9:6) He brought it into flesh, carried it about in His Own Person ("My peace") died to make it ours, left it as the heritage of His disciples upon earth, implants and maintains it by His Spirit in their hearts. Many a legacy is "left" that is never "given" to the legatee, many a gift destined that never reaches its proper object. But Christ is the Executor of His own Testament; the peace He *"leaves"* He *"gives";* Thus all is secure. **not as the world giveth**—in contrast with the world, He gives *sincerely, substantially, eternally*. **28. If ye loved me, ye would rejoice, because I said, I go unto the Father, for my Father is greater than I**—These words, which Arians and Socinians perpetually quote as triumphant evidence against the proper Divinity of Christ, really yield no intelligible sense on their principles. Were a holy *man* on his deathbed, beholding his friends in tears at the prospect of losing him, to say, "Ye ought rather to joy than weep for me, and would if ye really loved me, "the speech would be quite natural. But if they should ask him, *why* joy at his departure was more suitable than sorrow, would they not start back with astonishment, if not horror, were he to reply, *"Because my Father is greater than I?"* Does not this strange speech from Christ's lips, then, *presuppose such teaching* on His part as would make it extremely difficult for them to think He could gain anything by departing to the Father, and make it necessary for Him to say expressly that there was a sense in which He *could* do so? Thus, this startling explanation seems plainly intended to correct such misapprehensions as might arise from the emphatic and reiterated teaching of *His proper equality with the Father*—as if so Exalted a Person were incapable of any accession by transition from this dismal scene to a cloudless heaven and the very bosom of the Father—and by assuring them that this was *not* the case, to make them forget their own sorrow in His approaching joy. **30, 31. Hereafter I will not talk much with you**—'I have a little more to say, but My work hastens apace, and the approach of the adversary will cut it short.' **for the prince of this world**—See on ch. 12:31. **cometh**— with hostile intent, for a last grand attack, having failed in His first formidable assault (Luke 4) from which he "departed [only] *for a season*" (vs. 13). **and hath nothing in me**—*nothing of His own*—*nothing to fasten on*. Glorious saying! The *truth* of it is, that which makes the Person and Work of Christ the life of the world (Heb. 9:14; I John 3:5; II Cor. 5:21. **31. But that the world may know that I love the Father . . .**—The sense must be completed thus: 'But to the Prince of the world, though he has nothing in Me, I shall yield Myself up even unto death, that the world may know that I love and obey the Father, whose commandment it is that I give My life a ransom for many.' **Arise, let us go hence**—Did they then, at this stage of the discourse, leave the supper room, as some able interpreters conclude? If so, we think our Evangelist would have mentioned it: see ch. 18:1, which seems clearly to intimate that they then only left the upper room. But what do the words mean if not this? We think it was the dictate of that saying of earlier date, "I have a baptism to be baptized with, and *how am I straitened till it be accomplished!*"—a spontaneous and irrepressible expression of the deep eagerness of His spirit to get into the conflict, and that if, as is likely, it was responded to somewhat too literally by the guests who hung on His lips, in the way of a movement to depart, a wave of His hand, would be enough to show that He had yet more to say ere they broke up; and that disciple, whose pen was dipped in a love to his Master which made *their* movements of small consequence save when essential to the illustration of *His* words, would record this little outburst of the Lamb hastening to the slaughter, in the very midst of His lofty discourse; while the effect of it, if any, upon His hearers, as of no consequence, would naturally enough be passed over.

CHAPTER 15

Vss. 1-27. Discourse at the Supper table Continued. **1-8.** *The spiritual oneness of Christ and His people, and His relation to them as the Source of all their spiritual life and fruitfulness,* are here beautifully set forth by a figure familiar to Jewish ears (Isa. 5:1, etc.). **I am the true vine**—of whom the vine of *nature* is but a shadow. **my Father is the husbandman**—the great Proprietor of the vineyard, the Lord of the spiritual kingdom. (It is surely unnecessary to point out the claim to *supreme divinity* involved in this.) **2. Every branch in me that beareth not fruit ... every branch that beareth fruit**—As in a fruit tree, some branches may be *fruitful,* others quite *barren,* according as there is a *vital connection* between the branch and the stock, or *no vital connection;* so the disciples of Christ may be spiritually fruitful or the reverse, according as they are *vitally* and *spiritually connected* with Christ, or but *externally* and *mechanically attached* to Him. The fruitless He "taketh away" (see on vs. 6); the fruitful He "purgeth" (cleanseth, pruneth)—*stripping it,* as the husbandman does, *of what is rank* (Mark 4:19), "that it may bring forth more fruit"; a process often painful, but no less needful and beneficial than in the natural husbandry. **3. Now**—rather, 'Already,' **ye are clean through**—by reason of—**the word I have spoken to you**—already in a purified, fruitful condition, in consequence of the long action upon them of that searching "word" which was "as a refiner's fire" (Mal. 3:2, 3). **4. Abide in me, and I in you; as the branch cannot bear fruit of itself, except it abide in the vine ...**—As all spiritual fruitfulness had been ascribed to the mutual *inhabitation,* and living, active *interpenetration* (so to speak) of Christ and His disciples, so here the keeping up of this vital connection is made essential to continued fruitfulness. **5. without me**—apart, or vitally disconnected from Me. **ye can do nothing**—spiritually, acceptably. **6. If a man abide not in me, he is cast forth as a branch ... withered ... cast into the fire ... burned**—The one proper use of the vine is

to *bear fruit;* failing this, it is good for one other thing—*fuel.* (See Ezek. 15:1-5.) How awfully striking the figure, in this view of it! **7. If ye abide in me, and my words ... in you**—Mark the change from the inhabitation of *Himself* to that of His *words,* paving the way for the subsequent exhortations (vss. 9, 10). **ask what ye will, and it shall be done unto you**—because this indwelling of His words in them would secure the harmony of their askings with the divine will. **8. glorified that ye bear much fruit**—not only from His delight in it for its own sake, but as from 'the juices of the Living Vine.' **so shall ye be my disciples**—*evidence* your discipleship. **9-11. continue ye in my love**—not, 'Continue to love Me,' but, 'Continue in the possession and enjoyment of My love to you'; as is evident from the next words. **10. If ye keep my commandments, ye shall abide in my love**—the obedient spirit of true discipleship cherishing and attracting the continuance and increase of Christ's love; and this, He adds, was the secret even of His own abiding in His Father's love! **12-16. That ye love one another ...**—(See on ch. 13:34, 35). **13. Greater love hath no man than this, that a man lay down his life for his friends**—The emphasis lies not on "friends," but on *"laying down his life"* for them; i.e., 'One can show no greater regard for those dear to him than to give his life for them, and this is the love ye shall find in Me.' **14. Ye are my friends, if ye do whatsoever I command you**—hold yourselves in absolute subjection to Me. **15. Henceforth I call you not servants**—i.e., *in the sense explained* in the next words; for servants He still calls them (vs. 20), and they delight to call themselves so, in the sense of being "under law to Christ" (I Cor. 9:20). **the servant knoweth not what his lord doeth**—knows nothing of his master's *plans* and *reasons,* but simply receives and executes his orders. **but ... friends, for all things that I have heard of my Father I have made known unto you**—admitted you to free, unrestrained fellowship, keeping back nothing from you which I have received to communicate. (Cf. Gen. 18:17; Ps. 25: 14; Isa. 50:4.) **16. Ye have not chosen me, but I ... you**—a wholesale memento after the lofty things He had just said about their mutual indwelling, and the unreservedness of the friendship they had been admitted to. **ordained**—appointed—**you, that ye should go and bring forth fruit**—i.e., give yourselves to it. **and that your fruit should remain**—showing itself to be an imperishable and ever growing principle. (Cf. Prov. 4:18; II John 8.) **that whatsoever ye shall ask ...**—(See on vs. 7). **17-21.** The substance of these important verses has occurred more than once before. (See on Matt. 10: 34-36; Luke 12:49-53 etc.). **22-25.** (See on ch. 9: 39-41.) **If I had not come and spoken unto them, they had not had sin**—*comparatively* none; all other sins being light compared with the rejection of the Son of God. **now they have no cloak for their sin**—rather, 'pretext.' **24. If I had not done ... the works which none other ... did**—(See on ch. 12:37). **25. that the word might be fulfilled ..., They hated me without a cause**—quoted from the Messianic Psalm 69:4, applied also in the same sense in ch. 2:17; Acts 1:20; Romans 11:9, 10; 15:3. **26, 27.**—(See on ch. 14:16, 17). **27. ye also shall bear witness**—rather, "are witnesses"; with reference indeed to their *future* witness-bearing, but putting the emphasis upon their *present* ample opportunities for acquiring their qualifications for that great office, inasmuch as they had been "with Him from the beginning." (See on Luke 1:2.)

CHAPTER 16

Vss. 1-33. DISCOURSE AT THE SUPPER TABLE CONCLUDED. **1-5. These things have I spoken unto you, that ye should not be offended**—both the *warnings* and the *encouragements* just given. **2. They shall put you out of the synagogue**—(ch. 9:22; 12:42). **the time cometh, that whosoever killeth you will think that he doeth God service**—The words mean *religious service*—'that he is offering a service to God.' (So Saul of Tarsus, Gal. 1:13, 14; Phil. 3:6.) **4. these things I said not . . . at**—from—**the beginning**—He *had* said it pretty early (Luke 6: 22), but not quite as in vs. 2. **because I was with you. 5. But now I go my way to him that sent me**—While He was with them, the world's hatred was directed chiefly against Himself; but His departure would bring it down upon them as His representatives. **and none of you asketh me, Whither goest thou?**—They *had* done so in a sort (ch. 13:36; 14:5); but He wished more intelligent and eager inquiry on the subject. **6, 7. But because I have said these things . . . , sorrow hath filled your heart**—Sorrow had too much paralyzed them, and He would rouse their energies. **7. It is expedient for you that I go away**—

> My Saviour, can it ever be
> That I should gain by losing thee?
> KEBLE

Yes. **for if I go not away, the Comforter will not come unto you, but if I depart, I will send him unto you**—(See on ch. 7:39; 14:16). **8. And when he is come, he will . . .**—This is one of the passages most pregnant with thought in the profound discourses of Christ; with a few great strokes depicting all and every part of the ministry of the Holy Ghost in the world—His operation with reference to individuals as well as the mass, on believers and unbelievers alike [OLSHAUSEN]. **he will reprove**—This is too weak a word to express what is meant. *Reproof* is indeed implied in the term employed, and doubtless the word begins with it. But *convict* or *convince* is the thing intended; and as the one expresses the work of the Spirit on the *unbelieving* portion of mankind, and the other on the *believing*, it is better not to restrict it to either. **9. Of sin, because they believe not on me**—As all sin has its root in unbelief, so the most aggravated form of unbelief is the rejection of Christ. The Spirit, however, in fastening this truth upon the conscience, does not *extinguish*, but, on the contrary, does *consummate and intensify, the sense of all other sins*. **10. Of righteousness, because I go to my Father, and ye see me no more**—Beyond doubt, it is *Christ's personal righteousness* which the Spirit was to bring home to the sinner's heart. The evidence of this was to lie in the great *historical fact*, that He had "gone to His Father and was no more visible to men":—for if His claim to be the Son of God, the Saviour of the world, had been a lie, how should the Father, who is "a jealous God," have raised such a blasphemer from the dead and exalted him to His right hand? But if He was the "Faithful and True Witness," the Father's "Righteous Servant," "His Elect, in whom His soul delighted," then was His departure to the Father, and consequent disappearance from the view of men, but the fitting consummation, the august reward, of all that He did here below, the seal of His mission, the glorification of the testimony which He bore on earth, by the reception of its Bearer to

the Father's bosom. This triumphant vindication of Christ's *rectitude* is to us divine evidence, bright as heaven, that He is indeed the Saviour of the world, God's Righteous Servant to justify many, because He bare their iniquities (Isa. 53:11). Thus the Spirit, in this clause, is seen convincing men that there is in Christ perfect relief under the sense of *sin* of which He had before convinced them; and so far from mourning over His absence from us, as an irreparable loss, we learn to glory in it, as the evidence of His perfect acceptance on our behalf, exclaiming with one who understood this point, "Who shall lay anything to the charge of God's elect? It is God that justifieth: Who is he that condemneth? It is Christ that died; *yea, rather, that is risen again, who is even at the right hand of God . . .*" (Rom. 8:33, 34). **11. Of judgment, because the prince of this world is judged**—By supposing that the *final judgment* is here meant, the point of this clause is, even by good interpreters, quite missed. The statement, "The prince of this world is *judged*," means, beyond all reasonable doubt, the same as that in ch. 12:31, "Now shall the prince of this world be *cast out"*; and both mean that his dominion over men, or his power to enslave and so to ruin them, is destroyed. The death of Christ "judged" or judicially overthrew him, and he was thereupon "cast out" or expelled from his usurped dominion (Heb. 2:14: I John 3:8; Col. 2:15). Thus, then, the Spirit shall bring home to men's conscience: (1) the sense of *sin,* consummated in the rejection of Him who came to "take away the sin of the world"; (2) the sense of perfect relief in the *righteousness* of the Father's Servant, now fetched from the earth that spurned Him to that bosom where from everlasting He had dwelt; and (3) the sense of emancipation from the fetters of Satan, whose *judgment* brings to men liberty to be holy, and transformation out of servants of the devil into sons and daughters of the Lord Almighty. To one class of men, however, all this will carry *conviction* only; they "will not come to Christ"—revealed though He be to them as the life-giving One—that they may have life. Such, abiding voluntarily under the dominion of the prince of this world, are *judged in his judgment,* the visible consummation of which will be at the great day. To another class, however, this blessed teaching will have another issue—translating them out of the kingdom of darkness into the kingdom of God's dear Son. **12-15. when he, the Spirit of truth, is come . . . he shall not speak of himself**—i.e., *from* Himself, but, like Christ Himself, "what He hears," what is given Him to communicate. **he will show you things to come**—referring specially to those revelations which, in the Epistles partially, but most fully in the Apocalypse, open up a vista into the Future of the Kingdom of God, whose horizon is the everlasting hills. **14. He shall glorify me; for he shall receive of mine and show it unto you**—Thus the whole design of the Spirit's office is to glorify Christ—not in His own Person, for this was done by the Father when He exalted Him to His own right hand—but in the view and estimation of men. For this purpose He was to *"receive of Christ"*—all the truth relating to Christ—*"and show it unto them,"* or make them to discern it in its own light. The *subjective* nature of the Spirit's teaching—the discovery to the souls of men of what is Christ *outwardly*—is here very clearly expressed; and, at the same time, the vanity of looking for revelations of the Spirit which shall do anything beyond throwing light in the soul upon what Christ Himself is, and taught, and did upon earth. **15. All things that the Father hath are mine** —a plainer expression than this of *absolute community* with the Father in all things cannot be conceived, though the "all things" here have reference to the things of the Kingdom of Grace, which the Spirit was to receive that He might show it to us. We have here a wonderful glimpse into the *inner relations of the Godhead.* **16-22. A little while, and ye shall not see me; and again a little while, and ye shall see me, because I go to the Father**—The joy of the world at their not seeing Him seems to show that His removal from them by *death* was what He meant; and in that case, their joy at again seeing Him points to their transport at His reappearance amongst them on His *Resurrection,* when they could no longer doubt His identity. At the same time the sorrow of the widowed Church in the absence of her Lord in the heavens, and her transport at His personal return, are certainly here expressed. **23-28. In that day**—of the dispensation of the Spirit (as in ch. 14:20). **ye shall ask**—inquire of—**me nothing**—by reason of the fulness of the Spirit's teaching (ch. 14:26; 16:13; and cf. I John 2: 27). **24. Hitherto have ye asked nothing in my name**—for "prayer *in the name of* Christ, and prayer to Christ, presuppose His *glorification*" [OLS-HAUSEN]. **ask**—when I am gone, "in My name." **25. in proverbs**—in obscure language, opposed to "showing plainly"—i.e., by the Spirit's teaching. **26. I say not . . ., I will pray the Father for you**— as if He were not of *Himself* disposed to aid you: Christ does pray the Father for His people, but not for the purpose of inclining an *unwilling* ear. **27. For the Father himself loveth you, because ye have loved me**—This love of theirs is that which is called forth by God's eternal love in the gift of His Son *mirrored* in the hearts of those who believe, and resting on His dear Son. **28. I came forth from the Father . . .**—i.e., 'And ye are right, for I have indeed so come forth,and shall soon return whence I came.' This echo of the truth, alluded to in the preceding verse, seems like *thinking aloud,* as if it were grateful to His own spirit on such a subject and at such an hour. **29, 30. His disciples said, . . . now speakest thou plainly, and speakest no proverb**—hardly more so than before; the time for perfect plainness was yet to come; but having caught a glimpse of His meaning (it was nothing more), they eagerly express their satisfaction, as if glad to make anything of His words. How touchingly does this show both the simplicity of their hearts and the infantile character of their faith! **31-33. Jesus answered . . ., Do ye now believe?**—i.e., 'It is well ye do, for it is soon to be tested, and in a way ye little expect.' **the hour cometh, yea, is now come, that ye shall be scattered, every man to his own, and shall leave me alone; and yet I am not alone**—A deep and awful sense of *wrong* experienced is certainly expressed here, but how lovingly! That He was not to be utterly deserted, that there was One who would not forsake Him, was to Him matter of ineffable support and consolation; but that He should be without all *human* countenance and cheer, who as Man was exquisitely sensitive to the law of sympathy, would fill themselves with as much *shame,* when they afterwards recurred to it, as the Redeemer's heart in His hour of need with pungent *sorrow.* "I looked for some to take pity, but there was none; and for comforters, but I found none" (Ps. 69:20). **because the Father is with me**—how near, and with what sustaining power, who can express? **33. These things I have**

spoken unto you—not the immediately preceding words, but this whole discourse, of which these were the very last words, and which He thus winds up. **that in me ye might have peace**—in the sublime sense before explained. (See on ch. 14:27.) **In the world ye shall have tribulation**—specially arising from its deadly opposition to those who "are not of the world, but chosen out of the world." So that the "peace" promised was far from an unruffled one. **I have overcome the world**—not only *before* you, but *for* you, that ye may be able to do the same (I John 5:4, 5).

CHAPTER 17

Vss. 1-26. THE INTERCESSORY PRAYER. (See on ch. 14:1.) Had this prayer *not* been recorded, what reverential reader would not have exclaimed, Oh, to have been within hearing of such a prayer as that must have been, which wound up the whole of His past ministry and formed the point of transition to the dark scenes which immediately followed! But here it is, and with such signature of the Lips that uttered it that we seem rather to hear it from Himself than read it from the pen of His faithful reporter. **1-3. These words spake Jesus, and lifted up his eyes**—"John very seldom depicts the gestures or looks of our Lord, as here. But this was an occasion of which the impression was indelible, and the upward look could not be passed over" [ALFORD]. **Father, the hour is come**—See on ch. 13:31, 32. **glorify thy Son**—Put honor upon Thy Son, by countenancing, sustaining, and carrying Him through that "hour." **2. given—gavest—him power over all flesh**—(See on Matt. 11:27; 28:18-20). **give eternal life to as many as . . .**—lit., "to all that which thou hast given him." (See on ch. 6:37-40.) **3. this is**—that—**life eternal, that they might—may know . . .**—This life eternal, then, is not mere conscious and unending existence, but a life of acquaintance with God in Christ (Job 22:21). **thee, the only true God**—the sole personal living God; in glorious contrast equally with heathen *polytheism,* philosophic *naturalism,* and mystic *pantheism.* **and Jesus Christ whom thou hast sent**—This is the only place where our Lord gives Himself this compound name, afterwards so current in apostolic preaching and writing. Here the terms are used in their strict signification—"JESUS," because He "*saves* His people from their sins"; "CHRIST," as *anointed* with the measureless fulness of the Holy Ghost for the exercise of His saving offices (see on Matt. 1:16); "WHOM THOU HAST SENT," in the plenitude of Divine Authority and Power, to save. "The very juxtaposition here of *Jesus Christ* with *the Father* is a proof, by implication, of our Lord's Godhead. The knowledge of *God and a creature* could not be eternal life, and such an association of the one with the other would be inconceivable" [ALFORD]. **4, 5. I have glorified thee on the earth**—rather, "I glorified" (for the thing is conceived as now *past*). **I have finished**—(I finished)—**the work which thou gavest me to do**—It is very important to preserve in the translation the *past* tense, used in the original, otherwise it might be thought that the work already "*finished*" was only what He had done *before uttering that prayer;* whereas it will be observed that our Lord speaks throughout as already beyond this present scene (vs. 12, etc.), and so must be supposed to include in His "finished work" the "decease which He was to accomplish at Jerusalem." **5. And now**—in return. **glorify thou me**—The "*I*

Thee" and *"Thou Me"* are so placed in the original, each beside its fellow, as to show that A PERFECT RECIPROCITY OF SERVICES of the Son to the Father first, and then of the Father to the Son in return, is what our Lord means here to express. **with the glory which I had with thee before the world was** —when "in the beginning the Word was *with God"* (ch. 1:1), "the only-begotten Son *in the bosom of the Father"* (ch. 1:18). With this pre-existent glory, which He veiled on earth, He asks to be reinvested, the design of the veiling being accomplished—not, however, simply as before, but *now in our nature.* **6-8.** From praying for Himself He now comes to pray for His disciples. **I have manifested**—I manifested—**thy name**—His whole character towards mankind. **to the men thou gavest me out of the world** (See on ch. 6:37-40). **8. they ... have known surely that I came out from thee**—(See on ch. 16:30, 31). **9-14. I pray for them**—not as individuals merely, but as representatives of all such in every succeeding age (see on vs. 20). **not for the world**—for they had been given Him *"out of* the world" (vs. 6), and had been already transformed into the very *opposite* of it. The things sought for them, indeed, are applicable only to such. **10. all mine are thine, and thine are mine**— lit., "All My things are Thine and Thy things are Mine." (On this use of the *neuter* gender, see on ch. 6:37-40.) Absolute COMMUNITY OF PROPERTY between the Father and the Son is here expressed as nakedly as words can do it. (See on vs. 5.) **11. I am no more in the world**—(see on vs. 4) **but these are in the world**—i.e., Though My struggles are at an end, theirs are not; though I have gotten beyond the scene of strife, I cannot sever Myself in spirit from them, left behind and only just entering on their great conflict. **Holy Father**—an expression He nowhere else uses. *"Father"* is His wonted appellation, but *"Holy"* is here prefixed, because His appeal was to that perfection of the Father's nature, to "keep" or preserve them from being tainted by the unholy atmosphere of "the world" they were still in. **keep through thine own name**—rather, 'in thy name'; in the exercise of that gracious and holy character for which He was known. **that they may be one**—See on vs. 21. **12. I kept**—guarded—**them in thy name**—acting as Thy Representative on earth. **none of them is lost, but the son of perdition**—It is not implied here that the son of perdition was one of those whom the Father had given to the Son, but rather the contrary (ch. 13:18) [WEBSTER and WILKINSON]. It is just as in Luke 4:26, 27, where we are not to suppose that the woman of *Sarepta* (in Sidon) was one of the widows of *Israel,* nor Naaman the *Syrian* one of the lepers in *Israel,* though the language—the same as here—might *seem* to express it. **son of perdition**—doomed to it (II Thess. 2:3; Mark 14:21). **13. I speak in the world, that they might have my joy fulfilled in themselves**—i.e., Such a strain befits rather the upper sanctuary than the scene of conflict; but I speak so *"in the world,"* that My joy, the joy I experience in knowing that such intercessions are to be made for them by their absent Lord, may be tasted by those who now hear them, and by all who shall hereafter read the record of them,' **15-19. I pray not that thou shouldest take them out of the world**—for that, though it would secure their own safety, would leave the world unblessed by their testimony. **but ... keep them from the evil**—all evil in and of the world. **16. They are not of the world, even as I am not of the world**—(See on ch. 15:18, 19). This is reiterated here, to pave the way for the prayer which

follows. **17. Sanctify them**—As the former prayer, *"Keep* them," was *negative,* asking *protection* for them from the poisonous element which surrounded and pressed upon their renewed nature, so this prayer, *"Sanctify* them," is positive, asking the *advancement and completion* of their begun sanctification. **through**—in—**thy truth**—God's revealed truth, as the medium or element of sanctification; a statement this of immense importance. **thy word is truth**—(Cf. ch. 15:3; Col. 1:5; Eph. 1:13). **18. As thou hast sent**—sentest—**me into the world, even so have I also sent**—sent I also—**them into the world** —As their mission was to carry into effect the purposes of their Master's mission, so our Lord speaks of the *authority* in both cases as *co-ordinate.* **19. And for their sakes I sanctify**—consecrate—**myself, that they also might**—may—**be sanctified**—consecrated. The only difference between the application of the same term to Christ and the disciples is, as applied to Christ, that it means *only* to "consecrate"; whereas, in application to the disciples, it means to consecrate with the *additional idea* of previous sanctification, since nothing but what is holy can be presented as an offering. The whole self-sacrificing work of the disciples appears here as a mere *result* of the offering of Christ [OLSHAUSEN]. **through** 'in—**the truth**—Though the article is wanting in the original here, we are not to translate, as in the margin, "*truly* sanctified"; for the reference seems plainly to be to "the truth" mentioned in vs. 17. (See there.) **20-23. Neither pray I for these alone**—This very important explanation, uttered in condescension to the hearers and readers of this prayer in all time, is meant not merely of what follows, but of the whole prayer. **them also which shall believe**—The majority of the best MSS. read "which believe," all future time being viewed as *present,* while the present is viewed as past and gone. **21. that they all may be one, as thou, Father, art in me, and I in thee, that they may be one in us**—*The indwelling Spirit of the Father and the Son* is the one perfect bond of union, knitting up into a living unity, first all believers amongst themselves; next, this unity into one still higher, with the Father and the Son. (Observe, that Christ *never mixes Himself up with His disciples as He associates Himself with the Father,* but says I in THEM and THEY in US.) **that the world may believe that thou hast sent**—sentest—**me**—So the grand impression upon the world at large, that the mission of Christ is divine, is to be made by *the unity of His disciples.* Of course, then, it must be something that shall be *visible* or perceptible to the world. What is it, then? Not certainly a merely formal, mechanical unity of ecclesiastical machinery. For as that may, and to a large extent does, exist in both the Western and Eastern churches, with little of the Spirit of Christ, yea much, much with which the Spirit of Christ cannot dwell so instead of convincing the world *beyond its own pale* of the divinity of the Gospel, it generates infidelity to a large extent within its own bosom. But the Spirit of Christ, illuminating, transforming, and reigning in the hearts of the genuine disciples of Christ, drawing them to each other as members of one family, and prompting them to loving co-operation for the good of the world—this is what, when sufficiently glowing and extended, shall force conviction upon the world that Christianity is divine. Doubtless, the more that differences among Christians disappear—the more they can agree even in minor matters—the impression upon the world may be expected to be greater. But it is not *dependent* upon this; for living and loving oneness in Christ is sometimes more touchingly seen even amidst and in spite of minor differences, than where no such differences exist to try the strength of their deeper unity. Yet till this living brotherhood in Christ shall show itself strong enough to destroy the sectarianism, selfishness, carnality, and apathy that eat out the heart of Christianity in all the visible sections of it, in vain shall we expect the world to be overawed by it. It is when "the Spirit shall be poured upon us from on high," as a Spirit of truth and love, and upon all parts of the Christian territory alike, melting down differences and heart-burnings, kindling astonishment and shame at past unfruitfulness, drawing forth longings of catholic affection, and yearnings over a world lying in wickedness, embodying themselves in palpable forms and active measures—it is then that we may expect the effect here announced to be produced, and then it will be irresistible. *Should not Christians ponder these things? Should not the same mind be in them which was also in Christ Jesus about this matter? Should not His prayer be theirs?* **22. And the glory which thou gavest**—hast given—**me I have given them, that they may be one, even as we are one**—The last clause shows the meaning of the first. It is not the *future* glory of the heavenly state, but the secret of that *present* unity just before spoken of; *the glory*, therefore, *of the indwelling Spirit of Christ;* the glory of an accepted state, of a holy character, of every grace. **23. I in them, and thou in me, that they may be made perfect in one**—(See on vs. 21). **24-26. Father, I will**—The majesty of this style of speaking is quite transparent. No petty criticism will be allowed to fritter it away in any but superficial or perverted readers. **be with me where I am**—(See on ch. 14:3). **that they may behold my glory which thou hast given me**—(See on vs. 5.) Christ regards it as glory enough for us to be admitted to see and gaze for ever upon *His* glory! This is 'the beatific vision'; but it shall be no mere vision, for "we shall be like Him, because we shall see Him as He is" (I John 3:2). **25. O righteous Father, the world hath not known thee**—knew thee not. **but I have known**—knew—**thee, and these have known**—knew—**that thou hast sent**—sentest—**me**—As before He said "*Holy* Father," when desiring the display of that perfection on His disciples (vs. 11), so here He styles Him "*Righteous* Father," because He is appealing to His righteousness or justice, to make a distinction between those two diametrically opposite classes—"*the world*," on the one hand, which would not "know the Father, though brought so nigh to it in the Son of His love, and, on the other, *Himself*, who recognized and owned Him, *and even His disciples*, who owned His mission from the Father. **26. And I have declared**—I made known or communicated—**thy name**—in His past ministry. **and will declare it**—in yet larger measure, by the gift of the Holy Ghost at Pentecost and through all succeeding ages. **that the love wherewith thou hast loved**—lovedst—**me may be in them, and I in them**—This eternal love of the Father, resting first on Christ, is by His Spirit imparted to and takes up its permanent abode in all that believe in Him; and "He abiding in them and they in Him" (ch. 15:5), they are "*one Spirit*." "With this lofty thought the Redeemer closes His prayer for His disciples, and in them for His Church through all ages. He has compressed into the last moments given Him for conversation with His own the most sublime and glorious sentiments ever uttered by mortal lips. But hardly has the

sound of the last word died away, when He passes with the disciples over the brook Kedron to Gethsemane—and the bitter conflict draws on. The seed of the new world must be sown in Death, that thence Life may spring up" [OLSHAUSEN].

CHAPTER 18

VSS. 1-13. BETRAYAL AND APPREHENSION OF JESUS. **1-3. over the brook Kedron**—a deep, dark ravine, to the northeast of Jerusalem, through which flowed this small storm-brook or winter-torrent, and which in summer is dried up. **where was a garden**—at the foot of the Mount of Olives, "called Gethsemane; i.e., olive press (Matt. 26:30, 36). **2. Judas . . . knew the place, for Jesus ofttimes**—see ch. 8:1; Luke 21:37—**resorted thither with his disciples**—The baseness of this abuse of knowledge in Judas, derived from admission to the closest privacies of his Master, is most touchingly conveyed here, though nothing beyond bare narrative is expressed. Jesus, however, knowing that in this spot Judas would expect to find Him, instead of avoiding it, hies Him thither, as a Lamb to the slaughter. "No man taketh My life from Me, but I lay it down of Myself" (ch. 10:18). Besides, the scene which was to fill up the little breathing-time, the awful interval, between the Supper and the Apprehension—like the "silence in heaven for about the space of half an hour" between the breaking of the Apocalyptic Seals and the peal of the Trumpets of war (Rev. 8:1)—the AGONY—would have been too terrible for the upper room; nor would He cloud the delightful associations of the *last Passover* and the *first Supper* by pouring out the anguish of His soul there. The garden, however, with its amplitude, its shady olives, its endeared associations, would be congenial to His heart. Here He had room enough to retire—first, from eight of them, and then from the more favored three; and here, when that mysterious scene was over, the stillness would only be broken by the tread of the traitor. **3. Judas then**—"He that was called Judas, one of the Twelve," says Luke, in language which brands him with peculiar infamy, as *in* the sacred circle while in no sense *of* it. **a band of men**—"the *detachment* of the Roman cohort on duty at the festival for the purpose of maintaining order" [WEBSTER and WILKINSON]. **officers from the chief priests and Pharisees**—captains of the temple and armed Levites. **lanterns and torches**—It was full moon, but in case He should have secreted Himself somewhere in the dark ravine, they bring the means of exploring its hiding-places—little knowing whom they had to do with. "Now he that betrayed Him had given them a sign, saying, Whomsoever I shall kiss, that same is He, hold Him fast" (Matt. 26:48). The cold-bloodedness of this speech was only exceeded by the deed itself. "And Judas went before them [Luke 22:47], and forthwith he came to Jesus, and said, Hail, Master, and kissed Him" (Matt. 26:49; cf. Exod. 4:27; 18:7; Luke 7:45). The impudence of this atrocious deed shows how thoroughly he had by this time mastered all his scruples. If the dialogue between our Lord and His captors was *before* this, as some interpreters think it was, the kiss of Judas was purely gratuitous, and probably to make good his right to the money; our Lord having presented Himself unexpectedly before them, and rendered it unnecessary for any one to point Him out. But a comparison of the narratives seems to show that our Lord's "coming forth" to the band was *subsequent* to the interview of Judas. "And Jesus said unto him, Friend"—not the endearing term "friend" (in ch. 15:15), but "companion," a word used on occasions of remonstrance or rebuke (as in Matt. 20:13; 22: 12)—"Wherefore art thou come?" (Matt. 26:50). "Betrayest thou the Son of man with a kiss"—imprinting upon the foulest act the mark of tenderest affection? What *wounded feeling* does this express! Of this Jesus showed Himself on various occasions keenly susceptible—as all generous and beautiful natures do. **4-9. Jesus . . . , knowing all things that should come**—were coming—**upon him, went forth**—from the shade of the trees, probably, into open view, indicating His sublime preparedness to meet His captors. **Whom seek ye?**—partly to prevent a rush of the soldiery upon the disciples [BENGEL]; and see Mark 14:51, 52, as showing a tendency to this: but still more as part of that courage and majesty which so overawed them. He would not wait to be *taken*. **5. They answered . . . , Jesus of Nazareth**—just the sort of blunt, straightforward reply one expects from military men, simply acting on their instructions. **I am He**—(See on ch. 6:20). **Judas . . . stood with them**—No more is recorded here of *his* part of the scene, but we have found the gap painfully supplied by all the other Evangelists. **6. As soon then as he said unto them, I am He, they went backward**—recoiled. **and fell to the ground**—struck down by a power such as that which smote Saul of Tarsus and his companions to the earth (Acts 26:14). It was the glorious effulgence of the majesty of Christ which overpowered them. "This, occurring before His surrender, would show His *power* over His enemies, and so the *freedom* with which He gave Himself up" [MEYER]. **7. Then asked he them again, Whom seek ye?**—Giving them a door of escape from the guilt of a deed which *now* they were able in some measure to understand. **Jesus of Nazareth**—The stunning effect of His first answer wearing off, they think only of the necessity of executing their orders. **8. I have told you that I am He: if therefore ye seek me, let these go their way**—Wonderful self-possession, and consideration for others, in such circumstances! **9. That the saying might be fulfilled which he spake, Of them which thou gavest me have I lost none**—The reference is to such sayings as ch. 6:39; 17:12; showing how conscious the Evangelist was, that in reporting his Lord's former sayings, he was giving them not in *substance* merely, but in *form* also. Observe, also, how the preservation of the disciples on this occasion is viewed as part that *deeper preservation* undoubtedly intended in the saying quoted. **10, 11. Then Simon Peter, having a sword, drew it, and smote the high priest's servant, and cut off his right ear. The servant's name was Malchus**—None of the other Evangelists mention the name either of the ardent disciple or of his victim. John being "known to the high priest" (vs. 15), the mention of the servant's name by *him* is quite natural, and an interesting mark of truth in a small matter. As to the *right* ear, specified both here and in Luke, the man was "likely foremost of those who advanced to seize Jesus, and presented himself in the attitude of a combatant; hence his right side would be exposed to attack. The blow of Peter was evidently aimed vertically at his head" [WESTER and WILKINSON]. **11. Then said Jesus**—"Suffer ye thus far" (Luke 22:51). **Put up thy sword into the sheath: the cup which my Father hath given me, shall I not drink it?**—This expresses

both the feelings which struggled in the Lord's breast during the Agony in the garden—*aversion to the cup* viewed *in itself*, but, *in the light of the Father's will*, perfect *preparedness to drink it*. (See on Luke 22:39-46.) Matthew adds to the address to Peter the following:—"For all they that take the sword shall perish by the sword" (Matt. 26:52)—i.e., 'Those who take the sword must run all the risks of human warfare; but Mine is a warfare whose weapons, as they are not carnal, are attended with no such hazards, but carry certain victory.' "Thinkest thou that I cannot now"—even after things have proceeded so far—"pray to My Father, and He shall presently give Me"—rather, 'place at My disposal'—"more than twelve legions of angels"; with allusion, possibly, to the one angel who had, in His agony, "appeared to Him from heaven strengthening Him" (Luke 22:43); and in the precise number, alluding to the *twelve* who needed the help, Himself and His eleven disciples. (The full complement of a legion of Roman soldiers was six thousand.) "But how then shall the scripture be fulfilled that thus it must be?" (Matt. 26:53, 54.) He could not suffer, according to the Scripture, if He allowed Himself to be delivered from the predicted death. "And He touched his ear and healed him" (Luke 22:51); for "the Son of man came not to destroy men's lives, but to save them" (Luke 9. 56), and, even while they were destroying His, to save theirs. **12. Then the band . . . took Jesus**—but not till He had made them feel that "no man took His life from Him, but that He laid it down of Himself." **13. And led him away**—"In that hour," says Matthew (26:55, 56), and probably now, on the way to judgment. when the crowds were pressing upon Him, "said Jesus to the multitudes, Are ye come out as against a thief, with swords and staves, for to take Me"—expressive of the indignity which He felt to be thus done to Him—"I sat daily with you in the temple, and ye laid no hold on Me. But this" (adds Luke 22:53) "is your hour and the power of darkness." Matthew continues—"But all this was done that the scriptures of the prophets might be fulfilled. Then all the disciples forsook Him and fled" (Matt. 26:56)—thus fulfilling His prediction (Mark 14:27; ch. 16:32).

13-27. JESUS BEFORE ANNAS AND CAIAPHAS—FALL OF PETER. **13, 14. And led him away to Annas first**—(See on Luke 3:2, and on Matt. 26:57). **15-18. Simon Peter followed Jesus**—Natural though this was, and safe enough, had he only "watched and prayed that he enter not into temptation," as his Master bade him (Matt. 26:41), it was, in his case, a fatal step. **and . . . another disciple**—Rather, the other disciple"—our Evangelist himself, no doubt. **known unto the high priest**—(See on vs. 10). **went in with Jesus into the palace of the high priest. 16. But Peter stood at the door without**—by preconcerted arrangement with his friend till he should get access for him. **Then went out that other . . . and spake to her that kept the door, and brought in Peter**—The *naturalness* of these small details is not unworthy of notice. This other disciple first made good his own entrance on the score of acquaintance with the high priest; this secured, he goes forth again, now as a privileged person, to make interest for Peter's admission. But thus our poor disciple is in the coils of the serpent. The next steps will best be seen by *inverting* verses 17 and 18. **18. And the servants and officers**—the menials and some of the "band" that "took Jesus." **stood there, who had made**—'having made'—**a fire of coals, for it was cold, and** they warmed themselves—"John alone notices the material (charcoal) of which the fire was made, and the reason for a fire—the coldness of the night" [WEBSTER and WILKINSON]. "Peter went in and sat with the servants to see the end (Matt. 26:58), and warmed himself at the fire" (Mark 14:54). These two statements are extremely interesting. His wishing to "see the end," or issue of these proceedings, was what led him into the palace, for he evidently feared the worst. But once in, the serpent coil is drawn closer; it is a cold night, and why should not he take advantage of the fire as well as others? Besides, in the talk of the crowd about the all-engrossing topic, he may pick up something which he would like to hear. "And as Peter was beneath in the palace" (Mark 14:66). Matthew (26:69) says, "sat *without* in the palace." According to Oriental architecture, and especially in large buildings, as here, the street door—or heavy folding gate through which single persons entered by a wicket kept by a porter—opened by a passage or "porch" (Mark 14:68) into a quadrangular *court,* here called the "palace" or *hall,* which was *open above,* and is frequently *paved* with flagstones. In the center of this court the "fire" would be kindled (in a brazier). At the upper end of it, probably, was the chamber in which the trial was held, *open to the court* and *not far from the fire* (Luke 22:61), but on a higher level; for Mark says the court was *"beneath"* it. The ascent was, perhaps, by a short flight of steps. This explanation will make the intensely interesting details more intelligible. **17. Then saith the damsel that kept the door**—"one of the maids of the high priest," says Mark (14:66). "When she saw Peter warming himself, she looked upon him and said" (Mark 14:67). Luke is more graphic (22:56)—She "beheld him as he sat by the fire (lit., 'the light'), and earnestly looked on him (fixed her gaze upon him), and said." "His demeanor and timidity, which must have vividly showed themselves, as it so generally happens, leading to the recognition of him" [OLSHAUSEN]. **Art thou not also one of this man's disciples?**—i.e., thou as well as "that other disciple," whom she knew to be one, but did not challenge, perceiving that he was a privileged person. **He saith, I am not**—"He denied before them all, saying, I know not what thou sayest" (Matt. 26:70)—a common form of point-blank denial; "I know [supply 'Him'] not, neither understand I what thou sayest" (Mark 14:68); "Woman, I know Him not" (Luke 22:57). This was THE FIRST DENIAL. "And he went out into the porch [thinking, perhaps, to steal away], *and the cock crew,*" (Mark 14:68). **19-21. The high priest ... asked Jesus of his disciples, and of his doctrine**—probably to entrap Him into some statements which might be used against Him at the trial. From our Lord's answer it would seem that "His disciples" were understood to be some secret party. **20. I spake**—have spoken—**openly to the world**—See ch. 7:4. **I ever taught in the synagogues and in the temple, whither the Jews always resort**—courting publicity, though with sublime noiselessness. **in secret have I said**—spake I—**nothing**—i.e., nothing of any different nature; all His private communications with the Twelve being but explanations and developments of His public teaching. (Cf. Isa. 45:19; 48:16). **21. Why askest thou me? ask them which heard me ... they know what I ... said**—This seems to imply that He saw the attempt to draw Him into selfcrimination, and resented it by falling back upon the right of every accused party

to have some charge laid against Him by competent witnesses. **22. struck Jesus with the palm ... Answerest Thou the high priest so**—(See Isa. 50:6; and cf. Acts 23:2). **23. If I have spoken ...**—'if I spoke' evil, in reply to the high priest. **if well**—He does not say "If *not*" evil, as if His reply were merely unobjectionable: *"well"* seems to challenge more than this as due to His remonstrance [BENGEL]. This shows that Matthew 5:39 is not to be taken to the letter. **24-27. Now Annas had sent him bound unto Caiaphas**—Our translators so render the words, understanding that the foregoing interview took place before *Caiaphas;* Annas, declining to meddle with the case, having sent Him to Caiaphas *at once.* But the words here literally are, "Annas sent Him [not *'had* sent Him] to Caiaphas"—and the "now" being of doubtful authority. Thus read, the verse affords no evidence that He was sent to Caiaphas *before* the interview just recorded, but implies rather the contrary. We take this interview, then, with some of the ablest interpreters, to be a preliminary and non-official one with *Annas,* at an hour of the night when Caiaphas' Council could not convene; and one that ought not to be confounded with that solemn one recorded by the other Evangelists, when all were assembled and witnesses called. But *the building in which both met with Jesus appears to have been the same, the room only being different, and the court, of course, in that case, one.* **25. And Simon Peter was standing and warming himself. They said therefore ..., Art thou not also one of his disciples?**—In Matthew 26:71 the *second* charge was made by "another maid, when he was gone out into the porch," who "saw him, and said unto them that were there, This [fellow] was also with Jesus of Nazareth." So also Mark 14:69. But in Luke 22:58 it is said, "After a little while" (from the time of the first denial), "another [*man*] saw him, and said, Thou art also of them." Possibly it was thrown at him by more than one; but these circumstantial variations only confirm the truth of the narrative. **He denied it, and said, I am not**—in Matthew 26:72, "He denied *with an oath,* I do not know the man." This was THE SECOND DENIAL. **26. One of the servants of the high priest, being his kinsman, whose ear Peter cut off, saith, Did not I see thee in the garden with him**—No doubt his relationship to Malchus drew attention to the man who smote him, and this enabled him to identify Peter. "Sad reprisals!" [BENGEL]. The other Evangelists make his detection to turn upon his *dialect.* "After a while ['about the space of one hour after,' Luke 22:59] came unto him they that stood by and said to Peter, Surely thou also art one of them, for thy speech betrayeth thee" (Matt. 26:73). "Thou art a Galilean, and thy speech agreeth thereto" (Mark 14:70; and so Luke 22:59). The Galilean dialect had a more *Syrian* cast than that of Judea. *If Peter had held his peace,* this peculiarity had not been observed; but hoping, probably, to put them off the scent by joining in the *fireside talk,* he only thus revealed himself. **27. Peter then denied again**—But, if the challenge of Malchus' kinsman was made simultaneously with this on account of his Galilean dialect, it was no simple denial; for Matthew 26:74 says, "Then began he to *curse and to swear,* saying, I know not the man." So Mark 14:71. This was THE THIRD DENIAL. **and immediately**—"while he yet spake" (Luke 22:60). **the cock crew**—As Mark is the only Evangelist who tells us that our Lord predicted that the cock should crow *twice* (ch. 14:30), so he only mentions that it *did* crow twice (vs. 72). The other Evangelists, who tell us merely that our Lord predicted that "before the cock should *crow* he would deny Him thrice" (Matt. 26:34; Luke 22:34; John 13:38), mention only *one actual* crowing, which was Mark's last. This is something affecting in this Evangelist —who, according to the earliest tradition (confirmed by internal evidence), derived his materials so largely from Peter as to have been styled his "*interpreter,*" being the *only one* who gives both the sad prediction and its still sadder fulfilment *in full*. It seems to show that Peter himself not only retained through all his after-life the most vivid recollection of the circumstances of his fall, but that he was willing that others should know them too. The immediately *subsequent* acts are given in full only in Luke (22:61, 62): "And the Lord turned and looked upon Peter," from the hall of judgment to the court, in the way already explained. But who can tell what lightning flashes of wounded love and piercing reproach shot from that "look" through the eye of Peter into his heart! "And Peter remembered the word of the Lord, how He had said unto him, Before the cock crow, thou shalt deny Me thrice. And Peter went out and wept bitterly." How different from the sequel of Judas' act! Doubtless the hearts of the two men towards the Saviour were perfectly different from the first; and the treason of Judas was but the consummation of the wretched man's resistance of the blaze of light in the midst of which he had lived for three years, while Peter's denial was but a momentary obscuration of the heavenly light and love to his Master which ruled his life. But the immediate cause of the revulsion, which made Peter "weep bitterly," was, beyond all doubt, this heart-piercing "look" which his Lord gave him. And remembering the Saviour's own words at the table, "Simon, Simon, Satan hath desired to have you that he may sift you as wheat, *but I have prayed* [rather, 'I prayed'] *for thee that thy faith fail not*" (see on Luke 22:31, 32), may we not say that *this prayer fetched down all that there was in that "look"* to pierce and break the heart of Peter, to keep it from despair, to work in it "repentance unto salvation not to be repented of," and at length, under other healing touches, to "restore his soul?" (See on Mark 16:7.)

28-40. JESUS BEFORE PILATE. N.B. *Our Evangelist, having given the interview with Annas, omitted by the other Evangelists, here omits the trial and condemnation before Caiaphas, which the others had recorded.* (See on Mark 14:53-65.) [The notes broken off there at vs. 61 are here concluded. (Mark 14.) 61. "The high priest asked Him, Art Thou the Christ, the Son of the blessed?" —Matthew says the high priest *put Him upon solemn oath,* saying, I adjure Thee by the living God that Thou tell us whether Thou be the Christ, the Son of God" (26:63). This rendered an answer by our Lord legally necessary (Lev. 5:1). Accordingly, 62. "Jesus said, I am" ("Thou hast said," Matt. 26:64). In Luke 22:67, 68, some other words are given, "If I tell you, ye will not believe; and if I also ask you, ye will not answer Me, nor let Me go." This seems to have been uttered *before* giving His direct answer, as a calm remonstrance and dignified protest against the prejudgment of His case and the unfairness of their mode of procedure. "and ye shall see the Son of man ..."—This concluding part of our Lord's answer is given somewhat more fully by Matthew and Luke. "Nevertheless I say unto you, Hereafter [rather, 'From henceforth'] shall ye see the

Son of man sitting on the right hand of power, and coming in the clouds of heaven" (Matt. 26:64; Luke 22:69).—i.e., I know the scorn with which ye are ready to meet such an avowal: To your eyes, which are but eyes of flesh, there stands at this bar only a mortal like yourselves, and He at the mercy of the ecclesiastical and civil authorities: "*Nevertheless,*" a day is coming when ye shall see another sight: Those eyes, which now gaze on Me with proud disdain, shall see this very prisoner at the right hand of the Majesty on high, and coming in the clouds of heaven: Then shall the judged One be revealed as the Judge, and His judges in this chamber appear at His august tribunal; then shall the *unrighteous* judges be *impartially* judged; and while they are wishing that they had never been born, He for whom they now watch as their Victim shall be greeted with the hallelujahs of heaven, and the welcome of Him that sitteth upon the throne! 63, 64. "Then the high priest rent his clothes, and saith, What need we any further witnesses? Ye have heard the blasphemy"—"of his own mouth" (Luke 22:71); an affectation of religious horror. "What think ye?"—'Say, what verdict would ye pronounce.' "They all condemned Him to be guilty of death"—of a capital crime. (See Lev. 24: 16.) 65. "And some began to spit on Him" ("Then did they spit in His face," Matt. 26:67). See Isaiah 50:6. "And to cover His face, and to buffet Him, and to say unto Him, Prophesy"—or 'divine' "unto us, Thou Christ, who is he that smote Thee?" The sarcasm in styling Him "*the Christ,*" and as such demanding of Him the perpetrator of the blows inflicted upon Him, was in them as infamous as to Him it was stinging. "and the servants did strike him with the palms of their hands"—"And many other things blasphemously spake they against him" (Luke 22:65). This general statement is important, as showing that virulent and varied as were the *recorded* affronts put upon Him, they are but *a small specimen* of what He endured on that black occasion.]—**28. Then led they Jesus from Caiaphas to the hall of judgment**—but not till "in the morning the chief priests held a consultation with the elders and scribes and the whole council against Him to put Him to death, and bound Him" (Matt. 27:1; and see on Mark 15:1). The word here rendered "hall of judgment" is from the Latin, and denotes 'the palace of the governor of a Roman province.' **they themselves went not into the judgment hall lest they should be defiled**—by contact with ceremonially unclean Gentiles. **but that they might eat the passover**—If this refer to the principal part of the festival, the eating of the lamb, the question is, how our Lord and His disciples came to eat it the night before; and, as it was an *evening* meal, how ceremonial defilement contracted in the *morning* would unfit them for partaking of it, as after 6 o'clock it was reckoned a new day. These are questions which have occasioned immense research and learned treatises. But as the usages of the Jews appear to have somewhat varied at different times, and our present knowledge of them is not sufficient to clear up all difficulties, they are among the not very important questions which probably will never be entirely solved. **29-32. Pilate went out to them, and said, What accusation bring ye against this man?**—State your charge. **30. If he were not a malefactor, we would not have delivered him up unto thee**—They were conscious they *had no case* of which Pilate could take cognizance, and therefore insinuate that they had already found Him worthy of death by their own law; but not having the power, under the Roman government, to carry their sentence into execution, they had come merely for his sanction. **32. That the saying ... might be fulfilled which he spake, signifying what death he should die**—i.e., by *crucifixion* (ch. 12:32, 33; Matt. 20:19); which being a Roman mode of execution, could only be carried into effect by order of the governor. (The Jewish mode in such cases as this was by *stoning*.) **33-38. Pilate ... called Jesus, and said ..., Art thou the King of the Jews?**—In Luke 23:2 they charge our Lord before Pilate with "perverting the nation, and forbidding to give tribute to Cæsar, saying that He Himself is Christ a king." Perhaps this was what occasioned Pilate's question. **34. Jesus answered ..., Sayest thou this of thyself, or did others tell it thee of me?**—an important question for our Lord's case, to bring out whether the word *"King"* were meant in a *political* sense, with which Pilate had a right to deal, or whether he were merely *put up* to it by His accusers, who had no claims to charge Him but such as were of a purely *religious* nature, with which Pilate had nothing to do. **35. Pilate answered, Am I a Jew? Thine own nation and the chief priests delivered thee to me: What hast thou done?**—i.e., Jewish questions I neither understand nor meddle with; but Thou art here on a charge which, though it *seems* only Jewish, *may* yet involve treasonable matter: As *they* state it, I cannot decide the point; tell me, then, what procedure of Thine has brought Thee into this position.' In modern phrase, Pilate's object in this question was merely to determine the *relevancy* of the charge. **36. Jesus answered, My kingdom is not of this world**—He does not say 'not *over*,' but 'not of this world'—i.e., in its *origin* and *nature;* therefore 'no such kingdom as need give thee or thy master the least alarm.' **if my kingdom were of this world, then would my servants fight, that I should not be delivered to the Jews**—"A very convincing argument; for if His servants did not fight to prevent their King from being delivered up to His enemies, much less would they use force for the establishment of His kingdom" [WEBSTER and WILKINSON]. **but now**—but the fact is. **is my kingdom not from hence**—Our Lord only says whence His kingdom is *not*—first simply affirming it, next giving proof of it, then reaffirming it. This was all that Pilate had to do with. The *positive* nature of His kingdom He would not obtrude upon one who was as little able to comprehend it, as entitled officially to information about it. (It is worthy of notice that the "MY," which occurs *four* times in this one verse—*thrice* of His *kingdom*, and *once* of His *servants*—is put in the emphatic form.) **37. Art thou a king then?**—There was no sarcasm or disdain in this question [as THOLUCK, ALFORD, and others, allege], else our Lord's answer would have been different. Putting emphasis upon *"thou,"* his question betrays a mixture of *surprise* and *uneasiness,* partly at the possibility of there being, after all, something dangerous under the claim, and partly from a certain awe which our Lord's demeanor probably struck into him. **Thou sayest that I am a king**—It is even so. **To this end was I** ('have I been') **born, and for this cause came I**—am I come—**into the world, that I may bear witness to the truth**—His *birth* expresses His manhood; His *coming into the world*, His existence before assuming humanity: The truth, then, here affirmed, though Pilate would catch little of it, was that *His Incarnation was expressly in order to the assumption of Royalty in our nature.* Yet, instead of

saying, He came to be a King, which is His meaning, He says He came to *testify to the truth.* Why this? Because, in such circumstances it required a noble courage not to flinch from His royal claims; and our Lord, *conscious that He was putting forth that courage,* gives a turn to His confession expressive of it. It is to this that Paul alludes, in those remarkable words to Timothy: "I charge thee before God, who quickeneth all things, and before Christ Jesus, who, *in the presence* of Pontius Pilate, witnessed *the good confession"* (I Tim. 6:13). This one act of our Lord's life, His courageous witness-bearing before the governor, was selected as an encouraging example of the *fidelity* which Timothy ought to display. As the Lord [says OLSHAUSEN beautifully] owned Himself *the Son of God* before the most exalted theocratic council, so He confessed His *regal dignity* in presence of the representative of the highest political authority on earth. **Every one that is of the truth heareth my voice**—Our Lord here not only affirms that His word had in it a self-evidencing, self-recommending power, but gently insinuated the *true secret of the growth and grandeur of His kingdom*—as A KINGDOM OF TRUTH, in its highest sense, into which all souls who have learned to live and count all things but loss for the truth are, by a most heavenly attraction, drawn as into their proper element; THE KING of whom Jesus is, fetching them in and ruling them by His captivating power over their hearts. **38. Pilate saith unto him, What is truth?**—i.e., 'Thou stirrest the question of questions, which the thoughtful of every age have asked, but never man yet answered.' **And when he had said this**—as if, by putting such a question, he was getting into interminable and unseasonable inquiries, when this business demanded rather prompt action—**he went out again unto the Jews**—thus missing a noble opportunity for himself, and giving utterance to that consciousness of the want of all intellectual and moral certainty, which was the feeling of every thoughtful mind at that time. "The only certainty," says the elder PLINY, "is that nothing is certain, nor more miserable than man, nor more proud. The fearful laxity of morals at that time must doubtless be traced in a great degree to this skepticism. The revelation of the eternal truth alone was able to breathe new life into ruined human nature, and that in the apprehension of complete redemption" [OLSHAUSEN]. **and saith unto them**—in the hearing of our Lord, who had been brought forth—**I find in him no fault**—no crime. This so exasperated "the chief priests and elders" that, afraid of losing their prey, they poured forth a volley of charges against Him, as appears from Luke 23:4, 5: on Pilate's affirming His innocence, "they were *the more fierce,* saying, He stirreth up the people, teaching throughout all Jewry, beginning from Galilee to this place." They see no hope of getting Pilate's sanction to His death unless they can fasten upon Him a charge of conspiracy against the government; and as *Galilee* was noted for its turbulence (Luke 13:1; Acts 5:37), and our Lord's ministry lay chiefly there, they artfully introduce it to give color to their charge. "And the chief priests accused Him of *many things,* but He answered nothing (Mark 15.3). Then said Pilate unto Him, Hearest Thou not how many things they witness against Thee? And He answered him to never a word, insomuch that the governor marvelled greatly" (Matt. 27:13, 14). See on Mark 15:3-5. In his perplexity, Pilate, hearing of Galilee, bethinks himself of the expedient of sending Him to Herod, in the hope of thereby further shaking off responsibility in the case. See on Mark 15:6, and on Luke 23:6-12. The return of the prisoner only deepened the perplexity of Pilate, who, "calling together the chief priests, rulers, and people," tells them plainly that not one of their charges against "this man" had been made good, while even Herod, to whose jurisdiction he more naturally belonged, had done nothing to Him: He "will therefore chastise and release him" (Luke 23:13-16). **39. But ye have a custom that I should release one unto you at the passover . . .**—See on Mark 15:7-11. "On the typical import of the choice of Christ to suffer, by which Barabbas was set free, see Leviticus 16, particularly vss. 5-10, where the subject is the *sin offering* on the great day of atonement" [KRAFFT in LUTHARDT].

CHAPTER 19

VSS. 1-16. JESUS BEFORE PILATE—SCOURGED—TREATED WITH OTHER SEVERITIES AND INSULTS—DELIVERED UP, AND LED AWAY TO BE CRUCIFIED. **1-3. Pilate took Jesus and scourged him**—in hope of appeasing them. (See on Mark 15:15.) "And the soldiers led Him away into the palace, and they call the whole band" (Mark 15:16)—the body of the military cohort stationed there—to take part in the mock coronation now to be enacted. **2. the soldiers platted a crown of thorns, and put it on his head**—in mockery of a regal *crown*. **and they put on him a purple robe**—in mockery of the *imperial purple;* first "stripping him" (Matt. 27:28) of His own outer garment. The robe may have been the "gorgeous" one in which Herod arrayed and sent Him back to Pilate (Luke 23:11). "And they put a reed into His right hand" (Matt. 27:29)—in mockery of the regal *scepter.* "And they bowed the knee before Him" (Matt. 27:29). **3. And said, Hail, King of the Jews!**—doing Him derisive homage, in the form used on approaching the emperors. "And they spit upon Him, and took the reed and smote Him on the head" (Matt. 27:30). The best comment on these affecting details is to *cover the face.* **4, 5. Pilate . . . went forth again, and saith . . . , Behold, I bring**—am bringing, i.e., going to bring—**him forth to you, that ye may know I find no fault in him**—and, by scourging Him and allowing the soldiers to make sport of Him, have gone as far to meet your exasperation as can be expected from a judge. **5. Then Jesus came forth, wearing the crown of thorns, and the purple robe. And Pilate saith unto them, Behold the man!**—There is no reason to think that *contempt* dictated this speech. There was clearly a struggle in the breast of this wretched man. Not only was he reluctant to surrender to mere clamor an innocent man, but a feeling of anxiety about His mysterious claims, as is plain from what follows, was beginning to rack his breast, and the object of his exclamation seems to have been to *move their pity.* But, be *his* meaning what it may, those three words have been eagerly appropriated by all Christendom, and enshrined for ever in its heart as a sublime expression of its calm, rapt admiration of its suffering Lord. **6, 7. When the chief priests . . . saw him, they cried out**—their fiendish rage kindling afresh at the sight of Him—**Crucify him, crucify him**—(See on Mark 15:14). **Pilate saith unto them, Take ye him, and crucify him; for I find no fault in him**—as if this would relieve *him* of the responsibility of the deed, who, by surrendering Him, incurred it all!

7. The Jews answered him, We have a law, and by our law he ought to die, because he made himself the Son of God—Their criminal charges having come to nothing, they give up that point, and as Pilate was throwing the whole responsibility upon them, they retreat into their own Jewish law, by which, as claiming equality with God (see on ch. 5:18 and 8:59), He ought to die; insinuating that it was Pilate's duty, even as civil governor, to protect their law from such insult. **8-11. When Pilate . . . heard this saying, he was the more afraid**—the name "SON OF GOD," the lofty sense evidently attached to it by His Jewish accusers, the dialogue he had already held with Him, and the dream of his wife (Matt. 27:19), all working together in the breast of the wretched man. **9. and went again into the judgment hall, and saith to Jesus, Whence art thou?**—beyond all doubt a question relating not to His *mission* but to His personal *origin.* **Jesus gave him no answer**—He had said enough; the time for answering such a question was past; the weak and wavering governor is already on the point of giving way. **10. Then saith Pilate unto him, Speakest thou not to me?**—The "me" is the emphatic word in the question. He falls back upon the *pride of office,* which doubtless tended to blunt the workings of his conscience. **knowest thou not that I have power to crucify thee, and have power to release thee?**—said to work upon Him at once by *fear* and by *hope.* **11. Thou couldest**—rather 'shouldst'—**have no power at all against me**—neither to crucify nor to release, nor to do anything whatever against Me [BENGEL]. **except it were**—'unless it had been'—**given thee from above**—i.e., 'Thou thinkest too much of thy power, Pilate: against Me that power is none, save what is meted out to thee by special divine appointment, for a special end.' **therefore he that delivered me unto thee**—Caiaphas, too wit—but he only as representing the Jewish authorities as a body. **hath the greater sin**—as having better opportunities and more knowledge of such matters. **21-16. And from thenceforth**—particularly this speech, which seems to have filled him with awe, and redoubled his anxiety. **Pilate sought to release him**—i.e., to gain their *consent* to it, for he could have done it at once on his authority. **but the Jews cried**—seeing their advantage, and not slow to profit by it. **If thou let this man go, thou art not Cæsar's friend . . .**—"This was equivalent to a threat of *impeachment,* which we know was much dreaded by such officers as the procurators, especially of the character of Pilate or Felix. It also consummates the treachery and disgrace of the Jewish rulers, who were willing, for the purpose of destroying Jesus, to affect a zeal for the supremacy of a foreign prince" (See vs. 15.) [WEBSTER and WILKINSON]. **When Pilate . . . heard that, . . . he brougt Jesus forth, and sat down in**—['upon']—**the judgment seat**—that he might pronounce sentence against the Prisoner, on this charge, the more solemnly—**in a place called the Pavement**—a tesselated pavement, much used by the Romans—**in the Hebrew, Gabbatha**—from its being *raised.* **14. It was the preparation**—i.e., the day before the Jewish sabbath. **and about the sixth hour**—The true reading here is probably, "the *third* hour"—or 9 A.M.—which agrees best with the whole series of events, as well as with the other Evangelists. **he saith to the Jews, Behold your King!**—Having now made up his mind to yield to them, he takes a sort of quiet revenge on them by this irony, which he knew would sting them. This only reawakens their cry to despatch Him. **15. crucify your King?**

... We have no king but Cæsar—"Some of those who thus cried died miserably in rebellion against Cæsar forty years afterwards. But it suited their present purpose" [ALFORD]. **16. Then delivered he him therefore unto them to be crucified ...**—(See on Mark 15:15).

17-30. CRUCIFIXION AND DEATH OF THE LORD JESUS. **17. And he bearing his cross**—(See on Luke 23:26). **went forth**—Cf. Hebrews 13:11-13, "without the camp"; "without the gate." On arriving at the place, "they gave Him vinegar to drink mingled with gall [wine mingled with myrrh, Mark 15:23], and when He had tasted thereof, He would not drink" (Matt. 27:34). This potion was stupefying, and given to criminals just before execution, to deaden the sense of pain.

Fill high the bowl, and spice it well, and pour
The dews oblivious: for the Cross is sharp,
The Cross is sharp, and He
Is tenderer than a lamb.
                                        [KEBLE]

But *our Lord would die with every faculty clear, and in full sensibility to all His sufferings.*

Thou wilt feel all, that Thou may'st pity all;
And rather would'st Thou wrestle with strong pain
    Than overcloud Thy soul,
    So clear in agony,
Or lose one glimpse of Heaven before the time,
    O most entire and perfect Sacrifice,
        Renewed in every pulse.
                                        [KEBLE]

18. they crucified him, and two others with him—"malefactors" (Luke 23:33), "thieves" (rather "robbers," Matt. 27:38; Mark 15:27). **on either side one and Jesus in the midst**—a hellish expedient, to hold Him up as the worst of the three. But in this, as in many other of their doings, "the scripture was fulfilled, which saith (Isa. 53:12), *And he was numbered with the transgressors*"—(Mark 15: 28)—though the prediction reaches deeper. "Then said Jesus"—['probably while being nailed to the CROSS'] [OLSHAUSEN], "FATHER, FORGIVE THEM, FOR THEY KNOW NOT WHAT THEY DO" (Luke 23:34)—and again the Scripture was fulfilled which said, "And He made intercession for the transgressors" (Isa. 53:12), though this also reaches deeper. (See Acts 3:17; 13:27; and cf. I Tim. 1:13). Often have we occasion to observe how our Lord is the first to fulfil His own precepts—thus furnishing the right interpretation and the perfect Model of them. (See on Matt. 5:44.) How quickly was it seen in "His martyr Stephen," that though He had left the earth in Person, His Spirit remained behind, and Himself could, in some of His brightest lineaments, be reproduced in His disciples! (Acts 7:60.) And what does the world in every age owe to these few words, spoken *where* and *as* they were spoken! **19-22. Pilate wrote a title, and put it on the cross ... Jesus of Nazareth, the King of the Jews ... and it was written in Hebrew**—or Syro-Chaldaic, the language of the country—**and Greek**—the current language—**and Latin**—the official language. These were the chief languages of the earth, and this secured that all spectators should be able to read it. Stung by this, the Jewish ecclesiastics entreat that it may be so altered as to express, not His real dignity, but His false claim to it. But Pilate thought he had yielded quite enough to them; and having intended expressly to spite and insult them by this title, for having got him to act against his own sense of justice, he peremptorily refused them. And thus, amidst the conflicting passions of men, was proclaimed, in the chief tongues of mankind, from the Cross itself and in circumstances which threw upon it a lurid yet grand light, the truth which drew the Magi to His manger, and will yet be owned by all the world! **23, 24. Then the soldiers, when they had crucified Jesus, took his garments, and made four parts; to every soldier**—the four who nailed Him to the cross, and whose perquisite they were. **a part, and also his coat**—the Roman *tunic,* or close-fitting vest. **without seam, woven from the top throughout**—"perhaps denoting considerable skill and labor as necessary to produce such a garment, the work probably of one or more of the women who ministered in such things unto Him, Luke 8:3" [WEBSTER and WILKINSON]. **24. Let us not rend it, but cast lots ..., whose it shall be, that the scripture might be fulfilled which saith, They parted my raiment among them; and for my vesture they did cast lots ...** (Psalm 22:18). That a prediction so exceedingly specific—distinguishing one piece of dress from others, and announcing that while *those* should be parted amongst several, *that* should be given by lot to one person—that such a prediction should not only be fulfilled to the letter, but by a party of heathen military, without interference from either the friends or the enemies of the Crucified One, is surely worthy to be ranked among the wonders of this all-wonderful scene. Now come the *mockeries,* and from four different quarters:—(1) "And *they that passed by* reviled Him, wagging their heads" in ridicule (Ps. 22:7; 109:25; cf. Jer. 18:16; Lam. 2:15). "Ah!"—'Ha,' an exclamation here of derision. "Thou that destroyest the temple, and buildest it in three days, save Thyself and come down from the cross" (Matt. 27:39, 40; Mark 15:29, 30). "It is evident that our Lord's saying, or rather this *perversion* of it (for He claimed not to *destroy,* but to *rebuild* the temple destroyed by them) had greatly exasperated the feeling which the priests and Pharisees had contrived to excite against Him. It is referred to as the principal fact brought out in evidence against Him on the trial (cf. Acts 6:13, 14), as an offense for which He deserved to suffer. And it is very remarkable that now *while it was receiving its real fulfilment,* it should be made more public and more impressive by the insulting proclamation of His enemies. Hence the importance attached to it after the resurrection, ch. 2:22" [WEBSTER and WILKINSON]. (2) "Likewise also the *chief priests,* mocking Him, *with the scribes and elders,* said, He saved others, Himself He cannot save." There was a deep truth in this, as in other taunts; for *both* He could not do, having "come to give *His* life a ransom for *many.*" No doubt this added an unknown sting to the reproach. "If He be the king of Israel, let Him now come down from the cross, and we will believe Him." *No, they would not;* for those who resisted the evidence from the resurrection of Lazarus, and from His own resurrection, were beyond the reach of any amount of merely *external* evidence. "He trusted in God that He would deliver him; let Him deliver Him now if He will have Him [or 'delight in Him,'] cf. Ps. 18:19; Deut. 21:14]; for He said, I am the Son of God" (Matthew 27:41-43). We thank you, O ye chief priests, scribes, and elders, for this triple testimony, unconsciously borne by you, to our Christ: first to *His habitual trust in God,* as a feature in His character so marked and palpable that even ye found upon it your impotent taunt; next, to His identity with the Sufferer of the 22d Psalm, whose very words (vs. 8) ye unwittingly appropriate, thus *serving yourselves heirs* to the dark office and impotent malignity of Messiah's enemies; and again, to the true sense of that august title which He took to Himself, "THE SON OF GOD," which He rightly interpreted at the very first (see on ch. 5:18) as a claim to that *oneness of nature* with Him, and *dearness to Him*, which a son has to his father. (3) "And *the soldiers* also mocked Him, coming to Him and offering Him vinegar, and saying, If thou be the king of the Jews, save Thyself" (Luke 23:36, 37). They insultingly offer to share with Him their own vinegar, or sour wine, the usual drink of Roman soldiers, it being about the time of their midday meal. In the taunt of the soldiers we have one of those *undesigned coincidences* which so strikingly verify these historical records. While the ecclesiastics deride Him for calling Himself, "the *Christ*, the *King of Israel*, the *Chosen*, the *Son of God*," the soldiers, to whom all such phraseology was mere Jewish jargon, make sport of Him as a pretender to *royalty* ("KING of the Jews"), an office and dignity which it belonged to them to comprehend. "*The thieves* also, which were crucified with Him, cast the same in His teeth" (Matt. 27:44; Mark 15:32). Not *both* of them, however, as some commentators unnaturally think we must understand these words; as if some sudden change came over the *penitent* one, which turned him from an unfeeling railer into a trembling petitioner. The plural "thieves" need not denote more than the *quarter* or *class* whence came this last and cruelest taunt—i.e., 'Not only did scoffs proceed from the *passers-by*, the *ecclesiastics*, the *soldiery*, but even from His *fellow sufferers*,' a mode of speaking which no one would think necessarily meant both of them. Cf. Matthew 2:20, "*They* are dead which sought the child's life," meaning *Herod;* and Mark 9:1, "There be *some* standing here," where it is next to certain that only John, the youngest and last survivor of the apostles, is meant. And is it conceivable that this penitent thief should have first himself reviled the Saviour, and then, on his views of Christ suddenly changing, he should have turned upon his fellow sufferer and fellow reviler, and rebuked him not only with dignified sharpness, but in the language of *astonishment* that he should be capable of such conduct? Besides, there is a deep calmness in all that he utters, extremely unlike what we should expect from one who was the subject of a mental revolution so sudden and total. On the scene itself, see on Luke 23:29-43. **25-27. Now there stood by the cross of Jesus his mother, and his mother's sister, Mary, wife of Cleophas**—This should be read, as in *margin*, "Clopas," the same as "Alpheus" (Matt. 10:3). The "Cleopas" of Luke 24:18 was a different person. **26. When Jesus ... saw his mother, and the disciple whom he loved, standing by, he saith to his mother,** WOMAN, BEHOLD THY SON! **27. Then saith he to the disciple,** BEHOLD THY MOTHER! —What forgetfulness of self, what filial love, and to the "mother" and "son" what parting words! **from that hour ... took her to his own home**—or, home with him; for his father Zebedee and his mother Salome were both alive, and the latter here present (Mark 15:40). See on Matthew 13:55. Now occurred the supernatural *darkness*, recorded by all the other Evangelists, but not here. "Now from the sixth hour (12, noon) there was darkness over all the land unto the ninth hour" (Matt. 27:45). No ordinary eclipse of the sun could have occurred at this time, it being then *full moon*, and

this obscuration lasted about *twelve times* the length of any ordinary eclipse. (Cf. Exod. 10:21, 23). Beyond doubt, the divine intention of the portent was to invest this darkest of all tragedies with a gloom expressive of its real character. "And about the ninth hour Jesus cried, ELI, ELI, LAMA SABACTHANI ... *My God, My God, why hast Thou forsaken Me?*" (Matt. 27:46). As the darkness commenced at the sixth hour, the second of the Jewish hours of prayer, so it continued till the ninth hour, *the hour of the evening sacrifice*, increasing probably in depth, and *reaching its deepest gloom at the moment of this mysterious cry*, when the flame of the one great "Evening Sacrifice" was burning fiercest. The words were made to His hand. They are the opening words of a Psalm (the 22d) full of the last "sufferings of Christ and the following glories" (I Pet. 1:11). "FATHER," was the cry in the first prayer which He uttered on the cross, for matters had not then come to the worst. "Father" was the cry of His last prayer, for matters had then passed their worst. But at this crisis of His sufferings, "Father" does not issue from His lips, for the light of a Father's countenance was then mysteriously eclipsed. He falls back, however, on a title expressive of His *official* relation, which, though lower and more distant in itself, yet when grasped in pure and naked faith was mighty in its claims, and rich in psalmodic associations. And what deep earnestness is conveyed by the redoubling of this title! But as for the cry itself, it will never be fully comprehended. An absolute desertion is not indeed to be thought of; but a total eclipse of the *felt* sense of God's presence it certainly expresses. It expresses *surprise*, as under the experience of something not only *never before known*, but *inexplicable* on the footing which had till then subsisted between Him and God. *It is a question which the lost cannot utter.* They are forsaken, *but they know why.* Jesus is forsaken, but *does not know and demands to know why.* It is thus *the cry of conscious innocence*, but of innocence unavailing to draw down, at that moment, the least token of approval from the unseen Judge—innocence whose only recognition at that moment lay in the thick surrounding gloom which but reflected the horror of great darkness that invested His own spirit. *There was indeed a cause for it*, and He knew it too—the "why" must not be pressed so far as to exclude this. *He must taste this bitterest of the wages of sin "who did no sin."* But that is not the point now. In Him there was no cause at all (ch. 14:30) and He takes refuge in the glorious fact. When no ray from above shines in upon Him, He strikes a light out of His own breast. If God will not own Him, He shall own Himself. On the rock of His unsullied allegiance to Heaven He will stand, till the light of Heaven returns to His spirit. And it is near to come. While He is yet speaking, the fierceness of the flame is beginning to abate. One incident and insult more, and the experience of one other predicted element of suffering, and the victory is His. The incident, and the insult springing out of it, is the misunderstanding of the cry, for we can hardly suppose that it was anything else. "Some of them that stood there, when they heard that, said, This man calleth for Elias" (Matthew 27:47). **28-30. After this, Jesus knowing that all things were now accomplished**—i.e., the moment for the fulfilment of the last of them; for there was one other small particular, and the time was come for that too, in consequence of the burning thirst which the fevered state of His frame occasioned

(Ps. 22:15). **that the scripture**—Ps. 69:21—**might be fulfilled, saith, I thirst.** Now there was set a vessel full of vinegar—see on the offer of the soldiers vinegar, above—**and they**—"one of them," (Matt. 27:48). **29. filled a sponge with vinegar, and put it upon**—a stalk of—**hyssop, and put it to his mouth**—Though a stalk of this plant does not exceed eigtheen inches in length, it would suffice, as the feet of crucified persons were not raised high. "The rest said, Let be"—[i.e., as would seem, 'Stop that officious service'] "let us see whether Elias will come to save Him" (Matt. 27:49). This was the last cruelty He was to suffer, but it was one of the most unfeeling. "And when Jesus had cried with a loud voice" (Luke 23:46). This *"loud voice,"* noticed by three of the Evangelists, does not imply, as some able interpreters contend, that our Lord's strength was so far from being exhausted that He needed not to die then, and surrendered up His life sooner than Nature required, merely because it was the appointed time. It was indeed the appointed time, but time that He should be "crucified *through weakness*" (I Cor. 13:4), and Nature was now reaching its utmost exhaustion. But just as even His own dying saints, particularly the martyrs of Jesus, have sometimes had such gleams of coming glory immediately before breathing their last, as to impart to them a strength to utter their feelings which has amazed the bystanders, so this *mighty voice* of the expiring Redeemer was nothing else but the exultant spirit of the Dying Victor, receiving the fruit of His travail just about to be embraced, and nerving the organs of utterance to an ecstatic expression of its sublime feelings (not so much in the *immediately* following words of tranquil surrender, in Luke, as in the *final* shout, recorded only by John): "FATHER, INTO THY HANDS I COMMEND MY SPIRIT!" (Luke 23:46). Yes, the darkness is past, and the true light now shineth. His soul has emerged from its mysterious horrors; *"My God"* is heard no more, but in unclouded light He yields sublime into His *Father's* hands the infinitely precious spirit—using here also the words of those matchless Psalms (31:5) which were ever on His lips. "As the Father receives the spirit of Jesus, so Jesus receives those of the faithful" (Acts 7:59) [BENGEL]. And now comes the expiring mighty shout—**30. It is finished! and he bowed his head and gave up the ghost.** What is finished? The Law is fulfilled as never before, nor since, in His "obedience unto death, even the death of the cross"; Messianic prophecy is accomplished; Redemption is completed; "He hath finished the transgression, and made reconciliation for iniquity, and brought in everlasting righteousness, and sealed up the vision and prophecy, and anointed a holy of holies"; He has inaugurated the kingdom of God and given birth to a new world.

31-42. BURIAL OF CHRIST. **31-37. the preparation**—sabbath eve. **that the bodies should not remain**—over night, against the Mosaic law (Deut. 21:22, 23). **on the sabbath day, for that sabbath day was an high**—or 'great'—**day**—the first day of unleavened bread, and, as concurring with an ordinary sabbath, the most solemn season of the ecclesiastical year. Hence their peculiar jealousy lest the law should be infringed. **besought Pilate that their legs might be broken**—to hasten their death, which was done in such cases with clubs. **33. But when they came to Jesus, and saw that he was dead already**—there being in *His* case elements of suffering, unknown to the malefactors, which might naturally hasten His death, lingering though it al-

ways was in such cases, not to speak of His *previous* sufferings. **they brake not his legs**—a fact of vast importance, as showing that the *reality* of His death was visible to those whose business it was to see to it. The *other* divine purpose served by it will appear presently. **34. But one of the soldiers**—to make assurance of the fact doubly sure—**with a spear pierced his side**—making a wound deep and wide, as indeed is plain from ch. 20:27, 29. Had life still remained, it must have fled now—**and forthwith came thereout blood and water**—"It is now well known that the effect of long-continued and intense agony is frequently to produce a secretion of a colorless lymph within the pericardium (the membrane enveloping the heart), amounting in many cases to a very considerable quantity" [WEBSTER and WILKINSON]. **35. And he that saw it bare record**—hath borne witness—**and his witness is true, and he knoweth that he saith true, that ye might believe**—This solemn way of referring to his own testimony in this matter has no reference to what he says in his Epistle about Christ's "coming by water and blood" (see on I John 5:6), but is intended to call attention both to the fulfilment of Scripture in these particulars, and to the undeniable evidence he was thus furnishing of the *reality* of Christ's death, and consequently of His resurrection; perhaps also to meet the growing tendency, in the Asiatic churches, to deny the reality of our Lord's body, or that "Jesus Christ is come in the flesh" (I John 4:1-3). **36. that the scripture should be fulfilled, A bone of him shall not be broken**—The reference is to the paschal lamb, as to which this ordinance was stringent (Exod. 12:46; Num. 9: 12. Cf. I Cor. 5:7). But though we are to see here the fulfilment of a very definite typical ordinance, we shall, on searching deeper, see in it *a remarkable divine interposition to protect the sacred body of Christ from the last indignity after He had finished the work given Him to do.* Every imaginable indignity had been permitted *before that,* up to the moment of His death. But no sooner is that over than an Unseen hand is found to have provided against the clubs of the rude soldiers coming in contact with that temple of the Godhead. Very different from such violence was that *spear-thrust,* for which not only doubting Thomas would thank the soldier, but intelligent believers in every age, to whom the certainty of their Lord's death and resurrection is the life of their whole Christianity. **37. And again another scripture saith, They shall look on him whom they pierced**—The quotation is from Zechariah 12:10; not taken as usual from the Septuagint (the current Greek version), which here is all wrong, but direct from the Hebrew. And there is a remarkable nicety in the choice of the words employed both by the prophet and the Evangelist for "piercing." The word in Zechariah means to *thrust through* with spear, javelin, sword, or any such weapon. In that sense it is used in all the ten places, besides this, where it is found. How suitable this was to express the action of the Roman soldier, is manifest; and our Evangelist uses the exactly corresponding word, which the Septuagint certainly does not. Very *different is the other word* for *"pierce"* in Psalm 22:16, "*They pierced my hands and my feet."* The word there used is one signifying to *bore* as with an awl or hammer. How striking are these small niceties! **38-40. Joseph of Arimathea**—"a rich man" (Matt. 27:57), thus fulfilling Isaiah 53:9; "an honorable counsellor," a member of the Sanhedrim, and of good condition, "which also waited for the kingdom of God" (Mark

15:43), a devout expectant of Messiah's kingdom; "a good man and a just, the same had not consented to the counsel and deed of them" (Luke 23:50, 51–he had gone the length, perhaps, of dissenting and protesting in open council against the condemnation of our Lord); "who also himself was Jesus' disciple" (Matt. 27:57). **being a disciple of Jesus, but secretly, for fear of the Jews**–"He went in boldly unto Pilate" (Mark 15:43)–lit., "having taken courage went in," or "had the boldness to go in." Mark alone, as his manner is, notices the *boldness* which this required. The act would without doubt identify him *for the first time* with the disciples of Christ. Marvellous it certainly is, that one who while Jesus was yet alive merely refrained from condemning Him, not having the courage to espouse His cause by one positive act, should, now that He was dead, and His cause apparently dead with Him, summon up courage to go in personally to the Roman governor and ask permission to take down and inter the body. But if this be the first instance, it is not the last, that *a seemingly dead Christ has wakened a sympathy which a living one had failed to evoke. The heroism of faith is usually kindled by desperate circumstances, and is not seldom displayed by those who before were the most timid, and scarce known as disciples at all.* "And Pilate marvelled if he were"–rather "wondered that he was" "already dead." "And calling the centurion, he asked him whether He had been any while dead"–Pilate could hardly credit what Joseph had told him, that He had been dead "some time," and, before giving up the body to His friends, would learn how the fact stood from the centurion, whose business it was to oversee the execution. "And when he knew it of the centurion," that it was as Joseph had said, "he gave"–rather 'made a gift of'–"the body to Joseph"; struck, possibly, with the rank of the petitioner and the dignified boldness of the petition, in contrast with the spirit of the other party and the low rank to which he had been led to believe all the followers of Christ belonged. Nor would he be unwilling to show that he was not going to carry this black affair any farther. But, whatever were Pilate's motives, two most blessed objects were thus secured: (1) *The reality of our Lord's death was attested* by the party of all others most competent to decide on it, and certainly free from all bias–the officer in attendance–in full reliance on whose testimony Pilate surrendered the body: (2) The dead Redeemer, thus delivered out of the hands of His enemies, and committed by the supreme political authority to the care of His friends, was thereby protected from all further indignities; a thing most befitting indeed, now that His work was done, but impossible, so far as we can see, if His enemies had been at liberty to do with Him as they pleased. How wonderful are even the minutest features of this matchless History! **39. also Nicodemus, which at the first came to Jesus by night**–"This remark corresponds to the secrecy of Joseph's discipleship, just noticed, and calls attention to the similarity of their previous character and conduct, and the remarkable change which had now taken place" [WEBSTER and WILKINSON]. **brought . . . myrrh and aloes, about an hundred pounds weight**–an immense quantity, betokening the greatness of their love, but part of it probably intended as a layer for the spot on which the body was to lie. (See II Chron. 16:14) [MEYER]. **40. Then took they the body of Jesus, and wound it in linen clothes with the spices, as the manner of the Jews is to bury**–the mixed and pulverized myrrh and aloes shaken into the folds, and the entire body, thus swathed, wrapt in an outer covering of "clean linen cloth" (Matt. 27:59). Had the Lord's own friends had the least reason to think that the spark of life was still in Him, would *they* have done this? But even if one could conceive them mistaken, could anyone have lain thus enveloped for the period during which He was in the grave, and life still remained? Impossible. When, therefore, He walked forth from the tomb, we can say with the most absolute certainty, "Now is Christ *risen from the dead*, and become the first fruits of them that slept" (I Cor. 15:20). No wonder that the learned and the barbarians alike were prepared to die for the name of the Lord Jesus; for such evidence was to the unsophisticated resistless. (No mention is made of *anointing* in this operation. No doubt it was a hurried proceeding, for fear of interruption, and because it was close on the sabbath, the women seem to have set this as their proper task "as soon as the sabbath should be past" (Mark 16:1). But as the Lord graciously held it as undesignedly anticipated by Mary at Bethany (Mark 14:8), so this was probably all the anointing, in the strict sense of it, which He received. **41, 42. Now in the place where he was crucified there was a garden, and in the garden a new sepulchre**–The choice of this tomb was, on *their* part, dictated by the double circumstance that it was so near at hand, and by its belonging to a friend of the Lord; and as there was need of haste, even they would be struck with the providence which thus supplied it. "There laid they Jesus therefore, because of the Jew's preparation-day, for the sepulchre was nigh at hand." But there was one recommendation of it which probably would not strike them; but God had it in view. Not its being "hewn out of a rock" (Mark 15:46), accessible only at the entrance, which doubtless would impress them with its security and suitableness. But it was "a *new* sepulchre" (vs. 41), "*wherein never man before was laid*" (Luke 23:53): and Matthew (27:60) says that Joseph laid Him "in *his own new tomb*, which he had hewn out in the rock"–doubtless for his own use, though the Lord had higher use for it. Thus as He rode into Jerusalem on an ass "*whereon never man before had sat*," so now He shall lie in a tomb *wherein never man before had lain*, that from these specimens it may be seen that in all things He was "SEPARATE FROM SINNERS."

CHAPTER 20

Vss. 1-18. MARY'S VISIT TO THE SEPULCHRE, AND RETURN TO IT WITH PETER AND JOHN–HER RISEN LORD APPEARS TO HER. **1, 2. The first day . . . cometh Mary Magdalene early . . .**–(See on Mark 16:1-4; and Matt. 28:1, 2). **she runneth and cometh to Simon Peter, and to the other disciple whom Jesus loved, and saith unto them, They have taken away the Lord out of the sepulchre**–Dear disciple! thy dead Lord is to thee "the Lord" still. **3-10. Peter therefore went forth, and that other disciple, and came first to the sepulchre.**–These particulars have a singular air of artless truth about them. Mary, in her grief, runs to the two apostles who were soon to be so closely associated in proclaiming the Saviour's resurrection, and they, followed by Mary, hasten to see with their own eyes. The younger disciple outruns the older; love haply supplying swifter wings. He stoops, he gazes in, but enters not the open sepulchre, held back probably by a reverential fear. The bolder Peter, coming up, goes in at once, and is rewarded with bright evidence of what had happened. **6-7. seeth the linen clothes lie**—lying—**And the napkin, that was about his head, not lying with the linen clothes**—not loosely, as if hastily thrown down, and indicative of a hurried and disorderly removal—**but wrapped**—folded—**together in a place by itself**—showing with what grand tranquillity "the Living One" had walked forth from "the dead" (Luke 24: 5). "Doubtless the two attendant angels (vs. 12) did this service for the Rising One, the one disposing of the linen clothes, the other of the napkin" [BENGEL]. **8. Then went in . . . that other disciple which came first to the sepulchre**—The repetition of this, in connection with his not having gone in till after Peter, seems to show that at the moment of penning these words the advantage which each of these loving disciples had of the other was present to his mind. **and he saw and believed**—Probably he means, though he does not say, that he believed in his Lord's resurrection more immediately and certainly than Peter. **9. For as yet they knew**—i.e., understood—**not the scripture that he must rise again from the dead.**—In other words, they believed in His resurrection at first, not because they were prepared by Scripture to expect it; but *facts* carried resistless conviction of it in the first instance to their minds, and furnished a key to the Scripture predictions of it. **11-15. But Mary stood without at the sepulchre weeping . . .**—Brief was the stay of those two men. But Mary, arriving perhaps by another direction after they left, lingers at the spot, weeping for her missing Lord. As she gazes through her tears on the open tomb, she also ventures to stoop down and look into it, when lo! "two angels in white" (as from the world of light, and see on Matt. 28:3) appear to her in a "sitting" posture, "as having finished some business, and awaiting some one to impart tidings to" [BENGEL]. **12. one at the head, and the other at the feet where the body of Jesus had lain**—not merely proclaiming silently the *entire* charge they had had of the body of Christ [quoted in LUTHARDT], but rather, possibly, calling mute attention to the narrow space within which the Lord of glory had contracted Himself; as if they would say, Come, see within what limits, marked off by the interval here between us two, *the Lord* lay! But she is in tears, and these suit not the scene of so glorious an Exit. They are going to point out to her the incongruity. **13. Woman, why weepest thou?**—You would think the vision too much for a lone woman. But absorbed in the one Object of her affection and pursuit, she speaks out her grief without fear. **Because . . .**—i.e., Can I choose but weep, when "they have taken away . . ." repeating her very words to Peter and John. On this she turned herself and saw Jesus Himself standing beside her, but took Him for the gardener. Clad therefore in some such style He must have been. But if any ask, as too curious interpreters do, whence He got those habiliments, we answer [with OLSHAUSEN and LUTHARDT] where the two angels got theirs. Nor did the voice of His first words disclose Him to Mary—"Woman, why weepest thou? whom seekest thou?" He will *try* her ere he *tell* her. She answers not the stranger's question, but comes straight to her point with him. **15. Sir, if thou have borne him hence**—borne *whom?* She says not. She can think only of *One,* and thinks others must understand her. It reminds one of the question of the Spouse, "Saw ye him whom my soul loveth?" (Song of Sol. 3:3.)

tell me where thou hast laid him, and I will take him away—Wilt thou, dear fragile woman? But it is the language of sublime affection, that thinks itself fit for anything if once in possession of its Object. It is enough. Like Joseph, He can no longer restrain Himself (Gen. 45:1). **16, 17. Jesus saith unto her, Mary**—It is not now the distant, though respectful, "Woman." It is the oft-repeated name, uttered, no doubt, with all the wonted manner, and bringing a rush of unutterable and overpowering associations with it. **She turned herself, and saith to him, Rabboni!**—But that single word of transported recognition was not enough for woman's full heart. Not knowing the change which had passed upon Him, she hastens to express by her action what words failed to clothe; but she is checked. **17. Jesus saith unto her, Touch me not, for I am not yet ascended to my Father**—Old familiarities must now give place to new and more awful yet sweeter approaches; but for these the time has not yet come. This seems the spirit, at least, of these mysterious words, on which much difference of opinion has obtained, and not much that is satisfactory said. **but go to my brethren**—(Cf. Matt. 28:10; Heb. 2:11, 17). That He had still our Humanity, and therefore "*is not ashamed to call us brethren,*" is indeed grandly evidenced by these words. But it is worthy of most reverential notice, that *we nowhere read of anyone who presumed to call Him Brother.* "My brethren: Blessed Jesus, who are these? Were they not Thy followers? yea, Thy forsakers? How dost Thou raise these titles with Thyself! At first they were Thy *servants;* then *disciples;* a little before Thy death, they were Thy *friends;* now, after Thy resurrection, they were Thy *brethren.* But oh, mercy without measure! how wilt Thou, how canst Thou call *them* brethren whom, in Thy last parting, Thou foundest fugitives? Did they not run from Thee? Did not one of them rather leave his inmost coat behind him than not be quit of Thee? And yet Thou sayest, 'Go, tell My brethren! It is not in the power of the sins of our infirmity to unbrother us' " [BISHOP HALL]. **I ascend unto my Father and your Father, and to my God and your God**—words of incomparable glory! Jesus had called God habitually His *Father,* and on one occasion, in His darkest moment, His *God.* But both are here united, expressing that full-orbed relationship which embraces in its vast sweep at once Himself and His redeemed. Yet, note well, He says not, *Our* Father and *our* God. All the deepest of the Church fathers were wont to call attention to this, as expressly designed to distinguish between what God is to Him and to us—*His Father essentially, ours not so: our God essentially, His not so: His God only in connection with us: our God only in connection with Him.* **18. Mary Magdalene came and told the disciples that she had seen the Lord, and that he had spoken these things unto her**—*To a woman was this honor given to be the first that saw the risen Redeemer,* and *that woman was not His mother.* (See on Mark 16:9.)

19-23. JESUS APPEARS TO THE ASSEMBLED DISCIPLES. 19-23. the same day at evening, the first day of the week, the doors being shut where the disciples were assembled for fear of the Jews, came Jesus—plainly not by the ordinary way of entrance. **and saith unto them Peace be unto you**—not the mere *wish* that even His own exalted peace might be theirs (ch. 14:27), but conveying it into their hearts, even as He "opened their understandings to understand the scriptures" (Luke 24:45). **20. And**

when he had so said, he showed them his hands and his side—not only as *ocular* and *tangible* evidence of the *reality* of His resurrection (see on Luke 24:37-43), but as through "the *power* of that resurrection" dispensing all His peace to men. **Then were the disciples glad when they saw the Lord.   21. Then said Jesus**—prepared now to listen to Him in a new character. **Peace be unto you. As my Father hath sent me, so send I you**—(See on ch. 17:18).   **22. he breathed on them**—a symbolical conveyance to them of the Spirit.   **and saith, Receive ye the Holy Ghost**—an earnest and first fruits of the more copious Pentecostal effusion.   **23. Whose soever sins ye remit, they are remitted unto them . . .**—In any *literal* and *authoritative* sense *this power was never exercised by one of the apostles,* and plainly *was never understood by themselves as possessed by them or conveyed to them.* (See on Matthew 16:19.)   The power to intrude upon the relation between men and God cannot have been given by Christ to His ministers in any but a *ministerial* or *declarative* sense—as the authorized interpreters of His word, while in the *actings* of His ministers, the real nature of the power committed to them is seen in the exercise of *church discipline.*

24-29.   JESUS AGAIN APPEARS TO THE ASSEMBLED DISCIPLES.   **24, 25. But Thomas** (see on ch. 14: 16) . . . **was not with them when Jesus came**—why, we know not, though we are loath to think [with STIER, ALFORD and LUTHARDT] it was *intentional,* from sullen despondency.   The fact merely is here stated, as a loving apology for his slowness of belief.   **25. We have seen the Lord**—This way of speaking of Jesus (as vs. 20 and 21:7), so suited to His resurrection-state, was soon to become the prevailing style.   **Except I see in his hands the print of the nails, and put my finger into the print of the nails, and thrust my hand into his side, I will not believe**—The very form of this speech betokens the strength of the unbelief.   "It is not, *If I shall see I shall believe,* but, *Unless I shall see I will not believe;* nor does he expect to see, although the others tell him they had" [BENGEL].   How Christ Himself viewed this state of mind, we know from Mark 16: 14, "He upbraided them with their unbelief and hardness of heart because they believed not them which had seen Him after He was risen."   But whence sprang this pertinacity of resistance in *such* minds?   Not certainly from reluctance to believe, but as in Nathanael (see on ch. 1:46) from mere dread of mistake in so vital a matter.   **26-29. And after eight days**—i.e., on the eighth, or first day of the preceding week.   They probably met every day during the preceding week, but their Lord designedly reserved His second appearance among them till the recurrence of His resurrection day, that He might thus inaugurate the delightful sanctities of THE LORD'S DAY (Rev. 1:10).   **disciples were within, and Thomas with them . . . Jesus . . . stood in the midst, and said, Peace be unto you.   27. Then saith he to Thomas, Reach hither . . . behold . . . put it into my side, and be not faithless, but believing**— "There is something rhythmical in these words, and they are purposely couched in the words of Thomas himself, to put him to shame" [LUTHARDT].   But with what condescension and gentleness is this done!   **28. Thomas answered and said unto him, My Lord and my God**—That Thomas did *not* do what Jesus invited him to do, and what he had made the condition of his believing, seems plain from vs. 29 ("Because thou hast *seen* Me, thou hast believed").   He is overpowered, and the glory of Christ now breaks upon him in a flood.   His ex-

clamation surpasses all that had been yet uttered, nor can it be surpassed by anything that ever will be uttered in earth or heaven.   On the striking parallel in Nathanael, see on ch. 1:49.   The Socinian invasion of the supreme divinity of Christ here manifestly taught—as if it were a mere call upon God in a fit of astonishment—is beneath notice, save for the profanity it charges upon this disciple, and the straits to which it shows themselves reduced.   **29. because thou hast seen me, thou hast believed**—words of measured commendation, but of indirect and doubtless painfully-felt rebuke: i.e., 'Thou hast indeed believed; it is well: it is only on the evidence of thy senses, and after peremptorily refusing all evidence short of that.'   **blessed they that have not seen, and yet have believed**— "Wonderful indeed and rich in blessing for us who have not seen Him, is this closing word of the Gospel" [ALFORD].

30, 31.   FIRST CLOSE OF THIS GOSPEL.   The connection of these verses with the last words of vs. 29 is beautiful: i.e., And indeed, as the Lord pronounced them blessed who not having seen Him have yet believed, so for that one end have the whole contents of this Gospel been recorded, that all who read it may believe on Him, and believing, have life in that blessed name.   30. many other signs—miracles.   **31. But these are written**—as sufficient specimens.   **the Christ, the Son of God**— the one His *official,* the other His *personal,* title. **believing . . . may have life**—(See on ch. 6:51-54).

CHAPTER 21

Vss. 1-23.   SUPPLEMENTARY PARTICULARS.   (That this chapter was added by another hand has been asserted, against clear evidence to the contrary, by some late critics, chiefly because the Evangelist had *concluded* his part of the work with ch. 20:30, 31.   But neither in the Epistles of the New Testament, nor in other good authors, is it unusual to insert supplementary matter, and so have more than one conclusion).   **1, 2. Jesus showed**—manifested—**himself again . . . and on this wise he manifested himself**—This way of speaking shows that after His resurrection He appeared to them but *occasionally, unexpectedly,* and in a way quite *unearthly,* though yet *really* and *corporeally.*   **2. Nathanael**—(See on Matt. 10:3).   **3-6. Peter saith unto them, I go a fishing**—(See on Luke 5:11).   **that night . . . caught nothing**—as at the first miraculous draught (see on Luke 5:5); no doubt so ordered that the miracle might strike them the more by contrast.   The same principle is seen in operation throughout much of Christ's ministry, and is indeed a great law of God's spiritual procedure with His people.   **4. Jesus stood**—(Cf. ch. 20:19, 26).   **but the disciples knew not it was Jesus**—Perhaps there had been some considerable interval since the last manifestation, and having agreed to betake themselves to their secular employment, they would be unprepared to expect Him.   **5. Children**—This term would not necessarily identify Him, being not unusual from any superior; but when they did recognize Him, they would feel it sweetly like Himself.   **have ye any meat?**—provisions, supplies, meaning *fish.*   **They answered . . ., No**—This was in His wonted style, making them *tell* their case, and so the better prepare them for what was coming.   **6. he said unto them, Cast the net on the right side of the ship**—no doubt, by this very specific direction, intending to reveal to them His knowledge of the deep and power over it. **7-11. that disciple whom Jesus loved, said, It is the Lord**—again having the advantage of his brother in quickness of recognition (see on ch. 20:8), to be followed by an alacrity in Peter *all his own*. **he was naked**—his vest only on, worn next the body. **cast himself into the sea** —the shallow part, not more than a hundred yards from the water's edge (vs. 8), not meaning therefore to swim, but to get sooner to Jesus than in the full boat which they could hardly draw to shore. **8. the other disciples came in a little ship**—by ship. **9. they saw**—'see'—**a fire of coals, and fish laid thereon, and bread**—By comparing this with I Kings 19:6, and similar passages, the unseen agency by which Jesus made this provision will appear evident. **10. Jesus saith unto them, Bring of the fish ye have now caught**—Observe the double supply thus provided—His and theirs. The meaning of this will perhaps appear presently. **11. Peter went up**—into the boat; went aboard. **and drew the net to land full of great fishes, an hundred and fifty and three; and for all there were so many, yet was not the net broken**—The manifest reference here to the former miraculous draught (Luke 5:1-11) furnishes the key to this scene. There the draught was *symbolical* of the success of their future ministry: While "Peter and all that were with him were astonished at the draught of the fishes which they had taken, Jesus said unto him, Fear not, from henceforth thou shalt catch men." Nay, when first called, in the act of "casting their net into the sea, for they were fishers," the same *symbolic* reference was made to their secular occupation: "Follow Me, and I will make you fishers of men" (Matt. 4:18, 19). Here, then, if but the same symbolic reference be kept in view, the design of the whole scene will, we think, be clear. The *multitude* and the *size* of the fishes *they* caught symbolically foreshadowed the vast success of their now fast approaching ministry, and this only as a beginning of successive draughts, through the agency of a Christian ministry, till, "as the waters cover the sea, the earth should be full of the knowledge of the Lord." And whereas, at the first miraculous draught, the net "was breaking" through the weight of what it contained—expressive of *the difficulty with which, after they had "caught men," they would be able to retain, or keep them from escaping back into the world*—while here, "for all they were so many, yet was not the net broken," are we not reminded of such sayings as these (chap. 10:28): "I give unto My sheep eternal life, and they shall never perish, neither shall any pluck them out of My hand" [LUTHARDT]? But it is not through the agency of a Christian ministry that all true disciples are gathered. Jesus Himself, by unseen methods, gathers some, who afterwards are recognized by the constituted fishers of men, and mingle with the fruit of their labors. And are not these symbolized by that portion of our Galilean repast which the fishers found, in some unseen way, made ready to their hand? **12-14. none ... durst ask him, Who art thou, knowing it was the Lord**—implying that they *would* have liked Him just to say, "It is I"; but having such convincing *evidence* they were afraid of being "upbraided for their unbelief and hardness of heart" if they ventured to put the question. **13. Jesus ... taketh [the] bread, and giveth them, and [the] fish likewise**—See on Luke 24:30. **14. This is the third time that Jesus showed himself**—was manifested—**to his disciples**—His *assembled* disciples; for if we reckon His appearances to individual disciples, they were more. **15-17.**

when they had dined, Jesus saith—Silence appears to have reigned during the meal; unbroken on *His* part, that by their mute observation of Him they might have their assurance of His identity the more confirmed; and on *theirs,* from reverential shrinking to speak till He did. **15. Simon, son of Jonas, lovest thou me more than these?**—referring lovingly to those sad words of Peter, shortly before denying his Lord, "Though *all men* shall be offended because of Thee, *yet will I never* be offended" (Matt. 26:33), and intending by this allusion to bring the whole scene vividly before his mind and put him to shame. **Yea, Lord; thou knowest that I love thee** —He adds not, "more than these," but prefixes a touching appeal to the Saviour's own omniscience for the truth of his protestation, which makes it a totally different kind of speech from his former. **He saith unto him, Feed my lambs**—It is surely wrong to view this term as a mere diminutive of affection, and as meaning the same thing as "the sheep" [WEBSTER and WILKINSON]. It is much more according to usage to understand by the "lambs" *young and tender* disciples, whether in age or Christian standing (Isa. 40:11; I John 2:12, 13), and by the "sheep" the more *mature*. Shall we say (with many) that Peter was here reinstated in office? Not exactly, since he was not actually excluded from it. But after such conduct as his, the deep wound which the honor of Christ had received, the stain brought on his office, the damage done to his high standing among his brethren, and even his own comfort, in prospect of the great work before him, required some such renewal of his call and re-establishment of his position as this. **16. He saith to him ... the second time ... lovest thou me ...**—In this repetition of the question, though the wound was meant to be reopened, the words *"more than these"* are not repeated; for Christ is a *tender* as well as *skilful* Physician, and Peter's silence on that point was confession enough of his sin and folly. On Peter's repeating his protestation in the same words, our Lord rises higher in the manifestation of His restoring grace. **Feed**—keep—**my sheep**—It has been observed that the word here is studiously changed, from one signifying simply to *feed,* to one signifying to *tend* as a shepherd, denoting the *abiding* exercise of that vocation, and in its highest functions. **17. He saith unto him the third time, Simon, son of Jonas, lovest thou me? Peter was grieved because he said the third time ...** —This was the Physician's deepest incision into the wound, while yet smarting under the two former probings. Not till now would Peter discern the object of this succession of thrusts. The *third* time reveals it all, bringing up such a rush of dreadful recollections before his view, of his "*thrice* denying that he knew Him," that he feels it to the quick. It was fitting that he should; it was meant that he should. But this accomplished, the painful dialogue concludes with a delightful "Feed My sheep"; as if He should say, 'Now, Simon, the last speck of the cloud which overhung thee since that night of nights is dispelled: Henceforth thou art to Me and to My work as if no such scene had ever happened' **18, 19. When thou wast young**—embracing the whole period of life to the verge of old age. **thou girdedst thyself, and walkedst whither thou wouldest**—wast thine own master. **when ... old thou shalt stretch forth thine hands**—to be bound for execution, though not necessarily meaning *on a cross*. There is no reason, however, to doubt the very early tradition that Peter's death was by crucifixion. **19. This spake he, signifying by what**

death he should glorify God—not, therefore, a mere prediction of the manner of his *death,* but of the *honor* to be conferred upon him by dying for his Master. And, indeed, beyond doubt, this prediction was intended to follow up his triple restoration:—'Yes, Simon, thou shalt not only feed My lambs, and feed My sheep, but after a long career of such service, shalt be counted worthy to die for the name of the Lord Jesus.' **And when he had spoken this, he saith unto him, Follow me**—By thus connecting the utterance of this prediction with the invitation to follow Him, the Evangelist would indicate the deeper sense in which the call was understood, not merely to go along with Him at that moment, but to come after Him, *"taking up his cross."* **20, 21. Peter, turning about**—showing that he followed immediately as directed. **seeth the disciple whom Jesus loved following; which also leaned on Jesus' breast at supper, and said, Lord, which is he that betrayeth thee?**—The Evangelist makes these allusions to the peculiar familiarity to which he had been admitted on the most memorable of all occasions, perhaps lovingly to account for Peter's somewhat forward question about him to Jesus; which is the rather probable, as it was at Peter's suggestion that he put the question about the traitor which he here recalls (ch. 13:24, 25). **21. Peter ... saith to Jesus, Lord, and what shall this man do?**—What of this man? or, How shall it fare with him? **22, 23. Jesus saith to him, If I will that he tarry till I come, what is that to thee? follow thou me**—From the fact that John alone of the Twelve survived the destruction of Jerusalem, and so witnessed the commencement of that series of events which belongs to "the last days," many good interpreters think that this is a virtual prediction of fact, and not a mere supposition. But this is very doubtful, and it seems more

natural to consider our Lord as intending to give *no positive indication* of John's fate at all, but to signify that this was a matter which belonged to the Master of both, who would disclose or conceal it as He thought proper, and that Peter's part was to mind his own affairs. Accordingly, in "follow thou Me," the word *"thou"* is emphatic. Observe the absolute disposal of human life which Christ claims: *"If I will* that he tarry till I come . . . ." **23. Then went this saying abroad among the brethren, that that disciple should not die**—into which they the more easily fell from the prevalent expectation that Christ's second coming was then near at hand. **yet Jesus said not unto him, He shall not die**—The Evangelist is jealous for His Master's honor, which his death might be thought to compromise if such a misunderstanding should not be corrected.

24, 25. FINAL CLOSE OF THIS GOSPEL. **24. This is the disciple which testifieth of these things, and wrote these things**—thus identifying the author of this book with all that it says of this disciple. **we know that his testimony is true**—(Cf. ch. 19:35). **25. And there are many other things which Jesus did**—(Cf. ch. 20:30, 31). **if ... written every one, I suppose**—an expression used to show that what follows is not to be pressed too far. **even the world itself would not hold the books ...**—not a *mere* hyperbolical expression, unlike the sublime simplicity of this writer, but intended to let his reader know that, even now that he had done, he felt his materials so far from being exhausted, that he was still running over, and could multiply "Gospels" to almost any extent within the strict limits of what "Jesus did." But in the *limitation* of these matchless histories, in point of number, there is as much of that divine wisdom which has presided over and pervades the living oracles, as in their *variety* and *fulness.*

CHRONOLOGICAL TABLE OF THE PARABLES OF CHRIST

PARABLES	WHERE SPOKEN	WHERE RECORDED
The two debtors	[Capernaum.]	Luke 7:40–43.
The strong man armed	Galilee	Matt. 12:29; Mark 3:27; Luke 11:21, 22.
The unclean spirit	Galilee	Matt. 12:43–45; Luke 11:24–26.
The sower	Seashore of Galilee	Matt. 13:3–9, 18–23; Mark 4:3–9, 14–20; Luke 8:5–8, 11–15.
The tares and wheat	Seashore of Galilee	Matt. 13:24–30, 36–43.
The mustard seed	Seashore of Galilee	Matt. 13:31, 32; Mark 4:30–32; Luke 13:18, 19.
The seed growing secretly	Seashore of Galilee	Mark 4:26–29.
The leaven	Seashore of Galilee	Matt. 13:33; Luke 13:20, 21.
The hid treasure	Seashore of Galilee	Matt. 13:44.
The pearl of great price	Seashore of Galilee	Matt. 13:45, 46.
The draw net	Seashore of Galilee	Matt. 13:47–50.
The unmerciful servant	Capernaum	Matt. 18:21–35.
The good Samaritan	Near Jerusalem	Luke 10:29–37.
The friend at midnight	Near Jerusalem	Luke 11:5–8.
The rich fool	Galilee	Luke 12:16–21.
The barren fig tree	Galilee	Luke 13:6–9.
The great supper	Perea	Luke 14:15–24.
The lost sheep	Perea	Matt. 18:12–14; Luke 15:3–7.
The lost piece of money	Perea	Luke 15:8–10.
The prodigal son	Perea	Luke 15:11–32.
The good shepherd	Jerusalem	John 10:1–18.
The unjust steward	Perea	Luke 16:1–8.
The rich man and Lazarus	Perea	Luke 16:19–31.
The profitable servants	Perea	Luke 17:7–10.
The importunate widow	Perea	Luke 18:1–8.
The Pharisees and publicans	Perea	Luke 18:9–14.
The laborers in the vineyard	Perea	Matt. 20:1–16.
The pounds	Jericho	Luke 19:11–27.
The two sons	Jerusalem	Matt. 21:28–32.
The wicked husbandmen	Jerusalem	Matt. 21:33–44; Mark 12:1–12; Luke 20:9–18.
The marriage of the king's son	Jerusalem	Matt. 22:1–14.
The ten virgins	Mount of Olives	Matt. 25:1–13.
The talents	Mount of Olives	Matt. 25:14–30.

CHRONOLOGICAL TABLE OF THE MIRACLES OF CHRIST

On the order of some of our Lord's Miracles and Parables, the data being scanty, considerable difference obtains.

MIRACLES	WHERE WROUGHT	WHERE RECORDED
Water made wine	Cana	John 2:1–11.
Traders cast out of the temple	Jerusalem	John 2:13–17.
Nobleman's son healed	Cana	John 4:46–54.
First miraculous draught of fishes	Sea of Galilee	Luke 5:1–11.
Leper healed	Capernaum	Matt. 8:2–4; Mark 1:40–45; Luke 5:12–15.
Centurion's servant healed	Capernaum	Matt. 8:5–13; Luke 7:1–10.
Widow's son raised to life	Nain	Luke 7:11–17.
Demoniac healed	Capernaum	Mark 1:21–28; Luke 4:31–37.
Peter's mother-in-law healed	Capernaum	Matt. 8:14, 15; Mark 1:29–31; Luke 4:38, 39.
Paralytic healed	Capernaum	Matt. 9:2–8; Mark 2:1–12; Luke 5:17–26.
Impotent man healed	Jerusalem	John 5:1–16.
Man with withered hand healed	Galilee	Matt. 12:10–14; Mark 3:1–6; Luke 6:6–11.
Blind and dumb demoniac healed	Galilee	Matt. 12:22–24; Luke 11:14.
Tempest stilled	Sea of Galilee	Matt. 8:23–27; Mark 4:35–41; Luke 8:22–25.
Demoniacs dispossessed	Gadara	Matt. 8:28–34; Mark 5:1–20.
Jairus' daughter raised to life	Capernaum }	Matt. 9:18–26; Mark 5:22–24; Luke 8:41–56.
Issue of blood healed	Near Capernaum }	
Two blind men restored to sight	Capernaum	Matt. 9:27–31.
Dumb demoniac healed	Capernaum	Matt. 9:32–34.
Five thousand miraculously fed	Decapolis	Matt. 14:13–21; Mark 6:31–44; Luke 9:10–17; John 6:5–14.
Jesus walks on the sea	Sea of Galilee	Matt. 14:22–33; Mark 6:45–52; John 6:15–21.
Syrophœnician's daughter healed	Coasts of Tyre and Sidon	Matt. 15:21–28; Mark 7:24–30.
Deaf and dumb man healed	Decapolis	Mark 7:31–37.
Four thousand fed	Decapolis	Matt. 15:32–39; Mark 8:1–9.
Blind man restored to sight	Bethsaida	Mark 8:22–26.
Demoniac and lunatic boy healed	Near Cæsarea Philippi	Matt. 17:14–21; Mark 9:14–29; Luke 9:37–43.
Miraculous provision of tribute	Capernaum	Matt. 17:24–27.
The eyes of one born blind opened	Jerusalem	John 9:1–41.
Woman, of 18 years' infirmity, cured	[Perea]	Luke 13:10–17.
Dropsical man healed	[Perea]	Luke 14:1–6.
Ten lepers cleansed	Borders of Samaria	Luke 17:11–19.
Lazarus raised to life	Bethany	John 11:1–46
Two blind beggars restored to sight	Jericho	Matt. 20:29–34; Mark 10:46–52; Luke 18:35–43.
Barren fig tree blighted	Bethany	Matt. 21:12, 13, 18, 19; Mark 11:12–24.
Buyers and sellers again cast out	Jerusalem	Luke 19:45, 46.
Malchus' ear healed	Gethsemane	Matt. 26:51–54; Mark 14:47–49; Luke 22:50, 51; John 18:10, 11.
Second draught of fishes	Sea of Galilee	John 21:1–14.

THE ACTS OF

THE APOSTLES

INTRODUCTION

THIS book is to the Gospels what the fruit is to the tree that bears it. In the Gospels we see the corn of wheat falling into the ground and dying: in the Acts we see it bringing forth much fruit (John 12:24). There we see Christ purchasing the Church with His own blood: here we see the Church, so purchased, rising into actual existence; first among the Jews of Palestine, and next among the surrounding Gentiles, until it gains a footing in the great capital of the ancient world—sweeping majestically from Jerusalem to Rome. Nor is this book of less value as an Introduction to the Epistles which follow it, than as a Sequel to the Gospels which precede it. For without this history the Epistles of the New Testament—presupposing, as they do, the historical circumstances of the parties addressed, and deriving from these so much of their freshness, point, and force—would in no respect be what they now are, and would in a number of places be scarcely intelligible.

The genuineness, authenticity, and canonical authority of this book were never called in question within the ancient Church. It stands immediately after the Gospels, in the catalogues of the *Homologoumena*, or universally acknowledged books of the New Testament (see "Introduction" to our larger *Commentary*, Vol. V, pp. iv, v). It was rejected, indeed, by certain heretical sects in the second and third centuries—by the Ebionites, the Severians (see EUSEBIUS, *Ecclesiastical History*, 4:29), the Marcionites, and the Manicheans: but the totally uncritical character of their objections (see "Introduction" above referred to, pp. xiii, xiv) not only deprives them of all weight, but indirectly shows on what solid grounds the Christian Church had all along proceeded in recognizing this book.

In our day, however, its authenticity has, like that of all the leading books of the New Testament, been made the subject of keen and protracted controversy. DE WETTE, while admitting Luke to be the author of the entire work, pronounces the earlier portion of it to have been drawn up from unreliable sources (*Einleitung*, 2a and 2C). But the Tubingen school, with BAUR at their head, have gone much farther. As their fantastic theory of the post-Joannean date of the Gospels could not pretend even to a hearing so long as the authenticity of the Acts of the Apostles remained unshaken, they contend that the earlier portion of this work can be shown to be unworthy of credit, while the latter portion is in flat contradiction to the Epistle to the Galatians —which this school regard as unassailable—and bears internal evidence of being a designed distortion of facts for the purpose of setting up the catholic form which Paul gave to Christianity in opposition to the narrow Judaic but original form of it which Peter preached, and which after the death of the apostles was held exclusively by the sect of the Ebionites. It is painful to think that anyone should have spent so many years, and, aided by learned and acute disciples in different parts of the argument, should have expended so much learning, research, and ingenuity in attempting to build up a hypothesis regarding the origination of the leading books of the New Testament which outrages all the principles of sober criticism and legitimate evidence. As a school, this party at length broke up: its head, after living to find himself the sole defender of the theory as a whole, left this earthly scene complaining of desertion. While some of his associates have abandoned such heartless studies altogether for the more congenial pursuits of philosophy, others have modified their attacks on the historical truth of the New Testament records, retreating into positions into which it is not worth while to follow them, while others still have been gradually approximating to sound principles. The one compensation for all this mischief is the rich additions to the apologetical and critical literature of the books of the New Testament, and the earliest history of the Christian Church, which it has drawn from the pens of THIERSCH, EBRARD, and many others. Any allusions which it may be necessary for us to make to the assertions of this school will be made in connection with the passages to which they relate—in Acts, I Corinthians, and Galatians.

The manifest connection between this book and the third Gospel—of which it professes to be simply the continuation by the same author—and the striking similarity which marks the style of both productions, leave no room to doubt that the early Church was right in ascribing it with one consent to Luke. The difficulty which some fastidious critics have made about the sources of the earlier portion of the history has no solid ground. That the historian himself was an eyewitness of the earliest scenes—as HUG concludes from the circumstantiality of the narrative—is altogether improbable: but there were hundreds of eyewitnesses of some of the scenes, and enough of all the rest, to give to the historian, partly by oral, partly by written testimony, all the details which he has embodied so graphically in his history; and it will appear, we trust, from the commentary, that DE WETTE's complaints of confusion, contradiction, and error in this portion are without foundation. The same critic, and one or two others, would ascribe to Timothy those later portions of the book in which the historian speaks in the first person plural—"we"; supposing him to have taken notes of all that passed under his own eye, which Luke embodied in his history just as they stood. It is impossible here to refute this gratuitous hypothesis in detail; but the reader will find it done by EBRARD (*Gospel History*, sect. 110, CLARK's translation; sect. 127 of the original work, *Wissenschaftliche Kritik der Evangel. Geschichte*, 1850), and by DAVIDSON ("Introduction to New Testament," Vol. II, pp. 9–21.)

The undesigned coincidences between this History and the Apostolic Epistles have been brought out and handled, as an argument for the truth of the facts thus attested, with unrivalled felicity by PALEY in his *Horæ Paulinæ*, to which Mr. BIRKS has made a number of ingenious additions in his *Horæ Apostolicæ*. Exception has been taken to some of these by JOWETT (*St. Paul's Epistles*, Vol. I, pp. 108ff.), not without a measure of reason in certain cases—for our day, at least—though even he admits that in this line of evidence the work of PALEY, taken as a whole, is unassailable.

Much has been written about the object of this history. Certainly "the Acts of the Apostles" are but very partially recorded. But for this title the historian is not responsible. Between the two extremes—of supposing that the work has no plan at all, and that it is constructed on an elaborate and complex plan, we shall probably be as near the truth as is necessary if we take the design to be to record the diffusion of Christianity and the rise of the Christian Church, first among the Jews of Palestine, the seat of the ancient Faith, and next among the surrounding Gentiles, with Antioch for its headquarters, until, finally, it is seen waving over imperial Rome, foretokening its universal triumph. In this view of it, there is no difficulty in accounting for the almost exclusive place which it gives to the labors of Peter in the first instance, and the all but entire disappearance from the history both of him and of the rest of the Twelve after the great apostle of the Gentiles came upon the stage—like the lesser lights on the rise of the great luminary.

CHAPTER 1

Vss. 1-11. INTRODUCTION—LAST DAYS OF OUR LORD UPON EARTH—HIS ASCENSION. **1, 2. former treatise**—Luke's Gospel. **Theophilus**—(See on Luke 1:3). **began to do and teach**—a very important statement, dividing the work of Christ into two great branches: the one embracing His work *on earth,* the other His subsequent work *from heaven;* the one in His own Person, the other by His Spirit; the one the "beginning," the other the continuance of the same work; the one complete when He sat down at the right hand of the Majesty on high, the other to continue till His second appearing; the one recorded in "The Gospels," the *beginnings* only of the other related in this book of "The Acts." "Hence the grand history of what Jesus did and taught does not conclude with His departure to the

Father; but Luke now begins it in a higher strain; for all the subsequent labors of the apostles are just an exhibition of *the ministry of the glorified Redeemer Himself,* because they were acting under His authority, and He was the principle that operated in them all" [OLSHAUSEN]. **after he, through the Holy Ghost, had given commandments...**—referring to the charge recorded in Matthew 28:18-20; Mark 16:15-18; Luke 24:44-49. It is worthy of notice that nowhere else are such communications of the risen Redeemer said to have been given "through the Holy Ghost." In general, this might have been said of all He uttered and all He did in His official character; for it was for this very end that God "gave not the Spirit by measure unto Him" (John 3:34). But after His resurrection, as if to signify the new relation in which He now stood to the Church, He signalized His first meeting with the assembled disciples by *breathing* on them (immediately after dispensing to them His *peace*) and saying, *"Receive ye the Holy Ghost,"* thus anticipating the donation of the Spirit from His hands (see on John 20:21, 22); and on the same principle His parting charges are here said to have been given "through the Holy Ghost," as if to mark that He was now all redolent with the Spirit; that what had been husbanded, during His suffering work, for His own necessary uses, had now been set free, was already overflowing from Himself to His disciples, and needed but His ascension and glorification to flow all forth. (See on John 7:39.) **3-5. showed himself alive**—As the author is about to tell us that *"the resurrection of the Lord Jesus"* was the great burden of apostolic preaching, so the subject is here fitly introduced by an allusion to the primary evidence on which that great fact rests, the repeated and undeniable manifestations of Himself in the body to the assembled disciples, who, instead of being predisposed to believe it, had to be overpowered by the resistless evidence of their own senses, and were slow of yielding even to this (Mark 16:14). **after his passion**—or, suffering. This primary sense of the word "passion" has fallen into disuse; but it is nobly consecrated in the phraseology of the Church to express the Redeemer's final endurances. **seen of them forty days**—This important specification of time occurs here only. **speaking of**—rather 'speaking'—**the things pertaining to the kingdom of God** —till now only in germ, but soon to take visible form; the earliest and the latest burden of His teaching on earth. **4. should not depart from Jerusalem**—because the Spirit was to glorify the existing economy, by descending on the disciples at its metropolitan seat, and at the next of its great festivals after the ascension of the Church's Head; in order that "out of Zion might go forth the law, and the word of the Lord from Jerusalem" (Isa. 2: 3; and cf. Luke 24:49). **5. ye shall be baptized with the Holy Ghost not many days hence**—*ten* days hence, as appears from Leviticus 23:15, 16; but it was expressed thus indefinitely to exercise their faith. **6-8. wilt thou at this time restore the kingdom to Israel?**—Doubtless their carnal views of Messiah's kingdom had by this time been modified, though how far it is impossible to say. But, as they plainly looked for *some* restoration of the kingdom to Israel, so they are neither rebuked nor contradicted on this point. **7. It is not for you to know the times . . .**—implying not only that this was *not* the time, but that the question was irrelevant to their present business and future work. **8. receive power**—See Luke 24:49. **and ye shall be witnesses unto me . . . in Jerusalem . . . in all Judea . . . and unto the uttermost part of the earth**—*This order of apostolic preaching and success supplies the proper key to the plan of the Acts,* which relates first the progress of the Gospel "in Jerusalem, and all Judea and Samaria" (ch. 1 to ch. 9), and then "unto the uttermost part of the earth" (ch. 10 to ch. 28). **9-11. while they beheld, he was taken up**—See on Luke 24:50-53. Lest it should be thought He had disappeared when they were looking in some other direction, and so was only *concluded* to have gone up to heaven, it is here expressly said that *"while they were looking"* He was taken up, and a cloud received Him *out of their sight."* So Elijah, "If thou *see me* when I am taken from thee" (II Kings 2:10); "And Elisha *saw it"* (vs. 12). (See on Luke 9:32.) **10. while they looked steadfastly toward heaven**—following Him with their eager eyes, in

rapt amazement. Not, however, as a mere fact is this recorded, but as a part of that resistless evidence of their senses on which their whole subsequent testimony was to be borne. **two men in white apparel**—angels in human form, as in Luke 24:4. **11. Ye men of Galilee, why stand ye gazing up into heaven . . .**—'as if your now glorified Head were gone from you never to return: He is coming again; not another, but "this same Jesus"; and "as ye have seen Him go, in the like manner shall He come"—as *personally,* as *visibly,* as *gloriously;* and let the joyful expectation of this coming swallow up the sorrow of that departure.'

12-26. RETURN OF THE ELEVEN TO JERUSALEM— PROCEEDINGS IN THE UPPER ROOM TILL PENTECOST. **12-14. a sabbath day's journey**—about 2000 cubits. **went up into an upper room**—perhaps the same "large upper room" where with their Lord they had celebrated the last Passover and the first Supper (Luke 22:12). **where abode**—not lodged, but had for their place of rendezvous. **Peter . . .**—See on Matthew 10:2-4. **14. continued with one accord**—knit by a bond stronger than death. **in prayer and supplication**—for the promised baptism, the need of which in their orphan state would be increasingly felt. **and Mary the mother of Jesus**— distinguished from the other "women," but "so as to exclude the idea of her having any pre-eminence over the disciples. We find her with the rest in prayer to her glorified Son [WEBSTER and WILKINSON]. *This is the last mention of her in the New Testament.* The fable of the *Assumption of the Virgin* has no foundation even in tradition [ALFORD]. **with his brethren**—See on John 7:3-5. **15-26. in those days**—of expectant prayer, and probably towards the close of them, when the nature of their future work began more clearly to dawn upon them, and the Holy Ghost, already "breathed" on the Eleven (John 20:22), was stirring in Peter, who was to be the leading spirit of the infant community (Matt. 16:19). **the number . . . about an hundred and twenty**—Many, therefore, of the "500 brethren" who saw their risen Lord "at once" (I Cor. 15:6), must have remained in Galilee. **18. falling headlong . . .**—This information supplements, but by no means contradicts, what is said in Matthew 27:5. **20. his bishopric**—or 'charge.' The words are a combination of Psalms 69:25 and 109:8; in which the apostle discerns a greater than David, and a worse than Ahithophel and his fellow conspirators against David. **21. all the time the Lord Jesus went in and out among us**—in the close intimacies of a three years' public life. **22. Beginning from the baptism of John**—by whom our Lord was not only Himself baptized, but first officially announced and introduced to his own disciples. **unto that same day when he was taken up from us, must one be ordained to be a witness with us of his resurrection**—How clearly is the primary office of the apostles here expressed: (1) to testify, from personal observation, to the one great fact of "the resurrection of the Lord Jesus"; (2) to show how his glorified His whole previous life, of which they were constant observers, and established His divine claims. **23. they appointed**—'put up' in nomination; meaning not the Eleven but the whole company, of whom Peter was the spokesman. **two**—The choice would lie between a very few. **24. prayed and said, Thou, Lord . . .**—"The word 'Lord,' placed absolutely, denotes in the New Testament almost universally THE SON; and the words, 'Show whom Thou hast chosen,' are decisive. The apostles are just Christ's messengers: It is He that sends them, and of Him they bear witness. Here, therefore, we have the first example of a prayer offered to the exalted Redeemer; furnishing indirectly the strongest proof of His divinity" [OLSHAUSEN]. **which knowest the hearts of all men** —See John 2:24, 25; 21:15-17; Revelation 2:23. **25. that he might go to his own place**—A euphemistic or softened expression of the awful future of the traitor, implying not only destined habitation but congenial element. **26. was numbered**— 'voted in' by general suffrage. **with the eleven apostles**—completing the broken Twelve.

CHAPTER 2

Vss. 1-13. DESCENT OF THE SPIRIT—THE DISCIPLES SPEAK WITH TONGUES—AMAZEMENT OF THE MULTITUDE. **1-4. when the day of Pentecost was fully come**—The fiftieth from the morrow after the first Passover sabbath (Lev. 23:15, 16). **with one accord**—the solemnity of the day, perhaps, unconsciously raising their expectations. **2. And suddenly there came a sound from heaven, as of a rushing mighty wind ...**—"The whole description is so picturesque and striking that it could only come from an eyewitness" [OLSHAUSEN]. The suddenness, strength, and diffusiveness of the sound strike with deepest awe the whole company, and thus complete their preparation for the heavenly gift. Wind was a familiar emblem of the Spirit (Ezek. 37:9; John 3:8; 20:22). But this was not a rush of actual wind. It was only a sound *"as of"* it. **3. cloven tongues, like as of fire ...**—'disparted tonques,' i.e., tongue-shaped, flamelike appearances, rising from a common center or root, and resting upon each of that large company:—beautiful visible symbol of the burning energy of the Spirit now descending in all His plenitude upon the Church, and about to pour itself through every tongue, and over every tribe of men under heaven! **4. they ... began to speak with ... tongues ...**—real, living languages, as is plain from what follows. The thing uttered, probably the same by all, was "the wonderful works of God," perhaps in the inspired words of the Old Testament evangelical hymns; though it is next to certain that the speakers themselves understood nothing of what they uttered (see on I Cor. 14). **5-11. there were dwelling at Jerusalem Jews, devout men out of every nation**—not, it would seem, permanently settled there (see vs. 9), though the language seems to imply more than a temporary visit to keep this one feast. **9. Parthians ...**—Beginning with the farthest east, the Parthians, the enumeration proceeds farther and farther westward till it comes to Judea; next come the western countries, from Cappadocia to Pamphylia; then the southern, from Egypt to Cyrene; finally, apart from all geographical consideration, Cretes and Arabians are placed together. This enumeration is evidently designed to convey an impression of universality [BAUMGARTEN].
14-36. PETER, FOR THE FIRST TIME, PUBLICLY PREACHES CHRIST. **14-21. Peter, standing up with the eleven**—in advance, perhaps, of the rest. **15. these are not drunken**—meaning, not the Eleven, but the body of the disciples. **but the third hour** —9 A.M. (see Eccles. 10:16; Isa. 5:11; I Thess. 5:17). **17. in the last days**—meaning, the days of the Messiah (Isa. 2:2); as closing all preparatory arrangements, and constituting the final dispensation of God's kingdom on earth. **pour out of my Spirit**— in contrast with the mere drops of all preceding

time. **upon all flesh**—hitherto confined to the seed of Abraham. **sons ... daughters ... young men ... old men ... servants ... handmaidens**—without distinction of sex, age, or rank. **see visions ... dream dreams**—This is a mere accommodation to the ways in which the Spirit operated under the ancient economy, when the prediction was delivered; for in the New Testament, visions and dreams are rather the exception than the rule. **19. I will show wonders ...**—referring to the signs which were to precede the destruction of Jerusalem (see on Luke 21: 25-28). **21. whosoever shall call on the name of the Lord shall be saved**—This points to the permanent establishment of the economy of salvation, which followed on the breaking up of the Jewish state. **22-28. a man approved of God**—rather, 'authenticated,' 'proved,' or 'demonstrated to be from God.' **by miracles ... which God did by him**—This is not a low view of our Lord's miracles, as has been alleged, nor inconsistent with John 2: 11, but is in strict accordance with His progress from humiliation to glory, and with His own words in John 5:19. This view of Christ is here dwelt on to exhibit to the Jews the whole course of Jesus of Nazareth as the ordinance and doing of *the God of Israel* [ALFORD]. **23. determinate counsel and foreknowledge**—God's fixed plan and perfect foresight of all the steps involved in it. **ye have taken, and by wicked hands have crucified and slain**— How strikingly is the criminality of Christ's murderers here presented in harmony with the eternal purpose to surrender Him into their hands! **24. was not possible he should be holden of it**—Glorious saying! It was indeed impossible that "the Living One" should remain "among the dead" (Luke 24:5); but here, the impossibility seems to refer to the prophetic assurance that He should not see corruption. **27. wilt not leave my soul in hell** —in its disembodied state (see on Luke 16:23). **neither ... suffer thine Holy One to see corruption** —in the grave. **28. Thou hast made known to me the ways of life**—i.e., resurrection-life. **thou shalt make me full of joy with thy countenance**—i.e., in glory; as is plain from the whole connection and the actual words of the 16th Psalm. **29-36. David ... is ... dead and buried ...**—Peter, full of the Holy Ghost, sees in this 16th Psalm, one Holy Man, whose life of high devotedness and lofty spirituality is crowned with the assurance, that though He taste of death, He shall rise again without seeing corruption, and be admitted to the bliss of God's immediate presence. Now as this was palpably untrue of David, it could be meant only of One other, even of Him whom David was taught to expect as the final Occupant of the throne of Israel. (Those, therefore, and they are many, who take David himself to be the subject of this Psalm, and the words quoted to refer to Christ only *in a more eminent* sense, nullify the whole argument of the apostle.) The Psalm is then affirmed to have had its only proper fulfilment in JESUS, of whose resurrection and ascension they were witnesses, while the glorious effusion of the Spirit by the hand of the ascended One, setting an infallible seal upon all, was even then witnessed by the thousands who stood listening to Him. A further illustration of Messiah's ascension and session at God's right hand is drawn from Psalm 110:1, in which David cannot be thought to speak of himself, seeing he is still in his grave. **36. Therefore**—i.e., to sum up all. **let all the house of Israel**—for in this first discourse the appeal is formally made to the whole house of Israel, as the then existing Kingdom of God. **know**

assuredly—by indisputable facts, fulfilled predictions, and the seal of the Holy Ghost set upon all. **that God hath made**—for Peter's object was to show them that, instead of interfering with the arrangements of the God of Israel, these events were His own high movements. **this same Jesus, whom ye have crucified**—"The sting is at the close" [BENGEL]. To prove to them merely that Jesus was the Messiah might have left them all unchanged in heart. But to convince them that He whom they had crucified had been by the right hand of God exalted, and constituted the "LORD" whom David in spirit adored, to whom every knee shall bow, and the CHRIST of God, was to bring them to "look on Him whom they had pierced and mourn for Him." **37-40. pricked in their hearts**—the begun fulfilment of Zechariah 12:10, whose full accomplishment is reserved for the day when "all Israel shall be saved" (see on Rom. 11). **what shall we do?**—This is that beautiful spirit of genuine compunction and childlike docility, which, discovering its whole past career to have been one frightful mistake, seeks only to be set right for the future, be the change involved and the sacrifices required what they may. So Saul of Tarsus (ch. 9:6). **38. Repent**—The word denotes *change of mind,* and here includes the reception of the Gospel as the proper issue of that revolution of mind which they were then undergoing. **baptized . . . for the remission of sins**—as the visible seal of that remission. **39. For the promise**—of the Holy Ghost, through the risen Saviour, as the grand blessing of the new covenant. **all afar off**—the Gentiles (as in Eph. 2:17, but "to the Jew first." **40. with many other words did he testify and exhort** —Thus we have here but a summary of Peter's discourse; though from the next words it would seem that only the more practical parts, the home appeals, are omitted. **Save yourselves from this untoward generation**—as if Peter already foresaw the hopeless impenitence of the nation at large, and would have his hearers hasten in for themselves and secure their own salvation.

41-47. BEAUTIFUL BEGINNINGS OF THE CHRISTIAN CHURCH. **41-47. they that gladly received his word were baptized**—"It is difficult to say how 3000 could be baptized in one day, according to the old practice of a complete submersion; and the more as in Jerusalem there was no water at hand except Kidron and a few pools. The difficulty can only be removed by supposing that they already employed sprinkling, or baptized in houses in large vessels. Formal submersion in rivers, or larger quantities of water, probably took place only where the locality conveniently allowed it" [OLSHAUSEN]. **the same day there were added to them about 3000 souls**—fitting inauguration of the new kingdom, as an economy of the Spirit! **42. continued steadfastly in**—'attended constantly upon.' **the apostles' doctrine**—'teaching'; giving themselves up to the instructions which, in their raw state, would be indispensable to the consolidation of the immense multitude suddenly admitted to visible discipleship. **fellowship**—in its largest sense. **breaking of bread**—not certainly in the Lord's Supper alone, but rather in frugal repasts taken together, with which the Lord's Supper was probably conjoined until abuses and persecution led to the discontinuance of the common meal. **prayers**—probably, stated seasons of it. **43. fear came upon every soul**—A deep awe rested upon the whole community. **44. all that believed were together, and had all things common**—(See on ch. 4:34-37).

46. daily . . . in the temple—observing the hours of Jewish worship—**and breaking bread from house to house**—Rather, 'at home' (*margin*), i.e., in *private,* as contrasted with their *temple*-worship, but in some stated place or places of meeting. **eat their meat with gladness**—'exultation'—**and singleness of heart. 47. Praising God**—"Go thy way, eat thy bread with joy, and drink thy wine with a merry heart, *for God now accepteth thy works*" (Eccles. 9:7, see also on ch. 8:39). **having favour with all the people**—commending themselves by their lovely demeanor to the admiration of all who observed them. **And the Lord**—i.e., JESUS, as the glorified Head and Ruler of the Church. **added**—kept adding; i.e., to the visible community of believers, though the words "to the Church" are wanting in the most ancient MSS. **such as should be saved**—Rather, 'the saved,' or 'those who were being saved.' "The young Church had but few peculiarities in its outward form, or even in its doctrine: the single discriminating principle of its few members was that they all recognized the crucified Jesus of Nazareth as the Messiah. This confession would have been a thing of no importance, if it had only presented itself as a naked declaration, and would never in such a case have been able to form a community that would spread itself over the whole Roman empire. It acquired its value only through the power of the Holy Ghost, passing from the apostles as they preached to the hearers; for He brought the confession from the very hearts of men (I Cor. 12:3), and like a burning flame made their souls glow with love. By the power of this Spirit, therefore, we behold the first Christians not only in a state of active fellowship, but also internally changed: the narrow views of the natural man are broken through; they have their possessions in common, and they regard themselves as one family" [OLSHAUSEN].

CHAPTER 3

Vss. 1-26. PETER HEALS A LAME MAN AT THE TEMPLE GATE—HIS ADDRESS TO THE WONDERING MULTITUDE. **1-11. Peter and John**—already associated by their Master, first with James (Mark 1: 29; 5:37; 9:2), then by themselves (Luke 22:8; and see John 13:23, 24). Now we find them constantly together, but John (yet young) only as a silent actor. **went up**—were going up, were on their way. **2. a certain man lame from his mother's womb**—and now "above 40 years old" (ch. 4:22)—**was carried**—was wont to be carried. **4. Peter fastening his eyes on him with John, said, Look on us. 5. And he gave heed**—that, through the eye, faith might be aided in its birth. **6. Silver and gold have I none, but such as I have give I thee.**—What a lofty superiority breathes in these words! **In the name of Jesus Christ of Nazareth rise up and walk.**—These words, uttered with supernatural power, doubtless begat in this poor man the faith that sent healing virtue through his diseased members. **7. And he took . . . and lifted him up**—precisely what his Lord had done to his own mother-in-law (Mark 1:31). **his feet**—'soles'—**and ankle bones . . .**—the technical language of a physician (Col. 4:14). **8. leaping up, stood . . . walked . . . entered the temple walking, leaping, and praising God**—Every word here is emphatic, expressing the perfection of the cure, as vs. 7 its immediateness. **9. all the people saw him . . .**—as they assembled at the hour of public prayer, in the temple courts; so that the miracle had the utmost publicity. **10. they knew that it was he which sat for alms ...** —(Cf. John 9:8). **11. the lame man ... held ...**— This is human nature. **all the people ran together unto them in the porch ...**—How vividly do these graphic details bring the whole scene before us! Thus was Peter again furnished with a vast audience, whose wonder at the spectacle of the healed beggar clinging to his benefactors prepared them to listen with reverence to his words. **12-16. why marvel at this?**—For miracles are marvels only in relation to the limited powers of man. **as though by our own power or holiness we had made this man to walk.**—Neither the might nor the merit of the cure are due to us, mere agents of Him whom we preach. **13. The God of Abraham ...** —See on ch. 2:22, 36. **hath glorified his Son Jesus** —rather, 'his Servant Jesus,' as the same word is rendered in Matthew 12:18, but in that high sense in which Isaiah applies it always to Messiah (Isa. 42:1; 49:6; 52:13; 53:11). When 'Son' is intended a different word is used. **whom ye delivered up ...** —With what heroic courage does Peter here charge his auditors with the heaviest of all conceivable crimes, and with what terrific strength of language are these charges clothed! **15. killed the Prince of life**—Glorious paradox, but how piercing to the conscience of the auditors. **16. his name, through faith in his name, hath made this man strong ...**— With what skill does the apostle use the miracle both to glorify his ascended Lord and bring the guilt of His blood more resistlessly home to his audience! **17-21. And now, brethren.**—Our preacher, like his Master, "will not break the bruised reed." His heaviest charges are prompted by love, which now hastens to assuage the wounds it was necessary to inflict. **I wot**—'know.' **through ignorance ye did it**—(See *marginal reference*). **18. that Christ**—The best MSS. read, 'that His Christ'— **should suffer**—The doctrine of a SUFFERING MESSIAH was totally at variance with the current views of the Jewish Church, and hard to digest even by the Twelve, up to the day of their Lord's resurrection. Our preacher himself revolted at it, and protested against it, when first nakedly announced, for which he received a terrible rebuke. Here he affirms it to be the fundamental truth of ancient prophecy realized unwittingly by the Jews themselves, yet by a glorious divine ordination. How great a change had the Pentecostal illumination wrought upon his views! **19. when the times of refreshing shall come**—rather, 'in order that the times of refreshing may come'; that long period of repose, prosperity and joy, which all the prophets hold forth to the distracted Church and this miserable world, as eventually to come, and which is here, as in all the prophets, made to turn upon the national conversion of Israel. **20. he shall send Jesus Christ**—The true reading is, 'He shall send your predestinated [or foreordained] Messiah, Jesus.' **21. until the times**—embracing the whole period between the ascension and the second advent of Christ. **restitution of all things**—comprehending, probably, the rectification of all the disorders of the fall. **22-26. a prophet ... like unto me**—particularly in *intimacy of communication with God* (Num. 12:6-8), *and as the mediatorial Head of a new order of things* (Heb. 3:2-6). Peter takes it for granted that, in the light of all he had just said, it would be seen at once that One only had any claim to be that Prophet. **him shall ye hear in all things ...**—This part of the prediction is emphatically added, in order to shut up the au-

dience to the obedience of faith, on pain of being finally "cut off" from the congregation of the righteous (Ps. 1:1). **24. foretold of these days**—of Messiah; all pointing to "the time of reformation" (Heb. 9:10), though with more or less distinctness. **25. Ye are the children ... of the covenant**—and so the natural heirs of its promises. **in thy seed ...**— (See on Gal. 3:8, etc.). **26. God, having raised up** —not from the dead, but having provided, prepared, and given. **his Son Jesus**—'His Servant Jesus' (see on vs. 13). **sent him to bless you**—lit., 'sent Him blessing you,' as if laden with blessing. **in turning away every one of you from his iniquities**—i.e., 'Hitherto we have all been looking too much for a Messiah who should shed outward blessings upon the nation generally, and through it upon the world. But we have learned other things, and now announce to you that the great blessing with which Messiah has come laden is the turning away of every one of you from his iniquities.' With what divine skill does the apostle, founding on resistless facts, here drive home to the conscience of his auditors their guilt in crucifying the Lord of Glory; then soothe their awakened minds by assurances of forgiveness on turning to the Lord, and a glorious future as soon as this shall come to pass, to terminate with the Personal Return of Christ from the heavens whither He has ascended; ending all with warnings, from their own Scriptures, to submit to Him if they would not perish, and calls to receive from Him the blessings of salvation.

CHAPTER 4

Vss. 1-13. PETER AND JOHN BEFORE THE SANHEDRIM. **1-12. the captain**—of the Levitical guard— **of the temple**—annoyed at the disturbance created around it. **and the Sadducees**—who "say that there is no resurrection" (ch. 23:8), irritated at the apostles "preaching through [rather, 'in'] Jesus the resurrection from the dead"; for the resurrection of Christ, if a fact, effectually overthrew the Sadducean doctrine. **4. the number of the men**—or males, exclusive of women; though the word sometimes includes both. **about five thousand**—and this in Jerusalem, where the means of detecting the imposture or crushing the fanaticism, if such it had been, were within everyone's reach, and where there was every inducement to sift it to the bottom. **5. their rulers ...**—This was a regular meeting of the Sanhedrim (see on Matt. 2:4). **6. Annas ... and Caiaphas**—(See on Luke 3:2). **John and Alexander**—of whom nothing is known. **7. By what power or ... name have ye done this**—thus admitting the reality of the miracle, which afterwards they confess themselves unable to deny (vs. 16). **8. Then, filled with the Holy Ghost, said**— (See Mark 13:11; Luke 21:15). **10. Be it known unto you ... and to all the people of Israel**—as if emitting a formal judicial testimony to the entire nation through its rulers now convened. **by the name of Jesus ...**—(See on ch. 3:13, etc). **even by him doth this man stand before you whole**—for from vs. 14 it appears that the healed man was at that moment before their eyes. **11. This is the stone which was set at naught of you builders ...**— This application of Psalm 118:22, already made by our Lord Himself before some of the same "builders" (Matt. 21:42), is here repeated with peculiar propriety after the deed of rejection had been consummated, and the rejected One had, by His exaltation to the right hand of the Majesty on high, become "the head of the corner." **12. Neither is there salvation in any other; for there is none other name under heaven given among men whereby we must be saved**—How sublimely does the apostle, in these closing words, shut up these rulers of Israel to Jesus for salvation, and in what universal and emphatic terms does he hold up his Lord as the one Hope of men! **13-17. perceived that they were unlearned and ignorant men**—i.e., uninstructed in the learning of the Jewish schools, and of the common sort; men in private life, untrained to teaching. **took knowledge of them that they had been with Jesus**—recognized them as having been in His company; remembering possibly, that they had seen them with Him [Meyer, Bloomfield, Alford]; but, more probably, perceiving in their whole bearing what identified them with Jesus: i.e., 'We thought we had got rid of Him; but lo! He reappears in these men, and all that troubled us in the Nazarene Himself has yet to be put down in these His disciples.' What a testimony to these primitive witnesses! Would that the same could be said of their successors! **16. a notable miracle ... done by them is manifest to all ... in Jerusalem; and we cannot deny it**—And why should we wish to deny it, O ye rulers, but that ye hate the light, and will not come to the light lest your deeds should be reproved? **17. But that it spread no further ... let us straitly**—strictly—**threaten ... that they speak henceforth to no man in this name**—Impotent device! Little knew they the fire that was burning in the bones of those heroic disciples. **18-22. Whether it be right ... to hearken to you more than ... God, judge ye. 20. For we cannot but speak the things which we have seen and heard**—There is here a wonderful union of sober, respectful appeal to the better reason of their judges, and calm, deep determination to abide the consequences of a constrained testimony, which betokens a power above their own resting upon them, according to promise. **21. finding nothing how they might punish them, because of the people**—not at a loss for a pretext, but at a loss how to do it so as not to rouse the opposition of the people.

23-37. Peter and John, Dismissed from the Sanhedrim, Report the Proceedings to the Assembled Disciples—They Engage in Prayer—The Astonishing Answer and Results. 23-30. being let go, they went to their own company—Observe the two opposite classes, representing the two interests which were about to come into deadly conflict. **24. they lifted up their voice**—the assembled disciples, on hearing Peter's report. **with one accord**—the breasts of all present echoing every word of this sublime prayer. **Lord**—See on Luke 2:29. Applied to God, the term expresses absolute authority. **God which hast made heaven and earth**—against whom, therefore, all creatures are powerless. **25. by the mouth of ... David**—to whom the Jews ascribed the 2d Psalm, though anonymous; and internal evidence confirms it. David's spirit sees with astonishment "the heathen, the people, the kings and princes of the earth," in deadly combination against the sway of Jehovah and *His Anointed* (his Messiah, or Christ), and asks "why" it is. This fierce confederacy our praying disciples see in full operation, in the "gathering together of Herod and Pilate, the Gentiles (the Roman authority), and the people of Israel, against God's holy Child ('Servant') Jesus." (See on ch. 3:13). The best ancient copies read, after "were gathered together," '*in this city*,' which probably answers to "upon my holy hill of Zion," in the Psalm. **28.**

thy hand and thy counsel determined ... to be done—i.e., "Thy counsel" determined to be done by "Thy hand." **29. now, Lord, behold their threatenings**—Recognizing in the threatenings of the Sanhedrim a declaration of war by the combined powers of the world against their infant cause, they seek not enthusiastically to hide from themselves its critical position, but calmly ask the Lord of heaven and earth to "look upon their threatenings." **that with all boldness they may speak thy word**—Rising above self, they ask only fearless courage to testify for their Master, and divine attestation to their testimony by miracles of healing, etc., in His name. **31-37. place was shaken**—glorious token of the commotion which the Gospel was to make (ch. 17:6; cf. 16:26), and the overthrow of all opposing powers in which this was to issue. **they were all filled with the Holy Ghost, and spake ...**—The Spirit rested upon the entire community, first, in the very way they had asked, so that they "spake the word with boldness" (vss. 29, 31); next, in melting down all selfishness, and absorbing even the feeling of individuality in an intense and glowing realization of Christian unity. The community of goods was but an outward expression of this, and natural in such circumstances. **33. with great power**—effect on men's minds. **great grace was upon them all**—The grace of God copiously rested on the whole community. **35. laid ... at the apostles' feet**—sitting, it may be, above the rest. But the expression may be merely derived from that practice, and here meant figuratively. **36. Joses ...**—This is specified merely as an eminent example of that spirit of generous sacrifice which pervaded all. **son of consolation**—no doubt so surnamed from the character of his ministry. **a Levite**—who, though as a tribe having no inheritance, might and did acquire property as individuals (Deut. 18:8). **Cyprus**—a well-known island in the Mediterranean.

CHAPTER 5

Vss. 1-11. Ananias and Sapphira. "The first trace of a shade upon the bright form of the young Church. Probably among the new Christians a kind of holy rivalry had sprung up, every one eager to place his means at the disposal of the apostles" [Olshausen]. Thus might the newborn zeal of some outrun their abiding principle, while others might be tempted to seek credit for a liberality which was not in their character. **2. kept back part of the price, his wife also being privy to it**—The coolness with which they planned the deception aggravated the guilt of this couple. **brought a certain part**—pretending it to be the whole proceeds of the sale. **3-6. why hath Satan filled**—'why ... fill—'why hast thou suffered him to fill'—**thine heart ...**—so criminally entertaining his suggestion? Cf. vs. 4, "why hast thou conceived this thing in thine heart?" And see John 13:2, 27. **to lie to the Holy Ghost**—to men under His supernatural illumination. **4. While it remained, was it not thine own? and after it was sold, was it not in thine own power?**—from which we see how purely voluntary were all these sacrifices for the support of the infant community. **not lied to men but God**—to men so entirely the instruments of the directing Spirit that the lie was rather told to Him: language clearly implying both the distinct *personality* and the proper *divinity* of the Holy Ghost. **5 Ananias ... gave up the ghost ... great fear came on all that heard these** things—on those without the Christian circle; who, instead of disparaging the followers of the Lord Jesus, as they might otherwise have done on the discovery of such hypocrisy, were awed at the manifest presence of Divinity among them, and the mysterious power of throwing off such corrupt matter which rested upon the young Church. **6. the young men**—some of the younger and more active members of the church, not as office-bearers, nor coming forward now for the first time, but who probably had already volunteered their services in making subordinate arrangements. In every thriving Christian community such volunteers may be expected, and will be found eminently useful. **7-11. Tell me whether ye sold the land for so much**—naming the sum. **9. How is it that ye have agreed together**—See on vs. 2. **to tempt the Spirit** *try* whether they could escape detection by that omniscient Spirit of whose supernatural presence with the apostles they had had such full evidence. **feet of them that buried thy husband are at the door**—How awfully graphic! **10. buried her by her husband**—The later Jews buried before sunset of the day of death. **11. great fear on all the church . . .**—This effect on the Christian community itself was the chief design of so startling a judgment; which had its counterpart, as the sin itself had, in *Achan* (Josh. 7), while the *time*—at the commencement of a new career—was similar.

12-26. THE PROGRESS OF THE NEW CAUSE LEADS TO THE ARREST OF THE APOSTLES—THEY ARE MIRACULOUSLY DELIVERED FROM PRISON, RESUME THEIR TEACHING, BUT ALLOW THEMSELVES TO BE CONDUCTED BEFORE THE SANHEDRIM. **12.** Solomon's **Porch**—See on John 10:23. **13-16. of the rest durst no man join himself . . .**—Of the unconverted none ventured, after what had taken place, to profess discipleship; but yet their number continually increased. **15. into the streets**—'in every street.' **on beds and couches**—The words denote the softer couches of the rich and the meaner cribs of the poor [BENGEL]. **shadow of Peter . . . might overshadow some of them**—Cf. ch. 19:12; Luke 8: 46. So Elisha. Now the predicted greatness of Peter (Matt. 16:18), as the directing spirit of the early Church, was at its height. **17-23. sect of the Sadducees**—See on ch. 4:2 for the reason why this is specified. **19. by night**—the same night. **20. all the words of this life**—beautiful expression for that Life in the Risen One which was the burden of their preaching. **21. entered into the temple . . .** —How self-possessed! the indwelling Spirit raising them above fear. **called . . . all the senate . . .**—an unusually general convention, though hastily summoned. **23. the prison . . . shut . . . keepers . . . before the doors, but . . . no man within**—the reverse of the miracle in ch. 16:26; a similar contrast to that of the nets at the miraculous draughts of fishes (Luke 5:6; and John 21:11). **24-26. they doubted** —'were in perplexity.' **26. without violence, for they feared . . .**—hardened ecclesiastics, all unawed by the miraculous tokens of God's presence with the apostles, and the fear of the mob only before their eyes!

27-42. SECOND APPEARANCE AND TESTIMONY BEFORE THE SANHEDRIM—ITS RAGE CALMED BY GAMALIEL—BEING DISMISSED, THEY DEPART REJOICING, AND CONTINUE THEIR PREACHING. **27, 28. ye have filled Jerusalem with your doctrine**—noble testimony to the success of their preaching, and (for the reason mentioned on ch. 4:4) to the truth of their testimony, from reluctant lips! **intend to bring this man's blood upon us**—They avoid naming Him whom Peter gloried in holding up [BENGEL]. In speaking thus, they seem to betray a disagreeable recollection of their own recent imprecation, "His blood be upon us . . ." (Matt. 27:25), and of the traitor's words as he threw down the money, "I have sinned in that I have betrayed innocent blood" (Matt. 27:4). **29, 30. Then Peter . . .**—See on ch. 2:22, and on ch. 3:13, etc. **31. Prince and a Saviour**—the first word expressing that *Royalty* which all Israel looked for in Messiah, the second the *Saving* character of it which they had utterly lost sight of. Each of these features in our Lord's work enters into the other, and both make one glorious whole (cf. ch. 3:15; Heb. 2:10). **to give**—dispensing as a "Prince." **repentance and remission of sins**—as a "Saviour"; "repentance" embracing all that change which issues in the faith which secures "forgiveness" (cf. ch. 2:38; 20:21). How gloriously is Christ here exhibited; not, as in other places, as the *Medium*, but as the *Dispenser* of all spiritual blessings! **32, 33. we are his witnesses . . . and the Holy Ghost**—They as competent human witnesses to facts, and the Holy Ghost as attesting them by undeniable miracles. **33. cut to the heart and took**—'were taking'—**counsel to slay them**—How different this feeling and the effect of it from that "pricking of the heart" which drew from the first converts on the day of Pentecost the cry, "Men and brethren, what shall we do?" (ch. 2:37). The words used in the two places are strikingly different. **34. Then stood up . . . Gamaliel**—in all probability one of that name celebrated in the Jewish writings for his wisdom, the son of Simeon (possibly the same who took the infant Saviour in his arms, Luke 2:25-35), and grandson of Hillel, another celebrated rabbi. He died eighteen years before the destruction of Jerusalem [LIGHTFOOT]. **35-39. Theudas**—not the same with a deceiver of that name whom Josephus mentions as heading an insurrection some twelve years after this [*Antiquities*, 20. 5. 1], but some other of whom he makes no mention. Such insurrections were frequent. **37. Judas of Galilee**—See on Luke 2:2, and 13:1-3 [JOSEPHUS, *Antiquities*, 13. 1. 1]. **38. if . . . of men, it will come to naught**—This neutral policy was true wisdom, in the then temper of the council. But individual neutrality is hostility to Christ, as He Himself teaches (Luke 11:23). **40-42. beaten them**—for disobeying their orders (cf. Luke 23:16). **departed . . . rejoicing that they were counted worthy to suffer shame for his name**—'thought worthy by God to be dishonored by man' (Matt. 5: 12; I Pet. 4:14, 16) [WEBSTER and WILKINSON]. *This was their first taste of persecution,* and it felt sweet for His sake whose disciples they were. **42. in every house**—in private. (See on ch. 2:46.) **ceased not to preach Jesus Christ**—i.e., Jesus (to be the) Christ.

CHAPTER 6

Vss. 1-7. FIRST ELECTION OF DEACONS. **1. the Grecians**—the Greek-speaking Jews, mostly born in the provinces. **the Hebrews**—those Jews born in Palestine who used their native tongue, and were wont to look down on the "Grecians" as an inferior class. **were neglected**—'overlooked' by those whom the apostles employed, and who were probably of the Hebrew class, as being the most numerous. The complaint was in all likelihood well founded, though we cannot suspect the distributors of intentional partiality. "It was really just an emulation of love, each party wishing to have their own poor taken care of in the best manner" [OLSHAUSEN]. **the daily ministration**—the daily distribution of alms or of food, probably the latter. **2-4. the multitude** —the general body of the disciples. **It is not reason** —The word expresses dislike; i.e. 'We cannot submit.' **to leave the word of God**—to have our time and attention withdrawn from preaching; which, it thus appears, they regarded as their primary duty. **to serve tables**—oversee the distribution of provisions. **3. look ye out among you**—i.e., ye, "the multitude," from among yourselves. **seven men of honest report**—good reputation (ch. 10:22; I Tim. 3: 7). **full of the Holy Ghost**—not full of miraculous gifts, which would have been no qualification for the duties required, but *spiritually gifted* (although on two of them miraculous power did rest). **and wisdom**—discretion, aptitude for practical business. **whom we may appoint**—for while the *election* was vested in the Christian people, the *appointment* lay with the apostles, as spiritual rulers. **4. we will give ourselves to prayer**—public prayer, as along with preaching their great work. **5. Stephen . . .**— As this and the following names are all Greek, it is likely they were all of the "Grecian" class, which would effectually restore mutual confidence. **6. when they had prayed, they laid their hands on them**—the one proclaiming that all official gifts flowed from the Church's glorified Head, the other symbolizing the communication of these to the chosen office-bearers through the recognized channels. **7. word of God increased . . . disciples multiplied in Jerusalem greatly**—prosperity crowning the beautiful spirit which reigned in this mother community. **a great company of the priests were obedient . . .**—This was the crowning triumph of the Gospel, whose *peaceful* prosperity was now at its greatest height. After Stephen's teaching and trial made it clear that sacerdotal interests could not stand with the Gospel, such priestly accessions became rare indeed. Note (1) how easily misunderstandings may arise among the most loving and devoted followers of the Lord Jesus: but (2) How quickly and effectually such misunderstandings may be healed, where honest intentions, love, and wisdom reign: (3) What a beautiful model for imitation is furnished by the class here complained of, who, though themselves the majority, chose the new office-bearers from amongst the complaining minority! (4) How superior to the lust of power do the apostles here show themselves to be, in not only divesting themselves of the immediate superintendence of temporal affairs in the Christian community, but giving the choice of those who were to be entrusted with it to the disciples at large! (5) How little of formal organization did the apostles give to the Church at first, and when an emergency arose which demanded something more, how entirely was the remedy suggested by the reason of the thing! (6) Though the new office-bearers are not expressly called *Deacons* here, it is universally admitted that this was the first institution of that order in the Church; the success of the expedient securing its permanency, and the qualifications for "the office of a Deacon" being laid down in one of the apostolical Epistles immediately after those of "a Bishop" (I Tim. 3:8-13).

8-15. STEPHEN ARRAIGNED BEFORE THE SANHEDRIM. **8. And Stephen . . .**—The foregoing narrative seems to be only an introduction to what follows. **full of faith**—rather, 'of grace,' as the best MSS.read. **9, 10. synagogue of the Libertines**—Jewish freedmen; manumitted Roman captives, or the children of such, expelled from Rome (as appears from Jo-

SEPHUS and TACITUS), and now residing at Jerusalem. **Cyrenians**—Jews of Cyrene, in Libya, on the coast of Africa. **them of Cilicia**—amongst whom may have been Saul of Tarsus (ch. 7:58; 21:39). **and of Asia**—See on ch. 16:6. **10. not able to resist the wisdom and the spirit by which he spake**— What he said, and the power with which he spake it, were alike resistless. **11-14. blasphemous words against Moses**—doubtless referring to the impending disappearance of the whole Mosaic system. **and against God**—This must refer to the supreme dignity and authority which he claimed for Christ, as the head of that new economy which was so speedily to supersede the old (cf. ch. 7:56, 59, 60). **15. as . . . the face of an angel**—a play of supernatural radiance attesting to all who beheld his countenance the divine calm of the spirit within.

CHAPTER 7

Vss. 1-60. DEFENSE AND MARTYRDOM OF STEPHEN. In this long defense Stephen takes a much wider range, and goes less directly into the point raised by his accusers, than we should have expected. His object seems to have been to show (1) that so far from disparaging, he deeply reverenced, and was intimately conversant with, the whole history of the ancient economy; and (2) that in resisting the erection of the Gospel kingdom they were but treading in their fathers' footsteps, the whole history of their nation being little else than one continued misapprehension of God's high designs towards fallen man and rebellion against them. **1-5. The God of glory**—A magnificent appellation, fitted at the very outset to rivet the devout attention of his audience; denoting not that visible glory which attended many of the divine manifestations, but the glory of those manifestations themselves, of which this was regarded by every Jew as the fundamental one. It is the glory of absolutely free grace. **appeared unto our father Abraham before he dwelt in Charran, and said . . .**—Though this first call is not expressly recorded in Genesis, it is clearly implied in Genesis 15:7 and Nehemiah 9:7; and the Jewish writers speak the same language. **4. when his father was dead, he removed into this land**—Though Abraham was in Canaan before Terah's death, his settlement in it as the land of promise is here said to be after it, as being in no way dependent on the family movement, but a transaction purely between Jehovah and Abraham himself. **6-8. four hundred years**— using round numbers, as in Genesis 15:13, 16 (see on Gal. 3:17). **after that shall they come forth, and serve me in this place**—Here the promise to Abraham (Gen. 15:16), and that to Moses (Exod. 3:12), are combined; Stephen's object being merely to give a rapid summary of the leading facts. **8. the covenant of circumcision**—i.e., the covenant of which circumcision was the token. **and so**—i.e., according to the terms of this covenant, on which Paul reasons (Gal. 3). **the twelve patriarchs**—so called as the founders of the twelve tribes of Israel. **9-16. the patriarchs, moved with envy, sold Joseph into Egypt, but God was with him**—Here Stephen gives his first example of *Israel's opposition to God's purposes, in spite of which and by means of which those purposes were accomplished.* **14. threescore and fifteen souls**—according to the Septuagint version of Genesis 46:27, which Stephen follows, including the five children and grandchildren of Joseph's two sons. **17. But when**—rather, 'as'—the **time of the promise**—i.e., for its fulfilment. **the**

people grew and multiplied in Egypt—For more than 200 years they amounted to no more than seventy-five souls; how prodigious, then, must have been their multiplication during the latter two centuries, when 600,000 men, fit for war, besides women and children, left Egypt! **20-22. In which time**—of deepest depression. **Moses was born**—the destined deliverer. **exceeding fair**—lit., 'fair to God' (*Margin*), or, perhaps, divinely 'fair' (see on Heb. 11:23). **22. mighty in words**—Though defective in utterance (Exod. 4:10); his recorded speeches fully bear out what is here said. **and deeds**—referring probably to unrecorded circumstances in his early life. If we are to believe JOSEPHUS, his ability was acknowledged ere he left Egypt. **23-27.** In verses 23, 30, and 36, the life of Moses is represented as embracing three periods, of forty years each; the Jewish writers say the same; and though this is not expressly stated in the Old Testament, his age at death, 120 years (Deut. 34:7), agrees with it. **23. it came into his heart to visit his brethren**—his heart yearning with love to them as God's chosen people, and heaving with the consciousness of a divine vocation to set them free. **24. avenged him that was oppressed, and smote the Egyptian**—going farther in the heat of his indignation than he probably intended. **25. For he supposed his brethren would have understood...**—and perhaps imagined this a suitable occasion for rousing and rallying them under him as their leader; thus anticipating his work, and so running unsent. **but they understood not**—Reckoning on a spirit in them congenial with his own, he had the mortification to find it far otherwise. This furnishes to Stephen another example of *Israel's slowness to apprehend and fall in with the divine purposes of love.* **26. next day he showed himself unto them as they strove**—Here, not an Israelite and an Egyptian, but two parties in Israel itself, are in collision with each other; Moses, grieved at the spectacle, interposes as a mediator; but his interference, as unauthorized, is resented by the party in the wrong, *whom Stephen identifies with the mass of the nation* (vs. 35), just as Messiah's own interposition had been spurned. **28, 29. Wilt thou kill me, as thou didst the Egyptian yesterday?**—Moses had thought the deed unseen (Exod. 2:12), but it now appeared he was mistaken. **Then fled Moses...**—for "when Pharaoh heard this thing, he sought to slay Moses" (Exod. 2:15). **30-34. an angel of the Lord**—rather, 'the Angel of the Covenant,' who immediately calls Himself JEHOVAH (cf. vs. 38). **35-41. This Moses whom they refused, saying, Who made thee a ruler and a judge...**—Here, again, *"the stone which the builders refused is made the head of the corner"* (Ps. 118:22). **37. This is that Moses which said..., A prophet... him shall ye hear**—This is quoted to remind his Moses-worshipping audience of the grand testimony of their faithful lawgiver, that *he himself was not the last and proper object of the Church's faith, but only a humble precursor and small model of Him to whom their absolute submission was due.* **38. in the church**—the collective body of God's chosen people; hence used to denote the whole body of the faithful under the Gospel, or particular sections of them. **This is he that was in the church in the wilderness, with the angel... and with our fathers**—alike near to the Angel of the Covenant, from whom he received all the institutions of the ancient economy, and to the people, to whom he faithfully reported the living oracles and among whom he set up the prescribed institutions. *By this high testimony to Moses, Stephen rebuts the* main charge for which he was on trial. **39. To whom our fathers would not obey...**—Here he shows that *the deepest dishonor done to Moses came from the nation that now professed the greatest jealousy for his honor.* **in their hearts turned back... into Egypt**—In this Stephen would have his hearers read the downward career on which they were themselves entering. **42-50. gave them up**—judicially. **as... written in the book of the prophets**—the twelve minor prophets, reckoned as one: the passage is from Amos 5:25. **42. have ye offered to me... sacrifices?**—The answer is, Yes, but as if ye did it not; for "neither did ye offer to Me only, nor always, nor with a perfect and willing heart" [BENGEL]. **43. Yea, ye took up the tabernacle of Molech...**—Two kinds of idolatry are charged upon the Israelites: that of the golden calf and that of the heavenly bodies; Molech and Remphan being deities, representing apparently the divine powers ascribed to nature, under different aspects. **carry you beyond Babylon**—the well-known region of the captivity of Judah; while "Damascus" is used by the prophet (Amos 5:27), whither the ten tribes were carried. **44. Our fathers had the tabernacle of witness in the wilderness**—which aggravated the guilt of that idolatry in which they indulged, with the tokens of the divine presence constantly in the midst of them. **45. which... our fathers that came after**—rather (*Margin*) "having received it by succession," i.e., the custody of the tabernacle from their ancestors. **brought in with Jesus**—or Joshua. **into the possession**—rather, 'at the taking possession of [the territory of] the Gentiles.' **unto the days of David**—for till then Jerusalem continued in the hands of the Jebusites. But Stephen's object in mentioning David is to hasten from the tabernacle which he set up, to the temple which his son built, in Jerusalem; and this only to show, from their own Scripture (Isa. 66:1, 2), that *even that temple, magnificent though it was, was not the proper resting-place of Jehovah upon earth;* as his audience and the nations had all along been prone to imagine. (What that resting-place was, even *"the contrite heart, that trembleth at God's word,"* he leaves to be gathered from the prophet referred to.) **51-53. Ye stiffnecked... ye do always resist the Holy Ghost...**—It has been thought that symptoms of impatience and irritation in the audience induced Stephen to cut short his historical sketch. But as little farther light could have been thrown upon Israel's obstinacy from subsequent periods of the national history on the testimony of their own Scriptures, we should view this as the *summing up,* the brief import of the whole Israelitish history—*grossness of heart, spiritual deafness, continuous resistance of the Holy Ghost, down to the very council before whom Stephen was pleading.* **52. Which of...**—*Deadly hostility to the messengers of God,* whose high office it was to tell of "the Righteous One," that well-known prophetic title of Messiah (Isa. 53:11; Jer. 23:6, etc), and this *consummated by the betrayal and murder of Messiah Himself,* on the part of those now sitting in judgment on the speaker, are the still darker features of the national character depicted in these withering words. **53. Who have received the law by the disposition**—'at the appointment' or 'ordination,' i.e., by the ministry—**of angels, and have not kept it**—This closing word is designed to shut up those idolizers of the law under the guilt of high disobedience to it, aggravated by the august manner in which they had received it. **54-56. When they heard these things they were cut to the heart...**—

If they could have *answered* him, how different would have been their temper of mind! **55. But he, being full of the Holy Ghost, looked up steadfastly into heaven, and saw the glory of God**—You who can transfer to canvas such scenes as these, in which the rage of hell grins horribly from men, as they sit condemned by a frail prisoner of their own, and see heaven beaming from his countenance and opening full upon his view—I envy you, for I find no words to paint what, in the majesty of the divine text, is here so simply told. "But how could Stephen, in the council-chamber, see heaven at all? I suppose this question never occurred but to critics of narrow soul, one of whom [MEYER] conjectures that he saw it through the window! and another, of better mould, that the scene lay in one of the courts of the temple" [ALFORD]. As the sight was witnessed by Stephen alone, the opened heavens are to be viewed as revealed to his bright beaming spirit. **and Jesus standing on the right hand of God**—Why "*standing*," and not *sitting*, the posture in which the glorified Saviour is elsewhere represented? Clearly, to express the eager interest with which He watched from the skies the scene in that council chamber, and the full tide of His Spirit which He was at that moment engaged in pouring into the heart of His heroical witness, till it beamed in radiance from his very countenance. **56. I see ... the Son of man standing ...**—This is the only time that our Lord is by human lips called THE SON OF MAN after His ascension (Rev. 1:13; 14:14 are not instances). And why here? Stephen, full of the Holy Ghost, speaking now not of himself at all (vs. 55), but entirely by the Spirit, is led to repeat the very words in which Jesus Himself, *before this same council*, had foretold His glorification (Matt. 26:64), assuring them that that exaltation of the SON OF MAN which they should hereafter witness to their dismay, was already begun and actual [ALFORD]. **57, 58. Then they cried out ... and ran upon him with one accord**—To men of their mould and in their temper, Stephen's last seraphic words could but bring matters to extremities, though that only revealed the diabolical spirit which they breathed. **58. cast him out of the city** (according to Lev. 24:14; Num. 15:35; I Kings 21:13; and see Heb. 13:12. **and stoned**—'proceeded to stone' him. The actual stoning is recorded in next verse. **and the witnesses**—whose hands were to be first upon the criminal (Deut. 17:7). **laid down their clothes**—their loose outer garments, to have them taken charge of. **at a young man's feet whose name was Saul**—How thrilling is this our first introduction to one to whom Christianity—whether as developed in the New Testament or as established in the world—owes more perhaps than to all the other apostles together! Here he is, having perhaps already a seat in the Sanhedrim, some 30 years of age, in the thick of this tumultuous murder of a distinguished witness for Christ, not only "consenting unto his death" (ch. 8:1), but doing his own part of the dark deed. **59, 60. calling upon God and saying, Lord Jesus ...**—An unhappy supplement of our translators is the word "God" here; as if, while addressing the Son, he was really calling upon the Father. The sense is perfectly clear without any supplement at all—"calling upon [invoking] and saying, Lord Jesus"; Christ being the Person directly invoked and addressed by name (cf. 9:14). Even GROTIUS, DE WETTE, MEYER, etc. admit this, adding several other examples of direct prayer to Christ; and PLINY, in his well-known letter to the Emperor Trajan (A.D. 110 or 111), says it was part of the regular Christian

service to sing, in alternate strains, a hymn to Christ as God. **Lord Jesus, receive my spirit**—In presenting to Jesus the identical prayer which He Himself had on the cross offered to His Father, Stephen renders to his glorified Lord absolute divine worship, in the most sublime form, and at the most solemn moment of his life. In this commitment of his spirit to Jesus, Paul afterwards followed his footsteps with a calm, exultant confidence that with Him it was safe for eternity (II Tim. 1:12). **60. cried with a loud voice**—with something of the gathered energy of his dying Lord (see on John 19: 16-30). **Lord**—i.e., JESUS, beyond doubt, whom he had just before addressed as Lord. **lay not this sin to their charge**—Comparing this with nearly the same prayer of his dying Lord, it will be seen how very richly this martyr of Jesus had drunk into his Master's spirit, in its divinest form. **he fell asleep** —*never said of the death of Christ.* (See on I Thess. 4:14.) How bright the record of this first martyrdom for Christ, amidst all the darkness of its perpetrators; and how many have been cheered by it to like faithfulness even unto death!

CHAPTER 8

Vss. 1-4. PERSECUTION CONTINUED, IN WHICH SAUL TAKES A PROMINENT PART—HOW OVERRULED FOR GOOD—**1. Saul was consenting unto his death**—The word expresses hearty approval. **they were all scattered abroad**—all the leading Christians, particularly the preachers, agreeably to their Lord's injunctions (Matt. 10:23), though many doubtless remained, and others (as appears by ch. 9:26-30) soon returned. **except the apostles**—who remained, not certainly as being less exposed to danger, but, at whatever risk, to watch over the infant cause where it was most needful to cherish it. **2. and devout men**—pious Jews, probably, impressed with admiration for Stephen and secretly inclined to Christianity, but not yet openly declared. **3. Saul ... entering into every house**—like as inquisitor [BENGEL]. **haling men and women ...**—See his own affecting confessions afterwards (ch. 22:4; 26:9, 10; I Cor. 15:9; Gal. 1:13; Phil. 3:6; I Tim. 1:13). **they that were scattered abroad went everywhere preaching**—Though solemnly enjoined to do this (Luke 24: 47; ch. 1:8), they would probably have lingered at Jerusalem, but for this besom of persecution which swept them out. How often has the rage of Christ's enemies thus "turned out rather unto the furtherance of the Gospel" (see Phil. 1:12, 13).

5-25. SUCCESS OF PHILIP'S PREACHING IN SAMARIA—CASE OF SIMON MAGUS. **5. Then Philip**—not the apostle of that name, as was by some of the Fathers supposed; for besides that the apostles remained at Jerusalem, they would in that case have had no occasion to send a deputation of their own number to lay their hands on the baptized disciples [GROTIUS]. It was the deacon of that name, who comes next after Stephen in the catalogue of the seven, probably as being the next most prominent. The persecution may have been directed especially against Stephen's colleagues [MEYER]. **the city of Samaria**—or 'a city of Samaria'; but the former seems more likely. "It furnished the bridge between Jerusalem and the world" [BAUMGARTEN]. **6-8. the people with one accord gave heed to ... Philip**—the way being prepared perhaps by the fruits of our Lord's sojourn, as He Himself seems to intimate (see on John 4:31-38). But "we may mark the providence of God in sending a Grecian, or a Hellenistic Jew, to a people who from national antipathy would have been unlikely to attend to a *native* of Judea" [WEBSTER and WILKINSON]. **8. great joy in that city**—over the change wrought on it by the Gospel, as well as the cures which attested its divine character. **9-13. used sorcery**—magical arts. **some great one ... the great power of God** —a sort of incarnation of divinity. **To whom all gave heed ... because of long time he had bewitched them**—This, coupled with the rapidity with which they deserted him and attached themselves to Philip, shows the ripeness of Samaria for some religious change. **12. were baptized, both men and women** —the detection of Simon's frauds helping to extend and deepen the effects of Philip's preaching. **13. Then Simon himself believed also**—Left without followers, he thinks it best to join the man who had fairly outstripped him, not without a touch of real conviction. **and ... was baptized**—What a light does this throw on what is called *Baptismal Regeneration!* **he continued with Philip**—'was in constant attendance upon' him. **14-17. the apostles ... sent Peter and John**—showing that they regarded Peter as no more than their own equal. **15, 16. prayed ... they might receive the Holy Ghost. (For only they were baptized in the name of the Lord Jesus.)**—As the baptism of adults presupposed "the renewing of the Holy Ghost" (Titus 3:5-7; I Cor. 12:13), of which the profession of faith had to be taken for evidence, this communication of the Holy Ghost by the laying on of the apostles' hands was clearly a *superadded* thing; and as it was only *occasional,* so it was invariably *attended with miraculous manifestations* (see ch. 10:44, where it followed Peter's preaching; and ch. 19:1-7, where, as here, it followed the laying on of hands). In the present case an important object was served by it—"the sudden appearance of a body of baptized disciples in Samaria, by the agency of one who was not an apostle, requiring the presence and power of apostles to perform their special part as the divinely appointed founders of the Church" [ALFORD]. Beautiful, too, was the spectacle exhibited of Jew and Samaritan, one in Christ. **18-24. offered them money**—Hence the term *simony,* to denote trafficking in sacred things, but chiefly the purchase of ecclesiastical offices. **19. that on whomsoever I lay hands, he may receive the Holy Ghost**—*Spiritual ambition* here shows itself the key to this wretched man's character. **20. Thy money perish with thee**—i.e., 'Accursed be thou and thy money with thee.' It is the language of mingled horror and indignation, not unlike our Lord's rebuke of Peter himself (Matt. 16:23). **21. Thou hast neither part nor lot ... thy heart is not right ...**—This is the fidelity of a minister of Christ to one deceiving himself in a very awful manner. **22. Repent ... pray ... if perhaps the thought of thine heart may be forgiven**—this expression of doubt being designed to impress upon him the greatness of his sin, and the need of alarm on his part. **23. in the gall of bitterness and ... bond of iniquity**—expressing both the awfulness of his condition and the captivity to it in which he was held. **24. Pray ye to the Lord for me**—Peter had urged him to pray for himself: he asks those wonder-working men to do it for him; having no confidence in the prayer of faith, but thinking that those men possessed some peculiar interest with heaven. **that none of these things come upon me**—not that the thought of his wicked heart might be forgiven him, but only that the evils threatened might be averted from him. While this throws great light on Peter's view of his melancholy case, it shows that Christianity, as something divine, still retained its

hold of him. (Tradition represents him as turning out a great heresiarch, mingling Oriental or Grecian philosophy with some elements of Christianity.) **25. and they**—Peter and John—**when they had ... preached**—in the city where Philip's labors had been so richly blessed—**returned ... and preached ... in many villages of the Samaritans**—embracing the opportunity of their journey back to Jerusalem to fulfil their Lord's commission to the whole region of Samaria (ch. 1:8).

26-40. THE ETHIOPIAN EUNUCH. "With this narrative of the progress of the Gospel among the Samaritans is connected another which points to the diffusion of the doctrine of the Cross among the remotest nations. The simplicity of the chamberlain of Meroe forms a remarkable contrast with the craft of the magician just described" [OLSHAUSEN]. **26-28. the angel of the Lord**—rather, 'an angel.' **go ... south, the way that goeth down from Jerusalem to Gaza**—There was such a road, across Mount Hebron, which Philip might take without going to Jerusalem (as VON RAUMER's *Palæstina* shows) **which is desert**—i.e., *the way;* not Gaza itself, which was the southernmost city of Palestine, in the territory of the ancient Philistines. To go from a city, where his hands had been full of work, so far away on a desert road, could not but be staggering to the faith of Philip, especially as he was kept in ignorance of the object of the journey. But like Paul, he "was not disobedient to the heavenly vision"; and like Abram, "he went out not knowing whither he went" (ch. 26:19; Heb. 11:8). **27. a man of Ethiopia**—Upper Egypt, Meroe. **an eunuch of great authority**—Eunuchs were generally employed for confidential offices in the East, and to some extent are still. **Candace**—the family name of the queens of Upper Egypt, like Pharaoh, Cæsar, etc. (as appears from classic authors). **had come to Jerusalem to worship**—i.e., to keep the recent feast of Pentecost, as a Gentile proselyte to the Jewish faith. (See Isa. 56:3-8, and John 12:20). **28. Was returning**—Having come so far, he not only stayed out the days of the festival, but prolonged his stay till now. It says much for his fidelity and value to his royal mistress that he had such liberty. But the faith in Jehovah and love of His worship and word, with which he was imbued, sufficiently explain this. **and sitting in his chariot, read Esaias**—Not contented with the statutory services in which he had joined, he beguiles the tedium of the journey homeward by reading the Scriptures. But this is not all; for as Philip "heard him read the prophet Esaias," he must have been reading aloud and not (as is customary still in the East) so as merely to be audible, but in a louder voice than he would naturally have used if intent on his own benefit only: evidently therefore he was *reading to his charioteer.* **29-31. the Spirit said**—by an unmistakable voice within, as in ch. 10:19; 16:6, 7. **go near and join this chariot**—This would reveal to Philip the hitherto unknown object of his journey, and encourage him to expect something. **30. Understandest thou what thou readest?**—To one so engaged this would be deemed no rude question, while the eager appearance of the speaker, and the question itself, would indicate a readiness to supply any want of insight that might be felt. **31. How can I, except some man guide me?**—Beautiful expression at once of humility and docility; the invitation to Philip which immediately followed, to "come up and sit with him," being but the natural expression of this. **32, 33. The place ... was this, He was led as a sheep ...** —One cannot but wonder that this, of all predictions of Messiah's sufferings in the Old Testament the most striking, should have been that which the eunuch was reading before Philip joined him. He could hardly miss to have heard at Jerusalem of the sufferings and death of Jesus, and of the existence of a continually increasing party who acknowledged Him to be the Messiah. But his question to Philip, whether the prophet in this passage meant himself or some other man, clearly shows that he had not the least idea of any connection between this prediction and those facts. **34-38. And the eunuch answered, I pray thee ...**—The respect with which he here addresses Philip was prompted by his reverence for one whom he perceived to be his superior in divine things; his own worldly position sinking before this. **35. Then Philip opened his mouth**—(See on Matt. 5:2). **began at the same scripture**—founding on it as his text. **preached unto him Jesus**—showing Him to be the glorious Burden of this wonderful prediction, and interpreting it in the light of the facts of His history. **See, here is water**—more simply, 'Behold water!' as if already his mind filled with light and his soul set free, he was eagerly looking out for the first water in which he might seal his reception of the truth and be enrolled among the visible disciples of the Lord Jesus. **what doth hinder me to be baptized?**—Philip had probably told him that this was the ordained sign and seal of discipleship, but the eunuch's question was likely the first proposal of its application in this case. (Verse 37 is wanting in the principal MSS. and most venerable versions of the New Testament. It seems to have been added from the formularies for baptism which came into current use). **38. they went down both into the water, and he baptized him ...**—probably laving the water upon him, though the precise mode is neither certain nor of any consequence. **39, 40. the Spirit of the Lord caught away Philip**—To deny [as MEYER, OLSHAUSEN, BLOOMFIELD] the miraculous nature of Philip's disappearance, is vain. It stands out on the face of the words, as just a repetition of what we read of the ancient prophets, in I Kings 18:12; II Kings 2:16. And the same word (as BENGEL remarks) is employed to express a similar idea in II Corinthians 12:2, 4; I Thessalonians 4:17. **the eunuch saw him no more**—nor, perhaps, for very joy, cared to see him [BENGEL]. **and he went on his way rejoicing** —He had found Christ, and the key to the Scriptures; his soul was set free, and his discipleship sealed; he had lost his teacher, but gained what was infinitely better: He felt himself a new man, and "his joy was full." Tradition says he was the first preacher of the Gospel in Ethiopia; and how, indeed, could he choose but "tell what the Lord had done for his soul"? Yet there is no certainty as to any historical connection between his labors and the introduction of Christianity into that country. **40. Philip was found**—i.e., 'found himself,' 'made his appearance:' an expression confirming the miraculous manner of his transportation. **at Azotus**— the ancient Ashdod. **preached in all the cities**— along the coast, proceeding northward. **till he came to Cæsarea**—fifty-five miles northwest of Jerusalem, on the Mediterranean, just south of Mount Carmel; and so named by Herod, who rebuilt it, in honor of Cæsar Augustus. Henceforth we lose sight of zealous and honored Philip, as by and by we shall lose sight even of Peter. As the chariot of the Gospel rolls on, other agents are raised up, each suited to his work. But "he that soweth and he that reapeth shall rejoice together." (See on John 4:31-38).

CHAPTER 9

Vss. 1-25. CONVERSION OF SAUL, AND BEGINNINGS OF HIS MINISTRY. **1. Saul, yet breathing out threatenings and slaughter against the disciples of the Lord ...**—The emphatic "yet" is intended to note the remarkable fact, that up to this moment his blind persecuting rage against the disciples of the Lord burned as fiercely as ever. (In the teeth of this, NEANDER and OLSHAUSEN picture him deeply impressed with Stephen's joyful faith, remembering passages of the Old Testament confirmatory of the Messiahship of Jesus, and experiencing such a violent struggle as would inwardly prepare the way for the designs of God towards him. Is not dislike, if not unconscious disbelief, of *sudden conversion* at the bottom of this?) The word "slaughter" here points to cruelties not yet recorded, but the particulars of which are supplied by himself nearly thirty years afterwards: "And I persecuted this way *unto the death*" (ch. 22:4); "and when they were *put to death,* I gave my voice [vote] against them. And I punished them oft in every synagogue, and compelled them to [did my utmost to make them] blaspheme; and being exceedingly mad against them, I persecuted them even unto strange [foreign] cities" (ch. 26:10, 11). All this was *before* his present journey. **2. desired ... letters**—of authorization. **to Damascus**—the capital of Syria and the great highway between eastern and western Asia, about 130 miles northeast of Jerusalem; the most ancient city perhaps in the world, and lying in the center of a verdant and inexhaustible paradise. It abounded (as appears from JOSEPHUS, Wars, II. 20, 2) with Jews, and with Gentile proselytes to the Jewish faith. Thither the Gospel had penetrated; and Saul, flushed with past successes, undertakes to crush it out. **that if he found any of this way, whether men or women**—Thrice are *women* specified as objects of his cruelty, as an aggravated feature of it (ch. 8:3; 22:4; and here). **3. he came near Damascus**—so ch. 22:6. Tradition points to a bridge near the city as the spot referred to. Events which are the turning points in one's history so imprint themselves upon the memory that circumstances the most trifling in themselves acquire by connection with them something of their importance, and are recalled with inexpressible interest. **suddenly**—At what time of day, it is not said; for artless simplicity reigns here. But he himself emphatically states, in one of his narratives, that it was *"about noon"* (ch. 22:6), and in the other, *"at midday"* (ch. 26:13), when there could be no deception. **there shined round about him a light from heaven**— "a great light" (he himself says) "above the brightness of the sun," then shining in its full strength. **4-6. he fell to the earth**—and his companions with him (ch. 26:14), who "saw the light" (ch. 22:9). **and heard a voice saying unto him**—"in the Hebrew tongue" (ch. 26:14)—**Saul, Saul**—a reduplication full of tenderness [DE WETTE]. Though his name was soon changed into "Paul," we find him, in both his own narratives of the scene, after the lapse of so many years, retaining the original form, as not daring to alter, in the smallest detail, the overpowering words addressed to him. **why persecutest thou me?**—No language can express the affecting character of this question, addressed from the right hand of the Majesty on high to an infuriated, persecuting mortal. (See Matthew 25:45, and that whole judgment scene.) **5. Who art thou, Lord?**—"Jesus knew Saul ere Saul knew Jesus" [BENGEL]. The term "Lord" here is an indefinite term of respect for some unknown but august speaker. That Saul *saw* as well as *heard* this glorious Speaker, is expressly said by Ananias (vs. 17; 22:14), by Barnabas (ch. 9:27), and by himself (ch. 26:16); and in claiming apostleship, he explicitly states that he had "*seen* the Lord" (I Cor. 9:1; 15:8), which can refer only to this scene. **I am Jesus whom thou persecutest** —The "I" and "thou" here are touchingly emphatic in the original; while the term "Jesus" is purposely chosen, to convey to him the thrilling information that the hated name which he sought to hunt down —"*the Nazarene*," as it is in ch. 22:8—was now speaking to him from the skies, "crowned with glory and honor" (see ch. 26:9). **It is hard for thee to kick against the pricks. 6. And he, trembling and astonished, said, Lord, what wilt thou have me to do? And the Lord said**—(The most ancient MSS. and versions of the New Testament lack all these words *here;* but they occur in ch. 26:14 and ch. 22: 10, from which they appear to have been inserted here.) The metaphor of an ox, only driving the goad deeper by kicking against it, is a classic one, and here forcibly expresses, not only the vanity of all his measures for crushing the Gospel, but the deeper wound which every such effort inflicted upon himself. The question, What shall I do, Lord?" or, "Lord, what wilt Thou have me to do?" indicates a state of mind singularly interesting (see on ch. 2: 37). Its elements seem to be these: (1) Resistless conviction that "Jesus whom he persecuted," now speaking to him, was "Christ the Lord." (See on Gal. 1:15, 16). (2) As a consequence of this, that not only all his religious views, but his whole religious character, had been an entire mistake; that he was up to that moment fundamentally and wholly wrong. (3) That though his whole future was now a blank, he had absolute confidence in Him who had so tenderly arrested him in his blind career, and was ready both to take in all His teaching and to carry out all His directions. (See more on vs. 9). **Arise, and go into the city, and it shall be told thee, . . .**—See on ch. 8:26-28. **7. the men . . . stood speechless**—This may mean merely that they remained so; but if the *standing* posture be intended, we have only to suppose that though at first they "all fell to the earth" (ch. 26:14), they arose of their own accord while Saul yet lay prostrate. **hearing a**—rather 'the'—**voice**—Paul himself says, "they heard not the voice of Him that spake to me" (ch. 22:9). But just as "the people that stood by *heard*" the voice that saluted our Lord with recorded words of consolation and assurance, and yet *heard not* the articulate words, but thought "it thundered" or that some "angel spake to Him" (John 12:28, 29)—so these men heard the *voice* that spake to Saul, but heard not the *articulate words.* Apparent discrepancies like these, in the different narratives of the same scene in one and the same book of Acts, furnish the strongest confirmation both of the facts themselves and of the book which records them. **8. Saul arose . . . and when his eyes were opened, he saw no man**—after beholding the Lord, since he "could not see for the glory of that light" (ch. 22:11), he had involuntarily closed his eyes to protect them from the glare; and on opening them again he found his vision gone. "It is not said, however, that he was *blind,* for it was no punishment" [Bengel]. **9. And he was three days without sight, and neither did eat nor drink**—i.e., according to the Hebrew mode of computation: he took no food during the remainder of that day, the entire day following, and so much of the subsequent day as elapsed before the visit of Ananias. Such a pe-

riod of entire abstinence from food, in that state of mental absorption and revolution into which he had been so suddenly thrown, is in perfect harmony with known laws and numerous facts. But what three days those must have been! "Only one other space of three days' duration can be mentioned of equal importance in the history of the world" [Hows]. Since Jesus had been revealed not only to his *eyes* but to his *soul* (see on Gal. 1:15, 16), the double conviction must have immediately flashed upon him, that his whole reading of the Old Testament hitherto had been wrong, and that the system of legal righteousness in which he had, up to that moment, rested and prided himself was false and fatal. What materials these for spiritual exercise during those three days of total darkness, fasting, and solitude! On the one hand, what self-condemnation, what anguish, what death of legal hope, what difficulty in believing that in such a case there could be hope at all; on the other hand, what heartbreaking admiration of the grace that had "pulled him out of the fire," what resistless conviction that there must be a purpose of love in it, and what tender expectation of being yet honored, as a chosen vessel, to declare what the Lord had done for his soul, and to spread abroad the savor of that Name which he had so wickedly, though ignorantly, sought to destroy—must have struggled in his breast during those memorable days! Is it too much to say that all that profound insight into the Old Testament, that comprehensive grasp of the principles of the divine economy, that penetrating spirituality, that vivid apprehension of man's lost state, and those glowing views of the perfection and glory of the divine remedy, that beautiful ideal of the loftiness and the lowliness of the Christian character, that large philanthropy and burning zeal to spend and be spent through all his future life for Christ, which distinguish the writings of this chiefest of the apostles and greatest of men, were all quickened into life during those three successive days? **10-16. a certain disciple . . . named Ananias**—See on ch. 22: 12. **to him said the Lord**—i.e., Jesus. (See vss. 13, 14, 17.) **11. go into the street . . . called Straight**— There is still a street of this name in Damascus, about half a mile in length, running from east to west through the city [Maundrell]. **and inquire in the house of Judas for one called Saul of Tarsus** —There is something touching in the minuteness of these directions. Tarsus was the capital of the province of Cilicia, lying along the northeast coast of the Mediterranean. It was situated on the river Cydnus, was a "large and populous city" (says Xenophon, and see ch. 21:39), and under the Romans had the privilege of self-government. **behold, he prayeth**—"breathing out" no longer "threatenings and slaughter," but struggling desires after light and life in the Persecuted One. Beautiful note of encouragement as to the frame in which Ananias would find the persecutor! **12. And hath seen in a vision a man named Ananias . . .**—Thus, as in the case of Cornelius and Peter afterwards, there was a mutual preparation of each for each. But we have no account of the vision which Saul had of Ananias coming unto him and putting his hands upon him for the restoration of his sight, save this interesting allusion to it in the vision which Ananias himself had. **13. Ananias answered, Lord, I have heard by many of this man . . .**—"The objections of Ananias, and the removal of them by the Lord, display in a very touching manner the childlike relation of the believing soul to its Redeemer. The Saviour speaks with Ananias as a man does with his friend"

[OLSHAUSEN]. **how much evil he hath done to thy saints**– "*Thy* saints," says Ananias to Christ; therefore Christ is God [BENGEL]. So, in the very next verse, Ananias describes the disciples as "those that called on Christ's name." See on ch. 7:59, 60; and cf. I Corinthians 1:2. **14. here he hath authority . . .** –so that the terror not only of the great persecutor's name, but of this commission to Damascus, had travelled before him from the capital to the doomed spot. **15. Go thy way**–Do as thou art bidden, without gainsaying. **he is a chosen vessel**– a word often used by Paul in illustrating God's sovereignty in election (Rom. 9:21-23; II Cor. 4:7; II Tim. 2:20, 21 [ALFORD]. Cf. Zech. 3:2). **16. I will show him**–(see ch. 20:23, 24; 21:11). **how great things he must suffer for my name**–i.e., Much he has done against that Name; but now, when I show him what great things he must suffer for that Name, he shall count it his honor and privilege. **17-19. Ananias went his way, and putting his hands on him, said, Brother Saul**–How beautifully childlike is the obedience of Ananias to "the heavenly vision!" **the Lord, even Jesus**–This clearly shows in what sense the term "Lord" is used in this book. It is JESUS that is meant, as almost invariably in the Epistles also. **who appeared unto thee in the way**– This knowledge by an inhabitant of Damascus of what had happened to Saul before entering it, would show him at once that this was the man whom Jesus had already prepared him to expect. **and be filled with the Holy Ghost**–which Ananias probably, without any express instructions on that subject, took it for granted would descend upon him; and not necessarily after his baptism [BAUMGARTEN, WEBSTER and WILKINSON]–for Cornelius and his company received it before theirs (ch. 10:44-48)– but perhaps immediately after the recovery of his sight by the laying on of Ananias' hands **18. there fell from his eyes as it were scales**–"This shows that the blindness as well as the cure was supernatural. Substances like scales would not form naturally in so short a time" [WEBSTER and WILKINSON]. And the *medical* precision of Luke's language here is to be noted. **was baptized**–as directed by Ananias (ch. 22:16). **19. when he had received meat, he was strengthened**–for the exhaustion occasioned by his three days' fast would not be the less real, though unfelt during his struggles. (See on Matt. 4:2). **Then was Saul certain days with the disciples at Damascus**–making their acquaintance, in another way than either he or they had anticipated, and regaining his tone by the fellowship of the saints; but not certainly in order to learn from them what he was to teach, which he expressly disavows (Gal. 1:12, 16). **20-22. preached Christ . . . that he is the Son of God**–rather, "preached Jesus," according to all the most ancient MSS. and versions of the New Testament (so vs. 21, "all that call on this name," i.e., *Jesus;* and vs. 22, "proving that this" *Jesus* "is very *Christ*"). **23. And after many days were fulfilled, the Jews took counsel to kill him**–*Had we no other record than this, we should have supposed that what is here related took place while Saul continued at Damascus after his baptism. But in Galatians 1:17, 18 we learn from Paul himself that he "went into Arabia, and returned again unto Damascus," and that from the time of his first visit to the close of his second, both of which appear to have been short, a period of three years elapsed; either three full years, or one full year and part of two others. (See on Gal. 1: 16-18.) That such a blank should occur in the Acts, and be filled up in Galatians, is not more* remarkable than that the flight of the Holy Family into Egypt, their stay there, and their return thence, recorded only by Matthew, should be so entirely passed over by Luke, that if we had only his Gospel, we should have supposed that they returned to Nazareth immediately after the presentation in the temple. (Indeed in one of his narratives, ch. 22: 16, 17, Paul himself takes no notice of this period.) *But wherefore this journey?* Perhaps (1) because he felt a period of repose and partial seclusion to be needful to his spirit, after the violence of the change and the excitement of his new occupation. (2) To prevent the rising storm which was gathering against him from coming too soon to a head. (3) To exercise his ministry in the Jewish synagogues, as opportunity afforded. On his return, refreshed and strengthened in spirit, he immediately resumed his ministry, but soon to the imminent hazard of his life. **24, 25. they watched the gates night and day to kill him**–The full extent of his danger appears only from his own account (II Cor. 11:32): "In Damascus, the governor under Aretas the king kept the city of the Damascenes with a garrison, desirous to apprehend me"; the exasperated Jews having obtained from the governor a military force, the more surely to compass his destruction. **25. Then the disciples . . . by night let him down** "through a window" (II Cor. 11:33) **by the wall**– Such overhanging windows in the walls of Eastern cities were common, and are to be seen in Damascus to this day.

26-31. SAUL'S FIRST VISIT TO JERUSALEM AFTER HIS CONVERSION. **26. And when Saul was come to Jerusalem**–"three years after" his conversion, and particularly "to see Peter" (Gal. 1:18); no doubt because he was the leading apostle, and to communicate to him the prescribed sphere of his labors, specially to "the Gentiles." **he assayed to join himself to the disciples**–simply as one of them, leaving his apostolic commission to manifest itself. **they were all afraid of him . . .** –knowing him only as a persecutor of the faith; the rumor of his conversion, if it ever was cordially believed, passing away during his long absence in Arabia, and the news of his subsequent labors in Damascus perhaps not having reached them. **27. But Barnabas . . . brought him to the apostles**–i.e., to Peter and James; for "other of the apostles saw I none," says he fourteen years after (Gal. 1:18, 19). Probably none of the other apostles were there at the time (ch. 4:36). Barnabas being of Cyprus, which was within a few hours' sail of Cilicia, and annexed to it as a Roman province, and Saul and he being Hellenistic Jews and eminent in their respective localities, they may very well have been acquainted with each other before this [Hows]. What is here said of Barnabas is in fine consistency with the "goodness" ascribed to him (ch. 11:24), and with the name "son of consolation," given him by the apostles (ch. 4:36); and after Peter and James were satisfied, the disciples generally would at once receive him. **how he had seen the Lord . . . and he** –the Lord–**had spoken to him**–i.e., how he had received his commission direct from the Lord Himself. **28, 29. And he was with them, coming in and going out at Jerusalem**–for fifteen days, lodging with Peter (Gal. 1:18). **29. disputed against the Grecians**–See on ch. 6:1; addressing himself specially to them, perhaps, as being of his own class, and that against which he had in the days of his ignorance been the fiercest. **they went about to slay him**–Thus was he made to feel, throughout his whole course, what he himself had made others so cruelly to feel, *the cost of discipleship.* **30. they brought him down to Cæsarea**—on the coast (see on ch. 8:40); accompanying him thus far. But Paul had another reason than his own apprehension for quitting Jerusalem so soon. "While he was praying in the temple, he was in a trance," and received express injunctions to this effect. (See on ch. 22:17-21.) **and sent him forth to Tarsus**—In Galatians 1:21 he himself says of this journey, that he "came into the regions of Syria and Cilicia"; from which it is natural to infer that instead of sailing direct for Tarsus, he landed at Seleucia, travelled thence to Antioch, and penetrated from this northward into Cilicia, ending his journey at Tarsus. As this was his first visit to his native city since his conversion, so it is not certain that he ever was there again. (See on ch. 11:25, 26.) It probably was now that he became the instrument of gathering into the fold of Christ those "kinsmen," that "sister," and perhaps her "son," of whom mention is made in ch. 23:16, etc.; Rom. 16:7, 11, 21 [Hows].

31. FLOURISHING STATE OF THE CHURCH IN PALESTINE AT THIS TIME. **31. Then had all the churches rest**—rather, 'the Church,' according to the best MSS. and versions. But this rest was owing not so much to the conversion of Saul, as probably to the Jews being engrossed with the emperor Caligula's attempt to have his own image set up in the temple of Jerusalem (JOSEPHUS, *Antiquities,* 18:8; 1, etc.). **throughout all Judea, and Galilee, and Samaria**—This incidental notice of distinct churches already dotting all the regions which were the chief scenes of our Lord's ministry, and that were best able to test the facts on which the whole preaching of the apostles was based, is extremely interesting. "The fear of the Lord" expresses their holy walk; "the comfort of the Holy Ghost," their "peace and joy in believing," under the silent operation of the blessed Comforter.

32-43. PETER HEALS ENEAS AT LYDDA, AND RAISES TABITHA TO LIFE AT JOPPA. The historian now returns to Peter, in order to introduce the all-important narrative of Cornelius (ch. 10). The occurrences here related probably took place during Saul's sojourn in Arabia. **32-35. as Peter passed throughout all quarters**—not now fleeing from persecution, but peacefully visiting the churches. **to the saints which dwelt at Lydda**—about five miles east of Joppa. **34. And Peter said unto him, Eneas, Jesus Christ maketh thee whole**—See on ch. 3:6. **make thy bed**—See on John 5:8. **35. all that dwelt at Lydda and Saron**—(or "Sharon," a rich vale between Joppa and Cæsarea). **saw him, and turned to the Lord**—i.e., there was a general conversion in consequence. **35-39. at Joppa**—the modern *Jaffa,* on the Mediterranean, a very ancient city of the Philistines, afterwards still the seaport of Jerusalem, from which it lies distant forty-five miles to the northwest. **Tabitha . . . Dorcas**—the Syro-Chaldaic and Greek names for an *antelope* or *gazelle,* which, from its loveliness, was frequently employed as a proper name for women [MEYER, OLSHAUSEN]. Doubtless the interpretation, as here given, is but an echo of the remarks made by the Christians regarding her—how well her character answered to her name. **full of good works and alms-deeds**—eminent for the activities and generosities of the Christian character. **37. when they had washed**—according to the custom of civilized nations towards the dead. **in an**—rather, 'the'—**upper chamber**—(cf. I Kings 17:19). **38. the disciples sent unto Peter**—showing that the disciples

generally did not possess miraculous gifts [BENGEL]. **39. all the widows**—whom she had clad or fed. **stood by him weeping, and showing the coats and garments which Dorcas had made**—i.e., (as the tense implies), showing these as specimens only of what she *was in the habit of making.* **40-43. Peter put them all forth, and kneeled down**—the one in imitation of his Master's way (Luke 8:54; and cf. II Kings 4:33); the other, in striking contrast with it. The *kneeling* became the lowly servant, but not the Lord Himself, *of whom it is never once recorded that he knelt in the performance of a miracle.* **opened her eyes, and when she saw Peter, she sat up**—The graphic minuteness of detail here imparts to the narrative an air of charming reality. **41. he gave her his hand, and lifted her up**—as his Lord had done to his own mother-in-law (Mark 1:31). **43. with one Simon a tanner**—a trade regarded by the Jews as half unclean, and consequently disreputable, from the contact with dead animals and blood which was connected with it. For this reason, even by other nations, it is usually carried on at some distance from towns; accordingly, Simon's house was "by the seaside" (ch. 10:6). Peter's lodging there shows him already to some extent above Jewish prejudice.

CHAPTER 10

Vss. 1-48. ACCESSION AND BAPTISM OF CORNELIUS AND HIS PARTY; OR, THE FIRST FRUITS OF THE GENTILES. We here enter on an entirely new phase of the Christian Church, the "opening of the door of faith to the Gentiles"; in other words, the recognition of Gentile, on terms of perfect equality with Jewish, discipleship without the necessity of circumcision. Some beginnings appear to have been already made in this direction (see on ch. 11: 20, 21); and Saul probably acted on this principle from the first, both in Arabia and in Syria and Cilicia. But had he been the prime mover in the admission of uncircumcised Gentiles into the Church, the Jewish party, who were never friendly to him, would have acquired such strength as to bring the Church to the verge of a disastrous schism. But on Peter, "the apostle" specially "of the circumcision," was conferred the honor of initiating this great movement, as before of the first admission of Jewish believers. (See on Matt. 16: 19.) After this, however, one who had already come upon the stage was to eclipse this "chiefest of the apostles." **1, 2. Cæsarea**—See on ch. 8:40. **the Italian band**—a cohort of Italians, as distinguished from native soldiers, quartered at Cæsarea, probably as a bodyguard to the Roman procurator who resided there. An ancient coin makes express mention of such a cohort in Syria. (AKERMAN'S *Numismatic Illustrations of the New Testament.*) **2. A devout man . . .**—an uncircumcised Gentile proselyte to the Jewish faith, of whom there were a very great number at this time; a distinguished proselyte, who had brought his whole household establishment under the hallowing influence of the Jewish faith and the regular observance of its principal seasons of worship. **gave much alms to the people**—i.e., the *Jewish* people, on the same principle as another centurion before him (Luke 7:5); thinking it no "great thing," if they had "sown unto him spiritual things, that they should reap his carnal things" (I Cor. 9:11). **prayed to God alway**—at the stated daily seasons. (See on vs. 3.) **3-6. saw . . . evidently**—'distinctly.' **the ninth hour**

of the day—three o'clock, the hour of the evening sacrifice. But he had been "fasting until that hour" (vs. 30), perhaps from the sixth hour (vs. 9). **4. What is it, Lord?**—language which, tremulously though it was uttered, betokened childlike reverence and humility. **Thy prayers and thine alms**—The way in which both are specified is emphatic. The one denotes the spiritual outgoing of his soul to God, the other its practical outgoing to men. **are come up for a memorial before God**—i.e., as a *sacrifice* well-pleasing unto God, as an odor of a sweet smell (Rev. 8:4). **5. send to Joppa...for one Simon...**—(See on ch. 9:11). **7, 8. when the angel...was departed, he called**—immediately doing as directed, and thereby showing the simplicity of his faith. **a devout soldier of them that waited on him continually**—of the "soldiers under him," such as the centurion at Capernaum had (Matt. 8: 9). Who this "devout soldier" was, can only be matter of conjecture. Da Costa (*Four Witnesses*) gives a number of ingenious reasons for thinking that, having attached himself henceforth to Peter—whose influence in the composition of the second Gospel is attested by the earliest tradition, and is stamped on that Gospel itself—he is no other than the Evangelist *Mark*. **9-16. upon the housetop**—the flat roof, the chosen place in the East for cool retirement. **the sixth hour**—noon. **a trance**—differing from the "vision" of Cornelius, in so far as the things seen had not the same *objective* reality, though both were supernatural. **12. all manner of four-footed beasts...**—i.e., the *clean* and the *unclean* (ceremonially) all mixed together. **14. Not so, Lord**—See *Marginal* reference. **I have never eaten anything that is common**—i.e., *not sanctified* by divine permission to eat of it, and so "unclean." "The distinction of meats was a sacrament of national distinction, separation, and consecration" [Webster and Wilkinson]. **15. What God hath cleansed, that call not thou common**—The ceremonial distinctions are at an end, and Gentiles, ceremonially separated from the chosen people (vs. 28), and debarred from that access to God in the visible ordinances of His Church which they enjoyed, are now on a perfect equality with them. **16. done thrice**—See Genesis 41:32. **17-24. while Peter doubted...what this should mean, behold, the three men...stood before the gate...and asked**—'were inquiring,' i.e., in the act of doing so. The preparations here made—of Peter for his Gentile visitors, as of Cornelius for him—are devoutly to be noted. But besides this, at the same moment, "the Spirit" expressly informs him that three men were inquiring for him, and bids him unhesitatingly go with them, as sent by Him. **21. I am he whom ye seek**—This seems to have been said without any communication being made to Peter regarding the men or their errand. **22. they said, Cornelius... a just man...**—fine testimony this from his own servants. **of good report among all the nation of the Jews**—specified, no doubt, to conciliate the favorable regard of the Jewish apostle. **to hear words of thee**—See on ch. 11:14. **23. called them in and lodged them**—thus partially anticipating this fellowship with Gentiles. **Peter went...with them, and certain brethren**—six in number (ch. 11: 12). **from Joppa**—as witnesses of a transaction which Peter was prepared to believe pregnant with great consequences. **24. Cornelius...called together his kinsmen and near friends**—implying that he had been long enough at Cæsarea to form relationships there and that he had intimate friends there whose presence he was not ashamed to invite

to a religious meeting of the most solemn nature. **25-29. as Peter was coming in, Cornelius met him**—a mark of the highest respect. **fell down at his feet, and worshipped him**—In the East this way of showing respect was customary not only to kings, but to others occupying a superior station; but among the Greeks and Romans it was reserved for the gods. Peter, therefore, declines it as due to no mortal [Grotius]. *"Those who claim to have succeeded Peter, have not imitated this part of his conduct"* [Alford] (therein only verifying II Thess. 2:4, and cf. Rev. 19:10; 22:9). **28. Ye know it is...unlawful...for...a Jew to keep company, or come unto one of another nation...**—There was no express prohibition to this effect, and to a certain extent intercourse was certainly kept up. (See the Gospel history, towards the end.) But intimate social fellowship was not practiced, as being adverse to the spirit of the law. **29. I ask therefore...**—The whole speech is full of dignity, the apostle seeing in the company before him a new brotherhood, into whose devout and inquiring minds he was divinely directed to pour the light of new truth. **30-33. Four days ago**—the messengers being despatched on the first; on the second reaching Joppa (vs. 9); starting for Cæsarea on the third; and on the fourth arriving. **33. we are all here present before God, to hear all things that are commanded thee of God**—Beautiful expression of entire preparedness to receive the expected divine teaching through the lips of this heaven-commissioned teacher, and delightful encouragement to Peter to give free utterance to what was doubtless already on his lips! **34, 35. Peter opened his mouth**—See on Matthew 5:2. **Of a truth I perceive**—i.e., 'I have it now demonstrated before mine eyes.' **that God is no respecter of persons**—Not, 'I see there is no capricious *favoritism* with God,' for Peter would never imagine such a thing; but (as the next clause shows), 'I see that God has respect only to *personal character and state* in the acceptance of men, national and ecclesiastical distinctions being of no account.' **But in every nation**—not (observe), in every *religion;* according to a common distortion of these words. **he that feareth him, and worketh righteousness**—This being the well-known phraseology of the Old Testament in describing the truly godly man, within the pale of revealed religion, it cannot be alleged that Peter meant it to denote a merely *virtuous* character, in the heathen sense; and as Peter had learned enough, from the messengers of Cornelius and from his own lips, to convince him that the whole religious character of this Roman officer had been moulded in the Jewish faith, there can be no doubt that the apostle intended to describe exactly such saintship—in its internal spirituality and external fruitfulness—as God had already pronounced to be genuine and approved. And since to such "He giveth more grace," according to the law of His Kingdom (Jas. 4:6; Matt. 25: 29), He sends Peter, not to be the instrument of his *conversion*, as this is very frequently called, but simply to "show him the way of God more perfectly," as before to the devout Ethiopian eunuch. **36-38. the word...sent unto the children of Israel** —for to them (he would have them distinctly know) the Gospel was first preached, even as the facts of it took place on the special theater of the ancient economy. **preaching peace by Jesus Christ**—the glorious sum of all Gospel truth (I Cor. 1:20-22). **he is Lord of all**—exalted to embrace under the canopy of His peace, Jew and Gentile alike, whom the blood of His Cross had cemented into one reconciled and accepted family of God (Eph. 2:13-18). **37. That word ... ye know**—The facts, it seems, were too notorious and extraordinary to be unknown to those who mixed so much with Jews, and took so tender an interest in all Jewish matters as they did; though, like the eunuch, they knew not the significance of them. **which was published throughout all Judea, and began from Galilee**—See Luke 4:14, 37, 44; 7:17; 9:6; 23:5. **after the baptism which John preached**—See on ch. 1:22. **38. Now God anointed Jesus of Nazareth**—rather, 'Jesus of Nazareth (as the burden of that "published word"), how God anointed Him.' **with the Holy Ghost and with power**—i.e., at His baptism, thus visibly proclaiming Him MESSIAH, "the Lord's Christ." See Luke 4:18-21. For it is not His unction for personal holiness at His incarnation that is referred to—as many of the Fathers and some moderns take it—but His investiture with the insignia of the Messianic office, in which He presented Himself after His baptism to the acceptance of the people. **went about doing good**—holding up the *beneficent* character of all His miracles, which was their predicted character (Isa. 35:5, 6, etc.). **healing all that were oppressed of the devil**—whether in the form of demoniacal possessions, or more indirectly, as in her "whom Satan had bound with a spirit of infirmity eighteen years" (Luke 13:16); thereby showing Himself the Redeemer from all evil. **for God was with him**—Thus gently does the apostle rise to the supreme dignity of Christ with which he closes, accommodating himself to his hearers. **39-43. we are witnesses of all ... he did**—not objects of superstitious reverence, but simply *witnesses* to the great historical facts on which the Gospel is founded. **slew and hanged**—i.e., slew by hanging—**on a tree**—So ch. 5:30 (and see on Gal. 3:13). **40-41. showed him openly; Not to all the people**—for it was not fitting that He should subject Himself, in His risen condition, to a second rejection in Person. **but unto witnesses chosen before of God, ... to us, who did eat and drink with him after he rose ...**—Not the less certain, therefore, was the fact of His resurrection, though withholding Himself from general gaze in His risen body. **he which was ordained of God to be the Judge of quick and dead**—He had before proclaimed Him "Lord of all," for the dispensing of *"peace"* to all alike; now he announces Him in the same supreme lordship, for the exercise of *judgment* upon all alike. On this divine ordination, see John 5:22, 23, 27; ch. 17:31. Thus we have here all Gospel truth in brief. But, *forgiveness through this exalted One* is the closing note of Peter's beautifully simple discourse. **43. To him give all the prophets witness**—i.e., This is the burden, generally of the prophetic testimony. It was fitter thus to give the spirit of their testimony, than to quote them in detail on such an occasion. But let this apostolic statement of the evangelical import of the Old Testament writings be devoutly weighed by those who are disposed to rationalize away this element in the Old Testament. **whosoever believeth in him**—This was evidently said with special reference to the Gentile audience then before him, and formed a noble practical conclusion to the whole discourse. **44-45. While Peter yet spake ..., the Holy Ghost fell**—by visible and audible manifestation (vs. 46). **45. they of the circumcision ... were astonished, ... because that on the Gentiles also was poured out ...**—without circumcision. **46. heard them speak with tongues and magnify God**—As on the day of Pentecost it was no empty miracle, no mere

speaking of foreign languages, but utterance of "the wonderful works of God" in tongues to them unknown (ch. 2:11), so here; but more remarkable in this case, as the speakers were perhaps less familiar with the Old Testament songs of praise. **46-48. Then answered Peter, Can any man forbid water ... which have received the Holy Ghost ...**—Mark, he does not say, They have received the Spirit, what need have they for water? but, Having the living discipleship imparted to them and visibly stamped upon them, what objection can there be to admitting them, by the seal of baptism, into the full fellowship of the Church? **who have received the Holy Ghost as well as we**—and are thus, in all that is essential to salvation, on a level with ourselves. **48. he commanded them to be baptized**—not doing it with his own hands, as neither did Paul, save on rare occasions (I Cor. 1:14-17; cf. ch. 2:38, and John 4:2). **prayed ... him to tarry certain days**—"golden days" [BENGEL], spent, doubtless, in refreshing Christian fellowship, and in imparting and receiving fuller teaching on the several topics of the apostle's discourse.

CHAPTER 11

Vss. 1-18. PETER VINDICATES HIMSELF BEFORE THE CHURCH IN JERUSALEM FOR HIS PROCEDURE TOWARDS THE GENTILES. **1-11. the apostles and brethren ... in Judea**—rather, 'throughout Judea.' **2. they ... of the circumcision**—not the Jewish Christians generally, for here there were no other, but such as, from their jealousy for "the middle wall of partition" which circumcision raised between Jew and Gentile, were *afterwards* known as "they of the circumcision." They doubtless embraced apostles as well as others. **3-4. Thou wentest in .... But Peter rehearsed the matter ...**—These objectors scruple not to demand from Peter, though the first among the apostles, an explanation of his conduct; nor is there any insinuation on Peter's part of disrespect towards his authority in that demand—a manifest proof that such authority was unknown both to the complainers and to himself. **12-18. we entered the man's house**—No mention of Cornelius' name, much less of his high position, as if that affected the question. To the charge, "Thou wentest in to *men* uncircumcised," he simply speaks of the uncircumcised *"man"* to whom he had been divinely sent. **13. seen an angel**—lit., 'the angel,' for the rumor took that definite shape. **14. Who shall tell thee words whereby thou and all thy house shall be saved**—The historian makes the angel express this much more generally (ch. 10:6). So also the subsequent report of it by the deputies and by Cornelius himself to Peter (ch. 10:22, 32). But as Peter tarried with Cornelius certain days, and they doubtless talked over the wonderful scene together, perhaps this fuller and richer form of what the angel said was given to Peter; or the apostle himself may have *expressed* what the angel certainly *designed* by directing them to send for him. Observe, "salvation" is here made to hang upon *"words,"* i.e., the Gospel message concerning Christ. But on the "salvation" of Cornelius, see on ch. 10:34, 35. On that of his "house," see on Luke 19:10. **16-17. Then remembered I the word ... John ... baptized with water; but ye shall be baptized with the Holy Ghost. Forasmuch then ...**—i.e., 'Since God Himself has put them on a level with ourselves, by bestowing on them what the Lord Jesus pronounced the higher baptism of the Holy Ghost, would it not have been to withstand God if I had withheld from them the lower baptism of water, and kept aloof from them as still "unclean?" ' **18. held their peace and glorified God**—Well had it been if, when Paul afterwards adduced equally resistless evidence in justification of the same line of procedure, this Jewish party had shown the same reverential and glad submission! **Then hath God also granted to the Gentiles...**—rather, 'granted to the Gentiles also.' (See a similar misplacement of "also" in Heb. 12:1.) To "*grant* repentance unto life"—i.e., 'such as issues in life' (cf. II Cor. 7:10, "repentance unto salvation")—is more than to be willing to pardon upon repentance [GROTIUS]. The case of Cornelius is so manifestly one of *grace* reigning in every stage of his religious history, that we can hardly· doubt that this was just the feature of it which they meant here to express. *And this is the grace that reigns in every conversion.*

19-24. THE GOSPEL BEING PREACHED TO GENTILES AT ANTIOCH ALSO, BARNABAS IS SENT THITHER FROM JERUSALEM, WHO HAILS THEIR ACCESSION AND LABORS AMONG THEM. **19-24. they which were scattered abroad upon the persecution that arose about Stephen**—and who "went everywhere preaching the word" (ch. 8:4). **travelled as far as Phenice**—that part of the Mediterranean coast which, commencing a little north of Cæsarea, stretches northwards for upwards of 100 miles, halfway to Antioch. **and Cyprus**—See on ch. 4:36. An active commercial intercourse subsisted between Phenice and Cyprus. **and Antioch**—near the head of the northeast coast of the Mediterranean, on the river Orontes, and containing a large colony of Jews, to whose religion there were there numerous proselytes. "It was almost an Oriental Rome, in which all the forms of the civilized life of the empire found some representative; and through the two first centuries of the Christian era it was what Constantinople became afterwards, 'the Gate of the East' " [HOWS]. **20. some of them were men of Cyprus and Cyrene**—(see on Luke 23:26); as Lucius, mentioned in ch. 13:1. **spake unto the Grecians**—rather, "the *Greeks*," i.e., uncircumcised Gentiles (as the true reading beyond doubt is). The Gospel had, from the first, been preached to "the Grecians" or Greek-speaking *Jews*, and these "men of Cyprus and Cyrene" were themselves "Grecians." How, then, can we suppose that the historian would note, as something new and singular (vs. 22), that some of the dispersed Christians preached to *them?* **21. a great number believed**—Thus the accession of Cornelius and his party was not the first admission of uncircumcised Gentiles into the Church. (See on ch. 10:1.) Nay, we read of no influence which the accession of Cornelius and his house had on the further progress of the Gospel among the Gentiles; whereas there here open upon us operations upon the Gentiles from quite a different quarter, and attended with ever growing success. The only great object served by the case of Cornelius was *the formal recognition of the principles which that case afterwards secured.* (See on ch. 15.) **22. sent... Barnabas... as far as Antioch**—implying that even on the way to Antioch he found churches to visit [OLSHAUSEN]. It was in the first instance, no doubt, a mission of inquiry; and no one could be more suitable to inquire into the proceedings of those Cyprians and Cyrenians than one who was himself a "Grecian" of Cyprus (ch. 4:36), and "a son of consolation." **23. when he... had seen the grace of God**—in the

new converts. **was glad**—owned and rejoiced in it at once as divine, though they were uncircumcised. **exhorted them all that with purpose of heart**—as opposed to a hasty and fickle discipleship—**they would cleave unto the Lord**—the Lord Jesus. **24. For he was a good man**—The sense of "good" here is plainly "large-hearted," "liberal-minded," rising above narrow Jewish sectarianism, and that because, as the historian adds, he was "full of the Holy Ghost and of faith." **and much people were added unto the Lord**—This proceeding of Barnabas, so full of wisdom, love, and zeal, was blessed to the great increase of the Christian community in that important city.

25, 26. BARNABAS, FINDING THE WORK IN ANTIOCH TOO MUCH FOR HIM, GOES TO TARSUS FOR SAUL—THEY LABOR THERE TOGETHER FOR A WHOLE YEAR WITH MUCH SUCCESS, AND ANTIOCH BECOMES THE HONORED BIRTHPLACE OF THE TERM CHRISTIAN. **25. Then departed Barnabas to Tarsus for to seek Saul**—Of course, this was after the hasty despatch of Saul to Tarsus, no doubt by Barnabas himself among others, to escape the fury of the Jews at Jerusalem. And as Barnabas was the first to take the converted persecutor by the hand and procure his recognition as a disciple by the brethren at Jerusalem (ch. 9:27), so he alone seems at that early period to have discerned in him those peculiar endowments by virtue of which he was afterwards to eclipse all others. Accordingly, instead of returning to Jerusalem, to which, no doubt, he sent accounts of his proceedings from time to time, finding that the mine in Antioch was rich in promise and required an additional and powerful hand to work, he leaves it for a time, takes a journey to Tarsus, "finds Saul" (seemingly implying—not that he lay hid [BENGEL], but that he was engaged at the time in some preaching circuit—see on ch. 15:23), and returns with him to Antioch. Nor were his hopes disappointed. As co-pastors, for the time being, of the Church there, they so labored that the Gospel, even in that great and many-sided community, achieved for itself a name which will live and be gloried in as long as this world lasts, as the symbol of all that is most precious to the fallen family of man:—"*The disciples were called* CHRISTIANS *first in Antioch.*" This name originated not within, but without, the Church; not with their *Jewish* enemies, by whom they were styled "Nazarenes" (ch. 24:5), but with the *heathen* in Antioch, and (as the form of the word shows) with the *Romans*, not the *Greeks* there [OLSHAUSEN]. It was not at first used in a good sense (as ch. 26:28, and I Pet. 4:16 show), though hardly framed out of contempt [as DE WETTE, BAUMGARTEN, etc.]; but as it was a noble testimony to the light in which the Church regarded Christ—honoring Him as their only Lord and Saviour, dwelling continually on His name, and glorying in it—so it was felt to be too apposite and beautiful to be allowed to die.

27-30. BY OCCASION OF A FAMINE, BARNABAS AND SAUL RETURN TO JERUSALEM WITH A CONTRIBUTION FOR THE RELIEF OF THEIR SUFFERING BRETHREN. **27. came prophets from Jerusalem**—inspired teachers, a class we shall afterwards frequently meet with, who sometimes, but not necessarily, foretold future events. They are classed next to apostles (I Cor. 12:28, 29; Eph. 4:11). **28. that there should be great dearth throughout all the world**—the whole Roman empire. **which came to pass in the days of Claudius Cæsar**—Four famines occurred during his reign. This one in Judea and the adjacent countries took place, A.D. 41 [JOSEPHUS,

Antiquities, 20:2, 5]. *An important date for tracing out the chronology of the Acts.* (But this subject is too difficult and extensive to admit of being handled here.) **29. Then the disciples, every man according to his ability, determined to send relief . . . .**—This was the pure prompting of Christian love, which shone so bright in those earliest days of the Gospel. **30. sent it to the elders**—an office well known to be borrowed from the synagogue; *after the model of which, and not at all of the temple, the Christian Churches were constituted by the apostles.* **by the hands of Barnabas and Saul**—This was Saul's SECOND VISIT TO JERUSALEM after his conversion.

CHAPTER 12

Vss. 1-19. PERSECUTION OF THE CHURCH BY HEROD AGRIPPA I—MARTYRDOM OF JAMES AND MIRACULOUS DELIVERANCE OF PETER. **1-3. Herod the king**—grandson of Herod the Great, and son of Aristobulus. He at this time ruled over all his father's dominions. PALEY has remarked the accuracy of the historian here. For thirty years before this there was no king at Jerusalem exercising supreme authority over Judea, nor was there ever afterwards, save during the three last years of Herod's life, within which the transactions occurred. **2. killed James . . . with the sword**—beheaded him; a most ignominious mode of punishment, according to the Jews. Blessed martyr! Thou hast indeed "drunk of thy Lord's cup, and hast been baptized with his baptism." (See on Mark 10:38-40.) A grievous loss this would be to the Church; for though nothing is known of him beyond what we read in the Gospels, the place which he had as one of the three whom the Lord admitted to His closest intimacy would lead the Church to look up to him with a reverence and affection which even their enemies would come to hear of. They could spring only upon one more prized victim; and flushed with their first success, they prevail upon Herod to seize him also. **3. because he saw it pleased the Jews**—Popularity was the ruling passion of this Herod, not naturally so cruel as some of the family [JOSEPHUS, *Antiquities,* 19:7, 3]. **to take Peter also**—whose loss, at this stage of the Church, would have been, so far as we can see, irreparable. **Then were the days of unleavened bread**—seven in number, during which, after killing and eating the Passover, no leaven was allowed in Jewish houses (Exod. 12). **4. delivered him to four quaternions of soldiers**—i.e., to four parties of four each, corresponding to the four Roman watches; two watching in prison and two at the gates, and each party being on duty for the space of one watch. **intending after Easter**—rather, after the Passover; i.e., after the whole festival was over. (The word in our King James Version is an ecclesiastical term of later date, and ought not to have been employed here.) **to bring him forth to the people**—for execution; for during "the days of unleavened bread," or the currency of any religious festival, the Jews had a prejudice against trying or putting anyone to death. **5, 6. prayer was made without ceasing**—rather (*Margin*), 'instant,' 'earnest,' 'urgent'; as in Luke 22:44; ch. 26: 7; and I Peter 4:8 (see *Greek*). **of the church unto God for him**—not in public assembly, for it was evidently not safe to meet thus; but in little groups in private houses, one of which was Mary's (vs. 12). And this was kept up during all the days of unleavened bread. **6. And when Herod would have brought him forth**—'was going to bring him forth.' **the same night**—but a few hours before the intended execution. Thus long were the disciples kept waiting; their prayers apparently unavailing, and their faith, as would seem from the sequel, waxing feeble. Such, however, is the *law* of God's procedure (Deut. 32:36, and see on John 21:3). **Peter was sleeping between two soldiers, bound with two chains**—Roman prisoners had a chain fastened at one end to the wrist of their right hand, and at the other to the wrist of a soldier's left hand, leaving the right arm of the keeper free in case of any attempt to escape. For greater security the prisoner was sometimes, as here, chained to two soldiers, one on each side. (See ch. 21:23.) Ye think your prey secure, bloodthirsty priests and thou obsequious tyrant who, to "please the Jews," hast shut in this most eminent of the servants of Christ within double gates, guarded by double sentinels, while double keepers and double chains seem to defy all rescue! So thought the chief priests, who "made the sepulchre of the Lord sure, sealing the stone and setting a watch." But "He that sitteth in heaven shall laugh at you." Meanwhile, "Peter is sleeping!" In a few hours he expects a stingless death; "neither counts he his life dear unto him, so that he may finish his course with joy and the ministry which he has received of the Lord Jesus." In this frame of spirit he has dropped asleep, and lies the picture of peace. **7-11. the angel of the Lord**—rather, 'an angel'—**came upon him**—so in Luke 2:9, expressive of the unexpected nature of the visit. **smote Peter on the side . . . Arise up quickly. And his chains fell off . . . Gird thyself . . . And so he did . . . Cast thy garment**—tunic, which he had thrown off for the night—**about thee . . . follow me**—In such graphic minuteness of detail we have a charming mark of reality: while the rapidity and curtness of the orders, and the promptitude with which they were obeyed, betoken the despatch which, in the circumstances, was necessary. **9. wist not that it was true; but thought he saw a vision**—So little did the apostle look for deliverance! **10. first and the second ward . . . the iron gate that leadeth unto the city**—We can only conjecture the precise meaning of all this, not knowing the position of the prison. **passed on through one street; and forthwith the angel departed from him**—when he had placed him beyond pursuit. Thus "He disappointeth the devices of the crafty, so that their hands cannot perform their enterprise" (Job 5:12). **11. when Peter was come to himself**—recovered from his bewilderment, and had time to look back upon all the steps that had followed each other in such rapid succession. **Now I know of a surety, that the Lord hath sent his angel, and hath delivered me . . .**—another evidence that Peter expected nothing but to seal his testimony with his blood on this occasion. **12-17. he came to the house of Mary . . .**—who "must have had a house of some pretensions to receive a large number; and, accordingly, we read that her brother Barnabas (Col. 4:10) was a person of substance (ch. 4:37). She must also have been distinguished for faith and courage to allow such a meeting in the face of persecution" [WEBSTER and WILKINSON]. To such a house it was natural that Peter should come. **mother of John . . . Mark**—so called to distinguish him from the apostle of that name, and to distinguish her from the other Marys. **where many were gathered together praying**—doubtless for Peter's deliverance, and continuing, no doubt, on this the last of the days of unleavened bread, which was their last hope, all night in prayer to God. **13. came to hearken**—not to open; for neither was it a time nor an hour of night for that, but to listen who was there. **opened not for gladness, but ran in and told . . .**—How exquisite is this touch of nature! **15. Thou art mad**—one of those exclamations which one can hardly resist on hearing what seems far 'too good to be true.' **she constantly affirmed**—kept steadfastly affirming'—**that it was even so. Then said they, It is his angel**—his disembodied spirit, his ghost; anything, in fact, rather than himself. Though this had been the burden of their fervent prayers during all the days of unleavened bread, they dispute themselves out of it as a thing incredible. Still, it is but the unbelief of the disciples who "believed not *for joy* and wondered" at the tidings of their Lord's resurrection. How often do we pray for what we can hardly credit the bestowment of, when it comes in answer to our prayers! This, however, argues not so much hard unbelief as that kind of it incident to the best in this land of shadows, which perceives not so clearly as it might how very near heaven and earth, the Lord and His praying people, are to each other. **16. Peter continued knocking**—delay being dangerous. **17. But he, beckoning . . . with his hand to hold their peace**—a lively touch this. In the hubbub of joyful and wondering interrogatories there might mingle reflections, thrown out by one against another, for holding out so long against the testimony of Rhoda; while the emotion of the apostle's own spirit would be too deep and solemn to take part in such demonstrations or utter a word till, with his hand, he had signified his wish for perfect silence. **Go show these things unto James and to the brethren**—Whether James the son of Alpheus, one of the Twelve, usually known as "James the Less," and "James the Lord's brother" (Gal. 1:19), were the same person; and if not, whether the James here referred to was the former or the latter, critics are singularly divided, and the whole question is one of the most difficult. To us, it appears that there are strong reasons for thinking that they were *not* the same person, and that the one here meant, and throughout the Acts, is *the apostle* James. (But on this more hereafter.) James is singled out, because he had probably begun to take the oversight of the Church in Jerusalem, which we afterwards find him exercising (ch. 15). **And he departed, and went into another place**—according to his Lord's express command (Matt. 10:23). When told, on a former miraculous liberation from prison, to go and speak unto the people (ch. 5:20), he did it; but in this case to present himself in public would have been to tempt God by rushing upon certain destruction. **18, 19. as soon as it was day . . .**—His deliverance must have been during the fourth watch (three to six A.M.); else he must have been missed by the keepers at the change of the watch [WIES]. **examined the keepers**—who, either like the keepers of our Lord's sepulchre, had "shaken and become as dead men" (Matt. 28:4), or had slept on their watch and been divinely kept from awaking. **commanded that they should be put to death**—Impotent vengeance!

20-25. HEROD'S MISERABLE END—GROWING SUCCESS OF THE GOSPEL—BARNABAS AND SAUL RETURN TO ANTIOCH. **20. Herod was . . . displeased with them of Tyre and Sidon**—for some reason unknown; but the effect on their commercial relations made the latter glad to sue for peace. **their country was nourished by the king's country**—See I Kings 5:11; Ezra 3:7; Ezekiel 27:17. Perhaps the famine

(ch. 11:28) made them the more urgent for reconciliation. **21, 23. And upon a set day Herod . . . made an oration unto them**—to the Tyrians and Sidonians especially. **the people gave a shout . . .**—JOSEPHUS' account of his death is remarkably similar to this (*Antiquities,* xix, 8. 2). Several cases of such deaths occur in history. Thus was this wretched man nearer his end than he of whom he had thought to make a public spectacle. **24. But the word grew . . .**—i.e., Not only was the royal representative ignominiously swept from the stage, while his intended victim was spared to the Church, but the cause which he and his Jewish instigators sought to crush was only furthered and glorified. How full of encouragement and consolation is all this to the Christian Church in every age! **25. Barnabas and Saul returned from Jerusalem**—where, it thus appears, they had remained during all this persecution. **when they had fulfilled their ministry**—or service; that mentioned on ch. 11:29, 30. **took with them John . . . Mark**—(See on vs. 12), not to be confounded with the second Evangelist, as is often done. As his uncle was Barnabas, so his spiritual father was Peter (I Peter 5:13).

CHAPTER 13

CHAPTERS 13, 14

PAUL'S FIRST MISSIONARY JOURNEY In Company with Barnabas

Vss. 1-3. BARNABAS AND SAUL, DIVINELY CALLED TO LABOR AMONG THE GENTILES, ARE SET APART AND SENT FORTH BY THE CHURCH AT ANTIOCH. The first seven chapters of this book might be entitled, *The Church among the Jews;* the next five (ch. 8-12), *The Church in Transition from Jews to Gentiles;* and the last sixteen (ch. 13-28), *The Church among the Gentiles* [BAUMGARTEN]. "Though Christianity had already spread beyond the limits of Palestine, still the Church continued a stranger to *formal* missionary effort. Casual occurrences, particularly the persecution at Jerusalem (ch. 8:2), had hitherto brought about the diffusion of the Gospel. It was from Antioch that teachers were first sent forth with the definite purpose of spreading Christianity, and organizing churches, with regular institutions (ch. 14:23)" [OLSHAUSEN]. **1. there were . . . certain prophets**—see on ch. 11: 27—**and teachers; as Barnabas . . .**—implying that there were others there, besides; but, according to what appears the true reading, the meaning is simply that those here mentioned were in the Church at Antioch as prophets and teachers. **Simeon . . . Niger**—of whom nothing is known. **Lucius of Cyrene**—(See on ch. 2:20. He is mentioned, in Romans 16:21, as one of Paul's kinsmen. **Manaen** —or Menahem, the name of one of the kings of Israel (II Kings 15:14). **which had been brought up with**—or, the foster brother of—**Herod the tetrarch**—i.e., Antipas, who was himself "brought up with a certain private person at Rome" [JOSEPHUS, *Antiquities,* 117, 1, 3]. How differently did these two foster brothers turn out—the one, abandoned to a licentious life and stained with the blood of the most distinguished of God's prophets, though not without his fits of reformation and seasons of remorse; the other, a devoted disciple of the Lord Jesus and prophet of the Church at Antioch! But this is only what may be seen in every age: "Even so, Father, for so it seemeth good in Thy sight.'

If the courtier, whose son, at the point of death, was healed by our Lord (John 4:46) was of Herod's establishment, while Susanna's husband was his steward (Luke 8:3), his foster brother's becoming a Christian and a prophet is something remarkable. **and Saul**—last of all, but soon to become first. Henceforward this book is almost exclusively occupied with him; and his impress on the New Testament, on Christendom, and on the world is paramount. **2. As they ministered to the Lord**—The word denotes the performance of *official* duties of any kind, and was used to express the priestly functions under the Old Testament. Here it signifies the corresponding ministrations of the Christian Church. **and fasted**—As this was done in other cases on special occasions (vss. 3, 14, 23), it is not improbable that they had been led to expect some such prophetic announcement at this time. **the Holy Ghost said**—through some of the prophets mentioned in vs. 1. **Separate me**—So Romans 1:1. **for the work whereunto I have called them**—by some communication, perhaps, to themselves: in the case of Saul at least, such a designation was indicated from the first (ch. 22:21). N.B. While the *personality* of the Holy Ghost is manifest from this language, His supreme *divinity* will appear equally so by comparing it with Hebrews 5:4. **3. laid their hands on them**—(See on ch. 6:6)—"recommending them to the grace of God for the work which they had to fulfil" (ch. 14:26). **sent them away**—with the double call—of *the Spirit* first, and next of *the Church*. So clothed, their mission is thus described: "They being sent forth by the Holy Ghost." Have we not here for all time the true principle of appointment to sacred offices?

4-12. ARRIVING IN CYPRUS, THEY PREACH IN THE SYNAGOGUES OF SALAMIS—AT PAPHOS, ELYMAS IS STRUCK BLIND, AND THE GOVERNOR OF THE ISLAND IS CONVERTED. **4, 5. departed unto Seleucia**—the seaport of Antioch, from which it lay nearly due west fifteen miles, and five from the Mediterranean shore, on the river Orontes. **thence sailed to Cyprus**—whose high mountain summits are easily seen in clear weather from the coast [COLONEL CHESNEY in Hows]. "Four reasons may have induced them to turn in first to this island: (1) Its nearness to the mainland; (2) It was the native place of Barnabas, and since the time when Andrew found his brother Simon, and brought him to Jesus, and 'Jesus loved Martha, and her sister, and Lazarus,' family ties had not been without effect on the progress of the Gospel. (3) It could not be unnatural to suppose that the truth would be welcomed in Cyprus when brought by Barnabas and his kinsman Mark, to their own connections or friends. The Jews were numerous in Salamis. By sailing to that city, they were following the track of the synagogues; and though their mission was chiefly to the Gentiles, their surest course for reaching them was through the proselytes and Hellenizing Jews. (4) Some of the Cypriotes were already Christians. Indeed, no one place out of Palestine, except Antioch, had been so honorably associated with the work of successful evangelization" [Hows]. **5. and when they were at Salamis**—the Grecian capital of the island, on the eastern side, and not many hours' sail from Seleucia. At this busy mercantile port immense numbers of Jews were settled, which accounts for what is here said, that they had more than one synagogue, in which Barnabas and Saul preached, while other cities had one only. **they had ... John** [Mark] **to their minister**—'for their officer.' (See on Luke 4:20.) With what fruit they preached here

is not said. Probably their feeling was what Paul afterwards expressed at Antioch in Pisidia (vs. 46). **6. when they had gone through the isle unto Paphos** —on the opposite or west side of the island, about 100 miles by land, along the south coast; the Roman capital, where the governor resided. **they found a ... sorcerer**—one of a numerous class of impostors who, at this time of general unbelief, were encouraged even by cultivated Romans. **7. Which was with the deputy**—properly, *'the proconsul.'* This name was reserved for the governors of settled provinces, which were placed under the Roman Senate, and is never given in the New Testament to Pilate, Felix, or Festus, who were but *procurators,* or subordinate administrators of unsettled, imperial, military provinces. Now as Augustus reserved Cyprus for himself, its governor would in that case have been not a proconsul, but simply a procurator, had not the emperor afterwards restored it to the Senate, as a Roman historian [DIO CASSIUS] expressly states. In most striking confirmation of this minute accuracy of the sacred historian, coins have actually been found in the island, stamped with the names of *proconsuls,* both in Greek and Latin [AKERMAN's *Numismatic Illustrations of the New Testament*]. (GROTIUS and BENGEL, not aware of this, have missed the mark here.) **Sergius Paulus, a prudent** —intelligent—**man**—who thirsting for truth, sent for Barnabas and Saul, desiring ("earnestly desiring") to hear the Word of God. **8-12. But Elymas**—or 'the wise—**for so is his name by interpretation**—the word is from the *Arabic*—**withstood them**—perceiving, probably, how eagerly the proconsul was drinking in the word, and fearing a dismissal. (Cf. II Tim. 3:8.) **9. Then Saul ... also ... called Paul**— and henceforward Paul only; a softening of his former name, in accommodation to Roman ears, and (as the word signifies "little") probably with allusion as elsewhere to his insignificance of stature and appearance (II Cor. 10:1, 10) [WEBSTER and WILKINSON]. **filled with the Holy Ghost**—the Spirit coming mightily upon him. **set his eyes on him and said**—Henceforward Barnabas sinks into the background. The whole soul of his great colleague, now drawn out, as never before, shoots, by the lightning gaze of his eye, through the dark and tortuous spirit of the sorcerer. What a picture! **10. full of all subtlety**—referring to his magic arts. **and all malice**—The word signifies 'readiness for anything,' knavish dexterity. **thou child of the devil ...enemy of all righteousness**—These were not words of passion, for immediately before uttering them, it is said he was "filled with the Holy Ghost" [CHRYSOSTOM]. **wilt thou not cease to pervert the right ways of the Lord**—referring to his having to that hour made a trade of leading his fellow creatures astray. **11. the hand of the Lord is upon thee, and thou shalt be blind for a season**—the judgment being mercifully designed to lead him to repentance. The tradition that it did is hardly to be depended on. **there fell on him a mist ...**—This is in Luke's *medical* style. **12. Then the deputy, when he saw what was done, believed, being astonished at the doctrine of the Lord**—so marvellously attested; cf. Mark 1:27. What fruit, if any, followed this remarkable conversion, or how long after it the missionaries remained at Paphos, we know not.

13-52. AT PERGA JOHN MARK FORSAKES THEM— AT ANTIOCH, IN PISIDIA, PAUL PREACHES WITH GLORIOUS EFFECT—THE JEWS, ENRAGED, EXPEL THEM OUT OF THEIR COASTS. **13. they came to Perga in Pamphylia**—The distance from Paphos to Attalia, on the Gulf of Pamphylia (see on ch. 14:25), sailing in a northwest direction, is not much greater than from Seleucia to Salamis on the east. Perga was the metropolis of Pamphylia, on the river Cestrus, and about seven miles inland from Attalia. **and John departing from them returned to Jerusalem**—As Paul afterwards peremptorily refused to take Mark with him on his second missionary journey, because he "had departed [or 'fallen off'] from them and had not gone with them to the work" (ch. 15:38), there can be no doubt that he had either wearied of it or been deterred by the prospect of the dangers which lay before him. (But see on ch. 15:37, etc.). **14. departed from Perga**—apparently without making any stay or doing any work: cf. the different language of ch. 14:25, and see immediately below. **came to Antioch in Pisidia**—usually so called, to distinguish it from Antioch in Syria, from which they had started, though it actually lies in Phrygia, and almost due north from Perga. It was a long journey, and as it lay almost entirely through rugged mountain-passes, while "rivers burst out at the base of huge cliffs, or dash down wildly through narrow ravines," it must have been a perilous one. The whole region was, and to this day is, infested by robbers, as ancient history and modern travels abundantly attest; and there can be but little doubt that to this very journey Paul many years after alludes, when he speaks amidst his "journeyings often," of his *"perils of rivers"* (as the word is), and his *"perils of robbers"* (II Cor. 11:26). If this journey were taken in May—and earlier than that the passes would have been blocked up with snow—it would account for their not staying at Perga, whose hot streets are then deserted; "men, women, and children, flocks, herds, camels, and asses, all ascending at the beginning of the hot season from the plains to the cool basin-like hollows on the mountains, moving in the same direction with our missionaries" [Hows]. **15-17. Then Paul stood up, and beckoning with his hand**—as was his manner on such occasions (ch. 21:40; and see ch. 26:1). **Men of Israel, and ye that fear God**—by the latter expression meaning religious proselytes, who united with the Jews in all acts of ordinary worship. **and exalted the people when they dwelt as strangers in Egypt**—by marvellous interpositions for them in their deepest depression. **18-22. forty years suffered he their manners**—rather, according to what appears the true reading, 'cherished he them' (as a nurse the infant in her bosom). **20. after that he gave ... judges ... about the space of four hundred and fifty years**—As this appears to contradict I Kings 6:1, various solutions have been proposed. Taking the words as they stand in the *Greek,* thus, 'after that, by the space of 450 years, He gave judges,' the meaning may be, that about 450 years elapsed from the time of the covenant with Abraham *until* the period of the judges; which is historically correct, the word 'about' showing that chronological exactness was not aimed at. But taking the sense to be as in our version, that it was the period of the judges itself which lasted about 450 years, this statement also will appear historically correct, if we include in it the interval of subjection to foreign powers which occurred during the period of the judges, and understand it to describe the whole period from the settlement of the tribes in Canaan to the establishment of royalty. Thus, from the Exodus to the building of the temple were 592 years [Josephus, *Antiquities,* 8. 3. 1]; deduct forty years in the wilderness; twenty-five years of Joshua's rule [Josephus, *Antiquities,* 5. 1. 29]; forty years of Saul's reign (vs. 2); forty of David's and the first

four years of Solomon's reign (I Kings 6:1), and there remain, just 443 years; or, in round numbers, 'about 450 years.' **21. God gave ... them Saul ... of the tribe of Benjamin**—That the speaker was himself of the same name and of the same tribe, has often been noticed as in all likelihood present to the apostle's mind while speaking. **forty years**—With this length of Saul's reign (not mentioned in the Old Testament), Josephus coincides (*Antiquities* 6. 14. 9). **22. I have found David ...**—This quotation is the substance of Psalm 89:20; I Samuel 13:14; and perhaps also of Psalm 78:70-72. **23-25. Of this man's seed hath God, according to ... promise, raised unto Israel a Saviour, Jesus**—The emphasis on this statement lies: (1) in the *seed* from which Christ sprang—David's—and the *promise* to that effect, which was thus fulfilled; (2) on the *character* in which this promised Christ was given of God—"a Saviour." His personal name "Jesus" is emphatically added, as designed to express that very character. (See on Matt. 1:21.) **26-31. children ... of Abraham, and whosoever among you feareth God**—Gentile proselytes—**to you is the word of this salvation sent**—both being regarded as one class, as "the Jew first," to whom the Gospel was to be addressed in the first instance. **27. For they that dwell at Jerusalem, and their rulers, because they knew him not ...**—The apostle here speaks as if the more immediate guilt of Christ's death lay with the rulers and people of the metropolis, to which he fondly hoped that those residing at such a distance as Antioch would not set their seal. **28. found no cause of death**—though they *sought* it (Matt. 26:59, 60). **29. they took him down ... and laid him in a sepulchre**—Though the burial of Christ was an act of honor and love to Him by the disciples to whom the body was committed, yet since His enemies looked after it and obtained a guard of soldeirs to keep watch over it as the remains of their own victim, the apostle regards this as the last manifestation on their part of enmity to the Saviour, that they might see how God laughed all their precautions to scorn by "raising Him from the dead." **31. he was seen many days of them which came up with him from Galilee to Jerusalem, ...**—i.e., by those who, having gone out and in with Him in closest intimacy during all His public ministry, which lay chiefly in Galilee, and having accompanied Him on His last journey to Jerusalem, could not possibly be mistaken as to the identity of the risen One, and were therefore unexceptionable and sufficient witnesses. **32, 33. God hath fulfilled the same**—'hath completely fulfilled.' **in that he hath raised up Jesus again**—lit., 'raised up'; but the meaning is (notwithstanding the contrary opinion of many excellent interpreters) *"from the dead";* as the context plainly shows. **as it is written in the second psalm**—in many MSS. 'the first Psalm'; what we call the first being regarded by the ancient Jews as only an introduction to the Psalter, which was considered to begin with the second. **this day have I begotten thee**—As the apostle in Romans 1:4 regards the resurrection of Christ merely as the *manifestation* of a prior Sonship, which he afterwards (ch. 8:32) represents as *essential,* it is plain that this is his meaning here. (Such *declarative* meaning of the verb 'to be' is familiar to every reader of the Bible.) See i.e., John 15:8, "So shall ye be," i.e., *be seen* to be "My disciples." It is against the whole sense of the New Testament to ascribe the *origin* of Christ's Sonship to His resurrection. **34-37. now no more to return to corruption**—i.e., to the grave where death reigns; and cf.

Romans 6:9, "Christ being raised from the dead dieth no more, *death hath no more dominion over him.*" **I will give you the sure mercies of David**—(Isa. 55:3). The word rendered "mercies" is peculiar, denoting the *sanctity* of them, as comprehending the whole riches of the new covenant; while the other word, "sure," points to the *certainty* with which they would, through David's Seed, be at length all substantiated. See on John 1:14. But how do these words prove the resurrection of Christ? "They presuppose it; for since an eternal kingdom was promised to David, the Ruler of this kingdom could not remain under the power of death. But to strengthen the indefinite prediction by one more definite, the apostle adduces Psalm 16:10, of which Peter had given the same explanation (see on ch. 2:27, 30, 31), both apostles denying the possibility of its proper reference to David" [OLSHAUSEN]. **36. For David, after he had served his own generation by the will of God**—rather, 'served,' in his own generation, the will (or 'counsel') of God; yielding himself an instrument for the accomplishment of God's high designs, and in this respect being emphatically "the man after God's own heart." This done, he 'fell asleep, and was gathered to his fathers, and saw corruption.' David, therefore (argues the apostle), could not be the subject of his own prediction, which had its proper fulfilment only in the resurrection of the uncorrupted body of the Son of God, emphatically God's "Holy One." **38-41. the forgiveness of sins**—the first necessity of the sinner, and so the first experienced blessing of the Gospel. **39. by him all that believe are justified from all things**—The sense requires that a pause in the sentence be made here: 'By him the believer is absolved from all charges of the law.' What follows—**from which ye could not be justified by the law of Moses**—is not an *exceptional* but an *explanatory* clause. The meaning is not, 'Though the law justifies from many things, it cannot justify from all things, but Christ makes up all deficiencies"; but the meaning is, 'By Christ the believer is justified from all things, whereas the law justifies from nothing.' (N.B. The deeper sense of justification, the *positive* side of it, is reserved for the Epistles, addressed to the justified themselves: and whereas it is the *resurrection* of Christ here, and throughout the Acts chiefly, which is dwelt on, because the first thing in order to bring peace to the guilty through Christ was to establish His Messiahship by His resurrection, in the Epistles to believers His *death* as the way of reconciliation is fully unfolded.) **40. Beware, therefore . . .**—By this awful warning of the Old Testament the apostle would fain "shut them up unto the faith." **41. ye will not believe though a man declare it unto you**—i.e., even on unexceptionable testimony. The words, from Habakkuk 1:5, were originally a merciful but fruitless warning against the approaching destruction of Jerusalem by the Chaldeans and the Babylonish captivity. As such nothing could more fitly describe the more awful calamity impending over the generation which the apostle addressed. **42, 43. And when the Jews were gone out of the synagogue, the Gentiles besought that these words might be preached to them the next sabbath**—rather (according to what is beyond doubt the true reading), 'Now, as they were going out [of the synagogue], they besought'—i.e., not the Gentiles, whose case comes in afterwards, but the mixed congregation of Jews and proselytes, to whom the discourse had been addressed, entreated to have another hearing of such truths; those of them, that is, who had been

impressed. 'And after the breaking up of the synagogue, many of' both classes, Jews and religious proselytes, followed Paul and Barnabas (observe, from this time forward, the inverted order of these names; except ch. 14:14; 13:7; 12:25; on which see). These had evidently been won to the Gospel by what they had heard, and felt a clinging to their spiritual benefactors. **who, speaking to them**—following up the discourse in the synagogue by some further words of encouragement. **persuaded them to continue in the grace of God**—which they had experienced through the Gospel. (Cf. ch. 11:23.) **44-48. the next sabbath came almost the whole city together to hear the word of God**—the intervening days having been spent in further inquiry and instruction, and the excitement reaching the Gentiles, who now for the first time crowded, along with the usual worshippers, into the synagogue. **45. But when the Jews**—those zealots of exclusive Judaism—**saw the multitudes, they were filled with envy**—rather, 'indignation,' and broke out in their usual manner. **contradicting and blaspheming**—There is nothing more awful than Jewish fury and execration of the name of Jesus of Nazareth, when thoroughly roused. **46. Then Paul and Barnabas waxed bold, and said, . . .**—This is in the highest style of a last and solemn protestation. **It was necessary that the word should first have been spoken to you**—See the direction of Christ in Luke 24:47; also Romans 1:16. **since ye judge yourselves unworthy of everlasting life**—pass sentence upon yourselves. **47. For so hath the Lord commanded us, saying . . .**—These and other predictions must have been long before this brought vividly home to Paul's mind in connection with his special vocation to the Gentiles. **I have set thee**—i.e., Messiah; from which Paul inferred that he was but following out this destination of his Lord, in transferring to the Gentiles those "unsearchable riches" which were now by the Jews rejected and despised. **48. when the Gentiles heard this, they were glad**—to perceive that their accession to Christ was a matter of divine arrangement as well as apostolic effort. **and glorified the word of the Lord**—by a cordial reception of it. **and as many as were ordained to eternal life believed**—a very remarkable statement, which cannot, without force, be interpreted of anything lower than this, that *a divine ordination to eternal life is the cause*, not the effect, *of any man's believing.* **49-52. And the word of the Lord was published throughout all the region**—implying some stay in Antioch and missionary activity in its vicinity. **the devout and honourable women**—female proselytes of distinction, jaundiced against the new preachers by those Jewish ecclesiastics to whom they had learned to look up. The potent influence of the female character both for and against the truth is seen in every age of the Church's history. **expelled them**—an easier thing than to refute them. **shook off the dust of their feet against them**—as directed (Matt. 10:14). **came unto Iconium**—a populous city about forty-five miles southeast from Pisidian Antioch: at the foot of Mount Taurus; on the borders of Lycaonia, Phrygia, and Pisidia; and in later times largely contributing to the consolidation of the Turkish empire. **the disciples**—who, though not themselves expelled, had to endure sufferings for the Gospel, as we learn from ch. 14:22—**were filled with joy and with the Holy Ghost**—who not only raised them above shame and fear, as professed disciples of the Lord Jesus, but filled them with holy and elevated emotions.

CHAPTER 14

Vss. 1-7. MEETING WITH SIMILAR SUCCESS AND SIMILAR OPPOSITION AT ICONIUM, PAUL AND BARNABAS FLEE FOR THEIR LIVES TO LYSTRA AND DERBE, AND PREACH THERE. "After this detailed account of Paul's labors at Pisidian Antioch, Luke subjoins only brief notices of his further labors, partly because from the nature of the case his discourses must have embraced nearly the same topics, and partly because the consequences that resulted assumed quite a similar shape" [OLSHAUSEN]. **1. they went both together into the synagogue**—Though Paul was now the prominent speaker and actor, yet in everything Barnabas went along with him. **a ... multitude ... of the Greeks believed**—meaning probably the religious proselytes, as opposed to "the Gentiles" mentioned vs. 2. **3. Long time therefore abode the**y—because in spite of opposition they were meeting with so much success. **speaking boldly in the Lord**—rather, 'in dependence on the Lord,' i.e., on their glorified Head. **who gave testimony to the word of his grace**—a notable definition of the Gospel, whose whole burden is GRACE. **and granted**—granting,' i.e., who confirmed the Gospel by granting miraculous attestation to it. (The "and" is wanting in the best MSS.) **5. an assault made ... to stone them**—rather here, 'an impetuous movement' with a view to stoning them: for in II Corinthians 11:25, Paul says, "*Once* I was stoned," and that was at Lystra, as expressly related in vs. 19. (PALEY'S remarks—*Horæ Paulinæ*—on this singular coincidence between the Epistle and the history are very striking.) **fled**—(See Matt. 10:23). **6. unto Lystra and Derbe**—the one some twenty miles to the south, the other some sixty miles to the east of Iconium, somewhere near the bases of what are called the Black Mountains and the roots of Mount Taurus; but their exact position has not yet been discovered.

8-21. AT LYSTRA, PAUL HEALING A CRIPPLE, THE PEOPLE ARE SCARCE RESTRAINED FROM SACRIFICING TO THEM AS GODS, BUT AFTERWARDS, THEIR MINDS BEING POISONED, THEY STONE PAUL, LEAVING HIM FOR DEAD—WITHDRAWING TO DERBE, THEY PREACH AND TEACH THERE. There being no mention of the synagogue at Lystra, it is probable there were too few Jews there to form one. **8-10. there sat there a certain man ... a cripple from his mother's womb. ... The same heard Paul speak**—in the open air and (vs. 11) to a crowd of people. **who steadfastly beholding him**—as he did Elymas the sorcerer when about to work a miracle on him. **and perceiving that he had faith to be healed**—Paul may have been led by the sight of this cripple to dwell on the Saviour's miracles of healing, and His present power; and perceiving from the eagerness with which the patient drank in his words, that he was prepared to put his own case into the Redeemer's hands, the Spirit of the glorified Physician came all upon Paul, and "with a loud voice" he bade him "stand upright upon his feet." The effect was instantaneous—he sprang to his feet "and walked." **11-13. in the speech of Lycaonia**—whether a corruption of the Greek tongue, which was well enough understood in this region, or the remains of some older tongue, is not known. **The gods are come down to us in the likeness of men**—the language of an unsophisticated people. But "that which was a superstition in Lycaonia, and for which the whole creation groaned, became a reality at Bethlehem" [WEBSTER and WILKINSON]. **they called Barnabas, Jupiter**—the father of the gods, from his commanding mien

(CHRYSOSTOM thinks). **and Paul, Mercurius**—the god of eloquence and the messenger and attendant of Jupiter, in the heathen mythology. **the priest of Jupiter, which was**—i.e., whose temple stood—**before their city, brought oxen and garlands**—to crown the victims and decorate, as on festive occasions, the porches. **14-18. when ... Barnabas and Paul heard**—Barnabas is put first here, apparently as having been styled the "Jupiter" of the company—**they rent their clothes and ran in**—rather (according to the true reading), ran forth—**among the people, crying out, ... Sirs, why do ye these things?**—This was something more than that abhorrence of idolatry which took possession of the Jews as a nation from the time of the Babylonish captivity: it was that delicate sensibility to everything which affects the honor of God which Christianity, giving us in God a reconciled Father, alone can produce; making the Christian instinctively feel himself to be wounded in all dishonor done to God, and filling him with mingled horror and grief when such gross insults as this are offered to him. **We ... are men of like passions ...**—How unlike either imposture or enthusiasm is this, and how high above all self-seeking do these men of Christ show themselves to be! **unto the living God**—This is the most glorious and distinctive of all the names of God. It is the familiar phraseology of the Old Testament, which, in such contrast with all that is to be found within the literature of heathenism, is shown to be, with its sequel, the New Testament, the one Book of the true religion. **who made heaven, and earth, and the sea, and all ... therein**—This idea of *creation*, utterly unknown alike to rude and to cultivated heathenism, would not only define what was meant by "the living God," but open up a new world to the more thoughtful part of the audience. **Who in times past suffered all nations to walk in their own ways**—i.e., without extending to them the revelation vouchsafed to the seed of Abraham, and the grace attending it; cf. ch. 17:30; I Corinthians 1:21. Yet not without guilt on their part was this privation (Rom. 1:20, etc.). **17. Nevertheless he left not himself without witness**—Though the heinousness of idolatry is represented as so much less in the heathen, by how much they were outside the pale of revealed religion, he takes care to add that the heathen have divine "witness" enough to leave them "without excuse." **he did good**—scattering His beneficence everywhere and in a thousand forms. **rain from heaven, and fruitful seasons**—on which human subsistence and all human enjoyment depend. In Lycaonia, where, as ancient writers attest, rain is peculiarly scarce, this allusion would have all the greater effect. **filling our hearts with food and gladness**—a natural colloquialism, the heart being gladdened by the food supplied to the body. **with these sayings scarce restrained they the people that they had not done sacrifice to them**—In spite of this, and Peter's repudiation of all such honor (ch. 10:26), how soon idolatrous tendencies began to show themselves in the Christian Church, at length to be systematized and enjoined in the Church of Rome! **came thither Jews from Antioch and Iconium**—Furious zeal that would travel so far to counteract the missionaries of the Cross! **persuaded the people**—'the multitudes.' **and having stoned Paul**—See on vs. 5. Barnabas they seem to have let alone; Paul, as the prominent actor and speaker, being the object of all their rage. The words seem to imply that it was the Jews who did this; and no doubt they took the lead (vs. 19), but it was the act of the instigated and fickle multitudes

along with them.   **drew him out of the city**—By
comparing this with ch. 7:58 it will be seen that the
Jews were the chief actors in this scene.   **as the
disciples stood round about him**—sorrowing.   So
his labors here had not been in vain: "Disciples"
had been gathered, who now rallied around the
bleeding body.   And *one appears to have been
gained on this occasion, of far more importance
than all the rest*—TIMOTHEUS.   See on ch. 16:1-3.
(It could scarcely have been at the *subsequent* visit,
vs. 21, for the reason given in II Timothy 3:10, 11;
while at the *third* visit, ch. 16:1-3, he was already a
Christian.)   **he rose up**—It is possible that this recovery was natural; the insensibility occasioned by
such treatment as he had received sometimes passing away of itself, and leaving the patient less hurt
than appeared.   But certainly the impression naturally left on the mind by the words is that the
restoration was miraculous; and so the best interpreters understand the words.   This is confirmed
by what follows—**came into the city**—Noble intrepidity!   **next day he departed with Barnabas to
Derbe**—a journey for which he could hardly be fit
if his recovery had been natural.   (See as to Derbe,
on vs. 6.)   **and when they had preached . . . to that
city and had taught many**—rather, "had made many
disciples" (*margin*); but probably without suffering
any persecution, as Derbe is not mentioned along
with Antioch, Iconium, and Lystra (II Tim. 3:11).
   21-28. PAUL AND BARNABAS RETRACE THEIR STEPS,
RETURN TO ANTIOCH IN SYRIA, AND THUS COMPLETE
THEIR FIRST MISSIONARY JOURNEY.   **21, 22. they
returned . . . to Lystra, Iconium, and Antioch, confirming the souls . . .**—At Derbe, Paul was not far
from the well-known pass which leads down from
the central tableland to Cilicia and Tarsus.   But
his thoughts did not center in an earthly home.   He
revisited the places where he had been reviled and
persecuted, but where he had left as sheep in the
desert the disciples whom his Master had enabled
him to gather.   They needed building up and
strengthening in the faith, comforting in the midst
of their inevitable suffering, and fencing round by
permanent institutions.   Undaunted therefore by
the dangers that awaited them, our missionaries
return to them, using words of encouragement
which none but the founders of a true religion would
have ventured to address to their earliest converts,
that "we can only enter into the kingdom of God
by passing through much tribulation" [HOWS].
23, 24. when they had ordained them elders—lit.,
'chosen by show of hands.'   But as that would
imply that this was done by the apostles' own
hands, many render the word, as in our version,
"ordained."   Still, as there is no evidence in the
New Testament that the word had then lost its
proper meaning, as this is beyond doubt its meaning in II Corinthians 8:19, and as there is indisputable evidence that the concurrence of the people
was required in all elections to sacred office in the
earliest ages of the Church, it is perhaps better to
understand the words to mean, 'when they had
made a choice of elders,' i.e., superintended such
choice on the part of the disciples.   **and had prayed
with fasting**—lit., 'fastings,' thus setting them solemnly apart.   This last clause confirms our interpretation of the former.   For if "ordination" was by
prayer and fasting (see ch. 13:3), why should it be
said they first "ordained elders," and after that
"prayed with fasting"?   Whereas if the first clause
refer to the *choice* and the second to the *ordination*,
all is natural.   **they commended**—'committed'—
them—i.e., all these churches.   **to the Lord**—Jesus.

25. when they had preached the word in Perga—
now doing what, for some reason, they had not
done on their former visit, but probably with no
visible fruit.   **they went down into Attalla**—a seaport on the Gulf of Pamphylia, drawing to itself
the commerce of Egypt and Syria.   **26. sailed to
Antioch, from whence they had been recommended**
—See on ch. 13:3.   **27. when they had gathered the
church together, they rehearsed all that God had
done with them . . .**—As their call and mission had
been solemn and formal, in the presence of and by
the Church as well as the Holy Ghost, they duti-
fully, and no doubt with eager joy, convened the
church and gave their report of "all that God had
done with them," i.e., by and for them.   **and how**—
in particular—**he had opened the door of faith to the
Gentiles**—to such even as before had not been proselytes.   (See on ch. 11:21; and on the language, see
I Cor. 16:9; II Cor. 2:12; Col. 4:3.)   The ascribing directly to God of such access to the Gentiles is
to be noted.   **28. there they abode long time**—'no
little time.'   From the commencement of the mission till they left Antioch to go up to attend the
council at Jerusalem, some four or five years
elapsed; and as the missionary journey would probably occupy less than two years, the rest of the
time would be the period of their stay at Antioch.
(But see Chronological Table.)

CHAPTER 15

   VSS. 1-35.   COUNCIL AT JERUSALEM TO DECIDE
ON THE NECESSITY OF CIRCUMCISION FOR THE GEN-
TILE CONVERTS.   **1, 2. certain men**—See the description of them in Galatians 2:4.   **Paul and Barnabas**
—now the recognized heads of the Church at Antioch—**had no small dissension and disputation with
them, they determined**—i.e., the church did—**that
Paul and Barnabas, and certain others of them**—
Titus was one (Gal. 2:1); probably as an uncircumcised Gentile convert endowed with the gifts of the
Spirit.   He is not mentioned in the Acts, but only
in II Corinthians, Galatians, II Timothy, and the
Epistle addressed to him [ALFORD].   **they determined that Paul and Barnabas should go up to Jerusalem . . . about this question**—That such a deputation should be formally despatched by the Church
of Antioch was natural, as it might be called the
mother church of Gentile Christianity.   **3-6. being
brought on their way by the church**—a kind of official escort.   **they passed through Phenice**—See on
ch. 11:19.   **and Samaria, declaring the conversion
of the Gentiles, and they caused great joy to the
brethren**—As the converts in those parts were Jewish (ch. 11:19), their spirit contrasts favorably with
that of others of their nation.   **And when they were
come to Jerusalem**—This was Paul's THIRD VISIT
TO JERUSALEM after his conversion, and *on this occasion took place what is related in* Galatians 2:1-
10.   (See there.)   **were received of the church, and
the apostles and elders**—evidently at a meeting formally convened for this purpose: the deputation being
one so influential, and from a church of such note.
**they declared all things that God had done with
them.**   See on ch. 14:14-27.   **6. the apostles and
elders came together to consider of this**—but in
presence, as would seem, of the people (vss. 12, 22,
23).   **7. Peter . . .**—This is the last mention of him
in the Acts, and one worthy of his standing, as formally pronouncing, from the divine decision of the
matter already in his own case, in favor of the
views which all of Paul's labors were devoted to

establishing. **a good while ago**—probably about fifteen years before this. **made choice ... that the Gentiles by my mouth**—See on ch. 11:21. **8. God, which knoweth the hearts**—implying that the real question for admission to full standing in the visible Church is *the state of the heart.* Hence, though that cannot be known by men, no principle of admission to church privileges which *reverses* this can be sound. **9. put no difference between us and them: purifying their hearts by faith**—"Purification" here refers to "sprinkling (of the conscience by the blood of Jesus) from dead works to serve the living God." (See on I Cor. 6:11.) How rich is this brief description of the inward revolution wrought upon the genuine disciples of the Lord Jesus! **10. why tempt**—'try,' 'provoke'—**ye God**—by standing in the way of His declared purpose. **to put a yoke upon the neck of the disciples ...** He that was circumcised became thereby bound to keep the whole law. (See Gal. 5:1-6.) It was not then the mere yoke of burdensome ceremonies, but of an obligation which the more earnest and spiritual men became, the more impossible they felt it to fulfil. (See Rom. 3:5; Gal. 2:4, etc.). **11. through the grace of the Lord Jesus**—i.e., by that only. **we shall be saved, even as they**—circumcision in our case being no advantage, and in their case uncircumcision no loss; but *grace* doing all for both, and the same for each. **12. Then all ... gave audience to Barnabas and Paul**—On this order of the names here, see on vs. 25. **declaring what miracles and signs God wrought among the Gentiles by them**—This detail of facts, immediately following up those which Peter had recalled to mind, would lead all who waited only for divine teaching to see that God had Himself pronounced the Gentile converts to be disciples in as full standing as the Jews, without circumcision; and the attesting *miracles* to which Paul here refers would tend, in such an assembly to silence opposition. **13. James answered, saying ....**—Whoever this James was (see on Gal. 1:19), he was the acknowledged head of the church at Jerusalem, and here, as president of the assembly, speaks last, winding up the debate. His decision, though given as his own judgment only, could not be of great weight with the opposing party, from his conservative reverence for all Jewish usages within the circle of Israelitish Christianity. **14-17. Simeon**—a Hebrew variation of Simon, as in II Peter 1:1; (*Gr.*) the Jewish and family name of Peter. **hath declared how God at the first**—answering to Peter's own expression "a good while ago" (vs. 7). **did visit the Gentiles to take out of them**—in the exercise of His adorable sovereignty. **a people for**—the honor of—**his name**—or for His glory. **15. to this agree the words of the prophets**—generally; but those of Amos (ch. 9:11) are specified (nearly as in the Septuagint version). The point of the passage lies in the predicted purpose of God, under the new economy, that "the heathen" or "Gentiles" should be "called by His name," or have "His name called upon them." By the "building again of the fallen tabernacle of David," or restoring its decayed splendor, is meant that only and glorious recovery which it was to experience under David's "son and Lord." **18, 19. Known unto God are all his works from the beginning**—He who announced these things so long before, and He who had now brought them to pass, were one and the same; so that they were no novelty. **Wherefore, my sentence**—or 'judgment'—**is, that we trouble not**—with Jewish obligations—**them which from among the Gentiles are turned to God**—rather, 'are turning.' The work is

regarded as in progress, and indeed was rapidly advancing. **20. But ... that they abstain from pollutions of idols**—i.e., things polluted by having been offered in sacrifice to idols. The heathen were accustomed to give away or sell portions of such animals. From such food James would enjoin the Gentile converts to abstain, lest it should seem to the Jews that they were not entirely weaned from idolatry. **and from fornication**—The characteristic sin of heathendom, unblushingly practiced by all ranks and classes, and the indulgence of which on the part of the Gentile converts would to Jews, whose Scriptures branded it as an abomination of the heathen, proclaim them to be yet joined to their old idols. **and from things strangled**—which had the blood in them. **and from blood**—in every form, as peremptorily forbidden to the Jews, and the eating of which, therefore, on the part of the Gentile converts, would shock their prejudices. See on vss. 28, 29. **21. For Moses of old time hath in every city them that preach him ... every sabbath day**—thus keeping alive in every Jew those feelings which such practices would shock, and which, therefore, the Gentile converts must carefully respect if the oneness of both classes in Christ was to be practically preserved. The wisdom of these suggestions commended itself to all present. **22, 23. Judas surnamed Barsabas**—therefore not the apostle "Judas the brother of James" (ch. 1:13), surnamed "Thaddeus" (Matt. 10:3); nor can it be shown that he was a brother of "Joseph called Barsabas" (ch. 1:23). But nothing is known of him beyond what is here said. **and Silas**—the same as "Silvanus" in the Epistles. He became Paul's companion on his second missionary journey (vs. 40). **chief men among the brethren**—selected purposely as such, to express the honor in which they held the church at Antioch, and the deputies they had sent to the council, and, as the matter affected all Gentile converts, to give weight to the written decision of this important assembly. They were "prophets," vs. 32 (and see on ch. 11:27), and as such doubtless their eminence in the church at Jerusalem had been obtained. **And they wrote ... by them**—This is the first mention in the New Testament history of *writing* as an element in its development. And the combination here of written and oral transmission of an important decision reminds us of the first occasion of writing mentioned in the Old Testament, where a similar combination occurs (Exod. 17:14). But whereas *there* it is the deep *difference* between Israel and the Gentiles which is proclaimed, *here* it is the *obliteration of that difference* through faith in the Lord Jesus [BAUMGARTEN]. **greeting**—The only other place in the New Testament where this word occurs (except in the letter of Lysias, ch. 23: 26) is James 1:1, which seems to show that both letters were drawn up by the same hand [BENGEL]. **the Gentiles in Antioch, and Syria, and Cilicia**—showing that churches then existed in Cilicia as well as Syria, which owed their existence, in all likelihood, to Paul's labors during the interval between his return to Tarsus (ch. 9:30) and his departure in company with Barnabas for Antioch (see on ch. 11:25, 26). **24-27. Forasmuch as we have heard that certain which went out from us have troubled you with words**—without authority or even knowledge of the church at Jerusalem, though they belonged to it, and probably pretended to represent its views. **subverting your souls**—Such strong language is evidently designed to express indignation at this attempt, by an unauthorized party, to bring the whole Christian Church under judicial and legal bondage. **our beloved Barnabas and Paul**—Barnabas is put first here, and in vs. 12, on account of his former superior position in the church at Jerusalem (see ch. 9:27; 11:22)—an evidence this that we have the document precisely as written, as also of the credibility of this precious history. **Men that have hazarded**—lit., 'rendered up,' as in *will* they did—**their lives for the name of our Lord Jesus Christ**—Noble testimony to those beloved men! It was doubtless prompted more immediately by the narrative they had just listened to from their own lips (vs. 12), and judiciously inserted in this letter, to give them the highest weight as the bearers of it, along with their own deputies. **Judas and Silas ... shall tell you the same ... by mouth**—Mark here how considerate and tender it was to send men who would be able to say of Barnabas and Paul what could not be expected to come from themselves. **28, 29. For it seemed good to the Holy Ghost and to us ...**—The One, inwardly guiding to and setting His seal on the decision come to; the other, the external ecclesiastical authority devoutly embracing, expressing, and conveying to the churches that decision:—a great principle this for the Church in all time. **to lay upon you no greater burden than these necessary things ... from which if ye keep yourselves, ye shall do well**—The whole language of these prohibitions, and of vss. 20, 21, implies that they were designed as concessions to Jewish feelings on the part of the Gentile converts, and not as things which were all of unchanging obligation. The only cause for hesitation arises from "fornication" being mixed up with the other three things; which has led many to regard the whole as permanently prohibited. But the remarks on vs. 20 may clear this. The then state of heathen society in respect of all the four things seems the reason for so mixing them up. **30-33. they rejoiced for the consolation**—As the same word is in the next verse properly rendered "exhorted," the meaning probably is 'rejoiced for the exhortation' (*margin*), or advice; so wise in itself and so contrary to the imposition attempted to be practiced upon them by the Judaizers. **Judas and Silas, being prophets themselves**—i.e., inspired teachers—**exhorted the brethren with many words**—'much discourse'—**and confirmed them**—opening up, no doubt, the great principle involved in the controversy now settled, of gratuitous salvation, or the purification of the heart by faith alone (as expressed by Peter, vss. 9, 11), and dwelling on the necessity of harmony in principle and affection between the Gentile disciples and their Jewish brethren. **were let go in peace**—with peace, as the customary parting salutation. **34, 35. it pleased Silas**—Silas determined—**to abide there still**—(The authorities against the insertion of this verse are strong. It may have been afterwards added to explain vs. 40). Doubtless the attraction to Antioch for Silas was Paul's presence there, to whom he seems to have now formed that permanent attachment which the sequel of this book and Paul's Epistles show to have existed. **Paul ... and Barnabas continued in Antioch, teaching**—to the disciples—**and preaching**—to those without—**the word of the Lord, with many others**—other laborers—**also**—How rich must Antioch at this time have been in the ministrations of the Gospel! (*For a painful scene on this occasion between Paul and Peter, see* Gal. 2:11, etc.).

36-46. DISSENSION BETWEEN PAUL AND BARNABAS—THEY PART COMPANY TO PROSECUTE SEPARATE MISSIONARY TOURS. **And some days after**—How long is a matter of conjecture. **Paul said to Barna-**

bas, **Let us go again and visit our**—the true reading is, the—**brethren in every city where we have preached ... and see how they do**—whether they were advancing or declining, etc.: a pattern for churches and successful missionaries in every age. ("Reader, how stands it with thee?") [BENGEL]. "Paul felt that he was not called to spend a peaceful, though laborious life at Antioch, but that his true work was far off among the Gentiles." We notice here, for the first time, a trace of that tender solicitude for his converts, that earnest longing to see their faces, which appears in the letters which he wrote afterwards, as one of the most remarkable and attractive features of his character. He thought, doubtless, of the Pisidians and Lycaonians, as he thought afterwards at Athens and Corinth of the Thessalonians, from whom he had been lately "taken in presence, not in heart, night and day praying exceedingly that he might see their face and perfect that which was lacking in their faith" [Hows]. **John ... Mark**—his nephew (Col. 4:10). **But Paul thought not good to take him with them who departed from them**—i.e., who *had* departed; but the word is stronger than this—'who stood aloof' or 'turned away' from them—**from Pamphylia, and went not with them to the work**—the work yet before them. The allusion is to what is recorded in ch. 13:13 (on which see). **And the contention was so sharp between them**—such was the 'irritation,' or 'exacerbation'—**that they departed asunder one from the other**—Said they not truly to the Lystrians that they were "men of like passions with them"; (Ch. 14:15.) But *who was to blame*? (1) That John Mark had either tired of the work or shrunk from the dangers and fatigues that yet lay before them, was undeniable; and Paul concluded that what he had done he might, and probably would, do again. Was he wrong in this? (See Prov. 25:19.) But (2) To this Barnabas might reply that no rule was without exception; that one failure, in a young Christian, was not enough to condemn him for life; that if near relationship might be thought to warp his judgment, it also gave him opportunities of knowing the man better than others; and that as he was himself anxious to be allowed another trial (and the result makes this next to certain), in order that he might wipe out the effect of his former failure and show what "hardness he could now endure as a good soldier of Jesus Christ," his petition ought not to be rejected. Now, since John Mark *did* retrieve his character in these respects, and a reconciliation took place between Paul and him, so cordial that the apostle expresses more than once the confidence he had in him and the value he set upon his services (Col. 4:10, 11; II Tim. 4:11), it may seem that events showed Barnabas to be in the right, and Paul too harsh and hasty in his judgment. But, in behalf of Paul, it may well be answered, that not being able to see into the future he had only the unfavorable past to judge by; that the gentleness of Barnabas (ch. 4:36; 11:24) had already laid him open to imposition (see on Gal. 2:13), to which near relationship would in this case make him more liable; and that in refusing to take John Mark on this missionary journey he was not judging his Christian character nor pronouncing on his fitness for future service, but merely providing in the meantime against being again put to serious inconvenience and having their hands weakened by a possible second desertion. On the whole, then, it seems clear that each of these great servants of Christ had something to say for himself, in defense of the position which they respectively took up; that while Barnabas was quite able to appreciate the grounds on which Paul proceeded, Paul was not so competent to judge of the considerations which Barnabas probably urged; that while Paul had but one object in view, to see that the companion of their arduous work was one of thoroughly congenial spirit and sufficient nerve, Barnabas, over and above the same desire, might not unreasonably be afraid for the soul of his nephew, lest the refusal to allow him to accompany them on their journey might injure his Christian character and deprive the Church of a true servant of Jesus Christ; and that while both sought only the glory of their common Master, each looked at the question at issue, to some extent, through the medium of his own temperament, which grace sanctifies and refines, but does not destroy—*Paul,* through the medium of absolute devotion to the cause and kingdom of Christ, which, warm and womanly as his affections were, gave a tinge of lofty sternness to his resolves where that seemed to be affected; *Barnabas,* through the medium of the same singleness of heart in Christ's service, though probably not in equal strength (Gal. 2:13), but also of a certain natural gentleness which, where a Christian relative was concerned, led him to attach more weight to what seemed for his spiritual good than Paul could be supposed to do. In these circumstances, it seems quite possible that they might have amicably 'agreed to differ,' each taking his own companion, as they actually did. But the 'paroxysm' (as the word is), the 'exacerbation' which is expressly given as the cause of their parting, shows but too plainly, that human infirmity amidst the great labors of the Church at Antioch at length sundered those who had sweetly and lovingly borne together the heat and burden of the day during a protracted tour in the service of Christ. "Therefore let no man glory in men" (I Cor. 3:21). As for John Mark, although through his uncle's warm advocacy of his cause he was put in a condition to dissipate the cloud that hung over him, how bitter to him must have ever afterwards been the reflection that it was his culpable conduct which gave occasion to whatever was sinful in the strife between Paul and Barnabas, and to a separation in action, though no doubt with a mutual Christian regard, between those who had till then wrought nobly together! How watchful does all this teach Christians, and especially Christian ministers and missionaries, to be against giving way to rash judgment and hot temper towards each other, especially where on both sides the glory of Christ is the ground of difference! How possible is it that in such cases both parties may, on the question at issue, be more or less in the right! How difficult is it even for the most faithful and devoted servants of Christ, differing as they do in their natural temperament even under the commanding influence of grace, to see even important questions precisely in the same light! And if, with every disposition to yield what is unimportant, they still feel it a duty each to stand to his own point, how careful should they be to do it lovingly, each pursuing his own course without disparagement of his Christian brother! And how affectingly does the Lord overrule such difference of judgment and such manifestations of human infirmity, by making them "turn out rather unto the furtherance of the Gospel"; as in this case is eminently seen in the two missionary parties instead of one, not travelling over the same ground and carrying their dispute over all the regions of their former loving labors, but dividing the field between them! **and so Barnabas took Mark, and sailed unto Cyprus; and Paul chose Silas** (see on vs. 34)—going two and two, as the Twelve and the Seventy (Mark 6:7; Luke 10:1). **and departed, being recommended ... to the grace of God** —(no doubt by some solemn service; see ch. 13:3), as in ch. 14:26. It does not follow from the historian's silence that Barnabas was not so recommended, too; for this is the last mention of Barnabas in the history, whose sole object now is to relate the proceedings of Paul. Nor does it seem quite fair [with De Wette, Meyer, Hows, Alford, Hacket, Webster and Wilkinson, etc.] to conclude from this that the Church at Antioch took that marked way of showing their sympathy with Paul in opposition to Barnabas. **41. and he went through Syria and Cilicia, confirming the churches**—"It is very likely that Paul and Barnabas made a deliberate and amicable arrangement to divide the region of their first mission between them; Paul taking the *continental,* and Barnabas the *insular,* part of the proposed visitation. If Barnabas visited Salamis and Paphos, and if Paul (travelling westward), after passing through Derbe, Lystra, and Iconium, went as far as Antioch in Pisidia, the whole circuit of the proposed visitation was actually accomplished, for it does not appear that any converts had been made at Perga and Attalia" [Hows]. "This second missionary tour appears to have proceeded at first solely from the desire of visiting the churches already planted. In the end, however, it took a much wider sweep, for it brought the apostle to Europe" [Olshausen].

CHAPTER 16

PAUL'S SECOND MISSIONARY JOURNEY

Chapters 15:41 to 18:22

Chaps. 15:41 to 16:5. Visitation of the churches Formerly Established, Timotheus Here Joining the Missionary Party. Ch. 15:41. **he went through Syria and Cilicia** (see on vs. 23) —Taking probably the same route as when despatched in haste from Jerusalem to Tarsus, he then went by land (see on ch. 9:30). Ch. 16. **1-5. Then came he to Derbe and Lystra; and, behold, a certain disciple was there**—i.e., at Lystra (not Derbe, as some conclude from ch. 20:4). **named Timotheus**—See on ch. 14:20. As Paul styles him "his own son in the faith" (I Tim. 1:2), he must have been gained to Christ at the apostle's first visit; and as Paul says he "had fully known his persecutions which came on him at Lystra" (II Tim. 3:10, 11), he may have been in that group of disciples that surrounded the apparently lifeless body of the apostle outside the walls of Lystra, and that at a time of life when the mind receives its deepest impressions from the spectacle of innocent suffering and undaunted courage [Hows]. His would be one of "the souls of the disciples confirmed" at the apostle's second visit, "exhorted to continue in the faith, and" warned "that we must through much tribulation enter into the kingdom of God" (ch. 14: 21, 22). **the son of a certain ... Jewess**—"The unfeigned faith which dwelt first in his grandmother Lois" descended to "his mother Eunice," and thence it passed to this youth (II Tim. 1:5), who "from a child knew the Holy Scriptures" (II Tim. 3:15). His gifts and destination to the ministry of Christ had already been attested (I Tim. 1:18; 4:14); and though some ten years after this Paul speaks of him as still young (I Tim. 4:12), "he was already well reported of by the brethren that were at Lystra and Iconium" (vs. 2), and consequently must have been well known through all that quarter. **but his father was a Greek**—Such mixed marriages, though little practiced, and disliked by the stricter Jews in Palestine, must have been very frequent among the Jews of the dispersion, especially in remote districts, where but few of the scattered people were settled [Hows]. **Him would Paul have to go forth with him**—This is in harmony with all we read in the Acts and Epistles of Paul's affectionate and confiding disposition. He had no relative ties which were of service to him in his work; his companions were few and changing; and though Silas would supply the place of Barnabas, it was no weakness to yearn for the society of one who might become, what Mark once appeared to be, a *son* in the Gospel [Hows]. And such he indeed proved to be, the most attached and serviceable of his associates (Phil. 2:19-23; I Cor. 4:17; 16:10, 11; I Thess. 3:1-6). His double connection, with the Jews by the mother's side and the Gentiles by the father's, would strike the apostle as a peculiar qualification for his own sphere of labor. "So far as appears, Timothy is the first Gentile who after his conversion comes before us as a regular missionary; for what is said of Titus (Gal. 2:3) refers to a later period" [WIES]. But before his departure, Paul **took and circumcised him**—a rite which every Israelite might perform. **because of the Jews . . . for they knew all that his father was a Greek**—This seems to imply that the father was no proselyte. Against the wishes of a Gentile father no Jewish mother was, as the Jews themselves say, permitted to circumcise her son. We thus see why all the religion of Timothy is traced to the female side of the family (II Tim. 1:5). "Had Timothy not been circumcised, a storm would have gathered round the apostle in his farther progress. His fixed line of procedure was to act on the cities through the synagogues; and to preach the Gospel to the Jew first and then to the Gentile. But such a course would have been impossible had not Timothy been circumcised. He must necessarily have been repelled by that people who endeavored once to murder Paul because they imagined he had taken a Greek into the temple (ch. 21:29). The very intercourse of social life would have been almost impossible, for it was still 'an abomination' for the circumcised to eat with the uncircumcised" [Hows]. In refusing to compel Titus afterwards to be circumcised (Gal. 2:3) at the bidding of Judaizing Christians, as necessary to salvation, he only vindicated "the truth of the Gospel" (Gal. 2:5); in circumcising Timothy, "to the Jews he became as a Jew that he might gain the Jews." Probably Timothy's ordination took place now (I Tim. 4:14; II Tim. 1:6); and it was a service, apparently, of much solemnity—"before many witnesses" (I Tim. 6:12). **And as they went through the cities, they delivered . . . the decrees. . . . And so were the churches established in the faith, and increased in number daily**—not the churches, but the number of their members, by this visit and the written evidence laid before them of the triumph of Christian liberty at Jerusalem, and the wise measures there taken to preserve the unity of the Jewish and Gentile converts.

6-12. THEY BREAK NEW GROUND IN PHRYGIA AND GALATIA—THEIR COURSE IN THAT DIRECTION BEING MYSTERIOUSLY HEDGED UP, THEY TRAVEL WESTWARD TO TROAS, WHERE THEY ARE DIVINELY DIRECTED TO MACEDONIA—THE HISTORIAN HIMSELF HERE JOINING THE MISSIONARY PARTY, THEY EMBARK FOR NEAPOLIS, AND REACH PHILIPPI. **6-8. Now when they had gone throughout Phrygia and the region of Galatia**—proceeding in a northwesterly direction. At this time must have been formed "the churches of Galatia" (Gal. 1:2; I Cor. 16:1); founded, as we learn from the Epistle to the Galatians (particularly ch. 4:19), by the apostle Paul, and which were already in existence when he was on his *third* missionary journey, as we learn from ch. 18:23, where it appears that he was no less successful in Phrygia. *Why* these proceedings, so interesting as we should suppose, are not here detailed, it is not easy to say; for the various reasons suggested are not very satisfactory: e.g., that the historian had not joined the party [ALFORD]; that he was in haste to bring the apostle to Europe [OLSHAUSEN]; that the main stream of the Church's development was from Jerusalem to Rome, and the apostle's labors in Phrygia and Galatia lay quite out of the line of that direction [BAUMGARTEN]. **and were forbidden of the Holy Ghost**—speaking by some prophet, see on ch. 11:27. **to preach the word in Asia**—not the great Asiatic continent, nor even the rich peninsula now called Asia Minor, but only so much of its western coast as constituted the Roman province of Asia. **After they were come to Mysia**—where, as being part of Roman Asia, they were forbidden to labor (vs. 8)—**they assayed**—or attempted—**to go into**—or, towards—**Bithynia**—to the northeast. **but the Spirit**—speaking as before—**suffered them not**—probably because, (1) Europe was ripe for the labors of this missionary party; and (2) other instruments were to be honored to establish the Gospel in the eastern regions of Asia Minor, especially the apostle Peter (see I Pet. 1:1). By the end of the first century, as testified by Pliny the governor, Bithynia was filled with Christians. "This is the first time that the Holy Ghost is expressly spoken of as determining the course they were to follow in their efforts to evangelize the nations, and it was evidently designed to show that whereas hitherto the diffusion of the Gospel had been carried on in unbroken course, connected by natural points of junction, it was now to take a leap to which it could not be impelled but by an immediate and independent operation of the Spirit; and though primarily, this intimation of the Spirit was only negative, and referred but to the immediate neighborhood, we may certainly conclude that Paul took it for a sign that a new epoch was now to commence in his apostolic labors" [BAUMGARTEN]. **came down to Troas**—a city on the northeast coast of the Ægean Sea, the boundary of Asia Minor on the west; the region of which was the scene of the great Trojan war. **9, 10. a vision appeared to Paul in the night**—while awake, for it is not called a dream. **There stood a man of Macedonia, and prayed him, saying, Come over into Macedonia, and help us**—Stretching his eye across the Ægean Sea, from Troas on the northeast, to the Macedonian hills, visible on the northwest, the apostle could hardly fail to think this the destined scene of his future labors; and, if he retired to rest with this thought, he would be thoroughly prepared for the remarkable intimation of the divine will now to be given him. This visional Macedonian discovered himself by what he said. But it was a cry not of conscious *desire* for the Gospel, but of deep *need* of it and unconscious *preparedness* to receive it, not only in that region, but, we may well say, throughout all that western empire which Macedonia might be said to represent. It was a virtual confession "that the highest splendor of heathendom, which we must recognize in the arts of Greece and in the polity and imperial power of Rome, had arrived at the end of all its resources. God had left the Gentile peoples to walk in their own ways (ch. 14:2). They had sought to gain salvation for themselves; but those who had carried it farthest along the paths of natural development were now pervaded by the feeling that all had indeed been vanity. This feeling is the simple, pure result of all the history of heathendom. And Israel, going along the way which God had marked out for him, had likewise arrived at his end. At last he is in a condition to realize his original vocation, by becoming the guide who is to lead the Gentiles unto God, the only Author and Creator of man's redemption; and Paul is in truth the very person in whom this vocation of Israel is now a present divine reality, and to whom, by this nocturnal apparition of the Macedonian, the preparedness of the heathen world to receive the ministry of Israel towards the Gentiles is confirmed" [BAUMGARTEN]. *This voice cries from heathendom still to the Christian Church, and never does the Church undertake the work of missions, nor any missionary go forth from it, in the right spirit, save in obedience to this cry.* **and after he had seen the vision, immediately we endeavoured to go into Macedonia**—The "we," here first introduced, is a modest intimation that the historian himself had now joined the missionary party. (The modern objections to this are quite frivolous.) Whether Paul's broken health had anything to do with this arrangement for having "the beloved physician" with him [WIES], can never be known with certainty; but that he would deem himself honored in taking care of so precious a life, there can be no doubt. **11, 12. Therefore loosing from Troas, we came**—lit., 'ran'—**with a straight course**—i.e., 'ran before the wind.' **to Samothracia** —a lofty island on the Thracian coast, north from Troas, with an inclination westward. The wind must have set in strong from the south or southsoutheast to bring them there so soon, as the current is strong in the opposite direction, and they afterwards took five days to what they now did in two (ch. 20:6) [HOWS]. **next day to Neapolis**—on the Macedonian, or rather Thracian, coast, about sixty-five miles from Samothracia, and ten from Philippi, of which it is the harbor. **Philippi . . . the chief**—rather, perhaps, 'the first'—**city of that part of Macedonia**—The meaning appears to be—the first city one comes to, proceeding from Neapolis. The sense given in our version hardly consists with fact. **a colony**—i.e., possessing all the privileges of Roman citizenship, and, as such, both exempted from scourging and (in ordinary cases) from arrest, and entitled to appeal from the local magistrate to the emperor. Though the Pisidian *Antioch* and *Troas* were also "colonies," the fact is mentioned in this history of Philippi only on account of the frequent references to Roman privileges and duties in the sequel of the chapter.

12-34. AT PHILIPPI, LYDIA IS GAINED AND WITH HER HOUSEHOLD BAPTIZED—AN EVIL SPIRIT IS EXPELLED, PAUL AND SILAS ARE SCOURGED, IMPRISONED, AND MANACLED, BUT MIRACULOUSLY SET FREE, AND THE JAILER WITH ALL HIS HOUSEHOLD CONVERTED AND BAPTIZED. **12, 13. we were in that city abiding certain days**—waiting till the sabbath came round: their whole stay must have extended to some weeks. As their rule was to begin with the Jews and proselytes, they did nothing till the time when they knew that they would convene for worship. **on the sabbath day**—the first after their arrival, as the words imply. **we went out of the city**—rather, as the true reading is, 'outside of the (city) gate.' **by a river-side**—one of the small streams which gave name to the place ere the city was founded by Philip of Macedon. **where prayer was wont to be made**—or a prayer meeting held. It is plain there was no synagogue at Philippi (contrast ch. 17:1), the number of the Jews being small. The meeting appears to have consisted wholly of women, and these not all Jewish. The neighborhood of streams was preferred, on account of the ceremonial washings used on such occasions. **we sat down and spake unto the women . . .**—a humble congregation, and simple manner of preaching. *But here and thus were gathered the first fruits of Europe unto Christ, and they were of the female sex,* of whose accession and services honorable mention will again and again be made. **14, 15. Lydia**—a common name among the Greeks and Romans. **a seller of purple, of the city of Thyatira**—on the confines of Lydia and Phrygia. The Lydians, particularly the inhabitants of Thyatira, were celebrated for their dyeing, in which they inherited the reputation of the Tyrians. Inscriptions to this effect, yet remaining, confirm the accuracy of our historian. This woman appears to have been in good circumstances, having an establishment at Philippi large enough to accommodate the missionary party (vs. 15), and receiving her goods from her native town. **which worshipped God**—i.e., was a proselyte to the Jewish faith, and as such present at this meeting. **whose heart the Lord opened**—i.e., the Lord Jesus (see vs. 15; and cf. Luke 24:45; Matt. 11:27). **that she attended to the things . . . spoken by Paul**—"showing that the inclination of the heart towards the truth originates not in the will of man. The first disposition to turn to the Gospel is a work of grace" [OLSHAUSEN]. Observe here the place assigned to 'giving attention' or 'heed' to the truth—that species of attention which consists in having the whole mind engrossed with it, and in apprehending and drinking it in, in its vital and saving character. **And when . . . baptized . . . and her household**—probably without much delay. The mention of baptism here for the first time in connection with the labors of Paul, while it was doubtless performed on all his former converts, indicates a special importance in this first European baptism. Here also is the first mention of a Christian *household.* Whether it included children, also in that case baptized, is not explicitly stated; but the presumption, as in other cases of household baptism, is that it did. Yet the question of infant baptism must be determined on other grounds; and such incidental allusions form only part of the historical materials for ascertaining the practice of the Church. **she besought us, saying, If ye have judged me to be faithful to the Lord**—the Lord Jesus; i.e., 'By the faith on Him which ye have recognized in me by baptism.' There is a beautiful modesty in the expression. **And she constrained us**—The word seems to imply that they were reluctant, but were overborne. **16-18. as we went to prayer**—The words imply that it was *on their way to the usual place of public prayer,* by the river side, that this took place; therefore not on the same day with what had just occurred. **a . . . damsel**—a female servant, and in this case a slave (vs. 19). **possessed of a spirit of divination**—or, of

Python, i.e., a spirit supposed to be inspired by the Pythian Apollo, or of the same nature. The reality of this demoniacal possession is as undeniable as that of any in the Gospel history. **These men are servants of the most high God . . .**—Glorious testimony! But see on Luke 4:41. **this did she many days**—i.e., on many successive occasions when on their way to their usual place of meeting, or when engaged in religious services. **Paul being grieved**—for the poor victim; grieved to see such power possessed by the enemy of man's salvation, and grieved to observe the malignant design with which this high testimony was borne to Christ. **19. when her masters saw that the hope of their gains was gone, they caught Paul and Silas**—as the leading persons—**and drew them into the market-place**—or Forum, where the courts were—**to the magistrates, saying . . .**—We have here a full and independent confirmation of the reality of this supernatural cure, since on any other supposition such conduct would be senseless. **20. These men, being Jews**—objects of dislike, contempt, and suspicion by the Romans, and at this time of more than usual prejudice. **do exceedingly trouble our city**—See similar charges, ch. 17:6; 24:5; 1 Kings 18:17. There is some color of truth in all such accusations, in so far as the Gospel, and generally the fear of God, as a reigning principle of human action, is in a godless world a thoroughly *revolutionary* principle. How far external commotion and change will in any case attend the triumph of this principle depends on the breadth and obstinacy of the resistance it meets with. **21. And teach customs, which are not lawful for us to receive, neither to observe, being Romans**—Here also there was a measure of truth; as the introduction of new gods was forbidden by the laws, and this might be thought to apply to any change of religion. But the whole charge was pure hypocrisy; for as these men would have let the missionaries preach what religion they pleased if they had not dried up the source of their gains, so they conceal the real cause of their rage under color of a zeal for religion, and law, and good order: so ch. 17:6,7; and 19:25, 27. **22. the multitude rose up together against them**—so ch. 19:28, 34; 21:30; Luke 23:18. **the magistrates rent off their**—Paul's and Silas'—**clothes**—i.e., ordered the lictors, or rod-bearers, to tear them off, so as to expose their naked bodies (see on vs. 37). The word expresses the roughness with which this was done to prisoners preparatory to whipping. **and commanded to beat them**—without any trial (vs. 37), to appease the popular rage. Thrice, it seems, Paul endured this indignity (II Cor. 11:25). **23, 24. when they had laid many stripes upon them**—the bleeding wounds from which they were not washed till it was done by the converted jailer (vs. 33). **charged the jailer . . . who . . . thrust them into the inner prison**—"pestilential cells, damp and cold, from which the light was excluded, and where the chains rusted on the prisoners. One such place may be seen to this day on the slope of the Capitol at Rome" [Hows]. **made their feet fast in the stocks**—an instrument of torture as well as confinement, made of wood bound with iron, with holes for the feet, which were stretched more or less apart according to the severity intended. (Origen at a later period, besides having his neck thrust into an iron collar, lay extended for many days with his feet apart in the rack.) Though jailers were proverbially unfeeling, the manner in which the order was given in this case would seem to warrant all that was done. **25. And at midnight**

Paul and Silas prayed and sang praises—lit., 'praying, were singing praises'; i.e., while engaged in pouring out their hearts in prayer, had broken forth into singing, and were hymning loud their joy. As the word here employed is that used to denote the Paschal hymn sung by our Lord and His disciples after their last Passover (Matt. 26:30), and which we know to have consisted of Psalms 113-118, which was chanted at that festival, it is probable that it was portions of the Psalms, so rich in such matter, which our joyous sufferers chanted forth; nor could any be more seasonable and inspiring to them than those very six Psalms, which every devout Jew would no doubt know by heart. *"He giveth songs in the night"* (Job 35:10). Though their bodies were still bleeding and tortured in the stocks, their spirits, under 'the expulsive power of a new affection,' rose above suffering, and made the prison walls resound with their song. "In these midnight hymns, by the imprisoned witnesses for Jesus Christ, the whole might of Roman injustice and violence against the Church is not only set at naught, but converted into a foil to set forth more completely the majesty and spiritual power of the Church, which as yet the world knew nothing of. And if the sufferings of these two witnesses of Christ are the beginning and the type of numberless martyrdoms which were to flow upon the Church from the same source, in like manner the unparalleled triumph of the Spirit over suffering was the beginning and the pledge of a spiritual power which we afterwards see shining forth so triumphantly and irresistibly in the many martyrs of Christ who were given up as a prey to the same imperial might of Rome" [Neander in Baumgarten]. **and the prisoners heard them**—lit 'were listening to them,' i.e., when the astounding events immediately to be related took place; not asleep, but wide awake and rapt (no doubt) in wonder at what they heard. **26-28. And suddenly there was a great earthquake**—in answer, doubtless, to the prayers and expectations of the sufferers that, for the truth's sake and the honor of their Lord, some interposition would take place. **every one's bands**—i.e., the bands of all the prisoners—**were loosed**—not by the earthquake, of course, but by a miraculous energy accompanying it. By this and the joyous strains which they had heard from the sufferers, not to speak of the change wrought on the jailer, these prisoners could hardly fail to have their hearts in some measure opened to the truth; and this part of the narrative seems the result of information afterwards communicated by one or more of these men. **the keeper . . . awaking . . . drew . . . his sword, and would have killed himself . . .**—knowing that his life was forfeited in that case (ch. 12:19; and cf. 27:42). **But Paul cried with a loud voice**—the better to arrest the deed—**Do thyself no harm, for we are all here**—What divine calmness and self-possession! No elation at their miraculous liberation, or haste to take advantage of it; but one thought filled the apostle's mind at that moment—anxiety to save a fellow creature from sending himself into eternity, ignorant of the only way of life; and his presence of mind appears in the assurance which he so promptly gives to the desperate man, that his prisoners had none of them fled as he feared. But how, it has been asked by skeptical critics, could Paul in his inner prison know what the jailer was about to do? In many conceivable ways, without supposing any supernatural communication. Thus, if the jailer slept at the door of "the inner prison," which suddenly flew open when the earthquake shook the foundations of the building; if, too, as may easily be conceived, he uttered some cry of despair on seeing the doors open; and, if the clash of the steel, as the affrighted man drew it hastily from the scabbard, was audible but a few yards off, in the dead midnight stillness, increased by the awe inspired in the prisoners by the miracle—what difficulty is there in supposing that Paul, perceiving in a moment how matters stood, after crying out, stepped hastily to him, uttering the noble entreaty here recorded? Not less flat is the question, why the other liberated prisoners did not make their escape:—as if there were the smallest difficulty in understanding how, under the resistless conviction that there must be something supernatural in their instantaneous liberation without human hand, such wonder and awe should possess them as to take away for the time not only all desire of escape, but even all thought on the subject. **29, 30. Then he called for a light, and sprang in . . . and fell down before Paul and Silas, and brought them out and said**—How graphic this rapid succession of minute details, evidently from the parties themselves, the prisoners and the jailer, who would talk over every feature of the scene once and again, in which the hand of the Lord had been so marvellously seen. **Sirs, what must I do to be saved?**—If this question should seem in advance of any light which the jailer could be supposed to possess, let it be considered (I) that the "trembling" which came over him could not have arisen from any fear for the safety of his prisoners, for they were all there; and if it had, he would rather have proceeded to secure them again than leave them, to fall down before Paul and Silas. For the same reason it is plain that his trembling had nothing to do with any account he would have to render to the magistrates. Only one explanation of it can be given—that he had become all at once alarmed about his spiritual state, and that though, a moment before, he was ready to plunge into eternity with the guilt of self-murder on his head, without a thought of the sin he was committing and its awful consequences, his unfitness to appear before God, and his need of salvation, now flashed full upon his soul and drew from the depths of his spirit the cry here recorded. If still it be asked how it could take such definite shape, let it be considered (2) that the jailer could hardly be ignorant of the nature of the charges on which these men had been imprisoned, seeing they had been publicly whipped by order of the magistrates, which would fill the whole town with the facts of the case, including that strange cry of the demoniac from day to day—"These men are the servants of the most high God, which *show unto us the way of salvation*"—words proclaiming not only the divine commission of the preachers, but the news of salvation they were sent to tell, the miraculous expulsion of the demon and the rage of her masters. All this, indeed, would go for nothing with such a man, until roused by the mighty earthquake which made the building to rock; then despair seizing him at the sight of the open doors, the sword of self-destruction was suddenly arrested by words from one of those prisoners such as he would never imagine could be spoken in their circumstances—words evidencing something divine about them. Then would flash across him the light of a new discovery; "That was a true cry which the Pythoness uttered, 'These men are the servants of the most high God, which show unto us the way of salvation! That I now must know, and from them, as divinely sent to me, must I learn that 'way

of salvation!'" Substantially, this is the cry of every awakened sinner, though the degree of light and the depths of anxiety it expresses will be different in each case. **31-34. Believe on the Lord Jesus Christ, and thou shalt be saved**—The brevity, simplicity, and directness of this reply are, in the circumstances, singularly beautiful. Enough at that moment to have his faith directed simply to the Saviour, with the assurance that this would bring to his soul the needed and sought salvation—the *how* being a matter for after teaching. **thou shalt be saved, and thy house**—See on Luke 19:10. **And they spake unto him the word of the Lord**—unfolding now, doubtless, more fully what "the Lord Jesus Christ" was to whom they had pointed his faith, and what the "salvation" was which this would bring him. **and to all that were in his house**—who from their own dwelling (under the same roof no doubt with the prison) had crowded round the apostles, aroused first by the earthquake. (From their addressing the Gospel message "to all that were in the house" it is not necessary to infer that it contained no children, but merely that as it contained adults besides the jailer himself, so to all of these, as alone of course fit to be addressed, they preached the word.) **And he took them**—the word implies change of place—**the same hour of the night, and washed their stripes**—in the well or fountain which was within or near the precincts of the prison [Hows]. The mention of "the same hour of the night" seems to imply that they had to go forth into the open air, which, unseasonable as the hour was, they did. These bleeding wounds had never been thought of by the indifferent jailer. But now, when his whole heart was opened to his spiritual benefactors, he cannot rest until he has done all in his power for their bodily relief. **and was baptized, he and all his, straightway**—probably at the same fountain, since it took place "straightway"; the one washing on his part being immediately succeeded by the other on theirs. **And when he had brought them into his house, he set meat before them and rejoiced, believing**—i.e., as the expression implies, 'rejoiced because he had believed'—**in God**—as a converted heathen, for the faith of a *Jew* would not be so expressed [ALFORD]. **with all his house**—the wondrous change on himself and the whole house filling his soul with joy. "This is the second house which, in the Roman city of Philippi, has been consecrated by faith in Jesus, and of which the inmates, by hospitable entertainment of the Gospel witnesses, have been sanctified to a new beginning of domestic life, pleasing and acceptable to God. The first result came to pass in consequence simply of the preaching of the Gospel; the second was the fruit of a testimony sealed and ennobled by suffering" [BAUMGARTEN]. **35, 36. when it was day, the magistrates sent the sergeants, saying, Let those men go**—The cause of this change can only be conjectured. When the commotion ceased, reflection would soon convince them of the injustice they had done, even supposing the prisoners had been entitled to no special privileges; and if rumor reached them that the prisoners were somehow under supernatural protection, they might be the more awed into a desire to get rid of them. **the keeper**—overjoyed to have such orders to execute—**told this . . . to Paul . . . now therefore . . . go in peace**—Very differently did Paul receive such orders. **37. Paul said unto them**—to the sergeants who had entered the prison along with the jailer, that they might be able to report that the men had departed. **They

have beaten us openly—The *publicity* of the injury done them, exposing their naked and bleading bodies to the rude populace, was evidently the most stinging feature of it to the apostle's delicate feeling, and to this accordingly he alludes to the Thessalonians, probably a year after: "Even after we had suffered before, and *were shamefully entreated* (or 'insulted') as ye know at Philippi" (I Thess. 2:2). **uncondemned**—unconvicted on trial—**being Romans** —see on ch. 22:28—**and cast us into prison**—both illegal. Of Silas' citizenship, if meant to be included, we know nothing. **and now do they thrust** —hurry—**us out**—see Mark 9:38, *Greek*—**privily?**—Mark the intended contrast between the *public* insult they had inflicted and the *private* way in which they ordered them to be off. **nay verily**—no, indeed—**but let them come themselves and fetch us out**—by open and formal act, equivalent to a public declaration of their innocence. **38. they feared when they heard they were Romans**—their authority being thus imperilled; for they were liable to an action for what they had done. **39, 40. And they came**—in person—**and besought them**—not to complain of them. What a contrast this suppliant attitude of the prætors of Philippi to the tyrannical air with which they had the day before treated the preachers! (See Isa. 60:14; Rev. 3:9.) **brought them out**—conducted them forth from the prison into the street, as insisted on—**and desired**—'requested'—**them to depart out of the city**—perhaps fearing again to excite the populace. **And they went out of the prison**—Having attained their object—to vindicate their civil rights, by the infraction of which in this case the Gospel in their persons had been illegally affronted—they had no mind to carry the matter farther. Their citizenship was valuable to them only as a shield against unnecessary injuries to their Master's cause. What a beautiful mixture of *dignity* and *meekness* is this! Nothing secular, which may be turned to the account of the Gospel, is morbidly disregarded; in any other view, nothing of this nature is set store by:—an example this for all ages. **and entered into the house of Lydia**—as if to show by this leisurely proceeding that they had not been made to leave, but were at full liberty to consult their own convenience. **and when they had seen the brethren**—not only her family and the jailer's, but probably others now gained to the Gospel. **they comforted them**—rather, perhaps, 'exhorted' them, which would include comfort. *"This assembly of believers in the house of Lydia was the first church that had been founded in Europe"* [BAUMGARTEN]. **and departed**—but not all; for two of the company remained behind (see on ch. 17:14): *Timotheus*, of whom the Philippians "learned the proof" that he honestly cared for their state, and was truly likeminded with Paul, "serving with him in the Gospel as a son with his father" (Phil. 2:19-23); and *Luke*, "whose praise is in the Gospel," though he never praises himself or relates his own labors, and though we only trace his movements in connection with Paul, by the change of a pronoun, or the unconscious variation of his style. In ch. 17 the narrative is again in the *third* person, and the pronoun is not changed to the *second* till we come to ch. 20:5. The modesty with which Luke leaves out all mention of his own labors need hardly be pointed out. We shall trace him again when he rejoins Paul in the same neighborhood. His vocation as a physician may have brought him into connection with these contiguous coasts of Asia and Europe, and he may (as Mr. SMITH suggests, "Ship-

wreck," etc.) have been in the habit of exercising his professional skill as a surgeon at sea [Hows].

CHAPTER 17

Vss. 1-15. At Thessalonica the Success of Paul's Preaching Endangering His Life, He is Despatched by Night to Berea, Where His Message Meets with Enlightened Acceptance—A Hostile Movement from Thessalonica Occasions His Sudden Departure from Berea—He Arrives at Athens. **1. when they had passed through Amphipolis**—thirty-three miles southwest of Philippi, on the river Strymon, and at the head of the gulf of that name, on the northern coast of the Ægean Sea. **and Apollonia**—about thirty miles southwest of Amphipolis; but the exact site is not known. **they came to Thessalonica**—about thirty-seven miles due west from Apollonia, at the head of the Thermaic (or Thessalonian) Gulf, at the northwestern extremity of the Ægean Sea; the principal and most populous city in Macedonia. "We see at once how appropriate a place it was for one of the starting-points of the Gospel in Europe, and can appreciate the force of what Paul said to the Thessalonians within a few months of his departure from them: 'From you, the word of the Lord sounded forth like a trumpet, not only in Macedonia and Achaia, but in every place,' " (I Thess. 1; 8) [Hows]. **where was a synagogue of the Jews** - implying that (as at Philippi) there was none at Amphipolis and Apollonia. **2-4. Paul, as his manner was**—always to begin with the Jews. **went in unto them**—In writing to the converts but a few months after this, he reminds them of the courage and superiority to indignity, for the Gospel's sake, which this required after the shameful treatment he had so lately experienced at Philippi (I Thess. 2:2). **Opening and alleging that Christ must needs have suffered . . .**—His preaching, it seems, was chiefly expository, and designed to establish from the Old Testament Scriptures (1) that the predicted Messiah was to be a suffering and dying, and therefore a rising, Messiah; (2) that this Messiah was none other than Jesus of Nazareth. **consorted**—cast in their lot—**with Paul and Silas**—Cf. II Corinthians 8:5. **of the chief women**—female proselytes of distinction. From the First Epistle to the Thessalonians it appears that the converts were nearly all Gentiles; not only such as had before been proselytes, who would be gained in the synagogue, but such as up to that time had been idolaters (I Thess. 1:9, 10). During his stay, while Paul supported himself by his own labor (I Thess. 2:9; II Thess. 3:7-9), he received supplies once and again from the Philippians, of which he makes honorable acknowledgment (Phil. 4:15, 16). **5-9. the Jews . . . moved with envy**—seeing their influence undermined by this stranger. **lewd fellows of the baser sort**—better, perhaps, 'worthless market-people,' i.e., idle loungers about the market place, of indifferent character. **gathered a company**—rather, 'having raised a mob'—**assaulted the house of Jason** —with whom Paul and Silas abode (vs. 7), one of Paul's kinsmen, apparently (Rom. 16:21), and from his name, which was sometimes used as a Greek form of the word *Joshua* [GROTIUS], probably a Hellenistic Jew. **sought to bring them**—Jason's lodgers—**out to the people. And when they found them not, they drew Jason and certain brethren unto the rulers**—lit., 'the politarchs'; the very name given to the magistrates of Thessalonica in an inscription on a still remaining arch of the city—so minute is the accuracy of this history. **crying, These that have turned the world upside down** —See on ch. 16:20. **all do contrary to the decrees of Cæsar . . .**—meaning, probably, nothing but what is specified in the next words. **saying . . . there is another king, one Jesus**—See on John 19:12. **having taken security of Jason and of the other**—'the others'—probably making them deposit a money pledge that the preachers should not again endanger the public peace. **10-12. the brethren immediately sent away Paul and Silas by night**—for it would have been as useless as rash to attempt any further preaching at that time, and the conviction of this probably made his friends the more willing to pledge themselves against any present continuance of missionary effort. **to Berea**—fifty or sixty miles southwest of Thessalonica; a town even still of considerable population and importance. **These were more noble than those in Thessalonica**—The comparison is between *the Jews* of the two places; for the triumphs of the Gospel at Thessalonica were mostly among the Gentiles. See on vss. 2-4. **in that they received the word with all readiness of mind**—heard it not only without prejudice, but with eager interest, "in an honest and good heart" (Luke 8:17), with sincere desire to be taught aright (see John 7:17). Mark the "nobility" ascribed to this state of mind. **searched the scriptures daily whether those things were so**—whether the *Christian* interpretation which the apostle put upon the Old Testament Scriptures was the true one. **Therefore many of them believed**—convinced that Jesus of Nazareth whom Paul preached was indeed the great Promise and Burden of the Old Testament. From this it is undeniable, (1) that *the people*, no less than the ministers of the Church, *are entitled and bound to search the Scriptures;* (2) that *they are entitled and bound to judge, on their own responsibility, whether the teaching they receive from the ministers of the Church is according to the word of God;* (3) that *no faith but such as results from personal conviction ought to be demanded, or is of any avail.* **of honourable women which were Greeks, and of men**—which were Greeks—**not a few** —"The upper classes in these European-Greek and Romanized towns were probably better educated than those of Asia Minor" [WEBSTER and WILKINSON]. **the Jews of Thessalonica . . . came thither also**—"like hunters upon their prey, as they had done before from Iconium to Lystra" [Hows]. **13, 14. immediately the brethren**—the converts gathered at Berea. **sent away Paul**—as before from Jerusalem (ch. 9:30), and from Thessalonica (vs. 10). How long he stayed at Berea we know not; but as we know that he longed and expected soon to return to the Thessalonians (I Thess. 2:17), it is probable he remained some weeks at least, and only abandoned his intention of revisiting Thessalonica at that time when the virulence of his enemies there, stimulated by his success at Berea, brought them down thither to counterwork him. **to go as it were to the sea**—rather, perhaps, 'in the direction of the sea.' Probably he delayed fixing his next destination till he should reach the coast, and the providence of God should guide him to a vessel bound for the destined spot. Accordingly, it was only on arriving at Athens, that the convoy of Berean brethren, who had gone thus far with him, were sent back to bid Silas and Timothy follow him thither. **Silas and Timotheus abode there still** —"to build it up in its holy faith, to be a comfort and support in its trials and persecutions, and to

give it such organization as might be necessary" [Hows]. Connecting this with the apostle's leaving Timothy and Luke at Philippi on his own departure (see on ch. 16:40), we may conclude that this was his fixed plan for cherishing the first beginnings of the Gospel in European localities, and organizing the converts. Timotheus must have soon followed the apostle to Thessalonica, the bearer, probably, of one of the Philippian "contributions to his necessity" (Phil. 4:15, 16), and from thence he would with Silas accompany him to Berea. **15. Silas and Timotheus to come to him with all speed**—He probably wished their company and aid in addressing himself to so new and great a sphere as Athens. Accordingly it is added that he "waited for them" there, as if unwilling to do anything till they came. That they did come, there is no good reason to doubt (as some excellent critics do). For though Paul himself says to the Thessalonians that he "thought it good to be left at Athens alone" (I Thess. 3:1), he immediately adds that he "sent Timotheus to establish and comfort them" (vs. 2); meaning, surely, that he despatched him from Athens back to Thessalonica. He had indeed sent for him to Athens; but, probably, when it appeared that little fruit was to be reaped there, while Thessalonica was in too interesting a state to be left uncherished, he seems to have thought it better to send him back again. (The other explanations which have been suggested seem less satisfactory.) Timotheus rejoined the apostle at Corinth (ch. 18: 5).

16-34. PAUL AT ATHENS. **16, 17. wholly given to idolatry**—'covered with idols'; meaning the city, not the inhabitants. PETRONIUS, a contemporary writer at Nero's court, says satirically that it was easier to find a god at Athens than a man. This "stirred the spirit" of the apostle. "The first impression which the masterpieces of man's taste for art left on the mind of St. Paul was a revolting one, since all this majesty and beauty had placed itself between man and his Creator, and bound him the faster to his gods, who were not God. Upon the first contact, therefore, which the Spirit of Christ came into with the sublimest creations of human art, the judgment of the Holy Ghost—through which they have all to pass—is set up as 'the strait gate,' and this must remain the correct standard for ever" [BAUMGARTEN]. **therefore disputed**—or, discussed— **he in the synagogue with the Jews.** The sense is not, 'Therefore went he to the Jews,' because the Gentile Athenians were steeped in idolatry; but, 'Therefore set he himself to lift up his voice to the idol-city, but, as his manner was, he began with the Jews.' **and with the devout persons**—Gentile proselytes. After that, **in the market**—the *Agora*, or place of public concourse—**daily with them that met with him**—or 'came in his way.' **18-21. certain . . . of the Epicureans**—a well-known school of *atheistic materialists,* who taught that pleasure was the chief end of human existence; a principle which the more rational interpreted in a refined sense, while the sensual explained it in its coarser meaning. **and of the Stoics**—a celebrated school of *severe and lofty pantheists,* whose principle was that the universe was under the law of an iron necessity, the spirit of which was what is called the Deity: and that a passionless conformity of the human will to this law, unmoved by all external circumstances and changes, is the perfection of virtue. While therefore the Stoical was in itself superior to the Epicurean system, both were alike hostile to the Gospel. "The two enemies it has ever had to contend with are the two ruling principles of the Epicureans and Stoics—*Pleasure and Pride"* [Hows]. **What will this babbler say?** The word, which means 'a pickerup of seeds,' birdlike, is applied to a gatherer and retailer of scraps of knowledge, a prater; a general term of contempt for any pretended teacher. **a setter forth of strange gods**— 'demons,' but in the Greek (not Jewish) sense of '*objects of worship.*' **because he preached Jesus and the resurrection**—Not as if they thought he made these to be two divinities: the strange gods were *Jehovah* and *the Risen Saviour*, ordained to judge the world. **they took him, and brought him to Areopagus**—"the hill where the most awful court of judicature had sat from time immemorial to pass sentence on the greatest criminals, and to decide on the most solemn questions connected with religion. No place in Athens was so suitable for a discourse on the mysteries of religion" [Hows]. The apostle, however, was not here on his *trial*, but to expound more fully what he had thrown out in broken conversations in the Agora. **all the Athenians . . . spent their time in nothing else but to tell or hear some new thing**—lit., 'newer thing,' as if what was new becoming presently stale, they craved something still more new [Bengel]. This lively description of the Athenian character is abundantly attested by their own writers. **22. Then Paul stood . . . and said**—more graphically, 'standing in the midst of Mars' hill, said." This prefatory allusion to the position he occupied shows the writer's wish to bring the situation vividly before us [Baumgarten]. **I perceive that in all things ye are too superstitious**—rather (with most modern interpreters and the ancient Greek ones), 'in all respects extremely reverential' or 'much given to religious worship,' a conciliatory and commendatory introduction, founded on his own observation of the symbols of devotion with which their city was covered, and from which all Greek writers, as well as the apostle, inferred the exemplary religiousness of the Athenians. (The authorized translation would imply that only *too much* superstition was wrong, and represents the apostle as repelling his hearers in the very first sentence; whereas the whole discourse is studiously courteous.) **23. as I passed by and beheld your devotions**—rather, 'the objects of your devotion,' referring, as is plain from the next words, to their works of art consecrated to religion. **I found an altar . . . To the**—or 'an'—**unknown god**—erected, probably, to commemorate some divine interposition, which they were unable to ascribe to any known deity. That there were such altars, Greek writers attest; and on this the apostle skilfully fastens at the outset, as the text of his discourse, taking it as evidence of that dimness of religious conception which, in virtue of his better light, he was prepared to dissipate. **Whom therefore ye ignorantly worship**—rather, 'Whom, therefore, knowing Him not, ye worship,' alluding to "The Unknown God." **him declare**—announce —**I unto you**—*This is like none of his previous discourses, save that to the idolaters of Lycaonia* (ch. 14:15-17). His subject is not, as in the synagogues, the Messiahship of Jesus, but THE LIVING GOD, in opposition to the materialistic and pantheistic polytheism of Greece, which subverted all true religion. Nor does he come with *speculation* on this *profound subject*—of which they had had enough from others—but an authoritative "announcement" of Him after whom they were groping; not giving Him any name, however, nor even naming the Saviour Himself, but unfolding the true character

of both as they were able to receive it. **24, 25. God that made the world and all . . . therein**—The most profound philosophers of Greece were unable to conceive any real distinction between God and the universe. Thick darkness, therefore, behooved to rest on all their religious conceptions. To dissipate this, the apostle sets out with a sharp statement of the fact of *creation* as the central principle of all true religion—not less needed now, against the transcendental idealism of our day. **seeing he is Lord**—or Sovereign—**of heaven and earth**—holding in free and absolute subjection all the works of His hands; presiding in august royalty over them, as well as pervading them all as the principle of their being. How different this from the blind Force or Fate to which all creatures were regarded as in bondage! **dwelleth not in temples made with hands**—This thought, so familiar to Jewish ears (I Kings 8:27; Isa. 66:1, 2; ch. 7:48), and so elementary to Christians, would serve only more sharply to define to his heathen audience the spirituality of that living, personal God, whom he "announced" to them. **Neither is worshipped with hands**—ministered unto, served by—**men's hands, as though he needed anything**—No less familiar as this thought also is to us, even from the earliest times of the Old Testament (Job 35:6, 8; Ps. 16:2, 3; 50: 12-14; Isa. 40:14-18), it would pour a flood of light upon any candid heathen mind that heard it. **seeing he**—He Himself—**giveth to all life, and breath, and all things**—The Giver of all cannot surely be dependent for aught upon the receivers of all (1 Chron. 29:14). This is the culminating point of a pure Theism. **26, 27. and hath made of one blood all nations of men to dwell on all the face of the earth**—Holding with the Old Testament teaching, that in the blood is the life (Gen. 9:4; Lev. 17:11; Deut. 12:23), the apostle sees this lifestream of the whole human race to be one, flowing from one source [Baumgarten]. **and hath determined the times before appointed, and the bounds of their habitation**—The apostle here opposes both Stoical Fate and Epicurean Chance, ascribing the *periods* and *localities* in which men and nations flourish to the sovereign will and prearrangements of a living God. **That they should seek the Lord**—That is the high end of all these arrangements of Divine Power, Wisdom, and Love. **if haply they might feel after him**—as men groping their way in the dark—**and find him**—a lively picture of the murky atmosphere of Natural Religion—**though he be not far from every one of us**—The difficulty of finding God outside the pale of revealed religion lies not in His distance from us, but in our distance from Him through the blinding effect of sin. **28. For in him we live, and move, and have our being**—or, more briefly, 'exist').—This means, not merely, "Without Him we have no *life*, nor that *motion* which every inanimate nature displays, nor even *existence* itself" [Meyer], but that God is the living, immanent Principle of all these in men. **as certain also of your own poets have said, For we are also his offspring**— the first half of the fifth line, word for word, of an astronomical poem of Aratus, a Greek countryman of the apostle, and his predecessor by about three centuries. But, as he hints, the same sentiment is to be found in other Greek poets. They meant it doubtless in a *pantheistic* sense; but the truth which it expresses the apostle turns to his own purpose— to teach a pure, personal, spiritual Theism. (Probably during his quiet retreat at Tarsus, ch. 9:30, revolving his special vocation to the Gentiles, he gave himself to the study of so much Greek literature as might be turned to Christian account in his future work. Hence this and his other quotations from the Greek poets, I Cor. 15:33; Titus 1:12). **29. Forasmuch then as we are the offspring of God, we ought not to think**—*The courtesy of this language is worthy of notice*—**that the Godhead is like unto gold, or silver, or stone, graven by art and man's device**—('graven by the art or device of man'). One can hardly doubt that the apostle would here point to those matchless monuments of the plastic art, in gold and silver and costliest stone, which lay so profusely beneath and around him. The more intelligent pagan Greeks no more pretended that these sculptured gods and goddesses were real deities, or even their actual likenesses, than Romanist Christians do their images; and Paul doubtless knew this; yet here we find him condemning all such efforts visibly to represent the invisible God. How shamefully inexcusable then are the Greek and Roman churches in paganizing the worship of the Christian Church by the encouragement of pictures and images in religious service! (In the eighth century, the second council of Nicea decreed that the image of God was as proper an object of worship as God Himself.) **30. the times of this ignorance God winked at**—literally (and far better), 'overlooked,' i.e., bore with, without interposing to punish it, otherwise than suffering the debasing tendency of such worship to develop itself (cf. ch. 14:16, and see on Rom. 1:24, etc.). **but now**—that a new light was risen upon the world. **commandeth**—That duty—all along lying upon man estranged from his Creator, but hitherto only silently recommending itself and little felt—is now peremptory.' **all men every where to repent**—(cf. Col. 1:6, 23; Titus 1:11)—a tacit allusion to the narrow precincts of favored Judaism, within which immediate and entire repentance was ever urged. The word "repentance" is here used (as in Luke 13: 3, 5; 15:10) in its most comprehensive sense of "repentance unto life." **31. Because he hath appointed a day in the which he will judge the world** —Such language beyond doubt teaches that the judgment will, in its essence, be a solemn judicial assize held upon all mankind *at once*. "Aptly is this uttered on the Areopagus, the seat of judgment" [BENGEL]. **by that man whom he hath ordained**—cf. John 5:22, 23, 27; ch. 10:42. **whereof he hath given assurance unto all men, in that he hath raised him from the dead**—the most patent evidence to mankind at large of the judicial authority with which the Risen One is clothed. **32-34. when they heard of the resurrection of the dead, some mocked**—As the Greek religion was but the glorification of the present life, by the worship of all its most beauteous forms, the Resurrection, which presupposes the vanity of the present life, and is nothing but life out of the death of all that sin has blighted, could have no charm for the true Greek. It gave the deathblow to his fundamental and most cherished ideas; nor until these were seen to be false and fatal could the Resurrection, and the Gospel of which it was a primary doctrine, seem otherwise than ridiculous. **So Paul departed**—Whether he would have opened, to any extent, the Gospel scheme in this address, if he had not been interrupted, or whether he reserved this for exposition afterwards to earnest inquirers, we cannot tell. Only the speech is not to be judged of as quite complete. others said, **We will hear thee again of this** —"an idle compliment to Paul and an opiate to their consciences, such as we often meet with in our own day. They probably, like Felix, feared to hear

more, lest they should be constrained to believe unwelcome truths" (ch. 24:25; and cf. Matt. 13:15) [WEBSTER and WILKINSON]. **Howbeit certain men clave unto him**—Instead of mocking or politely waiving the subject, having listened eagerly, they joined themselves to the apostle for further instruction; and so they "believed." **Dionysius the Areopagite**—a member of that august tribunal. Ancient tradition says he was placed by the apostle over the little flock at Athens. "Certainly the number of converts there and of men fit for office in the Church was not so great that there could be much choice" [OLSHAUSEN]. **a woman named Damaris**—not certainly one of the apostle's audience on the Areopagus, but won to the faith either before or after. Nothing else is known of her. Of any further labors of the apostle at Athens, and how long he stayed, we are not informed. Certainly he was not driven away. But "it is a serious and instructive fact that the mercantile populations of Thessalonica and Corinth received the message of God with greater readiness than the highly educated and polished Athenians. Two letters to the Thessalonians, and two to the Corinthians, remain to attest the flourishing state of those churches. But we possess no letter written by Paul to the Athenians; and we do not read that he was ever in Athens again" [HOWS].

CHAPTER 18

Vss. 1-22. PAUL'S ARRIVAL AND LABORS AT CORINTH, WHERE HE IS REJOINED BY SILAS AND TIMOTHY, AND, UNDER DIVINE ENCOURAGEMENT, MAKES A LONG STAY—AT LENGTH, RETRACING HIS STEPS, BY EPHESUS, CÆSAREA, AND JERUSALEM, HE RETURNS FOR THE LAST TIME TO ANTIOCH, THUS COMPLETING HIS SECOND MISSIONARY JOURNEY. **1-4. came to Corinth**—rebuilt by Julius Cæsar on the isthmus between the Ægean and Ionian Seas; the capital of the Roman province of Achaia, and the residence of the proconsul; a large and populous mercantile city, and the center of commerce alike for East and West; having a considerable Jewish population, larger, probably, at this time than usual, owing to the banishment of the Jews from Rome by Claudius Cæsar (vs. 2). Such a city was a noble field for the Gospel, which, once established there, would naturally diffuse itself far and wide. **a Jew . . . Aquila . . . with his wife Priscilla**—From these Latin names one would conclude that they had resided so long in Rome as to lose their Jewish family names. **born in Pontus**—the most easterly province of Asia Minor, stretching along the southern shore of the Black Sea. From this province there were Jews at Jerusalem on the great Pentecost (ch. 2:9), and the Christians of it are included among "the strangers of the dispersion," to whom Peter addressed his first Epistle (I Pet. 1:1). Whether this couple were converted before Paul made their acquaintance, commentators are much divided. They may have brought their Christianity with them from Rome [OLSHAUSEN], or Paul may have been drawn to them merely by like occupation, and, lodging with them, have been the instrument of their conversion [MEYER]. They appear to have been in good circumstances, and after travelling much, to have eventually settled at Ephesus. The Christian friendship now first formed continued warm and unbroken, and the highest testimony is once and again borne to them by the apostle. **Claudius . . .**—This edict is almost certainly that mentioned by SUETONIUS, in his life of this emperor (ch. 25). **tentmakers**—manufacturers, probably, of those hair-cloth tents supplied by the goats of the apostle's native province, and hence, as sold in the markets of the Levant, called *cilicium*. Every Jewish youth, whatever the pecuniary circumstances of his parents, was taught some trade (see on Luke 2:42), and Paul made it a point of conscience to work at that which he had probably been bred to, partly that he might not be burdensome to the churches, and partly that his motives as a minister of Christ might not be liable to misconstruction. To both these he makes frequent reference in his Epistles. **the Greeks**—i.e., Gentile proselytes; for to the heathen, as usual, he only turned when rejected by the Jews (vs. 6). **5, 6. And when Silas and Timotheus were come from Macedonia**—i.e., from Thessalonica, whither Silas had probably accompanied Timothy when sent back from Athens (see on ch. 17:15). **Paul was pressed in the spirit**—rather (according to what is certainly the true reading) 'was pressed with the word'; expressing not only his zeal and assiduity in preaching it, but some inward *pressure* which at this time he experienced in the work (to convey which more clearly was probably the origin of the common reading). What that pressure was we happen to know, with singular minuteness and vividness of description, from the apostle himself, in his first Epistles to the Corinthians and Thessalonians (I Cor. 2:1-5; I Thess. 3:1-10). He had come away from Athens, as he remained there, in a depressed and anxious state of mind, having there met, for the first time, with unwilling Gentile ears. He continued, apparently for some time, laboring alone in the synagogue of Corinth, full of deep and anxious solicitude for his Thessalonian converts. His early ministry at Corinth was colored by these feelings. Himself deeply humbled, his power as a preacher was more than ever felt to lie in demonstration of the Spirit. At length Silas and Timotheus arrived with exhilarating tidings of the faith and love of his Thessalonian children, and of their earnest longing again to see their father in Christ; bringing with them also, in token of their love and duty, a pecuniary contribution for the supply of his wants. This seems to have so lifted him as to put new life and vigor into his ministry. *He now wrote his* FIRST EPISTLE TO THE THESSALONIANS, in which the "pressure" which resulted from all this strikingly appears. (See Introduction to First Thessalonians.) Such emotions are known only to the ministers of Christ, and, even of them, only to such as "travail in birth until Christ be formed in" their hearers. **Your blood be upon your own heads...**—See Ezekiel 33:4, 9. **from henceforth I will go unto the Gentiles**—Cf. ch. 13: 46. **7, 8. he departed thence, and entered into a certain man's house, named Justus**—not changing his lodging, as if Aquila and Priscilla up to this time were with the opponents of the apostle [ALFORD], but merely ceasing any more to testify in the synagogue, and henceforth carrying on his labors in this house of Justus, which "joining hard to the synagogue," would be easily accessible to such of its worshippers as were still open to light. Justus, too, being probably a proselyte, would more easily draw a mixed audience than the synagogue. From this time forth conversions rapidly increased. **Crispus, the chief ruler of the synagogue, believed on the Lord with all his house**—an event felt to be so important that the apostle deviated from his usual practice (I Cor. 1:14-16) and baptized him, as well

as Caius (Gaius) and the household of Stephanas, with his own hand [HOWS]. **many of the Corinthians... believed and were baptized**—The beginning of the church gathered there. **9-11. Then spake the Lord to Paul... by a vision, Be not afraid ...no man shall set on thee to hurt thee...**—From this it would seem that these signal successes were stirring up the wrath of the unbelieving Jews, and probably the apostle feared being driven by violence, as before, from this scene of such promising labor. He is reassured, however, from above. **I have much people in this city**—"whom in virtue of their election to eternal life He already designates as His" (cf. ch. 13:48) [BAUMGARTEN]. **continued there a year and six months**—the whole period of this stay at Corinth, and not merely up to what is next recorded. *During some part of this period he wrote his* SECOND EPISTLE TO THE THESSALONIANS. (See Introduction to Second Thessalonians.) **12-17. when Gallio was the deputy**—'the proconsul.' See on ch. 13:7. He was brother to the celebrated philosopher Seneca, the tutor of Nero, who passed sentence of death on both. **contrary to the**—Jewish—**law**—probably in not requiring the Gentiles to be circumcised. **If it were a matter of wrong or wicked lewdness**—any offense punishable by the magistrate. **if it be a question of words and names, and of your law... I will be no judge...**—in this only laying down the proper limits of his office. **drave them...**—annoyed at such a case. **all the Greeks**—the Gentile spectators. **took Sosthenes**—perhaps the successor of Crispus, and certainly the head of the accusing party. It is very improbable that this was the same Sosthenes as the apostle afterwards calls "his brother" (I Cor. 1:1). **and beat him before the judgment-seat**—under the very eye of the judge. **And Gallio cared for none of those things**—nothing loath, perhaps, to see these turbulent Jews, for whom probably he felt contempt, themselves getting what they hoped to inflict on another, and indifferent to whatever was beyond the range of his office and case. His brother eulogizes his loving and lovable manners. Religious indifference, under the influence of an easy and amiable temper, reappears from age to age. **18. Paul... tarried... yet a good while**—During his long residence at Corinth, Paul planted other churches in Achaia (II Cor. 1:1). **then took ...leave of the brethren, and sailed...into**—rather, 'for'—**Syria**—to Antioch, the starting point of all the missions to the Gentiles, which he feels to be for the present concluded. **with him Priscilla and Aquila**—In this order the names also occur in vs. 26 (according to the true reading); cf. Rom. 16: 3 and II Tim. 4:19, which seem to imply that the wife was the more prominent and helpful to the Church. Silas and Timotheus doubtless accompanied the apostle, as also Erastus, Gaius, and Aristarchus (ch. 19:22, 29). Of Silas, as Paul's associate, we read no more. His name occurs last in connection with Peter and the churches of Asia Minor [WEBTER and WILKINSON]. **having shorn his head in Cenchrea**—the eastern harbor of Corinth, about ten miles distant, where a church had been formed (Rom. 16:1). **for he**—Paul—**had a vow**—That it was the Nazarite vow (Num. 6) is not likely. It was probably one made in one of his seasons of difficulty or danger, in prosecution of which he cuts off his hair and hastens to Jerusalem to offer the requisite sacrifice within the prescribed thirty days (JOSEPHUS, *Jewish War*, 2. 15. 1). This explains the haste with which he leaves Ephesus (vs. 21), and the subsequent observance, on the recommendation of the brethren, of a similar vow (ch. 21:24). This one at Corinth was voluntary, and shows that even in heathen countries he systematically studied the prejudices of his Jewish brethren. **19. he came to Ephesus**—the capital of the Roman province of Asia. (See Introduction to Epistle to Ephesians.) It was a sail, right across from the west to the east side of the Ægean Sea, of some eight or ten days, with a fair wind. **left them**—Aquila and Priscilla—**there, but he himself entered into the synagogue**—merely taking advantage of the vessel putting in there. **and reasoned with the Jews**—the *tense* here not being the usual one denoting *continuous* action (as in ch. 17:2; 18:4), but that expressing *a transient act.* He had been forbidden to preach the word in Asia (ch. 16:6), but he would not consider that as precluding this passing exercise of his ministry when Providence brought him to its capital; nor did it follow that the prohibition was still in force. **20. when they desired him to tarry**—The Jews seldom rose against the Gospel till the successful preaching of it stirred them up, and there was no time for that here. **21. I must ... keep this feast**—probably Pentecost, presenting a noble opportunity of preaching the Gospel. **but I will return**—the fulfilment of which promise is recorded in ch. 19:1. **22. And when he had landed at Cæsarea**—where he left the vessel. **and gone up**—i.e., to Jerusalem—**and saluted the church**—In these few words does the historian despatch the apostle's FOURTH VISIT TO JERUSALEM after his conversion. The expression "going *up*" is invariably used of a journey to the metropolis; and thence he naturally "went *down* to Antioch." Perhaps the vessel reached too late for the feast, as he seems to have done nothing in Jerusalem beyond "saluting the Church," and privately offering the sacrifice with which his vow (vs. 18) would conclude. It is left to be understood, as on his arrival from his first missionary tour, that "when he was come, and had gathered the church together, he rehearsed all that God had done with him" (ch. 14:27) on this his *second missionary journey.*

23. Ch. 21:16. PAUL'S THIRD AND LAST MISSIONARY JOURNEY—HE VISITS THE CHURCHES OF GALATIA AND PHRYGIA. **and after he had spent some time there**—but probably not long. **he departed**—little thinking, probably, he was never more to return to Antioch. **went over all ... Galatia and Phrygia in order**—visiting the several churches in succession. See on ch. 16:6. Galatia is mentioned first here, as he would come to it first from Antioch. It was on this visitation that he ordained the weekly collection (I Cor. 16:1, 2), which has been since adopted generally, and converted into a public usage throughout Christendom. Timotheus and Erastus, Gaius and Aristarchus, appear to have accompanied him on this journey (ch. 19:22, 29; II Cor. 1: 1), and from II Corinthians we may presume, Titus also. The details of this visit, as of the former (ch. 16:6), are not given.

24-28. EPISODE CONCERNING APOLLOS AT EPHESUS AND IN ACHAIA. This is one of the most interesting and suggestive incidental narratives in this precious history. **24, 25, a ... Jew named Apollos**—a contraction from Apollonius. **born at Alexandria**—the celebrated city of Egypt on the southeastern shore of the Mediterranean, called after its founder, Alexander the Great. Nowhere was there such a fusion of Greek, Jewish, and Oriental peculiarities, and an intelligent Jew educated in that city could hardly fail to manifest all these elements in his mental character. **eloquent**—turning his Alexandrian culture to high account. **and mighty in the scriptures**—his eloquence enabling him to express clearly and enforce skilfully what, as a Jew, he had gathered from a diligent study of the Old Testament Scriptures. **came to Ephesus**—on what errand is not known. **This man was instructed in the way of the Lord ... knowing only the baptism of John**—He was instructed, probably, by some disciple of the Baptist, in the whole circle of John's teaching concerning Jesus, but no more: he had yet to learn the new light which the outpouring of the Spirit at Pentecost had thrown upon the Redeemer's death and resurrection; as appears from ch. 19:2, 3. **being fervent in the spirit**—His heart warm, and conscious, probably, of his gifts and attainments, he burned to impart to others the truth he had himself received. **he spake and taught diligently**—rather, 'accurately' (it is the same word as is rendered "perfectly" in vs. 26). **26. speak boldly in the synagogue, whom when Aquila and Priscilla heard**—joying to observe the extent of Scripture knowledge and evangelical truth which he displayed, and the fervency, courage, and eloquence with which he preached the truth. **they took him unto them**—privately—**and expounded unto him the way of God more perfectly**—opening up those truths, to him as yet unknown, on which the Spirit had shed such glorious light. (In what appears to be the true reading of this verse, Priscilla is put before Aquila, as in vs. 18, on which see; she being probably the more intelligent and devoted of the two.) One cannot but observe how providential it was that this couple should have been left at Ephesus when Paul sailed thence for Syria; and no doubt it was chiefly to pave the way for the better understanding of this episode that the fact is expressly mentioned by the historian in vs. 19. We see here also an example of not only *lay* agency (as it is called), but *female* agency of the highest kind and with the most admirable fruit. Nor can one help admiring the humility and teachableness of so gifted a teacher in sitting at the feet of a Christian woman and her husband. **27, 28. And when he was disposed**—'minded,' 'resolved'—**to pass into Achaia**—of which Corinth, on the opposite coast (see on vs. 1), was the capital; there to proclaim that Gospel which he now more fully comprehended. **the brethren**—We had not before heard of such gathered at Ephesus. But the desire of the Jews to whom Paul preached to retain him among them for some time (vs. 20), and his promise to return to them (vs. 21), seem to indicate some drawing towards the Gospel, which, no doubt, the zealous private labors of Priscilla and Aquila would ripen into discipleship. **wrote, exhorting the disciples to receive him**—a beautiful specimen of 'letters of recommendation' (as ch. 15: 23, 25-27, and see II Cor. 3:1); by which, as well as by interchange of deputations, etc., the early churches maintained active Christian fellowship with each other. **when he was come, helped them much**—was a great acquisition to the Achaian brethren. **which believed through grace**—one of those incidental expressions which show that *faith's being a production of God's grace in the heart* was so current and recognized a truth that it was taken for granted, as a necessary consequence of the general system of grace, rather than expressly insisted on. (It is against the natural order of the words to read them, as BENGEL, MEYER, and others, do, 'helped through grace those who believed.') **For he mightily convinced the Jews**—The word is very strong: 'stoutly bore them down in argument,' 'vigorously argued them down', and the *tense* implies that he *continued* to do it, or that this was the characteristic of his ministry. **showing by the scriptures that Jesus was Christ**—Rather, that the Christ (or Messiah) was Jesus. This expression, when compared with vs. 25, seems to imply a richer testimony than with his partial knowledge he was at first able to bear; and the power with which he bore down all opposition in argument is that which made him such an acquisition to the brethren. Thus his ministry would be as good as another visitation to the Achaian churches by the apostle himself (see I Cor. 3:6) and the more as, in so far as he was indebted for it to Priscilla and Aquila, it would have a decidedly *Pauline* cast.

CHAPTER 19

Vss. 1-41. SIGNAL SUCCESS OF PAUL AT EPHESUS. **1-3. while Apollos was at Corinth**—where his ministry was so powerful that a formidable party in the Church of that city gloried in his type of preaching in preference to Paul's (I Cor. 1:12; 3:4), no doubt from the marked infusion of Greek philosophic culture which distinguished it, and which the apostle studiously avoided (I Cor. 2:1-5). **Paul having passed through the upper coasts**—'parts,' the interior of Asia Minor, which, with reference to the seacoast, was elevated. **came to Ephesus**—thus fulfilling his promise (ch. 18:21). **finding certain disciples**—in the same stage of Christian knowledge as Apollos at first, newly arrived, probably, and having had no communication as yet with the church at Ephesus. **Have ye received the Holy Ghost since ye believed?**—rather, 'Received ye the Holy Ghost when ye believed?' implying, certainly, that the one did not of necessity carry the other along with it (see on ch. 8:14-17). Why this question was asked, we cannot tell; but it was probably in consequence of something that passed between them from which the apostle was led to suspect the imperfection of their light. **We have not so much as heard whether there be any Holy Ghost**—This cannot be the meaning, since the personality and office of the Holy Ghost, in connection with Christ, formed an especial subject of the Baptist's teaching. Literally, the words are, 'We did not even hear whether the Holy Ghost was (given); meaning, at the time of their baptism. That the word 'given' is the right supplement, as in John 7:39, seems plain from the nature of the case. **4. Then said Paul, John . . . baptized with the baptism of**—water unto —**repentance, saying unto the people, that they should believe on him which should come after him** —i.e., who should baptize with the Holy Ghost. The point of contrast is not between John and Christ personally, but between the *water* baptism of John unto *repentance*, and the promised baptism of *the Spirit* from the hands of his coming Master unto *new life*. As to all the facts, or at least the significancy, of this baptism, which made the whole life and work of Christ another thing from what it was conceived to be before it was vouchsafed, these simple disciples were unenlightened. **5-7. When they heard this**—not the mere words reported in vs. 4, but *the subject expounded* according to the tenor of those words. **they were baptized**—not however by Paul himself (I Cor. 1:14). **in the name of the Lord Jesus**—into the whole fulness of the new economy, as now opened up to their believing minds. **And when Paul had laid his hands upon them,.. . they spake with tongues . . .**—See on ch. 10:44, 45. **8-10. he went into the synagogue and spake boldly**

for . . . three months . . .—See on ch. 17:2, 3. **when divers**—'some'—**were hardened . . .**—implying that others, probably a large number, believed. **spake evil of that way before the multitude, he departed**—from the synagogue, as at Corinth (ch. 18:7). **and separated the disciples**—withdrawing to a separate place of meeting, for the sake both of the converts already made, and the unsophisticated multitude. **disputing**—'discoursing' or 'discussing'—**daily in the school**—or lecture hall—**of one Tyrannus**—probably a converted teacher of rhetoric or philosophy. **this continued . . . two years**—in addition to the former three months. See on ch. 20:31. But during some part of this period he must have paid a second unrecorded visit, since the one next recorded (see on ch. 20:2, 3) is twice called his *third* visit (II Cor. 12:14 13:1). See on II Corinthians 1:15, 16, which might seem inconsistent with this. The passage across was quite a short one (see on ch. 18:19). Towards the close of this long stay at Ephesus, as we learn from I Corinthians 16:8, he wrote his FIRST EPISTLE TO THE CORINTHIANS; also (though on this opinions are divided) the EPISTLE TO THE GALATIANS. (See Introduction to those Epistles.) And just as at Corinth his greatest success was after his withdrawal to a separate place of meeting (ch. 18:7-10), so at Ephesus. **so that all they which dwelt in**—the Roman province of—**Asia heard the word of the Lord Jesus, both Jews and Greeks**—This is the "great door and effectual opened unto him" while resident at Ephesus (I Cor. 16:9, which induced him to make it his headquarters for so long a period. The unwearied and varied character of his labors here are best seen in his own subsequent address to the elders of Ephesus (ch. 20:17, etc.). And thus Ephesus became the "ecclesiastical center for the entire region, as indeed it remained for a very long period" [BAUMGARTEN]. Churches arose at Colosse, Laodicea, and Hierapolis eastward, either through his own labors or those of his faithful helpers whom he sent out in different directions, Epaphras, Archippus, Philemon (Col. 1:7; 4:12-17; Philemon 23). **11, 12. God wrought special**—no ordinary—**miracles by the hands of Paul**—implying that he had not been accustomed to work such. **So that from his body were brought unto the sick handkerchiefs or aprons, . . .**—Cf. ch. 5:15, 16, very different from the magical acts practiced at Ephesus. "*God* wrought these miracles" merely "*by the hands of Paul*"; and the very exorcists (vs. 13), observing that the name of Jesus was the secret of all his miracles, hoped, by aping him in this, to be equally successful; while the result of all in the "magnifying of the Lord Jesus" (vs. 17) showed that in working them the apostle took care to hold up Him whom he *preached* as the source of all the miracles which he *wrought*. **13. vagabond Jews**—simply, 'wandering Jews,' who went from place to place practicing exorcism, or the art of conjuring evil spirits to depart out of the possessed. That such a power did exist, for some time at least, seems implied in Matthew 12:27. But no doubt this would breed imposture; and the present case is very different from that referred to in Luke 9:49, 50. **We adjure you by Jesus whom Paul preacheth**—a striking testimony to the power of Christ's name in Paul's mouth. **14-17. seven sons of . . . Sceva . . . chief of the priests**—head, possibly, of one of the 24 courts. **the evil spirit answered, Jesus I know**—'recognize'—**and Paul I know**—'know intimately,' in contrast to them, whom he altogether disowns—**but who are ye? And the man in whom the evil spirit was**—Mark the clear line of demarkation here between *"the evil spirit* which answered and said" and *"the man in whom the evil spirit was."* The reality of such possessions could not be more clearly expressed. **leaped on them . . . so that they fled . . . naked and wounded**—This was so appalling a testimony at once against those profane impostors and in favor of Paul and the Master whom he preached, that we wonder not that it spread to "all the Jews and Greeks at Ephesus, that fear fell on them," and that "the name of the Lord Jesus was magnified." **19, 20. many that believed came and confessed . . . their deeds**—the dupes of magicians, etc., acknowledging how shamefully they had been deluded, and how deeply they had allowed themselves to be implicated in such practices. **Many of them . . . which used curious arts**—The word signifies things 'overdone'; significantly applied to arts in which laborious but senseless incantations are practiced. **brought their books**—containing the mystic formularies. **and burned them before all** —The *tense,* here used graphically, expresses progress and continuance of the conflagration. **counted the price . . . and found it fifty thousand pieces of silver**—probably about $10,000 (presuming it to be the *drachma).* From their nature they would be costly, and books then bore a value above any standard we are familiar with. The scene must have been long remembered at Ephesus, as a strong proof of honest conviction on the part of the sorcerers and a striking triumph of Jesus Christ over the powers of darkness. The workers of evil were put to scorn, like Baal's priests on Carmel, and the word of God mightily grew and prevailed [Hows]. **21, 22. After these things were ended**—completed, implying something like a natural finish to his long period of labor at Ephesus. **Paul purposed . . . when he had passed through Macedonia and Achaia, to go to Jerusalem . . . After I have been there, I must see Rome also**—Mark here the vastness of the apostle's missionary plans. They were all fulfilled, though he "saw Rome" only as a prisoner. **So he sent into Macedonia . . . Timotheus and Erastus** —as his pioneers, in part to bring "them into remembrance of his ways which were in Christ" (I Cor. 4:17 and I Cor. 16:10), partly to convey his mind on various matters. After a brief stay he was to return (I Cor. 16:11). It is very unlikely that this Erastus was "the chamberlain of the city" of Corinth, of that name (Rom. 16:23). **he himself stayed in**—the province of—**Asia for a season**— i.e., at Ephesus, its chief city. (Asia is mentioned in contrast with Macedonia in the previous clause.) **23. the same time**—of Paul's proposed departure. **about that**—'the'—**way**—So the new religion seemed then to be designated (ch. 9:2; 22:4; 24:14). **24-26. silver shrines for**—'of'—**Diana**—small models of the Ephesian temple and of the shrine or chapel of the goddess, or of the shrine and statue alone, which were purchased by visitors as memorials of what they had seen, and were carried about and deposited in houses as a charm. (The models of the chapel of *our Lady of Loretto,* and such like, which the Church of Rome systematically encourages, are such a palpable imitation of this heathen practice that it is no wonder it should be regarded by impartial judges as *Christianity paganized.)* **gain to the craftsmen**—the master-artificers. **Whom he called together with the workmen of like occupation** —rather, 'with the workmen (or fabricators) of such articles,' meaning the artisans employed by the master-artificers, all who manufactured any kind of memorial of the temple and its worship for sale. **ye see and hear**—The evidences of it were to be

seen, and the report of it was in everybody's mouth. **that not alone at Ephesus, but almost throughout all Asia, this Paul hath . . . turned away much people** —Noble testimony this to the extent of Paul's influence! **saying that they be no gods which are made with hands**—The universal belief of *the people* was that they were gods, though the more intelligent regarded them only as habitations of Deity, and some, probably, as mere aids to devotion. It is exactly so in the Church of Rome. **27. So that not only this our craft is in danger . . . but . . .**—i.e., 'that indeed is a small matter; but there is something far worse.' So the masters of the poor Pythoness put forward the *religious revolution* which Paul was attempting to effect at Philippi, as the sole cause of their zealous alarm, to cloak the self-interest which they felt to be touched by his success (ch. 16:19-21). In both cases religious zeal was the hypocritical pretext; self-interest, the real moving cause of the opposition made. **also the temple of the great goddess Diana . . . despised, and her magnificence . . . destroyed, whom all Asia and the world worshippeth**—It was reckoned one of the wonders of the world. It was built about 550 B.C., of pure white marble, and though burned by a fanatic on the night of the birth of Alexander the Great, 356 B.C., was rebuilt with more splendor than before. It was 425 feet long by 220 broad, and the columns, 127 in number, were sixty feet in height, each of them the gift of a king, and thirty-six of them enriched with ornament and color. It was constantly receiving new decorations and additional buildings, statues, and pictures by the most celebrated artists, and kindled unparalleled admiration, enthusiasm, and superstition. *Its very site is now a matter of uncertainty.* The little wooden image of Diana was as primitive and rude as its shrine was sumptuous; not like the *Greek* Diana, in the form of an imposing huntress, but quite Asiatic, in the form of a manybreasted female (emblematic of the manifold ministrations of Nature to man), terminating in a shapeless block. Like some other far-famed idols, it was believed to have fallen from heaven (vs. 35), and models of it were not only sold in immense numbers to private persons, but set up for worship in other cities [Hows]. What power must have attended the preaching of that one man by whom the deathblow was felt to be given to their gigantic and witching superstition! **28, 29. Great is Diana of the Ephesians**—the civic cry of a populace so proud of their temple that they refused to inscribe on it the name of Alexander the Great, though he offered them the whole spoil of his Eastern campaign if they would do it [STRABO in Hows] **having caught Gaius and Aristarchus**—disappointed of Paul, as at Thessalonica (ch. 17:5, 6). They are mentioned in ch. 20:4; 27:2; Rom. 16:23; I Cor. 1:14; and probably III John 1. If it was in the house of Aquila and Priscilla that he found an asylum (see I Cor. 16:9), that would explain Romans 16:3, 4, where he says of them that "for his life they laid down their own necks" [Hows]. **rushed . . . into the theatre**—a vast pile, whose ruins are even now a wreck of immense grandeur [SIR C. FELLOWES, *Asia Minor,* 1839] **30-34. when Paul would have entered in**—with noble forgetfulness of self—**unto the people** —the *demos,* i.e., the people met in public assembly. **the disciples suffered him not**—The *tense* used implies only that they were *using their efforts* to restrain him; which might have been unavailing but for what follows. **And certain of the chief of Asia**—lit., 'And certain also of the Asiarchs.' These were wealthy and distinguished citizens of the principal towns of the Asian province, chosen annually, and ten of whom were selected by the proconsul to preside over the games celebrated in the month of May (the same month which Romanism dedicates to *the Virgin*). It was an office of the highest honor and greatly coveted. Certain of these, it seems, were favorably inclined to the Gospel, at least were Paul's "friends," and knowing the passions of a mob, excited during the festivals, "sent (a message) to him desiring him not to adventure himself into the theater." **they drew Alexander out of the multitude, the Jews putting him forward**—rather, 'some of the multitude urged forward Alexander, the Jews thrusting him forward.' As the blame of such a tumult would naturally be thrown upon the Jews, who were regarded by the Romans as the authors of all religious disturbances, they seem to have put forward this man to clear them of all responsibility for the riot. (BENGEL'S conjecture, that this was Alexander the coppersmith, II Tim. 4:14, has little to support it.) **beckoned with the hand**—cf. ch. 13:16; 21:40. **would have made his defence**—'offered to speak in defense.' **But when they knew he was a Jew, all with one voice, for the space of two hours, cried out, Great is Diana . . .**—The very appearance of a Jew had the opposite effect to that intended. To prevent him obtaining a hearing, they drowned his voice in one tumultuous shout in honor of their goddess, which rose to such frantic enthusiasm as took two hours to exhaust itself. **35-41. when the town-clerk**—keeper of the public archives, and a magistrate of great authority. **had appeased**—'calmed'—**the people**—'the multitude'—which the very presence of such an officer would go far to do. **he said . . . what man . . . knoweth not that the city of the Ephesians is a worshipper of the great goddess Diana**—lit., 'the *neocoros* or warden.' The word means 'temple-sweeper'; then, 'temple-guardian.' Thirteen cities of Asia had an interest in the temple, but Ephesus was honored with the charge of it. (Various cities have claimed this title with reference to *the Virgin* or certain *saints*) [WEBSTER and WILKINSON]. **and of the image which fell down from Jupiter**—'from the sky' or 'from heaven.' See on vs. 27. "With this we may compare various legends concerning images and pictures in the Romish Church, such as the traditional likenesses of Christ, which were said to be 'not made with hands' " [WEBSTER and WILKINSON]. **Seeing that these things cannot be spoken against . . .**—Like a true legal man, he urges that such was notoriously the constitution and fixed character of the city, with which its very existence was all but bound up. Did they suppose that all this was going to be overturned by a set of itinerant orators? Ridiculous! What did they mean, then, by raising such a stir? **For ye have brought hither these men, which are neither robbers of churches**—'temple-plunderers,' or sacrilegious persons. **nor yet blasphemers of your goddess**—This is a remarkable testimony, showing that the apostle had, in preaching against idolatry, studiously avoided (as at Athens) insulting the feelings of those whom he addressed—a lesson this to missionaries and ministers in general. **if Demetrius have a matter**—of complaint—**against any man, the law is open**—rather, 'the court-days are being held.' **and there are deputies**—lit., 'proconsuls' (see on ch. 13:7); i.e., probably, the proconsul and his council, as a court of appeal. **if ye inquire**—'have any question.' **concerning other matters**—of a public nature. **For we**—the public authorities—**are in danger of being called in question**—by our superiors.

CHAPTER 20

Vss. 1-12. PAUL FULFILS HIS PURPOSE OF PROCEEDING AGAIN TO MACEDONIA AND GREECE—RETURNING THENCE, ON HIS ROUTE FOR JERUSALEM, HE REVISITS PHILIPPI AND TROAS—HIS MINISTRATIONS AT TROAS. This section of the apostle's life, though peculiarly rich in material, is related with great brevity in the History. Its details must be culled from his own Epistles. **1, 2. departed**—after Pentecost (I Cor. 16:8). **to go into Macedonia**—in pursuance of the *first* part of his plan ch. 19:21). From his Epistles we learn; (1) That, as might have been expected from its position on the coast, he revisited Troas (II Cor. 2:12; see on ch. 16:8). (2) That while on his former visit he appears to have done no missionary work there, he now went expressly "to preach Christ's Gospel," and found "a door opened unto him of the Lord" there, which he entered so effectually as to lay the foundation of a church there (6, 7). (3) That he would have remained longer there but for his uneasiness at the non-arrival of Titus, whom he had despatched to Corinth to finish the collection for the poor saints at Jerusalem (I Cor. 16:1, 2; II Cor. 8:6), but still more, that he might bring him word what effect his first Epistle to that church had produced. (He had probably arranged that they should meet at Troas.) (4) That in this state of mind, afraid of something wrong, he "took leave" of the brethren at Troas, and went from thence into Macedonia.

It was, no doubt, the city of PHILIPPI that he came to (landing at Nicopolis, its seaport, see on ch. 16: 11, 12), as appears by comparing II Corinthians 11: 9, where "Macedonia" is named, with Philippians 4:15, where it appears that Philippi is meant. Here he found the brethren, whom he had left on his former visit in circumstances of such deep interest, a consolidated and thriving church, generous and warmly attached to their father in Christ; under the superintendence, probably, of our historian, "the beloved physician" (see on ch. 16:40). All that is said by our historian of this Macedonian visit is that "he went over those parts and gave them much exhortation." (5) Titus not having reached Philippi as soon as the apostle, "his flesh had no rest, but he was troubled on every side: without were fightings, within were fears" (II Cor. 7:5). (6) At length Titus arrived, to the joy of the apostle, the bearer of better tidings from Corinth than he had dared to expect (II Cor. 7:6, 7, 13), but checkered by painful intelligence of the efforts of a hostile party to undermine his apostolic reputation there (II Cor.). (7) Under the mixed feelings which this produced, he wrote—from Macedonia, and probably Philippi—*his* SECOND EPISTLE TO THE CORINTHIANS (see Introduction to II Corinthians); despatching Titus with it, and along with him two other unnamed deputies, expressly chosen to take up and bring their collection for the poor saints at Jerusalem, and to whom he bears the beautiful testimony, that they were "the glory of Christ" (II Cor. 8:22, 23). (8) It must have been at this time that he penetrated as far as to the confines of "Illyricum," lying along the shores of the Adriatic (Rom. 15:19). He would naturally wish that his second Letter to the Corinthians should have some time to produce its proper effect ere he revisited them, and this would appear a convenient opportunity for a northwestern circuit, which would enable him to pay a passing visit to the churches at Thessalonica and Berea, though of this we have no record. On his way southward to Greece, he would preach the

Gospel in the intermediate regions of Epirus, Thessaly, and Bœotia (see Rom. 15:19), though of this we have no record. **he came into Greece**—or Achaia, in pursuance of the *second* part of his plan (ch. 19:21). **3. And there abode three months**—Though the province only is here mentioned, it is the city of CORINTH that is meant, as the province of "Macedonia" (vs. 1) meant the city of Philippi. Some rough work he anticipated on his arrival at Corinth (II Cor. 10:1-8, 11; 13:1-10) though he had reason to expect satisfaction on the whole; and as we know there were other churches in Achaia besides that at Corinth (II Cor. 1:1; 11:10), he would have time enough to pay them all a brief visit during the three months of his stay there. This period was rendered further memorable by the despatch of *the* EPISTLE TO THE ROMANS, written during his stay at Corinth and sent by "Phœbe, a servant [deaconess] of the Church at Cenchrea" (see on ch. 18:3), a lady apparently of some standing and substance, who was going thither on private business. (See on Rom. 16:1 and Introduction to Epistles to Romans.) **And when the Jews laid wait for him, as he was about to sail into Syria**—He had intended to embark, probably at Cenchrea, the eastern harbor of the city, for Palestine, on his route to Jerusalem, the *third* part of his plan (ch. 19:21). But having detected some conspiracy against his life by his bitter Jewish enemies as at Damascus (ch. 9:22-25) and Jerusalem (ch. 9:29, 30), he changed his plan and determined "to return" as he had come, "through Macedonia." As he was never more to return to Corinth, so this route would bring him, for the last time, face to face with the attached disciples of *Berea, Thessalonica,* and *Philippi.* **4, 5. there accompanied him into**—the province of—**Asia, Sopater of Berea**—The true reading, beyond doubt, is, 'Sopater [the son] of Pyrrhus of Berea.' Some think this mention of his father was to distinguish him from Sosipater (the same name in fuller form), mentioned in Romans 16:21. But that they were the same person seems more probable. **of the Thessalonians, Aristarchus**—See on ch. 19:29. **and Secundus**—of whom nothing else is known. **Gaius of Derbe**—Though the Gaius of ch. 19:29 is said to be of "Macedonia," and this one "of Derbe," there is no sufficient reason for supposing them different persons; on the contrary, Romans 16:23 (cf. with III John 1, where there is hardly any reason to doubt that the same Gaius is addressed) seems to show that though he spent an important part of his Christian life away from his native Derbe, he had latterly retired to some place not very far from it. **and Timotheus**—not probably of Derbe, as one might suppose from this verse, but of Lystra (see on ch. 16:1); both being so associated in his early connection with the apostle that the mention of the one in the previous clause would recall the other on the mention of his name. **and of Asia, Tychicus and Trophimus**—The latter was an Ephesian, and probably the former also. They seem to have put themselves, from this time forward, at the apostle's disposal, and to the very last been a great comfort to him (Eph. 6:21, 22; Col. 4:7, 8; ch. 21:29; II Tim. 4:12, 20). From the mention of the places to which each of these companions belonged, and still more the order in which they occur, we are left to conclude that they were deputies from their respective churches, charged with taking up and bringing on the collection for the poor saints at Jerusalem, first at Berea, next at Thessalonica, then at Philippi [Hows], *where we gather that our historian himself rejoined the party* (from the resumption at vs. 5 of

the "us," dropped at ch. 16:17), by whom the Philippian collection would naturally be brought on **5, 6. These going before**—perhaps to announce and prepare for the apostle's coming. **tarried for us at Troas. And we sailed . . . from Philippi after the days of unleavened bread**—(i.e., the Passover). This, compared with I Corinthians 16:8, shows that the three months spent at Corinth (vs. 3) were the winter months. **came . . . to Troas**—for the third and last time. (See on ch. 16:8, and on vs. 1.) **in the five days**—As it might have been done in two days, the wind must have been adverse. The vivid style of one now present will be here again observed. **where we abode seven days**—i.e., arriving on a Monday, they stayed over the Jewish sabbath and the Lord's Day following; Paul occupying himself, doubtless, in refreshing and strengthening fellowship with the brethren during the interval. **7. upon the first day of the week, when the disciples came together**—This, compared with I Corinthians 16:2, and other similar allusions, plainly indicates that the Christian observance of the day afterwards distinctly called "the Lord's Day," was already a fixed practice of the churches. **Paul preached**—discoursed. The *tense* implies continued action—'kept discoursing.' **8. there were many lights in the upper chamber**—not a mere piece of graphic detail by an eyewitness [HACKETT, HOWS], but mentioned, probably, as increasing the heat and contributing to drowsiness [WEBSTER and WILKINSON], as the next clause seems to show. **9. in a**—'the'—**window**—or window-seat, of recess. **fell down from the third loft**—'story'—**and was taken up dead**—"The window projected (according to the side of the room where it was situated) either over the street or over the interior court; so that in either case he fell on the hard earth or pavement below." **10-12. Paul . . . fell on him**—like Elisha (II Kings 4:34). **his life is in him**—now restored; cf. Mark 5:39. **broken bread and eaten**—with what a mixture of awe and joy after such an occurrence! **and eaten**—denoting a common repast, as distinguished from the breaking of the eucharistic bread. **and talked a long while, even till break of day.** How lifelike this record of dear Christian fellowship, as free and gladsome as it was solemn! ((See Eccles. 9:7.)

13-38. CONTINUING HIS ROUTE TO JERUSALEM, HE REACHES MILETUS, WHENCE HE SENDS FOR THE ELDERS OF EPHESUS—HIS FAREWELL ADDRESS TO THEM. **13, 14. we . . . sailed** (from Troas) **unto Assos; there . . . to take in Paul: for so had he appointed, minding himself to go afoot**—'to go by land.' (See on Mark 6:33.) In sailing southward from Troas to Assos, one has to round Cape Lectum, and keeping due east to run along the northern shore of the Gulf of Adramyttium, on which it lies. This is a sail of nearly forty miles; whereas by land, cutting right across, in a southeasterly direction, from sea to sea, by that excellent Roman road which then existed, the distance was scarcely more than half. The one way Paul wished his companions to take, while he himself, longing perhaps to enjoy a period of solitude, took the other, joining the ship, by appointment, at Assos. **came to Mitylene**—the capital of the beautiful and classical island of Lesbos, which lies opposite the eastern shore of the Ægean Sea, about thirty miles south of Assos; in whose harbor they seem to have lain for the night. **15, 16. came the next day over against Chios**—now Scio: one of the most beautiful of those islands between which and the coast the sail is so charming. They appear not to have touched at it. **next day we arrived**—'touched' or 'put in'—**at Samos**—another island coming quite close to the mainland, and about as far south of Chios as it is south of Lesbos. **tarried**—for the night—**at Trogyllium**—an anchorage on the projecting mainland, not more than a mile from the southern extremity of the island of Samos. **next day we came to Miletus**—on the mainland; the ancient capital of Ionia, near the mouth of the Meander. **For Paul had determined to sail by**—or 'sail past'—**Ephesus**—He was right opposite to it when approaching Chios. **because he would not spend time in Asia**—the Asian province of which Ephesus was the chief city. **for he hasted, if . . . possible . . . to be at Jerusalem the day of Pentecost**—as a suitable season for giving in the great collection from all the western churches, for keeping the feast, and clearing his apostolic position with the Church, then represented in large number at Jerusalem. The words imply that there was considerable ground to doubt if he would attain this object—for more than three of the seven weeks from Passover to Pentecost had already expired—and they are inserted evidently to explain why he did not once more visit Ephesus. **17. from Miletus he sent to Ephesus, and called the elders of the church**—As he was now some forty miles south of Ephesus, we might think that more time would be lost by sending thus far for the elders to come to him, than by going at once to Ephesus itself, when so near it. But if unfavorable winds and stormy weather had overtaken them, his object could not have been attained, and perhaps he was unwilling to run the risk of detention at Ephesus by the state of the church and other causes. Those here called "*elders*" or "presbyters," are in vs. 28 called "*bishops.*" (See note there.) The identity of presbyters and bishops in the New Testament is beyond all reasonable dispute. **18. Ye know . . . after what manner I have been with you at all seasons**—For the Christian integrity and fidelity of his whole official intercourse with them he appeals to themselves. **19. Serving the Lord**—Jesus—**with all humility . . . and many tears and temptations**—Self-exaltation was unknown to him, and ease of mind: He "sowed in tears," from anxieties both on account of the converts from whom he "travailed in birth," and of the Jews, whose bitter hostility was perpetually plotting against him, interrupting his work and endangering his life. **20. kept back**—timidly withheld from fear of consequences. **nothing that was profitable**—edification directing all. **have taught you publicly, and from house to house**—Did an *apostle,* whose functions were of so wide a range, not feel satisfied without *private* as well as public ministrations? How then must *pastors* feel? [BENGEL]. **21. Testifying both to Jews and . . . Greeks**—laboring under a common malady, and recoverable only by a common treatment—**repentance toward God, and faith toward our Lord Jesus Christ**—See on ch. 5:31. REPENTANCE, as distinguished from *faith,* is that state of the "honest and good heart" which arises from a discovery of one's contrariety to the righteous demands of the divine law. This is said to be "*toward God,*" because seeing Him to be the party dishonored by sin, it feels all its acknowledgments and compunctions to be properly due to Him, as the great Lawgiver, and directs them to Him accordingly; condemning, humbling itself, and grieving before Him, looking also to Him as its only Hope of deliverance. FAITH is said to be "*toward our Lord Jesus Christ,*" because in that frame of mind just described it eagerly credits the testimony of relief divinely provided in Christ, gladly embraces the overtures of reconciliation in Him, and

directs all its expectations of salvation, from its first stage to its last, to Him as the one appointed Medium of all grace from God to a sinful world. Thus we have here a brief summary of all Gospel preaching. And it is easy to see why repentance is here put before faith; for the former must of necessity precede the latter. There *is* a repentance subsequent to faith, the fruit of felt pardon and restoration. It was this which drew the tears with which the Saviour's feet were once so copiously moistened. (Luke 7:37, 38, 47; and cf. Ezek. 16: 63.) But that is not the light in which it is here presented. **22, 23. And now, behold, I**—"I"—is emphatic here. **bound in the spirit**—cf. ch. 19:21. This internal pressure, unattended with any knowledge of "what was to befall him there," was the result of that higher guidance which shaped all his movements. **Save that the Holy Ghost witnesseth in every city . . .**—by prophetic utterances from city to city, as in ch. 11:4; 21:10, 11. Analogous premonitions of coming events are not unknown to the general method of God's providence. They would tend to season the apostle's spirit. **24. But none of these things move me, neither . . .**—In this noble expression of absolute dedication to the service of Christ and preparedness for the worst that could befall him in such a cause, note (1) his jealousy for the peculiar character of his mission, as *immediately from Christ Himself,* on which all the charges against him turned; (2) the burden of that Gospel which he preached—GRACE; it was "the Gospel of the Grace of God." **25-27. I know that ye all . . . shall see my face no more**—not an inspired prediction of what was certainly to be, but what the apostle, in his peculiar circumstances, fully expected. Whether, therefore, he ever did see them again, is a question to be decided purely on its own evidence. **I am pure from the blood of all men**—(Ch. 18:6; and cf. I Sam. 12:3, 5; Ezek. 3:17-21; 33:8, 9). **For I have not shunned to declare . . . all the counsel of God** —God's way of salvation, and His kingdom of souls saved by His Son Jesus Christ. See Luke 7:30. **28. Take heed . . . unto yourselves**—Cf. I Tim. 3: 2-7; 4:16; 6:11. **and to all the flock**—Cf. Hebrews 13:17. Observe here how the *personal* is put before the *pastoral* care. **over . . . which the Holy Ghost hath made you**—Cf. John 20:22, 23; Ephesians 4:8, 11, 12; Revelation 3:1. (Ch. 14:23 shows that the apostle did not mean to exclude *human* ordination.) **overseers**—or, as the same word is *everywhere else* rendered in our version, 'bishops.' The *English Version* has hardly dealt fair in this case with the sacred text, in rendering the word "overseers," whereas it ought here, as in all other places, to have been 'bishops,' in order that the fact of elders and bishops having been originally and apostolically synonymous, might be apparent to the ordinary English reader, which now it is not [ALFORD]. The distinction between these offices cannot be certainly traced till the second century, nor was it established till late in that century. **to feed the church of God**—or, 'the Church of the Lord.' Which of these two readings of the text is the true one, is a question which has divided the best critics. The evidence of MSS. preponderates in favor of 'THE LORD'; some of the most ancient Versions, though not all, so read; and *Athanasius,* the great champion of the supreme Divinity of Christ early in the fourth century, says the expression 'Church of God' is unknown to the Scriptures. Which reading, then, does the *internal* evidence favor? As 'Church of God' occurs nine times elsewhere in Paul's writings, and 'Church of the Lord' nowhere, the probability, it is said, is that he used his wonted phraseology here also. But if he did, it is extremely difficult to see how so many early transcribers should have altered it into the quite unusual phrase, 'Church of the Lord'; whereas, if the apostle did use this latter expression, and the historian wrote it so accordingly, it it easy to see how transcribers might, from being so accustomed to the usual phrase, write it 'Church of God.' On the whole, therefore, we accept the *second* reading as most probably the true one. But see what follows. **which he hath purchased**—'made His own,' 'acquired—**with his own blood**—'His own' is emphatic: 'That glorified Lord who from the right hand of power in the heavens is gathering and ruling the Church, and by His Spirit, through human agency, hath set you over it, cannot be indifferent to its welfare in your hands, seeing He hath given for it His own most precious blood, thus making it His own by the dearest of all ties.' The transcendent sacredness of the Church of Christ is thus made to rest on the dignity of its Lord and the consequent preciousness of that blood which He shed for it. And as the sacrificial atoning character of Christ's death is here plainly *expressed*, so His supreme dignity is *implied* as clearly by the second reading as it is *expressed* by the first. What a motive to *pastoral fidelity* is here furnished! **29, 30. after my departing shall grievous wolves enter in among you**—Two classes of coming enemies are here announced, the one more external to themselves, the other bred in the bosom of their own community; both were to be teachers, but the one, "grievous wolves," not sparing, i.e., making a prey of the flock; the other, simply sectarian "perverters" of the truth, with the view of drawing a party after them. Perhaps the one pointed to that subtle poison of Oriental Gnosticism which we know to have very early infected the Asiatic churches; the other to such Judaizing tendencies as we know to have troubled nearly all the early churches. See the Epistles to the *Ephesians, Colossians,* and *Timothy,* also those to the seven churches of Asia (chs. 2 and 3). But watchfulness against *all* that tends to injure and corrupt the Church is the duty of its pastors in every age. **31. by the space of three years**—speaking in round numbers; for it was nearer three than two years. **I ceased not to warn every one night and day with tears**—What an appeal to be able to make! "And if this was an apostle's part, how much more a pastor's!" [BENGEL]. **32-35. I commend you to God**—the almighty Conservator of His people. **and to the word of his grace**—that message of His pure grace (vs. 24) by the faith of which He keeps us (I Pet. 1:5). **which**—i.e., God —**is able to build you up, and to give you an inheritance . . .**—Observe how salvation—not only in its *initial stages* of pardon and regeneration, but in all its *subsequent stages* of "up-building," even to its *consummation* in the final inheritance—is here ascribed to the "ability" of God to bestow it, as in Romans 16:25; Ephesians 3:20; particularly Jude 24; and cf. II Timothy 1:12, where *the same thing is ascribed to Christ.* **among all them which are sanctified**—Sanctification is here viewed as the final character and condition of the heirs of glory, regarded as one saved company. **these hands**—doubtless holding them up, as before Agrippa in chains (ch. 26:29). **have ministered unto my necessities, and to them that were with me**—See ch. 18:3; and I Corinthians 4:12; 9:6, written from Ephesus; also I Thessalonians 2:9. **that so labouring**—as I have done, for others, as well as myself—**ye ought to support the weak, and to remember the words of**

the Lord Jesus, how he—'how Himself'—**said, It is more blessed to give than to receive**—This golden saying, snatched from oblivion, and here added to the Church's abiding treasures, is apt to beget the wish that more of what issued from those Lips which "dropped as an honeycomb," had been preserved to us. But see on John 21:25. **36-38. he kneeled down and prayed with them all . . .**—Nothing can be more touching than these three concluding verses, leaving an indelible impression of rare ministerial fidelity and affection on the apostle's part, and of warm admiration and attachment on the part of these Ephesian presbyters. Would to God that such scenes were more frequent in the Church!

CHAPTER 21

Vss. 1-16. SAILING FROM EPHESUS, THEY LAND AT TYRE, AND THENCE SAILING TO PTOLEMAIS, THEY PROCEED BY LAND TO CÆSAREA AND JERUSALEM. **1. we were gotten**—'torn'—**from them**—expressing the difficulty and pain of the parting. **with a straight course**—running before the wind, as ch. 16:11. **unto Coos**—Cos, an island due south from Miletus, which they would reach in about six hours, and coming close to the mainland. **the day following unto Rhodes**—another island, some fifty miles to the southeast, of brilliant classic memory and beauty. **thence unto Patara**—a town on the magnificent mainland of Lycia, almost due east from Rhodes. It was the seat of a celebrated oracle of Apollo. **2. And finding a ship**—their former one going no farther, probably—**to Phœnica**—See on ch. 11:19. **went abroad**—One would almost think this extracted from a journal of the voyage, so graphic are its details. **3. when we . . . discovered**—'sighted,' as the phrase is—**Cyprus, we left it on the left hand**—i.e., steered southeast of it, leaving it on the northwest. **sailed into**—'unto'—**Syria, and landed at Tyre**—the celebrated seat of maritime commerce for East and West. It might be reached from Patara in about two days. **there the ship was to unlade her burden** —which gave the apostle time for what follows. **4-6. finding disciples**—finding out the disciples,— implying some search. They would expect such, from what is recorded, ch. 11:19. Perhaps they were not many; yet there were gifted ones among them. **who said to Paul . . . that he should not go up to Jerusalem**—See on ch. 20:23; also on vss. 11-14. **they all brought us on our way with wives and children . . . and we kneeled down on the shore and prayed**—See on ch. 20:36-38. Observe here that the *children* of these Tyrian disciples not only were taken along with their parents, but must have joined in this act of solemn worship. See on Ephesians 6:1. **7. when we had finished our course**—completing the voyage—**from Tyre, we came**—which they would do the same day—**to Ptolemais**—anciently called Accho (Judg. 1:31), now St. Jean d'Acre, or Acre. **and saluted the brethren, and abode . . .**— disciples gathered probably as at Tyre, on the occasion mentioned (ch. 11:19). **8-10. next day we [that were of Paul's company] departed**—(The words in brackets are omitted in the best MSS. They were probably added as the connecting words at the head of some church lessons.) **and came to Cæsarea**—a run along the coast, southward, of some thirty miles. **Philip the evangelist**—a term answering apparently very much to our *missionary* [Hows], by whose ministry such joy had been diffused over Samaria, and the Ethiopian eunuch had been baptized (ch. 8). **one of the seven**—deacons, who had "purchased to himself a good degree" (I Tim. 3: 13). He and Paul now meet for the first time, some twenty-five years after that time. **the same man had four daughters . . . which did prophesy**—fulfilling Joel 2:28 (see ch. 2:18). This is mentioned, it would seem, merely as a high distinction divinely conferred on so devoted a servant of the Lord Jesus, and probably indicates the high tone of religion in his family. **tarried there many**—'a good many'—**days**—Finding himself in good time for Pentecost at Jerusalem, he would feel it a refreshing thing to his spirit to hold Christian communion for a few days with such a family. **there came down from Judea**—the news of Paul's arrival having spread—**a certain prophet . . . Agabus**—no doubt the same as in ch. 11:28. **11-14. So shall the Jews bind the man that owneth this girdle . . .**—For though the Romans did it, it was at the Jews' instigation (vs. 33; ch. 28:17). Such dramatic methods of announcing important future events would bring the old prophets to remembrance. (Cf. Isa. 20:2, etc.; Jer. 13:1, and Ezek. 5:1, etc.). This prediction and that at Tyre (vs. 4) were intended, not to prohibit him from going, but to put his courage to the test and when he stood the test, to deepen and mature it. **we and they at that place** (the Cæsarean Christians) **besought him**—even with tears, vs. 13—**not to go to Jerusalem. Then Paul answered, What mean ye to weep and to break mine heart**—Beautiful union of manly resoluteness and womanly tenderness, alike removed from mawkishness and stoicism! **I am ready not to be bound only**—'If that is all, let it come.' **but to die . . .**—It was well he could add this, for he had that also to do. **15, 16, we took up our carriages**—'our baggage'—**and went up to Jerusalem**—for the *fifth* time after his conversion, thus concluding *his third missionary tour,* which proved his *last,* so far as recorded; for though he accomplished the fourth and last part of the missionary plan sketched out (ch. 19:21)—"After I have been at Jerusalem, I must also see Rome"—it was as "a prisoner of Jesus Christ." **went with us . . . and brought with them**—rather, 'brought us to'. **Mnason of Cyprus, an old disciple . . .**—not an *aged* disciple, but probably 'a disciple of old standing,' perhaps one of the 3000 converted on the day of Pentecost, or, more likely still, drawn to the Saviour Himself during his lifetime. He had come, probably, with the other Cyprians (ch. 11:20), to Antioch, "preaching the Lord Jesus unto the Grecians," and now he appears settled at Jerusalem. **17-40. PAUL REPORTS THE EVENTS OF HIS THIRD MISSIONARY JOURNEY—IN THE TEMPLE, PURIFYING HIMSELF FROM A JEWISH VOW, HE IS SEIZED BY A MOB AND BEATEN TO THE DANGER OF HIS LIFE—THE UPROAR BECOMING UNIVERSAL, THE ROMAN COMMANDANT HAS HIM BROUGHT IN CHAINS TO THE FORTRESS, FROM THE STAIRS OF WHICH HE IS PERMITTED TO ADDRESS THE PEOPLE.** The apostle was full of anxiety about this visit to Jerusalem, from the numerous prophetic intimations of danger awaiting him, and having reason to expect the presence at this feast of the very parties from whose virulent rage he had once and again narrowly escaped with his life. Hence we find him asking the Roman Christians to wrestle with him in prayer, "for the Lord Jesus Christ's sake, and for the love of the Spirit, *that he might be delivered from them that believed not in Judea,*" as well as "that his service which he had for Jerusalem (the great collection for the poor saints there) might be accepted of the saints" (Rom. 15:30, 31). **17-19. the brethren re-**ceived us gladly—the disciples generally, as distinguished from the official reception recorded in vs. 18. **Paul went in with us unto James; and all the elders were present**—to "report himself" formally to the acknowledged head of the church at Jerusalem, and his associates in office. See on ch. 15:13. Had any other of the apostles been in Jerusalem on that occasion, it could hardly fail to have been noted. **he declared particularly**—in detail—**what God had wrought among the Gentiles by his ministry**—as on previous occasions (ch. 14:27; and see Rom. 15:15); no doubt referring to the insidious and systematic efforts of the Judaizing party in a number of places to shrivel the Church of Christ into a Jewish sect, and his own counter-procedure. **20-25. they glorified the Lord . . .**—constrained to justify his course, notwithstanding the Jewish complexion of the Christianity of Jerusalem. **they are informed . . . that thou teachest all the Jews which are among the Gentiles**—those residing in heathen countries—**to forsake Moses . . .**—This calumny of the unbelieving Jews would find easy credence among the Christian zealots for Judaism. **we have four men**—Christian Jews, no doubt. **which have a vow**—perhaps kept ready on purpose. **be at charges with them**—i.e., defray the expense of the sacrifices legally required of them, along with his own, which was deemed a mark of Jewish generosity. **touching the Gentiles . . . we have written and concluded that they observe no such things . . .**—This shows that with all their conciliation to Jewish prejudice, the Church of Jerusalem was taught to adhere to the decision of the famous council held there (ch. 15). **26. to signify**—i.e., announce to the priest—**the accomplishment of the days of purification . . .**—See on Numbers 6:14-21. **27-30. the Jews . . . of Asia**—in all likelihood those of *Ephesus* (since they recognized Trophimus apparently as a townsman, vs. 29, embittered by their discomfiture (ch. 19:9, etc.). **Trophimus**—See on ch. 20:4. **took Paul, and drew him out of the temple; and forthwith the doors were shut**—that the murder they meant to perpetrate might not pollute that holy place. **31. tidings came**—lit., 'went up,' i.e., to the fortress of Antonia, where the commandant resided. See on vs. 32. This part of the narrative is particularly graphic. **the chief captain**—'the chiliarch,' or tribune of the Roman cohort, whose full number was 1,000 men. **33. commanded him to be bound with two chains**—See on ch. 12. **34. some cried one thing**—The difficulty would be so to state his crimes as to justify their proceedings to a Roman officer. **to be carried into the castle**—rather, perhaps, 'the barracks,' or that part of the fortress of Antonia appropriated to the soldiers. The fort was built by Herod on a high rock at the northwest corner of the great temple area, and called after Mark Antony. **35, 36. Away with him**—as before of his Lord (Luke 23:18; John 19:15). **37-40. Art not thou that Egyptian . . .**—The form of the question implies that the answer is to be in the negative, and is matter of some surprise: 'Thou art not then . . . .?' **madest an uproar . . .**—The narrative is given in JOSEPHUS (*Jewish War,* ii, 8. 6; and 13. 5), though his two allusions and ours seem to refer to different periods of the rebellion. **a citizen of no mean city**—See on ch. 16:37. **stood on the stairs**—"What nobler spectacle than that of Paul at this moment! There he stood, bound with two chains, ready to make his defense to the people. The Roman commander sits by, to enforce order by his presence. An enraged populace look up to him from below. Yet in the midst of so many dangers, how self-possessed is he, how tranquil!"

[CHRYSOSTOM (or in his name) in HACKET]. **a great silence**—the people awed at the permission given him by the commandant, and seeing him sitting as a listener. **in the Hebrew tongue**—the Syro-Chaldaic the vernacular tongue of the Palestine Jews since the captivity.

CHAPTER 22

Vss. 1-30. PAUL'S DEFENSE FROM THE STAIRS OF THE FORTRESS—THE RAGE OF THE AUDIENCE BURSTING FORTH, THE COMMANDANT HAS HIM BROUGHT INTO THE FORT TO BE EXAMINED BY SCOURGING, BUT LEARNING THAT HE IS A ROMAN, HE ORDERS HIS RELEASE AND COMMANDS THE SANHEDRIM TO TRY HIM. **1, 2. when they heard . . . the Hebrew tongue** —see on ch. 21:40—**they kept the more silence**—They could have understood him in Greek, and doubtless fully expected the renegade to address them in that language, but the sound of their holy mother tongue awed them into deeper silence. **3. a Jew of Tarsus, brought up in this city, at the feet**—See on Luke 10: 39—**of Gamaliel**—(See on ch. 5:24); a fact of great importance in the apostle's history, standing in the same relation to his future career as Moses' education in the Egyptian court to the work for which he was destined. **the perfect manner of the law of the fathers**—the strictest form of traditional Judaism. **zealous**—'a zealot'—**toward God as ye all are this day**—his own former murderous zeal against the disciples of the Lord Jesus being merely reflected in their present treatment of himself. **4. I persecuted . . .**—See on ch. 9:1, 2, 5-7. **the high priest**—still alive—**doth bear me witness, and all the estate of the elders**—the whole Sanhedrim. **8. Jesus of Nazareth**—the Nazarene. See on ch. 9:5. **9-11. they that were with me**—See on ch. 9:7, etc. **12. Ananias, a devout man, according to the law, having a good report of all the Jews which dwelt there**—One would not know from this description of Ananias that he was a Christian at all, the apostles object being to hold him up as unexceptionable, even to the most rigid Jews. **13-15. The God of our fathers hath chosen thee**—studiously linking the new economy upon the old, as but the sequel of it; both having one glorious Author. **that thou shouldest . . . see that**—'the'—**Just One**—cf. ch. 3:14; 7:52. **hear the voice of his mouth**—in order to place him on a level with the other apostles, who had "seen the [risen] Lord." **16. be baptized and wash away thy sins**—This way of speaking arises from baptism being the visible seal of remission. **calling on the name of the Lord**—rather, 'having called,' i.e., *after* having done so; referring to the confession of Christ which *preceded* baptism, as ch. 8:37. **17-21. it came to pass . . .**—This thrilling dialogue between the glorified Redeemer and his chosen vessel is nowhere else related. **when I was come again to Jerusalem**—on the occasion mentioned in ch. 9:26-29. **while I prayed in the temple**—He thus calls their attention to the fact that after his conversion he kept up his connection with the temple as before. **get . . . quickly out of Jerusalem**—cf. ch. 9:29—**for they will not receive thy testimony . . . And I said, Lord, they know . . .**—'Can it be, Lord, that they will resist the testimony of one whom they knew so well as among the bitterest of all against Thy disciples, and whom nothing short of resistless evidence could have turned to Thee?' **Depart for I will send thee far hence unto the Gentiles**—i.e., 'Enough; thy testimony is not to be thrown away upon Jerusalem; the Gentiles, afar off, are thy peculiar sphere.' **22, 23. gave him audience to this word . . . then . . . Away with such a fellow from the earth . . .**—Their national prejudices lashed into fury at the mention of a mission to the Gentiles, they would speedily have done to him as they did to Stephen, but for the presence and protection of the Roman officer. **24-26. examined by scourging**—according to the Roman practice. **that he might know wherefore they cried so**—Paul's speech being to him in an unknown tongue, he concluded from the horror which it kindled in the vast audience that he must have been guilty of some crime. **Paul said to the centurion that stood by**—to superintend the torture and receive the confession expected to be wrung from him. **Is it lawful for you to scourge a man that is a Roman . . .**—See on ch. 16:37. **27-29. art thou a Roman?**—showing that this being of Tarsus, which he had told him before (ch. 21:39) did not necessarily imply that he was a Roman citizen. **With a great sum obtained I this freedom** —Roman citizenship was bought and sold in the reign of Claudius, we know, at a high price: at a subsequent date, for next to nothing. But to put in a false claim to this privilege was a capital crime. **I was [free] born**—born to it, by purchase, or in reward of services, on the part of his father or some ancestor. **chief captain feared . . .**—See on ch. 16: 38. **30. commanded the chief priests and all their council to appear**—i.e., the Sanhedrim to be formally convened. Note here the power to order a Sanhedrim to try this case, assumed by the Roman officers and acquiesced in on their part.

CHAPTER 23

Vss. 1-10. PAUL'S DEFENSE BEFORE THE SANHEDRIM DIVIDES THE RIVAL FACTIONS, FROM WHOSE VIOLENCE THE COMMANDANT HAS THE APOSTLE REMOVED INTO THE FORTRESS. **1. Paul, earnestly beholding the council**—with a look of conscious integrity and unfaltering courage, perhaps also recognizing some of his early fellow pupils. **I have lived in all good conscience before God until this day**—The word has an indirect reference to the 'polity' or "commonwealth of Israel," of which he would signify that he had been, and was to that hour, an honest and God-fearing member. **2. the high priest . . . commanded . . . to smite him on the mouth**—a method of silencing a speaker common in the East to this day [HACKET]. But for a judge thus to treat a prisoner on his trial, for merely prefacing his defense by a protestation of his integrity, was infamous. **3, 4. God shall smite thee**—as indeed He did; for he was killed by an assassin during the Jewish war (JOSEPHUS, *Jewish War,* ii. 17. 9). **thou whited wall**—i.e., hypocrite (Matt. 23:27). This epithet, however, correctly describing the man, must not be defended as addressed to a judge, though the remonstrance which follows—"for sittest thou . . ."—ought to have put him to shame. **5. I wist not . . . that he was the high priest**—All sorts of explanations of this have been given. The high priesthood was in a state of great confusion and constant change at this time (as appears from JOSEPHUS), and the apostle's long absence from Jerusalem, and perhaps the manner in which he was habited or the seat he occupied, with other circumstances to us unknown, may account for such a speech. But if he was thrown off his guard by an insult which touched him to the quick, "what can surpass the grace with which he recovered his self-possession, and the frankness with which he acknowledged his error? If his conduct in yielding to the momentary impulse was not that of Christ Himself under a similar provocation (John 18:22, 23), certainly the manner in which he atoned for his fault was *Christlike*" [HACKET]. **6-9. when Paul perceived**—from the discussion which plainly had by this time arisen between the parties—**that the one part were Sadducees, and the other Pharisees, he cried out**—raising his voice above both parties—**I am a Pharisee, the son of a Pharisee**—The true reading seems to be, 'the son of Pharisees,' i.e., belonging to a family who from father to son had long been such—**of the hope and resurrection of the dead**—i.e., not the vague hope of immortality, but the definite expectation of the resurrection—**I am called in question**—By this adroit stroke, Paul engages the whole Pharisaic section of the council in his favor; the doctrine of a resurrection being common to both, though they would totally differ in their *application* of it. This was, of course, quite warrantable, and the more so as it was already evident that no impartiality in trying his cause was to be looked for from such an assembly. **the Sadducees say . . . there is no resurrection, neither angel, nor spirit**—See on Luke 20:37. **the scribes . . . of the Pharisees' part . . . strove, saying, We find no evil in this man, but**—as to those startling things which he brings to our ears—**if a spirit or an angel hath spoken to him**—referring, perhaps, to his trance in the temple, of which he had told them (ch. 22:17). They put this favorable construction upon his proceedings for no other reason than that they had found him one of their own party. They care not to inquire into the *truth* of what he alleged, over and above their opinions, but only to explain it away as something not worth raising a noise about. (The following words, "Let us not fight against God," seem not to belong to the original text, and perhaps are from ch. 5:39. In this case, either the meaning is, 'If he has had some divine communication, *what of that?*' or, the conclusion of the sentence may have been drowned in the hubbub, which the next verse shows to have been intense). **10. the chief captain, fearing lest Paul should have been pulled to pieces . . . commanded the soldiers to go down and take him by force . . .**—This shows that the commandant was not himself present, and further, that instead of the Sanhedrim trying the cause, the proceedings quickly consisted in the one party attempting to seize the prisoner, and the other to protect him.

11-35. IN THE FORTRESS PAUL IS CHEERED BY A NIGHT VISION—AN INFAMOUS CONSPIRACY TO ASSASSINATE HIM IS PROVIDENTIALLY DEFEATED, AND HE IS DESPATCHED BY NIGHT WITH A LETTER FROM THE COMMANDANT TO FELIX AT CÆSAREA, BY WHOM ARRANGEMENTS ARE MADE FOR A HEARING OF HIS CAUSE. **11. the night following**—his heart perhaps sinking, in the solitude of his barrack ward, and thinking perhaps that all the predictions of danger at Jerusalem were now to be fulfilled in his death there. **the Lord**—i.e., Jesus—**stood by him . . . Be of good cheer, Paul; for as thou hast testified of me in Jerusalem, so must thou . . . also at Rome**—i.e., 'Thy work in Jerusalem is done, faithfully and well done; but thou art not to die here; thy purpose next to "see Rome" (ch. 19:21) shall not be disappointed, and there also must thou bear witness of Me.' As this vision was not unneeded now, so we shall find it cheering and upholding him throughout all that befell him up to his arrival there. **12-14. bound themselves under a curse . . . that they would neither eat . . . till they had killed Paul**—Cf. II Samuel 3:35;

I Samuel 14:24. **15. Now . . . ye with the council signify to the chief captain . . . as though . . .**—That these high ecclesiastics fell in readily with this infamous plot is clear. What will not unscrupulous and hypocritical religionists do under the mask of religion? The narrative bears unmistakable internal marks of truth. **or ever he come near**—Their plan was to assassinate him on his way down from the barracks to the council. The case was critical, but He who had pledged His word to him that he should testify for Him at Rome provided unexpected means of defeating this well-laid scheme. **16-22. Paul's sister's son**—See on ch. 9:30. If he was at this time residing at Jerusalem for his education, like Paul himself, he may have got at the schools those hints of the conspiracy on which he so promptly acted. **Then Paul called one of the centurions**—Though divinely assured of safety, he never allows this to interfere with the duty he owed to his own life and the work he had yet to do. (See on ch. 27:22-25, 31.) **took him by the hand**—This shows that he must have been quite in his boyhood, and throws a pleasing light on the kind-hearted impartiality of this officer. **and now are they ready, looking for a promise from thee**—Thus, as is so often the case with God's people, not till the last moment, when the plot was all prepared, did deliverance come. **23, 24. two hundred soldiers**—a formidable guard for such an occasion; but Roman officials felt their honor concerned in the preservation of the public peace, and the danger of an attempted rescue would seem to require it. The force at Jerusalem was large enough to spare this convoy. **the third hour of the night**—nine o'clock. **beasts . . . set Paul on**—as relays, and to carry baggage. **unto Felix, the governor**—the procurator. See on ch. 24:24, 25. **25-30. Claudius**—the Roman name he would take on purchasing his citizenship. **Lysias**—his Greek family name. **the most excellent governor**—an honorary title of office. **came I with an army**—rather, 'with the military.' **perceived to be accused of questions of their law . . .**—Amidst all his difficulty in getting at the charges laid against Paul, enough, no doubt, come out to satisfy him that the whole was a question of religion, and that there was no case for a civil tribunal. **gave commandment to his accusers . . . to say before thee**—This was not done when he wrote, but would be before the letter reached its destination. **31, 32. brought him . . . to Antipatris**—nearly forty miles from Jerusalem, on the way to Cæsarea; so named by Herod in honor of his father, Antipater. **On the morrow they**—the infantry—**left the horsemen**—themselves no longer needed as a guard. The remaining distance was about twenty-five or twenty-six miles. **34, 35. asked of what province he was**—the letter describing him as a Roman citizen. **I will hear thee**—The word means, 'give thee a full hearing.' **to be kept in Herod's judgment hall**—'prætorium,' the palace built at Cæsarea by Herod, and now occupied by the Roman procurators; in one of the buildings attached to which Paul was ordered to be kept.

CHAPTER 24

Vss. 1-27. PAUL, ACCUSED BY A PROFESSIONAL PLEADER BEFORE FELIX, MAKES HIS DEFENSE, AND IS REMANDED FOR A FURTHER HEARING. AT A PRIVATE INTERVIEW FELIX TREMBLES UNDER PAUL'S PREACHING, BUT KEEPS HIM PRISONER FOR TWO YEARS, WHEN HE WAS SUCCEEDED BY FESTUS. **1.**

after five days—or, on the fifth day from their departure from Jerusalem. **Ananias ... with the elders**—a deputation of the Sanhedrim. **a certain orator**—one of those Roman advocates who trained themselves for the higher practice of the metropolis by practicing in the provinces, where the Latin language, employed in the courts, was but imperfectly understood and Roman forms were not familiar. **informed ... against Paul**—'laid information,' i.e., put in the charges. **2-4. Seeing that by thee we enjoy great quietness ...**—In this fulsome flattery there was a semblance of truth: nothing more. Felix acted with a degree of vigor and success in suppressing lawless violence [JOSEPHUS, *Antiquities* xx. 8. 4; confirmed by TACITUS, *Ann.* xii. 54]. **by thy providence**—a phrase applied to the administration of the emperors. **5-8, a pestilent fellow**—a plague, or pest—**and a mover of sedition among all the Jews**—by exciting disturbances among them—**throughout the world**—See on Luke 2:1. This was the *first* charge; and true only in the sense explained on ch. 16:20. **a ringleader of the sect of the Nazarenes**—the *second* charge; and true enough. **hath gone about**—attempted—**to profane the temple**—the *third* charge; and entirely false. **we ... would have judged according to our law. But ... Lysias came upon us, and with great violence took him out of our hands**—a wilful falsehood and calumnious charge against a public officer. He had commanded the Sanhedrim to meet for no other purpose than to "judge him according to their law"; and only when, instead of doing so, they fell to disputing among themselves, and the prisoner was in danger of being "pulled in pieces of them" (ch. 23:10)—or as his own letter says "killed of them" (ch. 23:27)—did he rescue him, as was his duty, "by force" out of their hands. **Commanding his accusers to come unto thee**—Here they insinuate that, instead of troubling Felix with the case, he ought to have left it to be dealt with by the Jewish tribunal; in which case his life would soon have been taken. **by examining whom**—Lysias, as would seem (vs. 22)—**thyself mayest ...**—referring all, as if with confidence, to Felix. **the Jews assented ...**—See on ch. 23:15. **10. thou hast been many years a judge in this nation**—He had been in this province for six or seven years, and in Galilee for a longer period. Paul uses no flattery, but simply expresses his satisfaction at having to plead before one whose long official experience of Jewish matters would enable him the better to understand and appreciate what he had to say. **11. thou mayest understand**—canst easily learn—**that there are yet but twelve days since I went up to Jerusalem**—viz., 1. The day of his arrival in Jerusalem (ch. 21:15-17); 2. The interview with James (ch. 21:18-26); 3. The assumption of the vow (ch. 21:26); 4, 5, 6. Continuance of the vow, interrupted by the arrest (ch. 21: 27, etc); 7. Arrest of Paul (ch. 21:27); 8. Paul before the Sanhedrim (ch. 22:30; 23:1-10); 9. Conspiracy of the Jews and defeat of it (ch. 23:12-24), and despatch of Paul from Jerusalem on the evening of the same day (ch. 22:23, 31); 10, 11, 12, 13. The remaining period referred to (ch. 24:1) [MEYER]. This short period is mentioned to show how unlikely it was that he should have had time to do what was charged against him. **for to worship**—a very different purpose from that imputed to him. **12, 13. they neither found me ... Neither can they prove the things ...**—After specifying several particulars, he challenges proof of any one of the charges brought against him. So much for the charge of *sedition*. **14, 15. But this I confess to thee**—in which Felix would see no crime—**that after the way they call heresy**—literally, and better, 'a sect'—**so worship I the God of my fathers**—the ancestral God. Two arguments are contained here: (1) Our nation is divided into what they call *sects* —the sect of the Pharisees, and that of the Sadducees—all the difference between them and me is, that I belong to neither of these, but to another sect, or religious section of the nation, which from its Head they call *Nazarenes:* for this reason, and this alone, am I hated. (2) The Roman law allows every nation to worship its own deities; I claim protection under that law, worshipping the God of my ancestors, even as they, only of a different sect of the common religion. **believing all ...**—Here, disowning all opinions at variance with the Old Testament Scriptures, he challenges for the Gospel which he preached the authority of the God of their fathers. So much for the charge of *heresy*. **And have hope ... as they themselves ... allow, that there shall be a resurrection ...**—This appeal to the faith of his accusers shows that they were chiefly of the *Pharisees*, and that the favor of that party, to which he owed in some measure his safety at the recent council (ch. 23:6-9), had been quite momentary. **16. And herein**—On this account, accordingly; i.e., looking forward to that awful day (cf. II Cor. 5:10). **I exercise myself**—The "I" here is emphatic; 'Whatever they do, this is my study.' **to have always a conscience void of offence ...**— See ch. 23:1; II Corinthians 1:12; 2:17, etc.; i.e., 'These are the great principles of my life and conduct—how different from turbulence and sectarianism!' **17. Now after many**—several—**years**—absence from Jerusalem—**I came to bring alms to my nation**—referring to the collection from the churches of Macedonia and Greece, which he had taken such pains to gather. This only allusion in the Acts to what is dwelt upon so frequently in his own Epistles (Rom. 15:25, 26; I Cor. 16:1-4; II Cor. 8:1-4), throws a beautiful light on the truth of this History. (See PALEY's *Horæ Paulinæ*.) **and offerings**—connected with his Jewish vow: see next verse. **18-21. found me purified in the temple**—not polluting it, therefore, by my own presence, and neither gathering a crowd nor raising a stir: If then these Asiatic Jews have any charge to bring against me in justification of their arrest of me, why are they not here to substantiate it? **Or else let these ... here say**— 'Or, passing from all that preceded my trial, let those of the Sanhedrim here present say if I was guilty of aught there.' No doubt his hasty speech to the high priest might occur to them, but the provocation to it on his own part was more than they would be willing to recall. **Except ... this one voice ... Touching the resurrection ...**—This would recall to the Pharisees present their own inconsistency, in befriending him then and now accusing him. **22, 23. having more perfect knowledge of that**—'the'-*way*—See on ch. 19:23; and on vs. 10. **When Lysias ... shall come ... I will know ...**—Felix might have dismissed the case as a tissue of unsupported charges. But if from his interest in the matter he really wished to have the presence of Lysias and others involved, a brief delay was not unworthy of him as a judge. Certainly, so far as recorded, neither Lysias nor any other parties appeared again in the case. Verse 23, however, seems to show that *at that time* his prepossessions in favor of Paul were strong. **24, 25. Felix ... with his wife Drusilla ... a Jewess**—This beautiful but infamous woman was the third daughter of Herod Agrippa I, who was eaten of worms (see on ch. 12:

1), and a sister of Agrippa II, before whom Paul pleaded, ch. 26. She was "given in marriage to Azizus, king of the Emesenes, who had consented to be circumcised for the sake of the alliance. But this marriage was soon dissolved, after this manner: When Festus was procurator of Judea, he saw her, and being captivated with her beauty, persuaded her to desert her husband, transgress the laws of her country, and marry himself" [JOSEPHUS, *Antiquities*, xx. 7. 1. 2]. Such was this "wife" of Felix. **he sent for Paul and heard him concerning the faith in Christ**—Perceiving from what he had heard on the trial that the new sect which was creating such a stir was represented by its own advocates as but a particular development of the Jewish faith, he probably wished to gratify the curiosity of his Jewish wife, as well as his own, by a more particular account of it from this distinguished champion. And no doubt Paul would so far humor this desire as to present to them the great leading features of the Gospel. But from vs. 25 it is evident that his discourse took an entirely practical turn, suited to the life which his two auditors were notoriously leading. **And as he reasoned of righteousness**—with reference to the *public* character of Felix—**temperance**—with reference to his immoral life—**and judgment to come**—when he would be called to an awful account for both—**Felix trembled**—and no wonder. For, on the testimony of TACITUS, the Roman Annalist (vs. 9; xii. 54), he ruled with a mixture of cruelty, lust, and servility, and relying on the influence of his brother Pallas at court, he thought himself at liberty to commit every sort of crime with impunity. How noble the fidelity and courage which dared to treat of such topics in such a presence, and what withering power must have been in those appeals which made even a Felix to tremble! **Go thy way for this time; and when I have a convenient season I will call for thee**—Alas for Felix! This was his golden opportunity, but—*like multitudes still*—he missed it. Convenient seasons in abundance he found to call for Paul, but never again to "hear him concerning the faith in Christ," and writhe under the terrors of the wrath to come. Even in those moments of terror he had no thought of submission to the Cross or a change of life. The Word discerned the thoughts and intents of his heart, but that heart even then clung to its idols; even as Herod, who "did many things and heard John gladly," but in his best moments was enslaved to his lusts. How many Felixes have appeared from age to age! **26. He hoped ... that money should have been given him ... wherefore he sent for him the oftener, and communed with him**—Bribery in a judge was punishable by the Roman law, but the spirit of a slave (to use the words of TACITUS) was in all his acts, and his "communing with Paul"—as if he cared for either him or his message—simply added hypocrisy to meanness. The position in life of Paul's Christian visitors might beget the hope of extracting something from them for the release of their champion; but the apostle would rather lie in prison than stoop to this! **27. after two years**—What a trial to this burning missionary of Christ, to suffer such a tedious period of inaction! How mysterious it would seem! But this repose would be medicine to his spirit; he would not, and could not, be entirely inactive, so long as he was able by pen and message to communicate with the churches; and he would doubtless learn the salutary truth that even he was not essential to his Master's cause. That Luke wrote his Gospel during this period, under the

apostle's superintendence, is the not unlikely conjecture of able critics. **Porcius Festus**—Little is known of him. He died a few years after this [JOSEPHUS, *Antiquities*, xx. to 9. 1]. **came into Felix' room**—He was recalled, on accusations against him by the Jews of Cæsarea, and only acquitted through the intercession of his brother at court [JOSEPHUS, *Antiquities*, xx. 8, 10]. **Felix, willing to show the Jews a pleasure**—'to earn the thanks of the Jews,' which he did not. **left Paul bound** (ch. 26:29)—which does not seem to have been till then.

CHAPTER 25

Vss. 1-2. FESTUS, COMING TO JERUSALEM, DECLINES TO HAVE PAUL BROUGHT THITHER FOR JUDGMENT, BUT GIVES THE PARTIES A HEARING ON HIS RETURN TO CÆSAREA—ON FESTUS ASKING THE APOSTLE IF HE WOULD GO TO JERUSALEM FOR ANOTHER HEARING BEFORE HIM, HE IS CONSTRAINED IN JUSTICE TO HIS CAUSE TO APPEAL TO THE EMPEROR. **1-3. Festus ... after three days ... ascended ... to Jerusalem**—to make himself acquainted with the great central city of his government without delay. **Then the high priest**—a successor of him before whom Paul had appeared (ch. 23:2). **and the chief of the Jews**—and "the whole multitude of the Jews" (vs. 24) clamorously—**informed him against Paul ... desired favour**—in vs. 15, "judgment"—**against him**—It would seem that they had the insolence to ask him to have the prisoner executed even without a trial (vs. 16). **laying wait ... to kill him**—How deep must have been their hostility, when two years after the defeat of their former attempt, they thirst as keenly as ever for his blood! Their plea for having the case tried at Jerusalem, where the alleged offense took place, was plausible enough; but from vs. 10 it would seem that Festus had been made acquainted with their causeless malice, and that in some way which Paul was privy to. **4-6. answered that Paul should be kept**—rather, 'is in custody'—**at Cæsarea, and ... himself would depart shortly thither. Let them ... which among you are able, go down**—'your leading men.' **7. the Jews ... from Jerusalem**—clamorously, as at Jerusalem; see vs. 24. **many and grievous complaints against Paul**—From his reply, and Festus' statement of the case before Agrippa, these charges seem to have been a jumble of political and religious matter which they were unable to substantiate, and vociferous cries that he was unfit to live. Paul's reply, not given in full, was probably little more than a challenge to prove any of their charges, whether political or religious. **9, 10. Festus, willing to do the Jews a pleasure**—to ingratiate himself with them—**said, Wilt thou go up to Jerusalem, and ... be judged ... before me**—or, 'under my protection'. If this was meant in earnest, it was temporizing and vacillating. But, possibly, anticipating Paul's refusal, he wished merely to avoid the odium of refusing to remove the trial to Jerusalem. **Then said Paul, I stand at Cæsar's judgment seat**—i.e., I am already before the proper tribunal. This seems to imply that he understood Festus to propose handing him over to the Sanhedrim for judgment (and see on vs. 11), with a mere promise of protection from him. But from going to Jerusalem at all he was too well justified in shrinking, for there assassination had been quite recently planned against him. **to the Jews have I** done no wrong, as thou knowest very well—lit., 'better,' i.e., (perhaps), better than to press such a proposal. **if there be none of these things . . . no man may deliver me unto them**—The word signifies to 'surrender in order to gratify' another. **I appeal to Cæsar**—The right of appeal to the supreme power, in case of life and death, was secured by an ancient law to every Roman citizen, and continued under the empire. Had Festus shown any disposition to pronounce final judgment, Paul, strong in the consciousness of his innocence and the justice of a Roman tribunal, would not have made this appeal. But when the only other alternative offered him was to give his own consent to be transferred to the great hotbed of plots against his life, and to a tribunal of unscrupulous and bloodthirsty ecclesiastics whose vociferous cries for his death had scarcely subsided, no other course was open to him. **12. Festus**—little expecting such an appeal, but bound to respect it—**having conferred with the council**—his assessors in judgment, as to the admissibility of the appeal—**said, Hast thou**—for 'thou hast.' **to Cæsar shalt thou go**—as if he would add perhaps 'and see if thou fare better.'

13-27. HEROD AGRIPPA II, ON A VISIT TO FESTUS, BEING CONSULTED BY HIM ON PAUL'S CASE, DESIRES TO HEAR THE APOSTLE, WHO IS ACCORDINGLY BROUGHT FORTH. **13. King Agrippa**—great grandson of Herod the Great, and Drusilla's brother (see on ch. 24:24). On his father's awful death (ch. 12:23), being thought too young (17) to succeed, Judea, was attached to the province of Syria. Four years after, on the death of his uncle Herod, he was made king of the northern principalities of Chalcis, and afterwards got Batanea, Iturea, Trachonitis, Abilene, Galilee, and Perea, with the title of king. He died A.D. 100, after reigning fifty-one years. **and Bernice**—his sister. She was married to her uncle Herod, king of Chalcis, on whose death she lived with her brother Agrippa—not without suspicion of incestuous intercourse, which her subsequent licentious life tended to confirm. **came to salute Festus**—to pay his respects to him on his accession to the procuratorship. **14, 15. when there many**—'several'—**days, Festus declared Paul's cause**—taking advantage of the presence of one who might be presumed to know such matters better than himself; though the lapse of "several days" ere the subject was touched on shows that it gave Festus little trouble. **16-21. to deliver any man to die**—See on the word "deliver up', vs. 11. **as I supposed**—'suspected'—crimes punishable by civil law. **questions . . . of their own superstition**—rather 'religion' (see on ch. 17:22). It cannot be supposed that Festus would use the word in any discourteous sense in addressing his Jewish guest. **one Jesus**—"Thus speaks this miserable Festus of Him to whom every knee shall bow" [BENGEL]. **whom Paul affirmed**—kept affirming'—**was alive**—showing that the resurrection of the Crucified One had been the burden, as usual, of Paul's pleading. The insignificance of the whole affair in the eyes of Festus is manifest. **because I doubted of such manner of questions**—The "I" is emphatic—I, as a Roman judge, being at a loss how to deal with such matters. **the hearing of Augustus**—the imperial title first conferred by the Roman Senate on Octavius. **22-21. I would also hear**—'should like to hear'—**the man myself**—No doubt Paul was right when he said, "The king knoweth of these things . . . for I am persuaded that none of these things are hidden from him; for this thing was not done in a corner" (ch. 26:26). Hence his curiosity to see and

hear the man who had raised such commotion and was remodelling to such an extent the whole Jewish life. **when Agrippa was come, and Bernice, with great pomp**—in the same city in which their father, on account of his pride, had perished, eaten up by worms [WETST]. **with the chief captains**—See on ch. 21:32. JOSEPHUS (*Jewish War*, iii. 4. 2) says that five cohorts, whose full complement was 1000 men, were stationed at Cæsarea. **principal men of the city**—both Jews and Romans. "This was the most dignified and influential audience Paul had yet addressed, and the prediction (ch. 9:15) was fulfilled, though afterwards still more remarkably at Rome (ch. 27:24; II Tim. 4:16, 17" [WEBSTER and WILKINSON]. **I have no certain**—'definite'—**thing to write to my lord**—Nero. "The writer's accuracy should be remarked here. It would have been. a mistake to apply this term ('lord') to the emperor a few years earlier. Neither Augustus nor Tiberius would let himself be so called, as implying the relation of master and slave. But it had now come (rather, was coming) into use as one of the imperial titles" [HACKET].

CHAPTER 26

Vss. 1-32. PAUL'S DEFENSE OF HIMSELF BEFORE KING AGRIPPA, WHO PRONOUNCES HIM INNOCENT, BUT CONCLUDES THAT THE APPEAL TO CÆSAR MUST BE CARRIED OUT. This speech, though in substance the same as that from the fortress stairs of Jerusalem (ch. 22), differs from it in being less directed to meet the charge of apostasy from the Jewish faith, and giving more enlarged views of his remarkable change and apostolic commission, and the divine support under which he was enabled to brave the hostility of his countrymen. **1-3. Agrippa said**—Being a king he appears to have presided. **Paul stretched forth the hand**—chained to a soldier (vs. 29, and see on ch. 12:6). **I know thee to be expert . . .**—His father was zealous for the law, and he himself had the office of president of the temple and its treasures, and the appointment of the high priest [JOSEPHUS, *Antiquities*, 20. 1. 3]. **hear me patiently**—The idea of 'indulgently' is also conveyed. **4, 5. from my youth, which was at the first . . . at Jerusalem, know all the Jews; which knew me from the beginning**—plainly showing that he received his education, even from early youth, at Jerusalem. See on ch. 22:3. **if they would**—'were willing to'—**testify**—but this, of course, they were not, it being a strong point in his favor. **after the most straitest**—'the strictest'—**sect**—as the Pharisees confessedly were. This was said to meet the charge, that as a Hellenistic Jew he had contracted among the heathen lax ideas of Jewish peculiarities. **6, 7. I . . . am judged for the hope of the promise made . . . to our fathers**—'for believing that the promise of Messiah, the Hope of the Church (ch. 13:32; 28:20) has been fulfilled in Jesus of Nazareth risen from the dead.' **Unto which promise**—the fulfilment of it—**our twelve tribes**—James 1:1; and see on Luke 2:36. **instantly**—'intently'; see on ch. 12:5. **serving God**—in the sense of religious worship; see on "ministered," ch. 13:2. **day and night, hope to come**—The apostle rises into language as catholic as the thought—representing his despised nation, all scattered thought it now was, as twelve great branches of one ancient stem, in all places of their dispersion offering to the God of their fathers one unbroken worship, reposing on one great "promise" made of old unto their fathers, and sustained by one "hope" of "coming" to its fulfilment; the single point of difference between him and his countrymen, and the one cause of all their virulence against him, being, that his hope had found rest in One already come, while theirs still pointed to the future. **For which hope's sake, King Agrippa, I am accused of the Jews**–'I am accused of Jews, O king' (so the true reading appears to be); of all quarters the most surprising for such a charge to come from. The charge of *sedition* is not so much as alluded to throughout this speech. It was indeed a mere pretext. **8. Why should it be thought a thing incredible . . . that God should raise the dead?**–rather, 'Why is it judged a thing incredible if God raises the dead?' the case being viewed as an accomplished *fact*. No one dared to call in question the overwhelming evidence of the resurrection of Jesus, which proclaimed Him to be the Christ, the Son of God; the only way of getting rid of it, therefore, was to pronounce it incredible. But *why*, asks the apostle, *is it so judged?* Leaving this pregnant question to find its answer in the breasts of his audience, he now passes to his personal history. **9-15.** See on ch. 9:1, etc. and cf. ch. 22:4, etc. **16-18. But rise . . .**–Here the apostle appears to condense into one statement various sayings of his Lord to him in visions at different times, in order to present at one view the grandeur of the commission with which his Master had clothed him [ALFORD]. **a minister . . . both of these things which thou hast seen**–putting him on a footing with those "eye-witnesses and ministers of the word" mentioned in Luke 1:2. **and of those in which I will appear to thee**–referring to visions he was thereafter to be favored with; such as ch. 18:9, 10; 22:17-21; 23:11; II Corinthians 12, etc. (Gal. 1:12). **Delivering thee from the people**–(the Jews) and from the Gentiles. He was all along the object of Jewish malignity, and was at that moment in the hands of the Gentiles; yet he calmly reposes on his Master's assurances of deliverance from both, at the same time taking all precautions for safety and vindicating all his legal rights. **unto whom now I send thee**–The emphatic "I" here denotes the authority of the Sender [BENGEL]. **To open their eyes, and to turn them from darkness to light**–rather, 'that they may turn' (as in vs. 20), i.e., as the effect of their eyes being opened. The whole passage leans upon Isaiah 61: 1 (Luke 4:18). **and from the power of Satan**–Note the connection here between being "turned from darkness" and "from the power of Satan," whose whole power over men lies in keeping them *in the dark:* hence he is called "the ruler of the darkness of this world." See on II Corinthians 4: 4. **that they may receive forgiveness . . . and inheritance among the sanctified by faith that is in me** –Note: *Faith* is here made the instrument of salvation at once in its first stage, *forgiveness,* and its last, *admission to the home of the sanctified;* and the faith which introduces the soul to all this is emphatically declared by the glorified Redeemer to *rest upon Himself*–"FAITH, even THAT WHICH IS IN ME." And who that believes this can refrain from casting his crown before Him or resist offering Him supreme worship? **19-21. Whereupon, O King Agrippa, I was not disobedient unto the heavenly vision**–This musical and elevated strain, which carries the reader along with it, and doubtless did the hearers, bespeaks the lofty region of thought and feeling to which the apostle had risen while rehearsing his Master's communications to him

from heaven. **showed . . . to them of Damascus, and at Jerusalem**–omitting Arabia; because, beginning with the Jews, his object was to mention first the places where his former hatred of the name of Christ was best known: the mention of the Gentiles, so unpalatable to his audience, is reserved to the last. **repent and return to God, and do works meet for repentance**–a brief description of conversion and its proper fruits, suggested, probably, by the Baptist's teaching (Luke 3:7, 8). **22, 23. having obtained help**–'succor.' **from God**– 'that [which cometh] from God.' **I continue** –'stand,' 'hold my ground'–**unto this day, witnessing . . .**–i.e., This life of mine, so marvellously preserved, in spite of all the plots against it, is upheld for the Gospel's sake; therefore I "witnessed . . . ." **That Christ should suffer . . .**–The construction of this sentence implies that in regard to the question 'whether the Messiah is a suffering one, and whether, rising first from the dead, he should show light to the (Jewish) people and to the Gentiles,' he had only said what the prophets and Moses said should come. **24. Festus said with a loud voice**–surprised and bewildered. **Paul, thou art beside thyself, much learning doth make thee mad**–'is turning thy head.' The union of flowing Greek, deep acquaintance with the sacred writings of his nation, reference to a resurrection and other doctrines to a Roman utterly unintelligible, and, above all, lofty religious earnestness, so strange to the cultivated, cold-hearted skeptics of that day– may account for this sudden exclamation. **25, 26. I am not mad, most noble Festus, but . . .** Can anything surpass this reply, for readiness, self-possession, calm dignity? Every word of it refuted the rude charge, though Festus, probably, did not intend to hurt the prisoner's feelings. **the king knoweth . . .**–See on vss. 1-3. **27-29. believest thou the prophets? I know that thou believest**–The courage and confidence here shown proceeded from a vivid persuasion of Agrippa's knowledge of the *facts* and faith in the *predictions* which they verified; and the king's reply is the highest testimony to the correctness of these presumptions and the immense power of such bold yet courteous appeals to conscience. **Almost**–or, 'in a little time'–**thou persuadest me to be a Christian**–Most modern interpreters think the ordinary translation inadmissible, and take the meaning to be, 'Thou thinkest to make me with little persuasion (or small trouble) a Christian–but I am not to be so easily turned. But the apostle's *reply* can scarcely suit any but the sense given in our authorized version, which is that adopted by CHRYSOSTOM and some of the best scholars since. The objection on which so much stress is laid, that the word "Christian" was at that time only a term of contempt, has no force except on the other side; for taking it in that view, the sense is, 'Thou wilt soon have me one of that despised sect.' **I would to God . . .**–What unequalled magnanimity does this speech breathe! Only his Master ever towered above this. **not only . . . almost . . . but altogether**–or, 'whether soon or late,' or 'with little or much difficulty. **except these bonds**–doubtless holding up his two chained hands (see on ch. 12:6): which in closing such a noble utterance must have had an electrical effect. **30-32. when he had thus spoken, the king rose**–not over-easy, we may be sure. **This man might have been set at liberty if he had not appealed to Cæsar**–It would seem from this that such appeals, once made, behooved to be carried out.

CHAPTER 27

Vss. 1-44. THE VOYAGE TO ITALY—THE SHIP-WRECK AND SAFE LANDING AT MALTA. **1. we should sail . . .**—The "we" here reintroduces the historian as one of the company. Not that he had left the apostle from the time when he last included himself —ch. 21:18—but the apostle was parted from him by his arrest and imprisonment, until now, when they met in the ship. **delivered Paul and certain other prisoners**—State prisoners going to be tried at Rome; of which several instances are on record. **Julius**—who treats the apostle throughout with such marked courtesy (vss. 3, 43; ch. 28:16), that it has been thought [BENGEL] he was present when Paul made his defense before Agrippa (see ch. 25:23), and was impressed with his lofty bearing. **a centurion of Augustus' band**—the Augustan cohort, an honorary title given to more than one legion of the Roman army, implying, perhaps, that they acted as a bodyguard to the emperor or procurator, as occasion required. **2. a ship of**—belonging to— **Adramyttium**—a port on the northeast coast of the Ægean Sea. Doubtless the centurion expected to find another ship, bound for Italy, at some of the ports of Asia Minor, without having to go with this ship all the way to Adramyttium; and in this he was not disappointed. See on vs. 6. **meaning to sail by the coasts**—'places'—**of Asia**—a coasting vessel, which was to touch at the ports of proconsular Asia. **[one] Aristarchus, a Macedonian of Thessalonica, being with us**—rather, 'Aristarchus the Macedonian . . .' The word "one" should not have been introduced here by our translators, as if this name had not occurred before; for we find him seized by the Ephesian mob as a "man of *Macedonia* and Paul's companion in travel" (ch. 19:29) and as a *"Thessalonian"* accompanying the apostle from Ephesus on his voyage back to Palestine (ch. 20:4). Here both these places are mentioned in connection with his name. After this we find him at Rome with the apostle (Col. 4:10; Philemon 24). **3. next day we touched at Sidon**—To reach this ancient and celebrated Mediterranean port, about seventy miles north from Cæsarea, in one day, they must have had a fair wind. **Julius courteously**— (see on vs. 1)—**gave him liberty to go to his friends**— no doubt disciples, gained, it would seem, by degrees, all along the Phœnician coast since the first preaching there (see on ch. 11:19; and 21:4). **to refresh himself**—which after his long confinement would not be unnecessary. Such small personal details are in this case extremely interesting. **4. when we had launched**—'set sail'—**from thence, we sailed under Cyprus, because the winds were contrary**—The wind blowing from the westward, probably with a touch of the north, which was adverse, they sailed *under the lee* of Cyprus, keeping it on their *left*, and steering between it and the mainland of Phœnicia. **5. when we had sailed over the Sea of Cilicia and Pamphylia**—coasts with which Paul had been long familiar, the one, perhaps, from boyhood, the other from the time of his first missionary tour—**we came to Myra, a city of Lycia**—a port a little east of Patara (see on ch. 21:1). **6. there . . . found a ship of Alexandria, sailing into Italy, and he put us therein**—(See on vs. 2). As Egypt was the granary of Italy, and this vessel was laden with wheat (vs. 35), we need not wonder it was large enough to carry 276 souls, passengers and crew together (vs. 37). Besides, the Egyptian merchantmen, among the largest in the Mediterranean, were equal to the largest merchantmen in our day.

It may seem strange that on their passage from Alexandria to Italy they should be found at a Lycian port. But even still it is not unusual to stand to the north towards Asia Minor, for the sake of the current. **7. sailed slowly many days**— owing to contrary winds—**and scarce**—'with difficulty'—**were come over against Cnidus**—a town on the promontory of the peninsula of that name, having the island of Coos (see on ch. 21:1) to the west of it. But for the contrary wind they might have made the distance from Myra (130 miles) in one day. They would naturally have put in at Cnidus, whose larger harbor was admirable, but the strong westerly current induced them to run south. **under** —the lee of—**Crete**—See on Titus 1:5. **over against Salmone**—the cape at the eastern extremity of the island. **8. And hardly passing it**—'with difficulty coasting along it,' from the same cause as before, the westerly current and head winds. **came to . . . the Fair Havens**—an anchorage near the center of the south coast, and a little east of Cape Matala, the southern most point of the island. **nigh whereunto was the city Lasea**—identified by the REV. GEORGE BROWN [SMITH'S *Voyages and Shipwreck of St. Paul*, App. iii., 2d Ed., 1856. To this invaluable book commentators on this chapter, and these notes, are much indebted]. **9, 10. when much time was spent**—since leaving Cæsarea. But for unforeseen delays they might have reached the Italian coast before the stormy season. **and when sailing** —the navigation of the open sea—**was now dangerous, because the fast was now . . . past**—that of the day of atonement, answering to the end of *September* and beginning of *October*, about which time the navigation is pronounced unsafe by writers of authority. Since all hope of completing the voyage during that season was abandoned, the question next was, whether they should winter at Fair Havens, or move to Port Phenice, a harbor about forty miles to the westward. Paul assisted at the consultation and strongly urged them to winter where they were. **Sirs, I perceive, that this voyage will be with hurt and much damage . . .**—not by any divine communication, but simply in the exercise of a good judgment aided by some experience. The event justified his decision. **11. Nevertheless the centurion believed the master and owner . . . more than . . . Paul**—He would naturally think them best able to judge, and there was much to say for their opinion, as the bay at Fair Havens, being open to nearly one-half of the compass, could not be a good winter harbor. **12. Phenice**—'Phenix,' now called *Lutro*—**which lieth toward the southwest and northwest**—If this means that it was open to the west, it would certainly not be good anchorage. It is thought therefore to mean that a *wind from* that quarter would lead into it, or that it lay in an *easterly* direction from such a wind [SMITH]. The next verse seems to confirm this. **13. when the south wind blew softly, supposing they had attained their purpose**—With such a wind they had every prospect of reaching their destination in a few hours. **14, 15. a tempestuous**—'typhonic'—**wind**— i.e., like a *typhon* or tornado, causing a whirling of the clouds, owing to the meeting of opposite currents of air. **called Euroclydon**—The true reading appears to be *Euro-aquilo*, or east-northeast, which answers all the effects here ascribed to it. **could not bear up into**—'face'—**the wind, we let her drift**— before the gale. **16, 17. under**—the lee of—**a certain**—'small'—**island . . . Clauda**—southwest of Crete, now called *Gonzo;* about twenty-three miles to leeward. **we had much work to come by**—i.e., to hoist up and secure—**the boat**—now become necessary. But why was this difficult? Independently of the gale, raging at the time, the boat had been towed between twenty and thirty miles after the gale sprang up, and could scarcely fail to be filled with water [SMITH]. **undergirding the ship**—i.e., passing four or five turns of a cable-laid rope round the hull or frame of the ship, to enable her to resist the violence of the seas, an operation rarely resorted to in modern seamanship. **fearing lest they should fall into the quicksands**—'be cast ashore' or 'stranded upon the Syrtis,' the *Syrtis Major,* a gulf on the African coast, southwest of Crete, the dread of mariners, owing to its dangerous shoals. **they strake**—'struck'—**sail**—This cannot be the meaning, for to strike sail would have driven them directly towards the Syrtis. The meaning must be, 'lowered the gear' (appurtenances of every kind); here, perhaps, referring to the lowering of the heavy mainyard with the sail attached to it [SMITH]. **18-20. cast out with our own hands**—passengers and crew together—**the tackling of the ship**—whatever they could do without that carried weight. This further effort to lighten the ship seems to show that it was now in a *leaking* condition, as will presently appear more evident. **neither sun nor stars appeared in many**—'several'—**days**—probably most of the fourteen days mentioned in vs. 27. This continued thickness of the atmosphere prevented their making the necessary observations of the heavenly bodies by day or by night; so that they could not tell where they were. **all hope that we should be saved was taken away**—"Their exertions to subdue the leak had been unavailing; they could not tell which way to make for the nearest land, in order to run their ship ashore, the only resource for a sinking ship: but unless they did make the land, they must founder at sea. Their apprehensions, therefore, were not so much caused by the fury of the tempest, as by the state of the ship" [SMITH]. From the inferiority of ancient to modern naval architecture, leaks were sprung much more easily, and the means of repairing them were fewer than now. Hence the far greater number of shipwrecks from this cause. **21-26. But after long abstinence**—See on vs. 33. "The hardships which the crew endured during a gale of such continuance, and their exhaustion from laboring at the pumps and hunger, may be imagined, but are not described" [SMITH]. **Paul stood forth in the midst of them, and said, Sirs, ye should have hearkened to me . . .**—not meaning to reflect on them for the past, but to claim their confidence for what he was now to say . . . . **there stood by me this night the angel of God**—as in ch. 16:9 and 23:11). **whose I am**—I Cor. 6:19, 20—**and whom I serve**—in the sense of *worship* or *religious consecration* (see on ch. 13:2). **saying, Fear not, Paul: thou must be brought before Cæsar and, lo, God hath given thee all . . . that sail with thee**—While the crew were toiling at the pumps, Paul was wrestling in prayer, not for himself only and the cause in which he was going a prisoner to Rome, but with true magnanimity of soul for all his shipmates; and God heard him, "giving him" (remarkable expression!) all that sailed with him. "When the cheerless day came he gathered the sailors (and passengers) around him on the deck of the laboring vessel, and raising his voice above the storm" [HOWS], reported the divine communication he had received; adding with a noble simplicity, *"for I believe God"* that it shall be even as it was told me," and encouraging all on board to "be of good cheer" in the same confidence. What a contrast to this is the speech of Cæsar in similar circumstances to his pilot, bidding him keep up his spirit because he carried Cæsar and Cæsar's fortune! [PLUTARCH.] The Roman general knew no better name for the Divine Providence, by which he had been so often preserved, than *Cæsar's fortune* [HUMPHRY]. From the explicit particulars—that the ship would be lost, but not one that sailed in it, and that they "must be cast on a certain island"—one would conclude a visional representation of a total wreck, a mass of human beings struggling with the angry elements, and one and all of those whose figures and countenances had daily met his eye on deck, standing on some unknown island shore. From what follows, it would seem that Paul from this time was regarded with a deference akin to awe. **27-29. when the fourteenth night was come**—from the time they left Fair Havens—**as we were driven**—drifting—**up and down in Adria**—the *Adriatic,* that sea which lies between Greece and Italy. **about midnight the shipmen deemed**—no doubt from the peculiar sound of the breakers—**that they drew near some country** —'that some land was approaching them.' This nautical language gives a graphic character to the narrative. **they cast four anchors out of the stern** —The ordinary way was to cast the anchor, as now, from the *bow:* but ancient ships, built with both ends alike, were fitted with hawseholes in the stern, so that in case of need they could anchor either way. And when the fear was, as here, that they might fall on the rocks *to leeward,* and the intention was to run the ship ashore as soon as daylight enabled them to fix upon a safe spot, the very best thing they could do was to anchor by the stern [SMITH]. In stormy weather two anchors were used, and we have instances of four being employed, as here. **and wished**—'anxiously' or 'devoutly wished'—**for day**—the remark this of one present, and with all his shipmates alive to the horrors of their condition. "The ship might go down at her anchors, or the coast to leeward might be iron-bound, affording no beach on which they could land with safety. Hence their anxious longing for day, and the ungenerous but natural attempt, not peculiar to ancient times, of the seamen to save their own lives by taking to the boat" [SMITH]. **30. as the shipmen were about to flee out of the ship**—under cover of night—**when they had let down the boat . . . as though they would . . . cast anchors out of the foreship**—'bow'—rather, 'carry out' anchors, to hold the ship fore as well as aft. "This could have been of no advantage in the circumstances, and as the pretext could not deceive a seaman, we must infer that the officers of the ship were parties to the unworthy attempt, which was perhaps detected by the nautical skill of St. Luke, and communicated by him to St. Paul" [SMITH]. **31. Paul said to the centurion and to the soldiers**— the only parties now to be trusted, and whose own safety was now at stake. **except ye abide in the ship ye cannot be saved**—The soldiers and passengers could not be expected to possess the necessary seamanship in so very critical a case. The flight of the crew, therefore, might well be regarded as certain destruction to all who remained. *In full assurance of ultimate safety, in virtue of a* DIVINE *pledge, to all in the ship, Paul speaks and acts throughout this whole scene in the exercise of a sound judgment as to the indispensable* HUMAN *conditions of safety;* and as there is no trace of any feeling of inconsistency between these two things in his mind, so even the centurion, under whose orders the soldiers acted on Paul's views, seems never to have felt perplexed by the twofold aspect, divine and human, in which the same thing presented itself to the mind of Paul. *Divine agency and human instrumentality are in all the events of life quite as much as here.* The only difference is that the one is for the most part shrouded from view, while the other is ever naked and open to the senses. **32. Then the soldiers cut off the ropes of the boat**—already lowered—**and let her fall off**—let the boat drift away. **33-37. while day was coming on**—'until it should be day'; i.e., in the interval between the cutting off of the boat and the approach of day, which all were "anxiously looking for" (vs. 29). **Paul**—now looked up to by all the passengers as the man to direct them—**besought them all to take meat**—'partake of a meal'—**saying, This is the fourteenth day ye have tarried**—'waited for a breathingtime.' **having eaten nothing**—i.e., taken no regular meal. The impossibility of cooking, the occupation of all hands to keep down leakage, etc., sufficiently explain this, which is indeed a common occurrence in such cases. **I pray you to take some meat, for this is for your health, for there shall not a hair fall from . . . any of you**—On this beautiful union of confidence in the divine pledge and care for the whole ship's health and safety see on vs. 31. **when he had thus spoken he took bread**—assuming the lead—**and gave thanks to God in presence of them all**—an impressive act in such circumstances, and fitted to plant a testimony for the God he served in the breasts of all. **when he had broken it, he began to eat**—not understood by the Christians in the ship as a lovefeast, or celebration of the Lord's Supper, as some think, but a meal to recruit exhausted nature, which Paul shows them by his own example how a Christian partakes of. **Then were they all of good cheer, and they also took some meat**—'took food'; the first full meal since the commencement of the gale. Such courage in desperate circumstances as Paul here showed is wonderfully infectious. **38-40. when they had eaten enough . . .**—With fresh strength after the meal, they make a third and last effort to lighten the ship, not only by pumping, as before, but by throwing the whole cargo of wheat into the sea (see on vs. 6). **when it was day they knew not the land**—This has been thought surprising in sailors accustomed to that sea. But the scene of the wreck is remote from the great harbor, and possesses no marked features by which it could be recognized, even by a native if he came unexpectedly upon it [SMITH], not to speak of the rain pouring in torrents (ch. 28:2), which would throw a haze over the coast even after day broke. Immediately on landing they knew where they were (ch. 28:1). **discovered a creek with a shore**—Every creek of course, must have a shore; but the meaning is, a *practicable* shore, in a nautical sense, i.e., one with a smooth beach, in contradistinction to a rocky coast (as vs. 41 shows). **into which they were minded, if . . . possible, to thrust the ship**—This was their one chance of safety. **taken up the anchors, they committed themselves to the sea**—The *Marg.* is here evidently right, 'cut the anchors (away), they left them in the sea.' **loosed the rudder bands**—Ancient ships were steered by two large paddles, one on each quarter. When anchored by the stern in a gale, it would be necessary to lift them out of the water and secure them by lashings or rudder bands, and to loose these when the ship was again got under way [SMITH]. **hoised up the mainsail**—rather, 'the foresail,' the best possible sail that could be set in the circumstances. How necessary must

the crew have been to execute all these movements, and how obvious the foresight which made their stay indispensable to the safety of all on board (see on vs. 31)! **41. falling into a place where two seas met**—SMITH thinks this refers to the channel, not more than 100 yards broad, which separates the small island of Salmone from Malta, forming a communication between the sea inside the bay and that outside. **the fore part stuck fast, and remained immovable**—"The rocks of Malta disintegrate into extremely minute particles of sand and clay, which, when acted upon by the currents or surface agitation, form a deposit of tenacious clay; but, in still waters, where these causes do not act, mud is formed; but it is only in creeks, where there are no currents, and at such a depth as to be undisturbed by the waves, that the mud occurs. A ship, therefore, impelled by the force of a gale, into a creek, with such a bottom, would strike a bottom of mud, graduating into tenacious clay, into which the fore part would fix itself, and be held fast, while the stern was exposed to the force of the waves" [SMITH]. **hinder part was broken**—The *continued action* denoted by the tense here is to be noted—'was fast breaking,' going to pieces. **42-44. the soldiers' counsel was to kill the prisoners, lest any . . . should escape**—Roman cruelty, which made the keepers answerable for their prisoners with their own lives, is here reflected in this cruel proposal. **the centurion . . .**—Great must have been the influence of Paul over the centurion's mind to produce such an effect. All followed the swimmers in committing themselves to the deep, and according to the divine pledge and Paul's confident assurance given them, every soul got safe to land—yet without miracle. (While the graphic minuteness of this narrative of the shipwreck puts it beyond doubt that the narrator was himself on board, the great number of *nautical phrases*, which all critics have noted, along with the *unprofessional* air which the whole narrative wears, agrees singularly with all we know and have reason to believe of "the beloved physician"; see on ch. 16:40.)

CHAPTER 28

VSS. 1-31. THE WINTERING AT MALTA, AND NOTABLE OCCURRENCES THERE—PROSECUTION OF THE VOYAGE TO ITALY AS FAR AS PUTEOLI, AND LAND JOURNEY THENCE TO ROME—SUMMARY OF THE APOSTLE'S LABORS THERE FOR THE TWO FOLLOWING YEARS. **1. knew the island was called Melita**—See on ch. 27:39. The opinion that this island was not Malta to the south of Sicily, but Meleda in the Gulf of Venice—which till lately had respectable support among competent judges—is now all but exploded; examination of all the places on the spot, and of all writings and principles bearing on the question, by gentlemen of the highest qualification, particularly SMITH (see on ch. 27:41), having set the question, it may now be affirmed, at rest. **2. the barbarous people**—so called merely as speaking neither the Greek nor the Latin language. They were originally Phœnician colonists. **showed us no little**—'no ordinary'—**kindness, for they kindled a fire, and received us every one, because of the present rain**—'the rain that was on us'—not now first falling, but then falling heavily—**and because of the cold**—welcomed us all, drenched and shivering, to these most seasonable marks of friendship. In this these "barbarians" contrast favorably with many since, bearing the Christian name. The lifelike style of the narrative here and in the following verses gives it a great charm. **3. when Paul had gathered a bundle of sticks**–'a quantity of dry sticks.' The vigorous activity of Paul's character is observable in this comparatively trifling action [WEBSTER and WILKINSON]. **and laid them on the fire, there came a viper out of the heat**–Having laid itself up among the sticks on the approach of the cold winter season, it had suddenly recovered from its torpor by the heat. **and fastened**–its fangs–**on his hand**–Vipers dart at their enemies sometimes several feet at a bound. They have now disappeared from Malta, owing to the change which cultivation has produced. **4-6. No doubt this man is a murderer**–His chains, which they would see, might strengthen the impression. **whom . . . vengeance suffereth not to live**–They believed in a *Supreme, Resistless, Avenging Eye and Hand,* however vague their notions of *where* it resided. **shook off the beast and felt no harm**–See Mark 16:18. **they looked**–'continued looking'–**when he should have swollen or fallen down dead**–familiar with the effects of such bites–**and saw no harm come to him, they changed their minds, and said . . . he was a god**–from "a murderer" to "a god," as the Lycaonian greeting of Paul and Silas from "sacrificing to them" to "stoning them" (ch. 14:13, 19). What has not the Gospel done for the uncultivated portion of the human family, while its effects on the educated and refined, though very different, are not less marvellous! Verily it is God's chosen restorative for the human spirit, in all the multitudinous forms and gradations of its lapsed state. **7, 8. possessions of the chief man**–'the first man'–**of the island**–He would hardly be so styled in the lifetime of his father, if his distinction was that of the *family.* But it is now ascertained that this was the proper *official* title of the Maltese representative of the Roman prætor to Sicily, to whose province Malta belonged; two inscriptions having been discovered in the island, one in Greek, the other in Latin, containing the same words which Luke here employs. **who received us**–of Paul's company, but doubtless including the "courteous" Julius–**and lodged us three days courteously**–till proper winter lodgings could be obtained for them. **the father of Publius lay sick of a fever**–'fevers.' The word was often thus used in the plural number, probably to express *recurring attacks.* **and of a bloody flux**–'of dysentery.' (The *medical* accuracy of our historian's style has been observed here.) **to whom Paul entered in, and prayed**–thereby precluding the supposition that any charm resided in himself. **and laid his hands on him, and healed him**–Thus, as our Lord rewarded Peter for the use of his boat (Luke 5:3, 4, etc.), so Paul richly repays Publius for his hospitality. Observe the fulfilment here of two things predicted in Mark 16:18–the "taking up serpents," and "recovering of the sick by laying hands on them." **9. this . . . done, others . . . came and were healed**–'kept coming to [us] and getting healed,' i.e., during our stay, not all at once [WEBSTER and WILKINSON]. **10. who also honoured us . . . and when we departed they laded us . . .**– This was not taking hire for the miracles wrought among them (Matt. 10:8), but such grateful expressions of feeling, particularly in providing what would minister to their comfort during the voyage, as showed the value they set upon the presence and labors of the apostle among them, and such as it would have hurt their feelings to refuse. Whether any permanent effects of this three months' stay of the greatest of the apostles were left at Malta, we

cannot certainly say. But though little dependence is to be placed upon the tradition that Publius became bishop of Malta and afterwards of Athens, we may well believe the accredited tradition that the beginnings of the Christian Church at Malta sprang out of this memorable visit. **11. we departed in a ship of Alexandria**–(see on ch. 27:6)–**which had wintered in the isle**–no doubt driven in by the same storm which had wrecked on its shores the apostle's vessel–an incidental mark of consistency in the narrative. **whose sign**–or 'figurehead'; the figure, carved or painted on the bow, which gave name to the vessel. Such figureheads were anciently as common as now. **was Castor and Pollux**–the tutelar gods of mariners, to whom all their good fortune was ascribed. St. Anthony is substituted for them in the modern superstitions of Mediterranean (Romanist) sailors. They carry his image in their boats and ships. It is highly improbable that two ships of Alexandra should have been casually found, of which the owners were able and willing to receive on board such a number of passengers (ch. 27:6). We may then reasonably conceive that it was compulsory on the owners to convey soldiers and state travellers [WEBSTER and WILKINSON]. **12, 13. landing at Syracuse**–the ancient and celebrated capital of Sicily, on its eastern coast, about eighty miles, or a day's sail, north from Malta. **we tarried there three days**–probably from the state of the wind. Doubtless Paul would wish to go ashore, to find out and break ground among the Jews and proselytes whom such a mercantile center would attract to it; and if this was allowed at the outset of the voyage (ch. 27:3), much more readily would it be now when he had gained the reverence and confidence of all classes with whom he came in contact. At any rate we cannot wonder that he should be regarded by the Sicilians as the founder of the Church of that island. **from thence we fetched a compass**–i.e., proceeded circuitously, or *tacked,* working to windward probably, and availing themselves of the sinuosities of the coast, the wind not being favorable [SMITH]. What follows confirms this. **and came to Rhegium** –now *Reggio,* a seaport on the southwest point of the Italian coast, opposite the northeast point of Sicily, and at the entrance of the narrow straits of Messina. **after one day the south wind blew**– a south wind having sprung up'; being now favored with a fair wind, for want of which they had been obliged first to stay three days at Syracuse, and then to tack and put in for a day at Rhegium. **the next day to Puteoli**–now *Pozzuoli,* situated on the northern part of the magnificent bay of Naples about 180 miles north of Rhegium, a distance which they might make, running before their "south wind," in about twenty-six hours. The Alexandrian corn ships enjoyed a privilege peculiar to themselves, of not being obliged to strike their topsail on landing. By this they were easily recognized as they hove in sight by the crowds that we find gathered on the shore on such occasions [HOWS]. **14, 15. Where we found brethren**–not "*the* brethren" (see on ch. 21:4), from which one would conclude they did not expect to find such [WEBSTER and WILKINSON]. **and were desired**–'requested'–**to tarry with them seven days**–If this request came from Julius, it may have proceeded partly from a wish to receive instructions from Rome and make arrangements for his journey thither, partly from a wish to gratify Paul, as he seems studiously and increasingly to have done to the last. One can hardly doubt that he was influenced by both considerations. However this may be, the apostle had thus an opportunity of spending a Sabbath with the Christians of the place, all the more refreshing from his long privation in this respect, and as a seasoning for the unknown future that lay before him at the metropolis. **so we went toward Rome. And from thence, when the brethren**–of Rome–**heard of us**–by letter from Puteoli, and probably by the same conveyance which took Julius' announcement of his arrival. **they came to meet us as far as Appii Forum**–a town forty-one miles from Rome. **and the Three Taverns**–thirty miles from Rome. Thus they came to greet the apostle in two parties, one stopping short at the nearer, the other going on to the more distant place. **whom when Paul saw, he thanked God**–for such a welcome. How sensitive he was to such Christian affection all his Epistles show (Rom. 1:9, etc.). **and took courage**–his long-cherished purpose to "see Rome" (ch. 19:21), there to proclaim the unsearchable riches of Christ, and the divine pledge that in this he should be gratified (ch. 23:11), being now about to be auspiciously realized. **16. when we came to Rome**–the renowned capital of the ancient world, situated on the Tiber. **the centurion delivered the prisoners to the captain of the guard**–the *Prætorian Prefect*, to whose custody, as commander of the Prætorian guard, the highest military authority in the city, were committed all who were to come before the emperor for trial. Ordinarily there were two such prefects; but from A.D. 51 to 62, one distinguished general–*Burrus Aframus,* who had been Nero's tutor–held that office; and as our historian speaks of *"the* captain," as if there were but one, it is thought that this fixes the apostle's arrival at Rome to be not later than the year 62 [WIES]. But even though there had been two when Paul arrived, he would be committed only to one of them, who would be *"the* captain" who got charge of him. (At most, therefore, this can furnish no more than confirmation to the chronological evidence otherwise obtained.) **but Paul was suffered to dwell by himself with a**–'the'–**soldier that kept**–'guarded'–**him**–(See on ch. 12:6). This privilege was allowed in the case of the better class of prisoners, not accused of any flagrant offense, on finding security–which in Paul's case would not be difficult among the Christians. The extension of this privilege to the apostle may have been due to the terms in which Festus wrote about him; but far more probably it was owing to the high terms in which Julius spoke of him, and his express intercession in his behalf. It was overruled, however, for giving the fullest scope to the labors of the apostle compatible with confinement at all. As the soldiers who kept him were relieved periodically, he would thus make the personal acquaintance of a great number of the Prætorian guard; and if he had to appear before the Prefect from time to time, the truth might thus penetrate to those who surrounded the emperor, as we learn, from Philippians 1:12, 13, that it did. **17-20. Paul called the chief of the Jews together**–Though banished from the capital by Claudius, the Jews enjoyed the full benefit of the toleration which distinguished the first period of Nero's reign, and were at this time in considerable numbers, wealth, and influence settled at Rome. We have seen that long before this a flourishing Christian Church existed at Rome, to which Paul wrote his Epistle (see on ch. 20:3), and the first members of which were probably Jewish converts and proselytes. (See Introduction to Epistle to Romans.) **yet was I delivered prisoner from Jerusalem into the hands**

of the Romans–the Roman authorities, Felix and Festus. **I was constrained to appeal . . . not that I had aught to accuse my nation of**–'I am here not as their accuser, but as my own defender, and this not of choice but necessity.' His object in alluding thus gently to the treatment he had received from the Jews was plainly to avoid whatever might irritate his visitors at the first; especially as he was not aware whether any or what information against him had reached their community. **For this cause . . . have I called for you . . . because . . . for the hope of Israel**–see on 26:6, 7–**I am bound with this chain**–'This cause is not so much mine as yours; it is the nation's cause; all that is dear to the heart and hope of Israel is bound up with this case of mine.' From the touching allusions which the apostle makes to his chains, before Agrippa first, and here before the leading members of the Jewish community at Rome, at his first interview with them, one would gather that his great soul felt keenly his being in such a condition; and it is to this keenness of feeling, under the control of Christian principle, that we owe the noble use which he made of it in these two cases. **21, 22. We neither received letters out of Judea concerning thee . . .**–We need not suppose (with THOLUCK and others) that there was any dishonest concealment here. The distinction made between himself, against whom they heard nothing, and his "sect," as "everywhere spoken against," is a presumption in favor of their sincerity; and there is ground to think that as the case took an unexpected turn by Paul's appealing to Cæsar, so no information on the subject would travel from Jerusalem to Rome in advance of the apostle himself. **we desire**–'deem it proper'–**to hear of thee what thou thinkest**–what are thy sentiments, views, etc. The apparent freedom from prejudice here expressed may have arisen from a prudent desire to avoid endangering a repetition of those dissensions about Christianity to which, probably, SUETONIUS alludes, and which had led to the expulsion of the Jews under Claudius [HUMPHRY]. See on ch. 18:2. **23, 24. there came many**–'considerable numbers'–**into his lodging**–The word denotes one's place of stay as a *guest* (Philemon 22), not "his own hired house," mentioned in vs. 30. Some Christian friends–possibly Aquila and Priscilla, who had returned to Rome (Rom. 16:3), would be glad to receive him, though he would soon find himself more at liberty in a house of his own. **to whom he expounded and testified the kingdom of God**–opening up the great spiritual principles of that kingdom in opposition to the contracted and secular views of it entertained by the Jews. **persuading them concerning Jesus**–as the ordained and predicted Head of that kingdom. **out of the law . . . and the prophets**–drawing his materials and arguments from a source mutually acknowledged. **from morning till evening**–"Who would not wish to have been present?" exclaims BENGEL; but virtually we *are* present while *listening* to those Epistles which he *dictated* from his prison at Rome, and to his other epistolary expositions of Christian truth against the Jews. **and some believed . . . some not** –What simplicity and candor are in this record of a result repeated from age to age where the Gospel is presented to a promiscuous assemblage of sincere and earnest inquirers after truth, frivolous worldlings, and prejudiced bigots! **25-29. when they**–the Jews–**agreed not among themselves**–the discussion having passed into one between the two parties into which the visitors were now divided, respecting the arguments and conclusions of the apostle. **they**

departed—the material of discussion being felt by both parties to be exhausted. **after Paul had spoken one word**—one solemn parting testimony, from those Scriptures regarded by both alike as "the Holy Ghost speaking" to Israel. **Hearing, ye shall hear . . .**—See on Matthew 13:13-15; and John 12:38-40. With what pain would this stern saying be wrung from him whose "heart's desire and prayer to God for Israel was that they might be saved," and who "had great heaviness and continual sorrow in his heart" on their account (Rom. 10:1; 9:2)! **the salvation of God is sent to the Gentiles, and they will hear**—See on ch. 13:44-48. "This 'departure to the Gentiles' he had intimated to the perverse Jews at *Antioch* (ch. 13:46), and at *Corinth* (ch. 18:6); now at *Rome:* thus in *Asia, Greece,* and *Italy*" [BENGEL]. **the Jews departed, and had great** —'much'—**reasoning among themselves**—"This verse is wanting in many MSS. [and omitted by several recent editors], but certainly without reason. Probably the words were regarded as superfluous, as they seem to tell us what we were told before, that Paul 'departed' (see vs. 25). But in vs. 25 it is the breaking off of the discourse that is meant, here the final departure from the house" [OLSHAUSEN]. **30. in his own hired house**—(see on vs. 23), yet still in custody, for he only "received all that *came to him";* and it is not said that he went to the synagogue or anywhere else. **with all confidence, no man forbidding him**—enjoying, in the uninterrupted exercise of his ministry, all the liberty of a *guarded* man.

Thus closes this most precious monument of the beginnings of the Christian Church in its march from east to west, among the Jews first, whose center was Jerusalem; next among the Gentiles, with Antioch for its headquarters; finally, its banner is seen waving over imperial Rome, foretokening its universal triumphs. That distinguished apostle whose conversion, labors, and sufferings for "the faith which once he destroyed" occupy more than half of this History, it leaves a prisoner, unheard, so far as appears, for two years. His accusers, whose presence was indispensable, would have to await the return of spring before starting for the capital, and might not reach it for many months; nor, even when there, would they be so sanguine of success—after Felix, Festus, and Agrippa had all pronounced him innocent—as to be impatient of delay. And if witnesses were required to prove the charge advanced by Tertullus, that he was "a mover of sedition among all the Jews throughout the [Roman] world" (ch. 24:5), they must have seen that unless considerable time was allowed them the case would certainly break down. If to this be added the capricious delays which the emperor himself might interpose, and the practice of Nero to hear but one charge at a time, it will not seem strange that the historian should have no proceedings in the case to record for two years. Begun, probably, before the apostle's arrival, its progress at Rome under his own eye would furnish exalted employment, and beguile many a tedious hour of his two years' imprisonment. Had the case come on for hearing during this period, much more if it had been disposed of, it is hardly conceivable that the History should have closed as it does. But if,

at the end of this period, the Narrative only wanted the decision of the case, while hope deferred was making the heart sick (Prov. 13:12), and if, under the guidance of that Spirit whose seal was on it all, it seemed of more consequence to put the Church at once in possession of this History than to keep it back indefinitely for the sake of what might come to be otherwise known, we cannot wonder that it should be wound up as it is in its two concluding verses. All that we know of the apostle's proceedings and history beyond this must be gathered from the *Epistles of the Imprisonment*—Ephesians, Philippians, Colossians, and Philemon—written during this period, and the *Pastoral Epistles*—to Timothy and Titus, which, in our judgment, are of subsequent date. From the former class of Epistles we learn the following particulars: (1) That the trying restraint laid upon the apostle's labors by his imprisonment had only turned his influence into a new channel; the Gospel having in consequence penetrated even into the palace, and pervaded the city, while the preachers of Christ were emboldened; and though the Judaizing portion of them, observing his success among the Gentiles, had been led to inculcate with fresh zeal their own narrower Gospel, even this had done much good by extending the truth common to both (see on Phil. 1:12-18; 4:22); (2) That as in addition to all his other labors, "the care of all the churches pressed upon him from day to day" (II Cor. 11:28), so with these churches he kept up an active correspondence by means of letters and messages, and on such errands he lacked not faithful and beloved brethren enough ready to be employed—*Luke; Timotheus; Tychicus;* (John) *Mark; Demas; Aristarchus; Epaphras; Onesimus; Jesus,* called Justus; and, for a short time, *Epaphroditus.* (See on Col. 4:7, 9-12, 14; Philemon 23, 24; and Introduction to Ephesians, Philippians, and Philemon.) That the apostle suffered martyrdom under Nero at Rome has never been doubted. But that the appeal which brought him to Rome issued in his liberation, that he was at large for some years thereafter and took some wide missionary circuits, and that he was again arrested, carried to Rome, and then executed—was the undisputed belief of the early Church, as expressed by CHRYSOSTOM, JEROME, and EUSEBIUS, in the fourth century, up to CLEMENT of Rome, the "fellow laborer" of the apostle himself (Phil. 4:3), in the first century. The strongest possible confirmation of this is found in the Pastoral Epistles, which bear marks throughout of a more advanced state of the Church, and more matured forms of error, than can well have existed at any period before the appeal which brought the apostle to Rome; which refer to movements of himself and Timothy that cannot without some straining (as we think) be made to fit into any prior period; and which are couched in a manifestly riper style than any of his other Epistles. (See Introduction to Timothy and Titus, and *Notes.*) All this has been called in question by modern critics of great research and acuteness [PETAVIUS, LARDNER, DE WETTE, WIESELER, DAVIDSON, and others]. But those who maintain the ancient view are of equal authority and more numerous, while the weight of argument appears to us to be decidedly on their side.

CHRONOLOGICAL TABLE OF THE PRINCIPAL EVENTS CONNECTED WITH THE LIFE OF THE APOSTLE PAUL

Certainty in these dates is not to be had, the notes of time in the Acts being few and vague. It is only by connecting those events of secular history which it records, and the dates of which are otherwise tolerably known to us—such as the famine under Claudius Cæsar (ch. 11:28), the expulsion of the Jews from Rome by the same emperor (ch. 18:2), and the entrance of Porcius Festus upon his procuratorship (ch. 24:27), with the intervals specified between some occurrences in the apostle's life and others (such as ch. 20:31; 24:27; 28:30; and Gal. 1 and 2)—that we can thread our way through the difficulties that surround the chronology of the apostle's life, and approximate to certainty. Immense research has been brought to bear upon the subject, but, as might be expected, the learned are greatly divided. Every year has been fixed upon as the probable date of the apostle's conversion from A.D. 31 [BENGEL] to A.D. 42 [EUSEBIUS]. But the weight of authority is in favor of dates ranging between 35 and 40, a difference of not more than five years; and the largest number of authorities is in favor of the year 37 or 38. Taking the former of these, to which opinion largely inclines, the following Table will be useful to the student of apostolic history:

A.D. 37	PAUL'S CONVERSION	Acts 9:1
„ 40	*First* Visit to Jerusalem	„ 9:26; Gal. 1:18
„ 42–44	*First* Residence at Antioch	„ 11:25–30
„ 44	*Second* Visit to Jerusalem	„ 11:30; 12:25
„ 45–47	FIRST MISSIONARY JOURNEY	„ 13:2; 14: 26
„ 47–51	*Second* Residence at Antioch	„ 14:28
	Third Visit to Jerusalem	„ 15:2–30; Gal. 2:1–10
		(on which see *Notes*)
„ 51, 53, or 54	SECOND MISSIONARY JOURNEY	„ 15:36, 40; 18:22
„ 53 or 54.	*Fourth* Visit to Jerusalem	„ 18:21, 22
	Third Residence at Antioch	„ 18:22, 23
„ 54–58	THIRD MISSIONARY JOURNEY	„ 16:23; 21:15
„ 58	{ *Fifth* Visit to Jerusalem }	„ 21:15; 23:35
	{ Arrest and Imprisonment at Cæsarea }	
„ 60 (Aut.)— }	Voyage to and Arrival in Rome	„ 27:1; 28:16
„ 61 (Spring) } . . .		
„ 63	Release from Imprisonment	„ 28:30
	At Crete, Colosse, Macedonia, Corinth, Nicopolis, Dalmatia, Troas I & II Tim. and Tit.	
„ 63–65, or 66, or possibly as late as		
„ 66–68	Martyrdom at Rome	

THE EPISTLE OF PAUL THE APOSTLE TO THE

ROMANS

INTRODUCTION

THE GENUINENESS of the Epistle to the Romans has never been questioned. It has the unbroken testimony of all antiquity, up to Clement, the apostle's "fellow laborer in the Gospel, whose name was in the Book of Life" (Phil. 4:3), and who quotes from it in his undoubted Epistle to the Corinthians, written before the close of the first century. The most searching investigations of modern criticism have left it untouched.

WHEN and WHERE this Epistle was written we have the means of determining with great precision, from the Epistle itself compared with the Acts of the Apostles. Up to the date of it the apostle had never been at Rome (ch. 1:11, 13, 15). He was then on the eve of visiting Jerusalem with a pecuniary contribution for its Christian poor from the churches of Macedonia and Achaia, after which his purpose was to pay a visit to Rome on his way to Spain (ch. 15:23–28). Now this contribution we know that he carried with him from Corinth, at the close of his third visit to that city, which lasted three months (Acts 20:2, 3; 24:17). On this occasion there accompanied him from Corinth certain persons whose names are given by the historian of the Acts (Acts 20:4), and four of these are expressly mentioned in our Epistle as being with the apostle when he wrote it—Timotheus, Sosipater, Gaius, and Erastus (ch. 16:21, 23). Of these four, the third, Gaius, was an inhabitant of Corinth (I Cor. 1:14), and the fourth, Erastus, was "chamberlain of *the city*" (ch. 16:23), which can hardly be supposed to be other than Corinth. Finally, Phœbe, the bearer, as appears, of this Epistle, was a deaconess of the Church at Cenchrea, the eastern port of Corinth (ch. 16:1). Putting these facts together, it is impossible to resist the conviction, in which all critics agree, that Corinth was the place from which the Epistle was written, and that it was despatched about the close of the visit above mentioned, probably in the early spring of the year 58.

The FOUNDER of this celebrated church is unknown. That it owed its origin to the apostle Peter, and that he was its first bishop, though an ancient tradition and taught in the Church of Rome as a fact not to be doubted, is refuted by the clearest evidence, and is given up even by candid Romanists. On that supposition, how are we to account for so important a circumstance being passed by in silence by the historian of the Acts, not only in the narrative of Peter's labors, but in that of Paul's approach to the metropolis, of the deputations of Roman "brethren" that came as far as Appii Forum and the Three Taverns to meet him, and of his two years' labors there? And how, consistently with his declared principle—not to build on another man's foundation (ch. 15:20)—could he express his anxious desire to come to them that he might have some fruit among them also, even as among other Gentiles (ch. 1:13), if all the while he knew that they had the apostle of the circumcision for their spiritual father? And how, if so, is there no salutation to Peter among the many in this Epistle? or, if it may be thought that he was known to be elsewhere at that particular time, how does there occur in all the Epistles which our apostle afterwards wrote from Rome not one allusion to such an origin of the church at Rome? The same considerations would seem to prove that this church owed its origin to no prominent Christian laborer; and this brings us to the much-litigated question.

For WHAT CLASS of Christians was this Epistle principally designed—Jewish or Gentile? That a large number of Jews and Jewish proselytes resided at this time at Rome is known to all who are familiar with the classical and Jewish writers of that and the immediately subsequent periods; and that those of them who were at Jerusalem on the day of Pentecost (Acts 2:10), and formed probably part of the three thousand converts of that day, would on their return to Rome carry the glad tidings with them, there can be no doubt. Nor are indications wanting that some of those embraced in the salutations of this Epistle were Christians already of long standing, if not among the earliest converts to the Christian faith. Others of them who had made the apostle's acquaintance elsewhere, and who, if not indebted to him for their first knowledge of Christ, probably owed much to his ministrations, seemed to have charged themselves with the duty of cherishing and consolidating the work of the Lord in the capital. And thus it is not improbable that up to the time of the apostle's arrival the Christian community at Rome had been dependent upon subordinate agency for the increase of its numbers, aided by occasional visits of stated preachers from the provinces; and perhaps it may be gathered from the salutations of the last chapter that it was up to that time in a less organized, though far from less flourishing state, than some other churches to whom the apostle had already addressed Epistles. Certain it is, that the apostle writes to them expressly as a Gentile Church (ch. 1:13, 15; 15:15, 16); and though it is plain that there were Jewish Christians among them, and the whole argument presupposes an intimate acquaintance on the part of his readers with the leading principles of the Old Testament, this will be sufficiently explained by supposing that the bulk of them, having before they knew the Lord been Gentile proselytes to the Jewish faith, had entered the pale of the Christian Church through the gate of the ancient economy.

It remains only to speak briefly of the PLAN and CHARACTER of this Epistle. Of all the undoubted Epistles of our apostle, this is the most elaborate, and at the same time the most glowing. It has just as much in common with a theological treatise as is consistent with the freedom and warmth of a real letter. Referring to the headings which we have prefixed to its successive sections, as best exhibiting the progress of the argument and the connection of its points, we here merely note that its first great topic is what may be termed *the legal relation of man to God* as a violater of His holy law, whether as merely written on the heart, as in the case of the heathen, or, as in the case of the Chosen People, as further known by external revelation; that it next treats of that legal relation as wholly *reversed* through believing connection with the Lord Jesus Christ; and that its third and last great topic is *the new life* which accompanies this change of relation, embracing at once a blessedness and a consecration to God which, rudimentally complete already, will open, in the future world, into the bliss of immediate and stainless fellowship with God. The bearing of these wonderful truths upon the condition and destiny of the Chosen People, to which the apostle next comes, though it seem but the practical application of them to his kinsmen according to the flesh, is in some respects the deepest and most difficult part of the whole Epistle, carrying us directly to the eternal springs of Grace to the guilty in the sovereign love and inscrutable purposes of God; after which, however, we are brought back to the historical platform of the visible Church, in the calling of the Gentiles, the preservation of a faithful Israelitish remnant amidst the general unbelief and fall of the nation, and the ultimate recovery of all Israel to constitute, with the Gentiles in the latter day, one catholic Church of God upon earth. The remainder of the Epistle is devoted to sundry practical topics, winding up with salutations and outpourings of heart delightfully suggestive.

CHAPTER 1

Vss. 1-17. INTRODUCTION. 1. Paul—see on Acts 13:9—**a servant of Jesus Christ**—The word here rendered "servant" means 'bond-servant,' or one subject to the will and wholly at the disposal of another. In this sense it is applied to the disciples of Christ at large (I Cor. 7:21-23), as in the Old Testament to all the people of God (Isa. 66:14). But as, in addition to this, the prophets and kings of Israel were *officially* "the servants of the Lord" (Josh. 1:1; Ps. 18, title), the apostles call themselves, in the same official sense, "the servants of Christ" (as here, and Phil. 1:1; Jas. 1:1; II Pet. 1:1; Jude 1), expressing such absolute subjection and devotion to the Lord Jesus as they would never have yielded to a mere creature. (See on vs. 7; and on John 5:22, 23.) **called to be an apostle**—when first he "saw the Lord"; the indispensable qualification for apostleship. (See on Acts 9:5; 22:14; I

Cor. 9:1.) **separated unto the**—preaching of the—**gospel**—neither so late as when "the Holy Ghost said, *Separate* me Barnabas and Saul" (Acts 13:2), nor so early as when "*separated* from his mother's womb" (see on Gal. 1:15). He was called at one and the same time to the faith and the apostleship of Christ (Acts 26:16-18). **of God**—i.e., the Gospel of which God is the glorious Author. (So ch. 15: 16; I Thess. 2:2, 8, 9; I Pet. 4:17.) **2. Which he had promised afore...in the holy scriptures**—Though the Roman Church was Gentile by nation (see on vs. 13), yet as it consisted mostly of proselytes to the Jewish faith (see *Introduction* to this Epistle), they are here reminded that in embracing Christ they had not cast off, but only the more profoundly yielded themselves to, Moses and the prophets (Acts 13:32, 33). **3, 4. Concerning his Son Jesus Christ our Lord**—the grand burden of this "Gospel of God." **made of the seed of David**—as, according to "the holy scriptures," He behooved to be. (See on Matt. 1:1.) **according to the flesh**—i.e., in His *human* nature (cf. ch. 9:5, and John 1:14); implying, of course, that He had *another* nature, of which the apostle immediately proceeds to speak. **And declared**—lit., 'marked off,' 'defined,' 'determined,' i.e., 'shown,' or 'proved.' **to be the Son of God**—Observe how studiously the language changes here. He "*was* MADE [says the apostle] of the seed of David, according to the flesh"; but He was *not* made, He was only "*declared* [or proved] *to* BE the Son of God." So John 1:1, 14, "In the beginning WAS the Word . . . and the Word *was* MADE flesh"; and Isaiah 9:6, "Unto us *a Child* is BORN, unto us *a Son* is GIVEN." Thus the Sonship of Christ is in no proper sense a *born* relationship to the Father, as some, otherwise sound divines, conceive of it. By His birth in the flesh, that Sonship, which was essential and uncreated, merely effloresced into palpable manifestation. (See on Luke 1:35; Acts 13:32, 33.) **with power**—This may either be connected with "declared," and then the meaning will be 'powerfully declared' [LUTHER, BEZA, BENGEL, FRITZSCHE, ALFORD, etc.]; or (as in our version, and as we think rightly) with "the Son of God," and then the sense is, 'declared to be the Son of God in possession of that "power" which belonged to Him as the only-begotten of the Father, no longer shrouded as in the days of His flesh, but "by His resurrection from the dead" gloriously displayed and henceforth to be for ever exerted in this nature of ours" [VULGATE, CALVIN, HODGE, PHILIPPI, MEHRING, etc.]. **according to the spirit of holiness**—If "according to the flesh" means here, 'in His human nature,' this uncommon expression must mean 'in His *other* nature,' which we have seen to be that "of the Son of God"—an eternal, uncreated nature. This is here styled the "*spirit*," as an impalpable and immaterial nature (John 4:24), and "the spirit of *holiness*," probably in absolute contrast with that "likeness, of sinful flesh" which He assumed. One is apt to wonder that if this be the meaning, it was not expressed more simply. But if the apostle had said 'He was declared to be the Son of God according to *the Holy Spirit,*' the reader would have thought he meant '*the Holy Ghost';* and it seems to have been just to avoid this misapprehension that he used the rare expression, "the spirit of holiness." **5. By whom**—as the ordained channel—**we have received grace**—the whole "grace that bringeth salvation"—**and apostleship**—for the publication of that "grace," and the organization of as many as receive it into churches of visible discipleship. (We prefer thus taking them as two distinct things, and not, with some good interpreters, as one—'the grace of apostleship.') **for obedience to the faith**—rather, 'for the obedience of faith'—i.e., in order to men's yielding themselves to the belief of God's saving message, which is the highest of all obedience. **for his name**—that He might be glorified. **6. Among whom are ye also**—i.e., along with others; for the apostle ascribes nothing special to the Church of Rome (cf. I Cor. 14:36) [BENGEL]. **the called**—see on ch. 8:30—**of Christ Jesus**—i.e., either called '*by* Him' (John 5:25), or the called '*belonging* to Him'; 'Christ's called ones.' Perhaps this latter sense is best supported, but one hardly knows which to prefer. **7. beloved of God**—(Cf. Deut. 33:12; Col. 3:12). **Grace** . . . (See on John 1:14). **and peace**—the peace which Christ made through the blood of His cross (Col. 1:20), and which reflects into the believing bosom . . . "the peace of God which passeth all understanding" (Phil. 4:7). **from God our Father, and the Lord Jesus Christ**—"Noth-

ing speaks more decisively for the divinity of Christ than these juxtapositions of Christ with the eternal God, which run through the whole language of Scripture, and the derivation of purely divine influences from Him also. The name of no man can be placed by the side of the Almighty. He only, in whom the Word of the Father who is Himself God became flesh, may be named beside Him; for men are commanded to honor Him even as they honor the Father (John 5:23)" [OLSHAUSEN]. **8. your faith is spoken of throughout the whole world**—This was quite practicable through the frequent visits paid to the capital from all the provinces; and the apostle, having an eye to the influence they would exercise upon others, as well as their own blessedness, given thanks for such faith to "his God through Jesus Christ," as being the source, according to his theology of faith, as of all grace in men. **9. For God . . . whom I serve**—the word denotes religious service—**with my spirit**—from my inmost soul—**in the gospel of his Son**—to which Paul's whole religious life and official activity were consecrated—**is my witness, that without ceasing I make mention of you always in my prayers**—so for the Ephesians (Eph. 1:15, 15); so for the Philippians (Phil. 1:3, 4); so for the Colossians (Col. 1:3, 4); so for the Thessalonians (I Thess. 1:2, 3). What catholic love, what all-absorbing spirituality, what impassioned devotion to the glory of Christ among men! **10. Making request, if by any means now at length I may have a prosperous journey by the will of God, to come to you**—Though long anxious to visit the capital, he met with a number of providential hindrances (vs. 13; ch. 15:22; and see on Acts 19:21; 23:11, 28:15); insomuch that *nearly a quarter of a century* elapsed, after his conversion, ere his desire was accomplished, and that only as "a prisoner of Jesus Christ." Thus taught that his whole future was in the hands of God, he makes it his continual prayer that at length the obstacles to a happy and prosperous meeting might be removed. **11, 12. For I long to see you, that I may impart to you some spiritual gift**—not any supernatural gift, as the next clause shows, and cf. I Corinthians 1:7. **to the end that ye may be established; That is, that I may be comforted together with you by the mutual faith both of you and me**—"Not wishing to 'lord it over their faith,' but rather to be a 'helper of their joy,' the apostle corrects his former expressions: my desire is to instruct you and do you good, that is, for us to instruct and do one another good: in giving I shall also receive" [JOWETT]. "Nor is he insincere in so speaking, for there is none so poor in the Church of Christ who may not impart to us something of value: it is only our malignity and pride that hinder us from gathering such fruit from every quarter" [CALVIN]. How "widely different is the apostolic style from that of the court of Papal Rome!" [BENGEL.] **13. oftentimes I purposed to come unto you, but was let**—hindered—**hitherto**—chiefly by his desire to go first to places where Christ was not known (ch. 15:20-24). **that I might have some fruit**—of my ministry—**among you also, even as among other Gentiles**—The GENTILE origin of the Church at Rome is here so explicitly stated, that those who conclude, merely from the Jewish strain of the argument, that they must have been mostly Israelites, decide in opposition to the apostle himself. (But see *Introduction* to this Epistle.) **14, 15. I am debtor both to the**—cultivated—**Greeks and to the**—rude—**Barbarians . . . So, as much as in me is, I am ready to preach the gospel to you that are at Rome also**—He feels himself under an all-subduing obligation to carry the gospel to all classes of mankind, as adapted to and ordained equally for all (I Cor. 9:16). **16. For I am not ashamed of the gospel**—(The words, "of Christ," which follow here, are not found in the oldest and best MSS.) This language implies that it required some courage to bring to 'the mistress of the world' what "to the Jews was a stumbling block and to the Greeks foolishness." But its inherent glory, as God's life-giving message to a dying world, so filled his soul, that, like his blessed Master, he "despised the shame." **for** IT IS THE POWER OF GOD UNTO SALVATION TO EVERY ONE THAT BELIEVETH—Here and in the next verse the apostle announces the great theme of his ensuing argument; SALVATION, the one overwhelming necessity of perishing men; this revealed IN THE GOSPEL MESSAGE; and that message so *owned and honored of God as to carry,* in the proclamation of it, GOD'S OWN POWER TO SAVE EVERY SOUL THAT EMBRACES IT, Greek and Barbarian, wise and unwise alike. **17. For therein is the righteousness of God revealed**—that is (as the whole argument of the Epistle shows), GOD'S JUSTIFYING RIGHTEOUSNESS. **from faith to faith**—a difficult clause. Most interpreters (judging from the sense of such phrases elsewhere) take it to mean, 'from one degree of faith to another.' But this agrees ill with the apostle's design, which has nothing to do with the progressive stages of faith, but solely with faith itself as the appointed way of receiving God's "righteousness." We prefer, therefore, to understand it thus: 'The righteousness of God is in the gospel message, revealed (to be) from (or "by") faith to (or "for") faith,' that is, 'in order to be by faith received.' (So substantially, MELVILLE, MEYER, STUART, BLOOMFIELD, etc.). **as it is written**—Habakkuk 2:4—**The just shall live by faith**—This golden maxim of the Old Testament is thrice quoted in the New Testament—here; Galatians 3:11; Hebrews 10:38—showing that the gospel way of 'LIFE BY FAITH,' so far from disturbing, only continued and developed the ancient method. On the foregoing verses, note (1) What manner of persons ought the ministers of Christ to be, according to the pattern here set up: absolutely subject and officially dedicated to the Lord Jesus; separated unto the gospel of God, which contemplates the subjugation of all nations to the faith of Christ: debtors to all classes, the refined and the rude, to bring the gospel to them all alike, all shame in the presence of the one, as well as pride before the other, sinking before the glory which they feel to be in their message; yearning over all faithful churches, not lording it over them, but rejoicing in their prosperity, and finding refreshment and strength in their fellowship! (2) The peculiar features of the gospel here brought prominently forward should be the devout study of all who preach it, and guide the views and the taste of all who are privileged statedly to hear it: that it is "the gospel of God," as a message from heaven, yet not absolutely new, but on the contrary, only the fulfilment of Old Testament promise, that not only is Christ the great theme of it, but Christ in the very nature of God as His own Son, and in the nature of men as partaker of their flesh—the Son of God now in resurrection-power and invested with authority to dispense all grace to men, and all gifts for the establishment and edification of the Church, Christ the righteousness provided of God for the justification of all that believe in His name; and that in this glorious Gospel, when preached as such, there resides the very power of God to save Jew and Gentile alike who embrace it. (3) While

Christ is to be regarded as the ordained *Channel* of all grace from God to men (vs. 8), let none imagine that His proper divinity is in any respect compromised by this arrangement, since He is here expressly associated with "God the Father," in prayer for "grace and peace" (including all spiritual blessings) to rest upon this Church (vs. 7). (4) While this Epistle teaches, in conformity with the teaching of our Lord Himself, that all salvation is suspended upon *faith,* this is but half a truth, and will certainly minister to self-righteousness, if dissociated from another feature of the same truth, here explicitly taught, that this faith is *God's own gift* —for which accordingly in the case of the Roman believers, he "thanks his God through Jesus Christ" (vs. 8). (5) Christian fellowship, as indeed all real fellowship, is a mutual benefit; and as it is not possible for the most eminent saints and servants of Christ to impart any refreshment and profit to the meanest of their brethren without experiencing a rich return into their bosoms, so just in proportion to their humility and love will they feel their need of it and rejoice in it.

18. WHY THIS DIVINELY PROVIDED RIGHTEOUSNESS IS NEEDED BY ALL MEN. **For the wrath of God**—His holy displeasure and righteous vengeance against sin—**is revealed from heaven**—in the consciences of men, and attested by innumerable outward evidences of a moral government. **against all ungodliness**—i.e., their whole *irreligiousness,* or their living without any conscious reference to God, and proper feelings towards Him. **and unrighteousness of men**—i.e., all their *deviations from moral rectitude* in heart, speech, and behavior. (So these terms must be distinguished when used together, though, when standing alone, either of them includes the other.)

18-32. THIS WRATH OF GOD, REVEALED AGAINST ALL INIQUITY, OVERHANGS THE WHOLE HEATHEN WORLD. **18. who hold**—rather, 'hold down,' 'hinder,' or 'keep back'—**the truth in unrighteousness**—The apostle, though he began this verse with a comprehensive proposition regarding men in general, takes up in the end of it only one of the two great divisions of mankind, to whom he meant to apply it; thus gently sliding into his argument. But before enumerating their actual iniquities, he goes back to the origin of them all, their stifling the light which still remained to them. As darkness overspreads the mind, so impotence takes possession of the heart, when the "still small voice" of conscience is first disregarded, next thwarted, and then systematically deadened. Thus "the truth" which God left with and in men, instead of having free scope and developing itself, as it otherwise would, was obstructed (cf. Matt. 6:22, 23; Eph. 4:17, 18). **19. Because that which may be**—rather, 'which is'—**known of God is manifest in them; for God hath showed it unto them**—The sense of this pregnant statement the apostle proceeds to unfold in the next verse. **20. For the invisible things of him from**—or 'since'—**the creation of the world are clearly seen**—the mind brightly beholding what the eye cannot discern—**being understood by the things that are made**—Thus, the outward creation is not the *parent* but the *interpreter* of our faith in God. That faith has its primary sources within our own breast (vs. 19); but it becomes *an intelligible and articulate conviction* only through what we observe around us ("by the things which are made," vs. 20). And thus are the inner and the outer revelation of God the complement of each other, making up between them one universal and immovable conviction *that God is.* (With this striking apostolic statement agree the latest conclusions of the most profound speculative students of Theism.) **even his eternal power and Godhead**—both that there *is* an Eternal Power, and that this is not a mere blind force, or pantheistic 'spirit of nature,' but the power of a living *Godhead.* **so that they are without excuse**—all their degeneracy being a voluntary departure from truth thus brightly revealed to the unsophisticated spirit. **21. Because that, when they knew God**—that is, while still retaining some real knowledge of Him, and ere they sank down into the state next to be described—**they glorified him not as God, neither were thankful**—neither yielded the *adoration* due to Himself, nor rendered the *gratitude* which His beneficence demanded—**but became vain** —(cf. Jer. 2:5)—**in their imaginations**—thoughts, notions, speculations, regarding God; cf. Matt. 15:19; Luke 2:35; I Cor. 3:20, Greek—**and their foolish**— 'senseless,' 'stupid'—**heart**—i.e., their whole inner man—**was darkened**—How instructively is the downward progress of the human soul here traced! **22, 23. Professing themselves**—'boasting,' or 'pretending to be—**wise, they became fools**—"It is the invariable property of error in morals and religion, that men take credit to themselves for it and extol it as wisdom. So the heathen" (I Cor. 1:21) [Tholuck]. **and changed** —or 'exchanged'—**the glory of the uncorruptible God into**—or 'for'—**an image . . . like to corruptible man**—The allusion here is doubtless to the *Greek* worship, and the apostle may have had in his mind those exquisite chisellings of the human form which lay so profusely beneath and around him as he stood on Mars' Hill; and "beheld their devotions." (See on Acts 17:29.) But as if that had not been a deep enough degradation of the living God, there was found 'a lower deep' still. **and to birds, and four-footed beasts, and to creeping things**—referring now to the *Egyptian* and *Oriental* worship. In the face of these plain declarations of the *descent* of man's religious belief from loftier to ever lower and more debasing conceptions of the Supreme Being, there are expositors of this very Epistle (as Reiche and Jowett), who, believing neither in any fall from primeval innocence, nor in the noble traces of that innocence which lingered even after the fall and were only by degrees obliterated by wilful violence to the dictates of conscience, maintain that man's religious history has been all along a struggle to *rise,* from the lowest forms of nature worship, suited to the childhood of our race, into that which is more rational and spiritual. **24. Wherefore God also**—in righteous retribution—**gave them up**—This divine abandonment of men is here strikingly traced in three successive stages, at each of which the same word is used (vs. 24; vs. 26; and vs. 28, where the word is rendered "gave over"). "As they deserted God, God in turn deserted them; not giving them divine (i.e., supernatural) laws, and suffering them to corrupt those which were human; not sending them prophets, and allowing the philosophers to run into absurdities. He let them do what they pleased, even what was in the last degree vile, that those who had not honored God, might dishonor themselves" [Grotius]. **25. Who changed the truth of God into a lie**—i.e., the truth concerning God into idol falsehood. **and worshipped and served the creature more than the Creator**—Professing merely to worship the Creator *by means of* the creature, they soon came to lose sight of the Creator *in* the creature. How aggravated is the guilt of the Church of Rome, which, under the same flimsy pretext, does shamelessly what the heathen are here condemned for doing, and with light which the heathen never had! **who is blessed for ever! Amen**—By this doxology the apostle instinctively relieves the horror which the penning of such things excited within his breast; an example to such as are called to expose like dishonor done to the blessed God. **26, 27. For this cause God gave them up**—See on vs. 24. **for even their women**—that sex whose priceless jewel and fairest ornament is modesty, and which, when that is once lost, not only becomes more shameless than the other sex, but lives henceforth only to drag the other sex down to its level. **did change . . .**—The practices here referred to, though too abundantly attested by classic authors, cannot be further illustrated, without trenching on things which "ought not to be named among us as become the saints." But observe how vice is here seen consuming and exhausting itself. When the passions, scourged by violent and continued indulgence in *natural* vices, became impotent to yield the craved enjoyment, resort was had to artificial stimulants by the practice of *unnatural* and monstrous vices. How early these were in full career, in the history of the world, the case of Sodom affectingly shows; and because of such abominations, centuries after that, the land of Canaan "spued out" its old inhabitants. Long before this chapter was penned, the Lesbians and others throughout refined Greece had been luxuriating in such debasements; and as for the Romans, Tacitus, speaking of the emperor Tiberius, tells us that new words had then to be coined to express the newly invented stimulants to jaded passion. No wonder that, thus sick and dying as was this poor humanity of ours under the highest earthly culture, its many-voiced cry for the balm in Gilead, and the Physician there, "Come over and help us," pierced the hearts of the missionaries of the Cross, and made them "not ashamed of the Gospel of Christ!" **and receiving in themselves that recompense of their error which was meet**—alluding to the many physical and moral ways in which, under the righteous government of God, vice was made self-avenging. **28-31. gave them over**—or 'up'—see on vs. 24). **to do those things which are not convenient**—in the old sense of that word, i.e., 'not becoming,' 'indecorous,' 'shameful.' **haters of God**—The word usually signifies 'God-hated,' which some here prefer, in the sense of 'abhorred of the Lord'; expressing the detestableness of their character in His sight (cf. Prov. 22:14; Ps. 73:20). But the active sense of the word, adopted in our version and by the majority of expositors, though rarer, agrees perhaps better with the context. **32. Who knowing**—from the voice of conscience, ch. 2:14, 15—**the judgment of God**—the stern law of divine procedure—**that they which commit such things are worthy of death**—here used in its widest known sense, as the uttermost of divine vengeance against sin: see Acts 28:4. **not only do the same**—which they might do under the pressure of temptation and in the heat of passion. **but have pleasure in them that do them**—deliberately set their seal to such actions by encouraging and applauding the doing of them in others. This is the climax of our apostle's charges against the heathen; and certainly, if the things are in themselves as black as possible, this settled and unblushing satisfaction at the practice of them, apart from all the blinding effects of present passion, must be regarded as the darkest feature of human depravity.—On this section, note, (1) "The wrath of God" against sin has all the dread reality of a "revelation from heaven" sounding in the consciences of men, in the self-inflicted miseries of the wicked, and in the vengeance which God's moral government, sooner or later, takes upon all who outrage it; so this "wrath of God" is not confined to high-handed crimes, or the grosser manifestations of human depravity, but is "revealed" against all violations of divine law of whatever nature— "against all ungodliness" as well as "unrighteousness of men," against all disregard of God in the conduct of life as well as against all deviations from moral rectitude; and therefore, since no child of Adam can plead guiltless either of "ungodliness" or of "unrighteousness," to a greater or less extent, it follows that every human being is involved in the awful sweep of "the wrath of God" (vs. 18). The apostle places this terrible truth in the forefront of his argument on justification by faith, that upon the basis of *universal condemnation* he might rear the edifice of a free, world-wide salvation; nor can the Gospel be scripturally preached or embraced, save as the good news of salvation to those that are all equally "lost." (2) We must not magnify the supernatural revelation which God has been pleased to make of Himself, through Abraham's family to the human race, at the expense of that older, and, in itself, lustrous revelation which He has made to the whole family of man through the medium of their own nature and the creation around them. Without the latter, the former would have been impossible, and those who have not been favored with the former will be without excuse, if they are deaf to the voice and blind to the glory of the latter (vss. 19, 20). (3) Wilful resistance of light has a retributive tendency to blunt the moral perceptions and weaken the capacity to apprehend and approve of truth and goodness; and thus is the soul prepared to surrender itself, to an indefinite extent, to error and sin (vs. 21, etc.). (4) Pride of wisdom, as it is a convincing evidence of the want of it, so it makes the attainment of it impossible (vs. 22; and cf. Matt. 11:25; I Cor. 3:18-20). (5) As idolatry, even in its most plausible forms, is the fruit of unworthy views of the Godhead, so its natural effect is to vitiate and debase still further the religious conceptions; nor is there any depth of degradation too low and too revolting for men's ideas of the Godhead to sink to, if only their natural temperament and the circumstances they are placed in be favorable to their unrestrained development (vss. 23, 25). The apostle had Greece and Egypt in his eye when he penned this description. But all the paganisms of the East at this day attest its accuracy, from the more elaborate idolatry of India and the simpler and more stupid idolatry of China down to the childish rudiments of nature worship prevalent among the savage tribes. Alas! Christendom itself furnishes a melancholy illustration of this truth; the constant use of material images in the Church of Rome and the materialistic and sensuous character of its entire service (to say nothing of the less offensive but more stupid service of the Greek Church,) debasing the religious ideas of millions of nominal Christians, and lowering the whole character and tone of Christianity as represented within their immense pale. (6) Moral corruption invariably follows religious debasement. The grossness of pagan idolatry is only equalled by the revolting character and frightful extent of the immoralities which it fostered and consecrated (vss. 24, 26, 27). And so strikingly is this to be seen in all its essential features in the East at this day, that (as HODGE says) the missionaries have frequently been accused by the natives of having forged the whole of the

latter part of this chapter, as they could not believe that so accurate a description of themselves could have been written eighteen centuries ago. The kingdoms of Israel and Judah furnish a striking illustration of the inseparable connection between religion and morals. Israel corrupted and debased the worship of Jehovah, and the sins with which they were charged were mostly of the grosser kind —intemperance and sensuality: the people of Judah, remaining faithful to the pure worship, were for a long time charged mostly with formality and hypocrisy; and only as they fell into the idolatries of the heathen around them, did they sink into their vices. And may not a like distinction be observed between the two great divisions of Christendom, the Popish and the Protestant? To test this, we must not look to Popery, surrounded with, and more or less influenced by, the presence and power of Protestantism; nor to Protestantism under every sort of disadvantage, internal and external. But look at Romanism where it has unrestrained liberty to develop its true character, and see whether impurity does not there taint society to its core, pervading alike the highest and the lowest classes; and then look at Protestantism where it enjoys the same advantages, and see whether it be not marked by a comparatively high standard of social virtue. (7) To take pleasure in what is sinful and vicious for its own sake, and knowing it to be such, is the last and lowest stage of human recklessness (vs. 32). But (8) this knowledge can never be wholly extinguished in the breast of men. So long as reason remains to them, there is still a small voice in the worst of men, protesting, in the name of the Power that implanted it, "that they which do such things are worthy of death" (vs. 32).

CHAPTER 2

Vss. 1-29. THE JEW UNDER LIKE CONDEMNATION WITH THE GENTILE. From those *without*, the apostle now turns to those *within* the pale of revealed religion, the self-righteous Jews, who looked down upon the uncovenanted heathen as beyond the pale of God's mercies, within which they deemed themselves secure, however inconsistent their life may be. Alas! what multitudes wrap themselves up in like fatal confidence, who occupy the corresponding position in the Christian Church! **4. the goodness of God leadeth thee to repentance** —i.e., is designed and adapted to do so. **5. treasurest up unto thyself wrath against**—rather 'in'— **the day of wrath**—i.e., wrath to come on thee in the day of wrath. What an awful idea is here expressed—that the sinner himself is amassing, like hoarded treasure, an ever accumulating stock of divine wrath, to burst upon him in "the day of the revelation of the righteous judgment of God!" And this is said not of the reckless, but of those who boasted of their purity of faith and life. **7-10. To them who . . .**—The substance of these verses is that the final judgment will turn upon *character* alone. **by patient continuance in well-doing . . .**— Cf. Luke 8:15: "That on the good ground are they, which in an honest and good heart, having heard the word, keep it, and bring forth fruit *with patience";* denoting the *enduring* and *progressive* character of the new life. **But unto them that are contentious, and do not obey the truth . . .**—referring to such keen and determined resistance to the Gospel as he himself had too painfully witnessed on the part of his own countrymen. (See Acts 13:

44-46; 17:5, 13; 18:6, 12; and cf. I Thess. 2:15, 16.) **indignation and wrath**—in the bosom of a sin-avenging God. **Tribulation and anguish**—the *effect* of these in the sinner himself.**to the Jew first**—first in perdition if unfaithful; but if obedient to the truth, first in salvation (vs. 10). **11, 12. For as many as have sinned**—not 'as many as have sinned *at all*,' but, 'as many as are *found in sin*' at the judgment of the great day (as the whole context shows). **without law**—i.e., without the advantage of a positive Revelation. **shall also perish without law**—exempt from the charge of rejecting or disregarding it. **and as many as have sinned in the law**—within the pale of a positive, written Revelation. **shall be judged by the law**—tried and condemned by the higher standard of that written Revelation. **13-15. For not the hearers . . .**—As touching the Jews, in whose ears the written law is continually resounding, the condemnation of as many of them as are found sinners at the last involves no difficulty; but even as respects the heathen, who are strangers to the law in its positive and written form—since they show how deeply it is engraven on their moral nature, which witnesses within them for righteousness and against iniquity, accusing or condemning them according as they violate or obey its stern dictates—their condemnation also for all the sin in which they live and die will carry its dreadful echo in their own breasts. **their thoughts the meanwhile accusing or else excusing**—i.e., perhaps by turns doing both. **16. In the day . . .**—Here the unfinished statement of vs. 12 is resumed and closed. **shall judge the secrets of men**—here specially referring to the unfathomed depths of hypocrisy in the self-righteous whom the apostle had to deal with. (See Eccles. 12:14; I Cor. 4:5.) **according to my gospel**—to my teaching as a preacher of the Gospel. **7-24. Behold**—'But if' is, beyond doubt, the true reading here. (It differs but in a single letter from the received reading, and the sense is the same.) **approvest the things that are excellent**—*Margin*, 'triest the things that differ.' Both senses are good, and indeed the former is but the result of the latter action. (See on Phil. 1:10.) **hast the form of knowledge and of the truth in the law**—not being left, as the heathen are, to vague conjecture on divine things, but favored with definite and precise information from heaven. **thou that abhorrest idols**—as the Jews did ever after their captivity, though bent on them before—**dost thou commit sacrilege?**—not, as some excellent interpreters, 'dost thou rob idol-temples?' but more generally, as we take it, 'dost thou profane holy things?' (as in Matt. 21:12, 13, and in other ways). **as it is written**—(See *Marginal reference*.) **25-29. For circumcision**—i.e., One's being within the covenant of which circumcision was the outward sign and seal. **verily profiteth, if thou keep the law**—if the inward reality correspond to the outward sign. **but if . . .**—i.e., 'Otherwise, thou art no better than the uncircumcised heathen.' **Therefore if the uncircumcision keep the . . . law . . .**—Two mistaken interpretations, we think, are given of these words: *First*, that the case here supposed is an impossible one, and put merely for illustration [HALDANE, CHALMERS, HODGE]; *second* that it is the case of the heathen who may and do please God when they act, as has been and is done, up to the light of nature [GROTIUS, OLSHAUSEN, etc.]. The first interpretation is, in our judgment, unnatural; the second, opposed to the apostle's own teaching. But the case here put is, we think, such as that of Cornelius (Acts 10), who, though outside the *external* pale of God's covenant,

yet having come to the knowledge of the truths contained in it, do manifest the grace of the covenant without the seal of it, and exemplify the character and walk of Abraham's children, though not called by the name of Abraham. Thus, this is but another way of announcing that God was about to show the insufficiency of the mere badge of the Abrahamic covenant, by calling from among the Gentiles a seed of Abraham that had never received the seal of circumcision (see on Gal. 5:6); and this interpretation is confirmed by all that follows. **he is not a Jew which is one outwardly . . .**—In other words, the name of "Jew" and the rite of "circumcision" were designed but as outward symbols of a separation from the irreligious and ungodly world unto holy devotedness in heart and life to the God of salvation. Where this is realized, the signs are full of significance; but where it is not, they are worse than useless. Note, (1) It is a sad mark of depravity when all that is designed and fitted to melt within hardens the heart (vs. 4, and cf. II Pet. 3:9; Eccles. 8:11). (2) Amidst all the inequalities of religious opportunity measured out to men, and the mysterious bearing of this upon their character and destiny for eternity, the same great principles of judgment, in a form suited to their respective discipline, will be applied to all, and perfect equity will be seen to reign throughout every stage of the divine administration (vss. 11-16). (3) "The law written on the heart" (vss. 14, 15)—or the Ethics of Natural Theology—may be said to be the one deep foundation on which all revealed religion reposes; and see on ch. 1:19, 20, where we have what we may call its other foundation—the Physics and Metaphysics of Natural Theology. The testimony of these two passages is to the theologian invaluable, while in the breast of every teachable Christian it wakens such deep echoes as are inexpressibly solemn and precious. (4) High religious professions are a fearful aggravation of the inconsistencies of such as make them (vss. 17-24). See II Samuel 12:14. (5) As no external privileges, or badge of discipleship, will shield the unholy from the wrath of God, so neither will the want of them shut out from the kingdom of heaven such as have experienced without them that change of heart which the seals of God's covenant were designed to mark. In the sight of the great Searcher of hearts, the Judge of quick and dead, the renovation of the character in heart and life is all in all. In view of this, have not all baptized, sacramented disciples of the Lord Jesus, who "profess that they know God, but in works deny Him," need to tremble—who, under the guise of friends, are "the enemies of the cross of Christ"?

CHAPTER 3

Vss. 1-8. JEWISH OBJECTIONS ANSWERED. **1, 2. What advantage then hath the Jew?**—i.e., 'If the final judgment will turn solely on the state of the heart, and this may be as good in the Gentile *without*, as in the Jew *within*, the sacred enclosure of God's covenant, what better are we Jews for all our advantages? *Answer:* **Much every way; chiefly, because**—(rather, 'first, that')—**unto them were committed the oracles of God**—This remarkable expression, denoting 'divine communications' in general, is transferred to the Scriptures to express their *oracular*, divine, authoritative character. **3, 4. For what if some did not believe?**—It is the unbelief of the great body of the nation which the apostle points at; but as it sufficed for his argument to put the supposition thus gently, he uses this word "some" to soften prejudice. **shall their unbelief make the faith**—or, faithfulness—**of God of none effect?**—'nullify,' 'invalidate' it. **God forbid**—lit., *'Let it not be,'* i.e., 'Away with such a thought'—a favorite expression of our apostle, when he would not only repudiate a supposed consequence of his doctrine, but express his abhorrence of it. "The Scriptures do not authorize such a use of God's name as must have been common among the English translators of the Bible" [HODGE]. **yea, let God be**—held—**true, and every man a liar**—i.e., even though it should follow from this that every man is a liar. **when thou art judged**—so in Psalm 51:4, according to the LXX; but in the *Hebrew* and in our version, 'when thou judgest.' The general sentiment, however, is the same in both—that we are to vindicate the righteousness of God, at whatever expense to ourselves. **5, 6. But if ...** —Another objection: 'It would appear, then, that the more faithless we are, so much the more illustrious will the fidelity of God appear; and in that case, for Him to take vengeance on us for our unfaithfulness would be (to speak as men profanely do) unrighteousness in God.' *Answer:* **God forbid; for then how shall God judge the world?**—i.e., 'Far from us be such a thought; for that would strike down all future judgment. **7, 8. For if the truth of God ...**—A further illustration of the same sentiment: i.e., 'Such reasoning amounts to this—which indeed we who preach salvation by free grace are slanderously accused of teaching—that the more evil we do, the more glory will redound to God; a damnable principle.' (Thus the apostle, instead of refuting this principle, thinks it enough to hold it up to execration, as one that shocks the moral sense.)—On this brief section, Note (1) Mark the place here assigned to the Scriptures. In answer to the question, "What advantage hath the Jew?" or, "What profit is there of circumcision?" those holding Romish views would undoubtedly have laid the stress upon the *priesthood,* as the glory of the Jewish economy. But in the apostle's esteem, "the oracles of God" were the jewel of the ancient Church (vss. 1, 2). (2) God's eternal purposes and man's free agency, as also the doctrine of salvation by grace and the unchanging obligations of God's law, have ever been subjected to the charge of inconsistency by those who will bow to no truth which their own reason cannot fathom. But amidst all the clouds and darkness which in this present state envelop the divine administration and many of the truths of the Bible, such broad and deep principles as are here laid down, and which shine in their own luster, will be found the sheet-anchor of our faith. "Let God be true, and every man a liar"; and as many advocates of salvation by grace as say, "Let us do evil that good may come," "their damnation is just."

9-20. THAT THE JEW IS SHUT UP UNDER LIKE CONDEMNATION WITH THE GENTILE IS PROVED BY HIS OWN SCRIPTURE. **9. are we better than they?**—'do we excel them?' **No, in no wise**—Better off the Jews certainly were, for having the oracles of God to *teach* them better; but as they *were* no better, that only aggravated their guilt. **10-12. As it is written ...**—(Ps. 14:1-3; 53:1-3). These statements of the Psalmist were indeed suggested by particular manifestations of human depravity occurring under his own eye; but as this only showed what man, when unrestrained, is in his present condition, they were quite pertinent to the apostle's purpose. **13-18. Their ...**—From generals, the apostle here comes to particulars, culling from different parts of Scripture passages which speak of depravity as it affects *the different members of the body;* as if to show more affectingly how "from the sole of the foot even to the head there is no soundness" in us. **Their throat is an open sepulchre**—(Ps. 5:9); i.e., 'What proceeds out of their heart, and finds vent in speech and action through the throat, is like the pestilential breath of an open grave.' **with their tongues they have used deceit**—(Ps. 5:9); i.e., 'That tongue which is man's glory (Ps. 16:9; 57:8) is prostituted to the purposes of deception.' **the poison of asps is under their lips**—(Ps. 140:3): i.e., 'Those lips which should "drop as an honey-comb," and "feed many," and "give thanks unto His name" (Canticles 4:11; Prov. 10:21; Heb. 13:15), are employed to secrete and to dart deadly poison.' **Whose mouth ...**—(Ps. 10:7): i.e., 'That mouth which should be "most sweet" (Canticles 5:16), being "set on fire of hell" (Jas. 3:6), is filled with burning wrath against those whom it should only bless.' **Their feet are swift to shed blood**—(Prov. 1:16; Isa. 59:7): i.e., 'Those feet, which should "run the way of God's commandments" (Ps. 119:32), are employed to conduct men to deeds of darkest crime.' **Destruction and misery are in their ways; and the way of peace have they not known**—This is a supplementary statement about men's *ways,* suggested by what had been said about the "feet," and expresses the mischief and misery which men scatter in their path, instead of that peace which, as strangers to it themselves, they cannot diffuse. **There is no fear of God before their** EYES—(Ps. 36:1): i.e., 'Did the eyes but "see Him who is invisible" (Heb. 11:27), a reverential awe of Him with whom we have to do would chasten every joy and lift the soul out of its deepest depressions; but to all this the natural man is a stranger.' How graphic is this picture of human depravity, finding its way through each several organ of the body into the life: but how small a part of the "desperate wickedness" that is *within* (Jer. 17:9) "proceedeth *out of* the heart of man!" (Mark 7:21-23; Ps. 19:12.) **19. Now we know that what ... the law**—i.e., the Scriptures, considered as a law of duty—**saith, it saith to them that are under the law**—of course, therefore, to the Jews. **that every mouth**—opened in self-justification—**may be stopped, and all the world may become**—i.e., be seen to be, and own itself—**guilty**—and so condemned—**before God. 20. Therefore by the deeds of**—obedience to—**the law there shall no flesh be justified**—i.e., be held and treated as righteous; as is plain from the whole scope and strain of the argument. **in his sight**—at His bar (Ps. 143:2). **for by the law is the knowledge of sin**—See on ch. 4:15; 7:7; I John 3:4).—Note: How broad and deep does the apostle in this section lay the foundations of his great doctrine of Justification by free grace—in the disorder of man's whole nature, the consequent universality of human guilt, the condemnation, by reason of the breach of divine law, of the whole world, and the impossibility of justification before God by obedience to that violated law! Only when these humiliating conclusions are accepted and felt, are we in a condition to appreciate and embrace the grace of the Gospel, next to be opened up.

21-26. GOD'S JUSTIFYING RIGHTEOUSNESS, THROUGH FAITH IN JESUS CHRIST, ALIKE ADAPTED TO OUR NECESSITIES AND WORTHY OF HIMSELF. **21-23. But now the righteousness of God**—see on ch. 1:17 —**without the law**—i.e., a righteousness to which our obedience to the law contributes nothing whatever (vs. 28; Gal. 2:16). **is manifested, being witnessed** —attested—**by the law and the prophets**—the Old Testament Scriptures. Thus this justifying righteousness, though *new*, as only now fully disclosed, is an *old* righteousness, predicted and foreshadowed in the Old Testament. **by faith of**—i.e., in—**Jesus Christ unto all and upon all them that believe**— i.e., perhaps, brought nigh *"unto* all" men the Gospel, and actually *"upon* all" believing men, as theirs in possession [LUTHER and others]; but most interpreters understand both statements of believers as only a more emphatic way of saying that all believers, without distinction or exception, are put in possession of this gratuitous justification, purely by faith in Christ Jesus. **for there is no difference; for all have sinned**—Though men differ greatly in the *nature* and *extent* of their sinfulness, there is absolutely no difference between the best and the worst of men, in the *fact* that "all have sinned," and so underlie the wrath of God. **and come short of the glory**—or 'praise'—**of God**—i.e., 'have failed to earn His approbation' (cf. John 12:43, *Greek*). So the best interpreters. **24. justified freely**—without anything done on our part to deserve—**by his grace** —His free love—**through the redemption that is in Christ Jesus**—a most important clause; teaching us that though justification is quite gratuitous, it is not a mere *fiat* of the divine will, but based on a "Redemption," i.e., 'the payment of a Ransom,' in Christ's death. That this is the sense of the word 're-demption,' when applied to Christ's death, will appear clear to any impartial student of the passages where it occurs. **25, 26. Whom God hath set forth to be a propitiation**—or 'propitiatory sacrifice'— **through faith in his blood**—Some of the best interpreters, observing that "faith *upon*" is the usual phrase in Greek, not "faith *in*" Christ, would place a comma after "faith," and understand the words as if written thus: "to be a propitiation, in His blood, through faith." But "faith *in* Christ" is used in Galatians 3:26 and Ephesians 1:15; and "faith in His blood" is the natural and appropriate meaning here. **to declare his righteousness for the remission**—rather, 'pretermission' or 'passing by'—**of sins** —'the sins'—**that are past**—not the sins committed by the believer before he embraces Christ, but the sins committed under the old economy, before Christ came to "put away sin by the sacrifice of Himself." **through the forbearance of God**—God not *remitting* but only *forbearing* to punish them, or passing them by, until an adequate atonement for them should be made. In thus not imputing them, God *was* righteous, but He was not *seen* to be so; there was no "manifestation of His righteousness" in doing so under the ancient economy. But now that God can "set forth" Christ as a "propitiation for sin through faith in His blood," the righteousness of His procedure in passing by the sins of believers before, and in now remitting them, is "manifested," declared, brought fully out to the view of the whole world. (Our translators have unfortunately missed this glorious truth, taking "the sins that are past" to mean the past sins of believers —committed before faith—and rendering, by the word "remission," what means only a 'passing by'; thus making it appear that "remission of sins" is "through the forbearance of God," which it certainly is not.) **To declare ... at this time**—now for the first time, under the Gospel—**his righteousness: that he might be just, and the justifier of him that believeth in Jesus**—Glorious paradox! 'Just in punishing,' and 'merciful in pardoning,' men can understand; but 'just in justifying the guilty,' startles

them. But the propitiation through faith in Christ's blood resolves the paradox and harmonizes the discordant elements. For in that "God hath made Him to be sin for us who knew no sin," *justice* has full satisfaction; and in that "we are made the righteousness of God in Him," *mercy* has her heart's delight!—Note (1) One way of a sinner's justification is taught in the Old Testament and in the New alike: only more dimly during the twilight of Revelation; in unclouded light under its perfect day (vs. 21). (2) As there is no difference in the *need,* so is there none in the *liberty to appropriate* the provided salvation. The best need to be saved by faith in Jesus Christ; and the worst only need that. On this common ground all saved sinners meet here, and will stand for ever (vss. 22-24). (3) It is on the atoning blood of Christ, as the one propitiatory sacrifice which God hath set forth to the eye of the guilty, that the faith of the convinced and trembling sinner fastens for deliverance from wrath. Though he knows that he is "justified freely, by God's grace," it is only because it is "through the *redemption* that is in Christ Jesus" that he is able to find peace and rest even in this (vs. 25). (4) The strictly accurate view of believers under the Old Testament is not that of a company of *pardoned* men, but of men whose sins, put up with and passed by in the meantime, awaited a *future expiation* in the fulness of time (vss. 25, 26; see on Luke 9:31; and on Heb. 9:15; and 11:39, 40).

27-31. INFERENCES FROM THE FOREGOING DOCTRINES, AND AN OBJECTION ANSWERED. Inference first: *Boasting is excluded by this, and no other way of justification.* **27, 28. Where is boasting then? ... excluded. By what law?**—on what principle or scheme?—**of works? Nay; but by the law of faith. Therefore we conclude ...** —It is the unavoidable tendency of dependence upon our own works, less or more, for acceptance with God, to beget a spirit of "boasting." But that God should encourage such a spirit in sinners, by any procedure of His, is incredible. This therefore stamps falsehood upon every form of 'justification by works,' whereas the doctrine that.

> Our faith *receives* a righteousness
> That makes the sinner just,

manifestly and entirely excludes "boasting"; and this is the best evidence of its truth. Inference second: *This and no other way of salvation is adapted alike to Jew and Gentile.* **29. Is he the God of the Jews only? ...**—The way of salvation must be one equally suited to the whole family of fallen man: but the doctrine of justification by faith is the only one that lays the basis of a Universal Religion; this therefore is another mark of its truth. **30. it is one God who shall justify**—'has unchangeably fixed that He shall justify'—**the circumcision by**—'of'—**faith, and the uncircumcision through faith** —probably this is but a varied statement of the same truth for greater emphasis (see on vs. 22); though BENGEL thinks that the justification of the Jews, as the born heirs of the promise, may be here purposely said to be *"of* faith," while that of the Gentiles, previously "strangers to the covenants of promise," may be said to be *"through* faith," as thus admitted into a new family. *Objection.* **31. Do we then make void the law through faith?**— 'Does this doctrine of justification by faith, then, dissolve the obligation of the law? If so, it cannot be of God. But away with such a thought, for it does just the reverse.' **God forbid: yea, we estab-**

lish the law—It will be observed here, that, important as was this objection, and opening up as it did so noble a field for the illustration of the peculiar glory of the Gospel, the apostle does no more here than indignantly repel it, intending at a subsequent stage of his argument (ch. 6) to resume and discuss it at length.—Note (1) It is a fundamental requisite of all true religion that it tend to humble the sinner and exalt God; and every system which breeds self-righteousness, or cherishes boasting, bears falsehood on its face (vss. 27, 28). (2) The fitness of the Gospel to be a universal religion, beneath which the guilty of every name and degree are invited and warranted to take shelter and repose, is a glorious evidence of its truth (vss. 29, 30). (3) The glory of God's law, in its eternal and immutable obligations, is then only fully apprehended by the sinner, and then only is it enthroned in the depths of his soul, when, believing that "He was made sin for him who knew no sin," he sees himself "made the righteousness of God in Him." Thus do we not make void the law through faith: yea, we establish the law. (4) This chapter, and particularly the latter part of it, "is the proper seat of the Pauline doctrine of Justification, and the grand proof-passage of the Protestant doctrine of the Imputation of Christ's righteousness and of Justification not on account of, but through faith alone" [PHILIPPI]. To make good this doctrine, and reseat it in the faith and affection of the Church, was worth all the bloody struggles that it cost our fathers, and it will be the wisdom and safety, the life and vigor of the churches, to "stand fast in this liberty wherewith Christ hath made them free, and not be again entangled"—in the very least degree—"with the yoke of bondage."

CHAPTER 4

Vss. 1-25. THE FOREGOING DOCTRINE OF JUSTIFICATION BY FAITH ILLUSTRATED FROM THE OLD TESTAMENT. First: *Abraham was justified by faith.* **1-3. What shall we say then that Abraham, our father as pertaining to the flesh, hath found?**—i.e., (as the order in the original shows), 'hath found, as pertaining to ("according to," or "through") the flesh'; meaning, 'by all his natural efforts or legal obedience.' **For if Abraham were justified by works, he hath whereof to glory; but not before God**—'If works were the ground of Abraham's justification, he would have matter for boasting; but as it is perfectly certain that he hath none in the sight of God, it follows that Abraham could not have been justified by works.' And to this agree the words of Scripture. **For what saith the Scripture? Abraham believed God, and it**—his faith—**was counted to him for righteousness**—Gen. 15.6. Romish expositors and Arminian Protestants make this to mean that God accepted Abraham's act of believing as a substitute for complete obedience. But this is at variance with the whole spirit and letter of the apostle's teaching. Throughout this whole argument, *faith* is set in direct opposition to *works*, in the matter of justification—and even in the next two verses. The meaning, therefore, cannot possibly be that the mere act of believing—which is as much a work as any other piece of commanded duty (John 6:29; I John 3:23)—was counted to Abraham for all obedience. The meaning plainly is that Abraham believed in the promises which embraced Christ (Gen. 12:3; 15:5, etc.), as we believe in Christ Himself; and in both cases, faith is

merely the instrument that puts us in possession of the blessing gratuitously bestowed. **4, 5. Now to him that worketh**—as a servant for wages—**is the reward not reckoned of grace**—as a matter of favor—**but of debt**—as a matter of right. **But to him that worketh not**—who, despairing of acceptance with God by "working" for it the work of obedience, does not attempt it—**but believeth on him that justifieth the ungodly**—casts himself upon the mercy of Him that justifieth those who deserve only condemnation. **his faith ...**—See on vs. 3. Second: *David sings of the same justification.* **6-8. David also describeth**—'speaketh,' 'pronounceth'—**the blessedness of the man unto whom the Lord imputeth righteousness without works**—whom, though void of all good works, He, nevertheless, regards and treats as righteous. **Saying, Blessed ...** —(Ps. 32:1, 2). David here sings in express terms only of "transgression forgiven, sin covered, iniquity not imputed"; but as the negative blessing necessarily includes the positive, the passage is strictly in point. **9-12. Cometh this blessedness then ...**—i.e., 'Say not, All this is spoken of the *circumcised*, and is therefore no evidence of God's *general* way of justifying men; for Abraham's justification took place long before he was circumcised, and so could have no dependence upon that rite: nay, "the sign of circumcision" was given to Abraham as "a seal" (or token) of the (justifying) righteousness which he had *before* he was circumcised; in order that he might stand forth to every age as *the parent believer*—the model man of justification by faith—after whose type, as the first public example of it, all were to be moulded, whether Jew or Gentile, who should thereafter believe to life everlasting.' **13-15. For the promise ...**—This is merely an enlargement of the foregoing reasoning, applying to the *law* what had just been said of *circumcision*. **that he should be the heir of the world**—or, that "all the families of the earth should be blessed in him." **was not to Abraham or to his seed through the law**—in virtue of obedience to the law—**but through the righteousness of faith**—in virtue of his simple faith in the divine promises. **For if they which are of the law be heirs**—If the blessing is to be earned by obedience to the law. **faith is made void**—the whole divine method is subverted. **Because the law worketh wrath**—has nothing to give to those who break it but condemnation and vengeance. **for where there is no law, there is no transgression**—It is just the law that makes transgression, in the case of those who break it; nor can the one exist without the other. **16, 17. Therefore ...**—A general summary: 'Thus justification is by *faith,* in order that it is purely *gracious* character may be seen, and that all who follow in the steps of Abraham's faith—whether of his natural seed or no—may be assured of the like justification with the parent-believer.' **As it is written ...**— (Gen. 17:5). This is quoted to justify his calling Abraham the "father of us all," and is to be viewed as a parenthesis. **before**—i.e., 'in the reckoning of' **—him whom he believed**—i.e., 'Thus Abraham, in the reckoning of Him whom he believed, is the father of us all, in order that all may be assured, that doing as he did, they shall be treated as he was.' **even God, quickeneth the dead**—The nature and greatness of that faith of Abraham which we are to copy is here strikingly described. What he was required to believe being above nature, his faith had to fasten upon God's power to surmount physical incapacity, and call into being what did not then exist. But God having made the promise,

Abraham believed Him in spite of those obstacles. This is still further illustrated in what follows. **18-22. Who against hope**—when no ground for hope appeared. **believed in hope**—i.e., cherished the believing expectation. **that he might become the father of many nations, according to that which was spoken, So**—i.e., Such "as the stars of heaven," Gen. 15:5—**shall thy seed be . . . he considered not . . .**—paid no attention to those physical obstacles, both in himself and in Sarah, which might seem to render the fulfilment hopeless. **He staggered**—hesitated—**not . . . but was strong in faith, giving glory to God**—as able to make good His own word in spite of all obstacles. **And being fully persuaded . . .**—i.e., the glory which Abraham's faith gave to God consisted in this, that, firm in the persuasion of God's ability to fulfil his promise, no difficulties shook him. **And therefore it was imputed . . .**—'Let all then take notice that this was not because of anything meritorious in Abraham, but merely because he so *believed*.' **23-25. Now . . .**—Here is the application of this whole argument about Abraham: These things were not recorded as mere historical facts, but as illustrations for all time of God's method of justification by faith. **to whom it shall be imputed, if we believe in him that raised up Jesus our Lord from the dead**—in Him that *hath* done this, even as Abraham believed that God *would* raise up a seed in whom all nations should be blessed. **Who was delivered for**—'on account of'—**our offences**—i.e., in order to expiate them by His blood. **and raised again for**—'on account of,' i.e., in order to—**our justification**—As His resurrection was the divine assurance that He had "put away sin by the sacrifice of Himself," and the crowning of His whole work, our justification is fitly connected with that glorious act. *Note,* (1) The doctrine of justification by works, as it generates self-exaltation, is contrary to the first principles of all true religion (vs. 2; and see on ch. 3:21-26, *Note* 1). (2) The way of a sinner's justification has been the same in all time, and the testimony of the Old Testament on this subject is one with that of the New (vs. 3, etc., and see on ch. 3:27-31, *Note* 1). (3) Faith and works, in the matter of justification, are opposite and irreconcilable, even as grace and debt (vss. 4, 5; and see on ch. 11:6). If God "justifies the ungodly," works cannot be, in any sense or to any degree, the ground of justification. For the same reason, the first requisite, in order to justification, must be (under the conviction that we are "ungodly") to despair of it by works; and the next, to "believe in Him that justifieth the ungodly"—that hath a justifying righteousness to bestow, and is ready to bestow it upon those who deserve none, and to embrace it accordingly. (4) The sacraments of the Church were never intended, and are not adapted, to *confer* grace, or the blessings of salvation, upon men. Their proper use is to set a divine *seal* upon *a state already existing,* and so, they *presuppose,* and do not *create* it (vss. 8-12). As circumcision merely "sealed" Abraham's already existing acceptance with God, so with the sacraments of the New Testament. (5) As Abraham is "the heir of the world," all nations being blessed in him, through his Seed Christ Jesus, and justified solely according to the pattern of his faith, so the transmission of the true religion and all the salvation which the world will ever experience shall yet be traced back with wonder, gratitude, and joy, to that morning dawn when "the God of glory appeared unto our father Abraham, when he was in Mesopotamia, before he dwelt in Charran," Acts 7:

2 (vs. 13). (6) Nothing gives more glory to God than simple faith in His word, especially when all things seem to render the fulfilment of it hopeless (vss. 18-21). (7) All the Scripture examples of faith were recorded on purpose to beget and encourage the like faith in every succeeding age (vss. 23, 24; and cf. ch. 15:4). (8) *Justification,* in this argument, cannot be taken—as Romanists and other errorists insist—to mean a change upon men's *character;* for besides that this is to confound it with *Sanctification,* which has its appropriate place in this Epistle, the whole argument of the present chapter—and nearly all its more important clauses, expressions, and words—would in that case be unsuitable, and fitted only to mislead. Beyond all doubt it means exclusively a change upon men's *state* or *relation to God;* or, in scientific language, it is an *objective,* not a *subjective* change—a change from guilt and condemnation to acquittal and acceptance. And the best evidence that this is the key to the whole argument is, that it opens all the wards of the many-chambered lock with which the apostle has enriched us in this Epistle.

CHAPTER 5

Vss. 1-11. THE BLESSED EFFECTS OF JUSTIFICATION BY FAITH. The *proof* of this doctrine being now concluded, the apostle comes here to treat of its *fruits,* reserving the full consideration of this topic to another stage of the argument (ch. 8). **1. Therefore being**—'having been'—**justified by faith, we have peace with God . . .**—If we are to be guided by MS. authority, the true reading here, beyond doubt, is, 'Let us have peace'; a reading, however, which most reject, because they think it unnatural to exhort men to *have* what it belongs to God to *give,* because the apostle is not here giving exhortations, but stating matters of fact. But as it seems hazardous to set aside the decisive testimony of MSS., as to what the apostle *did* write, in favor of what we merely think he *ought* to have written, let us pause and ask—If it be the privilege of the justified to "*have* peace with God," why might not the apostle begin his enumeration of the fruits of justification by calling on believers to 'realize' this peace as belonged to them, or cherish the joyful consciousness of it as their own? And if this is what he has done, it would not be necessary to continue in the same style, and the other fruits of justification might be set down simply as matters of fact. This "peace" is first a change in God's relation to us; and next, as the consequence of this, a change on our part towards Him. God, on the one hand, has "reconciled us to Himself by Jesus Christ" (II Cor. 5:18); and we, on the other hand, setting our seal to this, "are reconciled to God" (II Cor. 5:20). The "propitiation" is the meeting-place; there the controversy on both sides terminates in an honorable and eternal "peace." **2. By whom also we have**—'have had'—**access by faith into this grace**—favor with God—**wherein we stand**—i.e., 'To that same faith which *first* gave us "peace with God" we owe our introduction into that *permanent standing* in the favor of God which the justified enjoy.' As it is difficult to distinguish this from the peace first mentioned, we regard it as merely an additional phase of the same [MEYER, PHILIPPI, MEHRING], rather than something new [BEZA, THOLUCK, HODGE]. **and rejoice**—'glory,' 'boast,' 'triumph'—'rejoice' is not strong enough. **in hope of the glory of God**—See on "hope," vs. 4. **3, 4. we glory in**

tribulation also; knowing that tribulation worketh patience–Patience is the quiet endurance of what we cannot but wish removed, whether it be the withholding of promised good (ch. 8:25), or the continued experience of positive ill (as here). There is indeed a patience of unrenewed nature, which has something noble in it, though in many cases the offspring of pride, if not of something lower. Men have been known to endure every form of privation, torture, and death, without a murmur and without even visible emotion, merely because they deemed it unworthy of them to sink under unavoidable ill. But this proud, stoical hardihood has nothing in common with the *grace* of patience–which is either the meek endurance of ill because it is of God (Job 1:21, 22; 2:10), or the calm waiting for promised good till His time to dispense it come (Heb. 10:36); in the full persuasion that such trials are divinely appointed, are the needed discipline of God's children, are but for a definite period, and are not sent without abundant promises of "songs in the night." If such be the "patience" which "tribulation worketh," no wonder that **patience worketh experience**–rather 'proof,' as the same word is rendered in II Corinthians 2:9; 13:3; Philippians 2:22; i.e., experimental *evidence* that we have "believed through grace." **and experience** –'proof'–**hope**–"of the glory of God," as prepared for us. Thus have we hope in two distinct ways, and at two successive stages of the Christian life: *first,* immediately on believing, along with the sense of peace and abiding access to God (vs. 1); *next,* after the reality of this faith has been "proved," particularly by the patient endurance of trials sent to test it. We first get it by looking *away from ourselves* to the Lamb of God; next by looking *into* or *upon ourselves* as transformed by that "looking unto Jesus." In the one case, the mind acts (as they say) *objectively;* in the other, *subjectively.* The one is (as divines say) the *assurance of faith;* the other, the *assurance of sense.* **5. And hope maketh not ashamed**–putteth not to shame, as empty hopes do–**because the love of God**–i.e., not 'our love to God,' as the Romish and some Protestant expositors (following some of the Fathers) represent it; but clearly 'God's love to us'–as most expositors agree. **is shed abroad**–lit., 'poured forth,' i.e., copiously diffused (cf. John 7:38; Titus 3:6). **by the Holy Ghost which is**–rather 'was'– **given unto us**–i.e., at the great Pentecostal effusion, which is viewed as the formal donation of the Spirit to the Church of God, for all time and for each believer. (*The Holy Ghost is here first introduced in this Epistle.*) It is as if the apostle had said, 'And how can this hope of glory, which as believers we cherish, put us to shame, when we feel God Himself, by His Spirit given to us, drenching our hearts in sweet, all-subduing sensations of His wondrous love to us in Christ Jesus?" This leads the apostle to expatiate on the amazing character of that love. **6-8. For when we were yet without strength**–i.e., powerless to deliver ourselves, and so ready to perish. **in due time**–at the appointed season–**Christ died for the ungodly**–Three signal properties of God's love are here given: First, "Christ died *for the ungodly,*" whose character, so far from meriting any interposition in their behalf, was altogether repulsive to the eye of God; second, He did this "when they were *without strength*"– with nothing between them and perdition but that self-originating divine compassion; third, He did this "*at the due time,*" when it was most fitting that it should take place (cf. Gal. 4:4). The two former

of these properties the apostle now proceeds to illustrate. **For scarcely for a righteous man**–a man of simply *unexceptionable* character–**will one**–'any one'–**die: yet peradventure for a good man**–a man who, besides being unexceptionable, is *distinguished for goodness,* a benefactor to society–**some**–'some one'–**would**–rather 'doth'–**even dare to die**– "Scarce an instance occurs of selfsacrifice for one merely upright; though for one who makes himself a blessing to society there *may* be found an example of such noble surrender of life" [So BENGEL, OLS-HAUSEN, THOLUCK, ALFORD, PHILIPPI]. (To make the "righteous" and the "good" man here to mean the same person, and the whole sense to be that "though rare, the case may occur, of one making a sacrifice of life for a worthy character" [as CALVIN, BEZA, FRITZSCHE, JOWETT], is extremely flat. **But God commendeth**–'setteth off,' 'displayeth'–in glorious contrast with all that men will do for each other. **his love toward us, in that, while we were yet sinners**–i.e., in a state not of positive "goodness," nor even of negative "righteousness," but on the contrary, "sinners," a state which His soul hateth. **Christ died for us**–Now comes the overpowering inference, emphatically redoubled. **9, 10. Much more then, being**–'having been'–**now justified by his blood, we shall be saved from wrath through him. For if, when we were enemies, we were reconciled to God by the death of his Son, much more, being now**–'having now been'–**reconciled, we shall be saved by his life**–i.e., 'If that part of the Saviour's work which cost Him His blood, and which had to be wrought for persons incapable of the least sympathy either with His love or His labors in their behalf–even our "justification," our "reconciliation"–is already completed; how much more will He do all that remains to be done, since He has it to do, not by death-agonies any more, but in untroubled "life," and no longer for enemies, but for friends–from whom, at every stage of it, He receives the grateful response of redeemed and adoring souls?' To be "saved from wrath through Him," denotes here the whole work of Christ towards *believers,* from the moment of justification, when the wrath of God is turned away from them, till the Judge on the great white throne shall discharge that wrath upon them that "obey not the Gospel of our Lord Jesus Christ"; and that work may all be summed up in "keeping them from falling, and presenting them faultless before the presence of His glory with exceeding joy" (Jude 24): thus are they "saved from wrath through Him." **11. And not only so, but we also joy**–rather, 'glory'–**in God through our Lord Jesus Christ, by** –'through'–**whom we have now received the atonement**–rather, 'the reconciliation' (*Margin*), as the same word is rendered in vs. 10 and in II Corinthians 5:18, 19. (In fact, the earlier meaning of the English word 'atonement' was "the *reconciliation* of two estranged parties") [TRENCH]. The foregoing effects of justification were all benefits to ourselves, calling for gratitude; this last may be termed a purely disinterested one. Our first feeling towards God, after we have found peace with Him, is that of clinging gratitude for so costly a salvation; but no sooner have we learned to cry, Abba, Father, under the sweet sense of reconciliation, than "gloriation" in Him takes the place of dread of Him, and now He appears to us "altogether lovely!"–On this section, *note* (1) How gloriously does the Gospel evince its divine origin by basing all acceptable obedience on "peace with God," laying the foundations of this peace in a righteous "justification" of the sinner "through our Lord Jesus Christ," and making this the entrance to a permanent standing in the divine favor, and a triumphant expectation of future glory! (vss. 1, 2). Other peace, worthy of the name, there is none; and as those who are strangers to it rise not to the enjoyment of such high fellowship with God, so they have neither any taste for it nor desire after it. (2) As only believers possess the true secret of patience under trials, so, although "not joyous but grievous" in themselves (Heb. 12:17), when trials divinely sent afford them the opportunity of evidencing their faith by the grace of patience under them, they should "count it all joy" (vss. 3, 4; and see Jas. 1:2, 3). (3) "Hope," in the New Testament sense of the term, is not a lower degree of faith or assurance (as many now say, I *hope* for heaven, but am not *sure* of it); but invariably means 'the confident expectation of future good.' It presupposes faith; and what faith *assures* us will be ours, hope accordingly *expects*. In the nourishment of this hope, the soul's look *outward* to Christ for the ground of it, and *inward* upon ourselves for evidence of its reality, must act and react upon each other (vs. 2 and vs. 4 compared). (4) It is the proper office of the Holy Ghost to beget in the soul the full conviction and joyful consciousness of the love of God in Christ Jesus to sinners of mankind, and to ourselves in particular; and where this exists, it carries with it such an assurance of final salvation as cannot deceive (vs. 5). (5) The *justification* of sinful men is not in virtue of their amendment, but of "the *blood* of God's Son"; and while this is expressly affirmed in vs. 9, our *reconciliation* to God by the *"death* of His Son," affirmed in vs. 10, is but a variety of the same statement. In both, the blessing meant is the *restoration of the sinner to a righteous standing* in the sight of God; and in both, the meritorious ground of this, which is intended to be conveyed, is the *expiatory sacrifice* of God's Son. (6) Gratitude to God for redeeming love, if it could exist without delight in God Himself, would be a selfish and worthless feeling; but when the one rises into the other—the transporting sense of eternal "reconciliation" passing into "gloriation in God" Himself—then the lower is sanctified and sustained by the higher, and each feeling is perfective of the other (vs. 11).

12-21. COMPARISON AND CONTRAST BETWEEN ADAM AND CHRIST IN THEIR RELATION TO THE HUMAN FAMILY. (This profound and most weighty section has occasioned an immense deal of critical and theological discussion, in which every point, and almost every clause, has been contested. We can here but set down what appears to us to be the only tenable view of it as a whole and of its successive clauses, with some slight indication of the grounds of our judgment). **12. Wherefore**—i.e., Things being so; referring back to the whole preceding argument. **as by one man**—Adam. **sin**—considered here in its guilt, criminality, penal desert. **entered into the world, and death by**—as the penalty of—**sin; and so death passed upon all men, for that all have sinned**—rather, 'all sinned,' i.e., in that one man's first sin. Thus death reaches every individual of the human family, as the penalty due to *himself*. [So, in substance, BENGEL, HODGE, PHILIPPI.] Here we should have expected the apostle to finish his sentence, in some such way as this: 'Even so, by one man righteousness has entered into the world, and life by righteousness.' But, instead of this, we have a digression, extending to five verses, to illustrate the important statement of

vs. 12; and it is only at vs. 18 that the comparison is resumed and finished. **13-14. For until the law sin was in the world**—i.e., during all the period from Adam "until the law" of Moses was given, God continued to treat men as sinners. **but sin is not imputed where there is no law**—'There must therefore have been a law during that period, because sin *was* then imputed'; as is now to be shown. **Nevertheless death reigned from Adam to Moses, even over them that had not sinned after the similitude of Adam's transgression**—But who are they?—a much contested question. *Infants* (say some), who being guiltless of *actual sin*, may be said not to have sinned in the way that Adam did [AUGUSTIN, BEZA, HODGE]. But why should infants be specially connected with the period "from Adam to Moses," since they die alike in every period? And if the apostle meant to express here the death of infants, why has he done it so enigmatically? Besides, the death of infants is comprehended in the universal mortality on account of the first sin, so emphatically expressed in vs. 12; what need then to specify it here? and why, if not necessary, should we presume it to be meant here, unless the language unmistakably point to it—which it certainly does not? The meaning then must be, that 'death reigned from Adam to Moses, even over those that had not, like Adam, transgressed against a positive commandment, threatening death to the disobedient.' (So most interpreters.) In this case, the particle "even," instead of specifying one particular class of those who lived "from Adam to Moses" (as the other interpretation supposes), merely explains what it was that made the case of those who died from Adam to Moses worthy of special notice—namely, that 'though unlike Adam and all since Moses, those who lived between the two had no positive threatening of death for transgression, "nevertheless, death reigned *even over them.*"' **who is the figure**—or, 'a type'—**of him that was to come**—Christ. "This clause is inserted on the first mention of the name 'Adam, the *one man* of whom he is speaking, to recall the purpose for which he is treating of him, as *the figure of Christ"* [ALFORD]. The point of analogy intended here is plainly the *public character* which both sustained, neither of the two being regarded in the divine procedure towards men as mere *individual* men, but both alike as *representative* men. (Some take the proper supplement here to be "Him [that is] to come"; understanding the apostle to speak from his own time, and to refer to Christ's second coming [FRITZSCHE, DE WETTE, ALFORD]. But this is unnatural, since the analogy of the second Adam to the first has been in full development ever since "God exalted Him to be a Prince and a Saviour," and it will only remain to be consummated at His second coming. The simple meaning is, as nearly all interpreters agree, that Adam is a type of Him who was to come after him in the same public character, and so to be "the second Adam.") **15. But**—'Yet,' 'Howbeit'—**not as the offence**—'trespass'—**so also is the free gift**—or 'the gracious gift,' 'the gift of grace.' The two cases present points of contrast as well as resemblance. **For if ...**—rather, 'For if through the offense of the one the many died (i.e., in that one man's first sin), much more did the grace of God, and the free gift by grace, even that of the one man, Jesus Christ, abound unto the many.' By "the many" is meant the *mass* of mankind represented respectively by Adam and Christ, as opposed, not to *few,* but to "the one" who represented them. By "the free gift" is meant (as in vs. 17) the glorious gift of *justifying righteousness;* this is expressly distinguished from "the grace of God," as the *effect* from the *cause;* and both are said to "abound" towards us in Christ—in what sense will appear in the next two verses. And the "much more," of the one case than the other, does not mean that we get much more of good by Christ than of evil by Adam (for it is not a case of quantity at all); but that we have much more reason to expect, or it is much more agreeable to our ideas of God, that the many should be benefited by the merit of one, than that they should suffer for the sin of one; and if the latter has happened, *much more* may we assure ourselves of the former [PHILIPPI, HODGE]. **16. And not as it was by one that sinned, so is the gift**—'Another point of contrast may be mentioned.' **for the judgment**—'sentence'—**was by one**—rather, 'was of one,' meaning not 'one man, but, as appears from the next clause, 'one offense'—**to condemnation, but the free gift**—'gift of grace'—**is of many offences unto justification**—a glorious point of contrast. 'The condemnation by Adam was for *one sin;* but the justification by Christ is an absolution not only from the guilt of that first offense, mysteriously attaching to every individual of the race, but from the *countless offenses* into which, as a germ lodged in the bosom of every child of Adam, it unfolds itself in his life.' This is the meaning of "grace *abounding* towards us in the *abundance of the gift* of righteousness." It is a grace not only rich in its *character,* but rich in *detail;* it is a "righteousness" not only rich in *a complete justification* of the guilty, condemned sinner; but rich in the *amplitude of the ground* which it covers, leaving no one sin of any of the justified uncancelled, but making him, though loaded with the guilt of myriads of offenses, "the righteousness of God in Christ." **17. For if by**—'the'—**one man's offence death reigned by one**—'through the one'—**much more shall they which receive**—'the'—**abundance of grace and of the gift of**—justifying—**righteousness ... reign in life by one**—'through the one'—**Jesus Christ**—We have here the two ideas of vs. 15 and vs. 16 sublimely combined into one, as if the subject had grown upon the apostle as he advanced in his comparison of the two cases. Here, for the first time in this section, he speaks of that LIFE which springs out of justification, in contrast with the death which springs from sin and follows condemnation. The proper idea of it therefore is, 'Right to live'—'Righteous life'—life possessed and enjoyed with the good will, and in conformity with the eternal law, of "Him that sitteth on the Throne"; life therefore in its widest sense—life in the whole man and throughout the whole duration of human existence, the life of blissful and loving relationship to God in soul and body, for ever and ever. It is worthy of note, too, that while he says death "reigned over" us through Adam, he does not say Life "reigns over us" through Christ; lest he should seem to invest this new life with the very attribute of death—that of fell and malignant tyranny, of which we were the hapless victims. Nor does he say Life reigns *in* us, which would have been a scriptural enough idea; but, which is much more pregnant, "*We* shall reign in life." While *freedom* and *might* are implied in the figure of "reigning," "life" is represented as the glorious territory or atmosphere of that reign. And by recurring to the idea of vs. 16, as to the "many offenses" whose complete pardon shows "the abundance of grace and of the gift of righteousness," the whole statement is to this effect: 'If one man's one offense let loose against us the tyrant power of

Death, to hold us as its victims in helpless bondage, "much more," when we stand forth enriched with God's "abounding grace" and in the beauty of a complete absolution from countless offenses, shall we expatiate in a life divinely owned and legally secured, "reigning" in exultant freedom and unchallenged might, through that other matchless "One," Jesus Christ!' (On the import of the *future* tense in this last clause, see on vs. 19, and on ch. 6. 5.) **18. Therefore**—now at length resuming the unfinished comparison of vs. 12, in order to give *formally* the concluding member of it, which had been done once and again *substantially,* in the intermediate verses. **as by the offence of one judgment came**—or, more simply, 'it came'—**upon all men to condemnation; even so by the righteousness of one the free gift came**—rather, 'it came'—**upon all men to justification of life**—[So CALVIN, BENGEL, OLSHAUSEN, THOLUCK, HODGE, PHILIPPI]. But better, as we judge: 'As through one offense it [came] upon all men to condemnation; even so through one righteousness [it came] upon all men to justification of life'—[So BEZA, GROTIUS, FERME, MEYER, DE WETTE, ALFORD, REVISED VERSION]. In this case, the apostle, resuming the statement of vs. 12, expresses it in a more concentrated and vivid form—suggested no doubt by the expression in vs. 16, "through one offense," representing Christ's whole work, considered as the ground of our justification, as "ONE RIGHTEOUSNESS." (Some would render the peculiar word here employed, 'one righteous act' [ALFORD, etc.]; understanding by it Christ's *death* as the one redeeming act which reversed the one undoing act of Adam. But this is to limit the apostle's idea too much; for as the same word is properly rendered "righteousness" in ch. 8:4, where it means "the righteousness of the law as fulfilled by us who walk not after the flesh, but after the Spirit," so here it denotes Christ's whole "obedience unto death," considered as the one meritorious ground of the reversal of the condemnation which came by Adam. But on this, and on the expression, "all men," see on vs. 19. The expression "justification of life," is a vivid combination of two ideas already expatiated upon, meaning 'justification entitling to and issuing in the rightful possession and enjoyment of life'). **19. For ...**—better, 'For as by the one man's disobedience the many were made sinners, even so by the obedience of the One shall the many be made righteous.' On this great verse observe: *First,* By the "obedience" of Christ here is plainly not meant more than what divines call His *active* obedience, as distinguished from His sufferings and death; it is the entire work of Christ in its *obediential* character. Our Lord Himself represents even His death as His great act of obedience to the Father: "This commandment (i.e., to lay down and resume His life) have I received of My Father" (John 10:8). *Second,* The significant word twice rendered "*made,*" does not signify to *work a change upon* a person or thing, but to *constitute* or *ordain,* as will be seen from all the places where it is used. Here, accordingly, it is intended to express that *judicial act* which holds men, in virtue of their connection with Adam, as sinners; and, in connection with Christ, as righteous. *Third,* The change of *tense* from the past to the future—"as through Adam we *were* made sinners, so through Christ we *shall be* made righteous"—delightfully expresses the enduring character of the act, and of the economy to which such acts belong, in contrast with the for-ever-past ruin of believers in Adam. (See on ch. 6:5.) *Fourth,* The "all men" of vs. 18 and the "many" of vs. 19 are the same party, though under a slightly different aspect. In the latter case, the contrast is between the *one* representative (Adam—Christ) and the *many* whom he represented; in the former case, it is between the one *head* (Adam—Christ) and the *human race,* affected for death and life respectively by the actings of that one. Only in this latter case it is the redeemed family of man that is alone in view; it is *humanity* as actually lost, but also as actually saved, as ruined and recovered. Such as refuse to fall in with the high purpose of God to constitute His Son a "second Adam," the Head of a new race, and as impenitent and unbelieving finally perish, have no place in this section of the Epistle, whose sole object is to show how God repairs in the second Adam the evil done by the first. (Thus the doctrine of *universal restoration* has no place here. Thus too the forced interpretation by which the "justification of all" is made to mean a justification merely in *possibility* and *offer* to all, and the "justification of the many" to mean the *actual* justification of as many as believe [ALFORD, etc.], is completely avoided. And thus the harshness of comparing a *whole* fallen family with a recovered *part* is got rid of. However true it be in *fact* that part of mankind is not saved, this is not the *aspect* in which the subject is here presented. It is *totals* that are compared and contrasted; and it is the *same total* in two successive conditions—namely, *the human race* as ruined in Adam and recovered in Christ). **20, 21. Moreover the law**—'The law, however.' The Jew might say, If the whole purposes of God towards men center in Adam and Christ, where does "the law" come in, and what was the use of it? *Answer:* It **entered**—But the word expresses an important idea besides 'entering.' It signifies, 'entered incidentally,' or 'parenthetically.' (In Galatians 2: 4 the same word is rendered, 'came in *privily.*') The meaning is, that the promulgation of the law at Sinai was no primary or essential feature of the divine plan, but it was "added" (Gal. 3:19) for a subordinate purpose—the more fully to reveal the evil occasioned by Adam, and the need and glory of the remedy by Christ, **that the offence might abound**—(or, 'be multiplied'). But what offense? Throughout all this section 'the offense' (four times repeated besides here) has one definite meaning, namely, 'the one first offense of Adam'; and this, in our judgment, is its meaning here also: 'All our multitudinous breaches of the law are nothing but *that one first offense,* lodged mysteriously in the bosom of every child of Adam as an *offending principal,* and *multiplying itself* into myriads of particular offenses in the life of each.' What was one *act* of disobedience in the head has been converted into a vital and virulent *principle* of disobedience in all the members of the human family, whose every act of wilful rebellion proclaims itself the child of the original transgression. **But where sin abounded**—or, 'was multiplied'—**grace did much more abound**—rather, 'did exceedingly abound,' or 'superabound.' The comparison here is between the multiplication of one offense into countless transgressions, and such an overflow of grace as more than meets that appalling case. **That as sin** —Observe, the word "offense" is no more used, as that had been sufficiently illustrated; but—what better befitted this comprehensive summation of the whole matter—the great general term *sin.* **hath reigned unto death**—rather, 'in death,' triumphing and (as it were) revelling in that complete destruction of its victims. **even so might grace reign**—In

vss. 14, 17 we had the reign of *death* over the guilty and condemned in Adam; here it is the reign of the mighty *causes* of these—of SIN which clothes Death a Sovereign with venomous *power* (I Cor. 15:56) and with awful *authority* (ch. 6:23), and of GRACE, the grace which originated the scheme of salvation, the grace which "sent the Son to be the Saviour of the world," the grace which "made Him to be sin for us who knew no sin," the grace which "makes us to be the righteousness of God in Him," so that "we who receive *the abundance of grace* and of the gift of righteousness do reign in life by One, Jesus Christ!" **through righteousness**—not *ours* certainly ('the obedience of Christians,' to use the wretched language of GROTIUS) nor yet exactly 'justification' [STUART, HODGE]; but rather, 'the (justifying) righteousness of Christ' [BEZA, ALFORD, and in substance, OLSHAUSEN, MEYER]; the same which in vs. 19 is called His "obedience," meaning His whole mediatorial work in the flesh. This is here represented as the *righteous medium* through which grace reaches its objects and attains all its ends, the stable throne from which Grace as a Sovereign dispenses its saving benefits to as many as are brought under its benign sway. **unto eternal life**—which is salvation in its highest form and fullest development for ever. **by Jesus Christ our Lord**—Thus, on that "Name which is above every name," the echoes of this hymn to the glory of "Grace" die away, and "Jesus is left alone." On reviewing this golden section of our Epistle, the following additional remarks occur: (1) If this section does not teach that the whole race of Adam, standing in him as their federal head, 'sinned in him and fell with him in his first transgression,' we may despair of any intelligible exposition of it. The apostle, after saying that Adam's sin introduced death into the world, does not say "and so death passed upon all men for that" *Adam* "sinned," but "for that *all* sinned." Thus, according to the teaching of the apostle, 'the death of all is for the sin of all'; and as this cannot mean the personal sins of each individual, but some sin of which unconscious infants are guilty equally with adults, it can mean nothing but the one 'first transgression' of their common head, regarded as *the sin of each* of his race, and punished, as such, with death. It is vain to start back from this imputation to all of the guilt of Adam's first sin, as wearing the appearance of *injustice.* For not only are all other theories liable to the same objection, in some other form—besides being inconsistent with the text—but the actual *facts of human nature,* which none dispute, and which cannot be explained away, involve essentially the same difficulties as the great *principle* on which the apostle here explains them. If we admit this principle, on the authority of our apostle, a flood of light is at once thrown upon certain features of the divine procedure, and certain portions of the divine oracles, which otherwise are involved in much darkness; and if the principle itself seem hard to digest, it is not harder than the *existence of evil,* which, as a fact, admits of no dispute, but, as a feature in the divine administration, admits of no explanation in the present state. (2) What is called *original sin*—or that depraved tendency to evil with which every child of Adam comes into the world—is not formally treated of in this section (and even in ch. 7, it is rather its nature and operation than its connection with the first sin which is handled). But indirectly, this section bears testimony to it; representing the one original offense, unlike every other, as having an *enduring vitality* in the bosom of every child of Adam, as a principle of disobedience, whose virulence has gotten it the familiar name of 'original sin.' (3) In what sense is the word *"death"* used throughout this section? Not certainly as mere *temporal* death, as Arminian commentators affirm. For as Christ came to undo what Adam did, which is all comprehended in the word "death," it would hence follow that Christ has merely dissolved the sentence by which soul and body are parted in death; in other words, merely procured the resurrection of the body. But the New Testament throughout teaches that the salvation of Christ is from a vastly more comprehensive "death" than that. But neither is death here used merely in the sense of *penal evil,* i.e., 'any evil inflicted in punishment of sin and for the support of law' [HODGE]. This is too indefinite, making death a mere figure of speech to denote 'penal evil' in general—an idea foreign to the simplicity of Scripture—or at least making death, strictly so called, only one part of the thing meant by it, which ought not to be resorted to if a more simple and natural explanation can be found. By "death" then, in this section, we understand the sinner's *destruction,* in the only sense in which he is capable of it. Even temporal death is called "destruction" (Deut. 7:23; I Sam. 5:11, etc.), as extinguishing all that men regard as life. But a destruction extending to the *soul* as well as the body, and *into the future world,* is clearly expressed in Matthew 7:13; II Thessalonians 1:9; II Peter 3:16, etc. This is the penal "death" of our section, and in this view of it we retain its proper sense. Life—as a state of enjoyment of the favor of God, of pure fellowship with Him, and voluntary subjection to Him—is a blighted thing from the moment that sin is found in the creature's skirts; in that sense, the threatening, "In the day that thou eatest thereof thou shalt surely die," was carried into immediate effect in the case of Adam when he fell; who was thenceforward "dead while he lived." Such are all his posterity from their birth. The separation of soul and body in temporal death carries the sinner's "destruction" a stage farther; dissolving his connection with that world out of which he extracted a pleasurable, though unblest, existence, and ushering him into the presence of his Judge—first as a disembodied spirit, but ultimately in the body too, in an enduring condition—"to be punished (and this is the final state) with *everlasting destruction* from the presence of the Lord, and from the glory of His power." This final extinction in soul and body of all that constitutes life, but yet eternal consciousness of a blighted existence—this, in its amplest and most awful sense, is "DEATH"! Not that Adam understood all that. It is enough that he understood "the day" of his disobedience to be the terminating period of his blissful "life." In that simple idea was wrapt up all the rest. But that he should comprehend its *details* was not necessary. Nor is it necessary to suppose all that to be intended in every passage of Scripture where the word occurs. Enough that all we have described is in the bosom of the *thing,* and will be realized in as many as are not the happy subjects of the Reign of Grace. Beyond doubt, the whole of this is intended in such sublime and comprehensive passages as this: "God ... gave His ... Son that whosoever believeth in Him *might not PERISH, but have everlasting LIFE"* (John 3:16). And should not the untold horrors of that "DEATH"—already "reigning over" all that are not in Christ, and hastening to its consummation—quicken our flight into "the second Adam," that having "received the abundance of grace and of the

gift of righteousness, we may reign in LIFE by the One, Jesus Christ"?

CHAPTER 6

Vss. 1-11. THE BEARING OF JUSTIFICATION BY GRACE UPON A HOLY LIFE. **1. What ...**—The subject of this *third* division of our Epistle announces itself at once in the opening question, "Shall we (or, as the true reading is, 'May we,' 'Are we to') continue in sin, that grace may abound?" Had the apostle's doctrine been that salvation depends *in any degree* upon our good works, no such objection to it could have been made. Against the doctrine of a purely gratuitous justification, the objection is plausible; nor has there ever been an age in which it has not been urged. That it *was* brought against the apostles, we know from ch. 3: 8; and we gather from Galatians 5:13; I Peter 2:16; Jude 4, that some did give occasion to the charge; but that it was a total perversion of the doctrine of Grace the apostle here proceeds to show. **2. God forbid**—'That be far from us'; the instincts of the new creature revolting at the thought. **How shall we, that are dead ...**—lit., and more forcibly, 'We who died to sin (as presently to be explained), how shall we live any longer therein?' **3. Know ye not, that so many of us as were baptized into Jesus Christ**—cf. I Corinthians 10:2—**were baptized into his death?**—sealed with the seal of heaven, and as it were formally entered and articled, to all the *benefits* and all the *obligations* of Christian discipleship in general, and of His *death* in particular. And since He was "made sin" and "a curse for us" (II Cor. 5:21; Gal. 5:13), "bearing our sins in His own body on the tree," and "rising again for our justification" (ch. 4:25; I Pet. 2:24), our whole sinful case and condition, thus taken up into His Person, has been brought to an end in His death. Whoso, then, has been baptized into Christ's death has formally surrendered the whole state and life of sin, as in Christ a dead thing. He has sealed himself to be not only "the righteousness of God in Him," but "a new creature"; and as he cannot be in Christ to the one effect and not to the other, for they are one thing, he has bidden farewell, by baptism into Christ's death, to his entire connection with sin. "How," then, "can he live any longer therein?" The two things are as contradictory in the fact as they are in the terms. **4. Therefore we are**—rather, 'were' (it being a past act, completed at once). **buried with him, by baptism into death**—(The *comma* we have placed after "him" will show what the sense is. It is not, 'By baptism we are buried with Him into death,' which makes no sense at all; but, 'By baptism with Him into death we are buried with Him'; in other words, 'By the same baptism which publicly enters us into His *death,* we are made partakers of His *burial* also. To leave a dead body unburied is represented, alike in heathen authors as in Scripture, as the greatest indignity (Rev. 11:8, 9). It was fitting, therefore, that Christ, after "dying for our sins according to the Scriptures," should "descend into the lower parts of the earth" (Eph. 4:9). As this was the last and lowest step of His humiliation, so it was the honorable dissolution of His last link of connection with that life which He laid down for us; and we, in being "buried with Him by our baptism into His death," have by this public act severed our last link of connection with that whole sinful condition and life which Christ brought to an end in His death.

that like as Christ was raised from the dead by the glory of the Father—i.e., by such a forthputting of the Father's *power* as was the effulgence of His whole glory—**even so we also**—as risen to a new life with Him—**should walk in newness of life**—But what is that "newness?" Surely if our *old* life, now dead and buried with Christ, was wholly sinful, the *new*, to which we rise with the risen Saviour, must be altogether a holy life; so that every time we go back to "those things whereof we are now ashamed" (vs. 21), we belie our resurrection with Christ to newness of life, and "forget that we have been purged from our old sins" (II Pet. 1:9). Whether the mode of baptism by immersion is alluded to in this verse, as a kind of symbolical burial and resurrection, does not seem to us of much consequence. Many interpreters think it is, and it may be so. But as it is not clear that baptism in apostolic times was exclusively by immersion (see on Acts 2:41), so *sprinkling* and *washing* are indifferently used in the New Testament to express the cleansing efficacy of the blood of Jesus. And just as the woman with the issue of blood got virtue out of Christ by simply *touching* Him, so the essence of baptism seems to lie in the simple *contact* of the element with the body, symbolizing living contact with Christ crucified; the mode and extent of suffusion being indifferent and variable with climate and circumstances). **5. For if we have been planted together** —lit., 'have become formed together.' (The word is used here only.) **in the likeness of his death, we shall be also in the likeness of his resurrection**— i.e., 'Since Christ's death and resurrection are inseparable in their efficacy, union with Him in the one carries with it participation in the other, for privilege and for duty alike.' The *future* tense is used of participation in His resurrection, because this is but partially realized in the present state. (See on ch. 5:19.) **6, 7. Knowing this . . .**—The apostle now grows more definite and vivid in expressing the sin-destroying efficacy of our union with the crucified Saviour. **that our old man**—'our old selves'; i.e., '*all that we were* in our old unregenerate condition, before union with Christ' (cf. Col. 3:9, 10; Eph. 4:22-24; Gal. 2:20; 5:24; 6:14). **is**—rather, 'was'—**crucified with him**—in order—**that the body of sin**—not a figure for 'the *mass* of sin'; nor the '*material body,*' considered as the seat of sin, which it is not; but (as we judge) for 'sin as it dwells in us in our present *embodied* state, under the law of the fall.' **might be destroyed**—(in Christ's death)—to the end— **that henceforth we should not serve**—'be in bondage to'—**sin**. For he that is dead—rather, 'hath died'— **is freed**—'hath been set free'—**from sin**—lit., 'justified,' 'acquitted,' 'got his discharge from sin.' As death dissolves all claims, so the whole claim of sin, not only to "reign unto death," but to keep its victims in sinful bondage, has been discharged once for all, by the believer's penal death in the death of Christ; so that he is no longer a "*debtor* to the flesh to live after the flesh" (ch. 8:12). **8. Now if we be dead**—'if we died'—**with Christ . . .**—See on vs. 5. **9-11. Christ being raised from the dead dieth no more; death hath no more dominion over him**— Though Christ's death was in the most absolute sense a voluntary act (Jas. 10:17, 18; Acts 2:24), that voluntary surrender gave death such rightful "dominion over *Him*" as dissolved its dominion over *us*. But this once past, "death hath," even in that sense, "dominion over Him no more." **For in that he died, he died unto**—i.e., in obedience to the claims of—**sin once**—for all—**but in that he liveth, he liveth unto**—in obedience to the claims of—**God**—

There never, indeed, was a time when Christ did not "live unto God." But in the days of His flesh He did so under the continual burden of sin "laid on Him" (Isa. 53:6; II Cor. 5:21); whereas, now that He has "put away sin by the sacrifice of Himself," He "liveth unto God," the acquitted and accepted Surety, unchallenged and unclouded by the claims of sin. **Likewise**—even as your Lord Himself— **reckon ye also yourselves to be dead indeed**—'dead on the one hand')—**unto sin, but alive unto God through Jesus Christ**—(The words, "our Lord," at the close of this verse, are wanting in the best MSS.) Note (1) "Antinomianism is not only an error; it is a falsehood and a slander" [HODGE]. That "we should continue in sin that grace may abound," not only is never the deliberate sentiment of any real believer in the doctrine of Grace, but is abhorrent to every Christian mind, as a monstrous abuse of the most glorious of all truths (vs. 1). (2) As the death of Christ is not only the expiation of guilt, but the death of sin itself in all who are vitally united to Him; so the resurrection of Christ is the resurrection of believers, not only to acceptance with God, but to newness of life (vss. 2-11). (3) In the light of these two truths, let all who name the name of Christ "examine themselves whether they be in the faith."

12-23. WHAT PRACTICAL USE BELIEVERS SHOULD MAKE OF THEIR DEATH TO SIN AND LIFE TO GOD THROUGH UNION TO THE CRUCIFIED SAVIOUR. Not content with showing that his doctrine has no tendency to relax the obligations to a holy life, the apostle here proceeds to enforce these obligations. **12. Let not sin therefore**—as a Master—**reign**—(The reader will observe that wherever in this section the words "Sin," "Obedience," "Righteousness," "Uncleanness," "Iniquity," are figuratively used, to represent a *Master*, they are here printed in capitals, to make this manifest to the eye, and so save explanation.) **in your mortal body, that ye should obey it**—sin—**in the lusts thereof**—"the lusts of the body," as the *Greek* makes evident. (The other reading, perhaps the true one, 'that ye should obey the lusts thereof,' comes to the same thing.) The "body" is here viewed as the instrument by which all the sins of the heart become facts of the outward life, and as itself the seat of the lower appetites; and it is called "our *mortal* body," probably to remind us how unsuitable is this reign of sin in those who are "alive from the dead." But the reign here meant is the unchecked dominion of sin *within* us. Its outward acts are next referred to. **13. Neither yield ye your members instruments of unrighteousness unto Sin, but yield yourselves**—this is the great surrender—**unto God as those that are alive from the dead, and**—as the fruit of this—**your members**—till now prostituted to sin—**instruments of righteousness unto God**—But what if indwelling sin should prove too strong for us? The reply is: But it will not. **14. For Sin shall not have dominion over you** —as the slaves of a tyrant lord—**for ye are not under the law, but under grace**—The force of this glorious assurance can only be felt by observing the grounds on which it rests. To be "under the law" is, first, to be under its claim to entire obedience; and so, next under its curse for the breach of these. And as all power to obey can reach the sinner only through *Grace,* of which the law knows nothing, it follows that to be "under the law" is, finally, to be shut up under an *inability to keep it,* and consequently to be the *helpless slave of sin.* On the other hand, to be "under grace," is to be under the glorious canopy and saving effects of that "grace which reigns through righteousness unto eternal life through Jesus Christ our Lord" (see on ch. 5:20, 21). The curse of the law has been completely lifted from off them; they are made "the righteousness of God in Him"; and they are "alive unto God through Jesus Christ." So that, as when they were "under the law," Sin *could not but* have dominion over them, so now that they are "under grace," Sin *cannot* but be subdued under them. If before, Sin resistlessly triumphed, Grace will now be more than conqueror. **15, 16. What then? . . . Know ye not**—it is a dictate of common sense—**that to whom ye yield yourselves servants to obey**—with the view of obeying him—**his servants ye are to whom ye obey**—to whom ye yield that obedience—**whether of Sin unto death**—i.e., 'issuing in death,' in the awful sense of ch. 8:6, the sinner's final condition—**or of Obedience unto righteousness**—i.e., obedience resulting in a righteous character, as the enduring condition of the servant of new Obedience (I John 2:17; John 8:34; II Pet. 2:19; Matt. 6:24). **17. But God be thanked, that ye were the servants of Sin**—i.e., that this is a state of things now past and gone. **but ye have obeyed from the heart that form of doctrine which was delivered you**—rather (*Margin*), 'whereunto ye were delivered,' or cast, as in a mould. The idea is, that the teaching to which they had heartily yielded themselves had stamped its own impress upon them. **18. Being then**—'And being'; it is the continuation and conclusion of the preceding sentence; not a new one—**made free from Sin, ye became the servants of**—'servants to'—**Righteousness**—The case is one of emancipation from entire servitude to one Master ᴛo entire servitude to another, whose property we are (see on ch. 1:1). There is no middle state of personal independence; for which we were never made, and to which we have no claim. When we would not that God should reign over us, we were in righteous judgment "sold under Sin"; now being through grace "made free from Sin," it is only to become "servants to Righteousness," which is our true freedom. **19. I speak after the manner of men**—descending, for illustration, to the level of common affairs. **because of the infirmity of your flesh**—the weakness of your spiritual apprehension. **for as ye have yielded**—'as ye yielded,' the thing being viewed as now past—**your members servants to Uncleanness and to Iniquity unto**—the practice of—**iniquity; even so now yield your members servants to Righteousness unto holiness**—rather, 'unto (the attainment of) sanctification,' as the same word is rendered in II Thessalonians 2:13; I Corinthians 1:30; I Peter 1:2: —i.e., 'Looking back upon the *heartiness* with which ye served Sin, and the *lengths* ye went to be stimulated now to like zeal and like exuberance in the service of a better Master.' **20. For when ye were the servants**—'were servants'—**of Sin, ye were free from**—rather, 'in respect of'—**Righteousness**— Difficulties have been made about this clause where none exist. The import of it seems clearly to be this:—'Since no servant can serve "two masters," much less where their interests come into deadly collision, and each demands the whole man, so, while ye were in the service of Sin ye were in no proper sense the servants of Righteousness, and never did it one act of real service: whatever might be your conviction of the claims of Righteousness, your real services were all and always given to Sin: Thus had ye full proof of the nature and advantages of Sin's service.' The searching question with which this is followed up, shows that this is the meaning. **21. What fruit had ye then in those things whereof ye are now ashamed? for the end of those things is death**—What permanent *advantage,* and what abiding *satisfaction,* have those things yielded? The apostle answers his own question:— 'Abiding satisfaction, did I ask? They have left only a sense of *"shame."* Permanent advantage? "The end of them is *death*."' By saying they were *"now* ashamed," he makes it plain that he is not referring to that disgust at themselves, and remorse of conscience by which those who are the most helplessly "sold under sin" are often stung to the quick; but that ingenuous feeling of self-reproach, which pierces and weighs down the children of God, as they think of the dishonor which their past life did to His name, the ingratitude it displayed, the violence it did to their own conscience, its deadening and degrading effects, and the death—"the second death"—to which it was dragging them down, when mere Grace arrested them. (On the sense of "death" here, see on ch. 5:12-21, *Note* 3, and on vs. 16: see also Rev. 21:8—The change proposed in the pointing of this verse: 'What fruit had ye then? things whereof ye are now ashamed" [LUTHER, THOLUCK, DE WETTE, PHILIPPI, ALFORD, etc.], seems unnatural and uncalled for. The ordinary pointing has at least powerful support [CHRYSOSTOM, CALVIN, BEZA, GROTIUS, BENGEL, STUART, FRITZSCHE]). **22. But now**—as if to get away from such a subject were unspeakable relief— **being made free from Sin, and become servants to God**—in the absolute sense intended throughout all this passage—**ye have**—not 'ought to have,' but 'do have,' in point of fact—**your fruit unto holiness**— 'sanctification,' as in vs. 19; meaning that *permanently holy state and character* which is built up out of the whole "fruits of righteousness," which believers successively bring forth. They "have their fruit" *unto* this, i.e., all *going towards* this blessed result. **and the end everlasting life**—as the final state of the justified believer; the beatific experience not only of complete exemption from the fall with all its effects, but of the perfect life of acceptance with God, and conformity to His likeness, of unveiled access to Him, and ineffable fellowship with Him through all duration. **23. For the wages of sin is death; but the gift of God is eternal life through**—'in'—**Jesus Christ our Lord**—This concluding verse—as pointed as it is brief—contains the marrow, the most fine gold, of the Gospel. As the laborer is worthy of his hire, and feels it to be his due —his own of right— so is death the due of sin, the wages the sinner has well wrought for, his own. But "eternal life" is in no sense or degree the wages of our righteousness; we do nothing whatever to earn or become entitled to it, and never can: it is therefore, in the most absolute sense, "THE GIFT OF GOD." Grace reigns in the bestowal of it in every case, and that "in Jesus Christ our Lord," as the righteous Channel of it. In view of this, who that hath tasted that the Lord is gracious can refrain from saying, "Unto Him that loved us, and washed us from our sins in His own blood, and hath made us kings and priests unto God and His Father, to Him be glory and dominion for ever and ever. Amen!" (Rev. 1:5, 6). Note (1) As the most effectual refutation of the oft-repeated calumny, that the doctrine of Salvation by grace encourages to continue in sin, is the holy life of those who profess it, let such ever feel that the highest service they can render to that Grace which is all their hope, is to "yield themselves unto God, as those that are alive from the dead, and their members instruments of righteousness unto God" (vss. 12, 13).

By so doing they will "put to silence the ignorance of foolish men," secure their own peace, carry out the end of their calling, and give substantial glory to Him that loved them. (2) The fundamental principle of Gospel-obedience is as original as it is divinely rational; that 'we are set free from the law in order to keep it, and are brought graciously under servitude to the law in order to be free' (vss. 14, 15, 18). So long as we know no principle of obedience but the terrors of the law, which condemns all the breakers of it, and knows nothing whatever of grace, either to pardon the guilty or to purify the stained, we are shut up under a moral impossibility of genuine and acceptable obedience: whereas when Grace lifts us out of this state, and through union to a righteous Surety, brings us into a state of conscious reconciliation, and loving surrender of heart to a God of salvation, we immediately feel the glorious *liberty to be holy,* and the assurance that "Sin shall not have dominion over us" is as sweet to our renewed tastes and aspirations as the ground of it is felt to be firm, "because we are not under the Law, but under Grace." (3) As this most momentous of all transitions in the history of a man is wholly of God's free grace, the change should never be thought, spoken, or written of but with lively thanksgiving to Him who so loved us (vs. 17). (4) Christians, in the service of God, should emulate their former selves in the zeal and steadiness with which they served sin, and the length to which they went in it (vs. 19). (5) To stimulate this holy rivalry, let us often "look back to the rock whence we were hewn, the hole of the pit whence we were digged," in search of the enduring advantages and permanent satisfactions which the service of Sin yielded; and when we find to our "shame" only gall and wormwood, let us follow a godless life to its proper "end," until, finding ourselves in the territories of "death," we are fain to hasten back to survey the service of Righteousness, that new Master of all believers, and find Him leading us sweetly into abiding "holiness," and landing us at length in "everlasting life" (vss. 20-22). (6) Death and life are before all men who hear the Gospel: the one, the natural issue and proper reward of sin; the other, the absolutely free "GIFT OF GOD" to sinners, "in Jesus Christ our Lord." And as the one is the *conscious* sense of the hopeless loss of all blissful existence, so the other is the conscious possession and enjoyment of all that constitutes a rational creature's highest "life" for evermore (vs. 23). Ye that read or hear these words, "I call heaven and earth to record this day against you, that I have set before you life and death, blessing and cursing, therefore choose life, that both thou and thy seed may live!" (Deut. 30:19).

CHAPTER 7

Vss. 1-25. SAME SUBJECT CONTINUED. **1-6.** *Relation of Believers to the Law and to Christ.* Recurring to the statement of ch. 6:14, that believers are "not under the law but under grace," the apostle here shows *how* this change is brought about, and what holy consequences follow from it. **1. I speak to them that know the law**—of Moses to whom, though not themselves Jews (see on ch. 1:13), the Old Testament was familiar. **2, 3. if her husband be dead**—'die' So vs. 3. **she be married**—'joined.' So vs. 4. **4. Wherefore . . . ye also are become dead** —rather, 'were slain'—**to the law by the body of**

Christ—through His slain body. The apostle here departs from his usual word "died," using the more expressive phrase 'were slain,' to make it clear that he meant their being "crucified with Christ" (as expressed in ch. 6:3-6, and Gal. 2:20. **that ye should be married to another, even to him that is**—'was'—**raised from the dead**—to the intent—**that we should bring forth fruit unto God**—It has been thought that the apostle should here have said that 'the *law* died to us,' not 'we to the law,' but that he purposely inverted the figure, to avoid the harshness to Jewish ears of *the death of the law* [CHRYSOSTOM, CALVIN, HODGE, PHILIPPI, etc.]. But this is to mistake the apostle's design in employing this figure, which was merely to illustrate the general principle that '*death dissolves legal obligation.*' It was essential to his argument that *we,* not the law, should be the dying party, since it is we that are "crucified with Christ," and not the law. This death dissolves our marriage obligation to the law, leaving us at liberty to contract a new relation—to be joined to the Risen One, in order to spiritual fruitfulness, to the glory of God [BEZA, OLSHAUSEN, MEYER, ALFORD, etc.]. The confusion, then, is in the expositors, not the text; and it has arisen from not observing that, like Jesus Himself, believers are here viewed as having a double life—the old sin-condemned life, which they lay down with Christ, and the new life of acceptance and holiness to which they rise with their Surety and Head; and all the issues of this new life, in Christian obedience, are regarded as the "fruit" of this blessed union to the Risen One. How such holy fruitfulness was impossible before our union to Christ, is next declared. **5. For when we were in the flesh**—in our unregenerate state, as we came into the world. See on John 3:6; and ch. 8:5-9. **the motions**—'passions' (*Margin*), 'affectious' (as in Gal. 5:24), or 'stirrings.' **of sins**—i.e., 'prompting to the commission of sins.' **which were by the law**—by occasion of the law, which fretted, irritated our inward corruption by its prohibitions. See on vss. 7-9. **did work in our members**—the members of the body, as the instruments by which these inward stirrings find vent in action, and become facts of the life. See on ch. 6: 6. **to bring forth fruit unto death**—death in the sense of ch. 6:21. Thus hopeless is all holy fruit before union to Christ. **6. But now**—See on the same expression in ch. 6:22, and cf. James 1:15. **we are delivered from the law**—The word is the same which, in ch. 6:6 and elsewhere, is rendered "destroyed," and is but another way of saying (as in vs. 4) that "we were *slain* to the law by the body of Christ"; language which, though harsh to the ear, is designed and fitted to impress upon the reader the *violence* of that death of the Cross, by which, as by a deadly wrench, we are "delivered from the law." **that being dead wherein we were held**—It is now universally agreed that the true reading here is, 'being dead to that wherein we were held.' The received reading has no authority whatever, and is inconsistent with the strain of the argument; for the death spoken of, as we have seen, is not the *law's,* but ours, through union with the crucified Saviour. **that we should**—'so as to' or 'so that we'—**serve in newness of spirit**—'in the newness of the spirit' **and not in the oldness of the letter**—not in our old way of literal, mechanical obedience to the divine law, as a set of external rules of conduct, and without any reference to the state of our hearts; but in that new way of spiritual obedience which, through union to the risen Saviour, we have learned to render (cf. ch. 2:29; II Cor. 3:6). **7-25.** *False Inferences re-*

garding the Law Repelled. And first, vss. 7-13, In the case of the UNREGENERATE. **7, 8. What . . . then? Is the law sin? God forbid!**—'I have said that when we were in the flesh the law stirred our inward corruption, and was thus the occasion of deadly fruit: Is then the law *to blame* for this? Far from us be such a thought.' **Nay**—'On the contrary' (as in ch. 8:37; I Cor. 12:22; *Greek*). **I had not known sin but by the law**—It is important to fix what is meant by *"sin"* here. It certainly is not 'the general nature of sin' [ALFORD, etc.], though it be true that this is learned from the law; for such a sense will not suit what is said of it in the following verses, where the meaning is the same as here. The only meaning which suits all that is said of it in this place is 'the *principle* of sin in the heart of fallen man.' The sense, then, is this: 'It was by means of the law that I came to know what a virulence and strength of sinful propensity I had within me.' The *existence* of this it did not need the law to reveal to him; for even the heathens recognized and wrote of it. But the dreadful nature and desperate power of it the law alone discovered—in the way now to be described. **for I had not known lust, except . . .**—Here the same Greek word is unfortunately rendered by three different English ones—"lust"; "covet"; "concupiscence"—which obscures the meaning. By using the word "lust" only, in the wide sense of all 'irregular desire,' or every outgoing of the heart towards anything forbidden, the sense will best be brought out; thus, 'For I had not known lust, except the law had said, Thou shalt not lust; But sin, taking ('having taken') occasion by the commandment (that one which forbids it), wrouᵍht in me all manner of lusting.' This gives a deeper view of the tenth commandment than the mere words suggest. The apostle saw in it the prohibition not only of desire after *certain things there specified,* but of 'desire after *everything divinely forbidden'*; in other words, all 'lusting' or 'irregular desire.' It was this which "he had not known but by the law." The law forbidding all such desire so stirred his corruption that it wrought in him "all manner of lusting"—desire of every sort after what was forbidden. **For without the law**—i.e., before its extensive demands and prohibitions come to operate upon our corrupt nature. **sin was**—rather, 'is'—**dead**—i.e., the sinful principle of our nature lies so dormant, so torpid, that its virulence and power are unknown, and to our feeling it is as good as "dead." **9. For I was alive without the law once**—'In the days of my ignorance, when, in this sense, a stranger to the law, I deemed myself a righteous man, and, as such, entitled to life at the hand of God.' **but when the commandment came**—forbidding all irregular desire; for the apostle sees in this the spirit of the whole law. **sin revived**—'came to life'; in its malignity and strength it unexpectedly revealed itself, as if sprung from the dead. **and I died**—'saw myself, in the eye of a law never kept and not to be kept, a dead man.' **10, 11. And**—thus—**the commandment, which was . . .**—designed—**to**—give—**life**—through the keeping of it—**I found to be unto death**—through breaking it. **For sin**—my sinful nature—**taking occasion by the commandment, deceived me**—or 'seduced me'—drew me aside into the very thing which the commandment forbade. **and by it slew me**—'discovered me to myself to be a condemned and gone man' (cf. vs. 9, "I *died*"). **12, 13. Wherefore**—'So that'—**the law is**—'is indeed'—**good, and the commandment**—that one so often referred to, which forbids all lusting—**holy, and just, and good. Was then that which

is good made**—'Hath then that which is good become'—**death unto me? God forbid**—i.e., 'Does the *blame* of my death lie with the good law? Away with such a thought.' **But sin**—became death unto me, to the end—**that it might appear sin**—that it might be seen in its true light—**working death in**—rather, 'to'—**me by that which is good, that sin by the commandment might become exceeding sinful**—'that its enormous turpitude might stand out to view, through its turning God's holy, just, and good law into a provocative to the very things which is forbids.' So much for *the law in relation to the unregenerate,* of whom the apostle takes himself as the example; first, in his ignorant, self-satisfied condition; next, under humbling discoveries of his inability to keep the law, through inward contrariety to it; finally, as self-condemned, and already, in law, a dead man. Some inquire to what period of his recorded history these circumstances relate. But there is no reason to think they were wrought into such conscious and explicit discovery at any period of his history before he "met the Lord in the way"; and though, "amidst the multitude of his thoughts within him" during his memorable three day's blindness immediately after that, such views of the law and of himself would doubtless be tossed up and down till they *took shape* much as they are here described (see on Acts 9:9) we regard this whole description of his inward struggles and progress rather as the *finished result* of all his past recollections and subsequent reflections on his unregenerate state, which he throws into historical form only for greater vividness. But now the apostle proceeds to repel false inferences *regarding the law,* secondly: vss. 14-25, In the case of the REGENERATE; taking himself here also as the example. **14. For we know that the law is spiritual**—in its demands. **but I am carnal**—fleshly (see on vs. 5), and as such, incapable of yielding spiritual obedience. **sold under sin**—enslaved to it. The "I" here, though of course not the *regenerate,* is neither the *unregenerate,* but the sinful principle of the renewed man, as is expressly stated in vs. 18. **15, 16. For . . .**—better, 'For that which I do I know not'; i.e., 'In obeying the impulses of my carnal nature I act the slave of another will than my own as a renewed man? **for . . .** rather, 'for not what I would (wish, desire) that do I, but what I hate that I do. But if what I would not that I do, I consent unto the law that it is good—the judgment of my inner man going along with the law.' **17. Now then it is no more I**—*my renewed self*—**that do it**—'that work it'—**but sin which dwelleth in me**—that principle of sin that still has its abode in me. To explain this and the following statements, as many do [even BENGEL and THOLUCK], of the sins of unrenewed men against their better convictions, is to do painful violence to the apostle's language, and to affirm of the unregenerate what is untrue. That coexistence and mutual hostility of "flesh" and "spirit" in the same renewed man, which is so clearly taught in ch. 8:4, etc., and in Galatians 5:16, etc., is the true and only key to the language of this and the following verses. (It is hardly necessary to say that the apostle means not to disown the blame of yielding to his corruptions, by saying, "it is not he that does it, but sin that dwelleth in him." Early heretics thus abused his language; but the whole strain of the passage shows that his sole object in thus expressing himself was to bring more vividly before his readers the conflict of two opposite principles, and how entirely, as a new man—honoring from his inmost soul the law of God—he condemned and renounced his corrupt nature, with its affections and lusts, its stirrings and its outgoings, root and branch). **18. For . . .**—better, 'For I know that there dwelleth not in me, that is in my flesh, any good.' **for to will**—'desire' —**is present with me; but to perform that which is good**—the supplement "how," in our version, weakens the statement—**I find not**—Here, again, we have the *double self* of the renewed man; 'In me dwelleth no good; but this corrupt self is not my true self; it is but sin dwelling in my real self, as a renewed man.' **19, 21. For . . .**—The conflict here graphically described between a self that 'desires' to do good and a self that in spite of this does evil, cannot be the struggles between conscience and passion in the *unregenerate*, because the description given of this "desire to do good" in the verse immediately following is such as cannot be ascribed, with the least show of truth, to any but the *renewed*. **22. For I delight in the law of God after the inward man**—'from the bottom of my heart.' The word here rendered "delight" is indeed stronger than "consent" in vs. 16; but both express a state of mind and heart to which the unregenerate man is a stranger. **23. But I see another**—it should be 'a different'—**law in my members**—see on vs. 5—**warring against the law of my mind, and bringing me into captivity to the law of sin which is in my members**—In this important verse, observe, first, that the word "law" means *an inward principle of action, good or evil, operating with the fixedness and regularity of a law.* The apostle found two such laws within him; the one "the law of sin in his members," called (in Gal. 5:17, 24) "the flesh which lusteth against the spirit," "the flesh with the affections and lusts," i.e., the sinful principle in the regenerate; the other, "the law of the mind," or the holy principle of the renewed nature. Second, when the apostle says he "sees" the one of these principles "warring against" the other, and "bringing him into captivity" to itself, *he is not referring to any actual rebellion going on within him while he was writing, or to any captivity to his own lusts then existing.* He is simply describing the two conflicting principles, and pointing out what it was the inherent property of each to aim at bringing about. Third, when the apostle describes himself as *"brought into captivity"* by the triumph of the sinful principle of his nature, he clearly speaks in the person of a *renewed man.* Men do not feel themselves to be in captivity in the territories of their own sovereign and associated with their own friends, breathing a congenial atmosphere, and acting quite spontaneously. But here the apostle describes himself, when drawn under the power of his sinful nature, as forcibly seized and reluctantly dragged to his enemy's camp, from which he would gladly make his escape. This ought to settle the question, whether he is here speaking as a regenerate man or the reverse. **24. O wretched man that I am! who shall deliver me from the body of this death?**—The apostle speaks of the "body" here with reference to "the law of sin" which he had said was "in his members," but merely as the instrument by which the sin of the heart finds vent in action, and as itself the seat of the lower appetites (see on ch. 6:6, and on vs 5); and he calls it "the body of *this* death," as feeling, at the moment when he wrote, the horrors of that death (ch. 6:21, and vs. 5) into which it dragged him down. But the language is not that of a sinner newly awakened to the sight of his lost state; it is the cry of a living but agonized believer, weighed down under a burden which is not himself, but which he longs to shake off from his renewed self. Nor

does the question imply ignorance of the way of relief at the time referred to. It was designed only to prepare the way for that outburst of thankfulness for the divinely provided remedy which immediately follows. **25. I thank God**—the Source—**through Jesus Christ**—the Channel of deliverance. **So then** —to sum up the whole matter—**with the mind**—the mind indeed—**I myself serve the law of God, but with the flesh the law of sin**—'Such then is the unchanging character of these two principles within me. God's holy law is dear to my renewed mind, and has the willing service of my new man; although that corrupt nature which still remains in me listens to the dictates of sin.' Note (1) This whole chapter was of essential service to the Reformers in their contendings with the Church of Rome. When the divines of that corrupt church, in a Pelagian spirit, denied that the sinful principle in our fallen nature, which they called 'Concupiscence,' and which is commonly called 'Original Sin,' had the nature of *sin* at all, they were triumphantly answered from this chapter, where—both in the first section of it, which speaks of it in the unregenerate, and in the second, which treats of its presence and actings in believers—it is explicitly, emphatically, and repeatedly called "*sin*." As such, they held it to be *damnable*. (See the Confessions both of the Lutheran and Reformed churches.) In the following century, the orthodox in Holland had the same controversy to wage with 'the Remonstrants' (the followers of Arminius), and they waged it on the field of this chapter. (2) Here we see that *Inability* is consistent with *Accountability.* (See vs. 18; Gal. 5:17.) "As the Scriptures constantly recognize the truth of these two things, so are they constantly united in Christian experience. Everyone feels that he cannot do the things that he would, yet is sensible that he is guilty for not doing them. Let any man test his power by the requisition to love God perfectly at all times. Alas! how entire our inability! Yet how deep our self-loathing and self-condemnation!" [HODGE]. (3) If the first sight of the Cross by the eye of faith kindles feelings never to be forgotten, and in one sense never to be repeated—like the first view of an enchanting landscape—the experimental discovery, in the latter stages of the Christian life, of its power to beat down and mortify inveterate corruption, to cleanse and heal from longcontinued backslidings and frightful inconsistencies, and so to triumph over all that threatens to destroy those for whom Christ died, as to bring them safe over the tempestuous seas of this life into the haven of eternal rest—is attended with yet more heart-affecting wonder draws forth deeper thankfulness, and issues in more exalted adoration of Him whose work Salvation is from first to last (vss. 24, 25). (4) It is sad when such topics as these are handled as mere questions of biblical interpretation or systematic theology. Our great apostle could not treat of them apart from personal experience, of which the facts of his own life and the feelings of his own soul furnished him with illustrations as lively as they were apposite. When one is unable to go far into the investigation of indwelling sin, without breaking out into an, "O wretched man that I am!" and cannot enter on the way of relief without exclaiming "I thank God through Jesus Christ our Lord," he will find his meditations rich in fruit to his own soul, and may expect, through Him who presides in all such matters, to kindle in his readers or hearers the like blessed emotions (vss. 24, 25). So be it even now, O Lord!

CHAPTER 8

Vss. 1-39. CONCLUSION OF THE WHOLE ARGUMENT
—THE GLORIOUS COMPLETENESS OF THEM THAT ARE
IN CHRIST JESUS. In this surpassing chapter the
several streams of the preceding argument meet and
flow in one "river of the water of life, clear as
crystal, proceeding out of the throne of God and of
the Lamb," until it seems to lose itself in the ocean
of a blissful eternity.

FIRST: *The Sanctification of Believers* (vss. 1-13).
1. There is therefore now . . .—referring to the immediately preceding context [OLSHAUSEN, PHILIPPI,
MEYER, ALFORD, etc.]. The subject with which ch.
7 concludes is still under consideration. The scope
of the four opening verses is to show how "the law
of sin and death" is deprived of its power to bring
believers again into bondage, and how the holy law
of God receives in them the homage of a living
obedience [CALVIN, FRASER, PHILIPPI, MEYER, AL-
FORD, etc.]. **no condemnation to them which are
in Christ Jesus**—As Christ, who "knew no sin," was,
to all legal effects, "made sin for us," so are we, who
believe in Him, to all legal effects, "made the righteousness of God in Him" (II Cor. 5:21); and thus,
one with Him in the divine reckoning, there is to
such "NO CONDEMNATION." (Cf. John 3:18; 5:24;
ch. 5:18, 19.) But this is no mere legal *arrangement*: it is a union in *life;* believers, through the
indwelling of Christ's Spirit in them, having one
life with Him, as truly as the head and the members of the same body have one life. **who walk not
after the flesh, but after the Spirit**—The evidence
of MSS. seems to show that this clause formed no
part of the original text of this verse, but that the
first part of it was early introduced, and the second
later, from vs. 4, probably as an explanatory comment, and to make the transition to vs. 2 easier.
**2. For the law of the Spirit of life in Christ Jesus
hath made me free**—rather, 'freed me'—referring to
the time of his conversion, when first he believed—
from the law of sin and death—It is the Holy Ghost
who is here called "the Spirit of *life*," as opening
up in the souls of believers a fountain of spiritual
life (see on John 7:38, 39); just as He is called "the
Spirit of truth," as "guiding them into all truth"
(John 16:13), and "the Spirit of counsel and might,
the spirit of knowledge and the fear of the Lord"
(Isa. 11:2), as the inspirer of these qualities. And
He is called "the Spirit of life *in Christ Jesus*," because it is as members of Christ that He takes up
His abode in believers, who in consequence of this
have one life with their Head. And as the word
"law" here has the same meaning as in ch. 7:23,
namely, 'an inward principle of action, operating
with the fixedness and regularity of a law,' it thus
appears that *"the law of the Spirit of life in Christ
Jesus"* here means, 'that new principle of action
which the Spirit of Christ has opened up within us
—the law of our new being.' This *"sets us free,"*
as soon as it takes possession of our inner man,
"from the law of sin and death" i.e., from the enslaving power of that corrupt principle which carries death in its bosom. The "strong man armed"
is overpowered by the "stronger than he"; the weaker principle is dethroned and expelled by the more
powerful; the principle of spiritual life prevails
against and brings into captivity the principle of
spiritual death—"leading captivity captive." If this
be the apostle's meaning, the whole verse is to this
effect: That the triumph of believers over their inward corruption, through the power of Christ's
Spirit in them, *proves* them to be in Christ Jesus,

and as such absolved from condemnation. But
this is now explained more fully. **3, 4. For what
the law could not do . . .**—a difficult and much controverted verse. But it is clearly, we think, the
law's inability to *free us from the dominion of sin*
that the apostle has in view; as has partly appeared
already (see on vs. 2), and will more fully appear
presently. The law could irritate our sinful nature
into more virulent action, as we have seen in ch.
7:5, but it could not secure its own fulfilment. How
that is accomplished comes now to be shown. **in
that it was weak through the flesh**—i.e., having to
address itself to us through a corrupt nature, too
strong to be influenced by mere commands and
threatenings. **God . . .**—The sentence is somewhat
imperfect in its structure, which occasions a certain
obscurity. The meaning is, that *whereas* the law
was powerless to secure its own fulfilment for the
reason given, God took the method now to be described for attaining that end. **sending**—'having
sent'—**his own Son**—This and similar expressions
plainly imply that Christ was God's "OWN SON" *before* He was sent—that is, in His own proper Person, and independently of His mission and appearance in the flesh (see on ch. 8:32; Gal. 4:4); and if
so, He not only has the *very nature* of God, even
as a son of his father, but is essentially *of* the Father, though in a sense too mysterious for any language of ours properly to define (see on ch. 1-4).
And this peculiar relationship is put forward here
to *enhance the greatness* and *define the nature* of
the relief provided, as coming *from beyond the precincts of sinful humanity altogether,* yea, *immediately from the Godhead itself*. **in the likeness of
sinful flesh**—lit., "of the flesh of sin"; a very remarkable and pregnant expression. He was made in
the reality of our flesh, but only in the *likeness* of
its sinful condition. He took our nature as it is in
us, compassed with infirmities, with nothing to distinguish Him as man from sinful men, save that
He was without sin. Nor does this mean that He
took our nature with all its properties save one;
for sin is *no property of humanity at all,* but only
the disordered state of our souls, as the fallen family of Adam; a disorder affecting, indeed, and overspreading our entire nature, but still purely *our own*.
and for sin—lit., 'and about sin'; i.e., 'on the business
of sin.' The expression is purposely a general one,
because the design was not to speak of Christ's mission to *atone* for sin, but in virtue of that atonement to *destroy its dominion* and *extirpate it altogether* from believers. We think it wrong, therefore, to render the words (as in *Margin*) 'by a sacrifice for sin' (suggested by the language of the LXX
and approved by CALVIN, etc.); for this sense is too
definite, and makes the idea of *expiation* more prominent than it is. **condemned sin**—'condemned it to
lose its power over men [BEZA, BENGEL, FRASER,
MEYER, THOLUCK, PHILIPPI, ALFORD]. In this glorious sense our Lord says of His approaching death
(John 12:31), "Now is the *judgment* of this world;
now shall the *prince of this world* be *cast out*", and
again (see on John 16:11), "When He (the Spirit)
shall come, He shall convince the world of . . . judgment, because the prince of this world is *judged,*"
i.e., condemned to let go his hold of men, who,
through the Cross, shall be emancipated into the
liberty and power to be holy. **in the flesh**—i.e., in
human nature, henceforth set free from the grasp
of sin. **That the righteousness of the law**—'the
righteous demand', 'the requirement' [ALFORD], or
'the precept' of the law; for it is not precisely the
word so often used in this Epistle to denote 'the

righteousness which justifies' (ch. 1:17; 3:21; 4:5, 6; 5:17, 18, 21), but another form of the same word, intended to express the *enactment* of the law, meaning here, we believe, the practical obedience which the law calls for. **might be fulfilled in us**—or, as we say, '*realized* in us.' **who walk**—the most ancient expression of *the bent of one's life*, whether in the direction of good or of evil (Gen. 48:15; Ps. 1:1; Isa. 2:5; Mic. 4:5; Eph. 4:17; I John 1:6, 7). **not after**—i.e., according to the dictates of—**the flesh, but after the spirit**—From vs. 9 it would seem that what is more immediately intended by "the spirit" here is *our own mind* as renewed and actuated by the Holy Ghost. **5. For they that are after the flesh**—i.e., under the influence of the fleshly principle—**do mind**—give their attention to (Phil. 3:19)—**the things of the flesh . . .**—Men must be under the predominating influence of one or other of these two principles, and, according as the one or the other has the mastery, will be the complexion of their life, the character of their actions. **6. For**—a mere particle of transition here [THOLUCK], like 'but' or 'now.' **to be carnally minded**—lit., 'the mind' or 'minding of the flesh' (*Margin*); i.e., the pursuit of fleshly ends. **is death**—not only 'ends in' [ALFORD, etc.], but even now 'is'; carrying death into its bosom, so that such are "dead while they live" (I Tim. 5:6; Eph. 2:1, 5) [PHILIPPI]. **but to be spiritually minded**—'the mind' or 'minding of the spirit'; i.e., the pursuit of spiritual objects. **is life and peace**—not "life" only, in contrast with the "death" that is in the other pursuit, but "peace"; it is the very element of the soul's deepest repose and true bliss. **7. Because the carnal mind is enmity against God**—The desire and pursuit of carnal ends is a state of enmity to God, wholly incompatible with true life and peace in the soul. **for it is not subject**—'doth not submit itself'—**to the law of God, neither indeed can be**—In such a state of mind there neither is nor can be the least subjection to the law of God. Many things may be done which the law requires, but nothing either is or can be done *because* God's law requires it, or purely to please God. **8. So then**—nearly equivalent to 'And so.' **they that are in**—and, therefore, under the government of—**the flesh cannot please God**—having no obediential principle, no desire to please Him. **9. But ye are not in the flesh, but in the spirit, if so be that the Spirit of God dwell in you**—This does not mean, 'if the *disposition* or *mind* of God dwell in you; but 'if *the Holy Ghost* dwell in you' (see I Cor. 6:11, 19; 3:16, etc.). (It thus appears that to be "in the spirit" means here to be under the dominion of *our own renewed mind;* because the indwelling of God's Spirit is given as the evidence that we are "in the spirit.") **Now**—'But'—**if any man have not the Spirit of Christ**—Again, this does not mean 'the *disposition* or *mind* of Christ,' but the Holy Ghost; here called "the Spirit of Christ," just as He is called "the Spirit of life in Christ Jesus" (see on vs. 2). It is as "the Spirit of Christ" that the Holy Ghost takes possession of believers, introducing into them all the gracious, dovelike disposition which dwelt in Him (Matt. 3:16; John 3:34). Now if any man's heart be void, not of such dispositions, but of the blessed Author of them, "the Spirit of Christ"—**he is none of his**—even though intellectually convinced of the truth of Christianity, and in a general sense influence by its spirit. Sharp, solemn statement this! **10, 11. And if Christ be in you**—by His indwelling Spirit in virtue of which we have *one life* with him. **the body**—'the body indeed.' **is dead because of**—'by reason of'—**sin;**

but the spirit is life because—or, 'by reason'—**of righteousness**—The word 'indeed,' which the original requires, is of the nature of a concession—'I grant you that the body is dead . . . and so far redemption is incomplete, *but . . .*'; i.e., 'If Christ be in you by His indwelling Spirit, though your "bodies" have to pass through the stage of "death" in consequence of the first Adam's "sin," your spirit is instinct with new and undying "life," brought in by the "righteousness" of the second Adam' [THOLUCK, MEYER, and ALFORD in part, but only HODGE entirely]. **But**—'And'—**if the Spirit of him that raised up Jesus from the dead dwell in you**—i.e., 'If He dwell in you as the Spirit of the Christ-raising One,' or, 'in all the *resurrection-power* which He put forth in raising Jesus.' **he that raised up Christ from the dead**—Observe the change of name from JESUS, as the historical Individual whom God raised from the dead, to CHRIST, the same Individual, considered as the Lord and Head of all His members, or of redeemed Humanity [ALFORD]. **shall also quicken**—rather, 'shall quicken even'—**your mortal bodies by**—the true reading appears to be 'by reason of'—**his Spirit that dwelleth in you**—; 'Your bodies indeed are not exempt from the death which sin brought in; but your spirits even now have in them an undying life, and if the Spirit of Him that raised up Jesus from the dead dwell in you, even these bodies of yours, though they yield to the last enemy and the dust of them return to the dust as it was, shall yet experience the same resurrection as that of their living Head, in virtue of the indwelling of the same Spirit in you that quickened Him.' **12, 13. Therefore, brethren, we are debtors, not to the flesh, to live after the flesh**—'Once we were sold under sin (ch. 7:14); but now that we have been set free from that hard master and become servants to Righteousness (ch. 6:22), we owe nothing to the flesh, we disown its unrighteous claims and are deaf to its imperious demands.' Glorious sentiment! **For if ye live after the flesh, ye shall die**—in the sense of ch. 6:21—**but if ye through the Spirit do mortify the deeds of the body**—see on ch. 7:23—**ye shall live**—in the sense of ch. 6:22. The apostle is not satisfied with assuring them that they are under no *obligations* to the flesh, to hearken to its suggestions, without reminding them where it will end if they do; and he uses the word "mortify" (put to death) as a kind of play upon the word "die" just before. 'If *ye* do not kill sin, *it* will kill you. But he tempers this by the bright alternative, that if they do, through the Spirit, mortify the deeds of the body, such a course will infallibly terminate in "life" everlasting. And this leads the apostle into a new line of thought, opening into his final subject, the "glory" awaiting the justified believer. Note (1) "There can be no safety, no holiness, no happiness, to those who are out of Christ: No *safety*, because all such are under the condemnation of the law (vs. 1); no *holiness*, because such only as are united to Christ have the spirit of Christ (vs. 9); no *happiness*, because to be 'carnally minded is death' (vs. 6)' [HODGE]. (2) The sanctification of believers, as it has its whole foundation in the atoning death, so it has its living spring in the indwelling of the Spirit of Christ (vss. 2-4). (3) "The bent of the thoughts, affections, and pursuits, is the only decisive test of character (vs. 5)" [HODGE]. (4) No human refinement of the carnal mind will make it spiritual, or compensate for the absence of spirituality. "Flesh" and "spirit" are essentially and unchangeably opposed; nor can the carnal mind, as such, be brought into real subjection to the law of God (vss. 5-7). Hence (5) the estrangement of God and the sinner is mutual. For as the sinner's state of mind is "enmity against God" (vs. 7), so in this state he "cannot please God" (vs. 8). (6) Since the Holy Ghost is, in the same breath, called indiscriminately "the Spirit of God," "the Spirit of Christ," and "Christ" Himself (as an indwelling life in believers), the *essential unity* and yet Personal *distinctness* of the Father, the Son, and the Holy Ghost, in the one adorable Godhead must be believed, as the only consistent explanation of such language (vss. 9-11). (7) The consciousness of spiritual life in our renewed souls is a glorious assurance of resurrection life in the body also, in virtue of the same quickening Spirit whose inhabitation we already enjoy (vs. 11). (8) Whatever professions of spiritual life men may make, it remains eternally true that "if we live after the flesh we shall die," and only "if we through the Spirit do mortify the deeds of the body we shall live" (vs. 13, and cf. Gal. 6:7, 8; Eph. 5:6; Phil. 3:18, 19; I John 3:7, 8).

SECOND: *The Sonship of Believers--Their future Inheritance--The Intercession of the Spirit for Them* (vss. 14-27). **14. For as many as are led by the Spirit of God, they . . .** —'these are sons of God'. Hitherto the apostle has spoken of the Spirit simply as a *power* through which believers mortify sin: now he speaks of Him as a gracious, loving *Guide*, whose "leading"—enjoyed by all in whom is the Spirit of God's dear Son—shows that they also are "sons of God." **15. For . . .**—'For ye received not (at the time of your conversion) the spirit of bondage,' i.e., 'The spirit ye received was not a spirit of bondage.' **again**—gendering—**to fear**—as under the law which "worketh wrath", i.e., 'Such was your condition before ye believed, living in legal bondage, haunted with incessant forebodings under a sense of unpardoned sin. But it was not to perpetuate that wretched state that ye received the Spirit.' **but ye have received**—'ye received'—**the spirit of adoption, whereby**—rather, 'wherein'—**we cry, Abba, Father**—The word "cry" is emphatic, expressing the spontaneousness, the strength, and the exuberance of the final emotions. In Galatians 4:6 this cry is said to proceed from *the Spirit* in us, drawing forth the filial exclamation in our hearts. Here, it is said to proceed from *our own hearts* under the vitalizing energy of the Spirit, as the very element of the new life in believers (cf. Matt. 10:19, 20; and see on vs. 4). "Abba" is the *Syro-Chaldaic* word for "Father"; and the *Greek* word for that is added, not surely to tell the reader that both mean the same thing, but for the same reason which drew both words from the lips of Christ Himself during his agony in the garden (Mark 14:36). He, doubtless, loved to utter His Father's name in both the accustomed forms; beginning with His cherished mother tongue, and adding that of the learned. In this view the use of both words here has a charming simplicity and warmth. **16. The Spirit itself**—It should be 'Himself' (see on vs. 26). **beareth witness with our spirit, that we are the children**—'are children'—**of God**—The testimony of our own spirit is borne in that cry of *conscious sonship*, "Abba, Father"; but we are not therein alone; for the Holy Ghost within us, yea, even in that very cry which it is His to draw forth, sets His own distinct seal to ours; and thus, "in the mouth of two witnesses" the thing is established. The apostle had before called us "*sons of God*," referring to our *adoption*; here the word changes to "children," referring to our *new birth*. The one expresses the *dignity* to which we are *admitted;* the other the *new*

life which we *receive*. The latter is more suitable here; because a son by *adoption* might not be heir of the property, whereas a son by *birth* certainly is, and this is what the apostle is now coming to. **17. And if children, then heirs**—'heirs also'. **heirs of God**—of our Father's kingdom. **and joint-heirs with Christ**—as the "First-born among many brethren" (vs. 29), and as "Heir of all things." **if so be that we suffer**—'provided we be suffering with Him' —**that we may be also glorified together**—with Him. This necessity of conformity to Christ in suffering in order to participate in His glory, is taught alike by Christ Himself and by His apostles (John 12:24-26; Matt. 16:24, 25; II Tim. 2:12). **18. For I reckon that the sufferings of this present time are not worthy to be compared with the glory which shall be revealed in us**—i.e., 'True, we must suffer with Christ, if we would partake of His glory; but what of that? For if such sufferings are set over against the coming glory, they sink into insignificance.' **19-22. For . . .**—'The apostle, fired with the thought of the future glory of the saints, pours forth this splendid passage, in which he represents the whole creation groaning under its present degradation, and looking and longing for the revelation of this glory as the end and consummation of its existence' [HODGE]. **the earnest expectation**—(cf. Phil. 1:20). **of the creature**—rather, 'the creation.' **waiteth for the manifestation**—'is waiting for the revelation.' **of the sons of God**—i.e., "for the redemption of their bodies" from the grave (vs. 23), which will reveal their sonship, now hidden (cf. Luke 20:36; Rev. 21:7). **For the creature**—'the creation'—**was made subject to vanity, not willingly**—i.e., through no natural principle of decay. The apostle, personifying creation, represents it as only submitting to the vanity with which it was smitten, on man's account, in obedience to that superior power which had mysteriously linked its destinies with man's. And so he adds—**but by reason of him who hath subjected the same**—'who subjected it'—**in hope; because**—or 'in hope that'—**the creature itself also**—'even the creation itself'—**shall be delivered from the bondage of corruption**—its bondage to the principle of decay—**into the glorious liberty**—rather, 'the liberty of the glory'—**of the children of God**—i.e., the creation itself shall, in a glorious sense, be delivered into that freedom from debility and decay in which the children of God, when raised up in glory, shall expatiate: into this freedom from corruptibility the creation itself shall, in a glorious sense, be delivered [So CALVIN, BEZA, BENGEL, THOLUCK, OLSHAUSEN, DE WETTE, MEYER, PHILIPPI, HODGE, ALFORD, etc.]. If for man's sake alone the earth was cursed, it cannot surprise us that it should share in his recovery. And if so, to represent it as sympathizing with man's miseries, and as looking forward to his complete redemption as the period of its own emancipation from its present sin-blighted condition, is a beautiful thought, and in harmony with the general teaching of Scripture on the subject. (See on II Pet. 3:13.) **23. And not only they, but ourselves also**—or 'not only [so], but even we ourselves'—i.e., besides the inanimate creation. **which have the first-fruits of the Spirit**—or, 'the Spirit as the first-fruits' of our full redemption (cf. II Cor. 1:22), moulding the heart to a heavenly frame and attempering it to its future element. **even we ourselves**—though we have so much of heaven already within us. **groan within ourselves**—under this "body of sin and death," and under the manifold "vanity and vexation of spirit" that are written upon every object and every pursuit and every enjoyment under the sun. **waiting for the**—manifestation of our—**adoption, to wit, the redemption of our body**—from the grave: "not (be it observed) the deliverance of ourselves from the body, but the redemption of the body itself from the grave" [BENGEL]. **24. For we are saved by hope**—rather, 'For in hope we are saved'; i.e., it is more a salvation in hope than as yet in actual possession. **but hope that is seen is not hope**—for the very meaning of hope is, the expectation that something now *future* will become *present*. **for what a man seeth, why doth he yet hope for?**—the latter ending when the other comes. **25. But if we hope for that we see not, then do we with patience wait for it**—i.e., then, patient waiting for it is our fitting attitude. **26, 27. Likewise the Spirit also . . .**—or, 'But after the like manner doth the Spirit also help . . . **our infirmities**—rather (according to the true reading), 'our infirmity'; not merely the one infirmity here specified, but *the general weakness of the spiritual life* in its present state, of which one example is here given. **for we know not what we should pray for as we ought**—It is not the proper *matter* of prayer that believers are at so much loss about, for the fullest directions are given them on this head: but to ask for the right things "as they ought" is the difficulty. This arises partly from the dimness of our spiritual vision in the present veiled state, while we have to "walk by faith, not by sight" (see on I Cor. 13:9; and on II Cor. 5:7), and the large admixture of the ideas and feelings which spring from the fleeting objects of sense that there is in the very best views and affections of our renewed nature; partly also from the necessary imperfection of all human language as a vehicle for expressing the subtle spiritual feelings of the heart. In these circumstances, how can it be but that much uncertainty should surround all our spiritual exercises, and that in our nearest approaches and in the freest outpourings of our hearts to our Father in heaven, doubts should spring up within us whether our *frame* of mind in such exercises is altogether befitting and well pleasing to God? Nor do these anxieties subside, but rather deepen, with the depth and ripeness of our spiritual experience. **But the Spirit**—rather, 'Himself.' (See end of vs. 27)—**maketh intercession for us with groanings which cannot be uttered**—i.e., which cannot be expressed in articulate language. Sublime and affecting ideas, for which we are indebted to this passage alone! 'As we struggle to express in articulate language the desires of our hearts and find that our deepest emotions are the most inexpressible, we "groan" under this felt inability. But not in vain are these groanings. For "the Spirit Himself" is in them, giving to the emotions which He Himself has kindled the only language of which they are capable; so that though on our part they are the fruit of impotence to utter what we feel, they are at the same time the intercession of the Spirit Himself in our behalf.' **And**—rather, 'But,' inarticulate though these groanings be—**he that searcheth the hearts knoweth what is the mind of the Spirit, because he**—the Spirit—**maketh intercession for the saints according to the will of God**—As the Searcher of hearts, He watches the surging emotions of them in prayer, and knows perfectly what the Spirit means by the groanings which He draws forth within us, because that blessed Intercessor pleads by them only for what God Himself designs to bestow. Note (1) Are believers "led by the Spirit of God" (vs. 14)? How careful then should they be not to "grieve the Holy Spirit of God" (Eph. 4:30)! Cf. Psalm 32:8, 9: "I will . . .

guide thee with Mine eye. *Be not* (then) *as the horse, or as the mule . . .*" (2) "The spirit of bondage," to which many Protestants are "all their lifetime subject," and the 'doubtsome faith' which the Popish Church systematically inculcates, are both rebuked here, being in direct and painful contrast to that "spirit of adoption," and that witness of the Spirit, along with our own spirit, to the fact of our sonship, which it is here said the children of God, as such, enjoy (vss. 15, 16). (3) As suffering with Christ is the ordained preparation for participating in this glory, so the insignificance of the one as compared with the other cannot fail to lighten the sense of it, however bitter and protracted (vss. 17, 18). (4) It cannot but swell the heart of every intelligent Christian to think that if external nature has been mysteriously affected for evil by the fall of man, it only awaits his completed recovery, at the resurrection, to experience a corresponding emancipation from its blighted condition into undecaying life and unfading beauty (vss. 19-23). (5) It is not when believers, through sinful "quenching of the Spirit," have the fewest and faintest glimpses of heaven, that they sigh most fervently to be there; but, on the contrary, when through the unobstructed working of the Spirit in their hearts, "the firstfruits" of the glory to be revealed are most largely and frequently tasted, then, and just for that reason, is it that they "groan within themselves" for full redemption (vs. 23). For thus they reason: If such be the drops, what will the ocean be? If thus "to see through a glass darkly" be so very sweet, what will it be to "see face to face?" If when "my Beloved stands behind our wall, looking forth at the windows, showing Himself through the lattice" (Canticles 2:9)—that thin veil which parts the seen from the unseen—if He is even thus to me "Fairer than the children of men," what shall He be when He stands confessed before my undazzled vision, the Only-begotten of the Father in my own nature, and I shall be like Him, for I shall see Him as He is? (6) "The patience of hope" (I Thess. 1:3) is the fitting attitude for those who with the joyful consciousness that they are already *"saved"* (II Tim. 1:9; Titus 3:5), have yet the painful consciousness that they are saved but *in part:* or, "that being justified by His grace, they are made (in the present state) heirs according to the hope (only) of eternal life," Titus 3:7 (vss. 24, 25). (7) As prayer is the breath of the spiritual life, and the believer's only effectual relief under the "infirmity" which attaches to his whole condition here below, how cheering is it to be assured that the blessed Spirit, cognizant of it all, comes in aid of it all; and in particular, that when believers, unable to articulate their case before God, can at times do nothing but lie "groaning" before the Lord, these inarticulate groanings are the Spirit's own vehicle for conveying into "the ears of the Lord of Sabaoth" their whole case; and come up before the Hearer of prayer as the Spirit's own intercession in their behalf, and that they are recognized by Him that sitteth on the Throne, as embodying only what His own "will" determined before to bestow upon them (vss. 26, 27)! (8) What a view do these two verses (vss. 26, 27) give of the relations subsisting between the Divine Persons in the economy of redemption, and the harmony of their respective operations in the case of each of the redeemed!

THIRD: *Triumphant Summary of the Whole Argument* (vss. 28-39). **28. And**—or, 'Moreover,' or 'Now'; noting a transition to a new particular. **we know . . .**—The order in the original is more striking: "We know that to them that love God" (cf. I Cor. 2:9; Eph. 6:24; Jas. 1:12; 2:5) "all things work together for good [even] to them who are the called (rather, 'who are called') according to His (eternal) purpose." Glorious assurance! And this, it seems, was a "household word," a "known" thing, among believers. This working of all things for good is done quite naturally to "them that love God", because such souls, persuaded that He who gave His own Son for them cannot but mean them well in all His procedure, learn thus to take in good part whatever He sends them, however trying to flesh and blood: and to them who are the called, according to "His purpose," all things do in the same intelligible way "work together for good"; for, even when "He hath His way in the whirlwind," they see "His chariot paved with love" (Canticles 3:10). And knowing that it is in pursuance of an eternal *"purpose"* of love that they have been *"called* into the fellowship of His Son Jesus Christ" (I Cor. 1:9), they naturally say within themselves, 'It cannot be that He "of whom, and through whom, and to whom are all things," should suffer that purpose to be thwarted by anything really adverse to us, or that He should not make all things, dark as well as light, crooked as well as straight, to co-operate to the furtherance and final completion of His high design.' **29. For**—as touching this "calling according to his purpose"—**whom he did foreknow he also did predestinate**—foreordain. In what sense are we to take the word "foreknow" here? 'Those who He foreknew would repent and believe,' say *Pelagians* of every age and every hue. But this is to thrust into the text what is contrary to the whole spirit, and even letter, of the apostle's teaching (see ch. 9:11; II Tim. 1:9). In ch. 11:2, and Psalm 1:6, God's "knowledge" of His people cannot be restricted to a mere foresight of future events, or acquaintance with what is passing here below. Does "whom He did foreknow," then, mean 'whom He foreordained?' Scarcely, because both 'foreknowledge' and 'foreordination' are here mentioned, and the one as the *cause* of the other. It is difficult indeed for our limited minds to distinguish them as states of the Divine Mind towards men; especially since in Acts 2:23 "the counsel" is put *before* "the foreknowledge of God," while in I Peter 1:2 "election" is said to be *"according to* the foreknowledge of God." But probably God's foreknowledge of His own people means His *peculiar, gracious, complacency in them,* while His "predestinating" or "foreordaining" them signifies His fixed *purpose,* flowing from this, to "save them and call them with an holy calling" (II Tim. 1:9). **to be conformed to the image of his Son**—i.e., to be His sons after the pattern, model, or image of *His* Sonship in our nature. **that he might be the first-born among many brethren**—"The First-born," the Son by nature; His "many brethren," sons by adoption: He, in the Humanity of the Only-begotten of the Father, bearing our sins on the accursed tree; they in that of mere men ready to perish by reason of sin, but redeemed by His blood from condemnation and wrath, and transformed into His likeness: He "the First-born from the dead"; they "that sleep in Jesus," to be in due time "brought with Him"; "The First-born," now "crowned with glory and honor"; His "many brethren," "when He shall appear, to be like Him, for they shall see Him as He is." **30. Moreover**—'And,' or 'Now'; explanatory of the foregoing verse—'In "predestinating us to be conformed to the image of His Son" in final glory, He settled all the successive steps of it. Thus—**whom**

he did predestinate, them he also called—The word "called" (as Hodge and others truly observe) is never in the Epistles of the New Testament applied to those who have only the *outward invitation* of the Gospel (as in Matt. 20:16; 22:14). It always means 'internally, effectually, savingly called.' It denotes the *first great step* in personal salvation and answers to "conversion." Only the word *conversion* expresses the *change of character* which then takes place, whereas this "calling" expresses the *divine authorship* of the change, and the *sovereign power* by which we are summoned, Matthew-like, Zaccheus-like, out of our old, wretched, perishing condition, into a new, safe, blessed life. **and whom he**—thus—**called, them he also justified**—brought into the definite state of reconciliation already so fully described. **and whom he justified, them he also glorified**—brought to final glory (vss. 17, 18). Noble climax, and so rhythmically expressed! And all this is viewed as past; because, starting from the past decree of "predestination to be conformed to the image of God's Son" of which the other steps are but the successive unfoldings—all is beheld as one entire, eternally completed salvation. **31. What shall we then say to these things?**—'We can no farther go, think, wish' [BENGEL]. This whole passage, to vs. 34, and even to the end of the chapter, strikes all thoughtful interpreters and readers, as transcending almost every thing in language, while OLSHAUSEN notices the 'profound and colossal' character of the thought. **If God be for us, who can be against us?** If God be *resolved* and *engaged* to bring us through, all *our* enemies must be *His;* and "Who would set the briers and thorns against Him in battle? He would go through them. He would burn them together" (Isa. 27:4). What strong consolation is here! Nay, but the great Pledge of all has already been given; for, **32. He**—rather, 'He surely.' (It is a pity to lose the emphatic particle of the original.) **that spared not**—'withheld not,' 'kept not back.' This expressive phrase, as well as the whole thought, is suggested by Genesis 22:12, where Jehovah's touching commendation of Abraham's conduct regarding his son Isaac seems designed to furnish something like a glimpse into the spirit of His own act in *surrendering* His own Son. "Take now (said the Lord to Abraham) thy *son,* thine *only, whom thou lovest,* and . . . offer him for a burnt offering" (Gen. 22:2); and only when Abraham had all but performed that loftiest act of self-sacrifice, the Lord interposed, saying, "Now I know that thou fearest God, seeing thou HAST NOT WITHHELD THY SON, THINE ONLY SON, from Me." In the light of this incident, then, and of this language, our apostle can mean to convey nothing less than this, that in "not sparing His own Son, but delivering Him up," or surrendering Him, God exercised, in His *Paternal* character, a mysterious act of *Self-sacrifice,* which, though involving none of the *pain* and none of the *loss* which are inseparable from the very idea of self-sacrifice on our part, was not less real, but, on the contrary, as far transcended any such acts of ours as His nature is above the creature's. But this is inconceivable if Christ be not God's "own (or proper) Son," partaker of His very nature, as really as Isaac was of his father Abraham's. In that sense, certainly, the Jews charged our Lord with making Himself "equal with God" (see on John 5:18), which He in reply forthwith proceeded, not to disown, but to illustrate and confirm. Understand Christ's Sonship thus, and the language of Scripture regarding it is intelligible and harmonious; but take it to be an *artificial* relationship, ascribed to Him in virtue either of His miraculous birth, or His resurrection from the dead, or the grandeur of His works, or all of these together—and the passages which speak of it neither explain of themselves nor harmonize with each other. **delivered him up**—not to *death* merely (as many take it), for that is too narrow an idea here, but 'surrendered Him' in the most comprehensive sense; cf. John 3:16, "God so loved the world that He GAVE His only-begotten Son." **for us all**—i.e., for all believers alike; as nearly every good interpreter admits must be the meaning here. **how shall he not**—how can we conceive that He should not. **with him also**—rather, 'also with Him.' (The word "also" is often so placed in our version as to obscure the sense; see on Heb. 12:1.) **freely give us all things?**—all other gifts being not only immeasurably *less* than this Gift of gifts, but virtually *included in it.* **33, 34. Who shall lay anything to the charge of**—or, 'bring any charge against.' **God's elect?**—the first place in this Epistle where believers are styled "the *elect.*" In what sense this is meant will appear in next chapter. **yea rather, that is risen again**—to make good the purposes of His death. Here, as in some other cases, the apostle delightfully corrects himself (see Gal. 4:9; and on ch. 1:12); not meaning that the resurrection of Christ was of more saving value than His death, but that having "put away sin by the sacrifice of Himself"—which though precious to us was to Him of unmingled bitterness—it was incomparably more delightful to think that He was again *alive,* and living to see to the efficacy of His death in our behalf. **who is even**—'also'—**at the right hand of God**—The right hand of the king was anciently the seat of honor (cf. I Sam. 20:25; I Kings 2:19; Ps. 45:9), and denoted participation in the royal power and glory (Matt. 20:21). The classical writings contain similar allusions. Accordingly Christ's sitting at the right hand of God—predicted in Psalm 110:1, and historically referred to in Mark 16:19; Acts 2: 33; 7:56; Ephesians 1:20; Colossians 3:1; I Peter 3: 22; Revelation 3:21—signifies the *glory* of the exalted Son of man, and the *power* in the government of the world in which He participates. Hence it is called "sitting on the right hand of *Power*" (Matt. 26:64), and "sitting on the right hand of the *Majesty* on high" (Heb. 1:3) [PHILIPPI]. **who also maketh intercession for us**—using all His boundless *interest* with God in our behalf. This is the top of the climax. "His *Session* at God's right hand denotes His *power* to save us; His *Intercession,* His *will* to do it" [BENGEL]. But how are we to conceive of this intercession? Not certainly as of one pleading 'on bended knees and with outstretched arms,' to use the expressive language of CALVIN. But yet, neither is it merely a figurative intimation that the power of Christ's redemption is continually operative [THOLUCK], or merely to show the fervor and vehemence of His love for us [CHRYSOSTOM]. It cannot be taken to mean less than this: that the glorified Redeemer, conscious of His claims, expressly *signifies His will* that the efficacy of His death should be made good to the uttermost, and signifies it in some such royal style as we find Him employing in that wonderful Intercessory Prayer which He spoke *as from within the veil* (see on John 17:11, 12): "Father, I WILL that they also whom Thou hast given Me be with Me where I am" (see on John 17:24). But *in what form* this will is expressed is as undiscoverable as it is unimportant. **35, 36. Who shall separate us from the love of Christ?** This does not mean 'our love to Christ,' as

if, Who shall hinder us from loving Christ? but 'Christ's love to us,' as is clear from the closing words of the chapter, which refer to the same subject. Nor would the other sense harmonize with the scope of the chapter, which is to exhibit the ample ground of the believer's confidence in Christ. "It is no ground of confidence to assert, or even to feel, that we will never forsake Christ; but it is the strongest ground of assurance to be convinced that His love will never change" [HODGE]. **shall tribulation . . .** 'None of these, nor all together, how terrible soever to the flesh, are tokens of God's wrath, or the least ground for doubt of His love.' From whom could such a question come better than from one who had himself for Christ's sake endured so much? (See II Cor. 11:11-33; I Cor. 4:10-13.) The apostle says not (remarks CALVIN nobly) 'What,' but "Who," just as if all creatures and all afflictions were so many gladiators taking arms against the Christians [THOLUCK]. **As it is written, For thy sake . . .**—Psalm 44:22—quoted as descriptive of what God's faithful people may expect from their enemies *at any period* when their hatred of righteousness is roused, and there is nothing to restrain it (see Gal. 4:29). **37. Nay, in all these things we are more than conquerors, through him that loved us**—not, "We are so far from being conquered by them, that they do us much good" [HODGE]; for though this be true, the word means simply, 'We are pre-eminently conquerors.' See on ch. 5:20. And so far are they from "separating us from Christ's love," that it is just "through Him that loved us" that we are victorious over them. **38, 39. For I am persuaded, that neither death, nor life, nor angels, nor principalities, nor powers**—whether good or bad. But as the bad are not called "angels," or "principalities," or "powers," save with some addition to show that such are meant (Matt. 25:41; Col. 2:15; Eph. 6: 12; II Pet. 2:4—except perhaps I Cor. 6:3), probably the *good* are meant here, but merely as the same apostle *supposes* an angel from heaven to preach a false gospel. (So the best interpreters.) **nor things present, nor things to come**—no condition of the present life and none of the unknown possibilities of the life to come. **nor any other creature**—rather, 'created thing'—any other thing in the whole created universe of God—**shall be able to separate us . . .**—"All the terms here are to be taken in their most general sense, and need no closer definition. The indefinite expressions are meant to denote all that can be thought of, and are only a rhetorical paraphrase of the conception of *allness*" [OLSHAUSEN]. **from the love of God, which is in Christ Jesus our Lord**—Thus does this wonderful chapter, with which the argument of the Epistle properly closes, leave us who are "justified by faith" in the arms of everlasting Love, whence no hostile power or conceivable event can ever tear us. "Behold what manner of love is this?" And "what manner of persons ought we to be," who are thus "blessed with all spiritual blessings in Christ?"—Note (1) There is a glorious consistency between the eternal purposes of God and the free agency of men, though the link of connection is beyond human, perhaps created, apprehension (vs. 28). (2) How ennobling is the thought that the complicated movements of the divine government of the world are all arranged in expressed furtherance of the "good" of God's chosen (vs. 28)! (3) To whatever conformity to the Son of God in dignity and glory, believers are or shall hereafter be raised, it will be the joy of everyone of them, as it is most fitting, "that in all things

He should have the pre-eminence" (Col. 1:18), (vs. 29). (4) "As there is a beautiful harmony and necessary connection between the several doctrines of grace, so must there be a like harmony in the character of the Christian. He cannot experience the joy and confidence flowing from his election without the humility which the consideration of its being gratuitous must produce; nor can he have the peace of one who is justified without the holiness of one who is saved" (vss. 29, 30) [HODGE]. (5) However difficult it may be for finite minds to comprehend the emotions of the Divine Mind, let us never for a moment doubt that in "not sparing His own Son, but delivering Him up for us all," God made a real sacrifice of all that was dearest to His heart, and that in so doing He meant for ever to assure His people that all other things which they need— inasmuch as they are nothing to this stupendous gift, and indeed but the necessary sequel of it—will in due time be forthcoming (vs. 32). (6) In return for such a sacrifice on God's part, what can be considered too great on ours? (7) If there could be any doubt as to the meaning of the all-important word "JUSTIFICATION" in this Epistle—whether, as the Church of Rome teaches, and many others affirm, it means '*infusing* righteousness into the unholy, so as to *make* them righteous,' or, according to Protestant teaching, '*absolving, acquitting,* or *pronouncing righteous* the guilty' vs. 33 ought to set such doubt entirely at rest. For the apostle's question in this verse is, "Who shall *bring a charge against* God's elect?" In other words, 'Who shall *pronounce*' or '*hold them guilty?*' seeing that "God *justifies*" them: showing beyond all doubt, that to "justify" was intended to express precisely the opposite of 'holding guilty'; and consequently (as CALVIN triumphantly argues) that it means '*to absolve from the charge of guilt.*' (8) If there could be any reasonable doubt in what light the *death* of Christ is to be regarded in this Epistle, vs. 34 ought to set that doubt entirely at rest. For there the apostle's question is, Who shall "*condemn*" God's elect, since "Christ *died*" for them; showing beyond all doubt (as PHILIPPI justly argues) that it was the *expiatory* (character of that death which the apostle had in view. (9) What an affecting view of the love of Christ does it give us to learn that His greatest *nearness* to God and most powerful *interest* with Him—as "seated on His right hand"—is employed in behalf of His people here below (vs. 34)! (10) "The whole universe, with all that it contains, so far as it is good, is the friend and ally of the Christian; and, so far as it is evil, is more than a conquered foe" (vss. 35-39), [HODGE]. (11) Are we who "have tasted that the Lord is gracious," both "kept by the *power* of God through faith unto salvation" (I Pet. 1:5), and embraced in the arms of Invincible *Love?* Then surely, while "building ourselves up on our most holy faith," and "praying in the Holy Ghost," only the more should we feel constrained to "*keep ourselves in the love of God,* looking for the mercy of our Lord Jesus Christ unto eternal life" (Jude 20,21).

CHAPTER 9

Vss. 1-33. THE BEARING OF THE FOREGOING TRUTHS UPON THE CONDITION AND DESTINY OF THE CHOSEN PEOPLE—ELECTION—THE CALLING OF THE GENTILES. Too well aware that he was regarded as a traitor to the dearest interests of his people (Acts 21:33; 22:22; 25:24), the apostle opens this

division of his subject by giving vent to his real feelings with extraordinary vehemence of protestation. **1, 2. I say the truth in Christ**—as if steeped in the spirit of Him who wept over impenitent and doomed Jerusalem (cf. ch. 1:9; II Cor. 12:19; Phil. 1:8). **my conscience bearing me witness in the Holy Ghost**—'my conscience as quickened, illuminated, and even now under the direct operation of the Holy Ghost.' **That I have . . .**—'That I have great grief (or, sorrow) and unceasing anguish in my heart'—the bitter hostility of his nation to the glorious Gospel, and the awful consequences of their unbelief, weighing heavily and incessantly upon his spirit. **3. For I could wish that myself were accursed from Christ for**—'in behalf of'—**my brethren, my kinsmen according to the flesh**—In proportion as he felt himself severed from his nation, he seems to have realized all the more vividly their natural relationship. To explain away the wish here expressed, as too strong for any Christian to utter or conceive, some have rendered the opening words, 'I *did* wish,' referring it to his former unenlightened state; a sense of the words too tame to be endured: others unwarrantably soften the sense of the word "accursed." But our version gives the true import of the original; and if it be understood as the language rather of "strong and indistinct emotions than of definite ideas" [HODGE], expressing passionately how he felt his whole being swallowed up in the salvation of his people, the difficulty will vanish, and we shall be reminded of the similar idea so nobly expressed by Moses (Exod. 32:32). **4. Who are Israelites**—See ch. 11:1; II Corinthians 11:22; Philippians 3:5. **to whom pertaineth**—'whose is'—**the adoption**—It is true that, compared with the new economy, the old was a state of minority and pupilage, and so far that of a bond-servant (Gal. 4:1-3); yet, compared with the state of the surrounding heathen, the choice of Abraham and his seed was a real separation of them to be a *Family of God* (Exod. 4:22; Deut. 32: 6; Isa. 1:2; Jer. 31:9; Hos. 11:1; Mal. 1:6). **and the glory**—that "glory of the Lord," or 'visible token of the Divine Presence in the midst of them,' which rested on the ark and filled the tabernacle during all their wanderings in the wilderness; which in Jerusalem continued to be seen in the tabernacle and temple, and only disappeared when, at the Captivity, the temple was demolished, and the sun of the ancient economy began to go down. This was what the Jews called the "*Shekinah.*" **and the covenants**—"the covenants of promise" to which the Gentiles before Christ were "strangers" (Eph. 2:12); meaning the *one covenant* with Abraham in its successive *renewals* (see Gal. 3:16, 17). **and the giving of the law**—from Mount Sinai, and the possession of it thereafter, which the Jews justly deemed their peculiar honor (Deut. 26:18, 19; Ps. 147:19, 20; ch. 2:17). **and the service of God**—or, of the sanctuary, meaning the whole divinely instituted religious service, in the celebration of which they were brought so nigh unto God. **and the promises**—the great Abrahamic promises, successively unfolded, and which had their fulfilment only in Christ; (see Heb. 7:6; Gal. 3:16, 21; Acts 26:6, 7). **5. Whose are the fathers**—here, probably, the three great fathers of the covenant—Abraham, Isaac, and Jacob—by whom God condescended to name Himself (Exod. 8:6, 13; Luke 20:37). **and**—most exalted privilege of all, and as such, reserved to the last—**of whom as concerning the flesh**—see on ch. 1:3—**Christ came**— or, 'is Christ'—**who is over all, God**—rather, 'God over all.' **blessed for ever. Amen**—To get rid of the bright testimony here borne to the supreme divinity of Christ, various expedients have been adopted: (1) To place a period, either after the words "concerning the flesh Christ came," rendering the next clause as a doxology to the Father—"God who is over all be blessed for ever"; or after the word "all"-thus, "Christ came, who is over all: God be blessed . . . ." [ERASMUS, LOCKE, FRITZSCHE, MEYER, JOWETT, etc.]. But it is fatal to this view, as even *Socinus* admits, that in other Scripture doxologies the word "Blessed" *precedes* the name of God on whom the blessing is invoked (thus: "Blessed be God," Ps. 68:35; "Blessed be the Lord God, the God of Israel," Ps. 72:18). Besides, any such doxology here would be 'unmeaning and frigid in the extreme'; the sad subject on which he was entering suggesting anything but a doxology, even in connection with Christ's Incarnation [ALFORD]. (2) To transpose the words rendered 'who is'; in which case the rendering would be, 'whose (i.e., the fathers') is Christ according to the flesh' [CRELLIUS, WHISTON, TAYLOR, WHITBY]. But this is a desperate expedient, in the face of all MS. authority; as is also the conjecture of GROTIUS and others, that the word "God" should be omitted from the text. It remains then, that we have here no doxology at all, but a naked statement of fact, that while Christ is "of" the Israelitish nation *"as concerning the flesh,"* He is *in another respect* "God over all, blessed for ever." (In II Cor. 11:31 the very Greek phrase which is here rendered "who is," is used in the same sense; and cf. ch. 1:25, *Greek.*) In this view of the passage, as a testimony to the supreme divinity of Christ, besides all the orthodox fathers, some of the ablest modern critics concur [BENGEL, THOLUCK, STUART, OLSHAUSEN, PHILIPPI, ALFORD, etc.] **6. Not as though the word of God had taken none effect**—'hath fallen to the ground,' i.e., failed: cf. Luke 16:17, *Greek.* **for they are not all Israel which are of Israel**—better, 'for not all they which are of Israel are Israel.' *Here the apostle enters upon the profound subject of* ELECTION, *the treatment of which extends to the end of ch. 11*—'Think not that I mourn over the total loss of Israel; for that would involve the failure of God's word to Abraham; but not all that belong to the natural seed, and go under the name of "Israel," are *the* Israel of God's irrevocable choice.' The difficulties which encompass this subject lie not in the apostle's teaching, which is plain enough, but in the truths themselves, the evidence for which, taken by themselves, is overwhelming, but whose perfect harmony is beyond human comprehension in the present state. The great source of error here lies in hastily inferring [as THOLUCK and others], from the apostle's taking up, at the close of this chapter, the calling of the Gentiles in connection with the rejection of Israel, and continuing this subject through the two next chapters, that the Election treated of in the body of this chapter is *national*, not *personal* Election, and consequently is Election merely to *religious advantages*, not to *eternal salvation.* In that case, the argument of vs. 6, with which the subject of Election opens, would be this: 'The choice of Abraham and his seed has not failed; because though Israel has been rejected, *the Gentiles* have taken their place; and God has a right to choose what nation He will to the privileges of His visible kingdom.' But so far from this, the Gentiles are not so much as mentioned at all till towards the close of the chapter; and the argument of this verse is, that 'all Israel *is not* rejected, but only a portion of it, the remainder being *the* "Israel" whom God has

chosen in the exercise of His sovereign right.' And that this is a choice not to mere external privileges, but to eternal salvation, will abundantly appear from what follows. **7-9. Neither, because they are the seed of Abraham, are they all children**—'Not in the line of mere fleshly descent from Abraham does the election run; else Ishmael, Hagar's child, and even Keturah's children, would be included, which they were not.' **but**—the true election are such of Abraham's seed as God unconditionally chooses, as exemplified in that promise. **In Isaac shall thy seed be called**—(Gen. 21:12). **10-13. And not only so; but when Rebecca . . .**—It might be thought that there was a natural reason for preferring the child of Sarah, as being Abraham's true and first wife, both to the child of Hagar, Sarah's maid, and to the children of Keturah, his second wife. But there could be no such reason in the case of Rebecca, Isaac's only wife; for the choice of her son Jacob was the choice of one of two sons by the same mother and of the younger in preference to the elder, and before either of them was born, and consequently before either had done good or evil to be a ground of preference: and all to show that the sole ground of distinction lay in the unconditional choice of God—*"not of works, but of Him that calleth."* **14. What shall we say then? Is there unrighteousness with God? God forbid**—This is the first of two objections to the foregoing doctrine, that God chooses one and rejects another, not on account of their works, but purely in the exercise of His own good pleasure: '*This doctrine is inconsistent with the justice of God.*' The answer to this objection extends to vs. 19, where we have the second objection. **15. For he saith to Moses**—Exod. 33:19—**I will have mercy on whom I will have**—'on whom I have'—**mercy, and I will have compassion on whom I will have**—'on whom I have'—**compassion**—'There can be no unrighteousness in God's choosing whom He will, for to Moses He expressly claims the right to do so.' Yet it is worthy of notice that this is expressed in the positive rather than the negative form: not, 'I will have mercy on *none but whom I will*'; but, 'I will have mercy on *whomsoever* I will.' **16. So then it is not of him that willeth**—hath the inward *desire*—**nor of him that runneth**—maketh active *effort*—(cf. I Cor. 9:24, 26; Phil. 2:16; 3:14). Both these are indispensable to salvation, yet salvation is owing to neither, but is purely "of God that showeth mercy." See on Philippians 2: 12, 13, "Work out your own salvation with fear and trembling: for it is God which, *out of His own good pleasure*, worketh in you both to *will* and to *do*." **17. For the scripture saith to Pharaoh**—observe here the light in which the Scripture is viewed by the apostle. **Even for this same**—'this very'—**purpose have I raised**—'raised I'—**thee up . . .**—The apostle had shown that God claims the right to choose whom He will: here he shows by an example that God punishes whom He will. But "God did not make Pharaoh wicked; He only forbore to make him good, by the exercise of special and altogether unmerited grace" [HODGE]. **that I might**—'may'—**show my power in thee**—It was not that Pharaoh was worse than others that he was so dealt with, but "in order that he might become a monument of the penal justice of God, and it was with a view to this that God provided that the evil which was in him should be manifested in this definite form" [OLSHAUSEN]. **and that my name might**—'may'—**be declared**—'proclaimed'—**in all the earth**—"This is the principle on which all punishment is inflicted, that the true character of the Divine Lawgiver should be known. This is of all objects, where God is concerned, the highest and most important; in itself the most worthy, and in its results the most beneficent" [HODGE]. **18. Therefore hath he**—'So then he hath.' The result then is that He hath—**mercy on whom he will have mercy, and whom he will he hardeneth**—by judicially abandoning them to the hardening influence of sin itself (Ps. 81:11, 12; ch. 1:24, 26, 28; Heb. 3:8, 13), and of the surrounding incentives to it (Matt. 24:12; I Cor. 15:38; II Thess. 2:17). **19.** *Second objection* to the doctrine of Divine Sovereignty: **Thou shalt say then unto me, Why**—'Why then' is the true reading—**doth he yet find fault? for who hath resisted**—'Who resisteth'—**his will?**—i.e., '*This doctrine is incompatible with human responsibility*'; If God chooses and rejects, pardons and punishes, whom He pleases, why are those blamed who, if rejected by Him, cannot help sinning and perishing? This objection shows quite as conclusively as the former the real nature of the doctrine objected to—that it is Election and Non-election to eternal salvation prior to any difference of personal character; this is the only doctrine that could suggest the objection here stated, and to this doctrine the objection *is* plausible. What now is the apostle's answer? It is twofold. *First:* 'It is irreverence and presumption in the creature to arraign the Creator.' **20, 21. Nay but, O man, who art thou that repliest against God? Shall the thing formed say to him that formed it, Why hast thou made**—'didst thou make'—**me thus**—(Isa. 45:9)? **Hath not the potter power over the clay; of the same lump to make one vessel unto honour, and another to dishonour?**—"The objection is founded on ignorance or misapprehension of the relation between God and His sinful creatures; supposing that He is under obligation to extend His grace to all, whereas He is under obligation to none. All are sinners, and have forfeited every claim to His mercy; it is therefore perfectly competent to God to spare one and not another, to make one vessel to honor and another to dishonor. But it is to be borne in mind that Paul does not here speak of God's right over His creatures *as creatures,* but *as sinful creatures:* as he himself clearly intimates in the next verses. It is the cavil of a sinful creature against his Creator that he is answering, and he does so by showing that God is under no obligation to give His grace to any, but is as sovereign as in fashioning the clay" [HODGE]. But, *Second:* 'There is nothing unjust in such sovereignty.' **22, 23. What if God, willing to show**—'designing to manifest'—**his wrath**—His holy displeasure against sin—**and to make his power**—to punish it—**known, endured with much long-suffering the vessels of wrath**—i.e., 'destined to wrath'; just as "vessels of mercy," in the next verse, mean 'vessels destined to mercy'; compare Ephesians 2:3, "children of wrath." **fitted for destruction**—It is well remarked by STUART that the "difficulties which such statements involve are not to be got rid of by softening the language of one text, while so many others meet us which are of the same tenor; and even if we give up the Bible itself, so long as we acknowledge an omnipotent and omniscient God we cannot abate in the least degree from any of the difficulties which such texts make." Be it observed, however, that if God, as the apostle teaches, expressly "designed to manifest His wrath, and to make His power (in the way of wrath) known," it could only be by punishing some, while He pardons others; and if the choice between the two classes was not to be founded, as our apostle also teaches, on their own doings but on God's good pleasure, the decision

behooved ultimately to rest with God. Yet, even in the necessary punishment of the wicked, as HODGE observes, so far from proceeding with undue severity, the apostle would have it remarked that God "endures with much long-suffering" those objects of His righteous displeasure. **and that he might make known the riches of his glory on the vessels of mercy**—that 'glorious exuberance of Divine mercy' which was manifested in choosing and eternally arranging for the salvation of sinners. **24. even us, whom he hath called** . . . —'Whom he hath also called, even us . . . , in not only "*afore preparing*," but in due time effectually "*calling* us." **not of the Jews** . . . —better, 'not from among Jews only, but also from among Gentiles.' *Here for the first time in this chapter the calling of the Gentiles is introduced;* all before having respect, not to the substitution of the called Gentiles for the rejected Jews, but to the choice of one portion and the rejection of another of the same Israel. Had Israel's rejection been total, God's promise to Abraham would *not* have been fulfilled by the substitution of the Gentiles in their room; but Israel's rejection being only partial, the preservation of a "remnant," in which the promise was made good, was but "according to the election of grace." And now, for the first time, the apostle tells us that along with this elect remnant of *Israel*, it is God's purpose to "take out of the *Gentiles* a people for His name" (Acts 28:14); and that subject, thus introduced, is now continued to the end of ch. 11. **25. As he saith also in Osee**—'Hosea.' **I will call them my people, which were not my people; and her beloved, which was not beloved**—quoted, though not quite to the letter, from Hosea 2:23, a passage relating immediately, not to the heathen, but to the kingdom of the ten tribes; but since they had sunk to the level of the heathen, who were "not God's people," and in that sense "not beloved," the apostle legitimately applies it to the heathen, as "aliens from the commonwealth of Israel and strangers to the covenants of promise" (so I Pet. 2:10). **26. And**—another quotation from Hosea 1:10—**it shall come to pass, that in the place where it was said unto them, Ye are not my people; there shall they be called the children**—'called sons'—**of the living God**—The expression, 'in the place where . . . there,' seems designed only to give greater emphasis to the gracious change here announced, from divine exclusion to divine admission to the privileges of the people of God. **27-29. Esaias also crieth**—('But Isaiah crieth')—an expression denoting a solemn testimony openly borne (John 1:15; 7:28, 37; 12:44; Acts 23:6; 24:41). **concerning Israel, Though the number of the children**—'sons'—**of Israel be as the sand of the sea, a**—'the'—**remnant**—i.e., the elect remnant *only*—**shall be saved: For he will finish the work, and cut**—'is finishing the reckoning, and cutting'—**it short in righteousness; because a short work**—'reckoning'—**will the Lord make upon the earth**—Isaiah 10:22, 23, as in the LXX. The sense given to these words by the apostle may seem to differ from that intended by the prophet. But the sameness of sentiment in both places will at once appear, if we understand those words of the prophet, "the consumption decreed shall overflow with righteousness," to mean that while a remnant of Israel should be graciously spared to return from captivity, "the decreed consumption" of the impenitent majority should be "replete with righteousness," or illustriously display God's righteous vengeance against sin. The "short reckoning" seems to mean the speedy completing of His word, both in cutting off the one portion and saving the other. **And as Esaias said**—'hath said'—**before**—i.e., probably in an earlier part of his book, namely, Isaiah 1:9. **Except the Lord of Sabaoth**—i.e., 'The Lord of Hosts': the word is *Hebrew,* but occurs so in the Epistle of James (ch. 5:4), and has thence become naturalized in our Christian phraseology. **had left us a seed**—meaning a 'remnant'; small at first, but in due time to be a seed of plenty (cf. Ps. 22:30, 31; Isa. 6:12, 13). **we had been**—'become'—**as Sodom . . .**—But for this precious seed, the chosen people would have resembled the cities of the plain, both in degeneracy of character and in merited doom. **30, 31. What shall we say then?**—'What now is the result of the whole?' The result is this—very different from what one would have expected—**That the Gentiles, which followed not after righteousness, have attained**—'attained'—**to righteousness, even the righteousness of faith**—As we have seen that "the righteousness of faith" is the righteousness which *justifies* (see on ch. 3:22, etc.), this verse must mean that 'the Gentiles, who while strangers to Christ were quite indifferent about acceptance with God, having embraced the Gospel as soon as it was preached to them, experienced the blessedness of a justified state.' **but Israel, which followed**—'following'—**after the law of righteousness, hath not attained**—'attained not'—**unto the law of righteousness**—The word "law" is used here, we think, in the same sense as in ch. 7:23, to denote 'a principle of action'; i.e., 'Israel, though sincerely and steadily aiming at acceptance with God, nevertheless missed it.' **32, 33. Wherefore? Because they sought it not by faith, but as it were**—rather simply, 'as'—**by the works of the law**—as if it were thus attainable, which justification is not: Since, therefore, it is attainable only by faith, they missed it. **for**—it is doubtful if this particle was originally in the text—**they stumbled at that stumbling stone**—better, 'against the stone of stumbling,' meaning *Christ.* But in this they only did—**as it is written**—Isa. 8:14; 28:16)—**Behold . . .**—Two Messianic predictions are here combined, as is not unusual in quotations from the Old Testament. Thus combined, the prediction brings together both the classes of whom the apostle is treating: those to whom Messiah should be only a stone of stumbling, and those who were to regard Him as the Cornerstone of all their hopes. Thus expounded, this chapter presents no serious difficulties, none which do not arise out of the subject itself, whose depths are unfathomable; whereas on every other view of it the difficulty of giving it any consistent and worthy interpretation is in our judgment insuperable. Note, (1) To speak and act "in Christ," with a conscience not only illuminated, but under the present operation of the Holy Ghost, is not peculiar to the supernaturally inspired, but is the privilege, and ought to be the aim, of every believer (vs. 1). (2) Grace does not destroy, but only intensify and elevate, the feelings of nature; and Christians should study to show this (vss. 2, 3). (3) To belong to the visible Church of God, and enjoy its high and holy distinctions, is of the sovereign mercy of God, and should be regarded with devout thankfulness (vss. 4, 5). (4) Yet the most sacred external distinctions and privileges will avail nothing to salvation without the heart's submission to the righteousness of God (vss. 31-33). (5) What manner of persons ought "God's elect" to be—in *humility,* when they remember that He hath saved them and called them, not according to their works, but according to His own purpose and grace, given them in Christ Jesus before the world began (II Tim. 1:9); in *thankful-*

ness, for "Who maketh thee to differ, and what hast thou that thou didst not receive?" (I Cor. 4:7); in *godly jealousy* over themselves; remembering that "God is not mocked," but "whatsoever a man soweth that shall he also reap" (Gal. 6:7); in *diligence* "to make our calling and election sure" (II Pet. 1:10); and yet in calm *confidence* that "whom God predestinates, and calls, and justifies, them (in due time) He also glorifies" (ch. 8:30). (6) On all subjects which from their very nature lie beyond human comprehension, it will be our wisdom to set down what God says in His word, and has actually done in His procedure towards men, as indisputable, even though it contradict the results at which in the best exercise of our limited judgment we may have arrived (vss. 14-23). (7) Sincerity in religion, or a general desire to be saved, with assiduous efforts to do right, will prove fatal as a ground of confidence before God, if unaccompanied by implicit submission to His revealed method of salvation (vss. 31-33). (8) In the rejection of the great mass of the chosen people, and the inbringing of multitudes of estranged Gentiles, God would have men to see a law of His procedure, which the judgment of the great day will more vividly reveal—that "the last shall be first and the first last" (Matt. 20:16).

CHAPTER 10

Vss. 1-21. Same Subject Continued—How Israel Came to Miss Salvation, and the Gentiles to Find It. **1. Brethren, my heart's desire**—The word here expresses 'entire complacency,' that in which the heart would experience full satisfaction. **and prayer**—'supplication'—**to God for Israel**—'for them' is the true reading; the subject being continued from the close of the preceding chapter. **is, that they may be saved**—'for their salvation.' Having before poured forth the anguish of his soul at the general unbelief of his nation and its dreadful consequences (ch. 9:1-3), he here expresses in the most emphatic terms his desire and prayer for their salvation. **2. For I bear them record**—or, 'witness,' as he well could from his own sad experience—**that they have a zeal of**—'for'—**God, but not according to knowledge**—(Cf. Acts 22:3; 26:9-11; Gal. 1:13, 14). He alludes to this well-meaning of his people, notwithstanding their spiritual blindness, not certainly to excuse their rejection of Christ and rage against His saints, but as some ground of hope regarding them. (See I Tim. 1:13). **3. For they being ignorant of God's righteousness**—i.e., for the justification of the guilty (see on ch. 1:17)—**and going about**—'seeking'—**to establish their own righteousness, have not submitted themselves to the righteousness of God**—The apostle views the general rejection of Christ by the nation as one act. **4. For Christ is the end**—the object or aim—**of the law for**—justifying—**righteousness to every one that believeth**—i.e., contains within Himself all that the law demands for the justification of such as embrace Him, whether Jew or Gentile (Gal. 3:24). **5-10. For Moses describeth the righteousness which is of the law, That the man that doeth**—'hath done'—**those things**—which it commands—**shall live in them**—(Lev. 28:5). This is the one way of justification and life—by "the righteousness which is of (or, by our own obedience to) the law." **But the**—justifying—**righteousness which is of faith speaketh on this wise**—'speaketh thus'—its language or import is to this effect (quoting in substance Deut. 30:13, 14). **Say not in thine heart, Who shall ascend into heav-**

en? that is, to bring Christ down . . . —i.e., 'Ye have
not to sigh over the impossibility of attaining to
justification; as if one should say, oh! if I could but
get someone to mount up to heaven and fetch me
down Christ, there might be some hope, but since
that cannot be, mine is a desperate case.'   or, Who
shall descend . . . —another case of impossibility,
suggested by Proverbs 30:4, and perhaps also Amos
9:2—probably proverbial expressions of impossibility (cf. Ps. 139:7-10; Prov. 24:7, etc.).   But what
saith it? It saith—continuing the quotation from
Deuteronomy 30:14—The word is nigh thee—easily
accessible.   in thy mouth—when thou confessest
Him.   and in thine heart—when thou believest on
Him.   Though it is of *the law* which Moses more
immediately speaks in the passage quoted, yet it is
of the law as Israel shall be brought to look upon
it when the Lord their God shall circumcise their
heart "to love the Lord their God with all their
heart" (vs. 6); and thus, in applying it, the apostle
(as OLSHAUSEN truly observes) is not merely appropriating the language of Moses, but keeping in the
line of his deeper thought.   that is, the word of
faith, which we preach—i.e., the word which men
have to believe for salvation (cf. I Tim. 4:6).   That
if thou shalt . . . —So understanding the words, the
apostle is here giving the language of the true
method of justification; and this sense we prefer
[with CALVIN, BEZA, FERME, LOCKE, JOWETT].   But
able interpreters render the words, 'For,' or 'Because
if thou shalt . . . , [VULGATE, LUTHER, DE WETTE,
STUART, PHILIPPI, ALFORD, REVISED VERSION]. In
this case, these are the apostle's own remarks, confirming the foregoing statements as to the simplicity
of the gospel method of salvation.   confess with
thy mouth the Lord Jesus—i.e., probably, 'If thou
shalt confess Jesus [to be] the Lord,' which is the
proper manifestation or evidence of faith (Matt. 10:
32; I John 4:15).   This is put first merely to correspond with the foregoing quotation—"in thy mouth
and in thine heart."   So in I Pet. 1:10 the "calling
of believers" is put before their "election," as that
which is first "made sure," although in point of
time it comes after it.   and shalt believe in thine
heart that God hath raised—'that God raised'—him
from the dead . . . —See on ch. 4:25.   In the next
verse the two things are placed in their natural
order.   For with the heart man believeth unto—
justifying—righteousness; and with the mouth confession is made unto salvation—This confession of
Christ's name, especially in times of persecution,
and whenever obloquy is attached to the Christian
profession, is an indispensable test of discipleship.
11-13. For the scripture saith—in Isaiah 28:16, a
glorious Messianic passage.   Whosoever believeth
on him shall not be ashamed—Here, as in ch. 9:33,
the quotation is from the LXX, which renders those
words of the original, "shall not make haste" i.e.,
fly for escape, as from conscious danger), 'shall not
be put to shame,' which comes to the same thing.
For there is no difference—or 'distinction'—between
Jew and Greek; for the same Lord over all—i.e.,
not *God* [as CALVIN, GROTIUS, OLSHAUSEN, HODGE],
but *Christ,* as will be seen, we think, by comparing
vss. 9, 12, 13 and observing the apostle's usual style
on such subjects. [So CHRYSOSTOM, MELVILLE,
BENGEL, MEYER, DE WETTE, FRITZSCHE, THOLUCK,
STUART, ALFORD, PHILIPPI.] is rich—a favorite Pauline term to express the exuberance of that saving
grace which is in Christ Jesus.   unto all that call
upon him—This confirms the application of the preceding words to *Christ;* since to call upon the name
of the Lord Jesus is a customary expression.   (See

Acts 7:59, 60; 9:14, 21; 22:16; I Cor. 1:2; II Tim.
2:22).   For saith the scripture whosoever—The
expression is emphatic, 'Everyone whosoever'—shall
call upon the name of the Lord shall be saved—
Joel 2:32; quoted also by Peter, in his great Pentecostal sermon (Acts 2:21), with evident application
to Christ.   14, 15. How then shall they call on him
in whom they have not believed? and . . . believe in
him of whom they have not heard? and . . . hear
without a preacher? and . . . preach except . . .
sent?—i.e., 'True, the same Lord over all is rich unto
all alike that call upon Him.   But this calling implies believing, and believing hearing, and hearing
preaching, and preaching *a mission to preach:* Why,
then, take ye it so ill, O children of Abraham, that
in obedience to our heavenly mission (Acts 26:16-18)
we preach among *the Gentiles* the unsearchable
riches of Christ?'   as it is written—(Isa. 52:7).
How beautiful are the feet of them that preach the
gospel of peace . . . —The whole chapter of Isaiah
from which this is taken, and the three that follow,
are so richly Messianic, that there can be no doubt
"the glad tidings" there spoken of announce a more
glorious release than of Judah from the Babylonish
captivity, and the very feet of its preachers are
called "beautiful" for the sake of their message.
16, 17. But they have not all obeyed the gospel—
i.e., the Scripture hath prepared us to expect this
sad result.   For Esaias saith, Lord, who hath believed our report?—i.e., 'Where shall one find a believer?'   The prophet speaks as if next to none
would believe: The apostle softens this into "They
have not all believed."   So then faith cometh by
hearing, and hearing by the word of God—'This is
another confirmation of the truth that faith supposes the hearing of the Word, and this a commission to preach it.'   18. But I say, Have they
not heard?—'Did they not hear?'   Can Israel,
through any region of his dispersion, plead ignorance of these glad tidings?   Yes, verily, their
sound went—'their voice went out'—into all the
earth, and their words unto the end of the world—
These beautiful words are from Psalm 19:4.
Whether the apostle quoted them as in their primary intention applicable to his subject [as OLSHAUSEN,
ALFORD, etc.], or only "used scriptural language to
express his own ideas, as is done involuntarily almost by every preacher in every sermon" [HODGE],
expositors are not agreed.   But though the latter
may seem the more natural since "the rising of the
Sun of righteousness upon the world" (Mal. 4:2),
"the Day-spring from on high visiting us, giving
light to them that sat in darkness, and guiding our
feet into the way of peace" (Luke 1:78, 79), must
have been familiar and delightful to the apostle's
ear, we cannot doubt that the irradiation of the
world with the beams of a better Sun by the universal diffusion of the Gospel of Christ, must have a
mode of speaking quite natural, and to him scarcely
figurative.   19. But I say, Did not Israel know?—
know, from their own Scriptures, of God's intention
to bring in the Gentiles?   First—i.e., First in the
prophetic line [DE WETTE].   Moses saith . . . —'I
will provoke you to jealousy ('against') [them that
are] not a nation, and against a nation without understanding will I anger you' (Deut. 32:21).   In this
verse God warns His ancient people that because
they had (that is, in aftertimes would) moved Him
to jealousy with their "no-gods," and provoked Him
to anger with their vanities, He in requital would
move them to jealousy by receiving into His favor
a "no-people," and provoke them to anger by adopting a nation void of understanding.   20. But Esaias

is very bold, and saith—i.e., is still plainer, and goes even the length of saying—I was found of them that sought me not—until I sought them—I was made—'became'—manifest unto them that asked not after me—until the invitation from Me came to them. That the calling of the Gentiles was meant by these words of the prophet (Isa. 65:1) is manifest from what immediately follows, "I said, Behold Me, behold Me, unto a nation that was not called by My name." 21. But to—rather, 'with regard to'—Israel he saith, All day—'All the day'—long I have stretched out—'did I stretch forth'—my hands—the attitude of gracious entreaty. unto a disobedient and gainsaying people—These words, which immediately follow the announcement just quoted of the calling of the Gentiles, were enough to forewarn the Jews both of God's purpose to eject them from their privileges, in favor of the Gentiles, and of the cause of it on their own part.—Note, (1) Mere sincerity, and even earnestness in religion—though it may be some ground of hope for a merciful recovery from error—is no excuse, and will not compensate, for the deliberate rejection of saving truth, when in the providence of God presented for acceptance (vss. 1-3; and see on ch. 9, *Note* 7). (2) The true cause of such rejection of saving truth, by the otherwise sincere, is the prepossession of the mind by some false notions of its own. So long as the Jews "sought to set up their own righteousness," it was in the nature of things impossible that they should "submit themselves to the righteousness of God"; the one of these two methods of acceptance being in the teeth of the other (vs. 3). (3) The essential terms of salvation have in every age been the same: "Whosoever will" is invited to "take of the water of life freely," Revelation 22:17 (vs. 13). (4) How will the remembrance of the simplicity, reasonableness, and absolute freeness of God's plan of salvation overwhelm those that perish from under the sound of it (vss. 4-13). (5) How piercingly and perpetually should that question—"How shall they hear without a preacher?"—sound in the ears of all churches, as but the apostolic echo of their Lord's parting injunction, "Preach the Gospel to every creature" (Mark 16:15), and how far below the proper standard of love, zeal, and self-sacrifice must the churches as yet be, when with so plenteous a harvest the laborers are yet so few (Matt. 9:37, 38), and that cry from the lips of pardoned, gifted, consecrated men—"Here am I, send me" (Isa. 6:8), is not heard everywhere (vss. 14, 15)! (6) The blessing of a covenant relation to God is the irrevocable privilege of no people and no Church; it can be preserved only by fidelity, on our part, to the covenant itself (vs. 19). (7) God is often found by those who apparently are the farthest from Him, while He remains undiscovered by those who think themselves the nearest (vss. 20, 21). (8) God's dealings even with reprobate sinners are full of tenderness and compassion; all the day long extending the arms of His mercy even to the disobedient and gainsaying. This will be felt and acknowledged at last by all who perish, to the glory of God's forbearance and to their own confusion (vs. 21).

CHAPTER 11

Vss. 1-36. Same Subject Continued and Concluded—The Ultimate Inbringing of All Israel, to Be, with the Gentiles, One Kingdom of God on the Earth. 1. I say then, Hath—'Did'—God cast away his people? God forbid—Our Lord did indeed announce that "the kingdom of God should be *taken from* Israel" (Matt. 21:41); and when asked by the Eleven, after His resurrection, if He would at that time "*restore* the kingdom to Israel," His reply is a virtual admission that Israel was in some sense already out of covenant (Acts 1:9). Yet here the apostle teaches that, in two respects, Israel was *not* "cast away"; First, Not *totally;* Second, Not *finally.* First, Israel is not *wholly* cast away. for I also am an Israelite—See Phil. 3:5, and so a living witness to the contrary. of the seed of Abraham—of pure descent from the father of the faithful. of the tribe of Benjamin—Phil. 3:5), that tribe which, on the revolt of the ten tribes, constituted, with Judah, the one faithful kingdom of God (I Kings 12:21), and after the captivity was, along with Judah, the kernel of the Jewish nation (Ezra 4:1; 10:9). 2-4. God hath—'did'—not cast away his people—i.e., *wholly.* which he foreknew—On the word "foreknew," see on ch. 8:29. Wot—i.e., 'Know'—ye not that the scripture saith—lit., 'in,' i.e., in the section which relates to—Elias? how he maketh intercession—'pleadeth'—against Israel—(The word "saying," which follows, as also the particle "and" before "digged down," should be omitted, as without MSS. authority.) and I am left alone—'I only am left.' seven thousand, that have not bowed the knee to Baal—not "the image of Baal," according to the supplement of our version. 5. Even so at this present time—'in this present season'; this period of Israel's rejection. (See Acts 1:7, *Greek.*) there is—'there obtains,' or 'hath remained.' a remnant according to the election of grace—, 'As in Elijah's time the apostasy of Israel was not so universal as it seemed to be, and as he in his despondency concluded it to be, so now, the rejection of Christ by Israel is not so appalling in extent as one would be apt to think: There is now, as there was then, a faithful remnant; not however of persons naturally better than the unbelieving mass, but of persons graciously chosen to salvation.' (See I Cor. 4:7; II Thess. 2:13.) This establishes our view of the argument on Election in ch. 9, as not being an election of Gentiles in the place of Jews, and merely to religious advantages, but a sovereign choice of some of Israel itself, from among others, to believe and be saved. (See on ch. 9:6.) 6. And ...—better, 'Now if it (the election) be by grace, it is no more of works; for [then] grace becomes no more grace: but if it be of works ...' (The authority of ancient MSS. against this latter clause, as superfluous and not originally in the text, though strong, is not sufficient, we think, to justify its exclusion. Such seeming redundancies are not unusual with our apostle). The general position here laid down is of vital importance: That there are but two possible sources of salvation—men's works, and God's grace; and that these are so essentially distinct and opposite, that salvation cannot be of any combination or mixture of both, but must be wholly either of the one or of the other. (See on ch. 4, *Note* 3. 7-10. What then?—How stands the fact? Israel hath not obtained that which he seeketh for—better, 'What Israel is in search of (i.e., Justification, or acceptance with God—see on ch. 9:31); this he found not; but the election (the elect remnant of Israel) found it, and the rest were hardened,' or judicially given over to the 'hardness of their own hearts.' as it is written—Isa. 29:10, and Deut. 29: 4—God hath given—'gave'—them the spirit of slumber—'stupor'. unto this—'this present'—day. And David saith—Psalm 69:23, which in such a Messianic psalm must be meant of the rejecters of

Christ. **Let their table** . . .—i.e., Let their very blessings prove a curse to them, and their enjoyments only sting and take vengeance on them. **Let their eyes be darkened . . . and bow down their back alway**—expressive either of the *decrepitude,* or of the *servile condition,* to come on the nation through the just judgment of God. The apostle's object in making these quotations is to show that what he had been compelled to say of the then condition and prospects of his nation was more than borne out by their own Scriptures. But, SECONDLY, God has not cast away His people *finally.* The illustration of this point extends from vs. 11 to vs. 31. **11. I say then, Have they stumbled**—'Did they stumble'—**that they should fall? God forbid; but**—the supplement "rather" is better omitted—**through their fall**—lit., 'trespass,' but here best rendered 'false step' [DE WETTE]; not "fall," as in our version. **salvation is come to the Gentiles, to provoke them to jealousy** —Here, as also in ch. 10:19 (quoted from Deut. 32: 21), we see that emulation is a legitimate stimulus to what is good. **12. Now if the fall of them**—'But if their trespass,' or 'false step'—**be the riches of the**—Gentile—**world**—as being the occasion of their accession to Christ. **and the diminishing of them**—i.e., the reduction of the *true* Israel to so small a remnant—**the riches of the Gentiles; how much more their fulness!**—i.e., their full recovery (see on vs. 26); i.e., 'If an event so untoward as Israel's fall was the occasion of such unspeakable good to the Gentile world, of how much greater good may we expect an event so blessed as their full recovery to be productive?' **13. I speak**—'am speaking'—**to you Gentiles**—another proof that this Epistle was addressed to Gentile believers. (See on ch. 1:13.) **I magnify**—'glorify'—**mine office**—The clause beginning with "inasmuch" should be read as a parenthesis. **If . . . I may provoke** . . . (See on vs. 11). **my flesh**—Cf. Isa. 58:7. **15. For if the casting away of them**—The apostle had denied that they were cast away (vs. 1); here he affirms it. But both are true; they *were* cast away, though neither totally nor finally, and it is of this partial and temporary rejection that the apostle here speaks. **be the reconciling of the**—Gentile—**world, what shall the receiving of them be, but life from the dead?**—The reception of the whole family of Israel, scattered as they are among all nations under heaven, and the most inveterate enemies of the Lord Jesus, will be such a stupendous manifestation of the power of God upon the spirits of men, and of His glorious presence with the heralds of the Cross, as will not only kindle devout astonishment far and wide, but so change the dominant mode of thinking and feeling on all spiritual things as to seem like a *resurrection from the dead.* **16. For**—'But'—**if the first fruit be holy, the lump is also holy; and if the root** . . ., **so the branches**—The Israelites were required to offer to God the first fruits of the earth—both in their raw state, in a sheaf of newly reaped grain (Lev. 23:10, 11), and in their prepared state, made into cakes of dough (Num. 15:19-21)—by which the whole produce of that season was regarded as *hallowed.* It is probable that the latter of these offerings is here intended, as to it the word "lump" best applies; and the argument of the apostle is, that as the separation unto God of Abraham, Isaac, and Jacob, from the rest of mankind, as the parent stem of their race, was as real an offering of first fruits as that which hallowed the produce of the earth, so, in the divine estimation, it was as real a separation of the mass or "lump" of that nation in all time to God. The figure of the "root" and its "branches" is of like

import—the consecration of the one of them extending to the other, **17, 18. And if**—rather, 'But if'; i.e., 'If notwithstanding this consecration of Abraham's race to God. **some of the branches**—The mass of the unbelieving and rejected Israelites are here called "some," not, as before, to meet Jewish prejudice (see on ch. 3:3, and on "not all" in ch. 10:16), but with the opposite view of checking Gentile pride. **and thou, being a wild olive, wert**—'wast'—**graffed in among them**—Though it is more usual to graft the superior cutting upon the inferior stem, the opposite method, which is intended here, is not without example. **and with them partakest**—'wast made partaker,'—along with the branches left, the believing remnant—**of the root and fatness of the olive tree**—the rich grace secured by covenant to the true seed of Abraham—**boast not against the** —rejected—**branches. But if thou**—'do'—**boast**—remember that—**thou bearest not**—'it is not thou that bearest'—**the root, but the root thee**—'If the branches may not boast over the root that bears them, then may not the Gentile boast over the seed of Abraham; for what is thy standing, O Gentile, in relation to Israel, but that of a branch in relation to the root? From Israel hath come all that thou art and hast in the family of God; for "salvation is of the Jews" (John 4:22). **19-21. Thou wilt say then**—as a plea for boasting—**The branches were broken off, that I might be graffed in. Well**—'Be it so, but remember that'—**because of unbelief they were broken off, and thou standest**—not as a Gentile, but solely—**by faith**—But as faith cannot live in those "whose soul is lifted up" (Hab. 2:4)—**Be not high-minded, but fear**—(Prov. 28:14; Phil. 2:12); **for if God spared not the natural branches**—sprung from the parent stem—**take heed lest he also spare not thee**—a mere wild graft. The former might, beforehand, have been thought very improbable; but, after that, no one can wonder at the latter. **22, 23. Behold therefore the goodness and severity of God: on them that fell, severity—in rejecting the** chosen seed—**but toward thee, goodness**—'God's goodness' is the true reading' i.e., His sovereign goodness in admitting thee to a covenant standing who before wert a "stranger to the covenants of promise" (Eph. 2:12-20). **if thou continue in his goodness**—in believing dependence on that pure goodness which made thee what thou art. **otherwise** . . . **And they also**—'Yea, and they'—**if they abide not still in unbelief, shall be graffed in: for God is able to graff them in again**—This appeal to the *power* of God to effect the recovery of His ancient people implies the vast difficulty of it—which all who have ever labored for the conversion of the Jews are made depressingly to feel. That intelligent expositors should think that this was meant of *individual* Jews, reintroduced from time to time into the family of God on their believing on the Lord Jesus, is surprising; and yet those who deny the *national* recovery of Israel must and do so interpret the apostle. But this is to confound the two things which the apostle carefully distinguishes. Individual Jews have been at all times admissible, and have been admitted, to the Church through the gate of faith in the Lord Jesus. This is the "remnant, *even at this present time,* according to the election of grace," of which the apostle, in the first part of the chapter, had cited himself as one. But here he manifestly speaks of something *not* then existing, but to be looked forward to as a great future event in the economy of God, the reingrafting of *the nation as such,* when they "abide not in unbelief." And though this is here spoken of merely as a supposition (if their unbelief shall cease)—in order to set it over against the other supposition, of what will happen to the Gentiles if they shall not abide in the faith—the supposition is turned into an explicit prediction in the verses following. **24. For if thou wert cut**—'wert cut off'—**from the olive tree, which is wild by nature, and wast graffed contrary to nature into a good olive tree; how much more shall these ...**—This is just the converse of vs. 21: 'As the excision of the merely *engrafted* Gentiles through unbelief is a thing much more to be expected than was the excision of the *natural* Israel, before it happened; so the restoration of Israel, when they shall be brought to believe in Jesus, is a thing far more in the line of what we should expect, than the admission of the Gentiles to a standing which they never before enjoyed.' **25. For I would not ... that ye should be ignorant of this mystery**—The word "mystery," so often used by our apostle, does not mean (as with us) something incomprehensible, but 'something before kept secret, either wholly or for the most part, and now only fully disclosed' (cf. ch. 16:25; I Cor. 2:7-10; Eph. 1:9, 10; 3:3-6, 9, 10). **lest ye should be wise in your own conceits**—as if ye alone were in all time coming to be the family of God. **that blindness**—'hardness'—**in part is happened to**—'hath come upon'—**Israel**—i.e., hath come partially, or upon a portion of Israel. **until the fulness of the Gentiles be**—'have'—**come in**—i.e., not the general conversion of the world to Christ, as many take it; for this would seem to contradict the latter part of this chapter, and throw the national recovery of Israel too far into the future: besides, in vs. 15, the apostle seems to speak of the receiving of Israel, not as following, but as contributing largely to bring about the general conversion of the world—but, 'until the Gentiles have had their *full* time of the visible Church all to themselves while the Jews are out, which the Jews had till the Gentiles were brought in.' (See Luke 21:24.) **26, 27. And so all Israel shall be saved**—To understand this great statement, as some still do, merely of such a gradual inbringing of *individual* Jews, that there shall at length remain none in unbelief, is to do manifest violence both to it and to the whole context. It can only mean the ultimate ingathering of Israel as a *nation*, in contrast with the present "remnant." [So THOLUCK, MEYER, DE WETTE, PHILIPPI, ALFORD, HODGE]. Three confirmations of this now follow: two from the prophets, and a third from the Abrahamic covenant itself. *First,* **as it is written, There shall come out of Sion the Deliverer, and shall**—or, according to what seems the true reading, without the "and"—'He shall'—**turn away ungodliness from Jacob**—The apostle, having drawn his illustrations of man's *sinfulness* chiefly from Psalm 14 and Isaiah 59, now seems to combine the language of the same two places regarding Israel's *salvation* from it [BENGEL]. In the one place the Psalmist longs to see the "salvation of Israel coming *out of Zion*" (Ps. 14:7); in the other, the prophet announces that "the Redeemer (or, "Deliverer") shall come *to* (or *for*) Zion" (Isa. 59:20). But as all the glorious manifestations of Israel's God were regarded as issuing out of Zion, as the seat of His manifested glory (Ps. 20:2; 110:2;. Isa. 31:9), the turn which the apostle gives to the words merely adds to them that familiar idea. And whereas the prophet announces that He "shall come *to* (or, '*for*') them that turn from transgression in Jacob," while the apostle makes Him say that He shall come "to turn away ungodliness *from* Jacob," this is taken

from the LXX version, and seems to indicate a different reading of the original text. The sense, however, is substantially the same in both. *Second,* **For**—rather, 'and' (again); introducing a new quotation. **this is my covenant with them**—lit., 'this is the covenant from me unto them." **when I shall take away their sins**—This, we believe, is rather a brief summary of Jeremiah 31:31-34 than the express words of any prediction. Those who believe that there are no predictions regarding the literal Israel in the Old Testament, that stretch beyond the end of the Jewish economy, are obliged to view these quotations by the apostle as mere adaptations of Old Testament language to express his own predictions [ALEXANDER on Isaiah, etc.]. But how forced this is, we shall presently see. **28, 29. As concerning the Gospel they are enemies for your sakes**—i.e., they are regarded and treated as enemies (in a state of exclusion through unbelief, from the family of God) for the benefit of you Gentiles; in the sense of vss. 11, 15. **but as touching the election**—of Abraham and his seed—**they are beloved**—*even in their state of exclusion*—**for the fathers' sakes. For the gifts and calling**—'and the calling'—**of God are without repentance**—'not to be,' or 'cannot be repented of.' By the "*calling* of God," in this case, is meant that sovereign act by which God, in the exercise of His free choice, "called" Abraham to be the father of a peculiar people; while "the *gifts* of God" here denote the articles of the covenant which God made with Abraham, and which constituted the real distinction between his and all other families of the earth. Both these, says the apostle, are irrevocable; and as the point for which he refers to this at all is the *final destiny* of the Israelitish nation, it is clear that the *perpetuity through all time of the Abrahamic covenant* is the thing here affirmed. And lest any should say that though Israel, *as a nation,* has no destiny at all under the Gospel, but as a people disappeared from the stage when the middle wall of partition was broken down, yet the Abrahamic covenant still endures in the *spiritual* seed of Abraham, made up of Jews and Gentiles in one undistinguished mass of redeemed men under the Gospel—the apostle, as if to preclude that supposition, expressly states that the very Israel who, as concerning the Gospel, are regarded as "enemies for the Gentiles' sakes," are "*beloved for the fathers' sakes*"; and it is in proof of this that he adds, "For the gifts and the calling of God are without repentance." But in what sense are the now unbelieving and excluded children of Israel "beloved for the fathers' sakes"? Not merely from ancestral *recollections,* as one looks with fond interest on the child of a dear friend for that friend's sake [DR. ARNOLD]—a beautiful thought, and not foreign to Scripture, in this very matter (see II Chron. 20:7; Isa. 41:8)—but it is from ancestral *connections* and *obligations,* or their lineal descent from and oneness in covenant with the fathers with whom God originally established it. In other words, the natural Israel—not "the *remnant* of them according to the election of grace," but THE NATION, sprung from Abraham according to the flesh—are still an elect people, and as such, "beloved." The very same love which chose the fathers, and rested on the fathers as a parent stem of the nation, still rests on their descendants at large, and will yet recover them from unbelief, and reinstate them in the family of God. **30, 31. For as ye in times past have not believed**—or, 'obeyed'—**God**—that is, yielded not to God "the obedience of faith," while strangers to Christ. **yet now have obtained mercy**

through—by occasion of—**their unbelief**—(See on vss. 11, 15, 28). **even so have these**—the Jews—**now not believed**—or, 'now been disobedient'—**that through your mercy**—the mercy shown to you—**they also may obtain mercy**—Here is an entirely new idea. The apostle has hitherto dwelt upon the unbelief of the Jews as making way for the faith of the Gentiles— the exclusion of the one occasioning the reception of the other; a truth yielding to generous, believing Gentiles but mingled satisfaction. Now, opening a more cheering prospect, he speaks of the mercy shown to the Gentiles as a means of Israel's recovery; which seems to mean that it will be by the instrumentality of believing Gentiles that Israel as a nation is at length to "look on Him whom they have pierced and mourn for Him," and so to "obtain mercy." (See II Cor. 3:15, 16.) **32. For God hath concluded them all in unbelief**—'hath shut them all up to unbelief'—**that he might have mercy upon all**—i.e., those "all" of whom he had been discoursing; the Gentiles first, and after them the Jews [FRITZSCHE, THOLUCK, OLSHAUSEN, DE WETTE, PHILIPPI, STUART, HODGE]. Certainly it is not 'all mankind individually' [MEYER, ALFORD]; for the apostle is not here dealing with individuals, but with those great divisions of mankind, Jew and Gentile. And what he here says is that God's purpose was to shut each of these divisions of men to the experience first of an humbled, condemned state, without Christ, and then to the experience of His mercy in Christ. **33. Oh, the depth . . .**— The apostle now yields himself up to the admiring contemplation of the grandeur of that divine plan which he had sketched out. **of the riches both of the wisdom and knowledge of God**—Many able expositors render this, 'of the riches and wisdom and knowledge . . .' [ERASMUS, GROTIUS, BENGEL, MEYER, DE WETTE, THOLUCK, OLSHAUSEN, FRITZSCHE, PHILIPPI, ALFORD, REVISED VERSION]. The words will certainly bear this sense, "the depth of God's riches." But "the riches of God" is a much rarer expression with our apostle than the riches of this or that perfection of God; and the words immediately following limit our attention to the unsearchableness of God's "*judgments,*" which probably means His decrees or plans (Ps. 119:75), and of "His *ways,*" or the method by which He carries these into effect. [So LUTHER, CALVIN, BEZA, HODGE, etc.] Besides, all that follows to the end of the chapter seems to show that while the *Grace* of God to guilty men in Christ Jesus is presupposed to be the whole theme of this chapter, that which called forth the special admiration of the apostle, after sketching at some length the divine purposes and methods in the bestowment of this grace, was "the depth of the riches of God's *wisdom and knowledge*" in these purposes and methods. The "knowledge," then, points probably to the vast sweep of divine comprehension herein displayed; the "wisdom" to that fitness to accomplish the ends intended, which is stamped on all this procedure. **34, 35. For who hath known the mind of the Lord?**— See Job 15:8; Jeremiah 23:18. **or who hath been his counsellor**—See Isaiah 40:13, 14. **or who hath first given to him, and it shall be recompensed to him**—'and shall have recompense made to him— **again**—see Job 35:7, and 41:11. These questions, it will thus be seen, are just quotations from the Old Testament, as if to show how familiar to God's ancient people was the great truth which the apostle himself had just uttered, that God's plans and methods in the dispensation of His Grace have a reach of comprehension and wisdom stamped upon them

which finite mortals cannot fathom, much less could ever have imagined, before they were disclosed. **36. For of him, and through him, and to him, are all things: to whom**—'to Him'—**be glory for ever. Amen**—Thus worthily—with a brevity only equalled by its sublimity—does the apostle here sum up this whole matter. "OF Him are all things," as their eternal Source: "THROUGH HIM are all things," inasmuch as He brings all to pass which in His eternal counsels He purposed: "TO Him are all things," as being His own last End; the manifestation of the glory of His own perfections being the ultimate, because the highest possible, design of all His procedure from first to last.—On this rich chapter, Note (1) It is an unspeakable consolation to know that in times of deepest religious declension and most extensive defection from the truth, the lamp of God has never been permitted to go out, and that a faithful remnant has ever existed—a remnant larger than their own drooping spirits could easily believe (vss. 1-5). (2) The preservation of this remnant, even as their separation at the first, is all of mere grace (vss. 5, 6). (3) When individuals and communities, after many fruitless warnings, are abandoned of God, they go from bad to worse (vss. 7-10). (4) God has so ordered His dealings with the great divisions of mankind, "that no flesh should glory in His presence." Gentile and Jew have each in turn been "shut up to unbelief," that each in turn may experience the "mercy" which saves the chief of sinners (vss. 11-32). (5) As we are "justified by faith," so are we "kept by the power of God through faith"—faith alone—unto salvation (vss. 20-32). (6) God's covenant with Abraham and his natural seed is a perpetual covenant, in equal force under the Gospel as before it. Therefore it is, that the Jews as a nation still survive, in spite of all the laws which, in similar circumstances, have either extinguished or destroyed the identity of other nations. And therefore it is that the Jews as a nation will yet be restored to the family of God, through the subjection of their proud hearts to Him whom they have pierced. And as believing Gentiles will be honored to be the instruments of this stupendous change, so shall the vast Gentile world reap such benefit from it, that it shall be like the communication of life to them from the dead. (7) Thus has the Christian Church the highest motive to the establishment and vigorous prosecution of *missions to the Jews;* God having not only promised that there shall be a remnant of them gathered in every age, but pledged Himself to the final ingathering of the whole nation assigned the honor of that ingathering to the Gentile Church, and assured them that the event, when it does arrive, shall have a life-giving effect upon the whole world (vss. 12-16, 26-31). (8) Those who think that in all the evangelical prophecies of the Old Testament the terms "Jacob," "Israel," etc., are to be understood solely of *the Christian Church,* would appear to read the Old Testament differently from the apostle, who, from the use of those very terms in Old Testament prophecy, draws arguments to prove that God has mercy in store for *the natural Israel* (vss. 26, 27). (9) Mere intellectual investigations into divine truth in general, and the sense of the living oracles in particular, as they have a hardening effect, so they are a great contrast to the spirit of our apostle, whose lengthened sketch of God's majestic procedure towards men in Christ Jesus ends here in a burst of *admiration,* which loses itself in the still loftier frame of *adoration* (vss. 33-36).

CHAPTER 12

Vss. 1-21. Duties of Believers, General and Particular. The doctrinal teaching of this Epistle is now followed up by a series of exhortations to practical duty. And *first,* the all-comprehensive duty. **1. I beseech you therefore**—in view of all that has been advanced in the foregoing part of this Epistle. **by the mercies of God**—those mercies, whose free and unmerited nature, glorious Channel, and saving fruits have been opened up at such length. **that ye present**—See on ch. 6:13, where we have the same exhortation and the same word there rendered "yield" (as also in vss. 16, 19). **your bodies**—i.e., 'yourselves in the body,' considered as the organ of the inner life. As it is through the body that all the evil that is in the unrenewed heart comes forth into palpable manifestation and action, so it is through the body that all the gracious principles and affections of believers reveal themselves in the outward life. Sanctification extends to the whole man (I Thess. 5:23, 24). **a living sacrifice**—in glorious contrast to the legal sacrifices, which, save as they were *slain,* were no sacrifices at all. The death of the one "Lamb of God, taking away the sin of the world," has swept all dead victims from off the altar of God, to make room for the redeemed themselves as "living sacrifices" to Him who made "Him to be sin for us"; while every outgoing of their grateful hearts in praise, and every act prompted by the love of Christ, is itself a sacrifice to God of a sweet-smelling savor (Heb. 13:15, 16). **holy**—As the Levitical victims, when offered without blemish to God, were regarded as holy, so believers, "yielding themselves to God as those that are alive from the dead, and their members as instruments of righteousness unto God, are, in His estimation, not ritually but really "holy," and so—**acceptable**—'wellpleasing'—**unto God**—not as the Levitical offerings, merely as appointed symbols of spiritual ideas, but objects, intrinsically, of divine complacency, in their renewed character, and endeared relationship to Him through His Son Jesus Christ. **which is your reasonable**—rather, 'rational' —**service**—in contrast, not to the senselessness of idol worship, but to the offering of irrational victims under the law. In this view the presentation of ourselves, as living monuments of redeeming mercy, is here called "our rational service"; and surely it is the most rational and exalted occupation of God's reasonable creatures. So II Peter 1:5, "to offer up *spiritual sacrifices,* acceptable to God through Jesus Christ." **2. And be ye not conformed to this world** —Cf. Eph. 2:2; Gal. 1:4, *Greek.* **but be ye transformed**—or, 'transfigured' (as in Matt. 17:2; and II Cor. 3:18, *Greek*). **by the renewing of your mind** —not by a mere outward disconformity to the ungodly world, many of whose actions in themselves may be virtuous and praiseworthy; but by such an inward spiritual transformation as makes the whole life new—new in its motives and ends, even where the actions differ in nothing from those of the world —new, considered as a whole, and in such a sense as to be wholly unattainable save through the constraining power of the love of Christ. **that ye may prove**—i.e., experimentally. (See on the word "experience" in ch. 5:4, and cf. I Thess. 5:10, where the sentiment is the same.) **what is that**—'the'— **good, and acceptable**—'well pleasing'—**and perfect, will of God**—We prefer this rendering [with Calvin] to that which many able critics [Tholuck, Meyer, De Wette, Fritzsche, Philippi, Alford, Hodge] adopt—'that ye may prove,' or 'discern the will of God, [even] what is good, and acceptable, and perfect.' God's will is *"good,"* as it demands only what is essentially and unchangeably good (ch. 7: 10); it is *"well pleasing,"* in contrast with all that is arbitrary, as demanding only what God has eternal complacency in (cf. Mic. 6:8, with Jer. 9:24); and it is *"perfect,"* as it required nothing else than the perfection of God's reasonable creature, who, in proportion as he attains to it, reflects God's own perfection. Such then is the great general duty of the redeemed—self-consecration, in our whole spirit and soul and body to Him who hath called us into the fellowship of His Son Jesus Christ. Next follow specific duties, chiefly social; beginning with Humility, the chiefest of all the graces— but here with special reference to spiritual gifts. **3. For I say**—authoritatively—**through the grace given unto me**—as an apostle of Jesus Christ; thus exemplifying his own precept by modestly falling back on that office which both warranted and required such plainness towards all classes. **to every man that is among you, not to think . . .**—It is impossible to convey in good English the emphatic play, so to speak, which each word here has upon another: 'not to be high-minded above what he ought to be minded, but so to be minded as to be sober-minded [Calvin, Alford]. This is merely a strong way of characterizing all undue self-elevation. **according as God hath dealt to every man the measure of faith** —Faith is here viewed as the inlet to all the other graces, and so, as the receptive faculty of the renewed soul—i.e., 'as God hath given to each his particular capacity to take in the gifts and graces which He designs for the general good.' **4, 5. For as we have many members . . .**—The same diversity and yet unity obtains in the body of Christ, whereof all believers are the several members, as in the natural body. **6-8. Having then gifts differing according to the grace given to us**—Here, let it be observed, all the gifts of believers alike are viewed as communications of mere *grace.* **whether**—we have the gift of—**prophecy**—i.e., of inspired teaching (as in Acts 15:32). Anyone speaking with divine authority—whether with reference to the past, the present, or the future—was termed a prophet (Exod. 7:1). **let us prophesy according to the proportion of faith** —rather, 'of our faith.' Many Romish expositors and some Protestant (as Calvin and Bengel, and, though, hesitatingly, Beza and Hodge), render this 'the analogy of faith,' understanding by it 'the general tenor' or 'rule of faith,' divinely delivered to men for their guidance. But this is against the context, whose object is to show that, as all the gifts of believers are according to their respective capacity for them, they are not to be puffed up on account of them, but to use them purely for their proper ends. **Or ministry, let us wait on**—be occupied with'—**our ministering**—The word here used imports any kind of service, from the dispensing of the word of life (Acts 6:4) to the administering of the temporal affairs of the Church (Acts 6:1-3). The latter seems intended here, being distinguished from "prophesying," "teaching," and "exhorting." **or he that teacheth**—Teachers are expressly distinguished from prophets, and put after them, as exercising a lower function (Acts 13:1; I Cor. 12:28, 29). Probably it consisted mainly in opening up the evangelical bearings of Old Testament Scripture; and it was in this department apparently that Apollos showed his power and eloquence (Acts 18:24). **or he that exhorteth**—Since all preaching, whether by apostles, prophets, or teachers, was followed up by exhortation (Acts 11:23; 14:22; 15:32, etc.), many think that no specific class is here in view. But if liberty was given to others to exercise themselves occasionally in exhorting the brethren, generally, or small parties of the less instructed, the reference may be to them. **he that giveth**—in the exercise of private benevolence probably, rather than in the discharge of diaconal duty. **with simplicity**—so the word probably means. But as simplicity seems enjoined in the next clause but one of this same verse, perhaps the meaning here is, 'with liberality,' as the same word is rendered in II Corinthians 8:2; 9:11. **he that ruleth**—whether in the Church or his own household. See I Timothy 3:4, 5, where the same word is applied to both. **with diligence**—with earnest purpose. **he that showeth mercy, with cheerfulness**—not only without grudging either trouble or pecuniary relief, but feeling it to be "more blessed to give than to receive," and to help than be helped. **9. Let love be without dissimulation**—'Let your love be unfeigned' (as in II Cor. 6:6; I Pet. 2:22; and see I John 3:18). **Abhor that which is evil; cleave to that which is good**—What a lofty tone of moral principle and feeling is here inculcated! It is not, Abstain from the one, and do the other; nor, Turn away from the one, and draw to the other; but, Abhor the one, and cling, with deepest sympathy, to the other. **10. Be** . . .—better, 'In brotherly love be affectionate one to another; in [giving, or showing] honor, outdoing each other.' The word rendered "prefer" means rather 'to go before,' 'take the lead,' i.e., 'show an example.' How opposite is this to the reigning morality of the heathen world! and though Christianity has so changed the spirit of society, that a certain beautiful disinterestedness and self-sacrifice shines in the character of not a few who are but partially, if at all under the transforming power of the Gospel, it is only those whom "the love of Christ constrains to live not unto themselves," who are capable of thoroughly acting in the spirit of this precept. **11. not slothful in business**—The word rendered "business" means 'zeal,' 'diligence,' 'purpose'; denoting the energy of action. **serving the Lord**—i.e., the Lord Jesus (see Eph. 6:5-8). Another reading—'serving the time,' or 'the occasion'—which differs in form but very slightly from the received reading, has been adopted by good critics [LUTHER, OLSHAUSEN, FRITZSCHE, MEYER]. But as MS. authority is decidedly against it, so is internal evidence; and comparatively few favor it. Nor is the sense which it yields a very Christian one. **12. rejoicing** . . .—Here it is more lively to retain the order and the verbs of the original: 'In hope, rejoicing; in tribulation, enduring; in prayer, persevering.' Each of these exercises helps the other. If our "hope" of glory is so assured that it is a rejoicing hope, we shall find the spirit of "endurance in tribulation" natural and easy; but since it is "prayer" which strengthens the faith that begets hope and lifts it up into an assured and joyful expectancy, and since our patience in tribulation is fed by this, it will be seen that all depends on our "perseverance in prayer." **13. given to hospitality**—i.e., the entertainment of strangers. In times of persecution, and before the general institution of houses of entertainment, the importance of this precept would be at once felt. In the East, where such houses are still rare, this duty is regarded as of the most sacred character [HODGE]. **14. Bless**—i.e., Call down by prayer a blessing on—**them which persecute you** . . .—This is taken from the Sermon on the Mount, which, from the allusions made to it, seems to have been the storehouse of Christian

morality among the churches. **15. Rejoice with them that rejoice; weep**—the "and" should probably be omitted—**with them that weep**—What a beautiful spirit of sympathy with the joys and sorrows of others is here inculcated! But it is only one charming phase of the unselfish character which belongs to all living Christianity. What a world will ours be when this shall become its reigning spirit! Of the two, however, it is more easy to sympathize with another's sorrows than his joys, because in the one case he *needs* us; in the other not. But just for this reason the latter is the more disinterested, and so the nobler. **16. Be**—'Being'—**of the same mind one toward another**—The feeling of the common bond which binds all Christians to each other, whatever diversity of station, cultivation, temperament, or gifts may obtain among them, is the thing here enjoined. This is next taken up in detail. **Mind not**—'not minding'—**high things**—i.e., Cherish not ambitious or aspiring purposes and desires. As this springs from selfish severance of our own interests and objects from those of our brethren, so it is quite incompatible with the spirit inculcated in the preceding clause. **but condescend**—'condescending'—**to men of low estate**—or (as some render the words), 'inclining unto the things that be lowly.' But we prefer the former. **Be not wise in your own conceits**—This is just the application of the caution against high-mindedness to the estimate we form of our own mental character. **17. Recompense**—'Recompensing' . . .—see on vs. 14. **Provide**—'Providing'—**things honest**—'honorable'—**in the sight of all men**—The idea (which is from Prov. 3:4) is the care which Christians should take so to demean themselves as to command the respect of all men. **18. If it be possible**—i.e., If others will let you—**as much as lieth in you**—or, 'dependeth on you' —**live peaceably**—or, 'be at peace'—**with all men**—The impossibility of this in some cases is hinted at, to keep up the hearts of those who, having done their best unsuccessfully to live in peace, might be tempted to think the failure was *necessarily* owing to themselves. But how emphatically expressed is the injunction to let nothing on our part prevent it! Would that Christians were guiltless in this respect! **19-21. avenge not** . . .—see on vs. 14. **but rather give place unto wrath**—This is usually taken to mean, 'but give room or space for wrath to spend itself.' But as the context shows that the injunction is to leave vengeance to God, "wrath" here seems to mean, not the *offense*, which we are tempted to avenge, but the *avenging wrath* of God (see II Chron. 24:18), which we are enjoined to await, or give room for. (So the best interpreters). **if thine enemy hunger** . . .—This is taken from Proverbs 25:21, 22, which without doubt supplied the basis of those lofty precepts on that subject which form the culminating point of the Sermon on the Mount. **in so doing thou shalt heap coals of fire on his head**—As the heaping of "coals of fire" is in the Old Testament the figurative expression of divine vengeance (Ps. 140:10; 11:6. etc.), the true sense of these words seems to be, 'That will be the most effectual vengeance—a vengeance under which he will be fain to bend [So ALFORD, HODGE, etc.]. The next verse confirms this. **Be not overcome of evil**—for then you are the conquered party. **but overcome evil with good**—and then the victory is yours; you have subdued your enemy in the noblest sense.— Note (1) The redeeming mercy of God in Christ is, in the souls of believers, the living spring of all holy obedience (vs. 1). (2) As redemption under the Gospel is not by irrational victims, as under the law, but "by the precious blood of Christ" (I Pet. 1:18, 19), and, consequently, is not ritual but real, so the sacrifices which believers are now called to offer are all "living sacrifices"; and these—summed up in self-consecration to the service of God—are "holy and acceptable to God," making up together "our rational service" (vs. 1). (3) In this light, what are we to think of the so-called 'unbloody sacrifice of the mass, continually offered to God as a propitiation for the sins both of the living and the dead,' which the adherents of Rome's corrupt faith have been taught for ages to believe is the highest and holiest act of Christian worship—in direct opposition to the sublimely simple teaching which the Christians of Rome first received (vs. 1)- (4) Christians should not feel themselves at liberty to be conformed to the world, if only they avoid what is manifestly sinful; but rather, yielding themselves to the transforming power of the truth as it is in Jesus, they should strive to exhibit before the world an entire renovation of heart and life (vs. 2). (5) What God would have men to be, in all its beauty and grandeur, is for the first time really apprehended, when "written not with ink, but with the Spirit of the living God, not on tables of stone, but on the fleshy tables of the heart," II Corinthians 3: 3 (vs. 2). (6) Self-sufficiency and lust of power are peculiarly unlovely in the vessels of mercy, whose respective graces and gifts are all a divine trust for the benefit of the common body and of mankind at large (vss. 3, 4). (7) As forgetfulness of this has been the source of innumerable and unspeakable evils in the Church of Christ, so the faithful exercise by every Christian of his own peculiar office and gifts, and the loving recognition of those of his brethren, as all of equal importance in their own place, would put a new face upon the visible Church, to the vast benefit and comfort of Christians themselves and to the admiration of the world around them (vss. 6-8). (8) What would the world be, if it were filled with Christians having but one object in life, high above every other—to "serve the Lord" —and throwing into this service 'alacrity' in the discharge of all duties, and abiding "warmth of spirit" (vs. 11)! (9) Oh, how far is even the living Church from exhibiting the whole character and spirit, so beautifully portrayed in the latter verses of this chapter (vss. 12-21)! What need of a fresh baptism of the Spirit in order to this! And how "fair as the moon, clear as the sun, and terrible as an army with banners," will the Church become, when at length instinct with this Spirit! The Lord hasten it in its time!

CHAPTER 13

Vss. 1-14. SAME SUBJECT CONTINUED—POLITICAL AND SOCIAL RELATIONS—MOTIVES. **1, 2. Let every soul**—every man of you—**be subject unto the higher powers**—or, 'submit himself to the authorities that are above him.' **For there is no power**—'no authority'—**but of God: the powers that be are**—'have been' —**ordained of God. Whosoever therefore resisteth the power**—'So that he that setteth himself against the authority'—**resisteth the ordinance of God; and they that resist shall receive to themselves damnation**—or, 'condemnation,' according to the old sense of that word; that is, not from the magistrate, but from God, whose authority in the magistrate's is resisted. **3, 4. For rulers are not a terror to good works**—'to the good work,' as the true reading appears to be—**but to the evil ... he beareth not the**

sword in vain—i.e., the symbol of the magistrate's authority to punish. **5. Wherefore ye must needs be subject, not only for wrath**—for fear of the magistrate's vengeance—**but also for conscience' sake**— from reverence for God's authority. It is of *Magistracy in general*, considered as a divine ordinance, that this is spoken: and the statement applies equally to all forms of government, from an unchecked despotism—such as flourished when this was written, under the Emperor Nero—to a pure democracy. The inalienable right of all subjects to endeavor to alter or improve the form of government under which they live is left untouched here. But since Christians were constantly charged with turning the world upside down, and since there certainly were elements enough in Christianity of moral and social revolution to give plausibility to the charge, and tempt noble spirits, crushed under misgovernment, to take redress into their own hands, it was of special importance that the pacific, submissive, loyal spirit of those Christians who resided at the great seat of political power, should furnish a visible refutation of this charge. **6, 7. For, for this cause pay ye**—rather, 'ye pay'—**tribute also**—i.e., "This is the reason why ye pay the contributions requisite for maintaining the civil government." **for they are God's ministers, attending continually upon**—'to'—**this very thing. Render therefore to all their dues**—From magistrates the apostle now comes to other officials, and from them to men related to us by whatever tie. **tribute**—land tax. **custom**—mercantile tax. **fear**—reverence for superiors. **honour**—the respect due to persons of distinction. **8. Owe no man anything, but to love one another**—"Acquit yourselves of all obligations except love, which is a debt that must remain ever due" [HODGE]. **for he that loveth another hath fulfilled the law**—[or the law itself is but love in manifold action, regarded as matter of duty. **9. For this, ...**—better thus: 'For the [commandments], Thou shalt not kill, Thou shalt not commit adultery, Thou shalt not steal, Thou shalt not covet, and whatever other commandment [there may be], it is summed up ... (The clause, "Thou shalt not bear false witness," is wanting in all the most ancient MSS.) The apostle refers here only to the second table of the law, as love to our neighbor is what he is treating of. **10. Love worketh no ill to his**—or, 'one's'—**neighbour: therefore ...**—As love, from its very nature, studies and delights to please its objects, its very existence is an effectual security against our wilfully injuring him. Next follow some general motives to the faithful discharge of all these duties. **11. And that**—rather, 'And this' [do]— knowing the time, that now it is high time—lit., 'the hour has already come.' **to awake out of sleep**— of stupid, fatal indifference to eternal things. **for now is our salvation**—rather, 'the salvation,' or simply 'salvation'—**nearer than when we**—first—**believed**—This is in the line of all our Lord's teaching, which represents the decisive day of Christ's second appearing as at hand, to keep believers ever in the attitude of wakeful expectancy, but without reference to the *chronological* nearness or distance of that event. **12. The night**—of evil—**is far spent, the day**—of consummated triumph over it—**is at hand: let us therefore cast off**—as a dress—**the works of darkness**—all works holding of the kingdom and period of darkness, with which, as followers of the risen Saviour, our connection has been dissolved. **and let us put on the armour of light**—described at length in Ephesians 6:11-18. **13. Let us walk honestly**—'becomingly,' 'seemingly'—**as in the day**—

'Men choose the night for their revels, but our night is past, for we are all the children of the light and of the day (I Thess. 5:5): let us therefore only do what is fit to be exposed to the light of such a day.' **not in rioting and drunkenness**–varied forms of intemperance; denoting revels in general, usually ending in intoxication. **not in chambering and wantonness**–varied forms of impurity; the one pointing to definite acts, the other more general. **not in strife and envying**–varied forms of that venomous feeling between man and man which reverses the law of love. **14. But**–to sum up all in one word–**put ye on the Lord Jesus Christ**–in such wise that Christ only may be seen in you (see II Cor. 3:3; Gal. 3:27; Eph. 4:24). **and make no provision**–'take no forethought'–**for the flesh, to fulfil the lust [thereof]**–'Direct none of your attention to the cravings of your corrupt nature, how you may provide for their gratification.'–Note, (1) How gloriously adapted is Christianity for human society in all conditions! As it makes war directly against no specific forms of government, so it directly recommends none. While its holy and benign principles secure the ultimate abolition of all iniquitous government, the reverence which it teaches for magistracy, under whatever form, as a divine institution, secures the loyalty and peaceableness of its disciples, amid all the turbulence and distractions of civil society, and makes it the highest interest of all states to welcome it within their pale, as in this as well as every other sense–"the salt of the earth, the light of the world" (vss. 1-5). (2) Christianity is the grand specific for the purification and elevation of all the social relations; inspiring a readiness to discharge all obligations, and most of all, implanting in its disciples that love which secures all men against injury from them, inasmuch as it is the fulfilling of the law (vss. 6-10). (3) The rapid march of the kingdom of God, the advanced stage of it at which we have arrived, and the ever-nearing approach of the perfect day–nearer to every believer the longer he lives–should quicken all the children of light to redeem the time, and, seeing that they look for such things, to be diligent, that they may be found of Him in peace, without spot and blameless (II Pet. 3:14). (4) In virtue of 'the expulsive power of a new and more powerful affection,' the great secret of persevering holiness in all manner of conversation will be found to be "Christ IN US, the hope of glory" (Col. 1:27), and Christ ON US, as the character in which alone we shall be able to shine before men (II Cor. 3:8) (vs. 14).

CHAPTER 14

Vss. 1-23. SAME SUBJECT CONTINUED–CHRISTIAN FORBEARANCE. The subject here, and on to ch. 15: 13, *is the consideration due from stronger Christians to their weaker brethren;* which is but the great law of love (treated of in ch. 13) in one particular form. **1. Him that is weak in the faith**–rather, 'in faith'; i.e., not 'him that is weak in the truth believed' [CALVIN, BEZA, ALFORD, etc.], but (as most interpreters agree), 'him whose faith wants that firmness and breadth which would raise him above small scruples.' (See on vss. 22, 23.) **receive ye**–to cordial Christian fellowship–**but not to doubtful disputations**–rather, perhaps, 'not to the deciding of doubts,' or 'scruples;' i.e., not for the purpose of arguing him out of them: which indeed usually does the reverse; whereas to receive him to full brotherly

confidence and cordial interchange of Christian affection is the most effectual way of drawing them off. Two examples of such scruples are here specified, touching Jewish *meats* and *days.* "The strong," it will be observed, are those who knew these to be abolished under the Gospel; "the weak" are those who had scruples on this point. **2. one believeth that he may eat all things**–See Acts 10:16. **another, who is weak, eateth herbs**–restricting himself probably to a vegetable diet, for fear of eating what might have been offered to idols, and so would be unclean. (See I Cor. 8.) **3. Let not him that eateth despise**–look down superciliously upon–**him that eateth not; and let not him that eateth not judge**–sit in judgment censoriously upon–**him that eateth: for God hath received him**–as one of His dear children, who in this matter acts not from laxity, but religious principle. **4. Who art thou that judgest another man's**–rather, 'another's'–**servant?** –i.e., CHRIST'S, as the whole context shows, especially vss. 8, 9. **Yea . . .**–'But he shall be made to stand, for God is able to make him stand'; i.e., to make good his standing, not at the day of judgment, of which the apostle treats in vs. 10, but in the true fellowship of the Church *here,* in spite of thy censures. **5. One man esteemeth one day above another: another esteemeth every day**–The supplement "alike" should be omitted, as injuring the sense. **Let every man be fully persuaded in his own mind** –be guided in such matters by conscientious conviction. **6. He that regardeth the day, regardeth it to the Lord**–the Lord CHRIST, as before–**and he . . . not, to the Lord he doth not**–each doing what he believes to be the Lord's will. **He that eateth, eateth to the Lord, for he giveth God thanks; and he that eateth not, to the Lord he eateth not, and giveth God thanks**–The one gave thanks to God for the flesh which the other scrupled to use; the other did the same for the herbs to which, for conscience' sake, he restricted himself. From this passage about the observance of days, ALFORD unhappily infers that such language could not have been used if the *sabbath law* had been in force under the Gospel in any form. Certainly it could not, if the sabbath were merely one of the Jewish festival days; but it will not do to take this for granted merely because it was observed *under* the Mosaic economy. And certainly, if the sabbath was more ancient than Judaism; if, even under Judaism, it was enshrined among the eternal sanctities of the Decalogue, uttered, as no other parts of Judaism were, amidst the terrors of Sinai; and if the Lawgiver Himself said of it when on earth, "The Son of man is LORD EVEN OF THE SABBATH DAY" (see Mark 2:28)–it will be hard to show that the apostle must have meant it to be ranked by his readers among those vanished Jewish festival days, which only "weakness" could imagine to be still in force–a weakness which those who had more light ought, out of love, merely to bear with. **7, 8. For none of us**–Christians–**liveth to himself**–(See II Cor. 5:14, 15), to dispose of himself or shape his conduct after his own ideas and inclinations. **and no man**–'and none'–of us Christians–**dieth to himself. For whether we live, we live unto the Lord**–the Lord CHRIST; see next verse–**and whether we die, we die unto the Lord; whether we live therefore, or die, we are the Lord's**–Nothing but the most vivid explanation of these remarkable words could make them endurable to any Christian ear, if Christ were a *mere creature.* For Christ is here–in the most emphatic terms, and yet in the most unimpassioned tone–held up as the supreme Object of the Christian's life, and of his death too;

and that by the man whose horror of creature-worship was such, that when the poor Lycaonians would have worshipped him, he rushed forth to arrest the deed, directing them to "the living God," as the only legitimate Object of worship (Acts 14:15). Nor does Paul *teach* this here, but rather *appeals* to it as a known and recognized fact, of which he had only to remind his readers.   And since the apostle, when he wrote these words, had never been at Rome, he could only know that the Roman Christians would assent to this view of Christ, because it was *the common teaching of all the accredited preachers of Christianity, and the common faith of all Christians.* **9. For to this end Christ both ...** —The true reading here is, To this end Christ died and lived ['again']—**that he might be Lord both of the dead and**—'and of the'—**living**—The grand object of His death was to *acquire* this absolute Lordship over His redeemed, both in their living and in their dying, as His of right. **10. But why ...**—The original is more lively:—'But thou (the weaker believer), why judgest thou thy brother? And thou again (the stronger), why despisest thou thy brother?' **for we shall all**—the strong and the weak together—**stand before the judgment seat of Christ**—All the most ancient and best MSS. read here, 'the judgment seat of God.'   The present reading doubtless crept in from II Corinthians 5:10, where "the judgment seat of *Christ*" occurs.   But here "the judgment seat of *God*" seems to have been used, with reference to the quotation and the inference in the next two verses.   **11, 12. For it is written**—Isaiah 45:23—**As I live, saith the Lord**—*Hebrew,* JEHOVAH —**every knee shall bow to me, and every tongue shall confess to God**—consequently, shall bow to the award of God upon their character and actions.   **So then**—infers the apostle—**every one of us shall give account of himself to God**—Now, if it be remembered that all this is adduced quite incidentally, to show that CHRIST is the absolute Master of all Christians, to rule their judgments and feelings towards each other while "living," and to dispose of them "dying," the testimony which it bears to the absolute Divinity of Christ will appear remarkable. On any other view, the quotation to show that we shall all stand before the judgment seat of *God* would be a strange proof that Christians are all amenable to *Christ.* **13. Let us not therefore judge** —'assume the office of judge over'—**one another; but judge this rather ...** —a beautiful sort of play upon the word 'judge,' meaning, 'But let this be your judgment, not to put a stumbling block....' **14, 15. I know, and am persuaded by**—or rather, 'in'— **the Lord Jesus**—as "having the mind of Christ" (I Cor. 2:16).   **that there is nothing unclean of itself** —Hence it is that he calls those "the strong" who believed in the abolition of all ritual distinctions under the Gospel. (See Acts 10:15.) **but**—'save that'—**to him that esteemeth anything to be unclean, to him it is unclean**—'and therefore, though *you* can eat of it without sin, *he cannot.*' **But if thy brother be grieved**—has his weak conscience hurt—**with thy meat**—rather, 'because of meat.' The word "meat" is purposely selected as something contemptible in contrast with the tremendous risk run for its sake. Accordingly, in the next clause, that idea is brought out with great strength. **Destroy not him with**—'by' —**thy meat for whom Christ died**—"The worth of even the poorest and weakest brother cannot be more emphatically expressed than by the words, 'for whom Christ died' " [OLSHAUSEN].   The same sentiment is expressed with equal sharpness in I Corinthians 8:11. *Whatever tends to make anyone*

violate his conscience tends to the destruction of his soul; and he who helps, whether wittingly or no, to bring about the one is guilty of aiding to accomplish the other. **16, 17. Let not then your good**—i.e., this liberty of yours as to Jewish meats and days, well founded though it be—**be evil spoken of**—for the evil it does to others. **For the kingdom of God**—or, as we should say, Religion; i.e., the proper business and blessedness for which Christians are formed into a community of renewed men in thorough subjection to God (cf. I Cor. 4:20). **is not meat and drink**—'eating and drinking'—**but righteousness, and peace, and joy in the Holy Ghost**—a beautiful and comprehensive division of living Christianity.   The first—"righteousness"—has respect to *God,* denoting here 'rectitude,' in its widest sense (as in Matt. 6:33);   the second—"peace"—has respect to *our neighbors,* denoting 'concord' among brethren (as is plain from vs. 19; cf. Eph. 4:3; Col. 3:14, 15); the third—"joy in the Holy Ghost"—has respect to *ourselves.*   This phrase, 'joy in the Holy Ghost,' represents Christians as so thinking and feeling under the workings of the Holy Ghost, that their joy may be viewed rather as that of the blessed Agent who inspires it than their own (cf. I Thess. 1:6).   **18. For he that is in these things**—'in this,' meaning this threefold life. **serveth Christ**—Here again observe how, though we do these three things as a "kingdom of *God,*" yet it is "*Christ*" that we serve in so doing; the apostle passing here from God to Christ as naturally as before from Christ to God—in a way to us inconceivable, if Christ had been viewed as a mere creature (cf. II Cor. 8:21).   **is acceptable to God, and approved of men**—these being the things which God delights in, and men are constrained to approve.   (Cf. Prov. 3:4; Luke 2:52; Acts 2:47; 19: 20.) **19. the things ...** —more simply, 'the things of peace, and the things of mutual edification.' **20. For**—'For the sake of'—**meat destroy not the work of God**—See on vs. 15. The apostle sees in whatever tends to violate a brother's conscience the *incipient* destruction of God's work (for every converted man is such)—on the same principle as "he that hateth his brother is a murderer" (I John 3:15). **All things indeed are pure**—'clean'; the ritual distinctions being at an end. **but it is evil to that man** —there is criminality in the man—**who eateth with offence**—i.e., so as to stumble a weak brother. **21. It is good not to eat flesh, nor to drink wine, nor any thing**—'nor to do any thing'—**whereby**—'wherein'—**thy brother stumbleth, or is offended, or is made weak**—rather, 'is weak.'   These three words, it has been remarked, are each intentionally weaker than the other:—'Which may cause a brother to stumble, or even be obstructed in his Christian course, nay—though neither of these may follow— wherein he continues weak; unable wholly to disregard the example, and yet unprepared to follow it.'   But this injunction to abstain from *flesh,* from *wine,* and from *whatsoever* may hurt the conscience of a brother, must be properly understood. Manifestly, the apostle is treating of the regulation of the Christain's conduct with reference simply to the prejudices of the weak in faith; and his directions are to be considered not as *prescriptions for one's entire lifetime,* even to promote the good of men on a large scale, but simply as cautions against the too free use of Christian liberty in matters where other Christians, through weakness, are not persuaded that such liberty is divinely allowed. How far the *principle* involved in this may be legitimately extended, we do not inquire here; but ere we consider that question, it is of great importance to fix how far it is here actually expressed, and what is the precise nature of the illustrations given of it. **22. Hast thou faith**—on such matters? **have it to thyself**—within thine own breast—**before God**—a most important clause. It is not mere *sincerity*, or a private *opinion*, of which the apostle speaks; it is conviction as to what is the truth and will of God. If thou hast formed this conviction in the sight of God, keep thyself in this frame before Him. Of course, this is not to be over-pressed, as if it were wrong to discuss such points at all with our weaker brethren. All that is here condemned is such a zeal for small points as endangers Christian love. **Happy is he that condemneth not himself in that which he alloweth**—allows himself to do nothing, about the lawfulness of which he has scruples; does only what he neither knows nor fears to be sinful. **23. And**—rather, 'But'—**he that doubteth is damned**—See on the word "damnation," ch. 13:2. **if he eat, because he eateth not of faith**—See on the meaning of "faith" here, vs. 22. **for whatsoever is not of faith is sin**—a maxim of unspeakable importance in the Christian life.—Note, (1) Some points in Christianity are unessential to Christian fellowship; so that though one may be in error upon them, he is not on that account to be excluded either from the communion of the Church or from the full confidence of those who have more light. This distinction between essential and non-essential truths is denied by some who affect more than ordinary zeal for the honor and truth of God. But they must settle the question with our apostle. (2) Acceptance with God is the only proper criterion of right to Christian fellowship. Whom God receives, men cannot lawfully reject (vss. 3, 4). (3) As there is much selfpleasing in setting up narrow standards of Christian fellowship, so one of the best preservatives against the temptation to do this will be found in the continual remembrance that CHRIST is the one Object for whom all Christians live, and to whom all Christians die; this will be such a living and exalted bond of union between the strong and the weak as will overshadow all their lesser differences and gradually absorb them (vss. 7-9). (4) The consideration of the common judgment seat at which the strong and the weak shall stand together will be found another preservative against the unlovely disposition to sit in judgment one on another (vss. 10-12). (5) How brightly does the supreme Divinity of Christ shine out in this chapter! The exposition itself supersedes further illustration here. (6) Though forbearance be a great Christian duty, indifference to the distinction between truth and error is not thereby encouraged. The former is, by the lax, made an excuse for the latter. But our apostle, while teaching "the strong" to bear with "the weak," repeatedly intimates in this chapter where the truth really lay on the points in question, and takes care to call those who took the wrong side "the weak" (vss. 1, 2, 14). (7) With what holy jealousy ought the purity of the conscience to be guarded, since every deliberate violation of it is incipient perdition (vss. 15, 20)! Some, who seem to be more jealous for the honor of certain doctrines than for the souls of men, enervate this terrific truth by asking how it bears upon the 'perseverance of the saints'; the advocates of that doctrine thinking it necessary to explain away what is meant by "destroying the work of God" (vs. 20), and "destroying him for whom Christ died" (vs. 15), for fear of the doctrinal consequences of taking it nakedly; while the opponents of that doctrine are ready to ask, How could the apostle have used such language

if he had believed that such a catastrophe was impossible? The true answer to both lies in dismissing the question as impertinent. The apostle is enunciating a great and eternal principle in Christian Ethics—that *the wilful violation of conscience contains within itself a seed of destruction;* or, to express it otherwise, that the total destruction of the work of God in the renewed soul, and, consequently, the loss of that soul for eternity, needs only the carrying out to its full effect of such violation of the conscience. Whether such effects *do* take place, in point of fact, the apostle gives not the most distant hint here; and therefore that point must be settled elsewhere. But, beyond all doubt, as the position we have laid down is emphatically expressed by the apostle, so the interests of all who call themselves Christians require to be proclaimed and pressed on every suitable occasion. (8) Zeal for comparatively small points of truth is a poor substitute for the substantial and catholic and abiding realities of the Christian life (vss. 17, 18). (9) "Peace" among the followers of Christ is a blessing too precious to themselves, and, as a testimony to them that are without, too important, to be ruptured for trifles, even though some lesser truths be involved in these (vss. 19, 20). Nor are those truths themselves disparaged or endangered thereby, but the reverse. (10) Many things which are lawful are not expedient. In the use of any liberty, therefore, our question should be, not simply, Is this lawful? but even if so, Can it be used with safety to a brother's conscience?—How will it affect my brother's soul (vs. 21)? It is permitted to no Christian to say with Cain, "Am I my brother's keeper?" (Gen. 4:9.) (11) Whenever we are in doubt as to a point of duty —where abstinence is manifestly sinless, but compliance not clearly lawful—the safe course is ever to be preferred, for to do otherwise is itself sinful. (12) How exalted and beautiful is the Ethics of Christianity—by a few great principles teaching us how to steer our course amidst practical difficulties, with equal regard to Christian liberty, love, and confidence!

CHAPTER 15

Vss. 1-13. SAME SUBJECT CONTINUED AND CONCLUDED. **1. We then that are strong**—on such points as have been discussed, the abolition of the Jewish distinction of meats and days under the Gospel. See on ch. 14:14, 20. **ought . . . not to please ourselves**—ought to think less of what we may lawfully do than of how our conduct will affect others. **2, 3. Let every one of us**—lay himself out to—**please his neighbour**—not indeed for his mere gratification, but—**for his good**—with a view—**to his edification. For even Christ pleased not**—lived not to please—**himself; but, as it is written**—(Ps. 69:9)—**The reproaches . . .** —see Mark 10:42-45. **4. For whatsoever things were written aforetime were written for our learning**—'instruction'—**that we through . . .** —'through the comfort and the patience of the Scriptures'—**might have hope**—i.e., 'Think not that because such portions of Scripture relate immediately to Christ, they are inapplicable to you; for though Christ's sufferings, as a Saviour, were exclusively His own, the *motives* that prompted them, the *spirit* in which they were endured, and the *general principle* involved in His whole work—self-sacrifice for the good of others—furnish our most perfect and beautiful model; and so all Scripture relating to these is for our instruction; and since the duty of *forbearance,* the strong with the weak, requires "patience," and this again needs "comfort," all those Scriptures which tell of *patience* and *consolation,* particularly of the patience of Christ, and of the consolation which sustained Him under it, are our appointed and appropriate nutriment, ministering to us "*hope*" of that blessed day when these shall no more be needed.' See on ch. 4, *Note* 7. (For the same connection between "patience and hope" see on ch. 12:12, and I Thess. 1:3). **5, 6. Now the God of patience and consolation**—Such beautiful names of God are taken from the graces which He inspires: as "the God of hope" (vs. 13), "the God of peace" (vs. 33).—**grant you to be like minded**—'of the same mind'—**according to Christ Jesus**—It is not mere unanimity which the apostle seeks for them; for unanimity in evil is to be deprecated. But it is "*according to Christ Jesus*"—after the sublimest model of Him whose all-absorbing desire was to do, "not His own will, but the will of Him that sent Him" (John 6:38). *That . . .* —rather, 'that with one accord ye may with one mouth glorify the God and Father of our Lord Jesus Christ'; the mind and the mouth of all giving harmonious glory to His name. What a prayer! And shall this never be realized on earth? **7. Wherefore** —returning to the point—**receive ye one another . . . to the glory of God**—If Christ received us, and bears with all our weaknesses, well may we receive and compassionate one with another, and by so doing God will be glorified. **8-12.** Now—'For' is the true reading: the apostle is merely assigning an additional motive to Christian forbearance. **I say that Jesus Christ was**—'hath become'—**a minister of the circumcision**—a remarkable expression, meaning 'the Father's Servant for the salvation of the circumcision (or, of Israel).' **for the truth of God**—to make good the veracity of God towards His ancient people. **to confirm the**—Messianic—**promises made unto the fathers**—To cheer the Jewish believers, whom he might seem to have been disparaging, and to keep down Gentile pride, the apostle holds up Israel's salvation as the primary end of Christ's mission. But next after this, Christ was sent—**that the Gentiles might glorify God for his mercy**—A number of quotations from the Old Testament here follow, to show that God's plan of mercy embraced, from the first, the Gentiles along with the Jews. **as it is written**—(Ps. 18:49)—**I will confess to**—i.e., glorify—**thee among the Gentiles . . . And again**—(Deut. 32:43, though there is some difficulty in the *Heb.*)—**Rejoice, ye Gentiles**—along— **with his people**—Israel. **And again**—(Ps. 117:1)—**Praise the Lord, all ye Gentiles; and laud him, all ye people**—'peoples'—the various nations outside the pale of Judaism. **And again, Esaias saith**—(Isa. 11:10)—**There shall be a**—'the'—**root of Jesse**—meaning, not 'He from whom Jesse sprang,' but 'He that is sprung from Jesse' (i.e., Jesse's son David)—see Revelation 22:16. **and he that shall rise . . .** —So the LXX in substantial, though not verbal, agreement with the original. **13. Now . . .** —This seems a concluding prayer, suggested by the whole preceding subject matter of the epistle. **the God of hope**—(see on vs. 5)—**fill you with all joy and peace in believing**—the native truth of that *faith* which is the great theme of this epistle (cf. Gal. 5:22). **that ye may abound in hope**—"of the glory of God." (See on ch. 5:1.) **through the power of the Holy Ghost**—to whom, in the economy of redemption, it belongs to inspire believers with all gracious affections.—On the foregoing portion, note, (1) No Christian is at liberty to regard himself as an isolated disciple of

the Lord Jesus, having to decide questions of duty and liberty solely with reference to himself. As Christians are one body in Christ, so the great law of love binds them to act in all things with tenderness and consideration for their brethren in "the common salvation" (vss. 1, 2). (2) Of this unselfishness CHRIST is the perfect model of all Christians (vs. 3). (3) Holy Scripture is the divine storehouse of all furniture for the Christian life, even in its most trying and delicate features (vs. 4). (4) The harmonious glorification of the God and Father of our Lord Jesus Christ by the whole body of the redeemed, as it is the most exalted fruit of the scheme of redemption, so it is the last end of God in it (vss. 5-7).

14-33. CONCLUSION: IN WHICH THE APOSTLE APOLOGIZES FOR THUS WRITING TO THE ROMAN CHRISTIANS, EXPLAINS WHY HE HAD NOT YET VISITED THEM, ANNOUNCES HIS FUTURE PLANS, AND ASKS THEIR PRAYERS FOR THE COMPLETION OF THEM. **14, 15. And . . .** —rather, 'Now I am persuaded, my brethren, even I myself, concerning you'—**that ye also yourselves are full of goodness**—of inclination to all I have been enjoining on you—**filled with all knowledge**—of the truth expounded—**and able**—without my intervention—**to admonish one another. Nevertheless, I have written the more boldly unto you in some sort**—'measure'—**as putting you in mind, because of the grace that is given to me of God**— as an apostle of Jesus Christ. **16. that I should be the**—rather, 'a'—**minister**—The word here used is commonly employed to express the office of the priesthood, from which accordingly the figurative language of the rest of the verse is taken. **of Jesus Christ**—'Christ Jesus,' according to the true reading —**to the Gentiles**—a further proof that the Epistle was addressed to a *Gentile* church. (See on ch. 1: 13.) **ministering the gospel of God**—As the word here is a still more priestly one, it should be rendered, 'ministering as a priest in the Gospel of God.' **that the offering up of the Gentiles**—as an oblation to God, in their converted character— **might be acceptable, being sanctified by the Holy Ghost**—the end to which the ancient offerings typically looked. **17. I have therefore whereof I may glory**—or (adding the article, as the reading seems to be), 'I have my glorying.' **through**—'in'—**Christ Jesus in those things which pertain to God**—the things of the ministry committed to me of God. **18-22. For I will not dare to speak of any**—'to speak aught'—**of those things which Christ hath not wrought by me**—a modest, though somewhat obscure form of expression, meaning, 'I will not dare to go beyond what Christ *hath* wrought by me'—in which form accordingly the rest of the passage is expressed. Observe here how Paul ascribes all the success of his labors to the activity of the living Redeemer, working in and by him. **by word and deed**—by preaching and working; which latter he explains in the next clause. **through mighty**—lit., 'in the power of—**signs and wonders**—i.e., glorious miracles. **by the power of the Spirit of God**—'the Holy Ghost,' as the true reading seems to be. This seems intended to explain the efficacy of the word preached, as well as the working of the miracles which attested it. **so that from Jerusalem, and round about unto**—'as far as'—**Illyricum**—to the extreme northwestern boundary of Greece. It corresponds to the modern Croatia and Dalmatia (II Tim. 4:10). See Acts 20:1, 2. **I have fully preached the gospel of Christ. Yea . . .** —rather, 'Yet making it my study (cf. II Cor. 5:9; I Thess. 4:11, *Greek*) so to preach the Gospel, not where Christ was [already] named, that I might not build upon another man's foundation: but (might act) as it is written, To whom no tidings of Him came, they shall see . . ., **For which cause**—'Being so long occupied with this missionary work, I have been much (or, 'for the most part') hindered . . . , (See on ch. 1:9-11.) **23, 24. But now having no more place**—'no longer having place,'—i.e., unbroken ground, where Christ has not been preached—**and having a great desire**—'a longing'—**these many years to come unto you**—(see, as before, on ch. 1:9-11)—**whensoever I take my journey into Spain**—Whether this purpose was ever accomplished has been much disputed, as no record of it nor allusion to it anywhere occurs. Those who think our apostle was never at large after his first imprisonment at Rome will of course hold that it never was; while those who are persuaded, as we are, that he underwent a second imprisonment, prior to which he was at large for a considerable time after his first, incline naturally to the other opinion. **I will come to you**—If these words were not originally in the text, and there is weighty evidence against them, they must at least be inserted as a necessary supplement. **in my journey . . .** —'as I pass through by you, to be set forward on my journey thither, if first I be somewhat filled with your company': i.e., 'I should indeed like to stay longer with you than I can hope to do, but I must, to some extent at least, have my fill of your company.' **25-27. But now I go to Jerusalem to minister**—'ministering'—**to the saints**—in the sense immediately to be explained. **For . . .** —better, 'For Macedonia and Achaia have thought good to make a certain contribution for the poor of the saints which are at Jerusalem.' (See Acts 24: 17.) 'They have thought it good; and their debtors verily they are'; i.e., 'And well they may, considering what the Gentile believers owe to their Jewish brethren.' **For if the Gentiles have been made partakers of their spiritual things, their duty is also** —'they owe it also'—**to minister unto them in carnal things**—(Cf. I Cor. 9:11; Gal. 6:6; and see Luke 7:4; Acts 10:2). **28, 29. When therefore I have . . . sealed**—i.e., delivered over safely—**to them this fruit** —of the faith and love of the Gentile converts—**I will come**—'come back,' or 'return'—**by you into Spain**—See on vs. 24. **And I am sure**—'I know'—**that . . . I shall come in the fulness of the blessing of Christ**—Such, beyond all doubts, is the true reading, the words "of the gospel" being in hardly any MSS. of antiquity and authority. Nor was the apostle mistaken in this confidence, though his visit to Rome was in very different circumstances from what he expected. See Acts 28:16-31. **30. Now I beseech you, brethren, for the Lord Jesus Christ's sake, and for the love of the Spirit**—or, 'by the Lord Jesus Christ, and by the love of the Spirit'—not the love which the Spirit bears to us, but that love which He kindles in the hearts of believers towards each other; i.e. 'By that Saviour whose name is alike dear to all of us and whose unsearchable riches I live only to proclaim, and by that love one to another which the blessed Spirit diffuses through all the brotherhood, making the labors of Christ's servants a matter of common interest to all—I beseech you'—**that ye strive together with me in your prayers to God for me**—implying that he had his grounds for anxious fear in this matter. **31. That I may be delivered from them that do not believe**—'that do not obey,' i.e., the truth, by believing it; as in ch. 2:8. **in Judea**—He saw the storm that was gathering over him in Judea, which, if at all, would certainly burst upon his head when he reached the capital;

and the event too clearly showed the correctness of these apprehensions. **and that my service which I have for Jerusalem**—See on vss. 25-28. **may be accepted by**—'prove acceptable to'—**the saints**—Nor was he without apprehension lest the opposition he had made to the narrow jealousy of the Jewish converts against the free reception of their Gentile brethren, should make this gift of theirs to the poor saints at Jerusalem less welcome than it ought to be. He would have the Romans therefore to join him in wrestling with God that this gift might be gratefully received, and prove a cement between the two parties. But further. **32. That I may come unto you with**—'in'—**joy by the will of God** (Acts 18:21; I Cor. 4:19; 16:7; Heb. 6:3; Jas. 4:15—**and may with you be refreshed**—rather, 'with you refresh myself,' after all his labors and anxieties, and so be refitted for future service. **33. Now the God of peace be with you all. Amen**—The peace here sought is to be taken in its widest sense: the peace of reconciliation to God, first, "through the blood of the everlasting covenant" (Heb. 13:20; I Thess. 5: 23; II Thess. 3:16; Phil. 4:9); then the peace which that reconciliation diffuses among all the partakers of it (I Cor. 14:33; II Cor. 13:11; and see on ch. 16:20); more widely still, that peace which the children of God, in beautiful imitation of their Father in Heaven, are called and privileged to diffuse far and wide through this sin-distracted and divided world (ch. 22:18; Matt. 5:9; Heb. 12: 14; Jas. 3:18).—*Note,* (1) Did "the chiefest of the apostles" apologize for writing to a Christian church which he had never seen, and a church that he was persuaded was above the need of it, save to "stir up their pure minds by way of remembrance" (II Pet. 1:13; 3:1); and did he put even this upon the sole plea of apostolic responsibility (vss. 14-16)? What a contrast is thus presented to hierarchical pride, and in particular to the affected humility of the bishop of this very Rome! How close the bond which the one spirit draws between ministers and people—how wide the separation produced by the other! (2) There is in the Christian Church no real priesthood, and none but figurative sacrifices. Had it been otherwise, it is inconceivable that the 16th verse of this chapter should have been expressed as it is. Paul's only priesthood and sacrificial offerings lay, first, in ministering to them as "the apostle of the Gentiles," not the sacrament with the 'real presence' of Christ in it, or the sacrifice of the mass, but "the Gospel of God," and then, when gathered under the wing of Christ, presenting them to God as a grateful offering, "being sanctified [not by sacrificial gifts, but] by the Holy Ghost." (See Heb. 13:9-16.) (3) Though the debt we owe to those by whom we have been brought to Christ can never be discharged, we should feel it a privilege when we render them any lower benefit in return (vss. 26, 27). (4) Formidable designs against the truth and the servants of Christ should, above all other ways of counteracting them, be met by combined prayer to Him who rules all hearts and controls all events; and the darker the cloud, the more resolutely should all to whom Christ's cause is dear "strive together in their prayers to God" for the removal of it (vss. 30, 31). (5) Christian fellowship is so precious that the most eminent servants of Christ, amid the toils and trials of their work, find it refreshing and invigorating; and it is no good sign of any ecclesiastic, that he deems it beneath him to seek and enjoy it even amongst the humblest saints in the Church of Christ (vss. 24, 32).

CHAPTER 16

Vss. 1-27. Conclusion, Embracing Sundry Salutations and Directions, and a Closing Prayer. **1. I commend unto you Phœbe our sister, which is a servant**—or 'deaconess'—**of the church which is at Cenchrea**—The word is Cenchreæ, the eastern part of Corinth (Acts 18:18). That in the earliest churches there were deaconesses, to attend to the wants of the female members, there is no good reason to doubt. So early at least as the reign of Trajan, we learn from Pliny's celebrated letter to that emperor—A.D. 110, or 111—that they existed in the Eastern churches. Indeed, from the relation in which the sexes then stood to each other, something of this sort would seem to have been a necessity. Modern attempts, however, to revive this office have seldom found favor; either from the altered state of society, or the abuse of the office, or both. **2. Receive her in the Lord**—i.e., as a genuine disciple of the Lord Jesus. **as**—'so as'—**becometh saints**—so as saints should receive saints. **assist her in whatsoever business she hath**—'may have'—**need of you**—some private business of her own. **for she hath been a succourer of many, and of myself also**—(See Ps. 41:1-3; II Tim. 1:16-18). **3-5. Salute Priscilla**—The true reading here is 'Prisca' (as in II Tim. 4:19), a contracted form of Priscilla, as "Silas" of "Silvanus." **and Aquila my helpers**—The wife is here named before the husband (as in Acts 18:18, and vs. 26, according to the true reading; also in II Tim. 4:19), probably as being the more prominent and helpful to the Church. **who have for my life laid down**—'who did for my life lay down'—**their own necks**—i.e., risked their lives; either at Corinth (Acts 18:6, 9, 10), or more probably at Ephesus (Acts 19:30, 31; and cf. I Cor. 15:32). They must have returned from Ephesus (where we last find them in the history of the Acts) to Rome, whence the edict of Claudius had banished them (Acts 18:2); and doubtless, if not the principal members of that Christian community, they were at least the most endeared to our apostle. **unto whom not only I give thanks, but also all the churches of the Gentiles**—whose special apostle this dear couple had rescued from imminent danger. **5. Likewise the church that is in their house**—The Christian assembly that statedly met there for worship. "From his occupation as tent-maker, he had probably better accommodations for the meetings of the church than most other Christians" [Hodge]. Probably this devoted couple had written to the apostle such an account of the stated meetings at their house, as made him feel at home with them, and include them in this salutation, which doubtless would be read at their meetings with peculiar interest. **Salute my well beloved Epænetus, who is the first fruits**—i.e., the first convert—**of Achaia unto Christ**—The true reading here, as appears by the MSS., is 'the first fruits of Asia unto Christ'—i.e., Proconsular Asia (see Acts 16:6). In I Corinthians 16:15 it is said that "the household of Stephanas was the first fruit of Achaia"; and though if Epænetus was one of that family, the two statements might be reconciled according to the received text, there is no need to resort to this supposition, as that text is in this instance without authority. Epænetus, as the first believer in that region called Proconsular Asia, was dear to the apostle. (See Hos. 9:10; and Mic. 7:1). None of the names mentioned from vss. 5-15 are otherwise known. One wonders at the number of them, considering that the writer had never been at Rome. But as Rome

was then the center of the civilized world, to and from which journeys were continually taken to the remotest parts, there is no great difficulty in supposing that so active a travelling missionary as Paul would, in course of time, make the acquaintance of a considerable number of the Christians then residing at Rome. **6. Greet**—or 'salute'—**Mary, who bestowed much labour on us**—labor, no doubt, of a womanly kind. **7. Andronicus and Junia**—or, as it might be, 'Junias,' a contracted form of 'Junianus'; in this case, the word is a man's name. But if, as is more probable, the word be, as in our version, "Junia," the person meant was no doubt either the wife or the sister of Andronicus. **my kinsmen**—or, 'relatives.' **and my fellow prisoners**—on what occasion, it is impossible to say, as the apostle elsewhere tells us that he was "in prisons more frequent" (II Cor. 11:23). **which are of note among the apostles**—Those who think the word "apostle" is used in a lax sense, in the Acts and Epistles, take this to mean 'noted apostles' [Chrysostom, Luther, Calvin, Bengel, Olshausen, Tholuck, Alford, Jowett]; others, who are not clear that the word "apostle" is applied to any without the circle of the Twelve, save where the connection or some qualifying words show that the literal meaning of 'one sent' is the thing intended, understand by the expression used here, 'persons esteemed by the apostles' [Beza, Grotius, De Wette, Meyer, Fritzsche, Stuart, Philippi, Hodge]. And of course, if "Junia" is to be taken for a woman, this latter must be the meaning. **who also were in Christ before me**—The apostle writes as if he envied them this priority in the faith. And, indeed, if to be "in Christ" be the most enviable human condition, the earlier the date of this blessed translation, the greater the grace of it. This latter statement about Andronicus and Junia seems to throw some light on the preceding one. Very possibly they may have been among the first fruits of Peter's labors, gained to Christ either on the day of Pentecost or on some of the succeeding days. In that case they may have attracted the special esteem of those apostles who for some time resided chiefly at Jerusalem and its neighborhood; and our apostle, though he came late in contact with the other apostles, if he was aware of this fact, would have pleasure in alluding to it. **8. Amplias**—a contracted form of 'Ampliatus'—**my beloved in the Lord**—an expression of dear Christian affection. **9, 10. Urbane**—rather, 'Urbanus.' It is a man's name. **our helper**—'fellow labourer'—**in Christ. Salute Apelles approved**—'the approved'—**in Christ**—or, as we should say, 'that tried Christian'; a noble commendation. **Salute them which are of Aristobulus' household**—It would seem, from what is said of Narcissus in the following verse, that this Aristobulus himself had not been a Christian; but that the Christians of his household simply were meant; very possibly some of his slaves. **11. Salute Herodion, my kinsman**—(See on vs. 7), **Greet them that be of the household of Narcissus, which are in the Lord**—which implies that others in his house, including probably himself, were not Christians. **12. Salute Tryphena and Tryphosa, who labour in the Lord**—two active women. **Salute the beloved Persis**—another woman—**which laboured much in the Lord**—referring probably, not to official services, such as would fall to the deaconesses, but to such higher Christian labors—yet within the sphere competent to woman—as Priscilla bestowed on Apollos and others (Acts 18:18). **13. Salute Rufus, chosen**—'the chosen'—**in the Lord**—meaning, not 'who is one of the elect,' as every believer is, but 'the choice' or 'precious one' in the Lord. (See I Pet. 2:4; II John 13.) We read in Mark 15:21 that Simon of Cyrene, who was compelled to bear our Lord's cross, was "the father of Alexander and Rufus." From this we naturally conclude that when Mark wrote his Gospel, Alexander and Rufus must have been well known as Christians among those by whom he expected his Gospel to be first read; and, in all likelihood, this was that very "Rufus"; in which case our interest is deepened by what immediately follows about his mother. **and**—salute **—his mother and mine**—The apostle calls her "his own mother," not so much as our Lord calls every elderly woman believer His mother (Matt. 12:49, 50), but in grateful acknowledgment of her motherly attentions to himself, bestowed no doubt for his Master's sake, and the love she bore to his honored servants. To us it seems altogether likely that the conversion of Simon the Cyrenian dated from that memorable day when "passing [casually] by, as he came from the country" (Mark 15:21), "they compelled him to bear the" Saviour's cross. Sweet compulsion, if what he thus beheld issued in his *voluntarily* taking up his own cross! Through him it is natural to suppose that his wife would be brought in, and that this believing couple, now "heirs together of the grace of life" (I Peter 3:7), as they told their two sons, Alexander and Rufus, what honor had unwittingly been put upon their father at that hour of deepest and dearest moment to all Christians, might be blessed to the inbringing of both of them to Christ. In this case, supposing the elder of the two to have departed to be with Christ ere this letter was written, or to have been residing in some other place, and Rufus left alone with his mother, how instructive and beautiful is the testimony here borne to her! **14, 15. Salute Asyncritus . . .**—These have been thought to be the names of ten less notable Christians than those already named. But this will hardly be supposed if it be observed that they are divided into two pairs of five each, and that after the first of these pairs it is added, "and the brethren which are with them," while after the second pair we have the words, "and all the saints which are with them." This perhaps hardly means that each of the five in both pairs had "a church at his house," else probably this would have been more expressly said. But at least it would seem to indicate that they were each a center of some few Christians who met at his house—it may be for further instruction, for prayer, for missionary purposes, or for some other Christian objects. These little peeps into the rudimental forms which Christian fellowship first took in the great cities, though too indistinct for more than conjecture, are singularly interesting. Our apostle would seem to have been kept minutely informed as to the state of the church at Rome, both as to its membership and its varied activities, probably by Priscilla and Aquila. **16. Salute one another with an holy kiss**—So I Corinthians 16:20; I Thessalonians 5:26; I Peter 5:14. The custom prevailed among the Jews, and doubtless came from the East, where it still obtains. Its adoption into the Christian churches, as the symbol of a higher fellowship than it had ever expressed before, was probably as immediate as it was natural. In this case the apostle's desire seems to be that on receipt of his epistle, with its salutations, they should in this manner expressly testify their Christian affection. It afterwards came to have a fixed place in the church service, immediately after the celebration of the Supper, and continued long in use. In such matters, however,

the state of society and the peculiarities of different places require to be studied. **The churches of Christ salute you**—The true reading is, 'All the churches'; the word "all" gradually falling out, as seeming probably to express more than the apostle would venture to affirm. But no more seems meant than to assure the Romans in what affectionate esteem they were held by the churches generally; all that knew he was writing to Rome having expressly asked their own salutations to be sent to them. (See vs. 19.) **17. Now I beseech you, brethren, mark them which cause divisions and offences contrary to the doctrine which ye have learned**—'which ye learned'—**and avoid them**—The fomentors of "divisions" here referred to are probably those who were unfriendly to the truths taught in this epistle, while those who caused "offenses" were probably those referred to in ch. 14:15 as haughtily disregarding the prejudices of the weak. The direction as to both is, first, to "mark" such, lest the evil should be done ere it was fully discovered; and next, to "avoid" them (cf. II Thess. 3:6, 14), so as neither to bear any responsibility for their procedure, nor seem to give them the least countenance. **18. For they that are such serve not our Lord Jesus Christ** —'our Lord Christ' appears to be the true reading. **but their own belly**—not in the grosser sense, but as 'living for low ends of their own' (cf. Phil. 3:19). **and by good words and fair speeches deceive the simple**—the unwary, the unsuspecting. (See Prov. 14:15.) **19. For your obedience**—i.e., tractableness—**is come abroad unto all. I am glad therefore on your behalf**—'I rejoice therefore over you,' seems the true reading. **but yet I would have you wise unto that which is good, and simple**—'harmless,' as in Matthew 10:16, from which the warning is taken—**concerning**—'unto'—**evil**—'Your reputation among the churches for subjection to the teaching ye have received is to me sufficient ground of confidence in you; but ye need the serpent's wisdom to discriminate between transparent truth and plausible error, with that guileless simplicity which instinctively cleaves to the one and rejects the other.' **20. And the God of peace shall bruise Satan under your feet shortly**—The apostle encourages the Romans to persevere in resisting the wiles of the devil with the assurance that, as good soldiers of Jesus Christ, they are "shortly" to receive their discharge, and have the satisfaction of "putting their feet upon the neck" of that formidable enemy—symbol familiar, probably, in all languages to express not only the completeness of the defeat, but the abject humiliation of the conquered foe. (See Josh. 10:24; II Sam. 22:41; Ezek. 21:29; Ps. 91:13.) Though the apostle here styles Him who is thus to bruise Satan, the God of peace," with special reference to the "divisions" (vs. 17) by which the church at Rome was in danger of being disturbed, this sublime appellation of God has here a wider sense, pointing to the whole "purpose for which the Son of God was manifested, to destroy the works of the devil" (I John 3:8); and indeed this assurance is but a reproduction of the first great promise, that the Seed of the woman should bruise the Serpent's head (Gen. 3:15). **The grace of our Lord Jesus Christ be with you. Amen**—The "Amen" here has no MS. authority. What comes after this, where one would have expected the epistle to close, has its parallel in Philippians 4:20, etc., and being in fact common in epistolary writings, is simply a mark of genuineness. **21. Timotheus, my work-fellow**—'my fellow labourer'; see Acts 16:1-5. The apostle mentions him here rather than in the opening address to this church, as he had not been at Rome [BENGEL]. **and Lucius**—not Luke, for the fuller form of 'Lucas' is not 'Lucius' but 'Lucanus.' The person meant seems to be "Lucius of Cyrene," who was among the "prophets and teachers" at Antioch with our apostle, before he was summoned into the missionary field (Acts 13:1). **and Jason**—See Acts 17:5. He had probably accompanied or followed the apostle from Thessalonica to Corinth. **Sosipater**—See Acts 20:4. **22. I, Tertius, who wrote this** —'the'—**epistle**—as the apostle's amanuensis, or penman—**salute you in the Lord**—So usually did the apostle dictate his epistles, that he calls the attention of the Galatians to the fact that to them he wrote with his own hand (Gal. 6:11). But this Tertius would have the Romans to know that, far from being a mere scribe, his heart went out to them in Christian affection; and the apostle, by giving his salutation a place here, would show what sort of assistants he employed. **23. Gaius mine host, and**—the host—**of the whole church**—See Acts 20:4. It would appear that he was one of only two persons whom Paul baptized with his own hand (cf. III John 1). His Christian hospitality appears to have been something uncommon. **Erastus the chamberlain**—'treasurer'—**of the city**—doubtless of Corinth. (See Acts 19:22; II Tim. 4:20.) **and Quartus a brother**—rather, 'the' or 'our brother'; as Sosthenes and Timothy are called (I Cor. 1:1, and II Cor. 1:1 *(Greek)*. Nothing more is known of this Quartus. **24. The grace,...**—a repetition of the benediction precisely as in vs. 20, save that it is here invoked on them "all." **25. Now to him that is of power**—more simply, as in Jude 24, 'to Him that is able'—**to stablish**—confirm, or uphold—**you, according to my gospel, and the preaching of Jesus Christ**—i.e., in conformity with the truths of that Gospel which I preach, and not I only, but all to whom has been committed "the preaching of Jesus Christ."—**according to the revelation of the mystery** —see on ch. 11:25—**which was kept secret since the world began**—lit., 'which hath been kept in silence during eternal ages'. **26. But is now made manifest** —The reference here is to that peculiar feature of the Gospel economy which Paul himself was specially employed to carry into practical effect and to unfold by his teaching—the introduction of the Gentile believers to an equality with their Jewish brethren, and the new, and, to the Jews, quite unexpected form which this gave to the whole Kingdom of God (cf. Eph. 3:1-10, etc.). This the apostle calls here a mystery hitherto undisclosed, in what sense the next verse will show, but now fully unfolded; and his prayer for the Roman Christians, in the form of a doxology to Him who was able to do what he asked, is that they might be established in the truth of the Gospel, not only in its essential character, but specially in that feature of it which gave themselves, as Gentile believers, their whole standing among the people of God. **and by the scriptures of the prophets, according to the commandment of the everlasting God, made known to all nations for**—in order to—**the obedience of faith** —Lest they should think, from what he had just said, that God had brought in upon his people so vast a change on their condition without giving them any previous notice, the apostle here adds that, on the contrary, "the Scriptures of the prophets" contain all that he and other preachers of the Gospel had to declare on these topics, and indeed that the same "everlasting God," who "from eternal ages" had kept these things hid, had given "commandment" that they should now, according to the

tenor of those prophetic Scriptures, be imparted to every nation for their believing acceptance. **27. to God,...**—'To the only wise God through Jesus Christ, be'—lit., 'to whom be'; i.e., 'to Him, I say, be the glory for ever. Amen.' At its outset, this is an ascription of glory to the *power* that could do all this; at its close it ascribes glory to the *wisdom* that planned and that presides over the gathering of a redeemed people out of all nations. The apostle adds his devout "Amen," which the reader—if he has followed him with the astonishment and delight of him who pens these words—will fervently echo.—On this concluding section of the Epistle, note (1) In the minute and delicate manifestations of Christian feeling, and lively interest in the smallest movements of Christian life, love, and zeal, which are here exemplified, combined with the grasp of thought and elevation of soul which this whole Epistle displays, as indeed all the writings of our apostle, we have the secret of much of that grandeur of character which has made the name of Paul stand on an elevation of its own in the estimation of enlightened Christendom in every age, and of that influence which under God, beyond all the other apostles, he has already exercised, and is yet destined to exert, over the religious thinking and feeling of men. Nor can any approach him in these peculiarities without exercising corresponding influence on all with whom they come in contact (vss. 1-16). (2) "The wisdom of the serpent and the harmlessness of the dove"—in enjoining which our apostle here only echoes the teaching of his Lord (Matt. 10:16)—is a combination of properties the rarity of which among Christians is only equalled by its vast importance. In every age of the Church there have been real Christians whose excessive study of the serpent's wisdom has so sadly trenched upon their guileless simplicity, as at times to excite the distressing apprehension that they were no better than wolves in sheep's clothing. Nor is it to be denied, on the other hand, that, either from inaptitude or indisposition to judge with manly discrimination of character and of measures, many eminently simple, spiritual, devoted Christians, have throughout life exercised little or no influence on any section of society around them. Let the apostle's counsel on this head (vs. 19) be taken as a study, especially by young Christians, whose character has yet to be formed, and whose permanent sphere in life is but partially fixed; and let them prayerfully set themselves to the combined exercise of both those qualities. So will their Christian character acquire solidity and elevation, and their influence for good be proportionally extended. (3) Christians should cheer their own and each other's hearts, amidst the toils and trials of their protracted warfare, with the assurance that it will have a speedy and glorious end; they should accustom themselves to regard all opposition to the progress and prosperity of Christ's cause—whether in their own souls, in the churches with which they are connected, or in the world at large—as just "Satan" in conflict, as ever, with Christ their Lord; and they should never allow themselves to doubt that "the God of peace" will "shortly" give them the neck of their Enemy, and make them to bruise the Serpent's head (vs. 20). (4) As Christians are held up and carried through solely by divine power, working through the glorious Gospel, so to that power, and to the wisdom that brought that Gospel nigh to them, they should ascribe all the glory of their stability now, as they certainly will of their victory at last (vss. 25-27). (5) "Has the everlasting God" "commanded" that the Gospel "mystery," so long kept hid but now fully disclosed, shall be "made known to all nations for the obedience of faith" (vs. 26)? Then, what "necessity is laid upon" all the churches and every Christian, to send the Gospel "to every creature!" And we may rest well assured that the prosperity or decline of churches, and of individual Christians, will have not a little to do with their faithfulness or indifference to this imperative duty.

The ancient subscription at the end of this epistle —though of course of no authority—appears to be in this case quite correct.

THE FIRST EPISTLE OF PAUL THE APOSTLE TO THE

CORINTHIANS

INTRODUCTION

The AUTHENTICITY of this Epistle is attested by Clement of Rome (*Ep. to Corinth.* c. 47), Polycarp (*Ep. to Philipp.* c. 11), and Irenæus (*Adversus Hæres* 4, 27, 3). The city to which it was sent was famed for its wealth and commerce, which were chiefly due to its situation between the Ionian and Ægean Seas on the isthmus connecting the Peloponese with Greece. In Paul's time it was the capital of the province Achaia and the seat of the Roman proconsul (Acts 18:12). The state of morals in it was notorious for debauchery, even in the profligate heathen world; so much so that "to Corinthianize" was a proverbial phrase for "to play the wanton"; hence arose dangers to the purity of the Christian Church at Corinth. That Church was founded by Paul on his first visit (Acts 18:1–17).

He had been the instrument of converting many Gentiles (ch. 12:2), and some Jews (Acts 18:8), notwithstanding the vehement opposition of the countrymen of the latter (Acts 18:5), during the year and a half in which he sojourned there. The converts were chiefly of the humbler classes (ch. 1:26, etc.). Crispus (ch. 1:14; Acts 18:8), Erastus, and Gaius (Caius) were, however, men of rank (Rom. 16:23). A variety of classes is also implied in ch. 11:22. The risk of contamination by contact with the surrounding corruptions, and the temptation to a craving for Greek philosophy and rhetoric (which Apollos' eloquent style rather tended to foster, Acts 18:24, etc.) in contrast to Paul's simple preaching of Christ crucified (ch. 2:1, etc.), as well as the opposition of certain teachers to him, naturally caused him anxiety. Emissaries from the Judaizers of Palestine boasted of "letters of commendation" from Jerusalem, the metropolis of the faith. They did not, it is true, insist on circumcision in refined Corinth, where the attempt would have been hopeless, as they did among the simpler people of Galatia; but they attacked the apostolic authority of Paul (ch. 9:1, 2; II Cor. 10:1, 7, 8), some of them declaring themselves followers of Cephas, the chief apostle, others boasting that they belonged to Christ Himself (ch. 1:12; II Cor. 10:7), while they haughtily repudiated all subordinate teaching. Those persons gave out themselves for apostles (II Cor. 11:5, 13). The ground taken by them was that Paul was not one of the Twelve, and not an eyewitness of the Gospel facts, and durst not prove his apostleship by claiming sustenance from the Christian Church. Another section avowed themselves followers of Paul himself, but did so in a party spirit, exalting the minister rather than Christ. The followers of Apollos, again, unduly prized his Alexandrian learning and eloquence, to the disparagement of the apostle, who studiously avoided any deviation from Christian simplicity (ch. 2:1–5). In some of this last philosophizing party there may have arisen the Antinomian tendency which tried to defend theoretically their own practical immorality: hence their denial of the future resurrection, and their adoption of the Epicurean motto, prevalent in heathen Corinth, "Let us eat and drink, for to-morrow we die" (ch. 15). Hence, perhaps, arose their connivance at the incestuous intercourse kept up by one of the so-called Christian body with his stepmother during his father's life. The household of Chloe informed Paul of many other evils: such as contentions, divisions, and lawsuits brought against brethren in heathen law courts by professing Christians; the abuse of their spiritual gifts into occasions of display and fanaticism; the interruption of public worship by simultaneous and disorderly ministrations, and decorum violated by women speaking unveiled (contrary to Oriental usage), and so usurping the office of men, and even the holy communion desecrated by greediness and revelling on the part of the communicants. Other messengers, also, came from Corinth, consulting him on the subject of (1) the controversy about meats offered to idols; (2) the disputes about celibacy and marriage; (3) the due exercise of spiritual gifts in public worship; (4) the best mode of making the collection which he had requested for the saints at Jerusalem (ch. 16:1, etc.). Such were the circumstances which called forth the First Epistle to the Corinthians, the most varied in its topics of all the Epistles.

In ch. 5:9, "I wrote unto you in an Epistle not to company with fornicators," it is implied that Paul had written a previous letter to the Corinthians (now lost). Probably in it he had also enjoined them to make a contribution for the poor saints at Jerusalem, whereupon they seem to have asked directions as to the mode of doing so, to which he now replies (ch. 16:2). It also probably announced his intention of visiting them on his way to Macedonia, and again on his return from Macedonia (II Cor. 1:15, 16), which purpose he changed on hearing the unfavorable report from Chloe's household (ch. 16:5–7), for which he was charged with fickleness (II Cor. 1:17). In the first Epistle which we have, the subject of fornication is alluded to only in a summary way, as if he were rather replying to an excuse set up after rebuke in the matter, than introducing it for the first time [ALFORD]. Preceding this former letter, he seems to have paid a *second* visit to Corinth.

For in II Cor. 12:4; 13:1, he speaks of his intention of paying them a *third* visit, implying he had already *twice* visited them. See also *Notes* on II Cor. 2:1; 13:2; also 1:15, 16. It is hardly likely that during his three years' sojourn at Ephesus he would have failed to revisit his Corinthian converts, which he could so readily do by sea, there being constant maritime intercourse between the two cities. This second visit was probably a short one (cf. ch. 16:7); and attended with pain and humiliation (II Cor. 2:1; 12:21), occasioned by the scandalous conduct of so many of his own converts. His milder censures having then failed to produce reformation, he wrote briefly directing them "not to company with fornicators." On their misapprehending this injunction, he explained it more fully in the Epistle, the first of the two extant (ch. 5:9, 12). That the *second* visit is not mentioned in Acts is no objection to its having really taken place, as that book is fragmentary and omits other leading incidents in Paul's life; e.g., his visit to Arabia, Syria, and Cilicia (Gal. 1:17-21).

The PLACE OF WRITING is fixed to be Ephesus (ch. 16:8). The subscription in *English Version*, "From Philippi," has no authority whatever, and probably arose from a mistaken translation of ch. 16:5, "For *I am passing through* Macedonia." At the time of writing Paul implies (ch. 16:8) that he intended to leave Ephesus after Pentecost *of that year*. He really did leave it about Pentecost (A.D. 57). Cf. Acts 19:20. The allusion to Passover imagery in connection with our Christian Passover, Easter (ch. 5:7), makes it likely that the season was about Easter. Thus the date of the Epistle is fixed with tolerable accuracy, about Easter, certainly before Pentecost, in the third year of his residence at Ephesus, A.D. 57. For other arguments, see CONYBEARE and HOWSON's *Life and Ep. of St. Paul.*

The Epistle is written in the name of Sosthenes "[our] brother." BIRKS supposes he is the same as the Sosthenes, Acts 18:17, who, he thinks, was converted subsequently to that occurrence. He bears no part in the Epistle itself, the apostle in the very next verses (vss. 4, etc.) using the first person: so Timothy is introduced, II Cor. 1:1. The bearers of the Epistle were probably Stephanas, Fortunatus, and Achaicus (see the subscription), whom he mentions (ch. 16:17, 18) as with him then, but who he implies are about to return back to Corinth; and therefore he commends them to the regard of the Corinthians.

CHAPTER 1

Vss. 1-31. THE INSCRIPTION; THANKSGIVING FOR THE SPIRITUAL STATE OF THE CORINTHIAN CHURCH; REPROOF OF PARTY DIVISIONS: HIS OWN METHOD OF PREACHING ONLY CHRIST. **1. called to be**—Found in some, not in others, of the oldest MSS. Possibly inserted from Romans 1:1; but as likely to be genuine. Translate, lit., "a called apostle" [CONYBEARE and HOWSON]. **through the will of God**—not because of my own merit. Thus Paul's call as "an apostle by the will of God," while constituting the ground of the authority he claims in the Corinthian Church (cf. Gal. 1:1), is a reason for humility on his own part (ch. 15:8, 10) [BENGEL]. In assuming the ministerial office a man should see he does so not of his own impulse, but by the will of God (Jer. 23:21); Paul if left to his own will would never have been an apostle (Rom. 9:16). **Sosthenes**—See my *Introduction*. Associated by Paul with himself in the inscription, either in modesty, Sosthenes being his inferior [CHRYSOSTOM], or in order that the name of a "brother" of note in Corinth (Acts 18:17) might give weight to his Epistle and might show, in opposition to his detractors that he was supported by leading *brethren*. Gallio had driven the Jews who accused Paul from the judgment seat. The Greek mob, who disliked Jews, took the opportunity then of beating Sosthenes the ruler of the Jewish synagogue, while Gallio looked on and refused to interfere, being secretly pleased that the mob should second his own contempt for the Jews. Paul probably at this time had showed sympathy for an adversary in distress, which issued in the conversion of the latter. So Crispus also, the previous chief ruler of the synagogue had been converted. Saul the persecutor turned into Paul the apostle, and Sosthenes the leader in persecution against that apostle, were two trophies of divine grace that, side by side, would appeal with double power to the Church at Corinth [BIRKS]. **2. church of God**—He calls it so notwithstanding its many blots. Fanatics and sectaries vainly think to anticipate the final sifting of the wheat and tares (Matt. 13:27-30). It is a dangerous temptation to think there is no church where there is not apparent perfect purity. He who thinks so, must at last separate from all others and think himself the only holy man in the world, or establish a peculiar sect with a few hypocrites. It was enough for Paul in recognizing the Corinthians as a church, that he saw among them evangelical doctrine, baptism, and the Lord's Supper" [CALVIN]. It was the Church *of God*, not of this or of that favorite leader [CHRYSOSTOM]. **at Corinth**—a church at dissolute Corinth—what a paradox of grace! **sanctified**—*consecrated*, or *set apart as holy to God in* (by union with) *Christ Jesus*. In the *Greek* there are no words "to them that are"; translate simply, "men sanctified." **called to be saints**—rather, "called saints"; saints by calling: applied by Paul to *all* professing members of the Church. As "sanctified in Christ" implies the fountain sources of holiness, the believer's original sanctification in Christ (ch. 6:11; Heb. 10:10, 14; I Pet. 1:2) in the purposes of God's grace, so "called saints" refers to their actual *call* (Rom. 8:30), and the end of that call that they should be holy (I Pet. 1:15). **with all that in every place call upon ... Christ**—The Epistle is intended for these also, as well as for the Corinthians. The true CATHOLIC CHURCH (a term first used by IGNATIUS, *ad Smyrnæos*, c. 8): not consisting of those who call themselves from Paul, Cephas, or any other eminent leader (vs. 12), but of all, wherever they be, who call on Jesus as their Saviour in sincerity (cf. II Tim. 2:22). Still a general unity of discipline and doctrine in the several churches is implied in ch. 4:17; 7:17 11-16; 14-33, 36. The worship due to God is here attributed to Jesus (cf. Joel 2:32; Matt. 4:10; Acts 9:14). **both theirs and ours**—"in every place which is their home ... and our home also"; this is added to include the Christians throughout Achaia, not residing in Corinth, the capital (II Cor. 1:1). Paul feels the home of his converts to be also his own. Cf. a similar phrase in Romans 16:13 [CONYBEARE and HOWSON]. "Ours" refers to Paul and Sosthenes, and the Corinthians' home [ALFORD]. BEZA better explains, "Both their Lord and our Lord." All believers have one and the same Lord (ch. 8:6; Eph. 4:5); a virtual reproof of the divisions of the Corinthians, as if Christ were divided (vs. 13). **3. peace**—peculiarly needed in the

Corinthian church, on account of its dissensions. On this verse see Romans 1:7. **4.** He puts the causes for praise and hope among them in the foreground, not to discourage them by the succeeding reproof, and in order to appeal to their better selves. **my God**–(Rom. 1:8; Phil. 1:3). **always**–(Cf. Phil. 1:4). **the grace . . . given you**–(Cf. vs. 7). **by . . . Christ**–lit., IN *Jesus Christ* given you as members in Christ. **5. utterance**–ALFORD from MENOCHIUS translates, "doctrine." Ye are rich in *preachers* or the *preaching* of the word, and rich in *knowledge* or *apprehension* of it: lit. (the) *word* (preached).' *English Version* (as in II Cor. 8:7) is better: for Paul, purposing presently to dwell on the *abuse* of the two gifts on which the Corinthians most prided themselves, *utterance* (speech) and *knowledge* (ch. 1:20; 3:18; 4:19; ch. 13 and 14), previously gains their goodwill by congratulating them on *having* those gifts. **6.** According as the testimony of (of, and concerning) Christ (who is both the object and author of this testimony [BENGEL]; ch. 2:1; I Tim. 2:6; II Tim. 1:8) was confirmed *among* [ALFORD] you; i.e., by God, through my preaching and through the miracles accompanying it (ch. 12:3; Mark 16:20; II Cor. 1:21, 22; Gal. 3:2, 5; Eph. 4:7, 8; Heb. 2:4). God *confirmed* (cf. Phil. 1:7; Heb. 2:3), or gave effect to the Gospel among (or better as *English Version*, "in") the Corinthians *by their accepting it* and setting their seal to its truth, through the inward power of His Spirit, and the outward gifts and miracles accompanying it [CALVIN]. **7. ye come behind**–are inferior to other Christians elsewhere [GROTIUS]. **in no gift**–not that all had all gifts, but different persons among them had different gifts (ch. 12. 4, etc.). **waiting for . . . coming of . . . Christ**–The crowning proof of their "coming behind in no gift." *Faith, hope*, and *love*, are all exercised herein (cf. II Tim. 4:8; Titus 2:13). "Leaving to others their MEMENTO MORI (remember death), do thou earnestly cherish this joyous expectation of the Lord's coming" [BENGEL]. The *Greek* verb implies, "to expect constantly, not only for a certain time, but even to the end till the expected event happens" (Rom. 8:19, [TITTM., *Synonyms*]. **8. Who**–God, vs. 4 (not Jesus Christ, vs. 7, in which case it would be "in *His* day"). **unto the end**–viz., "the coming of Christ." **blameless in the day of . . . Christ**–(I Thess. 5:23). After that day there is no danger (Eph. 4:30; Phil. 1: 6). Now is our day to work, and the day of our enemies to try us: then will be the day of Christ, and of His glory in the saints [BENGEL]. **9. faithful**–to His promises (Phil. 1:6; I Thess. 5:24). **called**–according to His purpose (Rom. 8:28). **unto . . . fellowship of . . . Jesus**–to be fellow heirs with Christ (Rom. 8:17-28), like Him sons of God and heirs of glory (Rom. 8:30; II Thess. 2:14; I Pet. 5:10; I John 1:3). CHRYSOSTOM remarks that the name of Christ is oftener mentioned in this than in any other Epistle, the apostle designing thereby to draw them away from their party admiration of particular teachers to Christ alone. **10. Now**–Ye already have *knowledge, utterance*, and *hope*, maintain also *love*. **brethren**–The very title is an argument for *love*. **by . . . Christ**–whom Paul wishes to be all in all to the Corinthians, and therefore names Him so often in this chapter. **speak . . . same thing**–not speaking different things as ye do (vs. 12), in a spirit of variance. **divisions**–lit., "splits," "breaches." **but**–"but rather." **perfectly joined together**–the opposite word to "divisions." It is applied to *healing a wound*, or *making whole a rent*. **mind . . . judgment**–the view taken by the

understanding, and the *practical decision* arrived at [CONYBEARE and HOWSON], as to what is to be done. The *mind*, within, refers to things to be believed: the *judgment* is displayed outwardly in things to be done [BENGEL]. *Disposition–opinion* [ALFORD]. **11.** (Ch. 11:18.) **by them . . . of . . . house of Chloe** –They seem to have been alike in the confidence of Paul and of the Corinthians. The Corinthians "wrote" to the apostle (ch. 7:1), consulting him concerning certain points; marriage, the eating of things offered to idols, the decorum to be observed by women in religious assemblies. But they said not a syllable about the enormities and disorders that had crept in among them. *That* information reached Paul by other quarters. Hence his language about those evils is, "It hath been declared unto me . . ."; "It is reported commonly" (ch. 5:1, 2). All this he says *before* he refers to their *letter*, which shows that the latter did not give him any intimation of those evils. An undesigned proof of genuineness [PALEY's *Horæ Paulinæ*]. Observe his prudence: He names the family, to let it be seen that he made his allegation not without authority: he does not name the individuals, not to excite odium against them. He tacitly implies that the information ought rather to have come to him directly from their presbyters, as they had consulted him about matters of less moment. **contentions**– not so severe a word as "divisions," lit., schisms (*Margin*, vs. 10). **12. this I say**–this is what *I mean* in saying "contentions" (vs. 11). **every one of you saith**–Ye say severally, "glorying in men" (vs. 31; ch. 3:21, 22), one, I am of Paul; another, I am of Apollos. . . . Not that they formed *definite* parties, but they individually betrayed the *spirit* of party in contentions under the name of different favorite teachers. Paul will not allow himself to be flattered even by those who made his name their party cry, so as to connive at the dishonor thereby done to Christ. These probably were converted under his ministry. Those alleging the name of Apollos, Paul's successor at Corinth (Acts 18:24, etc), were persons attracted by his rhetorical style (probably acquired in Alexandria, ch. 3:6), as contrasted with the "weak bodily presence" and "contemptible speech" of the apostle. Apollos, doubtless, did not willingly foster this spirit of undue preference (ch. 4:6, 8); nay, to discourage it, he would not repeat his visit just then (ch. 16:12). **I of Cephas**–probably Judaizers, who sheltered themselves under the name of Peter, the apostle of the circumcision ("Cephas" is the *Hebrew*, "Peter" the *Greek* name; John 1:42; Gal. 2:11, etc.): the subjects handled in chs. 7-9 were probably suggested as matters of doubt by them. The church there began from the Jewish synagogue, Crispus the chief ruler, and Sosthenes his successor (probably), being converts. Hence some Jewish leaven, though not so much as elsewhere, is traceable (II Cor. 11:22). *Petrism* afterwards sprang up much more rankly at Rome. If it be wrong to boast "I am of Peter," how much more so to boast "I am of the Pope!" [BENGEL]. **I of Christ**–A fair pretext used to slight the ministry of Paul and their other teachers (ch. 4:8; II Cor. 10:7-11). **13. Is Christ divided?**–into various parts (one under one leader, another under another) [ALFORD]. The unity of His body is not to be cut in pieces, as if all did not belong to Him, the One Head. **was Paul crucified for you?**–In the *Greek* the interrogation implies that a strong negative answer is expected: "Was it Paul (*surely you will not say so*) that was crucified for you?" In the former question the majesty of "CHRIST" (the Anointed One of God) implies the impossibility of His being "divided." in the latter, *Paul's* insignificance implies the impossibility of his being the head of redemption, "crucified for" them, and giving his name to the redeemed. This, which is true of Paul the *founder* of the Church of Corinth, holds equally good of Cephas and Apollos, who had not such a claim as Paul in the Corinthian Church. **crucified ... baptized**—The cross claims us for Christ, as redeemed by Him; baptism, as dedicated to Him. **in the name**—rather, "*into* the name" (Gal. 3:27), implying the *incorporation* involved in the idea of baptism. **14. I thank God's providence now, who so ordered it that I baptized none of you but Crispus** (the former ruler of the synagogue, Acts 18:8) **and Gaius** (written by the Romans *Caius,* the host of Paul at Corinth, and of the church, Rom. 16:23; a person therefore in good circumstances. Baptizing was the office of the deacons (Acts 10:48) rather than of the apostles, whose office was that of establishing and superintending generally the churches. The deacons had a better opportunity of giving the necessary *course of instruction preparatory to baptism.* Crispus and Gaius were probably among the first converts, and hence were baptized by Paul himself, who founded the church. **15. Lest**—not that Paul had this reason at the time, but God so arranged it that none might say [Alford]. **16. household of Stephanas**—"The first fruits of Achaia," i.e., among the first converted there (ch. 16:15, 17). It is likely that such "households" included infants (Acts 16:33). The history of the Church favors this view, as infant baptism was the usage from the earliest ages. **17.** Paul says this not to depreciate baptism; for he exalts it most highly (Rom. 6:3). He baptized some first converts; and would have baptized more, but that his and the apostles' peculiar work was to preach the Gospel, to found by their autoptic testimony particular churches, and then to superintend the churches in general. **sent me**—lit., "as an apostle." **not to baptize**—even in Christ's name, much less in my own. **not with wisdom of words**—or *speech; philosophical reasoning* set off with *oratorical language* and secular learning, which the Corinthians set so undue a value upon (vs. 5; ch. 2:1, 4) in Apollos, and the want of which in Paul they were dissatisfied with (II Cor. 10:10). **cross of Christ**—the sum and substance of the Gospel (vs. 23; ch. 2:2), Christ crucified. **be made of none effect**—lit., "be made void" (Rom. 4:14); viz., by men thinking more of the human reasonings and eloquence in which the Gospel was set forth, than of the Gospel itself of Christ crucified, the sinner's only remedy, and God's highest exhibition of love. **18. preaching ...**—lit., "the word," or speech as to the cross; in contrast to the "wisdom of *words*" (so called), vs. 17. **them that perish**—rather, "them that are perishing", viz., by preferring human "wisdom of words" to the doctrine of the "cross of Christ." It is not the final state that is referred to; but, "them that are in the way of perishing." So also in II Corinthians 2:15, 16. **us which are saved**—In the *Greek* the collocation is more modest, "to them that are being saved (that are in the way of salvation) as," i.e., to which class *we* belong. **power of God**—which includes in it that it is the wisdom of God" (vs. 24). God's powerful instrument of salvation; the highest exhibition of God's power (Rom. 1:16). What seems to the world "weakness" in God's plan of salvation (vs. 25), and in its mode of delivery by His apostle (ch. 2:3) is really His mighty "power." What seems "foolishness" because wanting man's "wis-

dom of words" (vs. 17), is really the highest "wisdom of God" (vs. 24). **19. I will destroy**—slightly altered from the LXX, Isaiah 29:14. The *Hebrew* is, "The wisdom of the wise shall perish, and the understanding of their prudent men shall be hid." Paul by inspiration gives the sense of the Spirit, by making God the cause of their *wisdom perishing,* etc., "*I* will destroy," etc. **understanding of the prudent**—lit., "of the understanding ones." **20. Where**—nowhere; for God "brings them to naught" (vs. 19). **the wise**—generally. **the scribe**—Jewish [Alford]. **the disputer**—Greek [Alford]. Cf. the Jew and Greek of this world contrasted with the godly wise, vss. 22, 23. Vitringa thinks the reference is to the Jewish discourses in the synagogue, *daraschoth,* from a *Hebrew* root "to dispute." Cf. "questions," Acts 26:3; Titus 3:9. If so, "wise" refers to *Greek* wisdom (cf. vs. 22). Paul applies Isaiah 33:18 here in a higher sense; there the primary reference was to temporal deliverance, here to external; vs. 22, which is in threefold opposition to vs. 18 there, sanctions this higher application; the Lord in the threefold character being the sole ground of glorying to His people. **of this world ... of this world**—rather, "dispensation (or *age*) ..., world"; the *Greek* words are distinct. The former is here *this age* or *worldly order of things* in a moral point of view, as opposed to the Christian dispensation or order of things. The latter is the *world* viewed externally and cosmically. **made foolish**—shown the world's philosophy to be folly, because it lacks faith in Christ crucified [Chrysostom]. Has treated it as folly, and not used its help in converting and saving men (vss. 26, 27) [Estius]. **21. after that**—rather, "whereas." **in the wisdom of God**—in the wise arrangement of God. **world by wisdom**—rather, "by *its* wisdom," or *its philosophy* (John 1:10; Rom. 1:28). **knew not God**—whatever other knowledge it attained (Acts 17:23, 27). The deistic theory that man can by the light of nature discover his duty to God, is disproved by the fact that man *has* never discovered it without revelation. All the stars and moon cannot make it day; that is the prerogative of the sun. Nor can nature's highest gifts make the moral day arise; that is the office of Christ. Even the Jew missed this knowledge, in so far as he followed after mere carnal *world* wisdom. **it pleased God**—Paul refers to Jesus' words (Luke 10:21). **by the foolishness of preaching**—by that preaching which the world (unbelieving Jews and Gentiles alike) deem *foolishness.* **save them that believe**—(Rom. 1:16). **22. For**—lit., "Since", seeing that. This verse illustrates how the "preaching" of Christ crucified came to be deemed "foolishness" (vs. 21). **a sign**—The oldest MSS. read "signs." The *singular* was a later correction from Matthew 12:38; 16:1; John 2:18. The signs the Jews craved for were not mere miracles, but direct tokens from heaven that Jesus was Messiah (Luke 11:16). **Greeks seek ... wisdom**—viz., a philosophic demonstration of Christianity. Whereas Christ, instead of *demonstrative* proof, demands *faith* on the ground of *His word,* and of a reasonable amount of evidence that the alleged revelation is His word. Christianity begins not with solving intellectual difficulties, but with satisfying the heart that longs for forgiveness. Hence not the refined Greeks, but the theocratic Jews were the chosen organ for propagating revelation. Again, intellectual Athens (Acts 17: 18-21, etc.) received the Gospel less readily than commercial Corinth. **23. we**—Paul and Apollos. **Christ crucified**—The *Greek* expresses not the mere fact of His crucifixion, but the *permanent character* acquired by the transaction, whereby He is now a Saviour (Gal. 3:1) [GREEN]. A Messiah (Christ) crucified was the stone on which the Jews stumbled (Matt. 21:44). The opposition of Jew and Gentile alike shows that a religion so seemingly contemptible in its origin could not have succeeded if it had not been divine. **unto the Greeks**—the oldest MSS. read "unto the *Gentiles.*" **24. called**—(cf. vs. 26). The same class as the "us which are (being) saved" (vs. 18); the elect, who have obeyed the call; called effectually (Rom. 8:28, 30). **Christ**—"Crucified" is not here added, because when the offense of the cross is overcome, "Christ" is received in all His relations, not only in His cross, but in His life and His future kingdom. **power**—so meeting all the reasonable requirements of the Jews who sought "a sign." The cross (the death of a slave), which to the Jews (looking for a temporal Messiah) was a "stumbling block," is really "the power of God" to the salvation of all who believe. **wisdom of God**—so really exhibiting, and in the highest degree (if they would but see it), that which the Greeks sought after—*wisdom* (Col. 2:3). **25. foolishness of God**—i.e., God's plan of salvation which men deem "foolishness." **weakness of God**—Christ "crucified through weakness" (II Cor. 13:4, the great *stumbling block* of the Jews), yet "living by the *power* of God." So He *perfects strength* out of the *weakness* of His servants (ch. 2:3; II Cor. 12:9). **26. ye see**—rather, from the prominence of the verb in the *Greek*, "see" or "consider" (imperative) [ALFORD from VULGATE and IRENÆUS]. **your calling . . . are called**—Instead of the words in italics, supplied by *English Version*, supply, "were your callers." What Paul is dwelling on (cf. vss. 27, 28) is the weakness of the instrumentality which the Lord employed to convert the world [HINDS and WHATELY; so ANSELM]. However, *English Version* accords well with vs. 24. "The whole history of the expansion of the Church is a progressive victory of the ignorant over the learned, the lowly over the lofty, until the emperor himself laid down his crown before the cross of Christ" [OLSHAUSEN]. **wise . . . after the flesh**—the wisdom of this world acquired by human study without the Spirit. (Contrast Matt. 16:17.) **27. the foolish things**—a general phrase for *all persons and things foolish.* Even *things* (and those, too, *foolish things*) are chosen by God to confound *persons*, (and those too persons who are *wise*). This seems to me the force of the change from neuter to masculine. **to confound**—The *Greek* is stronger, "*that* He might confound (or put to shame)." God confounds the wise by effecting through His instruments, without human wisdom, that the worldly wise, with it, cannot effect, viz., to bring men to salvation. **chosen . . . chosen**—The repetition indicates the gracious deliberateness of God's purpose (Jas. 2:5). **28. yea, and things which are not**—*Yea* is not in the *Greek*. Also some of the oldest MSS. omit "and." Thus the clause, "things which are not" (are regarded as naught), is in apposition with "foolish . . . weak . . . base (i.e., lowborn) and despised things." God has chosen all four, though regarded as *things that are not,* to bring to naught things that are. **29. no flesh . . . glory**—For they who try to glory (boast) because of human greatness and wisdom, are "confounded" or *put to shame* (vs. 27). Flesh, like "the flower of the field," is beautiful, but frail (Isa. 40:6). **in his presence**—We are to glory not *before* Him, but in Him [BENGEL]. **30. But . . . ye**—in contrast to them that "glory" in worldly wisdom and greatness. **of him are**—not of yourselves (Eph. 2:8), but of Him

(Rom. 11:36). *From* Him ye are (i.e., have spiritual life, who once were spiritually among the "things which are not." vs. 28). **in Christ**—by living union with Him. Not "in the flesh" (vss. 26, 29). **of God**—*from* God; emanating *from* Him and sent by Him. **is made unto us**—*has been made* to us, to our eternal gain. **wisdom**—unattainable by the worldly mode of seeking it (vss. 19, 20; contrast Col. 2:3; Prov. 8; Isa. 9:6). By it we become "wise unto salvation," owing to His *wisdom* in originating and executing the plan, whereas once we were "fools." **righteousness**—the ground of our justification (Jer. 23:5, 6; Rom. 4:25; II Cor. 5:21); whereas once we were "weak" (Rom. 5:6). Isaiah 42:21; 45:24. **sanctification**—by His Spirit; whereas formerly we were "base." Hereafter our righteousness and sanctification alike shall be both perfect and inherent. Now the righteousness wherewith we are justified is perfect, but not inherent; that wherewith we are sanctified is inherent, but not perfect [HOOKER]. Now sanctification is perfect in principle, but not in attainment. These two are joined in the *Greek* as forming essentially but *one* thing, as distinguished from the "wisdom" in *devising* and executing the plan for us ("abounded toward us in all wisdom," Eph. 1:8), and "redemption," the *final completion* of the scheme in the deliverance of the body (the position of "redemption" last shows that this limited sense is the one intended here). Luke 21:28; Romans 8:23; Ephesians 1:14; 4:30. **redemption**—whereas once we were "despised." **31. glory in . . Lord**—(Jer. 9:23, 24)—in opposition to "flesh glorying in His presence" (vs. 29). In contrast to morbid slavish self-abasement, Paul joins with humility the elevating consciousness of our true dignity in Christ. He who glories is to glory in the Lord, not in the flesh, nor in the world.

CHAPTER 2

Vss. 1-16. PAUL'S SUBJECT OF PREACHING, CHRIST CRUCIFIED, NOT IN WORLDLY, BUT IN HEAVENLY, WISDOM AMONG THE PERFECT. **1. And I**—"So I" [CONYBEARE] as one of the "foolish, weak, and despised" instruments employed by God (ch. 1:27, 28); "glorying in the Lord," not in man's wisdom (ch. 1:31). Cf. ch. 1:23, "We." **when I came**—(Acts 18:1, etc.). Paul might, had he pleased, have used an ornate style, having studied secular learning at Tarsus of Cilicia, which Strabo preferred as a school of learning to Athens or Alexandria; here, doubtless, he read the *Cilician* Aratus' poems (which he quotes, Acts 17:28), and Epimenides (Titus 1:12), and Menander (I Cor. 15:33). Grecian intellectual development was an important element in preparing the way for the Gospel, but it failed to regenerate the world, showing that for this a superhuman power is needed. Hellenistic (Grecizing) Judaism at Tarsus and Alexandria was the connecting link between the schools of Athens and those of the Rabbis. No more fitting birthplace could there have been for the apostle of the Gentiles than Tarsus, free as it was from the warping influences of Rome, Alexandria, and Athens. He had at the same time *Roman* citizenship, which protected him from sudden violence. Again, he was reared in the *Hebrew divine law* at Jerusalem. Thus, as the three elements, Greek cultivation, Roman polity (Luke 2:1), and the divine law given to the Jews, combined just at Christ's time, to prepare the world for the Gospel, so the same three, by God's marvellous providence, met together in the apostle to the Gentiles [CONYBEARE and HOWSON]. **testimony of God**—"the testimony *of Christ*" (ch. 1:6); therefore Christ is God. **2.** The *Greek* implies, "The only definite thing that I made it my business to know among you, was to know Jesus Christ (His person) and Him crucified (His office)" [ALFORD], not exalted on the earthly throne of David, but executed as the vilest malefactor. The historical fact of Christ's crucifixion had probably been put less prominently forward by the seekers after human wisdom in the Corinthian church, to avoid offending learned heathens and Jews. Christ's *person* and Christ's *office* constitute the sum of the Gospel. **3.** I—the *preacher:* as vs. 2 describes the *subject,* "Christ crucified," and vs. 4 the *mode* of preaching: "my speech . . . not with enticing words," "but in demonstration of the Spirit." **weakness**—personal and bodily (II Cor. 10:10; 12:7, 9; Gal. 4:13). **trembling**—(cf. Phil. 2:12). Not *personal fear,* but a *trembling anxiety to perform a duty;* anxious conscientiousness, as proved by the contrast to "eye service" (Eph. 6:5) [CONYBEARE and HOWSON]. **4. my speech**—in private. **preaching**—in public [BENGEL]. ALFORD explains it, *My discourse* on doctrines, and *my preaching* or announcement of facts. **enticing**—rather, "persuasive." **man's wisdom**—"man's" is omitted in the oldest authorities. Still "wisdom" does refer to *man's* wisdom. **demonstration of . . . Spirit . . .**—*Persuasion* is man's means of moving his fellow man. God's means is *demonstration,* leaving no doubt, and inspiring implicit faith, by the powerful working of the Spirit (then exhibited both outwardly by miracles, and inwardly by working on the heart, now in the latter and the more important way only, (Matt. 7:29; Acts 6:10; Heb. 4:12; cf. also Rom. 15:19). The same simple power accompanies divine truth now, producing certain persuasion and conversion, when the Spirit demonstrates by it. **5. stand in . . . wisdom of men**—rest on it, owe its origin and continuance to it. **6, 7.** Yet the Gospel preaching, so far from being at variance with true "wisdom," is a wisdom infinitely higher than that of the wise of the world. **we speak**—resuming "we" (preachers, I, Apollos, etc.) from "we preach" (ch. 1:28), only that here, "we speak" refers to something less public (cf. vss. 7.13, "mystery" "hidden") than "we preach," which is public. For "wisdom" here denotes not the whole of Christion doctrine, but its sublimer and deeper principles. **perfect**—Those *matured in Christian experience and knowledge* alone can understand the true superiority of the Christian wisdom which Paul preached. Distinguished not only from *worldly* and *natural* men, but also from *babes,* who though "in Christ" retain much that is "carnal" (ch. 3:1, 2), and cannot therefore understand the deeper truths of Christianity (ch. 14:20; Phil. 3:15; Heb. 5:14). Paul does not mean by the "mystery" or "hidden wisdom (vs. 7) some *hidden tradition distinct from the Gospel* (like the Church of Rome's *disciplina arcani* and doctrine of reserve), but the *unfolding* of the treasures of knowledge, once hidden in God's counsels, but *now* announced to all, which would be intelligently comprehended in proportion as the hearer's inner life became perfectly transformed into the image of Christ. Cf. instances of such "mysteries," i.e., deeper Christian truths, not preached at Paul's first coming to Corinth, when he confined himself to the fundamental elements (vs. 2), but now spoken to the "perfect" (ch. 15:51; Rom. 11:25; Eph. 3:5, 6). "Perfect" is used not of *absolute perfection,* but relatively to "babes," or those less ripe in Christian growth (cf. Phil. 3:12,

15, with I John 2:12-14). "God" (vs. 7) is opposed to the world, the apostles to "the princes [great and learned men] of this world" (vs. 8; cf. ch. 1:20) [BENGEL]. **come to naught**—nothingness (ch. 1:28). They are transient, not immortal. Therefore, their wisdom is not real [BENGEL]. Rather, translate with ALFORD, "Which *are being brought* to naught," viz., by God's choosing the "things which are not (the *weak and despised things of the Gospel*), to bring to naught (the same verb as here) things that are" (ch. 1:28). **7. wisdom of God**—emphatically contrasted with the wisdom *of men* and *of this world* (vss. 5, 6). **in a mystery**—connected in construction with "we speak": We speak as dealing with a mystery; i.e. not something *to be kept hidden,* but what heretofore was so, but is *now revealed.* Whereas the pagan mysteries were revealed only to a chosen few, the Gospel mysteries were made known to all who would obey the truth. "If our Gospel be *hid,* it is hid to them that are *lost*" (II Cor. 4:3), "whom the God of this world hath *blinded.*" Ordinarily we use "mystery" in reference to those from whom the knowledge is *withheld;* the apostles, in reference to those to whom it is *revealed* [WHATELY]. It is hidden before it is brought forward, and when it is brought forward it still remains hidden to those that are imperfect [BENGEL]. **ordained**—lit., "foreordained" (cf. vs. 9), "prepared for them that love Him." **before the world**—rather, "before *the ages*" (of time), i.e., from eternity. This infinitely antedates worldly wisdom in antiquity. It was before not only the wisdom of the world, but eternally before the world itself and its ages. **to our glory**—ours both now and hereafter, from "the Lord of *glory*" (vs. 8), who *brings to naught* "the princes of this world." **8. Which**—wisdom. The strongest proof of the natural man's destitution of heavenly wisdom. **crucified . . . Lord of glory**—implying the inseparable connection of Christ's humanity and His divinity. The Lord of glory (which He had in His own right before the world was, John 17:4, 24) was crucified. **9. But**—(it has happened) as it is written. **Eye hath not seen . . .**—ALFORD translates, "The things which eye saw not, . . . the things which God prepared . . ., to us God revealed through His Spirit." Thus, however, the "but" of vs. 10 is ignored. Rather construe, as ESTIUS, "('We speak,' supplied from vs. 8), things which eye saw not (heretofore), . . . things which God prepared. . . . But God revealed them to us . . . ." The quotation is not a verbatim one, but an inspired *exposition* of the "wisdom" (vs. 6, from Isa. 64:4). The exceptive words, "O God, *beside* (i.e., except) Thee," are not quoted directly, but are virtually expressed in the exposition of them (vs. 10), "None *but thou,* O God, seest these mysteries, and *God hath revealed them to us by His Spirit.*" **entered**—lit., "come up into the heart." A Hebraism (cf. *Margin,* Jer. 3:16). In Isaiah 64 it is "Prepared (lit., 'will do') for him that *waiteth for* Him"; here, "for them that *love* Him." For Isaiah spake to them who *waited for* Messiah's appearance as future; Paul, to them *who love Him* as having actually appeared (I John 4:19); cf. vs. 12, "the things that are freely given to us of God" [BENGEL]. **10. revealed . . . by . . . Spirit**—The inspiration of thoughts (so far as truth essential to salvation is concerned) makes the *Christian* (ch. 3:16; 12:3 Matt. 16:17; John 16:13; I John 2:20, 27); that of *words,* the PROPHET (II Sam. 23:1, 2; I Kings 13:1, 5), "by the *word* of the Lord" (vs. 13; John 20:30, 31; II Pet. 1:21). The secrets of revelation are secret to some, not because those who know them will not reveal them (for indeed, the very notion of *revelation* implies an unveiling of what had been veiled), but because those to whom they are announced have not the will or power to comprehend them. Hence the Spirit-taught alone know these secrets (Ps. 25:14; Prov. 3:32; John 7:17; 15:15). **unto us**—the "perfect" or fully matured in Christian experience (vs. 6). Intelligent men may understand the outline of doctrines; but without the Holy Spirit's revelation to the heart, these will be to them a mere outline—a skeleton, correct perhaps, but wanting life [*Cautions for the Times*, xiv.], (Luke 10:21). **the Spirit searcheth**—working in us and with our spirits (cf. Rom. 8:16, 26, 27). The Old Testament shows us God (the Father) for us. The Gospels, God (the Son) with us. The Acts and Epistles, God (the Holy Ghost) in us [MONOD], (Gal. 3:14). **deep things of God**—(Ps. 92:5). His divine nature, attributes, and counsels. The Spirit delights to explore the infinite depths of His own divine mind, and then reveal them to us, according as we are capable of understanding them (Deut. 29:29). This proves the personality and Godhead of the Holy Ghost. Godhead cannot be separated from the Spirit of God, as manhood cannot be separated from the Spirit of man [BENGEL]. **11. what man ...**—lit., "who of *men* knoweth the things of a *man,* save the spirit of that man?" **things of God knoweth no man**—rather, "*none* knoweth," not angel or man. This proves the impossibility of any knowing the things of God, save by the Spirit of God (who alone knows them, since even in the case of man, so infinitely inferior in mind to God, none of his fellow men, but his own spirit alone knows the things hidden within him). **12. we ... received, not ... spirit of ... world**—the personal evil "spirit that now worketh in the children of disobedience" (Eph. 2:2). This spirit is natural in the unregenerate, and needs not to be *received.* **Spirit which is of God**—i.e., which comes from God. We have received it only by the *gift* of God, whose Spirit it is, whereas our own spirit is the spirit that is in us men (vs. 11). **that we might know ... things ... freely given ... of God**—present experimental knowledge, to our unspeakable comfort, of His deep mysteries of wisdom, and of our future possession of the good "things which God hath prepared for them that love Him" (vs. 9). **13. also**—We not only *know* by the Holy Ghost, but *we also speak* the "things freely given to us of God" (vs. 12). **which the Holy Ghost teacheth**—The old MSS. read "the Spirit" simply, without "Holy." **comparing spiritual things with spiritual**—expounding the Spirit-inspired Old Testament Scripture, by comparison with the Gospel which Jesus by the same Spirit revealed [GROTIUS]; and conversely illustrating the Gospel mysteries by comparing them with the Old Testament types [CHRYSOSTOM]. So the *Greek* word is translated, "comparing" (II Cor. 10:12). WAHL (*Clavis*) translates, *"explaining* (as the *Greek* is translated, Gen. 40:8, LXX) to spiritual (i.e., Spirittaught) men, spiritual things (the things which we ourselves are taught by the Spirit)." Spirit-taught men alone can comprehend spiritual truths. This accords with vss. 6, 9, 10, 14, 15; ch. 3:1. ALFORD translates, "Putting together (combining) spirituals with spirituals"; i.e., attaching spiritual *words* to spiritual *things,* which we should not do, if we were to use words of worldly wisdom to expound spiritual things (so vss. 1, 4; I Pet. 4:11). Perhaps the generality of the neuters is designed to comprehend these several notions by implication. Comparing, or combining, spirituals

with spirituals; implying both that spiritual things are only suited to spiritual persons (so "things" comprehended *persons,* ch. 1:27), and also that spiritual truths can only be combined with spiritual (not worldly-wise) words; and lastly, spirituals of the Old and New Testaments can only be understood by mutual comparison or combination, not by combination with worldly "wisdom," or natural perceptions (ch. 1:21, 22; 2:1, 4-9; cf. Ps. 119:18). **14. natural man**—lit., "a man of animal soul." As contrasted with the *spiritual* man, he is governed by the animal soul, which overbears his *spirit,* which latter is without the Spirit of God (Jude 19). So the *animal (English Version,* "natural") body, or body led by the lower animal nature (including both the mere human fallen *reason* and *heart*), is contrasted with the Spiritquickened body (ch. 15:44-46). The *carnal* man (the man led by bodily appetites, and also by a self-exalting spirit, estranged from the divine life) is closely akin; so too the "earthly." "Devilish," or "demon-like"; "led by an evil spirit," is the awful character of such a one, in its worst type (Jas. 3:15). **receiveth not**—though they are offered to him, and are "worthy of being *received* by all men" (I Tim. 1:15). **they are foolishness unto him**—whereas he seeks "wisdom" (ch. 1:22). **neither can he**—Not only *does* he not, but **he** *cannot* know them, and therefore has no wish to "receive" them (Rom. 8:7). **15. He that is spiritual** —lit., "*the* spiritual (man)." In vs. 14, it is "*A* [not '*the,*' as *English Version*] natural man." *The* spiritual is *the* man distinguished above his fellow men, as he in whom the Spirit rules. In the unregenerate, the spirit which ought to be the organ of the Holy Spirit (and which is so in the regenerate), is overridden by the animal soul, and is in abeyance, so that such a one is never called "spiritual." **judgeth all things**—and persons, by their true standard (cf. ch. 6:2-4; I John 4:1), in so far as he is spiritual. "Discerneth ... is discerned," would better accord with the translation of the same *Greek* (vs. 14). Otherwise for "discerned," in vs. 14, translate, "judged of," to accord with the translation, "judgeth ... is judged" in this 15th verse. He has a practical insight into the verities of the Gospel, though he is not infallible on all theoretical points. If an individual may have the Spirit without being infallible, why may not the Church have the Spirit, and yet not be infallible (a refutation of the plea of Rome for the Church's infallibility, from Matt. 28: 20; John 16:13)? As the believer and the Church have the Spirit, and are yet not therefore impeccable, so he and the Church have the Spirit, and yet are not infallible or impeccable. He and the Church are both infallible and impeccable, only in proportion to the *degree* in which they are led by the Spirit. The Spirit leads into all truth and holiness; but His influence on believers and on the Church is as yet partial. Jesus alone, who had the Spirit without measure (John 3:34), is both infallible and impeccable. Scripture, because it was written by men, who while writing were infallibly inspired, is unmixed truth (Prov. 28:5; I John 2:27). **16. For**—proof of vs. 15, that the spiritual man "is judged of no man." In order to judge the spiritual man, the ordinary man must "know the mind of the Lord." But "who of ordinary men knows" that? **that he may instruct him**—i.e., so as to be able to set Him right as His counsellor (quoted from Isa. 40:13, 14). So the LXX translates the *Greek* verb, which means to "prove," in Acts 9:22. Natural men who judge spiritual men, living according to the mind of God ("We have the mind of Christ"), are virtually wishing to instruct God, and bring Him to another mind, as counsellors setting to right their king. **we have the mind of Christ**—in our degree of capability to apprehend it. Isaiah 40 refers to JEHOVAH: therefore, as it is applied here to *Christ,* He is Jehovah.

CHAPTER 3

Vss. 1-23. PAUL COULD NOT SPEAK TO THEM OF DEEP SPIRITUAL TRUTHS, AS THEY WERE CARNAL, CONTENDING FOR THEIR SEVERAL TEACHERS; THESE ARE NOTHING BUT WORKERS FOR GOD, TO WHOM THEY MUST GIVE ACCOUNT IN THE DAY OF FIERY JUDGMENT. THE HEARERS ARE GOD'S TEMPLE, WHICH THEY MUST NOT DEFILE BY CONTENTIONS FOR TEACHERS, WHO, AS WELL AS ALL THINGS, ARE THEIRS, BEING CHRIST'S. **1. And I**—i.e., as the natural (animal) man cannot receive, so *I also could not speak unto you* the deep things of God, *as I* would *to the spiritual; but* I was compelled to speak to you *as* I would *to* MEN OF FLESH. The oldest MSS. read this for "carnal." The former (lit., "fleshy") implies men wholly *of flesh,* or *natural. Carnal,* or *fleshly,* implies not they were *wholly natural* or unregenerate (ch. 2:14), but that they had much of a *carnal tendency;* e.g., their divisions. Paul had to speak to them *as* he would to men *wholly natural,* inasmuch as they are *still carnal* (vs. 3) in many respects, notwithstanding their conversion (ch. 1:4-9). **babes**—contrasted with the *perfect* (fully matured) *in Christ* (Col 1:28; cf. Heb. 5:13, 14). This implies they were not men wholly *of flesh,* though carnal in tendencies. They had life in Christ, but it was weak. He blames them for being still in a degree (not *altogether,* cf. ch. 1:5, 7; therefore he says "*as*") *babes* in Christ, when by this time they ought to have "come unto a perfect man, unto the measure of the stature of the fulness of Christ" (Eph. 4:13). In Romans 7:14, also the oldest MSS. read, "I am a man *of flesh.*" **2.** (Heb. 5:12.) **milk**—the elementary "principles of the doctrine of Christ." **3. envying**—jealousy, *rivalry.* As this refers to their *feelings,* "strife" refers to their *words,* and "divisions" to their *actions* [BENGEL]. There is a gradation, or ascending climax: *envying* had produced *strife,* and strife *divisions* (factious parties) [GROTIUS]. His language becomes severer now as He proceeds; in ch. 1:11 he had only said "contentions," he now multiplies the words (cf. the stronger term, ch. 4:6, than in ch. 3:21). **carnal**—For "strife" is a "work of the flesh" (Gal. 5:20). The "flesh" includes all feelings that aim not at the glory of God, and the good of our neighbor, but at gratifying self. **walk as men**—as unregenerate men (cf. Matt. 16:23). "After the flesh, not after the Spirit" of God, as becomes you as regenerate by the Spirit (Rom. 8:4; Gal. 5:25, 26). **4.** (Ch. 1:12.) **are ye not carnal**—The oldest MSS. read, "Are ye not *men?*" i.e., "walking as men" unregenerate (vs. 3). **5. Who then**—Seeing then that ye severally strive so for your favorite teachers, "Who is (of what intrinsic power and dignity) Paul?" If so great an apostle reasons so of himself, how much more does humility, rather than self-seeking, become ordinary ministers! **Paul ... Apollos**—The oldest MSS. read in the reverse order, "Apollos" ... "Paul." He puts Apollos before himself in humility. **but ministers ...**—The oldest MSS. have no "but." "Who is Apollos ... Paul? (mere) ministers (a lowly word appropriate here, *servants*), by whom (not '*in whom*'; *by whose ministrations*) ye believed." **as ... Lord gave to**

every man—i.e., to the several hearers, for it was GOD that "gave the increase" (vs. 6). **6. I ... planted, Apollos watered**—(Acts 18:1; 19:1). Apollos at his own desire (Acts 18:27) was sent by the brethren to Corinth, and there followed up the work which Paul had begun. **God gave the increase**—i.e., the growth (vs. 10; Acts 18:27). "Believed through *grace.*" Though ministers are nothing, and God all in all, yet God works by instruments, and promises the Holy Spirit in the faithful use of means. This is the dispensation of the Spirit, and ours is the ministry of the Spirit. **7. neither is he that ... anything ... but God**—viz., is all in all. "God" is emphatically last in the Greek, "He that giveth the increase (namely), GOD." Here follows a parenthesis from vs. 8 to vs. 21, where "Let no man glory in men" stands in antithetic contrast to "God" here. **8. one**—essentially in their aim they are *one,* engaged in one and the same ministry; therefore they ought not to be made by you the occasion of forming separate parties. **and every man**—rather "*but* every man." Though in their service or ministry, they are essentially "one," yet every minister is separately responsible in "*his own*" work, and "shall receive *his own* (emphatically repeated) reward, according to *his own* labor." The *reward* is something over and above personal salvation (vss. 14, 15; II John 8). He shall be rewarded according to, not his success or the amount of work done, but "according to his own labor." It shall be said to him, "Well done, thou good and (not *successful,* but) *faithful* servant, enter thou into the joy of thy Lord" (Matt. 25:23). **9.** Translate, as the *Greek* collocation of words, and the emphasis on "God" thrice repeated, requires, "For (in proof that "each shall receive reward according to his own labor," viz., from God) it is of God that we are the fellow workers (laboring *with,* but *under,* and *belonging to* Him as His servants, II Cor. 5:20; 6:1; cf. Acts 15:4; *Note,* I Thess. 3:2) of God that ye are the field (or tillage), of God that ye are the building" [ALFORD]. "Building" is a new image introduced here, as suited better than that of husbandry, to set forth the different kinds of teaching and their results, which he is now about to discuss. "To edify" or "build up" the Church of Christ is similarly used (Eph. 2:21, 22; 4:29). **10. grace ... given unto me**—Paul puts this first, to guard against seeming to want humility, in pronouncing himself "a WISE master builder," in the clause following [CHRYSOSTOM]. The "grace" is that "given" to him in common with all Christians (vs. 5), only proportioned to the work which God had for him to do [ALFORD]. **wise**—i.e., skilful. His *skill* is shown in his *laying a foundation.* The unskilful builder lays none (Luke 6:49). Christ is the foundation (vs. 11). **another**—who ever comes after me. He does not name *Apollos;* for he speaks generally of *all successors,* whoever they be. His warning, "Let every man (every *teacher*) take heed how ..." refers to other successors rather than Apollos, who doubtless did not, as they, build wood, hay, etc., on the foundation (cf. ch. 4: 15). "I have done my part, let them who follow me see (so the *Greek* for "take heed") to theirs" [BENGEL]. **how**—with what material [ALFORD]. How far *wisely,* and in builder-like style (I Pet. 4: 11). **buildeth thereupon**—Here the *building* or *superstructure* raised *on* Christ the "foundation," laid by Paul (ch. 2:2) is not, as in Ephesians 2:20, 21, the Christian Church made up of believers, the "lively stones" (I Peter 2:5), but *the doctrinal and practical teaching* which the teachers who succeeded Paul, superadded to his first teaching; not that they taught what was false, but their teaching was subtle and speculative reasoning, rather than solid and simple truth. **11.** (Isa. 28:16; Acts 4:12; Eph. 2:20.) **For**—my warning ("take heed . . ." vs. 10) is as to the superstructure ("buildeth *thereupon*"), not as to *the foundation:* "For other *foundation* can no man lay, than that which has (already) been laid (by God) Jesus Christ," the person, not the mere abstract doctrine about Him, though the latter also is included;*Jesus,* GOD-SAVIOUR; *Christ,* MESSIAH or ANOINTED. **can**—A man *can* not lay any other, since the only one recognized by God has been already laid. **12. Now**—rather, "But." The image is that of a building on a solid foundation, and partly composed of durable and precious, partly of perishable, materials. The "gold, silver, precious stones," which all can withstand fire (Rev. 21:18, 19), are *teachings* that will stand the fiery test of judgment; "wood, hay, stubble," are those which cannot stand it; not positive heresy, for that would destroy the foundation, but teaching mixed up with human philosophy and Judaism, curious rather than useful. Besides the *teachings,* the superstructure represents also the *persons* cemented to the Church by them, the reality of whose conversion, through the teachers' instrumentality, will be tested at the last day. Where there is the least grain of real gold of faith, it shall never be lost (I Pet. 1:7; cf. ch. 4:12). On the other hand, the lightest straw feeds the fire [BENGEL] (Matt. 5:19). **13. Every man's work**—each teacher's superstructure on the foundation. **the day**—of the Lord (ch. 1:8; Heb. 10:25; I Thess. 5:4). The article is emphatic, "*The* day," i.e., the great day of days, the long expected day. **declare it**—old English for "make it clear" (ch. 4:4). **it shall be revealed by fire**—it, i.e., "every man's work." Rather, "*He*," the Lord, whose day it is (II Thess. 1:7, 8). Translate lit., "*is being revealed* (the present in the *Greek* implies the *certainty* and *nearness* of the event, Rev. 22:10, 20) in fire" (Mal. 3:3; 4:1). The *fire* (probably *figurative* here, as the *gold, hay,* etc.) is not *purgatory* (as Rome teaches, i.e., *purificatory* and *punitive*), but *probatory,* not restricted to those dying in "venial sin"; the supposed *intermediate class* between those entering heaven at once, and those dying in mortal sin who go to hell, but *universal,* testing the godly and ungodly alike (II Cor. 5:10; cf. Mark 9:49). This fire is not till the *last* day, the supposed fire of purgatory begins *at death.* The fire of Paul is to try the *works,* the fire of purgatory the *persons,* of men. Paul's fire causes "loss" to the sufferers; Rome's purgatory, great gain, viz., heaven at last to those purged by it, if only it were true. Thus this passage, quoted by Rome for, is altogether against, purgatory. "It was not this doctrine that gave rise to prayers for the dead; but the practice of praying for the dead [which crept in from the affectionate but mistaken solicitude of survivors] gave rise to the doctrine" [WHATELY]. **14. abide**—abide the testing fire (Matt. 3:11, 12). **which he hath built thereupon**—which he built *on the foundation.* **reward**—*wages,* as a builder, i.e., teacher. His converts built on Christ the foundation, through his faithful teaching, shall be his "crown of rejoicing" (II Cor. 1:14; Phil. 2: 16; I Thess. 2:19). **15. If . . . be burnt**—if any *teacher's* work consist of such materials as the fire will destroy [ALFORD]. **suffer loss**—i.e., forfeit the special "reward"; not that he shall lose salvation (which is altogether a *free gift,* not a "reward" or wages), for he remains still on the foundation (vs.

12; II John 6). **saved; yet so as by fire**—rather, "so as *through* fire" (Zech. 3:2; Amos 4:11; Jude 23). "Saved, yet *not without* fire" (Rom. 2:27) [BENGEL]. As a builder whose building, not the foundation, is consumed by fire, escapes, but with the loss of his work [ALFORD]; as the shipwrecked merchant, though he has lost his merchandise, is saved, though having to pass *through* the waves [BENGEL]. Malachi 3:1, 2; and 4:1, give the key to explain the imagery. The "Lord suddenly coming to His temple" in flaming "fire," all the parts of the building which will not stand that fire will be consumed; the builders will escape with personal salvation, but with the loss of their work, through the midst of the conflagration [ALFORD]. Again, a distinction is recognized between minor and fundamental doctrines (if we regard the superstructure as representing the *doctrines* superadded to the elementary essentials); a man may err as to the former, and yet be saved, but not so as to the latter (cf. Phil. 3:15). **16. Know ye not**—It is no new thing I tell you, in calling you "God's building"; ye know and ought to remember, ye are the noblest kind of building, "the temple of God." **ye**—all Christians form together one vast temple. The expression is not, "ye are *temples,*" but "ye are *the temple*" collectively, and "lively stones" (I Pet. 2:5) individually. **God . . . Spirit**—God's indwelling, and that of the Holy Spirit, are one; therefore the Holy Spirit is God. No literal "temple" is recognized by the New Testament in the Christian Church. The only one is the spiritual temple, the whole body of believing worshippers in which the Holy Spirit dwells (ch. 6: 19; John 4:23, 24). The *synagogue,* not the temple, was the model of the Christian house of worship. The temple was the *house of sacrifice,* rather than of prayer. Prayers in the temple were silent and individual (Luke 1:10; 18:10-13), not joint and public, nor with reading of Scripture, as in the synagogue. The temple, as the name means (from a *Greek* root "to dwell"), was the earthly *dwelling place of God,* where alone He put His name. The synagogue (as the name means an *assembly*) was the place for assembling men. God now too has His earthly temple, not one of wood and stone, but the congregation of believers, the "living stones" on the "spiritual house." Believers are all spiritual priests in it. Jesus Christ, our High Priest, has the only literal priesthood (Mal. 1:11; Matt. 18:20; I Pet. 2: 5) [VITRINGA]. **17. If any . . . defile . . . destroy**—rather as the *Greek* verb is the same in both cases, "*destroy* . . . destroy." God repays in kind by a righteous retaliation. The destroyer shall himself be destroyed. As temporal death was the penalty of marring the material temple (Lev. 16:2; Dan. 5: 2, 3, 30), so eternal death is the penalty of marring the spiritual temple—the Church. The *destroyers* here (vss. 16, 17), are distinct from the *unwise* or unskilful builders (vss. 12, 15); the latter held fast the "foundation" (vs. 11), and, therefore, though they lose their work of superstructure and the special reward, yet they are themselves saved; the destroyers, on the contrary, assailed with false teaching the foundation, and so subvert the temple itself, and shall therefore be destroyed. (See *Note,* vs. 10), [ESTIUS and NEANDER]. I think Paul passes here from the teachers to all the members of the Church, who, by profession, are "priests unto God" (Exod. 19:6; I Pet. 2:9; Rev. 1:6). As the Aaronic priests were doomed to die if they violated the old temple (Exod. 28:43), so any Christian who violates the sanctity of the spiritual temple, shall perish eternally (Heb. 12:14; 10:26, 31). **holy**—inviolable

(Hab. 2:20). which *temple* ye are—rather, "the which (i.e., holy) are ye" [ALFORD], and, therefore, want of holiness on the part of any of you (or, as ESTIUS, "to tamper with *the foundation* in *teaching* you") is a violation of the temple, which cannot be let to pass with impunity. GROTIUS supports *English Version.* 18. seemeth—i.e., *is, and is regarded by* himself and others. wise in this world— wise in mere worldly wisdom (ch. 1:20). let him become a fool—by receiving the Gospel in its unworldly simplicity, and so *becoming a fool in the world's sight* [ALFORD]. Let him *no longer think* himself wise, but seek the true wisdom from God, bringing his understanding into captivity to the obedience of faith [ESTIUS]. 19. with God—*in the judgment of* God. it is written—in Job 5:13. The formula of quoting SCRIPTURE used here, establishes the canonicity of Job. He taketh...wise in... own craftiness—proving the "foolishness" of the world's wisdom, since it is made by God the very snare to catch those who think themselves so wise. Lit., "He who taketh..." the whole of the sentence not being quoted, but only the part which suited Paul's purpose. 20. Quotation from Psalm 94:11. There it is *of men;* here it is "of the wise." Paul by inspiration states the class of men whose "thoughts" (or rather, "reasonings," as suits the *Greek* and the sense of the context) the Spirit designated in the Psalm, "vanity," viz., the "proud" (vs. 2) and worldly-wise, whom God in vs. 8 calls "fools," though they "boast themselves" of their *wisdom* in pushing their interests (vs. 4). 21. let no man glory in men—resuming the subject from vs. 4; cf. ch. 1:12 and 31, where the true object of glorying is stated: "He that glorieth, let him glory in THE LORD." Also ch. 4:6, "That no one of you be puffed up for one against another." For all things —not only *all men.* For you to glory thus in men, is lowering yourselves from your high position as heirs of *all things.* All men (including your teachers) belong to Christ, and therefore to you, by your union with Him; He makes them and all things work together for your good (Romans 8:28). Ye are not for the sake of them, but they for the sake of you (II Cor. 4:5, 15). They belong to you, not you to them. 22. Enumeration of some of the "all things." The teachers, in whom they gloried, he puts first (ch. 1:12). He omits after "Cephas" *or Christ* (to whom exclusively some at Corinth, ch. 1:12, professed to belong); but, instead, substitutes "ye are Christ's" (vs. 23). world...life...death ...things present...things to come—Not only shall they not "separate you from the love of God in Christ" (Rom 8:38, 39), but they "all are yours," i.e., are for you (Rom. 8:28), and belong to you, as they belong to Christ your Head (Heb. 1:2). things present—"things *actually* present" [ALFORD]. 23. ye are Christ's—not Paul's, or Apollos', or Cephas' (ch. 11:3; Matt. 23: 8-10). "Neither be ye called masters; for one is your Master, even Christ" (Rom. 14:8). Not merely a particular section of you, but ye all are Christ's (ch. 1:12). Christ is God's—(ch. 11:3). God is the ultimate end of all, even of Christ, His co-equal Son (ch. 15:28; Phil. 2:6-11).

CHAPTER 4

VSS. 1-21. TRUE VIEW OF MINISTERS: THE JUDGMENT IS NOT TO BE FORESTALLED; MEANWHILE THE APOSTLES' LOW STATE CONTRASTS WITH THE CORINTHIANS' PARTY PRIDE, NOT THAT PAUL WOULD SHAME THEM, BUT AS A FATHER WARN THEM; FOR WHICH

END HE SENT TIMOTHY, AND WILL SOON COME HIM-SELF. 1. account...us—Paul and Apollos. ministers of Christ—not heads of the Church in whom ye are severally to glory (ch. 1:12); the headship belongs to Christ alone; we are but His servants ministering to you (ch. 1:13; 3:5, 22). stewards— (Luke 12:42; I Pet. 4:10). Not the depositories of grace, but dispensers of it ("rightly dividing" or *dispensing it*), so far as God gives us it, to others. The chazan, or *overseer,* in the synagogue answered to the *bishop* or "angel" of the Church, who called seven of the synagogue to read the law every sabbath, and *oversaw* them. The parnasin of the synagogue, like the ancient "deacon" of the Church, took care of the poor (Acts 6) and subsequently preached in subordination to the presbyters or bishops, as Stephen and Philip did. The Church is not the appendage to the priesthood; but the minister is the steward of God to the Church. Man shrinks from too close contact with God; hence he willingly puts a priesthood between, and would serve God by deputy. The pagan (like the modern Romish) priest was rather to conceal than to explain "the mysteries of God." The minister's office is to "preach" (lit., "proclaim as a herald," Matt. 10:27) the deep truths of God ("mysteries," heavenly truths, only known by revelation), so far as they have been revealed, and so far as his hearers are disposed to receive them. JOSEPHUS says that the Jewish religion made known to all the people the mysteries of their religion, while the pagans concealed from all but the "initiated" few, the mysteries of theirs. 2. Moreover—The oldest MSS. read, "Moreover here" (i.e., on earth). The contrast thus is between man's usage as to stewards (vs. 2), and God's way (vs. 3). Though *here* below, *in the case of stewards, inquiry is made, that one man be found* (i.e., proved to be) faithful; yet God's steward awaits no such *judgment* of man, in man's day, but the Lord's judgment in His great day. Another argument against the Corinthians for their partial preferences of certain teachers for their gifts: whereas what God requires in His stewards is *faithfulness* (I Sam. 3:20; Heb. 3:5; *Margin*); as indeed is required in earthly stewards, but with this difference (vs. 3), that God's stewards await not man's judgment to test them, but the testing which shall be in the day of the Lord. 3. it is a very small thing—lit., "it amounts to a very small matter"; not that I despise *your* judgment, but as compared with God's, it almost comes to nothing. judged...of man's judgment—lit., "man's *day,*" contrasted with the day (ch. 3:13) of the Lord (vs. 5; I Thess. 5:4). "The day of man" is here put before us as a *person* [WAHL]. All days previous to the day of the Lord *are man's days.* EMESTI translates the thrice recurring *Greek* for "judged...judge... judgeth" (vs. 4), thus: To me for my part (though capable of being found faithful) it is a very small matter that I should *be approved of* by man's judgment; yea, I do not even *assume the right of judgment and approving* myself—but He that *has the right, and is able to* judge on my case (the Dijudicator), is the Lord. 4. by myself—Translate, "I am conscious to myself of no (ministerial) unfaithfulness." BENGEL explains the *Greek* compound, "*to decide in judgments on* one in relation to others," not simply to *judge.* am I not hereby justified—Therefore conscience is not an infallible guide. Paul did not consider his so. This verse is directly against the judicial power claimed by the priests of Rome. 5. Disproving the judicial power claimed by the Romish priesthood in the confessional. **Therefore**—as the Lord is the sole Decider or Dijudicator. **judge**—not the same *Greek* word as in vss. 3, 4, where the meaning is to *approve of*, or *decide on*, the merits of one's case. Here all **judgments** in general are forbidden, which would, on our part, presumptuously forestall God's prerogative of final *judgment*. **Lord**—Jesus Christ, whose "ministers" we are (vs. 1), and who is to be the judge (John 5:22, 27; Acts 10:42; 17:31). **manifest ... hearts**—Our judgments now (as those of the Corinthians respecting their teachers) are necessarily defective; as we only see the outward *act*, we cannot see the *motives* of "hearts." "Faithfulness" (vs. 2) will hereby be estimated, and the "Lord" will "justify," or the reverse (vs. 4), according to the state of the *heart*. **then shall every man have praise**—(ch. 3:8; I Sam. 26:23; Matt. 25:21, 23; 28). Rather, "*his due* praise," not exaggerated praise, such as the Corinthians heaped on favorite teachers; "the praise" (so the *Greek*) due for acts estimated by the motives. "Then," not before: therefore wait till *then* (Jas. 5:7). **6. And**—"Now," marking transition. **in a figure transferred to myself**—i.e., I have represented under the persons of Apollos and myself what really holds good of all teachers, making us two a *figure* or *type* of all the others. I have mentioned us two, whose names have been used as a party cry; but under our names I mean others to be understood, whom I do not name, in order not to shame you [ESTIUS]. **not to think ...**—The best MSS. omit "think." Translate, "That in us (as your example) ye might learn (this), not (to go) beyond what is written." Revere the *silence* of Holy Writ, as much as its *declarations:* so you will less dogmatize on what is not expressly revealed (Deut. 29:29). **puffed up for one**—viz., "for one (favorite minister) against another." The *Greek* indicative implies, "That ye be not puffed up *as ye are*." **7.** Translate, "Who distinguisheth thee (above another)?" Not thyself, but God. **glory, as if thou hadst not received it**—as if it was to thyself, not to God, thou owest the receiving of it. **8.** Irony. Translate, "*Already* ye are filled full (with spiritual food), *already* ye are rich, ye have seated yourselves upon your throne as kings, without us." The emphasis is on "already" and "without us"; ye act as if ye needed no more to "hunger and thirst after righteousness," and as if already ye had reached the "kingdom" for which Christians have to strive and suffer. Ye are so puffed up with your favorite teachers, and your own fancied spiritual attainments in knowledge through them, that ye feel like those "filled full" at a feast, or as a "rich" man priding himself in his riches: so ye feel ye can now do "without us," your first spiritual fathers (vs. 15). They forgot that before the "kingdom" and the "*fulness* of joy," at the marriage feast of the Lamb, must come the cross, and suffering, to every true believer (II Tim. 2:5, 11, 12). They were like the self-complacent Laodiceans (Rev. 3:17; cf. Hosea 12:8). *Temporal* fulness and riches doubtless *tended* in some cases at Corinth, to generate this spiritual self-sufficiency; the contrast to the apostle's literal "hunger and thirst" (vs. 11) proves this. **I would ... ye did reign**—Translate, "I would indeed ...." I would truly it were so, and that your kingdom had really begun. **that we also might reign with you**—(II Cor. 12:14). "I seek not yours, but you." Your spiritual prosperity would redound to that of us, your fathers in Christ (ch. 9: 23). When you reach the kingdom, you shall be our "crown of rejoicing, in the presence of our Lord Jesus" (I Thess. 2:19). **9. For**—assigning the

reason for desiring that the "reign" of himself and his fellow apostles with the Corinthians were come; viz., the present afflictions of the former. **I think** —The Corinthians (ch. 3:18) "seemed" to (lit., as here, "thought") themselves "wise in this world." Paul, in contrast, "thinks" that God has sent forth him and his fellow ministers "last," i.e., the lowest in this world. The apostles fared worse than even the prophets, who, though sometimes afflicted, were often honored (II Kings 1:10; 5:9; 8:9, 12). **set forth**—as a spectacle or gazing-stock. **us the apostles**—Paul includes Apollos with the apostles, in the broader sense of the word; so Romans 16:7; II Corinthians 8:23 (*Greek* for "messengers," *apostles*). **as it were appointed to death**—as criminals condemned to die. **made a spectacle**—lit., "a theatrical spectacle." So the *Greek* in Hebrews 10: 33, "made a *gazing-stock* by reproaches and afflictions." Criminals "condemned to die," in Paul's time, were exhibited as a gazing-stock to amuse the populace in the amphitheater. They were "set forth last" in the show, to fight with wild beasts. This explains the imagery of Paul here. (Cf. TERTULLIAN, *de Pudicitia*, ch. 14.) **the world**—to the whole world, including "both angels and men"; "the whole family in heaven and earth" (Eph. 3: 15). As Jesus was "seen of angels" (I Tim. 3:16), so His followers are a spectacle to the holy angels who take a deep interest in all the progressive steps of redemption (Eph. 3:10; I Pet. 1:12). Paul tacitly implies that though "last" and lowest in the world's judgment, Christ's servants are deemed by angels a spectacle worthy of their most intense regard [CHRYSOSTOM]. However, since "the world" is a comprehensive expression, and is applied in this Epistle to the evil especially (ch. 1:27, 28), and since the spectators (in the image drawn from the amphitheater gaze at the show with savage delight, rather than with sympathy for the sufferers, I think *bad* angels are included, besides *good* angels. ESTIUS makes the bad *alone* to be meant. But the generality of the term "angels," and its frequent use in a good sense, as well as Ephesians 3:10; I Peter 1:12, incline me to include *good* as well as *bad* angels, though, for the reasons stated above, the bad may be principally meant. **10.** Irony. How much your lot (*supposing it real*) is to be envied, and ours to be pitied. **fools**—(ch. 1:21; 3:18; cf. Acts 17:18; 26:24.) **for Christ's sake ... in Christ** —Our connection with Christ only entails on us the lowest ignominy, "ON ACCOUNT OF," or, "FOR THE SAKE OF" Him, as "fools"; yours gives you full fellowship IN Him as "wise" (i.e., *supposing you really are all you seem*, ch. 3:18). **we ... weak ... ye ... strong**—(ch. 2:3; II Cor. 13:9). **we ... despised**—(II Cor. 10:10) because of our "weakness," and our not using worldly philosophy and rhetoric, on account of which ye Corinthians and your teachers are (seemingly) so "honorable." Contrast with "despised" the "ye (*Galatians*) despised not my temptation ... in my flesh." **11.** (IICor. 11:23-27.) **naked**—i.e., insufficiently clad (Rom. 8:35). **buffeted**—as a *slave* (I Pet. 2:20), the reverse of the state of the Corinthians, "reigning as *kings*" (Acts 23:2). So Paul's master before him was "buffeted" as a slave, when about to die a slave's death (Matt. 26:67). **12. working with our own hands**—viz., "even unto this present hour" (vs. 11). This is not stated in the *narrative* of Paul's proceedings at *Ephesus*, from which city he wrote this Epistle (though it is expressly stated of him *at Corinth*, cf. Acts 18:3, and 19). But in his *address* to the Ephesian elders at Miletus (Acts 20:34), he says,

"Ye yourselves know that these hands have ministered unto my necessities . . . ." The undesignedness of the coincidence thus indirectly brought out is incompatible with forgery. **13. defamed, we entreat**–viz., God for our defamers, as Christ enjoined (Matt. 5:10, 44) [GROTIUS]. We reply gently [ESTIUS]. **filth**–"the refuse" [CONYBEARE and HOWSON], the *sweepings* or *rubbish* thrown out after a cleaning. **of all things**–not of the "world" only. **14. warn**–rather, **"admonish" as a father** uses "admonition" to "beloved sons," not provoking them to wrath (Eph. 6:4). The Corinthians might well be "ashamed" at the disparity of state between the father, Paul, and his spiritual children themselves. **15. ten thousand**–implying that the Corinthians had more of them than was desirable. **instructors**–*tutors* who had the care of rearing, but had not the rights, or peculiar affection, of the father, who alone had begotten them spiritually. **in Christ**–Paul admits that these "instructors" were not mere legalists, but *evangelical* teachers. He uses, however, a stronger phrase of himself in begetting them spiritually, "In Christ Jesus," implying both the Saviour's *office and person*. As Paul was the means of spiritually *regenerating* them, and yet "baptized none of them save Crispus, Gaius, and the household of Stephanas," regeneration cannot be inseparably *in* and *by* baptism (ch. 1:14-17). **16. be ye followers of me**–lit., "imitators," viz., in my ways, which be in Christ (vs. 17; ch. 11:1), not in my crosses (vss. 8-13; Acts 26:29; Gal. 4:12). **17. For this cause**–that ye may the better "be followers of me" (vs. 16), through his admonitions. **sent . . . Timotheus**–(ch. 16:10; Acts 19:21, 22). "Paul purposed . . . when he had passed through Macedonia and *Achaia*, to go to Jerusalem. So he sent into Macedonia Timotheus and Erastus." Here it is not expressly said that he sent Timothy into Achaia (of which Corinth was the capital), but it is *implied*, for he sent him with Erastus *before him*. As he therefore purposed to go into Achaia himself, there is every probability they were to go thither also. They are said only to have been sent into Macedonia, because it was the country to which they went immediately from Ephesus. The undesignedness of the coincidence establishes the genuineness of both the Epistle and the history. In both, Timothy's journey is closely connected with Paul's own (cf. vs. 19). Erastus is not specified in the Epistle, probably because it was Timothy who was charged with Paul's orders, and possibly Erastus was a Corinthian, who, in accompanying Timothy, was only returning home. The seeming discrepancy at least shows that the passages were not taken from one another [PALEY's *Horæ Paulinæ*]. **son**–i.e., converted by me (cf. vs. 14, 15; Acts 14:6, 7; with 16:1, 2; I Tim. 1:2, 18; II Tim. 1:2). Translate, "My son, beloved and faithful in the Lord." **bring you into remembrance**–Timothy, from his spiritual connection with Paul, as converted by him, was best suited to *remind* them of the apostle's walk and teaching (II Tim. 3:10), which they in some respects, though not altogether (ch. 11:2), had forgotten. **as I teach . . . in every church**–an argument implying that what the Spirit directed Paul to teach "everywhere" else, must be necessary at Corinth also (ch. 7:17). **18. some . . . as though I would not come**–He guards against some misconstruing (as by the Spirit he foresees they will, when his letter shall have arrived) his sending Timothy, "as though" he "would not come" (or, "were not coming") himself. A *puffed-up* spirit was the besetting sin of the Corinthians (cf.

ch. 1:11; 5:2). **19.** ALFORD translates, "But come I will"; an emphatical negation of their supposition (vs. 18). **shortly**–after Pentecost (ch. 16:8). **if the Lord will**–a wise proviso (Jas. 4:15). He does not seem to have been able to go as soon as he intended. **and will know**–take cognizance of. **but the power**–I care not for their high-sounding "speech," "but" what I desire to know is "their power," whether they be really powerful in the Spirit, or not. The predominant feature of Grecian character, a love for power of *discourse*, rather than that of godliness, showed itself at Corinth. **20. kingdom of God is not in word**–Translate, as in vs. 19, to which the reference is "speech." Not empty "speeches," but the manifest "power" of the Spirit attests the presence of "the kingdom of God" (the *reign of the Gospel* spiritually), in a church or in an individual (cf. ch. 2:1, 4; I Thess. 1:5). **21. with a rod, or in love**–The *Greek* preposition is used in both clauses; must I come IN displeasure to exercise the *rod,* or IN love, and the Spirit of meekness (Isa. 11:4; II Cor. 13:3)?

CHAPTER 5

Vss. 1-13. THE INCESTUOUS PERSON AT CORINTH: THE CORINTHIANS REPROVED FOR CONNIVANCE, AND WARNED TO PURGE OUT THE BAD LEAVEN. QUALIFICATION OF HIS FORMER COMMAND AS TO ASSOCIATION WITH SINNERS OF THE WORLD. **1. commonly** –rather, "actually" [ALFORD]. Absolutely [BENGEL]. "It is reported," implies, that the Corinthians, though they "wrote" (ch. 7:1) to Paul on other points, gave him no information on those things which bore against themselves. These latter matters reached the apostle indirectly (ch. 1:11). **so much as named**–The oldest MSS. and authorities omit "named": "Fornication of such a gross kind as (exists) not even among the heathen, so that one (of you) hath (in concubinage) his father's wife," i.e., his stepmother, while his father is still alive (II Cor. 7:12; cf. Lev. 18:8). She was perhaps a heathen, for which reason he does not direct his rebuke against her (cf. vss. 12, 13). ALFORD thinks "have" means *have in marriage:* but the connection is called "fornication," and neither Christian nor Gentile *law* would have sanctioned such a *mariage,* however Corinth's notorious profligacy might wink at the concubinage. **2. puffed up**–with your own wisdom and knowledge, and the eloquence of your favorite teachers: at a time when ye ought to be "mourning" at the scandal caused to religion by the incest. Paul *mourned* because they did not mourn (II Cor. 2:4). We ought to *mourn* over the transgressions of others, and *repent* of our own (II Cor. 12:21) [BENGEL]. **that**–ye have not felt such mourning as would lead to the result *that* . . . . **taken away from among you**–by excommunication. The incestuous person was hereby brought to bitter repentance, in the interval between the sending of the first and second Epistles (II Cor. 2:5-10). Excommunication in the Christian Church corresponded to that in the Jewish synagogue, in there being a lighter and heavier form: the latter an utter separation from church fellowship and the Lord's house, the former exclusion from the Lord's Supper only but not from the Church. **3. as absent**–The best MSS. read, "being absent." **present in spirit** –(II Kings 5:26; Col. 2:5). **so done**–rather, "perpetrated," as the *Greek* word here is stronger than that for "done" in vs. 2. "So," i.e., so scandalously while called a brother. **4. In the name of our Lord**

Jesus Christ—By His authority and as representing His *person* and will (II Cor. 2:10). Join this with "to deliver such a one unto Satan" (vs. 5). The clause, "When ye have been gathered together and my spirit (wherein I am 'present,' though 'absent in body,' (vs. 3), with the power of our Lord Jesus," stands in a parenthesis between. Paul speaking of himself uses the word "spirit"; of Christ, "power." Christ's power was promised to be present with HIS Church "gathered together in His name" (Matt. 18: 18-20): and here Paul by inspiration gives a special promise of his apostolic spirit, which in such cases was guided by the Holy Spirit, ratifying their decree passed according to his *judgment* ("I have judged," vs. 3), as though he were present in person (John 20:21-23; (II Cor. 13:3-10). This power of infallible judgment was limited to the apostles; for they alone had the power of working miracles as their credentials to attest their infallibility. Their successors, to establish their claim to the latter, must produce the former (II Cor. 12:2). Even the apostles in ordinary cases, and where not specially and consciously inspired, were fallible (Acts 8:13, 23; Gal. 2:11-14). **5.** Besides excommunication (of which the Corinthians themselves had the power), Paul delegates here to the Corinthian Church *his own* special power as an apostle, of inflicting corporeal disease or death in punishment for sin ("to deliver to Satan such an one," i.e., so heinous a sinner). For instances of this power, see Acts 5:1-11; 13:11; I Tim. 1:20. As Satan receives power at times to try the godly, as Job (Job 2:4-7) and Paul (II Cor. 12:7; cf. also as to Peter, Luke 22:31), much more the ungodly. Satan, the "accuser of the brethren" (Rev. 12:10) and the "adversary" (I Pet. 5:8), demands the sinner for punishment on account of sin (Zech. 3:1). When God lets Satan have his way, He is said to "deliver the sinner unto Satan" (cf. Ps. 109:6). Here it is not finally; but for the affliction of the body with disease, and even *death* (ch. 11:30, 32), so as to *destroy fleshly lust.* He does not say, "for the destruction of the *body*," for *it* shall share in redemption (Rom. 8:23); but of the corrupt "flesh" which "cannot inherit the kingdom of God," and the lusts of which had prompted this offender to incest (Rom. 7:5; 8:9, 10). The "destruction of the flesh" answers to "*mortify* the deeds of the *body*" (Rom. 8:13), only that the latter is done by one's self, the former is effected by chastisement from God (cf. I Pet. 4:6). **the spirit . . . saved**—the spiritual part of man, in the believer the organ of the Holy Spirit. Temporary affliction often leads to permanent salvation (Ps. 83:16). **6.** Your glorying in your own attainments and those of your favorite teachers (ch. 3:21; 4:19; 5:2), while all the while you connive at such a scandal, is quite unseemly. **a little leaven leaveneth . . . whole lump**—(Gal. 5:9), viz., with *present* complicity in the guilt, and the danger of future contagion (ch. 15:33; II Tim. 2:17). **7. old leaven** —The remnant of the "old" (Eph. 4:22-24) heathenish and natural corruption. The image is taken from the extreme care of the Jews in searching every corner of their houses, and "purging out" every particle of leaven from the time of killing the lamb before the Passover (Deut. 16:3, 4). So Christians are continually to search and purify their hearts (Ps. 139:23, 24). **as ye are unleavened**—normally, and as far as your Christian calling is concerned: free from the leaven of sin and death (ch. 6:11). Paul often grounds exhortations on the assumption of Christian professors' *normal* state as realized (Rom. 6:3, 4) [ALFORD]. Regarding the

Corinthian Church as the Passover "unleavened lump" or mass, he entreats them to correspond in fact with this their normal state. "For Christ our Passover (Exod. 12:5-11, 21-23; John 1:29) *has been (English Version,* "is") sacrificed for us"; i.e., as the Jews *began* the days of unleavened bread with the slaying of the Passover lamb, so, Christ our Passover *having been already slain,* let there be no leaven of evil in you who are the "unleavened lump." Doubtless he alludes to the Passover which had been two or three weeks before kept by the Jewish Christians (ch. 16:8): the Gentile Christians probably also refraining from leavened bread at the love feasts. Thus the Jewish Passover naturally gave place to our Christian Easter. The time however, of *keeping feast* (metaphorical; i.e., *leading the Christian life of joy* in Christ's finished work, cf. Prov. 15:15) among us Christians, corresponding to the Jewish Passover, is not limited, as the latter, to one season, but is ALL our time; for the transcendent benefits of the once-for-all completed sacrifice of *our* Passover Lamb extends to all the time of our lives and of this Christian dispensation; in no part of our time is the leaven of evil to be admitted. **For even**—an additional reason, besides that in vs. 6, and a more cogent one for purging out every leaven of evil; viz., that Christ has been already sacrificed, whereas the old leaven is yet unremoved, which ought to have been long ago purged out. **8. not . . . old leaven**—of our unconverted state as Jews or heathen. **malice**—the opposite of "sincerity," which allows no leaven of evil to be mixed up with good (Matt. 16:6). **wickedness** —the opposite of "truth," which allows not evil to be mistaken for good. The *Greek* for "malice" means the evil *habit* of mind; "wickedness," the *outcoming* of the same in word and deed. The *Greek* for "sincerity" expresses literally, a thing which, when examined *by the sun's light,* is found pure and unadulterated. **9. I wrote . . . in an epistle** —rather, "in the Epistle": a former one not now extant. That Paul does not refer to the *present* letter is proved by the fact that no direction "not to company with fornicators" occurs in the previous part of it; also the words, "in an (or *the*) epistle," could not have been added if he meant, "I have just written" (II Cor. 10:10). "*His letters*" (*plural*; not applying to merely *one*) confirm this. II Corinthians 7:8 also refers to our *first* Epistle, just as here a *former* letter is referred to by the same phrase. Paul probably wrote a former brief reply to inquiries of the Corinthians: our first Epistle, as it enters more fully into the same subject, has superseded the former, which the Holy Spirit did not design for the guidance of the Church in general, and which therefore has not been preserved. See my *Introduction.* **10.** Limitation of the prohibition alluded to in vs. 9. As in dissolute Corinth to "company with no fornicators . . ." would be almost to company with none in the (unbelieving) world; ye need not *utterly* ("altogether") forego intercourse with fornicators, etc., of the unbelieving world (cf. ch. 10:27; John 17:15; I John 5:18, 19). As "fornicators" sin against themselves, so "extortioners" against their neighbors, and "idolaters" against God. The attempt to get "out of the world," in violation of God's will that believers should remain in it but keep themselves from its evil, led to monasticism and its consequent evils. **11. But now I have written**—"Now" does not express *time,* but "*the case being so,*" viz., that to avoid fornicators, etc., *of the world,* you would have to leave the world altogether, which would be absurd. So "now" is used in Hebrews 11:16. Thus we avoid making the apostle *now* retract a command which he had before given. **I have written**—i.e., my meaning in the letter I wrote was .... **a brother** —contrasted with a "fornicator, etc., *of the world*" (vs. 10). There is less danger in associating with open worldlings than with carnal professors. Here, as in Ephesians 5:3, 5, "covetousness" is joined with "fornication": the common fount of both being "the fierce and ever fiercer longing of the creature, which has turned from God, to fill itself with the inferior objects of sense" [TRENCH, *Syn. New Testament*]. Hence "idolatry" is associated with them: and the covetous man is termed an "idolater" (Num. 25:1, 2). The Corinthians did not fall into open idolatry, but ate things offered to idols, so making a compromise with the heathen; just as they connived at fornication. Thus this verse prepares for the precepts in ch. 8:4, etc. Cf. the similar case of fornication, combined with a similar idolatrous compromise, after the pattern of Israel with the Midianites (Rev. 2:14). **no not to eat**—not to sit at the same table with such; whether at the love feasts (*agapæ*) or in private intercourse, much more at the Lord's table: at the last, too often now the guests "are not as children in one family, but like a heterogeneous crowd of strangers in an inn" [BENGEL] (cf. Gal. 2:12; II John 10:11). **12. what have I to do**—You might have easily understood that my concern is not with unbelievers *outside* in the Church, but that I referred to those within it. **also** —Implying, *Those within* give me enough to do without those outside. **do not ye . . .**—Ye judge your fellow citizens, not strangers: much more should I [BENGEL]. Rather, Is it not *your duty* to judge them that are within? *God* shall judge them that are without: do you look at home [GROTIUS]. God is the Judge of the salvation of the heathen, not we (Rom. 2:12-16). Paul here gives an anticipatory censure of their going to law with saints before heathen tribunals, instead of judging such causes among themselves within. **13. put away from among yourselves that wicked**—Sentence of excommunication in language taken from Deuteronomy 24:7.

CHAPTER 6

Vss. 1-11. LITIGATION OF CHRISTIANS IN HEATHEN COURTS CENSURED: ITS VERY EXISTENCE BETRAYS A WRONG SPIRIT: BETTER TO BEAR WRONG NOW, AND HEREAFTER THE DOERS OF WRONG SHALL BE SHUT OUT OF HEAVEN. **1. Dare**—This word implies treason against Christian brotherhood [BENGEL]. **before the unjust**—The Gentile judges are here so termed by an epithet appropriate to the subject in question, viz., one concerning *justice*. Though all Gentiles were not altogether *unjust*, yet in the highest view of justice which has regard to God as the Supreme Judge, they are so: Christians, on the other hand, as regarding God as the only Fountain of justice, should not expect justice from them. **before . . . saints**—The Jews abroad were permitted to refer their disputes to Jewish *arbitrators* (JOSEPHUS, *Antiquities*, 14:10, 17). So the Christians were allowed to have Christian arbitrators. **2. Do ye not know**—as a truth universally recognized by Christians. Notwithstanding all your glorying in your "knowledge," ye are acting contrary to it (ch. 1:4, 5; 8:1). The oldest MSS. have "Or" before "know ye not"; i.e., "What! (expressing surprise) know ye not . . . ." **saints . . .**

judge—i.e., "rule," including *judgment:* as assessors of Christ. Matthew 19:28, "judging," i.e., "ruling over." (Cf. Ps. 49:14; Dan. 7:22, 27; Rev. 2:26; 3:21; 20:4.) There is a distinction drawn by able expositors between the saints who *judge* or *rule*, and the world which is ruled by them: as there is between the elected (Matt. 20:23) twelve apostles who sit on thrones judging, and the twelve tribes of Israel that are judged by them. To *reign*, and to be *saved*, are not necessarily synonymous. As Jehovah employed angels to carry the law into effect when He descended on Sinai to establish His throne in Israel, so at His coming the saints shall administer the kingdom for, and under, Him. The nations of the earth, and Israel the foremost, in the flesh, shall, in this view, be the *subjects* of the rule of the Lord and His saints in glorified bodies. The mistake of the Chiliasts was that they took the merely carnal view, restricting the kingdom to the terrestrial part. This part shall have place with the accession of spiritual and temporal blessings such as Christ's presence must produce. Besides this earthly glory, there shall be the heavenly glory of the saints reigning in transfigured bodies, and holding such blessed intercourse with mortal men, as angels had with men of old, and as Christ, Moses, and Elias, in glory had with Peter, James, and John, in the flesh at the transfiguration (II Tim. 2:12; II Pet. 1:16-18). But here the "world" seems to be the unbelieving world that is to be "condemned" (ch. 11:22), rather than the whole world, including the subject nations which are to be brought under Christ's sway; however, it may include *both* those to be condemned, with the bad angels, and those about to be brought into obedience to the sway of Christ with His saints. Cf. Matthew 25:32, 40, "all nations," "these my brethren" on the thrones with Him. The event will decide the truth of this view. **judged by you**—or, *before* you (cf. ch. 3:22). **smallest matters**—The weightiest of earthly questions at issue are infinitely *small* compared with those to be decided on the judgment day. **3. judge angels**—viz., *bad* angels. We who are now "a spectacle to angels" shall then "judge angels." The saints shall join in approving the final sentence of the Judge on them (Jude 6). Believers shall, as administrators of the kingdom under Jesus, put down all rule that is hostile to God. Perhaps, too, *good* angels shall then receive from the Judge, with the approval of the saints, higher honors. **4. judgments**—i.e., cases for judgment. **least esteemed**—lit., "those of no esteem." Any, however low in the Church, rather than the heathen (ch. 1:28). Questions of earthly property are of secondary consequence in the eyes of true Christians, and are therefore delegated to those in a secondary position in the Church. **5. your shame**—Thus he checks their *puffed-up* spirit (ch. 5:2; cf. ch. 15:34). To shame you out of your present unworthy course of litigation before the heathen, I have said (vs. 4), "Set the least esteemed in the Church to judge." Better even this, than your present course. **Is it so?** —Are you in such a helpless state that . . . ? **not a wise man**—though ye admire "wisdom" so much on other occasions (ch. 1:5, 22). Paul alludes probably to the title, "cachain," or *wise man*, applied to each Rabbi in Jewish councils. **no, not one**—not even one, amidst so many reputed among you for wisdom (ch. 3:18; 4:6). **shall be able**—when applied to. **brethren**—lit., "brother"; i.e., judge between brother and brother. As each case should arise, the arbitrator was to be chosen from the body of the church, such a wise person as had the charism, or gift, of church government. **6. But**—emphatically answering the question in the end of vs. 5 in the negative. Translate, "Nay . . . ." **7. utterly a fault**—lit., "a shortcoming" (not so strong as *sin*). Your going to law at all is a falling short of your high privileges, not to say your doing so *before unbelievers*, which aggravates it. **rather take wrong**—(Prov. 20:22; Matt. 5:39, 40); i.e., "suffer yourselves to be wronged." **8. ye**—emphatic. *Ye*, whom your Lord commanded to return good for evil, *on the contrary*, "do wrong (by taking away) and defraud" (by retaining what is entrusted to you; or "defraud" marks the *effect* of the "wrong" done, viz., the *loss* inflicted). Not only do ye not bear, but ye inflict wrongs. **9. unrighteous**—Translate, "Doers of wrong": referring to vs. 8 (cf. Gal. 5:21). **kingdom of God**—which is a kingdom of *righteousness* (Rom. 14:17). **fornicators**—alluding to ch. 5; also below, vss. 12-18. **effeminate**—self-polluters, who submit to unnatural lusts. **11. ye are washed**—The Greek middle voice expresses, "Ye have had yourselves washed." This washing implies the admission to the *benefits of Christ's salvation* generally; of which the parts are; (1) *Sanctification,* or the setting apart from the world, and adoption into the Church: so "sanctified" is used ch. 7:14; John 17:19. Cf. I Pet. 1:2, where it rather seems to mean the *setting apart* of one as *consecrated by the Spirit in the eternal purpose of God.* (2) *Justification* from condemnation through the righteousness of God in Christ by faith (Rom. 1:17). So PARÆUS. The order of *sanctification* before *justification* shows that it must be so taken, and not in the sense of *progressive* sanctification. "Washed" precedes both, and so must refer to the Christian's outward new birth of water, the sign of the inward setting apart to the Lord by the inspiration of the Spirit as the seed of new life (John 3:5; Eph. 5:26; Titus 3:5; Heb. 10:22). Paul (cf. the Church of England Baptismal Service), in charity, and faith in the ideal of the Church, presumes that baptism realizes its original design, and that those outwardly baptized inwardly enter into vital communion with Christ (Gal. 3:27). He presents the grand ideal which those alone realized in whom the inward and the outward baptism coalesced. At the same time he recognizes the fact that this in many cases does not hold good (vss. 8-10), leaving it to God to decide who are the really "washed," while he only decides on broad general principles. **in the name of . . . Jesus, and by the Spirit**—rather, "in the Spirit," i.e., by His *in*-dwelling. Both clauses belong to the three—"washed, sanctified, justified." **our God**—The "our" reminds them that amidst all his reproofs God is still the common God of himself and them.

12-20. REFUTATION OF THE ANTINOMIAN DEFENSE OF FORNICATION, AS IF IT WAS LAWFUL BECAUSE MEATS ARE SO. **12. All things are lawful unto me**—These, which were Paul's own words on a former occasion (to the Corinthians, cf. ch. 10:23, and Gal. 5:23), were made a pretext for excusing the eating of meats offered to idols, and so of what was generally connected with idolatry (Acts 15:29), "fornication" (perhaps in the letter of the Corinthians to Paul, ch. 7:1). Paul's remark had referred only to things *indifferent*: but they wished to treat fornication as such, on the ground that the existence of bodily appetites proved the *lawfulness* of their gratification. **me**—Paul giving himself as a sample of Christians in general. **but I**—whatever others do, *I will not* . . . . **lawful . . . brought under the power**—The *Greek* words are from the same

root, whence there is a play on the words: All things *are in* my *power,* but I will not be *brought under the power of any* of them (the "all things"). He who commits "fornication," steps aside from his own legitimate power or liberty, and is "brought under the power" of an harlot (vs. 15; cf. ch. 7:4). The "power" ought to be in the hands of the *believer,* not in the *things which he uses* [BENGEL]; else his liberty is forfeited; he ceases to be his own master (John 8:34-36; Gal. 5:13; I Pet. 2:16; II Pet. 2:19). Unlawful things ruin thousands; "lawful" things (unlawfully used), ten thousands. **13.** The argument drawn from the indifference of meats (ch. 8:8; Rom. 14:14, 17; cf. Mark 7:18; Col. 2:20-22) to that of fornication does not hold good. Meats doubtless are indifferent, since both they and the "belly" for which they are created are to be "destroyed" in the future state. But "the body is not (created) for fornication, but for the Lord, and the Lord for the body" (as its Redeemer, who hath Himself assumed the body): "And God hath raised up the Lord, and will also raise up us" (i.e., our bodies): therefore the "body" is not, like the "belly," after having served a temporary use, to be destroyed: Now "he that committeth fornication, sinneth against his own body (vs. 18). Therefore fornication is not indifferent, since it is a sin against one's own body, which, like the Lord for whom it is created, is not to be destroyed, but to be raised to eternal existence. Thus Paul gives here the germ of the three subjects handled in subsequent sections: (1) The relation between the sexes. (2) The question of meats offered to idols. (3) The resurrection of the body. **shall destroy**—at the Lord's coming to change the natural bodies of believers into spiritual bodies (ch. 15:44, 52). There is a real essence underlying the superficial phenomena of the present temporary organization of the body, and this essential germ, when all the particles are scattered, involves the future resurrection of the body incorruptible. **14.** (Rom. 8:11.) **raised up**—rather, "raised," to distinguish it from "will raise *up* us"; the *Greek* of the latter being a compound, the former a simple verb. Believers shall be raised up *out of* the rest of the dead (*Note,* Phil. 3:11); the first resurrection (Rev. 20:5). **us**—Here he speaks of the possibility of his being found in the grave when Christ comes; elsewhere, of his being possibly found alive (I Thess. 4:17). In either event, the Lord's coming rather than death is the great object of the Christian's expectation (Rom. 8:19). **15.** Resuming the thought in vs. 13, "the body is for the Lord" (ch. 12:27; Eph. 4:12, 15, 16; 5:30). **shall I then**—such being the case. **take**—spontaneously alienating them from Christ. For they cannot be at the same time "the members of an harlot," and "of Christ" [BENGEL]. It is a fact no less certain than mysterious, that moral and spiritual ruin is caused by such sins; which human wisdom (when untaught by revelation) held to be actions as blameless as eating and drinking [CONYBEARE and HOWSON]. **16.** Justification of his having called fornicators "members of an harlot" (vs. 15). **joined**—by carnal intercourse; lit., "cemented to": cleaving to. **one body**—with her. **saith he**—GOD speaking by Adam (Gen. 2:24; Matt. 19:5). "He which made them at the beginning said . . ." (Eph. 5:31). **17. one spirit**—with Him. In the case of union with a harlot, the fornicator becomes one "body" with her (not one "spirit," for the spirit which is normally the organ of the Holy Spirit in man, is in the carnal so overlaid with what is sensual that it is ignored altogether). But the believer not only has his body sanctified by union with Christ's body, but also becomes "one spirit" with Him (John 15:1-7; 17:21; II Pet. 1:4; cf. Eph. 5:23-32, and John 3:6). **18. Flee**—The only safety in such temptations is *flight* (Gen. 39:12; Job 31:1). **Every sin**—The *Greek* is forcible. *"Every sin whatsoever"* that a man doeth." Every *other* sin; even gluttony, drunkenness, and selfmurder are "without," i.e., comparatively external to the body (Mark 7:18; cf. Prov. 6: 30-32). He certainly injures, but he does not alienate the body itself; the sin is not terminated in the body; he rather sins against the perishing accidents of the body (as the "belly," and the body's present temporary organization), and against the soul than against the body in its permanent essence, designed "for the Lord." "But" the fornicator alienates that body which is the Lord's, and makes it one with a harlot's body, and so "sinneth against his own body," i.e., against the *verity* and *nature* of his body; not a mere *effect* on the body from without, but a *contradiction* of the truth of the body, wrought *within itself* [ALFORD]. **19.** Proof that "he that fornicates sinneth against his own **body" (vs. 18). your body**—not "bodies." As in ch. 3:17, he represented the whole company of believers (souls and bodies), i.e., the Church, as "the temple of God," the Spirit; so here, the *body* of each individual of the Church is viewed as the ideal "temple of the Holy Ghost." So John 17:23, which proves that not only the Church, but also each member of it, is "the temple of the Holy Ghost." Still though many the several members form one temple, the whole collectively being that which each is in miniature individually. Just as the Jews had one temple only, so in the fullest sense all Christian churches and individual believers form one temple only. Thus "YOUR [*plural*] body" is distinguished here from "HIS OWN [*particular* or *individual*] body" (vs. 18). In sinning against the latter, the fornicator sins against "your (ideal) body," that of "Christ," whose "members your bodies" are (vs. 15). In this consists the sin of fornication, that it is a sacrilegious desecration of God's temple to profane uses. The unseen, but much more efficient, Spirit of God in the spiritual temple now takes the place of the visible Shekinah in the old material temple. The whole man is the temple; the soul is the inmost shrine; **the understanding and** heart, the holy place; and the body, the porch and exterior of the edifice. Chastity is the guardian of the temple to prevent anything unclean entering which might provoke the indwelling God to abandon it as defiled [TERTULLIAN *de cultu fœminarum*]. None but God can claim a temple; here the Holy Ghost is assigned one; therefore the Holy Ghost is God. **not your own**—The fornicator treats his body as if it were "his own," to give to a harlot if he pleases (vs. 18; cf. vs. 20). But we have no right to alienate our body which is the Lord's. In ancient servitude the person of the servant was wholly the property of the master, not his own. *Purchase* was one of the ways of acquiring a slave. Man has *sold himself* to sin (I Kings 21:20; Rom. 7:14). Christ buys him to Himself, to serve Him (Rom. 6:16-22). **20. bought with a price**—Therefore Christ's blood is strictly a ransom paid to God's justice by the love of God in Christ for our redemption (Matt. 20:28; Acts 20:28; Gal. 3:13; Heb. 9:12; I Pet. 1:18, 19; II Pet. 2:1 Rev. 5:9). While He thus took off our obligation to punishment, He laid upon us a new obligation to obedience (ch. 7:22, 23). If we accept Him as our Prophet to reveal God to us, and our Priest to atone for us, we must also ac-

cept Him as our King to rule over us as wholly His, presenting every token of our fealty (Isa. 26:13). **in your body**—as "in" a temple (cf. John 13:32; Rom. 12:1; Phil. 1:20). **and in your spirit, which are God's**—not in the oldest MSS. and versions, and not needed for the sense, as the context refers *mainly* to the "body" (vss. 16, 18, 19). The "spirit" is *incidentally* mentioned in vs. 17, which perhaps gave rise to the interpolation, at first written in the margin, afterwards inserted in the text.

CHAPTER 7

Vss. 1-40. REPLY TO THEIR INQUIRIES AS TO MARRIAGE; THE GENERAL PRINCIPLE IN OTHER THINGS IS, ABIDE IN YOUR STATION, FOR THE TIME IS SHORT. **1.** The Corinthians in their letter had probably asked questions which tended to disparage marriage, and had implied that it was better to break it off when contracted with an unbeliever. **good**—i.e., "expedient," because of "the present distress"; i.e., the unsettled state of the world, and the likelihood of persecutions tearing rudely asunder those bound by marriage ties. Hebrews 13: 4, in opposition to ascetic and Romish notions of superior *sanctity* in celibacy, declares, "Marriage is HONORABLE IN ALL." Another reason why in some cases celibacy may be a matter of Christian *expediency* is stated in vss. 34, 35, "that ye may attend upon the Lord without distraction." But these are exceptional cases, and in exceptional times, such as those of Paul. **2.** Here the general rule is given *to avoid* **fornication**—More lit., *"on account of fornications,"* to which as being very prevalent at Corinth, and not even counted sins among the heathen, unmarried persons might be tempted. The *plural*, "fornications," marks irregular lusts, as contrasted with the *unity* of the marriage relation [BENGEL]. **let every man have**—a positive command to all who have not the gift of continency, in fact to the great majority of the world (vs. 5). The dignity of marriage is set forth by Paul (Eph. 5:25-32), in the fact that it signifies the mystical union between Christ and the Church. **3, 4.** *The duty of cohabitation on the part of the married.* **due benevolence**—The oldest MSS. read simply, "her due"; i.e., the conjugal cohabitation *due* by the marriage contract (cf. vs. 4). **4.** A paradox. She *hath not power over* her body, and yet it is *her own.* The *oneness of body* in which marriage places husband and wife explains this. The one complements the other. Neither without the other realizes the perfect ideal of man. **5. Defraud ... not**—viz., of the conjugal duty "due" (vs. 3; cf. LXX, Exod. 21:10). **except it be**—"unless perchance" [ALFORD]. **give yourselves to**—lit., "be at leisure for"; be *free from interruptions for;* viz., on some *special* "season," as the *Greek* for "time" means (cf. Exod. 19:15; Joel 2:16; Zech. 7:3). **fasting and prayer**—The oldest MSS. omit "fasting and"; an interpolation, evidently, of ascetics. **come together**—The oldest MSS. read, "be together," viz., in the regular state of the married. **Satan**—who often thrusts in his temptations to unholy thoughts amidst the holiest exercises. **for your incontinency**—*because of* your inability to "contain" (vs. 9) your natural propensities, which Satan would take advantage of. **6. by permission ... not of commandment**—not *by God's permission to me to say it:* but, "by way of permission to you, not as a commandment." "This" refers to the directions vss. 2-5. **7. even as I**—having the gift of continence (Matt. 19:11, 12). This wish does not hold good absolutely, else the extension of mankind and of the Church would cease; but relatively to "the present distress" (vs. 26). **8. to the unmarried**—in general, of both sexes (vss. 10, 11). **and widows**—in particular. **even as I**—unmarried (ch. 9:5). **9. if they cannot contain**—i.e., "have not continency." **burn**—with the secret flame of lust, which lays waste the whole inner man. [Cf. AUGUSTINE, *de Sancta Virginitate.*] The dew of God's grace is needed to stifle the flame, which otherwise would thrust men at last into hell-fire. **10. not I, but the Lord**—(Cf. vss. 12, 25, 40). In ordinary cases he writes on *inspired apostolic authority* (ch. 14:37); but here on the *direct* authority of the *Lord Himself* (Mark 10:11, 12). In both cases alike the things written are inspired by the Spirit of God "but not all for all time, nor all on the primary truths of the faith" [ALFORD]. **Let not the wife depart**—lit., "be separated from." Probably the separation on either side, whether owing to the husband or to the wife, is forbidden. **11. But and if she depart**—or "be separated." If the sin of separation has been committed, that of a new marriage is not to be added (Matt. 5:32). **be reconciled**—by appeasing her husband's displeasure, and recovering his good will. **let not ... husband put away ... wife**—In Matthew 5:32 the only exception allowed is, "saving for the cause of fornication." **12. to the rest**—the other classes (besides "the married," vs. 10, where both husband and wife are believers) about whom the Corinthians had inquired, viz., those involved in mixed marriages with unbelievers. **not the Lord**—by any direct command spoken by Him. **she be pleased**—*Greek,* "consents": implying his wish in the first instance, with which hers *concurs.* **13. the woman**—a believer. **let her not leave him**—"her husband," instead of "him," is the reading of the oldest MSS. The *Greek* for "leave" is the same as in vs. 12, "put away"; translate, "Let her not *put away* [i.e., part with] her husband." The wife had the power of effecting a divorce by Greek and Roman law. **14. sanctified**—Those inseparably connected with the people of God are *hallowed* thereby, so that the latter may retain the connection without impairing their own sanctity (cf. I Tim. 4:5); nay, rather imparting to the former externally some degree of their own hallowed character, and so preparing the way for the unbeliever becoming at last sanctified inwardly by faith. **by ... by**—rather, "in ... in"; i.e., in virtue of the marriage tie between them. **by the husband**—The oldest MSS. read, "by the brother." It is the fact of the husband being a "brother," i.e., a *Christian,* though the wife is not so, that sanctifies or hallows the union. **else ... children unclean**—i.e., beyond the hallowed pale of God's people: in contrast to "holy," i.e., all that is within the consecrated limits [CONYBEARE and HOWSON]. The phraseology accords with that of the Jews, who regarded the heathen as "unclean," and all of the elect nation as "holy," i.e., partakers of the holy covenant. Children were included in the covenant, as God made it not only with Abraham, but with his "seed after" him (Gen. 17:7). So the faith of one Christian parent gives to the children a near relationship to the Church, just as if both parents were Christians (cf. Rom. 11:16). Timothy, the bearer of this Epistle, is an instance in point (Acts 16:1). Paul appeals to the Corinthians as recognizing the principle, that the infants of heathen parents would not be admissible to Christian baptism, because there is no faith on the part of the parents; but where one parent is a be-

liever, the children are regarded as not aliens from, but admissible even in infancy as sharers in, the Christian covenant: for the Church presumes that the believing parent will rear the child in the Christian faith. Infant baptism tacitly superseded infant circumcision, just as the Christian Lord's day gradually superseded the Jewish sabbath, without our having any express command for, or record of, transference. The setting aside of circumcision and of sabbaths in the case of the Gentiles was indeed expressly commanded by the apostles and Paul, but the substitution of infant baptism and of the Lord's day were tacitly adopted, not expressly enacted. No explicit mention of it occurs till Irenæus in the third century; but no society of Christians that we read of disputed its propriety till 1500 years after Christ. Anabaptists would have us defer baptism till maturity as the child cannot understand the nature of it. But a child may be made heir of an estate: it is *his,* though incapable at the time of using or comprehending its advantage; he is not hereafter *to acquire the title and claim* to it. he will hereafter understand his claim, and be capable of employing his wealth: he will then, moreover, become responsible for the use he makes of it [ARCHBISHOP, WHATELY]. **15. if ... depart**—i.e., wishes for separation. Translate, "separateth himself": offended with her Christianity, and refusing to live with her unless she renounce it. **brother or a sister is not under bondage**—is not bound to renounce the faith for the sake of retaining her unbelieving husband [HAMMOND]. So Deuteronomy 13:6; Matthew 10:35-37; Luke 14:26. The believer does not lie under the same obligation in the case of a union with an unbeliever, as in the case of one with a believer. In the former case he is not bound not to separate, if the unbeliever separate or "depart," in the latter nothing but "fornication" justifies separation [PHOTIUS in *Æcumenius*]. **but God hath called us to peace**—Our Christian calling is one that tends to "peace" (Rom. 12:18), not quarrelling; therefore the believer should not ordinarily depart from the unbelieving consort (vss. 12-14), on the one hand; and on the other, in the exceptional case of the unbeliever desiring to depart, the believer is not bound to force the other party to stay in a state of continual discord (Matt. 5:32). Better still it would be not to enter into such unequal alliances at all (vs. 40; II Cor. 6:14). **16.** What knowest thou but that by staying with thy unbelieving partner thou mayest save him or her? Enforcing the precept to stay with the unbelieving consort (vss. 12-14). So Ruth the Moabitess became a convert to her husband's faith: and Joseph and Moses probably gained over their wives. So conversely the unbelieving husband may be won by the believing wife (I Pet. 3:1) [CALVIN]. Or else (vs. 15), if thy unbelieving consort wishes to depart, let him go, so that thou mayest live "in peace": for *thou canst not be sure of converting him,* so as to make it obligatory on thee at all costs to stay with him against his will [MENOCHIUS and ALFORD]. **16. save**—be the instrument of salvation to (Jas. 5:20). **17. But**—*Greek,* "If not." "Only." Caution that believers should not make this direction (vs. 16; as ALFORD explains it) a ground for separating *of themselves* (vss. 12-14). Or, *But if* there be *no* hope of gaining over the unbeliever, still let the general principle be maintained, "As *the Lord* hath allotted to each, as *God* hath called each, so let him walk" (so the *Greek* in the oldest reading); let him walk in the path allotted to him and wherein he was called. The heavenly calling does not set aside our earthly callings. **so ordain I in all churches**—Ye also therefore should obey. **18. not become uncircumcised**—by surgical operation (I Maccabees 1:15; Josephus, *Antiquities*, 12. 5. 1). Some Christians in excess of anti-Jewish feeling might be tempted to this. **let him not be circumcised**—as the Judaizing Christians would have him (Acts 15; Gal. 5:2). **19. Circumcision ... nothing, but ... keeping of ... commandments of God**—viz., is all in all. In Galatians 5:6 this "keeping of the commandments of God" is defined to be "faith which worketh by love"; and in Galatians 6:15, "a new creature." Circumcision was a commandment of God: but not for ever, as "love." **20. the same calling**—i.e., the *condition* from which he is called a Jew, a Greek, a slave, or a freeman. **21. care not for it**—Let it not be a trouble to thee that thou art a servant or slave. **use it rather**—Continue rather in thy state as a servant (vs. 20; Gal. 3:28; I Tim. 6:2). The *Greek*, "But if *even* thou mayest be made free, *use* it," and the context (vss. 20, 22) favors this view [Chrysostom, Bengel, and Alford]. This advice (if this translation be right) is not absolute, as the spirit of the Gospel is against slavery. What is advised here is, contentment under one's existing condition (vs. 24), though an undesirable one, since in our union with Christ all outward disparities of condition are compensated (vs. 22). Be not unduly impatient to cast off "*even*" thy condition as a servant *by unlawful means* (I Pet. 2:13-18); as, e.g., Onesimus did by fleeing (Philemon 10-18). The precept (vs. 23), "Become not (so the *Greek*) the servants of men," implies plainly that slavery is abnormal (cf. Lev. 25:42). "Men stealers," or slave dealers, are classed in I Timothy 1:10, with "murderers" and "perjurers." Neander, Grotius, etc., explain, "If called, being a slave, to Christianity, be content—but yet, if *also* thou canst be free (as a still *additional* good, which if thou canst not attain, be satisfied without it; but which, if offered to thee, is not to be despised), *make use of the opportunity of becoming free, rather than* by neglecting it to remain a slave." I prefer this latter view, as more according to the tenor of the Gospel, and fully justified by the *Greek*. **22. the Lord's freeman**—(Philemon 16)—rather, "freedman." Though a slave externally, spiritually *made free* by the Lord: from sin, John 8:36; from the law, Romans 8:2; from "circumcision," vs. 19; Galatians 5:1. **Christ's servant**—(ch. 9:21). Love makes Christ's service perfect freedom (Matt. 11:29,30; Gal. 5:13; I Peter 2:16). **23. be not ye**—*Greek*, "become not ye." Paul here changes from "thou" (vs. 21) to "ye.' Ye all are "bought" with the blood of Christ, whatever be your earthly state (ch. 6:20). "Become not servants to men," either externally, or spiritually; the former sense applying to the free alone: the latter to Christian freemen and slaves alike, that they should not be servile adherents to their party leaders at Corinth (ch. 3:21, 22; Matt. 23:8-10; II Cor. 11:20); nor indeed slaves to men generally, so far as their condition admits. The external and internal conditions, so far as is attainable, should correspond, and the former be subservient to the latter (cf. vss. 21, 32-35). **24. abide with God**—being chiefly careful of the footing on which he stands towards God rather than that towards men. This clause, "with God," limits the similar precept in vs. 20. A man may cease to "abide in the calling wherein he was called," and yet not violate the precept here. If a man's calling be not favorable to his "abiding with God" (retaining holy fellowship with Him), he may use lawful means to change

from it (cf. *Note*, vs. 21). **25. no commandment of the Lord: yet ... my judgment**—I have no *express revelation* from the Lord *commanding* it, but I give my *judgment* (opinion); viz., under the ordinary inspiration which accompanied the apostles in all their canonical writings (cf. vs. 40; ch. 14:37; I Thess. 4:15). The Lord inspires me in this case to give you only a *recommendation*, which you are free to adopt or reject—not a positive *command*. In the second case (vss. 10, 11) it was a positive command; for the Lord had already made known His will (Mal. 2: 14, 15; Matt. 5:31, 32). In the third case (vs. 12), the Old Testament commandment of God to put away strange wives (Ezra 10:3), Paul by the Spirit revokes. **mercy of the Lord**—(I Tim. 1:13). He attributes his apostleship and the gifts accompanying it (including inspiration) to God's grace alone. **faithful**—in dispensing to you the inspired directions received by me from the Lord. **26. I suppose**—"I consider." **this**—viz., "for a man so to be," i.e., in the same state in which he is (vs. 27). **for**—by reason of. **the present distress**—the distresses to which believers were then beginning to be subjected, making the married state less desirable than the single; and which would prevail throughout the world before the destruction of Jerusalem, according to Christ's prophecy (Matt. 24:8-21; cf. Acts 11:28). **27.** Illustrating the meaning of "so to be," vs. 26. Neither the married (those "bound to a wife") nor the unmarried (those "loosed from a wife") are to "seek" a change of state (cf. vss. 20, 24). **28. trouble in the flesh**—Those who marry, he says, shall incur "trouble in the flesh" (i.e., in their outward state, by reason of the present distress), not *sin*, which is the trouble of the *spirit*. **but I spare you**—The emphasis in the *Greek* is on "I." *My* motive in advising you so is, to "spare you" such trouble in the flesh. So Alford after Calvin, Bengel, and others. Estius from Augustine explains it, "I spare you further details of the inconveniences of matrimony, lest even the incontinent may at the peril of lust be deterred from matrimony: thus I have regard for your infirmity." The antithesis in the *Greek* of "I ... you" and "such" favors the former. **29. this I say**—A summing up of the whole, wherein he draws the practical inference from what precedes (ch. 15:50). **the time**—the *season* (so the *Greek*) of this present dispensation up to the coming of the Lord (Rom. 13:11). He uses the *Greek* expression which the Lord used in Luke 21:8; Mark 13:33. **short**—lit. "contracted." **it remaineth**—The oldest MSS. read, "The time (season) is shortened *as to what remains*, in order that both they ..."; i.e., the effect which the shortening of the time ought to have is, "that for the remaining time (henceforth), both they ...." The clause, "as to what remains," though in *construction* belonging to the previous clause, in *sense* belongs to the following. However, Cyprian and *Vulgate* support *English Version*. **as though they had none**—We ought to consider nothing as our own in real or permanent possession. **30. they that weep ... wept not**—(Cf. II Cor. 6:10). **they that buy ... possessed not**—(Cf. Isa. 24:1, 2). Christ specifies as the condemning sin of the men of Sodom not merely their open profligacy, but that "they bought, they sold," etc., as men whose all was in this world (Luke 17:28). "Possessed" in the *Greek* implies a *holding fast of a possession;* this the Christian will not do, for his "enduring substance" is elsewhere (Heb. 10:34). **31. not abusing it**—not abusing it by an *overmuch using* of it. The meaning of "abusing" here is, not so much *perverting,* as *using it to the full* [BENGEL]. We are to use it, not to *take our fill* of its pursuits as our chief aim (cf. Luke 10:40-42). As the planets while turning on their own axis, yet revolve round the sun; so while we do our part in our own worldly sphere, God is to be the center of all our desires. **fashion**—the present fleeting *form.* Cf. Psalm 39:6, "vain show"; Psalm 73:20, "a dream"; James 4:14, "a vapor." **passeth away**—not merely *shall pass away,* but *is* now actually *passing away.* The image is drawn from a *shifting* scene in a play represented on the stage (I John 2:17). Paul inculcates not so much the outward denial of earthly things, as the inward spirit whereby the married and the rich, as well as the unmarried and the poor, would be ready to sacrifice all for Christ's sake. **32. without carefulness**—I would have you to be not merely "without trouble," but "without distracting cares" (so the *Greek*). **careth**—if he uses aright the advantages of his condition. **34. difference also**—Not merely the unmarried and the married *man* differ in their respective duties, but *also* the *wife* and the *virgin.* Indeed a woman undergoes a greater change of condition than a man in contracting marriage. **35. for your own profit**—not to display *my* apostolic authority. **not . . . cast a snare upon you**—image from *throwing a noose* over an animal in hunting. Not that by hard injunctions I may entangle you with the fear of committing sin where there is no sin. **comely**—*befitting* under present circumstances. **attend upon**—lit., "assiduously wait on"; *sitting down* to the duty. Cf. Luke 10:39, Mary; Luke 2:37, "Anna . . . a widow, who departed not from the temple, but served God with fastings and prayers night and day" (I Tim. 5:5). **distraction**—the same *Greek* as "cumbered" (Luke 10:40, Martha). **36. behaveth . . . uncomely**—is not treating his daughter well in leaving her unmarried beyond the flower of her age, and thus debarring her from the lawful gratification of her natural feeling as a marriageable woman. **need so require**—if the exigencies of the case require it; viz., regard to the feelings and welfare of his daughter. Opposed to "having no necessity" (vs. 37). **let them marry**—the daughter and her suitor. **37. steadfast**—not to be turned from his purpose by the obloquy of the world. **having no necessity**—arising from the natural inclinations of the daughter. **power over his . . . will** —when, owing to his daughter's will not opposing his will, he has power to carry into effect his will or wish. **decreed**—determined. **38. her**—The oldest MSS. have "his own virgin daughter." **but**—The oldest MSS. have "and." **39. bound by the law**—The oldest MSS. omit "by the law." **only in the Lord**—Let her marry *only a Christian* (II Cor. 6:14). **40. happier**—(vss. 1, 28, 34, 35). **I think also**—"I also think"; just as you Corinthians and your teachers *think* much of your opinions, *so I also give my opinion* by inspiration; so in vs. 25, "my judgment" or opinion. *Think* does not imply doubt, but often a matter of well-grounded assurance (John 5:39).

CHAPTER 8

Vss. 1-13. On partaking of Meats Offered to Idols. **1.**Though to those knowing that an idol has no existence, the question of eating meats offered to idols (referred to in the letter of the Corinthians, cf. ch. 7:1) might seem unimportant, it is not so with some, and the infirmities of such should be respected. The portions of the victims not offered on the altars belonged partly to the priests, partly to the offerers; and were eaten at feasts in the temples and in private houses and were often sold in the markets; so that Christians were constantly exposed to the temptation of receiving them, which was forbidden (Num. 25:2; Ps. 106:28). The apostles forbade it in their decree issued from Jerusalem (Acts 15, and 21:25); but Paul does not allude here to that decree, as he rests his precepts rather on his own independent apostolic authority. **we know that we all have knowledge**—The Corinthians doubtless had referred to their "knowledge" (viz., of the indifference of meats, as in themselves having no sanctity or pollution). Paul replies, "We are aware that we all have [speaking *generally,* and so far as Christian *theory* goes; for in vs. 7 he speaks of some who *practically* have *not*] this knowledge." **Knowledge puffeth up**—when without "love." Here a parenthesis begins; and the main subject is resumed in the same words, vs. 4. "As concerning [touch ing] therefore the eating . . . ." "Puffing up" is to please self. "Edifying" is to please one's neighbor. Knowledge only says, All things are lawful for me; Love adds, But all things do not edify [BENGEL], (ch. 10:23; Rom. 14:15). **edifieth**—tends to *build up* the spiritual temple (ch. 3:9; 6:19). **2. And**—omitted in the oldest MSS. The absence of the connecting particle gives an emphatical sententiousness to the style, suitable to the subject. The first step to knowledge is to know our own ignorance. Without love there is only the *appearance* of knowledge. **knoweth**—The oldest MSS. read a *Greek* word implying *personal experimental acquaintance,* not merely *knowledge of a fact,* which the *Greek* of "we know" or *are aware* (vs. 1) means. **as he ought to know**—experimentally and in the way of "love." **3. love God**—the source of love to our neighbor (I John 4:11, 12, 20; 5:2). **the same**—lit., "this man"; he who loves, not he who "thinks that he knows," not having "charity" or love (vss. 1, 2). **is known of him**—is known with the knowledge of approval and is acknowledged by God as His (Ps. 1:6; Gal. 4:9; II Tim. 2:19). Contrast, "I never knew you" (Matt. 7:23). To love God is to know God; and he who thus knows God has been first known by God (cf. ch. 13:12; I Pet. 1:2). **4. As concerning . . .** —resuming the subject begun in vs. 1, "As touching . . . ." **idol is nothing**—has no true being at all, the god it represents is not a living reality. This does not contradict ch. 10:20, which states that they who worship idols, worship *devils;* for here it is the GODS *believed by the worshippers to be represented by the idols* which are denied to have any existence, not the devils which really under the idols delude the worshippers. **none other God**—The oldest MSS. omit the word "other"; which gives a clearer sense. **5.** "For even supposing there are (exist) gods so called (II Thess. 2:4), whether in heaven (as the sun, moon, and stars) or in earth (as deified kings, beasts, etc.), as there be (a recognized fact, Deut. 10:17; Ps. 135: 5; 136:2) gods many and lords many." Angels and men in authority are termed *gods* in Scripture, as exercising a divinely delegated power under God (cf. Exod. 22:9, with vs. 28; Ps. 82:1, 6; John 10:34, 35). **6. to us**—believers. **of whom**—from whom as Creator all things derive their existence. **we in him**—rather "we *for* Him," or "*unto* Him." God the FATHER is the end *for* whom and for whose glory believers live. In Colossians 1:16 all things are said to be created (not only "*by*" Christ, but also) "*for* Him" (CHRIST). *So entirely are the Father and Son one* (cf. Rom. 11: 36; Heb. 2:10). **one Lord**—contrasted with the "many lords" of heathendom (vs. 5). **by whom**—

(John 1:3; Heb. 1:2). **we by him**—as all things are *"of"* the Father by creation, so they (we believers especially) are restored *to* Him by the new creation (Col. 1:20; Rev. 21:5). Also, as all things are *by* Christ by creation, so they (we especially) are restored *by* Him by the new creation. **7. Howbeit**—Though to us who "have knowledge" (vss. 1, 4-6) all meats are indifferent, yet "this knowledge is not in all" in the same degree as we have it. Paul had admitted to the Corinthians that "we all have knowledge" (vs. 1), i.e., so far as Christian *theory* goes; but *practically* some have it not in the same degree. **with conscience**—an ancient reading; but other very old MSS. read "association" or "habit." In either reading the meaning is: Some Gentile Christians, whether from old *association* of ideas or misdirected *conscience*, when they ate such meats, ate them with some feeling as if the idol were something real (vs. 4), and had changed the meats by the fact of the consecration into something either holy or else polluted. **unto this hour**—after they have embraced Christianity; an implied censure, that they are not further advanced by this time in Christian "knowledge." **their conscience . . . is defiled**—by their eating it "as a thing offered to idols." If they ate it unconscious at the time that it had been offered to idols, there would be no defilement of conscience. But conscious of what it was, and not having such knowledge as other Corinthians boasted of, viz., that an idol is nothing and can therefore neither pollute nor sanctify meats, they by eating them sin against conscience (cf. Rom. 14:15-23). It was on the ground of Christian expediency, not to cause a stumbling block to "weak" brethren, that the Jerusalem decree against partaking of such meats (though indifferent *in themselves*) was passed (Acts 15). Hence he here vindicates it against the Corinthian asserters of an inexpedient liberty. **8. Other old MSS. read,** "Neither if we do not eat, are we the better: neither if we eat are we the worse": the language of the eaters who justified their eating thus [LACHMANN]. In *English Version* Paul admits that "meat neither *presents* [so the *Greek* for 'commendeth'] us as commended nor as disapproved before God": it does not affect our standing before God (Rom. 14:6). **9. this liberty of yours**—the watchword for lax Corinthians. The very indifference of meats, which I concede, is the reason why ye should "take heed" not to tempt weak brethren *to act against their conscience* (which constitutes sin, Rom. 14:22, 23). **10. if any man**—being weak. **which hast knowledge**—The very knowledge which thou pridest thyself on (vs. 1), will lead the weak after thy example to do that against his conscience, which thou doest without any scruple of conscience; viz., to eat meats offered to idols. **conscience of him which is weak**—rather, "His conscience, *seeing he* is weak" [ALFORD and others]. **emboldened**—lit., "built up." You ought to have *built up* your brother in good: but by your example your *building* him *up* is the emboldening him to violate his conscience. **11. shall . . . perish**—The oldest MSS. read "perisheth." A single act seemingly unimportant may produce everlasting consequences. The weak brother loses his faith, and if he do not recover it, his salvation [BENGEL] (Rom. 14:23). **for whom Christ died**—and for whose sake we too ought to be willing to die (I John 3:16). And yet professing Christians at Corinth virtually tempted their brethren to their damnation, so far were they from sacrificing aught for their salvation. Note here, that it is no argument against the dogma that *Christ*

died for all, even for those who perish, to say that thus He would have died *in vain* for many. Scripture is our rule, not our suppositions as to consequences. More is involved in redemption than the salvation of man: the *character of God* as at once just and loving is vindicated even in the case of the lost for they might have been saved, and so even in their case Christ has not died in vain. So the mercies of God's providence are not in vain, though many abuse them. Even the condemned shall manifest God's love in the great day, in that they too had the offer of God's mercy. It shall be the most awful ingredient in their cup that they might have been saved but would not: Christ died to redeem even them. **12. wound their weak conscience**—lit., *"smite* their conscience, being (as yet) *in a weak state."* It aggravates the cruelty of the act that it is committed on the weak, just as if one were to *strike an invalid.* **against Christ**—on account of the sympathy between Christ and His members (Matt. 25:40; Acts 9:4, 5). **13. meat**—Old English for "food" in general. **make . . . to offend**—*Greek,* "is a stumbling block to." **no flesh**—In order to ensure my avoiding flesh offered to idols, I would abstain from *all kinds of flesh,* in order not *to be a stumbling block* to my brother.

CHAPTER 9

Vss. 1-27. HE CONFIRMS HIS TEACHING AS TO NOT PUTTING A STUMBLING BLOCK IN A BROTHER'S WAY (ch. 8:13) BY HIS OWN EXAMPLE IN NOT USING HIS UNDOUBTED RIGHTS AS AN APOSTLE, SO AS TO WIN MEN TO CHRIST. **1. Am I not an apostle? am I not free?**—The oldest MSS. read the order thus, "Am I not free? am I not an apostle?" He alludes to ch. 8:9, "this liberty of yours": If you claim it, I appeal to yourselves as the witnesses, have not I also it? "Am I not free?" If you be so, much more I. For "am I not an apostle?" so that I can claim not only Christian, but also apostolic, liberty. **have I not seen Jesus**—*corporeally,* not in a mere vision: cf. ch. 15:8, where the fact of the resurrection, which he wishes to prove, could only be established by an actual bodily appearance, such as was vouchsafed to Peter and the other apostles. In Acts 9:7, 17 the contrast between "the men with him seeing *no man,"* and "Jesus that appeared unto thee in the way," shows that Jesus actually appeared to him in going to Damascus. His vision of Christ in the temple (Acts 22:17) was "in a trance." To be a witness of Christ's resurrection was a leading function of an apostle (Acts 1:22). The best MSS. omit "Christ." **ye my work in the Lord**—Your conversion is His workmanship (Eph. 2:10) through my instrumentality: the "seal of mine apostleship" (vs. 2). **2. yet doubtless**—*yet at least* I am such to you. **seal of mine apostleship**—Your conversion by my preaching, accompanied with miracles ("the signs of an apostle," Rom. 15:18, 19; II Cor. 12:12), and your gifts conferred by me (ch. 1:7), vouch for the reality of my apostleship, just as a seal set to a document attests its genuineness (John 3:33; Rom. 4:11). **3. to them that . . . examine me**—i.e., who call in question mine apostleship. **is this**—viz., that you are the seal of mine apostleship. **4. Have we not power**—*Greek,* "right," or lawful power, equivalent to "liberty" claimed by the Corinthians (ch. 8:9). The "we" includes with himself his colleagues in the apostleship. The *Greek* interrogative expresses, "You surely *won't* say (will you?) that we have *not* the power or right. . . ." **eat and drink**—without laboring with our hands (vss. 11, 13,

14). Paul's not exercising this right was made a plea by his opponents for insinuating that he was himself conscious he was no true apostle (II Cor. 12:13-16). **5. lead about a sister, a wife**–i.e., "a sister *as a wife";* "a sister" by faith, which makes all believers brethren and sisters in the one family of God: "a wife" by marriage covenant. Paul implies he did not exercise his undoubted right to marry and "lead about" a believer, for the sake of Christian expediency, as well to save the Church the expense of maintaining her in his wide circuits, as also that he might give himself more undistractedly to building up the Church of Christ (ch. 7:26, 32, 35). Contrast the Corinthians' want of self-sacrifice in the exercise of their "liberty" at the cost of destroying, instead of edifying, the Church (ch. 8: 9, 10; *Margin,* 11-13). **as other apostles**–implying that some of them had availed themselves of the power which they all had, of marrying. We know from Matthew 8:14, that Cephas (Peter) was a married man. A confutation of Peter's self-styled followers, the Romanists, who exclude the clergy from marriage. CLEMENS ALEXANDRINUS (*Stromata* or *Miscellanies,* 7. sec. 63) records a tradition that he encouraged his wife when being led to death by saying, "Remember, my dear one, the Lord." Cf. EUSEBIUS, *E. H.* 3. 30. **brethren of the Lord**–held in especial esteem on account of their relationship to Jesus (Acts 1:14; Gal. 1:9). James, Joses, Simon, and Judas. Probably *cousins* of Jesus: as cousins were termed by the Jews "brethren." ALFORD makes them literally *brothers* of Jesus by Joseph and Mary. **Cephas**–probably singled out as being a name carrying weight with one partisan section at Corinth. "If your favorite leader does so, surely so may I" (ch. 1:12; 3:22). **6. Barnabas**–long the associate of Paul, and, like him, in the habit of self-denyingly forbearing to claim the maintenance which is a minister's right. So Paul supported himself by tent-making (Acts 18:3; 20:34; I Thess. 2: 9; II Thess. 3:8). **7.** The minister is spiritually a soldier (II Tim. 2:3), a vine-dresser (ch. 3:6-8; Song of Sol. 1:6), and a shepherd (I Pet. 5:2, 4). **of the fruit**–The oldest MSS. omit "of." **8. as a man**–I speak thus not merely *according to human judgment,* but with the sanction of the divine law also. **9. ox . . . treadeth . . . corn**–(Deut. 25:4). In the East to the present day they do not after reaping carry the sheaves home to barns as we do, but take them to an area under the open air to be threshed by the oxen treading them with their feet, or else drawing a threshing instrument over them (cf. Mic. 4:13). **Doth God . . . care for oxen?**–rather, "Is it for the oxen that God careth?" Is the animal the ultimate object for whose sake this law was given? No. God does care for the lower animal (Ps. 36:6; Matt. 10:29), but it is with the ultimate aim of the welfare of *man,* the head of animal creation. In the humane consideration shown for the lower animal, we are to learn that still more ought it to be exercised in the case of man, the ultimate object of the law; and that the human (spiritual as well as temporal) laborer is worthy of his hire. **10. altogether**–Join this with "saith." "Does he (the divine lawgiver) by all means say it for our sakes?" It would be untrue, that God saith it *altogether* (in the sense of *solely*) for *our* sakes. But it is true, that He *by all means saith* it for our sakes as the ultimate object in the lower world. GROTIUS, however, translates, "mainly" or "especially," instead of *altogether.* **that**–"meaning that" [ALFORD]; lit., "because." **should plough**–*ought* to plough in hope. The obligation rests with the people not to

let their minister labor without remuneration. **he that thresheth in hope should be partaker of his hope**--The oldest MS. versions and Fathers read, "He that thresheth (*should* or *ought to thresh*) in the hope of partaking" (viz., *of the fruit of his threshing*). "He that plougheth," spiritually, is the first planter of a church in a place (cf. ch. 3:6, 9); "he that thresheth," the minister who tends a church already planted. **11. we . . . we**–emphatical in the *Greek.* WE, the same persons who have sown to you the infinitely more precious treasures of the *Spirit,* may at least claim in return what is the only thing *you* have to give, viz., the goods that nourish the *flesh* ("*your* carnal things"). **12. others**–whether true apostles (vs. 5) or false ones (II Cor. 11:20). **we rather**–considering our greater labors for you (II Cor. 11:23). **suffer all things**–without complaining of it. We desire to *conceal* (lit., "hold as a water-tight vessel") any distress we suffer from straitened circumstances. The same *Greek* is in ch. 13:7. **lest we . . . hinder . . . gospel**–not to *cause a hindrance to* its progress by giving a handle for the imputation of self-seeking, if we received support from our flock. The less of incumbrance and expense caused to the Church, and the more of work done, the better for the cause of the Gospel (II Tim. 2:4). **13. minister about holy things**–the Jewish priests and Levites. The *Greek* especially applies to the former, the priests *offering sacrifices.* **partakers with the altar**–a part of the victims going to the service of the altar, and the rest being shared by the priests (Lev. 7:6; Num. 18:6, etc.; Deut. 18:1, etc.). **14. Even so**–The only inference to be drawn from this passage is, not that the Christian ministry is of a sacrificial character as the Jewish priesthood, but simply, that as the latter was supported by the contributions of the people, so should the former. The stipends of the clergy were at first from voluntary offerings at the Lord's Supper. At the love feast preceding it every believer, according to his ability, offered a gift; and when the expense of the table had been defrayed, the bishop laid aside a portion for himself, the presbyters, and deacons; and with the rest relieved widows, orphans, confessors, and the poor generally [TERTULLIAN, *Apology,* ch. 39]. The stipend was in proportion to the dignity and merits of the several bishops, presbyters, and deacons [CYPRIAN, c. 4, ep. 6]. **preach . . . gospel**–plainly marked as the duty of the Christian minister, in contrast to the *ministering about sacrifices* (*Greek*) *and waiting at the altar* of the Jewish priesthood and Levites (vs. 13). If the Lord's Supper were a *sacrifice* (as the Mass is supposed to be), this 14th verse would certainly have been worded so, to answer to vs. 13. Note the same Lord Christ "ordains" the ordinances in the Old and in the New Testaments (Matt. 10:10; Luke 10:7). **15.** Paul's special gift of continency, which enabled him to abstain from marriage, and his ability to maintain himself without interrupting seriously his ministry, made that expedient to him which is ordinarily inexpedient; viz., that the ministry should not be supported by the people. What to him was a duty, would be the opposite to one, for instance, to whom God had committed a family, without other means of support. **I have used none of these things**–none of these "powers" or rights which I might have used (vss. 4-6, 12). **neither**–rather, "*Yet* I have *not* written." **so done unto me**–lit., "in my case": as is done in the case of a soldier, a planter, a shepherd, a ploughman, and a sacrificing priest (vss. 7, 10, 13). **make my glorying void**–deprive me of my privilege of preaching the Gospel without remuneration (II Corinthians 11:7-10). Rather than hinder the progress of the Gospel by giving any pretext for a charge of interested motives (II Cor. 12. 17, 18), Paul would "die" of hunger. Cf. Abraham's similar disinterestedness (Gen. 14:22, 23). **16. though I preach ... I have nothing to glory of**–i.e., If I preach the Gospel, and do so not gratuitously, I have no matter for "glorying." For the "necessity" that is laid on me to preach (cf. Jer. 20:9, and the case of Jonah) does away with ground for "glorying." The sole ground for the latter that I have, is my preaching *without charge* (vs. 18): since there is no necessity laid on me as to the latter, it is my voluntary act for the Gospel's sake. **17.** Translate, "If I be doing this (i.e., preaching) of my own accord (which I am not, for the "necessity" is laid on me which binds a servant to obey his master), I have a reward; but if (as is the case) involuntarily (Acts 9:15; 22:15; 26: 16; not of my own natural will, but by the constraining grace of God; Romans 9:16; I Tim. 1:13-16), I have had a dispensation (of the Gospel) entrusted to me" (and so can claim no "reward," seeing that I only "have done that which was my duty to do," Luke 17:10, but incur the "woe," vs. 16, if I fail in it). **18. What is my reward?**–The answer is in vs. 19; viz., that by making the Gospel without charge, where I might have rightfully claimed maintenance, I might "win the more." **of Christ**–The oldest MSS and versions omit these words. **abuse** –rather "that *I use* not *to the full* my power." This is his matter for "*glorying*"; the "*reward*" ultimately aimed at is the gaining of the more (vs. 19). The former, as involving the latter, is verbally made the answer to the question, "What is my reward?" But really the "reward" is that which is the ultimate aim of his preaching without charge, viz., that he may gain the more; it was for this end, not to have matter of glorying, that he did so. **19. free from all men**–i.e., from the power of all men. **gain the more**–i.e., *as many of them* ("all men") *as possible.* "Gain" is an appropriate expression in relation to a "reward" (I Thess. 2:19, 20); he therefore repeats it frequently (vss. 20-22). **20. I became as a Jew**–in things not defined by the *law*, but by Jewish usage. Not Judaizing in essentials, but in matters where there was no compromise of principle (cf. Acts 16:3; 21:20-26); an undesigned coincidence between the history and the Epistle, and so a sure proof of genuineness. **to them that are under the law, as under the law**–in things defined by *the law;* such as ceremonies not then repugnant to Christianity. Perhaps the reason for distinguishing this class from the former is that Paul himself belonged *nationally* to "the Jews," but did not in *creed* belong to the class of "them that are under the law." This view is confirmed by the reading inserted here by the oldest MSS., versions, and Fathers, "not being (i.e., parenthetically, 'not that I am') myself under the law." **21. To them ... without law**–i.e., without *revealed* law: the heathen (cf. Rom. 2:12 with vs. 15). **as without law**–not urging on them the ceremonies and "works of the law," but "the hearing of faith" (Gal. 3:2). Also discoursing in their own manner, as at Athens, with arguments from their own poets (Acts 17:28). **being not without law to God**–"While thus conforming to others in matters indifferent, taking care not to be *without law* in relation to God, but *responsible to law* (lit., IN LAW) in relation to Christ." This is the Christian's true position in relation to the world, to himself, and to God. Everything develops itself according to its proper law. So the

Christian, though no longer subject to the literal law as constraining him from without, is subject to an inward principle or law, the spirit of faith in Christ acting from within as the germ of a new life. He does not in the *Greek* (as in *English Version*) say "*under the law* (as he does in vs. 20) to Christ"; but uses the milder term, "in ... law," *responsible to law.* Christ was responsible to the law for us, so that we are no longer responsible to it (Gal. 3:13, 24), but to Him, as the members to the Head (ch. 7:22; Rom. 8:1-4; I Pet. 2:16). Christians serve Christ in newness of spirit, no longer in oldness of the letter (i.e., the old *external* law *as such*), Romans 7:4-6. To Christ, as man's Head, the Father has properly delegated His authority (John 5:22, 27); whence here he substitutes "Christ" for "God" in the second clause, "not without law to *God,* but under the law to *Christ.*" The law of Christ is the law of love (Gal. 6:2; cf. 5:13). **22. gain the weak** –i.e., establish, instead of being a stumbling block to inexperienced Christians (ch. 8:7). Romans 14: 1, "Weak in the faith." ALFORD thinks the "weak" are not Christians at all, for these have been already "won"; but those outside the Church, who are yet "without strength" to believe (Rom. 5:6). But when "weak" *Christians* are by the condescending love of stronger brethren kept from falling from faith, they are well said to be "gained" or won. **by all means ... some**–The gain of even "*some*" is worth the expenditure of "all means." He conformed himself to the feelings of each in the several classes, that out of them *all* he might *gain some.* **23. partaker thereof**–*Greek, "fellow partaker":* of the Gospel blessings promised at Christ's coming: "with" (not as *English Version,* "you": but) *them,* viz., with those thus "gained" by me to the Gospel. **24. Know ye not**–The Isthmian games, in which the foot race was a leading one, were of course well known, and a subject of patriotic pride to the Corinthians, who lived in the immediate neighborhood. These periodical games were to the Greeks rather a passion than a mere amusement: hence their suitableness as an image of Christian earnestness. **in a race**–*Greek,* "in a race course." **all ... one**– Although we knew that one alone could be saved, still it would be well worth our while to run [BENGEL]. Even in the Christian race not "all" who enter on the race win (ch. 10:1-5). **So run, that ye may obtain**–said parenthetically. These are the words in which the instructors of the young in the exercise schools (*gymnasia*) and the spectators on the race course exhorted their pupils to stimulate them to put forth all exertions. The *gymnasium* was a prominent feature in every Greek city. Every candidate had to take an oath that he had been ten months in training, and that he would violate none of the regulations (II Timothy 2:5; cf. I Tim. 4:7, 8). He lived on a strict self-denying diet, refraining from wine and pleasant foods, and enduring cold and heat and most laborious discipline. The "prize" awarded by the judge or umpire was a chaplet of green leaves; at the Isthmus, those of the indigenous pine, for which parsley leaves were temporarily substituted (vs. 25). The *Greek* for "obtain" is *fully obtain.* It is in vain to begin, unless we persevere to the end (Matt. 10:22; 24:13; Rev. 2:10). The "so" expresses, Run *with such perseverance* in the heavenly course, as "all" the runners exhibit in the earthly "race" just spoken of: *to the end that* ye may attain the prize. **25. striveth**–in wrestling: a still more severe contest than the foot race. **is temperate**–So Paul exercised self-denial, abstaining from claiming sustenance for the sake of the "reward," viz., to "gain the more" (vss. 18, 19). **corruptible**—*soon withering,* as being only of fir leaves taken from the fir groves which surrounded the Isthmian race course or stadium. **incorruptible**—(I Pet. 1:4; 5:4; Rev. 2:10). "Crown" here is not that of a king (which is expressed by a different *Greek* word, viz., "diadem"), but a *wreath* or *garland.* **26. I**—Paul returns to his main subject, *his own* self-denial, and his motive in it. **run, not as uncertainly**—not as a runner uncertain of the goal. Ye Corinthians gain no end in your entering idol temples or eating idol meats. But *I,* for my part, in all my acts, whether in my becoming "all things to all men," or in receiving no sustenance from my converts, have a definite end in view, viz., to "gain the more." I know what I aim at, and how to aim at it. He who runs with a clear aim, looks straightforward to the goal, makes it his sole aim, casts away every encumbrance (Heb. 12:1, 2), is indifferent to what the bystanders say, and sometimes even a fall only serves to rouse him the more [BENGEL]. **not as one that beateth the air**—instead of beating the adversary. Alluding to the *sciamachia* or *sparring in the school in sham-fight* (cf. ch. 14:9), wherein they struck out into the air as if at an imaginary adversary. The real adversary is Satan acting on us through the flesh. **27. keep under**—lit., "bruise the face under the eyes," so as to render it black and blue; so, to *chastise* in the most sensitive part. Cf. "*mortify* the deeds of the body," Romans 8:13; also I Pet. 2:11. It is not ascetic fasts or macerations of the body which are here recommended, but the *keeping under* of our natural self-seeking, so as, like Paul, to lay ourselves out entirely for the great work. **my body**—the old man and the remainders of lust in my flesh. "My body," so far as by the *flesh* it opposes the *spirit* [ESTIUS] (Gal. 5:17). Men may be severe to their bodies and yet indulge their lust. Ascetic "neglect of the body" may be all the while a more subtile "satisfying of the flesh" (Col. 2:23). Unless the soul keep the body under, the body will get above the soul. The body may be made a good servant, but is a bad master. **bring it into subjection**—or bondage, as a *slave* or servant *led away captive;* so the *Greek.* **preached**—lit., "heralded." He keeps up the image from the races. The *heralds* summoned the candidates for the foot race into the race course [PLATO, *Legg.* 8. 833], and placed the crowns on the brows of the conquerors, announcing their names [BENGEL]. They probably proclaimed also the laws of the combat; answering to the *preaching* of the apostles [ALFORD]. The The *Christian* herald is also a *combatant,* in which respect he is distinguished from the herald at the games. **a castaway**—failing shamefully of the prize myself, after I have *called* others to the contest. *Rejected* by God, the Judge of the Christian race, notwithstanding my having, by my preaching, led others to be accepted. Cf. the equivalent term, "reprobate," Jeremiah 6:30; II Corinthians 13:6. Paul implies, if such earnest, self-denying watchfulness over himself be needed still, with all his labors for others, to make his own calling sure, much more is the same needed by the Corinthians, instead of their going, as they do, to the extreme limit of Christian liberty.

CHAPTER 10

Vss. 1-33. DANGER OF FELLOWSHIP WITH IDOLATRY ILLUSTRATED IN THE HISTORY OF ISRAEL: SUCH FELLOWSHIP INCOMPATIBLE WITH FELLOWSHIP IN THE LORD'S SUPPER. EVEN LAWFUL THINGS ARE TO BE FORBORNE, SO AS NOT TO HURT WEAK BRETHREN. **1. Moreover**—The oldest MSS. read "for." Thus the connection with the foregoing chapter is expressed. Ye need to exercise self-denying watchfulness notwithstanding all your privileges, lest yc be castaways. FOR the Israelites with all their privileges were most of them castaways through want of it. **ignorant**—with all your boasted "knowledge." **our fathers**—The Jewish Church stands in the relation of parent to the Christian Church. **all**—Arrange as the *Greek,* "Our fathers were *all* under the *cloud*"; giving the "all" its proper emphasis. Not so much as one of so great a multitude was detained by force or disease (Ps. 105:37) [BENGEL]. Five times the "all" is repeated, in the enumeration of the five favors which God bestowed on Israel (vss. 1-4). Five times, correspondingly, they sinned (vss. 6-10). In contrast to the "all" stands "many (rather, 'the most') of them" (vs. 5). *All* of them had great privileges, yet *most* of them were castaways through lust. Beware you, having greater privileges, of sharing the same doom through a similar sin. Continuing the reasoning (ch. 9:24), "They which run in a race, run *all,* but *one* receiveth the prize." **under the cloud**—were continually *under the defense* of the pillar of cloud, the symbol of the divine presence (Exod. 13:21, 22; Ps. 105: 39; cf. Isa. 4:5). **passed through the sea**—by God's miraculous interposition for them (Exod. 14:29). **2. And**—"And so" [BENGEL]. **baptized unto Moses** —the servant of God and representative of the Old Testament covenant of the law: as Jesus, the Son of God, is of the Gospel covenant (John 1:17; Heb. 3:5, 6). The people were led to believe in Moses as God's servant by the miracle of the cloud protecting them, and by their being conducted under him safely through the Red Sea; therefore they are said to be "baptized unto" him (Exod. 14:31). "Baptized" is here equivalent to "*initiated*": it is used in accommodation to Paul's argument to the Corinthians; they, it is true, have been "baptized," but so also virtually were the Israelites of old; if the virtual baptism of the latter availed not to save them from the doom of lust, neither will the actual baptism of the former save them. There is a resemblance between the symbols also: for the cloud and sea consist of water, and as these took the Israelites out of sight, and then restored them again to view, so the water does to the baptized [BENGEL]. OLSHAUSEN understands "the cloud" and "the sea" as symbolizing the *Spirit* and *water* respectively (John 3:5; Acts 10:44-47). Christ is the pillar-cloud that screens us from the heat of God's wrath. Christ as "the light of the world" is our "pillar of fire" to guide us in the darkness of the world. As the rock when smitten sent forth the waters, so Christ, having been once for all smitten, sends forth the waters of the Spirit. As the manna bruised in mills fed Israel, so Christ, when "it pleased the Lord to bruise Him," has become our spiritual food. A strong proof of inspiration is given in this fact, that the *historical* parts of Scripture, without the consciousness even of the authors, are covert prophecies of the future. **3. same spiritual meat**—As the Israelites had the water from the rock, which answered to *baptism,* so they had the manna which corresponded to the other of the two Christian sacraments, the Lord's Supper. Paul plainly implies the *importance* which was attached to these two sacraments by all Christians in those days: "an inspired protest against those who lower their dignity, or deny their necessity" [ALFORD]. Still he guards against the other extreme of thinking the mere external possession of such privileges will ensure salvation. Moreover, had there been seven sacraments, as Rome teaches, Paul would have alluded to them, whereas he refers to only the two. He does not mean by "the same" that *the Israelites and we Christians* have the "same" sacrament; but that *believing and unbelieving* Israelites alike had "the same" spiritual privilege of the manna (cf. vs. 17). It was *"spiritual* meat" or food; because given by the power of God's spirit, not by human labor [GROTIUS and ALFORD]. Galatians 4:29, "born after the Spirit," i.e., supernaturally. Psalm 78:24, "corn of heaven" (Ps. 105:40). Rather, "spiritual" in its *typical* signification, Christ, the true Bread of heaven, being signified (John 6:32). Not that the Israelites clearly understood the signification; but believers among them would feel that in the type something more was meant; and their implicit and reverent, though indistinct, faith was counted to them for justification, of which the manna was a kind of sacramental seal. "They are not to be heard which feign that the old fathers did look only for transitory promises" (Article vii, Church of England), as appears from this passage (cf. Heb. 4: 2). **4. drink**—(Exod. 17:6). In Numbers 20:8, "the beasts" also are mentioned as having drunk. The literal water typified *"spiritual* drink," and is therefore so called. **spiritual Rock that followed them**—rather, *"accompanied* them." Not the literal rock (or its water) "followed" them, as ALFORD explains, as if Paul sanctioned the Jews' tradition (Rabbi Solomon on Num. 20:2) that the rock itself, or at least the stream from it, followed the Israelites from place to place (cf. Deut. 9:21). But Christ, the "Spiritual Rock" (Ps. 78:20, 35; Deut. 32:4, 15, 18, 30, 31, 37; Isa. 28:16; I Pet. 2:6), accompanied them (Exod. 33:15). "Followed" implies His *attending on* them to *minister to* them; thus, though mostly going *before* them, He, when occasion required it, *followed "behind"* (Exod. 14:19). He satisfied all alike as to their bodily thirst whenever they needed it; as on three occasions is expressly recorded (Exod. 15:24, 25; 17:6; Num. 20:8); and this drink for the body symbolized the spiritual drink from the Spiritual Rock (cf. John 4:13, 14; see *Note,* vs. 3). **5. But**—though they had so many tokens of God's presence. **many of them**—rather, "the majority of them"; "the whole part." All except Joshua and Caleb of the first generation. **not**—in the *Greek* emphatically standing in the beginning of the sentence: "Not," as one might have naturally expected, "with the more part of them was . . . ." **God**—whose judgment alone is valid. **for**—the event showed, they had not pleased God. **overthrown**—lit., "strewn in heaps." **in the wilderness**—far from the land of promise. **6. were**—*Greek,* "came to pass as." **our examples** —samples to us of what will befall us, if we also with all our privileges walk carelessly. **lust**—the fountain of all the four other offenses enumerated, and therefore put first (Jas. 1:14, 15; cf. Ps. 106: 14). A particular case of lust was that after flesh, when they pined for the fish, leeks, etc., of Egypt, which they had left (Num. 11:4, 33, 34). These are included in the "evil things," not that they are so in themselves, but they became so to the Israelites when they lusted after what God withheld, and were discontented with what God provided. **7. idolaters**—A case in point. As the Israelites *sat down* (a deliberate act), *ate,* and *drank* at the idol feast to the calves in Horeb, so the Corinthians were

in danger of idolatry by a like act, though not professedly worshipping an idol as the Israelites (ch. 8: 10, 11; 10:14, 20, 21; Exod. 32:6). He passes here from the first to the second person, as they alone (not he also) were in danger of idolatry, etc. He resumes the first person appropriately at the 16th verse. **some**—The multitude follow the lead of some bad men. **play**—with lascivious dancing, singing, and drumming round the calf (cf. "rejoiced," Acts 7:41). **8. fornication**—lit., Fornication was generally, as in this case (Num. 25), associated at the idol feasts with spiritual fornication, i.e., idolatry. This all applied to the Corinthians (ch. 5:1, 9; 6:9, 15, 18; ch. 8:10). Balaam tempted Israel to both sins with Midian (Rev. 2:14). Cf. ch. 8:7, 9, "stumbling block," "eat . . . thing offered unto . . . idol." **three and twenty thousand**—in Numbers 25:9 "twenty and four thousand." If this were a real discrepancy, it would militate rather against inspiration of the *subject matter* and *thought,* than against *verbal* inspiration. The solution is: Moses in Numbers includes all who died "in the plague"; Paul, all who died "in *one day"*; 1000 more may have fallen the next day [KITTO, *Biblical Cyclopædia*]. Or, the real number may have been between 23,000 and 24,000, say 23,500, or 23,600; when writing generally where the exact figures were not needed, one writer might quite veraciously give one of the two round numbers near the exact one, and the other writer the other [BENGEL]. Whichever be the true way of reconciling the seeming discrepant statements, at least the ways given above prove they are not really irreconcilable. **9. tempt Christ**—So the oldest *versions,* Irenæus (264), and *good* MSS. read. Some of the *oldest* MSS. read "Lord"; and one MS. only "God." If "Lord" be read, it will mean *Christ.* As "Christ" was referred to in one of the five privileges of Israel (vs. 4), so it is natural that He should be mentioned here in one of the five corresponding sins of that people. In Numbers 21:5 it is "spake against *God"* (whence probably arose the alteration in the one MS., I Cor. 10:9, "God," to harmonize it with Num. 21:5). As either "Christ" or "Lord" is the genuine reading, "Christ" must be "God." Cf. "Why do ye tempt the Lord?" (Exod. 17:2, 7. Cf. Rom. 14:11, with Isa. 45:22, 23). Israel's discontented complainings were temptings of Christ especially, the "Angel" of the covenant (Exod. 23:20, 21; 32:34; Isa. 63:9). Though they drank of "that Rock . . . Christ" (vs. 4), they yet complained for want of water (Exod. 17:2, 7). Though also eating the same spiritual meat (Christ, "the true manna," "the bread of life"), they yet murmured, "Our soul loatheth this light bread." In this case, being punished by the fiery serpents, they were saved by the brazen serpent, the emblem of *Christ* (cf. John 8:56; Heb. 11:26). The *Greek* for "tempt" means, *tempt or try, so as to wear out* the long-suffering of Christ (cf. Ps. 95:8, 9; Num. 14:22). The Corinthians were in danger of provoking God's long-suffering by walking on the verge of idolatry, through overweening confidence in their knowledge. **10. some of them . . . murmured**—upon the death of Korah and his company, who themselves were murmurers (Num. 16:41, 49). Their murmurs against Moses and Aaron were virtually murmurs against God (cf. Exod. 16:8, 10). Paul herein glances at the Corinthian murmurs against himself, the apostle of Christ. **destroyed**—14,700 perished. **the destroyer** —THE same destroying angel sent by God as in Exodus 12:23, and II Samuel 24:16. **11. Now . . . these things . . . ensamples**—resuming the thread of vs. 6. The oldest MSS. read, "by way of example." **the ends of the world**—lit., "of the ages"; the New Testament dispensation in its successive phases (*plural*, "ends") being the winding up of all former "ages." No new dispensation shall appear till Christ comes as Avenger and Judge; till then the "ends," being many, include various successive periods (cf. Heb. 9:26). As we live in the last dispensation, which is the consummation of all that went before, our responsibilities are the greater; and the greater is the guilt, Paul implies, to the Corinthians, which they incur if they fall short of their privileges. **12. thinketh he standeth**—stands and thinks that he stands [BENGEL]; i.e., stands "by faith" "well pleasing" to God; in contrast to vs. 5, "with many of them God was not well pleased" (Rom. 11:20). **fall**—from his place in the Church of God (cf. vs. 8, "fell"). Both temporally and spiritually (Rom. 14:4). Our security, so far as relates to God, consists in faith; so far as relates to ourselves, it consists in fear. **13.** Consolation to them, under their temptation; it is none but such as is "common to man," or "such as man can bear," "adapted to man's powers of endurance" [WAHL]. **faithful**—(Ps. 125:3; Isa. 27:3, 8; Rev. 3:10). "God is faithful" to the covenant which He made with you in calling you (I Thess. 5:24). To be *led into* temptation is distinct from *running* into it, which would be "tempting God" (vs. 9; Matt. 4:7). **way to escape**—(Jer. 29:11; II Pet. 2:9). The *Greek* is, "*the* way of escape"; the appropriate way of escape in each particular temptation; not an immediate escape, but one in due time, after patience has had her perfect work (Jas. 1:2-4,12). He "makes" the way of escape simultaneously with the temptation which His providence permissively aranges for His people. **to bear it**—*Greek*, "to bear up under it," or "against it." Not, He will take it away (II Cor. 12:7-9). **14.** Resuming the argument, vs. 7; ch. 8: 9, 10. **flee**—Do not tamper with it by doubtful acts, such as eating idol meats on the plea of Christian liberty. The only safety is in *wholly shunning* whatever borders on idolatry (II Cor. 6:16, 17). The Holy Spirit herein also presciently warned the Church against the idolatry, subsequently transferred from the idol feast to the Lord's Supper itself, in the figment of transubstantiation. **15.** Appeal to their own powers of *judgment* to weigh the force of the argument that follows: viz., that as the partaking of the Lord's Supper involves a partaking of the Lord Himself, and the partaking of the Jewish sacrificial meats involved a partaking of the altar of God, and, as the heathens sacrifice to devils, to partake of an idol feast is to have fellowship with devils. We cannot divest ourselves of the responsibility of "judging" for ourselves. The weakness of private judgment is not an argument against its use, but its abuse. We should the more take pains in searching the infallible word, with every aid within our reach, and above all with humble prayer for the Spirit's teaching (Acts 17:11). If Paul, an inspired apostle, not only permits, but urges, men to *judge* his sayings by Scripture, much more should the fallible ministers of the present visible Church do so. **To wise men**—refers with a mixture of irony to the Corinthian boast of "wisdom" (ch. 4:40; II Cor. 11:19). Here you have an opportunity of exercising your "wisdom" in judging "what I say." **16. The cup of blessing**—answering to the Jewish "cup of blessing," over which thanks were offered in the Passover. It was in doing so that Christ instituted this part of the Lord's Supper (Matt. 26. 27; Luke 22:17, 20). **we bless**—"we," not merely

ministers, but also the congregation. The minister "blesses" (i.e., *consecrates with blessing*) the cup, not by any priestly transmitted authority of his own, but as representative of the congregation, who virtually through him bless the cup. The consecration is the corporate act of the whole Church. The act of *joint blessing* by him and them (not "the cup" itself, which, as also "the bread," in the *Greek* is in the accusative), and the consequent drinking of it together, constitute the communion, i.e., the joint participation "of the blood of Christ." Cf. vs. 18, "They who eat . . . are partakers" (joint communicants). "Is" in both cases in this verse is literal, not *represents*. He who with faith partakes of the cup and the bread, partakes really but spiritually of the blood and body of Christ (Eph. 5:30, 32), and of the benefits of His sacrifice on the cross (cf. vs. 18). In contrast to this is to have "fellowship with devils" (vs. 20). ALFORD explains, "The cup . . . is the [joint] participation (i.e., that whereby the act of participation takes place) of the blood . . . ." It is the seal of our living union with, and a means of our partaking of, Christ as our Saviour (John 6:53-57). It is not said, "The cup . . . is *the blood*," or "the bread . . . is *the body*," but "is the *communion* [joint-participation] of the blood . . . body." If the bread be changed into the literal body of Christ, where is the sign of the sacrament? Romanists eat Christ "*in remembrance* of Himself." To drink literal *blood* would have been an abomination to Jews, which the first Christians were (Lev. 17:11, 12). *Breaking the bread* was part of the act of consecrating it, for thus was represented the crucifixion of Christ's body (I Cor. 11:24). The distinct specification of the bread and the wine disproves the Romish doctrine of concomitancy, and exclusion of the laity from the cup. **17. one bread**—rather, "loaf." One loaf alone seems to have been used in each celebration. **and one body**—Omit "and"; "one loaf [that is], one body." "We, *the many*" (viz., believers assembled; so the *Greek*), are one bread (by our partaking of the same loaf, which becomes assimilated to the substance of all our bodies; and so we become), one body" (with Christ, and so with one another). **we . . . all**—*Greek*, "the whole of us." **18. Israel after the flesh**—the literal, as distinguished from the spiritual, Israel (Rom. 2: 29; 4:1; 9:3; Gal. 4:29). **partakers of the altar**—and so *of God*, whose is the altar; they have fellowship in God and His worship, of which the altar is the symbol. **19, 20. What say I then?**—The inference might be drawn from the analogies of the Lord's Supper and Jewish sacrifices, that an idol is *really what the heathen thought it to be, a god,* and that in eating idol meats they had fellowship with the god. This verse guards against such an inference: "What would I say then? that a thing sacrificed to an idol is any real thing (in the sense that the heathen regard it), or that an idol is any real thing?" (The oldest MSS. read the words in this order. Supply "*Nay*";) "But [I say] that the things which the Gentiles sacrifice, they sacrifice to devils" (demons). Paul here introduces a new fact. It is true that, as I said, an idol has no reality in the sense that the heathen regard it, but it has a reality in another sense; heathendom being under Satan's dominion as "prince of this world," *he* and *his demons* are in fact the powers worshipped by the heathen, whether they are or are not conscious of it (Deut. 32:17; Lev. 17:7; II Chron. 11:15; Ps. 106. 37; Rev. 9:20). "Devil" is in the *Greek* restricted to Satan; "demons" is the term applied to his subordinate evil spirits. Fear, rather than love, is the motive of heathen worship (cf. the English word "panic," from PAN, whose human form with horns and cloven hoofs gave rise to the vulgar representations of Satan which prevail now); just as fear is the spirit of Satan and his demons (Jas. 2:19). **I would not that ye . . . have fellowship with devils**—by partaking of idol feasts (ch. 8:10). **21. Ye cannot . . .**—really and spiritually; though ye may outwardly (I Kings 18:21). **cup of devils**—in contrast to *the cup of the Lord.* At idol feasts libations were usually made from the cup to the idol first, and then the guests drank; so that in drinking they had fellowship with the idol. **the Lord's table**—The Lord's Supper is a feast on a *table*, not a sacrifice on an altar. Our only altar is the cross, our only sacrifice that of Christ once for all. The Lord's Supper stands, however, in the same relation, analogically, to Christ's sacrifice, as the Jews' sacrificial feasts did to their sacrifices (cf. Mal. 1:7, "altar . . . table of the Lord"), and the heathen idol feasts to their idolatrous sacrifices (Isa. 65:11). The heathen sacrifices were offered to idol nonentities, behind which Satan lurked. The Jews' sacrifice was but a shadow of the substance which was to come. Our one sacrifice of Christ is the only substantial reality; therefore, while the partaker of the Jew's sacrificial feast partook rather "of the altar" (vs. 18) than of GOD manifested fully, and the heathen idol-feaster had fellowship really with demons, the communicant in the Lord's Supper has in it a real communion of, or fellowship in, the body of Christ once sacrificed, and now exalted as the Head of redeemed humanity. **22. Do we provoke the Lord to jealousy?**—by dividing our fellowship between Him and idols (Ezek. 20:39). Is it our wish to provoke Him to assert His power? Deuteronomy 32:21 is before the apostle's mind [ALFORD], (Exod. 20:5). **are we stronger?**—that we can risk a contest with Him. **23. All things are lawful for me . . .**—Recurring to the Corinthian plea (ch. 6:12), he repeats his qualification of it. The oldest MSS. omit both times "for me." **edify not**—tend not to *build up* the spiritual temple, the Church, in faith and love. Paul does not appeal to the apostolic decision (Acts 15), which seems to have been not so much regarded outside of Palestine, but rather to the broad principle of true Christian freedom, which does not allow us to be governed by external things, as though, because we *can* use them, we *must* use them (ch. 6:12). Their use or non-use is to be regulated by regard to *edification.* **24.** (Vs. 33; ch. 13:5; Rom. 15:1, 2.) **25. shambles**—butchers' stalls; the flesh-market. **asking no question**—whether it has been offered to an idol or not. **for conscience' sake** —If on asking you should hear it had been offered to idols, a scruple would arise in your conscience which was needless, and never would have arisen had you asked no questions. **26.** The ground on which such eating without questioning is justified is, the earth and all its contents ("the fulness thereof," Ps. 20:1; 50:12), including all meats, belong to the Lord, and are appointed for our use; and where conscience suggests no scruple, all are to be eaten (Rom. 14:14, 20; I Tim. 4:4, 5; cf. Acts 10:15). **27. ye be disposed to go**—tacitly implying, they would be as well not to go, but yet not forbidding them to go (vs. 9) [GROTIUS]. The feast is not an idol feast, but a general entertainment, at which, however, there might be meat that had been offered to an idol. **for conscience' sake**—See *Note,* vs. 25. **28. if any man**—a weak Christian at table, wishing to warn his brother. **offered in sacrifice unto idols** —The oldest MSS. omit "unto idols." At a

heathen's table the expression, offensive to him, would naturally be avoided. **for conscience' sake**—not to cause a stumbling block to the conscience of thy weak brother (ch. 8:10-12). **for the earth is the Lord's, . . .**—not in the oldest MSS. **29. Conscience . . . of the other**—the weak brother introduced in vs. 28. **for why is my liberty judged of another man's conscience?**—Paul passes to the first person, to teach his converts by putting himself as it were in their position. The *Greek* terms for "the other" and "another" are distinct. *"The other" is the one with whom Paul's and his Corinthian converts' concern is; "another" is any other with whom he and they have no concern.* If a guest know the meat to be idol meat while I know it not, I have "liberty" to eat without being condemned by his "conscience" [GROTIUS]. Thus the "for . . ." is an argument for vs. 27, "Eat, asking no questions." Or, Why should I give occasion to the rash use of my liberty that another should condemn it [ESTIUS], or that my liberty should cause the destruction of my weak brother?" [MENOCHIUS.] Or, the words are those of the Corinthian objector (perhaps used in their letter, and so quoted by Paul), "Why is my liberty judged by another's conscience?" Why should not I be judged only by my own, and have liberty to do whatever it sanctions? Paul replies in vs. 31, Your doing so ought always to be limited by regard to what most tends "to the glory of God" [VATABLUS, CONYBEARE and HOWSON]. The first explanation is simplest; the "for . . ." in it refers to "not thine own" (i.e., "not *my* own," in Paul's change to the first person); I am to abstain only in the case of liability to offend *another's* conscience; in cases where *my own* has no scruple, I am not bound, in God's judgment, by any other conscience than my own. **30. For**—The oldest MSS. omit "For." **by grace**—rather, "thankfully" [ALFORD]. **I . . . be partaker**—I partake of the food set before me. **evil spoken of**—by him who does not use his liberty, but will eat nothing without scrupulosity and questioning whence the meat comes. **give thanks**—which consecrates all the Christian's acts (Rom. 14:6; I Tim. 4:3, 4). **31.** Contrast Zechariah 7:6; the picture of worldly men. The godly may "eat and drink," and it shall be well with him (Jer. 22:15, 16). **to the glory of God**—(Col. 3:17; I Pet. 4:11)—which involves our having regard to the edification of our neighbor. **32. Give none offence**—in things indifferent (ch. 8:13; Rom. 14:13; II Cor. 6:3); for in all essential things affecting Christian doctrine and practice, even in the smallest *detail*, we must not swerve from principle, whatever offense may be the result (ch. 1:23). Giving offense is unnecessary, if our own spirit cause it; necessary, if it be caused by the truth. **33. I please**—I try to please (ch. 9:19, 22; Rom. 15:2). **not seeking mine own**—(vs. 24). **many**—rather as *Greek*, "THE many."

CHAPTER 11

Vss. 1-34. CENSURE ON DISORDERS IN THEIR ASSEMBLIES: THEIR WOMEN NOT BEING VEILED, AND ABUSES AT THE LOVE-FEASTS. **1.** Rather belonging to the end of ch. 10, than to this chapter. **followers** —*Greek*, "imitators." **of Christ**—who did not please Himself (Rom. 15:3); but gave Himself, at the cost of laying aside His divine glory, and dying as man, for us (Eph. 5:2; Phil. 2:4, 5). We are to follow Christ first, and earthly teachers only so far as they follow Christ. **2.** Here the chapter ought to begin.

ye remember me in all things—in your *general* practice, though in the *particular* instances which follow ye fail. **ordinances**—*Greek*, "traditions," i.e., apostolic directions given by word of mouth or in writing (vs. 23; ch. 15:3; II Thess. 2:15). The reference here is mainly to *ceremonies:* for in vs. 23, as to the LORD'S SUPPER, which is not a mere ceremony, he says, not merely, "I *delivered* unto you," but also, "I *received* of the Lord"; here he says only, "I delivered to you." Romanists argue hence for oral traditions. But the difficulty is to know *what is a* genuine apostolic tradition intended for all ages. Any that can be *proved* to be such ought to be observed; any that cannot, ought to be rejected (Rev. 22:18). Those preserved in the written word alone can be proved to be such. **3.** The Corinthian women, on the ground of the abolition of distinction of sexes in Christ, claimed equality with the male sex, and, overstepping the bounds of propriety, came forward to pray and prophesy without the customary headcovering of females. The Gospel, doubtless, did raise women from the degradation in which they had been sunk, especially in the East. Yet, while on a level with males as to *the offer of, and standing in grace* (Gal. 3:28), their subjection in point of *order, modesty,* and *seemliness,* is to be maintained. Paul reproves here their unseemliness as to *dress:* in ch. 14:34, as to the retiring *modesty in public* which becomes them. He grounds his reproof here on the subjection of woman to man in the order of creation. **the head**—an appropriate expression, when he is about to treat of woman's appropriate *headdress* in public. **of every man ... Christ**—(Eph. 5:23). **of ... woman ... man**—(V.8; Gen. 3:16; I Tim. 2:11, 12; I Pet. 3:1, 5, 6). **head of Christ is God**—(ch. 3: 23; 15:27, 28; Luke 3:22, 38; John 14:28; 20:17; Eph. 3:9). "Jesus, therefore, must be of the same essence as God: for, since the man is the head of the woman, and since the head is of the same essence as the body, and God is the head of the Son, it follows the Son is of the same essence as the Father" [S. CHRYSOSTOM]. "The woman is of the essence of the man, and not made by the man; so, too, the Son is not made by the Father, but of the essence of the Father" [THEODORET, t. 3, p. 171]. **4. praying**—in public (vs. 17). **prophesying**—preaching in the Spirit (ch. 12:10). **having**—i.e., if he were to have: a supposed case to illustrate the impropriety in the *woman's* case. It was the Greek custom (and so that at Corinth) for men in worship to be uncovered; whereas the Jews wore the Talith, or veil, to show reverence before God, and their unworthiness to look on Him (Isa. 6:2); however, Maimonides (*Mishna*) excepts cases where (as in Greece) the custom of the place was different. **dishonoureth his head**—not as ALFORD, "Christ" (vs. 3): but literally, as "his head" is used in the beginning of the verse. *He dishonoreth his head* (the principal part of the body) by wearing a covering or veil, which is a mark of subjection, and which makes him look downwards instead of upwards to his Spiritual Head, Christ, to whom alone he owes subjection. Why, then, ought not man to wear the covering in token of his subjection to Christ, as the woman wears it in token of her subjection to man? "Because Christ is not seen: the man is seen; so the covering of him who is under Christ is not seen; of her who is under the man, is seen" [BENGEL]. (Cf. vs. 7.) **5. woman ... prayeth ... prophesieth** —This instance of women speaking in public worship is an extraordinary case, and justified only by the miraculous gifts which such women possessed

as their credentials; for instance, Anna the prophetess and Priscilla (so Acts 2:18). The ordinary rule to them is: silence in public (ch. 14:34, 35; I Tim. 2:11, 12). Mental receptivity and activity in family life are recognized in Christianity, as most accordant with the destiny of woman. This passage does not necessarily sanction women speaking in public. even though possessing miraculous gifts; but simply records what took place at Corinth, without expressing an opinion on it, reserving the censure of it till ch. 14:34, 35. Even those women endowed with prophecy were designed to exercise their gift, rather in other times and places, than the public congregation. **dishonoureth ... head**—in that she acts against the divine ordinance and the modest propriety that becomes her: in putting away the veil, she puts away the badge of her subjection to man, which is her true "honor"; for through him it connects her with Christ, the head of the man. Moreover, as the *head-covering* was the emblem of maiden modesty before man (Gen. 24:65), and conjugal chastity (Gen. 20:16); so, to *uncover the head* indicated withdrawal from the *power* of the husband, whence a suspected wife had her head *uncovered* by the priest (Num. 5:18). ALFORD takes "her head" to be man, her symbolical, not her literal head; but as it is literal in the former clause, it must be so in the latter one. **all one as if ... shaven** —As woman's hair is given her by nature, as her covering (vss. 15), to cut it off like a man, all admit, would be indecorous: therefore, to put away the head-covering, too, like a man, would be similarly indecorous. It is *natural* to her to have long hair for her covering: she ought, therefore, to add the other (the wearing of a head-covering) to show that she does of *her own will* that which *nature* itself teaches she ought to do, in token of her subjection to man. **6.** A woman would not like to be "shorn" or (what is worse) "shaven"; but if she chooses to be uncovered (unveiled) in front, let her be so also behind, i.e., "shorn." **a shame**—an unbecoming thing (cf. vss. 13-15). Thus the shaving of nuns is "a shame." **7-9.** Argument, also, from man's more immediate relation to God, and the woman's to man. **man ... image ... glory of God**—being created in God's "image," *first* and *directly:* the woman, *subsequently,* and *indirectly,* through the mediation of man. Man is the representative of God's "glory" this ideal of man being realized most fully in the Son of man (Ps. 8:4, 5; cf. II Cor. 8:23). Man is declared in Scripture to be both the "image," and in the "likeness," of God (cf. Jas. 3:9). But "image" alone is applied to the Son of God (Col. 1:15; cf. Heb. 1:3). "Express image," *Greek*, "the impress." The Divine Son is not merely "*like*" God, He is God of God, "being of one substance (essence) with the Father." [NICENE CREED]. **woman ... glory of ... man**—He does not say, also, "*the image* of the man." For the sexes differ: moreover, the woman is created in the *image of God*, as well as the man (Gen. 1:26, 27). But as the moon in relation to the sun (Gen. 37:9), so woman shines not so much with light direct from God, as with light derived from man, i.e., *in her order in creation;* not that she does not *in grace* come individually into *direct* communion with God; but even here much of her knowledge is mediately given her through man, on whom she is naturally dependent. **8. is of ... of**—*takes his being from* ("out of") ... *from:* referring to woman's original creation, "taken out of man" (cf. Gen. 2:23). The woman was made by God mediately through the man, who was, as it were, a veil or medium placed between her and God, and therefore, should wear the veil or head-covering in public worship, in acknowledgement of this subordination to man in the order of creation. The man being made immediately by God as His glory, has no veil between himself and God [FABER STAPULENSIS *in Bengel*]. **9. Neither**—rather, "For also"; *Another argument: The immediate object of woman's creation.* "The man was not created for the sake of the woman; but the woman for the sake of the man" (Gen. 2:18, 21, 22). Just as the Church, the bride, is made for Christ; and yet in both the natural and the spiritual creations, the bride, while made for the bridegroom, in fulfilling that end, attains her own true "glory," and brings "shame" and "dishonor" on herself by any departure from it (vss. 4, 6). **10. power on her head**—the kerchief: French *couvre-chef, head-covering, the emblem* of "power on her head"; the sign of her being under man's power, and exercising delegated authority under him. Paul had before his mind the root-connection between the *Hebrew* terms for "veil" *(radid)*, and subjection *(radad)*. **because of the angels**—who are present at our Christian assemblies (cf. Ps. 138:1, "gods," i.e., *angels*), and delight in the orderly subordination of the several ranks of God's worshippers in their respective places, the outward demeanor and dress of the latter being indicative of that inward humility which angels know to be most pleasing to their common Lord (ch. 4:9; Eph. 3:10; Eccles. 5:6). HAMMOND quotes Chrysostom, "Thou standest with angels; thou singest with them; thou hymnest with them; and yet dost thou stand laughing?" BENGEL explains, "As the angels are in relation to God, so the woman is in relation to man. God's face is uncovered; angels in His presence are veiled (Isa. 6:2). Man's face is uncovered; woman in His presence is to be veiled. For her not to be so, would, by its indecorousness, offend the angels (Matt. 18: 10, 31). She, by her weakness, especially needs their ministry; she ought, therefore, to be the more careful not to offend them." **11.** Yet neither sex is insulated and independent of the other in the Christian life [ALFORD]. The one needs the other in the sexual relation; and in respect to Christ ("in the Lord"), the man and the woman together (for neither can be dispensed with) realize the ideal of redeemed humanity represented by the bride, the Church. **12.** As the woman was formed *out of* (from) the man, even so is man born *by means of* woman; but all things (including both man and woman) are *from* God as their source (Rom. 11:36; II Cor. 5:18). They depend mutually each on the other, and both on him. **13.** Appeal to their own sense of decorum. **a woman ... unto God**—By rejecting the emblem of subjection (the head-covering), she passes at one leap in praying publicly beyond both the *man* and *angels* [BENGEL]. **14.** The fact that nature has provided woman, and not man, with long hair, proves that man was designed to be uncovered, and woman covered. The Nazarite, however, wore long hair lawfully, as being part of a vow sanctioned by God (Num. 6:5). Cf. as to Absalom, II Samuel 14:26, and Acts 18:18. **15. her hair ... for a covering**—Not that she does not need additional covering. Nay, her long hair shows she ought to cover her head as much as possible. The will ought to accord with nature [BENGEL]. **16.** A summary close to the argument by appeal to the universal custom of the churches. **if any ... seem**—The *Greek* also means *"thinks"* (fit) (cf. Matt. 3:9). If any man *chooses* (still after all my arguments) to be contentious. If any be

contentious and *thinks* himself *right* in being so. A reproof of the Corinthians' self-sufficiency and disputatiousness (ch. 1:20). **we**—apostles: or we of the Jewish nation, from whom ye have received the Gospel, and whose usages in all that is good ye ought to follow: Jewish women veiled themselves when in public, according to Tertullian [ESTIUS]. The former explanation is best, as the Jews are not referred to in the context: but he often refers to himself and his fellow apostles, by the expression, "we—us" (ch. 4:9, 10). **no such custom**—as that of women praying uncovered. Not as CHRYSOSTOM, "that of being contentious." The *Greek* term implies a *usage,* rather than a *mental habit* (John 18:39). The usage of true "churches" (plural: not, as Rome uses it, 'the Church,' as an abstract entity; but *'the churches,* as a number of *independent witnesses)* of God" (the churches which God Himself recognizes), is a valid argument *in the case of external rites,* especially, *negatively,* e.g., Such rites were not received among them, therefore, ought not to be admitted among us: but in questions of *doctrine,* or the *essentials of worship,* the argument is not valid [SCLATER] (ch. 7:17; 14: 33). **neither**—nor yet. Catholic usage is not an infallible test of *truth,* but a general test of *decency.* **17. in this**—which follows. **I declare**—rather, "I enjoin"; as the *Greek* is always so used. The oldest MSS. read literally "This I enjoin (you) not praising (you)." **that**—*inasmuch as: in that* you ... Here he qualifies his praise (vs. 2). "I said that I praised you for keeping the ordinances delivered to you; but I must now give injunction in the name of the Lord, on a matter in which I praise you not; viz., as to the Lord's Supper (vs. 23; ch. 14:37). **not for the better**—not so as to progress to what is better. **for the worse**—so as to retrograde to what is worse. The result of such "coming together" must be "condemnation" (vs. 34). **18. first of all**—In the first place. The "divisions" (*Greek, "schisms"*) meant, are not merely those of opinion (ch. 1:10), but in outward acts at the lovefeasts (*Agapæ*), (vs. 21). He does not follow up the expression, "in the first place," by "in the second place." But though not expressed, a *second* abuse was in his mind when he said, "In the first place," viz., THE ABUSE OF SPIRITUAL GIFTS, *which also created disorder in their assemblies* [ALFORD], (ch. 12:1; 14:23, 26, 33, 40). **in the church**—not the place of worship; for Isidore of Pelusium denies that there were such places specially set apart for worship in the apostles' times (*Epistle* 246.2). But, "in the assembly" or "congregation"; in convocation for worship, where especially love, order, and harmony should prevail. The very ordinance instituted for uniting together believers in one body, was made an occasion of "divisions" (schisms). **partly**—He hereby excepts the innocent. "I am unwilling to believe *all* I hear, but *some* I cannot help believing" [ALFORD]: while my love is unaffected by it [BENGEL]. **19. heresies**—Not merely "schisms" or "divisions" (vs. 18), which are *"recent dissensions of the congregation through differences of opinion"* [AUGUSTINE, *Con. Crescon. Don.* 2. 7, quoted by *French Synonyms, New Testament*], but also "heresies," i.e., "schisms which have now become *inveterate"*; "Sects" [CAMPBELL, vol. 2, pp. 126, 127]: so Acts 5:17; 15:5 translate the same *Greek.* At present there were dissensions at the love-feasts; but Paul, remembering Jesus' words (Matt. 18:7; 24:10, 12; Luke 17:1) foresees "there must be (come) also" *matured separations,* and established parties in secession, as separatists. The "must be" arises from sin in professors necessarily bearing its natural fruits: these are overruled by God to the probation of character of both the godly and the ungodly, and to the discipline of the former for glory. "Heresies" had not yet its technical sense ecclesiastically, referring to doctrinal errors: it means *confirmed schisms*. St. Augustine's rule is a golden rule as regards questions of heresy and catholicity: "In doubtful questions, liberty; in essentials, unity; in all things, charity." **that ... approved may be made manifest**—through the *disapproved* (reprobates) becoming manifested (Luke 2:35; I John 2:19). **20. When ... therefore**—Resuming the thread of discourse from vs. 18. *this* **is not to**—rather, "there is no such thing as eating the LORD's Supper"; *it is not possible* where each is greedily intent only on devouring "HIS OWN supper," and some are excluded altogether, not having been waited for (vs. 33), where some are "drunken," while others are "hungry" (vs. 21). The lovefeast usually preceded the Lord's Supper (as eating the Passover came before the Lord's Supper at the first institution of the latter). It was a club-feast, where each brought his portion, and the rich, extra portions for the poor; from it the bread and wine were taken for the Eucharist; and it was at it that the excesses took place, which made a *true* celebration of the Lord's Supper during or after it, with true discernment of its solemnity, out of the question. **21. one taketh before** *other*—the rich "before" the poor, who had no supper of their own. Instead of "tarrying for one another" (vs. 33); hence the precept (ch. 12: 21, 25). **his own supper**—"His own" belly is his God (Phil. 3:19); "the *Lord's* Supper," the spiritual feast, never enters his thoughts. **drunken**—The one has more than is good for him, the other less [BENGEL]. **22. What!**—*Greek*, "For." **houses**—(cf. vs. 34)—"at home." That is the place to satiate the appetite, not the assembly of the brethren [ALFORD]. **despise ye the church of God**—*the congregation* mostly composed of the poor, whom "GOD hath chosen," however ye show contempt for them (Jas. 2:5); cf. "of God" here, marking the true honor of the Church. **shame them that have not**—viz., *houses* to eat and drink in, and who, therefore, ought to have received their portion at the love-feasts from their wealthier brethren. **I praise you not**—resuming the words (vs. 17). **23.** His object is to show the unworthiness of such conduct from the dignity of the holy supper. **23. I**—Emphatic in the *Greek*. It is not *my own* invention, but the Lord's institution. **received of the Lord**—by immediate revelation (Gal. 1:12; cf. Acts 22:17, 18; II Cor. 12:1-4). The renewal of the institution of the Lord's Supper by special revelation to Paul enhances its solemnity. The similarity between Luke's and Paul's account of the institution, favors the supposition that the former drew his information from the apostle, whose companion in travel he was. Thus, the undesigned coincidence is a proof of genuineness. **night**—the time fixed for the Passover (Exod. 12:6): though the time for the Lord's Supper is not fixed. **betrayed**—With the traitor at the table, and death present before His eyes, He left this ordinance as His last gift to us, to commemorate His death. Though about to receive such an injury from man, He gave this pledge of His amazing love to man. **24. brake**—The *breaking* of the bread involves its *distribution* and reproves the Corinthian mode at the love-feast, of "every one taking before other his own supper." **my body ... broken for you**—"given" (Luke 22:19) for you (*Greek*, "in your behalf"), and "broken," so

as to be distributed among you. The oldest MSS. omit "broken," leaving it to be supplied from "brake." The two old versions, Memphitic and Thebaic, read from Luke, "given." The literal "body" could not have been meant; for Christ was still sensibly present among His disciples when He said, "This is My body." They *could* only have understood Him symbolically and analogically: As this bread is to your bodily health, so My body is to the spiritual health of the believing communicant. The words, Take, eat," are not in the oldest MSS. **25. when he had supped**—*Greek*, "after the eating of supper," viz., the Passover supper which preceded the Lord's Supper, as the love-feast did subsequently. Therefore, you Corinthians ought to separate common meals from the Lord's Supper [BENGEL]. **the new testament**—or "covenant." The cup is the parchment-deed, as it were, on which My new covenant, or last will is written and sealed, making over to you all blessings here and hereafter. **in my blood**—ratified by MY blood: "not by the blood of goats and calves" (Heb. 9:12).—**as oft as**—*Greek*, "as many times soever": implying that it is an ordinance *often* to be partaken of. **in remembrance of me**—Luke expresses this, which is understood by Matthew and Mark. Paul twice records it as suiting his purpose. The old sacrifices brought *sins* continually to remembrance (Heb. 10:1, 3). The Lord's Supper brings to remembrance *Christ* and His sacrifice once for all for the full and final *remission of sins*. **26. For**—in proof that the Lord's Supper is "in remembrance" of Him. **show**—*announce publicly*. The *Greek* does not mean to dramatically *represent*, but "ye publicly profess each of you, the Lord has died FOR ME" [WAHL]. This word, as "is" in Christ's institution (vss. 24, 25), implies not *literal* presence, but a *vivid realization, by faith*, of Christ in the Lord's Supper, as a living person, not a mere abstract dogma, "bone of our bone, and flesh of our flesh" (Eph. 5:30; cf. Gen. 2:23); and ourselves "members of His body, of His flesh, and of His bones," "our sinful bodies made clean by His body (once for all offered), and our souls washed through His most precious blood" [*Church of England Prayer Book*]. "Show," or "announce," is an expression applicable to *new* things; cf. "show" as to the Passover (Exod. 13:8). So the Lord's death ought always to be fresh in our memory; cf. in heaven, Revelation 5:6. That the Lord's Supper is in *remembrance* of Him, implies that He is bodily absent, though spiritually present, for we cannot be said to commemorate one absent. The fact that we not only show the Lord's death in the supper, but *eat* and *drink* the pledges of it, could only be understood by the Jews, accustomed to such feasts after propitiatory sacrifices, as implying our *personal appropriation* therein of the benefits of that death. **till he come**—when there shall be no longer need of symbols of His body, the body itself being manifested. The *Greek* expresses the *certainly* of His coming. Rome teaches that we eat Christ present corporally, "till He come" corporally; a contradiction in terms. The shew-bread, lit., "bread of the presence," was in the sanctuary, but not in the Holiest Place (Heb. 9:1-8); so the Lord's Supper in heaven, the antitype to the Holiest Place, shall be superseded by Christ's own bodily presence; then the wine shall be drunk "anew" in the Father's kingdom, by Christ and His people together, of which heavenly banquet, the Lord's Supper is a spiritual foretaste and specimen (Matt. 26:29). Meantime, as the shewbread was placed *new*, every sabbath, on the table before the

Lord (Lev. 24:5-8); so the Lord's death was *shown,* or announced *afresh* at the Lord's table the first day of every week in the primitive Church. We are now "priests unto God" in the dispensation of Christ's spiritual presence, antitypical to the HOLY PLACE: the perfect and eternal dispensation, which shall not begin till Christ's coming, is antitypical to the HOLIEST PLACE, which Christ our High Priest alone in the flesh as yet has entered (Heb. 9:6, 7); but which, at His coming, we, too, who are believers, shall enter (Rev. 7:15; 21:22). The supper joins the two closing periods of the Old and the New dispensations. The first and second comings are considered as *one* coming, whence the expression is not "return," but "come" (cf., however, John 14:3). **27. eat and drink**—So one of the oldest MSS. reads. But three or four equally old MSS., the *Vulgate* and Cyprian, read, "or." Romanists quote this reading in favor of communion in one kind. This consequence does not follow. Paul says, "Whosoever is guilty of unworthy conduct, *either* in eating the bread, *or* in drinking the cup, is guilty of the body and blood of Christ." Impropriety in only *one* of the two elements, vitiates true communion in *both.* Therefore, in the end of the verse, he says, not "body *or* blood," but "body and blood." Any who takes the bread without the wine, *or* the wine without the bread, *"unworthily"* communicates, and so "is guilty of Christ's body and blood"; for he disobeys Christ's express command to partake of both. If we do not partake of the sacramental symbol of the Lord's death worthily, we share in the guilt of that death. (Cf. "crucify to themselves the Son of God afresh," Heb. 6:6.) *Unworthiness in the person,* is not what ought to exclude any, but *unworthily communicating:* However unworthy we be, if we examine ourselves so as to find that we penitently believe in Christ's Gospel, we may worthily communicate. **28. examine**—Greek, "prove" or "test" his own state of mind in respect to Christ's death, and his capability of "discerning the Lord's body" (vss. 29, 31). Not auricular confession to a priest, but self-examination is necessary. **so**—after due self-examination. **of . . . of**—In vs. 27, where the receiving was *unworthily,* the expression was, "eat this bread, drink . . . cup" without "of." Here the "of" implies due circumspection in communicating [BENGEL]. **let him eat**—His self-examination is not in order that he may stay away, but that he may eat, i.e., communicate. **29. damnation**—A mistranslation which has put a stumbling block in the way of many in respect to communicating. The right translation is "judgment." The *judgment* is described (vss. 30-32) as temporal. **not discerning**—*not duty judging: not distinguishing in judgment* (so the *Greek:* the sin and its punishment thus being marked as corresponding) from common food, the sacramental pledges of the Lord's body. Most of the oldest MSS. omit "Lord's" (see vs. 27). Omitting also "unworthily," with most of the oldest MSS., we must translate, "He that eateth and drinketh, eateth and drinketh judgment to himself, IF he discern not the body" (Heb. 10:29). The Church is "the body of *Christ*" (ch. 12:27). The Lord's body is *His literal body* appreciated and discerned by the soul in the faithful receiving, and not present in the elements themselves. **30. weak . . . sickly**—He is "weak" who has *naturally* no strength: "sickly," who has *lost his strength* by disease [TITTM. *Synonyms*]. **sleep**—are being lulled in death: not a violent death; but one the result of sickness, sent as the Lord's chastening for the individual's salvation, the mind

being brought to a right state on the sick bed (vs. 31). **31. if we would judge ourselves**—Most of the oldest MSS. read "But," not "For." Translate also literally "If we duly judged ourselves, we should not be (or *not have been*) judged," i.e., we should escape (or *have escaped*) our present judgments. In order to *duly judge* or "discern [appreciate] the Lord's body," we need to "duly judge ourselves." A prescient warning against the dogma of priestly absolution after full confession, as the necessary preliminary to receiving the Lord's Supper. **32. chastened**—(Rev. 3:19). **with the world**—who, being bastards, are without chastening (Heb. 12:8). **33. tarry one for another**—In contrast to vs. 21. The expression is not, "Give a share to one another," for all the viands brought to the feast were *common* property, and, therefore, they should "tarry" till all were met to partake together of the common feast of fellowship [THEOPHYL]. **34. if any . . . hunger** —so as not to be able to "tarry for others," let him take off the edge of his hunger at home [ALFORD] (vs. 22). **the rest**—"the other questions you asked me as to the due celebration of the Lord's Supper." Not other questions in *general;* for he does subsequently set in order other general questions in this Epistle.

CHAPTER 12

Vss. 1-31. THE USE AND THE ABUSE OF SPIRITUAL GIFTS, ESPECIALLY PROPHESYING AND TONGUES. This is the *second* subject for correction in the Corinthian assemblies: the *"first"* was discussed (ch. 11: 18-34). **1. spiritual gifts**—the signs of the Spirit's continued efficacious presence in the Church, which is Christ's body, the complement of His incarnation, as the body is the complement of the head. By the love which pervades the whole, the gifts of the several members, forming reciprocal complements to each other, tend to the one object of perfecting the body of Christ. The ordinary and permanent gifts are comprehended together with the extraordinary, without distinction specified, as both alike flow from the divine indwelling Spirit of life. The extraordinary gifts, so far from making professors more peculiarly *saints* than in our day, did not always even *prove* that such persons were in a safe state at all (Matt. 7:22). They were needed at first in the Church: (1) as a pledge to Christians themselves who had just passed over from Judaism or heathendom, that God was in the Church; (2) for the propagation of Christianity in the world; (3) for the edification of the Church. Now that we have the whole *written* New Testament (which they had not) and Christianity established as the result of the miracles, we need no further miracle to attest the truth. So the pillar of cloud which guided the Israelites was withdrawn when they were sufficiently assured of the Divine Presence, the manifestation of God's glory being thenceforward enclosed in the Most Holy Place [ARCHBISHOP WHATELY]. Paul sets forth in order: I. The unity of the body (vss. 1-27). II. The variety of its members and functions (vss. 27-30). III. The grand principle for the right exercise of the gifts, viz., love (vs. 31, and ch. 13). IV. The comparison of the gifts with one another (ch. 14). **I would not have you ignorant**—with all your boasts of "knowledge" at Corinth. If ignorant now, it will be your own fault, not mine (ch. 14:38). **2. (Eph. 2:11.) that ye were** —The best MSS. read, "That WHEN ye were"; thus "ye were" must be supplied before "carried away"

—Ye were blindly transported hither and thither at the will of your false guides. **these dumb idols**—Greek, "*the* idols which are dumb"; contrasted with the living God who "speaks" in the believer by His Spirit (vs. 3, etc.). This gives the reason why the Corinthians needed instruction as to spiritual gifts, viz., their past heathen state, wherein they had no experience of intelligent spiritual powers. When blind, ye went to the *dumb*. **as ye were led**—The Greek is, rather, "as ye might (happen to) be led," viz., on different occasions. The heathen oracles led their votaries at random, without any definite principle. **3.** The negative and positive criteria of inspiration by the Spirit—the rejection or confession of Jesus as Lord [ALFORD] (I John 4:2; 5:1). Paul gives a test of truth against the Gentiles; John, against the false prophets. **by the Spirit**—rather, as Greek, "IN the Spirit"; that being the power pervading him, and the element *in* which he speaks [ALFORD], (Matt. 16:17; John 15:26). **of God ... Holy**—The same Spirit is called at one time "the Spirit of GOD"; at another, "the HOLY Ghost," or "Holy Spirit." Infinite *Holiness* is almost synonymous with *Godhead*. **speaking ... say**—"Speak" implies the act of utterance; "say" refers to that which is uttered. Here, "say" means a *spiritual* and *believing* confession of Him. **Jesus**—not an abstract doctrine, but the historical, living God-man (Rom. 10:9). **accursed**—as the Jews and Gentiles treated Him (Gal. 3:13). Cf. "to curse Christ" in the heathen PLINY's letter (*Ep.* 10. 97). The spiritual man feels Him to be the Source of all blessings (Eph. 1:3) and to be severed from Him is to be accursed (Rom. 9:3). **Lord**—acknowledging himself as His servant (Isa. 26:13). "Lord" is the LXX *translation* for the incommunicable Hebrew name JEHOVAH. **4. diversities of gifts**—i.e., varieties of spiritual endowments peculiar to the several members of the Church: cf. "dividing to every man severally" (vs. 11). **same Spirit**—The Holy Trinity appears here: the *Holy Spirit* in this verse; *Christ* in vs. 5; and *the Father* in vs. 6. The terms "gifts," "administrations," and "operations," respectively correspond to the Divine Three. *The Spirit* is treated of in vs. 7, etc.; *the Lord*, in vs. 12, etc.; *God*, in vs. 28. (Cf. Eph. 4:4-6.) **5, 6.** "Gifts" (vs. 4), "administrations" (the various *functions* and *services* performed by those having the gifts, cf. vs. 28), and "operations" (the actual *effects* resulting from both the former, through the universally operative power of the one Father who is "above all, through all, and in us all"), form an ascending climax [HENDERSON, *Inspiration*]. **same Lord**—whom the Spirit glorifies by these *ministrations* [BENGEL]. **6. operations**—(Cf. vs. 10). **same God ... worketh**—by His Spirit *working* (vs. 11). **all in all**—all of them (the "gifts") in all the persons (who possess them). **7. But**—Though all the gifts flow from the *one* God, Lord, and Spirit, the "manifestation" by which the Spirit acts (as He is hidden in Himself), varies in each individual. **to every man**—*to each* of the members of the Church *severally*. **to profit withal**—*with a view to the profit* of the whole body. **8-10.** Three classes of gifts are distinguished by a distinct Greek word for "another" (*a distinct class*), marking the three several *genera: allo* marks the species, *hetero* the genera (cf. Greek, ch. 15:39-41). I. Gifts of intellect, viz., (1) wisdom; (2) knowledge. II. Gifts dependent on a special *faith*, viz., that of miracles (Matt. 17:20): (1) healings; (2) workings of miracles; (3) prophecy of future events; (4) discerning of spirits, or the divinely given faculty of distinguishing between those really inspired, and those who

pretended to inspiration. III. Gifts referring to the *tongues:* (1) diverse kinds of tongues; (2) interpretation of tongues. The catalogue in vs. 28 is not meant strictly to harmonize with the one here, though there are some particulars in which they correspond. The three genera are summarily referred to by single instances of each in ch. 13:8. The first genus refers more to believers; the second, to unbelievers. **by ... by ... by**—The first in Greek is, "By means of," or "through the operation of"; the second is, "according to" the disposing of (cf. vs. 11); the third is, "in," i.e., *under the influence of* (so the *Greek,* Matt. 22:43; Luke 2:27). **word of wisdom**—the ready *utterance* of (for imparting to others, Eph. 6:19) *wisdom,* viz., new revelations of the divine wisdom in redemption, as contrasted with human philosophy (ch. 1:24; 2:6, 7; Eph. 1:8; 3:10; Col. 2:3). **word of knowledge**—ready *utterance supernaturally* imparted of truths ALREADY REVEALED (in this it is distinguished from "the word of wisdom," which related to NEW revelations). Cf. ch. 14:6, where "revelation" (answering to "wisdom" here) is distinguished from "knowledge" [HENDERSON]. *Wisdom* or *revelation* belonged to the "prophets"; *knowledge,* to the "teachers." *Wisdom* penetrates deeper than *knowledge. Knowledge* relates to things that are to be done. *Wisdom,* to things eternal: hence, *wisdom* is not, like *knowledge,* said to "pass away" (ch. 13:8), [BENGEL]. **9. faith**—not of doctrines, but of miracles: confidence in God, by the impulse of His Spirit, that He would enable them to perform any required miracle (cf. ch. 13:2; Mark 11:23; Jas. 5:15). Its nature, or principle, is the same as that of saving faith, viz., reliance on God; the producing cause, also, in the same, viz., a power altogether supernatural (Eph. 1:19, 20). But the objects of faith differ respectively. Hence, we see, saving faith does not save by its instrinsic merit, but by the merits of Him who is the obpect of it. **healing**—Greek plural, "healings"; referring to different kinds of disease which need different kinds of healing (Matt. 10:1). **10. working of miracles**—As "healings" are miracles, those here meant must refer to miracles of special and extraordinary POWER (so the Greek for "miracles" means); e.g., healings might be effected by human skill in course of time; but the raising of the dead, the infliction of death by a word, the innocuous use of poisons, etc., are *miracles of special power.* Cf. Mark 6:5; Acts. 19:11. **prophecy**—Here, probably, not in the wider sense of public teaching by the Spirit (ch. 11:4, 5; 14:1-5, 22-39); but, as its position between "miracles" and a "discerning of spirits" implies, *the inspired disclosure of the future* (Acts 11:27, 28; 21:11; I Tim. 1:18), [HENDERSON]. It depends on "faith" (vs. 9; Rom. 12:6). The *prophets* ranked next to the *apostles* (vs. 28; Eph. 3:5; 4:11). As *prophecy* is part of the whole scheme of redemption, an inspired insight into the obscurer parts of the existing Scriptures, was the necessary preparation for the miraculous foresight of the future. **discerning of spirits**—discerning between the operation of God's Spirit, and the evil spirit, or unaided human spirit (ch. 14: 29; cf. I Tim. 4:1; I John 4:1). **kinds of tongues**—the power of speaking *various languages:* also a *spiritual language unknown to man, uttered in ecstasy* (ch. 14:2-12). This is marked as a distinct genus in the *Greek,* "To another and a *different* class." **interpretation of tongues**—(ch. 14:13, 26, 27). **11. as he will**—(vs. 18; Heb. 2:4). **12, 13.** Unity, not unvarying uniformity, is the law of God in the world of grace, as in that of nature. As the many members of the body compose an organic whole and none can be dispensed with as needless, so those variously gifted by the Spirit, compose a spiritual organic whole, the body of Christ, into which all are baptized by the one Spirit. **of that one body**—Most of the oldest MSS. omit "one." **so also is Christ**—i.e, the whole Christ, *the head and body*. So Psalm 18:50, "His anointed (Messiah or Christ), David (the antitypical David) and His seed." **by ... Spirit ... baptized**—lit., "in"; in virtue of; through. The *designed* effect of baptism, which is realized when not frustrated by the unfaithfulness of man. **Gentiles**—lit., "Greeks." **all made to drink into one Spirit**—The oldest MSS. read, "Made to drink of one Spirit," omitting "into" (John 7:37). There is an indirect allusion to the Lord's Supper, as there is a direct allusion to baptism in the beginning of the verse. So the "Spirit, the water, and the blood" (I John 5:8), similarly combine the two outward signs with the inward things signified, the Spirit's grace. **are ... have been**—rather as *Greek*, "were ... were" (the past tense). **14.** Translate, "For the body *also*." The analogy of the body, not consisting exclusively of one, but of many members, illustrates the mutual dependence of the various members in the one body, the Church. The well-known fable of the belly and the other members, spoken by Menenius Agrippa, to the seceding commons [LIVY, 2. 32], was probably before Paul's mind, stored as it was with classical literature. **15.** The humbler members ought not to disparage themselves, or to be disparaged by others more noble (vss. 21, 22). **foot ... hand**—The humble speaks of the more honorable member which most nearly resembles itself: so the "ear" of the "eye" (the nobler and more commanding member, Num. 10:31), (vs. 16). As in life each compares himself with those whom he approaches nearest in gifts, not those far superior. The *foot* and *hand* represent men of active life; the *ear* and *eye*, those of contemplative life. **17.** Superior as the *eye* is, it would not do if it were the sole member to the exclusion of the rest. **18. now**—as the case really is. **every one**—each severally. **19. where were the body**—which, by its very idea, "hath many members" (vss. 12, 14), [ALFORD]. **20. now**—as the case really is: in contrast to the supposition (vs. 19; cf. vs. 18). **many members**—mutually dependent. **21.** The higher cannot dispense with the lower members. **22. more feeble**—more susceptible of injury: e.g., the brain, the belly, the eye. Their very feebleness, so far from doing away with the need for them, calls forth our greater care for their preservation, as being felt "necessary." **23. less honourable**—"We think" the feet and the belly "less honorable," though not really so in the nature of things. **bestow ... honour**—*putting* shoes *on* (*Margin*) the feet, and clothes to cover the belly. **uncomely parts** —the secret parts: the poorest, though unclad in the rest of the body, cover these. **24. tempered ... together**—on the principle of mutual compensation. **to that part which lacked**—to the deficient part [ALFORD], (vs. 23). **25. no schism** (cf. vs. 21)— no disunion; referring to the "divisions" noticed (ch. 11:18). **care one for another**—i.e., *in behalf of* one another. **26. And**—Accordingly. **all ... suffer with it**—"When a thorn enters the heel, the whole body feels it, and is concerned: the back bends, the belly and thighs contract themselves, the hands come forward and draw out the thorn, the head stoops, and the eyes regard the affected member with intense gaze" [CHRYSOSTOM]. **rejoice with it** —"When the head is crowned, the whole man feels

honored, the mouth expresses, and the eyes look, gladness" [CHRYSOSTOM]. **27. members in particular**—i.e., severally members of it. Each church is in miniature what the whole aggregate of churches is collectively, "the body of Christ" (cf. ch. 3:16): and its individual components are members, every one in his assigned place. **28. set ... in the church** —as He has "set the members ... in the body" (vs. 18). **first apostles**—above even the *prophets*. Not merely the *Twelve*, but others are so called, e.g., Barnabas, etc. (Rom. 16:7). **teachers**—who taught, for the most part, truths already revealed; whereas. the *prophets* made new revelations and spoke all their prophesyings under the Spirit's influence. As the teachers had the "word of knowledge," so the prophets "the word of wisdom" (vs. 8). Under "teachers" are included "evangelists and pastors." **miracles**—lit., "powers" (vs. 10): ranked below "teachers," as the function of *teaching* is more edifying, though less dazzling than working miracles. **helps, governments**—lower and higher departments of "ministrations" (vs. 5); as instances of the former, deacons whose office it was to *help* in the relief of the poor, and in baptizing and preaching, subordinate to higher ministers (Acts 6:1-10; 8:5-17); also, others who *helped* with their time and means, in the Lord's cause (cf. ch. 13:3; Num. 11:17). The Americans similarly use "helps" for "*helpers*." And, as instances of the latter, *presbyters*, or *bishops*, whose office it was to *govern* the Church (I Tim. 5:17; Heb. 13:17, 24). These officers, though now ordinary and permanent, were originally specially endowed with the Spirit for their office, whence they are here classified with other functions of an inspired character. Government (lit., *guiding the helm* of affairs), as being occupied with external things, notwithstanding the outward status it gives, is ranked by the Spirit with the lower functions. Cf. "He that giveth (answering to 'helps')—he that ruleth" (answering to "governments") (Rom. 12:8). Translate, lit., "Helpings, governings" [ALFORD]. **diversities of tongues**—(vs. 10). "*Divers* kinds of tongues." **29. Are all?**—Surely not. **31. covet earnestly**—*Greek*, "emulously desire." Not in the spirit of *discontented* "coveting." The Spirit "divides to every man severally *as He will*" (vs. 1); but this does not prevent men *earnestly seeking*, by prayer and watchfulness, and cultivation of their faculties, the *greatest* gifts. BEZA explains, "Hold in the highest estimation"; which accords with the distinction in his view (ch. 14:1) between "*follow after charity—zealously esteem* spiritual gifts"; also with (vss. 11, 18) the sovereign will with which the Spirit distributes the gifts, precluding individuals from desiring gifts not vouchsafed to them. But see the *Note*, ch. 14:1. **the best gifts**—Most of the oldest MSS. read, "the *greatest gifts*." **and yet**— *Greek*, "and *moreover*." *Besides* recommending your zealous desire for the greatest gifts, I am about to show you a something still more excellent (lit., "a way most waylike") to desire, "the way of love" (cf. ch. 14:1). This love, or "charity," includes both "faith" and "hope" (ch. 13:7), and bears the same fruits (ch. 13) as the ordinary and permanent fruits of the Spirit (Gal. 5:22-24). Thus "long-suffering," cf. vs. 4; "faith," vs. 7; "joy," vs. 6; "meekness," vs. 5; "goodness," vs. 5; "gentleness," vs. 4 (the *Greek* is the same for "is kind"). It is the work of the Holy Spirit, and consists in love to God, on account of God's love in Christ to us, and as a consequence, love to man, especially to the brethren in Christ (Rom. 5:5; 15:30). This is more to be desired than gifts (Luke 10:20).

CHAPTER 13

Vss. 1-13. CHARITY OR LOVE SUPERIOR TO ALL GIFTS. The New Testament psalm of love, as the 45th Psalm (see its title) and Canticles in the Old Testament. **1. tongues**—from these he ascends to "prophecy" (vs. 2); then, to "faith"; then to benevolent and self-sacrificing deeds: a climax. He does not except even himself, and so passes from addressing *them* ("unto you," ch. 12:31, to putting the case in his own person, "Though I . . ." **speak with the tongues**—with the eloquence which was so much admired at Corinth (e.g., Apollos, Acts 18: 24; cf. ch. 1:12; 3:21, 22), and with the command of various languages, which some at Corinth abused to purposes of mere ostentation (ch. 14:2, etc.). **of angels**—higher than men, and therefore, it is to be supposed, speaking a more exalted language. **charity**—the principle of the ordinary and more important gifts of the Spirit, as contrasted with the extraordinary gifts (ch. 12). **sounding . . . tinkling**—*sound* without soul or feeling: such are "tongues" without *charity*. **cymbal**—Two kinds are noticed (Ps. 150:5), the loud or *clear*, and the *highsounding* one: hand cymbals and finger cymbals, or castanets. The sound is sharp and piercing. **2. mysteries**—(Rom. 11:25 16:25). *Mysteries* refer to the deep counsels of God hitherto secret, but now revealed to His saints. *Knowledge*, to truths long known. **faith . . . remove mountains**—(Matt. 17:20; 21:21). The practical power of the will elevated by faith [NEANDER]; confidence in God that the miraculous result will surely follow the exercise of the will at the secret impulse of His Spirit. Without "love" prophecy, knowledge, and faith, are not what they seem (cf. ch. 8:1, 2; Matt. 7:22; Jas. 2:41, cf. vs. 8), and so fail of the heavenly reward (Matt. 6:2). Thus Paul, who teaches justification by faith only (Rom. 3:4, 5; Gal. 2:16; 3:7-14), is shown to agree with James, who teaches (Jas. 2:24) "by works" (i.e., by LOVE, which is the "spirit" of faith, Jas. 2:26) a man is justified, "and not by faith only." **3. bestow . . . goods . . . poor**—lit., "dole out in food" all my goods; one of the highest functions of the "helps" (ch. 12:28). **give . . . body to be burned** lit., "to such a degree as that I should be burned." As the three youths did (Dan. 3:28), "yielded their bodies" (cf. II Cor. 12:15). These are most noble exemplifications of love in giving and in suffering. Yet they may be without love; in which case the "goods" and "body" are given, but not the *soul*, which is the sphere of love. Without the soul God rejects all else, and so rejects the man, who is therefore "profited" nothing (Matt. 16:26; Luke 9:23-25). Men will fight for Christianity, and die for Christianity, but not live in its spirit, which is *love*. **4. suffereth long**—under provocations of *evil from* others. The negative side of *love*. **is kind**—the positive side. Extending *good* to others. Cf. with love's features here those of the "wisdom from above" (Jas. 3:17). **envieth**—The *Greek* includes also *jealousy*. **vaunteth not**—in words, even of gifts which it really possesses; an indirect rebuke of those at Corinth who used the gift of tongues for mere display. **not puffed up**—with party zeal, as some at Corinth were (ch. 4:6). **5. not . . . unseemly**—*is not uncourteous*, or inattentive to civility and propriety. **thinketh no evil**—*imputeth not evil* [ALFORD]; lit., "*the* evil" which actually is there (Prov. 10:12; I Pet. 4:8). Love makes allowances for the falls of others, and is ready to put on them a charitable construction. Love, so far from devising evil against another, excuses "*the* evil" which

another inflicts on her [ESTIUS]; *doth not meditate upon evil* inflicted by another [BENGEL]; and in doubtful cases, takes the more charitable view [GROTIUS]. **6. rejoiceth in the truth**—rather, "rejoiceth *with* the truth." Exults not at the perpetration of iniquity (unrighteousness) by others (cf. Gen. 9:22, 23), but rejoices when the truth rejoices; sympathizes with it in its triumphs (II John 4). See the opposite (II Tim. 3:8), "Resist the truth." So "the truth" and "unrighteousness" are contrasted (Rom. 2:8). "The truth" is the Gospel truth, the inseparable ally of love (Eph. 4:15; II John 12). The false charity which compromises "the truth" by glossing over "iniquity" or unrighteousness is thus tacitly condemned (Prov. 17:15). **7. Beareth all things**—without speaking of what it has to bear. The same *Greek* verb as in ch. 9:12. It *endures without divulging* to the world personal distress. Literally said of *holding fast* like a watertight vessel; so the charitable man *contains himself* in silence from giving vent to what selfishness would prompt under personal hardship. **believeth all things**—unsuspiciously believes all that is not palpably false, all that it can with a good conscience believe to the credit of another. Cf. James 3:17, "easy to be entreated"; *Greek*, "easily persuaded." **hopeth**—what is good of another, even when others have ceased to hope. **endureth**—persecutions in a patient and loving spirit. **8. never faileth**—never is to be out of use; it always holds its place. **shall fail . . . vanish away**—The same *Greek* verb is used for both; and that different from the *Greek* verb for "faileth." Translate, "Shall be done away with," i.e., shall be dispensed with at the Lord's coming, being superseded by their more perfect heavenly analogues; for instance, *knowledge* by *intuition*. Of "tongues," which are still more temporary, the verb is "shall *cease*." A primary fulfilment of Paul's statement took place when the Church attained its maturity; then "tongues" entirely "ceased," and "prophesyings" and "knowledge," so far as they were supernatural gifts of the Spirit, were superseded as no longer required when the ordinary preaching of the word, and the Scriptures of the New Testament collected together, had become established institutions. **9, 10. in part**—partially and imperfectly. Cf. a similar contrast to the "perfect man," "the measure of the stature of the fulness of Christ" (Eph. 4:11-13). **that which is in part**—fragmentary and isolated. **11. When . . . a child**—(ch. 3:1; 14:20). **I spake**—alluding to "tongues." **understood**—or, "had the sentiments of." Alluding to "prophecy." **I thought**—*Greek* "reasoned" or "judged"; alluding to "knowledge." **when I became . . . I put away**—rather, "now that I am become a man, I have done away with the things of the child." **12. now**—in our present state. **see**—an appropriate expression, in connection with the "prophets" of *seers* (I Sam. 9:9). **through a glass**—i.e., in a mirror; the reflection *seeming* to the eye to be behind the mirror, so that we see it *through* the mirror. Ancient mirrors were made of polished brass or other metals. The contrast is between the inadequate knowledge of an object gained by seeing it reflected in a dim mirror (such as ancient mirrors were), compared with the perfect idea we have of it by seeing itself directly. **darkly**—lit., "in enigma." As a "mirror" conveys an image to the *eye*, so an "enigma" to the *ear*. But neither "eye nor ear" can fully represent (though the believer's soul gets a small revelation now of) "the things which God hath prepared for them that love Him" (ch. 2:9). Paul alludes to Numbers 12:8, "not in *dark* speeches"; LXX, "not in *enigmas*." Compared with the *visions* and *dreams* vouchsafed to other prophets, God's communications with Moses were "not in enigmas." But compared with the intuitive and direct vision of God hereafter, even the revealed word now is "a dark discourse," or a shadowing forth *by enigma* of God's reflected likeness. Cf. II Pet. 1:19, where the "light" or *candle* in a dark place stands in contrast with the "day" dawning. God's word is called a *glass* or mirror also in II Corinthians 3:18. **then**—"when that which is perfect is come" (vs. 10). **face to face**—not merely "mouth to mouth" (Num. 12:8). Genesis 32:30 was a type (John 1:50, 51). **know ... known**—rather as *Greek*, "*fully* know ... *fully* known." Now we *are known by*, rather than *know*, God (ch. 8:3; Gal. 4:9). **13. And now**—Translate, "*But* now." "In this present state" [HENDERSON]. Or, "now" does not express time, but *opposition*, as in ch. 5:11, "the case being so" [GROTIUS]; whereas *it is the case that* the *three* gifts, "prophecy," "tongues," and "knowledge" (cited as specimens of the whole class of gifts) "fail" (vs. 8), *there abide* permanently only *these three—faith, hope, charity*. In one sense *faith* and *hope* shall be done away, faith being superseded by sight, and hope by actual fruition (Rom. 8:24; II Cor. 5:7); and charity, or love, alone never faileth (vs. 8). But in another sense, "faith and hope," as well as "charity," ABIDE; viz., after the extraordinary gifts have ceased; for those three are *necessary and sufficient for salvation at all times*, whereas the extraordinary gifts are not at all so; cf. the use of "abide," ch. 3:14. *Charity*, or love, is connected specially with the Holy Spirit, who is the bond of the loving union between the brethren (Rom. 15:30; Col. 1:8). *Faith* is towards God. *Hope* is in behalf of ourselves. *Charity* is love to God creating in us love towards our neighbor. In an unbeliever there is more or less of the three opposites—unbelief, despair, hatred. Even hereafter *faith* in the sense of *trust in God* "abideth"; also "hope," in relation to ever new joys in prospect, and at the anticipation of ever increasing blessedness, sure never to be disappointed. But love alone in every sense "abideth"; it is therefore "the greatest" of the three, as also because it presupposes "faith," which without "love" and its consequent "works" is dead (Gal. 5:6; Jas. 2:17, 20). **but**—rather, "and"; as there is not so strong opposition between charity and the other two, faith and hope, which like it also "abide."

CHAPTER 14

Vss. 1-25. SUPERIORITY OF PROPHECY OVER TONGUES. **1. Follow after charity**—as your first and chief aim, seeing that it is "the greatest" (ch. 13:13). **and desire**—Translate, "Yet (as a *secondary* aim) desire zealously (*Note*, ch. 12:31) spiritual gifts." **but rather**—"*but chiefly* that ye may prophesy" (speak and exhort under inspiration) (Prov. 29:18; Acts 13:1; I Thess. 5:20), whether as to future events, i.e., strict *prophecy*, or explaining obscure parts of Scripture, especially the prophetical Scriptures or illustrating and setting forth questions of Christian doctrine and practice. Our modern *preaching* is the successor of *prophecy*, but without the inspiration. Desire zealously this (prophecy) *more* than any other spiritual gift; or *in preference to* "tongues" (vs. 2, etc.) [BENGEL]. **2. speaketh ... unto God**—who alone understands *all* languages. **no man understandeth**—generally speaking; the few

who have the gift of interpreting tongues are the exception. **in the spirit**—as opposed to "the understanding" (vs. 14). **mysteries**—unintelligible to the hearers, exciting their wonder, rather than instructing them. Corinth, being a mart resorted to by merchants from Asia, Africa, and Europe, would give scope amidst its mixed population for the exercise of the gift of tongues; but its legitimate use was in an audience understanding the tongue of the speaker, not, as the Corinthians abused it, in mere display. **3. But**—on the other hand. **edification**—of which the two principal species given are "exhortation" to remove *sluggishness*, "comfort" or *consolation* to remove *sadness* [BENGEL]. Omit "to." **4. edifieth himself**—as he understands the meaning of what the particular "tongue" expresses; but "the church," i.e., the congregation, does not. **5.** Translate, "Now I wish you all to speak with tongues (so far am I from thus speaking through having any objection to tongues), but rather IN ORDER THAT (as my ulterior and higher wish for you) ye should prophesy." Tongues must therefore mean . *languages*, not ecstatic, unintelligible rhapsodie (as NEANDER fancied): for Paul could never "wish" for the latter in their behalf. **greater** —because *more useful*. **except he interpret**—the unknown tongue which he speaks, "that the Church may receive edifying" (*building up*). **6.** Translate, "*But* now"; seeing there is no edification without interpretation. **revelation ... prophesying**—corresponding one to the other; "revelation" being the supernatural *unveiling* of divine truths to man, "prophesying" the enunciation to men of such revelations. So "knowledge" corresponds to "doctrine," which is the gift of *teaching* to others our knowledge. As the former pair refers to specially *revealed mysteries*, so the latter pair refers to the *general obvious truths of salvation*, brought from the common storehouse of believers. **7.** Translate, "And things without life-giving sound, whether pipe or harp, YET (*notwithstanding their giving sound*) if they give not a distinction in the tones (i.e., notes) how ...?" **what is piped or harped**—i.e., what tune is played on the pipe or harp. **8.** Translate, "For if *also*," an *additional* step in the argument. **uncertain sound**—having no definite meaning: whereas it ought to be so marked that one succession of notes on the trumpet should summon the soldiers to attack; another, to retreat; another, to some other evolution. **9. So ... ye**—who have life; as opposed to "things without life" (vs. 7). **by the tongue**—the language which ye speak in. **ye shall speak**—Ye will be speaking into the air, i.e., *in vain* (ch. 9:26). **10. it may be**—i.e., perhaps, speaking by conjecture. "It may chance" (ch. 15:37). **so many**—as may be enumerated by investigators of such matters. Cf. "so much," used generally for a definite number left undefined (Acts 5:8; also II Sam. 12:8). **kinds of voices**—kinds of articulate speech. **without signification**—*without articulate voice* (i.e., distinct meaning). *None is without its own voice*, or mode of speech, *distinct* from the rest. **11. Therefore**—seeing that none is without meaning. **a barbarian**—a foreigner (Acts 28:2). Not in the depreciatory sense as the term is now used, but one *speaking a foreign language*. **12. zealous**—emulously desirous. **spiritual** *gifts*—lit., "spirits"; i.e., emanations from the one Spirit. **seek that ye may excel to**—Translate, "Seek *them*, that ye may abound *in them* to the edifying...." **13.** Explain, "Let him who speaketh with a tongue [unknown] *in his prayer* (or, *when praying*) *strive* that he may interpret" [ALFORD]. This explanation of "pray" is needed by its logical connection with "prayer in an unknown tongue" (vs. 14). Though his words be unintelligible to his hearers, let him in them pray that he may obtain the gift of interpreting, which will make them "edifying" to "the church" (vs. 12). **14. spirit**—my higher being, the *passive* object of the Holy Spirit's operations, and the instrument of prayer in the unknown tongue, distinguished from the "understanding," the *active* instrument of thought and reasoning; which in this case must be "unfruitful" in edifying others, since the vehicle of expression is unintelligible to them. On the distinction of *soul* or *mind* and *spirit*, see Ephesians 4:23; Hebrews 4:12. **15. What is it then?** —What is my determination thereupon? **and**—rather as *Greek*, "but"; I will not only pray with my spirit, which (vs. 14) might leave the understanding unedified, BUT with the understanding also [ALFORD and ELLICOTT]. **pray with the understanding also**—and, by inference, I will keep silence altogether if I cannot pray with the understanding (so as to make myself understood by others). A prescient warning, *mutatis mutandis,* against the Roman and Greek practice of keeping liturgies in dead languages, which long since have become unintelligible to the masses; though their forefathers spoke them at a time when those liturgies were framed for *general* use. **16. Else . . . thou**—He changes from the *first* person, as he had just expressed *his own* resolution, "*I* will pray with the understanding," whatever "thou" doest. **bless**—the highest kind of prayer. **occupieth the room of the unlearned**—one who, whatever other gifts he may possess, yet, as wanting the gift of interpretation, is reduced by the speaking in an unknown tongue to the position of one unlearned, or "a private person." **say Amen**— Prayer is not a vicarious duty done by others *for* us; as in Rome's liturgies and masses. We must join *with* the leader of the prayers and praises of the congregation, and say aloud our responsive "A-men" in assent, as was the usage of the Jewish (Deut. 27:15-26; Neh. 8:6) and Christian primitive churches [JUSTIN MART., *Apol.* 2. 97]. **17. givest thanks**—The prayers of the synagogue were called "eulogies," because to each prayer was joined a *thanksgiving.* Hence the prayers of the Christian Church also were called *blessings* and *giving of thanks.* This illustrates Colossians 4:2; I Thessalonians 5:17, 18. So the *Kaddisch* and *Keduscha,* the synagogue formulæ of "hallowing" the divine "name" and of prayer for the "coming of God's kingdom," answer to the Church's Lord's Prayer, repeated often and made the foundation on which the other prayers are built [TERTULLIAN, *de Oratione*]. **18. tongues**—The oldest MSS. have the singular, "in a tongue [foreign]." **19. I had rather** —The *Greek* verb more literally expresses this meaning, "I WISH to speak five words with my understanding (rather) than ten thousand words in an unknown tongue"; even the two thousandth part of ten thousand. The *Greek* for "I would rather," would be a different verb. Paul would NOT wish at all to speak "ten thousand words in an unknown tongue." **20. Brethren**—an appellation calculated to conciliate their favorable reception of his exhortation. **children in understanding**—as preference of gifts abused to nonedification would make you (cf. ch. 3:1; Matt. 10:16; Rom. 16:19; Eph. 4: 14). The *Greek* for "understanding" expresses the will of one's *spirit,* Romans 8:6 (it is not found elsewhere); as the "heart" is the will of the "soul." The same *Greek* is used for "minded" in Romans 8:6. **men**—full-grown. Be childlike, not childish. **21.**

In the law—as the whole Old Testament is called, being all of it the law of God. Cf. the citation of the Psalms as the "law," John 10:34. Here the quotation is from Isaiah 28:11, 12, where God virtually says of Israel, This people hear Me not, though I speak to them in the language with which they are familiar; I will therefore speak to them in other tongues, namely, those of the foes whom I will send against them; but even then they will not hearken to Me; which Paul thus applies, Ye see that it is a penalty to be associated with men of a strange tongue, yet ye impose this on the Church [GROTIUS]; they who speak in foreign tongues are like "children" just "weaned from the milk" (Isa. 28:9), "with stammering lips" speaking unintelligibly to the hearers, appearing ridiculous (Isa. 28:14), or as babbling drunkards (Acts 2:13), or madmen (vs. 23). **22.** Thus from Isaiah it appears, reasons Paul, that "tongues" (unknown and uninterpreted) are not a sign mainly intended for believers (though at the conversion of Cornelius and the Gentiles with him, tongues were vouchsafed to him and them to confirm their faith), but mainly to be a *condemnation* to those, the majority, who, like Israel in Isaiah's day, reject the sign and the accompanying message. Cf. "Sign . . . will they not hear Me" (vs. 21). "Sign" is often used for a *condemnatory* sign (Ezek. 4:3, 4; Matt. 12:39-42). Since they *will* not understand, they *shall* not understand. **prophesying . . . not for them that believe not, but . . . believe**—i.e., prophesying has no effect on them that are radically and obstinately like Israel (Isa. 28:11, 12), unbelievers, but on them that are either in receptivity or in fact believers; it makes believers of those not wilfully unbelievers (vs. 24, 25; Rom. 10: 17), and spiritually nourishes those that already believe. **23. whole . . . all . . . tongues**—The more there are assembled, and the more that speak in unknown tongues, the more will the impression be conveyed to strangers "coming in" from curiosity ("unbelievers"), or even from a better motive ("unlearned"), that the *whole* body of worshippers is a mob of fanatical "madmen"; and that "the Church is like the company of builders of Babel after the confusion of tongues, or like the cause tried between two deaf men before a deaf judge, celebrated in the Greek epigram" [GROTIUS]. **unlearned**— having some degree of faith, but not gifts [BENGEL]. **24. all**—one by one (vs. 31). **prophesy**—speak the truth by the Spirit intelligibly, and not in unintelligible tongues. **one**—"anyone." Here *singular;* implying that this effect, viz., *conviction by all,* would be produced on *anyone,* who might happen to enter. In vs. 23 the *plural* is used; "unlearned or unbelievers"; implying that however many there might be, not one would profit by the tongues; yea, their being many would confirm them in rejecting the sign, as many unbelieving men together strengthen one another in unbelief; individuals are more easily won [BENGEL]. **convinced**—convicted in conscience; said of the "one that believeth not" (John 16:8, 9). **judged**—His secret character is opened out. "Is searched into" [ALFORD]. Said of the "one unlearned" (cf. ch. 2:15). **25. And thus**—omitted in the oldest MSS. and versions. **secrets of his heart made manifest**—He sees his own inner character opened out by the sword of the Spirit (Heb. 4:12; Jas. 1:23), the word of God, in the hand of him who prophesieth. Cf. the same effect produced on Nebuchadnezzar (Dan. 2:30 and end of verse 47). No argument is stronger for the truth of religion than its manifestation of men to themselves in their true character. Hence hearers even now often think the preacher must have aimed his sermon particularly at them. **and so**—convicted at last, judged, and manifested to himself. Cf. the effect on the woman of Samaria produced by Jesus' unfolding of her character to herself (John 4:19, 29). **and report**—to his friends at home, as the woman of Samaria did. Rather, as the *Greek* is, "He will worship God, *announcing*," i.e., openly avowing then and there, "that God is in you of a truth," and by implication that the God who is in you is of a truth the God.

26-40. RULES FOR THE EXERCISE OF GIFTS IN THE CONGREGATION. **26. How is it then?**—rather, "*What then* is the true rule to be observed as to the use of gifts?" Cf. vs. 15, where the same *Greek* occurs. **a psalm**—extemporary, inspired by the Spirit, as that of Mary, Zechariah, Simeon, and Anna (Luke 1 and 2). **a doctrine**—to impart and set forth to the congregation. **a tongue . . . a revelation**—The oldest MSS. transpose the order: "revelation . . . tongue"; "interpretation" properly following "tongue" (vs. 13). **Let all things be done unto edifying**—The general rule under which this particular case falls; an answer to the question at the beginning of this verse. Each is bound to obey the ordinances of his church not adverse to Scripture. See Article XXXIV, Church of England Prayer Book. **27. let it be by two**—at each time, in one assembly; not more than two or three might speak with tongues at each meeting. **by course**—in turns. **let one interpret**—one who has the gift of interpreting tongues; and not more than one. **28. let him**—the speaker in unknown tongues. **speak to himself, and to God**—(cf. vss. 2, 4)—privately and not in the hearing of others. **29. two or three**—at one meeting (he does not add "at the most," as in vs. 27, lest he should seem to "quench prophesyings," the most edifying of gifts), and these "one by one," in turn (vs. 27, "by course," and vs. 31). Paul gives here similar rules to the prophets, as previously to those speaking in unknown tongues. **judge**—by their power of "discerning spirits" (ch. 12:10), whether the person prophesying was really speaking under the influence of the Spirit (cf. ch. 12:3; I John 4:1-3). **30. If any thing**—Translate, "*But* if any thing." **another that sitteth by**—a hearer. **let the first hold his peace**—Let him who heretofore spoke, and who came to the assembly furnished with a previous ordinary (in those times) revelation from God (vs. 26), give place to him who at the assembly is moved to prophesy by a sudden revelation from the Spirit. **31. For ye may**—rather, "For ye *can* [if ye will] all prophesy one by one," giving way to one another. The "for" justifies the precept (vs. 30), "let the first hold his peace." **32. And**—following up the assertion in vs. 31, "Ye can (if ye will) prophesy one by one," i.e., restrain yourselves from speaking all together; "and the spirits of the prophets," i.e., their own spirits, acted on by the Holy Spirit, are not so hurried away by His influence, as to cease to be under their own control; they can if they will hear others, and not demand that they alone should be heard uttering communications from God. **33.** In all the churches of the saints God is a God of peace; let Him not among you be supposed to be a God of confusion [ALFORD]. Cf. the same argument in ch. 11:16. LACHMANN and others put a full stop at "peace," and connect the following words thus: "As in all churches of the saints, let your women keep silence in your churches." **34.** (I Tim. 2:11, 12.) For women to speak in public would be an act of independence, as if they were not subject to their husbands (cf. ch. 11:3; Eph. 5:22 Titus 2:5; I Pet.

3:1). For "under obedience," translate, "in *subjection*" or "*submission*," as the *Greek* is translated (Eph. 5:21, 22, 24). **the law**—a term applied to the whole Old Testament; here, Genesis 3:16. **35.** Anticipation of an objection. Women may say, "But if we do not understand something, may we not 'ask' a question publicly so as to 'learn'? Nay, replies Paul, if you want information, 'ask' not in public, but 'at home'; ask not other men, but 'your own particular (so the *Greek*) husbands.'" **shame**—indecorous. **36. What!**—*Greek*, "Or." Are you about to obey me? *Or*, if you set up your judgment above that of other churches. I wish to know, do you pretend that your church is the first church FROM which the gospel word came, that you should give the law to all others? Or are you the only persons UNTO whom it has come? **37. prophet**—the species. **spiritual**—the genus: spiritually endowed. The followers of Apollos prided themselves as "spiritual" (ch. 3:1-3; cf. Gal. 6:1). Here *one capable of discerning spirits* is specially meant. **things that I write . . . commandments of the Lord**—a direct assertion of inspiration. Paul's words as an apostle are Christ's words. Paul appeals not merely to one or two, but *to a body of men*, for the reality of three facts about which no body of men could possibly be mistaken: (1) that his having converted them was not due to mere eloquence, but to the "demonstration of the Spirit and of power"; (2) that part of this demonstration consisted in the communication of miraculous power, which they were then exercising so generally as to require to be corrected in the irregular employment of it; (3) that among these miraculous gifts was one which enabled the "prophet" or "spiritual person" to decide whether Paul's Epistle was Scripture or not. He could not have written so, unless the facts were *notoriously true:* for he takes them for granted, as consciously known by the whole body of men whom he addresses [HINDS *on Inspiration*]. **38. if any man be ignorant**—wilfully; not wishing to recognize these ordinances and my apostolic authority in enjoining them. **let him be ignorant**—I leave him to his ignorance: it will be at his own peril; I feel it a waste of words to speak anything further to convince him. An argument likely to have weight with the Corinthians, who admired "knowledge" so much. **39. covet**—earnestly desire. Stronger than "forbid not"; marking how much higher he esteemed "prophecy" than "tongues." **40. Let . . .**—The oldest MSS. read, "*But* let. . . ." This verse is connected with vs. 39, "But (while *desiring prophecy,* and *not forbidding tongues*) let all things be done decently." "Church government is the best security for Christian liberty" [J. NEWTON]. (Cf. vss. 23, 26-33.)

CHAPTER 15

Vss. 1-58. THE RESURRECTION PROVED AGAINST THE DENIERS OF IT AT CORINTH. Christ's resurrection rests on the evidence of many eyewitnesses, including Paul himself, and is the great fact preached as the groundwork of the Gospel: they who deny the resurrection in general, must deny that of Christ, and the consequence of the latter will be, that Christian preaching and faith are vain. **1. Moreover**—"Now" [ALFORD and ELLICOTT]. **I declare**—lit., "I make known": it implies some degree of reproach that it should be now necessary to make it known to them afresh, owing to some of them "not having the knowledge of God" (vs. 34). Cf. Galatians 1:

11. wherein ye stand—wherein ye now take your stand. This is your present actual privilege, if ye suffer not yourselves to fall from your high standing. **2. ye are saved**—rather, "ye are being saved." **if ye keep in memory what I preached unto you**— Able critics, BENGEL and others, prefer connecting the words thus, "I declare unto you the Gospel (vs. 1) in what words I preached it unto you." Paul reminds them, or rather makes known to them, as if anew, not only the fact of the Gospel, but also *with what words,* and *by what arguments,* he preached it to them. Translate in that case, "if ye hold it fast." I prefer arranging as *English Version,* "By which ye are saved, if ye hold fast (in memory and personal appropriation) *with what speech* I preached it unto you." **unless**—which is impossible, your faith is vain, in resting on Christ's resurrection as an objective reality. **3. I delivered unto you**—A short creed, or summary of articles of faith, was probably even then existing; and a profession in accordance with it was required of candidates for baptism (Acts 8:37). **first of all**—lit., "among the foremost points" (Heb. 6:2). The atonement is, in Paul's view, of primary importance. **which I ... received**—from Christ Himself by special revelation (cf. ch. 11:23). **died for our sins**— i.e., to atone FOR them; *for* taking away *our sins* (I John 3:5; cf. Gal. 1:4): "gave Himself for our sins" (Isa. 53:5; II Cor. 5:15; Titus 2:14). The "for" here does not, as in some passages, imply vicarious substitution, but "in behalf of" (Heb. 5:3; I Pet. 2:24). It does not, however, mean merely "on account of," which is expressed by a different *Greek* word (Rom. 4:25), (though in *English Version* translated similarly, "for"). **according to the scriptures**—which "cannot be broken." Paul puts the testimony of *Scripture* above that of those who saw the Lord after His resurrection [BENGEL]. So our Lord quotes Isaiah 53:12, in Luke 22:37; cf. Psalm 22:15, etc.; Daniel 9:26. **4. buried ... rose again**—His burial is more closely connected with His resurrection than His death. At the moment of His death, the power of His inextinguishable life exerted itself (Matt. 27:52). The grave was to Him not the destined receptacle of corruption, but an apartment fitted for entering into life (Acts 2:26-28) [BENGEL]. **rose again**—*Greek,* "hath risen": the state thus begun, and its consequences, still continue. **5. seen of Cephas**—Peter (Luke 24:34). **the twelve**—The round number for "the Eleven" (Luke 24:33, 36). "The Twelve" was their ordinary appellation, even when their number was not full. However, very possibly Matthias was present (Acts 1:22, 23). Some of the oldest MSS. and versions read, "the Eleven": but the best on the whole, "the Twelve." **6. five hundred**—This appearance was probably on the mountain (Tabor, according to tradition), in Galilee, when His most solemn and public appearance, according to His special promise, was vouchsafed (Matt. 26:32; 28:7, 10, 16). He "appointed" this place, as one remote from Jerusalem, so that believers might assemble there more freely and securely. ALFORD'S theory of *Jerusalem* being the scene, is improbable; as such a multitude of believers could not, with any safety, have met in one place in the metropolis, after His crucifixion there. The number of disciples (Acts 1:15) at Jerusalem shortly after, was one hundred and twenty, those in Galilee and elsewhere not being reckoned. Andronicus and Junius were, perhaps, of the number (Rom. 16:7): they are said to be "among the apostles" (who all were witnesses of the resurrection, Acts 1:22). **remain unto this present**—and, therefore, may be sifted thoroughly to ascertain the trustworthiness of their testimony. **fallen asleep**—in the sure hope of *awaking* at the resurrection (Acts 7:60). **7. seen of James**—the Less, the brother of our Lord (Gal. 1:19). The Gospel according to the Hebrews, quoted by JEROME (*Catalogus Scriptorum Ecclesiasticorum,* p. 170 D.), records that "James swore he would not eat bread from the hour that he drank the cup of the Lord, till he should see Him rising again from the dead." **all the apostles**—The term here includes many others besides "the Twelve" already enumerated (vs. 5): perhaps the seventy disciples (Luke 10) [CHRYSOSTOM]. **8. one born out of due time**— *Greek,* "the one abortively born": the abortion in the family of the apostles. As a child *born before the due time* is puny, and though born alive, yet not of the proper size, and scarcely worthy of the name of man, so "I am *the least* of the apostles," scarcely "meet to be called an apostle"; a supernumerary taken into the college of apostles out of regular course, not led to Christ by long instruction, like a natural birth, but by a sudden power, as those prematurely born [GROTIUS]. Cf. the similar image from childbirth, and by the same spiritual power, the resurrection of Christ (I Pet. 1:3). "*Begotten again* by the *resurrection* of Jesus." Jesus' appearance to Paul, on the way to Damascus, is the one here referred to. **9. least**—The name, "Paulus," in Latin, means *least.* **I persecuted the church**— Though God has forgiven him, Paul can hardly forgive himself at the remembrance of his past sin. **10. by ... grace ... and his grace**—The repetition implies the prominence which God's *grace* had in his mind, as the sole cause of his marvellous conversion and subsequent labors. Though "not meet to be called an apostle," grace has given him, in Christ, the meetness needed for the office. Translate as the *Greek,* "His grace which was (showed) *towards* me." **what I am**—occupying the honorable office of an apostle. Contrast with this the self-sufficient prayer of another Pharisee (Luke 18:11). **but I laboured**—by God's grace (Phil. 2:16). **than they all**—than any of the apostles (vs. 7). **grace of God ... with me**—Cf. "the Lord working *with* them" (Mark 16:20). The oldest MSS. omit "which was." The "not I, but grace," implies, that though the human will concurred *with* God when brought by His Spirit into conformity with His will, yet "grace" so preponderated in the work, that his own co-operation is regarded as nothing, and grace as virtually the sole agent. (Cf. ch. 3:9; Matt. 10:20; II Cor. 6:1; Phil. 2:12, 13.) **11. whether it were I or they**—(the apostles) who "labored more abundantly" (vs. 10) in preaching, such was the substance of our preaching, viz., the truths stated in vss. 3, 4. **12. if**—Seeing that it is an admitted fact that Christ is announced by us eyewitnesses as having risen from the dead, how is it that some of you deny that which is a necessary consequence of Christ's resurrection, viz., the general resurrection? **some**— Gentile reasoners (Acts 17:32; 26:8) who would not believe it because they did not see "how" it could be (vss. 35, 36). **13.** If there be no general resurrection, which is the consequent, then there can have been no resurrection of Christ, which is the antecedent. The head and the members of the body stand on the same footing: what does not hold good of them, does not hold good of Him either: His resurrection and theirs are inseparably joined (cf. vss. 20-22; John 14:19). **14. your faith ... vain** —(vs. 11). The *Greek* for "vain" here is, *empty, unreal:* in vs. 17, on the other hand, it is, *without* *use, frustrated.* The principal argument of the first preachers in support of Christianity was that God had raised Christ from the dead (Acts 1:22; 2:32; 4: 10, 33; 13:37; Rom. 1:4). If this fact were false, the faith built on it must be false too. **15. testified of God**—i.e., concerning God. The rendering of others is, "against God" [*Vulgate,* ESTIUS, GROTIUS]: the *Greek* preposition with the genitive implies, not direct antagonism (as the accusative would mean), but *indirect* to *the dishonor of* God. *English Version* is probably better. **if so be**—as they assert. It is not right to tell untrue stories, though they are told and seem for the glory of God (Job 13:7). **16.** The repetition implies the unanswerable force of the argument. **17. vain**—Ye are, by the very fact (supposing the case to be as the skeptics maintained), *frustrated* of all which "your faith" appropriates: Ye are still under the everlasting condemnation of your sins (even in the *disembodied* state which is here referred to), from which Christ's resurrection is our justification (Rom. 4:25): "saved *by his life*" (Rom. 5:10). **18. fallen asleep in Christ**—in communion with Christ as His members. "In Christ's case the term used is *death,* to assure us of the reality of His suffering; in our case, *sleep,* to give us consolation: In His case, His resurrection having actually taken place, Paul shrinks not from the term death; in ours, the resurrection being still only a matter of hope, he uses the term *falling asleep*" [PHOTIUS, *Questiones Amphilochiæ,* 197]. **perished** —Their souls are lost; they are in misery in the unseen world. **19.** If our hopes in Christ were limited to this life only, we should be, of all men, most to be pitied; viz., because, while others live unmolested, we are exposed to every trial and persecution, and, after all, are doomed to bitter disappointment in our most cherished hope; for all our hope of salvation, even of the soul (not merely of the body), hangs on the resurrection of Christ, without which His death would be of no avail to us (Eph. 1:19, 20; I Pet. 1:3). The heathen are "without hope" (Eph. 2:12; I Thess. 4:13). We should be even worse, for we should be also without present enjoyment (ch. 4:9). **20. now**—as the case really is. **and become**—omitted in the oldest MSS. **the first fruits**—the earnest or pledge, that the whole resurrection harvest will follow, so that our faith is not vain, nor our hope limited to this life. The time of writing this Epistle was probably about the Passover (ch. 5:7); the day after the Passover sabbath was that for offering *the first fruits* (Lev. 23: 10, 11), and the same was the day of Christ's resurrection: whence appears the appropriateness of the image. **21. by man ... by man**—The first fruits are of the same nature as the rest of the harvest; so Christ, the bringer of life, is of the same nature as the race of men to whom He brings it; just as Adam, the bringer of death, was of the same nature as the men on whom he brought it. **22. in Adam all**—in union of nature with Adam, as representative head of mankind in their fall. **in Christ ... all**—in union of nature with Christ, the representative head of mankind in their recovery. The life brought in by Christ is co-extensive with the death brought in by Adam. **23. But every man in his own order**— rather, "rank": the *Greek* is not in the abstract, but concrete: image from troops, "each in his own regiment." Though all shall rise again, let not any think all shall be saved; nay, each shall have his proper place, Christ first (Col. 1:18), and after Him the godly who die in Christ (I Thess. 4:16), in a separate band from the ungodly, and then "the end," i.e., the resurrection of the rest of the dead.

Christian churches, ministers, and individuals seem about to be judged first "at His coming" (Matt. 25: 1-30); then "all the nations" (Matt. 25:31-46). Christ's own flock shall share His glory "at His coming," which is not to be confounded with "the end," or general judgment (Rev. 20:4-6, 11-15). The latter is not in this chapter specially discussed, but only the first resurrection, viz., that of the saints: not even the judgment of Christian hollow professors (Matt. 25:1-30) at His coming, is handled, but only the glory of them "that are Christ's," who alone in the highest sense "obtain the resurrection from the dead" (Luke 14:14; 20:35, 36; Phil. 3:11, see *Note*). The second coming of Christ is not a mere *point* of time, but a *period* beginning with the resurrection of the just at His appearing, and ending with the general judgment. The ground of the universal resurrection is the union of all mankind in nature with Christ, their representative Head, who has done away with death, by His own death in their stead: the ground of the resurrection of believers is not merely this, but their personal union with Him as *their* "Life" (Col. 3:4), effected *causatively* by the Holy Spirit, and *instrumentally* by faith as the *subjective,* and by ordinances as the *objective* means. **24. Then**—after that: next in the succession of "orders" or "ranks." **the end**—the general resurrection, and final judgment and consummation (Matt. 25:46). **delivered up ... kingdom to ... Father**—(Cf. John 13:3). Seeming at variance with Daniel 7:14, "His dominion is an *everlasting* dominion which *shall not pass away.*" *Really,* His giving up of the *mediatorial* kingdom to the Father, when the end for which the mediatorial economy was established has been accomplished, is altogether in harmony with its continuing everlastingly. The change which shall then take place, shall be in the *manner* of administration, not in the *kingdom* itself; God shall then come into *direct* connection with the earth, instead of mediatorially, when Christ shall have fully and finally removed everything that severs asunder the holy God and a sinful earth (Col. 1:20). The glory of God is the final end of Christ's mediatorial office (Phil. 2:10, 11). His co-equality with the Father is independent of the latter, and prior to it, and shall, therefore, continue when its function shall have ceased. His manhood, too, shall everlastingly continue, though, as now, subordinate to the Father. The *throne of the Lamb* (but no longer mediatorial) as well as *of* God, shall be in the heavenly city (Rev. 22:3; cf. 3: 21). The unity of the Godhead, and the unity of the Church, shall be simultaneously manifested at Christ's second coming. Cf. Zephaniah 3:9; Zechariah 14:9; John 17:21-24. The oldest MSS. for "*shall have* delivered up," read, "*delivereth* up," which suits the sense better. It is "when He *shall have* put down all rule," that "He *delivereth* up the kingdom to the Father." **shall have put down all rule**—the effect produced during the millenary reign of Himself and His saints (Ps. 110:1; 8:6; 2:6-9), to which passages Paul refers, resting his argument on the two words, "all" and "until," of the Psalmist: a proof of verbal inspiration of Scripture (cf. Rev. 2: 26, 27). Meanwhile, He "rules in the midst of His enemies" (Ps. 110:2). He is styled "the King" when He takes His great power (Matt. 25:34; Rev. 11:15, 17). The *Greek* for "put down" is, "*done away with,*" or "brought to naught." "All" must be subject to Him, whether openly opposed powers, as Satan and his angels, or kings and angelic principalities (Eph. 1:21). **25. must**—because Scripture foretells it. **till**—There will be no further need of

His mediatorial kingdom, its object having been realized. **enemies under his feet**—(Luke 19:27; Eph. 1:22). **26. shall be**—Greek, *"is* done away with" (Rev. 20:14; cf. 1:18). It is to believers especially this applies (vss. 55-57); even in the case of unbelievers, death is done away with by the general resurrection. Satan brought in *sin,* and *sin* brought in *death!* So they shall be destroyed (rendered utterly powerless) in the same order (vs. 56; Heb. 2: 14; Rev. 19:20; 20:10, 14). **27. all things**—including death (cf. Eph. 1:22; Phil. 3:21; Heb. 2:8; I Pet. 3:22). It is said, *"hath* put," for what God has said is the same as if it were already done, so sure is it. Paul here quotes the 8th Psalm in proof of his previous declaration, "For (it is written), *'He hath put all things under His feet.'* " **under his feet**—as His footstool (Ps. 110:1). In perfect and lasting subjection. **when he**—viz., God, who by His Spirit inspired the Psalmist. **28. Son . . . himself . . . subject**—not as the creatures are, but as a Son *voluntarily subordinate* to, though co-equal with, the Father. In the mediatorial kingdom, the Son had been, in a manner, distinct from the Father. Now, His kingdom shall merge in the Father's, with whom He is one; not that there is thus any derogation from His honor; for the Father Himself wills "that all should honor the Son, as they honor the Father" (John 5:22, 23; Heb. 1:6). **God . . . all in all**—as Christ is all in all (Col. 3:11; cf. Zech. 14:9). *Then,* and not till then, *"all* things," without the least infringement of the divine prerogative, shall be subject to the Son, and the Son subordinate to the Father, while co-equally sharing His glory. Contrast Psalm 10:4; 14:1. Even the saints do not fully realize God as their "all" (Ps. 73:25) now, through desiring it; then each shall feel, *God is all to me.* **29. Else**—if there be no resurrection. **what shall they do?**—How wretched is their lot! **they . . . which are baptized for the dead**—third person; a class distinct from that in which the apostle places himself, "we" (vss. 30); first person. ALFORD thinks there is an allusion to a practice at Corinth of baptizing a living person *in behalf of* a friend who died unbaptized; thus Paul, without giving the least sanction to the practice, uses an *ad hominem* argument from it against its practicers, some of whom, though using it, denied the resurrection: "What account can they give of their practice; why are they at the trouble of it, if the dead rise not?" [So Jesus used an *ad hominem* argument, Matthew 12:27.] But if so, it is strange there is no direct censure of it. Some Marcionites adopted the practice at a later period, probably from taking this passage, as AL-FORD does; but, generally, it was unknown in the Church. BENGEL translates, "over (immediately upon) the dead," i.e., who will be gathered to the dead *immediately after* baptism. Cf. Job 17:1, "the graves are ready for me." The price they get for their trouble is, that they should be gathered to the dead for ever (vss. 13, 16). Many in the ancient Church put off baptism till near death. This seems the better view; though there may have been some rites of symbolical baptism at Corinth, now unknown, perhaps grounded on Jesus' words (Matt. 20:22, 23), which Paul here alludes to. The best punctuation is, "If the dead rise not at all, why are they then baptized *for them"* (so the oldest MSS. read the last words, instead of "for the dead")? **30. we**—apostles (vs. 9; ch. 4:9). A gradation from those who could only for a little time enjoy this life (i.e., those baptized at the point of death), to *us,* who could enjoy it longer, if we had not renounced the world for Christ [BENGEL]. **31. by your rejoic-**

ing—*by the glorying which I have concerning you,* as the fruit of my labors in the Lord. Some of the earliest MSS. and fathers read "our," with the same sense. BENGEL understands "your rejoicing," to be *the enjoyable state of the Corinthians,* as contrasted with his dying daily to give his converts *rejoicing* or *glorying* (ch. 4:8; II Cor. 4:12, 15; Eph. 3:13; Phil. 1:26). But the words, "which I have," favor the explanation—'*the rejoicing which I have over you.*' Many of the oldest MSS. and *Vulgate* insert "brethren" here. **I die daily**—This ought to stand first in the sentence, as it is so put prominently forward in the *Greek.* I am day by day in sight of death, exposed to it, and expecting it (II Cor. 4:11, 12; 1:8, 9; 11:23). **32. Punctuate thus:** "If after the manner of men I have fought with beasts at Ephesus, what advantageth it me? If the dead rise not, let us eat and drink . . ." [BENGEL]. If *"merely as a man"* (with the mere human hope of the present life; not with the Christian's hope of the resurrection; answering to "If the dead rise not," the parallel clause in the next sentence), I have fought with men resembling savage beasts. Heraclitus, of Ephesus, had termed his countrymen "wild beasts" 400 years before. So Epimenides called the Cretians (Titus 1:12). Paul was still at Ephesus (ch. 16:8), and there his life was daily in danger (ch. 4:9; cf. II Cor. 1:8). Though the tumult (Acts 19:29, 30) had *not yet taken place* (for after it he set out *immediately* for Macedonia), this Epistle was written evidently just before it, when the storm was gathering; "many adversaries" (ch. 16:9) were already menacing him. **what advantageth it me?**—seeing I have renounced all that, *"as a mere man,"* might compensate me for such sufferings, gain, fame, etc. **let us eat . . .**—Quoted from LXX, (Isa. 22:13), where the prophet describes the reckless self-indulgence of the despisers of God's call to mourning, Let us enjoy the good things of life now, for it soon will end. Paul imitates the language of such skeptics, to reprove both their theory and practice. "If men but persuade themselves that they shall die like the beasts, they soon will live like beasts too" [SOUTH]. **33. evil communications corrupt good manners**—a current saying, forming a verse in Menander, the comic poet, who probably took it from Euripides (SOCRATES, *Historia Ecclesiastica,* 3. 16). "Evil communications" refer to intercourse with those who deny the resurrection. Their notion seems to have been that the resurrection is merely spiritual, that sin has its seat solely in the body, and will be left behind when the soul leaves it, if, indeed, the soul survive death at all. **good**—not only *good-natured,* but *pliant.* Intimacy with the profligate society around was apt to corrupt the principles of the Corinthians. **34. Awake**—lit., *"out of the sleep"* of carnal intoxication into which ye are thrown by the influence of these skeptics (vs. 32; Joel 1:5). **to righteousness**—in contrast with "sin" in this verse, and *corrupt manners* (vs. 33). **sin not**—Do not give yourselves up to sinful pleasures. The *Greek* expresses a continued state of abstinence from sin. Thus, Paul implies that they who live in sinful pleasures readily persuade themselves of what they wish, viz., that there is to be no resurrection. **some**—the same as in vs. 12. **have not the knowledge of God**—*and so know not His power* in the resurrection (Matt. 22:29). Stronger than "are ignorant of God." An habitual *ignorance:* wilful, in that they prefer to keep their sins, rather than part with them, in order to *know* God (cf. John 7:17; I Pet. 2:15). **to your shame**—that you Corinthian Christians, who boast of your *knowledge,* should have among you, and maintain intercourse with, those so practically ignorant of God, as to deny the resurrection. **35. How**—It is folly to deny a fact of REVELATION, because we do not know the *"how."* Some measure God's power by their petty intelligence, and won't admit, *even on His assurance,* anything which they cannot explain. Ezekiel's *answer of faith* to the question is the truly wise one (Ezek. 37:3). So Jesus argues not on principles of philosophy, but wholly from "the power of God," as declared by the Word of God (Matt. 19:26; Mark 10:27; 12:23; Luke 18:27). **come**— The dead are said to *depart,* or to be *deceased:* those rising again to *come.* The objector could not understand *how* the dead are to rise, and with *what kind of a body* they are to come. Is it to be the same body? If so, how is this, since the resurrection bodies will not eat or drink, or beget children, as the natural bodies do? Besides, the latter have mouldered into dust. *How* then can they rise again? If it be a different body, how can the personal identity be preserved? Paul answers, In one sense it will be the same body, in another, a distinct body. It will be a body, but a spiritual, not a natural, body. **36. fool**—with all thy boasted philosophy (Ps. 14:1). **that which thou**—"thou," emphatical: appeal to the objector's *own* experience: "The seed which *thou thyself* sowest." Paul, in this verse and in vs. 42, answers the question of vs. 35, "How?" and in vss. 37-41 and 43, the question, "With *what kind* of body?" He converts the very objection (the death of the natural body) into an argument. Death, so far from preventing *quickening,* is the necessary prelude and prognostication of it, just as the seed "is not quickened" into a new sprout with increased produce, "except it die" (except a dissolution of its previous organization takes place). Christ by His death for us has not given us a reprieve from death as to the life which we have from Adam; nay, He permits the law to take its course on our fleshly nature; but He brings from Himself new spiritual and heavenly life out of death (vs. 37). **37. not that body that shall be**—a *body* beautiful and no longer a "bare grain" [BENGEL]. No longer without stalk or ear, but clothed with blade and ears, and yielding many grains instead of only one [GROTIUS]. There is not an identity of all the particles of the old and the new body. For the perpetual transmutation of matter is inconsistent with this. But there is a hidden germ which constitutes the identity of body amidst all outward changes: the outward accretions fall off in its development, while the germ remains the same. Every such germ ("seed," vs. 38) "shall have its own body," and be instantly recognized, just as each plant now is known from the seed that was sown (see *Note,* ch. 6:13). So Christ by the same image illustrated the truth that His death was the necessary prelude of His putting on His glorified body, which is the ground of the regeneration of the many who believe (John 12:24). Progress is the law of the spiritual, as of the natural world. Death is the avenue not to mere *revivification* or *reanimation,* but to *resurrection* and *regeneration* (Matt. 19:28; Phil. 3:21). Cf. *"planted,"* etc., Romans 6:5. **38. as it hath pleased him**—at creation, when He gave *to each of the* (kinds of) *seeds* (so the *Greek* is for "to every seed") *a body of its own* (Gen. 1:11, "after its kind," suited to its species). So God can and will give to the blessed at the resurrection *their own* appropriate *body,* such *as it pleases Him,* and such as is suitable to their glorified state: a body peculiar to the individual, sub-

stantially the same as the body sown. **39-41.** Illustrations of the suitability of bodies, however various, to their species: the flesh of the several species of animals; bodies celestial and terrestrial; the various kinds of light in the sun, moon, and stars, respectively. **flesh**—animal organism [DE WETTE]. He implies by the word that our resurrection bodies shall be in some sense really flesh, not mere phantoms of air [ESTIUS]. So some of the oldest creeds expressed it, "I believe in the resurrection of the *flesh.*" Cf. as to Jesus' own resurrection body, Luke 24:39; John 20:27; to which *ours shall be made like,* and therefore shall be *flesh,* but not of animal organism (Phil. 3:21) and liable to corruption. But vs. 50 below implies, it is not "flesh and blood" in the animal sense we now understand them; for these "shall not inherit the kingdom of God." **not the same**—not flesh of the same nature and excellency. As the kinds of flesh, however widely differing from one another, do not cease to be flesh, so the kinds of bodies, however differing from one another, are still bodies. All this is to illustrate the difference of the new celestial body from its terrestrial seed, while retaining a substantial identity. **beasts**—quadrupeds. **another of fishes ... another of birds**—Most of the oldest MSS. read thus, "another FLESH of *birds* ... another of *fishes":* the order of nature. **40. celestial bodies**— not the sun, moon, and stars, which are first introduced in vs. 41, but *the bodies of angels,* as distinguished from the bodies of earthly creatures. **the glory of the celestial**—(Luke 9:26). **glory of ... terrestrial**—(Matt. 6:28, 29; I Pet. 1:24). **41. one glory of ... sun ... another ... of ... moon**—The analogy is not to prove different degrees of glory among the blessed (whether this may be, or not, *indirectly* hinted at), but this: As the various fountains of *light,* which is so similar in its aspect and properties, differ (the sun from the moon, and the moon from the stars; *and even* one star from another star, though all seem so much alike); so there is nothing unreasonable in the doctrine that *our present bodies* differ from *our resurrection bodies,* though still continuing *bodies.* Cf. the same simile, appropriate especially in the clear Eastern skies (Dan. 12:3; Matt. 13:43). Also that of *seed* in the same parable (Matt. 13:24; Gal. 6:7, 8). **42. sown**—Following up the image of *seed.* A delightful word instead of *burial.* **in corruption** —*liable to corruption: corruptible:* not merely a prey *when dead* to corruption; as the contrast shows, "raised in incorruption," i.e., *not liable to corruption, incorruptible.* **43. in dishonour**—answering to "our *vile* body" (Phil. 3:21); lit., "our body of humiliation": liable to various humiliations of disease, injury, and decay at last. **in glory**—the garment of incorruption (vss. 42, 43) like His glorious body (Phil. 4:21), which we shall put on (vss. 49, 53; II Cor. 5:2-4). **in weakness**—liable to infirmities (II Cor. 13:4). **in power**—answering to a "spiritual body" (vs. 44; cf. Luke 1:17, "Spirit and power"). Not liable to the weaknesses of our present frail bodies (Isa. 33:24; Rev. 21:4). **44. a natural body**—lit., *"an animal body,"* a body moulded in its organism of "flesh and blood" (vs. 50) to suit the animal soul which predominates in it. The Holy Spirit *in the spirit* of believers, indeed, is an earnest of a superior state (Rom. 8:11), but meanwhile *in the body* the animal soul preponderates; hereafter the Spirit shall predominate, and the animal soul be duly subordinate. **spiritual body**—a body wholly moulded by the Spirit, and its organism not conformed to the lower and animal

(Luke 20:35, 36), but to the higher and spiritual, life (cf. ch. 2:14; I Thess. 5:23). **There is . . .**—The oldest MSS. read, "IF there is a natural (or *animal-souled*) body, there is *also* a spiritual body." It is no more wonderful a thing, that there should be a body fitted to the capacities and want of man's highest part, his spirit (which we see to be the case), than that there should be one fitted to the capacities and wants of his subordinate part, the animal soul [ALFORD]. **45. so**—in accordance with the distinction just mentioned between the natural or *animal-souled* body and the *spiritual* body. **it is written** —(Gen. 2:7)—"Man became (was made to become) a living soul," i.e., endowed with *an animal soul*, the living principle of his body. **the last Adam**— the LAST Head of humanity, who is to be fully manifested in *the last day*, which is *His* day (John 6:39). He is so called in Job 19:25; see my *Note* there (cf. Rom. 5:14). In contrast to "the last," Paul calls "man" (Gen. 2:7) "the FIRST Adam." **quickening**—not only living, but *making alive* (John 5:21; 6:33, 39, 40, 54, 57, 62, 63; Rom. 8:11). As the *natural* or *animal-souled* body (vs. 44) is the fruit of our union with the first Adam, an *animal-souled* man, so the *spiritual* body is the fruit of our union with the second Adam, who is the quickening Spirit (II Cor. 3:17). As He became representative of the whole of humanity in His union of the two natures, He exhausted in His own person the sentence of death passed on all men, and giveth spiritual and everlasting life to whom He will. **46. afterward**—Adam had a soul not necessarily mortal, as it afterwards became by sin, but "a *living* soul," and destined to live for ever, if he had eaten of the tree of life (Gen. 3:22); still his body was but an *animal-souled* body, not a *spiritual* body, such as believers shall have; much less was he a "life-giving spirit," as Christ. His soul had the germ of the Spirit, rather than the fulness of it, such as man shall have when restored "body, soul, and spirit," by the second Adam (I Thess. 5:23). As the first and lower Adam came before the second and heavenly Adam, so the animal-souled body comes first, and must die before it be changed into the spiritual body (i.e., that in which the Spirit predominates over the animal soul). **47. of the earth** —inasmuch as being sprung from the earth, he is "earthy" (Gen. 2:7; 3. 19, "dust thou art"); i.e., not merely earthly or born *upon* the earth, but *terrene,* or *of earth;* lit., "of *heaped* earth" or clay. Adam means *red earth.* **the Lord**—omitted in the oldest MSS. and versions. **from heaven**—(John 3:13, 31). Humanity in Christ is generic. In Him man is impersonated in his true ideal as God originally designed him. Christ is the representative man, the federal head of redeemed man. **48. As is the earthy**—viz., Adam. **they . . . that are earthy**—All Adam's posterity in their *natural* state (John 3:6, 7). **the heavenly**—Christ. **they . . . that are heavenly**— His people in their regenerate state (Phil. 3:20, 21). As the former precedes the latter state, so the *natural bodies* precede the *spiritual bodies.* **49. as** —Greek, "even as" (see Gen. 5:3). **we shall also bear**—or wear as a garment [BENGEL]. The oldest MSS. and versions read, "We must also bear," or "let us also bear." It implies the divine appointment (cf. "must," vs. 53) and faith assenting to it. An exhortation, and yet implying a promise (so Rom. 8:29). The conformity to the image of the heavenly Representative man is to be begun here in our souls, in part, and shall be perfected at the resurrection in both bodies and souls. **50.** (See *Notes*, vss. 37, 39.) "Flesh and blood" of the same

animal and corruptible nature as our present (vs. 44) *animal-souled* bodies, cannot inherit the kingdom of God. Therefore the believer acquiesces gladly in the unrepealed sentence of the holy law, which appoints the death of the present body as the necessary preliminary to the resurrection body of glory. Hence he "dies daily" to the flesh and to the world, as the necessary condition to his regeneration here and hereafter (John 3:6; Gal. 2:20). As the being *born of the flesh* constitutes a child of Adam, so the being *born of the Spirit* constitutes a child of God. **cannot**—Not merely is the change of body *possible,* but it is *necessary.* The spirit extracted from the dregs of wine does not so much differ from them, as the glorified man does from the mortal man [BENGEL] of mere animal flesh and blood (Gal. 1:16). The resurrection body will be still a body though spiritual, and substantially retaining the personal identity; as is proved by Luke 24:39; John 20:27, compared with Philippians 3:21. **the kingdom of God**—which is not at all merely animal, but altogether spiritual. *Corruption* doth not *inherit,* though it is the way to, *incorruption* (vss. 36, 52, 53). **51. Behold**—Calling attention to the "mystery" heretofore hidden in God's purposes, but now revealed. **you**—emphatical in the *Greek;* I show (*Greek,* "tell," viz., *by the word of the Lord,* I Thess. 4:15) YOU, who think you have so much knowledge, "a mystery" (cf. Rom. 11:25) which your reason could never have discovered. Many of the old MSS. and Fathers read, "We shall all sleep, but we shall not all be changed"; but this is plainly a corrupt reading, inconsistent with I Thessalonians 4:15, 17, and with the apostle's argument here, which is that a *change* is necessary (vs. 53). *English Version* is supported by some of the oldest MSS. and Fathers. The *Greek* is literally "We all shall not sleep, but . . . ." The putting off of the corruptible body for an incorruptible by an instantaneous *change* will, in the case of "the quick," stand as equivalent to death, appointed to all men (Heb. 9:27); of this Enoch and Elijah are types and forerunners. The "we" implies that Christians in that age and every successive age since and hereafter were designed to stand waiting, as if Christ might come again in their time, and as if they might be found among "the quick." **52. the last trump**— at the sounding of the trumpet *on the last day* [VATABLUS] (Matt. 24:31; I Thess. 4:16). Or the Spirit by Paul hints that the other trumpets mentioned subsequently in the Apocalypse shall precede, and that this shall be the *last* of all (cf. Isa. 27:13; Zech. 9:14). As the law was given with the sound of a trumpet, so the final judgment according to it (Heb. 12:19; cf. Exod. 19:16). As the Lord ascended "with the sound of a trumpet" (Ps. 47:5), so He shall descend (Rev. 11:15). The trumpet was sounded to convoke the people on solemn feasts, especially on the first day of the seventh month (the type of the *completion* of time; *seven* being the number for *perfection;* on the tenth of the same month was the atonement, and on the fifteenth the feast of tabernacles, commemorative of completed salvation out of the spiritual Egypt, cf. Zech. 14:18, 19); cf. Ps. 50:1-7. Cf. His calling forth of Lazarus from the grave "with a loud voice," John 11:43, with 5:25, 28. **and**—immediately, in consequence. **53. this**—pointing to his *own* body and that of those whom he addresses. **put on**—as a garment (II Cor. 5:2, 3). **immortality**— Here only, besides I Timothy 6:16, the word "immortality" is found. Nowhere is the immortality of the *soul,* distinct from the body, taught; a notion which many erroneously have derived from heathen philosophers. Scripture does not contemplate the anomalous state brought about by death, as the consummation to be earnestly looked for (II Cor. 5:4), but the resurrection. **54. then**—not before. Death has as yet *a sting* even to the believer, in that his *body* is to be under its power till the resurrection. But then the sting and power of death shall cease for ever. **Death is swallowed up in victory** —In *Hebrew* of Isaiah 25:8, from which it is quoted, "*He* (Jehovah) *will swallow up* death in victory"; i.e., *for ever:* as "in victory" often means in *Hebrew* idiom (Jer. 3:5; Lam. 5:20). Christ will swallow it up *so altogether victoriously* that it shall never more regain its power (cf. Hos. 6:2; 13:14; II Cor. 5:4; Heb. 2:14, 15; Rev. 20:14; 21:4). **55.** Quoted from Hos. 13:14, substantially; but freely used by the warrant of the Spirit by which Paul wrote. The *Hebrew* may be translated, "O death, where are thy plagues? Where, O Hades, is thy destruction?" The LXX, "Where is thy victory (lit., *in a lawsuit*), O death? Where is thy sting, O Hades?" "Sting" answers to the *Hebrew* "plagues," viz., a poisoned *sting* causing *plagues*. Appropriate, as to the old serpent (Gen. 3; Num. 21:6). "Victory" answers to the *Hebrew* "destruction." Cf. Isaiah 25:7, "*destroy . . .* veil *. . . over all nations,*" viz., *victoriously destroy* it; and to "in victory" (vs. 54), which he triumphantly repeats. The "where" implies their past victorious destroying power and sting, now gone for ever; obtained through Satan's triumph over man in Eden, which enlisted God's law on the side of Satan and death against man (Rom. 5:12, 17:21). The souls in Hades being freed by the resurrection, death's sting and victory are gone. For "O grave," the oldest MSS .and versions read, "O death," the second time. **56.** If there were no sin, there would be no death. Man's transgression of the law gives death its lawful power. **strength of sin is the law**—Without the law sin is not perceived or imputed (Rom. 3:20; 4:15; 5:13). The law makes sin the more grievous by making God's will the clearer (Rom. 7:8-10). Christ's people are no longer "under the law" (Rom. 6:14). **57. to God**—The victory was in no way due to ourselves (Ps. 98:1). **giveth**—a present certainty. **the victory**—which death and Hades ("the grave") had aimed at, but which, notwithstanding the opposition of them, as well as of the law and sin, we have gained. The repetition of the word (vss. 54, 55) is appropriate to the triumph gained. **58. beloved**— Sound doctrine kindles Christian *love*. **steadfast** —not turning aside from the faith of the resurrection *of yourselves*. **unmovable**—not turned aside by *others* (vs. 12; Col. 1:23). **the work of the Lord** —the promotion of Christ's kingdom (Phil. 2:30). **not in vain**—as the deniers of the resurrection would make it (vss. 14, 17). **in the Lord**—applying to the whole sentence and its several clauses: Ye, as being in the Lord by faith, know that your labor in the Lord (i.e., labor according to His will) is not to be without its reward in the Lord (through His merits and according to His gracious appointment).

CHAPTER 16

Vss. 1-24. Directions as to the Collection for the Judean Christians: Paul's Future Plans: He Commends to Them Timothy, Apollos, etc. Salutations and Conclusions. **1. collection for the saints**—at Jerusalem (Rom. 15:26) and in Judea (Acts 11:29, 30; 24:17; cf. II Cor. 8:4; 9:1, 12). He

says "saints" rather than "the poor," to remind the Corinthians that in giving, it is to *the Lord's people,* their own *brethren in the faith*. Towards the close of the national existence of the Jews, Judea and Jerusalem were harassed with various troubles, which in part affected the Jewish Christians. The community of goods which existed among them for a time gave temporary relief but tended ultimately to impoverish all by paralyzing individual exertion (Acts 2:44), and hence was soon discontinued. A beautiful fruit of grace it was, that he who had by persecutions robbed many of their all (Acts 26:10), should become the foremost in exertions for their relief. **as I have given**—rather, "*gave* order," viz., during my journey through Galatia, that mentioned in Acts 18:23. The churches of Galatia and Phrygia were the last which Paul visited before writing this Epistle. He was now at Ephesus, and came thither immediately from visiting them (Acts 18:23; 19:1). That he had not been silent in Galatia on contributions for the poor, appears from the hint let fall in his Epistle to that church (Gal. 2:10): an undesigned coincidence and mark of genuineness [PALEY'S *Horæ Paulinæ*]. He proposes the Galatians as an example to the Corinthians, the Corinthians to the Macedonians, the Corinthians and Macedonians to the Romans (Rom 15:26, 27; II Cor. 9:2). There is great force in example. **2. first day of . . . week**—already kept sacred by Christians as the day of the Lord's resurrection, the beginning day both of the physical and of the new spiritual creations: it gradually superseded the Jewish sabbath on the seventh day (Ps. 118:22-24; John 20:19, 26; Acts 20:7; Rev. 1:10). So the beginning of the year was changed from autumn to spring when Israel was brought out of Egypt. Three annual feasts, all typical of Christian truths, were directed to be kept on the first day of the week: the feast of the wave offering of the first sheaf, answering to the Lord's resurrection; Pentecost, or the feast of weeks, typical of the fruits of the resurrection in the Christian Church (Lev. 23: 11, 15, 16, 36); the feast of tabernacles at harvest, typical of the ingathering of the full number of the elect from one end of heaven to the other. Easter was directed to be kept as a holy sabbath (Exod. 12:16). The Christian Sabbath commemorates the respective works of the Three Persons of the Triune God—creation, redemption (the resurrection), and sanctification (on Pentecost the Holy Ghost being poured out). Jesus came to fulfil the Spirit of the Law, not to cancel it, or to lower its standard. The primary object of the sabbath is *holiness*, not merely rest: "Remember that thou keep *holy* the sabbath day." Cf. Genesis 2:3, "God *blessed* and *sanctified* it, because . . . in it He had rested . . . ." The word "Remember" implies that it was in existence *before* the giving of the law from Sinai, and refers to its institution in Paradise (cf. Exod. 16:22, 23, 26, 30). "Six days shalt thou labor": the *spirit* of the command is fulfilled whether the six days' labor be on the last six days or on the first. A perpetual sabbath would doubtless be the highest Christian ideal; but living in a world of business where the Christian ideal is not yet realized, if a law of definite times was necessary in Paradise, it is still more so now. **every one of you**—even those in limited circumstances. **lay by him**—though there be not a weekly *public* collection, each is *privately* to set apart *a definite proportion of his weekly income* for the Lord's cause and charity. **in store**—abundantly: the earnest of a better store *laid up* for the giver (I Tim. 6:19). **as God hath prospered him**—lit., "whatsoever he may be prospered in," or "may by prosperity have acquired" [ALFORD], (Matt. 25:15-29; II Cor. 8:12). **that there be no gatherings when I come**—that they may not *then* have to be made, when your and my time ought to be employed in more directly spiritual things. When men give once for all, not so much is given. But when each *lays by* something every Lord's day, more is collected than one would have given at once [BENGEL]. **3. approve by your letters**—rather translate, "Whomsoever ye shall approve, them will I send *with* letters": viz., letters to several persons at Jerusalem, which would be their credentials. There could be no need of letters *from them* before Paul's coming, if the persons recommended were *not to be sent off before it.* Lit., "by letters"; an abbreviated expression for "I will send, recommending them by letters" [GROTIUS]. If *English Version* be retained, the sense will be, "When I come, I will send those whom by your letters, *then to be given them,* ye shall approve." But the antithesis (opposition or contrast) to Paul himself (vs. 4) favors GROTIUS' view. So "by" means *with* (Rom. 2:27); and the Greek for "by" is translated, with (II Cor. 2:4). **liberality**—lit., *gracious or free gift* (II Cor. 8:4). **4. meet**—"worth while." If your collections be large enough to be *worth* an apostle's journey (a stimulus to their liberality), I will accompany them *myself* instead of giving them *letters* credential (vs. 3; cf. Acts 20:1-4). **with me**—to guard against all possible suspicion of evil (II Cor. 8:4, 19-21). **5-7.** His first intention had been (II Cor. 1:15, 16) to pass through them (Corinth) to Macedonia, and again return to them from Macedonia, and so to Judea; this he had announced in the lost epistle (ch. 5:9); now having laid aside this intention (for which he was charged with levity, II Cor. 1:17, etc., whereas it was through lenity, II Cor. 1:23; 2:1), he announces his second plan of "not seeing them now by the way," but "passing through Macedonia" first on his way to them, and then "tarrying a while," and even "abiding and wintering with them." **for I do pass**—as much as to say, "This is what I at last *resolve upon*" (not as the erroneous subscription of the Epistle represents it, as if he was THEN at Philippi, *on his way through* Macedonia); implying that there had been some previous communication upon the subject of the journey, and also that there had been some indecisiveness in the apostle's plan [PALEY]. In accordance with his second plan, we find him in Macedonia when II Corinthians was written (II Cor. 2:13; 8:1; 9:2, 4), and on his way to Corinth (II Cor. 12:14; 13:1; cf. Acts 20:1, 2). "Pass through" is opposed to "abide" (vs. 6). He was *not yet* in Macedonia (as vs. 8 shows), but at Ephesus; but he was *thinking* of *passing through* it (not *abiding* as he purposed to do at Corinth). **6.** He did "abide and even winter" for the three WINTER months in Greece (Corinth), Acts 20:3, 6; from which passage it seems that Paul probably left Corinth about a month before the "days of unleavened bread" or the Passover (so as to allow time to touch at Thessalonica and Berea, from which cities two of his companions were; as we read he did at Philippi; so that thus the three months at Corinth would be December, January, and February [BIRKS, *Horæ Apostolicæ*]. **ye**—emphatical in the Greek. **whithersoever I go**—He purposed to go to Judea (II Cor. 1:16) from Corinth, but his plans were not positively fixed as yet (*Note*, vs. 4; cf. Acts 19:21). **7. I will not see you now by the way**—lit., "I do not wish to see you this time in passing"; i.e., to pay you now what would have to be a merely

passing visit as I did in the second visit (II Cor. 12:14). In contrast to "a while," i.e., *some time,* as the *Greek* might better be translated. **but**—The oldest MSS. read "for." **8. at Ephesus**—whence Paul writes this Epistle. Cf. vs. 19, "Asia," wherein Ephesus was. **until Pentecost**—He seems to have stayed as he here purposes: for just when the tumult which drove him away broke out, he was already intending to leave Ephesus (Acts 19:21, 22). Combined with ch. 5:7, 8, this verse fixes the date of this Epistle to a few weeks before Pentecost, and very soon after the Passover. **9. door**—(II Cor. 2:12). An *opening* for the extension of the Gospel. Wise men are on the watch for, and avail themselves of, *opportunities.* So *"door* of hope," Hosea 2:15. "Door of faith," Acts 14:27. "An open door," Revelation 3:8. "A door of utterance," Colossians 4:3. "Great," i.e., extensive. "Effectual," i.e., *requiring great labors* [ESTIUS]; or *opportune for effecting great results* [BEZA]. **many adversaries**—who would block up the way and prevent us from entering the open door. Not here false teachers, but open adversaries: both Jews and heathen. After Paul, by his now long-continued labors at Ephesus, had produced effects which threatened the interests of those whose gains were derived from idolatry, "many adversaries" arose (Acts 19:9-23). Where great good is, there evil is sure to start up as its antagonist. **10. Now**—rather, "But." Therefore Timothy was not the *bearer* of the Epistle; for it would not then be said, "IF Timothy come." He must therefore have been *sent* by Paul from Ephesus *before* this Epistle was written, to accord with ch. 4:17-19; and yet the passage here implies that Paul did not expect him to arrive at Corinth till *after* the letter was received. He tells them how to treat him "if" he should arrive. Acts 19:21, 22 clears up the difficulty: Timothy, when sent from Ephesus, where this Epistle was written, did not proceed direct to Corinth, but *went first to Macedonia;* thus though sent before the letter, he might not reach Corinth till after it was received in that city. The undesigned coincidence between the Epistle and the history, and the clearing up of the meaning of the former (which does not mention the journey to Macedonia at all) by the latter, is a sure mark of genuineness [PALEY's *Horæ Paulinæ*]. It is not certain that Timothy actually reached Corinth; for in Acts 19:22 only *Macedonia* is mentioned; but it does not follow that though Macedonia was the immediate object of his mission, Corinth was not the ultimate object. The "IF Timothy come," implies uncertainty. II Corinthians 1:1 represents him with Paul in *Macedonia;* and II Corinthians 12:18, speaking of *Titus* and others sent to Corinth, does not mention Timothy, which it would have probably done, had one so closely connected with the apostle as Timothy was, stayed as his delegate at Corinth. The mission of Titus then took place, when it became uncertain whether Timothy could go forward from Macedonia to Corinth, Paul being anxious for *immediate* tidings of the state of the Corinthian Church. ALFORD argues that if so, Paul's adversaries would have charged him with fickleness in this case also (II Cor. 1:17), as in the case of his own change of purpose. But Titus was sent *directly* to Corinth, so as to arrive there before Timothy could by the route through Macedonia. Titus' presence would thus make amends for the disappointment as to the intended visit of Timothy and would disarm adversaries of a charge in this respect (II Cor. 7:6, 7). **without fear**—Referring perhaps to a nervous timidity in Timothy's character (I Tim. 3:15; 5:22, 24). His *youth* would add to this feeling, as well as his country, Lystra, likely to be despised in refined Corinth. **11. despise**—This charge is not given concerning any other of the many messengers whom Paul sent. I Timothy 4:12 accounts for it (cf. Ps. 119:141). He was a *young man,* younger probably than those usually employed in the Christian missions; whence Paul apprehending lest he should, on that account, be exposed to contempt, cautions him, "Let no man despise thy youth" [PALEY's *Horæ Paulinæ*]. **conduct**—set him on his way with every mark of respect, and with whatever he needs (Titus 3:13). **in peace**—(Acts 15:33; Heb. 11:31). "Peace" is the salutation of kindness and respect in the East; and so it stands for every blessing. Perhaps here there is too a contrast between "peace" and the "contentions" prevalent at Corinth (ch. 1:11). **I look for him**—He and Titus were appointed to meet Paul in Troas, whither the apostle purposed proceeding from Ephesus (II Cor. 2:12, 13). Paul thus claims their respect for Timothy as one whom he felt so necessary to himself as "look for" to him [THEOPHYL]. **with the brethren**—Others besides Erastus accompanied Timothy to Macedonia (cf. vs. 12; Acts 19:22). **12. Apollos, I greatly desired . . . to come unto you**—He says this lest they should suspect that he from jealousy prevented Apollos' coming to them; perhaps they had expressly requested Apollos to be sent to them. Apollos was not at Ephesus when Paul wrote (cf. vs. 19, and ch. 1:1). Probably Apollos' unwillingness to go to Corinth at this time was because, being aware of the undue admiration of his rhetorical style which led astray many at Corinth, he did not wish to sanction it (ch. 1:12, 3:4). Paul's noble freedom from all selfish jealousy led him to urge Apollos to go; and, on the other hand, Apollos, having heard of the abuse of his name at Corinth to party purposes, perseveringly refused to go. Paul, of course, could not state in his letter particularly these reasons in the existing state of division prevalent there. He calls Apollos "brother" to mark the unity that was between the two. **with the brethren**—who bear this letter (vs. 17). (See subscription added to the Epistle.) CONYBEARE thinks Titus was one of the bearers of this first letter (II Cor. 8:6, 16-24; 12:18). ALFORD thinks "the brethren" here may be the same as in vs. 11. **convenient time**—Apollos did return to Corinth when their divisions were moderated [JEROME], and so it was a more seasonable time. **13.** He shows that they ought to make their hopes of salvation to depend not on Apollos or any other teacher; that it rests with themselves. "Watch ye": for ye are slumbering. "Stand": for ye are like men tottering. "Quit you like men; be strong": for ye are effeminate (vs. 14). "Let all your things be done with charity" (ch. 8:1; 13:1): not with strifes as at present [CHRYSOSTOM]. "In the faith" which was assailed by some (ch. 15:1, 2, 12-17). **15. first fruits of Achaia**—the first Achæan converts (cf. Rom. 16:5). The image is from the *first fruits* offered to the Lord (Lev. 23:10; cf. ch. 15:20). The members of this family had been baptized by Paul himself (ch. 1:16). **addicted themselves to the ministry of the saints**—Translate, "Set themselves, (i.e., voluntarily) to minister unto the saints" (cf. II Cor. 8:4). **16. That ye**—Translate, "That ye also," viz., in your turn . . . in return for their self-devotion [ALFORD]. **helpeth with**—them. **laboureth**—by himself. **17. Fortunatus . . . Achaicus**—probably of Stephanas' household. **that . . . lacking on**

your part—So far as you were unable *yourselves* to "*refresh* my spirit," in that you are absent from me, "they have supplied" by coming to me from you, and so supplying the means of intercourse between you and me. They seem to have carried this letter back; see the subscription below: hence the exhortations, vss. 16, 18, as though they would be at Corinth when the Epistle arrived. **18. refreshed my spirit and yours**—"yours" will be refreshed on receiving this letter, by knowing that "my spirit is refreshed" by their having come to me from you; and (perhaps) by the good report they gave of many of you (ch. 1:4-8); *my refreshment of spirit* redounds to *yours,* as being my disciples (II Cor. 7:13; cf. Zech. 6:8). **acknowledge**—render them due acknowledgments by a kind reception of them: I Thessalonians 5:12, "know" them in their true worth and treat them accordingly. **19. Asia**—not all Asia Minor, but *Lydian Asia* only, of which Ephesus was the capital. **much**—with especial affection. **Aquila . . . Priscilla**—(Cf. Acts 18:2; Rom. 16:3, 4). Originally driven out of Italy by Claudius, they had come to Corinth (whence their salutation of the Corinthians is appropriate here), and then had removed with Paul from Corinth to Ephesus (Acts 18:2, 18, 19, 26); here, as at Rome subsequently, they set up a Church (or assembly of believers) at their house (Rom. 16: 3, 5). A pattern to Christian husbands and wives. Their Christian self-devoting love appears wherever they were (Rom. 16:3, 4). Even the gifted Apollos, so highly admired at Corinth, owed much of his knowledge to them (Acts 18:24-26). In vs. 20, "All the brethren" (i.e., the whole Church) seem to be distinguished from "the church that is in their house," which was but a partial and private assembly out of the general Church at Corinth. NEANDER thinks Romans 16:23 refers to "*the whole Church*" *meeting at the house of Gaius* (cf. Col. 4: 15). "Synagogue" implies an assembly in general, without reference to the character or motives of its members. "Church," like the *Hebrew Kahal.* implies an assembly *legally* convened; as, for instance, the Jews met as a body politic to receive the law (hence Stephen calls it "the *Church* in the wilderness," Acts 7:38), and having a legal bond of union. Christ's followers when dispersed from one another cease to be a *congregation* (synagogue), but still are a *Church,* having the common bond of union to the same Head by the same faith and hope [VITRINGA, *Synagogue and Temple*]. From this we may explain Paul's entering "*into every house* and haling men and women": he would in searching for Christians go to their several "houses" of prayer. **in the Lord**—They pray for all blessings on you from *the Lord,* the source of every good [GROTIUS]. ALFORD explains, "in a Christian manner," as mindful of your common Lord. "In the Lord" seems to me to refer to *their union together in Christ,* their prayers for one another's good being in virtue of that union. **20. holy kiss** —the token of the mutual love of Christians, especially at the Lord's Supper (cf. Rom. 16:16; I Thess. 5:26), "in which all the dissensions of the Corinthians would be swallowed up" [BENGEL]. **21. salutation . . . with mine own hand**—He therefore dictated all the rest of the Epistle. **22.** A solemn closing warning added *in his own hand* as in Ephesians 6:24; Colossians 4:18. **22. the Lord**—who ought to be "loved" above Paul, Apollos, and all other teachers. Love to one another is to be in connection with love to Him above all. IGNATIUS (*Epistola ad Romanos* 7) writes of Christ, "My love has been crucified" (cf. Song of Solomon 2:7). **Jesus Christ**—omitted in the oldest MSS. **let him be Anathema**—*accursed* with that curse which the Jews who call Jesus "accursed" (ch. 12:3) are bringing righteously on their own heads [BENGEL]. So far from "saluting" him, I bid him be *accursed*. **Maranatha**—*Syriac* for, "the Lord cometh." A motto or watchword to urge them to preparedness for the Lord's coming; as in Philippians 4:5, "The Lord is at hand." **23. The grace . . .**—This is the salutation meant in vs. 21; and from which unbelievers (vs. 22; cf. II John 10:11) are excluded [BENGEL]. **24. My love . . .**—After having administered some severe rebukes, he closes with expressions of "love": his very rebukes were prompted by *love*, and therefore are altogether in harmony with the profession of love here made: it was *love in Christ Jesus*, and therefore embraced "*all*" who loved Him.

The subscription represents the Epistle as written from *Philippi*. Verse 8 shows it was written *at Ephesus*. BENGEL conjectures that perhaps, however, it was *sent* from Philippi (vs. 5), because the deputies of the Corinthians had accompanied Paul thither. From Ephesus there was a road to Corinth above Philippi.

THE SECOND EPISTLE OF PAUL THE APOSTLE TO THE

CORINTHIANS

INTRODUCTION

THE following reasons seem to have induced Paul to write this Second Epistle to the Corinthians: (1) That he might explain the reasons for his having deferred to pay them his promised visit, by taking Corinth as his way to Macedonia (I Cor. 4:19; ch. 1:15, 16; cf. I Cor. 16:5); and so that he might set forth to them his apostolic walk in general (ch. 1:12, 24; 6:3–13; 7:2). (2) That he might commend their obedience in reference to the directions in his First Epistle, and at the same time direct them now to forgive the offender, as having been punished sufficiently (ch. 2:1–11; 7:6–16). (3) That he might urge them to collect for the poor saints at Jerusalem (ch. 8:1–9, 15). (4) That he might maintain his apostolic authority and reprove gainsayers.

The external testimonies for *its genuineness* are IRENÆUS, *Hæreses* 3, 7, 1; ATHENAGORAS, *De resurrectione mortuorum;* CLEMENT of Alexandria, *Stromata* 3, sec. 94; 4, sec. 101; TERTULLIAN, *De pudicitia*, ch. 13.

The TIME OF WRITING was after Pentecost, A.D. 57, when Paul left Ephesus for Troas. Having stayed in the latter place for some time preaching the Gospel with effect (ch. 2:12), he went on to Macedonia, being eager to meet Titus there, having been disappointed in his not coming to Troas, as had been agreed on between them. Having heard from him the tidings he so much desired of the good effect produced on the Corinthians by his First Epistle, and after having tested the liberality of the Macedonian churches (ch. 8:1), he wrote this Second Epistle, and then went on to Greece, where he abode for three months; and then, after travelling by land, reached Philippi on his return at Passover or Easter, A.D. 58 (Acts 20:1–6). So that this Epistle must have been written about autumn, A.D. 57.

Macedonia was THE PLACE from which it was written (ch. 9:2, where the present tense, "I boast," or "am boasting," implies his presence *then* in Macedonia). In Asia (Lydian Asia) he had undergone some great peril of his life (ch. 1:8, 9), whether the reference be [PALEY] to the tumult at Ephesus (Acts 19:23–41), or, as ALFORD thinks, to a dangerous illness in which he despaired of life. Thence he passed by Troas to Philippi, the first city which would meet him in entering Macedonia. The importance of the Philippian Church would induce him to stay there some time; as also his desire to collect contributions from the Macedonian churches for the poor saints at Jerusalem. His anxiety of mind is recorded (ch. 7:5) as occurring *when he came into Macedonia*, and therefore must have been at *Philippi*, which was the first city of Macedonia in coming from Troas; and here, too, from ch. 7:6, compared with v. 5, must have been the scene of his receiving the comforting tidings from Titus. "Macedonia" is used for *Philippi* in II Cor. 11:9, as is proved by comparison with Phil. 4:15, 16. So it is probably used here (ch. 7:5). ALFORD argues from ch. 8:1, where he speaks of the "grace bestowed on the *churches* (plural) of Macedonia," that Paul must have visited *other* churches in Macedonia, besides Philippi, when he wrote, e.g., Thessalonica, Berea, etc., and that Philippi, the *first* on his route, is less likely to have been the scene of his writing than the *last* on his route, whichever it was, perhaps Thessalonica. But Philippi, as being the chief town of the province, was probably the place to which all the collections of the churches were sent. Ancient tradition, too (as appears from the subscription to this Epistle), favors the view that Philippi was the place from which this Epistle was sent by the hands of Titus who received, besides, a charge to prosecute at Corinth the collection which he had begun at his first visit (ch. 8:6).

The STYLE is most varied, and passes rapidly from one phase of feeling to another; now joyous and consolatory, again severe and full of reproof; at one time gentle and affectionate, at another, sternly rebuking opponents and upholding his dignity as an apostle. This variety of style accords with the warm and earnest character of the apostle, which nowhere is manifested more beautifully than in this Epistle. His bodily frailty, and the chronic malady under which he suffered, and which is often alluded to (ch. 4:7; 5:1–4; 12:7–9; cf. *Note*, 1:8), must have been especially trying to one of his ardent temperament. But besides this, was the more pressing anxiety of the "care of all the churches." At Corinth, as elsewhere, Judaizing emissaries wished to bind legal fetters of letter and form (cf. ch. 3:3-18) on the freedom and catholicity of the Church. On the other hand, there were free-thinkers who defended their immorality of practice by infidel theories (I Cor. 15:12, 32-36). These were the "fightings without," and "fears within" (ch. 7:5, 6) which agitated the apostle's mind until Titus brought him comforting tidings from Corinth. Even then, while the majority at Corinth had testified their repentance, and, as Paul had desired, excommunicated the incestuous person, and contributed for the poor Christians of Judea, there was still a minority who, more contemptuously than ever, resisted the apostle. These accused him of crafty and mercenary motives, as if he had personal gain in view in the collection being made; and this, notwithstanding his scrupulous care to be above the possibility of reasonable suspicion, by having others besides himself to take charge of the money. This insinuation was palpably inconsistent with their other charge, that he could be no true apostle, as he did not claim maintenance from the churches which he founded. Another accusation they brought of cowardly weakness; that he was always threatening severe measures without daring to execute them (ch. 10:8-16; 13:2); and that he was vacillating in his teaching and practice, circumcising Timothy, and yet withholding circumcision from Titus; a Jew among the Jews, and a Greek among the Greeks. That most of these opponents were of the Judaizing party in the Church, appears from ch. 11:22. They seem to have been headed by an emissary from Judea ("he that cometh," ch. 11:4), who had brought "letters of commendation" (ch. 3:1) from members of the Church at Jerusalem, and who boasted of his purity of Hebrew descent, and his close connection with Christ Himself (ch. 11:13, 23). His partisans contrasted his high pretensions with the timid humility of Paul (I Cor. 2:3); and his rhetoric with the apostle's plain and unadorned style (ch. 11:6, 10:10, 13). It was this state of things at Corinth, reported by Titus, that caused Paul to send him back forthwith thither with this Second Epistle, which is addressed, not to Corinth only (I Cor. 1:2), but to all the churches also in Achaia (ch. 1:1), which had in some degree been affected by the same causes as affected the Corinthian Church. The widely different tone in different parts of the Epistle is due to the diversity which existed at Corinth between the penitent majority and the refractory minority. The former he addresses with the warmest affection; the latter with menace and warning. Two deputies, chosen by the churches to take charge of the contribution to be collected at Corinth, accompanied Titus (ch. 8:18, 19, 22).

CHAPTER 1

Vss. 1-24. The Heading; Paul's Consolations in Recent Trials in Asia; His Sincerity Towards the Corinthians; Explanation of His Not Having Visited Them as He Had Purposed. **1. Timothy our brother**—When writing *to* Timothy himself, he calls him "my son" (I Tim. 1:18). Writing *of* him, "brother," and "my beloved son" (I Cor. 4:17). He had been sent before to Macedonia, and had met Paul at Philippi, when the apostle passed over from Troas to Macedonia (cf. ch. 2:12, 13; *Notes,* I Cor. 16:10, 11). **in all Achaia**—comprising Hellas and the Peloponese. The Gentiles themselves, and Annæus Gallio, the proconsul (Acts 18), strongly testified their disapproval of the accusation brought by the Jews against Paul. Hence, the apostle was enabled to labor in the whole province of Achaia with such success as to establish several churches there (I Thess. 1:8; II Thess. 1:4), where, writing from Corinth, he speaks of the "churches," viz., not only the Corinthian, but others also—Athens, Cenchrea, and, perhaps, Sicyon, Argos, etc. He addresses "the Church in Corinth," *directly,* and all "the saints" in the province, *indirectly.* In Galatians 1:2 all the "*churches*" are addressed *directly* in the same circular Epistle. Hence, here he does not say, *all the churches,* but "all the saints." **3.** This thanksgiving for his late deliverance forms a suitable introduction for conciliating their favorable reception of his reasons for not having fulfilled his promise of visiting them (vss. 15-24). **Father of mercies**—i.e., the Source of all mercies (cf. Jas. 1:17; Rom. 12:1). **comfort**—which flows from His "mercies" experienced. Like a true man of faith, he mentions "mercies" and "comfort," before he proceeds to speak of *afflictions* (vss. 4, 5, 6). The "tribulation" of believers is not inconsistent with God's mercy, and does not beget in them suspicion of it; nay, in the end they feel that He is "the God of all comfort," i.e., who imparts *the only true and perfect* comfort *in every instance* (Ps. 146:3, 5, 8; Jas. 5:11). **4. us**—idiomatic for *me* (I Thess. 2:18). **that we may ... com-**

fort them which are in any trouble—Translate, as the *Greek* is the same as before, "tribulation." The apostle lived, not to himself, but to the Church; so, whatever graces God conferred on him, he considered granted not for himself alone, but that he might have the greater ability to help others [Calvin]. So participation in all the afflictions of man peculiarly qualified Jesus to be man's comforter in all his various afflictions (Isa. 50:4-6; Heb. 4:15). **5. sufferings**—standing in contrast with "salvation" (vs. 6); as "tribulation" (distress of mind), with *comfort* or "consolation." **of Christ**—Cf. Colossians 1:24. The *sufferings* endured, whether by Himself, or by His Church, with which He considers Himself identified (Matt. 25:40, 45; Acts 9:4; I John 4:17-21). Christ calls His people's sufferings His own suffering: (1) because of the sympathy and mystical union between Him and us (Rom. 8:17; I Cor. 4:10); (2) They are borne for His sake; (3) They tend to His glory (Eph. 4:1; I Pet. 4:14, 16). **abound in us**—Greek, "abound *unto* us." The order of the *Greek* following words is more forcible than in *English Version,* "Even so through Christ aboundeth also our comfort." The *sufferings* (plural) are many; but the *consolation* (though singular) swallows up them all. Comfort preponderates in this Epistle above that in the first Epistle, as now by the effect of the latter most of the Corinthians had been much impressed. **6. we ... afflicted ... for your consolation**—exemplifying the communion of saints. Their hearts were, so to speak, mirrors reflecting the likenesses of each other (Phil. 2:26, 27) [Bengel]. Alike the afflictions and the consolations of the apostle tend, as in him so in them, as having communion with him, to their consolation (vs. 4 and ch. 4:15). The *Greek* for "afflicted" is the same as before, and ought to be translated, "Whether we *be in tribulation.*" **which is effectual**—lit., worketh effectually. **in the enduring ...**—i.e., in enabling you to endure "the same sufferings which we also suffer." Here follows, in the oldest MSS. (not as *English Version* in the beginning of vs. 7), the clause, And our hope is steadfast on your behalf." **7. so** *shall ye be*—rather,

"So *are* ye." He means, there *is* a community of consolation, as of suffering, between me and you. **8, 9.** Referring to the imminent risk of life which he ran in Ephesus (Acts 19:23-41) when the whole multitude were wrought up to fury by Demetrius, on the plea of Paul and his associates having assailed the religion of Diana of Ephesus. The words (vs. 9), "we had the sentence of death in ourselves," mean, that *he looked upon himself as a man condemned to die* [PALEY]. ALFORD thinks the danger at Ephesus was comparatively so slight that it cannot be supposed to be the subject of reference here, without exposing the apostle to a charge of cowardice, very unlike his fearless character; hence, he supposes Paul refers to some deadly *sickness* which he had suffered under (vss. 9, 10). But there is little doubt that, had Paul been found by the mob in the excitement, he would have been torn in pieces; and probably, besides what Luke in Acts records, there were other dangers of an equally distressing kind, such as, "lyings in wait of the Jews" (Acts 20:19), his ceaseless foes. They, doubtless, had incited the multitude at Ephesus (Acts 19:9), and were the chief of the "many adversaries" and "[wild] beasts," which he had to fight with there (I Cor. 15:32; 16:9). His weak state of health at the time combined with all this to make him regard himself as all but dead (ch. 11: 29; 12:10). What makes my supposition probable is, that the very cause of his not having visited Corinth directly as he had intended, and for which he proceeds to apologize (vss. 15-23), was, that there might be time to see whether the evils arising there not only from Greek, but from *Jewish* disturbers of the Church (ch. 11:29), would be checked by his first Epistle; there not being fully so was what entailed on him the need of writing this second Espistle. His not specifying this here *expressly* is just what we might expect in the outset of this letter; towards the close, when he had won their favorable hearing by a kindly and firm tone, he gives a more distinct reference to Jewish agitators (ch. 11:22). **above strength**—i.e., ordinary, natural powers of endurance. **despaired**—as far as human help or hope from man was concerned. But in respect to help from God we were "not in despair" (ch. 4:8). **9. But**—"Yea." **in God which raiseth the dead**—We had so given up all thoughts of life, that our only hope was fixed on the coming resurrection; so in I Corinthians 15:32 his hope of the resurrection was what buoyed him up in contending with foes, savage as wild beasts. Here he touches only on the doctrine of the resurrection, taking it for granted that its truth is admitted by the Corinthians, and urging its bearing on their practice. **10. doth deliver**—The oldest MSS. read, "will deliver," viz., as regards *immediately imminent* dangers. "In whom we trust that He will also (so the *Greek*) yet deliver us," refers to the *continuance* of God's delivering help *hereafter*. **11. helping together by prayer for us**—rather, "helping together on our behalf by your *supplication*"; the words "for us" in the *Greek* following "helping together," not "prayer." **that for the gift . . .**—lit., "That on the part of many persons the gift (lit., gift of grace; the mercy) bestowed *upon us* by means of (i.e., through the prayers of) many may be offered thanks for (may have thanks offered for it) on our behalf." **12. For**—reason why he may confidently look for their prayers for him. **our rejoicing**—*Greek*, "our glorying." Not that he glories in the testimony of his conscience, as something *to boast of;* nay, this testimony is itself the thing *in which* his glorying

consists. **in simplicity**—Most of the oldest MSS. read, "in holiness." *English Version* reading is perhaps a gloss from Ephesians 6:5 [ALFORD]. Some of the oldest MSS. and versions, however, support it. **godly sincerity**—lit., "sincerity of God"; i.e., sincerity as in the presence of God (I Cor. 5:8). We *glory* in this in spite of all our adversities. *Sincerity* in *Greek* implies the non-admixture of any foreign element. He had no sinister or selfish aims (as some insinuated) in failing to visit them as he had promised: such aims belonged to his adversaries, not to him (ch. 2:17). "Fleshly wisdom" suggests tortuous and insincere courses; but the "grace of God," which influenced him by God's gifts (Rom. 12:3; 15:15), suggests holy straightforwardness and sincere faithfulness to promises (vss. 17-20), even as God is faithful to His promises. The prudence which subserves selfish interests, or employs unchristian means, or relies on human means more than on the Divine Spirit, is "fleshly wisdom." **in the world**—even in relation to the world at large, which is full of disingenuousness. **more abundantly to you-ward**—(Ch. 2:4). His greater love to them would lead him to manifest, especially to them, proofs of his sincerity, which his less close connection with *the world* did not admit of his exhibiting towards it. **13. We write none other things** (in this Epistle) than what ye read (in my former Epistle [BENGEL]; *present*, because the Epistle *continued still* to be read in the Church as an apostolic rule). CONYBEARE and HOWSON think Paul had been suspected of writing privately to some individuals in the Church in a different strain from that of his public letters; and translates, "I write nothing else to you but what ye read *openly* (the *Greek* meaning, "ye *read aloud*," viz., when Paul's Epistles were publicly read in the congregation, I Thess. 5:27); yea, and what you acknowledge *inwardly*." **or acknowledge**—*Greek*, "or even acknowledge." The *Greek* for "read" and for "acknowledge" are words kindred in sound and root. I would translate, "None other things than what ye know by reading (by comparing my former Epistle with my present Epistle), or even know as a matter of fact" (viz., the consistency of my acts with my words). **even to the end**—of my life. Not excluding reference to *the day of the Lord* (end of vs. 14; I Cor. 4:5). **14. in part**—In contrast to "even to the end": the testimony *of his life* was not yet completed [THEOPHYL. and BENGEL]. Rather, "in part," i.e., some of you, not all [GROTIUS, ALFORD]. So in ch. 2:5; Romans 11:25. The majority at Corinth had shown a willing compliance with Paul's directions in the first Epistle: but some were still refractory. Hence arises the difference of tone in different parts of this Epistle. See *Introduction.* **your rejoicing**—your subject of *glorying* or *boast.* "Are" (not merely *shall be*) implies the present recognition of one another as a subject of mutual *glorying:* that *glorying* being about to be realized in its fulness "in the day (of the coming) of the Lord Jesus." **15. in this confidence**—of my character for sincerity being "acknowledged" by you (vss. 12-14). **was minded**—I was intending. **before**—"to come unto you before" visiting Macedonia (where he now was). Cf. *Note,* I Corinthians 16: 5; also 4:18, which, combined with the words here, implies that the insinuation of some at Corinth, that he would not come at all, rested on the fact of his having thus *disappointed* them. His change of intention, and ultimate resolution of going through Macedonia first, took place before his sending Timothy from Ephesus into Macedonia, and therefore

(I Cor. 4:17) before his writing the first Epistle. Cf. Acts 19:21, 22 (the order there is "Macedonia and Achaia," not *Achaia, Macedonia*); 20:1, 2. **that ye might have a second benefit**—one in going to, the other in returning from, Macedonia. The "benefit" of his visits consisted in the grace and spiritual gifts which he was the means of imparting (Rom. 1:11, 12). **16.** This intention of visiting them *on the way* to Macedonia, as well as after having passed through it, must have reached the ears of the Corinthians in some way or other—perhaps in the lost Epistle (I Cor. 4:18; 5:9). The sense comes out more clearly in the *Greek* order, "By you to pass into Macedonia, and from Macedonia to come again unto you." **17. use lightness**—Was I guilty of levity? viz., by promising more than I performed. **or ... according to the flesh, that with me there should be yea, yea ... nay, nay?**—The "or" expresses a different alternative: Did I act with levity, or (on the other hand) do I purpose what I purpose like worldly (fleshly) men, so that my "yea" must at all costs be yea, and my "nay" nay [BENGEL, WINER, CALVIN], (Matt. 14:7, 9)? The repetition of the "yea" and "nay" hardly agrees with ALFORD'S view, "What I purpose do I purpose according to the changeable purposes of the fleshly (worldly) man, that there may be with me the yea yea, and the nay nay (i.e., both affirmation and negation concerning the same thing)? The repetition will thus stand for the single yea and nay, as in Matthew 5: 37; James 5:12. But the latter passage implies that the double "yea" here is not equivalent to the single "yea": BENGEL's view, therefore, seems preferable. **18.** He adds this lest they might think his DOCTRINE was changeable like his *purposes* (the change in which he admitted in vs. 17, while denying that it was due to "lightness," and at the same time implying that *not* to have changed, where there was good reason, would have been to imitate the *fleshly-minded* who at all costs obstinately hold to their purpose). **true**—*Greek,* "faithful" (I Cor. 1:9). **our word**—the *doctrine* we preach. **was not**—The oldest MSS. read "*is* not." **yea and nay**—i.e., inconsistent with itself. **19.** Proof of the unchangeableness of the doctrine from the unchangeableness of the subject of it, viz., Jesus Christ. He is called "the Son of God" to show the impossibility of change in One who is co-equal with God himself (cf. I Sam. 15:29; Mal. 3:6). **by me ... Silvanus and Timotheus**—The Son of God, though preached by different preachers, was one and the same, unchangeable. *Silvanus* is contracted into *Silas* (Acts 15:22; cf. I Pet. 5:12). **in him was yea**—*Greek,* "*is made* yea in Him"; i.e., our preaching of the Son of God is confirmed as true in Him (i.e., *through* Him; through the miracles wherewith He has confirmed our preaching) [GROTIUS]; or rather, by the witness of the Spirit which He has given (vss. 21, 22) and of which miracles were only one, and that a subordinate manifestation. **20.** Rather, How many soever be the promises of God, in Him is the "yea" ("*faithfulness in His word*": contrasted with the "yea and nay," vs. 19, i.e., *inconstancy as to one's word*). **and in him Amen**—The oldest MSS. read, "*Wherefore through* Him is *the* Amen"; i.e., In Him is *faithfulness* ("yea") to His word, "wherefore through Him" is the immutable verification of it ("Amen"). As "yea" is His *word*, so "Amen" is His *oath*, which makes our assurance of the fulfilment doubly sure. Cf. "two immutable things (viz., His word and His oath) in which it was impossible for God to lie" (Heb. 6:18; Rev. 3:14). The whole range of Old Testament and New Testa-

ment promises are secure in their fulfilment for us in Christ. **unto the glory of God by us**—*Greek,* "for glory unto God by us" (cf. ch. 4:15), i.e., by our ministerial labors; by us His promises, and His unchangeable faithfulness to them, are proclaimed. CONYBEARE takes the "Amen" to be the Amen at the close of thanksgiving: but then "by us" would have to mean what it cannot mean here, "by us *and you.*" **21. stablisheth us ... in Christ**—i.e., in the faith of Christ—in believing in Christ. **anointed us** —As "Christ" is the "Anointed" (which His name means), so "He hath *anointed* (*Greek, chrisas*) us, ministers and believing people alike, with the Spirit (vs. 22; I John 2:20, 27). Hence we become "a sweet savor of Christ" (ch. 2:15). **22.** sealed—A *seal* is a token assuring the possession of property to one; "sealed" here answers to "stablisheth us" (vs. 21; I Cor. 9:2). **the earnest of the Spirit**—i.e., the Spirit as the earnest (i.e., money given by a purchaser as a pledge for the full payment of the sum promised). The Holy Spirit is given to the believer now as a first instalment to assure him his full inheritance as a son of God shall be his hereafter (Eph. 1:13, 14). "*Sealed* with that Holy Spirit of promise which is the *earnest* of our inheritance until the redemption of the purchased possession" (Rom. 8:23). The Spirit is the pledge of the fulfilment of "all the promises" (vs. 20). **23. Moreover I** —*Greek,* "But *I* (for my part)," in contrast to GOD who hath assured us of *His* promises being hereafter fulfilled certainly (vss. 20-22). **call God**—the all-knowing One, who avenges wilful unfaithfulness to promises. **for a record upon my soul**—As a witness *as to* the secret purposes of my soul, and a witness *against* it, if I lie (Mal. 3:5). **to spare you**—in order not to come in a rebuking spirit, as I should have had to come to you, if I had come *then*. **I came not as yet**—*Greek,* "no longer"; i.e., I *gave up my purpose of then* visiting Corinth. He wished to give them time for repentance, that he might not have to use severity towards them. Hence he sent Titus before him. Cf. ch. 10:10, 11, which shows that his detractors represented him as threatening what he had not courage to perform (I Cor. 4:18, 19). **24. Not for that**—i.e., Not that. "*Faith*" is here emphatic. He had "dominion" or a right to control them in matters of *discipline,* but in matters of "*faith*" he was only a "*fellow helper* of their joy" (viz., in believing, Rom. 15:13; Phil. 1:25). The *Greek* is, "Not that we *lord it* over your faith." This he adds to soften the magisterial tone of vs. 23. His desire is to cause them not *sorrow* (ch. 2:1, 2), but "*joy.*" The *Greek* for "helpers" implies a mutual leaning, one on the other, like the mutually supporting buttresses of a sacred building. "By faith (Rom. 11:20) ye stand"; therefore it is that I bestow such pains in "helping" your faith, which is the source of all true "joy" (Rom. 15:13). I want nothing more, not to *lord it over your faith.*

CHAPTER 2

Vss. 1-17. REASON WHY HE HAD NOT VISITED THEM ON HIS WAY TO MACEDONIA; THE INCESTUOUS PERSON OUGHT NOW TO BE FORGIVEN; HIS ANXIETY TO HEAR TIDINGS OF THEIR STATE FROM TITUS, AND HIS JOY WHEN AT LAST THE GOOD NEWS REACHES HIM. **1. with myself**—in contrast to "you" (ch. 1: 23). The same antithesis between Paul and them appears in vs. 2. **not come again ... in heaviness** —"sorrow"; implying that he had *already* paid them *one* visit *in sorrow* since his coming for the first time to Corinth. At that visit he had warned them "he would not spare if he should come again" (*Notes,* ch. 13:2; cf. ch. 12:14; 13:1). See *Introduction* to the first Epistle. The "in heaviness" implies *mutual* pain; they grieving him, and he them. Cf. vs. 2, "I make you sorry," and vs. 5, "If any have caused grief (sorrow)." In this verse he accounts for having postponed his visit, following up ch. 1:23. **2. For**—proof that he shrinks from causing them *sorrow* ("heaviness"). **if I**—The "I" is emphatic. Some detractor may say that *this* (vs. 1) is not my reason for not coming as I proposed; since I showed no scruple in causing "heaviness," or *sorrow*, in my Epistle (the first Epistle to the Corinthians). But I answer, If *I* be the one to cause you sorrow, it is not that I have any pleasure in doing so. Nay, my object was that he "who was made sorry by me" (viz., *the Corinthians in general*, vs. 3; but with tacit reference to *the incestuous person in particular*) should repent, and so "make me glad," as has actually taken place; "for . . . who is he then that . . . ?" **3. I wrote this same unto you**—viz., that I would not come to you *then* (vs. 1), as, if I were to come then, it would have to be "in heaviness" (causing *sorrow* both to him and them, owing to their impenitent state). He refers to the first Epistle (cf. I Cor. 16:7; cf. 4:19, 21; 5:2-7, 13) **sorrow from them of whom I ought to rejoice**—i.e., *sorrow* from their impenitence, when he ought, on the contrary, to have *joy* from their penitent obedience. The latter happy effect was produced by his first Epistle, whereas the former would have been the result, had he *then* visited them as he had originally proposed. **having confidence . . . that my joy is the joy of you all**—trusting that you, too, would feel that there was sufficient reason for the postponement, if it interfered with our mutual joy [ALFORD]. The communion of saints, he feels confident in them "ALL" (his charity overlooking, for the moment the small section of his detractors at Corinth, I Cor. 13:7), will make *his joy* (vs. 2) *their joy.* **4.** So far from my change of purpose being due to "lightness" (ch. 1:17), I wrote my letter to you (vs. 3) "out of much affliction (*Greek,* 'trouble') and anguish of heart, and with many tears." **not that ye should be grieved**—Translate, "be made sorry," to accord with the translation, vs. 2. My ultimate and main object was, "not that ye might be made sorry," but that through sorrow you might be led to repentance, and so to joy, redounding both to you and me (vss. 2, 3). I made you sorry before going to you, that when I went it might not be necessary. He is easily made sorry, who is admonished by a friend himself weeping [BENGEL]. **that ye might know the love**—of which it is a proof to rebuke sins openly and in season [ESTIUS], (Ps. 141:5; Prov. 27:6). "Love" is the source from which sincere reproof springs; that the Corinthians might ultimately recognize this as his motive, was the apostle's aim. **which I have more abundantly unto you**—who have been particularly committed to me by God (Acts 18:10; I Cor. 4:15; 9:2). **5. grief . . . grieved**—Translate as before, "sorrow . . . made sorry." The "any" is a delicate way of referring to the incestuous person. **not . . . me, but in part**—He has grieved me only in part (cf. ch. 1:14; Rom. 11:25), i.e., *I am not the sole party aggrieved; most of you,* also, were aggrieved. **that I may not overcharge**—that I may not unduly lay the weight of the charge on you all, which I should do, if I made myself to be the sole party aggrieved. ALFORD punctuates, "He hath not made sorry me, but in part (that I press not too heavily; viz., on him) you

all." Thus "you all" is in contrast to "me"; and "*in part*" is explained in the parenthetical clause. **6. Sufficient**—without increasing it, which would only drive him to despair (vs. 7), whereas the object of the punishment was, "that (his) spirit might be saved" in the last day. **to such a man**—a milder designation of the offender than if he had been *named* [MEYER]. Rather, it expresses estrangement from *such a one* who had caused such grief to the Church, and scandal to religion (Acts 22:22; I Cor. 5:5). **this punishment**—His being "delivered to Satan for the destruction of the flesh"; not only excommunication, but bodily disease (*Notes,* I Cor. 5:4, 5). **inflicted of many**—rather, "by the majority" (the more part of you). Not by an individual priest, as in the Church of Rome, nor by the bishops and clergy alone, but by the whole body of the Church. **7. with overmuch sorrow**—*Greek,* "with HIS overmuch sorrow." **8. confirm your love toward him**—by giving effect in act, and showing in deeds your love; viz., by restoring him to your fellowship and praying for his recovering from the sickness penally inflicted on him. **9. For**—Additional reason why they should restore the offender, viz., as a "proof" of their obedience "in all things"; now in *love,* as previously in *punishing* (vs. 6), at the apostle's desire. Besides his other reasons for deferring his visit, he had the further view, though, perhaps, unperceived by them, of making an experiment of their fidelity. This accounts for his deferring to give, in his Epistle, the *reason* for his change of plan (resolved on before writing it). This full discovery of his motive comes naturally from him now, in the second Epistle, after he had seen the success of his measures, but would not have been a seasonable communication before. All this accords with reality, and is as remote as possible from imposture [PALEY'S *Horæ Paulinæ*]. The interchange of feeling is marked (vs. 4), "I wrote . . . that *ye* might know the love . . .": here, "I did write, that *I* might know the proof of *you.*" **10.** Another encouragement to their taking on themselves the responsibility of restoring the offender. They may be assured of Paul's apostolic sanction to their doing so. **for if I forgave anything, to whom I forgave it**—The oldest MSS. read, "For even what I have forgiven, if I have forgiven anything." **for your sakes** *forgave* **I it**—He uses the past tense, as of a thing already determined on; as in I Corinthians 5:3, "I have judged already"; or, as speaking generally of forgiveness granted, or to be granted. It is for your sakes I have forgiven, and do forgive, that the Church (of which you are constituent members) may suffer no hurt by the loss of a soul, and that ye may learn leniency as well as faithfulness. **in the person of Christ**—representing Christ, and acting by His authority: answering to I Corinthians 5:4, "In the name of our Lord Jesus Christ . . . my spirit, with the power of our Lord Jesus Christ." **11.** Lit., "That we may have no advantage gained over us by Satan," viz., by letting one of our members be lost to us through despair, we ourselves furnishing Satan with the weapon, by our repulsive harshness to one now penitent. The loss of a single sinner is a common loss; therefore, in vs. 10, he said, "for your sakes." Paul had "delivered" the offender "to Satan for the destruction of the flesh, that the Spirit might be saved" (I Cor. 5:5). Satan sought to destroy the spirit also: to let him do so, would be to give him an advantage, and let him *overreach* us. **not ignorant of his devices**—"Ignorant" and "devices" are words akin in sound and root in *Greek:* we are not without *knowledge* of his *knowing* schemes. **12.** Paul expected to meet Titus at Troas, to receive the tidings as to the effect of his first Epistle on the Corinthian Church; but, disappointed in his expectation *there,* he passed on to Macedonia, where he met him at last (ch. 7:5, 6, 7) The *history* (Acts) does not record his passing through Troas, in going from Ephesus *to* Macedonia; but it does in coming *from* that country (Acts 20:6); also, that he had disciples there (Acts 20:7), which accords with the *Epistle* (ch. 2:12, "a door was opened unto me of the Lord"). An undesigned coincidence marking genuineness [PALEY'S *Horæ Paulinæ*]. Doubtless Paul had fixed a time with Titus to meet him at Troas; and had desired him, if detained so as not to be able to be at Troas at that time, to proceed at once to Macedonia to Philippi, the next station on his own journey. Hence, though a wide door of Christian usefulness opened to him at Troas, his eagerness to hear from Titus the tidings from Corinth, led him not to stay longer there when the time fixed was past, but he hastened on to Macedonia to meet him there [BIRKS]. **to preach**—lit., "for the Gospel." He had been at Troas before, but the vision of a man from Macedonia inviting him to come over, prevented his remaining there (Acts 16:8-12). On his return to Asia, after the longer visit mentioned here, he stayed seven days (Acts 20:6). **and**—i.e., *though* Paul would, under ordinary circumstances, have gladly stayed in Troas. **door ... opened ... of the Lord**—Greek, "*in* the Lord," i.e., in His work, and by His gracious Providence. **13. no rest in my spirit** —rather, "no rest *for* my spirit" (Gen. 8:9). As here his "spirit" had no rest; so in ch. 7:5, his "flesh." His "spirit" under the Holy Spirit, hence, concluded that it was not necessary to avail himself of the "door" of usefulness at Troas any longer. **taking ... leave of them**—the disciples at Troas. **14. Now**—Greek, "But." Though we left Troas disappointed in not meeting Titus there, and in having to leave so soon so wide a door, "thanks be unto God," we were triumphantly blessed in both the good news of you from Titus, and in the victories of the Gospel everywhere in our progress. The cause of triumph cannot be restricted (as AL- FORD explains) to the former; for "always," and "in every place," show that the latter also is intended. **causeth us to triumph**—The *Greek,* is rather, as in Colossians 2:15, "triumphs over us": "leadeth us in triumph." Paul regarded himself as a signal trophy of God's victorious power in Christ. His Almighty Conqueror was leading him about, through all the cities of the Greek and Roman world, as an illustrious example of His power at once to subdue and to save. The foe of Christ was now the servant of Christ. As to be led in triumph by man is the most miserable, so to be led in triumph by God is the most glorious, lot that can befall any [TRENCH]. Our only true triumphs are God's triumphs over us. His defeats of us are our only true victories [ALFORD]. The image is taken from the triumphal procession of a victorious general. The *additional* idea is perhaps included, which distinguishes God's triumph from that of a human general, that the captive is brought into *willing* obedience (ch. 10:5) to Christ, and so *joins in the triumph:* God "leads him in triumph" as one not merely *triumphed over,* but also as one *triumphing over* God's foes with God (which last will apply to the apostle's triumphant missionary progress under the leading of God). So BENGEL: "*Who shows us in triumph,* not [merely] as conquered, but as the ministers of His victory. Not only the

victory, but the open 'showing' of the victory is marked: for there follows, *Who maketh manifest.*" **savour**—retaining the image of a triumph. As the approach of the triumphal procession was made known by the *odor* of incense scattered far and wide by the incense-bearers in the train, so God "makes manifest by us" (His now at once triumphed over and triumphing captives, cf. Luke 5:10, "Catch," lit., "Take captive so as to preserve alive") the sweet savor of the knowledge of Christ, the triumphant Conqueror (Col. 2:15), everywhere. As the *triumph* strikes the eyes, so the savor the nostrils; thus every sense feels the power of Christ's Gospel. This *manifestation* (a word often recurring in his Epistles to the Corinthians, cf. I Cor. 4:5) refutes the Corinthian suspicions of his *dishonestly,* by reserve, *hiding* anything from them (vs. 17; ch. 4:2). **15.** The order is in *Greek,* "For (it is) of Christ (that) we are a sweet savor unto God"; thus, the "for" justifies his previous words (vs. 14), "the savor of HIS (Christ's) knowledge." We not only scatter the savor, but "we *are* the sweet savor" itself (Song of Sol. 1:3; cf. John 1:14, 16; Eph. 5:2; I John 2:27). **in them that are saved**—rather, "that *are being* saved ... that are perishing" (*Note,* I Cor. 1:18). As the light, though it blinds in darkness the weak, is for all that still light; and honey, though it taste bitter to the sick, is in itself still sweet; so the Gospel is still of a sweet savor, though many perish through unbelief [CHRYSOSTOM, *Homilies,* 5. 467]. (ch. 4:3, 4, 6). As some of the conquered foes led in triumph were put to death when the procession reached the capitol, and to them the smell of the incense was the "savor of death unto death," while to those saved alive, it was the "savor of life," so the Gospel was to the different classes respectively. **in them**—in the case of them. "Those being saved" (ch. 3:1, to 4:2): "Those that are perishing" (ch. 4:3- 5). **16. savour of death unto death ... of life unto life**—*an odor* arising *out of death* (a mere announcement of a *dead* Christ, and a virtually lifeless Gospel, in which light unbelievers regard the Gospel message), *ending* (as the just and natural consequence) *in death* (to the unbeliever); (but to the believer) *an odor* arising *out of life* (i.e., the announcement of a risen and *living* Saviour), *ending in life* (to the believer) (Matt. 21:44; Luke 2:34; John 9: 39). **who is sufficient for these things?**—viz., for diffusing aright everywhere the savor of Christ, so diverse in its effects on believers and unbelievers. He here prepares the way for one purpose of his Epistle, viz., to vindicate his apostolic mission from its detractors at Corinth, who denied his sufficiency. The *Greek* order puts prominently foremost the momentous and difficult task assigned to him, "For these things, who is sufficient?" He answers his own question (ch. 3:5, 6), "Not that we are *sufficient* of ourselves, but our *sufficiency* is of God, who hath made us *able* (*Greek,* 'sufficient') ministers ...." **17. not as many**—(ch. 11:18; Phil. 2:21). Rather, "*the* many," viz., *the* false teachers of whom he treats (chs. 10-12, especially ch. 11:13; I Thess. 2:3). **which corrupt**—Greek, "adulterating, as hucksters do wine for gain" (ch. 4:2; Isa. 1:22; II Pet. 2:3, "Make *merchandise* of you"). **as of sincerity ... as of God**—as one speaking from (out of) sincerity, as from (i.e., by the command of, and so in dependence on) God. **in Christ**—as united to Him in living membership, and doing His work (cf. ch. 12:19). The *whole* Gospel must be delivered such as it is, without concession to men's corruptions, and without selfish aims, if it is to be blessed with success (Acts 20:27).

CHAPTER 3

Vss. 1-18. THE SOLE COMMENDATION HE NEEDS TO PROVE GOD'S SANCTION OF HIS MINISTRY HE HAS IN HIS CORINTHIAN CONVERTS: HIS MINISTRY EXCELS THE MOSAIC, AS THE GOSPEL OF LIFE AND LIBERTY EXCELS THE LAW OF CONDEMNATION. **1.** Are we beginning again to recommend ourselves (ch. 5:12) (as some of them might say he had done in his first Epistle; or, a reproof to "some" who had *begun* doing so)! **commendation**—recommendation. (Cf. ch. 10:18.) The "some" refers to particular persons of the "many" (ch. 2:17) teachers who opposed him, and who came to Corinth with letters of recommendation from other churches; and when leaving that city obtained similar letters from the Corinthians to other churches. The 13th canon of the Council of Chalcedon (A.D. 451) ordained that "clergymen coming to a city where they were unknown, should not be allowed to officiate without letters commendatory from their own bishop." The history (Acts 18:27) confirms the existence of the custom here alluded to in the Epistle: "When Apollos was disposed to pass into Achaia [Corinth], *the brethren* [of Ephesus] *wrote,* exhorting the disciples to receive him." This was about two years before the Epistle, and is probably *one* of the instances to which Paul refers, as many at Corinth boasted of their being followers of Apollos (I Cor. 1:12). **2. our epistle**—of recommendation. **in our hearts**—not letters borne merely *in the hands.* Your conversion through my instrumentality, and your faith which is "known of all men" by widespread report (I Cor. 1:4-7), and which is written by memory and affection on my inmost heart and is borne about wherever I go, is my letter of recommendation (I Cor. 9:2). **known and read**—words akin in root, sound, and sense (so ch. 1:13). "Ye are *known* to be my converts by general knowledge: then ye are *known* more particularly by your reflecting my doctrine in your Christian life." The handwriting is first "known," then the Epistle is "read" [GROTIUS] (ch. 4:2; I Cor. 14:25). There is not so powerful a sermon in the world, as a consistent Christian life. The eye of the world takes in more than the ear. Christians' lives are the only religious books the world reads. IGNATIUS (*ad Ephesum,* ch. 10) writes, "Give unbelievers the chance of believing through you. Consider yourselves employed by God; your lives the form of language in which He addresses them. Be mild when they are angry, humble when they are haughty; to their blasphemy oppose prayer without ceasing; to their inconsistency, a steadfast adherence to your faith." **3. declared**—The letter is written so legibly that it can be "read by all men" (vs. 2). Translate, "Being manifestly shown to be an Epistle of Christ"; a letter coming manifestly from Christ, and "ministered by us," i.e., carried about and presented by us as (ministering) bearers to those (the world) for whom it is intended: Christ is the Writer and the Recommender, ye are the letter recommending us. **written not with ink, but with the Spirit of the living God**—Paul was the ministering pen or other instrument of writing, as well as the ministering bearer and presenter of the letter. "Not with ink" stands in contrast to the letters of commendation which "some" at Corinth (vs. 1) used. "Ink" is also used here to include all outward materials for writing, such as the Sinaitic tables of stone were. These, however, were not written with ink, but "graven" by "the finger of God" (Exod. 31:18; 32:16). Christ's Epistle (His believing members

converted by Paul) is better still: it is written not merely with the *finger,* but with the *"Spirit* of the *living God";* it is not the "ministration of death" as the law, but of the *"living* Spirit" that "giveth life" (vss. 6-8). **not in**—not *on* tables (tablets) of stone, as the ten commandments were written (vs. 7). **in fleshy tables of the heart**—ALL the best MSS. read, "On [your] *hearts* [which are] tables of flesh." Once your hearts were spiritually what the tables of the law were physically, tables of stone, but God has "taken away the stony heart out of your flesh, given you a heart of flesh" (*fleshy,* not *fleshly,* i.e., carnal; hence it is written, "out of your *flesh*" i.e., your *carnal* nature), Ezek. 11:19; 36:26. Cf. vs. 2, "As ye are our Epistle written in our hearts," so Christ has in the first instance made you "His Epistle written with the Spirit in (on) your hearts." I bear on my heart, as a testimony to all men, that which Christ has by His Spirit written in your heart [ALFORD]. (Cf. Prov. 3:3; 7:3; Jer. 31:31-34). This passage is quoted by PALEY (*Horæ Paulinæ*) as illustrating one peculiarity of Paul's style, viz., his *going off at a word into a parenthetic reflection:* here it is on the word "Epistle." So "savor," ch. 2:14-17. **4. And**—Greek, "But." "Such confidence, however (viz., of our 'sufficiency,' vss. 5, 6; ch. 2:16 [to which he reverts after the parenthesis], as ministers of the New Testament, 'not fainting,' ch. 4:1), we have through Christ (not through ourselves, cf. vs. 18) toward God" (i.e., in our relation to God and His work, the ministry committed by Him to us, for which we must render an account to Him). Confidence toward God is solid and real, as looking to Him for the strength needed now, and also for the reward of grace to be given hereafter. Cf. Acts 24:15, "hope toward God." Human confidence is unreal in that it looks to man for its help and its reward. **5.** The *Greek* is, "Not that we are (even yet after so long experience as ministers) sufficient to think anything OF ourselves as (coming) FROM ourselves; but our sufficiency is (derived) FROM God." *"From"* more definitely refers to the *source* out of which a thing comes; "of" is more general. **to think**—Greek, to "reason out" or "devise"; *to attain to* sound preaching *by our reasonings* [THEODORET]. The "we" refers here to *ministers* (II Pet. 1:21). **anything**—even the least. We cannot expect too little from man, or too much from God. **6. able**—rather, as the *Greek* is the same, corresponding to vs. 5, translate, *"sufficient* as ministers" (Eph. 3:7; Col. 1:23). **the new testament**—"the new *covenant"* as contrasted with the *Old* Testament or covenant (I Cor. 11:25; Gal. 4:24). He reverts here again to the contrast between the law on "tables of stone," and that "written by the Spirit on fleshly tables of the heart" vs. 3). **not of the letter**—joined with "ministers"; ministers not of *the mere literal precept,* in which the old law, as then understood, consisted; "but of the Spirit," i.e., *the spiritual holiness* which lay under the old law, and which the new covenant brings to light (Matt. 5:17-48) with new *motives* added, and a new *power* of obedience imparted, viz., the Holy Spirit (Rom. 7:6). Even in *writing the letter* of the New Testament, Paul and the other sacred writers were ministers *not of the letter, but of the spirit.* No piety of spirit could exempt a man from the yoke of the letter of each legal ordinance under the Old Testament; for God had appointed this as the way in which He chose a devout Jew to express his state of mind towards God. Christianity, on the other hand, makes the spirit of our outward observances everything, and the letter a secondary consideration (John 4:24).

Still the moral law of the ten commandments, being written by the finger of God, is as obligatory now as ever; but put more on the Gospel spirit of "love," than on the letter of a servile obedience, and in a deeper and fuller spirituality (Matt. 5:17-48; Rom. 13:9). No literal precepts could fully comprehend the wide range of holiness which LOVE, the work of the Holy Spirit, under the Gospel, suggests to the believer's heart instinctively from the word understood in its deep spirituality. **letter killeth**—by bringing home the knowledge of guilt and its punishment, *death;* vs. 7, "ministration of death" (Rom. 7:9). **spirit giveth life**—The spirit of the Gospel when brought home to the heart by the Holy Spirit, gives new spiritual life to a man (Rom. 6.4, 11). This "spirit of life" is for us in Christ Jesus (Rom. 8:2, 10), who dwells in the believer as a "quickening" or "life-giving Spirit" (I Cor. 15:45). Note, the spiritualism of rationalists is very different. It would admit no "stereotyped revelation," except so much as man's own inner instrument of revelation, the conscience and reason, can approve of: thus making the conscience judge of the written word, whereas the apostles make the written word the judge of the conscience (Acts 17:11; I Pet. 4:1). True spirituality rests on the whole written word, applied to the soul by the Holy Spirit as the only infallible interpreter of its far-reaching spirituality. The *letter* is nothing without the *spirit*, in a subject essentially spiritual. The *spirit* is nothing without the *letter,* in a record substantially historical. **7. the ministration of death**—the legal dispensation, summed up in the Decalogue, which denounces *death* against man for transgression. **written** *and* **engraven in stones**—There is no "and" in the *Greek.* The literal translation is, "The ministration of death *in letters,*" of which "engraven on stones" is an explanation. The preponderance of oldest MSS. is for the *English Version* reading. But one (perhaps the oldest existing MS.) has "in the letter," which refers to the preceding words (vs. 6), "*the letter* killeth," and this seems the probable reading. Even if we read as *English Version,* "The ministration of death (written) in letters," alludes to *the literal precepts* of the law as only bringing us the knowledge of sin and "*death,*" in contrast to "*the Spirit*" in the Gospel bringing us "*life*" (vs. 6). The opposition between "the letters" and "the Spirit" (vs. 8) confirms this. This explains why the phrase in *Greek* should be "in letters," instead of the ordinary one which *English Version* has substituted, "written *and.*" **was glorious**—lit., "was made (invested) *in glory,*" glory was the atmosphere with which it was encompassed. **could not steadfastly behold**—lit., "fix their eyes on." Exodus 34:30, "The skin of his face shone; and they were AFRAID *to come nigh him.*" "Could not," therefore means here, *for* FEAR. The "glory of Moses' countenance" on Sinai passed away when the occasion was over: a type of the transitory character of the dispensation which he represented (vs. 11), as contrasted with the permanency of the Christian dispensation (vs. 11). **8. be rather glorious**—lit., "be rather (i.e., still more, invested) in glory." "Shall be," i.e., shall be found to be in part now, but fully when the glory of Christ and His saints shall be revealed. **9. ministration of condemnation**—the law regarded in the "letter" which "killeth" (vs. 6; Rom. 7:9-11). The oldest existing MS. seems to read as *English Version.* But most of the almost contemporary MSS., versions, and Fathers, read, "If to the ministration of condemnation there be glory." **the ministration of righteousness**—the Gospel, which especially reveals

the righteousness of God (Rom. 1:17), and imputes righteousness to men through faith in Christ (Rom. 3:21-28; 4:3, 22-25), and imparts righteousness by the Spirit (Rom. 8:1-4). **exceed**—"abound." **10.** *For even* the ministration of condemnation, the law, vs. 7 (*which has been glorified* at Sinai in Moses' person), *has* now (*English Version* translates less fitly, "*was made . . .* had") *lost its glory in this respect by reason of the surpassing glory* (of the Gospel): as the light of the stars and moon fades in the presence of the sun. **11. was glorious**—lit., "was with glory"; or "marked *by glory.*" **that which remaineth**—abideth (Rev. 14:6). Not "the ministry," but the Spirit, and His accompaniments, life and righteousness. **is glorious**—lit., "is *in glory.*" The *Greek* "with" or "by" is appropriately applied to that of which the glory was *transient.* "In" to that of which the glory is permanent. The contrast of the Old and New Testaments proves that Paul's chief opponents at Corinth were Judaizers. **12. such hope**—of the future glory, which shall result from the ministration of the Gospel (vss. 8, 9). **plainness of speech**—openness; without reserve (ch. 2:17; 4:2). **13.** We use no disguise, "as Moses put a veil over his face, that the children of Israel might not look steadfastly upon the end of that which was to be done away" [ELLICOTT and others]. The view of Exodus 34:30-35, according to LXX is adopted by Paul, that Moses in going in to speak to God *removed the veil till* he came out *and had spoken to the people;* and then *when he had done speaking,* he put on the veil *that they might not look on the end,* or the fading, *of that transitory glory.* The veil was the symbol of *concealment,* put on directly after Moses' speaking; so that God's revelations by him were interrupted by intervals of concealment [ALFORD]. But ALFORD's view does not accord with vs. 7; the Israelites "could not look steadfastly on the face of Moses for the glory of his countenance". Plainly Moses' veil was put on *because of* their not having been able to "look steadfastly at him." Paul here (vs. 13) passes from the literal fact to the truth symbolized by it, the blindness of Jews and Judaizers to the ultimate end of the law: stating that Moses *put on the veil that they might not look steadfastly at* (Christ, Rom. 10:4) *the end of that* (law) *which* (like Moses' glory) *is done away.* Not that *Moses* had this *purpose;* but often God attributes to His prophets the purpose which He has Himself. Because the Jews *would not see,* God judicially gave them up *so as not to see.* The glory of Moses' face is antitypically Christ's glory shining behind the veil of legal ordinances. The veil which has been taken off to the believer is left on to the unbelieving Jew, so that he should not see (Isa. 6: 10; Acts 28:26, 27). He stops short at the letter of the law, not seeing the end of it. The evangelical glory of the law, like the shining of Moses' face, cannot be borne by a carnal people, and therefore remains veiled to them until the Spirit comes to take away the veil (vss. 14-17) [CAMERON]. **14-18.** Parenthetical: *Of Christians in general.* He resumes the subject of *the ministry,* ch. 4:1. **14 minds**—*Greek,* "mental perceptions"; "understandings." **blinded**—rather, "hardened." The opposite to "looking steadfastly at the end" of the law (vs. 13). *The veil on Moses' face* is further typical of *the veil that is on their hearts.* **untaken away . . . which** *veil*—rather, "the same veil . . . remaineth untaken away [lit., *not unveiled*], so that they do not see THAT it (not the *veil* as *English Version,* but 'THE OLD TESTAMENT,' or covenant of legal ordinances) is done away (vss. 7, 11, 13) in Christ" or, as BEN-

GEL, "Because it is done away in Christ," i.e., it is not done away save in Christ: the veil *therefore* remains untaken away from them, *because* they will not come to Christ, who does away, with the law as a mere letter. If they once saw that the law is done away in Him, the veil would be no longer on their hearts in reading it publicly in their synagogues (so "reading" means, Acts 15: 21). I prefer the former. **15. the veil is**—rather, "*a* veil *lieth* upon their *heart*" (Their understanding, affected by the corrupt will, John 8: 43; I Cor. 2:14). The Tallith was worn in the synagogue by every worshipper, and to this veil hanging over the breast there may be an indirect allusion here (*Note*, I Cor. 11:4): the apostle making it symbolize the spiritual veil on their heart. **16.** Moses took off the veil on entering into the presence of the Lord. So as to the Israelites whom Moses represents, "whensoever their heart (it) *turns* (not as *English Version*, 'shall turn') to the Lord, the veil is [by the very fact] (not as *English Version*, '*shall be*') taken away." Exodus 34:34 is the allusion; not Exodus 34:30, 31, as ALFORD thinks. Whenever the Israelites turn to the Lord, who is the Spirit of the law, the veil is taken off their hearts in the presence of the Lord: as the literal veil was taken off by Moses in going before God: no longer resting on the dead letter, *the veil,* they by the Spirit commune with God and with the inner spirit of the Mosaic covenant (which answers to the glory of *Moses' face unveiled* in God's presence). **17. the Lord**—Christ (vss. 14, 16; ch. 4:5). **is that Spirit**—is THE Spirit, viz., *that Spirit* spoken of in vs. 6, and here resumed after the parenthesis (vss. 7-16): Christ is the Spirit and "end" of the Old Testament, who giveth life to it, whereas "the letter killeth" (I Cor. 15:45; Rev. 19:10, end). **where the Spirit of the Lord is**—in a man's "heart", vs. 15; Rom. 8:9, 10). **there is liberty**—(John 8:36). "There," and *there only.* Such cease to be slaves to the letter, which they were while the veil was on their heart. They are free to serve God in the Spirit, and rejoice in Christ Jesus (Phil. 3:3): they have no longer the spirit of bondage, but of free sonship (Rom. 8:15; Gal. 4:7). "Liberty" is opposed to the letter (of the legal ordinances), and to the veil, the badge of slavery: also to the *fear* which the Israelites felt in beholding Moses' *glory unveiled* (Exod. 34:30; I John 4:18). **18. But we all**—Christians, as contrasted with the Jews who have a *veil* on their hearts, answering to Moses' veil on his face. He does not resume reference to *ministers* till ch. 4:1. **with open face**—Translate, "with *unveiled* face" (the *veil* being removed at conversion): contrasted with "hid" (ch. 4:3). **as in a glass**—in a mirror, viz., the Gospel which reflects the glory of God and Christ (ch. 4: 4; I Cor. 13:12; Jas. 1:23, 25). **are changed into the same image**—viz., the image of Christ's glory, spiritually now (Rom. 8:29; I John 3:3); an earnest of the bodily change hereafter (Phil. 3:21). However many they be, believers all reflect the *same* image of Christ more or less: a proof of the truth of Christianity. **from glory to glory**—from one degree of glory to another. As Moses' face caught a reflection of God's glory from being in His presence, so believers are changed into His image by beholding Him. **even as . . .**—Just such a transformation "*as*" was to be expected from "the Lord the Spirit" (not as *English Version*, "the Spirit of the Lord") [ALFORD] (vs. 17): "who receives of the things of Christ, and shows them to us" (John 16:14; Rom. 8:10, 11). (Cf. as to hereafter, Ps. 17:15; Rev. 22:4.)

CHAPTER 4

Vss. 1-18. HIS PREACHING IS OPEN AND SINCERE, THOUGH TO MANY THE GOSPEL IS HIDDEN; for he preaches Christ, not himself: the human vessel is frail that God may have the glory; yet, though frail, faith and the hope of future glory sustain him amidst the decay of the outward man. **1. Therefore**—Greek, "For this cause": Because we have the liberty-giving Spirit of the Lord, and with unveiled face behold His glory (ch. 3:17, 18). **seeing we have this ministry**—"The ministration of the Spirit" (ch. 3:8, 9): the ministry of such a spiritual, liberty-giving Gospel: resuming ch. 3:6, 8. **received mercy**—from God, in having had *this ministry* conferred on us (ch. 3:5). The sense of "mercy" received from God, makes men active for God (I Tim. 1:11-13). **we faint not**—in boldness of speech and action, and patience in suffering (vss. 2, 8-16, etc.). **2. renounced**—lit., "bid farewell to." **of dishonesty**—rather, "of shame." "I am not *ashamed* of the Gospel of Christ" (Rom. 1:16). Shame would lead to *hiding* (vs. 3); whereas "we use great plainness of speech" (ch. 3:12; "by *manifestation* of the truth." Cf. ch. 3:3, "*manifestly declared.*" He refers to the disingenuous artifices of "many" teachers at Corinth (ch. 2:17; 3:1; 11:13-15). **handling ... deceitfully** —so "corrupt" or *adulterate* "the word of God" (ch. 2:17; cf. I Thess. 2:3, 4). **commending**—recommending ourselves: recurring to ch. 3:1. **to**—to the verdict of. **every man's conscience**—(ch. 5:11). Not to men's carnal judgment, as those alluded to (ch. 3:1). **in the sight of God**—(ch. 2:17; Gal. 1: 10). **3. But if**—Yea, even if (as I grant is the case). **hid**—rather (in reference to ch. 3:13-18), "veiled." "Hid" (*Greek,* Col. 3:3) is said of that withdrawn from view altogether. "Veiled," of a thing within reach of the eye, but *covered* over so as not to be seen. So it was in the case of Moses' face. **to them**—in the case only of them: for *in itself* the Gospel is quite plain. **that are lost**—rather, "that are perishing" (I Cor. 1:18). So the same cloud that was "light" to the people of God, was "darkness" to the Egyptian foes of God (Exod. 14:20). **4. In whom**—Translate, "In whose case." **god of this world**—The worldly *make him their God* (Phil. 3:19). He is, *in fact,* the prince of the power of the air, *the spirit that ruleth in the children of disobedience*" (Eph. 2:2). **minds**—"understandings": "mental perceptions," as in ch. 3:14. **them which believe not**—the same as "them that are lost" (or "are perishing"). Cf. II Thessalonians 2:10-12. SOUTH quaintly says, "when the malefactor's eyes are covered, he is not far from his execution" (Esther 7:8). Those perishing unbelievers are not merely *veiled,* but blinded (ch. 3:14, 15): *Greek,* not "blinded," but "*hardened.*" **light of the glorious gospel of Christ**—Translate, "The illumination (*enlightening:* the *propagation* from those already enlightened, to others *of the light*) of the Gospel of the glory of Christ." "The glory of Christ" is not a mere *quality* (as "glorious" would express) of the Gospel; it is its very *essence and subject matter.* **image of God**—implying identity of nature and essence (John 1:18; Col. 1:15; Heb. 1:3). He who desires to see "the glory of God," may see it "in the face of Jesus Christ" (vs. 6; I Tim. 6:14-16). Paul here recurs to ch. 3:18. Christ is "the image of God," into which "same image" we, looking on it in the mirror of the Gospel, are changed by the Spirit; but this image is not visible to those blinded by Satan [ALFORD]. **5. For**—Their blindness is not our fault, as if we had selfseeking aims in our preaching. **preach ... Christ ... the Lord**—rather, "Christ *as Lord,*" and ourselves as your servants. ... "*Lord,*" or *Master,* is the correlative term to "servants." **6. For**—proof that we are true servants of Jesus unto you. **commanded the light**—*Greek,* "By speaking the word, commanded light" (Gen. 1:3). **hath shined**—rather, *as Greek,* "is He who shined." (It *is God) who commanded* light, etc., *that shined,* etc., (Job 37:15): Himself our Light and Sun, as well as the Creator of light (Mal. 4:2; John 8:12). The physical world answers to the spiritual. **in our hearts**—in themselves dark. **to give the light**—i.e., to propagate *to others* the light, etc., *which is in us* (cf. *Note,* vs. 4). **the glory of God**—answering to "the glory of Christ" (*Note,* vs. 4). **in the face of Jesus Christ**—Some of the oldest MSS. retain "Jesus." Others omit it. Christ is the manifestation of the glory of God, as His image (John 14:9). The allusion is still to the brightness on Moses' "face." The only true and full manifestation of God's brightness and glory is "in the face of Jesus" (Heb. 1:3). **7.** "Lest any should say, How then is it that we continue to enjoy *such unspeakable glory* in a mortal body? Paul replies, this very fact is one of the most marvellous proofs of God's power, that an earthen vessel could bear such splendor and keep *such a treasure*" [CHRYSOSTOM, *Homilies,* 8. 496, A.]. The treasure or "the light of the knowledge of the glory of God." The fragile "earthen vessel" is the *body,* the "outward man" (vs. 16; cf. vs. 10), liable to afflictions and death. So the light in Gideon's pitchers, the type (Judg. 7:16-20, 22). The ancients often kept their treasures in jars or vessels of earthenware. "There are earthen vessels which yet may be clean; whereas a golden vessel may be filthy" [BENGEL]. **that the excellency of the power ...**—that the *power* of the ministry (the Holy Spirit), in respect to its surpassing "excellency," exhibited in winning souls (I Cor. 2:4) and in sustaining us ministers, might be ascribed solely to God, we being weak as earthen vessels. God often allows the vessel to be chipped and broken, that the excellency of the treasure contained, and of the power which that treasure has, may be all His (vss. 10, 11; John 3:30). **may be of God ... not of us**—rather, as *Greek,* "may be *God's* (may be seen and be thankfully (vs. 15) acknowledged to *belong* to God), and not (to come) *from us.*" The power not merely comes *from* God, but *belongs* to Him continually, and is to be ascribed to him. **8.** *Greek,* "BEING hard pressed, yet not inextricably straitened; reduced to inextricable straits" (nominative to "we have,' vs. 7). **on every side**—*Greek,* "in every respect" (cf. vs. 10, "always"; ch. 7:5). This verse expresses *inward* distresses; next verse, *outward* distresses (ch. 7:5). "*Without* were fightings; *within* were fears." The first clause in each member of the series of contrasted participles, implies the *earthiness of the vessels;* the second clause, *the excellency of the power.* **perplexed, but not in despair**—*Greek,* "not utterly perplexed." As *perplexity* refers to the future, so "troubled" or "hard pressed" refers to the present. **9. not forsaken**—by God and man. Jesus was forsaken by both; so much do His sufferings exceed those of His people (Matt. 27:46). **cast down**—or "struck down"; not only "persecuted," i.e., *chased* as a deer or bird (I Sam. 26:20), but actually *struck down* as with a dart in the chase (Heb. 11:35-38). The *Greek* "always" in this verse means, "throughout the whole time"; in vs. 11 the *Greek* is different, and means, "at every time," "in every case when the occasion occurs." **bearing about in the body the dying of the Lord Jesus**—i.e., having my body

exposed to being put to death in the cause of Jesus (the oldest MSS. omit "the Lord"), and having in it the marks of such sufferings, I thus bear about wheresoever I go, an image of the suffering Saviour in my own person (vs. 11; ch. 1:5; cf. I Cor. 15:31). Doubtless, Paul was exposed to more dangers than are recorded in Acts (cf. ch. 7:5; 11:26). The *Greek* for "the dying" is lit., "the being made a *corpse*", such Paul regarded his body, yet a corpse which shares in the life-giving power of Christ's resurrection, as it has shared in His dying and death. **that the life also of Jesus might be made manifest in our body**—rather, "may be." The name "Jesus," by itself is often repeated here as Paul seems, amidst sufferings, peculiarly to have felt its sweetness. In vs. 11 the same words occur with the variation, "in our *mortal flesh.*" The fact of a dying, corpse-like body being sustained amidst such trials, manifests that "the (resurrection) life also," as well as the dying, "of Jesus," exerts its power in us. I thus bear about in my own person an image of the risen and *living,* as well as of the suffering, Saviour. The "our" is added here to "body," though not in the beginning of the verse. "For the body is *ours* not so much in death, as in life" [BENGEL]. **11. we which live**—in the power of Christ's "life" manifested in us, in our whole man, body as well as spirit (Rom. 8:10, 11; *Note,* vs. 10; cf. ch. 5:15). Paul regards his preservation amidst so many exposures to "death," by which Stephen and James were cut off, as a standing miracle (ch. 11:23). **delivered unto**—not by chance; by the ordering of Providence, who shows "the excellency of His power" (vs. 7), in *delivering unto* DEATH His living saints, that He may manifest LIFE also in their dying flesh. "Flesh," the very element of decay (not merely their "body"), is by Him made to manifest *life.* **12.** The *"death"* of Christ manifested in the continual "perishing of our outward man" (vs. 16), works peculiarly in us, and is the means of working *spiritual "life"* in you. The *life* whereof we witness in our bodily *dying,* extends beyond ourselves, and is brought by our very dying to you. **13.** Translate as *Greek,* "BUT having ..." i.e., not withstanding the trials just mentioned, we having ... **the same spirit of faith, according as it ...**—Cf. Romans 8:15, on the usage of "spirit of ..." The Holy Spirit acting on our spirit. Though "death worketh in us, and life in you" (vs. 12), yet *as we have the same spirit of faith as you,* we therefore [believingly] look for the same immortal *life* as you [ESTIUS], and *speak* as we believe. ALFORD not so well translates, "The *same* ... faith *with that described* in the Scriptures" (Ps. 116:10). The balance of the sentence requires the parallelism to be this, "According to that which is written, I believed, and therefore have I spoken; we also believe, and therefore speak," viz., without fear, amidst "afflictions" and "deaths" (vs. 17). **14. Knowing**—by faith (ch. 5:1). **shall raise up us also**—at the resurrection (I Cor. 6:13, 14). **by Jesus**—The oldest MSS. have *"with* Jesus." **present us**—vividly picturing the scene before the eyes (Jude 24). **with you**—(ch. 1:14; I Thess. 2:19, 20; 3:13). **15. For**—Confirming his assertion "with you" (vs. 14), and "life ... worketh in you" (vs. 12). **all things**—whether the afflictions and labors of us ministers (vss. 8-11), or your prosperity (vs. 12; I Cor. 3:21, 22; 4:8-13). **for your sakes**—(II Tim. 2:10). **abundant grace ...**—rather, "That grace (*the* grace which preserves us in trials and works life in you), being made the greater (multiplied), by means of the greater number (of its recipients), may cause the thanksgiving to abound to ..." [CHRYSOSTOM] (ch.

1:11; 9:11, 12). The *Greek* is susceptible also of this translation, "That grace, being made the greater (multiplied) on account of the thanksgiving of the greater number (for grace already received), may abound (abundantly redound) to. . ." Thus the *Greek* for "abound" has not to be taken in an active sense, but in its ordinary neuter sense, and so the other *Greek* words. Thanksgiving invites more abundant grace (II Chron. 20:19-22; Ps. 18:3; 50: 23). **16. we faint not**—notwithstanding our sufferings. Resuming vs. 1. **outward man**—the body, the flesh. **perish**—"is wearing away"; "is wasted away" by afflictions. **inward man**—our spiritual and true being, the "life" which even in our mortal bodies (vs. 11) "manifests the life of Jesus." **is renewed**—"is being renewed," viz., with fresh "grace" (vs. 15), and "faith" (vs. 13), and hope (vss. 17, 18). **17. which is but for a moment**—"Our PRESENT light (burden of) affliction" (so the *Greek;* cf. Matt. 11:30), [ALFORD]. Cf. "*now for a season . . . in heaviness*" (I Pet. 1:6). The contrast, however, between this and the "ETERNAL weight of glory" requires, I think, the translation, "Which is but for *the present passing moment.*" So WAHL. "The *lightness* of affliction" (he does not *express* "burden" after "light"; the *Greek* is "the light of affliction") contrasts beautifully with the "*weight* of the glory." **worketh**—rather, "worketh out." **a far more exceeding and**—rather, "in a surpassing and still more surpassing manner" [ALFORD]; "more and more exceedingly" [ELLICOTT, TRENCH, and others]. *Greek,* "in excess and to excess." The glory exceeds beyond all measure the affliction. **18. look not at**—as our aim. **things . . . seen**—"earthly things" (Phil. 3:19). We mind not the things seen, whether affliction or refreshment come, so as to be seduced by the latter, or deterred by the former [CHRYSOSTOM]. **things . . . not seen**—not "the invisible things" of Romans 1:20, but the things which, though not seen now, shall be so hereafter. **temporal**—rather, "for a time"; in contrast to eternal. *English Version* uses "temporal" for *temporary.* The *Greek* is rightly translated in the similar passage, "the pleasures of sin *for a season.*"

CHAPTER 5

Vss. 1-21. THE HOPE (ch. 4:17, 18) OF ETERNAL GLORY IN THE RESURRECTION BODY. Hence arises his ambition to be accepted at the Lord's coming judgment. Hence, too, his endeavor to deal openly with men, as with God, in preaching; thus giving the Corinthians whereof to boast concerning him against his adversaries. His constraining motive is the transforming love of Christ, by whom God has wrought reconciliation between Himself and men, and has committed to the apostle the ministry of reconciliation. **1. For**—Assigning the reason for the statement (ch. 4:17), that *affliction* leads to *exceeding glory*. **we know**—assuredly (ch. 4:14; Job 19:25). **if**—For *all* shall not die; many shall be "changed" without "dissolution" (I Cor. 15:51-53). If this daily *delivering unto death* (ch. 3:11) should end in actual death. **earthly**—not the same as *earthy* (I Cor. 15:47). It stands in contrast to "in the heavens." **house of this tabernacle**—rather, "house of the tabernacle." "House" expresses more *permanency* than belongs to the body; therefore the qualification, "of the tabernacle" (implying that it is *shifting,* not stationary), is added (cf. Job 4:19; II Pet. 1:13, 14). It thus answers to the tabernacle in the wilderness. Its wooden frame and curtains wore out in course of time when Israel dwelt in Canaan, and a fixed temple was substituted for it. The temple and the tabernacle in all essentials were one; there was the same ark, the same cloud of glory. Such is the relation between the "earthly" body and the resurrection body. The Holy Spirit is enshrined in the believer's body as in a sanctuary (I Cor. 3:16). As the ark went first in taking down the wilderness tabernacle, so the soul (which like the ark is sprinkled with blood of atonement, and is the sacred deposit in the inmost shrine, II Tim. 1:12) in the dissolution of the body; next the coverings were removed, answering to the flesh; lastly, the framework and boards, answering to the bones, which are last to give way (Num. 4). Paul, as a *tentmaker*, uses an image taken from his trade (Acts 18:3). **dissolved**—a mild word for death, in the case of believers. **we have**—in *assured* prospect of possession, as certain as if it were in our hands, laid up "in the heavens" for us. The tense is *present* (cf. John 3:36; 6:47, "*hath*"). **a building of God**—rather "*from* God." A solid *building,* not a temporary *tabernacle* or *tent.* "*Our*" body stands in contrast to "*from God.*" For though our present body be also *from God,* yet it is not fresh and perfect from His hands, as our resurrection body shall be. **not made with hands**—contrasted with houses erected by *man's* hands (I Cor. 15:44-49). So Christ's body is designated, as contrasted with the tabernacle reared by Moses (Mark 14:58; Heb. 9:11). This "house" can only be the *resurrection body,* in contrast to the "earthly house of the tabernacle," our present body. The intermediate state is not *directly* taken into account. A comma should separate "eternal," and "in the heavens." **2. For in this**—*Greek,* "For *also* in this"; "herein" (ch. 8: 10). ALFORD takes it, "in this" tabernacle. Verse 4, which seems parallel, favors this. But the parallelism is sufficiently exact by making "in this we groan" refer generally to what was just said (vs. 1), viz., that we cannot obtain our "house in the heavens" except our "earthly tabernacle" be first dissolved by death. **we groan** (Rom. 8:23) under the body's weaknesses now and liability to death. **earnestly desiring to be clothed upon**—translate, "earnestly *longing* to have *ourselves clothed upon* . . .," viz., by being found *alive* at Christ's coming, and so to escape *dissolution* by death (vss. 1, 4), and to have our heavenly body put on over the earthly. The groans of the saints prove the existence of the longing desire for the heavenly glory, a desire which cannot be planted by God within us in vain, as doomed to disappointment. **our house**—different *Greek* from that in vs. 1; translate, "our habitation," "our domicile"; it has a more distinct reference to the *inhabitant* than the general term "house" (vs. 1) [BENGEL]. **from heaven**—This domicile is "*from heaven*" in its origin, and is to be brought to us by the Lord at His coming again "from heaven" (I Thess. 4:16). Therefore this "habitation" or "domicile" is not heaven itself. **3. If so be . . .**—Our "desire" holds good, should the Lord's coming find us alive. Translate, "If so be that having ourselves clothed (with our natural body, cf. vs. 4) we shall not be found naked" (stripped of our present body). **4. For**—resuming vs. 2. **burdened; not for that**—rather, "*in that* we desire *not* to have ourselves unclothed (of our present body), but clothed upon" (with our heavenly body). **that mortality . . .**—rather, "that what is mortal (our mortal part) may be swallowed up of (absorbed and transformed into) life." Believers shrink from, not the *consequences,* but the mere *act* of dying; especially as believing in the possibility of their being found alive at the Lord's coming (I Thess. 4:15), and so of having their mortal body absorbed into the immortal without death. Faith does not divest us of all natural feeling, but subordinates it to higher feeling. Scripture gives no sanction to the contempt for the body expressed by philosophers. **5. wrought us**—framed us by redemption, justification, and sanctification. **for the selfsame thing**—"unto" it; viz., unto what is mortal of us being swallowed up in life (vs. 4). **who also**—The oldest MSS. omit "also." **earnest of the Spirit**—(*Note*, ch. 1:22). It is the Spirit (as "the first fruits") who creates in us the groaning desire for our coming deliverance and glory (Rom. 8:23). **6.** Translate as *Greek,* "Being therefore always confident and knowing . . . ." He had intended to have made the verb to this nominative, "we are willing" (rather, "well content"), but digressing on the word "confident" (vss. 6, 7), he resumes the word in a different form, viz., as an assertion: "We are confident and well content." "Being confident . . . . we are confident" may be the *Hebraic* idiom of emphasis; as Acts 7:34, *Greek,* "Having seen, I have seen," i.e., I have *surely seen.* **always**—under all trials. BENGEL makes the contrast between "*always* confident" and "confident" especially at the prospect of being "absent from the body." We are confident as well *at all times,* as also most of all in the hope of a blessed departure. **whilst . . . at home . . . absent**—Translate as *Greek,* "While we sojourn *in our home* in the body, we are *away from our home* in the Lord." The image from a "house" is retained (cf. Phil. 3:20; Heb. 11: 13-16; 13:14). **7. we walk**—in our Christian course here on earth. **not by sight**—*Greek,* "not by appearance." Our life is governed by faith in our immortal hope; not by the outward specious *appearance* of present things [TITTM. *Synonyms*]. Cf. "apparently," LXX, "by appearance," Numbers 12:8. WAHL supports *English Version.* Ch. 4:18 also confirms it (cf. Rom. 8:24; I Cor. 13:12, 13). God has appointed in this life *faith* for our great duty, and in the next, vision for our reward [SOUTH] (I Pet. 1:8). **8. willing**—lit., "well content." Translate also, "To go (lit., *migrate*) from our home in the body, and to come to our home with the Lord." We should prefer to be found alive at the Lord's coming, and to be clothed upon with our heavenly body (vss. 2-4). But feeling, as we do, the sojourn in the body to be a separation from our true home "with the Lord," we prefer even dissolution by death, so that *in the intermediate disembodied state* we may go to be "with the Lord" (Phil. 1:23). "To be with Christ" (the disembodied state) is distinguished from Christ's coming to take us to *be with Him* in soul and body (I Thess. 5:14-17, "with the Lord"). Perhaps the disembodied spirits of believers have fulness of communion *with Christ* unseen; but not the mutual recognition of one another, until clothed with their visible bodies at the resurrection (cf. I Thess. 4:13-17), when they shall with joy recognize Christ's image in each other perfect. **9. Wherefore**—with such a sure "confidence" of being blessed, whether we die before, or be found alive at Christ's coming. **we labour**—lit., "make it our ambition"; the only lawful ambition. **whether present or absent**—whether we be found at His coming present in the body, or absent from it. **accepted**—*Greek,* "well-pleasing." **10. appear**—rather, "be made manifest," viz., in our true character. So "appear," *Greek,* "be manifested" (Col. 3:4; cf. I Cor. 4:5). We are at all times, even now, manifest to God; *then* we shall be so to the assembled

intelligent universe and to ourselves: for the judgment shall be not only in order to assign the everlasting portion to each, but to vindicate God's righteousness, so that it shall be manifest to all His creatures, and even to the conscience of the sinner himself. **receive**—His reward of grace proportioned to "the things done . . " (ch. 9:6-9; II John 8). Though salvation be of grace purely, independent of works, the saved may have a greater or less *reward,* according as he lives to, and labors for, Christ more or less. Hence there is scope for the holy "ambition" (*Note*, vs. 9; Heb. 6:10). This verse guards against the Corinthians supposing that *all* share in the house . . . "from heaven" (vss. 1, 2). There shall be a searching judgment which shall sever the bad from the good, according to their respective deeds, the *motive* of the deeds being taken into account, not the mere external act; faith and love to God are the sole motives recognized by God as sound and good (Matt. 12:36, 37; 25:35-45), **done in his body**—The *Greek* may be, "by the instrumentality of the body"; but *English Version* is legitimate (cf. *Greek,* Rom. 2:27). Justice requires that *substantially the same* body which has been the instrument of the unbelievers' sin, should be the object of punishment. A proof of the essential identity of the natural and the resurrection body. **11. terror of the Lord**—the coming judgment, so full of terrors to unbelievers [ESTIUS]. ELLICOTT and ALFORD, after GROTIUS and BENGEL, translate, "The fear of the Lord" (ch. 7:1; Eccl. 12:13; Acts 9:31; Rom. 3:18; Eph. 5:21). **persuade**—Ministers should use the terrors of the Lord to *persuade* men, not to rouse their enmity (Jude 23). BENGEL, ESTIUS, and ALFORD explain: "Persuade men" (by our whole lives, vs. 13), viz., of our integrity as ministers. But this would have been expressed after "persuade," had it been the sense. The connection seems as follows: He had been accused of seeking to please and win men, he therefore says (cf. Gal. 1:10), "It is as knowing the terror (or *fear*) of the Lord that we persuade men; but (whether *men* who hear our preaching recognize our sincerity or not) we are made manifest unto God as acting on such motives (ch. 4:2); and I trust also in your consciences." Those so "manifested" need have no "terror" as to their being "manifested (*English Version,* appear) before the judgment seat" (vs. 10). **12. For**—the reason why he leaves the manifestation of his sincerity in preaching to their consciences (ch. 3:1), viz., his not wishing to "commend" himself again. **occasion to glory**—(ch. 1:14), viz., as to our sincerity. **in appearance**—*Greek,* "face" (cf. I Sam. 16: 7). The false teachers gloried in their *outward appearance,* and in external recommendations (ch. 11: 18) their learning, eloquence, wisdom, riches, not in vital religion in their *heart.* Their conscience does not attest their inward sincerity, as mine does (ch. 1:12). **13. be**—rather as *Greek,* "have been." The contrast is between the single act implied by the past tense, "If we *have ever been* beside ourselves," and the habitual state implied by the present, "Or whether we *be* sober," i.e., *of sound mind.* **beside ourselves**—The accusation brought by Festus against him (Acts 26:24). The holy enthusiasm with which he spake of what God effected by His apostolic ministry, seemed to many to be *boasting madness.* **sober**—humbling myself before you, and not using my apostolic power and privileges. **to God . . . for your cause**—The glorifying of his office was not for his own, but for God's glory. The abasing of himself was in adaptation to their infirmity, to gain them to Christ (I Cor. 9:22). **14.**

For—Accounting for his being "beside himself" with enthusiasm: the love of Christ towards us (in His death for us, the highest proof of it, Rom. 5:6-8), producing in turn love in us to Him, and not mere "terror" (vs. 11). **constraineth us**—with irresistible power *limits* us to the one great object to the exclusion of other considerations. The *Greek* implies *to compress forcibly* the energies into one channel. Love is *jealous* of any rival object engrossing the soul (ch. 11:1-3). **because we thus judge**—lit., (as) "having judged thus"; implying a judgment formed at conversion, and ever since regarded as a settled truth. **that if**—i.e., that *since.* But the oldest MSS. omit "if." "That one died for all" (*Greek*, "in behalf of all"). Thus the following clause will be, "Therefore all (lit., '*the* all,' viz., for whom He 'died') died." *His* dying is just the same as if *they all died;* and in their so dying, they died to sin and self, that they might live to God their Redeemer, whose henceforth they are (Rom. 6:2-11; Gal. 2:20; Col. 3:3; I Pet. 4:1-3). **15. they which live**—in the present life (ch. 4:11, "we which live") [ALFORD]; or, they who are thus indebted to Him for life of soul as well as body [MENOCHIUS]. **died for them**—He does not add, "rose again for them," a phrase not found in Paul's language [BENGEL]. He died *in their stead,* He arose again *for their good,* "for (the effecting of) their justification" (Rom. 4:25), and that He might be their Lord (Rom. 14:7-9). ELLICOTT and ALFORD join "for them" with both "died" and "rose again"; as Christ's death is *our death,* so His resurrection is *our resurrection; Greek,* "Who for them died and rose again." **not henceforth**—*Greek,* "no longer"; viz., now that His death for them has taken place, and that they know that His death saves them from death eternal, and His resurrection life brings spiritual and everlasting life to them. **16. Wherefore**—because of our settled *judgment* (vs. 14), **henceforth**—since our knowing Christ's constraining love in His death for us. **know we no man after the flesh**—i.e., according to his mere worldly and external relations (ch. 11:18; John 8:15; Phil. 3:4), as distinguished from what he is *according to the Spirit,* as a "new creature" (vs. 17). For instance, the outward distinctions of Jew or Gentile, rich or poor, slave or free, learned or unlearned, are lost sight of in the higher life of those who are dead in Christ's death, and alive with Him in the new life of His resurrection (Gal. 2:6; 3:28). **yea, though**—The oldest MSS. read, "if even." **known Christ after the flesh**—Paul when a Jew had looked for a temporal reigning, not a spritual, Messiah. (He says "Christ," not *Jesus:* for he had not known personally Jesus in the days of His flesh, but he had looked for Christ or the Messiah.) When once he was converted he no longer "conferred with flesh and blood" (Gal. 1:16). He had this advantage over the Twelve, that as one born out of due time he had never known Christ save in His heavenly life. To the Twelve it was "expedient that Christ should go away" that the Comforter should come, and so they might know Christ in the higher spiritual aspect and in His new life-giving power, and not merely "after the flesh," in the carnal aspect of Him (Rom. 6:9-11; I Cor. 15:45; I Pet. 3:18; 4:1, 2). Doubtless Judaizing Christians at Corinth prided themselves on the mere fleshly (ch. 11:18) advantage of their belonging to Israel, the nation of Christ, or on their having seen Him in the flesh, and thence claimed superiority over others as having a nearer connection with Him (vs. 12; ch. 10:7). Paul here shows the true aim should be to know Him spiritually as new creatures (vss. 15, 17), and that outward relations towards Him profit nothing (Luke 18:19-21; John 16:7, 22; Phil. 3:3-10). This is at variance with both Romish Mariolatry and transubstantiation. Two distinct *Greek* verbs are used here for "know"; the first ("*know* we no man") means "to be personally acquainted with"; the latter ("known Christ . . . know . . . more") is to *recognize,* or estimate. Paul's *estimate* of Christ, or the expected Messiah, was carnal, but is so now no more. **17. Therefore**—connected with the words in vs. 16, "We know Christ no more after the flesh." As Christ has entered on His new heavenly life by His resurrection and ascension, so all who are "in Christ" (i.e., united to Him by faith as the branch is IN the vine) are new creatures (Rom. 6:9-11). "New" in the *Greek* implies a new nature quite different from anything previously existing, not merely *recent,* which is expressed by a different *Greek* word (Gal. 6:15). **creature**—lit., "creation," and so the *creature* resulting from the creation (cf. John 3: 3, 5; Eph. 2:10; 4:23; Col. 3:10, 11). As we are "in Christ," so "God was in Christ" (vs. 19): hence He is Mediator between God and us. **old things**—selfish, carnal views (cf. vs. 16) of ourselves, of other men, and of Christ. **passed away**—spontaneously, like the snow of early spring [BENGEL] before the advancing sun. **behold**—implying an allusion to Isaiah 43:19, and 65:17. **18. all**—THE, *Greek*—**things**—all our privileges in this new creation (vss. 14, 15). **reconciled us**—i.e., *restored us* ("the world," vs. 19) *to His* favor by satisfying the claims of justice against us. Our position judicially considered in the eye of the law is altered, not as though the mediation of Christ had made a change in God's character, nor as if the love of God was produced by the mediation of Christ; nay, the mediation and sacrifice of Christ was the provision of God's love, not its moving cause (Rom. 8:32). Christ's blood was the price paid at the expense of God Himself, and was required to reconcile the exercise of mercy with justice, not as separate, but as the eternally harmonious attributes in the one and the same God (Rom. 3:25, 26). The *Greek* "reconcile" is *reciprocally* used as in the *Hebrew* Hithpahel conjugation, *appease, obtain the favor of.* Matthew 5:24, "Be reconciled to thy brother"; i.e., take measures that he be reconciled to thee, as well as thou to him, as the context proves. *Diallagethi,* however (Matt. 5:24), implying *mutual* reconciliation, is distinct from *Katallagethi* here, the latter referring to the *change* of status wrought in *one* of the two parties. The manner of God reconciling the world to Himself is implied (vs. 19), viz., by His "not imputing their trespasses to them." God not merely, as subsequently, reconciles the world by inducing them to lay aside their enmity, but in the first instance, does so by satisfying His own justice and righteous enmity against sin (Ps. 7:11). Cf. I Sam. 29:4, "Reconcile himself unto his master"; not remove his own anger against his master, but his master's against him [ARCHBISHOP MAGEE, *Atonement*]. The reconciling of *men to God* by their laying aside their enmity is the consequence of God laying aside His just enmity against their sin, and follows at vs. 20). **to us**—ministers (vss. 19, 20). **19. God was in Christ, reconciling**—i.e., God was BY Christ (*in virtue of Christ's intervention*) reconciling. . . . "Was reconciling" implies the time when the act of reconciliation was being carried into effect (vs. 21), viz., when "God made Jesus, who knew no sin, to be sin for us." The compound of "was" and the participle "reconciling," instead of the imperfect (*Greek*), may also imply the *continuous* purpose of God, from before the foundation of the world, to reconcile man to Himself, whose fall was foreseen. The expression "IN Christ" for "*by* Christ" may be used to imply *additionally* that God was IN Christ (John 10:38; 14: 10), and so *by* Christ (the God-man) was reconciling.... The *Greek* for "by" or *through* Christ (the best MSS. omit "Jesus"), vs. 18, is different. "In" must mean here *in the person of* Christ. The *Greek Katallasson* implies "changing" or *altering* the judicial status from one of condemnation to one of justification. The *atonement* (*at-one-ment*), or *reconciliation*, is the removal of the bar to peace and acceptance with a holy God, which His righteousness interposed against our sin. The first step towards restoring peace between us and God was on God's side (John 3:16). The *change* therefore *now* to be effected must be on the part of offending man, God the offended One being already reconciled. It is man, not God, who now needs to be reconciled, and to lay aside his enmity against God (Rom. 5:10, 11). ("We have *received the atonement*" [*Greek*, "reconciliation"], cannot mean "We have received the laying aside of *our own* enmity.") Cf. Romans 3:24, 25. **the world**—all men (Col. 1:20; I John 2: 2). The *manner* of the reconciling is by His "not imputing to men their trespasses," but imputing them to Christ the Sin-bearer. There is no incongruity that a father should be offended with that son whom he loveth, and at that time offended with him when he loveth him. So, though God loved men whom He created, yet He was offended with them when they sinned, and gave His Son to suffer for them, that through that Son's obedience He might be reconciled to them [reconcile them to Himself, i.e., restore them WITH JUSTICE to His favor] [BISHOP PEARSON, *Creed*]. **hath committed unto us**—*Greek*, "hath put into our hands." "Us," i.e., ministers. **20. for Christ ... in Christ's stead**—The *Greek* of both is the same: translate in both cases "on Christ's behalf." **beseech ... pray**—rather, "entreat [plead with you] ... beseech." Such "beseeching" is uncommon in the case of "ambassadors," who generally stand on their dignity (cf. ch. 10:2; I Thess. 2: 6, 7). **be ye reconciled to God**—*English Version* here inserts "ye," which is not in the original, and which gives the wrong impression, as if it were emphatic thus: *God* is reconciled to you, be *ye* reconciled to God. The *Greek* expresses rather, God was the RECONCILER in Christ ... let this reconciliation then have its designed effect. *Be reconciled to God*, i.e., let God reconcile you to Himself (vss. 18, 19). **21. For**—omitted in the oldest MSS. The grand reason why they should be reconciled to God, viz., the great atonement in Christ provided by God, is stated without the "for" as being part of *the message of reconciliation* (vs. 19). **he**—God. **sin**—not *a sin offering*, which would destroy the antithesis to "righteousness," and would make "sin" be used in different senses in the same sentence: not *a sinful person*, which would be untrue, and would require in the antithesis "righteous men," not "righteousness"; but "sin," i.e., the representative *Sin-bearer* (vicariously) of *the aggregate sin* of all men past, present, and future. The sin of the world is *one*, therefore the *singular*, not the *plural*, is used; though its *manifestations* are manifold (John 1:29). "Behold the Lamb of God, that taketh away the SIN of the world." Cf. "made a curse for us," Galatians 3:13. **for us**—*Greek*, "in our behalf." Cf. John 3:14, Christ being represented by the brazen *serpent*, the *form*, but not the *substance*, of the old serpent.

At His death on the cross the sin-bearing for us was consummated. **knew no sin**—by personal experience (John 8:46) [ALFORD]. Hebrews 7:26; I Peter 2:22; I John 3:5. **might be made**—not the same *Greek* as the previous "made." Rather, "might become." **the righteousness of God**—Not merely righteous, but *righteousness* itself; not merely righteousness, but the *righteousness of God*, because Christ is God, and what He is we are (I John 4:17), and He is "made of God unto us righteousness." As our sin is made over to Him, so His righteousness to us (in His having fulfilled all the righteousness of the law for us all, as our representative (Jer. 23:6; I Cor. 1:30). The innocent was punished voluntarily as if guilty, that the guilty might be gratuitously rewarded as if innocent (I Peter 2:24). "Such are we in the sight of God the Father, as is the very Son of God himself" [HOOKER]. **in him**—by virtue of our standing in Him, and in union with Him [ALFORD].

CHAPTER 6

Vss. 1-18. HIS APOSTOLIC MINISTRY IS APPROVED BY FAITHFULNESS IN EXHORTATION, IN SUFFERINGS, IN EXHIBITION OF THE FRUITS OF THE HOLY GHOST: HIS LARGENESS OF HEART TO THEM CALLS FOR ENLARGEMENT OF THEIR HEART TO HIM. EXHORTATIONS TO SEPARATION FROM POLLUTION. **1. workers together** —with God (Acts 15:4; I Cor. 3:9). Not only as "ambassadors." **beseech**—entreat (ch. 5:20). He is describing his ministry, not exhorting directly. **you also**—rather, "WE ALSO (as well as God, ch. 5:20) beseech" or "entreat you": vss. 14, 15, on to ch. 7:1, is part of this entreaty or exhortation. **in vain**—by making the grace of God a ground for continuance in sin (vs. 3). By a life of sin, showing that the word of reconciliation has been *in vain*, so far as you are concerned (Heb. 12:15; Jude 4). "The grace of God" here, is "the reconciliation" provided by God's love (ch. 5:18, 19; cf. Gal. 2:2). **2. For**— God's own promise is the ground of our exhortation. **he saith**—*God the Father* saith to God the Son, and so to all believers who are regarded as one with Him. **heard thee**—In the eternal purposes of my love I have hearkened to thy prayer for the salvation of thy people (cf. John 17:9, 15, 20, 24). **accepted ... accepted**—The *Greek* of the latter is more emphatic, "well-accepted." What was "*an accepted* time" in the prophecy (Isa. 49:8, *Hebrew*, "in the season of grace") becomes "*the wellaccepted* time" in the fulfilment (cf. Ps. 69:13). As it is *God's* time of *receiving* sinners, *receive ye* His grace: *accept* (vs. 1) the word of reconciliation in His *accepted* time. **in the day of salvation**—"in *a* day of salvation" (Luke 4:18, 19, 21; 19:42; Heb. 3:7). **3.** Resuming the connection with vs. 1, interrupted by the parenthetical vs. 2. "Giving no offense" (cf. I Cor. 10:33), "approving ourselves," and all the other participles down to vs. 10, are nominatives to "we also entreat you" (vs. 1), to show the pains he took to enforce his exhortation by example, as well as precept [ALFORD]. "Offense" would be given, if we were without "patience" and the other qualifications which he therefore subjoins (cf. Rom. 14:13). **4.** Translate, to mark the true order of the *Greek* words, "in everything, as God's ministers recommending ourselves," i.e., that our hearers may give our *message* a favorable hearing, through our consistency in every respect, not that they may glorify us. Alluding to ch. 3:1, he implies, *We commend ourselves*, not like them by word, but by deed. **patience**—(ch. 12:12). Put first. "Pure-minded" follows (vs. 6). Three triplets of trials exercising the "patience" (patient endurance) follow: Afflictions (or "tribulations"), necessities, distresses (or "straits"); stripes, imprisonments, tumults; labors, watchings, fastings. The first triplet expresses afflictions generally; the second, those in particular arising from the violence of men; the third, those *which* he brought on himself directly or indirectly. **5. stripes**—(ch. 11:23, 24; Acts 16:23). **imprisonments**—(ch. 11:23). He had been, doubtless, elsewhere imprisoned besides at Philippi when he wrote this Epistle. **tumults**—(Acts 13:50; 14:5, 19; 16:22; and recently 19:23-41). **labours**—in the cause of Christ (ch. 11:23; Rom. 16:12). **watchings**—(ch. 11:27). Sleepless nights. **fastings**—The context here refers to his *trials*, rather than *devotional exercises* (cf. ch. 11:27). Thus "foodlessness" would seem to be the sense (cf. I Cor. 4:11, Phil. 4:12). But the usual sense of the *Greek* is *fasts*, in the strict sense; and in ch. 11:27 it is spoken of independently of "hunger and thirst." (Cf. Luke 2:37; Acts 10:30; 14:23.) However, Matthew 15:32; Mark 8:3, justify the sense, more favored by the context, *foodlessness,* though a rare use of the word. GAUSSEN remarks "The apostles combine the highest offices with the humblest exterior: as everything in the Church was to be cast in the mould of death and resurrection, the cardinal principle throughout Christianity." **6. By...by...**—rather, as *Greek,* "In...in," implying not the instrument, but the sphere or element in which his ministry moved. **knowledge**—spiritual: in Gospel mysteries, unattainable by mere reason (I Cor. 2:6-16; II Cor. 3:6, 17, 18). **long-suffering... kindness**—associated with "charity" or "*love*" (I Cor. 13:4), as here. **by the Holy Ghost**—in virtue of His influences which produce these graces, and other gifts, "love unfeigned" being the foremost of them. **7. By the word of truth, by the power of God**—rather, "In... in...." As to "the word of truth" (cf. ch. 4:2; Col. 1:5), and "the (miraculous) power of God" (ch. 4:7); I Corinthians 2:4, "in demonstration of the Spirit and of power." **by the armour**—*Greek,* "through" or "by means of the armor." "Righteousness," which is the *breastplate* alone in Ephesians 6:13-17, here is made the *whole* Christian panoply (cf. ch. 10:4). **on... right... and... left**—i.e., guarding on every side. **8.** Translate, "*Through glory* and dishonor" (disgrace), viz., from *those in authority,* and accruing to us *present.* "By," or "*through* evil report and good report," from *the multitude,* and affecting us *absent* [BENGEL]. Regarded "as deceivers" by those who, *not knowing* (vs. 9), *dishonor* and give us an *evil report;* "as true," by those who "know" (vs. 9) us in the real "glory" of our ministry. In proportion as one has more or less of *glory* and *good report,* in that degree has he more or less of *dishonor* and *evil report.* **9. unknown... yet well known**—"unknown" in our true character to those who "evil report" of us, "well known" to those who hold us in "good report" (vs. 8). CONYBEARE explains, "Unknown by men, yet *acknowledged by God*" (I Cor. 13:12). Perhaps *both* God and men (believers) are intended as knowing him (ch. 5:11, and 11:6). **dying... live**—(ch. 1:9; 4:10, 11; 11:23). Cf. GAUSSEN'S remark, *Note,* vs. 5. "Behold" calls attention to the fact as something beyond all expectation. **chastened... not killed**—realizing Psalm 118:18. **10.** The "as" no longer is used to express the opinion of his adversaries, but the real state of him and his fellow laborers. **making many rich**—Spiritually (I Cor. 1:5), after the example of our Lord, who "by His

poverty made many rich" (ch. 8:9). **having nothing**—Whatever of earthly goods we have, and these are few, we have as though we had not; as tenants removable at will, not owners (I Cor. 7:30). **possessing all things**—The *Greek* implies *firm possession, holding fast in possession* (cf. I Cor. 3:21, 22). The things both of the present and of the future are, in the truest sense, the believer's in possession, for he possesses them all in Christ, his lasting possession, though the full *fruition* of them is reserved for the future eternity. **11. mouth... open unto you**—I use no concealment, such as some at Corinth have insinuated (ch. 4:2). I use all freedom and openness of speech to you as to beloved friends. Hence he introduces here, "O Corinthians" (cf. Phil. 4:15). The *enlargement* of his *heart* towards them (ch. 7:3) produced his *openness* of *mouth,* i.e., his unreserved expression of his inmost feelings. As an unloving man is *narrow* in heart, so the apostle's heart is *enlarged* by love, so as to take in his converts at Corinth, not only with their graces, but with their many shortcomings (cf. I Kings 4:29; Ps. 119:32; Isa. 60:5). **12.** Any constraint ye feel towards me, or narrowness of heart, is not from want of largeness of heart on my part towards you, but from want of it on your part towards me; "bowels," i.e., affections (cf. ch. 12:15). **not straitened in us**—i.e., for want of room in our hearts to take you in. **13.** Translate, "As a recompense in the same kind... be enlarged also yourselves" [ELLICOTT]. "In the same way" as my heart is enlarged towards you (vs. 11), and "as a recompense" for it (Gal. 4:12). **I speak as unto my children**—as children would naturally be expected to *recompense* their parents' love with similar love. **14. Be not**—*Greek,* "*Become* not." **unequally yoked**—"yoked with one alien in spirit." The image is from the symbolical precept of the law (Lev. 19: 19), "Thou shalt not let thy cattle gender with a diverse kind"; or the precept (Deut. 22:10), "Thou shalt not plough with an ox and an ass together." Cf. Deuteronony 7:3, forbidding marriages with the heathen; also I Corinthians 7:39. The believer and unbeliever are utterly *heterogeneous.* Too close intercourse with unbelievers in other relations also is included (vs. 16; I Cor. 8:10; 10:14). **fellowship** —lit., "share," or "participation." **righteousness**—the state of the believer, justified by faith. **unrighteousness**—rather, as always translated elsewhere, "iniquity"; the state of the unbeliever, the fruit of unbelief. **light**—of which believers are the children (I Thess. 5:5). **15. Belial**—*Hebrew,* "worthlessness, unprofitableness, wickedness." As Satan is opposed to God, and Antichrist to Christ; Belial being here opposed to Christ, must denounce all manner of Antichristian uncleanness [BENGEL]. **he that believeth with an infidel**—Translate, "a believer with an unbeliever." **16. agreement**—accordance of sentiments (cf. I Kings 18:21; Eph. 5:7, 11). **the temple of God**—i.e., you believers (I Cor. 3:16; 6:19). **with idols**—Cf. Dagon before the ark (I Sam. 5:24). **as**—"*even as* God said." Quotation from Leviticus 26:12; Jeremiah 31:33; 32:38; Ezekiel 37:26, 27; cf. Matthew 28:20; John 14:23. **walk in them**—rather, *among* them. As "dwell" implies the divine *presence,* so "walk," the divine *operation.* God's dwelling in the body and soul of saints may be illustrated by its opposite, demoniacal possession of body and soul. **my people**—rather, "they shall be *to me* a people." **17.** Quoted from Isaiah 52:11, with the freedom of one inspired, who gives variations sanctioned by the Holy Spirit. **be ye separate** —"be separated" (Hos. 4:17). **touch not the unclean** thing—rather, "*anything* unclean" (ch. 7:1; Mic. 2: 10). *Touching* is more polluting, as implying participation, than seeing. **receive you**—The *Greek* implies, "to myself"; as persons heretofore out of doors, but now admitted *within* (ch. 5:1-10). With this accords the clause, "Come *out from among them*," viz., so as to be received to me. So Ezekiel 20:41, "I will accept you"; and Zephaniah 3:19; "gather her that was driven out." "The intercourse of believers with the world should resemble that of angels, who, when they have been sent a message from heaven, discharge their office with the utmost promptness, and joyfully fly back home to the presence of God" (I Cor. 7:31; 5:9, 10). **18.** Translate, "I will be to you *in the relation of* a Father, and ye shall be *to me in the relation of* sons. . . ." This is a still more endearing relation than (vs. 16), "I will be their *God*, and they . . . My *people*." Cf. the promise to Solomon (I Chron. 28:6; Isa. 43:6; Rev. 21:3, 7; Jer. 31:1, 9). **Lord Almighty**—*The Lord the Universal Ruler:* nowhere else found but in Revelation. The greatness of the Promiser enhances the greatness of the promises.

CHAPTER 7

Vss. 1-16. Self-Purification Their Duty Resulting from the Foregoing. His Love to Them, and Joy at the Good Effects on Them of His Former Epistle, as Reported by Titus. **1. cleanse ourselves**—This is the conclusion of the exhortation (ch. 6:1, 14; I John 3:3; Rev. 22:11). **filthiness** —"the unclean thing" (ch. 6:17). **of the flesh**—for instance, *fornication*, prevalent at Corinth (I Cor. 6:15-18). **and spirit**—for instance, *idolatry*, direct or indirect (I Cor. 6:9; 8:1, 7; 10:7, 21, 22). The spirit (Ps. 32:2) receives pollution through the flesh, the instrument of uncleanness. **perfecting holiness** —The *cleansing away* impurity is a positive step towards holiness (ch. 6:17). It is not enough to begin; the end crowns the work (Gal. 3:3; 5:7; Phil. 1:6). **fear of God**—often conjoined with the consideration of the most glorious promises (ch. 5:11; Heb. 4:1). Privilege and promise go hand in hand. **2. Receive us**—with *enlarged* hearts (ch. 6:13). **we have wronged . . . corrupted . . . defrauded no man**—(cf. vs. 9). This is the ground on which he asks their reception of (making room for) him in their hearts. We *wronged* none by an undue exercise of apostolic authority; vs. 13 gives an instance in point. We have corrupted none, viz., by beguilements and flatteries, while preaching "another Gospel," as the false teachers did (ch. 11:3, 4). We have defrauded none by "making a gain" of you (ch. 12:17). Modestly he leaves them to supply the *positive* good which he had done; suffering all things himself that they might be benefited (vss. 9, 12; ch. 12:13). **3.** In excusing myself, I do not accuse you, as though you suspected me of such things [Menochius], or as though you were guilty of such things; for I speak only of the false apostles "Estius and *Greek* commentators]. Rather, "as though you were ungrateful and treacherous" [Beza]. **I . . . said before**—in ch. 6:11, 12; cf. Phil. 1:7. **die and live with you** —the height of friendship. I am ready to die and live with you and for you (Phil. 1:7, 20, 24; 2:17, 18). Cf. as to Christ, John 10:11. **4. boldness of speech**—(cf. ch. 6:11). **glorying of you**—Not only do I speak with unreserved openness *to you*, but I *glory* (boast) *greatly to others in your behalf*, in speaking *of you*. **filled with comfort**—at the report of Titus (vss. 6, 7, 9, 13; ch. 1:4). **exceeding joyful**

—*Greek*, I *overabound* with joy (vss. 7, 9, 16). **our tribulation**—described in vs. 5; also in ch. 4:7, 8; 6: 4, 5. **5.** *Greek*, "For also" (for "*even*"). This verse is thus connected with ch. 2:12, 13, "When I came to Troas, I had no rest in my *spirit*"; so "*also*" now, when I came to Macedonia, my "*flesh*" had no rest (he, by the term "flesh," excepts his *spiritual* consolations) from "fightings with adversaries 'without'" (I Cor. 5:12), and from fears for the Corinthian believers "within" the Church, owing to "false brethren" (ch. 11:26). Cf. ch. 4:8; Deuteronomy 32:25, to which he seems to allude. **6.** Translate in the order required by the *Greek*, "But he that comforteth those that are cast down, even God." Those that are of an high spirit are not susceptible of such comfort. **7. when he told us**— *Greek*, "telling us." We shared in the comfort which Titus felt in recording your desire (vs. 13). *He* rejoiced in telling the news; *we* in hearing them [Alford]. **earnest desire**—*Greek*, "longing desire," viz., *to see me* [Grotius]; or, in general, *towards me, to please me*. **mourning**—over your own remissness in not having immediately punished the sin (I Cor. 5:1, etc.) which called forth my rebuke. **fervent mind**—*Greek*, "zeal" (cf. vs. 11; John 2:17). **toward me**—*Greek*, "for me"; for my sake. They *in Paul's behalf* showed the zeal against the sin which Paul would have shown had he been present. **rejoiced the more**—more than before, at the mere coming of Titus. **8. with a letter**—*Greek*, "in the letter" viz., the first Epistle to the Corinthians. **I do not repent, though I did repent**—Translate, "I do not *regret* it, though I did *regret* it." The *Greek* words for *regret* and *repent* are distinct. Paul was almost regretting, through parental tenderness, his having used rebukes calculated to grieve the Corinthians; but now that he has learned from Titus the salutary effect produced on them, he no longer regrets it. **for I perceive**—This is explanatory of "I did repent" or "regret it," and is parenthetical ("for I perceive that *that* Epistle did make you sorry, though it was but for a season"). **9. Now I rejoice** —Whereas "I did repent" or regret having made you sorry by my letter, I rejoice now, not that ye were caused sorrow, but that your sorrow resulted in your repentance. **ye sorrowed**—rather, as before, "ye were made sorry." **after a godly manner**—lit., "according to God," i.e., your sorrow having regard to God, and rendering your mind conformable to God (Rom. 14:22; I Pet. 4:6). **that**—Translate in *Greek* order, "*to the end that* (cf. ch. 11:9) ye might in nothing receive damage from us," which ye would have received, had your sorrow been other than that "after a godly manner" (vs. 10). **10. worketh . . . worketh**—In the best *Greek* reading the translation is, "worketh (simply) . . . worketh *out*." "Sorrow" is not repentance, but, where it is "godly," "worketh" it; i.e., *contributes* or *tends to* it (the same *Greek* word is in Rom. 13:10). The "sorrow of the world" (i.e., such as is felt by the worldly) "worketh *out*," as its *result at last*, (eternal) death (the same *Greek* verb is in ch. 4:17, where see the *Note*). **repentance . . . not to be repented of**—There is not in the *Greek* this play on words, so that the word qualified is not "repentance" merely, but "repentance unto salvation"; this, he says, *none will ever regret*, however attended with "sorrow" at the time. "*Repentance*" implies a *coming to a right mind*; "regret" implies merely uneasiness of feeling at the past or present, and is applied even to the *remorse* of Judas (Matt. 27:3; *Greek*, "stricken with remorse," not as *English Version*, "repented himself"); so that, though always accompanying repentance, it is not always accompanied by repentance. "Repentance" removes the impediments in the way of "salvation" (to which "death," viz., of the soul, is opposed). "The sorrow of the world" is not at the *sin* itself, but at its *penal consequences:* so that the tears of pain are no sooner dried up, than the pleasures of ungodliness are renewed. So Pharaoh, Exodus 9:27, 28-30; and Saul, I Sam. 15: 23-30. Cf. Isaiah 9:13; Revelation 16:10, 11. Contrast David's "godly sorrow," II Samuel 12:13, and Peters, Matthew 26:75. **11.** Confirmation of vs. 10 from the Corinthians' own experience. **carefulness**–solicitude, lit., "diligence," opposed to their past negligence in the matter. **in you**–*Greek* "for you." **yea**–not only "carefulness" or *diligence*, but also "clearing of yourselves," viz., to me by Titus: anxiety to show you disapproved of the deed. **indignation**–against the offender. **fear**–of the wrath of God, and of sinning any more [SCLATER and CALVIN]; fear of Paul [GROTIUS], (I Cor. 4:2, 19-21). **vehement desire**–longing for restoration to Paul's approval [CONYBEARE and HOWSON]. "Fear" is in spite of one's self. "Longing desire" is spontaneous, and implies strong love and an aspiration for correction [CALVIN]. "Desire" *for the presence of Paul*, as he had given them the hope of it (I Cor. 4:19; 16:5) [GROTIUS and ESTIUS]. **zeal**–for right and for God's honor against what is wrong. Or, "for the good of the soul of the offender" [BENGEL]. **revenge**–*Translate*, "Exacting of punishment" (I Cor. 5:2, 3). Their "carefulness" was exhibited in the six points just specified: "clearing of themselves," and "indignation" in relation to themselves; "fear" and "vehement desire" in respect to the apostle; "zeal" and "revenge" in respect to the offender [BENGEL]; *(cf.* vs. 7). **In all**–the respects just stated. **clear**–*Greek*, "pure," viz., from complicity in the guilty deed. "Approved yourselves," *Greek*, "commended yourselves." Whatever suspicion of complicity rested on you (I Cor. 5:2, 6) through your former remissness, you have cleared off by your present strenuousness in reprobating the deed. **12. though I wrote unto you**–"making you sorry with my letter" (vs. 8). **his cause that suffered wrong**–the father of the incestuous person who had his father's wife (I Cor. 5:1). The father, thus it seems, was alive. **that our care for you . . .**–Some of the oldest MSS. read thus, "That YOUR care for US might be made manifest unto you. . . ." But the words, "unto you," thus, would be rather obscure; still the obscurity of the genuine reading may have been the very reason for the change being made by correctors into the reading of *English Version*. ALFORD explains the reading: "He wrote in order to bring out their zeal on his behalf (i.e., to obey his command), and make it manifest *to themselves* in God's sight, i.e., to bring out *among them* their zeal to regard and obey him." But some of the oldest MSS. and versions (including the *Vulgate* and old *Italian*) support *English Version*. And the words, "to you," suit it better than the other reading. Ch. 2:4, "I wrote . . . that ye might know the love which *I* have more abundantly *unto you*," plainly accords with it, and disproves ALFORD's assertion that *English Version is inconsistent with the fact* as to the purpose of his letter. His writing, he says, was not so much for the sake of the individual offender, or the individual offended, but from his "earnest care" or concern for the welfare of the Church. **13.** The oldest MSS. read thus, "Therefore *(Greek,* "for this *cause*," viz., because our aim has been attained) we have been (*English Version*, "were," is not so accurate) comforted; yea (*Greek,*

"but"), in OUR comfort we exceedingly the more joyed for the joy of Titus . . ." (cf. vs. 7). **14. anything**–i.e., at all. **I am not ashamed**–"I am not put to shame," viz., by learning from Titus that you did not realize the high character I gave him of you. **as . . . all things . . . in truth, even so our boasting . . . is found a truth**–As our speaking *in general* to you was true (ch. 1:18), so our *particular* boasting to Titus *concerning you* is now, by his report, proved to be truth (cf. ch. 9:2). Some oldest MSS. read expressly, "concerning you"; this in either reading is the *sense*. **15. his inward affection** –lit., bowels (cf. ch. 6:12; Phil. 1:8; 2:1; Col. 3:12). **obedience**–(ch. 2:9). **fear and trembling**–with trembling anxiety to obey my wishes, and fearful lest there should be aught in yourselves to offend him and me (vs. 11; cf. I Cor. 2:3). **16. therefore** –omitted in the oldest MSS. The conclusion is more emphatical without it. **that I have confidence in you in all things**–rather, as *Greek,* "that in everything I *am of good courage concerning* (lit., in the case of) you," as contrasted with my former doubts concerning you.

CHAPTER 8

Vss. 1-24. THE COLLECTION FOR THE SAINTS; THE READINESS OF THE MACEDONIANS A PATTERN TO THE CORINTHIANS; CHRIST THE HIGHEST PATTERN; EACH IS TO GIVE WILLINGLY AFTER HIS ABILITY; TITUS AND TWO OTHERS ARE THE AGENTS ACCREDITED TO COMPLETE THE COLLECTION. **1. we do you to wit**–*we make known to you.* **the grace of God bestowed on the churches of Macedonia**– Their liberality was not of themselves naturally, but of God's grace bestowed on them, and enabling them to be the instrument of God's "grace" to others (vss. 6, 19). The importance given in this Epistle to the collection, arose as well from Paul's engagement (Gal. 2:10), as also chiefly from his hope to conciliate the Judaizing Christians at Jerusalem to himself and the Gentile believers, by such an act of love on the part of the latter towards their Jewish brethren. **2. trial of affliction**–The *Greek* expresses, "in affliction (or, "tribulation") which *tested* them"; lit., "in a great testing of affliction." **abundance of their joy**–The greater was the depth of their poverty, the greater was the abundance of their joy. A delightful contrast in terms, and triumph, in fact, of spirit over flesh. **their deep poverty**–*Greek*, "their poverty down to the death of it." **abounded unto the riches . . .**–another beautiful contrast in terms: their *poverty* had the effect, not of producing stinted gifts, but of "abounding in the *riches* of liberality" (not as *Margin,* "simplicity"; though the idea of *singleness* of motive to God's glory and man's good, probably enters into the idea); (cf. Rom. 12:8, and *Margin;* ch. 9:11, *Note,* 13; Jas. 1:5). **3-5. they were willing**–rather, supply from vs. 5, the ellipsis thus, "According to their power . . . yea, and beyond their power, THEY GAVE." **of themselves**–not only not being besought, but themselves beseeching us. **4. that we would receive**–omitted in the oldest MSS. Translate therefore, "Beseeching of us . . . the grace and fellowship of (i.e., to grant them *the favor of sharing in*) the ministering unto the saints." The Macedonian contributions must have been from Philippi, because Philippi was the only church that contributed to Paul's support (Phil. 4:10, 15, 16). **5. And** *this they did,* **not as we hoped**–Translate, "And not as we hoped (i.e., far beyond our hopes), but their own selves gave they first to the Lord."

"First," not indicating priority of time, but first of all, *above all in importance*. The giving of themselves takes precedence of their other gifts, as being the motive which led them to the latter (Rom. 15: 16). **by the will of God**—not *"according to* the will of God," but *"moved by* the will of God, who made them willing" (Phil. 2:13). It is therefore called (vs. 1), "the grace of God." **6. Insomuch that**—As we saw the Macedonians' alacrity in giving, we could not but exhort Titus, that as we collected in Macedonia, so he in Corinth should complete the work of collecting which he had already begun there, lest ye, the wealthy people of Corinth, should be outdone in liberality by the poor Macedonians. **as he had begun**—*Greek,* "previously begun," viz., the collection at Corinth, *before* the Macedonians began to contribute, during the visit to Corinth from which he had just returned. **finish in you the same grace**—complete among you this act of grace or beneficence on your part. **also**—as well as other things which he had to do among them [ALFORD]. **7. in faith**—(ch. 1:24). **utterance**—(*Note,* I Cor. 1: 5). Not as ALFORD, "doctrine" or "word." **knowledge**—(I Cor. 8:1). **diligence**—in everything that is good. **your love to us**—lit., "love from you (i.e., on your part) in us" (i.e., which has us for its object; which is felt *in the case of* us). **8. not by commandment**—"not by way of commandment." **by the occasion of the forwardness of others, and . . .**—rather, "But by (mention of) the forwardness of others (as an inducement to you), and to prove (lit., proving) the sincerity of your love." The *Greek* is *"by means of,"* not *"on account of* the forwardness . . . ." BENGEL, ELLICOTT, and others translate, *"By means of* the forwardness of others, proving the sincerity of your love ALSO." The former is the simpler construction in the *Greek.* **9. ye know the grace**—the act of gratuitous love whereby the Lord emptied Himself of His previous heavenly glory (Phil. 2:6, 7) for your sakes. **became poor**—Yet this is not demanded of you (vs. 14); but merely that, without impoverishing yourselves, you should relieve others with your abundance. If the Lord did so much more, and at so much heavier a cost, for your sakes; much more may you do an act of love to your brethren at so little a sacrifice of self. **might be rich**—in the heavenly glory which constitutes His riches, and all other things, so far as is really good for us (cf. I Cor. 3: 21, 22). **10. advice**—Herein he does not (as some misinterpret the passage) disclaim inspiration for the advice he gives; but under the Spirit, states that it is his "opinion" [ALFORD] or "judgment" [ELLI-COTT, and others], not a *command,* that so their offering might be free and spontaneous. **this**—my giving you an *advice,* not a command. **who have begun before**—"seeing that ye have begun *before"* the Macedonian churches; "a year ago" should be connected with this clause. **not only to do, but also to be forward**—There were three steps: (1) the *forwardness,* more literally, "the will"; (2) the *setting about* it, lit., "doing it"; (3) *completion* of it [ALFORD]. In the two former, not only the *act,* but the *intention,* the Corinthians *preceded the Macedonians.* BENGEL explains, "Not only to do" FOR THE PAST YEAR, "but also to be forward" or *willing* FOR THIS YEAR. ELLICOTT translates, "already," instead of "before": "Ye began already a year ago, not only to do, but also to be forward." It appears hence, that something had been done in the matter a year before; other texts, however, show the collection was not yet paid (cf. vs. 11 and ch. 9:5, 7). This agrees with one, and only one.

supposition, viz., that every man had laid by in store the fund from which he was afterwards to contribute, the very case which is shown by I Cor. 16:2 to have existed [PALEY's *Horæ Paulinæ*]. **11. perform**—"complete the doing also" (*Note,* vs. 10). **a readiness to will**—*Greek,* "the readiness *of* will"; referring to vs. 10, where the *Greek* for "to be forward," ought to be translated as here, "to will." **performance**—"completion" [ALFORD]. The godly should show the same zeal to finish, as well as to begin well, which the worldly exhibit in their undertakings (Jer. 44:25). **12. For**—Following up the rule "out of that which ye have" (vs. 11), and no more. **a willing mind**—rather, as *Greek,* "the readiness," viz., to will, referring to vs. 11. **accepted** —*Greek* "favorably accepted." **according to that a man hath**—The oldest MSS. omit "a man." Translate, "According to whatsoever it have"; the *willing mind,* or "readiness" to will, is personified [ALFORD]. Or better, as BENGEL, *"He is* accepted according to whatsoever he have"; so ch. 9:7, The Lord loveth a cheerful *giver."* Cf. as to David, I Kings 8:18. God accepts the will for the deed. He judges not according to what a man has the opportunity to do, but according to what he would do if he had the opportunity (cf. Mark 14:8; and the widow's mite, Luke 21:3, 4). **13. For**—Supply from vs. 8, "I speak." My aim is not that others (viz., the saints at Jerusalem) may be relieved at the cost of your being "distressed" (so the *Greek* for "burdened"). The golden rule is, "Love thy neighbour *as thyself,"* not *more* than thyself. **14. by an equality**—"by the rule of equality" [ALFORD]: lit., "out of equality." **now at this time**—*Greek,* "at the present juncture" or season. **that their abundance also**—The *Greek* being distinct from the previous "that," translate, "in order that," viz., *at another season,* when your relative circumstances may be reversed. The reference is solely to *temporal* wants and supplies. Those, as BENGEL, who quote Romans 15:27 for interpreting this of spiritual supplies from the Jews to the Gentiles, forget that Romans 15:27 refers to the *past* benefit spiritually, which the Jews have conferred on the Gentiles, as a motive to *gratitude* on the part of the latter, not to a *prospective* benefit to be looked for from the former, which the text refers to. **15. Exodus 16:18; LXX.** As God gave an equal portion of manna to all the Israelites, whether they could gather much or little; so Christians should promote by liberality an equality, so that none should need the necessaries of life while others have superfluities. "Our luxuries should yield to our neighbor's comforts; and our comforts to his necessities" [J. HOWARD]. **16, 17.** Returning to the subject of vs. 6. **for you**—Translate, "Which put the same earnest care for you into the heart of Titus," as was in myself. My care for you led me to *"desire"* him (vss. 6 and 17, "exhortation," the same *Greek*); but Titus had of himself the same care, whence he "accepted (gladly) my exhortation" (vs. 17) to go to you (vs. 6). **being more forward**—more earnest than to need such exhortation. **he went**—*Greek,* "went forth." *We* should say, *he is going* forth; but the ancients put the *past* tense in letterwriting, as the things will have been past by the time that the correspondent, receives the letter. "Of his own accord," i.e., it is true he has been exhorted by me to go, but he shows that he has anticipated my desires, and already, "of his own accord," has desired to go. **18. the brother, whose praise is in the gospel**—whose praise is known in connection with the Gospel: *Luke* may be meant; not that "the Gospel" here refers to his *written*

Gospel; but the language implies some one well known throughout the churches, and at that time with Paul, as Luke then was (Acts 20:6). Not a Macedonian, as appears from ch. 9:4. Of all Paul's "companions in travel" (vs. 19; Acts 19:29), Luke was the most prominent, having been his companion in preaching the Gospel at his first entrance into Europe (Acts 16:10). The fact that the person here referred to was "chosen of the churches" as their trustee to travel with Paul in conveying the contribution to Jerusalem, implies that he had resided among them some time before: this is true of Luke, who after parting from Paul at Philippi (as he marks by the change from "we" to "they," Acts 16) six years before, is now again found in his company in Macedonia. In the interim he had probably become so well known that "his praise was throughout all the churches." Cf. ch. 12:18; Philemon 24. He who is faithful in the Gospel will be faithful also in matters of inferior importance [BENGEL]. **19. not** *that* **only**—not only praised in all the churches. **chosen**—by vote: so the *Greek*. **of the churches**—therefore these companions of Paul are called "messengers of the churches" (vs. 23). **to travel**—to Jerusalem. **with this grace**—*Greek*, "in the case of this grace," or "*gift.*" **to the glory of the same Lord**—The oldest MSS. omit "same." **declaration of your ready mind**—The oldest MSS. read, "our," not *your*. This and the previous clause, "to the glory of the same Lord," do not follow "administered by us," but "chosen of the churches to travel...." The union of the brother with Paul in this affair of the collection was done to guard against suspicions injurious "to the glory" of the Lord. It was also done in order to produce a "readiness" on the part of Paul and the brother to undertake the office which each, by himself, would have been less ready to undertake, for fear of suspicions arising (vs. 20) as to their appropriation of any of the money. **20. Avoiding**—taking precautions against this. **in this abundance**—*in the case of this abundance.* **21.** LXX (Prov. 3:4; Rom. 12:17). The oldest MSS. read, "For we provide." **honest things**—"*things* honorable" **22.** This *second* brother, BIRKS supposes to be Trophimus: for a Macedonian is not meant (ch. 9:4) probably the same as was sent before with Titus (ch. 12:18); and therefore sent from Ephesus, and probably an Ephesian: all this is true of Trophimus. **oftentimes ... in many things**—Join and translate as in the *Greek*, "many times in many things." **upon the great confidence which I have in you**—"through the great confidence WHICH HE HAS towards you" [ALFORD]. BENGEL better supports *English Version*, "We have sent ... through the confidence WHICH WE FEEL in regard to your liberality." **23. fellow helper concerning you**—*Greek*, "fellow worker towards you." **our brethren**—the two mentioned in vss. 18 and 22. **messengers**—rather, as the *Greek*, "apostles": in the less strict sense (Acts 14:14). **of the churches**—sent by the churches, as we are by the Lord (Phil. 2:25). There was in the synagogue an ecclesiastical officer, called "the angel of the Church," whence the title seems derived (cf. Rev. 2:1). **24.** The oldest MSS. read "[continue] *manifesting* to them in the face of the churches the manifestation of your love, and of our boasting on your behalf."

CHAPTER 9

VSS. 1-15. REASONS FOR HIS SENDING TITUS. THE GREATER THEIR BOUNTIFULNESS, THE MORE SHALL BE THE RETURN OF BLESSING TO THEM, AND THANKSGIVING TO GOD. **1. For**—connected with ch. 8:16: "Show love to the messengers of the churches; for as concerns the ministration for the saints, it is superfluous for me to write to you who are so forward already." **write**—emphatical: It is superfluous to *write,* for you will have witnesses present [BENGEL]. **2. ready a year ago**—to send off the money, owing to the apostle's former exhortation (I Cor. 16:1, 2). **your zeal**—*Greek,* "the zeal from you," i.e., on your part; propagated from you to others. **provoked**—i.e., stimulated. **very many**—*Greek,* "the greater number," viz., of the Macedonians. **3. have I sent**—we should say, "I send"; whereas **the** ancients put it in the past, the time which it would be by the time that the letter arrived. **the brethren** —(ch. 8:18, 22)—Titus and the two others. **should be in vain in this behalf**—"should be proved futile *in this particular,*" however true in general (ch. 7:4). A tacit compliment, softening the sharp monition. **as I said**—as I was saying (vs. 2). **4. if they of Macedonia**—rather as *Greek,* "if Macedonians." **unprepared**—with your collection; see vs. 2, "ready," *Greek,* "prepared." **we, not to say ye**—*Ye* would naturally feel more ashamed for yourselves, than we (who boasted of you) would for you. **confident boasting**—The oldest MSS. read simply "confidence," viz., in your liberality. **5. that they would go before**—Translate, "that they *should ....*" **whereof ye had notice before**—rather, "promised before"; "long announced by me to the Macedonians" (vs. 2) [BENGEL]. "Your promised bounty" [ELLICOTT and others]. **not as** *of* **covetousness**—Translate, "not as matter of covetousness," which it would be, if you gave niggardly. **6.** *I say*—ELLICOTT and others supply the ellipsis thus: "But *remember* this." **bountifully**—lit., "*with,*" or "*in blessings.*" The word itself implies a *beneficent spirit in the giver* (cf. vs. 7, end), and the *plural* implies the *abundance* and liberality of the gifts. "The reaping shall correspond to the proportions and spirit of the sowing" [BENGEL]. Cf. Ezekiel 34:26, "Showers of blessing." **7. according as he purposeth in his heart**—Let the full consent of the free will go with the gift [ALFORD]. Opposed to "of necessity," as "grudgingly" is opposed to "a *cheerful* giver" (Prov. 22:9; 11:25; Isa. 32:8). **8. all grace**—even in external goods, and even while ye bestow on others [BENGEL]. **that**—"in order that." God's gifts are bestowed on us, not that we may have them to ourselves, but that we may the more "abound in good works" to others. **sufficiency**—so as not to need the help of others, having yourselves from God "bread for your food" (vs. 10). **in all things**—*Greek,* "in everything." **every good work** —of charity to others, which will be "your seed sown" (vs. 10). **9. As it is written**—realizing the highly blessed character portrayed in Psalm 112:9. **He**—the "good man" (Ps. 112:5). **dispersed**—as seed sown with full and open hand, without anxious thought in what direction each grain may fall. It is implied also that he *has* always what he may disperse [BENGEL]. So in Psalm 112:9. **the poor** —The *Greek* word is found here only in New Testament, "one in straitened circumstances, who earns his bread by labor." The word usually employed means "one so poor as to live by begging." **his righteousness**—Here "beneficence": the evidence of his being *righteous* before God and man. Cf. Deuteronomy 24:13; Matthew 6:1, "alms"; *Greek,* "righteousness." **remaineth**—unexhausted and unfailing. **10.** Translate, as in Isaiah 55:10, "He that ministereth (supplieth) seed to the sower and bread for food" (lit., "bread for *eating*"). **minister—**rather future, as the oldest MSS., "*Shall* minister (supply) and multiply." **your seed—**your means for liberality. **the fruits of your righteousness—**the heavenly rewards for your Christian charity (Matt. 10:42). Righteousness shall be itself the reward, even as it is the thing rewarded (Hos. 10:12; Matt. 5:6; 6:33). **11.** Cf. vs. 8. **bountifulness—***Greek,* "single-minded liberality." Translated "simplicity," Romans 12:8. **causeth through us—**lit., "worketh through us"; i.e., through our instrumentality as the distributors. **thanksgiving—**on the part of the recipients. **12.** *Greek,* "The *ministration* of this *public* service (on your part) is not only *still further* supplying the wants of the saints (besides the supplies from other quarters), but is abounding also (viz., in respect to relieving the necessities of others in poverty through many thanksgivings to God." **13. by—**through occasion of. **experiment—**Translate, "the experience" [ELLICOTT and others]. Or, "the experimental proof" of your Christian character, afforded by "this ministration." **they—**the recipients. **for your professed subjection—***Greek,* "for the subjection of your profession"; i.e., your subjection in accordance with your profession, in relation to the Gospel. Ye yield yourselves in willing subjection to the Gospel precepts, evinced in acts, as well as in profession. *your* **liberal distribution—***Greek,* "the liberality of your contribution in relation to them . . . ." **14.** Translate, "Themselves also with prayer for you, longing after you on account of the exceeding grace of God (resting) upon you." *English Version* is, however, good sense: They glorify God (vs. 13) by the experimental proof, etc., "and by their prayer for you." But the *Greek* favors the former. **15. his unspeakable gift—**the gift of His own Son, which includes all other inferior gifts (ch. 8:9; Rom. 8:32). If we have received from God "His unspeakable gift," what great thing is it, if we give a few perishing gifts for His sake?

CHAPTER 10

Vss. 1-18. HE VINDICATES HIS APOSTOLIC AUTHORITY AGAINST THOSE WHO DEPRECIATED HIM FOR HIS PERSONAL APPEARANCE. HE WILL MAKE HIS POWER FELT WHEN HE COMES. HE BOASTS NOT, AS THEY, BEYOND HIS MEASURE. **1. I Paul myself—**no longer "we," "us," "our" (ch. 9:11): *I* who am represented by depreciators as "base," I, the same Paul, *of my own accord* "beseech you"; or rather "entreat," "exhort" you *for your sake.* As "I beseech you" (a distinct *Greek* verb, vs. 2) *for my sake.* **by the meekness and gentleness of Christ—**He mentions these graces of Christ especially (Ps. 18:35; Matt. 11:29), as on account of his imitation of them in particular he was despised [GROTIUS]. He entreats them by these, in order to show that though he must have recourse to more severe measures, he is naturally inclined to gentle ones after Christ's example [MENOCHIUS]. "Meekness" is more in the mind internally; "gentleness" in the external behavior, and in relation to others; for instance, the condescending *yieldingness* of a superior to an inferior, the former not insisting on his strict rights [TRENCH]. BENGEL explains it, "By the meekness and gentleness *derived by me from Christ,*" not from my own nature: he objects to understanding it of *Christ's* meekness and gentleness, since nowhere else is "gentleness" attributed to Him. But though the exact *Greek* word is not ap-

plied to Him, the idea expressed by it is (cf. Isa. 40:11; Matt. 12:19, 20). **in presence—**in personal appearance when present with you. **base—***Greek,* "lowly"; timid, humbly diffident: opposed to "bold." "Am" stands here by ironical concession for "am reputed to be" (cf. vs. 10). **2. I beseech you—**Intimating that, as he can *beseech* in letters, so he can be severe in their presence. **that I may not be—**that I may not *have to* be bold . . . . **with that confidence—***that authoritative sternness.* **I think—**I *am minded* to be. **as if we walked according to the flesh—**His Corinthian detractors judged of him by themselves, as if he were influenced by fleshly motives, the desire of favor or fear of giving offense, so as not to exercise his authority when present. **3. For—**Reason why they should regard him "beseeching" them (vs. 2) not to oblige him to have recourse to "bold" and stern exercise of authority. "We walk IN the flesh," and so *in weakness:* but not "ACCORDING TO the flesh" (vs. 2). Moreover, though we WALK in it, we do not WAR according to it. A double contrast or antithesis. "They who accuse us of walking after the flesh, shall find [to their cost] that we do not *war* after the flesh; therefore compel us not to use our weapons" [ALFORD]. **4.** A confutation of those who try to propagate their creed by force and persecution (cf. Luke 9:54-56). **weapons—**for punishing offending members (vs. 6; I Cor. 4:21; 5:5, 13); boldness of speech, ecclesiastical discipline (vs. 8; ch. 13:10), the power of the word, and of the sacraments, the various extraordinary gifts of the Spirit. **carnal—**Translate, "fleshly," to preserve the allusion to vss. 2, 3. **mighty through God—***Greek,* "mighty to God," i.e., mighty before God: not humanly, but divinely powerful. The power is not ours, but God's. Cf. "fair to God," i.e., divinely fair (*Margin,* Acts 7:20). Also above (ch. 2:15), "*unto God* a sweet savor." "The efficacy of the Christian religion proves its truth" [BENGEL]. **pulling down—**As the *Greek* is the same as in vs. 5, translate, "casting down." Cf. Jeremiah 1:10: the inspired servants of God inherit the commission of the Old Testament prophets. **strongholds—**(Prov. 21:22)—viz., in which sinners entrench themselves against reproof; all that opposes itself to Christ; the learning, and eloquence, and philosophical subtleties on which the Corinthians prided themselves. So Joshua's trumpet blast was "mighty" under God to overthrow the walls of Jericho. **5. imaginations** —rather, "reasonings." Whereas "thought" expresses men's own *purpose* and determination of living after their own pleasure [TITTM]. **high thing** —So it ought to be translated (Rom. 8:39). A distinct *Greek* word from that in Ephesians 3:18, "height," and Revelation 21:16, which belongs to God and heaven from whence we receive nothing hurtful. But "high thing" is not so much "height" as *something made high,* and belongs to those regions of air where the powers of darkness "exalt themselves" against Christ and us (Eph. 2:2; 6:12; II Thess. 2:4). **exalteth itself—**II Thessalonians 2:4 supports *English Version* rather than the translation of ELLICOTT, etc., "is lifted up." Such were the *high towers* of Judaic self-righteousness, philosophic speculations, and rhetorical sophistries, the "knowledge" so much prized by many (opposed to "the knowledge of God"), which endangered a section of the Corinthian Church. **against the knowledge of God—**True knowledge makes men humble. Where there is exaltation of self, there knowledge of God is wanting [BENGEL]. Arrange the words following thus: "Bringing every thought (i.e., *intent of the mind or will*) into captivity to the obedience of Christ," i.e., to obey Christ. The three steps of the apostle's spiritual warfare are: (1) It demolishes what is opposed to Christ; (2) It leads captive; (3) It brings into obedience to Christ (Rom. 1:5; 16:26). The "reasonings" (*English Version*, "imaginations") are utterly "cast down." The "mental intents" (*English Version*, "thoughts") are taken willing captives, and tender the voluntary obedience of faith to Christ the Conqueror. **6.** Translate, "Having ourselves (i.e., *being*) in readiness to exact punishment for all disobedience . . . ." We have this in store for the disobedient: it will be brought into action in due time. **when your obedience . . .** —He charitably assumes that most of the Corinthian Church will act obediently; therefore he says "YOUR obedience." But perhaps some will act otherwise; in order, therefore, to give all an opportunity of joining the obedient, he will not prematurely exact punishment, but wait until the full number of those gathered out to Christ has been "completed," and the remainder have been proved incorrigible. He had acted already so at Corinth (Acts 18:6-11; cf. Exod. 32:34: Matt. 13:28-30). **7.** Do ye regard mere outward appearance (mere external recommendations, personal appearance, voice, manner, oratory of teachers *present face to face,* such as they admired in the false teachers to the disparagement of Paul, vs. 10; *Note,* ch. 5:12)? Even in *outward bearing* when I shall be *present* with you (in contrast to "by *letters,*" vs. 9) I will show that I am more really armed with the authority of Christ, than those who arrogate to themselves the title of being peculiarly "Christ's" (I Cor. 1:12). A Jewish emissary seems to have led this party. **let him of himself think this again** —He may "of himself," without needing to be taught it in a more severe manner, by "thinking again," arrive at "this" conclusion, "that even as . . . ." Paul modestly demands for himself only an equal place with those whom he had begotten in the Gospel [BENGEL]. **8.** "For even if I were to boast somewhat more exceedingly (than I do, vss. 3-6) of our (apostolic) authority (vs. 6; ch. 13:10) . . . I should not be put to shame (by the fact; as I should be if my authority proved to be without foundation: my threats of punishment not being carried into effect). **for edification . . . not for . . . destruction**— *Greek,* "for building up . . . not for . . . CASTING DOWN" (the same *Greek* as in vs. 5): the image of a building as in vss. 4, 5. Though we "cast down reasonings," this is not in order to destroy, but really to *build up* ("edify"), by removing those things which are hindrances to edification, and testing what is unsound, and putting together all that is true in the building [CHRYSOSTOM]. **9.** I say this lest I should seem to be terrifying you, as children, with empty threats [BENGEL]. ESTIUS explains, "I might boast more of my authority, *but I forbear to do so,* that I may not seem as if . . . ." But this ellipsis is harsh: and vss. 10, 11 confirm BENGEL'S view. **10. letters**—implying that there had been already more letters of Paul received by the Corinthians than the one we have, viz., I Corinthians; and that they contained strong reproofs. **say they** —*Greek,* "says one," "such a one" (vs. 11) seems to point to some definite individual. Cf. Galatians 5: 10; a similar slanderer was in the Galatian Church. **weak**—(ch. 12:7; I Cor. 2:3). There was nothing of majesty or authority in his manner; he bore himself tremblingly among them, whereas the false teachers spoke with authoritative bearing and language. **11. think this**—"consider this." **such *will we be***—or "are," in general, not merely shall we be at our next visit. **12.** "We do not presume (irony) to judge ourselves among, or in comparison with, some of them that commend themselves." The charge falsely brought against him of *commending himself* (ch. 3:1; 5:12), really holds good of the false teachers. The phrase, "judge ourselves of the number," is drawn from the testing of athletes and senators, the "approved" being set down on the roll [WAHL]. **measuring themselves by themselves**— "*among* themselves": to correspond to the previous verb, "judge ourselves *among* them." Instead of measuring themselves by the public standard, they measure themselves by one made by themselves: they do not compare themselves with others who excel them, but with those like themselves: hence their high self-esteem. The one-eyed is easily king among the blind. **are not wise**—with all their boasted "wisdom" (I Cor. 1:19-26), they are anything but "wise." **13. not boast . . . without . . . measure**—*Greek,* "to unmeasured bounds." There is no limit to a man's high opinion of himself, so long as he measures himself by himself (vs. 13) and his fellows, and does not compare himself with his superiors. It marks the *personal* character of this Epistle that the word "boast" occurs twenty-nine times in it, and only twenty-six times in all the other Epistles put together. Undeterred by the charge of vanity, he felt he must vindicate his apostolic authority by facts [CONYBEARE and HOWSON]. It would be to "boast of things without our measure," were we to boast of conversions made by "other men's labors" (vs. 15). **distributed**—apportioned [ALFORD]. **a measure**—as a measure [ALFORD]. **to reach**—"that we should reach as far as even to you": not that he meant to go no further (vs. 16; Rom. 15:20-24). Paul's "measure" is the *apportionment* of his sphere of Gospel labors *ruled* for him by God. A "rule" among the so-called "apostolic canons" subsequently was, that no bishop should appoint ministers beyond his own limits. At Corinth no minister ought to have been received without Paul's sanction, as Corinth was *apportioned* to him by God as *his apostolic sphere.* The Epistle here incidentally, and therefore undesignedly, confirms the independent history, the Acts, which represents Corinth as the extreme limit as yet of his preaching, *at which he had stopped,* after he had from Philippi passed southward successively through Amphipolis, Apollonia, Thessalonica, Berea, and Athens [PALEY'S *Horæ Paulinæ*]. **14.** "We are not stretching ourselves beyond our measure, *as* (we should be) *if* we did not reach unto you: (but we do), for as far as even to you have we come in preaching the Gospel." **15.** "Not boasting to unmeasured bounds (i.e., not exceeding our own bounds by boasting) of (lit., "in") other men's labors." **when**—"AS your faith goes on increasing." The cause of his not yet reaching with the Gospel the regions beyond Corinth, was the weakness as yet of their faith. He desired not to leave the Corinthians before the proper time, and yet not to put off preaching to others too long. **enlarged by you**—*Greek,* "in your case." Our success in your case will give us an important step towards further progress beyond you (vs. 16). **according to our rule**—according to our divinely assigned apportionment of the area or sphere of our work; for "we stretch not ourselves beyond our measure" (vs. 14). **abundantly**—*Greek,* "unto exceeding abundance": so as to exceed the limits we have yet reached (vs. 16). **16. To**—i.e., *so as to* preach . . . beyond you (and) not to boast . . . . **in another man's line of things made ready to our hand**—Do not connect "line of things . . ."; but "boast of things . . ." To make this clearer, arrange the words thus, "Not to boast as to things (already made by the preaching of others) ready to our hand in another man's line (i.e., within the line, or sphere of labor, apportioned by God to another)." **17. glorieth**—Translate, to accord with vs. 16, "boasteth." In contrast to his opponents' practice of boasting in another's line or sphere, Paul declares the only true boasting is in the Lord (I Cor. 1:31; 15:10). **18.** (Prov. 27:2.) **whom the Lord commendeth**—to whom the Lord has given as His "Epistle of commendation," the believers whom he has been the instrument of converting: as was Paul's case (ch. 3:1-3). **is approved**—can stand the test of the final trial. A metaphor from testing metals (Rom. 16:10; I Cor. 11:19). So on the other hand those finally rejected by the Lord are termed "*reprobate* silver" (Jer. 6:30).

CHAPTER 11

Vss. 1-33. Through Jealousy over the Corinthians, Who Made More Account of the False Apostles than of Him, He Is Obliged to Commend Himself as in Many Respects Superior. **1. Would to God**—Translate as *Greek*, "I would that." **bear with me**—I may ask not unreasonably to be borne with; not so the false apostles (vss. 4, 20). **my**—not in the oldest MSS. **folly**—The *Greek* is a milder term than that for "foolishness" in I Corinthians 3:19; Matthew 5:22; 25:2. The *Greek* for "folly" here implies *imprudence;* the *Greek* for "foolishness" includes the idea of *perversity* and *wickedness.* **and indeed bear**—A request (so vs. 16). But the *Greek* and the sense favor the translation, "But indeed (I need not wish it, for) ye *do* bear with me"; still I wish you to bear with me further, while I enter at large into self-commendations. **2. For I am jealous**—The justification of his self-commendations lies in his zealous care lest they should fall from Christ, to whom he, as "the friend of the Bridegroom" (John 3:29), has espoused them; in order to lead them back from the false apostles to Christ, he is obliged to boast as an apostle of Christ, in a way which, but for the motive, would be "folly." **godly jealousy**—lit., "jealousy of God" (cf. ch. 1:12, "godly sincerity," lit., "sincerity of God"). "If I am immoderate, I am immoderate to God" [Bengel]. A jealousy which has God's honor at heart (I Kings 19:10). **I . . . espoused you**—Paul uses a *Greek* term applied properly to *the bridegroom,* just as he ascribes to himself "jealousy," a feeling properly belonging to the husband; so entirely does he identify himself with Christ. **present** *you as* **a chaste virgin to Christ**—at His coming, when the heavenly *marriage* shall take place (Matt. 25:6; Rev. 19:7, 9). What Paul here says he desires to do, viz., "present" the Church as "a chaste virgin" to Christ, *Christ Himself* is said to do in the fuller sense. Whatever ministers do effectively, is really done by Christ (Eph. 5:27-32). The *espousals* are going on now. He does not say "chaste virgins"; for not individual members, but the whole body of believers conjointly constitute the Bride. **3. I fear**—(ch. 12:20)—not inconsistent with love. His source of fear was their yielding character. **subtilty**—the utter foe of the "simplicity" which is intent on ONE object, Jesus, and seeks none "other," and no "other" and different Spirit (vs. 4); but loves him with tender SINGLENESS OF AFFECTION. Where Eve first gave way, was in mentally harboring for a moment the possibility insinuated by the serpent, of God not having her truest interests at heart, and of this "other" professing friend being more concerned for her than God. **corrupted**—so as to lose their virgin purity through seducers (vs. 4). The same *Greek* stands for "minds" as for "thoughts" (ch. 10:5, where see *Note*); *intents of the will,* or *mind.* The oldest MSS., after "simplicity," add, "and the purity" or "chastity." **in Christ**—rather, "that is *towards* Christ." **4. if . . .**—which in *fact* is impossible. However, if it were possible, ye might then bear with them (see *Note,* vs. 1). But there can be no *new Gospel;* there is but the *one* which I first preached; therefore it ought not to be "borne" by you, that the false teachers should attempt to supersede me. **he that cometh**—the high-sounding title assumed by the false teachers, who arrogated Christ's own peculiar title (**Greek,** Matt. 11:3, and Heb. 10:37), "He that is coming." Perhaps he was leader of the party which assumed peculiarly to be "Christ's" (ch. 10:7; I Cor. 1:12); hence his assumption of the title. **preacheth . . . receive**—is preaching . . . ye are receiving. **Jesus**—the "Jesus" of Gospel *history.* He therefore does not say "Christ," which refers to the *office.* **another . . . another**—*Greek,* "another Jesus . . . a *different* Spirit . . . a *different* Gospel." *Another* implies a distinct individual of the same kind; *different* implies one quite distinct in kind. **which ye have not received**—from us. **spirit . . . received . . . gospel . . . accepted**—The will of man is passive in RECEIVING the "Spirit"; but it is actively concurrent with the will of God (which goes before to give the good will) in ACCEPTING the "Gospel." **ye might well bear with him**—There would be an excuse for your conduct, though a bad one (for ye ought to give heed to no Gospel other than what ye have already heard from me, Gal. 1:6, 7); but the false teachers do not even pretend they have "another Jesus" and a "different Gospel" to bring before you; they merely try to supplant me, your accredited Teacher. Yet ye not only "bear with" them, but prefer them. **5. For**—My claim is superior to that of the false teachers, "For . . . ." **I suppose**—I reckon [Alford]. **I was not**—*Greek,* "That I have not been, and am not." **the very chiefest apostles**—James, Peter, and John, the witnesses of Christ's transfiguration and agony in Gethsemane. Rather, "those overmuch apostles," those *surpassers of the apostles* in their own esteem. This sense is proved by the fact that the context contains no comparison between him and the apostles, but only between him and the false teachers; vs. 6 also alludes to these, and not to the apostles; cf. also the parallel phrase, "false apostles" (*Note,* vs. 13, and ch. 12:11) [Alford]. **6. rude**—*Greek,* "a common man"; a "laic"; not rhetorically trained; unskilled in finish of diction. I Corinthians 2:1-4, 13; ch. 10:10, 11, shows his *words* were not without *weight,* though his "speech" was deficient in oratorical artifice. "Yet I am not so in my knowledge" (ch. 12:1-5; Eph. 3:1-5). **have been . . . made manifest**—Read with the oldest MSS., "We have made things (Gospel truths) manifest," thus showing our "knowledge." *English Version* would mean, I leave it to yourselves to decide whether I be rude in speech . . .: for we have been thoroughly (lit., "in everything") made manifest among you (lit., "in respect to you"; "in relation to you"). He had not by reserve kept back his "knowledge" in divine mysteries from them (ch. 2: 17; 4:2; Acts 20:20, 27). **in all things**—The *Greek* rather favors the translation, "among all men"; the sense then is, we have manifested the whole truth among all men with a view to your benefit [AL-FORD]. But the *Greek* in Philippians 4:12, "In each thing and in all things," sanctions *English Version*, which gives a clearer sense. **7. Have I**—lit., "OR have I?" Connected with last verse, "Or will any of you make it an objection that I have preached to you gratuitously?" He leaves their good feeling to give the answer, that this, so far from being an objection, was a decided superiority in him above the false apostles (I Cor. 9:6-15). **abasing myself**—in my mode of living, waiving my right of maintenance, and earning it by manual labor; perhaps with slaves as his fellow laborers (Acts 18:3; Phil. 4:12). **ye ... exalted**—spiritually, by your admission to Gospel privileges. **because**—"in that." **gospel of God**—"of God" implies its divine glory to which they were admitted. **freely**—"without charge." **8. I robbed**—i.e., took from them in order to spare you more than what was their fair share of contribution to my maintenance, e.g., the Philippian Church (Phil. 4:15, 16). **wages**—"subsidy." **to do you service**—*Greek,* "with a view to ministration to you"; cf. "supplied" (*Greek, "in addition"*), vs. 9, implying, he *brought with him* from the Macedonians, supplies towards his maintenance at Corinth; and (vs. 9) *when those resources failed* ("when I wanted") he received a *new supply,* while there, from the same source. **9. wanted**—"was in want." **chargeable**—*Greek,* "burdensome," lit., "to torpify," and so to *oppress.* JEROME says it is a Cilician word (ch. 12:14, 16). **the brethren which came**—rather, as *Greek,* "the brethren *when they came.*" Perhaps Timotheus and Silas (Acts 8: 1, 5). Cf. Philippians 4:15, 16, which refers to donations received from the Philippians (who were in Macedonia) at two distinct periods ("once and again"), one at Thessalonica, the other after his departure from Macedonia, that is, when he came into Achaia to Corinth (from the church in which city he would receive no help); and this "in the beginning of the Gospel," i.e., at its first preaching in these parts. Thus all three, the two Epistles and history, mutually, and no doubt undesignedly, coincide; a sure test of genuineness. **supplied**—*Greek,* "supplied in addition," viz., in addition to their former contributions; or as BENGEL, in addition to the supply obtained by my own manual labor. **10.** *Greek,* "There is (the) truth of Christ in me that . . ." (Rom. 9:1). **no man shall stop me of**—The oldest MSS. read, "This boasting shall not *be shut* (i.e., stopped) *as regards me.*" "Boasting is as it were personified . . . shall not have its mouth stopped as regards me" [ALFORD]. **11.** Love is often offended at its favors being not accepted, as though the party to whom they are offered wished to be under no obligation to the offerer. **12. I will do**—I will *continue* to decline help. **occasion**—*Greek, "the* occasion," viz., of misrepresenting my motives, which would be afforded to my detractors, if I accepted help. **that wherein they glory, they may be found even as we**—BENGEL joins this clause with "the occasion," viz., *of glorying* or *boasting;* the occasion "that they may be found (a point wherein they glory) even as we," i.e., quite as disinterested, or virtually, quite as gain-seeking and self-seeking. It cannot mean that the false teachers taught gratuitously even as Paul (cf. vs. 20; I Cor. 9:12). AL-FORD less clearly explains by reference to vs. 18, etc., where the "glorying" here is taken up and described as "glorying after the flesh"; thus it means, that in the matters of which they boast they may be found even as we, i.e., we may be cn a fair and equal footing; that there may be no *adventitious*

comparisons made between us, arising out of *misrepresentations* of my course of procedure, but that in every matter of boasting we may be fairly compared and judged by *facts;* FOR (vs. 13) realities they have none, no weapons but misrepresentation, being *false apostles.* **13. For**—reason why he is unwilling they should be thought like him [BENGEL]. **such**—they and those like them. **false apostles**—those "overmuch apostles" (*Note*, vs. 5) are no apostles at all. **deceitful workers**—pretending to be "workmen" for the Lord, and really seeking their own gain. **14. is transformed**—rather, "transforms himself" (cf. Job 1:6); habitually; the first occasion of his doing so was in tempting Eve. "Himself" is emphatical: If their master *himself,* who is the "prince of darkness," the most alien to light, does so, it is less marvellous in the case of them who are his servants (Luke 22:54; Eph. 6:12). **15. no great thing**—no difficult matter. **if his ministers also**—as well as himself. **righteousness**—answering to "light" (vs. 14); the manifestation wherewith God reveals Himself in Christ (Matt. 6:33; Rom. 1:17). **end**—The test of things is *the* end which strips off every specious *form* into which Satan's agents may now "transform" themselves (ch. Phil. 3:19, 21). **according to their works**—not according to their pretensions. **16. I say again**—again taking up from vs. 1 the anticipatory apology for his boasting. **if otherwise**—but if ye will not grant this; if ye will think me a fool. **yet as a fool**—"yet even as a fool receive me"; grant me the indulgent hearing conceded even to one suspected of folly. The *Greek* denotes one who does not rightly use his mental powers; not having the idea of blame necessarily attached to it; one deceived by foolish vanities, yet boasting himself [TITTM.], (vss. 17, 19). **that I**—The oldest MSS. read, "that I, *too,*" viz., *as well as they,* may boast myself. **17. not after the Lord**—By *inspired guidance* he excepts this "glorying" or "boasting" from the inspired authoritativeness which belongs to all else that he wrote; even this boasting, though undesirable in itself, was permitted by the Spirit, taking into account its aim, viz., to draw off the Corinthians from their false teachers to the apostle. Therefore this passage gives no proof that any portion of Scripture is uninspired. It merely guards against his boasting being made a justification of boasting in general, which is not ordinarily "after the Lord," i.e., consistent with Christian humility. **foolishly**—*Greek,* "in foolishness." **confidence of boasting**—(ch. 9:4). **18. many**—including the "false teachers." **after the flesh**—as fleshly men are wont to boast, viz., of external advantages, as their birth, doings, etc. (cf. vs. 22). **I will glory also**—i.e., I also will boast of such fleshly advantages, to show you that even in these I am not their inferiors, and therefore ought not to be supplanted by them in your esteem; though these are not what I desire to glory in (ch. 10:17). **19. gladly**—willingly. Irony. A plea why they should "bear with" (vs. 1) him in his folly, i.e., boasting; ye are, in sooth, so "wise" (I Cor. 4:8, 10; Paul's real view of their wisdom was very different, I Cor. 3:1-4) yourselves that ye can "bear with" the folly of others more complacently. Not only *can* ye do so, but ye *are actually* doing this and more. **20. For**—Ye may well "bear with" fools; *for* ye even "bear with" oppressors. Translate, "Ye bear with them." **a man**—as the false apostles do. **bring you into bondage**—to himself. Translate "brings," not "bring"; for the case is not merely a supposed case, but a case actually then occurring. Also "devours" (viz., by exactions, Matt. 23:24; Ps. 53:

4), "takes," "exalts," "smites." **take** *of you*—So the Greek for "take" is used for "take away from" (Rev. 6:4). ALFORD translates, as in ch. 12:16, "*catches* you." **exalt himself**—under the pretext of apostolic dignity. **smite you on the face**—under the pretext of divine zeal. The height of insolence on their part, and of servile endurance on yours (I Kings 22:24; Neh. 13:25; Luke 22:64; Acts 23:2; I Tim. 3:3). **21. as concerning reproach**—rather, "by way of dishonor (i.e., *self-disparagement*) I say it." **as though we ... weak**—in not similarly (vs. 20) showing our *power* over you. "An ironical reminiscence of his own abstinence when among them from all these acts of self-exaltation at their expense" (as if such abstinence was weakness) [ALFORD]. The "we" is emphatically contrasted with the false teachers who so oppressively displayed their power. I speak so as though WE had been weak when with you, because we did not show our power this way. Howbeit (we are not really weak; for), whereinsoever any is bold ... , I am bold also. **22. Hebrews ... Israelites ... the seed of Abraham**—A climax. "Hebrews," referring to the *language* and *nationality;* "Israelites," to the *theocracy* and *descent from Israel,* the "prince who prevailed with God" (Rom. 9:4); "the seed of Abraham," to the *claim to a share in the Messiah* (Rom. 11:1; 9:7). Cf. Philippians 3:5, "An Hebrew of the Hebrews," not an Hellenist or Greekspeaking Jew, but a Hebrew in tongue, and sprung from Hebrews. **23. I speak as a fool**—rather, as *Greek,* "I speak as if *beside myself";* stronger than "as a fool." **I am more**—viz., in respect to the credentials and manifestations of my ministry, more faithful and self-denying; and richer in tokens of God's recognition of my ministry. Old authorities read the order thus, "In prisons above measures, in stripes more abundantly" (*English Version,* less accurately, "more frequent"). Acts 16:23-40 records one case of his imprisonment with stripes. CLEMENT (I *Epistle to Corinthians*) describes him as having suffered bonds seven times. **in death oft**—(ch. 4:10; Acts 9:23; 13:50; 14:5, 6, 19; 17:5, 13). **24.** Deuteronomy 25:3 ordained that not more than forty stripes should be inflicted. To avoid exceeding this number, they gave one short of it: thirteen strokes with a treble lash [BENGEL]. This is one of those minute agreements with Jewish usage, which a forger would have not been likely to observe. **25.** The beating by Roman magistrates at Philippi (Acts 16:23) is the only one recorded in Acts, which does not profess to give a complete journal of his life, but only a sketch of it in connection with the design of the book, viz., to give an outline of the history of the Gospel Church from its foundation at Jerusalem, to the period of its reaching Rome, the capital of the Gentile world. **once was I stoned**—(Acts 14:19). **thrice ... shipwreck**—before the shipwreck at Melita (Acts 27). Probably in some of his voyages from Tarsus, where he stayed for some time after his conversion, and from which, as being a seafaring place, he was likely to make missionary voyages to adjoining places (Acts 9:30; 11:25; Gal. 1:21). **a night and a day ... in the deep**—probably in part swimming or in an open boat. **26. In**—rather, "By": connected with vs. 23, but now not with "in," as there, and as in vs. 27, where again he passes to the idea of surrounding circumstances or environments [ALFORD, ELLICOTT and others]. **waters**—rather, as *Greek,* "rivers," viz., perils by the flooding of rivers, as on the road often traversed by Paul between Jerusalem and Antioch, crossed as it is by the torrents rushing down from Lebanon. So

the traveller Spon lost his life. **robbers**—perhaps in his journey from Perga to Antioch in Pisidia. Pisidia was notorious for robbers; as indeed were all the mountains that divided the high land of Asia from the sea. **the heathen**—Gentiles. **in the city**—Damascus, Acts 9:24, 25; Jerusalem, Acts 9:29; Ephesus, Acts 19:23. **false brethren**—(Gal. 2:4). **27. fastings**—*voluntary,* in order to kindle devotions (Acts 13:2, 3; 14:23; I Cor. 9:27); for they are distinguished from "hunger and thirst," which were *involuntary* [GROTIUS]. See, however, *Note,* ch. 6: 5. The context refers solely to *hardships,* not to self-imposed devotional mortification. "Hunger and thirst" are not synonymous with "foodlessness" (as the *Greek* of "fasting" means), but are its consequences. **cold ... nakedness**—"cold" resulting from "nakedness," or insufficient clothing, as the *Greek* often means: as "hunger and thirst" result from "foodlessness." (Cf. Acts 28:2; Rom. 8:35.) "When we remember that he who endured all this was a man constantly suffering from infirm health (II Cor. 4:7-12; 12:7-10; Gal. 4:13, 14), such heroic self-devotion seems almost superhuman [CONYBEARE and HOWSON]. **28. without**—"Beside" trials falling on me *externally,* just recounted, there is "that which cometh upon me (lit., *the impetuous concourse to me* of business; properly, *a crowd rising up against one again and again, and ready to bear him down*), the care of all the churches" (including those not yet seen in the flesh, Col. 2:1): an *internal* and more weighty anxiety. But the oldest MSS., for "that which cometh," read, "the *pressure*": "the *pressing care-taking*" or "inspection that is upon me daily." ALFORD translates, "Omitting what is BESIDES"; viz., those other trials *besides* those recounted. But the *Vulgate,* ESTIUS, and BENGEL, support *English Version.* **the care**—The *Greek* implies, "my *anxious solicitude* for all the churches." **29. I ... weak**—in condescending sympathy with the weak (I Cor. 9:22). "*Care* generates sympathy, which causes the minister of Christ personally to enter into the feelings of all his people, as if he stood in their position, so as to accommodate himself to all" [CALVIN]. **offended** —by some stumbling block put in his way by others: the "weak" is most liable to be "offended." **I burn not**—The "I" in the *Greek* is emphatic, which it is not in the former clause, "I am not weak." I not only enter into the feeling of the party offended, but *I* burn with indignation at the offender, *I myself* taking up his cause as my own. "Who meets with a stumbling block and I am not disturbed even more than himself" [NEANDER]. **30. glory of ... infirmities**—A striking contrast! *Glorying* or *boasting of* what others make matter of shame, viz., *infirmities;* for instance, his humbling mode of escape in a basket (vs. 33). A character utterly incompatible with that of an enthusiast (cf. ch. 12:5, 9, 10). **31.** This solemn asseveration refers to what follows. The persecution at Damascus was one of the first and greatest, and having no human witness of it to adduce to the Corinthians, as being a fact that happened long before and was known to few, he appeals to God for its truth. Luke (Acts 9:25) afterwards recorded it (cf. Gal. 1:20), [BENGEL]. It may ALSO refer to the revelation in ch. 12:1, standing in beautiful contrast to his humiliating escape from Damascus. **32. governor**—*Greek,* "Ethnarch": a Jewish officer to whom heathen rulers gave authority over Jews in large cities where they were numerous. He was in this case under Aretas, king of Arabia. Damascus was in a Roman province. But at this time, A.D. 38 or 39, three years after

Paul's conversion, A.D. 36, Aretas, against whom the Emperor Tiberius as the ally of Herod Agrippa had sent an army under Vitellius, had got possession of Damascus on the death of the emperor, and the consequent interruption of Vitellius' operations. His possession of it was put an end to immediately after by the Romans [NEANDER]. Rather, it was granted by Caligula (A.D. 38) to Aretas, whose predecessors had possessed it. This is proved by our having no Damascus coins of Caligula or Claudius, though we do have of their immediate imperial predecessors and successors [ALFORD].

CHAPTER 12

VSS. 1-21. REVELATIONS IN WHICH HE MIGHT GLORY: BUT HE RATHER GLORIES IN INFIRMITIES, AS CALLING FORTH CHRIST'S POWER: SIGNS OF HIS APOSTLESHIP: HIS DISINTERESTEDNESS: NOT THAT HE IS EXCUSING HIMSELF TO THEM; BUT HE DOES ALL FOR THEIR GOOD, LEST HE SHOULD FIND THEM NOT SUCH AS HE DESIRED, AND SO SHOULD HAVE TO BE SEVERE AT HIS COMING. **1.** He proceeds to illustrate the "glorying in infirmities" (ch. 11:30). He gave one instance which might expose him to ridicule (ch. 11:33); he now gives another, but this one connected with a glorious revelation of which it was the sequel: but he dwells not on the glory done to himself, but on the *infirmity* which followed it, as displaying Christ's power. The oldest MSS. read, "I MUST NEEDS boast (or glory) though it be not expedient; *for* I will come." The "for" gives a proof that it is "not expedient to boast": I will take the case of revelations, in which if anywhere boasting might be thought harmless. "Visions" refers to things *seen:* "revelations," to things heard (cf. I Sam. 9:15) or *revealed* in any way. In "visions" their signification was not always vouchsafed; in "revelations" there was always an unveiling of truths before hidden (Dan. 2:19, 31). All parts of Scripture alike are matter of *inspiration;* but not all of *revelation.* There are degrees of revelation; but not of inspiration. **of**—i.e., *from* the Lord; Christ, vs. 2. **2.** Translate, "I know," not "I knew." **a man**—meaning *himself.* But he purposely thus distinguishes between the *rapt and glorified* person of vss. 2, 4, and *himself* the infirmity-laden victim of the "thorn in the flesh" (vs. 7). Such glory belonged not to *him,* but the *weakness* did. Nay, he did not even know whether he was in or out of the body when the glory was put upon him, so far was the glory from being *his* [ALFORD]. His spiritual self was his highest and truest self: the flesh with its infirmity merely his temporary self (Rom. 7:25). Here, however, the latter is the prominent thought. **in Christ**—a Christian (Rom. 16:7). **above**—rather, simply "fourteen years ago." This Epistle was written A.D. 55-57. Fourteen years before will bring the vision to A.D. 41-43, the time of his second visit to Jerusalem (Acts 22:17). He had long been intimate with the Corinthians, yet had never mentioned this revelation before: it was not a matter lightly to be spoken of. **I cannot tell**—rather as *Greek,* "I know not." If *in the body,* he must have been caught up bodily; if *out of the body,* as seems to be Paul's *opinion,* his spirit must have been caught up out of the body. At all events he recognizes the possibility of conscious receptivity in disembodied spirits. **caught up**—(Acts 8:39). **to the third heaven**—"*even to....*" These *raptures* (note the *plural,* "visions," "revelations") had two degrees: first he was *caught up* "to

the third heaven," and from thence to "Paradise" (vs. 4) [CLEMENS ALEXANDRINUS, *Stromata* 5. 427], which seems to denote an inner recess of the third heaven [BENGEL] (Luke 23:43; Rev. 2:7). Paul was permitted not only to "hear" the things of Paradise, but to *see* also in some degree the things of the third heaven (cf. "visions," vs. 1). The occurrence TWICE of "whether in the body ..., I know not, God knoweth," and of "lest I should be exalted above measure," marks two stages in the revelation. "Ignorance of the *mode* does not set aside the certain knowledge of the *fact.* The apostles were ignorant of many things" [BENGEL]. The first heaven is that of the clouds, the *air;* the second, that of the stars, *the sky;* the third is spiritual (Eph. 4:10). **3.** Translate, "I *know.*" **out of** —Most of the oldest MSS. read "apart from." **4. unspeakable**—not in themselves, otherwise Paul could not have heard them; but as the explanation states, "which it is not lawful ... to utter" [ALFORD]. They were designed for Paul's own consolation, and not for communication to others. Some heavenly words are communicable (Exod. 34: 6; Isa. 6:3). These were not so. Paul had not the power adequately to utter; nor if he had, would he have been permitted; nor would earthly men comprehend them (John 3:12; I Cor. 2:9). A man may hear and know more than he can speak. **5. of myself**—concerning myself. Self is put in the background, except in respect to his infirmities. His glorying in his other self, to which the revelations were vouchsafed, was not in order to give glory to his fleshly self, but to bring out in contrast the "infirmities" of the latter, that Christ might have all the glory. **6. For**—Not but that I might glory as to "myself" (vs. 5); "FOR if I should desire to glory, I shall not be a fool"; for I have things to glory, or boast of which are good matter for glorying of (not mere external fleshly advantages which when he gloried in (ch. 11) he termed such glorying "folly," ch. 11:1, 16, 17). **think of me**— Greek, "form his estimate respecting me." **heareth of me**—Greek, "heareth aught from me." Whatever haply he heareth from me in person. If on account of healing a cripple (Acts 14:12, 13), and shaking off a viper (Acts 28), the people thought him a god, what would they have not done, if he had disclosed those revelations? [ESTIUS.] I wish each of you to estimate me by "what he sees" my *present* acts and "hears" my teaching to be; not by my boasting of *past* revelations. They who allow themselves to be thought of more highly than is lawful, defraud themselves of the honor which is at God's disposal [BENGEL] (John 5:44; 12: 43). **7. exalted above measure**—Greek, "overmuch uplifted." How dangerous must self-exaltation be, when even the apostle required so much restraint! [BENGEL]. **abundance**—Greek, "the excess"; exceeding greatness. **given ... me**—viz., by God (Job 5:6; Phil. 1:29). **thorn in the flesh**—(Num. 33. 55; Ezek. 28:24). ALFORD thinks it to be the same bodily affliction as in Galatians 4:13, 14. It certainly was something personal, affecting him individually, and not as an apostle: causing at once *acute pain* (as "thorn" implies) and *shame* ("buffet": as slaves are *buffeted,* I Pet. 2:20). **messenger of Satan**—who is permitted by God to afflict His saints, as Job (Job 2:7; Luke 13:16). **to buffet me**—In Greek, *present:* to buffet me even now continuously. After experiencing the state of the blissful angels, he is now exposed to the influence of an evil angel. The chastisement from hell follows soon upon the revelation from heaven. As his *sight* and *hearing* had been ravished with heavenly "revelations," so his *touch* is pained with the "thorn in the flesh." **8. For**—"concerning this thing." **thrice**—To his first and second prayer no answer came. To his third the answer came, which satisfied his faith and led him to bow his will to God's will. So Paul's master, Jesus, *thrice* prayed on the Mount of Olives, in resignation to the Father's will. The thorn seems (from vs. 9, and *Greek*, vs. 7, "that he *may* buffet me") to have continued with Paul when he wrote, lest still he should be "overmuch lifted up." **the Lord**—Christ. Escape from the cross is not to be sought even indirectly from Satan (Luke 4:7). "Satan is not to be asked to spare us" [BENGEL]. **9. said**—lit., "He hath said," implying that His answer is enough [ALFORD]. **is sufficient**—The trial must endure, but the grace shall also endure and never fail thee [ALFORD], (Deut. 33:25). The Lord puts the words into Paul's mouth, that following them up he might say, "O Lord, Thy grace is sufficient for me" [BENGEL]. **my strength**—*Greek*, "power." **is made perfect**—has its most perfect manifestation. **in weakness**—Do not ask for sensible strength, FOR My power is perfected in man's "strengthlessness" (so the *Greek*). The "for" implies, thy "strengthlessness" (the same *Greek* as is translated "weakness"; and in vs. 10, "infirmities") is the very element in which My "power" (which moves coincident with "My grace") exhibits itself more perfectly. So that Paul instead of desiring the infirmity to "depart," "rather" henceforth "*glories* in infirmities, that the power of Christ may rest (*Greek*, 'tabernacle upon', cover my infirmity all over as with a tabernacle; cf. *Greek*, John 1:12) upon" him. This effect of Christ's assurance on him appears, ch. 4:7; I Corinthians 2:3, 4; cf. I Peter 4:14. The "My" is omitted in some of the oldest MSS.; the sense is the same, "power" (referring to God's power) standing absolutely, in contrast to "weakness" (put absolutely, for man's weakness). Paul often repeats the word "weakness" or "infirmity" (chs. 11, 12, and 13) as being Christ's own word. The Lord has more need of our weakness than of our strength: our strength is often His rival; our weakness, His servant, drawing on His resources, and showing forth His glory. Man's extremity is God's opportunity; man's security is Satan's opportunity. God's way is not to take His children out of trial, but to give them strength to bear up against it (Ps. 88:7; John 17:15). **10. take pleasure in**—too strongly. Rather as the *Greek*, "I am well contented in." **infirmities**—the *genus*. Two pairs of *species* follow, partly coming from "Satan's messenger," partly from men. **reproaches**—"insults." **when**—in all the cases just specified. **then**—then especially. **strong**—"*powerful*" in "the *power of Christ*," vs. 9; ch. 13:4; Heb. 11:34). **11. in glorying**—omitted in the oldest MSS. "I am become a fool." He sounds a retreat [BENGEL]. **ye**—emphatic. "It is YE who have compelled me; for I ought to have been commended by you," instead of having to commend myself. **am I behind**—rather as *Greek*, "was I behind" when I was with you? **the very chiefest**—rather, as in ch. 11:5, "those overmuch apostles." **though I be nothing**—in myself (I Cor. 15:9, 10). **12. Truly ...** —There is understood some such clause as this, "And yet I have not been commended by you." **in all patience, in signs ...**—The oldest MSS. omit "in." "Patience" is not one of the "signs," but the element IN which they were wrought: endurance of opposition which did not cause me to leave off working [ALFORD]. Translate, "IN ... patience, BY

signs ...." His mode of expression is modest, putting himself, the worker, in the background, "were wrought," not "*I* wrought." As the *signs* have not been transmitted to us, neither has the apostleship. The apostles have no literal successors (cf. Acts 1:21, 22). **mighty deeds**—palpable works of divine omnipotence. The silence of the apostles in fourteen Epistles, as to miracles, arises from the design of those Epistles being hortatory, not controversial. The passing allusions to miracles in seven Epistles prove that the writers were not enthusiasts to whom *miracles* seem the most important thing. *Doctrines* were with them the important matter, save when convincing adversaries. In the seven Epistles the mention of miracles is not *obtrusive*, but marked by a calm air of assurance, as of facts *acknowledged on all hands*, and therefore unnecessary to dwell on. This is a much stronger proof of their reality than if they were formally and obtrusively asserted. Signs and wonders is the regular formula of the Old Testament, which New Testament readers would necessarily understand of supernatural works. Again, in the Gospels the miracles are so inseparably and congruously tied up with the history, that you cannot deny the former without denying the latter also. And then you have a greater difficulty than ever, viz., *to account for the rise of Christianity;* so that the infidel has something infinitely more difficult to believe than that which he rejects, and which the Christian more rationally accepts. **13. wherein you were inferior** —i.e., were treated with less consideration by me than were other churches. **I myself**—*I made a gain of you* neither *myself*, nor *by* those others *whom I sent, Titus* and others (vss. 17, 18). **wrong**—His declining support from the Corinthians might be regarded as the denial to them of a privilege, and a mark of their spiritual inferiority, and of his looking on them with less confidence and love (cf. ch. 11:9, 11). **14. the third time**—See *Introduction* to First Corinthians. His *second* visit was probably a short one (I Cor. 16:7), and attended with humiliation through the scandalous conduct of some of his converts (cf. vs. 21; ch. 2:1). It was probably paid during his three years' sojourn at Ephesus, from which he could pass so readily by sea to Corinth (cf. ch. 1:15, 16; 13:1, 2). The context here implies nothing of a *third preparation* to come; but, "I am coming, and the third time, and will not burden you this time any more than I did at my *two previous visits*" [ALFORD]. **not yours, but you**—(Phil. 4:17). **children ... parents**—Paul was their spiritual father (I Cor. 4:14, 15). He does not, therefore, seek earthly *treasure* from them, but *lays up* the best *treasure* (viz., spiritual) "for their souls" (vs. 15). **15. I will ... spend**—all I have. **be spent** —all that I am. This is more than even natural parents do. They "lay up *treasures* for their children." But I spend not merely my treasures, but *myself*. **for you**—*Greek*, "for your souls"; not for your mere bodies. **the less I be loved**—Love rather descends than ascends [BENGEL]. Love him as a true friend who seeks your good more than your good will. **16. I did not burden you**—The "I" in the *Greek* is emphatic. A possible insinuation of the Corinthians is hereby anticipated and refuted: "But, you may say, granted that *I* did not burden you *myself;* nevertheless, being crafty, I caught you (in my net) with guile"; viz., made a gain of you *by means of others* (I Thess. 2:3). **17.** Paul's reply: You know well I did not. My associates were as distinterested as myself. An important rule to all who would influence others for good. **I desired Titus**—viz., to go unto you. Not the mission mentioned ch. 8:6, 17, 22; but a mission previous to this Epistle, probably that from which he had just returned announcing to Paul their penitence (ch. 7:6-16). **a brother**—rather "OUR (lit., "the") brother"; one well known to the Corinthians, and perhaps a Corinthian; probably one of the two mentioned in ch. 8:18, 22. **same spirit**—inwardly. **steps**—outwardly. **19. Again**—The oldest MSS. read, "*This long time* ye think that we are excusing ourselves unto you? (Nay.) It is *before God* (as opposed to 'unto you') that we speak in Christ" (ch. 2:17). *English Version Greek* text was a correction from ch. 3:1; 5:12. **20. For**—Assigning cause why they needed to be thus spoken to "for their edification"; viz., his fear that at his coming he should find them "not such as he would," and so he should be found by them "such as they would not" like, viz., severe in punishing misconduct. **debates**—*Greek*, "strifes," "contentions." **envyings**—The oldest MSS. read "envying," *singular*. **strifes**—"factions," "intrigues," "factious schemes" [WAHL]. *Ambitious self-seeking;* from a *Greek* root, "*to work for hire.*" **backbitings, whisperings**—*open* "slanderings," and "whispering backbitings" (Gal. 5:20). **swellings**—arrogant elation; puffing up of yourselves. Jude 16, "great swelling words" (II Pet. 2:18). **21. my God**—*his* God, however trying the humiliation that was in store for him. **will humble me**—The indicative implies that the supposition *will actually be so.* The faithful pastor is "humbled" at, and "bewails" the falls of his people, as though they were his own. **sinned already**—before my last coming [BENGEL], i.e., before the second visit which he paid, and in which he had much at Corinth to rebuke. **have not repented**—shall not have repented [ALFORD]. **uncleanness**—for example, of married persons (I Thess. 4:7). **fornication**—among the unmarried.

CHAPTER 13

Vss. 1-14. HE THREATENS A SEVERE PROOF OF HIS APOSTOLIC AUTHORITY, BUT PREFERS THEY WOULD SPARE HIM THE NECESSITY FOR IT. **This is the third time I am coming to you**—not merely *preparing* to come to you. This proves an *intermediate visit* between the two recorded in Acts 18:1; 20:2. **In the mouth of two or three witnesses shall every word be established**—Quoted from Deuteronomy 19:15, LXX. "I will judge not without examination, nor will I abstain from punishing upon due evidence" [CONYBEARE and HOWSON]. I will no longer be among you "in all patience" towards offenders (ch. 12:12). The apostle in this case, where ordinary testimony was to be had, does not look for an immediate revelation, nor does he order the culprits to be cast out of the church before his arrival. Others understand the "two or three witnesses" to mean *his two or three visits* as establishing either (1) the truth of the facts alleged against the offenders, or (2) the reality of his threats. I prefer the first explanation to either of the two latter. **2. Rather, "I have already said** (at my second visit), and tell you (now) beforehand, AS (I did) WHEN I WAS PRESENT THE SECOND TIME, SO also NOW in my absence (the oldest MSS. omit the 'I write,' which here wrongly follows in *English Version Greek* text) to them which heretofore have sinned (viz., before my second visit, ch. 12:21), and to all others" (who have sinned since my second visit, or are in danger of sinning). The *English Version,* "as if I

were present the *second* time," viz., this next time, is quite inconsistent with vs. 1, "this is the *third* time I am coming to you," as Paul could not have called the same journey at once "the second" and "the third time" of his coming. The antithesis between "the second time" and "now" is palpable. **if I come again...**—i.e., *whensoever I come again* (Acts 20:2). These were probably the very words of his former threat which he now repeats again. **3. Since**—The reason why he will not spare: Since ye challenge me to give a "proof" that Christ speaks in me. It would be better if ye would "*prove* your own selves" (vs. 5). This disproves the assertion of some that Scripture nowhere asserts the infallibility of its writers when writing it. **which**—"who" (Christ.) **is not weak**—in relation to you, by me and in this very Epistle, in exercising upon you strong discipline. **mighty in you**—has given many proofs of His power in miracles, and even in punishing offenders (ch. 5:11, 20, 21). Ye have no need to put me to the proof in this, as long ago Christ has exhibited great proofs of His power by me among you (ch. 12:12) [GROTIUS]. It is therefore not me, but Christ, whom ye wrong: it is His patience that ye try in despising my admonitions, and derogating from my authority [CALVIN]. **4. though**—omitted in some of the oldest MSS.; then translate, "For He was even crucified..." **through weakness**—*Greek,* "from weakness"; i.e., His assumption of our weakness was the source, or necessary condition, *from* which the possibility of His crucifixion flowed (Heb. 2:14; Phil. 2:7, 8). **by**—*Greek,* "from"; "owing to." **the power of God**—the Father (Rom. 1:4; 6:4; Eph. 1:20). **weak in him**—i.e., in virtue of our union with Him, and after His pattern, weakness predominates in us for a time (exhibited in our "infirmities" and weak "bodily presence," ch. 10:10; 12:5, 9, 10; and also in our not putting into immediate exercise our power of punishing offenders, just as Christ for a time kept in abeyance His power). **we shall live with him**—not only hereafter with Him, free from our present infirmities, in the resurrection life (Phil. 3:21), but presently in the exercise of our apostolic authority against offenders, which flows to us *in respect to you* from *the power of God,* however "weak" we now seem to you. "With Him," i.e., even as He now exercises His power in His glorified resurrection life, after His weakness for a time. **5. Examine**—*Greek,* "Try (make trial of) yourselves." **prove your own selves**—This should be your first aim, rather than "seeking a proof of Christ speaking *in me*" (vs. 3). **your own selves**—I need not speak much in proof of Christ being in me, your minister (vs. 3), for if ye try *your own selves* ye will see that Christ is also in you [CHRYSOSTOM], (Rom. 8:10). Finding Christ dwelling in yourselves by faith, ye may well believe that He speaks in me, by whose ministry ye have received this faith [ESTIUS]. To doubt it would be the sin of Israel, who, after so many miracles and experimental proofs of God's presence, still cried (Exod. 17:7), "Is the Lord among us or not?" (Cf. Mark 8:11). **except ye be reprobates**—The *Greek* softens the expression, "*somewhat* reprobates," i.e., not *abiding the "proof"* (alluding to the same word in the context); *failing when tested.* Image from metals (Jer. 6:30; Dan. 5:27; Rom. 1:28). **6. we...not reprobates**—not *unable to abide* the "*proof*" to which ye put us (vs. 6). "I trust that" your own Christianity will be *recognized* by you (observe, "ye shall *know*," answers to "*know* your own selves," vs. 5) as sufficient "proof" that ye are not reprobates, but that "Christ speaks in me," without needing a proof from me more trying to yourselves. If ye doubt my apostleship, ye must doubt your own Christianity, for ye are the fruits of my apostleship. **7. I pray**—The oldest MSS. read, "we pray." **not that we should appear approved**—not to gain credit for ourselves, your ministers, by your Christian conduct; but for your good [ALFORD]. The antithesis to "reprobates" leads me to prefer explaining with BENGEL, "We do *not* pray *that* we may appear *approved*," by restraining you when ye do evil; "but that ye should do what is *right*" (*English Version*, "honest"). **though we be as reprobates**—though we be thereby deprived of the occasion for exercising our apostolic power (viz., in punishing), and so may appear "as reprobates" (*incapable of affording proof* of Christ speaking in us). **8.** Our apostolic power is given us that we may use it not against, but for the furtherance of, the truth. Where you are free from fault, there is no scope for its exercise: and this I desire. Far be it from me to use it against the innocent, merely in order to increase my own power (vs. 10). **9. are glad**—*Greek,* "rejoice." **when we are weak**—having no occasion for displaying our power; and so seeming "weak," as being compassed with "infirmities" (ch. 10:10; 11:29, 30). **ye ... strong**—"mighty" in faith and the fruits of the Spirit. **and**—not in the oldest MSS. **we wish**—*Greek,* "pray for." **your perfection**—lit., "perfect restoration"; lit., that of a dislocated limb. Cf. vs. 11, "Be perfect," the same *Greek* word; also in I Corinthians 1:10, "perfectly joined together"; Eph. 4:12, "the perfecting of the saints." **10. Therefore**—because I wish the "sharpness" to be in my *letters* rather than in *deeds* [CHRYSOSTOM]. **edification ... not to destruction**—*for building up ... not for casting down.* To "use sharpness" would seem to be *casting down,* rather than *building up;* therefore he prefers not to have to use it. **11. farewell**—meaning in *Greek* also "rejoice"; thus in bidding farewell he returns to the point with which he set out, "we are helpers of your *joy*" (ch. 1:24; Phil. 4:4). **Be perfect**—Become perfect by filling up what is lacking in your Christian character (Eph. 4:13). **be of good comfort**—(ch. 1:6; 7:8-13; I Thess. 4:18). **14.** The benediction which proves the doctrine of the Divine Trinity in unity. "The grace of Christ" comes first, for it is only by it we come to "the love of God" the Father (John 14:6). The variety in the order of Persons proves that "in this Trinity none is afore or after other" [ATHANAS, *Creed*]. **communion**—joint fellowship, or participation, in the same Holy Ghost, which joins in one catholic Church, His temple, both Jews and Gentiles. Whoever has "the fellowship of the Holy Ghost," has also "the grace of our Lord Jesus Christ," and "the love of God"; and vice versa. For the three are inseparable, as the three Persons of the Trinity itself [CHRYSOSTOM]. The doctrine of the Trinity was not revealed clearly and fully till Christ came, and the whole scheme of our redemption was manifested in Him, and we know the Holy Three in One more *in their relations to us* (as set forth summarily in this benediction), than in their *mutual relations to one another* (Deut. 29:29). **Amen**—omitted in the oldest MSS. Probably added subsequently for the exigencies of public joint worship.

THE EPISTLE OF PAUL THE APOSTLE TO THE

GALATIANS

INTRODUCTION

THE internal and external evidence for *Paul's authorship* is conclusive. The style is characteristically Pauline. The superscription, and allusions to the apostle of the Gentiles in the first person, throughout the Epistle, establish the same truth (ch. 1:1, 13–24; 2:1–14). His authorship is also upheld by the unanimous testimony of the ancient Church: cf. IRENÆUS, *adversus Hæreses* 3, 7, 2 (Gal. 3:19); POLYCARP (Phil. ch. 3) quotes Galatians 4:26 and 6:7; JUSTIN MARTYR, or whoever wrote the *Oratio ad Græcos*, alludes to Gal. 4:12 and 5:20.

The Epistle was written "TO THE CHURCHES OF GALATIA" (ch. 1:2), a district of Asia Minor, bordering on Phrygia, Pontus, Bithynia, Cappadocia, and Paphlagonia. The inhabitants (Gallo-gærci, contracted into Galati, another form of the name Kelts) were Gauls in origin, the latter having overrun Asia Minor after they had pillaged Delphi, about 280 B.C. and at last permanently settled in the central parts, thence called Gallo-græcia or Galatia. Their character, as shown in this Epistle, is in entire consonance with that ascribed to the Gallic race by all writers. CÆSAR, B. G., 4, 5, "The infirmity of the Gauls is that they are fickle in their resolves and fond of change, and not to be trusted." So THIERRY [quoted by ALFORD], "Frank, impetuous, impressible, eminently intelligent, but at the same time extremely changeable, inconstant, fond of show, perpetually quarrelling, the fruit of excessive vanity." They received Paul at first with all joy and kindness; but soon wavered in their allegiance to the Gospel and to him, and hearkened as eagerly now to Judaizing teachers as they had before to him (ch. 4:14–16). The apostle himself had been the first preacher among them (Acts 16:6; Gal. 1:8; 4:13 [see *Note; "on account of* infirmity of flesh I preached unto you at the first": implying that sickness detained him among them]); and had then probably founded churches, which at his subsequent visit he "strengthened" in the faith (Acts 18:23). His first visit was about A.D. 51, during his second missionary journey. JOSEPHUS (*Antiquities,* 16:62) testifies that many Jews resided in Ancyra in Galatia. Among these and their brethren, doubtless, as elsewhere, he began his preaching. And though subsequently the majority in the Galatian churches were Gentiles (ch. 4:8, 9), yet these were soon infected by Judaizing teachers, and almost suffered themselves to be persuaded to undergo circumcision (ch. 1:6; 3:1, 3; 5:2, 3; 6:12, 13). Accustomed as the Galatians had been, when heathen, to the mystic worship of Cybele (prevalent in the neighboring region of Phrygia), and the theosophistic doctrines connected with that worship, they were the more readily led to believe that the full privileges of Christianity could only be attained through an elaborate system of ceremonial symbolism (ch. 4:9–11; 5:7–12). They even gave ear to the insinuation that Paul himself observed the law among the Jews, though he persuaded the Gentiles to renounce it, and that his motive was to keep his converts in a subordinate state, excluded from the full privileges of Christianity, which were enjoyed by the circumcised alone (ch. 5:11; 4:16, cf. with 2:17); and that in "becoming all things to all men," he was an interested flatterer (ch. 1:10), aiming at forming a party for himself: moreover, that he falsely represented himself as an apostle divinely commissioned by Christ, whereas he was but a messenger sent by the Twelve and the Church at Jerusalem, and that his teaching was now at variance with that of Peter and James, "pillars" of the Church, and therefore ought not to be accepted.

His PURPOSE, then, in writing this Epistle was: (1) to defend his apostolic authority (ch. 1:11–19; 2:1–14); (2) to counteract the evil influence of the Judaizers in Galatia (chs. 3 and 4), and to show that their doctrine destroyed the very *essence of* Christianity, by lowering its spirituality to an outward ceremonial system; (3) to give exhortation for the strengthening of Galatian believers in faith towards Christ, and in the fruits of the Spirit (chs. 5 and 6). He had already, face to face, testified against the Judaizing teachers (ch. 1:9; 4:16; Acts 18:23); and now that he has heard of the continued and increasing prevalence of the evil, he writes *with his own hand* (ch. 6:11: a labor which he usually delegated to an amanuensis) this Epistle to oppose it. The sketch he gives in it of his apostolic career confirms and expands the account in Acts and shows his independence of human authority, however exalted. His protest against Peter in ch. 2:14–21), disproves the figment, not merely of papal, but even of that apostle's supremacy; and shows that Peter, save when specially inspired, was fallible like other men.

There is much in common between this Epistle and that to the Romans on the subject of justification by faith only, and not by the law. But the Epistle to the Romans handles the subject in a didactic and logical mode, without any special reference; this Epistle, in a controversial manner, and with special reference to the Judaizers in Galatia.

The STYLE combines the two extremes, sternness (ch. 1; 3:1–5) and tenderness (ch. 4:19, 20), the characteristics of a man of strong emotions, and both alike well suited for acting on an impressible people such as the Galatians were. The beginning is abrupt, as was suited to the urgency of the question and the greatness of the danger. A tone of sadness, too, is apparent, such as might be expected in the letter of a warm-hearted teacher who had just learned that those whom he loved were forsaking his teachings for those of perverters of the truth, as well as giving ear to calumnies against himself.

The TIME OF WRITING was *after* the visit to Jerusalem recorded in Acts 15:1, etc.; i.e., A.D. 50, if that visit be, as seems probable, identical with that in ch. 2:1. Further, as ch. 1:9 ("as we said *before*"), and 4:16 ("Have [ALFORD] I *become* your enemy?" viz., at my second visit, whereas I was welcomed by you at my first visit), refer to his second visit (Acts 18:23); this Epistle must have been written after the date of that visit (the autumn of A.D. 54). Ch. 4:13, "Ye know how . . . I preached . . . at the first" (*Greek*, "at the former time"), implies that Paul, at the time of writing, had been *twice* in Galatia; and ch. 1:6, "I marvel that ye are *so soon* removed," implies that he wrote not long after having left Galatia for the second time; probably in the early part of *his residence at Ephesus* (Acts 18:23; 19:1, etc., from A.D. 54, the autumn, to A.D. 57, Pentecost) [ALFORD]. CONYBEARE and HOWSON, from the similarity between this Epistle and that to the Romans, the same line of argument in both occupying the writer's mind, think it was *not written till his stay at Corinth* (Acts 20:2, 3), during the winter of 57–58, whence he wrote his Epistle to the Romans; and certainly, in the theory of the earlier writing of it from Ephesus, it does seem unlikely that the two Epistles to the Corinthians, so dissimilar, should intervene between those so similar as the Epistles to the Galatians and Romans; or that the Epistle to the Galatians should intervene between the second to the Thessalonians and the first to the Corinthians. The decision between the two theories rests on the words, "so soon." If these be not considered inconsistent with little more than three years having elapsed since his second visit to Galatia, the argument, from the similarity to the Epistle to the Romans, seems to me conclusive. This to the Galatians seems written on the urgency of the occasion, tidings having reached him at Corinth from Ephesus of the Judaizing of many of his Galatian converts, in an admonitory and controversial tone, to maintain the great principles of Christian liberty and justification by faith only; that to the Romans is a more deliberate and systematic exposition of the same central truths of theology, subsequently drawn up in writing to a Church with which he was personally unacquainted. See *Note*, ch. 1:6, for BIRKS's view. PALEY (*Horæ Paulinæ*) well remarks how perfectly adapted the conduct of the argument is to the historical circumstances under which the Epistle was written! Thus, that to the Galatians, a Church which Paul had founded, he puts mainly upon *authority;* that to the Romans, to whom he was not personally known, entirely upon *argument.*

CHAPTER 1

Vss. 1-24. SUPERSCRIPTION. GREETINGS. THE CAUSE OF HIS WRITING IS THEIR SPEEDY FALLING AWAY FROM THE GOSPEL HE TAUGHT. DEFENSE OF HIS TEACHING: HIS APOSTOLIC CALL INDEPENDENT OF MAN. Judaizing teachers had persuaded the Galatians that Paul had taught them the new religion imperfectly, and at second hand; that the founder of their church himself possessed only a deputed commission, the seal of truth and authority being in the apostles at Jerusalem: moreover, that whatever he might profess among them, he had himself at other times, and in other places, given way to the doctrine of circumcision. To refute this, he appeals to the history of his conversion, and to the manner of his conferring with the apostles when he met them at Jerusalem; that so far was his doctrine from being derived from them, or they from exercising any superiority over him, that they had simply assented to what he had already preached among the Gentiles, which preaching was communicated, not by them to him, but by himself to them [PALEY]. Such an apologetic Epistle could not be a later forgery, the objections which it meets only coming out incidentally, not being obtruded as they would be by a forger; and also being such as could only arise in the earliest age of the Church, when Jerusalem and Judaism still held a prominent place. **1. apostle**—in the earliest Epistles, the two to the Thessalonians, through humility, he uses no title of authority; but associates with him "Silvanus and Timotheus"; yet here, though "brethren" (vs. 2) are with him, he does not *name* them but puts his own name and apostleship prominent; evidently because his apostolic commission needs now to be vindicated against deniers of it. **of**—*Greek,* "from." Expressing the *origin* from which his mission came, "not from *men,*" but from Christ and the Father (understood) as the source. "By" expresses the immediate operating agent in the call. Not only was the call *from* God as its ultimate source, but *by* Christ and the Father as the immediate agent in calling him (Acts 22:15, and 26:16-18). The laying on of Ananias' hands (Acts 9:17) is no objection to this; for that was but a sign of the fact, not an assisting cause. So the Holy Ghost calls him specially (Acts 13:2, 3); he was an apostle *before* this special mission. **man**—singular; to mark the contrast to "Jesus Christ." The opposition between "Christ" and "man," and His name being put in closest connection with God the Father, imply His Godhead. **raised him from the dead**—implying that, though he had not seen Him in His humiliation as the other apostles (which was made an objection against him), he had seen and been *constituted an apostle by Him in His resurrection power* (Matt. 28:18; Rom. 1:4, 5). Cf. as to the ascension, the consequence of the resurrection, and the cause of His giving "apostles," Ephesians 4:11. He rose again, too, for our *justification* (Rom. 4:25); thus Paul prepares the way for the prominent subject of the Epistle, justification in Christ, not by the law. **2. all the brethren**—I am not alone in my doctrine; all my colleagues in the Gospel work, travelling with me (Acts 19:29, Gaius and Aristarchus at Ephesus; Acts 20:4, Sopater, Secundus, Timotheus, Tychicus, Trophimus, some, or all of these), join with me. Not that these were *joint authors* with Paul of the Epistle; but joined him in the *sentiments* and *salutations.* The phrase, "all the brethren," accords with a date when he had many travelling companions, he and they having to bear jointly the collection to Jerusalem [CONYBEARE and HOWSON]. **the churches**—Pessinus and Ancyra were the principal cities; but doubtless there were many other churches in Galatia (Acts 18:23; I Cor. 16:1). He does not attach any honorable title to the churches here, as elsewhere, being displeased at their Judaizing. See I Corinthians; I Thessalonians, etc. The first Epistle of Peter is addressed to Jewish Christians sojourning in Galatia (I Pet. 1:1), among other places mentioned. It is interesting thus to find the apostle of the circumcision, as well as the apostle of the uncircumcision, once at issue (ch. 2:7-15), co-operating to build up the same churches. **3. from** . . . *from*—Omit the second "from." The *Greek* joins God the Father and our Lord Jesus Christ in closet union, by there being but the one preposition. **4. gave himself**—(ch. 2:20)—unto death, as an offering. Found only in this and the Pastoral Epistles. The *Greek* is different in Ephesians 5:25 (*Note*). **for our sins**—which enslaved us to the present evil world. **deliver us from this**—*Greek,* "out of the* . . ." The Father and Son are each said to "deliver us. . . ." (Col. 1:13); but the Son, not the Father, *"gave Himself for" us* in order to do so, and make us citizens of a better world (Phil. 3:20). The Galatians in desiring to return to legal bondage are, he

implies, renouncing the *deliverance* which Christ wrought for us. This he more fully repeats in ch. 3:13. "Deliver" is the very word used by the Lord as to His deliverance of Paul himself (Acts 26:17): an undesigned coincidence between Paul and Luke. **world**—*Greek,* "age"; *system* or *course* of the world, regarded from a religious point of view. The present *age* opposes the "glory" (vs. 5) of God, and is under the authority of the Evil One. The "ages of ages" (*Greek,* vs. 5) are opposed to "the present evil age." **according to the will of God and our Father**—*Greek,* "of Him who is at once God [the sovereign Creator] and our Father" (John 6:38, 39; 10:18, end). Without merit of ours. His sovereignty as "GOD," and our filial relation to Him as "OUR FATHER," ought to keep us from blending our own legal notions (as the Galatians were doing) with His will and plan. This paves the way for his argument. **5. be glory**—rather, as Greek, "be *the* glory"; the glory which is peculiarly and exclusively His. Cf. Ephesians 3:21, *Note.* **6.** Without the usual expressions of thanksgiving for their faith, etc., he vehemently plunges into his subject, zealous for "the glory" of God (vs. 5), which was being disparaged by the Galatians falling away from the pure Gospel of the "grace" of God. **I marvel**—implying that he had hoped better things from them, whence his sorrowful surprise at their turning out so different from his expectations. **so soon**—after my last visit; when I hoped and thought you were untainted by the Judaizing teachers. If this Epistle was written from Corinth, the interval would be a little more than three years, which would be "soon" to have fallen away, if they were apparently sound at the time of his visit. Ch. 4:18, 20 may imply that he saw no symptom of unsoundness *then,* such as he hears of in them *now.* But *English Version* is probably not correct there. See *Note,* also see *Introduction.* If from Ephesus, the interval would be not more than one year. BIRKS holds the Epistle to have been written from Corinth after his FIRST visit to Galatia; for this agrees best with the "so soon" here: with ch. 4:18, "It is good to be zealously affected always in a good thing, and not only when I am present with you." If they had persevered in the faith during three years of his first absence, and only turned aside after his second visit, they could not be charged justly with adhering to the truth only when he was present; for his first absence was longer than both his visits, and they would have obeyed longer in his *"absence"* than in his *"presence."* But if their decline had begun immediately after he left them, and before his return to them, the reproof will be just. But see *Note,* ch. 4:13. **removed**—Translate, "are being removed," i.e., ye are *suffering yourselves so soon* (whether from the time of my last visit, or from the time of the first temptation held out to you) [PARÆUS] *to be removed* by Jewish seducers. Thus he softens the censure by implying that the Galatians were tempted by seducers from without, with whom the chief guilt lay; and the present, "ye are *being* removed," implies that their seduction was only in process of being effected, not that it was actually effected. WAHL, ALFORD, and others take the *Greek* as middle voice. "ye are removing" or "passing over." "Shifting your ground" [CONYBEARE and HOWSON]. But thus the point of Paul's oblique reference to their misleaders is lost; and in Hebrews 7:12 the *Greek* is used passively, justifying its being taken so here. On the impulsiveness and fickleness of the Gauls (another form of Kel-t-s, the progenitors of the Erse, Gauls, Cymri, and Belgians), whence the Galatians sprang, see *Introduction* and CÆSAR, B. G. 3. 19. **from him that called you**—God the Father (vs. 15; ch. 5:8; Rom. 8:30; I Cor. 1:9; I Thess. 2:12; 5:24). **into**—rather, as *Greek,* "IN the grace of Christ," as the *element in* which, and the *instrument by* which, God calls us to salvation. Cf. *Note,* I Corinthians 7:15; Romans 5:15, "the gift by (*Greek,* 'in') grace (*Greek, 'the grace*') of (the) one man." "The grace of Christ," is Christ's gratuitously purchased and bestowed justification, reconciliation, and eternal life. **another**—rather, as *Greek,* "a second and *different* gospel," i.e., into a *so-called* gospel, different altogether from the only true Gospel. **7. another** —A distinct *Greek* word from that in vs. 6. Though I called it a gospel (vs. 6), it is not really so. There is really but *one* Gospel, and no *other* gospel, **but** —Translate, "Only that there are some that trouble you . . ." (ch. 5:10, 12). All I meant by the "different gospel" was nothing but a perversion by "some" of the one Gospel of Christ. **would pervert**—*Greek,* "wish to pervert"; they could not really pervert the Gospel, though they could pervert Gospel professors (cf. ch. 4:9, 17, 21; 6:12, 13; Col. 2:18). Though acknowledging Christ, they insisted on circumcision and Jewish ordinances and professed to rest on the authority of other apostles, viz., Peter and James. But Paul recognizes no gospel, save the pure Gospel. **8. But**—however weighty they may seem "who trouble you." Translate as *Greek,* "Even though we," viz., I and the brethren with me, weighty and many as we are (vss. 1, 2). The *Greek* implies a case supposed which never has occurred. **angel**—in which light ye at first received me (cf. ch. 4:14; I Cor. 13:1), and whose authority is the highest possible next to that of God and Christ. A new revelation, even though seemingly accredited by miracles, is not to be received if it contradict the already existing revelation. For God cannot contradict Himself (Deut. 13:1-3; I Kings 13:18; Matt. 24:24; II Thess. 2:9). The Judaizing teachers sheltered themselves under the names of the great apostles, James, John, and Peter: "Do not bring these names up to me, for even if an *angel.* . . ." Not that he means, the apostles really supported the Judaizers: but he wishes to show, when the truth is in question, respect of persons is inadmissible [CHRYSOSTOM]. **preach**—i.e., "should preach." **any other gospel . . . than**—The *Greek* expresses not so much "any other gospel *different* from what we have preached," as, "any gospel BESIDE that which we preached." This distinctly opposes the traditions of the Church of Rome, which are at once *besides* and *against* (the *Greek* includes both ideas) the written Word, our only *attested rule.* **9. said before**—when we were visiting you (so "before" means, II Cor. 13:2). Cf. ch. 5:2, 3, 21. Translate, "If any man *preacheth* unto you any gospel BESIDE that which. . . ." Observe the indicative, not the subjunctive or conditional mood, is used, "preacheth," lit., "furnisheth you with any gospel." The *fact* is assumed, not merely supposed as a contingency, as in vs. 8, "preach," or "should preach." This implies that he had already observed (viz., during his last visit) the machinations of the Judaizing teachers: but his *surprise* (vs. 6) *now* at the Galatians being misled by them, implies that they had not apparently been so *then.* As in vs. 8 he had said, "which we preached," so here, with an augmentation of the force, "which ye received"; acknowledging that they had truly *accepted it.* **accursed**—The opposite appears in ch. 6:16. **10. For**—accounting for the strong language he has just used. **do I *now***—resuming the "now" of vs. 9. "Am I

now persuading men?" [ALFORD], i.e., conciliating. Is what I have *just now* said a sample of men-pleasing, of which I am accused? His adversaries accused him of being an interested flatterer of men, "becoming all things to all men," to make a party for himself, and so observing the law among the Jews (for instance, circumcising Timothy), yet persuading the Gentiles to renounce it (ch. 5:11) (in order to flatter those, really keeping them in a subordinate state, not admitted to the full privileges which the circumcised alone enjoyed). NEANDER explains the "now" thus: Once, when a Pharisee, I was actuated only by a regard to human authority and to please men (Luke 16:15; John 5:44), but NOW I teach as responsible to God alone (I Cor. 4:3). **or God?**—Regard is to be had to God alone. **for if I yet pleased men**—The oldest MSS. omit "for." "If I were still pleasing men . . ." (Luke 6:26; John 15:19; I Thess. 2:4; Jas. 4:4; I John 4:5). On "yet," cf. ch. 5:11. **servant of Christ**—and so pleasing Him in all things (Titus 2:9; Col. 3:22). **11. certify** —I made known to you as to the Gospel which was preached by me, that it is not after man, i.e., not *of by,* or *from* man (vss. 1, 12). It is *not according* to man; not influenced by mere human considerations, as it would be, if it were of human origin. **brethren**—He not till now calls them so. **12.** Translate, "For *not even* did I *myself* (any more than the other apostles) receive it from man, *nor* was I taught it (by man)." "Received it," implies the absence of labor in acquiring it. "Taught it," implies the labor of learning. **by the revelation of Jesus Christ** —Translate, "by revelation of [i.e., from] Jesus Christ." By His revealing it to me. Probably this took place during the three years, in part of which he sojourned in Arabia (vss. 17, 18), in the vicinity of the scene of the giving of the law; a fit place for such a revelation of the Gospel of grace, which supersedes the ceremonial law (ch. 4:25). He, like other Pharisees who embraced Christianity, did not at first recognize its independence of the Mosaic law, but combined both together. Ananias, his first instructor, was universally esteemed for his legal piety and so was not likely to have taught him to sever Christianity from the law. This severance was partially recognized after the martyrdom of Stephen. But Paul received it by special revelation (I Cor. 11: 23; 15:3; I Thess. 4:15). A vision of the Lord Jesus is mentioned (Acts 22:18), at his first visit to Jerusalem (vs. 18); but this seems to have been subsequent to the revelation here meant (cf. vss. 15-18), and to have been confined to giving a particular command. The vision "fourteen years before" (II Cor. 12:1) was in A.D. 43, still later, six years after his conversion. Thus Paul is an independent witness to the Gospel. Though he had recived no instruction from the apostles, but from the Holy Ghost, yet when he met them his Gospel exactly agreed with theirs. **13. heard**—even before I came among you. **conversation**—"my former way of life." **Jews' religion**—The term, "Hebrew," expresses the *language;* "Jew," the *nationality,* as distinguished from the Gentiles; "Israelite," the highest title, the religious privileges, as a member of the theocracy. **the church**—Here singular, marking its unity, though constituted of many particular churches, under the one Head, Christ. **of God**—added to mark the greatness of his sinful alienation from God (I Cor. 15:19). **wasted**—laid it waste: the opposite of "building it up." **14. profited**—*Greek,* "I was becoming a proficient"; "I made progress." **above**—beyond. **my equals**—*Greek,* "Of mine own age, among my countrymen." **tradi-**

tions of my fathers—viz., those of the Pharisees, Paul being "a Pharisee, and son of a Pharisee" (Acts 23:6; 26:5). "MY fathers," shows that it is not to be understood generally of the traditions *of the nation*. 15. separated—"set me apart": in the purposes of His electing love (cf. Acts 9:15; 22:14), in order to show in me *His "pleasure,"* which is the farthest point that any can reach in inquiring the causes of his salvation. The actual "separating" or "setting apart" to the work marked out for him, is mentioned in Acts 13:2; Romans 1:1. There is an allusion, perhaps, in the way of contrast, to the derivation of Pharisee from *Hebrew, pharash,* "separated." I was once a socalled Pharisee or *Separatist,* but God had *separated* me to something far better. from . . . womb—Thus merit in me was out of the question, in assigning causes for His call (Rom. 9:11). Grace is the sole cause (Ps. 22:9; 71: 6; Isa. 49:1, 5; Jer. 1:5; Luke 1:15). called me—on the way to Damascus (Acts 9). 16. reveal his Son in me—within me, in my inmost soul, by the Holy Spirit (ch. 2:20). Cf. II Corinthians 4:6, "shined in our hearts." The revealing of His Son by me to the Gentiles (so translate for "heathen") was impossible, unless He had first revealed His Son *in me;* at first on my conversion, but especially at the subsequent revelation from Jesus Christ (vs. 12), whereby I learned the Gospel's independence of the Mosaic law. that I might preach—the present in the *Greek,* which includes the idea "that I *may* preach Him," implying an office still *continuing.* This was the main commission. entrusted to him (ch. 2:7, 9). immediately—connected chiefly with "I went into Arabia" (vs. 17). It denotes the sudden fitness of the apostle. So Acts 9:20, "*Straightway* he preached Christ in the synagogue." I conferred not—*Greek,* "I had not further (viz., in addition to revelation) recourse to . . . for the purpose of consulting." The divine revelation was sufficient for me [BENGEL]. flesh and blood—(Matt. 16:17). 17. went I up—Some of the oldest MSS. read, "went away." to Jerusalem—the seat of the apostles. into Arabia—This journey (not recorded in Acts) was during the whole period of his stay at Damascus, called by Luke (Acts 9:23), "many [*Greek,* a considerable number of] days." It is curiously confirmatory of the legitimacy of taking "many days" to stand for "three years," that the same phrase exactly occurs in the same sense in I Kings 2: 38, 39. This was a country of the *Gentiles;* here doubtless he preached as he did before and after (Acts 9:20, 22) at Damascus: thus he shows the independence of his apostolic commission. He also here had that comparative retirement needed, after the first fervor of his conversion, to prepare him for the great work before him. Cf. Moses (Acts 7:29, 30). His familiarity with the scene of the giving of the law, and the meditations and revelations which he had there, appear in ch. 4:24, 25; Hebrews 12:18. See *Note,* vs. 12. The Lord from heaven communed with him, as He on earth in the days of His flesh communed with the other apostles. returned —*Greek* "returned back again." 18. after three years—dating from my conversion, as appears by the contrast to "immediately" (vs. 16). This is the same visit to Jerusalem as in Acts 9:26, and at this visit occurred the vision (Acts 22:17, 18). The incident which led to his leaving Damascus (Acts 9: 25; II Cor. 11:33) was not the main *cause* of his going *to Jerusalem.* So that there is no discrepancy in the statement here that he went "to see Peter"; or rather, as *Greek,* "to make the acquaintance of";

"to become personally acquainted with." The two oldest MSS. read, "Cephas," the name given Peter elsewhere in the Epistle, the *Hebrew* name; as *Peter* is the *Greek* (John 1:42). Appropriate to the view of him here as the apostle especially of the Hebrews. It is remarkable that Peter himself, in his Epistles, uses the *Greek* name *Peter,* perhaps to mark his antagonism to the Judaizers who would cling to the Hebraic form. He was prominent among the apostles, though James, as bishop of Jerusalem, had the chief authority there (Matt. 16:18). abode—or "tarried" [ELLICOTT]. fifteen days—only fifteen days; contrasting with the long period of *three years,* during which, previously, he had exercised an independent commission in preaching: a fact proving on the face of it, how little he owed to Peter in regard to his apostolical authority or instruction. The *Greek* for "to see," at the same time implies *visiting a person important to know,* such as Peter was. The plots of the Jews prevented him staying longer (Acts 9:29). Also, the vision directing him to depart to the Gentiles, for that the people of Jerusalem would not receive his testimony (Acts 22:17, 18). 19. Cf. Acts 9:27, 28, wherein Luke, as an historian, describes more generally what Paul, the subject of the history, himself details more particularly. The history speaks of "apostles"; and Paul's mention of a *second* apostle, besides Peter, reconciles the Epistle and the history. At Stephen's martyrdom, and the consequent persecution, the other ten apostles, agreeably to Christ's directions, seem to have soon (though not *immediately,* Acts 8:14) left Jerusalem to preach elsewhere. James remained in charge of the mother church, as its bishop. Peter, the apostle of the circumcision, was present during Paul's fifteen days' stay; but he, too, presently after (Acts 9:32), went on a circuit through Judea. James, the Lord's brother—This designation, to distinguish him from James the son of Zebedee, was appropriate while that apostle was alive. But before Paul's second visit to Jerusalem (ch. 2:1; Acts 15), he had been beheaded by Herod (Acts 12:2). Accordingly, in the subsequent mention of James here (ch. 2:9, 12), he is not designated by this distinctive epithet: a minute, undesigned coincidence, and proof of genuineness. James was the Lord's brother, not in our strict sense, but in the sense, "cousin," or "kinsman" (Matt. 28:10; John 20:17). His brethren are never called "sons of Joseph," which they would have been had they been the Lord's brothers strictly. However, cf. Psalm 69:8, "I am an alien to *my mother's children.*" In John 7:3, 5, the "brethren" who believed not in Him may mean His *near relations,* not including the two of His brethren, i.e., relatives (James and Jude) who were among the Twelve apostles. Acts 1:14, "His brethren," refer to Simon and Joses, and others (Matt. 13:55) of His kinsmen, who were not apostles. It is not likely there would be two pairs of brothers named alike, of such eminence as James and Jude; the likelihood is that the apostles James and Jude are also the writers of the Epistles, and the brethren of Jesus. James and Joses were sons of Alpheus and Mary, sister of the Virgin Mary. 20. Solemn asseveration that his statement is true that his visit was but for fifteen days and that he saw no apostle save Peter and James. Probably it had been reported by Judaizers that he had received a long course of instruction from the apostles in Jerusalem from the first; hence his earnestness in asserting the contrary facts. 21. I came into . . . Syria and Cilicia— "preaching the faith" (vs. 23), and so, no doubt, founding the churches in Syria and Cilicia, which he subsequently confirmed in the faith (Acts 15:23, 41). He probably went first to Cæsarea, the main seaport, and thence by sea to Tarsus of Cilicia, his native place (Acts 9:30), and thence to Syria; Cilicia having its geographical affinities with Syria, rather than with Asia Minor, as the Tarsus mountains separate it from the latter. His placing "Syria" in the order of words before "Cilicia," is due to Antioch being a more important city than Tarsus, as also to his longer stay in the former city. Also "Syria and Cilicia," from their close geographical connection, became a generic geographical phrase, the more important district being placed first [CONYBEARE and HOWSON]. This sea journey accounts for his being "unknown by face to the churches of Judea" (vs. 22). He passes by in silence his *second* visit, with alms, to Judea and Jerusalem (Acts 11:30); doubtless because it was for a limited and special object, and would occupy but a few days (Acts 12:25), as there raged at Jerusalem at the time a persecution in which James, the brother of John, was martyred, and Peter was in prison, and James seems to have been the only apostle present (Acts 12:17); so it was needless to mention this visit, seeing that he could not at such a time have received the instructions which the Galatians alleged he had derived from the primary fountains of authority, the apostles. **22.** So far was I from being a disciple of the apostles, that I was even *unknown in the churches of Judea* (excepting Jerusalem, Acts 9:26-29), which were the chief scene of their labors. **23.** Translate as *Greek,* "They were hearing": tidings were brought them from time to time [CONYBEARE and HOWSON]. **he which persecuted us in times past**—"our former persecutor" [ALFORD]. The designation by which he was known among Christians still better than by his name "Saul." **destroyed**—*Greek,* "was destroying." **24. in me**—"in my case." "Having understood the entire change, and that the former wolf is now acting the shepherd's part, they received occasion for joyful thanksgiving to God in respect to me" [THEODORET]. How different, he implies to the Galatians, *their* spirit from *yours!*

CHAPTER 2

Vss. 1-21. HIS CO-ORDINATE AUTHORITY AS APOSTLE OF THE CIRCUMCISION RECOGNIZED BY THE APOSTLES. PROVED BY HIS REBUKING PETER FOR TEMPORIZING AT ANTIOCH: HIS REASONING AS TO THE INCONSISTENCY OF JUDAIZING WITH JUSTIFICATION BY FAITH. **1.** Translate, "After fourteen years"; viz., from Paul's conversion inclusive [ALFORD]. In the fourteenth year from his conversion [BIRKS]. The same visit to Jerusalem as in Acts 15 (A.D. 50), when the council of the apostles and Church decided that Gentile Christians need not be circumcised. His omitting allusion to that decree is; (1) Because his *design* here is to show the Galatians his own independent apostolic authority, whence he was not likely to support himself by their decision. Thus we see that general councils are not above apostles. (2) Because he argues the point upon principle, not authoritative decisions. (3) The decree did not go the length of the position maintained here: the council did not impose Mosaic ordinances; the apostle maintains that the Mosaic institution itself is at an end. (4) The Galatians were Judaizing, not because the Jewish law was imposed by authority of the Church as *necessary to Christianity,* but

because they thought it necessary to be observed by those who aspired to *higher perfection* (ch. 3:3; 4:21). The decree would not at all disprove their view, and therefore would have been useless to quote. Paul meets them by a far more direct confutation, "Christ is of *no effect* unto you whosoever are justified by the law" (ch. 5:4), [PALEY]. **Titus ... also**—specified on account of what follows as to him, in vs. 3. Paul and Barnabas, *and others,* were deputed by the Church of Antioch (Acts 15:2) to consult the apostles and elders at Jerusalem on the question of circumcision of Gentile Christians. **2. by revelation**—not from being absolutely dependent on the apostles at Jerusalem, but by independent divine "revelation." Quite consistent with his at the same time, being a deputy from the Church of Antioch, as Acts 15:2 states. He by this *revelation* was led to suggest the sending of the deputation. Cf. the case of Peter being led by vision, and at the same time by Cornelius' messengers, to go to Cæsarea, Acts 10. **I ... communicated unto them** —viz., "to the apostles and elders" (Acts 15:2): to the apostles in particular (vs. 9). **privately**—that he and the apostles at Jerusalem might decide previously on the principles to be adopted and set forward before the public council (Acts 15). It was necessary that the Jerusalem apostles should know beforehand that the Gospel Paul preached to the Gentiles was the same as theirs, and had received divine confirmation in the results it wrought on the Gentile converts. He and Barnabas related to the *multitude,* not the nature of the doctrine they preached (as Paul did privately to the apostles), but only the miracles vouchsafed in *proof* of God's sanctioning their preaching to the Gentiles (Acts 15:12). **to them ... of reputation**—James, Cephas, and John, and probably some of the "elders"; vs. 6, "those who seemed to be somewhat." **lest ...**— "lest I should be running, or have run, in vain"; i.e., that they might see that I am not running, and have not run, in vain. Paul does not *himself* fear lest he be running, or had run, in vain; but lest he should, if he gave them no explanation, *seem* so *to them.* His race was the swift-running proclamation of the Gospel to the Gentiles (cf. "run," *Margin,* for "Word ... have free course," II Thess. 3:1). His running would have been in vain, had circumcision been necessary, since he did not require it of his converts. **3. But**—So far were they from regarding me as running in vain, that "*not even* Titus who was with me, who was a Greek (and therefore uncircumcised), was compelled to be circumcised." So the *Greek* should be translated. The "false brethren," vs. 4 ("certain of the sect of the Pharisees which believed," Acts 15:5), demanded his circumcision. The apostles, however, constrained by the firmness of Paul and Barnabas (vs. 5), did not compel or insist on his being circumcised. Thus they virtually sanctioned Paul's course among the Gentiles and admitted his independence as an apostle: the point he desires to set forth to the Galatians. Timothy, on the other hand, as being a proselyte of the gate, and son of a Jewess (Acts 16:1), he circumcised (Acts 16:3). Christianity did not interfere with Jewish usages, regarded merely as social ordinances, though no longer having their religious significance, in the case of Jews and proselytes, while the Jewish polity and temple still stood; after the overthrow of the latter, those usages naturally ceased. To have insisted on Jewish usages for *Gentile* converts, would have been to make them essential parts of Christianity. To have rudely violated them at first in the case of *Jews,* would have been inconsistent with that charity which (in matters indifferent) is made all things to all men, that by all means it may win some (I Cor. 9:22; cf. Rom. 14:1-7, 13-23). Paul brought Titus about with him as a living example of the power of the Gospel upon the uncircumcised heathen. **4. And that**—i.e., What I did concerning Titus (viz., by not permitting him to be circumcised) was not from contempt of circumcision, but "on account of the false brethren" (Acts 15:1, 24) who, had I yielded to the demand for his being circumcised, would have perverted the case into a proof that I deemed circumcision necessary. **unawares**—"in an underhand manner brought in." **privily**—stealthily. **to spy out**—as foes in the guise of friends, wishing to destroy and rob us of—**our liberty**—from the yoke of the ceremonial law. If they had found that we circumcised Titus through fear of the apostles, they would have made that a ground for insisting on imposing the legal yoke on the Gentiles. **bring us into bondage**—The *Greek* future implies the *certainty* and *continuance* of the bondage as the result. **5.** *Greek,* "To whom not even for an hour did we yield by subjection." ALFORD renders the *Greek* article, "*with* THE subjection required of us." The sense rather is, We would willingly have yielded for *love* [BENGEL] (if no principle was at issue), but not in the way of *subjection,* where "the truth of the Gospel" (vs. 14; Col. 1:5) was at stake (viz., the fundamental truth of justification by faith only, without the works of the law, contrasted with another Gospel, ch. 1:6). Truth precise, unaccommodating, abandons nothing that belongs to itself, admits nothing that is inconsistent with it [BENGEL]. **might continue with you**—Gentiles. We defended for your sakes your true faith and liberties, which *you* are now renouncing. **6.** *Greek,* "From those who . . . ." He meant to complete the sentence with "I derived no special advantage"; but he alters it into "they . . . added nothing to me." **accepteth** —so as to show any partiality; "respecteth no man's person" (Eph. 6:9). **seemed to be somewhat**—i.e., not that they *seemed* to be what they *were not,* but "*were reputed as persons of some consequence*"; not insinuating a doubt but that they were justly so reputed. **in conference added**—or "imparted"; the same *Greek* as in ch. 1:16, "I conferred not with flesh and blood." As I did not by conference impart to them aught at my conversion, so they now did not impart aught additional to me, above what I already knew. This proves to the Galatians his independence as an apostle. **7. contrariwise**—on the contrary. So far from *adding any* new light to ME, THEY gave in THEIR adhesion to the new path on which Barnabas and I, by independent revelation, had entered. So far from censuring, they gave a hearty approval to my independent course, viz., the innovation of preaching the Gospel without circumcision to the Gentiles. **when they saw**—from the effects which I showed them, were "wrought" (vs. 8; Acts 15:12). **was committed unto me**—*Greek,* "I was entrusted with . . . , as Peter was with . . . . **gospel of the uncircumcision**—i.e., of the Gentiles, who were to be converted without circumcision being required. **circumcision . . . unto Peter**—Peter had originally opened the door to the Gentiles (Acts 10 and 15:7). But in the ultimate apportionment of the spheres of labor, the Jews were assigned to him (cf. I Pet. 1:1). So Paul on the other hand wrote to the Hebrews (cf. also Col. 4:11), though his main work was among the Gentiles. The non-mention of Peter in the list of names, presciently through the Spirit, given in Romans 16, shows that

Peter's residence at Rome, much more primacy, was *then* unknown. The same is palpable from the sphere here assigned to him. **8. he**—God (I Cor. 12:6). **wrought effectually**—i.e., made the preached word efficacious to conversion, not only by sensible miracles, but by the secret mighty power of the Holy Ghost. **in Peter**—ELLICOTT and others, translate, "*For* Peter." GROTIUS translates as *English Version.* **to**—with a view to. **was mighty**—Translate as before, the *Greek* being the same, "wrought effectually." **in me**—"for (or 'in') me *also.*" **9. James**—placed first in the oldest MSS., even before Peter, as being bishop of Jerusalem, and so presiding at the council (Acts 15). He was called "the Just," from his strict adherence to the law, and so was especially popular among the Jewish party though he did not fall into their extremes; whereas Peter was somewhat estranged from them through his intercourse with the Gentile Christians. To each apostle was assigned the sphere best suited to his temperament: to James, who was tenacious of the law, the Jerusalem Jews; to Peter, who had opened the door to the Gentiles but who was Judaically disposed, the Jews of the dispersion; to Paul, who, by the miraculous and overwhelming suddenness of his conversion, had the whole current of his early Jewish prejudices turned into an utterly opposite direction, the Gentiles. Not separately and individually, but collectively the apostles together represented Christ, the One Head, in the apostleship. The twelve foundation stones of various colors are joined together to the one great foundation stone on which they rest (I Cor. 3:11; Rev. 21: 14, 19, 20). John had got an intimation in Jesus' lifetime of the admission of the Gentiles (John 12: 20-24). **seemed**—i.e., *were reputed to be* (Note, vss. 2, 6) **pillars,** i.e., weighty supporters of the Church (cf. Prov. 9:1; Rev. 3:12). **perceived the grace . . . given unto me**—(II Pet. 3:15). **gave to me and Barnabas the right hands of fellowship**— recognizing me as a *colleague* in the apostleship, and that the Gospel I preached by special revelation to the Gentiles was the same as theirs. Cf. the phrase, Lamentations 5:6; Ezekiel 17:18. **heathen** —the Gentiles. **10. remember the poor**—of the *Jewish* Christians in Judea, then distressed. Paul and Barnabas had already done so (Acts 11:23-30). **the same**—the very thing. **I . . . was forward**—or "zealous" (Acts 24:17; Rom. 15:25; I Cor. 16:1; II Cor. 8 and 9). Paul was zealous for good works, while denying justification by them. **11. Peter**— "Cephas" in the oldest MSS. Paul's withstanding Peter is the strongest proof that the former gives of the independence of his apostleship in relation to the other apostles, and upsets the Romish doctrine of Peter's supremacy. The apostles were not always inspired; but were so always in *writing* the Scriptures. If then the inspired men who *wrote* them were not invariably at other times infallible, much less were the uninspired men who kept them. The Christian fathers may be trusted generally as witnesses to facts, but not implicitly followed in matters of opinion. **come to Antioch**—then the citadel of the Gentile Church: where first the Gospel was preached to *idolatrous Gentiles,* and where the name "Christians" was first given (Acts 11:20, 26), and where Peter is said to have been subsequently bishop. The question at Antioch was not whether the Gentiles were admissible to the Christian covenant without becoming circumcised—that was the question settled at the Jerusalem council just before—but whether the Gentile Christians were to be admitted to *social intercourse with the Jewish*

Christians without conforming to the Jewish institution. The Judaizers, soon after the council had passed the resolutions recognizing the equal rights of the Gentile Christians, repaired to Antioch, the scene of the gathering in of the Gentiles (Acts 11: 20-26), to witness, what to Jews would look so extraordinary, the receiving of men to communion of the Church without circumcision. Regarding the proceeding with prejudice, they explained away the force of the Jerusalem decision; and probably also desired to watch whether the *Jewish* Christians among the Gentiles violated the law, which that decision did not verbally sanction *them* in doing, though giving the Gentiles latitude (Acts 15:19). **to be blamed**—rather, "(self)-condemned"; his act at one time condemning his contrary acting at another time. **2. certain**—men: perhaps James' view (in which he was not infallible, any more than Peter) was that the Jewish converts were still to observe Jewish ordinances, from which he had decided with the council the *Gentiles* should be free (Acts 15:19). NEANDER, however, may be right in thinking these self-styled delegates from James were not really from him. Acts 15:24 favors this. "Certain from James," may mean merely that they came from the Church at Jerusalem under James' bishopric. Still James' leanings were to legalism, and this gave him his influence with the Jewish party (Acts 21:18-26). **eat with ... Gentiles**—as in Acts 10:10-20, 48, according to the command of the vision (Acts 11:3-17). Yet after all, this same Peter, through fear of man (Prov. 29:25), was faithless to his own so distinctly avowed principles (Acts 15:7-11). We recognize the same old nature in him as led him, after faithfully witnessing for Christ, yet for a brief space, to deny Him. "Ever the first to recognize, and the first to draw back from great truths" [ALFORD]. An undesigned coincidence between the Gospels and the Epistle in the consistency of character as portrayed in both. It is beautiful to see how earthly misunderstandings of Christians are lost in Christ. For in II Peter 3:15, Peter praises the very Epistles of Paul which he knew contained his own condemnation. Though apart from one another and differing in characteristics, the two apostles were one in Christ. **withdrew**—*Greek*, "*began* to withdraw...." This implies a *gradual drawing back;* "separated," *entire severance.* **13. the other**—*Greek,* "the rest." **Jews**—Jewish Christians. **dissembled likewise**—*Greek*, "joined in hypocrisy," viz., in living as though the law were necessary to justification, through fear of man, though they knew from God their Christian liberty of eating with Gentiles, and had availed themselves of it already (Acts 11:2-17). The case was distinct from that in I Corinthians chs. 8-10; Romans 14. It was not a question of liberty, and of bearing with others' infirmities, but one affecting the essence of the Gospel, whether the Gentiles are to be virtually "compelled to live as do the Jews," in order to be justified (vs. 14). **Barnabas also**—"Even Barnabas": one least likely to be led into such an error, being with Paul in first preaching to the idolatrous Gentiles: showing the power of bad example and numbers. In Antioch, the capital of Gentile Christianity and the central point of Christian missions, the controversy first arose, and in the same spot it now broke out afresh; and here Paul had first to encounter the party that afterwards persecuted him in every scene of his labors (Acts 15:30-35). **14. walked not uprightly**—lit., "straight": "were not walking with straightforward steps." Cf. ch. 6:16. **truth of the gospel**—which teaches that justification

by legal works and observances is inconsistent with redemption by Christ. Paul alone here maintained the truth against Judaism, as afterwards against heathenism (II Tim. 4:16, 17). **Peter**—"Cephas" in the oldest MSS. **before ... all**—(I Tim. 5:20). **If thou ...**—"If thou, although being a Jew (and therefore one who might seem to be more bound to the law than the Gentiles), livest (habitually, without scruple and from conviction, Acts 15:10, 11) as a Gentile (freely eating of every food, and living in other respects also as if legal ordinances in no way justify, vs. 12), and not as a Jew, *how* (so the oldest MSS. read, for "why") is it that thou art compelling (virtually, by thine example) the Gentiles to live as do the Jews?" (lit., *to Judaize,* i.e., to keep the ceremonial customs of the Jews: What had been formerly obedience to the law, is now mere *Judaism*). The high authority of Peter would constrain the Gentile Christians to regard Judaizing as necessary to all, since Jewish Christians could not consort with Gentile converts in communion without it. **15, 16.** Connect these verses together, and read with most of the oldest MSS. "But" in the beginning of vs. 16: "We (I and thou, Peter) by nature (not by proselytism), Jews, and not sinners as (Jewish language termed the Gentiles) from among the Gentiles, YET (lit., BUT) knowing that ... even we (resuming the 'we' of vs. 15, 'we also,' as well as the Gentile sinners; casting away trust in the law), have believed ...." **not justified by the works of the law**—as the GROUND of justification. "The works of the law" are those which have the law for their object—which are wrought to fulfil the law [ALFORD]. **but by**—Translate, "But only (in no other way save) *through* faith *in* Jesus Christ," as the MEAN and instrument of justification. **Jesus Christ**—In the second case, read with the oldest MSS., "Christ Jesus," the *Messiahship* coming into prominence in the case of *Jewish* believers, as "Jesus" does in the first case, referring to the general proposition. **justified by the faith of Christ** —i.e., by Christ, the object of faith, as the ground of our justification. **for by the works of the law shall no flesh be justified**—He rests his argument on this as an axiom in theology, referring to Psalm 143:2, "Moses and Jesus Christ; The law and the promise; Doing and believing; Works and faith; Wages and the gift; The curse and the blessing—are represented as diametrically opposed" [BENGEL]. The moral law is, in respect to justification, *more legal* than the ceremonial, which was an elementary and preliminary Gospel: So "Sinai" (ch. 4:24), which is more famed for the Decalogue than for the ceremonial law, is made pre-eminently the type of legal bondage. Thus, justification by the law, whether the moral or ceremonial, is excluded (Rom. 3:20). **17.** *Greek,* "But if, seeking to be justified IN (i.e., *in* believing *union with*) Christ (who has in the Gospel theory fulfilled the law for us), we (you and I) ourselves also *were* found (in *your* and *my former* communion with Gentiles) sinners (such as from the Jewish standpoint that now we resume, we should be regarded, since we have cast aside the law, thus having put ourselves in the same category as the Gentiles, who, being without the law, are, in the Jewish view, 'sinners," vs. 15), is therefore Christ, the minister of sin?" (Are we to admit the conclusion, in this case inevitable, that Christ having failed to justify us by faith, so has become to us the minister of sin, by putting us in the position of "sinners," as the Judaic theory, if correct, would make us, along with all others who are "without the law," Romans 2:14; I Corinthians 9:21; and with whom, by eating with them, we have identified ourselves?) The Christian mind revolts from so shocking a conclusion, and so, from the theory which would result in it. The whole sin lies, not with Christ, but with him who would necessitate such a blasphemous inference. But his false theory. though *"seeking"* from Christ, we have not "found" salvation (in contradiction to Christ's own words, Matt. 7:7), but "have been ourselves also (like the Gentiles) *found"* to be "sinners," by having entered into communion with Gentiles (vs. 12). **18.** *Greek,* "For if the things which I overthrew (by the faith of Christ), those very things I build up again (viz., legal righteousness, by subjecting myself to the law), I prove myself (lit., 'I commend myself') a transgressor." Instead of commending yourself as you sought to do (vs. 12, end), you merely commend yourself as a transgressor. The "I" is intended by Paul for *Peter* to take to himself, as it is *his* case, not Paul's own, that is described. A "transgressor" is another word for "sinner" (in vs. 17), for "sin is the *transgression* of the law." You, Peter, by now asserting the law to be obligatory, are proving yourself a "sinner," or "transgressor," in your having set it aside by living as the Gentiles, and with them. Thus you are debarred by transgression from justification by the law, and you debar yourself from justification by Christ, since in your theory He becomes a minister of sin. **19.** Here Paul seems to pass from his *exact words* to Peter, to the *general purport* of his argument on the question. However, his direct address to the Galatians seems not to be resumed till ch. 3:1, "O foolish Galatians...." **For**—But I am not a "transgressor" by forsaking the law. "For...." Proving his indignant denial of the consequence that "Christ is the minister of sin" (vs. 17), and of the premises from which it would follow. Christ, so far from being the minister of sin and death, is the establisher of righteousness and life. I am entirely in Him [BENGEL]. **I**—here emphatical. *Paul himself,* not *Peter,* as in the "I" (vs. 18). **through the law**—which was my "schoolmaster to bring me to Christ" (ch. 3:24); both by its terrors (ch. 3:13; Rom. 3:20) driving me to Christ, as the refuge from God's wrath against sin, and, when spiritually understood, teaching that itself is not permanent, but must give place to Christ, whom it prefigures as its scope and end (Rom. 10:4); and drawing me to Him by its promises (in the prophecies which form part of the Old Testament law) of a better righteousness, and of God's law written in the heart (Deut. 18:15-19; Jer. 31:33; Acts 10:43). **am dead to the law**—lit., "I died to the law," and so *am* dead to it, i.e., am passed from under its power, in respect to non-justification or condemnation (Col. 2:20; Rom. 6:14; 7:4, 6); just as a woman, once married and bound to a husband, ceases to be so bound to him when death interposes, and may be lawfully married to another husband. So by believing union to Christ in His death, we, being considered dead with Him, are severed from the law's past power over us (cf. ch. 6:14; I Cor. 7:39; Rom. 6:6-11; I Pet. 2:24). **live unto God**—(Rom. 6:11; II Cor. 5:15; I Pet. 4:1, 2). **20. I am crucified**—lit., "I have been crucified with Christ." This more particularizes the foregoing. "I am dead" (vs. 19; Phil. 3:10). **nevertheless I live; yet not I**—*Greek,* "nevertheless I live, no longer (indeed) I." Though crucified I live; (and this) no longer that old man such as I once was (cf. Rom. 7:17). No longer Saul the Jew (ch. 5:24; Col. 3:11, but "another man"; cf. I Sam. 10:6). ELLICOTT and others translate, "*And* it is no longer I that live, but Christ that

liveth in me." But the plain antithesis between "crucified" and "live," requires the translation, "nevertheless." **the life which I now live**—as contrasted with my life before conversion. **in the flesh** —My life seems to be a mere animal life "in the flesh," but this is not my true life; "it is but the mask of life under which lives another, viz., Christ, who is my true life" [LUTHER]. **I live by the faith ...**— *Greek,* "IN faith (viz.), that of (i.e., which rests on) the Son of God." "In faith," answers by contrast to "in the flesh." *Faith,* not *the flesh,* is the real element in which I live. The phrase, "the Son of God," reminds us that His Divine Sonship is the source of His life-giving power. **loved me**—His eternal gratuitous **love** is the link that unites me to the Son of God, and His "giving Himself for me," is the strongest proof of that love. **21. I do not frustrate the grace of God**—I do not *make it void,* as thou, Peter, art doing by Judaizing. **for**—justifying the strong expression "frustrate," or "make void." **is dead in vain**—*Greek,* "Christ died needlessly," or "without just cause." Christ's having died, shows that the law has no power to justify us; for if the law can justify or make us righteous, the death of Christ is superfluous [CHRYSOSTOM].

CHAPTER 3

Vss. 1-29. REPROOF OF THE GALATIANS FOR ABANDONING FAITH FOR LEGALISM. JUSTIFICATION BY FAITH VINDICATED: THE LAW SHOWN TO BE SUBSEQUENT TO THE PROMISE: BELIEVERS ARE THE SPIRITUAL SEED OF ABRAHAM, WHO WAS JUSTIFIED BY FAITH. THE LAW WAS OUR SCHOOLMASTER TO BRING US TO CHRIST, THAT WE MIGHT BECOME CHILDREN OF GOD BY FAITH. **1. that ye should not obey the truth**—omitted in the oldest MSS. **bewitched**—fascinated you so that you have lost your wits. THEMISTIUS says the Galatians were naturally very acute in intellect. Hence, Paul wonders they could be so misled in this case. **you**— emphatical. "YOU, before whose eyes Jesus Christ hath been graphically set forth (lit., *in writing,* viz., by vivid *portraiture* in preaching) among you, crucified" (so the sense and *Greek* order require rather than *English Version*). As Christ was "crucified," so ye ought to have been by faith *"crucified"* with Christ," and so "dead to the law" (ch. 2:19, 20). Reference to the "eyes" is appropriate, as *fascination* was supposed to be exercised through the eyes. The sight of Christ crucified ought to have been enough to counteract all fascination. **2.** "Was it by the works of the law that ye received the Spirit (manifested by outward miracles, vs. 5; Mark 16:17; Heb. 2:4; and by spiritual graces, vs. 14; Gal. 4:5, 6; Eph. 1:13), or by the hearing of faith?" The "only" implies, "I desire, omitting other arguments, to rest the question on *this alone";* I who was your *teacher,* desire now to "learn" this one thing from you. The epithet "Holy" is not prefixed to "Spirit" because that epithet is a joyous one, whereas this Epistle is stern and reproving [BENGEL]. **hearing of faith**—Faith consists not in *working,* but in *receiving* (Rom. 10:16, 17). **3. begun**—the Christian life (Phil. 1:6). **in the Spirit**—Not merely was Christ crucified "graphically set forth" in my preaching, but also "the Spirit" confirmed the word preached, by imparting His spiritual gifts. "Having thus begun" with the receiving His *spiritual* gifts, "are ye now *being* made perfect" (so the *Greek*), i.e., are ye *seeking* to be made perfect with *fleshly* ordinances of the law? [ESTIUS.] Cf. Romans 2:28; Philippians 3:3; Hebrews 9:10. Having begun in the Spirit, i.e., the Holy Spirit ruling your spiritual life as its "essence and active principle" [ELLICOTT], in contrast to "the flesh," the element in which the law works [ALFORD]. Having begun your Christianity in the Spirit, i.e., in the divine life that proceeds from faith, are ye seeking after something higher still (the perfecting of your Christianity) in the sensuous and the earthly, which cannot possibly elevate the inner life of the Spirit, viz., outward ceremonies? [NEANDER.] No doubt the Galatians thought that they were going more deeply into the Spirit; for the flesh may be easily mistaken for the Spirit, even by those who have made progress, unless they continue to maintain a pure faith [BENGEL]. **4. Have ye suffered so many things—** viz., persecution from Jews and from unbelieving fellow countrymen, incited by the Jews, at the time of your conversion. **in vain**—*fruitlessly, needlessly,* since ye might have avoided them by professing Judaism [GROTIUS]. Or, shall ye, by falling from grace, lose the reward promised for all your sufferings, so that they shall be "in vain" (ch. 4:11; I Cor. 15:2, 17-19, 29-32; II Thess. 1:5-7; II John 8)? **yet** rather, "If it be *really* (or 'indeed') in vain" [ELLICOTT]. "If, as it must be, what I have said, 'in vain,' is really the fact" [ALFORD]. I prefer understanding it as a mitigation of the preceding words. I hope better things of you, for I trust you will return from legalism to grace; if *so,* as I confidently expect, you will not have "suffered so many things in vain" [ESTIUS]. For "God has given you the Spirit and has wrought mighty works among you" (vs. 5; Heb. 10:32-36) [BENGEL]. **5. He ... that ministereth**—or "supplieth," God (II Cor. 9:10). He who *supplied and supplies* to you the Spirit *still,* to the present time. These miracles do not prove grace to be in the heart (Mark 9:38, 39). He speaks of these miracles as a matter of *unquestioned notoriety* among those addressed; an undesigned proof of their genuineness (cf. I Cor. 12). **worketh miracles among you**—rather, "IN you," as ch. 2:8; Matthew 14:2; Ephesians 2:2; Philippians 2:13; at your conversion and since [ALFORD]. **doeth he it by the works of the law**—i.e., as a consequence *resulting from* (so the *Greek*) the works of the law (cf. vs. 2). This cannot be because the law was then unknown to you when you received those gifts of the Spirit. **6.** The answer to the question in vs. 5 is here taken for granted, *It was by the hearing of faith:* following this up, he says, "Even as Abraham believed ..." (Gen. 15:4-6; Rom. 4:3). God supplies unto you the Spirit as the result of faith, not works, just as Abraham obtained justification by faith, not by works (vss. 6, 8, 16; ch. 4:22, 26, 28). Where justification is, there the Spirit is, so that if the former comes *by faith,* the latter must also. **7. they which are of faith**—as the source and starting point of their spiritual life. The same phrase is in the *Greek* of Romans 3:26. **the same**—*these, and these alone,* to the exclusion of all the other descendants of Abraham. **children**—*Greek,* "sons" (vs. 29). **8. And**—*Greek,* "Moreover." **foreseeing** —One great excellency of Scripture is, that in it all points liable ever to be controverted, are, with prescient wisdom, decided in the most appropriate language. **would justify**—rather, "justifieth." Present indicative. It is now, and at all times, God's *one* way of justification. **the heathen**—rather, "the Gentiles"; or "the nations," as the same *Greek* is translated at the end of the verse. God justifieth the *Jews,* too, "by faith, not by works." But he specifies *the Gentiles* in particular here, as

it was *their* case that was in question, the Galatians being Gentiles. **preached before the gospel**—"announced beforehand the Gospel." For the "promise" was substantially the Gospel by anticipation. Cf. John 8:56; Hebrews 4:2. A proof that "the old fathers did not look only for transitory promises" (Article VII, Church of England). Thus the Gospel, in its essential germ, is older than the law though the full development of the former is subsequent to the latter. **In thee**—not "in thy seed," which is a point not here raised; but strictly "in thee," as followers of thy faith, it having first shown the way to justification before God [ALFORD]; or "in thee," as Father of the promised seed, viz., Christ (vs. 16), who is the Object of faith (Gen. 22:18; Ps. 72:17), and imitating thy faith (see *Note,* vs. 9). **all nations**—or as above, "all *the Gentiles*" (Gen. 12:3; 18:18; 22:18). **be blessed**—an act of grace, not something earned by works. The blessing of justification was to Abraham by faith in the promise, not by works. So to those who follow Abraham, the father of the faithful, the blessing, i.e., justification, comes purely by faith in Him who is the subject of the promise. **9. they**—and they alone. **of faith**—*Note,* vs. 7, beginning. **with** — together with. **faithful**—implying what it is in which they are "blessed together with him," viz., faith, the prominent feature of his character, and of which the result to all who like him have it, is justification. **10.** Confirmation of vs. 9. They who depend on the works of the law cannot share the blessing, for they are under the curse "written," Deuteronomy 27:26, LXX. PERFECT *obedience* is required by the words, "in all things." CONTINUAL *obedience* by the word, "continueth." No man renders this obedience (cf. Rom. 3:19, 20). It is observable, Paul quotes Scripture to the Jews who were conversant with it, as in Epistle to the Hebrews, as *said* or *spoken;* but to the Gentiles, as *written.* So Matthew, writing for Jews, quotes it as *said,* or *spoken;* Mark and Luke, writing for Gentiles, as *written* (Matt. 1:22; Mark 1:2; Luke 2: 22, 23) [TOWNSON]. **11. by the law**—*Greek,* "IN the law." Both *in* and *by* are included. The syllogism in this verse and vs. 12, is, according to Scripture, "The just shall live by faith." But the law is not of faith, but of doing, or works (i.e., does not make faith, but works, the conditional ground of justifying). Therefore "in," or "by the law, no man is justified before God" (whatever the case may be *before men,* Rom. 4:2),—not even if he could, which he cannot, keep the law, because the Scripture element and conditional mean of justification is *faith.* **The just shall live by faith**—(Rom. 1:17; Hab. 2:4). Not as BENGEL and ALFORD, "He who is just by faith shall live." The *Greek* supports *English Version.* Also the contrast is between "live *by faith*" (viz., as the ground and source of his justification), and "live *in them,*" viz., in his doings or works (vs. 12), as the *conditional element wherein* he is justified. **12. doeth**—Many depended on the law although they did not keep it; but without doing, saith Paul, it is of no use to them (Rom. 2:13, 17, 23; 10: 5). **13.** Abrupt exclamation, as he breaks away impatiently *from* those who would involve us again in the curse of the *law,* by seeking justification in it, *to* "Christ," who "has redeemed us from its curse." The "us" refers primarily to the JEWS, to whom the law principally appertained, in contrast to "the Gentiles" (vs. 14; cf. ch. 4:3, 4). But it is not *restricted* solely to the Jews, as ALFORD thinks; for these are the representative people of the world at large, and their "law" is the embodiment of what

God requires of the whole world. The curse of its non-fulfilment affects the Gentiles through the Jews; for the law represents that righteousness which God requires of all, and which, since the Jews failed to fulfil, the Gentiles are equally unable to fulfil. Verse 10, "As many as are of the works of the law, are under the curse," refers plainly, not to *the Jews only*, but to all, even Gentiles (as the Galatians), who seek justification by the law. The Jews' law represents the universal law which condemned the Gentiles, though with less clear consciousness on their part (Rom. 2). The revelation of God's "wrath" by the law of conscience, in some degree prepared the Gentiles for appreciating redemption through Christ when revealed. The curse had to be removed from off the heathen, too, as well as the Jews, in order that the blessing, through Abraham, might flow to them. Accordingly, the "we," in "that *we* might receive the promise of the Spirit," plainly refers to both Jews and Gentiles. **redeemed us**—*bought us off* from our former bondage (ch. 4:5), and "from the curse" under which all lie who trust to the law and the works of the law for justification. The Gentile Galatians, by putting themselves under the law, were involving themselves in the curse from which Christ has redeemed the Jews primarily, and through them the Gentiles. The ransom price He paid was His own precious blood (I Pet. 1:18, 19; cf. Matt. 20:28; Acts 20:28; I Cor. 6:20; 7:23; I Tim. 2:6; II Peter 2:1; Rev. 5:9). **being made**—*Greek*, "having become." **a curse for us**—Having become what we were, *in our behalf*, "a curse," that we might cease to be a curse. Not merely *accursed* (in the concrete), but *a curse* in the abstract, *bearing the universal curse of the whole human race*. So II Corinthians 5:21, "Sin for us," not *sinful*, but bearing the whole sin of our race, regarded as *one* vast aggregate of sin. See *Note* there. "Anathema" means "set apart to God," to His glory, but to the person's own destruction. "*Curse*," an execration. **written**—Deuteronomy 21:23. Christ's bearing the *particular* curse of hanging on the tree, is a sample of the *general* curse which He representatively bore. Not that the Jews put to death malefactors by hanging; but *after* having put them to death otherwise, in order to brand them with peculiar ignominy, they *hung* the bodies on a tree, and such malefactors were accursed by the law (cf. Acts 5:30; 10:39). God's providence ordered it so that to fulfil the prophecy of the curse and other prophecies, Jesus should be crucified, and so *hang* on the tree, though that death was not a Jewish mode of execution. The Jews accordingly, in contempt, call Him "the *hanged* one," *Tolvi*, and Christians, "worshippers of the hanged one"; and make it their great objection that He died the accursed death [TRYPHO, in *Justin Martyr*, p. 249; I Pet. 2:24]. Hung between heaven and earth as though unworthy of either! **14.** The intent of "Christ becoming a curse for us"; "To the end that upon the Gentiles the blessing of Abraham (i.e., *promised to* Abraham, viz., justification by faith) might come in Christ Jesus" (cf. vs. 8). **that we might receive the promise of the Spirit**—the promised Spirit (Joel 2: 28, 29; Luke 24:49). This clause follows not the clause immediately preceding (for *our receiving the Spirit* is not the result of the *blessing of Abraham coming on the Gentiles*), but "Christ hath redeemed us . . ." **through faith**—not by works. Here he resumes the thought in vs. 2. "The Spirit from without, kindles within us some spark of faith whereby we lay hold of Christ, and even of the

Spirit Himself, that He may dwell within us" [FLACIUS]. **15. I speak after the manner of men**— I take an illustration from a merely human transaction of everyday occurrence. **but a man's covenant**—whose purpose it is far less important to maintain. **if it be confirmed**—when once it hath been ratified. **no man disannulleth**—"none setteth aside," not even the author himself, much less any second party. None does so who acts in common equity. Much less would the righteous God do so. *The law* is here, by personification, regarded as a second person, distinct from, and subsequent to, *the promise of God*. *The promise* is everlasting, and more peculiarly belongs to God. *The law* is regarded as something extraneous, afterwards introduced, exceptional and temporary (vss. 17-19, 21-24). **addeth**—None addeth new conditions "making" the covenant "of none effect" (vs. 17). So legal Judaism could make no alteration in the fundamental relation between God and man, already established by the promises to Abraham; it could not add as a new condition the observance of the law, in which case the fulfilment of the promise would be attached to a condition impossible for man to perform. The "covenant" here is one of free grace, a *promise* afterwards carried into effect in the Gospel. **16.** This verse is parenthetical. The covenant of promise was not "spoken" (so *Greek* for "made") to Abraham alone, but "to Abraham and his seed"; to the latter especially; and this means Christ (and that which is inseparable from Him, the *literal Israel*, and the *spiritual*, His body, the Church). Christ not having come when the law was given, the covenant could not have been then fulfilled, but awaited the coming of Him, the Seed, to whom it was spoken. **promises**— plural, because the same promise was often repeated (Gen. 12:3, 7; 15:5, 18; 17:7; 22:18), and because it involved many things; earthly blessings to the literal children of Abraham in Canaan, and spiritual and heavenly blessings to his spiritual children; but both promised to Christ, "the Seed" and representative Head of the literal and spiritual Israel alike. In the spiritual seed there is no distinction of Jew or Greek; but to the literal seed, the promises still in part remain to be fulfilled (Rom. 11:26). The covenant was not made with "many" seeds (which if there had been, a pretext might exist for supposing there was one seed before the law, another under the law; and that those sprung from one seed, say the Jewish, are admitted on different terms, and with a higher degree of acceptability, than those sprung from the Gentile seed), but with the one seed; therefore, the promise that in Him "all the families of the earth shall be blessed" (Gen. 12:3), joins in this one Seed, Christ, Jew and Gentile, as fellow heirs on the same terms of acceptability, viz., by grace through faith (Rom. 4:13); not to some by promise, to others by the law, but to all alike, circumcised and uncircumcised, constituting but one seed in Christ (Rom. 4:16). The law, on the other hand, contemplates the Jews and Gentiles as distinct seeds. God makes a covenant, but it is one of promise; whereas the law is a covenant of works. Whereas the law brings in a mediator, a third party (vss. 19, 20), God makes His covenant of promise with the one seed, Christ (Gen. 17:7), and embraces others only as they are identified with, and represented by, Christ. **one ... Christ**— not in the exclusive sense, the man Christ *Jesus*, but "Christ" (*Jesus* is not added, which would limit the meaning), including *His people* who are *part of Himself*, the Second Adam, and Head of redeemed humanity. Verses 28, 29 prove this, "Ye are all ONE in Christ Jesus" (Jesus is added here as the person is indicated). "And *if* ye be Christ's, ye are Abraham's SEED, heirs according to *the promise.*" **17. this I say**—"this is what I mean," by what I said in vs. 15. **confirmed ... of God**—"*ratified by* God" (vs. 15). **in Christ**—rather, "unto Christ" (cf. vs. 16). However, *Vulgate* and the old *Italian* versions translate as *English Version.* But the oldest MSS. omit the words altogether. **the law which was** —*Greek,* "which came into existence 430 years after" (Exod. 12:40, 41). He does not, as in the case of "the covenant," add "*enacted by God*" (John 1:17). The dispensation of "the promise" began with the call of Abraham from Ur into Canaan, and ended on the last night of his grandson Jacob's sojourn in Canaan, the *land of promise.* The dispensation of the law, which engenders bondage, was beginning to draw on from the time of his entrance into Egypt, the land of bondage. It was to Christ in him, as in his grandfather Abraham, and his father Isaac, not to him or them as persons, the promise was spoken. On the day following the last repetition of the promise orally (Gen. 46: 1-6), at Beershaba, Israel passed into Egypt. It is from the end, not from the beginning of the dispensation of promise, that the interval of 430 years between it and the law is to be counted. At Beersheba, after the covenant with Abimelech, Abraham called on the everlasting God, and the well was confirmed to him and his seed as an everlasting possession. Here God appeared to Isaac. Here Jacob received the promise of the blessing, for which God had called Abraham out of Ur, repeated for the last time, on the last night of his sojourn in the land of promise. **cannot**—*Greek,* "doth not disannul." **make ... of none effect**—The promise would become so, if the power of conferring the inheritance be transferred from it to the law (Rom. 4:14). **18. the inheritance**—all the blessings to be inherited by Abraham's literal and spiritual children, according to the promise made to him and to his Seed, Christ, justification and glorification (ch. 4:7; Rom. 8:17; I Cor. 6:9). **but God ...**—The *Greek* order requires rather, "But to Abraham it was by promise that God hath given it." The conclusion is, *Therefore the inheritance is not of, or from, the law* (Rom. 4:14). **19.** "Wherefore then serveth the law?" as it is of no avail for justification, is it either useless, or contrary to the covenant of God? [CALVIN.] **added**—to the original covenant of promise. This is not inconsistent with vs. 15, "No man addeth thereto"; for there the kind of *addition* meant, and therefore denied, is one that would add *new conditions,* inconsistent with the grace of the covenant of promise. The law, though misunderstood by the Judaizers as doing so, was really added for a different purpose, viz., "because of (or as the *Greek,* 'for the sake of') the transgressions," i.e., to bring out into clearer view *the transgressions* of it (Rom. 7:7-9); to make men more fully conscious of their *sins,* by being perceived as *transgressions of the law,* and so to make them long for the promised Saviour. This accords with vss. 23, 24; Romans 4:15. The meaning can hardly be "*to check* transgressions," for the law rather stimulates the corrupt heart to disobey it (Rom. 5:20; 7:13). **till the seed**—*during the period up to the time when the* seed came. The law was a preparatory dispensation for the Jewish nation (Rom. 5:20; *Greek,* "the law came in *additionally* and *incidentally*"), intervening between the promise and its fulfilment in Christ. **come**—(Cf.

"faith *came,*" vs. 23). **the promise**—(Rom. 4:21). **ordained**—*Greek,* "constituted" or "disposed." **by angels**—as the *instrumental enactors* of the law [ALFORD] God delegated the law to angels as something rather alien to Him and severe (Acts 7:53; Heb. 2:2, 3; cf. Deut. 33:2, "He came with ten thousands of saints," i.e., angels, Ps. 68:17). He reserved "the promise" to Himself and dispensed it according to His own goodness. **in the hand of a mediator**—viz., Moses. Deuteronomy 5:5, "I stood *between* the Lord and you": the very definition of a mediator. Hence the phrase often recurs, "By the hand of Moses." In the giving of the law, the "angels" were representatives of God; Moses, as mediator, represented the people. **20.** "Now a mediator cannot be of one (but must be of *two* parties whom he mediates between); but God is one" (not two: owing to His essential *unity* not admitting of an intervening party between Him and those to be blessed; but as the ONE Sovereign, His own representative, giving the blessing *directly* by *promise* to Abraham, and, in its fulfilment, to Christ, "the Seed," without new condition, and without a mediator such as the law had). The conclusion understood is, *Therefore a mediator cannot appertain to God;* and consequently, the law, with its inseparable appendage of a mediator, cannot be the normal way of dealing of God, the one, and unchangeable God, who dealt with Abraham by *direct* promise, as a sovereign, not as one forming a compact with another party, with conditions and a mediator attached thereto. God would bring man into immediate communion with Him, and not have man separated from Him by a mediator that keeps back from access, as Moses and the legal priesthood did (Exod. 19:12, 13, 17, 21-24; Heb. 12:19-24). The law that thus interposed a mediator and conditions between man and God, was an exceptional state limited to the Jews, and parenthetically preparatory to the Gospel, God's normal mode of dealing, as He dealt with Abraham, viz., *face to face directly;* by *promise* and *grace,* and not conditions; *to all nations united* by faith *in the one seed* (Eph. 2:14, 16, 18), and not to one people to the exclusion and severance from the ONE common Father, of all other nations. It is no objection to this view, that the Gospel, too, has a mediator (I Tim. 2:5). For Jesus is not a mediator separating the two parties in the covenant of promise or grace, as Moses did, but ONE in both nature and office with both *God* and *man* (cf. "God in Christ," vs. 17): representing the whole universal manhood (I Cor. 15:22, 45, 47), and also bearing in Him "all the fulness of the Godhead." Even His mediatorial office is to cease when its purpose of reconciling all things to God shall have been accomplished (I Cor. 15:24); and God's ONENESS (Zech. 14:9), as "all in all," shall be fully manifested. Cf. John 1:17, where the two mediators— Moses, the severing mediator of legal conditions, and Jesus, the uniting mediator of grace—are contrasted. The Jews began their worship by reciting the *Schemah,* opening thus, "Jehovah our God is ONE Jehovah"; which words their Rabbis (as JARCHIUS) interpret as teaching not only the unity of God, but the future *universality of His Kingdom* on earth (Zeph. 3:9). Paul (Rom. 3:30) infers the same truth from the ONENESS of God (cf. Eph. 4:4-6). He, as being One, unites all believers, without distinction, to Himself (vss. 8, 16, 28; Eph. 1:10; 2: 14; cf. Heb. 2:11) in direct communion. The unity of God involves the unity of the people of God, and also His dealing directly without intervention of a mediator. **21.** "Is the *law* (which involves a mediator) against the promises of God (which are without a mediator, and *rest on God* alone and immediately)? God forbid." **life**—The law, as an externally prescribed rule, can never internally impart spiritual life to men naturally dead in sin, and change the disposition. If the law had been a law capable of giving *life*, "verily (in very reality, and not in the mere fancy of legalists) righteousness would have been by the law" (for where life is, there righteousness, its *condition*, must also be). But the law does not *pretend* to give life, and therefore not righteousness; so there is no opposition between the law and the promise. Righteousness can only come through the promise to Abraham, and through its fulfilment in the Gospel of grace. **22. But**—as the law cannot give life or righteousness [ALFORD]. Or the "But" means, So far is *righteousness* from being of the law, that the *knowledge of sin* is rather what comes of the law [BENGEL]. **the scripture**—which began to be written after the time of the promise, at the time when the law was given. The *written* letter was needed so as PERMANENTLY to convict man of disobedience to God's command. Therefore he says, "the Scripture," not the "Law." Cf. vs. 8, "Scripture," for "the God of the Scripture." **concluded**—"shut up," under condemnation, as in a prison. Cf. Isaiah 24: 22, "As prisoners gathered in the pit and shut up in the prison." Beautifully contrasted with "the liberty wherewith Christ makes free," which follows, vss. 7, 9, 25, 26; ch. 5:1; Isaiah 61:1. **all**—Greek neuter, "the universe of things": the whole world, man, and all that appertains to him. **under sin**—(Rom. 3:9, 19; 11:32). **the promise**—*the inheritance promised* (vs. 18). **by faith of Jesus Christ**—i.e., which is by faith in Jesus Christ. **might be given**—The emphasis is on "given": that it might be a free *gift;* not something earned by the works of the law (Rom. 6:23). **to them that believe** —to them that have "the faith of (in) Jesus Christ" just spoken of. **23. faith**—viz., that just mentioned (vs. 22), of which Christ is the object. **kept**—Greek, "kept in ward": the effect of the "shutting up" (vs. 22; ch. 4:2; Rom. 7:6). **unto**—"with a view to the faith . . . ." We were, in a manner, morally forced to it, so that there remained to us no refuge but faith. Cf. the phrase, Psalm 78:50; *Margin*, 31:8. **which should afterwards . . .**—"which was afterwards to be revealed." **24.** *"So that* the law *hath been* (i.e., hath *turned out to be*) our schoolmaster (or "tutor," lit., "pedagogue": this term, among the Greeks, meant a faithful servant entrusted with the care of the boy from childhood to puberty, to keep him from evil, physical and moral, and accompany him to his amusements and studies) to guide us unto Christ," with whom we are no longer "shut up" in bondage, but are freemen. "Children" (lit., *infants*) need such *tutoring* (ch. 4:3). **might be**— rather, "that we *may* be justified by faith"; which we could not be till Christ, the object of faith, had come. Meanwhile the law, by outwardly checking the sinful propensity which was constantly giving fresh proof of its refractoriness—as thus the consciousness of the power of the sinful principle became more vivid, and hence the sense of need both of forgiveness of sin and freedom from its bondage was awakened—the law became a "schoolmaster to guide us unto Christ" [NEANDER]. The *moral* law shows us what we ought to do, and so we learn our inability to do it. In the *ceremonial* law we seek, by animal sacrifices, to answer for our not having done it, but find dead victims no satisfaction for the sins of living men, and that outward purifying will

not cleanse the soul; and that therefore we need an infinitely better Sacrifice, the antitype of all the legal sacrifices. Thus delivered up to the *judicial* law, we see how awful is the doom we deserve: thus the law at last leads us to Christ, with whom we find righteousness and peace. *"Sin, sin!* is the word heard again and again in the Old Testament. Had it not there for centuries rung in the ear, and fastened on the conscience, the joyful sound, 'grace for grace,' would not have been the watchword of the New Testament. This was the end of the whole system of sacrifices" [THOLUCK]. **25.** "But *now that* faith is come . . . ." Moses the lawgiver cannot bring us into the heavenly Canaan though he can bring us to the border of it. At that point he is superseded by Joshua, the type of Jesus, who leads the true Israel into their inheritance. The law leads us to Christ, and there its office ceases. **26. children**—Greek, "sons." **by**—Greek, "through faith." "Ye all" (Jews and Gentiles alike) are no longer *children* requiring a *tutor,* but SONS emancipated and walking at liberty. **27. baptized into Christ**—(Rom. 6:3). **have put on Christ**—Ye *did, in that very act* of being baptized into Christ, *put on,* or clothe yourselves with, Christ: so the *Greek* expresses. Christ is to you the *toga virilis* (the Roman garment of the full-grown man, assumed when ceasing to be a child) [BENGEL]. GATAKER defines a Christian, "One who has put on Christ." The argument is, By baptism ye have put on Christ; and therefore, He being the Son of God, ye become sons by adoption, by virtue of His Sonship by generation. This proves that baptism, *where it answers to its ideal,* is not a mere empty sign, but a means of spiritual transference from the state of legal condemnation to that of living union with Christ, and of sonship through Him in relation to God (Rom. 13: 14). Christ alone can, by baptizing with His Spirit, make the inward grace correspond to the outward sign. But as He promises the blessing in the faithful use of the means, the Church has rightly presumed, in charity, that such is the case, nothing appearing to the contrary. **28.** There is in this sonship by faith in Christ, no class privileged above another, as the Jews under the law had been above the Gentiles (Rom. 10:12; I Cor. 12:13; Col. 3:11). **bond nor free**—Christ alike belongs to both by faith; whence he puts "bond" *before* "free." Cf. *Notes,* I Cor. 7:21, 22; Eph. 6:8. **neither male nor female** —rather, as *Greek,* "there is *not* male *and* female." There is no distinction into male and female. Difference of sex makes no difference in Christian privileges. But under the law the male sex had great privileges. Males alone had in their body circumcision, the sign of the covenant (contrast *baptism* applied to male and female alike); they alone were capable of being kings and priests, whereas all of either sex are now "kings and priests unto God" (Rev. 1:6); they had prior right to inheritances. In the resurrection the relation of the sexes shall cease (Luke 20:35). **one**—Greek, "one man"; masculine, not neuter, viz., "one new man" in Christ (Eph. 2:15). **29. and heirs**—The oldest MSS. omit "and." Christ is "Abraham's seed" (vs. 16): ye are "one in Christ" (vs. 28), and one with Christ, as having "put on Christ" (vs. 27); therefore YE are "Abraham's seed," which is tantamount to saying (whence the "and" is omitted), ye are "heirs according to the *promise*" (not "by the *law*," vs. 18); for it was to Abraham's seed that the inheritance was promised (vs. 16). Thus he arrives at the same truth which he set out with (vs. 7). But one new "seed" of a righteous succession could be found.

One single faultless grain of human nature was found by God Himself, the source of a new and imperishable seed: "the seed" (Ps. 22:30) who receive from Him a new nature and name (Gen. 3:15; Isa. 53:10, 11; John 12:24). In Him the lineal descent from David becomes extinct. He died without posterity. But He lives and shall reign on David's throne. No one has a legal claim to sit upon it but Himself, He being the only living direct representative (Ezek. 21:27). His spiritual seed derive their birth from the travail of His soul, being born again of His word, which is the incorruptible seed (John 1:12; Rom. 9:8; I Peter 1:23).

CHAPTER 4

Vss. 1-31. The Same Subject Continued: Illustration Of Our Subjection to the Law Only till Christ Came, from the Subjection of an Heir to His Guardian till He Is of Age. Peter's Good will to the Galatians Should Lead Them to the Same Good will to Him as They Had at First Shown. Their Desire To Be under the Law Shown by the Allegory of Isaac and Ishmael to Be Inconsistent with Their Gospel Liberty. 1-7. The fact of God's sending His Son to redeem us who were under the law (vs. 4), and sending the Spirit of His Son into our hearts (vs. 6), confirms the conclusion (ch. 3:29) that we are "heirs according to the promise." the heir—(ch. 3:29). It is not, as in earthly inheritances, the death of the father, but our Father's sovereign will simply that makes us heirs. child—Greek, "one under age." differeth nothing . . .—i.e., has no more freedom than a slave (so the Greek for "servant" means). He is not at his own disposal. lord of all—by title and virtual ownership (cf. I Cor. 3:21, 22). 2. tutors and governors—rather, "guardians (of the person) and stewards" (of the property.) Answering to "the law was our schoolmaster" or "tutor" (ch. 3: 24). until the time appointed of the father—in His eternal purposes (Eph. 1:9-11). The Greek is a legal term, expressing a time defined by law, or testamentary disposition. 3. we—the Jews primarily, and inclusively the Gentiles also. For the "we" in vs. 5 plainly refers to both Jew and Gentile believers. The Jews in their bondage to the law of Moses, as the representative people of the world, include all mankind virtually amenable to God's law (Rom. 2: 14, 15; cf. ch. 3:13, 23, Notes). Even the Gentiles were under "bondage," and in a state of discipline suitable to nonage, till Christ came as the Emancipator. were in bondage—as "servants" (vs. 1). under the elements—or "rudiments"; rudimentary religion teaching of a non-Christian character: the elementary lessons of outward things (lit., "of the [outward] world"); such as the legal ordinances mentioned, vs. 10 (Col. 2:8, 20). Our childhood's lessons [Conybeare and Howson]. Lit., The letters of the alphabet (Heb. 5:12). 4. the fulness of the time—viz., "the time appointed by the Father" (vs. 2). Cf. Note, Ephesians 1:10; Luke 1:57; Acts 2:1; Ezekiel 5:2. "The Church has its own ages" [Bengel]. God does nothing prematurely, but, foreseeing the end from the beginning, waits till all is ripe for the execution of His purpose. Had Christ come directly after the fall, the enormity and deadly fruits of sin would not have been realized fully by man, so as to feel his desperate state and need of a Saviour. Sin was fully developed. Man's inability to save himself by obedience to the law, whether that

of Moses, or that of conscience, was completely manifested; all the prophecies of various ages found their common center in this particular time; and Providence, by various arrangements in the social and political, as well as the moral world, had fully prepared the way for the coming Redeemer. God often permits physical evil long before he teaches the remedy. The smallpox had for long committed its ravages before inoculation, and then vaccination, was discovered. It was essential to the honor of God's law to permit evil long before He revealed the full remedy. Cf. "the set time" (Ps. 102:13). was come—Greek, "came." sent forth—Greek, "sent forth out of heaven from Himself" [Alford and Bengel]. The same verb is used of the Father's sending forth the Spirit (vs. 6). So in Acts 7:12. Cf. with this verse, John 8:42; Isaiah 48:16. his—emphatical. "His own Son." Not by adoption, as we are (vs. 5); nor merely His Son by the anointing of the Spirit which God sends into the heart (vs. 6; John 1:18). made of a woman—"made" is used as in I Cor. 15:45, "The first man, Adam, was made a living soul," Greek, "made to be (born) of a woman." The expression implies a special interposition of God in His birth as man, viz., causing Him to be conceived by the Holy Ghost. So Estius. made under the law—"made to be under the law." Not merely as Grotius and Alford explain, "Born subject to the law as a Jew." But "made" by His Father's appointment, and His own free will, "subject to the law," to keep it all, ceremonial and moral, perfectly for us, as the Representative Man, and to suffer and exhaust the full penalty of our whole race's violation of it. This constitutes the significance of His circumcision, His being presented in the temple (Luke 2:21, 22, 27; cf. Matt. 5:17), and His baptism by John, when He said (Matt. 3:15), "Thus it becometh us to fulfil all righteousness." 5. To—Greek, "That He might redeem." them . . . under the law—primarily the Jews; but as these were the representative people of the world, the Gentiles, too, are included in the redemption (ch. 3:13). receive—The Greek implies the suitableness of the thing as long ago predestined by God. "Receive as something destined or due" (Luke 23:41; II John 8). Herein God makes of sons of men sons of God, inasmuch as God made of the Son of God the Son of man [St. Augustine on Ps. 52]. 6. because ye are sons . . .—The gift of the Spirit of prayer is the consequence of our adoption. The Gentile Galatians might think, as the Jews were under the law before their adoption, that so they, too, must first be under the law. Paul, by anticipation, meets this objection by saying, Ye are sons, therefore ye need not be as children (vs. 1) under the tutorship of the law, as being already in the free state of "sons" of God by faith in Christ (ch. 3:26), no longer in your nonage (as "children," vs. 1). The Spirit of God's only Begotten Son in your hearts, sent from, and leading you to cry to, the Father, attests your sonship by adoption: for the Spirit is the "earnest of your inheritance" (Rom. 8:15, 16; Eph. 1:13). "It is because ye are sons that God sent forth" (the Greek requires this translation, not "hath sent forth") into our (so the oldest MSS. read for "your," in English Version) hearts the Spirit of His son, crying, "Abba, Father" (John 1:12). As in vs. 5 he changed from "them," the third person, to "we," the first person, so here he changes from "ye," the second person, to "our," the first person: this he does to identify their case as Gentiles, with his own and that of his believing fellow countrymen, as Jews. In another point of view, though not the immediate one intended by the context, this verse expresses, "Because ye *are* sons (already in God's electing purpose of love), God sent forth the Spirit of His Son into your hearts . . .": God thus, by sending His Spirit in due time, actually conferring that sonship which He already regarded as a present reality ("are") because of His purpose, even before it was actually fulfilled. So Hebrews 2: 13, where "the children" are spoken of as existing in His purpose, before their actual existence. **the Spirit of his Son**—By faith ye are one with the Son, so that what is His is yours; His Sonship ensures your sonship; His Spirit ensures for you a share in the same. "If any man have not the Spirit of Christ, he is none of His" (Rom. 8:9). Moreover, as the Spirit of God proceeds from God the Father, so the Spirit of the Son proceeds from the Son: so that the Holy Ghost, as the Creed says, "proceedeth from the Father and the Son." The Father was not *begotten:* the Son is *begotten* of the Father; the Holy Ghost *proceeding* from the Father and the Son. **crying**—Here the SPIRIT is regarded as the *agent* in praying, and the believer as *His organ.* In Romans 8:15, "The Spirit of adoption" is said to be that whereby WE cry, "Abba, Father"; but in Romans 8:26, "The SPIRIT ITSELF maketh intercession for us with groanings which cannot be uttered." The believers' prayer is His prayer: hence arises its acceptability with God. **Abba, Father**—The Hebrew says, "Abba" (a *Hebrew* term), the Greek, "Father" (*"Pater,"* a *Greek* term in the original), both united together in one Sonship and one cry of faith, "Abba, Father." So "Even so (*'Nai,' Greek*), Amen" (*Hebrew*), both meaning the same (Rev. 1: 7). Christ's own former cry is the believers' cry, "Abba, Father" (Mark 14:36). **7. Wherefore**— Conclusion inferred from vss. 4-6. **thou**—individualizing and applying the truth to each. Such an individual appropriation of this comforting truth God grants in answer to them who cry, "Abba, Father." **heir of God through Christ**—The oldest MSS. read, "an heir through God." This combines on behalf of man, the whole before-mentioned agency of THE TRINITY: the Father sent His Son and the Spirit; the Son has freed us from the law; the Spirit has completed our sonship. Thus the redeemed are heirs THROUGH the Triune GOD, not through the law, nor through fleshly descent [WINDISCHMANN in ALFORD]; (ch. 3:18 confirms this). **heir**—confirming ch. 3:29; cf. Romans 8:17. **8-11.** appeal to them not to turn back from their privileges as free sons, to legal bondage again. **then**—when ye were "servants" (vs. 7). **ye knew not God**—not opposed to Romans 1:21. The heathen *originally knew* God, as Romans 1:21 states, but did not choose to retain God in their knowledge, and so corrupted the original truth. They *might* still *have* known Him, in a measure, from His works, but as a matter of fact they knew Him not, so far as His eternity, His power as the Creator, and His holiness, are concerned. **are no gods**—i.e., have no existence, such as their worshippers attribute to them, in the nature of things, but only in the corrupt imaginations of their worshippers (*Notes,* I Cor. 8:4; 10:19, 20; II Chron. 13:9). Your "service" was a different bondage from that of the Jews, which was a true service. Yet theirs, like yours, was a burdensome yoke; how then is it ye wish to resume the yoke after that God has transferred both Jews and Gentiles to a free service? **9. known God or rather are known of God**—*They* did not first know and love God, but *God* first, in His electing love, knew and loved them as His, and

therefore attracted them to the saving knowledge of Him (Matt. 7:23; I Cor. 8:3; II Tim. 2:19; cf. Exod. 33:12, 17; John 15:16; Phil. 3:12). God's great grace in this made their fall from it the more heinous. **how**—expressing indignant wonder at such a thing being possible, and even actually occurring (ch. 1:6). "How is it that ye turn back again?" **weak**—powerless to *justify:* in contrast to the justifying power of faith (ch. 3:24; cf. Heb. 7:18). **beggarly**—contrasted with the *riches* of the inheritance of believers in Christ (Eph. 1:18). The state of the "child" (vs. 1) is weak, as not having attained manhood; "beggarly," as not having attained the inheritance. **elements**—"rudiments." It is as if a schoolmaster should go back to learning the A, B, C's [BENGEL]. **again**—There are two *Greek* words in the original. "Ye desire again, *beginning afresh,* to be in bondage." Though the Galatians, as Gentiles, had never been under the Mosaic yoke, yet they had been under "the elements of the world" (vs. 3): the common designation for the Jewish and Gentile systems alike, in contrast to the Gospel (however superior the Jewish was to the Gentile). Both systems consisted in outward worship and cleaved to sensible forms. Both were in bondage to *the elements of sense,* as though these could give the justification and 'sanctification which the inner and spiritual power of God alone could bestow. **ye desire**—or "will." *Will-worship* is not acceptable to God (Col. 2:18, 23). **10.** To regard the observance of certain days as in itself meritorious as a work, is alien to the free spirit of Christianity. This is not incompatible with observing the Sabbath or the Christian Lord's day as obligatory, though *not as a work* (which was the Jewish and Gentile error in the observance of days), but as a holy mean appointed by the Lord for attaining the great end, holiness. The whole life alike belongs to the Lord in the Gospel view, just as the whole world, and not the Jews only, belong to Him. But as in Paradise, so now one portion of time is needed wherein to draw off the soul more entirely from secular business to God (Col. 2:16). "Sabbaths, new moons, and set feasts" (I Chron. 23:31; II Chron. 31:3), answer to "days, months, times." "Months," however, may refer to the *first* and *seventh* months, which were sacred on account of the number of feasts in them. **times**—*Greek,* "seasons," viz., those of the three great feasts, the Passover, Pentecost, and Tabernacles. **years**—The sabbatical year was about the time of writing this Epistle, A.D. 48 [BENGEL]. **11.** lest—*Greek,* "lest haply." My fear is not for my own sake, but for yours. **12. be as I am**—"As I have in my life among you cast off Jewish habits, so do ye; for I am become as ye are," viz., in the nonobservance of legal ordinances. "The fact of my laying them aside among Gentiles, shows that I regard them as *not at all contributing to justification* or *sanctification.* Do you regard them in the same light, and act accordingly." His observing the law among the Jews was not inconsistent with this, for he did so only in order to win them, without compromising principle. On the other hand, the Galatian Gentiles, by adopting legal ordinances, showed that they regarded them as needful for salvation. This Paul combats. **ye have not injured me at all**—viz., at the period when I first preached the Gospel among you, and when I made myself as you are, viz., living as a Gentile, not as a Jew. *You at that time did me no wrong;* "ye did not despise my temptation in the flesh" (vs. 14): nay, you "received me as an angel of God." Then in vs. 16, he asks, "Have I then, *since* that time, become your enemy by telling you the truth?" **13. how through infirmity** —rather, as *Greek*, "Ye know that *because* of an infirmity of *my* flesh I preached. . . ." He implies that bodily sickness, having detained him among them, contrary to his original intentions, was the occasion of his preaching the Gospel to them. **at the first**—lit., "at the *former* time"; implying that at the time of writing he had been *twice* in Galatia. See my *Introduction*: also vs. 16, and ch. 5:21, *Notes*. His sickness was probably the same as recurred more violently afterward, "the thorn in the flesh" (II Cor. 12:7), which also was overruled to good (II Cor. 12:9, 10), as the "infirmity of the flesh" here. **14. my temptation**—The oldest MSS. read, "your temptation." My infirmity, which was, or might have been, a "temptation," or *trial, to you,* ye despised not, i.e., ye were not tempted by it to despise me and my message. Perhaps, however, it is better to punctuate and explain as LACHMANN, connecting it with vs. 13, "And (ye know) your temptation (i.e., the temptation to which ye were exposed through the infirmity) which was in my flesh. Ye despised not (through *natural* pride), nor rejected (through *spiritual* pride), but received me. . . ." "Temptation does not mean here, as we now use the word, *tendency to an evil habit,* but BODILY TRIAL." **as an angel of God**—as a heaven-inspired and sent *messenger* from God: *angel* means messenger (Mal. 2:7). Cf. the phrase, II Samuel 19:27, a Hebrew and Oriental one for a person to be received with the highest respect (Zech. 12:8). An angel is free from the *flesh, infirmity,* and *temptation.* **as Christ**—being Christ's representative (Matt. 10:40). Christ is Lord of angels. **15. Where . . .**—*Of what value* was your *congratulation* (so the *Greek* for "blessedness" expresses) of yourselves, on account of your having among you me, the messenger of the Gospel, considering how entirely you have veered about since? Once you counted yourselves *blessed* in being favored with my ministry. **ye would have plucked out your own eyes**—one of the dearest members of the body—so highly did you value me: a proverbial phrase for the greatest selfsacrifice (Matt. 5:29). CONYBEARE and HOWSON think that this particular form of proverb was used with reference to a weakness in Paul's eyes, connected with a nervous frame, perhaps affected by the brightness of the vision described, Acts 22:11; II Corinthians 12:1-7. "You would have torn out your own eyes to supply the lack of mine." The divine power of Paul's words and works, contrasting with the feebleness of his person (II Cor. 10:10), powerfully at first impressed the Galatians, who had all the impulsiveness of the Keltic race from which they sprang. Subsequently they soon changed with the fickleness which is equally characteristic of Kelts. **16.** Translate, "Am I *then* become your enemy (an enemy in your eyes) *by telling* you the truth" (ch. 2:5, 14)? He plainly did not incur their enmity at his *first visit,* and the words here imply that he had *since then,* and *before* his now writing, incurred it: so that the occasion of his *telling* them the unwelcome truth, must have been at his second visit (Acts 18:23, see my *Introduction*). The fool and sinner hate a reprover. The righteous love faithful reproof (Ps. 141:5; Prov. 9:8). **17. They**—your flatterers: in contrast to Paul himself, who *tells* you the truth. **zealously**—zeal in proselytism was characteristic especially of the Jews, and so of Judaizers (ch. 1:14; Matt. 23:15; Rom. 10:2). **affect you**— i.e., court you (II Cor. 11:2. **not well**—not in a

good way, or for a good end. Neither the *cause* of their zealous courting of you, nor the *manner,* is what it ought to be. **they would exclude you**— "They wish to shut you out" from the kingdom of God (i.e., they wish to persuade you that as uncircumcised Gentiles, you are shut out from it), "that ye *may zealously court them,*" i.e., become circumcised, as zealous followers of themselves. ALFORD explains it, that their wish was to shut out the Galatians from the general community, and attract them as a separate clique to their own party. So the English word "exclusive," is used. **18. good to be zealously affected**—rather, to correspond to "zealously court" in vs. 18, "to be zealously courted." I do not find fault with them for zealously courting you, nor with you for being *zealously courted*: provided it be "in a good cause" (translate so), "it is a good thing" (I Cor. 9:20-23). My reason for saying the "not well" (vs. 17: the *Greek* is the same as that for "good," and "in a good cause," in vs. 28), is that their *zealous courting of you* is not in a good cause. The older interpreters, however, support *English Version* (cf. ch. 1:14). **always**—Translate and arrange the words thus, "*At all times,* and not only when I am present with you." I do not desire that *I* exclusively should have the privilege of zealously courting you. Others may do so in my absence with my full approval, if only it be in a good cause, and if Christ be faithfully preached (Phil. 1: 15-18). **19. My little children**—(I Tim. 1:18; II Tim. 2:1; I John 2:1). My relation to you is not merely that of one *zealously courting* you (vss. 17, 18), but that of a *father* to his *children* (I Cor. 4: 15). **I travail in birth**—i.e., like a mother in pain till the birth of her child. **again**—a second time. The former time was when I was "present with you" (vs. 18; cf. *Note,* vs. 13). **Christ be formed in you** —that you may live nothing but Christ, and think nothing but Christ (ch. 2:20), and glory in nothing but Him, and His death, resurrection, and righteousness (Phil. 3:8-10; Col. 1:27). **20.** Translate as *Greek,* "I could wish." If circumstances permitted (which they do not), I would gladly be with you [M.STUART]. **now**—as I was twice already. Speaking face to face is so much more effective towards loving persuasion than writing (II John 12; III John 13, 14). **change my voice**—as a mother (vs. 19): adapting my tone of voice to what I saw in person your case might need. This is possible to one present, but not to one in writing [GROTIUS and ESTIUS]. **I stand in doubt of you**—rather, "I am perplexed about you," viz., how to deal with you, what kind of words to use, gentle or servere, to bring you back to the right path. **21. desire**—of your own accord madly courting that which must condemn and ruin you. **do ye not hear**—do ye not consider the mystic sense of Moses' words? [GROTIUS.] The law itself sends you away from itself to Christ [ESTIUS]. After having sufficiently maintained his point by argument, the apostle confirms and illustrates it by an inspired allegorical exposition of historical facts, containing in them general laws and types. Perhaps his reason for using allegory was to confute the Judaizers with their own weapons: subtle, mystical, allegorical interpretations, unauthorized by the Spirit, were their favorite arguments, as of the Rabbins in the synagogues. Cf. the Jerusalem Talmud, *Tractatu Succa, cap. Hechalil.* Paul meets them with an allegorical exposition, not the work of fancy, but sanctioned by the Holy Spirit. History, if properly understood. contains in its complicated phenomena, simple and *continually recurring divine laws.* The history of the elect people, like their legal ordinances, had, besides the literal, a typical meaning (cf. I Cor. 10:1-4; 15:45, 47; Rev. 11:8). Just as the extra-ordinarily-born Isaac, the gift of grace according to promise, supplanted, beyond all human calculations, the naturally-born Ishmael, so the new theocratic race, the spiritual seed of Abraham by promise, the Gentile, as well as Jewish believers, were about to take the place of the natural seed, who had imagined that to them exclusively belonged the kingdom of God. **22.** (Gen. 16:3-16; 21:2.) **Abraham**—whose sons ye wish to be (cf. Rom. 9:7-9). **a bond maid ... a free woman**—rather, as *Greek,* 'the bond maid ... *the* free woman. **23. after the flesh**—born according to the usual course of nature: in contrast to Isaac, who was born "by virtue of *the* promise" (so the *Greek*), as the efficient cause of Sarah's becoming pregnant out of the course of nature (Rom. 4:19). Abraham was to lay aside all confidence in *the flesh* (after which Ishmael was born), and to live by faith alone in *the promise* (according to which Isaac was miraculously born, contrary to all calculations of flesh and blood). **24. are an allegory**—rather, "are allegorical," i.e., have *another besides the literal* meaning. **these are the two covenants**—"these [women] are (i.e., *mean*; omit 'the' with all the oldest MSS.) two covenants." As among the Jews the bondage of the mother determined that of the child, the children of the free covenant of promise, answering to Sarah, are free; the children of the legal covenant of bondage are not so. **one from**—i.e., *taking his* origin *from* Mount Sinai. Hence, it appears, he is treating of the moral law (ch. 3:19) chiefly (Heb. 12:18). Paul was familiar with the district of Sinai in Arabia (ch. 1:17), having gone thither after his conversion. At the gloomy scene of the giving of the Law, he learned to appreciate, by contrast, the grace of the Gospel, and so to cast off all his past legal dependencies. **which gendereth**—i.e., *bringing forth children* unto bondage. Cf. the phrase (Acts 3:25), *"children of the covenant which God made ... saying unto Abraham."* **Agar** i.e., Hagar. **25.** Translate, "For this *word,* Hagar, is (imports) Mount Sinai in Arabia" (i.e., among the Arabians—*in the Arabian tongue*). So CHRYSOSTOM explains. HARAUT, the traveller, says that to this day the Arabians call Sinai, "Hadschar," i.e., *Hagar,* meaning *a rock* or *stone.* Hagar twice fled into the desert of Arabia (Gen. 16 and 21): from her the mountain and city took its name, and the people were called Hagarenes. Sinai, with its rugged rocks, far removed from the promised land, was well suited to represent the law which inspires with terror, and the spirit of bondage. **answereth**—lit., "stands in the same rank with"; "she corresponds to." **Jerusalem which now is**—i.e., the Jerusalem of the Jews, having only a present temporary existence, in contrast with the spiritual Jerusalem of the Gospel, which in germ, under the form of the *promise,* existed ages before, and shall be for ever in ages to come. **and**—The oldest MSS. read, *"For* she is in bondage." As Hagar was in bondage to her mistress, so Jerusalem that now is, is in bondage to the law, and also to the Romans: her civil state thus being in accordance with her spiritual state [BENGEL]. **26.** This verse stands instead of the sentence which we should expect, to correspond to vs. 24, "One from Mount Sinai," viz., *the other covenant* from the heavenly mount above, which is (answers in the allegory to) Sarah. **Jerusalem ... above**—Hebrews 12:22, "the heavenly Jerusalem." "New Jerusalem, which cometh down out of heaven from my God" (Rev. 3:12; 21:2). Here *"the*

Messianic theocracy, which before Christ's second appearing is *the Church,* and after it, Christ's kingdom of glory" [MEYER]. **free**—as Sarah was; as opposed to "she is in bondage" (vs. 25). **all**—omitted in many of the oldest MSS., though supported by some. **"Mother of us,"** viz., *believers* who are already members of the invisible Church, the heavenly Jerusalem, hereafter to be *manifested* (Heb. 12:22). **27.** (Isa. 54:1.) **thou barren**—Jerusalem above: the spiritual Church of the Gospel, the fruit of "the promise," answering to *Sarah,* who bore not "after the flesh": as contrasted with the law, answering to Hagar, who was fruitful in the ordinary course of nature. Isaiah speaks primarily of Israel's restoration after her longcontinued calamities; but his language is framed by the Holy Spirit so as to reach beyond this to the spiritual Zion: including not only the Jews, the natural descendants of Abraham and children of the law, but also *the Gentiles.* The spiritual Jerusalem is regarded as "barren" while the law trammeled Israel, for she then had no spiritual children of the Gentiles. **break forth**—into crying. **cry**—shout for joy. **many more**—Translate as *Greek,* "Many are the children of the desolate (the New Testament Church made up in the greater part from the Gentiles, *who once had not the promise,* and so was destitute of God as her husband), more than of her which hath an (*Greek,* 'THE') husband" (the Jewish Church having GOD for her *husband,* Isa. 54:5; Jer. 2:2). Numerous as were the children of the legal covenant, those of the Gospel covenant are more so. The force of the *Greek* article is, "Her who has THE husband of which the other is destitute." **28. we**—The oldest MSS. and versions are divided between "we" and "ye." "We" better accords with vs. 26, "mother of us." **children of promise**—not children *after the flesh,* but through the promise (vss. 23, 29, 31). "We *are"* so, and ought to wish to continue so. **29. persecuted**—Ishmael "mocked" Isaac, which contained in it the germ and spirit of persecution (Gen. 21:9). His mocking was probably directed against Isaac's piety and faith in God's promises. Being the older by natural birth, he haughtily prided himself above him that was born by promise: as Cain hated Abel's piety. **him ... born after the Spirit**—The language, though referring primarily to Isaac, born in a spiritual way (viz., by the promise or word of God, rendered by His Spirit efficient out of the course of nature, in making Sarah fruitful in old age), is so framed as especially to refer to believers justified by Gospel grace through faith, as opposed to carnal men, Judaizers, and legalists. **even so it is now**—(ch. 5:11; 6:12, 17; Acts 9:29; 13:45, 49, 50; 14:1, 2, 19; 17:5, 13; 18:5, 6). The Jews persecuted Paul, not for preaching Christianity in opposition to heathenism, but for preaching it as distinct from Judaism. Except in the two cases of Philippi and Ephesus (where the persons beginning the assault were pecuniarily interested in his expulsion), he was nowhere set upon by the Gentiles, unless they were first stirred up by the Jews. The coincidence between Paul's Epistles and Luke's history (the Acts) in this respect, is plainly undesigned, and so a proof of genuineness (see PALEY's *Horæ Paulinæ*). **30.** Genesis 21:10, 12, where Sarah's words are, "shall not be heir with *my son, even with Isaac."* But what was there said literally, is here by inspiration expressed in its allegorical spiritual import, applying to the New Testament believer, who is antitypically "the son of the free woman." In John 8: 35, 36, Jesus refers to this. **Cast out**—from the house and inheritance: literally, Ishmael; spiritually, the carnal and legalists. **shall not be heir**—The *Greek* is stronger, *"must not* be heir," or "inherit." **31. So then**—The oldest MSS. read, "Wherefore." This is the conclusion inferred from what precedes. In ch. 3:29 and 4:7, it was etstablished that we, New Testament believers, are "heirs." If, then, we are heirs, "we are not children of the bond woman (whose son, according to Scripture, was 'not to be heir,' vs. 30), but of the free woman" (whose son was, according to Scripture, to be heir). For we are not "cast out" as Ishmael, but accepted as sons and heirs.

CHAPTER 5

Vss. 1-26. PERORATION. EXHORTATION TO STAND FAST IN THE GOSPEL LIBERTY, JUST SET FORTH, AND NOT TO BE LED BY JUDAIZERS INTO CIRCUMCISION, OR LAW JUSTIFICATION: YET THOUGH FREE, TO SERVE ONE ANOTHER BY LOVE: TO WALK IN THE SPIRIT, BEARING THE FRUIT THEREOF, NOT IN THE WORKS OF THE FLESH. **1.** The oldest MSS. read, "in liberty (so ALFORD, MOBERLEY, HUMPHRY, and ELLICOTT. But as there is no *Greek* for 'in,' as there is in translating in I Cor. 16:13; Phil. 1:27: 4:1, I prefer 'It is FOR freedom that') Christ hath made us free (not *in*, or *for*, a state of bondage). Stand fast, therefore, and be not entangled again *in* a yoke of bondage" (viz., the law, ch. 4:24; Acts 15:10). On "again," see *Note*, ch. 4:9. **2. Behold**—i.e., Mark what I say. **I Paul**—Though you now think less of my authority, I nevertheless give my name and personal authority as enough by itself to refute all opposition of adversaries. **if ye be circumcised**—not as ALFORD, "If you will *go on being* circumcised." Rather, "If ye suffer yourselves to be circumcised," viz., under the notion of its being necessary to *justification* (vs. 4: Acts 15:1). Circumcision here is not regarded simply by itself (for, viewed as a mere *national* rite, it was practiced for conciliation's sake by Paul himself, Acts 16:3), but as the symbol of *Judaism* and *legalism in general*. If this be necessary, then the Gospel of grace is at an end. If the latter be the way of justification, then Judaism is in no way so. **Christ … profit … nothing**—(ch. 2:21). For righteousness of works and justification by faith cannot co-exist. "He who is circumcised [for justification] is so as fearing the law, and he who fears, disbelieves the power of grace, and he who disbelieves can profit nothing by that grace which he disbelieves [CHRYSOSTOM]. **3. For**—*Greek*, "Yea, more"; "Moreover." **I testify … to every man**—as well as "unto you" (vs. 2). **that is circumcised**—that submits to be circumcised. Such a one became a "proselyte of righteousness." **the whole law**—impossible for man to keep even in part, much less *wholly* (Jas. 2:10); yet none can be justified by the law, unless he keep it *wholly* (ch. 3: 10). **4.** Lit., "Ye have become void from Christ," i.e., your connection with Christ has become void (vs. 2). Romans 7:2, "*Loosed* from the law," where the same *Greek* occurs as here. **whosoever of you are justified**—"are being justified," i.e., are *endeavoring* to be justified. **by the law**—*Greek*, "IN the law," as the element *in* which justification is to take place. **fallen from grace**—Ye no longer "*stand*" in grace (Rom. 5:2). Grace and legal righteousness cannot co-exist (Rom. 4:4, 5: 11:6). Christ, by circumcision (Luke 2:21), undertook to obey all the law, and fulfil all righteousness for us: any, therefore, that now seeks to fulfil the law for himself in any degree for justifying righteousness, severs him-

self from the grace which flows from Christ's fulfilment of it, and becomes "a debtor to do the whole law" (vs. 3). The decree of the Jerusalem council had said nothing so strong as this; it had merely decided that Gentile Christians were not bound to legal observances. But the Galatians, while not pretending to be so *bound,* imagined there was an efficacy in them to merit a higher degree of *perfection* (ch. 3:3). This accounts for Paul not referring to the decree at all. He took much higher ground. See PALEY's *Horæ Paulinæ.* The natural mind loves outward fetters, and is apt to forge them for itself, to stand in lieu of holiness of heart. **5. For** —proof of the assertion, "fallen from grace," by contrasting with the case of *legalists,* the "hope" of *Christians.* **through the Spirit**—*Greek*, rather, "by the Spirit": in opposition to *by the flesh* (ch. 4:29), or fleshly ways of justification, as circumcision and legal ordinances. "We" is emphatical, and contrasted with "whosoever of you would be justified by the law" (vs. 4). **the hope of righteousness**— "We wait for the (realization of the) hope (which is the fruit) of the righteousness (i.e., justification which comes) by (lit., *from—out of*) faith," Rom. 5:1, 4, 5; 8:24, 25, "Hope … we with patience *wait for* it." This is a farther step than being "justified"; not only are we this, but "wait for the hope" which is connected with it, and is its full consummation. "Righteousness," in the sense of justification, is by the believer once for all already attained: but the consummation of it in future perfection above is the object of *hope* to be *waited for:* "the crown of righteousness laid up" (II Tim. 4:8): "the hope laid up for you in heaven" (Col. 1:5; I Pet. 1:3). **6. For**—confirming the truth that it is "by faith" (vs. 5). **in Jesus Christ**—*Greek*, "in Christ Jesus." In union with *Christ* (the ANOINTED Saviour), that is, *Jesus* of Nazareth. **nor uncircumcision**—This is levelled against those who, being not legalists, or Judaizers, think themselves Christians on this ground alone. **faith which worketh by love** *Greek*, "working. …" This corresponds to "a new creature" (ch. 6:15), as its definition. Thus in vss. 5, 6, we have the three, "faith," "hope," and "love." The *Greek* expresses, "Which effectually worketh"; which exhibits its *energy* by love (so I Thess. 2:13). *Love* is not joined with *faith* in justifying, but is the principle of the works which follow after justification by faith. Let not legalists, upholding circumcision, think that the essence of the law is set at naught by the doctrine of justification by faith only. Nay, "all the law is fulfilled in one word—love," which is the principle on which "faith worketh" (vs. 14). Let them, therefore, seek this "faith," which will enable them truly to fulfil the law. Again, let not those who pride themselves on uncircumcision think that, because the law does not justify, they are free to walk after "the flesh" (vs. 13). Let them, then, seek that "love" which is inseparable from true faith (Jas. 2:8, 12-22). Love is utterly opposed to the enmities which prevailed among the Galatians (vss. 15, 20). The Spirit (vs. 5) is a Spirit of "faith" and "love" (cf. Rom. 14:17; I Cor. 7:19). **7.** Translate, "Ye were running well" in the Gospel race (I Cor. 9:24-26; Phil. 3:13, 14). **who … —**none whom you ought to have listened to [BENGEL]: alluding to the Judaizers (cf. ch. 3:1). **hinder**—The *Greek* means, lit., "hinder by breaking up a road." **not obey the truth**—not submit yourselves to the true Gospel way of justification. **8. This persuasion**—*Greek*, "*The* persuasion," viz., to which you are yielding. There is a play on words in the original, the *Greek* for *persuasion* being akin to "*obey*" (vs. 7). This persuasion which ye have *obeyed*. **cometh not of**–i.e. "from". Does not emanate from Him, but from an enemy. **that calleth you**–(*V.* 13: ch. 1:6; Phil. 3:14; I Thess. 5:24). The calling is the rule of the whole race [BENGEL]. **9. A little leaven**–the *false teaching* of the Judaizers. A small portion of legalism, if it be mixed with the Gospel, corrupts its purity. To add legal ordinances and works in the least degree to justification by faith, is to undermine "the whole." So "leaven" is used of *false doctrine* (Matt. 16:12; cf. 13:33). In I Corinthians 5:6 it means the corrupting influence of one bad *person;* so BENGEL understands it here to refer to the person (vss. 7, 8, 10) who misled them. Ecclesiastes 9:18, "One sinner destroyeth much good" (I Cor. 15:33). I prefer to refer it to false *doctrine,* answering to "persuasion" (vs. 8). **10.** *Greek,* "I (emphatical: "*I on my part*") have confidence in the Lord *with regard to* you (II Thess. 3:4), that ye will be none otherwise minded" (than what by this Epistle I desire you to be, Phil. 3:15). **but he that troubleth you**–(ch. 1:7; Acts 15:24; Josh. 7:25; I Kings 18:17, 18). Some one, probably, was prominent among the seducers, though the denunciation applies to them all (ch. 1:7; 4:17). **shall bear**–as a heavy burden. **his**–*his due and inevitable* judgment from God. Paul distinguishes the case of the seduced, who were misled through thoughtlessness, and who, now that they are set right by him, he confidently hopes, in God's goodness, will return to the right way, from that of the seducer who is doomed to judgment. **whosoever he be**–whether great (ch. 1:8) or small. **11.** Translate, "If I am still preaching (as I did before conversion) circumcision, why am I still persecuted?" The Judaizing troubler of the Galatians had said, "Paul himself preaches circumcision," as is shown by his having circumcised Timothy (Acts 16:3; cf. also Acts 20:6; 21:24). Paul replies by anticipation of their objection, As regards myself, the fact that I am still persecuted by the Jews shows plainly that I do *not* preach circumcision; for it is just because I preach Christ crucified, and not the Mosaic law, as the sole ground of justification, that they persecute me. If for conciliation he lived as a Jew among the Jews, it was in accordance with his principle enunciated (I Cor. 7:18, 20; 9:20). Circumcision, or uncircumcision, are things indifferent in themselves; their lawfulness or unlawfulness depends on the *animus* of him who uses them. The Gentile Galatians' animus in circumcision could only be their supposition that it influenced favorably their standing before God. Paul's living as a Gentile among Gentiles, plainly showed that, if he lived as a Jew among Jews, it was not that he thought it meritorious before God, but as a matter indifferent, wherein he might lawfully conform as a *Jew by birth* to those with whom he was, in order to put no needless stumbling block to the Gospel in the way of his countrymen. **then**–Presuming that I did so, "then," in that case, "the offense of (stumbling block, I Cor. 1:23 occasioned to the Jews by) the cross has become done away." Thus the Jews' accusation against Stephen was not that he preached Christ crucified, but that "he spake blasphemous words against this holy place and *the law.*" They would, in some measure, have borne the former, if he had mixed with it justification in part by circumcision and the law, and if he had, through the medium of Christianity, brought converts to Judaism. But if justification in any degree depended on legal ordinances, Christ's crucifixion in that degree was unnecessary, and could profit nothing (vss. 2, 4).

Worldly Wiseman, of the town of Carnal Policy, turns Christian out of the narrow way of the Cross, to the house of Legality. But the way to it was up a mountain, which, as Christian advanced, threatened to fall on him and crush him, amidst flashes of lightning from the mountain (*Pilgrim's Progress;* Heb. 12:18-21). **12. they ... which trouble you**– Translate, as the *Greek* is different from vs. 10, "they who are *unsettling* you." **were even cut off**– even as they desire your foreskin to be *cut off* and cast away by circumcision, so would that *they were even cut off* from your communion, being worthless as a castaway foreskin (ch. 1:7, 8; cf. Phil. 3:2). The fathers, JEROME, AMBROSE, AUGUSTINE, and CHRYSOSTOM, explain it, "Would that they would even cut themselves off," i.e., cut off not merely the foreskin, but the whole member; if *circumcision* be not enough for them, then let them have *excision* also; an outburst hardly suitable to the gravity of an apostle. But vss. 9, 10 plainly point to *excommunication* as the judgment threatened against the troublers; and danger of the bad "leaven" spreading, as the reason for it. **13.** The "ye" is emphatical, from its position in the *Greek,* "Ye brethren"; as opposed to those legalists "who trouble you." **unto liberty**–The *Greek* expresses, "on a footing of liberty." The *state* or *condition* in which ye have been called to salvation, is one of liberty. Gospel liberty consists in three things, freedom from the Mosaic yoke, from sin, and from slavish fear. **only ...**–Translate, "Only turn not *your* liberty into an occasion for the flesh." Do not give the flesh the handle or pretext (Rom. 7:8, "occasion") for its indulgence which it eagerly seeks for; do not let it make Christian "liberty" its pretext for indulgence (vss. 16:17; I Pet. 2:16; II Pet. 2:19; Jude 4). **but by love serve one another**–*Greek,* "Be servants (be in bondage) to one another." If ye must be *servants,* then *be servants to one another in love.* While free as to legalism, be *bound* by Love (the article in the *Greek* personifies love in the abstract) to serve one another (I Cor. 9:19). Here he hints at their unloving strifes springing out of lust of power. "For the lust of power is the mother of heresies" [CHRYSOSTOM]. **14. all the law**–*Greek,* "the whole law," viz., the Mosaic law. *Love to God* is presupposed as the root from which *love to our neighbor* springs; and it is in this tense the latter *precept* (so "word" means here) is said to be the fulfilling of "*all* the law" (Lev. 19:18). Love is "the law of Christ" (ch. 6:2; Matt. 7:12; 22:39, 40; Rom. 13:9, 10). **is fulfilled**–Not as received text "is being fulfilled," but as the oldest MSS. read, "has been fulfilled"; and so "receives its full perfection," as rudimentary teachings are fulfilled by the more perfect doctrine. The law only united Israelites together; the Gospel unites all men, and that in relation to God [GROTIUS]. **15. bite**–*backbite* the character. **devour**–the substance by injuring, extortion, etc. (Hab. 1:13; Matt. 23:14; II Cor. 11:20). **consumed ...**–Strength of soul, health of body, character, and resources, are all consumed by broils [BENGEL]. **16. This I say then** –Repeating in other words, and explaining the sentiment in vs. 13, "What I mean is this." **Walk in the Spirit**–*Greek,* "By (the rule of) the (Holy) Spirit." Cf. vss. 16-18, 22, 25; ch. 6:1-8, with Romans 7:22; 8:11. The best way to keep tares out of a bushel is to fill it with wheat. **the flesh**–the natural man, out of which flow the evils specified (vss. 19-21). The spirit and the flesh mutually exclude one another. It is promised, not that we should have no evil lusts, but that we should "not *fulfil*" them. If the spirit that is in us can be at ease under sin, it is not a spirit that comes from the Holy Spirit. The gentle dove trembles at the sight even of a hawk's feather. **17. For**—the reason why walking by the Spirit will exclude fulfilling the lusts of the flesh, viz., their mutual contrariety. **the Spirit**—not "lusteth," but "tendeth (or some such word is to be supplied) against the flesh." **so that ye cannot do the things that ye would**—The Spirit strives against the flesh and its evil influence; the flesh against the Spirit and His good influence, *so that neither the one nor the other can be fully carried out into action.* "But" (vs. 18) where "the Spirit" prevails, the issue of the struggle no longer continues doubtful (Rom. 7:15-20) [BENGEL]. The *Greek* is, "that ye may not do the things that ye would." "The flesh and Spirit are contrary one to the other," *so that* you must distinguish what proceeds from the Spirit, and what from the flesh; and *you must not fulfil what you desire according to the carnal self,* but what the Spirit within you desires [NEANDER]. But the antithesis of vs. 18 ("But . . ."), where the conflict is *decided,* shows, I think, that here vs. 17 contemplates the inability both for fully accomplishing the *good* we "would," owing to the opposition of the *flesh,* and for doing the *evil* our flesh would desire, owing to the opposition of *the Spirit* in the awakened man (such as the Galatians are assumed to be), until we yield ourselves wholly by the Spirit to "walk by the Spirit" (vss. 16, 18). **18.** "If ye *are* led (give yourselves up to be led) *by* (*Greek*) the Spirit, ye are not under the law." For ye are not working the works of the flesh (vss. 16, 19-21) which bring one "under the law" (Rom. 8:2, 14). The "Spirit makes free from the law of sin and death" (vs. 23). The law is made for a fleshly man, and for the works of the flesh (I Tim. 1:9), "not for a righteous man" (Rom. 6:14, 15). **19-23.** Confirming vs. 18, by showing the contrariety between the works of the flesh and the fruit of the Spirit. **manifest**—The hidden *fleshly* principle betrays itself palpably by its works, so that these are not hard to discover, and leave no doubt that they come not from the Spirit. **which are these**—*Greek,* "such as," for instance. **Adultery**—omitted in the oldest MSS. **lasciviousness**—rather, "wantonness" petulance, capricious insolence; it may display itself in "lasciviousness," but not necessarily or constantly so (Mark 7:21, 22. where it is not associated with fleshly lusts) [TRENCH]. "Works" (in the plural) are attributed to the "flesh," because they are divided, and often at variance with one another, and even when taken each one by itself, betray their fleshly origin. But the *"fruit* of the Spirit" (vs. 23) is singular, because, however manifold the results, they form one harmonious whole. The results of the flesh are not dignified by the name "fruit"; they are but "works" (Eph. 5:9, 11). He enumerates those fleshly *works* (committed against our neighbor, against God, and against ourselves) to which the Galatians were most prone (the Kelts have always been prone to disputations and internal strifes); and those manifestations of the *fruit* of the Spirit most needed by them (vss. 13, 15). This passage shows that "the flesh" does not mean merely *sensuality,* as opposed to *spirituality:* for "divisions" in the catalogue here do not flow from sensuality. The identification of "the natural (*Greek, animal-souled)* man," with the "carnal" or *fleshly* man (I Cor. 2:14), shows that "the flesh" expresses *human nature as estranged from God.* TRENCH observes, as a proof of our fallen state, how much richer is every vocabulary in words for sins, than in those for graces. Paul enumerates *seventeen* "works of

the flesh," only *nine* manifestations of "the fruit of the Spirit" (cf. Eph. 4:31). **20. witchcraft**—sorcery; prevalent in Asia (Acts 19:19; cf. Rev. 21). **hatred** —*Greek,* "hatreds." **variance**—*Greek,* "strife"; singular in the oldest MSS. **emulations**—in the oldest MSS. singular, "emulation," or rather, "jealousy"; for the sake of one's own advantage. "Envyings" (vs. 21) are even without advantage to the person himself [BENGEL]. **wrath**—*Greek,* plural, "passionate outbreaks" [ALFORD]. **strife**—rather as *Greek,* "factions," "cabals"; derived from a *Greek* root, meaning "a worker for hire": hence, *unworthy means for compassing ends, factious practices.* **seditions**—"dissensions," as to secular matters. **heresies**—as to sacred things (*Note,* I Cor. 11:19). Self-constituted *parties;* from a *Greek* root, to *choose.* A *schism* is a more recent split in a congregation from a difference of opinion. *Heresy* is a schism become inveterate [AUGUSTINE, *Con. Crescon. Don.,* 2, 7]. **21. tell . . . before**—viz., before the event. **I . . . told you in time past**—when I was with you. **you**—who, though maintaining justification by the law, are careless about keeping the law (Rom. 2:21-23). **not inherit . . . kingdom of God**—(I Cor. 6:9, 10; Eph. 5:5). **22. love**—the leader of the band of graces (I Corinthians 13). **gentleness**—*Greek,* "benignity," conciliatory to others; whereas "goodness," though ready to do good, has not such *suavity* of manner [JEROME]. ALFORD translates, "kindness." **faith**—"faithfulness"; opposed to "heresies" [BENGEL]. ALFORD refers to I Corinthians 13:7, "Believeth all things": *faith* in the widest sense, toward God and man. "Trustfulness" [CONYBEARE and HOWSON]. **23. temperance**—The *Greek* root implies *self-restraint* as to one's desires and lusts. **against such** —not *persons,* but things, as in vs. 21. **no law**—confirming vs. 18, "Not under the law" (I Tim. 1:9, 10). The law itself commands love (vs. 14); so far is it from being "against such." **24.** The oldest MSS. read, "They that are of Christ Jesus"; they that belong to Christ Jesus; being "led by (His) Spirit" (vs. 18). **have crucified the flesh**—They nailed it to the cross once for all when they became Christ's, on believing and being baptized (Rom. 6:3, 4): they keep it *now* in a state of crucifixion (Rom. 6:6): so that the Spirit can produce in them, comparatively uninterrupted by it, "the fruit of the Spirit" (vs. 22). "Man, by faith, is dead to the former standing-point of a sinful life, and rises to a new life (vs. 25) of communion with Christ (Col. 3:3). The act by which *they have crucified the flesh with its lust,* is already accomplished ideally in principle. But the practice, or outward conformation of the life, must harmonize with the tendency given to the inward life" (vs. 25) [NEANDER]. We are to be executioners, dealing cruelly with the body of sin, which has caused the acting of all cruelties on Christ's body. **with the affections**—Translate, "with its passions." Thus they are dead to the law's condemning power, which is only for the fleshly, and their lusts (vs. 23). **25. in . . . in**—rather, as *Greek,* "If we live (*Note,* vs. 24) BY the Spirit, let us also walk (vs. 16; ch. 6:16) BY the Spirit." Let our life in practice correspond to the ideal inner principle of our spiritual life, viz., our standing by faith as dead to, and severed from, sin, and the condemnation of the law. "Life by (or in) the Spirit" is not an occasional influence of the Spirit, but an abiding state, wherein we are continually alive, though sometimes sleeping and inactive. **26.** *Greek,* "Let us not BECOME." While not asserting that the Galatians are *"vainglorious"* now, he says they are liable to *become* so. **provoking one another**—an effect of "vaingloriousness" on the *stronger*: as "envying" is its effect on the *weaker*. A danger common both to the orthodox and Judaizing Galatians.

CHAPTER 6

Vss. 1-18. Exhortations Continued; To Forbearance and Humility; Liberality to Teachers and in General. Postscript and Benediction. **1. Brethren**—An expression of kindness to conciliate attention. Translate as *Greek,* "If a man *even* be overtaken" (i.e., caught in the very act [Alford and Ellicott]*.* before he expects: unexpectedly). Bengel explains the "before" in the *Greek* compound verb, "If a man be overtaken in a fault *before ourselves";* If another has *really* been overtaken in a fault *the first;* for often he who is *first to find fault,* is the very one who has *first transgressed.* **a fault**—*Greek,* "a transgression," "a fall"; such as a falling back into legal bondage. Here he gives monition to those who have not so fallen, "the spiritual," to be not "vainglorious" (ch. 5:26), but forbearing to such (Rom. 15:1). **restore**—The *Greek* is used of a dislocated limb, reduced to its place. Such is the tenderness with which we should treat a fallen member of the Church in restoring him to a better state. **the spirit of meekness**—*the meekness* which is the gift *of the Holy Spirit* working in our spirit (ch. 5:22, 25). "Meekness" is that temper of spirit towards God whereby we accept His dealings without disputing; then, towards men, whereby we endure meekly their provocations, and do not withdraw ourselves from the burdens which their sins impose upon us [Trench]. **considering thyself**—Transition from the plural to the singular. When congregations are addressed collectively, each individual should take home the monition *to himself.* **thou also be tempted**—as is likely to happen to those who reprove others without meekness (cf. Matt. 7:2-5; II Tim. 2:25*;* Jas. 2:13). **2.** If ye, legalists, must "bear burdens," then instead of legal burdens (Matt. 23:4), "bear one another's burdens," lit., "weights." Distinguished by Bengel from "burden," vs. 4 (a different *Greek* word, "load"): "weights" exceed the strength of those under them; "burden" is proportioned to the strength. **so fulfil**—or as other old MSS. read, "so ye will fulfil," *Greek,* "fill up," "thoroughly fulfil." **the law of Christ**—viz., "love" (ch. 5:14). Since ye desire "the law," then fulfil the law of Christ, which is not made up of various minute observances, but whose sole "burden" is "love" (John 13:34; 15:12); Romans 15:3 gives Christ as the example in the particular duty here. **3.** Self-conceit, the chief hindrance to forbearance and sympathy towards our fellow men, must be laid aside. **something**—possessed of some spiritual pre-eminence, so as to be exempt from the frailty of other men. **when he is nothing**—The *Greek* is subjective: "Being, if he would come to himself, and look on the real fact, nothing" [Alford] (vss. 2, 6; Rom. 12:3; I Cor. 8:2). **deceiveth himself**—lit., "he mentally deceives himself." Cf. James 1:26, "deceiveth his own heart." **4. his own work**—not merely his own *opinion* of himself. **have rejoicing in himself alone**—Translate, "Have *his* (matter for) glorying in regard to himself alone, and not in regard to another" (viz., not in regard to his neighbor, by comparing himself with whom, he has fancied he has matter for boasting as that neighbor's superior). Not that really a man by looking to "himself alone" is likely to find cause for glorying in himself. Nay, in vs. 5, he speaks of a "burden"

or *load,* not of matter for glorying, as what really belongs to each man. But he refers to *the idea those* whom he censures *had of themselves:* they *thought* they had cause for "glorying" in themselves, but it all arose from unjust self-conceited comparison of themselves with others, instead of looking at home. The only true glorying, if glorying it is to be called, is in the testimony of a good conscience, glorying in the cross of Christ. **5.** For (by this way, vs. 4, of proving himself, not depreciating his neighbor by comparison) each man shall bear his own "burden," or rather, "*load*" (viz., of sin and infirmity), the *Greek* being different from that in vs. 2. This verse does not contradict vs. 2. There he tells them to bear with others' "burdens" of infirmity in sympathy; here, that self-examination will make a man to feel he has enough to do with "his own load" of sin, without comparing himself boastfully with his neighbor. Cf. vs. 3. Instead of "thinking himself to be something," he shall feel the "load" of his own sin: and this will lead him to bear sympathetically with his neighbor's burden of infirmity. Æsop says a man carries two bags over his shoulder, the one with his own sins hanging behind, that with his neighbor's sins in front. **6.** From the mention of bearing one another's burdens, he passes to one way in which those burdens may be borne—by ministering out of their earthly goods to their spiritual teachers. The "but " in the *Greek,* beginning of this verse, expresses this: I said, Each shall bear his own burden; but I do not intend that he should not think of others, and especially of the wants of his ministers. **communicate unto him**—"impart a share unto his teacher": lit., *him that teacheth catechetically.* **in all good things**—in every kind of the good things *of this life,* according as the case may require (Rom. 15:27; I Cor. 9:11, 14). **7. God is not mocked**—The *Greek* verb is, literally, to sneer with the nostrils drawn up in contempt. God does not suffer Himself to be imposed on by empty words: He will judge according to works, which are seeds sown for eternity of either joy or woe. Excuses for illiberality in God's cause (vs. 6) seem valid before men, but are not so before God (Ps. 50: 21). **soweth**—especially of his resources (II Cor. 9:6). **that**—*Greek,* "this"; this and nothing else. **reap**—at the harvest, the end of the world (Matt. 13: 39). **8.** Translate, "He that soweth *unto his own* flesh," with a view to fulfilling its desires. He does not say, "*His* spirit," as he does say, "His flesh." For in ourselves we are not spiritual, but carnal. The flesh is devoted to *selfishness.* **corruption**—i.e., destruction (Phil. 3:19). Cf. as to the deliverance of believers from "corruption" (Rom. 8:21). The use of the term "corruption" instead, implies that *destruction* is not an *arbitrary* punishment of fleshly-mindedness, but is its *natural* fruit; the corrupt flesh producing corruption, which is another word for destruction: corruption is the fault, and corruption the punishment (*Note,* I Cor. 3:17: II Pet. 2:12). Future life only expands the seed sown here. Men cannot mock God because they can deceive themselves. They who sow tares cannot reap wheat. They alone reap life eternal who sow to the Spirit (Ps. 126:6; Prov. 11:18; 22:8; Hos. 8: 7; 10:12; Luke 16:25; Rom. 8:11; Jas. 5:7). **9.** (II Thess. 3:13.) And when we do good, let us also persevere in it without fainting. **in due season**—in its own proper season, God's own time (I Tim. 6:15). **faint not**—lit., "be relaxed." Stronger than "be not weary." *Weary of well-doing* refers to the will; "faint not" to relaxation of the powers [Bengel]. No one should faint, as in an earthly harvest sometimes happens. **10.** Translate, *"So then, according* as (i.e., in proportion as) we have *season* (i.e., opportunity), let us *work* (a distinct *Greek* verb from that for "do," in vs. 9) *that which is* (in each case) *good."* As thou art able, and while thou art able, and when thou art able (Eccles. 9:10). We have now the "season" for *sowing,* as also there will be hereafter the "due season" (vs. 9) for *reaping.* The whole life is, in one sense, the "seasonable opportunity" to us; and, in a narrower sense, there occur in it more especially convenient seasons. The latter are sometimes lost in looking for still more convenient seasons (Acts 24:25). We shall not always have the opportunity "we have" now. Satan is sharpened to the greater zeal in injuring us, by the shortness of his time (Rev. 12:12). Let us be sharpened to the greater zeal in well-doing by the shortness of ours. **them who are of the household** —Every right-minded man does well to the members of his own family (I Tim. 5:8); so believers are to do to those of the household of faith, i.e., those whom *faith* has made members of "the household of God" (Eph. 2:19); "the house of God" (I Tim. 3:15; I Pet. 4:17). **11.** Rather, "See *in how large letters* I have written." The *Greek* is translated "how great" in Hebrews 7:4, the only other passage where it occurs in the New Testament. Owing to his weakness of eyes (ch. 4:15) he wrote in large letters. So JEROME. All the oldest MSS. are written in uncial, i.e., capital letters, the *cursive,* or small letters, being of more recent date. Paul seems to have had a difficulty in writing, which led him to make the uncial letters larger than ordinary writers did. The mention of these is as a token by which they would know that he wrote the whole Epistle with his own hand; as he did also the pastoral Epistle, which this Epistle resembles in style. He usually dictated his Epistles to an amanuensis, excepting the concluding salutation, which he wrote himself (Rom. 16:22; I Cor. 16:21). This letter, he tells the Galatians, he writes with his own hand, no doubt in order that they may see what a regard he had for them, in contrast to the Judaizing teachers (vs. 12), who sought only their own ease. If *English Version* be retained, the words, "how large a letter" (lit., "in how large letters"), will not refer to the length of the Epistle *absolutely,* but that it was a large one for *him* to have written with his own hand. NEANDER supports *English Version,* as more appropriate to the earnestness of the apostle and the tone of the Epistle: "How *large"* will thus be put for "how *many."* **12.** Contrast between his zeal in their behalf, implied in vs. 11, and the zeal for self on the part of the Judaizers. **make a fair show**—(II Cor. 5:12). **in the flesh**—in outward things. **they**—it is "these" who.... **constrain you** —by example (vs. 13) and importuning. **only lest** —"only that they may not..." (cf. ch. 5:11). **suffer persecution**—They escaped in a great degree the Jews' bitterness against Christianity and the offense of the cross of Christ, by making the Mosaic law a necessary preliminary; in fact, making Christian converts into Jewish proselytes. **13.** Translate, "For not even do they who submit to circumcision, keep the law themselves (Rom. 2:17-23), but they wish you (emphatical) to be circumcised," etc. They arbitrarily selected circumcision out of the whole law, as though observing it would stand instead of their non-observance of the rest of the law. **that they may glory in your flesh**—viz., in the outward change (opposed to *an inward change wrought by the* SPIRIT) which they have effected in bringing you over to their own Jewish-Christian party. **14.** Translate, "But *as for me* (in opposition to those gloriers 'in your flesh,' vs. 13), God forbid that I.... **in the cross**—the atoning death on the cross. Cf. Philippians 3:3, 7, 8, as a specimen of his glorying. The "cross," the great object of shame to them, and to all carnal men, is the great object of glorying to me. For by it, the worst of deaths, Christ has destroyed all kinds of death [AUGUSTINE, *Tract* 36, on John, sec. 4]. We are to testify the power of Christ's death working in us, after the manner of crucifixion (ch. 5:24; Rom. 6.5, 6). **our**—He reminds the Galatians by this pronoun, that *they* had a share in the "Lord Jesus Christ" (the full name is used for greater solemnity), and therefore ought to glory in Christ's cross, as he did. **the world**—inseparably allied to the "flesh" (vs. 13). Legal and fleshly ordinances are merely outward, and "elements of the world" (ch. 4:3). **is**—rather, as *Greek,* "has been crucified to me" (ch. 2:20). He used "crucified" for *dead* (Col. 2:20, "dead with Christ"), to imply his oneness with Christ *crucified* (Phil. 3: 10): "the fellowship of His sufferings being made conformable unto His death." **15. availeth**—The oldest MSS. read, "is" (cf. ch. 5:6). Not only are they of no *avail,* but they *are nothing."* So far are they from being matter for "glorying," that they are "nothing." But Christ's cross is "all in all," as a subject for glorying, in "the new creature" (Eph. 2: 10, 15, 16). **new creature**—(II Cor. 5:17). A *transformation by the renewal of the mind* (Rom. 12:2). **16. as many**—contrasting with the "as many," vs. 12. **rule**—lit., *a straight rule,* to detect crookedness; so a rule of life. **peace**—from God (Eph. 2:14-17; 6:23). **mercy**—(Rom. 15:9). **Israel of God**—not the Israel after the flesh, among whom those teachers wish to enrol you; but the spiritual seed of Abraham by faith (ch. 3:9, 29; Rom. 2:28, 29; Phil. 3:3). **17. let no man trouble me**—by opposing my apostolic authority, seeing that it is stamped by a sure seal, viz., "I (in contrast to the Judaizing teachers who gloried in the flesh) bear" (as a high mark of honor from the King of kings). **the marks**—properly, marks branded on slaves to indicate their owners. So Paul's scars of wounds received for Christ's sake, indicate to whom he belongs, and in whose free and glorious service he is (II Cor. 11:23-25). The Judaizing teachers gloried in the circumcision mark in the flesh of *their followers;* Paul glories in the marks of suffering for Christ on *his own* body (cf. vs. 14; Phil. 3:10; Col. 1:24). **the Lord**—omitted in the oldest MSS. **18. Brethren** —Place it, as *Greek,* last in the sentence, before the "Amen." After much rebuke and monition, he bids them farewell with the loving expression of *brotherhood* as his last parting word (*Note,* ch. 1:6). **be with your spirit**—which, I trust, will keep down the *flesh* (I Thess. 5:23; II Tim. 4:22; Philemon 25).

THE EPISTLE OF PAUL THE APOSTLE TO THE

EPHESIANS

INTRODUCTION

THE headings (ch. 1:1), and ch. 3:1, show that this Epistle claims to be that of Paul. This claim is confirmed by, the testimonies of IRENÆUS, *Hæreses* 5:2, 3, and 1:8, 5; CLEMENS ALEXANDRINUS, *Stromata*, 4, sec. 65, and *Pæd.* 1, sec. 8; ORIGEN, *adv. Cels.* 4, 211. It is quoted by VALENTINUS A.D. 120, viz., ch. 3:14–18, as we know from HIPPOLYTUS' *Refut. of Hæres.*, p. 193. POLYCARP, *Ep. Philipp.*, ch. 12, testifies to its canonicity. So TERTULLIAN, *adv. Marcion* 5, 17. IGNATIUS, *Eph.* 12, which alludes to the frequent and affectionate mention made by Paul of the Christian state, privileges, and persons of the Ephesians in his Epistle.

Two theories, besides the ordinary one, have been held on the question, *to whom* the Epistle is addressed. GROTIUS, after the heretic Marcion, maintains that it was addressed to the Church at Laodicea, and that *it* is the Epistle to which Paul refers in Col. 4:16. But the Epistle to the Colossians was probably written *before* that to the Ephesians, as appears from the parallel passages in Ephesians bearing marks of being expanded from those in Colossians; and Marcion seems to have drawn his notion, as to our Epistle, from Paul's allusion (Col. 4:16) to an Epistle addressed by him to the Laodiceans. ORIGEN and CLEMENT of Alexandria, and even TERTULLIAN, who refers to Marcion, give no sanction to his notion. No single MS. contains the heading, "to the saints that are at Laodicea." The very resemblance of the Epistle to the Ephesians, to that to the Colossians, is against the theory; for if the former were really the one addressed to Laodicea (Col. 4:16), Paul would not have deemed it necessary that the churches of Colosse and Laodicea should interchange Epistles. The greetings, moreover (Col. 4:15), which he sends *through the Colossians to the Laodiceans*, are quite incompatible with the idea that Paul wrote an Epistle *to the Laodiceans* at the same time, and by the same bearer, Tychicus (the bearer of our Epistle to the Ephesians, as well as of that to Colosse); for who, under such circumstances, would not send the greetings *directly* in the letter to the party saluted? The letter to Laodicea was evidently written some time *before* that to Colosse, Archbishop USHER has advanced the second theory: That it was an *encyclical* letter headed, as in MS. B., "to the saints that are . . . and to the faithful," the name of each Church being inserted in the copy sent to it; and that its *being sent to Ephesus first*, occasioned its being entitled, as now, the Epistle to the Ephesians. ALFORD makes the following objections to this theory: (1) It is at variance with the spirit of the Epistle, which is clearly addressed to one set of persons throughout, co-existing in one place, and as one body, and under the same circumstances. (2) The improbability that the apostle, who in two of his Epistles (II Corinthians and Galatians) has so plainly specified their encyclical character, should have here omitted such specification. (3) The still greater improbability that he should have, as on this hypothesis must be assumed, written a circular Epistle to a district, of which ʌEphesus was the commercial capital, addressed to various churches within that district, yet from its very contents (as by the opponents' hypothesis) not admitting of application to the Church of that metropolis, in which he had spent so long a time, and to which he was so affectionately bound. (4) The inconsistency of this hypothesis with the address of the Epistle, and the universal testimony of the ancient Church. The absence of personal greetings is not an argument for either of the two theories; for similarly there are none in Galatians, Philippians, I and II Thessalonians, I Timothy. The better he knows the parties addressed, and the more general and solemn the subject, the less he seems to give of these individual notices. Writing, as he does in this Epistle, on the constitution and prospects of Christ's universal Church, he refers the Ephesians, as to personal matters, to the bearer of the Epistle, Tychicus (ch. 6:21, 22). As to the omission of "which are at Ephesus" (ch. 1:1), in MS. B., so "in Rome" (Rom. 1:7) is omitted in some old MSS.: it was probably done by churches *among whom it was read*, in order to generalize the reference of its contents, and especially where the subject of the Epistle is catholic. The words are found in the margin of B., from a first hand; and are found in all the oldest MSS. and versions.

Paul's first visit to Ephesus (on the seacoast of Lydia, near the river Cayster) is related in Acts 18:19–21. The work, begun by his disputations with the Jews in his short visit, was carried on by Apollos (Acts 18:24–26), and Aquila and Priscilla (26). At his second visit, after his journey to Jerusalem, and thence to the east regions of Asia Minor, he remained at Ephesus "three years" (Acts 19:10, the "two years" in which verse are only *part* of the time, and Acts 20:31); so that the founding and rearing of this Church occupied an unusually large portion of the apostle's time and care; whence his language in this Epistle shows a warmth of feeling, and a free outpouring of thought, and a union in spiritual privileges and hope between him and them (ch. 1:3, etc.), such as are natural from one so long and so intimately associated with those whom he addresses. On his last journey to Jerusalem, he sailed by Ephesus and summoned the elders of the Ephesian Church to meet him at Miletus, where he delivered his remarkable farewell charge (Acts 20:18–35).

This Epistle was addressed to the Ephesians during the early part of his imprisonment at Rome, immediately after that to the Colossians, to which it bears a close resemblance in many passages, the apostle having in his mind generally the same great truths in writing both. It is an undesigned proof of genuineness that the two Epistles, written about the same date, and under the same circumstances, bear a closer mutual resemblance than those written at distant dates and on different occasions. Cf. ch. 1:7 with Colossians 1:14; ch. 1:10 with Colossians 1:20; ch. 3:2 with Colossians 1:25; ch. 5:19 with Colossians 3:16; ch. 6:22 with Colossians 4:8; ch. 1:19; 2:5 with Colossians 2:12, 13; ch. 4:2–4 with Colossians 3:12–15; ch. 4:16 with Colossians 2:19; ch. 4:32 with Colossians 3:13; ch. 4:22–24 with Colossians 3:9, 10; ch. 5:6–8 with Colossians 3:6–8;

ch. 5:15, 16 with Colossians 4:5; ch. 6:19, 20 with Colossians 4:3, 4; ch. 5:22–33; 6:1–9 with Colossians 3:18; ch, 4:24, 25 with Colossians 3:9; ch. 5:20–22 with Colossians 3:17, 18. Tychicus and Onesimus were being sent to Colosse, the former bearing the two Epistles to the two churches respectively, the latter furnished with a letter of recommendation to Philemon, his former master, residing at Colosse. The date was probably about four years after his parting with the Ephesian elders at Miletus (Acts 20), about A.D. 62, before his imprisonment had become of the more severe kind, which appears in his Epistle to the Philippians. From ch. 6:19, 20 it is plain he had at the time, though a prisoner, some degree of freedom in preaching, which accords with Acts 28:23, 30, 31, where he is represented as receiving at his lodgings all inquirers. His imprisonment began in February A.D. 61 and lasted "two whole years" (Acts 28:30) at least, and perhaps longer.

The Church of Ephesus was made up of converts partly from the Jews and partly from the Gentiles (Acts 19:8–10). Accordingly, the Epistle so addresses a Church constituted (ch. 2:14–22). Ephesus was famed for its idol temple of Artemis or Diana, which, after its having been burnt down by Herostratus on the night that Alexander the Great was born (355 B.C.), was rebuilt at enormous cost and was one of the wonders of the world. Hence, perhaps, have arisen his images in this Epistle drawn from a beautiful temple: the Church being in true inner beauty that which the temple of the idol tried to realize in outward show (ch. 2:19–22). The Epistle (ch. 4:17; 5:1–13) implies the profligacy for which the Ephesian heathen were notorious. Many of the same expressions occur in the Epistle as in Paul's address to the Ephesian elders. Cf. ch. 1:6, 7 and 2:7, as to "grace," with Acts 20:24, 32: this may well be called "the Epistle of the grace of God" [ALFORD]. Also, as to his "bonds," ch. 3:1, and 4:1 with Acts 20:22, 23. Also ch. 1:11, as to "the counsel of God," with Acts 20:27. Also ch. 1:14, as to "the redemption of the purchased possession," with Acts 20:28. Also ch. 1:14, 18; ch. 2:20, and ch. 5:5, as to "building up" the "inheritance," with Acts 20:32.

The object of the Epistle is "to set forth the ground, the course, and the aim and end of THE CHURCH OF THE FAITHFUL IN CHRIST. He speaks to the Ephesians as a type or sample of the Church universal" [ALFORD]. Hence, "the Church" throughout the Epistle is spoken of in the singular, not in the plural, "churches." The Church's foundation, its course, and its end, are his theme alike in the larger and smaller divisions of the whole Epistle. "Everywhere the foundation of the Church is in *the will of the Father;* the course of the Church is by *the satisfaction of the Son;* the end of the Church is the *life in the Holy Spirit*" [ALFORD]. Cf. respectively ch. 1:11; ch. 2:5; ch. 3:16. This having been laid down as a matter of doctrine (this part closing with a sublime doxology, ch. 3:14–21), is then made the ground of practical exhortations. In these latter also (from ch. 4:1, onward), the same threefold division prevails, for the Church is represented as founded on the counsel of "God the Father, who is above all, through all, and in all," reared by the "one Lord," Jesus Christ, through the "one Spirit" (ch. 4:4–6, etc.), who give their respective graces to the several members. These last are therefore to exercise all these graces in the several relations of life, as husbands, wives, servants, children, etc. The conclusion is that we must put on "the whole armor of God" (ch. 6:13).

The sublimity of the STYLE and LANGUAGE corresponds to the sublimity of the subjects and exceeds almost that of any part of his Epistles. It is appropriate that those to whom he so wrote were Christians long grounded in the faith. The very sublimity is the cause of the difficulty of the style, and of the presence of peculiar expressions occurring, not found elsewhere.

CHAPTER 1

Vss. 1-23. INSCRIPTION: ORIGIN OF THE CHURCH IN THE FATHER'S ETERNAL COUNSEL, AND THE SON'S BLOODSHEDDING: THE SEALING OF IT BY THE SPIRIT. THANKSGIVING AND PRAYER THAT THEY MAY FULLY KNOW GOD'S GRACIOUS POWER IN CHRIST TOWARDS THE SAINTS. **1. by**—rather, "*through* the will of God": called to the apostleship through that same "will" which originated the Church (vss. 5, 9, 11; cf. Gal. 1:4). **which are at Ephesus**—See *Introduction.* **to the saints ... and to the faithful**—The same persons are referred to by both designations, as the *Greek* proves: "to those who are saints, and faithful in Christ Jesus." The *sanctification* by God is here put before man's *faith.* The twofold aspect of salvation is thus presented, God's grace in the first instance *sanctifying* us, (i.e., setting us apart in His eternal purposes as holy unto Himself); and our faith, by God's gift, laying hold of salvation (II Thess. 2:13; I Pet. 1:2). **2.** (Rom. 1:7; I Cor. 3; II Cor. 1:2; Galatians 1:3.) **3.** The doxologies in almost all the Epistles imply the real sense of grace experienced by the writers and their readers (I Pet. 1:3). From vs. 3 to vs. 14 sets forth summarily the Gospel of the grace of God: the FATHER'S work of love, vs. 3 (choosing us to *holi-* ness, vs. 4; to *sonship,* vs. 5; to *acceptance,* vs. 6): the SON'S, vs. 7 (*redemption,* vs. 7; *knowledge of the*

mystery of His will, vs. 9; *an inheritance,* vs. 11); the HOLY SPIRIT'S, vs. 13 (*sealing,* vs. 13; giving an *earnest* of the inheritance, vs. 14). **the God and Father of...Christ**—and so the God and Father of us who are in Him (John 20:17). God is "the God" of the *man* Jesus, and "the Father" of the *Divine Word.* The *Greek* is, "*Blessed* us," not "hath blessed us"; referring to the past original counsel of God. As in creation (Gen. 1:22) so in redemption (Gen. 12:3; Matt. 5:3-11; 25:34) God "blesses" His children; and that not in mere *words,* but in *acts.* **us**—all Christians. **blessings**—*Greek,* "blessing." "All," i.e., "*every possible* blessing for time and eternity, which *the Spirit* has to besow" (so "spiritual" means; not "spiritual," as the term is now used, as opposed to *bodily*). **in heavenly places**—a phrase five times found in this Epistle, and not elsewhere (vs. 20; ch. 2:6; 3:10; 6:12); *Greek,* "in *the* heavenly places." Christ's ascension is the means of introducing us into the heavenly places, which by our sin were barred against us. Cf. the change made by Christ (Col. 1:20; ch. 1:20). While Christ in the flesh was in the form of a *servant,* God's people could not realize fully their heavenly privileges as *sons.* Now "our *citizenship* (*Greek*) is in heaven" (Phil. 3:20), where our High Priest is ever "blessing" us. Our "treasures" are there (Matt. 6:20, 21); our aims and affections (Col. 3: 1, 2); our hope (Col. 1: 5; Titus 2:13); our inheritance (I Pet. 1:4). The gift of the Spirit itself, the source of the "spiritual blessing," is by virtue of Jesus having ascended thither (ch. 4:8). **in Christ**—the center and source of all blessing to us. **4. hath chosen us**—Greek, *"chose* us out for Himself" (viz., *out of* the world, Gal. 1:4): referring to His original choice, spoken of as *past.* **in him**—The repetition of the idea, "in Christ" (vs. 3), implies the paramount importance of the truth that it is *in Him,* and by virtue of union to Him, the Second Adam, the Restorer ordained for us from everlasting, the Head of redeemed humanity, believers have all their blessings (ch. 3: 11). **before the foundation of the world**—This assumes the eternity of the Son of God (John 17:5, 24), as of the election of believers in Him (II Tim. 1:9; II Thess. 2:13). **that we should be holy**—positively (Deut. 14:2). **without blame**—negatively (ch. 5:27; I Thess. 3:13). **before him**—It is to Him the believer looks, walking as in His presence, before whom he looks to be accepted in the judgment (Col. 1:22; cf. Rev. 7:15). **in love**—joined by BENGEL and others with vs. 5, "in love having predestinated us. . . ." But *English Version* is better. The words qualify the whole clause, "that we should be holy . . . before Him." Love, lost to man by the fall, but restored by redemption, is the root and fruit and sum of all holiness (ch. 5:2; I Thess. 3:12, 13). **5. predestinated**—more special in respect to the *end* and precise *means,* than "chosen" or *elected.* We are "chosen" *out of the rest of the world;* "predestinated" *to all things that secure the inheritance* for us (vs. 11; Rom. 8:29). *"Foreordained."* **by Jesus**—Greek, "through Jesus." **to himself**—the Father (Col. 1:20). ALFORD explains, "adoption . . . *into* Himself," i.e., so that we should be *partakers of the divine nature* (II Pet. 1:4). LACHMANN reads, "unto Him." The context favors the explanation of CALVIN: God has regard *to Himself* and the glory of His grace (vss. 6, 12, 14) as His ultimate end. He had one only begotten Son, and He was pleased *for His own glory,* to choose out of a lost world many to become His adopted sons. Translate, *"unto* Himself." **the good pleasure of his will**—So the *Greek* (Matt. 11:26; Luke 10:21). We cannot go beyond "the good pleasure of His will" in searching into the causes of our salvation, or of any of His works (vs. 9). (Job 33:13.) Why needest thou philosophize about an imaginary world of optimism? Thy concern is to take heed that thou be not bad. There was nothing in us which deserved His love (vss. 1, 9, 11) [BENGEL]. **6.** (Vss. 7, 17, 18.) The end aimed at (Ps. 50:23), i.e., that the glory of His grace may be praised by all His creatures, men and angels. **wherein**—Some of the oldest MSS. read, *"which."* Then translate, "which He graciously bestowed on us." But *English Version* is supported by good MSS. and the oldest versions. **us accepted**—a kindred *Greek* word to "grace": *charitos, echaritosen:* translate, "graciously accepted"; "made us subjects of His grace"; "embraced us in the arms of His grace" (Rom. 3:24; 5: 15). **in the beloved**—pre-eminently so called (Matt. 3:17; 17:5; John 3:35; Col. 1:13). *Greek,* "Son of His love." It is only "IN HIS BELOVED" that He loves us (vs. 3; I John 4:9, 10). **7. In whom**—"the Beloved" (vs. 6; Rom. 3:24). **we have**—as a *present* possession. **redemption**—Greek, *"our* (lit., *'the')* redemption"; THE redemption which is the grand subject of all revelation, and especially of the New Testament (Rom. 3:24), viz., from the power, guilt, and penal consequences of sin (Matt. 1:21). If a man were unable to redeem himself from being a bond servant, his kinsman might redeem him (Lev.

25:48). Hence, antitypically the Son of God became the Son of man, that as our kinsman He might redeem us (Matt. 20:28). Another "redemption" follows, viz., that "of the purchased possession" hereafter (vs. 14). **through his blood**—(ch. 2:13)—as the instrument; the propitiation, i.e., the consideration (devised by His own love) for which He, who was justly angry (Isa. 12:1), becomes propitious to us; the expiation, the price paid to divine justice for our sin (Acts 20:28; Rom. 3:25; I Cor. 6:20; Col. 1:20; I Pet. 1:18, 19). **the forgiveness of sins**—Greek, "the remission of *our transgressions":* not merely *"pretermission,"* as the *Greek* (Rom. 3: 25) ought to be translated. This "remission," being the explanation of "redemption," includes not only deliverance from sin's penalty, but from its pollution and enslaving power, negatively; and the reconciliation of an offended God, and a satisfaction unto a just God, positively. **riches of his grace**—(ch. 2:7)—"the exceeding riches of His grace." Cf. vs. 18, and ch. 3:16, "according to the riches of His glory": so that "grace" is His "glory." **8.** Rather, "which He made to abound towards us." **all wisdom and prudence**—"wisdom" in devising the plan of redeeming mankind; "prudence" in executing it by the means, and in making all the necessary arrangements of Providence for that purpose. Paul attributes to the Gospel of God's grace "all" possible "wisdom and prudence," in opposition to the boasts of wisdom and prudence which the unbelieving Jews and heathen philosophers and false apostles arrogated for their teachings. Christ crucified, though esteemed "foolishness" by the world, is "the wisdom of God" (I Cor. 1:18-30). Cf. ch. 3:10, "the *manifold* wisdom of God. **9.** "He hath abounded," or "made (grace) to abound toward us" (vs. 8), *in that He made known* to us, viz., experimentally, in our hearts. **the mystery**—God's purpose of redemption hidden heretofore in His counsels, but now revealed (ch. 6:19; Rom. 16:25; Col. 1:26, 27). This "mystery" is not like the heathen mysteries, which were imparted only to the initiated few. All Christians are the initiated. Only unbelievers are the uninitiated. **according to his good pleasure**—showing the cause why "He hath made known to us the mystery," viz., His own loving "good pleasure" toward us; also the *time* and *manner* of His doing so, are according to His good pleasure. **purposed**—(Vs. 11). **in himself**—God the Father. BENGEL takes it, "in *Him,"* i.e., *Christ,* as in vss. 3, 4. But the proper name, "in *Christ,"* vs. 10, immediately after, is inconsistent with His being here meant by the pronoun. **10.** Translate, *"Unto* the dispensation of the fulness of the times," i.e., "which He purposed in Himself" (vs. 9) *with a view to* the economy of (the gracious *administration* belonging to) the fulness of the times (Greek, "fit times," "seasons"). More comprehensive than "the fulness of the time" (Gal. 4:4). The whole of the Gospel *times* (plural) is meant, with the benefits to the Church *dispensed* in them severally and successively. Cf. "the ages to come" (ch. 2:7). "The ends of the ages" (Greek, I Cor. 10:11); "the times (same *Greek* as here, 'the seasons,' or 'fitly appointed times') of the Gentiles" (Luke 21:24); "the seasons which the Father hath put in His own power" (Acts 1:7); "the times of restitution of all things which God hath spoken by the prophets since the world began" (Acts 3:20, 21). The coming of Jesus at the first advent, "in the fulness of time," was *one* of these "times." The descent of the Holy Ghost, "when Pentecost was *fully come"* (Acts 2:1), was another. The testimony given by the apostles to Him "in due time" ("in its own seasons," *Greek*) (I Tim. 2:6) was another. The conversion of the Jews "when the *times* of the Gentiles are fulfilled," the second coming of Christ, the "restitution of all things," the millennial kingdom, the new heaven and earth, shall be severally instances of "the dispensation of the fulness of the times," i.e., "the dispensation of" the Gospel events and benefits belonging to their respective "times," when severally filled up or completed. God the Father, according to His own good pleasure and purpose, is the Dispenser both of the Gospel benefits and of their several fitting times (Acts 1:7). **gather together in one**—*Greek,* "sum up under one head"; "recapitulate." The "good pleasure which He purposed," was "to sum up all things (*Greek,* 'THE whole range of things') in Christ" (*Greek,* "the Christ," i.e., *His* Christ) [ALFORD]. God's purpose is to sum up the whole creation in Christ, the Head of angels, with whom He is linked by His invisible nature, and of men with whom He is linked by His humanity; of Jews and Gentiles; of the living and the dead (ch. 3:15); of animate and inanimate creation. Sin has disarranged the creature's relation of subordination to God. God means to gather up all together in Christ; or as Colossians 1:20 says, "By Him to reconcile all things unto Himself, whether things in earth or things in heaven." ALFORD well says, "The Church of which the apostle here mainly treats, is subordinated to Him in the highest degree of conscious and joyful union; those who are not His spiritually, in mere subjugation, yet consciously; the inferior tribes of creation unconsciously; but objectively, all are summed up in Him." **11. In whom**—by virtue of union to whom. **obtained an inheritance**—lit., "We were made to have an inheritance" [WAHL]. Cf. vs. 18, "*His* inheritance in the saints": as *His* inheritance is there said to be *in them,* so *theirs* is here said to be *in Him* (Acts 26: 18). However, vs. 12, "That we should BE TO ... His glory" (not "that we should *have*"), favors the translation of BENGEL, ELLICOTT, and others, "We were *made* an inheritance." So the literal Israel (Deut. 4:20; 9:29; 32:9). "Also" does not mean "we also," nor as *English Version,* "in whom also"; but, besides His having "made known to us His will," we were also "made His inheritance," or "we have also obtained an inheritance." **predestinated**—(Vs. 5). The foreordination of Israel, as the elect nation, answers to that of the spiritual Israelites, believers, to an eternal inheritance, which is the thing meant here. The "we" here and in vs. 12, means *Jewish* believers (whence the reference to the election of Israel nationally arises), as contrasted with "you" (vs. 13) *Gentile* believers. **purpose**—repeated from "purposed" (vs. 9; ch. 3:11). The Church existed in the mind of God eternally, before it existed in creation. **counsel of his ... will** —vs. 5, "the good pleasure of His will." Not arbitrary caprice, but infinite wisdom ("counsel") joined with sovereign will. Cf. his address to the same Ephesians in Acts 20:27, "All the counsel of God" (Isa. 28:29). Alike in the natural and spiritual creations, God is not an agent constrained by necessity. "Wheresoever counsel is, there is election, or else it is vain; where a will, there must be freedom, or else it is weak" [PEARSON]. **12.** (*V.* 6, 14.) **who first trusted in Christ**—rather (we Jewish Christians), "who have before hoped in *the* Christ": who before the Christ came, looked forward to His coming, waiting for the consolation of Israel. Cf. Acts 26:6, 7, "I am judged for *the hope of the promise made of God unto our fathers: unto which our*

twelve tribes, instantly serving God day and night, *hope to come.*" Acts 28:20, "*the hope of Israel*" [ALFORD]. Cf. vs. 18; ch. 2:12; 4:4. **13. In whom ye also**—Ye Gentiles. Supply as *English Version,* "trusted," from vs. 12; or "are." The priority of us Jews does not exclude you Gentiles from sharing in Christ (cf. Acts 13:46). **the word of truth**—the instrument of sanctification, and of the new birth (John 17:17; II Tim. 2:15; James. 1:18). Cf. Colossians 1:5, where also, as here, it is cannected with "hope." Also ch. 4:21. **sealed**—as God's confirmed children, by the Holy Spirit as the seal (Acts 19:1-6; Rom. 8:16, 23; *Note,* II Cor. 1:22; I John 3:24). A seal impressed on a document gives undoubted validity to the contract in it (John 3:33; 6: 27; cf. II Cor. 3:3). So the sense of "the love of God shed abroad in the heart by the Holy Ghost" (Rom. 5:5), and the sense of adoption given through the Spirit at regeneration (Rom. 8:15, 16), assure believers of God's good will to them. The Spirit, like a seal, impresses on the soul at regeneration the image of our Father. The "sealing" by the Holy Spirit is spoken of as *past* once for all. The witnessing to our hearts that we are the children of God, and heirs (vs. 11), is the Spirit's *present* testimony, the "earnest of the (coming) inheritance" (Rom. 8:16-18). **that Holy Spirit of promise**—rather, as the *Greek,* "The Spirit of promise, even the Holy Spirit": The *Spirit promised* both in the Old and New Testaments (Joel 2:28; Zech. 12:10; John 7:38, 39). "The word" *promised* the Holy Spirit. Those who "believed the word of truth" were sealed by the Spirit accordingly. **14. earnest** —the first instalment paid as a pledge that the rest will follow (Rom. 8:23; II Cor. 1:22). **until**—rather, "*Unto* the redemption ..."; joined thus, "ye were sealed (vs. 13) unto," i.e., *for the purpose of, and against,* the accomplishment of "the redemption," viz., not the *redemption* in its first stage, made by the blood of Christ, which secures our *title,* but, in its final completion, when the actual *possession* shall be ours, the full "redemption of the body" (Rom. 8:23), as well as of the soul, from every infirmity (ch. 4:30). The deliverance of the creature (the body, and the whole visible creation) from the bondage of corruption, and from the usurping prince of this world, into the glorious liberty of the children of God (Rom. 8:21-23; II Pet. 3:13). **of the purchased possession**—God's people *purchased* (acquired, *Greek*) as His *peculiar* (*Greek*) possession by the blood of Christ (Acts 20:28). We value highly that which we pay a high price for; so God, His Church (ch. 5:25, 26; I Pet. 1:18; 2:9; Mal. 3:17, *Margin,* "my *special* treasure"). **15. Wherefore**—because ye are in Christ and sealed by His Spirit (vss. 13, 14). **I also**—on my part, in return for God's so great benefits to *you.* **after I heard**—ever since I have heard. Not implying that he had only *heard* of their conversion: an erroneous argument used by some against the address of this Epistle to the Ephesians (*Note,* vs. 1); but referring to the report he had heard *since* he was with them, as to their Christian graces. So in the case of Philemon, his "*beloved fellow laborer*" (Philemon 1), he uses the same words (Philemon 4, 5). **your faith**—rather, as *Greek,* "the faith among you," i.e., which many (not all) of you have. **love unto all the saints** —of whatever name, simply because they are saints. A distinguishing characteristic of true Christianity (ch. 6:24). "*Faith* and *love* he often joins together. A wondrous pair" [CHRYSOSTOM]. Hope is added, vs. 18. **16.** (Col. 1:9.) **of you**—omitted in the oldest MSS. Then the translation may be as

English Version still, or as ALFORD, "making mention of *them*" (your "faith and love"). **17.** A fit prayer for all Christians. **the God of our Lord Jesus**—appropriate title here; as in vss. 20-22 he treats of *God's* raising *Jesus* to be Head over all things to the Church. Jesus Himself called the Father "*My God*" (Matt. 27:46). **the Father of glory**—(Cf. Acts 7:2). The Father of that infinite glory which shines in the face of Christ, who is "the glory" (the true Shekinah); through whom also "the glory of the inheritance" (vs. 18) shall be ours (John 17:24; II Cor. 3:7 to 4:6). **the spirit of wisdom**—whose attribute is infinite wisdom and who works wisdom in believers (Isa. 11:2). **and revelation**—whose function it is to *reveal* to believers spiritual mysteries (John 16:14, 15; I Cor. 2:10). **in the knowledge**—rather, as *Greek* (see *Note*, I Cor. 13:12), "in the *full knowledge* of Him," viz., God. **18. understanding**—The oldest MSS., versions, and Fathers, read "heart." Cf. the contrary state of unbelieving, the *heart* being in fault (ch. 4:18; Matt. 13:15). Translate, "Having the eyes of your heart enlightened" (ch. 5:14; Matt. 4:16). The first effect of the Spirit moving in the new creation, as in the original physical creation (Gen. 1:3; II Cor. 4: 6). So THEOPHILUS to AUTOLYCUS, 1. 3, "the ears of the heart." Where spiritual *light* is, there is *life* (John 1:4). The heart is "the core of life" [HARLESS], and the fountain of the thoughts; whence "the heart" in Scripture includes the *mind*, as well as the inclination. Its "eye," or inward vision, both receives and contemplates the light (Matt. 6:22, 23). The eye is the symbol of intelligence (Ezek. 1:18). **the hope of his calling**—the hope appertaining to His having called you; or, to the calling wherewith He has called you. **and**—omitted in the oldest MSS. and versions. **riches of the glory ...** —(Col. 1:27). **his inheritance in the saints**—The inheritance which he has in store in the case of the saints. I prefer explaining, "The inheritance which He has in his saints." (See *Note*, vs. 18; Deut. 32: 9.) **19. exceeding**—"surpassing." **power to us-ward who believe**—The whole of the working of His grace, which He is carrying on, and will carry on, in us who believe. By the term "saints" (vs. 18), believers are regarded as *absolutely perfected*, and so as being God's inheritance; in this verse, as in the course of *fighting* the good fight of faith. **according to**—in accordance with what might be expected from. **working**—*Greek*, "the energizing"; translate, "the effectual working" (ch. 3:7). The same superhuman power was needed and exerted to make us believe, as was needed and exerted to raise Christ from the dead (vs. 20). Cf. Philippians 3:10, "the power of His resurrection" (Col. 2:12; I Pet. 1:3-5). **of his mighty power**—*Greek*, "of the strength of His might." **20. in Christ**—as our "first fruits" of the resurrection, and Head, in virtue of God's mighty working in whom His power to us-ward is made possible and actual [ALFORD]. **when he raised him**—"in that He raised Him." The raising of Christ is not only an earnest of our bodies being hereafter raised, but has a spiritual power in it involving (by virtue of our living union with Him, as members with the Head) the resurrection, spiritually of the believer's soul now, and, consequently, of his body hereafter (Rom. 6:8-11; 8:11). The Son, too, as God (though not as man), had a share in raising His own human body (John 2:19; 10:17, 18). Also the Holy Spirit (Rom. 1:4; I Pet. 3:18). **set him**—*Greek*, "made Him sit." The glorious spirits *stand* about the throne of God, but they do not *sit at* God's right hand (Heb. 1:13). **at his own right hand**—(Ps. 110:1). Where He remains till all His enemies have been put under His feet (I Cor. 15:24). Being appointed to "rule in the midst of His enemies" during their rebellion (Ps. 110:2), He shall resign His commission after their subjection [PEARSON] (Mark 16:19; Heb. 1:3; 10:12). **in the heavenly places**—(vs. 3). As Christ has a literal body, heaven is not merely a state, but a *place;* and where He is, there His people shall be (John 14:3). **21.** *Greek,* "Far (or high) above all (ch. 4:10) principality (or rule, I Cor. 15:24), and authority, and power (Matt. 28:18), and dominion (or lordship)." Cf. Philippians 2:9; Colossians 1:16; Hebrews 7:26; I Peter 3:22. Evil spirits (who are similarly divided into various ranks, ch. 6:12), as well as angels of light, and earthly potentates, are included (cf. Rom. 8:38). Jesus is "King of kings, and Lord of lords" (Rev. 19:16). The higher is His honor, the greater is that of His people, who are His members joined to Him, the Head. Some philosophizing teachers of the school of Simon Magus, in Western Asia Minor, had, according to IRENÆUS and EPIPHANIUS, taught their hearers these names of various ranks of angels. Paul shows that the truest wisdom is to know Christ as reigning above them all. **every name**—every being whatever. "Any other creature" (Rom. 8:39). **in this world**—*Greek*, "age," i.e., the present *order of things.* "Things present ... things to come" (Rom. 8:38). **that ... to come** —"Names which now we know not, but shall know hereafter in heaven. We know that the emperor goes before all, though we cannot enumerate all the satraps and ministers of his court; so we know that Christ is set above all, although we cannot *name* them all" [BENGEL]. **22. put ... under**—*Greek,* "put in subjection under" (Ps. 8:6; I Cor. 15: 27). **gave ... to the church**—for her special advantage. The *Greek* order is emphatic: "HIM He gave as Head over all things to the Church." Had it been anyone save HIM, her Head, it would not have been the boon it is to the Church. But as *He* is Head over all things who is also her Head (and she the body), all things are hers (I Cor. 3:21-23). He is OVER ("far above") all things; in contrast to the words, "TO *the Church,*" viz., *for her advantage.* The former are subject; the latter is joined with Him in His dominion over them. "Head" implies not only His dominion, but our union; therefore, while we look upon Him at the right hand of God, we see ourselves in heaven (Rev. 3:21). For the Head and body are not severed by anything intervening, else the body would cease to be the body, and the Head cease to be the Head [PEARSON from CHRYSOSTOM]. **23. his body**—His mystical and spiritual, not literal, body. Not, however, merely figurative, or metaphorical. He is really, though spiritually, the Church's Head. His life is her life. She shares His crucifixion and His consequent glory. He possesses everything, His fellowship with the Father, His fulness of the Spirit, and His glorified manhood, not merely for Himself, but *for her,* who has a membership of His body, of His flesh, and of His bones (ch. 5:30). **fulness**—"the filled-up receptacle" [EADIE]. The Church is *dwelt in and filled by Christ.* She is the receptacle, not of His inherent, but of His *communicated, plenitude* of gifts and graces. As His is the "fulness" (John 1: 16; Col. 1:19; 2:9) inherently, so she is His "fulness" by His impartation of it to her, in virtue of her union to Him (ch. 5:18; Col. 2:10). "The *full manifestation* of His being, penetrated by His life" [CONYBEARE and HOWSON]. She is the continued revelation of His divine life in human form; *the fullest representative of His plenitude.* Not the angelic hierarchy, as false teachers taught (Col. 2:9, 10, 18), but Christ Himself is the "fulness of the God-head," and she represents Him. KOPPE translates less probably, "the whole universal multitude." **filleth all in all**—Christ as the Creator, Preserver, and Governor of the world, constituted by God (Col. 1:16-19), *fills all* the universe of things *with all* things. "Fills all creation with whatever it possesses" [ALFORD]. The *Greek* is, "filleth *for Himself.*"

CHAPTER 2

Vss. 1-22. GOD'S LOVE AND GRACE IN QUICKENING US, ONCE DEAD, THROUGH CHRIST. HIS PURPOSE IN DOING SO: EXHORTATION BASED ON OUR PRIVILEGES AS BUILT TOGETHER, AN HOLY TEMPLE, IN CHRIST, THROUGH THE SPIRIT. **1. And you**—"You also," among those who have experienced His mighty power in enabling them to believe (vss. 19-23). *hath he quickened*—supplied from the *Greek* (vs. 5). **dead**—spiritually (Col. 2:13). A living corpse: without the gracious presence of God's Spirit in the soul, and so unable to think, will, or do aught that is holy. **in trespasses . . . sins**—*in* them, as the element in which the unbeliever is, and through which he is dead to the true life. Sin is the death of the soul. Isaiah 9:2; John 5:25, "dead" (spiritually), I Timothy 5:6. "Alienated from the *life* of God" (ch. 4:18). Translate, as *Greek,* "in *your* trespasses . . . ." "Trespass" in *Greek,* expresses a FALL or LAPSE, such as the transgression of Adam whereby he fell. "Sin" (*Greek, "hamartia"*) implies innate *corruption* and ALIENATION from God (lit., *erring of the mind from the rule of truth*), exhibited in *acts* of sin (*Greek, "hamartemata"*). BENGEL refers "trespasses" to the Jews who had the law, and yet revolted from it; "sins," to the Gentiles who know not God. **2. the course of this world**—the career (lit., "the age," cf. Gal. 1:4), or present system of *this* world (I Cor. 2:6, 12; 3:18, 19, as opposed to "the world to come"): alien from God, and lying in the wicked one (I John 5:19). "The age" (which is something more external and ethical) regulates "the world" (which is something more external). **the prince of the power of the air**—the unseen God who lies underneath guiding "the course of this world" (II Cor. 4:4); ranging through the *air* around us: cf. Mark 4:4, "fowls of the air" (*Greek,* "heaven") i.e., (vs. 15), "Satan" and his demons. Cf. ch. 6:12; John 12:31. Christ's ascension seems to have cast Satan out of heaven (Rev. 12:5, 9, 10, 12, 13), where he had been heretofore the accuser of the brethren (Job 1). No longer able to accuse *in heaven* those justified by Christ, the ascended Saviour (Rom. 8:33, 34), he assails them on earth with all trials and temptations; and "we live in an atmosphere poisonous and impregnated with deadly elements. But a mighty purification of the air will be effected by Christ's coming" [AUBERLEN], for Satan shall be bound (Rev. 12:12, 13, 15, 17; 20:2, 3). "The power" is here used collectively for the "powers of the air"; in apposition with which "powers" stand the "spirits," comprehended in the singular, "the spirit," taken also collectively: the aggregate of the "seducing spirits" (I Tim. 4:1) which "work now (*still;* not merely, as in your case, 'in time *past*') in the sons of disobedience" (a Hebraism: men who are not merely by accident disobedient, but who are essentially *sons of disobedience* itself: cf. Matt. 3:7), and of which

Satan is here declared to be "the prince." The Greek does not allow "the spirit" to refer to *Satan,* "the prince" himself, but to *"the powers of the air"* of which he is prince. The powers of the air are the embodiment of that evil "spirit" which is the ruling principle of unbelievers, especially the heathen (Acts 26:18), as opposed to the spirit of the children of God (Luke 4:33). The potency of that "spirit" is shown in the "disobedience" of the former. Cf. Deuteronomy 32:20, "children in whom is no faith" (Isa. 30:9; 57:4). They disobey the Gospel both in faith and practice (II Thess. 1:8; II Cor. 2:12). **3. also we**—i.e., *we also.* Paul here joins himself in the same category with them, passing from the second person (vss. 1, 2) to the first person here. **all**—Jews and Gentiles. **our conversation**—"our way of life" (II Cor. 1:12; I Pet. 1:18). This expression implies an outwardly more *decorous* course, than the open "walk" in *gross sins* on the part of the majority of Ephesians in times past, the Gentile portion of whom may be specially referred to in vs. 2. Paul and his Jewish countrymen, though outwardly more seemly than the Gentiles (Acts 26:4, 5, 18), had been essentially like them in living to the unrenewed flesh, without the Spirit of God. **fulfilling**—*Greek,* "doing." **mind**—*Greek,* "our thoughts." Mental suggestions and purposes (independent of God), as distinguished from the blind impulses of "the flesh." **and were by nature** —He intentionally breaks off the construction, substituting "and we were" for "and being," to mark emphatically his and their *past* state by nature, as contrasted with their present state by grace. Not merely is it, we had our way of life fulfilling our fleshly desires, *and so being* children of wrath; but *we were by nature* originally "children of wrath," and so consequently had our way of life fulfilling our fleshly desires. "Nature," in *Greek,* implies that which has *grown* in us as the peculiarity of our being, growing with our growth, and strengthening with our strength, as distinguished from that which has been wrought on us by mere external influences: what is inherent, not acquired (Job 14:4; Ps. 51:5). An incidental proof of the doctrine of original sin. **children of wrath**—not merely "sons," as in the *Greek,* "sons of disobedience" (vs. 2), but "children" *by generation;* not merely *by adoption,* as "sons" might be. The *Greek* order more emphatically marks this innate corruption: "Those who in their (very) nature are children of wrath"; vs. 5, "grace" is opposed to "nature" here; and *salvation* (implied in vss. 5, 8, "saved") to "wrath." Cf. Article IX, Church of England Common Prayer Book. "Original sin (birth-sin), standeth not in the following of Adam, but is the fault and corruption of the nature of every man, naturally engendered of Adam [Christ was *supernaturally* conceived by the Holy Ghost of the Virgin], whereby man is very far gone from original righteousness, and is of his own nature inclined to evil; and therefore, in every person born into this world, it deserveth God's wrath and damnation." Paul shows that even the Jews, who boasted of their birth from Abraham, were by natural birth equally children of wrath as the Gentiles, whom the Jews despised on account of their birth from idolaters (Rom. 3:9; 5:12-14). "*Wrath* abideth" on all who disobey the Gospel in faith and practice (John 3:36). The phrase, "children of wrath," is a Hebraism, i.e., objects of God's wrath from childhood, in our natural state, as being born in the sin which God hates. So "son of death" (*Margin,* II Sam. 12:5); "son of perdition" (John 17:12; II Thess. 2:3). **as others**—*Greek,* "as the rest" of mankind are (I Thess. 4:13). **4. God, who is rich**—Greek "(as) *being* rich in mercy." **for** —i.e., "*because of* His great love." This was the *special* ground of God's saving us; as "rich in mercy" (cf. vs. 7; ch. 1:7; Rom. 2:4; 10:12) was the general ground. "*Mercy* takes away misery; *love* confers salvation" [BENGEL]. **5. dead in sins**—The best reading in the *Greek*, "dead in *our* (lit., '*the*') *trespasses.*" **quickened**—"vivified" spiritually, and consequences hereafter, corporally. There must be a spiritual resurrection of the soul before there can be a comfortable resurrection of the body [PEARSON] (John 11:25, 26; Rom. 8:11). **together with Christ**—The Head being seated at God's right hand, the body also sits there with Him [CHRYSOSTOM]. We are already seated there IN Him ("in Christ Jesus," vs. 6), and hereafter shall be seated *by* Him: IN Him already as in our Head, which is the ground of our hope; *by* Him hereafter, as by the conferring cause, when hope shall be swallowed up in fruition [PEARSON]. What God wrought in Christ, He wrought (by the very fact) in all united to Christ, and one with Him. **by grace ye are saved**—Greek, "Ye are in a saved state." Not merely "ye are being saved," but ye "are passed from death unto life" (John 5:24). Salvation is to the Christian not a thing to be waited for hereafter, but already realized (I John 3:14). The parenthetic introduction of this clause here (cf. vs. 8) is a burst of Paul's feeling, and in order to make the Ephesians feel that *grace* from first to last is the sole source of salvation; hence, too, he says "ye," not "we." **6. raised us up together**—with Christ. The "raising up" presupposes previous quickening of Jesus in the tomb, and of us in the grave of our sins. **made us sit together** —with Christ, viz., in His ascension. Believers are bodily in heaven in point of right, and virtually so in spirit, and have each their own place assigned there, which in due time they shall take possession of (Phil. 3:20, 21). He does not say, "*on the right hand* of God"; a prerogative reserved to Christ peculiarly; though they shall share His throne (Rev. 3:21). **in Christ Jesus**—Our union with Him is the ground of our present spiritual, and future bodily, resurrection and ascension. "Christ Jesus" is the phrase mostly used in this Epistle, in which the *office* of the Christ, the Anointed Prophet, Priest and King, is the prominent thought; when the Person is prominent, "Jesus Christ" is the phrase used. **7.** Greek, "That He might show forth (middle reflexive voice; for His own glory, ch. 1:6, 12, 14) in the ages which are coming on," i.e., the blessed *ages* of the Gospel which supersede "the *age* (Greek, for 'course') of this world" (vs. 2), and the past "ages" from which the mystery was hidden (Col. 1:26, 27). These good ages, though beginning with the first preaching of the Gospel, *and thenceforth continually succeeding one another,* are not consummated till the Lord's coming again (cf. ch. 1:21; Heb. 6:5). The words, "coming on," do not exclude *the time then present,* but imply simply the ages *following* upon Christ's "raising them up together" spiritually (vs. 6). **kindness**—"benignity." **through Christ**— rather, as *Greek*, "in Christ"; the same expression as is so often repeated, to mark that all our blessings center "IN HIM." **8. For**—illustrating "the exceeding riches of His grace in kindness," as in vs. 5, "Ye are in a saved state." **through faith**— the effect of the power of Christ's resurrection (ch. 1:19, 20; Phil. 3:10) whereby we are "raised together" with Him (vs. 6; Col. 2:12). Some of the oldest MSS. read, "through your (lit., '*the*') faith." The instrument or mean of salvation on the part of

the person saved; Christ alone is the *meritorious* agent. **and that**—viz., *the act of believing,* or "faith." "Of yourselves" stands in opposition to, "it is the gift of God" (Phil. 1:29). "That which I have said, 'through faith,' I do not wish to be understood so as if I excepted *faith* itself from *grace*" [ESTIUS]. "God justifies the believing man, not for the worthiness of his belief, but for the worthiness of Him in whom he believes" [HOOKER]. The initiation, as well as the increase, of faith, is from the Spirit of God, not only by an external proposal of the word, but by internal illumination in the soul [PEARSON]. Yet "faith" cometh by the means which man must avail himself of, viz., "hearing the word of God" (Rom. 10:17), and prayer (Luke 11: 13), though the blessing is wholly of God (I Cor. 3:6, 7). **9. Not of works**—This clause stands in contrast to "by grace," as is confirmed by Romans 4:4, 5; 11:6. **lest**—rather, as *Greek*, "that no man should boast" (Rom. 3:27; 4:2). **10. workmanship** —lit., "a thing of His making"; "handiwork." Here the spiritual creation, not the physical, is referred to (vss. 8, 9). **created**—having been created (ch. 4:24; Ps. 102:18; Isa. 43:21; II Cor. 5:5, 17). **unto good works**—"*for* good works." "Good works" cannot be performed until we are new "created unto" them. Paul never calls the works of the law "good works." We are not *saved by,* but *created unto,* good works. **before ordained**— Greek, "before made ready" (cf. John 5:36). God marks out for each in His purposes beforehand, the particular good works, and the time and way which He sees best. God both makes ready by His providence the opportunities for *the works,* and makes *us* ready for their performance (John 15:16; II Tim. 2:21). **that we should walk in them**—not "be saved" by them. Works do not justify, but the justified man works (Gal. 5:22-25). **11.** The *Greek* order in the oldest MSS. is, "That in time past (lit., *once*) ye . . . ." Such remembrance sharpens gratitude and strengthens faith (vs. 19) [BENGEL]. **Gentiles in the flesh**—i.e., Gentiles in respect to circumcision. **called Uncircumcision**—The Gentiles were called [in contempt], and *were,* the Uncircumcision; the Jews were called, but were not truly, the Circumcision [ELLICOTT]. **in the flesh made by hands**—as opposed to the true "circumcision of the heart in the Spirit, and not the letter" (Rom. 2:29), "made without the hands in putting off the body of the sins of the flesh by the circumcision of Christ" (Col. 2:11). **12. without Christ**—Greek, "*separate from* Christ"; having no part in Him; far from Him. A different *Greek* word (*aneu*) would be required to express, "Christ was not present with you" [TITTMANN]. **aliens**—Greek, "alienated from," not merely "separated from." The Israelites were cut off from the commonwealth of God, but it was as being self-righteous, indolent, and unworthy, not as *aliens* and *strangers* [CHRYSOSTOM]. The expression, "alienated from," takes it for granted that the Gentiles, before they had apostatized from the primitive truth, had been sharers in light and life (cf. ch. 4:18, 23). The hope of redemption through the Messiah, on their subsequent apostasy, was embodied into a definite "commonwealth" or *polity,* viz., that "of Israel," from which the Gentiles were alienated. Contrast vs. 13; ch. 3:6; 4:4, 5, with Psalm 147:20. **covenants of promise**—rather, ". . . of *the* promise," viz., "to thee and thy seed will I give this land" (Rom. 9:4; Gal. 3:16). The plural implies the several renewals of the covenant with Abraham, Isaac, and Jacob, and with the whole people at Sinai [ALFORD]. "The promise" is singular, to signify that the covenant, in reality, and substantially, is one and the same at all times, but only different in its accidents and external circumstances (cf. Heb. 1:1, "at sundry times and in divers manners"). **having no ... hope**—beyond this life (I Cor. 15:19). The CONJECTURES of heathen philosophers as to a future life were at best vague and utterly unsatisfactory. They had no divine "promise," and therefore no sure ground of "hope." Epicurus and Aristotle did not believe in it at all. The Platonists believed the soul passed through perpetual changes, now happy, and then again miserable; the Stoics, that it existed no longer than till the time of the general burning up of all things. **without God**—*Greek*, "atheists," i.e., they had not "God" in the sense we use the word, the Eternal Being who made and governs all things (cf. Acts 14:15, "Turn from these vanities unto *the living God* who made heaven, and earth, and the sea, and all things therein"), whereas the Jews had distinct ideas of God and immortality. Cf. also Galatians 4:8, "Ye knew not God ... ye did service unto them which are no gods" (I Thess. 4:5). So also pantheists are atheists, for an impersonal God is NO GOD, and an ideal immortality no immortality [THOLUCK]. **in the world**—in contrast to belonging to "the commonwealth of Israel." Having their portion and their all in this godless vain world (Ps. 17:14), from which Christ delivers His people (John 15:19; 17:14; Gal. 1:4). **13. now**—in contrast to "at that time" (vs. 12). **in Christ Jesus**—"Jesus" is here added, whereas the expression before (vs. 12) had been merely "Christ," to mark that they know Christ as the *personal* Saviour, "Jesus." **sometimes**—*Greek*, "aforetime." **far off** —the Jewish description of the Gentiles. Far off from God and from the people of God (vs. 17; Isa. 57:19; Acts 2:39). **are**—*Greek*, "have been." **by** —*Greek*, "in." Thus "the blood of Christ" is made the seal of a covenant IN which their nearness to God consists. In ch. 1:7, where the blood is more directly spoken of as the *instrument*, it is "*through* His blood" [ALFORD]. **14. he**—*Greek*, "Himself" alone, pre-eminently, and none else. Emphatical. **our peace**—not merely "Peacemaker," but "Himself" the price of our (Jews' and Gentiles' alike) peace with God, and so the bond of union between "both" in God. He took both into Himself, and reconciled them, united, to God, by His assuming our nature and our penal and legal liabilities (vs. 15; Isa. 9:5, 6; 53:5; Mic. 5:5; Col. 1:20). His title, "Shiloh," means the same (Gen. 49:10). **the middle wall of partition**—*Greek*, " ... of *the* partition" or "fence"; the *middle wall* which *parted* Jew and Gentile. There was a balustrade of stone which separated the court of the Gentiles from the holy place, which it was death for a Gentile to pass. But this, though incidentally alluded to, was but a symbol of the partition itself, viz., "the enmity" *between* "*both*" *and God* (vs. 15), the real cause of separation from God, and so the mediate cause of their separation from one another. Hence there was a twofold wall of partition, one the inner wall, severing the Jewish people from entrance to the holy part of the temple where the priests officiated, the other the outer wall, separating the Gentile proselytes from access to the court of the Jews (cf. Ezek. 44:7; Acts 21:28). Thus this twofold wall represented the Sinaitic law, which *both* severed all men, even the Jews, from access to God (through sin, which is the violation of the law), and also separated the Gentiles from the Jews. As the term "wall" implies the *strength* of the partition, so "fence" implies that it was easily removed by God

when the due time came. **15.** Rather, make "enmity" an apposition to "the middle wall of partition"; "Hath broken down the middle wall of partition (not merely as *English Version*, '*between us*,' but also *between all men and God*), to wit, the enmity (Rom. 8:7) by His flesh" (cf. vs. 16; Rom. 8:3). **the law of commandments** *contained* in—*Greek*, "the law of the commandments [consisting] in ordinances." This law was "the partition" or "fence," which embodied the expression of the "enmity" (the "wrath" of God against our sin, and our enmity to Him, vs. 3) (Rom. 4:15; 5:20; 7:10, 11; 8:7). Christ has in, or by, His crucified flesh, abolished it, so far as its condemning and enmity-creating power is concerned (Col. 2:14), substituting for it the law of love, which is the everlasting spirit of the law, and which flows from the realization in the soul of His love in His death for us. Translate what follows, "that He might make the two (Jews and Gentiles) into one new man." Not that He might merely reconcile the two to each other, but incorporate the two, reconciled in Him to God, into one new man; the old man to which both belonged, the enemy of God, having been slain in His flesh on the cross. Observe, too, ONE new man; we are all in God's sight but one in Christ, as we are but one in Adam [ALFORD]. **making peace**—primarily between all and God, secondarily between Jews and Gentiles; He being "our peace." This "peace-making" precedes its publication (vs. 17). **16.** Translate, "might altogether reconcile them both in one body (the Church, Col. 3:15) unto God through His cross." The *Greek* for "reconcile" (*apocatalaxe*), found only here and in Colossians 1:20, expresses not only a return to favor with one (*catallage*), but so to lay aside enmity that complete amity follows; to pass *from* enmity to *complete reconciliation* [TITTMANN]. **slain the enmity**—viz., that had been between man and God; and so that between Jew and Gentile which had resulted from it. By His being *slain*, He *slew* it (cf. Heb. 2:14). **thereby**—*Greek*, "therein"; "in" or "by the cross," i.e., His crucifixion (Col. 2:15). **17.** Translate, "He came and announced glad tidings of peace." "He came" of His own free love, and "announced peace" with His own mouth to the apostles (Luke 24:36; John 20:19, 21, 26); and by them to others, through His Spirit present in His Church (John 14:18). Acts 26:23 is strictly parallel; after His resurrection "He showed light to the people ('them that were nigh') and to the Gentiles" ("you that were afar off"), by His Spirit in His ministers (cf. I Pet. 3:19). **and to them**—The oldest MSS. insert "peace" again: "And peace to them." The repetition implies the joy with which both alike would dwell again and again upon the welcome word "peace." So Isaiah 57:19. **18.** Translate, "For it is through Him (John 14:6; Heb. 10:19) that we have *our* access (ch. 3:12; Rom. 5:2), both of us, in (i.e., united in, i.e., *by*, I Cor. 12: 13, *Greek*) one Spirit to the Father," viz., as our common Father, reconciled to both alike; whence flows the removal of all separation between Jew and Gentile. The *oneness* of "the Spirit," through which we both have our access, is necessarily followed by *oneness* of the body, the Church (vs. 16). The distinctness of persons in the Divine Trinity appears in this verse. It is also fatal to the theory of sacerdotal priests in the Gospel through whom alone the people can approach God. All alike, people and ministers, can draw nigh to God through Christ, their ever living Priest. **19. Now, therefore** —rather, "So then" [ALFORD]. **foreigners**—rather, "sojourners"; opposed to "members of the household," as "strangers" is to "fellow citizens." Philippians 3:19, 20, "conversation," *Greek,* "citizenship." **but**—The oldest MSS. add, "are." **with the saints**—"the commonwealth of (spiritual) Israel" (vs. 12). **of God**—THE FATHER; as JESUS CHRIST appears in vs. 20, and THE SPIRIT in vs. 22. **20.** Translate as *Greek,* "Built up upon . . ." (participle; *having been built up upon;* omit, therefore, "and are"). Cf. I Corinthians 3:11, 12. The same image in ch. 3:18, recurs in his address to the Ephesian elders (Acts 20:32), and in his Epistle to Timothy at Ephesus (I Tim. 3:15; II Tim. 2:19), naturally suggested by the splendid architecture of Diana's temple; the glory of the Christian temple is eternal and real, not mere idolatrous gaud. The image of a building is appropriate also to the Jew-Christians; as the temple at Jerusalem was the stronghold of Judaism; as Diana's temple, of paganism. **foundation of the apostles** . . .—i.e., upon their ministry and living example (cf. Matt. 16:18). Christ Himself, the only true Foundation, was the grand subject of their ministry, and spring of their life. As one with Him and His fellow workers, they, too, in a secondary sense, are called "foundations" (Rev. 21:14). The "prophets" are joined with them closely; for the expression is here not "*foundations* of the apostles and *the* prophets," but "*foundations* of the apostles and *prophets*." For the doctrine of both was essentially *one* (I Pet. 1:10, 11; Rev. 19:10). The apostles take the precedency (Luke 10:24). Thus he appropriately shows regard to the claims of the Jews and Gentiles: "the prophets" representing the old Jewish dispensation, "the apostles" the new. The "prophets" of the new also are included. BENGEL and ALFORD refer the meaning solely to these (ch. 3:5; 4:11). These passages imply, I think, that the New Testament prophets are not excluded; but the apostle's plain reference to Psalm 118:22, "the head stone of the corner," proves that the Old Testament prophets are a prominent thought. David is called a "prophet" in Acts 2:30. Cf. also Isaiah 28:16; another prophet present to the mind of Paul, which prophecy leans on the earlier one of Jacob (Gen. 49:24). The sense of the context, too, suits this: Ye were once aliens from the commonwealth of *Israel* (in the time of her *Old Testament prophets*), but now ye are members of the true Israel, built upon the foundation of her New Testament apostles and Old Testament prophets. Paul continually identifies his teaching with that of Israel's old prophets (Acts 26:22; 28:23). The costly foundation stones of the temple (I Kings 5:17) typified the same truth (cf. Jer. 51:26). The same stone is at once the cornerstone and the foundation stone on which the whole building rests. Paul supposes a stone or rock so large and so fashioned as to be both at once; supporting the whole as the foundation, and in part rising up at the extremities, so as to admit of the side walls meeting in it, and being united in it as the cornerstone [ZANCHIUS]. As the cornerstone, it is conspicuous, as was Christ (I Pet. 2:6), and coming in men's way may be stumbled over, as the Jews did at Christ (Matt. 21:42; I Pet. 2:7). **21. In whom**—as holding together the whole. **fitly framed**—so as exactly to fit together. **groweth** —"is growing" continually. Here an additional thought is added to the image; the Church has the *growth* of a living organism, not the mere *increase* of a building. Cf. I Peter 2:5; "*lively* stones . . . built up a spiritual house." Cf. ch. 4:16; Zechariah 6:12, "The *Branch* shall build the *temple* of the Lord," where similarly the growth of a branch, and the building of a temple, are joined. **holy**—being the "habitation *of God*" (vs. 22). So "in the Lord" (Christ) answers to "through the Spirit" (vs. 22; cf. ch. 3:16, 17). "Christ is the inclusive Head of all the building, the element in which it has its being and now its growth" [ALFORD]. **22. are builded together**—Translate, "are being builded together." **through**—*Greek,* "*in* the Spirit." God, by His Spirit *in* believers, has them for His habitation (I Cor. 3:16, 17; 6:19; II Cor. 6:16).

CHAPTER 3

VSS. 1-21. HIS APOSTOLIC OFFICE TO MAKE KNOWN THE MYSTERY OF CHRIST REVEALED BY THE SPIRIT: PRAYER THAT BY THE SAME SPIRIT THEY MAY COMPREHEND THE VAST LOVE OF CHRIST: DOXOLOGY ENDING THIS DIVISION OF THE EPISTLE. As the first chapter treated of THE FATHER'S office; and the second, THE SON'S, so this, that of THE SPIRIT. **1. of Jesus Christ**—*Greek,* "Christ Jesus." The *office* is the prominent thought in the latter arrangement; the *person,* in the former. He here marks the *Messiahship* of "Christ," maintained by him as the origin of his being a "prisoner," owing to the jealousy of the Jews being roused at his preaching it to *the Gentiles*. His very bonds were profitable to ("for" or "in behalf of you") Gentiles (vs. 13; II Tim. 2:10). He digresses at "For this cause," and does not complete the sentence which he had intended, until vs. 14, where he resumes the words, "For this cause," viz., because I know this your call of God as Gentiles (ch. 2:11-22), to be "fellow heirs" with the Jews (vs. 6), "I bow my knees to" the Father of our common Saviour (vss. 14, 15) to confirm you in the faith by His Spirit. "I Paul," expresses the agent employed by the Spirit to enlighten them, after he had been first enlightened himself by the same Spirit (vss. 3-5, 9). **2. If**—The *Greek* does not imply doubt: "Assuming (what I know to be the fact, viz.,) that ye have heard. . . ." "If, as I presume. . . ." The indicative in the *Greek* shows that no doubt is implied: "Seeing that doubtless. . . ." He by this phrase delicately reminds them of their having heard from himself, and probably from others subsequently, the fact. See *Introduction,* showing that these words do not disprove the address of this Epistle *to the Ephesians.* Cf. Acts 20:17-24. **the dispensation**—"The office of dispensing, as a steward, the grace of God which was (not 'is') given me to you-ward," viz., to dispense to you. **3. he made known**—The oldest MSS. read, "That by revelation *was* the mystery (viz., of the admission of the Gentiles, vs. 6; ch. 1:9) *made known* unto me (Gal. 1:12). **as I wrote afore**—viz., in this Epistle (ch. 1:9, 10), the words of which he partly repeats. **4. understand my knowledge**—"perceive my understanding" [ALFORD], or "intelligence." "When ye read," implies that, deep as are the mysteries of this Epistle, the way for all to understand them is to *read* it (II Tim. 3:15, 16). By *perceiving his understanding* of the mysteries, they, too, will be enabled to understand. **the mystery of Christ**—The "mystery" is Christ Himself, once hidden, but now revealed (Col. 1:27). **5. in other ages**—*Greek,* "generations." **not made known** —He does not say, "has not been *revealed.*" Making known by *revelation* is the source of making known by preaching [BENGEL]. The former was vouchsafed only to the prophets, in order that they might make known the truth so revealed to men in general. **unto the sons of men**—men in their state by birth, as contrasted with those illuminated "by the Spirit" (*Greek,* "IN the Spirit," cf. Rev. 1: 10), Matt. 16:17. **as**—The mystery of the call of the Gentiles (of which Paul speaks here) was not unknown to the Old Testament prophets (Isa. 56:6, 7; 49:6). But they did not know it with the same explicit distinctness "AS" it has been now known (Acts 10:19, 20; 11:18-21). They probably did not know that the Gentiles were to be admitted without circumcision or that they were to be on a level with the Jews in partaking of the grace of God. The gift of "the Spirit" in its fulness was reserved for the New Testament that Christ might thereby be glorified. The epithet, "holy," marks the special consecration of the New Testament "prophets" (who are here meant) by the Spirit, compared with which even the Old Testament prophets were but "sons of men" (Ezek. 2:3, and elsewhere). **6.** Translate, "That the Gentiles *are . . .*" "and *fellow members* of the same body, and *fellow* partakers of *the* (so the oldest MSS. read, not 'His') promise, in Christ *Jesus* (added in the oldest MSS.), *through* the Gospel." It is "in Christ Jesus" that they are made "fellow heirs" in the inheritance of GOD: "of the same body" under the Head, CHRIST JESUS; and "fellow partakers of the promise" in the communion of THE HOLY SPIRIT (ch. 1:13; Heb. 6:4). The Trinity is thus alluded to, as often elsewhere in this Epistle (ch. 2:19, 20, 22). **7. Whereof**—"of which" Gospel. **according to**—in consequence of, and in accordance with, "the gift of the grace of God." **given**—"which (gift of grace) was given to me by (*Greek,* 'according to,' as in vs. 20; ch. 1:19: as the result of, and in proportion to) the effectual working (*Greek,* 'energy,' or 'in-working') of His power." **8. am**—Not merely *was* I in times past, but I still am the least worthy of so high an office (cf. I Tim. 1:15, end). **least of all saints**—not merely "of all *apostles*" (I Cor. 15:9, 10). **is**—*Greek,* "has been given." **among**—omitted in the oldest MSS. Translate, "to *announce* to the Gentiles *the glad tidings of* the unsearchable (Job 5:9) riches," viz., of Christ's *grace* (ch. 1:7; 2:7). Romans 11: 33, "unsearchable" as a mine inexhaustible, whose treasures can never be fully explored (vss. 18, 19). **9. to make all men see**—*Greek,* "to enlighten all" (ch. 1:18; Ps. 18:28; Heb. 6:4). "All" (cf. Col. 1: 28). **fellowship**—The oldest MSS. read, "economy," or "dispensation" (cf. Col. 1:25, 26; and *Note,* ch. 1:10, above). "To make all see how it hath seemed good to God at this time to *dispense* (through me and others, His *stewards*) what heretofore was a mystery." ELLICOTT explains it, "the arrangement," or "regulation" of the mystery (the union of Jews and Gentiles in Christ) which was now to be humbly traced and acknowledged in the fact of its having secretly existed in the counsel of God, and now having been revealed to the heavenly powers by means of the Church. **from the beginning of the world**—*Greek,* "from (the beginning of) the ages." Cf. ch. 1:4; Romans 16:25; I Corinthians 2:7. The "ages" are the vast successive periods of time, marked by successive stages of creation and orders of beings. **in God**—"hidden in" His counsels (ch. 1:9). **created all things by Jesus Christ**—God's creation of the world and all things therein is the foundation of the rest of the "economy," which is freely dispensed according to the universal power of God [BENGEL]. As God created "the whole range of things" (so the *Greek*), physical and spiritual alike, He must have an absolute right to adjust all things as He will. Hence, we may see His right to keep the mystery of world-wide salvation in Christ "hidden in Him-

self," till his own good time for revealing it. The oldest MSS. omit "by Jesus Christ." **10.** The design of God in giving Paul grace to proclaim to the Gentiles the mystery of salvation heretofore hidden. **now**—first: opposed to "hidden from the beginning of the world" (vs. 5). **unto the principalities and**—*Greek* adds "the"—**powers**—unto the various orders of *good* angels primarily, as these dwell "in the heavenly places" in the highest sense; "known" to their adoring joy (1 Tim. 3:16; I Pet. 1:12). Secondarily, God's wisdom in redemption is made known to *evil* angels, who dwell "in heavenly places" in a lower sense, viz., the air (cf. ch. 2:2 with 6:12); "known" to their dismay (I Cor. 15: 24; Col. 2:15). **might be known**—Translate, "may be known." **by the church**—"by means of," or "through the Church," which is the "theater" for the display of God's manifold wisdom (Luke 15:10; I Cor. 4:9): "a spectacle (*Greek,* 'theater') to angels." Hence, angels are but our "fellow servants" (Rev. 19:10). **manifold wisdom**—though essentially one, as Christ 10). **manifold wisdom**—though essentially one, as Christ is one, yet varying the economy in respect to places, times, and persons (Isa. 55:8, 9; Heb. 1:1). Cf. I Pet. 4:10, "stewards of the manifold grace of God." Man cannot understand aright its single acts till he can survey them as a connected whole (I Cor. 13:12). The call of the Church is no haphazard remedy, or afterthought, but part of the eternal scheme, which, amidst manifold varieties of dispensation, is one in its end. **11. which he purposed**—*Greek,* "made." ELLICOTT translates, "wrought." **12.** Translate, "our boldness and our access (ch. 2:18) in confidence *through our* faith *in* Him." ALFORD quotes as an instance, Romans 8:38, etc. "THE access" (*Greek*) implies the formal introduction into the presence of a monarch. **13.** "I entreat you not to be dispirited." **for you**—in your behalf. **which is** —rather, "which *are* your glory," viz., inasmuch as showing that God loved you so much, as both to give His Son for you, and to permit His apostles to suffer "tribulations" for you [CHRYSOSTOM] in preaching the Gospel to the Gentiles. *Note,* vs. 1, "prisoner for you Gentiles." My tribulations are your spiritual "glory," as your faith is furthered thereby (I Cor. 4:10). **14. For this cause**—Resuming the thread of vs. 1, "For this cause." Because ye have such a standing in God's Church [ALFORD]. **bow my knees**—the proper attitude in humble prayer. Posture affects the mind, and is not therefore unimportant. See Paul's practice (Acts 20:36); and that of the Lord Himself on earth (Luke 22: 41). **unto the Father**—The oldest MSS. omit "of our Lord Jesus Christ." But *Vulgate* and some very old authorities retain them: vs. 15, "From whom," in either case, refers to "the Father" (*Patera*), as "family" (*patria*, akin in sound and etymology) plainly refers to Him. Still the foundation of all sonship is in Jesus Christ. **15. the whole family**—ALFORD, MIDDLETON, and others translate, "every family": alluding to the several *families* in heaven and in earth supposed to exist (THEOPHYLACT, ŒCUMENIUS, in SUICER, 2. 633), the apostle thus being supposed to imply that God, in His relation of Father to us His adopted children, is the great prototype of the paternal relation wherever found. But the idea that "the holy angels are bound up in spiritual *families* or *compaternities,*" is nowhere else in Scripture referred to. And Acts 2:36, where the article is similarly omitted, and yet the translation is, "*All the* house of Israel," shows that in New Testament *Greek* the translation is justifiable, *"all the* family," or *"the whole* family": which accords with Scripture views, that angels and men, the saints militant and those with God, are one holy family joined under the one Father in Christ, the mediator between heaven and earth (ch. 1:10; Phil. 2:10). Hence angels are termed our "brethren" (Rev. 19:10), and "sons of God" by creation, as we are by adoption (Job 38:7). The Church is part of the grand family, or kingdom, which comprehends, besides men, the higher spiritual world, where the archetype, to the realization of which redeemed man is now tending, is already realized. This universal idea of the "kingdom" of God as one divine community, is presented to us in the Lord's Prayer. By sin men were estranged, not only from God, but from that higher spiritual world in which the kingdom of God is already realized. As Christ when He reconciled men to God, united them to one another in a divine community (joined to Himself, the one Head), breaking down the partition wall between Jew and Gentile (ch. 2: 14), so also He joins them in communion with all those who have already attained that perfection in the kingdom of God, to which the Church on earth is aspiring (Col. 1:20) [NEANDER]. **is named**—derives its *origin* and its *name* as sons of God. To be named, and to be, are one with God. To bear God's name is to *belong to* God as *His own* peculiar people (Num. 6:27; Isa. 43:7; 44:5; Rom. 9:25, 26). **16. according to**—i.e. in abundance consonant to the riches of His glory; not "according to" the narrowness of our hearts. Colossians 1:11, "Strengthened with *all might according to His glorious power.*" **by**—*Greek,* "through"; "*by means of* His Spirit." **in**—The *Greek* implies, "infused into." **the inner man**—(ch. 4:22, 24; I Pet. 3:4)—"the hidden man of the heart." Not predicated of unbelievers, whose inward and outward man alike are carnal. But in believers, the "inner (new) man," their true self, stands in contrast to their old man, which is attached to them as a body of death daily being mortified, but not their true self. **17. That**—So that. **dwell**—abidingly make His abode (John 14:23). Where the Spirit is there Christ is (John 14:16, 18). **by faith**—*Greek,* "through faith," which opens the door of the *heart* to Jesus (John 3:20). It is not enough that He be on the tongue, or flit through the brain: the heart is His proper seat [CALVIN]. "You being rooted and grounded in love" (cf. vs. 19), is in the *Greek* connected with this clause, not with the clause, "that ye may be able to comprehend." "Rooted" is an image from a *tree;* "grounded" (*Greek,* "founded," "having your foundations resting on"), from a *building* (cf. *Note,* ch. 2:20, 21; Col. 1:23; 2:7). Contrast Matthew 13:6, 21. "Love," the first fruit of the Spirit, flowing from Christ's love realized in the soul, was to be the basis on which should rest their further comprehension of all the vastness of Christ's love. **18. May be able**—even still further. *Greek,* "May be *fully* able." **breadth ... length ... depth ... height** —viz., the full dimensions of the spiritual temple, answering to "the fulness of God" (vs. 19), to which the Church, according to its capacity, ought to correspond (cf. ch. 4:10, 13) as to "the fulness of *Christ.*" The "breadth" implies Christ's worldwide love, embracing all men; the "length" its being extended through all ages (vs. 21); the "depth," its profound wisdom which no creature can fathom (Rom. 11:33); the "height," its being beyond the reach of any foe to deprive us of (ch. 4:8) [BENGEL]. I prefer to understand "the breadth," etc., to refer to *the whole of the vast mystery of free salvation*

in Christ for all, Gentile and Jew alike, of which Paul had been speaking (vss. 3-9), and of which he now prays they may have a fuller comprehension. As subsidiary to this, and the most essential part of it, he adds, "and to know *the love of Christ*" (vs. 19). GROTIUS understands *depth* and *height* of God's goodness raising us from the lowest depression to the greatest height. **19. passeth**—surpasseth, exceeds. The paradox "to know ... which passeth knowledge," implies that when he says "know," he does not mean that we can *adequately* know; all we know is, that His love exceeds far our knowledge of it, and with even our fresh accessions of knowledge hereafter, will still exceed them. Even as God's power exceeds our thoughts (vs. 20). **filled with**—rather, as *Greek,* "filled even *unto* all the fulness of God" (this is the grand goal), i.e., filled, each according to your capacity, with the divine wisdom, knowledge, and love; *even as God is full,* and as Christ who dwells in your hearts, hath "all the fulness of the Godhead dwelling in Him bodily" (Col. 2:9). **20. unto us**—contrasted with *ourselves* and *our needs.* Translate, "that is able above all things (what is above all things) to do exceeding abundantly above what we ask or (even) think": *thought* takes a wider range than *prayers.* The word, *above,* occurs thrice as often in Paul's writings, as in all the rest of the New Testament, showing the warm exuberance of Paul's spirit. **according to the power**—the indwelling Spirit (Rom. 8:26). He appeals to their and his experience. **21.** Translate, "Unto Him be *the* glory (i.e., the whole glory of the gracious dispensation of salvation just spoken of) in the Church (as the theater for the manifestation of the glory, vs. 10) in Christ Jesus (as in Him all the glory centers, Zech. 6:13) to all the generations of eternal ages," lit., "of the age of the ages." Eternity is conceived as consisting of "ages" (these again consisting of "generations") endlessly succeeding one another.

CHAPTER 4

Vss. 1-32. EXHORTATIONS TO CHRISTIAN DUTIES RESTING ON OUR CHRISTIAN PRIVILEGES, AS UNITED IN ONE BODY, THOUGH VARYING IN THE GRACES GIVEN TO THE SEVERAL MEMBERS, THAT WE MAY COME UNTO A PERFECT MAN IN CHRIST. **1.** Translate, according to the *Greek* order, "I beseech you, therefore (seeing that such is your calling of grace, chs. 1, 2, 3). I the prisoner in the Lord" (i.e., imprisoned in the Lord's cause). What the world counted ignominy, he counts the highest honor, and he glories in his bonds for Christ, more than a king in his diadem [THEODORET]. His bonds, too, are an argument which should enforce his exhortation. **vocation**—Translate, "calling" to accord, as the *Greek* does, with "called" (vs. 4; ch. 1:18; Rom. 8: 28, 30). Colossians 3:15 similarly grounds Christian duties on our Christian "calling." *The exhortations of this part of the Epistle are built on the conscious enjoyment of the privileges mentioned in the former part.* Cf. ch. 4:32, with ch. 1:7; 5:1, with 1:5; 4:30, with 1:13; 5:15, with 1:8. **2, 3. lowliness**—In classic *Greek,* the meaning is *meanness* of *spirit:* the Gospel has elevated the word to express a Christian grace, viz., the esteeming of ourselves small, inasmuch as we are so; the thinking truly, and because truly, therefore lowlily, of ourselves [TRENCH]. **meekness**—that spirit in which we accept God's dealings with us without disputing and resisting; and also the accepting patiently of the injuries done us by men, out of the thought that they are permitted by God for the chastening and purifying of His people (II Sam. 16:11; cf. Gal. 6:1; II Tim. 2:25; Titus 3:2). It is only the *lowly*, humble heart that is also *meek* (Col. 3:12). As "lowliness and meekness" answer to "forbearing one another in love" (cf. "love," vss. 15, 16), so "long-suffering" answers to (vs. 4) "endeavoring (*Greek, 'earnestly'* or *'zealously giving diligence'*) to keep (maintain) the unity of the Spirit (the unity between men of different tempers, which flows from the presence of the Spirit, who is Himself 'one,' vs. 4) in (united in) the bond of peace" (the "bond" by which "peace" is maintained, viz., "love," Col. 3:14, 15 [BENGEL]; or, peace itself is the "bond" meant, uniting the members of the Church [AL-FORD]). **4.** In the apostle's creed, the article as to THE CHURCH properly follows that as to THE HOLY GHOST. To the Trinity naturally is annexed the Church, as the house to its tenant, to God His temple, the state to its founder [AUGUSTINE, *Enchir. ad Laurentium*, c. 15]. There is yet to be a Church, not merely potentially, but actually catholic or world-wide; then the Church and the world will be coextensive. Rome falls into inextricable error by setting up a mere man as a visible head, antedating that consummation which Christ, the true visible Head, at His appearing shall first realize. As the "SPIRIT" is mentioned here, so the "LORD" (Jesus), vs. 5, and "GOD the Father," vs. 6. Thus the Trinity is again set forth. **hope—here associated with** "the Spirit," which is the "earnest of our inheritance" (ch. 1:13, 14). As "faith" is mentioned, vs. 5, so "hope" here, and "love," vs. 2. The Holy Spirit, as the common higher principle of life (ch. 2:18, 22), gives to the Church its true unity. Outward uniformity is as yet unattainable; but beginning by having one mind, we shall hereafter end by having "one body." The true "body" of Christ (all believers of every age) is already "one," as joined to the one Head. But its unity is as yet not visible, even as the Head is not visible; but it shall appear when He shall appear (John 17:21-23; Col. 3:4). Meanwhile the rule is, "In essentials, unity; in doubtful questions, liberty; in all things, charity." There is more real unity where both go to heaven under different names than when with the same name one goes to heaven, the other to hell. Truth is the first thing: those who reach it, will at last reach unity, because truth is *one;* while those who seek unity as the first thing, may purchase it at the sacrifice of truth, and so of the soul itself. **of your calling**—the one "hope" *flowing from* our "calling," is the element "IN" which we are "called" to live. Instead of privileged classes, as the Jews under the law, a unity of dispensation was henceforth to be the common privilege of Jew and Gentile alike. Spirituality, universality, and unity, were *designed* to characterize the Church; and it shall be so at last (Isa. 2:2-4; 11:9, 13; Zeph. 3:9; Zech. 14:9). **5.** Similarly "faith" and "baptism" (the sacramental seal of faith) are connected Mark 16:16; Col. 2:12). Cf. I Corinthians 12:13, "Faith" is not here *that which we believe*, but the act of *believing*, the mean by which we apprehend the "one Lord." "Baptism" is specified, being the sacrament whereby we are *incorporated* into the "one body." Not the Lord's Supper, which is an act of matured communion on the part of those already incorporate, "a symbol of *union*, not of *unity*" [ELLICOTT]. In I Corinthians 10:17, where a breach of union was in question, it forms the rallying point [ALFORD]. There is not added, "One pope, one council, one form of govern-

ment" [*Cautions for Times*]. The Church is **one** in *unity* of *faith* (vs. 5; Jude 3); *unity of origination* (ch. 2:19-21); *unity of sacraments* (vs. 5; I Cor. 10: 17; 12:13); *unity of "hope"* (vs. 4; Titus 1:2); *unity of charity* (vs. 3); *unity (not uniformity) of discipline and government:* for where there is no order, no ministry with Christ as the Head, there is no Church [PEARSON, *Creed*, Article 9]. **6. above**—"*over* all." The "one God over all" (in His sovereignty and by His grace) is the grand source and crowning apex of unity (ch. 2:19, end). **through all**—by means of Christ "who filleth all things" (vs. 10; ch. 2:20, 21), and is "a propitiation" for all men (I John 2:2). **in you all**—The oldest MSS. omit "you." Many of the oldest versions and Fathers and old MSS. read, "in *us* all." Whether the pronoun be read or not, it must be understood (either from the "ye," vs. 4, or from the "us," vs. 7); for other parts of Scripture prove that the Spirit is not "in all" men, but only in believers (Rom. 8:9, 14). God is "Father" both by generation (as Creator) and regeneration (ch. 2:10; Jas. 1:17, 18; I John 5:1). **7. But**—Though "one" in our common connection with "one Lord, one faith, etc., one God," yet "each one of us" has assigned to him his own particular gift, to be used for the good of the whole: none is overlooked; none therefore can be dispensed with for the edifying of the Church (vs. 12). A motive to unity (vs. 3). Translate, "Unto *each* one of us was *the* grace (which was bestowed by Christ at His ascension, vs. 8) given according to . . . ." **the measure**—*the amount* "of the gift of Christ" (Rom. 12:3, 6). **8. Wherefore**—"For which reason," viz., in order to intimate that Christ, the Head of the Church, is the author of all these different gifts, and that giving of them is an act of His "grace" [ESTIUS]. **he saith**—God, whose word the Scripture is (Ps. 68:18). **When he ascended**—GOD is meant in the Psalm, represented by the ark, which was being brought up to Zion in triumph by David, after that "the Lord had given him rest round about from all his enemies" (II Sam. 6; 7:1; I Chron. 15). Paul quotes it of CHRIST ascending to heaven, who is therefore GOD. **captivity**—i.e., a band of captives. In the Psalm, the captive foes of David. In the antitypical meaning, the foes of Christ the Son of David, the devil, death, the curse, and sin (Col. 2: 15; II Pet. 2:4), led as it were in triumphal procession as a sign of the destruction of the foe. **gave gifts unto men**—in the Psalm, "*received* gifts *for* men," *Hebrew*, "among men," i.e., "thou hast received gifts" *to distribute among* men. As a conqueror distributes in token of his triumph the spoils of foes as gifts among his people. The impartation of the gifts and graces of the Spirit depended on Christ's ascension (John 7:39; 14:12). Paul stops short in the middle of the verse, and does not quote "that the Lord God might dwell \among *them*." This, it is true, is partly fulfilled in Christians being an "habitation of God through the Spirit" (ch. 2: 22). But the Psalm (vs. 16) refers to "the Lord dwelling in Zion *for ever*"; the ascension amidst attendant angels, having as its counterpart the second advent amidst "thousands of angels" (vs. 17), accompanied by the restoration of Israel (vs. 22), the destruction of God's enemies and the resurrection (vss. 20, 21, 23), the conversion of the kingdoms of the world to the Lord at Jerusalem (vss. 29-34). **9.** Paul reasons that (assuming Him to be God) His *ascent* implies a previous *descent;* and that the language of the Psalm can only refer to *Christ*, who first descended, then ascended. For God the Father does not ascend or descend. Yet the Psalm plainly refers to *God* (vss. 8, 17, 18). It must therefore be GOD THE SON (John 6:33, 62). As He declares (John 3:13), "No man hath ascended up to heaven, *but He that came down from heaven.*" Others, though they did not previously descend, have ascended; but none save *Christ* can be referred to in the Psalm as having done so; for it is of *God* it speaks. **lower parts of the earth**—The antithesis or contrast to "far above all heavens," is the argument of ALFORD and others, to show that this phrase means more than simply the *earth,* viz., the regions *beneath* it, even as He ascended not merely to the visible heavens, but "far above" them. Moreover, His design "that He might fill *all* things" (vs. 10, *Greek,* "the whole universe of things") may imply the same. But see *Note* on those words. Also the leading "captive" of the "captive band" ("captivity") of satanic powers, may imply that the warfare reached to *their habitation itself* (Ps. 63:9). Christ, as Lord of all, took possession first of the earth the unseen world beneath it (some conjecture that the region of the lost is in the central parts of our globe), then of heaven (Acts 2:27, 28). However, all we *surely* know is, that His soul at death descended to Hades, i.e., underwent the ordinary condition of departed spirits of men. The leading captive of satanic powers here, is not said to be at His descent, but *at His ascension;* so that no argument can be drawn from it for a descent to the abodes of Satan. Acts 2:27, 28, and Romans 10:7, favor the view of the reference being simply to His descent to *Hades.* So PEARSON *on Creed* (Phil. 2:10). **10. all heavens**—*Greek,* "all *the* heavens" (*Heb.* 7:26; 4:14), *Greek,* "passed *through* the heavens" to the throne of God itself. **might fill**—In *Greek,* the action is continued to the present time, both "*might*" and "may fill," viz., with His divine presence and Spirit, *not with His glorified body.* "Christ, as God, *is* present *everywhere;* as glorified man, He *can* be present *anywhere*" [ELLICOTT]. **11.** *Greek,* emphatical. "Himself" by His supreme power. "It is HE that gave. . . ." **gave some, apostles**—Translate, ". . . some to be apostles, and some to be prophets. . . ." The men who filled the office, no less than the office itself, were a divine gift [EADIE]. Ministers did not give themselves. Cf. with the list here, I Corinthians 12:10, 28. As the apostles, prophets, and evangelists were special and extraordinary ministers, so "pastors and teachers" are the ordinary stated ministers of a particular flock, including, probably, the bishops, presbyters, and deacons. Evangelists were itinerant preachers like our missionaries, as Philip the deacon (Acts 21:8); as contrasted with stationary "pastors and teachers" (II Tim. 4:5). The *evangelist* founded the Church; the *teacher* built it up in the faith already received. The "pastor" had the *outward rule* and *guidance* of the Church: the bishop. As to revelation, the "evangelist" testified infallibly of the past; the "prophet," infallibly of the future. The prophet derived all from the Spirit; the evangelist, in the special case of the Four, recorded matter of fact, cognizable to the senses, under the Spirit's guidance. No one form of Church polity as permanently *unalterable* is laid down in the New Testament though the apostolical order of bishops, or presbyters, and deacons, superintended by higher overseers (called bishops after the apostolic times), has the highest sanction of primitive usage. In the case of the Jews, a fixed model of hierarchy and ceremonial unalterably bound the people, most minutely detailed in the law. In the New Testament, the ab-

sence of minute directions for Church government and ceremonies, shows that a fixed model was not designed; the *general* rule is obligatory as to ceremonies, "Let all things be done decently and in order" (cf. Article 34, Church of England); and that a succession of ministers be provided, not self-called, but "called to the work by men who have public authority given unto them in the congregation, to call and send ministers into the Lord's vineyard" (Article 23). That the "pastors" here were the bishops and presbyters of the Church, is evident from Acts 20:28; I Peter 5:1, 2, where the *bishops'* and *presbyters'* office is said to be "to feed" the flock. The term, "shepherd," or "pastor," is used of guiding and *governing* and not merely *instructing,* whence it is applied to *kings,* rather than prophets or priests (Ezek. 34:23; Jer. 23:4). Cf. the names of princes compounded of *pharnas,* Hebrew, "pastor," Holophernes, Tissa-phernes (cf. Isa. 44:28). **12. For**—*with a view to;* the ultimate aim. "Unto." **perfecting**—The *Greek* implies *correcting* in all that is deficient, *instructing* and completing in number and all parts. **for**—a different *Greek* word; the immediate object. Cf. Romans 15:2, "Let every one . . . please his neighbor *for* his good *unto* edification." **the ministry**—*Greek,* "ministration"; without the article. The office of the ministry is stated in this verse. The good aimed at in respect to the Church (vs. 13). The way of growth (vss. 14, 15, 16). **edifying**—i.e., *building up* as the temple of the Holy Ghost. **13. come in**—rather, "attain unto." ALFORD expresses the *Greek order,* "Until we arrive all of us at the unity. . . . **faith and . . . knowledge**—Full unity of *faith* is then found, when all alike thoroughly *know* Christ, the object of faith, and that in His highest dignity as "the Son of God" [DE WETTE] (ch. 3:17, 19; II Pet. 1:5). Not even Paul counted himself to have fully "attained" (Phil. 3:12-14). Amidst the variety of the gifts and the multitude of the Church's members, its "faith" is to be ONE: as contrasted with the state of "children carried about with EVERY WIND OF DOCTRINE" (VS. 14). **perfect man**—unto the "*full-grown* man" (I Cor. 2: 6; Phil. 3:15; Heb. 5:14); the *maturity* of an *adult;* contrasted with children (vs. 14). Not "perfect *men";* for the many members constitute but *one* Church joined to the one Christ. **stature . . .**—The standard of spiritual "stature" is "the fulness of Christ," i.e., which Christ has (ch. 1:23; 3:19; .cf. Gal. 4:19); that the body should be worthy of the Head, the perfect Christ. **14.** Translate, "To the end that"; the aim of the bestowal of gifts stated negatively, as in vs. 13 it is stated positively. **tossed to and fro**—*inwardly,* even without wind; *like billows of the sea.* So the *Greek.* Cf. James 1:6. **carried about**—with every wind *from without.* **doctrine**—"teaching." The various *teachings* are the "winds" which keep them tossed on a sea of doubts (Heb. 13:9; cf. Matt. 11:7). **by**—*Greek,* "in"; expressing "the evil atmosphere *in* which the varying currents of doctrine exert their force" [ELLICOTT]. **sleight**—lit., "dice-playing." The player frames his throws of the dice so that the numbers may turn up which best suit his purpose. **of men**—contrasted with *Christ* (vs. 13). **and**—*Greek,* "in." **cunning craftiness, whereby they lie in wait to deceive**—Translate as *Greek,* "craftiness tending to the methodized system of deceit" ("the schemes of error") [ALFORD]. BENGEL takes "deceit," or "error," to stand for "the parent of error," Satan (cf. ch. 6:11): referring to his concealed mode of acting. **15. speaking the truth**—Translate, "holding the truth"; "following the truth"; opposed to "error" or "deceit" (vs. 14). **in love**—"Truth" is never to be sacrificed to so-called "charity"; yet it is to be maintained in charity. Truth in word and act, love in manner and spirit, are the Christian's rule (cf. vss. 21, 24). **grow up**—from the state of "children" to that of "full-grown men." There is growth only in the spiritually alive, not in the dead. **into him**—so' as to be more and more incorporated with Him, and become one with Him. **the head**—(ch. 1:22). **16.** (Col. 2:19) **fitly joined together**—"being fitly framed together," as in ch. 2:21; all the parts being in their proper position, and in mutual relation. **compacted**—implying *firm consolidation.* **by that which every joint supplieth**—*Greek,* "by means of every joint of the supply"; joined with "maketh increase of the body," not with "compacted." "By every ministering (supplying) joint." The joints are the points of union where the supply passes to the different members, furnishing the body with the materials of its growth. **effectual working**—(ch. 1: 19: 3:7). According to the effectual *working of grace* in each member (or else, rather, "according to *each several member's working*"), proportioned to the measure of its need of supply. **every part**—*Greek,* "each one part"; each individual part. **maketh increase**—Translate, as the *Greek* is the same as vs. 15, "maketh (carrieth on) the *growth* of the body." **17. therefore**—resuming the exhortation which he had begun with, "I *therefore* beseech you that ye *walk* worthy. . . ." (vs. 1). **testify in the Lord** —in whom (as our element) we do all things pertaining to the ministry (I Thess. 4:1 [ALFORD]; Rom. **9:1**). **henceforth . . . not**—*Greek,* "no longer"; resumed from vs. 14. **other**—*Greek,* "the *rest* of the Gentiles." **in the vanity . . .**—as their element: opposed to "in the Lord." "Vanity of mind" is the *waste* of the rational powers on worthless objects, of which idolatry is one of the more glaring instances. The root of it is departure from the knowledge of the true God (vss. 18, 19; Rom. 1:21; I Thess. 4:5). **18.** More lit., "Being darkened in their understanding," i.e., their *intelligence,* or *perceptions* (cf. ch. 5:8; Acts 26:18; I Thess. 5:4, 5). **alienated**—This and "darkened," imply that before the fall they (in the person of their first father) had been partakers of *life* and *light:* and that they had revolted from the primitive revelation (cf. ch. 2:12). **life of God**—that life whereby God lives in His own people: as He was the *life* and *light* in Adam before the irruption of death and darkness into human nature; and as He is the life in the regenerate (Gal. 2:20). "Spiritual life in believers is kindled from the life itself of God" [BENGEL]. **through**—rather as *Greek,* "*on account of* the ignorance," viz., of God. Wilful ignorance in the first instance, their fathers not "choosing to retain God in their knowledge." This is the beginning point of their misery (Acts 17: 30; Rom. 1:21, 23, 28; I Pet. 1:14). **because of**— "on account of." **blindness**—*Greek,* "hardness," lit., the hardening of the skin so as not to be sensible of touch. Hence a soul's *callousness to feeling* (Mark 3:5). Where there is spiritual "life" ("the life of God") there is feeling; where there is not, there is "hardness." **19. past feeling**—senseless, shameless, hopeless; the ultimate result of a long process of "hardening," or habit of sin (vs. 18). "Being past hope," or despairing, is the reading of the *Vulgate;* though not so well supported as *English Version* reading, "past feeling," which includes the absence of hope (Jer. 2:25; 18:12). **given themselves over**— In Romans 1:24 it is, *"God* gave them up to uncleanness." Their giving *themselves* to it was punished in kind, *God* giving them up to it by with-

drawing His preventing grace; their sin thus was made their punishment. They gave themselves up of their own accord to the slavery of their lust, to do all its pleasure, as captives who have ceased to strive with the foe. *God* gave them up to it, but not against their will; for *they* give themselves up to it [ZANCHIUS]. **lasciviousness** —"wantonness" [ALFORD]. So it is translated in Romans 13:13; II Peter 2:18. It does not necessarily include *lasciviousness;* but it means *intemperate,* reckless readiness for it, and for every self-indulgence. "The first beginnings of unchastity" [GROTIUS]. "Lawless insolence, and wanton caprice" [TRENCH]. **to work all uncleanness**—The *Greek* implies, "*with a deliberate view* to the working (as if it were their *work* or *business,* not a mere accidental fall into sin) of uncleanness *of every kind."* **with greediness**—*Greek,* "in greediness." *Uncleanness* and *greediness* of gain often go hand in hand (ch. 5:3, 5; Col. 3:5); though "greediness" here includes *all kinds* of *self-seeking.* **20. learned Christ**—(Phil. 3:10). To know Christ Himself, is the great lesson of the Christian life: this the Ephesians began to learn at their conversion. "Christ," in reference to His *office,* is here specified as the object of learning. "Jesus," in the following verse, as the *person.* **21. If so be that**—not implying doubt; assuming what I have no reason to doubt, that . . . . **heard him**—The Him is emphatic: heard *Himself,* not merely heard *about* Him. **taught by him**— *Greek,* "taught IN HIM," i.e., being in vital union with Him (Rom. 16:7). **as the truth is . . .**— Translate in connection with "taught"; "And in Him have been taught, according as is truth in Jesus." There is no article in the *Greek.* "Truth" is therefore used in the most comprehensive sense, truth in its essence, and highest perfection, in Jesus; "if *according as* it is thus in Him, ye have been so taught in Him"; in contrast to "the *vanity* of mind of the Gentiles" (vs. 17; cf. John 1:14, 17; 18:37). Contrast John 8:44. **22. That ye**—following "Ye have been taught" (vs. 21). **concerning the former conversation**—"in respect to your former way of life." **the old man**—your old unconverted nature (Rom. 6:6). **is corrupt according to the deceitful lusts**—rather, "which is being corrupted ('perisheth,' cf. Gal. 6:8, 'corruption,' i.e., *destruction*) according to (i.e., as might be expected from) the lusts of deceit." *Deceit* is personified; *lusts* are its servants and tools. In contrast to "the holiness of the truth," vs. 24, and "truth in Jesus," vs. 21; and answering to Gentile "vanity," vs. 17. Corruption and destruction are inseparably associated together. The man's old-nature-lusts are his own executioners, fitting him more and more for eternal corruption and death. **23. be renewed**—The *Greek* (*ananeousthai*) implies "the *continued* renewal in the *youth* of the new man." A different *Greek* word (*anakainousthai*) implies "renewal *from the old state."* **in the spirit of your mind**—As there is no *Greek* for "in," which there is at vs. 17, "*in* the vanity of their mind," it is better to translate, "*By* the Spirit of your mind," i.e., by your new spiritual nature; the restored and divinely informed leading principle of the mind. The "spirit" of man in New Testament is only then used in its proper sense, as worthy of its place and governing functions, when it is one spirit with the Lord. The natural, or animal man, is described as "not having the Spirit" (Jude 19) [ALFORD]. Spirit is not in this sense attributed to the unregenerate (I Thess. 5:23). **24. put on the new man**—Opposed to "the old man," which is to be "put off" (vs. 22). The *Greek* here (*kainon*) is different from that for "re-*new*-ed" (vs. 23). Put on not merely a *renovated* nature, but a new, i.e., altogether *different* nature, a changed nature (cf. Col. 3:10, *Note*). **after God . . .**—Translate, "Which hath been created (once for all: so the Greek aorist means: in Christ, ch. 2:10; so that in each believer it has not to be created again, but to be put on) after (the image of) God" (Gen. 1:27; Col. 3:10; I Pet. 1:15), etc. God's image in which the first Adam was originally created, is restored, to us far more gloriously in the second Adam, the image of the invisible God (II Cor. 4:4; Col. 1:15; Heb. 1:3). **in righteousness**—"IN" it as the *element* of the renewed man. **true holiness**—rather, as the *Greek*, "holiness *of the truth*"; holiness flowing from sincere following of "the truth of God" (Rom. 1:25; 3:7; 15:8): opposed to "the lusts *of deceit*" (*Greek*, vs. 22); cf. also vs. 21, "truth is in Jesus." "Righteousness" is in relation to our fellow men, the second table of the law; "Holiness," in relation to God, the first table; the religious observance of offices of piety (cf. Luke 1:75). In the parallel (Col. 3:10) it is, "renewed in *knowledge* after the image . . . ." As at Colosse the danger was from false pretenders to *knowledge,* the true "knowledge" which flows from renewal of the heart is dwelt on; so at Ephesus, the danger being from the corrupt morals prevalent around, the renewal in "holiness," contrasted with the Gentile "uncleanness" (vs. 19), and "righteousness," in contrast to "greediness," is made prominent. **25. Wherefore** —From the general character of "the new man," there will necessarily result the particular features which he now details. **putting away**—*Greek*, "having put away" *once for all.* **lying**—"falsehood": the abstract. "Speak ye truth each one with his neighbor," is quoted, slightly changed, from Zechariah 8:16. For "to," Paul quotes it "with," to mark our inner connection *with* one another, as "members *one of another*" [STIER]. Not merely members *of one body.* Union to one another in Christ, not merely the external command, instinctively leads Christians to fulfil mutual duties. One member could not injure or deceive another, without injuring himself, as all have a mutual and common interest. **26. Be ye angry, and sin not**—So the LXX, Psalm 4:4. Should circumstances arise to call for anger on your part, let it be as Christ's "anger" (Mark 3:5), without sin. Our natural feelings are not wrong when directed to their legitimate object, and when not exceeding due bounds. As in the future literal, so in the present spiritual, resurrection, no essential constituent is annihilated, but all that is a perversion of the original design is removed. Thus indignation at dishonor done to God, and wrong to man, is justifiable anger. *Passion* is sinful (derived from "passio," *suffering:* implying that amidst seeming energy. a man is really *passive,* the slave of his anger, instead of ruling it). **let not the sun go down upon your wrath**—"wrath" is absolutely forbidden; "anger" not so, though, like poison sometimes used as medicine, it is to be used with extreme caution. The sense is not, Your *anger* shall not be imputed to you if you put it away before nightfall; but "let no *wrath* (i.e., as the *Greek,* personal 'irritation' or 'exasperation') mingle with your 'anger,' even though the latter be righteous" [TRENCH, *Synonyms*]. "Put it away *before sunset*" (when the Jewish day began), is proverbial for put it away *at once* before *another day begin* (Deut. 24:15); *also* before you part with your brother for the night, perhaps never in this world to meet again. So JONA, "Let not night and anger

against anyone sleep with you, but go and conciliate the other party, though he have been the first to commit the offense." Let not your "anger" at another's wickedness verge into hatred, or contempt, or revenge [VATABLUS]. **27. Neither give place**—i.e., *occasion,* or *scope,* to the devil, by continuing in "wrath." The keeping of anger through the darkness of night, is giving place to the devil, the prince of darkness (ch. 6:12). **28.** *Greek,* "Let him that *stealeth.*" The imperfect or *past* tense is, however, mainly meant, though not to the exclusion of the present. "Let the stealing person steal no more." *Bandits* frequented the mountains near Ephesus. Such are meant by those called "thieves" in the New Testament. **but rather**—For it is not enough to cease from a sin, but the sinner must also enter on the path that is its very opposite [CHRYSOSTOM]. The thief, when repentant, should labor more than he would be called on to do, if he had never stolen. **let him labour**—Theft and idleness go together. **the thing which is good**—in contrast with theft, the thing which was evil in his past character. **with his hands**—in contrast with his former thievish use of his hands. **that he may have to give**—"that he may have *wherewith* to *impart.*" He who has stolen should exercise liberality beyond the restitution of what he has taken. Christians in general should make not selfish gain their aim in honest industry, but the acquisition of the means of greater usefulness to their fellow men; and the being independent of the alms of others. So Paul himself (Acts 20: 35; II Thess. 3:8) acted as he taught (I Thess. 4:11). **29. corrupt**—lit., "insipid," without "the salt of grace" (Col. 4:6), so *worthless* and then becoming *corrupt:* included in "foolish talking" (ch. 5:4). Its opposite is "that which is good to edifying." **communication**—language. **that which . . .**—*Greek,* "*whatever* is good." **use of edifying**—lit., "for edifying of the need," i.e., *for edifying where it is needed.* Seasonably edifying; according as the occasion and present needs of the hearers require, now censure, at another time consolation. Even words good in themselves must be introduced seasonably lest by our fault they prove injurious instead of useful. TRENCH explains, Not vague generalities, which would suit a thousand other cases equally well, and probably equally ill: our words should be as nails fastened in a sure place, words suiting the present time and the present person, being "for the edifying of the occasion" (Col. 4:6). **minister**—*Greek,* "give." The word spoken "gives grace to the hearers" when God uses it as *His* instrument for that purpose. **30. grieve not**—A condescension to human modes of thought most touching. Cf. "*vexed* His Holy Spirit" (Isa. 63:10; Ps. 78:40); "fretted me" (Ezek. 16:43: implying His tender love to us); and of hardened unbelievers, "resist the Holy Ghost" (Acts 7:51). This verse refers to *believers,* who grieve the Spirit by inconsistencies such as in the context are spoken of, corrupt or worthless conversation, etc. **whereby ye are sealed**—rather, "wherein (or 'IN whom') ye *were* sealed." As in ch. 1:13, believers are said to be sealed "*in*" Christ, so here" in *the Holy Spirit,*" who is one with Christ, and who reveals Christ in the soul: the *Greek* implies that the sealing was done already once for all. It is the *Father* "BY" whom believers, as well as the Son Himself, were sealed (John 6:27). The Spirit is represented as itself the *seal* (ch. 1:13, where see, for the image employed, the *Note*). Here the Spirit *is the element* IN *which* the believer is sealed, His gracious influences being the seal itself. **unto**—kept safely against the day of redemption, viz., of the *completion* of redemption in the deliverance of the body as well as the soul from all sin and sorrow (ch. 1:14; Luke 21:28; Rom. 8:23). **31. bitterness**—both of spirit and of speech: opposed to "kind." **wrath**—passion for a time: opposed to "tender-hearted." Whence BEN-GEL translates for "wrath," *harshness.* **anger**—lasting resentment: opposed to "forgiving one another." **clamour**—compared by CHRYSOSTOM to a horse carrying anger for its rider: "Bridle the horse, and you dismount its rider." "Bitterness" begets "wrath"; "wrath," "anger"; "anger," "clamor"; and "clamor," the more chronic "evil-speaking," slander, insinuations, and surmises of evil. "Malice" is the secret root of all: "fires fed within, and not appearing to bystanders from without, are the most formidable" [CHRYSOSTOM]. **32.** (Luke 7:42; Col. 3: 12.) **even as**—God hath shown Himself "kind, tender-hearted, and forgiving to you"; it is but just that you in turn shall be so to your fellow men, who have not erred against you in the degree that you have erred against God (Matt. 18:33). **God for Christ's sake**—rather as *Greek,* "God in Christ" (II Cor. 5:19). It is *in Christ* that God vouchsafes forgiveness to us. It cost God the death of His Son, as man, to forgive us. It costs us nothing to forgive our fellow man. **hath forgiven**—rather as *Greek, "forgave* you." God has, *once for all,* forgiven sin in Christ, as a *past historical fact.*

CHAPTER 5

Vss. 1-33. EXHORTATIONS TO LOVE: AND AGAINST CARNAL LUSTS AND COMMUNICATIONS. CIRCUMSPECTION IN WALK: REDEEMING THE TIME: BEING FILLED WITH THE SPIRIT: SINGING TO THE LORD WITH THANKFULNESS: THE WIFE'S DUTY TO THE HUSBAND RESTS ON THAT OF THE CHURCH TO CHRIST. **1. therefore**—seeing that "God in Christ forgave you" (ch. 4:32). **followers**—*Greek,* "imitators" of God, in respect to "love" (vs. 2): God's essential character (I John 4: 16). **as dear children**—*Greek,* "as children *beloved*"; to which vs. 2 refers, "As Christ also *loved* us" (I John 4:19). "We are sons of men, when we do ill; sons of God, when we do well" [AUGUSTINE, Ps. 52]; (cf. Matt. 5:44, 45, 48). Sonship infers an absolute necessity of *imitation,* it being vain to assume the title of son without any similitude of the Father [PEARSON]. **2. And**—in proof that you are so. **walk** —resuming ch. 4:1, "*walk* worthy of the vocation. ..." **as Christ ... loved us**—From the love of the Father he passes to the love of the Son, in whom God most endearingly manifests His love to us. **given himself for us**—*Greek,* "given Himself *up* (viz., to death, Gal. 2:20) for us," i.e., *in our behalf:* not here vicarious substitution, though that is *indirectly* implied, "in *our* stead." The offerer, and the offering that He offered, were one and the same (John 15:13; Rom. 5:8). **offering and a sacrifice**— "Offering" expresses *generally* His presenting Himself to the Father, as the Representative undertaking the cause of the whole of our lost race (Ps. 40:6-8), including His *life* of obedience; though not excluding His offering of His body for us (Heb. 10: 10). It is usually an *unbloody offering,* in the more limited sense. "Sacrifice" refers to His *death* for us exclusively. Christ is here, in reference to Psalm 40:6 (quoted again in Heb. 10:5), represented as the antitype of all the offerings of the law, whether the unbloody or bloody, eucharistical or propitiatory. **for a sweet-smelling savour**—*Greek,* "for an odor of a sweet smell," i.e., God is well pleased with the offering on the ground of its sweetness, and so is re-

conciled to us (ch. 1:6; Matt. 3:17; II Cor. 5:18, 19; Heb. 10:6-17). The ointment compounded of principal spices, poured upon Aaron's head, answers to the variety of the graces by which He was enabled to "offer Himself a sacrifice for a sweet-smelling savor." Another type, or prophecy by figure, was "the sweet savor" (*savor of rest, Margin*) which God smelled in Noah's sacrifice (Gen. 8:21). Again, as what Christ is, believers also are (I John 4:17), and ministers are: Paul says (II Cor. 2:17) "we are unto God a sweet savor of Christ." **3. once named**—*Greek,* "Let it not be even named" (vss. 4, 12). "Uncleanness" and "covetousness" are taken up again from ch. 4:19. The two are so closely allied that the *Greek* for "covetousness" *(pleonexia)* is used sometimes in Scripture, and often in the Greek Fathers, for sins of impurity. The common principle is the longing to fill one's desire with material objects of sense, outside of God. The expression, "not be even named," applies better to impurity, than to "covetousness." **4. filthiness**—obscenity in *act* or *gesture.* **foolish talking**—the *talk* of fools, which is folly and sin together. The *Greek* of it, and of "filthiness," occurs nowhere else in the New Testament. **nor**—rather, "or" (cf. vs. 3). **jesting**—*Greek,* "*eutrapelia*"; found nowhere else in the New Testament: implying strictly that *versatility* which turns about and adapts itself, without regard to principle, to the shifting circumstances of the moment, and to the varying moods of those with whom it may deal. Not scurrile buffoonery, but refined "persiflage" and "badinage," for which Ephesus was famed (PLAUTUS, *Miles Gloriosus,* 3.1, 42-52), and which, so far from being censured, was and is thought by the world a pleasant accomplishment. In Colossians 3:8, "filthy communication" refers to the *foulness;* "foolish talking," to the *folly;* "jesting," to the *false refinement* [and *trifling witticism,* TITTMANN] of discourse unseasoned with the salt of grace [TRENCH]. **not convenient**—"unseemly"; not such "as become saints" (vs. 3). **rather giving of thanks**—a happy play on sounds in *Greek, eucharistia* contrasted with *eutrapelia;* refined "jesting" and subtle humor sometimes offend the tender feelings of grace; "giving of thanks" gives that real cheerfulness of spirit to believers which the worldly try to get from "jesting" (vs. 19, 20; Jas. 5:13). **5. this ye know**—The oldest MSS. read, "Of this ye are sure knowing"; or as ALFORD, "This ye know being aware." **covetous ... idolater**—(Col. 3:5). The best reading may be translated, That is to say, lit., *which is* (in other words) *an idolater.* Paul himself had forsaken all for Christ (II Cor. 6:10; 11:27). Covetousness is worship of the creature instead of the Creator, the highest treason against the King of kings (I Sam. 15:3; Matt. 6:24; Phil. 3:19; I John 2:15). **hath**—The *present* implies the fixedness of the exclusion, grounded on the eternal verities of that kingdom [ALFORD]. **of Christ and of God**—rather, as one *Greek* article is applied to both, "of Christ and God," implying their perfect oneness, which is consistent only with the doctrine that Christ is God (cf. II Thess. 1:12; I Tim. 5:21; 6:13). **6. vain**—empty, unreal words, viz., palliations of "uncleanness," vss. 3, 4; Isaiah 5:20 (that it is natural to indulge in love), "covetousness" (that it is useful to society that men should pursue gain), and "jesting" (that it is witty and clever, and that God will not so severely punish for such things). **because of these things**—*uncleanness, covetousness,* etc. (vss. 3-5). **cometh**—present, not merely "shall come." Is as sure as if already come. **children**—

rather, "*sons* of disobedience" (ch. 2:2, 3). The children of unbelief in doctrine (Deut. 32:20) are "children of disobedience" in *practice,* and these again are "children of wrath." **7.** Here fellowship with wicked workers is forbidden; in vs. 11, with their wicked works. **8. sometimes**—"once." The emphasis is on "were." Ye ought to have no fellowship with sin, which is darkness, for your state as darkness is now PAST. Stronger than "in darkness" (Rom. 2:19). **light**—not merely "enlightened"; but *light* enlightening others (vs. 13). **in**—in union with the Lord, who is THE LIGHT. **children of light**—not merely "of the light"; just as "children of disobedience" is used on the opposite side; those whose distinguishing characteristic is *light.* PLINY, a heathen writing to Trajan, bears unwilling testimony to the extraordinary purity of Christians' lives, contrasted with the people around them. **9. fruit of the Spirit**—taken by transcribers from Galatians 5:22. The true reading is that of the oldest MSS., "The fruit of THE LIGHT"; in contrast with "the unfruitful works of darkness" (vs. 11). This verse is parenthetic. Walk as children of light, i.e., in all good works and words, "FOR the fruit of the light is [borne] in [ALFORD; but BENGEL, 'consists in'] all goodness [opposed to 'malice,' ch. 4:31], righteousness [opposed to 'covetousness,' vs. 3] and truth" [opposed to "lying," ch. 4:25]. **10. Proving**—construed with "walk" (vs. 8; Rom. 12:1, 2). As we prove a coin by the eye and the ear, and by using it, so by accurate and continued study, and above all by *practice* and experimental trial, we may prove or test "what is acceptable unto the Lord." This is the office of "light," of which believers are "children," to manifest what each thing is, whether sightly or unsightly. **11. unfruitful works of darkness**—Sins are terminated in themselves, and therefore are called "works," not "fruits" (Gal. 5:19, 22). Their only fruit is that which is not in a true sense fruit (Deut. 32:32), viz., "death" (Rom. 6:21; Gal. 6:8). Plants cannot bear "fruit" in the absence of light. Sin is "darkness," and its parent is *the prince of darkness* (ch. 6:12). Graces, on the other hand, as flourishing in "the light," are reproductive, and abound in fruits; which, as harmoniously combining in *one* whole, are termed (in the singular) "the FRUIT of the Spirit" (vs. 9). **rather...**—Translate as *Greek,* "rather *even* reprove them" (cf. Matt. 5:14-16). Not only "have no fellowship, but *even* reprove them," viz., in words, and in your deeds, which, shining with "the light," virtually reprove all that is contrary to light (vs. 13; John 3:19-21). "Have no fellowship," does not imply that we can avoid all intercourse (I Cor. 5:10), but "avoid such fellowship as will defile yourselves"; just as light, though it touch filth, is not soiled by it; nay, as light *detects* it, so, "even *reprove* sin." **12.** The *Greek* order is, "For the things done in secret by them, it is a shame even to speak of." The "for" gives his reason for "not naming" (cf. vs. 3) in detail the works of darkness, whereas he describes definitely (vs. 9) "the fruit of the light" [BENGEL]. "Speak of," I think, is used here as "speaking of *without reproving,*" in contrast to "even reprove them." Thus the "for" expresses this, Reprove them, for to *speak of* them *without reproving* them, is a shame (vs. 3). Thus "works of *darkness*" answers to "things done *in secret.*" **13. that are reproved**—rather, "when they are reproved," viz., by you (vs. 11). **whatsoever doth make manifest**—rather, "everything that is (i.e., suffers itself to be) made manifest (or 'shone upon,' viz., by your 'reproving,' vs. 11) is (thenceforth no longer 'darkness,' vs. 8, but)

light." The devil and the wicked will not suffer themselves to be made manifest by the light, but love darkness, though *outwardly* the light shines round them. Therefore, "light" has no transforming effect on *them,* so that they do not become light (John 3:19, 20). But, says the apostle, you being now light yourselves (vs. 8), by bringing to light through reproof those who are in darkness, will convert them to light. Your consistent lives and faithful reproofs will be your "armor of light" (Rom. 13:12) in making an inroad on the kingdom of darkness. **14. Wherefore**—referring to the whole foregoing argument (vss. 8, 11, 13). Seeing that light (spiritual) dispels the pre-existing darkness, He (God) saith ... (cf. the same phrase, ch. 4:8). **Awake**—The reading of all the oldest MSS. is "Up!" or, "Rouse thee!" a phrase used in stirring men to activity. The words are a paraphrase of Isaiah 60: 1, 2, not an exact quotation. The word "Christ," shows that in quoting the prophecy, he views it in the light thrown on it by its *Gospel fulfilment.* As Israel is called on to "awake" from its previous state of "darkness" and "death" (Isa. 59:10; 60:2), for that her Light is come; so the Church, and each individual is similarly called to awake. *Believers* are called on to "awake" out of *sleep; unbelievers,* to "arise" from the *dead* (cf. Matt. 25:5; Rom. 13: 11; I Thess. 5:6, with ch. 2:1). **Christ**—"the true light," "the Sun of righteousness." **give thee light** —rather, as *Greek,* "shall shine upon thee" (so enabling thee by being "made manifest" to become, and be, by the very fact, "light," vs. 13; then being so "enlightened," ch. 1:18, thou shalt be able, by "reproving," to enlighten others). **15. that**—rather as *Greek,* "See *how* ye walk...." The double idea is compressed into one sentence: "See (take heed) *how* ye walk," and "See *that* ye walk circumspectly." The *manner,* as well as the *act* itself, is included. See *how* ye are walking, with a view to your *being* circumspect (lit., *accurate, exact*) in your walk. Cf. Colossians 4:5, "Walk in *wisdom* (answering to 'as wise' here) toward them that are without" (answering to "circumspectly," i.e., *correctly, in relation to the unbelievers around,* not giving occasion of stumbling to any, but edifying all by a consistent walk). **not as fools**—*Greek,* "not as unwise, but as wise." **16. Redeeming the time**—(Col. 4:5). *Greek,* "Buying up for yourselves the seasonable time" (whenever it occurs) of good to yourselves and to others. Buying *off from* the vanities of "them that are without" (Col. 4:5), and of the "unwise" (here in Ephesians), the opportune time afforded to you for the work of God. In a narrower sense, *special favorable seasons for good,* occasionally presenting themselves, are referred to, of which believers ought diligently to avail themselves. This constitutes true "wisdom" (vs. 15). In a larger sense, *the whole season from the time that one is spiritually awakened,* is to be "redeemed" from vanity for God (cf. II Cor. 6:2; I Pet. 4:2-4). "Redeem" implies the preciousness of the opportune season, a jewel to be bought at any price. WAHL explains, "Redeeming for yourselves (i.e., availing yourselves of) the opportunity (offered you of acting aright), and commanding the time as a master does his servant." TITTMANN, "Watch the time, and make it your own so as to control it; as merchants look out for opportunities, and accurately choose out the best goods; serve not the time, but command it, and it shall do what you approve." So PINDAL, *Pythia,* 4. 509, "The time followed him as his servant, and was not as a runaway slave." **because the days are evil**—The days of life in general are so exposed to evil, as to make it necessary to make the most of the seasonable opportunity so long as it lasts (ch. 6:13 Gen. 47:9; Ps. 49:5; Eccles. 11:2; 12:1; John 12:35). Besides, there are many *special* evil days (in persecution, sickness, etc.) when the Christian is laid by in silence; therefore he needs the more to improve the seasonable times afforded to him (Amos 5:13), which Paul perhaps alludes to. **17. Wherefore**—seeing that ye need to walk so circumspectly, choosing and using the right opportunity of good. **unwise**—a different *Greek* word from that in vs. 15. Translate, "foolish," or "senseless." **understanding**—not merely *knowing* as a matter of fact (Luke 12:47), but *knowing with understanding.* **the will of the Lord**—as to how each opportunity is to be used. The Lord's will, ultimately, is our "sanctification" (I Thess. 4:3); and that "in every thing," meantime, we should "give thanks" (I Thess. 5:18; cf. above, vs. 10). **18. excess** —*worthless,* ruinous, reckless prodigality. **wherein** —not in the wine itself when used aright (I Tim. 5: 23), but in the "excess" as to it. **but be filled with the Spirit**—The effect in inspiration was that the person was "filled" with an ecstatic exhilaration, like that caused by wine; hence the two are here connected (cf. Acts 2:13-18). Hence arose the abstinence from wine of many of the prophets, e.g., John Baptist, viz., in order to keep distinct before the world the ecstasy caused by the Spirit, from that caused by wine. So also in ordinary Christians the Spirit dwells not in the mind that seeks the disturbing influences of excitement, but in the well-balanced prayerful mind. Such a one expresses his joy, not in drunken or worldly songs, but in Christian hymns of thankfulness. **19.** (Col. 3:16.) **to yourselves**—"to one another." Hence soon arose the antiphonal or responsive chanting of which PLINY writes to Trajan: "They are wont on a fixed day to meet before daylight [to avoid persecution] and to recite a hymn *among themselves by turns,* to Christ, as if being God." The Spirit gives true eloquence; wine, a spurious eloquence. **psalms**— generally accompanied by an instrument. **hymns** —in direct praise to God (cf. Acts 16:25; I Cor. 14: 26; Jas. 5:13). **songs**—the general term for lyric pieces; "spiritual" is added to mark their being here restricted to sacred subjects, though not merely to direct praises of God, but also containing exhortations, prophecies, etc. Contrast the drunken "songs," Amos 8:10. **making melody**—*Greek,* "playing and singing with an instrument." **in your heart**—not merely with the tongue; but the serious feeling of the heart accompanying the singing of the lips (cf. I Cor. 14:15; Ps. 47:7). The contrast is between the heathen and the Christian practice, "Let your songs be not the drinking songs of heathen feasts, but psalms and hymns; and their accompaniment, *not the music of the lyre,* but *the melody of the heart*" [CONYBEARE and HOWSON]. **to the Lord**—See Pliny's letter quoted above: "To *Christ* as God." **20. thanks . . . for all things**—even for adversities; also for blessings, unknown as well as known (Col. 3:17; I Thess. 5:18). **unto God and the Father**—the Fountain of every blessing in Creation, Providence, Election, and Redemption. **Lord Jesus Christ**—by whom all things, even distresses, become ours (Rom. 8:35, 37; I Cor. 3:20-23). **21.** (Phil. 2:3; I Peter 5:5.) Here he passes from our relations to God, to those which concern our fellow men. **in the fear of God**—All the oldest MSS. and authorities read, "in the fear of CHRIST." The believer passes from under the bondage of the law as a letter, to be "the servant of *Christ*" (I Cor. 7:

22), which, through the instinct of love to Him, is really to be "the Lord's freeman"; for he is "under the law to *Christ*" (I Cor. 9:21; cf. John 8:36). Christ, not the Father (John 5:22), is to be our judge. Thus reverential fear of displeasing Him is the motive for discharging our relative duties as Christians (I Cor. 10:22; II Cor. 5:11; I Pet. 2:13). **22.** (Ch. 6:9.) The Church's relation to Christ in His everlasting purpose, is the foundation and archetype of the three greatest of earthly relations, that of husband and wife (vss. 22-33), parent and child (ch. 6:1-4), master and servant (ch. 6:4-9). The oldest MSS. omit "submit yourselves"; supplying it from vs. 21, "Ye wives (submitting yourselves) unto your own husbands." "Your own" is an argument for submissiveness on the part of the wives; it is not a stranger, but *your own* husbands whom you are called on to submit unto (cf. Gen. 3:16; I Cor. 7:2; 14:34; Col. 3:18 Titus 2:5; I Pet. 3:1-7). Those subject ought to submit themselves, of whatever kind their superiors are. "Submit" is the term used of *wives:* "obey," of *children* (ch. 6:1), as there is a greater equality between wives and husbands, than between children and parents. **as unto the Lord**—Submissiveness is rendered by the wife to the husband under the eye of Christ, and so is rendered to Christ Himself. The husband stands to the wife in the relation that the Lord does to the Church, and this is to be the ground of her submission: though that submission is inferior in kind and degree to that which she owes Christ (vs. 24). **23.** (I Cor. 11:3.) **even as**—*Greek,* "as also." **and he is** —The oldest MSS. read, "Himself (being) Saviour. . . ." omitting "and," and "is." In Christ's case, the Headship is united with, nay gained by, His having SAVED the body in the process of redemption; so that (Paul implies) I am not alleging Christ's Headship as one entirely identical with that other, for He has a claim to it, and office in it, peculiar to Himself [ALFORD]. The husband is not saviour of the wife, in which particular Christ excels; hence, "But" (vs. 24) follows [BENGEL]. **24. Therefore**— Translate, as *Greek,* "But," or "Nevertheless," i.e., though there be the difference of headships mentioned in vs. 23, *nevertheless,* thus far they are one, viz., in the subjection or submission (the same *Greek* stands for "is *subject,*" as for "*submit,*" vss. 21, 22) of the Church to Christ, being the prototype of that of the wife to the husband. **their own**—not in most of the oldest MSS., and not needed by the argument. **in every thing**—appertaining to a husband's legitimate authority; "in the Lord" (Col. 3:18); everything not contrary to God. **25.** "Thou hast seen the measure of obedience; now hear also the measure of love. Do you wish your wife to obey you, as the Church is to obey Christ? Then have a solicitude for her as Christ had for the Church [vs. 23, 'Himself the Saviour of the body']; and if it be necessary to give thy life for her, or to be cut in ten thousand pieces, or to endure any other suffering whatever, do not refuse it; and if you suffer thus, not even so do you do what Christ has done; for you indeed do so being already united to her, but He did so for one that treated Him with aversion and hatred. As, therefore, He brought to His feet one that so treated Him, and that even wantonly spurned Him, by much tenderness of regard, not by threats, insults, and terror: so also do you act towards your wife, and though you see her disdainful and wantonly wayward, you will be able to bring her to your feet by much thoughtfulness for her, by love, by kindness. For no bound is more sovereign in binding than such bonds, especially in the case of husband

and wife. For one may constrain a servant by fear, though not even he is so to be bound to you; for he may readily run away. But the companion of your life, the mother of your children, the basis of all your joy, you ought to bind to you, not by fear and threats, but by love and attachment" [CHRYSOSTOM]. **gave himself**—*Greek*, "gave Himself *up*." **for it**—Translate, "for *her*." The relation of the Church to Christ is the ground of Christianity's having raised woman to her due place in the social scale, from which she was, and is, excluded in heathen lands. **26. sanctify**—i.e., consecrate her to God. Cf. John 17:19, meaning, "I *devote* Myself as a *holy* sacrifice, that My disciples also may be devoted or consecrated as holy in (through) the truth" [NEANDER] (Heb. 2:11; 10:10, *Note;* 13:12). **and cleanse** —rather, as *Greek*, "cleansing," without the "and." **with the washing of water**—rather as *Greek*, "with," or "by the *laver* of *the* water," viz., *the* baptismal water. So it ought to be translated in Titus 3:5, the only other passage in the New Testament where it occurs. As the bride passed through a purifying bath before marriage, so the Church (cf. Rev. 21:2). He speaks of baptism according to its high *ideal* and *design*, as if the inward grace accompanied the outward rite; hence he asserts of outward baptism whatever is involved in a believing appropriation of the divine truths it symbolizes, and says that Christ, by baptism, has purified the Church [NEANDER] (I Pet. 3:21). **by the word**—*Greek*, "IN the word." To be joined with "cleansing it," or "her." The "word of faith" (Rom. 10:8, 9, 17), of which confession is made in baptism, and which carries the real cleansing (John 15:3; 17:17) and regenerating power (I Pet. 1:23; 3:21) [ALFORD]. So AUGUSTINE, *Tract* 80, in John, "Take away the word, and what is the water save water? Add the word to the element, and it becomes a sacrament, being itself as it were the visible word." The regenerating efficacy of baptism is conveyed in, and by, the divine word alone. **27. he**—The oldest MSS. and authorities read, "That He might *Himself* present unto Himself the Church glorious," viz., as a bride (II Cor. 11:2). *Holiness* and *glory* are inseparable. "Cleansing" is the necessary preliminary to both. *Holiness* is *glory* internal; *glory* is *holiness* shining forth outwardly. *The laver* of baptism is the vehicle, but *the word* is the nobler and true instrument of the *cleansing* [BENGEL]. It is Christ that prepares the Church with the necessary ornaments of grace, for presentation to Himself, as the Bridegroom at His coming again (Matt. 25:1, etc.; Rev. 19:7; 21:2). **not having spot**—(Song of Sol. 4:7). The visible Church now contains clean and unclean together, like Noah's ark; like the wedding room which contained some that had, and others that had not, the wedding garment (Matt. 22:10-14; cf. II Tim. 2:20); or as the good and bad fish are taken in the same net because it cannot discern the bad from the good, the fishermen being unable to know what kind of fish the nets have taken under the waves. Still the Church is termed "holy" in the creed, in reference to her ideal and ultimate destination. When the Bridegroom comes, the bride shall be presented to Him wholly without spot, the evil being cut off from the body for ever (Matt. 13:47-50). Not that there are two churches, one with bad and good intermingled, another in which there are good alone; but one and the same Church in relation to different times, now with good and evil together, hereafter with good alone [PEARSON]. **28.** Translate, "So ought husbands *also* (thus the oldest MSS. read) to love their own (cf. *Note*, vs. 22) wives

as their own bodies." "He that loveth his own wife . . ." (vs. 28). So there is the same love and the same union of body between Christ and the Church (vss. 30, 32). **29. For**—Supply, and we all love ourselves: "For no man. . . ." **his own flesh** —(*V*. 31, end). **nourisheth**—*Greek*, "nourisheth it up," viz., to maturity. "Nourisheth," refers to food and internal sustenance; "cherisheth," to clothing and external fostering. **even as**—Translate, "even as also." **the Lord**—The oldest MSS. read, "Christ." Exodus 21:10 prescribes three duties to the husband. The two former (food and raiment) are here alluded to in a spiritual sense, by "nourisheth and cherisheth"; the third "duty of marriage" is not added in consonance with the holy propriety of Scripture language: its antitype is, "know the Lord" (Hos. 2:19, 20) [BENGEL]. **30. For**—*Greek*, "Because" (I Cor. 6:15). Christ nourisheth and cherisheth the Church as being of one flesh with Him. Translate, "Because we are members of His body (His literal body), *being* OF His flesh and of His bones" [ALFORD] (Gen. 2:23, 24). The *Greek* expresses, "Being formed *out of*," or "of the substance of His flesh." Adam's deep sleep, wherein Eve was formed from out of his opened side, is an emblem of Christ's death, which was the birth of the Spouse, the Church. John 12:24; 19:34, 35, to which verses 25, 26, 27 allude, as implying atonement by His *blood*, and sanctification by the "water," answering to that which flowed from His side (cf. also John 7:38, 39; I Cor. 6:11). As Adam gave Eve a new name, *Hebrew, Isha*, "woman," formed from his own rib, *Ish*, "man," signifying her formation from him, so Christ, Revelation 2:17; 3:12. Genesis 2:21, 23, 24 puts the *bones* first because the reference there is to the *natural* structure. But Paul is referring to the *flesh of Christ*. It is not our bones and flesh, but "*we*" that are *spiritually* propagated (in our soul and spirit now, and in the body hereafter, regenerated) from the manhood of Christ which has flesh and bones. We are members of His glorified body (John 6:53). The two oldest existing MSS., and *Coptic* or *Memphitic version*, omit "of His flesh and of His bones"; the words may have crept into the text through the Margin from Genesis 2:23, LXX. However, IRENÆUS, 294, and the old *Latin* and *Vulgate versions*, with some good old MSS., have them. **31. For this cause**—The propagation of the Church from Christ, as that of Eve from Adam, is the foundation of spiritual marriage. The natural marriage, wherein "a man leaves father and mother (the oldest MSS. omit 'his') and is joined unto his wife," is not the principal thing meant here, but *the spiritual marriage* represented by it, and on which it rests, whereby Christ left the Father's bosom to woo to Himself the Church out of a lost world: vs. 32 proves this: His earthly mother *as such*, also, He holds in secondary account as compared with His spiritual Bride (Luke 2:48, 49; 8:19-21; 11:27, 28). He shall again leave His Father's abode to consummate the union (Matt. 25:1-10; Rev. 19:7). **they two shall be one flesh**—So the Samaritan Pentateuch, LXX, etc., read (Gen. 2:24), instead of "they shall be one flesh." So Matthew 19:5. In natural marriage, husband and wife combine the elements of one perfect human being: the one being incomplete without the other. So Christ, as God-man, is pleased to make the Church, the body, a necessary adjunct to Himself, the Head. He is the archetype of the Church, from whom and according to whom, as the pattern, she is formed. He is her Head, as the husband is of the wife (Rom. 6:5; I Cor. 11:3; 15:45).

Christ will néver allow any power to sever Himself and His bride, indissolubly joined (Matt. 19:6; John 10:28, 29; 13:1). **32.** Rather, "This mystery is a great one." This *profound truth, beyond man's power of discovering,* but *now revealed,* viz., of the spiritual union of Christ and the Church, represented by the marriage union, is a great one, of deep import. See *Note,* vs. 30. So "mystery" is used of a divine truth not to be discovered save by revelation of God (Rom. 11:25; I Cor. 15:51). The *Vulgate* wrongly translates, "This is a great *sacrament,*" which is made the plea by the Romish Church (in spite of the blunder having been long ago exposed by their own commentators, CAJETAN and ESTIUS) for making marriage a *sacrament;* it is plain not marriage in general, but that of Christ and the Church, is what is pronounced to be a "great mystery," as the words following prove, "*I* [emphatic] say it in regard to Christ and to the Church" (so the *Greek* is best translated). "I, while I quote these words out of Scripture, use them in a higher sense" [CONYBEARE and HOWSON]. **33. Nevertheless** —not to pursue further the mystical meaning of marriage. Translate, as *Greek,* "Do ye also (as Christ does) severally each one so love. . . ." The words, "severally each one," refer to them in their *individual* capacity, contrasted with the previous *collective view* of the members of the Church as the bride of Christ.

CHAPTER 6

Vss. 1-24. MUTUAL DUTIES OF PARENTS AND CHILDREN: MASTERS AND SERVANTS: OUR LIFE A WARFARE: THE SPIRITUAL ARMOUR NEEDED AGAINST SPIRITUAL FOES. CONCLUSION. **1. obey**—stronger than the expression as to wives, "submitting," or "being subject" (ch. 5:21). *Obedience* is more unreasoning and implicit; *submission* is the willing *subjection* of an inferior in point of order to one who has a right to command. **in the Lord**—Both parents and children being Christians "in the Lord," expresses the *element* in which the obedience is to take place, and the *motive* to obedience. In Colossians 3:20, it is, "Children, obey your parents *in all things.*" This clause, "in the Lord," would suggest the due limitation of the obedience required (Acts 5:29; cf. on the other hand, the abuse, Mark 7:11-13). **right**—Even by *natural law* we should render obedience to them from whom we have derived life. **2.** Here the authority of *revealed law* is added to that of natural law. **which is . . . promise**—The "promise" is not made the *main* motive to obedience, but an incidental one. The main motive is, because it is God's will (Deut. 5:16, "Honor thy father and mother, *as the Lord thy God hath* COMMANDED *thee*"); and that it is so peculiarly, is shown by His accompanying it "*with a promise.*" **first** —in the decalogue with a *special* promise. The promise in the second commandment is a *general* one. Their duty is more expressly prescribed to children than to parents; for love descends rather than ascends [BENGEL]. This verse proves the law in the Old Testament is not abolished. **3. long on the earth**—In Exodus 20:12, "long upon the *land which the Lord thy God giveth thee,*" which Paul adapts to Gospel times, by taking away the local and limited reference peculiar to the Jews in Canaan. The godly are equally blessed in every land, as the Jews were in the land which God gave them. This promise is always fulfilled, either literally, or by the substitution of a higher blessing, viz., one spiritual and eternal (Job 5:26; Prov. 10:27). The

substance and essence of the law are eternally in force: its accidents alone (applying to Israel of old) are abolished (Rom. 6:15). **4. fathers**—including *mothers;* the fathers are specified as being the fountains of domestic authority. Fathers are more prone to passion in relation to their children than mothers, whose fault is rather over-indulgence. **provoke not**—irritate not, by vexatious commands, unreasonable blame, and uncertain temper [ALFORD]. Colossians 3:21, "lest they be discouraged." **nurture**—Greek, "discipline," viz., *training* by chastening in *act* where needed (Job 5:17; Heb. 12:7). **admonition**—training by *words* (Deut. 6:7; Prov. 22:6, *Margin,* "catechise"), whether of encouragement, or remonstrance, or reproof, according as is required [TRENCH]. Contrast I Samuel 3:13, *Margin.* **of the Lord**—such as the Lord approves, and by His Spirit dictates. **5. Servants**—lit., "slaves." **masters according to the flesh**—in contrast to your true and heavenly Master (vs. 4). A consolatory hint that the mastership to which they were subject, was but for a time [CHRYSOSTOM]; and that their real liberty was still their own (I Cor. 7:22). **fear and trembling**—not slavish terror, but (I Cor. 2:3, *Note;* II Cor. 7:15) an anxious eagerness to do your duty, and a fear of displeasing, as great as is produced in the ordinary slave by "threatenings" (vs. 9). **singleness**—without doublemindedness, or "eyeservice" (vs. 6), which seeks to please outwardly, without the sincere desire to make the master's interest at all times the first consideration (I Chron. 29:17; Matt. 6:22, 23; Luke 11:34). "Simplicity." **6.** (Col. 3:22.) Seeking to please their masters only so long as these have their eyes on them: as Gehazi was a very different man in his master's presence from what he was in his absence (II Kings 5). **men-pleasers**—not Christpleasers (cf. Gal. 1:10; I Thess. 2:4). **doing the will of God**—the unseen but ever present Master: the best guarantee for your serving faithfully your earthly master alike when present and when absent. **from the heart**—lit., *soul* (Ps. 111:1; Rom. 13:5). **7. good will**—expressing his feeling towards his master; as "doing the will of God from the heart" expresses the source of that feeling (Col. 3:23). "Good will" is stated by XENOPHON (*Economics*) to be the principal virtue of a slave towards his master: a real regard to his master's interest as if his own, a *good will* which not even a master's severity can extinguish. **8. any man doeth**—Greek, "any man shall have done," i.e., shall be found at the Lord's coming to have done. **the same**—in full payment, in heaven's currency. **shall . . . receive**—(II Cor. 5:10; Col. 3:25; but all of grace, Luke 17:10). **bond or free**—(I Cor. 7:22; 12:13; Gal. 3:28; Col. 3:11). Christ does not regard such distinctions in His present dealings of grace, or in His future judgment. The slave that has acted faithfully for the Lord's sake to his master, though the latter may not repay his faithfulness, shall have the Lord for his Paymaster. So the freeman who has done good for the Lord's sake, though man may not pay him, has the Lord for his Debtor (Prov. 19:17). **9. the same things**—*Mutatis mutandis.* Show the same regard to God's will, and to your servants' well-being, in your relation to them, as they ought to have in their relation to you. Love regulates the duties both of servants and masters, as one and the same light attempers various colors. Equality of nature and faith is superior to distinctions of rank [BENGEL]. Christianity makes all men brothers: cf. Leviticus 25:42, 43; Deuteronomy 15:12; Jeremiah 34:14 as to how the Hebrews were bound to treat their brethren in service; much more ought Christians to act with love. **threatening**—Greek, "*the* threatening" which masters commonly use. "Masters" in the *Greek,* is not so strong a term as "despots": it implies *authority,* but not absolute *domination.* **your Master also**—The oldest MSS. read, "the Master both of them and you": "their Master and yours." This more forcibly brings out the equality of slaves and masters in the sight of God. SENECA, *Thyestes,* 607, says, "Whatever an inferior dreads from you, this a superior Master threatens yourselves with: every authority here is under a higher above." As you treat your servants, so will He treat you. **neither ... respect of persons**—He will not, in judging, acquit thee because thou art a master, or condemn him because he is a servant (Acts 10:34; Rom. 2:11; Gal. 2:6; Col. 3:25; I Pet. 1:17). Derived from Deuteronomy 10:17; II Chronicles 19:7. **10. my brethren**—Some of the oldest MSS. omit these words. Some with *Vulgate* retain them. The phrase occurs nowhere else in the Epistle (see, however, vs. 23); if genuine, it is appropriate here in the close of the Epistle, where he is urging his fellow soldiers to the good fight in the Christian armor. Most of the oldest MSS. for "finally," read, "henceforward," or "from henceforth" (Gal. 6:17). **be strong**—Greek, "be strengthened." **in the power of his might**—*Christ's* might: as in ch. 1:19, it is *the Father's* might. **11. the whole armour**—the armor of light (Rom. 13:12); on the right hand and left (II Cor. 6:7). The panoply offensive and defensive. An image readily suggested by the Roman armory, Paul being now in Rome. Repeated emphatically, vs. 13. In Romans 13:14 it is, "Put ye on *the Lord Jesus Christ*"; in putting on Him, and the new man in Him, we put on "the whole armor of God." No opening at the head, the feet, the heart, the belly, the eye, the ear, or the tongue, is to be given to Satan. Believers have once for all overcome him; but on the ground of this fundamental victory gained over him, they are ever again to fight against and overcome him, even as they who once die with Christ have continually to mortify their members upon earth (Rom. 6:2-14; Col. 3:3, 5). **of God**—furnished by God; not our own, else it would not stand (Ps. 35:1-3). Spiritual, therefore, and mighty through God, not carnal (II Cor. 10:4). **wiles**—lit., "*schemes sought out*" for deceiving (cf. II Cor. 11:14). **the devil**—the ruling chief of the foes (vs. 12) organized into a kingdom of darkness (Matt. 12:26), opposed to the kingdom of light. **12.** *Greek,* "For our wrestling ('*the* wrestling' in which we are engaged) is not against flesh ...." Flesh and blood foes are Satan's mere tools, the real foe lurking behind them is Satan himself, with whom our conflict is. "Wrestling" implies that it is a hand-to-hand and foot-to-foot struggle for the mastery: to wrestle successfully with Satan, we must wrestle with GOD in irresistible prayer like Jacob (Gen. 32:24-29; Hos. 12:4). Translate, "*The* principalities ... *the* powers" (ch. 1:21; *Note,* 3:10; Col. 1:16). The same grades of powers are specified in the case of the demons here, as in that of angels there (cf. Romans 8:38; I Cor. 15:24; Col. 2:15). The Ephesians had practiced sorcery (Acts 19:19), so that he appropriately treats of evil spirits in addressing them. The more clearly any book of Scripture, as this, treats of the economy of the kingdom of light, the more clearly does it set forth the kingdom of darkness. Hence, nowhere does the satanic kingdom come more clearly into view than in the Gospels which treat of Christ, the true Light. **rulers of the**

darkness of this world—Greek, "age" or "course of the world." But the oldest MSS. omit "of world." Translate, "Against the world rulers of this (present) darkness" (ch. 2:2; 5:8; Luke 22:53; Col. 1:13). On Satan and his demons being "world rulers," cf. John 12:31; 14:30; 16:11; Luke 4:6; II Cor. 4:4; I John 5:19, *Greek,* "lieth in the wicked one." Though they be "world rulers," they are not the ruler of the universe; and their usurped rule of the world is soon to cease, when He shall "come whose right it is" (Ezek. 21:27). Two cases prove Satan not to be a mere subjective fancy: (1) Christ's temptation; (2) the entrance of demons into the swine (for these are incapable of such fancies). Satan tries to parody, or imitate in a perverted way, God's working (II Cor. 11:13, 14). So when God became incarnate, Satan, by his demons, took forcible possession of human bodies. Thus the demoniacally possessed were not peculiarly wicked, but miserable, and so fit subjects for Jesus' pity. Paul makes no mention of demoniacal possession, so that in the time he wrote, it seems to have ceased; it probably was restricted to the period of the Lord's incarnation, and of the foundation of His Church. **spiritual wickedness**—rather as *Greek,* "The spiritual *hosts of* wickedness." As three of the clauses describe the *power,* so this fourth, the *wickedness* of our spiritual foes (Matt. 12:45). **in high places**—Greek, "heavenly places": in ch. 2:2, "the air," where see the *Note.* The alteration of expression to "in heavenly places," is in order to mark the higher range of their powers than ours, they having been, up to the ascension (Rev. 12:5, 9, 10), dwellers "in the heavenly places" (Job 1:7), and being now in the regions of the air which are called the heavens. Moreover, pride and presumption are the sins *in heavenly places* to which they tempt especially, being those by which they themselves fell from heavenly places (Isa. 14:12-15). But believers have naught to fear, being "blessed with all spiritual blessings in the heavenly places" (ch. 1:3). **13. take ... of God**—not "make," God has done that: you have only to "take up" and put it on. The Ephesians were familiar with the idea of the gods giving armor to mythical heroes: thus Paul's allusion would be appropriate. **the evil day**—the day of Satan's special assaults (vss. 12, 16) in life and at the dying hour (cf. Rev. 3:10). We must have our armor always on, to be ready against the evil day which may come at any moment, the war being perpetual (Ps. 41:1, *Margin*). **done all**—rather, "accomplished all things," viz., necessary to the fight, and becoming a good soldier. **14. Stand**—The repetition in vss. 11, 14, shows that *standing,* i.e., *maintaining our ground,* not yielding or fleeing, is the grand aim of the Christian soldier. Translate as *Greek,* "Having girt about your loins with truth," i.e., with truthfulness, sincerity, a good conscience (II Cor. 1:12; I Tim. 1:5, 18; 3:9). Truth is the band that girds up and keeps together the flowing robes, so as that the Christian soldier may be unencumbered for action. So the Passover was eaten with the loins girt, and the shoes on the feet (Exod. 12:11; cf. Isa. 5:27; Luke 12:35). *Faithfulness* (LXX, "truth") is the girdle of Messiah (Isa. 11:5): so *truth* of His followers. **having on**—Greek, "having put on." **breastplate of righteousness**—Isaiah 59:17, similarly of Messiah. "Righteousness" is here joined with "truth," as in ch. 5:9: *righteousness* in works, *truth* in words [ESTIUS] (I John 3:7). Christ's righteousness inwrought in us by the Spirit. "Faith and love," i.e., faith working righteousness by love, are "the breastplate" in I

Thess. 5:8. **15.** Translate, "Having shod your feet" (referring to the sandals, or to the military shoes then used). **the preparation**—rather, "the preparedness," or "readiness of," i.e., arising from the "Gospel" (Ps. 10:17). Preparedness to do and suffer all that God wills; readiness for march, as a Christian soldier. **gospel of peace**—(cf. Luke 1:79; Rom. 10: 15). The "peace" within forms a beautiful contrast to the raging of the outward conflict (Isa. 26:3; Phil. 4:7). **16. Above all**—rather, "Over all"; so as to cover all that has been put on before. Three integuments are specified, the breastplate, girdle, and shoes; two defenses, the helmet and shield; and two offensive weapons, the sword and the spear (prayer). ALFORD translates, "Besides all," as the *Greek* is translated, Luke 3:20. But if it meant this, it would have come *last* in the list (cf. Col. 3: 14). **shield**—the large oblong oval door-like shield of the Romans, four feet long by two and a half feet broad; not the small round buckler. **ye shall be able**—not *merely* "ye may." The shield of faith will *certainly* intercept, and so "quench, all the fiery darts" (an image from the ancient fire-darts, formed of cane, with tow and combustibles ignited on the head of the shaft, so as to set fire to woodwork, tents, etc.) **of the wicked**—rather "of the EVIL ONE." Faith conquers him (I Pet. 5:9), and his darts of temptation to wrath, lust, revenge, despair, etc. It overcomes the world (I John 5:4), and so the prince of the world (I John 5:18). **17. take**—a different *Greek* word from that in vss. 13, 16; translate, therefore, "receive," "accept," viz., the helmet offered by the Lord, viz., "salvation" appropriated, as I Thessalonians 5:8, "Helmet, the hope of salvation"; not an uncertain hope, but one that brings with it no shame of disappointment (Rom. 5:5). It is subjoined to the shield of faith, as being its inseparable accompaniment (cf. Rom. 5:1, 5). The head of the soldier was among the principal parts to be defended, as on it the deadliest strokes might fall, and it is the head that commands the whole body. The head is the seat of the *mind,* which, when it has laid hold of the sure Gospel "hope" of eternal life, will not receive false doctrine, or give way to Satan's temptations to *despair.* God, by this hope, "lifts up the head" (Ps. 3:3; Luke 21:28). **sword of the Spirit**—i.e., furnished by the Spirit, who inspired the writers of the word of God (II Pet. 1:21). Again the Trinity is implied: the Spirit here; and Christ in "salvation" and God the Father, vs. 13 (cf. Heb. 4:12; Rev. 1: 16; 2:12). The two-edged sword, cutting both ways (Ps. 45:3, 5), striking some with conviction and conversion, and others with condemnation (Isa. 11:4; Rev. 19:15), is in the *mouth* of Christ (Isa. 49:2), in the *hand* of His saints (Ps. 149:6). Christ's use of this sword in the temptation is our pattern as to how we are to wield it against Satan (Matt. 4:4, 7, 10). There is no armor specified for the back, but only for the front of the body; implying that we must never turn our back to the foe (Luke 9:62); our only safety is in resisting ceaselessly (Matt. 4:11; Jas. 4: 7). **18. always**—*Greek,* "in every season"; implying *opportunity* and *exigency* (Col. 4:2). Paul uses the very words of Jesus in Luke 21:36 (a Gospel which he quotes elsewhere, in undesigned consonance with the fact of Luke being his associate in travel (I Cor. 11:23, etc.; I Tim. 5:18). Cf. Luke 18:1; Romans 12:12; I Thessalonians 5:17. **with all**—i.e., every kind of. **prayer**—a sacred term for *prayer* in general. **supplication**—a common term for a special kind of prayer [HARLESS], *an imploring request.* "Prayer" for obtaining blessings,

"supplication" for averting evils which we fear [GROTIUS]. **in the Spirit**—to be joined with "praying." It is he *in us,* as the Spirit of adoption, who prays, and enables us to pray (Rom. 8:15, 26; Gal. 4:6; Jude 20). **watching**—not sleeping (ch. 5:14; Ps. 88:13; Matt. 26:41). So in the temple a perpetual watch was maintained (cf. Anna, Luke 2:37). **thereunto**—"watching unto" (with a view to) prayer and supplication. **with**—*Greek,* "in." *Persevering constancy* ("perseverance") *and* (i.e., exhibited in) *supplication* are to be the element in which our watchfulness is to be exercised. **for all saints**—as none is so perfect as not to need the intercessions of his fellow Christians. **19. for me**—a different *Greek* preposition from that in vs. 18; translate, therefore, "on my behalf." **that I may open my mouth boldly**—rather, "that there may be given to me 'utterance,' or 'speech' *in the opening of my mouth* (when I undertake to speak; a formula used in *set and solemn* speech, Job 3:1; Dan. 10:16), so as *with boldness to make known* . . . ." etc. Bold plainness of speech was the more needed, as the Gospel is a "mystery" undiscoverable by mere reason, and only known by revelation. Paul looked for utterance to be *given* him; he did not depend on his natural or acquired power. The shortest road to any heart is by way of heaven; pray to God to open the door and to open your mouth, so as to avail yourself of every opening (Jer. 1:7, 8; Ezek. 3:8, 9, 11; II Cor. 4:13). **20. For**—*Greek,* as in vs. 19, "On behalf of which." **an ambassador in bonds**—a paradox. Ambassadors were held inviolable by the law of nations, and could not, without outrage to every sacred right, be put in chains. Yet Christ's "ambassador is in *a chain!*" The *Greek* is singular. The Romans used to bind a prisoner to a soldier by *a single chain,* in a kind of free custody. So Acts 28:16, 20, "I am bound with this *chain.*" The term, "bonds" (plural), on the other hand, is used when the prisoner's hands or feet were bound together (Acts 26:29); cf. Acts 12:6, where the plural marks the distinction. The singular is only used of the particular kind of custody described above; an undesigned coincidence [PALEY]. **21. that ye also**—as I have been discussing things relating to you, so that ye also may know about me (cf. Col. 4:7, 8). NEANDER takes it, "Ye also," as well as the Colossians (Col. 4:6). **my affairs**—*Greek,* "the things concerning me." **how I do**—how I fare. **Tychicus** —an Asiatic, and so a fit messenger bearing the respective Epistles to Ephesus and Colosse (Acts 20:4; II Tim. 4:12). **a . . .**—*Greek,* "the beloved brother"; the same epithet as in Colossians 4:7. **minister**—i.e., *servant.* **in the Lord**—in the Lord's work. **22. for the same purpose**—*Greek,* "for this very purpose." Colossians 4:8 is almost word for word the same as this verse. **our affairs**—*Greek,* "the things concerning us," viz., concerning myself. "Aristarchus, my fellow prisoner, and Marcus, sister's son to Barnabas" (Col. 4:10). **23. love with faith**—Faith is presupposed as theirs; he prays that love may accompany it (Gal. 5:6). **24.** Contrast the malediction on all who love Him not (I Cor. 16:22). **in sincerity**—*Greek,* "in incorruption," i.e., not as *English Version,* but "with an immortal (constant) love" [WAHL]. Cf. "that which is not corruptible" (I Pet. 3:4). Not a fleeting, earthly love, but a spiritual and eternal one [ALFORD]. Contrast Colossians 2:22, worldly things "which perish with the using." Cf. I Corinthians 9:25, "corruptible . . . *incorruptible* crown." "Purely," "holily" [ESTIUS], without the corruption of sin

(*Note,* I Cor. 3:17; II Pet. 1:4; Jude 10). Where the Lord Jesus has a true believer, there I have a brother [BISHOP M'ILWAINE]. He who is good enough for Christ, is good enough for me [R. HALL]. The differences of opinion among real Christians are comparatively small, and show that they are not following one another like silly sheep, each trusting the one before him. Their agreement in the main, while showing their independence as witnesses by differing in non-essentials, can only be accounted for by their being all in the right direction (Acts 15:8, 9; I Cor. 1:2; 12:3).

THE EPISTLE OF PAUL THE APOSTLE TO THE

PHILIPPIANS

INTRODUCTION

The INTERNAL EVIDENCE for the authenticity of this Epistle is strong. The style, manner of thought, and doctrine, accord with Paul's. The incidental allusions also establish his authorship. PALEY (*Horæ Paulinæ*, ch. 7) instances the mention of the object of Epaphroditus' journey to Rome, the Philippian contribution to Paul's wants, Epaphroditus' sickness (ch. 1:7; 2:25-30; 4:10-18), the fact that Timothy had been long with Paul at Philippi (ch. 1:1; 2:19), the reference to his being a prisoner at Rome now for a long time (ch. 1:12-14; 2:17-28), his willingness to die (cf. ch. 1:23, with II Cor. 5:8), the reference to the Philippians having *seen* his maltreatment at Philippi (ch. 1:29, 30; 2:1, 2).

The EXTERNAL EVIDENCE is equally decisive: POLYCARP, *ad Philippenses*, sec. 3 and 11; IRENÆUS, *adversus Hæreses*, 4. 18, sec. 4; CLEMENT OF ALEXANDRIA, *Pædagogus*, l. i., p. 107; The Epistle of the Churches of Lyons and Vienne," in EUSEBIUS' *Ecclesiastical History*, 5. 2; TERTULLIAN, *Resurrectio carnis*, c. 23; ORIGEN, *Celsus*, 1. 3., p. 122; CYPRIAN, *Testimonies against the Jews*, 3. 39.

Philippi was *the first* (*i.e.*, the farthest from Rome, and first which met Paul in entering Macedonia) Macedonian *city of the district*, called *Macedonia Prima* (so called as lying *farthest eastward*). The *Greek* (Acts 16:12) should not be translated "the *chief* city," as *English Version*, but as above [ALFORD]. Not it, but Thessalonica, was the *chief* city of the province, and Amphipolis, of the district called Macedonia Prima. It was a *Roman* "colony" (Acts 16:12), made so by Augustus, to commemorate his famous victory over Brutus and Cassius. A *colony* was in fact a portion of Rome itself transplanted to the provinces, an offshoot from Rome, and as it were a portrait of the mother city on a small scale [AULIUS GELLIUS, 16. 13]. Its inhabitants were Roman citizens, having the right of voting in the Roman tribes, governed by their own senate and magistrates, and not by the governor of the province, with the Roman law and Latin language.

Paul, with Silas and Timothy, planted the Gospel there (Acts 16:12, etc.), in his second missionary journey, A.D. 51. Doubtless he visited it again on his journey from Ephesus into Macedonia (Acts 20:1); and Acts 20:3, 6, expressly mentions his third visit on his return from Greece (Corinth) to Syria by way of Macedonia. His sufferings at Philippi (Acts 16:19, etc.) strengthened the Christian bond of union between him and his Philippian converts, who also, like him, were exposed to trials for the Gospel's sake (I Thess. 2:2). They alone sent supplies for his temporal wants, *twice* shortly after he had left them (Phil. 4:15, 16), and again a third time shortly before writing this Epistle (Phil. 4:10, 18; II Cor. 11:9). This fervent attachment on their part was, perhaps, also in part due to the fact that few Jews were in Philippi, as in other scenes of his labors, to sow the seeds of distrust and suspicion. There was no synagogue, but merely a Jewish *Proseucha*, or oratory, by the riverside. So that there only do we read of his meeting no opposition from Jews, but only from the masters of the divining damsel, whose gains had been put an end to by her being dispossessed.

Though the Philippian Church was as yet free from Judaizing influence, yet it needed to be forewarned of that danger which might at any time assail it from without (ch. 3:2); even as such evil influences had crept into the Galatian churches. In ch. 4:2, 3 we find a trace of the fact recorded in the history (Acts 16:13, 14), that *female* converts were among the first to receive the Gospel at Philippi.

As to the state of the Church, we gather from II Corinthians 8:1, 2 that its members were *poor*, yet most *liberal*; and from Philippians 1:28-30, that they were undergoing persecution. The only blemish referred to in their character was, on the part of some members, a tendency to dissension. Hence arise his admonitions against disputings (ch. 1:27; 2:1-4, 12, 14; 4:2).

The OBJECT of the Epistle is general: not only to thank the Philippians for their contribution sent by Epaphroditus, who was now in returning to take back the apostle's letter, but to express his Christian love and sympathy, and to exhort them to a life consonant with that of Christ, and to warn them against existing dissensions and future possible assaults of Judaizers from without. It is remarkable in this Epistle alone, as compared with the others, that, amidst many commendations, there are no express censures of those to whom it is addressed. No doctrinal error, or schism, has as yet sprung up; the only blemish hinted at is, that some of the Philippian Church were somewhat wanting in lowliness of mind, the result of which want was disputation. Two women, Euodias and Syntyche, are mentioned as having erred in this respect. The Epistle may be divided into *three* parts: I. Affectionate address to the Philippians; reference to his own state as a prisoner at Rome, and to theirs, and to his mission of Epaphroditus to them (chs. 1 and 2). Epaphroditus probably held a leading office in the Philippian Church, perhaps as a presbyter. After Tychicus and Onesimus had departed (A.D. 62), carrying the Epistles to the Ephesians, Colossians, and Philemon, Paul was cheered in his imprisonment by the arrival of Epaphroditus with the Philippian contribution. That faithful "brother, companion in labor, and fellow soldier" (ch. 2:25), had brought on himself by the fatigues of the journey a dangerous sickness (ch. 2:26, 30). But now that he was recovered, he "longed" (ch. 2:26) to return to his Philippian flock, and in person to relieve their anxiety on his behalf, in respect to his sickness; and the apostle gladly availed himself of the opportunity of writing to them a letter of grateful acknowledgments and Christian exhortations. II. Caution against Judaizing teachers, supported by reference to his own former and present feeling towards Jewish legalism (ch. 3). III. Admonitions to individuals, and to the Church in general, thanks for their seasonable aid, and concluding benedictions and salutations.

This Epistle was written from Rome during the imprisonment, the beginning of which is related in Acts 28:16, 20, 30, 31. The reference to "Cæsar's household" (ch. 4:22), and to the "palace" (ch. 1:13, *Greek, Prætorium*, probably, *the barrack of the Prætorian bodyguard*, attached to the palace of Nero) confirms this. It must have been during his *first* imprisonment at Rome, for the mention of the Prætorium agrees with the fact that it was during his first imprisonment he was in the custody of the Prætorian Prefect, and his situation, described in ch. 1:12–14, agrees with his situation in the first two years of his imprisonment (Acts 28:30, 31). The following reasons show, moreover, that it was written towards *the close* of that imprisonment: (1) He, in it, expresses his expectation of the immediate decision of his cause (ch. 2:23). (2) Enough time had elapsed for the Philippians to hear of his imprisonment, to send Epaphroditus to him, to hear of Epaphroditus' arrival and sickness, and send back word to Rome of their distress (ch. 2:26). (3) It must have been written after the three other Epistles sent from Rome, *viz.*, Colossians, Ephesians, and Philemon; for Luke is no longer with him (ch. 2:20); otherwise he would have been specified as saluting them, having formerly labored among them, whereas he is mentioned as with him, Colossians 4:14; Philemon 24. Again, in Ephesians 6:19, 20, his freedom to preach is implied: but in ch. 1:13–18, his bondage is dwelt on, and it is implied that, *not himself*, but *others*, preached, and made his imprisonment known. Again, in Philemon 22, he confidently anticipates his release, which contrasts with the more depressed anticipations of this Epistle. (4) A considerable time had elapsed since the beginning of his imprisonment, for "his bonds" to have become so widely known, and to have produced such good effects for the Gospel (ch. 1:13). (5) There is evidently an increase in the rigor of his imprisonment implied now, as compared with the early stage of it, as described in Acts 28; cf. ch. 1:29, 30; 2:27. History furnishes a probable clue to account for this increase of vigor. In the second year of Paul's imprisonment (A.D. 62), Burrus, the Prætorian Prefect, to whose custody he had been committed (Acts 28:16, "the captain of the guard"), died; and Nero the emperor having divorced Octavia, and married Poppœa, a Jewish proselytess (who then caused her rival, Octavia, to be murdered, and gloated over the head of her victim), exalted Tigellinus, the chief promoter of the marriage, a monster of wickedness, to the Prætorian Prefecture. It was then he seems to have been removed from his own house into the Prætorium, or barrack of the Prætorian guards, attached to the palace, for stricter custody; and hence he writes with less hopeful anticipations as to the result of his trial (ch. 2:17; 3:11). Some of the Prætorian guards who had the custody of him before, would then naturally make known his "bonds," in accordance with ch. 1:13; from the smaller Prætorian bodyguard at the palace the report would spread to the general permanent Prætorian camp, which Tiberius had established north of the city, outside of the walls. He had arrived in Rome, February, 61; the "two whole years (Acts 20:30) in his own hired house" ended February, 63, so that the date of this Epistle, written shortly after, evidently while the danger was imminent, would be about spring or summer, 63. The providence of God averted the danger. He probably was thought beneath the notice of Tigellinus, who was more intent on court intrigues. The death of Nero's favorite, Pallas, the brother of Felix, this same year, also took out of the way another source of danger.

The STYLE is abrupt and discontinuous, his fervor of affection leading him to pass rapidly from one theme to another (ch. 2:18, 19–24, 25–30; 3:1, 2, 3, 4–14, 15). In no Epistle does he use so warm expressions of love. In ch. 4:1 he seems at a loss for words sufficient to express all the extent and ardor of his affection for the Philippians: "My brethren dearly beloved and longed for, my joy and crown, so stand fast in the Lord, my dearly beloved." The mention of bishops and deacons in ch. 1:1 is due to the late date of the Epistle, at a time when the Church had begun to assume that order which is laid down in the Pastoral Epistles, and which continued the prevalent one in the first and purest age of the Church.

CHAPTER 1

Vss. 1-30. INSCRIPTION. THANKSGIVING AND PRAYERS FOR THE FLOURISHING SPIRITUAL STATE OF THE PHILIPPIANS. HIS OWN STATE AT ROME, AND THE RESULT OF HIS IMPRISONMENT IN SPREADING THE GOSPEL. EXHORTATION TO CHRISTIAN CONSISTENCY.
1. Timotheus—mentioned as being well known to the Philippians (Acts 16:3, 10-12), and now present with Paul. Not that Timothy had any share in writing the Epistle; for Paul presently uses the first person singular, "I," not "we" (vs. 3). The mention of his name implies merely that Timothy joined in affectionate remembrances to them. **servants of Jesus Christ**—The oldest MSS. read the order, "Christ Jesus." Paul does not call himself "an apostle," as in the inscriptions of other Epistles; for the Philippians needed not to be reminded of his

apostolic authority. He writes rather in a tone of affectionate familiarity. **all**—so vss. 4, 7, 8, 25; ch. 2:17, 26. It implies comprehensive affection which desired not to forget any one among them "all." **bishops**—synonymous with "presbyters"; as appears from the same persons being called "elders of the Church" at Ephesus (Acts 20:17), and "overseers" (Acts 20:28), *Greek*, "bishops." And Titus 1:5, cf. with vs. 7. This is the earliest letter of Paul where bishops and deacons are mentioned, and the only one where they are separately addressed in the salutation. This accords with the probable course of events, deduced alike from the letters and history. While the apostles were constantly visiting the churches in person or by messengers, regular pastors would be less needed; but when some were removed by various causes, provision for the permanent order of the churches would be needed. Hence the three pastoral letters, subsequent to this Epistle, give instruction as to the due appointment of bishops and deacons. It agrees with this new want of the Church, when other apostles were dead or far away, and Paul long in prison, that bishops and deacons should be prominent for the first time in the opening salutation. The Spirit thus intimated that the churches were to look up to their own pastors, now that the miraculous gifts were passing into God's ordinary providence, and the presence of the inspired apostles, the dispensers of those gifts, was to be withdrawn [PALEY's *Horæ Paulinæ*]. "Presbyter," implied the *rank;* "bishop," *the duties of the office* [NEANDER]. Naturally, when the apostles who had the chief supervision were no more, one among the presbyters presided and received the name "bishop," in the more restricted and modern sense; just as in the Jewish synagogue one of the elders presided as "ruler of the synagogue." Observe, the apostle addresses the Church (i.e., the congregation) more directly than its presiding ministers (Col. 4:17; I Thess. 5:12; Heb. 13:24; Rev. 1:4, 11). The bishops managed more the internal, the deacons the external, affairs of the Church. The plural number shows there was more than one bishop or presbyter, and more than one deacon in the Church at Philippi. **2. Grace ... peace**—The very form of this salutation implies the union of Jew, Greek, and Roman. The Greek salutation was "joy" (*chairein*), akin to the *Greek* for "grace" (*charis*). The Roman was "health," the intermediate term between *grace* and *peace*. The Hebrew was *"peace,"* including both temporal and spiritual prosperity. *Grace* must come first if we are to have true *peace*. **from ... from**—Omit the second "from": as in the *Greek,* "God our Father" and "the Lord Jesus Christ," are most closely connected. **3.** Translate, "In all my remembrance of you." **4. making request**—Translate, "making *my* request." **for you all**—The frequent repetition in this Epistle of "all" with "you," marks that Paul desires to declare his love for *all* alike, and will not recognize any divisions among them. **with joy**—the characteristic feature in this Epistle, as *love* is in that to the Ephesians (cf. vs. 18; ch. 2:2, 19, 28; 3:1; 4:1, 4). *Love* and *joy* are the two first fruits of the Spirit. *Joy* gives especial animation to prayers. It marked his high opinion of them, that there was almost everything in them to give him *joy,* and almost nothing to give him pain. **5.** Ground of his "thanking God" (vs. 3): "For your (continued) fellowship (i.e., real spiritual participation) in (lit., 'in regard to') the Gospel from the first day (of your becoming *partakers* in it) until now." Believers have the fellowship of the Son of God (I Cor. 1:9) and of the Father (I John 1:3) in the Gospel, by becoming partakers of "the fellowship of the Holy Ghost" (II Cor. 13:14), and exercise that fellowship by acts of communion, not only the communion of the Lord's Supper, but holy liberality to brethren and ministers (ch. 4:10, 15, *"communicated ... concerning giving";* II Cor. 9:13; Gal. 6:6; Heb. 13:16, "To communicate forget not"). **6. confident**—This confidence nerves prayers and thanksgivings (vss. 3, 4). **this very thing**—*the very thing* which he prays for (vs. 4) is the matter of his believing confidence (Mark 11:24; I John 5:14, 15). Hence the result is sure. **he which hath begun**—God (ch. 2:13). **a good work**—Any work that God begins, He will surely finish (I Sam. 3:12). Not even men begin a work at random. Much more the fact of His beginning the work is a pledge of

its completion (Isa. 26:12). So as to the particular work here meant, the *perfecting of their fellowship in the Gospel* (vs. 5; Ps. 37:24; 89:33; 138:8; John 10:28, 29; Rom. 8:29, 35-39; 11:1, 2; Heb. 6:17-19; Jas. 1:17; Jude 24). As God cast not off Israel for ever, though chastening them for a time, so He will not cast off the spiritual Israel (Deut. 33:3; Isa. 27:3, I Pet. 1:5). **perform it until**—"perfect it up to" [ALFORD, ELLICOTT, and others]. **the day of ... Christ**—(vs. 10). The Lord's coming, designed by God in every age of the Church to be regarded as near, is to be the goal set before believers' minds rather than their own death. **7. meet**—*Greek,* "just." **to think this**—to have the prayerful confidence I expressed (vss. 4-6). **of you**—lit., "in behalf of you." Paul's confident prayer *in their behalf* was that God would perfect His own good work of grace in them. **because ...**—Punctuate and translate, "Because I have you in my heart (so vs. 8); otherwise the *Greek* and the words immediately following in the verse, favor MARGIN, '*Ye* have *me* in *your* heart ... being partakers of my grace' (both, in my bonds, and in *my* defense and confirmation of the Gospel), you (I say) all being fellow partakers of my grace." This last clause thus assigns the reason why he has them *in his heart* (i.e., cherished in his love, II Cor. 3:2; 7:3), even in his bonds, and in his defense and confirmation of the Gospel (such as he was constantly making in private, Acts 28:17-23; his self-defense and confirmation of the Gospel being necessarily conjoined, as the *Greek* implies; cf. vs. 17), viz., "inasmuch as ye are fellow partakers of my grace": inasmuch as ye share with me in "the fellowship of the Gospel" (vs. 5), and have manifested this, both by suffering as I do for the Gospel's sake (vss. 28-30), and by imparting to me of your substance (ch. 4:15). It is natural and right for me thus confidently to pray in your behalf. (ELLICOTT, and others translate, "To be thus minded for you all"), because of my having you in my warmest remembrances even in my bonds, since you are sharers with me in the Gospel grace. Bonds do not bind love. **8.** Confirmation of vs. 7. **record**—i.e., *witness.* **in the bowels of Jesus Christ**—"Christ Jesus" is the order in the oldest MSS. My *yearning love* (so the *Greek* implies) to you is not merely from natural affection, but from devotedness to Christ Jesus. "Not Paul, but Jesus Christ lives in Paul; wherefore Paul is not moved in the bowels [i.e., the tender love, Jer. 31:20] of Paul, but of Jesus Christ" [BENGEL]. All real spiritual love is but a portion of Christ's love which yearns in all who are united to Him [ALFORD]. **9.** The subject of his prayer for them (vs. 4). **your love**—to Christ, producing love not only to Paul, Christ's minister, as it did, but also to one another, which it did not altogether so much as it ought (ch. 2:2; 4:2). **knowledge**—of doctrinal and practical truth. **judgment**—rather, "perception"; "perceptive sense." Spiritual perceptiveness: spiritual sight, spiritual hearing, spiritual feeling, spiritual taste. Christianity is a vigorous plant, not the hotbed growth of enthusiasm. "Knowledge" and "perception" guard love from being ill-judged. **10.** Lit., "With a view to your *proving* (and so approving and embracing) *the things that excel*" (Rom. 2:18); not merely things not bad, but the things best among those that are good; the things of more advanced excellence. Ask as to things, not merely, Is there no harm, but is there any good, and which is the best? **sincere**—from a *Greek* root. *Examined in the sunlight and found pure.* **without offence**—not stumbling; running the Christian race without falling through any stumbling block, i.e., temptation, in your way. **till** —rather, "unto," "against"; so that when the day of Christ comes, ye may be found pure and without offense. **11.** The oldest MSS. read the singular, "fruit." So Galatians 5:22 (see *Note*); regarding the works of righteousness, however manifold, as *one* harmonious whole, "the *fruit* of the Spirit" (Eph. 5:9); Jas. 3:18, "the fruit of righteousness" (Heb. 12:11); Rom. 6:22, "fruit unto holiness." **which are**—"which *is* by (*Greek, through*) Jesus Christ." Through His sending to us the Spirit from the Father. "We are wild and useless olive trees till we are graffed into Christ, who, by His living root, makes us fruit-bearing branches" [CALVIN]. **12. understand**—*Greek,* "know." The Philippians probably had feared that his imprisonment would hinder the spread of the Gospel; he therefore removes this fear. **the things which happened unto me**—*Greek,* "the things concerning me." **rather**—so far is my imprisonment from hindering the Gospel. Faith takes in a favorable light even what seems adverse [BENGEL] (vss. 19, 28; ch. 2:17). **13. my bonds in Christ**—rather as *Greek,* "So that my bonds *have become manifest in Christ,*" i.e., known, as endured in Christ's cause. **palace**—lit., "Prætorium," i.e., the barrack of the Prætorian guards attached to the palace of Nero, on the Palatine hill at Rome; not the general Prætorian camp outside of the city; for this was not connected with "Cæsar's household," which ch. 4:22 shows the Prætorium here meant was. The emperor was "Prætor," or Commander-in-Chief; naturally then the barrack of his bodyguard was called the Prætorium. Paul seems now not to have been at large in his own hired house, though chained to a soldier, as in Acts 28:16, 20, 30, 31, but in strict custody in the Prætorium; a change which probably took place on Tigellinus becoming Prætorian Prefect. See my *Introduction.* **in all other places**—so CHRYSOSTOM. Or else, "TO all the rest," i.e., "manifest to all the other" Prætorian soldiers stationed elsewhere, through the instrumentality of the Prætorian household guards who might for the time be attached to the emperor's palace, and who relieved one another in succession. Paul had been now upwards of two years a prisoner, so that there was time for his cause and the Gospel having become widely known at Rome. **14.** Translate as *Greek,* "And *that* (vs. 13) *most* of the brethren in the Lord ...." "In the Lord," distinguishes them from "brethren after the flesh," Jewish fellow countrymen. ELLICOTT translates, "*Trusting in the Lord.*" **by my bonds**—encouraged by my patience in bearing my bonds. **much more bold**—Translate as *Greek,* "are more abundantly bold." **15.** "Some indeed *are* preaching Christ even *for* envy, i.e., to carry out the *envy* which they felt towards Paul, on account of the success of the Gospel in the capital of the world, owing to his steadfastness in his imprisonment; they wished through envy to transfer the credit of its progress from him to themselves. Probably Judaizing teachers (Rom. 14; I Cor. 3:10-15; 9:1, etc.; II Cor. 11:1-4). **some also**—rather for—**good will**—answering to "the brethren" (vs. 14); some being *well disposed* to him. **16, 17.** The oldest MSS. transpose these verses, and read, "*These* (last) *indeed out of* love (to Christ and me), knowing (the opposite of 'thinking' below) that I am set (i.e., appointed by God, I Thess. 3:3) for the defense of the Gospel (vs. 7, not on my own account). But the others *out of* contention (or rather, 'a factious spirit'; 'cabal'; a spirit of intrigue, using unscrupu-

lous means to compass their end; *Note,* Gal. 5:20; 'self-seeking' [ALFORD]) *proclaim* (the *Greek* is not the same as that for 'preach,' but, '*announce*') Christ, not sincerely (answering to 'but of a spirit of intrigue,' or 'self-seeking'). Lit., 'not purely'; not with a pure intention; the Jewish leaven they tried to introduce was in order to *glorify themselves* (Gal. 6:12, 13; see, however, *Note,* vs. 18), thinking (but in vain) *to raise up* (so the oldest MSS. read) *tribulation* to my bonds." Their *thought* was, that taking the opportunity of my being laid aside, they would exalt themselves by their Judaizing preaching, and depreciate me and my preaching, and so cause me trouble of spirit in my bonds; they thought that I, like themselves, sought my own glory, and so would be mortified at their success over mine. But they are utterly mistaken; "I rejoice" at it (vs. 18), so far am I from being *troubled* at it. **18.** "What then?" What follows from this? Does this trouble me as they thought it would? "Notwithstanding" their unkind *thought* to me, and self-seeking intention, the cause I have at heart is furthered "every way" of preaching, "whether in pretense (with a by motive, vs. 16) or in truth (out of true 'love' to Christ, vs. 17), Christ is *proclaimed;* and therein I do rejoice, yea, and I will rejoice." From this it would seem that these self-seeking teachers in the main "proclaimed Christ," not "another Gospel," such as the Judaizers in Galatia taught (Gal. 1:6-8); but probably having some of the Jewish leaven (*Note,* vss. 15, 16, 17), their *chief* error was their selfseeking envious *motive,* not so much error of doctrine; had there been *vital* error, Paul would not have *rejoiced.* The *proclamation of* CHRIST, however done, roused attention, and so was sure to be of service. Paul could thus rejoice at the good result of their bad intentions (Ps. 76:10; Isa. 10:5, 7). **19. turn to my salvation**—"turn out *to me for* (or *unto*) salvation." This proclamation of Christ every way will turn out to *my spiritual good.* Christ, whose interests are my interests, being glorified thereby; and so the coming of His kingdom being furthered, which, when it does come, will bring completed "SALVATION" (Heb. 9:28) to me and all whose "earnest expectation" (vs. 20) is that Christ may be magnified in them. So far is their preaching from causing me, as they thought, *tribulation in my bonds* (vs. 16). Paul plainly quotes and applies to himself the very words of the LXX (Job 13:16), "This shall turn out to my salvation," which belong to all God's people of every age, in their tribulation (cf. Job 13:15). **through your prayer and the supply**—The *Greek* intimately joins the two nouns together, by having but one preposition and one article: "Through your prayer and (*the consequent*) supply of the Spirit of Jesus Christ" (obtained for me through your prayer). **20. According to my earnest expectation**—The *Greek* expresses, "expectation *with uplifted head* (Luke 21:28) *and outstretched neck.*" Romans 8:19 is the only other place in the New Testament that the word occurs. TITTMANN says, in both places it implies not mere *expectation,* but *the anxious desire of an anticipated prosperous issue in afflictive circumstances.* The subject of his earnest expectation which follows, answers to "my salvation" (vs. 19). **in nothing I shall be ashamed**—in nothing have reason to be ashamed of "my work for God, or His work in me" [ALFORD]. Or, "in nothing be *disappointed* in my *hope,* but that I may fully obtain it" [ESTIUS]. So "ashamed" is used in Romans 9:33. **all boldness**—"all" is opposed to "in nothing," as "boldness" is the opposite to "ashamed." **so now also**—when "my body" is "in bonds" (vs. 17). **Christ**—not Paul, "shall be magnified." **life, or by death**—Whatever be the issue, I cannot lose; I must be the gainer by the event. Paul was not omniscient; in the issue of things pertaining to themselves, the apostles underwent the same probation of faith and patience as we. **21. For**—in either event (vs. 20) I must be the gainer, "For to me . . . ." **to live is Christ**—whatever life, time, and strength, I have, is Christ's; Christ is the sole object for which I live (Gal. 2:20). **to die is gain**—not the act of dying, but as the *Greek* ("to have died") expresses, *the state after death.* Besides the glorification of Christ by my death, which is my primary object (vs. 20), the change of state caused by death, so far from being a matter of *shame* (vs. 20) or loss, as my enemies suppose, will be a positive "gain" to me. **22.** Rather as *Greek,* "But if to live in the flesh (if), this (I say, the continuance in life which I am undervaluing) be the fruit of my labor (i.e., be the condition in which the fruit of my ministerial labor is involved), *then* what I shall choose I know not" (I cannot determine with myself, if the choice were given me, both alternatives being great goods alike). So ALFORD and ELLICOTT. BENGEL takes it as *English Version,* which the *Greek* will bear by supposing an ellipsis, "If to live in the flesh (be my portion), this (continuing to live) is the fruit of my labor," i.e., this continuance in life will be the occasion of my bringing in "the fruit of labor," i.e., will be the occasion of "labors" which are their own "fruit" or reward; or, this my continuing "to live" will have this "fruit," viz., "labors" for Christ. GROTIUS explains "the fruit of labor" as an idiom for "worth-while"; If I live in the flesh, this is worth my while, for thus Christ's interest will be advanced, "For to me to live is Christ" (vs. 21; cf. ch. 2:30; Rom. 1:13). The second alternative, viz., dying, is taken up and handled, ch. 2:17, "If I be offered." **23. For**—The oldest MSS. read, "But." "I know not (vs. 22), BUT am in a strait (am perplexed) betwixt the two (viz., 'to live' and 'to die'), having the desire *for* departing (lit., *to loose* anchor, II Tim. 4: 6) and being with Christ; FOR (so the oldest MSS.) it is by far better"; or as the *Greek,* more forcibly, "by far *the more preferable*"; a double comparative. This refutes the notion of the soul being dormant during its separation from the body. It also shows that, while he regarded the Lord's advent as at all times near, yet that his death before it was a very possible contingency. The *partial* life eternal is in the interval between death and Christ's second advent; the *perfectional,* at that advent [BISHOP PEARSON]. *To depart* is better than to remain in the flesh; *to be with Christ is far, far better;* a New Testament hope (Heb. 12:24), [BENGEL]. **24. to abide**—to continue somewhat longer. **for you**—Greek, "on your account"; "for your sake." In order to be of service to *you,* I am willing to forego my entrance a little sooner into blessedness; heaven will not fail to be mine at last. **25.** Translate, "And being confident of this." **I know . . .**—by prophetical intimations of the Spirit. He did not yet know the issue, as far as *human appearances* were concerned (ch. 2:23). He doubtless returned from his first captivity to Philippi (Heb. 13:19; Philemon 22). **joy of faith**—*Greek,* "joy in your faith." **26.** Translate, "That your matter of glorying (or *rejoicing*) may abound in Christ Jesus in me (i.e., in my case; *in respect to me,* or *for me* who have been granted to your prayers, vs. 19) through my presence again among you." ALFORD makes the

"matter of glorying," *the possession of the Gospel,* received from Paul, which would abound, be assured and increased, by his presence among them; thus, "in me," implies that Paul is the worker of the material of abounding in Christ Jesus. But "my *rejoicing* over you" (ch. 2:16), answers plainly to "your *rejoicing* in respect to me" here. **27. Only** —Whatever happens as to my coming to you, or not, make this your one only care. By supposing this or that future contingency, many persuade themselves they will be such as they ought to be, but it is better always without evasion to perform present duties under present circumstances [BENGEL]. **let your conversation be**—(Cf. ch. 3:20.) The *Greek* implies, "Let your *walk as citizens* (viz., of the heavenly state; 'the city of the living God,' Heb. 12:22, 'the heavenly Jerusalem,' 'fellow citizens of the saints,' Eph. 2:19) be . . . ." **I . . . see . . . hear**—so vs. 30. "Hear," in order to include both alternatives, must include the meaning *know*. **your affairs**—your state. **in one spirit**—the fruit of partaking of the Holy Spirit (Eph. 4:3, 4). **with one mind**—rather as *Greek,* "*soul,*" the sphere of the affections; subordinate to the "Spirit," man's higher and heavenly nature. "There is sometimes natural antipathies among believers; but these are overcome, when there is not only unity of spirit, but also of *soul*" [BENGEL]. **striving together**—with united effort. **28. terrified**—lit., said of horses or other animals startled or suddenly scared; so of sudden *consternation* in general. **which**—your not being terrified. **evident token of perdition**—if they would only perceive it (II Thess. 1:5). It attests this, that in contending hopelessly against you, they are only rushing on to their own perdition, not shaking your united faith and constancy. **to you of salvation**—The oldest MSS. read, "of *your* salvation"; not merely *your temporal safety*. **29. For**—rather, a proof that this is an evident token from God of your salvation, "*Because* . . . ." **it is given** —*Greek,* "it *has been* granted *as a favor,*" or "gift of grace." Faith is the gift of God (Eph. 2:8), not wrought in the soul by the will of man, but by the Holy Ghost (John 1:12, 13). **believe on him**—"To believe *Him,*" would merely mean to believe He speaks the truth. "To believe *on Him,*" is to believe in, and trust through, Him to obtain eternal salvation. *Suffering for Christ* is not only not a mark of God's anger, but *a gift of His grace.* **30. ye saw in me**—(Acts 16:12, 19, etc.; I Thess. 2:2). I am "in nothing terrified by mine adversaries" (vs. 29), so ought not ye. The words here, "ye saw . . . and . . . hear," answer to "I come and *see* you, or else . . . *hear*" (vs. 27).

CHAPTER 2

VSS. 1-30. CONTINUED EXHORTATION: TO UNITY: TO HUMILITY AFTER CHRIST'S EXAMPLE, WHOSE GLORY FOLLOWED HIS HUMILIATION: TO EARNESTNESS IN SEEKING PERFECTION, THAT THEY MAY BE HIS JOY IN THE DAY OF CHRIST: HIS JOYFUL READINESS TO BE OFFERED NOW BY DEATH, SO AS TO PROMOTE THEIR FAITH. HIS INTENTION TO SEND TIMOTHY: HIS SENDING EPAPHRODITUS MEANTIME. **1.** The "therefore" implies that he is here expanding on the exhortation (ch. 1:27), "In one Spirit, with one mind" (*soul*). He urges *four influencing motives* in this verse, to inculcate the four Christian duties corresponding respectively to them (vs. 2). "That ye be *like-minded,* having the same *love,* of one accord, of one mind"; (1) "If there be (with you) *any consolation in Christ,*" i.e., any *consolation of which Christ is the source,* leading you to wish *to console me* in my afflictions borne for Christ's sake, ye owe it to me to grant my request "that ye be like-minded" [CHRYSOSTOM and ESTIUS]: (2) 'If there be any comfort of (i.e., flowing from) love," the adjunct of "consolation in Christ"; (3) "If any fellowship of (communion together as Christians, flowing from joint participation in) the Spirit" (II Cor. 13:14). As *Pagans* meant literally those who were of one village, and *drank of one fountain,* how much greater is the union which conjoins those who drink of the same Spirit! (I Cor. 12:4, 13) [GROTIUS]: (4) "If any bowels (tender emotions) and mercies" (compassions), the adjuncts of "fellowship of the Spirit." The opposites of the two pairs, into which the four fall, are reprobated, vss. 3, 4. **2. Fulfil**—i.e., Make full. I have joy in you, *complete* it by that which is still wanting, viz., *unity* (ch. 1:9). **likeminded**—lit., "that ye be of the same mind"; more general than the following "of one mind." **having the same love**—equally disposed to love and be loved. **being of one accord**—lit., "with united *souls.*" This pairs with the following clause, thus, "With united souls, being of one mind"; as the former two also pair together, "That ye be like-minded, having the same love." **3.** *Let nothing be done*—The italicized words are not in the *Greek.* Perhaps the ellipsis had better be supplied from the *Greek* (vs. 2), "*Thinking* nothing in the way of strife" (or rather, "factious intrigue," "self-seeking," *Note,* ch. 1:16). It is the *thought* which characterizes the action as good or bad before God. **lowliness of mind**—The *direct* relation of this grace is to God alone; it is the sense of dependence of the creature on the Creator as such, and it places all created beings in this respect on a level. The man "lowly of mind" as to his spiritual life is independent of men, and free from all slavish feeling, while sensible of his continual dependence on God. Still it INDIRECTLY affects his behavior toward his fellow men; for, conscious of his entire dependence on God for all his abilities, even as they are dependent on God for theirs, he will not pride himself on his abilities, or exalt self in his conduct toward others (Eph. 4:2; Col. 3:12) [NEANDER]. **let each esteem**—Translate as *Greek,* "esteeming each other superior to *yourselves.*" Instead of fixing your eyes on those points in which you excel, fix them on those in which your neighbor excels you: this is true "humility." **4.** The oldest MSS. read, "Not *looking each of you* (plural, *Greek*) on his own things (i.e., not *having regard* solely to them), but *each of you* on the things of others" also. Cf. vs. 21; also Paul's own example (ch. 1:24). **5.** The oldest MSS. read, "Have this mind in you. . . ." He does not put forward himself (see *Note,* vs. 4, and ch. 1:24) as an example, but Christ, THE ONE pre-eminently who sought not His own, but "humbled Himself" (vs. 8), first in taking on Him our nature, secondly, in humbling Himself further in that nature (Rom. 15: 3). **6.** Translate, "Who *subsisting* (or *existing,* viz., originally: the *Greek* is not the simple substantive verb, *to be*) in the form of God (the divine *essence* is not meant: but the *external self-manifesting characteristics of God,* the *form* shining forth from His glorious essence. The divine nature had infinite BEAUTY in itself, even without any creature contemplating that beauty: that beauty was 'the form of God'; as 'the *form* of a servant' (vs. 7), which is in contrasted opposition to it, takes for granted the *existence* of His human nature, so 'the form of God' takes for granted His divine nature [BENGEL], cf.

John 5:37; 17:5; Col. 1:15, 'Who is the IMAGE of the invisible God' at a time *before* 'every creature,' II Corinthians 4:4, *esteemed* (the same *Greek* verb as in vs. 3) His being *on an equality* with God "no (act of) robbery" or *self-arrogation;* claiming to one's self what does not belong to him. ELLICOTT, WAHL, and others have translated, "*A thing* to be grasped at," which would require the *Greek* to be *harpagma,* whereas *harpagmos* means the *act of* seizing. So *harpagmos* means in the only other passage where it occurs, PLUTARCH, *De educatione puerorum,* 120. The same insuperable objection lies against ALFORD's translation, "He regarded not as *self-enrichment* (i.e., an *opportunity for self-exaltation*) His equality with God." His argument is that the antithesis (vs. 7) requires it, "He used His equality with God as *an opportunity, not for self-exaltation,* but for self-abasement, or *emptying Himself.* But the antithesis is not between His *being on an equality with God,* and His *emptying Himself;* for He never emptied Himself of the fulness of His Godhead, or His "BEING *on an equality with God*"; but between His being "in the FORM (i.e., the outward glorious self-manifestation) of God," and His "taking on Him *the form of a servant,*" whereby He in a great measure emptied Himself of His precedent "form," or outward self-manifesting glory as God. Not "looking on His own things" (vs. 4), He, though existing in the form of God, He esteemed it no robbery to be on an equality with God, yet made Himself of no reputation. "Being on an equality with God," is not identical with "subsisting in the form of God"; the latter expresses the *external characteristics,* majesty, and beauty of the Deity, which "He emptied Himself of," to assume "the *form* of a servant"; the former, "HIS BEING," or NATURE, His already existing STATE OF EQUALITY with God, both the Father and the Son having the same ESSENCE. A glimpse of Him "in the form of God," previous to His incarnation, was given to Moses (Exod. 24:10, 11), Aaron, etc. **7. made himself of no reputation, and . . .and**—rather as the *Greek,* "*emptied* Himself, *taking* upon him the form of a servant, *being* made in the likeness of men." The two latter clauses (there being no conjunctions, "and—and," in the *Greek*) expresses *in what* Christ's "emptying of Himself" consists, viz., in "taking the form of a servant" (*Note,* Heb. 10:5; cf. Exod. 21:5, 6, and Ps. 40:6, proving that it was at the time when He assumed a *body,* He took "the form of a *servant*"), and in order to explain *how* He took "the form of a servant," there is added, by "being made in the likeness of men." His subjection to the law (Luke 2:21; Gal. 4:4) and to His parents (Luke 2:51), His low state as a carpenter, and carpenter's reputed son (Matt. 13:55; Mark 6: 3), His betrayal for the price of a bond-servant (Exod. 21:32), and slave-like death to relieve us from the slavery of sin and death, finally and chiefly, *His servant-like dependence as man on God,* while His divinity was not outwardly manifested (Isa. 49: 3, 7), are all marks of His "form as a servant." This proves: (1) He was in the form of a servant as soon as He was made man. (2) He was "in the form of God" *before* He was "in the form of a servant." (3) He did as really subsist in the divine nature, as in the form of a servant, or in the nature of man. For He was as much "in the form of God" as "in the form of a servant"; and was so in the form of God as "to be on an equality with God"; He therefore could have been none other than God; for God saith, "To whom will ye liken Me and make Me equal?" (Isa. 46:5), [BISHOP PEARSON]. His *empty-*

ing Himself presupposes His previous *plenitude of Godhead* (John 1:14; Col. 1:19; 2:9). He remained full of this; yet He bore Himself as if He were *empty.* **8. being found in fashion as a man**—*being already, by His "emptying Himself," in the form of a servant,* or likeness of man (Rom. 8:3), "He humbled Himself (still further by) *becoming* obedient *even* unto death (not as *English Version,* 'He humbled Himself *and became* . . .'; the *Greek* has no 'and,' and has the *participle,* not the verb), and that the death of the cross." "Fashion" expresses that He had the *outward guise, speech,* and *look.* In vs. 7, in the *Greek,* the emphasis is on *Himself* (which stands before the Greek verb), "He emptied *Himself," His divine self,* viewed in respect to what He had heretofore been; in vs. 8 the emphasis is on *"humbled"* (which stands before the *Greek* "Himself"); He not only "emptied Himself" of His previous "form of God," but submitted to *positive* HUMILIATION. He "became obedient," viz., to God, as His "servant" (Rom. 5:19; Heb. 5:8). Therefore *"God"* is said to "exalt" Him (vs. 9), even as it was God to whom He became voluntarily "obedient." "Even unto death" expresses the climax of His obedience (John 10:18). **9. Wherefore**—as the just consequence of His self-humiliation and obedience (Ps. 8:5, 6; 110:1, 7; Matt. 28:18; Luke 24:26; John 5:27; 10:17; Rom. 14:9; Eph. 1:20-22; Heb. 2:9). An intimation, that if we would hereafter be exalted, we too must, after His example. now humble ourselves (vss. 3, 5; ch. 3:21; I Pet. 5:5, 6). Christ emptied Christ; God exalted Christ as man to equality with God [BENGEL]. **highly exalted**—*Greek, "super-eminently* exalted" (Eph. 4:10). **given him** —*Greek,* "bestowed on Him." **a name**—along with the corresponding *reality,* glory and majesty. **which** —Translate, (viz.), "that which is above every name." The name "JESUS" (vs. 10), which is even now in glory His name of honor (Acts 9:5). "Above" not only men, but angels (Eph. 1:21). **10. at the name**—rather as *Greek,* "in the name." **bow**— rather, "bend," in token of worship. Referring to Isaiah 45:23; quoted also in Romans 14:11. To worship "in the name of Jesus," is to worship Jesus *Himself* (cf. vs. 11; Prov. 18:10), or *God in Christ* (John 16:23; Eph. 3:14). Cf. "Whosoever shall call upon *the name of the Lord* (i.e., whosoever shall call on *the Lord in His revealed character*) shall be saved" (Rom. 10:13; I Cor. 1:2); "all that call upon *the name of Jesus Christ our Lord*" (cf. II Tim. 2: 22); "call on the Lord"; Acts 7:59, "calling upon . . . and saying, Lord Jesus" (Acts 9:14, 21; 22:16). **of things in heaven**—angels. They worship Him not only as God, but as the ascended *God-man,* "Jesus" (Eph. 1:21; Heb. 1:6; I Pet. 3:22). **in earth**—men; among whom He tabernacled for a time. **under the earth**—the dead; among whom He was numbered once (Rom. 14:9, 11; Eph. 4:9, 10; Rev. 5:13). The demons and the lost may be included *indirectly,* as even they give homage, though one of fear, not love, to Jesus (Mark 3:11; Luke 8:31; Jas. 2:19, see *Note,* vs. 11). **11. every tongue**—Cf. "every knee" (vs. 10). *In every way* He shall be acknowledged as Lord (no longer as "servant," vs. 7). As none can fully do so "but by the Holy Ghost" (I Cor. 12:3), the spirits of good men who are dead, must be the class *directly* meant, vs. 10, "under the earth." **to the glory of God the Father**—the grand end of Christ's mediatorial office and kingdom, which shall cease when this end shall have been fully realized (John 5:19-23, 30; 17:1, 4-7; I Cor. 15:24-28. **12. Wherefore**—Seeing that we have in Christ such a specimen of glory resulting from

"obedience" (vs. 8) and humiliation, see that ye also be "obedient," and so *"your* salvation" shall follow your obedience. **as ye have . . . obeyed**—*"even as* ye have *been obedient."* viz., to God, as Jesus was "obedient" unto God (*Note,* vs. 8). **not as . . .**— "not *as if"* it were a matter to be done "in my presence only, but now (as things are) much more (with more earnestness) (in my absence)" (because my help is withdrawn from you) [ALFORD]. **work out** —carry out to its full perfection. "Salvation" is "worked in" (vs. 13; Eph. 1:11) believers by the Spirit, who enables them through faith to be justified *once for all;* but it needs, as a progressive work, to be "worked out" by obedience, through the help of the same Spirit, unto perfection (II Pet. 1:5-8). The sound Christian neither, like the formalist, rests in the means, without looking to the end, and to the Holy Spirit who alone can make the means effectual; nor, like the fanatic, hopes to attain the end without the means. **your own**—The emphasis is on this. Now that *I* am not present to further the work of your salvation, "work out *your own* salvation" yourselves the more carefully. Do not think this work cannot go on because I am absent; "for (vs. 13) it is God that worketh in you. . . ." In this case adopt a rule different from the former (vs. 4), but resting on the same principle of "lowliness of mind" (vs. 3), viz., "look each on *his own* things," instead of "disputings" with others (vs. 14). **salvation**—which is in "Jesus" (vs. 10), as His name (meaning God-Saviour) implies. **with fear and trembling**—the very feeling enjoined on "servants," as to what ought to accompany their "obedience" (Eph. 6:5). So here: See that, as "servants" to God, after the example of Christ, ye be so "with the fear and trembling" which becomes servants; not slavish fear, but *trembling anxiety not to fall short of the goal* (I Cor. 9:26, 27; Heb. 4:1, "Let us *fear,* lest a promise being left us of entering into His rest, any should come short of it"), *resulting from a sense of our human insufficiency, and from the consciousness that all depends on the power of God,* "who worketh both to will and to do" (Rom. 1:20). "Paul, though joyous, writes seriously" [J. J. WOLF]. **13. For**—encouragement to work: "For it is God who worketh in you," always present with you, though I be absent. It is not said, "Work out your own salvation, *though* it is God . . .," but, *"because* it is God who. . . ." The *will,* and the power *to work,* being first instalments of His grace, encourage us to make full proof of, and carry out to the end, the "salvation" which He has first "worked," and is still "working *in"* us, enabling us to "work it *out."* "Our will does nothing thereunto without grace; but grace is inactive without our will" [ST. BERNARD]. Man is, in different senses, entirely active, and entirely passive: *God producing all, and we acting all.* What He produced is our own acts. It is not that God does some, and we the rest. God does all, and we do all. God is the only proper author, we the only proper actors. Thus the same things in Scripture are represented as from God, and from us. God makes a new heart, and we are commanded to make us a new heart; not merely because we must use the means in order to the effect, but the effect itself is our act and our duty (Ezek. 11:19; 18:31; 36:26) [EDWARDS]. **worketh**—rather as *Greek,* "worketh *effectually."* We cannot of ourselves embrace the Gospel of grace: "the will" (Ps. 110:3; II Cor. 3:5) comes solely of God's gift to whom He will (John 6:44, 65); so also the power "to do" (rather, *"to work effectually,"* as the *Greek* is the same as that for "worketh in"), i.e., effectual

perseverance to the end, is wholly of God's gift (ch. 1:6; Heb. 13:21). **of his good pleasure**—rather as *Greek*, "FOR His good pleasure"; *in order to carry out* His sovereign gracious purpose towards you (Eph. 1:5, 9). **14. murmurings**—*secret murmurings* and complaints against your fellow men arising from selfishness: opposed to the example of Jesus just mentioned (cf. the use of the word, John 7:12, 13; Acts 6:1; I Peter 4:9; Jude 16). **disputings**—The *Greek* is translated "doubting" in I Tim. 2:8. But here referring to profitless "disputings" with our fellow men, in relation to whom we are called on to be "blameless and harmless" (vs. 15): so the *Greek* is translated, Mark 9:33, 34. These disputings flow from "vainglory" reprobated (vs. 3); and abounded among the Aristotelian philosophers in Macedon, where Philippi was. **15. blameless and harmless**—without either the repute of mischief, or the inclination to do it [ALFORD]. **sons**—rather as *Greek*, "the children of God" (Rom. 8:14-16). Imitation of our heavenly Father is the instinctive guide to our duty as His children, more than any external law (Matt. 5:44, 45, 48). **without rebuke**—"without (giving handle for) *reproach*." The whole verse tacitly refers by contrast to Deuteronomy 32:5, "Their *spot* . . . not . . . of His *children* . . . a *perverse* and *crooked* generation" (cf. I Pet. 2:12). **ye shine**—lit., "appear" [TRENCH]. "Show yourselves" (cf. Matt. 5:14-16; Eph. 5:8-13). **as lights in the world**—The *Greek* expresses "as *luminaries* in the world," as the sun and moon, "the lights," or "great lights," in the *material* world or in the firmament. LXX uses the very same *Greek* word in the passage, Genesis 1:14, 16; cf. *Note*, Revelation 21:11. **16. Holding forth**—to them, and so *applying* it (the common meaning of the *Greek;* perhaps here including also the other meaning, "holding *fast*"). The image of *light-bearers* or *luminaries* is carried on from vs. 15. As the heavenly luminaries' *light* is closely connected with the *life* of animals, so ye hold forth the light of Christ's "word" (received from me) which is the "life" of the Gentiles (John 1:4; I John 1:1, 5-7). Christ is "the Light of the world" (John 8:12); believers are only "lightbearers" reflecting His light. **that I may rejoice in**—lit., "*with a view to* (your being) a subject of rejoicing to me *against* the day of Christ" (ch. 4:1; II Cor. 1:14; I Thess. 2:19). **that I have not run in vain**—that it was not in vain that I labored for your spiritual good. **17. Yea, and if**—rather as *Greek*, "Yea, if even"; implying that he regarded the contingency as not unlikely: He had assumed the *possibility* of his being found alive at Christ's coming (for in every age Christ designed Christians to stand in preparedness for His coming as at hand): he here puts a supposition which he regards as more likely, viz., his own death before Christ's coming. **I be offered**—rather as *Greek*, "I am poured out." "I am made a libation." Present, not future, as the danger is threatening him *now*. As in sacrifices libations of wine were "*poured* upon" the offerings, so he represents his Philippian converts, offered through faith (or else their *faith* itself), as the sacrifice, and *his blood as the libation* "poured upon" it (cf. Rom. 15:16; II Tim. 4:6). **service**—*Greek*, "priest's ministration"; carrying out the image of a sacrifice. **I joy**—for myself (ch. 1: 21, 23). His expectation of release from prison is much fainter, than in the Epistles to Ephesians, Colossians, and Philemon, written somewhat earlier from Rome. The appointment of Tigellinus to be Prætorian Prefect was probably the cause of this change. See *Introduction*. **rejoice with you all**—ALFORD translates, "I *congratulate* you all," viz. on the

honor occurring to you by my blood being poured out on the sacrifice of your faith. If *they rejoiced* already (as *English Version* represents), what need of his urging them, "Do ye *also* joy." **18.** "Do ye also rejoice" at this honor to you, "and congratulate me" on my blessed "gain" (ch. 1:21). **19.** Vs. 22, "ye know the proof of him . . that . . . he hath served with me," implies that Timothy had been long with Paul at Philippi. Accordingly, in the history (Acts 16:1-4; 17:10, 14), we find them *setting out* together from Derbe in Lycaonia, and together again at Berea in Macedonia, near *the conclusion* of Paul's missionary journey: an *undesigned* coincidence between the Epistle and history, a mark of genuineness [PALEY]. From vss. 19-50, it appears Epaphroditus was to set out at once to allay the anxiety of the Philippians on his account, and at the same time bearing the Epistle; Timothy was to follow after the apostle's liberation was decided, when they could arrange their plans more definitely as to *where* Timothy should, on his return with tidings from Philippi, meet Paul, who was designing by a wider circuit, and slower progress, to reach that city. Paul's reason for sending Timothy so soon after having heard of the Philippians from Epaphroditus was that they were now suffering persecutions (ch. 1:28-30); and besides, Epaphroditus' delay through sickness on his journey to Rome from Philippi, made the tidings he brought to be of less recent date than Paul desired. Paul himself also hoped to visit them shortly. **But I trust**—Yet my death is by no means certain; yea, "I *hope* (*Greek*) in the Lord" (i.e., by the Lord's help). **unto you**—lit., "*for* you," i.e., to your satisfaction, not merely motion, *to you*. **I also**—that not only you "may be of good *courage*" (so *Greek*) on hearing of me (vs. 23), but "I also, when I know your state." **20.** His reason for sending Timothy above all others: I have none so "like-minded," lit., "like-souled," with myself as is Timothy. Cf. Deuteronomy 13:6, "Thy friend which is as thine own *soul*" (Ps. 55:14). Paul's second self. **naturally**—*Greek*, "genuinely"; "with *sincere* solicitude." A case wherein the Spirit of God so changed man's nature, that to be *natural* was with him to be *spiritual*: the great point to be aimed at. **21.** Translate as *Greek*, "*They* all" (viz., who are now with me, ch. 1:14, 17; ch. 4:21: such Demas, then with him, proved to be, Col. 4:14; cf. II Tim. 4:10; Philemon 24). **seek their own**—opposed to Paul's precept (vs. 4; I Cor. 10:24, 33; 13:5). This is spoken, by comparison with Timothy; for ch. 1: 16, 17 implies that some of those with Paul at Rome were genuine Christians, though not so self-sacrificing as Timothy. Few come to the help of the Lord's cause, where ease, fame, and gain have to be sacrificed. Most help only when Christ's gain is compatible with their own (Judg. 5:17, 23). **22.** Rare praise (Neh. 7:2). **as a son with the father**—Translate, "as a *child* (*serveth*) a *father*." **served with me**—When we might expect the sentence to run thus, "As a child *serveth a father*, so he *served me*"; he changes it to "served *with* me" in modesty; as Christians are not *servants* TO *one another*, but *servants of God* WITH *one another* (cf. ch. 3:17). **in the gospel**—*Greek*, "unto," or "*for* the Gospel." **23. so soon as I shall see**—i.e., so soon *as I shall have known for certain*. **24. also myself**—as well as Timothy. **25. I supposed**—"I thought it necessary." **to send**—It was properly a *sending* Epaphroditus *back* (ch. 4:18). But as he had come intending to stay some time with Paul, the latter uses the word "send" (cf. vs. 30). **fellow soldier**—in the "good fight" of faith (ch. 1:27, 30; II Tim. 2:3; 4:7). **your mes-**

senger—lit., "apostle." The "apostles" or "messengers *of the churches*" (Rom. 16:7; II Cor. 8:23), were distinct from the "apostles" specially commissioned *by Christ,* as the Twelve and Paul. **ministered to my wants**—by conveying the contributions from Phillippi. The *Greek leitourgon,* lit., implies *ministering in the ministerial office.* Probably Epaphroditus was a presbyter or else a deacon. **26. For**—reason for thinking it "necessary to send" "Epaphroditus. Translate as *Greek,* "*Inasmuch as he was longing* after you all." **full of heaviness**—The *Greek* expresses the being *worn out* and *overpowered with heavy grief.* **because that ye had heard that he had been sick**—rather, "that he *was* sick." He felt how exceedingly saddened you would be in hearing it; and he now is hastening to relieve your minds of the anxiety. **27.** Epaphroditus' sickness proves that the apostles had not ordinarily the *permanent* gift of miracles, any more than that of inspiration: both were vouchsafed to them only for each particular occasion, as the Spirit thought fit. **lest I should have sorrow upon sorrow**—viz., the sorrow of losing him by death, in addition to the sorrow of my imprisonment. Here only occurs anything of a sorrowful tone in this Epistle, which generally is most joyous. **29. Receive him**—There seems to be something behind respecting him. If extreme affection had been the sole ground of his "heaviness," no such exhortation would have been needed [ALFORD]. **in reputation**—"in honor." **30. for the work of Christ**—viz., the bringing of a supply to me, the minister of Christ. He was probably in a delicate state of health in setting out from Philippi; but at all hazards he undertook this service of Chirstian love, which cost him a serious sickness. **not regarding his life**—Most of the oldest MSS. read, "hazarding. . . ." **to supply your lack of service** —Not that Paul would imply, they lacked the *will:* what they "lacked" was the "*opportunity*" by which to send their accustomed bounty (ch. 4:10). "That which ye would have done if you could [but which you could not through absence], he did for you; therefore receive him with all joy" [ALFORD].

CHAPTER 3

Vss. 1-21. WARNING AGAINST JUDAIZERS: HE HAS GREATER CAUSE THAN THEY TO TRUST IN LEGAL RIGHTEOUSNESS, BUT RENOUNCED IT FOR CHRIST'S RIGHTEOUSNESS, IN WHICH HE PRESSES AFTER PERFECTION: WARNING AGAINST CARNAL PERSONS: CONTRAST OF THE BELIEVER'S LIFE AND HOPE. **1. Finally**—rather, not with the notion of time, but making a transition to another general subject, "Furthermore" [BENGEL and WAHL] as in I Thessalonians 4:1. Lit., "As to what remains. . . ." It is often used at the conclusion of Epistles for "finally" (Eph. 6:10, II Thess. 3:1). But it is not restricted to this meaning, as ALFORD thinks, supposing that Paul used it here intending to close his Epistle, but was led by the mention of the Judaizers into a more lengthened dissertation. **the same things**—concerning "rejoicing," the prevailing feature in this Epistle (ch. 1:18, 25; 2:17; 4:4, where, cf. the "again I say," with "the same things" here). **In the Lord**—marks the true ground of joy, in contrast with "having confidence in the flesh," or in any outward sensible matter of boasting (vs. 3). **not grievous**—"not irksome." **for you it is safe**—Spiritual *joy* is the best safety against error (vs. 2; Neh. 8:10, end). **2. Beware**—*Greek,* "Have your eye on" so as to beware of. Contrast "mark," or "observe," viz., so as to

follow vs. 17. **dogs**—*Greek,* "the dogs," viz., those impure persons "of whom I have told you often" (vs. 18, 19); "the abominable" (cf. Rev. 21:8, with 22:15; Matt. 7:6; Titus 1:15, 16): "dogs" in filthiness, unchastity, and snarling (Deut. 23:18; Ps. 59:6, 14, 15; II Pet. 2:22): especially "enemies of the cross of Christ" (vs. 18; Ps. 22:16, 20). The Jews regarded the Gentiles as "dogs" (Matt. 15:26); but by their own unbelief they have ceased to be the true Israel, and are become "dogs" (cf. Isa. 56:10, 11). **evil workers**—II Corinthians 11:13, "deceitful workers." Not simply "evildoers" are meant, but men who "worked," indeed, ostensibly for the Gospel, but worked for evil: "serving not our Lord, but their own belly" (vs. 19; cf. Rom. 16:18). Translate, "*The* evil *workmen,*" i.e., bad *teachers* (cf. II Tim. 2:15). **concision**—*Circumcision* had now lost its spiritual significance, and was now become to those who rested on it as any ground of justification, a senseless mutilation. Christians have the only true *circumcision,* viz., that of the heart; legalists have only "concision," i.e., *the cutting off of the flesh.* To make "cuttings in the flesh" was expressly prohibited by the law (Lev. 21:5): it was a Gentile-heathenish practice (I Kings 18:28); yet this, writes Paul indignantly, is what these *legalists* are virtually doing in violation of the law. There is a remarkable gradation, says BIRKS (*Horæ Apostolicæ*) in Paul's language as to circumcision. In his first recorded discourse (Acts 13:39), circumcision is not named, but implied as included in the law of Moses which cannot justify. Six or seven years later, in Epistle to Galatians (3:3), the first Epistle in which it is named, its spiritual inefficiency is maintained against those Gentiles who, beginning in the Spirit, thought to be perfected in the flesh. Later, in Epistle to Romans (2:28, 29), he goes farther, and claims the substance of it for every believer, assigning the shadow only of it to the unbelieving Jew. In Epistle to Colossians (2:11; 3:11), still later, he expounds more fully the true circumcision as the exclusive privilege of the believer. Last of all here, the very name is denied to the legalist, and a term of reproach is substituted, "concision," or *flesh-cutting.* Once obligatory on all the covenant people, then reduced to a mere national distinction, it was more and more associated in the apostle's experience with the open hostility of the Jews, and the perverse teaching of false brethren. **3.** "We are the (real) circumcision" (Rom. 2:25-29; Col. 2:11). **worship God in the Spirit**—The oldest MSS. read, "worship *by the Spirit of God*"; our religious *service* is rendered by the Spirit (John 4:23, 24). Legal worship was outward, and consisted in outward acts, restricted to certain times and places. Christian worship is *spiritual,* flowing from the inworkings of the Holy Spirit, not relating to certain isolated acts, but embracing the whole life (Rom. 12:1). In the former, men trusted in something human, whether descent from the theocratic nation, or the righteousness of the law, or mortification of "the flesh" ("Having confidence," or "glorying in the flesh") [NEANDER] (Rom. 1:9). **rejoice in Christ Jesus**—"make our *boast* in Christ Jesus," not in the law: the ground of their boasting. **have no confidence in the flesh**—but in the Spirit. **4.** "although *I* (emphatical) might have confidence *even* in the flesh." Lit., "I *having,*" but not using, "confidence in the flesh." **I more**—have more "whereof I might *have confidence* in the flesh." **5.** In three particulars he shows how he "might have confidence in the flesh" (vs. 4): (1) His pure Jewish blood. (2) His legal preciseness and high status as such. (3) His zeal for the law. The *Greek* is literally, "Being in circumcision an eighth-day person," i.e., not one circumcised in later life as a proselyte, but on the eighth day after birth, as the law directed in the case of Jew-born infants. **of the tribe of Benjamin** —son of Rachel, not of the maid servant [BENGEL]. **Hebrew of the Hebrews**—neither one or other parent being Gentile. The "Hebrew," wherever he dwelt, retained the *language* of his fathers. Thus Paul, though settled in Tarsus, a Greek city, calls himself a Hebrew. A "Grecian" or Hellenist, on the other hand, in the New Testament, is the term used for a *Greek-speaking* Jew [TRENCH]. **touching the law**— i.e., as to legal status and strictness. **a Pharisee**— "of the straitest sect" (Acts 26:5). **6. Concerning**— Translate as before and after, "*As touching* Zeal" (cf. Acts 22:3; 26:9). **blameless**—*Greek*, "having *become* blameless" as to *ceremonial* righteousness: having attained *in the eyes of man blameless* legal perfection. As to the holiness *before God*, which is the inner and truest spirit of the law, and which flows from "the righteousness of God by faith," he on the contrary declares (vss. 12-14) that he has *not* attained perfection. **7. gain**—rather as *Greek*, "gains"; including all possible advantages of outward status, which he had heretofore enjoyed. **I counted**—*Greek*, "I *have* counted for Christ's sake loss." He no longer uses the plural as in "gains"; for he counts them all but one great "loss" (Matt. 16:26; Luke 9:25). **8. Yea doubtless**—The oldest MSS. omit "doubtless" (*Greek*, "*ge*"): translate, "nay more." Not only "*have* I counted" *those* things just mentioned "loss for Christ's sake, but, moreover, I *even* DO count ALL things but loss...." **for the excellency**—*Greek*, "On account of the surpassing excellency (the super-eminence above them all) of the knowledge of Christ Jesus." **my Lord**— believing and loving appropriation of Him (Ps. 63: 1; John 20:28). **for whom**—"on account of whom." **I have suffered the loss**—not merely I "*counted*" them "loss," but have actually lost them. **all things** —The *Greek* has the article, referring to the preceding "all things"; "I have suffered the loss of *them all*." **dung**—*Greek*, "refuse (such as excrements, dregs, dross) *cast to the dogs*," as the derivation expresses. A "loss" is of something having value; but "refuse" is thrown away as not worthy of being any more touched or looked at. **win**—Translate, to accord with the translation, vs. 7, "*gain* Christ." A man cannot make other things his "gain" or chief confidence, and at the same time "gain Christ." He who loses all things, and even himself, on account of Christ, gains Christ: Christ is His, and He is Christ's (Song of Sol. 2:16; 6:3; Luke 9:23, 24; I Cor. 3:23). **9. be found in him**—"be found" at His coming again, living spiritually "in Him" as the element of my life. Once *lost*, I have been "found," and I hope to be perfectly "found" by Him (Luke 15:8). **own righteousness** ... **of the law**—(*V.* 6; Rom. 10:3, 5.) "Of," i.e., *from*. **righteousness** ... **of God by faith**—*Greek*, "which is *from* God (resting) *upon* faith." Paul was transported from legal bondage into Christian freedom at once, and without any gradual transition. Hence, the bands of Pharisaism were loosed instantaneously; and opposition to Pharisaic Judaism took the place of opposition to the Gospel. Thus God's providence fitly prepared him for the work of overthrowing all idea of legal justification. "The righteousness of faith," in Paul's sense, is the righteousness or perfect holiness of Christ appropriated by faith, as the *objective* ground of confidence for the believer, and also as a new *subjective* principle of life. Hence it

includes the essence of a new disposition, and may easily pass into the idea of sanctification, though the two ideas are originally distinct. It is not any arbitrary act of God, as if he treated as sinless a man persisting in sin, simply because he believes in Christ; but the *objective* on the part of God corresponds to the *subjective* on the part of man, viz., faith. The realization of the archetype of holiness through Christ contains the pledge that this shall be realized in all who are one with Him by faith, and are become the organs of His Spirit. Its germ is imparted to them in believing although the fruit of a life perfectly conformed to the Redeemer, can only be gradually developed in this life [NEANDER]. **10. That I may know him**—experimentally. The aim of the "righteousness" just mentioned. This verse resumes, and more fully explains, "the excellency of the knowledge of Christ" (vs. 8). To know HIM is more than merely to know a *doctrine* about Him. Believers are brought not only to redemption, but to the Redeemer Himself. **the power of his resurrection**—assuring believers of their justification (Rom. 4:25; I Cor. 15:17), and raising them up spiritually with Him, by virtue of their identification with Him in this, as in all the acts of His redeeming work for us (Rom. 6:4; Col. 2:12; 3:1). The power of the Divine Spirit, which raised Him from literal death, is the same which raises believers from spiritual death now (Eph. 1:19, 20), and shall raise their bodies from literal death hereafter (Rom. 8;11). **the fellowship of his sufferings**—by identification with Him in His sufferings and death, *by imputation;* also, in *actually* bearing the cross whatever is laid on us, after His example, and so "filling up that which is behind of the afflictions of Christ" (Col. 1:24); and in the *will* to bear aught for His sake (Matt. 10:38; 16:24; II Tim. 2:11). As He bore all our sufferings (Isa. 53:4), so we participate in His. **made conformable unto his death**—"conformed to the likeness of His death," viz., by continued sufferings for His sake, and mortifying of the carnal self (Rom. 8:29; I Cor. 15:31; II Cor. 4:10-12; Gal. 2:20). **11. If by any means**—not implying uncertainty of the issue, but the earnestness of the struggle of faith (I Cor. 9:26, 27), and the urgent need of jealous selfwatchfulness (I Cor. 10:12). **attain unto the resurrection of the dead**—The oldest MSS. read, "... the resurrection *from* (out of) the dead," viz., the first resurrection; that of believers at Christ's coming (I Cor. 15:23; I Thess. 4:15; Rev. 20:5, 6). The *Greek* word occurs nowhere else in the New Testament. "The power of Christ's resurrection" (Rom. 1:4), ensures the believer's attainment of the "resurrection from the (rest of the) dead" (cf. vss. 20, 21). Cf. "accounted worthy to *obtain the resurrection from the dead*" (Luke 20: 35). "The resurrection of the just" (Luke 14:14). **12.** Translate, "Not *that* I...." (I do *not* wish to be understood as saying *that*....) **attained**—"obtained," viz., a perfect knowledge of Christ, and of the power of His death, and fellowship of His sufferings, and a conformity to His death. **either were already perfect**—"or *am* already *perfected*," i.e., *crowned* with the garland of victory, my course *completed*, and *perfection absolutely reached*. The image is that of a *racecourse* throughout. See I Corinthians 9:24; Hebrews 12:23. See TRENCH, *Synonyms of New Testament*. **I follow after**—"I press on." **apprehend** ... **apprehended**—if *so be* that I may *lay hold on* that (viz., the *prize*, vs. 14) for which also *I was laid hold on* by Christ" (viz., at my conversion, Song of Sol. 1:4; I Cor. 13:12). **Jesus**—omitted in the oldest MSS. Paul was close to "apprehending" the prize (II Tim. 4:7, 8). Christ the Author, is also the Finisher of His people's "race." **13. I**—whatever others count as to themselves. He who counts himself perfect, must deceive himself by calling sin infirmity (I John 1:8); at the same time, each must *aim* at perfection, to be a Christian at all (Matt. 5:48). **forgetting those things ... behind**—*Looking back* is sure to end in *going back* (Luke 9:62): So Lot's wife (Luke 17:32). If in stemming a current we cease pulling the oar against it, we are carried back. God's word to us is as it was to Israel, "Speak unto the children of Israel that they go forward" (Exod. 14:15). The Bible is our landmark to show us whether we are progressing or retrograding. **reaching forth**—with hand and foot, like a runner in a race, and the body bent forward. The Christian is always humbled by the contrast between what he is and what he desires to be. The eye reaches before and draws on the hand, the hand reaches before and draws on the foot [BENGEL]. **unto**—towards (Heb. 6:1). **14. high calling**—lit., "the calling that is *above*" (Gal. 4:26; Col. 3:1): "the *heavenly* calling" (Heb. 3:1). "The prize" is "the crown of righteousness" (I Cor. 9:24; II Tim. 4:8). Revelation 2:10, "crown of life." I Peter 5:4, "a crown of glory that fadeth not away." "The high," or "heavenly calling," is not restricted, as ALFORD thinks, to Paul's own calling as an apostle by the summons of God from heaven; but *the common calling of all Christians to salvation in Christ,* which coming from heaven invites us to heaven, whither accordingly our minds ought to be uplifted. **15. therefore**—resuming vs. 3. "As many of us then, as are perfect," i.e., *full grown* (no longer "babes") in the Christian life (vs. 3, "worshipping God in the Spirit, and having no confidence in the flesh"), I Corinthians 2:6, fully established in things of God. Here, by "perfect," he means one *fully fit for running* [BENGEL]; knowing and complying with the *laws* of the course (II Tim. 2:5). Though "perfect" in this sense, he was not yet "made perfect" (*Greek*) in the sense intended in vs. 12, viz., "crowned with *complete* victory," and having attained *absolute perfection.* **thus minded**—having the mind which he had described, vss. 7-14. **otherwise minded**—having too high an opinion of yourselves as to your attainment of Christian *perfection.* "He who thinks that he has attained everything, hath nothing" [CHRYSOSTOM]. Probably, too, he refers to those who were tempted to think to attain to *perfection* by the law (Gal. 3:3): who needed the warning (vs. 3), "Beware of the concision," though on account of their former piety, Paul hopes confidently (as in Gal. 5:10) that God will reveal the path of right-mindedness to them. Paul taught externally God "reveals" the truth internally by His Spirit (Matt. 11:25; 16:17; I Cor. 3:6). **unto you**—who sincerely strive to do God's will (John 7:17; Eph. 1:17). **16.** The expectation of a new revelation is not to make you less careful in walking according to whatever degree of knowledge of divine things and perfection you have already attained. God makes further revelations to those who walk up to the revelations they already have (Hos. 6:3). **rule, let us mind the same thing**—omitted in the oldest MSS. Perhaps partly inserted from Galatians 6:16, and ch. 2:2. Translate then, "Whereunto we have attained, let us walk on (a military term, *march in order*) in the same" (the measure of knowledge already attained). **17. followers**—*Greek,* "imitators together." **of me**—as I am an *imitator of Christ* (I Cor. 11:1): Imitate me no farther than as I imitate Christ. Or as BENGEL

"My fellow imitators of God" or "Christ"; "imitators of Christ together with me" (*Note,* ch. 2:22; Eph. 5:1). **mark**—for imitation. **which walk so as ye have us for an ensample**—In *English Version* of the former clause, the translation of this clause is, "those who are walking so as ye have an example in us." But in BENGEL's translation, "inasmuch as," or "since," instead of "as." **18. many walk**—in such a manner. Follow not evildoers, because they are "many" (Exod. 23:2). Their numbers are rather a presumption against their being Christ's "little flock" (Luke 12:32). **often**—There is need of constant warning. **weeping**—(Rom. 9:2). A hard tone in speaking of the inconsistencies of professors is the very opposite of Paul's spirit, and David's (Ps. 119:136), and Jeremiah's (Jer. 13:17). The Lord and His apostles, at the same time, speak more strongly against empty professors (as the Pharisees), than against open scoffers. **enemies of the cross of Christ**—in their *practice,* not in doctrine (Gal. 6:14; Heb. 6:6; 10:29). **19. destruction**—everlasting at Christ's coming. Ch. 1:28, "perdition"; the opposite word is "Saviour" (vs. 20). **end**—fixed doom. **whose god is their belly**—(Rom. 16:18)—hereafter to be destroyed by God (I Cor. 6:13). In contrast to our "body" (vs. 21), which *our God,* the Lord Jesus, shall "fashion like unto His glorious body." Their belly is now pampered, our body now wasted; then the respective states of both shall be reversed. **glory is in their shame**—As "glory" is often used in the Old Testament for "God" (Ps. 106:20), so here it answers to "whose *God,*" in the parallel clause; and "shame" is the Old Testament term contemptuously given to an idol (Judg. 6:32, *Margin*). Hosea 4:7 seems to be referred to by Paul (cf. Rom. 1:32). There seems no allusion to circumcision, as no longer *glorious,* but a *shame* to them (vs. 2). The reference of the immediate context is to sensuality, and carnality in general. **mind earthly things**—(Rom. 8:5). In contrast to vs. 20; Col. 3:2. **20. our conversation** —rather, "our state" or "country"; *our citizenship: our life as citizens.* We are but *pilgrims* on earth; how *then* should we "mind earthly things?" (vs. 19; Heb. 11:9, 10, 13-16). Roman citizenship was then highly prized; how much more should the heavenly citizenship (Acts 22:28; cf. Luke 10:20)? **is**—*Greek,* "has its existence." **in heaven**—*Greek,* "in the heavens." **look for the Saviour, the Lord Jesus Christ**—"We wait for (so the same *Greek* is translated, Rom. 8:19) the Lord Jesus as a (i.e., in the capacity of a) Saviour" (Heb. 9:28). That He is "the Lord," now exalted above every name, assures our expectation (ch. 2:9-11). Our High Priest is gone up into the Holy of Holies not made with hands, there to atone for us; and as the Israelites stood outside the tabernacle, expecting Aaron's return (cf. Luke 1:21), so must we look unto the heavens expecting Christ thence. **21.** *Greek,* "Who shall *transfigure* the body *of our humiliation* (viz., in which our humiliation has place, II Cor. 4:10; Eph. 2:19; II Tim. 2:12), that it may be *conformed* unto the body *of His glory* (viz., in which His glory is manifested), according to the *effectual working* whereby...." Not only shall He come as our "Saviour," but also as our *Glorifier.* **even**—not only to make *the body* like His own, but "to subdue *all things,"* even death itself, as well as Satan and sin. He gave a sample of the coming *transfiguration* on the mount (Matt. 17:1, etc.). Not a change of *identity,* but of *fashion* or *form* (Ps. 17:15; I Cor. 15:51). Our spiritual resurrection now is the pledge of our bodily resurrection to glory hereafter (vs. 20;

Rom. 8:11). As Christ's glorified body was essentially identical with His body of humiliation; so our resurrection bodies as believers, since they shall be like His, shall be identical essentially with our present bodies, and yet "spiritual bodies" (I Cor. 15:42-44). Our "hope" is, that Christ, by His rising from the dead, hath obtained the power, and is become the pattern, of our resurrection (Mic. 2:13).

CHAPTER 4

Vss. 1-23. EXHORTATIONS: THANKS FOR THE SUPPLY FROM PHILIPPI: GREETING; AND CLOSING BENEDICTION. **1.** "Wherefore"; since we have such a glorious hope (ch. 3:20, 21). **dearly beloved**—repeated again at the close of the verse, implying that his great love to them should be a motive to their obedience. **longed for**—"yearned after" in your absence (ch. 1:8). **crown**—in the day of the Lord (ch. 2:16; I Thess. 2:19). **so**—as I have admonished you. **stand fast**—(Ch. 1:27). **2.** Euodia and Syntyche were two women who seem to have been at variance; probably deaconesses of the church. He repeats, "I beseech," as if he would admonish each separately, and with the utmost impartiality. **in the Lord**—the true element of Christian union; for those "in the Lord" by faith to be at variance, is an utter inconsistency. **3. And**—*Greek,* "Yea." **true yoke-fellow**—yoked with me in the same Gospel yoke Matt. 11:29, 30; cf. I Tim. 5:17, 18). Either Timothy, Silas (Acts 15:40; 16:19, *at Philippi*), or the chief bishop of Philippi. Or else the *Greek, Sunzugus,* or *Synzygus,* is a proper name: "Who art truly, as thy name means, a *yoke-fellow."* Certainly not *Paul's wife,* as I Corinthians 9:5 implies he had none. **help those women**—rather, as *Greek,* "help *them,"* viz., Euodia and Syntyche. "Cooperate with them" [BIRKS]; or as ALFORD, "Help in the work of their reconciliation." **which laboured with me**—"*inasmuch as* they labored with me." At Philippi, women were the first hearers of the Gospel, and Lydia the first convert. It is a coincidence which marks genuineness, that in this Epistle alone, special instructions are given to women who labored with Paul in the Gospel. In selecting the first teachers, those first converted would naturally be fixed on. Euodia and Syntyche were doubtless two of "the women who resorted to the riverside, where prayer was wont to be made" (Acts 16:13), and being early converted, would naturally take an active part in teaching other women called at a later period; of course not in public preaching, but in a less prominent sphere (I Tim. 2:11, 12). **Clement**—bishop of Rome shortly after the death of Peter and Paul. His Epistle from the Church of Rome to the Church of Corinth is extant. It makes no mention of the supremacy of the See of Peter. He was the most eminent of the apostolical fathers. ALFORD thinks that the Clement here was *a Philippian,* and not necessarily Clement, bishop of Rome. But ORIGEN (*Comment,* John 1:29) identifies the Clement here with the bishop of Rome. **in the book of life**—the register-book of those whose "citizenship is in heaven" (Luke 10:20; Phil. 3:20). Anciently, free cities had a roll-book containing the names of all those having the right of citizenship (cf. Exod. 32:32; Ps. 69:28; Ezek. 13:9; Dan. 12:1; Rev. 20:12; 21:27). **4.** (Isa. 61:10.) **alway**—even amidst the afflictions now distressing you (ch. 1:28-30). **again**—as he had already said, "Rejoice" (ch. 3:1). Joy is the predominant feature of the Epistle. **I say**—*Greek,* rather, "I *will* say." **5.**

moderation—from a *Greek* root, "to yield," whence *yieldingness* [TRENCH]; or from a root, "it is fitting," whence *"reasonableness of dealing"* [ALFORD], that considerateness for others, *not urging one's own rights to the uttermost,* but waiving a part, and thereby rectifying the injustices of justice. The archetype of this grace is God, who presses not the strictness of His law against us as we deserve (Ps. 130:3, 4); though having exacted the fullest payment for us from our Divine Surety. There are included in "moderation," *candor* and *kindliness.* Joy in the Lord raises us above rigorism towards others (vs. 5), and carefulness (vs. 6) as to one's own affairs. Sadness produces *morose harshness* towards others, and a troublesome spirit in ourselves. **Let ... be known**—i.e., in your conduct to others, let nothing inconsistent with "moderation" be seen. Not a precept to make a *display* of moderation. Let this grace "be known" to men in *acts;* let "your requests be made to God" in word (vs. 6). **unto all men**—even to the "perverse" (ch. 2:15), that so ye may win them. Exercise "forbearance" even to your persecutors. None is so ungracious as not to be kindly to someone, from some motive or another, on some occasion; the believer is to be so "unto all men" at all times. **The Lord is at hand**—The Lord's coming again speedily is the grand motive to every Christian grace (Jas. 5:8,9). Harshness to others (the opposite of "moderation") would be taking into our own hands prematurely the prerogatives of judging, which belongs to the Lord alone (I Cor. 4:5); and so provoking God to judge us by the strict letter of the law (Jas. 2:12, 13). **6.** Translate, "Be anxious about nothing." Care and prayer are as mutually opposed as fire and water [BENGEL]. **by prayer and supplication**—*Greek,* "by *the* prayer and *the* supplication" appropriate to each case [ALFORD]. *Prayer* for blessings; and the general term. *Supplication,* to avert ills; a special term, *suppliant entreaty* (*Note,* Eph. 6:18). **thanksgiving**—for every event, prosperity and affliction alike (I Thess. 5:18; Jas. 5:13). The Philippians might remember Paul's example at Philippi when in the innermost prison (Acts 16:25). Thanksgiving gives effect to prayer (II Chron. 20: 21), and frees from *anxious carefulness* by making all God's dealings matter for *praise,* not merely for *resignation,* much less *murmuring.* "Peace" is the companion of "thanksgiving" (vs. 7; Col. 3:15). **let your requests be made known unto God**—with generous, filial, unreserved confidence; not keeping aught back, as too great, or else too small, to bring before God, though you might feel so as to your fellow men. So Jacob, when fearing Esau (Gen. 32:9-12); Hezekiah fearing Sennacherib (II Kings 19:14; Ps. 37:5). **7. And**—The inseparable consequence of thus laying everything before God in "prayer with thanksgiving." **peace**—the dispeller of "anxious care" (vs. 6). **of God**—coming from God, and resting in God (John 14:27; 16:33; Col. 3:15). **passeth**—*surpasseth,* or *exceedeth,* all man's notional powers of understanding its full blessedness (I Cor. 2:9, 10; Eph. 3:20; cf. Prov. 3:17). **shall keep**—rather, "shall *guard";* shall keep as a well-garrisoned stronghold (Isa. 26:1, 3). The same *Greek* verb is used in I Peter 1:5. There shall be peace secure within, whatever outward troubles may besiege. **hearts and minds**—rather, "hearts (the *seat* of the thoughts) and *thoughts"* or purposes. **through**—rather as *Greek,* "in Christ Jesus." It is in Christ that we are "kept" or "guarded" secure. **8.** Summary of all his exhortations as to relative duties, whether as children or parents, husbands or wives, friends, neighbors, men in the intercourse of the world, etc. **true**—sincere, *in words.* **honest**—Old English for "seemly," viz., *in action;* lit., *grave, dignified.* **just**—towards *others.* **pure**—"chaste," in relation to *ourselves.* **lovely**—lovable (cf. Mark 10:21; Luke 7:4, 5). **of good report**—referring to the *absent* (ch. 1: 27); as "lovely" refers to what is lovable *face to face.* **if there be any virtue**—"whatever virtue there is" [ALFORD]. "Virtue," the standing word in heathen ethics, is found once only in Paul's Epistles, and once in Peter's (II Pet. 1:5); and this in uses different from those in heathen authors. It is a term rather earthly and human, as compared with the names of the spiritual graces which Christianity imparts; hence the rarity of its occurrence in the New Testament. Piety and true morality are inseparable. Piety is love with its face towards God; morality is love with its face towards man. Despise not anything that is good in itself; only let it keep its due place. **praise**—whatever is *praiseworthy;* not that Christians should make man's praise their aim (cf. John 12:43); but they should live so as to *deserve* men's praise. **think on**—have a continual regard to, so as to "do" these things (vs. 9) whenever the occasion arises. **9. both**—rather, "The things *also* which ye have learned . . . , these *practice";* the things which besides recommending them in words, have been *also* recommended *by my example,* carry into practice. **heard**—though ye have not yet sufficiently "received" them. **seen**—though ye have not as yet sufficiently "learned" them [BENGEL]. **and**—"and then," as the necessary result (vs. 7). Not only "the peace of God," but "the God of peace" Himself "shall be with you." **10. But**—transitional conjunction. But "now" to pass to another subject. **in the Lord**—He views everything with reference to Christ. **at the last**—"at last"; implying he was expecting their gift, not from a selfish view, but as a "fruit" of their faith, and to "abound" to their account (vss. 11, 17). Though long in coming, owing to Epaphroditus' sickness and other delays, he does not imply their gift was too late. **your care . . . hath flourished again**—*Greek,* "Ye have flourished again (*revived,* as trees sprouting forth *again* in spring) in your care *for me.*" **wherein ye were also careful**—in respect to which (*revival,* viz., the sending of a supply to me) "ye were also (all along) careful, but ye lacked opportunity"; whether from want of means or want of a messenger. Your "lack of service" (ch. 2:30), was owing to your having "lacked opportunity." **11. I have learned**—The *I* in *Greek* is emphatical. I leave it to others if they will, to be discontented. *I,* for my part, have learned, by the teaching of the Holy Spirit, and the dealings of Providence (Heb. 5:8), to be content in every state. **content**—The *Greek,* literally expresses "independent of others, and having *sufficiency in one's self.*" But Christianity has raised the term above the haughty *self-sufficiency* of the heathen Stoic to the *contentment* of the Christian, whose *sufficiency* is not in *self,* but in *God* (II Cor. 3:5; I Tim. 6:6, 8; Heb. 13:5; cf. Jer. 2:36; 45:5). **12. abased**—in low circumstances (II Cor. 4:8; 6:9, 10). **everywhere**—rather [ALFORD], "in each, and in all things." **instructed**—in the secret. Lit., "initiated" in a secret teaching, which is a *mystery* unknown to the world. **13. I can do all things**—*Greek,* "I have strength for all things"; not merely "how to be abased and how to abound." After special instances he declares his *universal* power—how triumphantly, yet how humbly! [MEYER.]

through Christ which strengtheneth me—The oldest MSS. omit "Christ"; then translate, "In *Him* who giveth me *power,*" i.e., by virtue of my living union and identification with Him, who is my strength (Gal. 2:20). Cf. I Timothy 1:12, whence probably, "Christ" was inserted here by transcribers. **14. He** here guards against their thinking from what he has just said, that he makes light of their bounty. **ye did communicate with my affliction**—i.e., ye made yourselves *sharers with* me in my present affliction, viz., by sympathy; of which sympathy your *contribution* is the proof. **15. Now**—"Moreover." Arrange as *Greek,* "Ye also know" (as well as I do myself). **in the beginning of the gospel**—dating from the *Philippian* Christian era; at the first preaching of the Gospel at Philippi. **when I departed from Macedonia**—(Acts 17:14). The Philippians had followed Paul with their bounty when he left Macedonia and came to Corinth. II Corinthians 11:8, 9 thus accords with the passage here, the dates assigned to the donation in both Epistles agreeing; viz., "in the *beginning* of the Gospel" here, and there, at the time of his *first* visit to Corinth [PALEY's *Horæ Paulinæ*]. However, the supply meant here is not that which he received at Corinth, but the supply sent to him when "in Thessalonica, once and again" (vs. 16), [ALFORD]. **as concerning giving and receiving**—In the account between us, "the giving" was all on your part; "the receiving" all on mine. **ye only**—We are not to wait for others in a good work, saying, "I will do so, when others do it." We must go forward, though *alone.* **16. even in Thessalonica**—"even" as early as when I had got no further than Thessalonica, ye sent me supplies for my necessities more than once. **17. a gift**—*Greek,* "*the* gift." Translate, "It is not that *I seek after the* gift, but *I do seek after the* fruit that *aboundeth* to your account"; what I do seek is your spiritual good, in the abounding of fruits of your faith which shall be put down to your account, against the day of reward (Heb. 6:10). **18. But**—Though "the gift" is not what I chiefly "seek after" (vs. 17), *yet* I am grateful for the gift, and hereby acknowledge it as ample for all my needs. Translate, "I have all" that I want, "and more than enough." Lit., as *English Version,* "I abound" over and above my needs. **I am full**—*Greek,* "I am filled full." **the odour of a sweet smell**—(*Note,* Eph. 5:2.) The figure is drawn from the sweet-smelling incense which was burnt along with the sacrifices; their gift being in faith was not so much to Paul, as *to God* (Matt. 25:40), before whom it "came up for a memorial" (Acts 10:4), sweet-smelling in God's presence (Gen. 8:21; Rev. 8:3, 4). **sacrifice acceptable**—(Heb. 13:16). **19. my**—Paul calls God here "my God," to imply that God would reward their bounty to His servant, by "fully supplying" (translate so, lit., *fill to the full*) their every "need" (II Cor. 9:8), even as they had "fully" supplied his "need" (vss. 16, 18). My Master will fully repay you; I cannot. The Philippians invested their bounty well since it got them such a glorious return. **according to his riches**—The measure of His supply to you will be the immeasurable "riches of His grace" (Eph. 1:7). **in glory**—These words belong to the whole sentence. "Glory" is the element IN which His rich grace operates; and it will be the element IN which He will "supply fully all your need." **by Christ Jesus**—by virtue of your being "IN" (so *Greek,* not "by") Christ Jesus, the Giver and Mediator of all spiritual blessings. **20. God and our Father**—Translate, "Unto *our God and*

Father." **be glory**—rather as the *Greek,* "be *the* glory." Not to us, but to Him be "*the* glory" alike of your gift, and of His gracious recompense to you. **21. Salute every saint**—*individually.* **greet**—salute you. **The brethren which are with me**—Perhaps Jewish believers are meant (Acts 28: 21). I think ch. 2:20 precludes our thinking of "closer friends," "colleagues in the ministry" [AL-FORD]; he had only one close friend with him, viz., Timothy. **22. they that are of Cæsar's household** —the slaves and dependents of Nero who had been probably converted through Paul's teaching while he was a prisoner in the Prætorian barrack attached to the palace. Philippi was a Roman "colony," hence there might arise a tie between the citizens of the mother city and those of the colony; especially between those of both cities who were Christians, converted as many of them were by the same apostle, and under like circumstances, he having been imprisoned at Philippi, as he now is at Rome. **23.** (Gal. 6:18.) **be with you all. Amen**—The oldest MSS. read, "Be with your spirit," and omit "Amen."

THE EPISTLE OF PAUL THE APOSTLE TO THE

COLOSSIANS

INTRODUCTION

The GENUINENESS of this Epistle is attested by JUSTIN MARTYR, *Contra Tryphonen,* p. 311, b., who quotes "the firstborn of every creature," in reference to Christ, from ch. 1:15. THEOPHILUS OF ANTIOCH, *to Autolychus,* 2. p. 100. IRENÆUS, 3. 14, 1, quotes expressly from this "Epistle to the Colossians" (ch. 4:14). CLEMENT OF ALEXANDRIA, *Stromata,* 1. p. 325, quotes ch. 1:28; also elsewhere he quotes ch. 1:9–11, 28; 2:2, etc.; 2:8; 3:12, 14; 4:2, 3, etc. TERTULLIAN, *De Præscriptione hæreticorum,* ch. 7, quotes ch. 2:8; and in *De Resurrectione carnis,* ch. 23, he quotes ch. 2:12, 20, and ch. 3:1, 2. ORIGEN, *Contra Celsus,* 5. 8, quotes ch. 2:18, 19.

Colosse (or, as it is spelt in the best MSS., "Colassæ") was a city of Phrygia, on the river Lycus, a branch of the Meander. The Church there was mainly composed of Gentiles (cf. ch. 2:13). ALFORD infers from ch. 2:1 (see *Note* there), that Paul had not seen its members, and therefore could not have been its founder, as THEO-DORET thought. Ch. 1:7, 8 suggests the probability that Epaphras was the first founder of the Church there. The date of its foundation must have been subsequent to Paul's visitation, "strengthening in order" all the church-es of Galatia and Phrygia (Acts 18:24); for otherwise we must have visited the Colossians, which ch. 2:1 implies he had not. Had Paul been their father in the faith, he would doubtless have alluded to the fact, as in I Corinthians 3:6, 10; 4:15; I Thessalonians 1:5; 2:1. It is only in the Epistles, Romans and Ephesians, and this Epistle, such allusions are wanting; in that to the Romans, because, as in this Church of Colosse, he had not been the instrument of their conversion; in that to the Ephesians, owing to the general nature of the Epistle. Probably during the "two years" of Paul's stay at Ephesus, when "*all which dwelt in Asia* heard the word of the Lord Jesus" (Acts 19:10, 26), Epaphras, Philemon, Archippus, Apphia and the other natives of Colosse, becoming converted at Ephesus, were subsequently the first sowers of the Gospel seed in their own city. This will account for their personal acquaintance with, and attachment to, Paul and his fellow ministers, and for his loving language as to them, and their counter salutations to him. So also with respect to "them at Laodicea", (ch. 2:1).

The OBJECT of the Epistle is to counteract Jewish false teaching, by setting before the Colossians their true standing in Christ alone (exclusive of all other heavenly beings), the majesty of His person, and the completeness of the redemption wrought by Him; hence they ought to be conformed to their risen Lord, and to exhibit that conformity in all the relations of ordinary life. Ch. 2:16, "new moon, sabbath days," shows that the false teaching opposed in this Epistle is that of *Judaizing* Christians. These mixed up with pure Christianity Oriental theosophy and angel worship, and the asceticism of certain sections of the Jews, especially the Essenes. Cf. JOSEPHUS, *Bell. Jud.,* 2. 8; 2. 13. These theosophists promised to their followers a deeper insight into the world of spirits, and a nearer approach to heavenly purity and intelligence, than the simple Gospel affords. CONYBEARE and HOWSON think that some Alexandrian Jew had appeared at Colosse, imbued with the Greek philosophy of Philo's school, combining with it the Rabbinical theosophy and angelology which afterwards was embodied in the Cabbala. Cf. JOSEPHUS, *Antiquities,* 12. 3, 4, from which we know that Alexander the Great had garrisoned the towns of Lydia and *Phrygia* with 2000 Mesopotamian and Babylonian *Jews* in the time of a threatened revolt. The Phrygians themselves had a mystic tendency in their worship of Cybele, which inclined them to receive the more readily the incipient Gnosticism of Judaizers, which afterward developed itself into the strangest heresies. In the Pastoral Epistles, the evil is spoken of as having reached a more deadly phase (I Tim. 4:1–3; 6:5), whereas he brings no charge of immorality in this Epistle: a proof of its being much earlier in date.

The PLACE from which it was written seems to have been Rome, during his first imprisonment there (Acts 28). In my *Introduction* to the Epistle to the Ephesians, it was shown that the three Epistles, Ephesians, Colossians, and Philemon, were sent at the same time, *viz.,* during the freer portion of his imprisonment, before the death of Burrus. Ch. 4:3, 4; Ephesians 6:19, 20, imply greater freedom than he had while writing to the Philippians, after the promotion of Tigellinus to be Prætorian Prefect. See *Introduction* to Philippians.

This Epistle, though *carried* by the same bearer, Tychicus, who bore that to the *Ephesians,* was *written* pre-viously to that Epistle; for many phrases similar in both appear in the more expanded form in the Epistle to the

Ephesians (cf. also *Note*, Eph. 6:21). The *Epistle to the Laodiceans* (ch. 4:16) was *written* before that to the Colossians, but probably was *sent* by him to Laodicea at the same time with that to the Church at Colosse.

The STYLE is peculiar: many *Greek* phrases occur here, found nowhere else. Cf. ch. 2:8, "*spoil* you"; "making a show of them openly" (ch. 2:15); "beguile of your reward," and "intruding" (vs. 18); "will-worship"; satisfying" (vs. 23); "filthy communication" (ch. 3:8); "rule" (ch. 3:15); "comfort" (ch. 4:11). The loftiness and artificial elaboration of style correspond to the majestic nature of his theme, the majesty of Christ's person and office, in contrast to the beggarly system of the Judaizers, the discussion of which was forced on him by the controversy. Hence arises his use of unusual phraseology. On the other hand, in the Epistle of the Ephesians, subsequently written, in which he was not so hampered by the exigencies of controversy, he dilates on the same glorious truths, so congenial to him, more at large, freely and uncontroversially, in the fuller outpouring of his spirit, with less of the elaborate and antithetical language of system, such as was needed in cautioning the Colossians against the particular errors threatening them. Hence arises the striking similarity of many of the phrases in the two Epistles written about the same time, and generally in the same vein of spiritual thought; while the peculiar phrases of the Epistle to the Colossians are such as are natural, considering the controversial purpose of that Epistle.

CHAPTER 1

Vss. 1-29. ADDRESS: INTRODUCTION: CONFIRMING EPAPHRAS' TEACHING: THE GLORIES OF CHRIST: THANKSGIVING AND PRAYER FOR THE COLOSSIANS: HIS OWN MINISTRY OF THE MYSTERY. **1. by the will of God**—*Greek*, "through . . ." (cf. *Note*, I Cor. 1:1). **Timothy**—(Cf. *Notes*, II Cor. 1:1; Phil. 1:1.) He was with Paul at the time of writing in Rome. He had been companion of Paul in his first tour through Phrygia, in which Colosse was. Hence the Colossians seem to have associated him with Paul in their affections, and the apostle joins him with himself in the address. Neither, probably, had *seen* the Colossian *Church* (cf. ch. 2:1); but had seen, during their tour through Phrygia, individual Colossians, as Epaphras, Philemon, Archippus, and Apphia (Philemon 2), who when converted brought the Gospel to their native city. **2. Colosse**—written in the oldest MSS., "Colasse." As "saints" implies union with God, so "the faithful brethren" union with Christian men [BENGEL]. **and the Lord Jesus Christ**—supported by some oldest MSS., omitted by others of equal antiquity. **3.** Thanksgiving for the "faith, hope, and love" of the Colossians. So in the twin Epistle sent at the same time and by the same bearer, Tychicus (Eph. 1:15, 16). **We**—I and Timothy. **and the Father**—So some of the oldest MSS. read. But others better omit the "and," which probably crept in from Ephesians 1:3. **praying always for you**—with thanksgiving (Phil. 4:6). See next verse. **4. Since we heard**—lit., "Having heard." The language implies that he had only heard of, and not *seen*, them (ch. 2:1). Cf. Romans 1:8, where like language is used of a Church which he had not at the time visited. **love . . . to all**—the absent, as well as those present [BENGEL]. **5. For**—to be joined with the words immediately preceding: "The love which ye have to all the saints *because* of (lit., *on account of*) the hope . . . ." The hope of eternal life will never be in us an inactive principle but will always produce "love." This passage is abused by Romanists, as if the hope of salvation depended upon works. A false argument. It does not follow that our hope is founded on our works because we are strongly stimulated to live well; since nothing is more effectual for this purpose than the sense of God's free grace [CALVIN]. **laid up**—a treasure *laid up* so as to be out of danger of being lost (II Tim. 4:8). *Faith, love*, and *hope* (vss. 4, 5), comprise the sum of Christianity. Cf. vs. 23, "the hope of the Gospel." **in heaven**—*Greek*, "in the heavens." **whereof ye heard before**—viz., at the time when it was preached to you. **in the word . . .**—That "hope" formed part of "the word of the truth of the Gospel" (cf. Eph. 1:13), i.e., part of the Gospel truth preached unto you. **6. Which is come unto you**—*Greek*, "Which is present among you," i.e., which has come to, and remains with, you. He speaks of the word as a living person *present* among them. **as it is in all the world**—*virtually*, as it was by this time preached in the leading parts of the then known world; *potentially*, as Christ's command was that the Gospel should be preached to all nations, and not be limited, as the law was, to the Jews (Matt. 13:38; 24:14; 28:19). However, the true reading, and that of the oldest MSS., is that which omits the following "and," thus (the "*it is*" of *English Version* is not in the original *Greek*): "As in all the world it is bringing forth fruit *and growing* (so the oldest MSS. read; *English Version* omits 'and growing,' without good authority), even as it doth in you also." Then what is asserted is not that the Gospel has been preached in all the world, but that it is *bearing fruits* of righteousness, and (like a tree *growing* at the same time that it is *bearing fruit*) *growing in numbers* of its converts in, or throughout, all the world. **heard of it**—rather, "heard *it*." **and knew**—rather, "came to know"; became *fully* experimentally *acquainted* with. **the grace of God in truth**—i.e., in its truth, and with true knowledge [ALFORD]. **7. As ye also learned**—"Also" is omitted in the oldest MSS. The insertion implied that those inserting it thought that *Paul* had preached the Gospel to the Colossians as well as Epaphras, Whereas the omission in the oldest MSS. implies that *Epaphras alone* was the founder of the Church at Colosse. **of**—"from Epaphras." **dear**—*Greek*, "beloved." **fellow servant**—viz., of Christ. In Philemon 23 he calls him "my fellow prisoner." It is possible that Epaphras may have been apprehended for his zealous labors in Asia Minor; but more probable that Paul gave him the title, as his faithful companion in his imprisonment (cf. *Note*, ch. 4:10, as to MEYER'S conjecture). **who is for you . . .**—Translate, "who is faithful in your behalf as a minister of Christ"; hinting that he is one not to be set aside for the new and erroneous teachers (ch. 2). Most of the oldest MSS. read, "for (or *in behalf of*) us." *Vulgate*, however, with one of the oldest MSS., supports *English Version*. **8. your love**—(vs. 4)—"to all the saints." **in the Spirit**—the sphere or element IN which alone true love is found; as distinguished from the state of those "in the flesh" (Rom. 8:9). Yet even they needed to be stirred up to greater love (ch. 3:12-14). Love is the first and chief fruit of the Spirit (Gal. 5:22). **9. we also**—on our part. **heard it**—(vs. 4). **pray**—Here he states what in *particular* he prays for; as in vs. 3 he stated *generally* the fact of his praying for them. **to desire**—"to make request." **might be filled**—rather, "*may* be filled"; a verb often found in this Epistle (ch. 4:12, 17). **knowledge**—*Greek*, "*full and accurate* knowledge." Akin to the *Greek* for "knew" (*Note*, vs. 6). **of his will**—as to how ye ought to walk (Eph. 5:17); as well as chiefly that "mystery of His will, according to His good pleasure which He purposed in Himself; that in the fulness of times He might gather together in one all things in Christ" (Eph. 1:9, 10); God's "will," whereby He eternally purposed to reconcile to Himself, and save men by Christ, not by angels, as the false teachers in some degree taught (ch. 2:18) [ESTIUS]. There seems to have been a want of *knowledge* among the Colossians; notwithstanding their general excellencies; hence he so often dwells on this subject (vs. 28; ch. 2:2, 3; 3:10, 13; 4:5, 6). On the contrary he less extols wisdom to the Corinthians, who were puffed up with the conceit of knowledge. **wisdom**—often mentioned in this Epistle, as opposed to the (false) "philosophy" and "show of wisdom" (ch. 2:8, 23; cf. Eph. 1:8). **understanding**—sagacity to discern what on each occasion is suited to the place and the time; its seat is "the understanding" or intellect; *wisdom* is more general and has its seat in the whole compass of the faculties of the soul [BENGEL]. "Wouldst thou know that the matters in the word of Christ are real things? Then never read them for mere knowledge sake." [Quoted by GAUSSEN.] Knowledge is desirable only when seasoned by "spiritual understanding." **10.** *Greek,* "So as to walk"; so that ye may walk. True knowledge of God's will is inseparable from walking conformably to it. **worthy of the Lord**—(Eph. 4:1). **unto**—so as in every way to be well-pleasing to God. **pleasing**—lit., "*desire of pleasing.*" **being fruitful**—*Greek*, "bearing fruit." This is the first manifestation of their "walking worthy of the Lord." The second is, "increasing (growing) in the knowledge of God" (or as the oldest MSS. read, "growing BY the full knowledge of God"); thus, as the *Gospel word* (vs. 6) was said to "bring forth fruit," and to "grow" in all the world, even as it did in the Colossians, ever since the day they *knew* the grace of God, so here it is Paul's prayer that *they* might continue to "bring forth fruit," and "grow" more and more *by the full knowledge* of God, the more that "knowledge" (vs. 9) was imparted to them. The full knowledge of God is the real *instrument* of enlargement in soul and life of the believer [ALFORD]. The third manifestation of their walk is (vs. 11), "Being strengthened with all might . . . ." The fourth is (vs. 12), "Giving thanks unto the Father . . . ." **11.** *Greek,* "Being made mighty with (lit., *in*) all might." **according to his glorious power**—rather, "according to the power (the characteristic of 'His glory,' here appropriate to Paul's argument, Eph. 1:19; 6:10; as its exuberant 'riches,' in Eph. 3:16) of His glory." His power is inseparable from His glory (Rom. 6:4). **unto all patience**—so as to attain to all *patient endurance;* persevering, enduring continuance in the faith, in spite of trials of persecutors, and seductions of false teachers. **long-suffering**—towards those whom one could repel. "Patience," or "endurance," is exercised in respect to those whom one cannot repel [CHRYSOSTOM]. **with joyfulness**—joyful endurance (Acts 16:25; Rom. 5:3, 11). **12.** *You* "giving thanks unto the Father." See *Note*, vs. 10; this clause is connected with "that ye may be filled" (vs. 9), and "that ye may walk" (vs. 10). The connection is not, "*We* do not cease to pray for you (vs. 9) giving thanks." **unto the Father**—of Jesus

Christ, and so *our* Father by adoption (Gal. 3:26; 4:4, 5, 6). **which hath made us meet**—*Greek,* "who *made* us meet." Not "*is making* us meet" by progressive growth in holiness; but *once for all made* us meet. It is not *primarily* the *Spirit's* work that is meant here, as the text is often used; but the *Father's* work in putting us by adoption, once for all, in a new standing, viz., *that of children.* The believers meant here were in different stages of progressive sanctification; but in respect to the meetness specified here, they all alike had it from the Father, in Christ His Son, being "complete in Him" (ch. 2:10). Cf. John 17:17; Jude 1, "sanctified by God *the Father";* I Corinthians 1:30. Still, *secondarily,* this once-for-all meetness contains in it the germ of sanctification, afterwards developed progressively in the life by the Father's Spirit in the believer. The Christian life of heavenliness is the first stage of heaven itself. There must, and will be, a *personal* meetness for heaven, where there is a *judicial* meetness. **to be partakers . . .**—*Greek,* "for the (or *our*) portion of the inheritance (Acts 20:32; 26:18; Eph. 1:11) of the saints in light." "Light" begins in the believer here, descending from "the Father of lights" by Jesus, "the true light," and is perfected in the kingdom of light, which includes knowledge, purity, love, and joy. It is contrasted here with the "darkness" of the unconverted state (vs. 13; cf. I Pet. 2:9). **13. from**—*Greek, "out of* the power," out of the sphere in which his power is exercised. **darkness**—blindness, hatred, misery [BENGEL]. **translated**—Those thus translated as to state, are also transformed as to character. Satan has an organized dominion with various orders of powers of evil (Eph. 2:2; 6:12). But the term "kingdom" is rarely applied to his usurped rule (Matt. 12:26); it is generally restricted to the kingdom of God. **his dear Son**—rather as *Greek,* "the Son of His love": the Son on whom His love rests (John 17:26; Eph. 1:6): contrasted with the "darkness" where all is hatred and hateful. **14.** (Eph. 1:7.) **redemption**—rather as *Greek, "our* redemption." **through his blood**—omitted in the oldest MSS.; probably inserted from Ephesians 1:7. **sins**—Translate as *Greek,* "our sins." The more general term: for which Ephesians 1:7, *Greek,* has, "our *transgressions*," the more special term. **15.** They who have experienced in themselves "redemption" (vs. 14), know Christ in the glorious character here described, as above the highest angels to whom the false teachers (ch. 2:18) taught worship was to be paid. Paul describes Him: (1) in relation to God and creation (vss. 15-17); (2) in relation to the Church (vss. 18-20). As the former regards Him as the Creator (vss. 15, 16) and the Sustainer (vs. 17) of the natural world; so the latter, as the source and stay of the new moral creation. **image**—exact likeness and perfect Representative. Adam was made "in the image of God" (Gen. 1:27). But Christ, the second Adam, perfectly reflected visibly "the invisible God" (I Tim. 1:17), whose glories the first Adam only in part represented. "Image" (*eicon*) involves "likeness" (*homoiosis*); but "likeness" does not involve "image." "Image" always supposes a prototype, which it not merely resembles, but from which it is drawn: the exact counterpart, as the reflection of the sun in the water: the child the living image of the parent. "Likeness" implies mere *resemblance*, not the exact *counterpart* and *derivation* as "image" expresses; hence it is nowhere applied to the Son, while "image" is here, cf. I Corinthians 11:7 [TRENCH]. (John 1:18; 14:9; II Cor. 4:4; I Tim. 3:16; Heb. 1:3.) Even before His incarnation He was the image of the invisible God, as the Word (John 1:1-3) by whom God created the worlds, and by whom God appeared to the patriarchs. Thus His *essential* character as *always* "the image of God," (1) before the incarnation, (2) in the days of His flesh, and (3) now in His glorified state, is, I think, contemplated here by the verb "is." **first-born of every creature**—Hebrews 1:6, "the first-begotten": "begotten of His Father before all worlds" [NICENE *Creed*]. Priority and superlative dignity is implied (Ps. 89:27). *English Version* might seem to favor Arianism, as if Christ were a creature. Translate, "Begotten (lit., born) *before* every creature," as the context shows, which gives the reason why He is so designated. "For . . ." (vss. 16, 17) [TRENCH]. This expression is understood by ORIGEN (so far is the *Greek* from favoring Socinian or Arian views) as declaring *the Godhead* of Christ, and is used by Him as a phrase to mark that *Godhead,* in contrast with His *manhood* (B. 2., sec. *contra Celsus*). The *Greek* does not strictly admit ALFORD's translation, "the first-born of all creation." **16. For**—Greek, "Because." This gives the proof that He is not included in the things created, but is the "first-begotten" before "every creature" (vs. 15), begotten as "the Son of God's love" (vs. 13), antecedently to all other emanations: "for" all these other emanations came from Him, and whatever was created, *was created by Him.* **by him**—rather as *Greek,* "in Him": as the conditional element, pre-existent and all-including: the creation of all things BY *Him* is expressed afterwards, and is a different fact from the present one, though implied in it [ALFORD]. God revealed Himself in the Son, the Word of the Father, *before all created existence* (vs. 15). That Divine Word carries IN *Himself the archetypes of all existences,* so that "IN *Him* all things that are in heaven and earth have been created." The "in Him" indicates that the Word is the ideal ground of all existence; the "*by* Him," below, that He is the *instrument* of actually realizing the divine idea [NEANDER]. His essential nature as the Word of the Father is not a mere appendage of His incarnation, but is the ground of it. The original relation of the Eternal Word to men "made in His image" (Gen. 1:27), is the source of the new relation to them by redemption, formed in His incarnation, whereby He restores them to His lost image. "*In Him*" implies something prior to "by" and "for Him" presently after: the three prepositions mark in succession the beginning, the progress, and the end [BENGEL]. **all things**—Greek, "*the* universe of things." That the *new creation* is not meant in this verse (as Socinians interpret), is plain; for *angels,* who are included in the catalogue, were not *new created* by Christ; and he does not speak of the new creation till vs. 18. The creation "of the things that are in the *heavens*" (so *Greek*) includes the creation of the *heavens themselves:* the former are rather named, since the inhabitants are more noble than their dwellings. Heaven and earth and all that is in them (I Chron. 29:11; Neh. 9:6; Rev. 10:6). **invisible**—the world of spirits: **thrones, or dominions** —lordships: the thrones are the greater of the two. **principalities, or powers**—rather, "*rules,* or *authorities*": the former are stronger than the latter (cf. *Note,* Eph. 1:21). The latter pair refer to offices *in respect to God's creatures:* "thrones and dominions" express exalted *relation to God,* they being the *chariots* on which He rides displaying His glory (Ps. 68:17). The existence of various orders of angels is established by this passage. **all things**—

Greek, "the whole universe of things." **were**—rather, to distinguish the *Greek* aorist, which precedes from the perfect tense here, "*have been* created." In the former case the creation was viewed as *a past act at a point of time,* or as done once for all; here it is viewed, not merely as one historic act of creation in the past, but as the *permanent result now and eternally continuing.* **by him**—as the instrumental Agent (John 1:3). **for him** —as the grand *End* of creation; containing in Himself the reason why creation is at all, and why it is as it is [ALFORD]. He is the *final* cause as well as the *efficient* cause. LACHMANN's punctuation of vss. 15-18 is best, whereby "the first-born of every creature" (vs. 15) answers to "the first-born from the dead" (vs. 18), the whole forming one sentence with the words ("All things were created by Him and for Him, and He is before all things, and by Him all things consist, and He is the Head of the body, the Church") intervening as a parenthesis. Thus Paul puts first, *the origination by Him of the natural creation;* secondly, *of the new creation.* The parenthesis falls into four clauses, two and two: the former two support the first assertion, "the first-born of every creature"; the latter two prepare us for "the first-born from the dead"; the former two correspond to the latter two in their form—"All things by Him . . . and He is," and "By Him all things . . . and He is." **17.** (John 8:58.) Translate as *Greek,* "And *He Himself* (the great HE) is (implying *divine essential being*) before all things," in *time,* as well as in dignity. Since He is before all things, He is *before even time,* i.e., *from eternity.* Cf. "the first-born of every creature" (vs. 15). **by him**—Greek, "IN Him" (as the conditional element of existence, vs. 16) [ALFORD]. **consist**—"subsist." Not only are called into being from nothing, but *are maintained in their present state.* The Son of God is the *Conserver,* as well as the *Creator* of all things [PEARSON]. BENGEL less probably explains, "All things in Him come together into one *system:* the universe found its completion in Him" (Isa. 41:4; Rev. 22:13). Cf. as to GOD, Romans 11:36: similar language; therefore *Christ* must be God. **18.** Revelation of Christ to the Church and the new creation, as the Originator of both. **he**—emphatical. Not angels in opposition to the false teachers' doctrine concerning angel-worship, and the power of Œons or (imaginary) spirit-emanations from God (ch. 2:10, 18). **head of the body, the church**— The Church is His body by virtue of His entering into communion corporeally with human nature [NEANDER], (Eph. 1:22). The same One who is the Head of all things and beings by creation, is also, by virtue of being "the first-born from the dead," and so "the first-fruits" of the new creation among men, the Head of the Church. **who is**—i.e., in that He is the Beginning [ALFORD]. Rather, this is *the beginning of a new paragraph.* As the former paragraph, which related to His originating the *physical* creation, began with "Who is" (vs. 15); so this, which treats of His originating the new creation, begins with "who is"; a parenthesis preceding, which closes the former paragraph, that parenthesis (see *Note,* vs. 16), including from "all things were created by Him," to "Head of the body, the Church." The *head* of kings and high priests was anointed, as the seat of the faculties, the fountain of dignity, and *original* of all the members (according to *Hebrew* etymology). So Jesus by His unction was designated as the *Head* of the body, the Church. **the beginning**—viz., of the new creation, as of the old (Prov. 8:22; John 1:1; cf. Rev. 1:8): the beginning of the Church of the first-born (Heb. 12: 23), as being Himself the "first-born from the dead" (Acts 26:23; I Cor. 15:20,23). Christ's primogeniture is threefold: (1) From eternity the "first-begotten" of the Father (vs. 15); (2) As the first-born of His mother (Matt. 1:25); (3) As the Head of the Church, mystically begotten of the Father, as it were to a new life, on the day of His resurrection, which is His "regeneration," even as His people's coming resurrection will be their "regeneration" (i.e., the resurrection which was begun in the soul, extended to the body and to the whole creation, Romans 8:21, 22) (Matt. 19:28; Acts 13:33; Rev. 1: 5). Sonship and resurrection are similarly connected (Luke 20:36; Rom. 1:4; 8:23; I John 3:2). Christ by rising from the dead is the efficient cause (I Cor. 15:22), as having obtained the power, and the exemplary cause, as being the pattern (Mic. 2: 13; Rom. 6:5; Phil. 3:21), of our resurrection: the resurrection of "the Head" involves consequentially that of the members. **that in all things**—He resumes the "all things" (vs. 20). **he might have the pre-eminence**—*Greek,* "He HIMSELF *may* (thus) become the One holding the first place," or, "take the precedency." Both ideas are included, priority in *time* and priority in *dignity:* now in the regenerated world, as before in the world of creation (vs. 15). "Begotten before every creature, or "first-born of every creature" (Ps. 89:27; John 3:13). **19.** *Greek,* "(God) was *well pleased* . . . ." **in him**—i.e., in the Son (Matt. 3:17). **all fulness**—rather as *Greek,* "all *the* fulness," viz., *of God,* whatever divine excellence is in God the Father (ch. 2:9; Eph. 3:19; cf. John 1:16; 3:34). The Gnostics used the term "fulness," for the assemblage of emanations, or angelic powers, coming from God. The Spirit presciently by Paul warns the Church, that the true "fulness" dwells in Christ alone. This assigns the reason why Christ takes precedence of every creature (vs. 15). For two reasons Christ is Lord of the Church: (1) Because the fulness of the divine attributes (vs. 19) dwells in Him, and so He has the *power* to govern the universe; (2) Because (vs. 20) what He has done for the Church gives Him the *right* to preside over it. **should . . . dwell**—as in a temple (John 2:21). *This indwelling of the Godhead in Christ* is the foundation of *the reconciliation* by Him [BENGEL]. Hence the "and" (vs. 20) connects as cause and effect the two things, *the Godhead in Christ,* and *the reconciliation by Christ.* **20.** The Greek order is, "And through Him (Christ) to reconcile again completely (see *Note,* Eph. 2:16) all things (*Greek,* 'the whole universe of things') unto Himself (unto God the Father, II Cor. 5:19), having made peace (God the Father having made peace) through the blood of His (Christ's) cross," i.e., shed by Christ *on* the cross: the price and pledge of our reconciliation with God. The Scripture phrase, "God reconciles man to Himself," implies that He takes away by the blood of Jesus the barrier which God's justice interposes against man's being in union with God (cf. *Note,* Rom. 5:10; II Cor. 5:18). So the LXX, I Samuel 29:4, "Wherewith should he reconcile himself unto his master," i.e., *reconcile his master* unto him by appeasing his wrath. So Matthew 5:23, 24. **by him**—"through Him" (the instrumental agent in the new creation, as in the original creation): emphatically repeated, to bring the person of Christ, as the Head of both creations alike, into prominence. **things in earth . . . in heaven**—Good angels, in one sense, do not need reconciliation to God; fallen angels are excluded from it (Jude 6). But probably redemp-

tion has effects on the world of spirits unknown to us. Of course, His reconciling *us,* and His reconciling *them,* must be by a different process, as He took not on Him the nature of angels, so as to offer a *propitiation* for them. But the effect of redemption on them, as He is *their* Head as well as *ours,* is that they are thereby *brought nearer God,* and so gain an increase of blessedness [ALFORD], and *larger views of the love and wisdom of God* (Eph. 3:10). All creation subsists in Christ, all creation is therefore affected by His propitiation: sinful creation is strictly "reconciled" from its enmity; sinless creation, comparatively distant from His unapproachable purity (Job 4:18; 15:15; 25:5), is lifted into nearer participation of Him, and in this wider sense is reconciled. Doubtless, too, man's fall, following on Satan's fall, is a segment of a larger circle of evil, so that the remedy of the former affects the standing of angels, from among whom Satan and his host fell. Angels thereby having seen the magnitude of sin, and the infinite cost of redemption, and the exclusion of the fallen angels from it, and the inability of any creature to stand morally in his own strength, are *now* put beyond the reach of falling. Thus BACON'S definition of Christ's Headship holds good: "The Head of *redemption* to man; the Head of *preservation* to angels." Some conjecture that Satan, when unfallen, ruled this earth and the pre-Adamic animal kingdom: hence his malice against man who succeeded to the lordship of this earth and its animals, and hence, too, his assumption of the form of a serpent, the subtlest of the animal tribes. Luke 19:38 states expressly "peace in heaven" as the result of finished redemption, as "peace on earth" was the result of its beginning at Jesus' birth (Luke 2:14). BENGEL explains the reconciliation to be that of not only God, but also *angels, estranged from men* because of man's enmity against God. Ephesians 1:10 accords with this: This is true, but only part of the truth: so ALFORD'S view also is but part of the truth. An actual *reconciliation* or *restoration of peace in heaven,* as well as on earth, is expressed by Paul. As long as that blood of reconciliation was not actually shed, which is opposed (Zech. 3:8, 9) to the accusations of Satan, but was only in promise, Satan could plead his right against men before God day and night (Job 1:6; Rev. 12: 10); hence he was in heaven till the ban on man was broken (cf. Luke 10:18). So here; the world of earth and heaven owe to Christ alone *the restoration of harmony after the conflict and the subjugation of all things under one Head* (cf. Heb. 11:23). Sin introduced discord not only on earth, but also in heaven, by the fall of demons; it brought into the abodes of holy angels, though not positive, yet privative loss, a retardation of their highest and most perfect development, harmonious gradation, and perfect consummation. Angels were no more able than men by themselves to overcome the peace-disturbers, and cast out the devils; it is only "by," or "through HIM," and "the blood of HIS cross," that *peace was restored even in heaven;* it is only after Christ has obtained the victory fully and legally, that Michael (Rev. 12:7-10) and his angels can cast out of heaven Satan and his demons (cf. ch. 2. 15). Thus the point of Paul's argument against angel-worship is, that angels themselves, like men, wholly depend on Christ, the sole and true object of worship [AUBERLEN]. **21.** The Colossians are included in this general reconciliation (cf. Eph. 2:1, 12). **sometime**—"once." **alienated**—from God and salvation: objectively *banished from* God, through the barrier which God's justice interposed against your sin: subjectively *estranged* through the alienation of your own wills from God. The former is the prominent thought (cf. Rom. 5:10), as the second follows, "enemies in your mind." "Actual *alienation* makes habitual 'enemies'" [BENGEL]. **in your mind**—Greek, "in your understanding" or "thought" (Eph. 2:3; 4:18). **by wicked works**—rather as Greek, "in *your* wicked works" (wicked works were the element *in* which your *enmity* subsisted). **yet now**—Notwithstanding the former alienation, *now* that Christ has come, *God* hath *completely reconciled*, or restored to His friendship *again* (so the Greek, cf. *Note*, vs. 20). **22. In the body of his flesh**—the element in which His reconciling sufferings had place. Cf. vs. 24, "afflictions of Christ *in my flesh*" (I Pet. 2:24). Angels who have not a "body of flesh" are not in any way our reconciling mediators, as your false teachers assert, but He, the Lord of angels, who has taken our *flesh*, that *in* it He might atone for our fallen manhood. **through death**—rather as Greek, "through *His* death" (which could only take place in a body like ours, of flesh, Heb. 2:14). This implies He took on Him our true and entire manhood. *Flesh* is the sphere in which His human sufferings could have place (cf. vs. 24; Eph. 2:15). **to present you**—(Eph. 5:27). The end of His reconciling atonement by death. **holy**—positively; and in relation to God. **unblamable ... unreprovable**—negatively. "Without blemish" (as the *former* Greek word is translated as to Jesus, our Head, I Pet. 1:19) *in one's self*. *Irreproachable* (the *Greek* for the *second* word, *one who gives no occasion for his being brought to a law court*) *is in relation to the world without*. *Sanctification*, as the fruit, is here treated of; *justification*, by Christ's reconciliation, as the tree, having preceded (Eph. 1:4; 5:26, 27; Titus 2:14). At the same time, our sanctification is regarded here as *perfect* in Christ, into whom we are grafted at regeneration or conversion, and who is "made of God unto us (perfect) sanctification" (I Cor. 1:30; I Pet. 1:2; Jude 1): not merely *progressive* sanctification, which is the *gradual development* of the sanctification which Christ is made to the believer from the first. **in his sight**—in God's sight, at Christ's appearing. **23. If**—"Assuming that ...": not otherwise shall ye be so presented at His appearing (vs. 22). **grounded**—Greek, "founded," "fixed on the *foundation*" (cf. *Note*, Eph. 3:17; Luke 6:48, 49). **settled**—"steadfast." "Grounded" respects the *foundation* on which believers rest; "settled," *their own steadfastness* (I Pet. 5:10). I Corinthians 15:58 has the same *Greek*. **not moved away**—by the false teachers. **the hope of the gospel**—(Eph. 1:18). **which ye have heard ... which was preached to every creature ... whereof I ... am ... a minister**—Three arguments against their being "moved away from the Gospel": (1) Their having heard it; (2) The universality of the preaching of it; (3) Paul's ministry in it. For "to (Greek, 'in') every creature," the oldest MSS. read, "in *all creation*." Cf. "in all the world," vs. 6; "all things ... in earth," vs. 20 (Mark 16:15): thus he implies that the Gospel from which he urges them *not to be moved*, has this mark of truth, viz., the universality of its announcement, which accords with the command and prophecy of Christ Himself (Matt. 24:14). By "*was* preached," he means not merely "*is being preached*," but *has been actually, as an accomplished fact, preached*. PLINY, not many years subsequently, in his famous letter to the Emperor Trajan (B. X., Ep. 97), writes, "Many of

every age, rank, and sex, are being brought to trial. For the contagion of that superstition [Christianity] has spread over not only cities, but villages and the country." **whereof I Paul am**—rather as Greek, "*was made* a minister." Respect for me, the minister of this world-wide Gospel, should lead you not to be moved from it. Moreover (he implies), the Gospel which ye heard from Epapharas, your "minister" (vs. 7), is the same of which "I was made a minister" (vs. 25; Eph. 3:7): if you be moved from it, ye will desert the teaching of the recognized ministers of the Gospel for unauthorized false teachers. **24. Who**—The oldest MSS. omit "who"; then translate, "Now I rejoice." Some very old MSS., and the best of the Latin versions, and *Vulgate*, read as *English Version*. To enhance the glory of Christ as paramount to all, he mentions his own sufferings for the Church of Christ. "Now" stands in contrast to "I *was made*," in the past time (vs. 23). **for you**—"on your behalf," that ye may be confirmed in resting solely on Christ (to the exclusion of angel-worship) by the glorification of Christ in my sufferings (Eph. 3:1). **fill up that which is behind**—lit., "the deficiencies"—all that are lacking of the afflictions of Christ (cf. *Note*, II Cor. 1:5). Christ is "afflicted in all His people's afflictions" (Isa. 63:9). "The Church is His body in which He is, dwells, lives, and therefore also suffers" [VITRINGA]. Christ was destined to endure certain afflictions in this figurative body, as well as in His literal; these were "that which is behind of the afflictions of *Christ*," which Paul "filled up." His own meritorious sufferings in expiation for sin were once for all completely filled up on the Cross. But His Church (His second Self) has her whole measure of afflictions fixed. The more Paul, a member, endured, the less remain for the rest of the Church to endure; the communion of saints thus giving them an interest in his sufferings. It is in reference to the Church's afflictions, which are "Christ's afflictions," that Paul here saith, "I fill up the deficiencies," or "what remain behind of the afflictions of Christ." She is afflicted to promote her growth in holiness, and her completeness in Christ. Not one suffering is lost (Ps. 56:8). All her members have thus a mutual interest in one another's sufferings (I Cor. 12:26). But Rome's inference hence, is utterly false that the Church has a stock treasury of the merits and satisfactions of Christ and His apostles, out of which she may dispense indulgences; the context has no reference to sufferings in *expiation of sin* and productive of *merit*. Believers should regard their sufferings less in relation to themselves as individuals, and more as parts of a grand whole, carrying out God's perfect plan. **25. am**—Greek, "I *was* made a minister": resuming vs. 23, "whereof I Paul was made a minister." **dispensation**—the *stewardship* committed to me to dispense in the house of God, the Church, to the whole family of believers, the goods of my Master (Luke 12:42; I Cor. 4:1, 2; 9:17; Eph. 3:2). **which is given**—Greek, "which *was* given." **for you**—with a view to you, Gentiles (vs. 27; Rom. 15:16). **to fulfil**—to bring it fully to all: the end of his stewardship: "fully preached" (Rom. 15:19). "The *fulness* of Christ (vs. 19), and of the times (Eph. 1:10) required him so to do" [BENGEL]. **26. the mystery**—(*Notes*, Eph. 1:9, 10; 3:5-9). The *mystery*, once hidden, now revealed, is redemption for the whole Gentile world, as well as for the Jews, "Christ in *you* (Gentiles) the hope of glory" (vs. 27). **from ages**—"from," according to ALFORD, refers to time, not "hidden from": from the time of the ages; still what is meant is that the mystery was hidden from *the beings living in those "ages."* The "ages" are the vast successive periods marked by successive orders of beings and stages of creation. *Greek,* "Æons," a word used by the Gnostics for angelic beings emanating from God. The Spirit by Paul presciently, in opposition to Gnostic error already beginning (ch. 2:18), teaches, that the mystery of redemption was hidden in God's purposes in Christ, alike from the *angelic beings* (cf. Eph. 3:10) of the pre-Adamic "ages," and from the subsequent *human* "generations." Translate as *Greek, "the ages . . . the* generations." **made manifest to his saints**—to His apostles and prophets primarily (Eph. 3:5), and through them to *all His saints.* **27. would**—rather as *Greek,* "willed," or *"was pleased* to make known." He resolves all into God's *good pleasure and will,* that man should not glory save in God's grace. **what**—How full and inexhaustible! **the riches of the glory of this mystery**—He accumulates phrase on phrase to enhance the greatness of the blessing in Christ bestowed by God on the Gentiles. Cf. ch. 2:3, "all the *treasures"* of *wisdom;* Ephesians 3:8, "the unsearchable *riches* of *Christ";* Ephesians 1:7, *"riches* of His *grace." "The glory* of this mystery" must be the glory which this once hidden, and now revealed, truth makes you Gentiles partakers of, partly now, but mainly when Christ shall come (ch. 3:4; Rom. 5:2; 8:17, 18; Eph. 1:18). This sense is proved by the following: "Christ in you the hope of *the (so Greek) glory."* The lower was the degradation of you Gentiles, the higher is the richness of the glory to which the mystery revealed now raises you. You were "without *Christ,* and having *no hope"* (Eph. 2:12). Now you have *"Christ* in you the *hope* of *the* glory" just mentioned. ALFORD translates, "Christ *among* you," to answer to "this mystery *among* the Gentiles." But the whole clause, "Christ IN you (Eph. 3:17) the hope of glory," answers to "this mystery," and not to the whole sentence, "this mystery *among* the Gentiles." What is *made known* "among you Gentiles" is, "Christ *in* you (now by faith as your *hidden* life, ch. 3:3; Gal. 2:20) the hope of glory" (your manifested life). The contrast (antithesis) between "CHRIST IN YOU" now as your *hidden* life, and "the hope of glory" hereafter to be *manifested,* requires this translation. **28. preach**—rather as *Greek,* "announce" or "proclaim." **warning . . . teaching**—"Warning" is connected with *repentance,* refers to one's *conduct,* and is addressed primarily to the *heart.* "Teaching" is connected with *faith,* refers to *doctrines,* and is addressed primarily to the *intellect.* These are the two heads of evangelical teaching. **every . . . every man**—without distinction of Jew or Gentile, great or small (Rom. 10:12, 13). **in all wisdom**—with all the wisdom *in our method of teaching* that we possess: so ALFORD. But vs. 9, and ch. 3:16, favor ESTIUS' view, which refers it to the *wisdom communicated to those being taught:* keeping back nothing, but instructing all in the perfect knowledge of the mysteries of faith which is the true *wisdom* (cf. I Cor. 2:6, 7; 12:8; Eph. 1:17). **present**—(*Note,* vs. 22)—at Christ's coming. **every man**—Paul is zealous lest the false teachers should seduce *one single* soul of Christ's people at Colosse. So each individual among them should be zealous for himself and his neighbor. Even one soul is of incalculable value. **perfect in Christ**—who is the *element in living union with* whom alone each believer can find *perfection:* per*fectly instructed* (Eph. 4:13) in doctrine, and *full grown* or *matured* in faith and practice. "Jesus"

is omitted in all the oldest MSS. **29. Whereunto**—viz., "to present every man perfect in Christ." **I also labour**—rather, "I labor also." I not only "proclaim" (*English Version,* "preach") Christ, but I *labor* also. **striving**—in "conflict" (ch. 2:1) of spirit (cf. Rom. 8:26). The same *Greek* word is used of Epaphras (ch. 4:12), *"laboring fervently* for you in prayers": lit., "agonizing," "striving as in the agony of a contest." So Jesus in Gethsemane when praying (Luke 22:44): so "strive" (the same *Greek* word, "agonize"), Luke 13:24. So Jacob *"wrestled"* in prayer (Gen. 32:24-29). Cf. "contention," *Greek,* "agony," or "striving earnestness," I Thessalonians 2:2. **according to his working**—Paul avows that he has power to "strive" in spirit for his converts, so far only as *Christ* works in him and by him (Eph. 3:20; Phil. 4:13). **mightily**—lit., "in power."

CHAPTER 2

VSS. 1-23. HIS STRIVINGS IN PRAYER FOR THEIR STEADFASTNESS IN CHRIST; FROM WHOM HE WARNS THEM NOT TO BE LED AWAY BY FALSE WISDOM. **1. For**—He explains in what respect he "labored *striving"* (ch. 1:29). Translate as *Greek,* "I *wish you to know how* great a conflict (the same *Greek* word as in ch. 1:29, *"agony* of a conflict" of fervent, anxious prayer; not conflict with the false teachers, which would have been impossible for him now in prison) I have for you." **them at Laodicea**—exposed to the same danger from false teachers as the Colossians (cf. ch. 4:16). This danger was probably the cause of his writing to Laodicea, as well as to Colosse. **not seen my face in the flesh**—including those in Hierapolis (ch. 4:13). Paul considered himself a "debtor" to all the Gentiles (Rom. 1:14). "His face" and presence would have been a "comfort" (vs. 2; Acts 20:38). Cf. ch. 1:4, 7, 8, in proof that he had not *seen,* but only *heard of* the Colossians. Hence he strives by earnest *conflict* with God in anxious prayer for them, to make up for the loss of his bodily presence among them. Though "absent in the *flesh,* I am with you in the *Spirit"* (vs. 5). **2.** Translate, "That their hearts *may* be comforted." The "their," compared with "you" (vs. 4), proves that in vs. 1 the words, "have not seen my face in the flesh," is a *general* designation of those for whom Paul declares he has "conflict," including the particular species, "you (Colossians) and them at Laodicea." For it is plain, the prayer "that *their* hearts may be comforted," must include in it the Colossians for whom he expressly says, "I have conflict." Thus it is an abbreviated mode of expression for, "That *your and their* hearts may be comforted." ALFORD translates, "confirmed," or allows "comforted" in its original radical sense *strengthened.* But the *Greek* supports *English Version:* the sense, too, is clear: *comforted* with the consolation of those whom Paul had not seen, and for whom, in consequence, he strove in prayerful conflict the more fervently; inasmuch as we are more anxious in behalf of absent, than present, friends [DAVENANT]. Their hearts would be comforted by "knowing what conflict he had for" them, and how much he is interested for their welfare; and also by being released from doubts on learning from the apostle, that the doctrine which they had heard from Epaphras was true and certain. In writing to churches which he had instructed face to face, he enters into particular details concerning them, as a father directing his children. But to those among whom he had not been in person, he treats of the more general truths of salvation. **being**—Translate as *Greek* in oldest MSS., "They being knit together." **in love**—the bond and element of perfect *knitting together;* the antidote to the dividing schismatical effect of false doctrine. Love to God and to one another in Christ. **unto**—the object and end of their being "knit together." **all riches**—*Greek,* "all *the* riches of the full assurance (I Thess. 1:5; Heb. 6:11; 10:22) of *the* (Christian) understanding." The accumulation of phrases, not only "understanding," but "the full assurance of understanding"; not only this, but "the *riches* of . . ."; not only this, but "*all* the riches of..." implies how he desires to impress them with the momentous importance of the subject in hand. **to**—Translate "unto." **acknowledgment**—The *Greek* implies, "full and accurate knowledge." It is a distinct *Greek* word from "knowledge," vs. 3. ALFORD translates, "thorough . . . knowledge." *Acknowledgment* hardly is strong enough; they did in a measure *acknowledge* the truth; what they wanted was the *full and accurate knowledge* of it (cf. *Notes,* ch. 1:9, 10; Phil. 1:9). **of God, and of the Father and of Christ**—The oldest MSS. omit "and of the Father, and of"; then translate, "Of God (viz.), Christ." Two very old MSS. and *Vulgate* read, "Of God the Father of Christ." **3.** Translate in the *Greek* order, "In whom (not as ALFORD, 'in which' *mystery;* Christ is Himself the 'mystery' (vs. 2; I Tim. 3:16), and to Christ the relative refers) are all the treasures of wisdom and knowledge hidden." The "all" here, answers to "all" in vs. 2; as "treasures" answer to the "riches"; it is from the *treasures* that *the riches* (vs. 2) are derived. "Are" is the predicate of the sentence; all the treasures ARE in Him; *hidden* is predicated of the state or manner in which they are in Him. Like a mine of unknown and inexhaustible wealth, the *treasures* of wisdom are all in Him *hidden,* but not in order to remain so; they only need to be explored for you to attain "unto the riches" in them (vs. 2); but until you, Colossians, press after attaining *the full knowledge* (see *Note,* vs. 2) of them, they remain "hidden." Cf. the parable, Matthew 13:44, "treasure hid." This sense suits the scope of the apostle, and sets aside ALFORD's objection that "the treasures are not hidden, but revealed." "Hidden" plainly answers to "mystery" (vs. 2), which is designed by God, if we be faithful to our privileges, not to remain *hidden,* but to be revealed (cf. I Cor. 2:7, 8). Still as the mine is unfathomable, there will, through eternity, be always fresh treasures in Him to be drawn forth from their hidden state. **wisdom**—general, and as to *experimental* and *practical* truth; whence comes "understanding" (vs. 2). **knowledge**—*special* and *intellectual,* in regard to *doctrinal* truth; whence comes "the full knowledge" (vs. 2). **4. And**—"Now." Cf. with "lest any man . . ." vss. 8, 16, 18. He refers to the blending of Judaism with Oriental philosophy, and the combination of this mixture with Christianity. **enticing words**—plausible as wearing the guise of *wisdom* and *humility* (vss. 18, 23). **5. For** —argument against their suffering themselves to be *beguiled,* drawn from a regard to his personal authority as though he were present. **joying and beholding**—beholding with joy. **order**—your *good order;* answering to "knit together" (vs. 2) as a well-organized body; the same *Greek* as that for "*knit together,*" is used of the body" of the Church "*compacted,*" in Ephesians 4:16. Cf. I Corinthians 14: 33, 40. **steadfastness**—*Greek,* "the firm (or *solid*) *foundation.*" As "order" expresses the outward aspect of the Church; so "steadfastness" expresses

the inner basis on which their Church rested. The *Greek* literally implies not an abstract quality, but the *thing* in the concrete; thus their "faith" here is *the solid thing* which constituted the *basis* of their Church. **6.** "As therefore ye received (once for all; the aorist tense; from Epaphras) Jesus *the* Christ *as your* Lord (cf. I Cor. 12:3; II Cor. 4:5; Phil. 3:8), so walk in Him." He says not merely, "Ye received" the doctrine of Christ, but "Jesus" Himself; this is the essence of faith (John 14:21, 23; Gal. 1:16). Ye have received once for all the Spirit of *life* in Christ; carry into practice that life in your *walk* (Gal. 5:25). This is the main scope of the Epistle. **7. Rooted**— (Eph. 3:17). **built up**—*Greek,* "*being* builded up." As "rooted" implies their *vitality;* so "builded up," massive *solidity.* As in the Song of Solomon, when one image is not sufficient to express the varied aspects of divine truth, another is employed to supply the idea required. Thus "walking," a third image (vs. 6), expresses the thought which "rooted" and "built," though each suggesting a thought peculiar to itself, could not express, viz., onward *motion.* "Rooted" is in the *past* tense, implying their first *conversion* and vital grafting "in Him." "Built up" is *present* (in the *Greek*), implying their progressive *increase* in religion by union with Him. Ephesians 2:20 refers to the *Church;* but the passage here to their *individual* progress in edification (Acts 20:32). **stablished**—confirmed. **as**—"even as." **abounding therein with thanksgiving**—advancing to fuller maturity (cf. vs. 2) in the faith, "with thanksgiving" to God as the gracious Author of this whole blessing. **8.** Translate, "Beware (lit., 'Look' well) lest there *shall be* (as I fear there is: the *Greek* indicative expresses this) any man (pointing to some known emissary of evil, Gal. 1:7) *leading you away as his spoil* (not merely gaining spoil out of you, but making *yourselves* his spoil) through (by means of) his philosophy," etc. The apostle does not condemn *all* philosophy, but "*the* philosophy" (so *Greek*) of the Judæic-oriental heretics at Colosse, which afterwards was developed into Gnosticism. You, who may have "the *riches* of *full* assurance" and "the *treasures* of wisdom," should not suffer yourselves to be led away as a *spoil* by *empty,* deceitful philosophy: "riches" are contrasted with spoil; "full" with "vain," or *empty* (vss. 2, 3, 9). **after**—"according to." **tradition of men**—opposed to, "the fulness of *the Godhead.*" Applied to *Rabbinical traditions,* Mark 7:8. When men could not make revelation even *seem* to tell about deep mysteries which they were curious to pry into, they brought in human philosophy and pretended traditions to help it, as if one should bring a lamp to the sundial to find the hour [*Cautions for times,* p. 85]. The false teachers boasted of a higher wisdom in theory, transmitted by tradition among the initiated; in practice they enjoined asceticism, as though matter and the body were the sources of evil. Phrygia (in which was Colosse) had a propensity for the mystical and magical, which appeared in their worship of Cybele and subsequent Montanism [NEANDER]. **rudiments of the world**—(*Note,* Gal. 4:3). "The rudiments" or elementary lessons "of the (outward) world," such as legal ordinances; our Judaic childhood's lessons (vss. 11, 16, 20; Gal. 4:1-3). But NEANDER, the *elements of the world,*" in the sense, *what is earthly, carnal and outward,* not "the rudiments of religion," in Judaism and heathenism. **not after Christ**—Their boasted higher "philosophy" is but human tradition, and a cleaving to the carnal and worldly, and not to Christ. Though acknowledging Christ nominally, in spirit they by their doctrine deny Him. **9. For**—"Because." *Their* philosophy" (vs. 8) is not "after Christ," as all true philosophy is, everything which comes not from, and tends not to, Him, being a delusion; "For in Him (alone) dwelleth" *as in a temple.* . . . **the fulness**—(ch. 1:19; John 14:10). **of the Godhead**—The *Greek* (*theotes*) means the ESSENCE and NATURE *of the Godhead*, not merely the *divine perfections* and attributes of Divinity (*Greek*, "theiotes"). He, as man, was not merely God-like, but in the fullest sense, GOD. **bodily**—not merely as before His incarnation, but now "bodily in Him" as the incarnate word (John 1:14, 18). Believers, by union with Him, partake of His fulness of the divine nature (John 1:16; *Note,* Eph. 3:19; II Pet. 1:4). **10. And**—And *therefore;* and so. Translate in the *Greek* order, "Ye are in Him (by virtue of union with Him) *filled full*" of all that you need (John 1:16). Believers receive of the divine unction which flows down from their Divine Head and High Priest (Ps. 133: 2). He is *full of* the "fulness" itself; we, *filled* from Him. Paul implies, Therefore ye Colossians need no supplementary sources of grace, such as the false teachers dream of. Christ is "the Head of all *rule and authority*" (so the *Greek*), Ephesians 1:10; He, therefore, alone, not these subject "authorities" also, is to be adored (vs. 18). **11.** Implying that they did not need, as the Judaizers taught, the outward rite of circumcision, since they had already the inward spiritual reality of it. **are**—rather, as the *Greek*, "Ye *were* (once for all) circumcised (spiritually, at your conversion and baptism, Rom. 2:28, 29; Phil. 3:3) with a (so the *Greek*) circumcision made without hands"; opposed to "the circumcision in the flesh *made by hands*" (Eph. 2:11). Christ's own body, by which the believer is sanctified, is said to be "not made with hands" (Mark 14:58; Heb. 9:11; cf. Dan. 2:45). **in putting off**—rather as *Greek*, "in your putting off"; as an old garment (Eph. 4:22); alluding to the putting off the foreskin in circumcision. **the body of the sins of the flesh**—The oldest MSS. read, "the body of the flesh," omitting "of the sins," i.e., "the body," of which the prominent feature is *fleshiness* (cf. Rom. 8:13, where "flesh" and "the body" mutually correspond). This fleshly body, in its sinful aspect, is put off in baptism (where baptism answers its ideal) as the seal of regeneration where received in repentance and faith. In circumcision the *foreskin* only was put off; in Christian regeneration "the *body* of the flesh" is spiritually put off, at least it is so in its ideal conception, however imperfectly believers *realize* that ideal. **by**—*Greek,* "in." This spiritual circumcision is realized in, or by, union with Christ, whose "circumcision," whereby He became responsible for us to keep the whole law, is imputed to believers for justification; and union with whom, in all His vicarious obedience, including HIS CIRCUMCISION, is the source of our sanctification. ALFORD makes it explanatory of the previous, "a circumcision made without hands," viz., "the circumcision brought about by your union with Christ." The former view seems to me better to accord with 12; ch. 3:1, 3, 4, which similarly makes the believer, by spiritual union with Christ, to have personal fellowship in the several states of Christ, viz., His death, resurrection, and appearing in glory. Nothing was done or suffered by our Mediator as such, but may be acted in our souls and represented in our spirits. PEARSON'S view, however, is that of ALFORD. JOSHUA, the type (not Moses in the wilderness), circumcised the Israelites in Canaan (Josh. 5: 2-9) the second time: the people that came out of

Egypt having been circumcised, and afterwards having died in the wilderness; but those born after the Exodus not having been so. Jesus, the Antitype, is the author of the true circumcision, which is therefore called "the circumcision of Christ" (Rom. 2: 29). As Joshua was "Moses' minister," so Jesus, "minister" of the circumcision for the truth of God" unto the Gentiles (Rom. 15:8). **12.** Translate, "*Having been* buried with Him in *your* baptism." The past participle is here coincident in time with the preceding verb, "ye were (*Greek*) circumcised." Baptism is regarded as the burial of the old carnal life, to which the act of immersion symbolically corresponds; and in warm climates where *immersion* is safe, it is the mode most accordant with the significance of the ordinance; but the spirit of the ordinance is kept by affusion, where immersion would be inconvenient or dangerous; to insist on literal immersion in all cases would be mere legal ceremonialism (Rom. 6:3, 4). **are risen**—rather as *Greek*, *were raised* with Him." **through the faith of** . . .—*by means of your* faith *in* the operation of God; so "faith of," for "faith *in*" (Eph. 3:12; Phil. 3:9). Faith in God's mighty operation in raising again Jesus, is saving faith (Rom. 4:24; 10:9); and it is wrought in the soul by His same "mighty working" whereby He "raised Jesus from the dead" (Eph. 1:19, 20). BENGEL seems to me (not as ALFORD understands him) to express the latter sense, viz., "Through the faith which is *a work of* the operation of God who. . . ." Ephesians 1:19, 20 accords with this; the same mighty power of God is exercised in raising one spiritually dead to the life of faith, as was "wrought in Christ when God raised Him literally from the dead." However, "faith of" *usually* is "faith in" (Rom. 3:22); but there is no grammatical impropriety in understanding it "the faith which is the effect of the operation of God" (Eph. 2:8; I Thess. 2:13). As His literal resurrection is the ground of the power put forth in our spiritual resurrection now, so it is a pledge of our literal resurrection hereafter (Rom. 8:11). **13. you, being dead**—formerly (Eph. 2:1, 2); even as Christ was among the dead, before that God raised Him "from the dead" (vs. 12). **sins**—rather as *Greek* is translated at end of this verse, "trespasses," lit., "fallings aside" from God's ways; actual transgressions, as that of Adam. **uncircumcision of your flesh**—your not having put off the old fleshly nature, the carnal foreskin, or *original sin,* which now by spiritual circumcision, i.e., conversion and baptism, you have put off. **he quickened**—GOD "quickened together with Him" (CHRIST). Just as Christ's resurrection proved that He was delivered from the sin laid on Him, so our spiritual quickening proves that we have been forgiven our sins (I Pet. 3:22; 4:1, 2). **forgiven you**—So *Vulgate* and HILARY. But the oldest MSS. read, "us," passing from the particular persons, the Colossians, to the general Church (ch. 1:14; Eph. 1:7). **all trespasses**—*Greek,* "all *our* trespasses." **14. Blotting out**—*Greek,* "Having wiped out"; coincident in time with "having forgiven you" (vs. 13); hereby having *cancelled* the law's indictment against you. The law (including especially the *moral* law, wherein lay the chief difficulty in obeying) is abrogated to the believer, as far as it was a compulsory, accusing code, and as far as "righteousness" (justification) and "life" were sought for by it. It can only produce outward works, not inward obedience of the will, which in the believer flows from the Holy Spirit in Him (Rom. 3:21; 7:2, 4; Gal. 2:19). **the handwriting of ordinances**—rather, "IN ordinances" (*Note,* Eph. 2:

15); "the law of commandments contained in ordinances." "The handwriting" (alluding to the Decalogue, the representative of the law, *written by the hand* of God) is *the whole law,* the obligatory bond, under which all lay; the Jews primarily were under the bond, but they in this respect were the representative people of the world (Rom. 3:19); and in their inability to keep the law was involved the inability of the Gentiles also, in whose hearts "the work of the law was written" (Rom. 2:15); and as they did not keep this, they were condemned by it. **that was against us ... contrary to us**—Greek "adversary to us"; so it is translated, Hebrews 10:27. "Not only was the law *against us* by its demands, but also an *adversary* to us by its accusations" [BENGEL]. TITTMANN explains the *Greek,* "having a *latent* contrariety to us"; not *open designed* hostility, but virtual unintentional opposition through *our* frailty; not through any opposition in *the law itself* to our good (Rom. 7:7-12, 14; I Cor. 15:56, Gal. 3:21; Heb. 10:3). The "WRITING" is part of "that which was contrary to us"; for "the *letter* killeth" (*Note,* II Cor. 3:6). **and took it**—Greek, and hath taken it out of the way" (so as to be no longer a hindrance to us), by "nailing it to *the* cross." Christ, by bearing the curse of the broken law, has redeemed us from its curse (Gal. 3:13). In His person nailed to the cross, the law itself was nailed to it. One ancient mode of cancelling bonds was by striking a nail through the writing: this seems at that time to have existed in Asia [GROTIUS]. The bond cancelled in the present case was the obligation lying against the Jews as representatives of the world, and attested by their *amen,* to keep the whole law under penalty of the curse (Deut. 27:26; Neh. 10:29). **15.** ALFORD, ELLICOTT, and others translate the *Greek* to accord with the translation of the same *Greek,* ch. 3:9, "Stripping off from Himself the principalities and the powers:" GOD put off from Himself *the angels,* i.e., their ministry, not employing them to be promulgators of the Gospel in the way that He had given the law by their "disposition" or ministry (Acts 7:53; Gal. 3:19; Heb. 2:2, 5): God manifested Himself without a veil in Jesus. "THE principalities and THE powers" refers back to vs. 10, Jesus, "the Head of all principality and power," and ch. 1: 16. In the sacrifice of Jesus on the cross, God subjected all the principalities, etc., to Jesus, declaring them to be powerless as to His work and His people (Eph. 1:21). Thus Paul's argument against those grafting on Christianity Jewish observances, along with angel worship, is, whatever part angels may be supposed to have had under the law, now at an end, God having put the legal dispensation itself away. But the objection is, that the context *seems* to refer to a triumph over *bad angels:* in II Corinthians 2: 14, however, Christ's *triumph* over those subjected to Him, is not a triumph for destruction, but for their salvation, so that good angels *may* be referred to (ch. 1:20). But the *Greek* middle is susceptible of *English Version,* "having spoiled," or, lit. [TITTMANN], "having *completely* stripped," or "despoiled" *for Himself* (cf. Rom. 8:38; I Cor. 15:24; Eph. 6:2). *English Version* accords with Matt. 12:29; Luke 11: 22; Hebrews 2:14. Translate as the *Greek,* "The *rules and authorities."* **made a show of them openly**—at His ascension (*Notes,* Eph. 4:8; confirming *English Version* of this verse). **openly**—John 7:4; 11: 54, support *English Version* against ALFORD'S translation, "in openness of speech." **in it**—viz., His cross, or crucifixion: so the Greek fathers translate. Many of the Latins, "In *Himself,*" or "in Him." Ephesians 2:16 favors *English Version,*

"reconcile ... by *the cross,* having slain the enmity thereby." If "in Him," i.e., Christ, be read, still the Cross will be the place and means of God's triumph in Christ over the principalities (Eph. 1:20; 2:5). Demons, like other angels, were in heaven up to Christ's ascension, and influenced earth from their heavenly abodes. As heaven was not yet opened to man before Christ (John 3:13), so it was not yet shut against demons (Job 1:6 2:1). But at the ascension Satan and his demons were "judged" and "cast out" by Christ's obedience unto death (John 12:31; 16:11; Heb. 2:14; Rev. 12:5-10), and the Son of man was raised to the throne of God; thus His resurrection and ascension are a public solemn triumph over the principalities and powers of death. It is striking that the heathen oracles were silenced soon after Christ's ascension. **16. therefore**—because ye are complete in Christ, and God in Him has dispensed with all subordinate means as *essential* to acceptance with Him. **meat ... drink**—Greek, "eating ... .drinking" (Rom. 14:1-17). Pay no regard to any one who sits in judgment on you as to legal observances in respect to foods. **holyday** —*a feast* yearly. Cf. the three, I Chronicles 23:31. **new moon**—monthly. **the sabbath**—Omit "THE," which is not in the *Greek* (cf. *Note,* Gal. 4:10). "SABBATHS" (not "the sabbaths") of the day of atonement and feast of tabernacles have come to an end with the Jewish services to which they belonged (Lev. 23:32, 37-39). The weekly sabbath rests on a more permanent foundation, having been instituted in Paradise to commemorate the completion of creation in six days. Leviticus 23:38 expressly distinguished "the sabbath of the Lord" from the other sabbaths. A *positive* precept is *right because it is commanded,* and ceases to be obligatory when abrogated; a moral precept is *commanded* eternally, *because it is* eternally *right.* If we could keep a perpetual sabbath, as we shall hereafter, the positive precept of the sabbath, one in each week, would not be needed. Hebrews 4:9, "rests," Greek, "keeping of sabbath" (Isa. 66:23). But we cannot, since even Adam, in innocence, needed one amidst his earthly employments; therefore the sabbath is still needed and is therefore still linked with the other nine commandments, as obligatory in the spirit, though the letter of the law has been superseded by that higher spirit of love which is the essence of law and Gospel alike (Rom. 13:8-10). **17. things to come**—the blessings of the Christian covenant, the substance of which Jewish ordinances were but the type. Cf. "ages to come," i.e., the Gospel dispensation (Eph. 2:7). Hebrews 2:5, "the world to come." **the body is of Christ**—The *real substance* (of the blessings typified by the law) belongs to Christ (Heb. 8:5; 10:1). **18. beguile**—Translate, "Defraud you of your prize," lit., "to adjudge a prize out of hostility away from him who deserves it" [TRENCH]. "To be umpire in a contest to the detriment of one." This *defrauding of their prize* the Colossians would suffer, by letting any self-constituted *arbitrator* or *judge* (i.e., false teacher) draw them away from Christ," the righteous Judge" and Awarder of the prize (II Tim. 4:8; Jas. 1:12; I Pet. 5:4), to angel-worship. **in a voluntary humility**—So "will worship" (vs. 23). Lit., "Delighting [WAHL] in humility"; *loving* (so the *Greek* is translated, Mark 12: 38, "*love* to go in long clothing") to indulge himself *in a humility* of his own imposing: *a volunteer in humility* [DALLÆUS]. Not as ALFORD, "Let no one *of purpose* defraud you. ..." Not as GROTIUS, "If he ever so much wish" (to defraud you). For the participle "wishing" or "delighting," is one of the series, and stands in the same category as "intruding," "puffed up," "not holding"; and the *self-pleasing* implied in it stands in happy contrast to the (mock) *humility* with which it seems to me, therefore, to be connected. His "humility," so called, is a *pleasing of self*: thus it stands in parallelism to "his fleshly mind" (its real name, though *he* styles it "humility"), as "wishing" or "delighting" does to "puffed up." The *Greek* for "humility" is lit., "lowliness of *mind*," which forms a clearer parallel to "puffed up by his fleshly *mind*." Under pretext of humility, as if they durst not come directly to God and Christ (like the modern Church of Rome), they invoked angels: as Judaizers, they justified this on the ground that the law was given by angels. This error continued long in Phrygia (where Colosse and Laodicea were), so that the Council of Laodicea (A.D. 360) expressly framed its 35th canon against the *"Angelici"* (as AUGUSTINE, *Hœreses*, 39, calls them) or "invokers of angels." Even as late as THEODORET's time, there were oratories to Michael the archangel. The modern Greeks have a legend that Michael opened a chasm to draw off an inundation threatening the Colossian Christians. Once men admit the inferior powers to share invocation with the Supreme, the former gradually engrosses all our serious worship, almost to the exclusion of the latter; thus the heathen, beginning with adding the worship of other deities to that of the Supreme, ended with ceasing to worship Him at all. Nor does it signify much, whether we regard such as directly controlling us (the pagan view), or as only *influencing* the Supreme in our behalf (the Church of Rome's view); because we from whom I expect happiness or misery, becomes the uppermost object in my mind, whether he *give*, or only *procure* it [*Cautions for Times*]. Scripture opposes the idea of "patrons" or "intercessors" (I Tim. 2:5, 6). True Christian humility joins consciousness of utter personal demerit, with a sense of participation in the divine life through Christ, and in the dignity of our adoption by God. Without such humility, a false self-humiliation results, which displays itself in ceremonies and ascetic selfabasement (vs. 23), which after all is but spiritual pride under the mock guise of humility. Contrast "glorying in the Lord" (I Cor. 1:31). **intruding into...things which he hath not seen**—So very old MSS. and *Vulgate* and ORIGEN read. But the oldest MSS. and LUCIFER omit "not"; then translate, "haughtily treading on ('standing on' [ALFORD]) the things which he hath seen." TREGELLES refers this to *fancied* visions of angels. But if Paul had meant a *fancied seeing*, he would have used some qualifying word, as, "which he *seemed to* see," not "which he *hath* seen." Plainly the things were *actually* seen by him, whether of demoniacal origination (I Sam. 28:11-20), or phenomena resulting from natural causation, mistaken by him as if supernatural. Paul, not stopping to discuss the nature of the things so seen, fixes on the radical error, the tendency of such a one in all this to walk by SENSE (viz., what he *haughtily prides himself on having* SEEN), rather than by FAITH in the UNSEEN "Head" (vs. 19; cf. John 20:29; II Cor. 5:7; Heb. 11:1). Thus is the parallelism, "vainly puffed up" answers to "haughtily treading on," or "setting his foot on"; "his fleshly mind" answers to the things which he hath seen," since his fleshliness betrays itself in priding himself on *what he hath seen*, rather than on the *unseen* objects of *faith*. That the things seen may have been of demoniacal origination, appears from I Timothy 4:1, "Some shall depart from the *faith*, giving heed to seducing spirits and doctrines of devils" (*Greek*, "demons"). A warning to modern spiritualists. **puffed up**—implying that the previous so called "humility" (*Greek*, "lowliness of mind") was really a "puffing up." **fleshly mind**—*Greek*, "By the mind of his own flesh." The flesh, or sensuous principle, is the fountain head whence his mind draws its craving after religious objects of *sight*, instead of, in true *humility* as a member, "holding fast the (unseen) Head." **19.** Translate, "Not holding *fast* the Head." He who does not hold Christ solely and supremely above all others, does not hold Him at all [BENGEL]. The want of firm holding of Christ has set him loose to [pry into, and so] "tread haughtily on (pride himself on) things which he hath seen." Each must hold fast the Head for himself, not merely be attached to the other members, however high in the body [ALFORD]. **from which**—rather, "from whom." **the body**—i.e., all the members of the body (Eph. 4:16). **joints**—the points of union where the supply of nourishment passes to the different members, furnishing the body with the materials of growth. **bands**—the sinews and nerves which bind together limb and limb. Faith, love, and peace, are the spiritual bands. Cf. "knit together in love" (vs. 2; ch. 3:14; Eph. 4:3). **having nourishment ministered**—i.e., supplied to it continually. "Receiving ministration." **knit together**—The *Greek* is translated, "compacted," Ephesians 4:16: implying firm consolidation. **with the increase of God**—(Eph. 4:16)—i.e., *wrought by* God, the Author and Sustainer of the believer's spiritual life, in union with Christ, the Head (I Cor. 3:6); and tending to the honor of God, being worthy of Him, its Author. **20. Wherefore**—The oldest MSS. omit "Wherefore." **if ye be dead**—*Greek*, "if ye died (so as to be freed) from..." (cf. Rom. 6:2; 7:2, 3; Gal. 2:19). **rudiments of the world**—(vs. 8). Carnal, outward, worldly, legal ordinances. **as though living**—as though you were not dead to the world like your crucified Lord, into whose death ye were buried (Gal. 6:14; I Pet. 4:1, 2). **are ye subject to ordinances**—Why do ye submit to be made subject to ordinances? Referring to vs. 14: you are again being made subject to "ordinances," the "handwriting" of which had been "blotted out" (vs. 14). **21.** Cf. vs. 16, "meat...drink." He gives instances of the "ordinances" (vs. 20) in the words of their imposers. There is an ascending climax of superstitious prohibitions. The first *Greek* word (*hapse*) is distinguished from the third (*thiges*), in that the former means *close contact* and *retention*; the latter, *momentary contact* (cf. I Cor. 7:1; John 20:17, *Greek*, "Hold me not"; cling not to me"). Translate, "Handle not, *neither* taste, *nor even touch*." The three refer to meats. "Handle not" (a stronger term than "nor even *touch*"), "nor taste" with the *tongue*, "nor even touch," however slight the contact. **22. Which**—things, viz., the three things handled, touched, and tasted. **are to perish**—lit., "are constituted by their very nature) for perishing (or *destruction by corruption*) in (or *with*) their using up" (consumption). Therefore they cannot really and lastingly defile a man (Matt. 15:17; I Cor. 6:13). **after**—according to. Referring to vss. 20, 21. All these "ordinances" are according to human, not divine, injunction. **doctrines**—*Greek*, teachings." ALFORD translates, (doctrinal) "systems." **23. have**—*Greek*, "are having"; implying the *permanent* characteristic which these ordinances are supposed to have. **show of wisdom**—rather, "a *reputation* of wisdom" [ALFORD]. **will worship**—arbitrarily invented worship: *would-be* worship, devised by *man's own will*, not God's. So jealous is God of human will worship, that He struck Nadab and Abihu dead for burning strange incense (Lev. 10:1-3). So Uzziah was stricken with leprosy for usurping the office of priest (II Chron. 26:16-21). Cf. the will worship of Saul (I Sam. 13:8-14) for which he was doomed to lose his throne. This "voluntary worship" is the counterpart to their "voluntary humility" (vs. 18): both specious in appearance, the former seeming in religion to do even *more* than God requires (as in the dogmas of the Roman and Greek churches)', but really setting aside God's will for man's own; the latter seemingly self-abasing, but really proud of man's self-willed "humility" (*Greek*, "lowliness of mind"), while virtually rejecting the dignity of direct communion with Christ, the Head, by worshipping of angels. **neglecting of the body**—*Greek*, "not sparing of the body." This asceticism seems to have rested on the Oriental theory that matter is the source of evil. This also looked plausible (cf. I Cor. 9:27). **not in any honour**—of the body. As "neglecting of the body" describes asceticism *positively;* so this clause, *negatively.* Not paying any of that "honor" which is due to the body as redeemed by such a price as the blood of Christ. We should not degrade, but have a just estimation of ourselves, not in ourselves, but in Christ (Acts 13:46; I Cor. 3:21; 6:15; 7:23; 12:23, 24; I Thess. 4:4). True self-denial regards the spirit, and not the forms of ascetical self-mortification in "meats which profit not those occupied therein" (Heb. 13:9), and is consistent with Christian self-respect, the "honor" which belongs to the believer as dedicated to the Lord. Cf. "vainly," vs. 18. **to the satisfying of the flesh**—This expresses the *real* tendency of their human ordinances of bodily asceticism, voluntary humility, and will worship of angels. While seeming to *deny* self and the body, they really are *pampering* the flesh. Thus "satisfying of the *flesh*" answers to "puffed up by his *fleshly* mind" (vs. 18), so that "flesh" is used in its ethical sense, "the carnal nature" as opposed to the *spiritual;* not in the sense, "body." The *Greek* for "satisfying" implies *satiating to repletion,* or *to excess.* "A surfeit of the carnal sense is human tradition" [HILARY THE DEACON, in BENGEL]. Tradition puffs up; it clogs the heavenly perceptions. They put away true "honor" that they may "*satiate to the full* THE FLESH." Self-imposed ordinances gratify the flesh (viz., self-righteousness), though seeming to mortify it.

CHAPTER 3

Vss. 1-25. EXHORTATIONS TO HEAVENLY AIMS, AS OPPOSED TO EARTHLY, ON THE GROUND OF UNION TO THE RISEN SAVIOUR; TO MORTIFY AND PUT OFF THE OLD MAN, AND TO PUT ON THE NEW; IN CHARITY, HUMILITY, WORDS OF EDIFICATION, THANKFULNESS; RELATIVE DUTIES. **1. If ... then**—The connection with ch. 2:18, 23, is, he had condemned the "fleshly mind" and the "satiating to the full the flesh"; in contrast to this he now says, "If then ye have been once for all raised up (*Greek*, aorist) together with Christ" (viz., at your conversion and baptism, Rom. 6:4). **seek those things ... above**—(Matt. 6:33; Phil. 3:20.) **sitteth**—rather, as *Greek*, "Where Christ is, sitting on the right of God" (Eph. 1:20). The Head being quickened, the members are also quickened with Him. Where the Head is, there the members must be. The contrast is between the believer's former state, alive to the world but dead to God, and his present state, dead to the world but alive to

God; and between the earthly abode of the unbeliever and the heavenly abode of the believer (I Cor. 15:47, 48). We are already seated there *in* Him as our Head; and hereafter shall be seated *by* Him, as the Bestower of our bliss. As Elisha (II Kings 2:2) said to Elijah when about to ascend, "As the Lord liveth ... I will not leave thee"; so we must follow the ascended Saviour with the wings of our meditations and the chariots of our affections. We should trample upon and subdue our lusts that our conversation may correspond to our Saviour's condition; that where the eyes of apostles were forced to leave Him, thither our thoughts may follow Him (Matt. 6:21, John 12:32) [PEARSON]. Of ourselves we can no more ascend than a bar of iron lift itself up from the earth. But the love of Christ is a powerful magnet to draw us up (Eph. 2:5, 6). The design of the Gospel is not merely to give rules, but mainly to supply *motives* to holiness. **2.** Translate, "Set your *mind* on the things above, not on the things ..." (ch. 2:20). Contrast "who *mind* earthly things" (Phil. 3:19). Whatever we make an idol of, will either be a cross to us if we be believers, or a curse to us if unbelievers. **3.** The *Greek* aorist implies, "For ye have died once for all" (ch. 2:12; Rom. 6:4-7). It is not said, Ye must die practically to the world in order to become dead with Christ; but the latter is assumed as *once for all* having taken place in the regeneration; what believers are told is, Develop this spiritual life in practice. "No one longs for eternal, incorruptible, and immortal life, unless he be wearied of this temporal, corruptible, and mortal life" [AUGUSTINE]. **your life ... hid**—Psalm 83:3—like a seed buried in the earth; cf. "planted," Romans 6:5. Cf. Matthew 13:31 and 33, "like ... leaven ... *hid.*" As the glory of Christ now is hid from the world, so also the glory of believers' inner life, proceeding from communion with Him, is still hidden with Christ in God; but (vs. 4) when Christ, the Source of this life, shall manifest Himself in glory, then shall their hidden glory be manifest, and correspond in appearance to its original [NEANDER]. The Christian's secret communion with God will now at times make itself seen without his intending it (Matt. 5:14, 16); but his full manifestation is at Christ's manifestation (Matt. 13:43; Rom. 8:19-23). "It doth not yet appear (*Greek*, 'is not yet *manifested*') what we shall be" (I John 3:2; I Pet. 1:7). As yet Christians do not always recognize the "life" of one another, so *hidden* is it, and even at times doubt as to their own life, so weak is it, and so harassed with temptations (Ps. 51; Rom. 7). **in God**—to whom Christ has ascended. Our "life" is "laid up for" us in *God* (ch. 1:5), and is secured by the decree of Him who is invisible to the world (II Tim. 4:8). **4.** Translate, "When Christ shall *be manifested* who is our life (John 11:25; 14:6, 19), then shall ye also with Him *be manifested* in glory" (I Pet. 4:13). The *spiritual* life our souls have now in Him shall be extended to our *bodies* (Rom. 8:11). **then**—and not till then. Those err who think to find a perfect Church before then. The true Church is now militant. Rome errs in trying to set up a Church now regnant and triumphant. The true Church shall be visible as a perfect and reigning Church, when Christ shall be visibly manifested as her reigning Head. Rome having ceased to look for Him in patient faith, has set up a visible mockhead, a false anticipation of the millennial kingdom. The Papacy took to itself by robbery that glory which is an object of hope, and can only be reached by bearing the cross now. When the Church became a harlot, she ceased to be a bride who goes to meet her Bridegroom. Hence the millennial kingdom ceased to be looked for [AUBERLEN]. **5. Mortify**—*Greek,* "make a corpse of"; "make dead"; "put to death." **therefore**—(*Note,* vs. 3). Follow out to its necessary consequence the fact of your *having once for all* died with Christ spiritually at your regeneration, by daily "deadening your members," of which united "the body of the sins of the flesh" consists (cf. 2:11). "The members" to be mortified are the fleshly instruments of lust, in so far as the members of the body are abused to such purposes. Habitually repress and do violence to corrupt desires of which the members are the instruments (cf. Rom. 6:19; 8:13; Gal. 5:24, 25). **upon the earth**—where they find their support [BENGEL] (cf. vs. 2, "things on earth"). See Ephesians 5:3, 4. **inordinate affection**—"lustful passion." **evil concupiscence**—more general than the last [ALFORD], the disorder of the *external* senses; "lustful passion," *lust within* [BENGEL]. **covetousness**—marked off by the *Greek* article as forming a whole genus by itself, distinct from the genus containing the various species just enumerated. It implies a self-idolizing, grasping spirit; far worse than another *Greek* term translated "the love of money" (I Tim. 6:10). **which is** —i.e., inasmuch as it is "idolatry." Cf. *Note,* Ephesians 4:19, on its connection with sins of impurity. *Self* and *mammon* are deified in the heart instead of God (Matt. 6:24; *Note,* Eph. 5:5). **6.** (*Note,* Eph. 5:6.) **7. sometime**—"once." **walked ... when ye lived in them**—These sins were the very element in which ye "lived" (before ye became once for all dead with Christ to them); no wonder, then, that ye "*walked*" in them. Cf. on the opposite side, "*living*" in the Spirit," having as its legitimate consequence, "*walking* in the Spirit" (Gal. 5:25). The *living* comes first in both cases, the *walking* follows. **8. But now**—that ye are no longer *living* in them. **ye also**—like other believers; answering to "ye also" (vs. 7) like other unbelievers formerly. **put off**—"Do ye also put away all these," viz., those just enumerated, and those which follow [ALFORD]. **anger, wrath**—(*Note,* Eph. 4:31). **blasphemy**—rather, "reviling," "evil-speaking," as it is translated in Ephesians 4:31. **filthy communication**—The context favors the translation, "*abusive language,*" rather than impure conversation. "Foul language" best retains the ambiguity of the original. **9.** (Eph. 4: 22, 25.) **put off**—*Greek,* "*wholly* put off"; utterly renounced [TITTMANN]. **the old man**—the unregenerate nature which ye had before conversion. **his deeds**—habits of acting. **10. the new man**—(*Note,* Eph. 4:23). Here (*neon*) the *Greek,* means "the *recently*-put-on nature"; that lately received at regeneration (see *Note,* Eph. 4:23, 24). **which is renewed**—*Greek,* "which is being renewed" (*anakainoumenou*); viz., its development into a perfectly renewed nature is continually progressing to completion. **in knowledge**—rather as the *Greek,* "unto perfect knowledge" (*Notes,* ch. 1:6, 9, 10). Perfect knowledge of God excludes all sin (John 17:3). **after the image of him that created him**—viz., of God that created the *new man* (Eph. 2:10; 4:24). The new creation is analogous to the first creation (II Cor. 4:6). As man was then made in the image of God naturally, so now spiritually. But the image of God formed in us by the Spirit of God, is as much more glorious than that borne by Adam, as the Second Man, the Lord from heaven, is more glorious than the first man. Genesis 1:26, "Let us make man in our *image,* after our *likeness.*" The "image" is claimed for man, I Corinthians 11:7; the

"likeness," James 3:9. ORIGEN (*Principia* 3:6) taught, the *image* was something *in* which were all created, and which continued to man after the fall (Gen. 9:6). The *likeness* was something *towards* which man was created, that he might strive after it and attain it. TRENCH thinks God in the double statement (Gen. 1:26), contemplates both man's first creation and his being "*renewed* in knowledge after the image of Him that created Him." **11. Where**—Translate, "Wherein," viz., in the sphere of the renewed man. **neither ... nor ... nor ... nor** —Translate as *Greek,* "There is *no such thing as* Greek *and* Jew (the difference of privilege between those born of the natural seed of Abraham and those not, is abolished), circumcision *and* uncircumcision (the difference of legal standing between the circumcised and uncircumcised is done away, Gal. 6:15)—bondman, freeman." The present Church is one *called out of the flesh,* and the present *world-course* (Eph. 2:2), wherein such distinctions exist, to life in the Spirit, and to the future first resurrection: and this because Satan has such power now over the flesh and the world. At Christ's coming when Satan shall no longer rule the flesh and the world, the nations in the flesh, and the word in millennial felicity, shall be the willing subjects of Christ and His glorified saints (Dan. 7:14, 22, 27; Luke 19:17, 19; Rev. 20:1-6; 3:21). Israel in Canaan was a type of that future state when the Jews, so miraculously preserved distinct now in their dispersion, shall be the central Church of the Christianized world. As expressly as Scripture abolishes the distinction of Jew and Greek now as to religious privileges, so does it expressly foretell that in the coming new order of things, Israel shall be first of the Christian nations, not for her own selfish aggrandizement, but for their good, as the medium of blessing to them. Finally, after the millennium, the life that is in Christ becomes the power which transfigures *nature,* in the time of the new heaven and the new earth; as, before, it first transfigured the spiritual, then the political and social world. **Scythian**—heretofore regarded as more barbarian than the barbarians. Though the relation of bond and free actually existed, yet in relation to Christ, all alike were free in one aspect, and servants of Christ in another (I Cor. 7:22; Gal. 3:28). **Christ is all**—Christ absorbs in Himself all distinctions, being to all alike, everything that they need for justification, sanctification, and glorification (I Cor. 1:30; 3:21-23; Gal. 2:20). **in all** —who believe and are renewed, without distinction of person; the sole distinction now is, how much each draws from Christ. The unity of the divine life shared in by all believers, counterbalances all differences, even as great as that between the polished "Greek" and the rude "Scythian." Christianity imparts to the most uncivilized the only spring of sound, social and moral culture. **12. the elect of God**—There is no "the" in the *Greek,* "God's elect" (cf. Rom. 8:3; I Thess. 1:4). The order of the words "elect, holy, beloved," answers to the order of the things. *Election* from eternity precedes *sanctification* in time; the *sanctified,* feeling God's *love,* imitate it [BENGEL]. **bowels of mercies**—Some of the oldest MSS. read singular, "mercy." *Bowels* express the yearning compassion, which has its seat in the heart, and which we feel to act on our inward parts (Gen. 43:30; Jer. 31:20; Luke 1:78, *Margin*). **humbleness of mind**—True "lowliness of mind"; not the mock "humility" of the false teachers (ch. 2:23; Eph. 4:2, 32). **13. Forbearing**—as to present offenses. **forgiving**—as to past offenses. **quarrel**—rather as *Greek,* "cause of blame," "cause of complaint." **Christ**—who had so infinitely greater cause of complaint against us. The oldest MSS. and *Vulgate* read "the Lord." *English Version* is supported by one very old MS. and old versions. It seems to, have crept in from Ephesians 4:32. **14. above**—rather "over," as in Ephesians 6:16. Charity, which is the crowning grace, covering the multitude of others' sins (I Pet. 4:8), must *overlie* all the other graces enumerated. **which is**—i.e., *"for it is"*; lit., *"which thing is."* **bond of perfectness**—an upper garment which *completes* and keeps together the rest, which, without it, would be loose and disconnected. Seeming graces, where love is wanting, are mere hypocrisy. Justification by faith is assumed as already having taken place in those whom Paul addresses, vs. 12, "elect of God, holy . . . beloved," and ch. 2:12; so that there is no plea here for Rome's view of justification by works. Love and its works *"perfect,"* i.e., manifest the full maturity of faith developed (Matt. 5:44, 48). Love . . . be ye *perfect* . . . (Jas. 2:21, 22; I John 2:5). "If we love one another, God's love is *perfected* in us" (Rom. 13:8; I Cor. 13; I Tim. 1:5; I John 4:12). As to "bond," cf. ch. 2:2, *"knit together* in love" (Eph. 4:3), "keep the unity of the Spirit in the bond of peace." **15. peace of God**—The oldest MSS. and versions read, "The peace of CHRIST" (cf. Phil. 4:7). "The peace of GOD." Therefore Christ is God. Peace was His legacy to His disciples before He left them (John 14:27), "MY peace I give unto you." Peace is peculiarly His to give. Peace follows *love* (vs. 14; Eph. 4:2, 3). **rule**—lit., "sit as umpire"; the same *Greek* verb simple, as appears compounded (ch. 2:18). The false teacher, as a self-constituted *umpire,* defrauds you of your prize; but if the peace of Christ be your umpire ruling in your hearts, your reward is sure. "Let the peace of Christ act as umpire when anger, envy, and such passions arise; and restrain them." Let not those passions give the award, so that you should be swayed by them, but let Christ's peace be the decider of everything. **in your hearts**—Many wear a peaceful countenance and speak peace with the mouth, while war is *in their hearts* (Ps. 28:3; 55:21). **to the which**—i.e., with a view to which state of Christian peace (Isa. 26:3); I Cor. 7:15, "God hath called us to peace." **ye are called**—*Greek,* "ye were also called." The "also" implies that besides Paul's exhortation, they have *also* as a motive to "peace," their having been once for all called. **in one body**—(Eph. 4:4). The unity of the body is a strong argument for "peace" among the members. **be ye thankful**—for your "calling." Not to have "peace ruling in your hearts" would be inconsistent with the "calling in one body," and would be practical unthankfulness to God who called us (Eph. 5:4, 19, 20). **16.** The form which "thankfulness" (vs. 15) ought to take. **Let the word of Christ**—the Gospel *word* by which ye have been called. **richly**—(ch. 2:2; Rom. 15:14)—**in all wisdom** —ALFORD joins this clause with "teaching. . . ." not with "dwell in you," as *English Version,* for so we find in ch. 1:28, "teaching in all wisdom," and the two clauses will thus correspond, "In all wisdom teaching," and "in grace singing in your hearts" (so the *Greek* order). **and . . . and**—The oldest MSS. read "psalms, hymns, spiritual songs" (*Note,* Eph. 5:19). At the *Agapæ* or love-feasts, and in their family circles, they were to be so full of the Word of Christ *in the heart* that the mouth should give it utterance in hymns of instruction, admonition, and praise (cf. Deut. 6:7). TERTULLIAN, *Apology,* 39, records that at the love-feasts, after the water had been furnished for the hands and the lights been

lit, according as any had the power, whether by his remembrance of Scripture, or by his powers of composition, he used to be invited to sing praises to God for the common good. Paul contrasts (as in Eph. 5:18, 19) the songs of Christians at their social meetings, with the bacchanalian and licentious songs of heathen feasts. Singing usually formed part of the entertainment at Greek banquets (cf. Jas. 5:13). **with grace**—*Greek,* "IN grace," the element in which your singing is to be: *"the* grace" of the indwelling Holy Spirit. This clause expresses the seat and source of true psalmody, whether in private or public, viz., the *heart* as well as the voice; singing (cf. vs. 15, "peace . . . rule *in your hearts"),* the psalm of love and praise being in the heart before it finds vent by the lips, and even when it is not actually expressed by the voice, as in closet-worship. The *Greek* order forbids *English Version,* "with grace in your hearts"; rather, "singing in your hearts." **to the Lord**—The oldest MSS. read, "to God." **17.** Lit., "And everything whatsoever we do . . . do all . . ."; this includes *words* as well as *deeds.* **in the name of the Lord Jesus**—*as disciples called by His name as His,* seeking His guidance and help, and desiring to act so as to gain His approval (Rom. 14:8; I Cor. 10:31; II Cor. 5:15; I Pet. 4:11). Cf. "in the Lord," vss. 18, and 11, "Christ is *all."* **God and the Father**—The oldest MSS. omit "and," which seems to have crept in from Ephesians 5:20. **by him**—*Greek,* "through Him" as the channel of His grace to us, and of our thanksgiving to Him (John 14:6, end). **18. unto your own husbands**—The oldest MSS. omit "own," which crept in from Ephesians 5:22. **as it is fit in the Lord**—*Greek, "was* fit," implying that there was at Colosse some degree of failure in fulfilling this duty, "as it was your duty to have done as disciples of the Lord." **19.** (Eph. 5:22-33.) **be not bitter**—ill-tempered and provoking. Many who are polite abroad, are rude and bitter at home because they are not afraid to be so there. **20.** (Eph. 6:1.) **unto the Lord**—The oldest MSS. read, "IN the Lord," i.e., this is acceptable to God when it is done *in the Lord,* viz., from the principle of faith,and as disciples in union with the Lord. **21.** (Eph. 6:4.) It is a different *Greek* verb, therefore translate here, *"irritate* not." By perpetual fault-finding "children" are "discouraged" or "disheartened." A broken-down spirit is fatal to youth [BENGEL]. **22.** (Eph. 6:5, 6.) This is to fear God, when, though none sees us, we do no *evil:* but if we do evil, it is not God, but men, whom we fear. **singleness**—*"simplicity* of *heart."* **fearing God**—The oldest MSS. read, "the Lord." **23. And** —omitted in the oldest MSS. (cf. Eph. 6:7, 8). Cf. the same principle in the case of all men, Hezekiah (II Chron. 31:21; Rom. 12:11). **do, do it**—two distinct *Greek* verbs, "Whatsoever ye *do, work at* it" (or *labor at* it). **heartily**—not from servile constraint, but with hearty good will. **24. the reward of the inheritance**—"Knowing that it is from the Lord (the ultimate source of reward), ye shall receive the compensation (or recompense, which will make ample amends for your having no earthly possession, as slaves now) consisting of the inheritance" (a term excluding the notion of meriting it by *works:* it is all of grace, Rom. 4:14; Gal. 3:18). **for ye serve**—The oldest MSS. omit "for," then translate as *Vulgate,* "Serve ye the Lord Christ;" cf. vs. 23, "To the Lord and not unto men" (I Cor. 7:22, 23). **25. But**—The oldest MSS. read, "for," which accords with "serve ye . . ." (vs. 24), the oldest reading: the *for* here gives a motive for obeying the precept. He addresses the slaves: Serve ye the

Lord Christ, and leave your wrongs in His hands to put to rights: (translate), "For he that doeth wrong shall receive *back the wrong* which he hath done (by just retribution in kind), and there is no respect of persons" with the Great Judge in the day of the Lord. He favors the master no more than the slave (Rev. 6:15).

CHAPTER 4

Vss. 1-18. Exhortations Continued. To Prayer: Wisdom in Relation to the Unconverted: As to the Bearers of the Epistle, Tychicus and Onesimus: Closing Salutations. **1.** give—*Greek* "render": lit., "afford." **equal**—i.e., as the slaves owe their duties to you, so you *equally* owe to them your duties as masters. Cf. "ye masters do the *same* things" (*Note,* Eph. 6:9). Alford translates, "fairness," "equity," which gives a large and liberal interpretation of justice in common matters (Philemon 16). **knowing**—(Ch. 3:24). **ye also**—as well as they. **2. Continue**—*Greek,* "Continue perseveringly," "persevere" (Eph. 6:18), "watching *thereunto*"; here, "watch *in the same,*" or "*in it,*" i.e., in prayer: watching against the indolence as to prayer, and in prayer, of our corrupt wills. **with thanksgiving**—for everything, whether joyful, or sorrowful, mercies temporal and spiritual, national, family, and individual (I Cor. 14:17; Phil. 4:6; I Thess. 5:18). **3. for us**—myself and Timothy (ch. 1:1). **a door of utterance**—Translate, "a door for the word." Not as in Ephesians 6:19, where power of "utterance" is his petition. Here it is an opportunity for *preaching the word,* which would be best afforded by his release from prison (I Cor. 16:9; II Cor. 2:12; Philemon 22; Rev. 3:8). **to speak**—so that we may speak. **the mystery of Christ**—(Ch. 1:27). **for which ... also**—*on account of which I am* (not only "an ambassador," Eph. 6: 20, but) also in *bonds.* **4.** Alford thinks that Paul asks their prayers for his release as if it were the *only* way by which he could "make it (the Gospel) manifest" as he ought. But while this is *included* in their subject of prayer, Philippians 1:12, 13, written somewhat later in his imprisonment, clearly shows that "a door for the word" could be opened, and was opened, for its *manifestation,* even while he remained imprisoned (cf. II Tim. 2:9). **5.** (*Notes,* Eph. 5:15, 16.) **in wisdom**—practical Christian prudence. **them ... without**—Those not in the Christian brotherhood (I Cor. 5:12; I Thess. 4:12). The brethren, through love, will make allowances for an indiscreet act or word of a brother; the world will make none. Therefore be the more on your guard in your intercourse with the latter, lest you be a stumbling block to their conversion. **redeeming the time**—The *Greek* expresses, buying up for yourselves, and *buying off* from worldly vanities the *opportunity,* whenever it is afforded you, of good to yourselves and others. "*Forestall the opportunity,* i.e., to buy up an article out of the market, so as to make the largest profit from it" [Conybeare and Howson]. **6. with grace**—*Greek,* "in grace" as its element (ch. 3:16; Eph. 4:29). Contrast the case of those "of the world" who "therefore *speak of the world*" (I John 4:5). Even the smallest leaf of the believer should be full of the sap of the Holy Spirit (Jer. 17:7, 8). His conversation should be cheerful without levity, serious without gloom. Cf. Luke 4:22; John 7:46, as to Jesus' speech. **seasoned with salt**—i.e., the *savor*

of fresh and lively spiritual wisdom and earnestness, excluding all "corrupt communication," and also tasteless *insipidity* (Matt. 5:13; Mark 9:50; Eph. 4: 29). Cf. all the sacrifices *seasoned with salt* (Lev. 2:13). Not far from Colosse, in Phrygia, there was a salt lake, which gives to the image here the more appropriateness. **how ye ought to answer every man**—(I Pet. 3:15). **7. Tychicus**—(*Note,* Eph. 6:2). **who is a beloved brother**—rather, "the beloved brother"; the article "the" marks him as *well known to them.* **8. for the same purpose**—*Greek,* "for this very purpose." **that he might know your estate**—Translate, "that he may know your state": answering to vs. 7. So one very old MS. and *Vulgate* read. But the oldest MSS. and the old Latin versions, "that ye may know our state." However, the latter reading seems likely to have crept in from Ephesians 6:22. Paul was the more anxious to know the state of the Colossians, on account of the seductions to which they were exposed from false teachers; owing to which he had "great conflict for" them (ch. 2:1). **comfort your hearts**—distressed as ye are by my imprisonment, as well as by your own trials. **9. Onesimus**—the slave mentioned in the Epistle to Philemon 10, 16, "a brother beloved." **a faithful ... brother**—rather, "the faithful brother," he being known to the Colossians as the slave of Philemon, their fellow townsman and fellow Christian. **one of you**—belonging to your city. **They shall make known unto you all things**—*Greek,* "all the things here." This substantial repetition of "all my state shall Tychicus declare unto you," strongly favors the reading of *English Version* in vs. 8, "that *he* might (may) know your state," as it is unlikely the same thing should be stated *thrice.* **10. Aristarchus**—a Macedonian of Thessalonica (Acts 27:2), who was dragged into the theater at Ephesus, during the tumult with Gaius, they being "Paul's companions in travel." He accompanied Paul to Asia (Acts 20:4), and subsequently (Acts 27:2) to Rome. He was now at Rome with Paul (cf. Philemon 23: 24). As he is here spoken of as Paul's "fellow prisoner," but in Philemon 24 as Paul's "fellow laborer"; and vice versa, Epaphras in Philemon 23, as his "fellow prisoner," but here (ch. 1:7) "fellow servant," Meyer in Alford, conjectures that Paul's friends voluntarily shared his imprisonment by turns, Aristarchus being his fellow prisoner when he wrote to the Colossians, Epaphras when he wrote to Philemon. The *Greek* for "fellow prisoner" is literally, *fellow captive,* an image from prisoners taken in warfare, Christians being "fellow soldiers" (Phil. 2:25; Philemon 2), whose warfare is "the good fight of faith." **Mark**—John Mark (Acts 12: 12, 25); the Evangelist according to tradition. **sister's son**—rather, "cousin," or "kinsman to Barnabas"; the latter being the better known is introduced to designate Mark. The relationship naturally accounts for Barnabas' selection of Mark as his companion when otherwise qualified; and also for Mark's mother's house at Jerusalem being the place of resort of Christians there (Acts 12:12). The family belonged to *Cyprus* (Acts 4:36); this accounts for Barnabas' choice of Cyprus as the first station on their journey (Acts 13:4), and for Mark's accompanying them readily so far, it being the country of his family; and for Paul's rejecting him at the second journey for not having gone further than Perga, in Pamphylia, but having gone thence home to his mother at Jerusalem (Matt. 10:37) on the first journey (Acts 13:13). **touching whom**—viz., Mark. **ye received commandments**—possibly *before* the writing of this Epistle; or the "commandments" were *verbal* by Tychicus, and *accompanying this letter*, since the *past* tense was used by the ancients (where we use the present) in relation to the time which it would be when the letter was read by the Colossians. Thus (Philemon 19), "I have written," for "I write." The substance of them was, "If he come unto you, receive him." Paul's rejection of him on his second missionary journey, because he had turned back at Perga on the first journey (Acts 13:13; 15:37-39), had caused an alienation between himself and Barnabas. Christian love soon healed the breach; for here he implies his restored confidence in Mark, makes honorable allusion to Barnabas, and desires that those at Colosse who had regarded Mark in consequence of that past error with suspicion, should now "receive" him with kindness. Colosse is only about 110 miles from Perga, and less than 20 from the confines of Pisidia, through which province Paul and Barnabas preached on their return during the same journey. Hence, though Paul had not personally visited the Colossian Church, they knew of the past unfaithfulness of Mark; and needed this recommendation of him, after the temporary cloud on him, so as to receive him, now that he was about to visit them as an evangelist. Again, in Paul's last imprisonment, he, for the last time, speaks of Mark (II Tim. 4:11). **11. Justus**—i.e., *righteous; a* common name among the Jews; *Hebrew, tzadik* (Acts 1:23). **of the circumcision**—This implies that Epaphras, Luke, and Demas (vss. 12, 14) were *not* of the circumcision. This agrees with Luke's Gentile name (the same as Lucanus), and the Gentile aspect of his Gospel. **These only ...**—viz., of the Jews. For the Jewish teachers were generally opposed to the apostle of the Gentiles (Phil. 1:15). Epaphras, etc., were also fellow laborers, but Gentiles. **unto**—i.e., in promoting the Gospel kingdom. **which have been**—*Greek,* "which have been *made,*" or "have become," i.e., *inasmuch as* they have become a comfort to me. The *Greek* implies *comfort* in forensic dangers; a different *Greek* word expresses comfort in domestic affliction [BENGEL]. **12. Christ**—The oldest MSS. add "Jesus." **labouring fervently**—As the *Greek,* is the same, translate, "striving earnestly" (*Note,* ch. 1: 29; 2:1), lit., *striving as in the agony of a contest.* **in prayers**—Translate as *Greek,* "in *his* prayers." **complete**—The oldest MSS. read, "fully assured." It is translated, "fully persuaded," Rom. 4:21; 14:5. In the expression "perfect," he refers to what he has already said, ch. 1:28; 2:2; 3:14. "Perfect" implies the attainment of the *full maturity* of a Christian. BENGEL joins "in all the will of God" with "stand." **13. a great zeal**—The oldest MSS. and *Vulgate* have "much *labor.*" **for you**—lest you should be seduced (ch. 2:4); a motive why you should be anxious for yourselves. **them that are in Laodicea ... Hierapolis**—churches probably founded by Epaphras, as the Church in Colosse was. Laodicea, called from Laodice, queen of Antiochus II, on the river Lycus, was, according to the subscription to I Timothy, "the chiefest city of Phrygia Pacatiana." All the three cities were destroyed by an earthquake in A.D. 62 [TACITUS, *Annals,* 14. 27] Hierapolis was six Roman miles north of Laodicea. **14.** It is conjectured that Luke "the beloved physician" (the same as the Evangelist), may have first become connected with Paul professionally attending on him in the sickness under which he labored in Phrygia and Galatia (in which latter place he was detained by sickness), in the early part of that journey wherein Luke first is found in his company (Acts

16:10; cf. *Note,* Gal. 4:13). Thus the allusion to his medical profession is appropriate in writing to men of Phrygia. Luke ministered to Paul in his last imprisonment (II Tim. 4:11). **Demas**—included among his "fellow laborers" (Philemon 24), but afterwards a deserter from him through love of this world (II Tim. 4:10). He alone has here no honorable or descriptive epithet attached to his name. Perhaps, already, his real character was betraying itself. **15. Nymphas**—of Laodicea. **church ... in his house**—So old MSS. and *Vulgate* read. The oldest read, "THEIR house"; and one MS., "HER house," which makes Nymphas a woman. **16. the epistle from Laodicea**—viz., the Epistle which I wrote to the Laodiceans, and which you will get *from* them on applying to them. Not the Epistle to the Ephesians. See INTRODUCTIONS to the Epistles to the Ephesians and Colossians. The Epistles from the apostles were publicly read in the church assemblies. IGNATIUS, ad *Ephesum* 12; POLYCARP, *ad Philippenses,* 3. 11, 12; CLEMENT, *ad Corinthios* 1. 47; I Thessalonians 5:27; Revelation 1:3, "Blessed is *he* that *readeth,* and *they that hear.*" Thus, they and the Gospels were put on a level with the Old Testament, which was similarly read (Deut. 31:11). The Holy Spirit inspired Paul to write, besides those extant, other Epistles which He saw necessary for *that* day, and for particular churches; and which were not so for the Church of all ages and places. It is possible that as the Epistle to the Colossians was to be read for the edification of other churches besides that of Colosse; so the Epistle to the Ephesians was to be read in various churches besides Ephesus, and that Laodicea was the last of such churches before Colosse, whence he might designate the Epistle to the Ephesians here as "the Epistle *from* Laodicea." But it is equally possible that the Epistle meant was one to the Laodiceans themselves. **17. say to Archippus**—*The Colossians* (not merely the clergy, but the laymen) are directed, "Speak ye to Archippus." This proves that Scripture belongs to the laity as well as the clergy; and that laymen may profitably admonish the clergy in particular cases when they do so in meekness. BENGEL suggests that Archippus was perhaps prevented from going to the Church assembly by weak health or age. The word, "fulfil," accords with his ministry being near its close (ch. 1:25; cf. Philemon 2). However, "fulfil" may mean, as in II Timothy 4:5, "*make full proof* of thy ministry." "Give all diligence to follow it out fully"; a monition perhaps needed by Archippus. **in the Lord**—The element in which every work of the Christian, and especially the Christian minister, is to be done (vs. 7; I Cor. 7:39; Phil. 4:2). **18.** Paul's autograph salutation (so I Cor. 16:21; II Thess. 3:17), attesting that the preceding letter, though written by an amanuensis, is from himself. **Remember my bonds**—Already in this chapter he had mentioned his "bonds" (vs. 3), and again vs. 10, an incentive why they should love and pray (vs. 3) for him; and still more, that they should, in reverential obedience to his monitions in this Epistle, shrink from the false teaching herein stigmatized, remembering what a conflict (ch. 2:1) he had in their behalf amidst his *bonds.* "When we read of his chains, we should not forget that they moved over the paper as he wrote; his [right] hand was chained to the [left hand of the] soldier who kept him" [ALFORD]. **Grace be with you**—*Greek,* "THE grace" which every Christian enjoys in some degree, and which flows from God in Christ by the Holy Ghost (Titus 3:15; Heb. 13:25)

THE FIRST EPISTLE OF PAUL THE APOSTLE TO THE

THESSALONIANS

INTRODUCTION

The AUTHENTICITY of this Epistle is attested by IRENÆUS, *Adversus Hæreses*, 5. 6, 1, quoting ch. 5:23; CLEMENT OF ALEXANDRIA, *Pædagogus*, 1. 88, quoting ch. 2:7; TERTULLIAN, *De Resurrectione carnis*, sec. 24, quoting ch. 5:1; CAIUS in EUSEBIUS' *Ecclesiastical History*, 6. 20; ORIGEN, *Contra Celsus*, 3.

The OBJECT OF THE EPISTLE.—Thessalonica was at this time capital of the Roman second district of Macedonia (LIVY, 45. 29). It lay on the bay of Therme, and has always been, and still is, under its modern name Saloniki, a place of considerable commerce. After his imprisonment and scourging at Philippi, Paul (ch. 2:2) passed on to Thessalonica; and in company with Silas (Acts 17:1–9) and Timotheus (Acts 16:3; 17:14, cf. with ch. 1:1; 3:1–6; II Thess. 1:1) founded the Church there. The Jews, as a body, rejected the Gospel when preached for three successive sabbaths (Acts 17:2); but some few "believed and consorted with Paul and Silas, and of the devout (i.e., proselytes to Judaism) Greeks a great multitude, and of the chief women not a few." The believers received the word joyfully, notwithstanding trials and persecutions (ch. 1:6; 2:13) from their own countrymen and from the Jews (ch. 2:14–16). His stay at Thessalonica was doubtless not limited to the three weeks in which were the three sabbaths specified in Acts 17:2; for his laboring there with his hands for his support (ch. 2:9; II Thess. 3:8), his receiving supplies there more than once from Philippi (Phil. 4:16), his making many converts from the Gentiles (ch. 1:9; and as two oldest MSS. read, Acts 17:4, "of the devout *and* of the Greeks a great multitude," Acts 17:4), and his appointing ministers,—all imply a longer residence. Probably as at Pisidian Antioch (Acts 13:46), at Corinth (Acts 18:6, 7), and at Ephesus (Acts 19:8, 9), having preached the Gospel to the Jews, when they rejected it, he turned to the Gentiles. He probably thenceforth held the Christian meetings in the house of Jason (Acts 17:5), perhaps "the kinsman" of Paul mentioned in Romans 16:21. His great subject of teaching to them seems to have been the coming and kingdom of Christ, as we may infer from ch. 1:10; 2:12, 19; 3:13; 4:13–18; 5:1–11, 23, 24; and that they should walk worthy of it (ch. 2:12; 4:1). And it is an undesigned coincidence between the two Epistles and Acts 17:5, 9, that the very charge which the assailants of Jason's house brought against him and other brethren was, "These do contrary to the decrees of Cæsar, saying that there is another *king*, one Jesus." As in the case of the Lord Jesus Himself (John 18:33–37; 19:12; cf. Matt. 26:64), they perverted the doctrine of the coming kingdom of Christ into a ground for the charge of treason against Cæsar. The result was, Paul and Silas were obliged to flee under the cover of night to Berea; Timothy had probably preceded him (Acts 17:10, 14). But the Church had been planted, and ministers appointed; nay, more, they virtually became missionaries themselve· for which they possessed facilities in the extensive commerce of their city, and both by word and example were extending the Gospel in Macedonia, Achaia, and elsewhere (ch. 1:7, 8). From Berea, also. Paul, after having planted a Scripture-loving Church, was obliged to flee by the Thessalonian Jews who followed him thither. Timothy (who seems to have come to Berea separately from Paul and Silas, cf. Acts 17:10, with 14) and Silas remained there still, when Paul proceeded by sea to Athens. While there he more than once longed to visit the Thessalonians again, and see personally their spiritual state, and "perfect that which was lacking in their faith" (ch. 3:10); but "Satan (probably using the Thessalonian Jews as his instruments, John 13:27) hindered" him (ch. 2:18; cf. Acts 17:13). He therefore sent Timotheus, who seems to have followed him to Athens from Berea (Acts 17:15), immediately on his arrival to Thessalonica (ch. 3:1); glad as he would have been of Timothy's help in the midst of the cavils of Athenian opponents, he felt he must forego that help for the sake of the Thessalonian Church. Silas does not seem to have come to Paul *at Athens* at all, though Paul had desired him and Timothy to "come to him with all speed" (Acts 17:15); but seems with Timothy (who came from Thessalonica called for him at Berea) to have joined Paul *at Corinth* first; cf. Acts 18:1, 5, "When Silas and Timothy were come from *Macedonia*." The Epistle makes no mention of Silas *at Athens*, as it does of Timothy (ch. 3:1).

Timothy's account of the Thessalonian Church was highly favorable. They abounded in faith and charity and reciprocated his desire to see them (ch. 3:6–10). Still, as nothing human on earth is perfect, there were some defects. Some had too exclusively dwelt on the doctrine of Christ's coming kingdom, so as to neglect the sober-minded discharge of present duties (ch. 4:11, 12). Some who had lost relatives by death, needed comfort and instruction in their doubts as to whether they who died before Christ's coming would have a share with those found alive in His kingdom then to be revealed. Moreover, also, there had been committed among them sins against chastity and sobriety (ch. 5:5–7), as also against charity (ch. 4:3–10; 5:13, 15). There were, too, symptoms in some of want of respectful love and subordination to their ministers; others treated slightingly the manifestations of the Spirit in those possessing His gifts (ch. 5:19). To give spiritual admonition on these subjects, and at the same time commend what deserved commendation, and to testify his love to them, was the object of the Epistle.

The PLACE OF WRITING IT was doubtless Corinth, where Timothy and Silas rejoined him (Acts 18:5) soon after he arrived there (cf. ch. 2:17) in the autumn of A.D. 52.

The TIME OF WRITING was evidently immediately after having received from Timothy the tidings of their state (ch. 3:6) in the winter of A.D. 52, or early in 53. For it was written not long after the conversion of the Thessalonians (ch. 1:8, 9), while Paul could speak of himself as only *taken from them for a short season* (ch. 2:17). Thus this Epistle was *first in date of all Paul's extant Epistles*. The Epistle is written in the joint names of Paul,

1329

Silas, and Timothy, the three founders of the Thessalonian Church. The plural first person "we," is used everywhere, except in ch. 2:18; 3:5; 5:27. "We" is the true reading, ch. 4:13. The *English Version* "I," in ch. 4:9; 5:1, 23, is not supported by the original [EDMUNDS].

The STYLE is calm and equable, in accordance with the subject matter, which deals only with Christian duties in general, taking for granted the great doctrinal truths which were not as yet disputed. There was no deadly error as yet to call forth his more vehement bursts of feeling and impassioned argument. The earlier Epistles, as we should expect, are moral and practical. It was not until Judaistic and legalizing errors arose at a later period that he wrote those Epistles (e.g., Romans and Galatians) which unfold the cardinal doctrines of grace and justification by faith. Still, later the Epistles from his Roman prison confirm the same truths. And last of all, the Pastoral Epistles are suited to the more developed ecclesiastical constitution of the Church, and give directions as to bishops and deacons, and correct abuses and errors of later growth.

The prevalence of the Gentile element in this Church is shown by the fact that these two Epistles are among the very few of Paul's writings in which no quotation occurs from the Old Testament.

CHAPTER 1

Vss. 1-10. ADDRESS: SALUTATION: HIS PRAYER-FUL THANKSGIVING FOR THEIR FAITH, HOPE, AND LOVE. THEIR FIRST RECEPTION OF THE GOSPEL, AND THEIR GOOD INFLUENCE ON ALL AROUND. **1. Paul**—He does not add "an apostle," because in their case, as in that of the Philippians (*Note*, Philippians 1:1), his apostolic authority needs not any substantiation. He writes familiarly as to faithful friends, not but that his apostleship was recognized among them (ch. 2:6). On the other hand, in writing to the Galatians, among whom some had called in question his apostleship, he strongly asserts it in the superscription. An undesigned propriety in the Epistles, evincing genuineness. **Silvanus**—a "chief man among the brethren" (Acts 15:22), and a "prophet" (vs. 32), and one of the deputies who carried the decree of the Jerusalem council to Antioch. His age and position cause him to be placed before "Timothy," then a youth (Acts 16:1; I Timothy 4:12). Silvanus (the Gentile expanded form of "Silas") is called in I Pet. 5:12, "a faithful brother" (cf. II Cor. 1:19). They both aided in planting the Thessalonian Church, and are therefore included in the address. This, the first of Paul's Epistles, as being written before various evils crept into the churches, is without the censures found in other Epistles. So realizing was their Christian faith, that they were able hourly to look for the Lord Jesus. **unto the church**—not merely as in the Epistles to Romans, Ephesians, Colossians, Philippians, "to the saints," or "the faithful at Thessalonica." Though as yet they do not seem to have had the *final* Church organization under *permanent* "bishops" and deacons, which appears in the later Epistles (*Note*, Phil. 1:1; and II Timothy). Yet he designates them by the honorable term "Church," implying their status as not merely isolated believers, but a corporate body with spiritual rulers (ch. 5:12; II Cor. 1:1; Gal. 1:2). **in**—implying *vital union*. **God the Father**—This marks that they were no longer *heathen*. **the Lord Jesus Christ**—This marks that they were not *Jews*, but Christians. **Grace be unto you, and peace**—that ye may have in God that *favor* and *peace* which men withhold [ANSELM]. This is the salutation in all the Epistles of Paul, except the three pastoral ones, which have "grace, mercy, and peace." Some of the oldest MSS. support, others omit the clause following, "from God our Father and the Lord Jesus Christ." It may have crept in from I Corinthians 1:3; II Corinthians 1:2. **2.** (Rom. 1:9; II Tim. 1:3.) The structure of the sentences in this and the following verses, each successive sentence repeating with greater fulness the preceding, characteristically marks Paul's abounding love and thankfulness in

respect to his converts, as if he were seeking by words heaped on words to convey some idea of his exuberant feelings towards them. **We**—I, Silvanus, and Timotheus. Romans 1:9 supports ALFORD in translating, "making mention of you in our prayers without ceasing" (vs. 3). Thus, "without ceasing," in the second clause, answers in parallelism to "always," in the first. **3. work of faith**—*the working reality of your faith*; its alacrity in *receiving* the truth, and in *evincing* itself by its fruits. Not an otiose assent; but a *realizing, working faith*; not "in word only," but in *one* continuous chain of "work" (singular, not plural, *works*), vss. 5-10; James 2:22. So "the work of faith" in I Thessalonians 1:11 implies its *perfect development* (cf. Jas. 1:4). The other governing substantives similarly mark respectively the characteristic manifestation of the grace which follows each in the genitive. *Faith, love,* and *hope,* are the three great Christian graces (ch. 5:8; I Cor. 13:13). **labour of love**—The *Greek* implies *toil,* or *troublesome labor,* which we are stimulated by love to bear (ch. 2:9); Rev. 2:2). For instances of self-denying *labors of love,* see Acts 20:35; Romans 16:12. Not here *ministerial* labors. Those who shun trouble for others, *love* little (cf. Heb. 6:10). **patience**—Translate, "*endurance* of hope"; the *persevering endurance* of trials which flows from "hope." Romans 15:4 shows that "patience" also nourishes "hope." **hope in our Lord Jesus**—lit., "hope of our Lord Jesus," viz., of His coming (vs. 10): a hope that looked forward beyond all present things for the manifestation of Christ. **in the sight of God**—Your "faith, hope, and love" were not merely such as would pass for genuine *before men,* but "in the sight of God," the Searcher of hearts [GOMARUS]. Things are really what they are before God. BENGEL takes this clause with "remembering." Whenever we *pray,* we *remember before God* your faith, hope, and love. But its separation from "remembering" in the order, and its connection with "your . . . faith . . ." make me to prefer the former view. **and . . .**—The *Greek* implies, "in the sight of *Him who is* [at once] God and our Father." **4. Knowing**—Forasmuch as we know. **your election of God**—The *Greek* is rather, "beloved by God"; so Romans 1:7; II Thessalonians 2:13. "Your election" means that *God has elected you* as individual believers to eternal life (Rom. 11:5, 7; Col. 3:12; II Thess. 2:13). **5. our gospel**—viz., the Gospel which we preached. **came**—*Greek,* "was made," viz., by God, its Author and Sender. God's having made our preaching among you to be attended with such "power," is the proof that you are "elect of God" (vs. 4). **in power**—in the efficacy of the Holy Spirit clothing us with power (see end of verse; Acts 1:8; 4:33; 6:5, 8) in preaching the Gospel, and making it in you the power of God unto salvation (Rom. 1:16). As "power" produces *faith;* so "the Holy Ghost," *love;* and "much assurance" (Col. 2:2, *full persuasion*), *hope* (Heb. 6: 11), resting on faith (Heb. 10:22). So *faith, love,* and *hope* (vs. 3). **as ye know**—answering to the "knowing," i.e., *as* WE *know* (vs. 4) your character as *the elect of God,* so YE *know* ours as *preachers.* **for your sake**—The purpose herein indicated is not so much that of the apostles, as that of *God.* "You know what *God enabled us to be ... how mighty in preaching the word ...* for your sakes ... thereby proving that He had *chosen* (vs. 4) you for His own" [ALFORD]. I think, from ch. 2:10-12, that, in "what manner of men we were among you," besides the *power in preaching,* there is included also Paul's and his fellow missionaries' whole *conduct* which confirmed their preaching; and in this sense, the "for your sake" will mean "in order to win you." This, though not the sole, yet would be a strong, motive to holy circumspection, viz., so as to win those without (Col. 4:5; cf. I Cor. 9:19-23). **6. And ye**—answering to *"For our* Gospel," vs. 5. **followers**—*Greek,* "imitators." The Thessalonians in their turn became "ensamples" (vs. 7) for others to *imitate.* **of the Lord**—who was the apostle of the Father, and taught the word, which He brought from heaven, under adversities [BENGEL]. This was the point in which they imitated Him and His apostles, *joyful* witness for *the word in much affliction:* the second proof of their *election of God* (vs. 4); vs. 5 is the first (see *Note,* vs. 5). **received the word in much affliction**—(ch. 2:14; 3:2-5; Acts 17:5-10). **joy of**—i.e., *wrought* by "the Holy Ghost." "The oil of gladness" wherewith the Son of God was "anointed above His fellows" (Ps. 45:7), is the same oil with which He, by the Spirit, anoints His fellows too (Isa. 61:1, 3; Rom. 14:17; I John 2:20, 27). **7. ensamples**—So some of the oldest MSS. read. Others, "ensample" (singular), the whole Church being regarded as *one.* The *Macedonian* Church of Philippi was the only one in Europe converted before the Thessalonians. Therefore he means their past conduct is an ensample to all believers now; of whom he specifies those "in Macedonia" because he had been there since the conversion of the Thessalonians, and had left Silvanus and Timotheus there; and those in "Achaia," because he was now at Corinth in Achaia. **8. from you sounded ... the word of the Lord**—not that they actually became missionaries: but they, by the *report* which spread abroad of their "faith" (cf. Rom. 1:8), and by Christian merchants of Thessalonica who travelled in various directions, bearing "the word of the Lord" with them, were *virtually* missionaries, recommending the Gospel to all within reach of their influence by word and by example (vs. 7). In "sounded," the image is that of a trumpet filling with its clear-sounding echo all the surrounding places. **to Godward**—no longer directed to idols. **so that we need not to speak any thing**—to them in praise of your faith; "for (vs. 9) they themselves" (the people in Macedonia, Achaia, and in every place) know it already. **9.** Strictly there should follow, "For they themselves show of you ..."; but, instead, he substitutes that which was the instrumental cause of the Thessalonians' conversion and faith, "for they themselves show of us what manner of entering in we had *unto you";* cf. vs. 5, which corresponds to this former clause, as vs. 6 corresponds to the latter clause. "And how ye turned from idols to serve the living ... God...." Instead of *our* having "to speak any thing" to them (in Macedonia and Achaia) in your praise (vs. 8), "they *themselves* (**have the**

start of us in speaking of you, and) *announce concerning* (so the *Greek* of 'show of' means) us, what manner of (how effectual an) entrance we had unto you" (vs. 5; ch. 2:1). **the living and true God**—as opposed to the *dead* and *false* gods from which they had "turned." In the *English Version* reading, Acts 17:4, "of *the devout Greeks* a great multitude," no mention is made, as here, of the conversion of *idolatrous* Gentiles at Thessalonica; but the reading of some of the oldest MSS. and *Vulgate* singularly coincides with the statement here: "Of the devout AND of Greeks (viz., *idolaters*) a great multitude"; so in vs. 17, "the devout persons," i.e., Gentile proselytes to Judaism, form a separate class. PALEY and LACHMANN, by distinct lines of argument, support the "AND." **10.** This verse distinguishes them from the *Jews,* as vs. 9 from the *idolatrous* Gentiles. To wait for the Lord's coming is a sure characteristic of a true believer, and was prominent amidst the graces of the Thessalonians (I Cor. 1:7, 8). His *coming* is seldom called his *return* (John 14:3); because the two advents are regarded as different phases of the same coming; and the second coming shall have features altogether new connected with it, so that it will not be a mere repetition of the first, or a mere coming *back again.* **his Son ... raised from the dead**—the grand proof of His divine *Sonship* (Rom. 1:4). **delivered**—rather as *Greek,* "who *delivereth us.*" Christ has once for all *redeemed* us; He is *our Deliverer* ALWAYS. **wrath to come**—(ch. 5:9; Col. 3:6).

CHAPTER 2

Vss. 1-20. HIS MANNER OF PREACHING, AND THEIRS OF RECEIVING, THE GOSPEL; HIS DESIRE TO HAVE REVISITED THEM FRUSTRATED BY SATAN. **1. For**—confirming ch. 1:9. He discusses the manner of his fellow missionaries' preaching among them (ch. 1:5, and former part of vs. 9) from vs. 1 to vs. 12; and the Thessalonians' reception of the word (cf. ch. 1:6, 7, and latter part of vs. 9) from vss. 13 to 16. **yourselves**—Not only do strangers report it, but *you* know it to be true [ALFORD] "yourselves." **not in vain**—*Greek,* "not vain," i.e., it was full of "power" (ch. 1:5). The *Greek* for "was," expresses rather "hath been and is," implying the *permanent* and continuing character of his preaching. **2. even after that we had suffered before**—at Philippi (Acts 16): a circumstance which would have deterred mere natural, unspiritual men from further preaching. **shamefully entreated**—ignominiously scourged (Acts 16:22, 23). **bold**—(Acts 4:29; Eph. 6:20). **in our God**—The ground of our boldness in speaking was the realization of God as "OUR God." **with much contention**—i.e., lit., as of *competitors in a contest:* striving earnestness (Col. 1:29; 2:1). But here *outward* conflict with persecutors, rather than *inward* and mental, was what the missionaries had to endure (Acts 17:5, 6; Phil. 1:30). **3. For**—The ground of his "boldness" (vs. 2), his freedom from all "deceit, uncleanness, and guile"; *guile,* before God, *deceit* (*Greek,* "imposture"), towards men (cf. II Cor. 1:12; 2:17 Eph. 4:14); *uncleanness,* in relation to one's self (impure motives of carnal self-gratification in gain, vs. 5), or lust; such as actuated false teachers of the Gentiles (Phil. 1:16; II Pet. 2: 10, 14; Jude 8; Rev. 2:14, 15). So Simon Magus and Cerinthus taught [ESTIUS]. **exhortation**—The *Greek* means "consolation" as well as "exhortation." The same Gospel which exhorts comforts. Its first lesson to each is that of peace in believing amidst outward and inward sorrows. It comforts them that mourn (cf. vs. 11; Isa. 61:2, 3; II Cor. 1:3, 4). **of**—*springing from—having its source in*—deceit, etc. **4. as**—according as; even as. **allowed**—*Greek*, "We have been approved on trial," "deemed fit." This word corresponds to "God which *trieth* our hearts" below. This approval as to sincerity depends solely on the grace and mercy of God (Acts 9:15; I Cor. 7:25; II Cor. 3:5; I Tim. 1:11, 12). **not as pleasing** —not as persons who seek to please men; characteristic of false teachers (Gal. 1:10). **5. used we flattering words**—lit., "become (i.e., have we been found) in (the use of) language of flattery"; the resource of those who try to "please men." **as ye know**—"Ye know" as to whether I *flattered* you; as to "covetousness," GOD, the Judge of the heart, alone can be "my witness." **cloak of**—i.e., any specious guise under which I might cloak "covetousness." **6.** Lit., "Nor of men (have we been found, vs. 5) seeking glory." The "of" here represents a different *Greek* word from "of" in the clause "*of* you . . . *of* others." ALFORD makes the former (*Greek, ex*) express the *abstract ground* of the glory; the latter (*apo*) the *concrete object* from which it was to come. The former means "originating from"; the latter means "on the part of." Many teach heretical novelties, though not for fain, yet for "glory." Paul and his associates were free even from this motive [GROTIUS], (John 5:44). **we might have been burdensome**—i.e., by claiming maintenance (vs. 9; II Cor. 11:9; 12:16; II Thess. 3:8). As, however, "glory" precedes, as well as "covetousness," the reference cannot be *restricted* to the latter, though I think it is not *excluded*. Translate, "when we might have borne heavily upon you," by pressing you *with the weight* of *selfglorifying authority*, and *with the burden* of our *sustenance*. Thus the antithesis is appropriate in the words following, "But we were *gentle* (the opposite of *pressing weightily*) among you" (vs. 7). On *weight* being connected with authority, cf. *Note, II Corinthians* 10:10, "His letters are *weighty*" (I Cor. 4:21). AL-FORD'S translation, which *excludes* reference to his right of claiming *maintenance* ("when we might have stood on our *dignity*"), seems to me disproved by vs. 9, which uses *the same Greek word* unequivocally for "chargeable." Twice he received supplies from Philippi while at Thessalonica (Phil. 4:16). **as the apostles**—i.e., as being apostles. **7. we were** —*Greek*, "we were *made*" by God's grace. **gentle** —*Greek*, "*mild* in bearing with the faults of others" [TITTMANN]; one, too, who is gentle (though firm) in reproving the erroneous opinions of others (II Tim. 2:24). Some of the oldest MSS. read, "we became *little children*" (cf. Matt. 18:3, 4). Others support the *English Version* reading, which forms a better antithesis to vss. 6, 7, and harmonizes better with what follows; for he would hardly, in the same sentence, compare himself both to the "infants" or "little children," and to "a nurse," or rather, "suckling mother." *Gentleness* is the fitting characteristic of *a nurse*. **among you**—*Greek*, "in the midst of you," i.e., in our intercourse with you being *as one of yourselves*. **nurse**—a suckling mother. **her** —*Greek*, "her own children" (cf. vs. 11). So Galatians 4:19. **8. So**—to be joined to "we were willing"; "*As* a nurse cherisheth . . . „so we were willing . . ." [ALFORD]. But BENGEL, "So," i.e., *seeing that we have such affection for you*. **being affectionately destrous**—The oldest reading in the *Greek* implies, lit., *to connect one's self with another;* to be closely *attached* to another. **willing**—The *Greek* is stronger, "we were *well content*"; "we would *gladly* have

imparted. . . ." "even our own *lives*" (so the *Greek* for "souls" ought to be translated); as we showed in the sufferings we endured in giving you the Gospel (Acts 17). As a nursing mother is ready to impart not only her milk to them, but her life for them, so we not only imparted gladly the spiritual milk of the word to you, but risked our own lives for your spiritual nourishment, imitating Him who laid down His life for His friends, the greatest proof of love (John 15:13). **ye were**—*Greek*, "ye were become," as having become our spiritual children. **dear**—*Greek*, "dearly beloved." **9. labour and travail**—The *Greek* for "labor" means *hardship in bearing;* that for "travail," *hardship in doing;* the former, toil with the utmost solicitude; the latter, the being wearied with fatigue [GROTIUS]. ZANCHIUS refers the former to *spiritual* (see ch. 3:5), the latter to *manual* labor. I would translate, "weariness (so the *Greek* is translated, II Cor. 11:27) and travail" (hard labor, *toil*). **for**—omitted in the oldest MSS. **labouring**—*Greek*, "working," viz., at tent-making (Acts 18:3). **night and day**—The Jews reckoned the day from sunset to sunset, so that "night" is put before "day" (cf. Acts 20:31). Their labors with their hands for a scanty livelihood had to be engaged in not only by day, but by night also, in the intervals between spiritual labors. **because we would not be chargeable**—*Greek*, "*with a view to* not *burdening* any of you" (II Cor. 11:9, 10). **preached unto you**—*Greek*, "unto and among you." Though but "three Sabbaths" are mentioned, Acts 17:2, these refer merely to the time of his preaching *to the Jews in the synagogue*. When rejected by them as a body, after having converted a few Jews, he turned to the Gentiles; of these (whom he preached to in a place distinct from the synagogue) "a great multitude believed" (Acts 17:4, where the oldest MSS. read, "of the devout [proselytes] AND Greeks a great multitude"); then after he had, by labors continued *among the Gentiles* for some time, gathered in many converts, the Jews, provoked by his success, assaulted Jason's house, and drove him away. His receiving "once and again" supplies from Philippi, implies a longer stay at Thessalonica than three weeks (Phil. 4:16). **10. Ye are witnesses** —as to our outward conduct. **God**—as to our inner motives. **holily**—towards God. **justly**—towards men. **unblamably**—in relation to ourselves. **behaved ourselves**—*Greek*, "were made to be," viz., by God. **among you that believe**—rather, "*before* (i.e., in the eyes of) you that believe"; whatever we may have seemed in the eyes of the unbelieving. As vs. 9 refers to their outward occupation in the world; so vs. 10, to their character among believers. **11. exhorted and comforted**—*Exhortation* leads one to do a thing willingly; *consolation*, to do it joyfully [BENGEL], (ch. 5:14). Even in the former term, "exhorted," the *Greek* includes the additional idea of *comforting* and *advocating* one's cause: "encouragingly exhorted." Appropriate in this case, as the Thessalonians were in sorrow, both through persecutions, and also through deaths of friends (ch. 4:13). **charged**—"conjured solemnly," lit., "testifying"; *appealing solemnly* to you before God. **every one of you**—in private (Acts 20:20), as well as publicly. The minister, if he would be useful, must not deal merely in generalities, but must individualize and particularize. **as a father**—with mild gravity. The *Greek* is, "*his own* children." **12. worthy of God**—"worthy *of the Lord*" (Col. 1:10); "worthily *of the saints*" (Rom. 16:2, *Greek*): ". . . *of the Gospel*" (Phil. 1:27) ". . . . *of the vocation* wherewith ye are called" (Eph. 4:1). Inconsistency would cause God's name to be "blasphemed among the Gentiles" (Rom. 2:24). The *Greek* article is emphatical, "Worthy of THE God who is calling you." **hath called**—So one of the oldest MSS. and *Vulgate.* Other oldest MSS., "Who *calleth* us." **his kingdom** —to be set up at the Lord's coming. **glory**—that ye may share His glory (John 17:22; Col. 3:4). **13. For this cause**—Seeing ye have had such teachers (vss. 10, 11, 12) [BENGEL], "we also (as well as 'all that believe' in Macedonia and Achaia) thank God without ceasing ('always' . . . 'in our prayers,' ch. 1: 2), that when ye received the word of God which ye heard from us (lit., 'God's word of hearing from us,' Rom. 10:16, 17), ye accepted it not as the word of men, but, even as it is truly, the word of God." ALFORD omits the "as" of *English Version.* But the "as" is required by the clause, "even as it is truly." "Ye accepted it, not (*as*) the word of men (which it might have been *supposed* to be), but (as) the word of God, *even as it really is.*" The *Greek* for the first "received," implies simply the hearing of it; the *Greek* of the second is "accepted," or "welcomed" it. The proper object of faith, it hence appears, is *the word of God,* at first oral, then for security against error, written (John 20:30, 31; Rom. 15:4; Gal. 4:30). Also, that faith is *the work of divine grace,* is implied by Paul's *thanksgiving.* **effectually worketh also in you that believe**—"Also," besides your accepting it with your hearts, it evidences itself in your lives. It shows its *energy* in its practical effects on you; for instance, working in you patient endurance in trial (vs. 14; cf. Gal. 3:5; 5:6). **14. followers**—*Greek,* "imitators." Divine *working* is most of all seen and felt in affliction. **in Judea**—The churches of Judea were naturally the patterns to other churches, as having been the first founded, and that on the very scene of Christ's own ministry. Reference to them is specially appropriate here, as the Thessalonians, with Paul and Silas, had experienced from Jews in their city persecutions (Acts 17:5-9) similar to those which "the churches in Judea" experienced from Jews in that country. **in Christ Jesus**—not merely "in God"; for the synagogues of the Jews (one of which the Thessalonians were familiar with, Acts 17:1) were also *in God.* But the Christian churches alone were not only *in God,* as the Jews in contrast to the Thessalonian idolaters were, but also *in Christ,* which the Jews were not. **of your own countrymen**—including primarily the Jews settled at Thessalonica, from whom the persecution originated, and also the Gentiles there, instigated by the Jews; thus, "fellow countrymen" (the *Greek* term, according to HERODIAN, implies, not the *enduring* relation of fellow citizenship, but sameness of country *for the time being*), including naturalized Jews and native Thessalonians, stand in contrast to the pure "Jews" in Judea (Matt. 10:36). It is an undesigned coincidence, that Paul at this time was suffering persecutions of the Jews at Corinth, whence he writes (Acts 18:5, 6, 12); naturally his letter would the more vividly dwell on Jewish bitterness against Christians. **even as they**—(Heb. 10:32-34). There was a *likeness* in respect to *the nation* from which both suffered, viz., Jews, and those *their own countrymen;* in the *cause* for which, and in the *evils* which, they suffered, and also in the steadfast *manner* in which they suffered them. Such sameness of fruits, afflictions, and experimental characteristics of believers, in all places and at all times, is a subsidiary evidence of the truth of the Gospel. **15. the Lord Jesus**—rather as *Greek,* "Jesus THE LORD." This enhances the glaring enormity of their sin, that

in killing Jesus they killed the LORD (cf. Acts 3:14, 15). **their own**—omitted in the oldest MSS. **prophets**—(Matt. 21:33-41; 23:31-37; Luke 13:33). **persecuted us**—rather as *Greek* (see *Margin*), "By persecution drove us out" (Luke 11:49). **please not God** —i.e., they do not *make it their aim to* please God. He implies that with all their boast of being God's peculiar people, they all the while are "no pleasers of God," as certainly as, by the universal voice of the world, which even they themselves cannot contradict, they are declared to be perversely "contrary to all men." JOSEPHUS, *Apion* 2. 14, represents one calling them "Atheists and Misanthropes, the dullest of barbarians"; and TACITUS, *Histories,* 5. 5, "They have a hostile hatred of all other men." However, the *contrariety to all men* here meant is, *in that they* "forbid us to speak to the Gentiles that they may be saved" (vs. 16). **16. Forbidding**— *Greek,* "Hindering us from speaking. . . ." **to fill up their sins alway**—Tending thus "to the filling up (the full measure of, Gen. 15:16; Dan. 8:23; Matt. 23:32) their sins at all times," i.e., *now as at all former times.* Their hindrance of the Gospel preaching to the Gentiles was the last measure added to their continually accumulating iniquity, which made them fully ripe for vengeance. **for**— Greek, "but." "But," they shall proceed no further, for (II Tim. 3:8) "the"divine "wrath *has* (so the *Greek*) come upon (overtaken unexpectedly; the past tense expressing the speedy certainty of the divinely destined stroke) them to the uttermost"; not merely partial wrath, but wrath to its full extent, "even to the finishing stroke" [EDMUNDS]. The past tense implies that the fullest visitation of wrath was already begun. Already in A.D. 48, a tumult had occurred at the Passover in Jerusalem, when about 30,000 (according to some) were slain; a foretaste of the whole vengeance which speedily followed (Luke 19:43, 44; 21:24). **17. But we**—resumed from vs. 13; in contrast to *the Jews,* vss. 15, 16. **taken** —rather as *Greek,* "severed (violently, Acts 17:7-10) from you," as parents bereft of their children. So "I will not leave you comfortless," *Greek,* "orphanized" (John 14:18). **for a short time**—lit., "for the space of an hour." "When we had been severed from you but a very short time (perhaps alluding to the suddenness of his unexpected departure), we the more abundantly (the shorter was our separation; for the desire of meeting again is the more vivid, the more recent has been the parting) endeavored..." (Cf. II Tim. 1:4.) He does not hereby, as many explain, anticipate a short separation from them, which would be a false anticipation; for he did not soon revisit them. The *Greek* past participle also forbids their view. **18. Wherefore**—The oldest MSS. read, "Because," or "Inasmuch as." **we would**—*Greek, "we wished* to come"; we intended to come. **even I Paul**—My fellow missionaries as well as myself wished to come; I can answer for *myself* that I intended it more than once. His slightly distinguishing himself here from his fellow missionaries, whom throughout this Epistle he associates with himself in the plural, accords with the fact that Silvanus and Timothy stayed at Berea when Paul went on to Athens; where subsequently Timothy joined him, and was thence sent *by Paul alone* to Thessalonica (ch. 3:1). **Satan hindered us**—On a different occasion "the Holy Ghost, the Spirit *of Jesus*" (so the oldest MSS. read), Acts 16:6, 7, forbad or hindered them in a missionary design; here it is *Satan,* acting perhaps by wicked men, some of whom had already driven him out of Thessalonica (Acts 17:13, 14; cf. John 13:27), or else by some more direct "messenger of Satan—a thorn in the flesh" (II Cor. 12:7; cf. 11:14). In any event, the Holy Ghost and the providence of God overruled Satan's opposition to further His own purpose. *We* cannot, in each case, define whence hindrances in good undertakings arise; *Paul* in this case, by inspiration, was enabled to say; the hindrance was from Satan. GROTIUS thinks Satan's mode of hindering Paul's journey to Thessalonica was by instigating the Stoic and Epicurean philosophers to cavil, which entailed on Paul the necessity of replying, and so detained him; but he seems to have left Athens leisurely (Acts 17:33, 34; 18:1). The *Greek* for "hindered" is lit., "to cut a trench between one's self and an advancing foe, to prevent his progress"; so Satan opposing the progress of the missionaries. **19. For**—giving the reason for his earnest desire to see them. **Are not even ye in the presence of ... Christ**—"Christ" is omitted in the oldest MSS. Are not even ye (viz., among others; the "even" or "also," implies that not *they alone* will be his crown) our hope, joy, and crown of rejoicing before Jesus, when He shall come (II Cor. 1:14; Phil. 2:16; 4:1)? The "hope" here meant is his hope (in a lower sense), that these his converts might be found in Christ at His advent (ch. 3:13). Paul's *chief* "hope" was JESUS CHRIST (I Tim. 1:1). **20.** Emphatical repetition with increased force. Who but ye and our other converts are our *hope*, etc., *hereafter*, at Christ's coming? For it is *ye who* ARE now *our glory and joy*.

CHAPTER 3

Vss. 1-13. PROOF OF HIS DESIRE AFTER THEM IN HIS HAVING SENT TIMOTHY: HIS JOY AT THE TIDINGS BROUGHT BACK CONCERNING THEIR FAITH AND CHARITY: PRAYERS FOR THEM. **1. Wherefore**—because of our earnest love to you (ch. 2:17-20). **forbear**—"endure" the suspense. The *Greek* is lit. applied to a watertight vessel. When we could no longer contain ourselves in our yearning desire for you. **left at Athens alone**—See my *Introduction*. This implies that he sent Timothy *from Athens,* whither the latter had followed him. However, the "we" favors ALFORD's view that the determination to send Timothy was formed during the hasty consultation of Paul, Silas, and Timothy, *previous to his departure from Berea,* and that then he with them "resolved" to be "left alone" at Athens, when he should arrive there: Timothy and Silas not accompanying him, but remaining at Berea. Thus the "I," vs. 5, will express that the *act* of sending Timothy, when he arrived at Athens, was *Paul's,* while the determination that Paul should be left alone at Athens, was that of the brethren as well as himself, at Berea, whence he uses, vs. 1, "we." The non-mention of Silas at Athens implies that he did not follow Paul to Athens as was at first intended; but Timothy did. Thus the history, Acts 17:14, 15, accords with the Epistle. The word "left behind" (*Greek*) implies that Timothy had been with him *at Athens*. It was an act of self-denial for their sakes that Paul deprived himself of the presence of Timothy at Athens, which would have been so cheering to him in the midst of philosophic cavillers; but from love to the Thessalonians, he is well content to be left all "alone" in the great city. **2. minister of God and our fellow labourer**—Some oldest MSS. read, "fellow workman with God"; others, "minister of God." The former is probably genuine, as copyists probably altered it to the latter to avoid the bold phrase, which, however, is sanctioned by I Corinthians 3:9;

II Corinthians 6:1. *English Version* reading is not well supported, and is plainly compounded out of the two other readings. Paul calls Timothy "our *brother*" here; but in I Corinthians 4:17, "my *son*." He speaks thus highly of one so lately ordained, both to impress the Thessalonians with a high respect for the delegate sent to them, and to encourage Timothy, who seems to have been of a timid character (I Tim. 4:12; 5:23). "Gospel ministers do the work of God *with* Him, *for* Him, and *under* Him" [EDMUNDS]. **establish**—*Greek,* "confirm." In II Thessalonians 3:3, GOD is said to stablish": He is the true establisher: ministers are His "instruments." **concerning**—*Greek,* "in behalf of," i.e., *for the furtherance* of your faith. The *Greek* for "comfort" includes also the idea, "exhort." The Thessalonians in their trials needed both (vs. 3; cf. Acts 14: 22). **3. moved**—"shaken," "disturbed." The *Greek* is lit. said of dogs *wagging* the tail in fawning on one. Therefore TITTMANN explains it, "That no man should, amidst his calamities, be *allured* by the *flattering* hope of a more pleasant life to abandon his duty." So ELSNER and BENGEL, "cajoled out of his faith." In afflictions, relatives and opponents combine with the ease-loving heart itself in flatteries, which it needs strong faith to overcome. **yourselves know**—We always candidly told you so (vs. 4; Acts 14:22). None but a religion from God would have held out such a trying prospect to those who should embrace it, and yet succeed in winning converts. **we**—Christians. **appointed thereunto**—by God's counsel (ch. 5:9). **4. that we should suffer**—*Greek,* "that we are about (we are sure) to suffer" according to the *appointment* of God (vs. 3). **even as**—"*even* (exactly) as it *both* came to pass *and* ye know"; ye know *both* that it came to pass, *and* that we foretold it (cf. John 13:19). The correspondence of the event to the prediction powerfully confirms faith: "Forewarned, forearmed" [EDMUNDS]. The repetition of "ye know," so frequently, is designed as an argument, that being forewarned of coming affliction, they should be less readily "moved" by it. **5. For this cause**—Because I know of your "tribulation" having actually begun (vs. 4). **when I**—*Greek,* "when I *also* (as well as Timothy, who, Paul delicately implies, was equally anxious respecting them, cf. "we," vs. 1), could no longer contain myself" (*endure* the suspense). **I sent**—Paul was the actual sender; hence the "I" here: Paul, Silas, and Timothy himself had agreed on the mission already, before Paul went to Athens: hence the "we," (vs. 1 *Note*). **to know**—to learn the state of your faith, whether it stood the trial (Col. 4:8). **lest ... have tempted ... and ... be**—The indicative is used in the former sentence, the subjunctive in the latter. Translate therefore, "To know ... *whether haply* the tempter *have* tempted you (the indicative implying that he supposed such *was* the case), and *lest* (in that case) our labor *may prove to be in* vain" (cf. Gal. 4:11). Our labor in preaching would in that case be vain, so far as *ye* are concerned, but not as concerns *us* in so far as *we* have sincerely labored (Isa. 49:4; I Cor. 3:8). **6. Join** "now" with "come"; "But Timotheus having *just now come* from you unto us" [ALFORD]. Thus it appears (cf. Acts 18:5) Paul is writing from Corinth. **your faith and charity**—(ch. 1:3; cf. II Thess. 1:3, whence it seems their faith subsequently increased still more). *Faith* was the solid foundation: *charity* the cement which held together the superstructure of their practice on that foundation. In that *charity* was included their "good (kindly) remembrance" of their teachers. **desiring greatly**—*Greek,* "having a yearning desire for." **we also**—The desires of loving friends for one another's presence are reciprocal. **7. over you** —in respect to you. **in**—in the midst of: notwithstanding "all our distress (*Greek*, 'necessity') and affliction," viz., external trials at Corinth, whence Paul writes (cf. vs. 6, with Acts 18:5-10). **8. now** —as the case is; seeing ye stand fast. **we live**—we flourish. It *revives us* in our affliction to hear of your steadfastness (Ps. 22:26; II John 3:4). **if**—implying that the vivid joy which the missionaries "now" feel, *will continue* if the Thessalonians continue steadfast. They still needed exhortation, vs. 10; therefore he subjoins the conditional clause, "if ye . . . (Phil. 4:1). **9. what . . .**—*what sufficient* thanks? **render . . . again**—in return for His goodness (Ps. 116:12). **for you**—"concerning you." **for all the joy**—on account of all the joy. It was "comfort," vs. 7, now it is more, viz., *joy*. **for your sakes**—on your account. **before our God**—It is a joy which will bear God's searching eye: a joy as in the presence of God, not selfseeking, but disinterested, sincere, and spiritual (cf. ch. 2:20; John 15:11). **10. Night and day**—(*Note*, ch. 2:9). Night is the season for the saint's holiest meditations and prayers (II Tim. 1:3). **praying**—connected with, "we joy"; we joy while we pray; or else as ALFORD, *What thanks can we render to God while we pray?* The *Greek* implies a *beseeching* request. **exceedingly**—lit., **"more than exceeding abundantly"** (cf. Eph. 3:20). **that which is lacking**—Even the Thessalonians had points in which they needed improvement [BENGEL], (Luke 17:5). Their doctrinal views as to the nearness of Christ's coming, and as to the state of those who had fallen asleep, and their practice in some points, needed correction (ch. 4:1-9). Paul's method was to begin by commending what was praiseworthy, and then to correct what was amiss; a good pattern to all admonishers of others. **11.** Translate, *"May God Himself, even* our Father (there being but one article in the *Greek*, requires this translation, 'He who is at once God and our Father'), direct. . . . "The "Himself" stands in contrast with "we" (ch. 2:18); *we* desired to come but could not through Satan's hindrance; but if God *Himself* direct our way (as we pray), none can hinder Him (II Thess. 2:16, 17). It is a remarkable proof of *the unity of the Father and Son*, that in the *Greek* here, and in II Thessalonians 2:16, 17, the verb is *singular*, implying that the subject, the Father and Son, are but *one in essential Being*, not in mere unity of will. Almost all the chapters in both Epistles to the Thessalonians are sealed, each with its own prayer (ch. 5:23; II Thess. 1:11; 2:16; 3:5, 16) [BENGEL]. Paul does not think the prosperous issue of a journey an unfit subject for prayer (Rom. 1:10; 15:32) [EDMUNDS]. His prayer, though the answer was deferred, in about five years afterwards was fulfilled in his return to Macedonia. **12.** The "you" in the *Greek* is emphatically put *first;* "But" (so the *Greek* for "and") what concerns "YOU," whether we come or not, "may the Lord make you to increase and abound in love. . . ." The *Greek* for "increase" has a more *positive* force; that for "abound" a more *comparative* force, "make you *full* (supplying "that which is lacking," vs. 10) and even abound." "The Lord" may here be the Holy Spirit; so the Three Persons of the Trinity will be appealed to (cf. vs. 13), as in II Thessalonians 3:5. So the Holy Ghost is called "the Lord" (II Cor. 3:17). "Love" is the fruit of the Spirit (Gal. 5:22), and His office is "to stablish in holiness" (vs. 13; I Pet. 1:2). **13. your hearts**—which are naturally the spring and seat of unholiness. **before God, even**

our Father—rather, "before Him who is at once God and our Father." Before not merely men, but Him who will not be deceived by the mere show of holiness, i.e., may your holiness be such as will stand His searching scrutiny. **coming**—*Greek,* "presence," or "arrival." **with all his saints**—including both the holy angels and the holy elect of men (ch. 4:14; Dan. 7:10; Zech. 14:5; Matt. 25:31; II Thess. 1:7). The saints are "His" Acts 9:13). We must have "holiness" if we are to be numbered with His holy ones or "saints." On "unblamable," cf. Revelation 14:5. This verse (cf. vs. 12) shows that "love" is the spring of true "holiness" (Matt. 5:44-48; Rom. 13:10; Col. 3:14). God is He who really "stablishes"; Timothy and other ministers are but instruments (vs. 2) in "stablishing."

CHAPTER 4

VSS. 1-18. EXHORTATIONS TO CHASTITY; BROTHERLY LOVE; QUIET INDUSTRY; ABSTINENCE FROM UNDUE SORROW FOR DEPARTED FRIENDS, FOR AT CHRIST'S COMING ALL HIS SAINTS SHALL BE GLORIFIED. **1. Furthermore**—*Greek,* "As to what remains." Generally used towards the close of his Epistles (Eph. 6:10; Phil. 4:8). **then**—with a view to the *love* and *holiness* (ch. 3:12, 13) which we have just prayed for in your behalf, we now give you exhortation. **beseech**—"ask" as if it were a personal favor. **by . . .**—rather as *Greek,* "IN the Lord Jesus"; in communion with the Lord Jesus, as Christian ministers dealing with Christian people [EDMUNDS]. **as ye . . . received**—when we were with you (ch. 2:13). **how**—*Greek,* the "how," i.e., *the manner.* **walk and . . . please God**—i.e., *"and so* please God," viz., by your walk; in contrast to the Jews who "please not God" (ch. 2:15). The oldest MSS. add a clause here, "even as also ye do walk" (cf. ch. 4:10; 5:11). These words, which he was able to say of them with truth, conciliate a favorable hearing for the precepts which follow. Also the expression, "abound *more and more,"* implies that there had gone before a recognition of their already in some measure *walking so.* **2. by the Lord Jesus**—by His authority and direction, not by our own. He uses the strong term, "commandments," in writing to this Church not long founded, knowing that they would take it in a right spirit, and feeling it desirable that they should understand he spake with divine authority. He seldom uses the term in writing subsequently, when his authority was established, to other churches. I Corinthians 7:10; 11:17; and I Timothy 1:5 (vs. 18, where the subject accounts for the strong expression) are the exceptions. "The Lord" marks His paramount authortiy, requiring implicit obedience. **3. For**—enforcing the assertion that his "commandments" were "by (the authority of) the Lord Jesus" (vs. 2). Since "this is the will of God," let it be your will also. **fornication**—not regarded as a sin at all among the heathen, and so needing the more to be denounced (Acts 15:20). **4. know**—by moral self-control. **how to possess his vessel**—rather as *Greek,* "how to *acquire* (get for himself) *his own* vessel," i.e., that each should have *his own wife* so as to avoid fornication (vs. 3; I Cor. 7:2). The emphatical position of "his own" in the *Greek,* and the use of "vessel" for *wife,* in I Pet. 3:7, and in common Jewish phraseology, and the correct translation "acquire," all justify this rendering. **in sanctification**—(Rom. 6:19; I Cor. 6:15, 18). Thus, "his own" stands in opposition to dishonoring his brother by lusting after *his* wife (vs. 6). **honour—** (Heb. 13:4) contrasted with "*dishonor* their own bodies" (Rom. 1:24). **5. in the lust—***Greek,* "passion"; which implies that such a one is unconsciously the *passive* slave of lust. **which know not God—**and so know no better. Ignorance of true religion is the parent of unchastity (Eph. 4:18, 19). A people's morals are like the objects of their worship (Deut. 7:26; Ps. 115:8; Rom. 1:23, 24). **6. go beyond—**transgress the bounds of rectitude in respect to his brother. **defraud—**"overreach" [ALFORD]; "take advantage of" [EDMUNDS]. **in any matter—**rather as *Greek,* "in *the* matter"; a decorous expression for the matter now in question; the conjugal honor of his neighbor as a husband, vs. 4; vs. 7 also confirms this view; the word "brother" enhances the enormity of the crime. It is your *brother* whom you wrong (cf. Prov. 6:27-33). **the Lord—**the coming Judge (II Thess. 1:7, 8). **avenger —**the Righter. **of all such—***Greek,* "concerning all *these things"*; in all such cases of wrongs against a neighbor's conjugal honor. **testified—***Greek,* "constantly testified [ALFORD]. **7. unto—***Greek,* "for the purpose of." **unto—**rather as *Greek,* "in"; marking that "holiness" is the element in which our calling has place; in a sphere of holiness. *Saint* is another name for Christian. **8. despiseth . . .—** *Greek,* "setteth at naught" such engagements imposed on him in his calling, vs. 7; in relation to his "brother," vs. 6. He who doth so, "sets at naught not man (as for instance his brother), but God" (Ps. 51:4). Or, as the *Greek* verb (Luke 10:16; John 12:48) is used of *despising* or *rejecting* God's minister, it may mean here, "He who despiseth" or "rejecteth" these our ministerial precepts. **who hath also given unto us—**So some oldest MSS. read, but most oldest MSS. read, "Who (without 'also') *giveth* (present) unto *you*" (not "us"). **his Spirit—** *Greek,* "His own Spirit, the Holy (One)"; thus emphatically marking "holiness" (vs. 7) as the end for which the *Holy* (One) is being given. "Unto you," in the *Greek,* implies that the Spirit is being given *unto, into* (put *into* your hearts), *and among* you (cf. ch. 2:9; Eph. 4:30). "Giveth" implies that sanctification is not merely a work once for all accomplished in the past, but a *present progressive* work. So the Church of England Catechism, "*sanctifieth* (present) all the elect people of God." "His own" implies that as He gives you that which is essentially identical with Himself, He expects you should become like Himself (I Pet. 1:16; II Pet. 1:4). **9. brotherly love . . .—**referring here to acts of brotherly kindness in relieving distressed brethren. Some oldest MSS. support *English Version* reading, "YE have"; others, and those the weightiest, read, "WE have." *We* need not write, as *ye yourselves* are taught, and that by *God;* viz., in the heart by the Holy Spirit (John 6:45; Heb. 8:11; I John 2:20, 27). **to love—***Greek,* "with a view to," or "to the end of your loving one another." Divine teachings have their confluence in love [BENGEL]. **10. And indeed —***Greek,* "For even." **11. study to be quiet—***Greek,* "*make it your ambition* to be quiet, and to do *your own business.*" In direct contrast to the world's ambition, which is, "to make a great stir," and "to be busybodies" (II Thess. 3:11, 12). **work with your own hands—**The Thessalonian converts were, it thus seems, chiefly of the *working* classes. Their expectation of the immediate coming of Christ led some enthusiasts among them to neglect their daily work and be dependent on the bounty of others. See end of vs. 12. The expectation was right in so far as that the Church should be always looking for

Him; but they were wrong in making it a ground for neglecting their daily work. The evil, as it subsequently became worse, is more strongly reproved in II Thessalonians 3:6-12. **12. honestly—**in the Old English sense, "becomingly," as becomes your Christian profession; not bringing discredit on it in the eyes of the outer world, as if Christianity led to sloth and poverty (Rom. 13:13; I Pet. 2:12). **them . . . without—**outside the Christian Church (Mark 4:11). **have lack of nothing—**not have to beg from others for the supply of your wants (cf. Eph. 4:28). So far from needing to beg from others, we ought to work and get the means of supplying the need of others. Freedom from pecuniary embarrassment is to be desired by the Christian on account of the liberty which it bestows. **13.** The leading topic of Paul's preaching at Thessalonica having been the coming *kingdom* (Acts 17:7), some perverted it into a cause for fear in respect to friends lately deceased, as if these would be excluded from the glory which those found alive alone should share. This error Paul here corrects (cf. ch. 5:10). **I would not—**All the oldest MSS. and versions have "*we* would not." My fellow labourers (Silas and Timothy) and myself desire that ye should not be ignorant. **them which are asleep—**The oldest MSS. read *present tense,* "them which are *sleeping"*; the same as "the dead in Christ" (vs. 16), to whose bodies (Dan. 12:2, not their *souls;* Eccl. 12:7; II Cor. 5:8) death is a calm and holy sleep, from which the resurrection shall waken them to glory. The word "cemetery" means *a sleeping-place.* Observe, the glory and chief hope of the Church are not to be realized at death, but at the Lord's coming; one is not to anticipate the other, but all are to be glorified together at Christ's coming (Col. 3:4; Heb. 11:40). Death affects the mere individual; but the coming of Jesus the whole Church; at death our souls are invisibly and individually with the Lord; at Christ's coming the whole Church, with all its members, in body and soul, shall be visibly and collectively with Him. As this is offered as a consolation to mourning relatives, *the mutual recognition of the saints* at Christ's coming is hereby implied. **that ye sorrow not, even as others—***Greek,* "the rest"; all the rest of the world besides Christians. Not all natural *mourning* for dead friends is forbidden: for the Lord Jesus and Paul sinlessly gave way to it (John 11:31, 33, 35; Phil. 2:27); but sorrow as though there were "no hope," which indeed the heathen had not (Eph. 2:12): the Christian *hope* here meant is that of *the resurrection.* Psalm 16:9, 11; 17:15; 73:24; Proverbs 14:32, show that the Old Testament Church, though not having the hope *so bright* (Isa. 38:18, 19), yet *had* this hope. Contrast CATULLUS, 5. 4, "When once our brief day has set, we must sleep one everlasting night." The sepulchral inscriptions of heathen Thessalonica express the hopeless view taken as to those once dead: as ÆSCHYLUS writes, "Of one once dead there is no resurrection." Whatever glimpses some heathen philosophers, had of the existence of the soul after death, they had none whatever of the body (Acts 17:18, 20, 32). **14. For if—**confirmation of his statement, vs. 13, that the removal of *ignorance* as to the sleeping believers would remove undue grief respecting them. See vs. 13, "hope." Hence it appears our *hope* rests on our *faith* ("if we believe"). "As surely as we all believe that Christ died and rose again (the very doctrine specified as taught at Thessalonica, Acts 17:3), *so also* will God bring *those laid to sleep by Jesus* with Him" (Jesus. So the order and balance of the members of the *Greek* sentence require us to translate). Believers are laid in sleep by Jesus, and so will be brought back from sleep with Jesus in His train when He comes. The disembodied souls are not here spoken of; the reference is to the sleeping *bodies*. The facts of Christ's experience are repeated in the believer's. He died and then rose: so believers shall die and then rise with Him. But in His case *death* is the term used, I Corinthians 15:3, 6, etc.; in theirs, *sleep;* because His death has taken for them the sting from death. The same Hand that shall raise them is that which *laid them to sleep*. "Laid to sleep by Jesus," answers to "dead in Christ" (vs. 16). **15. by the word of the Lord**—Greek, "in," i.e., *in virtue* of a direct revelation from the Lord to me. So I Kings 20:35. This is the "mystery," a truth once hidden, now revealed, which Paul shows (I Cor. 15:51, 52). **prevent**—i.e., "anticipate." So far were the early Christians from regarding their departed brethren as *anticipating* them in entering glory, that they needed to be assured that those who remain to the coming of the Lord "will not anticipate them that are asleep." The "we" means *whichever of us* are alive and remain unto the coming of the Lord. The Spirit designed that believers in each successive age should live in continued expectation of the Lord's coming, not knowing but that *they* should be among those found alive at His coming (Matt. 24:42). It is a sad fall from this blessed hope, that *death* is looked for by most men, rather than the coming of our Lord. Each successive generation in its time and place represents the generation which shall actually survive till His coming (Matt. 25:13; Rom. 13:11; I Cor. 15:51; Jas. 5:9; I Pet. 4:5, 6). The Spirit subsequently revealed by Paul that which is not inconsistent with the expectation here taught of the Lord's coming at any time; viz., that His coming would not be until there should be a "falling away first" (II Thess. 2:2, 3); but as symptoms of this soon appeared, none could say but that still this precursory event might be realized, and so the Lord come in his day. Each successive revelation fills in the details of the general outline first given. So Paul subsequently, while still looking mainly for the Lord's coming to clothe him with his body from heaven, looks for going to be with Christ in the meanwhile (II Cor. 5:1-10; Phil. 1:6, 23; 3:20, 21; 4:5). EDMUNDS well says, The "we" is an affectionate identifying of ourselves with our fellows of all ages, as members of the same body, under the same Head, Christ Jesus. So Hosea 12:4, "God spake with *us* in Bethel," i.e., with Israel. "*We* did rejoice," i.e., Israel at the Red Sea (Ps. 66:6). Though neither Hosea, nor David, was alive at the times referred to, yet each identifies himself with those that were present. **16. himself**—in all the Majesty of His presence in person, not by deputy. **descend** —even as He ascended (Acts 1:11). **with**—Greek, "in," implying one concomitant circumstance attending His appearing. **shout**—Greek, "signal shout," "war shout." Jesus is represented as a victorious King, giving the word of command to the hosts of heaven in His train for the last onslaught, at His final triumph over sin, death, and Satan (Rev. 19:11-21). **the voice of ... archangel**—distinct from the "signal shout." Michael is perhaps meant (Jude 9; Rev. 12:7), to whom especially is committed the guardianship of the people of God (Dan. 10:13). **trump of God**—the trumpet blast which usually accompanies God's manifestation in glory (Exod. 19:16; Ps. 47:5); here the last of the three accompaniments of His appearing: as the trumpet was used to convene God's people to their solemn

convocations (Num. 10:2, 10; 31:6), so here to summon God's elect together, preparatory to their glorification with Christ (Ps. 50:1-5; Matt. 24:31; I Cor. 15:52). **shall rise first**—previously to the living being "caught up." The "first" here has no reference to the *first* resurrection, as contrasted with that of "the rest of the dead." That reference occurs elsewhere (Matt. 13:41, 42, 50; John 5:29; I Cor. 15: 23, 24; Rev. 20:5, 6); it simply stands in opposition to "then," vs. 17. FIRST, "the *dead* in Christ" shall rise, THEN the *living* shall be caught up. The Lord's people alone are spoken of here. **17. we which are alive ... shall be caught up**—after having been "changed in a moment" (I Cor. 15:51, 52). Again he says, "we," recommending thus the expression to Christians of all ages, each generation bequeathing to the succeeding one a continually increasing obligation to look for the coming of the Lord. [EDMUNDS]. **together with them**—all together: the raised dead, and changed living, forming one joint body. **in the clouds**—Greek, "in clouds." The same honor is conferred on them as on their Lord. As He was taken in a cloud at His ascension (Acts 1:9), so at His return with clouds (Rev. 1:7), they shall be caught up in clouds. The clouds are His and their triumphal chariot (Ps. 104:3; Dan. 7:13). ELLICOTT explains the Greek, "robed round by upbearing clouds" (*Aids to Faith*). **in the air**—rather, "*into* the air"; caught up *into* the region just above the earth, where the *meeting* (cf. Matt. 25:1, 6) shall take place between them ascending, and their Lord descending towards the earth. Not that the air is to be the place of their *lasting abode* with Him. **and so shall we ever be with the Lord**—no more parting, and no more going out (Rev. 3:12). His point being established, that the dead in Christ shall be on terms of equal advantage with those found alive at Christ's coming, he leaves undefined here the other events foretold elsewhere (as not being necessary to his discussion), Christ's reign on earth with His saints (I Cor. 6:2, 3), the final judgment and glorification of His saints in the new heaven and earth. **18. comfort one another**—in your mourning for the dead (vs. 13).

CHAPTER 5

Vss. 1-28. THE SUDDENNESS OF CHRIST'S COMING A MOTIVE FOR WATCHFULNESS: VARIOUS PRECEPTS: PRAYER FOR THEIR BEING FOUND BLAMELESS, BODY, SOUL, AND SPIRIT, AT CHRIST'S COMING: CONCLUSION. **1. times**—the general and indefinite term for chronological periods. **seasons**—the *opportune times* (Dan. 7:12; Acts 1:7). *Time* denotes quantity; *season*, quality. *Seasons* are parts of *times*. **ye have no need**—those who watch do not need to be told *when* the hour will come, for they are always ready [BENGEL]. **cometh**—present: expressing its *speedy* and awful *certainty*. **2. as a thief in the night**—The apostles in this image follow the parable of their Lord, expressing how the Lord's coming shall take men by surprise (Matt. 24:43; II Pet. 3:10). "The *night* is wherever there is quiet unconcern" [BENGEL]. "At midnight" (perhaps figurative: to some parts of the earth it will be *literal* night), Matthew 25:6. The thief not only gives no notice of his approach but takes all precaution to prevent the household knowing of it. So the Lord (Rev. 16:15). *Signs* will precede the coming, to confirm the patient hope of the watchful believer; but the coming itself shall be sudden at last (Matt. 24-32-36; Luke 21:25-32, 35). **3. they**—the men of the world.

Verses 5, 6; ch. 4:13, "others," all the rest of the world save Christians. **Peace**—(Judg. 18:7, 9, 27, 28; Jer. 6:14; Ezek. 13:10). **then**—*at the very moment* when they least expect it. Cf. the case of Belshazzar, Daniel 5:1-5, 6, 9, 26-28; Herod, Acts 12:21-23. **sudden**—"unawares" (Luke 21:34). **as travail**—"As *the* labor pang" comes in an instant on the woman when otherwise engaged (Ps. 48:6; Isa. 13:8). **shall not escape**—Greek, "shall not at all escape." Another awful feature of their ruin: there shall be then no possibility of shunning it however they desire it (Amos 9:2, 3; Rev. 6:15, 16). **4. not in darkness**—not in darkness of understanding (i.e., spiritual ignorance) or of the moral nature (i.e., a state of sin), Ephesians 4:18. **that**—Greek, "in order that"; with God results are all purposed. **that day**—Greek, "THE day"; the *day* of the Lord (Heb. 10:25, "*the* day"), in contrast to "darkness." **overtake**—unexpectedly (cf. John 12:35). **as a thief**—The two oldest MSS. read, "as (the daylight overtakes) *thieves*" (Job 24:17). Old MSS. and *Vulgate* read as *English Version*. **5.** The oldest MSS. read, "FOR ye are all. . . ." Ye have no reason for fear, or for being taken by surprise, by the coming of the day of the Lord: "*For* ye are all sons (so the Greek) of light and sons of day"; a *Hebrew* idiom, implying that *sons* resemble their fathers, so you are in *character* light (intellectually and morally illuminated in a spiritual point of view), Luke 16:8; John 12:36. **are not of**—i.e., *belong not to* night nor darkness. The change of person from "ye" to "we" implies this: *Ye* are sons of light because ye are Christians; and *we*, Christians, are not of night nor darkness. **6. others**—Greek, "the rest" of the world: the unconverted (ch. 4:13). "Sleep" here is worldly apathy to spiritual things (Rom. 13:11; Eph. 5:14); in vs. 7, ordinary *sleep;* in vs. 10, death. **watch**—for Christ's coming; lit., "be wakeful." The same Greek occurs in I Corinthians 15:34; II Timothy 2:26. **be sober**—refraining from carnal indulgence, mental or sensual (I Pet. 5:8). **7.** This verse is to be taken in the literal sense. Night is the time when sleepers sleep, and drinking men are drunk. To sleep by day would imply great indolence; to be drunken by day, great shamelessness. Now, in a spiritual sense, "we Christians profess to be day people, not night people; therefore our work ought to be day work, not night work; our conduct such as will bear the eye of day, and such has no need of the veil of night" [EDMUNDS], (vs. 8). **8.** *Faith, hope,* and *love,* are the three pre-eminent graces (ch. 1:3; I Cor. 13:13). We must not only be awake and sober, but also *armed;* not only watchful, but also guarded. The armor here is only *defensive;* in Ephesians 6:13-17, also *offensive.* Here, therefore, the reference is to the Christian means of being *guarded* against being surprised by the day of the Lord as a thief in the night. The *helmet* and *breastplate* defend the two vital parts, the head and the heart respectively. "With head and heart right, the whole man is right" [EDMUNDS]. The head needs to be kept from error, the heart from sin. For "the breastplate of righteousness," Ephesians 6:14, we have here "the breastplate of faith and love"; for the righteousness which is imputed to man for justification, is "faith working by love" (Rom. 4:3, 22-24; Gal. 5:6). "Faith," as the motive *within,* and "love," exhibited in *outward* acts, constitute the perfection of *righteousness.* In Ephesians 6:17 the helmet is "salvation"; here, "the *hope* of salvation." In one aspect "salvation" is a present possession (John 3:36; 5:24; I John 5:13); in another, it is a matter of "hope" (Rom. 8:24, 25). Our Head primarily wore the "breastplate of righteousness" and "helmet of salvation," that we might, by union with Him, receive both. **9. For**—assigning the ground of our "hopes" (vs. 8). **appointed us**—Translate, "set" (Acts 13:47), in His everlasting purpose of love (ch. 3:3; II Tim. 1:9). Contrast Romans 9:22; Jude 4. **to**—i.e., *unto* wrath. **to obtain**—Greek, "to the acquisition of salvation"; said, according to BENGEL, of one saved out of a general wreck, when all things else have been lost: so of the elect saved out of the multitude of the lost (II Thess. 2:13, 14). The fact of God's "appointment" of His grace "through Jesus Christ" (Eph. 1:5), takes away the notion of our being able to "acquire" salvation *of ourselves.* Christ "acquired (so the *Greek* for 'purchased') the Church (and its salvation) with His own blood" (Acts 20:28); each member is said to be appointed by God to the "acquiring of salvation." In the primary sense, God does the work; in the secondary sense, man does it. **10. died for us**—Greek, "in our behalf." **whether we wake or sleep**—whether we be found at Christ's coming awake, i.e., alive, or asleep, i.e., in our graves. **together**—*all* of us *together;* the living not preceding the dead in their glorification "with Him" at His coming (ch. 4:13). **11. comfort yourselves**—Greek, "one another." Here he reverts to the same consolatory strain as in ch. 4:18. **edify one another**—rather as Greek, "edify (ye) the one the other"; "edify," lit., "build up," viz., in faith, hope, and love, by discoursing together on such edifying topics as the Lord's coming, and the glory of the saints (Mal. 3:16). **12. beseech**—"Exhort" is the expression in vs. 14; here, "we beseech you," as if it were a personal favor (Paul making the cause of the Thessalonian presbyters, as it were, his own). **know**—to have a regard and respect for. Recognize their office, and treat them accordingly (cf. I Cor. 16:18) with reverence and with liberality in supplying their needs (I Tim. 5:17). The Thessalonian Church having been newly planted, the ministers were necessarily novices (I Tim. 3:6), which may have been in part the cause of the people's treating them with less respect. Paul's practice seems to have been to ordain elders in every Church soon after its establishment (Acts 14:23). **them which labour . . . are over . . . admonish you**—not three classes of ministers, but one, as there is but one article common to the three in the Greek. "Labor" expresses their laborious life; "are over you," their pre-eminence as presidents or superintendents ("bishops," i.e., overseers, Phil. 1:1, "them that have rule over you," lit., *leaders,* Heb. 13:17; "pastors," lit., *shepherds,* Eph. 4:11); "admonish you," one of their leading functions; the *Greek* is "put in mind," implying not arbitrary authority, but gentle, though faithful, admonition (II Tim. 2:14, 24, 25; I Pet. 5:3). **in the Lord**—Their presidency over you is *in divine things;* not in worldly affairs, but in things appertaining to the Lord. **13. very highly**—Greek, "exceeding abundantly." **for their work's sake**—The high nature of their work alone, the furtherance of your salvation and of the kingdom of Christ, should be a sufficient motive to claim your reverential love. At the same time, the word "work," teaches ministers that, while claiming the reverence due to their office, it is not a sinecure, but a "work"; cf. "*labor*" (even to *weariness:* so the *Greek*), vs. 12. **be at peace among yourselves**—The "and" is not in the original. Let there not only be peace between ministers and their flocks, but also no party rivalries among yourselves, one contending in behalf of some one favorite minister, another in behalf of another

(Mark 9:50; I Cor. 1:12; 4:6). **14. brethren**—This exhortation to "warm (*Greek*, 'admonish,' as in vs. 12) the unruly (those 'disorderly' persons, II Thessalonians 3:6, 11, who would not work, and yet expected to be maintained, lit., said of soldiers who will *not* remain *in their ranks*, cf. ch. 4:11; also those insubordinate as to Church discipline, in relation to those 'over' the Church, vs. 12), comfort the feeble-minded" (the *faint-hearted*, who are ready to sink "without hope" in afflictions, ch. 4:13, and temptations), applies to all clergy and laity alike, though primarily the duty of the clergy (who are meant in vs. 12). **support**—lit., "lay fast hold on so as to support." **the weak**—spiritually. Paul practiced what he preached (I Cor. 9:22). **be patient toward all men**—There is no believer who needs not the exercise of patience "toward" him; there is none to whom a believer ought not to show it; many show it more to strangers than to their own families, more to the great than to the humble; but we ought to show it "toward *all men*" [BENGEL]. Cf. "the long-suffering of our Lord" (II Cor. 10:1; II Pet. 3:15). **15.** (Rom. 12:17; I Pet. 3:9.) **unto any man**—whether unto a Christian, or a heathen, however great the provocation. **follow**—as a matter of earnest pursuit. **16, 17.** In order to "rejoice evermore," we must "pray without ceasing." He who is wont to thank God for all things as happening for the best, will have continuous joy [THEOPHYLACT]. Ephesians 6:18; Philippians 4:4, 6, "Rejoice *in the Lord* ... by prayer and supplication with thanksgiving"; Romans 14:17, "*in the Holy Ghost*"; Romans 12: 12, "*in hope*"; Acts 5:41, "*in being counted worthy to suffer shame for Christ's name*"; James 1:2, *in falling "into divers temptations."* The *Greek* is, "Pray *without intermission*"; without allowing prayerless gaps to intervene between the times of prayer. **18.** In every thing—even what *seems* adverse: for nothing is *really* so (cf. Rom. 8:28; Eph. 5:20). See Christ's example (Matt. 15:36; 26:27; Luke 10:21; John 11:41). **this**—That ye should "rejoice evermore, pray without ceasing, (and) in every thing give thanks," "is the will of God in Christ Jesus (as the Mediator and Revealer of that will, observed by those who are *in Christ* by faith, cf. Phil. 3:14) concerning you." *God's will* is the believer's law. LACHMANN rightly reads commas at the end of the three precepts (vss. 16, 17, 18), making "this" refer to all three. **19. Quench not**—the Spirit being a holy *fire:* "where the Spirit is, He burns" [BENGEL] (Matt. 3:11; Acts 2:3;7:51). Do not throw cold water on those who, under extraordinary inspiration of the Spirit, stand up to speak with tongues, or reveal mysteries, or pray in the congregation. The enthusiastic exhibitions of some (perhaps as to the nearness of Christ's coming, exaggerating Paul's statement, II Thess. 2:2, By *spirit*), led others (probably the presiding ministers, who had not always been treated with due respect by enthusiastic novices, vs. 12), from dread of enthusiasm, to discourage the free utterances of those really inspired, in the Church assembly. On the other hand, the caution (vs. 21) was needed, not to receive "all" pretended revelations as divine, without "proving" them. **20. prophesyings**—whether exercised in inspired teaching, or in predicting the future. "Despised" by some as beneath "tongues," which seemed most miraculous; therefore declared by Paul to be a greater gift than tongues, though the latter were more showy (I Cor. 14:5). **21, 22.** Some of the oldest MSS. insert "But." You ought indeed not to "quench" the manifestations of "the Spirit," nor "despise prophesyings"; "but," at the same time, do

not take "all" as genuine which professes to be so; "prove (test) all" such manifestations. The means of testing them existed in the Church, in those who had the "discerning of spirits" (I Cor. 12:10; 14: 29; I John 4:1). Another sure test, which we also have, is, to try the professed revelation whether it accords with Scripture, as the noble Bereans did (Isa. 8:20; Acts 17:11; Gal. 1:8, 9). This precept negatives the Romish priest's assumption of infallibly laying down the law, without the laity having the right, in the exercise of private judgment, to test it by Scripture. LOCKE says, Those who are for laying aside reason in matters of revelation, resemble one who would *put out his eyes* in order to use a *telescope*. **hold fast that which is good**—Join with this clause with the next clause (vs. 22), not merely with the sentence preceding. As the result of your "proving all things," and especially all *prophesyings*, "*hold fast* (Luke 8:15; I Cor. 11:2; Heb. 2:1) the good, and *hold yourselves aloof from* every appearance of evil" ("*every evil species*" [BENGEL and WAHL]). Do not accept even a professedly spirit-inspired communication, if it be at variance with the truth taught you (II Thess. 2:2). TITTMANN supports *English Version*, "from every evil *appearance*" or "semblance." The context, however, does not refer to *evil appearances* IN OURSELVES which we ought to abstain from, but to *holding ourselves aloof from every evil appearance* IN OTHERS; as for instance, in the pretenders to spirit-inspired prophesyings. In many cases the Christian should *not* abstain from what has the *semblance* ("appearance") of evil, though really good. Jesus healed on the sabbath, and ate with publicans and sinners, acts which wore the *appearance* of evil, but which were not to be abstained from on that account, being really good. I agree with TITTMANN rather than with BENGEL, whom ALFORD follows. The context favors this sense: However *specious* be the *form* or *outward appearance* of such would-be prophets and their prophesyings, hold yourselves aloof from every such form when it is evil, lit., "Hold yourselves aloof from every evil appearance" or "form." **23. the very God**—rather as the *Greek*, "the God of peace *Himself*"; who can do for you by His own power what *I* cannot do by all my monitions, nor *you* by all your efforts (Rom. 16:20; Heb. 13:20), viz., keep you from all evil, and give you all that is good. **sanctify you**—for *holiness* is the necessary condition of "peace" (Phil. 4:6-9). **wholly**—*Greek*, (so that you should be) "perfect in every respect" [TITTMANN]. **and**—i.e., "*and* so (omit 'I pray God'; not in the *Greek*) may your . . . spirit and soul and body be preserved. . . ." **whole**—A different *Greek* word from "wholly." Translate, "entire"; with none of the integral parts wanting [TITTMANN]. It refers to man in his normal integrity, as originally designed; an ideal which shall be attained by the glorified believer. All three, spirit, soul, and body, each in its due place, constitute man "entire." The "spirit" links man with the higher intelligences of heaven, and is that highest part of man which is receptive of the quickening Holy Spirit (I Cor. 15: 47). In the unspiritual, the spirit is so sunk under the lower animal *soul* (which it ought to keep under) that such are termed "animal" (*English Version*, "sensual," having merely the *body* of organized matter, and the *soul* the immaterial animating essence), having *not the Spirit* (cf. I Cor. 2:14; *Notes*, 15:44; 46-48; John 3:6). The unbeliever shall rise with an *animal* (soul-animated) *body*, but not like the believer with a *spiritual* (spirit-endued) body like Christ's (Rom. 8:11). **blameless unto**—rather as

Greek, "blamelessly (so as to be in a blameless state) at the coming of Christ." In *Hebrew,* "peace" and "wholly" (perfect in every respect) are kindred terms; so that the prayer shows what the title "God of peace" implies. BENGEL takes "wholly" as *collectively,* all the Thessalonians without exception, so that no one should fail. And "whole" (entire),, *individually,* each one of them entire, with "spirit, soul, and body." The mention of the preservation of the *body* accords with the subject (ch. 4:16). TRENCH better regards "wholly" as meaning, "having perfectly attained the moral *end,"* viz., to be a full-grown man in Christ. "Whole," *complete,* with no grace which ought to be wanting in a Christian. **24. Faithful**—to His covenant promises (John 10:27-29; I Cor. 1:9; 10:23; Phil. 1:6). **he that calleth you**—God, the caller of His people, will cause His calling not to fall short of its designed end. **do it**—preserve and present you blameless at the coming of Christ (vs. 23; Rom. 8:30; I Pet. 5:10). You must not look at the foes before and behind, on the right hand and on the left, but to God's faithfulness to His promises, God's zeal for His honor, and God's love for those whom He calls. **25.** Some oldest MSS. read, "Pray ye *also* for (lit., *concerning*) us"; make us and our work the subject of your prayers, even as *we* have been just praying for you (vs. 23). Others omit the "also." The clergy need much the prayers of their flocks. Paul makes the same request in the Epistles to Romans, Ephesians, Philippians, Colossians, Philemon, and in II Corinthians; not so in the Epistles to Timothy and Titus, whose intercessions, as his spiritual sons, he was already sure of; nor in the Epistles, I Corinthians and Galatians, as these Epistles abound in rebuke. **26.** Hence it appears this Epistle was first handed to the elders, who communicated it to "the brethren." **holy kiss**—pure and chaste. "A kiss of charity" (I Pet. 5:14). A token of Christian fellowship in those days (cf. Luke 7:45; Acts 20:37), as it is a common mode of salutation in many countries. The custom

hence arose in the early Church of passing the kiss through the congregation at the. holy communion (JUSTIN MARTYR, *Apology,* 1. 65; *Apostolic Constitutions,* 2. 57), the men kissing the men, and the women the women, in the Lord. So in the Syrian Church each takes his neighbor's right hand and gives the salutation, "Peace." **27. I charge**—*Greek,* "I adjure you." **read unto all**—viz., publicly in the congregation at a particular time. The *Greek* aorist implies a single act done at a particular time. The earnestness of his adjuration implies how solemnly important he felt this divinely inspired message to be. Also, as this was the FIRST of the Epistles of the New Testament, he makes this the occasion of a solemn charge, that so its being publicly read should be a sample of what should be done in the case of the others, just as the Pentateuch and the Prophets were publicly read under the Old Testament, and are still read in the synagogue. Cf. the same injunction as to the public reading of the Apocalypse, the LAST of the New Testament canon (Rev. 1:3). The "all" includes women and children, and especially those who could not read it themselves (Deut. 31:12; Josh. 8:33-35). What Paul commands with an adjuration, Rome forbids under a curse [BENGEL]. Though these Epistles had difficulties, the laity were all to hear them read (I Pet. 4:11; II Pet. 3:10; even the very young, II Tim. 1:5; 3:15). "Holy" is omitted before "brethren" in most of the oldest MSS., though some of them support it. **28.** (*Note,* II Cor. 13:14.) Paul ends as he began (ch. 1:1), with "grace." The oldest MSS. omit "Amen," which probably was the response of the Church after the public reading of the Epistle.

The subscription is a comparatively modern addition. The Epistle was not, as it states, written from Athens, but from Corinth; for it is written in the names of Silas and Timothy (besides Paul), who did not join the apostle before he reached the latter city (Acts 18:5).

THE SECOND EPISTLE OF PAUL THE APOSTLE TO THE

T H E S S A L O N I A N S

INTRODUCTION

Its GENUINENESS is attested by POLYCARP (*Epistola ad Philippenses,* sec. 11), who alludes to ch. 3:15. JUSTIN MARTYR, *Dialogue with Tryphonen* (p. 193. 32), alludes to ch. 2:3. IRENÆUS (3. ch. 7., sec. 2) quotes ch. 2:8. CLEMENT OF ALEXANDRIA quotes ch. 3:2, as Paul's words (*Stromata,* 1. 5., p. 554; *Pædagogus,* 1. 17). TERTULLIAN (*De Resurrectio carnis,* ch. 24) quotes ch. 2:1, 2, as part of Paul's Epistle.

DESIGN.—The accounts from Thessalonica, after the sending of the first Epistle, represented the faith and love of the Christians there as on the increase; and their constancy amidst persecutions unshaken. One error of doctrine, however, resulting in practical evil, had sprung up among them. The apostle's description of Christ's sudden second coming (I Thess. 4:13, etc., and 5:2), and the *possibility* of its being at any time, led them to believe it was *actually* at hand. Some professed to know by "the Spirit" (ch. 2:2) that it was so; and others alleged that Paul had said so when with them. A letter, too, purporting to be from the apostle to that effect, seems to have been circulated among them. (That ch. 2:2 refers to such a spurious letter, rather than to Paul's first Epistle, appears likely from the statement, ch. 3:17, as to his autograph salutation being the mark whereby his genuine letters might be known.) Hence some neglected their daily business and threw themselves on the charity of others, as if their sole duty was to wait for the coming of the Lord. This error, therefore, needed rectifying, and forms a leading topic of the second Epistle. He in it tells them (ch. 2), that before the Lord shall come, there must first be a great *apostasy,* and *the Man of Sin* must be revealed; and that the Lord's sudden coming is no ground for neglecting daily business; that to do so would only bring scandal on the Church, and was contrary to his own practice among them (ch. 3:7-9), and that the faithful must withdraw themselves from such disorderly professors (ch. 3:6, 10–15). Thus, there are *three* divisions of the Epistle: (1) Ch. 1:1–12. Commendations of the Thessalonians' faith, love, and patience, amidst persecutions. (2) Ch. 2:1–17. The error as to the immediate coming of Christ corrected, and the previous rise and downfall of the Man of Sin foretold. (3) Ch. 3:1–16. Exhortations to orderly conduct in their whole walk, with prayers for them to the God of peace, followed by his autograph salutation and benediction.

DATE OF WRITING.—As the Epistle is written in the joint names of Timothy and Silas, as well as his own, and as these were with him while at Corinth, and not with him for a long time subsequently to his having left that city (cf. Acts 18:18, with 19:22; indeed, as to Silas, it is doubtful whether he was ever subsequently with Paul), it follows, the *place* of writing must have been Corinth, and the *date*, during the one "year and six months" of his stay there, Acts 18:11 (viz., beginning with the autumn of A.D. 52, and ending with the spring of A.D. 54), say about six months after his first Epistle, early in A.D. 53.

STYLE.—The style is not different from that of most of Paul's other writings, except in the prophetic portion of it (ch. 2:1–12), which is distinguished from them in subject matter. As is usual in his more solemn passages (for instance, in the denunciatory and prophetic portions of his Epistles, e.g., cf. Col. 2:8, 16, with vs. 3; I Cor. 15:24–28, with 8, 9; Rom. 1:18, with vss. 8, 10), his diction here is more lofty, abrupt, and elliptical. As the former Epistle dwells mostly on the second Advent in its aspect of glory to the sleeping and the living saints (I Thess. 4 and 5), so this Epistle dwells mostly on it in its aspect of everlasting destruction to the wicked and him who shall be the final consummation of wickedness, the Man of Sin. So far was Paul from laboring under an erroneous impression as to Christ's speedy coming, when he wrote his first Epistle (which rationalists impute to him), that he had distinctly told them, when he was with them, the same truths as to the apostasy being about first to arise, which he now insists upon in this second Epistle (ch. 2:5). Several points of coincidence occur between the two Epistles, confirming the genuineness of the latter. Thus, cf. ch. 3:2, with I Thessalonians 2:15, 16; again, ch. 2:9, the Man of Sin "coming after the working of Satan," with I Thessalonians 2:18; 3:5, where Satan's incipient work as the *hinderer* of the Gospel, and *the tempter*, appears; again, mild *warning* is enjoined, I Thessalonians 5:14; but, in this second Epistle, when the evil had grown worse, stricter discipline (ch. 3:6, 14): "withdraw from" the "company" of such.

Paul probably visited Thessalonica on his way to Asia subsequently (Acts 20:4), and took with him thence Aristarchus and Secundus: the former became his "companion in travel" and shared with him his perils at Ephesus, also those of his shipwreck, and was his "fellow prisoner" at Rome (Acts 27:2; Col. 4:10; Philemon 24). According to tradition he became bishop of Apamea.

CHAPTER 1

Vss. 1–12. ADDRESS AND SALUTATION: INTRODUCTION: THANKSGIVING FOR THEIR GROWTH IN FAITH AND LOVE, AND FOR THEIR PATIENCE IN PERSECUTIONS, WHICH ARE A TOKEN FOR GOOD EVERLASTING TO THEM, AND FOR PERDITION TO THEIR ADVERSARIES AT CHRIST'S COMING: PRAYER FOR THEIR PERFECTION. **1. in God our Father**—still more endearing than the address, I Thessalonians 1:1 "in God THE Father." **2. from God our Father**—So some oldest MSS. read. Others omit "our." **3. We are bound**—Greek, "We owe it as a debt" (ch. 2:13). They had prayed for the Thessalonians (I Thess. 3:12) that they might "increase and abound in love"; their prayer having been heard, it is a small but a bounden return for them to make, to thank God for it. Thus, Paul and his fellow missionaries practice what they preach (I Thess. 5:18). In I Thessalonians 1:3, their thanksgiving was for the Thessalonians' faith, love, and patience"; here, for their *exceeding growth* in *faith*, and for their *charity abounding*. **We are bound**—expresses the duty of thanksgiving from its subjective side as an inward conviction. "As it is meet," from the *objective* side as something answering to the state of circumstances [ALFORD]. Observe the exact correspondence of the prayer (I Thess. 3:12, "The Lord make you to *abound* in love") and the answer, "The love of every one of you all toward each other aboundeth" (cf. I Thess. 4:10). **meet**—right. **4. glory in you**—make our boast of you, lit., "in your case." "Ourselves" implies that not merely did they hear others speaking of the Thessalonians' faith, but they, the missionaries *themselves,* boasted of it. Cf. I Thessalonians 1:8, wherein the apostle said, their faith was so well known in various places, that he and his fellow missionaries had no need to speak of it; but here he says, so abounding

is their love, combined with faith and patience, that he and his fellow missionaries *themselves,* make it a matter of glorying in the various churches elsewhere (he was now at Corinth in Achaia, and boasted there of the faith of the Macedonian churches, II Cor. 10:15–17; 8:1, at the same time giving the glory to the Lord), not only looking forward to glorying thereat at Christ's coming (I Thess. 2:19), but doing so even now. **patience**—in I Thessalonians 1:3, "patience *of hope.*" Here *hope* is tacitly implied as the ground of their patience; vss. 5, 7 state the object of their hope, viz., the kingdom for which they suffer. **tribulations**—lit., "pressures." The Jews were the instigators of the populace and of the magistrates against Christians (Acts 17:6, 8). **which ye endure**—Greek, "are (now) enduring." **5. Which**—Your *enduring* these tribulations is a "token of the righteous judgment of God," manifested in your being enabled to endure them, and in your adversaries thereby filling up the measure of their guilt. The judgment is even now begun, but its consummation will be at the Lord's coming. David (Ps. 73:1–14) and Jeremiah (12:1–4) were perplexed at the wicked prospering and the godly suffering. But Paul, by the light of the New Testament, makes this fact a matter of consolation. It is a *proof* (so the *Greek*)of the future judgment, which will set to rights the anomalies of the present state, by rewarding the now suffering saint, and by punishing the persecutor. And even now "the Judge of all the earth does right" (Gen. 18:25); for the godly are in themselves sinful and need chastisement to amend them. What they suffer unjustly at the hands of cruel men they suffer justly at the hands of God; and they have their evil things here that they may escape condemnation with the world and have their good things hereafter (Luke 16:25; I Cor. 11:32) [EDMUNDS]. **that ye may be counted worthy**—expressing the purpose of God's "righteous judgment" as regards you. **for which**—*Greek, "in behalf of* which ye are also suffering" (cf. Acts 5: 41; 9:16; Phil. 1:29). "Worthy" implies that, though men are justified by faith, they shall be judged "according to their works" (Rev. 20:12; cf. I Thess. 2:12; I Pet. 1:6, 7; Rev. 20:4). The "also" implies the connection between *the suffering for the kingdom* and *being counted worthy* of it. Cf. Romans 8:17, 18. **6. seeing it is a righteous thing** —This justifies the assertion above of there being a *"righteous* judgment" (vs. 5), viz., "seeing that it is (lit., 'if at least,' 'if at all events it is') a *righteous* thing with (i.e., in the estimation of) God" (which, as we all feel, it certainly is). Our own innate feeling of what is just, in this confirms what is revealed. **recompense**—requite *in kind,* viz., *tribulation* to them that trouble you *(affliction* to those that *afflict* you); and to you who are *troubled, rest from trouble.* **7. rest**—governed by "to recompense" (vs. 6). The *Greek* is lit., "relaxation"; loosening of the *tension* which had preceded; *relaxing* of the strings of endurance now so tightly drawn. The *Greek* word for "rest," Matthew 11: 28, is distinct, viz., *cessation* from labor. Also, Hebrews 4:9, "A keeping of sabbath." **with us**— viz., Paul, Silas, and Timothy, the writers, who are troubled like yourselves. **when**—at the time when . . .; not sooner, not later. **with his mighty angels**—rather as the *Greek,* "with the angels of His might," or "power," i.e., the angels who are the ministers by whom He makes His might to be recognized (Matt. 13:41, 52). It is not *their* might, but His might, which is the prominent thought **8. In flaming fire**—*Greek,* "In flame of fire"; or, as other oldest MSS. read, *in fire of flame.* This *flame of fire* accompanied His manifestation in the bush (Exod. 3:2); also His giving of the law at Sinai (Exod. 19:18). Also it shall accompany His revelation at His advent (Dan. 7:9, 10), symbolizing His own bright glory and His consuming vengeance against His foes (Heb. 10:27; 12:29; II Pet. 3:7, 10). **taking**—lit., *"giving"* them, as their portion, "vengeance." **know not God**—the Gentiles primarily (Ps. 79:6; Gal. 4:8; I Thess. 4:5); not of course those *involuntarily* not knowing God, but those *wilfully* not knowing Him, as Pharaoh, who might have known God if he would, but who boasted "I know not the Lord" (Exod. 5:2); and as the heathen persecutors who might have known God by the preaching of those whom they persecuted. Secondarily, all who "profess to know God but in works deny Him" (Titus 1:16). **obey not the gospel**— primarily the unbelieving Jews (Rom. 10:3, 16); secondarily, all who obey not the truth (Rom. 2:8). **Christ**—omitted by some of the oldest MSS., and retained by others. **9. Who**—*Greek,* "persons who . . . ." **destruction from the presence of the Lord**—driven *far from* His presence [ALFORD]. The sentence *emanating from Him* in person, sitting as Judge [BENGEL], and *driving them far from* Him (Matt. 25:41; Rev. 6:16; 12:14; cf. I Pet. 3:12; Isa. 2:10, 19). "The presence of the Lord" is the source whence the sentence goes forth; "the glory of His power" is the instrument whereby the sentence is carried into execution [EDMUNDS]. But ALFORD better interprets the latter clause (see vs. 10), driven "from the manifestation of His power *in the glorification of His saints." Cast out from the presence of the Lord* is the idea at the root of eternal death, the law of evil left to its unrestricted working, without one counteracting influence of the presence of God, who is the source of all light and holiness (Isa. 66:24; Mark 9:44). **10.** "When He shall have

come." **glorified in his saints**—as the element and mirror IN which His glory shall shine brightly (John 17:10). **admired in all them that believe**—*Greek,* "them that *believed."* Once they *believed,* now they *see:* they had taken His word on trust. Now His word is made good and they need faith no longer. With *wonder* all celestial intelligences (Eph. 3:10) shall see and *admire* the Redeemer on account of the excellencies which He has wrought in them. **because . . .**—Supply for the sense, among whom (viz., those who shall be found to have believed) *you,* too, shall be; "because our testimony unto (so the *Greek* for 'among') you was believed" (and was not rejected as by those "who obey not the Gospel," vs. 8). The early preaching of the Gospel was not abstract discussions, but a *testimony* to facts and truths experimentally known (Luke 24: 48; Acts 1:8). *Faith* is defined by Bishop PEARSON as "an assent unto truths, credible upon the testimony of God, delivered unto us by the apostles and prophets" (originally delivering their testimony orally, but now in their writings). "Glorified in His saints" reminds us that *holiness* is *glory* in the bud; *glory* is *holiness* manifested. **11. Wherefore** —*Greek,* "With a view to which," viz., His glorification in you as His saints. **also**—We not only anticipate the coming glorification of our Lord *in His saints,* but we also pray concerning (so the *Greek)* YOU. **our God**—whom we serve. **count you worthy**—The prominent position of the "YOU" in the *Greek* makes it the emphatic word of the sentence. May *you* be found among the saints whom God shall count worthy of their calling (Eph. 4:1)! There is no dignity in us independent of God's calling of us (II Tim. 1:9). *The calling* here is not merely the first actual call, but the whole of God's electing act, originating in His "purpose of grace given us in Christ before the world began," and having its consummation in glory. **the good pleasure of . . .**—on the part of God [BENGEL]. **faith**—on your part. ALFORD refers the former clause, "good pleasure . . . ," also to *man,* arguing that the *Greek* for "goodness" is never applied to God, and translates, "All [i.e., every possible] *right purpose of goodness."* WAHL, "All *sweetness* of goodness," i.e., impart in full to you all the refreshing delights of goodness. I think that, as in the previous and parallel clause, "calling" refers to GOD'S purpose; and as the *Greek* for "good pleasure" mostly is used of *God,* we ought to translate, "fulfil (His) *every gracious purpose* of goodness" *(on your part),* i.e., fully perfect in you all goodness according to *His gracious purpose.* Thus, "the *grace* of our God," vs. 12, corresponds to *God's* "good pleasure" here, which confirms the *English Version,* just as "the grace of the *Lord Jesus* Christ" is parallel to "work of *faith,"* as Christ especially is the object of faith. "The work of faith"; *Greek,* (no article; supply from the previous clause *all) work* of faith"; faith manifested by *work,* which is its perfected development (Jas. 1:4; cf. *Note, I* Thess. 1:3). *Working reality of faith.* **with power** —*Greek,* "in power," i.e., *"powerfully fulfil* in you" (Col. 1:11). **12. the name of our Lord Jesus**—Our Lord Jesus *in His manifested personality* as the God-man. **in you, and ye in him**—reciprocal glorification; cf. Isaiah 28:5, *"The Lord of hosts shall* be . . . a crown of glory and . . . a diadem of beauty unto . . . . His people," with Isaiah 62:3, *"Thou* (Zion) shalt be a crown of glory in the hand of the Lord, and a royal diadem . . ." (John 21:10; Gal. 1:24; I Pet. 4:14). The believer's graces redound to Christ's glory, and His glory, as their Head, reflects glory on them as the members. **the grace of our God and the Lord Jesus Christ**—There is but one *Greek* article to both, implying the inseparable unity of God and the Lord Jesus.

CHAPTER 2

Vss. 1-17. Correction of Their Error as to Christ's Immediate Coming. The Apostasy That Must Precede It. Exhortation to Steadfastness, Introduced with Thanksgiving for Their Election by God. **1. Now**—rather, "But"; marking the transition from his prayers *for* them to entreaties *to* them. **we beseech you**—or "entreat you." He uses affectionate entreaty, rather than stern reproof, to win them over to the right view. **by**—rather, "with respect to"; as the *Greek* for "of" (II Cor. 1:8). **our gathering together unto him**—the consummating or final gathering together of the saints to Him at His coming, as announced, Matthew 24:31; I Thessalonians 4:17. The *Greek* noun is nowhere else found except in Hebrews 10: 25, said of *the assembling together* of believers for *congregational* worship. Our instinctive fears of the judgment are dispelled by the thought of being gathered together UNTO HIM ("even as the hen gathereth her chickens under her wings"), which ensures our safety. **2. soon**—on trifling grounds, without due consideration. **shaken**—lit., "tossed" as ships tossed by an agitated sea. Cf. for the same image, Ephesians 4:14. **in mind**—rather as the *Greek*, "*from* your mind," i.e., from your mental steadfastness on the subject. **troubled**—This verb applies to *emotional* agitation; as "shaken" to *intellectual*. **by spirit**—by a *person professing* to have the *spirit* of prophecy (I Cor. 12:8-10, I John 4:1-3). The Thessalonians had been warned (I Thess. 5:20, 21) to "prove" such professed prophesyings, and to "hold fast (only) that which is good." **by word**—*of mouth* (cf. vss. 5, 15); some word or saying alleged to be that of Paul, orally communicated. If oral tradition was liable to such perversion in the apostolic age (cf. a similar instance, John 21:23), how much more in our age! **by letter as from us**—purporting to be from us, whereas it is a forgery. Hence he gives a test by which to know his genuine letters (ch. 3:17). **day of Christ**—The oldest MSS. read, "day of *the Lord*." **is at hand**—rather, "is *immediately imminent*," lit., "is *present*;" "is *instantly* coming." Christ and His apostles always taught that the day of the Lord's coming *is at hand;* and it is not likely that Paul would imply anything contrary here; what he denies is, that it is so *immediately imminent, instant*, or *present*, as to justify the neglect of everyday worldly duties. Chrysostom, and after him Alford, translates, "is [already] present" (cf. II Tim. 2:18), a kindred error. But in II Timothy 3:1, the same *Greek* verb is translated "come." Wahl supports this view. The *Greek* is usually used of actual presence; but is quite susceptible of the translation, "is all but present." **3. by any means**—*Greek*, "in any manner." Christ, in Matthew 24:4, gives the same warning in connection with the same event. He had indicated three ways (vs. 2) in which they might be deceived (cf. other ways, vs. 9, and Matthew 24:5, 24). **a falling away**—rather as the *Greek*, "*the* falling away," or "apostasy," viz., *the* one of which "I told you" before (vs. 5), "when I was yet with you," and of which the Lord gave some intimation (Matt. 24:10-12; John 5:43). **that man of sin be revealed** —The *Greek* order is, "And there have been re-

vealed the man of sin." As Christ was first in *mystery*, and afterwards *revealed* (I Tim. 3:16), so Antichrist (the term used I John 2:18; 4:3) is first in mystery, and afterwards shall be developed and revealed (vss. 7-9). As righteousness found its embodiment in Christ, "the Lord our righteousness," so "sin" shall have its embodiment in "the man of sin." *The hindering* power meanwhile restrains its manifestation; when that shall be removed, then this manifestation shall take place. The articles, "*the* apostasy," and "*the* man of sin," may also refer to their being *well known as foretold* in Daniel 7:8, 25, "the little horn speaking great words against the Most High, and thinking to change times and laws"; and 11:36, the wilful king who "shall exalt and magnify himself above every god, and shall speak marvellous things against the God of gods; neither shall he regard any god." **the son of perdition**—a title applied besides to Judas (the traitor, John 17:12), and to none else. Antichrist (the second "beast" coming up out of the earth; therefore he shall at first be "like a lamb, while he speaks as a dragon" (Rev. 13:11); "coming in peaceably and by flatteries," "working deceitfully," but "his heart shall be against the holy covenant" (Dan. 11:21, 23, 28, 30). Seeds of "the falling away" soon appear (I Tim. 4:1-3), but the full development and concentration of these antiChristian elements in one person are still to appear. Contrast the King of Zion's coming as Jesus: **(1)** righteous or *just;* (2) having *salvation;* (3) *lowly;* whereas Antichrist is: (1) "the man of (the embodiment of) *sin;* (2) the son of *perdition;* (3) *exalting himself* above all that is worshipped. He is *the son of perdition*, as consigning many to it, and finally doomed to it himself (Rev. 17:18, 11). "He whose essence and inheritance is perdition" [Alford]. As "the *kingdom* of heaven" is first brought before us in the abstract, then in the concrete, the *King*, the Lord Jesus; so here, first we have (vs. 7) "the mystery of *iniquity*," then "the *iniquitous one*" (vs. 8). Doubtless "the apostasy" of *Romanism* (the abstract) is one of the greatest instances of the working of *the mystery of iniquity*, and its blasphemous claims for the Pope (the concrete) are forerunners of the final concentration of blasphemy in *the man of sin*, who shall not merely, as the Pope, usurp God's honor as *vicegerent* of God, but *oppose* God openly at last. **4.** Daniel 11:36, 37 is here referred to. The words used there as to Antiochus Epiphanes, Paul implies, shall even be more applicable to the man of sin, who is the New Testament actual Antichrist, as Antiochus was the Old Testament typical Antichrist. The previous world kingdoms had each one extraordinary person as its representative head and embodiment (thus Babylon had Nebuchadnezzar, Dan. 2:38, end; Medo-Persia had Cyrus; Greece had Alexander, and Antiochus Epiphanes, the forerunner of Antichrist); so the fourth and last world kingdom, under which we now live, shall have one final head, the concentrated embodiment of all the *sin* and *lawless iniquity* which have been in pagan and papal Rome. Rome's final phase will probably be an unholy alliance between idolatrous superstition and godless infidelity. **Who opposeth and exalteth himself**—There is but one *Greek* article to both participles, implying that the reason why he *opposeth himself* is in order that he may *exalt himself above* .... Alford takes the former clause absolutely, "He that withstands (Christ)," i.e., Antichrist (I John 2: 18). As at the conclusion of the Old Testament period, Israel apostate allied itself with the heathen world power against Jesus and His apostles (Luke 23:12; and at Thessalonica, Acts 17:5-9), and was in righteous retribution punished by the instrumentality of the world power itself (Jerusalem being destroyed by Rome), Daniel 9:26, 27; so the degenerate Church (become an "harlot"), allying itself with the godless world power (the "beast" of Revelation) against vital religion (i.e., the harlot sitting on the beast), shall be judged by that world power which shall be finally embodied in Antichrist (Zech. 13:8, 9; 14:2; Rev. 17:16, 17). In this early Epistle, the apostate Jewish Church as the harlot, and pagan Rome as the beast, form the historical background on which Paul draws his prophetic sketch of the apostasy. In the Pastoral Epistles, which were later, this prophecy appears in connection with Gnosticism, which had at that time infected the Church. The harlot (the apostate Church) is first to be judged by the beast (the world power) and its kings (Rev. 17:16); and afterwards the beasts and their allies (with the personal Antichrist at their head, who seems to rise after the judgment on the harlot, or apostate Church) shall be judged by the coming of Jesus Himself (Rev. 19: 20). Anti-Christian tendencies produce different Antichrists: these separate Antichrists shall hereafter find their consummation in an individual exceeding them all in the intensity of his evil character [AUBERLEN]. But judgment soon overtakes him. He is necessarily *a child of death,* immediately after his *ascent* as *the beast out of the bottomless pit going into perdition* (Rev. 17:8, 11). Idolatry of self, spiritual pride, and *rebellion against God,* are his characteristics; as *Christ-worship, humility,* and *dependence on God,* characterize Christianity. He not merely *assumes* Christ's character (as the "false Christs." Matt. 24:24), but "*opposes*" Christ. The *Greek* implies one *situated on an opposite side* (cf. I John 2:22; II John 7). One who, on the destruction of every religion, shall seek to establish his own throne, and for God's great truth, "God is man," to substitute his own lie, "Man is God" [TRENCH]. **above all that is called God**—(I Cor. 8: 5). The Pope (for instance, Clement VI) has even commanded the angels to admit into Paradise, without the alleged pains of purgatory, certain souls. But still this is only a foreshadowing of the Antichrist, who will not, as the Pope, act *in God's name,* but *against* God. **or that is worshipped**—Rome here again gives a presage of Antichrist. The *Greek* is *Sebasma;* and *Sebastus* is the *Greek* for Augustus, who was worshipped as the secular ruler and divine vicegerent. The papacy has risen on the overthrow of *Cæsar's* power. Antichrist shall exalt himself above *every* object of worship, whether on earth as the Cæsar, or in heaven as God. The various prefigurations of Antichrist, Mohammed, Rome, Napoleon, and modern infidel secularism, contain only *some,* not *all,* his characteristics. It is the union of all in some one person that shall form the full Antichrist, as the union in one Person, Jesus, of all the types and prophecies constituted the full Christ [OLSHAUSEN]. **in the temple of God ... that he is God**—"He will reign a time, times, and half a time" (Dan. 7:25), i.e., three and a half years, and will sit *in the temple at Jerusalem;* then the Lord shall come from heaven and cast him into the lake of fire and shall bring to the saints the times of their reigning, the seventh day of hallowed rest, and give to Abraham the promised inheritance" [IRENÆUS, *Adversus Hœreses,* 30. 4]. **showing himself**—with blasphemous and arrogant DISPLAY (cf. a type, Acts 12:21-23). The earliest

Fathers unanimously looked for a personal Antichrist. Two objections exist to Romanism being regarded *the* Antichrist, though probably Romanism will leave its *culmination* in him: (1) So far is Romanism from *opposing all that is called God,* that adoration of gods and lords many (the Virgin Mary and saints) is a leading feature in it, (2) the papacy has existed for more than twelve centuries, and yet Christ is not come, whereas the prophecy regards the final Antichrist as short-lived, and soon going to perdition through the coming of Christ (Rev. 17:18, 11). Gregory the Great declared against the patriarch of Constantinople, that whosoever should assume the title of "universal bishop" would be "the forerunner of Antichrist." The papacy fulfilled this his undesigned prophecy. The Pope has been called by his followers, "Our Lord God the Pope"; and at his inauguration in St. Peter's, seated in his chair upon the high altar, which is treated as his footstool, he has vividly foreshadowed him who "exalteth himself above all that is called God." An objection fatal to interpreting *the temple of God* here *as the Church* (I Cor. 3:16, 17; 6:19) is, the apostle would never designate the *apostate* anti-Christian Church "the temple *of* God." It is likely that, as Messiah was revealed among the Jews at Jerusalem, so Antimessiah shall appear among them when restored to their own land, and after they have rebuilt their *temple at Jerusalem.* Thus Daniel 11:41, 45 (see my *notes* there), corresponds, "He shall enter the glorious land (Judea), and he shall plant the tabernacles of his palaces between the seas in *the glorious holy mountain";* and then (Dan. 12:1) "Michael, the great prince, shall stand up" to deliver God's people. Cf. *Note,* Daniel 9:26, 27. Also the king of Assyria, type of Antichrist (Isa. 14:12-14). "Lucifer" (a title of Messiah, assumed by Antichrist, Rev. 22: 16); "I will exalt my throne above the stars of God." "I will sit upon the *mount of the congregation* (i.e., God's place of meeting His people of old, the temple), *in the sides of the north* (Ps. 48:2); I will be like the Most High." Revelation 11:1, 2, "The temple of God ... the holy city" (viz., Jerusalem, Matt. 4:5), cf. Psalm 68:18, 29, referring to a period since Christ's ascension, therefore not yet fulfilled (Isa. 2:1-3; Ezek., chs. 40-44; Zech. 14:16-20; Mal. 3:1). "In the temple of God," implies that it is an *internal,* not an exernal, enemy which shall assail the Church. Antichrist shall, the first three and a half years of the prophetical week, keep the covenant, then break it and usurp divine honors in the midst of the week. Some think Antichrist will be a Jew. At all events he will, "by flatteries," bring many, not only of the Gentiles, but also of "the tribes" of Israel (so the *Greek* for "kindreds," Rev. 11:8, 9), to own him as their long-looked-for Messiah, in the same "city where our Lord was crucified." "Sitteth" here implies his occupying the place of power and majesty in opposition to Him who "sitteth on the right hand of the Majesty on high" (Heb. 1:3), and who shall come to "sit" there where the usurper had sat (Matt. 26:64). *Note,* Dan. 9:27; Rev. 11:2, 3, 9, 11. Cf. Ezekiel 38:2, 3, 6, 9, 10, 13, 14, 16, as to Tyre, the type of Antichrist, characterized by similar blasphemous arrogance. **5. Remember ...**—confuting those who represent Paul as having labored under error as to Christ's immediate coming when writing his first Epistle, and as now correcting that error. **I told you**—more than once, lit., "I was telling," or "used to tell." **6. now ye know**—by my having told you. The power must have been one "known" to the

Thessalonians. **what withholdeth**—that which *holds* him *back;* "keeps him in check": the power that has restrained the man of sin from his full and final development, is *the moral and conservative influence of political states* [OLSHAUSEN]: *the fabric of human polity* as a *coercive* power; as "he who now letteth" refers to *those who rule tnat polity* by which the great upbursting of godlessness is kept down [ALFORD]. The "what withholdeth" refers to the *general hindrance;* "he who now letteth," to *the person in whom that hindrance is summed up.* Romanism, as a forerunner of Antichrist, was thus kept in check by *the Roman emperor* (the then representative of the coercive power) until Constantine, having removed the seat of empire to Constantinople, the Roman bishop by degrees first raised himself to precedency, then to primacy, and then to sole empire above the secular power. The historical fact from which Paul starts in his prediction was probably the emperor Claudius' expulsion of the Jews, the representative of the anti-Christian adversary in Paul's day, from Rome, thus "withholding" them in some degree in their attacks on Christianity; this suggested the principle holding good to the end of time, and about to find its final fulfilment in the removal of *the withholding person* or *authority,* whereupon Antichrist in his worst shape shall start up. **that he might be**—Greek, "in order that": ye know that which keeps him back, in God's purposes, from being sooner manifested, *"in order that he may be revealed in his own* time" (i.e., the time appointed by God to him as his proper time for being manifested), not sooner (cf. Dan. 11:35). The removal of the withholding power will be when the civil polity, derived from the Roman empire, which is to be, in its last form, divided into ten kingdoms (Rev. 17:3, 11-13), shall, with its leading representative head for the time being ("he who now letteth," Greek, "withholdeth," as in vs. 6), yield to the prevalent godless "lawlessness" with "the lawless one" as its embodiment. *The elect Church* and *the Spirit* cannot well be, as DE BURGH suggests, the *withholding* power meant; for both shall never be *wholly* "taken out of the way" (Matt. 28:20). However, the testimony of *the elect Church,* and the *Spirit* in her, are the great hindrance to the rise of the apostasy; and it is possible that, though the Lord shall have a faithful few even then, yet the full energy of the Spirit in *the visible* Church, counteracting the energy or "working" of "the mystery of lawlessness" by the testimony of the elect, shall have been so far "taken out of the way," or *set aside,* as to admit the manifestation of "the lawless one"; and so DE BURGH'S view may be right (Luke 18:8; Rev. 11:3-12). This was a power of which the Thessalonians might easily "know" through Paul's instruction. **7. the mystery of iniquity**—the counterwork to "the mystery of godliness" (I Tim. 3:16). Anti-Christianity *latently* working, as distinguished from its final *open* manifestation. "Mystery" in Scripture means, not what remains always a secret, but that which is for a while hidden, but in due time manifested (cf. Eph. 3:4, 5). Satan will resort to a mode of opposition more conformed to the then imminent "appearing" and "presence" of the Saviour, and will anticipate Him with a last effort to maintain the dominion of the world [DE BURGH], just as at His first advent he rushed into open opposition, by taking possession of the bodies of men. "Iniquity," *Greek, lawlessness;* defiant rejection of God's *law* (cf. *Note,* Zech. 5:9, 10). *"Wickedness"* (translated by the LXX by the same *Greek,* meaning "lawlessness," which

Paul employs here), embodied there as a woman, answers to "the mystery of iniquity," here embodied finally in "the man of sin": as the former was ultimately banished for ever from the Holy Land to her own congenial soil, Babylon, so iniquity and the man of sin shall fall before Michael and the Lord Himself, who shall appear as the Deliverer of His people (Dan. 12:1-3; Zech. 14:3-9). Cf. Matthew 12:43. The Jewish nation dispossessed of the evil spirit, the demon of idolatry being cast out through the Babylonian captivity, receives ultimately a worse form of the evil spirit, Christ-opposing self-righteousness. Also, the Christian Church in course of time taken possession of by the demon of Romish idolatry, then dispossessed of it by the Reformation, then its house "garnished" by hypocrisy, secularity, and rationalism, but "swept empty" of living faith, then finally apostatizing and repossessed by "the man of sin," and *outwardly* destroyed for a brief time (though even then Christ shall have witnesses for Him among both the Jews, Zech. 13:9, and Gentiles, Matt. 28:20), when Christ shall suddenly come (Dan. 11:32-45; Luke 18:7, 8). **already**—(II John 9:10; Col. 2:18-23; I Tim. 4:1)— cf. "even now already" (I John 2:18; 4:3) as distinguished from "in his own time" of being revealed *hereafter.* Antiquity, it appears from hence, is not a justification for unscriptural usages or dogmas, since these were "already," even in Paul's time, beginning to spring up: the written word is the only sure test. "Judaism infecting Christianity is the fuel; the mystery of iniquity is the spark." "It is one and the same impurity diffusing itself over many ages" [BENGEL]. **only he who now letteth** *will let*—The italicized words are not in the *Greek.* Therefore, translate rather, "only (i.e., the continuance of *the* MYSTERY of iniquity-working will be *only*) until he who now *withholdeth* (the same *Greek* as in vs. 6) be taken out of the way." "Only (*waiting,* Heb. 10:13) until he . . . ." Then it will work no longer in *mystery,* but in open manifestation. **8.** Translate, "the lawless one"; the embodiment of all the godless "lawlessness" which has been working in "mystery" for ages (vs. 7): "the man of sin" (vs. 3). **whom the Lord**—Some of the oldest MSS. read, "the Lord *Jesus.*" How awful that He whose very name means *God-Saviour,* should appear as the Destroyer; but the *salvation* of the Church requires the destruction of her foe. As the reign of Israel in Canaan was ushered in by judgments on the nations for *apostasy* (for the Canaanites were originally worshippers of the true God: thus Melchisedek, king of Salem, was the "priest of the most high God," Gen. 14:18: Ammon and Moab came from righteous Lot), so the Son of David's reign in Zion and over the whole earth, is to be ushered in by judgments on the apostate Christian world. **consume . . . and . . . destroy**—So Daniel 7:26, "consume and destroy"; Daniel 11:45. He shall "consume" him by His mere breath (Isa 11:4; 30:33): the sentence of judgment being the sharp sword that goeth out of His mouth (Rev. 19: 15, 21). Antichrist's manifestation and destruction are declared in the same breath; at his greatest height he is nearest his fall, like Herod his type (Isa. 1:24-27; Acts 12:20-23). As the advancing fire, while still at a distance consumes little insects [CHRYSOSTOM] by its mere heat, so Christ's mere approach is enough to consume Antichrist. The mere "appearance of the coming" of the Lord of glory is sufficient to show to Antichrist his perfect nothingness. He is seized and "cast alive into the lake of fire" (Rev. 19:20). So the world kingdoms, and the kingdom of the beast, give place to that of the Son of man and His saints. The *Greek* for "destroy" means "abolish" (the same *Greek* is so translated, II Tim. 1:10); i.e., cause every vestige of him to disappear. Cf. as to Gog attacking Israel and destroyed by Jehovah (Ezek. 38 and 39), so as not to leave a vestige of him. **with the brightness of his coming**—*Greek*, "the *manifestation* (or *appearance*) of His *presence*": the first outburst of His advent—the first gleam of His presence—is enough to *abolish* utterly all traces of Antichrist, as darkness disappears before the dawning day. Next, his adherents are "slain with the sword out of His mouth" (Rev. 19:21). BENGEL's distinction between "the appearance of His coming" and the "coming" itself is not justified by I Timothy 6:14; II Timothy 1:10; 4:1, 8; Titus 2:13, where the same *Greek* for "*appearing*" (*English Version*, here "the brightness") plainly refers to *the coming itself*. The expression, "*manifestation* (appearing) of His presence," is used in awful contrast to the *revelation* of the wicked one in the beginning of the verse. **9. whose coming**—The same *Greek* as was used for *the* Lord's coming (vs. 8) or personal "presence." **is**—in its essential character. **after**—*according to* the working ("energy") of Satan, as opposed to the *energy* or *working* of the Holy Spirit in the Church (*Note*, Eph. 1:19). As Christ is related to God, so is Antichrist to Satan, his visible embodiment and manifestation: Satan works through him. Revelation 13:2, "The dragon gave him (the beast) his power . . . seat . . . great authority." **lying wonders** —lit., "wonders" or "prodigies of falsehood." His "power, signs, and wonders," all have *falsehood* for their base, essence, and aim (John 8:44), [ALFORD]. In Matthew 24:24 Jesus implies that the miracles shall be real, though demoniac, such mysterious effects of the powers of darkness as we read of in the case of the Egyptian sorcerers, not such as Jesus performed in their character, power, or aim; for they are against the revealed Word, and therefore not to be accepted as evidences of truth; nay, on the authority of that sure Word of prophecy (here, and Matt. 24:24), to be known and rejected as wrought in support of *falsehood* (Deut. 13:1-3, 5; Gal. 1:8, 9; Rev. 13:11-15; 19:20). The same three *Greek* words occur for *miracles of Jesus* (Acts 2:22, and Heb. 2:4); showing that as the Egyptian magicians imitated Moses (II Tim. 3:1-8), so Antichrist will try to imitate Christ's works as a "sign," or *proof* of divinity. **10. deceivableness**—rather as *Greek*, "deceit of (to promote) unrighteousness" (vs. 12). **in**—The oldest MSS. and versions omit "in." Translate. "*unto* them that *are perishing*" (II Cor. 2:15, 16; 4:3): the victims of him whose very name describes his *perishing* nature, "the son of perdition"; in contrast to *you* whom (vs. 13) "God hath from the beginning chosen to *salvation* through *sanctification* of the Spirit and belief of the truth." **because**—lit., "in requital for"; in just retribution for their having no *love* for the truth which was within their reach (on account of its putting a check on their bad passions), and for their having "pleasure in unrighteousness" (vs. 12; Rom. 1:18); they are *lost* because they loved not, but rejected, the truth which would have *saved* them. **received not** —*Greek*, "welcomed not"; admitted it not cordially. **love of the truth**—not merely love of *truth*, but love of THE *truth* (and of Jesus who is *the* Truth, in opposition to Satan's "lie," vss. 9, 11; John 8:42-44), can *save* (Eph. 4:21). We are required not merely to assent to, but to *love* the truth (Ps. 119:97). The Jews rejected Him who came in His divine Father's name; they will receive Antichrist coming in *his* own name (John 5:43). Their pleasant sin shall prove their terrible scourge. **11. for this cause**— because "they received not the love of the truth." The best safeguard against error is "the love of the truth." **shall send**—*Greek*, "sends," or "is sending"; the "delusion" is already beginning. God judicially sends hardness of heart on those who have rejected the truth, and gives them up in righteous judgment to Satan's delusions (Isa. 6:9, 10; Rom. 1:24-26, 28). They first cast off the love of the truth, then God gives them up to Satan's delusions, then they settle down into "believing the lie": an awful climax (I Kings 22:22, 23; Ezek. 14:9; Job 12: 16; Matt. 24:5, 11; I Tim. 4:1). **strong delusion**— *Greek*, "the powerful working of error," answering to the energizing "working of Satan" (vs. 9); the same expression as is applied to the Holy Ghost's operation in believers: "powerful" or "effectual (energizing) working" (Eph. 1:19). **believe a lie**— rather, "*the* lie" which Antichrist tells them, appealing to his miracles as proofs of it . . . . (vs. 9). **12. they all . . . damned**—rather as *Greek*, "that *all* . . . ." He here states the general proposition which applies specially to Antichrist's adherents. Not all in the Church of Rome, or other anti-Christian systems, shall be damned, but only "all who believed not the truth" *when offered to them*, "but had pleasure in unrighteousness" (Rom. 1:32; 2:8). Love of *unrighteousness* being the great obstacle to *believing the truth*. **13. But**—In delightful contrast to the damnation of the lost (vs. 12) stands the "salvation" of Paul's converts. **are bound**—in duty (ch. 1:3). **thanks . . . to God**—not to ourselves, your ministers, nor to you, our converts. **beloved of the Lord**—Jesus (Rom. 8:37; Gal. 2:20; Eph. 5:2, 25). Elsewhere *God the Father* is said to love us (vs. 16; John 3:16; Eph. 2:4; Col. 3:12). Therefore Jesus and the Father are one. **from the beginning**—"before the foundation of the world" (Eph. 1:4; cf. I Cor. 2:7; II Tim. 1:9); in contrast to those that shall "worship the beast, whose names are not written in the book of life of the Lamb slain from the foundation of the world" (Rev. 13:8). Some of the oldest MSS. read as *English Version*, but other oldest MSS. and *Vulgate* read, "as *first fruits*." The Thessalonians were among the first converts in Europe (cf. Rom. 16:5; I Cor. 16:15). In a more general sense, it occurs in James 1:18; Revelation 14:4; so I understand it here including the more restricted sense. **chosen you**—The *Greek*, is not the ordinary word for "elected," implying His eternal *selection*; but *taken for Himself*, implying His having *adopted* them in His eternal purpose. It is found in the LXX (Deut. 7:7; 10:15). **through**— rather as *Greek*, "*in* sanctification" as the element in which *the choice to salvation* had place (cf. I Pet. 1: 2), standing in contrast to the "unrighteousness," the element in which Antichrist's followers are given over by God to *damnation* (vs. 12). **of the Spirit** —wrought by the Spirit who sanctifies all the elect people of God, first by eternally consecrating them to perfect holiness in Christ, once for all, next by progressively imparting it. **belief of the truth**— contrasted with "believed not the truth" (vs. 12). **14. you**—The oldest MSS. read, "us." **by our gospel**—"*through*" the Gospel which we preach. **to . . . glory**—In vs. 13 it was "salvation," i.e., deliverance from all evil, of body and soul (I Thess. 5:9); here it is positive good, even "glory," and that "the glory of our Lord Jesus" Himself, which believers are privileged to share with Him (John 17:22, 24; Rom. 8:17, 29; II Tim. 2:10). **15. Therefore**—God's sovereign choice of believers, so far from being a ground for inaction on their part, is the strongest incentive to action and perseverance in it. Cf. the argument, Philippians 2:12, 13, "Work out *your own* salvation, FOR it is God which worketh in you . . . ." We cannot fully explain this in *theory;* but to the sincere and humble, the *practical* acting on the principle is plain. "Privilege first, duty afterwards" [EDMUNDS]. **stand fast**—so as not to be "shaken or troubled" (vs. 2). **hold**—so as not to let go. Adding nothing, subtracting nothing [BENGEL]. The Thessalonians had not held fast his oral instructions but had suffered themselves to be imposed upon by pretended spirit-revelations, and words and letters pretending to be from Paul (vs. 2), to the effect that "the day of the Lord was instantly imminent." **traditions**—truths *delivered* and *transmitted* orally, or in writing (ch. 3:6; I Cor. 11:2; *Greek,* "traditions"). The *Greek* verb from which the noun comes, is used by Paul in I Corinthians 11:23; 15:3. From the *three* passages in which "tradition" is used in a good sense, Rome has argued for her accumulation of *uninspired* traditions, virtually overriding God's Word, while put forward as of co-ordinate authority with it. She forgets the *ten* passages (Matt. 15:2, 3, 6; Mark 7:3, 5, 8, 9, 13; Gal. 1:14; Col. 2:8) stigmatizing *man's uninspired* traditions. Not even the apostles' sayings were all inspired (e.g., Peter's dissimulation, Gal. 2:11-14), but only when they claimed to be so, as in their words afterwards embodied in their canonical writings. Oral inspiration was necessary in their case, until the canon of the written Word should be complete; they proved their possession of inspiration by miracles wrought in support of the new revelation, which revelation, moreover, accorded with the existing Old Testament revelation; an additional test needed besides miracles (cf. Deut. 13: 1-6; Acts 17:11). When the canon was complete, the infallibility of the living men was transferred to the written Word, now the sole unerring guide, interpreted by the Holy Spirit. Little else has come down to us by the most *ancient* and *universal* tradition save this, the all-sufficiency of Scripture for salvation. Therefore, by tradition, we are constrained to cast off all tradition not contained in, or not provable by, Scripture. The Fathers are valuable *witnesses to historical facts,* which give force to the *intimations* of Scripture: such as the Christian Lord's day, the baptism of infants, and the genuineness of the canon of Scripture. Tradition (in the sense of *human testimony*) cannot establish a *doctrine,* but can *authenticate a fact,* such as the facts just mentioned. Inspired tradition, in Paul's sense, is not a supplementary oral tradition completing *our* written Word, but it is identical with the written Word *now* complete; then the latter not being complete, the tradition was necessarily in part oral, in part written, and continued so until, the latter being complete before the death of St. John, the last apostle, the former was no longer needed. Scripture is, according to Paul, the complete and sufficient rule in all that appertains to making "the man of God *perfect, throughly furnished* unto *all* good works" (II Tim. 3:16, 17). It is by leaving Paul's God-inspired tradition for human traditions that Rome has become the forerunner and parent of the Antichrist. It is striking that, from this very chapter denouncing Antichrist, she should draw an argument for her "traditions" by which she fosters anti-Christianity. Because the apostles' oral word was as trustworthy as their written word, it by no means follows that the oral

word of those *not apostles* is as trustworthy as the *written* word of those who were apostles or inspired evangelists. No tradition of the apostles except their written word, can be *proved* genuine on satisfactory evidence. We are no more bound to accept implicitly the Fathers' interpretations of Scripture, because we accept the Scripture canon on their testimony, than we are bound to accept the Jews' interpretation of the Old Testament, because we accept the Old Testament canon on their testimony. **our epistle**—as distinguished from a "letter AS from us," vs. 2, viz., that purports to be from us, but is not. He refers to his first Epistle to the Thessalonians. **16, 17. himself**—by His own might, as contrasted with our feebleness; ensuring the efficacy of our prayer. Here *our Lord Jesus* stands first; in I Thessalonians 3:11. "God our Father." **which . . . loved us**—in the work of our redemption. Referring both to *our Lord Jesus* (Rom. 8:37; Gal. 2: 20) and *God our Father* (John 3:16). **everlasting consolation**—not transitory, as worldly consolations in trials (Rom. 8:38, 39). This for all time present, and then "good hope" for the future [ALFORD]. **through grace**—rather as *Greek* "IN grace"; to be joined to "hath given." Grace is the element *in* which the gift was made. **Comfort your hearts**—unsettled as you have been through those who announced the immediate coming of the Lord. **good word and work**—The oldest MSS. invert the order, "work and word." *Establishment* in these were what the young converts at Thessalonica needed, not fanatical teaching (cf. I Cor. 15:58).

CHAPTER 3

Vss. 1-18. HE ASKS THEIR PRAYERS: HIS CONFIDENCE IN THEM: PRAYER FOR THEM: CHARGES AGAINST DISORDERLY IDLE CONDUCT; HIS OWN EXAMPLE: CONCLUDING PRAYER AND SALUTATION. **1. Finally**—lit., "As to what remains." **may have free course**—lit., "may run"; spread rapidly without a drag on the wheels of its course. That the new-creating word may "run" as "swiftly" as the creative word at the first (Ps. 147:15). The opposite is the word of God being "bound" (II Tim. 2:9). **glorified**—by sinners accepting it (Acts 13:48; Gal. 1:23, 24). Contrast "evil spoken of" (I Pet. 4:14). **as it is with you**—(I Thess. 1:6; 4:10; 5:11). **2. that we . . . be delivered from unreasonable . . . men**—lit., men *out of place, inept,* unseemly: *out of the way bad:* more than ordinarily bad. An undesigned coincidence with Acts 18:5-9. Paul was now at Corinth, where the JEWS "opposed themselves" to his preaching: in answer to his prayers and those of his converts at Thessalonica and elsewhere, "the Lord, in vision," assured him of exemption from "the hurt," and of success in bringing in "much people." On the unreasonable, out-of-the-way perversity of the Jews, as known to the Thessalonians, see I Thessalonians 2:15, 16. **have not faith** —or as *Greek,* "the faith" of the Christian: the only antidote to what is "unreasonable and wicked." The Thessalonians, from their ready acceptance of the Gospel (I Thess. 1:5, 6), might think "all" would similarly receive it; but the Jews were far from having such a readiness to believe the truth. **3. faithful**—alluding to "faith" (vs. 2): though many will not believe, the Lord (other very old MSS. read "God") is still to be believed in as faithful to His promises (I Thess. 5:24; II Tim. 2:13). *Faith* on the part of man answers to faithfulness on the part of God. **stablish you**—as he had prayed (ch. 2:17). Though it was on himself that wicked men were making their onset, he turns away from asking the Thessalonians' prayers for HIS deliverance (vs. 2: so unselfish was he, even in religion), to express his assurance of THEIR establishment in the faith, and preservation from evil. This assurance thus exactly answers to his prayer for them (ch. 2:17), "Our Lord. . . *stablish* you in every good word and work." He has before his mind the Lord's Prayer, "Lead us not into temptation, but deliver us from evil"; where, as here, the translation may be, "from the evil one"; the great hinderer of "every good word and work." Cf. Matthew 13:19, "the wicked one." **4. we have confidence in the Lord**—as "faithful" (vs. 3). Have confidence in no man when left to himself [BENGEL]. **that ye both do**—Some of the oldest MSS. insert a clause, "that ye both have done" before, "and are doing, and will do." He means the *majority* by "ye," not *all* of them (cf. vs. 11; ch. 1:3; I Thess. 3:6). **5.** If "the Lord" be here the Holy Ghost (II Cor. 3:17), the three Persons of the Trinity will occur in this verse. **love of God**—love to God. **patient waiting for Christ**—rather as *Greek*, "the patience (endurance) of Christ," viz., which Christ showed [ALFORD] (ch. 2:4; I Thess. 1:3). ESTIUS, however, supports *English Version* (cf. Rev. 1:9; 3:10). At all events, this grace, "patience," or *persevering endurance*, is connected with the "hope" (I Thess. 1:3, 10) of *Christ's coming.* In ALFORD's translation we may compare Hebrews 12: 1, 2, "Run with *patience* (*endurance*) . . . looking to JESUS . . . who, for the joy that was before Him, *endured* the cross"; so WE are to endure, as looking for the hope to be realized at His coming (Heb. 10: 36, 37). **6. we command you**—Hereby he puts to a particular test their obedience in general to his *commands,* which obedience he had recognized in vs. 4. **withdraw**—lit., "to furl the sails"; as we say, *to steer clear of* (cf. vs. 14). Some had given up labor as though the Lord's day was immediately coming. He had enjoined mild censure of such in I Thessalonians 5:14, "*Warn* . . . the unruly"; but now that the mischief had become more confirmed, he enjoins stricter discipline, viz., withdrawal from their company (cf. I Cor.. 5:11; II John 10:11): not a formal sentence of excommunication, such as was subsequently passed on more heinous offenders (as in I Cor. 5:5; I Tim. 1:20). He says "brother," i.e., professing Christian; for in the case of unprofessing heathen, believers needed not be so strict (I Cor. 5: 10-13). **disorderly**—Paul plainly would not have sanctioned the *order* of Mendicant Friars, who reduce such a "disorderly" and lazy life to a system. Call it not an *order,* but a *burden* to the community (BENGEL, alluding to the *Greek,* vs. 8, for "be chargeable," lit., "be a burden"). **the tradition**—the oral instruction which he had given to them when present (vs. 10), and subsequently committed to writing (I Thess. 4:11, 12). **which he received of us**—Some oldest MSS. read, "*ye* received"; others, "*they* received." The *English Version* reading has no very old authority. **7. how ye ought to follow us**—how ye ought to live so as *to* "imitate (so the *Greek* for 'follow') *us*" (cf. *Note,* I Cor. 11:1; I Thess. 1:6). **8. eat any man's bread**—*Greek,* "eat bread *from* any man," i.e., live at anyone's expense. Contrast vs. 12, "*eat* THEIR OWN bread." **wrought**—(Acts 20: 34). In both Epistles they state they maintained themselves by labor; but in this second Epistle they do so in order to offer themselves herein as an example to the idle; whereas, in the first, their object in doing so is to vindicate themselves from all imputation of mercenary motives in preaching the

Gospel (I Thess. 2:5, 9) [EDMUNDS]. They preached gratuitously though they might have claimed maintenance from their converts. **labour and travail**—"toil and hardship" (*Note,* I Thess. 2:9). **night and day**—scarcely allowing time for repose. **chargeable** —*Greek,* "a burden," or "burdensome." The Philippians did not regard it as a *burden* to contribute to his support (Phil. 4:15, 16), sending to him while he was in this very Thessalonica (Acts 16:15, 34, 40). Many Thessalonians, doubtless, would have felt it a privilege to contribute, but as he saw some idlers among them who would have made a pretext of his example to justify themselves, he waived his right. His reason for the same course at Corinth was to mark how different were his aims from those of the false teachers who sought their own lucre (II Cor. 11:9, 12, 13). It is at the very time and place of writing these Epistles that Paul is expressly said to have *wrought at tent-making* with Aquila (Acts 18: 3); an undesigned coincidence. **9.** (I Cor. 9:4-6, etc.; Gal. 6:6.) **10. For even**—Translate, "For *also.*" We not only set you the example, but gave a positive "command." **commanded**—*Greek* imperfect, "We were commanding"; we kept charge of you. **would not work**—*Greek, "is unwilling* to work." BENGEL makes this to be the argument: not that such a one is to have his food withdrawn from him by others; but he proves from the necessity of *eating* the necessity of *working;* using this pleasantry, Let him who will not work *show himself an angel,* i.e., do without food as the angels do (but since he cannot do without food, then he ought to be not unwilling to work). It seems to me simpler to take it as a punishment of the idle. Paul often quotes good adages current among the people, stamping them with inspired approval. In the *Hebrew, Bereshith Rabba,* the same saying is found; and in the book *Zeror,* "He who will not work before the sabbath, must not eat on the sabbath." **11. busy bodies**—In the *Greek* the similarity of sound marks the antithesis, "Doing none of their own business, yet overdoing in the business of others." Busy about everyone's business but their own. "Nature abhors a vacuum"; so if not doing one's own business, one is apt to meddle with his neighbor's business. Idleness is the parent of busybodies (I Tim. 5:13). Contrast I Thessalonians 4:11. **12. by**—The oldest MSS. read, "IN the Lord Jesus." So the *Greek,* I Thessalonians 4:1, implying the sphere wherein such conduct is appropriate and consistent. "We exhort you thus, as *ministers* IN *Christ,* exhorting our people IN Christ." **with quietness**—quiet industry; laying aside restless, bustling, intermeddling officiousness (vs. 11). **their own**—bread earned by themselves, not another's bread (vs. 8). **13. be not weary**—The oldest MSS. read, "Be not cowardly in"; do not be wanting in strenuousness in doing well. EDMUNDS explains it: Do not *culpably* neglect to do well, viz., with patient industry do your duty in your several callings. In contrast to the "disorderly, not-working busybodies" (vs. 11; cf. Gal. 6:9). **14. note that man**—mark him in your own mind as one to be avoided (vs. 6). **that he may be ashamed**—*Greek,* "made to turn and look into himself, and so be put to shame." Feeling himself shunned by godly brethren, he may become ashamed of his course. **15. admonish him as a brother**—not yet excommunicated (cf. Lev. 19:17). Do not shun him in contemptuous silence, but tell him why he is so avoided (Matt. 18: 15; I Thess. 5:14). **16. Lord of peace**—Jesus Christ. The same title is given to Him as to the Father, "the GOD of peace" (Rom. 15:33; 16:20; II Cor. 13:11). An appropriate title in the prayer here, where the harmony of the Christian community was liable to interruption from the "disorderly." The *Greek* article requires the translation, "Give you *the* peace" which it is "His to give." "Peace" outward and inward, here and hereafter (Rom. 14:17). **always**—unbroken, not changing with outward circumstances. **by all means**—*Greek,* "in every way." Most of the oldest MSS. read, "in every *place";* thus he prays for their peace *in all times* ("always") *and places.* **Lord be with you all**—May He bless you not only with *peace,* but also with His *presence* (Matt. 28:20). Even the disorderly brethren (cf. vs. 15, "a brother") are included in this prayer. **17.** The Epistle was written by an amanuensis (perhaps Silas or Timothy), and only the closing salutation written by Paul's "own hand" (cf. Rom. 16:22; I Cor. 16:21; Col. 4:18). Wherever Paul does not subjoin this autograph salutation, we may presume he wrote the whole Epistle himself (Gal. 6:11). **which**—*which* autograph salutation. **the token**—to distinguish genuine Epistles from spurious ones put forth in my name (ch. 2:2). **in every epistle**—Some think he signed his name to every Epistle with his own hand; but as there is no trace of this in any MSS. of *all* the Epistles, it is more likely that he alludes to *his writing with his own hand in closing every Epistle,* even in those Epistles (Romans, II Corinthians, Ephesians, Philippians, I Thessalonians) wherein he does not specify his having done so. **so I write**—so I sign my name: this is a specimen of my *handwriting,* by which to distinguish my geniune letters from forgeries. **18.** He closes every Epistle by praying for GRACE to those whom he addresses. **Amen**—omitted in the oldest MSS. It was doubtless the response of the congregation after hearing the Epistle read publicly; hence it crept into copies.

The Subscription is spurious, as the Epistle was written not "from Athens," but from *Corinth.*

THE PASTORAL EPISTLES OF PAUL THE APOSTLE TO

TIMOTHY AND TITUS

INTRODUCTION

GENUINENESS.—The ancient Church never doubted of their being canonical and written by Paul. They are in the Peschito-Syriac version of the second century. MURATORI's *Fragment on the Canon of Scripture,* at the close of the second century, acknowledges them as such. IRENÆUS, *Adversus Hæreses,* 1. and 3. 3. 3; 4. 16. 3; 2. 14. 8; 3. 11. 1; 1. 16. 3, quotes I Timothy 1:4, 9; 6:20; II Timothy 4:9–11; Titus 3:10. CLEMENT OF ALEXANDRIA, *Stromata* 2. 457; 3. 534, 536; 1. 350, quotes I Timothy 4:1, 20; II Timothy, as to *deaconesses;* Titus, 1:12. TERTULLIAN, *De præscriptione Hæreticorum,* 25. and 6, quotes I Timothy 6:20; II Timothy 1:14; I Timothy 1:18; 6:13, etc.; II Timothy 2:2; Titus 3:10, 11. EUSEBIUS includes the three in the "universally acknowledged" Scriptures. Also THEOPHILUS OF ANTIOCH (*ad Autolycus,* 3. 14), quotes I Timothy 2:1, 2; Titus 3:1, and CAIUS (in EUSEBIUS, *Ecclesiastical History,* 6. 20) recognizes their authenticity. CLEMENT OF ROME, in the end of the first century, in his first *Epistle to Corinthians,* ch. 29, quotes I Timothy 2:8. IGNATIUS, in the beginning of the second century, in *Epistle to Polycarp,* sec. 6, alludes to II Timothy 2:4. POLYCARP, in the beginning of the second century (*Epistle to Philippians,* ch. 4), alludes to II Timothy 2:4; and in ch. 9 to II Timothy 4:10. HEGISIPPUS, in the end of the second century, in EUSEBIUS, *Ecclesiastical History,* 3. 32, alludes to I Timothy 6:3, 20. ATHENAGORAS, in the end of the second century, alludes to I Timothy 6:16. JUSTIN MARTYR, in the middle of the second century (*Dialogue contra Tryphonen,* 47), alludes to Titus 3:4. The Gnostic MARCION alone rejected these Epistles.

The HERESIES OPPOSED in them form the transition stage from Judaism, in its ascetic form, to Gnosticism, as subsequently developed. The references to Judaism and legalism are clear (I Tim. 1:7; 4:3; Titus 1:10, 14; 3:9). Traces of beginning Gnosticism are also unequivocal (I Tim. 1:4). The Gnostic theory of a twofold principle from the beginning, evil as well as good, appears in germ in I Timothy 4:3, etc. In I Timothy 6:20 the term *Gnosis* ("science") itself occurs. Another Gnostic error, viz., that "the resurrection is past," is alluded to in II Timothy 2:17, 18. The Judaism herein opposed is not that of the earlier Epistles, which upheld the law and tried to join it with faith in Christ for justification. It first passed into that phase of it which appears in the Epistle to the Colossians, whereby will worship and angel worship were superadded to Judaizing opinions. Then a further stage of the same evil appears in the Epistle to the Philippians (3:2, 18, 19), whereby *immoral practice* accompanied false doctrine as to the resurrection (cf. II Tim. 2:18, with I Cor. 15:12, 32, 33). This descent from legality to superstition, and from superstition to godlessness, appears more matured in the references to it in these Pastoral Epistles. The false teachers now know not the true use of *the law* (I Tim. 1:7, 8), and further, have p*ut away good conscience* as well as *the faith* (I Tim. 1:19; 4:2); *speak lies in hypocrisy,* are *corrupt in mind,* and regard *godliness as a means of earthly gain* (I Tim. 6:5; Titus 1:11); *overthrow the faith* by heresies *eating as a canker, saying* the *resurrection is past* (II Tim. 2:17, 18), *leading captive silly women, ever learning yet never knowing the truth, reprobate as Jannes and Jambres* (II Tim. 3:6, 8), *defiled, unbelieving, professing to know God, but in works denying Him, abominable, disobedient, reprobate* (Titus 1:15, 16). This description accords with that in the Catholic Epistles of St. John and St. Peter, and, in the Epistle to the Hebrews. This fact proves the later date of these Pastoral Epistles as compared with Paul's earlier Epistles. The Judaism reprobated herein is not that of an earlier date, so scrupulous as to the law; it was now tending to immortality of practice. On the other hand, the Gnosticism opposed in these Epistles is not the *anti-Judaic* Gnosticism of a later date, which arose as a consequence of the overthrow of Judaism by the destruction of Jerusalem and the temple, but it was the intermediate phase between Judaism and Gnosticism, in which the Oriental and Greek elements of the latter were in a kind of amalgam with Judaism, just prior to the overthrow of Jerusalem.

The DIRECTIONS AS TO CHURCH GOVERNORS and ministers, "bishop-elders, and deacons," are such as were natural for the apostle, in prospect of his own approaching removal, to give to Timothy, the president of the Church at Ephesus, and to Titus, holding the same office in Crete, for securing the due administration of the Church when he should be no more, and at a time when heresies were rapidly springing up. Cf. his similar anxiety in his address to the Ephesian elders (Acts 20:21–30). The Presbyterate (elders; *priest* is a contraction from presbyter) and Diaconate had existed from the earliest times in the Church (Acts 6:3; 11:30; 14:23). Timothy and Titus, as superintendents or overseers (so *bishop* subsequently meant), were to exercise the same power in ordaining elders *at Ephesus* which the apostle had exercised in his *general* supervision of all the Gentile churches.

The PECULIARITIES OF MODES OF THOUGHT AND EXPRESSION, are such as the *difference of subject and circumstances of those addressed* and *those spoken of* in these Epistles, as compared with the other Epistles, would lead us to expect. Some of these peculiar phrases occur also in Galatians, in which, as in the Pastoral Epistles, he, with his characteristic fervor, attacks the false teachers. Cf. I Timothy 2:6; Titus 2:14, "gave Himself for us," with Galatians 1:4; I Timothy 1:17; II Timothy 4:18, "for ever and ever," with Galatians 1:5: "before God," I Timothy 5:21; 6:13; II Timothy 2:14; 4:1, with Galatians 1:20: "a pillar." I Timothy 3:15, with Galatians 2:9: "mediator," I Timothy 2:5, with Galatians 3:20: "in due season," I Timothy 2:6; 6. 15; Titus 1:3 with Galatians 6:9.

TIME AND PLACE OF WRITING.—The First Epistle to Timothy was written not long after Paul had left Ephesus for Macedon (ch. 1:3). Now, as Timothy was in Macedon with Paul (II Cor. 1:1) on the occasion of Paul's having passed from Ephesus into that country, as recorded, Acts 19:22; 20:1, whereas the First Epistle to Timothy contemplates a longer stay of Timothy in Ephesus, MOSHEIM supposes that Paul was nine *months* of the "three years" stay mostly at Ephesus (Acts 20:31) in Macedonia, and elsewhere [perhaps Crete], (the mention of only "three months" and "two years," Acts 19:8, 10, favors this, the remaining nine months being spent elsewhere); and that during these nine months Timothy, in Paul's absence, superintended the Church of Ephesus. It is not likely that Ephesus and the neighboring churches should have been left long without church officers and church organization, rules respecting which are given in this Epistle. Moreover, Timothy was still "a youth" (I Tim. 4:12), which he could hardly be called *after* Paul's first imprisonment, when he must have been at least thirty-four years of age. Lastly, in Acts 20:25, Paul asserts his *knowledge* that *the Ephesians should not all see his face again,* so that I Timothy 1:3 will thus refer to his sojourn at Ephesus, recorded in Acts 19:10, whence he passed into Macedonia. But the difficulty is to account for the false teachers having sprung up almost immediately (according to this theory) after the foundation of the Church. However, his visit recorded in Acts 19 was not his first visit. The beginning of the Church at Ephesus was probably made at his visit a year before (Acts 18:19–21). Apollos, Aquila and Priscilla, carried on the work (Acts 18:24–26). Thus, as to the sudden growth of false teachers, there was time enough for their springing up, especially considering that the first converts at Ephesus were under Apollos' imperfect Christian teachings at first, imbued as he was likely to be with the tenets of Philo of Alexandria, Apollos' native town, combined with John the Baptist's Old Testament teachings (Acts 18:24–26). Besides Ephesus, from its position in Asia, its notorious voluptuousness and sorcery (Acts 19:18, 19), and its lewd worship of Diana (answering to the Phœnician Ashtoreth), was likely from the first to tinge Christianity in some of its converts with Oriental speculations and Asiatic licentiousness of practices. Thus the phenomenon of the phase of error presented in this Epistle, being *intermediate between Judaism and later Gnosticism* (see above), would be such as might occur at an early period in the *Ephesian* Church, as well as later, when we know it had open "apostles" of error (Rev. 2:2, 6), and Nicolaitans infamous in practice. As to the close connection between this First Epistle and the Second Epistle (which must have been written at the close of Paul's life), on which ALFORD relies for his theory of making the First Epistle also written at the close of Paul's life, the similarity of circumstances, the person addressed being one and the same, and either in Ephesus at the time, or at least connected with Ephesus as its church overseer, and having heretics to contend with of the same stamp as in the First Epistle, would account for the connection. There is not so great identity of tone as to compel us to adopt the theory that some years *could not* have elapsed between the two Epistles.

However, all these arguments against the later date may be answered. This First Epistle may refer not to the *first* organization of the Church under its bishops, or elders and deacons, but to the *moral qualifications* laid down at a later period for those officers when scandals rendered such directions needful. Indeed, the object for which he left Timothy at Ephesus he states (I Tim. 1:3) to be, not to organize the Church for the first time, but to restrain the false teachers. The directions as to the choice of fit elders and deacons refer to the filling up of vacancies, not to their first appointment. The fact of there existing an institution for Church widows implies an established organization. As to Timothy's "youth," it may be spoken of *comparatively young* compared with Paul, now "the aged" (Philemon 9), and with some of the Ephesian elders, senior to Timothy *their overseer.* As to Acts 20:25, we know not but that "all" of the elders of Ephesus called to Miletus "never saw Paul's face" afterwards, as he "knew" (doubtless by inspiration) would be the case, which obviates the need of ALFORD's lax view, that Paul was wrong in this his positive inspired anticipation (for such it was, not a mere boding surmise as to the future). Thus he probably visited Ephesus again (I Tim. 1:3; II Tim. 1:18; 4:20, he would hardly have been *at Miletum,* so near Ephesus, without visiting Ephesus) after his first imprisonment in Rome, though all the Ephesian elders whom he had addressed formerly at Miletus did not again see him. The general similarity of subject and style, and of the *state of the* Church between the two Epistles, favors the view that they were near one another in date. Also, against the theory of the early date is the difficulty of defining, when, during Paul's two or three years' stay at Ephesus, we can insert an absence of Paul from Ephesus long enough for the requirements of the case, which imply a lengthened stay and superintendence of Timothy at Ephesus (see, however, I Tim. 3:14, on the other side) after having been "left" by Paul there. Timothy did not stay there when Paul left Ephesus (Acts 19:22; 20:1; II Cor. 1:1). In I Timothy 3:14, Paul says, "I write, hoping to come unto thee *shortly*," but on the earlier occasion of his passing from Ephesus to Macedon he had no such expectation, but had planned to spend the summer in Macedon, and the winter in Corinth, (I Cor. 16:6). The expression *"Till I come"* (I Tim. 4:13), implies that Timothy was not to leave his post till Paul should arrive; this and the former objection, however, do not hold good against MOSHEIM's theory. Moreover, Paul in his farewell address to the Ephesian elders *prophetically anticipates* the rise of false teachers *hereafter* of their own selves; therefore this First Epistle, which speaks of their *actual* presence at Ephesus, would naturally seem to be not prior, but subsequent, to the address, i.e., will belong to the later date assigned. In the Epistle to the Ephesians no notice is taken of the Judæo-Gnostic errors, which would have been noticed had they been really in existence; however, they are alluded to in the contemporaneous sister Epistle to Colossians (Col. 2).

Whatever doubt must always remain as to the date of the First Epistle, there can be hardly any as to that of the Second Epistle. In II Timothy 4:13, Paul directs Timothy to bring the books and cloak which the apostle had left at Troas. Assuming that the visit to Troas referred to is the one mentioned in Acts 20:5-7, it will follow that the cloak and parchments lay for about seven years at Troas, that being the time that elapsed between the visit and Paul's first imprisonment at Rome: a very unlikely supposition, that he should have left either unused for so long. Again, when, during his first Roman imprisonment, he wrote to the Colossians (Col. 4:14) and Philemon (Phil. 24), Demas was with him; but when he was writing II Timothy 4:10, Demas had forsaken him from love of this world, and gone to Thessalonica. Again, when he wrote to the Ephesians, Colossians, Philippians, and Philemon, he had good hopes of a speedy liberation; but here in II Timothy 4:6-8, he anticipates immediate death, having been at least once already tried (II Tim. 4:16). Again, he is in this Epistle represented as in closer confinement than he was when writing those former Epistles in his first imprisonment (even in the Philippians, which represent him in greater uncertainty as to his life, he cherished the hope of soon being delivered, Phil. 2:24; II Tim. 1:16–18; 2:9; 4:6–8, 16). Again (II Tim. 4:20), he speaks of having left Trophimus sick at Miletum. This could not have been on the occasion, Acts 20:15. For Trophimus was with Paul at Jerusalem shortly afterwards (Acts 21:29). Besides, he would thus be made to speak of an event six or seven years after its occurrence, as a recent event: moreover, Timothy was, on that occasion of the apostle being at Miletum, with Paul, and therefore needed not to be informed of Trophimus' sickness there (Acts 20:4–17). Also, the statement (ch. 4:20), "Erastus abode at Corinth," implies that Paul had shortly before been at Corinth, and left Erastus there; but Paul had not been at Corinth for several years before his first imprisonment, and in the interval Timothy had been with him, so that he did not need to write subsequently about that visit. He must therefore have been liberated after his first imprisonment (indeed, Hebrews 13:23, 24, expressly proves that the writer was in *Italy* and *at liberty*), and resumed his apostolic journeyings, and been imprisoned at Rome again, whence shortly before his death he wrote Second Timothy.

EUSEBIUS, *Chronicles, anno* 2083 (beginning October, A.D. 67), says, "Nero, to his other crimes, added the persecution of Christians: under him the apostles Peter and Paul consummated their martyrdom at Rome." So JEROME, *Catalogus Scriptorum Ecclesiasticorum*, "In the fourteenth year of Nero, Paul was beheaded at Rome for Christ's sake, on the same day as Peter, and was buried on the Ostian Road, in the thirty-seventh year after the death of our Lord." ALFORD reasonably conjectures the Pastoral Epistles were written near this date. The interval was possibly filled up (so CLEMENT OF ROME states that Paul preached as far as "to the extremity of the west") by a journey to Spain (Rom. 15:24, 28), according to his own original intention. MURATORI's *Fragment on the Canon* (about A.D. 170) also alleges Paul's journey into Spain. So EUSEBIUS, CHRYSOSTOM, and JEROME. Be that as it may, he seems shortly before his second imprisonment to have visited Ephesus, where a new body of elders governed the Church (Acts 20:25), say in the latter end of A.D. 66, or beginning of 67. Supposing him thirty at his conversion, he would now be upwards of sixty, and older in constitution than in years, through continual hardship. Even four years before he called himself "Paul the aged" (Philemon 9).

From Ephesus he went into Macedonia (I Tim. 1:3). He may have written the First Epistle to Timothy from that country. But his use of "went," not "came," in I Timothy 1:3, "When I went into Macedonia," implies he was not there when writing. Wherever he was, he writes uncertain how long he may be detained from coming to Timothy (I Tim. 3:14, 15). BIRKS shows the probability that he wrote from Corinth, between which city and Ephesus the communication was rapid and easy. His course, as on both former occasions, was from Macedon to Corinth. He finds a coincidence between I Timothy 2:11–14, and I Corinthians 14:34, as to women being silent in Church; and I Timothy 5:17, 18, and I Corinthians 9:8–10, as to the maintenance of ministers, on the same principle as the Mosaic law, that the ox should not be muzzled that treadeth out the corn; and I Timothy 5:19, 20, and II Corinthians 13:1–4, as to charges against elders. It would be natural for the apostle *in the very place where these directions had been enforced*, to reproduce them in his letter.

The date of the Epistle to Titus must depend on that assigned to First Timothy, with which it is connected in subject, phraseology, and tone. There is no difficulty in the Epistle to Titus, *viewed by itself*, in assigning it to the earlier date, viz., before Paul's first imprisonment. In Acts 18:18, 19, Paul, in journeying from Corinth to Palestine, for some cause or other landed at Ephesus. Now we find (Titus 3:13) that Apollos in going from Ephesus to Corinth was to touch *at Crete* (which seems to coincide with Apollos' journey from Ephesus to Corinth, recorded in Acts 18:24, 27; 19:1); therefore it is not unlikely that Paul may have taken Crete similarly on his way between Corinth and Ephesus; or, perhaps been driven out of his course to it in one of his three shipwrecks spoken of in II Corinthians 11:25, 26; this will account for his taking Ephesus on his way from Corinth to Palestine, though out of his regular course. At Ephesus Paul may have written the Epistle to Titus [HUG]; there he probably met Apollos and gave the Epistle to Titus to his charge, before his departure for Corinth by way of Crete, and before the apostle's departure for Jerusalem (Acts 18:19–21, 24). Moreover, on Paul's way back from Jerusalem and Antioch, he travelled some time in Upper Asia (Acts 19:1); and it was then, probably, that his intention to "winter at Nicopolis" was realized, there being a town of that name between Antioch and Tarsus, lying on Paul's route to Galatia (Titus 3:12). Thus, First Timothy will, in this theory, be placed two and a half years later (Acts 20:1; cf. I Tim. 1:3).

ALFORD's argument for classing the Epistle to Titus with First Timothy, as written after Paul's first Roman imprisonment, stands or falls with his argument for assigning First Timothy to that date. Indeed, HUG's unobjectionable argument for the earlier date of the Epistle to Titus, favors the early date assigned to First Timothy, which is so much akin to it, if other arguments be not thought to counterbalance this. The Church of Crete had been just founded (Titus 1:5), and yet the same heresies are censured in it as in Ephesus, which shows that no argument, such as ALFORD alleges against the earlier date of First Timothy, can be drawn from them (Titus 1:10, 11, 15, 16; 3:9, 11). But vice versa, if, as seems likely from the arguments adduced, the First Epistle to Timothy be assigned to the later date, the Epistle to Titus must, from similarity of style, belong to the same period. ALFORD traces Paul's last journey *before his second imprisonment* thus: To Crete (Titus 1:5), Miletus (II Tim. 4:20), Colosse (fulfilling his intention, Philemon 22), Ephesus (I Tim. 1:3; II Tim. 1:18), from which neighborhood he wrote the Epistle to Titus; Troas, Macedonia, Corinth (II Tim. 4:20), Nicopolis (Titus 3:12) *in Epirus*, where he had intended to winter; a place in which, as being a Roman colony, he would be free from tumultuary violence, and yet would be more open to a direct attack from foes in the metropolis, Rome. Being known in Rome as the leader of the Christians, he was probably [ALFORD] arrested as implicated in causing the fire in A.D. 64, attributed by Nero to the Christians, and was sent to Rome by the Duumvirs of Nicopolis. There he was imprisoned as a common malefactor (II Tim. 2:9); his Asiatic friends deserted him, except Onesiphorus (II Tim. 1:16). Demas, Crescens, and Titus, left him. Tychicus he had sent to Ephesus. Luke alone remained with him (II Tim. 4:10–12). Under the circumstances he writes the Second Epistle to Timothy, most likely while Timothy was at Ephesus (II Tim. 2:17; cf. I Tim. 1:20; II Tim. 4:13), begging him to come to him before winter (II Tim. 4:21), and anticipating his own execution soon (II Tim. 4:6). Tychicus was perhaps the bearer of the Second Epistle (II Tim. 4:12). His defense was not made before the emperor, for the latter was then in Greece (II Tim. 4:16, 17). Tradition represents that he died by the sword, which accords with the fact that his Roman citizenship would exempt him from torture; probably late in A.D. 67 or A.D. 68, the last year of Nero.

Timothy is first mentioned, Acts 16:1, as dwelling in Lystra (not Derbe, cf. Acts 20:4). His mother was a Jewess named Eunice (II Tim. 1:5); his father, "a Greek" (i.e., a Gentile). As Timothy is mentioned as "a disciple" in Acts 16:1, he must have been converted before, and this by Paul (I Tim. 1:2), probably at his former visit to Lystra (Acts 14:6); at the same time, probably, that his Scripture-loving mother, Eunice, and grandmother, Lois, were converted to Christ from Judaism (II Tim. 3:14, 15). Not only the good report given as to him by the brethren of Lystra, but also his origin, partly Jewish, partly Gentile, adapted him specially for being Paul's assistant in missionary work, laboring as the apostle did in each place, firstly among the Jews, and then among the Gentiles. In order to obviate Jewish prejudices, he first circumcised him. He seems to have accompanied Paul in his tour through Macedonia; but when the apostle went forward to Athens, Timothy and Silas remained in Berea. Having been sent back by Paul to visit the Thessalonian Church (I Thess. 3:2), he brought his report of it to the apostle at Corinth (I Thess. 3:6). Hence we find his name joined with Paul's in the addresses of both the Epistles to Thessalonians, which were written at Corinth. We again find him "ministering to" Paul during the lengthened stay at Ephesus (Acts 19:22). Thence he was sent before Paul into Macedonia and to Corinth (I Cor. 4:17; 16:10). He was with Paul when he wrote the Second Epistle to Corinthians (II Cor. 1:1); and the following winter in Corinth, when Paul sent from thence his Epistle to the Romans (Rom. 16:21). On Paul's return to Asia through Macedonia, he went forward and waited for the apostle at Troas (Acts 20:3–5). Next we find him with Paul during his imprisonment at Rome, when the apostle wrote the Epistles to Colossians (Col. 1:1), Philemon (Philemon 1), and Philippians (Phil. 1:1). He was imprisoned and set at liberty about the same time as the writer of the Hebrews (Heb. 13:23). In the Pastoral Epistles, we find him mentioned as left by the apostle at Ephesus to superintend the Church there (I Tim. 1:3). The last notice of him is in the request which Paul makes to him (II Tim. 4:21) to "come before winter," i.e. about A.D. 67 [ALFORD]. EUSEBIUS, *Ecclesiastical History*, 3. 42, reports that he was first bishop of Ephesus; and NICOPHORUS, *Ecclesiastical History*, 3. 11, represents that he died by martyrdom. If then, St. John, as tradition represents, resided and died in that city, it must have been *at a later period*. Paul himself ordained or consecrated him with laying on of his own hands, and those of the presbytery, in accordance with prophetic intimations given respecting him by those possessing the prophetic gift (I Tim. 1:18; 4:14; II Tim. 1:6). His self-denying character is shown by his leaving home at once to accompany the apostle, and submitting to circumcision for the Gospel's sake; and also by his abstemiousness (noted in I Tim. 5:23) notwithstanding his bodily infirmities, which would have warranted a more generous diet. Timidity and a want of self-confidence and boldness in dealing with the difficulties of his position, seem to have been a defect in his otherwise beautiful character as a Christian minister (I Cor. 16:10; I Tim. 4:12; II Tim. 1:7).

The DESIGN of the First Epistle was: (1) to direct Timothy to charge the false teachers against continuing to teach other doctrine than that of the Gospel (I Tim. 1:3–20; cf. Rev. 2:1–6); (2) to give him instructions as to the orderly conducting of worship, the qualifications of bishops and deacons, and the selection of widows who should, in return for Church charity, do appointed service (I Tim. 2 to 6:2); (3) to warn against covetousness, a sin prevalent at Ephesus, and to urge to good works (I Tim. 6:3–19).

CHAPTER 1

Vss. 1-20. Address: Paul's Design in Having Left Timothy at Ephesus, viz., to Check False Teachers; True Use of the Law; Harmonizing with the Gospel; God's Grace in Calling Paul, Once a Blasphemer, to Experience and to Preach It; Charges to Timothy. **1. by the commandment of God**—the authoritative *injunction*, as well as the commission, of God. In the earlier Epistles the phrase is, "by the *will* of God." Here it is expressed in a manner implying that a necessity was laid on him to act as an apostle, not that it was merely at his option. The same expression occurs in the doxology, probably written long after the Epistle itself [Alford] (Rom. 16:26). **God our Saviour**—The Father (ch. 2:3; 4:10; Luke 1:47; II Tim. 1:9; Titus 1:3; 2:10; 3:4; Jude 25). It was a Jewish expression in devotion, drawn from the Old Testament (cf. Ps. 106:21). **our hope**—(Col. 1:27; Titus 1:2; 2:13). **2. my own son**—lit., "a *genuine* son" (cf. Acts 16:1; I Cor. 4:14-17). See *Introduction.* **mercy**—added here, in addressing Timothy, to the ordinary salutation, "Grace unto you (Rom. 1:7; I Cor. 1:3,etc.), and peace." In Galatians 6: 16, "peace and *mercy*" occur. There are many similarities of style between the Epistle to the Galatians and the Pastoral Epistles (see *Introduction*); perhaps owing to his there, as here, having, as a leading object in writing, the correction of false teachers, especially as to the right and wrong use of the *law* (vs. 9). If the earlier date be assigned to I Timothy, it will fall not long after, or before (according as the Epistle to the Galatians was written at Ephesus or at Corinth) the writing of the Epistle to the Galatians, which also would account for some similarity of style. "Mercy" is grace of a more tender kind, exercised towards the *miserable*, the experience of which in one's own case especially fits for the Gospel ministry. Cf. as to Paul himself (vss. 14, 16; I Cor. 7:25; II Cor. 4:1; Heb. 2:17) [Bengel]. He did not use "mercy" as to the churches, because "mercy" in all its fulness already existed towards them; but in the case of an individual minister, fresh measures of it were continually needed. "Grace" has reference to the *sins* of men; "mercy" to their *misery*. God extends His *grace* to men as they are guilty; His *mercy* to them as they are miserable [Trench]. **Jesus Christ**—The oldest MSS. read the order, "Christ Jesus." In the Pastoral Epistles "Christ" is often put before "Jesus," to give prominence to the fact that the *Messianic* promises of the Old Testament, well known to Timothy (II Tim. 3: 15), were fulfilled in Jesus. **3.** Timothy's superintendence of the Church at Ephesus was as *locum tenens* for the apostle, and so was temporary. Thus, the office of superintending overseer, needed for a time at Ephesus or Crete, in the absence of the presiding apostle, subsequently became a permanent institution on the removal, by death, of the apostles who heretofore superintended the churches. The first title of these overseers seems to have been "angels" (Rev. 1:20). **3. As I besought thee to remain**—He meant to have added, "*so* I still beseech thee," but does not complete the sentence until he does so *virtually*, not formally, at vs. 18. **at Ephesus**—Paul, in Acts 20:25, declared to the Ephesian elders, "I *know* that ye all shall see my face no more." If, then, as the balance of arguments seems to favor (see *Introduction*), this Epistle was written subsequently to Paul's first imprisonment, the apparent discrepancy between his prophecy and the event may be reconciled by considering that the

terms of the former were not that *he* should never visit *Ephesus* again (which this verse implies he did), but that *they all* should "see his face no more." I cannot think with Birks, that this verse is compatible with his theory, that Paul did not actually visit Ephesus, though in its immediate neighborhood (cf. ch. 3:14; 4:13). The corresponding conjunction to "as" is not given, the sentence not being completed till it is virtually so at vs. 18. **I besought**—a mild word, instead of authoritative command, to Timothy, as a fellow helper. **some**—The indefinite pronoun is *slightly* contemptuous as to them (Gal. 2:12; Jude 4), [Ellicott]. **teach no other doctrine**—than what I have taught (Gal. 1:6-9). His prophetic bodings some years before (Acts 20:29, 30) were now being realized (cf. ch. 6:3). **4. fables**—legends about the origin and propagation of angels, such as the false teachers taught at Colosse (Col. 2:18-23). "Jewish fables" (Titus 1:14). "Profane, and old wives' fables" (ch. 4:7; II Tim. 4:4). **genealogies**—not merely such civil genealogies as were common among the Jews, whereby they traced their descent from the patriarchs, to which Paul would not object, and which he would not as here class with "fables," but Gnostic genealogies of spirits and aeons, as they called them, "Lists of Gnostic emanations" [Alford]. So Tertullian, *Adversus Valentinianos*, c. 3, and Irenæus, *Præf.* The Judaizers here alluded to, while maintaining the perpetual obligation of the Mosaic law, joined with it a theosophic ascetic tendency, pretending to see in it mysteries deeper than others could see. The *seeds, not the fullgrown* Gnosticism of the post-apostolic age, then existed. This formed the transition stage between Judaism and Gnosticism. "Endless" refers to the tedious unprofitableness of their lengthy genealogies (cf. Titus 3:9). Paul opposes to their "aeons," the "King of *the aeons* (so the *Greek*, vs. 17), whom be glory throughout the aeons of aeons." The *word* "aeons" was probably not used in the technical sense of the latter Gnostics as yet; but "the only wise God" (vs. 17), by anticipation, confutes the subsequently adopted notions in the Gnostics' own phraseology. **questions**—of mere speculation (Acts 25:20), not practical; generating merely curious discussions. "Questions and strifes of words" (ch. 6:4): "to no profit" (II Tim. 2:14); "gendering strifes" (II Tim. 2:23). "Vain jangling" (vss. 6, 7) of would-be "teachers of the law." **godly edifying**—The oldest MSS. read, "*the dispensation* of God," the Gospel dispensation of God towards man (I Cor. 9:17), "which is (has) its element) in faith." Conybeare translates, "The exercising of *the stewardship* of God" (I Cor. 9:17). He infers that the false teachers in Ephesus were presbyters, which accords with the prophecy, Acts 20:30. However, the oldest Latin versions, and Irenæus and Hilary, support *English Version* reading. Cf. vs. 5, "faith unfeigned." **5. But**—in contrast to the doctrine of the false teachers. **the end**—the aim. **the commandment**—*Greek*, "of the charge" which you ought to urge on your flock. Referring to the same *Greek* word as in vss. 3, 18; here, however, in a larger sense, as including *the Gospel* "dispensation of God" (*Notes*, vs. 4 and vs. 11). which was the sum and substance of the "charge" committed to Timothy wherewith he should "charge" his flock. **charity**—love; the sum and end of the law and of the Gospel alike, and that wherein the Gospel is the fulfilment of the spirit of the law in its every essential jot and tittle (Rom. 13:10). The foundation is *faith* (vs. 4), the "end" is *love* (vs. 14; Titus 3:15). **out of**—springing as from a fountain. **pure heart**—a heart purified by faith (Acts 15:9; II Tim. 2:22; Titus 1:15). **good conscience**—a conscience cleared from guilt by the effect of sound faith in Christ (vs. 19; ch. 3:9; II Tim. 1:3; I Pet. 3:21). Contrast I Timothy 4:2; Titus 1:15; cf. Acts 23:1. John uses "heart," where Paul would use "conscience." In Paul the understanding is the seat of *conscience;* the *heart* is the seat of *love* [BENGEL]. A good conscience is joined with sound faith; a bad conscience with unsoundness in the faith (cf. Heb. 9:14). **faith unfeigned**—not a hypocritical, dead, and unfruitful faith, but faith working by love (Gal. 5:6). The false teachers drew men off from such a loving, working, real faith, to profitless, speculative "questions" (vs. 4) and jangling (vs. 6). **6. From which**—viz., from a pure heart, good conscience, and faith unfeigned, the well-spring of love. **having swerved**—lit., "having missed the mark (the 'end') to be aimed at." It is translated, "erred," ch. 6:21; II Tim. 2:18. Instead of aiming at and attaining the graces above named, they "have turned aside (ch. 5:15; II Tim. 4:4; Heb. 12:13) unto vain jangling"; lit., "vain talk," about the law and genealogies of angels (vs. 7; Titus 3:9; 1:10); I Timothy 6:20, "vain babblings and oppositions." It is the greatest vanity when divine things are not truthfully discussed (Rom. 1: 21) [BENGEL]. **7.** Sample of their "vain talk" (vs. 6). **Desiring**—They are *would-be* teachers, not really so. **the law**—the Jewish law (Titus 1:14; 3:9). The Judaizers here meant seem to be distinct from those impugned in the Epistles to the Galatians and Romans, who made the works of the law necessary to justification in opposition to Gospel grace. The Judaizers here meant corrupted the law with "fables," which they pretended to found on it, subversive of morals as well as of truth. Their error was not in maintaining the *obligation* of the law, but in *abusing* it by fabulous and immoral interpretations of, and additions to, it. **neither what they say, nor whereof**—neither understanding *their own assertions,* nor the *object* itself about which they make them. They understand as little about the one as the other [ALFORD]. **8. But**—"*Now* we know" (Rom. 3:19; 7:14). **law is good**—in full agreement with God's holiness and goodness. **if a man**—primarily, *a teacher;* then, every Christian. **use it lawfully**—in its lawful place in the Gospel economy, viz., not as a means of a "righteous man" attaining higher perfection than could be attained by the Gospel alone (ch. 4:8; Titus 1:14), which was the perverted use to which the false teachers put it, but as a means of awakening the sense of sin in the ungodly (vss. 9, 10; cf. Rom. 7:7-12; Gal. 3:21). **9. law is not made for a righteous man**—not for one standing by faith in the righteousness of Christ put on him for justification,and imparted inwardly by the Spirit for sanctification. "One not forensically amenable to the law" [ALFORD]. For *sanctification,* the law gives no inward power to fulfil it; but ALFORD goes too far in speaking of the righteous man as "not morally needing the law." Doubtless, in proportion as he is inwardly led by the Spirit, the justified man needs not the law, which is only an outward rule (Rom. 6:14; Gal. 5:18, 23). But as the justified man often does not give himself up wholly to the inward leading of the Spirit, he *morally* needs the outward *law* to show him his sin and God's requirements. The reason why the ten commandments have no power to condemn the Christian, is not that they have no *authority* over him, but because Christ has fulfilled them as our surety (Rom. 10:4). **disobedient**—Greek, "not subject"; insubordinate; it is translated "unruly," Titus 1:6,

10; "lawless and disobedient" refer to opposers of the *law,* for whom it is "enacted" (so the *Greek,* for "is made"). **ungodly and ... sinners**—Greek, he who does *not reverence* God, and he who *openly sins* against Him; the opposers of *God,* from the law comes. **unholy and profane**—those inwardly *impure,* and those deserving exclusion from the outward participation in services of the sanctuary; sinners against the third and fourth commandments. **murderers**—or, as the *Greek* may mean, 'smiters' of fathers and ... mothers; sinners against the fifth commandment. **manslayers**—sinners against the sixth commandment. **10. whoremongers ...**—sinners against the seventh commandment. **men-stealers**—i.e., slave dealers. The most heinous offense against the eighth commandment. No stealing of a man's goods can equal in atrocity the stealing of a man's liberty. Slavery is not directly assailed in the New Testament; to have done so would have been to revolutionize violently the existing order of things. But Christianity teaches principles sure to undermine, and at last overthrow it, wherever Christianity has had its natural development (Matt. 7: 12). **liars ... perjured**—offenders against the ninth commandment. **if there be any other thing ...**—answering to the tenth commandment in its widest aspect. He does not particularly specify it because his object is to bring out the *grosser* forms of transgression; whereas the tenth is deeply spiritual, so much so indeed, that it was by it that the sense of sin, in its subtlest form of "lust," Paul tells us (Rom. 7:7), was brought home to his own conscience. Thus, Paul argues, these *would-be teachers of the law,* while boasting of a higher perfection through it, really bring themselves down from the Gospel elevation to the level of the grossly "lawless," for whom, not for Gospel believers, the law was designed. And in actual practice the greatest sticklers for the law as the means of moral perfection, as in this case, are those ultimately liable to fall utterly from the morality of the law. Gospel grace is the only true means of sanctification as well as of justification. **sound**—*healthy,* spiritually *wholesome* (ch. 6:3; II Tim. 1:13; Titus 1:13; 2:2), as opposed to *sickly, morbid* (as the *Greek* of "doting" means, ch. 6:4), and "canker" (II Tim. 2:17). "The doctrine," or "teaching, which is according to godliness" (ch. 6:3). **11. According to the glorious gospel**—The *Christian's freedom from the law as a sanctifier, as well as a justifier,* implied in the previous, vss. 9, 10, is what this vs. 11 is connected with. This exemption of the righteous from the law, and assignment of it to the lawless as its true object, is "according to the Gospel *of the glory* (so the *Greek,* cf. *Note,* II Cor. 4:4) of the blessed God." The Gospel manifests God's glory (Eph. 1:17; 3:16) in accounting "righteous" the believer, through the righteousness of Christ, without "the law" (vs. 9); and in imparting that righteousness whereby he loathes all those sins against which (vss. 9, 10) the law is directed. The term, "blessed," indicates at once *immortality* and *supreme happiness.* The supremely blessed One is He from whom all blessedness flows. This term, as applied to GOD, occurs only here and in ch. 6:15: appropriate in speaking here of the Gospel blessedness, in contrast to the *curse* on those under the law (vs. 9; Gal. 3:10). **committed to my trust**—Translate as in the *Greek* order, which brings into prominent emphasis *Paul,* "committed in trust to me"; in contrast to the kind of law-teaching which *they* (who had no Gospel commission), the false teachers, *assumed to themselves* (vs. 8; Titus 1:3). **12.** The honor done him in having the Gospel ministry committed to him suggests the digression to what he once was, no better (vs. 13) than those lawless ones described above (vss. 9, 10), when the grace of our Lord (vs. 14) visited him. **and**—omitted in most (not all) of the oldest MSS. **I thank**—*Greek,* "I have (i.e., feel) gratitude." **enabled me**—the same *Greek* verb as in Acts 9:22, "Saul increased the more in strength." An undesigned coincidence between Paul and Luke, his companion. *Enabled me,* viz., for the ministry. "It is not in my own strength that I bring this doctrine to men, but as strengthened and nerved by Him who saved me" [THEODORET]. Man is by nature "without strength" (Rom. 5:6). True conversion and calling confer power [BENGEL]. **for that** —the main ground of his "thanking Christ." **he counted me faithful**—He foreordained and foresaw that I would be faithful to the trust committed to me. Paul's *thanking* God for this shows that the merit of his faithfulness was due solely to God's grace, not to his own natural strength (I Cor. 7:25). *Faithfulness* is the quality required in a steward (I Cor. 4:2). **putting me into**—rather as in I Thessalonians 5:9, "appointing me (in His sovereign purposes of grace) unto the ministry" (Acts 20:24). **13. Who was before**—*Greek,* "Formerly being a blasphemer." "*Notwithstanding that I was* before a blasphemer . . ." (Acts 26:9, 11). **persecutor**—Gal. 1:13). **injurious**—*Greek,* "insulter"; one who acts injuriously from arrogant contempt of others. Translate, Romans 1:30, "despiteful." One who added insult to injury. BENGEL translates, "a despiser." I prefer the idea, *contumelious to others* [WAHL]. Still I agree with BENGEL that "blasphemer" is against *God,* "persecutor," against holy *men,* and "insolently injurious" includes, with the idea of injuring others, that of insolent "uppishness" [DONALDSON] in relation to *one's self.* This threefold relation to God, to one's neighbor, and to one's self, occurs often in this Epistle (vss. 5, 9, 14; Titus 2:12). **I obtained mercy**—God's mercy, and Paul's want of it, stand in sharp contrast [ELLICOTT]; *Greek,* "I was made the object of mercy." The sense of mercy was perpetual in the mind of the apostle (cf. *Note,* vs. 2). Those who have felt mercy can best have mercy on those out of the way (Heb. 5:2, 3). **because I did it ignorantly**—*Ignorance* does not in itself deserve pardon; but it is a less culpable cause of unbelief than pride and wilful hardening of one's self against the truth (John 9:41; Acts 26:9). Hence it is Christ's plea of intercession for His murderers (Luke 23:34); and it is made by the apostles a mitigating circumstance in the Jews' sin, and one giving a hope of a door of repentance (Acts 3:17; Rom. 10:2). The "because . . ." does not imply that ignorance was a sufficient reason for *mercy* being bestowed; but shows how it was possible that such a sinner could obtain mercy. The positive ground of mercy being shown to him, lies solely in the compassion of God (Titus 3:5). The ground of the *ignorance* lies in the *unbelief,* which implies that this ignorance is not unaccompanied with guilt. But there is a great difference between his honest zeal for the law, and a wilful striving against the Spirit of God (Matt. 12:24-32; Luke 11:52) [WIESINGER]. **14. And**—*Greek,* "But." Not only so (was *mercy* shown me), but. . . . **the grace**—by which "I obtained mercy" (vs. 13). **was exceeding abundant**—*Greek,* "superabounded." Where sin abounded, grace did much more abound" (Rom. 5:20). **with faith**—*accompanied with* faith, the opposite of "unbelief" (vs. 13). **love**—in contrast to "a blasphemer, persecutor, and injurious." **which is in Christ**—as

its element and home [ALFORD]: here as its source whence it flows to us. **15. faithful**—worthy of credit, because "God" who says it "is faithful" to His word (I Cor. 1:9; I Thess. 5:24; II Thess. 3:3; Rev. 21:5; 22:6). This seems to have become an axiomatic *saying* among Christians the phrase, "faithful saying," is peculiar to the Pastoral Epistles (ch. 2:11; 4:9; Titus 3:8). Translate as *Greek,* "Faithful is the saying." **all**—all possible; full; to be received by all, and with all the faculties of the soul, mind, and heart. Paul, unlike the false teachers (vs. 7), *understands what he is saying, and whereof he affirms;* and by his simplicity of style and subject, setting forth the grand fundamental truth of salvation through Christ, confutes the false teachers' abstruse and unpractical speculations (I Cor. 1:18-28; Titus 2:1). **acceptation**—*reception* (as of a boon) into the heart, as well as the understanding, with all gladness; this is faith acting on the Gospel offer, and welcoming and appropriating it (Acts 2: 41). **Christ**—as promised. **Jesus**—as manifested [BENGEL]. **came into the world**—which was full of sin (John 1:29; Rom. 5:12; I John 2:2). This implies His pre-existence. John 1:9, *Greek,* "the true Light that, *coming into the world,* lighteth every man." **to save sinners**—even notable sinners like Saul of Tarsus. His instance was without a rival since the ascension, in point of the greatness of the sin, and the greatness of the mercy: that the consenter to Stephen, the proto-martyr's death, should be the successor of the same! **I am**—not merely, "I *was* chief" (I Cor. 15:9; Eph. 3:8; cf. Luke 18:13). To each believer his own sins must always appear, as long as he lives, greater than those of others, which he never can know as he can know his own. **chief**—the same *Greek* as in vs. 16, "first," which alludes to this 15th verse, Translate in both verses, "foremost." Well might he infer where there was mercy for *him,* there is mercy for all who will come to Christ (Matt. 18:11; Luke 19:10). **16. Howbeit** —*Greek,* "But"; contrasting his own conscious sinfulness with God's gracious visitation of him in mercy. **for this cause**—for this very purpose. **that in me**—in my case. **first**—"foremost." As I was "foremost" (*Greek* for *chief,* vs. 15) in sin, so God has made me the "foremost" sample of *mercy.* **show**—to His own glory (the middle *Greek,* voice), Ephesians 2:7. **all long-suffering**—*Greek,* "the whole (of His) long-suffering," viz., in bearing so long with me while I was a persecutor. **a pattern** —a sample (I Cor. 10:6, 11) to assure the greatest sinners of the certainty that they shall not be rejected in coming to Christ, since even Saul found mercy. So David made his own case of pardon, notwithstanding the greatness of his sin, a sample to encourage other sinners to seek pardon (Ps. 32:5, 6). The *Greek* for "pattern" is sometimes used for a "sketch" or outline—the filling up to take place in each man's own case. **believe on him**—Belief rests ON Him as the only foundation on which faith relies. **to life everlasting**—the ultimate aim which faith always keeps in view (Titus 1:2). **17.** A suitable conclusion to the beautifully simple enunciation of the Gospel, of which his own history is a living sample or pattern. It is from the experimental sense of grace that the doxology flows [BENGEL]. **the King, eternal**—lit., "King of the (eternal) ages." The LXX translates Exodus 15:18, "The Lord shall reign *for ages and beyond them.*" Psalm 145:13, *Margin,* "Thy kingdom is an everlasting kingdom," lit., "a kingdom of all ages." The "life everlasting" (vs. 16) suggested here "the King *eternal,*" or *everlasting.* It answers also to "for ever and ever" at the close, lit., "to the ages of the ages" (the countless succession of ages made up of ages). **immortal**—The oldest MSS. read, "incorruptible." *Vulgate*, however, and one very old MS. read as *English Version* (Rom. 1:23). **invisible**—(ch. 6:16; Exod. 33:20; John 1:18; Col. 1:15; Heb. 11:27). **the only wise God**—The oldest MSS. omit "wise," which probably crept in from Romans 16:27, where it is more appropriate to the context than here (cf. Jude 25). "The only Potentate" (ch. 6:15; Ps. 86:10; John 5:44). **for ever . . .**—See *Note*, above. The thought of eternity (terrible as it is to unbelievers) is delightful to those assured of grace (vs. 16) [BENGEL]. **18.** He resumes the subject begun at vs. 3. The conclusion (apodosis) to the foregoing, "*as I besought thee . . . charge*" (vs. 3), is here given, if not formally, at least substantially. **This charge**—viz., "that thou in them (so the *Greek*) mightest war," i.e., fulfil thy high calling, not only as a Christian, but as a *minister* officially, one function of which is, to "*charge* some that they teach no other doctrine" (vs. 3). **I commit**—as a sacred deposit (ch. 6:20; II Tim. 2:2) to be laid before thy hearers. **according to**—in pursuance of; in consonance with. **the prophecies which went before on thee**—the intimations given by prophets respecting thee at thy ordination, ch. 4:14 (as, probably, by Silas, a companion of Paul, and "a prophet," Acts 15:32). Such prophetical intimation, as well as the good report given of Timothy by the brethren (Acts 16:2), may have induced Paul to take him as his companion. Cf. similar prophecies as to others: Acts 13:1-3, in connection with laying on of hands; 11:28; 21:10, 11; cf. I Corinthians 12:10; 14:1; Ephesians 4:11. In Acts 20:28, it is expressly said that "*the Holy Ghost* had made them [the Ephesian presbyters] overseers." CLEMENT OF ROME, *Epistola ad Corinthios*, states it was the custom of the apostles "to make trial by the Spirit," i.e., by the "power of discerning," in order to determine who were to be overseers and deacons in the several churches planted. So CLEMENT OF ALEXANDRIA says as to the churches near Ephesus, that the overseers were marked out for ordination by a revelation of the Holy Ghost to St. John. **by them**—*Greek*, "in them"; arrayed as it were in them; armed with them. **warfare**—not the mere "fight" (ch. 6:12; II Tim. 4:7), but the *whole campaign;* the military service. Translate as *Greek*, not "*a*," but "*the* good warfare." **19. Holding**—Keeping hold of "faith" and "good conscience" (vs. 5); not "putting the latter away" as "some." *Faith* is like a very precious liquor; *a good conscience* is the clean, pure glass that contains it [BENGEL]. The loss of *good conscience* entails the *shipwreck of faith*. Consciousness of sin [unrepented of and forgiven] kills the germ of faith in man [WIESINGER]. **which**—*Greek* singular, viz., "good conscience," not "faith" also; however, the result of *putting away* good conscience is, one *loses* faith also. **put away**—a wilful act. They thrust it from them as a troublesome monitor. It reluctantly withdraws, extruded by force, when its owner is tired of its importunity, and is resolved to retain his sin at the cost of losing it. One cannot be on friendly terms with it and with sin at one and the same time. **made shipwreck**—"with respect to THE faith." *Faith* is the vessel in which they had professedly embarked, of which "good conscience" is the anchor. The ancient Church often used this image, comparing the course of faith to navigation. The *Greek* does not imply that one having once had *faith* makes shipwreck of it, but that they who put away good conscience "make shipwreck with

respect to THE faith." **20. Hymeneus**—There is no difficulty in supposing him to be the Hymeneus of II Timothy 2:17. Though "delivered over to Satan" (the lord of all outside the Church, Acts 26: 18, and the executor of wrath, when judicially allowed by God, on the disobedient, I Cor. 5:5; II Cor. 12:7), he probably was restored to the Church subsequently, and again troubled it. Paul, as an apostle, though distant at Rome pronounced the sentence to be executed at Ephesus, involving, probably, the excommunication of the offenders (Matt. 18:17, 18). The sentence operated not only spiritually, but also physically, sickness, or some such visitation of God, falling on the person excommunicated, in order to bring him to repentance and salvation. Alexander here is probably "the coppersmith" who did Paul "much evil" when the latter visited Ephesus. The "delivering him to Satan" was probably the consequence of his *withstanding* the apostle (II Tim. 4:14, 15); as the same sentence on Hymeneus was the consequence of his "saying that the resurrection is past already" (II Tim. 2:18; his putting away *good conscience*, naturally producing *shipwreck concerning* FAITH, vs. 19. If one's religion better not his morals, his moral deficiencies will corrupt his religion. The rain which falls pure from heaven will not continue pure if it be received in an unclean vessel [ARCHBISHOP WHATELY]). It is possible that he is the Alexander, *then* a Jew, put forward by the Jews, doubtless against Paul, at the riot in Ephesus (Acts 19:33). **that they may**—not "might"; implying that the effect still continues—the sentence is as yet unremoved. **learn**—*Greek*, "be disciplined," viz., by *chastisement* and suffering. **blaspheme**—the name of God and Christ, by doings and teachings unworthy of their Christian profession (Rom. 2:23, 24; Jas. 2:7). Though the apostles had the power of excommunication, accompanied with bodily inflictions, miraculously sent (II Cor. 10:8), it does not follow that fallible ministers now have any power, save that of excluding from church fellowship notorious bad livers.

CHAPTER 2

VSS. 1-15. PUBLIC WORSHIP. DIRECTION AS TO INTERCESSIONS FOR ALL MEN, SINCE CHRIST IS A RANSOM FOR ALL. THE DUTIES OF MEN AND WOMEN RESPECTIVELY IN RESPECT TO PUBLIC PRAYER. WOMAN'S SUBJECTION; HER SPHERE OF DUTY. **1. therefore**—taking up again the general subject of the Epistle in continuation (II Tim. 2:1). "What I have therefore to say to thee by way of a *charge* (ch. 1:3, 18), is . . . ." **that, first of all . . . be made**—ALFORD takes it, "I *exhort first of all to make.*" "First of all," doubtless, is to be connected with "I exhort"; what I *begin* with (for special reasons), is . . . . As the destruction of Jerusalem drew near, the Jews (including those at Ephesus) were seized with the dream of freedom from every yoke; and so virtually "blasphemed" (cf. ch. 1:20) God's name by "speaking evil of dignities" (ch. 6:1; II Pet. 2:10; Jude 8). Hence Paul, in opposition, gives prominence to the injunction that prayer be made for *all* men, especially for *magistrates* and *kings* (Titus 3:1-3) [OLSHAUSEN]. Some professing Christians looked down on all not Christians, as doomed to perdition; but Paul says *all men* are to be prayed for, as Christ died for all (vss. 4-6). **supplications**—a term implying the suppliant's *sense of need*, and of *his own insufficiency.* **prayers**—

implying devotion. **intercessions**—properly *the coming near to God* with childlike confidence, generally *in behalf of another.* The accumulation of terms implies prayer in its every form and aspect, according to all the relations implied in it. **2. For kings**—an effectual confutation of the adversaries who accused the Christians of disaffection to the ruling powers (Acts 17:7; Rom. 13:1-7). **all ... in authority**—lit., " ... in eminence"; in stations of eminence. The "quiet" of Christians was often more dependent on subordinate rulers, than on the supreme king; hence, "*all* ... in authority" are to be prayed for. **that we may lead**—that we may be blessed with such good government as to lead ...; or rather, as *Greek*, "to *pass*" or "spend." The prayers of Christians for the government bring down from heaven peace and order in a state. **quiet** —not troubled *from without.* **peaceable**—"tranquil"; not troubled *from within* [OLSHAUSEN]. "He is *peaceable* (*Greek*) who makes no disturbance; he is *quiet* (*Greek*) who is himself free from disturbance" [TITTMANN]. **in all godliness**—"in all (possible ... requisite) *piety*" [ALFORD]. A distinct *Greek* word, vs. 10, expresses "godliness." **honesty** *Greek*, "gravity" (Titus 2:2, 7), "decorum," or propriety of conduct. As "piety" is in relation to *God*, "gravity" is propriety of behavior among men. In the Old Testament the Jews were commanded to pray for their heathen rulers (Ezra 6: 10; Jer. 29:7). The Jews, by Augustus' order, offered a lamb daily for the Roman emperor, till near the destruction of Jerusalem. The Jewish Zealots, instigated by Eleazar, caused this custom to cease [JOSEPHUS, *B. J.*, 2. 17], whence the war originated, according to JOSEPHUS. **3. this**—praying for all men. **in the sight of God**—not merely *before men*, as if it were their favor that we sought (II Cor. 8:21). **our Saviour**—a title appropriate to the matter in hand. He who is "our Saviour" *is willing that all should be saved* (vs. 4; Rom. 5:18); therefore we should meet the will of God in behalf of others, by praying for the salvation of all men. More would be converted if we would pray more. He has actually saved *us* who believe, being "*our* Saviour." He is willing that all should be saved, even those who do not as yet believe, if they will believe (cf. ch. 4:10; Titus 2:11). **4.** "Imitate God." Since He wishes that all should be saved, do you also wish it; and if you wish it, pray for it. For prayer is the instrument of effecting such things [CHRYSOSTOM]. Paul does not say, "He wishes *to save* all"; for then he *would* have saved all in matter of fact; but "will have all men to be saved," implies the possibility of man's accepting it (through God's prevenient grace) or rejecting it (through man's own perversity). Our prayers ought to include *all,* as God's grace included *all.* **to come**—They are not forced. **unto the knowledge**—*Greek,* "the *full* knowledge" or "recognition" (*Note,* I Cor. 13:12; Phil. 1:9). **the truth**—the saving truth as it is in, and by, Jesus (John 17:3, 17). **5. For there is one God**—God's *unity* in essence and purpose as a proof of His comprehending all His human children alike (created in His image) in His offer of grace (cf. the same argument from His unity, Rom. 3:30; Gal. 3:20); therefore all are to be prayed for. Verse 4 is proved from vs. 5; vs. 1, from vs. 4. The *one God* is common to all (Isa. 45:22; Acts 17:26). The one Mediator is mediator between God and all men potentially (Rom. 3:29; Eph. 4. 5, 6; Heb. 8:6; 9:15; 12:24). They who have not this one God by one Mediator, have none: lit., a "go-between." The Greek order is not "*and* one mediator," but "one

mediator *also* between .... While God will have all men to be saved by knowing God and the Mediator, there is a legitimate, holy order in the exercise of that will wherewith men ought to receive it. All mankind constitute, as it were, ONE MAN before God [BENGEL]. **the man**—rather "man," absolutely and generically: not a mere *individual man:* the Second Head of humanity, representing and embodying in Himself *the whole human race and nature.* There is no "the" in the *Greek.* This epithet is thus the strongest corroboration of his argument, viz., that Christ's mediation affects the whole race, since there is but the one Mediator, designed as the Representative Man for all men alike (cf. Rom. 5:15; I Cor. 8:6; II Cor. 5:19; Col. 2:14). His being "man" was necessary to His being a Mediator, sympathizing with us through experimental knowledge of our nature (Isa. 50:4; Heb. 2:14; 4:15). Even in nature, almost all blessings are conveyed to us from God, not immediately, but through the mediation of various agents. The effectual intercession of Moses for Israel (Numbers 14, and Deuteronomy 9); of Abraham for Abimelech (Gen. 20:7); of Job for his friends (Job 42:10), the mediation being PRESCRIBED *by God* while declaring His purposes of forgiveness: all prefigure the grand mediation for all by the one Mediator. On the other hand, ch. 3:16 asserts that He was also *God.* **6. gave himself**—(Titus 2:14). Not only *the Father* gave Him for us (John 3:16); but *the Son* gave Himself (Phil. 2:5-8). **ransom**— properly of a captive slave. Man was the captive slave of Satan, sold under sin. He was unable to ransom himself, because absolute obedience is due to God, and therefore no act of ours can satisfy for the least offense. Leviticus 25:48 allowed one sold captive to be redeemed by one of his brethren. The Son of God, therefore, became man in order that, being made like unto us in all things, sin only excepted, as our elder brother He should redeem us (Matt. 20:28; Eph. 1:7; I Pet. 1:18, 19). The *Greek* implies not merely *ransom*, but a *substituted* or *equivalent ransom:* the *Greek* preposition, "*anti*," implying reciprocity and vicarious substitution. **for all**—*Greek,* "in behalf of all": not merely for a privileged few; cf. vs. 1: the argument for *praying in behalf of all* is given here. **to be testified**—*Greek,* "the testimony (that which was to be testified of, I John 5:8-11) in its own due times," or *seasons,* i.e., in the times appointed by God for its being testified of (ch. 6:15; Titus 1:3). The oneness of the Mediator, involving the universality of redemption [which faith, however, alone appropriates], was the great subject of Christian testimony [ALFORD] (I Cor. 1:6; 2:1; II Thess. 1:10). **7. Whereunto**—For the giving of which testimony. **I am ordained**—lit., "I was set": the same *Greek,* as "puttting me ... " (ch. 1:12). **preacher**—lit., "herald" (I Cor. 1:21; 9:27; 15:11; II Tim. 1:11; Titus 1:3). He recurs to himself, as in ch. 1:16, in *himself* a living *pattern* or announcement of the Gospel, so here "a herald and teacher of (it to) the Gentiles" (Gal. 2:9; Eph. 3:1-12; Col. 1:23). The universality of his commission is an appropriate assertion here, where he is arguing to prove that prayers are to be made "for *all* men" (vs. 1). **I speak the truth ... and lie not**—a strong asseveration of his universal commission, characteristic of the ardor of the apostle, exposed to frequent conflict (Rom. 11:1; I Cor. 11:13). **in faith and verity** —rather, "in *the* faith and *the* truth." The sphere in which his ministry was appointed to be exercised was *the faith* and *the truth* (vs. 4): *the Gospel truth,* the subject matter of *the faith* [WIESINGER]. **8. I will**—The *active* wish, or desire, is meant. **that men**—rather as *Greek*, "that *the* men," as distinguished from "the women," to whom he has something different to say from what he said to the men (vss. 9-12; I Cor. 11:14, 15; 14:34, 35). The *emphasis*, however, is not on this, but on the precept of *praying*, resumed from vs. 1. **everywhere** —*Greek*, "in every place," viz., of public prayer. Fulfilling Malachi 1:11, "*In every place* . . . from the rising of the sun even unto the going down of the same . . . incense shall be offered unto My name"; and Jesus' words, Matthew 18:20; John 4:21, 23. **lifting up holy hands**—The early Christians turned up their palms towards heaven, as those craving help do. So also Solomon (I Kings 8:22; Ps. 141:2). The Jews washed their hands before prayer (Ps. 26:6). Paul figuratively (cf. Job 17:9; Jas. 4:8) uses language alluding to this custom here: so Isaiah 1:15, 16. The *Greek* for "holy" means hands *which have committed no impiety*, and *observed every sacred duty*. This (or at least the contrite desire to be so) is a needful qualification for effectual prayer (Ps. 24:3, 4). **without wrath**—*putting* it *away* (Matt. 5:23, 24; 6:15). **doubting**— —rather, "disputing," as the *Greek* is translated in Philippians 2:14. Such things *hinder prayer* (Luke 9:46; Rom. 14:1; I Pet. 3:7). BENGEL supports *English Version* (cf. an instance, II Kings 7:2; Matt. 14:31; Mark 11:22-24; Jas. 1:6). **9, 10.** The context requires that we understand these directions as to women, in relation to their deportment *in public worship*, though the rules will hold good on *other* occasions *also*. **in modest apparel**—"in seemly guise" [ELLICOTT]. The adjective means properly, *orderly, decorous*, becoming; the noun in secular writings means *conduct, bearing*. But here "apparel." Women are apt to love fine dress; and at Ephesus the riches of some (ch. 6:17) would lead them to dress luxuriously. The *Greek* in Titus 2:3 is a more general term meaning "deportment." **shamefacedness**—TRENCH spells this word according to its true derivation, "shamefastness" (that which is made fast by an honorable shame); as "steadfastness" (cf. vss. 11, 12). **sobriety**—"self-restraint" [ALFORD]. Habitual inner self-government [TRENCH]. I prefer ELLICOTT's translation, "sobermindedness": the well-balanced state of mind arising from habitual self-restraint. **with**—*Greek*, "in." **braided hair**—lit., "plaits," i.e., plaited hair: probably with the "gold and pearls" intertwined (I Pet. 3:3). Such gaud is characteristic of the spiritual harlot (Rev. 17:4). **10. professing**—*Greek*, "promising": engaging to follow. **with good works**—The *Greek* preposition is not the same as in vs. 9; "by means of"; "*through* good works." Their adorning is to be effected *by means of* good works: not that they are to be clothed *in*, or *with*, them (Eph. 2:10). Works, not words in public, is their province (vss. 8, 11, 12; I Pet. 3:1). *Works* are often mentioned in the Pastoral Epistles in order to oppose the loose living, combined with the loose doctrine, of the false teachers. The discharge of everyday duties is honored with the designation, "good works." **11. learn**—not "teach" (vs. 12; I Cor. 14:34). She should not even put questions in the public assembly (I Cor. 14:35). **with all subjection**—not "usurping authority" (vs. 12). She might teach, but not in public (Acts 18:26). Paul probably wrote this Epistle from Corinth, where the precept (I Cor. 14:34) was in force. **12. usurp authority**—"to lord it over the man" [ALFORD], lit., "to be an autocrat." **13. For**—reason of the precept; the original order of creation. **Adam . . . first**—before Eve, who was created *for him* (I Cor. 11:8, 9). **14. Adam was not deceived**—as Eve was *deceived* by the serpent; but was *persuaded* by his wife. Genesis 3:17, "hearkened unto . . . voice of . . . wife." But in Genesis 3:13, Eve says, "The *serpent beguiled* me." Being more easily deceived, she more easily deceives [BENGEL], (II Cor. 11:3). Last in being, she was first in sin—indeed, she alone was *deceived*. The subtle serpent knew that she was "the weaker vessel." He therefore tempted her, not Adam. She yielded to the temptations of sense and the *deceits of Satan;* he, to *conjugal* love. Hence, in the order of God's judicial sentence, the serpent, the prime offender, stands first; the woman, who was deceived, next; and the man, persuaded by his wife, last (Gen. 3:14-19). In Romans 5:12, Adam is represented as the first transgressor; but there no reference is made to Eve, and Adam is regarded as the head of the sinning race. Hence, as here, vs. 11, in Genesis 3:16, woman's "subjection" is represented as the consequence of her being deceived. **being deceived**—The oldest MSS. read the compound *Greek* verb for the simple, "Having been *seduced by deceit*": implying how *completely* Satan *succeeded in deceiving* her. **was in the transgression**—*Greek*, "*came to be* in the transgression": became involved in the existing state of transgression, lit., "the going beyond a command"; breach of a positive precept (Rom. 4:15). **15. be saved in child-bearing** *Greek*, "in (lit., *through*) (*her* lit., *the*) child-bearing." *Through*, or *by*, is often so used to express not *the means of* her salvation, but *the circumstances* AMIDST *which* it has place. Thus I Corinthians 3:15, "He . . . shall be saved: yet so as by (lit., *through*, i.e., amidst) fire": in spite of the fiery ordeal which he has necessarily to pass *through*, he shall be saved. So here, "*In spite of* the trial of childbearing which she passes *through* (as her portion of the curse, Gen. 3:16, 'in sorrow shalt thou *bring forth children*'), she shall be saved." Moreover, I think it is *implied* indirectly that the very curse will be turned into a condition favorable to her salvation, by her faithfully performing her part in doing and suffering what God has assigned to her, viz., *child-bearing* and home duties, *her* sphere, as distinguished from public teaching, which is not hers, but *man's* (vss. 11, 12). In this home sphere, not ordinarily in one of active duty for advancing the kingdom of God, which contradicts the position assigned to her by God, she will be saved on the same terms as all others, viz., by living faith. Some think that there is a reference to the Incarnation "through THE child-bearing" [*Greek*], the bearing of the child Jesus. Doubtless this is the ground of women's *child-bearing* in general becoming to them a blessing, instead of a curse; just as in the original prophecy (Gen. 3:15, 16) the promise of "the Seed of the woman" (the Saviour) stands in closest connection with the woman's being doomed to "sorrow" in "bringing forth children," her very *child-bearing*, though *in sorrow*, being the function assigned to her by God whereby the Saviour was born. This may be an ulterior reference of the Holy Spirit in this verse; but the primary reference required by the context is the one above given. "She shall be saved ([though] with child-bearing)," i.e., though suffering her part of the primeval curse in childbearing; just as a man shall be saved, though having to bear his part, viz., the sweat of the brow. **if they . . .**—"if *the women* (plural, taken out of "the woman," vs. 14, which is put for *the whole sex*) continue," or more lit., "shall (be found at the judgment to) have continued." **faith and charity**—the essential way to salvation (ch. 1:5). *Faith* is in relation to God. *Charity*, to our fellow man. *Sobriety*, to one's self. **sobriety**—"sober-mindedness" (*Note*, vs. 9, as contrasted with the unseemly forwardness reproved in vs. 11). Mental receptivity and activity in family life were recognized in Christianity as the destiny of woman. One reason alleged here by Paul, is the greater danger of self-deception in the weaker sex, and the spread of errors arising from it, especially in a class of addresses in which sober reflectiveness is least in exercise [NEANDER]. The case (Acts 21:9) was doubtless in private, not in public.

CHAPTER 3

VSS. 1-16. RULES AS TO BISHOPS (OVERSEERS) AND DEACONS. THE CHURCH, AND THE GOSPEL MYSTERY NOW REVEALED TO IT, ARE THE END OF ALL SUCH RULES. **1.** Translate as *Greek*, "Faithful is the saying." A needful preface to what follows: for the office of a bishop or overseer in Paul's day, attended as it was with hardship and often persecution, would not seem to the world generally a desirable and "good work." **desire**—lit., "stretch one's self forward to grasp"; "aim at": a distinct *Greek* verb from that for "desireth." What one does voluntarily is more esteemed than what he does when asked (I Cor. 16:15). This is utterly distinct from ambitious desires after office in the Church. (Jas. 3:1). **biship**—overseer: as yet identical with "presbyter" (Acts 20:17, 28; Titus 1:5-7). **good work**—lit., "honorable work." Not the honor associated with it, but the *work*, is the prominent thought (Acts 15:38; Phil. 2:30; cf. II Tim. 4:5). He who aims at the office must remember the high qualifications needed for the due discharge of its functions. **2.** The existence of Church organization and presbyters at Ephesus is presupposed (ch. 5:17, 19). The institution of Church widows (ch. 5) accords with this. The directions here to Timothy, the president or apostolic delegate, are as to filling up *vacancies* among the bishops and deacons, or *adding* to their number. New churches in the neighborhood also would require presbyters and deacons. Episcopacy was adopted in apostolic times as the most expedient form of government, being most nearly in accordance with Jewish institutions, and so offering the less obstruction through Jewish prejudices to the progress of Christianity. The synagogue was governed by presbyters, "elders" (Acts 4:8; 24:1), called also *bishops* or *overseers*. Three among them presided as "rulers of the synagogue," answering to "bishops" in the modern sense [LIGHTFOOT, *Horæ.*], and one among them took the lead. AMBROSE (in *Amularius de Officiis*, 2. 13, as also BINGHAM, *Ecclesiastical Antiquities*, 2. 11) says, "They who are now called bishops were originally called apostles. But those who ruled the Church after the death of the apostles had not the testimony of miracles, and were in many respects inferior. Therefore they thought it not decent to assume to themselves the name of apostles; but dividing the names, they left to presbyters the name of the *presbytery*, and they themselves were called *bishops*." "*Presbyter*" refers to the *rank;* "bishop," to the *office* or function. Timothy (though not having the name) exercised the power at Ephesus then, which bishops in the modern sense more recently exercised. **blameless**—"unexceptionable"; giving no *just* handle for blame. **hus-**

band of one wife—confuting the celibacy of Rome's priesthood. Though the Jews practiced polygamy, yet as he is writing as to a Gentile Church, and as polygamy was never allowed among even laymen in the Church, the ancient interpretation that the prohibition here is against polygamy in a candidate bishop is not correct. It must, therefore, mean that, though laymen might lawfully marry again, candidates for the episcopate or presbytery were better to have been married only *once*. As in ch. 5:9, "wife of one man," implies a woman married but once; so "husband of one wife" here must mean the same. The feeling which prevailed among the Gentiles, as well as the Jews (cf. as to Anna, Luke 2:36, 37), against a second marriage would, on the ground of expediency and conciliation in matters indifferent and not involving compromise of principle, account for Paul's prohibition here in the case of one in so prominent a sphere as a bishop or a deacon. Hence the stress that is laid in the context on *the repute* in which the candidate for orders is held among those over whom he is to preside (Titus 1: 16). The Council of Laodicea and the apostolic canons discountenanced second marriages, especially in the case of candidates for ordination. Of course second marriage being *lawful*, the undesirableness of it holds good only under special circumstances. It is implied there also, that he who has a wife and virtuous family, is to be preferred to a bachelor; for he who is himself bound to discharge the domestic duties mentioned here, is likely to be more attractive to those who have similar ties, for he teaches them not only by precept, but also by example (vss. 4, 5). The Jews teach, a priest should be neither unmarried nor childless, lest he be unmerciful [BENGEL]. So in the synagogue, "no one shall offer up prayer in public, unless he be married" [In *Colbo*, ch. 65; VITRINGA, *Synagogue*]. **vigilant**—lit., "sober"; ever on the watch, as sober men alone can be; keenly alive, so as to foresee what ought to be done (I Thess. 5:6-8). **sober**—sober-minded. **of good behaviour**—*Greek*, "orderly." "*Sober*" refers to the inward mind; "*orderly*," to the *outward* behavior, tone, look, gait, dress. The new man bears somewhat of a sacred festival character, incompatible with all confusion, disorder, excess, violence, laxity, assumption, harshness, and meanness (Phil. 4:8) [BENGEL]. **apt to teach**—(II Tim. 2:24). **3.** Not given to wine—The *Greek* includes *besides* this, not indulging in *the brawling, violent conduct towards others*, which proceeds from being given to wine. The opposite of "patient" or (*Greek*) "forbearing," reasonable to others (*Note*, Phil. 4:5). **no striker**—with either hand or tongue: not as some teachers pretending a holy zeal (II Cor. 11:20), answering to "not a brawler" or fighter (cf. I Kings 2:24; Neh. 13:25; Isa. 58:4; Acts 23:2; II Tim. 2:24, 25). **not covetous**—*Greek*, "not a lover of money," whether we have much or little (Titus 1:7). **4.** ruleth—*Greek*, "presiding over." **his own house**—children and servants, as contrasted with "the church" (house) of God (vss. 5, 15) which he may be called on to preside over. **having his children**—rather as *Greek*, "having children (who are) in subjection" (Titus 1:6). **gravity** propriety: *reverent* modesty on the part of the children [ALFORD]. The fact that *he has children* who are *in subjection to him in all gravity*, is the recommendation in his favor as one likely to rule well the Church. **5. For**—*Greek*, "But." **the church**—rather, "*a* church" or congregation. How shall he who cannot perform the lesser function, perform the greater and more difficult? **6. not a novice**—one just converted. This proves the Church of Ephesus was established now for some time. The absence of this rule in the Epistle to Titus, accords with the recent planting of the Church at Crete. *Greek, neophyte,* lit., "a young plant"; luxuriantly verdant (Rom. 6:5; 11:-17; I Cor. 3:6). The young convert has not yet been disciplined and matured by afflictions and temptations. Contrast Acts 21:16, "an old disciple." **lifted up with pride**—*Greek,* lit., "wrapt in smoke," so that, inflated with self-conceit and exaggerated ideas of his own importance, he cannot see himself or others in the true light (ch. 6: 4; II Tim. 3:4). **condemnation of the devil**—into the same condemnation as Satan fell into (vs. 7; II Tim. 2:26). Pride was the cause of Satan's condemnation (Job 38:15; Isa. 14:12-15; John 12:31; 16:11; II Pet. 2:4; Jude 6). It cannot mean condemnation or accusation *on the part of the devil.* The devil may bring a *reproach* on men (vs. 7), but he cannot bring them into *condemnation,* for he does not judge, but is judged [BENGEL]. **7. a good report** —*Greek,* "testimony." So Paul was influenced by the good report given of Timothy to choose him as his companion (Acts 16:2). **of them which are without**—from the as yet unconverted Gentiles around (I Cor. 5:12; Col. 4:5; I Thess. 4:12), that they may be the more readily won to the Gospel (I Pet. 2:12), and that the name of Christ may be glorified. Not even the former life of a bishop should be open to reproach [BENGEL]. **reproach and the snare of the devil**—*reproach* of men (ch. 5:14) proving the occasion of his falling into *the snare of the devil* (ch. 6:9; Matt. 22:15; II Tim. 2:26). The *reproach* continually surrounding him for former sins might lead him into *the snare* of becoming as bad as his reputation. Despair of recovering *reputation* might, in a weak moment, lead some into recklessness of living (Jer. 18:12). The reason why only moral qualities of a general kind are specified is, he presupposes in candidates for a bishopric the special gifts of the Spirit (ch. 4:14) and true faith, which he desires to be evidenced outwardly; also he requires qualifications *in a bishop* not so indispensable in others. **8.** The *deacons* were chosen by the voice of the people. CYPRIAN (*Epistle* 2. 5) says that good bishops never departed from the old custom of consulting the people. The deacons answer to the chazzan of the synagogue: the attendant *ministers,* or subordinate coadjutors of the presbyter (as Timothy himself was to Paul, ch. 4:6; Philemon 13; and John Mark, Acts 13:5). Their duty was to read the Scriptures in the Church, to instruct the catechumens in Christian truths, to assist the presbyters at the sacraments, to receive oblations, and to preach and instruct. As the chazzan covered and uncovered the ark in the synagogue, containing the law, so the deacon in the ancient Church put the covering on the communion table. (See CHRYSOSTOM, 19, *Homily* on Acts; THEOPHYLACT on Luke 19; and BALSAMAN on *Canon* 22, *Council of Laodicea.*) The appointing of "the seven" in Acts 6 is perhaps not meant to describe the *first* appointment of the deacons of the Church. At least the chazzan previously suggested the similar order of deacons. **double-tongued**—lit., "of double-speech"; saying one thing to this person, and another to that person [THEODORET]. The extensive personal intercourse that deacons would have with the members of the Church might prove a temptation to such a fault. Others explain it, "Saying one thing, thinking another" (Prov. 20:19; Gal. 2:13). I prefer the former. **not greedy of filthy lucre**— All gain is filthy (lit., "base") which is set before a

man as a by-end in his work for God [ALFORD] (I Pet. 5:2). The deacon's office of collecting and distributing alms would render this a necessary qualification. **9. the mystery of the faith**—*holding the faith,* which to the natural man remains *a mystery,* but which has been revealed by the Spirit to them (Rom. 16:25; I Cor. 2:7-10), *in a pure conscience* (ch. 1:5, 19). ("Pure," i.e., in which nothing base or foreign is intermixed [TITTMANN]). Though deacons were not ordinarily called on to preach (Stephen and Philip are not exceptions to this, since it was as *evangelists,* rather than as *deacons,* they preached), yet as being office-bearers in the Church, and having much intercourse with all the members, they especially needed to have this characteristic, which every Christian ought to have. **10.** "And moreover . . ." [ALFORD]. **be proved**—not by a period of probation, but by a searching inquiry, conducted by Timothy, the ordaining president (ch. 5:22), whether they be "blameless"; then when found so, "let them act as deacons." **blameless**— *Greek,* "unexceptionable"; as the result of public investigation unaccused [TITTMANN]. **11. their wives** —rather, "the women," i.e., *the deaconesses.* For there is no reason that special rules should be laid down as to the wives of the deacons, and not also as to the wives of the bishops or overseers. Moreover, if the wives of the deacons were meant, there seems no reason for the omission of "their" (not in the *Greek*). Also the *Greek* for "even so" (the same as for "likewise," vs. 8, and "in like manner," ch. 2:9), denotes a transition to another class of persons. Further, there were doubtless deaconesses at Ephesus, such as Phœbe was at Cenchrea (Rom. 16:1, "servant," *Greek,* "deaconess"), yet no mention is made of them in this Epistle if not here; whereas, supposing them to be meant here, ch. 3 embraces in due proportion all the persons in the service of the Church. Naturally after specifying the qualifications of the deacon, Paul passes to those of the kindred office, the deaconess. "Grave" occurs in the case of both. "Not slanderers" here, answers to "not double-tongued" in the deacons; so "not false accusers" (Titus 2:3). "Sober" here answers to "not given to much wine," in the case of the deacons (vs. 8). Thus it appears he requires the same qualifications in female deacons as in deacons, only with such modifications as the difference of sex suggested. PLINY, in his celebrated letter to Trajan, *calls* them "female ministers." **faithful in all things**—of life as well as faith. Trustworthy in respect to the alms committed to them and their other functions, answering to "not greedy of filthy lucre," vs. 8, in the case of the deacons. **12. husbands of one wife**—(*Note,* vs. 2). **ruling their children**—There is no article in the *Greek,* "ruling children"; implying that he regarded the *having children to rule* as a qualification (vs. 4; Titus 1:6). **their own houses**—as distinguished from "the Church of God" (*Note,* vs. 5). In the case of the deacons, as in that of the bishops, he mentions the first condition of receiving office, rather than the special qualifications for its discharge. The practical side of Christianity is the one most dwelt on in the Pastoral Epistles, in opposition to the heretical teachers; moreover, as the miraculous gifts began to be withdrawn, the safest criterion of efficiency would be the previous moral character of the candidate, the disposition and talent for the office being presupposed. So in Acts 6:3, a similar criterion was applied, "Look ye out among you seven men *of honest report.*" Less stress is laid on personal dignity in the case of the deacon than in that of the bishop (*Notes*, cf. vss. 2, 3). **13. purchase to themselves a good degree**—lit., "are *acquiring* . . . a . . . *step.*" Understood by many as "a higher step," i.e., promotion to the higher office of presbyter. But ambition of rising seems hardly the motive to faithfulness which the apostle would urge; besides, it would require the comparative, "a *better* degree." Then the *past* aorist participle, "they that used the office of deacon well," implies that the *present* verb, "*are acquiring* to themselves boldness," is the result of the completed action of using the diaconate well. Also, Paul would not probably hold out to every deacon the prospect of promotion to the presbytery in reward of his service. The idea of moving upwards in Church offices was as yet unknown (cf. Rom. 12:7, etc.; I Cor. 12:4-11). Moreover, there seems little connection between reference to a higher Church rank and the words "great boldness.' Therefore, what those who have faithfully discharged the diaconate acquire for themselves is "a good standing-place" [ALFORD] (a well-grounded *hope* of salvation) against the day of judgment, ch. 6:19; I Cor. 3:13, 14 (the figurative meaning of "degree" or "step," being the *degree of worth* which one has obtained in the eye of God [WIESINGER]); and boldness (resting on that *standing-place*), as well for preaching and admonishing others now (Eph. 6:19; a firm standing forth for the truth against error), as also especially in relation to God their coming Judge, before whom they may be boldly confident (Acts 24:16; I John 2:28; 3:21; 4:17; Heb. 4:16). **in the faith**—rather as *Greek*, "in faith," i.e., boldness resting on their own faith. **which is in Christ Jesus**—resting *in* Christ Jesus. **14. write I . . . hoping**—i.e., "though I hope to come unto thee shortly" (ch. 4:13). As his hope was not very confident (vs. 15), he provides for Timothy's lengthened superintendence by giving him the preceding rules to guide him. He now proceeds to give more general instructions to him as an evangelist, having a "gift" committed to him (ch. 4:14). **shortly**—*Greek*, "sooner,' viz., than is presupposed in the preceding directions given to him. See my *Introduction* on this verse. This verse best suits the theory that this First Epistle was not written after Paul's visit and departure from Ephesus (Acts 19 and 20) when he had resolved to winter at Corinth after passing the summer in Macedonia (I Cor. 16: 6), but after his first imprisonment at Rome (Acts 28); probably at Corinth, where he might have some thoughts of going on to Epirus before returning to Ephesus [BIRKS]. **15. But if I tarry long**—before coming to thee. **that**—i.e., I *write* (vs. 14) "that thou mayest know. . . ." **behave thyself**—in directing the Church at Ephesus (ch. 4:11). **the house of God**—the Church (Heb. 3:2, 5, 6; 10:21; I Pet. 4:17; I Cor. 3:16, "the temple of God"; Eph. 2:22). **which is**—i.e., inasmuch as it is. **the church** —"the congregation." The fact that the sphere of thy functions is "the congregation of the living God" (who is the ever living Master of the house, II Tim. 2:19, 20, 21), is the strongest motive to faithfulness in this *behavior as president* of a department of the house." *The living God* forms a striking contrast to the lifeless idol, Diana of Ephesus (I Thess. 1:9). He is the fountain of "truth," and the foundation of our "trust" (ch. 4:10). Labor directed to a particular Church is service to the one great house of God, of which each particular Church is a part, and each Christian a lively stone (I Pet. 2:5). **the pillar and ground of the truth**—evidently predicated of *the Church*, not of "the mystery of godliness" (an interpretation not started

till the 16th century; so BENGEL); for after two weighty predicates, "pillar and ground," and these substantives, the third, a much weaker one, and that an adjective, "confessedly," or "without controversy great," would not come. "Pillar" is so used metaphorically of the three apostles on whom principally the Jewish Christian Church depended (Gal. 2:9; cf. Rev. 3:12). The Church is "the pillar of the truth," as the continued existence (historically) of the truth rests on it; for it supports and preserves the word of truth. He who is of the truth belongs by the very fact to the Church. Christ is the alone ground of the truth in the highest sense (I Cor. 3: 11). The apostles are foundations in a secondary sense (Eph. 2:20; Rev. 21:14). The Church rests on the truth as it is in Christ; not the truth on the Church. But the truth *as it is in itself* is to be distinguished from the truth *as it is acknowledged in the world*. In the former sense it needs no *pillar*, but supports itself; in the latter sense, it needs the Church as its pillar, i.e., its supporter and preserver [BAUMGARTEN]. The importance of Timothy's commission is set forth by reminding him of the excellence of "the house" in which he serves; and this in opposition to the coming heresies which Paul presciently forewarns him of immediately after (ch. 4: 1). The Church is to be the stay of the truth and its conserver for the world, and God's instrument for securing its continuance on earth, in opposition to those heresies (Matt. 16:18; 28:20). The apostle does not recognize a Church which has not the truth, or has it only in part. Rome falsely claims the promise for herself. But it is not historical descent that constitutes a Church, but this only, to those heresies (Matt. 16:18; 28:20). The apostle does not recognize a Church which has not the intermediate; the "ground," or "basement" (similar to "foundation," II Tim. 2:19), the final support of the building [ALFORD]. It is no objection that, having called the Church before "the house of God," he now calls it the "pillar"; for the literal word "Church" immediately precedes the new metaphors: so the *Church*, or congregation of believers, which before was regarded as *the habitation of God*, is now, from a different point of view, regarded as the *pillar* upholding the truth. **16. And**—following up vs. 15: The pillar of the truth is the Church in which thou art required to minister; "AND (that thou mayest know how grand is that *truth* which the Church so upholds) confessedly (so the *Greek* for 'without controversy') great is the mystery of godliness: (viz.) HE WHO (so the oldest MSS. and versions read for 'God') was manifested in (the) flesh (He who) was justified in the Spirit. . . . There is set before us the whole dignity of Christ's person. If He were not essentially superhuman (Titus 2:13), how could the apostle emphatically declare that He was *manifested in* (the) *flesh*? [TREGELLES, *Printed text, Greek New Testament*.] (John 1:14; Phil. 2:7; I John 1:2; 4:2.) Christ, in all His aspects, is Himself "the mystery of godliness." He who before was hidden "with God" was made *manifest* (John 1:1, 14; Rom. 16:25, 26; Col. 1:26; II Tim. 1:10; Titus 2:11; 3:4; I John 3:5, 8). "Confessedly," i.e., by the universal confession of the members of "the "Church," which is in this respect the "pillar" or upholder "of *the truth*." **the mystery**—the divine scheme embodied in CHRIST (Col. 1:27), once hidden from, but now revealed to us who believe. **of godliness**—rather, "piety"; a different *Greek*, expresses godliness (ch. 2:10). In opposition to the *ungodliness* or *impiety* inseparable from error (*departure from the faith*: "doctrines of devils," "profane fables," ch. 4:1, 7; cf. ch. 6:3). To the victims of such error, the "mystery of piety" (i.e., Christ Himself) remains a *mystery unrevealed* (ch. 4:2). It is accessible only to "piety" (vs. 9): in relation to the pious it is termed a "mystery," though *revealed* (I Cor. 2:7-14), to imply the excellence of Him who is the surpassing essential subject of it, and who is Himself "wonderful" (Isa. 9:6, surpassing knowledge (Eph. 3:18, 19); cf. Ephesians 5:32. The apostle now proceeds to unfold this confessedly great mystery in its details. It is not unlikely that some formula of confession or hymn existed in the Church and was generally accepted, to which Paul alludes in the words *"confessedly* great is the mystery . . ." (to wit), "He who was manifested. . . ." Such hymns were then used (cf. Eph. 5:19; Col. 3: 16). PLINY, 1. 10, *Ep.* 97, "They are wont on a fixed day before dawn to meet and sing a hymn in alternate responses to Christ, *as being God";* and EUSEBIUS, *Ecclesiastical History,* 5. 28. The short unconnected sentences with the words similarly arranged, and the number of syllables almost equal, and the ideas antithetically related, are characteristics of a Christian hymn. The clauses stand in parallelism; each two are connected as a pair, and form an antithesis turning on the opposition of heaven to earth; the order of this antithesis is reversed in each new pair of clauses: *flesh* and *spirit, angels* and *Gentiles, world* and *glory;* and there is a correspondence between the first and the last clause: "manifested in the flesh, received up into glory" [WIESINGER]. **justified**—i.e., approved to be righteous [ALFORD]. Christ, while "in the flesh," seemed to be just such a one as men in the flesh, and in fact bore their *sins;* but by having died to sin, and having risen again, He gained for Himself and His people *justifying righteousness* (Isa. 50:8; John 16:10; Acts 22:14; Rom. 4:25; 6:7, 10; Heb. 9:28; I Pet. 3:18; 4:1; I John 2:1) [BENGEL]; or rather, as the antithesis to "was manifest in the flesh" requires, He was justified in the Spirit *at the same time* that He was manifest in the flesh, i.e., He was vindicated as divine "in His Spirit," i.e., in *His higher nature;* in contrast to "in the flesh," *His visible human nature.* This contrasted opposition requires "in the Spirit" to be thus explained: not "by the Spirit," as ALFORD explains it. So Romans 1:3, 4, "Made of the seed of David according to the flesh, and *declared to be the Son of God with power,* according to the Spirit of holiness, by the resurrection from the dead." So "justified" is used to mean *vindicated in one's true character* (Matt. 11:19; Luke 7:35; Rom. 3:4). His manifestation "in the flesh" exposed him to *misapprehension,* as though he were nothing more (John 6:41; 7:27). His *justification,* or vindication, *in respect to His Spirit* or higher being, was effected by ALL *that manifested that higher being,* His words (Matt. 7: 29; John 7:46), His works (John 2:11; 3:2), by His Father's testimony at His baptism (Matt. 3:17), and at the transfiguration (Matt. 17:5), and especially by His resurrection (Acts 13:33; Rom. 1:4), though not by this *exclusively,* as BENGEL limits it. **seen of angels**—answering to "preached unto the Gentiles" (or rather "among *the nations";* including the Jews), on the other hand (Matt. 28:19; Rom. 16:25, 26). "Angels saw the Son of God with us, not having seen Him before" [CHRYSOSTOM]: "not even they had seen His divine nature, which is not visible to any creature, but they saw Him incarnate" [THEODORET](Eph. 3:8, 10; I Pet. 1:12; cf. Col. 1:16, 20). What angels came to know by *seeing,* the nations learned by *preaching.* He is a new message to the

one class as well as to the other; in the wondrous union in His person of things most opposite, viz., heaven and earth, lies "the mystery" [WIESINGER]. If the *English Version,* "Gentiles," be retained, the antithesis will be between the *angels* who are so *near* the Son of God, the Lord of angels, and *the Gentiles* who were so utterly "afar off" (Eph. 2:17). **believed on in the world**—which lieth in wickedness (I John 2:15; 5:19). Opposed to "glory" (John 3:16, 17). This followed upon His being "preached" (Rom. 10:14). **received up into glory**—Greek, "in glory." However, *English Version* may be retained thus, "Received up (*so as now to be) in* glory," i.e., *into glory* (Mark 16:19; Luke 24:51; Acts 1:11). His reception in heaven answers to His reception on earth by being "believed on."

CHAPTER 4

Vss. 1-16. PREDICTION OF A COMING DEPARTURE FROM THE FAITH: TIMOTHY'S DUTY AS TO IT: GENERAL DIRECTIONS TO HIM. The "mystery of iniquity" here alluded to, and already working (II Thess. 2: 7), stands opposed to the "mystery of godliness" just mentioned (I Timothy 3:16). **1. Now**—Greek, "But." In contrast to the "mystery of godliness." **the Spirit**—speaking by the prophets in the Church (whose prophecies rested on those of the Old Testament, Dan. 7:25; 8:23, etc.; 11:30, as also on those of Jesus in the New Testament, Matt. 24:11-24), and also by Paul himself, II Thessalonians 2:3 (with whom accord II Pet. 3:3; I John 2:18; Jude 18). **expressly**—"in plain words." This shows that he refers to prophecies of the Spirit then lying before him. **in the latter times**—in the times *following* upon the times in which he is now writing. Not some remote future, but times *immediately subsequent,* the beginnings of the apostasy being already discernible (Acts 20:29): these are the forerunners of "the *last* days" (II Tim. 3:1). **depart from the faith**—The apostasy was to be within the Church, the faithful one becoming the harlot. In II Thessalonians 2:3 (written earlier), the apostasy of the Jews from God (joining the heathen against Christianity) is the groundwork on which the prophecy rises; whereas here, in the Pastoral Epistles, the prophecy is connected with Gnostic errors, the seeds of which had already been sown in the Church [AUBERLEN] (II Tim. 2:18). Apollonius Tyanæus, a heretic, came to Ephesus in the lifetime of Timothy. **giving heed**—(ch. 1:4; Titus 1:14). **seducing spirits**—working in the heretical teachers. I John 4:2, 3, 6, "the spirit of error," opposed to "the spirit of truth," "the Spirit" which "speaketh" in the true prophets against them. **doctrines of devils**—lit., "teachings of (i.e. suggested by) demons." James 3:15, "wisdom . . . devilish"; II Corinthians 11:15, "Satan's ministers." **2.** Rather translate, "Through (lit., 'in'; the element *in* which the apostasy has place) the hypocrisy of lying speakers"; this expresses the means *through* which "some shall (be led to) depart from the faith," viz., the feigned sanctity of the seducers (cf. "deceivers," Titus 1:10). **having their conscience seared**—Greek, "having *their own* conscience . . ," i.e., not only "speaking lies" *to others,* but also having *their own* conscience seared. Professing to lead others to holiness, *their* own conscience is all the while defiled. Bad consciences always have recourse to hypocrisy. As *faith* and a *good conscience* are joined (ch. 1:5); so *hypocrisy* (i.e., *unbelief,* Matt. 24:5, 51; cf. Luke 12:46) and a *bad conscience* here. THEODORET explains like *English Version,* "seared," as implying their extreme *insensibility;* the effect of cauterizing being to deaden sensation. The *Greek,* however, primarily means "branded" with the consciousness of crimes committed against their better knowledge and conscience, like so many scars burnt in by a branding-iron: Cf. Titus 1:15; 3:11, "condemned of himself." They are conscious of the brand within, and yet with a hypocritical show of sanctity, they strive to seduce others. As "a seal" is used in a good sense (II Tim. 2:19), so "a brand" in a bad sense. The image is taken from the branding of criminals. **3.** Sensuality leads to false spiritualism. Their own inward impurity is reflected in their eyes in the world without them, and hence their asceticism (Titus 1:14, 15) [WIESINGER]. By a spurious spiritualism (II Tim. 2:18), which made moral perfection consist in abstinence from outward things, they pretended to attain to a higher perfection. Matthew 19:10-12 (cf. I Cor. 7:8, 26, 38) gave a seeming handle to their "forbidding marriage" (contrast ch. 5:14); and the Old Testament distinction as to clean and unclean, gave a pretext for teaching to "abstain from meats" (cf. Col. 2:16, 17, 20-23). As these Judaizing Gnostics combined the harlot or apostate Old Testament Church with the beast (Rev. 17:3), or Gnostic spiritualizing anti-Christianity, so Rome's Judaizing elements (ch. 4:3) shall ultimately be combined with the open worldly-wise anti-Christianity of the false prophet or beast (ch. 6:20, 21; Col. 2:8; I John 4:1-3; Rev. 13:12-15). Austerity gained for them a show of sanctity while preaching false doctrine (Col. 2:23). EUSEBIUS (*Ecclesiastical History,* 4. 29) quotes from IRENÆUS (1. 28) a statement that Saturninus, Marcion, and the Encratites preached abstinence from marriage and animal meats. Paul prophetically warns against such notions, the seeds of which already were being sown (ch. 6:20; II Tim. 2:17, 18). **to be received**— *Greek,* "to be partaken of." **of them**—lit., (created and designed) *"for them."* Though *all* (even the unbelieving, Ps. 104:14; Matt. 5:45) are partakers in these foods created by God, "they which believe" alone fulfil God's design in creation *by partaking of them with thanksgiving;* as opposed to those who *abstain* from them, or in partaking of them, do not do so *with thanksgiving.* The unbelieving have not the designed use of such foods by reason of their "conscience being defiled" (Titus 1:15). The children of God alone "inherit the earth"; for obedience is the necessary qualification (as it was in the original grant of the earth to Adam), which they alone possess. **and know the truth**—explanatory and defining who are "they which believe." Translate as *Greek,* "and have *full* knowledge of the truth" (*Note,* Phil. 1:9). Thus he contradicts the assumption of superior *knowledge* and higher moral perfection, put forward by the heretics, on the ground of their abstinence from marriage and meats. "The *truth"* stands in opposition to their *"lies"* (vs. 2). **4, 5.** Translate as *Greek,* "Because" (expressing a reason resting on an *objective fact;* or, as here, a Scripture quotation)—"For" (a reason resting on something *subjective* in *the writer's mind).* **every creature ... good**—(Gen. 1:31; Rom. 14:14, 20). A refutation by anticipation of the Gnostic opposition to creation: the seeds of which were now lurking latently in the Church. Judaism (Acts 10: 11-16; I Cor. 10:25, 26) was the starting-point of the error as to meats: Oriental Gnosis added new elements. The old Gnostic heresy is now almost extinct; but its remains in the celibacy of Rome's priesthood, and in its fasts from animal meats, enjoined under the penalty of mortal sin, remain. **if ... with thanksgiving**—Meats, though pure in themselves, become impure by being received with an unthankful mind (Rom. 14:6; Titus 1:15). **5. sanctified**—"hallowed"; set apart as holy for the use of believing men: separated from "the creature," which is under *the bondage of vanity and corruption* (Romans 8:19, etc.). Just as in the Lord's Supper, the thanksgiving prayer sanctifies the elements, separating them from their naturally alien position in relation to the spiritual world, and transferring them to their true relation to the new life. So in *every* use of the creature, thanksgiving prayer has the same effect, and ought always to be used (I Cor. 10:30, 31). **by the word of God and prayer**—i.e., "by means of *intercessory* prayer" (so the *Greek)*— i.e., *consecratory* prayer in behalf of "the creature" or food—that prayer mainly consisting of "the word of God." The *Apostolic Constitutions,* 7. 49, give this ancient grace, almost wholly consisting of Scripture, "Blessed art thou, O Lord, who feedest me from my youth, who givest food to all flesh: Fill our hearts with joy and gladness, that we, having all sufficiency, may abound unto every good work in Christ Jesus our Lord, through whom glory, honour, and might, be to thee for ever. Amen." In the case of inspired men, "the word of God" would refer to *their* inspired prayers (I Kings 17:1; but as Paul speaks in general, including uninspired men's thanksgiving for meals, the "word of God" more probably refers to the *Scripture* words used in thanksgiving prayers. **6. If thou put ... in remembrance**—rather as *Greek,* "If thou *suggest* to (bring under the notice of) the brethren. . . ." **these things** —viz., the truths stated in vss. 4, 5, in opposition to the errors foretold, vss. 1-3. **minister**—"servant." **nourished up**—The *Greek* is *present,* not *past:* "continually *being* nourished in" (II Tim. 1:5; 3:14, 15). **the words of faith**—rather, ". . . of *the* faith" (cf. vs. 12). **good doctrine**—"the good *teaching."* Explanatory of "the faith," in opposition to the "teachings of demons" (*English Version,* "doctrines of devils," vs. 1) which Timothy was to counteract. Cf. "sound doctrine" (ch. 1:10; 6:3; Titus 1:9; 2:1). **whereunto thou hast attained**—"the *course* of which thou hast *followed";* hast *followed along* by tracing its course and accompanying it [ALFORD]. Thou hast begun to follow up [BENGEL]. The same *Greek* occurs, "thou hast fully known" (II Tim. 3: 10), "having had perfect understanding" (Luke 1: 3). It is an undesigned coincidence that the *Greek* verb is used only by Paul and *Paul's companion,* Luke. **7. refuse**—reject, avoid, *have nothing to do with* (II Tim. 2:23; Titus 3:10.) **old wives' fables** —anile myths (ch. 1:4, 9; Titus 1:14). They are "profane," because leading away from "godliness" or "piety" (ch. 1:4-7; 6:20; II Tim. 2:16; Titus 1:1, 2). **exercise thyself**—lit., "exercise thyself" as one undergoing training in a gymnasium. Let thy self-discipline be not in ascetical exercises as the false teachers (vss. 3, 8; cf. II Tim. 2:22, 23; Heb. 5:14; 12:11), but with a view to godliness or "piety" (ch. 6:11, 12). **8. profiteth little**—*Greek,* "profiteth to (but) a small extent." Paul does not deny that fasting and abstinence from conjugal intercourse for a time, with a view to reaching the inward man through the outward, do profit somewhat, Acts 13: 3; I Corinthians 7:5, 7; 9:26, 27 (though in its degenerate form, asceticism, dwelling solely on what is outward, vs. 3, is not only not profitable but injurious). Timothy seems to have had a leaning to such outward self-discipline (cf. ch. 5:23). Paul, therefore, while not disapproving of this in its due proportion and place, shows the vast superiority of *godliness* or *piety*, as being *profitable* not merely "to a small extent," but unto *all* things; for, having its seat within, it extends thence to the whole outward life of a man. Not unto one portion only of his being, but to every portion of it, bodily and spiritual, temporal and eternal [ALFORD]. "He who has *piety* (which is 'profitable unto *all* things') wants nothing needed to his well-being, even though he be without those helps which, 'to a small extent,' *bodily exercise* furnishes" [CALVIN]. *"Piety,"* which is the *end* for which thou art to "exercise thyself" (vs. 7), is the essential thing: the means are secondary. **having promise ...**—Translate as *Greek,* "Having promise of life, that which now is, and that which is to come." "Life" in its truest and best sense now and hereafter (II Tim. 1:1). Length of life now so far as it is really good for the believer; life in its truest enjoyments and employments now, and life blessed and eternal hereafter (Matt. 6:33; Mark 10:29, 30). "Now in this time" (Ps. 84:11; 112: Rom. 8:28; I Cor. 3:21, 22, *"all* things are yours ... the world, life ... things present, things to come"). Christianity, which seems to aim only at our happiness hereafter, effectually promotes it here (ch. 6:6; II Pet. 1:3). Cf. Solomon's prayer and the answer (I Kings 3:7-13). **9.** (Ch. 1:15.) This verse (*Greek*), "faithful is the saying ..." confirms the assertion as to the "promise" attached to "godliness," vs. 8, and forms a prefatory introduction to vs. 10, which is joined to vs. 9 by "For." So II Timothy 2:11. Godly men seem to suffer loss as to this life: Paul hereby refutes the notion [BENGEL]. "God is the *Saviour* specially of those that believe" (vs. 10), both as to "the life that now is," and also as to "the life which is to come" (vs. 8). **10. therefore**—*Greek,* "with a view to this." *The reason why* "we both ('both' is omitted in the oldest MSS.) labor (endure hardship) and suffer reproach (some oldest MSS. read 'strive') is *because* we have rested, and do rest our hope, on the living (and therefore, *life-giving,* vs. 8) God." **Saviour**—even in this life (vs. 8). **specially of those that believe**—Their "labor and reproach" are not inconsistent with their having from the living God, their Saviour, even the present life (Mark 10:30, "a hundred fold now in this time ... with persecutions"), much more the life to come. If God is in a sense "Saviour" of unbelievers (ch. 2:4, i.e., is *willing* to be so *everlastingly,* and *is temporally here* their *Preserver* and *Benefactor*), much more of believers. He is the Saviour of all men *potentially* (ch. 1:15); of believers alone *effectually.* **11.** These truths, to the exclusion of those useless and even injurious teachings (vss. 1-8), while weighing well thyself, charge also upon others. **12. Let no man despise thy youth** —Act so as to be respected in spite of thy youth (I Cor. 16:11; Titus 2:15); cf. "youthful" as to Timothy (II Tim. 2:22). He was but a mere youth when he joined Paul (Acts 16:1-3). Eleven years had elapsed since then to the time subsequent to Paul's first imprisonment. He was, therefore, still young; especially in comparison with Paul, whose place he was filling; also in relation to elderly presbyters whom he should "entreat as a father" (ch. 5:1), and generally in respect to his duties in rebuking, exhorting, and ordaining (ch. 3:1), which ordinarily accord best with an elderly person (ch. 5:19). **be thou an example**—*Greek,* "*become a pattern*" (Titus 2:7); the true way of making men not to despise (slight, or disregard) thy youth. **in word**—in all that thou sayest in public and private. **conversation**—i.e., "behavior" the Old English sense of the word. **in charity ... faith**—the two cardinal principles of the Christian (Gal. 5:6). The oldest MSS. omit, "in spirit." **in purity**—simplicity of holy motive followed out in consistency of holy action [ALFORD] (ch. 5:22; II Cor. 6:6; Jas. 3:17; 4:8; I Pet. 1:22). **13. Till I come**—when Timothy's commission would be superseded for the time by the presence of the apostle himself (ch. 1:3; 3:14). **reading**—especially in the public congregation. The practice of reading Scripture was transferred from the Jewish synagogue to the Christian Church (Luke 4:16-20; Acts 13:15; 15:21; II Cor. 3:14). The New Testament Gospel and Epistles being recognized as inspired by those who had the gift of *discerning spirits,* were from the first, according as they were written, read along with the Old Testament in the Church (I Thess. 5:21, 27; Col. 4:16), [JUSTIN MARTYR, *Apology,* 1. 67]. I think that while *public reading* is the prominent thought, the Spirit intended also to teach that Scripture reading in private should be "the fountain of all wisdom from which pastors ought to draw whatever they bring before their flock" [ALFORD]. **exhortation**—addressed to the feelings and will with a view to the regulation of the conduct. **doctrine**—*Greek* (ministerial), "teaching" or *instruction.* Addressed to the understanding, so as to impart knowledge (ch. 6:2; Rom. 12:7, 8). Whether in public or private, *exhortation* and *instruction* should be based on *Scripture reading.* **14. Neglect not the gift**—by letting it lie unused. In II Timothy 1:6 the gift is represented as a *spark* of the Spirit lying within him, and sure to smoulder by neglect, the *stirring up* or keeping in lively exercise of which depends on the will of him on whom it is bestowed (Matt. 25:18, 25, 27, 28). The *charism* or spiritual gift, is that of the Spirit which qualified him for "the work of an evangelist" (Eph. 4:11; II Tim. 4:5), or perhaps *the gift of discerning spirits,* specially needed in his function of ordaining, as overseer [BISHOP HINDS]. **given thee** —by God (I Cor. 12:4, 6). **by prophecy**—i.e., by the Holy Spirit, at his general ordination, or else consecration, to the special see of Ephesus, speaking through the prophets God's will to give him the graces needed to qualify him for his work (ch. 1:18; Acts 13:1-3). **with ... laying on of ... hands**—So in Joshua's case (Num. 27:18-20; Deut. 34:9). The gift was connected with the symbolical act of laying on hands. But the *Greek* "with" implies that the *presbyter's* laying on hands was the mere *accompaniment* of the conferring of the gift. "By" (II Tim. 1:6) implies that *Paul's* laying on his hands was the actual *instrument* of its being conferred. **of the presbytery**—In II Timothy 1:6 the apostle mentions only *his own* laying on of hands. But there his aim is to remind Timothy specially of the part he himself took in imparting to him the gift. Here he mentions the fact, quite consistent with the other, that the neighboring presbyters took part in the ordination or consecration, he, however, taking the foremost part. Paul, though having the general oversight of the elders everywhere, was an elder himself (I Pet. 5:1; II John 1). The Jewish council was composed of the elders of the Church (the presbytery, Luke 22:66; Acts 22:5), and a presiding rabbi; so the Christian Church was composed of apostles, elders, and a president (Acts 15:16). As the president of the synagogue was of the same order as his presbyters, so the bishop was of the same order as his presbyters. At the ordination of the president of the synagogue there were always three presbyters present to lay on hands, so the early Church canons required three bishops to be present at the consecration of a bishop. As the president of the synagogue, so the bishop of the Church alone could ordain, he acting as the representative, and in the name of the whole presbytery [VITRINGA]. So, in the Anglican Church, the bishop ordains, the presbyters or priests present joining with him in laying on hands. **15. Meditate**—*Greek, "Meditate* CAREFULLY *upon"* (Ps. 1:2; 119:15; cf. "Isaac," Gen. 24:63). **these things**—(vss. 12-14). As food would not nourish without digestion, which assimilates the food to the substance of the body, so spiritual food, in order to benefit us, needs to be appropriated by prayerful meditation. **give thyself wholly to**—lit., "BE *in* these things"; let them engross thee wholly; be wholly absorbed in them. *Entire selfdedication,* as in other pursuits, so especially in religion, is the secret of proficiency. There are changes as to all other studies, fashionable today, out of fashion tomorrow; this study alone is never obsolete, and when made the all-engrossing aim sanctifies all other studies. The exercise of the ministry threatens the spirit of the ministry, unless it be sustained within. The minister must be first his own scholar before he can be another's teacher. **profiting**—*Greek,* "progress" towards perfection in the Christian life, and especially towards the fullest realization of the ideal of a Christian minister (vs. 12). **may appear to all**—not for thy glory, but for the winning of souls (Matt. 5:16). **16. Take heed**—Give heed (Acts 3:5). **thyself, and ... doctrine**—"and unto thy teaching." The two requisites of a good pastor: His teaching will be of no avail unless his own life accord with it; and his own purity of life is not enough unless he be diligent in teaching [CALVIN]. This verse is a summary of vs. 12. **continue in them**—(II Tim. 3:14). **in doing this**—not "*by* doing this," as though he could save himself by works. **thou shalt ... save thyself, and them ...**—(Ezek. 33:9; Jas. 5:20). In performing faithfully his duty to others, the minister is promoting his own salvation. Indeed he cannot "give heed unto the teaching" of others, unless he be at the same time "giving heed unto himself."

CHAPTER 5

Vss. 1-25. GENERAL DIRECTIONS AS TO HOW TIMOTHY SHOULD DEAL WITH DIFFERENT CLASSES IN THE CHURCH. **1. an elder**—*in age;* probably not an elder *in the ministry;* these latter are not mentioned till vs. 17, "the elders that rule." Cf. Acts 2:17, "your old men," lit., "elders." Contrasted with "the younger men." As Timothy was admonished so to conduct himself as to give no man reason to *despise* his youth (ch. 4:12); so here he is told to bear in mind his youth, and to behave with the modesty which becomes a young man in relation to his elders. **Rebuke not**—lit., "Strike not hard upon"; *Rebuke not sharply;* a different word from "rebuke" in II Timothy 4:2. **entreat**—exhort. **as brethren**—and therefore equals; not lording it over them (I Pet. 5:1-3). **2. with all purity**—respectful treatment of the other sex will promote "purity." **3. Honour**—by setting on the church roll, as fit objects of charitable sustenance (vss. 9, 17, 18; Acts 6:1). So "honor" is used for *support* with necessaries (Matt. 15:4, 6; Acts 28:10). **widows indeed**—(vs. 16). Those really desolate; not like those (vs. 4) having children or relations answerable for their support, nor like those (in vs. 6) "who live in pleasure"; but such as, from their earthly desolation as to friends, are most likely to trust wholly in God,

persevere in continual prayers, and carry out the religious duties assigned to Church widows (vs. 5). Care for widows was transferred from the Jewish economy to the Christian (Deut. 14:29; 16:11; 24: 17, 19). **4. if any widow ...**—not "a widow indeed," as having children who ought to support her. **nephews**—rather, as *Greek,* "descendants," or "grandchildren" [HESYCHIUS]. "Nephews" in old English meant "grandchildren" [HOOKER, *Ecclesiastical Polity,* 5. 20]. **let them**—the children and descendants. **learn first**—ere it falls to the Church to support them. **to show piety at home**—filial piety towards their widowed mother or grandmother, by giving her sustenance. Lit., " ... towards *their own house."* "Piety is applied to the reverential discharge of filial duties; as the parental relation is the earthly representation of God our heavenly Father's relation to us. *"Their own"* stands in opposition to *the Church,* in relation to which the widow is comparatively a stranger. She has a claim on *her own* children, prior to her claim on the Church; let them fulfil this prior claim which she has on them, by sustaining her and not burdening the Church. **parents**—*Greek,* (living) "progenitors," i.e., their mother or grandmother, as the case may be. "Let them learn," implies that abuses of this kind had crept into the Church, widows claiming Church support though they had children or grandchildren able to support them. **good and**—The oldest MSS. omit. The words are probably inserted by a transcriber from ch. 2:3. **5. widow indeed, and desolate**—contrasted with her who has children or grandchildren to support her (vs. 4). **trusteth in God**—perfect tense in *Greek,* "hath rested, and doth rest her hope in God." This vs. 5 *adds another* qualification in a widow for Church maintenance, besides her being" desolate" or destitute of children to support her. She must be not one "that liveth in pleasure" (vs. 6), but one making God her main hope (the accusative in *Greek* expresses that God is *the ultimate aim whereto* her hope is *directed;* whereas, ch. 4:10, dative expresses hope *resting on* God as her present stay [WIESINGER]), and continuing constantly in prayers. Her destitution of children and of all ties to earth would leave her more unencumbered for devoting the rest of her days to God and the Church (I Cor. 7:33, 34). Cf. also "Anna a widow," who remained unmarried after her husband's death and "departed not from the temple, but served God with fastings and prayers day and night" (Luke 2:36, 37). Such a one, Paul implies, would be the fittest object for the Church's help (vs. 3); for such a one is promoting the cause of Christ's Church by her prayers for it. "Ardor in prayers flows from hoping confidence in God" [LEO]. **in supplications and prayers**—*Greek,* "in *her* supplications and prayers"; the former signifies *asking under a sense of need,* the latter, *prayer* (*Notes,* ch. 2:1; Phil. 4:6). **night and day**—another coincidence with Luke (Luke 18:7, "cry day and night"); contrast Satan's accusations "day and night" (Rev. 12:10). **6. she that liveth in pleasure**—the opposite of such a widow as is described in vs. 5, and therefore one utterly undeserving of Church charity. The *Greek* expresses *wanton prodigality* and excess [TITTMANN]. The root expresses *weaving* at a fast rate, and so lavish excess (*Note,* Jas. 5:5). **dead while she liveth**—dead in the Spirit while alive in the flesh (Matt. 8:22; Eph. 5: 14). **7. these things**—just now spoken (vss. 5, 6). **that they may be blameless**—viz., the widows supported by the Church. **8. But**—reverting to vs. 4, "If any (a general proposition; therefore including in its application *the widow's children* or *grand-children*) provide not for his own (relations in general), and especially for those of his own house (in particular), he hath (practically) denied the faith." Faith without love and its works is dead; "for the subject matter of faith is not mere opinion, but the grace and truth of God, to which he that believes gives up his spirit, as he that loves gives up his heart" [MACK]. If in any case a duty of love is plain, it is in relation to one's own relatives; to fail in so plain an obligation is a plain proof of want of love, and therefore of want of faith. "Faith does not set aside natural duties, but strengthens them" [BENGEL]. **worse than an infidel**—because even an infidel (or unbeliever) is taught by nature to provide for his own relatives, and generally recognizes the duty; the Christian who does not so, is worse (Matt. 5:46, 47). He has less excuse with his greater light than the infidel who may break the laws of nature. **9.** Translate, "As a widow (i.e., of the ecclesiastical order of *widowhood;* a kind of *female presbytery*), let none be enrolled (in the catalogue) who is less than sixty years old." These were not *deaconesses*, who were chosen at a younger age (forty was the age fixed at the Council of Chalcedon), and who had virgins (in a later age called *widows*) as well as widows among them, but a band of widows set apart, though not yet formally and finally, to the service of God and the Church. Traces of such a class appear in Acts 9:41. Dorcas herself was such a one. As it was expedient (*Note,* ch. 3:2; Titus 1:6) that the presbyter or bishop should have been but once married, so also in her case. There is a transition here to a new subject. The reference here cannot be, as in vs. 3, to *providing Church sustenance* for them. For the restriction to widows above sixty would then be needless and harsh, since many widows might be in need of help at a much earlier age; as also the rule that the widow must *not* have been *twice married*, especially since he himself, below (vs. 14) enjoins the younger widows to marry again; as also that she must have *brought up children.* Moreover, vs. 10 presupposes some competence, at least in past times, and so poor widows would be excluded, the very class requiring charity. Also, vs. 11 would then be senseless, for then their re-marrying would be a benefit, not an injury, to the Church, as relieving it of the burden of their sustenance. TERTULLIAN, *De Velandis Virginibus,* c. 9., HERMAS, *Shepherd,* B. 1. 2, and CHRYSOSTOM, *Homily* 31, mention such an order of ecclesiastical widowhood, each one not less than sixty years old, and resembling the presbyters in the respect paid to them, and in some of their duties; they ministered with sympathizing counsel to other widows and to orphans, a ministry to which their own experimental knowledge of the feelings and sufferings of the bereaved adapted them, and had a general supervision of their sex. *Age* was doubtless a requisite in *presbyters,* as it is here stated to have been in *presbyteresses,* with a view to their influence on the younger persons of their sex. They were supported by the Church, but not the only widows so supported (vss. 3, 4). **wife of one man**—in order not to throw a stumbling block in the way of Jews and heathen, who regarded with disfavor second marriages (*Note,* ch. 3:2; Titus 1:6). This is the force of "blameless," giving no offense, even in matters indifferent. **10. for good works**—Greek, "IN *honourable* (excellent) works"; the sphere or element *in* which the good report of her had place (Titus 2:7). This answers to ch. 3:7, as to the bishop or presbyter, "He must have a good

report of them which are without." **if**—if, in addition to being "well reported of," she .... **she ... brought up children**—either her own (ch. 3:4, 12), or those of others, which is one of the "good works"; a qualification adapting her for ministry to orphan children, and to mothers of families. **lodged strangers**—ch. 3:2, "given to hospitality" (Titus 1:8); in the case of *presbyters.* **washed ... saints' feet**—after the example of the Lord (John 13: 14); a specimen of the universal spirit of humbly "by love serving one another," which actuated the early Christians. **relieved the afflicted**—whether by pecuniary or other relief. **followed ... good**—(I Thess. 5:15; cf. instances in Matt. 25:35, 36). **11. younger**—than sixty years old (vs. 9). **refuse**—to take on the roll of presbyteress widows. **wax wanton**—lit., "over-strong" (II Chron. 26:16). **against Christ**—rebelling against Christ, their proper Bridegroom [JEROME]. **they will**—Greek, "they wish"; their *desire* is to marry again. **12. Having**—Bringing on themselves, and so *having* to bear as a burden (Gal. 5:10) *judgment* from God (cf. ch. 3:6), weighing like a load on them. **cast off their first faith**—viz., pledged to Christ and the service of the Church. There could be no hardship at the age of sixty or upwards in not marrying again (end of vs. 9), for the sake of serving better the cause of Christ as presbyteresses; though, to ordinary widows, no barrier existed against re-marriage (I Cor. 7:39). This is altogether distinct from Rome's unnatural vows of celibacy in the case of young marriageable women. The widow-presbyteresses, moreover, engaged to remain single, not as though single life were holier than married life (according to Rome's teaching), but because the interests of Christ's cause made it desirable (*Note,* ch. 3:2). They had pledged "their first faith" to Christ as presbyteress widows; they now wish to transfer their faith to a husband (cf. I Cor. 7:32, 34). **13. withal**—"at the same time, moreover." **learn**—usually in a good sense. But these women's "learning" is *idleness, trifling,* and *busybodies' tattle.* **wandering**—Greek, "going about." **from house to house**—of the members of the Church (II Tim. 3:6). "They carry the affairs of this house to that, and of that to this; they tell the affairs of all to all" [THEOPHYLACT]. **tattlers**—lit., "*trifling* talkers." In III John 10, translated "prating." **busybodies**—mischievously *busy;* inconsiderately *curious* (II Thess. 3:11). Acts 19:19, "curious," the same Greek. *Curiosity* usually springs from idleness, which is itself the mother of *garrulity* [CALVIN]. **speaking**—not merely "*saying.*" The *subject matter,* as well as the *form,* is involved in the Greek word [ALFORD]. **which they ought not**—(Titus 1: 11). **14. younger women**—rather, as ellipsis ought to be supplied, "the younger *widows,*" viz., younger widows in general, as distinguished from *the older widows taken on the roll of presbyteresses* (vs. 9). The "therefore" means *seeing that young widows are exposed to such temptations,* "I will," or "desire ..." (vss. 11-13). The precept here that they should marry again is not inconsistent with I Corinthians 7:40; for the circumstances of the two cases were distinct (cf. I Cor. 7:26). Here re-marriage is recommended as an antidote to *sexual passion, idleness,* and the other evils noted in vss. 11-13. Of course, where there was no tendency to these evils, marriage again would not be so requisite; Paul speaks of what is generally desirable, and supposing there should be danger of such evils, as was likely. "He does not impose *a law,* but points out *a remedy,* to younger widows" [CHRYS-

OSTOM]. **bear children**–(ch. 2:15)–thus gaining one of the qualifications (vs. 10) for being afterwards a presbyteress widow, should Providence so ordain it. **guide**–*Greek, "rule* the house" in the woman's due place; not *usurping authority* over the man (ch. 2: 12). **give none occasion**–lit., "starting-point": handle of reproach through the loose conduct of nominal Christians. **the adversary**–of Christianity, Jew or Gentile. Philippians 1:28; Titus 2:8, "He that is of the contrary part." Not *Satan,* who is introduced in a different relation (vs. 15.) **to speak reproachfully**–lit., "for the sake of reproach" (ch. 3:7; 6:1; Titus 2:5, 10). If the *handle* were given, *the adversary* would use it *for the sake of reproach.* The adversary is eager to exaggerate the faults of a few, and to lay the blame on the whole Church and its doctrines [BENGEL]. **15. For**–*For* in the case of some this result has already ensued; "Some (widows) are already turned aside after Satan," the seducer (not by falling away from the faith in general, but) by such errors as are stigmatized in vss. 11-13, sexual passion, idleness, etc., and so have *given occasion of reproach* (vs. 14). "Satan finds some mischief still for the idle hands to do." **16. If any . . . have widows**–of his family, however related to him. Most of the oldest MSS. and versions omit "man or," and read, "If any woman that believeth." But the Received text *seems* preferable. If, however, the weightiest *authorities* are to prevail, the sense will be: He was speaking of younger widows; He now says, If *any believing young widow* have widows related to her needing support, let her relieve them, thereby easing the Church of the burden, vss. 3, 4 (*there* it was *the children* and *grandchildren; here* it is *the young widow,* who, in order to avoid the evils of *idleness* and *wantonness,* the result of *idleness,* vss. 11, 13; Ezekiel 16:49, is to be diligent in good works, such as "relieving the afflicted," vs. 10, thus qualifying herself for being afterwards a *widow-presbyteress*). **let them**–rather as *Greek,* "let him," or "her"; "let such a one" (vs. 10). **be charged**–lit., "be *burdened*" with their support. **widows indeed**–really helpless and friendless (vss. 3, 4). **17.** The transition from the widow presbyteresses (vs. 9) to the presbyters here, is natural. **rule well**–lit., "preside well," with wisdom, ability, and loving faithfulness, over the flock assigned to them. **be counted worthy of double honour**–i.e., the honor which is expressed by gifts (vss. 3, 18) and otherwise. If a presbyter as such, in virtue of his office, is already worthy of honor, he who *rules well* is *doubly so* [WIESINGER] (I Cor. 9:14; Gal. 6:6; I Thess. 5:12). Not literally that a presbyter who rules well should get *double the salary* of one who does not rule well [ALFORD], or of a presbyteress widow, or of the deacons [CHRYSOSTOM]. "Double" is used for *large* in general (Rev. 18:6). **specially they who labour in the word and doctrine**–*Greek,* "teaching"; preaching of the word, and instruction, catechetical or otherwise. This implies that of the *ruling presbyters* there were two kinds, those who *labored in the word and teaching,* and those who did not. Lay presbyters, so called merely because of their *age,* have no place here; for both classes mentioned here alike are *ruling* presbyters. A college of presbyters is implied as existing in each large congregation. As in ch. 3 their qualifications are spoken of, so here the acknowledgments due to them for their services. **18. the scripture**–(Deut. 25:4; quoted before in I Cor. 9:9). **the ox that treadeth out**–*Greek, "An* ox *while treading." The labourer is worthy of his reward**–or "hire"; quoted from Luke 10:7, whereas Matthew 10:10 has "his meat," or "food." If Paul extends the phrase, "Scripture saith," to this second clause, as well as to the first, he will be hereby recognizing the Gospel of Luke, his own helper (whence appears the undesigned appositeness of the quotation), as inspired *Scripture.* This I think the correct view. The Gospel according to Luke was probably in circulation then about eight or nine years. However, it is possible "Scripture saith" applies only to the passage quoted from Deuteronomy 25:4; and then his quotation will be that of a common proverb, quoted also by the Lord, which commends itself to the approval of all, and is approved by the Lord and His apostle. **19. Against an elder**–a presbyter of the Church. **receive not**–"entertain not" [ALFORD]. **but before two or three witnesses**–A *judicial conviction* was not permitted in Deuteronomy 17:6; 19:15, except on the testimony of at least two or three witnesses (cf. Matt. 18:16; John 8:17; II Cor. 13:1; I John 5:6, 7). But Timothy's *entertaining an accusation* against anyone is a different case, where the object was not judicially to punish, but to admonish: here he might *ordinarily* entertain it *without the need of two or three witnesses;* but not in the case of an elder, since the more earnest an elder was to *convince gainsayers* (Titus 1:9), the more exposed would he be to vexatious and false accusations. How important then was it that Timothy should not, without strong testimony, entertain a charge against presbyters, who should, in order to be efficient, be "blameless" (ch. 3:2; Titus 1:6). Verses 21, 24 imply that Timothy had the power of judging in the Church. Doubtless he would not *condemn* any save on the testimony of two or three witnesses, but in ordinary cases he would cite them, as the law of Moses also allowed, though there were only one witness. But in the case of elders, he would require two or three witnesses before even citing them; for their character for innocence stands higher, and they are exposed to envy and calumny more than others [BENGEL]. "Receive" does not, as ALFORD thinks, include both citation and conviction, but means only the former. **20. Them that sin**–whether presbyters or laymen. **rebuke before all**–publicly before the Church (Matt. 18:15-17; I Cor. 5:9-13; Eph. 5:11). Not until this "rebuke" was disregarded was the offender to be excommunicated. **others . . . fear**–that other members of the Church may have a wholesome fear of offending (Deut. 13:11; Acts 5: 11). **21. I charge thee**–rather as *Greek,* "I adjure thee"; so it ought to be translated (II Tim. 4:1). **before**–*"in the presence of* God." **Lord**–omitted in the oldest MSS. *God the Father, and Christ the Son,* will testify against thee, if thou disregardest my injunction. He vividly sets before Timothy *the last judgment,* in which God shall be revealed, and Christ seen face to face with His angels [BENGEL]. **elect angels**–an epithet of reverence. The objects of divine electing love (I Pet. 2:6). Not only *"elect"* [according to the everlasting purpose of God] in contradistinction to *the reprobate* angels (II Pet. 2:4), but also to mark the excellence of the angels in general [as God's chosen ministers, "holy angels," "angels of light"], and so to give more solemnity to their testimony [CALVIN] as witnesses to Paul's adjuration. Angels take part by action and sympathy in the affairs of the earth (Luke 15: 10; I Cor. 4:9). **these things**–the injunctions, vss. 19, 20. **without preferring one before another**–rather as *Greek, "prejudice";* "judging before" hearing all the facts of a case. There ought to be judgment, but not prejudging. Cf. "suddenly," vs. 22, also vs. 24. **partiality**—*in favor of* a man, as "prejudice" is bias *against* a man. Some of the oldest MSS. read, "in the way of *summoning* (brethren) *before a* (heathen) *judge."* But *Vulgate* and other good authorities favor the more probable reading in *English Version.* **22. Lay hands**—i.e., ordain (ch. 4:14; II Tim. 1:6; Titus 1:5). The connection is with vs. 19. The way to guard against scandals occurring in the case of presbyters is, be cautious as to the character of the candidate before ordaining him; this will apply to other Church officers so ordained, as well as to presbyters. Thus, this clause refers to vs. 19, as next clause, "neither be partaker of other men's sins," refers to vs. 20. ELLICOTT and WIESINGER understand it of *receiving back into Church fellowship* or *absolution, by laying hands on those who had been "rebuked"* (vs. 20) *and then excommunicated* (Matt. 18:17); vs. 20 favors this. But as in ch. 4:14, and Acts 6:6, 13:3; II Tim. 1:6, the laying on of hands is used of *ordination* (cf. however as to *confirmation,* Acts 8: 17), it seems better to take it so here. **suddenly**—hastily: vss. 24, 25 show that waiting for a time is salutary. **neither be partaker of other men's sins**—by negligence in ordaining ungodly candidates, and so becoming in some degree responsible for their sins. Or, there is the same transition from the *elders* to *all in general* who may sin, as in vss. 19, 20. Be not a partaker in other men's sins by not "rebuking them that sin before all," as well as those that are candidates for the presbytery, as also all "that sin." **keep thyself pure**—"thyself" is emphatic. "Keep THYSELF" *clear* of participation in OTHER men's sin by not failing to *rebuke them that sin* (vs. 20). Thus the transition is easy to vs. 23, which is concerning Timothy *personally;* cf. also vs. 24. **23. no longer**—as a habit. This injunction to drink wine occasionally is a modification of the preceding "keep thyself pure." The presbyter and deacon were enjoined to be "not given to wine" (ch. 3:3, 8). Timothy seems to have had a tendency to undue ascetical strictness on this point (cf. *Note,* ch. 4:8; cf. the Nazarene vow, Num. 6:1-4; John Baptist, Luke 1:15; Rom. 14). Paul therefore modifies the preceding words, "keep thyself pure," virtually saying, "Not that I mean to enjoin that kind of purity which consists in asceticism, nay, *be no longer a water-drinker,"* i.e., no longer drink *only* water, but *use a little wine,* as much as is needed for thy health. So ELLICOTT and WIESINGER. ALFORD thus: Timothy was of a feeble frame *(Note,* I Cor. 16:10, 11), and prone to timidity in his duties as overseer where vigorous action was needed; hence Paul exhorts him to take all proper means to raise his bodily condition above these infirmities. God hereby commands believers to use all due means for preserving health, and condemns by anticipation the human traditions which among various sects have denied the use of wine to the faithful. **24.** Two kinds of sins are specified: those *palpably manifest* (so the *Greek* for "open beforehand" ought to be translated; so in Heb. 7:14, it is translated "evident"; lit., *"before" the eyes,* i.e., notorious), further explained as "going before to judgment"; and those which follow after the men ("some men they, i.e., their sins, follow after"), viz., not going beforehand, loudly accusing, but hidden till they come to the judgment: so vs. 25, *the good works* are of two classes: those *palpably manifest* (translate so, instead of "manifest beforehand") and "those that are otherwise," i.e., not *palpably manifest.* Both alike "cannot be hid"; the former class

in the case of bad and good are *manifest* already; the latter class in the case of both are not manifest now, but shall be so at *the final judgment.* **going before to judgment**—as heralds; crying sins which accuse their perpetrator. The connection seems to me this: He had enjoined Timothy, vs. 20, "Rebuke *them that sin* before all": and in vs. 22, "Neither be partaker of other men's sins," by ordaining ungodly men; having then by a digression at the clause, "keep thyself pure," guarded against an ascetical error of Timothy in fancying purity consisted in asceticism, and having exhorted him to use wine for strengthening him in his work, he returns to the subject of his being vigorous as an overseer in *rebuking sin,* whether in presbyters or people, and in avoiding participation in men's sins by ordaining ungodly candidates. He says, therefore, there are two classes of *sins,* as there are two classes of *good works:* those palpably *manifest,* and those not so; the former are those on which thou shouldest act decidedly at once when called on, whether to rebuke in general, or to ordain ministers in particular; as to the latter, the final *judgment* alone can decide; however hidden now they "cannot be hid" then. This could only be said of *the final judgment* (I Cor. 4:5; therefore, ALFORD'S reference of this verse to *Timothy's judgment* in choosing elders must be wrong); all judgments before then are fallible. Thus he implies that Timothy can only be responsible if he connive at *manifest,* or evident sins; not that those *that are otherwise* shall escape judgment at last: just as in the case of *good works,* he can only be responsible for taking into account in his judgments those which are patent to all, not those secret good works which nevertheless will not remain hidden at the final judgment.

CHAPTER 6

Vss. 1-21. EXHORTATIONS AS TO DISTINCTIONS OF CIVIL RANK; THE DUTY OF SLAVES, IN OPPOSITION TO THE FALSE TEACHINGS OF GAIN-SEEKERS; TIMOTHY'S PURSUIT IS TO BE GODLINESS, WHICH IS AN EVERLASTING POSSESSION: SOLEMN ADJURATION TO DO SO AGAINST CHRIST'S COMING; CHARGE TO BE GIVEN TO THE RICH. CONCLUDING EXHORTATION. **1. servants** —to be taken as predicated thus, "Let as many as are under the yoke (as) slaves" (Tit. 2:9). The exhortation is natural as there was a danger of Christian slaves inwardly feeling above their heathen masters. **their own masters**—The phrase "their own," is an argument for submissiveness; it is not *strangers,* but *their own masters* whom they are required to respect. **all honour**—*all* possible and fitting *honor;* not merely outward subjection, but that inward *honor* from which will flow spontaneously right outward conduct (*Note,* Eph. 5:22). **that the name of God**—by which Christians are called. **blasphemed**—Heathen masters would say, What kind of a God must be the God of the Christians, when such are the fruits of His worship (Rom. 2:24; Titus 2:5, 10)? **2. And**—rather, "But." The opposition is between those Christian slaves *under the yoke* of heathen, and *those that have believing masters* (he does not use the phrase "under the yoke" in the latter case, for service under believers is not a *yoke).* Connect the following words thus, "Let them (the slaves) not, because they (the masters) are brethren (and so *equals,* masters and slaves alike being Christians), despise them" (the masters). **but rather ...**—"but all the more (so much the more: with the greater good will) do them service because they (the masters) are faithful (i.e., believers) and beloved who receive (in the mutual *interchange* of relative duties between master and servant; so the *Greek*) the benefit" (*English Version* violates *Greek* grammer). This latter clause is parallel to, "because they are brethren"; which proves that "they" refers to the *masters,* not the *servants,* as TITTMANN takes it, explaining the verb in the common sense (Luke 1:54; Acts 20:35), "who *sedulously labor for* their (masters') benefit." The very term "benefit" delicately implies service done with the right *motive,* Christian "good will" (Eph. 6:7). If the common sense of the *Greek* verb be urged, the sense must be, "Because they (the masters) are faithful and beloved who *are sedulously intent on the benefiting*" of their servants. But PORPHYRY (*de abstin.* 1. 46) justifies the sense of the *Greek* verb given above, which also better accords with the context; for otherwise, the article "*the,*" will have nothing in the preceding words to explain it, whereas in my explanation above "*the* benefit" will be that of the slaves' *service.* **These things teach**— (ch. 4:11; Titus 2:15). **3. teach otherwise**—than I desire thee to "teach" (vs. 2). The *Greek* indicative implies, he puts not a merely supposed case, but one actually existing, ch. 1:3, "*Every one* who *teaches* otherwise," i.e., who teaches *heterodoxy.* **consent not**—*Greek,* "accede not to." **wholesome** —"sound" (ch. 1:10): opposed to the false teachers' words, *unsound* through profitless science and immorality. **words of our Lord Jesus Christ**—Paul's inspired words are not merely his own, but are also *Christ's* words. **4. He is proud**—lit., "wrapt in smoke"; filled with the fumes of self-conceit (ch. 3:6) while "knowing nothing," viz., of the doctrine which is according to godliness (vs. 3), though arrogating pre-eminent knowledge (ch. 1:7). **doting about**—lit., "sick about"; the opposite of "*wholesome*" (vs. 3). *Truth* is not the center *about* which his investigations move, but mere *word-strifes.* **questions**—of controversy. **strifes of words**—rather than about *realities* (II Tim. 2:14). These stand with them instead of "godliness" and "wholesome words" (vs. 3; ch. 1:4; Titus 3:9). **evil surmisings** —as to those who are of a different party from themselves. **5. Perverse disputings**—useless disputings. The oldest MSS. read, "lasting contests" [WIESINGER]; "incessant collisions" [ALFORD]. "Strifes of words" had already been mentioned so that he would not be likely to repeat the same idea (as in the *English Version* reading) again. **corrupt minds**—*Greek,* "of men corrupted (depraved) in mind." The inmost source of the evil is in the perverted mind (vs. 4; II Tim. 3:8; Titus 1:15). **destitute of the truth**—(Titus 1:14). They had had the truth, but through want of moral integrity and of love of the truth, they were misled by a pretended deeper gnosis (knowledge) and higher ascetical holiness, of which they made a trade [WIESINGER]. **supposing . . .**—The *Greek* requires, "supposing (regarding the matter in this point of view) that piety (so translated for 'godliness') is a means of gain" (i.e., a way of advancing one's worldly interests: a different *Greek* form, *poriswa,* expresses *the thing gained, gain*); not "that gain is godliness," as *English Version.* **from such withdraw thyself**—omitted in the oldest MSS. The connection with vs. 6 favors the omission of these words, which interrupt the connection. **6. But**—Though they err in this, there is a sense in which "piety is" not merely gain, but "*great* means of gain": not the *gaining* which they pursue, and which makes men to be *discontented* with their present possessions, and to use religion

as "a cloak of covetousness" (I Thess. 2:5) and *means of earthly gain,* but *the present and eternal gain* which *piety,* whose accompaniment is *contentment,* secures to the soul. WIESINGER remarks that Paul observed in Timothy a tendency to indolence and shrinking from the conflict, whence he felt (vs. 11) that Timothy needed cautioning against such temptation; cf. also the second Epistle. Not merely *contentment* is great gain (a sentiment of the heathen CICERO [*Parad.* 6], "the greatest and surest riches"), but "*piety* with contentment"; for piety not only feels no need of what it has not, but also has that which exalts it above what it has not [WIESINGER]. The *Greek* for *contentment* is translated "sufficiency" (II Cor. 9:8). But the adjective (Phil. 4:11) "content"; lit., "having a *sufficiency in one's self*" independent of others. "The Lord always supplies His people with what is necessary for them. True happiness lies in piety, but this *sufficiency* [supplied by God, with which moreover His people are *content*] is thrown into the scale as a kind of overweight" [CALVIN] (I Kings 17:1-16; Ps. 37:19; Isa. 33:6, 16; Jer. 37:21). **7. For**—confirming the reasonableness of "contentment." **and it is certain**—*Vulgate* and other old versions support this reading. The oldest MSS., however, omit "and it is certain"; then the translation will be, "We brought nothing into the world (to teach us to remember) that neither can we carry anything out" (Job 1:21; Eccles. 5:15). Therefore, we should have no gain-seeking anxiety, the breeder of discontent (Matt. 6:25). **8. And**—*Greek,* "But." In contrast to the greedy gain-seekers (vs. 5). **having** —so long as we have food. (The *Greek* expresses "food sufficient in each case for our continually recurring wants" [ALFORD]). It is implied that we, as believers, shall *have* this (Isa. 23:16). **raiment** —*Greek,* "covering"; according to some including a *roof to cover us,* i.e., a dwelling, as well as clothing. **let us be therewith content**—lit., "we shall be sufficiently provided"; "we shall be sufficed" [ALFORD]. **9. will be rich**—have more than "*food* and raiment." *Greek,* "*wish* to be rich"; not merely *are willing,* but are resolved, and earnestly *desire* to have riches at any cost (Prov. 28:20, 22). This *wishing* (not the riches themselves) is fatal to "contentment" (vs. 6). Rich men are not told to cast away their riches, but not to "trust" in them, and to "do good" with them (vss. 17, 18; Ps. 62:10). **fall into temptation**—not merely "are exposed to temptation," but actually "*fall into*" it. The *falling into* it is what we are to pray against, "Lead us not into temptation" (Jas. 1:14); such a one is already in a sinful state, even before any overt act of sin. The *Greek* for "temptation" and "gain" contains a play on sounds—*porasmus, peirasmus.* **snare**—a further step downwards (ch. 3:7). He falls into "the snare of the devil." **foolish**—irrational. **hurtful**—to those who fall into the snare. Cf. Ephesians 4:22, "deceitful lusts" which deceive to one's deadly hurt. **lusts**—With the one evil lust ("*wish* to be rich") many others join themselves: the one is the "root of all evils" (vs. 10). **which**—*Greek,* "whatever (lusts)." **drown**—an awful descending climax from "fall into"; this is the last step in the terrible descent (Jas. 1:15); translated "sink," Luke 5:7. **destruction . . . perdition**—*destruction* in general (temporal or eternal), and *perdition* in particular, viz., that of body and soul in hell. **10. the love of money**—not the money itself, but the *love* of it—the *wishing to be rich* (vs. 9)—"is a root (ELLICOTT and MIDDLETON: not as *English Version,* "*the* root") of all *evils.*" (So the *Greek* plural.) The wealthiest may be rich not in a bad sense; the poorest may covet to be so (Ps. 62:10). *Love of money* is not the sole root of evils, but it is a leading "root of bitterness" (Heb. 12:15), for "it destroys faith, the root of all that is good" [BENGEL]; its offshoots are "temptation, a snare, lusts, destruction, perdition." **coveted after** —lusted after. **erred from**—lit., "have been made to err from the faith" (ch. 1:19; 4:1). **pierced**—(Luke 2:35). **with . . . sorrows**—"pains": "thorns" of the parable (Matt. 13:22) which choke the word of "faith." "The prosperity of fools destroys them" (Prov. 1:32). BENGEL and WIE-SINGER make them the gnawings of conscience, pro-ducing remorse for wealth badly acquired; the harbingers of the future "perdition" (vs. 9). **11. But thou**—in contrast to the "some" (vs. 10). **man of God**—who hast God as thy true riches (Gen. 15: 1; Ps. 16:5; Lam. 3:24). Applying primarily to Timothy as a minister (cf. II Pet. 1:21), just as the term was used of Moses (Deut. 33:1), Samuel (I Sam. 9:6), Elijah, and Elisha; but, as the exhorta-tion is as to duties *incumbent also on all Christians*, the term applies secondarily to him (so II Tim. 3:17) as a Christian man *born of God* (Jas. 1:18; I John 5:1), no longer a *man of the world* raised above earthly things; therefore, God's property, not his own, bought with a price, and so having parted with all right in himself: Christ's work is to be *his* great work: he is to be Christ's living representative. **flee these things**—viz., "the love of money" with its evil results (vs. 9, 10). **follow after righteousness**—(II Tim. 2:22). **godliness**—"piety." *Righteousness* is more in relation to our fellow man; *piety* ("godli-ness") to God; *faith* is the root of both (*Note*, Titus 2:12). **love**—by which "faith worketh." **patience** —*enduring perseverance* amidst trials. **meekness**— The oldest MSS. read, "meek-spiritedness," viz., to-wards the opponents of the Gospel. **12. Fight the good fight**—BIRKS thinks this Epistle was written from Corinth, where contests in the national games recurred at stated seasons, which will account for the allusion here as in I Corinthians 9:24-26. Con-trast "strifes of words" (vs. 4). Cf. ch. 1:18; II Tim. 4:7. The "good profession" is connected with the "good fight" (Ps. 60:4). **lay hold on eternal life** —the crown, or garland, the prize of victory, laid hold of by the winner in the *good fight* (II Tim. 4: 7, 8; Phil. 3:12-14). "*Fight* (lit., 'strive') with such striving earnestness as to *lay hold on* the prize, *eternal life.*" **also**—not in the oldest MSS. **pro-fessed a good profession**—*Greek,* "didst confess THE good *confession,*" viz., *the Christian* confes-sion (as the *Greek* word is the same in this verse as that for "confession" in vs. 13, probably the *pro-fession* here is the confession *that Christ's kingdom is the kingdom of the truth,* John 18:36, 37), at thy being set apart to thy ministerial function (whether in general, or as overseer at Ephesus): the same oc-casion as is referred to in ch. 1:18; 4:14; II Tim. 1: 4. **before many witnesses**—who would testify against thee if thou shouldest fall away [BENGEL]. **13. quickeneth all things**—i.e., "maketh alive." But the oldest MSS. read, "preserveth alive"; as the same *Greek* means in Acts 7:19; cf. Nehemiah 9:6. He urges Timothy to faithfulness here by the present manifestation of God's power in preserving all things, as in vs. 14, by the future manifestation of God's power at the appearing of Christ. The assurance that "eternal life," vs. 12, will be the result of "fighting the good fight," rests on the ful-ness and power of Him who is the God of all life, present and to come. **witnessed**—It was the Lord's part to *witness*, Timothy's part to *confess* (or "pro-

fess," vs. 12) "*the* good confession" [BENGEL]. *The* confession was His testimony that He was King, and His kingdom that of *the truth* (vs. 15; *Note,* vs. 12; Matt. 27:11). Christ, in attesting, or bearing wit-ness to this truth, attested the truth of the whole of Christianity. Timothy's *profession,* or *confession,* included therefore the whole of the Christian truth. **14. keep this commandment**—*Greek,* "the com-mandment," i.e., the Gospel rule of life (ch. 1:5; John 13:34; II Pet. 2:21; 3:2). **without spot, un-rebukeable**—agreeing with "thou." Keep the com-mandment and so be without spot. . . . "Pure" (ch. 5:22; Eph. 5:27; Jas. 1:27; II Pet. 3:14). **until the appearing of . . . Christ**—*His coming in person* (II Thess. 2:8; Titus 2:13). Believers then used in their practice to set before themselves the day of Christ as near at hand; we, the hour of death [BEN-GEL]. The fact has in all ages of the Church been certain, the time as uncertain to Paul, as it is to us; hence, vs. 15, he says, "in His times": the Church's true attitude is that of continual expectation of her Lord's return (I Cor. 1:8; Phil. 1:6, 10). **15. in his times**—*Greek,* "His own [fitting] times" (Acts 1:7). The plural implies successive stages in the mani-festation of the kingdom of God, each having its own appropriate time, the regulating principle and knowledge of which rests with the Father (ch. 2: 6; II Tim. 1:9; Titus 1:3; Heb. 1:1). **he shall show** —"display": an expression appropriate in reference to His "APPEARING," which is stronger than His "coming," and implies its *visibility;* "manifest": *make visible* (cf. Acts 3:20): "He" is *the Father* (vs. 16). **blessed**—in Himself: so about to be the source of *blessing* to His people at Christ appearing, whence flows their "blessed hope" (ch. 1:11; Titus 2:13). **only**—(John 17:3; Rom. 16:27; Rev. 15:4). **King of kings**—elsewhere applied also to Jesus (Rev. 1:5; 17:14; 19:16). **16. Who only hath immortality** —in His own essence, not merely at the will of another, as all other immortal beings [JUSTIN MARTYR, *Quæst ad Orthod., 61*]. As He *hath im-mortality,* so will He give it to us who believe; to be out of Him is death. It is mere heathen philos-ophy that attributes to the soul indestructibility in itself, which is to be attributed solely to God's gift. As He hath life *in Himself,* so hath He given to the Son to have life *in Himself* (John 5:26). The term used in the New Testament for "immortal," which does not occur, is "incorruptible." "Immortality" is found in I Corinthians 15:53, 54. **dwelling in the light which no man can approach unto**—After *life* comes mention of *light,* as in John 1:4. That *light* is *unapproachable* to creatures, except in so far as they are admitted by Him, and as He goes forth to them [BENGEL]. It is *unapproachable* on account of its exceeding brightness [THEOPHYLACT]. If one cannot gaze steadfastly at the sun, which is but a small part of creation, by reason of its exceed-ing heat and power, how much less can mortal man gaze at the inexpressible glory of God [THEOPHY-LACT, *ad Autolycus*] (Ps. 104:2; I John 1:5). **no man hath seen**—(Exod. 23:20; John 1:18; Col. 1:15; Heb. 11:27; I John 4:12). Perhaps even in the per-fect state no creature shall fully see God. Still the saints shall, in some sense, have the blessedness of *seeing* Him, which is denied to mere *man* (Matt. 5: 8; I Cor. 13:12; I John 3:2; Rev. 22:4). **17. Resum-ing** the subject from above, vs. 5, 10. The im-mortality of God, alone rich in glory, and of His people through Him, is opposed to the lust of money (cf. vss. 14-16). From speaking of the *desire* to be rich, he here passes to those who *are* rich: (1) What ought to be their disposition; (2) What use they ought to make of their riches, and, (3) The consequences of their so using them. **rich in this world**—constrasted with the riches of the future kingdom to be the portion of believers at Christ's "appearing," vs. 14. **high-minded**—often the character of the rich (see Rom. 12:16). **trust**—*Greek,* "to have their trust resting." **in . . . in**—rather, "upon . . . upon," as the oldest MSS. **uncertain riches**—rather as *Greek,* "the *uncertainty of* riches." They who rest their trust on riches, rest trust on *uncertainty* itself (Prov. 23:5). Now they belong to one person, now to another, and that which has many masters is possessed by none [THEODORET]. **living God**—The best MSS. and versions omit "living." He who trusts in riches transfers to them the duty he owes to God [CALVIN]. **who giveth**—*Greek,* "affordeth." **all things richly**—temporal and eternal, for the body and for the soul. In order to be truly rich, seek to be blessed of, and in, God (Prov. 10:22; II Pet. 1:3). **to enjoy**—*Greek,* "for enjoyment." Not that the heart may cleave to them as its idol and *trust* (ch. 4:3). *Enjoyment* consists in giving, not in holding fast. Nonemployment should be far removed, as from man, so from his resources (Jas. 5:2, 3) [BENGEL]. **18. do good**—like God Himself (Ps. 119:68; Acts 14:17) and Christ (Acts 10:38). TITTMANN translates, "to do," or "act well"; as the *Greek* for "to be beneficent" is a distinct word, *agathopoiein.* **rich in good works**—so "rich in faith," which produces good works (Jas. 2:5). Contrasted with "rich in this world," vs. 17. Lit., it is "rich in honorable (right) works." *Greek, kalois, ergois,* are works good or *right* in themselves: *agathois,* good to another. **ready to distribute**—free givers [ALFORD]; the heart not cleaving to possessions, but ready to impart to others. **willing to communicate**—ready *contributors* [ALFORD]: liberal in admitting others to share our goods in *common with* ourselves (Gal. 6:6; Heb. 13:16). **19. Laying up in store**—"therefrom (i.e., by this means [ALFORD]; but BENGEL makes the *Greek apo* mean laying apart *against a future time*), laying up for themselves as a treasure" [ALFORD] (Matt. 6:19, 20). This is a treasure which we act wisely in *laying up in store,* whereas the wisest thing we can do with earthly treasures is "to distribute" them and give others a share of them (vs. 18). **good foundation**—(Note, ch. 3:13; Luke 6:48; I Cor. 3:11). The sure reversion of the future heavenly inheritance: earthly riches *scattered* in faith lay up in store a sure *increase* of heavenly riches. We gather by scattering (Prov. 11:24; 13:7; Luke 16:9). **that . . . eternal life**—The oldest MSS. and versions read, "*that which is really* life," its joys being solid and enduring (Ps. 16:11). The life that now is cannot be called so, its goods being unsubstantial, and itself a vapor (Jas. 4:14). "In order that ('with their feet so to speak on this foundation' [DE WETTE]) they may lay hold on that which is life indeed." **20, 21.** Recapitulatory conclusion: the main aim of the whole Epistle being here summarily stated. **20. O Timothy**—a personal appeal, marking at once his affection for Timothy, and his prescience of the coming heresies. **keep**—from spiritual thieves, and from enemies who will, while men sleep, sow tares amidst the good seed sown by the Son of man. **that which is committed to thy trust**—*Greek,* "the deposit" (ch. 1:18; II Tim. 1:12, 14; 2:2). *The true or sound doctrine* to be taught, as opposed to *the science falsely so called,* which leads to *error concerning the faith* (vs. 21). "It is not thine: it is another's property with which thou hast been entrusted: Diminish it not at all" [CHRYSOSTOM]

"That which was entrusted to thee, not found by thee; which thou hast received, not invented; a matter not of genius, but of teaching; not of private usurpation, but of public tradition; a matter brought to thee, not put forth by thee, in which thou oughtest to be not an enlarger, but a guardian; not an originator, but a disciple; not leading, but following. 'Keep,' saith he, 'the deposit'; preserve intact and inviolate the talent of the catholic faith. What has been entrusted to thee, let that same remain with thee; let that same be handed down by thee. Gold thou hast received, gold return. I should be sorry thou shouldest substitute aught else. I should be sorry that for gold thou shouldest substitute lead impudently, or brass fraudulently. I do not want the mere appearance of gold, but its actual reality. Not that there is to be no progress in religion in Christ's Church. Let there be so by all means, and the greatest progress; but then let it be real progress, not a change of the faith. Let the intelligence of the whole Church and its individual members increase exceedingly, provided it be only in its own kind, the doctrine being still the same. Let the religion of the soul resemble the growth of the body, which, though it develops its several parts in the progress of years, yet remains the same as it was essentially" [VINCENTIUS LIRINENSIS, A.D. 434]. **avoiding**—"turning away from" (cf. II Tim. 3:4). Even as they have "turned away from the truth" (ch. 1:6; 5:15; II Tim. 4:4). **profane**—(ch. 4:7; II Tim. 2:16). **vain**—*Greek,* "empty": mere "strifes of words," vs. 4, producing no moral fruit. **oppositions**—dialectic antithesis of the false teachers [ALFORD]. WIESINGER, not so probably, "oppositions to the sound doctrine." I think it likely germs existed already of the heresy of dualistic oppositions, viz., between the good and evil principle, afterwards fully developed in Gnosticism. Contrast Paul's just antithesis (ch. 3:16; 6:5, 6; II Tim. 2:15-23). **science falsely so called**—where there is not faith, there is not knowledge [CHRYSOSTOM]. There was true "knowledge," a special gift of the Spirit, which was abused by some (I Cor. 8:1; 12:8; 14:6). This gift was soon counterfeited by false teachers arrogating to themselves preeminently the gift (Col. 2:8, 18, 23). Hence arose the creeds of the Church, called *symbols,* i.e., in *Greek,* "watchwords," or a test whereby the orthodox might distinguish one another in opposition to the heretical. Perhaps here, vs. 20, and II Timothy 1:13, 14, imply the existence of some such brief formula of doctrine then existing in the Church; if so, we see a good reason for its not being written in Scripture, which is designed not to give dogmatic formularies, but to be the fountain whence all such formularies are to be drawn according to the exigencies of the several churches and ages. Probably thus a portion of the so-called apostle's creed may have had their sanction, and been preserved solely by tradition on this account. "The creed, handed down from the apostles, is not written on paper and with ink, but on fleshy tables of the heart" [JEROME, *adv. err. Johann. Hieros.,* ch. 9]. Thus, in the creed, contrary to the "oppositions" (the germs of which probably existed in the Church in Paul's latter days) whereby the aeons were *set off* in pairs, God is stated to be "the Father Almighty," or *all-governing* "maker of heaven and earth" [BISHOP HINDS]. **21. Which some professing**—viz., professing these *oppositions of science falsely so called.* **erred**—(*Note,* ch. 1:6; 2:11—lit., "missed the mark" (II Tim. 3:7, 8). True sagacity is inseparable from faith. **Grace**—*Greek,* "*the* grace," viz., of God, for which we Christians look, and in which we stand [ALFORD]. **be with thee**—He restricts the salutation to Timothy, as the Epistle was not to be read in public [BENGEL]. But the oldest MSS. read, "be with you"; and the "thee" may be a transcriber's alteration to harmonize with II Timothy 4:22; Titus 3:15. **Amen**—omitted in the oldest MSS.

THE SECOND EPISTLE OF PAUL THE APOSTLE TO

TIMOTHY

INTRODUCTION

PLACE OF WRITING.—Paul, in the interval between his first and second imprisonment, after having written First Timothy from Macedonia or Corinth [BIRKS] (if we are to adopt the opinion that First Timothy was written after his first imprisonment), returned to Ephesus, as he intended, by way of *Troas*, where he left the books, etc. (mentioned in ch. 4:13), with Carpus. From Ephesus he went to Crete for a short visit and returned, and then wrote to Titus. Next he went by Miletus to Corinth (ch. 4:20), and thence to Nicopolis (Titus 3:12), whence he proceeded to Rome. From his prison there he wrote the Second Epistle to Timothy, shortly before his martyrdom. It is not certain where Timothy was at this time. Some of the internal evidences favor the view of his having been then at Ephesus; thus the salutation of Priscilla and Aquila, who generally resided there (ch. 4:19); also that of the household of Onesiphorus, who is stated in ch. 1:16–18 to have ministered to Paul *at Ephesus*, a circumstance implying his residence there. Also, the Hymeneus of ch. 2:17 seems to be the same as the Hymeneus at Ephesus (I Tim. 1:20); and probably "Alexander the coppersmith" (ch. 4:14) is the same as the Alexander joined with Hymeneus (I Tim. 1:20), and possibly the same as the Alexander put forward by the Jews to clear themselves, not to befriend Paul, at the riot in *Ephesus* (Acts 19:33, 34). The difficulty is, on this supposition, how to account for ch. 4:12, 20: if Timothy was at Ephesus, why did he need to be told that *Paul had sent Tychicus to Ephesus?* or that *Paul had left Trophimus, himself an Ephesian* (Acts 21:29), *sick at Miletus*, which was only thirty miles from Ephesus? See, however, the *notes*, ch. 4:12, 20. Troas lay on the road to Rome from either Ephesus or Pontus, so that ch. 4:13 will accord with the theory of either Ephesus or any other place in the northwest of Asia Minor, being Timothy's place of sojourn at the time. Probably, he had the general superintendence of the Pauline churches in Asia Minor, in accordance with his mission combining the office of *evangelist*, or *itinerant missionary*, with that of *presiding overseer*. Ephesus was probably his headquarters.

TIME OF WRITING.—(1) Paul's first imprisonment, described in Acts 28, was much milder than that in which he was when writing Second Timothy. In the former, he had liberty to lodge in his own hired house, and to receive all comers, guarded only by a single soldier; in the latter, he was so closely confined that Onesiphorus with difficulty found him; he was chained, his friends had forsaken him, and he had narrowly escaped sentence of execution from the Roman emperor. Mediæval legends represent the Mamertine prison, or Tullianum, as the scene of his incarceration with Peter. But this is irreconcilable with the fact of Onesiphorus, Linus, Pudens, etc., having access to him. He was probably under military custody, as in his former imprisonment, though of a severer kind (ch. 1:16–18; 2:9; 4:6–8, 16, 17). (2) The visit to Troas (ch. 4:13) can hardly have been that mentioned in Acts 20:5–7, the last before his first imprisonment; for, if it were, the interval between that visit and the first imprisonment would be seven or eight years, a period most unlikely for him to have allowed to pass without sending for his cloak and parchments, when they might have been of service to him in the interim. (3) Paul's leaving Trophimus sick at Miletus (ch. 4:20), could not have been on the occasion mentioned in Acts 20:15; for, subsequent to that, Trophimus was with Paul in Jerusalem (Acts 21:29). (4) The words (ch. 4:20), "Erastus abode at Corinth," imply that Paul had shortly before been at Corinth, where he left Erastus. But before his first imprisonment, Paul had not been at Corinth for several years; and in the interval Timothy had been with him, so that Timothy did not need at a later period to be told about that visit (Acts 20:2, 4). For all these reasons the imprisonment, during which he wrote Second Timothy, is shown to be his second imprisonment. Moreover, Hebrews 13:23, 24, represents the writer (who was probably Paul) as *in Italy*, and *at liberty*. So CLEMENT OF ROME (B. 1. 5), the disciple of Paul, explicitly states, "In the east and west, Paul as a preacher instructed *the whole world* (i.e., the Roman empire) in righteousness, and having gone to *the extremity of the west*, and having borne witness before the rulers (of Rome), he so was removed from the world." This plainly implies that he fulfilled his design (Rom. 15:24–28) of a missionary journey *into Spain*. The canon of the New Testament, compiled about A.D. 170 (called MURATORI's *Canon*), also mentions "the journey of Paul from Rome to Spain." See ROUTH, *Reliq. Sacr.*, vol. 4, p. 1–12.

His martyrdom is universally said to have occurred in Nero's reign [EUSEBIUS, *Ecclesiastical History*, 2. 22; JEROME, *Catalogus Scriptorum*]. Five years thus seem to have elapsed between the first imprisonment, A.D. 63 (Acts 28), and his martyrdom, June A.D. 68, the last year of Nero's reign. He was probably arrested by the magistrates in Nicopolis (Titus 3:12) in Epirus, in the winter, on a double charge, first, of being one of the Christians who had conspired, it was alleged by Nero's partisans, to set fire to Rome, A.D. 64; secondly, of introducing a novel and unlawful religion. His friends all left him, except Luke: Demas from "love of this present world": the others from various causes (ch. 4:10, 11). On the first charge he seems to have been acquitted. His liberation from his first imprisonment took place in A.D. 63, the year before the great fire at Rome, which

Nero made the pretext for his persecution of the Christians. Every cruelty was heaped on them; some were crucified; some were arrayed in the skins of wild beasts and hunted to death by dogs; some were wrapped in pitch-robes and set on fire by night to illuminate the circus of the Vatican and gardens of Nero, while that monster mixed among the spectators in the garb of a charioteer. But now (A.D. 67 or 68) some years had elapsed since the first excitement which followed the fire. Hence, Paul, being a Roman citizen, was treated in his trial with a greater respect for the forms of the law, and hence was acquitted (ch. 4:17) on the first charge of having instigated the Christians to their supposed acts of incendiarism before his last departure from Rome. Alexander the coppersmith seems to have been a witness against him (ch. 4:14). Had he been condemned on the first charge, he would probably have been burnt alive, as the preceding martyrs were, for *arson*. His judge was the city Præfect. Clemens Romanus specifies that his trial was (not before the emperor, but) "before the rulers." No advocate ventured to plead his cause, no patron appeared for him, such as under ordinary circumstances might have aided him; for instance, one of the powerful Æmilian house, under which his family possibly enjoyed clientship (ch. 4:16, 17), whence he may have taken his name Paul. The place of trial was, probably, one of the great basilicas in the Forum, two of which were called the Pauline Basilicas, from L. Æmilius Paulus, who had built one and restored the other. He was remanded for the second stage of his trial. He did not expect this to come on until the following "winter" (ch. 4:21), whereas it took place about midsummer; if in Nero's reign, not later than June. In the interim Luke was his only constant companion; but one friend from Asia, Onesiphorus, had diligently sought him and visited him in prison, undeterred by the danger. Linus, too, the future bishop of Rome, Pudens, the son of a senator, and Claudia, his bride, perhaps the daughter of a British king (Note, ch. 4:21), were among his visitors; and Tychicus, before he was sent by Paul to Ephesus (ch. 4:12; perhaps bearing with him this Epistle).

Object of the Epistle.—He was anxious to see his disciple Timothy, before his death, and that Timothy should bring Mark with him (ch. 1:4; 4:9, 11, 21). But feeling how uncertain it was whether Timothy should arrive in time, he felt it necessary, also, to give him by letter a last warning as to the heresies, the germs of which were then being scattered in the Churches. Hence he writes a series of exhortations to faithfulness, and zeal for sound doctrine, and patience amidst trials: a charge which Timothy seems to have needed, if we are to judge from the apostle's earnestness in urging him to boldness in Christ's cause, as though Paul thought he saw in him some signs of constitutional timidity (ch. 2:2–8; 4:1–5; I Tim. 5:22, 23).

Paul's Death.—Dionysius, bishop of Corinth (quoted in Eusebius, *Ecclesiastical History*, 2. 25) about A.D. 170, is the earliest authority for the tradition that Peter suffered martyrdom at Rome "about the same time" as Paul, after having labored for some time there. He calls Peter and Paul "the founders of the Corinthian and Roman Churches." The Roman presbyter, Caius (about A.D. 200), mentions the tradition that Peter suffered martyrdom in the Vatican. But (1) Peter's work was *among the Jews* (Gal. 2:9), whereas Rome was a Gentile Church (Rom. 1:13. Moreover, (2) the First Epistle of Peter (1:1; 5:13) represents him as laboring *in Babylon* in Mesopotamia. (3) The silence concerning Peter of Paul's Epistles written in Rome, negatives the tradition of his having founded, or labored long at Rome; though it is *possible* he may have endured martyrdom there. His martyrdom, certainly, was not, as Jerome says, "on the same day" with that of Paul, else Paul would have mentioned Peter's being at Rome in ch. 4:11. The legend says that Peter, through fear, was fleeing from Rome at early dawn by the Appian Way, when he met our Lord, and falling at His feet, asked, Lord, whither goest thou? to which the Lord replied, I go again to be crucified. The disciple returned penitent and ashamed, and was martyred. The Church of *Domine quo vadis*, on the Appian Way, commemorates the supposed fact. Paul, according to Caius (quoted in Eusebius, *Ecclesiastical History*, 2. 25), suffered martyrdom *on the Ostian Way*. So also Jerome, who gives the date, the 14th year of Nero. It was common to send prisoners, whose death might attract too much notice at Rome, to some distance from the city, under a military escort, for execution; hence the soldier's *sword*, not the executioner's *axe*, was the instrument of his decapitation [Orosius, *Hist.*, 7. 7]. Paul appears, from Philippians 1, to have had his partisans even in the palace, and certainly must have exercised such an influence as would excite sympathy in his behalf, to avoid which the execution was ordered outside the city. Cf. Tacitus, *Hist.*, 4. 11. The Basilica of St. Paul, first built by Constantine, now stands outside Rome on the road to Ostia: before the Reformation it was under the protection of the kings of England, and the emblem of the order of the Garter is still to be seen among its decorations. The traditional spot of the martyrdom is the *Tre Fontane*, not far from the Basilica [Conybeare and Howson].

CHAPTER 1

Vss. 1-18. Address: Thankful Expression of Love and Desire to See Him: Remembrance of His Faith and That of His Mother and Grandmother. Exhortation to Stir Up the Gift of God in Him, and Not Shrink from Affliction, Enforced by the Consideration of the Freeness of God's Grace in Our Gospel Calling, and by the Apostle's Example. The Defection of Many: The Steadfastness of Onesiphorus. **1.** This Epistle is the last testament and swanlike death-song of Paul [Bengel]. **according to the promise of life . . . in Christ**—Paul's *apostleship* is *in order to carry into effect* this promise. Cf. "according to the faith . . . in hope of eternal life . . . promise . . ." (Titus 1:1, 2). This "promise of life

in Christ" (cf. vs. 10; ch. 2:8) was needed to nerve Timothy to fortitude amidst trials, and to boldness in undertaking the journey to Rome, which would be attended with much risk (vs. 8). **2. my dearly beloved son**—In I Timothy 1:2, and Titus 1:4, written at an earlier period than this Epistle, the expression used is in the *Greek*, "my *genuine* son." Alford sees in the change of expression an intimation of an altered tone as to Timothy, more of mere love, and less of confidence, as though Paul saw in him a want of firmness, whence arose the need of his *stirring up* afresh the faith and grace in Him (vs. 6). But this seems to me not justified by the *Greek* word *agapetos*, which implies the attachment of *reasoning* and *choice*, on the ground of *merit* in the one "beloved," not of merely *instinctive* love. See Trench, *Synonyms of New Testament*. **3.**

I thank—Greek, "I feel gratitude to God." **whom I serve from my forefathers**—whom I serve (Rom. 1:9) as did my forefathers. He does not mean to put on the same footing the Jewish and Christian service of God; but simply to assert his own conscientious service of God as he had received it from his progenitors (not Abraham, Isaac, etc., whom he calls "the fathers," not "progenitors" as the Greek is here; Rom. 9:5). The memory of those who had gone before to whom he is about to be gathered, is now, on the eve of death, pleasant to him; hence also, he calls to mind the faith of the mother and grandmother of Timothy; as he walks in the faith of his forefathers (Acts 23:1; 24:14; 26:6, 7; 28:20), so Timothy should persevere firmly in the faith of his parent and grandparent. Not only Paul, but the Jews who reject Christ, forsake the faith of their forefathers, who looked for Christ; when they accept Him, the hearts of the children shall only be returning to the faith of their forefathers (Mal. 4:6; Luke 1:17; Rom. 11:23, 24, 28). Probably Paul had, in his recent defense, dwelt on this topic, viz., that he was, in being a Christian, only following his *hereditary faith*. **that . . . I have remembrance of thee**—"how unceasing I make my mention concerning thee" (cf. Philemon 4). The cause of Paul's feeling thankful is, not that he remembers Timothy unceasingly in his prayers, but for what Timothy is in faith (vs. 5) and graces; cf. Romans 1:8, 9, from which supply the elliptical sentence thus, "I thank God [for thee, for God is my witness] whom I serve . . . that (or *how*) without ceasing I have remembrance (or *make mention*) of thee . . . ." **night and day**—(Note, I Tim. 5:5). **4. desiring**—Greek, "with *yearning* as for one much *missed*." **mindful of thy tears**—not only at our parting (Acts 20:37), but also often when under pious feelings. **that I may be filled with joy**—to be joined with "desiring to see thee" (Rom. 1:11, 12; 15:32). **5. When I call to remembrance . . .**—This increased his "desire to see" Timothy. The oldest MSS. read, "When I *called* to remembrance"; implying that some recent incident (perhaps the contrasted cowardice of the hypocrite Demas, who forsook him) had reminded him of the sincerity of Timothy's faith. **faith that is in thee**—ALFORD translates, "that *was* in thee." He remembers Timothy's faith in the *past* as a fact; its *present* existence in him is only matter of his confident *persuasion* or hope. **which**—Greek, "such as." **dwelt**—"made its dwelling" or abode (John 14:23). The past tense implies they were now dead. **first**—before it dwelt in thee. She was the furthest back of the progenitors of Timothy whom Paul knew. **mother** Eunice—a believing Jewess; but his father was a Greek, i.e., a heathen (Acts 16:1). The faith of the one parent sanctified the child (ch. 3:15; I Cor. 7: 14). She was probably converted at Paul's first visit to Lystra (Acts 14:6). It is an undesigned coincidence, and so a mark of truth, that in Acts 16:1 the belief of the mother *alone* is mentioned, just as here praise is bestowed on the faith of the mother, while no notice is taken of the father [PALEY's *Horæ Paulinæ*]. **and**—Greek, "but," i.e., notwithstanding appearances [ALFORD]. **persuaded that**—it dwells, or it shall dwell "in thee also." The mention of the faith of his mother and grandmother is designed as an incentive to stir up his faith. **6. Wherefore**—Greek, "For which cause," viz., because thou hast inherited, didst once possess, and I trust ["am persuaded"] still dost possess, such unfeigned faith [ALFORD]. **stir up**—lit., "rekindle," "revive the spark of"; the opposite to "quench" or

extinguish (I Thess. 5:19). Paul does not doubt the existence of real faith in Timothy, but he desires it to be put into active exercise. Timothy seems to have become somewhat remiss from being so long without Paul (ch. 2:22). **gift of God**—the spiritual grace received for his ministerial office, either at his original ordination, or at his consecration to the particular office of superintending the Ephesian Church (*Note*, I Tim. 4:14), imparting *fearlessness*, *power, love, and a sound mind* (vs. 7). **by the putting on of my hands**—In I Timothy 4:14, it is "*with by*] the laying on of the hands *of the presbytery*." The apostle was chief in the ordination, and to him "BY" is applied. The presbytery were his assistants; so "with," implying merely *accompaniment*, is said of them. Paul was the instrument in Timothy's ordination and reception of the grace then conferred; the presbyters were the concurrent participants in the act of ordination; so the Greek, *dia* and *meta*. So in ordinations by a bishop in our days, he does the *principal* act; they join in laying on hands *with* him. **7. For . . .**—implying that Timothy needed the exhortation "to stir up the gift of God in him," being constitutionally *timid*: "For God *did not give* us (so the Greek, viz., at our ordination or consecration) the spirit of *fear*." The spirit which He gave us, was not the spirit of timidity (lit., "cowardice," which is weakness), but of "power" (exhibited in a fearless "testimony" for Christ, vs. 8). "Power is the invariable accompaniment of the gift of *the Holy Ghost*. Luke 24:49; Acts 1:8; cf. 6:6, "full of faith and of the *Holy Ghost*," with vs. 8," full of faith and *power*." Fear is the result of "the spirit of bondage" (Rom. 8:15). Fear *within* exaggerates the causes of fear *without*. "The spirit of power" is the spirit of man dwelt in by the Spirit of God imparting *power*; this power "casteth out fear" from ourselves, and stimulates us to try to cast it out of others (I John 4:18). **love** —which moves the believer while "speaking the truth" with *power*, when giving his testimony for Christ (vs. 8), at the same time to do so "in love" (Eph. 4:15). **a sound mind**—The Greek, is rather, "the bringing of men to a sound mind" [WAHL]. BENGEL supports *English Version*, "a sound mind," or "sober-mindedness"; a duty to which a young man like Timothy especially needed to be exhorted (ch. 2:22; I Tim. 4:12; Titus 2:4, 6). So Paul urges him, in ch. 2:4, to give up worldly entanglements, which as *thorns* (Luke 8:14) choke the word. These three gifts are preferable to any miraculous powers whatever. **8. therefore**—seeing that God hath given us such a spirit, not that of *fear*. **Be not thou . . . ashamed**—I agree with ELLICOTT, in opposition to ALFORD, that the Greek subjunctive here, with the negative, implies action *completed at one time*, not *continued action*, which the present imperative would express; thus implying that Timothy had *not* decidedly *yet* evinced such feeling of *shame*; though I think, Paul, amidst the desertion of others who once promised fair, and from being aware of Timothy's constitutional *timidity* (*Note*, vs. 7), felt it necessary to stir him up and guard him against the possibility of unchristian dereliction of duty as to bold confession of Christ. *Shame* (vs. 8) is the companion of *fear* (vs. 7); if fear be overcome, false shame flees [BENGEL]. Paul himself (vs. 12), and Onesiphorus (vs. 16), were instances of fearless profession removing false shame. He presents in contrast sad instances of fear and shame (vs. 15). **of the testimony of our Lord**—of the testimony which thou art bound to give in the cause of our Lord; he says "our," to connect Timothy and himself together in the testimony which both should give for their common Lord. *The testimony which Christ gave before Pilate* (I Tim. 6:12, 13), is an incentive to the believer that he should, after His Lord's example, *witness a good testimony* or *confession*. **nor of me his prisoner**—The cause of God's servants is the cause of God Himself (Eph. 4:1). Timothy might easily be tempted to be ashamed of one in prison, especially as not only worldly shame, but great risk, attended any recognition of Paul the prisoner. **be thou partaker** —*with me*. **of the gospel**—rather, as *Greek*, "*for* the Gospel," i.e., suffered *for the Gospel* (ch. 2:3-5; Philemon 13). **according to the power of God**— exhibited in having *saved* and *called* us (vs. 9). God who has done the greater act of power (i.e., saved us), will surely do the less (carry us safe through *afflictions* borne *for the Gospel*). "Think not that thou hast to bear these afflictions by thine own power; nay, it is by the power of God. It was a greater exercise of power than His making the heaven, His persuading the world to embrace salvation" [CHRYSOSTOM]. **9. Who ... called us**—viz., God the Father (Gal. 1:6). The having "saved us" in His eternal purpose of "grace, given us in Christ before the world began," precedes his actual "calling" of us in due time with a call made effective to us by the Holy Spirit; therefore, "saved us" comes before "called us" (Rom. 8:28-30). **holy calling**— the actual call *to* a life of *holiness*. Hebrews 3:1, "heavenly calling" [TITTMANN, *Synonyms*]; whereas we were *sinners* and *enemies* (Eph. 1:18; 4:1). The call comes wholly *from* God and claims us wholly *for* God. "Holy" implies the *separation* of believers from the rest of the world unto God. **not according to**—not having regard to our works in His election and calling of grace (Rom. 9:11; Eph. 2:8, 9). **his own purpose**—The origination of salvation was of *His own purpose*, flowing from His own goodness, not for works of ours coming first, but wholly because of His own gratuitous, electing love [THEODORET and CALVIN]. **grace ... given us** —in His everlasting purpose, regarded as the same as when actually accomplished in due time. **in Christ**—believers being regarded by God as IN HIM, with whom the Father makes the covenant of salvation (Eph. 1:4; 3:11). **before the world began**— *Greek*, "before the times (periods) of ages"; the enduring ages of which no end is contemplated (I Cor. 2:7; Eph. 3:11). **10. But ... now ... manifest** —in contrast to its concealment heretofore in the eternal purpose of God "before the world began" (vs. 9; Col. 1:16; Titus 1:2, 3). **appearing**—the visible manifestation in the flesh. **abolished death** —*Greek*, "taken away *the power* from death" [TITTMANN]. The *Greek* article before "death" implies that Christ abolished death, not only in some particular instance, but in its very essence, being, and idea, as well as in all its aspects and consequences (John 11:26; Rom. 8:2, 38; I Cor. 15:26, 55; Heb. 2:14). The carrying out of the abolition of death into full effect is to be at the resurrection (Rev. 20: 14). The death of the body meanwhile is but temporary, and is made no account of by Christ and the apostles. **brought ... to light**—making visible by the Gospel what was before hidden in God's purpose. **life**—of the Spirit, acting first on the soul here, about to act on the body also at the resurrection. **immortality**—*Greek*, "incorruptibility" of the new life, not merely of the risen body [ALFORD], (Rom. 8:11). **through**—*by means of the Gospel*, which *brings to light the life and immortality* purposed by God from eternity, but manifested now

first to man by Christ, who in His own resurrection has given the pledge of His people's final triumph over death through Him. Before the Gospel revelation from God, man, by the light of nature, under the most favorable circumstances, had but a glimmering idea of the possibility of a future being of *the soul,* but not the faintest idea of the resurrection of *the body* (Acts 17:18, 32). If Christ were not "the life," the dead could never live; if He were not the resurrection, they could never rise; had He not the keys of hell and death (Rev. 1:18), we could never break through the bars of death or gates of hell [BISHOP PEARSON]. **11. Whereunto**—For the publication of which Gospel. **I am appointed**— *Greek,* "I *was* appointed." **preacher**—*Greek,* "herald." **teacher of the Gentiles**—(I Tim. 2:7). He brings forward his own example in this verse and vs. 12, as a pattern for Timothy, as a *public* "preacher," an "apostle," or *missionary* from place to place, and a "teacher" *in private* instructing His flock with patient perseverance. **12. For the which cause**—For the Gospel cause of which I was appointed a preacher (vss. 10, 11). **I also suffer**— besides my *active* work as a missionary. ELLICOTT translates, "I suffer even these things"; the sufferings attendant on my being a prisoner (vss. 8, 15). **I am not ashamed**—neither be thou (vs. 8). **for**—Confidence as to the future drives away shame [BENGEL]. **I know**—though the world knows Him not (John 10:14; 17:25). **whom** —I know what a *faithful,* promisekeeping God He is (ch. 2:13). It is not, I know *how* I have believed, but, I know WHOM I have believed; a feeble faith may clasp a strong Saviour. **believed**—rather, "trusted"; carrying out the metaphor of a depositor depositing his pledge with one whom he *trusts.* **am persuaded**—(Rom. 8:38). **he is able**—in spite of so many foes around me. **that which I have committed unto him**—*Greek,* "my deposit"; the body, soul, and spirit, which I have deposited in God's safe keeping (I Thess. 5:23; I Pet. 4:19). So Christ Himself in dying (Luke 23:46). "God deposits with us His word; we deposit with God our spirit" [GROTIUS]. There is one deposit [His revelation] committed by God to us, which we ought to keep (vss. 13, 14) and transmit to others (ch. 2:2); there is another committed by God to us, which we should commit to His keeping, viz., ourselves and our heavenly portion. **that day**—the day of His appearing (vs. 18; ch. 4:8). **13. Hold fast the form** —rather as *Greek,* "Have (i.e., keep) a *pattern* of sound (*Greek,* 'healthy') words which thou hast heard from me, in faith and love." "Keep" suits the reference to a *deposit* in the context. The secondary position of the verb in the *Greek* forbids our taking it so strongly as *English Version,* "Hold fast." The *Greek* for "form" is translated "pattern" in I Timothy 1:16, the only other passage where it occurs. Have such a *pattern* drawn from my *sound* words, in opposition to the *unsound* doctrines so current at Ephesus, *vividly impressed* (WAHL translates it "delineation"; the verb implies "to make *a lively and lasting impress*") on thy mind. **in faith and love**—the element IN which my sound words had place, and in which thou art *to have the vivid impression* of them as thy *inwardly delineated pattern,* moulding conformably thy outward profession. So nearly BENGEL explains, I Timothy 3:9. **14.** Translate as *Greek,* "That goodly deposit keep through the Holy Ghost," viz., "the sound words which I have committed to thee" (vs. 13; ch. 2:2). **in us**—in all believers, not merely in you and me. The indwelling Spirit enables us to keep from the robbers of the soul the deposit of His word committed to us by God. **15. all they which are in Asia** —Proconsular Asia; "all who are there *now, when they were in Rome* (not "*be*" or *are*, but) turned from me" then; were "ashamed of my chain," in contrast to ONESIPHORUS; did not stand with me but forsook me (ch. 4:16). It is possible that the occasion of their turning from him was at his apprehension in Nicopolis, whither they had escorted him on his way to Rome, but from which they turned back to Asia. A hint to Timothy, now in Asia, not to be like them, but to imitate rather ONESIPHORUS, and to come to him (ch. 4:21). **Phygellus and Hermogenes**—specified perhaps, as being persons from whom such pusillanimous conduct could least be expected; or, as being well known to Timothy, and spoken of before in conversations between him and Paul, when the latter was in Asia Minor. **16. The Lord give mercy**—even as ONESIPHORUS had abounded in works of *mercy*. **the house of One-siphorus**—He himself was then absent from Ephesus, which accounts for the form of expression (ch. 4:19). His *household* would hardly retain his name after the master was dead, as BENGEL supposes him to have been. Nowhere has Paul prayers for the dead, which is fatal to the theory, favored by ALFORD also, that he was dead. God blesses not only the righteous man himself, but all his household. **my chain**—Paul in the second, as in his first imprisonment, was bound by a chain to the soldier who guarded him. **17. found me**—in the crowded metropolis. So in turn "may he *find* mercy of the Lord in that day" when the whole universe shall be assembled. **18. grant unto him**— as well as "unto his house" (vs. 16). **the Lord**— who rewards a kindness done to His disciples as if done to Himself (Matt. 25:45). **of**—*from* the Lord; "the Lord" is emphatically put instead of "from Himself," for solemnity and emphasis (II Thess. 3: 5). **in how many things**—"how many acts of ministry he rendered." **unto me**—omitted in the oldest MSS., so that the "ministered" may include services rendered *to others* as well as to Paul. **very well**—rather as *Greek,* "Thou knowest better" (than I can tell thee, seeing that thou art more of a regular resident at Ephesus).

CHAPTER 2

Vss. 1-26. EXHORTATIONS; TO FAITHFULNESS AS A GOOD SOLDIER OF CHRIST; ERRORS TO BE SHUNNED; THE LORD'S SURE FOUNDATION; THE RIGHT SPIRIT FOR A SERVANT OF CHRIST. **1. Thou therefore**—following my example (ch. 1:8, 12), and that of ONE-SIPHORUS (ch. 1:16-18), and shunning that of those who forsook me (ch. 1:15). **my son**—*Children* ought to imitate their father. **be strong**—lit., "be invested with *power*." Have power, and show thyself to have it; implying an abiding state of power. **in the grace**—the *element* IN which the believer's strength has place. Cf. ch. 1:7, "God hath given us the spirit of *power*." **2. among**—*Greek,* "through," i.e., with the attestation (lit., "intervention") of many witnesses, viz., the presbyters and others present at his ordination or consecration (I Tim. 4:14; 6:12). **commit**—in trust, as a *deposit* (ch. 1:14). **faithful**—the quality most needed by those having a trust committed to them. **who**—*Greek,* "(persons) *such as* shall be competent to teach (them to) others also." Thus the way is prepared for inculcating the duty of faithful endurance (vss. 3-13). Thou shouldest consider as a motive to endurance, that thou hast not only to

keep the deposit for thyself, but to transmit it unimpaired to others, who in their turn shall fulfil the same office. This is so far from supporting oral tradition *now* that it rather teaches how precarious a mode of preserving revealed truth it was, depending, as it did, on the trustworthiness of each individual in the chain of succession; and how thankful we ought to be that *God Himself* has given *the written Word*, which is exempt from such risk. **3. Thou therefore endure hardness**—The oldest MSS. have no "*Thou therefore*," and read, "Endure hardship *with*" (me). "Take thy share in suffering" [CONYBEARE and HOWSON]. **4.** "No one while serving as a soldier." **the affairs . . .**—"the businesses of life" [ALFORD]; mercantile, or other than military. **him who hath chosen him**—the general who at the first enlisted him as a soldier. Paul himself worked at tent-making (Acts 18:3). Therefore what is prohibited here is, not all other save religious occupation, but the becoming *entangled,* or over-engrossed therewith. **5. And**—"Moreover." **strive for masteries**—"strive in the games" [ALFORD]; viz., the great national games of Greece. **yet is he not crowned, except**—even though he gain the victory. **strive lawfully**—observing all the conditions of both the contest (keeping within the bounds of the course and stript of his clothes) and the preparation for it, viz., as to selfdenying diet, anointing, exercise, self-restraint, chastity, decorum, etc. (I Cor. 9:24-27). **6. must be first partaker**—The right of *first partaking of the fruits* belongs to him *who* is *laboring;* do not thou, therefore, relax thy labors, as thou wouldest be foremost in partaking of the reward. CONYBEARE explains "first," *before the idler.* **7.** Consider the force of the illustrations I have given from the soldier, the contender in the games, and the husbandmen, as *applying to thyself in thy ministry.* **and the Lord give thee . . .**—The oldest MSS. read, "*for* the Lord *will give* thee understanding." Thou canst understand my meaning so as personally to apply it to thyself; for the Lord will give thee understanding when thou seekest it from Him "in all things." Not intellectual perception, but personal appropriation of the truths metaphorically expressed, was what he needed to be given him by the Lord. **8.** Rather as *Greek,* "Remember Jesus Christ, raised from the dead." Remember Christ risen, so as to follow Him. As He was raised after death, so if thou wouldest share His risen "life," thou must now share His "death" (vs. 11). The *Greek* perfect passive participle, implies a *permanent character* acquired by Jesus as *the risen* Saviour, and *our permanent interest in Him as such.* Christ's resurrection is put prominently forward as being the truth now assailed (vs. 18), and the one best calculated to stimulate Timothy to steadfastness in sharing Paul's sufferings for the Gospel's sake (*Note,* vs. 3). **of the seed of David**—The one and only genealogy (as contrasted with the "endless genealogies," (I Tim. 1: 4) worth thinking of, for it proves Jesus to be the Messiah. The absence of the article in the *Greek,* and this formula, "of the seed of David" (cf. Rom. 1:3), imply that the words were probably part of a recognized short oral creed. In His death He assured us of His humanity; by His resurrection, of His divinity. That He was not crucified for *His own* sin appears from His resurrection; that He was crucified shows that He bore sin, *on* Him, though not *in* Him. **my gospel**—that which I always taught. **9. Wherein**—in proclaiming which Gospel. **suffer trouble**—lit., "evil." I am a sufferer of evil as though I were a doer of evil. **bonds**—(ch. 1:16).

word . . . not bound—Though my person is bound, my tongue and my pen are not (ch. 4:17; Acts 28: 31). Or he alludes not merely to *his own* proclamation of the Gospel, though in chains, but to the freedom of its circulation *by others,* even though his power of circulating it is now prescribed (Phil. 1: 18). He also hints to Timothy that he being free ought to be the more earnest in the service of it. **10. Therefore**—Because of the anxiety I feel that the Gospel should be extended; that anxiety being implied in vs. 9. **endure**—not merely "I passively *suffer,*" but "I actively and perseveringly *endure,*" and "am ready to endure patiently all things." **the elect's sakes**—for the sake of the Church: all the members of Christ's spiritual body (Col. 1:24). **they . . . also**—as well as myself: both God's elect not yet converted and those already so. **salvation . . . glory**—not only *salvation* from wrath, but *glory* in *reigning* with Him eternally (vs. 12). *Glory* is the full expansion of *salvation* (Acts 2:47; Rom. 8: 21-24, 30; Heb. 9:28). So *grace* and *glory* (Ps. 84: 12). **11.** *Greek,* "Faithful is the saying." **For**— "For" the fact is so that, "if we be dead with Him (the *Greek* aorist tense implies *a state once for all entered into in past times* at the moment of regeneration, Rom. 6:3, 4, 8; Col. 2:12), we shall also live with Him." The symmetrical form of "the saying," vss. 11-13, and the rhythmical balance of the parallel clauses, makes it likely, they formed part of a Church hymn (*Note,* I Tim. 3:16), or accepted formula, perhaps first uttered by some of the Christian "prophets" in the public assembly (I Cor. 14:26). The phrase "faithful is the saying," which seems to have been the usual formula (cf. I Tim. 1:15; 3:1; 4:9; Titus 3:8) in such cases, favors this. **12. suffer**—rather, as the *Greek* is the same as in vs. 10, "If we endure (with Him)," (Rom. 8:17). **reign with him**—The peculiar privilege of the elect Church now suffering with Christ, then to reign with Him (*Note,* I Cor. 6:2). *Reigning* is something more than mere *salvation* (Rom. 5:17; Rev. 3:21; 5:10; 20:4, 5). **deny**—*with the mouth.* As "believe" *with the heart follows,* vs. 12. Cf. the opposite, "confess with thy mouth" and "believe in thine heart" (Rom. 10:9, 10). **he also will deny us**—(Matt. 10:33). **13. believe not**—"If we are unbelievers (lit., 'unfaithful'), He remains *faithful*" (Deut. 7:9, 10). The oldest MSS. read, *"For* He cannot (it is an *impossibility* that He should) deny Himself." *He* cannot be unfaithful to His word that He will deny those who deny Him, though *we* be not faithful to our profession of faith in Him (Rom. 3:3). Three things are impossible to God, to die, to lie, and to be deceived [AUGUSTINE, *Symbolism ad Catechumenos,* 1. 1], (Heb. 6:18). This impossibility is not one of infirmity, but of infinite power and majesty. Also, indirectly, comfort is suggested to believers, that He is faithful to His promises to them; at the same time that apostates are shaken out of their self-deceiving fancy, that because they change, Christ similarly may change. A warning to Timothy to be steadfast in the faith. **14. them**—those over whom thou dost preside (Titus 3:1). **charging**—*Greek,* "testifying continually": "adjuring them." **before the Lord**—(I Tim. 5:21). **that they strive not about words**—rather, "strive with words": "not to have a (mere) *war of words*" (vss. 23, 24; I Tim. 6:4) where the most vital matters are at stake (vss. 17, 18; Acts 18:15). The oldest MSS. put a stop at "charging them before the Lord" (which clause is thus connected with "put them in remembrance") and read the imperative, "Strive not thou in words . . . ." **to no profit**—not

qualifying "words"; but *Greek* neuter, in apposition with "strive in words," "(a thing tending) to no profit," lit., "profitable for nothing"; the opposite of "meet for the master's use" (vs. 21). **to the subverting**—sure to subvert (overturn) the hearers: the opposite of "edifying" (building up) (II Cor. 13:10). **15. Study**—*Greek,* "Be earnest," or "diligent." **to show**—*Greek,* "present," as in Romans 12:1. **thyself**—as distinguished from those whom Timothy was to charge (vs. 14). **approved**—tested by trial: opposed to "reprobate" (Titus 1:16). **workman**—alluding to Matthew 20:1 etc. **not to be ashamed**—by his work not being "approved" (Phil. 1:20). Contrast "deceitful workers" (II Cor. 11: 13). **rightly dividing**—"rightly handling" [*Vulgate*]; "rightly administering" [ALFORD]; lit., cutting "straight" or "right": the metaphor being from a father or a steward (I Cor. 4:1) *cutting* and *distributing* bread among his children [VITRINGA and CALVIN], (Luke 12:42). LXX, Proverbs 3:6 and 11:5, use it of "making one's way": so BENGEL here takes Paul to mean that Timothy may *make ready a straight way for* "the word of truth," and may himself walk straight forward according to this line, turning neither to the right nor to the left, "teaching no other doctrine" (I Tim. 1:3). The same image of a *way* appears in the *Greek* for "increase" (*Note,* vs. 16). The opposite to "rightly handling," or "dispensing," is, II Corinthians 2:17, "corrupt the word of God." **truth**—*Greek,* "the truth" (cf. vs. 18). **16. shun**—lit., "stand above," separate from, and superior to. **vain**—opposed to "the truth" (vs. 15). **babblings**—with loud voice: opposed to the temperate "word" (Titus 3:9). **increase**—*Greek,* advance"; lit., "strike forward": an image from pioneers *cutting* away all obstacles *before* an advancing army. They pretend *progress;* the only kind of *progress* they make is to a greater pitch of impiety. **more ungodliness**—*Greek,* "a greater degree of impiety." **17. will eat**—lit., "will have pasture." The consuming progress of mortification is the image. They pretend to give rich spiritual *pasture* to their disciples: the only *pasture* is that of a spiritual cancer feeding on their vitals. **canker**—a "cancer" or "gangrene." **Hymeneus**—(*Note,* I Tim. 1:20). After his excommunication he seems to have been re-admitted into the Church and again to have troubled it. **18. erred**—*Greek,* "missed the aim" (*Note,* I Tim. 6:21). **is past already**—has already taken place. The beginnings of the subsequent Gnostic heresy already existed. They "wrested" (II Pet. 3:16) Paul's own words (Rom. 6:4; Eph. 2:6 Col. 2:12) "to their own destruction," as though the resurrection was merely the spiritual raising of souls from the death of sin. Cf. I Corinthians 15:12, where he shows all our hopes of future glory rest on the literal reality of the resurrection. To believe it past (as the Seleucians or Hermians did, according to AUGUSTINE, *Ep.* 119. 55, *ad Januarium,* sec. 4), is to deny it in its true sense. **overthrow**—trying to subvert "the foundation" on which alone faith can rest secure (vs. 19; cf. Titus 1:11). **19. Nevertheless**—Notwithstanding the subversion of *their* faith, "the firm foundation of *God* standeth" fast (so the *Greek* ought to be translated). The "foundation" here is "the Church" [ALFORD]; "the ground" or basement support "of the truth" (I Tim. 3:15), Christ Himself being the ultimate "foundation" (I Cor. 3:11). In the steadfast standing of *the Church* there is involved the steadfast certainty of the *doctrine* in question (vs. 18). Thus the "house" (vs. 20) answers to the "foundation"; it is made up of the elect whom "the Lord knoweth" (acknowledgeth, recognizes, Ps. 1:6; Matt. 7:23; John 10:14; I Cor. 8:3) as "His," and who persevere to the end, though others "err concerning the faith" (Matt. 24:24; John 10:28; Rom. 10:38, 39; I John 2:19). BENGEL takes "the foundation" to be *the immovable faithfulness of God* (to His promises to His elect [CALVIN]). This contrasts well with the *erring from the faith* on the part of the reprobate, vs. 18. Though *they deny the faith, God abates not His faithfulness* (cf. vs. 13). **having**—seeing that it has [ELLICOTT]. **seal**—"inscription": indicating *ownership* and *destination*; inscriptions were often engraven on a "foundation" stone (Rev. 21:14) [ALFORD]. This will agree with the view that "the foundation" is *the Church* (Eph. 2:20). If it be taken God's *immovable faithfulness*, the "seal" will be regarded as attached to His covenant promise, with the inscription or legend, on one side of its round surface, "The Lord knoweth (it is 'knew' in LXX, Num. 16:5, to which Paul here alludes, altering it for his purpose by the Spirit) them that are His"; on the observe side, "Let every one that nameth (as *his* Lord, Ps. 20:7, or preacheth in His name, Jer. 20:9) Christ. . . ." **depart**—*Greek,* "stand aloof." **from iniquity** —(Isa. 52:11). In both clauses there may be an allusion to Num. 16:5, 26, LXX. God's part and man's part are marked out. God chooseth and knoweth His elect; our part is to believe, and by the Spirit depart from all iniquity, an unequivocal proof of our being the Lord's (cf. Deut. 29:29; Luke 13:23-27). St. Lucian when asked by his persecutors, "Of what country art thou?" replied, "I am a Christian." "What is your occupation?" "I am a Christian." "Of what family?" "I am a Christian." [CHRYSOSTOM, *Orationes,* 75.] He cannot be honored with the name Christian, who dishonors by iniquity, Christ, the Author of the name. Blandina's refreshment amidst her tortures was to say," I am a Christian, and *with us Christians no evil is done*" [EUSEBIUS, *Ecclesiastical History,* 5. 1]. Apostasy from the faith is sure soon to be followed by indulgence in iniquity. It was so with the false teachers (ch. 3:2-8, 13). **20. in a great house**—i.e., the visible professing Christian Church (I Tim. 3:15). Paul is speaking, not of those without, but of the [visible] family of God [CALVIN]. So the parable of the sweep net (Matt. 13:47-49) gathering together of every kind, good and bad: as the good and bad cannot be distinguished while under the waves, but only when brought to shore, so believers and unbelievers continue in the same Church, until the judgment makes the everlasting distinction. "The ark of Noah is a type of the Church; as in the former there were together the leopard and the kid, the wolf and the lamb; so in the latter, the righteous and sinners, vessels of gold and silver, with vessels of wood and earth" [JEROME, *contra Luciferianos,* 302] (cf. Matt. 20:16). **vessels of gold . . . silver**—precious and able to endure fire. **of wood and earth**—worthless, fragile, and soon burnt (II Cor. 3:12-15; 15:47). **some . . . some**—the former . . . the latter. **to dishonour**—(Prov. 16:4; Rom. 9:17-23). **21. If a man . . . purge himself from these**—The *Greek* expresses "If one (e.g., thou, Timothy) purify himself (so as to separate) *from among these*" (*vessels* unto dishonor). **sanctified**—set apart as wholly consecrated to the Lord. **and meet**— Some oldest MSS. omit "and." **the master's**—the Lord's. Paul himself was such a vessel: once one among those of earth, but afterwards he became by grace one of gold. **prepared unto every good work** —(Ch. 3:17; Titus 3:1). Contrast Titus 1:16. **22.**

Flee—There are many lusts from which our greatest safety is in *flight* (Gen. 39:12). Avoid occasions of sin. From the abstemious character of Timothy (I Tim. 5:23) it is likely that not animal indulgences, but the impetuosity, rash self-confidence, hastiness, strife, and vainglory of young men (I John 2:14-16), are what *he* is here warned against: though the Spirit probably intended the warning to include *both* in its application to the Church *in general.* **also**— Greek, "But"; in contrast to "every good work," vs. 21. **youthful**—Timothy was a youth (I Tim. 4:12). **righteousness**—the opposite of "iniquity," i.e., unrighteousness (vs. 19; cf. I Tim. 6:11). **peace, with . . .**—rather put no comma, "*peace with them* that call on the Lord out of a pure heart" (I Tim. 1:5; Eph. 6:5; Col. 3:22). We are to *love* all men, but it is not possible to be at *peace* with all men, for this needs community of purpose and opinion; they alone who call on the Lord sincerely [as contrasted with the false teachers who had only the form of godliness, ch. 3:5, 8; Titus 1:15, 16] have this community [THEODORET]. (Rom. 12:18). **23.** (Titus 3:9.) **unlearned**—*Greek,* "undisciplined"; not tending to promote the discipline of faith and morals (Prov. 5:23). "Uninstructive"; in contrast with "instructing" (vs. 25), and "wise unto salvation" (ch. 3:15). **avoid**—"decline." **24. not strive**—"The servant of the Lord" must imitate his master in not *striving contentiously,* though uncompromising in earnestly contending for the faith (Jude 3; Matt. 12:19). **gentle unto all men**—"patient" (*Greek,* "patient in bearing wrongs") in respect to adversaries. He is to be *gentle* so that he may occasion no evils; *patient* so that he may endure evils. **apt to teach**—implying not only solid teaching and ease in teaching, but patience and assiduity in it [BENGEL]. **25. instructing**—*Greek,* "disciplining," *instructing with correction,* which those who deal in "*uninstructive*" or "undisciplined questions" need (*Notes,* vs. 23; I Tim. 1:20). **those that oppose themselves**—*Greek,* "oppositely affected"; those of a different opinion. **if . . . peradventure**—*Greek,* "if at any time." **repentance**—which they need as antecedent to *the full knowledge* (so the *Greek* for "*acknowledgment*") *of the truth* (I Tim. 2:4), their minds being corrupted (ch. 3:8), and their lives immoral. The cause of the spiritual ignorance which prompts such "questions" is moral, having its seat in the *will,* not in the intellect (John 7:17). Therefore repentance is their first need. That, not man, but God alone can "give" (Acts 5:31). **26. recover themselves**—*Greek,* "awake to soberness," viz., from the spiritual intoxication whereby they have fallen into the snare of the devil. **the snare**—(Eph. 6:11, "the wiles of the devil"; I Tim. 3:7; 6:9). **taken captive by him at his will**— *so as to follow the will of* "THAT" (the *Greek* emphatically marks Satan thus) foe. However, different *Greek* pronouns stand for "him" and "his"; and the *Greek* for "taken captive" means not "captured *for destruction,*" but "*for being saved alive,*" as in Luke 5:10, "Thou shalt catch men to save them unto life"; also there is no article before the *Greek* participle, which the *English Version* "who are taken captive," would require. Therefore, translate, "That they may awake . . ., taken as saved (and willing) captives by him (the servant of the Lord, vs. 24), so as to follow the will of HIM (the Lord, vs. 24, or "God," vs. 25." There are here two evils, the "snare" and *sleep,* from which they are delivered: and two goods to which they are translated, *awaking* and *deliverance.* Instead of Satan's thrall comes the free and willing *captivity of obedience* to Christ (II Cor. 10:5). It is God who goes before, *giving repentance* (vs. 25); then the work of His servant following is sure to be crowned with success, leading the convert henceforth to "live to the will of God" (Acts 22:14; I Pet. 4:2).

CHAPTER 3

Vss. 1-17. Coming Evil Days: Signs of Evil Already: Contrast in the Doctrine and Life of Paul, Which Timothy Should Follow in Accordance with His Early Training in Scripture. **1. also**—*Greek,* "but." **last days**—preceding Christ's second coming (II Pet. 3:3; Jude 18). "The *latter* times," I Timothy 4:1, refer to a period not so remote as "the *last* days," viz., the long days of papal and Greek anti-Christianity. **perilous**—lit., *"difficult* times," in which it is difficult to know what is to be done: "grievous times." **shall come**—*Greek,* "shall be imminent"; "shall come unexpectedly" [Bengel]. **2. men**—in the professing Church. Cf. the catalogue, Romans 1:29, etc., where much the same sins are attributed to heathen men; it shall be a relapse into virtual heathendom, with all its beastlike propensities, whence the symbol of it is "a beast" (Rev. 13:1, 11, 12, etc.; 17:3, 8, 11). **covetous**—Translate, "money-loving," a distinct *Greek* word from that for "covetous" (*Note,* Col. 3:5). The cognate *Greek* substantive (I Tim. 6:10) is so translated, "the *love of money* is a (*Greek,* not "the") root of all evil." **boasters**—empty boasters [Alford]; boasting of having what they have not. **proud**—overweening: lit., *showing* themselves *above* their fellows. **blasphemous**—rather, "evil-speakers," revilers. **disobedient to parents**—The character of the times is even to be gathered especially from the manners of the young [Bengel]. **unthankful**—The obligation to *gratitude* is next to that of *obedience* to parents. **unholy**—irreligious [Alford]; inobservant of the offices of piety. **3. truce-breakers**—rather as the *Greek* is translated in Romans 1:31, "implacable." **false accusers**—slanderers (I Tim. 3:11; Titus 2:3). **incontinent, fierce**—at once both soft and hard: incontinently indulging themselves, and inhuman to others. **despisers ...**—"no lovers of good" [Alford]; the opposite of "a lover of good" (Titus 1:8). **4. heady**—precipitate in action and in passion. **high-minded**—lit., "puffed up" with pride, as with smoke blinding them. **lovers of pleasure ... God**—Love of pleasure destroys the love and sense of God. **5. form**—outward semblance. **godliness**—piety. **denying**—rather as *Greek,* "having denied," i.e., renounced. **the power** —the living, regenerating, sanctifying influence of it. **turn away**—implying that some of such characters, forerunners of the last days, were already in the Church. **6. of this sort**—*Greek,* "of these," such as were described (vs. 5). **creep into**—stealthily. **laden with sins**—(Isa. 1:4)—applying to the "silly women" whose consciences are burdened with sins, and so are a ready prey to the false teachers who promise ease of conscience if they will follow them. A bad conscience leads easily to shipwreck of faith (I Tim. 1:19). **divers lusts**—not only animal lusts, but passion for change in doctrine and manner of teaching; the running after fashionable men and fashionable tenets, drawing them in the most opposite directions [Alford]. **7. Ever learning**—some new point, for mere curiosity, to the disparagement of what they seemed to know before. **the knowledge**—*Greek,* "the *perfect* knowledge"; the only safeguard against further novelties. Gnosticism laid hold especially of the female sex [Irenæus, 1. 13. 3.]: so Roman Jesuitism. **8. Now**—*Greek,*

"But"; it is no wonder there should be now such opponents to the truth, for their prototypes existed in ancient times [Alford]. **Jannes ... Jambres**—traditional names of the Egyptian magicians who resisted Moses (Exod. 7:11, 22), derived from "the unwritten teaching of the Jews" [Theodoret]. In a point so immaterial as the names, where Scripture had not recorded them, Paul takes the names which general opinion had assigned the magicians. Eusebius, *Præparatio Evangelica,* quotes from Numenius, "Jannes and Jambres were *sacred scribes* (a lower order of priests in Egypt) skilled in magic." Hiller interprets Jannes from the Abyssinian language *a trickster,* and Jambres *a juggler* (Acts 13:8). **resist**—"withstand," as before. They did so by trying to rival Moses' miracles. So the false teachers shall exhibit lying wonders in the last days (Matt. 24:24; II Thess. 2:9; Rev. 13:14, 15). **reprobate**—*incapable of testing* the truth (Rom. 1:28) [Bengel]. Alford takes passively, "not abiding the test"; rejected on being tested (Jer. 6:30). **9. they shall proceed no further**—Though *for a time* (ch. 2:16) "they shall *advance* or *proceed* (*English Version,* 'increase') unto more ungodliness," yet there is a *final* limit beyond which they shall not be able to "proceed further" (Job 38:11; Rev. 11:7, 11). They themselves shall "wax worse and worse" (vs. 13), but they shall at last be for ever prevented from seducing others. "Often malice proceeds deeper down, when it cannot extend itself" [Bengel]. **their folly**—lit., "dementation": *wise* though they think themselves. **shall be manifest**—*Greek,* "shall be brought forth from concealment into open day" [Bengel], (I Cor. 4:5). **as theirs ... was**—as that of those magicians was, when not only could they no longer try to rival Moses in sending boils, but the boils fell upon themselves: so as to the lice (Exod. 8:18; 9:11). **10. fully known**—lit., "fully followed up" and traced; viz., with a view to following me as thy pattern, so far as I follow Christ; the same *Greek* as in Luke 1:3, "*having had perfect understanding of* all things." His pious mother Eunice and grandmother Lois would recommend him to *study fully* Paul's Christian course as a pattern. He had not been yet the companion of Paul at the time of the apostle's persecutions in Antioch, Iconium, and Lystra (Acts 13:50; 14:5, 19), but is first mentioned as such Acts 16:1-3. However, he was "a disciple" already, when introduced to us in Acts 16:1-3; and as Paul calls him "my own son in the faith," he must have been converted by the apostle previously; perhaps in the visit to those parts three years before. Hence arose Timothy's knowledge of Paul's persecutions, which were the common talk of the churches in those regions about the time of his conversion. The *incidental* allusion to them here forms an *undesigned coincidence* between the history and the Epistle, indicating genuineness [Paley's *Horæ Paulinæ*]. A forger of Epistles from the Acts would never allude to Timothy's *knowledge* of persecutions, when that knowledge is not expressly mentioned in the history, but is only arrived at by indirect inference; also the omission of *Derbe* here, in the Epistle, is in minute accordance with the fact that in Derbe *no persecution* is mentioned in the history, though *Derbe and Lystra* are commonly mentioned together. The reason why he mentions his persecutions before Timothy became his companion, and not those subsequent, was because Timothy was familiar with the latter as an eyewitness and Paul needed not to remind him of them, but the former Timothy had *traced up* by seeking the information from others, especially as the date and scene of them was the date and scene of his own conversion. **doctrine**—"teaching." **manner of life**—"conduct," "behavior." **purpose**—The *Greek* is elsewhere usually used of *God's* "purpose." But here, as in Acts 11:23, of Paul's determined "purpose of heart in cleaving unto the Lord." My *set aim*, or *resolution*, in my apostolic function, and in every action is, not my selfish gain, but the glory of God in Christ. **long-suffering**—towards my adversaries, and the false teachers; towards brethren in bearing their infirmities; towards the unconverted, and the lapsed when penitent (ch. 4:2; II Cor. 6:6; Gal. 5:22; Eph. 4:2; Col. 3:12). **charity**—*love* to all men. **patience**—"endurance"; *patient continuance* in well-doing amidst adversities (vs. 11; Rom. 2:7). **11. afflictions**—"sufferings." **which**—*Greek*, "such as." **in Antioch**—of Pisidia (Acts 13:14, 50, 51). **Iconium**—(Acts 14:1-5). **Lystra**—(Acts 14:6, 19). **what**—How grievous. **out of ... all ... Lord delivered me**—(ch. 4:17; Ps. 34:17; II Cor. 1:10). An encouragement to Timothy not to fear persecutions. **12. Yea, and**—an additional consideration for Timothy: if he *wishes to live godly in Christ*, he must make up his mind to encounter persecution. **that will ...**—*Greek*, "all whose *will is to* live ..." So far should persecution be from being a stumbling block to Timothy, he should consider it a mark of the pious. So the same *Greek* is used of the same thing, Luke 14:28, 33, "intending (*Greek*, *wishing*) to build a tower ... counteth the cost." **live godly in Christ**—(Gal. 2:20; Phil. 1:21). There is no godliness (*Greek*, *piously*") or *piety* out of Christ. The world easily puts up with the mask of a religion which depends on itself, but the piety which derives its vigor directly from Christ is as odious to modern Christians as it was to the ancient Jews [BENGEL]. **shall suffer persecution**—and will not decline it (Gal. 5:11). BISHOP PEARSON proves the divine origination of Christianity from its success being inexplicable on the supposition of its being of human origin. The nature of its doctrine was no way likely to command success: (1) it condemns all other religions, some established for ages; (2) it enjoins precepts ungrateful to flesh and blood, the mortifying of the flesh, the love of enemies, and the bearing of the cross; (3) it enforces these seemingly unreasonable precepts by promises seemingly incredible; not good things such as afford complacency to our senses, but such as cannot be obtained till after this life, and presuppose what then seemed impossible, the resurrection; (4) it predicts to its followers what would seem sure to keep most of the world from embracing it, *persecutions*. **13.** Reason why persecutions must be expected, and these becoming worse and worse as the end approaches. The breach between light and darkness, so far from being healed, shall be widened [ALFORD]. **evil men**—in contrast to the "godly" (vs. 12). **seducers**—lit., "conjurors." Magical arts prevailed at Ephesus (Acts 19:19), and had been renounced by many Ephesians on embracing Christianity: but now when Paul was writing to Ephesus, symptoms of a return to *conjuring* tricks appeared: an undesigned coincidence [BURTON]. Probably *sorcery* will characterize the final apostasy (Rev. 13:15; 18:23; 22:15). **wax worse**—lit., "advance in the direction of worse" (*Note*, vs. 9). Not contradictory to that verse: there the *diffusion* of the evil was spoken of; here its *intensity* [ALFORD]. **deceiving, and being deceived**—He who has once begun to deceive others, is the less easily able to recover himself from error, and the

more easily embraces in turn the errors of others [BENGEL]. **14. But ... thou**—Whatever they may do. Resuming the thread begun at vs. 10. **learned**—from me and thy mother and grandmother (ch. 1:5; 2:2). **assured of**—from Scripture (vs. 15). **of whom**—plural, not singular, in the oldest MSS., "from what teachers." Not only from me, but from Lois and Eunice. **15. from a child**—lit., "from an infant." The tender age of the first dawn of reason is that wherein the most lasting impressions of faith may be made. **holy scriptures**—The Old Testament taught by his *Jewish* mother. An undesigned coincidence with ch. 1:5; Acts 16:1-3. **able**—in themselves: though through men's own fault they often do not *in fact* make men savingly alive. **wise unto salvation**—i.e., *wise* unto the attainment of salvation. Contrast "folly" (vs. 9). *Wise* also in extending it to others. **through faith**—as the *instrument* of this wisdom. Each *knows* divine things only as far as *his own experience* in himself extends. He who has not faith, has not *wisdom* or *salvation*. **which is in**—i.e., rests on Christ Jesus. **16. All scripture**—*Greek*, "Every Scripture," i.e., Scripture in its every part. However, *English Version* is sustained, though the *Greek* article be wanting, by the technical use of the term "Scripture" being so well known as not to need the article (cf. *Greek*, Eph. 3:15; 2:21). The *Greek* is never used of *writings* in general, but only of the sacred Scriptures. The position of the two *Greek* adjectives closely united by "and," forbids our taking the one as an epithet, the other as predicated and translated as ALFORD and ELLICOTT. "Every Scripture given by inspiration of God is *also* profitable." *Vulgate* and the best MSS., favor *English Version*. Clearly the adjectives are so closely connected that as surely as one is a predicate, the other must be so too. ALFORD admits his translation to be harsh, though legitimate. It is better with *English Version* to take it in a construction legitimate, and at the same time *not harsh*. The *Greek*, "God-inspired," is found nowhere else. Most of the New Testament books were written when Paul wrote this his latest Epistle; so he includes in the clause "All Scripture is God-inspired," not only the *Old Testament*, in which alone Timothy was taught when a child (vs. 15), but the New Testament books according as they were recognized in the churches which had men gifted with "discerning of spirits," and so able to distinguish really inspired utterances, persons, and so their writings from spurious. Paul means, "All Scripture is God-inspired *and therefore* useful"; because *we* see no utility in any words or portion of it, it does not follow it is not God-inspired. It is *useful*, because *God-inspired*, not *God-inspired*, because useful. One reason for the article not being before the *Greek*, "Scripture," may be that, if it had, it *might* be supposed that it limited the sense to the *hiera grammata*, "Holy Scriptures" (vs. 15) *of the Old Testament*, whereas here the assertion is more general: "*all* Scripture" (cf. *Greek*, II Pet. 1:20). The translation, "all Scripture that is God-inspired is also useful," would imply that there is some *Scripture* which is not God-inspired. But this would exclude the appropriated sense of the word "Scripture"; and who would need to be told that "all divine Scripture is *useful*" ("profitable")? Hebrews 4:13 would, in ALFORD'S view, have to be rendered, "All naked things are *also* open to the eyes of Him ...": so also I Timothy 4:4, which would be absurd [TREGELLES *on Daniel*]. KNAPP well defines inspiration, "An extraordinary divine agency upon teachers while giving instruction, whether oral or written, by which they were taught how and what they should speak or write" (cf. II Sam. 23:1; Acts 4:25; II Pet. 1:21). The *inspiration* gives the divine *sanction* to all the words of Scripture, though those words be the utterances of the individual writer, and only in special cases *revealed* directly by God (I Cor. 2:13). *Inspiration* is here predicated of the *writings,* "all Scripture," not of the persons. The question is not *how* God has done it; it is as to the *word,* not the *men* who wrote it. What we must believe is that He *has* done it, and that all the sacred writings are every where inspired, though not all alike matter of special *revelation:* and that even the very *words* are stamped with divine sanction, as Jesus used them (e.g. in the temptation and John 10:34, 35), for deciding all questions of doctrine and practice. There are degrees of *revelation* in Scripture, but not of *inspiration.* The sacred writers did not even always know the full significancy of their own God-inspired words (I Pet. 1:10, 11, 12). Verbal inspiration does not mean mechanical dictation, but all "Scripture is (so) inspired by God," that everything in it, its narratives, prophecies, citations, the whole—ideas, phrases, and words—are such as He saw fit to be there. The *present* condition of the text is no ground for concluding against the *original text* being inspired, but is a reason why we should use all critical diligence to restore the original inspired text. Again, inspiration may be accompanied by revelation or not, but it is as much needed for writing *known* doctrines or facts authoritatively, as for communicating *new* truths [TREGELLES]. The omission here of the substantive verb is, I think, designed to mark that, not only the Scripture *then* existing, but what was *still to be written till the canon should be completed,* is included as God-inspired. The Old Testament law was the schoolmaster to bring us to Christ; so it is appropriately said to be "able to make *wise* unto salvation through faith in Jesus Christ": the term *wisdom* being appropriated to a knowledge of the relations between the Old and New Testaments, and opposed to the pretended *wisdom* of the false teachers (I Tim. 1:7, 8). **doctrine**—*Greek,* "teaching," i.e., *teaching the ignorant dogmatic* truths which they cannot otherwise know. He so uses the Old Testament, Romans 1:17. **reproof**—"refutation," *convicting the erring* of their error. Including *polemical* divinity. As an example of this use of the Old Testament, cf. Gal. 3:6, 13, 16. "Doctrine and reproof" comprehend the *speculative* parts of divinity. Next follow the *practical:* Scripture is profitable for: (1) *correction* (*Greek,* "setting one right"; cf. an example, I Cor. 10:1-10) and *instruction* (*Greek,* "disciplining," as a father does his child, *Note,* ch. 2:25; Eph. 6:4; Heb. 12:5, 11, or "training" by instruction, warning, example, kindnesses, promises, and chastisements; cf. an example, I Cor. 5:13). Thus the whole science of theology is complete in Scripture. Since Paul is speaking of Scripture in general and in the notion of it, the only *general* reason why, in order to *perfecting* the godly (vs. 17), it should extend to *every department* of revealed truth, must be that it was intended to be the *complete and sufficient rule* in all things touching perfection. See Article VI, *Common Prayer Book.* **in**—*Greek,* "instruction *which is in* righteousness," as contrasted with the "instruction" in worldly rudiments (Col. 2:20, 22). **17. man of God**—(*Note,* I Tim. 6:11). **perfect, throughly furnished**—*Greek,* "thoroughly perfected," and so "perfect." The man of God is perfectly accoutred out of Scripture for his work,

whether he be a minister (cf. ch. 4:2 with ch. 3:16) or a spiritual layman. No oral tradition is needed to be added.

CHAPTER 4

Vss. 1-22. SOLEMN CHARGE TO TIMOTHY TO DO HIS DUTY ZEALOUSLY, FOR TIMES OF APOSTASY ARE AT HAND, AND THE APOSTLE IS NEAR HIS TRIUMPHANT END: REQUESTS HIM TO COME AND BRING MARK WITH HIM TO ROME, AS LUKE ALONE IS WITH HIM, THE OTHERS HAVING GONE: ALSO HIS CLOAK AND PARCHMENTS: WARNS HIM AGAINST ALEXANDER: TELLS WHAT BEFELL HIM AT HIS FIRST DEFENSE: GREETINGS: BENEDICTION. **1. charge**—*Greek,* "adjure." **therefore**—omitted in the oldest MSS. **the Lord Jesus Christ**—The oldest MSS. read simply, "Christ Jesus." **shall judge**—His *commission* from God is mentioned, Acts 10:42; his resolution to do so, I Peter 4:5; the execution of his commission, here. **at his appearing**—The oldest MSS. read, "and" for "at"; then translate, "(I charge thee *before God . . .*) and *by* His appearing." **and his kingdom**—to be set at His appearing, when we hope to reign with Him. His kingdom is real now, but not visible. It shall then be both real *and visible* (Luke 22:18, 30; Rev. 1:7 11:15; 19:6). *Now* he reigns *in the midst of His enemies* expecting till they shall be overthrown (Ps. 110:2; Heb. 10:13). *Then* He shall reign with His adversaries prostrate. **2. Preach** lit., "proclaim as a herald." The term for the discourses in the synagogue was *daraschoth;* the corresponding *Greek* term (implying dialectical style, dialogue, and discussion, Acts 17:2, 18; 18:4, 19) is applied in Acts to *discourses* in the Christian Church. JUSTIN MARTYR, *Apology* 2, describes the order of public worship, "On Sunday all meet and the writings of the apostles and prophets are read; then the president delivers a discourse; after this all stand up and pray; then there is offered bread and wine and water; the president likewise prays and gives thanks, and the people solemnly assent, saying, Amen." The bishops and presbyters had the right and duty to preach, but they sometimes called on deacons, and even laymen, to preach. EUSEBIUS, *Ecclesiastical History,* 6. 19; in this the Church imitated the synagogue (Luke 4:17-22; Acts 13:15, 16). **be instant**—i.e., urgent, earnest, in the whole work of the ministry. **in season, out of season**—i.e., at all seasons; whether they regard your speaking as seasonable or unseasonable. "Just as the fountains, though none may draw from them, still flow on; and the rivers, though none drink of them, still run; so must we do all on our part in speaking, though none give heed to us" [CHRYSOSTOM, *Homily,* 30., vol. 5., p. 221]. I think with CHRYSOSTOM, there is included also the idea of times whether seasonable or unseasonable *to Timothy himself;* not merely when convenient, but when inconvenient to thee, night as well as day (Acts 20:31), in danger as well as in safety, in prison and when doomed to death as well as when at large, not only in church, but everywhere and on all occasions, whenever and wherever the Lord's work requires it. **reprove**—"convict," "confute." **with . . .**—*Greek,* "IN (the element in which the exhortation ought to have place) all long-suffering (ch. 2:24, 25; 3:10) and *teaching*"; cf. ch. 2:24, "apt to teach." The *Greek* for "doctrine" here is *didache,* but in ch. 3:16 *didascalia.* "*Didascalia*" is what one receives; *didache* is what is communicated [TITTMANN]. **3. they** —professing Christians. **sound doctrine**—*Greek,* "the sound (*Note,* I Tim. 1:10) doctrine" (*didascal-*

ias) or "teaching," viz., of the Gospel. Presently follows the concrete, teachers." **after their own lusts**—Instead of regarding the will of God they dislike being interrupted in their lusts by true teachers. **heap**—one on another: an indiscriminate mass of false teachers. Variety delights itching ears. "He who despises sound teaching, leaves sound teachers; they seek instructors like themselves" [BENGEL]. It is the corruption of the people in the first instance, that creates priestcraft (Exod. 32:1). **to themselves**—such as will suit their depraved tastes; *populus vult decipi, et decipiatur*—"the people wish to be deceived, so let them be deceived." "Like priest, like people" (I Kings 12:31; Hos. 4:9). **itching**—like to hear teachers who give them mere pleasure (Acts 17:19-21), and do not offend by truths grating to their ears. They, as it were, tickle with pleasure the levity of the multitude [CICERO], who come as to a theater to hear what will delight their ears, not to learn [SENECA, Ep. 10. 8] what will do them good. "Itch in the ear is as bad in any other part of the body, and perhaps worse" [SOUTH]. **4.** The ear brooks not what is opposed to the man's lusts. **turned**—Greek, "turned aside" (I Tim. 1:6). It is a righteous retribution, that when men *turn away* from the truth, they should be *turned to* fables (Jer. 2:19). **fables**—(I Tim. 1:4). **5.** I am no longer here to withstand these things; be thou a worthy successor of me, no longer depending on me for counsel, but thine own master, and swimming without the corks [CALVIN]; follow my steps, inherit their result, and the honor of their end [ALFORD]. **watch thou**—lit., "with the wakefulness of one *sober*." **in all things**—on all occasions and under all circumstances (Titus 2:7). **endure affliction**—suffer hardships [ALFORD]. **evangelist**—a missionary bishop preacher, and teacher. **make full proof of**—fulfil in all its requirements, leaving nothing undone (Acts 12:25; Rom. 15:19; Col. 4:17). **6.** *Greek,* "For I am already being offered"; lit., as a *libation;* appropriate to the shedding of *his blood.* Every sacrifice began with an initiatory libation on the victim's head (*Note,* cf. Phil. 2:17). A motive to stimulate Timothy to faithfulness—the departure and final blessedness of Paul; it is the end that crowns the work [BENGEL]. As the time of his departure was indicated to Peter, so to Paul (II Pet. 1:14). **my departure**—lit., "loosing anchor" (*Note,* Phil. 1:23). *Dissolution.* **7.** "I have striven the good strife"; the *Greek* is not restricted to a *fight,* but includes any competitive *contest,* e.g., that of the racecourse (I Tim. 6:12 [ALFORD]; I Cor. 9:24, etc.; Heb. 12:1, 2). **kept the faith**—the Christian faith committed to me as a believer and an apostle (cf. ch. 1:14; Rev. 2:10; 3:10). **8. a crown**—rather as *Greek,* "*the* crown." The "henceforth" marks the decisive moment; he looks to his state in a threefold aspect: (1) The past "I have fought"; (2) The immediate present; "there is laid up for me". (3) The future "the Lord will give in that day" [BENGEL]. **crown**—a crown, or garland, used to be bestowed at the Greek national games on the successful competitor in wrestling, running, etc. (cf. I Pet. 5:4; Rev. 2:10). **of righteousness**—The reward is *in recognition of righteousness* wrought in Paul by God's Spirit; the crown is prepared for the righteous; but it is a crown *which consists in righteousness. Righteousness will be its own reward* (Rev. 22:11). Cf. Exodus 39:30. A man is justified gratuitously by the merits of Christ through faith; and when he is so justified God accepts his works and honors them with a reward which is not their due, but is given of grace. "So great is God's good-

ness to men that He wills that their works should be merits, though they are merely His own gifts" [*Ep.* POPE CELESTINE I., 12]. **give**—Greek, "shall award" in righteous requital as "Judge" (Acts 17:31; II Cor. 5:10; II Thess. 1:6, 7). **in that day**—not until His appearing (ch. 1:12). The partakers of the first resurrection may receive a *crown* also *at the last day,* and obtain in that general assembly of all men, a *new* award of praise. The favorable sentence passed on the "brethren" of the Judge, who sit with Him on His throne, is in Matthew 25:40, taken for granted as *already* awarded, when that affecting those who benefited them is being passed [BENGEL]. The former, the elect Church who reign with Christ in the millennium, are fewer than the latter. The *righteous* heavenly Judge stands in contrast to the unrighteous earthly judges who condemned Paul. **me**—individual appropriation. *Greek,* "not only to me." **them that love**—Greek, "have loved, and do love"; *habitual* love and desire for Christ's appearing, which presupposes *faith* (cf. Heb. 9:28). Cf. the sad contrast, vs. 10, "having *loved* this present world." **9.** (vs. 21; ch. 1:4, 8.) Timothy is asked to come to be a comfort to Paul, and also to be strengthened by Paul, for carrying on the Gospel work after Paul's decease. **10. Demas**—once a "fellow laborer" of Paul, along with Mark and Luke (Col. 4:14; Philemon 24). His motive for forsaking Paul seems to have been love of worldly ease, safety, and comforts at home, and disinclination to brave danger with Paul (Matt. 13:20, 21, 22). CHRYSOSTOM implies that Thessalonica was his home. **Galatia**—One oldest MS. supports the reading "Gaul." But most oldest MSS., etc., "Galatia." **Titus**—He must have therefore left Crete after "setting in order" the affairs of the churches there (Titus 1:5). **Dalmatia**—part of the Roman province of Illyricum on the coast of the Adriatic. Paul had written to him (Titus 3:12) to come to him in the winter to Nicopolis (in Epirus), intending in the spring to preach the Gospel in the adjoining province of Dalmatia. Titus seems to have gone thither to carry out the apostle's intention, the execution of which was interrupted by his arrest. Whether he went of his own accord, as is likely, or was sent by Paul, which the expression "is departed" hardly accords with, cannot be positively decided. Paul here speaks only of his personal attendants having forsaken him; he had still friends among the Roman Christians who visited him (ch. 4:21), though they had been afraid to stand by him at his trial (vs. 16). **11. Take**—Greek, "take up" on thy journey (Acts 20:13, 14). John Mark was probably in, or near, Colosse, as in the Epistle to the Colossians (Col. 4:10), written two years before this, he is mentioned as about to visit them. Timothy was now absent from Ephesus and somewhere in the interior of Asia Minor; hence he would be sure to fall in with Mark on his journey. **he is profitable to me for the ministry**—Mark had been under a cloud for having forsaken Paul at a critical moment in his missionary tour with Barnabas (Acts 15:37-40; 13:5, 13). Timothy had subsequently occupied the same post in relation to Paul as Mark once held. Hence Paul, appropriately here, wipes out the past censure by high praise of Mark and guards against Timothy's making self-complacent comparisons between himself and Mark, as though he were superior to the latter (cf. Philemon 24). Demas apostatizes. Mark returns to the right way, and is no longer unprofitable, but is profitable for the Gospel ministry (Philemon 11). **12. And**—Greek, "But." Thou art to come to me, *but* Tychicus I have sent to Ephesus to supply thy place (if thou so willest it) in presiding over the Church there in thy absence (cf. Titus 3:12). It is possible Tychicus was the bearer of this Epistle, though the omission of "to thee" is rather against this view. **13. cloak . . . I left**—probably obliged to leave it in a hurried departure from Troas. **Carpus**—a faithful friend to have been entrusted with so precious deposits. The mention of his "cloak," so far from being unworthy of inspiration, is one of those graphic touches which sheds a flood of light on the last scene of Paul's life, on the confines of two worlds; in this wanting a cloak to cover him from the winter cold, in that covered with the righteousness of saints, "clothed upon with his house from heaven" [GAUSSEN]. So the inner vesture and outer garment of Jesus, Paul's master, are suggestive of most instructive thought (John 19). **books**—He was anxious respecting these that he might transmit them to the faithful, so that they might have the teaching of his writings when he should be gone. **especially the parchments**—containing perhaps some of his inspired Epistles themselves. **14. Alexander the coppersmith**—or "smith" in general. Perhaps the same as the Alexander (I Tim. 1:20, *Note*) at Ephesus. Excommunicated then he subsequently was restored, and now vented his personal malice because of his excommunication in accusing Paul before the Roman judges, whether of incendiarism or of introducing a new religion. See my *Introduction*. He may have been the Alexander put forward by the Jews in the tumult at Ephesus (Acts 19: 33, 34). **reward**—The oldest MSS. read, "*shall reward*," or "requite him." Personal revenge certainly did not influence the apostle (vs. 16, end). **15. our words**—the arguments of us Christians for our common faith. Believers have a common cause. **16. At my first answer**—i.e., "defense" in court, at my first public examination. Timothy knew nothing of this, it is plain, till Paul now informs him. But during his *former* imprisonment at Rome, Timothy was with him (Phil. 1:1, 7). This must have been, therefore, a *second* imprisonment. He must have been set free before the persecution in A.D. 64, when the Christians were accused of causing the conflagration in Rome; for, had he been a prisoner then, he certainly would not have been spared. The tradition [EUSEBIUS, 2. 25] that he was finally *beheaded*, accords with his not having been put to death in the persecution, A.D. 64, when *burning to death* was the mode by which the Christians were executed, but subsequently to it. His "first" trial in his second imprisonment seems to have been on the charge of complicity in the conflagration; his absence from Rome may have been the ground of his acquittal on that charge; his final condemnation was probably on the charge of introducing a new and unlawful religion into Rome." **stood with me**—*Greek*, "came forward with me" [ALFORD] as a friend and advocate. **may [it] not be laid to their charge**—The position of "their," in the *Greek*, is emphatic. "May it not be laid to THEIR charge," for they were intimidated; *their* drawing back from me was not from bad disposition so much as from fear; it is sure to be laid to the charge of those who intimidated them. Still Paul, like Stephen, would doubtless have offered the same prayer for his persecutors themselves (Acts 7:60). **17. the Lord**—the more because *men* deserted me. **stood with me**—stronger than "came forward with me" (*Greek*, vs. 16). **strengthened**—*Greek*, "*put strength in me.*" **by me**—"through me"; through my means. One single occasion is often of the greatest moment.

the preaching—"the Gospel proclamation." **might be fully known**—might be fully made (*Note,* vs. 5). **that all the Gentiles**—present at my trial, "might hear" the Gospel proclaimed then. Rome was the capital of the Gentile world, so that a proclamation of the truth to the Romans was likely to go forth to the rest of the Gentile world. **I was delivered out of the mouth of the lion**—viz., Satan, the roaring, devouring lion (Luke 22:31; I Pet. 5:8). I was prevented falling into his snare (ch. 2:26; Ps. 22: 21; II Pet. 2:9); vs. 18 agrees with this interpretation, "The Lord shall *deliver* me *from every evil work,*" viz., both from evil and the evil one, as the *Greek* of the Lord's Prayer expresses it. It was not deliverance from Nero (who was called *the lion*) which he rejoiced in, for he did not fear *death* (vss. 6-8), but deliverance from the temptation, through fear, to deny His Lord: so ALFORD. **18. And the Lord shall . . .**—Hope draws its conclusions from the past to the future [BENGEL]. **will preserve me**—lit., "will save" (Ps. 22:21), "will bring me safe to." Jesus is the Lord and the Deliverer (Phil. 3:20; I Thess. 1:10: He saves from evil; He gives good things. **heavenly kingdom**—*Greek*, "His kingdom which is a heavenly one." **to whom . . .**—*Greek*, "to whom be *the* glory unto the ages of ages." The very *hope* produces a doxology: how much greater will be the doxology which the actual *enjoyment* shall produce! [BENGEL]. **19. Prisca and Aquila**—(Acts 18:2, 3; Rom. 16:3, 4; I Cor. 16:19, written from Ephesus, where therefore Aquila and Priscilla must then have been). **household of Onesiphorus**—If he were dead at the time, the "household" would not have been called "the household *of Onesiphorus.*" He was probably *absent* (*Note,* ch. 1:16). **20.** In order to depict his desertion, he informs Timothy that Erastus, one of his usual companions (Acts 19:22, possibly the same Erastus as in Rom. 16:23, though how he could leave his official duties for missionary journeys is not clear), stayed behind at Corinth, his native place, or usual residence, of which city he was "chamberlain," or city steward and treasurer (Rom. 16:23); and Trophimus he left behind at Miletus sick. (See on his former history, Acts 20:4; 21:29.) This verse is irreconcilable with the imprisonment from which he writes being the *first:* for he did not pass by Corinth or Miletus on his way to Rome when about to be imprisoned for the first time. As Miletus was near Ephesus, there is a presumption that Timothy was *not* at Ephesus when Paul wrote, or he would not need to inform Timothy of Trophimus lying sick in his immediate neighborhood. However, Trophimus may not have been still at Miletus at the time when Paul wrote, though he had left him there on his way to Rome. Prisca and Aquila were most likely to be at *Ephesus* (vs. 19), and he desires Timothy to *salute them:* so also Onesiphorus' household (ch. 1:18). Paul had not the power of healing at will (Acts 19:12), but as the Lord allowed him. **21. before winter**—when a voyage, according to ancient usages of navigation, would be out of the question: also, Paul would need his "cloak" against the winter (vs. 13). **Pudens . . . Claudia**—afterwards husband and wife (according to MARTIAL IV, 13; XI, 54), he a Roman knight, she a Briton, surnamed *Rufina.* TACITUS, *Agricola,* 14, mentions that territories in southeast Britain were given to a British king; Cogidunus, in reward for his fidelity to Rome, A.D. 52, while Claudius was emperor. In 1772 a marble was dug up at Chichester, mentioning Cogidunus with the surname Claudius, added from his patron, the emperor's name; and *Pudens* in connection with Cogidunus, doubtless his father-in-law. His daughter would be Claudia, who seems to have been sent to Rome for education, as a pledge of the father's fidelity. Here she was under the protection of Pomponia, wife of Aulus Plautius, conqueror of Britain. Pomponia was accused of *foreign superstitions*, A.D. 57 [TACITUS, *Annals*, 3. 32], probably *Christianity*. She probably was the instrument of converting Claudia, who took the name *Rufina* from her, that being a cognomen of the Pomponian gens (cf. Rom. 16:13, *Rufus*, a Christian). Pudens in Martial and in the Chichester inscription, appears as a *pagan;* but perhaps he or his friends concealed his Christianity through fear. Tradition represents *Timothy*, a son

of Pudens, as taking part in converting the Britons. **Linus**—put third; therefore not at this time yet, as he was afterwards, *bishop*. His name being here inserted between Pudens and Claudia, implies the two were not yet married. "Eubulus" is identified by some with Aristobulus, who, with his converts, is said to have been among the first evangelists of Britain. Paul himself, says CLEMENT, "visited *the farthest west* [perhaps Britain, certainly *Spain*], and was martyred under the rulers at Rome," who were Nero's vicegerents in his absence from the city. **22. Grace be with you**—plural in oldest MSS., "with YOU," i.e., thee and the members of the Ephesian and neighboring churches.

THE EPISTLE OF PAUL TO

TITUS

INTRODUCTION

GENUINENESS.—CLEMENT OF ROME quotes it (*Epistola ad Corinthios*, c. 2); IRENÆUS (3. 3, sec. 4) refers to it as Paul's; THEOPHILUS, *ad Autolycus*, 3., sec. 14, quotes it as Scripture. Cf. CLEMENT OF ALEXANDRIA, *Stromata*, 1. 299; TERTULLIAN, *Præscriptione Hæreticorum*, 6.

TIME AND PLACE OF WRITING.—This Epistle seems to have been written from Corinth [BIRKS], subsequently to his first imprisonment, when Paul was on his way to Nicopolis (ch. 3:12) in Epirus, where he purposed passing the winter, shortly before his martyrdom, A.D. 67. BIRKS thinks, from the similarity of the Epistle to Titus and First Timothy, that both were written from the same place, Corinth, and at dates not widely apart; First Timothy shortly after coming to Corinth, before he had planned a journey to Epirus, the Epistle to Titus afterwards. The journey to Crete and Ephesus for the bearers of his letters would be easy from Corinth, and he could himself thence easily pass into Epirus. He had shortly before visited Crete, wherein a Church existed (though without due organization), the first foundation of which he may have partly laid at his former visit (Acts 27:7, etc.), when on his way to his first imprisonment at Rome. That he returned to the East after his first imprisonment appears most probable from Philippians 2:24; Philemon 22. However, there may have been seeds of Christianity sown in Crete, even before his first visit, by the Cretans who heard Peter's preaching on Pentecost (Acts 2:11).

OCCASION OF WRITING.—Corrupt elements soon showed themselves in the Cretan Church, similar to those noticed in the Epistles to Timothy, as existing in the Ephesian Church, Judaism, false pretensions to science, and practical ungodliness. Paul, on his late visit, had left Titus in Crete to establish Church government, and ordain *presbyters* (*deacons* are not mentioned). Titus had been several times employed by Paul on a mission to the Corinthian Churches, and had probably thence visited Crete, which was within easy reach of Corinth. Hence the suitableness of his selection by the apostle for the superintendence of the Cretan Church. Paul now follows up with instructions by letter those he had already given to Titus in person on the qualifications of elders, and the graces becoming the old, the young, and females, and warns him against the unprofitable speculations so rife in Crete. The national character of the Cretans was low in the extreme, as EPIMENIDES, quoted in ch. 1:12, paints it. LIVY, 44. 45, stigmatizes their *avarice*; POLYBIUS, 6. 46. 9, their *ferocity* and *fraud*; and 6. 47. 5, their *mendacity*, so much so, that "to Cretanize" is another name for *to lie*: they were included in the proverbial three infamous initials K or C, "Cappadocia, Crete, Cilicia."

NOTICES OF TITUS.—It is strange that he is never mentioned by this name in Acts, and there seems none of those mentioned in that book who exactly answers to him. He was a Greek, and therefore a Gentile (Gal. 2:1, 3), and converted by Paul (ch. 1:4). He accompanied the apostle on the deputation sent from the Church of Antioch to Jerusalem, to consult the apostles respecting the circumcision of Gentile converts (Acts 15:2); and, agreeably to the decree of the council there, was not circumcised. He was in company with Paul at Ephesus, whence he was sent to Corinth to commence the collection for the Jerusalem saints, and to ascertain the effect of the First Epistle on the Corinthians (II Cor. 7:6–9; 8:6; 12:18), and there showed an unmercenary spirit. He next proceeded to Macedon, where he joined Paul, who had been already eagerly expecting him at Troas (II Cor. 2:12, 13, "Titus my brother"; 7:6). He was then employed by the apostle in preparing the collection for the poor saints in Judea, and became the bearer of the Second Epistle to the Corinthians (II Cor. 8:16, 17, 23). Paul in it calls him "my partner and fellow helper concerning you." His being located in Crete (Titus 1:5) was subsequent to Paul's first imprisonment, and shortly before the second, about A.D. 67, ten years subsequent to the last notice of him in Second Corinthians, A.D. 57. He probably met Paul, as the apostle desired, at Nicopolis; for his subsequent journey into Dalmatia, thence (or else from Rome, whither he may have accompanied Paul) would be more likely, than from the distant Crete (II Tim. 4:10, written *subsequently to the Epistle to Titus*). In the unsettled state of things then, Titus' episcopal commission in Crete was to be but temporary, Paul requiring the presence of Titus with himself, whenever Artemas or Tychicus should arrive in Crete and set him free from his duties there.

Tradition represents him to have died peaceably in Crete, as archbishop of Gortyna, at an advanced age.

CHAPTER 1

Vss. 1-16. Address: For What End Titus Was Left in Crete. Qualifications for Elders: Gainsayers in Crete Needing Reproof. **1. servant of God**—not found elsewhere in the same connection. In Romans 1:1 it is "servant of Jesus Christ" (Gal. 1:10; Phil. 1:1; cf. Acts 16:17; Rev. 1:1; 15:3). In Romans 1:1, there follows, "called to be an *apostle*," which corresponds to the general designation of the office first, "*servant of* God," here, followed by the special description, "*apostle* of *Jesus Christ*." The full expression of his apostolic office answers, in both Epistles, to the design, and is a comprehensive index to the contents. The *peculiar* form here would never have proceeded from a forger. **according to the faith**—rather, "for," "with a view to subserve the faith"; this is the object of my apostleship (cf. vss. 4, 9; Rom. 1:5). **the elect**—for whose sake we ought to endure all things (II Tim. 2:10). This election has its ground, not in anything belonging to those thus distinguished, but in the purpose and will of God from everlasting (II Tim. 1:9; Rom. 8:30-33; cf. Luke 18:7; Eph. 1:4; Col. 3:12). Acts 13:48 shows that all faith on the part of the elect, rests on the divine foreordination: they do not become *elect* by their faith, but receive *faith*, and so become believers, because they are *elect*. **and the acknowledging of the truth**—"and (for promoting) the *full knowledge* of the truth," i.e., the Christian truth (Eph. 1:13). **after godliness**—i.e., which belongs to *piety:* opposed to the knowledge which has not for its object the truth, but error, doctrinal and practical (vss. 11, 16; I Tim. 6:3); or even which has for its object mere earthly truth, not growth in the divine life. "Godliness," or "piety," is a term peculiar to the Pastoral Epistles: a fact explained by the apostle having in them to combat doctrine tending to "ungodliness" (II Tim. 2:16; cf. ch. 2:11, 12). **2. In hope of eternal life**—connected with the whole preceding sentence. That whereon rests my aim as an apostle to promote *the elect's faith and full knowledge of the truth,* is, "the hope of eternal life" (ch. 2:13; 3:7; Acts 23:6; 24:15; 28:20). **that cannot lie**—(Rom. 3:4; 11:29; Heb. 6:18). **promised before the world began**—a contracted expression for "*purposed* before the world began (lit., before the ages of time), and *promised* actually in time," the promise springing from the eternal purpose; as in II Timothy 1:9, the *gift* of grace was the result of the eternal purpose "before the world began." **3. in due times**—Greek, "in *its own seasons,*" the seasons appropriate to it, and fixed by God for it (Acts 1:7). **manifested**—implying that the "promise," vs. 2, had lain hidden in His eternal purpose heretofore (cf. Col. 1:26; II Tim. 1:9, 10). **his word**—equivalent to "eternal life" (vs. 2; John 5:24; 6:63; 17:3, 17). **through preaching**—Greek, "in preaching," or rather as Alford (*Note,* cf. II Tim. 4:17), "in the (Gospel) *proclamation* (the thing preached, the Gospel) with which I was entrusted." **according to**—in pursuance of (cf. I Tim. 1:1). **of God our Saviour**—rather as Greek, "of *our Saviour God.*" God is predicated of *our Saviour* (cf. Jude 25; Luke 1:47). Also Psalm 24:5; Isaiah 12:2; 45:15, 21, LXX. Applied to Jesus, vs. 4; ch. 2:13; 3:6; II Timothy 1:10. **4. Titus, mine own son**—Greek, "my *genuine* child" (I Tim. 1:2), i.e., converted by my instrumentality (I Cor. 4:17; Philemon 10). **after the common faith**—a genuine son in respect to (in virtue of) the faith *common* to all the people of God, comprising in a common brotherhood Gentiles as well as Jews, therefore embracing Titus a Gentile (II Pet. 1:1; Jude 3). **Grace, mercy, and peace**—"mercy" is omitted in some of the oldest MSS. But one of the best and oldest MSS. supports it (*Notes,* cf. I Tim. 1:2; II Tim. 1:2). There are many similarities of phrase in the Pastoral Epistles. **the Lord Jesus Christ**—The oldest MSS. read only "Christ Jesus." **our Saviour**—found thus added to "Christ" only in Paul's *Pastoral Epistles,* and in II Pet. 1:1, 11; 2:20; 3:18. **5. I left thee**—"I left thee *behind*" [Alford] when I left the island: *not* implying *permanence* of commission (cf. I Tim. 1:3). **in Crete**—now Candia. **set in order**—rather as *Greek,* "that thou mightest *follow up* (the work begun by me), setting right the things that are wanting," which I was unable to complete by reason of the shortness of my stay in Crete. Christianity, doubtless, had long existed in Crete: there were some Cretans among those who heard Peter's preaching on Pentecost (Acts 2:11). The number of Jews in Crete was large (vs. 10), and it is likely that those scattered in the persecution of Stephen (Acts 11:19) preached to them, as they did to the Jews of Cyprus, etc. Paul also was there on his voyage to Rome (Acts 27:7-12). By all these instrumentalities the Gospel was sure to reach Crete. But until Paul's later visit, after his first imprisonment at Rome, the Cretan Christians were without Church organization. This Paul began, and had commissioned (before leaving Crete) Titus to go on with, and now reminds him of that commission. **ordain**—rather, "appoint," "constitute." **in every city**—"from city to city." **as I ... appointed thee**—i.e., as I directed thee; prescribing as well the *act* of constituting elders, as also the *manner* of doing so, which latter includes the qualifications required in a presbyter presently stated. Those called "elders" here are called "bishops" in vs. 7. *Elder* is the term of *dignity* in relation to the college of presbyters; *bishop* points to the *duties* of his office in relation to the flock. From the unsound state of the Cretan Christians described here, we see the danger of the want of Church government. The appointment of presbyters was designed to check idle *talk* and speculation, by setting forth the "faithful word." **6.** (*Notes,* cf. I Tim. 3:2-4.) The thing dwelt on here as the requisite in a bishop, is a good reputation among those over whom he is to be set. The immorality of the Cretan professors rendered this a necessary requisite in one who was to be a *reprover:* and their unsoundness in doctrine also made needful great steadfastness in the faith (vss. 9, 13). **having faithful children**—i.e., *believing* children. He who could not bring his children to faith, how shall he bring others? [Bengel.] Alford explains, "established in the faith." **not accused**—not merely not riotous, but "not (even) accused of riot" ("profligacy" [Alford]; "dissolute life" [Wahl]). **unruly**—*insubordinate;* opposed to "in subjection" (I Tim. 3:4). **7. For ... must**—The emphasis is on "must." The reason why I said "blameless" is the very idea of a "bishop" (an overseer of the flock); he here substitutes for "presbyter" the term which expresses his *duties*) involves the *necessity* for such blamelessness, if he is to have influence over the flock. **steward of God**—The greater the master is, the greater the virtues required in His servant [Bengel], (I Tim. 3:15); the Church is God's house, over which the minister is set as a steward (Heb. 3:2-6; I Pet. 4:10, 17). Note: ministers are not merely *Church* officers, but God's stewards; Church government is of divine appointment. **not self-willed**—lit., "self-pleasing"; unaccommodating to others; *harsh,* the opposite of "a lover of hospitality" (vs. 6); so

Nabal (I Sam. 25); self-loving and imperious; such a spirit would incapacitate him for *leading* a willing flock, instead of *driving*. **not given to wine**—(Notes, I Tim. 3:3, 8). **not given to filthy lucre**—not making the Gospel a means of gain (I Tim. 3:3, 8). In opposition to those "teaching for filthy lucre's sake" (vs. 11; I Tim. 6:5; I Pet. 5:2). **8. lover of hospitality**—needed especially in those days (Rom. 12:13; I Tim. 3:2; Heb. 13:2; I Pet. 4:9; III John 5). Christians travelling from one place to another were received and forwarded on their journey by their brethren. **lover of good men**—Greek, "a lover of (all that is) good," men or things (Phil. 4:8, 9). **sober** towards *one's self;* "discreet"; self-restrained" [ALFORD], (*Note,* I Tim. 2:9). **just**—towards *men.* **holy**—towards *God* (*Note,* I Thess. 2:10). **temperate**—"One having his passions, tongue, hand and eyes, at command" [CHRYSOSTOM]; "continent." **9. Holding fast**—Holding firmly to (cf. Matt. 6:24; Luke 16:13). **the faithful**—true and trustworthy (I Tim. 1:15). **word as he has been taught**—lit., "the word (which is) according to the teaching" which he has received (cf. I Tim. 4:6, end; II Timothy 3: 14). **by**—Translate as Greek, "to exhort *in* doctrine (*instruction*) which is sound"; *sound doctrine* or *instruction* is the element IN which his *exhorting* is to have place. On "sound" (peculiar to the Pastoral Epistles), see I Timothy 1:10; 6:3. **convince**—rather, "reprove" [ALFORD], (vs. 13). **10. unruly**—"insubordinate." **and**—omitted in the oldest MSS. "There are many unruly persons, vain talkers, and deceivers"; "unruly" being predicated of both *vain talkers* and deceivers. **vain talkers**—opposed to "holding fast the faithful word" (vs. 9). "Vain jangling" (I Tim. 1:6); "foolish questions, unprofitable and vain" (ch. 3:9). The source of the evil was corrupted Judaism (vs. 14). Many Jews were then living in Crete, according to JOSEPHUS; so the Jewish leaven remained in some of them after conversion. **deceivers**—lit., "deceivers of the minds of others" (*Greek,* Gal. 6:3). **11. mouths . . . stopped**—lit., "muzzled," "bridled" as an unruly beast (cf. Ps. 32:9). **who**—Greek, "(seeing that they are) such men as"; or "inasmuch as they" [ELLICOTT]. **subvert . . . houses**—"overthrowing" their "faith" (II Tim. 2: 18). "They are the devil's levers by which he subverts the houses of God" [THEOPHYL ACT]. **for filthy lucre**—(I Tim. 3:3, 6; 6:5). **12. One**—Epimenides of Phæstus, or Gnossus, in Crete, about 600 B.C. He was sent for to purify Athens from its pollution occasioned by Cylon. He was regarded as a diviner and *prophet*. The words here are taken probably from his treatise *"concerning oracles."* Paul also quotes from two other heathen writers, ARATUS (Acts 17:28) and MENANDER (I Cor. 15:33), but he does not honor them so far as even to mention their names. **of themselves . . . their own**—which enhances his authority as a witness. "To Cretanize" was proverbial for *to lie;* as "to Corinthianize" was for *to be dissolute.* **alway liars**—not merely *at times,* as every natural man is. Contrast vs. 2, "God that *cannot lie.*" They love "fables" (vs. 14); even the heathen poets laughed at their lying assertion that they had in their country the sepulchre of Jupiter. **evil beasts**—rude, savage, cunning, greedy. Crete was *a country without wild beasts.* Epimenides' sarcasm was that its human inhabitants supplied the place of wild beasts. **slow bellies**—indolent through pampering their bellies. *They themselves* are called "bellies," for that is the member for which they live (Rom. 16:18; Phil. 3: 19). **13. This witness**—"This testimony (though coming from a Cretan) is true." **sharply**—Gentle-

ness would not reclaim so perverse offenders. **that they**—that *those seduced* by the false teachers may be brought back to *soundness* in the faith. Their malady is strifes about words and questions (ch. 3: 9; I Tim. 6:4). **14. Jewish fables**—(Notes, I Tim. 1:4; 4:7; II Tim. 4:4). These formed the transition stage to subsequent Gnosticism; as yet the error was but profitless, and not tending to godliness, rather than openly opposed to the faith. **commandments of men**—as to *ascetic* abstinence (vs. 15; Mark 7:7-9; Col. 2:16, 20-23; I Tim. 4:3). **that turn from the truth**—whose characteristic is that they turn away from the truth (II Tim. 4:4). **15. all things**—external, "are pure" in themselves; the distinction of *pure* and *impure* is not in the things, but in the disposition of him who uses them; in opposition to "the commandments of men" (vs. 14), which forbade certain things as if impure intrinsically. "To the pure" inwardly, i.e., those purified in heart by *faith* (Acts 15:9; Rom. 14:20; I Tim. 4:3), all outward things are pure; all are open to their use. Sin alone touches and defiles the soul (Matt. 23:26; Luke 11:41). **nothing pure**—either within or without (Rom. 14:23). **mind**—their mental sense and intelligence. **conscience**—their moral consciousness of the conformity or discrepancy between their motives and acts on the one hand, and God's law on the other. A conscience and a mind defiled are represented 'as the source of the errors opposed in the Pastoral Epistles (I Tim. 1:19; 3:9; 6:5). **16. They profess**—i.e., *make a profession* acknowledging God. He does not deny their theoretical knowledge of God, but that they *practically* know Him. **deny him**—the opposite of the previous "profess" or "confess" Him (I Tim. 5:8; II Tim. 2: 12; 3:5). **abominable**—themselves, though laying so much stress on the contracting of abomination from outward things (cf. Lev. 11:10-13; Rom. 2:22). **disobedient**—to God (ch. 3:3; Eph. 2:2; 5:6). **reprobate**—rejected as worthless *when tested* (Notes, Rom. 1:28; I Cor. 9:27; II Tim. 3:8).

CHAPTER 2

Vss. 1-15. DIRECTIONS TO TITUS: HOW TO EXHORT VARIOUS CLASSES OF BELIEVERS: THE GRACE OF GOD IN CHRIST OUR GRAND INCENTIVE TO LIVE GODLY. **1. But . . . thou**—in contrast to the reprobate seducers stigmatized in ch. 1:11, 15, 16. "He deals more in exhortations, because those intent on useless questions needed chiefly to be recalled to the study of a holy, moral life; for nothing so effectually allays men's wandering curiosity, as the being brought to recognize those duties in which they ought to exercise themselves" [CALVIN]. **speak** —without restraint: contrast ch. 1:11, "mouths . . . stopped." **doctrine**—"instruction" or "teaching." **2. sober**—Translated "vigilant," as *sober* men alone can be (I Tim. 3:2). But "sober" here answers to "not given to wine," vs. 3; ch. 1:7. **grave**—"dignified"; behaving with *reverent propriety.* **temperate** —"self-restrained"; "discreet" [ALFORD], (ch. 1:8; I Tim. 2:9). **faith . . . charity** [love] **. . . patience**—combined in I Timothy 6:11. "Faith, hope, charity" (I Cor. 13:13). "Patience," Greek, "enduring perseverance," is the attendant on, and is supported by, "hope" (I Cor. 13:7; I Thess. 1:3). It is the grace which especially becomes *old men,* being the fruit of ripened experience derived from trials overcome (Rom. 5:3). **3. behaviour**—"deportment." **as becometh holiness**—"as becometh women consecrated to God" [WAHL]: being by our Christian calling priestesses unto God (Eph. 5:3; I Tim. 2:10). "Observant of sacred decorum" [BENGEL]. **not false accusers**—not slanderers: a besetting sin of some elderly women. **given to much wine**—the besetting sin of the Cretans (ch. 1:12). Lit., "enslaved to much wine." Addiction to wine is *slavery* (Rom. 6:16; II Pet. 2:19). **teachers**—in private: not in public (I Cor. 14:34; I Tim. 2:11, 12); influencing for good the younger women by precept and example. **4. to be sober**—*Greek*, "self-restrained," "discreet"; the same *Greek* as in vs. 2, "temperate." (But see *Note* vs. 2; cf. *Note*, II Tim. 1:7.) ALFORD therefore translates, "That they school [admonish in their duty] the young women to be lovers of their husbands . . ." (the foundation of all domestic happiness). It was judicious that Titus, a young man, should admonish the young women, not directly, but through the older women. **5. keepers at home**—as "guardians of the house," as the *Greek* expresses. The oldest MSS. read, "*Workers* at home": active in household duties (Prov. 7:11; I Tim. 5:13). **good**—kind, *beneficent* (Matt. 20:15; Rom. 5:7; I Pet. 2:18). Not churlish and niggardly, but thrifty as housewives. **obedient**—rather "submissive," as the *Greek* is translated; (see *Notes*, Eph. 5:21, 22, 24). **their own**—marking the duty of subjection which they owe them, as being *their own* husbands (Eph. 5:22; Col. 3:18). **blasphemed**—"evil spoken of." That no reproach may be cast on the Gospel, through the inconsistencies of its professors (vs. 8, 10; Rom. 2:24; I Tim. 5:14; 6:1). "Unless we are virtuous, blasphemy will come through us to the faith" [THEOPHYLACT]. **6. Young**—*Greek*, "The younger men." **soberminded**—self-restrained [ALFORD]. "Nothing is so hard at this age as to overcome pleasures and follies" [CHRYSOSTOM]. **7. In**—*with respect to* all things. **thyself a pattern**—though but a young man thyself. All teaching is useless unless the teacher's example confirm his word. **in doctrine**—*in* thy ministerial *teaching* (showing) *uncorruptness*, i.e., *untainted purity* of motive on thy part (cf. II Cor. 11: 3), so as to be "a pattern" to all. As "gravity," etc., refers to Titus himself, so "uncorruptness"; though, doubtless, uncorruptness of *the doctrine* will be sure to follow as a consequence of the Christian minister being of simple, uncorrupt integrity himself. **gravity**—dignified seriousness in setting forth the truth. **sincerity**—omitted in the oldest MSS. **8. speech**—discourse in public and private ministrations. **he that is of the contrary part**—the adversary (ch. 1:9; II Tim. 2:25), whether he be heathen or Jew. **may be ashamed**—put to confusion by the power of truth and innocence (cf. vss. 5, 10; I Tim. 5:14; 6:1). **no evil thing**—*in our acts*, or demeanor. **of you**—So one of the oldest MSS. Other very old MSS. read, "of us," Christians. **9. servants**—"slaves." **to please them well**—"to give satisfaction" [ALFORD]. *To be complaisant in everything;* to have that zealous desire to gain the master's goodwill which will anticipate the master's wish and do even more than is required. The reason for the frequent recurrence of injunctions to slaves to *subjection* (Eph. 6:5, etc.; Col. 3:22; I Tim. 6:1, etc.; I Pet. 2:18) was, that in no rank was there more danger of the doctrine of the *spiritual* equality and freedom of Christians being misunderstood than in that of slaves. It was natural for the slave who had become a Christian, to forget his place and put himself on a *social* level with his master. Hence the charge for each to abide in the sphere in which he was when converted (I Cor. 7:20-24). **not answering again**—*in contradiction* to the master: so the *Greek*, "not contradict-

ing" [WAHL]. **10. Not purloining**—*Greek*, "Not *appropriating*" what does not belong to one. It means "keeping back" dishonestly or deceitfully (Acts 5:2, 3). **showing**—manifesting in acts. **all**—all possible. **good**—really good; not so in mere appearance (Eph. 6:5, 6; Col. 3:22-24). "The heathen do not judge of the Christian's doctrines from the doctrine, but from his actions and life" [CHRYSOSTOM]. Men will write, fight, and even die for their religion; but how few *live* for it! Translate, "That they may adorn the doctrine of our Saviour God," i.e., God the Father, the originating author of salvation (cf. *Note*, I Tim. 1:1). God deigns to have His Gospel-doctrine adorned even by slaves, who are regarded by the world as no better than beasts of burden. "Though the service be rendered to an earthly master, the honor redounds to God, as the servant's goodwill flows from the fear of God" [THEOPHYLACT]. Even slaves, low as is their status, should not think the influence of their example a matter of no consequence to religion: how much more those in a high position. His love in being "our Saviour" is the strongest ground for our adorning His doctrine by our lives. This is the force of "For" in vs. 11. **11. the grace of God**—God's *gratuitous favor* in the scheme of redemption. **hath appeared**—*Greek*, "hath been *made to appear*," or "*shine* forth" (Isa. 9:2; Luke 1:79). "hath been *manifested*" (ch. 3:4), after having been long hidden in the loving counsels of God (Col. 1:26; II Tim. 1:9, 10). The image is illustrated in Acts 27:20. The grace of God hath now been embodied in Jesus, the *brightness* of the Father's glory, *manifested* as the "Sun of righteousness," "the Word made flesh." The Gospel dispensation is hence termed "the day" (I Thess. 5:5, 8; there is a double "appearing," that of "grace" here, that of "glory," vs. 13; cf. Rom. 13:12). Connect it not as *English Version*, but, "The grace . . . that *bringeth salvation to all men* hath appeared," or "been manifested" (I Tim. 2:4; 4:10). Hence God is called "our *Saviour*" (vs. 10). The very name *Jesus* means the same. **to all**—of whom he enumerated the different classes (vss. 2-9): even to servants; to us Gentiles, once aliens from God. Hence arises our obligation to all men (ch. 3:2). **12. Teaching**—*Greek*, "disciplining us." Grace exercises *discipline*, and is imparted in connection with disciplining chastisements (I Cor. 11:32; Heb. 12:6, 7). The education which the Christian receives from "the grace" of God is a discipline often trying to flesh and blood: just as children need disciplining. The *discipline* which it exercises *teaches* us to *deny ungodliness and worldly lusts, and to live soberly, righteously, and godly, in this present world* (Greek, "age," or course of things) where such self-discipline is needed, seeing that its spirit is opposed to God (ch. 1:12, 16; I Cor. 1:20; 3:18, 19): in the coming world we may gratify every desire without need of self-discipline, because all desires there will be conformable to the will of God. **that**—*Greek*, "in order that"; the end of the "disciplining" is "*in order that . . .* we may live soberly. . . ." This point is lost by the translation, "*teaching* us." **denying . . . lusts**—(Luke 9:23). The *Greek* aorist expresses "denying *once for all.*" We deny them when we withhold our consent from them, when we refuse the delight which they suggest, and the act to which they solicit us, nay, tear them up by the roots out of our soul and mind [ST. BERNARD, *Serm.* 11]. **worldly lusts**—The *Greek* article expresses, "*the* lusts of the world," "*all* worldly lusts" [ALFORD], (Gal. 5:16; Eph. 2:3; I John 2:15-17; 5: 19). The *world* (*cosmos*) will not come to an end when this present *age* (*aeon*) or course of things shall end. **live soberly, righteously, and godly**—the *positive* side of the Christian character; as "denying ...lusts" was the *negative.* "Soberly," i.e., *with self-restraint,* in relation to *one's self;* "righteously" or *justly,* in relation to our *neighbor;* "godly" or *piously,* in relation to *God* (not merely *amiably* and *justly,* but something higher, *godly,* with love and reverence toward God). These three comprise our "disciplining" in *faith* and *love,* from which he passes to *hope* (vs. 13). **13.** (Phil. 3:20, 21). **Looking for**—with constant *expectation* (so the *Greek*) and with joy (Rom. 8:19). This will prove the antidote to worldly lusts, and the stimulus to "live in this present world" conformably to this *expectation.* The *Greek* is translated, "waiting for," in Luke 2: 25. **that**—*Greek,* "the." **blessed**—bringing blessedness (Rom. 4:7, 8). **hope**—i.e., object of hope (Rom. 8:24; Gal. 5:5; Col. 1:5). **the glorious appearing**—There is but one *Greek* article to both "hope" and "appearing," which marks their close connection (the *hope* being about to be realized only at the *appearing* of Christ). Translate, "*The* blessed hope *and manifestation* (cf. *Note,* vs. 11) *of the glory.*" The *Greek* for "manifestation" is translated "brightness" in II Thessalonians 2:8. As His "coming" (*Greek, parousia*) expresses the fact; so "brightness, appearing," or "manifestation" (*epiphaneia*) expresses His personal *visibility* when He shall come. **the great God and our Saviour Jesus**—There is but one *Greek* article to "God" and "Saviour," which shows that both are predicated of one and the same Being. "Of Him who is at once the great God and our Saviour." Also (2) "appearing" (*epiphaneia*) is never by Paul predicated of God the Father (John 1:18; I Tim. 6:16), or even of "His glory" (as ALFORD explains it): it is *invariably* applied to CHRIST's coming, to which (at His first advent, cf. II Tim. 1:10) the kindred verb "appeared" (*epephanee*), vs. 11, refers (I Tim. 6:14; II Tim. 4:1, 8). Also (3) in the context (vs. 14) there is no reference to the Father, but to Christ alone; and here there is no occasion for reference to *the Father* in the exigencies of the context. Also (4) the expression "great God," as applied to Christ, is in accordance with the context, which refers to *the glory of His appearing;* just as "the true God" is predicated of Christ, I John 5:20. The ·phrase occurs nowhere else in the New Testament, but often in the Old Testament. Deuteronomy 7:21; 10:17, predicated of Jehovah, who, as their manifested Lord, led the Israelites through the wilderness, doubtless the Second Person in the Trinity. Believers now look for the manifestation of His glory, inasmuch as they shall share in it. Even the Socinian explanation, making "the great God" to be *the Father,* "our Saviour," *the Son,* places God and Christ *on an equal relation* to "the glory" of the future appearing: a fact incompatible with the notion that Christ is not divine; indeed it would be blasphemy so to couple any mere created being with God. **14. gave himself**—"The forcible 'Himself, His whole self, the greatest gift ever given,' must not be overlooked." **for us**—*Greek,* "in our behalf." **redeem us**—*deliver us from bondage by paying the price* of His precious blood. An appropriate image in addressing bond servants (vss. 9, 10). **from all iniquity**—the essence of sin, viz., "transgression of the law": in bondage to which we were till then. The aim of His redemption was to redeem us, not merely from the penalty, but from the being of all iniquity. Thus he reverts to the "teaching" in righteousness, or *disciplining* effect of the grace of God that bringeth

salvation (vss. 11, 12). **peculiar**—*peculiarly His own,* as Israel was of old. **zealous**—in doing and promoting "good works." **15. with all authority**—Translate, "authoritativeness" (cf. "sharply," ch. 1: 13). **Let no man despise thee**—Speak with such vigor as to command respect (I Tim. 4:12). Warn them with such authority that no one may *think himself above* (so the *Greek* lit.) the need of admonition [TITTMANN, *Synonyms of New Testament*].

CHAPTER 3

VSS. 1-15. WHAT TITUS IS TO TEACH CONCERNING CHRISTIANS' BEHAVIOR TOWARDS THE WORLD: HOW HE IS TO TREAT HERETICS: WHEN AND WHERE HE IS TO MEET PAUL. SALUTATION. CONCLUSION. **1. Put them in mind**—as they are in danger of forgetting their duty, though knowing it. The opposition of Christianity to heathenism, and the natural disposition to rebellion of the Jews under the Roman empire (of whom many lived in Crete), might lead many to forget practically what was a recognized Christian principle in theory, submission to the powers that be. Diodorus Siculus mentions the tendency of the Cretans to riotous insubordination. **to be subject**—"willingly" (so the *Greek*). **principalities . . . powers**—*Greek,* magistracies ... authorities.'. **to obey**—the *commands* of "magistrates"; not necessarily implying *spontaneous* obedience. *Willing* obedience is implied in "ready to every good work." Cf. Romans 13:3, as showing that obedience to the magistracy would tend to good works, since the magistrate's aim *generally* is to favor the good and punish the bad. Contrast "disobedient" (vs. 3). **2. To speak evil of no man**—especially, not of "dignities" and magistrates. **no brawlers**—"not quarrelsome," not attacking others. **gentle**—towards those who attack us. Yielding, considerate, not urging one's rights to the uttermost, but forbearing and kindly (*Note,* Phil. 4: 5). Very different from the *innate greediness* and spirit of aggression towards others which characterized the Cretans. **showing**—in acts. **all**—all possible. **meekness**—(*Note,* II Cor. 10:1)—the opposite of passionate severity. **unto all men**—The duty of Christian conduct towards *all men* is the proper consequence of the universality of God's grace to all men, so often set forth in the pastoral Epistles. **3. For**—Our own past sins should lead us to be lenient towards those of others. "Despise none, for such wast thou also." As the penitent thief said to his fellow thief, "Dost thou not fear God ... seeing that thou art in the same condemnation." **we**—Christians. **were**—Contrast vs. 4, "But when," i.e., *now:* a favorite contrast in Paul's writing, that between our *past* state by nature, and our *present* state of deliverance from it by grace. As God treated us, we ought to treat our neighbor. **sometimes**—once. **foolish**—wanting right reason in our course of living. Irrational. The exact picture of human life without grace. Grace is the sole remedy for foolishness. **disobedient**—to God. **deceived**—led astray. The same *Greek,* "out of the way" (Heb. 5:2). **serving**—*Greek,* "in bondage to," serving as *slaves.*" **divers**—The cloyed appetite craves constant variety. **pleasures**—of the flesh. **malice**—malignity. **hateful . . . hating**—correlatives. Provoking the hatred of others by their detestable character and conduct, and in turn hating them. **4.** To show how little reason the Cretan Christians had to be proud of themselves, and despise others not Christians (*Notes,* vss. 2, 3). It is to the "kindness and love of God," not to their own merits, that they owe salvation. **kindness**—Greek, "goodness," "benignity," which manifests His *grace*. **love** . . . **toward man**—teaching us to have such "love (benevolence) toward *man*" (*Greek*, "philanthropy"), "showing all meekness unto all *men*" (vs. 2), even as God had "*toward man*" (ch. 2:11); opposed to the "hateful and hating" characteristics of unrenewed men, whose wretchedness moved God's *benevolent kindness*. **of God our Saviour**—Greek, "of our Saviour God," viz., the Father (ch. 1:3), who "saved us" (vs. 5) "through Jesus Christ our Saviour" (vs. 6). **appeared**—Greek, "was made to appear"; was manifested. **5. Not by**—Greek, "Out of"; "not as a result springing *from* works. . . ." **of righteousness** —Greek, "in righteousness," i.e., wrought *in a state of righteousness;* as "deeds . . . wrought *in* God." There was an utter absence in us of the element ("righteousness") in which alone righteous works could be done, and so necessarily an absence of the works. "We neither did works of righteousness, nor were saved in consequence of them; but His goodness did the whole" [THEOPHYLACT]. **we**—emphatically opposed to "His." **mercy**—the prompting cause of our salvation individually: "*In pursuance of* His mercy." His *kindness* and *love to man* were manifested in redemption once for all wrought by Him for mankind *generally;* His *mercy* is the prompting cause for our *individual* realization of it. *Faith* is presupposed as the instrument of our being "saved"; our being so, then, is spoken of as an *accomplished fact. Faith* is not mentioned, but only *God's* part. as Paul's object here is not to describe man's new state, but the saving agency of *God* in bringing about that state, *independent of all merit on the man's part (Note,* vs. 4). **by**—Greek, "through"; by means of. **the washing**—rather, "the laver," i.e., the baptismal font. **or regeneration**— *designed* to be the visible instrument of regeneration. "The apostles are wont to draw an argument from the sacraments to prove the thing therein signified, because it ought to be a recognized principle among the godly, that God does not mark us with empty signs, but by His power inwardly makes good what He demonstrates by the outward sign. Wherefore baptism is congruously and truly called *the laver of regeneration.* We must connect the sign and thing signified, so as not to make the sign empty and ineffectual; and yet not, for the sake of honoring the sign, to detract from the Holy Spirit what is peculiarly His" [CALVIN], (I Pet. 3:21). Adult candidates for baptism are presupposed to have had repentance and faith (for Paul often assumes in faith and charity that those addressed are what they profess to be, though in fact some of them were not so, I Cor. 6:11), in which case baptism would be the visible "laver or regeneration" to them, "faith being thereby *confirmed,* and grace *increased,* by virtue of prayer to God" (Church of England, Article 27). Infants are *charitably presumed* to have received a grace in connection with their Christian descent, in answer to the *believing* prayers of their parents or guardians presenting them for baptism, which grace is visibly sealed and increased by baptism, "the laver of regeneration." They are *presumed* to be then regenerated, until years of developed consciousness prove whether they have been *actually* so or not. "Born of (from) water and (no 'of' in *Greek*) the Spirit." The Word is the *remote* and *anterior* instrument of the new birth; Baptism, the *proximate* instrument. The Word, the instrument to the *individual;* Baptism, in relation to the *Society* of Christians. The laver of

cleansing stood outside the door of the tabernacle, wherein the priest had to wash before entering the Holy Place; so we must wash in the laver of regeneration before we can enter the Church, whose members are "a royal priesthood." "Baptism by the Spirit" (whereof water baptism is the designed accompanying seal) makes the difference between Christian baptism and that of John. As Paul presupposes the outward Church as the visible community of the redeemed, so he speaks of baptism on the supposition that it answers to its idea; that all that is inward belonging to its completeness accompanied the outward. Hence he here asserts of outward baptism whatever is involved in the believing appropriation of the divine facts which it symbolizes, whatever is realized when baptism fully corresponds to its original design. So Galatians 3:27; language holding good only of those in whom the inward living communion and outward baptism coalesce. "Saved us" applies fully to those truly regenerate alone; in a general sense it may include many who, though put within reach of salvation, shall not finally be saved. "Regeneration" occurs only once more in New Testament, Matthew 19:28, i.e., *the new brith of the heaven and earth* at Christ's second coming to renew all material things, the human body included, when the creature, now travailing in labor-throes to the birth, shall be delivered from the bondage of corruption into the glorious liberty of the children of God. Regeneration, which now begins in the believer's soul, shall then be extended to his body, and thence to all creation. **and renewing**—not "*the laver* ('washing') of renewing," but "and BY the renewing . . ." following "saved us." To make "renewing of the Holy Ghost" follow "the laver" would destroy the balance of the clauses of the sentence, and would make baptism the seal, not only of *regeneration,* but also of the subsequent process of *progressive* sanctification ("renewing of the Holy Ghost"). *Regeneration* is a thing once for all done; *renewing* is a process daily proceeding. As "the washing," or "laver," is connected with "*regeneration,*" so the "renewing of the Holy Ghost" is connected with "shed on us abundantly" (vs. 6). **6. Which**—the Holy Ghost. **he shed** —Greek, "poured out"; not only on the Church in general at Pentecost, but also "on us" individually. This *pouring out* of the Spirit comprehends the grace received before, in, and subsequently to, baptism. **abundantly**—Greek, "richly" (Col. 3:16). **through Jesus Christ**—the channel and Mediator of the gift of the Holy Ghost. **our Saviour**—immediately; as the Father is mediately "our Saviour." The Father is the author of our salvation and saves us by Jesus Christ. **7. That . . .**—the purpose which He aimed at in having "saved us" (vs. 5), viz., "That being (having been) justified (*accounted righteous through faith at our 'regeneration,'* and *made righteous* by the daily 'renewing of the Holy Ghost') by His grace (as opposed to *works,* vs. 5) we should be made heirs." **his grace**—Greek, "the grace of the former," i.e., *God* (vs. 4; Rom. 5:15). **heirs**— (Gal. 3:29). **according to the hope of eternal life** —Ch. 1:2, and also the position of the *Greek* words, confirm *English Version,* i.e., *agreeably to* the hope of eternal life; the eternal inheritance fully satisfying the hope. BENGEL and ELLICOTT explain it, "*heirs of eternal life,* in the way of hope," i.e., not yet in actual possession. Such a *blessed hope,* which once was not possessed, will lead a Christian to practice holiness and meekness toward others, the lesson especially needed by the Cretans. **8.** Greek, "faithful is the saying." A formula peculiar to the Pastoral Epistles. Here "the saying" is the statement (vss. 4-7) as to the gratuitousness of God's gift of salvation. Answering to the "Amen." **these things ...**—Greek "concerning these things (the truths dwelt on, vss. 4-7; not as *English Version*, what follow), I will that thou affirm (*insist*) strongly and *persistently, in order that* they who have *believed God* (the *Greek* for 'believed *in* God' is different, John 14:1. 'They who have learnt to credit God' in what He saith) may be careful ('solicitously sedulous'; *diligence is necessary*) *to* maintain (lit., 'to set before themselves so as to sustain') good works." No longer applying their *care* to "unprofitable" and unpractical speculations (vs. 9). **these things**—These results of doctrine ("good works" are "good and profitable unto men," whereas no such practical results flow from "foolish questions." So GROTIUS and WIESINGER. But ALFORD, to avoid the tautology, "these (good works) are good unto men," explains, "these *truths*' (vss. 4-7). **9. avoid**—stand aloof from. Same *Greek*, as in *Note*, II Timothy 2:16. **foolish**—Greek, "insipid"; producing no moral fruit. "Vain talkers." **genealogies** —akin to the "fables" (see *Note*, I Tim. 1:4). Not so much direct heresy as yet is here referred to, as profitless discussions about genealogies of aeons, etc., which ultimately led to Gnosticism. Synagogue discourses were termed *daraschoth*, i.e., discussions. Cf. "*disputer* of this world (*Greek*, 'dispensation')." **strivings about the law**—about the authority of the "commandments of men," which they sought to confirm by the law (ch. 1:14; *Note*, I Tim. 1:7), and about the mystical meaning of the various parts of the law in connection with the "genealogies." **10. heretic**—*Greek* "heresy," originally meant a *division* resulting from individual self-will; the individual doing and teaching what he *chose*, independent of the teaching and practice of the Church. In course of time it came to mean definitely "heresy" in the modern sense; and in the later Epistles it has almost assumed this meaning. The heretics of Crete, when Titus was there, were in doctrine followers of their own self-willed "questions" reprobated in vs. 9, and immoral in practice. **reject**—decline, avoid; not formal excommunication, but, "have nothing more to do with him," either in admonition or intercourse. **11. is ... subverted**—"is become perverse." **condemned of himself**—He cannot say, no one told him better; continuing the same after frequent admonition, he is self-condemned. "He sinneth" wilfully against knowledge. **12. When I shall send**—have sent—**Artemas or Tychicus**—to supply thy place in Crete. Artemas is said to have been subsequently bishop of Lystra. Tychicus was sent twice by Paul from Rome to Lesser Asia in his first imprisonment (which shows how well qualified he was to become Titus' successor in Crete); Ephesians 6:21; and in his second, II Timothy 4:12. Tradition makes him subsequently bishop of Chalcedon, in Bithynia. **Nicopolis**—"the city of victory," called so from the battle of Actium, in Epirus. This Epistle was probably written from Corinth in the autumn. Paul purposed a journey through Œtolia and Acarnania, into Epirus, and there "to winter." See my *Introduction* to the Pastoral Epistles. **13. Bring ... on their journey**—Enable them to proceed forward by supplying necessaries for their journey. **Zenas**—the contracted form of Zenodorus. **lawyer**—a Jewish "scribe," who, when converted, still retained the title from his former occupation. A *civil* lawyer. **Apollos**—with Zenas, probably the bearers of this Epistle. In I Cor. 16:12, Apollos is mentioned as purposing to visit Corinth; his now being at Corinth (on the theory of Paul being at Corinth when he wrote) accords with this purpose. Crete would be on his way either to Palestine or his native place, Alexandria. Paul and Apollos thus appear in beautiful harmony in that very city where their names had been formerly the watchword of unchristian party work. It was to avoid this party rivalry that Apollos formerly was unwilling to visit Corinth though Paul desired him. HIPPOLYTUS mentions Zenas as one of the Seventy, and afterwards bishop of Diospolis. **14. And ... also**—Greek, "But ... also." Not only *thou*, but let others also of "our" fellow believers (or "whom we have gained over at Crete") with thee. **for necessary uses**—*to supply the necessary wants* of Christian missionaries and brethren, according as they stand in need in their journeys for the Lord's cause. Cf. ch. 1:8, "a lover of hospitality." **15. Greet**—"*Salute* them that love us in the faith." All at Crete had not this *love* rooted in *faith*, the true bond of fellowship. A salutation peculiar to this Epistle, such as no forger would have used. **Grace**—Greek, "*The* grace," viz., *of God*. **with you all**—not that the Epistle is addressed to *all* the Cretan Christians, but Titus would naturally impart it to his flock.

THE EPISTLE OF PAUL TO

PHILEMON

INTRODUCTION

The testimonies to its authenticity are—ORIGEN, *Homily 19, on Jerem.*, vol. 1., p. 185, *Ed. Huet.*, cites it as the letter of Paul to Philemon concerning ONESIMUS; TERTULLIAN, *against Marcion*, 5. 21. "The brevity of this Epistle is the sole cause of its escaping the falsifying hands of Marcion"; EUSEBIUS, *Ecclesiastical History*, 3. 25, mentions it among "the universally acknowledged Epistles of the canon"; JEROME, *Prœmium in Philemonem*, vol. iv., p. 442, argues for it against those who objected to its canonicity on the ground of its subject being beneath an apostle to write about. IGNATIUS, *Eph.* 2., and *Magnes.* 12, seems to allude to Philemon 20. Cf Epistle to POLYCARP (chs. 1 and 6). Its brevity is the cause of its not being often quoted by the Fathers. PALEY, *Horæ Paulinæ*, has shown striking proofs of its authenticity in the undesigned coincidences between it and the Epistle to the Colossians.

PLACE AND TIME OF WRITING.—This Epistle is closely linked with the Epistle to the Colossians. Both were carried by the same bearer, ONESIMUS (with whom, however, Tychicus is joined in the Epistle to the Colossians), Colossians 4:9. The persons sending salutations are the same, except one, Jesus called *Justus* (Col. 4:11). In both alike Archippus is addressed (vs. 2; Col. 4:17). Paul and Timothy stand in the headings of both. And in both Paul appears as a prisoner (vs. 9; Col. 4:18). Hence it follows, it was written at the same time and place as the Epistle to the Colossians (which was about the same time as the Epistle to the Ephesians), viz., at Rome, during Paul's first imprisonment, A.D. 61 or 62.

OBJECT.—ONESIMUS, of Colosse ("one of you," Col. 4:9), slave of Philemon, had fled from his master to Rome, after having probably defrauded him (vs. 18). He there was converted to Christianity by Paul, and being induced by him to return to his master, he was furnished with this Epistle, recommending him to Philemon's favorable reception, as being now no longer a mere servant, but also a brother in Christ. Paul ends by requesting Philemon to prepare him a lodging, as he trusted soon to be set free and visit Colosse. This Epistle is addressed also to Apphia, supposed from its domestic subject to have been Philemon's wife, and Archippus (a minister of the Colossian Church, Col. 4:17), for the same reason, supposed to be a near relative.

Onesimus in the Apostolical Canons (73), is said to have been emancipated by his master. The Apostolical Constitutions (7. 46) state that he was consecrated by Paul, bishop of Berea, in Macedonia, and that he was martyred at Rome. IGNATIUS, *Epistola ad Ephesum*, ch. 1, speaks of him as bishop of the Ephesians.

STYLE.—It has been happily termed, from its graceful and delicate urbanity, "the polite Epistle." Yet there is nothing of insincere compliment, miscalled politeness by the world. It is manly and straightforward, without misrepresentation or suppression of facts; at the same time it is most captivatingly persuasive. ALFORD quotes Luther's eloquent description, "This Epistle showeth a right, noble, lovely example of Christian love. Here we see how St. Paul layeth himself out for the poor Onesimus, and with all his means pleadeth his cause with his master, and so setteth himself as if he were Onesimus, and had himself done wrong to Philemon. Yet all this doeth he, not with force, as if he had right thereto, but he stripped himself of his right, and thus enforceth Philemon to forego his right also. Even as Christ did for us with God the Father, thus also doth St. Paul for Onesimus with Philemon: for Christ also stripped Himself of His right, and by love and humility enforced [?] the Father to lay aside His wrath and power, and to take us to His grace for the sake of Christ, who lovingly pleadeth our cause, and with all His heart layeth Himself out for us; for we are all His Onesimi, to my thinking."

Vs. 1-25. ADDRESS. THANKSGIVING FOR PHILEMON'S LOVE AND FAITH. INTERCESSION FOR ONESIMUS. CONCLUDING REQUEST AND SALUTATIONS. This Epistle affords a specimen of the highest wisdom as to the manner in which Christians ought to manage social affairs on more exalted principles. **1. prisoner of Jesus Christ**—one whom Christ's cause has made a prisoner (cf. "in the bonds of the Gospel," (vs. 13). He does not call himself, as in other Epistles, "Paul an apostle," as he is writing familiarly, not authoritatively. **our ... fellow labourer**—in building up the Church at Colosse, while we were at Ephesus. See my *Introduction* to Colossians. **2. Apphia**—the Latin "Appia"; either the wife or some close relative of Philemon. She and Archippus, if they had not belonged to his family, would not have been included with Philemon in the address of a letter on a domestic matter. **Archippus**—a minister of the Colossian Church (Col. 4:17). **fellow soldier**—(II Tim. 2:3). **church in thy house**—In the absence of a regular church building, the houses of particular saints were used for that purpose. Observe Paul's tact in associating with Philemon those associated by kindred or Christian brotherhood with his *house*, and not going beyond it. **4. always**—joined by ALFORD with, "I thank my God." **5. Hearing**—the ground of his thanksgiving. It is a delicate mark of authenticity, that he says "hearing" as to churches and persons whom he had not seen or *then* visited. Now Colosse, Philemon's place of residence, he had never yet seen. Yet vs. 19 here implies that Philemon was his convert. Philemon, doubtless, was converted at Ephesus, or in some other place where he met Paul. **love and faith**—The theological order is first *faith* then *love*, the fruit of faith. But he purposely puts Philemon's *love* in the first place, as it is to an act of love that he is exhorting him. **toward ... toward**—different *Greek*, words: "towards" ... "unto." *Towards* implies simply direction; *unto*, to the advantage of thee. **6. That ...**—The aim of my thanksgiving and prayers for thee is, *in order*

that the. . . . **the communication of thy faith** —the imparting of it and its fruits (viz., acts of love and beneficence: as Heb. 13:16, "to communicate," i.e., to impart a share) *to others;* or, *the liberality to others flowing from thy faith* (so the *Greek* is translated, "liberal distribution," II Cor. 9:13). **effectual by**—*Greek*, "in"; the element in which his liberality had place, i.e., may be *proved by acts in. . . .* **acknowledging**—*Greek*, "the thorough knowledge," i.e., the experimental or practical *recognition*. **of every good thing which is in you**—The oldest MSS. read, "which is in US," i.e., the practical recognition of every grace which is in us *Christians,* in so far as we realize the Christian character. In short, that thy faith may by acts be proved to be "a faith which worketh by love." **in Christ Jesus**—rather as *Greek,* "*unto* Christ Jesus," i.e., to the glory of Christ Jesus. Two of the oldest MSS. omit "Jesus." This verse answers to vs. 5, "thy love and faith toward all saints"; Paul never ceases to mention him in his prayers, *in order that* his faith may still further show its power in his relation to others, by exhibiting every grace which is in Christians to the glory of Christ. Thus he paves the way for the request in behalf of Onesimus. **7. For**—a reason for the prayer, vss. 4-6. **we have**—*Greek,* "we had." **joy and consolation**—joined in II Corinthians 7:4. **saints are refreshed by thee**—His house was open to them. **brother**—put last, to conciliate his favorable attention to the request which follows. **8. Wherefore**—Because of my love to thee, I prefer to "*beseech*," rather than "enjoin," or *authoritatively command.* **I might ... enjoin**—in virtue of the obligation to *obedience* which Philemon lay under to Paul, as having been converted through his instrumentality. **in Christ**—the element in which his boldness has place. **9. for love's sake**—mine to thee, and [what ought to be] thine to Onesimus. Or, that Christian love of which thou showest so bright an example (vs. 7). **being such an one**—Explain, *Being such a one* as thou knowest me to be, viz., *Paul* (the founder of so many churches, and an apostle of Christ, and thy father in the faith)*the aged* (a circumstance calculated to secure thy respect for anything I request), *and now also a prisoner of Jesus Christ* (the strongest claim I have on thy regard: if for no other reason, at least in consideration of this, through commiseration gratify me). **10. I beseech thee**—emphatically repeated from vs. 9. In the *Greek,* the name "Onesimus" is skilfully put last, he puts first a favorable description of him before he mentions the name that had fallen into so bad repute with Philemon. "I beseech thee for my son, whom I have begotten in my bonds, Onesimus." Scripture does not sanction slavery, but at the same time does not begin a political crusade against it. It sets forth *principles of love* to our fellow men which were sure (as they have done) in due time to undermine and overthrow it, without violently convulsing the then existing political fabric, by stirring up slaves against their masters. **11. Which ... was ... unprofitable**—belying his name Onesimus, which means "profitable." Not only was he "unprofitable," but positively injurious, having "wronged" his master. Paul uses a mild expression. **now profitable**—Without godliness a man has no station. *Profitable* in spiritual, as well as in *temporal* things. **12. mine own bowels**—as dear to me as my own heart [ALFORD]. Cf. vs. 17, "as myself." The object of my most intense affection as that of a parent for a child. **13. I**—emphatical. I for my part. Since *I* had such implicit trust in him as to desire to keep him with me for his services, *thou* mayest. **I would have retained**—different *Greek* from the "would," vs. 14, "I could have *wished,*" "I was *minded*" here; but "I was not *willing,*" vs. 14. **in thy stead**—that he might supply in your place all the services to me which you, if you were here, would render in virtue of the love you bear to me (vs. 19). **bonds of the gospel**—my bonds endured for the Gospel's sake (vs. 9). **14. without thy mind**—i.e., consent. **should not be as**—"should not appear as a matter of necessity, but of free will." Had Paul kept Onesimus, however willing to gratify Paul Philemon might be, he would have no opportunity given him of showing he was so, his leave not having been asked. **15. perhaps**—speaking in human fashion, yet as one believing that God's Providence probably (for we cannot dogmatically define the hidden purposes of God in providence) overruled the past evil to ultimately greater good to him. This thought would soften Philemon's indignation at Onesimus' past offense. So Joseph in Genesis 45:5. **departed**—lit., "was parted from thee"; a softening term for "ran away," to mitigate Philemon's wrath. **receive him**—*Greek,* "have him for thyself in full possession" (*Note,* Phil. 4:18). The same *Greek* as in Matthew 6:2. **for ever**—in this life and in that to come (cf. Exod. 21:6). Onesimus' time of absence, however long, was but a short "hour" (so *Greek*) compared with the everlasting devotion henceforth binding him to his master. **16.** No longer as a mere servant or slave (though still he is that), but above a servant, so that thou shalt derive from him not merely the services of a slave, but higher benefits: a *servant* "in the flesh," he is a *brother* "in the Lord." **beloved, specially to me**—who am his spiritual father, and who have experienced his faithful attentions. Lest Philemon should

dislike Onesimus being called "brother," Paul first recognizes him as a brother, being the spiritual son of the same God. **much more unto thee**—to whom he stands in so much nearer and more lasting relation. **17. a partner**—in the Christian fellowship of faith, hope, and love. **receive him as myself**—resuming "receive him that is mine own bowels." **18.** *Greek,* "But it (thou art not inclined to 'receive him' because) he hath wronged thee"; a milder term than "robbed thee." Onesimus seems to have confessed some such act to Paul. **put that on mine account**—I am ready to make good the loss to thee if required. The latter parts of vss. 19, 21, imply that he did not expect Philemon would demand it. **19. with mine own hand**—not employing an amanuensis, as in other Epistles: a special compliment to Philemon which he ought to show his appreciation of by granting Paul's request. Contrast Colossians 4:18, which shows that the Epistle to the Colossian Church, accompanying this Epistle, had only its closing "salutation" written by Paul's own hand. **albeit ...**—lit., "that I may not say ... not to say...." **thou owest ... even thine own self**—not merely thy possessions. For to my instrumentality thou owest thy salvation. So the debt which "he oweth thee" being transferred upon me (I making myself responsible for it) is cancelled. **20. let me**—"me" is emphatic: "Let *me* have profit (so *Greek* 'for joy,' *onaimen,* referring to the name *Onesimus,* 'profitable') from *thee,* as *thou* shouldst have had from Onesimus"; for "thou owest thine own self to me." **in the Lord**—not in worldly gain, but in thine increase in the graces of the Lord's Spirit [ALFORD]. **my bowels**—my heart. Gratify my feelings by granting this request. **in the Lord**—The oldest MSS. read, *"in Christ,"* the element or sphere in which this act of Christian love naturally ought to have place. **21. Having confidence in thy obedience**—to my apostolic authority, if I were to "enjoin" it (vs. 8), which I do not, preferring to beseech thee for it as a favor (vs. 9). **thou wilt also do more**—towards Onesimus: hinting at his possible manumission by Philemon, *besides* being kindly received. **22.** This prospect of Paul's visiting Colosse would tend to secure a kindly reception for Onesimus, as Paul would know in person how he had been treated. **your ... you**—referring to Philemon, Apphia, Archippus, and the Church in Philemon's house. The same expectation is expressed by him, Philippians 2:23, 24, written in the same imprisonment. **23.** The same persons send salutations in the accompanying Epistle, except that "Jesus Justus" is not mentioned here. **Epaphras, my fellow prisoner**—He had been sent by the Colossian Church to inquire after, and minister to, Paul, and possibly was cast into *prison* by the Roman authorities on suspicion. However, he is not mentioned as a *prisoner* in Colossians 4:12, so that "fellow prisoner" here may mean merely one who was a faithful companion to Paul in his imprisonment, and by his society put himself in the position of a prisoner. So also "Aristarchus, my fellow prisoner," Colossians 4:10, may mean. BENSON conjectures the meaning to be that on some *former* occasion these two were Paul's "fellow prisoners," *not at the time.* **25. be with your spirit**—(Gal. 6:18; II Timothy 4:22).

THE EPISTLE OF PAUL THE APOSTLE TO THE

HEBREWS

INTRODUCTION

CANONICITY AND AUTHORSHIP.—CLEMENT OF ROME, at the end of the first century (A.D.), copiously uses it, adopting its words just as he does those of the other books of the New Testament; not indeed giving to either the term "Scripture," which he reserves for the Old Testament (the canon of the New Testament not yet having been formally established), but certainly not ranking it below the other New Testament acknowledged Epistles. As our Epistle claims *authority* on the part of the writer, CLEMENT's adoption of extracts from it is virtually sanctioning its authority, and this in the apostolic age. JUSTIN MARTYR quotes it as divinely authoritative, to establish the titles "apostle," as well as "angel," as applied to the Son of God. CLEMENT OF ALEXANDRIA refers it expressly to Paul, on the authority of PANTÆNUS, chief of the Catechetical school in Alexandria, in the middle of the second century, saying, that as Jesus is termed in it the "apostle" sent to the Hebrews, Paul, through humility, does not in it call himself apostle of the Hebrews, being apostle to the Gentiles. CLEMENT also says that Paul, as the Hebrews were prejudiced against him, prudently omitted to put forward his name in the beginning; also, that it was originally written in *Hebrew* for the Hebrews, and that Luke translated it into *Greek* for the Greeks, whence the style is similar to that of Acts. He, however, quotes frequently the words of the existing Greek Epistle as Paul's words. ORIGEN similarly quotes it as Paul's Epistle. However, in his Homilies, he regards the style as distinct from that of Paul, and as "more Grecian," but the thoughts as the apostle's; adding that the "ancients who have handed down the tradition of its Pauline authorship, must have had good reason for doing so, though God alone knows the certainty who was the actual writer" (i.e., probably "transcriber" of the apostle's thoughts). In the African Church, in the beginning of the third century, TERTULLIAN ascribes it to Barnabas. IRENÆUS, bishop of Lyons, is mentioned in EUSEBIUS, as quoting from this Epistle, though without expressly referring to it to Paul. About the same period, CAIUS, the presbyter, in the Church of Rome, mentions only *thirteen* Epistles of Paul, whereas, if the Epistle to the Hebrews were included, there would be *fourteen*. So the canon fragment of the end of the second century, or beginning of the third, published by MURATORI, apparently omits mentioning it. And so the Latin Church did not recognize it as Paul's till a considerable time after the beginning of the third century. Thus, also, NOVATIAN OF ROME, CYPRIAN OF CARTHAGE, and VICTORINUS, also of the Latin Church. But in the fourth century, HILARY OF POITIERS (A.D. 368), LUCIFER OF CAGLIARI (A.D. 371), AMBROSE OF MILAN (A.D. 397) and other Latins, quote it as Paul's; and the fifth Council of Carthage (A.D. 419) formally reckons it among his fourteen Epistles.

As to the *similarity* of its *style to that of Luke's* writings, this is due to his having been so long the companion of Paul. CHRYSOSTOM, comparing Luke and Mark, says, "Each imitated his teacher: Luke imitated Paul flowing along with more than river-fulness; but Mark imitated Peter, who studied brevity of style." Besides, there is a greater predominance of Jewish feeling and familiarity with the peculiarities of the Jewish schools apparent in this Epistle than in Luke's writings. There is no clear *evidence* for attributing the authorship to him, or to Apollos, whom ALFORD upholds as the author. The grounds alleged for the latter view are its supposed Alexandrian phraseology and modes of thought. But these are such as any Palestinian Jew might have used; and Paul, from his Hebræo-Hellenistic education at Jerusalem and Tarsus, would be familiar with Philo's modes of thought, which are not, as some think, necessarily all derived from his Alexandrian, but also from his Jewish, education. It would be unlikely that the Alexandrian Church should have so undoubtingly asserted the Pauline authorship, if Apollos, *their own countryman*, had really been the author. The eloquence of its style and rhetoric, a characteristic of Apollos' at Corinth, whereas Paul there spoke in words unadorned by man's wisdom, are doubtless designedly adapted to the minds of those whom Paul in this Epistle addresses. To the Greek Corinthians, who were in danger of idolizing human eloquence and wisdom, he writes in an unadorned style, in order to fix their attention more wholly on the Gospel itself. But the Hebrews were in no such danger. And his Hebræo-Grecian education would enable him to write in a style attractive to the Hebrews at Alexandria, where Greek philosophy had been blended with Judaism. The *Septuagint* translation framed at Alexandria had formed a connecting link between the latter and the former; and it is remarkable that all the quotations from the Old Testament, excepting two (ch. 10:30; 13:5), are taken from the LXX. The fact that the peculiarities of the LXX are interwoven into the argument proves that the Greek Epistle is an original, not a translation; had the original been Hebrew, the quotations would have been from the *Hebrew* Old Testament. The same conclusion follows from the plays on similarly sounding words in the Greek, and alliterations, and rhythmically constructed periods. CALVIN observes, If the Epistle had been written in Hebrew, ch. 9:15–17 would lose all its point, which consists in the play upon the double meaning of the *Greek diathece*, a "covenant," or a "testament," whereas the *Hebrew berith* means only "covenant."

Internal evidence favors the Pauline authorship. Thus the topic so fully handled in this Epistle, that Christianity is superior to Judaism, inasmuch as the reality exceeds the type which gives place to it, is a favorite one with Paul (cf. II Cor. 3:6–18; Gal. 3:23–25; 4:1-9, 21-31, wherein the allegorical mode of interpretation appears in its divinely sanctioned application—a mode pushed to an unwarrantable excess in the Alexandrian school). So the Divine Son appears in ch. 1:3, etc., as in other Epistles of Paul (Phil. 2:6; Col. 1:15–20), as *the Image*, or manifestation *of the Deity*. His lowering of Himself for man's sake similarly, cf. ch. 2:9, with II Corinthians 8:9; Phil. 2:7, 8. Also His final exaltation, cf. ch. 2:8; 10:13; 12:2, with I Corinthians 15:25, 27. The word "Mediator" is peculiar to Paul alone, cf. ch. 8:6, with Gal. 3:19, 20. Christ's death is represented as the sacrifice for sin prefigured by the Jewish sacrifices, cf. Rom. 3:22–26; I Corinthians 5:7, with Hebrews 7: to 10. The phrase, "God of Peace," is peculiar to Paul, cf. ch. 13:20; Romans 15:33; I Thessalonians 5:23. Also, cf. ch. 2:4, *Margin*, I Corinthians 12:4. Justification, or "righteousness by faith." appears in ch. 11:7; 10:38, as in Romans 1:17; 4:22; 5:1; Galatians 3:11; Philippians 3:9. The word of God is the "sword of the Spirit," cf. ch. 4:12, with, Ephesians 6:17. Inexperienced Christians are *children* needing *milk*, i.e., instruction in the *elements*, whereas riper Christians, as *full grown men*, require *strong meat*, cf. ch. 5:12, 13; 6:1, with I Corinthians 3:1, 2; 14, 20; Galatians 4:9; Colossians 3:14. Salvation is represented as a *boldness of access to God by Christ*, cf. ch. 10:19 with Romans 5:2; Ephesians 2:18; 3. 12. Afflictions are a *fight*, ch. 10:32; cf Philippians 1:30; Colossians 2:1. The Christian life is a *race*, ch 12:1; cf. I Corinthians 9:24; Philippians 3:12–14. The Jewish ritual is a *service*, Romans 9:4; cf. ch. 9:1, 6. Cf. "subject to bondage." ch. 2:15, with Galatians 5:1. Other characteristics of Paul's style appear in this Epistle; viz., a propensity "to go off at a word" and enter on a long parenthesis suggested by that word, a fondness for play upon words of similar sound, and a disposition to repeat some favorite word. Frequent appeals to the Old Testament, and quotations linked by "and again," cf. ch. 1:5; 2:12, 13, with Romans 15:9–12. Also quotations in a peculiar application, cf. ch. 2:8, with I Corinthians 15:27; Ephesians 1:22. Also the same passage quoted in a form not agreeing with the LXX, and with the addition "saith the Lord," not found in the *Hebrew*, in ch. 10:30; Romans 12:19.

The supposed Alexandrian (which are rather Philon-like) characteristics of the Epistle are probably due to the fact that the Hebrews were generally then imbued with the Alexandrian modes of thought of Philo, etc., and Paul, without coloring or altering Gospel truth "to the Jews, became (in style) as a Jew, that he might win the Jews" (I Cor. 9:20). This will account for its being recognized as Paul's Epistle in the Alexandrian and Jerusalem churches unanimously, to the Hebrews of whom probably it was addressed. Not one Greek father ascribes the Epistle to any but Paul, whereas in the Western and Latin churches, which it did not reach for some time, it was for long doubted, owing to its anonymous form, and generally less distinctively Pauline style. Their reason for not accepting it as Paul's, or indeed as canonical, for the first three centuries, was *negative*, insufficient evidence for it, not positive evidence against it. The positive evidence is generally for its Pauline origin. In the Latin churches, owing to their distance from the churches to whom belonged the Hebrews addressed, there was no generally received tradition on the subject. The Epistle was in fact but little known at all, whence we find it is not mentioned at all in the canon of *Muratori*. When at last, in the fourth century, the Latins found that it was received as Pauline and canonical on good grounds in the Greek churches, they universally acknowledged it as such.

The personal notices all favor its Pauline authorship, viz., his intention to visit those addressed, shortly, along with Timothy, styled "our brother," ch. 13:23; his being then in prison, ch. 13:19; his formerly having been imprisoned in Palestine, according to *English Version* reading, ch. 10:34; the salutations transmitted to them from believers of Italy, ch. 13:24. A reason for not prefixing the name may be the rhetorical character of the Epistle which led the author to waive the usual form of epistolary address.

DESIGN.—His aim is to show the superiority of Christianity over Judaism, in that it was introduced by one far higher than the angels or Moses, through whom the Jews received the law, and in that its priesthood and sacrifices are far less perfecting as to salvation than those of Christ; that He is the substance of which the former are but the shadow, and that the type necessarily gives place to the antitype; and that now we no longer are kept at a comparative distance as under the law, but have freedom of access through the opened veil, i.e., Christ's flesh; hence he warns them of the danger of apostasy, to which Jewish converts were tempted, when they saw Christians persecuted, while Judaism was tolerated by the Roman authorities. He infers the obligations to a life of faith, of which, even in the less perfect Old Testament dispensation, the Jewish history contained bright examples. He concludes in the usual Pauline mode, with practical exhortations and pious prayers for them.

HIS MODE OF ADDRESS is in it hortatory rather than commanding, just as we might have expected from Paul addressing the Jews. He does not write to the *rulers* of the Jewish Christians, for in fact there was no exclusively Jewish Church; and his Epistle, though primarily addressed to the Palestinian Jews, was intended to include the Hebrews of all adjoining churches. He inculcates obedience and respect in relation to their rulers (ch. 13:7, 17, 24); a tacit obviating of the objection that he was by writing this Epistle interfering with the prerogative of Peter the apostle of the circumcision, and James the bishop of Jerusalem. Hence arises his gentle and delicate mode of dealing with them (Heb. 13:22). So far from being surprised at discrepancy of style between an Epistle to Hebrews and Epistles to Gentile Christians, it is just what we should expect. The Holy Spirit guided him to choose means best suited to the nature of the ends aimed at. WORDSWORTH notices a peculiar Pauline *Greek* construction, Romans 12:9, lit., "Let your love be without dissimulation, ye abhorring . . . evil, cleaving to . . . good," which is found nowhere else save Hebrews 13:5, lit., "Let your conversation be without covetousness, ye being content with . . ." (a noun singular feminine nominative absolute, suddenly passing into a participle masculine nominative plural absolute). So in quoting Old Testament Scripture, the writer of the Epistle to the Hebrews quotes it as *a Jew* writing to Jews would, "God *spoke* to our fathers," not, "it is *written*." So ch. 13:18, "We trust we have a good conscience" is an altogether Pauline sentiment (Acts 23:1; 24:16; II Cor. 1:12; 4:2; II Tim. 1:3). Though he has not prefixed his name, he has given at the close his universal token to identify him, viz., his apostolic salutation, "Grace be with you all"; this "salutation with his own hand" he declared (II Thess. 3:17, 18) to be "his token in every Epistle"; so I Corinthians 16:21, 23; Colossians 4:18. The same prayer of greeting closes *every one* of his Epistles, and is not found in any one of the Epistles of the other apostles written in Paul's lifetime; but it is found in the last book of the New Testament Revelation, and subsequently in the Epistle of Clement of Rome. This proves that, by whomsoever the body of the Epistle was committed to writing (whether a mere amanuensis writing by dictation, or a companion of Paul by the Spirit's gift of *interpreting tongues*, I Cor. 12:10, transfusing Paul's Spirit-taught sentiments into his own Spirit-guided diction),

Paul at the close sets his seal to the whole as really his, and sanctioned by him as such. The churches of the East, and Jerusalem, their center, to which quarter it was first sent, received it as Paul's from the earliest times according to Cyril, Bishop of Jerusalem (A.D. 349). JEROME, though bringing with him from Rome the prejudices of the Latins against the Epistle to the Hebrews, aggravated, doubtless, by its seeming sanction of the Novatian heresy (ch. 6:4–6), was constrained by the force of facts to receive it as Paul's, on the almost unanimous testimony of all Greek Christians from the earliest times; and was probably the main instrument in correcting the past error of Rome in rejecting it. The testimony of the Alexandrian Church is peculiarly valuable, for it was founded by Mark, who was with Paul at Rome in his first confinement, when this Epistle seems to have been written (Col. 4:10), and who possibly was the bearer of this Epistle, at the same time visiting Colosse on the way to Jerusalem (where Mark's mother lived), and thence to Alexandria. Moreover, II Peter 3:15, 16, written shortly before Peter's death, and like his first Epistle written by him, "the apostle of the circumcision," to the *Hebrew* Christians dispersed in the East, says, "As our beloved brother Paul hath written *unto you*," i.e., to the *Hebrews*; also the words added, "As also in *all* his Epistles," distinguish the *Epistle to the Hebrews* from the rest; then he further speaks of it as on a level with "*other* Scriptures," thus asserting at once its Pauline authorship and divine inspiration. An interesting illustration of the power of Christian faith and love; Peter, who had been openly rebuked by Paul (Gal. 2:7–14), fully adopted what Paul wrote; there was no difference in the Gospel of the apostle of the circumcision and that of the apostle of the uncircumcision. It strikingly shows God's sovereignty that He chose as the instrument to confirm the *Hebrews*, Paul, *the apostle of the Gentiles*; and on the other hand, Peter to open the Gospel door to the *Gentiles* (Acts 10:1, etc.), though being *the apostle of the Jews*; thus perfect unity reigns amidst the diversity of agencies.

Rome, in the person of Clement of Rome, originally received this Epistle. Then followed a period in which it ceased to be received by the Roman churches. Then, in the fourth century, Rome retracted her error. A plain proof she is not unchangeable or infallible. As far as Rome is concerned, the Epistle to the Hebrews was not only lost for three centuries, but never would have been recovered at all but for the Eastern churches; it is therefore a happy thing for Christendom that Rome is not the Catholic Church.

It plainly was written before the destruction of Jerusalem, which would have been mentioned in the Epistle had that event gone before, cf. ch. 13:10; and probably to churches in which the Jewish members were the more numerous, as those in Judea, and perhaps Alexandria. In the latter city were the greatest number of resident Jews next to Jerusalem. In Leontopolis, in Egypt, was another temple, with the arrangements of which, WIESELER thinks the notices in this Epistle more nearly corresponded than with those in Jerusalem. It was from Alexandria that the Epistle appears first to have come to the knowledge of Christendom. Moreover, "the Epistle to the Alexandrians," mentioned in the Canon of *Muratori*, may possibly be this Epistle to the Hebrews. He addresses the Jews as peculiarly "the people of God" (ch. 2:17; 4:9; 13:12), "the seed of Abraham," i.e., as the primary stock on which Gentile believers are grafted, to which Romans 11:16–24 corresponds; but he urges them to come out of the carnal earthly Jerusalem and to realize their spiritual union to "the heavenly Jerusalem" (ch. 12:18–23; 13:13).

The use of Greek rather than Hebrew is doubtless due to the Epistle being intended, not merely for the Hebrew, but for the Hellenistic Jew converts, not only in Palestine, but elsewhere; a view confirmed by the use of the LXX. BENGEL thinks, probably (cf. II Pet. 3:15, 16, explained above), the Jews primarily, though not exclusively, addressed, were those who had left Jerusalem on account of the war and were settled in Asia Minor.

The notion of its having been originally in Hebrew arose probably from its Hebrew tone, method, and topics. It is reckoned among the Epistles, *not at first generally acknowledged*, along with James, II Peter, II and III John, Jude, and Revelation. A beautiful link exists between these Epistles and *the universally acknowledged* Epistles. Hebrews unites the ordinances of Leviticus with their antitypical Gospel fulfilment. James is the link between the highest doctrines of Christianity and the universal law of moral duty—a commentary on the Sermon on the Mount—harmonizing the decalogue law of Moses, and the revelation to Job and Elias, with the Christian law of liberty. Second Peter links the teaching of Peter with that of Paul. Jude links the earliest unwritten to the latest written Revelation. The two shorter Epistles to John, like Philemon, apply Christianity to the minute details of the Christian life, showing that Christianity can sanctify all earthly relations.

CHAPTER 1

Vss. 1-14. THE HIGHEST OF ALL REVELATIONS IS GIVEN US NOW IN THE SON OF GOD, WHO IS GREATER THAN THE ANGELS, AND WHO, HAVING COMPLETED REDEMPTION, SITS ENTHRONED AT GOD'S RIGHT HAND. The writer, though not inscribing his name, was well known to those addressed (ch. 13:19). For proofs of Paul being the author, see my *Introduction*. In the Pauline method, the statement of subject and the division are put before the discussion; and at the close, the practical follows the doctrinal portion. The ardor of Spirit in this Epistle, as in I John, bursting forth at once into the subject (without prefatory inscription of name and greeting), the more effectively strikes the hearers. The date must have been while the temple was yet standing, before its destruction, A.D. 70; some time before the martyrdom of Peter, who mentions this

Epistle of Paul (II Pet. 3:15, 16); at a time when many of the first *hearers* of the Lord were dead. **1. at sundry times**—*Greek,* "in many portions." All was not revealed to each one prophet; but one received one portion of revelation, and another another. To Noah the quarter of the world to which Messiah should belong was revealed; to Abraham, the nation; to Jacob, the tribe; to David and Isaiah, the family; to Micah, the town of nativity; to Daniel, the exact time; to Malachi, the coming of His forerunner, and His second advent; through Jonah, His burial and resurrection; through Isaiah and Hosea, His resurrection. Each only knew in part; but when that which was perfect came in Messiah, that which was in part was done away (I Cor. 13:12). **in divers manners**—e.g., internal suggestions, audible voices, the Urim and Thummim, dreams, and visions. "In one way He was seen by Abraham, in another by Moses, in another by Elias, and in another by Micah; Isaiah, Daniel, and Ezekiel, beheld different forms" [THEODORET] (cf. Num. 12: 6-8). The Old Testament revelations were fragmentary in substance, and manifold in form; the very *multitude* of prophets shows that they prophesied only *in part.* In Christ, the revelation of God is full, not in shifting hues of separated color, but Himself the pure light, uniting in His one person the whole spectrum (vs. 3). **spake**—the expression usual for a Jew to employ in addressing Jews. So Matthew, a Jew writing especially for Jews, quotes Scripture, not by the formula, "It is written," but "said. . . ." **in time past**—From Malachi, the last of the Old Testament prophets, for four hundred years, there had arisen no prophet, in order that the Son might be the more an object of expectation [BENGEL]. As God (the Father) is introduced as having *spoken* here; so God the Son, ch. 2:3; God the Holy Ghost, ch. 3:7. **the fathers**—the Jewish fathers. The Jews of former days (I Cor. 10:1). **by**—Greek, "in." A mortal king speaks *by* his ambassador, not (as the King of kings) *in* his ambassador. The Son is the last and highest manifestation of God (Matt. 21:34, 37); not merely a measure, as in the prophets, but the fulness of the Spirit of God dwelling in Him bodily (John 1:16; 3:34; Col. 2:9). Thus he answers the Jewish objection drawn from their prophets. Jesus is the end of all prophecy (Rev. 19:10), and of the law of Moses (John 1:17; 5:46). **2. in these last days**—In the oldest MSS. the *Greek* is, "At the last part of these days." The Rabbins divided the whole of time into "this age," or "world," and "the age to come" (ch. 2:5; 6:5). The days of Messiah were the transition period or "last part of these days" (in contrast to "in times past"), the close of the existing dispensation, and beginning of the final dispensation of which Christ's second coming shall be the crowning consummation. **by** *his* **Son**—Greek, "IN (His) Son" (John 14:10). The true "Prophet" of God. "His majesty is set forth: (1) *Absolutely* by the very name 'Son,' and by three glorious predicates, 'whom He hath appointed,' 'by whom He made the worlds,' 'who sat down on the right hand of the Majesty on high;' thus His course is described from the beginning of all things till he reached the goal (vss. 2, 3). (2) *Relatively,* in comparison with the angels, vs. 4; the *confirmation* of this follows, and the very name 'Son' is proved at vs. 5; the 'heirship,' vss. 6-9; the 'making the worlds,' vss. 10-12; the 'sitting at the right hand' of God, vss. 13, 14." His being made *heir* follows His *sonship,* and preceded His *making the worlds* (Prov. 8:22, 23; Eph. 3:11). As *the first begotten,* He is heir of the universe (vs. 6), which He made instrumentally, ch. 11:3, where "by the Word of God" answers to "by whom" (the Son of God) here (John 1:3). Christ was "appointed" (in God's eternal counsel) to creation as an office; and the universe so created was assigned to Him as a kingdom. He is "heir of all things" by right of creation, and especially by right of redemption. The promise to Abraham that he should be heir of the world had its fulfilment, and will have it still more fully, in Christ (Rom. 4:13; Gal. 3:16; 4:7). **worlds**—the inferior and the superior worlds (Col. 1:16). Lit., "ages" with all things and persons belonging to them; the universe, including all space and ages of time, and all material and spiritual existences. The *Greek* implies, He not only appointed His Son heir of all things before creation, but *He also* (better than "also He") made by Him the worlds. **3. Who being**—by pre-existent and essential being. **brightness of his glory**—Greek, the

effulgence of His glory. "Light of (from) light" [NICENE *Creed*]. "Who is so senseless as to doubt concerning the eternal being of the Son? For when has one seen light without effulgence?" [ATHANASIUS *against* ARIUS, *Orat.* 2]. "The sun is never seen without effulgence, nor the Father without the Son" [THEOPHYLACT]. It is *because* He is the brightness, etc., and *because* He upholds, etc., that He *sat down on the right hand,* etc. It was a return to His divine glory (John 6:62; 17:5; cf. *Wisd.* 7:25, 26, where similar things are said of wisdom). **express image** —"impress." But veiled in the flesh.

> The Sun of God in glory beams
> Too bright for us to scan;
> But we can face the light that streams
> For the mild Son of man. (II Cor. 3:18)

of his person—Greek, "of His substantial essence"; *hypostasis.* **upholding all things**—Greek, "*the* universe." Cf. Colossians 1:15, 17, 20, which enumerates the three facts in the same order as here. **by the word**—Therefore the Son of God is a Person; for He has the word [BENGEL]. *His* word is *God's* word (ch. 11:3). **of his power**—"The word" is the utterance which comes from His (the Son's) power, and gives expression to it. **by himself**—omitted in the oldest MSS. **purged**—Greek, "*made purification* of . . . sins," viz., in His atonement, which graciously covers the guilt of sin. "Our" is omitted in the oldest MSS. Sin was the great *uncleanness* in God's sight, of which He has effected the purgation by His sacrifice [ALFORD]. Our nature, as guilt-laden, could not, without our great High Priest's blood of atonement sprinkling the heavenly mercy seat, come into immediate contact with God. EBRARD says, "The mediation between man and God, who was present in the Most Holy Place, was revealed in three forms: (1) In sacrifices [typical propitiations for guilt]; (2) In the priesthood [the agents of those sacrifices]; (3) In the Levitical laws of purity [Levitical purity being attained by sacrifice positively, by avoidance of Levitical pollution negatively, the people being thus enabled to come into the presence of God without dying, Deuteronomy 5:26]" (Lev. 16). **sat down on the right hand of the Majesty on high**—fulfilling Psalm 110:1. This sitting of the Son at God's right hand was by the act of the Father (ch. 8:1; Eph. 1:20); it is never used of His pre-existing state coequal with the Father, but always of His exalted state as Son of man after His sufferings, and as Mediator for man in the presence of God (Rom. 8:34): a relation towards God and us about to come to an end when its object has been accomplished (I Cor. 15:28). **4. Being made . . . better**—by His exaltation by the Father (vss. 3, 13): in contrast to His being "made lower than the angels" (ch. 2:9). "Better," i.e., *superior* to. As "being" (vs. 3) expresses His essential being so "being made" (ch. 7:26) marks what He became in His assumed manhood (Phil. 2:6-9). Paul shows that His humbled form (at which the Jews might stumble) is no objection to His divine Messiahship. As the law was given by the ministration of angels and Moses, it was inferior to the Gospel given by the divine Son, who both is (vss. 4-14) as God, and has been made, as the exalted Son of man (ch. 2:5-18), much better than the angels. The manifestations of God by angels (and even by the angel of the covenant) at different times in the Old Testament, did not bring man and God into personal union, as the manifestation of God in human flesh does. **by inheritance obtained**—He always had the *thing* itself, viz., *Sonship;* but He "obtained by inheritance," according to the promise of the Father, *the name* "Son," whereby He is made known to men and angels. He is "the Son of God" is a sense far exalted above that in which angels are called "sons of God" (Job 1:6; 38:7). "The fulness of the glory of the peculiar name 'the Son of God,' is unattainable by human speech or thought. All appellations are but fragments of its glory—beams united in it as in a central sun. Revelation 19:12. *A name that no man knew but He Himself.*" **5. For**—substantiating His having "obtained a more excellent name than the angels." **unto which**—A frequent argument in this Epistle is derived from *the silence of Scripture* (vs. 13; ch. 2:16; 7:3, 14) [BENGEL]. **this day have I begotten thee**–(Ps. 2:7). Fulfilled at the resurrection of Jesus, whereby the Father "declared," i.e., made manifest His divine Sonship, heretofore veiled by His humiliation (Acts 13:33; Rom. 1:4). Christ has a fourfold right to the title "Son of God"; (1) By *generation,* as begotten of God; (2) By *commission,* as sent by God; (3) By *resurrection,* as "the first-begotten of the dead" (cf. Luke 20:36; Rom. 1:4; Rev. 1:5); (4) By *actual possession,* as heir of all [BISHOP PEARSON]. The Psalm here quoted applied primarily in a less full sense to Solomon, of whom God promised by Nathan to David, "I will be his father and he shall be my son." But as the whole theocracy was of Messianic import, the triumph of David over Hadadezer and neighboring kings (II Sam. 8; Psalm 2:2, 3, 9-12) is a type of God's ultimately subduing all enemies under His Son, whom He sets (*Hebrew,* "anointed," Ps. 2:6) on His "holy hill of Zion," as King of the Jews and of the whole earth, the antitype to Solomon, son of David. The "I" in *Greek* is emphatic; *I* the Everlasting Father have begotten Thee this day, i.e., on this day, the day of Thy being manifested as My Son, "the first-*begotten* of the dead" (Col. 1:18; Rev. 1:5), when Thou hast ransomed and opened heaven to Thy people. He had been always Son, but now first was manifested as such in His once humbled, now exalted manhood united to His Godhead. ALFORD refers "this day" to the *eternal* generation of the Son: the day in which the Son was begotten by the Father is an everlasting *today:* there never was a yesterday or past time to Him, nor a tomorrow or future time: "Nothing there is to come, and nothing past, but an eternal NOW doth ever last" (Prov. 30:4; John 10:30, 38; 16:28; 17:8). The communication of the divine essence in its fulness, involves eternal generation; for the divine essence has no beginning. But the context refers to a definite point of time, viz., that of His having entered on the *inheritance* (vs. 4). The "bringing the firstbegotten into the world" (vs. 6), is not subsequent, as ALFORD thinks, to vs. 5, but anterior to it (cf. Acts 2:30-35). **6. And**–*Greek,* "But." Not only this proves His superiority, BUT a more decisive proof is Psalm 97:7, which shows that not only at His resurrection, but also in prospect of His being *brought into the world* (cf. ch. 9:11; 10:5) as man, in His incarnation, nativity (Luke 2:9-14), temptation (Matt. 4:10, 11), resurrection (Matt. 28:2), and future second advent in glory, angels were designed by God to be subject to Him. Cf. I Tim. 3:16, "seen of angels"; God manifesting Messiah as one to be gazed at with adoring love by heavenly intelligences (Eph. 3:10; II Thess. 1:9, 10; I Pet. 3:22). The fullest realization of His Lordship shall be at His second coming (Ps. 97:7; I Cor. 15:24, 25; Phil. 2:9). "Worship Him all ye gods" ("gods," i.e., *exalted beings,* as

angels), refers to *God;* but it was universally admitted among the Hebrews that God would dwell, in a peculiar sense, in Messiah (so as to be in the Talmud phrase, "capable of being pointed to with the finger"); and so what was said of God was true of, and to be fulfilled in, Messiah. KIMCHI says that Psalms 93-101 contain in them the mystery of Messiah. God ruled the theocracy in and through Him. **the world**–subject to Christ (ch. 2:5). As "the first-begotten" He has the rights of *primogeniture* (Rom. 8:29); Col. 1:15, 16, 18). In Deuteronomy 32:43, the LXX has, "Let all the angels of God worship Him," words not now found in the Hebrew. This passage of the LXX may have been in Paul's mind as to the *form,* but the *substance* is taken from Psalm 97:7. The type David, in the Psalm 89:27 (quoted in vs. 5), is called "God's *first-born,* higher than the *kings* of the earth"; so the antitypical first-begotten, the son of David, is to be worshipped by all inferior *lords,* such as *angels* ("gods," Ps. 97:7); for He is "King of kings and Lord of lords" (Rev. 19:16). In the *Greek,* "again" is transposed; but this does not oblige us, as ALFORD thinks, to translate, "when He *again shall have introduced....*" viz., at Christ's second coming; for there is no previous mention of a *first* bringing in; and "again" is often used in quotations, not to be joined with the verb, but parenthetically ("that I may again quote Scripture"). *English Version* is correct (cf. Matt. 5:33; *Greek,* John 12:39). **7. of**—The *Greek* is rather, "In reference TO the angels." **spirits**–or "winds": Who employeth His angels as the winds, His ministers as the lightnings; or, He maketh His angelic ministers the directing powers of winds and flames, when these latter are required to perform His will. "Commissions them to assume the agency or form of flames for His purposes" [ALFORD]. *English Version,* "maketh His angels *spirits,*" means, He maketh them of a subtle, incorporeal nature, swift as the wind. So Psalm 18:10, "a *cherub . . .* the wings of the *wind.*" Verse 14, "ministering *spirits,*" favors *English Version* here. As "spirits" implies the windlike velocity and subtle nature of the *cherubim,* so "flame of fire" expresses the burning devotion and intense all-consuming zeal of the adoring *seraphim* (meaning "burning"), Isaiah 6:1. The translation, "maketh winds His messengers, and a flame of fire His *ministers* (!)," is plainly wrong. In the Psalm 104:3, 4, the subject in each clause comes first, and the attribute predicated of it second; so the *Greek* article here marks "angels" and "ministers" as the *subjects,* and "winds" and "flame of fire," *predicates, Schemoth Rabba* says, "God is called God of Zebaoth (the heavenly hosts), because He does what He pleases with His angels. When He pleases, He makes them to sit (Judg. 6:11); at other times to stand (Isa. 6:2); at times to resemble women (Zech. 5:9); at other times to resemble men (Gen. 18:2); at times He makes them 'spirits'; at times, fire." "Maketh" implies that, however exalted, they are but creatures, whereas the Son is the Creator (vs. 10): not *begotten from everlasting,* nor to be *worshipped,* as the Son (Rev. 14:7; 22:8, 9). **8. O God**—the *Greek* has the article to mark emphasis (Ps. 45:6, 7). **for ever ... righteousness**–*Everlasting duration* and *righteousness* go together (Ps. 45:2; 89:14). **a sceptre of righteousness**—lit., "a rod of rectitude," or "straightforwardness." The oldest MSS. prefix "and" (cf. Esther 4:11). **9. iniquity**–"unrighteousness." Some oldest MSS. read, "lawlessness." **therefore**—because God loves righteousness and hates iniquity. **God ... thy God**–JEROME, AUGUS-

TINE, and others translate Psalm 45:7, "O God, Thy God, hath anointed thee," whereby Christ is addressed as God. This is probably the true translation of the *Hebrew* there, and also of the *Greek* of Hebrews here; for it is likely the Son is addressed, "O God," as in vs. 8. The *anointing* here meant is not that at His baptism, when He solemnly entered on His ministry for us; but that with the "oil of gladness," or "exulting joy" (which denotes a *triumph,* and follows as the consequence of His manifested *love of righteousness* and *hatred of iniquity*), wherewith, after His triumphant completion of His work, He has been anointed by the Father above His fellows (not only above us, His fellow men, the adopted members of God's family. whom "He is not ashamed to call His brethren," but above the angels, fellow partakers in part with Him, though infinitely His inferiors, in the glories, holiness, and joys of heaven; "sons of God," and angel "messengers," though subordinate to the divine Angel—"Messenger of the covenant"). Thus He is antitype to Solomon, "chosen of all David's many sons to sit upon the throne of the kingdom of the Lord over Israel," even as His father David was chosen before all the house of his father's sons. The image is drawn from the custom of anointing guests at feasts (Ps. 23:5); or rather of anointing kings: not until His ascension did He assume *the kingdom* as Son of man. A fuller accomplishment is yet to be, when He shall be VISIBLY the anointed King over the whole earth (set by the Father) on His holy hill of Zion, Psalm 2:6, 8. So David, His type, was first anointed at Bethlehem (I Sam. 16: 13; Ps. 89:20); and yet again at Hebron, first over Judah (II Sam. 2:4), then over all Israel (II Sam. 5:3); not till the death of Saul did he enter on his actual kingdom; as it was not till after Christ's death that the Father set Him at His right hand far above all principalities (Eph. 1:20, 21). The 45th Psalm in its first meaning was addressed to Solomon; but the Holy Spirit inspired the writer to use language which in its fulness can only apply to the antitypical Solomon, the true Royal Head of the theocracy. **10. And**—In another passage (Ps. 102:25-27) He says. **in the beginning**—*English Version,* Psalm 102:25, "of old": *Hebrew,* "before," "aforetime." LXX, "in the beginning" (as in Gen. 1:1) answers by contrast to *the end* implied in "They shall perish. . . ." The *Greek* order here (not in the LXX) is, "Thou in the beginning, O Lord," which throws the "Lord" into emphasis. "Christ is preached even in passages where many might contend that the Father was principally intended" [BENGEL]. **laid the foundation of**—*"firmly* founded" is included in the idea of the *Greek.* **heavens**—plural: not merely one, but manifold, and including various orders of heavenly intelligences (Eph. 4:10). **works of thine hands**—the heavens, as a woven veil or curtain spread out. **11. They**—The earth and the heavens in their present state and form "shall perish" (ch. 12:26, 27; II Pet. 3:13). "Perish" does not mean *annihilation; just* as it did not mean so in the case of "the world that being overflowed with water, *perished*" under Noah (II Pet. 3:6). The covenant of the possession of the earth was renewed with Noah and his seed on the renovated earth. So it shall be after the perishing by fire (II Pet. 3:12, 13). **remainest**—*through* (so the *Greek*) all changes. **as . . . a garment**—(Isa. 51:6). **12. vesture**—*Greek,* "an enwrapping cloak." **fold them up** —So the LXX, Psalm 102:26; but the *Hebrew,* "*change* them." The Spirit, by Paul, treats the *Hebrew* of the Old Testament, with independence of handling, presenting the divine truth in various aspects; sometimes as here sanctioning the LXX (cf. Isa. 34:4; Rev. 6:14); sometimes the *Hebrew;* sometimes varying from both. **changed**—as one lays aside a garment to put on another. **thou art the same**—(Isa. 46:4; Mal. 3:6). The same in nature, therefore in covenant faithfulness to Thy people. **shall not fail**—*Hebrew,* "shall not end." Israel, in the Babylonian captivity, in Psalm 102, casts her hopes of deliverance on Messiah, the unchanging covenant God of Israel. **13.** Quotation from Psalm 110:1. The image is taken from the custom of conquerors putting the feet on the necks of the conquered (Josh. 10:24, 25). **14. ministering spirits**—referring to vs. 7, "spirits . . . ministers." They are incorporeal *spirits,* as God is, but *ministering* to Him as inferiors. **sent forth**—present participle: "being sent forth *"continually,* as their regular service in all ages. **to minister**—*Greek,* "unto (i.e., 'for') ministry." **for them**—*Greek, "on account of* the." Angels are sent forth on *ministrations to God and Christ,* not primarily to men, though *for the good* of "those who are about to inherit salvation" (so the *Greek*): the elect, who believe, or shall believe, for whom all things, angels included, work together for good (Rom. 8:28). Angels' ministrations are not properly rendered to men, since the latter have no power of commanding them, though their ministrations to God are often directed to the good of men. So the superiority of the Son of God to angels is shown. They "all," how ever various their ranks, "minister"; He is ministered to. They "*stand*" (Luke 1:19) before God, or are "*sent* forth" to execute the divine commands on behalf of them whom He pleases to save; He "*sits* on the right hand of the Majesty on high" (vss. 3, 13). He rules; they serve.

CHAPTER 2

VSS. 1-18. DANGER OF NEGLECTING SO GREAT SALVATION, FIRST SPOKEN BY CHRIST; TO WHOM, NOT TO ANGELS, THE NEW DISPENSATION WAS SUBJECTED; THOUGH HE WAS FOR A TIME HUMBLED BELOW THE ANGELS: THIS HUMILIATION TOOK PLACE BY DIVINE NECESSITY FOR OUR SALVATION. **1. Therefore**— Because Christ the Mediator of the new covenant is so far (ch. 1) above all angels, the mediators of the old covenant. **the more earnest**—*Greek,* "the more abundantly." **heard**—spoken by God (ch. 1:1); and by the Lord (vs. 3). **let them slip**—lit., "flow past them" (ch. 4:1). **2.** (Cf. vs. 3.) Argument a fortiori. **spoken by angels**—the Mosaic law spoken by the ministration of angels (Deut. 33:2; Ps. 68:17; Acts 7:53; Gal. 3:19). When it is said, Exodus 20:1, "God spake," it is meant He spake by angels as His mouthpiece, or at least angels repeating in unison with His voice the words of the Decalogue; whereas the Gospel was first spoken by the Lord alone. **was steadfast**—*Greek, "was made* steadfast," or "confirmed": was enforced by penalties on those violating it. **transgression**—by doing evil; lit., *overstepping* its bounds: a positive violation of it. **disobedience**—by neglecting to do good: a negative violation of it. **recompense**—(Deut. 32:35). **3. we** —who have received the message of salvation so clearly delivered to us (cf. ch. 12:25). **so great salvation**—embodied in Jesus, whose very name means "salvation," including not only deliverance from foes and from death, and the grant of temporal blessings (which the law promised to the obedient), but also grace of the Spirit, forgiveness of sins, and the promise of heaven, glory, and eternal life (vs. 10). **which**—"*inasmuch as it is a* salvation *which* began. . . ." **spoken by the Lord**—as the instrument of proclaiming it. Not as the law, spoken by the instrumentality of angels (vs. 2). Both law and Gospel came from God; the difference here referred to lay in *the instrumentality* by which each respectively was promulgated (cf. vs. 5). Angels recognize Him as "the Lord" (Matt. 28:6; Luke 2:11). **confirmed unto us**—not by penalties, as the law was *confirmed*, but by spiritual gifts (vs. 4). **by them that heard** *him*—(Cf. Luke 1: 2). Though Paul had a special and independent revelation of Christ (Gal. 1:16, 17, 19), yet he classes himself with those Jews whom he addresses, "unto us"; for like them in many particulars (e.g., the agony in Gethsemane, ch. 5:7), he was dependent for autoptic information on the twelve apostles. So the *discourses* of Jesus, e.g., the Sermon on the Mount, and the first proclamation of the Gospel kingdom by the Lord (Matt. 4:17), he could only know by the report of the Twelve: so the saying, "It is more blessed to give than to receive" (Acts 20:35). Paul mentions what they had *heard*, rather than what they had *seen*, conformably with what he began with, ch. 1:1, 2, "spake . . . spoken." Appropriately also in his Epistles to Gentiles, he dwells on his independent call to the apostleship of the Gentiles; in his Epistle to the Hebrews, he appeals to the apostles who had been long with the Lord (cf. Acts 1:21; 10:41): so in his sermon to the Jews in Antioch of Pisidia (Acts 13:31); and "he only appeals to the testimony of these apostles in a general way, in order that he may bring the Hebrews to the Lord alone" [BENGEL], not to become partisans of particular apostles, as Peter, the apostle of the circumcision, and James, the bishop of Jerusalem. This verse implies that the Hebrews of the *churches of Palestine and Syria* (or those of them dispersed in Asia Minor [BENGEL], I Pet. 1:1, or in Alexandria) were primarily addressed in this Epistle; for of none so well could it be said, the Gospel was confirmed to them by the immediate hearers of the Lord: the past tense, "was confirmed," implies some little time had elapsed since this testification by eyewitnesses. **4. them**—rather, "God also [as well as Christ, vs. 3] bearing witness to *it*" . . . "joining in attestation of it." **signs and wonders**—performed by Christ and His apostles. "Signs" and miracles, or other facts regarded as *proofs* of a divine mission; "wonders" are miracles viewed as prodigies, causing *astonishment* (Acts 2:22, 33); "powers" are miracles viewed as evidences of superhuman *power*. **divers miracles**—Greek, "varied (miraculous) *powers*" (II Cor. 12:12) granted to the apostles after the ascension. **gifts . . .**—Greek, "distributions." The gift of the Holy Spirit was given to Christ without measure (John 3:34), but to us it is distributed in various measures and operations (Rom. 12:3, 6, etc.; I Cor. 12:4-11). **according to his own will**—God's free and sovereign will, assigning one gift of the Spirit to one, another to another (Acts 5:32; Eph. 1:5). **5. For**—confirming the assertion, vss. 2, 3, that the new covenant was spoken by One higher than the mediators of the old covenant, viz., angels. Translate in the *Greek* order, to bring out the proper emphasis, "Not the angels hath He. . . . the **world to come**—implying, He *has* subjected to angels *the existing world,* the Old Testament dispensation (then still partly existing as to its framework), vs. 2, the political kingdom of the earth (Dan. 4:13; 10:13, 20, 21; 12:1), and the natural elements (Rev. 9:11; 16:4), and even individuals (Matt. 18:10). "The

world to come" is the new dispensation brought in by Christ, beginning in grace here, to be completed in glory hereafter. It is called "to come," or "about to be," as at the time of its being subjected to Christ by the divine decree, it was as yet a thing of the future, and is still so to us, in respect to its full consummation. In respect to the *subjecting* of all things to Christ in fulfilment of Psalm 8, the realization is still "to come." Regarded from the Old Testament standpoint, which looks prophetically forward to the New Testament (and the Jewish priesthood and Old Testament ritual were in force then when Paul wrote, and continued till their forcible abrogation by the destruction of Jerusalem), it is "the world to come"; Paul, as addressing Jews, appropriately calls it so, according to their conventional way of viewing it. We, like them, still pray, "Thy kingdom come"; for its *manifestation* in glory is yet future. "This world" is used in contrast to express the present fallen condition of the world (Eph. 2:2). Believers belong not to this present world-course, but by faith rise in spirit to "the world to come," making it a present, though internal, reality. Still, in the present world, natural and social, angels are mediately rulers under God in some sense: not so in the coming world: man in it, and the Son of man, man's Head, are to be supreme. Hence greater reverence was paid to angels by men in the Old Testament than is permitted in the New Testament. For man's nature is exalted in Christ now, so that angels are our "fellow servants" (Rev. 22:9). In their ministrations they stand on a different footing from that on which they stood towards us in the Old Testament. We are "brethren" of Christ in a nearness not enjoyed even by angels (vss. 10-12, 16). **6. But**—It is not to angels the Gospel kingdom is subject, BUT. . . . **one. . . testified**—the usual way of quoting Scripture to readers familiar with it. Psalm 8:5-7 praises Jehovah for exalting MAN, so as to subject all the works of God on earth to him: this dignity having been lost by the first Adam, is realized only in Christ the Son of man, the Representative Man and Head of our redeemed race. Thus Paul proves that it is to MAN, not to *angels,* that God has subjected the "world to come." In vss. 6-8, MAN is spoken of *in general* ("him . . . him . . . his"); then at vs. 9, first JESUS is introduced as fulfilling, as man, all the conditions of the prophecy, and passing through death Himself; and so consequently bringing us men, His "brethren," to "glory and honor." **What . . .**—How insignificant in himself, yet how exalted by God's grace! (Cf. Ps. 144:3). The *Hebrew, Enosh* and *Ben-Adam,* express "man" and "Son of man" in his weakness: "Son of man" is here used of *any* and *every child of man:* unlike, seemingly, the lord of creation, such as he was originally (Gen. 1 and 2), and such as he is designed to be (Ps. 8), and such as he actually is by title and shall hereafter more fully be in the person of, and in union with, Jesus, pre-eminently the Son of man (vs. 9). **art mindful** —as of one absent. **visitest**—*lookest after* him, as one present. **7. a little**—not as BENGEL, "a little *time.*" **than the angels**—Hebrew, "than God," *Elohim,* i.e., the abstract qualities of God, such as *angels* possess in an inferior form; viz., heavenly, spiritual, incorporeal natures. Man, in his original creation, was set next beneath them. So the man Jesus, though Lord of angels, when He emptied Himself of the externals of His Divinity (*Note,* Phil. 2:6, 7), was in His human nature "a little lower than the angels"; though this is not the primary reference here, but *man* in general. **crownedst him**

with glory and honour—as the appointed kingly vicegerent of God over this earth (Gen. 1 and 2). **and didst set him over the works of thy hands**—omitted in some of the oldest MSS.; but read by others and by oldest versions: so Psalm 8:6, "Thou madest him to have dominion over the works of thy hands." **8.** (I Cor. 15:27.) **For in that**—i.e., "For in that" *God saith in the 8th Psalm,* "He put *the* all things (so the *Greek, the* all things just mentioned) in subjection under him (man), He left nothing. . . . As no limitation occurs in the sacred writing, the "all things" must include heavenly, as well as earthly things (cf. I Cor. 3:21, 22). **But now**—As things now are, we see not yet *the* all things put under man. **9. But**—We see not *man* as yet exercising lordship over all things, "*but rather,* Him who was made a little lower than the angels (cf. Luke 22: 43), we behold (*by faith:* a different *Greek* verb from that for 'we *see,*' vs. 8, which expresses the impression which our eyes *passively* receive from objects around us; whereas, 'we behold,' or 'look at,' implies the *direction* and *intention* of one *deliberately* regarding something which he tries to see: so ch. 3:19; 10:25, *Greek*), viz., Jesus, on account of His suffering of death, crowned. . . ." He is already crowned, though unseen by us, save by faith; hereafter all things shall be subjected to Him visibly and fully. The ground of His exaltation is "on account of His having suffered death" (vs. 10; Phil. 2:8, 9). **that he by the grace of God**—(Titus 2:11; 3:4). The reading of ORIGEN, "That He *without God*" *(laying aside His Divinity;* or, for every being *save God;* or perhaps alluding to His having been temporarily "forsaken," as the Sin-bearer, by the Father on the cross), is not supported by the MSS. The "that . . ." is connected with "crowned with glory . . ." thus: His exaltation after sufferings is the *perfecting* or consummation of His work (vs. 10) for us: without it His death would have been ineffectual; with it, and from it, flows the result *that His tasting of death is available for* (in behalf of, for the good of) *every man.* He is crowned as the Head in heaven of our common humanity, presenting His blood as the all-prevailing plea for us. This coronation above makes His death applicable for *every* individual *man* (observe the singular; not merely "for all men"), ch. 4:14; 9:24; I John 2:2. "Taste death," implies His personal experimental undergoing of death: death of the body, and death (spiritually) of the soul, in His being forsaken of the Father. "As a physician first tastes his medicines to encourage his sick patient to take them, so Christ, when all men feared death, in order to persuade them to be bold in meeting it, tasted it Himself, though He had no need" [CHRYSOSTOM] (vss. 14, 15). **10. For**—giving a reason why "the grace of God" required that Jesus "should taste death." **it became him**—The whole plan was [not only not derogatory to, but] highly *becoming* God, though unbelief considers it a *disgrace* [BENGEL]. An answer to the Jews, and Hebrew Christians, whosoever, through impatience at the delay in the promised advent of Christ's glory, were in danger of apostasy, stumbling at Christ *crucified.* The Jerusalem Christians especially were liable to this danger. This scheme of redemption was altogether such a one as harmonizes with the love, justice, and wisdom of God. **for whom**—God the Father (Rom. 11:36; I Cor. 8:6; Rev. 4:11). In Colossians 1:16 the same is said of Christ. **all things**—*Greek,* "*the* universe of things," "*the* all things." He uses for "God," the periphrasis, "Him for whom . . . by whom are all things," to mark the becomingness

of Christ's suffering as the way to His being "perfected" as "Captain of our salvation," seeing that His is the way that pleased Him whose will and whose glory are *the end* of all things, and by whose *operation* all things exist. **in bringing**—The *Greek* is past, "having brought as He did," viz., *in His electing purpose* (cf. "ye *are* sons," viz., in His purpose, Gal. 4:6; Eph. 1:4), a purpose which is accomplished in Jesus being "perfected through sufferings." **many**—(Matt. 20:28)." The Church" (vs. 12), "the general assembly" (ch. 12:23). **sons**—no longer *children* as under the Old Testament law, but *sons* by adoption. **unto glory**—to share Christ's "glory" (vs. 9; cf. 7; John 17:10, 22, 24; Rom. 8: 21). Sonship, holiness (vs. 11), and glory, are inseparably joined. "Suffering," "salvation," and "glory," in Paul's writings, often go together (II Tim. 2:10). *Salvation* presupposes *destruction,* deliverance from which for us required Christ's "sufferings." **to make . . . perfect**—"to consummate"; to bring to consummated glory through sufferings, as the appointed avenue to it. "He who suffers for another, not only benefits him, but becomes himself the brighter and more perfect" [CHRYSOSTOM]. Bringing to the end of troubles, and to the *goal* full of glory: a metaphor from the contests in the public games. Cf. "It is finished," Luke 24:26; John 19:30. I prefer, with CALVIN, understanding, "to make perfect as a completed *sacrifice": legal* and *official,* not moral, *perfection* is meant: "to *consecrate*" (so the same *Greek* is translated ch. 7:28; cf. *Margin*) by the finished expiation of His death, as our perfect High Priest, and so our "Captain of salvation" (Luke 13:32). This agrees with vs. 11, "He that sanctifieth," i.e., consecrates them by Himself being made a consecrated offering for them. So ch. 10:14, 29; John 17:19: by the perfecting of His consecration for them in His death, He perfects their consecration, and so throws open access to glory (ch. 10:19-21; ch. 5:9; 9:9, accord with this sense). **captain of . . .**—lit., *Prince-leader:* as Joshua, not Moses, led the people into the Holy Land, so will our Joshua, or Jesus, lead us into the heavenly inheritance (Acts 13:39). The same *Greek* is in ch. 12:2, "*Author* of our faith." Acts 3:15, "*Prince* of life" (5:31). Preceding others by His example, as well as the originator of our salvation. **11. he that sanctifieth** —Christ who once for all consecrates His people to God (Jude 1, bringing them nigh to Him as the consequence) and everlasting glory, by having consecrated Himself for them in His being made "perfect (as their expiatory sacrifice) through sufferings" (vs. 10; ch. 10:10, 14, 29; John 17:17, 19). God in His electing love, by Christ's finished work, *perfectly* sanctifies them to God's service and to heaven *once for all:* then they are *progressively* sanctified by the transforming Spirit "Sanctification is glory working in embryo; glory is sanctification come to the birth, and manifested" [ALFORD]. **they who are sanctified**—*Greek,* "they that are being sanctified" (cf. the use of "sanctified," I Cor. 7:14). **of one**—Father, God: not in the sense wherein He is Father of *all* beings, as angels; for these are excluded by the argument (vs. 16); but as He is Father of His *spiritual human* sons, Christ the Head and elder Brother, and His believing people, the members of the body and family. Thus, this and the following verses are meant to justify his having said, "many *sons*" (vs. 10). "Of one" is not "of one father *Adam,*" or "*Abraham,*" as BENGEL and others suppose. For the Saviour's participation in the *lowness* of our humanity is not mentioned till vs.

14, and then as a consequence of what precedes. Moreover, "Sons *of God"* is, in Scripture usage, the dignity obtained by our union with Christ; and our *brotherhood* with Him flows from *God* being *His* and *our* Father. Christ's Sonship (by generation) in relation to God is reflected in the sonship (by adoption) of His brethren. **he is not ashamed**—though being the Son *of God,* since they have now by adoption obtained a like dignity, so that His majesty is not compromised by brotherhood with them (cf. ch. 11:16). It is a striking feature in Christianity that it unites such amazing contrasts as "our brother and our God" [THOLUCK]. "God makes of sons of men sons of God, because God hath made of the Son of God the Son of man" [ST. AUGUSTINE on Psalm 2]. **12.** (Psalm 22:22). Messiah declares the name of the Father, not known fully as Christ's Father, and therefore *their* Father, till after His crucifixion (John 20:17), among His brethren ("the Church," i.e., the congregation), that they in turn may praise Him (Ps. 22:23). At vs. 22, the 22d Psalm, which begins with Christ's cry, "My God, my God, why hast thou forsaken me?" and details minutely His sorrows, passes from Christ's sufferings to His triumph, prefigured by the same in the experience of David. **will I sing**—as leader of the choir (Ps. 8:2). **13. I will put my trust in him**—from the LXX, Isaiah 8:17, which immediately precedes the next quotation, "Behold, I and the children. . . ." The only objection is the following words, "and again," usually introduce a *new* quotation, whereas these two are parts of one and the same passage. However, this objection is not valid, as the two clauses express distinct ideas; "I will put my trust in Him" expresses His *filial* confidence in God as His Father, to whom He flees from His sufferings, and is not disappointed; which His believing brethren imitate, *trusting* solely in the Father through Christ, and not in their own merits. "Christ exhibited this 'trust,' not for Himself, for He and the Father are one, but for His own people" (vs. 16). Each fresh aid given Him assured Him, as it does them, of aid for the future, until the complete victory was obtained over death and hell Phil. 1:16 [BENGEL]. **Behold I and the children . . .** —(Isa. 8:18). "Sons" (vs. 10), "brethren" (vs. 12), and "children," imply His right and property in them from everlasting. He speaks of them as "children" of God, though not yet in being, yet considered as such in His *purpose,* and presents them before God the Father, who has given Him them, to be glorified with Himself. Isaiah (meaning "salvation of Jehovah") typically represented Messiah, who is at once Father and Son, Isaiah and Immanuel (Isa. 9:6). He expresses his resolve to rely, he and his children, not like Ahaz and the Jews on the Assyrian king, against the confederacy of Pekah of Israel, and Rezin of Syria, but on Jehovah; and then foretells the deliverance of Judah by God, in language which finds its antitypical full realization only in the far greater deliverance wrought by Messiah. Christ, the antitypical Prophet, similarly, instead of the human confidences of His age, Himself, and with Him GOD THE FATHER'S *children* (who are therefore *His* children, and so antitypical to *Isaiah's* children, though here regarded as His "brethren," cf. Isaiah 9:6; "Father" and "His *seed,"* 53:10) led by Him, trust wholly in God for salvation. The official words and acts of all the prophets find their antitype in the Great Prophet (Rev. 19:10), just as His kingly office is antitypical to that of the theocratic kings; and His priestly office to the types and rites of the Aaronic priesthood.

14. He who has thus been shown to be the "Captain (*Greek,* 'Leader') of salvation" to the "many sons," by *trusting* and *suffering* like them, must therefore become *man* like them, in order that His death may be efficacious for them [ALFORD]. **the children**—before mentioned (vs. 13); those existing in His eternal purpose, though not in actual being. **are partakers of**—lit., "have [in His purpose] been partakers" all in common. **flesh and blood**—*Greek* oldest MSS. have "blood and flesh." The inner and more important element, the *blood,* as the more immediate vehicle of the soul, stands before the more palpable element, the flesh; also, with reference to *Christ's blood-shedding* with a view to which He entered into community with our *corporeal* life. "The life of the *flesh* is in the *blood*; it is the blood that maketh an atonement for the soul" (Lev. 17:11, 14). **also**—*Greek,* "in a *somewhat* similar manner"; not *altogether* in a like manner. For He, unlike them, was conceived and born not in sin (ch. 4:15). But mainly "in like manner"; not in mere *semblance* of a body, as the Docetæ heretics taught. **took part of**—participated in. The forfeited inheritance (according to Jewish law) was ransomed by the nearest of kin; so Jesus became our nearest of kin by His assumed humanity, in order to be our Redeemer. **that through death**—which He could not have undergone as God but only by becoming man. Not by Almighty power but *"by His death"* (so the *Greek*) He overcame death. "Jesus suffering death overcame; Satan wielding death succumbed" [BENGEL]. As David cut off the head of Goliath with the giant's own sword wherewith the latter was wont to win his victories. Coming to redeem mankind, Christ made Himself a sort of hook to destroy the devil; for in Him there was His humanity to attract the devourer to Him, His divinity to pierce him, apparent weakness to provoke, hidden power to transfix the hungry ravisher. The Latin epigram says, *Mors mortis morti mortem nisi morte tulisset, Æternæ vitæ janua clausa foret.* "Had not death by death borne to death the death of Death, the gate of eternal life would have been closed." **destroy**—lit., "render powerless"; deprive of all power to hurt His people. "That thou mightest still the enemy and avenger" (Psalm 8:2). The same *Greek* verb is used in II Timothy 1:10, "abolished death." There is no more death for believers. Christ plants in them an undying seed, the germ of heavenly immortality, though believers have to pass through natural death. **power**—Satan is "strong" (Matt. 12:29). **of death**—implying that *death* itself is a *power* which, though originally foreign to human nature, now reigns over it (Rom. 5:12; 6:9). The power which death has Satan wields. The author of sin is the author of its consequences. Cf. "power of the enemy" (Luke 10:19). Satan has acquired over man (by God's law, Gen. 2:17; Rom. 6:23) the power of death by man's sin, death being the executioner of sin, and man being Satan's *"lawful* captive." Jesus, by dying, has made the dying His own (Rom. 14:9), and has taken the prey from the mighty. Death's power was manifest; he who wielded that power, lurking beneath it, is here expressed, viz., Satan. Wisdom 2:24, "By the envy of the devil, death entered into the world." **15. fear of death**—even before they had experienced its actual *power.* **all their lifetime**—Such a life can hardly be called life. **subject to bondage**—lit., "subjects *of* bondage"; not merely *liable to* it, but *enthralled in* it (cf. Rom. 8:15; Gal. 5:1). Contrast with this *bondage,* the *glory* of the "sons" (vs. 10). "Bondage" is defined by Aristotle, "The living not as one chooses"; "liberty," "the living as one chooses." Christ by delivering us from the curse of God against our sin, has taken from death all that made it formidable. Death, viewed apart from Christ, can only fill with horror, if the sinner dares to think. **16. For verily**—*Greek,* "For *as we all know*"; "For as you will doubtless grant." Paul probably alludes to Isaiah 41:8 Jeremiah 31:32, LXX, from which all *Jews* would know well that the fact here stated as to Messiah was what the prophets had led them to expect. **took not on him . . .**—rather, "It is not angels that He *is helping* (the present implies *duration*); but it is the seed of Abraham that He is *helping.*" The verb is lit., *to help by taking one by the hand,* as in ch. 8:9, "When I took them by the hand. . . ." Thus it answers to "succor," vs. 18, and "deliver," vs. 15. "Not angels," who have no flesh and blood, but "the children," who have "flesh and blood," He takes hold of to help by "Himself taking part of the same" (vs. 14). Whatever effect Christ's work may have on angels, He is not taking hold to help them by suffering in their nature to deliver them from death, as in our case. **seed of Abraham**—He views Christ's redemption (in compliment to the Hebrews whom he is addressing, and as enough for his present purpose) with reference to Abraham's seed, *the Jewish nation,* primarily; not that he excludes the Gentiles (vs. 9, "for every man"), who, when believers, are the seed of Abraham spiritually (cf. vs. 12; Ps. 22:22, 25, 27), but direct reference to them (such as is in Rom. 4:11, 12, 16; Gal. 3:7, 14, 28, 29) would be out of place in his present argument. It is the same argument for Jesus being the Christ which Matthew, writing his Gospel for the Hebrews, uses, tracing the genealogy of Jesus from Abraham, the father of the Jews, and the one to whom the promises were given, on which the Jews especially prided themselves (cf. Rom. 9:4, 5). **17. Wherefore**—*Greek,* "Whence." Found in *Paul's* speech, Acts 26:19. **in all things**—which are incidental to manhood, the being born, nourished, growing up, suffering. *Sin* is not, in the original constitution of man, a necessary attendant of manhood, so He had no sin. **it behooved him**—by moral necessity, considering what the justice and love of God required of Him as Mediator (cf. ch. 5:3), the office which He had voluntarily undertaken in order to "help" man (vs. 16). **his brethren**—(vs. 11)—"the seed of Abraham" (vs. 16), and so also the spiritual seed, His elect out of all mankind. **be . . .**—rather as *Greek,* "that He might *become* High Priest"; He was *called* so, when He was "made perfect by the things which He suffered" (vs. 10; ch. 5:8-10). He was actually *made* so, when He entered within the veil, from which last flows His ever continuing intercession as Priest for us. The death, as man, must first be, in order that the bringing in of the blood into the heavenly Holy Place might follow, in which consisted the expiation as High Priest. **merciful**—to "the *people*" deserving wrath by "sins." *Mercy* is a prime requisite in a priest, since his office is to help the wretched and raise the fallen: such *mercy* is most likely to be found in one who has a fellowfeeling with the afflicted, having been so once Himself (ch. 4:15); not that the Son of God needed to be taught by suffering to be merciful, but that in order to save us He needed to take our manhood with all its sorrows, thereby qualifying Himself, by experimental suffering with us, to be our sympathizing High Priest, and assuring us of His entire fellow-feeling with us in every sorrow. So in the main CALVIN remarks

here. **faithful**—true to God (ch. 3:5, 6) and to man (ch. 10:23) in the mediatorial office which He has undertaken. **high priest**—which Moses was not, though "faithful" (ch. 2). Nowhere, except in Psalm 110, Zechariah 6:13, and in this Epistle, is Christ expressly called a *priest.* In this Epistle alone His priesthood is professedly discussed; whence it is evident how necessary is this book of the New Testament. In Psalm 110, and Zechariah 6:13, there is added mention of the *kingdom* of Christ, which elsewhere is spoken of without the *priesthood,* and that frequently. On the cross, whereon as Priest He offered the sacrifice, He had the title "King" inscribed over Him [BENGEL]. **to make reconciliation for the sins**—rather as *Greek,* "to propitiate (in respect to) the sins"; "to expiate the sins." Strictly divine *justice* is "propitiated"; but God's *love* is as much from everlasting as His justice; therefore, lest Christ's sacrifice, or its typical forerunners, the legal sacrifices, should be thought to be antecedent to God's grace and love, neither are said in the Old or New Testament to have *propitiated* God; otherwise Christ's sacrifices might have been thought to have first induced God to love and pity man, instead of (as the fact really is) His love having *originated* Christ's sacrifice, whereby divine justice and divine love are harmonized. The sinner is brought by that sacrifice into God's favor, which by sin he had forfeited; hence his right prayer is, "God *be propitiated* (so the *Greek*) to me who am a sinner" (Luke 18:13). Sins bring death and "the fear of death" (vs. 15). He had no sin Himself, and "made reconciliation for the iniquity" of all others (Dan. 9:24). **of the people**—"the seed of Abraham" (vs. 16); the literal Israel first, and then (in the design of God), through Israel, the believing Gentiles, the spiritual Israel (I Pet. 2:10). **18. For**—explanation of how His being *made like His brethren in all things* has made Him *a merciful and faithful High Priest* for us (vs. 17). **in that**—rather as *Greek,* "wherein He suffered Himself; having been tempted, He is able to succor them *that are being tempted*" in the same temptation; and as "He was tempted (tried and afflicted) in *all* points," He is able (by the power of *sympathy*) to succor us in all possible temptations and trials incidental to man (ch. 4:16; 5:2). He is the antitypical Solomon, having for every grain of Abraham's seed (which were to be as the sand for number), "largeness of heart even as the sand that is on the seashore" (I Kings 4:29). "Not only as God He knows our trials, but also as man He knows them by experimental feeling."

CHAPTER 3

Vss. 1-19. THE SON OF GOD GREATER THAN MOSES, WHEREFORE UNBELIEF TOWARDS HIM WILL INCUR A HEAVIER PUNISHMENT THAN BEFELL UNBELIEVING ISRAEL IN THE WILDERNESS. As Moses especially was the prophet by whom "God in times past spake to the fathers," being the mediator of the law, Paul deems it necessary now to show that, great as was Moses, the Son of God is greater. EBRARD in ALFORD remarks, The angel of the covenant came in the name of God before Israel; Moses in the name of Israel before God; whereas the high priest came *both* in the name of God (bearing the name JEHOVAH on his forehead) before Israel, and in the name of Israel (bearing the names of the twelve tribes on his breast) before God (Exod. 28:9-29, 36, 38). Now Christ is above the angels, according to chs. 1 and 2 because (1) as Son of God

He is higher; and (2) because manhood, though originally lower than angels, is in Him exalted above them to the lordship of "the world to come," inasmuch as He is at once Messenger of God to men, and also atoning Priest-Representative of men before God (ch. 2:17, 18). Parallel with this line of argument as to His superiority to angels (ch. 1:4) runs that which here follows as to His superiority to Moses (ch. 3:3): (1) because as *Son* over the house; He is above the *servant* in the house (vss. 5, 6), just as the *angels* were shown to be but *ministering* (serving) spirits (ch. 1:14), whereas He is the *Son* (vss. 7, 8); (2) because the bringing of Israel into the promised rest, which was not finished by Moses, is accomplished by Him (ch. 4:1-11), through His being not merely a leader and lawgiver as Moses, but also a propitiatory High Priest (ch. 4:14; 5:10). **1. Wherefore**—*Greek,* "Whence," i.e., seeing we have such a sympathizing Helper you ought to "consider attentively," "contemplate"; fix your eyes and mind on Him with a view to profiting by the contemplation (ch. 12:2). The *Greek* word is often used by Luke, Paul's companion (Luke 12:24, 27). **brethren**—in Christ, the common bond of union. **partakers**—"of the Holy Ghost." **heavenly calling**—coming to us from heaven, and leading us to heaven whence it comes. Philippians 3:14, "the high calling"; *Greek* "the calling above," i.e., *heavenly.* **the Apostle and High Priest of our profession** —There is but one *Greek* article to both nouns, "Him who is at once Apostle and High Priest"— *Apostle,* as Ambassador (a higher designation than "angel"-*messenger*) sent by the Father (John 20:21), pleading the cause of *God with us; High Priest,* as pleading *our* cause *with God.* Both His Apostleship and High Priesthood are comprehended in the one title, *Mediator* [BENGEL]. Though the title "Apostle" is nowhere else applied to Christ, it is appropriate here in addressing Hebrews, who used the term of the delegates sent by the high priest to collect the temple tribute from Jews resident in foreign countries, even as Christ was Delegate of the Father to this world far off from Him (Matt. 21: 37). Hence as what applies to Him, applies also to His people, the Twelve are designated His apostles, even as He is the Father's (John 20:21). It was desirable to avoid designating Him here "angel," in order to distinguish His nature from that of angels mentioned before, though he is "the Angel of the Covenant." The "legate of the Church" (*Sheliach Tsibbur*) offered up the prayers in the synagogue in the name of all, and for all. So Jesus, the Apostle of our profession, is *delegated* to intercede for the Church before the Father. The words "of our profession," mark that it is not of the legal ritual, but of our Christian faith, that He is the High Priest. Paul compares Him as an *Apostle* to Moses; as High Priest to Aaron. He alone holds both offices combined, and in a more eminent degree than either, which those two brothers held apart. **profession**—"confession," corresponds to God having *spoken* to us by His Son, sent as Apostle and High Priest. What God proclaims we confess. **2.** He first notes the feature of *resemblance* between Moses and Christ, in order to conciliate the Hebrew Christians whom He addressed, and who still entertained a very high opinion of Moses; he afterwards brings forward Christ's superiority to Moses. **Who was faithful**—The *Greek* implies also that He still is faithful, viz., as our mediating High Priest, faithful to the trust God has assigned Him (ch. 2:17). So Moses *in* God's house (Num. 12:7). **appointed him**—"*made*

Him" HIGH PRIEST; to be supplied from the preceding context. *Greek,* "made"; so in ch. 5:5; I Samuel 12:6, *Margin;* Acts 2:36; so the *Greek* fathers. Not as ALFORD, with AMBROSE and the Latins, "*created* Him," i.e., as man, in His incarnation. The likeness of Moses to Messiah was foretold by Moses himself (Deut. 18:15). Other prophets only *explained Moses,* who was in this respect superior to them; but Christ was *like Moses,* yet superior. **3. For**—assigning the reason why they should "consider" attentively "Christ" (vs. 1), highly as they regard Moses who resembled Him in *faithfulness* (vs. 2). **was**—*Greek,* "has been." **counted worthy of more glory**—by God, when He exalted Him to His own right hand. The Hebrew Christians admitted the fact (ch. 1:13). **builded the house**—*Greek,* "inasmuch as He hath more honor than the house, who *prepared* it," or "*established* it" [ALFORD]. The *Greek* verb is used purposely instead of "builded," in order to mark that the building meant is not a literal, but a spiritual house: the Church both of the Old Testament and New Testament; and that the building of such a house includes all the *preparations* of providence and grace needed to furnish it with "living stones" and fitting "servants." Thus, as Christ the Founder and Establisher (in Old Testament as well as the New Testament) is greater than the house so established, including the servants, He is greater also than Moses, who was but a "servant." Moses, as a servant, is a portion of the house, and less than the house; Christ, as the Instrumental Creator of all things, must be God, and so greater than the house of which Moses was but a part. *Glory* is the result of *honor.* **4.** Someone must be the establisher of every house; Moses was not the establisher of the house, but a portion of it (but He who established all things, *and therefore* the spiritual house in question, is God). Christ, as being instrumentally the Establisher of all things, must be the Establisher of the house, and so greater than Moses. **5. faithful in all his house**—i.e., in all GOD's house (vs. 4). **servant**—not here the *Greek* for "slave," but "a ministering attendant"; marking the high office of Moses towards God, though inferior to Christ, a kind of *steward.* **for a testimony . . .**—in order that he might in his typical institutions give "testimony" to Israel "of the things" of the Gospel "which were to be spoken afterwards" by Christ (ch. 8:5; 9:8, 23; 10:1). **6. But Christ**—was and is faithful (vs. 2). **as a son over his own house**—rather, "over *His* (GOD's, vs. 4) house"; and therefore, as *the inference* from His being one with God, *over His own house.* So ch. 10:21, "having an High Priest over the house *of God.*" Christ enters His Father's house as the Master [OVER it], but Moses as a servant [IN it, vss. 2, 5] [CHRYSOSTOM]. An ambassador in the absence of the king is very distinguished —in the presence of the king he falls back into the multitude [BENGEL]. **whose house are we**—Paul and his Hebrew readers. One old MS., with *Vulgate* and LUCIFER, reads, "*which* house"; but the weightiest MSS. support *English Version* reading. **the rejoicing**—rather, "the matter of rejoicing." **of the hope**—"of *our* hope." Since all our good things lie in hopes, we ought so to hold fast our hopes as already to rejoice, as though our hopes were realized [CHRYSOSTOM]. **firm unto the end**—omitted in LUCIFER and AMBROSE, and in one oldest MS., but supported by most oldest MSS. **7-11.**—Exhortation from Psalm 95, not through unbelief to lose participation in the spiritual house. **Wherefore**—Seeing that we are the house of God if we hold fast our confidence ... (vs. 6). Jesus is "faithful," be not ye unfaithful (vss. 2, 12). The sentence beginning with "wherefore," interrupted by the parenthesis confirming the argument from Psalm 95, is completed at vs. 12, "Take heed ...." **Holy Ghost saith**—by the inspired Psalmist; so that the words of the latter are the words of God Himself. **Today**—at length; in David's day, as contrasted with the days of Moses in the wilderness, and the whole time since then, during which they had been rebellious against God's voice; as for instance, in the wilderness (vs. 8). The Psalm, each fresh time when used in public worship, by "today," will mean the particular day when it was, or is, used. **hear**—obediently. **his voice**—of grace. **8. Harden not your hearts**—This phrase here only is used of *man's* own act; usually of *God's* act (Rom. 9:18). When man is spoken of as the agent in hardening, the phrase usually is, "harden his neck," or "back" (Neh. 9:17). **provocation ... temptation**—Massah-meribah, translated in *Margin* "tentation ... chiding," or "strife" (Exod. 17:1-7). Both names seem to refer to that one event, the murmuring of the people against the Lord at Rephidim for want of water. The first offense especially ought to be guarded against, and is the most severely reproved, as it is apt to produce many more. Numbers 20: 1-13 and Deuteronomy 33:8 mention a second similar occasion in the wilderness of Sin, near Kadesh, also called Meribah. **in the day**—Greek, "according to the day of." **9. When**—rather, "Where," viz., in the wilderness. **your fathers**—The authority of the *ancients* is not conclusive [BENGEL]. **tempted me, proved me**—The oldest MSS. read, "tempted (Me) in the way of testing," i.e., *putting (Me) to the proof* whether I was able and willing to relieve them, not believing that I am so. **saw my works forty years**—They saw, without being led thereby to repentance, My works of power partly in affording miraculous help, partly in executing vengeance, forty years. The "forty years" joined in the *Hebrew* and LXX, and below, vs. 17, with "I was grieved," is here joined with "they saw." Both are true; for, during the same forty years that they were tempting God by unbelief, notwithstanding their seeing God's miraculous works, God was being grieved. The lesson intended to be hinted to the Hebrew Christians is, their "today" is to last only between the first preaching of the Gospel and Jerusalem's impending overthrow, viz., FORTY YEARS; exactly the number of years of Israel's sojourn in the wilderness, until the full measure of their guilt having been filled up all the rebels were overthrown. **10. grieved**—displeased. Cf. "walk contrary," Leviticus 26:24, 28. **that generation**—"*that*" implies alienation and estrangement. But the oldest MSS. read, "this." **said**—"*grieved*," or "displeased," at their first offense. Subsequently when they hardened their heart in unbelief still more, He *sware* in His *wrath* (vs. 11); an ascending gradation (cf. vss. 17, 18). **and they have not known**—Greek, "But these very persons ...." They perceived I was displeased with them, yet they, the same persons, did not a whit the more wish to know my ways [BENGEL]; cf. "but they," Psalm 106: 43. **not known my ways**—not known practically and believingly the ways in which I would have had them go, so as to reach My rest (Exod. 18:20). **11. So**—lit., "as." **I sware**—BENGEL remarks the oath of God preceded the forty years. **not**—lit., "If they shall enter ... (God do so to me and more also)," II Sam. 3:35. The *Greek* is the same, Mark 8:12. **my rest**—Canaan, primarily, their rest after

wandering in the wilderness: still, even when in it, they never *fully* enjoyed rest; whence it followed that the threat extended farther than the exclusion of the unbelieving from the literal land of rest, and that the rest promised to the believing in its full blessedness was, and is, yet future: Psalm 25:13; 37: 9, 11, 22, 29, and Christ's own beatitude (Matt. 5:5) all accord with this, vs. 9. **12. Take heed**—to be joined with "wherefore," vs. 7. **lest there be**—Greek (indicative), "lest there *shall* be"; lest there be, as I fear there is; implying that it is not merely a *possible* contingency, but that there is ground for thinking *it will be so.* **in any**—"in any one of you." Not merely ought all in general be on their guard, but they ought to be so concerned for the safety of *each one* member, as not to suffer any one to perish through their negligence [CALVIN]. **heart**—The *heart* is not to be trusted. Cf. vs. 10, "They do always err in their heart." **unbelief**—*faithlessness.* Christ is *faithful;* therefore, saith Paul to the Hebrews, we ought not to be *faithless* as our fathers were under Moses. **departing**—apostatizing. The opposite of "come unto" Him (ch. 4:16). God punishes such apostates in kind. He departs from them—the worst of woes. **the living God**—real: the distinctive characteristic of the God of Israel, not like the lifeless gods of the heathen; therefore One whose threats are awful realities. To apostatize from Christ is to apostatize from the living God (ch. 2:3). **13. one another**—Greek, "yourselves"; let each exhort himself and his neighbor. **daily**—Greek, "on each day," or "day by day." **while it is called Today**—while the "today" lasts (the day of grace, Luke 4:21, before the coming of the day of glory and judgment at Christ's coming, ch. 10:25, 37). Tomorrow is the day when idle men work, and fools repent. Tomorrow is Satan's today; he cares not what good resolutions you form, if only you fix them for tomorrow. **lest ... of you**—The "you" is emphatic, as distinguished from "your fathers" (vs. 9). "That from among you no one (so the *Greek* order is in some of the oldest MSS.) be hardened" (vs. 8). **deceitfulness**—causing you to "err in your heart." **sin**—unbelief. **14. For ...**—enforcing the warning, vs. 12. **partakers of Christ** —(Cf. vss. 1, 6). So "partakers of the Holy Ghost" (ch. 6:4). **hold**—Greek, "hold fast." **the beginning of our confidence**—i.e., the confidence (lit., *substantial, solid confidence*) of faith which we have begun (ch. 6:11; 12:2). A Christian so long as he is not *made perfect*, considers himself as a *beginner* [BENGEL]. **unto the end**—unto the coming of Christ (ch. 12:2). **15. While it is said**—connected with vs. 13, "exhort one another ... while it is said, Today": vs. 14, "for we are made partakers ...," being a parenthesis. "It entirely depends on yourselves that the invitation of the 95th Psalm be not a mere invitation, but also an actual enjoyment." ALFORD translates, "Since (i.e., for) it is said ...," regarding vs. 15 as a proof that we must "hold ... confidence ... unto the end," in order to be "partakers of Christ." **16. For some**—rather interrogatively, "For WHO was it that, when they had heard (referring to 'if ye will *hear*,' vs. 15), did provoke (God)?" The "For" implies, Ye need to take heed against unbelief: *for,* was it not because of unbelief that all our fathers were excluded (Ezek. 2:3)? "Some," and "not all," would be a faint way of putting his argument, when his object is to show the *universality* of the evil. Not merely *some,* but *all* the Israelites, for the solitary exceptions, Joshua and Caleb, are hardly to be taken into account in so general a statement. So vss. 17, 18, are interrogative: (1) the beginning of the provocation, soon after the departure from Egypt, is marked in vs. 16; (2) the forty years of it in the wilderness, vs. 17; (3) the denial of entrance into the land of rest, vs. 18. *Note,* cf. I Corinthians 10:5, "with the majority of them God was displeased." **howbeit**—"Nay (why need I put the question?), was it not all that came out of Egypt?" (Exod. 17:1, 2). **by Moses**—by the instrumentality of Moses as their leader. **17. But**—Translate, "Moreover," as it is not in contrast to vs. 16, but carrying out the same thought. **corpses**—lit., "limbs," implying that their bodies fell limb from limb. **18. to them that believed not**—rather as *Greek,* "to them that *disobeyed.*" *Practical* unbelief (Deut. 1:26). **19. they could not enter**—though desiring it.

CHAPTER 4

Vss. 1-16. The Promise of God's Rest Is Fully Realized through Christ: Let Us Strive to Obtain It by Him, Our Sympathizing High Priest. **1. Let us . . . fear**—not with slavish terror, but godly "fear and trembling" (Phil. 2:12). Since so many have fallen, we have cause to fear (ch. 3:17-19). **being left us**—still *remaining* to us after the others have, by neglect, lost it. **his rest**—God's heavenly rest, of which Canaan is the type. "Today" still continues, during which there is the danger of failing to reach the *rest.* "Today," rightly used, terminates in the *rest* which, when once obtained, is never lost (Rev. 3:12). A foretaste of the rest is given in the inward rest which the believer's soul has in Christ. **should seem to come short of it**—*Greek,* "to *have* come short of it"; *should be found,* when the great trial of all shall take place [ALFORD], to have fallen short of attaining the promise. The word "seem" is a mitigating mode of expression, though not lessening the reality. BENGEL and OWEN take it, Lest there should be any *semblance* or appearance of falling short. **2. gospel preached . . . unto them**—in type: the earthly Canaan, wherein they failed to realize perfect rest, suggesting to them that they should look beyond to the heavenly land of rest, to which *faith* is the avenue, and from which *unbelief* excludes, as it did from the earthly Canaan. **the word preached**—lit., "the word of hearing": *the word heard by them.* **not being mixed with faith in them that heard**—So the *Syriac* and the *Old Latin Versions,* older than any of our MSS., and LUCIFER, read, "As the world did not unite with the hearers in faith." The word heard being the food which, as the bread of life, must pass into flesh and blood through man's appropriating it to himself in faith. Hearing alone is of as little value as undigested food in a bad stomach [THOLUCK]. The whole of oldest *extant* MS. authority supports a different reading, "unmingled as *they* were (*Greek* accusative agreeing with 'them') in faith with its hearers," i.e., with its *believing, obedient* hearers, as Caleb and Joshua. So "hear" is used for "obey" in the context, vs. 7, "Today, if ye will hear His voice." The disobedient, instead of being blended in "the same body," separated themselves as Korah: a tacit reproof to like separatists from the Christian assembling together (ch. 10:25; Jude 19). **3. For**—justifying his assertion of the need of "faith," vs. 2. **we which have believed**—we who at Christ's coming shall be found to have believed. **do enter**—i.e., are to enter: so two of the oldest MSS. and LUCIFER and the old Latin. Two other oldest MSS. read, "Let us enter." **into rest**—*Greek,* "into *the* rest" which is promised in the 95th Psalm. **as he said**—God's

saying that *unbelief* excludes from entrance implies that *belief* gains an entrance into the rest. What, however, Paul mainly here dwells on in the quotation is that the promised "*rest*" has not *yet* been entered into. At vs. 11 he again, as in ch. 3:12-19 already, takes up *faith* as the indispensable qualification for entering it. **although . . .**—Although God had finished His works of creation and entered on *His* rest from creation long before Moses' time, yet under that leader of Israel another rest was promised, which most fell short of through unbelief; and although the rest in Canaan was subsequently attained under Joshua, yet long after, in David's days, God, in the 95th Psalm, still speaks of *the rest of God* as not yet attained. THEREFORE, there must be meant a rest *still future,* viz., that which "remaineth for the people of God" in heaven, vss. 3-9, when they shall rest from their works, as God did from His, vs. 10. The argument is to show that by "My rest," God means a future rest, not *for Himself,* but *for us.* **finished**—*Greek,* "brought into existence," "made." **4. he spake**—God (Gen. 2:2). **God did rest the seventh day**—a rest not ending with the seventh day, but beginning then and still continuing, into which believers shall hereafter enter. God's rest is not a rest necessitated by fatigue, nor consisting in idleness, but is that upholding and governing of which creation was the beginning [ALFORD]. Hence Moses records the end of each of the first six days, but not of the seventh. **from all his works**—*Hebrew,* Genesis 2:2, "from all His *work.*" God's "*work*" was *one,* comprehending, however, many "*works.*" **5. in this place**—In this passage of the Psalm again, it is implied that the rest was even then still future. **6. it remaineth**—still to be realized. **some must enter**—The denial of entrance to unbelievers is a virtual promise of entrance to those that believe. God wishes not His rest to be empty, but furnished with guests (Luke 14:23). **they to whom it was first preached entered not**—lit., "they who first (in the time of Moses) had the Gospel preached to them," viz., in type, as *Note,* vs. 2. **unbelief**—*Greek,* rather "disobedience" (*Note,* ch. 3:18). **7. Again**—*Anew* the promise recurs. Translate as the *Greek* order is, "He limited a certain day, 'Today.' " Here Paul interrupts the quotation by, "In (the Psalm of) David saying after so long a time" (after 500 years' possession of Canaan), and resumes it by, "as it has been said *before* (so the *Greek* oldest MS., *before,* viz., ch. 3:7, 15), Today if ye hear His voice . . ." [ALFORD]. **8.** Answer to the objection which might be made to his reasoning, viz., that those brought into Canaan by Joshua (so "Jesus" here means, as in Acts 7:45) did enter the *rest* of God. If the rest of God meant Canaan, God would not after their entrance into that land, have spoken (or speak [ALFORD]) of another (future) day of entering the rest. **9. therefore**—because God "speaks of another day" (*Note,* vs. 8). **remaineth**—still to be realized hereafter by the "some (who) must enter therein" (vs. 6), i.e., "the people of God." the true Israel who shall enter into *God's rest* ("My rest," vs. 3). God's rest was a Sabbatism; so also will ours be. **a rest**—*Greek,* "Sabbatism." In time there are many Sabbaths, but then there shall be the enjoyment and keeping of a Sabbath rest: one perfect and eternal. The "rest" in vs. 8 is *Greek catapausis; Hebrew, Noah;* rest from weariness, as the ark rested on Ararat after its tossings to and fro; and as Israel, under Joshua, enjoyed at last rest from war in Canaan. But the "rest" in this vs. 9 is the nobler and more exalted (*Hebrew*) "Sabbath" *rest;* lit., "cessation": rest from *work when finished* (vs. 4), as God rested (Rev. 16:17). The two ideas of "rest" combined, give the perfect view of the heavenly Sabbath. Rest from weariness, sorrow, and sin; and rest in the completion of God's new creation (Rev. 21:5). The whole renovated creation shall share in it; nothing will there be to break the Sabbath of eternity; and the Triune God shall rejoice in the work of His hands (Zeph. 3:17). Moses, the representative of the law, could not lead Israel into Canaan: the law leads us to Christ, and there its office ceases, as that of Moses on the borders of Canaan: it is Jesus, the antitype of Joshua, who leads us into the heavenly rest. This verse indirectly establishes the obligation of the Sabbath still; for the type continues until the antitype supersedes it: so legal sacrifices continued till the great antitypical Sacrifice superseded it, As then the antitypical heavenly Sabbath rest will not be till Christ, our Gospel Joshua, comes, to usher us into it, the typical earthly Sabbath must continue till then. The Jews call the future rest "the day which is all Sabbath." **10. For**—justifying and explaining the word "rest," or "Sabbatism," just used (*Note*, vs. 9). **he that is entered**—whosoever once enters. **his rest**—*God's* rest: the rest prepared *by God* for His people [Estius]. Rather, *His* rest: the *man's* rest: that assigned to him by God as *his*. The *Greek* is the same as that for "his own" immediately after. **hath ceased**—The *Greek* aorist is used of indefinite time, "*is wont to* cease," or rather, "rest": *rests*. The past tense implies at the same time the *certainty* of it, as also that in this life a kind of foretaste in Christ is already given [Grotius] (Jer. 6:16; Matt. 11:28, 29). Our highest happiness shall, according to this verse, consist in our being united in one with God, and moulded into conformity with Him as our archetype [Calvin]. **from his own works**—even from those that were good and suitable to the time of doing work. Labor was followed by rest even in Paradise (Gen. 2: 3, 15). The work and subsequent rest of God are the archetype to which we should be conformed. The argument is: He who once enters rest, rests from labors; but God's people have not yet rested from them, therefore they have not yet entered the rest, and so it must be still future. Alford translates, "He that entered into his (or else God's, but rather 'his'; Isa. 11:10, 'His rest': 'the joy *of the Lord*,' Matt. 25:21,23) rest (viz., *Jesus*, our Forerunner, vs. 14; ch. 6:20, 'The Son of God that *is passed through the heavens*': in contrast to Joshua the type, who did *not bring* God's people *into* the heavenly rest), he *himself* (*emphatical*) rested from his works (vs. 4), as God (did) from *His own*" (so the *Greek*, "works"). The argument, though generally applying to *anyone who has entered his rest*, probably alludes to *Jesus* in particular, the antitypical Joshua, who, having entered His rest at the Ascension, has ceased or rested from His work of the new creation, as God on the seventh day rested from the work of physical creation. Not that He has ceased to carry on the work of redemption, nay, He upholds it by His mediation; but He has ceased from those portions of the work which constitute the foundation; the sacrifice has been once for all accomplished. Cf. as to God's creation rest, once for all completed, and rested from, but now still upheld (*Note*, vs. 4). **11. Let us . . . therefore**—Seeing such a promise is before us, which we may, like them, fall short of through unbelief. **labour**—*Greek*, "strive diligently." **that rest**—which is still future and so glorious. Or, in Alford's transla-

tion of vs. 10, "That rest into which *Christ* has entered before" (vs. 14; ch. 6:20). **fall**—with the soul, not merely the body, as the rebel Israelites fell (ch. 3:17). **after the same example**—Alford translates, "fall *into* the same example." The less prominent place of the "fall" in the *Greek* favors this. The sense is, "lest any fall into such *disobedience* (so the *Greek* for 'unbelief' means) as they gave a sample of" [Grotius]. The Jews say, "The parents are a sign (warning) to their sons." **12. For**—Such *diligent striving* (vs. 11) is incumbent on us(for we have to do with a God whose "word" whereby we shall be judged, is heart-searching, and whose eyes are all-seeing (vs. 13). The qualities here attributed to *the word of God,* and the whole context, show that it is regarded in its judicial power, whereby it doomed the disobedient Israelites to exclusion from Canaan, and shall exclude unbelieving so-called Christians from the heavenly rest. The written Word of God is not the prominent thought here, though the passage is often quoted as if it were. Still the word of God (the same as that preached, vs. 2), used here in the broadest sense, but with special reference to its *judicial* power, includes the Word of God, the sword of the Spirit with double edge, one edge for convicting and converting some (vs. 2), and the other for condemning and destroying the unbelieving (vs. 14). Revelation 19:15 similarly represents the Word's judicial power as a sharp sword going out of Christ's mouth to *smite* the nations. The same word which is saving to the faithful (vs. 2) is destroying to the disobedient (II Cor. 2:15, 16). The personal Word, to whom some refer the passage, is not here meant: for He *is* not the sword, but *has* the sword. Thus reference to Joshua appropriately follows in vs. 8. **quick** —*Greek*, "living"; having living power, as "the rod of the mouth and the breath of the lips" of "the living God." **powerful**—*Greek*, "energetic"; not only *living*, but *energetically efficacious*. **sharper** —"more cutting." **two-edged**—sharpened at both edge and back. Cf. "sword of the Spirit . . . word of God" (Eph. 6:17). Its *double* power seems to be implied by its being "two-edged." "It judges all that is in the heart, for there it passes through, at once *punishing* [unbelievers] and searching" [both believers and unbelievers] [Chrysostom]. Philo similarly speaks of "God passing between the parts of Abraham's sacrifices [Gen. 15:17, where, however, it is a 'burning lamp' that passed between the pieces] with His word, which is the cutter of all things: which sword, being sharpened to the utmost keenness, never ceases to divide all sensible things, and even things not perceptible to sense or physically divisible, but perceptible and divisible by the word." Paul's early training, both in the Greek schools of Tarsus and the Hebrew schools at Jerusalem, accounts fully for his acquaintance with Philo's modes of thought, which were sure to be current among learned Jews everywhere, though Philo himself belonged to Alexandria, not Jerusalem. Addressing Jews, he by the Spirit sanctions what was true in their current literature, as he similarly did in addressing Gentiles (Acts 17:28). **piercing**—*Greek*, "coming through." **even to the dividing asunder of soul and spirit**—i.e., reaching through even to the separation of the animal *soul,* the lower part of man's incorporeal nature, the seat of animal desires, which he has in common with the brutes; cf. the same *Greek*, I Corinthians 2:14, "the natural [animalsouled] man" (Jude 19), from the spirit (the higher part of man, receptive of the Spirit of God, and allying him to heavenly beings).

and of the joints and marrow—rather, (*reaching even to*) "*both* the joints (so as to divide them) and marrow." Christ "knows what is in man" (John 2: 25): so His word reaches as far as to the most intimate and accurate knowledge of man's most hidden parts, feelings, and thoughts, dividing, i.e., *distinguishing* what is *spiritual* from what is *carnal* and *animal* in him, the *spirit* from the *soul:* so Proverbs 20:27. As the knife of the Levitical priest reached to dividing parts, closely united as the *joints* of the limbs, and penetrated to the innermost parts, as the *marrows* (the *Greek* is *plural*); so the word of God divides the closely joined parts of man's immaterial being, soul and spirit, and penetrates to the innermost parts of the spirit. The clause (reaching even to) "*both* the joints and marrow" is subordinate to the clause, "even to the dividing a-sunder of soul and spirit." (In the oldest MSS., as in *English Version*, there is no "both," as there is in the clause "*both* the joints *and* . . . , which marks the latter to be subordinate.) An image (appropriate in addressing Jews) from the literal dividing of joints, and penetrating to, so as to open out, the marrow, by the priest's knife, illustrating the previously mentioned spiritual "dividing of soul from spirit," whereby each (soul as well as spirit) is laid bare and "naked" before God; this view accords with vs. 13. Evidently "the dividing of the soul from the spirit" answers to the "joints" which *the sword, when it reaches* unto, *divides asunder,* as the "spirit" answers to the innermost "marrow." "Moses forms the soul, Christ the spirit. The soul draws with it the body; the spirit draws with it both soul and body." ALFORD's interpretation is clumsy, by which he makes the soul *itself,* and the spirit *itself,* to be divided, instead of the soul *from* the spirit: so also he makes not only the *joints* to be divided asunder, but the *marrow* also to be divided(?). The Word's dividing and far penetrating power has both a punitive and a healing effect. **discerner of the thoughts**—*Greek,* "capable of judging the purposes." **intents**—rather, "conceptions" [CRELLIUS]; "ideas" [ALFORD]. As the *Greek* for "thoughts" refers to the *mind* and *feelings,* so that for "intents," or rather "mental conceptions," refers to the *intellect.* **13. creature**—visible or invisible. **in his sight**—in *God's* sight (vs. 12). "God's wisdom, simply manifold, and uniformly multiform, with incomprehensible comprehension, comprehends all things incomprehensible." **opened**—lit., "thrown on the back so as to have the neck laid bare," as a victim with neck exposed for sacrifice. The *Greek* perfect tense implies that this is our *continuous* state in relation to God. "Show, O man, *shame* and *fear* towards thy God, for no veil, no twisting, bending, coloring, or disguise, can cover *unbelief*" (*Greek,* "disobedience," vs. 11). Let us, therefore, earnestly labor to enter the rest lest any fall through practical unbelief (vs. 11). **14. having, therefore . . .**—resuming ch. 2:17. **great**—as being "the Son of God, higher than the heavens" (ch. 7:26): the archetype and antitype of the legal high priest. **passed into the heavens**—rather, "passed *through* the heavens," viz., those which come between us and God, the aerial heaven, and that above the latter containing the heavenly bodies, the sun, moon, etc. These heavens were the veil which our High Priest *passed through* into the heaven of heavens, the immediate presence of God, just as the Levitical high priest passed through the veil into the Holy of Holies. Neither Moses, nor even Joshua, could bring us into this rest, but Jesus, as our Forerunner, already spiritually, and

hereafter in actual presence, body, soul, and spirit, brings His people into the heavenly rest. **Jesus**—the antitypical Joshua (vs. 8). **hold fast**—the opposite of "let slip" (ch. 2:1); and "fall away" (ch. 6: 6). As the *genitive* follows, the lit., sense is, "Let us *take hold* of our profession," i.e., of the faith and hope which are subjects of our profession and confession. The accusative follows when the sense is "hold fast" [TITTMANN]. **15. For**—the motive to "holding our profession" (vs. 14), viz., the sympathy and help we may expect from our High Priest. Though "great" (vs. 14), He is not above caring for us; nay, as being in all points one with us as to manhood, sin only excepted, He sympathizes with us in every temptation. Though exalted to the highest heavens, He has changed His place, not His nature and office in relation to us, His condition, but not His affection. Cf. Matthew 26:38, "watch with me": showing His desire in the days of His flesh for *the sympathy of those whom He loved:* so He now gives His suffering people *His sympathy.* Cf. Aaron, the type, bearing the names of the twelve tribes in the breastplate of judgment on his heart, when he entered into the holy place, for a memorial before the Lord continually (Exod. 28:29). **cannot be touched with the feeling of**—*Greek,* "cannot sympathize with our infirmities": our *weaknesses,* physical and moral (not sin, but liability to its assaults). He, though sinless, can sympathize with us sinners; His understanding more acutely perceived the forms of temptation than we who are weak can; His will repelled them as instantaneously as the fire does the drop of water cast into it. He, therefore, experimentally knew what power was needed to overcome temptations. He is capable of sympathizing, for He was at the same time tempted without sin, and yet truly tempted [BENGEL]. In Him alone we have an example suited to men of every character and under all circumstances. In sympathy He adapts himself to each, as if He had not merely taken on Him man's nature in general, but also the peculiar nature of that single individual. **but**—"nay, rather, He was (one) tempted" [ALFORD]. **like as we are**—*Greek,* "according to (our) similitude." **without sin**—*Greek, choris,* "*separate* from sin" (ch. 7:26). If the *Greek aneu* had been used, *sin* would have been regarded as the object absent from Christ the subject; but *choris* here implies that Christ, the *subject,* is regarded as separated from sin the object [TITTMANN]. Thus, throughout His temptations in their origin, process, and result, sin had nothing in Him; He was apart and separate from it [ALFORD]. **16. come**—rather as *Greek,* "approach," "draw near." **boldly**—*Greek,* "with confidence," or "freedom of speech" (Eph. 6:19). the **throne of grace**—God's throne is become to us a *throne of grace* through the mediation of our High Priest at God's right hand (ch. 8:1; 12:2). Pleading our High Priest Jesus' meritorious death, we shall always find God on a *throne of grace.* Contrast Job's complaint (Job 23:3-8) and Elihu's "IF . . ." (Job 33:23-28). **obtain**—rather, "receive." **mercy**—"Compassion," by its derivation (lit., fellow feeling from *community* of *suffering*), corresponds to the character of our High Priest "touched with the feeling of our infirmities" (vs. 15). **find grace**—corresponding to "throne *of grace.*" *Mercy* especially refers to the remission and removal of sins; *grace,* to the saving bestowal of spiritual gifts [ESTIUS]. Cf. Come unto Me . . . and I will *give* you rest (the rest *received* on first believing); take My yoke on you . . . and ye shall *find* rest (the continuing rest and peace *found* in daily submitting to Christ's easy yoke; the former answers to "*receive* mercy" here; the latter, to "*find* grace," Matt. 11:28, 29). **in time of need**—*Greek,* "seasonably." Before we are overwhelmed by the temptation; when we most need it, in temptations and persecutions; such as is suitable to the time, persons, and end designed (Ps. 104:27). A supply of grace is in store for believers against all exigencies; but they are only supplied with it according as the need arises. Cf. "in due time," Romans 5. 6. Not, as ALFORD explains, "help in time," i.e., *today,* while it is yet open to us; the accepted time (II Cor. 6:2). **help**—Cf. ch. 2:18, "He is able to *succor* them that are tempted."

CHAPTER 5

Vss. 1-14. CHRIST'S HIGH PRIESTHOOD; NEEDED QUALIFICATIONS; MUST BE A MAN; MUST NOT HAVE ASSUMED THE DIGNITY HIMSELF, BUT HAVE BEEN APPOINTED BY GOD; THEIR LOW SPIRITUAL PERCEPTIONS A BAR TO PAUL'S SAYING ALL HE MIGHT ON CHRIST'S MELCHISEDEC-LIKE PRIESTHOOD. **1. For**—substantiating ch. 4:15. **every**—i.e., every legitimate high priest; for instance, the Levitical, as he is addressing Hebrews, among whom the Levitical priesthood was established as the legitimate one. Whatever, reasons Paul, is excellent in the Levitical priests, is also in Christ, and besides excellencies which are not in the Levitical priests. **taken from among men**—not from among angels, who could not have a fellow feeling with us men. This qualification Christ has, as being, like the Levitical priest, *a man* (ch. 2:14, 16). Being "*from* men," He can be "*for* (i.e., in behalf of, for the good of) men." **ordained**—*Greek,* "constituted," "appointed." **both gifts**—to be joined with "for sins," as "sacrifices" is (the "both . . . and" requires this); therefore not the *Hebrew, mincha,* unbloody offerings, but animal whole burnt offerings, *spontaneously given.* "Sacrifices" are the animal sacrifices *due according to the legal ordinance* [ESTIUS]. **2. Who can**—*Greek,* "being able"; *not pleasing himself* (Rom. 15:3). **have compassion**—*Greek,* "estimate mildly," "feel leniently," or "moderately towards"; "to make allowance for"; not showing stern rigor save to the obstinate (ch. 10:28). **ignorant**—sins not committed in resistance of light and knowledge, but as Paul's past sin (I Tim. 1:13). No sacrifice was appointed for wilful sin committed with a high hand; for such were to be punished with death; all other sins, viz., ignorances and errors, were confessed and expiated with sacrifices by the high priest. **out of the way**—not deliberately and altogether wilfully erring, but deluded through the fraud of Satan and their own carnal frailty and thoughtlessness. **infirmity**—moral weakness which is sinful, and makes men capable of sin, and so requires to be expiated by sacrifices. This kind of "infirmity" Christ had not; He had the "infirmity" of body whereby He was capable of suffering and death. **3. by reason hereof**—"on account of this" infirmity. **he ought . . . also for himself, to offer for sins**—the Levitical priest ought; in this our High Priest is superior to the Levitical. The second "for" is a different *Greek* term from the first; "*in behalf of* the people . . . , *on account* of sins." **4. no man**—of any other family but Aaron's, according to the Mosaic law, can take to himself the office of high priest. This verse is quoted by some to prove the need of an apostolic succession of ordination in

the Christian ministry; but the reference here is to the *priesthood,* not the Christian *ministry.* The analogy in our Christian dispensation would warn ministers, seeing that God has separated them from the congregation of His people to bring them near Himself, and to do the service of His house, and to minister (as He separated the Levites, Korah with his company), that content with this, they should beware of assuming the sacrificial priesthood also, which belongs to Christ alone. The sin of Korah was, not content with the ministry as a Levite, he took the sacerdotal priesthood also. No Christian minister, as such, is ever called *Hiereus,* i.e., sacrificing priest. All Christians, without distinction, whether ministers or people, have a metaphorical, not a literal, priesthood. The sacrifices which they offer are spiritual, not literal, their bodies and the fruit of their lips, praises continually (ch. 13:15). Christ alone had a proper and true sacrifice to offer. The law sacrifices were typical, not metaphorical, as the Christian's, nor proper and true, as Christ's. In Roman times the Mosaic restriction of the priesthood to Aaron's family was violated. **5. glorified not himself**—did not assume the glory of the priestly office of Himself without the call of God (John 8:54). **but he that said**—i.e., the Father glorified Him or appointed Him to the priesthood. This appointment was involved in, and was the result of, the *Sonship* of Christ, which qualified Him for it. None but the divine Son could have fulfilled such an office (ch. 10:5-9). The connection of *Sonship* and *priesthood* is typified in the *Hebrew* title for *priests* being given to David's *sons* (II Sam. 8:18). Christ did not constitute *Himself* the Son of God, but was from everlasting the only-begotten *of the Father.* On His Sonship depended His glorification, and His being called of God (vs. 10), as Priest. **6.** He is here called simply "Priest"; in vs. 5, "High Priest." He is a *Priest* absolutely, because He stands alone in that character without an equal. He is "High Priest" in respect of the Aaronic type, and also in respect to us, whom He has made *priests* by throwing open to us access to God [BENGEL]. "The *order* of Melchisedec" is explained in ch. 7:15, "the *similitude* of Melchisedec." The priesthood is similarly combined with His kingly office in Zechariah 6:13. Melchisedec was at once man, priest, and king. Paul's selecting as the type of Christ one not of the stock of Abraham, on which the Jews prided themselves, is an intimation of Messianic universalism. **7. in the days of his flesh**—(ch. 2:14; 10:20). Verses 7-10 state summarily the subject about to be handled more fully in chs. 7 and 8. **when he had offered**—rather, "*in that* He *offered.*" His crying and tears were part of the experimental lesson of obedience which He submitted to learn from the Father (when God was qualifying Him for the high priesthood). "Who" is to be construed with "learned obedience" (or rather as *Greek,* "*His* obedience"; *the* obedience which we all know about). This all shows that "Christ glorified not Himself to be made an High Priest" (vs. 5), but was appointed thereto by the Father. **prayers and supplications**—*Greek,* "*both* prayers and supplications." In Gethsemane, where He prayed *thrice,* and on the cross, where He cried, My God, my God . . . , probably repeating inwardly *all* the 22d Psalm. "Prayers" refer to the mind: "supplications" also to the body [viz., the suppliant attitude] (Matt. 26:39) [BENGEL]. **with strong crying and tears**—The "tears" are an additional fact here communicated to us by the inspired apostle, not recorded in the Gospels, though implied. Matthew 26:37, "sorrowful and very heavy." Mark 14:33; Luke 22:44, "in an agony He prayed more earnestly . . . His sweat . . . great drops of blood falling down to the ground." Psalm 22:1 ("roaring . . . cry"), 2, 19, 21, 24; 69:3, 10, "I *wept*." **able to save him from death**—Mark 14:36, "All things are *possible* unto Thee" (John 12:27). His cry showed His entire participation of man's infirmity: His reference of His wish to the will of God, His sinless faith and obedience. **heard in that he feared**—There is no intimation in Psalm 22, or the Gospels that Christ prayed to be saved from the mere act of dying. What He feared was the hiding of the Father's countenance. His holy filial love must rightly have shrunk from this strange and bitterest of trials without the imputation of impatience. To have been passively content at the approach of such a cloud would have been, not faith, but sin. The cup of death He prayed to be freed from was, not corporal, but spiritual death, i.e., the (temporary) separation of His human soul from the light of God's countenance. His prayer was "heard" in His Father's strengthening Him so as to hold fast His unwavering faith under the trial (*My* God, *my* God, was still His filial cry under it. still claiming God as His, though God hid His face), and soon removing it in answer to His cry during the darkness on the cross, "My God, my God . . . ." But see below a further explanation of how He was heard. The *Greek* lit. is, "Was heard *from His fear*," i.e., so as to be saved from His fear. Cf. Psalm 22:21, which well accords with this, "Save me *from* the lion's mouth (His prayer): thou hast heard me *from* the horns of the unicorns." Or what better accords with the strict meaning of the *Greek* noun, "*in consequence of His* REVERENTIAL FEAR," i.e., in that He *shrank from* the horrors of separation from the bright presence of the Father, yet was *reverentially cautious* by no thought or word of impatience to give way to a shadow of distrust or want of perfect filial love. In the same sense ch. 12:28 uses the noun, and ch. 11:7 the verb. ALFORD somewhat similarly translates, "By reason of His reverent submission." I prefer "reverent *fear*." The word in derivation means the *cautious handling* of some precious, yet delicate vessel, which with ruder handling might easily be broken [TRENCH]. This fully agrees with Jesus' spirit, "If it be possible . . . *nevertheless not My will, but Thy will be done*"; and with the context, vs. 5, "Glorified not Himself to be made an High Priest," implying *reverent fear:* wherein it appears He had the requisite for the office specified vs. 4, "No man taketh this honor unto himself." ALFORD well says, What is true in the Christian's life, that what we ask from God, though He may not grant in the form we wish, yet He grants in His own, and that a better form, does not hold good in Christ's case; for Christ's real prayer, "not My will, but Thine be done," in consistency with His reverent fear towards the Father, was granted in the very form in which it was expressed, not in another. **8. Though He** WAS (so it ought to be translated: a positive admitted fact: not a mere supposition as *were* would imply) God's divine Son (whence, even in His agony, He so lovingly and often cried, *Father*, Matt. 26:39), yet He learned *His* (so the *Greek*) obedience, not from His Sonship, but from His sufferings. As the Son, He was always obedient to the Father's will; but *the* special obedience needed to qualify Him as our High Priest, He learned experimentally in practical suffering. Cf. Philippians 2:6-8, "*equal with God, but . . . took upon Him the form of a servant,* and became *obedient* unto death . . . ." He was *obedient* already before His passion, but He stooped to a still more humiliating and trying form of *obedience* then. The *Greek* adage is, *Pathemata mathemata*, "sufferings, disciplinings." *Praying* and *obeying*, as in Christ's case, ought to go hand in hand. **9. made perfect**—completed, brought to His goal of learning and suffering through death (ch. 2:10) [ALFORD], viz., at His glorious resurrection and ascension. **author**—*Greek*, "cause." **eternal salvation**—obtained for us in the *short* "days of Jesus' flesh" (vs. 7; cf. vs. 6, "for ever," Isa. 45: 17). **unto all . . . that obey him**—As Christ *obeyed* the Father, so must we *obey* Him by faith. **10. Greek**, rather, "*Addressed* by God (by the appellation) High Priest." Being formally recognized by God as High Priest at the time of His being "made perfect" (vs. 9). He was High Priest already *in the purpose of God* before His passion; but after it, when perfected, He was formally addressed so. **11.** Here he digresses to complain of the low spiritual attainments of the Palestinian Christians and to warn them of the danger of falling from light once enjoyed; at the same time encouraging them by God's faithfulness to persevere. At ch. 6:20 he resumes the comparison of Christ to Melchisedec. **hard to be uttered**—rather as *Greek*, "hard *of interpretation* to speak." Hard for me to state intelligibly to you owing to your dulness about spiritual things. Hence, instead of *saying many things*, he writes in comparatively *few words* (ch. 13:22). In the "we," Paul, as usual, includes Timothy with himself in addressing them. **ye are**—*Greek*, "ye have *become* dull" (the *Greek*, by derivation, means *hard to move*): this implies that *once*, when first "enlightened," they were earnest and zealous, but had *become* dull. That the Hebrew believers AT JERUSALEM were dull in spiritual things, and legal in spirit, appears from Acts 21:20-24, where James and the elders expressly say of the "thousands of Jews which believe," that "they are all *zealous of the law*"; **this** was at Paul's last visit to Jerusalem, after which this Epistle seems to have been written (vs. 12, *Note* on "for the time"). **12. for the time**—considering the long time that you have been Christians. Therefore this Epistle was not one of those written early. **which be the first principles**—*Greek*, "the *rudiments of the beginning* of." A Pauline phrase (*Notes*, Gal. 4:3, 9). Ye need not only to be taught *the first elements*, but also "*which they be*." They are therefore enumerated ch. 6:1, 2 [BENGEL]. ALFORD translates, "That *someone* teach you the rudiments"; but the position of the *Greek tina*, inclines me to take it interrogatively, "which," as *English Version, Syriac, Vulgate,* etc. **of the oracles of God**—viz., of the Old Testament: instead of seeing Christ as the end of the Old Testament Scripture, they were relapsing towards Judaism, so as not only not to be capable of understanding the typical reference to Christ of such an Old Testament personage as Melchisedec, but even much more elementary references. **are become**—through indolence. **milk . . . not . . . strong meat**—"Milk" refers to such fundamental first principles as he enumerates in ch. 6:1, 2. The *solid meat*, or *food*, is not absolutely necessary for preserving life, but is so for acquiring greater strength. Especially in the case of the Hebrews, who were much given to allegorical interpretations of their law, which they so much venerated, the application of the Old Testament types, to Christ and His High Priesthood, was calculated much to strengthen them in the Christian faith [LIMBORCH]. **13. useth**–*Greek,* "partaketh," i.e., taketh as *his portion.* Even strong men partake of milk, but do not make milk their chief, much less their sole, diet. **the word of righteousness**–the Gospel wherein "the righteousness of God is revealed from faith to faith" (Rom. 1:17), and which is called "the ministration of righteousness" (II Cor. 3:9). This includes the doctrine of *justification* and sanctification: the first *principles,* as well as the *perfection, of the doctrine of Christ:* the nature of the offices and person of Christ as the true Melchisedec, i.e., "King of *righteousness*" (cf. Matt. 3:15). **14. strong meat**–"solid food." **them . . . of full age**–lit., "perfect": akin to "perfection" (ch. 6:1). **by reason of use**–*Greek,* "habit." **senses**–organs of sense. **exercised**–similarly connected with "righteousness" in ch. 12:11. **to discern both good and evil**–as a child no longer an infant (Isa. 7:16): so able to distinguish between sound and unsound doctrine. The mere child puts into its mouth things hurtful and things nutritious, without discrimination: but not so the adult. Paul again alludes to their tendency not to discriminate, but to be carried about by strange doctrines, in ch. 13:9.

CHAPTER 6

Vss. 1-14. WARNING AGAINST RETROGRADING, WHICH SOON LEADS TO APOSTASY; ENCOURAGEMENT TO STEADFASTNESS FROM GOD'S FAITHFULNESS TO HIS WORD AND OATH. **1. Therefore**–Wherefore: seeing that ye ought not now to be still "babes" (ch. 5:11-14). **leaving**–getting further forward than the elementary "principles." "As in building a house one must never leave the foundation: yet to be always laboring in 'laying the foundation' would be ridiculous" [CALVIN]. **the principles of the doctrine**–*Greek,* "the word *of* the beginning," i.e., the discussion of the "first principles of Christianity (ch. 5:12). **let us go on**–*Greek,* "let us be borne forward," or "bear ourselves forward"; implying active exertion: press on. Paul, in teaching, here classifies himself with the Hebrew readers, or (as they ought to be) learners, and says, Let us together press forward. **perfection**–the matured knowledge of those who are "of full age" (ch. 5:14) in Christian attainments. **foundation of**–i.e., *consisting in* "repentance." **repentance from dead works** –viz., not springing from the *vital* principle of faith and love toward God, and so counted, like their doer, *dead* before God. This *repentance from dead works* is therefore paired with "faith toward God." The three pairs of truths enumerated are designedly such as JEWISH believers might in some degree have known from the Old Testament, but had been taught more clearly when they became Christians. This accounts for the omission of *distinct* specification of some essential first principle of Christian truth. Hence, too, he mentions "faith toward *God,*" and not *explicitly* faith toward *Christ* (though of course included). Repentance and faith were the first principles taught under the Gospel. **2. the doctrine of baptisms**–paired with "laying on of hands," as the latter followed on Christian baptism, and answers to the rite of *confirmation* in Episcopal churches. Jewish believers passed, by an easy transition, from Jewish *baptismal purifications* (ch. 9:10, "washings"), baptism of proselytes, and John's baptism, and legal imposition of hands, to their Christian analogues, *baptism,* and the subsequent

laying on of hands, accompanied by the gift of the Holy Ghost (cf. vs. 4). *Greek, baptismoi,* plural, including *Jewish* and *Christian baptisms,* are to be distinguished from *baptisma,* singular, *restricted* to Christian baptism. The six particulars here specified had been, as it were, *the Christian Catechism* of the Old Testament; and such Jews who had begun to recognize Jesus as the Christ immediately on the new light being shed on these fandamental particulars, were accounted as having the elementary *principles* of the doctrine of Christ [BENGEL]. The first and most obvious elementary instruction of Jews would be the *teaching* them the typical significance of their own ceremonial law in its Christian fulfilment [ALFORD]. **resurrection . . .**–held already by the Jews from the Old Testament: confirmed with clearer light in Christian *teaching* or "doctrine." **eternal judgment**–judgment fraught with eternal consequences either of joy or of woe. **3. will we do**–So some of the oldest MSS. read; but others, "Let us do." "This," i.e., "Go on unto perfection." **if God permit**–For even in the case of good resolutions, we cannot carry them into effect, save through God "working in us both to will and to do of His good pleasure" (Phil. 2:13). The "for" in vs. 4 refers to this: I say, if God permit, *for* there are cases where God does not permit, e.g., "it is impossible," etc. Without God's blessing, the cultivation of the ground does not succeed (vs. 7). **4. We** must "go on toward perfection"; for if we *fall away,* after having received enlightenment, it will be *impossible to renew* us *again to repentance.* **for those** –"in the case of those." **once enlightened**–once for all illuminated by the word of God taught in connection with "baptism" (to which, in vs. 2, as once for all done," once enlightened" here answers); cf. Ephesians 5:26. This passage probably originated the application of the term "illumination" to baptism in subsequent times. *Illumination,* however, was not supposed to be the inseparable accompaniment of *baptism:* thus CHRYSOSTOM says, "Heretics have *baptism,* not *illumination:* they are baptized in body, but not enlightened in soul: as Simon Magus was baptized, but not illuminated." That "enlightened" here means *knowledge of the word of truth,* appears from comparing the same *Greek* word "illuminated," ch. 10:32, with 26, where "knowledge of the truth" answers to it. **tasted of the heavenly gift**–tasted *for themselves.* As "enlightened" refers to the sense of *sight:* so here *taste* follows. "The heavenly gift"; *Christ* given by the Father and revealed by the enlightening word preached and written: as conferring peace in the remission of sins; and as the Bestower of the gift of the Holy Spirit (Acts 8:19, 20), **made partakers of the Holy Ghost**–specified as distinct from, though so inseparably connected with, "enlightened," and "tasted of the heavenly gift," Christ, as answering to "laying on of hands" after baptism, which was then generally accompanied with the impartation of *the Holy Ghost* in miraculous *gifts.* **5. tasted the good word of God**–distinct from "tasted OF (genetive) the heavenly gift"; we do not yet enjoy *all* the fulness of Christ, but only have a taste OF Him, the heavenly gift now; but believers may taste the *whole* word (accusative) of God already, viz., God's "good word" *of promise.* The Old Testament promise of Canaan to Israel typified "the good word of God's" promise of the heavenly rest (ch. 4). Therefore, there immediately follows the clause, "the powers of the world to come." As "enlightening" and "tasting of the heavenly gift," Christ, the Bread of Life, answers to FAITH: so "made partakers of the Holy Ghost," to CHARITY, which is the first fruit of the Spirit: and "tasted the good word of *God,* and the powers of the world to come," to HOPE. Thus the triad of privileges answers to the Trinity, the Father, Son, and Spirit, in their respective works toward us. "The world to come," is the Christian dispensation, viewed especially in its *future glories,* though already begun in grace here. The *world to come* thus stands in contrast to *course of this world,* altogether disorganized because God is not its spring of action and end. By faith, Christians make the world to come a present reality, though but a foretaste of the perfect future. The powers of this new spiritual world, partly exhibited in outward miracles at that time, and then, as now, especially consisting in the Spirit's inward quickening influences are the earnest of the coming inheritance above, and lead the believer who gives himself up to the Spirit to seek to live as the angels, to sit with Christ in heavenly places, to set the affections on things above, and not on things on earth, and to look for Christ's coming and the full manifestation of the world to come. This "world to come," in its future aspect, thus corresponds to "resurrection of the dead and eternal life" (vs. 2), the *first* Christian principles which the Hebrew believers had been taught, by the Christian light being thrown back on their Old Testament for their instruction (*Note,* vss. 1, 2). "The world to come," which, as to its "powers," exists already in the redeemed, will pass into a fully realized fact at Christ's coming (Col. 3:4). **6. If**—*Greek, And* (yet) have fallen away"; cf. a less extreme falling or declension, Galatians 5:4, "Ye are fallen from grace." Here an entire and wilful apostasy is meant; the Hebrews had not yet so fallen away; but he warns them that such would be the final result of retrogression, if, instead of "going on to perfection," they should need to learn again the first principles of Christianity (vs. 1). **to renew them again**—They have been "once" (vs. 4) already *renewed,* or made anew, and now they need to be *"renewed"* over "again." **crucify to themselves the Son of God**—"are crucifying to themselves" Christ, instead of, like Paul, *crucifying the world unto them by the cross of Christ* (Gal. 6:14). So in ch. 10:29, "trodden under foot the Son of God, and counted the blood of the covenant, wherewith . . . sanctified, an unholy thing." "The Son of God," marking His dignity, shows the greatness of their offense. **put him to an open shame**—lit., "make a public example of" Him, as if He were a malefactor suspended on a tree. What the carnal Israel did outwardly, those who fall away from light do inwardly, they virtually crucify again the Son of God; "they tear him out of the recesses of their hearts where He had fixed His abode and exhibit Him to the open scoffs of the world as something powerless and common" [BLEEK in ALFORD]. The Montanists and Novatians used this passage to justify the lasting exclusion from the Church of those who had once lapsed. The Catholic Church always opposed this view, and readmitted the lapsed on their repentance, but did not rebaptize them. This passage implies that persons may be in some sense "renewed," and yet fall away finally; for the words, "renew *again,*" imply that they have been, in *some* sense, *not the full sense,* ONCE RENEWED by the Holy Ghost; but certainly not that they are "the elect," for these can never fall away, being chosen unto everlasting life (John 10:28). The elect abide in Christ, hear and continuously obey His voice, and do not fall away. He who abides not in Christ, is cast forth as a withered

branch; but he who abides in Him becomes more and more free from sin; the wicked one cannot touch him; and he by faith overcomes the world. A *temporary* faith is possible, without one thereby being constituted one of the elect (Mark 4:16, 17). At the same time it does not limit God's grace, as if it were "impossible" *for God* to reclaim even such a hardened rebel so as yet to look on Him whom he has pierced. The impossibility rests in their having known in themselves once the power of Christ's sacrifice, and yet now rejecting it; there *cannot possibly* be any new means devised for their renewal afresh, and the means provided by God's love they now, after experience of them, deliberately and continuously reject; their conscience being seared, and they "twice dead" (Jude 12), are now past hope, except by a miracle of God's grace. "It is the curse of evil eternally to propagate evil" [THOLUCK]. "He who is led into the whole (?) compass of Christian experiences, may yet cease to abide in them; he who abides not in them, was, at the very time when he had those objective experiences, not *subjectively* true to them; otherwise there would have been fulfilled in him, 'Whosoever hath, to him shall be given, and he shall have more abundance' (Matt. 13:12), so that he would have abided in them and not have fallen away" [THOLUCK]. Such a one was never truly a Spirit-led disciple of Christ (Rom. 8:14-17). The sin against the Holy Ghost, though somewhat similar, is not identical with this sin; for *that* sin may be committed by those *outside* the Church (as in Matt. 12:24, 31, 32); this, only by those *inside.* **7. the earth**—rather as *Greek* (no article), "land." **which drinketh in**—*Greek,* "which *has* drunk in"; not merely receiving it on the surface. Answering to those who have enjoyed the privilege of Christian experiences, being in some sense renewed by the Holy Ghost; true alike of those who persevere and those who "fall away." **the rain that cometh oft upon it**—not merely falling *over* it, or *towards* it, but falling and resting *upon* it so as to *cover* it (the *Greek* genitive, not the accusative). The "oft" implies, on God's part, the riches of His abounding grace ("coming" spontaneously, and often); and, on the apostate's part, the wilful perversity whereby he has done continual despite to the oft-repeated motions of the Spirit. Cf. "How *often.*" Matthew 23:37. The rain of heaven falls both on the elect and the apostates. **bringeth forth** —as the *natural* result of "*having drunk in* the rain." See above. **herbs**—provender. **meet**—fit. Such as the master of the soil wishes. The opposite of "rejected," vs. 8. **by whom**—rather as *Greek,* "for (i.e., on account of) whom," viz., the lords of the soil; not the laborers, as *English Version,* viz., God and His Christ (I Cor. 3:9). The heart of man is the earth; man is the dresser; herbs are brought forth meet, not for the dresser, by whom, but for God, the owner of the soil, for whom it is dressed. The plural is general, *the owners whoever they may be;* here *God.* **receiveth**—"partaketh of." **blessing**—fruitfulness. Contrast God's curse causing unfruitfulness (Gen. 3:17, 18); also spiritually (Jer. 17:5-8). **from God**—Man's use of means is vain unless God bless (I Cor. 3:6, 7). **8. that which**—rather as *Greek* (no article), "But *if it* (the 'land' vs. 7) *bear*"; not so favorable a word as "bringeth forth," vs. 7, said of the good soil. **briers**—*Greek,* "thistles." **rejected**—after having been *tested;* so the *Greek* implies. *Reprobate . . . rejected* by the Lord. **nigh unto cursing**—on the verge of being given up to its own barrenness by the just curse of God. This "nigh" softens the severity of the previous "It is impossible . . ." (vss. 4, 6). The ground is not yet actually *cursed.* **whose**—"of which (*land*) the end is unto burning," viz., with the consuming fire of the last judgment; as the land of Sodom was given to "brimstone, salt, and *burning*" (Deut. 29: 23); so as to the ungodly (Matt. 3:10, 12; 7:19; 13: 30; John 15:6; II Pet. 3:10). Jerusalem, which had so resisted the grace of Christ, was then nigh unto cursing, and in a few years was burned. Cf. Matthew 22:7, "*burned* up their city" an earnest of a like fate to all wilful abusers of God's grace (ch. 10:26, 27). **9. beloved**—appositely here introduced; LOVE to you prompts me in the strong warnings I have just given, not that I entertain unfavorable thoughts of you; nay, I anticipate *better things* of you; *Greek* "the things which *are* better"; that ye are not *thorn-bearing,* or *nigh unto cursing,* and doomed *unto burning,* but heirs of *salvation* in accordance with God's faithfulness (ch. 6:10). **we are persuaded**—on good grounds; the result of proof. Cf. Romans 15:14, "I myself am persuaded of you, my brethren, that ye are full of *goodness.*" A confirmation of the Pauline authorship of this Epistle. **things that accompany**—*Greek,* "things that hold by," i.e., are close unto "salvation." Things that are linked unto salvation (cf. vs. 19). In opposition to "nigh unto cursing." **though**—*Greek,* "if even we thus speak." "For it is better to make you afraid with words, that ye may not suffer in fact." **10. not unrighteous**—not *unfaithful* to His own gracious promise. Not that we have any inherent *right to claim* reward; for (1) a *servant* has no merit, as he only does that which is his bounden duty; (2) our best performances bear no proportion to what we leave undone; (3) all strength comes from God; but God has *promised of His own grace* to reward the good works of His people (already accepted through faith in Christ); it is His *promise,* not our merits, which would make it *unrighteous* were He not to reward His people's works. God will be no man's debtor. **your work**—your whole Christian life of active obedience. **labour of love** —The oldest MSS. omit "labor of," which probably crept in from I Thess. 1:3. As "love" occurs here, so "hope," vs. 11, "faith," vs. 12; as in I Corinthians 13:13: the *Pauline* triad. By their *love* he sharpens their *hope* and *faith.* **ye have showed**— (Cf. ch. 10:32-34). **toward his name**—Your acts *of love to* the saints were done for His name's sake. The distressed condition of the Palestinian Christians appears from the collection for them. Though receiving bounty from other churches, and therefore not able to minister much by *pecuniary* help, yet those somewhat better off could minister to the greatest sufferers in their Church in various other ways (cf. II Tim. 1:18). Paul, as elsewhere, gives them the utmost credit for their graces, while delicately hinting the need of perseverance, a lack of which had probably somewhat begun to show itself. **11. And**—*Greek,* "But." **desire**—*Greek,* "*earnestly* desire." The language of fatherly affection, rather than command. **every one of you**— implying that *all* in the Palestinian churches had not shown the same diligence as some of those whom he praises in vs. 10. "He cares alike for great and small, and overlooks none." "Every one of them," even those dilligent in acts of LOVE (vs. 10), needed to be stimulated to *persevere* in the same diligence with a view to the full assurance of HOPE unto the end. They needed, besides love, patient perseverance, resting on *hope* and *faith* (ch. 10:36; 13:7). Cf. "the full assurance of faith," ch. 10:22; Romans 4:21; I Thessalonians 1:5. **unto**

the end—the coming of Christ. **12. be not**—*Greek,* "*become* not." In ch. 5:11, he said, "Ye have become dull (*Greek, slothful*) *of hearing*"; here he warns them not to become "slothful" *absolutely,* viz., also in mind and deed. He will not become slothful who keeps always *the end* in view; *hope* is the means of ensuring this. **followers**—*Greek,* "imitators"; so in Ephesians 5:1, *Greek;* I Corinthians 11:1. **patience**—*Greek,* "*long-suffering* endurance." There is the *long-suffering patience,* or *endurance of love,* I Corinthians 13:4, and that of *faith,* vs. 15. **them who . . . inherit the promises**—*Greek,* ". . . who *are inheriting* . . ."; to whom the promises are their inheritance. Not that they *have* actually entered on the *perfect* inheritance, which ch. 11:13, 39, 40 explicitly denies; though doubtless the dead in Christ have, in the disembodied soul, a foretaste of it; but "them (enumerated in ch. 11) who in every age have been, are, or shall be, *inheritors* of the promises"; of whom Abraham is an illustrious example (vs. 13). **13. For**—confirming the reasonableness of resting on "the promises" as infallibly sure, resting as they do on God's oath, by the instance of Abraham. "He now gives consolation, by *the oath of God's grace,* to those whom, in chs. 3 and 4, he had warned by the *oath* of God's 'wrath.' The oath of wrath did not primarily extend its force beyond the wilderness; but the oath of grace is in force for ever" [BENGEL]. **14 multiplying . . . multiply**—Hebraism for *superabundantly multiply.* **thee**—The increase of Abraham's *seed* is virtually an increase of *himself.* The argument here refers to Abraham *himself* as an example; therefore Paul quotes Genesis 22:17, "thee," instead of "thy seed." **15. so**—thus relying on the promise. **16. for confirmation**—not to be joined, as *English Version,* to "an oath"; but to "an end" [ALFORD]. I prefer, "The oath is to them, in respect to confirmation (of one's solemn promise or covenant; as here, *God's*), an end of all *contradiction*" (so the *Greek* is translated, ch. 12:3), or "gainsaying." This passage shows: (1) an oath is sanctioned even in the Christian dispensation as lawful; (2) that the limits to its use are, that it only be employed where it can *put an end to contradiction in disputes,* and *for confirmation* of a solemn promise. **17. Wherein**— i.e., *Which being the case* among men, God, in accommodation to their manner of confirming covenants, superadded to His sure *word* His *oath:* the "TWO immutable things" (vs. 18). **willing . . . counsel**—*Greek,* "willing . . . *will*"; words akin. Expressing the utmost benignity [BENGEL]. **more abundantly**—than had He not sworn. His word would have been amply enough; but, to make assurance doubly sure, He "interposed with an oath" (so the *Greek*). Lit., *He acted as Mediator,* coming between Himself and us; as if He were less, while He swears, than Himself by whom He swears [for the less among men usually swear by the greater]. Dost thou not yet believe, thou that hearest the promise? [BENGEL]. **heirs of promise**—not only Abraham's literal, but also his spiritual, seed (Gal. 3:29). **18, immutable**—Translate, as in vs. 17, "unchangeable." **impossible . . . to lie**—"*ever* to lie"; this is the force of the *Greek* aorist [ALFORD]. His not being able to deny Himself is a proof, not of weakness, but of strength incomparable. **consolation**—under doubts and fears, and so "encouragement," lit., "exhortation." **fled for refuge**—as if from a shipwreck; or, as one fleeing to one of the six cities of refuge. Kadesh, i.e., *holy,* implies the holiness of Jesus, our Refuge. Shechem, i.e., *shoulder,* the government is upon his shoulder (Isa.

9:6). Hebron, i.e., *fellowship,* believers are called into the fellowship of Christ. Bezer, i.e., *a fortress,* Christ is so to all who trust in Him. Ramoth, i.e., *high,* for Him hath God exalted with His right hand (Acts 5:31). Golan, i.e., *joy,* for in Him all the saints are justified and shall glory. **lay hold upon the hope**—i.e.,the object of our hope, as upon a preservative from sinking. **set before us**—as a prize for which we strive; a new image, viz., the race-course (ch. 12:1, 2). **19.** *Hope* is found represented on coins by an *anchor.* **sure and steadfast**—*sure* in respect to *us; steadfast,* or "firm" [ALFORD], in *itself.* Not such an *anchor* as will not keep the vessel from tossing, or an anchor unsound or too light [THEOPHYLACT]. **which entereth into that**—i.e., the place—**within the veil**—two images beautifully combined: I. The *soul* is *the ship;* the *world* the *sea:* the *bliss beyond* the world, *the distant coast;* the *hope* resting on faith, the *anchor* which prevents the vessel being tossed to and fro; the *encouraging consolation* through the *promise* and *oath* of God, the cable connecting the ship and anchor. II. The world is the fore-court; heaven, the Holy of Holies; Christ, the High Priest going before us, so as to enable us, after Him, and through Him, to enter within the veil. ESTIUS explains, As the anchor does not stay in the waters, but enters the ground hidden beneath the waters, and fastens itself in it, so hope, our anchor of the soul, is not satisfied with merely coming to the vestibule, i.e., is not content with merely earthly and visible goods, but penetrates even to those which are within the veil, viz., to the Holy of Holies, where it lays hold on God Himself, and heavenly goods, and fastens on them. "Hope, entering within heaven, hath made us already to be in the things promised to us, even while we are still below, and have not yet received them; such strength hope has, as to make those that are earthly to become heavenly." "The soul clings, as one in fear of shipwreck, to an anchor, and sees not whither the cable of the anchor runs—where it is fastened: but she knows that it is fastened behind the veil which hides the future glory." **veil**—Greek, *catapetasma;* the *second* veil which shut in the Holiest Place. The outer veil was called by a distinct *Greek* term. *calumma;* "the second (i.e., the inner) veil." **20.** The absence of the *Greek* article requires ALFORD'S translation, "Where, AS forerunner for us (i.e., in our behalf), entered Jesus" [*and is now:* this last clause is implied in the "where" of the *Greek,* which implies being IN a place: "whither" is understood to "entered," taken out of "where"; whither *Jesus entered,* and *where* He is now]. The "for us" implies that it was not for Himself. as God, He needed to enter there, but as our High Priest, representing and introducing us, His followers, opening the way to us, by His intercession with the Father, as the Aaronic high priest entered the Holiest Place once a year to make propitiation for the people. The first fruits of our nature are ascended, and so the rest is sanctified. Christ's ascension is our promotion: and whither the glory of the Head has preceded, thither the hope of the body, too, is called. We ought to keep festal day, since Christ has taken up and set in the heavens the first fruit of our lump, that is, the human flesh [CHRYSOSTOM]. As John Baptist was Christ's forerunner on earth, so Christ is ours in heaven.

CHAPTER 7

VSS. 1-28. CHRIST'S HIGH PRIESTHOOD AFTER THE ORDER OF MELCHISEDEC SUPERIOR TO AARON'S. **1.**

this Melchisedec—(ch. 6:20; Ps. 110:4). The verb does not come till vs. 3, "abideth." **king ... priest** —Christ unites these offices in their highest sense, and so restores the patriarchal union of these offices. **Salem**—Jerusalem, i.e., *seeing peace;* others make Salem distinct, and to be that mentioned (Gen. 33: 18; John 3:23). **the most high God**—called also "Possessor of heaven and earth" (Gen. 14:19, 22). This title of God, "the Most High," handed down by tradition from the primitive revelation, appears in the Phœnician god "Elion," i.e., *Most High.* It is used to imply that the God whom Melchisedec served is THE TRUE GOD, and not one of the gods of the nations around. So it is used in the only other cases in which it is found in the New Testament, viz., in the address of the demoniac, and the divining damsel constrained to confess that her own gods were false, and God the only true God. **who met Abraham**—in company with the king of Sodom (Gen. 14:17, 18). **slaughter**—perhaps *defeat,* as ALFORD translates. So Genesis 14:17 (cf. 15) may be translated. Arioch, king of Ellasar, lived and reigned after the disaster [BENGEL]. However, if Chedorlaomer and Amraphel and Tidal were slain, though Arioch survived, "*slaughter* of the kings" would be correct. **blessed him**—As priest he first blessed Abraham on God's part; next he blessed God on Abraham's part: a reciprocal blessing. Not a mere wish, but an authoritative and efficacious intercession as a priest. The Most High God's prerogative as "Possessor of heaven and earth," is made over to Abraham; and Abraham's glory, from his victory over the foe, is made over to God. A blessed exchange for Abraham (Gen. 14:19, 20). **2.** **gave**—Greek, "apportioned"; assigned as his portion. **tenth ... of all**—viz., the booty taken. The tithes given are closely associated with the priesthood: the mediating priest received them as a pledge of the giver's whole property being God's; and as he conveyed God's gifts to man (vs. 1, "blessed him"), so also man's gifts to God. Melchisedec is a sample of how God preserves, amidst general apostasy, an elect remnant. The meeting of Melchisedec and Abraham is the connecting link between to two dispensations, the patriarchal, represented by Melchisedec, who seems to have been *specially consecrated by God as a* KINGPRIEST, the highest form of that primitive system in which each father of a household was priest in it, and the Levitical, represented by Abraham, in which the priesthood was to be limited to one family of one tribe and one nation. The Levitical was parenthetical, and severed the kingdom and priesthood; the patriarchal was the true forerunner of Christ's, which, like Melchisedec's, *unites the kingship and priesthood,* and is not derived from other man, or transmitted to other man; but derived from God, and is transmitted in God to a never-ending perpetuity. Melchisedec's priesthood continueth in Christ for ever. For other points of superiority, see vss. 16-21. Melchisedec must have had some special consecration above the other patriarchs, as Abraham, who also exercised the priesthood; else Abraham would not have paid tithe to him as to a superior. His peculiar function seems to have been, by God's special call, KING-*priest;* whereas no other patriarch-priest was also a God-consecrated king. **first being** —Paul begins the mystical explanation of the historical fact (allegorical explanations being familiar to JEWS), by mentioning the significancy of the name. **righteousness**—not merely righteous: so Christ. *Hebrew Malchi* means *king: Tzedek, righteousness.* **King of Salem**—not only his own name, but that of the city which he ruled, had a typical significance, viz., *peace.* Christ is the true *Prince of peace.* The *peace* which He brings is the fruit of *righteousness.* **3. Without father . . .**—explained by "without genealogy" (so the *Greek* is for "without descent"); cf. vs. 6, i.e., his genealogy is *not known,* whereas a Levitical priest could not dispense with the proof of his descent. **having neither beginning of days nor end of life**—viz., history not having recorded his beginning nor end, as it has the beginning and end of Aaron. The *Greek* idiom expressed by "without father. . ." one whose parentage was humble or *unknown.* "Days" mean his time of discharging his *function.* So the eternity spoken of in Psalm 110:4 is that of the *priestly office* chiefly. **made like**—It is not said that he was absolutely "like." *Made like,* viz., in the particulars here specified. Nothing is said in Genesis of the end of his priesthood, or of his having had in his priesthood either predecessor or successor, which, in a typical point of view, represents Christ's eternal priesthood, without beginning or end. Aaron's *end* is recorded; Melchisedec's not: typically significant. "The Son of God" is not said to be made like unto Melchisedec, but Melchisedec to be "made like the Son of God." When ALFORD denies that Melchisedec was made like the Son of God *in respect of his priesthood,* on the ground that Melchisedec was *prior in time* to our Lord, he forgets that Christ's eternal priesthood was an archetypal reality *in God's purpose from everlasting,* to which Melchisedec's priesthood was "made like" in due time. The Son of God is the more ancient, and is the archetype: cf. ch. 8:5, where the heavenly things are represented as the *primary archetype of the Levitical ordinances.* The epithets, "without father, . . ." beginning of days, "nor end," "abideth continually," belong to Melchisedec only *in respect to his priesthood,* and in *so far as he is the type of the Son of God,* and are strictly true of Him alone. Melchisedec was, in his priesthood, "made like" Christ, as far as the imperfect type could represent the lineaments of the perfect archetype. "The portrait of a living man can be seen on the canvas, yet the man is very different from his picture." There is nothing in the account, Genesis 14, to mark Melchisedec as a superhuman being: he is classed with the other kings in the chapter as a living historic personage: not as ORIGEN thought, an angel; nor as the Jews thought, Shem, son of Noah; nor as CALMET, Enoch; nor as the Melchisedekites, that he was the Holy Ghost; nor as others, the Divine Word. He was probably of Shemitic, not Canaanite origin: the last independent representative of the original Shemitic population, which had been vanquished by the Canaanites, Ham's descendants. The greatness of Abraham then lay in hopes; of Melchisedec, in present possession. Melchisedec was the highest and last representative of the Noahic covenant, as Christ was the highest and ever enduring representative of the Abrahamic. Melchisedec, like Christ, unites in himself the *kingly and priestly* offices, which Abraham does not. ALFORD thinks the epithets are, in some sense, strictly true of Melchisedec *himself;* not merely in the typical sense given above; but that he had not, as mortal men have, a beginning or end of life (?). A very improbable theory, and only to be resorted to in the last extremity, which has no place here. With Melchisedec, whose priesthood probably lasted a long period, the priesthood and worship of the true God in Canaan ceased. He was first and last *king-priest* there, till Christ, the antitype; and therefore his

priesthood is said to last for ever, because it both lasts a long time, and lasts as long as the nature of the thing itself (viz., his life, and the continuance of God's worship in Canaan) admits. If Melchisedec were high priest for ever in a literal sense, then Christ and he would now still be high priests, and we should have two instead of one (!). THOLUCK remarks, "Melchisedec *remains* in so far as the type remains in the antitype, in so far as his priesthood remains in Christ." The *father* and *mother* of Melchisedec, as also his children, are not descended from Levi, as the Levitical priests (vs. 6) were required to be, and are not even mentioned by Moses. The wife of Aaron, Elisheba, the *mother* from whom the Levitical priests spring, is mentioned: as also Sarah, the original mother of the Jewish nation itself. As man, Christ had no *father;* as God, *no mother.* **4. consider**—not merely *see,* but *weigh with attentive contemplation,* the fact. **even**—"to whom (as his superior) Abraham *even* paid tithe (went so far as to pay tithe) of (consisting of, lit., 'from') *the best of the spoils*" (lit., "the top of the heap"; whether of corn, the first fruits of which, taken from the top, used to be consecrated to God; or of spoils, from the top of which the general used to take some portion for consecration to God, or for his own use). He paid "tithes of ALL," and those tithes were taken out of the topmast and best portion of the whole spoils. **the patriarch**—in the *Greek* emphatically standing at the end of the whole sentence: And this payer of tithe being no less a personage than "the patriarch," the first forefather and head of our Jewish race and nation See *Note,* vs. 3, on Melchisedec's superiority as specially consecrated *king-priest,* above the other *patriarch-priests.* **5. sons of Levi**—viz., those alone who belonged to the family of Aaron, to whom the priesthood was restricted. Tithes originally paid to the whole tribe of Levi, became at length attached to the priesthood. **according to the law**—sanctioned by Jehovah (ch. 9:19). **of their brethren**—with whom, in point of natural descent, they are on a level. **though . . .**—Though thus on a level by common descent from Abraham, they yet pay tithe to the Levites, whose brethren they are. Now the Levites are subordinate to the priests; and these again to Abraham, their common progenitor; and Abraham to Melchisedec. "How great" (vs. 4) then, must this Melchisedec be in respect to his priesthood, as compared with the Levitical, though the latter received tithes! and now unspeakably great must "the Son of God" be, to whom, as the sacerdotal archetype (in God's purpose), Melchisedec was made like! Thus compare the "consider," vs. 4, in the case of Melchisedec, the type, with the "consider" (*Greek,* "contemplate attentively," *Note,* ch. 3:1, a stronger word than here) in the case of Christ, the archetype. **6. he whose descent is not counted from them**—not from "the sons of Levi," as those "who receive the priesthood." This verse explains "without descent" (*Greek,* "genealogy" in both verses, vs. 3). He who needs not, as the Levitical priests, to be able to trace his genealogy back to Levi. **received**—*Greek,* "*hath* received tithes." **blessed**—*Greek,* "*hath* blessed." The perfect tense implies that the significance of the fact endures to the present time. **him that had**—"the possessor of the promises," Abraham's peculiar distinction and designation. Paul exalts Abraham in order still more to exalt Melchisedec. When Christ is the subject, the singular "promise" is used. "The promises" in the plural, refer to God's promise of greatness to himself and his seed, and of the possession of Canaan, twice repeated before the blessing of Melchisedec. As the priests, though above the people (vs. 7) whom it was their duty to "bless," were yet subordinate to Abraham; and as Abraham was subordinate to Melchisedec, who blessed him, Melchisedec must be much above the Levitical priests. **7.** The principle that the blesser is superior to him whom he blesses, holds good only in a blessing given with divine authority; not merely a prayerful wish, but one that is divinely efficient in working its purport, as that of the patriarchs on their children: so Christ's blessing, Luke 24:51; Acts 3: 26. **8.** Second point of superiority: Melchisedec's is an *enduring*, the Levitical a *transitory*, priesthood. As the law was a *parenthesis* between Abraham's dispensation of promise of grace, and its enduring fulfilment at Christ's coming (Rom. 5:20,*Greek*, "The law entered as something adscititious and by the way"): so the Levitical priesthood was parenthetical and temporary, between Melchisedec's typically enduring priesthood, and its antitypical realization in our ever continuing High Priest, Christ. **here**—in the *Levitical* priesthood. **there**—in the priesthood *after the order of Melchisedec*. In order to bring out the typical parallel more strongly, Paul substitutes, "He of whom it is witnessed that he liveth," for the more untypical, "He *who is made like to Him* that liveth." Melchisedec "liveth" merely in his *official* capacity, his priesthood being continued in Christ. Christ, on the other hand, is, in *His own person*, "ever living after the power of an endless life" (vss. 16, 25). Melchisedec's death not being recorded, is expressed by the positive term "liveth," for the sake of bringing into prominence the antitype, Christ, of whom alone it is strictly and perfectly true, "that He liveth." **9. as I may so say** —to preclude what he is about to say being taken in the mere literal sense; *I may say* that, *virtually*, Levi, in the person of his father Abraham, acknowledged Melchisedec's superiority, and paid tithes to him. **who receiveth tithes**—(Cf. vs. 5). **in Abraham**—*Greek*, "by means of (by the hand of) Abraham"; through Abraham. "Paid tithes," lit., "hath been tithed," i.e., been taken tithes of. **10. in the loins of his father**—i.e., *forefather* Abraham. *Christ* did not, in this sense, pay tithes in Abraham, for He never was in the loins of an earthly father [ALFORD]. Though, in respect to His mother, He was "of the fruit of (David's, and so of) Abraham's loins," yet, being supernaturally, without human father, conceived, as He is above the natural law of birth, so is he above the law of tithes. Only those born in the natural way, and so in sin, being under the curse, needed to pay tithe to the priest, that he might make propitiation for their sin. Not so Christ, who derived only His flesh, not also the taint of the flesh, from Abraham. BENGEL remarks, The blessings which Abraham had *before* meeting Melchisedec were the *general* promises, and the special one of a *natural seed*, and so of Levi; but the promises under which *Christ* was comprehended, and the faith for which Abraham was so commended, followed *after* Abraham's meeting Melchisedec, and being *blessed by him*: to which fact. Genesis 15:1, "*After* these things," calls our attention. This explains why Christ, the supernatural seed, is not included as paying tithes through Abraham to Melchisedec. **11. perfection**—absolute: "the bringing of man to his highest state, viz., that of salvation and sanctification." **under it**—The reading in the oldest MSS. is, "*Upon* it (i.e., on the ground of it as the basis, the priest having to administer the law, Malachi 2:7: it being presupposed) the people (ch.

9:19, '*all* the people') have received the law" (the *Greek* is *perfect*, not aorist; implying the people were still observing the law). **what further need**— (ch. 8:7). For God does nothing needless. **another** —rather as *Greek*, "that a *different* priest (one of a different order) should arise" (*anew*, vs. 15). **not be called**—*Greek*, "not be *said* (*to be*) after the order of Aaron," i.e., that, when spoken of in the Psalm 110:4, "He is not said to be (as we should expect, if the Aaronic priesthood was perfect) after the order of Aaron." **12. For**—the reason why Paul presses the words "after the order of Melchisedec" in Psalm 110:4, viz., because these presuppose a change or transference of the priesthood, and this carries with it a change also of the law (which is inseparably bound up with the priesthood, both stand and fall together, vs. 11). This is his answer to those who might object, What need was there of a new covenant? **13.** Confirming the truth that *a change is made of the law* (vs. 12), by another fact showing the distinctness of the new priesthood from the Aaronic. **these things**—(Ps. 110:4). **pertaineth** —*Greek*, "hath partaken of" (the perfect tense implies the *continuance* still of His manhood). **another**—"a *different* tribe" from that of Levi. **14. evident** —lit., "manifest before the eyes" as a thing indisputable; a proof that whatever difficulties may now appear, *then* Jesus Christ's genealogy labored under none. **our Lord**—the only place where this now common title occurs without "Jesus," or "Christ," except II Peter 3:15. **sprang**—as a plant, and a branch. **Judah**—Genesis 49:10; Luke 1:27, 39 (Hebron of Judah, where LIGHTFOOT thinks Jesus was conceived); 2:4, 5; Rev. 5:5. **of which tribe . . . priesthood**—"*in respect to* which tribe Moses spake nothing concerning priests" (so the oldest MSS. read, nothing to imply that priests were to be taken from it). **15.** Another proof that the law, or economy, is changed, viz., forasmuch as Christ is appointed Priest, "not according to the law of a carnal (i.e., a mere *outward*) commandment," but "according to the power of an *indissoluble* (so the *Greek*) life." The 110th Psalm appoints Him "for ever" (vs. 17). The Levitical law required a *definite carnal* descent. In contrast stands "the power"; Christ's spiritual, inward, living power of overcoming death. Not agreeably to a *statute* is Christ appointed, but according to an inward *living power*. **it**—the change of the law or economy, the statement (vss. 12, 18). **far more**—*Greek*, "more abundantly." **for that**—"seeing that," lit., "if"; so Romans 5:10. **after the similitude of Melchisedec**—answering to "after the order of Melchisedec" (ch. 5:10). The "order" cannot mean a *series of priests*, for Melchisedec neither received his priesthood from, nor transmitted it to, any other mere man; it must mean "answering to the *office* of Melchisedec." Christ's priesthood is similar to Melchisedec's in that it is "for ever" (vss. 16, 17). **another**—rather as *Greek*, "a different." **16. carnal . . . endless**—mutually contrasted. As "form" and "power" are opposed, II Timothy 3:5; so here "the law" and "power," cf. Romans 8:3, "The law was *weak* through the flesh"; and vs. 18, "weakness." "The law" is here not the law in general, but the *statute* as to the priesthood. "Carnal," as being only *outward* and *temporary*, is contrasted with "endless," or, as *Greek*, "indissoluble." Commandments is contrasted with "life." The *law* can give a *commandment*, but it cannot give *life* (vs. 19). But our High Priest's inherent "power," now in heaven, has in Him "life for ever"; ch. 9:14, "through the *eternal Spirit*"; ch. 7:25, "able" . . . "ever liveth" (John 5:26). It is in the power of His resurrection life, not of His earthly life, that Christ officiates as a Priest. **17. For**—proving His *life* to be "endless" or indissoluble (vs. 16). The emphasis is on "for ever." The oldest MSS. read, "*He is testified of,* that Thou art. . . . **18. there is**—Greek, "there takes place," according to Psalm 110:4. **disannuling**—a repealing. **of the commandment**—ordaining the Levitical priesthood. And, as the Levitical priesthood and the law are inseparably joined, since the former is repealed, the latter is so also (*Note,* vs. 11). **going before**—the legal ordinance introducing and giving place to the Christian, the antitypical and permanent end of the former. **weakness and unprofitableness**—The opposite of "power" (vs. 16). **19. For . . .** —justifying his calling the law *weak* and *unprofitable* (vs. 18). The law could not bring men to true justification or sanctification before God, which is the "perfection" that we all need in order to be accepted of Him, and which we have in Christ. **nothing**—not merely "no one," but "nothing." The law brought nothing to its perfected end; everything in it was introductory to its antitype in the Christian economy, which realizes the perfection contemplated; cf. "unprofitableness," vs. 18. **did**—rather connect with vs. 18, thus, "There takes place (by virtue of Ps. 110:4) a repealing of the commandment (on the one hand), but (on the other) *a bringing in afterwards* (the Greek expresses that there is a bringing in of something *over and above* the law; a *superinducing,* or *accession of something new,* viz., something better than the good things which the pre-existing law promised [WAHL]) of a better hope," not one weak and unprofitable, but, as elsewhere the Christian dispensation is called, "everlasting," "true," "the second," "more excellent," "different," "living," "new," "to come," "perfect." Cf. ch. 8:6, bringing us *near to God,* now in spirit, hereafter both in spirit and in body. **we draw nigh unto God**—the sure token of "perfection." *Weakness* is the opposite of this filial confidence of access. The access through the legal sacrifices was only symbolical and through the medium of a priest; that through Christ is immediate, perfect, and spiritual. **20. Another** proof of the superiority of Christ's Melchisedec-like priesthood; the oath of God gave a solemn weight to it which was not in the law-priesthood, which was not so confirmed. **he was made priest**—rather supply from vs. 22, which completes the sentence begun in this verse, vs. 21 being a parenthesis, "inasmuch as not without an oath *He was made surety of the testament* (for . . .), of so much better a testament hath Jesus been made the surety." **21.** Translate in the *Greek* order, "For they indeed (the existing legal priests) without the (solemn) *promise on* oath (so the *Greek* [TITTMANN]) are made priests." **by him**—God. **unto him**—the Lord, the Son of God (Ps. 110:1). **not repent**—never change His purpose. **after the order of Melchisedec**—omitted in some oldest MSS., contained in others. **22. surety**—ensuring in His own person the certainty of the covenant to us. This He did by becoming responsible for our guilt, by sealing the covenant with His blood, and by being openly acknowledged as our triumphant Saviour by the Father, who raised Him from the dead. Thus He is at once God's surety for man, and man's surety for God, and so Mediator between God and man (ch. 8:6). **better**—ch. 8:6; 13:20, "everlasting." **testament**—sometimes translated, "covenant." The *Greek* term implies that it is *appointed* by God, and comprises the relations and bearings partly of a *covenant,* partly of a *testament:* (1) the appointment made without the concurrence

of a second party, of somewhat concerning that second party; a last will or testament, so in ch. 9:16, 17; (2) a mutual agreement in which both parties consent. **23.** Another proof of superiority; the Levitical priests were many, as death caused the need of continually new ones being appointed in succession. Christ dies not, and so hath a priesthood which passes not from one to another. **were** —Greek, "are made." **many**—one after another; opposed to His "*unchangeable* (that does not pass from one to another) priesthood" (vs. 24). **not suffered to continue**—Greek, "hindered from *permanently* continuing," viz., *in the priesthood.* **24. he**—emphatic; Greek, "Himself." So in Psalm 110:4, "THOU art a *priest*"; singular, not *priests,* "many." **continueth**—Greek, simple verb, not the compound as in vs. 23. "Remaineth," viz., *in life.* **unchangeable**—Greek, "hath His priesthood unchangeable"; *not passing from one to another, intransmissible.* Therefore no earthly so-called apostolic succession of priests are His vicegerents. The Jewish priests had *successors* in office, because "they could not continue by reason of death." But this Man, because He liveth ever, hath no successor in office, not even Peter (I Pet. 5:1). **25. Wherefore**—Greek, "Whence"; inasmuch as "He remaineth *for ever.*" **also**—as a natural consequence flowing from the last, at the same time *a new and higher* thing [ALFORD]. **save**—His very name JESUS (vs. 22) meaning *Saviour* —**to the uttermost**—altogether, perfectly, so that nothing should be wanting afterwards for ever [TITTMANN]. It means "in any wise," "utterly," in Luke 13:11. **come unto God**—by faith. **by him**—*through Him* as their mediating Priest, instead of through the Levitical priests. **seeing he ever liveth** —resuming "He continueth ever," vs. 24; therefore "He is able to the uttermost"; He is not, like the Levitical priest, prevented by *death,* for "He ever liveth" (vs. 23). **to make intercession**—There was but the *one offering* on earth once for all. But his *intercession* for us in the heavens (vs. 26) is ever continuing, whence the result follows, that we can never be separated from the love of God in Christ. He *intercedes* only for those who come unto God through Him, not for the unbelieving world (John 17:9). As samples of His intercession, cf. the *prophetical* descriptions in the Old Testament. "By an humble omnipotency (for it was by His *humiliation* that He obtained *all* power), or omnipotent humility, appearing in the presence, and presenting His postulations at the throne of God [BISHOP PEARSON]. He was not only the offering, but the priest who offered it. Therefore, He has become not only a sacrifice, but an intercessor; His intercession being founded on His voluntary offering of Himself without spot to God. We are not only then in virtue of His sacrifice forgiven, but in virtue of the intercession admitted to favor and grace [ARCHBISHOP MAGEE]. **26. such**—as is above described. The oldest MSS. read, "also." "For to us (as *sinners;* emphatical) there was also becoming (besides the other excellencies of our High Priest) such an High Priest." **holy**—"pious" (a distinct Greek word from that for *holy,* which latter implies *consecration*) towards *God;* perfectly answering God's will in reverent piety (Ps. 16:10). **harmless** —lit., "free from evil" and guile, in relation to *Himself.* **undefiled**—not defiled by stain contracted from others, in relation to *men.* Temptation, to which He was exposed, left no trace of evil in Him. **separate**—rather, "*separated* from sinners," viz., in His heavenly state as our High Priest above, after He had been *parted from the earth,* as the Levitical[1] high priest was separated from the people in the sanctuary (whence he was not to go out), Lev. 21:12. Though justifying through faith the ungodly, He hath no contact with them *as such*. He is lifted above our sinful community, being "made higher than the heavens," at the same time that He makes believers *as such* (not as sinners), "to sit together (with Him) in heavenly places" (Eph. 2:6). Just as Moses *on the mount* was separated from and above the people, and alone with God. This proves Jesus is GOD. "Though innumerable lies have been forged against the venerable Jesus, none dared to charge Him with any intemperance" [ORIGEN]. **made**—Jesus WAS higher before (John 17:5), and as the God-MAN was *made* so by the Father after His humiliation (cf. ch. 1:4). **higher than the heavens** —for "He passed *through* [so the *Greek*] the heavens" (ch. 4:14). **27. daily**—"day by day." The priests *daily* offered sacrifices (ch. 9:6; 10:11; Exod. 29:38-42). The high priests took part in these daily-offered sacrifices only on festival days; but as they represented the whole priesthood, the daily offerings are here attributed to them; their exclusive function was to offer the atonement "once every year" (ch. 9:7), and "year by year continually" (ch. 10:1). The "daily" strictly belongs to *Christ*, not to the high priests, "who needeth not daily, as those high priests (*year by year*, and their subordinate priests daily), to offer...." **offer up**—The *Greek* term is peculiarly used of *sacrifices for sin*. The high priest's double offering on the day of atonement, the bullock for himself, and the goat for the people's sins, had its counterpart in the TWO lambs offered daily by the ordinary priests. **this he did**— not "died first for His own sins and then the people's," but *for the people's only*. The negation is twofold: He needeth not to offer (1) daily; nor (2) to offer for His own sins also; for He offered Himself a spotless sacrifice (vs. 26; ch. 4:15). The sinless alone could offer for the sinful. **once**—rather as *Greek*, "once for all." The sufficiency of the *one* sacrifice to atone for *all* sins *for ever*, resulted from its absolute spotlessness. **28. For**—reason for the difference stated in vs. 27, between His one sacrifice and their oft repeated sacrifices, viz., because of His entire freedom from the sinful *infirmity* to which they are subject. *He needed not, as they, to offer* FOR HIS OWN SIN; and being now exempt from death and "perfected for evermore," *He needs not to* REPEAT *His sacrifice.* **the word**—"the word" confirmed by "the oath." **which**—which *oath* was after the law, viz., in Psalm 110:4, abrogating the preceding law-priesthood. **the Son**—contrasted with "men." **consecrated**—*Greek*, "made perfect" once for all, as in ch. 2:10; 5:9, Notes. Opposed to "having infirmity." *Consecrated as a perfected priest* by His perfected sacrifice, and consequent anointing and exaltation to the right hand of the Father.

CHAPTER 8

Vss. 1-13. CHRIST, THE HIGH PRIEST IN THE TRUE SANCTUARY, SUPERSEDING THE LEVITICAL PRIESTHOOD; THE NEW RENDERS OBSOLETE THE OLD COVENANT. **1. the sum**—rather, "the principal point"; for the participle is present, not *past*, which would be required if the meaning were "the sum." "The chief point in (or, 'in the case'; so the *Greek*, ch. 9:10, 15, 17) the things which we are speaking," lit., "which are being spoken." **such**—so transcendently pre-eminent, viz., in this respect, that

"He is set on the right hand of...." Infinitely above all other priests in this one grand respect, He exercises His priesthood IN HEAVEN, not in the *earthly* "holiest place" (ch. 10:12). The Levitical high priests, even when they entered the Holiest Place once a year, only STOOD for a *brief space before the symbol* of God's throne; but Jesus SITS *on the throne* of the Divine Majesty in the heaven itself, and this *for ever* (ch. 10:11, 12). **2. minister** —The *Greek* term implies *priestly ministry* in the temple. **the sanctuary**—*Greek*, "the holy places"; the Holy of Holies. Here the heavenly sanctuary is meant. **the true**—the archetypal and antitypical, as contrasted with the typical and symbolical (ch. 9:24). *Greek alethinos* (used here) is opposed to that which does not fulfil its idea, as for instance, *a type; alethes*, to that which is untrue and unreal, as *a lie*. The measure of *alethes* is reality; that of *alethinos*, ideality. In *alethes* the idea corresponds to the thing; in *alethinos*, the thing to the idea [KALMIS in ALFORD]. **tabernacle**—(ch. 9:11). *His body*. Through His glorified body as the tabernacle, Christ passes into the heavenly "Holy of Holies," the immediate immaterial presence of God, where He intercedes for us. This tabernacle in which God dwells, is where God in Christ meets us who are "members of His body, of His flesh, and of His bones." This tabernacle answers to the heavenly Jerusalem, where God's *visible* presence is to be manifested to His perfected saints and angels, who are united in Christ the Head; in contradistinction to His personal *invisible* presence in the Holy of Holies unapproachable save to Christ. John 1:14, "Word...dwelt among us," *Greek*, "tabernacled." **pitched**—*Greek*, "fixed" firmly. **not man**—as Moses (vs. 5). **3. For**—assigning his reason for calling him "minister of the sanctuary" (vs. 2). **somewhat**—He does not offer again His *once for all* completed sacrifice. But as the high priest did *not* enter the Holy Place *without blood*, so Christ has entered the heavenly Holy Place *with His own blood*. That "blood of sprinkling" is in heaven. And is thence made effectual to sprinkle believers as the end of their election (I Pet. 1:2). The term "consecrate" as a priest, is lit., to *fill the hand*, implying that an offering is given into the hands of the priest, which it is his duty to present to God. If a man be a priest, he must have some gift in his hands to offer. Therefore, Christ, as a priest, has His blood as His oblation to offer before God. **4.** Implying that Christ's priestly office is exercised in heaven, not in earth; in the power of His resurrection life, not of His earthly life. **For**—The oldest MSS. read, "accordingly then." **if...**—"if He were on earth, He would *not even* (so the *Greek*) be a priest" (cf. ch. 7:13, 14); therefore, certainly, He could not exercise the high priestly function in the earthly Holy of Holies. **seeing that...**—"since there are" already, and exist now (the temple service not yet being set aside, as it was on the destruction of Jerusalem), "those (the oldest MSS. omit 'priests') who offer *the* (appointed) gifts according to (the) law." *Therefore, His sacerdotal "ministry" must be "in the heavens," not on earth* (vs. 1). "If His priesthood terminated on the earth, He would not even be a priest at all" [BENGEL]. I conceive that the denial here of Christ's priesthood *on earth* does not extend to the sacrifice on the cross which *He offered as a priest on earth;* but applies only to the crowning work of His priesthood, the *bringing of the blood into the Holy of Holies,* which He could not have done in the *earthly* Holy of Holies, as not being an Aaronic priest. The *place* (the heavenly Holy of Holies) was as essential to the atonement being made as the *oblation* (the blood). The body was burnt without the gate; but the sanctification was effected by the presentation of the blood within the sanctuary by the high priest. If on earth, He would not be a priest. *in the sense of the law of Moses* ("according to the law" is emphatic. **5. Who**—viz., the priests. **serve unto the example**—not "*after* the example," as BENGEL explains. But as in ch. 13:10, "serve the tabernacle," i.e., do it service: so "serve (the tabernacle which is but) *the outline* and shadow." The *Greek* for "example" is here taken for the *sketch, copy,* or *suggestive representation* of the heavenly sanctuary, which is the antitypical reality and primary archetype. "The mount" answers to *heaven,* ch. 12:22. **admonished**—The *Greek* especially applies to *divine responses* and *commands.* **to make**—"perfectly": so the *Greek.* **See**—Take heed, accurately observing the pattern, that so thou mayest make . . . . **saith he** —God. **the pattern**—an accurate representation, presented in vision to Moses, of the heavenly real sanctuary. Thus the earthly tabernacle was copy of a copy; but the latter accurately representing the grand archetypical original in heaven (Exod. 25: 40). **6. now**—not *time;* but "as it is." **more excellent ministry**—than any earthly ministry. **by how much**—in proportion as. **mediator**—coming between us and God, to carry into effect God's covenant with us. "The messenger (angel) of the covenant." **which**—*Greek,* "one which" [ALFORD]: *inasmuch as being one which.* **established**—*Greek,* "enacted as a law." So Romans 3:27, "law of faith"; and 8:2; 9:31, apply "law" to the Gospel covenant. It is implied hereby, the Gospel is founded on the law, in the spirit and essence of the latter. **upon**—resting upon. **better promises**—enumerated vss. 10, 11. The Old Testament promises were mainly of earthly, the New Testament promises, of heavenly blessings: the exact fulfilment of the earthly promises was a pledge of the fulfilment of the heavenly. "Like a physician who prescribes a certain diet to a patient, and then when the patient is beginning to recover, changes the diet, permitting what he had before forbidden; or as a teacher gives his pupil an elementary lesson at first, preparatory to leading him to a higher stage": so RABBI ALBO in his *Ikkarim.* Cf. Jeremiah 7:21, 22, which shows that God's original design in the old covenant ritual system was, that it should be pædagogical, as a schoolmaster leading and preparing men for Christ. **7.** Same reasoning as in ch. 7:11. **faultless**—perfect in all its parts, so as *not to be found fault with* as wanting anything which ought to be there: answering all the purposes of a law. The law in its *morality* was *blameless, Greek-amomos;* but *in saving us* it was defective, and so not *faultless, Greek-amemptos.* **should no place have been sought**—as it has to be now; and as it is sought in the prophecy (vss. 8-11). The old covenant would have anticipated all man's wants, so as to give no occasion for *seeking* something more perfectly adequate. Cf. on the phrase "place . . . sought," ch. 12:17. **8. finding fault with them**—the people of the old covenant, who were not made "faultless" by it (vs. 7); and whose *disregard* of God's covenant made Him to "*regard* them *not*" (vs. 9). The law is not *in itself* blamed, but *the people* who had not observed it. **he saith** —(Jer. 31:31-34; cf. Ezek. 11:19; 36:25-27). At Rama, the headquarters of Nebuzaradan, whither

the captives of Jerusalem had been led, Jeremiah uttered this prophecy of Israel's restoration under another David, whereby Rachel, wailing for her lost children, shall be comforted; literally in part fulfilled at the restoration under Zerubbabel, and more fully to be hereafter at Israel's return to their own land; spiritually fulfilled in the Gospel covenant, whereby God forgives absolutely His people's sins, and writes His law by His Spirit on the hearts of believers, the true Israel. "This prophecy forms the third part of the third trilogy of the three great trilogies into which Jeremiah's prophecies may be divided: Jeremiah 21-25, against the shepherds of the people; 26-29, against the false prophets; 30 and 31, the book of restoration" [DELITZSCH in ALFORD]. **Behold, the days come**—the frequent formula introducing a Messianic prophecy. **make**— *Greek,* "perfect"; "consummate." A suitable expression as to the new covenant, which perfected what the old could not (cf. end of vs. 9, with end of vs. 10). **Israel . . . Judah**—Therefore, the ten tribes, as well as Judah, share in the new covenant. As both shared the exile, so both shall share the literal and spiritual restoration. **9. Not according to . . .**—very different from, and far superior to, the old covenant, which only "worked wrath" (Rom. 4:15) through man's "not regarding" it. The new covenant enables us to obey by the Spirit's inward impulse producing love because of the forgiveness of our sins. **made with**—rather as *Greek,* "made to": the Israelites being only recipients, not co-agents [ALFORD] *with* God. **I took them by the hand**—as a father takes his child by the hand to support and guide his steps. "There are three periods: (1) that of the promise; (2) that of the pædagogical instruction; (3) that of fulfilment" [BENGEL]. The second, that of the pædagogical pupilage, began at the exodus from Egypt. **I regarded them not**—*English Version,* Jeremiah 31:32, translates, "Although *I was an husband unto* them." Paul's translation here is supported by LXX, *Syriac,* and GESENIUS, and accords with the kindred *Arabic.* The Hebrews *regarded not* God, so God, in righteous retribution, *regarded* them *not.* On "continued not in my covenant," SCHELLING observes: The law was in fact the mere *ideal* of a religious constitution: in *practice,* the Jews were throughout, before the captivity, more or less polytheists, except in the time of David, and the first years of Solomon [the type of Messiah's reign]. Even after the return from Babylon, idolatry was succeeded by what was not much better, formalism and hypocrisy (Matt. 12:43). The law was (1) a typical picture, tracing out the features of the glorious Gospel to be revealed; (2) it had a delegated virtue from the Gospel, which ceased, therefore, when the Gospel came. **10. make with**—*Greek,* "make unto." **Israel**—comprising the before disunited (vs. 8) ten tribes' kingdom, and that of Judah. They are united in the spiritual Israel, the elect Church, now: they shall be so in the literal restored kingdom of Israel to come. **I will put**—lit., "(I) giving." This is the first of the "better promises" (vs. 6). **mind**—their intelligent faculty. **in . . .** —rather, "ON their hearts." Not on tables of stone as the law (II Cor. 3:3). **write**—*Greek,* "inscribe." **I will be to them a God . . .**—fulfilled first in the outward kingdom of God. Next, in the inward Gospel kingdom. Thirdly, in the kingdom at once outward and inward, the spiritual being manifested outwardly (Rev. 21:3). Cf. a similar progression as to the priesthood (1) Exodus 19:6; (2) I Peter 2: 5; (3) Isaiah 61:6; Revelation 1:6. This progressive advance of the significance of the Old Testament institutions, etc., says THOLUCK, shows the *transparency* and prophetic character which runs throughout the whole. **11.** Second of the "better promises" (vs. 6). **they shall not**—"they shall not have to teach" [ALFORD]. **his neighbour**—So *Vulgate* reads; but the—oldest MSS. have "his (fellow) *citizen*." **brother**—a closer and more endearing relation than *fellow citizen*. **from the least to the greatest**—*Greek*, "from the little one to the great one." Zechariah 12:8, "He that is feeble among them shall be as David." Under the old covenant, the priest's lips were to keep knowledge, and at his mouth the people were to seek the law: under the new covenant, the Holy Spirit teaches every believer. Not that the mutual teaching of brethren is excluded while the covenant is being promulgated; but when once the Holy Spirit shall have fully taught all the remission of their sins and inward sanctification, then there shall be no further need of man teaching his fellow man. Cf. I Thessalonians 4:9; 5:1, an earnest of that perfect state to come. On the way to that perfect state every man should teach his neighbor. "The teaching is not hard and forced, because grace renders all teachable; for it is not the ministry of the letter, but of the spirit (II Cor. 3:6). The believer's firmness does not depend on the *authority* of human teachers. God Himself teaches" [BENGEL]. The New Testament is shorter than the Old Testament, because, instead of the *details* of an outward letter law, it gives the all-embracing *principles* of the spiritual law written on the conscience, leading one to spontaneous instinctive obedience in outward details. None save the Lord can teach effectually, "know the Lord." **12. For ...**—the *third* of "the better promises" (vs. 6). The *forgiveness of sins* is, and will be, the root of this new state of inward grace and knowledge of the Lord. Sin being abolished, sinners obtain grace. **I will be merciful** *Greek*, "propitious"; the *Hebrew, salach,* is always used of God only in relation to men. **and their iniquities**—not found in *Vulgate, Syriac, Coptic,* and one oldest *Greek* MS.; but most oldest MSS. have the words (cf. ch. 10:17). **remember no more**— Contrast the law, ch. 10:3. **13. he**—God. **made ... old**—"hath (at the time of speaking the prophecy) antiquated the first covenant." From the time of God's mention of a NEW covenant (since God's words are all realities) the first covenant might be regarded as ever dwindling away, until its complete abolition on the actual introduction of the Gospel. Both covenants cannot exist side by side. **Mark** how verbal inspiration is proved in Paul's argument turning wholly on the one word "NEW" (covenant), occurring but once in the Old Testament. **that which decayeth**—*Greek*, "that which is being antiquated," viz., at the time when Jeremiah spake. For in Paul's time, according to his view, the new had absolutely set aside the old covenant. The *Greek* for (*Kaine*) *New* (Testament) implies that it is *of a different kind* and *supersedes the old:* not merely *recent* (*Greek, nea*). Cf. Hosea 3:4, 5.

CHAPTER 9

Vss. 1-28. INFERIORITY OF THE OLD TO THE NEW COVENANT IN THE MEANS OF ACCESS TO GOD: THE BLOOD OF BULLS AND GOATS OF NO REAL AVAIL: THE BLOOD OF CHRIST ALL-SUFFICIENT TO PURGE AWAY SIN, WHENCE FLOWS OUR HOPE OF HIS APPEARING AGAIN FOR OUR PERFECT SALVATION. **1.**

Then verily—*Greek*, "Accordingly then." Resuming the subject from ch. 8:5. In accordance with the command given to Moses, "the first covenant had ...." **had**—not "has," for as a *covenant* it no longer existed, though its rites were observed till the destruction of Jerusalem. **ordinances**—of divine right and institution. **service**—worship. **a worldly sanctuary**—*Greek*, "its (lit., *the*) sanctuary worldly," mundane; consisting of the elements of the visible world. Contrasted with *the heavenly sanctuary*. Cf. vss. 11, 12, "not of this building," vs. 24. Material, outward, perishing (however precious its materials were), and also defective religiously. In vss. 2-5, *"the worldly sanctuary"* is discussed; in vs. 6, etc., the "ordinances of worship." The outer tabernacle the Jews believed, signified *this world;* the Holy of Holies, *heaven.* JOSEPHUS calls the outer, divided into two parts, "a secular and common place," answering to "the earth and sea"; and the inner holiest place, the third part, appropriated to God and not accessible to men. **2.** Defining "the worldly tabernacle." **a tabernacle**— "the tabernacle." **made**—built and furnished. **the first**—the anterior tabernacle. **candlestick ... table** —typifying *light* and *life* (Exod. 25:31-39). The candlestick consisted of a shaft and six branches of gold, seven in all, the bowls made like almonds, with a knop and a flower in one branch. It was carried in Vespasian's triumph, and the figure is to be seen on Titus' arch at Rome. The *table* of shittim wood, covered with gold, was for the shewbread (Exod. 25:23-30). **shew-bread**—lit., "the setting forth of the loaves," i.e., the loaves set forth: "the show of the bread" [ALFORD]. In the outer holy place: so the Eucharist continues until our entrance into the heavenly Holy of Holies (I Cor. 11:26). **which ...**—"which (tabernacle) is called the holy place," as distinguished from "the Holy of Holies." **3. And**—*Greek*, "But." **after**— behind: within. **second veil**—There were two veils or curtains, one before the Holy of Holies (*catapetasma*), here alluded to, the other before the tabernacle door (*calumma*). **called**—as opposed to "the true." **4. golden censer**—The *Greek*, must not be translated "altar of incense," for *it* was not in "the holiest" place "after the second veil," but in "the holy place"; but as in II Chronicles 26:19, and Ezekiel 8:11, "censer": so *Vulgate* and *Syriac.* This GOLDEN censer was only used on the day of atonement (other kinds of censers on other days), and is therefore associated with *the holiest place,* as being taken into it on that anniversary by the high priest. The expression "which had," does not mean that the golden censer was deposited there, for in that case the high priest would have had to go in and bring it out before burning incense in it; but that the golden censer was one of the articles *belonging to,* and used for, the yearly service in the holiest place. He virtually supposes (without specifying) the existence of the "altar of incense" in the anterior holy place, by mentioning *the golden censer* filled with incense from it: the incense answers to *the prayers of the saints;* and the altar though outside the holiest place, is connected with it (*standing close by the second veil, directly before the ark of the covenant*), even as we find an antitypical altar in heaven. The rending of the veil by Christ has brought the antitypes to the altar, candlestick, and shew-bread of the anterior holy place into the holiest place, heaven. In I Kings 6: 22, *Hebrew, the altar* is said to *belong to the oracle,* or holiest place (cf. Exod. 30:6). **ark**—of shittim wood, i.e., acacia. Not in the second temple, but in its stead was a stone basement (called "the stone of foundation"), three fingers high. **pot**—"golden," added in the LXX, and sanctioned by Paul. **manna**—an omer, each man's daily portion. In I Kings 8:9; II Chronicles 5:10, it is said there was nothing in the ark of Solomon's temple save the two stone tables of the law put in by Moses. But the expression that there was nothing THEN therein save the two tables, leaves the inference to be drawn that formerly were the other things mentioned by the Rabbis and by Paul here, the pot of manna (the memorial of God's providential care of Israel) and the rod of Aaron, the memorial of the lawful priesthood (Num. 17:3, 5, 7, 10). The expressions "before the Lord" (Exod. 16:32), and "before the testimony" (Num. 17:10) thus mean, IN the ark." "In," however, may be used here (as the corresponding *Hebrew* word) as to things *attached to* the ark as appendages, as the book of the law was put *"in the side of the ark,"* and so the golden jewels offered by the Philistines (I Sam. 6:8). **tables of the covenant**—(Deut. 9:9; 10:2). **5. over it**—over "the ark of the covenant." **cherubim**—representing the ruling powers by which God acts in the moral and natural world. (See my *Note,* Ezek. 1:6; 10:1.) Hence sometimes they answer to the ministering angels; but mostly to the elect redeemed, by whom God shall hereafter rule the world and set forth His manifold wisdom: redeemed humanity, combining in, and with itself, the highest forms of subordinate creaturely life; not angels. They stand on the mercy seat, and *on that ground* become the habitation of God, from which His glory is to shine upon the world. They expressly say, Revelation 5:8-10, "Thou hast *redeemed us.*" They are there *distinguished from the angels,* and associated with the elders. They were of one piece with the mercy seat, even as the Church is one with Christ: their sole standing is on the blood-sprinkled mercy seat; they gaze down at it as the redeemed shall for ever; they are "the habitation of God through the Spirit." **of glory** —The cherubim were *bearers* of the divine *glory,* whence, perhaps, they derive their name. The Shekinah, or cloud of *glory,* in which Jehovah appeared between the cherubim over the mercy seat, the lid of the ark, is doubtless the reference. THOLUCK thinks the twelve loaves of the shew-bread represent the twelve tribes of the nation, *presented as a community* before God consecrated to Him [just as in the Lord's Supper believers, the spiritual Israel, all partaking of the one bread, and becoming one bread and one body, present themselves before the Lord as consecrated to Him, I Cor. 10:16, 17]; the oil and light, the pure knowledge of the Lord, in which the covenant people are to shine [the *seven* (lights), implying perfection]; the ark of the covenant, the symbol of God's kingdom in the old covenant, and representing God dwelling among His own; the ten commandments in the ark, the law as the basis of union between God and man; the mercy seat covering the law and sprinkled with the blood of atonement for the collective sin of the people, God's mercy [in Christ] stronger than the law; the cherubim, the personified [redeemed] creation, looking down on the mercy seat, where God's mercy, and God's law, are set forth as the basis of creation. **mercy seat**—*Greek,* "the propitiatory": the golden cover of the ark, on which was sprinkled the blood of the propitiatory sacrifice on the day of atonement; the footstool of Jehovah, the meeting-place of Him and His people. **we cannot**—conveniently: besides what met the eye in

the sanctuary, there were spiritual realities symbolized which it would take too long to discuss in detail, our chief subject at present being the *priesthood* and the *sacrifices.* "Which" refers not merely to the cherubim, but to *all* the contents of the sanctuary enumerated in vss. 2-5. **6.** The use made of the sanctuary so furnished by the high priest on the anniversary of atonement. **ordained** —arranged. **always**—twice at the least every day, for the morning and evening care of the lamps, and offering of incense (Exod. 30:7, 8). **went**—*Greek,* "enter": present tense. **7. once every year**—the tenth day of the seventh month. He entered within the veil *on that day* twice at least. Thus "once" means here *on the one occasion only.* The two, or possibly more, entrances on that one day were regarded as parts of the one whole. **not without blood**—(ch. 8:3). **offered**—*Greek,* "offers." **errors**—*Greek,* "ignorances": "inadvertent errors." They might have known, as the law was clearly promulged, and they were bound to study it; so that their *ignorance* was culpable (cf. Acts 3: 17; Eph. 4:18; I Pet. 1:14). Though one's ignorance may mitigate one's punishment (Luke 12:48), it does not wholly exempt from punishment. **8. The Holy Ghost**—Moses himself did not comprehend the typical meaning (I Pet. 1:11, 12). **signifying**—by the typical exclusion of all from the holiest, save the high priest once a year. **the holiest of all**—heaven, the antitype. **the first tabernacle**—the anterior tabernacle, representative of the whole Levitical system. *While it* (the first tabernacle, and that which represents the Levitical system) *as yet "has a standing"* (so the Greek, i.e., "has continuance": "lasts"), *the way to heaven* (the antitypical "holiest place") *is not yet made manifest* (cf. ch. 10:19, 20). The Old Testament economy is represented by the holy place, the New Testament economy by the Holy of Holies. Redemption, by Christ, has opened the Holy of Holies (access to heaven by *faith* now, ch. 4:16; 7:19, 25; 10:19, 22; by *sight* hereafter, Isa. 33:24; Rev. 11: 19; 21:2, 3) to all mankind. The *Greek* for "not yet" (*me po*) refers to the mind of the Spirit: the Spirit intimating that men should *not think* the way was yet opened [TITTMANN]. The *Greek* negative, *ou po,* would deny the *fact* objectively; *me po* denies the thing subjectively. **9. Which**—"The which," viz., anterior tabernacle: "as being that which was" [ALFORD]. **figure**—*Greek,* "parable": *a parabolic setting forth of the character of the Old Testament.* **for**—"*in reference to the existing time.*" *The time of the temple worship really belonged to the Old Testament, but continued still in Paul's time and that of his Hebrew readers.* "The time of reformation" (vs. 10) stands in contrast to this, "the existing time"; though, in reality, "the time of reformation," the New Testament time, was now *present* and existing. So "the age *to come,*" is the phrase applied to the Gospel, because it was *present only to believers,* and its fulness even to them is still *to come.* Cf. vs. 11, "good things to come." **in which**—*tabernacle,* not *time,* according to the reading of the oldest MSS. Or translate, "according to which" *parabolic representation,* or *figure.* **were**—*Greek,* "are." **gifts**—unbloody oblations. **could not**—*Greek,* "cannot": are not able. **him that did the service**—any worshipper. The *Greek* is *latreuein, serve* God, which is all men's duty; not *leitourgein,* to serve in a *ministerial office.* **make . . . perfect**—perfectly remove the sense of guilt, and sanctify inwardly through love. **as pertaining to the conscience**—"in respect to the (moral-religious) consciousness." They can only reach as far as the outward flesh (cf. "*carnal* ordinances," vss. 10, 13, 14). **10.** *Which* —sacrifices. *stood*—consisted in [ALFORD]; or, *have attached to them* only things which appertain to the use of foods, etc. The rites of meats, etc., go *side by side* with the sacrifices [THOLUCK and WAHL]; cf. Colossians 2:16. **drinks**—(Lev. 10:9; 11:4). Usage subsequently to the law added many observances as to meats and drinks. **washings**— (Exod. 29:4). **and carnal ordinances**—One oldest MS., *Syriac* and *Coptic,* omit "and." "Carnal ordinances" stand in apposition to "sacrifices" (vs. 9). *Carnal* (outward, affecting only the *flesh*) is opposed to *spiritual.* Contrast "flesh" with "conscience" (vss. 13, 14). **imposed**—as a burden (Acts 15:10, 28) continually pressing heavy. **until the time of reformation**—*Greek,* "the *season* of *rectification,*" when the reality should supersede the type (ch. 8:8-12). Cf. "better," vs. 23. **11. But**—in contrast to "*could not* make . . . perfect" (vs. 9). **Christ**—The Messiah, of whom all the prophets foretold; not "Jesus" here. From whom the "reformation" (vs. 10), or *rectification,* emanates, which frees from the yoke of carnal ordinances, and which is being realized gradually now, and shall be perfectly in the consummation of the age (world) to come." "Christ . . . High Priest," exactly answers to Leviticus 4:5, "the priest that is anointed." **being come an . . .**—rather, "having come forward (cf. ch. 10:7, a different *Greek* word, picturesquely presenting Him before us) *as* High Priest." The Levitical priests must therefore retire. Just as on the day of atonement, no work was done, no sacrifice was offered, or priest was allowed to be in the tabernacle while the high priest went into the holiest place to make atonement (Lev. 16:17, 29). So not our righteousness, nor any other priest's sacrifice, but Christ alone atones; and as the high priest before offering incense had on common garments of a priest, but after it wore his holy garments of "glory and beauty" (Exod. 28) in entering the holiest, so Christ entered the heavenly holiest in His glorified body. **good things to come**—*Greek,* "*the* good things to come," ch. 10:1; "better promises," (ch. 8:6; the "eternal inheritance," vs. 15; I Peter 1:4; the "things hoped for," ch. 11:1. **by a . . . tabernacle**—joined with "He entered." Translate, "*Through the . . . tabernacle*" (of which we know) [ALFORD]. As the Jewish high priest passed *through* the anterior tabernacle into the holiest place, so Christ passed through *heaven* into the inner abode of the unseen and unapproachable God. Thus, "the tabernacle" here is the *heavens through* which He passed (*Note,* ch. 4:14). But "the tabernacle" is also the *glorified body* of Christ (*Note,* ch. 8:2), "not of this building" (not of the mere natural "*creation,* but of the spiritual and heavenly, *the new creation*"), the Head of the mystical body, the Church. *Through* this glorified body He passes into the heavenly holiest place (vs. 24), the immaterial, unapproachable presence of God, where He intercedes for us. *His glorified body,* as the meeting-place of God and all Christ's redeemed, and the angels, answers to *the heavens* through which He passed, and passes. His *body* is opposed to the *tabernacle,* as His blood to the blood of goats, etc. **greater**— as contrasted with the small dimensions of the earthly anterior tabernacle. **more perfect**—effective in giving pardon, peace, sanctification, and access to closest communion with God (cf. vs. 9, ch. 10:1). **not made with hands**—but by the Lord

Himself (ch. 8:2). **12. Neither**—"Nor yet." **by**—"through"; as the means of His approach. **goats . . . calves**—not a bullock, such as the Levitical high priest offered for himself, and a goat for the people, on the day of atonement (Lev. 16:6, 15), *year by year,* whence the plural is used, *goats . . . calves.* Besides the goat offered for the people the blood of which was sprinkled before the mercy seat, the high priest led forth a second goat, viz., the scapegoat; over it he confessed the people's sins, putting them on the head of the goat, which was sent as the sin-bearer into the wilderness out of sight, implying that the atonement effected by the goat sin offering (of which the ceremony of the scapegoat is a part, and not distinct from the sin offering) consisted in the transfer of the people's sins on the goat, and their consequent removal out of sight. The translation of sins on the victim usual in other expiatory sacrifices being omitted in the case of the slain goat, but employed in the case of the goat sent away, proved the two goats were regarded as one offering [ARCHBISHOP MAGEE]. Christ's death is symbolized by the slain goat; His resurrection to life by the living goat sent away. Modern Jews substitute in some places a *cock for* the goat as an expiation, the sins of the offerers being transferred to the entrails, and exposed on the housetop for the birds to carry out of sight, as the scapegoat did; the *Hebrew* for "man" and "cock" being similar, *gebher* [BUXTORF]. **by**—"through," as the means of His entrance; the key unlocking the heavenly Holy of Holies to Him. The *Greek* is forcible, "through THE blood of His own" (cf. vs. 23). **once**—"once for all." **having obtained**—having *thereby* obtained; lit., "found for Himself," as a thing of insuperable difficulty to all save Divine Omnipotence, self-devoting zeal, and love, to find. The access of Christ to the Father was arduous (ch. 5:7). None before had trodden the path. **eternal**—The entrance of our Redeemer, *once for all,* into the heavenly holiest place, secures *eternal* redemption to us; whereas the Jewish high priest's entrance was repeated year by year, and the effect temporary and partial, "On redemption," cf. Matt. 20:28; Eph. 1:7; Col. 1:14; I Tim. 2:5, Titus 2:14; I Pet. 1:19.

13-28. PROOF OF, AND ENLARGEMENT ON, THE "ETERNAL REDEMPTION" MENTIONED IN VS. 12. For His blood, offered by Himself, purifies not only outwardly, as the Levitical sacrifices on the day of atonement, but inwardly unto the service of the living God (vss. 13, 14). His death is the inaugurating act of the new covenant, and of the heavenly sanctuary (vss. 15-23). His entrance into the true Holy of Holies is the consummation of His once-for-all-offered sacrifice of atonement (vss. 24, 26); henceforth, His reappearance alone remains to complete our redemption (vss. 27, 28). **13. if**—as we know is the case; so the *Greek* indicative means. Argument from the less to the greater. If the blood of mere brutes could purify in any, however small a degree, how much more shall inward purification, and complete and eternal salvation, be wrought by the blood of Christ, in whom dwelt all the fulness of the Godhead? **ashes of an heifer**— (Num. 19:16-18). The type is full of comfort for us. The water of separation, made of the ashes of the red heifer, was the provision for removing ceremonial defilement whenever incurred *by contact with the dead.* As she was slain without the camp, so Christ (cf. ch. 13:11; Num. 19:3, 4). The ashes were laid by for constant use; so the continually cleansing effects of Christ's blood, once for all shed.

In our wilderness journey we are continually contracting defilement by contact with the spiritually dead, and with dead works, and need therefore continual application to the antitypical life-giving cleansing blood of Christ, whereby we are afresh restored to peace and living communion with God in the heavenly holy place. **the unclean**—*Greek,* "those defiled" on any particular occasion. **purifying**—*Greek,* "purity." **the flesh**—Their effect in themselves extended no further. The law had a carnal and a spiritual aspect; *carnal,* as an instrument of the Hebrew polity, God, their King, accepting, in minor offenses, expiatory victims instead of the sinner, otherwise doomed to death; spiritual, as *the shadow of good things to come* (ch. 10:1). The spiritual Israelite derived, in partaking of these legal rights, spiritual blessings not flowing from them, but from the great antitype. Ceremonial sacrifices released from *temporal penalties* and *ceremonial disqualifications;* Christ's sacrifice releases from *everlasting penalties* (vs. 12), and *moral impurities on the conscience* disqualifying from access to God (vs. 14). The purification of the *flesh* (the mere outward man) was by "sprinkling"; the *washing* followed by inseparable connection (Num. 19: 19). So *justification* is followed by *renewing.* **14. offered himself**—The voluntary nature of the offering gives it especial efficacy. He "through the eternal Spirit," i.e., His divine Spirit (Rom. 1:4, in contrast to His "flesh," vs. 3; *His Godhead,* I Tim. 3:16; I Pet. 3:18), "His inner personality" [ALFORD], which gave a free consent to the act, offered Himself. The animals offered had no *spirit* or will to consent in the act of sacrifice; they were offered *according to the law;* they had a life neither enduring, nor of any intrinsic efficacy. But He from eternity, with *His divine and everlasting Spirit,* concurred with the Father's will of redemption by Him. His offering began on the altar of the cross, and was completed in His entering the holiest place with His blood. The *eternity* and infinitude of His divine Spirit (cf. ch. 7:16) gives *eternal* ("*eternal* redemption," vs. 12, also cf. vs. 15) and infinite merit to His offering, so that not even the infinite justice of God has any exception to take against it. It was "through His most burning love, flowing from His eternal Spirit," that He offered Himself [ŒCOLAMPADIUS]. **without spot**—The animal victims had to be without *outward* blemish; Christ on the cross was a victim *inwardly* and *essentially* stainless (I Pet. 1:19). **purge**—purify from fear, guilt, alienation from Him, and selfishness, the source of *dead works* (vss. 22, 23). **your**—The oldest MSS. read "our." *Vulgate,* however, supports *English Version* reading. **conscience**—moral religious *consciousness.* **dead works**—All works done in the natural state, which is a state of sin, are *dead;* for they come not from living faith in, and love to, "the living God" (ch. 11:6). As contact with a dead body defiled ceremonially (cf. the allusion, "ashes of an heifer," vs. 13), so dead works defile the inner consciousness spiritually. **to serve**—*so as to* serve. The ceremonially unclean could not *serve* God in the outward communion of His people; so the unrenewed cannot serve God in spiritual communion. Man's works before justification, however lifelike they look, are dead, and cannot therefore be accepted before the living God. To have offered a dead animal to God would have been an insult (cf. Mal. 1:8); much more for a man not justified by Christ's blood to offer dead works. But those purified by Christ's blood in *living* faith do serve. (Rom. 12:1), and shall more fully serve

God (Rev. 22:3). **living God**—therefore requiring living spiritual service (John 4:24). **15. for this cause**—Because of the all-cleansing power of His blood, this fits Him to be Mediator (ch. 8:6, ensuring to both parties, God and us, the ratification) of the new covenant, which secures both forgiveness for the sins not covered by the former imperfect covenant or testament, and also an eternal inheritance to the called. **by means of death**—rather, as *Greek,* "death having taken place." At the moment that His death took place, the necessary effect is, "the called receive the (*fulfilment of the*) promise" (so Luke 24:49 uses "promise"; ch. 6:15; Acts 1:4); that moment divides the Old from the New Testament. The "called" are the elect "heirs," "partakers of the heavenly calling" (ch. 3:1). **redemption of . . . transgressions . . . under . . . first testament**—the transgressions of *all men* from Adam to Christ, first against the primitive revelation, then against the revelations to the patriarchs, then against the law given to Israel, the representative people of the world. The "first testament" thus includes the whole period from Adam to Christ, and not merely that of the covenant with Israel, which was a concentrated representation of *the covenant made with* (or *the first testament* given to) *mankind by sacrifice,* down from the fall to redemption. Before the *inheritance by the New Testament* (for here the idea of the "INHERITANCE," following as the result of Christ's "death," being introduced, requires the *Greek* to be translated "testament," as it was before *covenant*) could come in, there must be *redemption* of (i.e., deliverance from the penalties incurred by) the *transgressions* committed *under the first testament,* for the propitiatory sacrifices under the first testament reached only as far as removing outward ceremonial defilement. But in order to obtain the inheritance which is a reality, there must be a real propitiation, since God could not enter into covenant relation with us so long as past sins were unexpiated; Romans 3:24, 25, "a propitiation . . . His righteousness for the remission of sins that are past." **might**—*Greek,* "may receive," which previously they could not (ch. 11:39, 40). **the promise**—to Abraham. **16.** A general axiomatic truth; it is "*a* testament"; not *the* testament. The testator must die before his *testament* takes effect (vs. 17). This is a common meaning of the *Greek* noun *diathece.* So in Luke 22:29, "I appoint (by testamentary disposition; the cognate *Greek* verb *diatithemai*) unto you a kingdom, as my Father hath appointed unto me." The need of death before the testamentary appointment takes effect, holds good in Christ's relation as MAN to us; of course not in *God's* relation to Christ. **be**—lit., be borne": "be involved in the case"; *be inferred;* or else, "be brought forward in court," so as to give effect to the will. This sense (*testament*) of the *Greek diathece* here does not exclude its other secondary senses in the other passages of the New Testament: (1) a *covenant* between *two* parties; (2) an arrangement, or disposition, made by *God alone* in relation to us. Thus, Matthew 26:28 may be translated, "Blood of the *covenant";* for a *testament* does not require *blood* shedding. Cf. Exodus 24:8 (*covenant*), which Christ quotes, though it is probable He *included* in a sense "testament" also under the *Greek* word *diathece* (comprehending *both* meanings, "covenant" and "testament"), as this designation strictly and properly applies to the new dispensation, and is rightly applicable to the old also, not in itself, but when viewed as typifying the new, which is properly a *testament.* Moses

(Exod. 24:8) speaks of the same thing as [Christ and] Paul. Moses, by the term "covenant," does not mean aught save one concerning giving the heavenly *inheritance* typified by Canaan after the death of the *Testator*, which he represented by the sprinkling of blood. And Paul, by the term "testament," does not mean aught save one having *conditions* attached to it, one which is at the same time a *covenant* [POLI, *Synopsis*]; the conditions are fulfilled by Christ, not by us, except that we must *believe*, but even this God works in His people. THOLUCK explains, as elsewhere, "*covenant* . . . covenant . . . mediating victim"; the *masculine* is used of the victim personified, and regarded as mediator of the covenant; especially as in the new covenant a MAN (Christ) took the place of the victim. The covenanting parties used to pass between the divided parts of the sacrificed animals; but, without reference to this rite, the need of a *sacrifice* for establishing a covenant sufficiently explains this verse. Others, also, explaining the *Greek* as "covenant," consider that the death of the sacrificial victim represented in all covenants the death of both parties as *unalterably bound to the covenant*. So in the redemption-covenant, the death of Jesus symbolized the death of God (?) in the person of the mediating victim, and the death of man in the same. But the expression is not "there must be the death of *both parties* making the covenant," but *singular*, "of *Him* who *made* (aorist, past time; not 'of Him *making*') the testament." Also, it is "death," not "sacrifice" or "slaying." Plainly, the death is supposed to be *past* (aorist, "made"); and the fact of the death is *brought* (*Greek*) before court to give effect to the will. These requisites of a will, or testament, concur here: (1) a testator; (2) heirs; (3) goods; (4) the death of the testator; (5) the fact of the death *brought forward* in court. In Matthew 26:28 two other requisites appear: *witnesses*, the disciples; and a *seal*, the sacrament of the Lord's Supper, the sign of His *blood* wherewith the testament is primarily sealed. It is true the *heir* is ordinarily the *successor* of him who dies and so ceases to have the possession. But in this case Christ comes to life again, and is Himself (including all that He hath), in the power of His now endless life, His people's inheritance; in *His* being Heir (ch. 1:2), *they* are heirs. **17. after**—lit., "over," as we say "*upon* the death of the testators"; not as THOLUCK, "on the condition that slain sacrifices be there," which the *Greek* hardly sanctions. **otherwise**—"seeing that it is never availing" [ALFORD]. BENGEL and LACHMANN read with an interrogation, "Since, is it ever in force (surely not) while the testator liveth?" **18. Whereupon**—rather, "Whence." **dedicated**—"inaugurated." The Old Testament strictly and formally began on that day of inauguration. "Where the *disposition*, or *arrangement*, is ratified by the blood of another, viz., of animals, which cannot make a *covenant*, much less make a *testament*, it is not strictly a *testament*, where it is ratified by the death of him that makes the arrangement, it is strictly, *Greek diathece*, *Hebrew berith*, taken in a wider sense, a *testament*" [BENGEL]; thus, in vs. 18, referring to the old dispensation, we may translate, "the first (*covenant*)": or better, retain "the first (*testament*)," not that the old dispensation, *regarded by itself*, is a *testament*, but it is so when regarded as the *typical representative of the new*, which is strictly a *Testament*. **19. For**—confirming the general truth, vs. 16. **spoken . . . according to the law**—strictly adhering to every direction of "the law of commandments

contained in ordinances" (Eph. 2:15). Cf. Exodus 24:3, "Moses told the people *all the words of the Lord, and all the judgments;* and *all the people* answered with one voice . . . ." **the blood of calves**—*Greek,* "the calves," viz., those sacrificed by the "young men" whom he sent to do so (Exod. 24:5). The "peace offerings" there mentioned were "of *oxen*" (LXX, 'little calves'), and the "burnt offerings" were probably (though this is not specified), as on the day of atonement, *goats*. The law in Exodus sanctioned formally many sacrificial practices in use by tradition, from the primitive revelation long before. **with water**—prescribed, though not in Exodus 24, yet in other purifications; e.g., of the leper, and the water of separation which contained the ashes of the red heifer. **scarlet wool, and hyssop**—ordinarily used for purification. *Scarlet* or *crimson,* resembling blood: it was thought to be a peculiarly deep, fast dye, whence it typified sin (*Note,* Isa. 1:18). So Jesus wore a scarlet robe, the emblem of the deep-dyed sins He bore *on* Him, though He had none *in* Him. Wool was used as imbibing and retaining water; the hyssop, as a bushy, tufty plant (wrapt round with the scarlet wool), was used for sprinkling it. The wool was also a symbol of purity (Isa. 1:18). The *Hyssopus officinalis* grows on walls, with small lancet-formed woolly leaves, an inch long, with blue and white flowers, and a knotty stalk about a foot high. **sprinkled . . . the book**—viz., out of which he had read "every precept": the book of the testament or covenant. This sprinkling of the book is not mentioned in Exodus 24. Hence BENGEL translates, "And (having taken) the book itself (so Exod. 24:7), he both sprinkled all the people, and (vs. 21) moreover sprinkled the tabernacle." But the *Greek* supports *English Version*. Paul, by inspiration, supplies the particular specified here, not in Exodus 24:7. The sprinkling of the *roll* (so the *Greek* for "book") of the covenant, or testament, as well as of the people, implies that neither can *the law* be fulfilled, nor the people be purged from their sins, save by the sprinkling of the blood of Christ (I Pet. 1:2). Cf. vs. 33, which shows that there is something antitypical to the Bible in heaven itself (cf. Rev. 20:12). The *Greek*, "itself," distinguishes *the book itself* from the "precepts" in it which he "spake." **20.** Exodus 24:8, "*Behold* the blood of the covenant, which *the Lord* has made with you concerning all these words." The change is here made to accord with Christ's inauguration of the new testament, or covenant, as recorded in Luke 22:20, "This cup (is) the new Testament in My blood, which is shed for you": the only Gospel in which the "is" has to be supplied. Luke was *Paul's* companion, which accounts for the correspondence, as here too "is" has to be supplied. **testament**—(*Note*, vss. 16, 17). The *Greek diathece* means both "testament" and "covenant": the term "covenant" better suits the old dispensation, though the idea *testament* is included, for the old was one in its typical relation to the new dispensation, to which the term "testament" is better suited. Christ has sealed the testament with His *blood*, of which the Lord's Supper is the sacramental sign. The testator was represented by the animals slain in the old dispensation. In both dispensations the inheritance was bequeathed: in the new by One who has come in person and died; in the old by the same one, only typically and ceremonially present. See ALFORD's excellent *Note*. **enjoined unto you**—*commissioned* me to ratify *in relation to you*. In the old dispensation the condition to be fulfilled on the people's part is implied in the words, Exodus 24:8, "(Lord made with you) *concerning all these words.*" But here Paul omits this clause, as he includes the fulfilment of this condition of obedience to "all these words" in the new covenant, as part of God's promise, in ch. 8:8, 10, 12, whereby Christ fulfils all for our justification, and will enable us by putting His Spirit in us to fulfil all in our now progressive, and finally complete, sanctification. **21.** *Greek,* "And, moreover, *in like manner.*" The *sprinkling of the tabernacle with blood* is added by inspiration here to the account in Exodus 30:25-30; 40:9, 10, which mentions only Moses' anointing the tabernacle and its vessels. In Leviticus 8:10, 15, 30, the sprinkling of blood upon Aaron and his garments, and upon his sons, and upon the altar, is mentioned as well as the anointing, so that we might naturally infer, as JOSEPHUS has distinctly stated, that the tabernacle and its vessels were sprinkled with blood as well as being anointed: Leviticus 16. 16, 20, 33, virtually sanctions this inference. The tabernacle and its contents needed purification (II Chron. 29:21). **22.** almost—to be joined with "all things," viz., *almost all things* under the old dispensation. The exceptions to *all things being purified by blood* are, Exodus 19:10; Leviticus 15:5, etc., 16:26, 28; 22:6; Numbers 31:22-24. **without**—*Greek,* "apart from." **shedding of blood**—*shed* in the slaughter of the victim, and poured out at the altar subsequently. The *pouring out of the blood on the altar* is the main part of the sacrifice (Lev. 17:11), and it could not have place apart from the previous *shedding of* the blood in the slaying. Paul has, perhaps, in mind here, Luke 22:20, "This cup is the new testament in my blood, which is shed for you." **is**—*Greek,* "takes place": comes to pass. **remission**—of sins: a favorite expression of Luke, Paul's companion. Properly used of remitting a debt (Matt. 6:12; 18:27, 32); our sins are debts. On the truth here, cf. Leviticus 5:11-13, an exception because of poverty, confirming the general rule. **23.** **patterns**—"the suggestive representations"; the typical copies (*Note,* ch. 8:5). **things in the heavens**—the heavenly tabernacle and the things therein. **purified with these**—with the blood of bulls and goats. **heavenly things themselves**—the archetypes. Man's sin had introduced an element of disorder into the relations of God and His holy angels in respect to man. The *purification* removes this element of disorder and changes God's wrath against man in heaven (designed to be the place of God's revealing His grace to men and angels) into a smile of reconciliation. Cf. "peace in heaven" (Luke 19:38). "The uncreated heaven of God, though in itself untroubled light, yet needed a purification in so far as the light of love was obscured by the fire of wrath against sinful man" [DELITZSCH *in* ALFORD]. Contrast Revelation 12:7-10. Christ's atonement had the effect also of casting Satan out of heaven (Luke 10:18; John 12:31, cf. ch. 2:14). Christ's body, the true tabernacle (*Notes,* ch. 8:2; 9:11), as bearing our imputed sin (II Cor. 5:21), was consecrated (John 17:17, 19) and purified by the shedding of His blood to be the meeting-place of God and man. **sacrifices**—The plural is used in expressing the general proposition, though strictly referring to the *one* sacrifice of Christ once for all. Paul implies that His one sacrifice, by its matchless excellency, is equivalent to the Levitical many sacrifices. It, though but one, is manifold in its effects and applicability to many. **24.** Resumption more fully of the thought, "He entered in once into the holy place," vs. 12.

He has in vss. 13, 14, expanded the words "by his own blood," vs. 12; and in vss. 15-23, he has enlarged on "an High Priest of good things to come." **not ... into ... holy places made with hands**—as was the Holy of Holies in the earthly tabernacle (*Note,* vs. 11). **figures**—copies "of the true" holiest place, heaven, the original archetype (ch. 8:5). **into heaven itself**—the immediate presence of the invisible God beyond all the created heavens, *through* which latter Jesus passed (*Note,* ch. 4:14; I Tim. 6: 16). **now**—ever since His ascension in the present economy (cf. vs. 26). **to appear**—TO PRESENT HIMSELF; *Greek,* "to be made to appear." Mere man may have a vision through a medium, or veil, as Moses had (Exod. 33:18, 20-23). Christ alone beholds the Father without a veil, and is His perfect image. Through seeing HIM only can we see the Father. **in the presence of God**—*Greek,* "to the face of God." The saints shall hereafter see God's face in Christ (Rev. 22:4): the earnest of which is now given (II Cor. 3:18). Aaron, the Levitical high priest *for* the people, stood *before the ark* and only saw the *cloud,* the symbol of God's glory (Exod. 28:30). **for us**—in our behalf as our Advocate and Intercessor (ch. 7:25; Rom. 8:34; I John 2:1). "It is enough that Jesus should *show Himself for us* to the Father: the sight of Jesus satisfied God in our behalf. He brings before the face of God no offering which has exhausted itself, and, as only sufficing for a time, needs renewal; but He himself is in person, by virtue of the eternal Spirit, i.e., the imperishable life of His person, now and for ever freed from death, our eternally present offering before God" [DELITZSCH *in* ALFORD]. **25.** As in vs. 24, Paul said, it was not into the typical, but the true sanctuary, that Christ is entered; so now he says, that His sacrifice needs not, as the Levitical sacrifices did, to be repeated. Construe, *"Nor yet* did He enter for this purpose *that He may offer Himself often,"* i.e., *present Himself in the presence of God,* as the high priest does (Paul uses the *present tense,* as the legal service was then existing), year by year, on the day of atonement, entering the Holy of Holies. **with**—lit., "in." **blood of others**—*not his own,* as Christ did. **26. then**—in that case. **must ... have suffered**—rather as *Greek,* "It would have been necessary for Him often to suffer." In order to "offer" (vs. 25), or present Himself often before God in the heavenly holiest place, like the legal high priests making fresh renewals of this high priestly function. He would have had, and would have often to suffer. His *oblation* of Himself before God was once for all (i.e., the bringing in of His blood into the heavenly Holy of Holies), and therefore the preliminary *suffering* was once for all. **since the foundation of the world**—The continued sins of men, from their first creation, would entail a continual suffering on earth, and consequent oblation of His blood in the heavenly holiest place, *since the foundation of the world,* if the one oblation "in the fulness of time" were not sufficient. PHILO, *de Mon.,* p. 637, shows that the high priest of the Hebrews offered sacrifices for the whole human race. "If there had been greater efficacy in the repetition of the oblation, Christ necessarily would not have been so long promised, but would have been sent immediately after the foundation of the world to suffer, and offer Himself at successive periods" [GROTIUS]. **now**—as the case is. **once**—for all; without need of renewal. Rome's fiction of an UNBLOODY sacrifice in the mass, contradicts her assertion that the *blood* of Christ is present in the wine; and also confutes her assertion that the mass is propitiatory; for, if *unbloody*, it cannot be *propitiatory;* for *without shedding of blood there is no remission* (vs. 22). Moreover, the expression "once" for all here, and in vs. 28, and ch. 10:10, 12, proves the falsity of her view that there is a continually repeated offering of Christ in the Eucharist or mass. The offering of Christ was a thing once done that it might be thought of for ever (*Note;* cf. ch. 10:12). **in the end of the world**—Greek, "at the consummation of the ages"; the winding up of all the previous ages from the foundation of the world; to be followed by a new age (ch. 1:1, 2). The last age, beyond which no further age is to be expected before Christ's speedy second coming, which is the complement of the first coming; lit., "the ends of the ages"; Matthew 28:20 is lit., "the consummation of *the age*," or *world* (singular; not as here, plural, *ages*). Cf. "the fulness of times," Ephesians 1:10. **appeared**—Greek, "been manifested" on earth (I Tim. 3:16; I Pet. 1:20). *English Version* has confounded three distinct *Greek* verbs, by translating all alike, vss. 24, 26, 28, "appear." But, in vs. 24, it is "to present Himself," viz., *before God in the heavenly sanctuary;* in vs. 26, "been manifested" *on earth.* in vs. 28, "shall be seen" by all, and especially believers. **put away**—abolish; doing away sin's power as well by delivering men from its guilt and penalty, so that it should be powerless to condemn men, as also from its yoke, so that they shall at last sin no more. **sin**—singular number; all the sins of men of every age are regarded as *one mass* laid on Christ. He hath not only atoned for all *actual sins,* but destroyed *sin itself.* John 1:29, "Behold the Lamb of God that taketh away the *sin* (not merely *the sins:* singular, not plural) of the world." **by the sacrifice of himself**—Greek, "by (through) *His own* sacrifice"; not by "blood *of others*" (vs. 25). ALFORD loses this contrast in translating, "by His sacrifice." **27. as**—inasmuch as. **it is appointed**—Greek, "it is *laid up* (as our appointed lot)," Colossians 1:5. The word "appointed" (so *Hebrew seth* means) in the case of man, answers to "anointed" in the case of Jesus; therefore "the Christ," i.e., *the anointed,* is the title here given designedly. He is the representative man; and there is a strict correspondence between the history of *man* and that of *the Son of man.* The two most solemn facts of our being are here connected with the two most gracious truths of our dispensation, our death and judgment answering in parallelism to Christ's first coming to die for us, and His second coming to consummate our salvation. **once**—and no more. **after this the judgment**—viz., at Christ's appearing, to which, in vs. 28, "judgment" in this verse is parallel. Not, "after this comes the heavenly glory." The intermediate state is a state of joyous, or else agonizing and fearful, *expectation* of "judgment"; after the judgment comes the full and final state of joy, or else woe. **28. Christ**—Greek, "THE Christ"; the representative MAN; representing all men, as the first Adam did. **once offered**—not "often," vs. 25; just as "men," of whom He is the representative Head, are appointed by God *once* to die. He did not need to die again and again for each individual, or each successive generation of men, for He represents *all* men of every age, and therefore needed to die but once for all, so as to exhaust the penalty of death incurred by all. He was offered by the Father, His own "eternal Spirit" (vs. 14) concurring; as Abraham spared not Isaac, but offered him, the son himself unresistingly sub-

mitting to the father's will (Gen. 22). **to bear the sins**—referring to Isaiah 53:12, "He bare the sins of many," viz., *on Himself;* so "bear" means, Leviticus 24:15; Numbers 5:31; 14:34. The *Greek* is lit. "to bear up" (I Pet. 2:24). "Our sins were laid on Him. When, therefore, He was lifted up on the cross, He bare up our sins along with Him" [BENGEL]. **many**—not opposed to *all,* but to *few.* He, *the One,* was offered for *many;* and that *once for all* (cf. Matt. 20:28). **look for him**—*with waiting expectation even unto the end* (so the *Greek*). It is translated "wait for" in Romans 8:19, 23; I Cor. 1:7, which see. **appear**—rather, as *Greek,* "be seen." No longer in the alien "form of a servant," but in His own proper glory. **without sin**—apart from, separate from, sin. Not bearing the sin of many *on* Him as at His first coming (even then there was no sin *in* Him). That sin has been at His first coming once for all taken away, so as to need no repetition of His sin offering of Himself (vs. 26). At His second coming He shall have no more to do with sin. **unto salvation**—to bring in completed salvation; redeeming then the body which is as yet subject to the bondage of corruption. Hence, in Philippians 3:20 he says, "we look for THE SAVIOUR." Note, Christ's *prophetical* office, as the *divine Teacher,* was especially exercised during His earthly ministry; His *priestly* is now from His first to His second coming; His *kingly* office shall be fully manifested at, and after, His second coming.

CHAPTER 10

Vss. 1-39. CONCLUSION OF THE FOREGOING ARGUMENT. THE YEARLY RECURRING LAW SACRIFICES CANNOT PERFECT THE WORSHIPPER, BUT CHRIST'S ONCE-FOR-ALL OFFERING CAN. Instead of the daily ministry of the Levitical priests, Christ's service is perfected by the one sacrifice, whence He now sits on the right hand of God as a Priest-King, until all His foes shall be subdued unto Him. Thus the new covenant (ch. 8:8-12) is inaugurated, whereby the law is written on the heart, so that an offering for sin is needed no more. Wherefore we ought to draw near the Holiest in firm faith and love; fearful of the awful results of apostasy; looking for the recompense to be given at Christ's coming. **1.** Previously the *oneness* of Christ's offering was shown; now is shown its perfection as contrasted with the law sacrifices. **having**—inasmuch as it has but "the shadow, not the very image," i.e., not the exact likeness, reality, and full revelation, such as the Gospel has. The "image" here means the *archetype* (cf. ch. 9:24), the original, solid image [BENGEL] realizing to us those heavenly verities, of which the law furnished but *a shadowy outline* before. Cf. II Corinthians 3:13, 14, 18; the Gospel is the very setting forth by the Word and Spirit of the heavenly realities themselves, out of which it (the Gospel) is constructed. So ALFORD. As Christ is "*the express image* (Greek, 'impress') of the Father's person" (ch. 1:3), so the Gospel is the heavenly verities themselves manifested by revelation—*the* heavenly very *archetype,* of which the law was drawn as a sketch, or outline copy (ch. 8:5). The law was a continual process of acted prophecy, proving the divine design that its counterparts should come; and proving the truth of those counterparts when they came. Thus the imperfect and continued expiatory sacrifices before Christ foretend, and now prove, the reality of Christ's one perfect antitypical expiation. **good things to come**

—(ch. 9:11)—belonging to "the world (age) to come." *Good things* in part made present by faith to the believer, and to be fully realized hereafter in actual and perfect enjoyment. LESSING says, "As Christ's Church on earth is a prediction of the economy of the future life, so the Old Testament economy is a prediction of the Christian Church." In relation to the temporal good things of the law, the spiritual and eternal good things of the Gospel are "good things *to come.*" Colossians 2:17 calls legal ordinances "the shadow," and Christ "the body." **never**—at any time (vs. 11). **with those sacrifices**—rather, "with *the same* sacrifices. **year by year**—This clause in the *Greek* refers to the whole sentence, not merely to the words "which they the priests offered" (*Greek,* "offer"). Thus the sense is, not as *English Version,* but, *the law year by year, by the repetition of the same sacrifices, testifies its inability to perfect the worshippers;* viz., on the YEARLY *day of atonement.* The *"daily"* sacrifices are referred to, vs. 11. **continually**—*Greek,* "continuously," implying that they offer a toilsome and ineffectual *"continuous"* round of the "same" atonement-sacrifices *recurring* "year by year." **comers thereunto**—those so *coming unto* God, viz., the worshippers (the whole people) coming to God in the person of their representative, the high priest. **perfect**—fully meet man's needs as to justification and sanctification (*Note,* ch. 9:9). **2. For**—if the law could, by its sacrifices, have perfected the worshippers. **they**—the sacrifices. **once purged**—IF they were *once for all cleansed* (ch. 7: 27). **conscience**—"*consciousness* of sin" (ch. 9:9). **3. But**—so far from *those sacrifices ceasing to be offered* (vs. 2). **in . . .**—in the fact of their being offered, and in the course of their being offered on the day of atonement. Contrast vs. 17. **a remembrance**—a recalling to mind by the high priest's confession, on the day of atonement, of the sins both of each past year and of all former years, proving that the expiatory sacrifices of former years were not felt by men's consciences to have fully atoned for former sins; in fact, the expiation and remission were only legal and typical (vss. 4, 11). The Gospel remission, on the contrary, is so complete, that sins are "remembered no more" (vs. 17) by God. It is unbelief to "forget" this once-for-all purgation, and to fear on account of "former sins" (II Pet. 1:9). The believer, once for all *bathed,* needs only to "wash" his hands and "feet" of soils, according as he daily contracts them, in Christ's blood (John 13: 10). **4. For . . .**—reason why, necessarily, there is a continually recurring "remembrance of sins" in the legal sacrifices (vs. 3). *Typically,* "**the blood** of bulls," etc., sacrificed, had power; but it was only in virtue of the power of the one real antitypical sacrifice of Christ; they had no power *in themselves;* they were not the instrument of perfect vicarious atonement, but an exhibition of the need of it, suggesting to the faithful Israelite the sure hope of coming redemption, according to God's promise. **take away**—"take *off.*" The *Greek,* vs. 11, is stronger, explaining the weaker word here, "take away *utterly.*" The blood of beasts could not take away the sin of *man.* A MAN must do that (*Notes,* ch. 9:12-14). **5.** Christ's voluntary self-offering, in contrast to those inefficient sacrifices, is shown to fulfil perfectly "the will of God" as to our redemption, by completely atoning "for (our) sins." **Wherefore**—seeing that a nobler than animal sacrifices was needed to "take away sins." **when he cometh**—*Greek,* "coming." The time referred to is the period *before* His entrance into the world,

when the inefficiency of animal sacrifices for expiation had been proved [THOLUCK]. Or, the time is that between Jesus' first dawning of reason as a child, and the beginning of His public ministry, during which, being ripened in human resolution, He was intently devoting Himself to the doing of His Father's will [ALFORD]. But the time of "coming" is *present;* not "when He had come," but "when *coming* into the world"; so, in order to accord with ALFORD's view, "the world" must mean His PUBLIC ministry: when coming, or about to come, into *public.* The *Greek* verbs are in the past: "sacrifice . . . Thou *didst* not wish, but a body Thou *didst* prepare for Me"; and, "Lo, *I am come.*" Therefore, in order to harmonize these times, the present *coming,* or about to come, with the past, "A body Thou *didst* prepare for Me," we must either explain as ALFORD, or else, if we take the period to be *before* His actual arrival in the world (the earth) or *incarnation,* we must explain the *past* tenses to refer to God's *purpose,* which speaks of what He designed from eternity as though it were already fulfilled. "A body Thou didst prepare in Thy eternal counsel." This seems to me more likely than explaining "coming into the world," "*coming into public,*" or entering on His public ministry. David, in Psalm 40 (here quoted), reviews his past troubles and God's having delivered him from them, and his consequent desire to render willing obedience to God as more acceptable than sacrifices; but the Spirit puts into his mouth language finding its partial application to David, and its full realization only in the divine Son of David. "The more any son of man approaches the incarnate Son of God in position, or office, or individual spiritual experience, the more directly may his holy breathings in the power of Christ's Spirit be taken as utterances of Christ Himself. Of all men, the prophet-king of Israel resembled and foreshadowed Him the most" [ALFORD]. **a body hast thou prepared me**—*Greek,* "Thou didst *fit* for Me a body." "In Thy counsels *Thou didst determine to make for Me a body,* to be given up to death as a sacrificial victim" [WAHL]. In the *Hebrew,* Psalm 40:6, it is "mine ears hast thou opened," or "dug." Perhaps this alludes to the custom of *boring the ear of a slave who volunteers to remain under his master when he might be free.* Christ's assuming a human *body,* in obedience to the Father's will, in order to die the death of a slave (ch. 2:14), was virtually the same act of voluntary submission to service as that of a slave suffering his ear to be bored by his master. His *willing obedience to the Father's will* is what is dwelt on as giving especial virtue to His sacrifice (vss. 7, 9, 10). The *preparing,* or *fitting of a body* for Him, is not with a view to His mere incarnation, but to His expiatory *sacrifice* (vs. 10), as the *contrast* to "sacrifice and offering" requires; cf. also Rom. 7:4; Eph. 2:16; Col. 1:22. More probably "opened mine ears" means *opened mine inward ear,* so as to be attentively obedient to what God wills me to do, viz., to assume the body He has prepared for me for my sacrifice, so Job, *Margin,* 33:16; 36:10 (doubtless the boring of a slave's *ear* was the symbol of *such willing obedience*); Isaiah 50:5, "The Lord God hath opened mine ear," i.e., made me *obediently* attentive as a slave to his master. Others somewhat similarly explain, "Mine ears hast thou digged," or "*fashioned,*" not with allusion to Exodus 21:6, but to the true office of the ear—a willing, submissive attention to the voice of God (Isa. 50:4, 5). The forming of the ear implies the preparation of the body, i.e., the incarnation; this secondary idea, really in the *Hebrew,* though less prominent, is the one which Paul uses for his argument. In either explanation the idea of Christ taking on Him the form, and becoming *obedient as a servant,* is implied. As He assumed a body in which to make His self-sacrifice, so ought we *present* our *bodies a living sacrifice* (Rom. 12:1). **6. burnt offerings**—Greek, "*whole* burnt offerings." **thou·hast had no pleasure**—as if these could in themselves atone for sin: God had pleasure in (*Greek,* "approved," or "was *well pleased* with") them, in so far as they were an act of obedience to His positive command under the Old Testament, but not as having an intrinsic efficacy such as Christ's sacrifice had. Contrast Matthew 3:17. **7. I come**—rather, "I am come" (*Note,* vs. 5). "Here we have the creed, as it were, of Jesus: "*I am come* to fulfil the law, Matthew 5:17; to preach, Mark 1:38; to call sinners to repentance, Luke 5:32; to send a sword and to set men at variance, Matthew 10:34, 35; I came down from heaven to do the will of Him that sent me, John 6:38, 39 (so here, Psalm 40:7, 8); I am sent to the lost sheep of the house of Israel, Matthew 15:24; I am come into this world for judgment, John 9:39; I am come that they might have life, and might have it more abundantly, John 10:10; to save what had been lost, Matthew 18:11; to seek and to save that which was lost, Luke 19:10; cf. I Timothy 1:15; to save men's lives, Luke 9:56; to send fire on the earth, Luke 12:49; to minister, Matthew 20:28; as "the Light," John 12:46; to bear witness unto the truth, John 18:37.' See, reader, that thy Saviour obtain what He aimed at in thy case. Moreover, do thou for thy part say, why thou art come here? Dost thou, then, also, do the will of God? From what time? and in what way?" [BENGEL]. When the two goats on the day of atonement were presented before the Lord, that goat on which the lot of the Lord should fall was to be offered as a sin offering; and that lot was lifted up on high in the hand of the high priest, and then laid upon the head of the goat which was to die; so the *hand* of God *determined* all that was done to Christ. Besides the covenant of God with man through Christ's blood, there was another covenant made by the Father with the Son from eternity. The condition was, "If He shall make His soul an offering for sin, He shall see His seed . . ." (Isa. 53:19). The Son accepted the condition, "Lo, I come to do Thy will, O God" [BISHOP PEARSON]. Oblation, intercession, and benediction, are His three priestly offices. **in the volume . . .**—lit., "the roll": the parchment MS. being wrapped around a cylinder headed with knobs. Here, the Scripture "volume" meant is the 40th Psalm. "By this very passage 'written of Me,' I undertake to do Thy will [viz., that I should die for the sins of the world, in order that all who believe may be saved, not by animal sacrifices, vs. 6, but by My death]." This is the written contract of Messiah (cf. Neh. 9:38), whereby He engaged to be our surety. So complete is the inspiration of all that is written, so great the authority of the Psalms, that what David says is really what Christ then and there said. **8. he**—Christ. **Sacrifice . . .**—The oldest MSS. read, "*Sacrifices* and *offerings*" (plural). This verse combines the two clauses previously quoted distinctly, vss. 5, 6, in contrast to the sacrifice of Christ with which God was well pleased. **9. Then said he**—"At that time (viz., when speaking by David's mouth in the 40th Psalm) He hath said." The rejection of the legal sacrifices in-

volves, as its concomitant, the voluntary offer of Jesus to make the self-sacrifice with which God is well pleased (for, indeed, it was God's own "will" that He *came to do* in offering it: so that *this* sacrifice could not but be well pleasing to God). **I come**—"I am come." **taketh away**—"sets aside the first," viz., "the legal system of sacrifices" which God wills not. **the second**—"the will of God" (vss. 7, 9) that Christ should redeem us by His self-sacrifice. **10. By**—Greek, "In." So "in," and "through," occur in the same sentence, I Pet. 1:22, "Ye have purified your souls *in* obeying the truth *through* the Spirit." Also, I Peter 1:5, in the *Greek.* The "*in* (fulfilment of) which will" (cf. the use of *in,* in Ephesians 1:6, "wherein [in which grace] He hath made us accepted in the Beloved"), expresses the *originating* cause; "THROUGH the offering . . . of Christ," the *instrumental* or *mediatory* cause. The whole work of redemption flows from "the will" of God the Father, as the First Cause, who decreed redemption from before the foundation of the world. The "will" here (*boulema*) is His *absolute sovereign will.* His "good will" (*eudokia*) is a particular aspect of it. **are sanctified**—once for all, and as our *permanent state* (so the *Greek*). It is the finished work of Christ in having sanctified us (i.e., having translated us from a state of unholy alienation into a state of *consecration* to God, having "no more conscience of sin," vs. 2) once for all and permanently, not the process of gradual sanctification, which is here referred to. **the body**—"prepared" for Him by the Father (vs. 5). As the atonement, or reconciliation, is by the blood of Christ (Lev. 17. 11), so our *sanctification* (consecration to God, holiness and eternal bliss) is by the *body* of Christ (Col. 1:22). ALFORD quotes the *Book of Common Prayer Communion Service,* "that our sinful bodies may be *made clean by His body,* and our souls washed through His most precious blood." **once for all**—(ch. 7:27; 9:12, 26, 28; 10:12, 14). **11. And**—a new point of contrast; the frequent repetition of the sacrifices. **priest**—The oldest MSS. read, "high priest." Though he did not in person stand "daily" offering sacrifices, he did so by the subordinate priests of whom, as well as of all Israel, he was the representative head. So "daily" is applied to the high priests (ch. 7:27). **standeth**—the attitude of one ministering; in contrast to "*sat down* on the right hand of God," vs. 12, said of Christ; the posture of one being ministered to as a king. **which**—Greek, "the which," i.e., of such a kind as. **take away**—utterly; lit., "strip off all round." Legal sacrifices might, *in part,* produce the sense of forgiveness, yet scarcely even that (*Note,* vs. 4); but *entirely* to strip off one's guilt they never could. **12. this man**—emphatic (ch. 3:3). **for ever**—joined in *English Version* with "offered one sacrifice"; offered one sacrifice, the efficacy of which endures for ever; lit., "continuously," (cf. vs. 14). "The offering of Christ, once for all made, will continue the one and only oblation for ever; no other will supersede it" [BENGEL]. The mass, which professes to be the frequent repetition of one and the same sacrifice of Christ's body, is hence disproved. For not only is Christ's body one, but also *His offering is one,* and that inseparable from His suffering (ch. 9:26). The mass would be much the same as the Jewish sacrifices which Paul sets aside as abrogated, for they were anticipations of the one sacrifice, just as Rome makes masses continuations of it, in opposition to Paul's argument. A repetition would imply that the former once-for-all offering of the one sacrifice was imperfect, and so would be dishonoring to it (vss. 2, 18). Verse 14, on the contrary, says, "He hath PERFECTED FOR EVER them that are sanctified." If Christ offered Himself at the last supper, then He offered Himself again on the cross, and there would be *two* offerings; but Paul says there was only *one, once for all.* Cf. *Note,* ch. 9:26. *English Version* is favored by the usage in this Epistle, of putting the *Greek* "for ever" after that which it qualifies. Also, "one sacrifice for ever," stands in contrast to "the same sacrifices oftentimes" (vs. 11). Also, I Corinthians 15:25, 28, agrees with vss. 12, 13, taken as *English Version,* not joining, as ALFORD does, "for ever" with "sat down," for Jesus is to *give up* the mediatorial throne "when all things shall be subdued unto Him," and not to sit on it *for ever.* **13. expecting** —"waiting." *Awaiting* the execution of His Father's will, that all His foes should be subjected to Him. The Son *waits* till the Father shall "send Him forth to triumph over all His foes." He is now *sitting* at rest (vs. 12), invisibly reigning, and having His foes virtually, by right of His death, subject to Him. His present *sitting* on the unseen throne is a necessary preliminary to His coming forth to subject His foes openly. He shall then come forth to a visibly manifested kingdom and conquest over His foes. Thus He fulfils Psalm 110:1. This agrees with I Corinthians 15:23-28. He is, by His Spirit and His providence, now subjecting His foes to Him in part (Psalm 110). The subjection of His foes *fully* shall be at His second advent, and from that time to the general judgment (Revelation 19 and 20); then comes the subjection of Himself as Head of the Church to the Father (the mediatorial economy ceasing when its end shall have been accomplished), that God may be all in all. Eastern conquerors used to tread on the necks of the vanquished, as Joshua did to the five kings. So Christ's total and absolute conquest at His coming is symbolized. **be made his footstool**—lit., "be placed (rendered) footstool of His feet." **his enemies**—Satan and Death, whose strength consists in "sin"; this being taken away (vs. 12), the power of the foes is taken away, and their destruction necessarily follows. **14. For**—The sacrifice being "for ever" in its efficacy (vs. 12) needs no renewal. **them that are sanctified**—rather as *Greek,* "them that *are being* sanctified." The sanctification (consecration to God) of the elect (I Pet. 1:2) believers is perfect in Christ once for all (*Note,* vs. 10). (Contrast the law, ch. 7:19; 9:9; 10:1.) The development of that sanctification is progressive. **15.** The *Greek,* has "moreover," or "now." **is a witness**—of the truth which I am setting forth. The Father's witness is given ch. 5:10. The Son's, ch. 10:5. Now is added that of the Holy Spirit, called accordingly "the Spirit of grace," vs. 29. The testimony of all Three leads to the same conclusion (vs. 18). **for after that he had said . . .**—The conclusion to the sentence is in vs. 17, "*After* He had said before, This is the covenant that I will make with them (*with the house of Israel,* ch. 8:10; here extended to the spiritual Israel) . . . , saith the Lord; I will put (lit., "giving," referring to the *giving* of the law; not now as then, *giving into the hands,* but *giving*) My laws into their hearts ("mind," ch. 8:10) and in their minds ("hearts," ch. 8:10); I will *inscribe* (so the *Greek*) them (here He omits the addition quoted in ch. 8:10, 11, *I will be to them a God . . . , and they shall not teach every man his neighbor . . .*), and (i.e., *after He had said the foregoing,* HE THEN ADDS) their sins . . . will I remember no more." The great object of the quo-

tation here is to prove that, there being *in the Gospel covenant* "REMISSION of sins" (vs. 17), there is no more need of a sacrifice for sins. The object of the same quotation in ch. 8:8-13 is to show that, there being a "NEW covenant," the old is antiquated. **18. where remission of these is**—as there is under the Gospel covenant (vs. 17). "Here ends the finale (ch. 10:1-18) of the great tripartite arrangement (ch. 7:1-25; 7:26 to 9:12; 9:13 to 10:18) of the middle portion of the Epistle. Its great theme was Christ a High Priest for ever after the order of Melchisedec. What it is to be a high priest after the order of Melchisedec is set forth, ch. 7:1-25, as contrasted with the Aaronic order. That Christ, however, as High Priest, is Aaron's antitype in the true holy place, by virtue of His self-sacrifice here on earth, and Mediator of a better covenant, whose essential character the old only typified, we learn, ch. 7:26 to 9:12. And that Christ's selfsacrifice, offered through the Eternal Spirit, is of everlasting power, as contrasted with the unavailing cycle of legal offerings, is established in the third part, ch. 9:13 to 10:18; the first half of this last portion [ch. 9:13-28], showing that both our present possession of salvation, and our future completion of it, are as certain to us as that He is with God, ruling as a Priest and reigning as a King, once more to appear, no more as a bearer of our sins, but in glory as a Judge. The second half, ch. 10:1-18, reiterating the main position of the whole, the High Priesthood of Christ, grounded on His offering of Himself—its kingly character its eternal accomplishment of its end, confirmed by Psalms 40 and 110, and Jeremiah 31" [DELITZSCH in ALFORD]. **19.** Here begins the third and last division of the Epistle; *our duty now while waiting for the Lord's second advent.* Resumption and expansion of the exhortation (ch. 4:14-16; cf. vss. 22, 23 here) wherewith he closed the first part of the Epistle, preparatory to his great doctrinal argument, beginning at ch. 7:1. **boldness**—"free confidence," grounded on the consciousness that our sins have been forgiven. **to enter**—lit., "as regards the entering." **by**—*Greek,* "in"; it is *in* the blood of Jesus that our boldness to enter is grounded. Cf. Ephesians 3:12, "*In* whom we have boldness and access with confidence." It is His having once for all entered as our Forerunner (ch. 6:20) and High Priest (vs. 21), making atonement for us with His blood, which is continually there (ch. 12:24) before God, that gives us confident access. No priestly caste now mediates between the sinner and his Judge. We may come *boldly* with loving confidence, not with slavish fear, directly through Christ, the only mediating Priest. The minister is not officially nearer God than the layman; nor can the latter serve God at a distance or by deputy, as the natural man would like. Each must come for himself, and all are accepted when they come by the new and living way opened by Christ. Thus all Christians are, in respect to access directly to God, virtually high priests (Rev. 1:6). They draw nigh in and through Christ, the only proper High Priest (ch. 7:25). **20. which . . .**—The antecedent in the *Greek* is "the entering"; not as *English Version,* "way." Translate, "which (entering) He has consecrated (not as though it were already existing, but *has been the first to open,* INAUGURATED *as a new thing; Note,* ch. 9:18, where the *Greek* is the same) for us (as) a new (*Greek,* 'recent'; recently opened, Rom. 16:25, 26) and living way" (not like the lifeless way through the law offering of the blood of *dead* victims, but real, *vital,* and of perpetual efficacy, because the *living* and *life-giving* Saviour is that *way.* It is a *living hope* that we have, producing not *dead,* but *living,* works). Christ, the first fruits of our nature, has ascended, and the rest is sanctified thereby. "Christ's ascension is our promotion; and whither the glory of the Head hath preceded, thither the hope of the body, too, is called" [LEO]. **the veil** —As the *veil* had to be passed *through* in order to enter the holiest place, so the weak, human suffering *flesh* (ch. 5:7) of Christ's humanity (which veiled His God head) had to be passed through by Him in entering the heavenly holiest place for us; in putting off His *rent flesh,* the temple veil, its type, was simultaneously rent from top to bottom (Matt. 27: 51). Not His *body,* but His weak suffering *flesh,* was the veil; His body was the temple (John 2:19). **21. high priest**—As a different *Greek* term (*archiereus*) is used always elsewhere in this Epistle for "high priest," translate as *Greek* here, "A Great Priest"; one who is at once King and "Priest on His throne" (Zech. 6:13); a royal Priest, and a priestly King. **house of God**—the spiritual house, the Church, made up of believers, whose home is *heaven,* where Jesus now is (ch. 12:22, 23). Thus, by "the house of God," over which Jesus is, *heaven* is included in meaning, as well as the *Church,* whose home it is. **22.** (Ch. 4:16; 7:19.) **with a true heart**—without hypocrisy; "in truth, and with a perfect heart"; a heart thoroughly imbued with "the truth" (vs. 26). **full assurance**—(ch. 6:11)— with no doubt as to our acceptance when coming to God by the blood of Christ. As *"faith"* occurs here, so *"hope,"* and *"love,"* vss. 23, 24. **sprinkled from**—i.e., sprinkled *so as to be cleansed* from. **evil conscience**—a consciousness of guilt unatoned for, and uncleansed away (vs. 2; ch. 9:9). Both the *hearts* and the *bodies* are cleansed. The legal purifications were with blood of animal victims and with water, and could only cleanse the *flesh* (ch. 9: 13, 21). Christ's blood purifies the *heart* and conscience. The Aaronic priest, in entering the holy place, washed with *water* (ch. 9:19) in the brazen laver. Believers, as priests to God, are once for all washed in BODY (as distinguished from "hearts") at baptism. As we have an immaterial, and a material nature, the cleansing of both is expressed by "hearts" and "body," the inner and the outer man; so the whole man, material and immaterial. The baptism of the body, however, is not the mere putting away of material filth, nor an act operating by intrinsic efficacy, but the sacramental seal, applied to the outer man, of a spiritual washing (I Pet. 3: 21). "Body" (not merely "flesh," the *carnal* part, as II Cor. 7:1) includes the *whole* material man, which needs cleansing, as being redeemed, as well as the soul. The body, once polluted with sin, is washed, so as to be fitted like Christ's holy body, and by His body, to be spiritually a pure and living offering. On the "pure water," the symbol of consecration and sanctification, cf. John 19:34; I Corinthians 6:11; I John 5:6; Ezekiel 36:25. The perfects "having . . . hearts *sprinkled . . . body* (the *Greek* is singular) *washed,"* imply a continuing state produced by a once-for-all accomplished act, viz., our justification by faith through Christ's blood, and consecration to God, sealed sacramentally by the baptism of our body. **23.** Ch. 3:6, 14; 4:14. **profession**—*Greek,* "confession." **our faith**—rather as *Greek,* "our hope"; which is indeed *faith* exercised as to the future inheritance. *Hope* rests on faith, and at the same time quickens *faith,* and is the ground of our bold *confession* (I Pet. 3:15). *Hope* is similarly (vs. 22) connected with *purification* (I

John 3:3). **without wavering**—without declension (ch. 3:14), "steadfast unto the end." **he**—God is faithful to His promises (ch. 6:17, 18; 11:11; 12:26, 28; I Cor. 1:9; 10:13; I Thess. 5:24; I Thess. 3:3; see also Christ's promise, John 12:26); but man is too often unfaithful to his duties. **24.** Here, as elsewhere, *hope* and *love* follow *faith;* the Pauline triad of Christian graces. **consider**—with the mind attentively fixed on "one another" (*Note,* ch. 3:1), contemplating with continual consideration the characters and wants of our brethren, so as to render mutual help and counsel. Cf. "consider," Psalm 41:1, and ch. 12:15, "(All) looking diligently lest *any* fail of the grace of God." **to provoke**— *Greek,* "*with a view to provoking* unto love," instead of provoking to hatred, as is too often the case. **25. assembling of ourselves together**—The *Greek, episunagoge,* is only found here and II Thessalonians 2:1 (the gathering together of the elect to Christ at His coming, Matt. 24:31). The assembling or gathering of ourselves for Christian communion in private and public, is an earnest of our being gathered together to Him at His appearing. Union is strength; continual assemblings together beget and foster *love,* and give good opportunities for "provoking to good works," by "exhorting one another" (ch. 3:13). IGNATIUS says, "When ye frequently, and in numbers meet together, the powers of Satan are overthrown, and his mischief is neutralized by your likemindedness in the faith." To neglect such assemblings together might end in apostasy at last. He avoids the *Greek* term *sunagoge,* as suggesting the Jewish *synagogue* meetings (cf. Rev. 2:9). **as the manner of some is** —"manner," i.e., habit, custom. This gentle expression proves he is not here as yet speaking of *apostasy.* **the day approaching**—This, the shortest designation of the day of the Lord's coming, occurs elsewhere only in I Corinthians 3:13; a confirmation of the Pauline authorship of this Epistle. The Church being *in all ages* kept uncertain how soon Christ is coming, *the day* is, and has been, in each age, practically always near; whence, believers have been called on always to be watching for it as nigh at hand. The Hebrews were now living close upon one of those great types and foretastes of it, the destruction of Jerusalem (Matt. 24), "the bloody and fiery dawn of the great day; that day is the day of days, the ending day of all days, the settling day of all days, the day of the promotion of time into eternity, the day which, for the Church, breaks through and breaks off the night of the present world" [DELITZSCH in ALFORD]. **26.** Cf. on this and following verses, ch. 6:4, etc. There the warning was that if there be not diligence in progressing, a falling off will take place, and apostasy may ensue: here it is, that if there be lukewarmness in Christian communion, apostasy may ensue. **if we sin**—*Greek* present participle: if we be found *sinning,* i.e., not isolated acts, but a *state* of sin [ALFORD]. A violation not only of the *law,* but of the whole economy of the New Testament (vss. 28, 29). **wilfully**—presumptuously, *Greek* "willingly." After receiving "full knowledge (so the *Greek,* cf. I Tim. 2:4) of the truth," by having been "enlightened," and by having "tasted" a certain measure even of grace of "the Holy Ghost" (the Spirit of truth, John 14:17; and "the Spirit of grace," vs. 29): to *fall away* (as "sin" here means, ch. 3:12, 17; cf. ch. 6:6) and apostatize (ch. 3:12) to Judaism or infidelity, is not a sin of *ignorance,* or error ("*out of the way,*" the result) of infirmity, but a *deliberate sinning* against the Spirit (vs. 29; ch. 5:2): *such* sinning, where a consciousness of Gospel obligations not only was, but *is* present: a sinning presumptuously and preseveringly against Christ's redemption *for* us, and the Spirit of grace *in* us. "He only who stands high can fall low. A lively reference in the soul to what is good is necessary in order to be thoroughly wicked; hence, man can be more reprobate than the beasts, and the apostate angels than apostate man" [THOLUCK]. **remaineth no more sacrifice**—For there is but ONE Sacrifice that can atone for sin; they, after having fully known that sacrifice, deliberately reject it. **27. a certain**—an extraordinary and indescribable. The indefiniteness, as of something *peculiar of its kind*, makes the description the more terrible (cf. *Greek*, Jas. 1:18). **looking for**—"expectation": a later sense of the *Greek*. ALFORD strangely translates, as the *Greek* usually means elsewhere, "reception." The transition is easy from "giving a reception to" something or someone, to "looking for." Contrast the "expecting" (the very same *Greek* as here), vs. 13, which refutes ALFORD. **fiery indignation**—lit., "zeal of fire." Fire is personified: glow or ardor of fire, i.e., of Him who is "a consuming fire." **devour**—continually. **28.** Cf. ch. 2:2, 3; 12:25. **despised**—"set at naught" [ALFORD]: utterly and heinously violated, not merely some minor detail, but *the whole law and covenant*; e.g., by idolatry (Deut. 17:2-7). So here *apostasy* answers to such an utter violation of the old covenant. **died**—*Greek*, "dies": the normal punishment of such transgression, then still in force. **without mercy**—lit., "mercies": removal out of the pale of mitigation, or a respite of his doom. **under**—on the evidence of. **29. sorer**—*Greek*, "worse," viz., "punishment" (lit., "vengeance") than any mere temporal punishment of the body. **suppose ye**—an appeal to the Hebrews' reason and conscience. **thought worthy**—by God at the judgment. **trodden under foot the Son of God**—by "wilful" apostasy. So he treads under foot God Himself who "glorified His *Son* as an high priest" (ch. 5:5; 6:6). **an unholy thing**—lit., "common," as opposed to "sanctified." No better than the blood of a common man, thus involving the consequence that Christ, in claiming to be God, was guilty of blasphemy, and so deserved to die! **wherewith he was sanctified**—for Christ died even for him. "Sanctified," in the fullest sense, belongs only to the saved elect. But in some sense it belongs also to those who have gone a far way in Christian experience, and yet fall away at last. The higher such a one's past Christian experiences, the deeper his fall. **done despite unto**—by repelling in *fact*: as "blasphemy" is despite in *words* (Mark 3:29). "Of the Jews who became Christians and relapsed to Judaism, we find from the history of URIEL ACOSTA, that they required a blasphemy against Christ. 'They applied to Him epithets used against Molech the adulterous branch,' " etc. [THOLUCK]. **the Spirit of grace**—the Spirit that confers grace. "He who does not accept the benefit, insults Him who confers it. He hath made thee a son: wilt thou become a slave? He has come to take up His abode with thee; but thou art introducing evil into thyself" [CHRYSOSTOM]. "It is the curse of evil eternally to propagate evil: so, for him who profanes the Christ *without him*, and blasphemes the Christ *within him*, there is subjectively no renewal of a change of mind (ch. 6:6), and objectively no new *sacrifice for sins*" (ch. 10:26) [THOLUCK]. **30. him**—God, who enters no empty threats. **Vengeance belongeth unto me**—*Greek*, "To Me belong-eth vengeance": exactly according with *Paul's* quotation, Romans 12:19, of the same text. **Lord shall judge his people**—in grace, or else anger, according as each deserves: here, "judge," so as to punish the reprobate apostate; there, "judge," so as to interpose in behalf of, and save His people (Deut. 32. 36). **31. fearful . . . to fall into the hands . . .**—It is good like David *to fall into the hands of God*, rather than man, when one does so with filial *faith* in his father's love, though God *chastises* him. "It is fearful" to fall into His hands as a reprobate and presumptuous sinner doomed to His just vengeance as Judge (vs. 27). **living God**—therefore able to punish for ever (Matt. 10:28). **32.** As previously he has warned them by the awful end of apostates, so here he stirs them up by the remembrance of their own former faith, patience, and self-sacrificing love. So Revelation 2:3, 4. **call to remembrance** —habitually: so the present tense means. **illuminated**—"enlightened": come to "the knowledge of the truth" (vs. 26) in connection with baptism (*Note*, ch. 6:4). In spiritual baptism, Christ, who is "the Light," is put on. "On the one hand, we are not to sever the sign and the grace signified where the sacrifice truly answers its designs; on the other, the glass is not to be mistaken for the liquor, nor the sheath for the sword" [BENGEL]. **fight of**—i.e., *consisting of* afflictions. **33.** The persecutions here referred to seem to have been endured by the Hebrew Christians at their first conversion, not only in Palestine, but also in Rome and elsewhere, the Jews in every city inciting the populace and the Roman authorities against Christians. **gazing-stock**—as in a *theater* (so the *Greek*): often used as the place of punishment in the presence of the assembled multitudes. Acts 19:29; I Corinthians 4:9, "Made a *theatrical* spectacle to the world." **ye became**—of your own accord: attesting your Christian sympathy with your suffering brethren. **companions of**—sharers in affliction with. **34. ye had compassion on me in my bonds**—The oldest MSS. and versions omit "me," and read, "Ye both sympathized with *those in bonds* (answering to the last clause of vs. 33; cf. ch. 13:3, 23; 6:10), and accepted (so the *Greek* is translated in ch. 11:35) with joy (Jas. 1:2; *joy* in tribulations, as exercising faith and other graces, Rom. 5:3; and the pledge of the coming glory, Matt. 5:12) the plundering of your (own) goods" (answering to the first clause of vs. 33). **in yourselves**—The oldest MSS. omit "in": translate, "knowing that ye have *for* (or *to*) *yourselves*." **better**—a heavenly (ch. 11:16). **enduring**—not liable to *spoiling*. **substance**—possession: peculiarly our own, if we will not *cast away* our birthright. **35-37.** Consequent exhortation to confidence and endurance, as Christ is soon coming. **Cast not away**—implying that they now have "confidence," and that it will not withdraw of itself, unless they "cast it away" wilfully (cf. ch. 3:14). **which**—*Greek*, "the which": inasmuch as being such as. **hath**—present tense: it is as certain as if you had it in your hand (vs. 37). It hath in reversion. **recompense of reward**—of grace not of debt: a reward of a kind which no mercenary selfseeker would seek: holiness will be its own reward; self-devoting unselfishness for Christ's sake will be its own rich recompense (*Note*, ch. 2:2; 11:26). **36. patience**—*Greek*, "waiting endurance," or "enduring perseverance": the kindred *Greek* verb in the LXX, Habakkuk 2:3, is translated, "*wait for* it" (cf. Jas. 5:7). **after ye have done the will of God**—"that whereas ye have done the will of God" hitherto (vss. 32-35), ye may now show also *patient, persevering en-*

durance, and so "receive the promise," i.e., the promised reward: eternal life and bliss commensurate with our work of faith and love (ch. 6:10-12). We must not only *do,* but also *suffer* (I Pet. 4:19). God first uses the *active* talents of His servants; then polishes the other side of the stone, making the *passive* graces shine, *patience, meekness,* etc. It may be also translated, "That ye may do the will of God, and receive ..." [ALFORD]: "patience" itself is a further and a persevering doing of "God's will"; otherwise it would be profitless and no real grace (Matt. 7:21). We should look, not merely for individual bliss now and at death, but for the great and general consummation of bliss of all saints, both in body and soul. **37, 38.** Encouragement to patient endurance by consideration of the shortness of the time till Christ shall come, and God's rejection of him that draws back, taken from Habakkuk 2:3, 4. **a little while**—(John 16:16). **he that shall come**—lit., "the Comer." In Habakkuk, it is *the vision* that is said to be about to come. *Christ,* being the grand and ultimate subject of all prophetical vision, is here made by Paul, under inspiration, the subject of the Spirit's prophecy by Habakkuk, in its final and exhaustive fulfilment. **38. just**—The oldest MSS. and *Vulgate* read, "*my* just man." God is the speaker: "He who is just in My sight." BENGEL translates, "The just shall live by *my faith*": answering to the *Hebrew,* Habakkuk 2:4; lit., "the just shall live by the faith *of Him*," viz., *Christ,* the final subject of "the vision," who "will not lie," i.e., disappoint. Here not merely the first beginning, as in Galatians 3:11, but the *continuance,* of the spiritual life of the justified man is referred to, as opposed to declension and apostasy. As the justified man receives his first spiritual life by faith, so it is *by faith* that he *shall* continue to *live* (Luke 4:4). The *faith* meant here is that fully developed living trust in the unseen (ch. 11:1) Saviour, which can keep men steadfast amidst persecutions and temptations (vss. 34-36). **but**—*Greek,* "and." **if** *any man* **draw back**—So the Greek admits: though it might also be translated, as ALFORD approves, "if *he* (the just man) draw back." Even so, it would not disprove the final perseverance of saints. For "the just man" in this latter clause would mean one seemingly, and in part really, though not savingly, "just" or *justified:* as in Ezekiel 18:24, 26. In the *Hebrew,* this latter half of the verse stands first, and is, "Behold, his soul which is lifted up, is not upright in him." Habakkuk states the *cause* of drawing back: *a soul lifted up,* and in self-inflated unbelief setting itself up against God. Paul, by the Spirit, states the *effect,* it *draws back.* Also, what in Habakkuk is, "His soul is not upright in him," is in Paul, "My soul shall have no pleasure in him." Habakkuk states the *cause,* Paul the effect: He who is not right in his own soul, does not stand right with God; God has no pleasure in him. BENGEL translates Habakkuk, "His soul is not upright in *respect to him,*" viz., Christ, the subject of "the vision," i.e., *Christ has no pleasure in him* (cf. ch. 12:25). Every flower in spring is not a fruit in autumn. **39.** A Pauline elegant turning-off from denunciatory warnings to charitable hopes of his readers (Rom. 8:12). **saving of the soul**—lit., "acquisition (or *obtaining*) of the soul." The kindred *Greek* verb is applied to Christ's *acquiring* the Church as the *purchase* of His blood (Acts 20:28). If we *acquire* or *obtain* our soul's salvation, it is through Him who has obtained it for us by His bloodshedding. "The unbelieving man *loses his soul:*

for not being God's, neither is he his own [cf. Matt. 16:26 with Luke 9:25]: faith saves the soul by linking it to God" [DELITZSCH *in* ALFORD].

CHAPTER 11

Vss. 1-40. DEFINITION OF THE FAITH JUST SPOKEN OF (ch. 10:39): EXAMPLES FROM THE OLD COVENANT FOR OUR PERSEVERANCE IN FAITH. **1.** *Description* of the great things which *faith* (in its widest sense: not here restricted to *faith* in the Gospel sense) does for us. Not a full *definition* of faith in its whole nature, but a description of its great characteristics in relation to the subject of Paul's exhortation here, viz., to perseverance. **substance ...** —It substantiates promises of God which we hope for, as future in fulfilment, making them present realities to us. However, the *Greek* is translated in ch. 3:14, "confidence"; and it also here may mean "sure confidence." So ALFORD translates. THOMAS MAGISTER supports *English Version,* "The whole thing that follows is virtually contained in the first principle; now the *first commencement* of the things hoped for is in us through the assent of faith, which virtually contains all the things hoped for." Cf. *Note,* ch. 6:5, "tasted ... powers of the world to come." Through faith, the future object of Christian hope, *in its beginning,* is already present. True faith infers the reality of the objects believed in and hoped for (vs. 6). HUGO DE ST. VICTOR distinguished *faith* from *hope.* By *faith* alone we are sure of eternal things that they ARE: but by *hope* we are confident that WE SHALL have them. All hope presupposes faith (Rom. 8:25). **evidence**—"demonstration": convincing proof to the believer: the soul thereby seeing what the eye cannot see. **things not seen**—the whole invisible and spiritual world: not things future and things pleasant, as the "things hoped for," but also the past and present, and those the reverse of pleasant. "Eternal life is promised to us, but it is when we are dead: we are told of a blessed resurrection, but meanwhile we moulder in the dust; we are declared to be justified, and sin dwells in us; we hear that we are blessed, meantime we are overwhelmed in endless miseries: we are promised abundance of all goods, but we still endure hunger and thirst; God declares He will immediately come to our help, but He seems deaf to our cries. What should we do if we had not faith and hope to lean on, and if our mind did not emerge amidst the darkness above the world by the shining of the Word and Spirit of God?" [CALVIN]. Faith is an assent unto truths credible upon the testimony of God [not on the *reasonableness* of the thing revealed, though by this we may judge as to whether it be what it professes, a genuine revelation], delivered unto us in the writings of the apostles and prophets. Thus Christ's ascension is the cause, and His absence the crown, of our faith: because He ascended, we the more believe, and because we believe in Him who hath ascended, our faith is the more accepted [BISHOP PEARSON]. Faith believes what it sees not; for if thou seest there is no faith; the Lord has gone away so as not to be seen: He is hidden that He may be believed; the yearning desire by faith after Him who is unseen is the preparation of a heavenly mansion for us; when He shall be seen it shall be given to us as the reward of faith [AUGUSTINE]. As Revelation deals with spiritual and invisible things exclusively, faith is the faculty needed by us, since it is the evidence of things not seen. By faith we venture our eternal interests on the bare word of

God, and this is altogether reasonable. **2. For**—So high a description of faith is not undeserved; for . . . [ALFORD]. **by it**—*Greek,* "in it": in respect to . . . in the matter of," it, "or, as *Greek* more emphatically, "this." **the elders**—as though still living and giving their powerful testimony to the reasonableness and excellence of faith (ch. 12:1). Not merely *the ancients,* as though they were people solely of the past; nay, they belong to the one and the same blessed family as ourselves (vss. 39, 40). *"The* elders," whom we all revere so highly. "Paul shows how we ought to seek in all its fulness, under the veil of history, the essential substance of the doctrine sometimes briefly indicated" [BENGEL]. "The elders," as "the fathers," is a title of honor given on the ground of their bright faith and practice. **obtained a good report**—*Greek,* "were testified of," viz., favorably (cf. ch. 7:8). It is a phrase of Luke, Paul's companion. Not only men, but God, gave testimony to their faith (vss. 4, 5, 39). Thus they being testified of themselves have become "witnesses" to all others (ch. 12:1). The earlier elders had their patience exercised for a long period of life: those later, in sharper afflictions. Many things which they hoped for and did not see, subsequently came to pass and were conspicuously seen, the event confirming faith [BENGEL]. **3. we understand**—We perceive with our spiritual intelligence the fact of the world's creation by God, though we see neither Him nor the act of creation as described in Genesis 1. The natural world could not, without revelation, teach us this truth, though it confirms the truth when apprehended by faith (Rom. 1:20). Adam is passed over in silence here as to his faith, perhaps as being the first who fell and brought sin on us all; though it does not follow that he did not repent and believe the promise. **worlds**—lit., "ages"; all that exists in time and space, visible and invisible, present and eternal. **framed**—"fitly formed and consolidated"; including the creation of the single parts and the harmonious organization of the whole, and the continual providence which maintains the whole throughout all ages. As creation is the foundation and a specimen of the whole divine economy, so faith in creation is the foundation and a specimen of all faith [BENGEL]. **by the word of God**—not here, the *personal* word (*Greek, logos.* John 1:1) but *the spoken word* (*Greek, rhema*); though by the instrumentality of the personal word (ch. 1:2). **not made . . .**—Translate as *Greek,* "so that not out of things which appear hath that which is seen been made"; not as in the case of all things which we see reproduced from previously existing and visible materials, as, for instance, the plant from the seed, the animal from the parent, etc., has the visible world sprung into being from apparent materials. So also it is implied in the first clause of the verse that the invisible spiritual worlds were framed not from previously existing materials. BENGEL explains it by distinguishing "appear," i.e., *begin to be seen* (viz., at creation), from *that which is seen* as already in existence, not merely *beginning* to be seen; so that the things seen were not made of the things which appear," i.e., which *begin to be seen by us in the act of creation.* We were not spectators of creation; it is by faith we perceive it. **4. more excellent sacrifice**—because offered in *faith.* Now *faith* must have some *revelation of God* on which it fastens. The revelation in this case was doubtless God's command to sacrifice *animals* ("the firstlings of the flock") in token of the forfeiture of men's life by sin, and as a type of the promised bruiser of the

serpent's head (Gen. 3:15), the one coming sacrifice; this command is implied in God's having made coats of skin for Adam and Eve (Gen. 3:21): for these skins must have been taken from animals slain *in sacrifice;* inasmuch as it was not for *food* they were slain, animal food not being permitted till after the flood; nor for mere *clothing,* as, were it so, clothes might have been made of the fleeces without the needless cruelty of killing the animal; but a coat of skin put on Adam from a sacrificed animal typified the covering or atonement (the *Hebrew* for *atone* means to *cover*) resulting from Christ's sacrifice. The *Greek* is more lit. rendered [KENNICOTT] by WICKLIFFE, "a *much more* sacrifice"; and by Queen Elizabeth's version "a greater sacrifice." A fuller, more ample sacrifice, that which partook more largely and essentially of the true nature and virtue of sacrifice [ARCHBISHOP MAGEE]. It was not any intrinsic merit in "the firstling of the flock" above "the fruit of the ground." It was God's appointment that gave it all its excellency as a sacrifice; if it had not been so, it would have been a presumptuous act of *will-worship* (Col. 2:23), and taking of a life which man had no right over before the flood (Gen. 9). The sacrifice seems to have been a holocaust, and the sign of the divine acceptance of it was probably the consumption of it by fire from heaven (Gen. 15:17). Hence, "to accept" a burnt sacrifice is in *Hebrew* "to turn it to ashes" (*Margin,* Ps. 20:3). A flame seems to have issued from the Shekinah, or flaming cherubim, east of Eden ("the presence of the Lord," Gen. 4:16), where the first sacrifices were offered. Cain, in unbelieving self-righteousness, presented merely a *thank offering,* not like Abel feeling his need of the propitiatory sacrifice appointed on account of sin. God "had respect (first) unto Abel, and (then) to his offering" (Gen. 4:4). Faith causes the believer's person to be accepted, and then his offering. Even an animal sacrifice, though of God's appointment, would not have been accepted, had it not been offered in faith. **he obtained witness**—*God* by fire attesting His acceptance of him as "righteous by faith." **his gifts** —the common term for *sacrifices,* implying that they must be freely *given.* **by it**—by faith exhibited in his animal sacrifice. **dead, yet speaketh**—His *blood crying from the ground* to God, shows how precious, because of his "faith," he was still in God's sight, even when dead. So he becomes a witness to us of the blessed effects of faith. **5.** *Faith* was the ground of his *pleasing God;* and his *pleasing God* was the ground of his *translation.* **translated**—(Gen. 5:22, 24). Implying a *sudden* removal (the same *Greek* as in Galatians 1:6) from mortality without death to immortality: such a CHANGE as shall pass over the living at Christ's coming (I Cor. 15:51, 52). **had this testimony**—viz., of Scripture; the *Greek* perfect implies that this testimony continues still: "he *has* been testified of." **pleased God**—The Scripture testimony virtually expresses that he *pleased God,* viz., "Enoch walked with God." LXX translates the *Hebrew* for "walked with God," Genesis 6:9, *pleased God.* **6. without**—*Greek,* "apart *from* faith": if one be destitute of faith (cf. Rom. 14:23). **to please**—Translate, as ALFORD does, the *Greek* aorist, "It is impossible to please God *at all"* (Rom. 8:8). Natural amiabilities and "works done before the grace of Christ are not pleasant to God, forasmuch as they spring not of faith in Jesus Christ; yea, rather, for that they are not done as God hath willed them to be done, we doubt not but they have the nature of sin" [Article XIII, *Book of Common Prayer*]. Works not rooted in God are splendid sins [AUGUSTINE]. **he that cometh to God** —as a worshipper (ch. 7:19). **must believe**—*once for all: Greek* aorist. **that God is**—IS: is the true self-existing Jehovah (as contrasted with all so-called gods, not gods, Gal. 4:8), the source of all being, though he sees Him not (vs. 1) as being "invisible" (vs. 27). So Enoch; this passage implies that he had not been favored with *visible* appearances of God, yet he *believed* in God's *being,* and in God's *moral government,* as the Rewarder of His diligent worshippers, in opposition to antediluvian skepticism. Also Moses was not so favored before he left Egypt the first time (vs. 27); still he believed. **and . . . is**—a different *Greek* verb from the former "is." Translate, "is eventually"; *proves to be;* lit., "becomes." **rewarder**—renderer of reward [AL-FORD]. So God proved to be to Enoch. The reward is *God Himself* diligently "sought" and "walked with" in partial communion here, and to be fully enjoyed hereafter. Cf. Genesis 15:1, "I am thy exceeding great reward." **of them**—and them only. **diligently seek**—*Greek,* "seek out" God. Cf. "seek early," Proverbs 8:17. Not only "ask" and "seek," but "knock," Matthew 7:7; cf. ch. 11:12; Luke 13: 24, "Strive" as in an agony of contest. **7. warned of God**—The same **Greek,** ch. 8:5, "admonished of God." **moved with fear**—not mere slavish fear, but as in *Note,* ch. 5:7; *Greek,* "reverential fear": opposed to the world's sneering disbelief of the revelation, and self-deceiving security. Join "by faith" with "prepared an ark" (I Pet. 3:20). **by the which** —faith. **condemned the world**—For since he believed and was saved, so might they have believed and been saved, so that their condemnation by God is by his case shown to be just. **righteousness which is by faith**—*Greek,* "according to faith." A Pauline thought. Noah is first called "righteous" in Genesis 6:9. Christ calls Abel so, Matthew 23:35. Cf. as to Noah's righteousness, Ezekiel 14:14, 20; II Peter 2:5, "a preacher of righteousness." Paul here makes *faith* the principle and ground of his righteousness. **heir**—the consequence of sonship which flows from faith. **8.** From the antediluvian saints he passes to the patriarchs of Israel, to whom "the promises" belonged. **called**—by God (Gen. 12:1). The oldest MSS. and *Vulgate* read, "He that was called Abraham," his name being changed from Abram to Abraham, on the occasion of God's making with him and his seed a covenant sealed by circumcision, many years after his call out of Ur. "By faith, he who was (afterwards) called Abraham (*father of nations,* Gen. 17:5, in order to become which was the design of God's bringing him out of Ur) obeyed (the command of God: to be understood in this reading), *so as to go out. . . ."* **which he should after receive**—He had not fully received even this promise when he went out, for it was not *explicitly* given him till he had reached Canaan (Gen. 12:1, 6, 7). When the promise of the land was given him the Canaanite was still in the land, and himself a stranger; it is in the new heaven and new earth that he shall receive his personal inheritance promised him; so believers sojourn on earth as strangers, while the ungodly and Satan lord it over the earth; but at Christ's coming that same earth which was the scene of the believer's conflict shall be the inheritance of Christ and His saints. **9. sojourned**—as a "stranger and pilgrim." **in**—*Greek,* "into," i.e., he went *into* it and sojourned there. **as in a strange country**—a country *not belonging to him,* but to others (so the *Greek*), Acts 7:5, 6. **dwelling in tabernacles**—*tents:* as *strangers* and *sojourners* do: moving from place to place, as having no

fixed possession of their own. In contrast to the abiding "city" (vs. 10). **with**—Their kind of dwelling being the same is a proof that their faith was the same. They all alike were content to wait for their good things hereafter (Luke 16:25). Jacob was fifteen years old at the death of Abraham. **heirs with him of the same promise**—Isaac did not inherit it from Abraham, nor Jacob from Isaac, but they all inherited it from God directly as "fellow heirs." In ch. 6:12, 15, 17, "the promise" means *the thing promised* as a thing in part *already attained*; but in this chapter "the promise" is of something still *future.* See, however, *Note* ch. 6; 12. **10. looked for**—*Greek,* "he was expecting"; waiting for with eager expectation (Rom. 8:19). **a city**—*Greek, "the* city," already alluded to. Worldly Enoch, son of the murderer Cain, was the first to build his *city* here: the godly patriarchs waited for their city hereafter (vs. 16; ch. 12:22; 13:14). **foundations**—*Greek, "the* foundations" which the *tents* had not, nor even men's present cities have. **whose builder and maker**—*Greek, "designer* [Eph. 1:4, 11] and master-builder," or *executor of the design.* The city is worthy of its Framer and Builder (cf. vs. 16; ch. 8:2). Cf. "found," *Note,* ch. 12. **11. also Sara herself**— though being the weaker vessel, and though at first she doubted. **was delivered of a child**—omitted in the oldest MSS.: then translate, "and that when she was past age" (Rom. 4:19). **she judged him faithful who had promised**—after she had ceased to doubt, being instructed by the angel that it was no jest, but a matter in serious earnest. **12. as good as dead**—lit., "deadened"; no longer having, as in youth, energetic vital powers. **stars . . . sand**—(Gen. 22:17). **13-16.** Summary of the characteristic excellencies of the patriarchs' faith. **died in faith**— died as *believers,* waiting for, not actually *seeing* as yet their good things promised to them. They were true to this principle of *faith* even unto, and especially in, their dying hour (cf. vs. 20). **These all**— beginning with "Abraham" (vs. 8), to whom *the promises were made* (Gal. 3:16), and who is alluded to in the end of vs. 13 and in vs. 15 [BENGEL and ALFORD]. But the "ALL" can hardly but include Abel, Enoch, and Noah. Now as these did not receive the promise of entering literal Canaan, *some other promise made in the first ages,* and often repeated, must be that meant, viz., the promise of a coming Redeemer made to Adam, viz., "the seed of the woman shall bruise the serpent's head." Thus the promises cannot have been merely temporal, for Abel and Enoch mentioned here received no temporal promise [ARCHBISHOP MAGEE]. This promise of eternal redemption is the inner essence of the promises made to Abraham (Gal. 3:16). **not having received**—It was this that constituted their "faith." If they had "received" THE THING PROMISED (so "the promises" here mean: the plural is used because of the *frequent renewal* of the promise to the patriarchs: verse 17 says he *did* receive the *promises,* but not *the thing promised*), it would have been *sight,* not *faith.* **seen them afar off**— (John 8:56). Christ, as the Word, was preached to the Old Testament believers, and so became the seed of life to their souls, as He is to ours. **and were persuaded of them**—The oldest MSS. omit this clause. **embraced them**—as though they were not "afar off," but within reach, so as to draw them to themselves and clasp them in their embrace. TRENCH denies that the Old Testament believers *embraced* them, for they only saw them *afar off:* he translates, "saluted them," as the homeward-bound mariner, recognizing from afar the well-known promontories of his native land. ALFORD translates, *"greeted* them." Jacob's exclamation, "I have waited for Thy salvation, O Lord" (Gen. 49: 18, is such a *greeting* of salvation from afar [DELITZSCH]. **confessed ... were strangers**—so Abraham to the children of Heth (Gen. 23:4); and Jacob to Pharaoh (Gen. 47:9; Ps. 119:19). Worldly men hold fast the world; believers sit loose to it. *Citizens of the world* do not confess themselves "strangers on the earth." **pilgrims**—*Greek,* "temporary (lit., by the way) sojourners." **on the earth**—contrasted with "an heavenly" (vs. 16): "our *citizenship* is in heaven" (*Greek:* ch. 10:34; Ps. 119:54; Phil. 3: 20). "Whosoever professes that he has a Father in heaven, confesses himself a stranger on earth; hence there is in the heart an ardent longing, like that of a child living among strangers, in want and grief, far from his fatherland" [LUTHER]. "Like ships in seas while *in, above* the world." **14. For** —proof that "faith" (vs. 13) was their actuating principle. **declare plainly**—make it plainly evident. **seek**—*Greek,* "seek *after";* implying the direction towards which their desires ever tend. **a country** —rather as *Greek,* "a fatherland." In confessing themselves *strangers* here, they evidently imply that they regard not this as their home or fatherland, but seek after another and a better. **15.** As Abraham, had he desired to leave his pilgrim life in Canaan, and resume his former fixed habitation in Ur, among the carnal and worldly, had in his long life ample opportunities to have done so; and so spiritually, as to all believers who came out from the world to become God's people, they might, if they had been so minded, have easily gone back. **16.** Proving the truth that the old fathers did not, as some assert, "look only for transitory promises" (Article VII, *Book of Common Prayer*). **now**—as the case is. **is not ashamed**—*Greek,* "is not ashamed of them." Not merely once did God call himself *their God,* but He is NOW not ashamed to have Himself called so, they being *alive* and abiding with Him where He is. For, by the law, God cannot come into contact with anything dead. None remained dead in Christ's presence (Luke 20:37, 38). He who is Lord and Maker of heaven and earth, and all things therein, when asked, What is Thy name? said, omitting all His other titles, "I am the God of Abraham, and the God of Isaac, and the God of Jacob" [THEODORET]. Not only is He *not ashamed,* but glories in the name and relation to His people. The "wherefore" does not mean that God's *good pleasure* is the meritorious, but the *gracious,* consequence of their obedience (that obedience being the result of His Spirit's work in them in the first instance). He first so "called" Himself, then they so called Him. **for**—proof of His being *"their God,"* viz., "He hath prepared (in His eternal counsels, Matt. 20:23, 25:34, and by the progressive acts of redemption, John 14:2) for them a city," the city in which He Himself reigns, so that their yearning *desires* shall not be disappointed (vss. 14,16). **a city**—on its garniture by God (cf. Rev. 21:10-27). **17. offered up**—lit., "hath offered up," as if the work and its praise were yet enduring [ALFORD]. As far as His intention was concerned, he did sacrifice Isaac; and in actual fact "he offered him," as far as the presentation of him on the altar as an offering to God is concerned. **tried**—*Greek,* "tempted," as in Genesis 22:1. *Put to the proof* of his faith. Not that God "tempts" *to sin,* but God "tempts" in the sense of *proving* or *trying* (Jas. 1:13-15). **and**— and so. **he that had received**—rather as *Greek,*

"accepted," i.e., *welcomed* and embraced by faith, not merely "had the promises," as in ch. 7:6. This added to the difficulty in the way of his faith, that it was in Isaac's posterity the promises were to be fulfilled; how then could they be fulfilled if Isaac were sacrificed? **offered up**—rather as *Greek,* "was offering up"; he was in the act of offering. **his only-begotten son**—Cf. Genesis 22:2, "Take now thy son, thine only son." EUSEBIUS, *Præparatio Evangelica.* 1. 10, and 4. 16, has preserved a fragment of a *Greek* translation of Sanchoniatho, which mentions a mystical sacrifice of the Phœnicians, wherein a prince in royal robes was the offerer, and his only son was to be the victim: this evidently was a tradition derived from Abraham's offering, and handed down through Esau or Edom, Isaac's son. Isaac was Abraham's "only-begotten son" in respect of Sarah and the promises: he sent away his other sons, by other wives (Gen. 25:6). Abraham is a type of the Father not sparing His only-begotten Son to fulfil the divine purpose of love. God nowhere in the Mosaic law allowed human sacrifices, though He claimed the firstborn of Israel as His. **18. Of whom** —rather as *Greek* "He (*Abraham,* not Isaac) TO whom it was said" [ALFORD]. BENGEL supports *English Version.* So ch. 1:7 uses the same *Greek* preposition, "unto," for "in respect to," or "of." This verse gives a difinition of the "only-begotten Son" (vs. 17). **in Isaac shall thy seed be called**— (Gen. 21:12). The posterity of Isaac alone shall be accounted as the seed of Abraham, which is the heir of the promises (Rom. 9:7). **19.** Faith answered the objections which reason brought against God's command to Abraham to offer Isaac, by suggesting that what God had promised He both could and would perform, however impossible the performance might seem (Rom. 4:20, 21). **able to raise** *him*—rather, in general, "able to raise from the dead." Cf. Romans 4:17, "God who quickeneth the dead." The quickening of Sarah's dead womb suggested the thought of God's power to raise even the dead, though no instance of it had as yet occurred. **he received him**—"received him back" [ALFORD]. **in a figure**—*Greek,* "in a parable." ALFORD explains, "Received him back, risen from that death which he had undergone in, under, *the figure of the ram.*" I prefer with BISHOP PEARSON, ESTIUS, and GREGORY of Nyssa, understanding the *figure* to be the representation which the whole scene gave to Abraham of Christ in His death (typified by Isaac's offering in intention, and the ram's actual substitution answering to Christ's vicarious death), and in His resurrection (typified by Abraham's receiving him back alive from the jaws of death, cf. II Cor. 1:9, 10); just as on the day of atonement the slain goat and the scapegoat together formed one joint rite representing Christ's death and resurrection. It was then that Abraham saw Christ's day (John 8:56): accounting God was able to raise even from the dead: from which state of the dead he received him back *as a type of the resurrection in Christ.* **20.** Jacob is put before Esau, as heir of the chief, viz., the *spiritual* blessing. **concerning things to come**—*Greek,* "*even* concerning things to come": not only concerning things present. Isaac, *by faith,* assigned to his sons things future, as if they were present. **21. both the sons**—*Greek,* "*each* of the sons" (Gen. 47:29, 48:8-20). He knew not Joseph's sons, and could not distinguish them by sight, yet *he did distinguish them by faith,* transposing his hands intentionally, so as to lay his right hand on the younger, Ephraim, whose posterity was to be greater than that of Manasseh: he also adopted these grandchildren as his own sons, after having transferred the right of primogeniture to Joseph (Gen. 48:22). **and worshipped...**—This did not take place in immediate connection with the foregoing, but before it, when Jacob made Joseph swear that he would bury him with his fathers in Canaan, not in Egypt. The assurance that Joseph would do so filled him with pious gratitude to God, which he expressed by raising himself on his bed to an attitude of *worship*. His faith, as Joseph's (vs. 22), consisted in his so confidentially anticipating the fulfilment of God's promise of Canaan to his descendants, as to desire to be buried there as his proper possession. **leaning upon the top of his staff**—Genesis 47:31, *Hebrew* and *English Version*, "upon the bed's head." LXX translates as Paul here. JEROME justly reprobates the notion of modern Rome, that Jacob *worshipped the top of Joseph's staff*, having on it an image of Joseph's power, to which Jacob bowed in recognition of the future sovereignty of his son's tribe, the father bowing to the son! The *Hebrew*, as translated in *English Version*, sets it aside: *the bed* is alluded to afterwards (Gen. 48:2; 49:33), and it is likely that Jacob turned himself in his *bed* so as to have his face toward the pillow, Isaiah 38:2 (there were no *bedsteads* in the East). Paul by adopting the LXX version, brings out, under the Spirit, *an additional fact*, viz., that the aged patriarch used *his own* (not Joseph's) *staff* to lean on in worshipping on his bed. The *staff*, too, was the *emblem of his pilgrim state* here on his way to his heavenly city (vss. 13, 14), wherein God had so wonderfully supported him. Genesis 32:10, "With my *staff* I passed over Jordan, and now I am become..." (cf. Exod. 12:11; Mark 6:8). In I Kings 1:47, the same thing is said of David's "bowing on his bed," an act of adoring thanksgiving to God for God's favor to his son before death. He omits the more leading blessing of the twelve sons of Jacob; because "he plucks only the flowers which stand by his way, and leaves the whole meadow full to his readers" [DE-LITZSCH *in* ALFORD]. **22. when he died**—"when dying." **the departing**—"the exodus" (Gen. 50:24, 25). Joseph's eminent position in Egypt did not make him regard it as his home: in faith he looked to God's promise of Canaan being fulfilled and desired that his bones should rest there: testifying thus: (1) that he had no doubt of his posterity obtaining the promised land: and (2) that he believed in the resurrection of the body, and the enjoyment in it of the heavenly Canaan. His wish was fulfilled (Josh. 24:32; Acts 4:16). **23. parents**—So the LXX has the plural, viz., Amram and Jochebed (Num. 26:59); but in Exod. 2:2, the mother alone is mentioned; but doubtless Amram sanctioned all she did, and secrecy being their object, he did not appear prominent in what was done. **a proper child**—Greek, "a comely child." Acts 7:20, "exceeding fair," *Greek*, "fair to God." The "faith" of his parents in saving the child must have had some divine revelation to rest on (probably at the time of his birth), which marked their "exceeding fair" babe as one whom God designed to do a great work by. His *beauty* was probably "the sign" appointed by God to assure their faith. **the king's commandment**—to slay all the males (Exod. 1:22). **24.** So far from *faith* being opposed to *Moses*, he was an eminent example of it [BENGEL]. **refused**—in believing self-denial, when he might possibly have succeeded at last to the throne of Egypt. Thermutis, Pharaoh's daughter, according to the tradition which Paul under the Spirit sanctions, adopted him, as

JOSEPHUS says, with the consent of the king. Josephus states that when a child, he threw on the ground the diadem put on him in jest, a presage of his subsequent formal rejection of Thermutis' adoption of him. Faith made him to prefer the adoption of the King of kings, unseen, and so to choose (vss. 25, 26) things, the very last which flesh and blood relish. **25.** He balanced the best of the world with the worst of religion, and decidedly chose the latter. "Choosing" implies a deliberate resolution, not a hasty impulse. He was forty years old, a time when the judgment is matured. **for a season**—If the world has "pleasure" (*Greek*, "enjoyment") to offer, it is but "for a season." If religion bring with it "affliction," it too is but for a season; whereas its "pleasures are for evermore." **26. Esteeming**—Inasmuch as he esteemed. **the reproach of Christ**—i.e., the reproach which falls on the Church, and which Christ regards as His own reproach, He being the Head, and the Church (both of the Old and New Testament) His body. Israel typified Christ; Israel's sufferings were Christ's sufferings (cf. II Cor. 1:5; Col. 1:24). As uncircumcision was Egypt's *reproach*, so circumcision was the badge of Israel's expectation of Christ, which Moses especially cherished, and which the Gentiles reproached Israel on account of. Christ's people's reproach will ere long be their great glory. **had respect unto...**—Greek, "turning his eyes away from other considerations, he fixed them on the (eternal) recompense" (vss. 39, 40). **27. not fearing the wrath of the king**—But in Exodus 2:14 it is said, "Moses feared, and fled from the face of Pharaoh." He was *afraid*, and fled from the danger where no duty called him to stay (to have stayed without call of duty would have been to tempt Providence, and *to sacrifice his hope of being Israel's future deliverer according to the divine intimations*; his great aim, Note, vs. 23). He *did not fear the king* so as to neglect his duty and not return when God called him. It was *in spite of the king's prohibition he left Egypt*, not fearing the consequences which were likely to overtake him if he should be caught, after having, in defiance of the king, left Egypt. If he had stayed and resumed his position as adopted son of Pharaoh's daughter, his slaughter of the Egyptian would doubtless have been connived at; but his resolution to take his portion with oppressed Israel, which he could not have done had he stayed, was the motive of his flight, and constituted the "faith" of this act, according to the express statement here. The exodus of Moses with Israel cannot be meant here, for it was made, not in defiance, but by the desire, of the king. Besides, the chronological order would be broken thus, the next particular specified here, viz., the institution of the *Passover*, having taken place *before the exodus*. Besides, it is Moses' *personal* history and faith which are here described. The faith of the people ("THEY passed") is not introduced till vs. 29. **endured**—steadfast in faith amidst trials. He had fled, *not* so much from *fear of Pharaoh*, as from a revulsion of feeling in finding God's people insensible to their high destiny, and from disappointment at not having been able to inspire them with those hopes for which he had sacrificed all his earthly prospects. This accounts for his strange reluctance and despondency when commissioned by God to go and arouse the people (Exod. 3:15; 4:1, 10-12). **seeing him...invisible**—as though he had not to do with men, but only with God, ever before his eyes by faith, though *invisible* to the bodily eye (Rom. 1:20; I Tim. 1:17; 6:16). Hence he feared not the wrath of *visible* man; the characteristic of *faith* (vs. 1; Luke 12: 4, 5). **28. kept**—Greek, "hath kept," the Passover being, in Paul's day, still observed. His *faith* here was his belief in the invisible God's promise that the destroying angel should *pass over*, and not *touch* the inmates of the blood-sprinkled houses (Exod. 12:23). "He acquiesced in the bare word of God where the thing itself was not apparent" [CALVIN]. **the first-born**—Greek neuter; *both of man and beast.* **29. they**—Moses and Israel. **Red Sea**—called so from its red seaweed, or rather from Edom (meaning "red"), whose country adjoined it. **which . . . assaying to do**—Greek, "of which (Red Sea) the Egyptians having made experiment." *Rashness* and *presumption* mistaken by many for *faith;* with similar rash presumption many rush into eternity. The same thing when done by the believer, and when done by the unbeliever, is not the same thing [BENGEL]. What was *faith* in Israel, was *presumption* in the Egyptians. **were drowned** —Greek, "were swallowed up," or "engulfed." They sank in the sands as much as in the waves of the Red Sea. Cf. Exodus 15:12, "the *earth* swallowed them." **30.** The soundings of trumpets, though one were to sound for ten thousand years, cannot throw down walls, but *faith* can do all things [CHRYSOSTOM]. **seven days**—whereas sieges often lasted for years. **31.** Rahab showed her "faith" in her confession, Joshua 2:9, 11, "I know that Jehovah hath given you the land; Jehovah your God, is God in heaven above, and in earth beneath." **the harlot**—Her former life adds to the marvel of her repentance, faith, and preservation (Matt. 21:31-32). **believed not**—Greek, "were disobedient," viz., to the will of God manifested by the miracles wrought in behalf of Israel (Josh. 2:8-11). **received** —in her house (Josh. 2:1, 4, 6). **with peace**—peaceably; so that they had nothing to fear in her house. Thus Paul, quoting the same examples (vss. 17, 31) for the power of *faith,* as James (2:21, 25; see my *Notes* there) does for justification by *works* evidentially, shows that in maintaining justification by faith alone, he means not a dead faith, but "faith which *worketh* by love" (Gal. 5:6). **32. the time**—suitable for the length of an Epistle. He accumulates collectively some out of many examples of faith. **Gedeon**—put before Barak, not chronologically, but as being more celebrated. Just as Samson for the same reason is put before Jephthae. The mention of Jephthae as an example of "faith," makes it unlikely he sacrificed the *life* of his daughter for a rash vow. David, the warrior king and prophet, forms the transition from warrior chiefs to the "prophets," of whom "Samuel" is mentioned as the first. **33. subdued kingdoms**—as David did (II Sam. 8:1, etc.); so also Gideon subdued Midian (Judg. 7). **wrought righteousness**—as Samuel did (I Sam. 8:9; 12:3-23 15:33); and David (II Sam. 8:15). **obtained promises**—as "the prophets" (vs. 32) did; for through them the promises were given (cf. Dan. 9:21) [BENGEL]. Rather, "obtained *the fulfilment* of promises," which had been previously the object of their *faith* (Josh. 21:45; I Kings 8:56). Indeed, Gideon, Barak, etc., also *obtained* the things which God promised. Not "*the* promises," which are still future (vss. 13, 39). **stopped the mouths of lions** —Note the words, "because he *believed* in his God." Also Samson (Judg. 14:6), David (I Sam. 17:34-37), Benaiah (II Sam. 23:20). **34. Quenched the violence of fire**—(Dan. 3:27). Not merely "quenched the fire," but "quenched the power (so the *Greek*) of the fire." Daniel 3 and 6 record the last miracles of the Old Testament. So the martyrs of the Ref-

ormation, though not escaping *the fire,* were delivered from its having *power* really or lastingly to hurt them. **escaped . . . sword**—So Jephthah (Judg. 12: 3); and so David escaped Saul's sword (I Sam. 18: 11; 19:10, 12); Elijah (I Kings 19:1, etc.; II Kings 6: 14). **out of weakness . . . made strong**—Samson (Judg. 16:28; 15:19). Hezekiah (Isa. 37 and 38). Milton says of the martyrs, "They shook the powers of darkness with the irresistible power of weakness." **valiant in fight**—Barak (Judg. 4:14, 15). And the Maccabees, the sons of Matthias, Judas, Jonathan, and Simon, who delivered the Jews from their cruel oppressor, Antiochus of Syria. **armies**—lit., "camps" referring to Judges 7:21. But the reference may be to the Maccabees having put to flight the Syrians and other foes. **35. Women received their dead raised**—as the widow of Zarephath (I Kings 17:17-24). The Shunammite (II Kings 4:17-35). The two oldest MSS. read, "They received women of aliens by raising their dead." I Kings 17:24 shows that the raising of the widow's son by Elijah led her to the faith, so that he thus *took* her into fellowship, an *alien* though she was. Christ, in Luke 4:26, makes especial mention of the fact that Elijah was sent to an alien from Israel, a woman of Sarepta. Thus Paul may quote this as an instance of Elijah's faith, that at God's command he went to a Gentile city of Sidonia (contrary to Jewish prejudices), and there, as the fruit of faith, not only raised her dead son, but *received* her as a convert into the family of God, as *Vulgate* reads. Still, *English Version* may be the right reading. **and**—Greek, "but"; in contrast to those raised *again* to life. **tortured**— "broken on the wheel." Eleazar (II Maccabees 6: 18, end; 19:20, 30). The sufferer was stretched on an instrument like a drumhead and scourged to death. **not accepting deliverance**—when offered to them. So the seven brothers, II Maccabees 7:9, 11, 14, 29, 36; and Eleazar, II Maccabees 6:21, 28, 30, "Though I might have been delivered from death, I endure these severe pains, being beaten." **a better resurrection**—than that of the women's children "raised to life again"; or, than the resurrection which their foes could give them by delivering them from death (Dan. 12:2; Luke 20:35; Phil. 3: 11). The fourth of the brethren (referring to Dan. 12:2) said to King Antiochus, "To be put to death by men, is to be chosen to look onward for the hopes which are of God, to be raised up again by Him; but for thee there is no resurrection to life." The writer of II Maccabees *expressly disclaims inspiration,* which prevents our mistaking Paul's allusion here to it as if it sanctioned the Apocrypha as inspired. In quoting Daniel, he quotes a book *claiming inspiration,* and so tacitly sanctions that claim. **36. others**—of a *different* class of confessors for the truth (the *Greek* is different from that for "others," vs. 35, *alloi, heteroi*). **trial**—testing their *faith.* **imprisonment**—as Hanani (II Chron. 16:10), imprisoned by Asa. Micaiah, the son of Imlah, by Ahab (I Kings 22:26, 27). **37. stoned**—as Zechariah, son of Jehoiada (II Chron. 24:20-22; Matt. 23:35). **sawn asunder**—as Isaiah was said to have been by Manasseh; but see my *Introduction* to Isaiah. **tempted**—by their foes, in the midst of their tortures, to renounce their faith; the most bitter aggravation of them. Or else, *by those of their own household,* as Job was [ESTIUS]; or by the fiery darts of Satan, as Jesus was in His last trials [GLASSIUS]. Probably it included all three; they were *tempted* in every possible way, by friends and foes, by human and satanic agents, by caresses and afflictions, by words and deeds, to forsake God, but in vain, through the power of faith. **sword**—lit., "they died in the murder of the sword." In vs. 34 the contrary is given as an effect of *faith,* "they escaped the edge of the sword." Both alike are marvellous effects of faith. In both accomplishes great things and suffers great things, without counting it suffering [CHRYSOSTOM]. Urijah was so slain by Jehoiakim (Jer. 26:23); and *the prophets* in Israel (I Kings 19:10). **in sheepskins**—as Elijah (I Kings 19:13, LXX). They were *white;* as the "goatskins" were *black* (cf. Zech. 13:4). **tormented**—*Greek,* "in evil state." **38. Of whom the world was not worthy**—So far from their being unworthy of living in the world, as their exile in deserts, etc., might seem to imply, "the world was not worthy of them." The world, in shutting them out, shut out from itself a source of blessing; such as Joseph proved to Potiphar (Gen. 39:5), and Jacob to Laban (Gen. 30:27). In condemning them, the world condemned itself. **caves**—lit., "chinks." Palestine, from its hilly character, abounds in *fissures* and caves, affording shelter to the persecuted, as the fifty hid by Obadiah (I Kings 18:4, 13) and Elijah (I Kings 19:8, 13); and Mattathias and his sons (I Maccabees 2:28, 29); and Judas Maccabeus (II Maccabees 5:27). **39. having obtained a good report**—*Greek,* "being borne witness of." *Though* they were so, yet "they received not the promise," i.e., the *final completion* of "salvation" *promised* at Christ's coming again (ch. 9:28); "the eternal inheritance" (ch. 9:15). Abraham did *obtain* the very thing *promised* (ch. 6:15) *in part,* viz., blessedness *in soul* after death, by virtue of faith in Christ about to come. The *full* blessedness of body and soul shall not be till the full number of the elect shall be accomplished, and all together, no one preceding the other, shall enter on the full glory and bliss. Moreover, in another point of view, "It is probable that some accumulation of blessedness was added to holy souls, when Christ came and fulfilled all things even as at His burial many rose from the dead, who doubtless ascended to heaven with Him" [FLACIUS *in* BENGEL] (cf. *Note,* Eph. 4:8). The *perfecting* of believers in title, and in respect to conscience, took place once for all, at the death of Christ, by virtue of His being made by death *perfect* as Saviour. Their *perfecting in soul* at, and ever after Christ's death, took place, and takes place at their death. But the universal and final perfecting will not take place till Christ's coming. **40. provided**—with divine forethought from eternity (cf. Gen. 22:8, 14). **some better thing for us**—(ch. 7:19) —than they had here. They had not in this world, "apart from us" (so the *Greek* is for "without us," i.e., they had to wait for us for), the clear revelation of the promised salvation actually accomplished, as we now have it in Christ; in their state, beyond the grave their *souls* also seem to have attained an increase of *heavenly* bliss on the death and ascension of Christ; and they shall not attain the full and final *glory in body and soul* (the regeneration of the creature), until the full number of the elect (including us with them) is completed. The Fathers, CHRYSOSTOM, etc., restricted the meaning of vss. 39, 40 to this last truth, and I incline to this view. The connection is, You, Hebrews, may far more easily exercise patience than Old Testament believers; for they had much longer to wait, and are still waiting until the elect are all gathered in; you, on the contrary, have not to wait for them" [ESTIUS]. I think his object in these verses (39, 40) is to warn Hebrew Christians against their tendency to relapse into *Judaism.* "Though the Old Testament worthies at-

tained such eminence by faith, they are not above us in privileges, but the reverse." It is not *we* who are perfected *with them,* but rather *they with us.* They *waited* for His coming; we enjoy Him as having come (ch. 1:1; 2:3). Christ's death, the means of *perfecting* what the Jewish *law could not perfect,* was reserved for our time. Cf. ch. 12:2, "*perfecter* (*Greek*) of our faith." Now that Christ is come, they in soul share our blessedness, being "the spirits of the just made perfect" (ch. 12:23); so ALFORD; however, see *Note* there. Ch. 9:12 shows that the blood of Christ, brought into the heavenly holy place by Him, first opened an entrance into heaven (cf. John 3:13). Still, the fathers were in blessedness by faith in the Saviour to come, at death (ch. 6:15; Luke 16:22).

CHAPTER 12

VSS. 1-29. EXHORTATION TO FOLLOW THE WITNESSES OF FAITH JUST MENTIONED: NOT TO FAINT IN TRIALS: TO REMOVE ALL BITTER ROOTS OF SIN: FOR WE ARE UNDER, NOT A LAW OF TERROR, BUT THE GOSPEL OF GRACE, TO DESPISE WHICH WILL BRING THE HEAVIER PENALTIES, IN PROPORTION TO OUR GREATER PRIVILEGES. **1. we also**—as well as those recounted in vs. 11. **are compassed about**—*Greek,* "have so great a cloud (a numberless multitude *above* us, like a cloud, 'holy and pellucid,' [CLEMENS ALEXANDRINUS]) of witnesses surrounding us." The image is from a "race," an image common even in Palestine from the time of the Græco-Macedonian empire, which introduced such Greek usages as national games. The "witnesses" answer to the spectators pressing round to see the competitors in their contest for the prize (Phil. 3:14). Those "witnessed of" (*Greek,* ch. 11: 5, 39) become in their turn "witnesses" in a twofold way: (1) attesting by their own case the faithfulness of God to His people [ALFORD] (ch. 6:12), some of them *martyrs* in the modern sense; (2) witnessing our struggle of faith; however, this second sense of "witnesses," though agreeing with the *image* here if it is to be pressed, is not *positively,* unequivocally, and *directly* sustained by Scripture. It gives vividness to the image; as the crowd of spectators gave additional spirit to the combatants, so the *cloud of witnesses* who have themselves been in the same contest, ought to increase our earnestness, testifying, as they do, to God's faithfulness. **weight**—As corporeal unwieldiness was, through a disciplinary diet, laid aside by candidates for the prize in racing; so carnal and worldly lusts, and all, whether from without or within, that would impede the heavenly runner, are the spiritual *weight* to be laid aside. "Encumbrance," *all superfluous weight;* the lust of the flesh, the lust of the eye, and the pride of life, and even harmless and otherwise useful things which would positively retard us (Mark 10:50, the blind man *casting away his garment* to come to Jesus; 9: 42-48; cf. Eph. 4:22; Col. 3:9, 10). **the sin which doth so easily beset us**—*Greek,* "sin which easily stands around us"; so LUTHER, "which always so clings to us"; "sinful propensity always surrounding us, ever present and ready" [WAHL]. It is not primarily "*the sin,*" etc., but *sin* in general, with, however, special reference to "apostasy," against which he had already warned them, as one to which they might *gradually* be seduced; the besetting sin of the Hebrews, UNBELIEF. **with patience**—*Greek,* "in persevering endurance" (ch. 10:36). On "run" cf. I Corinthians 9:24, 25. **2. Looking unto**—lit..

"Looking from afar" (*Note,* ch. 11:26); fixing the eyes upon Jesus seated on the throne of God. **author** —"Prince-leader." The same *Greek* is translated, "Captain (of salvation)," ch. 2:10; "Prince (of life)," Acts 3:15. Going before us as the Originator of our faith, and the Leader whose matchless example we are to follow always. In this He is distinguished from all those examples of faith in ch. 11. (Cf. I Cor. 11:1.) On His "faith" cf. ch. 2:13; 3:2. Believers have ever looked to Him (ch. 11:26; 13:8). **finisher**—*Greek,* "Perfecter," referring to ch. 11:40. **of our faith**—rather as *Greek,* "of *the* faith," including both His faith (as exhibited in what follows) and our faith. He fulfilled the ideal of faith Himself, and so, both as a vicarious offering and an example, He is the object of our faith. **for the joy . . . set before him**—viz., of presently after *sitting down at the right hand of the throne of God;* including besides His own personal joy, the joy of sitting there as a Prince and Saviour, to give repentance and remission of sins. The coming joy disarmed of its sting the present pain. **cross . . . shame** —the great stumbling block to the Hebrews. "Despised," i.e., disregarded. **3. For**—justifying his exhortation, "Looking unto Jesus." **consider**—by way of comparison with yourselves, so the *Greek.* **contradiction**—unbelief, and every kind of opposition (Acts 28:19). **sinners**—*Sin* assails us. Not *sin,* but *sinners,* contradicted Christ [BENGEL]. **be wearied and faint**—*Greek,* "lest ye weary fainting." Cf. Isaiah 49:4, 5, as a specimen of Jesus not being *wearied out* by the *contradiction* and strange unbelief of those among whom He *labored,* preaching as never man did, and exhibiting miracles wrought by His inherent power, as none else could do. **4. not yet resisted unto blood**—image from *pugilism,* as he previously had the image of a *race,* both being taken from the great national Greek games. Ye have suffered the loss of *goods,* and *been a gazing-stock by reproaches and afflictions;* ye have not shed your *blood* (*Note,* ch. 18:7). "The athlete who hath seen his own *blood,* and who, though cast down by his opponent, does not let his spirits be cast down, who as often as he hath fallen hath risen the more determined, goes down to the encounter with great hope" [SENECA]. **against sin**—*Sin* is personified as an adversary; sin, whether within you, leading you to *spare* your blood, or in our adversaries, leading them to *shed* it, if they cannot through your faithfulness even unto blood, induce you to apostatize. **5. forgotten**—"utterly," so the *Greek.* Cf. vss. 15-17, in which he implies how utterly *some* of them had forgotten God's word. His *exhortation* ought to have more effect on you than the cheers and exhortations of the spectators have on the competitors striving in the games. **which**—*Greek,* "the which," of which the following is a specimen [ALFORD]. **speaketh unto you**—as in *a dialogue* or *discourse,* so the *Greek,* implying God's loving condescension (cf. Isa. 1:18). **despise not**—lit., "Do not *hold of little account."* Betraying a *contumacious spirit of unbelief* (ch. 3:12), as "faint" implies a brokendown, weak, and *desponding spirit.* "Chastening" is to be borne with "subjection" (vs. 9); "rebuke" (more severe than *chastening*) is to be borne with *endurance* (vs. 7). "Some in adversity kick against God's will, others despond; neither is to be done by the Christian, who is peculiarly the child of God. To him such adverse things occur only by the decree of God, and that designed in kindness, viz., to remove the defilements adhering to the believer, and to exercise his patience" [GROTIUS]. **6.** (Rev. 3:19.) **and**—*Greek,* "yea and," "and moreover"; bringing

out an additional circumstance. **scourgeth**—which draws forth "blood" (vs. 4). **receiveth**—accepts. Takes to Himself as a son "in whom He *delighteth"* (Prov. 3:12). **7.** In vss. 7, 8 the need of "chastening" or "discipline" is inculcated; in vs. 9, the duty of those to whom it is administered. **If**—The oldest MSS. read, "With a view to chastening (i.e., since God's chastisement is with a view to your chastening, i.e., disciplinary amelioration) endure patiently"; so *Vulgate.* ALFORD translates it as indicative, not so well, "It is for chastisement that *ye are enduring."* **dealeth with you**—"beareth Himself toward you" in the very act of chastening. **what son is he**—"What son is there" even in ordinary life? Much more God as to His sons (Isa. 48:10; Acts 14:22). The most eminent of God's saints were the most afflicted. God leads them by a way they know not (Isa. 42:16). We too much look at each trial by itself, instead of taking it in connection with the whole plan of our salvation, as if a traveller were to complain of the steepness and roughness of one turn in the path, without considering that it led him into green pastures, on the direct road to the city of habitation. The New Testament alone uses the *Greek* term for education (*paideia*), to express "discipline" or *correction,* as of a *child* by a wise father. **8. if ye be without**—excluded from participation in chastisement, and wishing to be so. **all** —all *sons:* all the worthies enumerated in ch. 11: all the *witnesses* (vs. 1). **are**—*Greek,* "have been made." **then are ye bastards**—of whom their fathers take no care whether they are educated or not; whereas every rightminded father is concerned for the moral well-being of his legitimate son. "Since then not to be chastised is a mark of bastardy, we ought [not to refuse, but] rejoice in chastisement, as a mark of our genuine sonship" [CHRYSOSTOM]. **9. fathers . . . which corrected us**—rather as *Greek,* "We had the fathers of our flesh as correctors." **subjection**—See the punishment of insubordination, Deuteronomy 21:18. **Father of spirits**—contrasted with "the fathers of our flesh." "Generation by men is carnal, by God is spiritual" [BENGEL]. As "Father of spirits," He is both the Originator, and the Providential and Gracious Sustainer, at once of animal and spiritual life. Cf. "and LIVE," viz., spiritually; also vs. 10, "that we might be partakers of HIS holiness" (II Pet. 1:4). God is a spirit Himself, and the Creator of spirits like Himself, in contrast to men who are flesh, and the progenitors of flesh (John 3:6). Jesus our pattern "learned obedience" experimentally by suffering (ch. 5:8). **and live**—and so, thereby live spiritually and eternally. **10.** Showing wherein the chastisement of our heavenly Father is preferable to that of earthly fathers. **for a few days**—i.e., *with a view to* our well-being in *the few days* of our earthly life: so the *Greek.* **after their own pleasure**—*Greek,* "according to what seemed fit to themselves." Their rule of chastening is what may seem fit to their own often erring judgment, temper, or caprice. The two defects of human education are: (1) the prevalence in it of a view to the interests of our *short* earthly term of *days;* (2) the absence in parents of the unerring wisdom of our heavenly Father. "They err much at one time in severity, at another in indulgence [I Sam. 3:13; Eph. 6:4], and do not so much chasten as THINK they chasten" [BENGEL]. **that we might be partakers of his holiness**—becoming holy as He is holy (John 15:2). To become *holy* like God is tantamount to being educated for passing *eternity* with God (vs. 14; II Pet. 1:4). So this "partaking of

God's holiness" stands in contrast to the "few days" of this life, with a view to which earthly fathers generally educate their sons. **11. joyous...grievous**—*Greek,* "matter of joy...matter of grief." The objection that chastening is grievous is here anticipated and answered. It only seems so to those being chastened, whose judgments are confused by the present pain. Its ultimate *fruit* amply compensates for any temporary pain. The real object of the fathers in chastening is not that they find pleasure in the children's pain. Gratified wishes, our Father knows, would often be our real curses. **fruit of righteousness**—*righteousness* (in practice, springing from faith) is the *fruit* which chastening, the tree yields (Phil. 1:11). "Peaceable" (cf. Isa. 32:17): in contrast to the ordeal of conflict by which it has been won. "Fruit of righteousness to be enjoyed in peace after the conflict" [THOLUCK]. As the olive garland, the emblem of *peace* as well as *victory*, was put on the victor's brow in the games. **exercised thereby**—as athletes exercised in training for a contest. *Chastisement* is the *exercise* to give experience, and make the spiritual combatant irresistibly victorious (Rom. 5:3). "Oh, happy the servant for whose improvement his Lord is earnest, with whom he deigns to be angry, whom He does not deceive by dissembling admonition" (withholding admonition, and so leading the man to think he needs it not)! [TERTULLIAN, *de Pat.,* c. 11]. Observe the "afterwards"; *that* is the time often when God works. **12.** He addresses them as runners in a race, and pugilists, and warriors [CHRYSOSTOM]. The "wherefore" is resumed from vs. 1. **lift up**—In Isaiah 35:3, from which Paul here quotes, it is, "*Strengthen* ye the weak hands." The *hand* is the symbol of one's strength. ALFORD translates, "Put straight again the relaxed hands." *English Version* expresses the sense well. **feeble**—lit., "paralyzed"; a word used only by Luke, *Paul's* companion, in the New Testament. The exhortation has three parts: the first relates to *ourselves,* vss. 12, 13; the second, to *others,* vs. 14, "peace with all men"; the third, to *God,* "holiness, without which..." The first is referred to in vs. 15, "lest any man fail of the grace of God"; the second in the words, "lest any root of bitterness..."; the third in vs. 16, "Lest there be any fornicator or profane person...." This threefold relation often occurs in *Paul's* Epistles. Cf. *Note,* Titus 2:12, "soberly, righteously, and godly." The *Greek* active verb, not the middle or reflexive, requires the sense to be, Lift up not only *your own* hands and knees, but also those *of your brethren* (cf. vs. 15; Isa. 35:4). **13.** Quoted from Proverbs 4:26, LXX, "Make straight paths for thy feet." **straight**—i.e., leading by a straight road to joy and grace (vss. 1, 2, 15). Cease to "halt" between Judaism and Christianity [BENGEL]. **paths** —lit., "wheel tracks." Let your walk be so firm and so unanimous in the right direction that a plain track and "highway" may be thereby established for those who accompany and follow you, to perceive and walk in (Isa. 35:8) [ALFORD]. **that which is lame**—those "weak in the faith" (Rom. 14:1), having still Judaizing prejudices. **be turned out of the way**—(Prov. 4:27)—and, so missing the way, ¹ose the prize of "the race" (vs. 1). **rather he healed**—Proper exercise of itself contributes to health; the habit of walking straight onward in the right way tends to *healing.* **14. follow peace with all men**—with the brethren especially (Rom. 14:19), that so the "lame" among them be not "turned out of the way" (vs. 13), and that no one of them "fail of the grace of God" (vs. 15). **holiness**—a distinct *Greek*

word from God's "holiness" (vs. 10). Translate here "sanctification." His is absolute *holiness:* our part is to put on His holiness, becoming "holy as He is holy," by *sanctification.* While "following peace with all men," we are not so to seek to please them, as to make God's will and our sanctification a secondary object; this latter must be our first aim. (Gal. 1:10). **without which**—*Greek,* "apart from which." **no man shall see the Lord**—no man *as a son;* in heavenly glory (Rev. 22:3, 4). In the East, none but the greatest favorites are admitted to the honor of seeing the king (cf. II Sam. 14:24). The Lord being pure and holy, none but the pure and holy shall see Him (Matt. 5:8). Without holiness in them, they could not enjoy Him who is holiness itself (Zech. 14:20). The connection of *purity* with *seeing the Lord,* appears in I John 3:2, 3; Ephesians 5:5. Contrast vs. 16 (cf. I Thess. 4:3). In Matthew 24:30; Revelation 1:7, it is said that all shall see the Lord; but, that shall be as a *Judge,* not as their lasting portion and God, which is meant here. The *Greek* verb does not denote the mere action of seeing, but the seer's state of mind to which the object is presented: so in Matthew 5:8 they shall *truly comprehend* God [TITTMANN]. None but the holy could *appreciate* the holy God, none else therefore shall abide in His presence. "The bad shall only see Him in His form as *Son of man* [cf. Rev. 1:13, with 7; and Matt. 24:30; Acts 1:11; 17:31]; still it will be in the glory in which He shall judge, not in the lowliness in which He was judged. *His form as God,* wherein He is equal to the Father, without doubt the ungodly shall not see; for it is only 'the pure in heart who shall see God'" [AUGUSTINE]. "He shall come to judge, who stood before a judge. He shall come in the form in which He was judged, that they may see Him whom they pierced: He who was before hidden shall come manifested in power: He, as Judge, shall condemn the real culprits, who was Himself falsely made a culprit." **15. lest any ...fall**—*Greek,* "lest any (viz., through sloth in running) *failing,*" or "*falling short of* the grace of God...*trouble you.*" The image is taken from a company of travellers, one of whom lags behind, and so never reaches the end of the long and laborious journey [CHRYSOSTOM]. **root of bitterness**—not merely a "*bitter* root," which might possibly bring forth sweet fruits; this, a root whose *essence* is "*bitterness,*" never could. Paul here refers to Deuteronomy 29:18, "Lest there should be among you a root that beareth gall and wormwood" (cf. Acts 8:23). *Root of bitterness* comprehends every *person* (cf. vs. 16) and every *principle* of doctrine or practice so radically corrupt as to spread corruption all around. The only safety is in rooting out such a root of bitterness. **many**—rather, "*the many,*" i.e., the whole congregation. So long as it is hidden under the earth it cannot be remedied, but when it "springs up," it must be dealt with boldly. Still remember the caution (Matt. 13:26-30) as to rooting out *persons.* No such danger can arise in rooting out bad *principles.* **16. fornicator**—(ch. 13:4; I Cor. 10:8). **or profane**—*Fornication* is nearly akin to gluttony, Esau's sin. He *profanely* cast away his spiritual privilege for the gratification of his palate. Genesis 25:34 graphically portrays him. An example well fitted to strike needful horror into the Hebrews, whosoever of them, like Esau, were only sons of Isaac according to the flesh [BENGEL]. **for one morsel**—The smallness of the inducement only aggravates the guilt of casting away eternity for such a trifle, so far is it from being a claim for mercy (cf. Gen. 3:6). *One* single act has often the greatest power either for good or for evil. So in the cases of Reuben and Saul, for evil (Gen. 49:4; I Chron. 5:1; I Sam. 13:12-14); and, on the other hand, for good, Abraham and Phinehas (Gen. 12:1, etc.; 15:5, 6; Num. 25:6-15). **his birthright**— Greek, "his own (so the oldest MSS. read, intensifying the suicidal folly and sin of the act) rights of primogeniture," involving the high spiritual privilege of being ancestor of the promised seed, and heir of the promises in Him. The Hebrews whom Paul addressed, had, as Christians, the spiritual rights of primogeniture (cf. vs. 23): he intimates that they must exercise holy selfcontrol, if they wish not, like Esau, to forfeit them. **17. afterwards**—Greek, "even afterward." He despised his birthright, accordingly *also* he was despised and rejected when he wished to have the blessing. As in the believer's case, so in the unbeliever's, there is an "afterwards" coming, when the believer shall look on his past griefs, and the unbeliever on his past joys, in a very different light from that in which they were respectively viewed at the time. Cf. "Nevertheless afterward . . ." vs. 11, with the "afterward" here. **when he would**—when he *wished* to have. "He that will not when he may, when he will, shall have nay" (Prov. 1:24-30; Luke 13:34, 35; 19:42). **he was rejected**—not as to every blessing, but only that which would have followed the primogeniture. **he found no place of repentance**—The *cause* is here put for the *effect*, "repentance" for the object which Esau aimed at in his so-called *repentance,* viz., *the change of his father's determination* to give the chief blessing to Jacob. Had he *sought* real *repentance with tears* he would have *found* it (Matt. 7:7). But he did not find it because this was not what he sought. What proves his *tears* were not those of one seeking true repentance is, immediately after he was foiled in his desire, he resolved to murder Jacob! He shed tears, not for his sin, but for his suffering the penalty of his sin. His were tears of vain regret and remorse, not of repentance. "Before, he might have had the blessing without tears; afterwards, no matter how many tears he shed, he was rejected. Let us use the time" (Luke 18:27)! [BENGEL]. ALFORD explains "repentance" here, *a chance, by repenting, to repair* (i.e., to regain the lost blessing). I agree with him that the translation, instead of "repentance," "no place for *changing* HIS FATHER'S *mind*," is forced; though doubtless this is what was the true aim of the "repentance" which he sought. The language is framed to apply to *profane* despisers who wilfully cast away grace and *seek repentance* (i.e., not real; but *escape from the penalty* of their sin), but in vain. Cf. "afterward," Matthew 25:11, 12. Tears are no proof of real repentance (I Sam. 24:16, 17; contrast Ps. 56:8). **it**—*the blessing,* which was the real object of Esau, though ostensibly seeking "repentance." **18. For**— The fact that we are not under the law, but under a higher, and that the last dispensation, the Gospel, with its glorious privileges, is the reason why especially the Hebrew Christians should "look diligently . . ." (vss. 15, 16). **are not come**—Greek, "have not come near to." Alluding to Deuteronomy 4:11, "Ye *came near* and stood under the mountain; and the mountain burned with fire . . . with darkness, clouds, and thick darkness." "In your *coming near unto God*, it has not been to. . . ." **the mount**—The oldest MSS. and *Vulgate* omit "the mount." But still, "the mount" must be supplied from vs. 22. **that might be touched**—palpable and material. Not that any save Moses was allowed to touch it (Exod. 19:12, 13). The Hebrews drew near to the material

Mount Sinai with material bodies; we, to the spiritual mount in the spirit. The "darkness" was that formed by the clouds hanging round the mount; the "tempest" accompanied the thunder. **19. trumpet** —to rouse attention, and herald God's approach (Exod. 19:16). **entreated that the word should not be spoken**—lit., "that speech should not be added to them"; not that they refused to hear the word of God, but they wished that God should not Himself speak, but employ Moses as His mediating spokesman. "The voice of words" was the Decalogue, spoken by God Himself, a voice issuing forth, without *any* form being seen: after which "He *added* no more" (Deut. 5:22). **20. that which was commanded** —"the interdict" [TITTMANN]. A *stern interdictory mandate* is meant. **And**—rather, "Even if a beast (much more a man) touch. . . ." **or thrust through with a dart**—omitted in the oldest MSS. The *full* interdict in Exodus 19:12, 13 is abbreviated here; the beast alone, being put for "whether man or beast"; the *stoning,* which applies to the *human* offender, alone being specified, the beast's punishment, viz., the being *thrust through with a dart,* being left to be understood. **21. the sight**—the *vision* of God's majesty. **quake**—Greek, "I am in trembling"; "fear" affected his *mind;* "trembling," his body. Moses is not recorded in Exodus to have used these words. But Paul, by inspiration, supplies (cf. Acts 20:35; II Tim. 3:8) this detail. We read in Deuteronomy 9:19, LXX, of similar words used by Moses after breaking the two tables, through fear of God's anger at the people's sin in making the golden calves. He doubtless similarly "feared" in hearing the ten commandments spoken by the voice of Jehovah. **22. are come**—Greek, "have come near unto" (cf. Deut. 4:11). Not merely, ye *shall* come, but, *ye have already come.* **Mount Sion**—antitypical Sion, the heavenly Jerusalem, of which the spiritual invisible Church (of which the first foundation was laid in literal Zion, John 12:15; I Pet. 2:6) is now the earnest; and of which the restored literal Jerusalem hereafter shall be the earthly representative, to be succeeded by the everlasting and "new Jerusalem, coming down from God out of heaven" (Rev. 21:2-27; cf. ch. 11:10). **22, 23. to an innumerable company of angels, to the general assembly and church**—The *city* of God having been mentioned, the mention of its citizens follows. Believers being like the angels (Job 1:6; 38: 7), "sons of God," are so their "equals" (Luke 20: 36); and, being reconciled through Christ, are adopted into God's great and blessed family. For the full completion of this we pray (Matt. 6:10). *English Version* arrangement is opposed: (1) by "and" always beginning each new member of the whole sentence; (2) "general assembly and Church," form a kind of tautology; (3) "general assembly," or rather, "*festal* full assembly," "the jubilant full company" (such as were the Olympic games, celebrated with joyous singing, dancing, etc.), applies better to the *angels* above, ever hymning God's praises, than to the Church, of which a considerable part is now militant on earth. Translate therefore, "to myriads (ten thousands, cf. Deut. 33:2; Ps. 68: 17; Dan. 7:10; Jude 14; namely), the full festal assembly of angels, and the Church of the firstborn." Angels and saints together constitute the *ten thousands.* Cf. "*all* angels, *all nations*" Matthew 25: 31, 32. Messiah is pre-eminently "the First-born," or "First-begotten" (ch. 1:6), and all believers become so by adoption. Cf. the type, Leviticus 3: 12, 45, 50; I Peter 1:18. As the kingly and priestly succession was in the first-born, and as Israel was

God's "first-born" (Exod. 4:22; cf. 13:2), and a "kingdom of priests" to God (Exod. 19:6), so believers (Rev. 1:6). **written in heaven**—enrolled as citizens there. *All* those who at the coming of "God the Judge of all" (which clause therefore naturally follows), shall be found "written in heaven," i.e., *in the Lamb's book of life.* Though still fighting the good fight on earth, still, in respect to your destiny, and present life of *faith* which substantiates things hoped for, ye *are* already members of the heavenly citizenship. "We are one citizenship with angels; to which it is said in the psalm, *Glorious things are spoken of thee, thou city of God"* [AUGUSTINE]. I think ALFORD wrong in *restricting* "the Church of the first-born written in heaven," to those militant on earth; it is rather, *all* those who *at the Judge's coming* shall be found written in heaven (the true patent of heavenly nobility; contrast "written in the earth," Jer. 17:13, and Esau's profane sale of his birthright, vs. 16); these all, from the beginning to the end of the world, forming *one* Church to which every believer is already come. The *first-born* of Israel were "written" in a roll (Num. 3:40). **the spirits of just men made perfect**—at the resurrection, when the "JUDGE" shall appear, and believers' bliss shall be consummated by the union of the glorified *body* with the *spirit;* the great hope of the New Testament (Rom. 8:20-23; I Thess. 4:16). The place of this clause *after* "the JUDGE OF ALL," is my objection to BENGEL and ALFORD'S explanation, the souls of the just *in their separate state perfected.* Cf. (*Note*) ch. 11:39, 40, to which he refers here, and which I think confirms my view; those heretofore *spirits,* but now to be perfected by being clothed upon with the body. Still the phrase, *"spirits of* just men made perfect," not merely "just men made perfect," may favor the reference to the happy spirits in their separate state. The *Greek* is not "the *perfected spirits,"* but "the spirits of *the perfected just."* In no other passage are *the just* said to be *perfected* before the resurrection, and the completion of the full number of the elect (Rev. 6:11); I think, therefore, "spirits of the just," may here be used to express *the just whose predominant element in their perfected state shall be spirit.* So *spirit* and *spirits* are used of *a man* or *men in the body, under the influence of the spirit,* the opposite of *flesh* (John 3:6). The resurrection bodies of the saints shall be *bodies* in which the *spirit* shall altogether preponderate over the *animal soul* (Note, I Cor. 15:44). **24. new**—not the usual term (*kaine*) applied to the Christian covenant (ch. 9:15), which would mean *new* as *different from,* and superseding the *old;* but Greek, *nea,* recent, lately established, having the *freshness of youth,* as opposed to age. The mention of Jesus, *the Perfecter* of our faith (vs. 2), and Himself perfected through sufferings and death, in His resurrection and ascension (ch. 2:10; 5:9), is naturally suggested by the mention of "the just *made perfect"* at their resurrection (cf. ch. 7:22). Paul uses "Jesus," dwelling here on Him as the Person realized as our loving friend, not merely in His *official* character as the *Christ.* **and to the blood of sprinkling**—here enumerated as distinct from "Jesus." BENGEL reasonably argues as follows: His blood was entirely "poured out" of His body by the various ways in which it was shed, His bloody sweat, the crown of thorns, the scourging, the nails, and after death the spear, just as the blood was entirely poured out and extravasated from the animal sacrifices of the law. It was *incorruptible* (I Pet. 1:18, 19). No Scripture states it was again put into the Lord's body. At His ascension, as our

great High Priest, He entered the heavenly holiest place "BY His own blood" (not *after* shedding His blood, nor *with* the blood in His body, but), carrying it separately from his body (cf. the type, ch. 9:7, 12, 25; 13:11). Paul does not say, by the efficacy of His blood, but, "by *His own proper* blood" (ch. 9:12); not MATERIAL blood, but "the blood of Him who, through the eternal Spirit, offered Himself without spot unto God" (ch. 9:14). So in ch. 10:29, *the Son of God* and *the blood of the covenant wherewith* (the professor) *was sanctified,* are mentioned separately. Also in ch. 13:12, 20; also cf. ch. 10:19, with 21. So in the Lord's Supper (I Cor. 10:16; 11:24-26), *the body* and *blood* are separately represented. The blood itself, therefore, continues still in heaven before God, the perpetual ransom-price of "the eternal covenant" (ch. 13:20). Once for all Christ sprinkled the blood peculiarly for us at His ascension (ch. 9:12). But it is called "the blood of sprinkling," on account also of its continued use in heaven, and in the consciences of the saints on earth (ch. 9:14; 10:22; Isa. 52:15). This sprinkling is analogous to the sprinkled blood of the Passover. Cf. Revelation 5:6, "In the midst of the throne, a Lamb *as it had been slain."* His glorified body does not require meat, nor the circulation of the blood. His blood introduced into heaven took away the dragon's right to accuse. Thus Rome's theory of *concomitancy* of the blood with the body, the excuse for giving only the bread to the laity, falls to the ground. The mention of "the blood of sprinkling" naturally follows the mention of the "covenant," which could not be consecrated without *blood* (ch. 9:18, 22). **speaketh better things than that of Abel**—viz., than the sprinkling (the best MSS. read the article *masculine,* which refers to "sprinkling," not to "blood," which last is neuter) of blood by Abel in his sacrifice spake. This comparison between two *things of the same kind* (viz., Christ's sacrifice, and Abel's sacrifice) is more natural, than between two things different in kind and in results (viz., Christ's sacrifice, and Abel's own blood [ALFORD], which was not a sacrifice at all); cf. ch. 11:4; Genesis 4:4. This accords with the whole tenor of the Epistle, and of this passage in particular (vss. 18-22), which is to show the superiority of Christ's sacrifice and the new covenant, to the Old Testament sacrifices (of which Abel's is the first recorded; it, moreover, was testified to by God as acceptable to Him above Cain's), cf. ch. 9 and 10. The word "better" implies superiority to something that is good: both Abel's *own* blood was not at all good for the purpose for which Christ's blood was efficacious; nay, it cried for vengeance. So ARCHBISHOP MAGEE, HAMMOND, and KNATCHBULL. BENGEL takes "the blood of Abel" as put for *all* the blood shed on earth crying for vengeance, and greatly increasing the other cries raised by sin in the world; counteracted by the blood of Christ calmly speaking in heaven for us, and from heaven to us. I prefer MAGEE'S view. Be this as it may, to deny that Christ's atonement is truly a propitiation, overthrows Christ's priesthood, makes the sacrifices of Moses' law an unmeaning mummery, and represents Cain's sacrifice as good as that of Abel. **25. refuse not**—through unbelief. **him that speaketh**—God in Christ. As the *blood of sprinkling* is represented as *speaking* to God for us, vs. 24; so here God is represented as speaking to us (ch. 1:1, 2). His word now is the prelude of the last "shaking" of all things (vs. 27). The same word which is heard in the Gospel *from heaven,* will shake heaven and earth (vs. 26). **who refused him**—*Greek,* "refusing as they did." Their seemingly submissive entreaty that the word should not be spoken to them by God any more (vs. 19), covered over refractory hearts, as their subsequent deeds showed (ch. 3:16). **that spake**—*revealing with oracular warnings His divine will:* so the *Greek.* **if we turn away**—*Greek,* "we who turn away." The word implies greater refractoriness than "refused," or "declined." **him that speaketh from heaven**—God, by His Son in the Gospel, speaking from His heavenly throne. Hence, in Christ's preaching frequent mention is made of "the kingdom *of the heavens*" (*Greek,* Matt. 3:2). In the giving of the law God spake on earth (viz., Mount Sinai) by angels (ch. 2:2; cf. ch. 1:2). In Exodus 20:22, when God says, "I talked with you *from heaven,*" this passage in Hebrews shows that not the highest heavens, but the visible heavens, the clouds and darkness, are meant, out of which God by angels proclaimed the law on Sinai. **26. then shook**—when He gave the law on Sinai. **now**—under the Gospel. **promised**—The announcement of His coming to break up the present order of things, is to the ungodly a terror, to the godly a promise, the fulfilment of which they look for with joyful hope. **Yet once more**—Cf. my *Notes,* Haggai 2:6, 21, 22, both of which passages are condensed into one here. The shaking began at the first coming of Messiah; it will be completed at His second coming, prodigies in the world of nature accompanying the overthrow of all kingdoms that oppose Messiah. The *Hebrew* is lit., "it is yet one little," i.e., a single brief space till the series of movements begins ending in the advent of Messiah. Not merely the earth, as at the establishment of the Sinaitic covenant, but heaven also is to be shaken. The two advents of Messiah are regarded as one, the complete shaking belonging to the second advent, of which the presage was given in the shakings at the first advent: the convulsions connected with the overthrow of Jerusalem shadowing forth those about to be at the overthrow of all the God-opposed kingdoms by the coming Messiah. **27. this** *word,* **Yet once more** —So Paul, by the Spirit, sanctions the LXX rendering of Haggai 2:6, giving an additional feature to the prophecy in the *Hebrew,* as rendered in *English Version,* not merely that it shall be *in a little while,* but that it is to be "*once* more" as the final act. The stress of his argument is on the "ONCE." *Once for all; once and for ever.* "In saying 'once more,' the Spirit implies that something has already passed, and something else shall be which is to remain, and is no more to be changed to something else; for the *once* is exclusive, i.e., *not many times*" [ESTIUS]. **those things that are shaken**—the heaven and the earth. As the shaking is to be *total,* so shall the removal be, making way for the better things that are unremovable. Cf. the Jewish economy (the type of the whole present order of things) giving way to the new and abiding covenant: the forerunner of the everlasting order of bliss. **as of things … made**—viz., of this present *visible creation:* cf. II Corinthians 5:1; and ch. 9:11, "made with hands … of this creation," i.e., things so *made* at creation that they would not remain of themselves, but be removed. The new abiding heaven and earth are also *made* by God, but they are of a higher nature than the material creation, being made to partake of the divine nature of Him who is *not made:* so in this relation, as one with the uncreated God, they are regarded as not of the same class as the *things made.* The things *made* in the former sense do *not remain;* the things of the new heaven

and earth, like the uncreated God, "shall REMAIN before God" (Isa. 66:22). The Spirit, the seed of the new and heavenly being, not only of the believer's soul, but also of the future body, is an *uncreated* and immortal principle. **28. receiving**—as we do, in prospect and sure hope, also in the possession of the Spirit the first fruits. This is our privilege as Christians. **let us have grace**—"let us have thankfulness" [ALFORD after CHRYSOSTOM]. But (1) this translation is according to classical Greek, not Paul's phraseology for "to be thankful." (2) "To God" would have been in that case added. (3) "Whereby we may serve God," suits the *English Version* "grace" (i.e. Gospel grace, the work of the Spirit, producing faith exhibited in *serving God*), but does not suit "thankfulness." **acceptably**— *Greek,* "wellpleasingly." **reverence and godly fear** —The oldest MSS. read, "reverent caution and fear." *Reverent caution* (same *Greek* as in ch. 5:7; see *Note* there) lest we should offend God, who is of purer eyes than to behold iniquity. *Fear* lest we should bring destruction on ourselves. **29.** *Greek,* "For even": "for also"; introducing an *additional* solemn incentive to diligence. Quoted from Deuteronomy 4:24. **our God**—in whom we *hope,* is also to be *feared.* He is love; yet there is another side of His character; God has *wrath* against sin (ch. 10: 27, 31).

CHAPTER 13

Vss. 1-25. EXHORTATION TO VARIOUS GRACES, ESPECIALLY CONSTANCY IN FAITH, FOLLOWING JESUS AMIDST REPROACHES. CONCLUSION, WITH PIECES OF INTELLIGENCE AND SALUTATIONS. **1. brotherly love**—a distinct special manifestation of "charity" or "love" (II Pet. 1:7). The Church of Jerusalem, to which in part this Epistle was addressed, was distinguished by this grace, we know from Acts (cf. ch. 6:10; 10:32-34; 12:12, 13). **continue**—*Charity* will itself *continue.* See that it *continue with you.* **2.** Two manifestations of "brotherly love," *hospitality* and *care for those in bonds.* **Be not forgetful**—implying it was a duty which they all recognized, but which they might forget to act on (vss. 3, 7, 16). The enemies of Christianity themselves have noticed the practice of this virtue among Christians [JULIAN, *Ep.* 49]. **entertained angels unawares**—Abraham and Lot did so (Gen. 18:2; 19:1). To obviate the natural distrust felt of strangers, Paul says, an unknown guest may be better than he looks: he may be unexpectedly found to be as much a *messenger* of God for good, as the angels (whose name means *messenger*) are; nay more, if a Christian, he represents Christ Himself. There is a play on the same *Greek* word, *Be not forgetful* and *unaware; let not* the duty of hospitality to strangers *escape* you; for, by entertaining strangers, it has *escaped* the entertainers that they were entertaining angels. Not unconscious and forgetful of the duty, they have unconsciously brought on themselves the blessing. **3. Remember**—in prayers and acts of kindness. **bound with them**—by virtue of the unity of the members in the body under one Head, Christ (I Cor. 12:26). **suffer adversity**—*Greek,* "are in evil state." **being yourselves also in the body**—and so liable to the adversities incident to the natural body, which ought to dispose you the more to sympathize with them, not knowing how soon your own turn of suffering may come. "One experiences adversity almost his whole life, as Jacob; another in youth, as Joseph; another in manhood, as Job;

another in old age" [BENGEL]. **4. is . . .**—Translate, "Let marriage *be treated as* honorable": as vs. 5 also is an exhortation. **in all**—"in the case of all men": "among all." "To avoid fornication let EVERY MAN have his own wife" (I Cor. 7:2). Judaism and Gnosticism combined were soon about to throw discredit on marriage. The venerable Paphnutius, in the Council of Nice, quoted this verse for the justification of the married state. If one does not himself marry, he should not prevent others from doing so. Others, especially Romanists, translate, "in all *things*," as in vs. 18. But the warning being against lasciviousness, the contrast to "*whoremongers* and *adulterers*" in the parallel clause, requires the "in all" in this clause to refer to *persons.* **the bed undefiled**—Translate, as *Greek* requires "undefiled" to be a *predicate,* not an epithet, "And let the bed *be* undefiled." **God will judge**—Most whoremongers escape the notice of human tribunals; but God takes particular cognizance of those whom man does not punish. Gay immoralities will then be regarded in a very different light from what they are now. **5. conversation**—"manner of life." The love of filthy lust and the love of filthy lucre follow one another as closely akin, both alienating the heart from the Creator to the creature. **such things as ye have**—lit., "present things" (Phil. 4:11). **I will never leave thee, nor forsake thee**—A promise tantamount to this was given to Jacob (Gen. 28:15), to Israel (Deut. 31:6, 8), to Joshua (Josh. 1:5), to Solomon (I Chron. 28:20). It is therefore like a divine adage. What was said to them, extends also to us. He will neither withdraw His *presence* ("never leave thee") nor His *help* ("nor forsake thee") [BENGEL]. **6. may**—rather as *Greek,* expressing confidence actually. realized, "So that we boldly (confidently) *say*" (Ps. 56:4. 11; 118:6). Punctuate as both the *Hebrew* and the *Greek* require, "And (so) I will not fear: what (then) shall man do unto me?" **7. Remember**—so as to imitate: not to *invoke* in prayer, as Rome teaches. **have the rule** —rather, "who have *had* the rule over you": your spiritual leaders. **who**—*Greek,* "the which": such persons as. **have spoken unto you**—"spake" (so the *Greek* aorist means) during their lifetime. This Epistle was among those written later, when many of the heads of the Jerusalem Church had passed away. **whose faith**—even unto death: probably death by martyrdom, as in the case of the instances of *faith* in ch. 11:35. Stephen, James the brother of our Lord and bishop of Jerusalem, as well as James the brother of John (Acts 12:2), in the Palestinian Church, which Paul addresses, suffered martyrdom. **considering**—*Greek,* "looking up to," "diligently contemplating all over," as an artist would a model. **the end**—the termination, at death. The *Greek,* is used of *decease* (Luke 9:31; II Pet. 1:15). **of their conversation**—"manner of life": "religious walk" (Gal. 1:13; Eph. 4:22; I Tim. 4:12; Jas. 3:13). *Considering* how they manifested the soundness of their faith by their holy *walk,* which they maintained even to *the end of that walk* (their death by martyrdom). **8.** This verse is not, as some read it, in apposition with "the end of their conversation" (vs. 7), but forms the transition. "Jesus Christ, yesterday and to-day (is) the same, and (shall be the same) unto the ages" (i.e., unto all ages). The *Jesus Christ* (the full name being given, to mark with affectionate solemnity both His *person* and His *office*) who supported your spiritual *rulers* through life even unto their *end* "yesterday" (in times past),

being at once "the Author and the Finisher of their faith" (ch. 12:2), remains still the same Jesus Christ "to-day," ready to help you also, if like them **you** walk by "faith" in Him. Cf. "this same Jesus," Acts 1:11. He who *yesterday* (proverbial for the past time) suffered and died, is *today* in glory (Rev. 1:18). "As night comes between yesterday and to-day, and yet night itself is swallowed up by *yesterday* and *today,* so the *suffering* did not so interrupt the glory of Jesus Christ which was of yesterday, and that which is today, as not to continue to be the same. He is the same *yesterday,* before He came into the world, and *today,* in heaven. *Yesterday* in the time of our predecessors, and *today* in our age" [BENGEL]. So the doctrine is the *same,* not variable: this verse thus forms the transition between vs. 7 and vs. 9. He is always "the same" (ch. 1:12). The same in the Old and in the New Testament. **9. about**—rather, as oldest MSS. read, "carried *aside*"; viz., cf. Eph. 4:14. **divers**—differing from the one faith in the one and the same Jesus Christ, as taught by them who had the rule over you (vs. 7). **strange**—foreign to the truth. **doctrines**—"teachings." **established with grace; not with meats**—not with observances of Jewish distinctions between clean and unclean meats, to which ascetic Judaizers added in Christian times the rejection of some meats, and the use of others: noticed also by *Paul* in I Corinthians 8:8, 13; 6:13. Romans 14:17, an exact parallel to this verse: these are some of the "divers and strange doctrines" of the previous sentence. Christ's body offered once for all for us, is our true spiritual "meat" to "eat" (vs. 10), "the stay and the staff of bread" (Isa. 3:1), the mean of all "grace." **which have not profited** —Greek, "in which they who walked were not profited"; viz., in respect to justification, perfect cleansing of the conscience, and sanctification. Cf. on "walked," Acts 21:21; viz., with superstitious scrupulosity, as though the worship of God in itself consisted in such legal observances. **10.** Christianity and Judaism are so totally distinct, that "they who serve the (Jewish) tabernacle," have no right to eat our spiritual Gospel meat, viz., the Jewish priests, and those who follow their guidance in serving the ceremonial ordinance. He says, "serve *the tabernacle,*" not "serve IN the tabernacle." Contrast with this servile worship ours. **an altar**—the cross of Christ, whereon His body was offered. The Lord's table represents this altar, the cross; as the bread and wine represent the sacrifice offered on it. Our meat, which we by faith spiritually eat, is the flesh of Christ, in contrast to the typical ceremonial meats. The two cannot be combined (Gal. 5:2). That not a literal eating of the sacrifice of Christ is meant in the Lord's Supper, but a spiritual is meant, appears from comparing vs. 9 with vs. 10, "with GRACE, NOT with MEATS." **11, 12.** For just as "the bodies of those beasts whose blood is brought into the sanctuary by . . . are burned without the camp," so "Jesus also that . . . suffered without the gate" of ceremonial Judaism, of which His crucifixion outside the gate of Jerusalem is a type. **for**—reason why they who serve the tabernacle, are excluded from share in Christ; because His sacrifice is not like one of those sacrifices in which they had a share but answers to one which was "wholly burned" outside (the *Greek* is "burnt completely," "consumed by burning"), and which consequently they could not eat of. Leviticus 6:30, gives the general rule, "No sin offering whereof any of the blood is brought into the tabernacle of the congregation to reconcile withal in the holy place, shall be eaten; it shall be burnt in the fire." The sin offerings are twofold: the *outward,* whose blood was sprinkled on the outward altar, and of whose bodies the priests might eat; and the *inward,* the reverse. **the sanctuary**—here *the Holy of Holies,* into which the blood of the sin offering was brought on the day of atonement. **without the camp**—in which were the tabernacle and Levitical priests and legal worshippers, during Israel's journey through the wilderness; replaced afterwards by Jerusalem (containing the temple), outside of whose walls Jesus was crucified. **12. Wherefore Jesus**—In order that the Antitype might fulfil the type. **sanctify**—Though not brought into the temple "sanctuary" (vs. 11) His blood has been brought into the heavenly sanctuary, and "sanctifies the people" (ch. 2:11, 17), by cleansing them from sin, and consecrating them to God. **his own**—not blood of animals. **without the gate**—of Jerusalem; as if unworthy of the society of the covenant people. The fiery ordeal of His *suffering* on the cross, answers to the *burning* of the victims; thereby His mere fleshly life was completely destroyed, as their bodies were; the second part of His offering was His carrying His blood into the heavenly holiest before God at His ascension, that it should be a perpetual atonement for the world's sin. **13. therefore**—This "therefore" breathes the deliberate fortitude of believers [Bengel]. **without the camp**—"outside the legal polity" [Theodoret] of Judaism (cf. vs. 11) "Faith considers Jerusalem itself as a *camp,* not a *city* [Bengel]. He contrasts with the Jews, who serve an earthly sanctuary, the Christians to whom the altar in heaven stands open, while it is closed against the Jews. As Jesus suffered without the gate, so spiritually must those who desire to belong to Him, withdraw from the earthly Jerusalem and its sanctuary, as from this world in general. There is a reference to Exodus 33:7, when the tabernacle was moved *without the camp,* which had become polluted by the people's idolatry of the golden calves; so that "every one who sought the Lord went out unto *the tabernacle of the congregation* (as Moses called the tabernacle outside the camp), which was without the camp"; a lively type of what the Hebrews should do, viz., come out of the carnal worship of the earthly Jerusalem to worship God in Christ in spirit, and of what we all ought to do, viz., come out from all carnalism, worldly formalism, and mere sensuous worship, and know Jesus in His spiritual power apart from worldliness, seeing that "we have no continuing city" (vs. 14). **bearing**—as Simon of Cyrene did. **his reproach**—the reproach which He bare, and which all His people bear with Him. **14. here**—on earth. Those Hebrews who clung to the earthly sanctuary are representatives of all who cling to this earth. The earthly Jerusalem proved to be no "abiding city," having been destroyed shortly after this Epistle was written, and with it fell the Jewish civil and religious polity; a type of the whole of our present earthly order of things soon to perish. **one to come**—(ch. 2:5; 11:10, 14, 16; 12:22; Phil. 3:20). **15.** As the "altar" was mentioned in vs. 10, so the "sacrifices" here (cf. I Pet. 2:5, viz., *praise* and *doing good,* vs. 16). Cf. Psalm 119:108; Rom. 12:1. **By him**—as the Mediator of our prayers and praises (John 14:13, 14); not by Jewish observances (Ps. 50:14, 23; 69:30, 31; 107:22; 116:17). It was an old saying of the rabbis, "At a future time all sacrifices shall cease, but praises shall not cease." **praise**—for salvation. **continually**—not merely at fixed seasons, as those on which the legal sacrifices were offered, but throughout all our lives. **fruit of our lips**—(Isa. 57:19; Hos. 14:2). **giving thanks**—Greek, "confessing." Bengel remarks that the Hebrew, *todah,* is beautifully emphatic. It literally means "acknowledgment" or "confession." In praising a creature, we may easily exceed the truth; but in praising God we have only to go on *confessing* what He really is to us. Hence it is impossible to exceed the truth, and here is *genuine* praise. **16. But**—But the sacrifice of praise with the lips (vs. 15) is not enough; there must be also *doing good* (beneficence) and communicating (i.e., imparting a share of your means, Gal. 6:6) to the needy. **with such**—and not mere ritualistic sacrifices. **17. Obey them that have the rule over you**—(Cf. vss. 7, 24). This threefold mention of the *rulers* is peculiar to this Epistle. In other Epistles Paul includes the *rulers* in his exhortations. But here the address is limited to the *general body of the Church,* in contrast to the *rulers* to whom they are charged to yield reverent submission. Now this is just what might be expected when the apostle of the Gentiles was writing to the Palestine Christians, among whom James and the eleven apostles had exercised a more immediate authority. It was important he should not seem to set himself in opposition to their guides, but rather strengthen their hands; he claims no authority directly or indirectly over these rulers themselves [Birks]. "Remember" your deceased rulers (vs. 7). "Obey" your living rulers; nay, more, not only *obey* in cases where no sacrifice of self is required, and where you are *persuaded* they are right (so the *Greek,* for "obey"), but *"submit* yourselves" as a matter of dutiful *yielding,* when your judgment and natural will incline you in an opposite direction. **they**—on their part; so the *Greek.* As they do their part, so do you yours. So Paul exhorts, I Thessalonians 5:12, 13. **watch**—"are vigilant" (*Greek*). **for**—*Greek,* "in behalf of." **must give account**—The strongest stimulus to *watchfulness* (Mark 13:34-37). Chrysostom was deeply struck with these words, as he tells us (*De Sacerdotio,* B. 6), "The fear of this threat continually agitates my soul." **do it**—"watch for your soul's eternal salvation." It is a perilous responsibility for a man to have to give account for others' deeds, who is not sufficient for his own [Estius, from Aquinas]. I wonder whether it be possible that any of the rulers should be saved [Chrysostom]. Cf. Paul's address to the elders, Acts 20:28; I Corinthians 4:1-5, where also he connects ministers' responsibility with the account to be hereafter given (cf. I Pet. 5:4). **with joy**—at your obedience; anticipating, too, that you shall be their "joy" in the day of giving account (Phil. 4:1). **not with grief**—at your disobedience; apprehending also that in the day of account you may be among the lost, instead of being their crown of rejoicing. In giving account, the stewards are liable to blame if aught be lost to the Master. "Mitigate their toil by every office of attention and respect, that with alacrity, rather than with grief, they may fulfil their duty, arduous enough in itself, even though no unpleasantness be added on your part" [Grotius]. **that**—Grief in your pastors is *unprofitable for you,* for it weakens their spiritual power; nay, more, "the *groans* (so the *Greek* for 'grief') of other creatures are heard; how much more of pastors!" [Bengel]. So God will be provoked to avenge on you their "groaning" (*Greek*). If they must render God an account of their negligence, so must you for your ingratitude to them [Grotius]. **18. Pray**

for us—Paul usually requests the Church's intercessions for him in closing his Epistles, just as he begins with assuring them of his having them at heart in his prayers (but in this Epistle not till vss. 20, 21), Romans 15:30. "Us," includes both himself and his companions; he passes to himself alone, vs. 19. **we trust we have a good conscience**—in spite of your former jealousies, and the charges of my Jewish enemies at Jerusalem, which have been the occasion of my imprisonment at Rome. In refutation of the Jews' aspersions, he asserts in the same language as here his own *conscientiousness* before God and man, Acts 23:1-3; 24:16, 20, 21 (wherein he virtually implies that his reply to Ananias was not sinful impatience; for, indeed, it was a prophecy which he was inspired at the moment to utter, and which was fulfilled soon after). **we trust** *Greek,* "we are persuaded," in the oldest MSS. Good conscience produces confidence, where the Holy Spirit rules the conscience (Rom. 9:1). **honestly**—"in a *good* way." The same *Greek* word as "*good* conscience." *Lit.,* "rightly," "becomingly." **19. the rather**—*Greek,* "*I the more abundantly* beseech you." **to do this**—to pray for me. **that I may be restored to you**—(Philemon 22). It is here first in the letter he mentions himself, in a way so unobtrusive, as not to prejudice his Hebrew readers against him, which would have been the result had he commenced this as his other Epistles, with authoritatively announcing his name and apostolic commission. **20.** Concluding prayer. **God of peace**—So Paul, Romans 15:33; 16:20; II Corinthians 13:11; Philippians 4:9; I Thessalonians 5: 23; II Thessalonians 3:16. The Judaizing of the Hebrews was calculated to sow seeds of discord among them, of disobedience to their pastors (vs. 17), and of alienation towards Paul. *The God of peace* by giving unity of true doctrine, will unite them in mutual love. **brought again from the dead** —*Greek,* "brought up . . .": God brought the Shepherd; the Shepherd shall bring the flock. Here only in the Epistle he mentions the resurrection. He would not conclude without mentioning the connecting link between the two truths mainly discussed; the *one perfect sacrifice* and the *continual priestly intercession*—the depth of His humiliation and the height of His glory—the "altar" of the cross and the ascension to the heavenly Holy of Holies. **Lord Jesus**—the title marking His *person* and His *Lordship* over us. But vs. 21, "through Jesus *Christ*." His *office,* as the *Anointed* of the Spirit, making Him the medium of communicating the Spirit to us, the holy unction flowing down from the Head on the members (cf. Acts 2:36). **great**—(Ch. 4. 14.) **shepherd of the sheep**— A title familiar to his Hebrew readers, from their Old Testament (Isa. 63:11; LXX): primarily *Moses,* antitypically *Christ:* already compared together, ch. 3:2-7. The transition is natural from their earthly pastors (vs. 17), to the Chief Pastor, as in I Peter 5:1-4. Cf. Ezekiel 34:23 and Jesus' own words, John 10:2, 11, 14. **through the blood**—*Greek,* "in," *in virtue of* the blood (ch. 2:9); it was because of

His bloody death for us, that the Father raised and crowned Him with glory. The "blood" was the seal of the everlasting covenant entered into between the Father and Son; *in virtue of the Son's blood,* first Christ was raised, then Christ's people shall be so (Zech. 9:11, seemingly referred to here; Acts 20:28). **everlasting**—The *everlastingness* of the *covenant* necessitated the resurrection. This clause, "the blood of the everlasting covenant," is a summary retrospect of the Epistle (cf. ch. 9:12). **21. Make you perfect**—properly said of healing a rent; *join you together in perfect harmony* [BENGEL]. **to do his will, working in you**—(Ch. 10:36) —rather as *Greek,* "*doing* in you." Whatever good we *do,* God *does* in us. **well-pleasing in his sight**—(Isa. 53:10; Eph. 5:10). **through Jesus Christ**—"God *doing* (working) in you that . . . *through Jesus Christ*" (Phil. 1:11). **to whom**—to Christ. He closes as he began (ch. 1), with giving glory to Christ. **22. suffer the word**—The Hebrews not being the section of the Church assigned to Paul (but the Gentiles), he uses gentle entreaty, rather than authoritative command. **few words**— compared with what might be said on so important a subject. *Few,* in an Epistle which is more of a *treatise* than an Epistle (cf. I Pet. 5:12). On the seeming inconsistency with Galatians 6:11, cf. *Note* there. **23. our brother Timothy**—So Paul, I Corinthians 4:17; II Corinthians 1:1; Colossians 1:1; I Thessalonians 3:2. **is set at liberty**—from prison. So Aristarchus was imprisoned with Paul. BIRKS translates, "dismissed," "sent away," viz., on a mission to Greece, as Paul promised (Phil. 2:19). However, *some* kind of previous detention is implied before his being *let go* to Philippi. Paul, though now at large, was still *in Italy,* whence he sends the salutations of Italian Christians (vs. 24), waiting for Timothy to join him, so as to start for Jerusalem: we know from I Timothy 1:3, he and Timothy were together at Ephesus after his departing from Italy eastward. He probably left Timothy there and went to Philippi as he had promised. Paul implies that if Timothy shall not *come shortly,* he will start on his journey to the Hebrews at once. **24. all**—The Scriptures are intended for *all,* young and old, not merely for ministers. Cf. the different classes addressed, "wives," Ephesians 5:22; little children, I John 2:18; "all," I Peter 3:8; 5:5. He says here "all," for the Hebrews whom he addresses were not all in one place, though the Jerusalem Hebrews are chiefly addressed. **They of Italy**—not merely the brethren at Rome, but of other places in Italy. **25.** *Paul's* characteristic salutation in every one of his other thirteen Epistles, as he says himself, I Corinthians 16:21, 23; Colossians 4:18; II Thessalonians 3:17. It is found in no Epistle written by any other apostle in Paul's lifetime. It is used in Revelation 22:21, written subsequently, and in CLEMENT OF ROME. Being known to be his badge, it is not used by others in his lifetime. The *Greek* here is, "*The* grace (viz., of our Lord Jesus Christ) be with you all."

THE GENERAL EPISTLE OF

JAMES

INTRODUCTION

THIS is called by EUSEBIUS (*Ecclesiastical History*, 2. 23, about the year 330 A.D.) the first of the Catholic Epistles, i.e., the Epistles intended for general circulation, as distinguished from Paul's Epistles, which were addressed to particular churches or individuals. In the oldest MSS. of the New Testament extant, they stand *before* the Epistles of Paul. Of them, two only are mentioned by EUSEBIUS as *universally acknowledged* (*Homologoumena*), viz., the First Epistle of Peter, and the First Epistle of John. *All*, however, are found in every existing MS. of the whole New Testament.

It is not to be wondered at that Epistles not addressed to particular churches (and particularly one like that of James, addressed to the Israelite believers scattered abroad) should be for a time less known. The first mention of James' Epistle by name occurs early in the third century, in ORIGEN (*Comment.* on John 1. 19. 4. 306), who was born about 185, and died A.D. 254. CLEMENS ROMANUS (First Epistle to the Corinthians, ch. 10; cf. Jas. 2:21, 23; ch. 11, cf. Jas. 2:25; Heb. 11:31) quotes it. So also the Shepherd of Hermas quotes ch. 4:7. IRENÆUS (*Hæreses*, 4. 16. 2) is thought to refer to ch. 2:23. CLEMENS ALEXANDRINUS commented on it, according to CASSIODORUS. EPHREM SYRUS (*Opp. Græc.* 3. 51) quotes ch. 5:1. An especially strong proof of its authenticity is afforded by its forming part of the old *Syriac* version, which contains no other of *the disputed books* (*Antilegomena*, EUSEBIUS, 3. 25), except the Epistle to the Hebrews. None of the Latin fathers before the fourth century quote it; but soon after the Council of Nice it was admitted as canonical both by the East and West churches, and specified as such in the Councils of Hippo and Carthage (397 A.D.). This is just what we might expect; a writing known only partially at first, when subsequently it obtained a wider circulation, and the proofs were better known of its having been recognized in apostolic churches, having in them men endowed with the discernment of spirits, which qualified them for discriminating between inspired and uninspired writings, was universally accepted. Though *doubted* for a time, at last the disputed books (James, II Peter, II and III John, Jude, and Revelation) were universally and undoubtingly accepted, so that no argument for the Old Testament Apocrypha can be drawn from their case: as to *it* the Jewish Church had *no doubt*; it was *known not* to be inspired.

Luther's objection to it ("an Epistle of straw, and destitute of an evangelic character") was due to his mistaken idea that it (ch. 2) opposes the doctrine of justification by faith, and not by works, taught by Paul. But the two apostles, while looking at justification from distinct standpoints, perfectly harmonize and mutually complement the definitions of one another. Faith precedes love and the works of love; but without them it is dead. Paul regards faith in the justification of the sinner *before God*; James, in the justification of the believer *evidently before men*. The error which James meets was the Jewish notion that their possession and knowledge of the law of God would justify them, even though they disobeyed it (cf. ch. 1:22 with Rom. 2:17-25). Ch. 1:3 and 4:1, 12 seem plainly to allude to Romans 5:3; 6:13; 7:23; 14:4. Also the tenor of ch. 2 on "justification," seems to allude to Paul's teaching, so as to correct false Jewish notions of a different kind from those which he combatted, though not unnoticed by him also (Rom. 2:17, etc.).

Paul (Gal. 2:9) arranges the names "James, Cephas, John," in the order in which their Epistles stand. James who wrote this Epistle (according to most ancient writers) is called (Gal. 1:19), "the Lord's brother." He was son of Alpheus or Cleopas (Luke 24:13-18) and Mary, sister of the Virgin Mary. Cf. Mark 15:40 with John 19:25, which seems to identify the mother of James the Less with the wife of Cleopas, not with the Virgin Mary, Cleopas' wife's sister. Cleopas is the Hebrew, Alpheus the Greek mode of writing the same name. Many, however, as HEGESIPPUS [EUSEBIUS, *Ecclesiastical History*], distinguish "the Lord's brother" from the son of Alpheus. But the Gospel according to the Hebrews, quoted by JEROME, represents James, *the Lord's brother*, as present at the institution of the Eucharist, and therefore identical with the apostle James. So the Apocryphal Gospel of James. In Acts, James who is put foremost in Jerusalem after the death of James, the son of Zebedee, is not distinguished from James, the son of Alpheus. He is not mentioned as one of the Lord's brethren in Acts 1:14; but as one of the "apostles" (Gal. 1:19). He is called "the Less" (lit., "the little," Mark 15:40), to distinguish him from James, the son of Zebedee. ALFORD considers James, the brother of the Lord, the author of the Epistle, to have been the eldest of the sons of Joseph and Mary, after Jesus (cf. Matt. 13:55), and that James the son of Alpheus is distinguished from him by *the latter* being called "the Less," (i.e., junior. His arguments against the Lord's brother, the bishop of Jerusalem, being the apostle, are: (1) The Lord's brethren did not believe on Jesus at a time when the apostles had been already called (John 7:3, 5), therefore none of the Lord's brethren could be among the apostles (but it does not follow from John 7:3 that *no one* of them believed). (2) The apostles' commission was to preach the Gospel *everywhere*, not to be bishops in a particular locality (but it is unlikely that one not an apostle should be bishop of Jerusalem, to whom even apostles yield deference, Acts 15:13, 19; Galatians 1:19; 2:9, 12. The Saviour's last command to the apostles collectively to preach the Gospel everywhere, is not inconsistent with each having a particular sphere of labor in which he should be a missionary bishop, as Peter is said to have been at Antioch).

He was surnamed "the Just." It needed peculiar wisdom so to preach the Gospel as not to disparage the law. As bishop of Jerusalem writing to the twelve tribes, he sets forth the Gospel in its aspect of relation to the law, which the Jews so reverenced. As Paul's Epistles are a commentary on the doctrines flowing from the death and resurrection of Christ, so James's Epistle has a close connection with His teaching during His life on earth, especially His Sermon on the Mount. In both, the law is represented as fulfilled in love: the very language is palpably similar (cf. ch. 1:2 with Matt. 5:12; ch. 1:4 with Matt. 5:48; ch. 1:5; 5:15 with Matt. 7:7–11; ch. 6:13 with Matt. 5:7, and 6:14, 15; ch. 2:10 with Matt. 5:19; ch. 4:4 with Matt. 6:24; ch. 4:11 with Matt. 7:1, 2; ch. 5:2 with Matt. 6:19). The whole spirit of this Epistle breathes the same Gospel-*righteousness* which the Sermon on the Mount inculcates as the highest realization of the law. James's own character as "the Just," or *legally righteous*, disposed him to this coincidence (cf. ch. 1:20; 2:10; 3:18 with Matt. 5:20). It also fitted him for presiding over a Church still zealous for the law (Acts 21:18–24; Gal. 2:12). If any could win the Jews to the Gospel, he was most likely who presented a pattern of Old Testament righteousness, combined with evangelical faith (cf. also ch. 2:8 with Matt. 5:44, 48). Practice, not profession, is the test of obedience (cf. ch. 2:17; 4:17 with Matt. 7:21–23). Sins of the tongue, however lightly regarded by the world, are an offense against the law of love (cf. ch. 1:26; 3:2–18 with Matt. 5:22; also any swearing, ch. 5:12; cf. Matt. 5:33–37).

The absence of the apostolic benediction in this Epistle is probably due to its being addressed, not merely to the believing, but also indirectly to unbelieving, Israelites. To the former he commends humility, patience, and prayer; to the latter he addresses awful warnings (ch. 5:7–11; 4:9; 5:1–6).

James was martyred at the Passover. This Epistle was probably written just before it. The destruction of Jerusalem foretold in it (ch. 5:1, etc.), ensued a year after his martyrdom, A.D. 69. HEGESIPPUS (quoted in EUSEBIUS, 2. 23) narrates that he was set on a pinnacle of the temple by the scribes and Pharisees, who begged him to restrain the people who were in large numbers embracing Christianity. "Tell us," said they in the presence of the people gathered at the feast, "which is the door of Jesus?" James replied with a loud voice, "Why ask ye me concerning Jesus the Son of man? He sitteth at the right hand of power, and will come again on the clouds of heaven." Many thereupon cried, Hosanna to the Son of David. But James was cast down headlong by the Pharisees; and praying, "Father, forgive them, for they know not what they do," he was stoned and beaten to death with a fuller's club. The Jews, we know from Acts, were exasperated at Paul's rescue from their hands, and therefore determined to wreak their vengeance on James. The publication of his Epistle to the dispersed Israelites, to whom it was probably carried by those who came up to the periodical feasts, made him obnoxious to them, especially to the higher classes, because it foretold the woes soon about to fall on them and their country. Their taunting question, "Which is the door of Jesus?" (i.e., by what door will He come when He returns?), alludes to his prophecy, "the coming of the Lord draweth nigh . . . behold the Judge standeth before the *door*" (ch. 5:8, 9). Hebrews 13:7 probably refers to the martyrdom of James, who had been so long bishop over the Jewish Christians at Jerusalem, "Remember them which have (rather, 'had') the rule (spiritually) over you, who have spoken unto you the word of God; whose faith follow, considering *the end* of their conversation."

His inspiration as an apostle is expressly referred to in Acts 15:19, 25, "*My sentence* is . . .": "It seemed good to *the Holy Ghost and to us . . .*" His episcopal authority is implied in the deference paid to him by Peter and Paul (Acts 12:17; 21. 18; Gal. 1:19; 2:9). The Lord had appeared specially to him after the resurrection (I Cor. 15:7). Peter in his First Epistle (universally from the first received as canonical) tacitly confirms the inspiration of James's Epistle, by incorporating with his own inspired writings no less than ten passages from James. The "apostle of the circumcision," Peter, and the first bishop of Jerusalem, would naturally have much in common. Cf. ch. 1:1 with I Peter 1:1; ch. 1:2 with I Peter 1:6; 4:12, 13; ch. 1:11 with I Peter 1:24; ch. 1:18 with I Peter 1:3; ch. 2:7 with I Peter 4:14; ch. 3:13 with I Peter 2:12; ch. 4:1 with I Peter 2:11; ch. 4:6 with I Peter 5:5, 6; ch. 4:7 with I Peter 5:6, 9; ch. 4:10 with I Peter 5:6; ch. 5:20 with I Peter 4:6. Its being written in the purest Greek shows it was intended not only for the Jews at Jerusalem, but also for the Hellenistic, i.e., Greek-speaking, Jews.

The style is close, curt, and sententious, gnome following after gnome. A Hebraic character pervades the Epistle, as appears in the occasional poetic parallelisms (ch. 3:1–12). Cf. ch. 2:2, "Assembly," *Margin* "synnagogue." The images are analogical arguments, combining at once logic and poetry. Eloquence and persuasiveness are prominent characteristics.

The similarity to Matthew, the most Hebrew of the Gospels, is just what we might expect from the bishop of Jerusalem writing to Israelites. In it the higher spirit of Christianity is seen putting the Jewish law in its proper place. The law is enforced in its everlasting spirit, not in the letter for which the Jews were so zealous. The doctrines of grace, the distinguishing features of Paul's teaching to the Hellenists and Gentiles, are less prominent as being already taught by that apostle. James complements Paul's teaching, and shows to the Jewish Christians who still kept the legal ordinances down to the fall of Jerusalem, the spiritual principle of the law, viz., love manifested in obedience. To sketch "the perfect man" *continuing* in the Gospel *law of liberty*, is his theme.

CHAPTER 1

Vss. 1-27. INSCRIPTION: EXHORTATION ON HEARING, SPEAKING, AND WRATH. The last subject is discussed in ch. 3:13 to 4:17. **1. James**—an apostle of the circumcision, with Peter and John, James in Jerusalem, Palestine, and Syria; Peter in Babylon and the East; John in Ephesus and Asia Minor. Peter addresses the dispersed *Jews of Pontus, Galatia, and Cappadocia;* James, the *Israelites of the twelve tribes scattered abroad.* **servant of God**—not that he was not an *apostle;* for Paul, an apostle, also calls himself so; but as addressing the Israelites generally, including even indirectly the unbelieving, he in humility omits the title "apostle"; so Paul in writing to the Hebrews; similarly Jude, an apostle,

in his General Epistle. **Jesus Christ**—not mentioned again save in ch. 2:1; not at all in his speeches (Acts 15:14, 15, and 21:20, 21), lest his introducing the name of Jesus oftener should seem to arise from vanity, as being "the Lord's brother" [BENGEL]. His teaching being practical, rather than doctrinal, required less frequent mention of Christ's name. **scattered abroad**—lit., "which are in the dispersion." The dispersion of the Israelites, and their connection with Jerusalem as a center of religion, was a divinely ordered means of propagating Christianity. The pilgrim troops of the law became caravans of the Gospel [WORDSWORTH]. **greeting**—found in no other Christian letter, but in James and the Jerusalem Synod's Epistle to the Gentile churches; an undesigned coincidence and mark or genuineness. In the original Greek (*chairein*) for "greeting," there is a connection with the "joy" to which they are exhorted amidst their existing distresses from poverty and consequent oppression. Cf. Romans 15:26, which alludes to their poverty. **2. My brethren**—a phrase often found in James, marking community of nation and of faith. **all joy**—cause for the highest joy [GROTIUS]. Nothing but joy [PISCATOR]. Count *all* "divers temptations" to be *each* matter of *joy* [BENGEL]. **fall into**—unexpectedly, so as to be *encompassed by* them (so the original *Greek*). **temptations**—not in the limited sense of allurements to sin, but *trials* or distresses of any kind which test and purify the Christian character. Cf. "tempt," i.e., try, Genesis 22:1. Some of those to whom James writes were "sick," or otherwise "afflicted" (ch. 5:13). Every possible trial to the child of God is a masterpiece of strategy of the Captain of his salvation for his good. **3. the trying**—the *testing* or *proving* of your faith, viz., by "divers temptations." Cf. Romans 5:3, "*tribulation*" worketh patience, and patience *experience* (in the original *dokime*, akin to *dokimion*, "trying," here; there it is *experience:* here the "trying" or *testing,* whence experience flows). **patience**—The original implies more; *persevering endurance* and *continuance* (cf. Luke 8:15). **4.** Let endurance have a perfect *work* (taken out of the previous "*worketh* patience" or endurance), i.e., have its *full effect,* by showing the most perfect degree of endurance, viz., "joy in bearing the cross" [MENOCHIUS], and enduring to the end (Matt. 10:22), [CALVIN]. **ye may be perfect**—fully developed in all the attributes of a Christian character. For this there is required "joy" [BENGEL], as part of the "perfect work" of probation. The work of God in a man *is* the man. If God's teachings by patience have had a perfect work in you, *you* are perfect [ALFORD]. **entire**—that which has all *its parts complete, wanting no integral part;* I Thessalonians 5:23, "your whole (lit., 'entire') spirit, soul, and body"; as "perfect" implies *without a blemish in its parts.* **5.** *English Version* omits "But," which the *Greek* has, and which is important. "But (as this *perfect entireness wanting nothing* is no easy attainment) if any. . . ." **lack**—rather, as the Greek word is repeated after James's manner, from vs. 4, "*wanting* nothing," translate, "If any of you *want* wisdom," viz., the wisdom whereby ye may "count it all joy when ye fall into divers temptations," and "let patience have her perfect work." This "wisdom" is shown in its effects in detail, ch. 3:7. The highest wisdom, which governs patience alike in poverty and riches, is described in vss. 9, 10. **ask**—(Ch. 4:2). **liberally**—So the *Greek* is rendered by *English Version.* It is rendered *with simplicity,* Romans 12:8. God gives without adding aught which may take off from the graciousness of the gift [ALFORD]. God requires the same "simplicity" in His children ("eye . . . single," Matt. 6:22, lit., "simple"). **upbraideth not**—an illustration of God's giving *simply.* He gives to the humble suppliant without upbraiding him with his past sin and ingratitude, or his future abuse of God's goodness. The Jews pray, "Let me not have need of the gifts of men, whose gifts are few, but their upbraidings manifold; but give me out of Thy large and full hand." Cf. Solomon's prayer for "wisdom," and God's gift above what he asked, though God foresaw his future abuse of His goodness would deserve very differently. James has before his eye the Sermon on the Mount (see my *Introduction*). God hears every true prayer and grants either the thing asked, or else something better than it; as a good

physician consults for his patient's good better by denying something which the latter asks not for his good, than by conceding a temporary gratification to his hurt. **6. ask in faith**—i.e., the persuasion that God can and will give. James begins and ends with *faith.* In the middle of the Epistle he removes the hindrances to faith and shows its true character [BENGEL]. **wavering**—between belief and unbelief. Cf. the case of the Israelites, who seemed to partly believe in God's power, but leaned more to unbelief by "limiting" it. On the other hand, cf. Acts 10:20; Romans 4:20 ("*staggered not . . .* through unbelief," lit., as here, "*wavered not*"); I Timothy 2:8. **like a wave of the sea**—Isaiah 57:20; Ephesians 4:14, where the same *Greek* word occurs for "tossed to and fro," as is here translated, "driven with the wind," **driven with the wind**—from without. **tossed**—from within, by its own instability [BENGEL]. At one time cast on the shore of faith and hope, at another rolled back into the abyss of unbelief; at one time raised to the height of worldly pride, at another tossed in the sands of despair and affliction [WIESINGER]. **7. For**—resumed from "For" in vs. 6. **that man**—such a wavering self-deceiver. **think**—Real *faith* is something more than a mere *thinking* or *surmise.* **anything**—viz., of the things that he prays for: he does receive many things from God, food, raiment, etc., but these are the general gifts of His providence: of the things specially granted in answer to prayer, the waverer shall not receive "anything," much less wisdom. **8. double-minded**—lit., "double-souled," the one soul directed towards God, the other to something else. The *Greek* favors ALFORD'S translation, "He (the waverer, vs. 6) *is* a man double-minded, unstable . . ."; or better, BEZA'S. The words in this vs. 8 are in apposition with "that man," vs. 7; thus the "us," which is not in the original, will not need to be supplied, "A man double-minded, unstable in all his ways!" The word for "double-minded" is found here and in ch. 4:8, for the first time in Greek literature. It is not a *hypocrite* that is meant, but a *fickle,* "wavering" man, as the context shows. It is opposed to *the single eye* (Matt. 6:22). **9, 10.** Translate, "*But* let the brother . . .," i.e., the best remedy against *double-mindedness* is that Christian *simplicity* of spirit whereby the "brother," low in outward circumstances, may "rejoice" (answering to vs. 2) "in that he is exalted," viz., by being accounted a son and heir of God, his very sufferings being a pledge of his coming glory and crown (vs. 12), and the rich may rejoice "in that he is made low," by being stripped of his goods for Christ's sake [MENOCHIUS]; or in that he is made, by sanctified trials, lowly in spirit, which is true matter for rejoicing [GOMARUS]. The design of the Epistle is to reduce all things to an equable footing (ch. 2:1; 5:13). The "low," rather than the "rich," is here called "the brother" [BENGEL]. So far as one is merely "rich" in worldly goods, "he shall pass away"; in so far as his predominant character is that of a "brother," he "abideth for ever" (I John 2:17). This view meets all ALFORD'S objections to regarding "the rich" here as a "brother" at all. To avoid making the rich a brother, he translates, "But the rich glories in his humiliation," viz., in that which is really his debasement (his rich state, Phil. 3:19), just as the low is told to rejoice in what is really his exaltation (his lowly state). **11.** Taken from Isaiah 40:6-8. **heat**—rather, "the hot wind" from the (east or) south, which scorches vegetation (Luke 12:55). The "burning heat" of the sun is not at its *rising,* but rather at noon; whereas the scorching *Kadim* wind is often at sunrise (Jonah 4:8) [MID-

DLETON, *Greek Article*]. Matthew 20:12 uses the *Greek* word for "heat." Isaiah 40:7, *"bloweth upon it,"* seems to answer to "the hot *wind"* here. **grace of the fashion**—i.e., of the external appearance. **in his ways**—referring to the burdensome extent of the rich man's devices [BENGEL]. Cf. "his ways," i.e., his course of life, vs. 8. **12. Blessed**—Cf. the beatitudes in the Sermon on the Mount (Matt. 5:4, 10, 11). **endureth temptation**—not the "falling into divers temptations" (vs. 2) is the matter for "joy," but the *enduring* of temptation "unto the end." Cf. Job 5:17. **when he is tried**—lit., "when he has become tested" or "approved," when he has passed through the "trying" (vs. 3), his "faith" having finally gained the victory. **the crown**—not in allusion to the crown or garland given to winners in the games; for this, though a natural allusion for Paul in writing to the heathen, among whom such games existed, would be less appropriate for James in addressing the Jewish Christians, who regarded Gentile usages with aversion. **of life**—"life" constitutes the crown, lit., *the* life, the only true life, the highest and eternal life. The crown implies a *kingdom* (Ps. 21:3). **the Lord**—not found in the best MSS. and versions. The believer's heart fills up the omission, without the name needing to be mentioned. The "faithful One who promised" (Heb. 10:23). **to them that love him**—In II Timothy 4:8, "the crown of righteousness to them that love His appearing." Love produces patient *endurance:* none attest their love more than they who suffer for Him. **13. when . . . tempted**—tried by *solicitation to evil.* Heretofore the "temptation" meant was that of *probation by afflictions.* Let no one fancy that God lays upon him an inevitable necessity of sinning. God does not send trials on you in order to make you worse, but to make you better (vss. 16, 17). Therefore do not sink under the pressure of evils (I Cor. 10:13). **of God**—by agency proceeding *from* God. The *Greek* is not "tempted *by,"* but, "from," implying indirect agency. **cannot be tempted with evil . . .**—"Neither do any of our sins tempt God to entice us to worse things, nor does He tempt any *of His own accord"* (lit., "of Himself"; cf. the antithesis, vs. 18, *"Of His own will* He begat us" to holiness, so far is He from tempting us *of His own will)* [BENGEL]. God is said in Genesis 22:1 to have "tempted Abraham"; but there the *tempting* meant is that of *trying* or *proving,* not that of seducement. ALFORD translates according to the ordinary sense of the *Greek,* "God is *unversed* in evil." But as this gives a less likely sense, *English Version* probably gives the true sense; for ecclesiastical *Greek* often uses words in new senses, as the exigencies of the new truths to be taught required. **14. Every man, when tempted,** is so through being drawn away of (again here, as in vs. 13, the *Greek* for "of" expresses the actual *source,* rather than the agent of temptation) his own lust. The cause of sin is in ourselves. Even Satan's suggestions do not endanger us before they are made *our own.* Each one has *his own peculiar* (so the *Greek*) lust, arising from his own temperament and habit. Lust flows from the original birth-sin in man, inherited from Adam. **drawn away**—the *beginning* step in temptation: drawn away from truth and virtue. **enticed**—lit., "taken with a bait," as fish are. The *further progress:* the man *allowing himself* (as the *Greek* middle voice implies) *to be enticed* to evil [BENGEL]. "Lust" is here personified as the harlot that allures the man. **15.** The guilty union is committed by the will embracing the temptress. "Lust," the harlot, then, "brings forth sin,"

viz., of that kind to which the temptation inclines. Then *the particular sin* (so the *Greek* implies), "when it is completed, brings forth death," with which it was all along pregnant [ALFORD]. This "death" stands in striking contrast to the "crown of *life"* (vs. 12) which "patience" or *endurance* ends in, when it has its "perfect work" (vs. 4). He who will fight Satan with Satan's own weapons, must not wonder if he finds himself overmatched. Nip sin in the bud of lust. **16.** Do not err in attributing to God temptation to evil; nay (as he proceeds to show), "every good," all that is good on earth, comes from God. **17. gift . . . gift**—not the same words in *Greek:* the first, *the act of giving,* or the gift in its *initiatory* stage; the second, *the thing given, the boon, when perfected.* As the "good gift" stands in contrast to "sin" in its initiatory stage (vs. 15), so the "perfect boon" is in contrast to "sin when it is finished," bringing forth *death* (II Pet. 1:3). **from above**—(Cf. ch. 3:15). **Father of lights**—Creator *of the lights in heaven* (cf. Job. 38:28 [ALFORD]; Gen. 4:20, 21; Heb. 12:9). This accords with the reference to the changes in the light of the heavenly bodies alluded to in the end of the verse. Also, Father of the spiritual lights in the kingdom of grace and glory [BENGEL]. These were typified by the supernatural lights on the breastplate of the high priest, the Urim. As "God is light, and in Him is no darkness at all" (I John 1:5), He cannot in any way be the Author of sin (vs. 13), which is darkness (John 3:19). **no variableness . . . shadow of turning** —(Mal. 3:6). None of the alternations of light and shadow which the physical "lights" undergo, and which even the spiritual lights are liable to, as compared with God. "Shadow of turning," lit., the dark "shadow-mark" cast *from* one of the heavenly bodies, arising from its "turning" or revolution, e.g., when the moon is eclipsed by the shadow of the earth, and the sun by the body of the moon. BENGEL makes a climax, "no variation—not even the shadow of a turning"; the former denoting a change in the *understanding;* the latter, in the *will.* **18.** (John 1:13.) The believer's regeneration is the highest example of nothing but good proceeding from God. **Of his own will**—Of his own good pleasure (which shows that it is God's essential nature to do good, not evil), not induced by any external cause. **begat he us**—spiritually: a once-for-all accomplished act (I Pet. 1:3, 23). In contrast to "lust when it hath conceived, *bringeth forth* sin, and sin . . . *death"* (vs. 15). Life follows naturally in connection with *light* (vs. 17). **word of truth**—the Gospel. The objective mean, as *faith* is the appropriating mean of regeneration by the Holy Spirit as the efficient agent. **a kind of first fruits**—Christ is, in respect to the resurrection, "the first fruits" (I Cor. 15:20, 23): believers, in respect to regeneration, are, *as it were,* first fruits (image from the consecration of the first-born of man, cattle, and fruits to God; familiar to the Jews addressed), i.e., they are the first of God's regenerated creatures, and the pledge of the ultimate regeneration of the creation, Romans 8:19, 23, where also the Spirit, the divine agent of the believer's regeneration, is termed "the first fruits," i.e., the earnest that the regeneration now begun in the soul, shall at last extend to the body too, and to the lower parts of creation. Of all God's visible creatures, believers are the noblest part, and like the legal "first-fruits," sanctify the rest; for this reason they are much tried now. **19. Wherefore**—as your evil is of yourselves, but your good from God. However, the oldest MSS. and versions read thus: "YE KNOW IT (so Eph. 5:5; Heb.

12:17), my beloved brethren; BUT (consequently) let every man be swift to hear," i.e., docile in receiving "the word of truth" (vss. 18, 21). The true method of hearing is treated in vss. 21-27, and ch. 2. **slow to speak**—(Prov. 10:19; 17:27, 28; Eccles. 5:2). A good way of escaping one kind of temptation arising from ourselves (vs. 13). Slow to speak authoritatively as a master or teacher of others (cf. ch. 3:1): a common Jewish fault: slow also to speak such hasty things of God, as in vs. 13. Two ears are given to us, the rabbis observe, but only one tongue: the ears are open and exposed, whereas the tongue is walled in behind the teeth. **slow to wrath** —(ch. 3:13, 14; 4:5). Slow in becoming heated by debate: another Jewish fault (Rom. 2:8), to which much *speaking* tends. TITTMANN thinks not so much "wrath" is meant, as an *indignant* feeling of *fretfulness* under the calamities to which the whole of human life is exposed; this accords with the "divers temptations" in vs. 2. Hastiness of temper hinders hearing God's word; so Naaman, II Kings 5:11; Luke 4:28. **20.** Man's angry zeal in debating, as if jealous for the honor of God's righteousness, is far from working that which is really righteousness in God's sight. True "righteousness is sown in peace," not in wrath (ch. 3:18). The oldest and the received reading is "worketh," **produceth not.** best reading means "worketh," i.e., *practiceth* not: **21. lay apart**—"once for all" (so the *Greek*): as a filthy garment. Cf. Joshua's filthy garments, Zechariah 3:3, 5; Revelation 7:14. "Filthiness" is cleansed away by hearing the word (John 15:3). **superfluity of naughtiness**—*excess* (for instance, the *intemperate* spirit implied in "wrath," vss. 19, 20), which arises from *malice* (our natural, *evil disposition* towards one another). I Peter 2:1 has the very same words in the *Greek*. So "malice" is the translation, Ephesians 4:31; Colossians 3:8. "*Faulty* excess" [BENGEL] is not strong enough. Superfluous excess in *speaking* is also reprobated as "coming of *evil*" (the *Greek* is akin to the word for "naughtiness" here) in the Sermon on the Mount (Matt. 5:37), with which James' Epistle is so connected. **with meekness**—*in mildness* towards one another [ALFORD], the opposite to "wrath" (vs. 20): answering to "as new-born babes" (I Pet. 2:2). *Meekness,* I think, includes also a childlike, *docile, humble,* as well as an uncontentious, spirit (Ps. 25: 9; 45:4; Isa. 66:2; Matt. 5:5; 11:28-30; 18:3, 4; contrast Rom. 2:8). On "receive," applied to ground receiving seed, cf. Mark 4:20. Contrast Acts 17:11; I Thessalonians 1:6 with II Thessalonians 2:10. **engrafted word**—the Gospel *word,* whose proper attribute is to be *engrafted* by the Holy Spirit, so as to be livingly incorporated with the believer, as the fruitful shoot is with the wild natural stock on which it is engrafted. The law came to man only from without, and admonished him of his duty. The Gospel is *engrafted* inwardly, and so fulfils the ultimate design of the law (Deut. 6:6 11:18; Ps. 119: 11). ALFORD translates, "The *implanted* word," referring to the parable of the sower (Matt. 13). I prefer *English Version.* **able to save**—a strong incentive to correct our dulness in hearing the word: that word which we hear so carelessly, is able (instrumentally) to save us [CALVIN]. **souls**—your true selves, for the "body" is now liable to sickness and death: but the soul being now saved, both soul and body at last shall be so (ch. 5:15, 20). **22.** Qualification of the precept, "Be swift to *hear*": "Be ye doers . . . not hearers only"; not merely "*Do* the word," but "*Be* doers" systematically and continually, as if this was your regular business. James

here again refers to the Sermon on the Mount (Matt. 7:21-29). **deceiving your own selves**—by the logical fallacy (the *Greek* implies this) that the mere hearing is all that is needed. **23. For**—the logical self-deceit (vs. 22) illustrated. **not a doer**—more lit., "a notdoer" [ALFORD]. The true disciple, say the rabbis, learns in order that he may do, not in order that he may merely know or teach. **his natural face** —lit., "the countenance of his birth": the face he was born with. As a man may behold his *natural face* in a mirror, so the hearer may perceive his *moral* visage in God's Word. This faithful portraiture of man's soul in Scripture, is the strongest proof of the truth of the latter. In it, too, we see mirrored God's glory, as well as our natural vileness. **24. beholdeth**—more lit., "he *contemplated* himself and hath *gone* his way," i.e., no sooner has he contemplated his image than he is gone his way (vs. 11). "Contemplate" answers to hearing the word: "goeth his way," to relaxing the attention after hearing—letting the mind go elsewhere, and the interest of the thing heard pass away: then *forgetfulness* follows [ALFORD] (cf. Ezek. 33:31). "Contemplate" here, and in vs. 23, implies that, though cursory, yet some knowledge of one's self, at least for the time, is imparted in hearing the word (I Cor. 14:24). **and . . . and**—The repetition expresses hastiness joined with levity [BENGEL]. **forgetteth what manner of man he was**—in the mirror. Forgetfulness is no excuse (vs. 25; II Pet. 1:9). **25. looketh into**—lit., "stoopeth down to take a close look into." Peers into: stronger than "beholdeth," or "contemplated," vs. 24. A blessed curiosity if it be efficacious in bearing fruit [BENGEL]. **perfect law of liberty**—the Gospel rule of life, perfect and perfecting (as shown in the Sermon on the Mount, Matt. 5:48), and making us truly walk at liberty (Ps. 119:32, *Church of England Prayer Book Version*). Christians are to aim at a higher standard of holiness than was generally understood under the law. The *principle* of love takes the place of the letter of the law, so that by the Spirit they are free from the yoke of sin, and free to obey by spontaneous instinct (ch. 2:8, 10, 12; John 8:31-36; 15:14, 15; cf. I Cor. 7:22; Gal. 5:1, 13; I Pet. 2:16). The law is thus *not made void,* but *fulfilled.* **continueth therein**—contrasted with "goeth his way," vs. 24: continues both *looking into* the mirror of God's word, and doing its precepts. **doer of the work**— rather, "a doer of work" [ALFORD], an actual worker. **blessed in his deed**—rather, "in his *doing*"; in the very doing there is blessedness (Ps. 19:11). **26, 27.** An example of *doing work.* **religious . . religion**—The *Greek* expresses the *external service* or exercise *of religion,* "godliness" being the internal soul of it. "If any man *think himself to be* (so the *Greek*) religious, i.e., *observant of the offices of religion,* let him know these consist not so much in outward observances, as in such acts of mercy and humble piety (Mic. 6:7, 8) as *visiting the fatherless,* etc., and *keeping one's self unspotted from the world*" (Matt. 23:23). James does not mean that these *offices* are the great essentials, or sum total of religion; but that, whereas the law service was merely ceremonial, the very *services* of the Gospel consist in acts of mercy and holiness, and it has light for its *garment,* its very *robe* being righteousness [TRENCH]. The *Greek* word is only found in Acts 26:5, "after the straitest sect of our *religion* I lived a Pharisee." Colossians 2:18, "*worshipping* of angels." **bridleth not . . . tongue**—Discretion in speech is better than fluency of speech (cf. ch. 3:2, 3). Cf. Psalm 39:1. God alone can enable us to do so. James, in treating of the law, naturally notices this sin. For they who are free from grosser sins, and even bear the outward show of sanctity, will often exalt themselves by detracting others under the pretense of zeal, while their real motive is love of evil-speaking [CALVIN]. **heart**—It and the tongue act and react on one another. **27. Pure . . . and undefiled**—"Pure" is that love which has in it *no foreign admixture,* as self-deceit and hypocrisy. "Undefiled" is the means of its being "pure" [TITTMANN]. "Pure" expresses the *positive,* "undefiled" the *negative* side of religious service; just as *visiting the fatherless and widow* is the active, *keeping himself unspotted from the world,* the passive side of religious duty. This is the nobler shape that our religious exercises take, instead of the ceremonial offices of the law. **before God and the Father**—lit., "before Him who is (our) God and Father." God is so called to imply that if we would be like our Father, it is not by fasting, etc., for He does none of these things, but in being "merciful as our Father is merciful" [CHRYSOSTOM]. **visit**—in sympathy and kind offices to alleviate their distresses. **the fatherless**—whose "Father' is God (Ps. 68:5); peculiarly helpless. **and**—not in the *Greek;* so close is the connection between active works of mercy to others, and the maintenance of personal unworldliness of spirit, word, and deed; no copula therefore is needed. Religion in its rise interests us about *ourselves;* in its progress, about our *fellow creatures;* in its highest stage, about the honor of God. **keep himself**—with jealous watchfulness, at the same time praying and depending on God as alone able to keep us (John 17:15; Jude 24).

CHAPTER 2

Vss. 1-26. THE SIN OF RESPECT OF PERSONS: DEAD, UNWORKING FAITH SAVES NO MAN. **1-13.** James illustrates "the perfect law of liberty" (ch. 1:25) in one particular instance of a sin against it, concluding with a reference again to that law (vss. 12, 13). **1. brethren**—The equality of all Christians as "brethren," forms the groundwork of the admonition. **the faith of . . . Christ**—i.e., the Christian faith. James grounds Christian practice on Christian faith. *the Lord* **of glory**—So I Corinthians 2:8. As all believers, alike rich and poor, derive all their glory from their union with Him, "the Lord of glory," not from external advantages of worldly fortune, the sin in question is peculiarly inconsistent with His "faith." BENGEL, making no ellipsis of "the Lord," explains "glory" as in apposition with Christ who is THE GLORY (Luke 2:32); the true Shekinah glory of the temple (Rom. 9:4). *English Version* is simpler. The glory of Christ resting on the poor believer should make him be regarded as highly by "brethren" as his richer brother; nay, more so, if the poor believer has more of Christ's spirit than the rich brother. **with respect of persons**—lit., *"in respectings* of persons"; *in* the practice of partial preferences of persons in various ways and on various occasions. **2. assembly**—lit., "synagogue"; this, the latest honorable use, and the only *Christian* use of the term in the New Testament, occurs in James's Epistle, the apostle who maintained to the latest possible moment the bonds between the Jewish synagogue and the Christian Church. Soon the continued resistance of the truth by the Jews led Christians to leave the term to them exclusively (Rev. 3:9). The "synagogue" implies a mere *assembly* or congregation not necessarily

united by any common tie. "Church," a people bound together by mutual ties and laws, though often it may happen that the members are not assembled [TRENCH and VITRINGA]. Partly from James' Hebrew tendencies, partly from the Jewish Christian churches retaining most of the Jewish forms, this term "synagogue" is used here instead of the Christian term "Church" (*ecclesia,* derived from a root, "called out," implying the union of its members in spiritual bonds, independent of space, and called out into separation from the world); an undesigned coincidence and mark of truth. The people in the Jewish synagogue sat according to their rank, those of the same trade together. The introduction of this custom into Jewish Christian places of worship is here reprobated by James. Christian churches were built like the synagogues, the holy table in the east end of the former, as the ark was in the latter; the *desk* and *pulpit* were the chief articles of furniture in both alike. This shows the error of comparing the Church to the temple, and the ministry to the priesthood; the temple is represented by the whole body of worshippers; the church building was formed on the model of the synagogue. See VITRINGA, *Synagogue.* **2, 3.** "If there chance to have come" [ALFORD]. **goodly apparel . . . gay clothing**—As the *Greek,* is the same in both, translate both alike, "gay," or "splendid clothing." **have respect to him . . .**—though ye know not who he is, when perhaps he may be a heathen. It was the office of the deacons to direct to a seat the members of the congregation [CLEMENT, *Constitut.* 2. 57, 58]. **unto him**—not in the best MSS. Thus "thou" becomes more demonstratively emphatic. **there**—at a distance from where the good seats are. **here**—near the speaker. **under my footstool**—not literally so; but on the ground, down by my footstool. The poor man must either *stand,* or if he sits, *sit* in a degrading position. The speaker has a footstool as well as a good seat. **4. Are ye not . . . partial**—lit., "Have ye not made distinctions or "differences" (so as to prefer one to another)? So in Jude 22. **in yourselves**—in your minds, i.e., according to your carnal inclination [GROTIUS]. **are become judges of evil thoughts**—The *Greek* words for "judges" and for "partial," are akin in sound and meaning. A similar translation ought therefore to be given to both. Thus, either for "judges . . ." translate, *"distinguishers* of (i.e., *according to* your) evil thoughts"; or, do ye not *partially judge between* men, and are become *evilly-thinking judges* (Mark 7:21)? The "evil thoughts" are in the judges themselves; as in Luke 18:6, the *Greek,* "judge of injustice," is translated, "unjust judge." ALFORD and WAHL translate, "Did ye not *doubt"* (respecting your *faith,* which is inconsistent with the distinctions made by you between rich and poor)? For the *Greek* constantly means *"doubt"* in all the New Testament. So in ch. 1:6, "wavering." Matthew 21:21; Acts 10:20; Romans 4:20, "staggered not." The same play on the same kindred words occurs in the *Greek* of Romans 14: 10, 23, "judge . . . doubteth." The same blame of being a judge, when one ought to be an obeyer, of the law is found in ch. 4:11. **5. Hearken**—James *brings to trial* the self-constituted "judges" (vs. 4). **poor of this world**—The best MSS. read, "those poor *in respect to the* world." In contrast to "the rich in this world" (I Tim. 6:17). Not of course *all* the poor; but the poor, *as a class,* furnish more believers than the rich as a class. The rich, if a believer, renounces riches as his portion; the poor, if an unbeliever, neglects that which is the peculiar advantage of poverty (Matt. 5:3; I Cor. 1:26, 27, 28). **rich in faith**—*Their* riches consist *in faith.* Luke 12:21, "rich toward God." I Timothy 6:18, "rich in good works" (Rev. 2:9; cf. II Cor. 8:9). Christ's poverty is the source of the believer's riches. **kingdom . . . promised**—(Luke 12:32; I Cor. 2:9; II Tim. 4:8). **6.** The world's judgment of the poor contrasted with God's. **ye**—Christians, from whom better things might have been expected; there is no marvel that men of the world do so. **despised**—lit., "dishonored." To dishonor the poor is to dishonor those whom God honors, and so to invert the order of God [CALVIN]. **rich**—as a class. **oppress**—lit., "abuse their power against" you. **draw you**—Translate, "is it not *they* (those very persons whom ye partially prefer, vss. 1-4) that *drag* you" (viz., with violence) [ALFORD]. **before . . . judgment seats**—instituting persecutions for religion, as well as oppressive lawsuits, against you. **7.** "Is it not they that blaspheme . . . ?" as in vs. 6 [ALFORD]. Rich heathen must here chiefly be meant; for none others would directly blaspheme the name of Christ. Only *indirectly* rich Christians can be meant, who, by their inconsistency, *caused* His name *to be blasphemed;* so Ezekiel 36:21, 22; Romans 2:24. Besides, there were few rich Jewish Christians at Jerusalem (Rom. 15:26). They who dishonor God's name by wilful and habitual sin, "take (or *bear*) the Lord's name in vain" (cf. Prov. 30:9, with Exod. 20:7). **that worthy name**—which is "good before the Lord's saints" (Ps. 52:9; 54:6); which ye pray may be "hallowed" (Matt. 6:9), and "by which ye are called," lit., "which was invoked" (or, "called upon") by you" (cf. Gen. 48:16; Isa. 4:1, *Margin;* Acts 15:17), so that at your baptism "*into* the name" (so the *Greek,* Matt. 28:19) of Christ, ye became Christ's people (I Cor. 3:23). **8.** The *Greek* may be translated, "If, *however,* ye fulfil . . ." i.e., as ALFORD, after ESTIUS, explains, "*Still* I do not say, hate the rich (for their oppressions) and drive them from your assemblies; if you choose to observe the royal law . . . , well and good; but respect of persons is a breach of that law." I think the translation is, "If *in very deed* (or *indeed on the one hand*) ye fulfil the royal law . . . , ye do well, but if (on the other hand) ye respect persons, ye practice sin." The Jewish Christians boasted of, and rested in, the "law" (Acts 15:1; 21:18-24; Rom. 2:17; Gal. 2:12). To this the "indeed" alludes. "(Ye rest in the law): If *indeed* (then) ye fulfil it, ye do well; but if . . ." **royal**—the law that is king of all laws, being the sum and essence of the ten commandments. The great King, God, is love; His law is the royal law of love, and that law, like Himself, reigns supreme. He "is no respecter of persons"; therefore to respect persons is at variance with Him and His royal law, which is at once a law of love and of liberty (vs. 12). The law is the "whole"; "the (particular) Scripture" (Lev. 19:18) quoted is a part. To break a part is to break the whole (vs. 10). **ye do well**—being "blessed in your deed" ("doing," *Margin*) as a doer, not a forgetful hearer of the law (ch. 1:25). **9.** *Respect of persons* violates the command to *love all alike* "as thyself." **ye commit sin**—lit., "ye work sin," Matthew 7:23, to which the reference here is probably, as in ch. 1:22. Your *works* are sin, whatever boast of the law ye make in words (*Note,* vs. 8). **convinced**—*Old English* for "convicted." **as transgressors**—not merely of this or that particular command, but of the whole absolutely. **10.** The best MSS. read, "Whosoever *shall have kept* the whole law, and yet *shall have offended* (lit., 'stumbled'; not so

strong as 'fall,' Rom. 11:11) in one (point; here, the *respecting of persons*), is (hereby) become guilty of all." The law is one seamless garment which is rent if you but rend a part; or a musical harmony which is spoiled if there be one discordant note [TIRINUS]; or a golden chain whose completeness is broken if you break one link [GATAKER]. You thus break *the whole law,* though not the whole of the law, because you offend against *love,* which is the fulfilling of the law. If any part of a man be leprous, the whole man is judged to be a leper. God requires perfect, not partial, obedience. We are not to choose out parts of the law to keep, which suit our whim, while we neglect others. **11.** He is One who gave the whole law; therefore, they who violate His will in one point, violate it all [BENGEL]. The law and its Author alike have a complete unity. **adultery . . . kill**—selected as being the most glaring cases of violation of duty towards one's neighbor. **12.** Summing up of the previous reasonings. **speak** —referring back to ch. 1:19, 26; the fuller discussion of the topic is given ch. 3. **judged by the law of liberty**—(ch. 1:25)—i.e., the Gospel law of love, which is not a law of external constraint, but of internal, *free,* instinctive inclination. The law of liberty, through God's mercy, frees us from the curse of the law, that henceforth we should be free to love and obey willingly. If we will not in turn practice the law of love to our neighbor, that law of grace condemns us still more heavily than the old law, which spake nothing but wrath to him who offended in the least particular (vs. 13). Cf. Matthew 18:32-35; John 12:48; Revelation 6:16, "Wrath of the (merciful) Lamb." **13.** The converse of, "Blessed are the merciful, for they shall obtain mercy" (Matt. 5:7). Translate, "*The* judgment (which is coming on all of us) shall be without mercy to him who hath showed no mercy." It shall be such toward every one as every one shall have been [BENGEL]. "Mercy" here corresponds to "love," vs. 8. **mercy rejoiceth against judgment** —Mercy, so far from fearing judgment in the case of its followers, actually *glorifieth against* it, knowing that it cannot condemn them. Not that *their* mercy is the ground of their acquittal, but the mercy of God in Christ towards them, producing mercy on their part towards their fellow men, makes them to *triumph over judgment,* which all in themselves otherwise deserve. **14.** James here, passing from the particular case of "mercy" or "love" violated by "respect of persons," notwithstanding profession of the "faith of our Lord Jesus" (vs. 1), combats the Jewish tendency (transplanted into their Christianity) to substitute a lifeless, inoperative acquaintance with the letter of the law, for change of heart to practical holiness, as if justification could be thereby attained (Rom. 2:3, 13, 23). It seems hardly likely but that James had seen Paul's Epistles, considering that he uses the same phrases and examples (cf. vss. 21, 23, 25, with Rom. 4:3; Heb. 11:17, 31; and vss. 14, 24, with Rom. 3:28; Gal. 2:16). Whether James individually designed it or not, the Holy Spirit by him combats not Paul, but those who abuse Paul's doctrine. The teaching of both alike is inspired, and is therefore to be received without wresting of words; but each has a different class to deal with; Paul, self-justiciaries; James, Antinomian advocates of a mere notional faith. Paul urged as strongly as James the need of works as evidences of faith, especially in the later Epistles, when many were abusing the doctrine of faith (Titus 2:14; 3:8). "Believing and doing are blood relatives" [RUTHERFORD]. **What doth it**

profit–lit., "What is the profit?"   **though a man say** –James' expression is not, "If a mon have faith," but "if a man *say* he hath faith"; referring to a mere *profession* of faith, such as was usually made at baptism. Simon Magus so "*believed* and was baptized," and yet had "neither part nor lot in this matter," for his "heart," as his words and works evinced, was not right in the sight of God. AL-FORD wrongly denies that "say" is emphatic. The illustration, vs. 16, proves it is: "If one of you *say*" to a naked brother, "Be ye warmed, notwithstanding ye give not those things needful." The inoperative *profession* of sympathy answering to the inoperative *profession* of faith.   **can faith save him** –rather, "can such a faith (lit., "the faith") save him?"–*the* faith you pretend to: the empty name of boasted faith, contrasted with true fruit-producing faith. So that which self-deceivers claim is called "wisdom," though not true wisdom, ch. 3:15. The "him" also in the *Greek* is emphatic; the particular man who professes faith without having the works which evidence its vitality.   **15.** The *Greek* is, "*But* if . . .": the "But" taking up the argument against such a one as "said he had faith, and yet had not works," which are its fruits.   **a brother . . .** –a *fellow Christian,* to whom we are specially bound to give help, independent of our general obligation to help all our fellow creatures.   **be**– The *Greek* implies, "*be found,* on your access to them."   **16.** The habit of receiving passively sentimental impressions from sights of woe without carrying them out into active habits only hardens the heart.   **one of you**–James brings home the case to his hearers individually.   **Depart in peace**–as if all their wants were satisfied by the mere words addressed to them. The same words in the mouth of Christ, whose faith they said they had, were accompanied by efficient deeds of love.   **be . . . warmed**–with clothing, instead of being as heretofore "naked" (vs. 15; Job 31:20).   **filled**–instead of being "destitute of food" (Matt. 15:37).   **what doth it profit**–concluding with the same question as at the beginning, vs. 14. Just retribution: kind professions unaccompanied with corresponding acts, as they are of no "profit" to the needy object of them, so are of no profit to the professor himself. So faith consisting in mere profession is unacceptable to God, the object of faith, and profitless to the possessor.   **17. faith . . . being alone**– ALFORD joins "is dead *in itself.*" So BENGEL, "If the works which living faith produces have no existence, it is a proof that faith itself (lit., "in respect to itself) has no existence; i.e., that what one boasts of as faith, is *dead.*" "Faith" is said to be "dead *in itself,*" because when it has works it is *alive,* and it is discerned to be so, not in respect to its works, but in respect to *itself. English Version,* if retained, must not be understood to mean that faith can exist "alone" (i.e., severed from works), but thus: Even so *presumed* faith, if it have not works, is dead, being by itself "alone," i.e., severed from works of charity; just as the body would be "dead" if alone, i.e., severed from the spirit (vs. 26). So ESTIUS.   **18.** "*But* some *one will* say": so the *Greek.* This verse continues the argument from vss. 14, 16. One may *say* he has faith though he have not works. Suppose one were to *say* to a naked brother, "Be warmed," without giving him needful clothing. "*But* someone (entertaining right views of the need of faith having works joined to it) will say" (in opposition to the "say" of the professor).   **show me thy faith without thy works**–if thou canst; but thou canst not SHOW,

i.e., *manifest* or *evidence* thy alleged (vs. 14, "say") faith without works. "Show" does not mean here to *prove* to me, but *exhibit* to me. Faith is unseen save by God. To *show* faith to man, works in some form or other are needed: we are justified judicially by God (Rom. 8:33); meritoriously, by Christ (Isa. 53:11); mediately, by faith (Rom. 5:1); evidentially, by works. The question here is not as to the *ground* on which believers are justified, but about the *demonstration* of their faith: so in the case of Abraham. In Genesis 22:1 it is written, God did *tempt* Abraham, i.e., put to the *test of demonstration* the reality of his faith, not for the satisfaction of God, who already knew it well, but to *demonstrate* it before men. The offering of Isaac at that time, quoted here, vs. 21, formed no part of the *ground* of his justification, for he was justified previously on his simply believing in the promise of spiritual heirs, i.e., believers, numerous as the stars. He was then justified: that justification was *showed* or manifested by his offering Isaac forty years after. That work of faith *demonstrated,* but did not contribute to his justification. The tree *shows* its life by its fruits, but it was alive before either fruits or even leaves appeared.   **19. Thou**–emphatic. Thou self-deceiving claimant to faith without works.   **that there is one God**– rather, "that God is one": God's *existence,* however, is also asserted. The fundamental article of the creed of Jews and Christians alike, and the point of faith on which especially the former boasted themselves, as distinguishing them from the Gentiles, and hence adduced by James here.   **thou doest well**–so far good. But unless thy faith goes farther than an assent to this truth, "the evil spirits (lit., 'demons': 'devil' is the term restricted to *Satan,* their head) believe" so far in common with thee, "and (so far from being saved by such a faith) shudder" (so the *Greek*), Matt. 8:29; Luke 4:34; II Pet. 2:4; Jude 6; Rev. 20:10. Their faith only adds to their torment at the thought of having to meet Him who is to consign them to their just doom: so thine (Heb. 10:26, 27, it is not the faith of love, but of fear, that hath torment, I John 4: 18).   **20. wilt thou know**–"Vain" men are not *willing* to know, since they have no wish to *do* the will of God. James beseeches such a one to lay aside his perverse *unwillingness* to know what is palpable to all who are willing to do.   **vain**–who deceivest thyself with a delusive hope, resting on an unreal faith.   **without works**–The *Greek,* implies *separate from the* works [ALFORD] which ought to flow from it if it were real.   **is dead**– Some of the best MSS. read, "is idle," i.e., unavailing to effect what you hope, viz., to save you.   **21. Abraham . . . justified by works**–*evidentially,* and *before men* (see *Note,* vs. 18). In vs. 23, James, like Paul, recognizes the Scripture truth, that it was his *faith* that was counted to Abraham for righteousness in his justification before God.   **when he had offered**–rather, "when he offered" [ALFORD], i.e., brought as an offering at the altar; not implying that he actually offered him.   **22.** Or, "thou seest."   **how**–rather, "that." In the two clauses which follow, emphasize "faith" in the former, and "works" in the latter, to see the sense [BENGEL].   **faith wrought with his works**–for it was *by faith* he offered his son. Lit., "was working (at the time) with his works."   **by works was faith made perfect**–not was *vivified,* but attained its *fully consummated development,* and is *shown to be real.* So "my strength is *made perfect* in weakness," i.e., *exerts itself most perfectly,* shows how great it is

[CAMERON]: so I John 4:17; Hebrews 2:10; 5:9. The germ really, from the first, contains in it the fullgrown tree, but its perfection is not attained till it is matured fully. So ch. 1:4, "Let patience have her *perfect work,*" i.e., have its *full effect* by showing the most perfect degree of endurance, "that ye may be perfect," i.e., *fully developed* in the *exhibition* of the Christian character. ALFORD explains, "Received its realization, was entirely exemplified and filled up." So Paul, Phil. 2:12, "Work out your own salvation": the salvation was already in germ theirs in their free justification through faith. It needed to be *worked out* still to fully developed perfection in their life. **23. scripture was fulfilled**—Genesis 15:6, quoted by Paul, as realized in Abraham's justification by *faith;* but by James, as realized subsequently in Abraham's *work* of offering Isaac, which, he says, *justified* him. Plainly, then, James must mean by *works* the same thing as Paul means by *faith,* only that he speaks of faith at its manifested development, whereas Paul speaks of it in its germ. Abraham's offering of Isaac was not a mere act of obedience, but an act of faith. Isaac was the subject of the promises of God, that in him Abraham's seed should be called. The same God calls on Abraham to slay the subject of His own promise, when as yet there was no seed in whom those predictions could be realized. Hence James' saying that Abraham was justified by *such* a work, is equivalent to saying, as Paul does, that he was justified by faith itself; for it was in fact *faith expressed in action,* as in other cases saving faith is expressed in words. So Paul states as the mean of salvation faith *expressed.* The "Scripture" would not be "fulfilled," as James says it was, but contradicted by any interpretation which makes man's *works* justify him before God: for that Scripture makes no mention of works at all, but says that Abraham's *belief* was counted to him for righteousness. God, in the first instance, "justifies the *ungodly*" through faith; subsequently the believer is justified *before the world* as righteous through faith manifested in words and works (cf. Matt. 25:35-37 "the righteous," 40). The best authorities read, "But Abraham believed . . . ." **and he was called the Friend of God**—He was not so *called* in his lifetime, though he *was* so even then from the time of his justification; but he was *called* so, being recognized as such by all on the ground of his works of faith. "He was the *friend* (in an active sense), the *lover of God,* in reference to his works; and (in a passive sense) *loved by God* in reference to his justification by works. Both senses are united in John 15:14, 15" [BENGEL]. **24. justified and, not by faith only**—i.e., by "faith without (*separated* from: *severed from*) works," its proper fruits (*Note,* vs. 20). Faith to justify must, from the first, include obedience in germ (to be developed subsequently), though the former alone is the ground of justification. The scion must be grafted on the stock that it may live; it must bring forth fruit to prove that it does live. **25.** It is clear from the nature of Rahab's act, that it is not quoted to prove justification by works as such. She *believed* assuredly what her other countrymen disbelieved, and this in the face of every improbability that an unwarlike few would conquer well-armed numbers. In this belief she hid the spies at the risk of her life. Hence, Hebrews 11:31 names this as an example of *faith,* rather than of obedience. "By *faith* the *harlot* Rahab perished not with them that *believed* not." If an instance of obedience were wanting,

Paul and James would hardly have quoted a woman of previously bad character, rather than the many moral and pious patriarchs. But as an example of free grace justifying men through an *operative,* as opposed to a mere verbal *faith,* none could be more suitable than a saved "harlot." As Abraham was an instance of an illustrious man and the father of the Jews, so Rahab is quoted as a woman, and one of abandoned character, and a Gentile, showing that justifying faith has been manifested in those of every class. The nature of the works alleged is such as to prove that James uses them only as *evidences of faith,* as contrasted with a mere verbal profession: not works of charity and piety, but works the value of which consisted solely in their being proofs of faith: they were faith expressed in act, synonymous with *faith* itself. **messengers**—spies. **had received . . . had sent**—rather, "received . . . thrust them forth" (in haste and fear), [ALFORD]. **another way**—from that whereby they entered her house, viz., through the window of her house on the wall, and thence to the mountain. **26.** Faith is a spiritual thing: works are material. Hence we might expect *faith* to answer to the *spirit, works* to the *body.* But James reverses this. He therefore does not mean that faith in all cases answers to the body; but the FORM *of faith* without *the working reality* answers to the *body* without *the animating spirit.* It does not follow that *living faith* derives its life from works, as the body derives its life from the animating spirit.

CHAPTER 3

Vss. 1-18. DANGER OF EAGERNESS TO TEACH, AND OF AN UNBRIDLED TONGUE: TRUE WISDOM SHOWN BY UNCONTENTIOUS MEEKNESS. **1. be not**—lit., "become not": taking the office too hastily, and of your own accord. **many**—The office is a noble one; but few are fit for it. Few govern the tongue well (vs. 2), and only such as can govern it are fit for the office; therefore, "teachers" ought not to be many. **masters**—rather, "teachers." The Jews were especially prone to this presumption. The idea that faith (so called) without works (ch. 2) was all that is required, prompted "many" to set up as "teachers," as has been the case in all ages of the Church. At first all were allowed to teach in turns. Even their inspired gifts did not prevent liability to abuse, as James here implies: much more is this so when self-constituted teachers have no such miraculous gifts. **knowing**—as all might know. **we . . . greater condemnation**—James in a humble, conciliatory spirit, includes himself: if *we* teachers abuse the office, we shall receive greater condemnation than those who are mere hearers (cf. Luke 12:42-46). CALVIN, like *English Version,* translates, "masters" i.e., self-constituted *censors* and reprovers of others. Ch. 4:12 accords with this view. **2. all**—The *Greek* implies "all without exception": even the apostles. **offend not**—lit., "stumbleth not": is void of offence or *slip* in word: in which respect one is especially tried who sets up to be a "teacher." **3. Behold**—The best authorities read, "but if," i.e., *Now whensoever* (in the case) of horses (such is the emphatic position of "horses" in the *Greek*) we put *the* bits (so lit., "the customary bits") into their mouths that they may obey us, we turn about *also* their whole body. This is to illustrate how *man* turns about his whole body with the little tongue. "The same applies to the pen, which is the substitute for the tongue among the absent" [BENGEL]. **4.** Not only animals, but *even ships*. **the governor listeth**—lit., "the impulse of the steersman pleaseth." The feeling which moves the tongue corresponds with this. **5. boasteth great things**—There is *great* moment in what the careless think "little" things [BENGEL]. Cf. "a world," "the course of nature," "hell," vs. 6, which illustrate how the little tongue's great words produce great mischief. **how great a matter a little fire kindleth**—The best MSS. read, *"how little a fire kindleth how great a . . . ."* ALFORD, for "matter," translates, "forest." But GROTIUS translates as *English Version*, "material for burning": a pile of fuel. **6.** Translate, "The tongue, that world of iniquity, is a fire." As man's little world is an image of the greater world, the universe, so the tongue is an image of the former [BENGEL]. **so**—omitted in the oldest authorities. **is**—lit., "is constituted." "The tongue is (constituted), among the members, the one which defileth . . ." (viz., as fire defiles with its smoke). **course of nature**—"the orb (cycle) of creation." **setteth on fire . . . is set on fire**—habitually and continually. While a man inflames others, he passes out of his own power, being consumed in the flame himself. **of hell**—i.e., of the devil. *Greek,* "Gehenna"; found here only and in Matthew 5:22. James has much in common with the Sermon on the Mount (Prov. 16:27). **7. every kind**—rather, "every nature" (i.e., natural disposition and characteristic power). **of beasts**—i.e., quadrupeds of every disposition; as distinguished from the three other classes of creation, "birds, creeping things (the *Greek* includes not merely 'serpents,' as *English Version*), and things in the sea." **is tamed, and hath been**—is continually being tamed, and hath been so long ago. **of mankind**—rather, "by the nature of man": man's characteristic power taming that of the inferior animals. The dative in the *Greek* may imply, "Hath suffered itself to be brought into tame subjection TO the nature of men." So it shall be in the millennial world; even now man, by gentle firmness, may tame the inferior animal, and even elevate its nature. **8. no man**—lit., "no one of men": neither can a man control his neighbor's, nor even his own tongue. Hence the truth of vs. 2 appears. **unruly evil**—The *Greek,* implies that it is at once *restless* and *incapable of restraint.* Nay, though nature has hedged it in with a double barrier of the lips and teeth, it bursts from its barriers to assail and ruin men [ESTIUS]. **deadly**—lit., "death-bearing." **9. God**—The oldest authorities read, "Lord." "Him who is Lord and Father." The uncommonness of the application of "Lord" to the Father, doubtless caused the change in modern texts to "God" (ch. 1:27). But as Messiah is called "Father," Isaiah 9:6, so God the Father is called by the Son's title, "Lord": showing the unity of the Godhead. "Father" implies His *paternal* love; "Lord," His dominion. **men, which**—not "men *who";* for what is meant is not particular men, but men *generically* [ALFORD]. **are made after . . . similitude of God**—Though in a great measure man has lost the *likeness* of God in which he was originally made, yet enough of it still remains to show what once it was, and what in regenerated and restored man it shall be. We ought to reverence this remnant and earnest of what man shall be in ourselves and in others. "Absalom has fallen from his father's favor, but the people still recognize him to be the king's son" [BENGEL]. Man resembles in humanity the Son of man, "the express image of His person" (Heb. 1:3), cf. Genesis 1:26; I John 4:

20. In the passage, Genesis 1:26, "image" and "likeness" are distinct: "image," according to the Alexandrians, was something *in* which men were created, being common to all, and continuing to man after the fall, while the "likeness" was something *toward* which man was created, to strive after and attain it: the former marks man's physical and intellectual, the latter his moral pre-eminence. **10.** The tongue, says ÆSOP, is at once the best and the worst of things. So in a fable, a man with the same breath blows hot and cold. "Life and death are in the power of the tongue" (cf. Ps. 62:4). **brethren**—an appeal to their consciences by their *brotherhood* in Christ. **ought not so to be**—a mild appeal, leaving it to themselves to understand that such conduct deserves the most severe reprobation. **11. fountain**—an image of the *heart:* as the *aperture* (so the *Greek* for "place" is lit.) of the fountain is an image of man's *mouth.* The image here is appropriate to the scene of the Epistle, Palestine, wherein salt and bitter springs are found. Though "sweet" springs are sometimes found near, yet "sweet and bitter" (water) do not flow "at the same place" *(aperture).* Grace can make the same mouth that "sent forth the bitter" once, send forth the sweet for the time to come: as the wood (typical of Christ's cross) changed Marah's bitter water into sweet. **12.** Transition from the mouth to the heart. **Can the fig tree . . .**—implying that it is an *impossibility:* as before in vs. 10 he had said it *"ought* not so to be." James does not, as Matthew (7:16, 17), make the question, "Do men gather figs of *thistles?"* His argument is, No tree "can" bring forth *fruit inconsistent with its nature,* as e.g., the fig tree, olive berries: so if a man speaks bitterly, and afterwards speaks good words, the latter must be so only seemingly, and in hypocrisy, they *cannot* be real. **so can no fountain . . . salt . . . and fresh**—The oldest authorities read, "Neither can a salt (water spring) yield fresh." So the mouth that emits cursing, cannot really emit also blessing. **13.** **Who**—(Cf. Ps. 34:12, 13). All wish to appear "wise": few are so. **show**—"by works," and not merely by profession, referring to ch. 2:18. **out of a good conversation his works**—by *general* "good conduct" manifested in *particular* "works." "Wisdom" and "knowledge," without these being "shown," are as dead as faith would be without works [ALFORD]. **with meekness of wisdom**—with the meekness inseparable from true "wisdom." **14. if ye have**—*as is the case* (this is implied in the *Greek* indicative). **bitter**—Ephesians 4:31, "bitterness." **envying**—rather, "emulation," or lit., "zeal": kindly, generous emulation, or zeal, is not condemned, but that which is "bitter" [BENGEL]. **strife**—rather, "rivalry." **in your hearts**—from which flow your words and deeds, as from a fountain. **glory not, and lie not against the truth**—To *boast of your wisdom* is virtually a lying against the truth (the gospel), while your lives belie your glorying. Vs. 15; ch. 1:18, "The word of truth." Romans 2:17.23, speaks similarly of the same contentious Jewish Christians. **15. This wisdom**—in which ye "glory," as if ye were "wise" (vss. 13, 14). **descendeth not from above**—lit., "is not one descending . . .": "from the Father of lights" (true illumination and wisdom), ch. 1:17; through "the Spirit of truth," John 15:26. **earthly**—opposed to *heavenly.* Distinct from "earthy," I Corinthians 15:47. *Earthly* is what is IN the earth; *earthy,* what is of the earth. **sensual**—lit., "animal-like": the wisdom of the "natural" (the same *Greek*) man, not born again of God; "not having the Spirit"

(Jude 19). **devilish**—in its origin (from "hell," vs. 6; not from God, the Giver of true wisdom, ch. 1: 5), and also in its character, which accords with its origin. Earthly, sensual, and devilish, answer to the three spiritual foes of man, the world, the flesh, and the devil. **16. envying**—So *English Version* translates the *Greek,* which usually means "zeal"; "*emulation,*" in Romans 13:13. "The envious man stands in his own light. He thinks his candle cannot shine in the presence of another's sun. He aims directly at men, obliquely at God, who makes men to differ." **strife**—rivalry [ALFORD]. **confusion**—lit., "tumultuous anarchy": both in society (translated "commotions," Luke 21:9; "tumults," II Cor. 6:5), and in the individual mind; in contrast to the "peaceable" composure of true "wisdom," vs. 17. James does not honor such effects of this earthly wisdom with the name "fruit," as he does in the case of the wisdom from above. Vs. 18; cf. Galatians 5:19-22, "*works* of the flesh . . . *fruit* of the Spirit." **17. first pure**—lit., "chaste," "sanctified"; pure from all that is "earthly, sensual (animal), devilish" (vs. 15). This is put, "*first of all,*" before "peaceable" because there is an unholy peace with the world which makes no distinction between clean and unclean. Cf. "undefiled" and "unspotted from the world," ch. 1:27; 4:4, 8, "purify . . . hearts"; I Peter 1:22, "*purified . . . souls*" (the same *Greek*). Ministers must not preach before a purifying change of heart, "Peace," where there is no peace. Seven (the perfect number) characteristic peculiarities of true wisdom are enumerated. *Purity* or *sanctity* is put first because it has respect both to God and to ourselves; the six that follow regard our fellow men. Our first concern is to have in ourselves sanctity; our second, to be at peace with men. **gentle** "forbearing"; making allowances for others; lenient towards neighbors, as to the DUTIES they owe us. **easy to be entreated**—lit., "easily persuaded," tractable; not harsh as to a neighbor's FAULTS. **full of mercy**—as to a neighbor's MISERIES. **good fruits**—contrasted with "every evil work," vs. 16. **without partiality**—recurring to the warning against partial "respect to persons," ch. 2:1, 4, 9. ALFORD translates as the *Greek* is translated, ch. 1:6, "wavering," "*without doubting.*" But thus there would be an epithet referring to *one's self* inserted amidst those referring to one's conduct towards others. *English Version* is therefore better. **without hypocrisy**—Not as ALFORD explains from ch. 1:22, 26, "Without deceiving yourselves" with the name without the reality of religion. For it must refer, like the rest of the six epithets, to our relations to others; our peaceableness and mercy towards others must be "without dissimulation." **18.** "The peaceable fruit of righteousness." He says "righteousness"; because it is itself the true wisdom. As in the case of the earthly wisdom, after the characteristic description came its *results;* so in this verse, in the case of the heavenly wisdom. There the results were present; here, future. **fruit . . . sown**—Cf. Psalm 97: 11; Isaiah 61:3, "trees of righteousness." Anticipatory, i.e., the seed whose "fruit," viz., "righteousness," shall be ultimately reaped, is now "sown in peace." "Righteousness," now in germ, when fully developed as "fruit" shall be itself the everlasting *reward* of the righteous. As "sowing in peace" (cf. "*sown in* dishonor," I Cor. 15:43) produces the "fruit of righteousness," so conversely "the work" and "effect of righteousness" is "peace." **of them that make peace**—"by (implying also that it is *for* them, and *to* their good) them that work peace." They, and they alone, are "blessed."

"Peacemakers," not merely they who reconcile others, but who *work peace.* "Cultivate peace" [EST-IUS]. Those truly wise towards God, while peaceable and tolerant towards their neighbors, yet make it their chief concern to sow righteousness, not cloaking men's sins, but reproving them with such peaceable moderation as to be the physicians, rather than the executioners, of sinners [CALVIN].

CHAPTER 4

Vss. 1-17. AGAINST FIGHTINGS AND THEIR SOURCE; WORLDLY LUSTS; UNCHARITABLE JUDGMENTS, AND PRESUMPTUOUS RECKONING ON THE FUTURE. **1. whence**—The cause of quarrels is often sought in external circumstances, whereas internal lusts are the true origin. **wars . . .**—contrasted with the "peace" of heavenly wisdom. "Fightings" are the active carrying on of "wars." The best authorities have a second "whence" before "fightings." Tumults marked the era before the destruction of Jerusalem when James wrote. He indirectly alludes to these. The members are the first seat of war; thence it passes to conflict between man and man, nation and nation. **come they not . . .**—an appeal to their consciences. **lusts**—lit., "pleasures," i.e., the lusts which prompt you to "desire" (*Note,* vs. 2) *pleasures;* whence you seek self at the cost of your neighbor, and hence flow "fightings." **that war**—"campaign, as an army of soldiers encamped within" [ALFORD] the soul; tumultuously war against the interests of your fellow men, while lusting to advance self. But while warring thus against others they (without his knowledge) war against the soul of the man himself, and against the Spirit; therefore they must be "mortified" by the Christian. **2. Ye lust**—A different *Greek* word from that in vs. 1. "Ye desire"; lit., "ye set your *mind* (or heart) *on*" an object. **have not**—The lust of desire does not ensure the actual possession. Hence "ye kill" (not as *Margin,* without any old authority, "envy") to ensure possession. Not probably in the case of professing Christians of that day in a literal sense, but "kill and envy" (as the *Greek* for "desire to have" should be translated), i.e., harass and oppress through envy [DRUSIUS]. Cf. Zechariah 11:5, "slay"; *through envy, hate,* and desire to get out of your way, and so are "murderers" in God's eyes [ESTIUS]. If literal murder [ALFORD] were meant, I do not think it would occur so early in the series; nor had Christians then as yet reached so open criminality. In the Spirit's application of the passage to all ages, literal *killing* is included, flowing from the desire to possess so David and Ahab. There is a climax: "Ye desire," the individual lust for an object; "ye kill and envy," the feeling and action of individuals against individuals; "ye fight and war," the action of many against many. **ye have not, because ye ask not**—God promises to those who pray, not to those who fight. The petition of the lustful, murderous, and contentious is not recognized by God as *prayer.* If ye prayed, there would be no "wars and fightings." Thus this last clause is an answer to the question, vs. 1, "Whence come wars and fightings?" **3.** Some of them are supposed to say in objection, But we do "ask" (pray); cf. vs. 2. James replies, It is not enough to ask for good things, but we must ask with a good spirit and intention. "Ye ask amiss, that ye may consume *it* (your object of prayer) upon (lit., "in") your lusts (lit., "pleasures"); not that ye may have the things you need for the service of God. Contrast ch. 1:5 with Matthew

6:31, 32. If ye prayed aright, all your proper wants would be supplied; the improper cravings which produce "wars and fightings" would then cease. Even believers' prayers are often best answered when their desires are most opposed. **4.** The oldest MSS. omit "adulterers and," and read simply, "Ye adulteresses." God is the rightful husband; the men of the world are regarded collectively as one *adulteress,* and individually as *adulteresses.* **the world**—in so far as the men of it and their motives and acts are aliens to God, e.g., its selfish "lusts" (vs. 3), and covetous and ambitious "wars and fightings" (vs. 1). **enmity**—not merely "inimical"; a state of enmity, and that enmity itself. Cf. I John 2:15, "love . . . the world . . . the love of the Father." **whosoever . . . will be**—The *Greek* is emphatic, "shall *be resolved* to be." Whether he succeed or not, if his *wish* be to be the friend of the world, he *renders himself, becomes* (so the *Greek* for "is") by the very fact, "the enemy of God." Contrast "Abraham the friend of God." **5. in vain** —No word of Scripture can be so. The quotation here, as in Ephesians 5:14, seems to be not so much from a particular passage as one gathered by James under inspiration from the general tenor of such passages in both the Old and New Testaments, as Numbers 14:29; Proverbs 21:20; Galatians 5:17. **spirit that dwelleth in us**—Other MSS. read, "that God hath made to dwell in us" (viz., at Pentecost). If so translated, "Does the (Holy) Spirit that God hath placed in us lust to (towards) envy" (viz., as ye do in your worldly "wars and fightings")? Certainly not; ye are therefore walking in the flesh, not in the Spirit, while ye thus *lust towards,* i.e., *with envy* against one another. The friendship of the world tends to breed *envy;* the Spirit produces very different fruit. ALFORD attributes the epithet "with envy," in the unwarrantable sense of *jealously,* to the Holy Spirit: "The Spirit *jealously desires* us for His own." In *English Version* the sense is, "the (natural) spirit that hath its dwelling in us lusts with (lit., "to," or "towards") envy." Ye lust, and because ye have not what ye lust after (vss. 1, 2), ye envy your neighbor who has, and so the *spirit of envy* leads you on to "fight." James also here refers to ch. 3:14, 16. **6. But**—"Nay, rather." **he** —God. **giveth more grace**—ever increasing grace; the farther ye depart from "envy" [BENGEL]. **he saith**—The same God who causes His spirit to dwell in believers (vs. 5), by the Spirit also speaks in Scripture. The quotation here is probably from Proverbs 3:34; as probably Proverbs 21:10 was generally referred to in vs. 5. In *Hebrew* it is "scorneth the scorners," viz., those who think "Scripture speaketh in vain." **resisteth**—lit., "setteth Himself in array against"; even as they, like Pharaoh, set themselves against Him. God repays sinners in their own coin. "Pride" is the mother of "envy" (vs. 5); it is peculiarly satanic, for by it Satan fell. **the proud**—The *Greek* means in derivation one who *shows himself above* his fellows, and so lifts himself against God. **the humble**—the unenvious, uncovetous, and unambitious as to the world. Contrast vs. 4. **7. Submit to . . . God**—so ye shall be among "the humble," vs. 6; also vs. 10; I Peter 5:6. **Resist . . . devil**—Under his banner *pride* and *envy* are enlisted in the world; resist his temptations to these. Faith, humble prayers, and heavenly wisdom, are the weapons of resistance. The language is taken from warfare. "Submit" as a good soldier puts himself in complete subjection to his captain. "Resist," stand bravely against. **he will flee**— Translate, "he *shall* flee." For it is a promise of

God, not a mere assurance from man to man [ALFORD]. He shall flee worsted as he did from Christ. **8. Draw nigh to God**—So "cleave unto Him," Deuteronomy 30:20, viz., by prayerfully (vss. 2, 3) "resisting Satan," who would oppose our access to God. **he will draw nigh**—propitious. **Cleanse . . . hands**—the outward instruments of action. None but the cleanhanded can ascend into the hill of the Lord (justified through Christ, who alone was perfectly so, and as such "ascended" thither). **purify . . . hearts**—lit., "make chaste" of your spiritual *adultery* (vs. 4, i.e., worldliness) "your hearts": the inward source of all impurity. **double-minded**— divided between God and the world. The "double-minded" is at fault in *heart;* the *sinner* in his *hands* likewise. **9. Be afflicted . . .**—lit., "Endure misery," i.e., mourn over your wretchedness through sin. *Repent with deep sorrow* instead of your present laughter. A blessed *mourning.* Contrast Isaiah 22:12, 13; Luke 6:25. James does not add here, as in ch. 5:1, "howl," where he foretells the *doom of the impenitent* at the coming destruction of Jerusalem. **heaviness**—lit., "falling of the countenance," casting down of the eyes. **10. in the sight of the Lord**—as continually in the presence of Him who alone is worthy to be exalted: recognizing His presence in all your ways, the truest incentive to *humility.* The tree, to grow upwards, must strike its roots deep downwards; so man, to be exalted, must have his mind deep-rooted in humility. In I Peter 5:6, it is, Humble yourselves under the mighty hand of God, viz., in His dealings of Providence: a distinct thought from that here. **lift you up**—in part in this world, fully in the world to come. **11.** Having mentioned sins of the tongue (ch. 3), he shows here that *evil-speaking* flows from the same spirit of exalting self at the expense of one's neighbor as caused the "fightings" reprobated in this chapter (vs. 1). **Speak not evil**—lit., "Speak not against" one another. **brethren**—implying the inconsistency of such depreciatory speaking of one another in *brethren.* **speaketh evil of the law**—for the law in commanding, "Love thy neighbor as thyself" (ch. 2:8), virtually condemns evil-speaking and judging [ESTIUS]. Those who superciliously condemn the acts and words of others which do not please themselves, thus aiming at the reputation of sanctity, put their own moroseness in the place of the law, and claim to themselves a power of censuring above the law of God, condemning what the law permits [CALVIN]. Such a one acts as though the law could not perform its own office of *judging,* but he must fly upon the office [BENGEL]. This is the last mention of the law in the New Testament. ALFORD rightly takes the "law" to be the old moral law applied in its comprehensive spiritual fulness by Christ: "the law of liberty." **if thou judge the law, thou art not a doer . . . but a judge**—Setting aside the Christian *brotherhood* as all alike called to be *doers* of the law, in subjection to it, such a one arrogates the office of a *judge.* **12. There is one lawgiver**—The best authorities read in addition, "and judge." Translate, "There is One (alone) who is (at once) Lawgiver and Judge, (namely) He who is able to save and destroy." Implying, God alone is Lawgiver and therefore Judge, since it is He alone who can execute His judgments; our inability in this respect shows our presumption in trying to act as judges, as though we were God. **who art thou . . .** —The order in the *Greek* is emphatic, "But (inserted in oldest MSS.) thou, who art thou that . . .?" How rashly arrogant in judging thy fellows, and wresting from God the office which belongs to Him over thee and THEM alike! **another**—The oldest authorities read, "thy neighbor." **13. Go to now**—"Come now"; said to excite attention. **ye that say** —*boasting* of the morrow. **Today or tomorrow**—as if ye had the free choice of either day as a certainty. Others read, "Today *and* tomorrow." **such a city**—lit., "this the city" (viz., the one present to the mind of the speaker). *This city here.* **continue . . . a year**—rather, "spend one year." Their language implies that when this one year is out, they purpose similarly settling plans for to come [BENGEL]. **buy and sell**—Their plans for the future are all worldly. **14. what**—lit., "of what nature" is your life? i.e., how evanescent it is. **It is even**—Some oldest authorities read, "For ye are." BENGEL, with other old authorities, reads, "For it shall be, the future referring to the "morrow" (vss. 13-15). The former expresses, "Ye yourselves are transitory"; so everything of yours, even your life, must partake of the same transitoriness. Received text has no old authority. **and then vanisheth away**—"afterwards vanishing as it came"; lit., "afterwards (as it appeared), *so vanishing"* [ALFORD]. **15.** Lit., "instead of your saying . . ." This refers to "ye that say" (vs. 13). **we shall live**—The best MSS. read, "We shall *both* live *and* do. . . ." The boasters spoke as if *life, action,* and the particular kind of action were in their power, whereas all three depend entirely on the will of God. **16. now**—as it is. **rejoice in . . . boastings**—"ye boast in arrogant presumptions," viz., vain confident fancies that the future is certain to you (vs. 13). **rejoicing**—boasting [BENGEL]. **17.** The general principle illustrated by the particular example just discussed is here stated: knowledge without practice is imputed to a man as great and presumptuous sin. James reverts to the principle with which he started. Nothing more injures the soul than wasted impressions. Feelings exhaust themselves and evaporate, if not embodied in practice. As we will not act except we feel, so if we will not act out our feelings, we shall soon cease to feel.

CHAPTER 5

VSS. 1-20. WOES COMING ON THE WICKED RICH: BELIEVERS SHOULD BE PATIENT UNTO THE LORD'S COMING: VARIOUS EXHORTATIONS. **1. Go to now**—Come now. A phrase to call solemn attention. **ye rich**—who have neglected the true enjoyment of riches, which consists in doing good. James intends this address to rich Jewish unbelievers, not so much for themselves, as for the saints, that they may bear with patience the violence of the rich (vs. 7), knowing that God will speedily avenge them on their oppressors [BENGEL]. **miseries that shall come**—lit., "that are coming upon you" unexpectedly and swiftly, viz., at the coming of the Lord (vs. 7); primarily, at the destruction of Jerusalem; finally, at His visible coming to judge the world. **2. corrupted**—*about to be destroyed* through God's curse on your oppression, whereby your riches are accumulated (vs. 4). CALVIN thinks the sense is, Your riches perish without being of any use either to others or even to yourselves, for instance, your garments which are moth-eaten in your chests. **garments . . . moth-eaten**—referring to Matthew 6: 19, 20. **3. is cankered**—"rusted through" [ALFORD]. **rust . . . witness against you**—in the day of judgment; viz., that your riches were of no profit to any, lying unemployed and so contracting rust. **shall eat your flesh**—The rust which once ate your

riches, shall then gnaw your conscience, accompanied with punishment which shall prey upon your bodies for ever. **as . . . fire**—not with the slow process of *rusting,* but with the swiftness of consuming *fire.* **for the last days**—Ye have heaped together, not treasures as ye suppose (cf. Luke 12: 19), but wrath against the last days, viz., the coming judgment of the Lord. ALFORD translates more lit., *"In* these last days (before the coming judgment) ye laid up (worldly) treasure" to no profit, instead of repenting and seeking salvation (see *Note,* vs. 5). **4. Behold**—calling attention to their coming doom as no vain threat. **labourers**—lit., "workmen." **of you kept back**—So *English Version* rightly. Not as ALFORD, "crieth out *from* you." The "keeping back of the hire" was, *on the part* OF the rich, virtually an act of *"fraud,"* because the poor laborers were not immediately paid. The phrase is therefore not, "kept back *by* you," but *"of* you"; the latter implying *virtual,* rather than overt, fraud. James refers to Deuteronomy 24:14, 15, "At this day . . . give his *hire,* neither shall the sun go down upon it, lest he CRY against thee unto the Lord, and it be sin unto thee." Many sins "cry" to heaven for vengeance which men tacitly take no account of, as unchastity and injustice [BENGEL]. Sins peculiarly offensive to God are said to "cry" to Him. The rich ought to have given freely to the poor; their not doing so was sin. A still greater sin was their not paying their debts. Their greatest sin was not paying them to the poor, whose wages is their all. **cries of them**—a double cry; both that of the hire abstractly, and that of the laborers hired. **the Lord of sabaoth**—here only in the New Testament. In Romans 9:29 it is a quotation. It is suited to the Jewish tone of the Epistle. It reminds the rich who think the poor have no protector, that the Lord of the whole hosts in heaven and earth is the guardian and avenger of the latter. He is identical with the "coming Lord" Jesus (vs. 7). **5.** Translate, "Ye have luxuriated . . . and wantoned." The former expresses *luxurious effeminacy;* the latter, *wantonness* and *prodigality.* Their luxury was at the expense of the defrauded poor (vs. 4). **on the earth**—The same earth which has been the scene of your wantonness, shall be the scene of the judgment coming on you: instead of earthly delights ye shall have punishments. **nourished . . . hearts**—i.e., glutted your bodies like beasts to the full extent of your hearts' desire; ye live to eat, not eat to live. **as in a day of slaughter** —The oldest authorities omit "as." Ye are like beasts which eat to their hearts' content *on* the very day of their approaching slaughter, unconscious it is near. The phrase answers to "the last days," vs. 3, which favors ALFORD'S translation there, "in," not "for." **6. Ye have condemned . . . the just**—The *Greek* aorist expresses, "Ye are *accustomed* to condemn . . . the just." Their condemnation of Christ, "the Just," is foremost in James' mind. But all the innocent blood shed, and to be shed, is included, the Holy Spirit comprehending James himself, called "the Just," who was slain in a tumult. See my *Introduction.* This gives a peculiar appropriateness to the expression in this verse, the same "as the righteous (*just*) man" (vs. 16). The justice or righteousness of Jesus and His people is what peculiarly provoked the ungodly great men of the world. **he doth not resist you**—The very patience of the Just one is abused by the wicked as an incentive to boldness in violent persecution, as if they may do as they please with impunity. God doth "resist the proud" (ch. 4:6); but Jesus as man, "as a sheep is dumb before the shearers, so He opened not His mouth": so His people are meek under persecution. The day will come when God will resist (lit., "set Himself in array against") His foes and theirs. **7. Be patient therefore**—as judgment is so near (vss. 1, 3), ye may well afford to be "patient" after the example of the *unresisting Just one* (vs. 6). **brethren**—contrasted with the "rich" oppressors, vss. 1-6. **unto the coming of the Lord** —Christ, when the trial of your patience shall cease. **husbandman waiteth for**—i.e., patiently bears toils and delays through hope of the harvest at last. Its "preciousness" (cf. Ps. 126:6, "precious seed") will more than compensate for all the past. Cf. the same image, Galatians 6:3, 9. **hath long patience for it**—"over it," *in respect to* it. **until he receive**—"until *it* receive" [ALFORD]. Even if *English Version* be retained, the receiving of the early and latter rains is not to be understood as the object of his hope, but *the harvest* for which those rains are the necessary preliminary. The early rain fell at sowing time, about November or December; the latter rain, about March or April, to mature the grain for harvest. The latter rain that shall precede the coming spiritual harvest, will probably be another Pentecost-like effusion of the Holy Ghost. **8. coming ... draweth nigh**—The *Greek* expresses present time and a settled state. I Peter 4:7, "is at hand." We are to live in a continued state of expectancy of the Lord's coming, as an event *always* nigh. Nothing can more "stablish the heart" amidst present troubles than the realized expectation of His speedy coming. **9. Grudge not** —rather "Murmur not"; "grumble not." The *Greek* is lit., "groan": a half-suppressed murmer of impatience and harsh judgment, not uttered aloud or freely. Having exhorted them to patience in bearing wrongs from the wicked, he now exhorts them to a forbearing spirit as to the offenses given by brethren. Christians, who bear the former patiently, sometimes are impatient at the latter, though much less grievous. **lest ... condemned**— The best MS. authorities read, "judged." James refers to Matthew 7:1, "Judge not lest ye be *judged.*" To "murmur against one another" is virtually to *judge,* and so to become liable to be *judged.* **judge ... before the door**—referring to Matthew 24:33. The *Greek* is the same in both passages, and so ought to be translated here as there, "doors," plural. The phrase means "near at hand" (Gen. 4:7, which in the oldest interpretations [the Targums of Jonathan and Jerusalem] is explained, "thy sin is reserved *unto the judgment of the world to come.*" Cf. "the everlasting doors" (Ps. 24:7, whence He shall come forth). The Lord's coming to destroy Jerusalem is primarily referred to; and ultimately, His coming again visibly to judgment. **10. the prophets**—who were especially persecuted, and therefore were especially "blessed." **example of suffering affliction**—rather, simply, "of affliction," lit., "evil treatment." **11. count them happy**—(Matt. 5:10). **which endure**— The oldest authorities read, "which have endured," which suits the sense better than *English Version:* "Those who in past days, like the prophets and Job, have endured trials." Such, not those who "have lived in pleasure and been wanton on the earth" (vs. 5), are "happy." **patience**—rather, "endurance," answering to "endure": the *Greek* words similarly corresponding. Distinct from the *Greek* word for "patience," vs. 10. The same word ought to be translated, "endurance," ch. 1:3. He here reverts to the subject which he began with.

Job—This passage shows the history of him is concerning a real, not an imaginary person; otherwise his case could not be quoted as an example at all. Though he showed much of impatience, yet he always returned to this, that he committed himself wholly to God, and at last showed a perfect spirit of enduring submission. **and have seen**—(with the eyes of your mind). ALFORD translates from the old and genuine reading, "see also ...." The old reading is, however, capable of being translated as *English Version.* **the end of the Lord**—the end which the Lord gave. If Job had much to "endure," remember also Job's happy "end." Hence, learn, though much tried, to "endure to the end." **that**—ALFORD and others translate, "inasmuch as," "for." **pitiful ... of tender mercy**—The former refers to the *feeling;* the latter, to the *act.* His pity is shown in not laying on the *patient endurer* more trials than he is able to bear; His *mercy,* in His giving a happy "end" to the trials [BENGEL]. **12. But above all**—as swearing is utterly alien to the Christian meek "endurance" just recommended. **swear not**—through impatience, to which trials may tempt you (vss. 10, 11). In contrast to this stands the proper use of the tongue, vs. 13. James here refers to Matthew 5:34, etc. **let your yea be yea**— Do not use oaths in your everyday conversation, but let a simple affirmative or denial be deemed enough to establish your word. **condemnation**— lit., "judgment," viz., of "the Judge" who "standeth before the doors" (vs. 9). **13. afflicted**—referring to the "suffering affliction" (vs. 10). **let him pray**—not "swear" in rash impatience. **merry** —joyous in mind. **sing psalms**—of praise. Paul and Silas sang psalms even in affliction. **14. let him call for the elders**—not some *one* of the elders, as Roman Catholics interpret it, to justify their usage in *extreme unction.* The prayers of the elders over the sick would be much the same as though the whole Church which they represent should pray [BENGEL]. **anointing him with oil**— The usage which Christ committed to His apostles was afterwards continued with laying on of hands, as a token of the highest faculty of medicine in the Church, just as we find in I Corinthians 6:2 the Church's highest judicial function. Now that the miraculous gift of healing has been withdrawn for the most part, to use the sign where the reality is wanting would be unmeaning superstition. Cf. other apostolic usages now discontinued rightly, I Corinthians 11:4-15; 16:20. "Let them use oil who can by their prayers obtain recovery for the sick: let those who cannot do this, abstain from using the empty sign" [WHITAKER]. Romish extreme unction is administered to those *whose life is despaired of,* to heal the *soul,* whereas James' unction was to heal the body. CARDINAL CAJETAN (*Commentary*) admits that James cannot refer to extreme unction. Oil in the East, and especially among the Jews (see the Talmud, *Jerusalem* and *Babylon*), was much used as a curative agent. It was also a sign of the divine grace. Hence it was an appropriate sign in performing miraculous cures. **in the name of the Lord**—by whom alone the miracle was performed: men were but the instruments. **15. prayer**—He does not say *the oil* shall save: it is but the symbol. **save**—plainly not as Rome says, "save" *the soul,* but *heal* "the sick": as the words, "the Lord shall raise him up," prove. So the same *Greek* is translated, "made (thee) whole," Matthew 9:21, 22. **and if ... sins**—for not all who are sick are so because of some special sins. Here a case is supposed of one visited with sickness for special sins. **have**

committed—lit., *"be* in a state of *having committed* sins, i.e., be under the consequences of sins committed. **they**—rather, "it": *his having committed sins* shall be forgiven him. The connection of sin and sickness is implied in Isaiah 33:24; Matthew 9: 2-5; John 5:14. The absolution of the sick, retained in the Church of England, refers to the sins which the sick man confesses (vs. 16) and repents of, whereby outward scandal has been given to the Church and the cause of religion; not to sins in their relation to God, the only Judge. **16.** The oldest authorities read, "Confess, THEREFORE . . . ." Not only in the particular case of sickness, but universally confess. **faults**—your *falls* and *offenses,* in relation to one another. The word is not the same as *sins.* Matthew 5:23, 24; Luke 17:4, illustrate the precept here. **one to another**—not to the priest, as Rome insists. The Church of England *recommends* in certain cases. Rome *compels* confession in all cases. Confession is desirable in the case of (1) *wrong* done to a neighbor; (2) when under a troubled conscience we ask *counsel* of a godly minister or friend as to how we may obtain God's forgiveness and strength to sin no more, or when we desire their intercessory prayers for us ("Pray for one another"): "Confession may be made to anyone who can pray" [BENGEL]; (3) *open* confession of sin before the Church and the world, in token of penitence. Not *auricular* confession. **that ye may be healed**—of your bodily sicknesses. Also that, if your sickness be the punishment of sin, the latter being forgiven on intercessory prayer, "ye may be healed" of the former. Also, that ye may be healed spiritually. **effectual**—intense and fervent, not "wavering" (ch. 1:6), [BEZA]. "When *energized"* by the Spirit, as those were who performed miracles [HAMMOND]. This suits the collocation of the Greek words and the sense well. A righteous man's prayer is always heard generally, but his particular request for the *healing* of another was then likely to be granted when he was one *possessing a special charism of the Spirit.* ALFORD translates, "Availeth much *in its working."* The "righteous" is one himself careful to avoid "faults," and showing his faith by works (ch. 2:24). **17. Elias . . . like passions as we**—therefore it cannot be said that he was so raised above us as to afford no example applicable to common mortals like ourselves. **prayed earnestly**—lit., "prayed with prayer": Hebraism for *prayed intensely.* Cf. Luke 22:15,

"With desire I have desired," i.e., earnestly desired. ALFORD is wrong in saying, Elias' prayer that it might not rain "is not even hinted at in the Old Testament history." In I Kings 17:1 it is plainly implied, "As the Lord God of Israel liveth, *before whom I stand,* there shall not be dew nor rain these years, but *according to my word."* His prophecy of the fact was according to a divine intimation given to him in answer to prayer. In jealousy for God's honor (I Kings 19:10), and being of one mind with God in his abhorrence of apostasy, he prayed that the national idolatry should be punished with a national judgment, drought; and on Israel's profession of repentance he prayed for the removal of the visitation, as is implied in I Kings 18:39-42: cf. Luke 4:25. **three years . . .**—Cf. I Kings 18:1, "The third year," viz., from Elijah's going to Zarephath; the prophecy (vs. 1) was probably about five or six months previously. **18. prayed . . . and** —i.e., "and so." Mark the connection between the prayer and its accomplishment. **her fruit**—her usual and due fruit, heretofore withheld on account of sin. Three and a half years is the time also that the two witnesses prophesy who "have power to shut and open heaven that it rain not." **19.** The blessing of reclaiming an erring sinner by the mutual consent and intercessory prayer just recommended. **do err**—more lit., "be led astray." **the truth**—the Gospel doctrine and precepts. **one**—lit., "any"; as *"any"* before. *Everyone* ought to seek the salvation of *everyone* [BENGEL]. **20. Let him**—the converted—**know**—for his comfort, and the encouragement of others to do likewise. **shall save** —future. The salvation of the one so converted shall be manifested hereafter. **shall hide a multitude of sins**—not his own, but the sins of the converted. The *Greek* verb in the middle voice requires this. Proverbs 10:12 refers to charity "covering" the sins of others *before men;* James to one's effecting by the conversion of another that that other's sins be covered *before God,* viz., with Christ's atonement. He effects this by making the convert partaker in the Christian covenant for the remission of all sins. Though this hiding of sins was included in the previous "shall save," James expresses it to mark in detail the greatness of the blessing conferred on the penitent through the converter's instrumentality, and to incite others to the same good deed.

THE FIRST EPISTLE GENERAL OF

PETER

INTRODUCTION

ITS GENUINENESS is attested by II Peter 3:1. On the authority of II Peter, see the *Introduction.* Also by POLY-CARP (in EUSEBIUS, 4. 14), who, in writing to the Philippians, quotes many passages: in ch. 2 he quotes I Peter 1:13, 21, and 3:9; in ch. 5, I Peter 2:11. EUSEBIUS says of PAPIAS *(Ecclesiastical History,* 3. 39*)* that he, too, quotes Peter's First Epistle. IRENÆUS *(Hæreses,* 4. 9. 2) expressly mentions it; and in 4. 16. 5, I Peter 2:16. CLEMENT OF ALEXANDRIA, *Stromata,* 1. 3., p. 544, quotes I Peter 2:11, 12, 15, 16; and p. 562, I Peter 1:21, 22; and 4., p. 584, I Peter 3:14-17; and p. 585, I Peter 4:12-14. ORIGEN (in EUSEBIUS, *Ecclesiastical History,* 6. 25) mentions this Epistle; in *Homily* 7, on Joshua, vol. ii, p. 63, he mentions *both* Epistles; and *Comment.* on Psalm 3 and on John, he mentions I Peter 3:18-21. TERTULLIAN, *Scorp.,* c. 12, quotes expressly I Peter 2:20, 21; and ch. 14, I Peter 2:13, 17. EUSEBIUS states it as the opinion of those before him that this was among *the universally* *acknowledged* Epistles. The *Peschito Syriac Version* contains it. The fragment of the canon called MURATORI's omits it. Excepting this, and the Paulician heretics, who rejected it, all ancient testimony is on its side. The *internal evidence* is equally strong. The author calls himself the apostle Peter, ch. 1:1, and "a witness of Christ's sufferings," and an "elder," ch. 5:1. The energy of the style harmonizes with the warmth of Peter's character; and, as ERASMUS says, this Epistle is full of apostolic dignity and authority and is worthy of the leader among the apostles.

PETER'S PERSONAL HISTORY.—Simon, or Simeon, was a native of Bethsaida on the Sea of Galilee, son of Jonas or John. With his father and his brother Andrew he carried on trade as a fisherman at Capernaum, his subsequent place of abode. He was a married man, and tradition represents his wife's name as *Concordia* or *Perpetua*. CLEMENS ALEXANDRINUS says that she suffered martyrdom, her husband encouraging her to be faithful unto death, "Remember, dear, our Lord." His wife's mother was restored from a fever by Christ. He was brought to Jesus by his brother Andrew, who had been a disciple of John the Baptist, but was pointed to the Saviour as "the Lamb of God" by his master. Jesus, on first beholding him, gave him the name by which chiefly he is known, indicative of his subsequent character and work in the Church, "Peter" (*Greek*) or "Cephas" (*Aramaic*), *a stone*. He did not join our Lord finally until a subsequent period. The leading incidents in his apostolic life are well known: his walking on the troubled waters to meet Jesus, but sinking through doubting; his bold and clear acknowledgment of the divine person and office of Jesus, notwithstanding the difficulties in the way of such belief, whence he was then also designated as *the stone*, or *rock*; but his rebuke of his Lord when announcing what was so unpalatable to carnal prejudices, Christ's coming passion and death; his passing from one extreme to the opposite, in reference to Christ's offer to wash his feet; his self-confident assertion that *he* would never forsake his Lord, whatever others might do, followed by his base denial of Christ thrice with curses; his deep penitence; Christ's full forgiveness and prophecy of his faithfulness unto death, after he had received from him a profession of "love" as often repeated as his previous denial. These incidents illustrate his character as zealous, pious, and ardently attached to the Lord, but at the same time impulsive in feeling, rather than calmly and continuously steadfast. Prompt in action and ready to avow his convictions boldly, he was hasty in judgment, precipitate, and too self-confident in the assertion of his own steadfastness; the result was that, though he abounded in animal courage, his moral courage was too easily overcome by fear of man's opinion. A wonderful change was wrought in him by his restoration after his fall, through the grace of his risen Lord. His zeal and ardor became sanctified, being chastened by a spirit of unaffected humility. His love to the Lord was, if possible, increased, while his mode of manifesting it now was in doing and suffering for His name, rather than in loud protestations. Thus, when imprisoned and tried before the Sanhedrim for preaching Christ, he boldly avowed his determination to continue to do so. He is well called "the mouth of the apostles." His faithfulness led to his apprehension by Herod Agrippa, with a view to his execution, from which, however, he was delivered by the angel of the Lord.

After the ascension he took the lead in the Church; and on the descent of the Holy Spirit at Pentecost, he exercised the designed power of "the keys" of Christ's kingdom, by opening the door of the Church, in preaching, for the admission of thousands of Israelites; and still more so in opening (in obedience to a special revelation) an entrance to the "devout" (i.e., Jewish proselyte from heathendom) *Gentile*, Cornelius: the forerunner of the harvest gathered in from *idolatrous* Gentiles at Antioch. This explains in what sense Christ used as to him the words, "Upon this rock I will build my Church," viz., on the preaching of Christ, the true "Rock," by connection with whom only he was given the designation: a title shared in common on the same grounds by the rest of the apostles, as the first founders of the Church on Christ, "the chief cornerstone." A name is often given in Hebrew, not that the person is actually the thing itself, but has some special relation to it; as Elijah means *Mighty Jehovah*, so Simon is called Peter "the rock," not that he is so, save by connection with Jesus, the only true Rock (Isa. 28:16; I Cor. 3:11). As subsequently he identified himself with "Satan," and is therefore *called so*, in the same way, by his clear confession of Christ, the Rock, he became identified with Him, and is accordingly so called. It is certain that there is no instance on record of Peter's having ever claimed or exercised supremacy; on the contrary, he is represented as *sent* by the apostles at Jerusalem to confirm the Samaritans baptized by Philip the deacon; again at the council of Jerusalem, not he, but James the president, or leading bishop in the Church of that city, pronounced the authoritative decision: Acts 15:19, "My *sentence* is . . . A kind of primacy, doubtless (though certainly not supremacy), was given him on the ground of his age, and prominent earnestness, and boldness in taking the lead on many important occasions. Hence he is called "first" in enumerating the apostles. Hence, too, arise the phrases, "Peter and the Eleven," "Peter and the rest of the apostles"; and Paul, in going up to Jerusalem after his conversion, went to see Peter in particular.

Once only he again betrayed the same spirit of vacillation through fear of man's reproach which had caused his denial of his Lord. Though at the Jerusalem council he advocated the exemption of Gentile converts from the ceremonial observances of the law, yet he, after having associated in closest intercourse with the Gentiles at Antioch, withdrew from them, through dread of the prejudices of his Jewish brethren who came from James, and timidly dissembled his conviction of the religious equality of Jew and Gentile; for this Paul openly withstood and rebuked him: a plain refutation of his alleged *supremacy* and *infallibility* (except where specially inspired, as in writing his Epistles). In all other cases he showed himself to be, indeed, as Paul calls him, "a pillar." Subsequently we find him in "Babylon," whence he wrote this First Epistle to the Israelite believers of the dispersion, and the Gentile Christians united in Christ, in Pontus, Galatia, Cappadocia, Asia, and Bithynia.

JEROME (*De Scriptorum Ecclesiasticorum*, 1) states that "Peter, after having been bishop of Antioch, and after having preached to the believers of the circumcision in Pontus, etc. [plainly inferred from ch. 1:1], in the second year of Claudius went to Rome to refute Simon Magus, and for twenty-five years there held the episcopal chair, down to the last year of Nero, i.e., the 14th, by whom he was crucified with his head downwards, declaring himself unworthy to be crucified as his Lord, and was buried in the Vatican, near the triumphal way." EUSEBIUS,

Chron. Ann. 3, also asserts his episcopate at Antioch; his assertion that Peter founded that Church contradicts Acts 11:19–22. His journey to Rome to oppose Simon Magus arose from JUSTIN's story of the statue found at Rome (really the statue of the Sabine god, *Semo Sancus,* or Hercules, mistaken as if Simon Magus were worshipped by that name, "Simoni Deo Sancto"; found in the Tiber in 1574, or on an island in the Tiber in 1662), combined with the account in Acts 8:9–24. The twenty-five years' bishopric is chronologically impossible, as it would make Peter, at the interview with Paul at Antioch, to have been then for some years bishop of Rome! His crucifixion is certain from Christ's prophecy, John 21:18, 19. DIONYSIUS OF CORINTH (in EUSEBIUS, *Ecclesiastical History,* 2. 25) asserted in an epistle to the Romans that Paul and Peter planted both the Roman and Corinthian churches, and endured martyrdom in Italy at the same time. So TERTULLIAN, *Contra Marcion,* 4. 5, and *Præscriptio Hæreticorum,* c. 36, 38. Also CAIUS, the presbyter of Rome, in EUSEBIUS (*Ecclesiastical History,* 2. 25) asserts that some memorials of their martyrdom were to be seen at Rome on the road to Ostia. So EUSEBIUS, *Ecclesiastical History,* 2. 25, and *Demonstratio Evangelicæ,* 3. 116. So LACTANTIUS, *De Mortibus Persecutorum,* c. 2. Many of the details are palpably false; whether the *whole* be so or not is dubious, considering the tendency to concentrate at Rome events of interest. [ALFORD]. What is certain is, that Peter was not there before the writing of the Epistle to the Romans (A.D. 58). otherwise he would have been mentioned in it; nor during Paul's first imprisonment at Rome, otherwise he would have been mentioned in some one of Paul's many other Epistles written from Rome; nor during Paul's second imprisonment, at least when he was writing the Second Epistle to Timothy, just before his martyrdom. He *may* have gone to Rome after Paul's death, and, as common tradition represents, been imprisoned in the Mamertine dungeon, and crucified on the Janiculum, on the eminence of St. Pietro in Montorio, and his remains deposited under the great altar in the center of the famous basilica of St. Peter. AMBROSE (*Ep.* 33, *Ed. Paris,* 1586, p. 1022) relates that St. Peter, not long before his death, being overcome by the solicitations of his fellow Christians to save himself, was fleeing from Rome when he was met by our Lord, and on asking, "Lord, whither goest Thou?" received the answer, "I go to be crucified afresh." On this he returned and joyfully went to martyrdom. The church called "*Domine quo vadis,*" on the Appian Way, commemorates the legend. It is not unlikely that the whole tradition is built on the connection which existed between Paul and Peter. As Paul, "the apostle of the uncircumcision," wrote Epistles to Galatia, Ephesus, and Colosse, and to Philemon at Colosse, making the Gentile Christians the persons prominently addressed, and the Jewish Christians subordinately so; so, vice versa, Peter, "the apostle of the circumcision," addressed the same churches, the Jewish Christians in them primarily, and the Gentile Christians also, secondarily.

TO WHOM HE ADDRESSES THIS EPISTLE.—The heading, ch. 1:1, "to the elect strangers (spiritually *pilgrims*) *of the dispersion*" (*Greek*), clearly marks the Christians of the *Jewish* dispersion as prominently addressed, but still including also *Gentile* Christians as grafted into the Christian Jewish stock by adoption and faith, and so being part of the true Israel. Ch. 1:14; 2:9, 10; 3:6; and 4:3 clearly prove this. Thus he, the apostle of the circumcision, sought to unite in one Christ Jew and Gentile, promoting thereby the same work and doctrine as Paul the apostle of the uncircumcision. The provinces are named by Peter in the heading in the order proceeding from northeast to south and west. Pontus was the country of the Christian Jew Aquila. To Galatia Paul paid two visits, founding and confirming churches. Crescens, his companion, went there about the time of Paul's last imprisonment, just before his martyrdom. Ancyra was subsequently its ecclesiastical metropolis. Men of Cappadocia, as well as of "Pontus" and "Asia," were among the hearers of Peter's effective sermon on the Pentecost whereon the Spirit decended on the Church; these probably brought home to their native land the first tidings of the Gospel. Proconsular "Asia" included Mysia, Lydia, Caria, Phrygia, Pisidia, and Lyaconia. In Lycaonia were the churches of Iconium, founded by Paul and Barnabas; of Lystra, Timothy's birthplace, where Paul was stoned at the instigation of the Jews; and of Derbe, the birthplace of Gaius, or Caius. In Pisidia was Antioch, where Paul was the instrument of converting many, but was driven out by the Jews. In Caria was Miletus, containing doubtless a Christian Church. In Phrygia, Paul preached both times when visiting Galatia in its neighborhood, and in it were the churches of Laodicea, Hierapolis, and Colosse, of which last Church Philemon and Onesimus were members, and Archippus and Epaphras leaders. In Lydia was the Philadelphian Church, favorably noticed in Revelation 3:7, etc.; that of Sardis, the capital, and of Thyatira, and of Ephesus, founded by Paul, and a scene of the labors of Aquila and Priscilla and Apollos, and subsequently of more than two whole years' labor of Paul again, and subsequently censured for falling from its first love in Revelation 2:4. Smyrna of Ionia was in the same quarter, and as one of the seven churches receives unqualified praise. In Mysia was Pergamos. Troas, too, is known as the scene of Paul's preaching and raising Eutychus to life, and of his subsequently staying for a time with Carpus. Of "Bithynia," no Church is expressly named in Scripture elsewhere. When Paul at an earlier period "assayed to go into Bithynia," the Spirit suffered him not. But afterwards, we infer from ch. 1:1, the Spirit did impart the Gospel to that country, possibly by Peter's ministry, In government, these several churches, it appears from this Epistle (ch. 5:1, 2, "Feed . . ."), were much in the same states as when Paul addressed the Ephesian "elders" at Miletus (Acts 20:17, 28, "feed") in very similar language; elders or presbyter-bishops ruled, while the apostles exercised the general superintendence. They were exposed to persecutions, though apparently not systematic, but rather annoyances and reproach arising from their not joining their heathen neighbors in riotous living, into which, however, some of them were in danger of falling. The evils which existed among themselves, and which are therefore reproved, were ambition and lucre-seeking on the part of the presbyters (ch. 5:2, 3), evil thoughts and words among the members in general, and a want of sympathy and generosity towards one another.

HIS OBJECT seems to be, by the prospect of their heavenly portion and by Christ's example, to afford consolation to the persecuted, and prepare them for a greater approaching ordeal, and to exhort all, husbands, wives, servants, presbyters, and people, to a due discharge of relative duties, so as to give no handle to the enemy to reproach Christianity, but rather to win them to it, and so to establish them in "the true grace of God wherein they stand" (ch. 5:12). See, however, *note* there, on the oldest reading. ALFORD rightly argues that "exhorting and testifying" there, refer to Peter's *exhortations* throughout the Epistle grounded on *testimony* which he bears *to the Gospel truth, already well known to his readers by the teaching of Paul in those churches.* They were already introduced "into" (so the *Greek*, ch. 5:12) this *grace of God* as their safe *standing-ground.* Cf. I Corinthians 15:1, "I declare unto you the Gospel *wherein ye stand.*" Therefore he does not, in this Epistle, set forth a complete statement of this Gospel doctrine of grace, but falls back on it as already known. Cf. ch. 1:8, 18, "ye know"; 3:15; II Peter 3:1. Not that Peter servilely copies the style and mode of teaching of Paul, but as an independent witness in his own style attests the same truths. We may divide the Epistle into: (I) The inscription (ch. 1:1, 2). (II) The stirring-up of a pure feeling in believers as born again of God. By the motive of *hope* to which God has regenerated us (vss. 3–12); bringing forth the fruit of *faith*, considering the costly price paid for our redemption from sin (vss. 14–21). Being purified by the Spirit unto *love* of the brethren as begotten of God's eternal word, as spiritual priest-kings, to whom alone Christ is precious (vs. 22; ch. 2:10); after Christ's example in suffering, maintaining a good *conversation* in every relation (vs. 10; ch. 3:14), and a good *profession* of faith as having in view Christ's once-offered sacrifice, and His future coming to judgment (vs. 15; ch. 4:11); and exhibiting *patience* in *adversity*, as looking for future glorification with Christ, (I) in general as Christians, vs. 12–19; (2) each in his own sphere, ch. 5:1–11. "The title 'Beloved' marks the separation of the second part from the first, ch. 2:11; and of the third part from the second," ch. 4:12 [BENGEL]. (III). The conclusion.

TIME AND PLACE OF WRITING.—It was plainly before the open and *systematic* persecution of the later years of Nero had begun. That this Epistle was written after Paul's Epistles, even those written during his imprisonment at Rome, ending in A.D. 63, appears from the acquaintance which Peter in this Epistle shows he has with them. Cf. ch. 2:13 with I Timothy 2:2–4; 2:18 with Ephesians 6:5; 1:2 with Ephesians 1:4–7; 1:3 with Ephesians 1:3; 1:14 with Romans 12:2; 2:6–10 with Romans 9:32, 33; 2:13 with Romans 13:1–4; 2:16 with Galatians 5:13; 2:18 with Ephesians 6:5; 3:1 with Ephesians 5:22; 3:9 with Romans 12:17; 4:9 with Philippians 2:14 and Romans 12:13 and Hebrews 13:2; 4:10 with Romans 12:6–8; 5:1 with Romans 8:18; 5:5 with Ephesians 5:21; Philippians 2:3, 5–8; 5:8 with I Thessalonians 5:6; 5:14 with I Corinthians 16:20. Moreover, in ch. 5:13, Mark is mentioned as with Peter in Babylon. This must have been after Colossians 4:10 (A.D. 61–63), when Mark was with Paul at Rome, but intending to go to Asia Minor. Again, in II Timothy 4:11 (A.D. 67 or 68), Mark was in or near Ephesus, in Asia Minor, and Timothy is told to bring him to Rome. So that it is likely it was after this, viz., after Paul's martyrdom, that Mark joined Peter, and consequently that this Epistle was written. It is not likely that Peter would have entrenched on Paul's field of labor, the churches of Asia Minor, *during Paul's lifetime.* The death of the apostle of the uncircumcision, and the consequent need of someone to follow up his teachings, probably gave occasion to the testimony given by Peter to the same churches, collectively addressed, in behalf of the same truth. The relation in which the Pauline Gentile churches stood towards the apostles at Jerusalem favors this view. Even the Gentile Christians would naturally look to the spiritual fathers of the Church at Jerusalem, the center whence the Gospel had emanated to them, for counsel wherewith to meet the pretensions of Judaizing Christians and heretics; and Peter, always prominent among the apostles in Jerusalem, would even when elsewhere feel a deep interest in them, especially when they were by death bereft of Paul's guidance. BIRKS (*Horæ Evangelicae*) suggests that false teachers may have appealed from Paul's doctrine to that of James and Peter. Peter then would naturally write to confirm the doctrines of grace and tacitly show there was no difference between his teaching and Paul's. BIRKS prefers dating the Epistle A.D. 58, after Paul's second visit to Galatia, when Silvanus was with him, and so could not have been with Peter (A.D. 54), and before his imprisonment at Rome, when Mark was with him, and so could not have been with Peter (A.D. 62); perhaps when Paul was detained at Cæsarea, and so debarred from personal intercourse with those churches. I prefer the view previously stated. This sets aside the tradition that Paul and Peter suffered martyrdom together at Rome. ORIGEN'S and EUSEBIUS' statement that Peter visited the churches of Asia in person seems very probable.

The PLACE OF WRITING was doubtless Babylon on the Euphrates (ch. 5:13). It is most improbable that in the midst of writing matter-of-fact communications and salutations in a remarkably plain Epistle, the symbolical language of prophecy viz., "Babylon" for *Rome*) should be used. JOSEPHUS (*Antiquities*, 15. 2, 2; 3. 1) states that there was a *great multitude of Jews* in the Chaldean Babylon; it is therefore likely that "the apostle of the circumcision" would at some time or other visit them. Some have maintained that the Babylon meant was in Egypt because Mark preached in and around Alexandria after Peter's death, and therefore it is likely he did so along with that apostle in the same region previously. But no mention elsewhere in *Scripture* is made of this Egyptian Babylon, but only of the Chaldean one. And though towards the close of Caligula's reign a persecution drove the Jews thence to Seleucia, and a plague five years after still further thinned their numbers, yet this does not preclude their return and multiplication during the twenty years that elapsed between the plague and the writing of the Epistle. Moreover, the order in which the countries are enumerated, from northeast to south and west, is such as would be adopted by one writing from the Oriental Babylon on the Euphrates, not from Egypt or Rome. Indeed, COSMAS INDICOPLEUSTES, in the sixth century, understood the Babylon meant to be *outside* the Roman empire. Silvanus, Paul's companion, became subsequently Peter's, and was the carrier of this Epistle.

STYLE.—Fervor and practical truth, rather than logical reasoning, are the characteristics, of this Epistle, as they were of its energetic, warm-hearted writer. His familiarity with Paul's Epistles shown in the language accords with what we should expect from the fact of Paul's having "communicated the Gospel which he preached among the Gentiles" (as revealed specially to him) to Peter among others "of reputation". Individualities occur, such as baptism, "the answer of a good conscience toward God" (ch. 4:21); "consciousness of God" (*Greek*), ch. 2:19, as a motive for enduring sufferings; "living hope" (ch. 1:3); "an inheritance incorruptible, undefiled, and that fadeth not away" (ch. 1:4); "kiss of charity" (ch. 5:14). Christ is viewed less in relation to His past sufferings than as at present exalted and hereafter to be manifested in all His majesty. *Glory* and *hope* are prominent features in this Epistle (ch. 1:8), so much so that WEISS entitles him "the apostle of hope." The realization of future bliss as near causes him to regard believers as but "strangers" and "sojourners" here. Chastened fervor, deep humility, and ardent love appear, just as we should expect from one who had been so graciously restored after his grievous fall. "Being converted," he truly does "strengthen his brethren." His fervor shows itself in often repeating the same thought in similar words.

In some passages he shows familiarity with the Epistle of James, the apostle of special weight with the Jewish legalizing party, whose inspiration he thus confirms (cf. ch. 1:6, 7 with Jas. 1:2, 3; 1:24 with Jas. 1:10; 2:1 with Jas. 1:21; 4:8 with Jas. 5:20, both quoting Prov. 10:12; 5:5 with Jas. 4:6, both quoting Prov. 3:34). In most of these cases Old Testament quotations are the common ground of both. "Strong susceptibility to outward impressions, liveliness of feeling, dexterity in handling subjects, dispose natures like that of Peter to repeat afresh the thoughts of others" [STEIGER].

The diction of this Epistle and of his speeches in Acts is very similar: an undesigned coincidence, and so a mark of genuineness (cf. ch. 2:7 with Acts 4:11; 1:12 with Acts 5:32; 2:24 with Acts 5:30; 10:39; 5:1 with Acts 2:32; 3:15; 1:10 with Acts 3:18; 10:43; 1:21 with Acts 3:15; 10:40; 4:5 with Acts 10:42; 2:24 with Acts 3:19, 26).

There is, too, a recurrence to the language of the Lord at the last interview after His resurrection, recorded in John 21. Cf. "the Shepherd . . . of . . . souls," ch. 2:25; "Feed the flock of God," "the chief Shepherd," ch. 5:2, 4, with John 21:15–17; "Feed My lambs . . .sheep"; also "Whom . . . ye *love*," ch. 1:8; 2:7, with John 21:15–17; "lovest thou Me?" and II Peter 1:14, with John 21:18, 19. WIESINGER well says, "He who in loving impatience cast himself into the sea to meet the Lord, is also the man who most earnestly testifies to the hope of His return; he who dated his own faith from the sufferings of his Master, is never weary in holding up the suffering form of the Lord before his readers to comfort and stimulate them; he before whom the death of a martyr is in assured expectation, is the man who, in the greatest variety of aspects, sets forth the duty, as well as the consolation, of suffering for Christ; as a rock of the Church he grounds his readers against the storm of present tribulation on the true Rock of ages."

CHAPTER 1

Vss. 1-25. ADDRESS TO THE ELECTED OF THE GODHEAD: THANKSGIVING FOR THE LIVING HOPE TO WHICH WE ARE BEGOTTEN, PRODUCING JOY AMIDST SUFFERINGS: THIS SALVATION AN OBJECT OF DEEPEST INTEREST TO PROPHETS AND TO ANGELS: ITS COSTLY PRICE A MOTIVE TO HOLINESS AND LOVE, AS WE ARE BORN AGAIN OF THE EVER-ABIDING WORD OF GOD.
1. Peter—*Greek* form of Cephas, *man of rock*. **an apostle of Jesus Christ**—"He who preaches otherwise than as a messenger of Christ, is not to be heard; if he preach as such, then it is all one as if thou didst hear Christ speaking in thy presence" [LUTHER]. **to the strangers scattered**—lit., "sojourners *of the dispersion*"; only in John 7:35 and James 1:1, in New Testament, and LXX, Psalm 147:2, "the outcasts of Israel"; the designation peculiarly given to *the Jews* in their dispersed state throughout the world ever since the Babylonian captivity. These he, as the apostle of the circumcision, primarily addresses, but not in the limited temporal sense only; he regards their temporal condition as a shadow of their spiritual calling to be *strangers* and pilgrims on earth, looking for the heavenly Jerusalem as their home. So the *Gentile* Christians, as the spiritual Israel, are included secondarily, as having the same high calling. He (ch. 1:14; 2:10; 4:3) plainly refers to Christian *Gentiles* (cf. vs. 17; ch. 2:11). Christians, if they rightly consider their calling, must never settle themselves here, but feel themselves *travellers*. As the Jews in their *dispersion* diffused through the nations the knowledge of the one God, preparatory to Christ's first advent, so Christians, by their dispersion among the unconverted, diffuse the knowledge of Christ, preparatory to His second advent. "The children of God scattered abroad" constitute one whole in Christ, who "gathers them together in one," now partially and in Spirit, hereafter perfectly and visibly. "Elect," in the *Greek* order, comes before "strangers"; *elect*, in relation to heaven, *strangers*, in relation to the earth. The *election* here is that of individuals to eternal life by the sovereign grace of God, as the sequel shows. "While each is certified of his own election by the

Spirit, he receives no assurance concerning others, nor are we to be too inquisitive [John 21:21, 22]; Peter numbers them among the *elect*, as they carried the appearance of having been regenerated" [CALVIN]. He calls the whole Church by the designation strictly belonging only to the better portion of them [CALVIN]. The election to *hearing*, and that to *eternal life*, are distinct. Realization of our election is a strong motive to holiness. The minister invites all, yet he does not hide the truth that in none but the elect will the preaching effect eternal blessing. As the chief fruit of exhortations, and even of threatenings, redounds to "the elect"; therefore, at the outset, Peter addresses *them*. STEIGER translates, to "the elect pilgrims who form the dispersion in Pontus . . . ." The *order* of the provinces is that in which they would be viewed by one writing from the east from *Babylon* (ch. 5:13); from northeast southwards to Galatia, southeast to Cappadocia, then Asia, and back to Bithynia, west of Pontus. Contrast the order, Acts 2:9. He now was ministering to those same peoples as he preached to on Pentecost: "Parthians, Medes, Elamites, dwellers in Mesopotamia and Judea," i.e., the Jews now subject to the Parthians, whose capital was *Babylon*, where he labored in person; "dwellers in Cappadocia, Pontus, Asia, Phrygia, Bithynia," the Asiatic dispersion derived from Babylon, whom he ministers to by letter. **2. foreknowledge**—*foreordaining* love (vs. 20), inseparable from God's *foreknowledge*, the origin *from* which, and pattern *according to* which, election takes place. Acts 2:23, and Romans 11:2, prove "foreknowledge" to be *foreordination*. God's *foreknowledge* is not the perception of any ground of action out of Himself; still in it liberty is comprehended, and all absolute constraint debarred [ANSELM *in* STEIGER]. For so the Son of God was "foreknown" (so the *Greek* for "foreordained," vs. 20) to be the sacrificial Lamb, not against, or without His will, but His will rested in the will of the Father; this includes self-conscious action; nay, even cheerful acquiescense. The *Hebrew* and *Greek* "know" include *approval* and *acknowledging* as one's own. The *Hebrew* marks the oneness of *loving* and *choosing*, by having one word for both, *bachar* (LXX, *Greek, hairetizo*). Peter descends from the eternal "election" of God through the *new birth,* to the believer's "sanctification," that from this he might again raise them through the consideration of their *new birth* to a "living hope" of the heavenly "inheritance" [HEIDEGGER]. The divine three are introduced in their respective functions in redemption. **through**—*Greek,* "in", the element in which we are elected. The "election" of God realized and manifested itself "IN" their sanctification. Believers are "sanctified through the offering of Christ once for all" (Heb. 10:10). "Thou must believe and know that thou art holy; not, however, through thine own piety, but through the blood of Christ" [LUTHER]. This is the true sanctification of the Spirit, to obey the Gospel, to trust in Christ [BULLINGER]. **sanctification**—the Spirit's setting apart of the saint as consecrated to God. The execution of God's *choice* (Gal. 1:4). God the Father gives us salvation by gratuitous election; the Son earns it by His blood-shedding; the Holy Spirit applies the merit of the Son to the soul by the Gospel word [CALVIN]. Cf. Numbers 6:24-26, the Old Testament triple blessing. **unto obedience**—the result or *end aimed at* by God as respects us, the *obedience* which consists in faith, and that which flows from faith; "obeying the truth through the Spirit" (vs. 22). Romans 1:5, "obedience to the faith," and obedience the fruit of faith. **sprinkling . . .**—not in justification through the atonement once for all, which is expressed in the previous clauses, but (as the order proves) *the daily being sprinkled by Christ's blood, and so cleansed from all sin,* which is the privilege of one already justified and "walking in the light." **Grace**—the source of "peace." **be multiplied**—still further than already. Daniel 4:1, "Ye have now peace and grace, but still not in perfection; therefore, ye must go on increasing until the old Adam be dead" [LUTHER]. **3.** He begins, like Paul, in opening his Epistles with giving thanks to God for the greatness of the salvation; herein he looks forward (1) into the future (vss. 3-9); (2) backward into the past (vss. 10-12) [ALFORD]. **Blessed**—A distinct *Greek* word (*eulogetos,* "Blessed BE") is used of God, from that used of man (*eulogemenos,* "Blessed IS"). **Father**—This whole Epistle accords with the Lord's prayer; "Father," ch. 1:3, 14, 17, 23; 2:2; "Our," ch. 1:4, end; "In heaven," ch. 1:4; "Hallowed be Thy name," ch. 1:15, 16; 3:15; "Thy kingdom come," ch. 2:9; "Thy will be done," ch. 2:15; 3:17; 4:2, 19; "daily bread," ch. 5:7; "forgiveness of sins," ch. 4:8, 1; "temptation," ch. 4:12; "deliverance," ch. 4:18 [BENGEL]; cf. ch. 3:7 and 4:7, for allusions to *prayer.* Barak, Hebrew "bless," is lit. "kneel." God, as the original source of blessing, must be blessed through all His works. **abundant** —*Greek,* "much," "full." That God's "mercy" should meet *us,* guilty and enemies, proves its fulness. "Mercy" met our *misery;* "grace," our *guilt.* **begotten us again**—of the *Spirit* by the *word* (vs. 23); whereas we were children of wrath naturally, and *dead* in sins. **unto**—so that we have. **lively**—*Greek,* "living." It has life in itself, gives life, and looks for life as its object [DE WETTE]. *Living* is a favorite expression of Peter (vs. 23; ch. 2:4, 5). He delights in contemplating *life* overcoming death in the believer. *Faith* and *love* follow *hope* (vss. 8, 21, 22). "(Unto) a lively hope" is further explained by "(To) an inheritance incorruptible . . . fadeth not away," and "(unto) salvation . . . ready to be revealed in the last time." I prefer with BENGEL and STEIGER to join as in *Greek,* "Unto a

hope *living* (possessing life and vitality) *through* the resurrection of Jesus Christ." Faith, the subjective means of the spiritual resurrection of the soul, is wrought by the same power whereby Christ was raised from the dead. Baptism is an objective means (ch. 3:21). Its moral fruit is a new life. The connection of our sonship with the resurrection appears also in Luke 20:36; Acts 13:33. Christ's resurrection is the cause of ours, (1) as an efficient cause (I Cor. 15:22); (2) as an exemplary cause, all the saints being about to rise after the similitude of His resurrection. Our "hope" is, Christ rising from the dead hath ordained the power, and is become the pattern of the believer's resurrection. The soul, born again from its natural state into the life of grace, is after that born again unto the life of glory. Matthew 19:28, "regeneration, when the Son of man shall sit in the throne of His glory"; the resurrection of our bodies is a kind of coming out of the womb of the earth and entering upon immortality, a nativity into another life [BISHOP PEARSON]. The four causes of our salvation are; (1) the primary cause, God's mercy; (2) the proximate cause, Christ's death and resurrection; (3) the formal cause, our regeneration; (4) the final cause, our eternal bliss. As John is the disciple of *love,* so Paul of *faith,* and Peter of *hope.* Hence, Peter, most of all the apostles, urges the resurrection of Christ; an undesigned coincidence between the history and the Epistle, and so a proof of genuineness. Christ's resurrection was the occasion of his own restoration by Christ after his fall. **4. To an inheritance**—the object of our "hope" (vs. 3), which is therefore not a *dead,* but a *"living"* hope. The inheritance is the believer's already by title, being actually assigned to him; the entrance on its possession is future, and hoped for as a certainty. Being "begotten again" as a "son," he is an "heir," as earthly fathers *beget* children who shall *inherit* their goods. The *inheritance* is "salvation" (vss. 5, 9); "the grace to be brought at the revelation of Christ" (vs. 13); "a crown of glory that fadeth not away." **incorruptible**—not having within the germs of death. Negations of the imperfections which meet us on every side here are the chief means of conveying to our minds a conception of the heavenly things which "have not entered into the heart of man," and which we have not faculties now capable of fully knowing. Peter, sanguine, impulsive, and highly susceptible of outward impressions, was the more likely to feel painfully the deepseated *corruption* which, lurking under the outward splendor of the loveliest of earthly things, dooms them soon to rottenness and decay. **undefiled**—not stained as earthly goods by sin, either in the acquiring, or in the using of them; unsusceptible of any stain. "The rich man is either a dishonest man himself, or the heir of a dishonest man" [JEROME]. Even Israel's inheritance was *defiled* by the people's sins. Defilement intrudes even on our holy things now, whereas God's service ought to be undefiled. **that fadeth not away**—Contrast vs. 24. Even the most delicate part of the heavenly inheritance, its bloom, continues *unfading.* "In *substance* incorruptible; in *purity* undefiled; in *beauty* unfading" [ALFORD]. **reserved**—*kept up* (Col. 1:5, "laid up for you in heaven," II Tim. 4:8); *Greek* perfect, expressing a *fixed and abiding state,* "which has been and is reserved." The inheritance is in security, beyond risk, out of the reach of Satan, though we for whom it is reserved are still in the midst of dangers. Still, if we be believers, we too, as well as the inheritance, are "kept" (the same

Greek, John 17:12) by Jesus safely (vs. 5). **in heaven**–*Greek,* "in the heavens," where it can neither be destroyed nor plundered. It does not follow that, because it is *now* laid up in *heaven,* it shall not *hereafter* be on *earth* also. **for you**–It is secure not only in itself from all misfortune, but also from all alienation, so that no other can receive it in your stead. He had said US (vs. 3; he now turns his address to the elect in order to encourage and exhort them. **5. kept**–*Greek,* "who are being guarded." He answers the objection, Of what use is it that salvation is "reserved" for us in heaven, as in a calm secure haven, when we are tossed in the world as on a troubled sea in the midst of a thousand wrecks? [CALVIN]. As the inheritance is "kept" (vs. 4) safely for the far distant "heirs," so must they be "guarded" in their persons so as to be sure of reaching it. Neither shall it be wanting to them, nor they to it. "We are *guarded in the world* as our inheritance is *kept in heaven.*" This defines the "you" of vs. 4. The inheritance, remember, belongs only to those who "endure unto the end," being "guarded" by, or IN "the power of God, through *faith.*" Contrast Luke 8:13. God Himself is our sole *guarding power.* "It is His *power* which saves us from our enemies. It is His *long-suffering* which saves us from ourselves" [BENGEL]. Jude 1, "preserved in Christ Jesus"; Philippians 1:6; 4:7, "keep"; *Greek,* "guard," as here. This guarding is effected, on the part of God, by His "power," the efficient cause; on the part of man, "through faith," the effective means. **by**–*Greek,* "in." The believer lives spiritually *in* God, and in virtue of His power, and God lives in him. "In" marks that the cause is inherent in the means, working organically through them with living influence, so that the means, in so far as the cause works organically through them, exist also in the cause. The power of God which guards the believer is no external force working upon him from without with mechanical necessity, but the spiritual power of God in which he lives, and with whose Spirit he is clothed. It comes down on, and then dwells in him, even as he is in it [STEIGER]. Let none flatter himself he is being guarded by the power of God unto salvation, if he be not walking by faith. Neither speculative knowledge and reason, nor works of seeming charity, will avail, severed from *faith.* It is through faith that salvation is both received and kept. **unto salvation**–the final end of the new birth. "Salvation," not merely accomplished for us in title by Christ, and made over to us on our believing, but *actually manifested, and finally completed.* **ready to be revealed**–When Christ shall be revealed, it shall be revealed. The preparations for it are being made now, and began when Christ came: "All things are now *ready*"; the salvation is already accomplished, and only waits the Lord's time to be manifested: He "is ready to judge." **last time**–the last day, closing the day of grace; the day of judgment, of redemption, of the restitution of all things, and of perdition of the ungodly. **6. Wherein**–in which prospect of final salvation. **greatly rejoice**–"exult with joy": "are exuberantly glad." *Salvation* is realized by faith (vs. 9) as a thing so actually present as to cause exulting joy in spite of existing afflictions. **for a season**–*Greek,* "for a little time." **if need be**–"if it be God's will that it should be so" [ALFORD], for not all believers are afflicted. One need not invite or lay a cross on himself, but only "take up" the cross which God imposes ("his cross"). II Timothy 3:12 is not to be pressed too

far. Not every believer, nor every sinner, is tried with afflictions [THEOPHYLACT]. Some falsely think that notwithstanding our forgiveness in Christ, a kind of atonement, or expiation by suffering, is needed. **ye are in heaviness**–*Greek,* "ye were grieved." The "grieved" is regarded as *past,* the "exculting joy" present. Because the realized joy of the coming salvation makes the *present grief* seem as a thing of the *past.* At the first shock of affliction ye *were grieved,* but now by *anticipation* ye *rejoice,* regarding the present grief as past. **through**–*Greek,* "IN": the element in which the grief has place. **manifold**–many and of various kinds (ch. 4:12, 13). **temptations**–"trials" testing your faith. **7.** Aim of the "temptations." **trial**–testing, proving. That your *faith so proved* "may be found (aorist; *once for all,* as the result of its being proved on the judgment-day) unto (eventuating in) praise ..." viz., the praise to be bestowed by the Judge. **than that of gold**–rather "than gold." **though**–"which perisheth, YET is tried with fire." If gold, though perishing (vs. 18), is yet tried with fire in order to remove dross and test its genuineness, how much more does your faith, which shall never perish, need to pass through a fiery trial to remove whatever is defective, and to test its genuineness and full value? **glory**–"Honor" is not so strong as "glory." As "praise" is in *words, so* "honor" is in deeds: *honorary reward.* **appearing**–*Translate* as in vs. 13, "revelation." At Christ's revelation shall take place also the revelation of the sons of God (Rom. 8:19, "manifestation," *Greek,* "revelation"; I John 3:2, *Greek,* "manifested ... manifested," for "appear ... appear"). **8. not having seen, ye love**–though in other cases it is *knowledge* of the person that produces *love* to him. They are more "blessed that have not seen and yet have believed," than they who believed because they have seen. On Peter's own love to Jesus, cf. John 21:15-17. Though the apostles had seen Him, they now ceased to know Him merely after the flesh. **in whom**–connected with "believing": the result of which is "ye rejoice" (*Greek,* "exult"). **now**–*in the present state,* as contrasted with the *future* state when believers "shall see His face." **unspeakable**–(I Cor. 2:9.) **full of glory**–*Greek,* "glorified." A joy now already *encompassed with glory.* The "glory" is partly in present possession, through the presence of Christ, "the Lord of glory," in the soul; partly in assured anticipation. "The Christian's *joy* is bound up with *love* to Jesus: its ground is *faith;* it is not therefore either self-seeking or self-sufficient" [STEIGER]. **9. Receiving**–in sure anticipation; "the end of your faith," i.e., its crowning consummation, finally completed "salvation" (Peter here confirms Paul's teaching as to *justification by faith):* also receiving *now* the title to it and the first fruits of it. In the next verse (vs. 10) the "salvation" is represented as *already present,* whereas "the prophets" had it not as yet present. It must, therefore, in this verse, refer to the present: *Deliverance now from a state of wrath:* believers even now "receive salvation," though its full "revelation" is future. **of ... souls**–The immortal *soul* was what was lost, so "salvation" primarily concerns the soul; the *body* shall share in redemption hereafter; the *soul* of the believer is saved already: an additional proof that "receiving ... salvation" is here a thing present. **10.** The magnitude of this "salvation" is proved by the earnestness with which "prophets" and even "angels" searched into it. Even from the beginning of the world this salvation has been testified to by the Holy Spirit. **prophets**—Though there is no *Greek* article, yet *English Version* is right, *"the prophets"* generally (including all the Old Testament *inspired* authors), as *"the* angels" similarly refer to them in general. **inquired**—perseveringly: so the *Greek.* Much more is manifested to us than by diligent inquiry and search the prophets attained. Still it is not said, they searched *after* it, but *"concerning"* (so the *Greek* for "of") it. They were already certain of the redemption being about to come. They did not like us fully *see,* but they *desired* to see the one and the same Christ whom we fully see in spirit. "As Simeon was anxiously desiring previously, and tranquil in peace only when he had seen Christ, so all the Old Testament saints saw Christ only hidden, and as it were absent—absent not in power and grace, but inasmuch as He was not yet manifested in the flesh" [CALVIN]. The prophets, as *private individuals,* had to reflect on the hidden and far-reaching sense of their own prophecies; because their words, *as prophets, in their public function,* were not so much their own as the Spirit's, speaking by and in them: thus Caiaphas. A striking testimony to verbal inspiration; the *words* which the inspired authors wrote are God's words expressing the mind of the Spirit, which the writers themselves searched into, to fathom the deep and precious meaning, even as the believing readers did. "Searched" implies that they had determinate marks to go by in their search. **the grace that should come unto you**—viz., the grace of the New Testament: an earnest of **"the grace" of** perfected "salvation" "to be brought at the (second) revelation of Christ." Old Testament believers also possessed the grace of God; they were children of God, but it was as children in their nonage, so as to be like servants; whereas we enjoy the full privileges of adult sons. **11. what**—*Greek,* "In reference to* what, or what manner of time." *What* expresses the *time* absolutely: what was to be the era of Messiah's coming; *"what manner of time";* what events and features should characterize the time of His coming. The "or" implies that some of the prophets, if they could not as individuals discover the exact *time,* searched into its characteristic features and events. The *Greek* for "time" is *the season,* the epoch, the fit time in God's purposes. **Spirit of Christ ... in them**—(Acts 16:7, in oldest MSS., "the Spirit of Jesus"; Rev. 19:10.) So JUSTIN MARTYR says, "Jesus was He who appeared and communed with Moses, Abraham, and the other patriarchs." CLEMENS ALEXANDRINUS calls Him "the Prophet of prophets, and Lord of all the prophetical spirit." **did signify** —"did give intimation." **of**—*Greek,* "the sufferers (appointed) *unto* Christ," or *foretold in regard to Christ.* "Christ" *the anointed* Mediator whose *sufferings* are the price of our "salvation" (vss. 9, 10), and who is the channel of "the grace that should come unto you." **the glory**—*Greek,* "glories," viz., of His resurrection, of His ascension, of His judgment and coming kingdom, the necessary consequence of the sufferings. **that should follow** —*Greek,* "after these (sufferings)," ch. 3:18-22; 5:1. Since "the Spirit of Christ" is the *Spirit* of God, Christ is God. It is only because the Son of God was to become our Christ that He manifested Himself and the Father through Him in the Old Testament, and by the Holy Spirit, eternally proceeding from the Father and Himself, spake in the prophets. **12.** Not only was the future revealed to them, but this also, that these revelations of the future were given them not for themselves, but for our

good in Gospel times. This, so far from disheartening, only quickened them in unselfishly testifying in the Spirit for the partial good of their own generation (only of believers), and for the full benefit of posterity. Contrast in Gospel times, Revelation 22:10. Not that their prophecies were unattended with spiritual instruction as to the Redeemer to their own generation, but the full light was not to be given till Messiah should come; it was well that they should have this "revealed" to them, lest they should be disheartened in not clearly discovering with all their *inquiry and search* the full particulars of the coming "salvation." To Daniel (Dan. 9:25, 26) the "time" was revealed. *Our* immense privileges are thus brought forth by contrast with theirs, notwithstanding that they had the great honor of Christ's Spirit speaking in them; and this, as an incentive to still greater earnestness on our part than even they manifested (vs. 13, etc.). **us**—The oldest MSS. read "you," as in vs. 10. This verse implies that *we,* Christians, may understand the prophecies by the Spirit's aid in their most important part, viz., so far as they have been already fulfilled. **with the Holy Ghost sent down**—on Pentecost. The oldest MSS. omit *Greek* preposition *en,* i.e., "in"; then translate, "by." The Evangelists speaking by the Holy Spirit were infallible witnesses. "The Spirit of Christ" was in the prophets also (vs. 11), but not manifestly, as in the case of the Christian Church and its first preachers, "SENT down from heaven." How favored are we in being ministered to, as to "salvation," by prophets and apostles alike, the latter now announcing the same things as actually fulfilled which the former foretold. **which things**— "the things now reported unto you" by the evangelistic preachers "Christ's sufferings and the glory that should follow" (vss. 11, 12). **angels**—still higher than "the prophets" (vs. 10). Angels do not any more than ourselves possess an INTUITIVE knowledge of redemption. "To look into" in *Greek* is lit., "to bend over so as to look deeply into and see to the bottom of a thing." See *Note* on same word, James 1:25. As the cherubim stood bending over the mercy seat, the emblem of redemption, in the holiest place, so the angels intently gaze upon and desire to fathom the depths of "the great mystery of godliness, God manifest in the flesh, justified in the Spirit, *seen of angels."* Their "ministry to the heirs of salvation" naturally disposes them to wish to penetrate this mystery as reflecting such glory on the love, justice, wisdom, and power of their and our God and Lord. They can know it only through its manifestation in the Church, as they personally have not the direct share in it that we have. "Angels have only the contrast between good and evil, without the power of conversion from sin to righteousness: witnessing such conversion in the Church, they long to penetrate the knowledge of the means whereby it is brought about" [HOFMAN in ALFORD]. **13. Wherefore**— Seeing that the prophets ministered unto you in these high Gospel privileges which they did not themselves fully share in, though "searching" into them, and seeing that even angels "desire to look into" them, how earnest you ought to be and watchful in respect to them! **gird up ... loins**—referring to Christ's own words, Luke 12:35; an image taken from the way in which the Israelites ate the passover with the loose outer robe girded up about the waist with a girdle, as ready for a journey. Workmen, pilgrims, runners, wrestlers, and warriors (all of whom are types of the Christians), so gird themselves up, both to shorten the garment so as not to impede motion, and to gird up the body itself so as to be braced for action. The believer is to have his mind (mental powers) collected and always ready for Christ's coming. "Gather in the strength of your spirit" [HENSLER]. *Sobriety*, i.e., spiritual *self-restraint*, lest one be overcome by the allurements of the world and of sense, and patient *hopeful* waiting for Christ's revelation, are the true ways of "girding up the loins of the mind." **to the end**—rather, "perfectly," so that there may be nothing deficient in your hope, no *casting away of your confidence*. Still, there may be an allusion to the "end" mentioned in vs. 9. Hope so perfectly (*Greek, teleios*) as to reach unto *the end* (*telos*) of your faith and hope, viz., "the grace that is being brought unto you in (so the *Greek*) the revelation of Christ." As *grace* shall then be *perfected*, so you ought to *hope perfectly*. "Hope" is repeated from vs. 3. The two appearances are but different stages of the ONE great revelation of Christ, comprising the New Testament from the beginning to the end. **14.** From *sobriety of spirit* and *endurance of hope* he passes to *obedience, holiness,* and *reverential fear*. **As**—marking their present actual character as "born again" (vss. 3, 22). **obedient**—*Greek*, "children of obedience": children to whom *obedience* is their characteristic and ruling nature, as a child is of the same nature as the mother and father. Contrast Ephesians 5:6, "the children of disobedience." Cf. vs. 17, "obeying the Father" whose "children" ye are. Having the obedience of *faith* (cf. vs. 22) and so of *practice* (cf. vss. 16, 18). "Faith is the highest obedience, because discharged to the highest command" [LUTHER]. **fashioning**—The outward *fashion* (*Greek, schema*) is fleeting, and merely on the surface. The "form," or *conformation* in the New Testament, is something deeper and more perfect and essential. **the former lusts in**—which were characteristic of your state of ignorance of God: true of both Jews and Gentiles. The sanctification is first described negatively (vs. 14, "not fashioning yourselves . . ."; the putting off the old man, even in the outward *fashion*, as well as in the inward *conformation*), then positively (vs. 15, putting on the new man, cf. Eph. 4:22, 24). "Lusts" flow from the original birth-sin (inherited from our first parents, who by self-willed desire brought sin into the world), the *lust* which, ever since man has been alienated from God, seeks to fill up with earthly things the emptiness of his being; the manifold forms which the mother-lust assumes are called in the plural *lusts*. In the regenerate, as far as the *new man* is concerned, which constitutes his truest self, "sin" no longer exists; but in the flesh or old man it does. Hence arises the conflict, uninterruptedly maintained through life, wherein the new man in the main prevails, and at last completely. But the natural man knows only the combat of his lusts with one another, or with the law, without power to conquer them. **15.** Lit., "But (rather) after the pattern of Him who hath called you (whose characteristic is that He is) holy, be (*Greek*, 'become') ye yourselves also holy." God is our grand model. God's *calling* is a frequently urged motive in Peter's Epistles. Every one that begets, begets an offspring resembling himself [EPIPHANIUS]. "Let the acts of the offspring indicate similarity to the Father" [AUGUSTINE]. **conversation**—deportment, course of life: one's way of going about, as distinguished from one's internal nature, to which it must outwardly correspond.

Christians are already holy unto God by consecration; they must be so also in their *outward walk and behavior in all respects*. The outward must correspond to the inward man. **16.** *Scripture* is the true source of all authority in questions of doctrine and practice. **Be ye . . . for I am**—It is I with whom ye have to do. Ye are mine. Therefore abstain from Gentile pollutions. We are too prone to have respect unto men [CALVIN]. As I am the fountain of holiness, being holy in My *essence,* be ye therefore zealous to be *partakers* of holiness, that ye may be as I also am [DIDYMUS]. God is essentially holy: the creature is holy in so far as it is sanctified by God. God, in giving the command, is willing to give also the power to obey it, viz., through the sanctifying of the Spirit (vs. 2). **17. if**—i.e., "*seeing that* ye call on," for all the regenerate pray as *children* of God, "Our *Father* who art in heaven." **the Father**—rather, "Call upon as *Father* Him who without acceptance of persons (Acts 10:34; Rom. 2:11; Jas. 2:1, not accepting the Jew above the Gentile, II Chron. 19:7; Luke 20:21; properly said of a judge not biassed in judgment by respect of persons) judgeth . . . ." The Father judgeth by His Son, His Representative, exercising His delegated authority (John 5:22). This marks the harmonious and complete unity of the Trinity. **work**—Each man's *work* is *one* complete whole, whether good or bad. The particular works of each are manifestations of the general character of his lifework, whether it was of faith and love whereby alone we can please God and escape condemnation. **pass**—*Greek*, "conduct yourselves during." **sojourning**—The outward state of the Jews in their *dispersion* is an emblem of the *sojourner-like* state of all believers in this world, away from our true Fatherland. **fear**—reverential, not slavish. He who is your Father, is also your Judge—a thought which may well inspire reverential fear. THEOPHYLACT observes, A double fear is mentioned in Scripture: (1) *elementary,* causing one to become serious; (2) *perfective:* the latter is here the motive by which Peter urges them as sons of God to be obedient. *Fear* is not here opposed to *assurance,* but to carnal *security:* fear producing vigilant caution lest we offend God and backslide. "*Fear* and *hope* flow from the same fountain: *fear* prevents us from falling away from *hope*" [BENGEL]. Though *love* has no *fear* IN it, yet in our present state of imperfect love, it needs to have fear going ALONG WITH it as a subordinate principle. This fear drowns all other fears. The believer fears God, and so has none else to fear. Not to fear God is the greatest baseness and folly. The martyrs' more than mere human courage flowed from this. **18.** Another motive to reverential, vigilant *fear* (vs. 17) of displeasing God, the consideration of the costly price of our redemption from sin. Observe, it is *we* who are bought by the blood of Christ, not heaven. The blood of Christ is not in Scripture said to buy heaven for us: heaven is the "inheritance" (vs. 4) given to us as sons, by the promise of God. **corruptible**—Cf. vs. 7, "gold that perisheth," 23. **silver and gold**—*Greek,* "or." Cf. Peter's own words, Acts 3:6: an undesigned coincidence. **redeemed**—Gold and silver being liable to corruption themselves, can free no one from spiritual and bodily death; they are therefore of too little value. Contrast vs. 19, Christ's "*precious*" blood." The Israelites were ransomed with half a shekel each, which went towards purchasing the *lamb* for the daily sacrifice (Exod. 30:12-16; cf. Num. 3:44-51).

But the Lamb who redeems the spiritual Israelites does so "without money or price." Devoted by sin to the justice of God, the Church of the first-born is redeemed from sin and the curse with Christ's precious blood (Matt. 20:28; I Tim. 2:6; Titus 2:14; Rev. 5:9). In all these passages there is the idea of *substitution,* the giving of one for another by way of a ransom or equivalent. Man is "sold under sin" as a slave; shut up under condemnation and the curse. The ransom was, therefore, paid to the righteously incensed Judge, and was accepted as a vicarious satisfaction for our sin by God, inasmuch as it was His own love as well as righteousness which appointed it. An Israelite sold as a bond-servant for debt might be redeemed by one of his brethren. As, therefore, we could not redeem ourselves, Christ assumed our nature in order to become our nearest of kin and brother, and so our God or Redeemer. Holiness is the natural fruit of redemption "from our vain conversation"; for He *by* whom we are redeemed is also He *for* whom we are redeemed. "Without the righteous abolition of the curse, either there could be found no deliverance, or, what is impossible, the grace and righteousness of God must have come in collision" [STEIGER]; but now, Christ having borne the curse of our sin, frees from it those who are made God's children by His Spirit. **vain** —self-deceiving, unreal, and unprofitable: promising good which it does not perform. Cf. as to the Gentiles, Acts 14:15; Romans 1:21; Ephesians 4:17; as to human philosophers, I Corinthians 3:20; as to the disobedient Jews, Jeremiah 4:14. **conversation**—course of life. To know what our sin is we must know what it cost. **received by tradition from your fathers**—The Jews' traditions. "Human piety is a vain blasphemy, and the greatest sin that a man can commit" [LUTHER]. There is only one Father to be imitated, vs. 17; cf. Matthew 23:9, the same antithesis [BENGEL]. **19. precious**—of inestimable value. The *Greek* order is, "With precious blood, as of a lamb without blemish (*in itself*) and without spot (*contracted by contact with others*), [even the blood] of Christ." Though very man, He remained pure *in Himself* ("without blemish"), and uninfected by any impression of sin *from without* ("without spot"), which would have unfitted Him for being our atoning Redeemer: so the passover lamb, and every sacrificial victim; so too, the Church, the Bride, by her union with Him. As Israel's redemption from Egypt required the blood of the paschal lamb, so our redemption from sin and the curse required the blood of Christ; "foreordained" (vs. 20) from eternity, as the passover lamb was taken up on the tenth day of the month. **20.** God's eternal foreordination of Christ's redeeming sacrifice, and completion of it *in these last times for us,* are an additional obligation on us to our maintaining a holy walk, considering how great things have been thus done for us. Peter's language in the history corresponds with this here: an undesigned coincidence and mark of genuineness. Redemption was no afterthought, or remedy of an unforeseen evil, devised at the time of its arising. God's *foreordaining* of the Redeemer refutes the slander that, on the Christian theory, there is a period of 4000 years of nothing but an incensed God. God *chose us in Christ before the foundation of the world.* **manifest**—in His incarnation in the fulness of the time. He existed from eternity before He was *manifested.* **in these last times**—I Corinthians 10:11, "the ends of the world." This last dispensation, made up of "times" marked by

great changes, but still retaining a general unity, stretches from Christ's ascension to His coming to judgment. **21. by him**—Cf. "the *faith* which is *by Him,*" Acts 3:16. *Through* Christ: His Spirit, obtained for us in His resurrection and ascension, enabling us to believe. This verse excludes all who do not "by Him believe in God," and includes all of every age and clime that do. Lit., *"are believers* in God." *To believe* IN (*Greek, eis*) *God* expresses an *internal* trust: "by believing to love God, going INTO Him, and cleaving to Him, incorporated into His members. By this faith the ungodly is justified, so that *thenceforth* faith itself begins to work by love" [P. LOMBARD]. To *believe* ON (*Greek, epi,* or dative case) *God* expresses the confidence, which grounds itself *on* God, reposing ON Him. "Faith IN (*Greek, en*) His blood" (Rom. 3:25) implies that His blood is the element IN which faith has its proper and abiding place. Cf. with this verse, Acts 20:21, "Repentance toward (*Greek, eis,* 'into,' turning *towards* and *going into*) God and faith toward (*Greek, eis,* 'into') Christ": where, as there is but one article to both "repentance" and "faith," the two are inseparably joined as together forming one truth; where *repentance* is, there *faith* is; when one knows God the Father spiritually, then he must know the Son by whom alone we can come to the Father. In Christ we have life: if we have not the doctrine of Christ, we have not God. The only living way to God is through Christ and His sacrifice. **that raised him**—The raising of Jesus by God is the special ground of our "believing": (1) because by it God declared openly His acceptance of Him as our righteous substitute; (2) because by it and His glorification He received power, viz., the Holy Spirit, to impart to His elect "faith": the same power enabling us to believe as raised Him from the dead. Our faith must not only be in Christ, but BY and THROUGH Christ. "Since in Christ's resurrection and consequent dominion our safety is grounded, *there* 'faith' and 'hope' find their stay" [CALVIN]. **that your faith and hope might be in God**—the object and effect of *God's raising Christ.* He states what was the actual result and fact, not an exhortation, except *indirectly.* Your *faith* flows from His *resurrection;* your *hope* from God's having "given Him glory" (cf. vs. 11, "glories"). Remember God's having raised and glorified Jesus as the anchor of your faith and hope in God, and so keep alive these graces. Apart from Christ we could have only feared, not *believed* and *hoped* in God. Cf. vss. 3, 7-9, 13, on *hope* in connection with *faith; love* is introduced in vs. 22. **22. purified ... in obeying the truth**—Greek, "in *your* (or *the*) obedience of (i.e., *to*) the truth" (the Gospel way of salvation), i.e., in the fact of your *believing.* Faith purifies the heart as giving it the only pure motive, love to God (Acts 15:9; Rom. 1:5, *"obedience* to the faith"). **through the Spirit**—omitted in the oldest MSS. The Holy Spirit is the purifier by bestowing the obedience of faith (vs. 2; I Cor. 12:3). **unto**—with a view to: the proper result of the *purifying* of your hearts by faith. "For what end must we lead a chaste life? That we may thereby be saved? No: but for this, that we may serve our neighbor" [LUTHER]. **unfeigned**—ch. 2:1, 2, "laying aside ... *hypocrisies* ... sincere." **love of the brethren**—i.e., of Christians. *Brotherly love* is distinct from common *love.* "The Christian loves primarily those in Christ; secondarily, all who might be in Christ, viz., all men, as Christ as man died for all, and as he hopes that they, too, may become his Christian brethren" [STEIGER].

BENGEL remarks that as here, so in II Peter 1:5-7, "brotherly love" is preceded by the purifying graces, *"faith,* knowledge, and godliness," etc. Love to the brethren is the evidence of our regeneration and justification by faith. **love one another**—When the *purifying by faith into love of the brethren* has formed the *habit,* then the *act* follows, so that the "love" is at once *habit* and *act.* **with a pure heart** —The oldest MSS. read, "(love) from the heart." **fervently**—*Greek,* "intensely": with all the powers *on the stretch* (ch. 4:8). "Instantly" (Acts 26:7). **23.** Christian brotherhood flows from our new birth of an imperishable seed, the abiding word of God. This is the consideration urged here to lead us to exercise *brotherly love.* As natural relationship gives rise to natural affection, so spiritual relationship gives rise to spiritual, and therefore abiding love, even as the *seed* from which it springs is abiding, not transitory as earthly things. **of ... of ... by**—"The word of God" is not the material of the spiritual new birth, but its mean or medium. By means of the *word* the man receives the incorruptible *seed of the Holy Spirit,* and so becomes one "born again": John 3:3-5, "born *of water and the Spirit":* as there is but one *Greek* article to the two nouns, *the* close connection of the sign and the grace, or new birth signified is implied. The *word* is the remote and anterior instrument; *baptism,* the proximate and sacramental instrument. The word is the instrument in relation to the individual; baptism, in relation to the Church as a society (Jas. 1:18). We are born again *of the Spirit,* yet not without the use of means, but by the word of God. The word is not the begetting principle itself, but only that by which it works: the vehicle of the mysterious germinating power [ALFORD]. **which liveth and abideth for ever**—It is because the Spirit of God accompanies it that the word carries in it the germ of life. They who are so born again *live and abide for ever,* in contrast to those who sow to the flesh. "The Gospel bears incorruptible fruits, not dead works, because it is itself incorruptible [BENGEL]. The word is an eternal divine power. For though the voice or speech vanishes, there still remains the kernel, the truth comprehended in the voice. This sinks into the heart and is living; yea, it is God Himself. So God to Moses, Exodus 4:12, "I will be with thy mouth" [LUTHER]. The life is in *God,* yet it is communicated to us through the *word.* "The *Gospel* shall never cease, though its ministry shall" [CALOV]. The abiding *resurrection glory* is always connected with our *regeneration* by the Spirit. Regeneration beginning with renewing man's *soul* at the resurrection, passes on to the *body,* then to the whole world of nature. **24.** Scripture proof that the word of God lives for ever, in contrast to man's natural frailty. If ye were born again of flesh, corruptible seed, ye must also perish again as the grass; but now that from which you have derived life remains eternally, and so also will render you eternal. **flesh**—man in his mere earthly nature. **as**—omitted in some of the oldest MSS. **of man**—The oldest MSS. read, "of it" (i.e., of the flesh). "The glory" is the wisdom, strength, riches, learning, honor, beauty, art, virtue, and righteousness of the NATURAL man (expressed by "flesh"), which all are transitory (John 3:6), not OF MAN (as *English Version* reads) absolutely, for the glory of *man, in his true ideal* realized in the believer, is eternal. **withereth**—*Greek,* aorist: lit., "withered," i.e., is withered as a thing of the past. So also the *Greek* for "falleth" is *"fell* away," i.e.,

is fallen away: it no sooner is than it is gone. **thereof**—omitted in the best MSS. and versions. "The grass" is the *flesh:* "the flower" its *glory.* **25.** (Ps. 119:89.) **this is the word ... preached unto you**—That is eternal which is born of incorruptible seed (vs. 24): but ye have received the incorruptible seed, the word (vs. 25); therefore ye are born for eternity, and so are bound now to live for eternity (vss. 22, 23). Ye have not far to look for the word; it is among you, even the joyful Gospel message which we preach. Doubt not that the Gospel *preached to you* by our brother Paul, and which ye have embraced, is the eternal truth. Thus the *oneness* of Paul's and Peter's creed appears. See my *Introduction,* showing Peter addresses some of the same churches as Paul labored among and wrote to.

CHAPTER 2

Vss. 1-25. EXHORTATIONS: To guileless feeding on the word by the sense of their privileges as newborn babes, living stones in the spiritual temple built on Christ the chief cornerstone, and royal priests, in contrast to their former state: also to abstinence from fleshly lusts, and to walk worthily in all relations of life, so that the world without which opposes them may be constrained to glorify God in seeing their good works. Christ, the grand pattern to follow in patience under suffering for well-doing. **1. laying aside**—once for all: so the *Greek* aorist expresses as a garment *put off.* The exhortation applies to Christians alone, for in none else is the new nature existing which, as "the inward man" (Eph. 3:16) can cast off the old as an outward thing, so that the Christian, through the continual renewal of his inward man, can also exhibit himself externally as a new man. But to unbelievers the demand is addressed, that *inwardly,* in regard to the *nous* (mind), they must become changed, *meta-noeisthai (re-pent)* [STEIGER]. The "therefore" resumes the exhortation begun in ch. 1: 22. Seeing that ye are born again of an incorruptible seed, be not again entangled in evil, which "has no substantial being, but is an acting in contrariety to the being formed in us" [THEOPHYLACT]. "Malice," etc., are utterly inconsistent with the "love of the brethren," unto which ye have "purified your souls" (ch. 1:22). The vices here are those which offend against the BROTHERLY LOVE inculcated above. Each succeeding one springs out of that which immediately precedes, so as to form a *genealogy* of the sins against love. Out of *malice* springs *guile;* out of *guile, hypocrises* (pretending to be what we are not, and not showing what we really are; the opposite of "love unfeigned," and "without dissimulation"); out of *hypocrisies, envies* of those to whom we think ourselves obliged to play the hypocrite; out of *envies, evil-speaking,* malicious, envious detraction of others. *Guile* is the permanent *disposition; hypocrisies* the *acts* flowing from it. The guileless knows no envy. Cf. vs. 2, "sincere," *Greek, "guileless." "Malice* delights in another's hurt; *envy* pines at another's good; *guile* imparts duplicity to the heart; *hypocrisy* (flattery) imparts duplicity to the tongue; *evil-speakings* wound the character of another" [AUGUSTINE]. **2. newborn babes**—altogether without "guile" (vs. 1). As long as we are here we are "babes," in a specially tender relation to God (Isa. 40:11). The childlike spirit is indispensable if we would enter heaven. "Milk" is here not elementary truths in contradistinction to more advanced Christian truths, as in I Corinthians

3:2; Hebrews 5:12, 13; but in contrast to "guile, hypocrisies . . ." (vs. 1); the simplicity of *Christian doctrine in general* to the childlike spirit. The same "word of grace" which is the instrument in regeneration, is the instrument also of *building up.* "The mother of the child is also its natural nurse" [STEIGER]. The babe, instead of chemically analyzing, instinctively desires and feeds on the milk; so our part is not self-sufficient rationalizing and questioning, but simply receiving the truth in the love of it (Matt. 11: 25). **desire**—*Greek,* "have a yearning desire for," or "longing after," a natural impulse to the regenerate, "for as no one needs to teach newborn babes what food to take, knowing instinctively that a table is provided for them in their mother's breast," so the believer of himself thirsts after the word of God (Ps. 119). Cf. Tatius' language as to Achilles. **sincere**—*Greek,* "guileless." Cf. vs. 1, "laying aside *guile."* IRENÆUS says of heretics, They mix chalk with the milk. The article, "the," implies that besides *the well-known pure milk, the Gospel,* there is no other pure, unadulterated doctrine; it alone can make us *guileless* (vs. 1). **of the word**—Not as ALFORD, "spiritual," nor "reasonable," as *English Version* in Romans 12:1. The *Greek logos* in Scripture is not used of the *reason,* or *mind,* but of the WORD; the preceding context requires that "the word" should be meant here; the adjective *logikos* follows the meaning of the noun *logos,* "word." James 1:21, *"Lay apart* all filthiness . . . and receive with meekness *the engrafted* WORD," is exactly parallel, and confirms *English Version* here. **grow**—The oldest MSS. and versions read, "grow *unto salvation."* Being BORN *again unto salvation,* we are also to *grow unto salvation.* The end to which growth leads is perfected *salvation.* "Growth is the measure of the fulness of that, not only rescue from destruction, but positive blessedness, which is implied in *salvation"* [ALFORD]. **thereby**—*Greek, "in* it"; fed *on it; in its strength* (Acts 11:14). "The word is to be desired with appetite as the cause of life, to be swallowed in the hearing, to be chewed as cud is by rumination with the understanding, and to be digested by faith" [TERTULLIAN]. **3.** Peter alludes to Psalm 34:8. The first *tastes* of God's goodness are afterwards followed by fuller and happier experiences. A taste whets the appetite [BENGEL]. **gracious**—*Greek,* "good," benignant, kind; as God is revealed to us in Christ, "the Lord" (vs. 4), we who are born again ought so to be *good* and *kind* to the brethren (ch. 1:22). "Whosoever has not tasted the word to him it is not sweet it has not reached the heart; but to them who have experienced it, who with the heart believe, 'Christ has been sent *for me* and is become *my own;* my miseries are His, and His *life* mine,' it tastes sweet" [LUTHER]. **4. coming**—*drawing near* (same *Greek* as here, Hebrews 10:22) by faith continually; present tense: not having come once for all at conversion. **stone**—*Peter* (i.e., *a stone,* named so by Christ) desires that all similarly should be *living stones* BUILT ON CHRIST, THE TRUE FOUNDATION-STONE; cf. his speech in Acts 4:11. An undesigned coincidence and mark of genuineness. The Spirit foreseeing the Romanist perversion of Matthew 16:18 (cf. 16, "Son of the LIVING God," which coincides with his language here, "the LIVING stone"), presciently makes Peter himself to refuse it. He herein confirms Paul's teaching. Omit the *as unto* of *English Version.* Christ is positively termed the "living stone"; *living,* as having life in Himself from the beginning, and as raised from the dead to live evermore (Rev. 1:18) after His rejection

by men, and so the source of life to us. Like no earthly *rock,* He lives and gives life. Cf. I Corinthians 10:4, and the type, Exodus 17:6; Numbers 20:11. **disallowed**—rejected, reprobated; referred to also by Christ Himself: also by Paul; cf. the kindred prophecies, Isaiah 8:14; Luke 2:34. **chosen of God**—lit., *"with* (or *in the presence and judgment of)* God elect," or, "chosen out" (vs. 6). Many are alienated from the Gospel, because it is not everywhere in favor, but is on the contrary rejected by most men. Peter answers that, though rejected by men, Christ is peculiarly the *stone* of salvation honored by God, first so designated by Jacob in his deathbed prophecy. **5. Ye also, as lively stones**—partaking of the name and life which is in "THE LIVING STONE" (vs. 4; I Cor. 3:11). Many names which belong to Christ in the singular are assigned to Christians in the plural. He is "THE SON," "High Priest," "King," "Lamb"; they, "sons," "priests," "kings," "sheep," "lambs." So the Shulamite called from Solomon [BENGEL]. **are built up**—*Greek,* "are being built up," as in Ephesians 2:22. Not as ALFORD, "Be ye built up." Peter grounds his exhortations, vs. 2, 11, etc., on their conscious sense of their high privileges as *living stones in the course of being built up into a spiritual house* (i.e., the habitation of the Spirit"). **priesthood**—Christians are both the spiritual *temple* and the *priests* of the temple. There are two *Greek* words for "temple"; *hieron* (*the sacred place*), the whole building, including the courts wherein the sacrifice *was killed*; and *naos* (*the dwelling,* viz., of God), the inner shrine wherein God peculiarly manifested Himself, and where, in the holiest place, the *blood* of the slain sacrifice was presented before Him. All believers alike, and not merely ministers, are now the dwelling of God (and are called the *naos, Greek,* not the *hieron*) and priests unto God (Rev. 1:6). The minister is not, like the Jewish priest (*Greek, hiercus*), admitted nearer to God than the people, but merely for order's sake leads the spiritual services of the people. *Priest* is the abbreviation of *presbyter* in the *Church of England Prayer Book,* not corresponding to the Aaronic *priest* (*hiereus,* who offered *literal* sacrifices). Christ is the only literal *hiereus-priest* in the New Testament through whom alone we may always draw near to God. Cf. vs. 9, "a royal priesthood," i.e., *a body of priest-kings,* such as was Melchisedec. The Spirit never, in New Testament, gives the name *hiereus,* or *sacerdotal* priest, to ministers of the Gospel. **holy**—consecrated to God. **spiritual sacrifices**—not the literal one of the mass, as the Romish self-styled disciples of Peter teach. Cf. Isaiah 56:7, which cf. with *"acceptable* to God" here; Psalm 4:5; 50:14; 51:17, 19; Hosea 14:2; Philippians 4:18. "Among spiritual sacrifices the first place belongs to the general oblation of ourselves. For never can we offer anything to God until we have offered ourselves (II Cor. 8:5] in sacrifice to Him. There follow afterwards prayers, giving of thanks, alms-deeds, and all exercises of piety" [CALVIN]. Christian houses of worship are never called temples because the *temple* was a place for *sacrifice,* which has no place in the Christian dispensation; the Christian temple is the congregation of spiritual worshippers. The synagogue (where reading of Scripture and prayer constituted the worship) was the model of the Christian house of worship (cf. *Note,* Jas. 2:2, *Greek,* "synagogue"; Acts 15:21). Our sacrifices are those of prayer, praise, and self-denying services in the cause of Christ (vs. 9, end). **by Jesus Christ**—as our mediating High Priest before God. Connect these words with "offer up." Christ is both *precious* Himself and makes us *accepted* [BENGEL]. As the temple, so also the priesthood, is built on Christ (vss. 4, 5) [BEZA]. Imperfect as are our services, we are not with unbelieving timidity, which is close akin to refined self-righteousness, to doubt their acceptance THROUGH CHRIST. After extolling the dignity of Christians he goes back to CHRIST as the sole source of it. **6. Wherefore also**—The oldest MSS. read, "Because that." The statement above is so "*because* it is contained in Scripture." **Behold**—calling attention to the glorious announcement of His eternal counsel. **elect**—so also believers (vs. 9, "chosen," *Greek*, "*elect* generation"). **precious**—in *Hebrew*, Isaiah 28:16, "a cornerstone of preciousness." See all my *Note* there. So in vs. 7, Christ is said to be, to believers, "precious," *Greek*, "preciousness." **confounded**—same *Greek* as in Romans 9:33 (Peter here as elsewhere confirming Paul's teaching. See *Introduction*, also Rom. 10: 11,) "ashamed." In Isaiah 28:16, "make haste," i.e., flee in sudden panic, covered with the *shame* of confounded hopes. **7.** Application of the Scripture just quoted first to the believer, then to the unbeliever. On the opposite effects of the same Gospel on different classes, cf. John 9:39; II Corinthians 2: 15, 16. **precious**—*Greek*, "THE preciousness" (vs. 6). To you believers belongs *the preciousness* of Christ just mentioned. **disobedient**—to the faith, and so disobedient in practice. **the stone which ... head of ... corner**—(Ps. 118:22). Those who rejected the STONE were all the while in spite of themselves unconsciously contributing to its becoming Head of the corner. The same magnet has two poles, the one repulsive, the other attractive; so the Gospel has opposite effects on believers and unbelievers respectively. **8. stone of stumbling ...**—quoted from Isaiah 8:14. Not merely they *stumbled*, in that their prejudices were offended; but their stumbling implies the *judicial punishment* of their reception of Messiah; they hurt themselves in stumbling over the cornerstone, as "stumble" means in Jeremiah 13:16; Daniel 11:19. **at the word**—rather join "being disobedient to the word"; so ch. 3:1; 4:17. **whereunto**—to penal *stumbling*; to the judicial punishment of their unbelief. See above. **also**—an additional thought; God's ordination; not that God ordains or *appoints* them to *sin*, but they are given up to "the fruit of *their own* ways" according to the eternal counsel of God. The moral ordering of the world is altogether of God. God appoints the ungodly to be *given up unto* sin, and a *reprobate mind*, and its necessary penalty. "Were appointed," *Greek*, "set," answers to "*I* lay," *Greek*, "set," vs. 6. God, in the active, is said to *appoint* Christ and the elect [directly]. Unbelievers, in the passive, are said to be *appointed* [God acting less directly in the appointment of the sinner's awful course] [BENGEL]. God ordains the wicked to punishment, not to crime [J. CAPPEL]. "Appointed" or "set" (not here "FOREordained") refers, not to the eternal counsel so directly, as to the penal justice of God. Through the same Christ whom sinners rejected, they shall be rejected; unlike believers, they are by God *appointed unto wrath* as FITTED for it. The lost shall lay all the blame of their ruin on their own sinful perversity, not on God's decree; the saved shall ascribe all the merit of their salvation to God's electing love and grace. **9.** Contrast in the privileges and destinies of believers. Cf. the similar contrast with the preceding context. **chosen**—"elect" of God, even as Christ your Lord is. **generation**—implying the

unity of spiritual origin and kindred of believers as a class distinct from the world. **royal**—kingly. Believers, like Christ, the antitypical Melchisedec, are at once *kings* and *priests*. Israel, in a spiritual sense, was designed to be the same among the nations of the earth. The full realization on earth of this, both to the literal and the spiritual Israel, is as yet future. **holy nation**—antitypical to Israel. **peculiar people**—lit., "a people *for an acquisition*," i.e., whom God chose to be *peculiarly His:* Acts 20: 28, "purchased," lit., "acquired." God's "*peculiar treasure*" above others. **show forth**—*publish abroad*. Not *their own* praises but *His*. They have no reason to magnify themselves above others for once they had been in the same darkness, and only through God's grace had been brought to the light which they must henceforth *show forth* to others. **praises**—*Greek*, "virtues," "excellencies": His glory, *mercy* (vs. 10), *goodness* (*Greek*, vs. 3; Num. 14:17, 18; Isa. 63:7). The same term is applied to believers, II Pet. 1:5. **of him who hath called you**—(II Pet. 1:3). **out of darkness**—of heathen and even Jewish ignorance, sin, and misery, and so out of the dominion of the prince of darkness. **marvellous**—Peter still has in mind Ps. 118:23. **light**—It is called "His," i.e., God's. Only the (spiritual) *light* is created by God, not *darkness*. In Isaiah 45:7, it is physical darkness and evil, not moral, that God is said to *create*, the punishment of sin, not sin itself. Peter, with characteristic boldness, brands as *darkness* what all the world calls *light;* reason, without the Holy Spirit, in spite of its vaunted power, is spiritual darkness. "It cannot apprehend what faith is: there it is stark blind; it gropes as one that is without eyesight, stumbling from one thing to another, and knows not what it does" [LUTHER]. **10.** Adapted from Hosea 1:9, 10; 2:23. Peter plainly confirms Paul, who quotes the passage as implying the call of the Gentiles to become spiritually that which Israel had been literally, "the people of God." Primarily, the prophecy refers to literal Israel, hereafter to be fully that which in their best days they were only partially, God's people. **not obtained mercy**—lit., "who were men not compassionated." Implying that it was God's pure *mercy*, not their merits, which made the blessed change in their state; a thought which ought to kindle their lively *gratitude*, to be shown with their life, as well as their lips. **11.** As heretofore he exhorted them to walk worthily of their calling, in contradistinction to their own former walk, so now he exhorts them to glorify God before unbelievers. **Dearly beloved** —He gains their attention to his exhortation by assuring them of his love. **strangers and pilgrims**—(ch. 1:17). *Sojourners*, lit., settlers having a *house* in a city without being *citizens* in respect to the rights of citizenship; a picture of the Christian's position on earth; *and pilgrims,* staying for a time in a foreign land. FLACIUS thus analyzes the exhortation: (1) Purify your souls (a) as *strangers* on earth who must not allow yourselves to be kept back by earthly lusts, and (b) because these lusts war against the soul's salvation. (2) Walk piously among unbelievers (a) so that they may cease to calumniate Christians, and (b) may themselves be converted to Christ. **fleshly lusts**—enumerated in Galatians 5:19, etc. Not only the gross appetites which we have in common with the brutes, but all the thoughts of the unrenewed mind. **which**—*Greek*, "*the* which," i.e., inasmuch as being such as "war," etc. Not only do they impede, but they assail [BENGEL]. **the soul**—i.e., against the regenerated soul; such as were those now addressed. The regenerated soul is besieged by sinful lusts. Like Samson in the lap of Delilah, the believer, the moment that he gives way to fleshly lusts, has the locks of his strength shorn, and ceases to maintain that spiritual separation from the world and the flesh of which the Nazarite vow was the type. **12. conversation**—"behavior"; "conduct." There are two things in which "strangers and pilgrims" ought to bear themselves well: (1) the *conversation* or conduct, as subjects (vs. 13), servants (vs. 18), wives (ch. 3:1), husbands (ch. 3:7), all persons under all circumstances (vs. 8); (2) *confession* of the faith (ch. 3:15, 16). Each of the two is derived from *the will of God*. Our conversation should correspond to our Saviour's condition; this is in heaven, so ought that to be. **honest**— honorable, becoming, proper (ch. 3:16). Contrast "vain conversation," ch. 1:18. A good walk does not make us pious, but we must first be pious and believe before we attempt to lead a good course. Faith first receives from God, then love gives to our neighbor [LUTHER]. **whereas they speak against you**—*now* (vs. 15), that they may, nevertheless, at some time or other *hereafter* glorify God. The *Greek* may be rendered, "*Wherein* they speak against you . . . , that (*herein*) they may, by your good works, which *on a closer inspection they shall behold,* glorify God." The very works "which on more careful consideration, must move the heathen to praise God, are at first the object of hatred and raillery" [STEIGER]. **evildoers**—Because as Christians they could not conform to heathenish customs, they were accused of disobedience to all legal authority; in order to rebut this charge, they are told to *submit to every ordinance of man* (not sinful in itself). **by**—owing to. **they shall behold** —*Greek,* "they shall be *eyewitnesses of*"; "shall behold *on close inspection";* as opposed to their "ignorance" (vs. 15) of the true character of Christians and Christianity, by judging on mere hearsay. The same *Greek* verb occurs in a similar sense in ch. 3:2. "Other men *narrowly look at* (so the *Greek* implies) the actions of the righteous" [BENGEL]. TERTULLIAN contrasts the early Christians and the heathen: these delighted in the bloody gladiatorial spectacles of the amphitheater, whereas a Christian was excommunicated if he went to it at all. No Christian was found in prison for crime, but only for the faith. The heathen excluded slaves from some of their religious services, whereas Christians had some of their presbyters of the class of slaves. Slavery silently and gradually disappeared by the power of the Christian law of love, "Whatsoever ye would that men should do to you, do ye even so to them." When the pagans deserted their nearest relatives in a plague, Christians ministered to the sick and dying. When the Gentiles left their dead unburied after a battle and cast their wounded into the streets, the disciples hastened to relieve the suffering. **glorify**—forming a high estimate of the God whom Christians worship, from the exemplary conduct of Christians themselves. We must do good, not with a view to *our own* glory, but to the glory *of God.* **the day of visitation**—of God's grace; when God shall *visit* them *in mercy.* **13. every ordinance of man**—"every human institution" [ALFORD], lit., "every human *creation.*" For though of divine appointment, yet in the mode of nomination and in the exercise of their authority, earthly governors are but human institutions, being *of men,* and *in relation to men.* The apostle speaks as one raised above all human things. But lest they should think themselves so ennobled by faith as to be raised above subordination to human authorities, he tells

them to *submit themselves for the sake of Christ,* who desires you to be subject, and who once was subject to earthly rulers Himself, though having all things subject to Him, and whose honor is at stake in you as His earthly representatives. Cf. Romans 13:5, "Be subject for conscience' sake." **king**—The Roman emperor was "supreme" in the Roman provinces to which this Epistle was addressed. The Jewish zealots refused obedience. The distinction between "the king as supreme" and "governors sent by him" implies that "if the king command one thing, and the subordinate magistrate another, we ought rather to obey the superior" [AUGUSTINE *in* GROTIUS]. Scripture prescribes nothing upon the form of government, but simply subjects Christians to that everywhere subsisting, without entering into the question of the *right* of the rulers (thus the Roman emperors had by force seized supreme authority, and Rome had, by unjustifiable means, made herself mistress of Asia), because the *de facto* governors have not been made by chance, but by the providence of God. **14. governors**—subordinate to the emperor, "sent," or delegated by Cæsar to preside over the provinces. **for the punishment**— No tyranny ever has been so unprincipled as that some appearance of equity was not maintained in it; however corrupt a government be, God never suffers it to be so much so as not to be better than anarchy [CALVIN]. Although bad kings often oppress the good, yet that is scarcely ever done by public authority (and it is of what is done by public authority that Peter speaks), save under the mask of right. Tyranny harasses many, but anarchy overwhelms the whole state [HORNEIUS]. The only justifiable exception is in cases where obedience to the earthly king plainly involves disobedience to the express command of the King of kings. **praise of them that do well**—Every government recognizes the excellence of truly Christian subjects. Thus PLINY, in his letter to the Emperor Trajan, acknowledges, "I have found in them nothing else save a perverse and extravagant superstition." The recognition in the long run mitigates persecution (ch. 3:13). **15.** Ground of his directing them to *submit themselves* (vs. 13). **put to silence**—lit., "to muzzle," "to stop the mouth." **ignorance**—spiritual not having "the knowledge of God," and therefore ignorant of the children of God, and misconstruing their acts; influenced by mere appearances, and ever ready to open their mouths, rather than their eyes and ears. Their *ignorance* should move the believer's pity, not his anger. They judge of things which they are incapable of judging through unbelief (cf. vs. 12). Maintin such a walk that they shall have no charge against you, except touching your faith; and so their minds shall be favorably disposed towards Christianity. **16. As free**—as the Lord's freemen," connected with vs. 15, *doing well as* being *free.* "Well-doing" (vs. 15) is the natural fruit of being *freemen* of Christ, made free by "the truth" from the bondage of sin. Duty is enforced on us to guard against licentiousness, but the *way* in which it is to be fulfilled, is by love and the holy instincts of Christian liberty. We are given *principles,* not. *details.* **not using**—Greek, "not *as having* your liberty for a veil (cloak) of *badness,* but as the servants of God," and therefore bound to *submit to every ordinance of man* (vs. 13) which is of God's appointment. **17. Honour all men**—*according to whatever honor is due in each case.* Equals have a respect due to them. Christ has dignified our humanity by assuming it; therefore we should not dishonor, but be considerate to and honor our common humanity, even in the very humblest. The first "honor" is in the *Greek aorist* imperative, implying, "*In every case render promptly* every man's due" [ALFORD]. The second is in the *present*, implying, *Habitually and continually* honor the king. Thus the first is the general precept; the three following are its three great divisions. **Love**—present: *Habitually love* with the special and congenial affection that you ought to feel to brethren, besides the general *love* to all men. **Fear God . . . the king**—The king is to be *honored;* but God alone, in the highest sense, *feared*. **18. Servants**—*Greek*, "household servants": not here the *Greek* for "slaves." Probably including *freedmen* still remaining in their master's house. *Masters* were not commonly Christians: he therefore mentions only the duties of the *servants*. These were then often persecuted by their unbelieving masters. Peter's special object seems to be to teach them *submission*, whatever the character of the masters might be. Paul not having this as his prominent design, includes *masters* in his monitions. **be subject**—*Greek*, "being subject": the participle expresses a particular instance of the general exhortation to good conduct, vss. 11, 12, of which the first particular precept is given vs. 13, "Submit yourselves to every ordinance of man for the Lord's sake." The general exhortation is taken up again in vs. 16; and so the participle vs. 18, "being subject," is joined to the hortatory imperatives going before, viz., "abstain," "submit yourselves." "honor all men." **with**—*Greek*, "*in*." **all**—all possible: under all circumstances, such as are presently detailed. **fear**—the awe of one subject: God, however, is the ultimate object of the "fear": *fear* "for the Lord's sake" (vs. 13), not merely slavish fear of masters. **good**—kind. **gentle**—indulgent towards errors: considerate: yielding, not exacting all which justice might demand. **froward**—perverse: harsh. Those bound to obey must not make the disposition and behavior of the superior the measure of the fulfilment of their obligations. **19.** Reason for subjection even to froward masters. **thankworthy**—(Luke 6:33). A course out of the common, and especially *praiseworthy* in the eyes of God: not as Rome interprets, earning merit, and so a work of supererogation (cf. vs. 20). **for conscience toward God**—lit., "consciousness of God": from a conscientious regard to God, more than to men. **endure**—*Greek*, "patiently bear up under": as a superimposed burden [ALFORD]. **grief**—*Greek*, "griefs." **20. what**—*Greek*, "what kind of." **glory**—what peculiar *merit*. **buffeted**—the punishment of slaves, and suddenly inflicted [BENGEL]. **this is**—Some oldest MSS. read, "for." Then the translation is, "But if when . . . ye take it patiently (it is a glory), *for* this is. . . . **acceptable**—*Greek*, "thankworthy," as in vs. 19. **21.** Christ's example a proof that patient endurance under undeserved sufferings is acceptable with God. **hereunto**—to the patient endurance of unmerited suffering (ch. 3:9). Christ is an example to servants, even as He was once in "the form of a servant." **called**—with a heavenly calling, though slaves. **for us**—*His dying for us* is the highest exemplification of "doing well" (vs. 20). Ye must patiently suffer, being innocent, as Christ also innocently suffered (not for Himself, but *for us*). The oldest MSS. for "us . . . us," read, "you . . . for you." Christ's sufferings, while they are for an example, were also primarily sufferings "*for us*," a consideration which imposes an everlasting obligation on us to please Him. **leaving**—*behind:* so the *Greek:* on His departure to the Father, to His glory. **an example**—

Greek, "a copy," lit., "a writing copy" set by masters for their pupils. Christ's precepts and sermons were the *transcript* of His life. Peter *graphically* sets before servants those features especially suited to their case. **follow**—*close upon:* so the *Greek*. **his steps**—*footsteps*, viz., of His *patience* combined with *innocence*. **22.** Illustrating Christ's *well-doing* (vs. 20) though suffering. **did**—*Greek* aorist. Never in a single instance did" [ALFORD]. Quoted from Isaiah 53:9, end, LXX. **neither**—nor yet: not even [ALFORD]. Sinlessness as to the *mouth* is a mark of *perfection*. Guile is a common fault of servants. "If any boast of his innocency, Christ surely did not suffer as an evildoer" [CALVIN], yet He took it patiently (vs. 20). On Christ's sinlessness, cf. II Corinthians 5:21; Hebrews 7:26. **23.** Servants are apt to "answer again" (Titus 2:9). *Threats* of divine judgment against oppressors are often used by those who have no other arms, as for instance, slaves. Christ, who as Lord could have threatened with truth, never did so. **committed himself**—or *His cause*, as man in His suffering. Cf. the type, Jeremiah 11:20. In this Peter seems to have before his mind Isaiah 53:8. Cf. Romans 12: 19, on our corresponding duty. Leave your case in His hands, not desiring to make Him executioner of your revenge, but rather praying for enemies. God's *righteous judgment* gives tranquillity and consolation to the oppressed. **24. his own self**—there being *none other* but *Himself* who could have done it. His *voluntary* undertaking of the work of redemption is implied. The *Greek* puts in antithetical juxtaposition, OUR, and His OWN SELF, to mark the idea of *His substitution for us*. His "well-doing" in His sufferings is set forth here as an example to servants and to us all (vs. 20). **bare**—to sacrifice: *carried and offered up:* a sacrificial term. Isaiah 53:11, 12, "He *bare* the sin of many": where the *idea of bearing on Himself* is the prominent one; here the *offering in sacrifice* is combined with that idea. So the same *Greek* means in ch. 2:5. **our sins**—In *offering* or *presenting in sacrifice* (the *Greek* for "bare" implies) His body, Christ offered in it the *guilt* of our sins upon the cross, as upon the altar of God, that it might be expiated in Him, and so taken away from us. Cf. Isaiah 53:10, "Thou shalt make His soul an offering for sin." Peter thus means by "bare" what the Syriac takes two words to express, *to bear* and *to offer:* (1) He hath *borne* our sins laid upon Him [viz., their guilt, curse, and punishment]; (2) He hath so borne them that He *offered* them along with Himself on the altar. He refers to the animals upon which sins were first laid, and which were then *offered* thus laden [VITRINGA]. Sin or guilt among the Semitic nations is considered as a burden lying heavily upon the sinner [GESENIUS]. **on the tree**—the cross, the proper place for One on whom the *curse* was laid: this curse stuck to Him until it was legally (through His death as the guilt-bearer) destroyed in His body; thus the handwriting of the bond against us is cancelled by His death. **that we being dead to sins**—the effect of His death to "sin" in the aggregate, and to all particular "sins," viz., that we should be as entirely *delivered from* them, as a slave that is *dead* is delivered from service *to* his master. This is our spiritual *standing* through faith by virtue of Christ's death: our actual mortification of particular *sins* is in proportion to the degree of our effectually being made conformable to His death. "That we should *die to the sins* whose collected guilt Christ carried away in His death, and SO LIVE TO THE RIGHTEOUSNESS (cf. Isa. 53:11. 'My *righteous* servant shall *justify* many'), the gracious relation to God which He has brought in" [STEIGER]. **by whose stripes** [*Greek,* "stripe"] ye were healed—a paradox, yet true. "Ye servants (cf. 'buffeted,' 'the tree,' vss. 20, 24) often bear *the strife;* but it is not more than your Lord Himself bore; learn from Him patience in wrongful sufferings. **25.** (Isa. 53:6.) For—Assigning their natural need of *healing* (vs. 24). **now**—Now that the atonement for all has been made, the foundation is laid for *individual conversion:* so *"ye are returned,"* or *"have become converted* to. . . ." **Shepherd and Bishop**—The designation of the *pastors* and *elders* of the Church belongs in its fullest sense to the great Head of the Church, "the good Shepherd." As the *"bishop"* oversees (as the *Greek* term means), so "the *eyes of the Lord are over* the righteous" (ch. 3:12). He gives us His spirit and feeds and guides us by His word. "Shepherd," *Hebrew, Parnas,* is often applied to *kings,* and enters into the composition of names, as *Pharna*bazus.

CHAPTER 3

Vss. 1-22. RELATIVE DUTIES OF HUSBANDS AND WIVES: EXHORTATIONS TO LOVE AND FORBEARANCE: RIGHT CONDUCT UNDER PERSECUTIONS FOR RIGHTEOUSNESS' SAKE, AFTER CHRIST'S EXAMPLE, WHOSE DEATH RESULTED IN QUICKENING TO US THROUGH HIS BEING QUICKENED AGAIN, OF WHICH BAPTISM IS THE SACRAMENTAL SEAL. **1. Likewise**—*Greek,* "In like manner," as "servants" in their sphere; cf. the reason of the woman's subjection, I Corinthians 11:8-10; I Timothy 2:11-14. **your own**—enforcing the obligation: it is not strangers ye are required to *be subject to.* Every time that obedience is enjoined upon women to their husbands, the *Greek, idios,* "one's own peculiarly," is used, while the wives of men are designated only by *heauton,* "of themselves." Feeling the need of leaning on one stronger than herself, the wife (especially if joined to an *unbeliever*) might be tempted, though only spiritually, to enter into that relation with another in which she ought to stand to *her own* spouse (I Cor. 14:34, 35, "Let them ask *their own* [*idios*] husbands at home"); an attachment to the person of the teacher might thus spring up, which, without being in the common sense spiritual adultery, would still weaken in its spiritual basis the married relation [STEIGER]. **that, if**—*Greek,* "that even if." *Even if* you have a husband that obeys not the word (i.e., is an unbeliever). **without the word**—*independently of hearing the word preached,* the usual way of *faith* coming. But BENGEL, "without word," i.e., *without direct* Gospel *discourse* of the wives, "they *may* (lit., in oldest MSS., shall, which marks the almost objective *certainty* of the result) be won" indirectly. "Unspoken acting is more powerful than unperformed speaking" [ŒCUMENIUS]. "A soul converted is *gained* to itself, to the pastor, wife, or husband, who sought it, and to Jesus Christ; added to His treasury who thought not His own precious blood too dear to lay out for this gain" [LEIGHTON]. "The discreet wife would choose first of all to persuade her husband to share with her in the things which lead to blessedness; but if this be impossible, let her then alone diligently press after virtue, in all things obeying him so as to do nothing at any time against his will, except in such things as are essential to virtue and salvation" [CLEMENS ALEXANDRINUS]. **2. behold**—on narrowly looking into it, lit., "having closely observed." **chaste**—pure, spotless, free from all impurity. **fear**—*reverential,* to-

wards your husbands. Scrupulously pure, as opposed to the noisy, ambitious character of worldly women. **3.** Lit., "To whom let there belong [viz., as their peculiar ornament] not the outward adornment [usual in the sex which first, by the fall, brought in the need of covering, *Note,* ch. 5:5] of . . ." **plaiting**—artificial braiding, in order to attract admiration. **wearing**—lit., "putting round," viz., the head, as a diadem—the arm, as a bracelet—the finger, as rings. **apparel**—showy and costly. "Have the blush of modesty on thy face instead of paint, and moral worth and discretion instead of gold and emeralds" [MELISSA]. **4. But**—"Rather." The "outward adornment" of jewelry, etc., is forbidden, in so far as woman loves such things, not in so far as she uses them from a sense of propriety, and does not *abuse* them. Singularity mostly comes from pride and throws needless hindrances to religion in the way of others. Under costly attire there may be a humble mind. "Great is he who uses his earthenware as if it were plate; not less great is he who uses his silver as if it were earthenware" [SENECA *in* ALFORD]. **hidden**—*inner* man, which the Christian instinctively *hides* from public view. **of the heart**—*consisting in the heart* regenerated and adorned by the Spirit. This "inner man of the heart" is the subject of the verb "be," vs. 3, *Greek:* "Of whom let the inner man be," viz., the distinction or adornment. **in that**—consisting or standing *in that* as its element. **not corruptible**—not transitory, nor tainted with corruption, as all earthly adornments. **meek and quiet**—*meek,* not creating disturbances: *quiet,* bearing with tranquillity the disturbances caused by others. *Meek* in affections and feelings; *quiet* in words, countenance, and actions [BENGEL]. **in the sight of God**—who looks to inward, not merely outward things. **of great price** —The results of redemption should correspond to its costly price (ch. 1:19). **5. after this manner**—with the *ornament of a meek and quiet spirit* (cf. the portrait of the godly wife, Prov. 31:10-31). **trusted** —*Greek,* "hoped." "Holy" is explained by "hoped in (so as to be *united to, Greek*) God." Hope in God is the spring of true holiness [BENGEL]. **in subjection**—Their ornament consisted in their subordination. Vanity was forbidden (vs. 3) as being contrary to female *subjection.* **6. Sara**—an example of *faith.* **calling him lord**—(Gen. 18:12). **ye are**—*Greek,* "ye have become": "children" of Abraham and Sara by *faith,* whereas ye were Gentile aliens from the covenant. **afraid with any amazement**—*Greek,* "fluttering alarm," "consternation." *Act well, and be not thrown into sudden panic,* as weak females are apt to be, by any opposition from without. BENGEL *translates,* "Not afraid OF *any fluttering terror* coming from without" (vss. 13-16). So LXX, Proverbs 3:25 uses the same *Greek* word, which Peter probably refers to. Anger assails men; *fear,* women. You need fear no man in doing what is right: not thrown into fluttering agitation by any sudden outbreak of temper on the part of your unbelieving husbands, while you *do well.* **7. dwell** —*Greek,* "dwelling": connected with the verb, ch. 2:17, "Honor all." **knowledge**—Christian knowledge: appreciating the due relation of the sexes in the design of God, and acting with tenderness and forbearance accordingly: *wisely: with wise consideration.* **them . . . giving honour to the wife**—translate and punctuate the *Greek* rather, "dwelling according to knowledge with the female (*Greek adjective,* qualifying 'vessel'; not as *English Version,* a noun) as with the weaker vessel (*Note,* I Thess. 4:4). Both husband and wife are vessels in

God's hand, and of God's making, to fulfil His gracious purposes. Both weak, the woman the *weaker*. The sense of his own weakness, and that she, like himself, is God's *vessel* and fabric, ought to lead him to act with tender and wise consideration towards her who is the *weaker fabric*), giving (lit., '*assigning*,' '*apportioning*') honor as being also (besides being man and wife) heirs together . . ."; or, as the Vatican MS. reads, "as to those who are also (besides being your wives) fellow heirs." (The reason why the man should *give honor* to the woman is, because *God gives honor to both* as fellow heirs; cf. the same argument, vs. 9.) He does not take into account the case of an *unbelieving* wife, as she might yet believe. **grace of life**—God's *gracious gift of life* (ch. 1:4, 13). **that your prayers be not hindered**—by dissensions, which prevent *united* prayer, on which depends the blessing. **8.** *General* summary of relative duty, after having detailed *particular* duties from ch. 2:18. **of one mind**—as to the faith. **having compassion one of another**—*Greek,* "sympathizing" in the joy and sorrow of others. **love as brethren**—*Greek,* "loving the brethren." **pitiful**—towards the afflicted. **courteous**—genuine Christian politeness; not the tinsel of the world's politeness; stamped with *unfeigned love* on one side, and *humility* on the other. But the oldest MSS. read, "humble-minded." It is slightly different from "humble," in that it marks a *conscious effort* to be truly *humble*. **9. evil**—in deed. **railing**—in word. **blessing**—your revilers; participle, not a noun after "rendering." **knowing that**—The oldest MSS. read merely, "because." **are**—*Greek,* "were" called. **inherit a blessing**—not only passive, but also active; receiving spiritual blessing from God by faith, and in your turn blessing others from love [GERHARD *in* ALFORD]. "It is not in order to inherit a blessing that we must bless, but because our portion is blessing." No *railing* can injure you (vs. 13). Imitate God who *blesses* you. The first fruits of His *blessing* for eternity are enjoyed by the righteous even now (vs. 10) [BENGEL]. **10. will love**—*Greek,* "wishes to love." He who *loves life* (present and eternal), and *desires to continue to do so,* not involving himself in troubles which will make this life a burden, and cause him to forfeit eternal life. Peter confirms his exhortation, vs. 9, by Psalm 34:12-16. **refrain**—curb, lit., "cause to cease"; implying that our natural inclination and custom is to speak evil. "Men commonly think that they would be exposed to the wantonness of their enemies if they did not strenuously vindicate their rights. But the Spirit promises a life of blessedness to none but those who are gentle and patient of evils" [CALVIN]. **evil . . . guile**—First he warns against sins of the *tongue,* evil-speaking, and deceitful, double-tongued speaking; next, against *acts* of injury to one's neighbor. **11.** In oldest MSS., *Greek,* "*Moreover* (besides his *words,* in *acts*), let him." **eschew**—"turn from." **ensue**—*pursue* as a thing hard to attain, and that flees from one in this troublesome world. **12.** Ground of the promised present and eternal life of blessedness to the meek (vs. 10). The Lord's *eyes* are ever over them for good. **ears . . . unto their prayers**—(I John 5:14, 15). **face . . . against**—The *eyes* imply *favorable* regard; the *face* of the Lord *upon* (not as *English Version,* "against") them that do evil, implies that He narrowly observes them, so as not to let them really and lastingly hurt His people (cf. vs. 13). **13. wnu . . . will harm you**—This fearless confidence in God's protection from harm, Christ, the Head, in His sufferings realized; so His members. **if ye be**—

Greek, "if ye have *become.*" **followers**—The oldest MSS. read "emulous," "zealous of" (Titus 2:14). **good**—The contrast in *Greek* is, "Who will do you *evil,* if ye be zealous of *good*?" **14. But and if**—"But *if even.*" "The promises of *this* life extend only so far as it is expedient for us that they should be fulfilled" [CALVIN]. So he proceeds to state the exceptions to the promise (vs. 10), and how the truly wise will behave in such exceptional cases. "If ye should *suffer*"; if it should so happen; "suffer," a milder word than *harm*. **for righteousness**—"not the suffering, but the cause for which one suffers, makes the martyr" [AUGUSTINE]. **happy**—Not even can *suffering* take away your *blessedness,* but rather promotes it. **and**—*Greek,* "but." Do not impair your blessing (vs. 9) by *fearing* man's *terror* in your times of adversity. Lit., "Be not terrified with their terror," i.e., with that which they try to strike into you, and which strikes themselves when in adversity. This verse and v. 15 is quoted from Isaiah 8:12, 13. God alone is to be feared; he that fears God has none else to fear. **neither be troubled**—the threat of the law, Leviticus 26:36; Deuteronomy 28:65, 66; in contrast to which the Gospel gives the believer a heart assured of God's favor, and therefore unruffled, amidst all adversities. Not only be not *afraid,* but be not even *agitated*. **15. sanctify**—hallow; honor as holy, enshrining Him *in your hearts*. So in the Lord's Prayer, Matthew 6:9. God's holiness is thus glorified in our hearts as the dwelling-place of His Spirit. **the Lord God**—The oldest MSS. read "Christ." Translate, "Sanctify *Christ as Lord.*" **and**—*Greek,* "but," or "moreover." *Besides* this inward sanctification of God *in the heart, be also ready always to give . . . .* **answer**—an apologetic answer defending your faith. **to every man that asketh you**—The last words limit the universality of the "always"; not to a railer, but to everyone among the heathen who inquires honestly. **a reason**—a reasonable account. This refutes Rome's dogma, "I believe it, because the Church believes it." Credulity is believing without evidence; faith is believing on evidence. There is no repose for reason itself but in faith. This verse does not impose an obligation to bring forward a learned proof and logical defense of revelation. But as believers deny themselves, crucify the world, and brave persecution, they must be buoyed up by some strong "hope"; men of the world, having no such hope themselves, are moved by curiosity to *ask* the secret of this hope; the believer must be *ready* to give an *experimental account* "how this hope arose in him, what it contains, and on what it rests" [STEIGER]. **with**—The oldest MSS. read, "*but* with." Be ready, *but* with "meekness." Not pertly and arrogantly. **meekness**—(vs. 4.) The most effective way; not self-sufficient impetuosity. **fear**—due respect towards man, and reverence towards God, remembering His cause does not need man's hot temper to uphold it. **16. Having a good conscience**—the secret spring of *readiness to give account* of our *hope.* So *hope* and *good conscience* go together in Acts 24:15, 16. Profession without practice has no weight. But those who *have a good conscience* can afford to give an account of their hope "with meekness." **whereas**—(ch. 2:12). **they speak evil of you, as of evildoers**—One oldest MS. reads, "ye are spoken against," omitting the rest. **falsely accuse**—"calumniate"; the *Greek* expresses malice shown in deeds as well as in words. It is translated, "despitefully use," Matthew 5:44; Luke 6:28. **conversation**—life, conduct. **in Christ**—who is the very element of your life as Christians. "In

Christ" defines "good." It is your good walk *as Christians,* not as citizens, that calls forth malice (ch. 4:4, 5, 14). **17. better**—One may object, I would not bear it so ill if I had deserved it. Peter replies, it is *better* that you did not deserve it, in order that doing well and yet being spoken against, you may prove yourself a true Christian [GERHARD]. **if the will of God be so**—rather as the optative is in the oldest MSS., "if the will of God should will it so." Those who honor God's will as their highest law (ch. 2:15) have the comfort to know that suffering is God's appointment (ch. 4:19). So Christ Himself; our inclination does not wish it. **18.** Confirmation of vs. 17, by the glorious results of Christ's suffering innocently. **For**—"Because." That is "better," vs. 17, means of which we are rendered more like to Christ in death and in life; for His death brought the best issue to Himself and to us [BENGEL]. **Christ**—the Anointed *Holy* One of God; the *Holy* suffered for *sins,* the *Just* for the *unjust.* **also**—as well as yourselves (vs. 17). Cf. ch. 2:21; there His suffering was brought forward as an example to us; here, as a proof of the blessedness of suffering for well-doing. **once**—for all; never again to suffer. It is "better" for us also once to suffer with Christ, than for ever without Christ [BENGEL]. We now are suffering our "once"; it will soon be a thing of the past; a bright consolation to the tried. **for sins**—as though He had Himself committed them. He exposed Himself to death by His "confession," even as we are called on to "give an answer to him that asketh a reason of our hope." This was "welldoing" in its highest manifestation. As He suffered, "The Just," so we ought willingly to suffer, for *righteousness'* sake (vs. 14; cf. vss. 12. 17). **that he might bring us to God**—together with Himself in His ascension to the right hand of God (vs. 22). He brings us, "the unjust," justified together with Him into heaven. So the result of Christ's death is His *drawing men to Him;* spiritually now, in our having *access into the Holiest,* opened by Christ's ascension; literally hereafter. "Bring us," moreover, by the same steps of humiliation and exaltation through which He Himself passed. The several steps of Christ's progress from lowliness to glory are trodden over again by His people in virtue of their oneness with Him (ch. 4:1-3). "To God," is *Greek* dative (not the preposition and case), implying that *God wishes it* [BENGEL]. **put to death**—the means of His *bringing us to God.* **in the flesh**—i.e., *in respect to* the life of *flesh* and blood. **quickened by the Spirit**—The oldest MSS. omit the *Greek* article. Translate with the preposition "in," as the antithesis to the previous "*in* the flesh" requires, "IN spirit," i.e., in respect to His Spirit. "Put to death" in the former *mode of lifs*; "quickened" in the other. Not that His Spirit ever died and was *quickened,* or made alive again, but whereas He had lived after the manner of mortal men in the flesh, He *began to live a spiritual* "resurrection" (vs. 21) *life,* whereby He has the power to bring us to God. Two ways of explaining vss. 18, 19, are open to us: (1) "Quickened in Spirit," i.e., *immediately* on His release from the "flesh," the energy of His undying spirit-life was "quickened" by God the Father, into new modes of action, viz., "in the Spirit He *went* down (as subsequently He *went* up to heaven, vs. 22, the same *Greek* verb) and heralded [not *salvation,* as ALFORD, contrary to Scripture, which everywhere represents man's state, whether saved or lost, after death irreversible. Nor is any mention made of the *conversion* of the spirits in prison. See *Note,* vs. 20. Nor is the phrase here 'preached *the Gospel*' (*evan-*

gelizo), but 'heralded' (*ekeruxe*) or 'preached'; but simply *made the announcement* of His finished work; so the same *Greek* in Mark 1:45, 'publish,' confirming Enoch and Noah's testimony, and thereby declaring the virtual condemnation of their unbelief, and the salvation of Noah and believers; a sample of the similar opposite effects of the same work on *all* unbelievers, and believers, respectively; also a consolation to those whom Peter addresses, in their sufferings at the hands of unbelievers; specially selected for the sake of 'baptism,' its 'antitype' (vs. 21), which, as a seal, marks believers as separated from the rest of the doomed world] to the spirits (His *Spirit* speaking to the *spirits*) in prison (in Hades or Sheol, awaiting the judgment, II Pet. 2:4), which were of old disobedient when...." (2) The strongest point in favor of (I) is the position of "sometime," i.e., *of old,* connected with "disobedient"; whereas if the *preaching* or announcing were a thing long past, we should expect "sometime," or *of old,* to be joined to "went and preached." But this transposition may express that *their disobedience preceded His preaching.* The *Greek* participle expresses the reason of His *preaching,* "inasmuch as they were sometime disobedient" (cf. ch. 4:6). Also "went" seems to mean a *personal* going, as in vs. 22, not merely in spirit. But see the answer below. The objections are "quickened" must refer to Christ's *body* (cf. vs. 21, end), for as His *Spirit* never ceased to live, it cannot be said to be "quickened." Cf. John 5:21; Romans 8:11, and other passages, where "quicken" is used of the *bodily* resurrection. Also, **not** His *Spirit,* but His *soul,* went to Hades. His Spirit was commended by Him at death to His Father, and was thereupon "in Paradise." The theory—(1) would thus require that His descent to the spirits in prison should be *after* His resurrection! Cf. Ephesians 4:9, 10, which makes the *descent* precede the *ascent.* Also Scripture elsewhere is silent about such a heralding, though possibly Christ's death had immediate effects on the state of both the godly and the ungodly in Hades: the souls of the godly heretofore in comparative confinement, perhaps then having been, as some Fathers thought, translated to God's immediate and heavenly presence; but this cannot be *proved* from Scripture. Cf. however, John 3:13; Colossians 1:18. *Prison* is always used in a *bad* sense in Scripture. "Paradise" and "Abraham's bosom," the abode of good spirits in Old Testament times, are separated by a wide gulf from Hell or Hades, and cannot be called "prison." Cf. II Corinthians 12:2, 4, where "paradise" and the "third heaven" correspond. Also, why should the antediluvian unbelievers in particular be selected as the objects of His preaching in Hades? Therefore explain: "Quickened in spirit, in which (as distinguished from *in person*; the words "in which," i.e., *in spirit,* expressly obviating the objection that "went" implies a *personal going*) He went (in the person of Noah, "a preacher of righteousness," II Pet. 2:5; ALFORD's own *Note,* Eph. 2:17, is the best reply to his argument from "went" that a *local* going to Hades *in person* is meant. As "He CAME and preached peace" *by His Spirit* in the apostles and ministers after His death and ascension: so before His incarnation He preached in Spirit through Noah to the antediluvians, John 14: 18, 28; Acts 26:23. "Christ should show," lit., "*announce* light to the Gentiles") and preached unto the spirits in prison, i.e., the antediluvians, whose bodies indeed seemed free, but their spirits were in prison, shut up in the earth as one great condemned cell (exactly parallel to Isa. 24: 22, 23 "upon the earth

... they shall be gathered together as *prisoners* are gathered in the pit, and shall be shut up *in the prison* ..." [just as the fallen angels are judicially regarded as "in chains of darkness," though for a time now at large on the earth, I Pet. 2:4], where vs. 18 has a plain allusion to the flood, "the *windows from on high* are open," cf. Gen. 7:11); from this prison the only way of escape was that preached by Christ in Noah. Christ, who in our times came in the flesh, in the days of Noah preached *in Spirit* by Noah to the spirits then in prison (Isa. 61:1, end, "the Spirit of the Lord God hath sent me to *proclaim* the opening of the *prison* to them that are bound"). So in ch. 1:11, "the Spirit of Christ" is said to have testified in the prophets. As Christ suffered even to death by enemies, and was afterwards quickened in virtue of His "Spirit" (or divine nature, Rom. 1:3, 4; I Cor. 15:45), which henceforth acted in its full energy, the first result of which was the raising of His body (vs. 21, end) from the prison of the grave and His soul from Hades; so the same Spirit of Christ enabled Noah, amidst reproach and trials, to preach to the disobedient spirits fast bound in wrath. That Spirit in you can enable you also to suffer patiently now, looking for the resurrection deliverance. **20. once**—not in the oldest MSS. **when . . . the long-suffering of God waited in the days of Noah** —Oldest MSS. *Greek,* "*was continuing to* wait *on*" (if haply men in the 120 years of grace would repent until the *end* of His waiting came in their death by the flood. This refutes ALFORD's idea of a second day of grace having been given in Hades. Noah's days are selected, as the ark and the destroying flood answer respectively to "baptism" and the coming destruction of unbelievers by fire. **while the ark was a-preparing**—(Heb. 11:7). A long period of God's "long-suffering and waiting," as Noah had few to help him, which rendered the world's unbelief the more inexcusable. **wherein**—lit., "(by having entered) *into* which." **eight**—seven (the sacred number) with ungodly Ham. **few**—so now. **souls**—As this term is here used of *living* persons, why should not "spirits" also? Noah preached to their ears, but Christ *in spirit*, to their *spirits*, or spiritual natures. **saved by water**—The same water which drowned the unbelieving, buoyed up the ark in which the eight were saved. Not as some translate, "were brought safe *through* the water." However, the sense of the preposition may be as in I Corinthians 3:15, "they were safely preserved through the water," though having to be *in the water*. **21. whereunto**—The oldest MSS. read, "which": lit., "which (viz., *water*, in general; being) the antitype (of the water of the flood) is now saving (the salvation being not yet fully realized by us, cf. I Corinthians 10:1, 2, 5; Jude 5; *puts into a state of salvation*) us also (two oldest MSS. read 'you' for 'us': *You also*, as well as Noah and his party), to wit, baptism." Water saved Noah not of itself, but by sustaining the ark built in *faith* resting on God's word: it was to him the sign and mean of a kind of *regeneration* of the earth. The flood was for Noah a baptism, as the passage through the Red Sea was for the Israelites; by baptism in the flood he and his family were transferred from the old world to the new; from immediate destruction to lengthened probation; from the companionship of the wicked to communion with God; from the severing of all bonds between the creature and the Creator to the privileges of the covenant: so we by spiritual baptism. As there was a Ham who forfeited the privileges of the covenant, so many now. The antitypical water, viz., baptism, saves you also not of itself, nor the mere material water, but the spiritual thing conjoined with it, repentance and faith, of which it is the sign and seal, as Peter proceeds to explain. Cf. the union of the sign and thing signified, John 3:5; Ephesians 5:26; Titus 3:5; Hebrews 10:22; cf. I John 5:6. **not the . . .**—"flesh" bears the emphasis. "Not the putting away of the filth of *the flesh*" (as is done by a mere water baptism, unaccompanied with the Spirit's baptism, cf. Eph. 2: 11), but of the soul. It is the ark (Christ and His Spirit-filled Church), not the water, which is the instrument of salvation: the water only flowed round the ark; so not the mere water baptism, but the water when accompanied with the Spirit. **answer** —*Greek,* "interrogation"; referring to the *questions* asked of candidates for baptism; eliciting a confession of faith "toward God" and a renunciation of Satan [AUGUSTINE, *ad Catechumenos,* B. 4., c. 1; CYPRIAN, *Ep.* 7., *ad Rogatian*], which, when flowing from "a good conscience," assure one of being "saved." Lit., "a good conscience's interrogation (including the satisfactory *answer*) toward God." I prefer this to the translation of WAHL, ALFORD and others, "*inquiry of a good conscience after God*": not one of the parallels alleged, not even II Samuel 11:7, in the LXX, is strictly in point. Recent Byzantine *Greek* idiom (whereby the term meant: (1) the question; (2) the stipulation; (3) the engagement), easily flowing from the usage of the word as Peter has it, confirms the former translation. **by the resurrection of Jesus**—joined with "saves you": In so far as baptism applies to us the power of Christ's resurrection. As Christ's death unto sin is the source of the believer's death unto, and so deliverance from, sin's penalty and power; so His resurrection life is the source of the believer's new spiritual life. **22.** (Ps. 110:1; Rom. 8:34, 38; I Cor. 15: 24; Eph. 1:21; 3:10; Col. 1:16; 2:10-15.) The fruit of His patience in His voluntary endured and undeserved sufferings: a pattern to us, vss. 17, 18. **gone**—(Luke 24:51). Proving against rationalists an actual material ascension. Lit., "is on the right hand of God, *having gone* into heaven." The oldest MSS. of the *Vulgate* and the *Latin* Fathers, add what expresses the benefit to us of Christ's sitting on God's right hand, "Who is on the right hand of God, *having swallowed up death that we may become heirs of everlasting life*"; involving for us A STATE OF LIFE, saved, glorious, and eternal. The GREEK MSS., however, reject the words. Cf. with this verse Peter's speeches, Acts 2:32-35; 3:21, 26; 10: 40, 42.

CHAPTER 4

Vss. 1-19. LIKE THE RISEN CHRIST, BELIEVERS HENCEFORTH OUGHT TO HAVE NO MORE TO DO WITH SIN. *As the end is near, cultivate self-restraint, watchful prayerfulness, charity, hospitality, scriptural speech, ministering to one another according to your several gifts to the glory of God: Rejoicing patience under suffering.* **1. for us**—supported by some oldest MSS. and versions, omitted by others. **in the flesh**—in His mortal body of humiliation. **arm**—(Eph. 6:11, 13). **the same mind**—of suffering with patient willingness what God *wills* you to suffer. **he that hath suffered**—for instance, Christ first, and in His person the believer: a general proposition. **hath ceased**—lit., "has been made to cease," *has obtained* by the very fact of His having suffered once for all, *a cessation from sin*, which had heretofore lain on Him (Rom. 6:6-11, especially, vs. 7). The Christian is by faith one with Christ: as then Christ by death is judicially freed from sin; so the Christian who has in the person of Christ died, has no more to do with it judicially, and ought to have no more to do with it actually. "The flesh" is the sphere in which sin has place. **2. That he ...**—"That he (the believer, who has once for all obtained cessation from sin by suffering, in the person of Christ, viz., in virtue of his union with the crucified Christ) should no longer live the rest of his time in the flesh to the lusts of men, but to the will of God" as his rule. *"Rest of his time in the flesh"* (the *Greek* has the preposition "in" here, not in vs. 1 as to Christ) proves that the reference is here not to Christ, but to the believer, whose remaining time for glorifying God is short (vs. 3). "Live" in the truest sense, for heretofore he was *dead*. Not as ALFORD, "*Arm yourselves ... with a view no longer to live the rest of your time.*" **3. may suffice**—*Greek,* "is sufficient." Peter takes the lowest ground: for not even the past time ought to have been wasted in lust; but since you cannot recall it, at least lay out the future to better account. **us**—omitted in oldest MSS. **wrought**—*Greek,* "wrought out." **Gentiles**—heathen: which many of you were. **when ...**—"walking as ye have done [ALFORD] in *lasciviousness*"; the *Greek* means *petulant, immodest, wantonness,* unbridled conduct: not so much filthy lust. **excess of wine**—"wine-bibbings" [ALFORD]. **abominable**—"nefarious," "lawless idolatries," violating God's most sacred law; not that *all* Peter's readers (*Note,* ch. 1:1) *walked* in these, but many, viz., the Gentile portion of them. **4. Wherein**—In respect to which abandonment of your former *walk* (vs. 3). **run not with them**—eagerly, in troops [BENGEL]. **excess**—lit., "profusion"; a sink: stagnant water remaining after an inundation. **riot**—profligacy. **speaking evil**—charging you with pride, singularity, hypocrisy, and secret crimes (vs. 14; II Pet. 2:2). However, there is no "of you" in the *Greek,* but simply "blaspheming." It seems to me always to be used, either directly or indirectly, in the sense of *impious reviling against God, Christ, or the Holy Spirit,* and the Christian religion, not merely against men as such; *Greek,* vs. 14, below. **5. They who now call you to account falsely, shall have to give account themselves for this very evil-speaking (Jude 15), and be condemned justly. ready**—very speedily (vs. 7; II Pet. 3:10). Christ's coming is to the believer always near. **6. For**—giving the reason for vs. 5, "judge the *dead.*" **gospel preached also to ... dead**—as well as to them now living, and to them that shall be found alive at the coming of the Judge. "Dead" must be taken in the same literal sense as in vs. 5, which refutes the explanation "dead" *in sins.* Moreover, the absence of the *Greek* article does not necessarily restrict the sense of "dead" to particular dead persons, for there is no *Greek* article in vs. 5 also, where "the dead" is universal in meaning. The sense seems to be, Peter, as representing the true attitude of the Church in every age, expecting Christ at any moment, says, The Judge is ready to judge the quick and dead—*the dead,* I say, *for* they, too, in their lifetime, have had the Gospel preached to them, that so they might be judged at last in the same way as those living now (and those who shall be so when Christ shall come), viz.., "men in the flesh," and that they might, having escaped condemnation by embracing the Gospel so preached, live unto God in the spirit (though death has passed over their flesh), Luke 20:38, thus being made like Christ in death and in life (*Note,* ch. 3:18). He says, "live," not "made alive" or quickened; for they are

supposed to have been already "quickened together with Christ" (Eph. 2:5). This verse is parallel to ch. 3:19; cf. *Note* there. The Gospel, substantially, was "preached" to the Old Testament Church; though not so fully as to the New Testament Church. It is no valid objection that the Gospel has not been preached to *all* that shall be found dead at Christ's coming. For Peter is plainly referring only to those within reach of the Gospel, or who might have known God through His ministers in Old and New Testament times. Peter, like Paul, argues that those found *living* at Christ's coming shall have no advantage above the *dead* who shall then be raised, inasmuch as the latter *live unto,* or "according to," *God,* even already in His purpose. ALFORD's explanation is wrong, "that they might be judged according to men as regards the flesh," i.e., *be in the state of the completed sentence on sin,* which is *death after the flesh.* For "judged" cannot have a different meaning in this verse from what "judge" bears in vs. 5. "Live according to God" means, live a life with God, *such as God lives,* divine; as contrasted with "according to men in the flesh," i.e., a life such as men live in the flesh. **7.** Resuming the idea in vs. 5. **the end of all things**—and therefore also of the wantonness (vss. 3, 4) of the wicked, and of the sufferings of the righteous [BENGEL]. The nearness meant is not that of mere *time,* but that *before the Lord;* as he explains to guard against misapprehension, and defends God from the charge of procrastination: We live in the last dispensation, not like the Jews under the Old Testament. The Lord will come as a thief; He is "ready" (vs. 5) to judge the world at any moment; it is only God's long-suffering and His will that the Gospel should be preached as a witness to all nations, that induces Him to lengthen out the time which is with Him still as nothing. **sober**—"self-restrained." The opposite duties to the sins in vs. 3 are here inculcated. Thus "sober" is the opposite of "lasciviousness" (vs. 3). **watch**—*Greek,* "be soberly vigilant"; not intoxicated with worldly cares and pleasures. Temperance promotes *wakefulness* or watchfulness, and both promote prayer. Drink makes drowsy, and drowsiness prevents prayer. **prayer**—*Greek,* "prayers"; the end for which we should exercise vigilance. **8. above all things**—not that "charity" or *love* is placed above "prayer," but because *love* is the animating spirit, without which all other duties are dead. Translate as *Greek,* "Having your mutual (lit., 'towards yourselves') charity intense." He presupposes its existence among them; he urges them to make it more fervent. **charity shall cover the multitude ...**—The oldest MSS. have "covereth." Quoted from Proverbs 10: 12; cf. 17:9. "Covereth" so as not harshly to condemn or expose faults; but forbearingly to bear the other's burdens, forgiving and forgetting past offenses. Perhaps the *additional* idea is included, By prayer for them, *love tries to have them covered by God;* and so being the instrument of converting the sinner from his error, "covereth a (not 'the,' as *English Version*) multitude of sins"; but the former idea from Proverbs is the *prominent* one. It is not, as Rome teaches, "covereth" *his own* sins; for then the *Greek* middle voice would be used; and Proverbs 10:12 and 17:9 support the Protestant view. "As God with His love covers my sins if I believe, so must I also *cover the sins of my neighbor*" [LUTHER] Cf. the conduct of Shem and Japheth to Noah (Gen. 9:23), in contrast to Ham's exposure of his father's shame. We ought to cover others' sins only where love itself does not require the contrary. **9.** (Rom.

12:13; Heb. 13:2.) Not the spurious hospitality which passes current in the world, but the entertaining of those *needing* it, especially those exiled for the faith, as the representatives of Christ, and all hospitality to whomsoever exercised from genuine Christian love. **without grudging**–*Greek,* "murmuring." "He that giveth, let him do it with simplicity," i.e. open-hearted sincerity; with cordiality. Not secretly speaking against the person whom we entertain, or upbraiding him with the favor we have conferred in him. **10. every**–"even as *each* man hath received," in whatever degree, and of whatever kind. The Spirit's *gifts* (lit., "gift *of grace,*" i.e., *gratuitously* bestowed) are the common property of the Christian community, each Christian being but a steward for the edifying of the whole, not receiving the gift merely for his own use. **minister the same**–not discontentedly envying or disparaging *the gift of another.* **one to another**–*Greek* as in vs. 8, "towards yourselves"; implying that all form but one body, and in seeking the good of other members they are promoting the good of *themselves.* **stewards**–referring to Matthew 25:15, etc.; Luke 19:13-26. **11. If any . . . speak**–viz., as a prophet, or divinely taught *teacher* in the Church assembly. **the . . .**–The *Greek* has no article: "as oracles of God." This may be due to *Greek:* "God," having no article, it being a principle when a governed noun omits the *Greek* article that the governing noun should omit it, too. In Acts 7:38 also, the *Greek* article is wanting; thus *English Version,* "as *the* oracles of God," viz., *the Old Testament,* would be right, and the precept be similar to Romans 12:6, "prophesy according to *the analogy of the faith.*" But the context suits better thus, "Let him speak as (becomes one speaking) *oracles* OF GOD." His divinely inspired words are *not his own,* but *God's,* and as a *steward* (4:10) having them committed to him, he ought so to speak them. Jesus was the pattern in this respect (Matt. 7:29; John 12:49; 14:10; cf. Paul, II Cor. 2:17). Note, the very same term as is applied in the only other passages where it occurs (Acts 7:38; Rom. 3:2; Heb. 5:12), to the *Old Testament* inspired writings, is here predicated of the inspired *words* (the substance of which was afterwards committed to *writing*) of the *New Testament* prophets. **minister**–in *acts;* the other sphere of spiritual activity besides *speaking.* **as of** –"out of" the store of his "strength" (*Greek, physical* power in relation to outward service, rather than moral and intellectual "ability"; so in Mark 12:30). **giveth**–*Greek,* "supplieth"; originally said of a *choragus,* who *supplied* the chorus with all necessaries for performing their several parts. **that God in all things may be glorified**–the final end of all a Christian's acts. **through Jesus Christ**–the mediator through whom all our blessings come down to us, and also through whom all our praises ascend to God. Through Christ alone can God be glorified in us and our sayings and doings. **to whom**–Christ. **be**–*Greek,* "is." **for ever and ever**–*Greek,* "unto the ages of the ages." **12. strange**–they might th:nk it strange that God should allow His chosen children to be sore tried. **fiery trial**–like the fire by which metals are tested and their dross removed. The *Greek* adds, "in your case." **which is to try you**–*Greek,* "which is taking place for a trial to you." Instead of its "*happening* to you" as some strange and untoward *chance,* it "is taking place" with the gracious *design* of trying you; God has a wise design in it–a consolatory reflection. **13. inasmuch as**–The oldest MSS. read, "in proportion as"; "in as far as" ye by suffering are partakers of

Christ's sufferings, i.e., by faith enter into realizing fellowship with them; willingly for His sake suffering as He suffered. **with exceeding joy**–*Greek, "exulting* joy"; now ye *rejoice* amidst sufferings; then ye shall EXULT, for ever free from sufferings (ch. 1:6, 8). If we will not bear suffering for Christ now, we must bear eternal sufferings hereafter. **14. for**–*Greek,* "IN the name of Christ," viz., *as Christians* (vs. 16; ch. 3:14, above); "*in My name,* because *ye belong to Christ.*" The emphasis lies on this: vs. 15, "as a murderer, thief," etc., stands in contrast. Let your suffering be on account of Christ, not on account of evil-doing (ch. 2:20). **reproached**–*Reproach* affects noble minds more than loss of goods, or even bodily sufferings. **the spirit . . . upon you**–the same Spirit as rested on Christ (Luke 4:18). "The Spirit of glory" is *His* Spirit, for He is the "Lord *of glory"* (Jas. 2:1). Believers may well overcome the "*reproach*" (cf. Heb. 11:26), seeing that "the Spirit of *glory"* rests upon them, as upon Him. It cannot prevent the happiness of the righteous, if they are reproached for Christ, because they retain before God their *glory* entire, as having the Spirit, with whom *glory* is inseparably joined [CALVIN]. **and of God**–*Greek,* "and *the* (Spirit) of God"; implying that the *Spirit of glory* (which is Christ's Spirit) is at the same time also *the Spirit of God.* **on their part he is evil spoken of, but on your part he is glorified**–omitted in the two oldest *Greek* MSS. and *Syriac* and *Coptic* versions, but supported by one very old MS., *Vulgate, Sahidic, Cyprian,* etc. "Evil spoken of," lit., "blasphemed"; not merely do they "*speak against you,*" as in ch. 3:16, but *blasphemously mock* Christ and Christianity itself. **15. But**–*Greek,* "For." "Reproached *in the name of Christ*" I say (vs. 14), "FOR *let none . . . .*" **as . . . as . . . as . . . as**–the *as* twice in italics is not in the *Greek.* The second *Greek,* "as," distinguishes the class "busybody in other men's matters," from the previous class of delinquents. Christians, from mistaken zeal, under the plea of faithfulness, might readily step out of their own calling and make themselves judges of the acts of unbelievers. Lit., "a bishop in what is (not his own, but) another's" province; an allusion to the existing *bishops* or overseers of the Church; a self-constituted bishop in others' concerns. **16. a Christian**–the name given in contempt first at Antioch, Acts 11:26; 26:28; the only three places where the term occurs. At first believers had no distinctive name, but were called among themselves "brethren," Acts 6:3; "disciples," Acts 6:1; "those of the way," Acts 9:2; "saints," Romans 1:7; by the Jews (who denied that Jesus was the CHRIST, and so would never originate the name *Christian*), in contempt, "Nazarenes." At Antioch, where first *idolatrous* Gentiles (Cornelius, Acts 10, was not an idolater, but a proselyte) were converted, and wide missionary work began, they could be no longer looked on as a *Jewish sect,* and so *the Gentiles* designated them by the new name "Christians." The rise of the new name marked a new epoch in the Church's life, a new stage of its development, viz., its missions to the Gentiles. The idle and witty people of Antioch, we know from heathen writers, were famous for inventing nicknames. The date of this Epistle must have been when this had become the generally recognized designation *among Gentiles (it is never applied by Christians to each other,* as it was in after ages–an undesigned proof that the New Testament was composed when it professes), and when the name exposed one to reproach and suffering, though not seemingly as yet to *systematic* persecution. **let** him not be ashamed—though the world is ashamed of shame. To suffer for one's own faults is no honor (vs. 15; ch. 2:20),—for Christ, is no *shame* (vs. 14; ch. 3:13). **but let him glorify God**—not merely glory in persecution; Peter might have said as the contrast, "but let him esteem it an honor to himself"; but the honor is to be given *to God*, who counts him worthy of such an honor, involving exemption from the coming judgments on the ungodly. **on this behalf**—The oldest MSS. and *Vulgate* read, "in this *name*," i.e., in respect of suffering for such a name. **17.** Another ground of consolation to Christians. All must pass under the judgment of God; God's own household first, their chastisement being here, for which they should glorify Him as a proof of their membership in His family, and a pledge of their escape from the end of those whom the last judgment shall find disobedient to the Gospel. **the time**—*Greek*, "season," "fit time." **judgment must begin at the house of God**—the Church of living believers. Peter has in mind Ezekiel 9:6; cf. Amos 3:2; Jeremiah 25:29. Judgment is already begun, the Gospel word, as a "two-edged sword," having the double effect of saving some and condemning others, and shall be consummated at the last judgment. "When power is given to the destroyer, he observes no distinction between the righteous and the wicked; not only so, but he begins first at the righteous" [WETSTEIN from *Rabbins*]. But God limits the destroyer's power over His people. **if . . . at us, what shall the end be of them . . .**—If even the godly have chastening judgments now, how much more shall the ungodly be doomed to damnatory judgments at last. **gospel of God**—the very God who is to judge them. **18. scarcely**—Cf. "so as by fire," I Corinthians 3:15; having to pass through trying chastisements, as David did for his sin. "The righteous" man has always more or less of trial, but the issue is certain, and the entrance into the kingdom *abundant* at last. The "scarcely" marks the severity of the ordeal, and the unlikelihood (in a mere human point of view) of the righteous sustaining it; but the righteousness of Christ and God's everlasting covenant make it all sure. **ungodly**—having no regard for God; negative description. **sinner**—loving sin; positive; the same man is at once God-forgetting and sin-loving. **appear**—in judgment. **19.** General conclusion from vss. 17, 18. Seeing that the godly know that their sufferings are *by God's will*, to chasten them that they may not perish with the world, they have good reason to trust God cheerfully amidst sufferings, persevering *in well-doing*. **let them**—*Greek*, "let them *also*," "let *even* them," as well as those not suffering. Not only under ordinary circumstances, but *also* in time of *suffering, let* believers *commit*. . . . (Cf. *Note*, ch. 3:14.) **according to the will of God**—(*Note*, ch. 3:17). God's will that the believer should suffer (vs. 17), is for his good. One oldest MS. and *Vulgate* read, "in *well-doings*"; contrast ill-doings, vs. 15. Our committing of ourselves to God is to be, not in indolent and passive quietism, but accompanied with active *well-doings*. **faithful** —to His covenant promises. **Creator**—who is therefore also our Almighty Preserver. He, not we, must *keep* our souls. Sin destroyed the original spiritual relation between creature and Creator, leaving that only of government. Faith restores it; so that the believer, living to *the will of God* (ch. 4:2), rests implicitly on his *Creator's* faithfulness.

CHAPTER 5

Vss. 1-14. EXHORTATIONS TO ELDERS, JUNIORS, AND ALL IN GENERAL. PARTING PRAYER. CONCLUSION. **1. elders**—alike in office and age (vs 5). **I . . . also an elder**—To put one's self on a level with those whom we exhort, gives weight to one's exhortations (cf. II John 1). Peter, in true humility for the Gospel's sake, does not put forward his *apostleship* here, wherein he *presided over the elders*. In the apostleship the apostles have no successors, for "the signs of an apostle" have not been transmitted. The presidents over the presbyters and deacons, by whatever name designated, *angel, bishop,* or *moderator,* etc., though *of the same* ORDER *as the presbyters,* yet have virtually succeeded to a superintendency of the Church analogous to that exercised by the apostles (this superintendency and priority existed from the earliest times after the apostles [TERTULLIAN]; just as the Jewish synagogue (the model which the Church followed)'was governed by a council of presbyters, presided over by one of themselves, "the chief ruler of the synagogue." (Cf. VITRINGA, *Synagogue,* Part II, chs. 3 and 7.) **witness**—an *eyewitness* of Christ's sufferings, and so qualified to exhort you to believing patience in *suffering for well-doing* after His example (ch. 4:19; 2:20). This explains the "therefore" inserted in the oldest MSS., "I therefore exhort," resuming exhortation from ch. 4:19. His higher dignity as an *apostle* is herein delicately implied, as *eyewitnessing* was a necessary qualification for apostleship: cf. Peter's own speeches, Acts 1:21, 22; 2:32; 10:39. **also**—implying the righteous recompense corresponding to the sufferings. **partaker of the glory**—according to Christ's promise; an earnest of which was given in the transfiguration. **2. Feed**—*Greek,* "Tend as a shepherd," by discipline and doctrine. Lead, feed, heed; by prayer, exhortation, government, and example. The dignity is marked by the term *"elder";* the *duties* of the office, to *tend* or *oversee,* by *"bishop."* Peter has in mind Christ's injunction to him, "Feed (*tend*) My sheep . . . Feed (*pasture*) My lambs" (John 21:16). He invites the elders to share with him the same duty (cf. Acts 20:28). The flock is Christ's. **which is among you**—While having a concern for *all* the Church, your special duty is to feed that portion of it "which is among you." **oversight**—*Greek,* "bishopric," or duty of bishops, i.e., overseer. **not by constraint**—Necessity is laid upon them, but willingness prevents it being felt, both in undertaking and in fulfilling the duty [BENGEL]. "He is a true presbyter and minister of the counsel of God who doeth and teacheth the things of the Lord, being not accounted righteous merely because he is a presbyter, but because righteous, chosen into the presbytery" [CLEMENS ALEXANDRINUS]. **willingly**—One oldest MS., *Vulgate, Syriac,* and *Coptic,* add, "as God would have it to be done" (Rom. 8:27). **not for filthy lucre** —(Isa. 56:11; Titus 1:7). **of a ready mind**—promptly and heartily, without selfish motive of gain-seeking, as the Israelites gave their services *willing-heartedly* to the sanctuary. **3. being lords**—*Greek,* "lording it": implying pride and oppression. "Not that we have dominion over your faith." *God's* **heritage**—*Greek,* "the inheritances," i.e., the *portions* of the Church committed severally to your pastoral charge [BENGEL]. It is explained by "the flock" in the next clause. However, in vs. 2, "flock of God which is among you," answering to "(God's) heritages" (plural to express *the sheep* who are God's portion and inheritance, Deut. 32:9) committed to you, favors *English Version.* The flock, *as one whole,* is God's heritage, or *flock* in the singular. Regarded in relation to its *component sheep,* divided among several pastors, it is in the plural "heritages." Cf. Acts 1:17, 25, "part" (the same *Greek*). Bernard of Clairvaux, wrote to Pope Eugene, "Peter could not give thee what he had not: what he had he gave: the *care* over the Church, not *dominion.*" **being**—*Greek,* "becoming." **ensamples**—the most effective recommendation of precept (I Tim. 4:12). Titus 2:7, "patterns." So Jesus. "A monstrosity it is to see the highest rank joined with the meanest mind, the first seat with the lowest life, a grandiloquent tongue with a lazy life, much talking with no fruit" [BERNARD]. **4. And**—"And so": as the result of "being ensamples" (vs. 3). **chief Shepherd**—the title peculiarly Christ's own, not Peter's or the pope's. **when...shall appear**—*Greek,* "be manifested" (Col. 3:4). Faith serves the Lord while still unseen. **crown**—*Greek, stephanos,* a garland of *victory,* the prize in the Grecian games, woven of ivy, parsley, myrtle, olive, or oak. *Our* crown is distinguished from *theirs* in that it is "incorruptible" and "fadeth not away," as the leaves of theirs soon did. "The crown *of life.*" Not a *kingly* "crown" (a different *Greek* word, *diadema*): the prerogative of the Lord Jesus (Rev. 19:12). **glory**—*Greek,* "the glory," viz., *to be* then *revealed* (vs. 1; ch. 4:13). **that fadeth not away**—*Greek,* "amaranthine" (cf. ch. 1:4). **5. ye younger**—The *deacons* were originally the younger men, the *presbyters* older; but subsequently as presbyter expressed the *office* of Church ruler or teacher, so *Greek neoteros* means not (as lit.) *young men* in age, but *subordinate ministers* and servants of the Church. So Christ uses the term "younger." For He explains it by "he that doth serve," lit., "he that ministereth as a deacon"; just as He explains "the greatness" by "he that is chief," lit., "he that *ruleth,*" the very word applied to the *bishops* or *presbyters.* So "the young men" are undoubtedly the deacons of the Church of Jerusalem, of whom, as being all *Hebrews,* the Hellenistic Christians subsequently complained as neglecting their *Grecian* widows, whence arose the appointment of the *seven* others, *Hellenistic* deacons. So here, Peter, having exhorted the *presbyters,* or elders, not to lord it over those committed to them, adds, Likewise ye *neoters* or younger, i.e., subordinate ministers and deacons, submit cheerfully to the **command of the elders** [MOSHEIM]. There is no Scripture sanction for "younger" meaning *laymen* in general (as ALFORD explains): its use in this sense is probably of later date. The *"all of you"* that follows, refers to the *congregation* generally; and it is likely that, like Paul, Peter should notice, previous to the general congregation, the *subordinate ministers* as well as the *presbyters,* writing as he did to the same region (Ephesus), and to confirm the teaching of the apostle of the Gentiles. **Yea**—to sum up all my exhortations in one. **be subject**—omitted in the oldest MSS. and Versions, but TISCHENDORF quotes the *Vatican* MS. for it. Then translate, "Gird (ch. 1:13; 4:1) fast on humility (lowliness of mind) to one another." The verb is lit., "tie on with a fast knot" [WAHL]. Or, *"gird on* humility *as the slave dress (encomboma)":* as the Lord girded Himself with a towel to perform a servile office of humility and love, washing His disciples' feet, a scene in which Peter had played an important part, so that he would naturally have it before his mind. Cf. similarly vs. 2 with John 21:15-17. Clothing was the original badge of man's sin and shame. Pride caused the need of man's clothing, and pride still reigns in dress; the Christian therefore clothes himself in humility (ch. 3:3, 4). God provides him with the robe of Christ's righteousness, in order to receive which man must be stripped of pride. **God resisteth the proud**—Quoted, as James 4:6, from Proverbs 3:34. Peter had James before his mind, and gives his Epistle inspired sanction. Cf. vs. 9 with James 4:7, lit., "arrayeth Himself against." Other sins flee from God: pride alone opposeth itself to God; therefore, God also in turn *opposes Himself to* the proud [GERHARD in ALFORD]. Humility is the vessel of all graces [AUGUSTINE]. **6. under the mighty hand**—afflicting you (ch. 3:15): "accept" His chastisements, and turn to Him that smiteth you. He depresses the proud and exalts the humble. **in due time**—Wait humbly and patiently for His own fit time. One oldest MS. and *Vulgate* read, "In the season of visitation," viz., His visitation in mercy. **7. Casting**—*once for all:* so the *Greek* aorist. **care**—"anxiety." The advantage flowing from *humbling ourselves under God's hand* (vs. 6) is confident reliance on His goodness. Exemption from care goes along with humble submission to God. **careth for you**—lit., *"respecting you."* Care is a burden which faith casts off the man on his God. Cf. Psalm 22:10; 37:5; 55:22, to which Peter alludes; Luke 12:22, 37; Philippians 4:6. **careth**—not so strong a *Greek* word as the previous *Greek* "anxiety." **8.** Peter has in mind Christ's warning to himself to *watch* against *Satan,* from forgetting which he fell. **Be sober...vigilant**—"Care," i.e., *anxiety,* will intoxicate the soul; therefore be sober, i.e., self-restrained. Yet, lest this freedom from *care* should lead any to false security, he adds, "Be vigilant" against "your adversary." Let this be your "care." God provides, therefore do not be anxious. The devil seeks, therefore watch [BENGEL]. **because**—omitted in the oldest MSS. The broken and disjointed sentences are more fervid and forcible. LUCIFER of Cagliari reads as *English Version.* **adversary**—lit., "opponent in a court of justice" (Zech. 3:1). "Satan" means *opponent.* "Devil," *accuser* or slanderer (Rev. 12:10). "The enemy" (Matt. 13:39). "A murderer from the beginning" (John 8:44). He counteracts the Gospel and its agents. "The tempter." **roaring lion**—implying his violent and insatiable thirst for prey as a hungry lion. Through man's sin he got God's justice on his side against us; but Christ, our Advocate, by fulfilling all the demands of justice for us, has made our redemption altogether consistent with justice. **walketh about**—(Job 1:7; 2:2). So the children of the wicked one *cannot rest.* Evil spirits are in II Peter 2:4; Jude 6, said to be already in chains of darkness and in hell. This probably means that this is their doom *finally:* a doom already begun in part; though for a time they are permitted to roam in the world (of which Satan is prince), especially in the dark air that surrounds the earth. Hence perhaps arises the miasma of the air at times, as physical and moral evil are closely connected. **devour**—entangle in worldly "care" (vs. 7) and other snares, so as finally to destroy. Cf. Revelation 12:15, 16. **9.** (Luke 4:13; Eph. 6:11-17; Jas. 4:7.) **steadfast**—Cf. established in the truth," II Pet. 1:12. Satan's power exists only in respect to the unbelieving; the faithful he cannot hurt (I John 5:18). Faith gives strength to prayer, the great instrument against the foe (Jas. 1:6, etc.). **knowing...**—"encouragement not to faint in afflictions": your brethren suffer the same; nothing beyond the common lot of Christians befalls you (I Cor. 10:13). It is a sign of God's favor rather than displeasure, that Satan is allowed to harass you, as he did Job. Your fellow Christians have the same battle of faith and prayer against Satan. **are**—*are being accomplished* according to the appointment of God. **in the world**—lying in the wicked one, and therefore necessarily the scene of "tribulation" (John 16:33). **10.** Comforting assurance that God will finally "perfect" His work of "grace" in them, after they have undergone the necessary previous suffering. **But**—Only do you watch and resist the foe: God will perform the rest [BENGEL]. **of all grace**—(Cf. ch. 4:10). The God to whom as its source all grace is to be referred; who in grace completes what in grace He began. He from the first "called YOU (so the oldest MSS. read for 'us') unto (with a view to) glory." He will not let His purpose fall short of completion. If He does so in punishing, much more in grace. The three are fitly conjoined: the *call*, the *glory* to which we are called, and the way (*suffering*); the fourth is the ground of the calling, viz., *the grace of God in Christ*. **by**—Greek, "in." Christ is He *in virtue of* whom, and *in union with* whom, believers are called to glory. The opposite is "in the world" (vs. 9; John 16:33). **after that ye have suffered**—Join to "called you": *suffering*, as a necessary preliminary to *glory*, was contemplated in God's *calling*. **a while**—short and inconsiderable, as compared with the *glory*. **perfect...**—The two oldest MSS., and *Vulgate* and *Coptic* versions, read, "*shall* perfect (so that there shall be nothing *defective* in you), stablish, strengthen," and omit "settle," lit., "ground," or "fix on a foundation." ALFORD reads it in spite of the oldest MSS. The authority of the latter I prefer; moreover the climax seems to require rather a verb of *completing* the work of grace, than, as the *Greek* means, *founding* it. The *Greek* has, "shall HIMSELF perfect you": though you are called on to *watch* and *resist* the foe, God *Himself* must really do all in and through you. The same God who begins must *Himself* complete the work. The *Greek* for "stablish" (so as to be "steadfast in the faith," vs. 9) is the same as "strengthen," Luke 22:32. Peter has in mind Christ's charge, "When thou art converted, *strengthen* thy brethren." His exhortation accords with his name *Peter*, "Thou art *Peter*, and upon this *rock* I will build My Church." "Stablish," so as not to waver. "Strengthen" *with might in the inner man by His Spirit*, against the foe. **11. To him**—emphatic. To Him and Him alone: not to ourselves. Cf. "Himself," *Note*, vs. 10. **glory and**—omitted in the oldest MSS. and versions. **dominion**—Greek, "*the* might" shown in so "perfecting," you, vs. 10. **12. Silvanus**—Silas, the companion of Paul and Timothy: a suitable messenger by whom to confirm, as Peter here does, *Paul's* doctrine of "the true grace of God" in the same churches (cf. II Pet. 3:16). We never meet with Silvanus as Paul's companion after Paul's last journey to Jerusalem. His connection with Peter was plainly subsequent to that journey. **as I suppose**—Join "faithful unto you [STEIGER], as I suppose." Silvanus may have stood in a close relation to the churches in Asia, perhaps having taken the oversight of them after Paul's departure, and had afterwards gone to Peter, by whom he is now sent back to them with this Epistle. He did not *know*, by positive observation, *Silvanus' faithfulness to them*; he therefore says, "faithful *to you*, as I suppose," from the accounts I hear; not expressing doubt.

ALFORD joins "I have *written unto you*," which the *Greek* order favors. The seeming uncertainty, thus, is not as to Silvanus' faithfulness, which is strongly marked by the *Greek* article, but as to whether he or some other would prove to be the bearer of the letter, addressed as it was to five provinces, *all* of which Silvanus might not reach: "By Silvanus, that faithful brother, as *expect*, I have written to you" [BIRKS]. **briefly**—Greek, "in few (words)," as compared with the importance of the subject (Heb. 13:22). **exhorting**—not so much formally *teaching doctrines*, which could not be done in so "few words." **testifying**—bearing my testimony *in confirmation* (so the *Greek* compound verb implies) of that truth which ye have already heard from Paul and Silas (I John 2:27). **that this**—of which I have just written, and of which Paul before testified to you (whose testimony, now that he was no longer in those regions, was called in question probably by some; cf. II Peter 3:15, 16). II Peter 1:12, "the present truth," viz., the grace formerly promised by the prophets, and *now* manifested to you. "Grace" is the keynote of Paul's doctrine which Peter now confirms (Eph. 2:5, 8). Their sufferings for the Gospel made them to need some attestation and confirmation of the truth, that they should not fall back from it. **wherein ye stand**—The oldest MSS. read imperatively, "*Stand ye*." Lit., "*into* which (having been already admitted, ch. 1:8, 21; 2:7, 8, 9) stand (therein)." Peter seems to have in mind Paul's words (Rom. 5:2; I Cor. 15:1). "The grace wherein we stand must be true, and our standing in it true also" [BENGEL]. Cf. in STEIGER, "He began his Epistle with grace (ch. 1:2), he finishes it with grace, he has besprinkled the middle with grace, that in every part he might teach that the Church is not saved but by grace." **13. The ... at Babylon**—ALFORD, BENGEL, and others translate, "She that is elected together with you in Babylon," viz., *Peter's wife*, whom he *led about* with him in his missionary journeys. Cf. ch. 3:7, "*heirs together* of the grace of life." But why she should be called "elected together with you *in Babylon*," as if there had been no Christian woman in Babylon besides, is inexplicable on this view. In *English Version* the sense is clear: "That portion of *the whole dispersion* (ch. 1:1, *Greek*), or Church of Christianized Jews, with Gentile converts, which resides in Babylon." As Peter and John were closely associated, Peter addresses the Church in John's peculiar province, Asia, and closes with "your co-elect sister Church at *Babylon* saluteth you"; and John similarly addresses the "elect lady," i.e., *the Church in Babylon*, and closes with "the children of thine elect sister (the Asiatic Church) greet thee"; (cf. *Introduction* to II John). ERASMUS explains, "Mark *who is in the place of a son* to me": cf. Acts 12:12, implying Peter's connection with Mark; whence the mention of him in connection with *the Church* at Babylon, in which he labored under Peter before he went to Alexandria is not unnatural. PAPIAS reports from the presbyter John (B. 3.39), that Mark was interpreter of Peter, recording in his Gospel the facts related to him by Peter. Silvanus or Silas had been substituted for John Mark, as Paul's companion, because of Mark's temporary unfaithfulness. But now Mark restored is associated with Silvanus, Paul's companion, in Peter's esteem, as Mark was already reinstated in Paul's esteem. That Mark had a spiritual connection with the Asiatic churches which Peter addresses, and so naturally salutes them, appears from II Timothy 4:11; Colossians 4:10. **Babylon**

—The Chaldean Babylon on the Euphrates. See *Introduction*, ON THE PLACE OF WRITING this Epistle, in proof that *Rome* is not meant as Papists assert; cf. LIGHTFOOT *sermon.* How unlikely that in a *friendly salutation* the enigmatical title of Rome given in *prophecy* (John, Rev. 17:5), should be used! Babylon was the center from which the Asiatic *dispersion* whom Peter addresses was derived. PHILO (*Legat. ad Caium*, sec. 36) and JOSEPHUS (*Antiquities*, 15. 2. 2; 23. 12) inform us that Babylon contained a great many Jews in the apostolic age (whereas those at Rome were comparatively few, about 8000 (JOSEPHUS 17. 11); so it would naturally be visited by the apostle of the circumcision. It was the headquarters of those whom he had so successfully addressed on Pentecost, Acts 2:9, Jewish "Parthians . . . dwellers in Mesopotamia" (the Parthians were then masters of Mesopotamian Babylon); these he ministered to *in person.* His other hearers, the Jewish "dwellers in Cappadocia, Pontus, Asia, Phrygia, Pamphylia," he now ministers to by letter. The earliest distinct authority for Peter's martyrdom *at Rome* is DIONYSIUS, bishop of Corinth, in the latter half of the second century. The desirableness of representing Peter and Paul, the two leading apostles, as together founding the Church of the metropolis, seems to have originated the tradition. CLEMENT OF ROME (1 *Epistola ad Corinthias*, sec. 4. 5), often quoted for, is really against it. He mentions Paul and Peter together, but makes it as a *distinguishing* circumstance of Paul, that he preached both in the East and West, implying that Peter never was in the West. In II Peter 1:14, he says, "I must *shortly* put off this tabernacle," implying his martyrdom was near, yet he makes no allusion to Rome, or any intention of his visiting it. **14. kiss of charity** —Romans 16:16, "an *holy* kiss": the token of love to God and the brethren. *Love* and *holiness* are inseparable. Cf. the instance, Acts 20:37. **Peace** —Peter's closing salutation; as Paul's is, "Grace be with you," though he accompanies it with "peace be to the brethren." "Peace" (flowing from *salvation*) was Christ's own salutation after the resurrection, and from Him Peter derives it. **be with you all that are in Christ**—The oldest MSS. omit "Jesus." In Ephesians 6:24, addressed to the same region, the same limitation of the salutation occurs, whence, perhaps, Peter here adopts it. Contrast, "Be *with you all*," Romans 16:24; I Corinthians 16:33.

THE SECOND EPISTLE GENERAL OF

PETER

INTRODUCTION

AUTHENTICITY AND GENUINENESS.—If not a gross imposture, *its own internal witness* is unequivocal in its favor. It has *Peter's* name and apostleship in its heading: not only his surname, but his original name *Simon*, or *Simeon*, he thus, at the close of his life, reminding his readers who he originally was before his call. Again, in ch. 1:16–18, he mentions *his presence at the Transfiguration*, and *Christ's prophecy of his death!* and in ch. 3:15, *his brotherhood with Paul.* Again, in ch. 3:1, the author speaks of himself as author of the former Epistle: it is, moreover, addressed so as to *include* (but not to be restricted to) the same persons as the first, whom he presupposes to be acquainted with the writings of Paul, by that time recognized as "Scripture" (ch. 3:15, "the long-suffering of God," cf. Rom. 2:4). This necessarily implies *a late date*, when Paul's Epistles (including Romans) already had become generally diffused and accepted as Scripture in the Church. The Church of the fourth century had, besides the testimony which we have of the *doubts* of the earlier Christians, other external evidence which we have not, and which, doubtless, under God's overruling providence, caused them to accept it. It is hard to understand how a book palpably false (as it would be if Peter be not the author) could have been accepted in the Canon as finally established in the Councils of Laodicea, A.D. 360 (if the 59th article be genuine), Hippo, and Carthage in the fourth century (393 and 397). The whole tone and spirit of the Epistle disprove its being an imposture. He writes as one not speaking of himself, but *moved by the Holy Ghost* (ch. 1:21). An attempt at such a fraud in the first ages would have brought only shame and suffering, alike from Christians and heathen, on the perpetrator: there was then *no temptation to pious frauds* as in later times. That it must have been written in the earliest age is plain from the *wide gulf in style* which separates it and the other New Testament Scriptures from even the earliest and best of the post-apostolic period. DAILLE well says, "God has allowed a fosse to be drawn by human weakness around the sacred canon to protect it from all invasion."

Traces of acquaintance with it appear in the earliest Fathers. HERMAS, *Similes* 6. 4; cf. ch. 2:13, *Greek*, "*luxury* in the day . . . luxuriating with their own deceivings"; and *Shepherd*, *Vision* 3. 7, "They have left their true way" (cf. ch. 2:15); and *Vision* 4. 3, "Thou hast escaped this world" (cf. ch. 2:20). CLEMENT OF ROME, *ad Corinthios*, c. 7. 9 and 10, as to *Noah's preaching* and *Lot's* deliverance, "*the Lord* making it known that He does not abandon those that trust in Him, but appoints those otherwise inclined to *judgment*" (cf. ch. 2:5, 6, 7, 9). IRENÆUS A.D. 178 ("the day of the Lord is as a thousand years"), and JUSTIN MARTYR seem to allude to ch. 3:8. HIPPOLYTUS, *De Antichristo*, seems to refer to ch. 1:21, "*The prophets spake not of their own private* (individual) ability and *will*, but what was (revealed) to them alone by God." The difficulty is, neither TERTULIAN, CYPRIAN, CLEMENT OF ALEXANDRIA, nor the oldest Syriac (*Peschito*) version (the *later Syriac* has it), nor the fragment known as MURATORI's Canon, mentions it. The first writer who has expressly named it is ORIGEN, in the third century (*Homily* on Joshua; also 4th *Homily* on Leviticus, and 13th on Numbers), who names it "Scripture," quoting ch. 1:4; 2:16; however (in EUSEBIUS, *Ecclesiastical History*, 6. 25), he mentions that the Second Epistle was doubted by some. FIRMILIAN, bishop of Cappadocia, in *Epistle ad Cyprian* speaks of Peter's *Epistles* as warning us to avoid heretics (a monition which occurs in the *Second*, not the *First* Epistle). Now *Cappadocia* is one of the countries mentioned (cf. I Pet. 1:1 with ch. 3:1) as addressed; and it is striking, that from Cappadocia we get the earliest decisive testimony. "Internally it claims to be written by Peter, and this claim is confirmed by the Christians of that very region in whose custody it *ought* to have been found" [TREGELLES].

The books disputed (*Antilegomena*), as distinguished from those universally recognized (*Homologoumena*), are Epistles II Peter, James, II and III John, Jude, the Apocalypse, Epistle to Hebrews (cf. EUSEBIUS, *Ecclesiastical History*, 3. 3, 25). The *Antilegomena* stand in quite a different class from the *Spurious*; of these there was no dispute, they were universally rejected; *e.g.*, the Shepherd of Hermas, the Revelation of Peter, the Epistle of Barnabas. CYRIL OF JERUSALEM (A.D. 348) enumerates *seven* Catholic Epistles, including IJ Peter; so also GREGORY OF NAZIANZEN (A.D. 389), and EPIPHANIUS, A.D. 367. The oldest *Greek* MSS. extant (of the fourth century) contain the *Antilegomena*. JEROME, *De Viris Illustribus*, conjectured, from a supposed difference of style between the two Epistles, that Peter, being unable to write Greek, employed a different translator of his Hebrew dictation in the Second Epistle, and not the same as translated the First into Greek. Mark is said to have been his translator in the case of the Gospel according to Mark; but this is all gratuitous conjecture.

Much of the same views pervade both Epistles. In both alike he looks for the Lord's coming suddenly, and the end of the world (cf. ch. 3:8–10 with I Pet. 4:5); the inspiration of the prophets (cf. I Pet. 1:10–12 with ch. 1:19–21; 3:2); the new birth by the divine word a motive to abstinence from worldly lusts (I Pet. 1:22; 2:2; cf. ch. 1:4); also cf. I Peter 2:9 with ch. 1:3, both containing in the *Greek* the rare word "virtue" (I Pet. 4:17 with ch. 2:3).

It is not strange that *distinctive peculiarities of* STYLE should mark each Epistle, the design of both not being the same. Thus the *sufferings* of Christ are more prominent in the First Epistle, the object there being to encourage thereby Christian sufferers; the *glory* of the exalted Lord is more prominent in the Second, the object being to communicate fuller "knowledge" of Him as the antidote to the false teaching against which Peter warns his readers. Hence His title of redemption, "Christ," is the one employed in the First Epistle; but in the Second Epistle, "the Lord." *Hope* is characteristic of the First Epistle; *full knowledge*, of the Second Epistle. In the First Epistle he puts his *apostolic authority* less prominently forward than in the Second, wherein his design is to warn against false teachers. The same difference is observable in Paul's Epistles. Contrast I Thessalonians 1:1; II Thessalonians 1:1; Philippians 1:1, with Galatians 1:1; I Corinthians 1:1. The reference to Paul's writings as already existing in numbers, and as then a recognized part of *Scripture*, implies that this Epistle was written at a late date, just before Peter's death.

Striking verbal coincidences occur: cf. I Peter 1:19, end, with ch. 3:14, end; ch. 1:3, "His own," *Greek*, 2:16; 3:17 with I Peter 3:1, 5. The omission of the *Greek* article, I Peter 2:13 with ch. 1:21, 2:4, 5, 7. Moreover, two words occur, ch. 1:13, "tabernacle," i.e., the body, and 15, "decease," which at once remind us of the transfiguration narrative in the Gospel. Both Epistles refer to the deluge, and to Noah as the *eighth* that was saved. Though the First Epistle abounds in *quotations* of the Old Testament, whereas the Second contains none, yet *references* to the Old Testament occur often (ch. 1:21; 2:5–8, 15; 3:5, 6, 10, 13). Cf. *Greek*, I Peter 3:21, "putting away," with ch. 1:14; I Peter 1:17, *Greek*, "*pass* the time," with ch. 2:18; I Peter 4:3, "walked in," with ch. 2:10; 3:3; "called you," I Peter 1:15; 2:9; 5:10, with ch. 1:3.

Moreover, more verbal coincidences with the speeches of Peter in Acts occur in this *Second*, than in the *First* Epistle. Cf. *Greek*, "obtained," ch. 1:1 with Acts 1:17; ch. 1:6, *Greek*, "godliness," with Acts 3:12, the only passage where the term occurs, except in the Pastoral Epistles; and ch. 2:9 with Acts 10:2, 7; ch. 2:9, "punished," with Acts 4:21, the only places where the term occurs; ch. 3:2, the double genitive, with Acts 5:32; "the day of the Lord," ch. 3:10, with Acts 2:20, where only it occurs, except in I Thessalonians 5:2.

The testimony of Jude, 17, 18, is strong for its genuineness and inspiration, by adopting its very words, and by referring to it as received by the churches to which he, Jude, wrote, "Remember the words which were spoken before of the *apostles* of our Lord Jesus Christ; how that they told you *there should be mockers in the last time, who should walk after their own ungodly lusts*." Jude, therefore, must have written *after* II Peter, to which he plainly refers; not before, as ALFORD thinks. No less than eleven passages of Jude rest on similar statements of II Peter. Jude 2, cf. ch. 1:2; Jude 4, cf. ch. 2:1; Jude 6, cf. ch. 2:4; Jude 7, cf. ch. 2:6; Jude 8, cf. ch. 2:10; Jude 9, cf. ch. 2:11; Jude 11, cf. ch. 2:15; Jude 12, cf. ch. 2:17; Jude 16, cf. ch. 2:18; Jude 18, cf. ch. 2:1 and 3:3. Just in the same way Micah, ch. 4:1–4, leans on the somewhat earlier prophecy of Isaiah, whose inspiration he thereby confirms. ALFORD reasons that because Jude, in many of the passages akin to II Peter, is fuller than II Peter, he must be prior. This by no means follows. It is at least as likely, if not more so, that the briefer is the earlier, rather than the fuller. The dignity and energy of the style is quite consonant to what we should expect from the prompt and ardent foreman of the apostles. The difference of style between I and II Peter accords with the distinctness of the subjects and objects.

THE DATE, from what has been said, would be about A.D. 68 or 69, about a year after the first, and shortly before the destruction of Jerusalem, the typical precursor of the world's end, to which ch. 3 so solemnly calls attention, after Paul's ministry had closed (cf. *Greek* aorist, "wrote," past time, ch. 3:15), just before Peter's own death. It was written to *include* the same persons, and perhaps in, or about the same place, as the first. Being without salutations of individuals, and entrusted to the care of no one church, or particular churches as the first is, but directed generally "to them that have obtained like precious faith with us," it took a longer time in being recognized as canonical. Had Rome been the place of its composition or publication, it could hardly have failed to have had an early acceptance—an incidental argument against the tradition of Peter's martyrdom *at Rome*. The remote scene of its composition in Babylon, or else in some of the contiguous regions beyond the borders of the Roman empire, and of its circulation in Cappadocia, Pontus, etc., will additionally account for its tardy but at last universal acceptance in the catholic Church. The former Epistle, through *its more definite address*, was earlier in its general acceptance.

OBJECT.—In ch. 3:17, 18 the twofold design of the Epistle is set forth; viz., to guard his readers against "the error" of false teachers, and to exhort them to grow in experimental "knowledge of our Lord and Saviour." The ground on which this *knowledge* rests is stated, ch. 1:12–21, viz., the inspired testimony of apostles and prophets. The danger now, as of old, was about to arise from false teachers, who soon were to come among them, as Paul also (to whom reference is made, ch. 3:15, 16) testified in the same region. The grand antidote is "the *full knowledge* of our Lord and Saviour," through which we know God the Father, partake of His nature, escape from the pollutions of the world, and have entrance into Christ's kingdom. The aspect of Christ presented is not so much that of the past *suffering*, as of the future *reigning*, Saviour, His present *power*, and future new kingdom. This aspect is taken as best fitted to counteract the *theories* of the false teachers who should "deny" His *Lordship* and His *coming* again, the two very points which, as an *apostle and eyewitness*, Peter attests (His "power" and His "coming"); also, to counteract *their evil example in practice*, blaspheming the way of truth, despising governments, slaves to covetousness and filthy lusts of the flesh, while boasting of Christian freedom, and, worst of all, apostates from the truth. The *knowledge of Christ*, as being the knowledge of "the way of righteousness," "the right way," is the antidote of their bad practice. Hence "the preacher" of righteousness, Noah, and "righteous Lot," are instanced as escaping the destruction which overtook the "unjust" or "unrighteous"; and BALAAM is instanced as exemplifying the awful result of "unrighteousness" such as characterized the false teachers. Thus the Epistle forms one connected whole, the parts being closely bound together by mutual relation, and the end corresponding with the beginning; cf. ch. 3:14, 18 with ch. 1:2, in both "grace" and "peace" being connected with "the knowledge" of our Saviour; cf. also ch. 3:17 with 1:4, 10, 12; and ch. 3:18, "grow in grace and knowledge," with the fuller ch. 1:5–8; and ch. 2:21; and ch. 3:13, "righteousness," with ch. 1:1; and ch. 3:1 with ch. 1:13; and ch. 3:2 with ch. 1:19.

The *germs* of Carpocratian and Gnostic heresies already existed, but the actual manifestation of these heresies is spoken of as *future* (ch. 2:1, 2, etc.): another proof that this Epistle was written, as it professes, in the apostolic age, before the *development* of the Gnostic heresies in the end of the first and the beginning of the second centuries. The description is too general to identify the heresies with any particular one of the subsequent forms of heresy, but applies generally to them all.

Though altogether distinct in aim from the First Epistle, yet a connection may be traced. The neglect of the warnings to circumspection in the walk led to the evils foretold in the Second Epistle. Cf. the warning against the abuse of Christian *freedom*, I Peter 2:16 with ch. 2:19, "While they promise them *liberty*, they themselves are the *servants of corruption*"; also the caution against *pride*, I Peter 5:5, 6 with ch. 2:18, "they speak great swelling words of vanity."

CHAPTER 1

Vss. 1-21. ADDRESS: EXHORTATION TO ALL GRACES, AS GOD HAS GIVEN US, IN THE KNOWLEDGE OF CHRIST, ALL THINGS PERTAINING TO LIFE: CONFIRMED BY THE TESTIMONY OF APOSTLES, AND ALSO PROPHETS, TO THE POWER AND COMING OF CHRIST. **1. Simon**—the *Greek* form: in oldest MSS., "Symeon" (*Hebrew*, i.e., "hearing"), as in Acts 15: 14. His mention of his original name accords with the design of this Second Epistle, which is to warn against the coming false teachers, by setting forth the true "knowledge" of Christ on the testimony of the *original apostolic eyewitnesses* like himself. This was not required in the First Epistle. **servant**—"slave": so Paul, Romans 1:1. **to them ...**—He addresses a wider range of readers (*all* believers) than in the First Epistle, ch. 1, but means to include *especially* those addressed in the First Epistle, as ch. 3:1 proves. **obtained**—by grace. Applied by *Peter* to the receiving of the apostleship, lit., "by allotment": as the *Greek* is, Luke 1:9; John 19:24. They did not acquire it for themselves; the divine election is as independent of man's control, as the lot which is cast forth. **like precious**—"equally precious" to all: to those who believe, though not having seen Christ, as well as to Peter and those who have seen Him. For it lays hold of the same "exceeding great and *precious* promises," and the same "righteousness of God our Saviour." "The *common* salvation . . . the faith once delivered unto the saints" (Jude 3). **with us**—apostles and eyewitnesses (vs. 18). Though putting forward his *apostleship* to enforce his exhortation, he with true humility puts himself, as to "the faith," on a level with all other believers. The degree of faith varies in different believers; but *in respect to its objects*, present justification, sanctification, and future

glorification, it is common alike to all. Christ is to all believers "made of God wisdom, righteousness, sanctification, and redemption." **through**—*Greek*, "in." Translate, as the one article to both nouns requires, "the righteousness of *Him who is* (at once) *our God and* (our) Saviour." Peter, confirming Paul's testimony to the same churches, adopts Paul's inspired phraseology. The Gospel plan sets forth *God's righteousness*, which is Christ's righteousness, in the brightest light. Faith has its sphere IN it as its peculiar element: God is in redemption "righteous," and at the same time a "Saviour"; cf. Isaiah 45:21, "a *just* God and a *Saviour*." **2. Grace ... peace**—(I Pet. 1:2). **through**—*Greek*, "in": the sphere IN which alone *grace* and *peace* can be multiplied. **knowledge**—*Greek*, "full knowledge." **of God, and of Jesus our Lord**—The *Father* is here meant by "God," but the *Son* in vs. 1: marking how entirely one the Father and Son are (John 14:7-11). The *Vulgate* omits "of God and"; but oldest MSS. support the words. Still the prominent object of Peter's exhortation is "the knowledge *of Jesus our Lord*" (a phrase only in Rom. 4: 24), and, only secondarily, of the Father through Him (vs. 8; ch. 2:20; 3:18). **3. According as ...**—Seeing that [ALFORD]. "*As* He hath given us ALL things (needful) for life and godliness, (so) do you give us ALL diligence...." The oil and flame are given wholly of grace by God, and "taken" by believers: their part henceforth is to "trim their lamps" (cf. vss. 3, 4 with 5, etc.). **life and godliness** Spiritual *life* must exist first before there can be true *godliness*. Knowledge of God experimentally is the first step to *life* (John 17:3). The child must have vital breath first, and then cry to, and walk in the ways of, his father. It is not by *godliness* that we obtain *life*, but by *life*, godliness. To *life* stands opposed *corruption;* to *godliness*, lust (vs. 4). **called**

us—vs. 10—"calling" (I Pet. 2:9). **to glory and virtue** —rather, "*through* (His) glory." Thus *English Version* reads as one oldest MS. But other oldest MSS. and *Vulgate* read, "*By His own* (peculiar) glory and virtue"; being the explanation of "His divine power"; *glory* and *moral excellency* (the same attribute is given to God in I Peter 2:9, "praises," lit., "virtues" characterize God's "power." "Virtue," the standing word in heathen ethics, is found only once in Paul (Phil. 4:8), and in Peter in a distinct sense from its classic usage; it (in the heathen sense) is a term too low and earthly for expressing the gifts of the Spirit [TRENCH, *Synonyms*]. **4. Whereby** . . .— By His *glory* and *virtue:* His *glory* making the "promises" to be *exceeding great;* His *virtue* making them "precious" [BENGEL]. *Precious promises* are the object of *precious faith.* **given**—The *promises* themselves are a *gift:* for God's *promises* are as sure as if they were fulfilled. **by these**—*promises.* They are the object of faith, and even now have a sanctifying effect on the believer, assimilating him to God. Still more so, when they shall be *fulfilled.* **might** . . .—Greek, "that ye MAY become partakers of the divine nature," even now in part; hereafter perfectly; I John 3:2, "We shall be like Him." **the divine nature**—not God's essence, but His *holiness*, including His "glory" and "virtue," vs. 3; the opposite to "corruption through lust." Sanctification is the imparting to us of *God Himself* by the Holy Spirit in the soul. We by faith partake also of the material nature of Jesus (Eph. 5:30). The "divine *power"* enables us to be partakers of "the divine *nature.*" **escaped the corruption**—which involves in, and with itself, *destruction* at last of soul and body; on "escaped" as from a condemned cell, cf. ch. 2:18-20; Genesis 19:17; Colossians 1:13. **through** —Greek, "in." "The corruption in the world" has its seat, not so much in the surrounding elements, as in the "lust" or concupiscence of men's hearts. **5. And beside this**—rather, "And for this very reason," viz., "seeing that His divine power hath given unto us all things that pertain to life and godliness" (vs. 3). **giving**—lit., "introducing," side by side with God's *gift*, on your part "diligence." Cf. an instance, vs. 10; ch. 3:14; II Corinthians 7:11. **all** —all possible. **add**—lit., "minister additionally," or, abundantly (cf. *Greek,* II Cor. 9:10); said properly of the one who *supplied* all the equipments of a chorus. So accordingly, "there will be *ministered abundantly* unto you an entrance into the everlasting kingdom of our Saviour" (vs. 11). **to**—Greek, "in"; *in* the possession of *your faith, minister virtue.* Their *faith* (answering to "knowledge of Him," vs. 3) is presupposed as the gift of God (vs. 3; Eph. 2:8), and is not required to be *ministered* by *us; in* its exercise, *virtue* is to be, moreover, ministered. Each grace being assumed, becomes the steppingstone to the succeeding grace: and the latter in turn qualifies and completes the former. *Faith* leads the band; *love* brings up the rear [BENGEL]. The fruits of *faith* specified are *seven,* the perfect number. **virtue**—moral excellency; manly, strenuous energy, answering to the *virtue* (energetic excellency) of God. **and to**—Greek, "in"; "and in (the exercise of) your virtue knowledge," viz., practical discrimination of good and evil; intelligent appreciation of what is the will of God in each detail of practice. **6.** Greek, "And in your knowledge self-control." In the exercise of Christian *knowledge* or discernment of God's will, let there be the practical fruit of *self-control* as to one's lusts and passions. Incontinence weakens the mind; continence, or self-control, removes weakness and imparts strength [BENGEL].

"And in your self-control patient endurance" amidst sufferings, so much dwelt on in the First Epistle, chs. 2, 3 and 4. "And in your patient endurance godliness"; it is not to be mere stoical endurance, but united to [and flowing from] *God-trusting* [ALFORD]. **7.** "And in your godliness brotherly kindness"; not suffering your godliness to be moroseness, nor a sullen solitary habit of life, but kind, generous, and courteous [ALFORD]. Your natural affection and *brotherly kindness* are to be sanctified by *godliness.* "And in your brotherly kindness love," viz., to *all* men, even to enemies, in thought, word, and deed. From *brotherly kindness* we are to go forward to *love.* Cf. I Thessalonians 3:12, "Love one toward another (brotherly kindness), and toward all men" (charity). So *charity* completes the choir of graces in Colossians 3:14. In a retrograde order, he who has *love* will exercise *brotherly kindness;* he who has *brotherly kindness* will feel *godliness* needful; the *godly* will mix nothing stoical with his *patience*; to the patient, *temperance* is easy; the temperate weighs things well, and so has *knowledge;* knowledge guards against sudden impulse carrying away its *virtue* [BENGEL]. **8. be**—Greek, "subsist" i.e., supposing these things to have an actual *subsistence* in you; "be" would express the mere matter-of-fact *being* (Acts 16:20). **abound**—*more than in others;* so the *Greek.* **make**—"render," "constitute you," habitually, by the very fact of possessing these graces. **barren**—"inactive," and, as a field lying fallow and *unworked* (*Greek*), so *barren* and *useless.* **unfruitful in**—rather, ". . . . *in respect to,*" "The *full knowledge* (*Greek*) of Christ" is the goal towards which all these graces tend. As their *subsisting* in us constitutes us *not barren* or idle, so their *abounding* in us constitutes us *not unfruitful* in respect to it. It is through *doing* His will, and so becoming like Him, that we grow in *knowing* Him (John 7:17). **9. But**—Greek, "For." Confirming the need of these graces (vss. 5-8) by the fatal consequences of the want of them. **he that lacketh**— Greek, "he to whom these are not present." **blind** —as to the spiritual realities of the unseen world. **and cannot see afar off**—explanatory of "blind." He *closes his eyes* (*Greek*) as unable to see distant objects (viz., heavenly things), and fixes his gaze on present and earthly things which alone he can see. Perhaps a degree of *wilfulness* in the blindness is implied in the *Greek,* "closing the eyes," which constitutes its culpability; hating and rebelling against the light shining around him. **forgotten**— Greek, "contracted forgetfulness," wilful and culpable obliviousness. **that he was purged**—The continually present sense of one's sins having been once for all forgiven, is the strongest stimulus to every grace (Ps. 130:4). This once-for-all accomplished cleansing of unbelievers *at their* new birth is taught symbolically by Christ, John 13:10, Greek, "He that has been *bathed* (once for all) needeth not save to *wash* his feet (of the soils contracted in the daily walk), but is clean every whit (in Christ our righteousness)." "Once purged (with Christ's blood), we should have no more consciousness of sin" (as condemning us, Heb. 10:2) because of God's promise. Baptism is the sacramental pledge of this. **10. Wherefore**—seeking the blessed consequence of having, and the evil effects of not having, these graces (vss. 8, 9). **the rather**—the more earnestly. **brethren**—marking that it is affection for them which constrains him so earnestly to urge them. Nowhere else does he so address them, which makes his calling them so here the more emphatical. **give diligence**—The *Greek* aorist implies *one lifelong ef-*

fect [ALFORD]. **to make**—*Greek* middle voice; to make *so far as it depends on you;* to do *your part* towards making. "To make" absolutely and finally is God's part, and would be in the active. **your calling and election sure**—by "*ministering additionally in your faith virtue, and in your virtue knowledge* ..." God must work all these graces in us, yet not so that we should be mere *machines,* but *willing instruments* in His hands in making His election of us "secure." The *ensuring* of our *election* is spoken of not in respect to God, whose counsel is steadfast and everlasting, but in respect to *our part.* There is no uncertainty on His part, but on ours the only security is our *faith* in His promise and the fruits of the Spirit (vss. 5-7, 11). Peter subjoins *election* to *calling,* because the *calling* is the effect and proof of God's *election,* which goes before and is the main thing (Rom. 8:28, 30, 33, where God's "*elect*" are those "*predestinated,*" and election is "His *purpose,*" *according to* which He "called" them). We know His *calling* before His *election,* thereby *calling* is put first. **fall**—*Greek,* "stumble" and fall finally (Rom. 11:11). Metaphor from one *stumbling* in a race (I Cor. 9:24). **11. an entrance**—rather as *Greek,* "*the* entrance" which ye look for. **ministered**—the same verb as in vs. 5. *Minister* in your faith virtue and the other graces, so shall there be *ministered to you* the entrance into that heaven where these graces shine most brightly. The reward of grace hereafter shall correspond to the work of grace here. **abundantly**—*Greek,* "richly." It answers to "abound," vs. 8. If these graces *abound* in you, you shall have your entrance into heaven not merely "scarcely" (as he had said, I Pet. 4:18), nor "so as by fire," like one escaping with life after having lost all his goods, but in triumph without "stumbling and falling." **12. Wherefore**—as these graces are so necessary to your abundant entrance into Christ's kingdom (vss. 10, 11). **I will not be negligent**—The oldest MSS. read, "*I will be about* always to put you in remembrance" (an accumulated future: I will regard you as always needing to be reminded): cf. "I will endeavor," vs. 15. "I will be sure always to remind you" [ALFORD]. "Always"; implying the reason why he writes the second Epistle so soon after the first. He feels *there is likely* to be more and more need of admonition on account of the increasing corruption (ch. 2:1, 2). **in the present truth**—*the Gospel truth now present with you:* formerly promised to Old Testament believers as *about to be,* now in the New Testament *actually present* with, and in, believers, so that they are "established" in it as a "present" reality. Its importance renders frequent monitions never superfluous: cf. Paul's similar apology, Romans 15:14, 15. **13. Yea**—*Greek,* "But"; though "you know" the truth (vs. 12). **this tabernacle**—soon to be taken down (II Cor. 5:1): I therefore need *to make the most of my short time* for the good of Christ's Church. The zeal of Satan against it, the more intense *as his time is short,* ought to stimulate Christians on the same ground. **by**—*Greek,* "in" (cf. ch. 3:1). **14. shortly I must put off**—*Greek,* "the putting off (as a garment) of my tabernacle is speedy": implying a *soon approaching,* and also a *sudden* death (as a violent death is). Christ's words, John 21:18, 19, "When thou art old ...," were the ground of his "knowing," now that he was old, that his foretold martyrdom was near. Cf. as to Paul, II Timothy 4:6. Though a violent death, he calls it a "departure" (*Greek* for "decease," vs. 15), cf. Acts 7:60. **15. endeavour**—"use my diligence": the same *Greek* word as in vs. 10: this is the field in which my *diligence* has scope. Peter thus fulfils Christ's charge, "Feed My sheep." **decease** —"departure." The very word (exodus) used in the Transfiguration, Moses and Elias conversing about Christ's *decease (found nowhere else in the New Testament,* but Heb. 11:22, "the *departing* of Israel" out of Egypt, to which the saints' deliverance from the present bondage of corruption answers). "Tabernacle" is another term found here as well as there (Luke 9:31, 33): an undesigned coincidence confirming Peter's authorship of this Epistle. **that ye may be able**—by the help of this written Epistle; and perhaps also of Mark's Gospel, which Peter superintended. **always**—*Greek,* "on each occasion": as often as occasion may require. **to have ... in remembrance**—*Greek,* "to exercise remembrance of." Not merely "to remember," as sometimes we do, things we care not about; but "have them in (earnest) remembrance," as momentous and precious truths. **16. For**—reason why he is so earnest that the remembrance of these things should be continued after his death. **followed**—out in detail. **cunningly devised**—*Greek,* "devised by (*man's*) *wisdom*"; as distinguished from what *the Holy Ghost* teaches (cf. I Cor. 3:13). But cf. also ch. 2:3, "feigned words." **fables**—as the heathen mythologies, and the subsequent Gnostic "fables and genealogies," of which the germs already existed in the junction of Judaism with Oriental philosophy in Asia Minor. A precautionary protest of the Spirit against the rationalistic theory of the Gospel history being *myth.* **when we made known unto you**—not that Peter himself had *personally* taught the churches in Pontus, Galatia, etc., but he was one of the apostles whose testimony was borne to them, and to *the Church in general,* to whom this Epistle is addressed (ch. 1:1, *including,* but not *restricted, as* I *Peter,* to the churches in Pontus, etc.). **power**—the opposite of "fables"; cf. the contrast of "word" and "power," I Corinthians 4:20. A specimen of His *power* was given at the Transfiguration also of His "*coming*" again, and its attendant glory. The *Greek* for "coming" is always used of His *second* advent. A refutation of the scoffers (ch. 3:4): I, James and John, saw with our own eyes a mysterious sample of His coming glory. **were**—*Greek,* "were made." **eyewitnesses**—As initiated spectators of mysteries (so the *Greek*), we were admitted into His innermost secrets, viz., at the Transfiguration. **his**—emphatical (cf. *Greek*): "THAT great ONE'S *majesty.*" **17. received ... honour**—in the *voice* that spake to Him. **glory**—in the *light* which shone around Him. **came** *Greek,* "was borne": the same phrase occurs only in I Peter 1:13; one of several instances showing that the argument against the authenticity of this Second Epistle, from its dissimilarity of style as compared with I Peter, is not well founded. **such a voice**—as he proceeds to describe. **from the excellent glory**—rather as *Greek,* "by (i.e. uttered by) the magnificent glory" (i.e., by *God:* as His glorious manifested presence is often called by the Hebrews "the Glory," cf. "His Excellency," Deut. 33:26; Ps. 21:5). **in whom**—*Greek,* "*in regard to* whom" (accusative); but Matthew 17:5, "in whom" (dative) centers and rests My good pleasure. Peter also omits, as not required by his purpose, "hear Him," showing his independence in his inspired testimony. **I am**—*Greek* aorist, past time, "My good pleasure *rested* from eternity. **18. which came**—rather as *Greek,* "we heard borne from heaven." **holy mount** —as the Transfiguration mount came to be regarded, on account of the manifestation of Christ's divine glory there. **we**—emphatical: we, James and John, as well as myself. **We**—all believers. **a more sure**

—rather as *Greek,* "we have *the* word of prophecy more sure" (confirmed). Previously we knew its *sureness* by faith, but, through that visible specimen of its hereafter entire fulfilment, assurance is made *doubly sure.* Prophecy assures us that Christ's *sufferings,* now past, are to be followed by Christ's *glory,* still future: the Transfiguration gives us a pledge to make our faith still stronger, that "the day" of His glory will "dawn" ere long. He does not mean to say that "the word of prophecy," or Scripture, is surer than *the voice of God* heard at the Transfiguration, as *English Version;* for this is plainly not the fact. The fulfilment of *prophecy* so far in Christ's history makes us the *surer* of what is yet to be fulfilled, His consummated glory. The word was the "lamp (*Greek* for 'light') heeded" by Old Testament believers, until a gleam of the "day-dawn" was given at Christ's first coming, and especially in His Transfiguration. So the word is *a lamp* to us still, until "the day" burst forth fully at the second coming of "the Sun of righteousness." *The day,* when it dawns upon you, makes *sure* the fact that you saw correctly, though indistinctly, the objects revealed by *the lamp.* **whereunto**—to which word of prophecy, primarily the Old Testament in Peter's *day;* but now also in our day the New Testament, which, though brighter than the Old Testament (cf. I John 2:8, end), is but a *lamp* even still as compared with the brightness of the eternal day (cf. ch. 3:2). Oral teachings and traditions of ministers are to be tested by the written word (Acts 17:11). **dark**—The *Greek* implies *squalid,* having neither water nor light: such spiritually is the world without, and the smaller world (microcosm) within, the heart in its natural state. Cf. the "*dry places*" Luke 11:24 (viz., unwatered by the Spirit), through which the unclean spirit goeth. **dawn**—bursting *through* the darkness. **day star**—*Greek,* the morning star," as Revelation 22:16. The Lord Jesus. **in your hearts**—Christ's *arising in the heart* by His Spirit giving full assurance, creates spiritually full day in the heart, the means to which is prayerfully *giving heed to the word.* This is associated with the coming of *the day of the Lord,* as being the earnest of it. Indeed, even our *hearts* shall not *fully* realize Christ in all His unspeakable glory and felt presence, until He shall come (Mal. 4:2). Isaiah 66:14, 15, "When you see this, your *heart* shall rejoice ... For, behold, the Lord will come." However, TREGELLES' punctuation is best, "whereunto ye do well to take heed (as unto a light shining in a dark place, until the day have dawned and the morning star arisen) in your hearts." For the day has already dawned in the heart of believers; what they wait for is its visible manifestation at Christ's coming. **20.** "Forasmuch as ye know this" (I Pet. 1:18). **first**—the *foremost* consideration in studying the word of prophecy. Laying it down as a *first principle* never to be lost sight of. **is**—*Greek,* not the simple verb, *to be,* but *to begin to be,* "proves to be," "becometh." No prophecy is found to be the result of "private (the mere individual writer's uninspired) *interpretation*" (*solution*), and so *origination.* The *Greek* noun *epilusis,* does not mean in itself *origination;* but that which the sacred writer could not always fully *interpret,* though being the speaker or writer (as I Pet. 1:10-12 implies), was plainly not of his own, but of God's *disclosure, origination,* and *inspiration,* as Peter proceeds to add, "But holy men ... spake (and afterwards *wrote*) ... moved by the Holy Ghost": a reason why ye should "give" all "heed" to it. The parallelism to vs. 16 shows that "*private interpretation,*" con-

trasted with "moved by the Holy Ghost," here answers to "fables *devised by* (*human*) *wisdom,*" contrasted with "we were eyewitnesses of *His majesty,*" as attested by the "voice from God." The words of the prophetical (and so of all) Scripture writers were not mere words *of the individuals,* and therefore to be *interpreted by them,* but of "the Holy Ghost" by whom they were "moved." "Private" is explained, vs. 21, "by the will of man" (viz., the individual writer). In a secondary sense the text teaches also, as the word is the *Holy Spirit's,* it cannot be *interpreted* by its *readers* (any more than by its *writers* by their mere *private* human powers, but by the teaching of *the Holy Ghost* (John 16:14). "He who is the author of Scripture is its supreme interpreter" [GERHARD]. ALFORD translates, "springs not out of human interpretation," i.e., is not a prognostication made by a man *knowing what he means* when he utters it, but ... (John 11:49-52). Rightly: except that the verb is rather, *doth become,* or *prove to be.* It not being of private interpretation, you must "*give heed*" to it, looking for the *Spirit's* illumination "in your hearts" (cf. *Notes,* vs. 19). **21. came not in old time** —rather, "was never at any time borne" (to us). **by the will of man**—alone. Jeremiah 23:26, "prophets of the deceit *of their own heart.*" Cf. ch. 3:5, "willingly." **holy**—One oldest MS. has, "*men* FROM *God*": the emissaries from God. "Holy," if read, will mean because they had the Holy Spirit. **moved**—*Greek,* "borne" (along) as by a mighty wind: Acts 2:2, "*rushing* (the same *Greek*) wind": rapt out of themselves: still not in fanatical excitement (I Cor. 14:32). The *Hebrew nabi,* "prophet," meant an *announcer* or interpreter of God: he, as *God's spokesman,* interpreted not his own "private" will or thought, but God's "*Man of the Spirit*" (*Margin,* Hos. 9:7). "Thou testifiedst by Thy Spirit in Thy prophets." "Seer," on the other hand, refers to the *mode of receiving* the communications from God, rather than to the *utterance* of them to others. "Spake" implies that, both in its original oral announcement, and now even when in writing, it has been always, and is, *the living voice* of God *speaking* to us through His inspired servants. *Greek,* "borne (along)" forms a beautiful antithesis to "was borne." They were passive, rather than active instruments. The *Old Testament* prophets primarily, but including also *all* the inspired penmen, whether of the New or Old Testament (ch. 3:2).

CHAPTER 2

Vss. 1-22. FALSE TEACHERS TO ARISE: THEIR BAD PRACTICES AND SURE DESTRUCTION, FROM WHICH THE GODLY SHALL BE DELIVERED, AS LOT WAS. **1. But**—in contrast to the prophets "moved by the Holy Ghost" (ch. 1:21). **also**—as well as the true prophets (ch. 1:19-21). Paul had already testified the entrance of false prophets into the same churches. **among the people**—Israel: he is writing to believing *Israelites* primarily (*Note,* I Pet. 1:1). Such a "false prophet" was Balaam (vs. 15). **there shall be**—Already symptoms of the evil were appearing (vss. 9-22; Jude 4-13). **false teachers**—teachers of falsehood. In contrast to the true teachers, whom he exhorts his readers to give heed to (ch. 3:2). **who**—*such as* (lit., "the which") shall. **privily**—not at first openly and directly, but *by the way,* bringing in error *by the side* of the true doctrine (so the *Greek*): Rome objects, Protestants cannot point out the exact date of the beginnings of the false doctrines superadded to the original truth; we answer, Peter foretells us it would be so, that the first introduction of them would be stealthy and unobserved (Jude 4). **damnable**—lit., "of destruction"; entailing destruction (Phil. 3:19) on all who follow them. **heresies**—*selfchosen* doctrines, not emanating from God (cf. "will worship," Col. 2:23). **even**—going *even* to such a length as to *deny* both in teaching and practice. *Peter* knew, by bitter repentance, what a fearful thing it is to *deny* the Lord (Luke 22:61, 62). **denying**—Him whom, above all others, they ought to *confess*. **Lord**—"Master and Owner" (*Greek*), cf. Jude 4, *Greek*. Whom the true doctrine teaches to be their OWNER *by* right of purchase. Lit., "denying Him who bought them (that He should be thereby), their Master." **bought them**—Even the ungodly were bought by His "precious blood." It shall be their bitterest self-reproach in hell, that, as far as Christ's redemption was concerned, they might have been saved. The denial of His *propitiatory* sacrifice is included in the meaning (cf. I John 4:3). **bring upon themselves**—cf. "God *bringing in* the flood *upon* the world," vs. 5. Man brings upon himself the vengeance which God brings upon him. **swift** —swiftly descending: as the Lord's coming shall be swift and sudden. As the ground swallowed up Korah and Dathan, and "they went down *quick* into the pit." Cf. Jude 11, which is akin to this passage. **2. follow**—out: so the *Greek*. **pernicious ways**—The oldest MSS. and *Vulgate* read, "licentiousness" (Jude 4). False doctrine and immoral practice generally go together (vss. 18, 19). **by reason of whom**—"on account of whom," viz., the followers of the false teachers. **the way of truth shall be evil spoken of**—"blasphemed" by those without, who shall lay on Christianity itself the blame of its professors' evil practice. Contrast I Peter 2:12. **3. through . . .**—*Greek*, "IN covetousness" as their element (vs. 14, end). Contrast II Corinthians 11:20; 12:17. **of a long time**—in God's eternal purpose. "*Before of old* ordained to condemnation" (Jude 4). **lingereth not**—though sinners think it lingers; "is not idle." **damnation**— *Greek*, "destruction" (*Note*, vs. 1). Personified. **slumbereth not**—though sinners *slumber*. **4. if**— The apodosis or consequent member of the sentence is not expressed, but is virtually contained in vs. 9. If God in past time has punished the ungodly and saved His people, He will be sure to do so also in our days (cf. end of vs. 3). **angels**—the highest of intelligent creatures (cf. with this verse, Jude 6), yet not spared when they sinned. **hell**—*Greek*, "Tartarus": nowhere else in New Testament or LXX: equivalent to the usual *Greek*, *Gehenna*. Not inconsistent with I Peter 5:8; for though their final doom is *hell*, yet for a time they are permitted to roam beyond it in "the darkness of this world." Slaves of *Tartarus* (called "the abyss," or "deep," Luke 8: 31; "the bottomless pit," Revelation 9:11) may also come upon earth. Step by step they are given to Tartarus, until at last they shall be wholly bound to it. **delivered**—as the judge delivers the condemned prisoner to the officers (Rev. 20:2). **into chains**—(Jude 6). The oldest MSS. read, "dens," as ALFORD translates: the *Greek*, however, may, in Hellenistic *Greek*, mean "chains," as Jude expresses it. They are "reserved" unto hell's "mist of darkness" as their final "judgment" or doom, and meanwhile their exclusion from the light of heaven is begun. So the ungodly were considered as virtually "in prison," though at large on the earth,

from the moment that God's sentence went forth, though not executed till 120 years after. **5. eighth** —i.e., Noah, and seven others. Contrasted with the densely peopled "world of the ungodly." **preacher**—not only "righteous" himself (cf. vs. 8), but also "a preacher of righteousness": adduced by Peter against the *licentiousness* of the false teachers (vs. 2) who have no prospect before them but destruction, even as it overtook the ungodly world in Noah's days. **6. with . . .**—"TO overthrow" [ALFORD]. **ensample**—"of (the fate that should befall) those who in after time should live ungodly." Cf. Jude 7, "set forth for an example." **7. just**—righteous. **filthy conversation**—lit., "behavior in licentiousness" (Gen. 19:5). **the wicked**—*Greek*, "lawless": who set at defiance the *laws* of nature, as well as man and God. The Lord reminds us of Lot's faithfulness, but not of his sin in the cave: so in Rahab's case. **8. vexed**—*Greek*, "tormented." **9. knoweth how**—He is at no loss for means, even when men see no escape. **out**—not actually *from*. **temptations**—trials. **to be punished**—*Greek*, "being punished": as the fallen angels (vs. 4), actually under sentence, and awaiting its final execution. Sin is already its own penalty; hell will be its full development. **10. chiefly**—They *especially* will be punished (Jude 8). **after**—following after. **lust of uncleanness**—*defilement*: "hankering after polluting and unlawful use of the flesh" [ALFORD]. **government**—*Greek*, "lordship," "dominion" (Jude 8). **Presumptuous**—*Greek*, "Darers." *Self-will* begets *presumption*. Presumptuously daring. **are not afraid**—though they are so insignificant in might; *Greek*, "tremble not" (Jude 8, end). **speak evil of**—*Greek*, "blaspheme." **dignities**—*Greek*, "glories." **11. which are**—though they are. **greater**—than these blasphemers. Jude instances *Michael*. **railing accusation**—*Greek*, "blaspheming judgment" (Jude 9). **against them**—against "dignities," as for instance, the fallen angels: once exalted, and still retaining traces of their former power and glory. **before the Lord**—In the presence of the Lord, *the Judge*, in reverence, they abstain from judgment [BENGEL]. Judgment belongs to God, not the angels. How great is the dignity of the saints who, as Christ's assessors, shall hereafter judge angels! Meanwhile, *railing judgments*, though spoken with truth, *against dignities*, as being uttered irreverently, are of the nature of "blasphemies" (*Greek*: I Cor. 4:4, 5). If superior angels dare not, as being in the presence of God, the Judge, speak evil even of the bad angels, how awful the presumption of those who speak evil blasphemously of good "dignities." II Samuel 16: 7, 8, Shimei; Numbers 16:2, 3, Korah, and, referred to also in Jude 11; Numbers 12:8, "Were ye (Aaron and Miriam) *not afraid to speak evil* of My servant Moses?" The angels who sinned still retain the indelible impress of majesty. Satan is still "a strong man": "prince of this world"; and under him are "principalities, powers, rulers of the darkness of this world." We are to avoid irreverence in regard to them, not on their account, but on account of God. A warning to those who use Satan's name irreverently and in blasphemy. "When the ungodly curseth Satan, he curseth his own soul." **12.** (Jude 10:19). **But**—In contrast to the "angels," vs. 11. **brute**—*Greek*, "irrational." In contrast to *angels* that "excel in strength." **beasts**—*Greek*, "animals" (cf. Ps. 49:20). **natural**—transposed in the oldest MSS., "born natural," i.e., born naturally so: being *in their very nature* (i.e., naturally) as such (irrational animals), born to be taken and destroyed (*Greek*, "unto capture and destruction," or *corruption, Note,* Gal. 6:8; cf. end of this verse, "shall perish," lit., "shall be corrupted," in their own *corruption.* Jude 10, "*naturally . . . corrupt themselves,*" and so *destroy* themselves; for one and the same *Greek* word expresses *corruption,* the seed, and *destruction,* the developed fruit). **speak evil of**—*Greek*, "in the case of things which they understand not." Cf. the same presumption, the parent of subsequent Gnostic error, producing an opposite, though kindred, error, "the worshipping of good angels": Colossians 2:18, "*intruding into those things which he hath not seen.*" **13. receive**—"shall carry *off* as their due." **reward of**—i.e., *for* their "unrighteousness" [ALFORD]. Perhaps it is implied, *unrighteousness* shall be its own *reward* or punishment. "Wages of unrighteousness" (vs. 15) has a different sense, viz., *the earthly gain to be gotten by* "unrighteousness." **in the daytime**—Translate as *Greek*, "counting the luxury which is in the daytime (not restricted to *night,* as ordinary revelling. Or as *Vulgate* and CALVIN, 'the luxury which is *but for a day":* so Hebrews 11:25, 'the pleasures of sin *for a season";* and 12:16, Esau) to be pleasure," i.e., to be their chief good and highest enjoyment. **Spots**—*in themselves.* **blemishes**—disgraces: bringing *blame* (so the *Greek*) *on* the *Church* and on *Christianity* itself. **sporting themselves**—*Greek,* "luxuriating." **with**—*Greek,* "in." **deceivings**—or else passively, "deceits": *luxuries gotten by deceit.* Cf. Matthew 13:22, "Deceitfulness of riches"; Ephesians 4:22, "Deceitful lusts." While deceiving others, they are deceived themselves. Cf. with *English Version,* Philippians 3:19, "Whose glory is in their shame." "Their own" stands in opposition to "you": "While partaking of the *love-feast* (cf. Jude 12) with *you,*" they are at the same time "luxuriating in *their own* deceivings," or "deceits" (to which latter clause answers Jude 12, end: Peter presents the positive side, "they *luxuriate* in their own deceivings"; Jude, the negative, "feeding themselves *without fear"*). But several of the oldest MSS., *Vulgate, Syriac,* and *Sahidic Versions* read (as Jude), "In their own love feasts": "their own" will then imply that they pervert the *love feasts* so as to make them subserve *their own* self-indulgent purposes. **14. full of adultery**—lit., "full of an adulteress," as though they carried about adulteresses always dwelling in their eyes: the eye being the avenue of lust [HORNEIUS]. BENGEL makes the *adulteress* who fills their eyes, to be "alluring desire." **that cannot cease**—"that cannot *be made to cease* from sin." **beguiling**—"laying baits for." **unstable**—not firmly established in faith and piety. **heart**—not only the *eyes,* which are the channel, but the *heart,* the fountain head of lust. Job 31:7, "Mine *heart* walked after mine *eyes.*" **covetous practices**—The oldest MSS. read singular, "covetousness." **cursed children**—rather as *Greek,* "children of curse," i.e., devoted to the curse. *Cursing* and *covetousness,* as in Balaam's case, often go together: the curse he designed for Israel fell on Israel's foes and on himself. True believers *bless,* and curse not, and *so are blessed.* **15. have**—Some of the seducers are spoken of as already come, others as *yet to* come. **following**—out: so the *Greek.* **the way**—(Num. 22:23, 32; Isa. 56:11). **son of Bosor**—the same as *Beor* (Num. 22:5). This word was adopted, perhaps, because the kindred word *Basar* means *flesh;* and Balaam is justly termed *son of carnality,* as covetous, and the enticer of Israel to lust. **loved the wages of unrighteousness**—and therefore wished (in order to

gain them from Balak) to curse Israel whom God had blessed, and at last gave the hellish counsel that the only way to bring God's curse on Israel was to entice them to *fleshly lust* and *idolatry,* which often go together. **16. was rebuked**—*Greek,* "had a rebuke," or *conviction;* an *exposure* of his specious wickedness on his being *tested* (the root verb of the *Greek* noun means to "convict on testing"). **his**—*Greek,* "his own": his own beast convicted him of *his own* iniquity. **ass**—lit., "beast of burden"; the **ass** was the ordinary animal used in riding in Palestine. **dumb**—*Greek,* "voiceless-speaking in man's *voice";* marking the marvellous nature of the miracle. **forbade**—lit., "hindered." It was not the *words* of the ass (for it merely deprecated his beating it), but *the miraculous fact of its speaking at all,* which *withstood* Balaam's perversity in desiring to go after God had forbidden him in the first instance. Thus indirectly the ass, and directly the angel, *rebuked* his worse than asinine obstinacy; the ass *turned aside* at the sight of the angel, but Balaam, after God had plainly said, Thou shalt not go, persevered in wishing to go for gain; thus the ass, *in act, forbade* his madness. How awful a contrast—a *dumb beast* forbidding an *inspired prophet!* **17.** (Jude 12, 13.) **wells**—"clouds" in Jude; both *promising* (cf. vs. 19) water, but yielding none; so their "great swelling words" are found on trial to be but "vanity" (vs. 18). **clouds**—The oldest MSS. and versions read, "mists," *dark,* and not transparent and bright as "clouds" often are, whence the latter term is applied sometimes to the saints; fit emblem of the children of darkness. "Clouds" is a transcriber's correction from Jude 12, where it is appropriate, "clouds . . . without water" (promising what they do not perform); but not here, "mists driven along by a tempest." **mist**—*blackness;* "the *chilling horror* accompanying *darkness*" [BENGEL]. **18. allure**—*Greek,* "lay baits for." **through**—*Greek,* "in"; the *lusts of the flesh* being the element IN which they lay their baits. **much wantonness**—*Greek,* "by licentiousness"; the bait which they lay. **clean escaped**—*Greek,* "really escaped." But the oldest MSS. and *Vulgate* read, "scarcely," or "for but a little time"; scarcely have they escaped from them who live in error (the ungodly world), when they are allured by these seducers into sin again (vs. 20). **19. promise . . . liberty**—(Christian) —These promises are instances of their "great swelling words" (vs. 18). The *liberty* which they propose is such as fears not Satan, nor loathes the flesh. Pauline language, adopted by Peter here, and I Peter 2:16, *Note;* (cf. ch. 3:15; Rom. 6:16-22; 8:15, 21; Gal. 5:1, 13; cf. John 8:34). **corruption**—*Note,* vs. 12, "destroyed . . . perish . . . corruption." **of whom**—"by whatever . . . by the same . . . ." **20. after they**—*the seducers* "themselves" *have escaped* (vs. 19: *Note,* Heb. 6:46). **pollutions**—which bring "corruption" (vs. 19). **through**—*Greek,* "in." **knowledge**—*Greek,* "full and accurate knowledge." **the Lord and Saviour Jesus Christ**—solemnly expressing in full the great and gracious One from whom they fall. **latter end is worse . . . than the beginning**—Peter remembers Christ's words. "Worse" stands opposed to "better" (vs. 21). **21. the way of righteousness**—"the way of truth" (vs. 2). Christian doctrine, and "the knowledge of the Lord and Saviour." **turn**—back again; so the *Greek.* **from the holy commandment** —the Gospel which enjoins *holiness;* in opposition to their *corruption.* "Holy," not that it makes holy, but because it ought to be kept *inviolate* [TITTMANN]. **delivered**—once for all; admitting no turning back. **22. But**—You need not wonder at the event; for *dogs* and *swine* they were before, and dogs and swine they will continue. They "scarcely" (vs. 18) have escaped from their filthy folly, when they again are entangled in it. Then they seduce others who have in like manner "for a little time escaped from them that live in error" (vs. 18). Peter often quoted Proverbs in his First Epistle (1: 7; 2:17; 4:8, 18); another proof that both Epistles come from the same writer.

CHAPTER 3

Vss. 1-18. SURENESS OF CHRIST'S COMING, AND ITS ACCOMPANIMENTS, DECLARED IN OPPOSITION TO SCOFFERS ABOUT TO ARISE. GOD'S LONG-SUFFERING A MOTIVE TO REPENTANCE, AS PAUL'S EPISTLES SET FORTH; CONCLUDING EXHORTATION TO GROWTH IN THE KNOWLEDGE OF CHRIST. **1. now**—"This now a second Epistle I write." Therefore he had lately written the former Epistle. The seven Catholic Epistles were written by James, John, and Jude, shortly before their deaths; previously, while having the prospect of being still for some time alive, they felt it less necessary to write [BENGEL]. **unto you**—The Second Epistle, though more general in its address, yet *included* especially the same persons as the First Epistle was particularly addressed to. **pure**—lit., "pure when examined by sunlight"; "sincere." *Adulterated with no error.* Opposite to "having the understanding *darkened.*" ALFORD explains, The mind, will, and affection, in relation to the outer world, being turned to God [the *Sun* of the soul], and not obscured by fleshly and selfish regards. **by way of**—Greek, "in," *in putting you in remembrance* (ch. 1:12, 13). Ye already *know* (vs. 3); it is only needed that I *remind* you (Jude 5). **2. prophets**—of the Old Testament. **of us**—The oldest MSS. and *Vulgate* read, "And of the commandment of the Lord and Saviour (declared) by YOUR apostles" (so "apostle *of the Gentiles,*" Rom. 11:13)—the apostles *who live among you in the present time,* in contrast to the *Old Testament* "prophets." **3. Knowing this first**—from the word of the apostles. **shall come**—Their very *scoffing* shall confirm the truth of the prediction. **scoffers** —The oldest MSS. and *Vulgate* add, "(scoffers) *in* (i.e., with) *scoffing.*" As Revelation 14:2, "harping with harps." **walking after their own lusts**— (ch. 2:10; Jude 16, 18). Their own pleasure is their sole law, unrestrained by reverence for God. **4.** (Cf. Ps. 10:11; 73:11.) Presumptuous skepticism and lawless lust, setting nature and its so-called laws above the God of nature and revelation, and arguing from the past continuity of nature's phenomena that there can be no future interruption to them, was the sin of the antediluvians, and shall be that of the scoffers in the last days. **Where**— implying that it ought to have taken place before this, if ever it was to take place, but that it never will. **the promise**—which you, believers, are so continually looking for the fulfilment of (vs. 13). What becomes of the promise which you talk so much of? **his**—*Christ's;* the subject of prophecy from the earliest days. **the fathers**—to whom *the promise* was made, and who rested all their hopes on it. **all things**—in the *natural world;* skeptics look not beyond this. **as they were**—*continue as they do;* as we see them to continue. From the time of the promise of Christ's coming as Saviour and King being given to the fathers, down to the present time, all things continue, and have con-

tinued, *as they now are,* from "the beginning of creation." The "scoffers" here are not necessarily atheists, nor do they maintain that the world existed from eternity. They are willing to recognize a God, but not the God *of revelation.* They reason from seeming delay against the fulfilment of God's word at all. **5.** Refutation of their scoffing from Scripture history. **willingly**—wilfully; they do not *wish* to know. Their ignorance is voluntary. **they . . . are ignorant of**—in contrast to vs. 8, "Be not ignorant of this." Lit., in both verses, "This escapes THEIR notice (sagacious philosophers though they think themselves)"; "let this not escape YOUR notice." They obstinately shut their eyes to the Scripture record of the creation and the deluge; the latter is the very parallel to the coming judgment by fire, which Jesus mentions, as Peter doubtless remembered. **by the word of God** —not by a fortuitous concurrence of atoms [AL-FORD]. **of old**—Greek, "from of old"; from the first beginning of all things. A confutation of their objection, "all things continue as they were FROM THE BEGINNING OF CREATION." Before the flood, the same objection to the possibility of the flood might have been urged with the same plausibility: The heavens (sky) and earth have been FROM OF OLD, how unlikely then that they should not *continue* so! But, replies Peter, the flood came in spite of their reasonings; so will the conflagration of the earth come in spite of the "scoffers" of the last days, changing the whole order of things (the present "world," or as *Greek* means, "order"), and introducing the new heavens and earth (vs. 13). **earth standing out of**—Greek, "consisting of," i.e., "formed out of the water." The waters under the firmament were at creation gathered together into one place, and the dry land emerged *out of,* and above, them. **in . . .**—rather, "*by means of* the water," as a great instrument (along with *fire*) in the changes wrought on the earth's surface to prepare it for man. Held together BY the water. The earth arose *out of* the water *by the efficacy of the water* itself [TITTMANN]. **6. Whereby**—Greek, "By which" (plural). *By means of which* heavens and earth (in respect to the WATERS which flowed together *from both) the then world perished* (i.e., in respect to its *occupants,* men and animals, and its then existing *order:* not *was annihilated);* for in the flood "the fountains of the great deep were broken up" from *the earth* (1) below, and "the windows of *heaven*" (2) above "were opened." The earth was deluged by that water *out of* which it had originally risen. **7.** (Cf. Job 28:5, end.) **which are now**—"the postdiluvian visible world." In contrast to "that *then was,*" vs. 6. **the same**—Other oldest MSS. read, "His" (God's). **kept in store**—Greek, "treasured up." **reserved**—"kept." It is only God's constantly watchful providence which holds together the present state of things till His time for ending it. **8. be not ignorant**—as those scoffers are (vs. 5). Besides the refutation of them (vss. 5-7) drawn from the history of the deluge, here he adds another (addressed more to believers than to the mockers): God's delay in fulfilling His promise is not, like men's delays, owing to inability or fickleness in keeping His word, but through "long-suffering." **this one thing**—as the consideration *of chief importance* (Luke 10:42). **one day . . . thousand years**—Psalm 90:4: Moses there says, Thy *eternity,* knowing no distinction between a *thousand* years and a *day,* is the refuge of us creatures of a day. Peter views God's eternity in relation to the last day: that day seems to us, short-lived beings, long in coming, but *with the Lord* the interval is irrespective of the idea of long or short. His eternity exceeds all measures of time: to His divine knowledge all future things are present: His power requires not long delays for the performance of His work: His long-suffering excludes all impatient expectation and eager haste, such as we men feel. He is equally blessed in one day and in a thousand years. He can do the work of a thousand years in one day: so in vs. 9 it is said, "He is not slack," i.e., "slow": He has always the power to fulfil His "promise." **thousand years as one day**—No delay which occurs is long to God: as to a man of countless riches, a thousand dollars are as a single penny. God's æonologe (*eternal-ages* measurer) differs wholly from man's horologe (*hour-glass*). His gnomon (dial-pointer) shows all the hours at once in the greatest activity and in perfect repose. To Him the hours pass away, neither more slowly, nor more quickly, than befits His economy. There is nothing to make Him need either to hasten or delay the end. The words, "with the Lord" (Ps. 90:4, "In Thy sight"), silence all man's objections on the ground of his incapability of understanding this [BENGEL]. **9. slack**—slow, tardy, *late;* exceeding the due time, as though that time were already come. Hebrews 10:37, "will not *tarry*." **his promise**—which the scoffers cavil at. Verse 4, "Where is the promise?" It shall be surely fulfilled "according to His promise" (vs. 13). **some**—the "scoffers." **count**—His promise to be the result of "slackness" (tardiness). **long-suffering**—waiting until the full number of those appointed to "salvation" (vs. 15) shall be completed. **to us-ward**—The oldest MSS., *Vulgate, Syriac,* etc. read, "towards YOU." **any**—not desiring that any, yea, even that the scoffers, should perish, which would be the result if He did not give space for repentance. **come** —*go and be received to* repentance: the *Greek* implies there is *room* for their being *received* to repentance (cf. *Greek,* Mark 2:2; John 8:37). **10.** The certainty, suddenness, and concomitant effects, of the coming of the day of the Lord. FABER argues from this that the millennium, etc., must *precede* Christ's literal coming, not *follow* it. But "the day of the Lord" comprehends the whole series of events, beginning with the premillennial advent, and ending with the destruction of the wicked, and final conflagration, and general judgment (which last intervenes between the conflagration and the renovation of the earth). **will**— emphatical. But (in spite of the mockers, and notwithstanding the delay) *come and be present* the day of the Lord SHALL. **as a thief**—Peter remembers and repeats his Lord's image (Luke 12:39, 41) used in the conversation in which he took a part; so also Paul (I Thess. 5:2) and John (Rev. 3:3; 16: 15). **the heavens**—which the scoffers say shall "continue" as they are (vs. 4; Matt. 24:35; Rev. 21: 1). **with a great noise**—with a rushing noise, like that of a *whizzing* arrow, or the crash of a devouring flame. **elements**—*the component materials of the world* [WAHL]. However, as "the works" in the earth are mentioned separately from "the earth," so it is likely by "elements," mentioned after "the heavens," are meant "the works therein," viz., *the sun, moon, and stars* (as THEOPHILUS OF ANTIOCH, p. 22, 148, 228; and JUSTIN MARTYR, *Apology,* 2. 44, use the word "elements"): these, as at creation, so in the destruction of the world, are mentioned [BENGEL]. But as "elements" is not so used in Scripture *Greek,* perhaps it refers to *the component materials* of "the heavens," including *the heavenly*

bodies; it clearly belongs to the former clause, "the heavens," not to the following, "the earth . . . ." **melt**—be dissolved, as in vs. 11. **the works . . . therein**—of nature and of art. **11.** Your duty, seeing that this is so, is to be ever eagerly expecting the day of God. **then**—Some oldest MSS. substitute "thus" for "then": a happy refutation of the "thus" of the scoffers, vs. 4 (*English Version,* "AS they were," *Greek,* "thus"). **shall be**—*Greek,* "*are being* (in God's appointment, soon to be fulfilled) dissolved"; the present tense implying *the certainty* as though it were actually present. **what manner of men . . .**—exclamatory. How watchful, prayerful, zealous! **to be**—not the mere *Greek* substantive verb of existence (*einai*), but (*huparchein*) denoting a *state* or *condition* in which one is supposed to be [TITTMANN]. What holy men ye ought to be found to be, when the event comes! This is "the holy commandment" mentioned in vs. 2. **conversation . . . godliness**—*Greek,* plural: *behaviors* (towards men), *godlinesses* (or *pieties* towards God) in their *manifold* modes of manifestation. **12. hasting unto**—*with the utmost eargerness desiring* [WAHL], praying for, and contemplating, the coming Saviour as at hand. The *Greek may* mean "hastening (i.e., *urging onward* [ALFORD] the day of God"; not that God's eternal appointment of the time is changeable, but God appoints *us* as instruments of accomplishing those events which must be first before the day of God can come. By praying for His coming, furthering the preaching of the Gospel for a witness to all nations, and bringing in those whom "the long-suffering of God" waits to save, we *hasten the coming of the day of God.* The *Greek* verb is always in New Testament used as neuter (as *English Version* here), not active; but the LXX uses it *actively.* Christ says, "Surely I come quickly. Amen." *Our* part is to *speed forward* this consummation by praying, "Even so, come, Lord Jesus." **the coming**—*Greek,* "presence" of a *person:* usually, of the Saviour. **the day of God**—God has given many myriads of days to *men:* one shall be the great "day of God" Himself. **wherein**—rather as *Greek,* "on account of (or owing to) which" day. **heavens**—the upper and lower regions of the sky. **melt**—Our igneous rocks show that they were once in a liquid state. **13. Nevertheless**—"But": in contrast to the destructive effects of the day of God stand its constructive effects. As the flood was the baptism of the earth, eventuating in a renovated earth, partially delivered from "the curse," so the baptism with fire shall purify the earth so as to be the renovated abode of regenerated man, wholly freed from the curse. **his promise**—(Isa. 65:17; 66:22). The "we" is not emphatical as in *English Version.* **new heavens**—new atmospheric heavens surrounding the renovated earth. **righteousness**—*dwelleth* in that coming world as its essential feature, all pollutions having been removed. **14. that ye . . . be found of him**— "in His sight" [ALFORD], at His coming; plainly implying a *personal* coming. **without spot**—at the coming marriage feast of the Lamb, in contrast to ch. 2:13, "Spots they are and blemishes while they feast," not having on the King's pure wedding garment. **blameless**—(I Cor. 1:8; Phil. 1:10; I Thess. 3:13; 5:23). **in peace**—in all its aspects, towards God, your own consciences, and your fellow men, and as its consequence eternal *blessedness:* "the God of peace" will effect this for you. **15. account . . . the long-suffering . . . is salvation**—is designed for the salvation of those yet to be gathered into the Church: whereas those scoffers "count it (to be the result of) slackness" on the Lord's part (vs. 9). **our beloved brother Paul**—a beautiful instance of love and humility. Peter praises the very Epistles which contain his condemnation. **according to the wisdom given unto him**—adopting Paul's own language, I Corinthians 3:10, "*According to the* grace of God which is *given unto* me as a *wise* masterbuilder." Supernatural and inspired wisdom "GIVEN" him, not acquired in human schools of learning. **hath written**—*Greek* aorist, "wrote," as a thing wholly *past:* Paul was by this time either dead, or had ceased to minister to them. **to you**—*Galatians,* Ephesians, *Colossians,* the same region as Peter addresses. Cf. "in peace," vs. 14, a practical exhibition of which Peter now gives in showing how perfectly agreeing Paul (who wrote the Epistle to the *Galatians*) and he are, notwithstanding the event recorded (Gal. 2:11-14). Colossians 4 refers to *Christ's second coming.* The Epistle to the Hebrews, too (addressed not only to the Palestinian, but also secondarily to the Hebrew Christians everywhere), may be referred to, as Peter primarily (though not exclusively) addresses in both Epistles the *Hebrew* Christians of the dispersion (*Note*, I Pet. 1:1). Hebrews 9:27, 28; 10:25, 37, "speak of these things" (vs. 16) which Peter has been handling, viz., the coming of the day of the Lord, delayed through His "long-suffering," yet near and sudden. **16. also in all his epistles**—Romans 2:4 is very similar to vs. 15, beginning. The Pauline Epistles were by this time become the *common* property of all the churches. The "all" seems to imply they were now completed. The subject of the Lord's coming is handled in I Thessalonians 4: 13; 5:11; cf. vs. 10 with I Thessalonians 5:2. Still Peter distinguishes Paul's Epistle, or Epistles, "TO YOU," from "*all* his (*other*) Epistles," showing that certain definite churches, or particular classes of believers, are meant by "you." **in which**—*Epistles.* The oldest MSS. read the feminine relative (*hais*); not as Received Text (*hois*), "in which *things.*" **some things hard to be understood**—viz., in reference to Christ's coming, e.g., the statements as to the man of sin and the apostasy, before Christ's coming. "Paul seemed thereby to delay Christ's coming to a longer period than the other apostles, whence some doubted altogether His coming" [BENGEL]. Though there be some things hard to be understood, there are enough besides, plain, easy, and sufficient for perfecting the man of God. "There is scarce anything drawn from the obscure places, but the same in other places may be found most plain" [AUGUSTINE]. It is our own prejudice, foolish expectations, and carnal fancies, that make

Scripture difficult [JEREMY TAYLOR]. **unlearned**—Not those wanting *human* learning are meant, but those *lacking the learning imparted by the Spirit.* The humanly *learned* have been often most deficient in spiritual learning, and have originated many heresies. Cf. II Timothy 2:23, a different *Greek* word, "unlearned," lit., "untutored." When religion is studied as a science, nothing is more abstruse; when studied in order to know our duty and practice it, nothing is easier. **unstable**—not yet established in what they have learned; shaken by every seeming difficulty; who, in perplexing texts, instead of waiting until God by His Spirit makes them plain in comparing them with other Scriptures, hastily adopt distorted views. **wrest**—strain and twist (properly with a *hand screw*) what is straight in itself (e.g., II Tim. 2:18). **other scriptures**—Paul's Epistles were, therefore, by this time, recognized in the Church, as "Scripture": a term never applied in any of the fifty places where it occurs, save to the Old and New Testament sacred writings. Men in each Church having miraculous *discernment of spirits* would have prevented any uninspired writing from being put on a par with the Old Testament word of God; the apostles' lives also were providentially prolonged, Paul's and Peter's at least to thirty-four years after Christ's resurrection, John's to thirty years later, so that fraud in the canon is out of question. The three first Gospels and Acts are included in "the other Scriptures," and perhaps all the New Testament books, save John and Revelation, written later. **unto their own destruction**—not through Paul's fault (ch. 2:1). **17. Ye**—warned by the case of those "unlearned and unstable" persons (vs. 16). **knowing ... before**—the event. **led away with**—the very term, as Peter remembers, used by Paul of Barnabas' being "carried," *Greek,* "led away with" Peter and the other Jews in their hypocrisy. **wicked**—"lawless," as in ch. 2:7. **fall from**—(*grace,* Gal. 5:4: the true source of) "steadfastness" or *stability* in contrast with the "unstable" (vs. 16): "established" (ch. 1:12): all kindred *Greek* terms. Cf. Jude 20, 21. **18. grow**—Not only do not "fall from" (vs. 17), but *grow onward:* the true secret of not going backward. Ephesians 4:15, "Grow up into Him, the Head, Christ." **grace and ... knowledge of ... Christ**—"the grace and knowledge of Christ" [ALFORD rightly]: *the grace* of which *Christ* is the author, and *the knowledge* of which *Christ* is the object. **for ever**—*Greek,* "to the day of eternity": the day that has no end: "the day of the Lord," beginning with the Lord's coming.

THE FIRST GENERAL EPISTLE OF

JOHN

INTRODUCTION

AUTHORSHIP.—POLYCARP, the disciple of John (*ad Philippenses* c. 7), quotes ch. 4:3. EUSEBIUS (*Ecclesiastical History* 3. 39) says of PAPIAS, a hearer of John, and a friend of POLYCARP, "He used testimonies from the First Epistle of John." IRENÆUS, according to EUSEBIUS (*Ecclesiastical History* 5. 8), often quoted this Epistle. So in his work *Against Heresies* (3. 15. 5, 8) he quotes from John by name, ch. 2:18, etc.; and in 3. 16, 7, he quotes ch. 4:1-3; 5:1, and II John 7:8. CLEMENT OF ALEXANDRIA (*Stromata* 2. 66, p. 464) refers to ch. 5:16, as in

John's *larger Epistle*. See other quotations *Stromata* 3. 32, 42; 4. 102. TERTULLIAN (*Adversus Marcion* 5. 16) refers to ch. 4:1, etc.; *Adversus Praxean*, c. 15, to I John 1:1. See his other quotations, c. 28; and *Contra Gnosticos*, 12. CYPRIAN, *Epistle* 28 (24), quotes as John's, ch. 2:3, 4; and *De Oratione Domini* 5 quotes ch. 2:15–17; and *De Opere and Eleemos*,ch. 1:8; and *De Bene Patientiæ* 2 quotes ch. 2:6. MURATORI's fragment on the Canon states, "There are two of John (the Gospel and Epistle?) esteemed Catholic," and quotes ch. 1:3.. The *Peschito Syriac* contains it. ORIGEN (in EUSEBIUS 6. 25) speaks of the First Epistle as genuine, and "probably the second and third, though all do not recognize the latter two"; on the Gospel of John, tom. 13, vol. 2, he quotes ch. 1:5. DIONYSIUS OF ALEXANDRIA, ORIGEN's scholar, cites the words of this Epistle as those of the Evangelist John. EUSEBIUS, *Ecclesiastical History* 3. 24, says, John's first Epistle and Gospel are *acknowledged without question* by those of the present day, as well as by the ancients. So also JEROME, in *Catalogue Ecclesiasticorum Scriptorum*. The opposition of COSMAS INDICOPLEUSTES, in the sixth century, and that of MARCION because our Epistle was inconsistent with his views, are of no weight against such irrefragable testimony.

The internal evidence is equally strong. Neither the Gospel, nor this Epistle, can be pronounced an imitation; yet both, in style and modes of thought, are evidently of the same mind. The *individual* notices are not so numerous or obvious as in Paul's writings, as was to be expected in a *Catholic* Epistle; but such as there are accord with John's position. He implies his apostleship, and perhaps alludes to his Gospel, and the affectionate tie which bound him as an *aged* pastor to his spiritual "children"; and in ch. 2:18, 19; 4:1–3, he alludes to the false teachers as known to his readers; and in ch. 5:21 he warns them against the idols of the surrounding world. It is no objection against its authenticity that the doctrine of the *Word*, or divine second Person, existing from everlasting, and in due time made flesh, appears in it, as also in the Gospel, as opposed to the heresy of the Docetæ *in the second century*, who denied that our Lord *is come in the flesh*, and maintained He came only in outward *semblance*; for the same doctrine appears in Colossians 1:15–18; I Timothy 3:16; Hebrews 1:1–3; and the germs of Docetism, though not fully developed till the second century, were in existence in the first. The Spirit, presciently through John, puts the Church beforehand on its guard against the coming heresy.

TO WHOM ADDRESSED.—AUGUSTINE, *Quæst. Evang.*, 2. 39, says this Epistle was written to the *Parthians*. BEDE, in a prologue to the seven Catholic Epistles, says that Athanasius attests the same. By the *Parthians* may be meant the Christians living beyond the Euphrates in the Parthian territory, outside the Roman empire, "the Church at Babylon elected together with" the churches in the Ephesian region, the quarter to which Peter addressed his Epistles. As Peter addressed the flock which John subsequently tended (and in which Paul had formerly ministered), so John, Peter's close companion after the ascension, addresses the flock among whom Peter had been when he wrote. Thus "the elect lady" answers "to the Church elected together." See farther confirmation of this view in *Introduction* to II John. It is not necessarily an objection to this view that John never is known to have personally ministered in the Parthian territory. For neither did Peter personally minister to the churches in Pontus, Galatia, Cappadocia, Asia, Bithynia, though he wrote his Epistles to them. Moreover, in John's prolonged life, we cannot dogmatically assert that he did not visit the Parthian Christians, after Peter had ceased to minister to them, on the mere ground of absence of extant testimony to that effect. This is as probable a view as ALFORD's, that in the passage of Augustine, "to the Parthians," is to be altered by conjectural emendation; and that the Epistle is addressed to the churches at and around Ephesus, on the ground of the fatherly tone of affectionate address in it, implying his personal ministry among his readers. But his position, as probably the only surviving apostle, accords very well with his addressing, in a Catholic Epistle, a cycle of churches which he may not have specially ministered to in person, with affectionate fatherly counsel, by virtue of his general apostolic superintendence of all the churches.

TIME AND PLACE OF WRITING.—This Epistle seems to have been written subsequently to his Gospel as it assumes the reader's acquaintance with the Gospel facts and Christ's speeches, and also with the special aspect of the incarnate Word, as God *manifest in the flesh*, set forth more fully in his Gospel. The tone of address, as a father addressing his "*little children*" (the continually recurring term), accords with the view that this Epistle was written in John's old age, perhaps about A.D. 90. In ch. 2:18, "it is the last time," probably does not refer to any particular event (as the destruction of Jerusalem, which was now many years past) but refers to the nearness of the Lord's coming as proved by the rise of *Antichristian teachers*, the mark of *the last time*. It was the Spirit's purpose to keep the Church always expecting Christ as ready to come at any moment. The whole Christian age is *the last time* in the sense that no other dispensation is to arise till Christ comes. Cf. "these last days," Hebrews 1:2. Ephesus may be conjectured to be the place whence it was written. The controversial allusion to the germs of Gnostic heresy accord with Asia Minor being the *place*, and the last part of the apostolic age the *time*, of writing this Epistle.

CONTENTS.—The leading subject of the whole is, *fellowship with the Father* and *the Son* (ch. 1:3). Two principal divisions may be noted: (1) ch. 1:5 to 2:28: the theme of this portion is stated at the outset, "*God is light, and in Him is no darkness at all*"; consequently, in order to have fellowship with Him, we must *walk in light*; connected with which in the *confession* and subsequent *forgiveness of our sins* through *Christ's propitiation* and *advocacy*, without which forgiveness there could be no light or fellowship with God: a farther step in thus walking in the light is, positively *keeping God's commandments*, the sum of which is *love*, as opposed to *hatred*, the acme of disobedience to God's word: negatively, he exhorts them according to their several stages of spiritual growth, *children, fathers, young men*, in consonance with their privileges as *forgiven, knowing the Father*, and *having overcome the wicked one, not to love the world*, which is incompatible with the indwelling *of the love of the Father*, and to be on their guard against the *Antichristian* teachers already in the world, who were not of the Church, but of the world, against whom the true defense is, that his believing readers who have the *anointing* of God, should *continue to abide in the Son and in the Father*. (2) The second division (ch. 2:29 to 5:5) discusses the theme with which it opens, "*He is righteous*"; consequently (as in the first division), "*every one that doeth righteousness is born of Him*." *Sonship* in us involves our purifying ourselves as He is pure, even as we *hope to see, and therefore to be made like our Lord when He shall appear;* in this second, as in the first division, both a positive and a negative side are presented of "doing righteousness as He is righteous." involving a contrast between the children of God and the children of the devil. *Hatred* marks the latter; *love,* the former: this love gives assurance of acceptance with God for ourselves and our prayers, accompanied as they are (vs. 23) with obedience to His great commandment, to "believe on Jesus, and love one another"; the seal (vs. 24) of His dwelling in us and assuring our hearts, is the Spirit which He hath given us. In contrast to this (as in the first division), he warns against false spirits, the notes of which are, *denial of Christ,* and *adherence to the world. Sonship,* or birth of God, is then more fully described: its essential feature is unslavish, free *love to God, because God first loved us,* and *gave His Son to die for us.* and consequent *love to the brethren,* grounded on their being sons of God also like ourselves, and so *victory over the world:* this victory being gained only by the man who *believes in Jesus as the Son of God.* (3) *The conclusion* establishes this last central truth, on which rests our fellowship with God, *Christ's having come by the water* of baptism, *the blood* of atonement, and *the witnessing Spirit,* which *is truth.* As in the opening he rested this cardinal truth on the apostles' witness of the eye, the ear, and the touch, so now at the close he rests it on *God's witness,* which is accepted by the believer, in contrast with the unbeliever, who *makes God a liar.* Then follows his closing statement of his *reason for writing* (ch. 5:13; cf. the corresponding ch. 1:4, at the beginning), namely, that *believers in Christ the Son of God may know that they have* (now already) *eternal life* (the source of "joy," ch. 1:4; cf. similarly his object in writing the Gospel, John 20:31), and so have confidence as to their prayers being answered (corresponding to ch. 3:22 in the second part); for instance, their intercessions for a *sinning brother* (unless his sin be a *sin unto death*). He closes with a brief summing up of the instruction of the Epistle, the high dignity, sanctity, and safety from evil of the children of God in contrast to the sinful world, and a warning against *idolatry,* literal and spiritual: "Keep yourselves from idols."

Though the Epistle is not directly polemical, the *occasion* which suggested his writing was probably the rise of Antichristian teachers; and, *because* he knew the spiritual character of the several classes whom he addresses, *children, youths, fathers,* he feels it necessary to write to confirm them in the faith and joyful fellowship of the Father and Son, and to assure them of the reality of the things they believe, that so they may have the *full* privileges of believing.

STYLE.—His peculiarity is fondness for aphorism and repetition. His tendency to repeat his own phrase, arises partly from the affectionate, hortatory character of the Epistle; partly, also, from its Hebraistic forms abounding in parallel clauses, as distinguished from the Grecian and more logical style of Paul; also, from his childlike simplicity of spirit, which, full of his one grand theme, repeats, and dwells on it with fond delight and enthusiasm. Moreover as ALFORD well says, the appearance of uniformity is often produced by want of deep enough exegesis to discover the real differences in passages which seem to express the same. Contemplative, rather than argumentative, he dwells more on the general, than on the particular, on the inner, than on the outer, Christian life. Certain fundamental truths he recurs to again and again, at one time enlarging on, and applying them, at another time repeating them in their condensed simplicity. The thoughts do not march onward by successive steps, as in the logical style of Paul, but rather in circle drawn round one central thought which he reiterates, ever reverting to it, and viewing it, now under its positive, now under its negative, aspect. Many terms which in the Gospel are given as Christ's, in the Epistle appear as the favorite expressions of John, naturally adopted from the Lord. Thus the contrasted terms, "flesh" and "spirit," "light" and "darkness," "life" and "death," "abide in Him": fellowship with the Father and Son, and with one another," is a favorite phrase also, not found in the Gospel, but in Acts and Paul's Epistles. In him appears the harmonious union of opposites, adapting him for his high functions in the kingdom of God, contemplative repose of character, and at the same time ardent zeal, combined with burning, all-absorbing love: less adapted for active outward work, such as Paul's, than for spiritual service. He handles Christian verities not as abstract dogmas, but as living realities, personally enjoyed in fellowship with God in Christ, and with the brethren. Simple, and at the same time profound, his writing is in consonance with his spirit, unrhetorical and undialectic, gentle, consolatory, and loving: the reflection of the Spirit of Him on whose breast he lay at the last supper, and whose beloved disciple he was. EWALD in ALFORD, speaking of the "unruffled and heavenly repose" which characterizes this Epistle, says, "It appears to be the tone, not so much of a father talking with his beloved children, as of a glorified saint addressing mankind from a higher world. Never in any writing has the doctrine of heavenly love—a love working in stillness, ever unwearied, never exhausted—so thoroughly approved itself as in this Epistle."

JOHN'S PLACE IN THE BUILDING UP OF THE CHURCH.—As Peter founded and Paul propagated, so John completed the spiritual building. As the Old Testament puts prominently forward the *fear of God,* so John, the last writer of the New Testament, gives prominence to the *love of God.* Yet, as the Old Testament is not all limited to presenting the fear of God, but sets forth also His *love,* so John, as a representative of the New Testament, while breathing so continually the spirit of love, gives also the plainest and most awful warnings against sin, in accordance with his original character as Boanerges, "son of thunder." His mother was Salome, mother of the sons of Zebedee, probably sister to Jesus' mother (cf. John 19:25, "His mother's sister," with Matt. 27:56; Mark 15:40), so that he was cousin to our Lord; to his mother, under God, he may have owed his first serious impressions. Expecting as she did the Messianic kingdom in glory, as appears from her petition (Matt. 20:20-23), she doubtless tried to fill his young and ardent mind with the same hope. NEANDER distinguishes three leading tendencies in the development of the Christian doctrine, the Pauline, the Jacobean (between which the Petrine forms an intermediate link), and the Johannean. John, in common with James, was less disposed to the intellectual and dialectic cast of thought which distinguishes Paul. He had not, like the apostle of the Gentiles, been brought to faith and peace through severe conflict; but, like James, had reached his Christian individuality through a quiet development: James, however, had passed through a moulding in Judaism previously, which, under the Spirit, caused him to present Christian truth in connection with the law, in so far as the latter in its spirit, though not letter, is permanent, and not abolished, but established under the Gospel. But John, from the first, had drawn his whole spiritual development from the personal view of Christ, the model man, and from intercourse with Him. Hence, in his writings, everything turns on one simple contrast: divine *life* in communion with Christ; death in separation from Him, as appears from his characteristic phrases, "*life, light, truth; death, darkness, lie.*" "As James and Peter mark the gradual transition from spiritualized Judaism to the independent development of Christianity, and as Paul represents the independent development of Christianity in opposition to the Jewish standpoint, so the contemplative element of John reconciles the two, and forms the closing point in the training of the apostolic Church" [NEANDER].

CHAPTER 1

Vss. 1-10. THE WRITER'S AUTHORITY AS AN EYEWITNESS TO THE GOSPEL FACTS, HAVING SEEN, HEARD, AND HANDLED HIM WHO WAS FROM THE BEGINNING: HIS OBJECT IN WRITING:HIS MESSAGE. IF WE WOULD HAVE FELLOWSHIP WITH HIM, WE MUST WALK IN LIGHT, AS HE IS LIGHT. 1. Instead of a formal, John adopts a virtual address (cf. vs. 4). To wish *joy* to the reader was the ancient customary address. The sentence begun in vs. 1 is broken off by the parenthetic vs. 2, and is resumed at vs. 3 with the repetition of some words from vs. 1. **That which was**—not "began to be," but *was* essentially (*Greek, een,* not *egeneto*) before He was *manifested* (vs. 2); answering to "Him that is *from the beginning*" (ch. 2:13); so John's Gospel, 1:1, "In the beginning was the Word." Proverbs 8:23, "I was set up from everlasting, *from the beginning,* or ever the earth was." **we**—apostles. **heard ... seen ... looked upon ... handled**—a series rising in gradation. *Seeing* is a more convincing proof than *hearing* of; *handling,* than even *seeing.* "Have heard ... have seen" (perfects), as a possession *still abiding* with us; but in *Greek* (not as *English Version* "have," but simply) "looked upon" (not perfect, as of a *continuing* thing, but aorist, *past* time) while Christ the incarnate Word was still with us. "Seen," viz., His glory, as revealed in the Transfiguration and in His miracles; and His passion and death in a real body of flesh and blood. "Looked upon" as a wondrous spectacle steadfastly, deeply, contemplatively; so the *Greek.* Appropriate to John's contemplative character. **hands ... handled**—Thomas and the other disciples on distinct occasions after the resurrection. John himself had leaned on Jesus' breast at the last supper. Contrast the wisest of the heathen *feeling after* (the same *Greek* as here; *groping after* WITH THE HANDS) if haply they might find God. This proves against Socinians he is here speaking of the *personal incarnate Word,* not of Christ's *teaching* from the beginning of His official life. **of**—"concerning"; following "heard." "Heard" is the verb most applying to the purpose of the Epistle, viz. the truth which John had *heard concerning the Word of life,* i.e., (Christ) *the Word* who is *the life.* "Heard," viz., from Christ Himself, including all Christ's teachings about Himself. Therefore he puts "of," or "concerning," before "the word of life," which is inapplicable to any of the verbs except "heard"; also "heard" is the only one of the verbs which he resumes at vs. 5. **2. the life**—Jesus, "the Word of life." **was manifested**—who had previously been "with the Father." **show**—Translate as in vs. 3, "declare" (cf. vs. 5). *Declare* is the general term; *write* is the particular (vs. 4). **that eternal life**—*Greek,* "the life which is eternal." As the Epistle begins, so it ends with "eternal life," which we shall ever enjoy with, and in, Him who is "the life eternal." **which**—*Greek,* "the which," the beforementioned (vs. 1) life *which* was with the Father "from the beginning" (cf. John 1:1). This proves the distinctness of the First and Second Persons in the one Godhead. **3. That which we have seen and heard**—resumed from vs. 1, wherein the sentence, being interrupted by vs. 2, parenthesis, was left incomplete. **declare we unto you**—Oldest MSS. add *also; unto you also* who have not *seen* or *heard* Him. **that ye also may have fellowship with us**—that *ye also* who have not seen, *may* have the *fellowship* with us which we who have seen enjoy; what that fellowship consists in he proceeds to state, "Our fellowship is with the Father and with His Son." Faith realizes what we have not seen as spiritually visible; not till by faith we too have seen, do we know all the excellency of the true Solomon. He Himself is ours; He in us and we in Him. We are "partakers of the divine nature." We know God only by having fellowship with Him; He may thus be *known,* but not *comprehended.* The repetition of "with" before the "Son," distinguishes the *persons,* while the *fellowship* or *communion* with both *Father* and *Son,* implies their unity. It is not added "and with the Holy Ghost"; for it is *by* the Holy Ghost or Spirit of the Father and Son in us, that we are enabled to have *fellowship with the Father and Son* (cf. ch. 3:24). Believers enjoy the fellowship OF, but not WITH, the Holy Ghost. "Through Christ God closes up the chasm that separated Him from the human race, and imparts Himself to them, in the communion of the divine life" [NEANDER]. **4. these things**—and none other, viz., this whole Epistle. **write we unto you**—Some oldest MSS. omit "unto you," and emphasize "we." Thus the antithesis is between "we" (apostles and eye-witnesses) and "your." *We* write thus that *your joy* may be full. Other oldest MSS. and versions read "OUR joy," viz., *that our joy may be filled full by* bringing you also into fellowship with the Father and Son. (Cf. John 4:36, end; Phil. 2:2, "Fulfil ye my joy," 16; and 4:1; II John 8). It is possible that "your" may be a correction of transcribers to make this verse harmonize with John 15:11; 16:24; however, as John often repeats favorite phrases, he may do so here, so "your" may be from himself. So II John 12, "your" in oldest MSS. The authority of MSS. and versions on both sides here is almost evenly balanced. Christ Himself is the source, object, and center of His people's joy (cf. vs. 3,end); it is in *fellowship with* Him that we have *joy,* the fruit of faith. **5.** First division of the body of the Epistle (cf. *Introduction*). **declare**—*Greek,* "announce"; report in turn; a different *Greek* word from vs. 3. As the Son announced the message heard from the Father as His apostle, so the Son's apostles announce what they have heard from the Son. John nowhere uses the term "Gospel"; but the *witness* or *testimony, the word, the truth,* and here the *message.* **God is light**—What light is in the natural world, that God, the source of even material light, is in the spiritual, the fountain of wisdom, purity, beauty, joy, and glory. As all material life and growth depends on *light,* so all spiritual life and growth depends on GOD. As God here, so Christ, in ch. 2:8, is called "the true light."

no darkness at all—strong negation; *Greek,* "No, not even one speck of darkness"; no ignorance, error, untruthfulness, sin, or death. John heard this from Christ, not only in express words, but in His acted words, viz., His is whole manifestation in the flesh as "the brightness of the Father's *glory.*" Christ Himself was the embodiment of "the message," representing fully in all His sayings, doings, and sufferings, Him who is Light. 6. say—profess. have fellowship with him—(vs. 3). The essence of the Christian life. walk—in inward and outward action, whithersoever we turn ourselves [Bengel]. in darkness—*Greek,* "in *the* darkness"; opposed to "the light" (cf. ch. 2:8, 11). lie—(ch. 2:4). do not— —in *practice,* whatever we *say.* the truth—(Eph. (4: 21; John 3:21). 7. Cf. Ephesians 5:8, 11-14. "We walk"; "God is (*essentially* in His very nature as 'the light,' vs. 5) in the light." Walking *in the light,* the element in which God Himself is, constitutes the test of fellowship with Him. Christ, like us, *walked* in the light (ch. 2:6). Alford notices, Walking in the light as He is in the light, is no mere imitation of God, *but an identity in the essential element* of our daily walk with the essential element of God's eternal being. we have fellowship one with another—and of course *with God* (to be understood from vs. 6). Without having fellowship with God there can be no true and Christian fellowship one with another (cf. vs. 3). and—as the result of "walking in the light, as He is in the light." the blood of Jesus . . . cleanseth us from all sin—daily contracted through the sinful weakness of the flesh, and the power of Satan and the world. He is speaking not of justification through His blood once for all, but of the *present sanctification* ("cleanseth" is *present*) which the believer, *walking in the light* and having *fellowship with God and the saints,* enjoys as His privilege. Cf. John 13:10, *Greek,* "He that has been *bathed,* needeth not save to *wash* his feet, but is clean every whit." Cf. vs. 9, "*cleanse* us from all unrighteousness," a further step besides "*forgiving* us our sins." Christ's blood is the cleansing mean, whereby gradually, being already justified and in fellowship with God, we become *clean* from all sin which would mar our fellowship with God. Faith applies the cleansing, purifying blood. Some oldest MSS. omit "Christ"; others retain it. 8. *The confession of sins* is a necessary consequence of "walking in the light" (vs. 7). "If thou shalt confess thyself a sinner, the *truth* is in thee; for the *truth* is itself *light.* Not yet has thy life become perfectly light, as sins are still in thee, but yet thou hast already begun to be illuminated, because there is in thee confession of sins" [Augustine]. that we have no sin—"Have," not "have *had,*" must refer not to the past sinful life while unconverted, but to the *present* state wherein believers *have* sin even still. Observe, "sin" is in the singular; "(confess our) *sins*" (vs. 9) in the plural. *Sin* refers to the *corruption of the old man* still present in us, and the *stain* created by the actual *sins* flowing from that old nature in us. To confess our need of cleansing from *present* sin is essential to "walking in the light"; so far is the presence of some sin incompatible with our *in the main* "walking in light." But the believer hates, confesses, and longs to be delivered from all sin, which is *darkness.* "They who defend their sins, will see in the great day whether their sins can defend them." deceive ourselves—We cannot deceive God; we only make ourselves to err from the right path. the truth—(ch. 2:4). True faith. "The truth respecting God's holiness and our sinfulness, which is the very first spark of light

in us, has no place in us" [Alford]. 9. confess—with the lips, speaking from a contrite heart; involving also confession to our fellow men of offenses committed against them. he—God. faithful—to His own promises; "true" to His word. just—Not merely the mercy, but the *justice* or *righteousness* of God is set forth in the redemption of the penitent believer in Christ. God's promises of mercy, to which He is *faithful,* are in accordance with His *justice.* to—*Greek,* "in order that." His forgiving *us our sins and cleansing us from . . .* is in furtherance of the *ends* of His eternal *faithfulness* and *justice.* forgive—remitting the *guilt.* cleanse—purify from all filthiness, so that henceforth we more and more become free from the presence of sin through the Spirit of sanctification (cf. Heb. 9:14; and above, *Note,* vs. 7). unrighteousness—offensive to Him who "is just" or *righteous;* called "sin," vs. 7, because "sin is the transgression of the law," and the law is the expression of God's *righteousness,* so that *sin* is *unrighteousness.* 10. Parallel to vs. 8. we have not sinned—referring to the commission of actual *sins,* even after regeneration and conversion; whereas in vs. 8, "we have no sin," refers to the present Guilt remaining (until cleansed) from the *actual sins* committed, and to the sin of our corrupt old nature still adhering to us. The perfect "have . . . sinned" brings down the commission of sins to the present time, not merely sins committed *before,* but *since, conversion.* we make him a liar —a gradation; vs. 6, "we lie"; vs. 8, "we deceive ourselves"; worst of all, "we make Him a liar," by denying His word that all men are sinners (cf. ch. 5:10). his word is not in us—"His word," which is "the truth" (vs. 8), accuses us truly; by denying it we drive it from our hearts (cf. John 5:38). Our rejection of "His word" in respect to our being sinners, implies as the consequence our rejection of His word and will revealed in the law and Gospel *as a whole;* for these throughout rest on the fact that *we have sinned,* and *have sin.*

CHAPTER 2

Vss. 1-29. The Advocacy of Christ Is Our Antidote to Sin while Walking in the Light; for to Know God, We Must Keep His Commandments and love the Brethren, and Not Love the World, nor Give Heed to Antichrists, against Whom Our Safety Is through the Inward Anointing of God to Abide in God: So at Christ's Coming We Shall Not Be Ashamed. 1. (Ch. 5:18). My little children—The diminutive expresses the tender affection of an aged pastor and spiritual father. *My own dear children,* i.e., sons and daughters (*Note,* vs. 12). these things—(ch. 1:6-10). My purpose in writing what I have just written is not that you should abuse them as giving a license to sin but, on the contrary, "in order that ye may not sin at all" (the *Greek* aorist implying the absense not only of the habit, but of *single acts* of sin [Alford]). In order to "walk in the light" (ch. 1:5, 7), the first step is *confession of sin* (ch. 1:9), the next (ch. 2:1) is that we should *forsake all sin.* The divine purpose has for its aim, either to prevent the commission of, or to destroy sin [Bengel]. And . . .—connected with the former; *Furthermore,* "if any man sin," let him, while loathing and condemning it, not fear to go at once to God, the Judge, confessing it, for "we have an Advocate with Him." He is speaking of a believer's *occasional* sins of infirmity through Satan's fraud and malice. The use of "we" immediately afterwards implies that *we all* are *liable* to this, though not necessarily constrained to sin. **we have an advocate**–Advocacy is God's family blessing; other blessings He grants to good and bad alike, but justification, sanctification, continued intercession, and peace, He grants to His children alone. **advocate**–*Greek*, "paraclete," the same term as is applied to the Holy Ghost, as the "other Comforter"; showing the unity of the Second and Third Persons of the Trinity. Christ is the Intercessor *for us* above; and, in His absence, here below the Holy Ghost is the other Intercessor *in us*. Christ's *advocacy* is inseparable from the Holy Spirit's *comfort* and working in us, as the spirit of intercessory prayer. **righteous**–As our "advocate," Christ is not a mere suppliant petitioner. He pleads for us on the ground of *justice*, or *righteousness*, as well as mercy. Though He can say nothing good *of* us, He can say much *for* us. It is His *righteousness*, or obedience to the law, and endurance of its full penalty for us, on which He grounds His claim for our acquittal. The sense therefore is, "in that He is *righteous*"; in contrast to our *sin* ("if any man *sin*"). The Father, by raising Him from the dead, and setting Him at His own right, has once for all accepted Christ's claim for us. Therefore the accuser's charges against God's children are vain. "The righteousness of Christ stands on our side; **for God's righteousness is, in Jesus Christ, ours**" [LUTHER]. **2. And he**–*Greek*, "And Himself." He is our all-prevailing Advocate, because He is *Himself* "the propitiation"; abstract, as in I Corinthians 1:30: He is to us *all that is needed for propitiation* "in behalf of our sins"; *the propitiatory sacrifice*, provided by the Father's love, removing the estrangement, and appeasing the righteous wrath, on God's part, against the sinner. "There is no incongruity that a father should be *offended* with that son whom he loveth, and at that time offended with him when he *loveth* him" [BISHOP PEARSON]. The only other place in the New Testament where *Greek* "propitiation" occurs, is ch. 4:10; it answers in LXX to *Hebrew caphar*, to *effect an atonement* or *reconciliation* with God; and in Ezekiel 44:29, to the *sin offering*. In Romans 3:25, *Greek*, it is "propitiatory," i.e., the mercy seat, or lid of the ark whereon God, represented by the Shekinah glory above it, met His people, represented by the high priest who sprinkled the blood of the sacrifice on it. **and**–*Greek*, "yet." **ours**–believers: not *Jews*, in contrast to Gentiles; for he is not writing to Jews (ch. 5:21). **also for the sins of the whole world**–Christ's *advocacy* is limited to *believers* (vs. 1; ch. 1:7): His propitiation extends as widely as *sin* extends: *Note*, II Peter 2:1, "denying the Lord that *bought them*." "The *whole world*" cannot be restricted to the *believing* portion of the world (cf. ch. 4:14; and "the whole world," ch. 5:19). "Thou, too, art part of the world, so that thine heart cannot deceive itself and think, The Lord died for Peter and Paul, but not for me" [LUTHER]. **3. hereby**–*Greek*, "in this." "It is *herein*, and herein only, that we know (present) that we have knowledge of (perfect, once-for-all obtained and continuing *knowledge of*) Him" (vss. 4, 13, 14). Tokens whereby to discern grace are frequently given in this Epistle. The Gnostics, by the Spirit's prescient forewarning, are refuted, who boasted of *knowledge*, but set aside *obedience*. "Know Him," viz., as "the righteous" (vss. 1, 29); our "Advocate and Intercessor." **keep**–John's favorite word, instead of "do," lit. "watch," "guard," and "keep safe" as a precious thing; observing so as to keep. So Christ Himself. Not

faultless conformity, but hearty acceptance of, and willing subjection to, God's whole revealed will, is meant. **commandments**–*injunctions* of faith, love, and obedience. John never uses "the law" to express the rule of Christian obedience: he uses it as the Mosaic law. **4. I know**–*Greek*, "I have knowledge of (perfect) Him." Cf. with this verse ch. 1:8. **5.** Not merely repeating the proposition, vs. 3, or asserting the merely opposite alternative to vs. 4, but expanding the "know Him" of vs. 3, into "in Him, verily (not as a matter of vain boasting) is the love of (i.e. towards) God perfected," and "we are in Him." *Love* here answers to *knowledge* in vs. 3. In proportion as we love God, in that same proportion we *know* Him, and vice versa, until our *love and knowledge* shall attain their full maturity of perfection. **5. his word**–*His word* is one (*Note*, ch. 1:5), and comprises His "*commandments*," which are many (vs. 3). **hereby**–in our progressing towards this ideal of perfected love and obedience. There is a gradation: vs. 3, "*know* Him"; vs. 5, "we *are* in Him"; vs. 6, "*abideth* in Him"; respectively, *knowledge, fellowship, abiding constancy* [BENGEL]. **6. abideth**–implying a condition lasting, without intermission, and without end. **He that saith ... ought**–so that his deeds may be consistent with his words. **even as he**–Believers readily supply the name, their hearts being full of Him (cf. John 20:15). "Even as He walked" when on earth, especially in respect to *love*. John delights in referring to Christ as the model man, with the words, "Even as He...." "It is not Christ's walking on the sea, but His ordinary walk, that we are called on to imitate" [LUTHER]. **7. Brethren**–The oldest MSS. and versions read instead, "Beloved," appropriate to the subject here, *love*. **no new commandment**–viz., *love*, the main principle of walking *as Christ walked* (vs. 6), and that commandment, of which one exemplification is presently given, vss. 9, 10, *the love of brethren*. **ye had from the beginning**–from the time that ye first heard the Gospel word preached. **8. a new commandment**–It was "old," in that *Christians* as such had heard it *from the first;* but "new" (*Greek, kaine*, not *nea: new and different* from the *old* legal precept) in that it was first *clearly* promulgated with Christianity; though the inner *spirit* of the law was *love* even to enemies, yet it was enveloped in some bitter precepts which caused it to be temporarily almost unrecognized, till the Gospel came. Christianity first put *love to brethren* on the *new* and highest MOTIVE, instinctive love to Him who first loved us, constraining us to love all, even enemies, thereby walking in the steps of Him who loved us when enemies. So Jesus calls it "new," John 13:34, 35, "Love one another *as I have loved you*" (the new motive); 15:12. **which thing is true in him and in you**–"*In Christ* all things are always true, and were so from the beginning; but *in Christ and in us* conjointly *the commandment* [the love of brethren] *is then true* when we acknowledge the truth which is *in Him*, and have the same flourishing *in us*" [BENGEL]. ALFORD explains, "Which thing (*the fact that the commandment is a new one*) is true in Him and in you because the darkness is *passing away*, and the true light is now shining; i.e., the commandment *is a new one*, and this is true both in the case of Christ and in the case of you; because *in you* the darkness is passing away, and *in Him* the true light is shining; therefore, on both accounts, the command is a *new one*: new as regards you, because you are newly come from darkness into light; new as regards Him, because He uttered it when He came into the world to lighten every man, and began that shining which even now continues." I prefer, as BENGEL, to explain, The *new commandment* finds its *truth* in its practical *realization* in the walk of Christians in union with Christ. Cf. the use of "verily," vs. 5. John 4:42, "indeed"; 6:55. The repetition of "in" before "you," "in Him and in you," not "in Him and you," implies that the love-commandment finds its realization *separately:* first it did so "*in Him,*" and then it does so "in us," in so far as we now "also walk even as He walked"; and yet it finds its realization also *conjointly,* by the two being united in one sentence, even as it is by virtue of the love-commandment having been first fulfilled *in Him,* that it is also now fulfilled *in us,* through His Spirit in us: cf. a similar case, John 20: 17, "*My Father* and *your* Father"; by virtue of His being "*My* Father," He is also *your* Father. **darkness is past**—rather, as in ch. 2:17, "is passing away." It shall not be wholly "past" until "the Sun of right-eousness" shall arise *visibly;* "the light is now shining" *already,* though but partially until the day bursts forth. **9-11.** There is no mean between *light and darkness, love* and *hatred, life* and *death, God* and the *world:* wherever spiritual *life* is, however weak, there *darkness* and *death* no longer reign, and *love* supplants *hatred;* and Luke 9:50 holds good: wherever *life* is not, *there death, darkness, the flesh, the world, and hatred,* however glossed over and hidden from man's observation, prevail; and Luke 11: 23 holds good. "Where love is not, there hatred is; for the heart cannot remain a void" [BENGEL]. **in the light**—as his proper element. **his brother**—his neighbor, and especially those of the Christian brotherhood. The very title "brother" is a reason why love should be exercised. **even until now**—notwithstanding that "the true light already has begun to shine" (vs. 8). **10.** Abiding in *love* is *abiding* in *the light;* for the Gospel light not only illumines the understanding, but warms the heart into love. **none occasion of stumbling**—In contrast to, "He that hateth his brother is in darkness, and walketh in darkness, and knoweth not whither he goeth, because that darkness hath blinded his eyes." "In him who loves there is neither blindness nor *occasion of stumbling* [to himself]: in him who does not love, there is both *blindness* and occasion of stumbling. He who hates his brother, is both a stumbling block to himself, and stumbles against himself and everything within and without; he who loves has an unimpeded path" [BENGEL]. John has in mind Jesus' words, John 11:9, 10. ALFORD well says, "The light and the darkness are within ourselves; admitted into us by the eye, whose singleness fills the whole body with light." **11. is in darkness ...walketh**—"is" marks his continuing STATE: he has never come out of "the (so *Greek*) darkness"; "walketh" marks his OUTWARD WALK and acts. **whither**—*Greek,* "where"; including not only the destination *to which,* but the way *whereby.* **hath blinded**—rather as *Greek* aorist, "blinded" of old. Darkness not only surrounds, but blinds him, and that a blindness of long standing. **12. little children**—*Greek,* "little *sons,*" or "dear sons and daughters"; not the same *Greek* as in vs. 13, "little *children,*" "infants" (in age and standing). He calls ALL to whom he writes, "little *sons*" (ch. 2:1, *Greek;* 2:28; 3:18; 4:4; 5:21); but only in vss. 13 and 18 he uses the term "little children," or "infants." Our Lord, whose Spirit John so deeply drank into, used to His disciples (John 13:33) the term "little sons," or *dear sons and daughters;* but in John 21:5, "little children." It is an undesigned coincidence with the

Epistle here, that in John's Gospel somewhat similarly the classification, "lambs, sheep, sheep," occurs. **are forgiven**—"have been, and are forgiven you": ALL God's *sons and daughters* alike enjoy this privilege. **13, 14.** All three classes are first addressed in the present. "I write"; then in the past (aorist) tense, "I wrote" (not "I have written"; moreover, in the oldest MSS. and versions, in the end of vs. 13, it is past, "1 wrote," not as *English Version,* "I write"). Two classes, "fathers" and "young men," are addressed with the same words each time (except that the address to the *young men* has an addition expressing the source and means of their victory); but the "little sons" and "little children" are differently addressed. **have known**—and do know: so the *Greek* perfect means. The "I wrote" refers not to a former Epistle, but to this Epistle. It was an idiom to put the *past* tense, regarding the time from the *reader's* point of view; when he should receive the Epistle the writing would be *past.* When he uses "I write," he speaks from *his own* point of view. **him** *that is* **from the beginning**—Christ: "that which was from the beginning." **overcome**—The *fathers,* appropriately to their age, are characterized by *knowledge.* The *young men,* appropriately to theirs, by *activity in conflict.* The *fathers,* too, have *conquered;* but now their active service is past, and they and *the children* alike are characterized by *knowing* (the *fathers* know *Christ,* "Him that was from the beginning"; *the children* know the Father). The first thing that the *little children* realize is that God is their *Father;* answering in the parallel clause to "little sons . . . your sins are forgiven you for His name's sake," the universal first privilege of *all* those really-dear *sons* of God. Thus this latter clause includes *all,* whereas the former clause refers to those more especially who are in the *first* stage of spiritual life, "little children." Of course, these can only know *the Father* as theirs through *the Son* (Matt. 11:27). It is beautiful to see how the *fathers* are characterized as reverting back to the first great truths of spiritual childhood, and the sum and ripest fruit of advanced experience, the *knowledge of Him that was from the beginning* (twice repeated, vss. 13, 14). Many of them had probably known *Jesus* in person, as well as by faith. **14. young men . . . strong** —*made* so *out of* natural *weakness,* hence enabled to *overcome* "the strong man armed" through Him that is "stronger." Faith is the victory that overcomes the world. This term "overcome" is peculiarly John's, adopted from his loved Lord. It occurs sixteen times in the Apocalypse, six times in the First Epistle, only thrice in the rest of the New Testament. In order to overcome the world on the ground, and in the strength, of the blood of the Saviour, we must be willing, like Christ, to part with whatever of the world belongs to us: whence immediately after "ye have overcome the wicked one (the prince of the world)," it is added, "Love not the world, neither the things . . . in the world." **and . . .**—the secret of the young men's *strength:* the Gospel *word,* clothed with living power by the Spirit who *abideth* permanently in them; this is "the sword of the Spirit" wielded in prayerful waiting on God. Contrast the mere physical strength of young men, Isaiah 40:30, 31. *Oral teaching* prepared these youths for the profitable use of *the word* when *written.* "Antichrist cannot endanger you (vs. 18), nor Satan tear from you *the word of God.*" **the wicked one**—who, as "prince of this world," enthrals "the world" (vss. 15-17; ch. 5:19, *Greek,* "the wicked one"), especially the young. Christ came to destroy this "prince of the world". Believers achieve the first grand conquest over him when they pass from darkness to light, but afterwards they need to maintain a continual *keeping* of themselves from his assaults, looking to God by whom alone they are *kept* safe. BENGEL thinks John refers specially to the remarkable constancy exhibited by youths in Domitian's persecution. Also to the young man whom John, after his return from Patmos, led with gentle, loving persuasion to repentance. This youth had been commended to the overseers of the Church by John, in one of his tours of superintendency, as a promising disciple; he had been, therefore, carefully watched up to baptism. But afterwards relying too much on baptismal grace, he joined evil associates, and fell from step to step down, till he became a captain of robbers. When John, some years after, revisited that Church and heard of the youth's sad fall, he hastened to the retreat of the robbers, suffered himself to be seized and taken into the captain's presence. The youth, stung by conscience and the remembrance of former years, fied away from the venerable apostle. Full of love the aged father ran after him, called on him to take courage, and announced to him forgiveness of his sins in the name of Christ. The youth was recovered to the paths of Christianity, and was the means of inducing many of his bad associates to repent and believe [CLEMENS ALEXANDRINUS, *Quis dives salvus?* c. 4. 2; EUSEBIUS, *Ecclesiastical History*, Book 3. 20; CHRYSOSTOM, 1 *Exhortation to Theodore*, 11]. **15. Love not the world**—that *lieth in the wicked one* (ch. 5:19), whom ye young men *have overcome.* Having once for all, through *faith, overcome the world* (ch. 4:4; 5:4), carry forward the conquest by not loving it. "The world" here means "man, and man's world" [ALFORD], in his and its state as *fallen from God.* "God loved [with the love of *compassion*] the world," and we should feel the same kind of love for the fallen world; but we are *not* to love the world with *congeniality* and *sympathy* in its alienation from God; we cannot have this latter kind of love for the God-estranged world, and yet have also "the love of the Father in" us. **neither**—*Greek,* "nor yet." A man might deny in general that he *loved* the world, while keenly following some one of THE THINGS IN IT: its riches, honors, or pleasures; this clause prevents him escaping from conviction. **any man**—therefore the warning, though primarily addressed to the young, applies to *all.* **love of**—i.e., *towards* "the Father." The two, God and the (sinful) world, are so opposed, that both cannot be congenially loved at once. **16. all that is in the world**—can be classed under one or other of the three; the world contains these and no more. **lust of the flesh**—i.e., the lust which has its seat and source in our lower animal nature. Satan tried this temptation the first on Christ: Luke 4:3, "Command this stone that it be made *bread.*" Youth is especially liable to fleshly lusts. **lust of the eyes**—the avenue through which outward things of the world, riches, pomp, and beauty, inflame us. Satan tried this temptation on Christ when he showed Him the kingdoms of the world in a moment. By the lust of the eyes David (II Sam. 11:2) and Achan fell (Josh. 7:21). Cf. David's prayer, Psalm 119:37; Job's resolve, Psalm 31:1 Matthew 5:28. The only good of worldly riches to the possessor is the beholding them with the *eyes.* Cf. Luke 14:18, "I must go and SEE it." **pride of life** —lit., "arrogant assumption": vainglorious display. *Pride* was Satan's sin whereby he fell and forms the link between the two foes of man, the *world* (answering to "the lust of the eyes") and the *devil* (as

"the lust of the flesh" is the third foe). Satan tried this temptation on Christ in setting Him on the temple pinnacle that, in spiritual *pride* and *presumption,* on the ground of His Father's care, He should cast Himself down. The same three foes appear in the three classes of soil on which the divine seed falls: the wayside hearers, the *devil;* the thorns, *the world;* the rocky undersoil, *the flesh.* The world's awful *antitrinity,* the "lust of the flesh, the lust of the eyes, and the pride of life," similarly is presented in Satan's temptation of Eve: "When she saw that the tree was good for *food,* pleasant to the *eyes,* and a tree to be desired to make one *wise*" (one manifestation of "the pride of life," the desire to know above what God has revealed, Col. 2:8, the pride of unsanctified knowledge). **of**—does not spring *from* "the Father" (used in relation to the preceding "little children," vs. 12, or "little sons"). He who is born *of* God alone turns *to* God; he who is of the world turns to the world; the sources of love to God and love to the world, are irreconcilably distinct. **17. the world**—with all who are of the world worldly. **passeth away**—*Greek,* "is passing away" even now. **the lust thereof**—in its threefold manifestation (vs. 16). **he that doeth the will of God**—not his own *fleshly* will, or the will of the *world,* but that of God (vss. 3, 6), especially in respect to *love.* **abideth for ever**—"even as God also abideth for ever" (with whom the godly is one; cf. Ps. 55:19, "God, even He that abideth of old"): a true *comment,* which CYPRIAN and LUCIFER have added to the *text* without support of *Greek* MSS. In contrast to the three *passing* lusts of the world, the doer of God's will has three *abiding* goods, "riches, honor, and life" (Prov. 22:4). **18. Little children**—same *Greek* as vs. 13; children *in age.* After the *fathers* and *young men* were gone, "the last time" with its "many Antichrists" was about to come suddenly on *the children.* "In this *last hour* we all even still live" [BENGEL]. Each successive age has had in it some of the signs of "the last time" which precedes Christ's coming, in order to keep the Church in continual waiting for the Lord. The connection with vss. 15-17 is: There are coming those seducers who are of the world (ch. 4:5), and would tempt you to go out from us (vs. 19) and deny Christ (vs. 22). **as ye have heard**—from the apostles, preachers of the Gospel (e.g., II Thess. 2: 3-10; and in the region of Ephesus, Acts 20:29, 30). **shall come**—*Greek,* "cometh," viz., out of his own place. *Antichrist* is interpreted in two ways: a false Christ (Matt. 24:5, 24), lit., "*instead* of Christ"; or an *adversary* of Christ, lit., "*against* Christ." As John never uses *pseudo-Christ,* or "false Christ," for *Antichrist,* it is plain he means an *adversary of Christ,* claiming to himself what belongs to Christ, and wishing to substitute himself for Christ as the supreme object of worship. He *denies the Son,* not merely, like the pope, acts in the name of the Son, II Thessalonians 2:4, "Who *opposeth* himself (*Greek,* ANTI-*keimenos*) [to] all that is called God," decides this. For God's great truth, "God is man," he would substitute his own lie, "man is God" [TRENCH]. **are there**—*Greek,* "there have begun to be"; there have arisen. These "many Antichrists" answer to "the spirit of lawlessness (*Greek*) doth already work." The Antichristian principle appeared then, as now, in evil men and evil teachings and writings; but still "THE Antichrist" means a hostile *person,* even as "THE Christ" is a personal Saviour. As "cometh" is used of Christ, *so* here of Antichrist, the embodiment in his own person of all the Antichristian features and spirit of those "many

Antichrists" which have been, and are, his forerunners. John uses the singular of him. No other New Testament writer uses the term. He probably answers to "the little horn having the eyes of a man, and speaking great things" (Dan. 7:8, 20); "the man of sin, son of perdition" (II Thessalonians 2); "the beast ascending out of the bottomless pit" (Rev. 11: 7; 17:8), or rather, "the false prophet," the same as "the second beast coming up out of the earth" (Rev. 13:11-18; 16:13). **19. out from us**—from our Christian communion. Not necessarily a formal secession or *going out:* thus Rome has spiritually *gone out*, though formally still of the Christian Church. **not of us**—by spiritual fellowship (ch. 1:3). "They are like bad humors in the body of Christ, the Church: when they are vomited out, then the body is relieved; the body of Christ is now still under treatment, and has not yet attained the perfect soundness which it shall have only at the resurrection" [AUGUSTINE, *Ep. John, Tract* 3, 4]. **they would ... have continued**—implying the indefectibility of grace in the elect. "Where God's call is effectual, there will be sure perseverance" [CALVIN]. Still, it is no fatal necessity, but a "voluntary necessity" [DIDYMUS], which causes men to remain, or else go from the body of Christ. "We are either among the members, or else among the bad humors. It is of his own will that each is either an Antichrist, or in Christ" [AUGUSTINE]. Still God's actings in eternal election harmonize in a way *inexplicable to us*, with man's free agency and responsibility. It is men's own evil will that chooses the way to hell; it is God's free and sovereign grace that draws any to Himself and to heaven. To God the latter shall ascribe wholly their salvation from first to last: the former shall reproach themselves alone, and not God's decree, with their condemnation (ch. 3:9; 5: 18). **that they were not all of us**—This translation would imply *that some of the Antichrists are of us*! Translate, therefore, "that all (who are for a time among us) are not of us." Cf. I Corinthians 11:19, "There must be heresies among you, that they which are approved may be made manifest among you." For "were" some of the oldest MSS. read "are." Such occasions test who are, and who are not, the Lord's people. **20. But**—*Greek,* "And." He here states the means which they as believers have wherewith to withstand. *Antichrists* (vs. 18), viz., the *chrism* (so the *Greek:* a play upon similar sounds), or "anointing unguent," viz., the Holy Spirit (more plainly mentioned further on, as in John's style, ch. 3:24; 4:13; 5:6), which *they* ("ye" is emphatical in contrast to those apostates, vs. 19) have "from the Holy One, *Christ* (John 1:33; 3:34; 15:26; 16:14): "the righteous" (vs. 1), "pure" (ch. 3:3), "the Holy One" (Acts 3:14) "of God"; Mark 1:24. Those anointed of God in *Christ* alone can resist those anointed with the spirit of Satan, *Antichrists,* who would sever them from the Father and from the Son. Believers have the anointing Spirit from *the Father* also, as well as from the Son; even as the Son is anointed therewith by the Father. Hence the Spirit is the token that we are in the Father and in the Son; without it a man is none of Christ's. The material unguent of costliest ingredients, poured on the head of priests and kings, typified this spiritual unguent, derived from Christ, the Head, to us, His members. We can have no share in Him as *Jesus,* except we become truly *Christians,* and so be in Him as *Christ,* anointed with that unction from the Holy One. The Spirit poured on Christ, the Head, is by Him diffused through all the members. "It appears that we all are the body of *Christ,* be-

cause we all are anointed: and we all in Him are both *Christ's* and *Christ,* because in some measure the whole *Christ* is Head and body." **and**—therefore. **ye know all things**—needful for acting aright against Antichrist's seductions, and for Christian life and godliness. In the same measure as one hath *the Spirit,* in that measure (no more and no less) he knows all these things. **21. because ye know it, and that ...**—Ye not *only know* what is the truth (concerning the Son and the Father, vs. 13), but also are able to detect a lie as a thing opposed to the truth. For right (a straight line) is the index of itself and of what is crooked [ESTIUS]. The *Greek* is susceptible of ALFORD'S translation, "Because ye know it, and *because* no lie is of the truth" (lit., "every lie is excluded from being of the truth"). I therefore wrote (in this Epistle) to point out what the lie is, and who the liars are. **22. a liar**—*Greek,* "Who is the liar?" viz., guilty of *the* lie just mentioned (vs. 21). **that Jesus is the Christ**—the grand central truth. **He is Antichrist**—*Greek,* "*the* Antichrist"; not however here *personal,* but in the abstract; the ideal of Antichrist is "he that denieth the Father and the Son." To deny the latter is virtually to deny the former. Again, the truth as to the Son must be held in its integrity; to deny that Jesus is the Christ, or that He is the Son of God, or that He came in the flesh, invalidates the whole (Matt. 11:27). **23.** *Greek,* "Every one who denieth the Son, hath not the Father either" (ch. 4:2, 3): "inasmuch as God hath given Himself to us wholly to be enjoyed in Christ" [CALVIN]. **he**—*that acknowledgeth the Son hath the Father also*—These words ought not to be in italics, as though they were not in the original: for the oldest *Greek* MSS. have them. **hath**—viz., in his abiding possession as his "portion"; by living personal "fellowship." **acknowledgeth**—by open confession of Christ. **Let that**—truth respecting the Father and the Son, regarded as a seed not merely dropped in, but having taken root (ch. 3:9). **ye**—in the *Greek* standing emphatically at the beginning of the sentence. YE, therefore, *acknowledge the Son, and* so shall ye *have the Father also* (vs. 23). **from the beginning**—from the time of your first hearing the Gospel. **remain**—Translate as before, "abide." **ye also**—in your turn, as distinguished from "that which ye have heard," the seed *abiding in you.* Cf. vs. 27, "the anointing *abideth in you ...* ye shall *abide in Him.*" Having taken into us the living seed of the truth concerning the Father and the Son, we become transformed into the likeness of Him whose seed we have taken into us. **25. this is the promise**—*Eternal life* shall be the permanent consummation of thus *abiding in the Son and in the Father* (vs. 24). **he**—*Greek,* "Himself," Christ, "the Son" (cf. ch. 1:1). **promised**—(John 3:15, 36; 6:40, 47, 57; 17:2, 3). **26. These things**—(vss. 18-25). **have I written**—resumed from vs. 21 and vs. 14. **seduce you**—i.e., are trying to seduce or lead you into error. **27. But**—*Greek,* "And you (contrasting the believing readers with the *seducers;* the words "and you" stand prominent, the construction of the sentence following being altered, and no verb agreeing with 'and you' until 'need not') ... the anointing ..." (resumed from vs. 20). **received of him**—(John 1: 16). So we "are unto God a sweet savor of Christ." **abideth in you**—He tacitly thus admonishes them to say, when tempted by seducers, "The anointing abideth in us; we do not need a teacher [for we have the Holy Spirit as our teacher, Jer. 31:34; John 6:45; 16:13]; it teaches us the truth; in that teaching we will abide" [BENGEL]. **and**—and therefore.

God is sufficient for them who are taught of Him; they are independent of all others, though, of course, not declining the Christian counsel of faithful ministers. "Mutual communication is not set aside, but approved of, in the case of those who are partakers of the anointing in one body" [BENGEL]. **the same anointing**—which ye once for all received, and which now still abides in you. **of**—"concerning." **all things**—essential to salvation; the point under discussion. Not that the believer is made infallible, for no believer here receives the Spirit in all its fulness, but only the measure needful for keeping him from soul-destroying error. So the Church, though having the Spirit in her, is not infallible (for many fallible members can never make an infallible whole), but is kept from ever wholly losing the saving truth. **no lie**—as Antichristian teaching. **ye shall abide in him**—(vs. 24, end)—even as "the anointing abideth in you." The oldest MSS. read the imperative, "*abide* in Him." **28. little children**—*Greek,* "little sons," as in vs. 12; believers of every stage and age. **abide in him**—Christ. John repeats his monition with a loving appellation, as a father addressing dear children. **when**—lit., "if"; the uncertainty is not as to the fact, but *the time.* **appear**—*Greek,* "be manifested." **we**—both writer and readers. **ashamed before him**—lit., "*from* Him"; shrink back *from Him* ashamed. Contrast "boldness in the day of judgment," ch. 4: 17; cf. ch. 3:21; 5:14. In the Apocalypse (written, therefore, BENGEL thinks, subsequently), Christ's coming is represented as put off to a greater distance. **29.** *The heading of the second division of the Epistle:* "God is righteous; therefore, every one that doeth righteousness is born of Him." Love is the grand feature and principle of "righteousness" selected for discussion, ch. 2:29 to 3:3. **If ye know ... ye know**—distinct *Greek* verbs: "if ye *are aware* (are in possession of the knowledge) ... ye *discern* or apprehend also that...." Ye are already aware that *God* ("He" includes both "the Father," *of* whom the believer *is born* [end of this verse, and ch. 3:1], and "the Son," vss. 1, 23) *is righteous,* ye must necessarily, thereby, perceive also the consequence of that truth, viz., "that everyone that doeth righteousness (and he alone; lit., *the* righteousness such as the righteous God approves) is born of Him." The righteous produceth the righteous. We are never said to be *born* again *of Christ,* but of *God,* with whom Christ is one. HOLLAZ *in* ALFORD defines *the righteousness of God,* "It is the divine energy by whose power God wills and does all things which are conformable to His eternal law, prescribes suitable laws to His creatures, fulfils His promises to men, rewards the good, and punishes the ungodly." **doeth**—"For the graces (virtues) are practical, and have their being in being produced (in being exercised); for when they have ceased to act, or are only about to act, they have not even being" [ŒCUMENIUS] "God is righteous, and therefore the *source* of righteousness; when then a man doeth righteousness, we know that the source of his righteousness is God, that consequently he has acquired by new birth from God that righteousness which he had not by nature. We argue from his *doing righteousness,* to his being *born of God.* The error of Pelagians is to conclude that *doing righteousness* is a condition of *becoming* a child of God" [ALFORD most truly]. Cf. Luke 7:47, 50: Her much love *evinced* that her sins *were already* forgiven; not, were the *condition* of her sins being forgiven.

CHAPTER 3

Vss. 1-24. DISTINGUISHING MARKS OF THE CHILDREN OF GOD AND THE CHILDREN OF THE DEVIL. BROTHERLY LOVE THE ESSENCE OF TRUE RIGHTEOUSNESS. **1. Behold**—calling attention, as to some wonderful exhibition, little as the world sees to admire. This verse is connected with the previous ch. 2:29, thus: All our *doing* of *righteousness* is a mere sign that God, of His matchless love, has adopted us as children; it does not save us, but is a proof that we are saved of His grace. **what manner of**—of what surpassing excellence, how gracious on His part, how precious to us. **love ... bestowed**—He does not say that God hath given us some gift, but *love itself* and the fountain of all honors, the heart itself, and that not for our works or efforts, but of His grace [LUTHER]. **that**—"what manner of love"; resulting in, proved by, our being.... The immediate *effect aimed at* in the bestowal of this love is, "*that* we should be called children of God." **should be called**—should have received the privilege of such a glorious *title* (though seeming so imaginary to the world), along with the glorious *reality.* With God *to call* is to *make really to be.* Who so great as God? What nearer relationship than that of *sons?* The oldest MSS. add, "And we ARE SO" really. **therefore**—"on this account," because "we are (really) so." **us**—the children, like the Father. **it knew him not**—viz., the Father. "If they who regard not God, hold thee in any account, feel alarmed about thy state" [BENGEL]. Contrast ch. 5:1. The world's whole course is one great act of non-recognition of God. **2. Beloved**—by the Father, and therefore by me. **now**—in contrast to "not yet." We *now* already are really sons, though not recognized as such by the world, and (as the consequence) we look for the visible manifestation of our sonship, which *not yet* has taken place. **doth not yet appear**—*Greek,* "it hath not yet ('at any time'), *Greek* aorist) been visibly manifested what we shall be"—what further glory we shall attain by virtue of this our sonship. The "what" suggests a something inconceivably glorious. **but**—omitted in the oldest MSS. Its insertion in *English Version* gives a wrong antithesis. It is not, "*We do not yet know manifestly* what..., but we know...." *Believers have* some degree of the manifestation already, though the *world has* not. The connection is, The manifestation *to the world* of what we shall be, has not yet taken place; *we know* (in general; as a matter of *well-assured knowledge;* so the *Greek*) that when (lit., "if"; expressing no doubt as to the fact, but only as to the time; also implying the coming preliminary fact, on which the consequence follows, Mal. 1:6; John 14:3) He ("it," viz., that which is not yet manifested [ALFORD]) shall be manifested (vs. 5; ch. 2:28), we shall be like Him (Christ; all sons have a substantial resemblance to their father, and Christ, whom we shall be like, is "the express image of the Father's person," so that in resembling Christ, we shall resemble the Father). We *wait for the manifestation* (lit., the "apocalypse"; the same term as is applied to Christ's own manifestation) *of the sons of God.* After our natural birth, the new birth into the life of grace is needed, which is to be followed by the new birth into the life of glory; the two latter alike are termed "the regeneration" (Matt. 19:28). The resurrection of our bodies is a kind of coming out of the womb of the earth, and being born into another life. Our first temptation was that we should be like God in knowledge, and by that we fell; but being raised by Christ, we become truly like Him, by knowing Him as we are known, and by seeing Him as He is [PEARSON, *Creed*]. As the first immortality which Adam lost was to be able not to die, so the last shall be not to be able to die. As man's first free choice or will was to be able not to sin, so our last shall be not to be able to sin [AUGUSTINE, *Civit. Dei*, B. 22, c. 30]. The devil fell by aspiring to God's *power;* man, by aspiring to his *knowledge;* but aspiring after God's *goodness,* we shall ever grow in His likeness. The transition from *God* the Father to "He," "Him," referring to Christ (who alone is ever said in Scripture to be *manifested;* not the Father, John 1:18), implies the entire unity of the Father and the Son. **for . . .** —Continual beholding generates likeness (II Cor. 3: 18); as the face of the moon being always turned towards the sun, reflects its light and glory. **see him**—not in His innermost Godhead, but as manifested in Christ. None but the pure can see the infinitely Pure One. In all these passages the *Greek* is the same verb *opsomai;* not denoting the action of seeing, but the state of him to whose eye or mind the object is presented; hence the *Greek* verb is always in the middle or reflexive voice, to *perceive* and *inwardly appreciate* [TITTMANN]. Our spiritual bodies will appreciate and recognize spiritual beings hereafter, as our natural bodies now do natural objects. **3. this hope**—of being hereafter "like Him." *Faith* and *love,* as well as *hope,* occur in vss. 11, 23. **in**—rather, "(resting) *upon* Him"; grounded on His promises. **purifieth himself**—by Christ's Spirit in him (John 15:5, end). "Thou purifiest thyself, not of thyself, but of Him who comes that He may dwell in thee" [AUGUSTINE]. One's justification through faith is presupposed. **as he is pure**—unsullied with any uncleanness. The Second Person, by whom both the Law and Gospel were given. **4.** Sin is incompatible with birth from God (vss. 1-3). John often sets forth the same truth *negatively,* which he had before set forth *positively.* He had shown, birth from God involves self-purification; he now shows where sin, i.e., the want of self-purification, is, there is no birth from God. **Whosoever**—*Greek,* "Every one who." **committeth sin**—in contrast to vs. 3, "Every man that hath this hope in Him purifieth himself"; and vs. 7, "He that doeth righteousness." **transgresseth . . . the law**—*Greek,* "committeth transgression of law." God's law of purity; and so shows he has no such hope of being hereafter pure as God is pure, and, therefore, that he is not born of God. **for**—*Greek,* "and." **sin is . . . transgression of . . . law**—definition of *sin* in general. The *Greek* having the article to both, implies that they are convertible terms. The *Greek* "sin" (*hamartia*) is lit., "a missing of the mark." God's will being that mark to be ever aimed at. "By the law is the knowledge of sin." The crookedness of a line is shown by being brought into juxtaposition with a straight ruler. **5.** Additional proof of the incompatibility of sin and sonship; the very object of Christ's manifestation in the flesh was *to take away* (by one act, and entirely, aorist) all sins, as the scapegoat did typically. **and**—another proof of the same. **in him is no sin**—not "was," but "is," as in vs. 7, "He *is* righteous," and vs. 3, "He *is* pure." Therefore we are to be so. **6.** He reasons from Christ's own entire separation from sin, that those in him must also be separate from it. **abideth in him**—as the branch in the vine, by vital union living by His life. **sinneth not**—In so far as he abides in Christ, so far is he free from all sin. The ideal of the Christian. The life of sin and the life of God mutually exclude one another, just as darkness

and light. In matter of fact, believers do fall into sins (ch. 1:8-10; 2:1, 2); but all such sins are alien from the life of God, and need Christ's cleansing blood, without application to which the life of God could not be maintained. He sinneth not so long as he abideth in Christ. **whosoever sinneth hath not seen him**—*Greek* perfect, "has not seen, and does not see Him." Again the *ideal* of Christian intuition and knowledge is presented (Matt. 7:23). All sin as such is at variance with the notion of one regenerated. Not that "whosoever is betrayed into sins has never seen nor known God"; but *in so far* as sin exists, *in that degree* the spiritual intuition and knowledge of God do not exist in him. **neither** —"not even." To *see* spiritually is a further step than *to know;* for by *knowing* we come to *seeing* by vivid realization and experimentally. **7, 8.** The same truth stated, with the addition that he who sins is, so far as he sins, "of the devil." **let no man deceive you**—as Antinomians try to mislead men. **righteousness**—*Greek,* "*the* righteousness," viz., of Christ or God. **he that doeth . . . is righteous**–Not his *doing* makes him *righteous,* but his *being* right*eous* (justified by the righteousness of God in Christ, Rom. 10:3-10) makes him to do *righteousness;* an inversion common in familiar language, logical in reality, though not in form, as in Luke 7:47; John 8:47. Works do not justify, but the justified man works. We infer from his *doing righteousness* that he is already *righteous* (i.e., has the true and only principle of *doing righteousness,* viz., *faith*), and is therefore *born of God* (vs. 9); just as we might say, The tree that bears good fruit is a good tree, and has a living root; not that the fruit *makes* the tree and its root to be good, but it *shows* that they are so. **he**—Christ. **8. He that committeth sin is of the devil** —in contrast to "He that doeth righteousness," vs. 7. He is *a son of the devil* (vs. 10; John 8:44). John does not, however, say, "born of the devil." as he does "born of God," for "the devil begets none, nor does he create any; but whoever imitates the devil becomes a child of the devil by imitating him, not by proper birth" [AUGUSTINE, *Tract,* 4. 10]. From the devil there is not generation, but corruption [BENGEL]. **sinneth from the beginning**—from the time that any began to sin [ALFORD]; from the time that he became what he is, the devil. He seems to have kept his first estate only a very short time after his creation [BENGEL]. *Since the fall of man* [at the beginning *of our world*] *the devil is* (*ever*) *sinning* (this is the force of "sinneth"; he has sinned from the beginning, is the cause of all sins, and still goes on sinning; present). As the author of sin, and prince of this world, he has never ceased to seduce man to sin [LUECKE]. **destroy**—break up and do away with; bruising and crushing the serpent's head. **works of the devil**—sin, and all its awful consequences. John argues, Christians cannot do that which Christ came to destroy. **9. Whosoever is born of God**—lit., "Everyone that is begotten of God." **doth not commit sin**—His higher nature, as one born or begotten of God, doth not sin. *To be begotten of God* and *to sin,* are states mutually excluding one another. In so far as one sins, he makes it doubtful whether he be *born of God.* **his seed**—the living word of God, made by the Holy Spirit the seed in us of a new life and the continual mean of sanctification. **remaineth**—abideth in him (*Note,* cf. vs. 6; John 5:38). This does not contradict ch. 1:8, 9; the regenerate show the utter incompatibility of *sin* with *regeneration,* by cleansing away every sin into which they may be betrayed by the old nature, at once in the blood of Christ. **can-**

not sin, because he is born of God—"because it is *of God* that *he is born*" (so the *Greek* order, as compared with the order of the same words in the beginning of the verse); not "because he *was* born of God" (the *Greek* is perfect, which is *present* in meaning, not aorist); it is not said, Because a man was once for all born of God he never afterwards can sin; but, Because he is born of God, the seed abiding now in Him, he cannot sin; so long as it energetically abides, sin can have no place. Cf. Genesis 39:9, Joseph, "How CAN I do this great wickedness and sin against God?" The principle within me is at utter variance with it. The regenerate life is incompatible with sin, and gives the believer a hatred for sin in every shape, and an unceasing desire to resist it. "The child of God in this conflict receives indeed wounds daily, but never throws away his arms or makes peace with his deadly foe" [LUTHER]. The exceptional sins into which the regenerate are surprised, are owing to the new life-principle being for a time suffered to lie dormant, and to the sword of the Spirit not being drawn instantly. Sin is ever active, but no longer reigns. The *normal* direction of the believer's energies is against sin; the law of God after the inward man is the *ruling* principle of his true self though the old nature, not yet *fully* deadened, rebels and sins. Contrast ch. 5:18 with John 8:34; cf. Psalm 18:22, 23; 32:2, 3; 119:113, 176. The magnetic needle, the nature of which is always to point to the pole, is easily turned aside, but always re-seeks the pole. **10. children of the devil**—(*Note,* vs. 8; Acts 13:10). There is no middle class between the children of God and the children of the devil. **doeth not righteousness**—Contrast ch. 2:29. **he that loveth not his brother**—(ch. 4:8)—a particular instance of that *love* which is the sum and fulfilment of all righteousness, and the token (not loud professions, or even seemingly good works) that distinguishes God's children from the devil's. **11. the message**—"announcement," as of something good; not a mere *command,* as the law. The Gospel *message* of Him who loved us, announced by His servants, is, that we *love the brethren;* not here all mankind, but those who are our brethren in Christ, children of the same family of God, of whom we have been born anew. **12. who**—not in the Greek. **of that wicked one**—Translate, "*evil*" one," to accord with "Because his own works were *evil.*" Cf. vs. 8, "of the devil," in contrast to "of God," vs. 10. **slew he him? Because his own works were evil, and his brother's righteous**—through envy and hatred of his brother's piety, owing to which God accepted Abel's, but rejected Cain's offering. Enmity from the first existed between the seed of the woman and the seed of the serpent. **13. Marvel not**—The marvel would be if the world loved you. **the world**—of whom Cain is the representative (vs. 12). **hate you** —as Cain hated even his own brother, and that to the extent of murdering him. The world feels its bad works tacitly reproved by your good works. **14. We**—emphatical; hated though we be by the world, *we* know what the world knows not. **know** —as an assured fact. **passed**—*changed our state.* Colossians 1:13, "from the power of darkness . . . translated into the kingdom of His dear Son." **from death unto life**—lit., "*out of the* death (which enthrals the unregenerate) *into the* life" (of the regenerate). A palpable coincidence of language and thought, the beloved disciple adopting his Lord's words. **because we love the brethren**—the ground, not of our *passing over out of death into life,* but of our *knowing* that we have so. *Love,* on our

part, is the *evidence* of our justification and regeneration, not the *cause* of them. "Let each go to his own heart; if he find there love to the brethren, let him feel assured that he has passed from death unto life. Let him not mind that his glory is only hidden; when the Lord shall come, then shall he appear in glory. For he has vital energy, but it is still wintertime; the root has vigor, but the branches are as it were dry; within there is marrow which is vigorous, within are leaves, within fruits, but they must wait for summer" [AUGUSTINE]. **He that loveth not**—Most of the oldest MSS. omit "his brother," which makes the statement more general. **abideth**—still. **in death**—"in *the* (spiritual) death" (ending in eternal death) which is the state of all by nature. His want of *love* evidences that no saving change has passed over him. **15. hateth**—equivalent to "loveth not" (vs. 14); there is no medium between the two. "Love and hatred, like light and darkness, life and death, necessarily replace, as well as necessarily exclude, one another" [ALFORD]. **is a murderer**—because indulging in that passion, which, if followed out to its natural consequences, would make him one. "Whereas, vs. 16 desires us to lay down our lives for the brethren; *duels* require one (awful to say!) to risk *his own* life, rather than not deprive *another* of life" [BENGEL]. God regards the inward disposition as tantamount to the outward act which would flow from it. Whomsoever one hates, one wishes to be dead. **hath**—Such a one still "abideth in death." It is not his *future* state, but his *present,* which is referred to. He who hates (i.e., loveth not) his brother (vs. 14), cannot in this his present state have eternal life abiding in him. **16.** What true *love to the brethren* is, illustrated by the love of Christ to us. **Hereby**— Greek, "Herein." **the love** *of God*—The words "of God" are not in the original. Translate, "We arrive at the knowledge of love"; we apprehend what true love is. **he**—Christ. **and we**—on our part, if absolutely needed for the glory of God, the good of the Church, or the salvation of a brother. **lives**— Christ alone laid down His one *life* for us all; we ought to lay down our *lives* severally for the lives of the brethren; if not actually, at least virtually, by giving our time, care, labors, prayers, substance: "*Non nobis, sed omnibus.*" Our life ought not to be dearer to us than God's own Son was to Him. The apostles and martyrs acted on this principle. **17. this world's good**—lit., "livelihood" or substance. If we ought to lay down our *lives* for the brethren (vs. 16), how much more ought we not to withhold our *substance*? **seeth**—not merely *casually,* but deliberately *contemplates* as a spectator; Greek, "beholds." **shutteth up his bowels** *of compassion*— which had been momentarily opened by the *spectacle* of his brother's need. The "bowels" mean the *heart,* the seat of compassion. **how**—*How* is it possible that "the love of (i.e. *to*) God dwelleth (*Greek,* 'abideth') in him?" Our superfluities should yield to the necessities; our comforts, and even our necessaries in some measure, should yield to the extreme wants of our brethren. "Faith gives Christ to me; love flowing from faith gives me to my neighbor." **18.** When the venerable John could no longer walk to the meetings of the Church but was borne thither by his disciples, he always uttered the same address to the Church; he reminded them of that one commandment which he had received from Christ Himself, as comprising all the rest, and forming the distinction of the new covenant, "My little children, love one another." When the brethren present, wearied of hearing the same thing so often, asked why he always repeated the same thing, he replied, "Because it is the commandment of the Lord, and if this one thing be attained, it is enough" [JEROME]. **in word**—Greek, "*with* word . . . *with* tongue, but *in* deed and truth." **19. hereby**—Greek, "herein"; in our *loving in deed and in truth* (vs. 18). **we know** —The oldest MSS. have "we shall know," viz., if we fulfil the command (vs. 18). **of the truth**—that we are real disciples of, and belonging to, *the truth,* as it is in Jesus: begotten of God with the word of truth. Having herein *the truth* radically, we shall be sure not to love merely *in word and tongue.* (vs. 18). **assure**—lit., "persuade," viz., so as to cease to condemn us; satisfy the questionings and doubts of our consciences as to whether we be accepted *before* God or not (cf. Matt. 28:14; Acts 12:20, "*having made* Blastus their friend," lit., "persuaded"). The "heart," as the seat of the feelings, is our inward *judge; the conscience,* as the witness, acts either as our justifying advocate, or our condemning accuser, before God even now. John 8: 9, has "conscience," but the passage is omitted in most old MSS. John nowhere else uses the term "conscience." Peter and Paul alone use it. **before him**—as in the sight of Him, the omniscient Searcher of *hearts. Assurance* is designed to be the ordinary experience and privilege of the believer. **20.** LUTHER and BENGEL take this verse as consoling the believer whom his *heart condemns;* and who, therefore, like Peter, appeals from conscience to Him, who is *greater than conscience.* "Lord, Thou *knowest all things:* thou knowest that I love Thee." Peter's conscience, though condemning him of his sin in denying the Lord, assured him of his *love;* but fearing the possibility, owing to his past fall, of deceiving himself, he appeals to the all-knowing God: so Paul, I Corinthians 4:3, 4. So if we be believers, even *if our heart condemns us of sin in general,* yet having the one sign of sonship, *love,* we may still *assure our hearts* (some oldest MSS, read *heart,* vs. 19, as well as vs. 20), as knowing *that God is greater than our heart, and knoweth all things.* But thus the same *Greek* is translated "because" in the beginning, and "(we know) *that*" in the middle of the verse, and if the verse were consolatory, it probably would have been, "Because EVEN if our heart condemn us . . . ." Therefore translate, *"Because* (rendering the reason why it has been stated in vs. 19 to be so important to 'assure our hearts before Him') if our heart condemn (Greek, '*know* [aught] *against* us"; answering by contrast to 'we shall *know* that we are of the truth') us (it is) *because* God is greater than our heart and knoweth all things." If our heart judges us unfavorably, we may be sure that He, knowing more than our heart knows, judges us more unfavorably still [ALFORD]. A similar ellipsis ("it is") occurs in I Corinthians 14:27; II Corinthians 1:6; 8:23. The condemning testimony of our conscience is not alone, but is the echo of the voice of Him who is greater and knoweth all things. Our hypocrisy in *loving by word and tongue,* not in *deed and truth,* does not escape even our conscience, though weak and knowing but little, how much less God who knows all things! Still the consolatory view may be the right one. For the *Greek* for "we shall *assure* our hearts" (see *Note,* vs. 19), is *gain over, persuade* so as to be stilled, implying that there was a previous state of *self-condemnation by the heart* (vs. 20), which, however, is *got over* by the consolatory thought, "God is greater than my heart" which condemns me, and "knows all things" (*Greek ginoskei,* "knows," not *kataginoskei,* "condemns"), and therefore knows my

love and desire to serve Him, and knows my *frame* so as to pity my weakness of faith. This *gaining over* the heart to peace is not so advanced a stage as the *having* CONFIDENCE *towards God* which flows from a *heart condemning us not.* The first "because" thus applies to the two alternate cases, vss. 20, 21 (giving the ground of saying, that *having love we shall gain over,* or *assure our minds before Him,* vs. 19); the second "because" applies to the first alternate alone, viz., "if our heart condemn us." When he reaches the second alternate, vs. 21, he states it independently of the former "because" which had connected it with vs. 19, inasmuch as CONFIDENCE *toward God* is a farther stage than *persuading our hearts,* though always preceded by it. **21. Beloved**—There is no "But" contrasting the two cases, vss. 20, 21, because "Beloved" sufficiently marks the transition to the case of the brethren walking in the full confidence of *love* (vs. 18). The two results of our being able to "assure our hearts before Him" (vs. 19), and of "our heart condemning us not" (of insincerity as to *the truth* in general, and as to LOVE in particular) are, (1) confidence toward God; (2) a sure answer to our prayers. John does not mean that all whose hearts do not condemn them, are therefore safe before God; for some have their conscience seared, others are ignorant of the truth, and it is not only *sincerity,* but *sincerity in the truth* which can save men. Christians are those meant here: knowing Christ's precepts and testing themselves by them. **22. we receive**—as a matter of fact, according to His promise. Believers, as such, ask only what is in accordance with God's will; or if they ask what God wills not, they bow their will to God's will, and so God grants them either their request, or something better than it. **because we keep his commandments**—Cf. Psalm 66:18; 34:15; 145:18, 19. Not as though our merits earned a hearing for our prayers, but when we are believers in Christ, all our works of faith being the fruit of *His* Spirit in us, are "pleasing in God's sight"; and our prayers being the voice of the same Spirit of God in us, naturally and necessarily are answered by Him. **23.** Summing up of God's commandments under the Gospel dispensation in one commandment. **this is his commandment**—singular: for *faith* and *love* are not *separate* commandments, but are indissolubly united. We cannot truly *love* one another without *faith* in Christ, nor can we truly believe in Him without love. **believe**—*once for all; Greek* aorist. **on the name of his Son**—on all that is revealed in the Gospel concerning Him, and on Himself in respect to His person, offices, and atoning work. **as he**—as *Jesus* gave us commandment. **24. dwelleth in him**—The believer dwelleth in Christ. **and he in him**—Christ in the believer. Reciprocity. "Thus he returns to the great keynote of the Epistle, *abide in Him,* with which the former part concluded" (ch. 2:28). **hereby**—"herein we (believers) know that He abideth in us, viz., from (the presence in us of) the Spirit which He hath given us." Thus he prepares, by the mention of the true Spirit, for the transition to the false "spirit," ch. 4:1-6; after which he returns again to the subject of *love.*

CHAPTER 4

Vss. 1-21. TESTS OF FALSE PROPHETS. LOVE, THE TEST OF BIRTH FROM GOD, AND THE NECESSARY FRUIT OF KNOWING HIS GREAT LOVE IN CHRIST TO US. **1. Beloved**—the affectionate address wherewith he calls their attention, as to an important subject. **every spirit**—which presents itself in the person of a prophet. The Spirit of truth, and the spirit of error, speak by men's spirits as their organs. There is but one Spirit of truth, and one spirit of Antichrist. **try**—by the tests (vss. 2, 3). All believers are to do so: not merely ecclesiastics. Even an angel's message should be tested by the word of God: much more men's teachings, however holy the teachers may seem. **because . . .**—the reason why we must "try," or *test* the spirits. **many false prophets**—not "prophets" in the sense "foretellers," but organs of the spirit that inspires them, *teaching* accordingly either truth or error: "many Antichrists." **are gone out**—as if from God. **into the world**—said alike of good and bad prophets (II John 7). The world is easily seduced (vss. 4, 5). **2. Hereby**—"Herein." **know . . . the Spirit of God**—whether he be, or not, in those teachers professing to be moved by Him. **Every spirit**—i.e., *Every teacher* claiming inspiration by the HOLY SPIRIT. **confesseth**—The truth is taken for granted as established. Man is required to *confess* it, i.e., in his teaching to profess it openly. **Jesus Christ is come in the flesh**—a twofold truth confessed, that *Jesus* is the *Christ*, and that *He is come* (the *Greek* perfect implies not a mere past historical fact, as the aorist would, but also the *present continuance* of the fact and its blessed effects) *in the flesh* ("clothed with flesh": not with a mere *seeming* humanity, as the Docetæ afterwards taught: He therefore was, previously, something far above flesh). His *flesh* implies His *death* for us, for only by assuming flesh could He die (for as God He could not), Hebrews 2:9, 10, 14, 16; and His death implies His LOVE for us (John 15:13). To deny the reality of *His flesh* is to deny His love, and so cast away the root which produces all true love on the believer's part (vss. 9-11, 19). Rome, by the doctrine of the immaculate conception of the Virgin Mary, denies Christ's proper humanity. **3. confesseth not that Jesus Christ is come in the flesh**—IRENÆUS (3. 8), LUCIFER, ORIGEN, on Matthew 25:14, and *Vulgate* read, "Every spirit which *destroys* (sets aside, or does away with) Jesus (Christ)." CYPRIAN and POLYCARP support *English Version* text. The oldest extant MSS., which are, however, centuries after POLYCARP, read, "Every spirit that confesseth not (i.e., refuses to confess) Jesus" (in His person, and all His offices and divinity), omitting "is come in the flesh." **ye have heard**—from your Christian teachers. **already is it in the world**—in the person of *the false prophets* (vs. 1). **4. Ye**—emphatical: YE who confess Jesus: in contrast to "them," the false teachers. **overcome them**—(ch. 5:4, 5)—instead of being "overcome and brought into (spiritual) bondage" by them (II Pet. 2:19). John 10:8, 5, "the sheep did *not hear them*": "a stranger will they not follow, but will flee from him: for they know not the voice of strangers." **he that is in you**—*God*, of whom ye are. **he that is in the world**—the spirit of Antichrist, the devil, "the prince of this world." **5. of the world**—They derive their spirit and teaching from the world, "unregenerate human nature, ruled over and possessed by Satan, the prince of this world" [ALFORD]. **speak they of the world**—They draw the matter of their conversation from the life, opinions, and feelings of the world. **the world heareth them**—(John 15:18, 19). *The world loves its own.* **6. We**—*true teachers* of Christ: in contrast to *them.* **are of God**—and therefore *speak of God:* in contrast to "speak they of the world," vs. 5. **knoweth God**—as his Father, being a child "of

God" (ch. 2:13, 14). **heareth us**—Cf. John 18:37, "Every one that is of the truth, heareth My voice." **Hereby**—(vss. 2-6)—by their confessing, or not confessing, Jesus; by the kind of reception given them respectively by those who know God, and by those who are of the world and not of God. **spirit of truth**—*the Spirit* which comes from God and teaches *truth.* **spirit of error**—*the spirit* which comes from Satan and seduces into *error.* **7.** Resumption of the main theme (ch. 2:29). *Love,* the sum of *righteousness,* is the test of our being *born of God.* Love flows from a sense of God's love to us: cf. vs. 9 with ch. 3:16, which vs. 9 resumes; and vs. 13 with ch. 3:24, which similarly vs. 13 resumes. At the same time, vss. 7-21 is connected with the immediately preceding context, vs. 2 setting forth *Christ's incarnation, the great proof of God's love* (vs. 10). **Beloved**—an address appropriate to his subject, "love." **love**—*All love is from God* as its fountain: especially that embodiment of love, God manifest in the flesh. The *Father* also is *love* (vs. 8). The *Holy Ghost* sheds *love* as its first *fruit* abroad in the heart. **knoweth God**—spiritually, experimentally, and habitually. **8. knoweth not**—*Greek* aorist: not only *knoweth* not now, but never *knew, has not once for all known* God. **God is love**—There is no *Greek* article to *love,* but to *God;* therefore we cannot translate, *Love is God.* God is fundamentally and essentially LOVE: not merely *is loving,* for then John's argument would not stand; for the conclusion from the premises then would be this, *This man is not loving: God is loving; therefore he knoweth not God* IN SO FAR AS GOD IS LOVING; still he might know Him in His *other* attributes. But when we take *love* as God's essence, the argument is sound: *This man doth not love,* and *therefore knows not love: God is essentially love, therefore he knows not God.* **9. toward us**—*Greek,* "in our case." **sent**—*Greek,* "hath sent." **into the world**—a proof against Socinians, that the Son existed before He was "sent into the world." Otherwise, too, He could not have been our *life* (vs. 9), our *"propitiation"* (vs. 10), or our "Saviour" (vs. 14). It is the grand *proof* of God's love, His having sent *His only-begotten Son, that we might live through Him,* who is *the Life,* and who has redeemed our forfeited life; and it is also the grand *motive* to our mutual love. **10. Herein is love**—*love* in the abstract: *love,* in its highest ideal, is herein. The love was all on God's side, none on ours. **not that we loved God**—though so altogether worthy of love. **he loved us**—though so altogether unworthy of love. The *Greek* aorist expresses, Not that we *did* any act of love *at any time* to God, but that He *did* the act of love to us in sending Christ. **11.** God's love to us is the grand motive for our love to one another (ch. 3:16). **if**—as we all admit as a fact. **we . . . also**—as being *born of God,* and therefore resembling our Father who is love. In proportion as we appreciate God's love to us, we love Him and also *the brethren,* the children (by regeneration) of the same God, the representatives of the unseen God. **12.** *God, whom no man hath seen at any time,* hath appointed His children as the *visible* recipients of our outward kindness which flows from love to Himself, "whom *not* having *seen,* we love," cf. *Notes,* vss. 11, 19, 20. Thus vs. 12 explains why, instead (in vs. 11) of saying, "If God so loved us, we ought also to love *God,*" he said, "We ought also to love *one another.*" **If we love one another, God dwelleth in us**—for God is love; and it must have been from Him dwelling in us that we drew the real love we bear to the brethren (vss. 8, 16). John discusses this in vss. 13-16. **his love**—rather, "the love of (i.e., to) Him" (ch. 2:5), evinced by our love to His representatives, our brethren. **is perfected in us**—John discusses this in vss. 17-19. Cf. ch. 2:5, "is perfected," i.e., attains its proper maturity. **13. Hereby**—"Herein." The token vouchsafed to us of God's dwelling (*Greek*, "abide") in us, though we see Him not, is this, that He hath given us "of His Spirit" (ch. 3:24). Where the Spirit of God is, there God is. ONE Spirit dwells in the Church: each believer receives a measure "of" that Spirit in the proportion God thinks fit. *Love* is His first fruit (Gal. 5:22). In Jesus alone the Spirit dwelt without measure (John 3:34). **14. And we**—primarily, *we apostles*, Christ's appointed eyewitnesses to testify to the facts concerning Him. The internal evidence of the indwelling Spirit (vs. 13) is corroborated by the external evidence of the eyewitnesses to the fact of the Father having "sent His Son to be the Saviour of the world." **seen**—*Greek*, "contemplated," "attentively beheld" (*Note*, ch. 1:1). **sent**—*Greek*, "hath sent": not an entirely past fact (aorist), but one of which the effects continue (perfect). **15. shall confess**—once for all: so the *Greek* aorist means. **that Jesus is the Son of God**—and therefore "the Saviour of the world" (vs. 14). **16. And we**—*John and his readers* (not as vs. 14, *the apostles* only). **known and believed**—True *faith*, according to John, is a faith of *knowledge* and experience: true *knowledge* is a knowledge of *faith* [LUECKE]. **to us**—*Greek*, "in our case" (*Note*, vs. 9). **dwelleth**—*Greek*, "abideth." Cf. with this verse, vs. 7. **17, 18.** (Cf. ch. 3:19-21.) **our love**—rather as the *Greek*, "LOVE (in the abstract, the principle of love [ALFORD]) is made perfect (in its relations) *with us*." Love dwelling in us advances to its consummation *"with us"* i.e., as it is concerned *with us:* so *Greek.* Luke 1:58, "showed mercy upon (lit., 'with') her": II John 2, the truth "shall be *with us* for ever." **boldness**—"confidence": the same *Greek* as ch. 3:21, to which this passage is parallel. The opposite of "fear," vs. 18. *Herein* is our love perfected, viz., in *God dwelling in us, and our dwelling in God* (vs. 16), involving as its *result* "that we can have confidence (or *boldness*) in the day of judgment" (so terrible to all other men, Acts 24:25; Rom. 2:16). **because...**—The ground of our "confidence" is, "*because* even as He (Christ) is, we also are in this world" (and He will not, in that day, condemn those who are like *Himself*), i.e., we are *righteous* as He is righteous, especially in respect to that which is the sum of righteousness, *love* (ch. 3:14). Christ IS righteous, and *love* itself, in heaven: so are we, His members, who are still "in this world." Our oneness with Him even *now* in His exalted position above (Eph. 2:6), so that all that belongs to Him of righteousness, etc., belongs to us also by perfect imputation and progressive impartation, is the ground of our *love* being *perfected so that we can have confidence in the day of judgment.* We are *in*, not *of*, this world. **18.** *Fear* has no place in *love. Bold confidence* (vs. 17), based on *love*, cannot coexist with *fear. Love*, which, when *perfected*, gives *bold confidence*, casts out fear (cf. Heb. 2:14, 15). The design of Christ's propitiatory death was to *deliver* from this *bondage* of *fear.* **but**—"nay" [ALFORD]. **fear hath torment**—*Greek*, "punishment." Fear is always revolving in the mind the punishment deserved [ESTIUS]. Fear, by anticipating punishment [through consciousness of deserving it], has it even now, i.e., the foretaste of it. *Perfect love* is

incompatible with such a self-punishing *fear. Godly fear* of offending God is quite distinct from slavish fear of consciously deserved punishment. The latter *fear* is natural to us all until *love casts it out.* "Men's states vary: one is without fear and love; another, with fear without love; another, with fear and love; another, without fear with love" [BENGEL]. **19. him**—omitted in the oldest MSS. Translate, *We* (emphatical: WE on our part) love (in general: love alike *Him*, and *the brethren*, and *our fellow men*), because He (emphatical: answering to "we"; *because it was He who*) first loved us in sending His Son (*Greek* aorist of a definite act at a point of time). He was the first to love us: this thought ought to create in us *love casting out fear* (vs. 18). **20. loveth not...brother whom he hath seen, how can he love God whom he hath not seen**—It is easier for us, influenced as we are here by sense, to direct love towards one within the range of our senses than towards One unseen, appreciable only by faith. "Nature is prior to grace; and we by nature love things seen, before we love things unseen" [ESTIUS]. *The eyes are our leaders in love.* "Seeing is an incentive to love" [ŒCUMENIUS]. If we do not love *the brethren*, the visible representatives of *God,* how can we love God, the invisible One, *whose children they are?* The true ideal of man, lost in Adam, is realized in Christ, in whom God is revealed as He is, and man as he ought to be. Thus, by faith in Christ, we learn to love both the true God, and the true man, and so to love the brethren as bearing His image. **hath seen**—and continually sees. **21.** Besides the argument (vs. 20) from the common feeling of men, he here adds a stronger one from God's express *commandment* (Matt. 22:39). He who loves, will do what the object of his love wishes. **he who loveth God**—he who wishes to be regarded by God as loving Him.

CHAPTER 5

Vss. 1-21. WHO ARE THE BRETHREN ESPECIALLY TO BE LOVED (ch. 4:21); OBEDIENCE, THE TEST OF LOVE, EASY THROUGH FAITH, WHICH OVERCOMES THE WORLD. LAST PORTION OF THE EPISTLE. THE SPIRIT'S WITNESS TO THE BELIEVER'S SPIRITUAL LIFE. TRUTHS REPEATED AT THE CLOSE: FAREWELL WARNING. **1.** Reason why our "brother" (ch. 4:21) is entitled to such *love,* viz., because he is "born (begotten) of God": so that if we want to show our love to *God,* we must show it to God's visible representative. **Whosoever**—*Greek*, "Everyone that." He could not be our "Jesus" (God-Saviour) unless He were "the Christ"; for He could not reveal the way of salvation, except He were a *prophet:* He could not work out that salvation, except He were a *priest:* He could not confer that salvation upon us, except He were a *king:* He could not be *prophet, priest, and king,* except He were the Christ [PEARSON *on the Creed*]. **born**—Translate, "begotten," as in the latter part of the verse, the *Greek* being the same. Christ IS the "only-begotten Son" by *generation;* we become begotten sons of God by *regeneration* and adoption. **every one that loveth him that begat**—sincerely, not in mere profession (ch. 4:20). **loveth him also that is begotten of him**—viz., "his brethren" (ch. 4:21). **2. By**—*Greek*, "In." As our *love to the brethren* is the sign and test of our *love to God,* so (John here says) our *love to God* (tested by our "keeping his commandments") is, conversely, the ground and only true basis of *love to our brother*. **we know** —John means here, not the *outward* criteria of genuine brotherly love, but the *inward spiritual* criteria of it, *consciousness of love to God* manifested in a hearty keeping of His commandments. When we have this inwardly and outwardly confirmed *love to God*, we can *know* assuredly that we truly *love the children of God*. "*Love to one's brother* is prior, according to the order of nature (*Note*, ch. 4:20); *love to God* is so, according to the order of grace (ch. 5:2). At one time the former is more immediately known, at another time the latter, according as the mind is more engaged in human relations or in what concerns the divine honor" [ESTIUS]. John shows what true *love* is, viz., that which is referred to God as its first object. As previously John urged the effect, so now he urges the cause. For he wishes mutual love to be so cultivated among us, as that *God* should always be placed first [CALVIN]. **3. this is**—the *love* of God consists in this. **not grievous**—as so many think them. It is "the way of the transgressor" that "is hard." What makes them to the regenerate "not grievous," is *faith* which "overcometh the world" (vs. 4): in proportion as faith is strong, the grievousness of God's commandments to the rebellious flesh is overcome. The reason why believers feel any degree of irksomeness in God's commandments is, they do not realize fully by faith the privileges of their spiritual life. **4. For**—(*Note*, vs. 3). The reason why "His commandments are not grievous." Though there is a conflict in keeping them, the issue for the whole body of the regenerate is victory over every opposing influence; meanwhile there is a present joy to each believer in keeping them which makes them "not grievous." **whatsoever**— Greek, "*all* that is begotten of God." The neuter expresses *the universal whole*, or *aggregate of the regenerate*, regarded as one collective body John 3: 6; 6:37, 39, "where BENGEL remarks, that in Jesus' discourses, what the Father has given Him is called, in the singular number and neuter gender, *all* whatsoever; those who come to the *Son* are described in the masculine gender and plural number, *they all*, or singular, *every one*. The Father has given, as it were, the whole mass to the Son, that all whom He gave may be *one* whole: that *universal* whole the Son singly evolves, in the execution of the divine plan." **overcometh**—habitually. **the world**—all that is opposed to keeping the commandments of God, or draws us off from God, in this world, including our corrupt *flesh*, on which the world's blandishments or threats act, as also including Satan, *the prince of this world*. **this is the victory that overcometh**—Greek aorist: " ... that *hath* (already) *overcome* the world": the *victory* (where *faith* is) hereby is implied as having been *already obtained* (ch. 2:13; 4:4). **5. Who**—"Who" *else* "but he that believeth that Jesus is the Son of God—"the Christ" (vs. 1)? Confirming, by a triumphant question defying all contradiction, as an undeniable fact, vs. 4, that *the victory* which overcomes the world is *faith*. For it is by *believing* that we are made one with *Jesus the Son of God*, so that we partake of *His victory over the world*, and have dwelling in us One greater than he who is in the world (ch. 4:4). "Survey the whole world, and show me even one of whom it can be affirmed with truth that he overcomes the world, who is not a Christian, and endowed with this faith" [EPISCOPIUS *in* ALFORD]. **6. This**—the Person mentioned in vs. 5. This *Jesus*. **he that came by water and blood**—"by water," when His ministry was in-

augurated by baptism in the Jordan, and He received the Father's testimony to His Messiahship and divine *Sonship*. Cf. vs. 5, "believeth that Jesus is the *Son of God*," with John 1:33, 34, "The Spirit ... remaining on Him ... I saw and bare record that this is *the Son of God*"; and vs. 8, below, "there are three that bear *witness* in earth, the Spirit, and the water, and the blood." Corresponding to this is *the baptism of water and the Spirit* which He has instituted as a standing seal and mean of initiatory incorporation with Him. **and blood**— He came by "the blood of His cross" (so "by" is used, Heb. 9:12: "by," i.e., *with,* "His own blood He entered in once into the holy place"): a fact *seen* and so solemnly *witnessed to* by John. "These two past facts in the Lord's life are this abiding *testimony* to us, by virtue of the permanent application to us of their cleansing and atoning power." **Jesus Christ**—not a mere appellation, but a solemn assertion of the Lord's Person and Messiahship. **not by ...**—Greek, "not IN *the* water only, but IN *the* water and IN (so oldest MSS. add) *the* blood." As "*by*" implies the mean *through,* or *with,* which He came: so "*in,*" the element *in* which He came. "The" implies that *the water* and *the blood* were sacred and well-known symbols. John Baptist came only baptizing with water, and therefore was not the *Messiah*. Jesus came first to undergo Himself the double baptism of water and blood, and then to baptize us with the Spirit-cleansing, of which *water* is the sacramental seal, and with His atoning *blood,* the efficacy of which, once for all shed, is perpetual in the Church; and therefore is *the Messiah*. It was His shed *blood* which first gave *water baptism* its spiritual significancy. We are baptized *into His death*: the grand point of union between us and Him, and, through Him, between us and God. **it is the Spirit ...**—*The Holy Spirit* is an additional witness (cf. vs. 7), besides the *water* and the *blood,* to Jesus' *Sonship* and *Messiahship.* The Spirit attested these truths at Jesus' baptism by descending on Him, and throughout His ministry by enabling Him to speak and do what man never before or since has spoken or done; and "it is the Spirit that beareth witness" of Christ, now permanently in the Church: both in the inspired New Testament Scriptures, and in the hearts of believers, and in the spiritual reception of baptism and the Lord's Supper. **because the Spirit is truth**—It is His essential *truth* which gives His witness such infallible authority. **7. three**—Two or three witnesses were required by law to constitute adequate testimony. The only *Greek* MSS. *in any form* which support the words, "in heaven, the Father, the Word, and the Holy Ghost, and these three are one; and there are three that bear witness in earth," are the *Montfortianus* of Dublin, copied evidently from the *modern* Latin Vulgate; the *Ravianus,* copied from the *Complutensian Polyglot*; a MS. at Naples, with the words added in the margin by a recent hand; *Ottobonianus,* 298, of the fifteenth century, the *Greek* of which is a mere translation of the accompanying Latin. All the old versions omit the words. The oldest MSS. of the *Vulgate* omit them: the earliest *Vulgate* MS. which has them being *Wizanburgensis,* 99, of the eighth century. A scholium quoted in *Matthæi,* shows that the words did not arise from fraud; for in the words· in all *Greek* MSS., "there are *three* that bear record," as the Scholiast notices, the word "three" is *masculine,* because the three things (*the Spirit, the water,* and *the blood*) are SYMBOLS OF THE TRINITY. To this Cyprian, 196, also refers, "Of the *Father, Son* and

Holy Spirit, it is written, '*And these* three are one' (a unity)." There must be some mystical truth implied in using "*three*" (*Greek*) in the *masculine*, though the antecedents, "Spirit, water, and blood," are *neuter*. That THE TRINITY was the truth meant is a natural inference: the triad specified pointing to a still Higher Trinity; as is plain also from vs. 9, "the witness of GOD," referring to the *Trinity* alluded to in the Spirit, water, and blood. It was therefore first written as a *marginal* comment to complete the sense of the *text,* and then, as early at least as the eighth century, was introduced into the text of the *Latin Vulgate.* The testimony, however, could only be borne *on earth* to men, not in *heaven.* The marginal comment, therefore, that inserted "in heaven," was inappropriate. It is *on earth* that the context evidently requires the witness of the three, *the Spirit, the water,* and *the blood,* to be borne: mystically setting forth the divine *triune* witnesses, the Father, the Spirit, and the Son. LUECKE notices as internal evidence against the words, John never uses "the Father" and "the Word" as correlates, but, like other New Testament writers, associates "the Son" with "the Father," and always refers "the Word" to "God" as its correlate, not "the Father." VIGILIUS, at the end of the fifth century, is the first who quotes the disputed words as in the text; but no *Greek* MS. earlier than the fifteenth is extant with them. The *term* "Trinity" occurs first in the third century in TERTULLIAN, *adversus Praxean,* 3. **8. agree in one**—"tend unto one result"; their agreeing testimony to Jesus' Sonship and Messiahship they give by the sacramental grace in the *water* of baptism, received by the penitent believer, by the atoning efficacy of His *blood,* and by the internal witness of His *Spirit* (vs. 10): answering to the testimony given to *Jesus'* Sonship and Messiahship by His baptism, His crucifixion, and the Spirit's manifestations in Him (*Note,* vs. 6). It was by His *coming by water* (i.e., His baptism in Jordan) that Jesus was solemnly inaugurated in office, and revealed Himself as Messiah; this must have been peculiarly important in John's estimation, who was first led to Christ by the testimony of the Baptist. By the baptism then received by Christ, and by His redeeming *blood*-shedding, and by that which the Spirit of God, whose witness is infallible, has effected, and still effects, by Him, the *Spirit,* the *water,* and the *blood,* unite, as the threefold witness, to verify His divine Messiahship [NEANDER]. **9. If ...**—We do *accept* (and rightly so) the witness of veracious men, fallible though they be; much more ought we to accept *the* infallible witness of God (the Father). "The testimony of the Father is, as it were, the basis of the testimony of the Word and of the Holy Spirit; just as the testimony of *the Spirit* is, as it were, the basis of the testimony of *the water* and the *blood*" [BENGEL]. **for**—This principle applies in the present case, FOR .... **which**—in the oldest MSS., "*because* He hath given testimony concerning His Son." What that testimony is we find above in vss. 1, 5, "Jesus is the Christ, the Son of God"; and below in vss. 10, 11. **10. hath the witness**—of God, by His *Spirit* (vs. 8). **in himself**—God's Spirit dwelling in him and *witnessing* that "Jesus is the Lord," "the Christ," and "the Son of God" (vss. 1, 5). The witness of the Spirit *in* the believer *himself* to his own sonship is not here expressed, but follows as a consequence of believing the witness of God to Jesus' divine Sonship. **believeth not God**—credits not His *witness.* **made him a liar**—a consequence which many who virtually, or even avowedly, do not believe, may

well startle back from as fearful blasphemy and presumption (ch. 1:10). **believeth not the record**—*Greek,* "believeth not IN the record, or *witness.*" Refusal to *credit* God's testimony ("believeth not God") is involved in refusal *to believe* IN (to rest one's trust in) Jesus Christ, the object of God's *record* or *testimony.* "Divine *faith* is an assent unto something as credible upon the testimony of God. This is the highest kind of *faith;* because the object hath the highest credibility, because grounded upon the testimony of God, which is infallible" [PEARSON *on Creed*]. "The authority on which we believe is divine; the doctrine which we follow is divine" [LEO]. **gave**—*Greek,* "hath testified, and now testifies." **of**—concerning. **11. hath given**—*Greek,* aorist: "gave" once for all. Not only "*promised*" it. **life is in his Son**—essentially (John 1:4; 11:25; 14:6); bodily (Col. 2:9); operatively (II Tim. 1:10) [LANGE *in* ALFORD]. It is in the second Adam, the Son of God, that this *life* is secured to us, which, if left to depend on us, we should lose, like the first Adam. **12. the Son ... life**—*Greek,* "THE life." BENGEL remarks, The verse has two clauses: in the former the Son is mentioned without the addition "of God," for believers know *the Son:* in the second clause the addition "of God" is made, that unbelievers may know thereby what a serious thing it is not to have Him. In the former clause "has" bears the emphasis; in the second, *life.* To *have the Son* is to be able to say as the bride, "I am my Beloved's, and *my Beloved is mine.*" *Faith* is the mean whereby the regenerate HAVE Christ as a *present* possession, and in having Him *have life* in its germ and reality now, and shall have life in its fully developed manifestation hereafter. *Eternal life* here is: (1) *initial,* and is an earnest of that which is to follow; in the intermediate state (2) *partial,* belonging but to a part of a man, though that is his nobler part, the soul separated from the body; at and after the resurrection (3) *perfectional.* This life is not only natural, consisting of the union of the soul and the body (as that of the reprobate in eternal pain, which ought to be termed *death* eternal, not *life*), but also spiritual, the union of the soul to God, and supremely blessed for ever (for *life* is another term for *happiness*) [PEARSON *on Creed*]. **13. These things**—This Epistle. He, towards the close of his Gospel (John 20:30, 31), wrote similarly, stating his purpose in having written. In ch. 1:4 he states the object of his writing this Epistle to be, "that your joy may be full." To "*know that we have eternal life*" is the sure way to "joy in God." **13.** The oldest MSS. and versions read, "These things have I written unto you [omitting *that believe on the name of the Son of God*] that ye may know that ye have eternal life (cf. vs. 11), THOSE (of you I mean) WHO believe (not as *English Version* reads, *and that ye may believe*) on the name of the Son of God." *English Version,* in the latter clause, will mean, "that ye may *continue to believe ...*" (cf. vs. 12). **14. the confidence**—*boldness*" (ch. 4:17) in prayer, which results from *knowing that we have eternal life* (vs. 13; ch. 3:19, 22). **according to his will**—which is the believer's will, and which is therefore no restraint to his prayers. In so far as God's will is not our will, we are not abiding in faith, and our prayers are not accepted. ALFORD well says, If we *knew* God's will thoroughly, and *submitted* to it heartily, it would be impossible for us to ask anything for the spirit or for the body which He should not perform; it is this ideal state which the apostle has in view.

It is the *Spirit* who teaches us inwardly, and Himself in us asks according to the will of God. **15. hear**—*Greek,* "that He *heareth* us." **we have the petitions that we desired of him**—*We have,* as present possessions, everything *whatsoever we desired (asked) from Him.* Not one of our *past* prayers offered in faith, *according to His will,* is lost. Like Hannah, we can rejoice over them as granted even before the event; and can recognize the event when it comes to pass, as not from chance, but obtained by our past prayers. Cf. also Jehoshaphat's believing confidence in the issue of his prayers, so much so that he appointed singers to praise the Lord beforehand. **16. If any . . . see**—on any particular occasion; *Greek* aorist. **his brother**—a fellow Christian. **sin a sin**—in the act of sinning, and continuing in the sin: present. **not unto death**—provided that it is *not unto death.* **he shall give**—The *asker* shall be the means, by his intercessory prayer, of *God giving* life to the sinning brother. Kindly reproof ought to accompany his intercessions. *Life* was in process of being forfeited by the sinning brother when the believer's intercession obtained its restoration. **for them**—resuming the proviso put forth in the beginning of the verse. "Provided that the sin is not unto death." "Shall give life," I say, *to,* i.e., obtain life *"for* (in the case of) them that sin not unto death." **I do not say that he shall pray for it**—The *Greek* for "pray" means a REQUEST as of one on an equality, or at least on terms of familiarity, with him from whom the favor is sought. "The Christian intercessor for his brethren, John declares, shall not assume the authority which would be implied in making request for a sinner who has sinned the sin unto death (I Sam. 15:35; 16:1; Mark 3:29), that it might be forgiven him" [TRENCH, *Synonyms of New Testament*]. Cf. Deuteronomy 3:26. *Greek* "ask" implies the humble petition of an inferior; so that our Lord never uses it, but always uses (*Greek*) "request." Martha, from ignorance, once uses "ask" in His case (John 11:22). "Asking" for a brother sinning not unto death, is a humble petition in consonance with God's will. To "request" for a sin unto death [*intercede, as it were, authoritatively for it,* as though we were more merciful than God] would savor of presumption; prescribing to God in a matter which lies out of the bounds of our brotherly yearning (because one sinning unto death would thereby be demonstrated not to be, nor ever to have been, truly a brother, ch. 2:19), how He shall inflict and withhold His righteous judgments. Jesus Himself intercedes, not for the world which hardens itself in unbelief, but for those given to Him out of the world. **17.** "Every unrighteousness (even that of believers, cf. ch. 1:9; 3:4. Every coming short of *right*) is sin"; (but) not every sin is the sin unto death. **and there is a sin not unto death**—in the case of which, therefore, believers may intercede. *Death* and *life* stand in correlative opposition (vss. 11-13). *The sin unto death* must be one tending "towards" (so the *Greek*), and so resulting in, *death.* ALFORD makes it to be an appreciable ACT of sin, viz., *the denying Jesus to be the Christ, the Son of God* (in contrast to confess this truth, vss. 1, 5), ch. 2:19, 22; 4:2, 3; 5:10. Such wilful deniers of Christ are not to be received into one's house, or wished "God speed." Still, I think with BENGEL, not merely the *act,* but also the *state* of apostasy accompanying the *act,* is included—a "state of soul in which faith, love, and hope, in short, the new life, is extinguished." The chief commandment is *faith* and *love.* Therefore, the chief sin is that by which faith and love are destroyed. In the former case is *life;* in the latter, death. As long as it is not evident (*Note,* 'see,' vs. 16) that it is a sin unto death, it is lawful to pray. But when it is deliberate rejection of grace, and the man puts from him life thereby, how can others procure for him life?" Contrast James 5:14-18. Cf. Matthew 12:31, 32 as to the wilful rejection of Christ, and resistance to the Holy Ghost's plain testimony to Him as the divine Messiah. Jesus, on the cross, pleaded only for those who KNEW NOT *what they were doing* in crucifying Him, not for those wilfully resisting grace and knowledge. If we *pray for* the impenitent, it must be with humble reference of the matter to God's will, not with the intercessory *request* which we should offer for *a brother* when erring. **18.** (Ch. 3:9.) **We know**—Thrice repeated emphatically, to enforce the three truths which the words preface, as matters of the brethren's joint experimental knowledge. This vs. 18 warns against abusing vss. 16: 17, as warranting carnal security. **whosoever**—*Greek,* "every one who." Not only advanced believers, but *every one* who is born again, "sinneth not." **he that is begotten**—*Greek* aorist, "has been (once for all in *past* time) begotten of God"; in the beginning of the verse it is perfect. "Is begotten," or "born," as a *continuing* state. **keepeth himself**—the *Vulgate* translates, "The having been begotten of God keepeth HIM" (so one of the oldest MSS. reads: so ALFORD. Lit., "He having been begotten of God (nominative pendent), *it* (the divine generation implied in the nominative) keepeth him." So ch. 3:9, "His seed remaineth in him." Still, in *English Version* reading, God's working by His Spirit inwardly, and man's working under the power of that Spirit as a responsible agent, is what often occurs elsewhere. That *God* must *keep* us, if we are to *keep ourselves* from evil, is certain. Cf. John 17: 15 especially with this verse. **that wicked one toucheth him not**—so as to hurt him. In so far as he realizes his regeneration-life, the prince of this world *hath nothing in him* to fasten his deadly temptations on, as in Christ's own case. His divine regeneration has severed once for all his connection with the prince of this world. **19. world lieth in wickedness**—rather, "lieth in *the wicked one,*" as the *Greek* is translated in vs. 18; ch. 2:13, 14; cf. ch. 4:4; John 17:14, 15. The world *lieth* in the power of, and abiding in, the wicked one, as the resting-place and lord of his slaves; cf. "abideth in death," ch. 3:14; contrast vs. 20, "we are in Him that is true." While the believer has been delivered out of his power, the whole world *lieth* helpless and motionless still in it, just as it was; including the wise, great, respectable, and all who are not by vital union in Christ. **20.** Summary of our Christian privileges. **is come**—*is present, having come.* "HE IS HERE—all is full of Him—His incarnation, work, and abiding presence, is to us a living fact" [ALFORD]. **given us an understanding**—Christ's office is to give the inner spiritual understanding to discern the things of God. **that we may know**—Some oldest MSS. read, "(so) that *we know.*" **him that is true**—God, as opposed to every kind of *idol* or false god (vs. 21). Jesus, by virtue of His oneness with God, is also "He that is true" (Rev. 3:7). *even*—"we are in the true" God, *by virtue of being* "in His Son Jesus Christ." **This is the true God**—"*This* Jesus Christ (the last-named Person) is the true God" (identifying Him thus with the Father in His attribute, "the only true God," John 17:3, primarily attributed to the Father). **and eternal life**

—predicated of the Son of God; ALFORD wrongly says, He was *the life,* but not *eternal life.* The Father is indeed *eternal life* as its source, but the Son also is that *eternal life manifested,* as the very passage (ch. 1:2) which ALFORD quotes, proves against him. Cf. also vss. 11, 13. Plainly it is as the *Mediator of* ETERNAL LIFE *to us* that Christ is here contemplated. The *Greek* is, "The true God and eternal life is this" Jesus Christ, i.e., In believing in Him we believe in the true God, and have eternal life. The Son is called "He that is TRUE," Revelation 3:7, as here. This naturally prepares the way for warning against *false* gods (vs. 21). Jesus Christ is the only "express image of God's person" which is sanctioned, the only true visible

manifestation of God. All other representations of God are forbidden as *idols.* Thus the Epistle closes as it began (ch. 1:1, 2). **21.** Affectionate parting caution. **from idols**—Christians were then everywhere surrounded by *idolaters,* with whom it was impossible to avoid intercourse. Hence the need of being on their guard against any even indirect compromise or act of communion with idolatry. Some at Pergamos, in the region whence John wrote, fell into the snare of eating things sacrificed to idols. The moment we cease to abide "in Him that is true (by abiding) in Jesus Christ," we become part of "the world that lieth in the wicked one," given up to *spiritual,* if not in all places *literal, idolatry* (Eph. 5:5; Col. 3:5).

THE SECOND EPISTLE GENERAL OF

JOHN

INTRODUCTION TO THE SECOND AND THIRD EPISTLES

AUTHENTICITY.—That these two Epistles were written by the same author appears from their similarity of tone, style, and sentiments. That John, the beloved disciple, was the author of the Second and Third Epistles, as of the First Epistle, appears from IRENÆUS, *Adversus Hæreses,* 1. 16. 3, who quotes II John 10:11; and in 3. 16. 8, he quotes II John 7, mistaking it, however, as if occurring in I John. CLEMENT OF ALEXANDRIA (A.D. 192), *Stromata,* 2. 66, implies his knowledge of other Epistles of John besides the First Epistle; and in fragments of his *Adumbrations* (p. 1011), he says, "John's Second Epistle which was written to the virgins (*Greek, parthenous;* perhaps *Parthos* is what was meant) is the simplest; but it was written to a certain Babylonian named *the Elect lady.*" DIONYSIUS OF ALEXANDRIA (in EUSEBIUS, *Ecclesiastical History,* 7. 25) observes that John never names himself in his Epistles, "not even in the Second and Third Epistles, although they are short Epistles, but simply calls himself the presbyter," a confutation of those who think John *the apostle* distinct from John *the presbyter.* ALEXANDER OF ALEXANDRIA cites II John 10:11, as John's (SOCRATES, *Historia Ecclesiastica,* 1. 6). CYPRIAN, *De Hæreticis Baptizandis,* in referring to the bishops at the Council of Carthage, says, "John the apostle, in His Epistle, has said, if any come to you" (II John 10); so that this Epistle, and therefore its twin sister, III John, was recognized as apostolic in the North African Church. The MURATORI fragment is ambiguous. The Second and Third Epistles were not in the *Peschito* or old *Syriac* version; and COSMAS INDICOPLEUSTES in the sixth century says that in his time the Syriac Church only acknowledged three of the Catholic Epistles, I Peter, I John, and James. But EPHREM SYRUS quotes the Second Epistle of John. EUSEBIUS (*Ecclesiastical History*) reckons both Epistles among the *Antilegomena* or *controverted* Scriptures, as distinguished from the *Homologoumena* or *universally acknowledged* from the first. Still his own opinion was that the two minor Epistles were genuine, remarking, as he does in *Demonstratio Evangelica,* 3, 5, that in John's "*Epistles*" he does not mention his own name, nor call himself an apostle or evangelist, but an "elder" (II John 1; III John 1). ORIGEN (in EUSEBIUS, *Ecclesiastical History,* 6. 25) mentions the Second and Third Epistles, but adds, "*not all* admit [implying that *most* authorities do] their genuineness." JEROME (*De Viris Illustribus,* 9) mentions the two latter Epistles as attributed to John the presbyter, whose sepulcher was shown among the Ephesians in his day. But the designation "elder" was used of the apostles by others (e.g., PAPIAS, in EUSEBIUS, *Ecclesiastical History,* 3. 39), and is used by Peter, an apostle, of himself (I Peter 5:1). Why, then, should not John also use this designation of himself, in consonance with the humility which leads him not to name himself or his apostleship even in the First Epistle? The Antilegomena were generally recognized as canonical soon after the Council of Nice (A.D. 325). Thus CYRIL OF JERUSALEM, A.D. 349, enumerates fourteen Epistles of Paul, and seven Catholic Epistles. So GREGORY OF NAZIANZEN, in A.D. 389. The Councils of Hippo, 393, and Carthage, 397, adopted a catalogue of New Testament books exactly agreeing with our canon. So our oldest extant *Greek* MSS. The Second and Third Epistles of John, from their brevity (which ORIGEN notices), and the private nature of their contents, were less generally read in the earliest Christian assemblies and were also less quoted by the Fathers; hence arose their non-universal recognition at the first. Their private nature makes them the less likely to be spurious, for there seems no purpose in their forgery. The style and coloring too accord with the style of the First Epistle.

TO WHOM ADDRESSED.—The Third Epistle is directed to Gaius or Caius; whether Gaius of Macedonia (Acts 19:20), or Gaius of Corinth (Rom. 16:23; I Cor. 1:14), or Gaius of Derbe (Acts 20:4), it is hard to decide. MILL believes Gaius, bishop of Pergamos (*Apostolic Constitutions,* 7. 40), to be the person addressed in III John.

The address of the Second Epistle is more disputed. It opens, "The elder unto the *Elect lady.*" And it closes, "The children of thy *elect* sister greet thee." Now, I Peter 1:1, 2, addresses the *elect* in Asia, etc., and closes (I Pet. 5:13), "The Church that is *at Babylon, elected* together with you, saluteth you." Putting together these facts, with the quotations (above) from CLEMENT OF ALEXANDRIA, and the fact that the word "Church" comes from a *Greek* word (*kyriake*) cognate to the *Greek* for "lady" (*kyria*, belonging to the *Lord*, *kyrios*), WORDS-WORTH's view is probable. As Peter in Babylon had sent the salutations *of the elect Church* in the then *Parthian* (see above on CLEMENT OF ALEXANDRIA) *Babylon* to her *elect sister* in Asia, so John, the metropolitan president of the elect Church in Asia, writes to *the elect lady*, i.e., Church, in Babylon. NEANDER, ALFORD, and others, think the *Greek kyria* not to mean "lady," but to be her *proper name;* and that she had a "sister, a Christian matron," then with John.

DATE AND PLACE OF WRITING.—EUSEBIUS (*Ecclesiastical History*, 3. 25) relates that John, after the death of Domitian, returned from his exile in Patmos to Ephesus, and went on missionary tours into the heathen regions around, and also made visitations of the churches around, and ordained bishops and clergy. Such journeys are mentioned, II John 12; III John 10, 14. If EUSEBIUS be right, both Epistles must have been written after the Apocalypse, in his old age, which harmonizes with the tone of the Epistles, and in or near Ephesus. It was on one of his visitation tours that he designed to rebuke Diotrephes (III John 9, 10).

Vss. 1-13. ADDRESS: GREETING: THANKSGIVING FOR THE ELECT LADY'S FAITHFULNESS IN THE TRUTH: ENJOINS LOVE: WARNS AGAINST DECEIVERS, LEST WE LOSE OUR REWARD: CONCLUSION. **1. The elder**—In a familiar letter John gives himself a less authoritative designation than "apostle"; so I Peter 5. **1. lady**—BENGEL takes the *Greek* as a proper name *Kyria*, answering to the *Hebrew* "Martha." Being a person of influence, "deceivers" (vs. 7) were insinuating themselves into her family to seduce her and her children from the faith [TIRINUS], whence John felt it necessary to write a warning to her. (But see my *Introduction*, and I Pet. 5:13.) A particular *Church*, probably that at Babylon, was intended. "Church" is derived from *Greek Kuriake*, akin to *Kuria*, or *Kyria* here; the latter word among the Romans and Athenians means the same as *ecclesia*, the term appropriated to designate the *Church* assembly. **love in the truth**—Christian *love* rests on the Christian *truth* (vs. 3, end). Not merely "I love *in truth*," but "I love in THE truth." **all**—All Christians form one fellowship, rejoicing in the spiritual prosperity of one another. "The communion of love is as wide as the communion of faith" [ALFORD]. **2. For the truth's sake**—joined with "I love," vs. 1. "They who love *in* the truth, also love *on account of* the truth." **dwelleth in us, and shall be with us for ever**—in consonance with Christ's promise. **3. Grace be with you**—One of the oldest MSS. and several versions have "us" for *you.* The *Greek* is lit., "Grace *shall be* with us," i.e., with both *you and me.* A prayer, however, is implied besides a confident affirmation. **grace ... mercy ... peace**—"Grace" covers the sins of men; "mercy," their miseries. *Grace* must first do away with man's guilt before his misery can be relieved by *mercy.* Therefore *grace* stands before *mercy. Peace* is the result of both, and therefore stands third in order. Casting all our care on the Lord, with thanksgiving, maintains this peace. **the Lord**—The oldest MSS. and most of the oldest versions omit "the Lord." John never elsewhere uses this title in his Epistles, but "the Son of God." **in truth and love**—The element or sphere in which alone *grace, mercy,* and *peace,* have place. He mentions *truth* in vs. 4; *love,* in vs. 5. Paul uses FAITH and *love;* for *faith* and *truth* are close akin. **4. I found**—probably in one of his missionary tours of superintendence. See *Introduction*, at the end, and vs. 12; III John 10:14. **of thy children**—some. **in truth**—i.e., in *the* Gospel truth. **as**—even as. "The Father's commandment" is the standard of "the truth." **5. I beseech**—rather (cf. *Note*, I John 5:16), "I request thee," implying some degree of *authority.* **not ... new commandment**—It was *old* in that Christians heard it from the first in the Gospel preaching; *new,*

in that the Gospel rested love on the new principle of filial imitation of God who first loved us, and gave Jesus to die for *us;* and also, in that *love* is now set forth with greater clearness than in the Old Testament dispensation. Love performs both tables of the law, and is the end of the law and the Gospel alike (cf. *Note,* I John 2:7, 8). **that we**—implying that he already had love, and urging her to join him in the same Christian grace. This verse seems to me to decide that a *Church,* not an *individual lady,* is meant. For a man to urge a woman ("THEE"; not *thee and thy children*) that he and she should *love one another,* is hardly like an apostolic precept, however pure may be the love enjoined; but all is clear if "the lady" represent a *Church.* **6.** "Love is the fulfilling of the law," and the fulfilling of the law is the sure test of love. **This is the commandment**—*Greek,* "The commandment is this," viz., *love,* in which all God's other commandments are summed up. **7.** As *love* and *truth* go hand in hand (vss. 3, 4), he feels it needful to give warning against teachers of untruth. **For**—giving the reason why he dwelt on *truth* and on *love,* which manifests itself in keeping God's commandments (vs. 6). **many**—(I John 2:18; 4:1). **are entered**—The oldest MSS. read, "have *gone forth,*" viz., from us. **confess not ... Jesus ... in the flesh**—the token of Antichrist. **is come**—*Greek,* "coming." He who denies Christ's *coming* in the flesh, denies the *possibility* of the incarnation; he who denies that he *has come,* denies its *actuality.* They denied the possibility of a Messiah's appearing, or *coming,* in the flesh [NEANDER]. I think the *Greek* present participle implies *both* the first and the second advent of Christ. He is often elsewhere called *the Coming One* (*Greek*), Matthew 11:3; Hebrews 10:37. The denial of the reality of His manifestation in the flesh, at His first coming, and of His personal advent again, constitutes Antichrist. "The world *turns away* from God and Christ, busily intent upon its own husks; but to OPPOSE God and Christ is of the leaven of Satan" [BENGEL]. **This is a ...**—*Greek,* "This (such a one as has been just described) is *the* deceiver and *the* Antichrist." The *many* who in a degree fulfil the character, are forerunners of the final personal Antichrist, who shall concentrate in himself all the features of previous Antichristian systems. **8. Look to yourselves**—amidst the widespread prevalence of deception so many being led astray. So Christ's warning, Matthew 24:4, 5, 24. **we lose not ... we receive**—The oldest MSS. and versions read, "That YE lose not, but that YE receive." **which we have wrought**—So one oldest MS. reads. Other very old MSS., versions, and Fathers, read, "which YE have wrought." The *we* being seemingly the more difficult reading is less likely to have been a transcriber's alteration. Look that ye lose not the believing state of "truth and love," which WE (as God's workmen, II Cor. 6:1; II Tim. 2:15) were the instruments of working in you. **a full reward**—of grace not of debt. *Fully* consummated glory. If "which YE have wrought" be read with very old authorities, the reward meant is that of their "work (of faith) and labor of love." There are degrees of heavenly reward proportioned to the degrees of capability of receiving heavenly blessedness. Each vessel of glory hanging on Jesus shall be fully happy. But the larger the vessel, the greater will be its capacity for receiving heavenly bliss. He who with one pound made ten, received authority over ten cities. He who made five pounds received five cities; each according to his capacity of rule, and in proportion to his faithfulness. Cf. I Corinthians 15:41. "There is no half reward of the saints. It is either lost altogether, or received *in full; in full* communion with God" [BENGEL]. Still no service of minister or people shall fail to receive its reward. **9.** The *loss* (vs. 8) meant is here explained: the *not having God*, which results from *abiding not in the doctrine of Christ.* **transgresseth** —The oldest MSS. and versions read, "Every one who *takes the lead"*; lit., "goes," or "leads on before"; cf. John 10:4, "He goeth before them" (not the same *Greek*). Cf. III John 9, "Loveth to have the *pre-eminence.*" **hath not God**—(I John 2:23; 5:15). The second "of Christ" is omitted in the oldest MSS., but is understood in the sense. **He**— emphatical: *He and He alone.* **10. If there come any**—as a teacher or brother. The *Greek* is indicative, not subjunctive; implying that such persons *do actually come*, and *are sure to come;* when any comes, as there will. True love is combined with hearty renunciation and separation from all that is false, whether persons or doctrines. **receive him not . . . neither bid him God speed**—This is not

said of those who were always aliens from the Church, but of those who wish to be esteemed brethren, and subvert the true doctrine [GROTIUS]. The greeting salutation forbidden in the case of such a one is that *usual among Christian brethren* in those days, not a mere formality, but a token of *Christian brotherhood.* **11.** By wishing a false brother or teacher "God (or *good*) speed," you imply that he is capable as such of good speed and *joy* (the lit. meaning of the *Greek*), and that you wish him it while opposing Christ; so you identify yourself with "his evil deeds." The *Greek* of "partaker" is "having communion with." We cannot have communion with saints and with Antichrist at the same time. Here we see John's naturally fiery zeal directed to a right end. POLYCARP, the disciple of John, told contemporaries of IRENÆUS, who narrates the story on their authority, that on one occasion when John was about to bathe, and heard that Cerinthus, the heretic, was within, he retired with abhorrence, exclaiming, Surely the house will fall in ruins since the enemy of the truth is there. **12. I would not write**—A heart full of love pours itself out more freely face to face, than by letter. **paper**—made of Egyptian papyrus. Pens were then reeds split. **ink**—made of soot and water, thickened with gum. Parchment was used for the permanent MSS. in which the Epistles were preserved. Writing *tablets* were used merely for temporary purposes, as our slates. **face to face**— lit., "mouth to mouth." **full**—*Greek*, "filled full." Your joy will be complete in hearing from me in person the joyful Gospel truths which I now defer communicating till I see you. On other occasions his writing the glad truths was for the same purpose. **13.** ALFORD confesses that the non-mention of the "lady" herself here seems rather to favor the hypothesis that a *Church* is meant.

THE THIRD EPISTLE OF

JOHN

Vss. 1-14. ADDRESS: WISH FOR GAIUS' PROSPERITY: JOY AT HIS WALKING IN THE TRUTH. HIS HOSPITALITY TO THE BRETHREN AND STRANGERS THE FRUIT OF LOVE. DIOTREPHES' OPPOSITION AND AMBITION. PRAISE OF DEMETRIUS. CONCLUSION. **1. I**—emphatical: *I* personally, for my part. On Gaius or Caius, see *Introduction* before Second Epistle. **love in the truth**—(II John 1). "Beloved" is repeated often in this Epistle, indicating strong affection (vss. 1, 2, 5, 11). **2. above all things**— *Greek*, "concerning all things": so ALFORD: *in all respects.* But WAHL justifies *English Version* (cf. I Pet. 4:8). Of course, since his *soul's prosperity* is presupposed, "above all things" does not imply that John wishes Gaius' bodily health above that of his soul, but as the *first* object to be desired *next after spiritual health.* I know you are prospering in the concerns of your soul. I wish you similar prosperity in your body. Perhaps John had heard from the brethren (vs. 3) that Gaius was in bad health, and was tried in other ways (vs. 10), to which the wish, vs. 2, refers. **prosper**—in general. **be in health**—in particular. **3. testified of the truth**

that is in thee—*Greek*, "of (or *to*) thy truth": thy share of that truth in which thou walkest [ALFORD]. **even as thou**—in contrast to Diotrephes (vs. 9). **4. my children**—members of the Church: confirming the view that the "elect lady" is a Church. **5. faithfully**—an act becoming a faithful man. **whatsoever thou doest**—a distinct *Greek* word from the former "doest": translate, "workest": whatsoever work, or labor of love, thou dost perform. So Matthew 26: 10, "She hath wrought a good *work* upon me." **and to strangers**—The oldest MSS., "and that (i.e., and those brethren) strangers." The fact of the brethren whom thou didst entertain being "strangers," enhances the love manifested in the act. **6. borne witness of thy charity before the church**—to stimulate others by the good example. The brethren so entertained by Gaius were missionary evangelists (vs. 7); and, probably, in the course of narrating their missionary labors for the edification of the Church where John then was, incidentally mentioned the loving hospitality shown them by Gaius. **bring forward on their journey**—"if thou (*continue to*) forward on their journey" by giving them provisions for the way. **after a godly sort—** *Greek,* "in a manner worthy of God," whose ambassadors they are, and whose servant thou art. He who honors God's missionary servants (vs. 7), honors God. **7. his name's sake—**Christ's. **went forth—**as missionaries. **taking nothing—**refusing to *receive* aught by way of pay, or maintenance, though justly entitled to it, as Paul at Corinth and at Thessalonica. **Gentiles—**the Christians just gathered out by their labors from among the heathen. As Gaius himself was a *Gentile* convert, "the Gentiles" here must mean *the converts just made from the heathen,* the Gentiles to whom they had *gone forth.* It would have been inexpedient to have taken aught (the *Greek meden* implies, not that they *got* nothing, though they had desired it, but that it was of *their own choice* they *took nothing*) from the infant churches among the heathen: the case was different in receiving hospitality from Gaius. **8. We—**in contradistinction to "the Gentiles" or "heathen" referred to, vs. 7. **therefore—** as they take nothing from the Gentiles or heathen. **receive—**The oldest MSS. read, "take up." As they *take* nothing from the Gentiles, we ought to *take* them *up* so as to support them. **fellow helpers—** with them. **to the truth—**i.e., *to promote* the truth. **9. I wrote—**The oldest MSS. add "something": *a communication,* probably, on the subject of *receiving the brethren* with brotherly love (vss. 8, 10). That Epistle was not designed by the Spirit for the universal Church, or else it would have been preserved. **unto the church—**of which Gaius is a member. **loveth ... pre-eminence—**through ambition. Evidently occupying a high place in the Church where Gaius was (vs. 10). **among them—** *over* the members of the Church. **receiveth us not** —virtually, viz., by not *receiving* with love the brethren whom *we* recommended to be received (vss. 8, 10; cf. Matt. 10:40). **10. if I come—**(*V.* 14). **I will remember—**lit., "I will bring to mind" before all by stigmatizing and punishing. **prating—**with mere silly tattle. **neither doth he ... receive the brethren—**with hospitality. "The brethren" are the missionaries on their journey. **forbiddeth them that would—**receive them. **casteth them—**those that would receive the brethren, by excommunication from the Church, which his influence, as a leading man (vs. 9) in it, enabled him to do. NEANDER thinks that the missionaries were JEWS by birth, whence it is said in their praise they *took nothing from* THE GENTILES: in contrast to other Jewish missionaries who abused ministers' right of maintenance elsewhere, as Paul tells us, II Corinthians 11:22; Philippians 3:2, 5, 19. Now in the Gentile churches there existed an ultra-Pauline party of anti-Jewish tendency, the forerunners of Marcion: Diotrephes possibly stood at the head of this party, which fact, as well as this domineering spirit, may account for his hostility to the missionaries, and to the apostle John, who had, by the power of love, tried to harmonize the various elements in the Asiatic churches. At a later period, Marcion, we know, attached himself to Paul alone, and paid no deference to the authority of John. **11. follow not that which is evil—**as manifested in Diotrephes (vss. 9, 10). **but ... good—**as manifested in Demetrius (vs. 12). **is of God—**is born of God, who is good. **hath not seen God—**spiritually, not literally. **12. of all men—**who have had opportunity of knowing his character. **of the truth itself—**The Gospel standard of *truth* bears witness to him that he walks conformably to it, in acts of real love, hospitality to the brethren (in contrast to Diotrephes), etc. Cf. John 3:21 "He that doeth truth cometh to the light, that his deeds may be made manifest that they are wrought in God." **we also—**besides the testimony of "all men," and "of the truth itself." **ye know—**The oldest MSS. read, "thou knowest." **13. I will not—**rather as *Greek,* "I wish not ... to write" more. **14. face to face—**Greek, "mouth to mouth." **Peace—**peace inward of conscience, peace fraternal of friendship, peace supernal of glory [LYRA]. **friends—**a title seldom used in the New Testament, as it is absorbed in the higher titles of "brother, brethren." Still Christ recognizes the relation of *friend* also, based on the highest grounds, obedience to Him from love, and entailing the highest privileges, admission to the intimacy of the holy and glorious God, and sympathizing Saviour; so Christians have "friends" in Christ. Here in a friendly letter, mention of "friends" appropriately occurs. **by name—**not less than if their names were written [BENGEL].

THE GENERAL EPISTLE OF

JUDE

INTRODUCTION

AUTHOR.—He calls himself in the address "the servant of Jesus Christ, and brother of James." See *Introduction to the Epistle of James,* in proof of James the *apostle,* and James *the Lord's brother,* the bishop of Jerusalem, being one and the same person. Galatians 1:19 alone seems to me to prove this. Similarly, Jude the brother of our Lord, and Jude the apostle, seem to be one and the same. JEROME, *Contra Helvidium,* rightly maintains that by the Lord's brethren are meant his cousins, children of Mary and Cleophas (the same as Alphæus). From I Corinthians 9:5 (as "brethren of the Lord" stands between "other apostles" and "Cephas"), it seems natural to think that the *brethren of the Lord* are distinguished from the apostles only because *all* his brethren were not apostles, but only James and Jude. Jude's reason for calling himself "brother of Jesus," was that James, as bishop of Jerusalem, was better known than himself. Had he been, in the strict sense, *brother of our Lord,* he probably would have so entitled himself. His omission of *mention* of his *apostleship* is no proof that he was not an apostle; for so also James omits it in his heading; and Paul, in his Epistles to the Philippians, Thessalonians, and Philemon, omits it. Had the writer been a counterfeiter of the apostle Jude, he would doubtless have called himself an "apostle." He was called also Lebbæus and Thaddeus, probably to distinguish him from Judas Iscariot, the traitor. Lebbæus, from *Hebrew leeb*, "heart," means *courageous*. Thaddeus is the same as Theudas, from *Hebrew thad*, the "breast." Luke and John, writing later than Matthew, when there would be no confusion between him and Judas Iscariot, give his name Judas. The only circumstance relating to him recorded in the Gospels occurs in John 14:22, "Judas saith unto Him, not Iscariot, Lord, how is it that Thou wilt manifest Thyself unto us, and not unto the world?" JEROME (*Annotationes in Matthæum*) says that he was sent to Edessa, to Abgarus, king of Osroene, or Edessa, and that he preached in Syria, Arabia, Mesopotamia, and Persia, in which last country he suffered martyrdom. The story is told on EUSEBIUS' authority, that Abgarus, on his sickbed, having heard of Jesus' power to heal, sent to beg Him to come and cure him, to which the Lord replied, praising his faith, that though he had not seen the Saviour, he yet believed; adding, "As for what thou hast written, that I should come to thee, it is necessary that all those things for which I was sent should be fulfilled by Me in this place, and that having filled them I should be received up to Him that sent Me. When, therefore, I shall be received into heaven, I will send unto thee some one of My disciples who shall both heal thy distemper and give life to thee and those with thee." Thomas is accordingly said to have been inspired to send Thaddeus for the cure and baptism of Abgarus. The letters are said to have been shown Thaddeus among the archives of Edessa. It is possible such a message was verbally sent, and the substance of it registered in writing afterwards (cf. II Kings 5; and Matthew 15:22). HEGESIPPUS (*in* EUSEBIUS, *Ecclesiastical History*, 3. 20) states that when Domitian inquired after David's posterity, some grandsons of Jude, called the Lord's brother, were brought into his presence. Being asked as to their possessions, they said that they had thirty-nine acres of the value of 9000 denarii, out of which they paid him taxes, and lived by the labor of their hands, a proof of which they gave by showing the hardness of their hands. Being interrogated as to Christ and His kingdom, they replied that it was not of this world, but heavenly; and that it would be manifested at the end of the world, when He would come in glory to judge the living and the dead.

AUTHENTICITY.—EUSEBIUS, *Ecclesiastical History*, 3. 25, reckons it among the *Antilegomena* or *controverted* Scriptures, "though recognized by the majority." The reference to the contest of Michael, the archangel, with the devil, for the body of Moses, not mentioned elsewhere in the Old Testament, but found in the *apocryphal* "Book of Enoch," probably raised doubts as to its authenticity, as JEROME (*Catalogus Scriptorum Ecclesiasticorum*, 4) says. Moreover, its not being addressed to one particular Church, or individual, caused it not to be so immediately recognized as canonical. A counterfeiter would have avoided using what did not occur in the Old Testament, and which might be regarded as apocryphal.

As to the book of Enoch, if quoted by Jude, his quotation of a passage from it gives an inspired sanction only to *the truth of that passage*, not to the whole book; just as Paul, by inspiration, sanctions particular sentiments from Aratus, Epimenides, and Menander, but not all their writings. I think, rather as there is some slight variation between Jude's statement and that of the book of Enoch, that Jude, though probably not ignorant of the book of Enoch, stamps with inspired sanction the current tradition of the Jews as to Enoch's prophecies; just as Paul mentions the names of the Egyptian magicians, "Jannes and Jambres," not mentioned in the Old Testament. At all events, the prophecy ascribed to Enoch by Jude was really his, being sanctioned as such by this inspired writer. So also the narration as to the archangel Michael's dispute with Satan concerning the body of Moses, is by Jude's inspired authority (vs. 9) declared true. The book of Enoch is quoted by JUSTIN, MARTYR, IRENÆUS, CLEMENT OF ALEXANDRIA, etc. Bruce, the Abyssinian traveler, brought home three copies of it in *Ethiopic*, from Alexandria, of which Archbishop Lawrence, in 1821, gave an English translation. The *Ethiopic* was a version from the *Greek*, and the *Greek* doubtless a version from the *Hebrew*, as the names of the angels in it show. The Apostolic Constitutions, ORIGEN (*Contra Celsum*), JEROME, and AUGUSTINE, pronounce it not canonical. Yet it is in the main edifying, vindicating God's government of the world, natural and spiritual, and contradicting none of the Scripture statements. The name *Jesus* never occurs, though "Son of man," so often given to Messiah in the Gospels, is frequent, and terms are used expressive of His dignity, character, and acts, exceeding the views of Messiah in any other Jewish book. The writer seems to have been a Jew who had become thoroughly imbued with the sacred writings of Daniel. And, though many coincidences occur between its sentiments and the New Testament, the Messianic portions are not distinct enough to prove that the writer knew the New Testament. Rather, he seems to have immediately preceded Christ's coming, about the time of Herod the Great, and so gives us a most interesting view of believing Jews' opinions before the advent of our Lord. The Trinity is recognized, 60:13, 14. Messiah is "the elect One" existing from eternity, 48:2, 3, 5; "All kings shall fall down before Him, and worship and fix their hopes on this Son of man," 61:10–13. He is the object of worship, 48:3, 4; He is the supreme Judge, 60:10, 11; 68:38, 39. There shall be a future state of retribution, 93:8, 9; 94. 2, 4; chs. 95, 96, 99, 103. The eternity of future punishment, 103:5. VOLKMAR, *in* ALFORD, thinks the book was written at the time of the sedition of Barchochebas (A.D. 132), by a follower of Rabbi Akiba, the upholder of that impostor. This would make the book Antichristian in its origin. If this date be correct, doubtless it copied some things from Jude, giving them the Jewish, not the Christian, coloring.

EUSEBIUS (*Demonstratio Evangelica*, 3. 5) remarks, it accords with John's humility that in II and III John he calls himself "the elder." For the same reason James and Jude call themselves "servants of Jesus Christ." CLEMENS ALEXANDRINUS (*Adumbrations*, in Ep. Jud., p. 1007) says, "Jude, through reverential awe, did not call himself *brother*, but *servant*, of Jesus Christ, and brother of James."

TERTULLIAN (*De Cultu Fœminarum*, c. 3) cites the Epistle as that of the apostle James. CLEMENS ALEXANDRINUS quotes it (vss. 8, 17) as Scripture, *Stromata* 3. 2. 11; and (vs. 5) in *Pædagogus* 3, 8. 44. The MURATORI fragment asserts its canonicity [ROUTH, *Reliquiæ Sacræ*, 1. 306]. ORIGEN (*Commentary on Matthew* 13:55) says, "Jude wrote an Epistle of few lines, but one filled full of the strong words of heavenly grace." Also, in *Commentary* on Matthew 22:23, he quotes vs. 6; and on Matthew 18:10, he quotes vs. 1. He calls the writer "Jude the apostle," in the Latin remains of his works (cf. DAVIDSON, *Introduction* III. 498). JEROME (*Catalogus Scriptorum*

Ecclesiasticorum 4) reckons it among the Scriptures. Though the oldest MSS. of the *Peschito* omit it, Ephrem Syrus recognizes it. WORDSWORTH reasons for its genuineness thus: Jude, we know, died before John, i.e., before the beginning of the second century. Now EUSEBIUS (*Ecclesiastical History* 3. 32) tells us that James was succeeded in the bishopric of Jerusalem by Symeon his brother; and also that Symeon sat in that see till A.D. 107, when as a martyr he was crucified in his 120th year. We find that the Epistle to Jude was known in the East and West in the second century; it was therefore circulated in Symeon's lifetime. It never would have received currency such as it had, nor would Symeon have permitted a letter bearing the name of an apostle, his own brother Jude, brother of his own apostolical predecessor, James, to have been circulated, if it were not really Jude's.

TO WHOM ADDRESSED.—The references to Old Testament history, vss. 5, 7, and to Jewish tradition, vs. 14, etc., make it likely that *Jewish* Christians are the readers to whom Jude mainly (though including also *all* Christians, vs. 1) writes, just as the kindred Epistle, II Peter, is addressed primarily to the same class; cf. *Introductions* to I and II Peter. The persons stigmatized in it were not merely *libertines* (as ALFORD thinks), though no doubt that was one of their prominent characteristics, but heretics in *doctrine*, "denying the only Lord God, and our Saviour Jesus Christ." Hence he urges believers "earnestly to contend for *the faith* once delivered unto the saints." Insubordination, self-seeking, and licentiousness, the fruit of Antinomian teachings, were the evils against which Jude warns his readers; reminding them that, to build themselves in their most holy faith, and to pray in the Holy Ghost, are the only effectual safeguards. The same evils, along with mocking skepticism, shall characterize the last days before the final judgment, even as in the days when Enoch warned the ungodly of the coming flood. As Peter was in Babylon in writing I Peter 5:13, and probably also in writing II Peter (cf. *Introductions* to I and II Peter), it seems not unlikely that Jude addressed his Epistle primarily to *the Jewish Christians in and about Mesopotamian Babylon* (a place of great resort to the Jews in that day), or else to *the Christian Jews dispersed in Pontus, Galatia, Cappadocia, Asia, and Bithynia*, the persons addressed by Peter. For Jude is expressly said to have preached in *Mesopotamia* (JEROME, *Annotationes in Matthæum*), and his Epistle, consisting of only twenty-five verses, contains in them no less than eleven passages from II Peter (see the list in my *Introduction* to II Peter). Probably in vs. 4 he witnesses to the fulfilment of Peter's prophecy, "There *are* certain men *crept in unawares*, who were before of old ordained (rather as *Greek*, 'forewritten,' i.e., announced *beforehand* by the apostle Peter's *written* prophecy) to this *condemnation*, ungodly men *denying* the only Lord God, and our Lord Jesus Christ." Cf. II Peter 2:1, "There *shall* be false teachers among you who *privily* shall bring in *damnable* heresies, even *denying the Lord* that bought them, and bring upon themselves swift *destruction*." Also vss. 17, 18 plainly refers to *the very words* of II Peter 3:3, "Remember the words which were spoken before of the *apostles* of our Lord Jesus; how they told you there should be *mockers in the last time* who should *walk after their own ungodly lusts*." This proves, in opposition to ALFORD, that Jude's Epistle is later than Peter's (whose inspiration he thus confirms, just as Peter confirms Paul's, II Peter 3:15, 16), not vice versa.

TIME AND PLACE OF WRITING.—ALFORD thinks, that, considering Jude was writing to Jews and citing signal instances of divine vengeance, it is very unlikely he would have omitted to allude to the destruction of Jerusalem if he had written after that event which uprooted the Jewish polity and people. He conjectures from the tone and references that the writer lived in Palestine. But as to the former, negative evidence is doubtful; for neither does John allude in his Epistles, written after the destruction of Jerusalem, to that event. MILL fixes on A.D. 90, after the death of all the apostles save John. I incline to think from vss 17, 18 that some time had elapsed since the Second Epistle of Peter (written probably about A.D. 68 or 69) when Jude wrote, and, therefore. that the Epistle of Jude was written *after* the destruction of Jerusalem.

Vss. 1-25. ADDRESS: GREETING: HIS OBJECT IN WRITING: WARNING AGAINST SEDUCERS IN DOCTRINE AND PRACTICE FROM GOD'S VENGEANCE ON APOSTATES, ISRAEL, THE FALLEN ANGELS, SODOM AND GOMORRAH. DESCRIPTION OF THESE BAD MEN, IN CONTRAST TO MICHAEL: LIKE CAIN, BALAAM, AND CORE: ENOCH'S PROPHECY AS TO THEM: THE APOSTLES' FOREWARNING: CONCLUDING EXHORTATION AS TO PRESERVING THEIR OWN FAITH, AND TRYING TO SAVE OTHERS: DOXOLOGY. **1. servant of Jesus Christ**—as His minister and apostle. **brother of James**—who was more widely known as bishop of Jerusalem and "brother of the Lord" (i.e., either *cousin*, or stepbrother, being son of Joseph by a former marriage; for ancient traditions universally agree that Mary, Jesus' mother, continued perpetually a virgin). Jude therefore calls himself modestly "brother of James." See my *Introduction*. **to them ... sanctified by God the Father**—The oldest MSS. and versions, ORIGEN, LUCIFER, and others read, "beloved" for *sanctified*. If *English Version* be read, cf. Colossians 1:12; I Peter 1:2. The *Greek* is not "by," but "in." God the Father's *love* is the element IN which they are "beloved." Thus the conclusion, vs. 21, corresponds, "Keep yourselves *in* the love of God." Cf. "beloved of the Lord" II

Thessalonians 2:13. **preserved in Jesus Christ**—"kept." Translate not "in," but as *Greek*, "FOR Jesus Christ." "Kept *continually* (so the *Greek perfect* participle means) by God the Father for Jesus Christ," against the day of His coming. Jude, beforehand, mentions the source and guarantee for the final accomplishment of believers' salvation; lest they should be disheartened by the dreadful evils which he proceeds to announce [BENGEL]. **and called**—predicated of "them that are beloved in God the Father, and preserved in Jesus Christ: who are called." God's effectual *calling* in the exercise of His divine prerogative, guarantees their eternal safety. **2. Mercy**—in a time of wretchedness. Therefore *mercy* stands first; the mercy of *Christ* (vs. 21). **peace**—in the *Holy Ghost* (vs. 20). **love**—of *God* (vs. 21). The three answer to the divine Trinity. **be multiplied**—in you and towards you. **3.** Design of the Epistle (cf. vss. 20, 21). **all diligence**—(II Pet. 1:5). As the minister is to give *all diligence* to admonish, so the people should, in accordance with his admonition, give *all diligence* to have all Christian graces, and to make their calling sure. **the common salvation**—wrought by Christ. Cf. *Note*, "obtained LIKE precious faith," II Pet. 1:1. This *community of faith*, and of the object of faith, *salvation,* forms the ground of mutual exhortation by appeals to common hopes and fears. **it was needful for me**—rather, "I felt it necessary to write (now *at once;* so the *Greek* aorist means; the *present* infinitive 'to write,' which precedes, expresses merely the general fact of writing) exhorting you." The reason why he felt it necessary "to write *with exhortation,*" he states, vs. 4, "For there are certain men crept in. . . ." Having intended to write generally of *the common salvation,* he found it necessary from the existing evils in the Church, to write specially that they should *contend for the faith against* those evils. **earnestly contend**—Cf. Philippians 1:27, "striving together for the faith of the Gospel." **once . . .**—*Greek,* "*once for all* delivered. . . ." No other faith or revelation is to supersede it. A strong argument for resisting heretical innovators (vs. 4). Believers, like Nehemiah's workmen, with one hand "build themselves up in their most holy faith"; with the other they" contend earnestly for the faith" against its foes. **the saints** —all Christians, *holy* (i.e., consecrated to God) by their calling, and in God's design. **4. certain men** —implying disparagement. **crept in unawares**— stealthily and unlawfully. *Note,* II Peter 2:1, "*privily* shall bring in damnable heresies." **before . . . ordained**—*Greek,* "forewritten," viz., in Peter's prophecy vss. 17, 18; and in Paul's before that, I Tim. 4:1; II Tim. 3:1; and by implication in the judgments which overtook the apostate angels. The disobedient Israelites, Sodom and Gomorrah, Balaam and Core, and which are *written* "for an example" (vs. 7, and vss. 5, 6, 11). God's eternal character as the Punisher of sin, as set forth in Scripture "of old," is the ground on which such apostate characters are ordained to condemnation. Scripture is the reflection of God's book of life in which believers are "written among the living." "Forewritten" is applied also in Romans 15:4 to the things written in Scripture. Scripture itself reflects God's character from everlasting, which is the ground of His decrees from everlasting. BENGEL explains it as an abbreviated phrase for, "They were *of old fore*told by Enoch (vs. 14, who did not *write* his prophecies), and afterwards marked out by the *written* word." **to this condemnation**—Jude graphically puts their judgment as it were present before the eyes, "THIS." Enoch's prophecy comprises the "ungodly men" of the last days before Christ's coming to judgment, as well as their forerunners, the "ungodly men" before the flood, the type of the last judgment (Matt. 24:37-39; II Pet. 3:3-7). The disposition and the doom of both correspond. **the grace of our God**—A phrase for the Gospel especially sweet to believers who appropriate God in Christ as "*our* God," and so rendering the more odious the vile perversity of those who turn the Gospel state of grace and liberty into a ground of licentiousness, as if their exemption from the law gave them a license to *sin.* **denying the only Lord**—The oldest MSS., versions, and Fathers omit "God," which follows in *English Version.* Translate as the *Greek,* "the only Master"; here used of *Jesus Christ,* who is at once *Master* and "Lord" (a different *Greek* word). So II Peter 2:1, *Note.* By virtue of Christ's perfect oneness with the Father, He, as well as the Father, is termed "the ONLY" God and "MASTER." *Greek,* "Master," implies God's *absolute ownership* to dispose of His creatures as He likes. **5.** (Heb. 3:16; 4:13). **therefore**—Other oldest MSS. and *Vulgate* read, "But"; in contrast to the ungodly vs. 4. **though ye once**—rather, "once for all." Translate, "I wish to remind you, *as* knowing ALL (viz., *that I am re-*

ferring to; so the oldest MSS., versions, and Fathers) *once for all.*" *As* already they know all the facts once for all, he needs only to "remind" them. **the Lord**—The oldest MSS. and versions read, "Jesus." So "Christ" is said to have accompanied the Israelites in the wilderness; so perfectly is Jesus one with the God of the Israelite theocracy. **saved**—brought safely, and into a state of safety and salvation. **afterward**—*Greek,* "secondly"; in the next instance "destroyed them that believed not," as contrasted with His *in the first instance* having *saved* them. **6.** (II Pet. 2:4.) **kept not their first estate**—*Vulgate* translates, "their own *principality,*" which the fact of angels being elsewhere called "principalities," favors: "their own" implies that, instead of being content with the *dignity* once for all assigned to them under the Son of God, they aspired higher. ALFORD thinks the narrative in Genesis 6:2 is alluded to, not the fall of the devil and his angels, as he thinks "giving themselves over to fornication" (vs. 7) proves; cf. *Greek,* "in like manner *to these,*" viz., to the angels (vs. 6). It seems to me more natural to take "sons of God" (Gen. 6:2) of the Sethites, than of angels, who, as "spirits," do not seem capable of carnal connection. The parallel, II Peter 2:4, plainly refers to the fall of the apostate angels. And "in like manner *to these,*" vs. 7, refers to *the inhabitants of Sodom and Gomorrah,* "the cities about them" sinning "in like manner" as *they* did [ESTIUS and CALVIN]. Even if *Greek* "these," vs. 7, refer to *the angels,* the sense of "in like manner as these" will be, not that the angels carnally *fornicated* with the daughters of men, but that their ambition, whereby their affections went *away from* God and they fell, is in God's view a sin of like kind spiritually as Sodom's going *away* from God's order of nature after strange flesh; the sin of the apostate angels after their kind is analogous to that of the human Sodomites after their kind. Cf. the somewhat similar spiritual connection of *whoremongers* and *covetousness.* The apocryphal book of Enoch interprets Genesis 6:2 as ALFORD. But though Jude accords with it in some particulars, it does not follow that he accords with it in all. The Hebrews name the fallen angels Aza and Azael. **left**—on their own accord. **their own**—*Greek,* "their proper." **habitation**—heaven, all bright and glorious, as opposed to the "*darkness*" to which they now are doomed. Their ambitious designs seem to have had a peculiar connection with this earth, of which Satan before his fall may have been God's vicegerent, whence arises his subsequent connection with it as first the Tempter, then "the prince of this world." **reserved**—As the *Greek* is the same, and there is an evident reference to *their* having "*kept not* their first estate," translate, "He hath kept." Probably what is meant is, He hath kept them *in His purpose;* that is their sure doom; moreover, as yet, Satan and his demons roam at large on the earth. An earnest of their doom is their having been cast out of heaven, being already restricted to "the darkness of this present world," the "air" that surrounds the earth, their peculiar element now. They lurk in places of gloom and death, looking forward with agonizing fear to their final torment in the bottomless pit. He means not literal chains and darkness, but figurative in this present world where, with restricted powers and liberties, shut out from heaven, they, like condemned prisoners, await their doom. **7. Even as**—ALFORD translates, "I wish to remind you (vs. 5) *that.*" **Sodom . . .**—(II Pet. 2:6). **giving themselves over to fornication**—following fornication *extraordinarily,* i.e., *out of the* order of nature. On "in like manner *to them*" (*Greek*), cf. *Note,* vs. 6. Cf. on spiritual fornication, "go a *whoring from thee,*" Psalm 73: 27. **going after strange flesh**—departing from the course of nature, and going after that which is unnatural. In later times the most enlightened heathen nations indulged in the sin of Sodom without compunction or shame. **are set forth**—before our eyes. **suffering**—undergoing *to this present time;* alluding to the marks of volcanic fire about the Dead Sea. **the vengeance**—*Greek,* "righteous retribution." **eternal fire**—The lasting marks of the fire that consumed the cities irreparably, is a type of the eternal fire to which the inhabitants have been consigned. BENGEL translates as the *Greek* will admit, "*Suffering (the) punishment* (which they endure) as an example or *sample of eternal fire* (viz., that which shall consume the wicked)." Ezekiel 16:53-55 shows that Sodom's punishment, as a nation, is *not eternal.* Cf. also II Peter 2:6. **8. also**—rather, "In like manner nevertheless" (notwithstanding these warning examples) [ALFORD]. **these ... dreamers**—The *Greek* has not "*filthy*" of English Version. The clause, "these men dreaming" (i.e., in their dreams), belongs to all the verbs, "defile," "despise," and "speak evil." All sinners are spiritually asleep, and their carnal activity is as it were a *dream* (I Thess. 5:6, 7). Their *speaking evil of dignities* is because they are *dreaming,* and *know not what they are speaking evil of* (vs. 10). "As a man dreaming seems to himself to be seeing and nearing many things, so the natural man's lusts are agitated by joy, distress, fear, and the other passions. But he is a stranger to self-command. Hence, though he bring into play all the powers of reason, he cannot conceive the true liberty which the sons of light, who are awake and in the daylight; enjoy" [BENGEL]. **defile the flesh**—(*V.* 7). **dominion**—"lordship." **dignities**—lit., "glories." Earthly and heavenly *dignities.* **9. Michael, the archangel**—Nowhere in Scripture is the plural used, "archangels"; but only ONE, "archangel." The only other passage in the New Testament where it occurs, is I Thessalonians 4:16, where Christ is distinguished from the archangel, with whose voice He shall descend to raise the dead; they therefore err who confound Christ with Michael. The name means, *Who is like God?* In Daniel 10:13 he is called "One (*Margin, the first*) of the chief princes." He is the champion angel of Israel. In Revelation 12:7 the conflict between Michael and Satan is again alluded to. **about the body of Moses**—his literal body. Satan, as having the power of death, opposed the raising of it again, on the ground of Moses' sin at Meribah, and his murder of the Egyptian. That Moses' body was raised, appears from his presence with Elijah and Jesus (who were in the body) at the Transfiguration: the sample and earnest of the coming resurrection-kingdom, to be ushered in by Michael's standing up for God's people. Thus in each dispensation a sample and pledge of the future resurrection was given: Enoch in the patriarchal dispensation, Moses in the Levitical, Elijah in the prophetical. It is noteworthy that the same rebuke is recorded here as was used by the Angel of the Lord, or Jehovah the Second Person, in pleading for Joshua, the representative of the Jewish Church, against Satan, in Zechariah 3:2; whence some have thought that also here "the body of Moses" means the Jewish Church accused by Satan, before God, for its filthiness, on which ground he demands that divine justice should take its course against Israel, but is rebuked by the Lord who has "chosen Jerusalem": thus, as "the body of Christ" is *the Christian Church,* so "the body of Moses" is the Jewish Church. But the literal body is evidently here meant (though, secondarily, the Jewish Church is typified by Moses' body, as it was there represented by Joshua the high priest); and Michael, whose connection seems to be so close with Jehovah-Messiah on the one hand, and with Israel on the other, naturally uses the same language as his Lord. As Satan (*adversary* in court) or the devil (*accuser*) accuses alike the Church collectively and "the brethren" individually, so Christ pleads for us as our Advocate. Israel's, and all believers' full justification, and the accuser's being rebuked finally, is yet future. JOSEPHUS, *Antiquities,* 4. 8, states that God hid Moses' body, lest, if it had been exposed to view, it would have been made an idol of. Jude, in this account, either adopts it from the aprocryphal "assumption of Moses" (as ORIGEN, *concerning Principalities,* 3. 2, thinks), or else from the ancient tradition on which that work was founded. *Jude,* as inspired, could distinguish how much of the tradition was true, how much false. *We* have no such means of distinguishing, and therefore can be sure of no tradition, save that which is in the *written word.* **durst not**—from reverence for Satan's former *dignity* (vs. 8). **railing accusation**—*Greek,* "judgment of blasphemy," or *evil-speaking.* Peter said, Angels do not, in order to avenge themselves, rail at dignities, though ungodly, when they have to contend with them: Jude says that the archangel Michael himself did not rail even at the time when he fought with the devil, the prince of evil spirits—not from fear of him, but from reverence of God, whose delegated power in this world Satan once had, and even in some degree still has. From the word "disputed," or *debated in controversy,* it is plain it was a judicial contest. **10.** (II Peter 2:12.) **those things which**—*Greek,* "all things whatsoever they understand *not,*" viz., the things of the spiritual world. **but what ... naturally**—Connect thus, "*Whatever* (so the *Greek*) things naturally (by natural, blind instinct), as the unreasoning (so the *Greek*) animals, they know...." The *Greek* for the former "know" implies deeper knowledge; the latter "know," the mere perception of the "animal senses and faculties." **11. Woe**—*Note,* II Peter 2: 14, "*cursed* children." **Cain**—the murderer: the root of whose sin was hatred and envy of the godly, as it is the sin of these seducers. **ran greedily**—lit., "have been poured forth" like a torrent that has burst its banks. Reckless of what it costs, the loss of God's favor and heaven, on they rush after gain like Balaam. **perished in the gainsaying of Core**—(Cf. *Note,* vs. 12). When we read of Korah perishing by gainsaying, we read virtually also of these perishing in like manner through the same: for the same seed bears the same harvest. **12. spots**—So II Peter 2:13, *Greek, spiloi;* but here the *Greek* is *spilades,* which elsewhere, in secular writers, means *rocks,* viz., on which the Christian *love feasts* are in danger of being shipwrecked. The oldest MS. prefixes the article emphatically, "THE rocks." The reference to "clouds ... winds ... waves of the sea," accords with this image of *rocks. Vulgate* seems to have been misled by the similar sounding word to translate, as *English Version,* "spots"; cf. however, vs. 23, which favors *English Version,* if the *Greek* will bear it. Two oldest MSS., by the transcriber's effort to make Jude say the same as Peter, read here "deceivings" for "love feasts," but the weightiest MS. and authorities support *English Version* reading. The love feast accompanied the Lord's Supper (I Cor. 11, end). Korah the Levite, not satisfied with his *ministry,* aspired to the *sacrificing priest-hood* also: so ministers in the Lord's Supper have sought to make it a *sacrifice,* and themselves the *sacrificing* priests, usurping the function of our only Christian sacerdotal *Priest,* Christ Jesus. Let them beware of Korahs doom! **feeding themselves—***Greek,* "pasturing (tending) themselves." What they look to is the pampering of *themselves,* not the feeding of the flock. **without fear—**Join these words not as *English Version,* but with "feast." Sacred feasts especially ought to be celebrated *with fear.* Feasting is not faulty in itself [BENGEL], but it needs to be accompanied with *fear* of forgetting God, as Job in the case of his sons' feasts. **clouds—**from which one would expect refreshing rains. II Peter 2:17, "wells without water." Professors without practice. **carried about—**The oldest MSS. have "carried aside," i.e., out of the right course (cf. Eph. 4:14). **trees whose fruit withereth—**rather, "trees of the late (or *waning*) autumn," viz., when there are no longer leaves or fruits on the trees [BENGEL]. **without fruit—**having no good fruit of knowledge and practice; sometimes used of what is positively *bad.* **twice dead—**First when they cast their leaves in autumn, and seem during winter *dead,* but revive again in spring; secondly, when they are "plucked up by the roots." So these apostates, once dead in unbelief, and then by profession and baptism raised from the death of sin to the life of righteousness, but now having become *dead again* by apostasy, and so *hopelessly dead.* There is a climax. Not only *without leaves,* like *trees in late autumn,* but *without fruit:* not only so, but dead twice; and to crown all, "plucked up by the roots." **13. Raging—**wild. Jude has in mind Isaiah 57:29. **shame—**plural in *Greek,* "shames" (cf. Phil. 3:19). **wandering stars**—instead of moving on in a regular orbit, as lights to the world, bursting forth on the world like erratic comets, or rather, meteors of fire, with a strange glare, and then doomed to fall back again into the blackness of gloom. **14.** See *Introduction* on the source whence Jude derived this prophecy of Enoch. The Holy Spirit, by Jude, has sealed the truth of this much of the matter contained in the book of Enoch, though probably that book, as well as Jude, derived it from tradition (cf. *Note,* vs. 9). There are reasons given by some for thinking the book of Enoch copied from Jude rather than vice versa. It is striking how, from the first, prophecy hastened towards its consummation. The earliest prophecies of the Redeemer dwell on His second coming in glory, rather than His first coming in lowliness (cf. Gen. 3:15 with Rom. 16:20). Enoch, in his translation without death, illustrated that truth which he all his life preached to the unbelieving world, the certainty of the Lord's coming, and the resurrection of the dead, as the only effectual antidote to their skepticism and self-wise confidence in nature's permanence. **And Enoch—***Greek,* "Moreover, also Enoch. . . ." **seventh from Adam—***Seven* is the sacred number. In Enoch, freedom from death and the sacred number are combined: for every seventh object is most highly valued. Jude thus shows the antiquity of the prophecies. Cf. "of old," *Note,* vs. 4. There were only *five* fathers between Enoch and Adam. The *seventh* from Adam prophesied the things which shall close the *seventh age* of the world [BENGEL]. **of these—**in relation to these. The reference of his prophecies was not to the antediluvians alone, but to *all* the ungodly (vs. 15). His prophecy applied primarily indeed to the flood, but ultimately to the final judgment. **cometh—**lit., "came." Phophecy regards the future as certain as if it were *past.* **saints—**Holy angels (cf. Deut. 33:2; Dan. 7:10 Zech. 14:5; Matt. 25:31; Heb. 12:22). **15.** This verse and the beginning of Enoch's ᵖrophecy is composed in Hebrew poetic parallelism, the oldest specimen extant. Some think Lamech's speech, which is also in poetic parallelism, was composed in mockery of Enoch's prophecy: as Enoch foretold Jehovah's coming to judgment, so Lamech presumes on impunity in polygamy and murder (just as Cain the murderer seemed to escape with impunity). **convince—**convict. **hard speeches—**such as are noticed in vss. 8, 10, 16; Malachi 3:13, 14; contrast 16:17. **ungodly sinners** —not merely *sinners,* but proud *despisers of God: impious.* **against him—**They who speak against God's children are regarded by God as speaking *against Himself.* **16. murmurers—**in secret: *muttering murmurs* against God's ordinances and ministers in Church and state. Cf. vs. 8, "speak evil of dignities"; 15, "hard speeches"; against the Lord. **complainers—**never satisfied with their lot (Num. 11:1; cf. the penalty, Deut. 28:47, 48). **walking after their own lusts—**(vs. 18). The secret of their *murmuring* and *complaining* is the restless insatiability of their desires. **great swelling words—**(II Pet. 2:18). **men's persons—**their mere outward appearance and rank. **because of advantage—**for the sake of what they may gain from them. While they *talk great swelling words,* they are really mean and fawning towards those of wealth and rank. **17. But; beloved . . . ye—**in contrast to those reprobates, vs. 20, again. **remember—**implying that his readers had been contemporaries of the apostles. For Peter uses the very same formula in reminding the contemporaries of himself and the other apostles. **spoken before—**spoken already before now. **the apostles—**Peter (*Notes,* II Pet. 3:2, 3), and Paul before Peter (Acts 20:29; I Tim. 4:1; II Tim. 3:1). Jude does not exclude himself from the number of *the apostles* here, for in vs. 18, immediately after, he says, "they told you," not *us* (rather as *Greek,* "used to tell you" implying that Jude's readers were contemporaries of the apostles, who *used to tell* them). **18. mockers—**In the parallel, II Peter 3:3, the same *Greek* is translated, "scoffers." The word is found nowhere else in the New Testament. How ALFORD can deny that II Peter 3:2, 3 is referred to (at least in part), I cannot imagine, seeing that Jude quotes the very words of *Peter* as the words which *the apostles* used to speak to his (Jude's) readers. **walk after their own ungodly lusts—**lit., "after (according to) their own lusts *of ungodliness.*" **19. These be they—**showing that their characters are such as Peter and Paul had foretold. **separate themselves—**from Church communion in its vital, spiritual reality: for outwardly they took part in Church ordinances (vs. 12). Some oldest MSS. omit "themselves": then understand it, "separate," cast out members of the Church by excommunication (Isa. 65:5; 66:5; Luke 6:22; John 9:34; cf. "casteth them out of the Church," III John 10). Many, however, understand "themselves," which indeed is read in some of the oldest MSS. as *English Version* has it. Arrogant setting up of themselves, as having greater sanctity and a wisdom and peculiar doctrine, distinct from others, is implied. **sensual—**lit., "animal-souled": as opposed to the *spiritual,* or "having the Spirit." It is translated, "the *natural* man," I Corinthians 2:14. In the threefold division of man's being, *body, soul, and spirit,* the due state in God's design is, that "the spirit," which is the recipient of the Holy Spirit uniting man to God, should be first, and should rule the soul, which stands intermediate between *the body* and *spirit;* but in the *animal,* or *natural* man, the spirit is sunk into subserviency to the animal soul, which is earthly in its motives and aims. The "carnal" sink somewhat lower, for in these *the flesh,* the lowest element and corrupt side of man's bodily nature, reigns paramount. **having not the Spirit**—In the animal and natural man *the spirit,* his higher part, which ought to be the receiver of the Holy Spirit, is not so; and therefore, his spirit not being in its normal state, he is said *not to have the spirit* (cf. John 3:5, 6). In the completion of redemption the parts of redeemed man shall be placed in their due relation: whereas in the ungodly, *the soul* severed from *the spirit* shall have for ever animal life without union to God and heaven—a living death. **20.** Resuming vs. 17. **building up yourselves**—the opposite to the "separate themselves" (vs. 19): as "in the Holy Ghost" is opposed to "having not the Spirit." **on**—as *on* a foundation. *Building on* THE FAITH is equivalent to building on *Christ,* the object of faith. **praying in the Holy Ghost**—(Rom. 8:26; Eph. 6:18). The Holy Spirit teaches *what we are* to pray for, and *how.* None can pray aright save by being *in the Spirit,* i.e., in the element of His influence. CHRYSOSTOM states that, among the charisms bestowed at the beginning of the New Testament dispensation, was *the gift of prayer,* bestowed on someone who prayed in the name of the rest, and taught others to pray. Moreover, their prayers so conceived and often used, were received and preserved among Christians, and out of them forms of prayer were framed. Such is the origin of liturgies [HAMMOND]. **21.** In vss. 20, 21, Jude combines the Father, the Son, and the Holy Ghost: and *faith, hope,* and *love.* **Keep yourselves**—not in your own strength, but "in the love of God," i.e., *God's love to you* and all His believing children, the only guarantee for their being *kept* safe. Man's need of watching is implied; at the same time he cannot *keep* himself, unless God in His love keep him. **looking for**—in hope. **the mercy of our Lord Jesus Christ**—to be fully manifested at His coming. *Mercy* is usually attributed to the Father: here to the Son; so entirely one are they. **22, 23.** None but those who "keep themselves" are likely to "save" others. **have compassion**—So one oldest MS. reads. But two oldest MSS., *Vulgate,* etc., read, "convict"; "reprove to their conviction"; "confute, so as to convince." **making a difference**—The oldest MSS. and versions read the accusative for the nominative, "when separating themselves" [WAHL], referring to vs. 19; or "when contending with you," as the *Greek* is translated, vs. 9. **23. save with fear**—The oldest MSS. do not read "with fear" in this position: but after "snatching them out of the fire" (with which,

cf. Amos 4:11; I Cor. 3:15; Zech. 3:2, said of a most narrow escape), they add the following words, forming a THIRD class, "and others compassionate with (IN) fear." Three kinds of patients require three kinds of medical treatment. Ministers and Christians are said to "save" those whom they are made the instruments of saving; the *Greek* for "save" is present, therefore meaning "try to save." Jude already (vs. 9) had reference to the same passage (Zech. 3:1-3). The three classes are: (1) those who *contend with you* (accusative in oldest MSS.), whom you should *convict;* (2) those who are as brands already in *the fire,* of which hell-fire is the consummation: these you should *try to save by snatching them out;* (3) those who are objects of *compassion,* whom accordingly you should *compassionate* (and help if occasion should offer), but at the same time not let pity degenerate into connivance at their error. Your compassion is to be accompanied "with fear" of being at all defiled by them. **hating**—Even *hatred* has its legitimate field of exercise. Sin is the only thing which God hates: so ought we. **even the garment**—a proverbial phrase: avoiding the most remote contact with sin, and hating that which borders on it. As *garments* of the apostles wrought miracles of good in healing, so the very *garment* of sinners metaphorically, i.e., anything brought into contact with their pollution, is to be avoided. Cf. as to lepers and other persons defiled, Leviticus 13: 52-57; 15:4-17: the garments were held polluted; and anyone touching them was excluded, until purified, from religious and civil communion with the sanctified people of Israel. Christians who received at baptism the white garment in token of purity, are not to defile it by any approach to what is defiled. **24, 25.** Concluding doxology. **Now**—*Greek,* "But." **you**—ALFORD, on inferior authority, reads, "them." *You* is in contradistinction to those *ungodly men* mentioned above. **keep . . . from falling**—rather, "guard . . . (so as to be) *without falling,*" or *stumbling.* **faultless**—*Greek,* "blameless." **before the presence of his glory**—i.e., *before Himself,* when He shall be revealed in *glory.* **with exceeding joy**—lit., "with exultation" as of those who *leap* for joy. **To the only . . . God our Saviour**—The oldest MSS. add, "through Jesus Christ our Lord." The transcribers, fancying that "Saviour" applied to Christ alone, omitted the words. The sense is, To the only God (the Father) who is our Saviour through (i.e., by the mediation of) Jesus Christ our Lord. **dominion**—*Greek,* "might." **power** —*authority: legitimate power.* The oldest MSS. and *Vulgate,* after "power," have "before all the age," i.e., before all time as to the *past;* "and now," as to the present; "and to all the ages," i.e., *for ever,* as to the time to come.

THE REVELATION

OF ST. JOHN THE DIVINE

INTRODUCTION

AUTHENTICITY.—The author calls himself *John* (ch. 1:1, 4, 9; 22:8). JUSTIN MARTYR (*Dialogue,* p. 308, A.D. 139–161) quotes from the Apocalypse, as *John the apostle's* work, the prophecy of the millennium of the saints, to be followed by the general resurrection and judgment. This testimony of Justin is referred to also by EUSEBIUS (*Ecclesiastical History* 4. 18). JUSTIN, in the early part of the second century, held his controversy with Trypho, a learned Jew, at *Ephesus*, where John had been living thirty or thirty-five years before: he says that "the Revelation had been given to John, one of the twelve apostles of Christ." MELITO, bishop of *Sardis* (about A.D. 171), *one of the seven churches addressed*, a successor, therefore, of one of the seven angels, is said by EUSEBIUS (*Ecclesiastical History* 4. 26) to have written treatises on the Apocalypse *of John*. The testimony of the bishop of Sardis is the more impartial, as Sardis is one of the churches severely reproved (ch. 3:1). So also THEOPHILUS OF ANTIOCH (about A.D. 180), according to EUSEBIUS 4. 26, quoted testimonies from the Apocalypse of John. EUSEBIUS says the same of Apollonius, who lived in Asia Minor in the end of the second century. IRENÆUS (about A.D. 180), a hearer of Polycarp, the disciple of John, and supposed by ARCHBISHOP USHER to be the *angel of the Church of Smyrna*, is most decided again and again in quoting the Apocalypse as the work of the apostle John (*Hæreses* 4., 20. 11; 4., 21. 3; 4., 30. 4; 5., 36. 1; 5., 30. 3; 5., 35. 2). In 5., 30. 1, alluding to the mystical number of the beast, 666 (ch. 13:18), found in all old copies, he says, "We do not hazard a confident theory as to the name of Antichrist; for if it had been necessary that his name should be proclaimed openly at the present time, it would have been declared by him who saw the apocalyptic vision; *for it was seen at no long time back, but almost in our generation, towards the end of Domitian's reign.*" In his work *against heresies*, published ten years after Polycarp's martyrdom, he quotes the Apocalypse twenty times, and makes long extracts from it, as inspired Scripture. These testimonies of persons contemporary with John's immediate successors, and more or less connected with the region of the seven churches to which Revelation is addressed, are most convincing. TERTULLIAN, of North Africa (about A.D. 220), *Adversus Marcion* 3. 14, quotes the apostle John's descriptions in the Apocalypse of the sword proceeding out of the Lord's mouth (ch. 19:15), and of the heavenly city (ch. 21). Cf. *De Resurrectione* 27; *De Anima* 8, 9, etc.; *De Præscriptione Hæreticorum* 33. The MURATORI fragment of the canon (about A.D. 200) refers to John the apostle writing to the seven churches. HIPPOLYTUS, bishop of Ostia, near Rome (about A.D. 240), *De Antichristo*, p. 67, quotes ch. 17:1–18, as the writing of John the apostle. Among Hippolytus' works, there is specified in the catalogue on his statue, a treatise "on the Apocalypse and Gospel according to John." CLEMENT OF ALEXANDRIA (about A.D. 200), *Stromata* 6. 13, alludes to the twenty-four seats on which the elders sit as mentioned by John in the Apocalypse (ch. 4:5); also, in *Quis dives Salvus*, sec. 42, he mentions John's return from Patmos to Ephesus on the death of the Roman tyrant. ORIGEN (about A.D. 233), *Commentary on Matthew*, in EUSEBIUS (*Ecclesiastical History* 6. 25), mentions John as the author of the Apocalypse, without expressing any doubts as to its authenticity; also, in *Commentary on Matthew*, tom. 16. 6, he quotes ch. 1:9, and says, "John seems to have beheld the Apocalypse in the island of Patmos." VICTORINUS, bishop of Pettau in Pannonia, who suffered martyrdom under Diocletian in A.D. 303, wrote the earliest extant commentary on the Apocalypse. Though the *Old Syriac Peschito version* does not contain the Apocalypse, yet EPHREM SYRUS (about A.D. 378) frequently quotes the Apocalypse as canonical, and ascribes it to John.

Its *canonicity* and inspiration (according to a schollum of ANDREAS OF CAPPADOCIA) are attested by PAPIAS, a hearer of John, and associate of POLYCARP. PAPIAS was bishop of Hierapolis, near *Laodicea*, one of the seven churches. WORDSWORTH conjectures that a feeling of shame, on account of the rebukes of Laodicea in Revelation, may have operated on the Council of *Laodicea*, so as to omit Revelation from its list of books to be *read publicly*. (?) The Epistle of the churches of Lyons and Vienne to the churches of Asia and Phrygia (in EUSEBIUS, *Ecclesiastical History* 5. 1–3), in the persecution under M. Aurelius (A.D. 77) quotes ch. 1:5; 3:14; 14:4, and 22:11, as Scripture. CYPRIAN (about A.D. 250) also, in *Ep.* 13, quotes ch. 2:5 as Scripture; and in *Ep.* 25 he quotes ch. 3:21, as of the same authority as the Gospel. (For other instances, see ALFORD's *Prolegomena*, from whom mainly this summary of evidence has been derived.) ATHANASIUS, in his *Festival Epistle*, enumerates the Apocalypse among the *canonical* Scriptures, to which none must add, and from which none must take away. JEROME (in *Epistola ad Paulinum*) includes in the canon the Apocalypse, adding, "It has as many mysteries as words. All praise falls short of its merits. In each of its words lie hid manifold senses." Thus an unbroken chain of testimony down from the apostolic period confirms its canonicity and authenticity.

The ALOGI (*Epiphanius Hæreses* 51) and CAIUS the Roman presbyter (EUSEBIUS 3. 28), towards the end of the second and beginning of the third century, rejected John's Apocalypse on mere captious grounds. CAIUS, according to JEROME, *De Viris Illustribus*, about A.D. 210, attributed it to Cerinthus, on the ground of its supporting the millennial reign on earth. DIONYSIUS OF ALEXANDRIA mentions many before his time who rejected it because of its obscurity and because it seemed to support Cerinthus' dogma of an earthly and carnal kingdom; whence they attributed it to Cerinthus. This DIONYSIUS, scholar of ORIGEN, and bishop of Alexandria (A.D. 247), admits its inspiration (in EUSEBIUS, *Ecclesiastical History* 7. 10), but attributes it to some John distinct from John the apostle, on the ground of its difference of style and character, as compared with John's Gospel and Epistle, as also because the name John is several times mentioned in the Apocalypse, which is always kept back in both the Gospel and Epistle; moreover, neither does the Epistle make any allusion to the Apocalypse, nor the Apocalypse to the Epistle; and the style is not pure Greek, but abounds in barbarisms and solecisms. EUSEBIUS wavers in opinion (*Ecclesiastical History* 24. 39) as to whether it is, or is not, to be ranked among the undoubtedly canonical Scriptures. His antipathy to the millennial doctrine would give an unconscious bias to his judgment on the Apocalypse. CYRIL OF JERUSALEM (A.D. 386), *Catechesis* 4. 35, 36, omits the Apocalypse in enumerating the New Testament Scriptures to be read privately as well as publicly. "Whatever is not read in the churches, that do not even read by thyself; the apostles and ancient bishops of the Church who transmitted them to us were far wiser than thou art." Hence, we see that, in his day, the Apocalypse was not read in the churches. Yet in *Catechesis* 1. 4 he quotes ch. 2:7, 17; and in *Catechesis* 1., 15. 13 he draws the prophetical statement from ch. 17:11, that the king who is to humble the three kings (Dan. 7:8, 20) is the *eighth king*. In c. 15. and 27. he similarly quotes from ch. 12:3, 4. ALFORD conjectures that CYRIL had at some time changed his opinion, and that these references to the Apocalypse were slips of memory whereby he retained phraseology which belonged to his former, not his subsequent views. The sixtieth canon (if genuine) of the Laodicean

Council in the middle of the fourth century omits the Apocalypse from the canonical books. The Eastern Church in part doubted, the Western Church, after the fifth century, universally recognized, the Apocalypse. CYRIL OF ALEXANDRIA, *De Adoratione* 146, though implying the fact of some doubting its genuineness, himself undoubtedly accepts it as the work of St. John. ANDREAS OF CÆSAREA, in Cappadocia, recognized as genuine and canonical, and wrote the first entire and connected commentary on, the Apocalypse. The sources of doubt seem to have been, (1) the antagonism of many to the millennium, which is set forth in it; (2) its obscurity and symbolism having caused it not to be read in the churches, or to be taught to the young. But *the most primitive* tradition is unequivocal in its favor. In a word, the objective evidence is decidedly for it; the only arguments against it seem to have been subjective.

The personal notices of John in the Apocalypse occur ch. 1:1, 4, 9; 22:8. Moreover, the writer's addresses to the churches of Proconsular *Asia* (ch. 2:1) accord with the concurrent tradition, that after John's return from his exile in Patmos, at the death of DOMITIAN, under Nerva, he resided for long, and died at last in Ephesus, in the time of Trajan (EUSEBIUS, *Ecclesiastical History* 3. 20, 23). If the Apocalypse were not the inspired work of John, purporting as it does to be an address from their superior to the seven churches of Proconsular Asia, it would have assuredly been rejected *in that region;* whereas the earliest testimonies *in those churches* are all in its favor. One person alone was entitled to use language of authority such as is addressed to the seven angels of the churches—namely, John, as the last surviving apostle and superintendent of all the churches. Also, it accords with John's manner to assert the accuracy of his testimony both at the beginning and end of his book (cf. ch. 1:2, 3, and 22:8, with John 1:14; 21:24; I John 1:1, 2). Again, it accords with the view of the writer being an *inspired apostle* that he addresses the angels or presidents of the several churches in the tone of a *superior* addressing inferiors. Also, he commends the Church of Ephesus for trying and convicting "them which *say they are apostles,* and are not," by which he implies his own undoubted claim to apostolic inspiration (ch. 2:2), as declaring in the seven epistles Christ's will revealed through him.

As to the difference of style, as compared with the Gospel and Epistle, *the difference of subject* in part accounts for it, the visions of the seer, transported as he was above the region of sense, appropriately taking a form of expression abrupt, and unbound by the grammatical laws which governed his writings of a calmer and more deliberate character. Moreover, as being a Galilean Hebrew, John, in writing a Revelation akin to the Old Testament prophecies, naturally reverted to their Hebraistic style. ALFORD notices, among the features of resemblance between the styles of the Apocalypse and John's Gospel and Epistle: (1) the characteristic appellation of our Lord, peculiar to John exclusively, "the Word of God" (ch. 19:13; cf. John 1:1; I John 1:1). (2) the phrase, "he that overcometh" (ch. 2:7, 11, 17; 3:5, 12, 21; 12:11; 15:2; 17:14; 21:7; cf. John 16:33; I John 2:13, 14; 4:4; 5:4, 5). (3) The *Greek* term (*alethinos*) for "true," as opposed to that which is shadowy and unreal (ch. 3:7, 14; 6:10; 15:3; 16:7; 19:2, 9, 11; 21:5; 22:6). This term, found only once in Luke (Luke 16:11), four times in Paul (I Thess. 1:9; Heb. 8:2; 9:24; 10:22), is found nine times in John's Gospel (John 1:9; 4:23, 37; 6:32; 7:28; 8:16; 15:1; 17:3; 19:35), twice in John's First Epistle (I John 2:8; 5:20), and ten times in Revelation (ch. 3:7, 14; 6:10; 15:3; 16:7; 19:2, 9, 11; 21:5; 22:6). (4) The *Greek* diminutive for "Lamb" (*arnion,* lit., "lambkin") occurs twenty-nine times in the Apocalypse, and the only other place where it occurs is John 21:15. In John's writings alone is Christ called *directly* "the Lamb" (John 1:29, 36). In I Peter 1:19, He is called "as a lamb without blemish," in allusion to Isaiah 53:7. So the use of "witness," or "testimony" (ch. 1:2, 9; 6:9; 11:7, etc.; cf. John 1:7, 8, 15, 19, 32; I John 1:2; 4:14; 5:6–11). "Keep the word," or "commandments" (ch. 3:8, 10; 12:17; cf. John 8:51, 55; 14:15). The assertion of the same thing positively and negatively (ch. 2:2, 6, 8, 13; 3:8, 17, 18; cf. John 1:3, 6, 7, 20; I John 2:27, 28). Cf. also I John 2:20, 27 with ch. 3:18, as to the spiritual *anointing.* The seeming solecisms of style are attributable to that inspired elevation which is above mere grammatical rules, and are designed to arrest the reader's attention by the peculiarity of the phrase, so as to pause and search into some deep truth lying beneath. The vivid earnestness of the inspired writer, handling a subject so transcending all others, raises him above all servile adherence to ordinary rules, so that at times he abruptly passes from one grammatical construction to another, as he graphically sets the thing described before the eye of the reader. This is not due to ignorance of grammar, for he "has displayed a knowledge of grammatical rules in other much more difficult constructions" [WINER]. *The connection of thought* is more attended to than mere grammatical connection. Another consideration to be taken into account is that two-fifths of the whole being the recorded language of others, he moulds his style accordingly. Cf. TREGELLES' *Introduction to Revelation from Heathen Authorities.*

TREGELLES well says (*New Testament Historic Evidence*), "There is no book of the New Testament for which we have such clear, ample, and numerous testimonies in the second century as we have in favor of the Apocalypse. The more closely the witnesses were connected with the apostle John (as was the case with Irenæus), the more explicit is their testimony. That doubts should prevail in after ages must have originated either in ignorance of the earlier testimony, or else from some supposed intuition of what an apostle *ought* to have written. The objections on the ground of internal *style* can weigh nothing against the actual evidence. It is in vain to argue, a priori, that John *could* not have written this book when we have the evidence of several competent witnesses that he *did* write it."

RELATION OF THE APOCALYPSE TO THE REST OF THE CANON.—GREGORY NYSSEN, tom. 3, p. 601, calls Revelation "the last book of grace." It completes the volume of inspiration, so that we are to look for no further revelation till Christ Himself shall come. Appropriately the last book completing the canon was written by John, the last survivor of the apostles. The New Testament is composed of the historical books, the Gospels and Acts, the doctrinal Epistles, and the one prophetical book, Revelation. The same apostle wrote the last of the Gospels, and probably the last of the Epistles, and the only prophetical book of the New Testament. All the books of the New Testament had been written, and were read in the Church assemblies, some years before John's death. His life was providentially prolonged that he might give the final attestation to Scripture. About the year A.D. 100, the bishops of Asia (the angels of the seven churches) came to John at EPHESUS, bringing him copies of the three Gospels, Matthew, Mark, and Luke, and desired of him a statement of his apostolical judgment concerning them; whereupon he pronounced them authentic, genuine, and inspired, and at their request added his own Gospel to complete the fourfold aspect of the Gospel of Christ (cf. MURATORI's *Canon;* EUSEBIUS 3. 24; JEROME, *Præmium in Matthæum;* VICTORINUS on the *Apocalypse;* THEODORET, *Mopsuestia*). A Greek divine, quoted in ALLATIUS, calls Revelation "the seal of the whole Bible." The canon would be incomplete without Revelation. Scripture is a complete whole, its component books, written in a period ranging over 1500 years, being mutually connected. Unity of aim and spirit pervades the entire, so that the end is the necessary sequence of the middle, and the middle of the beginning. Genesis presents before us man and his bride in innocence and blessedness, followed by man's fall through Satan's subtlety, and man's consequent misery, his exclusion from Paradise and its tree of life and delightful rivers. Revelation presents, in reverse order, man first liable to sin and death, but afterwards made conqueror through the blood of the Lamb; the first Adam and Eve, represented by the second Adam, Christ, and the Church. His spotless bride, in Paradise, with free access to the tree of life and the crystal water of life that flows from the throne of God. As Genesis foretold the bruising of the serpent's head by the woman's seed, so Revelation declares the final accomplishment of that prediction (chs. 19, 20).

PLACE AND TIME OF WRITING.—The best authorities among the Fathers state that John was exiled under Domitian (IRENÆUS, 5, 30; CLEMENT OF ALEXANDRIA; EUSEBIUS, *Ecclesiastical History* 3. 20). VICTORINUS says that he had to labor in the mines of Patmos. At Domitian's death, A.D. 95, he returned to Ephesus under the Emperor Nerva. Probably it was immediately after his return that he wrote, under divine inspiration, the account of the visions vouchsafed to him in Patmos (ch. 1:2, 9). However, ch. 10:4 seems to imply that he wrote the visions immediately after seeing them. Patmos is one of the Sporades. Its circumference is about thirty miles. "It was fitting that when forbidden to go beyond certain bounds of the earth's lands, he was permitted to penetrate the secrets of heaven" [BEDE, *Explan. Apocalypse* on ch. 1]. The following arguments favor an earlier date, viz., under Nero: (1) EUSEBIUS in(*Evangelical Demonstrations*) unites in the same sentence John's banishment with the stoning of James and the beheading of Paul, which were *under Nero.* (2) CLEMENS ALEXANDRINUS' story of the robber reclaimed by John, after he had pursued, and with difficulty overtaken him, accords better with John then being a younger man than under Domitian, when he was 100 years old. ARETHAS, in the sixth century, applies the sixth seal to the destruction of Jerusalem (A.D. 70), adding that the Apocalypse was written before that event. So the *Syriac version* states he was banished by Nero the Cæsar. Laodicea was overthrown by an earthquake (A.D. 60) but was immediately rebuilt, so that its being called "rich and increased with goods" is not incompatible with this book having been written under the Neronian persecution (A.D. 64). But the possible allusions to it in Hebrews 10:37; cf. ch. 1:4, 8; 4:8; 22:12; Hebrews 11:10; cf. ch. 21:14; Hebrews 12:22, 23; cf. ch. 14:1; Hebrews 8:1, 2; cf. ch. 11:19; 15:5; 21:3; Hebrews 4:12; cf. ch. 1:16; 2:12, 16; 19:13, 15; Hebrews 4:9; cf. ch. 20; also I Peter 1:7, 13; 4:13, with ch. 1:1; I Peter 2:9 with ch. 5:10; II Timothy 4:8, with ch. 2. 26, 27; 3:21; 11:18; Ephesians 6:12, with ch. 12:7–12; Philippians 4:3, with ch. 3:5; 13:8, 17:8; 20:12, 15; Colossians 1:18, with ch. 1:5; I Corinthians 15:52, with ch. 10:7; 11:15–18, make a date before the destruction of Laodicea possible. Cerinthus is stated to have died before John; as then he borrowed much in his Pseudo-Apocalypse from John's, it is likely the latter was at an earlier date than Domitian's reign. See TILLOCH's *Introduction to Apocalypse.* But the Pauline benediction (ch. 1:4) implies it was written after Paul's death under Nero.

TO WHAT READERS ADDRESSED.—The inscription states that it is addressed to the seven churches of Asia, i.e., Proconsular Asia. John's reason for fixing on the number *seven* (for there were more than seven churches in the region meant by "Asia," for instance, Magnesia and Tralles) was doubtless because *seven* is the sacred number implying totality and universality: so it is implied that John, through the medium of the seven churches, addresses in the Spirit the Church of all places and ages. The Church in its various states of spiritual life or deadness, in all ages and places, is represented by the seven churches, and is addressed with words of consolation or warning accordingly. Smyrna and Philadelphia alone of the seven are honored with unmixed praise, as faithful in tribulation and rich in good works. Heresies of a decided kind had by this time arisen in the churches of Asia, and the love of many had waxed cold, while others had advanced to greater zeal, and one had sealed his testimony with his blood.

OBJECT.—It begins with admonitory addresses to the seven churches from the divine Son of man, whom John saw in vision, after a brief introduction which sets forth the main subject of the book, viz., to "show unto His servants things which must shortly come to pass" (chs. 1–3). From ch. 4 to the end is mainly prophecy, with practical exhortations and consolations, however, interspersed, similar to those addressed to the seven churches (the representatives of the universal Church of every age), and so connecting the body of the book with its beginning, which therefore forms its appropriate introduction.

Three schools of interpreters exist: (1) The Preterists, who hold that almost the whole has been fulfilled. (2) The Historical Interpreters, who hold that it comprises the history of the Church from John's time to the end of the world, the seals being *chronologically* succeeded, by the trumpets and the trumpets by the vials. (3) The Futurists, who consider almost the whole as yet future, and to be fulfilled immediately before Christ's second coming. The first theory was not held by any of the earliest Fathers, and is only held now by Rationalists, who limit John's vision to things within his own horizon, pagan Rome's persecutions of Christians, and its consequently anticipated destruction. The Futurist school is open to this great objection: it would leave the Church of Christ unprovided with prophetical guidance or support under her fiery trials for 1700 or 1800 years. Now God has said, "Surely He will do nothing, but He revealeth His secrets unto His servants the prophets." The Jews had a succession of prophets who guided them with the light of prophecy: what their prophets were to them, that the apocalyptic Scriptures have been, and are, to us.

ALFORD, following ISAAC WILLIAMS, draws attention to the parallel connection between the Apocalypse and Christ's discourse on the Mount of Olives, recorded in Matthew 24. The seals plainly bring us down to the second coming of Christ, just as the trumpets also do (cf. ch. 6:12–17; 8:1, etc.; 11:15), and as the vials also do (ch. 16:17): all three run parallel, and end in the same point. Certain "catchwords" (as WORDSWORTH calls them) connect the three series of symbols together. They do not succeed one to the other in historical and chronological sequence, but move side by side, the subsequent series filling up in detail the same picture which the preceding series had drawn in outline. So VICTORINUS (on ch. 7:2), the earliest commentator on the Apocalypse, says, "The order of the things said is not to be regarded, since often the Holy Spirit, when He has run to the end of the last time, again returns to the same times, and supplies what He has less fully expressed." And PRIMASIUS (*Ad Apocalypsin in fine*), "In the trumpets he gives a description by a pleasing *repetition*, as is his custom."

At the very beginning, John hastens, by anticipation (as was the tendency of all the prophets), to the grand consummation. Ch. 1:7, "Behold, He cometh with clouds . . ."; 8, 17, "I am the beginning and *the ending*—the first and *the last.*" So the seven epistles exhibit the same anticipation of the end. Ch. 3:12, "Him that overcometh, I will write upon Him the name of my God, and the name of the city of my God, which is new Jerusalem, which cometh down out of heaven"; cf. at the close, ch. 21:2. So also ch. 2:28, "I will give him the morning star"; cf. at the close, 22:16, "I am the bright and morning star."

Again, the *earthquake* that ensues on the opening of the sixth seal is one of the catchwords, i.e., a link connecting chronologically this sixth seal with the sixth trumpet (ch. 9:13; 11:13): cf. also the seventh vial, ch. 16:17, 18. The concomitants of the opening of the sixth seal, it is plain, in no full and exhaustive sense apply to any event, save the terrors which shall overwhelm the ungodly just before the coming of the Judge.

Again, *the beast out of the bottomless pit*, between the sixth and seventh trumpets, connects this series with the section, chs. 12, 13, 14, concerning the Church and her adversaries.

Again, the sealing of the 144,000 under the sixth seal connects this seal with the section, chs. 12–14.

Again, the loosing of the four winds by the four angels standing on the four corners of the earth, under the sixth seal, answers to the loosing of the *four* angels at the Euphrates, under the sixth trumpet.

Moreover, links occur in the Apocalypse connecting it with the Old Testament. For instance, the "mouth speaking great things," connects the *beast that blasphemes against God, and makes war against the saints*, with *the little horn*, or at last king, who, arising after the ten kings, shall *speak against the Most High, and wear out the saints;* also, cf. the "forty-two months" (ch. 13:5), or "a thousand two hundred and threescore days" (ch. 12:6), with the "time, times, and the dividing of time," of Daniel 7:25. "Moreover, the "forty-two months," ch. 11:2, answering to ch. 12:6 and 13:5, link together the period under the sixth trumpet to the section, chs. 12, 13, 14.

AUBERLEN observes, "The history of salvation is mysteriously governed by holy numbers. They are the scaffolding of the organic edifice. They are not merely outward indications of time, but indications of nature and essence. Not only nature, but history, is based in numbers. Scripture and antiquity put numbers as the fundamental forms of things, where we put ideas." As number is the regulator of the relations and proportions of the natural world, so does it enter most frequently into the revelations of the Apocalypse, which sets forth the harmonies of the supernatural, the immediately Divine. Thus the most supernatural revelation leads us the farthest into the natural, as was to be expected, seeing the God of nature and of revelation is one. *Seven* is the number for perfection (cf. ch. 1:4; 4:5, the *seven* Spirits before the throne; also, ch. 5:6, the Lamb's *seven* horns and *seven* eyes). Thus *the seven churches* represent the Church catholic in its totality. *The seven seals—trumpets—vials*, are severally a complete series each in itself, fulfilling perfectly the divine course of judgments. *Three and a half* implies a number opposed to the divine (seven), but broken in itself, and which, in the moment of its highest triumph, is overwhelmed by judgment and utter ruin. *Four* is the number of the world's extension; *seven* is the number of God's revelation in the world. In the *four* beasts of Daniel there is a recognition of some power above them, at the same time that there is a mimicry of the *four* cherubs of Ezekiel, the heavenly symbols of all creation in its due subjection to God (ch. 4:6–8). So the four corners of the earth, the four winds, the four angels loosed from the Euphrates, and Jerusalem lying "foursquare," represent worldwide extension. The sevenfoldness of the Spirits on the part of God corresponds with the fourfold cherubim on the part of the created. John, seeing more deeply into the essentially God-opposed character of the world, presents to us, not the *four* beasts of Daniel, but the *seven* heads of the beast, whereby it arrogates to itself the *sevenfold* perfection of *the Spirits of God;* at the same time that, with characteristic self-contradiction, it has *ten* horns, the number peculiar to the world power. Its unjust usurpation of the sacred number *seven* is marked by the addition of an *eighth* to the *seven* heads, and also by the beast's own number, 666, which in units, tens, and hundreds, verges upon, but falls short of, *seven*. The judgments on the world are complete in *six:* after the sixth seal and the sixth trumpet, there is a pause. When *seven* comes, there comes "the kingdom of our Lord and His Christ." Six is the number of the world given to judgment. Moreover, *six* is half of *twelve*, as *three and a half* is the half of *seven*. *Twelve* is the number of the Church: cf. the *twelve* tribes of Israel, the *twelve* stars on the woman's head (ch. 12:1), the *twelve* gates of new Jerusalem. *Six* thus symbolizes the world broken, and without solid foundation. Twice twelve is the number of the heavenly elders; twelve times twelve thousand the number of the sealed elect: the tree of life yields twelve manner of fruits. Doubtless, besides this symbolic force, there is a special chronological meaning in the numbers; but as yet, though a *commanded* subject of investigation, they have received no solution which we can be *sure* is the true one. They are intended to stimulate reverent inquiry, not to gratify idle speculative curiosity; and when the event shall have been fulfilled, they will show the divine wisdom of God, who ordered all things in minutely harmonious relations, and left neither the times nor the ways haphazard.

The arguments for the year-day theory are as follows: Daniel 9:24, "Seventy weeks are determined upon," where the *Hebrew* may be *seventy sevens;* but MEDE observes, the *Hebrew* word means always seven of *days,* and never seven of *years* (Lev. 12:5; Deut. 16:9, 10, 16). Again, the number of *years'* wandering of the Israelites was made to correspond to the number of *days* in which the spies searched the land, viz., *forty:* cf. "each day for a year," Numbers 14:33, 34. So in Ezekiel 4:5, 6, "I have laid upon thee the *years* of their iniquity, according to the number of the *days,* three hundred and ninety days . . . forty days: I have appointed thee *each day for a year.*" John, in Revelation itself, uses *days* in a sense which can hardly be literal. Ch. 2:10, "Ye shall have tribulation *ten days*": the persecution of *ten years* recorded by EUSEBIUS seems to correspond to it. In the year-day theory there is still quite enough of obscurity to exercise the patience and probation of faith, for we cannot say precisely *when* the 1260 years *begin:* so that this theory is quite compatible with Christ's words, "Of that day and hour knoweth no man." However, it is a difficulty in this theory that "a thousand years," in ch. 20:6, 7, can hardly mean 1000 by 360 days, i.e., 360,000 years. The first resurrection there must be literal, even as vs. 5 must be taken literally, "*the rest of the dead* lived not again until the thousand years were finished." To interpret the former spiritually would entail the need of interpreting the latter so, which would be most improbable; for it would imply that *the rest of the* (spiritually) *dead lived not* spiritually until the end of the thousand years, and then that they did come spiritually to life. I Corinthians 15:23, "they that are Christ's at His coming," confirms the literal view.

CHAPTER 1

VSS. 1-20. TITLE: SOURCE AND OBJECT OF THIS REVELATION: BLESSING ON THE READER AND KEEPER OF IT, AS THE TIME IS NEAR: INSCRIPTION TO THE SEVEN CHURCHES: APOSTOLIC GREETING: KEYNOTE, "BEHOLD HE COMETH" (cf. at the close, ch. 22:20, "Surely I come quickly"): INTRODUCTORY VISION OF THE SON OF MAN IN GLORY, AMIDST THE SEVEN CANDLESTICKS, WITH SEVEN STARS IN HIS RIGHT HAND. **1. Revelation**—an apocalypse or *unveiling* of those things which had been veiled. A *manifesto* of the kingdom of Christ. The travelling manual of the Church for the Gentile Christian times. Not a *detailed history* of the future, but a representation of the great epochs and chief powers in developing the kingdom of God in relation to the world. The Church-*historical* view goes counter to the great principle that Scripture interprets itself. Revelation is to teach us to understand the times, not the times to interpret to us the Apocalypse, although it is in the nature of the case that a reflex influence is exerted here and is understood by the prudent [AUBERLEN]. The book is in a series of parallel groups, not in chronological succession. Still there is an organic historical development of the kingdom of God. In this book all the other books of the Bible end and meet: in it is the consummation of all previous prophecy. Daniel foretells as to Christ and the Roman destruction of Jerusalem, and the last Antichrist. But John's Revelation fills up the intermediate period, and describes the millennium and final state beyond Antichrist. Daniel, as a godly statesman, views the history of God's people in relation to the *four world kingdoms.* John, as an apostle, views history from the *Christian Church aspect.* The term *Apocalypse* is applied to no Old Testament book. Daniel is the nearest approach to it; but what Daniel was told to *seal* and *shut up till the time of the end,* John, now that *the time is at hand* (vs. 3), is directed to *reveal.* **of Jesus Christ**—coming *from* Him. Jesus Christ, not John the writer, is the Author of the Apocalypse. Christ taught many things before His departure; but those which were unsuitable for announcement at that time He brought together into the Apocalypse [BENGEL]. Cf. His promise, John 15:15, "All things that I have heard of My Father, I have made known unto you"; also, John 16:13, "The Spirit of truth *will show* you things to come." The Gospels and Acts are the books, respectively, of His first advent, in the flesh, and in the Spirit; the Epistles are the inspired comment on them. The Apocalypse is the book of His second advent and the events pre-

liminary to it. **which God gave unto him**—The Father reveals Himself and His will in, and by, His Son. **to show**—The word recurs in ch. 22:6: so entirely have the parts of Revelation reference to one another. It is its peculiar excellence that it comprises in a perfect compendium future things, and these widely differing: things close at hand, far off, and between the two; great and little; destroying and saving; repeated from old prophecies and new; long and short, and these interwoven with one another, opposed and mutually agreeing; mutually involving and evolving one another; so that in no book more than in this would the addition, or taking away, of a single word or clause (ch. 22:18, 19), have the effect of marring the sense of the context and the comparison of passages together [BENGEL]. **his servants**—not merely to "His servant John," but to *all* His servants (cf. ch. 22:3). **shortly**—*Greek,* "speedily"; lit., "in," or "with speed." Cf. "the time is at hand," vs. 3; ch. 22:6, "shortly"; 7, "Behold, I come *quickly.*" Not that the things prophesied were according to man's computation near; but this word "shortly" implies a corrective of our estimate of worldly events and periods. Though a "thousand years" (ch. 20 at least are included, the time is declared to be *at hand.* Luke 18:8, "speedily." The Israelite Church hastened eagerly to the predicted end, which premature eagerness prophecy restrains (cf. Dan. 9). The Gentile Church needs to be reminded of the transitoriness of the world (which it is apt to make its home) and the nearness of Christ's advent. On the one hand Revelation says, "the time is at hand"; on the other, the succession of seals, etc., show that many intermediate events must first elapse. **he sent**—Jesus Christ sent. **by his angel**—joined with "sent." The angel does not come forward to "signify" things to John until ch. 17:1; 19:9, 10. Previous to that John receives information from others. Jesus Christ opens the Revelation, vss. 10, 11; ch. 4:1; in ch. 6:1 one of the four living creatures acts as his informant; in ch. 7:13, one of the elders; in ch. 10:8, 9, the Lord and His angel who stood on the sea and earth. Only at the end (ch. 17:1) does the one angel stand by Him (cf. Dan. 8:16; 9:21; Zech. 1:19). **2. bare record of**—"testified the word of God" in this book. Where we would say "*testifies*," the ancients in epistolary communications use the past tense. The word of God constitutes his testimony; vs. 3, "the words of this prophecy." **the testimony of Jesus**— "the Spirit of prophecy" (ch. 19:10). **and of all things that . . .**—The oldest MSS. omit "and." Translate, "whatsoever things he saw," in apposition with "the word of God and the testimony of

Jesus Christ." **3. he that readeth, and they that hear**—viz., the *public reader* in Church assemblies, and *his hearers*. In the first instance, he by whom John sent the book from Patmos to the seven churches, read it publicly: a usage most scriptural and profitable. A special *blessing* attends him who *reads* or *hears* the apocalyptic "prophecy" with a view to *keeping* the things therein (as there is but one article to "they that hear and keep those things," not two classes, but only one is meant: "they who not only hear, but also keep those things," Rom. 2:13); even though he find not the key to its interpretation, he finds a stimulus to faith, hope, and patient waiting for Christ. Note, the term "prophecy" has relation to the human medium or *prophet* inspired, here John: "Revelation" to the Divine Being who reveals His will, here Jesus Christ. God gave the revelation to Jesus: He by His angel revealed it to John, who was to make it known to the Church. **4. John**—the apostle. For none but he (supposing the writer an honest man) would thus sign himself nakedly without addition. As sole survivor and representative of the apostles and eye-witnesses of the Lord, he needed no designation save his name, to be recognized by his readers. **seven churches**—not that there were not more churches in that region, but the number *seven* is fixed on as representing *totality*. These *seven* represent the universal Church of all times and places. See TRENCH'S (*Epistles to Seven Churches*) interesting Note, ch. 1:20, on the number *seven*. It is the *covenant number*, the sign of God's covenant relation to mankind, and especially to the Church. Thus, the *seventh day*, sabbath (Gen. 2:3; Ezek. 20:12). Circumcision, the sign of the covenant, after *seven* days (Gen. 17:12). Sacrifices (Num. 23:1, 14:29; II Chron. 29:21). Cf. also God's acts typical of His covenant (Josh. 6:4, 15, 16; II Kings 5:10). The feasts ordered by *sevens* of time (Deut. 15:1; 16:9, 13, 15). It is a combination of *three*, the divine number (thus the Trinity: the thrice Holy, Isa. 6:3; the blessing, Num. 6:24-26), and *four* the number of the organized world in its extension (thus the *four* elements, the *four* seasons, the *four* winds, the *four* corners or quarters of the earth, the *four* living creatures, emblems of redeemed creaturely life, ch. 4:6; Ezek. 1:5, 6, with *four* faces and *four* wings each; the *four* beasts and *four* metals, representing the four world empires, Dan. 2:32, 33; 7:3; the *four*-sided Gospel designed for all quarters of the world; the sheet tied at *four* corners, Acts 10:11; the *four* horns, the sum of the world's forces against the Church, Zech. 1:18). In the Apocalypse, where God's covenant with His Church comes to its consummation, appropriately the number *seven* recurs still more frequently than elsewhere in Scripture. **Asia**—Proconsular, governed by a Roman proconsul: consisting of Phrygia, Mysia, Caria, and Lydia: the kingdom which Attalus III had bequeathed to Rome. **Grace ... peace**—Paul's apostolical greeting. In his Pastoral Epistles he inserts "mercy" in addition: so II John 3. **him which is ... was ... is to come**—a periphrasis for the incommunicable name JEHOVAH, the self-existing One, unchangeable. In *Greek* the indeclinability of the designation here implies His unchangeableness. Perhaps the reason why "He which is to come" is used, instead of "He that shall be," is because the grand theme of Revelation is the Lord's *coming* (vs. 7). Still it is THE FATHER as distinguished from "Jesus Christ" (vs. 5) who is here meant. But so one are the Father and Son that the designation, "which is to come," more immediately applicable to Christ, is used here

of the Father. **the seven Spirits which are before his throne**—The oldest MSS. omit "are." **before**—lit., "in the presence of." The Holy Spirit in His sevenfold (i.e., perfect, complete, and universal) energy. Corresponding to "the *seven* churches." One in His own essence, manifold in His gracious influences. The *seven* eyes resting on the stone laid by Jehovah (ch. 5:6). Four is the number of the creature world (cf. the fourtold cherubim); *seven* the number of God's revelation in the world. **5. the faithful witness**—of the truth concerning Himself and His mission as Prophet, Priest, and King Saviour. "He was *the faithful witness*, because all things that He heard of the Father He faithfully made known to His disciples. Also, because He taught the way of God in truth, and cared not for man, nor regarded the persons of men. Also, because the truth which He taught in words He confirmed by miracles. Also, because the testimony to Himself on the part of the Father He denied not even in death. Lastly, because He will give true testimony of the works of good and bad at the day of judgment" [RICHARD OF ST. VICTOR *in* TRENCH]. The nominative in *Greek* standing in apposition to the genitive, "Jesus Christ," gives majestic prominence to "the faithful witness." **the first-begotten of the dead**—(Col. 1:18). Lazarus rose to die again. Christ rose to die no more. The image is not as if the grave was the womb of His resurrection-birth [ALFORD]; but as Acts 13:33; Romans 1:4, treat Christ's *resurrection* as the epoch and event which fulfilled the Scripture, Psalm 2:7, "This day (at the resurrection) have I *begotten* Thee." It was then that His divine Sonship as the Godman was manifested and openly attested by the Father. So our resurrection and our manifested sonship, or generation, are connected. Hence "regeneration" is used of the *resurrection state* at the restitution of all things (Matt. 19:28). **the prince**—or Ruler. The kingship of the world which the tempter offered to Jesus on condition of doing homage to him, and so shunning the cross, He has obtained by the cross. "The kings of the earth" conspired against the Lord's Anointed (Ps. 2:2): these He shall break in pieces (Ps. 2:9). Those who are wise in time and kiss the Son shall *bring their glory* unto Him at His manifestation as King of kings, after He has destroyed His foes. **Unto him that loved us**—The oldest MSS. read the present, ". . . *loveth* us." It is His evercontinuing character, *He loveth us*, and ever shall love us. His love rests evermore on His people. **washed us**—The two oldest MSS. read, "freed (*loosed* as from a bond) us": so ANDREAS and PRIMASIUS. One very old MS., *Vulgate*, and *Coptic* read as *English Version*, perhaps drawn from ch. 7:4. "loosed us in (virtue of) His blood," being the *harder* reading to understand, is less likely to have come from the transcribers. The reference is thus to *Greek*, *lutron*, the ransom paid for our release (Matt. 20:28). In favor of *English Version* reading is the usage whereby the priests, before putting on the holy garments and ministering, *washed* themselves: so spiritually believers, as *priests* unto God, must first be *washed* in Christ's blood from every stain before they can serve God aright now, or hereafter minister as dispensers of blessing to the subject nations in the millennial kingdom, or minister before God in heaven. **6. And hath**—rather as *Greek*, "And (He) hath." **made us kings**—The oldest MSS. read, "a kingdom." One oldest MS. reads the dative, "for us." Another reads "us," accusative: so *Vulgate, Syriac, Coptic*, and *Andreas*. This seems preferable, "He made us (to be) a kingdom." So Exodus 19:6, "a kingdom of priests"; I Peter 2:9, "a royal priesthood." The saints shall constitate peculiarly a *kingdom* of God, and shall themselves be *kings* (ch. 5:10). They shall share His King-Priest throne in the millennial kingdom. The emphasis thus falls more on the *kingdom* than on *priests:* whereas in *English Version* reading it is equally distributed between both. This book lays prominent stress on the saints' *kingdom.* They are kings because they are priests: the priesthood is the continuous ground and legitimization of their kingship; they are kings in relation to man, priests in relation to God, serving Him day and night in His temple (ch. 7:15; 5:10). The priest-kings shall rule, not in an external mechanical manner, but simply in virtue of what they are, by the power of attraction and conviction overcoming the heart [AUBERLEN]. **priests**—who have preeminently the privilege of near access to the king. David's sons were priests (*Hebrew*), II Samuel 8:18. The distinction of *priests* and people, nearer and more remote from God, shall cease; all shall have nearest access to Him. All persons and things shall be holy to the Lord. **God and his Father**—There is but one article to both in the *Greek*, therefore it means, "Unto Him who is at once God and His Father." **glory and dominion**—*Greek*, "*the* glory and *the* might." The fuller threefold doxology occurs, ch. 4:9, 11; fourfold, ch. 5:13; Jude 25; sevenfold, ch.7:12 ; I Chronicles 29:11. Doxology occupies the prominent place above, which prayer does below. If we thought of *God's glory* first (as in the Lord's Prayer), and gave the secondary place to our needs, we should please God and gain our petitions better than we do. **for ever and ever**—*Greek*, "unto the ages." **7. with clouds**—*Greek*, "*the* clouds," viz., of heaven. "A cloud received Him out of their sight" at His ascension (Acts 1:9). His ascension corresponds to the manner of His coming again (Acts 1:11). Clouds are the symbols of *wrath* to sinners. **every eye**—His coming shall therefore be a personal, visible appearing. **shall see**—It is because they do not now *see* Him, they will not believe. Contrast John 20:29. **they** *also*—they *in particular;* "whosoever." Primarily, at His pre-millennial advent *the Jews,* who shall "look upon Him whom they have pierced," and mourn *in repentance*, and say, "Blessed is He that cometh in the name of the Lord." Secondarily, and here *chiefly,* at the general judgment all the ungodly, not only those who actually pierced Him, but those who did so by their sins, shall look with trembling upon Him. John is the only one of the Evangelists who records the *piercing* of Christ's side. This allusion identifies him as the author of the Apocalypse. The reality of Christ's humanity and His death is proved by His having been *pierced;* and the *water and blood* from His side were the antitype to the Levitical waters of cleansing and blood offerings. **all kindreds . . . shall wail**—all the unconverted at the general judgment; and especially at His pre-millennial advent, the Antichristian confederacy (Zech. 12:3-6, 9; 14:1-4; Matt. 24:30). *Greek,* "all the *tribes* of the *land,*" or "the earth." See the limitation to "all," ch. 13:8. Even the godly while rejoicing in His love shall feel penitential sorrow at their sins, which shall all be manifested at the general judgment. **because of**—*Greek,* "at," or "*in regard to* Him." **Even so, Amen**—Gods seal of His own word; to which corresponds the believer's prayer, ch. 22:20. The "even so" is *Greek;* "Amen" is *Hebrew.* To both Gentiles and Jews His promises and threats are unchangeable. **8.** *Greek,* "I am *the*

Alpha and *the* Omega." The first and last letters of the alphabet. God in Christ comprises all that goes between, as well as the first and last. **the beginning and the ending**—omitted in the oldest MSS., though found in *Vulgate* and *Coptic*. Transcribers probably inserted the clause from ch. 21:6. In Christ, Genesis, the Alpha of the Old Testament, and Revelation, the Omega of the New Testament, meet together: the last book presenting to us man and God reconciled in Paradise, as the first book presented man at the beginning innocent and in God's favor in Paradise. Accomplishing *finally* what I *begin*. Always the same; before the dragon, the beast, false prophet, and all foes. An anticipatory consolation to the saints under the coming trials of the Church. **the Lord**—The oldest MSS. read "the Lord God." **Almighty**—*Hebrew, Shaddai,* and *Jehovah Sabaoth,* i.e., of hosts; commanding all the hosts or powers in heaven and earth, so able to overcome all His Church's foes. It occurs often in Revelation, but nowhere else in the New Testament save II Corinthians 6:18, a quotation from Isaiah. **9. I John**—So "I Daniel" (Dan. 7:28; 9:2; 10:2). One of the many features of resemblance between the Old Testament and the New Testament apocalyptic seers. No other Scripture writer uses the phrase. **also**—as well as being an apostle. The oldest MSS. omit "also." In his Gospel and Epistles he makes no mention of his *name,* though describing himself as "the disciple whom Jesus loved." Here, with similar humility, though naming himself, he does not mention his apostleship. **companion**—*Greek,* "fellow partaker in the tribulation." Tribulation is the necessary precursor of the kingdom," therefore "the" is prefixed. This must be borne with "patient endurance." The oldest MSS. omit "in the" before "kingdom." All three are inseparable: *the tribulation, kingdom and endurance.* **patience**—Translate, "endurance." "Persevering, enduring continuance" (Acts 14:22); "the queen of the graces (virtues)" [CHRYSOSTOM]. **of . . .**—The oldest MSS. read "IN Jesus," or "Jesus Christ." It is IN Him that believers have the right to the *kingdom,* and the spiritual strength to enable them to *endure patiently* for it. **was**—*Greek,* "came to be." **in . . . Patmos**—now Patmo or Palmosa. See *Introduction* on this island, and John's exile to it under Domitian, from which he was released under Nerva. Restricted to a small spot on earth, he is permitted to penetrate the wide realms of heaven and its secrets. Thus John drank of Christ's cup, and was baptized with His baptism (Matt. 20:22). **for**—*Greek,* "for the sake of," "on account of"; so, "*because of* the word of God and . . . testimony." Two oldest MSS. omit the second "for"; thus "the Word of God" and "testimony of Jesus" are the more closely joined. Two oldest MSS. omit "Christ." The Apocalypse has been always appreciated most by the Church in adversity. Thus the Asiatic Church from the flourishing times of Constantine less estimated it. The African Church being more exposed to the cross always made much of it [BENGEL]. **10. I was**—*Greek,* "I came to be"; "I became," **in the Spirit**—in a state of ecstasy; the outer world being shut out, and the inner and higher life or spirit being taken full possession of by God's Spirit, so that an immediate connection with the invisible world is established. While the *prophet* "speaks" in the Spirit, the apocalyptic seer *is in* the Spirit in his whole person. The spirit only (that which connects us with God and the invisible world) is active, or rather recipient, in the apocalyptic state. With Christ this being "in the Spirit" was not the exception, but His continual state. **on the Lord's day**—Though forcibly detained from Church communion with the brethren in the sanctuary on the Lord's day, the weekly commemoration of the resurrection, John was holding spiritual communion with them. This is the earliest mention of *the term*, "the Lord's day." But the consecration of the day to worship, almsgiving, and the Lord's Supper, is implied in Acts 20:7; I Corinthians 16:2; cf. John 20:19-26. The name corresponds to "the Lord's Supper," I Corinthians 11:20. IGNATIUS seems to allude to "the Lord's day" (*ad Magnes*. 9), and IRENÆUS in the *Quæst, ad Orthod*. 115 (in JUSTIN MARTYR). JUSTIN MARTYR, *Apology*, 2. 98, etc., "On Sunday we all hold our joint meeting; for the first day is that on which God, having removed darkness and chaos, made the world, and Jesus Christ our Saviour rose from the dead. On the day before Saturday they crucified Him; and on the day after Saturday, which is Sunday, having appeared to His apostles and disciples, He taught these things." To the Lord's day PLINY doubtless refers (*Ex*. 97, B. 10), "The Christians on a *fixed day* before dawn meet and sing a hymn to Christ as God ..." TERTULLIAN, *De Coron*. 3, "On the Lord's day we deem it wrong to fast." MELITO, bishop of Sardis (second century), wrote a book *on the Lord's day* (EUSEBIUS 4. 26). Also, DIONYSIUS OF CORINTH, *in* EUSEBIUS, *Ecclesiastical History*, 4. 23, 8. CLEMENT OF ALEXANDRIA, *Stromata* 5. and 7. 12; ORIGEN, *c. Cels*. 8. 22. The theory that the *day of Christ's second coming* is meant, is untenable. "The day of the Lord" is different in the *Greek* from "the Lord's (an adjective) day," which latter in the ancient Church always designates our Sunday, though it is not impossible that the two shall coincide (at least in some parts of the earth), whence a tradition is mentioned in JEROME, on Matthew 25, that the Lord's coming was expected especially on the Paschal Lord's day. The visions of the Apocalypse, the seals, trumpets, and vials, etc., are grouped in *sevens*, and naturally begin on the first day of the seven, the birthday of the Church, whose future they set forth [WORDSWORTH]. **great voice**—summoning solemn attention; *Greek* order, "I heard a voice behind me great (loud) as (that) of a trumpet." The trumpet summoned to religious feasts, and accompanies God's revelations of Himself. **11. I am Alpha and Omega, the first and the last; and**—The oldest MSS, omit all this clause. **write in a book** —To this *book*, having such an origin, and to the other books of Holy Scripture, who is there that gives the weight which their importance demands, preferring them to the *many books* of the world? [BENGEL.] **seven churches**—As there were many other churches in Proconsular Asia (e.g., Miletus, Magnesia, Tralles), besides the seven specified, doubtless the number *seven* is fixed upon because of its mystical signification, expressing *totality* and *universality*. The words, "which are in Asia" are rejected by the oldest MSS., A, B, C, CYPRIAN, *Vulgate,* and *Syriac; Coptic* alone supports them of old authorities. These seven are representative churches; and, as a complex whole, ideally complete, embody the chief spiritual characteristics of the Church, whether as faithful or unfaithful, in all ages. The churches selected are not taken at random, but have a many-sided completeness. Thus, on one side we have Smyrna, a Church exposed to persecutions unto death; on the other Sardis, having a high *name* for spiritual *life and yet dead*. Again, Laodicea, in its own estimate *rich* and *having need of nothing,* with ample talents, yet *lukewarm* in Christ's

cause; on the other hand, Philadelphia, with but a *little strength,* yet *keeping* Christ's *word* and having an *open door* of usefulness *set before* it by Christ Himself. Again, Ephesus, intolerant of *evil* and of *false apostles,* yet having *left its first love;* on the other hand, Thyatira, abounding in *works, love, service, and faith,* yet *suffering* the false *prophetess* to *seduce* many. In another aspect, Ephesus in conflict with false freedom, i.e. fleshly licentiousness (the Nicolaitans); so also Pergamos in conflict with Balaam-like tempters to fornication and *idol-meats;* and on the other side, Philadelphia in conflict with the Jewish synagogue, i.e., legal bondage. Finally, Sardis and Laodicea without any active opposition to call forth their spiritual energies; a dangerous position, considering man's natural indolence. In the historic scheme of interpretation, which seems fanciful, Ephesus (meaning "the beloved" or "desired" [STIER]) represents the waning period of the apostolic age. Smyrna ("myrrh"), bitter suffering, yet sweet and costly perfume, the martyr period of the Decian and Diocletian age. Pergamos (a "castle" or "tower"), the Church possessing earthly power and decreasing spirituality from Constantine's time until the seventh century. Thyatira ("unwearied about sacrifices"), the Papal Church in the first half of the Middle Ages; like "Jezebel," keen about its so-called *sacrifice* of the mass, and slaying the prophets and witnesses of God. Sardis, from the close of the twelfth century to the Reformation. Philadelphia ("brotherly love"), the first century of the Reformation. Laodicea, the Reformed Church after its first zeal had become *luke-warm.* **12. see the voice**—i.e., ascertain whence the *voice* came; to *see* who was it from whom the *voice* proceeded. **that**—*Greek*, "of what kind it was which." The voice is that of God the Father, as at Christ's baptism and transfiguration, so here in presenting Christ as our High Priest. **spake**—The oldest MSS., versions, and Fathers read, "was speaking." **being**—"having turned." **seven . . . candlesticks**—"lamp-stands" [KELLY]. The stand holding the lamp. In Exodus 25:31, 32, the seven are united in ONE candlestick or lamp-stand, i.e., six arms and a central shaft; so Zechariah 4:2, 11. Here the seven are *separate* candlesticks, typifying, as that *one,* the entire Church, but now no longer as the Jewish Church (represented by the *one* sevenfold candlestick) restricted to one outward unity and one place; the several churches are mutually independent as to external ceremonies and government (provided all things are done to edification, and schisms or needless separations are avoided), yet one in the unity of the Spirit and the Headship of Christ. The candlestick is not light, but the bearer of light, holding it forth to give light around. The light is the Lord's, not the Church's; from Him she receives it. She is to be a lightbearer to His glory. The candlestick stood in the holy place, the type of the Church on earth, as the holiest place was type of the Church in heaven. The holy place's only light was derived from the candlestick, daylight being excluded; so the Lord God is the Church's only light; hers is the light of grace, not nature. "Golden" symbolizes at once the greatest *preciousness* and *sacredness;* so that in the *Zend Avesta* "golden" is synonymous with heavenly or divine [TRENCH]. **13.** His glorified form as man could be recognized by John, who had seen it at the Transfiguration. **in the midst**—implying Christ's continual presence and ceaseless activity *in the midst* of His people *on earth.* In ch. 4, when He appears *in heaven,* His insignia undergo a corresponding change yet even there the rainbow reminds us of His everlasting covenant with them. **seven**—omitted in two of the oldest MSS., but supported by one. **Son of man**—The form which John had seen enduring the agony of Gethsemane, and the shame and anguish of Calvary, he now sees glorified. His glory (as *Son of man*, not merely *Son of God*) is the result of His humiliation as *Son of man*. **down to the foot**—a mark of high rank. The garment and girdle seem to be emblems of His *priesthood*. Cf. Exodus 28:2, 4, 31; LXX. Aaron's robe and girdle were "for glory and beauty," and combined the insignia of royalty and priesthood, the characteristics of Christ's antitypical priesthood "after the order of Melchisedec." His being *in the midst of the candlesticks* (only seen in the *temple*), shows that it is as a *king-priest* He is so attired. This priesthood He has exercised ever since His ascension; and, therefore He here wears its emblems. As Aaron wore these insignia when He came forth from the sanctuary to bless the people (Lev. 16:4, 23, 24, the *chetoneth*, or holy linen coat), so when Christ shall come again, He shall appear in the similar attire of "beauty and glory" (*Margin*, Isa. 4:2). The angels are attired somewhat like their Lord (ch. 15:6). The ordinary girding for one actively engaged, was at *the loins;* but JOSEPHUS, *Antiquities* 3., 7. 2, expressly tells us that the Levitical priests were girt higher up, about the breasts or *paps*, appropriate to calm, majestic movement. The girdle bracing the frame together, symbolizes collected powers. *Righteousness* and *faithfulness* are Christ's girdle. The high priest's girdle was only interwoven with gold, but Christ's is all of gold; the antitype exceeds the type. **14.** *Greek*, "But," or "And." **like wool**—*Greek*, "like *white* wool." The *color* is the point of comparison; signifying *purity* and glory. (So in Isa. 1:18.) Not *age*, for hoary hairs are the sign of decay. **eyes...as...flame**—all-searching and penetrating like fire: at the same time, also, implying *consuming* indignation against sin, especially at His coming "in flaming fire, taking vengeance" on all the ungodly, which is confirmed as the meaning here, by Revelation 19: 11, 12. **15. fine brass**—*Greek*, *chalcolibanus*, derived by some from two *Greek* words, "brass" and "frankincense"; derived by BOCHART from *Greek*, *chalcos*, brass, and *Hebrew*, *libbeen*, to whiten; hence, "brass," which in the furnace has reached a *white* heat. Thus it answers to "burnished (flashing, or glowing) brass," Ezekiel 1:7; Revelation 10: 1, "His feet as pillars *of fire*." Translate, "*Glowing* brass, as if they had been made fiery (red-hot) in a furnace." The feet of the priests were bare in ministering in the sanctuary. So our great High Priest here. **voice as...many waters**—Ezekiel 43: 2; in Daniel 10:6, it is "like the voice of a *multitude*." As the Bridegroom's voice, so the bride's, ch. 14:2; 19:6; Ezekiel 1:24, the cherubim, or redeemed creation. His voice, however, is here regarded in its terribleness to His foes. Contrast Song of Solomon 2:8; 5:2, with which cf. ch. 3:20. **16. he had**—*Greek*, "having." John takes up the description from time to time, irrespective of the construction, *with separate strokes of the pencil* [ALFORD]. **in...right hand seven stars**—(vs. 20; ch. 2:1; 3:1). He holds them as a star-studded "crown of glory," or "royal diadem," in His hand: so Isaiah 62:3. He is their Possessor and Upholder. **out of...mouth went**—*Greek*, "going forth"; not wielded in the hand. His WORD is omnipotent in executing His will in punishing sinners. It is the sword of His Spirit. Reproof and punishment, rather than its converting winning power, is

the prominent point. Still, as He encourages the churches, as well as threatens, the former quality of the Word is not excluded. Its *two* edges (back and front) may allude to its double efficacy, condemning some, converting others. TERTULLIAN, *adv. Jud.*, takes them of *the Old and the New Testaments.* RICHARD OF ST. VICTOR, "the Old Testament cutting externally our *carnal*, the New Testament internally, our *spiritual* sins." **sword**—*Greek, romphaia*, the Thracian long and heavy broadsword: six times in Revelation, once only elsewhere in New Testament, viz., Luke 2:35. **sun...in his strength**—in unclouded power. So shall the righteous shine, reflecting the image of the Sun of righteousness. TRENCH notices that this description, sublime as a purely mental conception, would be intolerable if we were to give it an outward form. With the Greeks, æsthecial taste was the first consideration, to which all others must give way. With the Hebrews, truth and the full representation ideally of the religious reality were the paramount consideration, that representation being designed not to be outwardly embodied, but to remain a purely mental conception. This exalting of the essence above the form marks their deeper religious earnestness. **17.** So fallen is man that God's manifestation of His glorious presence overwhelms him. **laid his right hand upon me**—So the same Lord Jesus did at the Transfiguration to the three prostrate disciples, of whom John was one, saying, Be not afraid. The "touch" of His hand, as of old, imparted strength. **unto me**—omitted in the oldest MSS. **the first... the last**—(Isa. 41:4; 44:6; 48:12). From eternity, and enduring to eternity: "the First by creation, the Last by retribution: the First, because before Me there was no God formed; the Last, because after Me there shall be no other: the First, because from Me are all things; the Last, because to Me all things return" [RICHARD OF ST. VICTOR]. **18.** Translate as *Greek*, "And THE LIVING ONE": connected with last sentence, vs. 17. **and was**—*Greek*, "and (yet) I *became*." **alive for evermore**—*Greek*, "living unto the ages of ages": not merely "*I live*," but I have life, and am the source of it to My people. "To Him belongs *absolute* being, as contrasted with the *relative* being of the creature; others may *share*, He only *hath* immortality: *being in essence, not by mere participation, immortal* [THEODORET in TRENCH]. One oldest MS., with *English Version*, reads "A-men." Two others, and most of the oldest versions and Fathers, omit it. His having passed through death as one of us, and now living in the infinite plenitude of life, reassures His people, since through Him death is the gate of resurrection to eternal life. **have...keys of hell**—*Greek*, "Hades"; *Hebrew*, "Sheol." "Hell" in the sense, the *place of torment*, answers to a different *Greek* word, viz., *Gehenna*. I can release from *the unseen world of spirits* and from DEATH whom I *will.* The oldest MSS. read by transposition, "Death and Hades," or Hell." It is death (which came in by sin, robbing man of his immortal birthright, Rom. 5:12) that peoples Hades, and therefore should stand first in order. *Keys* are emblems of authority, opening and shutting at will "the gates of Hades" (Ps. 9:13, 14; Isa. 38:10; Matt. 16:18). **19.** The oldest MSS. read, "Write *therefore*" (inasmuch as I, the First and Last, have the keys of death, and vouchsafe to thee this vision for the comfort and warning of the Church). **things which are**—"the things which thou hast seen" are those narrated in this chapter (cf. vs. 11). "The things which are" imply the present state of things in the churches when John was writing, as represented in chs. 2 and 3. "The things which shall be hereafter," the things symbolically represented concerning the future history of chs. 4-22. ALFORD translates, *"What things they signify";* but the antithesis of the next clause forbids this, "the things which shall be hereafter," *Greek,* "which are about to come to pass." The plural *(Greek)* "are," instead of the usual *Greek* construction *singular,* is owing to *churches* and *persons* being meant by things" in the clause, "the things which are." **20. in**—*Greek,* "*upon* My right hand." **the mystery ... candlesticks**—in apposition to, and explaining, "the things which thou hast seen," governed by "Write." *Mystery* signifies the hidden truth, veiled under this symbol, and now revealed; its correlative is *revelation. Stars* symbolize lordship (Num. 24:17; cf. Dan. 12:3, of faithful teachers; ch. 8:10; 12:4; Jude 13). **angels**—not as ALFORD, from ORIGEN *Homily* 13 on Luke, and 20 on Numbers, the guardian angels of the churches, just as individuals have their guardian angels. For how could heavenly angels be charged with the delinquencies laid here to the charge of these angels? Then, if a human angel be meant (as the Old Testament analogy favors, Hag. 1:13, "the Lord's Messenger in the Lord's message"; Mal. 2:7; 3:1), *the bishop,* or superintendent pastor, must be the angel. For whereas there were many presbyters in each of the larger churches (as e.g., Ephesus, Smyrna, etc.), there was but *one* angel, whom, moreover, the Chief Shepherd and Bishop of souls holds responsible for the spiritual state of the Church under him. The term *angel,* designating an office, is, in accordance with the enigmatic symbolism of this book, transferred from the heavenly to the earthly superior ministers of Jehovah; reminding them that, like the heavenly angels above, they below should fulfil God's mission zealously, promptly and efficiently. "Thy will be done on earth, as it is in heaven!"

CHAPTER 2

Vss. 1-29. EPISTLES TO EPHESUS, SMYRNA, PERGAMOS, THYATIRA. Each of the seven epistles in this chapter and ch. 3, commences with, "I know thy works." Each contains a promise from Christ, "To him that overcometh." Each ends with, "He that hath an ear, let him hear what the Spirit saith unto the churches." The title of our Lord in each case accords with the nature of the address, and is mainly taken from the imagery of the vision, ch. 1. Each address has a threat or a promise, and most of the addresses have both. Their order seems to be ecclesiastical, civil, and geographical: Ephesus first, as being the Asiatic metropolis (termed "the light of Asia," and "first city of Asia"), the nearest to Patmos, where John received the epistle to the seven churches, and also as being that Church with which John was especially connected; then the churches on the west coast of Asia; then those in the interior. Smyrna and Philadelphia alone receive unmixed praise. Sardis and Laodicea receive almost solely censure. In Ephesus, Pergamos, and Thyatira, there are some things to praise, others to condemn, the latter element preponderating in one case (Ephesus), the former in the two others (Pergamos and Thyatira). Thus the main characteristics of the different states of different churches, in all times and places, are portrayed, and they are suitably encouraged or warned. **1. Ephesus**—famed for the temple of Diana, one of the seven wonders of the world. For three years Paul labored there. He

subsequently ordained Timothy superintending overseer or bishop there: probably his charge was but of a temporary nature. John, towards the close of his life, took it as the center from which he superintended the province. **holdeth**—*Greek,* "holdeth fast," as in vs. 25; ch. 3:11; cf. John 10:28, 29. The title of Christ here as "holding fast the seven stars (from ch. 1:16: only that, for *having* is substituted *holding fast* in His grasp), and walking in the midst of the seven candlesticks," accords with the beginning of His address to the *seven* churches representing the universal Church. *Walking* expresses His unwearied activity in the Church, guarding her from internal and external evils, as the high priest moved to and fro in the sanctuary. **2. I know thy works**—expressing His omniscience. Not merely "thy professions, desires, good resolutions" (ch. 14:13, end). **thy labour**—Two oldest MSS. omit "thy"; one supports it. The *Greek* means "labor *unto weariness.*" **patience**—persevering *endurance.* **bear**—*evil men* are a *burden* which the Ephesian Church regarded as intolerable. We are to "*bear* (the same *Greek,* Gal. 6:2) one another's burdens" in the case of *weak* brethren; but not to bear *false brethren.* **tried**—by experiment; not the *Greek* for "test," as I John 4:1. The apostolical churches had the miraculous gift of *discerning spirits.* Cf. Acts 20:28-30, wherein Paul presciently warned the *Ephesian* elders of the coming false teachers, as also in writing to Timothy at Ephesus. TERTULLIAN, *De baptism,* 17, and JEROME, *in Catal. Vir. Illustr. in Lucca* 7, record of John, that when a writing, professing to be a canonical history of the acts of Paul, had been composed by a presbyter of Ephesus, John convicted the author and condemned the work. So on one occasion he would not remain under the same roof with Cerinthus the heretic. **say they are apostles**—probably Judaizers. IGNATIUS, *Ad Ephesum* 6, says subsequently, "Onesimus praises exceedingly your good discipline that no heresy dwells among you"; and 9, "Ye did not permit those having evil doctrine to sow their seed among you, but closed your ears." **3. borne ... patience**—The oldest MSS. transpose these words. Then translate as *Greek,* "persevering endurance . . . borne." "Thou hast borne" My reproach, but "thou canst not bear the evil" (vs. 2). A beautiful antithesis. **and ... hast laboured, and hast not fainted**—The two oldest MSS. and oldest versions read, "and . . . hast not labored," omitting "and hast fainted." The difficulty which transcribers by *English Version* reading tried to obviate, was the seeming contradiction, "I know thy *labor . . .* and thou hast *not labored.*" But what is meant is, "Thou hast not been wearied out with labor." **4. somewhat ... because**—Translate, "I have against thee (this) *that ..."* It is not a mere "somewhat"; it is everything. How characteristic of our gracious Lord, that He puts foremost all He can find to approve, and only after this notes the shortcomings! **left thy first love** —to Christ. Cf. I Timothy 5:12, "cast off their first faith." See the Ephesians' first *love,* Ephesians 1:15. This epistle was written under Domitian, when thirty years had elapsed since Paul had written his Epistle to them. Their warmth of love had given place to a lifeless orthodoxy. Cf. Paul's view of faith so called without love, I Corinthians 13:2. **5. whence**—from what a height. **do the first works** —the *works* which flowed from thy *first love.* Not merely "feel thy first feelings," but do works flowing from the same principle as formerly, "faith which worketh by love." **I will come**—*Greek,* "I am coming" in special judgment on thee. **quickly**

-omitted in two oldest MSS., *Vulgate* and *Coptic versions:* supported by one oldest MS.). **remove thy candlestick out of his place**—I will take away the Church from Ephesus and remove it elsewhere. "It is removal of the candlestick, not extinction of the candle, which is threatened here; judgment for some, but that very judgment the occasion of mercy for others. So it has been. The seat of the Church has been changed, but the Church itself survives. What the East has lost, the West has gained. One who lately visited Ephesus found only three Christians there, and these so ignorant as scarcely to have heard the names of St. Paul or St. John" [TRENCH]. **6. But**—How graciously, after necessary censure, He returns to praise for our consolation, and as an example to *us*, that we would show, when we reprove, we have more pleasure in praising than in fault-finding. **hatest the deeds**—We should hate men's evil *deeds*, not hate the men themselves. **Nicolaitanes**—IRENÆUS, *Hæreses* 1. 26. 3; and TERTULLIAN, *Præscriptione Hæreticorum* 46, make these followers of Nicolas, one of *the seven* (honorably mentioned, Acts 6:3, 5). They (CLEMENS ALEXANDRINUS, *Stromata* 2. 20; 3. 4 and EPIPHANIUS, *Hæreses* 25) evidently confound the latter Gnostic Nicolaitanes, or followers of one Nicolaos, with those of Revelation. MICHAELIS' view is probable: Nicolaos (*conqueror of the people*) is the *Greek* version of Balaam, from *Hebrew Belang Am, Destroyer of the people.* Revelation abounds in such duplicate *Hebrew* and *Greek* names: as Apollyon, Abaddon: Devil, Satan: Yea (*Greek, Naï*), Amen. The name, like other names, Egypt, Babylon, Sodom, is symbolic. Cf. vss. 14, 15, which shows the true sense of Nicolaitanes; they are not a sect, but professing Christians who, like Balaam of old, tried to introduce into the Church a false freedom, i.e., licentiousness; this was a reaction in the opposite direction from Judaism, the first danger to the Church combated in the council of Jerusalem, and by Paul in the Epistle to Galatians. These symbolical Nicolaitanes, or followers of Balaam, abused Paul's doctrine of the grace of God into a plea for lasciviousness (II Pet. 2:15, 16, 19; Jude 4, 11 who both describe the same sort of seducers as followers of *Balaam*). The difficulty that they should appropriate a name branded with infamy in Scripture is met by TRENCH: The Antinomian Gnostics were so opposed to John as a Judaizing apostle that they would assume as a name of chiefest honor one which John branded with dishonor. **7. He that hath an ear**—This clause precedes the promise in the first three addresses, succeeds it in the last four. Thus the promises are enclosed on both sides with the precept urging the deepest attention as to the most momentous truths. Every man "hath an ear" naturally, but he alone will be able to hear spiritually to whom God has given "the hearing ear"; whose "ear God hath wakened" and "opened." Cf. "Faith, the ears of the soul" [CLEMENS ALEXANDRINUS]. **the Spirit saith**—What *Christ* saith, *the Spirit* saith; so one are the Second and Third Persons. **unto the churches**—not merely to the particular, but to the universal Church. **overcometh**—In John's Gospel (16:33) and First Epistle (2:13, 14, 5:4, 5) an object follows, viz., "the world," "the wicked one." Here, where the final issue is spoken of, *the conqueror* is named absolutely. Paul uses a similar image (I Cor. 9:24, 25; II Tim. 2:5; but not the same as John's phrase, except Rom. 12:21). **will I give**—as the Judge. The tree of life in Paradise, lost by the fall, is restored by the Redeemer. Allusions to it occur in Proverbs 3:18; 11:30; 13:12; 15:4, and

prophetically, ch. 22:2, 14; Ezekiel 47:12; cf. John 6:51. It is interesting to note how closely these introductory addresses are linked to the body of Revelation. Thus, *the tree of life* here, with ch. 22:1; deliverance from *the second death* (ch. 2:11), with ch. 20:14; 21:8; *the new name* (ch. 2:17), with ch. 14:1; *power over the nations,* with ch. 20:4; *the morning star* (ch. 2:28), with ch. 22:16; *the white raiment* (ch. 3:5), with ch. 4:4; 16:15; *the name in the book of life* (ch. 3:5), with ch. 13:8; 20:15; *the new Jerusalem* and its citizenship (ch. 3: 12), with ch. 21:10. **give . . . tree of life**—The thing promised corresponds to the kind of faithfulness manifested. They who refrain from Nicolaitane indulgences (vs. 6) and idol meats (vss. 14, 15), shall eat of meat infinitely superior, viz., the fruit of the tree of life, and the hidden manna (vs. 17). **in the midst of the paradise**—The oldest MSS. omit "the midst of." In Genesis 2:9 these words are appropriate, for there were *other* trees in the garden, but not *in the midst* of it. Here *the tree of life* is simply *in the paradise,* for no other tree is mentioned in it; in ch. 22:2 the tree of life is *"in the midst* of the street of Jerusalem"; from this the clause was inserted here. *Paradise* (a Persian, or else Semitic word), originally used of any garden of delight; then specially of Eden; then the temporary abode of separate souls in bliss; then "the Paradise *of God,"* the third heaven, the immediate presence of God. **of God**—(Ezek. 28:13). One oldest MS., with *Vulgate, Syriac,* and *Coptic,* and CYPRIAN, read, "MY God," as in ch. 3:12. So Christ calls God, *"My* God and your God" (John 20:17; cf. Eph. 1: 17.) God is *our* God, in virtue of being peculiarly *Christ's* God. The main bliss of Paradise is that it is the Paradise *of God;* God Himself dwelling there (ch. 21:3). **8. Smyrna**—in Ionia, a little to the north of Ephesus. POLYCARP, martyred in A.D. 168, eighty-six years after his conversion, was bishop, and probably "the angel of the Church in Smyrna" meant here. The allusions to persecutions and faithfulness unto death accord with this view. IGNATIUS (*Martyrium Ignatii,* 3), on his way to martyrdom in Rome, wrote to POLYCARP, then (A.D. 108) bishop of Smyrna; if his bishopric commenced ten or twelve years earlier, the dates will harmonize. TERTULLIAN, *Præscriptione Hæreticorum,* 32, and IRENÆUS, who had talked with POLYCARP in youth, tell us POLYCARP was consecrated bishop of Smyrna by St. John. **the first . . . the last . . . was dead . . . is alive**—The attributes of Christ most calculated to comfort the Church of Smyrna under its persecutions; resumed from ch. 1:17, 18. As death was to Him but the gate to life eternal, so it is to be to them (vs. 10, 11). **9. thy works, and**—omitted in two oldest MSS., *Vulgate,* and *Coptic.* Supported by one oldest MS. **tribulation**—owing to persecution. **poverty**—owing to "the spoiling of their goods." **but thou art rich**—in grace. Contrast Laodicea, *rich* in the world's eyes and her own, *poor* before God. "There are both poor rich-men, and rich poor-men in God's sight" [TRENCH]. **blasphemy of them**—blasphemous calumny of thee on the part of (or *arising from*) them. . . . **say they are Jews, and are not**—Jews by national descent, but not spiritually of "the true circumcision." The Jews blaspheme Christ as "the hanged one." As elsewhere, so at Smyrna they bitterly opposed Christianity; and at POLYCARP's martyrdom they joined the heathens in clamoring for his being cast to the lions; and when there was an obstacle to this, for his being burnt alive; and with their own hands they carried logs for the pile. **synagogue of Satan**—Only once is the term "synagogue" in the New Testament used of the Christian assembly, and that by the apostle who longest maintained the union of the Church and Jewish Synagogue. As the Jews more and more opposed Christianity, and it more and more rooted itself in the Gentile world, the term "synagogue" was left altogether to the former, and Christians appropriated exclusively the honorable term "Church"; contrast an earlier time when the Jewish theocracy is called "the Church in the wilderness." Cf.Numbers 16:3; 20:4, "congregation *of the Lord.*" Even in James 2:2 it is "*your* (not *the Lord's*) assembly." The *Jews,* who might have been "the Church of God," had now, by their opposition and unbelief, become the synagogue of Satan. So "the throne of Satan" (vs. 13) represents the *heathens'* opposition to Christianity; "the depths of Satan" (vs. 24), the opposition of *heretics.* **10. Fear none ...**—the oldest MSS. read, "Fear *not* those things. ..." "The Captain of our salvation never keeps back what those who faithfully witness for Him may have to bear for His name's sake; never entices recruits by the promise they shall find all things easy and pleasant there" [TRENCH]. **devil** —"the accuser." He acted, through Jewish *accusers* against Christ and His people. The conflict of the latter was not with mere flesh and blood, but with the rulers of the darkness of this world. **tried** —with *temptation* by "the devil." The same event is often both a *temptation* from the devil, and a *trial* from God—God sifting and winnowing the man to separate his chaff from his wheat, the devil sifting him in the hope that nothing but chaff will be found in him [TRENCH]. **ten days**—not the ten persecutions from Nero to Diocletian. LYRA explains *ten years* on the year-day principle. The *shortness* of the duration of the persecution is evidently made the ground of consolation. The time of trial shall be short, the duration of your joy shall be for ever. Cf. the use of "ten days" for a short time, Genesis 24:55; Numbers 11:19. *Ten* is the number of the world powers hostile to the Church; cf. the *ten* horns of the beast, ch. 13:1. **unto death**—so as even to endure death for My sake. **crown of life**—James 1:12; II Timothy 4:8, "crown of righteousness"; I Peter 5:4, "crown of glory." The *crown* is the *garland,* the mark of a *conqueror,* or of one *rejoicing,* or at a *feast;* but *diadem* is the mark of a KING. **11. shall not be hurt**—*Greek,* "shall not by any means (or possibly) be hurt." **the second death**— "the lake of fire." "The death in life of the lost, as contrasted with the life in death of the saved" [TRENCH]. The phrase "the second death" is peculiar to the Apocalypse. What matter about the first death, which sooner or later must pass over us, if we escape *the second death?* "It seems that they who die that death shall be *hurt* by it; whereas, if it were annihilation, and so a conclusion of their torments, it would be no way hurtful, but highly beneficial to them. But the living torments are the second death" [BISHOP PEARSON]. "The life of the damned is death" [AUGUSTINE]. Smyrna (meaning *myrrh*) yielded its sweet perfume in being bruised even to death. Myrrh was used in embalming dead bodies (John 19:39); was an ingredient in the holy anointing oil (Exod. 30:23); a perfume of the heavenly Bridegroom (Ps. 45:8), and of the bride (Song of Sol. 3:6). "Affliction, like it, is *bitter* for the time being, but *salutary;* preserving the elect from *corruption,* and *seasoning* them for immortality, and gives scope for the exercise of the *fragrantly breathing* Christian virtues" [VITRINGA]. POLYCARP'S noble words to his heathen judges who

wished him to recant, are well known: "Fourscore and six years have I served the Lord, and He never wronged me, how then can I blaspheme my King and Saviour?" Smyrna's faithfulness is rewarded by its candlestick not having been removed out of its place (vs. 5); Christianity has never wholly left it; whence the Turks call it, "Infidel Smyrna." **12.** TRENCH prefers writing *Pergamus,* or rather, *Pergamum,* on the river Caicus. It was capital of Attalus the Second's kingdom, which was bequeathed by him to the Romans, 133 B.C. Famous for its library, founded by Eumenes (197-159), and destroyed by Caliph Omar. *Parchment,* i.e., *Pergamena charta,* was here discovered for book purposes. Also famous for the magnificent temple of Esculapius, the healing god [TACITUS, *Annals,* 3. 63]. **he which hath the sharp sword with two edges**—appropriate to His address having a twofold bearing, a searching power so as to convict and convert some (vss. 13, 17), and to convict and condemn to punishment others (vss. 14-16, especially vs. 16; cf. also *Note,* ch. 1:16). **13. I know thy works**—Two oldest MSS. omit this clause; one oldest MS. retains it. **Satan's seat**—rather as the *Greek* is translated all through Revelation, "throne." Satan, in impious mimicry of God's heavenly throne, sets up his earthly throne (ch. 4:2). Esculapius was worshipped there under the serpent form; and Satan, the old serpent, as the instigator (cf. vs. 10) of fanatical devotees of Esculapius, and, through them, of the supreme magistracy at Pergamos, persecuted one of the Lord's people (Antipas) even to death. Thus, this address is an anticipatory preface to ch. 12:1-17; *Note,* "throne ... the dragon, Satan ... war with her seed," 5:9, 17. **even in those days**—Two oldest MSS. omit "even"; two retain it. **wherein**—Two oldest MSS. omit this (then translate, "in the days of Antipas, My faithful witness," or "martyr"); two retain it. Two oldest MSS.read, "My witness, MY faithful one"; two read as *English Version.* Antipas is another form for Antipater. SIMEON METAPHRASTES has a palpably legendary story, unknown to the early Fathers, that Antipas, in Domitian's reign, was shut up in a red-hot brazen bull, and ended his life in thanksgivings and prayers. HENGSTENBERG makes the name, like other apocalyptic names, symbolical, meaning one standing out "against all" for Christ's sake. **14. few**—in comparison of the *many* tokens of thy faithfulness. **hold the doctrine of Balaam**—"the *teaching* of Balaam," viz., that which he "taught Balak." Cf. "the counsel of Balaam," Numbers 31:16. "Balak" is dative in the *Greek,* whence BENGEL translates, "taught (the Moabites) for (i.e., to please) Balak." But though in Numbers it is not expressly said he taught *Balak,* yet there is nothing said inconsistent with his having done so; and JOSEPHUS, *Antiquities,* 4. 6. 6, says he did so. The dative is a Hebraism for the accusative. **children**—*Greek,* "*sons* of Israel." **stumbling block**—lit., that part of a trap on which the bait was laid, and which, when touched, caused the trap to close on its prey; then any entanglement to the foot [TRENCH]. **eat things sacrificed unto idols** —the act common to the Israelites of old, and the Nicolaitanes in John's day; he does not add what was peculiar to the Israelites, viz., that they *sacrificed* to idols. The temptation to eat idol meats was a peculiarly strong one to the Gentile converts. For not to do so involved almost a withdrawal from partaking of any social meal with the heathen around. For idol meats, after a part had been offered in sacrifice, were nearly sure to be on the heathen entertainer's table; so much so, that the

Greek "to kill" (*thuein*) meant originally "to sacrifice." Hence arose the decree of the council of Jerusalem forbidding to eat such meats; subsequently some at Corinth ate unscrupulously and *knowingly* of such meats, on the ground that the idol is nothing; others needlessly fortured themselves with scruples, lest *unknowingly* they should eat of them when they got meat from the market or in a heathen friend's house. Paul handles the question in I Corinthians 8 and 10:25-33. **fornication**—often connected with idolatry. **15. thou**—emphatic: "So THOU also hast," As Balak and the Moabites of old had Balaam and his followers literally, *so hast thou also them that hold the* same Balaamite or *Nicolaitane doctrine* spiritually or symbolically. Literal eating of idol meats and fornication in Pergamos were accompanied by spiritual idolatry and fornication. So TRENCH explains. But I prefer taking it, "THOU *also*," as well as Ephesus ("in like manner" as Ephesus; see below the oldest reading), hast ... Nicolaitanes, with this important difference, Ephesus, as a Church, *hates them* and casts them out, but thou "*hast them*," viz., in the Church. **doctrine**—teaching (*Note*, vs. 6): viz., to tempt God's people to idolatry. **which thing I hate**—It is sin not to hate what God hates. The Ephesian Church (vs. 6) had this point of superiority to Pergamos. But the three oldest MSS., and *Vulgate* and *Syriac,* read instead of "which I hate," "IN LIKE MANNER." **16.** The three oldest MSS. read, "Repent, *therefore*." Not only the Nicolaitanes, but the whole Church of Pergamos is called on to repent of not having *hated* the Nicolaitane teaching and practice. Contrast Paul, Acts 20:26. **I will come**—I am coming. **fight against them**—Greek, "war with them"; with the Nicolaitanes primarily; but including also *chastisement of the* whole Church at Pergamos: cf. "unto THEE." **with the sword of my mouth**—resumed from ch. 1:16, but with an allusion to the drawn *sword* with which the angel of the Lord confronted Balaam on his way to curse Israel: an earnest of *the sword* by which he and the seduced Israelites fell at last. The spriutal Balaamites of John's day are to be smitten with the Lord's spiritual sword, the word or "rod of His mouth." **17. to eat**—omitted in the three oldest MSS. **the hidden manna**—the heavenly food of Israel, in contrast to the idol meats (vs. 14). A pot of manna was laid up in the holy place "before the testimony." The allusion is here to this: probably also to the Lord's discourse (John 6:31-35). Translate, "the manna which is hidden." As the manna hidden in the sanctuary was by divine power preserved from corruption, so Christ in His incorruptible body has passed into the heavens, and is hidden there until the time of His appearing. Christ Himself is the manna "hidden" from the world, but revealed to the believer, so that he has already a foretaste of His preciousness. Cf. as to Christ's own hidden food on earth, John 4:32, 34, and Job 23:12. The full manifestation shall be at His coming. Believers are now hidden, even as their meat is hidden. As the manna in the sanctuary, unlike the other manna, was incorruptible, so the spiritual feast offered to all who reject the world's dainties for Christ is everlasting: an incorruptible body and life for ever in Christ at the resurrection. **white stone** ... **new name** ... **no man knoweth saving he** ...—TRENCH's explanation seems best. *White* is the color and livery of heaven. "New" implies something altogether renewed and heavenly. The white stone is a glistening diamond, the Urim borne by the high priest within the *choschen* or breastplate of judgment, with the

twelve tribes' names on the twelve precious stones, next the heart. The word *Urim* means light, answering to the color *white*. None but the high priest knew the name written upon it, probably the incommunicable name of God, "Jehovah." The high priest consulted it in some divinely appointed way to get direction from God when needful. The "new name" is *Christ's* (cf. ch. 3:12, "I will write upon him *My* new name"): some new revelation of Himself which shall hereafter be imparted to His people, and which they alone are capable of receiving. The connection with the "hidden manna" will thus be clear, as none save the high priest had access to the "manna hidden" in the sanctuary. Believers, as spiritual priests unto God, shall enjoy the heavenly antitypes to the hidden manna and the Urim stone. What they had peculiarly to contend against at Pergamos was the temptation to *idol meats,* and *fornication,* put in their way by Balaamites. As Phinehas was rewarded with "an everlasting priesthood" for his zeal against these very sins to which the Old Testament Balaam seduced Israel; so the heavenly high priesthood is the reward promised here to those zealous against the New Testament Balaamites tempting Christ's people to the same sins. **receiveth it**—viz., "the stone"; not "the new name"; see above. The "name that no man knew but Christ Himself," He shall hereafter reveal to His people. **18. Thyatira**—in Lydia, south of Pergamos. Lydia, the purple-seller of this city, having been conve.ted at Philippi, a Macedonian city (with which Thyatira, as being a Macedonian colony, had naturally much intercourse), was probably the instrument of first carrying the Gospel to her native town. John follows the geographical order here, for Thyatira lay a little to the left of the road from Pergamos to Sardis (STRABO, 13:4). **Son of God ... eyes like ... fire ... feet ... like fine brass**—or "glowing brass" (*Note*, ch. 1:14, 15, whence this description is resumed). Again His attributes accord with His address. The title "Son of God," is from Psalm 2:7, 9, which is referred to in vs. 27. The attribute, "eyes like a flame ..." answers to vs. 23, "I am He which searcheth the reins and hearts." The attribute, "feet like ... brass," answers to vs. 27, "as the vessels of a potter shall they be broken to shivers," He *treading* them *to pieces* with His strong feet. **19.** The oldest MSS. transpose the *English Version* order, and read, "faith and service." The four are subordinate to "thy works"; thus, "I know thy works, *even* the love and the faith (these two forming one pair, as 'faith works by love,' Gal. 5:6), and the service (*ministration* to the suffering members of the Church, and to all in spiritual or temporal need), and the endurance of (i.e., shown by) thee" (this pronoun belongs to all four). As *love* is inward, so *service* is its outward manifestation. Similarly, *faith* and persevering *edurance,* or "*patient continuance*" (the same Greek as here, Rom. 2:7) in well-doing," are connected. **and thy works; and the last**—Omit the second "and," with the three oldest MSS. and the ancient versions; translate, "And (I know) thy works which are last (to be) more in number than the first"; realizing I Thessalonians 4:1; the converse of Matthew 12:45; II Peter 2:20. Instead of retrograding from "the first works" and "first love," as Ephesus, Thyatira's *last works* exceeded her *first* (vss. 4, 5). **20. a few things**—omitted in the three oldest MSS. Translate then, "I have against thee *that....*" **sufferest**—The three oldest MSS. read, "lettest alone." **that woman**—Two oldest MSS. read, "THY wife"; two omit it. *Vulgate* and most ancient versions read as *English*

Version. The symbolical Jezebel was to the Church of Thyatira what Jezebel, Ahab's "wife," was to him. Some self-styled prophetess (or as the feminine in *Hebrew* is often used *collectively* to express a multitude, *a set of false prophets*), as closely attached to the Church of Thyatira as a *wife* is to a husband, and as powerfully influencing for evil that Church as Jezebel did Ahab. As Balaam, in Israel's early history, so Jezebel, daughter of Eth-baal, king of Sidon (I Kings 16:31, formerly priest of Astarte, and murderer of his predecessor on the throne, JOSEPHUS, *Contra Apion*, 1. 18), was the great seducer to idolatry in Israel's later history. Like her father, she was swift to shed blood. Wholly given to Baal-worship, like Eth-baal, whose name expresses his idolatry, she, with her strong will, seduced the weak Ahab and Israel beyond the calf-worship (which was a worship of the true God under the cherub-ox form, i.e., a violation of the second commandment) to that of Baal (a violation of the first commandment also). She seems to have been herself a priestess and prophetess of Baal. Cf. II Kings 9:22, 30, "*whoredoms* of . . . Jezebel and her *witchcrafts*" (impurity was part of the worship of the Phœnician Astarte, or Venus). Her spiritual counterpart at Thyatira lured God's "servants" by pretended utterances of inspiration to the same libertinism, fornication, and eating of idol meats, as the Balaamites and Nicolaitanes (vss. 6, 14, 15). By a false spiritualism these seducers led their victims into the grossest carnality, as though things done in the flesh were outside the true man, and were, therefore, indifferent. "The deeper the Church penetrated into heathenism, the more she herself became heathenish; this prepares us for the expressions 'harlot' and 'Babylon,' applied to her afterwards" [AUBERLEN]. **to teach and to seduce**—The three oldest MSS. read, "and she teaches and seduces," or "deceives." "Thyatira was just the reverse of Ephesus. There, much zeal for orthodoxy, but little love; here, activity of faith and love, but insufficient zeal for godly discipline and doctrine, a patience of error even where there was not a participation in it" [TRENCH]. **21. space**—*Greek,* "time." **of her fornication . . . she repented not**—The three oldest MSS. read, "and she *willeth* not *to repent of* (lit., 'out of', i.e., so as to come *out* of) *her fornication.*" Here there is a transition from *literal* to *spiritual* fornication, as appears from vs. 22. The idea arose from Jehovah's covenant relation to the Old Testament Church being regarded as a marriage, any transgression against which was, therefore, *harlotry, fornication,* or *adultery.* **22. Behold**—calling attention to her awful doom to come. **I will**—*Greek* present, "I cast her." **a bed**—The place of her sin shall be the place of her punishment. The bed of her sin shall be her bed of sickness and anguish. Perhaps a pestilence was about to be sent. Or the bed of the grave, and of the hell beyond, where the worm dieth not. **them that commit adultery with her**—spiritually; including both the eating of *idol meats* and *fornication.* "With her," in the *Greek,* implies *participation with* her in her adulteries, viz., by *suffering her* (vs. 20), or *letting* her *alone,* and so virtually encouraging her. Her punishment is distinct from theirs; she is to be cast into a *bed,* and her *children* to be *killed;* while those who make themselves partakers of her sin by tolerating her, are to be cast into *great tribulation.* **except they repent**—*Greek* aorist, "repent" *at once;* shall have repented by the time limited in My purpose. **their deeds**—Two of the oldest MSS. and most ancient versions read "her." Thus,

God's true servants, who by connivance, are incurring the guilt of *her deeds,* are distinguished from her. One oldest MS., ANDREAS, and CYPRIAN, support "their." **23. her children**—(Isa. 57:3; Ezek. 23: 45, 47). Her proper adherents; not those who *suffer* her, but those who are begotten of her. A distinct class from the last in vs. 22 (cf. *Note* there), whose sin was less direct, being that only of connivance. **kill . . . with death**—Cf. the disaster that overtook the literal Jezebel's votaries of Baal, and Ahab's sons, I Kings 18:40; II Kings 10:6, 7, 24, 25. *Kill with death* is a Hebraism for *slay with most sure and awful death;* so "dying thou shalt die" (Gen. 2:17). Not "die the common death of men" (Num. 16:29). **all the churches shall know**—implying that these addresses are designed for the catholic Church of all ages and places. So palpably shall God's hand be seen in the judgment on Thyatira, that the whole Church shall recognize it as God's doing. **I am he**—the "I" is strongly emphatical: "that it is *I* am He who. . . ." **searcheth . . . hearts**—God's peculiar attribute is given to Christ. The "reins" are the seat of the desires; the "heart," that of the thoughts. The *Greek* for "searcheth" expresses an accurate following up of all tracks and windings. **unto every one of you**—lit., "unto you, to each." **according to your works**—to be judged not according to the mere act as it appears to man, but with reference to the motive, *faith* and *love* being the only motives which God recognizes as sound. **24. you . . . and . . . the rest**—The three oldest MSS. omit "and"; translate then, "Unto you, the rest." **as many as have not**—not only do not *hold,* but are free from contact with. **and which**—The oldest MSS. omit "and"; translate, "whosoever." **the depths**—These false prophets boasted peculiarly of their *knowledge of mysteries* and *the deep things of God;* pretensions subsequently expressed by their arrogant title, *Gnostics* ("full of knowledge"). The Spirit here declares their so-called "depths," (viz., of knowledge of divine things) to be really "depths *of Satan";* just as in vs. 9, He says, instead of "the synagogue *of God,*" "the synagogue *of Satan.*" HENGSTENBERG thinks the teachers themselves professed to fathom *the depths of Satan,* giving loose rein to fleshly lusts, without being hurt thereby. They who thus think to fight Satan with his own weapons always find him more than a match for them. The words, "as they speak," i.e., "as they call them," coming after not only "depths," but "depths of Satan," seem to favor this latter view; otherwise I should prefer the former, in which case, "as they speak," or "call them," must refer to "depths" only, not also "depths *of Satan.*" The original sin of Adam was a desire to know EVIL *as well as good;* so in HENGSTENBERG'S view, those who professed to know "the depths of Satan." It is the prerogative of God alone to know evil fully, without being hurt or defiled by it. **I will put**—Two oldest MSS. have "I put," or "cast." One oldest MS. reads as *English Version.* **none other burden**—save abstinence from, and protestation against, these abominations; no "depths" beyond your reach, such as they teach, no new doctrine, but the old faith and rule of practice once for all delivered to the saints. Exaggerating and perfecting Paul's doctrine of grace without the law as the source of justification and sanctification, these false prophets rejected the law as a rule of life, as though it were an intolerable "burden." But it is a "light" burden. In Acts 15:28, 29, the very term "burden," as here, is used of abstinence from fornication and idol meats; to this the Lord here refers. **25. that which ye have** already—(Jude 3, end). **hold fast**—do not let go from your grasp, however false teachers may wish to wrest it from you. **till I come**—when your conflict with evil will be at an end. The *Greek* implies *uncertainty* as to when He shall come. **26. And**—implying the close connection of the promise to the conqueror that follows, with the preceding exhortation, vs. 25. **and keepeth**—*Greek,* "and he that keepeth." Cf. the same word in the passage already alluded to by the Lord, Acts 15:28, 29, end. **my works**—in contrast to "her (*English Version,* 'their') works" (vs. 22). The works which I command and which are the fruit of My Spirit. **unto the end**—(Matt. 24:13). The image is perhaps from the race, wherein it is not enough to enter the lists, but the runner must persevere *to the end.* **give power**—*Greek,* authority." over the nations—at Christ's coming the saints shall possess the kingdom "under the whole heaven"; therefore over this earth; cf. Luke 19:17, "have thou *authority* [the same *word* as here] over ten cities." **27.** From Psalm 2:8, 9. **rule**—lit., "rule as a shepherd." In Psalm 2:9 it is, "Thou shalt *break* them with a rod of iron." The LXX, pointing the *Hebrew* word differently, read as Revelation here. The *English Version* of Psalm 2:9 is doubtless right, as the parallel word, "dash in pieces," proves. But the Spirit in this case sanctions the *additional* thought as true, that the Lord shall mingle mercy to some, with judgment on others; beginning by destroying His Antichristian foes, He shall reign in love over the rest. "Christ shall rule them with a *scepter* of iron, to make them capable of being ruled with a scepter of gold; severity first, that grace may come after" [TRENCH, who thinks we ought to translate "SCEPTER" for "rod," as in Hebrews 1:8]. "Shepherd" is used in Jeremiah 6:3, of *hostile rulers;* so also in Zechariah 11:16. As severity here is the primary thought, "rule as a shepherd" seems to me to be used thus: He who would have shepherded them with a pastoral rod, shall, because of their hardened unbelief, shepherd them with a rod of iron. **shall they be broken**—So one oldest MS., *Vulgate, Syriac,* and *Coptic Versions* read. But two oldest MSS. read, "as the vessels of a potter *are* broken to shivers." *A potter's vessel dashed to pieces,* because of its failing to answer the design of the maker, is the image to depict God's sovereign power to give reprobates to destruction, not by caprice, but in the exercise of His righteous judgment. The saints shall be in Christ's victorious "armies" when He shall inflict the last decisive blow, and afterwards shall reign with Him. Having by faith "overcome the world," they shall also rule the world. **even as I**—"as I also have received of (from) My Father," viz., in Psalm 2:7-9. Jesus had refused to receive the kingdom without the cross at Satan's hands; He would receive it from none but the Father, who had appointed the cross as the path to the crown. As the Father has given the authority to Me over the heathen and uttermost parts of the earth, so I impart a share of it to My victorious disciple. **28. the morning star**—i.e., I will give unto him *Myself,* who am "the morning star" (ch. 22:16); so that reflecting My perfect brightness, he shall shine like Me, the morning star, and share My *kingly glory* (of which a *star* is the symbol, Num. 21:17; Matt. 2:2). Cf. vs. 17, "I will give him ... the hidden manna," i.e., *Myself,* who am that manna (John 6:31-33).

CHAPTER 3

Vss. 1-22. THE EPISTLES TO SARDIS, PHILADELPHIA, AND LAODICEA. **1. Sardis**—the ancient capital of Lydia, the kingdom of wealthy Crœsus, on the river Pactolus. The address to this Church is full of rebuke. It does not seem to have been in vain; for Melito, bishop of Sardis in the second century, was eminent for piety and learning. He visited Palestine to assure himself and his flock as to the Old Testament canon and wrote an epistle on the subject [EUSEBIUS, 4. 26]; he also wrote a commentary on the Apocalypse [EUSEBIUS, 4. 26; JEROME, *Catalogus Scriptorum Ecclesiasticorum,* 24]. **he that hath the seven Spirits of God**—i.e., He who hath all the fulness of the Spirit (ch. 1:4; 4:5; 5:6, with which cf. Zech. 3:9; 4:10, proving His Godhead). This attribute implies His infinite power by the Spirit to convict of sin and of a hollow profession. **and the seven stars**—(ch. 1:16, 20). His *having the seven stars,* or presiding ministers, flows, as a consequence, from His *having the seven Spirits,* or the fulness of the Holy Spirit. The human ministry is the fruit of Christ's sending down the gifts of the Spirit. *Stars* imply brilliancy and glory; the fulness of the Spirit, and the fulness of brilliant light in Him, form a designed contrast to the formality which He reproves. **name ... livest ... dead**—(I Tim. 5:6; II Tim. 3:5 Titus 1:16; cf. Eph. 2:1, 5; 5:14). "A name," i.e., a reputation. Sardis was famed among the churches for spiritual *vitality;* yet the Heart-searcher, who seeth not as man seeth, pronounces her *dead;* how great searchings of heart should her case create among even the best of us! Laodicea deceived herself as to her true state (vs. 17), but it is not written that she had a high *name* among the other churches, as Sardis had. **2. Be**—*Greek,* "Become," what thou art not, "watchful," or "wakeful," lit., "waking." **the things which remain**—Strengthen those thy remaining few graces, which, in thy spiritual deadly slumber, are not yet quite extinct [ALFORD]. "The things that remain" can hardly mean "the PERSONS that are not yet dead, but *are ready to die";* for vs. 4 implies that the "few" faithful ones at Sardis were not "ready to die," but were full of life. **are**—The two oldest MSS. read, "were ready," lit., "were about to die," viz., at the time when you "strengthen" them. This implies that "thou art dead," vs. 1, is to be taken with limitation; for those must have some life who are told to *strengthen the things that remain.* **perfect**—lit., "filled up in full complement"; Translate, "complete." Weighed in the balance of Him who requires living faith as the motive of works, and found wanting. **before God**—*Greek,* in the sight of God." The three oldest MSS., *Vulgate, Syriac,* and *Coptic,* read, "before (in the sight of) MY God"; Christ's judgment is God the Father's judgment. In the sight of men, Sardis had "a name of living": "so many and so great are the obligations of pastors, that he who would in reality fulfil even a third of them, would be esteemed holy by men, whereas, if content with that alone, he would be sure not to escape hell" [JUAN D'AVILA]. Note, in Sardis and Laodicea alone of the seven we read of no conflict with foes within or without the Church. Not that either had renounced the *appearance* of opposition to the world; but neither had the faithfulness to witness for God by word and example, so as to "*torment* them that dwelt on the earth" (ch. 11:10). **3. how thou hast received**—(Col. 2:6; I Thess. 4:1; I Tim. 6:20). What Sardis is to "remember" is, not *how* joyfully she had received originally the

Gospel message, but how the precious deposit was committed to her originally, so that she could not say, she had not "received and heard" it. The *Greek* is not aorist (as in ch. 2:4, as to Ephesus, "Thou *didst leave* thy first love"), but "thou hast received" (perfect), and still hast the permanent deposit of doctrine committed to thee. The word "keep" (so the *Greek* is for *English Version*, "hold fast") which follows, accords with this sense. "Keep" or observe the commandment which thou hast received and didst hear. **heard**—*Greek* aorist, "didst hear," viz., when the Gospel doctrine was committed to thee. TRENCH explains "how," *with what demonstration of the Spirit and power* from Christ's ambassadors the truth came to you, and how heartily and zealously you at first received it. Similarly BENGEL, "Regard to her former *character* (*how* it once stood) ought to guard Sardis against the future *hour, whatsoever* it shall be, proving fatal to her." But it is not likely that the Spirit repeats the same exhortation virtually to Sardis as to Ephesus. **If therefore**—seeing thou art so warned, if, nevertheless. . . . **come on thee as a thief**—in special judgment on thee as a Church, with the same stealthiness and as unexpectedly as shall be My visible second coming. As *the thief* gives no notice of his approach. Christ applies the language which in its fullest sense describes His second coming, to describe His coming in special judgments on churches and states (as Jerusalem, Matt. 24) these special judgments being anticipatory earnests of that great last coming. "The last day is hidden from us, that every day may be observed by us" [AUGUSTINE]. Twice Christ in the days of His flesh spake the same words (Matt. 24:42, 43; Luke 12:39, 40); and so deeply had His words been engraven on the minds of the apostles that they are often repeated in their writings (ch. 16:15; I Thess. 5:2, 4, 6; II Pet. 3:10). The Greek proverb was that "the feet of the avenging deities are shod with wool," expressing the noiseless approach of the divine judgments, and their possible nearness at the moment when they were supposed the farthest off [TRENCH]. **4.** The three oldest MSS. prefix "but," or "nevertheless" (notwithstanding thy spiritual deadness), and omit "even." **names**—persons *named* in the book of life (vs. 5) known by name by the Lord as His own. These had the reality corresponding to their name; not a mere *name* among men as *living*, while really *dead* (vs. 1). The gracious Lord does not overlook any exceptional cases of real saints in the midst of unreal professors. **not defiled their garments**—viz., the garments of their Christian profession, of which baptism is the initiatory seal, whence the candidates for baptism used in the ancient Church to be arrayed in white. Cf. also Ephesians 5:27, as to the spotlessness of the Church when she shall be presented to Christ; and ch. 19:8, as to the "fine linen, clean and white, the righteousness of the saints," in which it shall be granted to her to be arrayed; and "the wedding garment." Meanwhile she is not to sully her Christian profession with any defilement of flesh or spirit, but to "keep her garments." For no defilement shall enter the heavenly city. Not that any keep themselves here wholly free from defilement; but, as compared with hollow professors, the godly *keep themselves unspotted from the world;* and when they do contract it, they wash it away, so as to have their "robes white in the blood of the Lamb" (ch. 7:14). The *Greek* is not "to stain" (*Greek, miainein*), but to "defile," or besmear (*Greek, molunein*), Song of Solomon 5:3. **3. they shall walk with me in white**—The promised reward

accords with the character of those to be rewarded: keeping their *garments undefiled* and white through the blood of the Lamb now, they shall *walk with Him in while* hereafter. On "with me," cf. the very same words, Luke 23:43; John 17:24. "Walk" implies spiritual life, for only the living walk; also liberty, for it is only the free who walk at large. The grace and dignity of flowing long garments is seen to best advantage when the person "walks": so the graces of the saint's manifested character shall appear fully when he *shall serve* the Lord perfectly hereafter (ch. 22:3). **they are worthy**—with the worthiness (not their own, but that) which Christ has put on them (ch. 7:14). Ezekiel 16:14, "perfect through MY comeliness which I had put upon thee." Grace is glory in the bud. "The *worthiness* here denotes a congruity between the saint's *state of grace* on earth, and that of *glory*, which the Lord has appointed for them, about to be estimated by the law itself of grace" [VITRINGA]. Contrast Acts 13:46. **5. white**—not a dull white, but glittering, dazzling white [GROTIUS]. Cf. Matthew 13:43. The body transfigured into the likeness of Christ's body, and emitting beams of light reflected from Him, is probably the "white raiment" promised here. **the same**—*Greek,* "THIS man"; he and he alone. So one oldest MS. reads. But two oldest MSS., and most of the ancient versions, shall THUS be clothed. . . ." **raiment**—*Greek,* "garments." "He that overcometh" shall receive the same reward as they who "have not defiled their garments" (vs. 4); therefore the two are identical. **I will not**—*Greek,* "I will not by any means." **blot out . . . name out of . . . book of life**—of the heavenly city. A register was kept in ancient cities of their citizens: the names of the dead were of course erased. So those who have a *name that they live and are dead* (vs. 1), are blotted out of God's roll of the heavenly citizens and heirs of eternal *life;* not that in God's electing decree they ever were in His book of life. But, according to human conceptions, those who had a high name for piety would be supposed to be in it, and were, in respect to privileges, actually among those in the way of salvation; but these privileges, and the fact that they once might have been saved, shall be of no avail to them. As to the *book of life,* cf. ch. 13:8; 17:8; 20:12, 15; 21:27; Exod. 32:32; Psalm 69: 28; Daniel 12:1. In the sense of the *call,* many are enrolled among the *called* to salvation, who shall not be found among *the chosen* at last. The pale of salvation is wider than that of election. Election is fixed. Salvation is open to all and is pending (humanly speaking) in the case of those mentioned here. But ch. 20:15; 21:27, exhibit the book of the elect alone in the narrower sense, after the erasure of the others. **before . . . before**—*Greek,* "in the presence of." Cf. the same promise of Christ's confessing before His Father those who confessed Him, Matthew 10:32, 33; Luke 12:8, 9. He omits "in heaven" after "My Father," because there is, now that He is in heaven, no contrast between the Father *in heaven* and the Son *on earth.* He now sets His seal from heaven upon many of His words uttered on earth [TRENCH]. An undesigned coincidence, proving that these epistles are, as they profess, in their words, as well as substance, Christ's own addresses; not even tinged with the color of John's style, such as it appears in his Gospel and Epistles. The coincidence is mainly with the three other Gospels, and not with John's, which makes the coincidence more markedly undesigned. So also the clause, "He that hath an ear, let him hear," is not repeated from John's Gospel, but from the

Lord's own words in the three synoptic Gospels (Matt. 11:15; 13:9; Mark 4:9, 23; 7:16; Luke 8:8; 14:35). **6.** (Cf. *Note*, ch. 2:7.) **7. Philadelphia**—in Lydia, twenty-eight miles southeast of Sardis, built by Attalus Philadelphus, king of Pergamos, who died A.D. 138. It was nearly destroyed by an earthquake in the reign of Tiberius [TACITUS, *Annals*, 2. 47]. The connection of this Church with Jews there causes the address to it to have an Old Testament coloring in the images employed. It and Smyrna alone of the seven receive unmixed praise. **he that is holy**—as in the Old Testament, *"the Holy One* of Israel." Thus Jesus and the God of the Old Testament are one. None but God is absolutely holy (*Greek, hagios,* separate from evil and perfectly hating it). In contrast to "the synagogue of Satan" (vs. 9). **true**—*Greek, alethinos:* "VERY God," as distinguished from the false gods and from all those who *say that they are* what *they are not* (vs. 9): real, genuine. Furthermore, He *perfectly* realizes all that is involved in the names, GOD, *Light* (John 1:9; I John 2:8), *Bread* (John 6:32), the *Vine* (John 15:1); as distinguished from all typical, partial, and imperfect realizations of the idea. His nature answers to His name (John 17:3; I Thess. 1:9). The *Greek, alethes,* on the other hand, is "truth-speaking," "truthloving" (John 3:33; Titus 1:2). **he that hath the key of David**—the antitype of Eliakim, to whom the "key," the emblem of authority "over the house of David," was transferred from Shebna, who was removed from the office of chamberlain or treasurer, as unworthy of it. Christ, the Heir of the throne of David, shall supplant all the less worthy stewards who have abused their trust in God's spiritual house, and "shall reign over the house of Jacob," literal and spiritual (Luke 1:32, 33), "for ever," "as a Son over His own house" (Heb. 3:2-6). It rests with Christ to open or shut the heavenly palace, deciding who is, and who is not, to be admitted: as He also opens, or shuts, the prison, *having the keys of hell* (*the grave*) *and death* (ch. 1:18). The power of the keys was given to Peter and the other apostles, only when, and in so far as, Christ made him and them infallible. Whatever degrees of this power may have been committed to ministers, the supreme power belongs to Christ alone. Thus Peter rightly opened the Gospel door to the Gentiles (Acts 10; 11:17, 18; especially 14: 27, end). But he wrongly tried to shut the door in part again (Gal 2:11-18). Eliakim had "the key of the house of David laid upon his shoulder": Christ, as the antitypical David, Himself has the key of the supreme "government upon His shoulder." His attribute here, as in the former addresses, accords with His promise. Though "the synagogue of Satan," false "Jews" (vs. 9) try to "shut" the "door" which I "set open before thee"; "no man can shut it" (vs. 8). **shutteth**—So *Vulgate* and *Syriac Versions* read. But the four oldest MSS. read, "shall shut"; so *Coptic Version* and ORIGEN. **shutteth, and no man openeth**—Two oldest MSS., B, ℵ *Coptic Version,* and ORIGEN read, "shall open." Two oldest MSS., A, C. and *Vulgate Version* support *English Version* reading. **8. I have set**—*Greek,* "given": it is My gracious *gift* to thee. **open door** for evangelization; a door of spiritual usefulness. The *opening of a door* by Him to the Philadelphian Church accords with the previous assignation to Him of "the key of David." **and**—The three oldest MSS., A, B, C, and ORIGEN read, *"which* no man can shut." **for**—"because." **a little**—This gives the idea that Christ says, He sets before Philadelphia an open door because she has *some little* strength;

whereas the sense rather is, He does so because she has *"but little* strength": being consciously weak herself, she is the fitter object for God's power to rest on [so AQUINAS], that so the Lord Christ may have all the glory. **and hast kept**—*and* so, the *littleness of thy strength* becoming the source of Almighty power to thee, as leading thee to rest wholly on My great power, *thou hast kept My word.* GROTIUS makes "little strength" to mean that she had a Church *small in numbers and external resources:* "a little flock poor in worldly goods, and of small account in the eyes of men" [TRENCH]. So ALFORD. I prefer the view given above. The *Greek* verbs are in the aorist tense: "Thou didst keep . . . didst not deny My name": alluding to some particular occasion when her faithfulness was put to the test. **9. I will make**—*Greek* present, "I make," lit., "I give" (*Note,* vs. 8). The promise to Philadelphia is larger than that to Smyrna. To Smyrna the promise was that "the synagogue of Satan" should not prevail against the faithful in her: to Philadelphia, that she should even win over some of "the synagogue of Satan" to *fall on their faces and confess God is in her of a truth.* Translate, "(some) of the synagogue." For until Christ shall come, and *all* Israel then be saved, there is but "a remnant" being gathered out of the Jews "according to the election of grace." This is an instance of how Christ set before her an "open door," some of her greatest adversaries, the Jews, being brought to the obedience of the faith. Their *worshipping before her feet* expresses the convert's willingness to take the very lowest place in the Church, doing servile honor to those whom once they persecuted, rather than dwell with the ungodly. So the Philippian jailer before Paul. **10. patience**—"endurance." "The word of My endurance" is *My Gospel word,* which teaches *patient endurance* in expectation of my coming (ch. 1:9). *My endurance* is the endurance which I require, and which I practice. Christ Himself now *endures, patiently* waiting until the usurper be cast out, and all "His enemies be made His footstool." So, too, His Church, for the joy before her of sharing His coming kingdom, *endures patiently.* Hence, in vs. 11, follows, "Behold, I come quickly." **I also** —The reward is in kind: "because thou didst keep. . . ." "I also (on My side) will keep thee. . . . **from** —*Greek,* "(so as to deliver thee) *out of*," not to exempt *from* temptation. **the hour of temptation**—the appointed *season* of affliction and temptation (so in Deut. 4:34 the plagues are called "the temptations of Egypt"), lit., *"the* temptation": the sore temptation which is coming on: the time of great tribulation before Christ's second coming. **to try them that dwell upon the earth**—those who are of earth, earthy (ch. 8:13). "Dwell" implies that their *home* is earth, not heaven. *All mankind, except the elect* (ch. 13:8, 14). The temptation brings out the fidelity of those *kept* by Christ and hardens the unbelieving reprobates (ch. 9:20, 21; 16:11, 21). The particular persecutions which befell Philadelphia shortly after, were the earnest of the great last tribulation before Christ's coming, to which the Church's attention in all ages is directed. **11. Behold**—omitted by the three oldest MSS. and most ancient versions. **I come quickly**—the great incentive to persevering faithfulness, and the consolation under present trials. **that . . . which thou hast**—"The word of my patience," or "endurance" (vs. 10), which He had just commended them for keeping, and which involved with it the attaining of the kingdom; this they would lose if they yielded to the temptation of exchanging consistency and suffering for compromise and ease. **that no man take thy crown**—which otherwise thou wouldst receive: that no tempter cause thee to lose it: not that the tempter would thus secure it for himself (Col. 2:18). **12. pillar in the temple**—In one sense there shall be "no temple" in the heavenly city because there shall be no distinction of things into sacred and secular, for all things and persons shall be holy to the Lord. The city shall be all one great temple, in which the saints shall be not merely *stones*, as in the spiritual temple now on earth, but all eminent as *pillars:* immovably firm (unlike Philadelphia, the city which was so often shaken by earthquakes, STRABO, 12 and 13), like the colossal pillars before Solomon's temple, Boaz (i.e., "In it is strength") and Jachin ("It shall be established"): only that those pillars were outside, these shall be within the temple. **my God**—(*Note*, ch. 2:7). **go no more out**—The *Greek* is stronger, *never more at all*. As the elect angels are beyond the possibility of falling, being now under (as the Schoolmen say) "the blessed necessity of goodness," so shall the saints be. The door shall be once for all shut, as well to shut safely in for ever the elect, as to shut out the lost (Matt. 25:10; John 8:35; cf. Isa. 22:23, the type, Eliakim). They shall be priests for ever unto God (ch. 1:6). "Who would not yearn for that city out of which no friend departs, and into which no enemy enters?" [AUGUSTINE *in* TRENCH]. **write upon him the name of my God**—as belonging to God in a peculiar sense (ch. 7:3; 9:4; 14:1; and especially 23:4), therefore secure. As the name of Jehovah ("Holiness to the Lord") was on the golden plate on the high priest's forehead (Exod. 28:36-38); so the saints in their heavenly royal priesthood shall bear His name openly, as consecrated to Him. Cf. the caricature of this in the brand on the forehead of the beast's followers (ch. 13:16, 17), and on the harlot (ch. 17:5; cf. 20:4). **name of the city of my God**—as one of its citizens (ch. 21:2, 3, 10, which is briefly alluded to by anticipation here). The full description of the city forms the appropriate close of the book. The saint's citizenship is now hidden, but then it shall be manifested: he shall have *the right to enter in through the gates into the city* (ch. 22:14). This was the city which Abraham *looked for.* **new**—*Greek, kaine.* Not the old Jerusalem, once called "the holy city," but having forfeited the name. *Greek, nea*, would express that it had *recently come* into existence; but *Greek, kaine*, that which is *new and different*, superseding the worn-out old Jerusalem and its polity. "John, in the Gospel, applies to the old city the *Greek* name *Hierosolyma*. But in the Apocalypse, always, to the heavenly city the *Hebrew* name, *Hierousalem.* The *Hebrew* name is the original and holier one: the *Greek*, the recent and more secular and political one" [BENGEL]. **my new name**—at present incommunicable and only known to God: to be hereafter revealed and made the believer's own in union with God in Christ. Christ's name written on him denotes he shall be *wholly Christ's. New* also relates to Christ, who shall assume a *new* character (answering to His "new name") entering with His saints on a kingdom—not that which He had with the Father before the worlds, but that earned by His humiliation as Son of man. Gibbon, the infidel (*Decline and Fall*, ch. 64), gives an unwilling testimony to the fulfilment of the prophecy as to Philadelphia from a temporal point of view, Among the Greek colonies and churches of Asia, Philadelphia is still erect,—a *column* in a scene of

ruins—a pleasing example that the paths of honor and safety may sometimes be the same." **13.** (*Note*, ch. 2:7.) **14. Laodiceans**—The city was in the southwest of Phrygia, on the river Lycus, not far from Colosse, and lying between it and Philadelphia. It was destroyed by an earthquake, A.D. 62, and rebuilt by its wealthy citizens without the help of the state [TACITUS, *Annals* 14. 27]. This wealth (arising from the excellence of its wools) led to a self-satisfied, lukewarm state in spiritual things, as vs. 17 describes. See *Note* on Colossians 4:16, on the Epistle which is thought to have been written to the Laodicean Church by Paul. The Church in latter times was apparently flourishing; for one of the councils at which the canon of Scripture was determined was held in Laodicea in A.D. 361. Hardly a Christian is now to be found on or near its site. **the Amen**—(Isa. 65:16, *Hebrew*, "Bless Himself in the God of *Amen* . . . swear by the God of *Amen*," II Cor. 1:20). He who not only says, but is, *the Truth.* The saints used *Amen* at the end of prayer, or in assenting to the word of God; but none, save the Son of God, ever said, "Amen, I say unto you," for it is the language peculiar to God, who avers *by Himself.* The New Testament formula, "Amen, I say unto you," is equivalent to the Old Testament formula, *"as I live,* saith Jehovah." In John's Gospel alone He uses (in the *Greek*) the double "Amen," John 1:51; 3:3, etc.; in *English Version,"* Verily, verily." The title happily harmonizes with the address. His unchanging faithfulness as "the Amen" contrasts with Laodicea's wavering of purpose, "neither hot nor cold" (vs. 16). The angel of Laodicea has with some probability been conjectured to be Archippus, to whom, thirty years previously, Paul had already given a monition, as needing to be stirred up to diligence in his ministry. So the *Apostolic Constitutions*, 8. 46, name him as the first bishop of Laodicea: supposed to be the son of Philemon (Philemon 2). **faithful and true witness**—As "the Amen" expresses the unchangeable truth of His promises; so "the faithful the true witness," the truth of His revelations as to the heavenly things which He has seen and testifies. "Faithful," i.e., trustworthy (II Tim. 2:11, 13). "True" is here (*Greek, alethinos*) *not truth-speaking* (*Greek, alethes*), but "perfectly realizing all that is comprehended in the name *Witness"* (I Tim. 6:13). Three things are necessary for this: (1) to have seen with His own eyes what He attests; (2) to be competent to relate it for others; (3) to be willing truthfully to do so. In Christ all these conditions meet [TRENCH]. **beginning of the creation of God**—not he whom God created first, but as in Colossians 1:15-18 (cf. *Notes* there), the *Beginner* of all creation, its originating instrument. All creation would not be represented adoring Him, if He were but one of themselves. His being the Creator is a strong guarantee for His *faithfulness* as "the Witness and Amen." **15. neither cold**—The antithesis to "hot," lit., "boiling" ("fervent," Acts 18:25; Rom. 12:11; cf. Song of Sol. 8:6; Luke 24:32), requires that "cold" should here mean more than negatively *cold;* it is rather, positively *icy cold:* having never yet been warmed. The Laodiceans were in spritual things *cold* comparatively, but not *cold* as the world outside, and as those who had never belonged to the Church. The lukewarm state, if it be the transitional stage to a warmer, is a desirable state (for a little religion, if real, is better than none); but most fatal when, as here, an abiding condition, for it is mistaken for a safe state (vs. 17). This accounts for Christ's desiring that they were *cold* rather than *lukewarm*. For then there would not be the same "danger of mixed motive and disregarded principle" [ALFORD]. Also, there is more hope of the "cold," i.e., those who are of the world, and not yet warmed by the Gospel call; for, when called, they may become *hot* and fervent Christians: such did the once-*cold* publicans, Zaccheus and Matthew, become. But the *lukewarm* has been brought within reach of the holy fire, without being heated by it into *fervor:* having religion enough to lull the conscience in false security, but not religion enough to save the soul: as Demas, II Timothy 4. Such were the *halters between two opinions* in Israel (I Kings 18:21; cf. II Kings 17: 41; Matt. 6:24). **16. neither cold nor hot**—So one oldest MS., B., and *Vulgate* read. But two oldest MSS., *Syriac, and Coptic* transpose thus, "hot nor cold." It is remarkable that the *Greek* adjectives are in the masculine, agreeing with the angel, not feminine, agreeing with the Church. The Lord addresses the angel as the embodiment and representative of the Church. The chief minister is answerable for his flock if he have not faithfully warned the members of it. **I will**—*Greek,* "I am about to," "I am ready to": I have it in my mind: implying graciously the possibility of the threat not being executed, if only they repent at once. His dealings towards them will depend on theirs towards Him. **spue thee out of my mouth**—reject with righteous loathing, as Canaan spued out its inhabitants for their abominations. Physicians used *lukewarm* water to cause *vomiting. Cold* and *hot* drinks were common at feasts, but never *lukewarm.* There were hot and cold springs near Laodicea. **17.** Self-sufficiency is the fatal danger of a likewarm state (*Note,* vs. 15). **thou sayest**—virtually and mentally, if not in so many words. **increased with goods**—*Greek,* "have become enriched," implying self-praise in self-acquired riches. The Lord alludes to Hosea 12:8. The riches on which they prided themselves were spiritual riches; though, doubtless, their spiritual self-sufficiency ("I have need of nothing") was much fostered by their worldly wealth; as, on the other hand, *poverty of spirit* is fostered by *poverty* in respect to worldly riches. **knowest not that thou**—in particular above all others. The "THOU" in the *Greek* is emphatic. **art wretched**—*Greek,* "art *the* wretched one." **miserable**—So one oldest MSS. reads. But two oldest MSS. prefix "the." Translate, "*the* pitiable"; "the one especially to be pitied." How different Christ's estimate of men, from their own estimate of themselves, "I have need of nothing!" **blind**—whereas Laodicea boasted of a deeper than common *insight* into divine things. They were not absolutely *blind,* else *eye-salve* would have been of no avail to them; but *short-sighted.* **18.** Gentle and loving irony. Take *My* advice, thou who fanciest thyself *in need of nothing.* Not only art thou not in need of nothing, but art in need of the commonest necessaries of existence. He graciously stoops to their modes of thought and speech: Thou art a people ready to listen to any *counsel* as to how to *buy* to advantage; then, listen to My *counsel* (for I am "Counsellor," Isa. 9:6), buy of ME" (*in whom,* according to Paul's Epistle written to the neighboring Colosse and intended for the Laodicean Church also, Colossians 2:1, 3; 4:16, *are hidden all the treasures of wisdom and knowledge*). "Buy" does not imply that we can, by any work or merit of ours, *purchase* God's free gift; nay the very purchase money consists in the renunciation of all

self-righteousness, such as Laodicea had (vs. 17). "Buy" at the cost of thine own self-sufficiency (so Paul, Phil. 3:7, 8); and the giving up of all things, however dear to us, that would prevent our *receiving* Christ's salvation as a *free gift,* e.g., self and worldly desires. Cf. Isaiah 55:1, "Buy . . . without money and price." **of me**—the source of "unsearchable riches" (Eph. 3:8). Laodicea was a city of extensive money transactions [CICERO]. **gold tried in . . .**—lit., "*fired* (and fresh) *from* the fire," i.e., just fresh *from* the furnace which has proved its purity, and retaining its bright gloss. Sterling spiritual wealth, as contrasted with its counterfeit, in which Laodicea boasted itself. Having bought this *gold* she will be no longer *poor* (vs. 17). **mayest be rich**—*Greek,* ". . . enriched." **white raiment**—"garments." Laodicea's wools were famous. Christ offers infinitely whiter raiment. As "gold tried in the fire" expresses *faith* tested by fiery trials: so "white raiment," *Christ's righteousness* imputed to the believer in justification and imparted in sanctification. **appear**—*Greek,* "be manifested," viz., at the last day, when everyone without the wedding garment shall be discovered. To strip one, is in the East the image of putting to open shame. So also to clothe one with fine apparel is the image of doing him honor. Man can discover his shame, God alone can cover it, so that his nakedness shall not be manifested at last (Col. 3:10-14). Blessed is he whose sin is so *covered.* The hypocrite's shame may be manifested now; it must be so at last. **anoint . . . with eye-salve**—The oldest MSS. read, "(buy of Me) eye-salve (collyrium, a roll of ointment), *to anoint* thine eyes." Christ has for Laodicea an ointment far more precious than all the costly unguents of the East. The *eye* is here the conscience or inner light of the mind. According as it is sound and "single" (*Greek, haplous,* "simple"), or otherwise, the man sees aright spiritually, or does not. The Holy Spirit's unction, like the ancient eye-salve's, first smarts with conviction of sin, then heals. He opens our eyes first to ourselves in our wretchedness, then to the Saviour in His preciousness. TRENCH notices that the most sunken churches of the seven, viz., Sardis and Laodicea, are the ones in which alone are specified no opponents from without, nor heresies from within. The Church owes much to God's overruling Providence which has made so often internal and external foes, in spite of themselves, to promote His cause by calling forth her energies in contending for the faith once delivered to the saints. Peace is dearly bought at the cost of spiritual stagnation, where there is not interest enough felt in religion to contend about it at all. **19.** (Job 5:17; Prov. 3: 11, 12; Heb. 12:5, 6.) So in the case of Manasseh (II Chron. 33:11-13). **As many**—All. "He scourgeth every son whom He receiveth. And shalt thou be an exception? If excepted from suffering the scourge, thou art excepted from the number of the sons" [AUGUSTINE]. This is an encouragement to Laodicea not to despair, but to regard the rebuke as a token for good, if she profit by it. **I love**—Greek, *philo,* the love of gratuitous *affection,* independent of any grounds for esteem in the object loved. But in the case of Philadelphia (vs. 9), "I have loved thee" (*Greek, egapesa*) with the love of *esteem,* founded on the judgment. Cf. *Note* in my *English Gnomon* of BENGEL, John 21:15-17. **I rebuke**—The "I" in the *Greek* stands first in the sentence emphatically. *I* in My dealings, so altogether unlike man's, in the case of *all whom I love, rebuke.* The *Greek, elencho,* is the same verb as in John 16:8, "(the Holy Ghost) will *convince* (rebuke unto conviction) the world of sin." **chasten** —"chastise." The *Greek, paideu,* which in classical Greek means to *instruct,* in the New Testament means to *instruct by chastisement* (Heb. 12:5, 6). David was *rebuked unto conviction,* when he cried, "I have sinned against the Lord"; the *chastening* followed when his child was taken from him (II Sam. 12:13, 14). In the divine *chastening,* the sinner at one and the same time winces under the rod and learns righteousness. **be zealous**—habitually. Present tense in the *Greek,* of a *lifelong course of zeal.* The opposite of "lukewarm." The *Greek* by alliteration marks this: Laodicea had not been "hot" (*Greek, zestos*), she is therefore urged to "be zealous" (*Greek, zeleue*): both are derived from the same verb, *Greek, zeo,* "to boil." **repent** —*Greek* aorist: of an act to be *once for all done,* and *done at once.* **20. stand**—waiting in wonderful condescension and long-suffering. **knock**—(Song of Sol. 5:2). This is a further manifestation of His loving desire for the sinner's salvation. He who is Himself "the Door," and who bids us "knock" that it may be "opened unto" us, is first Himself to knock at the door of our hearts. If He did not knock first, we should never come to knock at His door. Cf. Song of Solomon 5:4-6, which is plainly alluded to here; the Spirit thus in Revelation sealing the canonicity of that mystical book. The spiritual state of the bride there, between *waking* and *sleeping,* slow to open the door to her divine lover, answers to that of the *lukewarm* Laodicea here. "Love in regard to men emptied (humbled) God; for He does not remain in His place and call to Himself the servant whom He loved, but He comes down Himself to seek him, and He who is allrich arrives at the lodging of the pauper, and with His own voice intimates His yearning love, and seeks a similar return, and withdraws not when disowned, and is not impatient at insult, and when persecuted still waits at the doors" [NICOLAUS CABASILAS in TRENCH]. **my voice**—He appeals to the sinner not only with His hand (His providences) *knocking,* but with His *voice* (His word read or heard; or rather, His Spirit inwardly applying to man's spirit the lessons to be drawn from His providence and His word). If we refuse to answer to His knocking at our door now, He will refuse to hear our knocking at His door hereafter. In respect to His second coming also, He is even now *at the door,* and we know not how soon He may *knock:* therefore we should always be ready to *open to Him immediately.* **if any man hear**—for man is not compelled by irresistible force: Christ *knocks,* but does not break open the door, though the violent take heaven by the force of prayer (Matt. 11:12): whosoever does hear, does so not of himself, but by the *drawings* of God's grace (John 6:44): *repentance* is Christ's gift (Acts 5:31). He *draws,* not drags. The Sun of righteousness, like the natural sun, the moment that *the door* is opened, pours in His light, which could not previously find an entrance. Cf. HILARY on Psalm 118:19. **I will come in to him** —as I did to Zaccheus. **sup with him, and he with me**—Delightful reciprocity! Cf. "dwelleth in me, and I in Him," John 6:56. Whereas, ordinarily, the admitted guest sups with the admitter, here the divine guest becomes Himself the host, for He is the bread of life, and the Giver of the marriage feast. Here again He alludes to the imagery of the Song of Solomon 4:16, where the Bride invites Him to *eat pleasant fruits,* even as He had first prepared a feast for her, "His fruit was sweet to my taste."

Cf. the same interchange, John 21:9-13, the feast being made up of the viands that Jesus brought, and those which the disciples brought. The consummation of this blessed intercommunion shall be at the Marriage Supper of the Lamb, of which the Lord's Supper is the earnest and foretaste. **21. sit with me in my throne**—(Ch. 2:26, 27; 20:6; Matt. 19:28; 20:23; John 17:22, 24; II Tim. 2.12). The same whom Christ had just before threatened to *spue out of His mouth,* is now offered *a seat with Him on His throne!* "The highest place is within reach of the lowest; the faintest spark of grace may be fanned into the mightiest flame of love" [TRENCH]. **even as I also**—Two thrones are here mentioned: (1)His Father's, upon which He now sits, and has sat since His ascension, after His victory over death, sin, the world; upon this none can sit save God, and the God-man Christ Jesus, for it is the incommunicable prerogative of God alone; (2) the throne which shall be peculiarly *His* as the once humbled and then glorified *Son of man,* to be set up over the whole earth (heretofore usurped by Satan) at His coming again; in this the *victorious* saints shall share (I Cor. 6:2). The transfigured elect Church shall with Christ judge and reign over the nations in the flesh, and Israel the foremost of them; ministering blessings to them as angels were the Lord's mediators of blessing and administrators of His government in setting up His throne in Israel at Sinai. This privilege of our high calling belongs exclusively to the present time while Satan reigns, when alone there is scope for conflict and for *victory* (II Tim. 2:11, 12). When Satan shall be bound (ch. 20.4), there shall be no longer scope for it, for all on earth shall know the Lord from the least to the greatest. This, the grandest and crowning promise, is placed at the end of all the seven addresses, to gather all in one. It also forms the link to the next part of the book, where the Lamb is introduced seated *on His Father's throne* (ch. 4:2, 3; 5:5, 6). The Eastern throne is broad, admitting others besides him who, as chief, occupies the center. TRENCH notices; The order of the promises in the seven epistles corresponds to that of the unfolding of the kingdom of God its first beginnings on earth to its consummation in heaven. To the faithful at Ephesus: (1) *The tree of life in the Paradise of God* is promised (ch. 2:7), answering to Genesis 2. (2) Sin entered the world and death by sin; but to the faithful at Smyrna it is promised, they *shall not be hurt by the second death* (ch. 2:11). (3) The promise of the *hidden manna* (ch. 2:17) to Pergamos brings us to the Mosaic period, the Church in the wilderness. (4) That to Thyatira, viz., triumph *over the nations* (ch. 2:26, 27), forms the consummation of the kingdom in prophetic type, the period of David and Solomon characterized by this *power of the nations.* Here there is a division, the seven falling into two groups, *four* and three, as often, e.g., the Lord's Prayer, three and four. The scenery of the last three passes from earth to heaven, the Church contemplated as triumphant, with its steps from glory to glory. (5) Christ promises to the believer of Sardis not to blot his name out of the book of life but to confess him before His Father and the angels at the judgment day, and clothe him with a glorified body of dazzling whiteness (vss. 4, 5). (6) To the faithful at Philadelphia Christ promises they shall be citizens of the new Jerusalem, fixed as immovable pillars there, where city and temple are one (vs. 12); here not only individual salvation is promised to the believer, as in the case of Sardis, but also privileges in the blessed communion of the Church triumphant. (7) Lastly, to the faithful of Laodicea is given the crowning promise, not only the two former blessings, but a seat with Christ on His throne, even as He has sat with His Father on His Father's throne (vs. 21).

CHAPTER 4

Vss. 1-11. VISION OF GOD'B THRONE IN HEAVEN; THE FOUR AND TWENTY ELDERS; THE FOUR LIVING CREATURES. Here begins the Revelation proper; and first, chs. 4 and 5 set before us the heavenly scenery of the succeeding visions, and God on His throne, as the *covenant God of His Church,* the Revealer of them to His apostle through Jesus Christ. The first great portion comprises the opening of the seals and the sounding of the trumpets (chs. 4 to 11). As the communication respecting the seven churches opened with a suitable vision of the Lord Jesus as Head of the Church, so the second part opens with a vision suitable to the matter to be revealed. The scene is changed from earth to *heaven.* **1. After this**—Greek, "After these things," marking the opening of the next vision in the succession. Here is the transition from "the things which are" (ch. 1:19), the existing state of the seven churches, as a type of the Church in general, in John's time, to "the things which shall be hereafter," viz., in relation to the time when John wrote. **I looked**—rather as *Greek,* "I saw" in vision; not as *English Version* means, I directed my *look* that way. **was**—Omit, as not being in the *Greek* **opened** "standing open"; not as though John saw it in the act of being opened. Cf. Ezekiel 1:1; Matthew 3: 16; Acts 7:56; 10:11. But in those visions the heavens opened, disclosing the visions to those below on earth. Whereas here, heaven, the temple of God, remains closed to those on earth, but John is transported in vision through an open door up into heaven, whence he can see things passing on earth or in heaven, according as the scenes of the several visions require. **the first voice which I heard**—the voice which I heard at first, viz., in ch. 1:10; *the former voice. was* **as it were**—Omit *was,* it not being in the *Greek.* "Behold" governs in sense both "a door . . ." and "the first voice. . . ." **Come up hither**—through the "open door." **be**—come to pass. **hereafter**—Greek, "after these things": after the present time (ch. 1:19). **2. And**—omitted in the two oldest MSS., *Vulgate, Syriac.* **I was . . .** —Greek, "I became in the Spirit" (*Note,* ch. 1:10): I was completely rapt in vision into the heavenly world. **was set**—not *was placed,* but *was situated,* lit., "lay." **one sat on the throne**—the Eternal Father: the Creator (vs. 11): also cf. vs. 8 with ch. 1:4, where also the Father is designated, "which is, and was, and is to come." When the Son, "the Lamb," is introduced, ch. 5:5-9, a *new* song is sung which distinguishes the *Sitter on the throne* from *the Lamb,* "*Thou* hast redeemed us to God," and vs. 13, "Unto Him that sitteth upon the throne, and unto the Lamb." So also in ch. 5:7, as in Daniel 7:13, the *Son of man* brought before *the Ancient of days* is distinguished from Him. The Father in essence is invisible, but in Scripture at times is represented as assuming a visible form. **3. was**—omitted in the two oldest MSS., but supported by *Vulgate* and *Coptic.* **to look upon**—Greek, "in sight," or "appearance." **jasper**—From ch. 21:11, where it is called *most precious,* which the *jasper*

was not, EBRARD infers it was a diamond. Ordinarily, the *jasper* is a stone of various wavy colors, somewhat transparent: in ch. 21:11 it represents watery crystalline brightness. The *sardine,* our cornelian, or else a fiery red. As the watery brightness represents God's holiness, so the fiery red His justice executing fiery wrath. The same union of white or watery brightness and fiery redness appears in ch. 1:14; 10:1; Ezekiel 1:4; 8:2; Daniel 7: 9. **rainbow round about the throne**—forming a complete circle (type of God's perfection and eternity: not a half circle as the earthly rainbow) surrounding the throne vertically. Its various colors, which combined form one pure solar ray, symbolize the varied aspects of God's providential dealings uniting in one harmonious whole. Here, however, the predominating color among the prismatic colors is green, the most refreshing of colors to look upon, and so symbolizing God's consolatory promises in Christ to His people amidst judgments on His foes. Moreover, the rainbow was the appointed token of God's covenant with all flesh, and His people in particular. Hereby God in type renewed to man the grant originally made to the first Adam. The antitype will be the "new heavens and the new earth" restored to redeemed man, just as the earth, after the destruction by the flood, was restored to Noah. As the rainbow was first reflected on the waters of the world's ruin, and continues to be seen only when a cloud is brought over the earth, so another deluge, viz., of fire, shall precede the new heavens and earth: the Lord, as here, on His throne, whence (vs. 5) proceed "lightnings and thunderings," shall issue the commission to rid the earth of its oppressors: but then, amidst judgment, when other men's hearts fail them for fear, the believer shall be reassured by the rainbow, the covenant token, round the throne (cf. DE BURGH, *Rev.*). The heavenly bow speaks of the shipwreck of the world through sin: it speaks also of calm and sunshine after the storm. The *cloud* is the regular token of God's and Christ's presence, e.g., in the tabernacle's holiest place; on Mount Sinai at the giving of the law; at the ascension (Acts 1:9); at His coming again (ch. 4:7). **4. seats**—rather as the *Greek* is translated in this very verse, "thrones," of course lower and smaller than the grand central *throne.* So ch. 16:10, "the seat (rather *throne*) of the beasts," in hellish parody of God's throne. **four and twenty elders**—Greek, "*the* four and twenty (or as one oldest MS., 'twenty-four') elders": the well-known elders [ALFORD]. But TREGELLES translates, "Upon the twenty-four thrones (*I saw:* omitted in two oldest MSS.) elders sitting": which is more probable, as the twenty-four *elders* were not mentioned before, whereas the twenty-four *thrones* were. They are not angels, for they have *white robes* and *crowns* of victory, implying a conflict and endurance, "Thou hast *redeemed us*": they represent the *Heads* of the **Old** and **New Testament** churches respectively, the Twelve Patriarchs (cf. ch. 7:5-8, not in their personal, but in their representative character), and Twelve Apostles. So in ch. 15:3, "the song of *Moses,* and of the *Lamb,*" the double constituents of the Church are implied, the Old Testament and the New Testament. "Elders" is the very term for *the ministry* both of the Old and New Testament, the Jewish and the catholic Gentile Church. The tabernacle was a "pattern" of the heavenly antitype; the holy place, a figure of HEAVEN ITSELF. Thus Jehovah's throne is represented by the mercy seat in the holiest, the Shekinah cloud over it.

"The seven lamps of fire before the throne" (vs. 5) are antitypical to the seven-branched candlestick also in the holiest, emblem of the manifold Spirit of God: "the sea of glass" (vs. 6) corresponds to the molten sea before the sanctuary, wherein the priests washed themselves before entering on their holy service; so introduced here in connection with the redeemed "priests unto God" (cf. *Note*, ch. 15:2). The "four living creatures" (vss. 6, 7) answer to the cherubim over the mercy seat. So the twenty-four throned and crowned elders are typified by the twenty-four chiefs of the twenty-four courses of priests, "*Governors* of the sanctuary, and governors of God" (I Chron. 24:5; 25). **5. proceeded**—*Greek*, "proceed." **thunderings and voices** —The two oldest MSS. transpose, "voices and thunderings." Cf. at the giving of the law on Sinai, Exodus 19:16. "The *thunderings* express God's threats against the ungodly: there are voices in the thunders (ch. 10:3), i.e., not only does He threaten generally, but also predicts *special* judgments" [GROTIUS]. **seven lamps ... seven Spirits** —The Holy Spirit in His sevenfold operation, as the light-and-life Giver (cf. ch. 5:6, *seven eyes ... the seven Spirits of God;* 1:4; 21:23 Ps. 119:105) and fiery purifier of the godly, and consumer of the ungodly (Matt. 3:11). **6.** Two oldest MSS., A, B, *Vulgate, Coptic,* and *Syriac* read, "*As it were* a sea of glass." **like ...crystal**—not imperfectly transparent as the ancient common glass, but like rock crystal. Contrast the turbid "many waters" on which the harlot "sitteth" (ch. 17). Cf. Job 37:18, "the sky ... as a molten looking-glass." Thus, primarily, the pure ether which separates God's throne from John, and from all things before it, may be meant, symbolizing the "purity, calmness, and majesty of God's rule" [ALFORD]. But see the analogue in the temple, the molten sea *before* the sanctuary (*Note*, vs. 4, above). There is in this sea depth and transparency, but not the fluidity and instability of the natural sea (cf. ch. 21:1). It stands solid, calm, and clear, God's *judgments* are called "a great deep" (Ps. 36:6). In ch. 15:2 it is a "sea of glass mingled with *fire*." Thus there is symbolized here the purificatory baptism of water and the Spirit of all who are made "kings and priests unto God." In ch. 15:2 the baptism with the fire of trial is meant. Through both all the kingpriests have to pass in coming to God: His *judgments*, which overwhelm the ungodly, they stand firmly upon, as on a solid sea of glass; able like Christ to walk on the sea, as though it were solid. **round about the throne**—one in the midst of each side of the throne. **four beasts**—The *Greek* for "beasts," ch. 13:1, 11, is different, *therion,* the symbol for the carnal man by opposition to God losing his true glory, as lord, under Him, of the lower creatures, and degraded to the level of the *beast.* Here it is *zoon*, "living creatures"; not *beast.* **7. calf**—"a steer"—[ALFORD]. The LXX often uses the *Greek* term here for an *ox* (Exod. 22:1; 29:10, etc.). **as a man**—The oldest MSS. have "as of a man." **8. about him**—*Greek*, "round about him." ALFORD connects this with the following sentence: "All round and within (their wings) they are (so two oldest MSS., A, B, and *Vulgate* read) full of eyes." John's object is to show that the six wings in each did not interfere with that which he had before declared, viz., that they were "full of eyes before and behind." The eyes were *round* the outside of each wing, and up the *inside* of each when half expanded, and of the part of body in that inward recess. **rest not**—lit.,

"have no rest." How awfully different the reason why the worshippers of the beast "have no rest day nor night," viz., "their torment for ever and ever " **Holy, holy, h**oly—The *"tris-hagion"* of the *Greek* liturgies. In Isaiah 6:3, as here, it occurs; also Psalm 99:3, 5, 9, where He is praised as "holy," (1) on account of His majesty (vs. 1) about to display itself; (2) His justice (vs. 4) already displaying itself; (3) His mercy (vss. 6-8) which displayed itself in times past. So here "Holy," as He "who was"; "Holy," as He "who is": "Holy," as He "who is to come." He showed Himself an object of holy worship in the past creation of all things: more fully He shows Himself so in governing all things: He will, in the highest degree, show Himself so in the consummation of all things. "Of (from) Him, through Him, and to Him, are all things: to whom be glory for ever. Amen." In Isaiah 6:3 there is added, "the whole EARTH is full of His glory." But in Revelation this is deferred until the glory of THE LORD fills *the earth*, His enemies having been destroyed [BENGEL]. **Almighty**—answering to "Lord of hosts" (Sabaoth), Isaiah 6:3. The cherubim here have *six* wings, like the seraphim in Isaiah 6; whereas the cherubim in Ezekiel 1:6 had *four* wings each. They are called by the same name, "living creatures." But whereas in Ezekiel each living creature has all four faces, here the four belong severally one to each. See my *Note*, Ezekiel 1:6. The four *living creatures* answer by contrast to the four world powers represented by four *beasts.* The Fathers identified them with the four Gospels, Matthew the lion, Mark the ox, Luke the man, John the eagle: these symbols, thus viewed, express not the personal character of the Evangelists, but the manifold aspect of *Christ* in relation to the world *(four* being the number significant of worldwide extension, e.g., the four quarters of the world) presented by them severally: the lion expressing *royalty,* as Matthew gives prominence to this feature of Christ; the ox, *laborious endurance,* Christ's prominent characteristic in Mark; man, *brotherly sympathy* with the whole race of man, Christ's prominent feature in Luke; the eagle, *soaring majesty,* prominent in John's description of Christ as the Divine Word. But here the context best suits the view which regards the *four living creatures* as representing the *redeemed election-Church* in its relation of ministering king-priests to God, and ministers of blessing to the redeemed earth, and the nations on it, and the animal creation, in which man stands at the head of all, *the lion* at the head of wild beasts, *the ox* at the head of tame beasts, *the eagle* at the head of birds and of the creatures of the waters. Cf. ch. 5:8-10, "Thou hast *redeemed us* by Thy blood *out of every kindred,* . . . and *hast made us unto our God kings and priests: and we shall reign on the earth";* and ch. 20:4, the partakers with Christ of the first resurrection, who conjointly with Him *reign* over the redeemed nations that are in the flesh. Cf. as to the happy and willing subjection of the lower animal world, Isaiah 11:6-8; 65:25; Ezekiel 34:25; Hosea 2:18. Jewish tradition says the "four standards" under which Israel encamped in the wilderness, to the east, Judah, to the north, Dan, to the west, Ephraim, to the south, Reuben, were respectively *a lion,* an *eagle,* an *ox,* and a *man,* while in the midst was the tabernacle containing the Shekinah symbol of the Divine Presence. Thus we have "the picture of that blessed period when—the earth having been fitted for being the kingdom of the Father—the court of heaven will be transferred to earth, and the 'tabernacle of God shall be with men' (ch. 21:3), and the whole world will be subject to a never-ending theocracy" (cf. DE BURGH, *Rev.*). The point of union between the two views given above is: Christ is the perfect realization of the ideal of man; Christ is presented in His fourfold aspect in the four Gospels respectively. The redeemed election-Church similarly, when in and through Christ (with whom she shall reign) she realizes the ideal of man, shall combine in herself human perfections having a fourfold aspect: (1) kingly righteousness with hatred of evil and judicial equity, answering to the "lion"; (2) laborious diligence in every duty, the "ox"; (3) human sympathy, the "man"; (4) the contemplation of heavenly truth, the "eagle." As the high-soaring intelligence, the *eagle,* forms the contrasted complement to practical labor, the *ox* bound to the soil; so holy judicial vengeance against evil, the *lion* springing suddenly and terribly on the doomed, forms the contrasted complement to human sympathy, the *man.* In Isaiah 6:2 we read, "Each had six wings: with twain he covered his face [in *reverence,* as not presuming to lift up his face to God], with twain he covered his feet [in humility, as not worthy to stand in God's holy presence], and with twain he did fly [in *obedient* readiness to do instantly God's command]." **9-11.** The ground of praise here is God's *eternity,* and God's *power* and *glory* manifested in the creation of all things for His pleasure. Creation is the foundation of all God's other acts of power, wisdom, and love, and therefore forms the first theme of His creatures' thanksgivings. The four living creatures take the lead of the twenty-four elders, both in this anthem, and in that *new song* which follows on the ground of their redemption (ch. 5:8-10). **9. when** —i.e., whensoever: as often as. A simultaneous giving of glory on the part of the beasts, and on the part of the elders. **give**—"shall give" in one oldest MS. **for ever and ever**—*Greek,* "unto the ages of the ages." **10. fall**—immediately. *Greek, "shall fall down":* implying that this ascription of praise *shall be* repeated onward to eternity. So also, "shall worship . . . *shall* cast their crowns," viz., in acknowledgment that all the merit of their *crowns* (not kingly *diadems,* but the *crowns* of conquerors) is due to Him. **11. O Lord**—The two oldest MSS., A, B, *Vulgate,* and *Syriac* add, "and our God." "Our" by virtue of creation, and especially redemption. One oldest MS., B, and *Syriac* insert "the Holy One." But another, A, *Vulgate,* and *Coptic* omit this, as *English Version* does. **glory . . .**—"the glory—*the honor—the* power." **thou**—emphatic in the *Greek:* "It is THOU who didst create." **all things** —*Greek,* "the all things": the universe. **for . . .**— *Greek,* "on account of"; "for the sake of Thy pleasure," or "will." *English Version* is good *Greek,* Though the context better suits, it was *because of Thy will,* that "they were" (so one oldest MS, A, *Vulgate, Syriac,* and *Coptic* read, instead of *English Version* "are": another oldest MS, B, reads, "They were *not,* and were created," were created out of nothing), i.e., *were existing,* as contrasted with their previous non-existence. With God to *will* is to effect: to determine is to perform. So in Genesis 1:3, "Let there be light, and there was light": in *Hebrew* an expressive tautology, the same word and tense and letters being used for "let there be," and "there was," marking the simultaneity and identity of the will and the effect. D. LONGINUS, *on the Sublime,* sec. 9, a heathen, praises this description of God's power by "the lawgiver of the Jews, no ordinary man," as one worthy of the

theme. **were created**—by Thy definite act of creation at a definite time.

CHAPTER 5

VSS. 1-14. THE BOOK WITH SEVEN SEALS: NONE WORTHY TO OPEN IT BUT THE LAMB: HE TAKES IT AMIDST THE PRAISES OF THE REDEEMED, AND OF THE WHOLE HEAVENLY HOST. **1. in . . .**—*Greek,* "(lying) *upon* the right hand . . . ." His right hand was open and on it lay the book. On God's part there was no withholding of His future purposes as contained in the book: the only obstacle to unsealing it is stated in vs. 3 [ALFORD]. **book**—rather, as accords with the ancient form of books, and with the *writing on the backside,* "a roll." The *writing on the back* implies fulness and completeness, so that nothing more needs to be added (ch. 22:18). The roll, or book, appears from the context to be *"the title-deed of man's inheritance"* [DE BURGH] redeemed by Christ, and contains the successive steps by which He shall recover it from its usurper and obtain actual possession of the kingdom already "purchased" for Himself and His elect saints. However, no portion of the roll is said to be *unfolded* and *read;* but simply the *seals* are successively *opened,* giving final access to its contents being read as a perfect whole, which shall not be until the events symbolized by the seals shall have been past, when Ephesians 3:10 shall receive its *complete* accomplishment, and the Lamb shall reveal God's providential plans in redemption in all their manifold beauties. Thus the opening of the seals will mean the successive steps by which God in Christ clears the way for the final opening and reading of the book at the visible setting up of the kingdom of Christ. Cf., at the grand consummation, ch. 20:12, "Another book was opened . . . the book of life"; 22:19. None is worthy to do so save the Lamb, for He alone as such has redeemed man's forfeited inheritance, of which *the book is the title-deed.* The question (vs. 2) is not (as commonly supposed), Who should reveal the destinies of the Church (for this any inspired prophet would be competent to do)? but, Who has the WORTH *to give man a new title to his lost inheritance?* [DE BURGH.] **sealed . . . seven seals**—*Greek,* "sealed up," or "firmly sealed." The number *seven* (divided into four, the world-wide number, and three, the divine) abounds in Revelation and expresses *completeness.* Thus, the *seven seals,* representing all power given to the Lamb; the *seven trumpets,* by which the world kingdoms are shaken and overthrown, and the Lamb's kingdom ushered in; and the *seven vials,* by which the beast's kingdom is destroyed. **2. strong**—(Ps. 103:20). His voice penetrated heaven, earth, and Hades (ch. 10:1-3). **2. no man**—*Greek,* "no one." Not merely *no man,* but also *no one* of any order of beings. **in earth** —*Greek,* "upon the earth." **under the earth**—viz., in Hades. **look thereon**—to look upon the contents, so as to read them. **4. and to read**—inserted in *English Version* Greek text without good authority. One oldest MS., ORIGEN, CYPRIAN, and HILARY omit the clause. "To read" would be awkward standing between "to open the book" and "to look thereon." John having been promised a revelation of "things which must be hereafter," *weeps* now at his earnest desire being apparently frustrated. He is a pattern to us to imitate, as an eager and teachable learner of the Apocalypse. **5. one of**— *Greek,* "one from among." The "elder" meant is, according to some (in LYRA), Matthew. With this accords the description here given of Christ, "the *Lion,* which is (so the *Greek*) of the tribe of Juda, the root of David"; the royal, David-descended, lion-aspect of Christ being that prominent in Matthew, whence the lion among the fourfold cherubim is commonly assigned to him. GERHARD *in* BENGEL thought Jacob to be meant, being, doubtless, one of those who rose with Christ and ascended to heaven (Matt. 27:52, 53). The elders in heaven round God's throne know better than John, still in the flesh, the far-reaching power of Christ. **Root of David**—(Isa. 11:1, 10). Not merely "a sucker come up from David's ancient root" (as ALFORD limits it), but also including the idea of His being Himself the root and origin of David: cf. these two truths brought together, Matthew 22:42-45. Hence He is called not merely *Son of David,* but also *David.* He is at once "the branch" of David, and "the root" of David, David's Son and David's Lord, the *Lamb* slain and therefore the *Lion* of Juda: about to reign over Israel, and thence over the whole earth. **prevailed**—*Greek,* "conquered": absolutely, as elsewhere (ch. 3:21): *gained the victory:* His past victory over all the powers of darkness entitles Him now to open the book. **to open**—i.e., *so as to open.* One oldest MS., B, reads, "He that openeth," i.e., whose office it is to open, but the weight of oldest authorities is with *English Version* reading, viz., A, *Vulgate, Coptic,* and ORIGEN. **6. I beheld, and, lo**—One oldest MS., A, omits "and, lo." Another, B, CYPRIAN, etc,. support, "and, lo," but omit, "and I beheld." **in the midst of the throne** —i.e., not *on* the throne (cf. vs. 7), but in the midst of the company (ch. 4:4) which was "round about the throne." **Lamb**—*Greek, arnion;* always found in Revelation exclusively, except in John 21:15 alone: it expresses *endearment,* viz., the endearing relation in which Christ now stands to us, as the consequence of His previous relation as the *sacrificial Lamb.* So also our relation to Him: He the *precious Lamb,* we His *dear lambs,* one with Him. BENGEL thinks there is in *Greek, arnion,* the idea of *taking the lead of the flock.* Another object of the form *Greek, arnion,* the Lamb, is to put Him in the more marked contrast to *Greek, therion,* the Beast. Elsewhere *Greek, amnos,* is found, applying to Him as the *paschal, sacrificial Lamb* (Isa. 53: 7, LXX; John 1:29, 36; Acts 8:32; I Pet. 1:19). **as it had been slain**—bearing marks of His past death wounds. He was standing, though bearing the marks of one slain. In the midst of heavenly glory Christ crucified is still the prominent object. **seven horns**—i.e., *perfect might,* "seven" symbolizing *perfection;* "horns," *might,* in contrast to the *horns* of the Antichristian world powers, ch. 17:3; etc.; Daniel 7:7, 20; 8:3. **seven eyes . . . the seven Spirits . . . sent forth**—So one oldest MS., A. But B reads, *"being sent forth."* As the *seven lamps* before the throne represent the Spirit of God immanent in the Godhead, so the *seven eyes* of the Lamb represent the same sevenfold Spirit profluent from the incarnate Redeemer in His world-wide energy. The *Greek* for "sent forth," *apostellomena,* or else *apestalmenoi,* is akin to the term "apostle," reminding us of the Spirit-impelled labors of Christ's apostles and minister throughout the world: if the present tense be read, as seems best, the idea will be that of those labors *continually going on* unto the end. "Eyes" symbolize His all-watchful and wise providence for His Church, and against her foes. **7.** The book lay on the open hand of Him that sat on the throne for any to take

who was found worthy [ALFORD]. The Lamb takes it from the Father in token of formal investiture into His universal and everlasting dominion as Son of man. This introductory vision thus presents before us, in summary, the consummation to which all the events in the seals, trumpets, and vials converge, viz., the setting up of Christ's kingdom visibly. Prophecy ever hurries to the grand crisis or end, and dwells on intermediate events only in their typical relation to, and representation of, the end. **8. had taken**—*Greek,* "took." **fell down before the Lamb**—who shares worship and the throne with the Father. **harps**—Two oldest MSS., A, B, *Syriac* and *Coptic* read, "a harp": a kind of guitar, played with the hand or a quill. **vials**—"bowls" [TREGELLES]: censers. **odours**—*Greek,* "incense." **prayers of saints**—as the angel offers their prayers (ch. 8:3) with incense (cf. Ps. 141:2). This gives not the least sanction to Rome's dogma of our praying to saints. Though *they* are employed by God in some way unknown to us to present our prayers (nothing is said of their *interceding* for us), yet *we* are told to pray only to Him (ch. 19:10; 22: 8, 9). *Their own* employment is praise (whence they all have *harps*): ours is prayer. **9. sung**—*Greek,* "sing": it is their blessed occupation continually. The theme of *redemption* is ever new, ever suggesting fresh thoughts of praise, embodied in the "new song." **us to God**—So MS. B, *Coptic, Vulgate,* and CYPRIAN. But A omits "us": and ℵ reads instead, "to *our* God." **out of**—the present election-church gathered *out of* the world, as distinguished from the peoples gathered to Christ as the subjects, not of an election, but of a general and world-wide conversion of all nations. **kindred . . . tongue . . . people . . . nation**—The number *four* marks world-wide extension: the four quarters of the world. For "kindred," translate as *Greek,* "tribe." This term and "people" are usually restricted to *Israel:* "tongue and nation" to the Gentiles (ch. 7:9; 11:9; 13:7, the oldest reading; 14:6). Thus there is here marked the election-Church gathered from Jews and Gentiles. In ch. 10:11, for "tribes," we find among the four terms "kings"; in 17:15, "multitudes." **10. made us**—A, B, ℵ, *Vulgate, Syriac,* and *Coptic* read, "them." The *Hebrew* construction of the third person for the first, has a graphic relation to *the redeemed,* and also has a more modest sound than *us,* priests [BENGEL]. **unto our God**—So B and ℵ read. But A omits the clause. **kings**—So B reads. But A, ℵ, *Vulgate, Coptic,* and CYPRIAN, read, "A kingdom." ℵ reads also "a priesthood" for *priests.* They who cast their crowns before the throne, do not call themselves *kings* in the sight of the great King (ch. 4:10, 11); though their priestly access has such dignity that their reigning on earth cannot exceed it. So in ch. 20:6 they are not called "kings" [BENGEL]. **we shall reign on the earth**—This is a new feature added to ch. 1:6. ℵ, *Vulgate,* and *Coptic* read, "They shall reign." A and B read, *"They reign."* ALFORD takes this reading and explains it of the Church EVEN NOW, in Christ her Head, reigning on the earth: "all things are being put under her feet, as under His; her kingly office and rank are asserted, even in the midst of persecution." But even if we read (I think the weightiest authority is against it), "They *reign*," still it is the prophetical present for the future: the seer being transported into the future when the full number of the redeemed (represented by the *four living creatures*) shall be complete and the visible *kingdom begins.* The saints do spiritually reign now; but certainly not as they shall when the prince of this world shall be bound (*Notes*, ch. 20:2-6). So far from *reigning on the earth* now, they are "made as the filth of the world and the offscouring of all things." In ch. 11:15, 18, the locality and time of the kingdom are marked. KELLY translates, "reign *over* the earth" (*Greek, epi tees gees*), which is justified by the *Greek* (LXX, Judg. 9:8; Matt. 2:22). The elders, though ruling *over the earth,* shall not necessarily (according to this passage) remain *on* the earth. But *English Version* is justified by ch. 3:10. "The elders were *meek,* but the flock of the meek independently is much larger" [BENGEL]. **11. I beheld**—the angels: who form the outer circle, while the Church, the object of redemption, forms the inner circle nearest the throne. The heavenly hosts ranged around gaze with intense love and adoration at this crowning manifestation of God's love, wisdom, and power. **ten thousand times ten thousand**—*Greek,* "myriads of myriads." **12. to receive power**—*Greek,* "*the* power." The remaining six (the whole being *seven,* the number for *perfection* and *completeness*) are all, as well as "power," ranged under the one *Greek* article, to mark that they form *one* complete aggregate belonging to God and His coequal, the Lamb. Cf. ch. 7:12, where each of all seven has the article. **riches**—both spiritual and earthly. **blessing**—ascribed praise: the *will* on the creature's part, though unaccompanied by the *power,* to return blessing for blessing conferred [ALFORD]. **13.** The universal chorus of creation, including the outermost circles as well as the inner (of saints and angels), winds up the doxology. The *full* accomplishment of this is to be when Christ takes His great power and reigns visibly. **every creature**—"all His works in all places of His dominion" (Ps. 103:22). **under the earth**—the departed spirits in Hades. **such as are**—So B and *Vulgate*. But A omits this. **in the sea**—*Greek,* "*upon* the sea": the sea animals which are regarded as being on the surface [ALFORD]. **all that are in them**—So *Vulgate* reads. A omits "all (things)" here (*Greek, panta*), and reads, "I heard *all* (*Greek, pantas*) saying": implying the harmonious concert of all in the four quarters of the universe. **Blessing . . .**—*Greek,* "*the* blessing, *the* honor, and *the* glory, and *the* might to *the* ages of *the* ages." The *fourfold* ascription indicates *world-wide* universality. **14. said**—So A, *Vulgate,* and *Syriac* read. But B and *Coptic* read, "(I heard) *saying*." **Amen**—So A reads. But B reads, "*the* (accustomed) Amen." As in ch. 4:11, the four and twenty elders asserted God's worthiness to receive the glory, as having *created all things,* so here the four living creatures ratify by their "Amen" the whole *creation's* ascription of glory to Him. **four and twenty**—omitted in the oldest MSS.: *Vulgate* supports it. **him that liveth for ever and ever**—omitted in all the MSS.: inserted by commentators from ch. 4:9. But there, where the thanksgiving is *expressed,* the words are appropriate; but here less so, as their worship is that of silent prostration. "Worshipped" (viz., God and the Lamb). So in ch. 11:1, "worship" is used absolutely.

CHAPTER 6

VSS. 1-17. THE OPENING OF THE FIRST SIX OF THE SEVEN SEALS. Cf. *Note,* ch. 5:1. Many (MEDE, FLEMING, NEWTON, etc.) hold that all these seals have been fulfilled, the sixth having been so

by the overthrow of paganism and establishment of Christianity under Constantine's edict, A.D. 312. There can, however, be no doubt that at least the sixth seal is future, and is to be at the coming again of Christ. The great objection to supposing the seals to be finally and exhaustively fulfilled (though, probably, particular events may be partial fulfilments typical of the final and fullest one), is that, if so, they ought to furnish (as the destruction of Jerusalem, according to Christ's prophecy, does) a strong external evidence of Revelation. But it is clear they cannot be used for this, as hardly any two interpreters of this school are agreed on what events constitute the fulfilment of each seal. Probably not isolated facts, but *classes* of events preparing the way for Christ's coming kingdom, are intended by the opening of the seals. The four living creatures severally cry at the opening of the first four seals, "Come," which fact marks the division of the *seven,* as often occurs in this sacred number, into *four* and *three.* **1. one of the seals**—The oldest MSS., A, B, C, *Vulgate,* and *Syriac* read, "one of the *seven* seals." **noise**—The three oldest MSS. read this in the nominative or dative, not the genitive, as *English Version,* "I heard one from among the four living creatures saying, as (it were) *the voice* (or, *as with the voice*) of thunder." The first living creature was like a *lion* (ch. 4:7): his voice is in consonance. Implying the lion-like boldness with which, in the successive great revivals, the faithful have *testified for Christ,* and especially a little before His coming shall testify. Or, rather, their earnestness in praying for *Christ's coming.* **Come and see**—One oldest MS., B, has "And see." But A, C, and *Vulgate* reject it. ALFORD rightly objects to *English Version* reading: "Whither was John to come? Separated as he was by the glassy sea from the throne, was he to cross it?" Contrast the form of expression, ch. 10:8. It is much more likely to be the cry of the redeemed to the Redeemer, "Come" and deliver the groaning creature from the bondage of corruption. Thus, vs. 2 is an answer to the cry, *went* (lit., "came") forth corresponding to "Come." "Come," says GROTIUS, is the living creature's address to John, *calling his earnest attention.* But it seems hard to see how "Come" by itself can mean this. Cf. the only other places in Revelation where it is used, ch. 4:1; 22:17. If the four living creatures represent the four Gospels, the "Come" will be their invitation to everyone (for it is not written that they addressed *John*) to *accept* Christ's salvation while there is time, as the opening of the seals marks a progressive step towards the end (cf. ch. 22:17). Judgments are foretold as accompanying the *preaching of the Gospel as a witness to all nations* (ch. 14:6-11; Matt. 24:6-14). Thus the invitation, "Come," here, is aptly parallel to Matthew 24:14. The opening of the first four seals is followed by judgments preparatory for His coming. At the opening of the fifth seal, the martyrs above express the same (vs. 9, 10; cf. Zech. 1:10). At the opening of the sixth seal, the Lord's coming is ushered in with terrors to the ungodly. At the seventh, the consummation is fully attained (ch. 11: 15). **2.** Evidently Christ, whether in person, or by His angel, preparatory to His coming again, as appears from ch. 19:11, 12. **bow**—(Ps. 45:4, 5). **crown**—*Greek, stephanos,* the garland or wreath of a *conqueror,* which is also implied by His *white horse,* white being the emblem of victory. In ch. 19:11, 12 the last step in His victorious progress is represented; accordingly there He wears *many* diadems (*Greek, diademata;* not merely *Greek, stephanoi,* crowns or wreaths), and is personally attended by the hosts of heaven. Cf. Zechariah 1 and 6; especially vs. 10 below, with Zechariah 1: 12; also cf. the colors of the four horses. **and to conquer**—i.e., so as to gain a lasting victory. All four seals usher in *judgments* on the earth, as the power which opposes the reign of Himself and His Church. This, rather than the work of conversion and conviction, is primarily meant, though doubtless, secondarily, the elect will be gathered out through His word and His judgments. **3. and see** —omitted in the three oldest MSS., A, B, C, and *Vulgate.* **4. red**—the color of *blood.* The color of the horse in each case answers to the mission of the rider. Cf. Matthew 10:24-36, "Think not I am come to send *peace* on earth; I came not to send *peace,* but a *sword."* The *white* horse of Christ's bloodless victories is soon followed, through man's perversion of the Gospel, by the *red* horse of bloodshed; but this is overruled to the clearing away of the obstacles to Christ's coming kingdom. The patient *ox* is the emblem of the second *living creature* who, at the opening of this seal, saith, "Come." The saints amidst judgments on the earth in patience "endure to the end." **that they should kill**— The *Greek* is indicative future, "that they may, as they also shall, kill one another." **5. Come and see**—The two oldest MSS., A, C. and *Vulgate* omit "and see." B retains the words. **black**—implying *sadness* and *want.* **had**—*Greek,* "having." **a pair of balances**—the symbol of scarcity of provisions, the bread being doled out by weight. **6. a voice**— Two oldest MSS., A, C, read, "*as it were* a voice." B reads as *English Version.* The voice is heard "in the midst of the four living creatures" (as Jehovah in the Shekinah cloud manifested His presence between the cherubim); because it is only for the sake of, and in connection with, His redeemed, that God mitigates His judgments on the earth. **A measure**—"A *chœnix."* While making food scarce, do not make it so much so that a *chœnix* (about a day's provision of wheat, variously estimated at two or three pints) shall not be obtainable "for a penny" (*denarius,* about twenty cents, probably the day's wages of a laborer). *Famine* generally follows the *sword.* Ordinarily, from sixteen to twenty measures were given for a denarius. The *sword, famine, noisome beasts,* and the *pestilence,* are God's four judgments on the earth. A spiritual famine, too, may be included in the judgment. The "Come," in the case of this third seal, is said by the third of the four living creatures, whose likeness is *a man* indicative of sympathy and human compassion for the sufferers. God in it tempers judgment with mercy. Cf. Matthew 24:7, which indicates the very calamities foretold in these seals, *nation rising against nation* (the sword), *famines, pestilences* (vs. 8), and *earthquakes* (vs. 12). **three measures of barley for a penny**—the cheaper and less nutritious grain, bought by the laborer who could not buy enough wheat for his family with his day's wages, a denarius, and, therefore, buys barley. **see thou hurt not the oil, and the wine**—the luxuries of life, rather than necessaries; the oil and wine were to be spared for the refreshment of the sufferers. **7. and see**—supported by B; omitted by A, C, and *Vulgate.* The *fourth living creature,* who was "like a flying eagle," introduces this seal; implying high-soaring intelligence, and judgment descending from on high fatally on the ungodly, as the king of birds on his prey. **8. pale**—"livid" [ALFORD]. **Death**—personified. **Hell**—*Hades* personified. **unto them**

—*Death* and *Hades.* So A, C read. But B and *Vulgate* read, "to him." **fourth part of the earth** —answering to the first four seals; his portion as one of the four, being a *fourth part.* **death**—pestilence; cf. Ezekiel 14:21 with the four judgments here, the *sword, famine, pestilence,* and *wild beasts;* the *famine* the consequence of the *sword; pestilence,* that of *famine;* and *beasts* multiplying by the consequent depopulation. **with the beasts**—*Greek,* "by"; more direct agency. These four seals are marked off from the three last, by the four living creatures introducing them with "Come." The calamities indicated are not restricted to one time, but extend through the whole period of Church history to the coming of Christ, before which last great and terrible day of the Lord they shall reach highest aggravation. The first seal is the summary, Christ going forth *conquering* till all enemies are subdued under Him, with a view to which the judgments subsequently specified accompany the *preaching of the Gospel for a witness to all nations.* **9.** The three last seals relate to the invisible, as the first four to the visible world; the fifth, to the martyrs who have died as believers; the sixth, to those who have died, or who shall be found at Christ's coming, unbelievers, viz., "the kings . . . great men . . . bondman . . . freeman"; the seventh, to the silence in heaven. The scene changes from earth to heaven; so that interpretations which make these three last consecutive to the first four seals, are very doubtful. **I saw**—in spirit. For souls are not naturally visible. **under the altar**—As the blood of sacrificial victims slain on the altar was poured *at the bottom of the altar,* so the souls of those sacrificed for Christ's testimony are symbolically represented as *under the altar,* in heaven; for the life or animal *soul* is in the *blood,* and blood is often represented as crying for vengeance (Gen. 4:10). The altar in heaven, antitypical to the altar of sacrifice, is Christ crucified. As it is the altar that sanctifies the gift, so it is Christ alone who makes our obedience, and even our sacrifice of life for the truth, acceptable to God. The sacrificial altar was not in the sanctuary, but outside; so Christ's literal sacrifice and the figurative sacrifice of the martyrs took place, not in the heavenly sanctuary, but outside, here on earth. The only altar in heaven is that antitypical to the temple altar of incense. The blood of the martyrs cries from the earth under Christ's cross, whereon they may be considered virtually to have been sacrificed; their souls cry from under the altar of incense, which is Christ in heaven, by whom alone the incense of praise is accepted before God. They are *under* Christ, in His immediate presence, shut up unto Him in joyful eager expectancy until He shall come to raise the sleeping dead. Cf. the language of II Maccabees 7:36 as indicating Jewish opinion on the subject. Our brethren who have now suffered a short pain are dead *under* (*Greek*) *God's covenant* of everlasting life. **testimony which they held**—i.e., which they bore, as committed to them to bear. Cf. ch. 12:17, "*Have* (same *Greek* as here) the testimony of Jesus." **10. How long**—*Greek,* "Until when?" As in the parable the woman (symbol of the Church) *cries day and night* to the unjust judge for justice against her adversary who is always oppressing her (cf. below, ch. 12:10); so the elect (not only on earth, but *under Christ's covering,* and in His presence in Paradise) *cry day and night* to God, who will assuredly, in His own time, avenge His and their cause, "though He bear *long* with them." These passages need not be *restricted* to some particular martyrdoms, but have been, and are receiving, and shall receive partial fulfilments, until their last exhaustive fulfilment before Christ's coming. So as to the other events foretold here. The glory even of those in Paradise will only be complete when Christ's and the Church's foes are cast out, and the earth will become Christ's kingdom at His coming to raise the sleeping saints. **Lord**–*Greek,* "Master"; implying that He has them and their foes and all His creatures as absolutely at His disposal, as a master has his *slaves;* hence, in vs. 11, *"fellow servants,"* or *fellow slaves* follows. **holy**–*Greek,* "the Holy one." **avenge**–"exact vengeance for our blood." **on**–*Greek,* "from them." **that dwell on the earth**–the ungodly, of earth, earthly, as distinguished from the Church, whose home and heart are even now in heavenly places. **11. white robes**–The three oldest MSS., A, B, C, read, "A white robe was given." **every one of**–One oldest MS., B, omits this. A and C read, "unto them, unto each," i.e., unto them severally. Though their joint cry for the riddance of the earth from the ungodly is not yet granted, it is intimated that it will be so in due time; meanwhile, *individually* they receive the white robe, indicative of light, joy, and triumphant victory over their foes; even as the Captain of their salvation goes forth on a *white* horse *conquering and to conquer;* also of purity and sanctity through Christ. MAIMONIDES says that the Jews used to array priests, when approved of, *in white robes;* thus the sense is, they are admitted among the blessed ones, who, as spotless priests, minister unto God and the Lamb. **should** –So C reads. But A and B, *"shall* rest." **a little season**–One oldest MS., B, omits "little." A and C support it. Even if it be omitted, is it to be inferred that the "season" is short as compared with eternity? BENGEL fancifully made a *season (Greek, chronus,* the word here used) to be one thousand one hundred and eleven one-ninth years, and a **time** (ch. 12:12, 14, **Greek, kairos**) to be a fifth of a *season,* i.e., two hundred and twenty-two two-ninths years. The only distinction in the *Greek* is, a *season (Greek, chronus)* is a sort of aggregate of *times. Greek, kairos,* a specific time, and so of short duration. As to their *rest,* cf. ch. 14:13 (the same *Greek, anapauomai*); Isa. 57:2; Dan. 12:13. **until their ... brethren ... be fulfilled**–in number. Until their full number shall have been completed. The number of the elect is definitely fixed: perhaps to fill up that of the fallen angels. But this is mere conjecture. The *full* blessedness and glory of all the saints shall be simultaneous. The earlier shall not anticipate the later saints. A and C read, "shall have been accomplished"; B and ℵ read, "shall have accomplished (their course)." **12.** As vss. 4, 6-8, the sword, famine, and pestilence, answer to Matthew 24:6, 7; and vss. 9, 10, as to martyrdoms, answer to Matthew 24:9, 10; so this passage, vss. 12, 17, answers to Matthew 24:29, 30, "the sun shall be darkened, and the moon shall not give her light, and the stars shall fall from heaven; ... then shall all the tribes of the earth mourn, and they shall see the Son of man coming"; imagery describing *the portents* of the immediate coming of the day of the Lord; but *not the coming itself* until the elect are sealed, and the judgments invoked by the martyrs descend on the earth, the sea, and the trees (ch. 7). **and, lo**–So A reads. But B and C omit "lo." **earthquake**–*Greek,* "shaking" of *the heavens,* the sea, and the dry land; the shaking of these mutable things being the necessary preliminary to the setting up of those *things which cannot be shaken.* This is one of the *catchwords*

[WORDSWORTH] connecting the sixth seal with the sixth trumpet (ch. 11:13) and the seventh vial (ch. 16:17-21); also the seventh seal (ch. 8:5). **sackcloth** –One kind, made of the "hair" of Cilician goats, was called "cilicium," or Cilician cloth, and was used for tents, etc. Paul, a Cilician, made such tents (Acts 18:3). **moon**–A, B, C, and oldest versions read, the whole moon"; the full moon; not merely the crescent moon. **as blood**–(Joel 2:31). **13. stars ... fell ... as a fig tree casteth her ... figs** –(Isa. 34:4, Nah. 3:12). The Church shall be then ripe for glorification, the Antichristian world for destruction, which shall be accompanied with mighty phenomena in nature. As to the stars falling to the earth, Scripture describes natural phenomena as they would appear to the spectator, not in the language of scientific accuracy; and yet, while thus adapting itself to ordinary men, it drops hints which show that it anticipates the discoveries of modern science. **14. departed**–*Greek,* "was *separated from*" its place; "was made to depart." Not as ALFORD, "parted *asunder";* for, on the contrary, it was rolled *together* as a scroll which had been open is rolled up and laid aside. There is no "asunder one from another" here in the *Greek,* as in Acts 15:39, which ALFORD copies. **mountain ... moved out of ... places**–(Ps. 121:1, *Margin;* Jer. 3:23; 4:24; Nah. 1:5). This total disruption shall be the precursor of the new earth, just as the pre-Adamic convulsions prepared it for its present occupants. **15. kings ... hid themselves**–Where was now the spirit of those whom the world has so greatly feared? [BENGEL]. **great men**–statesmen and high civil officers. **rich men ... chief captains** –The three oldest MSS., A, B, C, transpose thus, "chief captains ... rich men." **mighty**–The three oldest MSS, A, B, and C read, "strong" physically (Ps. 33:16). **in**–lit., "into"; ran *into,* so as to *hide themselves* in. **dens**–"caves." **16. from the face**–(Ps. 34:16). On the whole verse, cf. Hosea 10:8; Luke 23:30. **17.** Lit., "the day, the great (day)," which can only mean the last great day. After the Lord has exhausted all His ordinary judgments, the sword, famine, pestilence, and wild beasts, and still sinners are impenitent, the great day of the Lord itself shall come. Matthew 24 plainly forms a perfect parallelism to the six seals, not only in the events, but also in the order of their occurrence: vs. 3, the first seal; vs. 6, the second seal; vs. 7, the third seal; vs. 7, end, the fourth seal; vs. 9, the fifth seal, the persecutions and abounding iniquity under which, as well as consequent judgments accompanied with gospel preaching to all nations as a witness, are particularly detailed, vss. 9-28; vs. 29, the sixth seal. **to stand**–to stand justified, and not condemned before the Judge. Thus the sixth seal brings us to the verge of the Lord's coming. The ungodly "tribes of the earth" tremble at the signs of His immediate approach. But before He actually inflicts the blow in person, "the elect" must be "gathered " out.

CHAPTER 7

VSS. 1-17. SEALING OF THE ELECT OF ISRAEL. THE COUNTLESS MULTITUDE OF THE GENTILE ELECT. **1. And**–so B and *Syriac.* But A, C, *Vulgate,* and *Coptic* omit "and." **after these things**–A, B, C, and *Coptic* read, "after this." The two visions in this chapter come in as an episode *after* the sixth seal, and before the seventh seal. It is clear that, though "Israel" may elsewhere designate the spiritual Israel, "the elect (Church) on earth" [ALFORD], here, where the names of the tribes one by one are specified, these names cannot have any but the literal meaning. The second advent will be the time of *the restoration of the kingdom to Israel,* when *the times of the Gentiles shall have been fulfilled,* and the Jews shall at last say, "Blessed is He that cometh in the name of the Lord." The period of the Lord's absence has been a blank in the history of the Jews as a nation. As then Revelation is the Book of the Second Advent [DE BURGH], naturally mention of God's restored favor to Israel occurs among the events that usher in Christ's advent. **earth . . . sea . . . tree**—The judgments to descend on these are in answer to the martyrs' prayer under the *fifth* seal. Cf. the same judgments under the *fifth* trumpet, the sealed being exempt (ch. 9:4). **on any tree**—Greek, "*against* any tree" (*Greek, epi ti dendron:* but *on* the earth," *Greek, epi tees gees*). **2. from the east**—*Greek,* ". . . the rising of the sun." The quarter from which God's glory oftenest manifests itself. **3. Hurt not**—by letting loose the destructive winds. **till we have sealed the servants of our God**—parallel to Matthew 24:31, "His angels . . . shall gather together His elect from the four winds." God's love is such, that He *cannot do anything* in the way of judgment, till His people are secured from hurt (Gen. 19:22). Israel, at the eve of the Lord's coming, shall be found re-embodied as a nation; for its tribes are distinctly specified (Joseph, however, being substituted for Dan; whether because Antichrist is to come from Dan, or because Dan is to be Antichrist's especial tool [ARETAS, tenth century], cf. Gen. 49:17; Jer. 8:16; Amos 8:14; just as there was a Judas among the Twelve). Out of these tribes *a believing remnant* will be preserved from the judgments which shall destroy all the Antichristian confederacy (ch. 6:12 -17), and *shall be transfigured with the elect Church of all nations,* viz., 144,000 (or whatever number is meant by this symbolical number), who shall faithfully resist the seductions of Antichrist, while the rest of the nation, restored to Palestine in unbelief, are his dupes, and at last his victims. Previously to the Lord's judgments on Antichrist and his hosts, these latter shall destroy *two-thirds* of the nation, *one-third* escaping, and, by the Spirit's operation through affliction, turning to the Lord, which remnant shall form the nucleus on earth of the Israelite nation that is from this time to stand at the head of the millennial nations of the world. Israel's spiritual resurrection shall be "as life from the dead" to all the nations. As now a regeneration goes on here and there of individuals, so there shall then be a regeneration of nations universally, and this in connection with Christ's coming. Matthew 24:34, "this generation (the Jewish nation) shall not pass till all these things be fulfilled," which implies that Israel can no more *pass away* before Christ's advent, than Christ's own *words* can *pass away* (the same *Greek*), Matthew 24:35. So exactly Zechariah 13:8, 9; 14:2-4, 9-21; cf. 12:2-14; 13:1, 2. So also Ezekiel 8:17, 18; 9:1-7, especially vs. 4. Cf. also Ezekiel 10:2 with ch. 8:5, where the final judgments actually fall on the earth, with the same accompaniment, *the fire of the altar cast into the earth,* including the *fire scattered over the city.* So again, ch. 14:1, the same 144,000 appear on Zion with the Father's name in their forehead, at the close of the section, chs. 12, 13, 14, concerning the Church and her foes. Not that the saints are exempt from trial: vs. 14 proves the contrary; but their trials are distinct from the

destroying judgments that fall on the world; from these they are exempted, as Israel was from the plagues of Egypt, especially from the last, the Israelite doors having the protecting seal of the blood-mark. **foreheads**—the most conspicuous and noblest part of man's body; on which the helmet, "the hope of salvation," is worn. **4.** *Twelve*—is the number of the tribes, and appropriate to *the Church:* 3 by 4:3, the *divine* number, multiplied by 4, the number for *world-wide extension.* 12 by 12 implies *fixity and completeness,* which is taken a thousandfold in 144,000. A *thousand* implies *the world perfectly pervaded by the divine;* for it is *ten,* the world number, raised to the power of *three,* the number of God. **of all the tribes**—lit., "out of every tribe"; not 144,000 of each tribe, but the aggregate of the 12,000 *from every tribe.* **children**—Greek, "*sons* of Israel." Ch. 3:12; 21:12, are no objection, as ALFORD thinks, to the literal Israel being meant; for, in consummated glory, still the Church will be that "built on the foundation of the (*Twelve*) apostles (Israelites), Jesus Christ (an Israelite) being the chief cornerstone." Gentile believers shall have *the name of Jerusalem written on them,* in that they shall share the citizenship antitypical to that of the literal Jerusalem. **5-8.** Judah (meaning *praise*) stands first, as Jesus' tribe. Benjamin, the youngest, is last; and with him is associated second last, Joseph. Reuben, as originally first-born, comes next after Judah, to whom it gave place, having by sin lost its primogeniture-right. Besides the reason given above, another akin for the omission of Dan, is, its having been the first to lapse into idolatry (Judg. 18); for which same reason the name Ephraim, also (cf. Judg. 17: Hos. 4:17), is omitted, and Joseph substituted. Also, it had been now for long almost extinct. Long before, the Hebrews say [GROTIUS], it was reduced to the one family of Hussim, which perished subsequently in the wars before Ezra's time. Hence it is omitted in I Chronicles 4-8. Dan's small numbers are joined here to Naphtali's, whose brother he was by the same mother [BENGEL]. The twelve times twelve thousand sealed ones of Israel are the nucleus of transfigured humanity [AUBERLEN], to which the elect Gentiles are joined, "a multitude which no man could number," vs. 9 (i.e., the Church of Jews and Gentiles indiscriminately, in which the Gentiles are the predominant element, Luke 21:24. The word "tribes," *Greek,* implies that *believing Israelites* are in this *countless multitude).* Both are in heaven, yet ruling over the earth, as ministers of blessing to its inhabitants: while upon earth the world of nations is added to the kingdom of Israel. The twelve apostles stand at the head of the whole. The upper and the lower congregation, though distinct, are intimately associated. **9. no man**—Greek, "no one." **of all nations**—Greek, "OUT OF every nation." The human race is *one nation* by origin, but afterwards separated itself into *tribes, peoples,* and *tongues;* hence, the one singular stands first, followed by the three plurals. **kindreds**—Greek, "tribes." **people**—Greek, "peoples." The "first fruits unto the Lamb," the 144,000 (ch. 14:1-4) of Israel, are followed by a copious harvest of all nations, an election *out of* the Gentiles, as the 144,000 are an election out of Israel (*Note,* vs. 3). **white robes**—(*Note,* ch. 6:11; also ch. 3:5, 18; 4:4). **palms in . . . hands**—the antitype to Christ's entry into Jerusalem amidst the palm-bearing multitude. This shall be just when He is about to come visibly and take possession of His kingdom. The *palm branch* is the symbol of joy and triumph. It was used at the feast of tabernacles, on the fifteenth day of the seventh month, when they kept feast to God in thanksgiving for the ingathered fruits. The antitype shall be the completed gathering in of the harvest of the elect redeemed here described. Cf. Zechariah 14:16, whence it appears that the *earthly* feast of tabernacles will be renewed, in commemoration of Israel's preservation in her long wilderness-like sojourn among the nations from which she shall now be delivered, just as the original typical feast was to commemorate her dwelling for forty years in booths or tabernacles in the literal wilderness. **10. cried**—Greek, "cry," in the three oldest MSS., A, B, C, *Vulgate, Syriac,* and *Coptic.* It is their continuing, ceaseless employment. **Salvation**—lit., "THE salvation"; all the praise of our salvation be ascribed to our God. At the Lord's entry into Jerusalem, the type, similarly "salvation" is the cry of the palm-bearing multitudes. *Hosanna* means "save us now"; taken from Psalm 118:25, in which Psalm (vss. 14, 15, 21, 26) the same connection occurs between *salvation,* the *tabernacles* of the righteous, and the Jews' cry to be repeated by the whole nation at Christ's coming, "Blessed be He that cometh in the name of the Lord." **11.** The angels, as in ch. 5:11, in their turn take up the anthem of praise. There it was "*many* angels," here it is "*all* the angels." **stood** —"were standing" [ALFORD]. **12.** Greek, "*The* blessing, *the* glory, *the* wisdom, *the* thanksgiving, *the* honor, *the* power, *the* might [the doxology is *sevenfold,* implying its totality and completeness], *unto the ages of the ages.*" **13. answered**—viz., to my thoughts; spoke, asking the question which might have been expected to arise in John's mind from what has gone before. One of the twenty-four elders, representing the Old and New Testament ministry, appropriately acts as interpreter of this vision of the glorified Church. **What . . .**— Greek order, "These which are arrayed in white robes, WHO are they?" **14. Sir**—Greek, "Lord." B, C, *Vulgate, Syriac, Coptic* versions, and CYPRIAN read, "My Lord." A omits "My," as *English Version.* **thou knowest**—taken from Ezekiel 37:3. Comparatively ignorant ourselves of divine things, it is well for us to look upward for divinely communicated knowledge. **came**—rather as *Greek,* "come"; implying that they are *just come.* **great tribulation**—Greek, "THE great tribulation"; "the tribulation, the great one," viz., *the* tribulation to which the martyrs were exposed under the fifth seal, the same which Christ foretells as about to precede His coming (Matt. 24:21, *great tribulation*), and followed by the same signs as the sixth seal (Matt. 24:29, 30), cf. Daniel 12:1; including also retrospectively all *the tribulation* which the saints of all ages have had to pass through. Thus this seventh chapter is a recapitulation of the vision of the six seals, ch. 6, to fill up the outline there given in that part of it which affects the faithful of that day. There, however, their number was waiting to be completed, but here it is completed, and they are seen taken out of the earth before the judgments on the Antichristian apostasy; with their Lord, they, and all His faithful witnesses and disciples of past ages, wait for His coming and their coming to be glorified and reign together with Him. Meanwhile, in contrast with their previous sufferings, they are exempt from the hunger, thirst, and scorching heats of their life on earth (vs. 16), and are fed and refreshed by the Lamb of God Himself (vs. 17; ch. 14:1-4, 13); an earnest of their future

perfect blessedness in both body and soul united (ch. 21:4-6; 22:1-5). **washed . . . robes . . . white in the blood of . . . Lamb**—(ch. 1:5; Isa. 1:18; Heb. 9:14; I John 1:7; cf. Isa. 61:10; Zech. 3:3-5). Faith applies to the heart the purifying blood; once for all for justification, continually throughout the life for sanctification. **15. Therefore**—because they are so washed white; for without it they could never have entered God's holy heaven; ch. 22:14, "Blessed are those who *wash their robes* (the oldest MSS. reading), that they may have right to the tree of life, and may enter in through the gates into the city"; 21:27; Ephesians 5:26, 27. **before**— Greek, "in the presence of." Matthew 5:8; I Corinthians 13:12, "face to face." **throne . . . temple** —These are connected because we can approach the heavenly King only through priestly mediation; therefore, Christ is at once King and Priest on His throne. **day and night**—i.e., perpetually; as those approved of as priests by the Sanhedrim were clothed in white, and kept by turns a perpetual watch in the temple at Jerusalem; cf. as to the singers, I Chronicles 9:33, "day and night"; Psalm 134:1. Strictly "there is no night" in the heavenly sanctuary (ch. 22:5). **in his temple**—in what is the heavenly analogue to His temple on earth, for strictly there is "no temple therein" (ch. 21:22), "God and the Lamb are the temple" filling the whole, so that there is no distinction of sacred and secular places; the city is the temple, and the temple the city. Cf. ch. 4:8, "the four living creatures rest not *day and night,* saying, Holy . . ." **shall dwell among them**—rather (*Greek, scenosei ep' autous*), "shall be the tabernacle over them" (cf. ch. 21:3; Lev. 26:11 especially Isa. 4:5, 6; 8:14; 25: 4; Ezek. 37:27). His *dwelling among them* is to be understood as a secondary truth, besides what is expressed, viz., His being their *covert.* When once He *tabernacled among us* as the Word made *flesh,* He was in great lowliness; then He shall be in great glory. **16.** (Isa. 49:10.) **hunger no more** —as they did here. **thirst any more**—(John 4:13). **the sun**—literally, scorching in the East. Also, symbolically, the sun of persecution. **neither . . . light**—Greek, "by no means at all . . . light" (fall). **heat**—as the sirocco. **17. in the midst of the throne** —i.e., in the middle point in front of the throne (ch. 5:6). **feed**—Greek, "tend as a shepherd." **living fountains of water**—A, B, *Vulgate,* and CYPRIAN read, (eternal) "*life's* fountains of waters." "Living" is not supported by the old authorities.

CHAPTER 8

Vss. 1-13. SEVENTH SEAL. PREPARATION FOR THE SEVEN TRUMPETS. THE FIRST FOUR AND THE CONSEQUENT PLAGUES. **1. was**—Greek, "came to pass"; "began to be." **silence in heaven about . . . half an hour**—The last seal having been broken open, the book of God's eternal plan of redemption is opened for the Lamb to read to the blessed ones in heaven. The *half hour's silence* contrasts with the previous jubilant songs of *the great multitude,* taken up by the *angels* (ch. 7:9-11). It is the solemn introduction to the employments and enjoyments of the eternal Sabbath-rest of the people of God, commencing with the Lamb's reading the book heretofore sealed up, and which we cannot know till then. In ch. 10:4, similarly at the eve of the sounding of the seventh trumpet, when the seven thunders uttered their voices, John is forbidden to write them. The seventh trumpet (ch. 11:15-19) winds up God's vast plan of providence and grace in redemption, just as the seventh seal brings it to the same consummation. So also the seventh vial, ch. 16:17. Not that the seven seals, the seven trumpets, and the seven vials, though parallel, are repetitions. They each trace the course of divine action up to the grand consummation in which they all meet, under a different aspect. *Thunders, lightnings, an earthquake,* and *voices* close the seven thunders and the seven seals alike (cf. ch. 8:5, with ch. 11:19). Cf. at the seventh vial, the voices, thunders, lightnings, and earthquake, ch. 16:18. The *half-hour silence* is the brief pause GIVEN TO JOHN between the preceding vision and the following one, implying, on the one hand, the solemn introduction to the eternal sabbatism which is to follow the seventh seal; and, on the other, the silence which continued during the incense-accompanied prayers which usher in the first of the seven trumpets (ch. 8:3-5). In the Jewish temple, musical instruments and singing resounded during the whole time of the offering of the sacrifices, which formed the first part of the service. But at the offering of incense, solemn silence was kept (Ps. 62: 1, "My soul *waiteth* upon God." *Margin,* "is silent"; 65:1, *Margin),* the people praying secretly all the time. The *half-hour* stillness implies, too, the earnest adoring expectation with which the blessed spirits and the angels await the succeeding unfolding of God's judgments. A *short* space is implied; for even an *hour* is so used (ch. 17:12; 18: 10, 19). **2. the seven angels**—Cf. the apocryphal Tobit, 12:15, "I am Raphael, one of the seven holy angels which present the prayers of the saints, and which go in and out before the glory of the Holy One." Cf. Luke 1:19, "I am Gabriel, that stand in the presence of God." **stood**—*Greek,* "stand." **seven trumpets**—These come in during the time while the martyrs *rest until their fellow servants also, that should be killed as they were, should be fulfilled;* for it is *the inhabiters of the earth* on whom the judgments fall, on whom also the martyrs prayed that they should fall (ch. 6:10). *All* the ungodly, and not merely some one portion of them, are meant, all the opponents and obstacles in the way of the kingdom of Christ and His saints, as is proved by ch. 11:15, 18, end, at the close of the seven trumpets. The Revelation becomes more special only as it advances farther (ch. 13; 16:10; 17:18). By the seven trumpets the world kingdoms are overturned to make way for Christ's universal kingdom. The first four are connected together; and the last three, which alone have *Woe, woe, woe* (vss. 7-13). **3. another angel**—not Christ, as many think; for He, in Revelation, is always designated by one of His proper titles; though, doubtless, He is the only true High Priest, the Angel of the Covenant, standing before the golden altar of incense, and there, as Mediator, offering up His people's prayers, rendered acceptable before God through the incense of His merit. Here the angel acts merely as a *ministering spirit,* just as the twenty-four elders *have vials full of odors,* or incense, *which are the prayers of saints,* and which they present before the Lamb. How precisely their ministry, in perfuming the prayers of the saints and offering them on the altar of incense, is exercised, we know not, but we do know they are not to be prayed TO. If we send an offering of tribute to the king, the king's messenger is not allowed to appropriate what is due to the king alone. **there was given unto him**—The angel does not provide the incense; it is *given to him* by Christ, whose meritori-

ous obedience and death are the incense, rendering the saints' prayers well pleasing to God. It is not the saints who give the angel the incense; nor are their prayers identified with the incense; nor do they offer their prayers to him. Christ alone is the Mediator through whom, and to whom, prayer is to be offered. **offer it with the prayers**—rather as *Greek,* "give it TO the prayers," so rendering them efficacious as a *sweet-smelling savor* to God. Christ's merits alone can thus *incense* our prayers, though the angelic ministry be employed to attach this incense to the prayers. The saints' praying on earth, and the angel's incensing in heaven, are simultaneous. **all saints**—The prayers both of the saints in the heavenly rest, and of those militant on earth. The martyrs' cry is the foremost, and brings down the ensuing judgments. **golden altar** —antitype to the earthly. **4. the smoke ... which came with the prayers ... ascended up**—rather, "the smoke of the incense FOR (or *given* TO: 'given' being understood from vs. 3) the prayers of the saints ascended up, out of the angel's hand, in the presence of God." The angel merely burns the incense given him by Christ the High Priest, so that its smoke blends with the ascending prayers of the saints. The saints themselves are priests; and the angels in this priestly ministration are but *their fellow servants* (ch. 19:10). **5. cast it into the earth**—i.e., *unto* the earth: the hot coals off the altar cast on the earth, symbolize God's fiery judgments about to descend on the Church's foes in answer to the saints' incense-perfumed prayers which have just ascended before God, and those of the martyrs. How marvellous the power of the saints' prayers! **there were**—"there took place," or "ensued." **voices ... thunderings ...** —B places the "voices" after "thunderings." A places it after "lightnings." **6. sound**—blow the trumpets. **7.** The common feature of the first four trumpets is, the judgments under them affect *natural objects,* the accessories of life, the earth, trees, grass, the sea, rivers, fountains, the light of the sun, moon, and stars. The last three, the *woe-trumpets* (vs. 13), affect men's life with pain, death, and hell. The language is evidently drawn from the plagues of Egypt, five or six out of the ten exactly corresponding: the *hail,* the *fire* (Exod. 9:24), the WATER *turned to blood* (Exod. 7:19), the *darkness* (Exod. 10:21), the *locusts* (Exod. 10:12), and perhaps the *death* (ch. 9:18). Judicial retribution in kind characterizes the inflictions of the first four, those elements which had been abused punishing their abusers. **mingled with** —A, B, and *Vulgate* read, *Greek,* "... IN blood." So in the case of the second and third vials (ch. 16:3, 4). **upon the earth**—*Greek,* "*unto* the earth." A, B, *Vulgate,* and *Syriac* add, "And the third of the earth was burnt up." So under the third trumpet, the *third* of the rivers is affected: also, under the sixth trumpet, the *third* part of men are killed. In Zechariah 13:8, 9 this tripartite division appears, but the proportions reversed, two parts killed, only a third preserved. Here, vice versa, two-thirds escape, one-third is smitten. The fire was the predominant element. **all green grass**— no longer a third, but *all* is *burnt up.* **8. as it were** —not literally a mountain: a mountain-like burning mass. There is a plain allusion to Jeremiah 51: 25; Amos 7:4. **third part of the sea became blood** —In the parallel second vial, the *whole* sea (not merely *a third)* becomes *blood.* The overthrow of Jericho, the type of the Antichristian Babylon, after which Israel, under Joshua (the same name as *Jesus),* victoriously took possession of Canaan, the type of Christ's and His people's kingdom, is perhaps alluded to in the SEVEN *trumpets,* which end in the overthrow of all Christ's foes, and the setting up of His kingdom. On the *seventh* day, at the *seventh* time, when the *seven* priests blew the *seven* ram's horn trumpets, the people shouted, and the walls fell flat: and then ensued the *blood-shedding* of the foe. A mountain-like fiery mass would not naturally change water into blood; nor would the third part of *ships* be thereby destroyed. The symbolical interpreters take *the ships* here to be *churches.* For the *Greek* here for ships is not the common one, but that used in the Gospels of the apostolic vessel in which Christ taught: and the first churches were in the shape of an inverted ship: and the *Greek* for *destroyed* is also used of heretical *corruptings* (I Tim. 6:5). **10. a lamp**—*a torch.* **11.** The symbolizers interpret the *star fallen from heaven* as a chief minister (ARIUS, according to BULLINGER, BENGEL, and others; or some future false teacher, if, as is more likely, the event be still future) falling from his high place in the Church, and instead of shining with heavenly light as a *star,* becoming a torch lit with earthly fire and smouldering with smoke. And "wormwood," though medicinal in some cases, if used as ordinary water would not only be disagreeable to the taste, but also fatal to life: so "heretical wormwood changes the sweet Siloas of Scripture into deadly Marahs" [WORDSWORTH]. Contrast the converse change of bitter Marah water into sweet, Exodus 15:23. ALFORD gives as an illustration in a physical point of view, the conversion of water into *firewater* or *ardent* spirits, which may yet go on to destroy even as many as a third of the ungodly in the latter days. **12. third part**—not a *total* obscuration as in the sixth seal (ch. 6:12, 13). This *partial* obscuration, therefore, comes between the prayers of the martyrs under the fifth seal, and the last overwhelming judgments on the ungodly under the sixth seal, at the eve of Christ's coming. **the night likewise**—withdrew a third part of the light which the bright Eastern moon and stars ordinarily afford. **13. an angel**—A, B, *Vulgate, Syriac,* and *Coptic* read for "angel," which is supported by none of the oldest MSS., "an eagle": the symbol of judgment descending fatally from on high; the king of birds pouncing on the prey. Cf. this fourth trumpet and the flying *eagle* with the fourth seal introduced by the fourth living creature, "like a flying eagle," ch. 4:7; 6:7, 8: the aspect of Jesus as presented by the fourth Evangelist. *John* is compared in the cherubim (according to the primitive interpretation) to a flying eagle: *Christ's divine majesty* in this similitude is set forth in the Gospel according to John, His *judicial visitations* in the Revelation of John. Contrast "another angel," or *messenger,* with "the everlasting Gospel," ch. 14:6. **through the midst of heaven**—*Greek,* "in the mid-heaven," i.e., in the part of the sky where the sun reaches the *meridian:* in such a position as that the eagle is an object conspicuous to all. **the inhabiters of the earth**—the ungodly, the "men of the world," whose "portion is in this life," upon whom the martyrs had prayed that their blood might be avenged (ch. 6:10). Not that they sought personal revenge, but their zeal was for the honor of God against the foes of God and His Church. **the other**—*Greek, "the remaining* voices."

CHAPTER 9

VSS. 1-21. THE FIFTH TRUMPET: THE FALLEN STAR OPENS THE ABYSS WHENCE ISSUE LOCUSTS. THE SIXTH TRUMPET. FOUR ANGELS AT THE EUPHRATES LOOSED. **1.** The last three trumpets of the seven are called, from ch. 8:13, *the woe-trumpets.* **fall**—rather as *Greek,* "fallen." When John saw it, it was not in the act of *falling,* but had *fallen* already. This is a connecting link of this fifth trumpet with ch. 12:8, 9, 12, *"Woe to the inhabiters of the earth,* for the *devil* is *come down.* ..." Cf. Isaiah 14:12, "How art thou *fallen from heaven,* Lucifer, son of the morning!" **the bottomless pit**—*Greek,* "the pit of the abyss"; *the orifice of the hell* where Satan and his demons dwell. **3. upon**—*Greek,* "unto," or "into." **as the scorpions of the earth**—as contrasted with the "locusts" which come up *from hell,* and are not "of the earth." **have power**—viz., to sting. **4. not hurt the grass ... neither ... green thing ... neither ... tree**—the food on which they ordinarily prey. Therefore, not natural and ordinary locusts. Their natural instinct is supernaturally restrained to mark the judgment as altogether divine. **those men which** —*Greek,* "*the* men whosoever." **in ...**—*Greek,* "*upon* their forehead." Thus this fifth trumpet is proved to follow the *sealing* in ch. 7, under the sixth seal. None of the saints are hurt by these locusts, which is not true of the saints in Mohammed's attack, who is supposed by many to be meant by the locusts; for many true believers fell in the Mohammedan invasions of Christendom. **5. they ... they** —The subject changes: the first "they" is *the locusts;* the second is the *unsealed.* **five months**—the ordinary time in the year during which locusts continue their ravages. **their torment**—the torment of the sufferers. This fifth verse and vs. 6 cannot refer to an invading army. For an army would *kill,* and not merely *torment.* **6. shall desire**—*Greek,* "eagerly desire"; set their mind on. **shall flee**—So B, *Vulgate, Syriac,* and *Coptic* read. But A and ℵ read, "fleeth," viz., continually. In ch. 6:16, which is at a later stage of God's judgments, the ungodly seek annihilation, not from the torment of their suffering, but from fear of the face of the Lamb before whom they have to stand. **7. prepared unto battle**—*Greek,* "made ready unto war." Cf. *Note,* Joel 2:4, where the resemblance of locusts to horses is traced: the plates of a horse armed for battle are an image on a larger scale of the outer shell of the locust. **crowns**—(Nah. 3:17). ELLIOTT explains this of the *turbans* of Mohammedans. But how could turbans be "like gold?" ALFORD understands it of the head of the locusts actually ending in a crown-shaped fillet which resembled gold in its material. **as the faces of men**—The "as" seems to imply the locusts here do not mean *men.* At the same time they are not natural locusts, for these do not sting *men* (vs. 5). They must be supernatural. **8. hair of women**—long and flowing. An Arabic proverb compares the antlers of locusts to the hair of girls. EWALD *in* ALFORD understands the allusion to be to the hair on the legs or bodies of the locusts: cf. "rough caterpillars," Jeremiah 51:27. **as the teeth of lions**—(Joel 1:6, as to locusts). **9. as it were breastplates of iron**—not such as forms the thorax of the natural locust. **as ... chariots** (Joel 2:5-7). **battle**—*Greek,* "war." **10. tails like unto scorpions**—like unto *the tails of* scorpions. **and there were stings**—There is no oldest MS. for this reading. A, B, ℵ *Syriac,* and *Coptic* read, "and (they have) stings: and in their tails (is) their power (lit., 'authority': authorized power) to hurt." **11. And**–so *Syriac.* But A, B, and ℵ, omit "and." **had**–*Greek*, "have." **a king ... which is the angel**–*English Version*, agreeing with A, ℵ, reads the *(Greek)* article before "angel," in which reading we must translate, "They have as king over them *the* angel..." Satan (cf. vs. 1). Omitting the article with B, we must translate, "They have as king *an* angel...": one of the chief demons under Satan: I prefer from vs. 1, the former. **bottomless pit**– *Greek*, "abyss." **Abaddon**–i.e., *perdition* or *destruction* (Job 26:6; Prov. 27: 20). The locusts are supernatural instruments in the hands of Satan to torment, and yet not kill, the ungodly, under this fifth trumpet. Just as in the case of godly Job, Satan was allowed to torment with elephantiasis, but not to touch his *life.* In vs. 20, these two woe-trumpets are expressly called "plagues." ANDREAS OF CÆSAREA, A.D. 500, held, in his *Commentary on Revelation*, that the locusts mean *evil spirits* again permitted to come forth on earth and afflict men with various plagues. **12.** *Greek, "The* one woe." **hereafter**–*Greek*, "after these things." I agree with ALFORD and DE BURGH, that these *locusts from the abyss* refer to judgments about to fall on the ungodly immediately before Christ's second advent. None of the interpretations which regard them as past, are satisfactory. Joel 1:2-7; 2:1-11, is strictly parallel and expressly refers (2:11) to THE DAY OF THE LORD GREAT AND VERY TERRIBLE: vs. 10 gives the portents accompanying the day of the Lord's coming, *the earth quaking, the heavens trembling, the sun, moon, and stars, withdrawing their shining:* vs. 18. 31, 32, also point to the immediately succeeding deliverance of Jerusalem: cf. also, the previous last conflict in the valley of Jehoshaphat, and the dwelling of God thenceforth in Zion, blessing Judah. DE BURGH confines the locust judgment to *the Israelite land,* even as the sealed in ch. 7 are Israelites: not that there are not others sealed as elect in *the earth;* but that, the judgment being confined to *Palestine,* the sealed of *Israel alone* needed to be expressly excepted from the visitation. Therefore, he translates throughout, "the land" (i.e., of Israel and Judah), instead of "the earth." I incline to agree with him. **13. a voice**–lit., "*one* voice." **from**–*Greek*, "out of." **the four horns**–A, *Vulgate (Amiatinus* MS.), *Coptic,* and *Syriac* omit "four." B and CYPRIAN support it. The *four* horns together gave forth their voice, not diverse, but *one.* God's revelation (e.g., the Gospel), though in its aspects fourfold (*four* expressing *world-wide* extension: whence *four* is the number of the Evangelists), still has but one and the same voice. However, from the parallelism of this sixth trumpet to the fifth seal (ch. 6:9, 10), the martyrs' cry for the avenging of their blood from the altar reaching its consummation under the sixth seal and sixth trumpet, I prefer understanding this *cry from the four corners of the altar* to refer to the saints' prayerful cry from the four quarters of the world, *incensed* by the angel, and ascending to God from the golden altar of incense, and bringing down in consequence fiery judgments. omits the whole clause, "one from the four horns." **14. in ...**–*Greek, epi to potamo;* "on," or "at the great river." **Euphrates**–(Cf. ch. 16:12). The river whereat Babylon, the ancient foe of God's people was situated. Again, whether from the literal region of the Euphrates, or from the spiritual Babylon (*the apostate Church,* especially ROME), four angelic ministers of God's judgments shall go forth, as-

sembling an army of horsemen throughout the four quarters of the earth, to slay a third of men, the brunt of the visitation shall be on Palestine. **15. were**–"which had been prepared" [TREGELLES rightly]. **for an hour ...**–rather as *Greek*, "for (i.e., against) THE hour, and day, and month, and year," viz., appointed by God. The *Greek* article (*teen*), put once only before all the periods, implies that the hour in the day, and the day in the month, and the month in the year, and the year itself, had been definitely fixed by God. The article would have been omitted had a sum-total of periods been specified, viz., 391 years and one month (the period from A.D. 1281, when the Turks first conquered the Christians, to 1672, their last conquest of them, since which last date their empire has declined). **slay** –not merely to "hurt" (vs. 10), as in the fifth trumpet. **third part**–(*Note,* ch. 8:7-12). **of men**–viz., of earthy men, ch. 8:13, "inhabiters of the earth," as distinguished from God's sealed people (of which the sealed of Israel, ch. 7, form the nucleus). **16.** Cf. with these 200,000,000, Psalm 68:17; Daniel 7:10. The hosts here are evidently, from their numbers and their appearance (vs. 17), not merely *human* hosts, but probably *infernal,* though constrained to work out God's will (cf. vss. 1, 2). **and I heard**–A, B, ℵ, *Vulgate, Syriac, Coptic,* and CYPRIAN omit "and." **17. thus**–as follows. **of fire** –the *fiery color* of the breastplates answering to the *fire* which *issued* out of their *mouths.* **of jacinth** –lit., "of hyacinth color," the hyacinth of the ancients answering to our *dark blue iris:* thus, their *dark, dull-colored* breastplates correspond to the *smoke* out of their mouths. **brimstone**–*sulphur-colored:* answering to the *brimstone* or sulphur *out of their mouths.* **18. By these three**–A, B, C, and ℵ read (*apo for kupo*), "From"; implying the *direction* whence the slaughter came; not direct instrumentality as "by" implies. A, B, C, ℵ also add "plagues" after "three." *English Version* reading, which omits it, is not well supported. **by the fire**–*Greek*, "owing to the fire," lit., "out of." **19. their**–A, B, C and ℵ read, "the power *of the horses.*" **in their mouth**–whence *issued* the fire, smoke, and brimstone (vs. 17). Many interpreters understand the *horsemen* to refer to the myriads of Turkish cavalry arrayed in scarlet, blue, and yellow (*fire, hyacinth,* and *brimstone*), the *lion-headed horses* denoting their invincible courage, and *the fire* and *brimstone* out of their mouths, the gunpowder and artillery introduced into Europe about this time, and employed by the Turks; the tails, like serpents, having a venomous sting, the false religion of Mohammed supplanting Christianity, or, as ELLIOTT thinks, the Turkish pachas' horsetails, worn as a symbol of authority. (!) All this is very doubtful. Considering the parallelism of this sixth trumpet to the sixth seal, the likelihood is that events are intended immediately preceding the Lord's coming. "The false prophet" (as Isa. 9:15 proves), or second beast, having the horns of a lamb, but speaking as *the dragon,* who supports by lying miracles the final Antichrist, seems to me to be intended. Mohammed, doubtless, is a forerunner of him, but not the exhaustive fulfiller of the prophecy here: Satan will, probably, towards the end, bring out all the powers of hell for the last conflict (*Note,* "devils," vs. 20; cf. vss. 1, 2, 17, 18). **with them**–with the serpent heads and their venomous fangs. **20. the rest of the men**–i.e., the ungodly. **yet**–So A, *Vulgate, Syriac,* and *Coptic.* B and ℵ read, "did *not* even repent of," viz., so as to give up "the works ...." Like Pharaoh hardening his heart against repentance notwithstanding the plagues. **of their hands**—(Deut. 31:29). Especially the idols *made by their hands.* Cf. ch. 13:14, 15, "the image of the beast" ch. 19: 20. **that they should not**—So B reads. But A, C, and ℵ read. ". . . shall not": implying a prophecy of *certainty* that it shall be so. **devils**—*Greek,* "demons" which lurk beneath the idols which idolaters worship. **21. sorceries**—witchcrafts by means of *drugs* (so the *Greek*). One of the fruits of the unrenewed flesh: the sin of the heathen: about to be repeated by apostate Christians in the last days, ch. 22:15 "sorcerers." The heathen who shall have rejected the proffered Gospel and clung to their fleshly lusts, and apostate Christians who shall have relapsed into the same shall share the same terrible judgments. The worship of images was established in the East in A.D. 842. **fornication**— singular: whereas the other sins are in the plural. Other sins are perpetrated at intervals: those lacking purity of heart indulge in *one* perpetual fornication [BENGEL].

CHAPTER 10

Vss. 1-11. VISION OF THE LITTLE BOOK. As an episode was introduced between the sixth and seventh seals, so there is one here (ch. 10:1-11, 14) after the sixth and introductory to the seventh trumpet (ch. 21:15, which forms the grand consummation). The Church and her fortunes are the subject of this episode: as the judgments on the unbelieving *inhabiters of the earth* (ch. 8:13) were the exclusive subject of the fifth and sixth woe-trumpets. Ch. 6:11 is plainly referred to in vs. 6 below; in ch. 6:11 the martyrs crying to be avenged were told they must "rest yet for a little season" or *time:* in vs. 6 here they are assured, "There shall be no longer (any interval of) time"; their prayer shall have no longer to wait, but (vs. 7) *at the trumpet-sounding of the seventh angel* shall be consummated, and *the mystery of God* (His mighty plan heretofore hidden, but then to be revealed) *shall be finished.* The *little open book* (vss. 2, 9, 10) is given to John by the angel, with a charge (vs. 11) that he *must prophesy again concerning* (so the *Greek*) *peoples, nations, tongues, and kings:* which prophecy (as appears from ch. 11) affects those *peoples, nations, tongues, and kings* only in relation to ISRAEL AND THE CHURCH, who form the main object of the prophecy. **1. another mighty angel** —as distinguished from the *mighty angel* who asked as to the former and more comprehensive book (ch. 5:2), "Who is worthy to open the book?" **clothed with a cloud**—the emblem of God coming in judgment. **a**—A, B, C. and ℵ read "the"; referring to (ch. 4:3) *the rainbow* already mentioned. **rainbow upon his head**—the emblem of covenant mercy to God's people, amidst judgments on God's foes. Resumed from ch. 4:3 (see *Note* there). **face as . . . the sun**—(ch. 1:16 18:1). **feet as pillars of fire** —(ch. 1:15; Ezek. 1:7). The angel, as representative of Christ, reflects His glory and bears the insignia attributed in ch. 1:15, 16; 4:3, to Christ Himself. The *pillar of fire* by night led Israel through the wilderness, and was the symbol of God's presence. **2. he had**—*Greek,* "Having." **in his hand** in his left hand: as in vs. 5 (*Note*), he lifts up his *right hand to heaven.* **a little book**—a roll *little* in comparison with the "book" (ch. 5:1) which contained the *whole* vast scheme of God's purposes, not to be fully read till the final consummation. This other, a *less book,* contained only a portion

which John was now to make his own (vss. 9, 11), and then to use in prophesying to others. The New Testament begins with the word "book" (*Greek, biblus*), of which "the little book" (*Greek, biblaridion*) is the diminutive, "the little bible," the Bible in miniature. **upon the sea . . . earth**—Though the beast with seven heads is about to arise out of the *sea* (ch. 13:1), and the beast with two horns like a lamb (ch. 13:11) out of the *earth,* yet it is but for a time, and that *time shall no longer be* (vss. 6, 7) when once *the seventh trumpet is about to sound;* the angel with his right foot on the sea, and his left on the earth, claims both as God's, and as about soon to be cleared of the usurper and his followers. **3. as . . . lion**—Christ, whom the angel represents, is often so symbolized (ch. 5:5, "the Lion of the tribe of Juda"). **seven thunders**—*Greek, "the* seven thunders." They form part of the Apocalyptic symbolism; and so are marked by the article as *well known.* Thus *thunderings* marked the opening of the seventh seal (ch. 8:1, 5); so also at the seventh vial (ch. 16:17, 18). WORDSWORTH calls this *the prophetic use of the article; "the* thunders, of which more hereafter." Their full meaning shall be only known at the grand consummation marked by the seventh seal, the seventh trumpet (ch. 11:19), and the seventh vial. **uttered their**— *Greek,* "spake their own voices"; i.e., voices peculiarly *their own,* and not now revealed to men. **4. when**—ℵ reads, "Whatsoever things." But most MSS. support *English Version.* **uttered their voices** —A, B, C, and ℵ omit "their voices." Then translate, "had spoken." **unto me**—omitted by A, B, C, ℵ , and *Syriac.* **Seal up**—the opposite command to ch. 22:20. Even though at *the time of the end* the things *sealed* in Daniel's time were to be revealed, yet not so the voices of these thunders. Though heard by John, they were not to be imparted by him to others in this book of Revelation; so terrible are they that God in mercy withholds them, since "sufficient unto the day is the evil thereof." The godly are thus kept from morbid ponderings over the evil to come; and the ungodly are not driven by despair into utter recklessness of life. Alford adds another aim in concealing them, viz., "godly fear, seeing that the arrows of God's quiver are not exhausted." Besides the terrors foretold, there are others unutterable and more horrifying lying in the background. **5. lifted up his hand**—So A and *Vulgate* read. But B, C, ℵ *Syriac,* and *Coptic,* ". . . his *right* hand." It was customary to lift up the hand towards heaven, appealing to the God of truth, in taking a solemn oath. There is in this part of the vision an allusion to Daniel 12. Cf. vs. 4, with Daniel 12:4, 9; and these vss. 5, 6, end, with Daniel 12:7. But there the angel clothed in linen, and standing upon the waters, sware "a time, times, and a half" were to interpose before the consummation; here, on the contrary, the angel standing with his left foot on the earth, and his right upon the sea, swears *there shall be time no longer.* There he lifted up both hands to heaven; here he has *the little book* now *open* (whereas in Daniel *the book* is *sealed*) *in his left hand* (vs. 2), and he *lifts up* only *his right hand to heaven.* **6. liveth for ever and ever**—*Greek,* "liveth unto the ages of the ages" (cf. Dan. 12:7). **created heaven . . . earth . . . sea . . .** —This detailed designation of God as the Creator, is appropriate to the subject of the angel's oath, viz., the consummating of the mystery of God (vs. 7), which can surely be brought to pass by the same Almighty power that created all things, and by none else.

that there should be time no longer—*Greek*, "that time (i.e., an interval of time) no longer shall be." The martyrs shall have no longer a time to wait for the accomplishment of their prayers for the purgation of the earth by the judgments which shall remove their and God's foes from it (ch. 6:11). The appointed *season* or *time* of delay is at an end (the same *Greek* is here as in ch. 6:11, *chronus*). Not as *English Version* implies, Time shall end and eternity begin. 7. But—connected with vs. 6. "There shall be no longer time (i.e., delay), *but* in the days of the voice of the seventh angel, when he is about to (so the *Greek*) sound his trumpet (so the *Greek*), then (lit., "also"; which conjunction often introduces the consequent member of a sentence) the mystery of God is finished," lit., "has been finished"; the prophet regarding the future as certain as if it were past. A, C, ℵ, and *Coptic* read the past tense (*Greek, etelesthee*). B reads, as *English Version*, the future (*Greek, telesthee*). should be finished" (cf. ch. 11:15-18). Sweet consolation to the waiting saints! The seventh trumpet shall be sounded without further delay. **the mystery of God**—the theme of the "little book," and so of the remainder of the Apocalypse. What a grand contrast to the "mystery of iniquity—Babylon!" The mystery of God's scheme of redemption, once hidden in God's secret counsel and dimly shadowed forth in types and prophecies, but now more and more clearly revealed according as the Gospel-kingdom develops itself, up to its fullest consummation at the end. Then finally His servants shall praise Him most fully, for the glorious consummation of the mystery in having taken to Himself and His saints the kingdom so long usurped by Satan and the ungodly. Thus this verse is an anticipation of ch. 11:15-18. declared to—*Greek*, "declared the glad tidings to." "The mystery of God" is the *Gospel glad tidings*. The office of *the prophets* is to receive *the glad tidings* from God, in order to *declare* them to others. The final consummation is the great theme of the Gospel announced to, and by, the prophets (cf. Gal. 3:8). 8. spake . . . and said—So *Syriac* and *Coptic* read. But A, B, C, "(I heard) again speaking with me, and saying" (*Greek, lalousan . . . legousan*). little book—So ℵ and B read. But A and C, "the book." 9. I went—*Greek*, "I went *away*." John here leaves heaven, his standingpoint of observation heretofore, to be near the angel standing on the earth and sea. Give—A, B, C, and *Vulgate* read the infinitive, "Telling him *to give*." eat it up —appropriate its contents so entirely as to be assimilated with (as food), and become part of thyself, so as to impart them the more vividly to others. His finding the roll sweet to the taste at first, is because it was the Lord's will he was doing, and because, divesting himself of carnal feeling, he regarded God's will as always agreeable, however bitter might be the message of judgment to be announced. Cf. Psalm 40:8, *Margin*, as to Christ's inner complete appropriation of God's word. thy belly bitter—parallel to Ezekiel 2:10, "There was written therein lamentations, and mourning, and woe." as honey—(Ps. 19:10 119:103). Honey, sweet to the mouth, sometimes turns into bile in the stomach. The thought that God would be glorified (ch. 11:3-6, 11-18) gave him the sweetest pleasure. Yet, afterwards the *belly*, or carnal natural feeling, was embittered with grief at the prophecy of the coming bitter persecutions of the Church (ch. 11:7-10); cf. John 16:1, 2. The revelation of the secrets of futurity is *sweet* to one at first, but *bitter*

and distasteful to our natural man, when we learn the cross which is to be borne before the crown shall be won. John was grieved at the coming apostasy and the sufferings of the Church at the hands of Antichrist. 10. the little book—So A and C, but B, ℵ, and *Vulgate*, "the book." was bitter —*Greek*, "was embittered." 11. he said—A, B, and *Vulgate* read, "*they say* unto me"; an indefinite expression for "it was said unto me." Thou must— The obligation lies upon thee, as the servant of God, to prophesy at His command. again—as thou didst already in the previous part of this book of Revelation. before . . .—rather as *Greek* (*epilaois*), "*concerning* many peoples . . .", viz., in their relation to the Church. The eating of the book, as in Ezekiel's case, marks John's inauguration to his prophetical office—here to a fresh stage in it, viz., the revealing of the things which befall the holy city and the Church of God—the subject of the rest of the book.

CHAPTER 11

Vss. 1-19. Measurement of the Temple. The Two Witnesses' Testimony: Their Death, Resurrection, and Ascension: The Earthquake: The Third Woe: The Seventh Trumpet Ushers in Christ's Kingdom. Thanksgiving of the Twenty-four Elders. This eleventh chapter is a compendious summary of, and introduction to, the more detailed prophecies of the same events to come in chs. 12, 13, 14, 15, 16, 17, 18, 19, 20. Hence we find *anticipatory* allusions to the subsequent prophecies; cf. vs. 7, "the beast that ascendeth out of the bottomless pit" (not mentioned before), with the detailed accounts, ch. 13:1, 11; 17:8; also vs. 8, "the great city," with ch. 14:8; 17:1, 5; 18:10. 1. and the angel stood—omitted in A, *Vulgate*, and *Coptic*. Supported by B and *Syriac*. If it be omitted, the "reed" will, in construction, agree with "saying." So Wordsworth takes it. The *reed*, the canon of Scripture, the measuring reed of the Church, our rule of faith, *speaks*. So in ch. 16:7 *the altar* is personified as *speaking* (cf. *Note* there). The Spirit speaks in the canon of Scripture (the word *canon* is derived from *Hebrew*, *kaneh*, "a reed," the word here used; and John it was who completed the canon). So Victorinus, Aquinas, and Vitringa. "Like a rod," viz., straight: like a *rod of iron* (ch. 2:27), unbending, destroying all error, and that "cannot be broken." Ch. 2:27; Hebrews 1:8, *Greek*, "a rod of straightness," *English Version*, "a scepter of righteousness"; this is added to guard against it being thought that the *reed* was one "shaken by the wind." In the abrupt style of the Apocalypse, "saying" is possibly indefinite, put for "*one said*." Still Wordsworth's view agrees best with *Greek*. So the ancient commentator, Andreas of Cæsarea, in the end of the fifth century (cf. *Note*, vss. 3, 4). the temple—*Greek, naon* (as distinguished from the *Greek, hieron*, or temple in general), the Holy Place, "*the sanctuary*." the altar—of incense; for it alone was in *the sanctuary* (*Greek, naos*). The measurement of the Holy place seems to me to stand parallel to the sealing of the elect of Israel under the sixth seal. God's elect are symbolized by the sanctuary at Jerusalem (I Cor. 3:16, 17, where the same *Greek* word, *naos*, occurs for "temple," as here). Literal Israel in Jerusalem, and with the temple restored (Ezek. 40: 3, 5, where also the temple is measured with the measuring reed, 41, 42, 43, 44), shall stand at the head of the elect Church. The measuring implies at once the exactness of the proportions of the temple to be restored, and the definite completeness (not one being wanting) of the numbers of the Israelite and of the Gentile elections. The literal temple at Jerusalem shall be the typical forerunner of the heavenly Jerusalem, in which there shall be all temple, and *no* portion exclusively set apart as *temple*. John's accurately drawing the distinction in subsequent chapters between God's servants and those who bear the mark of the beast, is the way whereby he fulfils the direction here given him *to measure the temple*. The fact that the *temple* is distinguished from *them that worship therein*, favors the view that the spiritual temple, the Jewish and Christian Church, is not exclusively meant, but that the literal temple must also be meant. It shall be rebuilt on the return of the Jews to their land. Antichrist shall there put forward his blasphemous claims. The sealed elect of Israel, the head of the elect Church, alone shall refuse his claims. These shall constitute the true sanctuary which is here measured, i.e., accurately marked and kept by God, whereas the rest shall yield to his pretensions. WORDSWORTH objects that, in the twenty-five passages of the Acts, wherein the Jewish temple is mentioned, it is called *hieron*, not *naos*, and so in the apostolic Epistles; but this is simply because no occasion for mentioning *the literal Holy Place* (Greek, *naos*) occurs in Acts and the Epistles; indeed, in Acts 7:48, though not directly, there does occur the term, *naos*, indirectly referring to the Jerusalem temple *Holy Place*. In addressing Gentile Christians, to whom the literal Jerusalem *temple* was not familiar, it was to be expected the term, *naos*, should not be found in the literal, but in the spiritual sense. In vs. 19 *naos* is used in a *local* sense; cf. also ch. 14: 15, 17; 15:5, 8. **2. But**—*Greek*, "And." **the court ... without**—all outside *the Holy Place* (vs. 1). **leave out**—of thy measurement, lit., "cast out"; reckon as unhallowed. **it**—emphatic. *It* is not to be measured; whereas the Holy Place is. **given**—by God's appointment. **unto the Gentiles**—In the wider sense, there are meant here "the times of the Gentiles," wherein Jerusalem is "*trodden* down of the Gentiles," as the parallel, Luke 21:24, proves; for the same word is used here [*Greek, patein*], tread under foot." Cf. also Psalm 79:1; Isaiah 63:18. **forty ... two months**—(ch. 13:5). The same period as Daniel's "time, times, and half" (ch. 12:14); and vs. 3, and ch. 12:6, the woman a fugitive in the wilderness "a thousand two hundred and threescore days." In the wider sense, we may either adopt the year-day theory of 1260 years (on which, and the papal rule of 1260 years, see my *Notes, Dan.* 7:25; 8:14; 12-11), or rather, regard the 2300 days (Dan. 8:14), 1335 days (Dan. 12:11, 12). 1290 days, and 1260 days, as symbolical of the long period of the Gentile times, whether dating from the subversion of the Jewish theocracy at the Babylonian captivity (the *kingdom* having been never since restored to Israel), or from the last destruction of Jerusalem under Titus, and extending to the restoration of the theocracy at the coming of Him "whose right it is"; the different epochs marked by the 2300, 1335, 1290, and 1260 days, will not be fully cleared up till the grand consummation; but, meanwhile, our duty and privilege urge us to investigate them. Some one of the epochs assigned by many may be right but as yet it is uncertain. The times of the Gentile monarchies during Israel's *seven times* punishment, will probably, in the narrower sense (vs. 2), be succeeded by the much more restricted times of the personal Antichrist's

tyranny in the Holy Land. The long years of papal misrule may be followed by the short time of the man of sin who shall concentrate in himself all the apostasy, persecution, and evil of the various forerunning Antichrists, Antiochus, Mohammed, Popery, just before Christ's advent. His time shall be THE RECAPITULATION and open consummation of the "mystery of iniquity" so long leavening the world. Witnessing churches may be followed by witnessing individuals, the former occupying the longer, the latter, the shorter period. The *three and a half* (1260 days being three and a half years of 360 days each, during which the two witnesses prophesy in sackcloth) is the sacred number *seven* halved, implying the Antichristian world-power's time is broken at best; it answers to the *three and a half* years' period in which Christ witnessed for the truth, and the Jews, His own people, disowned Him, and the God-opposed world power crucified Him (cf. *Note*, Dan. 9:27). The three and a half, in a word, marks the time in which the earthly rules over the heavenly kingdom. It was the duration of Antiochus' treading down of the temple and persecution of faithful Israelites. The resurrection of the witnesses after three and a half days, answers to Christ's resurrection after three days. The world-power's times never reach the sacred fulness of seven times 360, i.e., 2520, though they approach to it in 2300 (Dan. 8:14). The forty-two months answer to Israel's forty-two sojournings (Num. 33:1-50) in the wilderness, as contrasted with the sabbatic rest in Canaan: reminding the Church that here, in the world wilderness, she cannot look for her sabbatic rest. Also, three and a half years was the period of the heaven being shut up, and of consequent famine, in Elias' time. Thus, three and a half represented to the Church the idea of toil, pilgrimage, and persecution. **3. I will give**—*power*—There is no "power" in the *Greek*, so that "give" must mean "give *commission*," or some such word. **my two witnesses**—*Greek*, "*the* two witnesses of me." The article implies that the two were well known at least to John. **prophesy**—preach under the inspiration of the Spirit, denouncing judgments against the apostate. They are described by symbol as "the two olive trees" and "the two candlesticks," or *lamp-stands*, "standing before the God of the earth." The reference is to Zechariah 4:3, 12, where two *individuals* are meant, Joshua and Zerubbabel, who ministered to the Jewish Church, just as the two olive trees emptied the oil out of themselves into the bowl of the candlestick. So in the final apostasy God will raise up two inspired witnesses to minister encouragement to the afflicted, though sealed, remnant. As *two* candlesticks are mentioned in vs. 4, but only *one* in Zechariah 4, I think the twofold Church, Jewish and Gentile, may be meant by the two candlesticks represented by the two witnesses: just as in ch. 7 there are described first the sealed of Israel, then those of all nations. But see *Note*, vs. 4. The actions of the two witnesses are just those of Moses when witnessing for God against Pharaoh (the type of Antichrist, the last and greatest foe of Israel), *turning the waters into blood*, and *smiting* with *plagues;* and of Elijah (the witness for God in an almost universal apostasy of Israel, a remnant of 7000, however, being left, as the 144,000 sealed, ch. 7) causing *fire* by his word to *devour the enemy*, and *shutting heaven, so that it rained not* for *three years and six months*, the very time (1260 days) during which the two witnesses prophesy. Moreover, the words "witness" and "prophesy" are usually applied to *individuals*, not to abstractions (cf. Ps. 52:8). DE BURGH thinks Elijah and Moses will again appear, as Malachi 4: 5, 6 seems to imply (cf. Matt. 17:11; Acts 3:21). Moses and Elijah appeared with Christ at the Transfiguration, which foreshadowed His coming millennial kingdom. As to Moses, cf. Deuteronomy 34:5, 6; Jude 9. Elias' genius and mode of procedure bears the same relation to the second coming of Christ, that John the Baptist's did to the first coming [BENGEL]. Many of the early Church thought the two witnesses to be Enoch and Elijah. This would avoid the difficulty of the dying a *second* time, for these have never yet died; but, perhaps, shall be the witnesses slain. Still, the *turning the water to blood, and the plagues* (vs. 6), apply best to *Moses* (cf. ch. 15:3, the song of *Moses*"). The transfiguration glory of Moses and Elias was not their permanent resurrection state, which shall not be till Christ shall come to glorify His saints, for He has precedence before all in rising. An objection to this interpretation is that those blessed departed servants of God would have to submit to death (vss. 7, 8), and this in Moses' case a *second* time, which Hebrews 9:27 denies. See my *Note*, Zechariah 4:11, 12, on the two witnesses as answering to "the two olive trees." The two olive trees are channels of the oil feeding the Church, and symbols of peace. The Holy Spirit is the oil in them. Christ's witnesses, in remarkable times of the Church's history, have generally appeared in pairs: as Moses and Aaron, the inspired civil and religious authorities; Caleb and Joshua; Ezekiel the priest and Daniel the prophet; Zerubbabel and Joshua. **in sackcloth**—the garment of prophets, especially when calling people to mortification of their sins, and to repentance. Their very exterior aspect accorded with their teachings: so Elijah, and John who came in His spirit and power. The *sackcloth* of the witnesses is a catch word linking this episode under the sixth trumpet, with the *sun black as sackcloth* (in righteous retribution on the apostates who rejected God's witnesses) under the sixth seal (ch. 6:12). **4. standing before the God of the earth**—A, B, C, *Vulgate, Syriac, Coptic,* and ANDREAS read "Lord" for "God": so Zechariah 4: 14. Ministering to (Luke 1:19), and as in the sight of Him, who, though now so widely disowned on *earth*, is its rightful King, and shall at last be openly recognized as such (vs. 15). The phrase alludes to Zechariah 4:10, 14, "the two anointed ones that stand by the Lord of the whole earth." · The article "the" marks this allusion. They are "the two candlesticks," not that they are the Church, the *one* candlestick, but as its representative *light-bearers* (*Greek*, Phil. 2:15, *phosteres*), and ministering for its encouragement in a time of apostasy. WORDSWORTH's view is worth consideration, whether it may not constitute a secondary sense: *the two witnesses, the olive trees,* are THE TWO TESTAMENTS ministering their *testimony* to the Church of the old dispensation, as well as to that of the new, which explains the two witnesses being called also *the two candlesticks* (the Old and New Testament churches; the candlestick in Zechariah 4 is but *one* as there was then but one Testament, and one Church, the Jewish). The Church in both dispensations has no light in herself, but derives it from the Spirit through the witness of the twofold word, the two olive trees: cf. (*Note*) vs. 1, which is connected with this, *the reed*, the *Scripture canon*, being the measure of the Church: so PRIMASIUS X, p. 314: the two witnesses preach in sackcloth, marking the

ignominious treatment which the word, like Christ Himself, receives from the world. So the twenty-four elders represent the ministers of the two dispensations by the double twelve. But vs. 7 proves that primarily the two Testaments cannot be meant; for these shall never be "killed," and never "shall have finished their testimony" till the world is finished. **5. will hurt**—*Greek*, "wishes," or "desires to hurt them." **fire ... devoureth**—(Cf. Jer. 5:14; 23:29). **out of their mouth**—not literally, but God makes their inspired denunciations of judgment to come to pass and *devour* their enemies. **if any man will hurt them**—twice repeated, to mark the *immediate certainty* of the accomplishment. **in this manner**—so in like manner as he tries to hurt them (cf. ch. 13:10). Retribution in kind. **6. These ... power**—*Greek*, "authorized power." **it rain not**—*Greek, huetos brechee,* "rain shower not," lit., "*moisten* not" (the earth). **smite ... with all plagues**—*Greek*, "with (lit., 'in') every plague." **7. finished their testimony**—The same verb is used of Paul's ending his ministry by a violent death. **the beast that ascended out of the bottomless pit**—*Greek*, "the wild beast ... the abyss." This beast was not mentioned before, yet he is introduced as "*the* beast," because he had already been described by Daniel (7:3, 11), and he is fully so in the subsequent part of the Apocalypse, viz., ch. 13:1; 17:8. Thus, John at once appropriates the Old Testament prophecies; and also, viewing his whole subject at a glance, mentions as familiar things (though not yet so to the reader) objects to be described hereafter by himself. It is a proof of the unity that pervades all Scripture. **make war against them**—alluding to Daniel 7:21, where the same is said of *the little horn* that sprang up among the ten horns on the fourth beast. **8. dead bodies**—So *Vulgate, Syriac,* and ANDREAS. But A, B, C, the oldest MSS., and *Coptic* read the singular, "dead body." The two fallen in one cause are considered as *one*. **the great city**—*eight* times in the Revelation elsewhere used of BABYLON (ch. 14:8; 16:19; 17:18; 18:10, 16, 18, 19, 21). In ch. 21:10 (*English Version* as to *the new Jerusalem*), the oldest MSS. omit "the great" before *city*, so that it forms no exception. It must, therefore, have an anticipatory reference to the mystical Babylon. **which**—*Greek*, "the which," viz., *the* city *which*. **spiritually**—in a spiritual sense. **Sodom**—The very term applied by Isaiah 1:10 to apostate Jerusalem (cf. Ezek. 16:48). **Egypt** —the nation which the Jews' besetting sin was to lean upon. **where ... Lord was crucified**—This identifies the city as Jerusalem, though the Lord was crucified *outside* of the city. EUSEBIUS mentions that the scene of Christ's crucifixion was enclosed within the city by Constantine; so it will be probably at the time of the slaying of the witnesses. "The beast [e.g., Napoleon and France's efforts] has been long struggling for a footing in Palestine; after his ascent from the bottomless pit he struggles much more" [BENGEL]. Some one of the Napoleonic dynasty may obtain that footing, and even be regarded as Messiah by the Jews, in virtue of his restoring them to their own land; and so may prove to be the last Antichrist. The difficulty is, how can Jerusalem be called "the great city," i.e., Babylon? By her becoming the world's capital of idolatrous apostasy, such as Babylon originally was, and then Rome has been; just as she is here called also "Sodom and Egypt." **also our**—A, B, C, ORIGEN, ANDREAS, and others read, "also their." Where *their Lord, also,* as well as they, was slain. Cf. ch. 18:24, where *the blood of* ALL *slain on earth* is said to be found IN BABYLON, just as in Matthew 23:35, Jesus saith that, "upon the Jews and JERUSALEM" (cf. vss. 37, 38) shall "come ALL the righteous blood shed upon earth"; whence it follows Jerusalem shall be the last capital of the world apostasy, and so receive the last and worst visitation of all the judgments ever inflicted on the apostate world, the earnest of which was given in the Roman destruction of Jerusalem. In the wider sense, in the Church-historical period, the Church being the sanctuary, all outside of it is the world, the great city, wherein all the martyrdoms of saints have taken place. *Babylon* marks its idolatry, *Egypt* its tyranny, *Sodom* its desperate corruption, *Jerusalem* its pretensions to sanctity on the ground of spiritual privileges, while all the while it is the murderer of Christ in the person of His members. All which is true of Rome. So VITRINGA. But in the more definite sense, *Jerusalem* is regarded, even in Hebrews (ch. 13:12-14), as the world city which believers were then to go forth from, in order to "seek one to come." **9. they**—rather, "(*some*) of the peoples." **peoples**—*Greek,* "peoples." **kindreds**—*Greek,* "tribes"; all save the elect (whence it is not said, *The peoples . . .,* but [some] *of the peoples . . .;* or, *some of the peoples . . . may refer to those of the nations . . ., who at the time shall hold possession of Palestine and Jerusalem*). **shall see**—So *Vulgate, Syriac,* and *Coptic.* But A, B, C, and ANDREAS, the present, "see," or rather (*Greek, blepousin*), "look upon." The prophetic present. **dead bodies**—So *Vulgate, Syriac,* and ANDREAS. But A, B, C, and *Coptic,* singular, as in vs. 8, "dead body." Three and a half days answer to the three and a half years (*Notes,* vss. 2, 3), the half of seven, the full and perfect number. **shall not suffer**—so B, *Syriac, Coptic,* and ANDREAS. But A, C, and *Vulgate* read, "do not suffer." **in graves**—so *Vulgate* and PRIMASIUS. But B, C, *Syriac, Coptic,* and ANDREAS, *singular;* translate, "into a sepulchre," lit., "a monument." Accordingly, in righteous retribution in kind, *the flesh* of the Antichristian hosts is not buried, but given to *all the fowls in midheaven* to eat (ch. 19:17, 18, 21). **10. they that dwell upon . . . earth**—those who belong to the earth, as its citizens, not to heaven (ch. 3:10; 8:13; 12:12; 13:8). **shall**—so *Vulgate, Syriac,* and *Coptic.* But A, B, and C read *the present;* cf. *Note,* vs. 9, on "shall not suffer." **rejoice over them**—The Antichristianity of the last days shall probably be under the name of philosophical enlightenment and civilization, but really man's deification of himself. Fanaticism shall lead Antichrist's followers to exult in having at last seemingly silenced in death their Christian rebukers. Like her Lord, the Church will have her dark passionweek followed by the bright resurrection morn. It is a curious historical coincidence that, at the fifth Lateran Council, May 5, 1514, no witness (not even the Moravians who were summoned) testified for the truth, as HUSS and JEROME did at Constance; an orator ascended the tribunal before the representatives of papal Christendom, and said, "There is no reclaimant, no opponent." LUTHER, on October 31, 1517, exactly three and a half years afterwards, posted up his famous theses on the church at Wittenberg. The objection is, the years are years of 365, not 360, days, and so two and a half days are deficient; but still the coincidence is curious; and if this prophecy be allowed other fulfilments, besides the final and literal one under the last Antichrist, this may reasonably be regarded as one. **send gifts one to another**—as was usual at a joyous

festival. **tormented them**—viz., with the plagues which they had power to inflict (vss. 5, 6); also, by their testimony against the earthly. **11.** Translate as *Greek,* "After *the* three days. . . ." **the Spirit of life**—the same which breathed *life* into Israel's dry bones, Ezekiel 37:10, 11 (where see my *Notes*), "Breath *came into* them." The passage here, as there, is closely connected with *Israel's* restoration as a nation to political and religious life. Cf. also concerning the same, Hosea 6:2, where Ephraim says, "After two days will He revive us; in the *third day* He will *raise* us *up,* and we shall *live* in His sight." **into**—so B and *Vulgate.* But A reads (*Greek, en autois*), "(so as to be) IN them." **stood upon their feet**—the very words in Ezekiel 37:10, which proves the allusion to be to *Israel's* resurrection, in contrast to "the times of the Gentiles" wherein these "tread under foot the holy city." **great fear**—such as fell on the soldiers guarding Christ's tomb at His resurrection (Matt. 28:4), when also there was a great earthquake (vs. 2). **saw** —*Greek,* "beheld." **12. they**—so A, C, and *Vulgate.* But B, *Coptic, Syriac,* and ANDREAS read, "I heard." **a cloud**—*Greek,* "the cloud"; which may be merely the generic expression for what we are familiar with, as we say "*the* clouds." But I prefer taking the article as definitely alluding to THE cloud which received Jesus at His ascension, Acts 1:9 (where there is no article, as there is no allusion to a previous cloud, such as there is here). As they resembled Him in their three and a half years' witnessing, their three and a half days lying in death (though not for exactly the same time, nor put in a tomb as He was), so also in their ascension is the translation and transfiguration of the sealed of Israel (ch. 7), and the elect of all nations, caught up out of the reach of the Antichristian foe. In ch. 14:14, 15, 16, He is represented as sitting on a *white cloud.* **their enemies beheld them**—and were thus openly convicted by God for their unbelief and persecution of His servants; unlike Elijah's ascension formerly, in the sight of friends only. The Church caught up to meet the Lord in the air, and transfigured in body, is justified by her Lord before the world, even as the manchild (Jesus) was "caught up unto God and His throne" from before *the dragon standing ready to devour the woman's child as soon as born.* **13.** "In that same (lit. 'the') hour." **great earthquake**—answering to the "great earthquake" under the sixth seal, just at the approach of the Lord (ch. 6:12). Christ was delivered unto His enemies on the fifth day of the week, and on the *sixth* was crucified, and on the sabbath rested; so it is under the sixth seal and sixth trumpet that the last suffering of the Church, begun under the fifth seal and trumpet, is to be consummated, before she enters on her seventh day of eternal sabbath. *Six* is the number of the world-power's greatest triumph, but at the same time verges on *seven,* the divine number, when its utter destruction takes place. Cf. "666" in ch. 13:18, "the number of the beast." **tenth part of the city fell**—i.e., of "the great city" (ch. 16:19; Zech. 14:2). Ten is the number of the *world kingdoms* (ch. 17:10-12), and the *beast's horns* (ch. 13:1), and the *dragon's* (ch. 12:3). Thus, in the Church-historical view, it is hereby implied that one of the ten apostate world kingdoms fall. But in the narrower view a tenth of Jerusalem under Antichrist falls. The nine-tenths remain and become when purified the center of Christ's earthly kingdom. **of men**—*Greek,* "names of men." The men are as accurately enumerated as if their names were given. **seven**

thousand—ELLIOTT interprets *seven chiliads* or provinces, i.e., the seven Dutch United Provinces lost to the papacy; and "names of men," titles of dignity, duchies, lordships, etc. Rather, *seven thousand* combine the two mystical perfect and comprehensive numbers *seven* and *thousand,* implying the *full and complete* destruction of the impenitent. **the remnant**—consisting of the Israelite inhabitants not slain. Their conversion forms a blessed contrast to ch. 16:9; and above, ch. 9:20, 21. These repeating (Zech. 12:10-14; 13:1), become in the flesh the loyal *subjects* of Christ reigning over the earth with His transfigured saints. **gave glory to the God of heaven**—which while apostates, and worshipping the beast's image, they had not done. **God of heaven**—The apostates of the last days, in pretended scientific enlightenment, recognize no *heavenly* power, but only the natural forces in the earth which come under their observation. His receiving up into *heaven* the two witnesses who had *power* during their time on earth *to shut heaven* from raining (vs. 6), constrained His and their enemies who witnessed it, to acknowledge *the God of heaven,* to be *God of the earth* (vs. 4). As in vs. 4 He declared Himself to be *God of the earth* by His two witnesses, so now He proves Himself to be *God of heaven* also. **14. The second woe**—that under the sixth trumpet (ch. 9:12-21), including also the prophecy, ch. 11:1-13: *Woe* to the world, joy to the faithful, as *their redemption draweth nigh.* **the third woe cometh quickly**—It is not mentioned in detail for the present, until first there is given a sketch of the history of the origination, suffering, and faithfulness of the Church in a time of apostasy and persecution. Instead of the third woe being detailed, the grand consummation is summarily noticed, the thanksgiving of the twenty-four elders in heaven for the establishment of *Christ's kingdom on earth,* attended with the *destruction of the destroyers of the earth.* **15. sounded** —with his trumpet. Evidently "the LAST trumpet." *Six* is close to *seven,* but does not reach it. The world judgments are complete in *six,* but by the fulfilment of *seven* the world kingdoms become Christ's. Six is the number of the world given over to judgment. It is half of *twelve,* the Church's number, as three and a half is half of seven, the divine number for completeness. BENGEL thinks the angel *here* to have been Gabriel, which name is compounded of *El,* GOD, and *Geber,* MIGHTY MAN (ch. 10:1). Gabriel therefore appropriately announced to Mary the advent of the *mighty God-man:* cf. the account of the *manchild's* birth which follows (ch. 12:1-6), to which this forms the transition though the seventh trumpet in time is subsequent, being the consummation of the historical episode, chs. 12 and 13. The seventh trumpet, like the seventh seal and seventh vial, being the consummation, is accompanied differently from the preceding six: not the consequences which follow on earth, but those IN HEAVEN, are set before us, the *great voices and thanksgiving of the twenty-four elders in heaven,* as the *half-hour's silence in heaven* at the seventh seal, and *the voice out of the temple in heaven, "It is done,"* at the seventh vial. This is parallel to Daniel 2:44, "The God *of heaven* shall set up a *kingdom,* which shall never be destroyed: and the kingdom shall not be left to other people, but it shall break to pieces all these *kingdoms,* and it shall stand for ever." It is the setting up of *Heaven's* sovereignty over the earth visibly, which, when invisibly exercised, was rejected by the earthly rulers heretofore. The dis-

tinction of worldly and spiritual shall then cease. There will be no beast in opposition to the woman. Poetry, art, science, and social life will be at once worldly and Christian. **kingdoms**—A, B, C, and *Vulgate* read the singular, "The *kingdom* (sovereignty) *of* (over) the world is our Lord's and His Christ's." There is no good authority for *English Version* reading. The *kingdoms* of the world give way to *the kingdom of* (over) *the world* exercised by Christ. The earth kingdoms are many: His shall be *one.* The appellation "Christ," *the Anointed,* is here, where His *kingdom* is mentioned appropriately for the first time used in Revelation. For it is equivalent to KING. Though priests and prophets also were *anointed,* yet this term is peculiarly applied to Him as King, insomuch that "the Lord's anointed" is His title as KING, in places where He is distinguished from the priests. The glorified Son of man shall rule mankind by His transfigured Church in heaven, and by His people Israel on earth: Israel shall be the priestly mediator of blessings to the whole world, realizing them first. **he**—not emphatic in the *Greek.* **shall reign for ever and ever**—Greek, "unto the ages of the ages." Here begins the millennial reign, the consummation of "the mystery of God" (ch. 10:7). **16. before God**—B and *Syriac* read, "before *the throne of* God." But A, C, *Vulgate,* and *Coptic* read as *English Version.* **seats**—Greek, "thrones." **17. thanks**—for the answer to our prayers·(ch. 6:10, 11) in *destroying them which destroy the earth* (vs. 18), thereby preparing the way for setting up the kingdom of Thyself and Thy saints. **and art to come** —omitted in A, B, C, *Vulgate, Syriac,* CYPRIAN, and ANDREAS. The consummation having actually come, they do not address Him as they did when it was still future, "Thou that art to come." Cf. vs. 18, "is come." From the sounding of the seventh trumpet He is to His people JAH, the ever present Lord, WHO IS, more peculiarly than JEHOVAH "who is, was, and *is to come.*" **taken to thyself thy great power**—"to Thee" is not in the *Greek.* Christ *takes* to Him the kingdom as His own of *right.* **18. the nations were angry**—alluding to Psalm 99:1, LXX, "The Lord is become King: let the peoples become *angry.*" Their anger is combined with *alarm* (Exod. 15:14; II Kings 19:28, "thy *rage against Me* is come up into Mine ears, I will put My hook in thy nose . . ."). Translate, as the *Greek* is the same. "The nations were *angered,* and Thy *anger* is come." How petty man's impotent *anger,* standing here side by side with that of the omnipotent God! **dead . . . be judged**—proving that this seventh trumpet is at the end of all things, when the judgment on Christ's foes and the reward of His saints, long prayed for by His saints, shall take place. **the prophets**—as, for instance, the two *prophesying witnesses* (vs. 3), and those who have showed them kindness for Christ's sake. Jesus shall come to effect by His presence that which we have looked for long, but vainly, in His absence, and by other means. **destroy them which destroy the earth**—Retribution in kind (cf. ch. 16:6; Luke 19:27). Daniel 7:14-18, my *Notes.* **19.** A similar solemn conclusion to that of the seventh seal, ch. 8:5, and to that of the seventh vial, ch. 16:18. Thus, it appears, the seven seals, the seven trumpets, and the seven vials, are not consecutive, but parallel, and ending in the same consummation. They present the unfolding of God's plans for bringing about the grand end under three different aspects, mutually complementing each other. **the temple** —the sanctuary or *Holy place* (Greek, *naos*), not the whole *temple* (*Greek, hieron*). **opened in heaven**—A and C read the article, "the temple of God *which is* in heaven, was opened." **the ark of his testament**—or ". . . His *covenant.*" As in the first verse the earthly sanctuary was *measured,* so here its heavenly antitype is laid open, and the antitype above to the *ark of the covenant* in the Holiest Place below is seen, the pledge of God's faithfulness to His covenant in saving His people and punishing their and His enemies. Thus this forms a fit close to the series of trumpet judgments and an introduction to the episode (chs. 12 and 13) as to His faithfulness to His Church. Here first His secret place, the heavenly sanctuary, is opened for the assurance of His people; and thence proceed His judgments in their behalf (ch. 14:15, 17; 15:5; 16:17), which the great company in heaven laud as "true and righteous." This then is parallel to the scene at the heavenly altar, at the close of the seals and opening of the trumpets (ch. 8:3),and at the close of the episode (chs. 12-15) and opening of the vials (ch. 15:7, 8). See *Note* at the opening of next chapter.

CHAPTER 12

Vss. 1-17. Vision of the Woman, Her Child, and the Persecuting Dragon. **1.** This episode (chs. 12, 13, 14, and 15) describes *in detail* the persecution of Israel and the elect Church by the beast, which had been *summarily* noticed, ch. 11:7-10, and the triumph of the faithful, and torment of the unfaithful. So also chs. 16-20 are the description in detail of the judgment on the beast, etc., summarily noticed in ch. 11:13, 18. The beast in vs. 3, etc., is shown not to be alone, but to be the instrument in the hand of a greater power of darkness, Satan. That this is so, appears from the time of ch. 11 being the period also in which the events of chs. 12 and 13 take place, viz., 1260 days (vss. 6, 14; ch. 13:5; cf. ch. 11:2, 3). **great**—in size and significance. **wonder**—*Greek,* "sign": significant of momentous truths. **in heaven**—not merely the sky, but the *heaven* beyond just mentioned, ch. 11:19; cf. vss. 7-9. **woman clothed with the sun . . . moon under her feet**—the Church, Israel first, and then the Gentile Church; clothed with Christ, "the Sun of righteousness." "Fair as the moon, clear as the sun." Clothed with the Sun, the Church is the bearer of divine supernatural light in the world. So the seven churches (i.e., the Church universal, the woman) are represented as lightbearing *candlesticks* (ch. 1). On the other hand, the *moon,* though standing above the sea and earth, is altogether connected with them and is an earthly light: *sea, earth,* and *moon* represent the worldly element, in opposition to the kingdom of God—heaven, the sun. The moon cannot disperse the darkness and change it into day: thus she represents the world religion (heathenism) in relation to the supernatural world. The Church has the moon, therefore, under her feet; but the stars, as heavenly lights, on her head. The devil directs his efforts against the stars, the angels of the churches, about hereafter to shine for ever. The twelve stars, the crown around her head, are the twelve tribes of Israel [AUBERLEN]. The allusions to *Israel* before accord with this: cf. ch. 11:19. "the temple of God"; "the ark of His testament." The ark lost at the Babylonian captivity, and never since found, is seen in the "temple of God opened in heaven," signifying that God now enters again into covenant with His ancient people.

The woman cannot mean, literally, the virgin mother of Jesus, for she did not flee into the wilderness and stay there for 1260 days, while the dragon persecuted the remnant of her seed (vss. 13-17) [DE BURGH]. The *sun, moon,* and *twelve stars,* are emblematical of Jacob, Leah, or else Rachel, and the twelve patriarchs, i.e., the Jewish Church: secondarily, the Church universal, having *under her feet,* in due subordination, the ever changing moon, which shines with a borrowed light, emblem of *the Jewish dispensation,* which is now in a position of inferiority, though supporting the woman, and also of the changeful things of this world, and having on her head the crown of twelve stars, the twelve apostles, who, however, are related closely to Israel's twelve tribes. The Church, in passing over into the Gentile world, is (1) persecuted; (2) then seduced, as heathenism begins to react on her. This is the key to the meaning of the symbolic woman, beast, harlot, and false prophet. *Woman* and *beast* form the same contrast as *the Son of man* and the *beasts* in Daniel. As the Son of man comes *from heaven,* so the woman is seen *in heaven* (vs. 1). The two beasts arise respectively *out of the sea* (cf. Dan. 7:3) and *the earth* (ch. 13:1, 11): their origin is not of heaven, but of earth earthy. Daniel beholds the heavenly Bridegroom coming visibly to reign. John sees the woman, the Bride, whose calling is heavenly, in the world, before the Lord's coming again. The characteristic of woman, in contradistinction to man, is her being subject, the surrendering of herself, her being receptive. This similarly is man's relation to God, to be subject to, and receive from, God. All autonomy of the human spirit reverses man's relation to God. Woman-like receptivity towards God constitutes *faith.* By it the *individual* becomes a child of God; the children *collectively* are viewed as "the woman." Humanity, in so far as it belongs to God, is the *woman.* Christ, the Son of the woman, is in vs. 5 emphatically called "the MAN-child" (*Greek, huios arrheen,* "male-child"). Though born of a woman, and under the law for man's sake, He is also the Son of God, and so the HUSBAND of the Church. As Son of the woman, He is "Son of man"; as *male-child,* He is Son of God, and Husband of the Church. All who imagine to have life in themselves are severed from Him, the Source of life, and, standing in their own strength, sink to the level of senseless *beasts.* Thus, the woman designates universally the kingdom of God; the beast, the kingdom of the world. The woman of whom Jesus was born represents *the Old Testament congregation of God.* The woman's travail-pains (vs. 2) represent the Old Testament believers' ardent longings for the promised Redeemer. Cf. the joy at His birth (Isa. 9:6). As new Jerusalem (called also "the woman," or "wife," ch. 21:2, 9-12), with its twelve gates, is the exalted and transfigured Church, so the woman with the twelve stars is the Church militant. **2. pained**—*Greek,* "tormented" (*basanizomene*). DE BURGH explains this of the bringing in of the first-begotten into the world AGAIN, when Israel shall at last welcome Him, and when "the man-child shall rule all nations with the rod of iron." But there is a plain contrast between the *painful travailing* of the woman here, and Christ's second coming to the Jewish Church, the believing remnant of Israel, "*Before she travailed* she brought forth . . . a MAN-CHILD," i.e., almost *without travail-pangs,* she receives (at His second advent), as if born to her, Messiah and a numerous seed. **3. appeared**—"was seen." **wonder**—

Greek; *semeion* "sign." **red**–So A and *Vulgate* read. But B, C, and *Coptic* read, "of fire." In either case, the *color* of the dragon implies his fiery rage as a *murderer from the beginning.* His representative, *the beast,* corresponds, *having seven heads and ten horns* (the number of horns on the fourth beast of Daniel 7:7; ch. 13:1. But there, *ten* crowns are on the *ten horns* (for before the end, the fourth empire is divided into *ten* kingdoms); here, *seven* crowns (rather, "diadems," *Greek, diademata*, not *stephanoi*, "wreaths") are *upon his seven heads.* In Daniel 7 the Antichristian powers up to Christ's second coming are represented by four beasts, which have among them *seven* heads, i.e., the first, second, and fourth beasts having *one* head each, the third, *four* heads. His universal dominion as prince of this fallen world is implied by the *seven diadems* (contrast the "many diadems on Christ's head," ch. 19:12, when coming to destroy him and his), the caricature of the *seven* Spirits of God. His worldly instruments of power are marked by the *ten horns,* ten being the number of the world. It marks his self-contradictions that he and the beast bear both the number *seven* (the divine number) and *ten* (the world number). **4. drew**–*Greek,* present, "draweth," "drags down." His *dragging down the stars* with *his tail* (lashed back and forward in his fury) implies his persuading to apostatize, like himself, and to become earthy, those angels and also once eminent human teachers who had formerly been heavenly (cf. vs. 1; ch. 1:20; Isa. 14:12). **stood**–"stands" [ALFORD]: perfect, *Greek, hesteken.* **ready to be delivered**–"about to bring forth." **for to devour ...**–"that when she brought forth, he might devour her child." So the dragon, represented by his agent Pharaoh (a name common to all the Egyptian kings, and meaning, according to some, *crocodile,* a reptile like the dragon, and made an Egyptian idol), was ready to devour Israel's *males* at the birth of the nation. Antitypically the true Israel, Jesus, when born, was sought for destruction by Herod, who slew all the *males* in and around Bethlehem. **5. man-child**–*Greek,* "a son, a male." On the deep significance of this term, cf. *Notes,* vss. 1, 2. **rule**–*Greek, poimainein,* "tend as a shepherd"; (see *Note,* ch. 2:27). **rod of iron**–A rod is for long-continued obstinacy until they submit themselves to obedience [BENGEL]: ch. 2:27; Psalm 2:9, which passages prove the Lord Jesus to be meant. Any interpretation which ignores this must be wrong. The *male son's* birth cannot be the origin of the Christian state (Christianity triumphing over heathenism under Constantine), which was not a divine child of the woman, but had many impure worldly elements. In a secondary sense, *the ascending of the witnesses up to heaven* answers to Christ's own ascension, "caught up unto God, and unto His throne": so also His ruling the nations with a rod of iron is to be shared in by believers (ch. 2:27). What took place primarily in the case of the divine Son of the woman, shall take place also in the case of those who are one with Him, the sealed of Israel (ch. 7), and the elect of all nations, about to be translated and to reign with Him over the earth at His appearing. **6. woman fled**–Mary's flight with Jesus into Egypt is a type of this. **where she hath**–So C reads. But A and B add "there." **a place**–that portion of the heathen world which has received Christianity professedly, viz., mainly the fourth kingdom, having its seat in the modern Babylon, Rome, implying that *all* the heathen world would not be Christianized in the

present order of things. **prepared of God**–lit., *"from* God." Not by human caprice or fear, but by the determined counsel and foreknowledge of God, the *woman,* the Church, *fled into the wilderness.* **they should feed her**–*Greek,* "nourish her." Indefinite for, "she should be fed." The heathen world, *the wilderness,* could not nourish the Church, but only afford her an outward shelter. Here, as in Daniel 4:26, and elsewhere, the third person plural refers to *the heavenly powers* who minister from God *nourishment* to the Church. As Israel had its time of first bridal love, on its first going out of Egypt into the wilderness, so the Christian Church's *wilderness*-time of *first love* was the apostolic age, when it was separate from the *Egypt* of this world, having no city here, but seeking one to come; having only a *place in the wilderness prepared of God* (vss. 6, 14). The harlot takes the world city as her own, even as Cain was the first builder of a *city,* whereas the believing patriarchs lived in *tents.* Then apostate Israel was the harlot and the young Christian Church the woman; but soon spiritual fornication crept in, and the Church in ch. 17 is no longer *the woman,* but *the harlot,* the *great Babylon,* which, however, has in it hidden the true people of God (ch. 18:4). The deeper the Church penetrated into heathendom, the more she herself became heathenish. Instead of overcoming, she was overcome by the world [AUBERLEN]. Thus, *the woman* is "the one inseparable Church of the Old and New Testament" [HENGSTENBERG], the stock of the Christian Church being Israel (Christ and His apostles being Jews), on which the Gentile believers have been *grafted,* and into which Israel, on her conversion, shall be grafted, as into *her own olive tree.* During the whole Church-historic period, or "times of the Gentiles," wherein "Jerusalem is trodden down of the Gentiles," there is no believing Jewish Church, and therefore, only the Christian Church can be "the woman." At the same time there is meant, secondarily, the preservation of the Jews during this Church-historic period, in order that Israel, who was once "the woman,"and of whom the *man-child* was born, may become so again at the close of the Gentile times, and stand at the head of the two elections, literal Israel, and spiritual Israel, the Church elected from Jews and Gentiles without distinction. Ezekiel 20:35, 36, "I will bring you into *the wilderness of the people* (Hebrew, *peoples*), and there will I plead with you ... like as I pleaded with your fathers in the wilderness of Egypt" (cf. my *Note* there): not a *wilderness* literally and locally, but spiritually a *state of discipline and trial* among the Gentile "*peoples*," during the long Gentile times, and one finally consummated in the last time of unparalleled trouble under Antichrist, in which the sealed remnant (ch. 7) who constitute "the woman," are nevertheless preserved "from the face of the serpent" (vs. 14). **thousand two hundred and threescore days**–anticipatory of vs. 14, where the persecution which caused her to flee is mentioned in its place: ch. 13 gives the details of the persecution. It is most unlikely that the transition should be made from the birth of Christ to the last Antichrist, without notice of the long intervening Church-historical period. Probably the 1260 days, or periods, representing this long interval, are RECAPITULATED on a shorter scale analogically during the last Antichrist's short reign. They are equivalent to three and a half years, which, as half of the divine number *seven,* symbolize the seeming victory of the world over the Church. As they include the whole *Gentile times* of *Jerusalem's being trodden of the Gentiles,* they must be much longer than 1260 years; for, above several centuries more than 1260 years have elapsed since Jerusalem fell. **7.** In Job 1 and 2, Satan appears among the sons of God, presenting himself before God in heaven, as the accuser of the saints: again in Zechariah 3:1, 2. But at Christ's coming as our Redeemer, he *fell from heaven,* especially when Christ suffered, rose again, and ascended to heaven. When Christ appeared before God as our Advocate, Satan, the accusing adversary, could no longer appear before God against us, but was *cast out judicially* (Rom. 8:33, 34). He and his angels henceforth range through the air and the earth, after a time (viz., the interval between the ascension and the second advent) about to be cast hence also, and bound in hell. That "heaven" here does not mean merely the air, but the abode of angels, appears from vss. 9, 10, 12; I Kings 22:19-22. **there was**—*Greek,* "there came to pass," or "arose." **war in heaven**—What a seeming contradiction in terms, yet true! Contrast the blessed result of Christ's triumph, Luke 19:38, "peace in heaven." Colossians 1:20, "made peace through the blood of His cross, by Him to *reconcile* all things unto Himself; whether ... things in earth, or things *in heaven.*" **Michael and his angels ... the dragon ... and his angels**—It was fittingly ordered that, as the rebellion arose from unfaithful angels and their leader, so they should be encountered and overcome by faithful angels and their archangel, in heaven. On earth they are fittingly encountered, and shall be overcome, as represented by the beast and false prophet, by the Son of man and His armies of human saints (ch. 19:14-21). The conflict on earth, as in Daniel 40, has its correspondent conflict of angels in heaven. Michael is peculiarly the prince, or presiding angel, of the Jewish nation. The conflict in heaven, though judicially decided already against Satan from the time of Christ's resurrection and ascension, receives its actual completion in the execution of judgment by the angels who cast out Satan from heaven. From Christ's ascension he has no standing-ground judicially against the believing elect. Luke 10:18, "I beheld (in the earnest of the future full fulfilment given in the subjection of the demons to the disciples) Satan as lightning fall from heaven." As Michael fought before with Satan about the body of the mediator of the old covenant (Jude 9), so now the mediator of the new covenant, by offering His sinless body in sacrifice, arms Michael with power to renew and finish the conflict by a complete victory. That Satan is not yet *actually* and *finally* cast out of heaven, though the *judicial* sentence to that effect received its ratification at Christ's ascension, appears from Ephesians 6:12, "spiritual wickedness in high (*Greek, heavenly*) places." This is the primary Church-historical sense here. But, through Israel's unbelief, Satan has had ground against that, the elect nation, appearing before God as its accuser. At the eve of its restoration, in the ulterior sense, his standing-ground in heaven against Israel, too, shall be taken from him, "the Lord that hath chosen Jerusalem" *rebuking* him, and casting him out from heaven actually and for ever by Michael, the prince, or presiding angel of the Jews. Thus Zechariah 3:1-9 is strictly parallel, Joshua, the high priest, being representative of his nation Israel, and Satan standing at God's right hand as adversary to resist Israel's justification. Then, and not till then, fully (vs. 10, "NOW ...") shall ALL *things be reconciled*

unto Christ IN HEAVEN (Col. 1:20), and there shall be p*eace in heaven* (Luke 19:38). **against**—A, B, and C read, "with." **8. prevailed not**—A and *Coptic* read, "*He* prevailed not." But B and C read as *English Version.* **neither**—A, B, and C read, "not even" (*Greek, oude*): a climax. Not only did they not prevail, but *not even their place was found any more in heaven.* There are four gradations in the ever deeper downfall of Satan: (1) He is deprived of his heavenly excellency, though having still access to heaven as man's accuser, up to Christ's first coming. As heaven was not fully yet opened to man (John 3:13), so it was not yet shut against Satan and his demons. The Old Testament dispensation could not overcome him. (2) From Christ, down to the millennium, he is judicially cast out of heaven as the accuser of the elect, and shortly before the millennium loses his power against Israel, and has sentence of expulsion fully executed on him and his by Michael. His rage on earth is consequently the greater, his power being concentrated on it, especially towards the end, when "he knoweth that he hath but a short time" (vs. 12). (3) He is bound during the millennium (ch. 20:1-3). (4) After having been loosed for a while, he is cast for ever into the lake of fire. **9. that old serpent**—alluding to Genesis 3:1, 4. **Devil**—the *Greek,* for "accuser," or "slanderer." **Satan** the *Hebrew* for "adversary," especially in a court of justice. The twofold designation, Greek and Hebrew, marks the twofold objects of his accusations and temptations, the elect Gentiles and the elect Jews. **world**—*Greek,* "habitable world." **10. Now**—*Now* that Satan has been cast out of heaven. Primarily fulfilled in part at Jesus' resurrection and ascension, when He said (Matthew 28:18), "All power [*Greek, exousia,* 'authority,' as here; see below] is given unto Me in heaven and in earth"; connected with vs. 5, "Her child was *caught up unto God and to His throne.*" In the ulterior sense, it refers to the eve of Christ's second coming, when Israel is about to be restored as mother-church of Christendom, Satan, who had resisted her restoration on the ground of her unworthiness, having been cast out by the instrumentality of Michael, Israel's angelic *prince* (*Note,* vs. 7). Thus this is parallel, and the necessary preliminary to the glorious event similarly expressed, ch. 11:15, "The kingdom of this world is become (the very word here, *Greek egeneto,* 'is come,' 'hath come to pass') our Lord's and His Christ's," the result of Israel's resuming her place. **salvation ...**—*Greek,* "*the salvation* (viz., fully, finally, and victoriously accomplished, Heb. 9:28; cf. Luke 3:6, yet future; hence, not till *now* do the blessed raise the fullest hallelujah for *salvation* to the Lamb, ch. 7:10; 19:1) *the power* (*Greek, dunamis*), and *the authority* (*Greek, exousia; legitimate power; see above*) of His Christ. **accused them before our God day and night**—Hence the need that the oppressed Church, *God's own elect* (like the widow, *continually coming,* so as even to *weary* the unjust judge), should cry day and night unto Him. **11. they**—emphatic in the *Greek.* "They" in particular. They and they alone. They were the persons who overcame. **overcame**—(Rom. 8:33, 34, 37; 16:20). **him**—(I John 2:14, 15). It is the same *victory* (a peculiarly Johannean phrase) over Satan and the world which the Gospel of John describes in the life of Jesus, his Epistle in the life of each believer, and his Apocalypse in the life of the Church. **by ...**—*Greek* (*dia to haima;* accusative, not genitive, as *English Version* would require, cf. Heb. 9:12), "on account *of* (on the ground of) the blood of the Lamb"; "because of . . ."; on account of and by virtue of its having been shed. Had that blood not been shed, Satan's accusations would have been unanswerable; as it is, that blood meets every charge. SCHÖTTGEN mentions the Rabbinical tradition that Satan accuses men all days of the year, except the day of atonement. TITTMANN takes the *Greek dia,* as it often means, *out of regard to* the blood of the Lamb; this was the impelling cause which *induced* them to undertake the contest *for the sake of* it; but the view given above is good Greek, and more in accordance with the general sense of Scripture. **by the word of their testimony**—*Greek,* "on account of the word of their testimony." On the ground of their faithful testimony, even unto death, they are constituted victors. Their testimony evinced their victory over him by virtue of the blood of the Lamb. Hereby they confess themselves worshippers of the slain Lamb and overcome the beast, Satan's representative; an anticipation of ch. 15:2, "them that had gotten the victory over the beast" (cf. ch. 13:15, 16). **unto**—*Greek, achri,* "even as far as." They carried their not-love of life *as far as even unto* death. **12. Therefore**—because Satan is cast out of heaven (vs. 9). **dwell**—lit., "tabernacle." Not only angels and the souls of the just with God, but also the faithful militant on earth, who already in spirit tabernacle in heaven, having their home and citizenship there, *rejoice* that Satan is cast out of their home. "Tabernacle" for *dwell* is used to mark that, though still on the earth, they in spirit are hidden "in the secret of God's *tabernacle.*" They belong not to the world, and, therefore, exult in judgment having been passed on the prince of this world. **the inhabiters of**—So ANDREAS reads. But A, B, and C omit. The words probably, were inserted from ch. 8:13. **is come down**—rather as *Greek, catebee,* "is *gone* down"; John regarding the heaven as his standing-point of view whence he looks down on the earth. **unto you**—*earth and sea,* with their inhabitants; those who lean upon, and essentially belong to, the *earth* (contrast John 3:7, *Margin,* with John 3:31; 8:23; Phil. 3:19, end; I John 4:5) and its *sea*-like troubled politics. Furious at his expulsion from heaven, and knowing that his time on earth is short until he shall be cast down lower, when Christ shall come to set up *His* kingdom (ch. 20:1, 2), Satan concentrates all his power to destroy as many souls as he can. Though no longer able to accuse the elect in heaven, he can tempt and persecute on earth. The more light becomes victorious, the greater will be the struggles of the powers of darkness; whence, at the last crisis, Antichrist will manifest himself with an intensity of iniquity greater than ever before. **short time**—*Greek, kairon,* "season": *opportunity* for his assaults. **13.** Resuming from vs. 6 the thread of the discourse, which had been interrupted by the episode, vss. 7-12 (giving in the invisible world the ground of the corresponding conflict between light and darkness in the visible world), this verse accounts for her *flight into the wilderness* (vs. 6). **14. were given**—by God's determinate appointment, not by human chances (Acts 9:11). **two**—*Greek,* "the two wings of *the* great eagle." Alluding to Exodus 19:4: proving that the Old Testament Church, as well as the New Testament Church, is included in "the woman." All believers are included (Isa. 40:30, 31). *The great eagle* is the world power; in Ezekiel 17:3, 7, *Babylon* and *Egypt:* in early Church history, *Rome,* whose standard was the eagle, turned by God's providence from being

hostile into a protector of the Christian Church. As "wings" express remote parts of the earth, the *two* wings may here mean the east and west divisions of the Roman empire. **wilderness**—the land of the heathen, the Gentiles: in contrast to Canaan, the *pleasant* and *glorious land.* God dwells in the glorious land; demons (the rulers of the heathen world, ch. 9:20; I Cor. 10:20), in the wilderness. Hence Babylon is called *the desert of the sea,* Isaiah 21:1-10 (referred to also in ch. 14:8; 18:2). Heathendom, in its essential nature, being without God, is a desolate *wilderness.* Thus, the woman's flight into the wilderness is the passing of the kingdom of God from the Jews to be among the Gentiles (typified by Mary's flight with her child from Judea into Egypt). The eagle flight is from Egypt into the wilderness. The *Egypt* meant is virtually stated (ch. 11:8) to be Jerusalem, which has become spiritually so by *crucifying our Lord.* Out of her the New Testament Church flees, as the Old Testament Church out of the literal Egypt; and as the true Church subsequently is called to flee out of Babylon (the woman become an harlot, i.e., the Church become apostate) [AUBERLEN]. **her place** —the chief seat of the then world empire, Rome. The Acts of the Apostles describe the passing of the Church from Jerusalem to Rome. The Roman protection was the eagle wing which often shielded Paul, the great instrument of this transmigration, and Christianity, from Jewish opponents who stirred up the heathen mobs. By degrees the Church had "her place" more and more secure, until, under Constantine, the empire became Christian. Still, all this Church-historical period is regarded as a wilderness time, wherein the Church is in part protected, in part oppressed, by the world power, until just before the end the enmity of the world power under Satan shall break out against the Church worse than ever. As Israel was in the wilderness forty years, and had forty-two stages in her journey, so the Church for *forty-two* months, three and a half years or *times* [lit., *seasons,* used for *years* in Hellenistic Greek (MŒRIS, the Atticist), *Greek, kairous,* Dan. 7:25; 12:7], or 1260 days (vs. 6) between the overthrow of Jerusalem and the coming again of Christ, shall be a wilderness sojourner before she reaches her millennial rest (answering to Canaan of old). It is possible that, besides this Church-historical fulfilment, there may be also an ulterior and narrower fulfilment in the restoration of Israel to Palestine, Antichrist for seven times (short periods analogical to the longer ones) having power there, for the former three and a half times keeping covenant with the Jews, then breaking it in the midst of the week, and the mass of the nation fleeing by a second Exodus into the wilderness, while a *remnant* remains in the land exposed to a fearful persecution (the "144,000 sealed of Israel," ch. 7, and 14:1, *standing with the Lamb,* after the conflict is over, *on Mount Zion:* "the first fruits" of a large company to be gathered to Him) [DE BURGH]. These *details* are very conjectural. In Daniel 7: 25; 12:7, the subject, as perhaps here, is the time of Israel's calamity. That seven times do not necessarily mean seven years, in which each day is a year, i.e., 2520 years, appears from Nebuchadnezzar's *seven times* (Dan. 4:23), answering to Antichrist, the beast's duration. **15, 16. flood**—*Greek,* "river" (cf. Exod. 2:3; Matt. 2:20; and especially Exod. 14). The *flood,* or river, is the stream of Germanic tribes which, pouring on Rome, threatened to destroy Christianity. But *the earth helped the woman,* by *swallowing up the flood.* The earth, as contradistinguished from water, is the world consolidated and civilized. The German masses were brought under the influence of Roman civilization and Christianity [AUBERLEN]. Perhaps it includes also, generally, the help given by earthly powers (those least likely, yet led by God's overruling providence to give help) to the Church against persecutions and also heresies, by which she has been at various times assailed. **17. wroth with** —Greek, "at." **went**—Greek, "went *away.*" **the remnant of her seed**—distinct in some sense from the woman herself. Satan's first effort was to root out the Christian Church, so that there should be no visible profession of Christianity. Foiled in this, he *wars* (ch. 11:7; 13:7) against the invisible Church, viz., "those who keep the commandments of God, and have the testimony of Jesus" (A, B, and C omit "Christ"). These are "the remnant," or *rest of her seed,* as distinguished from her seed, "the man-child" (vs. 5), on one hand, and from mere professors on the other. The Church, in her beauty and unity (Israel at the head of Christendom, the whole forming one perfect Church), is now not manifested, but awaiting the *manifestations of the sons of God* at Christ's coming. Unable to destroy Christianity and the Church as a whole, Satan directs his enmity against true Christians, the elect *remnant:* the others he leaves unmolested.

CHAPTER 13

Vss. 1-18. VISION OF THE BEAST THAT CAME OUT OF THE SEA: THE SECOND BEAST, OUT OF THE EARTH, EXERCISING THE POWER OF THE FIRST BEAST, AND CAUSING THE EARTH TO WORSHIP HIM. **1. I stood** So B, ℵ, and *Coptic* read. But A, C, *Vulgate,* and *Syriac,* "*He* stood." Standing on the sand of the *sea,* HE gave his power to the beast that rose out of the sea. **upon the sand of the sea**—where *the four winds* were to be seen *striving upon the great sea* (Dan. 7:2). **beast**—Greek, "wild beast." Man becomes "brutish" when he severs himself from God, the archetype and true ideal, in whose image he was first made, which ideal is realized by the man Christ Jesus. Hence, the world powers seeking **their** own glory, and not God's, are represented as *beasts;* and Nebuchadnezzar, when in self-deification he forgot that "the Most High ruleth in the kingdom of men," was driven among the beasts. In Daniel 7 there are *four* beasts: here the *one* beast expresses the sum-total of the God-opposed world power viewed in its universal development, not restricted to one manifestation alone, as Rome. This first beast expresses the world power attacking the Church more from without; the second, which is a revival of, and minister to, the first, is the world power as *the false prophet* corrupting and destroying the Church from within. **out of the sea**—(Dan. 7:3; cf. my *Note,* ch. 8:8)—out of the troubled waves of *peoples, multitudes, nations, and tongues.* The *earth* (vs. 11), on the other hand, means the consolidated, ordered world of nations, with its culture and learning. **seven heads and ten horns**—A, B, and C transpose, "ten horns and seven heads." The ten horns are now put first (contrast the order, ch. 12:3) because they are crowned. They shall not be so till the last stage of the fourth kingdom (the Roman), which shall continue until the fifth kingdom, Christ's, shall supplant it and destroy it utterly; this last stage is marked by the *ten toes* of the two feet of the image in Daniel 2. The *seven* implies the world power setting up itself

as God, and caricaturing the *seven* Spirits of God; yet its true character as God-opposed is detected by the number *ten* accompanying the seven. Dragon and beast both wear crowns, but the former on the heads, the latter on the horns (ch. 12:3; 13: 1). Therefore, both heads and horns refer to kingdoms; cf. ch. 17:7, 10, 12, "kings" representing the kingdoms whose heads they are. The *seven* kings, as peculiarly powerful—the great powers of the world—are distinguished from the *ten,* represented by the horns (simply called "kings," ch. 17:12). In Daniel, *the ten* mean the last phase of the world power, the fourth kingdom divided into *ten parts.* They are connected with the *seventh head* (ch. 17: 12), and are as yet future [AUBERLEN]. The mistake of those who interpret the beast to be Rome exclusively, and the *ten horns* to mean kingdoms which have taken the place of Rome in Europe already, is, the fourth kingdom in the image has TWO legs, representing the eastern as well as the western empire; the ten toes are not upon the one foot (the west), as these interpretations require, but on the two (east and west) together, so that any theory which makes the ten kingdoms belong to the west alone must err. If the ten kingdoms meant were those which sprung up on the overthrow of Rome, the ten would be accurately known, whereas twenty-eight different lists are given by so many interpreters, making in all sixty-five kingdoms! [TYSO in DE BURGH.] The seven heads are the seven world monarchies, Egypt, Assyria, Babylon, Persia, Greece, Rome, the Germanic empire, under the last of which we live [AUBERLEN], and which devolved for a time on Napoleon, after Francis, emperor of Germany and king of Rome, had resigned the title in 1806. FABER explains *the healing of the deadly wound* to be the revival of the Napoleonic dynasty after its overthrow at Waterloo. That secular dynasty, in alliance with the ecclesiastical power, the Papacy (vs. 11, etc.), being "the eighth head," and yet "of the seven" (ch. 17: 11), will temporarily triumph over the saints, until destroyed in Armageddon (ch. 19). A Napoleon, in this view, will be the Antichrist, restoring the Jews to Palestine, and accepted as their Messiah at first, and afterwards fearfully oppressing them. Antichrist, the summing up and concentration of all the world evil that preceded, is the eighth, but yet one of the seven (ch. 17:11). **crowns**—Greek, "diadems." **name of blasphemy**—So C, *Coptic,* and ANDREAS. A, B, and *Vulgate* read, "names ..." viz., a name on each of the heads; blasphemously arrogating attributes belonging to God alone (cf. *Note,* ch. 17:3). A characteristic of the *little horn* in Daniel 7:8, 20, 21; II Thessalonians 2:4. **2. leopard ... bear ... lion**—This beast unites in itself the God-opposed characteristics of the three preceding kingdoms, resembling respectively the *leopard, bear,* and *lion.* It rises up out of the *sea,* as Daniel's four beasts, and has *ten horns,* as Daniel's fourth beast, *and seven heads,* as Daniel's four beasts had in all, viz., one on the first, one on the second, four on the third, and one on the fourth. Thus it represents comprehensively in one figure *the world power* (which in Daniel is represented by four) *of all times and places,* not merely of one period and one locality, viewed as opposed to God; just as the *woman* is the Church of all ages. This view is favored also by the fact, that the beast is the vicarious representative of Satan, who similarly has *seven heads* and *ten horns:* a general description of his universal power in all ages and places of the world. Satan appears as a serpent, as being the archetype of the beast nature (ch. 12:9). "If the seven heads meant merely seven Roman emperors, one cannot understand why they alone should be mentioned in the original image of Satan, whereas it is perfectly intelligible if we suppose them to represent Satan's power on earth viewed collectively" [AUBERLEN]. **3. one of**—lit., "from among." **wounded . . . healed**—twice again repeated emphatically (vs. 12, 14); cf. ch. 17:8, 11, "the beast that *was, and is not, and shall ascend* out of the bottomless pit" (cf. vs. 11 below); the Germanic empire, the seventh head (revived in *the eighth*), as yet future in John's time (ch. 17:10). Contrast the change whereby Nebuchadnezzar, being humbled from his selfdeifying pride, was converted from his *beast*-like form and character to MAN'S form and true position towards God; symbolized by his *eagle wings being plucked*, and himself made to stand upon his feet as a *man* (Dan. 7:4). Here, on the contrary, the *beast's* head is not changed into a *human* head, but receives a deadly wound, i.e., the world kingdom which this head represents does not truly turn to God, but for a time its God-opposed character remains paralyzed ("as it were slain"; the very words marking the beast's outward resemblance to the Lamb, "as it were slain," *Notes*, ch. 5:6. Cf. also the second beast's resemblance to the *Lamb*, vs. 11). Though seemingly *slain* (*Greek* for "wounded"), it remains the beast still, to rise again in another form (vs. 11). The first six heads were heathenish, Egypt, Assyria, Babylon, Persia, Greece, Rome; the new seventh world power (the pagan German hordes pouring down on Christianized Rome), whereby Satan had hoped to stifle Christianity (ch. 11:15, 16), became itself Christianized (answering to the beast's, *as it were, deadly wound: it was slain*, and *it is not*, ch. 17:11). Its *ascent out of the bottomless pit answers* to the *healing of its deadly wound* (ch. 17:8). No essential change is noticed in Daniel as effected by Christianity upon the fourth kingdom; it remains essentially God-opposed to the last. The beast, *healed* of its temporary and external *wound*, now returns, not only from the *sea*, but from the *bottomless pit*, whence it draws new Antichristian strength of hell (vss. 3, 11, 12, 14; ch. 11:7; 17:8). Cf. the *seven evil spirits* taken into the temporarily dispossessed, and *the last state worse than the first*, Matthew 12:43-45. A new and worse heathenism breaks in upon the Christianized world, more devilish than the old one of the first heads of the beast. The latter was an apostasy only from the general revelation of God in nature and conscience; but this new one is from God's revelation of love in His Son. It culminates in Antichrist, the man of sin, the son of perdition (cf. ch. 17:11); II Thess. 2:3; cf. II Tim. 3:1-4, the very characteristics of old heathenism (Rom. 1:29-32) [AUBERLEN]. More than one wound seems to me to be meant, e.g., that under Constantine (when the pagan worship of the emperor's image gave way to Christianity), followed by the healing, when image worship and the other papal errors were introduced into the Church; again, that at the Reformation, followed by the lethargic *form of godliness without the power*, and about to end in the last great apostasy, which I identify with the second beast (vs. 11), Antichrist, the same seventh world power in another form. **wondered after**—followed with wondering gaze. **4. which gave**—A, B, C, *Vulgate, Syriac,* and ANDREAS read, *"because* he gave." **power**—*Greek, "the authority"* which it had; *its* authority. **Who is like unto the beast?**—The very language appropriated to

God, Exodus 15:11 (whence, in the *Hebrew,* the Maccabees took their name; the opponents of the Old Testament Antichrist, Antiochus); Psalm 35: 10; 71:19; 113:5; Micah 7:18; *blasphemously* (vss. 1, 5) assigned to the beast. It is a parody of the name "Michael" (cf. ch. 12:7), meaning, "Who is like unto God?" **5. blasphemies**—So ANDREAS reads. B reads "blasphemy." A, "blasphemous things" (cf. Dan. 7:8; 11:25). **power**—"authority"; *legitimate power (Greek, exousia).* **to continue**—*Greek, poiesai,* "to act," or "work." B reads, "to make *war*" (cf. vs. 4). But A, C, *Vulgate, Syriac,* and ANDREAS omit "war." **forty . . . two months**—*(Notes,* ch. 11:2, 3; 12:6). **6. opened . . . mouth**—The usual formula in the case of a set speech, or series of speeches. Vss. 6, 7 expand vs. 5. **blasphemy**—So B and ANDREAS. A and C read "blasphemies." **and them**—So *Vulgate, Coptic,* ANDREAS, and PRIMASIUS read. A and C omit "and": "them that dwell (lit., 'tabernacle') in heaven," mean not only angels and the departed souls of the righteous, but believers on earth who have their citizenship in heaven, and whose true life is hidden from the Antichristian persecutor in *the secret of God's tabernacle. Note,* ch. 12:12; John 3:7. **7. power**—*Greek,* "authority." **all kindreds . . . tongues . . . nations**—*Greek,* "every tribe . . . tongue . . . nation." A, B, C, *Vulgate, Syriac,* ANDREAS, and PRIMASIUS add "and people," after "tribe" or "kindred." **8. all that dwell upon the earth**—being of earth earthy; in contrast to "them that dwell in heaven." **whose names are not written**—A, B, C, *Syriac, Coptic,* and ANDREAS read singular, "(every one) whose *(Greek, hou;* but B, *Greek, hon,* plural) *name* is not written." **Lamb slain from the foundation of the world**—The *Greek* order of words favors this translation. He was *slain* in the Father's eternal counsels: cf. I Peter 1:19, 20, virtually parallel. The other way of connecting the words is, "Written from the foundation of the world in the book of life of the Lamb slain." So in ch. 17:8. The elect. The former is in the *Greek* more obvious and simple. "Whatsoever virtue was in the sacrifices, did operate through Messiah's death alone. As He was 'the Lamb slain from the foundation of the world,' so all atonements ever made were only effectual by His blood" [BISHOP PEARSON, *Creed*]. **9.** A general exhortation. Christ's own words of monition calling solemn attention. **10. He that leadeth into captivity**—A, B, C, and *Vulgate* read, "if any one (be) for captivity." **shall go into captivity**—*Greek* present, "goeth into captivity." Cf. Jeremiah 15:2, which is alluded to here. ℵ, B, and C read simply, "he goeth away," and omit "into captivity." But A and *Vulgate* support the words. **he that killeth with the sword, must be killed with the sword**—So B and C read. But A reads, "if any (is for) being (lit., 'to be') killed. . . ." As of old, so now, those to be persecuted by the beast in various ways, have their trials severally appointed them by God's fixed counsel. *English Version* is quite a different sense, viz., a warning to the persecutors that they shall be punished with retribution in kind. **Here**—"Herein": in bearing their appointed sufferings lies the *patient endurance . . . of the saints.* This is to be the motto and watchword of the elect during the period of the world kingdom. As the first beast is to be met by *patience* and *faith* (vs. 10), the second beast must be opposed by true *wisdom* (vs. 18). **11. another beast**—"the false prophet." **out of the earth**—out of society civilized, consolidated, and ordered, but still, with all its culture, of earth earthy: as distinguished from "the sea," the troubled agitations of various peoples out of which the world power and its several kingdoms have e-merged. *"The sacerdotal persecuting power, pagan and Christian;* the pagan priesthood making an image of the emperors which they compelled Christians to worship, and working wonders by magic and omens; the Romish priesthood, the inheritors of pagan rites, images, and superstitions, lamb-like in Christian professions, dragon-like in word and act" [ALFORD, and so the Spanish Jesuit, LACUNZA, writing under the name BEN EZRA]. As the first beast was like the Lamb in being, *as it were, wounded to death,* so the second is like the Lamb in having *two lamb-like horns* (its essential difference from the Lamb is marked by its having TWO, but the Lamb SEVEN horns, ch. 5:6). The former paganism of the world power, seeming to be wounded to death by Christianity, revives. In its second beast-form it is Christianized heathendom ministering to the former, and having earthly culture and learning to recommend it. The second beast's, or false prophet's rise, coincides in time with the healing of the beast's deadly wound and its revival (ch. 13:12-14). Its *manifold* character is marked by the Lord (Matt. 24:11, 24), *"Many false prophets shall rise,"* where He is speaking of the last days. As the former beast corresponds to the first four beasts of Daniel, so the second beast, or the false prophet, to the little horn starting up among the ten horns of the fourth beast. This Antichristian horn has not only the mouth of blasphemy (vs. 5), but also "the eyes of man" (Dan. 7:8): the former is also in the first beast (vss. 1, 5), but the latter not so. "The eyes of man" symbolize cunning and intellectual culture, the very characteristic of "the false prophet" (vss. 13-15; ch. 16:14). The first beast is physical and political; the second a spiritual power, the power of knowledge, *ideas* [the favorite term in the French school of politics], and scientific cultivation. Both alike are *beasts,* from below, not from above; faithful allies, worldly Antichristian wisdom standing in the service of the worldly Antichristian power: the dragon is both lion and serpent: might and cunning are his armory. The dragon gives his external power to the first beast (vs. 2), his spirit to the second, so that it *speaks as a dragon* (vs. 11). The second, arising *out of the earth,* is in ch. 11:7, and 17:8, said to *ascend out of the bottomless pit:* its very culture and world wisdom only intensify its infernal character, the pretense to superior knowledge and rationalistic philosophy (as in the primeval temptation, Gen. 3: 5, 7, "their EYES [as here] were opened") veiling the deification of nature, self, and man. Hence spring Idealism, Materialism, Deism, Pantheism, Atheism. Antichrist shall be the culmination. The Papacy's claim to the double power, secular and spiritual, is a sample and type of the twofold beast, that *out of the sea,* and that *out of the earth,* or *bottomless pit.* Antichrist will be the climax, and final form. PRIMASIUS OF ADRUMETUM, in the sixth century, says, "He feigns to be a lamb that he may assail the Lamb—the body of Christ." **12. power**—*Greek,* "authority." **before him**—"in his presence"; as ministering to, and upholding him. "The non-existence of the beast embraces the whole Germanic Christian period. The healing of the wound and return of the beast is represented [in regard to its *final* Antichristian manifestation though including also, meanwhile, its healing and return under Popery, which is baptized heathenism] in that principle which, since 1789, has manifested it-self in beast-like outbreaks" [AUBERLEN]. **which dwell therein**—the earthly-minded. The Church becomes the *harlot:* the world's political power, the Antichristian *beast;* the world's wisdom and civilization, *the false prophet.* Christ's three offices are thus perverted: the first beast is the false *kingship;* the harlot, the false *priesthood;* the second beast, the false *prophet.* The beast is the *bodily,* the false prophet the *intellectual,* the harlot the *spiritual* power of Antichristianity [AUBERLEN]. The *Old Testament Church* stood under the power of the beast, the heathen world power: *the Middle-Ages Church* under that of the harlot: *in modern times* the false prophet predominates. But in the last days all these God-opposed powers which have succeeded each other shall *co-operate,* and raise each other to the most terrible and intense power of their nature: *the false prophet causes men to worship the beast, and the beast carries the harlot.* These three forms of apostasy are reducible to two: *the apostate Church* and *the apostate world, pseudo-Christianity* and *Antichristianity,* the harlot and the beast; for the false prophet is also a beast; and the two beasts, as different manifestations of the same beast-like principle, stand in contradistinction to the harlot, and are finally judged together, whereas separate judgment falls on the harlot [AUBERLEN]. **deadly wound**—*Greek,* "wound of death." **13. wonders**—*Greek,* "signs." **so that**—so *great* that. **maketh fire**—*Greek,* "maketh even fire." This is the very miracle which the two witnesses perform, and which Elijah long ago had performed; this the beast from the bottomless pit, or the false prophet, mimics. Not merely tricks, but miracles of a demoniacal kind, and by demon aid, like those of the Egyptian magicians, shall be wrought, most calculated to deceive; wrought "after the working (*Greek,* 'energy') of Satan." **14. deceiveth them that dwell on the earth**—the earthly-minded, but not *the elect.* Even a miracle is not enough to warrant belief in a professed revelation unless that revelation be in harmony with God's already revealed will. **by the means of those miracles**—rather as *Greek,* "on account of* (because of; in consequence of) those miracles." **which he had power to do**—*Greek,* "which were given him to do." **in the sight of the beast**—"before him" (vs. 12). **which**—A, B, and C read, "who"; marking, perhaps, a personal Antichrist. **had**—So B and ANDREAS read. But A, C, and *Vulgate* read, "hath." **15. he had power**—*Greek,* "it was given to him." **to give life**—*Greek,* "breath," or "spirit." **image**—Nebuchadnezzar set up in Dura a golden *image* to be worshipped, probably of himself; for his dream had been interpreted, "Thou art this head of gold"; the three Hebrews who refused to worship the image were cast into a burning furnace. All this typifies the last apostasy. PLINY, in his letter to Trajan, states that he consigned to punishment those Christians who would not worship the emperor's *image* with incense and wine. So Julian, the apostate, set up his own image with the idols of the heathen gods in the Forum, that the Christians in doing reverence to it, might seem to worship the idols. So Charlemagne's image was set up for homage; and the Pope *adored* the new emperor (DUPIN, vol. 6, p. 126). Napoleon, the successor of Charlemagne, designed after he had first lowered the Pope by removing him to Fontainebleau, then to "make an idol of him" [*Memorial de Sainte Helene*]; keeping the Pope near him, he would, through the Pope's influence, have directed the religious, as well as the political world. The revived Napoleonic dynasty may, in some one representative, realize the project, becoming the beast supported by the false prophet (perhaps some openly infidel supplanter of the papacy, under a spiritual guise, after the harlot, or apostate Church, who is distinct from the second beast, has been stripped and judged by the beast, ch. 17:16); he then might have an image set up in his honor as a test of secular and spiritual allegiance. **speak**—"False doctrine will give a spiritual, philosophical appearance to the foolish apotheosis of the creature-ly personified by Antichrist" [AUBERLEN]. JEROME, on Daniel 7, says, Antichrist shall be "one of the human race in whom the whole of Satan shall dwell bodily." Rome's *speaking* images and winking pictures of the Virgin Mary and the saints are an earnest of the future demoniacal miracles of the false prophet in making the beast's or Antichrist's image to speak. **16. to receive a mark**—lit., "that they should give them a mark"; such a brand as masters stamp on their slaves, and monarchs on their subjects. Soldiers voluntarily punctured their arms with marks of the general under whom they served. Votaries of idols branded themselves with the idol's cipher or symbol. Thus Antiochus Epiphanes branded the Jews with the ivy leaf, the symbol of Bacchus (II Maccabees 6:7; III Maccabees 2:29). Contrast God's *seal* and *name in the foreheads of His servants*, ch. 7:3; 14:1; 22:4; and Galatians 6:17, "I bear in my body the marks of the Lord Jesus," i.e., I am His soldier and servant. The mark in the right hand and forehead implies the prostration of *bodily* and *intellectual* powers to the beast's domination. "In *the forehead* by way of profession; in the *hand* with respect to work and service" [AUGUSTINE]. **17. And**—So A, B, and *Vulgate* read. C, IRENÆUS, 316, *Coptic*, and *Syriac* omit it. **might buy**—Greek, "may be able to buy." **the mark, or the name**—Greek, "the mark (viz.), the name of the beast." The mark may be, as in the case of the sealing of the saints in the forehead, not a visible mark, but symbolical of allegiance. So the sign of the cross in Popery. The Pope's interdict has often shut out the excommunicate from social and commercial intercourse. Under the final Antichrist this shall come to pass in its most violent form. **number of his name**—implying that the name has some numerical meaning. **18. wisdom**—the armory against the second beast, as *patience and faith* against the first. Spiritual *wisdom* is needed to solve the *mystery* of iniquity, so as not to be beguiled by it. **count . . . for**—The "for" implies the possibility of our calculating or counting the beast's number. **the number of a man**—i.e., counted as men generally count. So the phrase is used in ch. 21:17. The number is the number of a *man*, not of *God;* he shall extol himself above the power of the Godhead, as the MAN *of sin* [AQUINAS]. Though it is an imitation of the divine name, it is only *human*. **six hundred threescore and six**—A and *Vulgate* write the numbers in full in the Greek. But B writes merely the three *Greek* letters standing for numbers, *Ch, X, St*. "C reads" 616, but IRENÆUS, 328, opposes this and maintains "666." IRENÆUS, in the second century, disciple of POLYCARP, John's disciple, explained this number as contained in the Greek letters of *Lateinos* (L being 30; A, 1; T, 300; E, 5; I, 10; N, 50; O, 70; S, 200). The Latin is peculiarly the language of the Church of Rome in all her official acts; the forced unity of language in ritual being the counterfeit of the true unity; the premature and spurious anticipation of the real unity, only to be realized at Christ's coming, when all the earth shall

speak "one language" (Zeph. 3:9). The last Antichrist may have a close connection with Rome, and so the name *Lateinos* (666) may apply to him. The *Hebrew* letters of *Balaam* amount to 666 [BUNSEN]; a type of the *false prophet*, whose characteristic, like Balaam's, will be high spiritual knowledge perverted to Satanic ends. The number *six* is the world number; in 666 it occurs in units, tens, and hundreds. It is next neighbor to the sacred *seven*, but is severed from it by an impassable gulf. It is *the number of the world given over to judgment;* hence there is a pause between the sixth and seventh seals, and the sixth and seventh trumpets. The judgments on the world are complete in *six;* by the fulfilment of *seven*, the kingdoms of the world become Christ's. As *twelve* is the number of the Church, so six, its half, symbolizes the world kingdom broken. The raising of the six to tens and hundreds (higher powers) indicates that the beast, notwithstanding his progression to higher powers, can only rise to greater ripeness for judgment. Thus 666, the judged world power, contrasts with the 144,000 sealed and transfigured ones (the Church number, twelve, squared and multiplied by 1000, the number symbolizing the world pervaded by God; ten, the world number, raised to the power of three the number of God) [AUBERLEN]. The "mark" (Greek, *charagma*) and "name" are one and the same. The first two radical letters of *Christ* (Greek, *Christos*), *Ch* and *R*, are the same as the first two of *charagma*, and were the imperial monogram of Christian Rome. Antichrist, personating Christ, adopts a symbol like, but not agreeing with, Christ's monogram, *Ch, X, St;* whereas the radicals in "Christ" are *Ch, R, St*. Papal Rome has similarly substituted the standard of *the Keys* for the standard of *the Cross;* so on the papal *coinage* (the image of power, Matt. 22:20). The two first letters of "Christ," *Ch, R,* represent *seven* hundred, the perfect number. The *Ch, X, St* represent an imperfect number, a triple *falling away* (apostasy) from *septenary* perfection [WORDSWORTH].

CHAPTER 14

Vss. 1-20. THE LAMB SEEN ON ZION WITH THE 144,000. THEIR SONG. THE GOSPEL PROCLAIMED BEFORE THE END BY ONE ANGEL: THE FALL OF BABYLON, BY ANOTHER: THE DOOM OF THE BEAST WORSHIPPERS, BY A THIRD. THE BLESSEDNESS OF THE DEAD IN THE LORD. THE HARVEST. THE VINTAGE. In contrast to the beast, false prophet, and apostate Church (ch. 13) and introductory to the announcement of judgments about to descend on them and the world (vss. 8-11, anticipatory of ch. 18:2-6), stand here the redeemed, "the divine kernel of humanity, the positive fruits of the history of the world and the Church" [AUBERLEN]. Chs. 14-16 describe the preparations for the Messianic judgment. As ch. 14 begins with *the 144,000 of Israel* (cf. ch. 7:4-8, no longer exposed to trial as then, but now triumphant), so ch. 15 begins with those who have *overcome* from among the Gentiles (cf. ch. 15:1-5 with ch. 7:9-17); the two classes of elect forming together the whole company of transfigured saints who shall reign with Christ. **1. a**—A, B, C, *Coptic*, and ORIGEN read, "*the*." **Lamb . . . on . . . Sion**—having left His position "in the midst of the throne," and now taking His stand *on Sion*. **his Father's name**—A, B, and C read, "*His name and* His Father's name." **in**—Greek, "upon."

God's and Christ's *name* here answers to the *seal* "upon their foreheads" in ch. 7:3. As the 144,000 of Israel are "the first fruits" (vs. 4), so "the harvest" (vs. 15) is the general assembly of Gentile saints to be translated by Christ as His first act in assuming His kingdom, prior to His judgment (ch. 16, the last seven vials) on the Antichristian world, in executing which His saints shall share. As Noah and Lot were taken seasonably out of the *judgment*, but exposed to the *trial* to the last moment [DE BURGH], so those who shall reign with Christ shall first suffer with Him, being delivered out of the *judgments*, but not out of the *trials*. The Jews are meant by "the saints of the Most High": against them Antichrist makes war, *changing their times and laws;* for true Israelites cannot join in the idolatry of the beast, any more than true Christians. The common affliction will draw closely together, in opposing the beast's worship, the Old Testament and New Testament people of God. Thus the way is paved for Israel's conversion. This last utter *scattering of the holy people's power* leads them, under the Spirit, to seek Messiah, and to cry at His approach, "Blessed is He that cometh in the name of the Lord." **2. from**—*Greek,* "out of." **voice of many waters**—as is the voice of Himself, such also is the voice of His people **I heard the voice of harpers**—A, B, C, and ORIGEN read, "the voice which I heard (was) as of harpers." **3. sung** —*Greek,* "sing." **as it were**—So A, C, and *Vulgate* read. It is "as it were" a *new song;* for it is, in truth, as old as God's eternal purpose. But B, *Syriac, Coptic,* ORIGEN, and ANDREAS omit these words. **new song**—(ch. 5:9, 10). The song is that of victory after conflict with the dragon, beast, and false prophet: never sung before, for such a conflict had never been fought before; therefore *new:* till now the kingdom of *Christ* on earth had been usurped; they sing the new song in anticipation of His blood-bought kingdom with His saints. **four beasts**—rather as *Greek,* "four living creatures." The harpers and singers evidently include the 144,000: so the parallel proves (ch. 15:2, 3), where the same act is attributed to *the general company of the saints,* the *harvest* (vs. 15) from all nations. Not as ALFORD, "the harpers and song are in heaven, but the 144,000 are on earth." **redeemed**—lit., "purchased." Not even the angels can learn that song, for they know not *experimentally* what it is to have "come out of the great tribulation, and washed their robes white in the blood of the Lamb" (ch. 7:14). **4. virgins**—spiritually (Matt. 25:1); in contrast to the apostate Church, Babylon (vs. 8), spiritually "a harlot" (ch. 17:1-5; Isa. 1:21; contrast II Cor. 11:2; Eph. 5:25-27). Their not being *defiled with women* means they were not led astray from Christian faithfulness by the tempters who jointly constitute the spiritual "harlot." **follow the Lamb whithersoever he goeth**—in glory, being especially near His person; the fitting reward of their following Him so fully on earth. **redeemed** —"purchased." *being* **the**—rather, "*as a* first fruit." Not merely a "first fruit" in the sense in which *all* believers are so, but Israel's 144,000 elect are the *first fruit,* the Jewish and Gentile elect Church is the *harvest;* in a further sense, the whole of the transfigured and translated Church which reigns with Christ at His coming, is the *first fruit,* and the consequent general ingathering of Israel and the nations, ending in the last judgment, is the full and final harvest. **5. guile**—So ANDREAS in one copy. But A, B, C, ORIGEN, and ANDREAS in other copies read, "falsehood." Cf. with *English Version* read-

ing Psalm 32:2; Isaiah 53:9; John 1:47. **for**—So B, *Syriac, Coptic,* ORIGEN, and ANDREAS read. But A and C omit. **without fault**—*Greek,* "blameless": in respect to the sincerity of their fidelity to Him. Not absolutely, and in themselves *blameless;* but regarded as such on the ground of His righteousness in whom alone they trusted, and whom they faithfully served by His Spirit in them. The allusion seems to be to Psalm 15:1, 2. Cf. vs. 1, "*stood on* Mount Sion." **before the throne of God**—A, B, C, *Syriac, Coptic,* ORIGEN, and ANDREAS omit these words. The oldest *Vulgate* MS. supports them. **6.** Here begins the portion relating to the Gentile world, as the former portion related to Israel. Before the *end* the Gospel is to be preached for a WITNESS *unto all nations:* not that all nations shall be converted, but all nations shall have had the opportunity given them of deciding whether they will be for, or against, Christ. Those thus *preached to* are "they that dwell (so A, *Coptic,* and *Syriac* read. But B, C, ORIGEN, *Vulgate,* CYPRIAN, 312, read, 'SIT,' cf. Matt. 4:16; Luke 1:79, having their *settled* home) on the earth," being of earth earthy: this last season of grace is given them, if yet they may repent, before "judgment" (vs. 7) descends: if not, they will be left without excuse, as the world which resisted the preaching of Noah in the 120 years "while the long-suffering of God waited." "So also the prophets gave the people a last opportunity of repentance before the Babylonian destruction of Jerusalem, and our Lord and His apostles before the Roman destruction of the holy city" [AUBERLEN]. The *Greek* for "unto" (*epi,* in A and C) means lit., "upon," or "over," or "in respect to" (Mark 9:12; Heb.7:13). So also "TO every nation" (*Greek, epi,* in A, B, C, *Vulgate, Syriac,* ORIGEN, ANDREAS, CYPRIAN, and PRIMASIUS). This, perhaps, implies that the Gospel, though diffused *over* the globe, shall not come savingly *unto* any save the elect. The world is not to be evangelized till Christ shall come: meanwhile, God's purpose is "to take out of the Gentiles a people for His name," to be witnesses of the effectual working of His Spirit during the counter-working of "the mystery of iniquity." **everlasting gospel**—the Gospel which announces the *glad tidings* of the *everlasting* kingdom of Christ, about to ensue immediately after the "judgment" on Antichrist, announced as imminent in vs. 7. As the former angel "flying through the midst of heaven" (ch. 8:13) announced "woe," so this angel "flying in the midst of heaven" announced joy. The three angels making this last proclamation of the Gospel, the fall of Babylon (vs .8), the harlot, and the judgment on the beast worshippers (vss. 9-11), the voice from heaven respecting the blessed dead (vs. 13), the vision of the Son of man on the cloud (vs. 11), the harvest (vs. 15), and the vintage (vs. 18), form the compendious summary, amplified in detail in the rest of the book. **7. Fear God**—the forerunner to embracing the *love* of God manifested in *the Gospel.* Repentance accompanies faith. **give glory to him**—and not to the beast (cf. ch. 13:4; Jer. 13:16). **the hour of his judgment** —"The hour" implies the *definite time.* "Judgment," not the general judgment, but that upon Babylon, the beast, and his worshippers (vss. 8-12). **worship him that made heaven**—not Antichrist (cf. Acts 14:15). **sea . . . fountains**—distinguished also in ch. 8:8, 10. **8. another**—so *Vulgate.* But A, B, *Syriac,* and ANDREAS add, "a second"; "another, a second angel." **Babylon**—here first mentioned; identical with *the harlot,* the apostate Church; distinct from *the beast,* and judged separately. **is fal-**

len—anticipation of ch. 18:2. A, *Vulgate, Syriac,* and ANDREAS support the second "is fallen." But B, C, and *Coptic* omit it. **that great city**—A, B, C, *Vulgate, Syriac,* and *Coptic* omit "city." Then translate, "Babylon the great." The ulterior and exhaustive fulfilment of Isaiah 21:9. **because**—so ANDREAS. But A, C, *Vulgate,* and *Syriac* read, "which." B and *Coptic* omit it. Even reading "which," we must understand it as giving the *reason* of her fall. **all nations**—A, B and C read, "all *the* nations." **the wine of the wrath of her fornication** —*the wine of the wrath* of God, the consequence *of her fornication.* As she made the nations drunk with the wine of her fornication, so she herself shall be made drunk with the wine of God's wrath. **9.** A, B, C, and ANDREAS read, "another, a third angel." Cf. with this verse ch. 13:15, 16. **10. The same**—*Greek,* "he also," as the just and inevitable retribution. **wine of ... wrath of God**—(Ps. 75:8). **without mixture**—whereas wine was so commonly *mixed* with water that to *mix* wine is used in *Greek* for to *pour out* wine; *this* wine of God's wrath is *undiluted;* there is no drop of water to cool its heat. Naught of grace or hope is blended with it. This terrible threat may well raise us above the fear of man's threats. This *unmixed* cup is already *mingled* and prepared for Satan and the beast's followers. **indignation**—*Greek, orges,* "abiding wrath." But the *Greek* for "wrath" above (*Greek, thumou*) is *boiling indignation,* from (*Greek, thuo*) a root meaning "to boil"; this is temporary ebullition of anger; that is lasting [AMMONIUS], and accompanied with a purpose of vengeance [ORIGEN on Ps. 2:5]. **tormented ... in the presence of ... angels**—(Ps. 49: 14; 58:10; 139:21; Isa. 66:24). God's enemies are regarded by the saints as their enemies, and when the day of probation is past, their mind shall be so entirely one with God's, that they shall rejoice in witnessing visibly the judicial vindication of God's righteousness in sinners' punishment. **11. for ever and ever**—*Greek,* "unto ages of ages." **no rest day nor night**—Contrast the very different sense in which the same is said of the four living creatures in heaven, "They rest not day and night, saying, Holy, holy, holy ..."; yet they do "rest" in another sense; they rest from sin and sorrow, weariness and weakness, trial and temptation (vs. 13); the lost have no rest from sin and Satan, terror, torment, and remorse. **12. Here ...**—resumed from ch. 13:10, where see the *Note.* In the fiery ordeal of persecution which awaits all who will not worship the beast, the *faith* and *patience* of the followers of *God and Jesus* shall be put to the test, and proved. **patience**—*Greek, hupomene,* "patient, persevering endurance." The second "here" is omitted in A, B, C, *Vulgate, Syriac, Coptic,* and PRIMASIUS. Translate, "Here is the endurance of the saints, who keep ...." **the faith of Jesus**—the faith which has Jesus for its object. **13.** Encouragement to cheer those persecuted under the beast. **Write**—to put it on record for ever. **Blessed**—in *resting from their toils,* and, in the case of the saints just before alluded to as persecuted by the beast, in *resting from persecutions.* Their full *blessedness* is now "from henceforth," i.e., FROM THIS TIME, when the judgment on the beast and the harvest gatherings of the elect are imminent. The time so earnestly longed for by former martyrs is now all but come; the full number of their fellow servants is on the verge of completion; they have no longer to "*rest* (the same *Greek* as here, *anapausis*) yet for a little season," their eternal *rest,* or *cessation* from toils (II Thessalonians 1:7; *Greek, anesis,* relaxation after hard-

ships. Heb. 4:9, 10, *sabbatism of rest;* and *Greek, catapausis,* akin to the *Greek* here) is close at hand now. They are *blessed* in being about to sit down to *the marriage supper of the Lamb* (ch. 19:9), and in having *part* in the *first resurrection* (ch. 20:6), and in *having right to the tree of life* (ch. 22:14). In vss. 14-16 follows the explanation of why they are pronounced "blessed" *now* in particular, viz., *the Son of man on the cloud* is just coming to gather them in as *the harvest* ripe for garner. **Yea, saith the Spirit**—The words of God the Father (the "voice from heaven") are echoed back and confirmed by the Spirit (speaking in the Word, ch. 2:7; 22:17; and in the saints, II Cor. 5:5; I Pet. 4:14). All "God's promises in Christ are yea" (II Cor. 1:20). **unto me**—omitted in A, B, C, *Vulgate, Syriac,* and *Coptic.* **that they may**—The *Greek* includes also the idea, They are blessed, *in that they* SHALL *rest from their toils* (so the *Greek*). **and**— So B and ANDREAS read. But A, C, *Vulgate,* and *Syriac* read "for." They rest from their toils *because* their time for toil is past; they enter on the *blessed rest because* of their faith evinced by their works which, therefore, "follow WITH (so the *Greek*) them." Their *works* are specified because respect is had to the coming judgment, wherein every man shall be "judged according to his works." His works do not go before the believer, nor even go by his side, but *follow* him at the same time that they go *with* him as a proof that he is Christ's. **14. crown**—*Greek, stephanon,* "garland" of victory; not His *diadem* as a king. The victory is described in detail, ch. 19:11-21. **one sat**—"one sitting," *Greek, cathemenon homoion,* is the reading of A, B, C, *Vulgate,* and *Coptic.* **15. Thrust in**—*Greek,* "Send." The angel does not command the "Son of man" (vs. 14), but is the mere messenger announcing to the Son the will of *God the Father,* in whose hands are kept *the times and the seasons.* **thy sickle**— alluding to Mark 4:29, where also it is "*sendeth* the sickle." The Son sends His sickle-bearing angel to reap the righteous when fully ripe. **harvest**— the harvest crop. By the *harvest*-reaping the elect righteous are gathered out; by the *vintage* the Antichristian offenders are removed out of the earth, the scene of Christ's coming kingdom. The Son of man Himself, with a golden crown, is introduced in the *harvest*-gathering of the elect, a mere angel in the *vintage* (vss. 18-20). **is ripe**—lit., "is dried." Ripe for glory. **16. thrust in**—*Greek,* "cast." **17. out of the temple ... in heaven**—(ch. 11:19). **18. from the altar**—upon which were offered the incense-accompanied prayers of all saints, which bring down in answer God's fiery judgment on the Church's foes, the *fire* being *taken from the altar and cast upon the earth.* **fully ripe**—*Greek,* "come to their acme"; ripe for punishment. **19.** "The vine" is what is the subject of judgment because its grapes are not what God looked for considering its careful culture, but "wild grapes' (Isa. 5). The apostate world of Christendom, not the world of heathendom who have not heard of Christ, is the object of judgment. Cf. the emblem, ch. 19: 15; Isaiah 63:2, 3; Joel 3:13. **20. without the city** —Jerusalem. The scene of the blood-shedding of Christ and His people shall be also the scene of God's vengeance on the Antichristian foe. Cf. the "horsemen," ch. 9:16, 17. **blood**—answering to the red wine. The slaughter of the apostates is what is here spoken of, not their eternal punishment. **even unto the horse bridles**—of the avenging "armies of heaven." **by the space of a thousand ... six hundred furlongs**—lit., "a thousand six hundred furlongs *off*" [W. KELLY]. Sixteen hundred is a square number; 4 by 4 by 100. The *four* quarters, north, south, east, and west, of the Holy Land, or else of the world (the completeness and universality of the world-wide destruction being hereby indicated). It does not exactly answer to the length of Palestine as given by JEROME, 160 Roman miles. BENGEL thinks the valley of Kedron, between Jerusalem and the Mount of Olives, is meant, the torrent in that valley being about to be discolored with blood to the extent of 1600 furlongs. This view accords with Joel's prophecy that the valley of Jehoshaphat is to be the scene of the overthrow of the Antichristian foes.

CHAPTER 15

Vss. 1-8. THE LAST SEVEN VIALS OF PLAGUES: SONG OF THE VICTORS OVER THE BEAST. **1. the seven last plagues**—*Greek,* "seven plagues which are the last." **is filled up**—lit., "was finished," or "consummated": the prophetical past for the future, the future being to God as though it were past, so sure of accomplishment is His word. This verse is the summary of the vision that follows: the angels do not actually receive the vials till vs. 7; but here, in vs. 1, by anticipation they are spoken of as *having* them. There are no more plagues after these until the Lord's coming in judgment. The destruction of Babylon (ch. 18) is the last: then in ch. 19 He appears. **2. sea of glass**—Answering to the molton sea or great brazen laver before the mercy seat of the earthly temple, for the purification of the priests; typifying the baptism of water and the Spirit of all who are made kings and priests unto God. **mingled with fire**—answering to the *baptism* on earth *with fire,* i.e., fiery trial, as well as with the Holy Ghost, which Christ's people undergo to purify them, as gold is purified of its dross in the furnace. **them that had gotten the victory over**—*Greek,* "those (coming) off from (the conflict with) the beast-conquerors." **over the number of his name** A, B, C, *Vulgate, Syriac,* and *Coptic* omit the words in *English Version,* "over his mark." *The mark,* in fact, is the *number of his name* which the faithful refused to receive, and so were victorious over it. **stand on the sea of glass**—ALFORD and DE BURGH explain "on (the shore of) the sea": *at the* sea. So the preposition, *Greek, epi,* with the accusative, is used for *at,* ch. 3:20. It has a pregnant sense: "standing" implies *rest, Greek epi* with the accusative implies motion *towards.* Thus the meaning is, Having come TO the sea, and now standing AT it. In Matthew 14:26, where Christ walks *on* the sea, the *Greek* oldest MSS. have the genitive, not the accusative as here. Allusion is made to the Israelites standing *on the shore at the Red Sea,* after having passed victoriously through it, and after the Lord had destroyed the Egyptian foe (type of Antichrist) in it. Moses and the Israelites' song of triumph (Exod. 15:1) has its antitype in the saints' "song of Moses and the Lamb" (vs. 3). Still *English Version* is consistent with good Greek, and the sense will then be: As the sea typifies the troubled state out of which the beast arose, and which is to be no more in the blessed world to come (ch. 21:1), so the victorious saints stand on it, having it *under their feet* (as the *woman* had the *moon,* ch. 12:1, see *Note*); but it is now no longer treacherous wherein the feet sink, but solid like glass, as it was under the feet of Christ, whose triumph and power the saints now share. Firm-

ness of footing amidst apparent instability is thus represented. They can stand, not merely as victorious Israel *at* the Red Sea, and as John *upon* the sand of the shore, but *upon the sea* itself, now firm, and reflecting their glory as glass, their past conflict shedding the brighter luster on their present triumph. Their happiness is heightened by the retrospect of the dangers through which they have passed. Thus this corresponds to ch. 7:14, 15. **harps of God**—in the hands of these heavenly *virgins,* infinitely surpassing the timbrels of Miriam and the Israelitesses. **3. song of Moses ... and ... the Lamb**—The New Testament song of the Lamb (i.e., the song which the Lamb shall lead, as being "the Captain of our salvation," just as Moses was leader of the Israelites, the song in which those who conquer through Him [Rom. 8:37] shall join, ch. 12:11) is the antitype to the triumphant Old Testament song of Moses and the Israelites at the Red Sea (Exod. 15). The Churches of the Old and New Testament are essentially one in their conflicts and triumphs. The two appear joined in this phrase, as they are in the twenty-four elders. Similarly, Isaiah 12 foretells the song of the redeemed (Israel foremost) after the second antitypical exodus and deliverance *at the Egyptian Sea.* The passage through the Red Sea under the pillar of cloud was Israel's baptism, to which the believer's baptism in trials corresponds. The elect after their trials (especially those arising from the beast) shall be taken up before the vials of wrath be poured on the beast and his kingdom. So Noah and his family were taken out of the doomed world before the deluge; Lot was taken out of Sodom before its destruction; the Christians escaped by a special interposition of Providence to Pella before the destruction of Jerusalem. As the pillar of *cloud* and *fire* interposed between Israel and the Egyptian foe, so that Israel was safely landed on the opposite shore before the Egyptians were destroyed; so the Lord, coming with *clouds* and in flaming *fire,* shall first catch up His elect people "in the clouds to meet Him in the air," and then shall with fire destroy the enemy. The Lamb leads the song in honor of the Father amidst the great congregation. This is the "new song" mentioned in ch. 14:3. The singing victors are the 144,000 of Israel, "the first fruits," and the general "harvest" of the Gentiles. **servant of God**—(Exod. 14:31; Num. 12:7; Josh. 22:5). The Lamb is more: He is the SON. **Great and marvellous are thy works ...**—part of Moses' last song. The vindication of the justice of God that so He may be glorified is the grand end of God's dealings. Hence His servants again and again dwell upon this in their praises (ch. 16:7; 19:2; Prov. 16:4; Jer. 10:10; Dan. 4:37). Especially at the judgment (Ps. 50:1-6; 145:17). **saints**—There is no MS. authority for this. A, B, *Coptic,* and CYPRIAN read, "of the NATIONS." C reads "of the ages," and so *Vulgate* and *Syriac.* The point at issue in the Lord's controversy with the earth is, whether He, or Satan's minion, the beast, is "the King of the nations"; here at the eve of the judgments descending on the kingdom of the beast, the transfigured saints hail Him as "the King of the nations" (Ezek. 21:27). **4. Who shall not**—*Greek,* "Who is there but must fear Thee?" Cf. Moses' song, Exodus 15:14-16, on the fear which God's judgments strike into the foe. **thee**—so *Syriac.* But A, B, C, *Vulgate,* and CYPRIAN reject "thee." **all nations shall come**—alluding to Psalm 22:27-31; cf. Isaiah 66:23; Jeremiah 16:19. The conversion of *all nations,* therefore, shall be when Christ shall come, and not till then; and the first moving cause will be Christ's *manifested judgments* preparing all hearts for receiving Christ's mercy. He shall effect by His presence what we have in vain tried to effect in His absence. The present preaching of the Gospel is gathering out the elect remnant; meanwhile "the mystery of iniquity" is at work, and will at last come to its crisis; then shall judgment descend on the apostates at the *harvest-end of this age* (*Greek*, Matt. 13:39, 40) when the tares shall be cleared out of the earth, which thenceforward becomes Messiah's kingdom. The confederacy of the apostates against Christ becomes, when overthrown with fearful judgments, the very means in God's overruling providence of preparing the nations not joined in the Antichristian league to submit themselves to Him. **judgment**—*Greek*, "righteousness." **5.** So ch. 11:19; cf. ch. 16:17. "The tabernacle of the testimony" appropriately here comes to view, where God's faithfulness in avenging His people with judgments on their foes is about to be set forth. We need to get a glimpse within the Holy place to "understand" the secret spring and the end of God's righteous dealings. **are**—lit., "were": the prophetical past for the immediate future. **5. behold**—omitted by A, B, C, *Syriac*, and ANDREAS. It is supported only by *Vulgate*, *Coptic*, and PRIMASIUS, but no MS. **6. having**—So B reads. But A and C, read "who have": not that they had them yet (cf. vs. 7), but they are by anticipation described according to their office. **linen**—So B reads. But A, C, and *Vulgate*, "a stone." On the principle that the harder reading is the one least likely to be an interpolation, we should read, "a stone pure ('and' is omitted in A, B, C, and ANDREAS), brilliant" (so the *Greek*): probably the diamond. With *English Version*, cf. Acts 1:10; 10:30. **golden girdles**—resembling the Lord in this respect (ch. 1:13). **7. one of the four beasts**—*Greek*, "living creatures." The presentation of the vials to the angels by one of the living creatures implies the ministry of the Church as the medium for manifesting to angels the glories of redemption (Eph. 3:10). **vials**—"bowls"; a broad shallow cup or bowl. The breadth of the vials in their upper part would tend to cause their contents to pour out *all at once*, implying the overwhelming suddenness of the woes. **full of . . . wrath**—How sweetly do the *vials full of odors*, i.e., the incense-perfumed prayers of the saints, contrast with these! **8. temple . . . filled**—Isaiah 6:4; cf. Exodus 40:34; II Chronicles 5:14, as to the earthly temple, of which this is the antitype. **the glory of God and . . . power**—then fully manifested. **no man was able to enter . . . the temple**—because of God's presence in His manifested glory and power during the execution of these judgments.

CHAPTER 16

Vss. 1-21. THE SEVEN VIALS AND THE CONSEQUENT PLAGUES. The trumpets shook the world kingdoms in a longer process; the vials destroy with a swift and sudden overthrow the kingdom of the beast in particular who had invested himself with the world kingdom. The Hebrews thought the Egyptian plagues to have been inflicted with but an interval of a month between them severally [BENGEL, referring to SEDER OLAM]. As Moses took ashes from an earthly common furnace, so angels, as priestly ministers in the heavenly temple, take holy fire in sacred vials or bowls, from the heavenly altar to pour down (cf. ch. 8:5). The same heavenly altar which would have kindled the sweet incense of prayer bringing down blessing upon earth, by man's sin kindles the fiery descending curse. Just as the river Nile, which ordinarily is the source of Egypt's fertility, became blood and a curse through Egypt's sin. **1. a great voice**—viz., God's. These seven vials (the detailed expansion of *the vintage*, ch. 14:18-20) being called "the last," must belong to the period just when the term of the beast's power has expired (whence reference is made in them all to the worshippers of the beast as the objects of the judgments), close to the end or coming of the Son of man. The first four are distinguished from the last three, just as in the case of the seven seals and the seven trumpets. The first four are more general, affecting the earth, the sea, springs, and the sun, not merely a portion of these natural bodies, as in the case of the trumpets, but the whole of them; the last three are more particular, affecting the throne of the beast, the Euphrates, and the grand consummation. Some of these particular judgments are set forth in detail in chs. 17-20. **out of the temple**—B and *Syriac* omit. But A, C, *Vulgate*, and ANDREAS support the words. **the vials**—so *Syriac* and *Coptic*. But A, B, C, *Vulgate*, and ANDREAS read, "the *seven* vials." **upon**—*Greek*, "into." **2. went**—*Greek*, "went away." **poured out**—So the angel cast fire into the earth previous to the series of trumpets (ch. 8:5). **upon**—*so Coptic*. But A, B, C, *Vulgate*, and *Syriac* read, "into." **noisome**—lit., "evil" (cf. Deut. 28:27, 35). The very same *Greek* word is used in the LXX as here, *Greek*, *helkos*. The reason why the sixth Egyptian plague is the *first* here is because it was directed against the Egyptian magicians, Jannes and Jambres, so that they could not stand before Moses; and so here the plague is sent upon those who in the beast worship had practiced sorcery. As they submitted to the mark of the beast, so they must bear the mark of the avenging God. Contrast ch. 7:3; Ezekiel 9:4, 6. **grievous**—distressing to the sufferers. **sore upon the men**—antitype to the sixth Egyptian plague. **which had the mark of the beast**—Therefore this first vial is subsequent to the period of the beast's rule. **3. angel**—So B and ANDREAS. But A, C, and *Vulgate* omit it. **upon**—*Greek*, "into." **became as . . . blood**—answering to another Egyptian plague. **of a dead man**—putrefying. **living soul**—So B and ANDREAS. But A, C, and *Syriac*, "soul of life" (cf. Gen. 1:30; 7:21, 22). **in the sea**—So B and ANDREAS. But A, C, and *Syriac* read, "(as respects) the things in the sea." **4.** Exodus 7:20. **angel**—so *Syriac*, *Coptic*, and ANDREAS. But A, B, C, and *Vulgate* omit it. **5. angel of the waters**—i.e., presiding over the waters. **O Lord**—omitted by A, B, C, *Vulgate*, *Syriac*, *Coptic*, and ANDREAS. **and shalt be**—A, B, C, *Vulgate*, and ANDREAS for this clause read, "(which art and wast) *holy*." The Lord is now no longer He that *shall* come, for He *is come* in vengeance and therefore the third of the three clauses found in ch. 1:4, 8; and 4:8 is here and in ch. 11:17 omitted. **judged thus**—lit., "these things." "Thou didst inflict this judgment." **6.** (Ch. 11:18, end; Gen. 9:6; Isa. 49:26.) An anticipation of ch. 18:20, 24; cf. ch. 13:15. **For**—A, B, C, and ANDREAS omit. **7. another out of**—omitted in A, C, *Syriac*, and *Coptic*. Translate then, "I heard the altar [personified] saying." On it the prayers of saints are presented before God: beneath it are the souls of the martyrs crying for vengeance on the foes of God. **8. angel**—so *Coptic* and ANDREAS. But A,

B, C, *Vulgate,* and *Syriac* omit it.   **upon**—not as in vss. 2, 3, "into."   **sun**—Whereas by the fourth trumpet the sun is darkened (ch. 8:12) in a third part, here by the fourth vial the sun's bright scorching power is intensified.   **power was given unto him**—rather, "unto *it,*" the sun.   **men**—Greek, "the men," viz., those who had the mark of the beast (vs. 2).   **9. men**—Greek, "*the* men."   **repented not to give him glory**—(ch. 9:20).   Affliction, if it does not melt, hardens the sinner.   Cf. the better result on others, ch. 11:13; 14:7; 15:4.   **10. angel**—omitted by A, B, C, *Vulgate,* and *Syriac.*   But *Coptic* and ANDREAS support it.   **seat**—Greek, "throne of the beast": set up in arrogant mimicry of God's throne; the dragon gave his throne to the beast (ch. 13:2).   **darkness**—parallel to the Egyptian plague of darkness, Pharaoh being the type of Antichrist (cf. ch. 15:2, 3, *Notes;* cf. the fifth trumpet, ch. 9:2).   **gnawed their tongues for pain**—Greek, "*owing to the* pain" occasioned by the previous plagues, rendered more appalling by the darkness. Or, as "gnashing of teeth" is one of the accompaniments of hell, so this "gnawing of their tongues" is through rage at the baffling of their hopes and the overthrow of their kingdom. They meditate revenge and are unable to effect it; hence their frenzy [GROTIUS]. Those in anguish, mental and bodily, bite their lips and tongues.   **11. sores**—This shows that each fresh plague was accompanied with the continuance of the preceding plagues: there was an accumulation, not a mere succession, of plagues.   **repented not**—(Cf. vs. 9).   **12. angel**—so *Coptic* and ANDREAS.   A, B, C, *Vulgate,* and *Syriac* omit.   **kings of the east**—Greek, "the kings who are from the rising of the sun."   Reference to *the Euphrates* similarly occurs in the sixth trumpet. The drying up of the *Euphrates,* I think, is to be taken figuratively, as *Babylon* itself, which is situated on it, is undoubtedly so, ch. 17:5.   The waters of the Euphrates (cf. Isa. 8:7, 8) are spiritual Babylon's, i.e., the apostate Church's (of which Rome is the chief, though not exclusive representative) spiritual and temporal powers.   The drying up of the waters of Babylon expresses the same thing as the ten kings stripping, eating, and burning the whore. The phrase, "way may be prepared for," is that applied to *the Lord's coming* (Isa. 40:3; Matt. 3:3; Luke 1:76).   He shall come *from the East* (Matt. 24:27; Ezek. 43:2, "the glory of the God of Israel came *from the way of the East*"): not alone, for His elect transfigured saints of Israel and the Gentiles shall accompany Him, who are "*kings* and *priests unto God*" (ch. 1:6).   As the Antichristian ten *kings* accompany the beast, so the saints accompany as *kings* the *King of kings* to the last decisive conflict.   DE BURGH and others take it of *the Jews,* who also were designed to be *a kingdom of priests to God* on earth.   They shall, doubtless, become priest-kings in the flesh to the nations in the flesh at His coming.   Abraham from the East (if Isa. 41:2, 8, 9, refers to him, and not Cyrus) conquering the Chaldean kings is a type of Israel's victorious restoration to the priest-kingdom.   Israel's exodus after the last Egyptian plagues typifies Israel's restoration after the spiritual Babylon, the apostate Church, has been smitten.   Israel's promotion to the priest-kingdom after Pharaoh's downfall, and at the Lord's descent at Sinai to establish the theocracy, typifies the restored kingdom of Israel at the Lord's more glorious descent, when Antichrist shall be destroyed utterly.   Thus, besides the transfigured saints, Israel secondarily may be meant by "the kings from the East" who shall accompany

the "King of kings" returning "from the way of the East" to reign over His ancient people.   As to the *drying up* again of the *waters* opposing His people's assuming the kingdom, cf. Isaiah 10:26; 11:11, 15; Zechariah 10:9-11.   The name Israel (Gen. 32:28) implies a *prince with God.*   Cf. Micah 4:8 as to the return of the kingdom to Jerusalem.   DURHAM, several centuries ago, interpreted the drying up of the Euphrates to mean the wasting away of the Turkish power, which has heretofore held Palestine, and so the way being prepared for Israel's restoration.   But as *Babylon* refers to the apostate Church, not to Mohammedanism, the drying up of the Euphrates (answering to Cyrus' overthrow of literal Babylon by marching into it through the dry channel of the Euphrates) must answer to the draining off of the apostate Church's resources, the Roman and Greek corrupt Church having been heretofore one of the greatest barriers by its idolatries and persecutions in the way of Israel's restoration and conversion.   The *kings of the earth* who are earthly (vs. 14), stand in contrast to the *kings from the East* who are heavenly.   **13. unclean spirits like frogs**—the antitype to the plague of frogs sent on Egypt.   The presence of the "unclean spirit" in the land (Palestine) is foretold, Zechariah 13:2, in connection with idolatrous *prophets.*   Beginning with infidelity as to Jesus Christ's coming in the flesh, men shall end in the grossest idolatry of the beast, the incarnation of all that is self-deifying and God-opposed in the world powers of all ages; having rejected Him that came in the Father's name, they shall worship one that comes in his own, though really the devil's representative; as frogs croak by night in marshes and quagmires, so these unclean spirits in the darkness of error teach lies amidst the mire of filthy lusts.   They talk of *liberty,* but it is not Gospel liberty, but license for lust.   There being *three,* as also *seven,* in the description of the last and worst state of the Jewish nation, implies a parody of the two divine numbers, *three* of the Trinity, and *seven* of the Holy Spirit (ch. 1:4).   Some observe that *three frogs* were the original arms of France, a country which has been the center of infidelity, socialism, and false spiritualism.   A and B read, "*as it were* frogs," instead of "*like* frogs," which is not supported by MSS.   The unclean spirit out of the mouth of *the dragon* symbolizes the proud infidelity which opposes God and Christ.   That out of the *beast's* mouth is the spirit of the world, which in the politics of men, whether lawless democracy or despotism, sets man above God.   That out of the mouth of the *false prophet* is lying spiritualism and religious delusion, which shall take the place of the harlot when she shall have been destroyed.   **the dragon**—Satan, who *gives his power and throne* (ch. 13:2) *to the beast.*   **false prophet**—distinct from the harlot, the apostate Church (of which Rome is the chief, though not sole, representative), ch. 17:1-3, 16; and identical with *the second beast,* ch. 13:11-15, as appears by comparing it with ch. 19:20 and ch. 13:13; ultimately consigned to the lake of fire with the first beast; as is also the dragon a little later (ch. 20:10).   The dragon, the beast, and the false prophet, "the mystery of iniquity," form a blasphemous Antitrinity, the counterfeit of "the mystery of godliness" God manifests in Christ, witnessed to by the Spirit.   The dragon acts the part of God the Father, assigning his authority to his representative the beast, as the Father assigns His to the Son.   They are accordingly jointly worshipped; cf. as to the Father and Son, John 5:23; as the ten-horned beast has its ten horns crowned with *diadems* (*Greek*, ch. 13: 1), so Christ has on His head *many diadems*. While the false prophet, like the Holy Ghost, speaks not of himself, but tells all men to worship the beast, and confirms his testimony to the beast by *miracles*, as the Holy Ghost attested similarly to Christ's divine mission. **14. devils**–*Greek*, "demons." **working miracles**–*Greek*, "signs." **go forth unto** –or "for," i.e., to tempt them to the battle with Christ. **the kings of the earth and . . .**–A, B, *Syriac*, and ANDREAS omit "of the earth and," which clause is not in any MS. Translate, "kings of the whole habitable world," who are "of this world," in contrast to "the kings of (from) the East" (the sunrising), vs. 12, viz., the saints to whom Christ *has appointed a kingdom*, and who are "children of light." God, in permitting Satan's *miracles*, as in the case of the Egyptian magicians who were His instruments in hardening Pharaoh's heart, gives the reprobate up to judicial delusion preparatory to their destruction. As Aaron's rod was changed into a serpent, so were those of the Egyptian magicians. Aaron turned the water into blood; so did the magicians. Aaron brought up frogs; so did the magicians. With the *frogs* their power ceased. So this, or whatever is antitypical to it, will be the last effort of the dragon, beast, and false prophet. **battle**–*Greek*, "war"; the final conflict for the kingship of the world described in ch. 19:17-21. **15.** The gathering of the world kings with the beast against the Lamb is the signal for Christ's coming; therefore He here gives the charge to be watching for His coming and clothed in the garments of justification and sanctification, so as to be accepted. **thief**–(Matt. 24:43; II Pet. 3:10), **they**–saints and angels. **shame**–lit., "unseemliness" (*Greek, aschemosunee*): Greek, I Corinthians 13:5: a different word from the *Greek* in ch. 3:18 (*Greek, aischunee*). **16. he**–rather, "they (the three unclean spirits) gathered them together." If *English Version* be retained, "He" will refer to *God* who gives them over to the delusion of the three unclean spirits; or else *the sixth angel* (vs. 12). **Armageddon**–*Hebrew, Har,* a mountain, and *Megiddo* in Manasseh in Galilee, the scene of the overthrow of the Canaanite kings by God's miraculous interposition under Deborah and Barak; the same as the great plain of Esdraelon. Josiah, too, as the ally of Babylon, was defeated and slain at Megiddo; and the mourning of the Jews at the time just before God shall interpose for them against all the nations confederate against Jerusalem, is compared to the mourning for Josiah at Megiddo. Megiddo comes from a root, *gadad*, "cut off," and means *slaughter*. Cf. Joel 3:2, 12, 14, where "the valley of Jehoshaphat" (meaning in *Hebrew*, "judgment of God") is mentioned as the scene of God's final vengeance on the God-opposing foe. Probably some great plain, antitypical to the valleys of Megiddo and Jehoshaphat, will be the scene. **17. angel** –so ANDREAS. But A, B, *Vulgate*, and *Syriac* omit it. **into**–so ANDREAS (*Greek, eis*). But A and B, "upon" (*Greek, epi*). **great**–so B, *Vulgate, Syriac, Coptic,* and ANDREAS. But A omits. **of heaven** –so B and ANDREAS But A, *Vulgate, Syriac,* and *Coptic* omit. **It is done**–"It is come to pass." God's voice as to the final consummation, as Jesus' voice on the cross when the work of expiation was completed, "It is finished." **18. voice . . . thunders . . . lightnings**–A has the order, "lightnings . . . voices . . . thunders." This is the same close as that of the seven seals and the seven thunders; but with the difference that they do not merely form

the conclusion, but introduce the consequence, of the last vial, viz., the utter destruction of Babylon and then of the Antichristian armies. **earthquake** –which is often preceded by a lurid state of air, such as would result from the vial poured upon it. **men were**–so B, *Vulgate, Syriac,* and ANDREAS. But A and *Coptic* read, "A man was." **so mighty**– *Greek*, "such." **19. the great city**–the capital and seat of the apostate Church, spiritual Babylon (of which Rome is the representative, if one literal city be meant). The city in ch. 11:8 (see *Note*), is probably distinct, viz., Jerusalem under Antichrist (*the beast*, who is distinct from *the harlot* or apostate Church). In ch. 11:13 only a *tenth* of Jerusalem falls whereas here the city (Babylon) "became (*Greek*) into three parts" by the earthquake. **cities of the nations**–other great cities in league with spiritual Babylon. **great . . . came in remembrance**–*Greek*, "Babylon the great was remembered" (ch. 18:5). It is now that the last call to escape from Babylon is given to God's people in her (ch. 18:4). **fierceness**–the *boiling over* outburst of His wrath (*Greek, thumou orgees*), cf. *Note*, ch. 14:10. **20.** Plainly parallel to ch. 6:14-17, and by anticipation descriptive of the last judgment. **the mountains**–rather as *Greek*, "there were found no mountains." **21. fell**–*Greek*, "descends." **upon men**–*Greek*, "*the* men." **men**– not those struck who died, but the rest. Unlike the result in the case of Jerusalem (ch. 11:13), where "the remnant . . . affrighted . . . gave glory to the God of heaven." **was**–*Greek*, "is."

CHAPTER 17

VSS. 1-18. THE HARLOT BABYLON'S GAUD: THE BEAST ON WHICH SHE RIDES, HAVING SEVEN HEADS AND TEN HORNS, SHALL BE THE INSTRUMENT OF JUDGMENT ON HER. As ch. 16:12 stated generally the vial judgment about to be poured on *the harlot*, Babylon's power, as chs. 17 and 18 give the same in detail, so ch. 19 gives in detail the judgment on the *beast* and the *false prophet*, summarily alluded to in ch. 16:13-15, in connection with the Lord's *coming*. **1. unto me**–A, B, *Vulgate, Syriac,* and *Coptic* omit. **many**–So A. But B, "*the* many waters" (Jer. 51:13); vs. 15, below, explains the sense. The whore is the apostate Church, just as *the woman* (ch. 12) is *the Church while faithful*. Satan having failed by violence, tries too successfully to seduce her by the allurements of the world; unlike her Lord, she was overcome by this temptation; hence she is seen *sitting on the scarlet-colored beast*, no longer the wife, but the harlot; no longer Jerusalem, but spiritually Sodom (ch. 11:8). **2. drunk with**–*Greek*, "owing to." It cannot be pagan Rome, but papal Rome, if a particular seat of error be meant, but I incline to think that the judgment (ch. 18:2) and the spiritual fornication (ch. 18:3), though finding their culmination in Rome, are not restricted to it, but comprise the whole apostate Church, Roman, Greek, and even Protestant, so far as it has been seduced from its "first love" (ch. 2:4) to Christ, the heavenly Bridegroom, and given its affections to worldly pomps and idols. The *woman* (ch. 12:1) is the congregation of God in its purity under the Old and New Testament, and appears again as the Bride of the Lamb, the transfigured Church prepared for the marriage feast. The woman, the invisible Church, is latent in the apostate Church, and is the Church militant; the Bride is the Church triumphant. **3. the wilderness**–

Contrast her in ch. 12:6, 14, having *a place in the wilderness*-world, but not a home; a sojourner here, looking for the city to come. Now, on the contrary, she is contented to have her portion in this moral wilderness. **upon a scarlet ... beast**—The same as in ch. 13:1, who there is described as here, "having seven heads and ten horns (therein betraying that he is representative of the dragon, ch. 12:3), and upon his heads names (so the oldest MSS. read) of blasphemy"; cf. also vss. 12-14, below, with ch. 19:19, 20, and ch. 17:13, 14, 16. Rome, resting on the world power and ruling it by the claim of supremacy, is the chief, though not the exclusive, representative of this symbol. As the dragon is fiery-*red*, so the beast is blood-red in color; implying its *blood-guiltiness*, and also deep-dyed sin. The *scarlet* is also the symbol of kingly authority. **full**—all over; not merely "on his heads," as in ch. 13:1, for its opposition to God is now about to develop itself in all its intensity. Under the harlot's superintendence, the world power puts forth blasphemous pretensions worse than in pagan days. So the Pope is placed by the cardinals *in God's temple on the altar to sit there,* and the cardinals *kiss the feet* of the Pope. This ceremony is called in Romish writers "the adoration." *Historie de Clerge,* Amsterd., 1716; and LETTENBURGH's *Notitia Curiæ Romanæ,* 1683, p. 125; HEIDEGGER, *Myst. Bab.,* 1, 511, 514, 537; a papal coin (*Numismata Pontificum,* Paris, 1679, p. 5) has the *blasphemous* legend, *"Quem creant, adorant."* *Kneeling* and *kissing* are the worship meant by John's word nine times used in respect to the rival of God (*Greek, proskunein*). *Abomination,* too, is the scriptural term for an idol, or any creature worshipped with the homage due to the Creator. Still, there is some check on the God-opposed world power while ridden by the harlot; the consummated Antichrist will be when, having destroyed her, the beast shall be revealed as the concentration and incarnation of all the self-deifying God-opposed principles which have appeared in various forms and degrees heretofore. "The Church has gained outward recognition by leaning on the world power which in its turn uses the Church for its own objects; such is the picture here of Christendom ripe for judgment" [AUBER-LEN]. The seven heads in the view of many are the seven successive forms of government of Rome: kings, consuls, dictators, decemvirs, military tribunes, emperors, the German emperors [WORDS-WORTH], of whom Napoleon is the successor (vs. 11). But see the view given, *Notes,* vss. 9, 10, which I prefer. The crowns formerly on the ten horns (ch. 13:1) have now disappeared, perhaps an indication that the ten kingdoms into which the Germanic-Slavonic world [*the old Roman empire, including the East as well as the West, the two legs of the image with five toes on each, i.e., ten in all*] is to be divided, will lose their monarchical form in the end [AUBERLEN]; but see vs. 12, which seems to imply crowned *kings.* **4.** The color scarlet, it is remarkable, is that reserved for popes and cardinals. Paul II made it penal for anyone but cardinals to wear hats of scarlet; cf. *Cæremoniale Rom.,* 3 sect. 5, c. 5. This book was compiled several centuries ago by Marcellus, a Romish archbishop, and dedicated to Leo X. In it are enumerated five different articles of dress of *scarlet* color. A vest is mentioned studded with *pearls.* The Pope's miter is of *gold* and *precious stones.* These are the very characteristics outwardly which Revelation thrice assigns to the harlot or Babylon. So Joachim an abbot from Calabria, about A.D. 1200, when

asked by Richard of England, who had summoned him to Palestine, concerning Antichrist, replied that "he was born long ago at Rome, and is now exalting himself above all that is called God." ROGER HOVEDEN, *Angl. Chron.,* 1. 2, and elsewhere, wrote, "The harlot arrayed in gold is the Church of Rome." Whenever and wherever (not in Rome alone) the Church, instead of being "clothed (as at first, ch. 12:1) with the sun" of heaven, is arrayed in earthly meretricious gauds, compromising the truth of God through fear, or flattery, of the world's power, science, or wealth, she becomes the harlot seated on the beast, and doomed in righteous retribution to be judged by the beast (vs. 16). Soon, like Rome, and like the Jews of Christ's and the apostles' time leagued with the heathen Rome, she will then become the persecutor of the saints (vs. 6). Instead of drinking her Lord's "cup" of suffering, she has "a cup full of abominations and filthinesses." Rome, in her medals, represents herself holding a cup with the self-condemning inscription, *"Sedet super universum."* Meanwhile the world power gives up its hostility and accepts Christianity externally; the beast gives up its God-opposed character, the woman gives up her divine one. They meet halfway by mutual concessions; Christianity becomes worldly, the world becomes Christianized. The gainer is the world; the loser is the Church. The beast for a time receives a *deadly wound* (ch. 13:3), but is not really transfigured; he will return worse than ever (vss. 11-14). The Lord alone by His coming can make the kingdoms of this world become the kingdoms of our Lord and His Christ. The "purple" is the badge of empire; even as in mockery it was put on our Lord. **decked**—lit., "gilded." **stones**—*Greek,* "stone." **filthiness**—A, B, and ANDREAS read, "the filthy (impure) things. **5. upon ... forehead ... name**—as harlots usually had. What a contrast to "HOLINESS TO THE LORD," inscribed on the miter *on* the high priest's *forehead!* **mystery**—implying a spiritual fact heretofore hidden, and incapable of discovery by mere reason, but now revealed. As the union of Christ and the Church is a "great mystery" (a spiritual truth of momentous interest, once hidden, now revealed, Eph. 5:31, 32), so the Church conforming to the world and thereby becoming a harlot is a counter "mystery" (or spiritual truth, symbolically now revealed). As iniquity in the harlot is a leaven working in *"mystery,"* and therefore called "the *mystery* of iniquity," so when she is destroyed, the iniquity heretofore working (comparatively) latently in her, shall be *revealed* in *the man of iniquity,* the open embodiment of all previous evil. Contrast the "mystery of God" and "godliness," ch. 10:7; I Timothy 3:16. It was Rome that crucified Christ; that destroyed Jerusalem and scattered the Jews; that persecuted the early Christians in pagan times, and Protestant Christians in papal times; and probably shall be again restored to its pristine grandeur, such as it had under the Cæsars, just before the burning of the harlot and of itself with her. So HIPPOLYTUS, *De Antichristo* (who lived in the second century), thought. Popery cannot be at one and the same time the "*mystery*" of iniquity," and the *manifested* or *revealed* Antichrist. Probably it will compromise for political power (vs. 3) the portion of Christianity still in its creed, and thus shall prepare the way for Antichrist's manifestation. The name Babylon, which in the image, Daniel 2, is given to the *head,* is here given to the harlot, which marks her as being connected with the fourth kingdom, Rome, the last part of the image. Benedict XIII, in his indiction for a jubilee, A.D. 1725, called Rome "the *mother* of all believers, and the mistress of all churches" (harlots like herself). The correspondence of syllables and accents in Greek is striking; *He porne kai to therion; He numphe kai to arnion.* The whore and the beast; the Bride and the Lamb. **of harlots** —Greek, "of *the* harlots and of *the* abominations." Not merely Rome, but Christendom as a whole, even as formerly Israel as a whole, has become a harlot. The invisible Church of true believers is hidden and dispersed in the visible Church. The boundary lines which separate harlot and woman are not denominational nor drawn externally, but can only be spiritually discerned. If Rome were the *only* seat of Babylon, much of the spiritual profit of Revelation would be lost to us; but the harlot "sitteth upon many waters" (vs. 1), and "ALL nations have drunk of the wine of her fornication" (vs. 2; ch. 18:3; "the earth," ch. 19:2). External extensiveness over the whole world and internal conformity to the world—worldliness in extent and contents—is symbolized by the name of the world city, "Babylon." As the sun shines on all the earth, thus the woman clothed with the sun is to let her light penetrate to the uttermost parts of the earth. But she, in externally Christianizing the world, permits herself to be seduced by the world; thus her universality or catholicity is not that of the *Jerusalem* which we look for ("the MOTHER of us all," ch. 21:2; Isa. 2:2-4; Gal. 4:26), but that of *Babylon,* the world-wide but harlot city! (As Babylon was destroyed, and the Jews restored to Jerusalem by Cyrus, so our Cyrus—a Persian name meaning the *sun*—the Sun of righteousness, shall bring Israel, literal and spiritual, to the holy Jerusalem at His coming. Babylon and Jerusalem are the two opposite poles of the spiritual world.) Still, the Romish Church is not only accidentally and as a matter of fact, but in virtue of its very PRINCIPLE, a harlot, the metropolis of whoredom, "the mother of harlots"; whereas the evangelical Protestant Church is, according to her principle and fundamental creed, a chaste woman; the Reformation was a protest of the woman against the harlot. The spirit of the heathen world kingdom Rome had, before the Reformation, changed the Church in the West into a *Church-State,* Rome; and in the East, into a *State-Church,* fettered by the world power, having its center in Byzantium; the Roman and Greek churches have thus fallen from the invisible spiritual essence of the Gospel into the elements of the world [AUBERLEN]. Cf. with the "woman" called "Babylon" here, the woman named "wickedness," or "lawlessness," "iniquity" (Zech. 5:7, 8, 11), carried to *Babylon;* cf. "the mystery of iniquity" and "the man of sin," "that *wicked* one," lit., "*the lawless one*" (II Thess. 2:7, 8; also Matt. 24:12). **6. martyrs**—witnesses. **I wondered with great admiration**—As the *Greek* is the same in the verb and the noun, translate the latter "wonder." John certainly did not *admire* her in the modern English sense. Elsewhere (vs. 8; ch. 13:3), all the earthly-minded ("they that dwell on the earth") *wonder* in admiration of the beast. Here only is John's *wonder* called forth; not the *beast,* but the woman sunken into the harlot, the Church become a world-loving apostate, moves his sorrowful astonishment at so awful a change. That the world should be beastly is natural, but that the faithful bride should become the whore is monstrous, and excites the same amazement in him as the same awful change in Israel excited in Isaiah and Jeremiah. "Hor-

rible thing" in them answers to "abominations" here. "*Corruptio optimi pessima*"; when the Church falls, she sinks lower than the godless world, in proportion as her right place is higher than the world. It is striking that in vs. 3, "woman" has not the article, "*the* woman," as if she had been before mentioned: for though identical in one sense with the *woman,* ch. 12, in another sense she is not. The elect are never perverted into apostates, and still remain as *the* true *woman* invisibly contained in the *harlot;* yet Christendom regarded as *the woman* has apostatized from its first *faith.* **8. beast . . . was, and is not**—(Cf. vs. 11). The time when the beast "is not" is the time during which it has "the deadly wound"; the time of *the seventh head* becoming Christian externally, when its beast-like character was put into suspension temporarily. The *healing of its wound* answers to its *ascending out of the bottomless pit.* The beast, or Antichristian world power, returns worse than ever, with satanic powers from hell (ch. 11:7), not merely from *the sea* of convulsed nations (ch. 13:1). Christian civilization gives the beast only a temporary wound, whence *the deadly wound* is always mentioned in connection with its being *healed up*, the non-existence of the beast in connection with its reappearance; and Daniel does not even notice any change in the world power effected by Christianity. We are endangered on one side by the spurious Christianity of the harlot, on the other by the open Antichristianity of the beast; the third class is Christ's little flock." **go**—So B, *Vulgate,* and ANDREAS read the future tense. But A and IRENÆUS, "goeth." **into perdition**—The continuance of this revived seventh (i.e., the eighth) head is short: it is therefore called "the son of perdition," who is essentially doomed to it almost immediately after his appearance. **names were**—so *Vulgate* and ANDREAS. But A, B, *Syriac,* and *Coptic* read the singular, "name is." **written in**—Greek, "*upon*." **which**—rather, "when they behold the beast *that* it was . . . . So *Vulgate.* **was, and is not, and yet is**—A, B, and ANDREAS read, ". . . and shall come" (lit., "be present," viz., again: *Greek, kai parestai*). The *Hebrew, tetragrammaton,* or sacred four letters in *Jehovah* "who is, who was, and who is to come," the believer's object of worship, has its contrasted counterpart in the beast "who was, and is not, and shall be present," the object of the earth's worship [BENGEL]. They exult with *wonder* in seeing that the beast which had seemed to have received its deathblow from Christianity, *is on the eve of reviving* with greater power than ever on the ruins of that religion which tormented them (ch. 11:10). **9.** Cf. ch. 13:18; Daniel 12:10, where similarly spiritual discernment is put forward as needed in order to understand the symbolical prophecy. **seven heads and seven mountains**—The connection between *mountains and kings* must be deeper than the mere outward fact to which incidental allusion is made, that Rome (the then world city) is on seven hills (whence heathen Rome had a national festival called *Septimontium,* the feast of the seven-hilled city [PLUTARCH]; and on the imperial coins, just as here, she is represented as a *woman seated on seven hills.* Coin of Vespasian, described by Captain SMYTH, *Roman Coins,* p. 310; ACKERMAN, 1, p. 87). The seven heads can hardly be at once seven *kings or kingdoms* (vs. 10), and seven geographical *mountains.* The true connection is, as the *head* is the prominent part of the body, so the *mountain* is prominent in the land. Like "sea" and "earth"and "waters . . . peoples" (vs. 15), so "mountains" have a symbolical meaning, viz., prominent seats of power. Especially such as are prominent hindrances to the cause of God (Ps. 68:16, 17; Isa. 40:4; 41:15; 49:11; Ezek. 35.2); especially Babylon (which geographically was in a *plain,* but spiritually is called a destroying *mountain,* Jer. 51:25), in majestic contrast to which stands Mount Zion, "the mountain of the Lord's house" (Isa. 2:2), and the heavenly mount; ch. 21:10, "a great and high mountain . . . and that great city, the holy Jerusalem." So in Daniel 2:35, the *stone* becomes a *mountain*—Messiah's universal kingdom supplanting the previous world kingdoms. As nature shadows forth the great realities of the spiritual world, so seven-hilled Rome is *a* representative of the seven-headed world power of which the dragon has been, and is the prince. The "seven kings" are hereby distinguished from the "ten kings" (vs. 12): the former are what the latter are not, "mountains," great seats of the world power. The seven universal God-opposed monarchies are Egypt (the first world power which came into collision with God's people,) Assyria, Babylon, Greece, Medo-Persia, Rome, the Germanic-Slavonic empire (the *clay* of the fourth kingdom mixed with its iron in Nebuchadnezzar's image, Dan. 2:33, 34, 42, 43, symbolizing this last head). These seven might seem not to accord with the seven heads in Daniel 7:4-7, *one* head on the first beast (Babylon), *one* on the second (Medo-Persia), *four* on the third (Greece; viz., Egypt, Syria, Thrace with Bithynia, and Greece with Macedon): but Egypt and Greece are in both lists. Syria answers to Assyria (from which the name Syria is abbreviated), and Thrace with Bithynia answers to the Gothic-Germanic-Slavonic hordes which, pouring down on Rome from the North, founded the Germanic-Slavonic empire. *The woman sitting on the seven hills* implies the Old and New Testament Church conforming to, and resting on, the world power, i.e., on all the seven world kingdoms. Abraham and Isaac dissembling as to their wives through fear of the kings of Egypt foreshadowed this. Cf. Ezekiel 16 and 23, on Israel's whoredoms with Egypt, Assyria, Babylon; and Matthew 7:24; 24:10-12, 23-26, on the characteristics of the New Testament Church's harlotry, viz., distrust, suspicion, hatred, treachery, divisions into parties, false doctrine. **10. there are**—Translate, "they (the seven heads) are seven kings." **five . . . one**—*Greek,* "the five . . . the one"; the first five of the seven are *fallen* (a word applicable not to *forms of government passing away,* but to the *fall* of once powerful empires: Egypt, Ezek. 29 and 30; Assyria and Nineveh, Nah. 3:1-19; Babylon, ch. 18: 2; Jer. 50 and 51; Medo-Persia, Dan. 8:3-7, 20-22; 10:13; 11:2; Greece, Dan. 11:4). *Rome* was "the one" existing in John's days. "Kings" is the Scripture phrase for *kingdoms,* because these kingdoms are generally represented in character by some one prominent head, as Babylon by Nebuchadnezzar, Medo-Persia by Cyrus, Greece by Alexander, etc. **the other is not yet come**—not as ALFORD, inaccurately representing ALBERLEN, *the Christian* empire *beginning with Constantine;* but, the *Germanic-Slavonic* empire *beginning* and continuing in its beastlike, i.e., HEATHEN Antichristian character for only "a short space." The time when it is said of it, "it is not" (vs. 11), is the *time* during which it is "wounded to death," and has the "deadly wound" ch. 13:3). The external Christianization of the migrating hordes from the North which descended on Rome, is the *wound* to the beast answering to the *earth swallowing up the flood* (heathen tribes)

sent by the dragon, Satan, to drown the woman, the Church. The emphasis palpably is on "a *short* space," which therefore comes first in the *Greek,* not on "he must continue," as if his *continuance for some* [considerable] *time* were implied, as ALFORD wrongly thinks. The time of external Christianization (while the beast's wound continues) has lasted for centuries, ever since Constantine. Rome and the Greek Church have partially healed the wound by image worship. **11. beast that . . . is not** —his beastly character being kept down by outward Christianization of the state until he starts up to life again as "the eighth" king, his "wound being healed" (ch. 13:3), Antichrist manifested in fullest and most intense opposition to God. The "he" is emphatic in the Greek. *He,* peculiarly and pre-eminently: answering to "the little horn" with eyes like the eyes of a man, and a mouth speaking great things, before whom *three of the ten horns were plucked up by the roots,* and to whom the whole ten "give their power and strength" (vss. 12, 13, 17). That a *personal* Antichrist will stand at the head of the Antichristian kingdom, is likely from the analogy of Antiochus Epiphanes, the Old Testament Antichrist, "the little horn" in Daniel 8:9-12; also, "the man of sin, son of perdition" (II Thess. 2:3-8), answers here to "goeth into perdition," and is applied to an individual, viz., Judas, in the only other passage where the phrase occurs (John 17:12). He is essentially a child of destruction, and hence he has but a little time ascended out of the bottomless pit, when he "goes into perdition" (vss. 8, 11). "While the Church passes through death of the flesh to glory of the Spirit, the beast passes through the glory of the flesh to death" [AUBERLEN]. **is of the seven**—rather "springs *out of* the seven." The eighth is not merely one of the seven restored, but a new power or person proceeding *out of* the seven, and at the same time embodying all the God-opposed features of the previous seven concentrated and consummated; for which reason there are said to be not *eight,* but only *seven* heads, for the eighth is the embodiment of all the seven. In the birth-pangs which prepare the "regeneration" there are *wars, earthquakes,* and *disturbances* [AUBERLEN], wherein Antichrist takes his rise ("sea," ch. 13:1; Mark 13:8; Luke 21:9-11). He does not *fall* like the other seven (vs. 10), but is *destroyed, going to* his own *perdition,* by the Lord in person. **12. ten kings . . . received no kingdom as yet; but receive power as kings . . . with the beast** —Hence and from vss. 14, 16, it seems that these ten kings or kingdoms, are to be contemporaries with the beast in its last or eighth form, viz., Antichrist. Cf. Daniel 2:34, 44, "the stone smote the image upon *his feet,*" i.e., upon the *ten* toes, which are, in vss. 41-44, interpreted to be "*kings.*" The ten kingdoms are not, therefore, ten which arose in the overthrow of Rome (heathen), but are to rise out of the last state of the fourth kingdom under the eighth head. I agree with ALFORD that the phrase "*as kings,*" implies that they reserve their kingly rights in their alliance with the beast, wherein "they give their power and strength unto" him (vs. 13). They have the *name* of kings, but not with undivided kingly power [WORDSWORTH]. See AUBERLEN's not so probable view, *Note,* vs. 3. **one hour**—a definite *time* of *short* duration, during which "the devil is come down to the inhabitant of the earth and of the sea, having great wrath, because he knoweth that he hath but a *short time.*" Probably the three and a half years (ch. 11:2, 3; 13:5). Antichrist is in existence long before the fall of

Babylon; but it is only at its fall he obtains the vassalage of the ten kings. He in the first instance imposes on the Jews as the Messiah, coming in his own name; then persecutes those of them who refuse his blasphemous pretensions. Not until the sixth vial, in the latter part of his reign, does he associate the ten kings with him in war with the Lamb, having gained them over by the aid of the spirits of devils working miracles. His connection with Israel appears from his sitting "in the temple of God" (II Thess. 2:4), and as the antitypical "abomination of desolation standing in the Holy place" (Dan. 9:27; 12:11; Matt. 24:15), and "in the city where our Lord was crucified" (ch. 11:8). It is remarkable that IRENÆUS (*Hær.* 5:25) and ST. CYRIL OF JERUSALEM (RUFFINUS, *Hist.,* 10. 37) prophesied that Antichrist would have his seat at Jerusalem and would restore the kingdom of the Jews. Julian the apostate, long after, took part with the Jews, and aided in building their temple, herein being Antichrist's forerunner. **13. one mind**—one *sentiment.* **shall give**—so *Coptic.* But A, B, and *Syriac,* "give." **strength**—*Greek,* "authority." They become his dependent allies (vs. 14). Thus Antichrist sets up to be *King of kings,* but scarcely has he put forth his claim when the true KING OF KINGS appears and dashes him down in a moment to destruction. **14. These shall ... war with the Lamb**—in league with the beast. This is a summary anticipation of ch. 19:19. This shall not be till *after* they have first executed judgment on the harlot (vss. 15, 16). **Lord of lords ...** —anticipating ch. 19:16. *are*—not in the *Greek.* Therefore translate, "And they that are with Him, called chosen, and faithful (shall overcome them, viz., the beast and his allied kings)." These have been with Christ in heaven unseen, but now appear with Him. **15.** (Vs. 1; Isa. 8:7.) An impious **parody of Jehovah** who "sitteth upon the flood" [ALFORD]. Also, contrast the "many waters" ch. 19:6, "Alleluia." The "peoples ..." here mark the universality of the spiritual fornication of the Church. The "tongues" remind us of the original Babel, the confusion of *tongues,* the beginning of Babylon, and the first commencement of idolatrous apostasy after the flood, as the tower was doubtless dedicated to the deified heavens. Thus, Babylon is the appropriate name of the harlot. The Pope, as the chief representative of the harlot, claims a double supremacy over all *peoples,* typified by the "two swords" according to the interpretation of Boniface VIII in the Bull, "*Unam Sanctam,*" and represented by the two keys: spiritual as the universal bishop, whence he is crowned with the miter; and temporal, whence he is also crowned with the tiara in token of his imperial supremacy. Contrast with the Pope's *diadems* the "many diadems" of Him who alone has claim to, and shall exercise when He shall come, the twofold dominion (ch. 19:12). **16. upon the beast**—But A, B, *Vulgate,* and *Syriac* read, "*and* the beast." **shall make her desolate**—having first dismounted her from her seat on the beast (vs. 3). **naked**—stripped of all her gaud (vs. 4). As Jerusalem used the world power to crucify her Saviour, and then was destroyed by that very power, Rome; so the Church, having apostatized to the world, shall have judgment executed on her first by the world power, the beast and his allies; and these afterwards shall have judgment executed on them by Christ Himself in person. So Israel leaning on Egypt, a broken reed, is pierced by it; and then Egypt itself is punished. So Israel's whoredom with Assyria and Babylon was punished by the

Assyrian and Babylonian captivities. So the Church when it goes a-whoring after the word as if *it* were the reality, instead of witnessing against its apostasy from God, is false to its profession. Being no longer a reality itself, but a sham, the Church is rightly judged by that world which for a time had used the Church to further its own ends, while all the while "hating" Christ's unworldly religion, but which now no longer wants the Church's aid. **eat her flesh**—*Greek* plural, "masses of flesh," i.e., "carnal possessions"; implying the fulness of carnality into which the Church is sunk. The judgment on the harlot is again and again described (ch. 18:1; 19:5); first by an "angel having great power" (ch. 18:1), then by "another voice from heaven" (ch. 18:4-20), then by "a mighty angel" (ch. 18:21-24). Cf. Ezekiel 16:37-44, orginally said of Israel, but further applicable to the New Testament Church when fallen into spiritual fornication. On the phrase, "eat ... flesh" for prey upon one's property, and injure the character and person, cf. Psalm 14: 4; 27:2; Jeremiah 10:25; Micah 3:3. The First Napoleon's Edict published at Rome in 1809, confiscating the papal dominions and joining them to France, and later the severance of large portions of the Pope's territory from his sway and the union of them to the dominions of the king of Italy, virtually through Louis Napoleon, are a first instalment of the full realization of this prophecy of the whore's destruction. "Her flesh" seems to point to her temporal dignities and resources, as distinguished from "herself" (*Greek*). How striking a retribution, that having obtained her first temporal dominions, the exarchate of Ravenna, the kingdom of the Lombards, and the state of Rome, by recognizing the *usurper* Pepin as lawful king of France, she should be stripped of her dominions by another usurper of France, the Napoleonic dynasty! **burn ... with fire**—the legal punishment of an abominable fornication. **17. hath put**—the prophetical past tense for the future. **fulfil**—*Greek,* "do," or "accomplish." The *Greek, poiesai,* is distinct from that which is translated, "fulfilled," *Greek, telesthesontai,* below. **his will**—*Greek,* "his mind," or *purpose;* while they think only of doing their own purpose. **to agree**—lit., "to do (or *accomplish*) one mind" **or** "**purpose**." A and *Vulgate* omit this clause, but B supports it. **the words of God**—foretelling the rise and downfall of the beast; *Greek, hoi logoi,* in A, B, and ANDREAS. *English Version* reading is *Greek, ta rhemata,* which is not well supported. No mere articulate utterances, but the efficient *words* of Him who is *the Word: Greek, logos.* **fulfilled**—(ch. 10:7). **18. reigneth**—lit., "*hath kingship* over the kings." The harlot cannot be a mere *city* literally, but is called so in a spiritual sense (ch. 11:8). Also the beast cannot represent a spiritual power, but a world power. In this verse the harlot is presented before us ripe for judgment. The 18th chapter details that judgment.

CHAPTER 18

Vss. 1-24. BABYLON'S FALL: GOD'S PEOPLE CALLED OUT OF HER: THE KINGS AND MERCHANTS OF THE EARTH MOURN, WHILE THE SAINTS REJOICE AT HER FALL. **1. And**—so *Vulgate* and ANDREAS. But A, B, *Syriac,* and *Coptic* omit "And." **power**—Greek, "authority." **lightened**—"illumined." **with** —*Greek,* "owing to." **2. mightily ... strong**—not supported by MSS. But A, B, *Vulgate, Syriac,* and

Coptic read, "with (lit., 'in' a mighty voice." **is fallen, is fallen**—so A, *Vulgate, Syriac,* and ANDRE-AS. But B and *Coptic* omit the second "is fallen" (Isa. 21:9; Jer. 51:8). This phrase is here prophet-ical of her fall, still future, as vs. 4 proves. **devils** —*Greek,* "demons." **the hold**—a keep or prison. **3. drunk**—ch. 14:8, from which perhaps "the wine" may have been interpolated. They have *drunk of her fornication,* the consequence of which will be *wrath* to themselves. But A, B, and C read, "(owing to the wrath of her fornication all nations) have *fallen.*" *Vulgate* and most versions read as *English Version,* which may be the right reading though not supported by the oldest MSS. Baby-lon, the whore, is destroyed before the beast slays the two witnesses (ch. 11), and then the beast him-self is destroyed. **the wine**—so B, *Syriac,* and *Coptic.* But A, C, and *Vulgate* omit. **abundance** —lit., "power." **delicacies**—*Greek,* "luxury." See *Note,* I Timothy 5:11, where the *Greek* verb "wax wanton" is akin to the noun here. Translate, "wanton luxury." The reference is not to earthly merchandise, but to spiritual wares, indulgences, idolatries, superstitions, worldly compromises, wherewith the harlot, i.e., the apostate Church, has made *merchandise* of men. This applies especially to Rome; but the *Greek,* and even in a less degree Protestant churches, are not guiltless. However, the *principle* of evangelical Protestantism is pure, but the *principle* of Rome and the Greek church is not so. **4. Come out of her, my people**—quoted from Jeremiah 50:8; 51:6, 45. Even in the Romish Church God has a people: but they are in great danger; their only safety is in coming out of her at once. So also in every apostate or world-conform-ing church there are some of God's invisible and true Church, who, if they would be safe, must come out. Especially at the eve of God's judgment on apostate Christendom: as Lot was warned to come out of Sodom just before its destruction, and Israel to come from about the tents of Dathan and A-biram. So the first Christians came out of Jeru-salem when the apostate Jewish Church was judged. "State and Church are precious gifts of God. But the State being desecrated to a different end from what God designed it, viz.. to govern for, and as under, God, becomes beastlike; the Church apos-tatizing becomes the harlot. The true woman is the kernel: beast and harlot are the shell: whenever the kernel is mature, the shell is thrown away" [AUBERLEN]. "The harlot is not Rome alone (though she is pre-eminently so), but every Church that has not Christ's mind and spirit. False Chris-tendom, divided into very many sects, is truly Babylon, i.e., confusion. However, in all Chris-tendom the true Jesus-congregation, the woman clothed with the sun, lives and is hidden. Corrupt, lifeless Christendom is the harlot, whose great aim is the pleasure of the flesh, and which is governed by the spirit of nature and the world" [HAHN in AUBERLEN]. The first justification of the woman is in her being called out of Babylon the harlot, as the culminating stage of the latter's sin, when judgment is about to fall: for apostate Christen-dom, Babylon, is not to be converted, but to be destroyed. Secondly, she has to pass through an ordeal of persecution from the beast, which purifies and prepares her for the transfiguration glory at Christ's coming (ch. 20:4; Luke 21:28). **be not partakers**—*Greek,* "have no *fellowship with* her sins." **that ye receive not of her plagues**—as Lot's wife, by lingering too near the polluted and doomed city. **5. her sins**—as a great heap. **reached**—*Greek,*

"reached so far as to come into close contact with, and to *cleave* unto." **6.** Addressed to the execution-ers of God's wrath. **Reward**—*Greek,* "repay." **she rewarded**—*English Version* reading adds "you" with none of the oldest MSS. But A, B, C, *Vul-gate, Syriac,* and *Coptic* omit it. She had not *rewarded* or *repaid* the world power for some in-jury which the world power had inflicted on her; but she had *given* the world power that which was its *due,* viz., spiritual delusions, because it did not like to retain God in its knowledge; the unfaithful Church's principle was, *Populus vult decipi, et decipiatur,* "The people like to be deceived, and let them be deceived." **double**—of sorrow. Con-trast with this the *double* of joy which Jerusalem shall receive for her past suffering (Isa. 61:7; Zech. 9:12); even as she has received *double* punishment for her sins (Isa. 40:2). **unto her**—So *Syriac, Coptic,* and ANDREAS. A, B, and C omit it. **in the cup**— (vs. 3; ch. 14:8; 17:4). **filled**—lit., mixed. **fill to her double**—of the Lord's cup of wrath. **7. How much**—i.e., in proportion as. **lived deliciously**— luxuriously: *Note,* vs. 3, where the *Greek* is akin. **sorrow**—*Greek,* "mourning," as for a dead husband. **I sit**—so *Vulgate.* But A, B, and C prefix "that." **I . . . am no widow**—for the world power is my hus-band and my supporter. **shall see no sorrow**— *Greek,* "mourning." "I am seated (*this long time*) . . . I *am* no widow . . . I *shall* see no sorrow," marks her complete unconcerned security as to the past, present, and future [BENGEL]. I shall never have to mourn as one bereft of her husband. As Babylon was queen of the East, so Rome has been queen of the West, and is called on Imperial coins "the *eternal* city." So Papal Rome is called by AMMIAN MARCELLIN, 15. 7. "Babylon is a former Rome, and Rome a latter Babylon. Rome is a daughter of Babylon, and by her, as by her mother, God has been pleased to subdue the world under one sway" [ST. AUGUSTINE]. As the Jew's restora-tion did not take place till Babylon's fall, so R. KIMCHI, on Obadiah, writes, "When Rome (Edom) shall be devastated, there shall be redemption to Is-rael." Romish idolatries have been the great stumbling blocks to the Jews' acceptance of Chris-tianity. **8. death**—on herself, though she thought herself secure even from the death of her husband. **mourning**—instead of her feasting. **famine**—instead of her *luxurious delicacies* (vss. 3, 7). **fire**—(*Note,* ch. 17:16). Literal fire may burn the literal city of Rome, which is situated in the midst of volcanic agencies. As the ground was cursed for Adam's sin, and the earth under Noah was sunk beneath the flood, and Sodom was burnt with fire, so may Rome be. But as the harlot is mystical (the whole faithless Church), the *burning* may be mainly mys-tical, symbolizing utter destruction and removal. BENGEL is probably right in thinking Rome will once more rise to power. The carnal, faithless, and worldly elements in all churches, Roman, Greek, and Protestant, tend towards one common center, and prepare the way for the last form of the beast, viz., Antichrist. The Pharisees were in the main sound in creed, yet judgment fell on them as on the unsound Sadduces and half-heathenish Samaritans. So faithless and adulterous, carnal, worldly Pro-testant churches, will not escape for their sound-ness of creed. **the Lord**—so B, C, *Syriac,* and AN-DREAS. But A and *Vulgate* omit. "Strong"—is the meaning of God's *Hebrew* name, EL. **judgeth**—But A, B, and C read the *past* tense (*Greek, krinas*), "who *hath judged* her": the prophetical past for the future: the charge in vs. 4 to God's people to *come* *out of her* implies that the judgment was not yet actually executed. **9. lived deliciously**—*Greek,* luxuriated. The faithless Church, instead of reproving, connived at the self-indulgent luxury of the great men of this world, and sanctioned it by her own practice. Contrast the world's *rejoicing* over the dead bodies of the two witnesses (ch. 11:10) who had tormented it by their faithfulness, with its *lamentations* over the harlot who had made the way to heaven smooth, and had been found a useful tool in keeping subjects in abject tyranny. Men's carnal mind relishes a religion like that of the apostate Church, which gives an opiate to conscience, while leaving the sinner license to indulge his lusts. **bewail her**—A, B, C, *Syriac, Coptic,* and CYPRIAN omit "her." **10.** God's judgments inspire fear even in the worldly, but it is of short duration, for the kings and great men soon attach themselves to the beast in its last and worst shape, as open Antichrist, claiming all that the harlot had claimed in blasphemous pretensions and more, and so making up to them for the loss of the harlot. **mighty**—*Rome* in *Greek* means *strength;* though that derivation is doubtful. **11. shall**—So. B. But A and C read the present, "weep and mourn." **merchandise**—*Greek,* "cargo": wares carried in *ships:* ship-lading (cf. vs. 17). Rome was not a commercial city, and is not likely from her position to be so. The *merchandise* must therefore be spiritual, even as the harlot is not literal, but spiritual. She did not witness against carnal luxury and pleasure-seeking, the source of the *merchants'* gains, but conformed to them (vs. 7). She cared not for the sheep, but for the wool. Professing Christian merchants in her lived as if this world not heaven, were the reality, and were unscrupulous as to the means of getting gain. Cf. Zechariah 5:4-11 (*Notes*), on the same subject, the judgment on mystical *Babylon's* merchants for unjust gain. All the merchandise here mentioned occurs repeatedly in the "Roman Ceremonial." **12.** (*Note,* ch. 17:4.) **stones . . . pearls**—*Greek,* "stone . . . pearl." **fine linen**—A, B, and C read *Greek, bussinou* for *bussou,* i.e., fine linen manufacture" [ALFORD]. The manufacture for which *Egypt* (the type of the apostate Church, ch. 11:8) was famed. Contrast "the fine linen" (Ezek. 16:10) put on Israel, and on the New Testament Church (ch. 19:8), the Bride, by God (Ps. 132:9). **thyine wood**—the *citrus* of the Romans: probably the *cypressus thyoyides,* or the *thuia articulata.* "Citron wood" [ALFORD]. A sweet-smelling tree of Cyrene in Lybia, used for incense. **all manner vessels**—*Greek,* "every vessel," or "furniture." **13. cinnamon**—designed by God for better purposes: being an ingredient in the holy anointing oil, and a plant in the garden of the Beloved (Song of Sol. 4:14); but desecrated to vile uses by the adulteress (Prov. 7:17). **odours**—of incense. A, C, *Vulgate,* and *Syriac* prefix "and amomium" (a precious hair ointment made from an Asiatic shrub). *English Version* reading is supported by *Coptic* and ANDREAS, but not oldest MSS. **ointments**—*Greek,* "ointment." **frankincense**—Contrast the true "incense" which God loves (Ps. 141: 2; Mal. 1:11). **fine flour**—the *similago* of the Latins [ALFORD]. **beasts**—of burden: cattle. **slaves**—*Greek,* "bodies." **souls of men**—(Ezek. 27:13). Said of *slaves.* Appropriate to the spiritual harlot, apostate Christendom, especially Rome, which has so often *enslaved* both *bodies* and *souls* of men. Though the New Testament does not directly forbid slavery, which would, in the then state of the world, have incited a slave revolt, it virtually con-

dems it, as here. Popery has derived its greatest gains from the sale of masses for *the souls of men* after death, and of indulgences purchased from the Papal chancery by rich merchants in various countries, to be retailed at a profit [MOSHEIM, III, 95. 96]. **14.** Direct address to Babylon. **the fruits that thy soul lusted after**—*Greek,* "thy autumn-ripe fruits of the lust (eager desire) of the soul." **dainty** —*Greek,* "fat": "sumptuous" in food. **goodly**— "splendid," "bright," in dress and equipage. **departed**—supported by none of our MSS. But A, B, C, *Vulgate, Syriac,* and *Coptic* read, "perished." **thou shalt**—A, C, *Vulgate,* and *Syriac* read, "They (men) *shall* no more find them at all." **15. of these things**—of the things mentioned, vss. 12, 13. **which** —"*who.*" **made rich by**—*Greek,* "derived riches *from* her." **stand afar off for the fear**—(Cf. vs. 10). **wailing**—*Greek,* "mourning." **16. And**—so *Vulgate* and ANDREAS. But A, B, and C omit. **decked**— lit., "gilded." **stones . . . pearls**—*Greek,* "stone . . . pearl." B and ANDREAS read "pearls." But A and C, "pearl." **17. is come to naught**—*Greek,* "is desolated." **shipmaster**—*Greek,* "steersman," or "pilot." **all the company in ships**—A, C, *Vulgate,* and *Syriac* read, "Every one who saileth to a place" (B has ". . . to *the* place") *every voyager. Vessels* were freighted with pilgrims to various shrines, so that in one month (A.D. 1300) 200,000 pilgrims were counted in Rome [D'AUBIGNE, *Reformation*]: a source of gain, not only to the Papal see, but to *shipmasters, merchants, pilots,* etc. These latter, however, are not restricted to those literally "shipmasters," etc., but mainly refer, in the mystical sense, to all who share in the spiritual traffic of apostate Christendom. **18. when they saw**—*Greek, horontes.* But A, B, C, and ANDREAS read, *Greek, blepontes,* "looking at." *Greek, blepo,* is to *use the eyes,* to *look:* the act of seeing without thought of the object seen. *Greek, horao,* refers to the thing *seen* or presented to the eyes [TITTMANN]. **smoke**—so B, C. But A reads "place." **What city is like**—Cf. the similar beast as to *the beast,* ch. 13: 4: so closely do the harlot and beast approximate one another. Contrast the attribution of this praise to God, to whom alone it is due, by *His* servants (Exod. 15:11). MARTIAL says of Rome, "Nothing is equal to her"; and ATHENÆUS, "She is the epitome of the world." **19. wailing**—"mourning." **that had ships**—A, B, and C read, "that had *their* ships": lit., "*the* ships." **costliness**—her costly treasures: abstract for concrete. **20. holy apostles**—So C reads. But A, B, *Vulgate, Syriac, Coptic,* and ANDREAS read, "Ye *saints and ye* apostles." **avenged you on her**—*Greek,* "judged your judgment on (lit., exacting it *from*) her." "There is more joy in heaven at the harlot's downfall than at that of the two beasts. For the most heinous of all sin is the sin of those who know God's word of grace, and keep it not. The worldliness of the Church is the most worldly of all worldliness. Hence, Babylon, in Revelation, has not only Israel's sins, but also the sins of the heathen; and John dwells longer on the abominations and judgments of the harlot than on those of the beast. The term 'harlot' describes the false Church's essential character. She retains her human shape as the *woman,* does not become a *beast:* she has the form of godliness, but denies its power. Her rightful lord and husband, Jehovah-Christ, and the joys and goods of His house, are no longer her all in all, but she runs after the visible and vain things of the world, in its manifold forms. The fullest form of her whoredom is, where the Church wishes to be itself a worldly power, uses politics and diplomacy, makes flesh her arm, uses unholy means for holy ends, spreads her dominion by sword or money, fascinates men by sensual ritualism, becomes 'mistress of ceremonies' to the dignitaries of the world, flatters prince or people, and like Israel, seeks the help of one world power against the danger threatening from another" [AUBERLEN]. *Judgment,* therefore, *begins with* the harlot, as in privileges *the house of God.* **21. a**— *Greek,* "one." **millstone**—Cf. the judgment on the Egyptian hosts at the Red Sea, Exodus 15:5, 10; Nehemiah 9:11, and the foretold doom of Babylon, the world power, Jeremiah 51:63, 64. **with violence** —*Greek,* "with impetus." This verse shows that this prophecy is regarded as still to be fulfilled. **22. pipers**—flute players. "Musicians," painters and sculptors, have desecrated their art to lend fascination to the sensuous worship of corrupt Christendom. **craftsman**—artisan. **23.** What a blessed contrast is ch. 22:5, respecting the city of God: "They need *no candle* (just as Babylon shall *no more* have *the light of a candle,* but for a widely different reason), for the Lord God giveth them light." **candle**—Translate as *Greek,* "lamp." **bridegroom** ... **bride** ... **no more** ... **in thee**—Contrast the heavenly city, with its *Bridegroom, Bride,* and blessed *marriage supper* (ch. 19:7, 9; 21:2, 9; Isa. 62:4, 5). **thy merchants were**—So most of the best authorities read. But A omits the *Greek* article before "merchants," and then translates, "The great men of ... were thy merchants." **sorceries**—*Greek,* "sorcery." **24.** Applied by Christ (Matt. 23:35) to apostate Jerusalem, which proves that not merely the literal city Rome, and the Church of Rome (though the *chief* representative of the apostasy), but the WHOLE of the faithless Church of both the Old and New Testament is meant by Babylon the harlot; just as the whole Church (Old and New Testament) is meant by "the woman" (ch. 12:1). As to literal *city,* ARINGHUS in BENGEL says, Pagan Rome was the *general shambles* for slaying the sheep of Jesus. FRED. SEYLER in BENGEL calculates that papal Rome, between A.D. 1540 and 1580, slew more than 900,000 Protestants. Three reasons for the harlot's downfall are given: (1) The *worldly greatness* of her *merchants,* which was due to unholy traffic in spiritual things. (2) Her *sorceries,* or juggling tricks, in which the false prophet that ministers to the beast in its last form shall exceed her; cf. "sorcerers" (ch. 21:8; 22:15), specially mentioned among those doomed to the lake of fire. (3) Her persecution of (Old Testament) "prophets" and (New Testament) "saints."

CHAPTER 19

Vss. 1-21. THE CHURCH'S THANKSGIVING IN HEAV-EN FOR THE JUDGMENT ON THE HARLOT. THE MAR-RIAGE OF THE LAMB: THE SUPPER: THE BRIDE'S PREP-ARATION: JOHN IS FORBIDDEN TO WORSHIP THE ANGEL: THE LORD AND HIS HOSTS COME FORTH FOR WAR: THE BEAST AND THE FALSE PROPHET CAST INTO THE LAKE OF FIRE: THE KINGS AND THEIR FOLLOW-ERS SLAIN BY THE SWORD OUT OF CHRIST'S MOUTH. 1. As in the case of the opening of the prophecy, ch. 4:8; 5:9, etc.; so now, at one of the great closing events seen in vision, the judgment on the harlot (described in ch. 18), there is a song of praise in heaven to God: cf. ch. 7:10, etc., toward the close of the seals, and ch. 11:15-18, at the close of the trumpets: ch. 15:3, at the saints' victory over the beast. **And**—so ANDREAS. But A, B, C, *Vulgate,*

Syriac, and *Coptic* omit. **a great voice**—A, B, C, *Vulgate, Coptic,* and ANDREAS read, "*as it were* a great voice." What a contrast to the lamentations ch. 18! Cf. Jeremiah 51:48. The *great* manifestation of God's power in destroying Babylon calls forth a *great voice* of praise *in heaven.* **people**— *Greek,* "multitude." **Alleluia**—*Hebrew,* "Praise ye JAH," or JEHOVAH: here first used in Revelation, whence ELLICOTT infers the *Jews* bear a prominent part in this thanksgiving. JAH is not a contraction of JEHOVAH, as it sometimes occurs jointly with the latter. It means "He who IS": whereas Jehovah is "He who will be, is, and was." It implies God experienced as a PRESENT help; so that "Hallelujah," says KIMCHI in BENGEL, is found first in the Psalms *on the destruction of the ungodly.* "Hallelu-Jah" occurs four times in this passage. Cf. Psalm 149: 4-9, which is plainly parallel, and indeed identical in many of the phrases, as well as the general idea. Israel, especially, will join in the Hallelujah, when "her warfare is accomplished" and her foe destroyed. **Salvation** ... —*Greek,* "The salvation ... the glory ... the power." **and honour**—so *Coptic.* But A, B, C, and *Syriac* omit. **unto the Lord our God**—so ANDREAS. But A, B, C, and *Coptic* read, "(Is) of our God," i.e., belongs to Him. **2. which did corrupt the earth**—*Greek,* "used to corrupt" continually. "Instead of opposing and lessening, she promoted the sinful life and decay of the world by her own earthliness, allowing the salt to lose its savor" [AUBERLEN]. **avenged**—*Greek,* "exacted in retribution." A particular application of the principle (Gen. 9:5). **blood of his servants**—literally shed by the Old Testament adulterous Church, and by the New Testament apostate Church; also virtually, though not literally, by all who, though called Christians, hate their brother, or love not the brethren of Christ, but shrink from the reproach of the cross, and show unkindness towards those who bear it. **3. again**—*Greek,* "a second time." **rose up**—*Greek,* "goeth up." **for ever and ever**—*Greek,* "to the ages of the ages." **4. beasts**—rather, "living creatures." **sat**—*Greek,* "sitteth." **5. out of**— *Greek,* "out from the throne" in A, B, C. **Praise our God**—Cf. the solemn act of praise performed by the Levites I Chronicles 16:36; 23:5, especially when the house of God was filled with the divine glory (II Chron. 5:13). **both**—omitted in A, B, C, *Vulgate, Coptic,* and *Syriac.* Translate as *Greek,* "*the* small and *the* great." **6. many waters**—Contrast the "many waters" on which the whore sitteth (ch. 17:1). This verse is the hearty response to the stirring call, "Alleluia! Praise our God" (vs. 4, 5). **the Lord God omnipotent**—*Greek,* "the Omnipotent." **reigneth**—lit., "reigned": hence *reigneth once for all.* His reign is a fact already established. Babylon, the harlot, was one great hindrance to His reign being recognized. Her overthrow now clears the way for His advent to reign; therefore, not merely Rome, but the whole of Christendom in so far as it is carnal and compromised Christ for the world, is comprehended in the term "harlot." The beast hardly arises when he at once "goeth into perdition": so that Christ is prophetically considered as already reigning, so soon does His advent follow the judgment on the harlot. **7. glad** ... **rejoice**—*Greek,* "rejoice ... exult." **give**—so B and ANDREAS. But A reads, "we *will* give." **glory**— *Greek,* "*the* glory." **the marriage of the Lamb is come**—The *full* and *final* consummation is at ch. 21:2-9, etc. Previously there must be the overthrow of the beast, etc., at the Lord's coming, the binding of Satan, the millennial reign, the loosing of

Satan and his last overthrow, and the general judgment. The elect-Church, the heavenly Bride, soon after the destruction of the harlot, is transfigured at the Lord's coming, and joins with Him in His triumph over the beast. On the emblem of the heavenly Bridegroom and Bride, cf. Matthew 22:2; 25:6, 10; II Corinthians 11:2. Perfect union with Him personally, and participation in His holiness; joy, glory, and kingdom, are included in this symbol of "marriage"; cf. Song of Solomon everywhere. Besides the *heavenly* Bride, the transfigured, translated, and risen Church, reigning *over* the earth with Christ, there is also the *earthly* bride, Israel, in the flesh, never yet *divorced*, though for a time separated, from her divine husband, who shall then be reunited to the Lord, and be the mother Church of the millennial earth, Christianized through her. Note, we ought, as Scripture does, restrict the language drawn from marriage-love to *the Bride,* the Church *as a whole;* not use it as individuals in our relation to Christ, which Rome does in the case of her nuns. Individually, believers are effectually-*called guests;* collectively, they constitute *the bride.* The harlot divides her affections among many lovers: the bride gives hers exclusively to Christ. **8. granted**—Though in one sense *she* "made herself ready," having by the Spirit's work in her put on "the wedding garment," yet in the fullest sense it is not she, but her Lord, who makes her ready by "*granting* to her that she be arrayed in fine linen." It is He who, by *giving Himself for* her, *presents her to Himself a glorious Church, not having spot, but holy and without blemish.* It is He also who *sanctifies* her, naturally vile and without beauty, *with the washing of water by the word,* and *puts His own comeliness on her,* which thus becomes hers. **clean and white**—so ANDREAS. But A and B transpose. Translate, "bright and pure"; at once brilliantly *splendid* and *spotless* as in the bride herself. **righteousness**—*Greek,* "righteousnesses"; distributively used. *Each* saint must have this righteousness: not merely be justified, as if the righteousness belonged to the Church *in the aggregate;* the saints together have *righteousnesses;* viz., He is *accounted as* "the Lord our righteousness" to each saint on his believing, their robes being made *white in the blood of the Lamb.* The righteousness of the saint is not, as ALFORD erroneously states, *inherent,* but is *imputed:* if it were otherwise, Christ would be merely enabling the sinner to justify himself. Romans 5:18 is decisive on this. Cf. Article XI, Church of England. The justification already given to the saints in title and unseen possession, is now GIVEN them *in manifestation: they* openly *walk with Christ in white.* To this, rather than to their primary justification on earth, the reference is here. Their justification before the apostate world, which had persecuted them, contrasts with the judgment and condemnation of the harlot. "Now that the harlot has fallen, the woman triumphs" [AUBERLEN]. Contrast with the *pure fine linen* (indicating the simplicity and purity) of the bride, the tawdry ornamentation of the harlot. Babylon, the apostate Church, is the antithesis to new Jerusalem, the transfigured Church of God. The woman (ch. 12), the harlot (ch. 17), the bride (ch. 19), are the three leading aspects of the Church. **9. He**—God by His angel *saith unto me.* **called**—effectually, not merely externally. The "unto," or into," seems to express this: not merely invited *to* (*Greek, epi*), but called INTO, so as to be *partakers of* (*Greek, eis*); cf. I Corinthians 1:9. **marriage supper**—*Greek,* "the supper of the marriage."

Typified by the Lord's Supper. **true**—*Greek,* "genuine"; veritable sayings which shall surely be fulfilled, viz., all the previous revelations. **10. at**—*Greek,* "before." John's intending to worship the angel here, as in ch. 22:8, on having revealed to him the glory of the new Jerusalem, is the involuntary impulse of adoring joy at so blessed a prospect. It forms a marked contrast to the sorrowful *wonder* with which he had looked on the Church in her apostasy as the harlot (ch. 17:6). It exemplifies the corrupt tendencies of our fallen nature that even John, an apostle, should have all but fallen into "voluntary humility and worshipping of angels," which Paul warns us against. **and of thy brethren** —i.e., *a fellow servant* of thy brethren. **have the testimony of Jesus**— (*Note,* ch. 12:17). **the testimony of**—i.e., *respecting* Jesus. **is the spirit of prophecy**—is the result of the same spirit of prophecy in you as in myself. We angels, and you apostles, all alike have the testimony of (bear testimony concerning) Jesus by the operation of one and the same Spirit, who enables me to show you these revelations and enables you to record them: wherefore we are *fellow servants,* not I your lord to be worshipped by you. Cf. ch. 22:9, "I am fellow servant of thee and of thy brethren *the prophets";* whence the "FOR the testimony . . ." here, may be explained as giving the reason for his adding "and (fellow servant) of thy brethren that have the testimony of Jesus." I mean, *of the prophets;* "for it is of *Jesus* that thy brethren, *the prophets,* testify by the Spirit in them." A clear condemnation of Romish invocation of saints as if they were our superiors to be adored. **11. behold a white horse; and he that sat upon him**—identical with ch. 6:2. Here as there he comes forth "conquering and to conquer." Compare the *ass*-colt on which He rode into Jerusalem. The *horse* was used for war: and here He is going forth to war with the beast. The *ass* is for peace. His riding on it into Jerusalem is an earnest of His reign in Jerusalem over the earth, as the *Prince of peace,* after all hostile powers have been overthrown. When the security of the world power, and the distress of the people of God, have reached the highest point, the Lord Jesus shall appear visibly from heaven to put an end to the whole course of the world, and establish His kingdom of glory. He comes to judge with vengeance the world power, and to bring to the Church redemption, transfiguration, and power over the world. Distinguish between this *coming* (Matt. 24:27, 29, 37, 39; *Greek, parousia*) and *the end,* or final judgment (Matt. 25:31; I Cor. 15:23). Powerful natural phenomena shall accompany His advent [AUBERLEN]. **12.** Identifying Him with the Son of man similarly described, ch. 1:14. **many crowns**—*Greek,* "diadems": not merely (*Greek, stephanoi*) garlands of victory, but royal crowns, as KING OF KINGS. Christ's diadem comprises all the diadems of the earth and of heavenly powers too. Contrast the papal tiara composed of three *diadems.* Cf. also the little horn (Antichrist) that overcomes the *three* horns or kingdoms, Daniel 7:8, 24 (*Quære, the Papacy?* or some *three* kingdoms that succeed the papacy, which itself, as a temporal kingdom, was made up at first of *three* kingdoms, the exarchate of Ravenna, the kingdom of the Lombards, and the state of Rome, obtained by Pope Zachary and Stephen II from Pepin, the usurper of the French dominion). Also, the *seven crowns* (diadems) *on the seven heads of the dragon* (ch. 12:3), and *ten diadems on the ten heads of the beast.* These usurpers claim the diadems which belong to Christ alone. **he had a name written**—B and *Syriac* insert, "He had *names written,* and a name written . . . meaning that *the names* of the dominion which each diadem indicated were *written* on them severally. But A, *Vulgate*, ORIGEN, and CYPRIAN omits the words, as *English Version.* **name . . . that no man knew but . . . himself**—(Judg. 13:18; I Cor. 2:9, 11; I John 3:2). The same is said of the "new name" of believers. In this, as in all other respects, the disciple is made like his Lord. The Lord's own "new name" is to be theirs, and to be "in their foreheads"; whence we may infer that His as yet *unknown* name also is written on His forehead; as the high priest had "Holiness to the Lord" inscribed on the miter on his brow. John saw it as "written," but *knew not* its meaning. It is, therefore, a name which in all its glorious significancy can be only understood when the union of His saints with Him, and His and their joint triumph and reign, shall be perfectly manifested at the final consummation. **13. vesture dipped in blood**—Isaiah 63:2 is alluded to here, and in vs. 15, end. There the *blood* is not His own, but that of His foes. So here the blood on His "vesture," reminding us of *His own blood* shed for even the ungodly who trample on it, is a premonition of the shedding of *their blood* in righteous retribution. He sheds the blood, not of the godly, as the harlot and beast did, but of the bloodstained ungodly, including them both. **The Word of God**—who made the world, is He also who under the same character and attributes shall make it anew. His title, *Son of God,* is applicable in a lower sense, also to His people; but "the Word of God" indicates His incommunicable Godhead, joined to His manhood, which He shall then manifest in glory. "The Bride does not fear the Bridegroom; her love casteth out fear. She welcomes Him; she cannot be happy but at His side. The Lamb [vs. 9, the aspect of Christ to His people at His coming] is the symbol of Christ in His gentleness. Who would be afraid of a lamb? Even a little child, instead of being scared, desires to caress it. There is nothing to make us afraid of God but sin, and Jesus is the *Lamb of God that taketh away the sin of the world.* What a fearful contrast is the aspect which He will wear towards His enemies! Not as the Bridegroom and the Lamb, but as the [avenging] judge and warrior stained in the blood of His enemies." **14. the armies . . . in heaven**—Cf. "the horse bridles," ch. 14:20. The glorified saints whom God "will bring with" Christ at His advent; cf. ch. 17:14, "they that are with Him, called, chosen, faithful"; as also "His mighty angels." **white and clean**—*Greek,* "pure." A, B, *Vulgate, Syriac,* and CYPRIAN omit "and," which ORIGEN and ANDREAS retain, as *English Version.* **15. out of his mouth . . . sword**—(ch. 1:16; 2:12, 16). Here in its *avenging* power, II Thessalonians 2:8, "consume with the Spirit *of His mouth*" (Isa. 11:4, to which there is allusion here); not in its convicting and converting efficacy (Eph. 6:17; Heb. 4:12, 13, where also the judicial keenness of the sword-like word is included). The Father commits the judgment to the Son. **he shall rule**—The HE is emphatic, He and none other, in contrast to the usurpers who have misruled on earth. "Rule," lit., "tend as a shepherd"; but here in a punitive sense. He, who would have *shepherded* them with pastoral rod and with the golden scepter of His love, shall dash them in pieces, as refractory rebels, with "a rod of iron." **treadeth . . . wine press**—(Isa. 63:3). **of the fierceness and wrath**—So ANDREAS reads. But A, B, *Vulgate, Coptic,* and ORIGEN

read, "of the fierceness (or *boiling indignation*) of the wrath," omitting "and." **Almighty**—The fierceness of Christ's wrath against His foes will be executed with the resources of omnipotence. **16.** "His name written on His vesture and on His thigh," was written partly on the vesture, partly on the thigh itself, at the part where in an equestrian figure the robe drops from the thigh. The *thigh* symbolizes Christ's humanity as having come, after the flesh, from the *loins* of David, and now appearing as the glorified "Son of man." On the other hand, His incommunicable divine name, "which no man knew," is on His head (vs. 12), [MENOCHIUS]. KING OF KINGS—Cf. ch. 17:14, in contrast with vs. 17, the beast being in attempted usurpation a *king of kings,* the ten kings delivering their kingdom to him. **17. an**—*Greek,* "one." **in the sun**—so as to be conspicuous in sight of the whole world. **to all the fowls**—(Ezek. 39:17-20). **and gather yourselves**—A, B, *Vulgate, Syriac, Coptic,* and ANDREAS read, "be gathered," omitting "and." **of the great God**—A, B, *Vulgate, Syriac, Coptic,* and ANDREAS read, "the great supper (i.e., banquet) of God." **18.** Contrast with this "supper," vs. 17, 18, *the marriage supper of the Lamb,* vs. 9. **captains** —*Greek,* "captains of thousands," i.e., *chief captains.* The "kings" are "the ten" who "give their power unto the beast." **free and bond**—specified in ch. 13:16, as "receiving the mark of the beast." The repetition of *flesh* (in the *Greek* it is plural: *masses of flesh*) five times in this verse, marks the gross *carnality* of the followers of the beast. Again, the giving of their flesh to the fowls to eat, is a righteous retribution for their not suffering *the dead bodies* of Christ's *witnesses to be put in graves.* **19. gathered together**—at Armageddon, under the sixth vial. For *"their* armies" in B and ANDREAS, there is found *"His* armies" in A. **war**—so ANDREAS. But A and B read, *"the* war," viz., that foretold. ch. 16:14; 17:4. **20. and with him . . .**— A reads, "and those with him." B reads, "and he who was with him, the false prophet." **miracles**— *Greek,* "the miracles (lit., "signs") recorded already (ch. 13:14) as wrought by *the second beast before* (lit., in sight of) *the first beast.* Hence it follows the *second beast* is identical with *the false prophet.* Many expositors represent the first beast to be the secular, the second beast to be the ecclesiastical power of Rome; and account for the change of title for the latter from the "other beast" to the "false prophet," is because by the judgment on the harlot, the ecclesiastical power will then retain nothing of its former character save the power to deceive. I think it not unlikely that the false prophet will be the successor of the spiritual pretensions of the papacy; while the beast in its last form as the fully revealed Antichrist will be the secular representative and embodiment of the fourth world kingdom, Rome, in its last form of intensified opposition to God. Cf. with this prophecy, Ezekiel 38:39; Daniel 2:34, 35, 44; 11:44, 45; 12:1; Joel 3:9-17; Zechariah 12; 13; 14. Daniel (7:8) makes no mention of the second beast, or false prophet, but mentions that "the little horn" has "the eyes of a man," i.e., cunning and intellectual culture; this is not a feature of the first beast in ch. 13, but is expressed by the Apocalyptic "false prophet," the embodiment of man's unsanctified knowledge, and the subtlety of the old serpent. The first beast is a political power; the second is a spiritual power— the power of ideas. But both are *beasts,* the worldly Antichristian wisdom serving the worldly Antichristian power. The dragon is both lion and serpent. As the first law in God's moral government is that "judgment should begin at the house of God," and be executed on the harlot, the faithless Church, by the world power with which she had committed spiritual adultery, so it is a second law that the world power, after having served as God's instrument of punishment, is itself punished. As the harlot is judged by the beast and the ten kings, so these are destroyed by the Lord Himself coming in person. So Zephaniah ch. 1 compared with ch. 2. And Jeremiah, after denouncing Jerusalem's judgment by Babylon, ends with denouncing Babylon's own doom. Between the judgment on the harlot and the Lord's destruction of the beast, will intervene that season in which earthly-mindedness will reach its culmination, and Antichristianity triumph for its short three and a half days during which the two witnesses lie dead. Then shall the Church be ripe for her glorification, the Antichristian world for destruction. The world at the highest development of its material and spiritual power is but a decorated carcass round which the eagles gather. It is characteristic that Antichrist and his kings, in their blindness, imagine that they can wage war against the King of heaven with earthly hosts; herein is shown the extreme folly of Babylonian confusion. The Lord's mere appearance, without any actual encounter, shows Antichrist his nothingness; cf. the effect of Jesus' appearance even in His humiliation, John 18:6 [AUBERLEN]. **had received**—rather as *Greek*, "received," *once for all.* **them ; that worshipped**—lit., "them worshipping" not an act *once for all done*, as the "received" implies, but those *in the habit of* "worshipping." **These both were cast . . . into a lake**— *Greek*, ". . . *the* lake of fire," Gehenna. Satan is subsequently cast into it, at the close of the outbreak which succeeds the millennium (ch. 20:10). Then Death and Hell, as well those not found at the general judgment "written in the book of life"; this constitutes "the second death." **alive**—a living death; not mere annihilation. "Their worm dieth not, their fire is not quenched." **21. the remnant**—*Greek*, "the rest," i.e., "the kings and their armies" (vs. 19) classed together in one indiscriminate mass. A solemn confirmation of the warning in Psalm 2:10.

CHAPTER 20

VSS. 1-15. SATAN BOUND, AND THE FIRST-RISEN SAINTS REIGN WITH CHRIST, A THOUSAND YEARS; SATAN LOOSED, GATHERS THE NATIONS, GOG AND MAGOG, ROUND THE CAMP OF THE SAINTS, AND IS FINALLY CONSIGNED TO THE LAKE OF FIRE; THE GENERAL RESURRECTION AND LAST JUDGMENT. **1.** The destruction of his representatives, the beast and the false prophet, to whom he had given his *power, throne,* and *authority,* is followed by the binding of Satan himself for a thousand years. **the key of the bottomless pit**—now transferred from Satan's hands, who had heretofore been permitted by God to use it in letting loose plagues on the earth; he is now to be made to feel himself the torment which he had inflicted on men, but his full torment is not until he is cast into "the lake of fire" (vs. 10). **2. that old**—ancient serpent (ch. 12:9). **thousand years**—As *seven* mystically implies universality, so a *thousand* implies *perfection,* whether in good or evil [AQUINAS *on* ch. 11]. *Thousand* symbolizes that the world is perfectly leavened and pervaded by the divine; since *thousand* is *ten,* the number of the world, raised to the *third* power, *three*

being the number of God [AUBERLEN]. It may denote *literally* also a *thousand years.* **3. shut him** —A, B, *Vulgate, Syriac,* and ANDREAS omit "him." **set a seal upon him**—*Greek*, "over him," i.e., sealed up the door of the abyss over his head. A surer seal to keep him from getting out than his seal over Jesus in the tomb of Joseph, which was burst on the resurrection morn. Satan's binding at this juncture is not arbitrary, but is the necessary consequence of the events (ch. 19:20); just as Satan's being cast out of heaven, where he had previously been the accuser of the brethren, was the legitimate judgment which passed on him through the death, resurrection, and ascension of Christ (ch. 12:7-10). Satan imagined that he had overcome Christ on Golgotha, and that His power was secure for ever, but the Lord in death overcame him, and by His ascension as our righteous Advocate cast out Satan, the accuser from heaven. Time was given on earth to make the beast and harlot powerful, and then to concentrate all his power in Antichrist. The Antichristian kingdom, his last effort, being utterly destroyed by Christ's mere appearing, his power on earth is at an end. He had thought to destroy God's people on earth by Antichristian persecutions (just as he had thought previously to destroy Christ); but the Church is not destroyed from the earth but is raised to rule over it, and Satan himself is shut up for a thousand years in the "abyss" (*Greek* for "bottomless pit"), the preparatory prison to the "lake of fire," his final doom. As before he ceased by Christ's ascension to be an accuser in heaven, so during the millennium he ceases to be the seducer and the persecutor on earth. As long as the devil rules in the darkness of the world, we live in an atmosphere impregnated with deadly elements. A mighty purification of the air will be effected by Christ's coming. Though sin will not be absolutely abolished—for men will still be in the flesh (Isa. 65:20)—sin will no longer be a universal power, for the flesh is not any longer seduced by Satan. He will not be, as now, "the god and prince of the world"—nor will the world "lie in the wicked one"—the flesh will become ever more isolated and be overcome. Christ will reign with His transfigured saints over men in the flesh [AUBERLEN]. This will be the manifestation of "the world to come," which has been already set up invisibly in the saints, amidst "this world" (II Cor. 4:4; Heb. 2:5; 5:5). The Jewish Rabbis thought, as the world was created in six days and on the *seventh* God rested, so there would be six millenary periods, followed by a sabbatical millennium. Out of seven years every seventh is the year of remission, so out of the seven thousand years of the world the seventh millenary shall be the millenary of remission. A tradition in the house of Elias, A.D. 200, states that the world is to endure 6000 years; 2000 before the law, 2000 under the law, and 2000 under Messiah. Cf. *Note* and *Margin,* Hebrews 4:9; ch. 14:13. PAPIAS, JUSTIN MARTYR, IRENÆUS, and CYPRIAN, among the earliest Fathers, all held the doctrine of a millennial kingdom on earth; not till millennial views degenerated into gross carnalism was this doctrine abandoned. **that he should deceive**—so A. But B reads, "that he deceive" (*Greek, plana,* for *planeesee*). **and**—so *Coptic* and ANDREAS. But A, B. and *Vulgate* omit "and." **4, 5. they sat**—the twelve apostles, and the saints in general. **judgment was given unto them**—(*Note*, Dan. 7:22). The office of judging was given to them. Though in one sense having to stand before the judgment seat of Christ, yet in another sense they "do not come into judgment (*Greek*), but have already passed from death unto life." **souls**—This term is made a plea for denying the literality of the first resurrection, as if the resurrection were the spiritual one of the *souls* of believers in this life; the life and reign being that of the soul raised in this life from the death of sin by vivifying faith. But "souls" expresses their disembodied state (cf. ch. 6:9) as John saw them at first; "and they lived" implies their *coming to life in the body again*, so as to be visible, as the phrase, vs. 5, "this is the first resurrection," proves; for as surely as "the rest of the dead lived not (again) until ..." refers to the *bodily* general resurrection, so must *the first resurrection* refer to the body. This also accords with I Corinthians 15: 23, "They that are Christ's at His coming." Cf. Psalm 49:11-15. From ch. 6:9, I infer that "souls" is here used in the strict sense of *spirits disembodied* when first seen by John; though doubtless "souls" is often used in general for *persons,* and even for *dead bodies.* **beheaded**—lit., "smitten with an axe"; a *Roman* punishment, though crucifixion, casting to beasts, and burning, were the more common modes of execution. The guillotine in revolutionary France was a revival of the mode of capital punishment of pagan imperial Rome. Paul was *beheaded,* and no doubt shall share *the first resurrection,* in accordance with his prayer that he "might attain unto the resurrection from out of the rest of the dead" (*Greek, exanastasis*). The above facts may account for the specification of this particular kind of punishment. **for ... for**—*Greek,* "for the sake of"; on account of"; "because of." **and which**—*Greek,* "and the *which.*" And prominent among this class (the beheaded), such as did not worship the beast. So ch. 1:7, *Greek,* "and the which," or "and such as," particularizes prominently among the general class those that follow in the description [TREGELLES]. The *extent* of the first resurrection is not spoken of here. In I Corinthians 15:23, 51; I Thessalonians 4:14 we find that all "in Christ" shall share in it. John himself was not "beheaded," yet who doubts but that he shall share in the first resurrection? The martyrs are put first, because most like Jesus in their sufferings and death, therefore nearest Him in their life and reign; for Christ indirectly affirms there are relative degrees and places of honor in His kingdom, the highest being for those who drink his cup of suffering. Next shall be those who have not bowed to the world power, but have looked to the things unseen and eternal. **neither**—"not yet." **foreheads ... hands**—*Greek,* "forehead ... hand." **reigned with Christ**—over the earth. **5. But**—B, *Coptic,* and ANDREAS read, "and." A and *Vulgate* omit it. **again**—A, B, *Vulgate, Coptic,* and AN-DREAS omit it. "Lived" is used for *lived again,* as in ch. 2:8. John saw them not only when restored to life, but when in the act of reviving [BENGEL]. **first resurrection**—"the resurrection of the just." Earth is not yet transfigured, and cannot therefore be the meet locality for the transfigured Church; but from heaven the transfigured saints with Christ rule the earth, there being a much freer communion of the heavenly and earthly churches (a type of which state may be seen in the forty days of the risen Saviour during which He appeared to His disciples), and they know no higher joy than to lead their brethren on earth to the same salvation and glory as they share themselves. The millennial reign on earth does not rest on an isolated passage of the Apocalypse, but all Old Testament prophecy goes on the same view (cf. Isa. 4:3; 11:9; 35:8).

Jesus, while opposing the carnal views of the kingdom of God prevalent among the Jews in His day, does not contradict, but confirms, the Old Testament view of a coming, earthly, Jewish kingdom of glory: beginning from within, and spreading itself now spiritually, the kingdom of God shall manifest itself outwardly at Christ's coming again. The papacy is a false anticipation of the kingdom during the Church-historical period. "When Christianity became a worldly power under Constantine, the hope of the future was weakened by the joy over present success" [BENGEL]. Becoming a harlot, the Church ceased to be a bride going to meet her Bridegroom; thus millennial hopes disappeared. The rights which Rome as a harlot usurped, shall be exercised in holiness by the Bride. They are "kings" because they are "priests" (vs. 6; ch. 1:6; 5:10); their priesthood unto God and Christ (ch. 7: 15) is the ground of their kingship in relation to man. Men will be willing subjects of the transfigured priest-kings, in the day of the Lord's power. Their power is that of attraction, winning the heart, and not counteracted by devil or beast. Church and State shall then be coextensive. Man created "to have dominion over earth" is to rejoice over *his* world with unmixed, holy joy. John tells us that, instead of the devil, the transfigured Church of Christ; Daniel, that instead of the heathen beast, the holy Israel, shall rule the world [AUBERLEN]. **6. Blessed**—(Cf. ch. 14:13; 19:9). **on such the second death hath no power**—even as it has none on Christ now that He is risen. **priests of God**—Apostate Christendom being destroyed, and the believing Church translated at Christ's coming, there will remain Israel and the heathen world, constituting the majority of men then alive, which, from not having come into close contact with the Gospel, have not incurred the guilt of rejecting it. These will be the subjects of a general conversion (ch. 11:15). "The veil" shall be taken off. Israel first, then from off "all people." The glorious events attending Christ's appearing, the destruction of Antichrist, the transfiguration of the Church, and the binding of Satan, will prepare the nations for embracing the Gospel. As *individual* regeneration goes on now, so there shall be a "regeneration" of *nations* then. Israel, as a nation, shall be "born at once—in one day." As *the Church* began at Christ's ascension, so the *kingdom* shall begin at His second advent. This is the humiliation of the modern civilized nations, that nations which they despise most, Jews and uncivilized barbarians, the negro descendants of Ham who from the curse of Noah have been so backward, Kush and Sheba, shall supplant and surpass them as centers of the world's history (cf. Deut. 32:21; Rom. 10:19; 11: 20, etc.). The Jews are our teachers even in New Testament times. Since their rejection revelation has been silent. The whole Bible. even the New Testament, is written by Jews. If revelation is to recommence in the millennial kingdom, converted Israel must stand at the head of humanity. In a religious point of view, Jews and Gentiles stand on an equal footing as both alike needing mercy; but as regards God's instrumentalities for bringing about His kingdom on earth, Israel is His chosen people for executing His plans. The Israelite priest-kings on earth are what the transfigured priest-kings are in heaven. There shall be a blessed chain of giving and receiving—God, Christ, the transfigured Bride the Church, Israel, the world of nations. A new time of revelation will begin by the outpouring of the fulness of the Spirit. Ezekiel (chs. 40-48), himself son of a priest, sets forth the priestly character of Israel; Daniel the statesman, its kingly character; Jeremiah (33:17-21), both its priestly and kingly character. In the Old Testament the whole Jewish national life was religious only in an external legal manner. The New Testament Church insists on inward renewal, but leaves its outward manifestations free. But in the millennial kingdom, all spheres of life shall be truly Christianized from within outwardly. The Mosaic ceremonial law corresponds to Israel's priestly office; the civil law to its kingly office: the Gentile Church adopts the moral law, and exercises the prophetic office by the word working inwardly. But when the royal and the priestly office shall be revived, then—the principles of the Epistle to the Hebrews remaining the same—also the ceremonial and civil law of Moses will develop its spiritual depths in the divine worship (cf. Matt. 5:17-19). At present is the time of preaching; but then the time of the *Liturgy of* converted souls forming "the great congregation" shall come. Then shall our present defective governments give place to perfect governments in both Church and State. Whereas under the Old Testament the Jews exclusively, and in the New Testament the Gentiles exclusively, enjoy the revelation of salvation (in both cases humanity being divided and separated), in the millennium both Jews and Gentiles are united, and the whole organism of mankind under the firstborn brother, Israel, walks in the light of God, and the full life of humanity is at last realized. Scripture does not view the human race as an aggregate of individuals and nationalities, but as an organic whole, laid down once for all in the first pages of revelation. (Gen. 9:25-27; 10:1, 5, 18, 25, 32; Deut. 32:8 recognizes the fact that from the first the division of the nations was made with a relation to Israel). Hence arises the importance of the Old Testament to the Church now as ever. Three grand groups of nations, Hamites, Japhetites, and Shemites, correspond respectively to the three fundamental elements in man—body, soul, and spirit. The flower of Shem, the representative of *spiritual* life, is Israel, even as the flower of Israel is He in whom all mankind is summed up, the second Adam (Gen. 12:1-3). Thus Israel is the mediator of divine revelations for all times. Even nature and the animal world will share in the millennial blessedness. As sin loses its power, decay and death will decrease [AUBERLEN]. Earthly and heavenly glories shall be united in the twofold election. Elect Israel in the flesh shall stand at the head of the earthly, the elect spiritual Church, the Bride, in the heavenly. These twofold elections are not merely for the good of the elect themselves, but for the good of those to whom they minister. The heavenly Church is elected not merely to salvation, but to rule in love, and minister blessings over the whole earth, as king-priests. The glory of the transfigured saints shall be felt by men in the flesh with the same consciousness of blessing as on the Mount of Transfiguration the three disciples experienced in witnessing the glory of Jesus, and of Moses and Elias, when Peter exclaimed, "It is good for us to be here"; in II Peter 1:16-18, the Transfiguration is regarded as the earnest of Christ's coming in glory. The privilege of "our high *calling* in Christ" is limited to the present time of Satan's reign; when he is bound, there will be no scope for suffering for, and so afterwards *reigning* with, Him (ch. 3: 21; cf. *Note*, I Cor. 6:2). Moreover, none can be saved in the present age and in the pale of the Christian Church who does not also reign with Christ hereafter, the necessary preliminary to which is suffering with Christ now. If we fail to lay hold of the crown, we lose all, "*the gift of grace* as well as the *reward of service*" [DE BURGH]. **7. expired** —*Greek*, "finished." **8. Gog and Magog**—(*Notes*, Ezek. 38 and 39). Magog is a general name for northern nations of Japheth's posterity, whose ideal head is Gog (Gen. 10:2). A has but one Greek article to "Gog and Magog," whereby the two, viz., the prince and the people, are marked as having the closest connection. B reads the second article before Magog wrongly. HILLER (*Onomasticon*) explains both words as signifying "lofty," "elevated." For "quarters" the *Greek* is "corners." **to battle**—*Greek*, "to *the* war," in A and B. But ANDREAS omits "the." **9. on the breadth of the earth**—so as completely to overspread it. Perhaps we ought to translate, ". . . . of the [holy] *land.*" **the camp of the saints . . . and the beloved city**—the camp of the saints encircling *the beloved city*, Jerusalem (Ecclesiasticus 24:11). Contrast "hateful" in Babylon (ch. 18:2; Deut. 32: 15, LXX). Ezekiel's prophecy of Gog and Magog (38 and 39) refers to the attack made by Antichrist on Israel *before* the millennium: but this attack is made *after* the millennium, so that "Gog and Magog" are mystical names representing the final adversaries led by Satan in person. Ezekiel's Gog and Magog come from *the north,* but those here come "from the four corners of the earth." *Gog* is by some connected with a *Hebrew* root, "covered." **from God**—so B, *Vulgate, Syriac, Coptic,* and ANDREAS. But A omits the words. Even during the millennium there is a separation between heaven and earth, transfigured humanity and humanity in the flesh. Hence it is possible that an apostasy should take place at its close. In the judgment on this apostasy the world of nature is destroyed and renewed, as the world of history was before the millennial kingdom; it is only then that the new heaven and new earth are realized in final perfection. The *millennial* new heaven and earth are but a foretaste of this everlasting state when the upper and lower congregations shall be no longer separate, though connected as in the millennium, and when new Jerusalem shall descend from God out of heaven. The inherited sinfulness of our nature shall be the only influence during the millennium to prevent the power of the transfigured Church saving all souls. When this time of grace shall end, no other shall succeed. For what can move him in whom the visible glory of the Church, while the influence of evil is restrained, evokes no longing for communion with the Church's King? As the history of the world of nations ended with the manifestation of the Church in visible glory, so that of mankind in general shall end with the great separation of the just from the wicked (vs. 12) [AUBERLEN]. **10. that deceived**—*Greek*, "that deceiveth." **lake of fire**—his final doom: as the bottomless pit" (vs. 1) was his temporary prison. **where**—so *Coptic.* But A, B, *Vulgate*, and *Syriac* read, "where *also.*" **the beast and the false prophet are**—(ch. 19:20). **day and night**—figurative for *without intermission* (ch. 22:5), such as now is caused by night interposing between day and day. The same phrase is used of the *external* state of the blessed (ch. 4:8). As the bliss of these is eternal, so the woe of Satan and the lost must be. As the beast and the false prophet led the former conspiracy against Christ and His people, so Satan in person heads the last conspiracy. Satan shall not be permitted to enter this Paradise regained, to show the perfect security of believers, unlike the first Adam whom Satan succeeded in robbing of Paradise; and shall, like Pharaoh at the Red Sea, receive in this last attempt his final doom. **for ever and ever**—Greek, "to the ages of the ages." **11. great**—in contrast to the "thrones," vs. 4. **white**—the emblem of purity and justice. **him that sat on it**—the Father [ALFORD]. Rather, the Son, to whom "the Father hath committed all judgment." God in Christ, i.e., the Father represented by the Son, is He before whose judgment seat we must all stand. The Son's mediatorial reign is with a view to prepare the kingdom for the Father's acceptance. When He has done that, He shall give it up to the Father, "that God may be all in all," coming into direct communion with His creatures, without intervention of a Mediator, for the first time since the fall. Heretofore Christ's *Prophetical* mediation had been prominent in His earthly ministry, His Priestly mediation is prominent now in heaven between His first and second advents, and His Kingly shall be so during the millennium and at the general judgment. **earth and heaven fled away**—The final conflagration, therefore, precedes the general judgment. This is followed by the new heaven and earth (ch. 21). **12. the dead**—"the rest of the dead" who did not share the first resurrection, and those who died during the millennium. **small and great**—B has "*the* small and *the* great." A, *Vulgate, Syriac,* and ANDREAS have "the great and the small." The wicked who had died from the time of Adam to Christ's second advent, and all the righteous and wicked who had died during and after the millennium, shall then have their eternal portion assigned to them. The godly who were transfigured and reigned with Christ during it, shall also be present, not indeed to have their portion assigned as if for the first time (for that shall have been fixed long before, John 5:24), but to have it *confirmed* for ever, and that God's righteousness may be vindicated in the case of both the saved and the lost, in the presence of an assembled universe. Cf. "*We* must ALL appear...." Romans 14:10; II Corinthians 5:10. The saints having been first pronounced just themselves by Christ out of "the book of life," shall sit as assessors of the Judge. Cf. Matthew 25:31, 32, 40, "*these* My brethren." God's omniscience will not allow the most insignificant to escape unobserved, and His omnipotence will cause the mightiest to obey the summons. The *living* are not specially mentioned: as these all shall probably first (before the destruction of the ungodly, vs. 9) be transfigured, and caught up with the saints long previously transfigured; and though present for the confirmation of their justification by the Judge, shall not then first have their eternal state assigned to them, but shall sit as assessors with the Judge. **the books ... opened**—(Dan. 7:10). The books of God's remembrance, alike of the evil and the good (Ps. 56:8; 139:4; Mal. 3:16): conscience (Rom. 2: 15, 16), the word of Christ (John 12:48), the law (Gal. 3:10), God's eternal counsel (Ps. 139:16). **book of life**—(ch. 3:5; 13:8; 21:27; Exod. 32:32, 33; Ps. 69:28; Dan. 12:1; Phil. 4:3). Besides the general book recording the works of all, there is a special book for believers in which their names are written, not for their works, but for the work of Christ *for,* and *in,* them. Therefore it is called, "*the Lamb's* book of life." Electing grace has singled them out from the general mass. **according to their works**—We are justified *by* faith, but judged *according to* (not *by*) our works. For the general judgment is primarily designed for the final

vindication of *God's righteousness before* the whole world, which in this checkered dispensation of good and evil, though really ruling the world, has been for the time less manifest. *Faith* is appreciable by God and the believer alone (ch. 2:17). But *works* are appreciable by all. These, then, are made the evidential test to decide men's eternal state, thus showing that God's administration of judgment is altogether righteous. **13. death and hell**—Greek, "Hades." The essential identity of the dying and risen body is hereby shown; for the *sea* and *grave* give up *their dead.* The body that sinned or served God shall, in righteous retribution, be the body also that shall suffer or be rewarded. The "sea" may have a symbolical [CLUVER *from* AUGUSTINE], besides the literal, meaning, as in ch. 8:8; 12:12; 13: 1; 18:17, 19; so "death" and "hell" are personifications (cf. ch. 21:1). But the literal sense need hardly be departed from: all the different regions wherein the bodies and souls of men had been, gave them up. **14.** Death and Hades, as personified representatives of the enemies of Christ and His Church, are said to be cast into the lake of fire to express the truth that Christ and His people shall never more die, or be in the state of disembodied spirits. **This is the second death**—"the lake of fire" is added in A, B, and ANDREAS. *English Version,* which omits the clause, rests on inferior MSS. In hell the ancient form of death, which was one of the enemies destroyed by Christ, shall not continue, but a death of a far different kind reigns there, "*everlasting* destruction from the presence of the Lord": an abiding testimony of the victory of Christ. **15.** The blissful lot of the righteous is not here specially mentioned as their bliss had commenced *before* the final judgment. Cf., however, Matthew 25:34, 41, 46.

CHAPTER 21

Vss. 1-27. THE NEW HEAVEN AND EARTH: NEW JERUSALEM OUT OF HEAVEN. The remaining two chapters describe the eternal and consummated kingdom of God and the saints on the new earth. As the world of nations is to be pervaded by divine influence in the millennium, so the world of nature shall be, not annihilated, but transfigured universally in the eternal state which follows it. The earth was cursed for man's sake; but is redeemed by the second Adam. *Now* is the Church; in the millennium shall be the kingdom; and after that shall be the new world wherein God shall be all in all. The "day of the Lord" and the conflagration of the earth are in II Peter 3 spoken of as if connected together, from which many argue against a millennial interval between His coming and the general conflagration of the old earth, preparatory to the new; but "day" is used often of a whole period comprising events intimately connected together, as are the Lord's second advent, the millennium, and the general conflagration and judgment. Cf. Genesis 2:4 as to the wide use of "day." Man's *soul* is redeemed by regeneration through the Holy Spirit now; man's *body* shall be redeemed at the resurrection; man's *dwelling-place,* His inheritance, the earth, shall be redeemed perfectly at the creation of the new heaven and earth, which shall exceed in glory the first Paradise, as much as the second Adam exceeds in glory the first Adam before the fall, and as man regenerated in body and soul shall exceed man as he was at creation. **1. the first**—i.e., the former. **passed away**—Greek, in A and B is "were departed" (*Greek, apeelthon,* not as in English Version, *pareelthe*). **was**—*Greek,* "is," which graphically sets the thing before our eyes as present. **no more sea**—The sea is the type of perpetual unrest. Hence our Lord rebukes it as an unruly hostile troubler of His people. It symbolized the political tumults out of which "the beast" arose, ch. 13:1. As the physical corresponds to the spiritual and moral world, so the absence of *sea,* after the metamorphosis of the earth by *fire,* answers to the unruffled state of solid peace which shall then prevail. The *sea,* though severing lands from one another, is now, by God's eliciting of good from evil, made the medium of communication between countries through navigation. Then man shall possess inherent powers which shall make the *sea* no longer necessary, but an element which would detract from a perfect state. A "river" and "water" are spoken of in ch. 22:1, 2, probably literal (i.e., with such changes of the natural properties of water, as correspond analogically to man's own transfigured body), as well as symbolical. The sea was once the element of the world's destruction, and is still the source of death to thousands, whence after the millennium, at the general judgment, it is specially said, "The *sea* gave up the dead . . . in it." Then it shall cease to destroy, or disturb, being removed altogether on account of its past destructions. **2. And I John**—"John" is omitted in A, B, *Vulgate, Syriac, Coptic,* and ANDREAS; also the "I" in the *Greek* of these authorities is not emphatic. The insertion of "I John" in the *Greek* would somewhat interfere with the close connection which subsists between "the new heaven and earth," vs. 1, and the "new Jerusalem" in this verse. **Jerusalem . . . out of heaven**—(ch. 3:12; Gal. 4:26, "Jerusalem which is above"; Heb. 11:10; 12:22; 13:14). The *descent* of the new Jerusalem *out of heaven* is plainly distinct from the *earthly* Jerusalem in which Israel in the flesh shall dwell during the millennium, and follows on the creation of the new heaven and earth. John in his Gospel always writes [*Greek*] *Hierosoluma* of the old city; in the Apocalypse always *Hierousaleem* of the heavenly city (ch. 3:12). *Hierousaleem* is a *Hebrew* name, the original and holy appellation. *Hierosoluma* is the common Greek term, used in a political sense. Paul observes the same distinction when refuting Judaism (Gal. 4:26; cf. 1:17, 18; 2:1; Heb. 12:22), though not so in the Epistles to Romans and Corinthians [BENGEL]. **bride**—made up of the blessed citizens of "the holy city." There is no longer merely a Paradise as in Eden (though there is that also, ch. 2:7), no longer a mere garden, but now *the city of God* on earth, costlier, statelier, and more glorious, but at the same time the result of labor and pains such as had not to be expended by man in dressing the primitive garden of Eden. "The lively stones" were severally in time laboriously chiselled into shape, after the pattern of "the Chief cornerstone," to prepare them for the place which they shall everlastingly fill in the heavenly Jerusalem. **3. out of heaven**—SO ANDREAS. But A and *Vulgate* read, "out of the throne." **the tabernacle**—alluding to the tabernacle of God in the wilderness (wherein many signs of His presence were given): of which this is the antitype, having previously been in heaven: ch. 11:19; 15:5, "the temple of the tabernacle of the testimony in heaven"; also 13:6. Cf. the contrast in Hebrews 9:23, 14, between "the patterns" and "the heavenly things themselves," between "the figures" and "the true." The earnest of the true and heavenly tabernacle was afforded

in the Jerusalem temple described in Ezekiel 40, etc., as about to be, viz., during the millennium. **dwell with them**—lit., "*tabernacle* with them"; the same *Greek* word as is used of the divine Son "*tabernacling* among us." Then He was in the weakness of the *flesh:* but at the new creation of heaven and earth He shall tabernacle among us in the glory of His manifested Godhead (ch. 22:4). **they**—in *Greek* emphatic, *"they"* (in particular). **his people**—*Greek,* "His *peoples":* "the nations of the saved" being all peculiarly His, as Israel was designed to be. So A reads. But B, *Vulgate, Syriac,* and *Coptic* read, "His *people":* singular. **God himself . . . with them**—realizing fully His name Immanuel. **4. all tears**—*Greek,* "every tear." **no more death**—*Greek,* "death shall be no more." Therefore it is not the millennium, for in the latter there is *death* (Isa. 65:20; I Cor. 15:26, 54, "the *last* enemy . . . destroyed is *death,*" ch. 20:14, *after* the millennium). **sorrow**—*Greek,* "mourning." **passed away**—*Greek,* "departed," as in vs. 1. **5. sat**—*Greek,* "sitteth." **all things new**—not -recent, but *changed from the old* (*Greek, kaina,* not *nea*). An earnest of this regeneration and transfiguration of nature is given already in the regenerate soul. **unto me**—so *Coptic* and ANDREAS. But A, B, *Vulgate,* and *Syriac* omit. **true and faithful**—SO ANDREAS. But A, B, *Vulgate, Syriac,* and *Coptic* transpose, "faithful and true" (lit., "genuine"). **6. It is done**—the same *Greek* as in ch. 16:17. "It is come to pass." So *Vulgate* reads with *English Version.* But A reads, "They (*these words,* vs. 5) are come to pass." All is as sure as if it actually had been fulfilled for it rests on the word of the unchanging God. When the consummation shall be, God shall rejoice over the work of His own hands, as at the completion of the first creation God saw *everything that He had made, and behold it was very good.* **Alpha . . . Omega**—*Greek* in A and B, "*the* Alpha . . . *the* Omega" (ch. 1:18). **give unto . . . athirst . . . water of life**—(ch. 22:17; Isa. 12:3; 55:1; John 4:13, 14; 7:37, 38). This is added lest any should despair of attaining to this exceeding weight of glory. In our present state we may drink of the stream, then we shall drink at the *Fountain.* **freely** —*Greek,* "gratuitously": the same *Greek* as is translated, "(They hated Me) without a cause," John 15:25. As *gratuitous* as was man's hatred of God, so *gratuitous* is God's love to man: there was every cause in Christ why man should love Him, yet man hated Him; there was every cause in man why (humanly speaking) God should have hated man, yet God loved man: the very reverse of what might be expected took place in both cases. Even in heaven our drinking at the Fountain shall be God's *gratuitous* gift. **7. He that overcometh**—another aspect of the believer's life: a conflict with sin, Satan, and the world is needed. *Thirsting* for salvation is the first beginning of, and continues for ever (in the sense of an appetite and relish for divine joys) a characteristic of the believer. In a different sense, the believer "shall never thirst." **inherit all things** —A, B, *Vulgate,* and CYPRIAN read, "*these* things," viz., the blessings described in this whole passage. With "all things," cf. I Corinthians 3:21-23. **I will be his God**—*Greek,* ". . . to him a God," i.e., all that is implied of blessing in the name "God." **he shall be my son**—"He" is emphatic: *He* in particular and in a peculiar sense, above others: *Greek,* "shall be *to me* a son," in fullest realization of the promise made in type to Solomon, son of David, and antitypically to the divine Son of David. **8. the fearful**—*Greek,* "the cowardly," who do not *quit* *themselves like men* so as to "overcome" in the good fight; who have the spirit of slavish "fear," not love, towards God; and who through fear of man are not bold for God, or "draw back." Cf. vs. 27; ch. 22:15. **unbelieving**—*Greek,* "faithless." **abominable**—who have drank of the harlot's "cup of abominations." **sorcerers**—one of the characteristics of Antichrist's time. **all liars**—*Greek,* "all *the* liars": or else "all *who are* liars"; cf. I Timothy 4:1, 2, where similarly *lying* and dealings with *spirits* and *demons,* are joined together as features of the latter times." **second death**—ch. 20:14: "*everlasting* destruction," II Thessalonians 1:9; Mark 9:44, 46, 48, "Where THEIR worm dieth not, and the fire is not quenched."**9.** The same angel who had shown John *Babylon the harlot,* is appropriately employed to show him in contrast *new Jerusalem, the Bride* (ch. 17:1-5). The angel so employed is the one that had the last seven plagues, to show that the ultimate blessedness of the Church is one end of the divine judgments on her foes. **unto me** —A, B, and *Vulgate* omit. **the Lamb's wife**—in contrast to her *who sat on many waters* (ch. 17:1), (i.e., intrigued with many peoples and nations of the world, instead of giving her undivided affections, as the Bride does, to the Lamb. **10.** The words correspond to ch. 17:3, to heighten the contrast of the bride and harlot. **mountain**—Cf. Ezekiel 40:2, where a similar vision is given from a *high mountain.* **that great**—omitted in A, B, *Vulgate, Syriac, Coptic,* and CYPRIAN. Translate then, "the holy city Jerusalem." **descending**—Even in the millennium the earth will not be a suitable abode for transfigured saints, who therefore shall then reign in heaven over the earth. But after the renewal of the earth at the close of the millennium and judgment, they shall *descend* from heaven to dwell on an earth assimilated to heaven itself. "From God" implies that "we (the city) are God's workmanship." **11. Having the glory of God**—not merely the Shekinah cloud, but God Himself as her glory dwelling in the midst of her. Cf. the type, the earthly Jerusalem in the millennium (Zech. 2:5; cf. vs. 23, below). **her light**—*Greek,* "light-giver": properly applied to the heavenly *luminaries* which diffuse light. Cf. *Note,* Philippians 2:15, the only other passage where it occurs. The "and" before "her light' is omitted in A, B, and *Vulgate.* **even like**—*Greek,* "as it were." **jasper**—representing *watery crystalline brightness.* **12. And**—A and B omit. Ezekiel 48:30-35, has a similar description, which implies that the millennial Jerusalem shall have its exact antitype in the heavenly Jerusalem which shall descend on the finally regenerated earth. **wall great and high**—setting forth the security of the Church. Also, the exclusion of the ungodly. **twelve angels**—guards of the twelve gates: an additional emblem of perfect security, while the gates being never shut (vs. 25) imply perfect liberty and peace. Also, angels shall be the brethren of the heavenly citizens. **names of . . . twelve tribes**—The inscription of the names on the gates implies that none but the spiritual Israel, God's elect, shall enter the heavenly city. As the millennium wherein *literal* Israel *in the flesh* shall be the mother Church, is the antitype to the Old Testament *earthly* theocracy in the Holy Land, so the *heavenly* new *Jerusalem* is the consummation antitypical to the *spiritual* Israel, the elect Church of Jews and Gentiles being now gathered out: as the spiritual Israel now is an advance upon the previous literal and carnal Israel, so the heavenly Jerusalem shall be much in advance of the millennial Jerusa-

lem. **13. On the north . . . on the south**—A, B, *Vulgate, Syriac,* and *Coptic* read, "*And* on the north *and* on the *south.* In Ezekiel 48:32, Joseph, Benjamin, Dan (for which Manasseh is substituted in ch. 7:6), are on the east. Reuben, Judah, Levi, are on the *north.* Simeon, Issachar, Zebulun, on the *south.* Gad, Asher, Naphtali, on the *west.* In Numbers 2, Judah, Issachar, Zebulun, are on the east. Reuben, Simeon, Gad, on the south. Ephraim, Manasseh, Benjamin, on the *west.* Dan, Asher, Naphtali, on the *north.* **14. twelve foundations**—Joshua, the type of Jesus, chose twelve men out of the people, to carry twelve stones over the Jordan with them, as Jesus chose twelve apostles to be the twelve foundations of the heavenly city, of which He is Himself the Chief cornerstone. Peter is not the only apostolic rock on whose preaching Christ builds His Church. Christ Himself is the true foundation: the twelve are foundations only in regard to their apostolic testimony concerning Him. Though Paul was an apostle besides the twelve, yet the mystical number is retained, 12 representing the Church, viz. 3, the divine number, multiplied by 4, the world number. **in them the names . . .**— As architects often have their names inscribed on their great works, so the names of the apostles shall be held in everlasting remembrance. *Vulgate* reads, "*in* them." But A, B, *Syriac, Coptic,* and ANDREAS read, "*upon* them." These authorities also insert "twelve" before "names." **15. had a golden reed**—so *Coptic.* But A, B, *Vulgate,* and *Syriac* read, "had (as) *a measure,* a golden reed." In ch. 11:2 the non-measuring of the outer courts of the temple implied its being given up to secular and heathen desecration. So here, on the contrary, the city being measured implies the entire consecration of every part, all things being brought up to the most exact standard of God's holy requirements, and also God's accurate guardianship henceforth of even the most minute parts of His holy city from all evil. **twelve thousand furlongs**—lit., "*to* 12,000 *stadii": one* thousand furlongs being the space between the several twelve gates. BENGEL makes the length of *each side* of the city to be 12,000 stadii. The stupendous height, length, and breadth being exactly alike, imply its faultless symmetry, transcending in glory all our most glowing conceptions. **17, hundred . . . forty . . . four cubits** —twelve times twelve: the Church-number squared. The wall is far beneath the height of the city. **measure of a man, that is, of the angel**—The ordinary measure used by *men* is the measure here used by the *angel,* distinct from "the measure of the sanctuary." Men shall then be *equal to the angels.* **18. the building**—"the "structure" [TREGELLES], *Greek, endomeesis.* **gold, like . . . clear glass**—Ideal gold, transparent as no gold here is [ALFORD]. Excellencies will be combined in the heavenly city which now seem incompatible. **19. And**—so *Syriac, Coptic,* and ANDREAS. But A, B, and *Vulgate* omit. Cf. vs. 14 with this verse; also Isaiah 54:11. **all manner of precious stones**—Contrast ch. 18:12 as to the harlot, Babylon. These precious stones constituted the "foundations." **chalcedony** —agate from Chalcedon: semi-opaque, sky-blue, with stripes of other colors [ALFORD]. **20. sardonyx** —a gem having the redness of the cornelian, and the whiteness of the onyx. **sardius**—(*Note,* ch. 4:3). **chrysolite**—described by PLINY as transparent and of a golden brightness, like our topaz: different from our pale green crystallized *chrysolite.* **beryl**—of a sea-green color. **topaz**—PLINY, 37. 32, makes it *green* and transparent, like our chrysolite. **chrysoprasus**

—somewhat pale, and having the purple color of the amethyst [PLINY, 37, 20, 21]. **jacinth**—The flashing violet brightness in the amethyst is diluted in the jacinth [PLINY, 37. 41]. **21. every several**—*Greek*, "each one severally." **22. no temple ... God ... the temple**—As God now dwells in the spiritual Church, His "temple" (*Greek, naos,* shrine; I Cor. 3:17; 6:19), so the Church when perfected shall dwell in Him as her "temple" (*naos:* the same *Greek*). As the Church was "His sanctuary," so He is to be their sanctuary. Means of grace shall cease when the end of grace is come. Church ordinances shall give place to the God of ordinances. Uninterrupted, immediate, direct, communion with Him and the Lamb (cf. John 4:23), shall supersede intervening ordinances. **23. in it**—so *Vulgate.* But A, B, and ANDREAS read, "(shine) *on* it," or lit., "*for her." **the light**—*Greek*, "the lamp" (Isa. 60:19, 20). The direct light of God and the Lamb shall make the saints independent of God's creatures, the sun and moon, for light. **24. of them which are saved ... in**—*A, B, Vulgate, Coptic,* and ANDREAS read, (the nations shall walk) "*by means* of her light"; omitting "of them which are saved." Her brightness shall supply them with light. **the kings of the earth**—who once had regard only to their glory, having been converted, now in the new Jerusalem do bring their glory into it, to lay it down at the feet of their God and Lord. **and honour**—so B, *Vulgate,* and *Syriac.* But A omits the clause. **25. not be shut ... by day**—therefore shall never be shut: for it shall *always* be day. Gates are usually shut by night: but in it shall be no night. There shall be continual free ingress into it, so as that all which is blessed and glorious may continually be brought into it. So in the millennial type. **26.** All that was truly glorious and excellent in the earth and its converted *nations* shall be gathered into it; and while all shall form *one* Bride, there shall be various orders among the redeemed, analogous to the divisions of *nations* on earth constituting the one great human family, and to the various orders of angels. **27. anything that defileth**—*Greek, koinoun.* A and B read [*koinon*], "anything *unclean.*" **in the Lamb's book of life**—*Note*, ch. 20:12, 15). As all the filth of the old Jerusalem was carried outside the walls and burnt there, so nothing defiled shall enter the heavenly city, but be burnt *outside* (cf. ch. 22:15). It is striking that the apostle of love, who shows us the glories of the heavenly city, is he also who speaks most plainly of the terrors of hell. On vss. 26, 27, ALFORD writes a *Note*, rash in speculation, about the heathen *nations*, above what is written, and not at all required by the sacred text: cf. my *Note*, vs. 26.

CHAPTER 22

Vss. 1-21. THE RIVER OF LIFE: THE TREE OF LIFE: THE OTHER BLESSEDNESSES OF THE REDEEMED. JOHN FORBIDDEN TO WORSHIP THE ANGEL. NEARNESS OF CHRIST'S COMING TO FIX MAN'S ETERNAL STATE. TESTIMONY OF JESUS, HIS SPIRIT, AND THE BRIDE, ANY ADDITION TO WHICH, OR SUBTRACTION FROM WHICH, SHALL BE ETERNALLY PUNISHED. CLOSING BENEDICTION. **1. pure**—A, B, *Vulgate,* and HILARY 22, omit. **water of life**—infinitely superior to the typical waters in the first Paradise (Gen. 2: 10-14); and even superior to those figurative ones in the millennial Jerusalem (Ezek. 47:1, 12; Zech. 14:8), as the matured fruit is superior to the flower. The millennial waters represent full Gospel grace;

these waters of new Jerusalem represent Gospel glory perfected. Their continuous flow from God, the Fountain of life, symbolizes the uninterrupted continuance of life derived by the saints, ever fresh, from Him: life in fulness of joy, as well as perpetual vitality. Like pure crystal, it is free from every taint: cf. ch. 4:6, "before the throne a sea of glass, like crystal." **clear**—*Greek,* "bright." **2.** The harmonious unity of Scripture is herein exhibited. The Fathers compared it to a ring, an unbroken circle, returning into itself. Between the events of Genesis and those at the close of the Apocalypse, at least 6000 or 7000 years intervene; and between Moses the first writer and John the last, about 1500 years. How striking it is that, as in the beginning we found Adam and Eve, his bride, in innocence in Paradise, then tempted by the serpent, and driven from the tree of life, and from the pleasant waters of Eden, yet not without a promise of a Redeemer who should crush the serpent; so at the close, the old serpent cast out for ever by the second Adam, the Lord from heaven, who appears with His Bride, the Church, in a better Paradise, and amidst better waters (vs. 1): the tree of life also is there with all its *healing* properties, not guarded with a flaming sword, but open to all who overcome (ch. 2:7), and there is no more curse. **street of it**—i.e., of the city. **on either side of the river**—ALFORD translates, "In the midst of the street of it (the city) and of the river, on one side and on the other" (for the second *Greek, enteuthen,* A, B, and *Syriac* read, *ekeithen:* the sense is the same; cf. *Greek,* John 19: 18); thus the trees were on each side in the middle of the space between the street and the river. But from Ezekiel 47:7, I prefer *English Version.* The antitype exceeds the type: in the first Paradise was only *one* tree of life; now there are "*very many* trees *at the bank of the river, on the one side and on the other.*" To make good sense, supposing there to be but *one* tree, we should either, as MEDE, suppose that the *Greek* for *street* is a *plain* washed on both sides by the river (as the first Paradise was washed on one side by the Tigris, on the other by the Euphrates), and that in the midst of the plain, which itself is in the midst of the river's branches, stood the tree: in which case we may translate, "In the midst of the street (plain) *itself,* and of the river (having two branches flowing) on this and on that side, was there the tree of life." Or else with DURHAM suppose, *the tree* was in the midst of the river, and extending its branches to both banks. But cf. Ezekiel 47:12, the millennial type of the final Paradise; which shows that there are several trees of the one kind, all termed "the tree of life." Death reigns now because of sin; even in the millennial earth sin, and therefore death, though much limited, shall not altogether cease. But in the final and heavenly city on earth, sin and death shall utterly cease. **yielded her fruit every month**—*Greek*, "according to each month"; each month had its own proper fruit, just as different seasons are now marked by their own productions; only that then, unlike now, there shall be *no season without its fruit,* and there shall be an endless variety, answering to *twelve,* the number symbolical of the worldwide Church (cf. *Notes*, ch. 12:1; 21:14). ARCHBISHOP WHATELY thinks that the tree of life was among the trees of which Adam *freely ate* (Gen. 2:9, 16, 17), and that his continuance in immortality was dependent on his *continuing* to eat of this tree; having forfeited it, he became liable to death; but still the effects of having eaten of it for a time showed themselves in the longevity of the patriarchs.

God could undoubtedly endue a tree with special medicinal powers. But Genesis 3:22 seems to imply, *man had not yet taken of the tree,* and that if he had, he would have lived for ever, which in his then fallen state would have been the greatest curse. **leaves ... for ... healing**–(Ezek. 47:9, 12). The *leaves* shall be the *health-giving* preventive securing the redeemed against, not healing them of, sicknesses, while "the fruit shall be for meat." In the millennium described in Ezekiel 47 and ch. 20, the Church shall give the Gospel-tree to the nations outside Israel and the Church, and so shall heal their spiritual malady; but in the *final* and *perfect* new Jerusalem here described, the state of all is eternally fixed, and no saving process goes on any longer (cf. vs. 11). ALFORD utterly mistakes in speaking of "nations outside," and "dwelling on the renewed earth, organized under kings, and saved by the influences of the heavenly city"(!) Cf. vss. 2, 10-27; the "nations" mentioned (ch. 21:24) are those which have long before, viz., in the millennium (ch. 11: 15), become the Lord's and His Christ's. **3. no more curse**–of which the earnest shall be given in the millennium (Zech. 14:11). God can only dwell where the curse and its cause, the cursed thing sin (Josh. 7:12), are removed. So there follows rightly, "But the throne of God and of the Lamb (who redeemed us from the curse, Gal. 3:10, 13) shall be in it." Cf. in the millennium, Ezekiel 48:35. **serve him**–with *worship* (ch. 7:15). **4. see his face** –revealed in divine glory, *in Christ Jesus.* They shall see and know Him with intuitive knowledge of Him, *even as they are known by Him* (I Cor. 13:9-12), and face to face. Cf. I Tim. 6:16, with John 14:9. God the Father can only be seen in Christ. **in**–*Greek, "on* their foreheads." Not only shall they personally and in secret (ch. 3:17) know their sonship, but they shall be known as sons of God to all the citizens of the new Jerusalem, so that the free flow of mutual love among the members of Christ's family will not be checked by suspicion as here. **5. there**–so ANDREAS. But A, B, *Vulgate,* and *Syriac* read, "(there shall be no night) any longer"; *Greek, eti,* for *ekei.* **they need**–A, *Vulgate,* and *Coptic* read the future, "they *shall* not have need." B reads, "(and there shall be) no need." **candle**–*Greek,* "lamp." A, *Vulgate, Syriac,* and *Coptic* insert "light *(of a candle,* or *lamp)."* B omits it. **of the sun**–so A. But B omits it. **giveth ... light**–"illumines." So *Vulgate* and *Syriac.* But A reads, *"shall* give light." **them**–so B and ANDREAS. But A reads, *"upon* them." **reign** –with a glory probably transcending that of their reign in heaven with Christ over the millennial nations in the flesh described in ch. 20:4, 6; that reign was but for a limited time, "a thousand years"; this final reign is "unto the ages of the ages." **6. These sayings are true**–thrice repeated (ch. 19:9; 21:5). For we are slow to believe that God is as good as He is. The news seems to us, habituated as we are to the misery of this fallen world, too good to be true [NANGLE]. They are no dreams of a visionary, but the realities of God's sure word. **holy**–so ANDREAS. But A, B, *Vulgate, Syriac,* and *Coptic* read, ("the Lord God of the) *spirits* (of the prophets.)" The Lord God who with His Spirit inspired their spirits so as to be able to prophesy. There is but one Spirit, but individual prophets, according to the measure given them [I Cor. 12: 4-11], had their own spirits [BENGEL] (I Pet. 1:11; II Peter 1:21). **be done**–*Greek,* "come to pass." **7.** "And" is omitted in *Coptic* and ANDREAS with *English Version,* but is inserted by A, B,

Vulgate and *Syriac.* **blessed**–(ch. 1:3). **8.** Both here and in ch. 19:9, 10, the apostle's falling at the feet of the angel is preceded by a glorious promise to the Church, accompanied with the assurance, that "These are the true sayings of God," and that those are "blessed" who keep them. Rapturous emotion, gratitude, and adoration, at the prospect of the Church's future glory transport him out of himself, so as all but to fall into an unjustifiable act; contrast his opposite feeling at the prospect of the Church's deep fall [AUBERLEN], ch. 17:6, where cf.the *Note,* and on ch. 19:9, 10. **saw and heard**–A, B, *Vulgate,* and *Syriac* transpose these verbs. Translate lit., "I John (was he) who heard and saw these things." It is observable that in ch. 19:10, the language is, "I fell before his feet to worship hini;" but here, "I fell down to worship (God?) *before the feet* of the angel." It seems unlikely that John, when once reproved, would fall into the very same error again. BENGEL's view, therefore, is probable; John had first intended to worship *the angel* (ch. 19:10), but now only *at his feet* intends to worship (God). The angel does not even permit this. **9.** Lit., "See not"; the abruptness of the phrase marking the angel's abhorrence of the thought of *his* being worshipped however indirectly. Contrast the fallen angel's temptation to Jesus, "Fall down and worship me" (Matt. 4:9). **for**–A, B, *Vulgate, Syriac, Coptic,* ANDREAS, and CYPRIAN omit "for"; which accords with the abrupt earnestness of the angel's prohibition of an act derogatory to God. **and of**–"and (the fellow servant) of thy brethren." **10. Seal not**–But in Daniel 12:4, 9 (cf. 8:26), the command is, "Seal the book," for the vision shall be "for many days." The fulfilment of Daniel's prophecy was distant, that of John's prophecy is near. The New Testament is the time of the end and fulfilment. The Gentile Church, for which John wrote his Revelation, needs more to be impressed with the shortness of the period, as it is inclined, owing to its Gentile origin, to conform to the world and forget the coming of the Lord. The Revelation points, on the one hand, to Christ's coming as distant, for it shows the succession of the seven seals, trumpets, and vials; on the other hand, it proclaims, "Behold, I come quickly." So Christ marked many events as about to intervene before His coming, and yet He also says "Behold, I come quickly," because our right attitude is that of continual prayerful watching for His coming (Matt. 25: 6, 13, 19; Mark 13:32-37 [AUBERLEN]; cf. ch. 1:3). **11. unjust**–"unrighteous"; in relation to one's fellow men; opposed to "righteous," or "just" (as the *Greek* may be translated) below. More literally, "he that *doeth unjustly,* let him *do unjustly* still." **filthy**–in relation to one's own soul as unclean before God; opposed to holy," consecrated to God as pure. A omits the clause, "He which is filthy let him be filthy still." But B supports it. In the letter of the Vienne and Lyons Martyrs (in EUSEBIUS) in the second century, the reading is, "He that is *lawless* (*Greek, anomos*) let him be lawless; and he that is righteous let him be righteous (lit., 'be justified') still." No MS. is so old. A, B, *Vulgate, Syriac, Coptic,* ANDREAS, and CYPRIAN read, "let him *do righteousness"* (I John 2:29; 3:7). The punishment of sin is sin, the reward of holiness is holiness. Eternal punishment is not so much an arbitrary law, as a result necessarily following in the very nature of things, as the fruit results from the bud. No worse punishment can God lay on ungodly men than to give them up to themselves.

The solemn lesson derivable from this verse is, Be converted now in the short time left (vs. 10, end) before "I come" (vss. 7, 12), or else you must remain unconverted for ever; sin in the eternal world will be left to its own natural consequences; holiness in germ will there develop itself into perfect holiness, which is happiness. **12. And**—none of our MSS. But A, B, *Vulgate, Syriac, Coptic*, and CYPRIAN omit it. **behold, I come quickly**—(Cf. vs. 7). **my reward is with me**—(Isa. 40:10; 62:11). **to give**—*Greek*, "to render." **every man**—*Greek*, "to *each*." **shall be**—so B in MAI. But B in TISCHENDORF, and *A, Syriac*, read, "is." **13. I am Alpha**—*Greek*, " . . . *the* Alpha and *the* Omega." A, B, *Vulgate, Syriac*, ORIGEN, and CYPRIAN transpose thus, "the First and the Last, the Beginning and the End." ANDREAS supports *English Version*. Cf. with these divine titles assumed here by the Lord Jesus, ch. 1:8, 17; 21:6. At the winding up of the whole scheme of revelation He announces Himself as the One *before whom and after whom there is no God*. **14. do his commandments**—so B, *Syriac, Coptic*, and CYPRIAN. But A, ℵ, and *Vulgate* read, (Blessed are they that) "*wash their robes*," viz., *in the blood of the Lamb* (cf. ch. 7:14). This reading takes away the pretext for the notion of salvation by works. But even *English Version* reading is quite compatible with salvation by grace; for God's first and grand Gospel "commandment" is to believe on Jesus. Thus our "right" to (*Greek*, "privilege" or "lawful authority over") the tree of life is due not to our doings, but to what He has done for us. The *right*, or *privilege*, is founded, not on our merits, but on God's grace. **through**—*Greek*, "by the gates." **15. But**—so *Coptic*. But A, B, HIPPOLYTUS, ANDREAS, and CYPRIAN omit. **dogs**—*Greek*, "the dogs"; the impure, filthy (vs. 11; cf. Phil. 3:2). **maketh**—including also "whosoever *practiceth* a lie" [W. KELLY]. **16. mine angel**—for Jesus is Lord of the angels. **unto you**—ministers and people in the seven representative churches, and, through you, to testify to Christians of all times and places. **root . . . offspring of David**—appropriate title here where assuring His Church of "the sure mercies of David," secured to Israel first, and through Israel to the Gentiles. *Root* of David, as being Jehovah; the offspring of David as man. David's Lord, yet David's son (Matt. 22:42-45). **the morning star**—that ushered in the day of grace in the beginning of this dispensation, and that shall usher in the everlasting day of glory at its close. **17.** Reply of the spiritual Church and John to Christ's words (vss. 7, 12, 16). **the Spirit**—in the churches and in the prophets. **the bride**—not here called "wife," as that title applies to her only when the full number constituting the Church shall have been completed. The invitation, "Come," only holds good while the Church is still but an affianced *Bride*, and not the actually wedded *wife*. However, "Come" may rather be the prayer of the Spirit in the Church and in believers in reply to Christ's "I come quickly," crying, Even so, "Come" (vss. 7, 12); vs. 20 confirms this view. The whole question of your salvation hinges on this, that you be able to hear with joy Christ's announcement, "I come," and to reply, "Come" [BENGEL]. Come to fully glorify Thy Bride. **let him that heareth**—i.e., let him that heareth the Spirit and Bride saying to the Lord Jesus, "Come," join the Bride as a true believer, become part of her, and so say with her to Jesus, "Come." On "heareth" means "obeyeth"; for until one has *obeyed* the Gospel call, he cannot pray to Jesus "Come"; so "hear" is used, ch. 1:3; John 10:16. Let him that hears and obeys Jesus'

voice (vs. 16; ch. 1:3) join in praying "Come." Cf. ch. 6:1, *Note*, 10. In the other view, which makes "Come" an invitation to sinners, this clause urges those who themselves hear savingly the invitation to address the same to others, as did Andrew and Philip after they themselves had heard and obeyed Jesus' invitation, "Come." **let him that is athirst come**—As the Bride, the Church, prays to Jesus, "Come," so she urges all whosoever *thirst* for participation in the full manifestation of redemption-glory at *His coming to us*, to COME in the meantime and drink of the living waters, which are the earnest of "the water of life pure as crystal . . . out of the throne of God of the Lamb" (vs. 1) in the regenerated heaven and earth. **And**—so *Syriac*. But A, B, *Vulgate*, and *Coptic* omit "and." **whosoever will**—i.e., is willing and desirous. There is a descending climax; Let him that *heareth* effectually and savingly Christ's voice, pray individually, as the Bride, the Church, does collectively, "Come, Lord Jesus" (vs. 20). Let him who, though not yet having actually *heard* unto salvation, and so not yet able to join in the prayer, "Lord Jesus, come, "still *thirsts* for it, *come* to Christ. Whosoever is even *willing*, though his desires do not yet amount to positive *thirsting*, let him take the water of life freely, i.e., gratuitously. **18. For**—None of our MSS. have this. A, B, *Vulgate*, and ANDREAS read, "I" emphatic in the *Greek*. "I testify." **unto these things**—A, B, and ANDREAS read, "unto them." **add . . . add**—just retribution in kind. **19. book**—None of our MSS. read this. A, B, ℵ, *Vulgate, Syriac*, and *Coptic* read, "(take away his part, i.e., portion) from the *tree* of life," i.e., shall deprive him of participation in the tree of life. **and from the things**—so *Vulgate*. But A, B, ℵ, *Syriac, Coptic*, and ANDREAS omit "and"; then "which are written in this book" will refer to "the holy city and the tree of life." As in the beginning of this book (ch. 1:3) a blessing was promised to the devout, obedient student of it, so now at its close a curse is denounced against those who add to, or take from, it. **20. Amen. Even so, come**—The Song of Solomon (8:14) closes with the same yearning prayer for Christ's coming. A, B, and ℵ omit "Even so," *Greek, nai:* then translate for *Amen*, "So be it, come, Lord Jesus"; joining the "Amen," or "So be it," not with Christ's saying (for He calls Himself the "Amen" at the beginning of sentences, rather than puts it as a confirmation at the end), but with John's reply. Christ's "I come," and John's "Come," are almost coincident in time; so truly does the believer reflect the mind of his Lord. **21. our** —so *Vulgate, Syriac*, and *Coptic*. But A, B, and ℵ omit. **Christ**—so B, *Vulgate, Syriac, Coptic*, and ANDREAS. But A and ℵ omit. **with you all**—so none of our MSS. B has, "with all the saints." A and *Vulgate* have, "with all." ℵ has, "with the saints." This closing benediction, Paul's mark in his Epistles, was after Paul's death taken up by John. The Old Testament ended with a "curse" in connection with the *law;* the New Testament ends with a blessing in union with the Lord Jesus. **Amen**—so B, ℵ, and ANDREAS. A and *Vulgate Fuldensis* omit it.

May the Blessed Lord who has caused all holy Scriptures to be written for our learning, bless this humble effort to make Scripture expound itself, and make it an instrument towards the conversion of sinners and the edification of saints, to the glory of His great name and the hastening of His kingdom! Amen.